BIOGRAPHY AND GENEALOGY MASTER INDEX 1992

The Gale Biographical Index Series

Biography and Genealogy Master Index
Second Edition, Supplements and Annual Volumes
(GBIS Number 1)

Children's Authors and Illustrators
Fourth Edition
(GBIS Number 2)

Author Biographies Master Index
Third Edition
(GBIS Number 3)

Journalist Biographies Master Index
(GBIS Number 4)

Performing Arts Biography Master Index
Second Edition
(GBIS Number 5)

Writers for Young Adults: Biographies Master Index
Third Edition
(GBIS Number 6)

Historical Biographical Dictionaries Master Index
(GBIS Number 7)

Twentieth-Century Author Biographies Master Index
(GBIS Number 8)

Artist Biographies Master Index
(GBIS Number 9)

Business Biography Master Index
(GBIS Number 10)

Abridged Biography and Genealogy Master Index
(GBIS Number 11)

ISSN 0730-1316

Gale Biographical Index Series
Number 1

BIOGRAPHY AND GENEALOGY MASTER INDEX 1992

A consolidated index to more than 450,000 biographical sketches in over 95 current and retrospective biographical dictionaries

Barbara McNeil, Editor

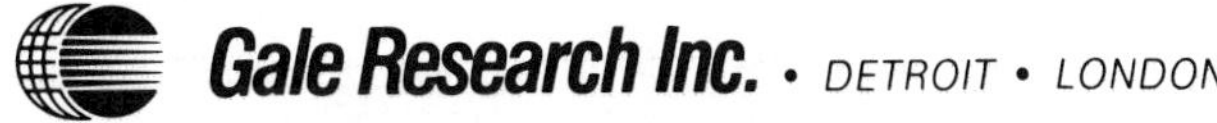

Senior Editor: Peter M. Gareffa
Editor: Barbara McNeil
Associate Editors: Miranda Herbert Ferrara, Karen D. Kaus, Paula K. Woolverton

Systems and Programming Supervisor: Theresa Rocklin

Data Entry Supervisor: Benita Spight
Data Entry Associates: Nancy S. Aiuto, Arlene Kevonian, Roger Moore

Production Manager: Mary Beth Trimper
Production Assistant: Shanna Heilveil

Art Director: Art Chartow
Keyliner: C. J. Jonik

The paper used in this publication meets the minimum requirements of American National Standard for Information Sciences—Permanence Paper for Printed Library Materials, ANSI Z39.48-1984 ∞™

Library of Congress Catalog Number 82-15700
ISBN 0-8103-4802-0
ISSN 0730-1316

Printed in the United States of America

Published simultaneously in the United Kingdom
by Gale Research International Limited
(An affiliated company of Gale Research Inc.)

Advisory Board
For
Biography and Genealogy Master Index

Contents

Introduction

Biography and Genealogy Master Index 1992 is the eleventh in a series of annual updates to the *Biography and Genealogy Master Index (BGMI)* base volumes published in 1981. Containing more than 450,000 citations, *BGMI 1992* provides an index to 150 volumes and editions of over 95 biographical dictionaries, including new editions of sources previously indexed as well as new titles. With the publication of *BGMI 1992*, the total number of biographical sketches indexed by the *BGMI* base set and its eleven updates exceeds 8,382,000. The chart at the conclusion of this introduction provides further details on *BGMI* publications already available and those planned for the future.

Concept and Scope

BGMI is a unique index that enables the user to determine which edition(s) of which publication to consult for biographical information. Almost as helpful, if there is no listing for a given individual in *BGMI* it reveals that there is no listing for that individual in any of the sources indexed. In cases where *BGMI* shows multiple listings for the same person, the user is able either to choose which source is the most convenient or to locate multiple sketches to compare and expand information furnished by a single listing.

Biographical sources indexed in *BGMI* are of several different types: 1) biographical dictionaries and who's whos, which supply information on a number of individuals; 2) subject encyclopedias, which include some biographical entries; 3) volumes of literary criticism, which may contain only a limited amount of biographical information but give critical surveys of a writer's works; and 4) indexes, which do not provide immediate information but refer the user to a body of information elsewhere.

Sources indexed by *BGMI* cover both living and deceased persons from every field of activity and from all areas of the world. The sources are predominantly current, readily available, "standard" reference books (for example, the Marquis Who's Who series); however, *BGMI* also includes important retrospective sources and general subject sources that cover both contemporary and noncontemporary people.

Although the majority of the sources indexed in *BGMI* covers individuals in the United States, this index also includes sources that cover individuals in foreign countries in such titles as *The Dictionary of National Biography* (Great Britain), *Dictionary of Canadian Biography*, and *Who's Who in the World*.

BGMI 1992, for example, indexes general works, both current and retrospective (*Biography Index, Current Biography Yearbook*). Also, included are sources on special subject areas such as literature (*Authors of Books for Young People, Dictionary of Scandinavian Literature, Hispanic Writers, World Authors*), art and architecture (*International Dictionary of Art and Artists, Who's Who in American Art*), business (*Contemporary American Business Leaders, Standard & Poor's Register of Corporations, Directors and Executives*), government and politics (*American Legislative Leaders, Biographical Directory of the United States Executive Branch*), and music (*Contemporary Musicians, The New Age Music Guide, Who's Who in New Country Music*). Other subject areas covered in *BGMI 1992* include parapsychology, psychiatry, science, sports, and theater and film.

How to Read a Citation

Each citation in *BGMI* gives the person's name followed by the years of birth and/or death as found in the source book. If a source has indicated that the dates may not be accurate, the questionable date(s) are followed by a question mark. If there is no year of birth, the death date is preceded by a lower case d. The codes for the books indexed follow the dates.

Walsh, William 1512?-1577 *DcNaB*

Sokoine, Edward d1984 *NewYTBS 84*

References to names that are identical in spelling and dates have been consolidated under a single name and date entry, as in the example below for *Bernard Goodwin*. When a name appears in more than one edition or volume of an indexed work, the title code for the book is given only once and is followed by the various codes for the editions in which the name appears.

Goodwin, Bernard 1907- *IntMPA 81, -82, -84,*
WhoAm 80, -82, -84, WhoWor 82

Another feature of the *BGMI* updates is the portrait indicator. If the source has a portrait or photograph of the person, this is indicated by the abbreviation *[port]* after the source code.

Daniel, C William 1925- *WhoCan 84 [port]*

A list of the works indexed in *BGMI 1992*, and the codes used to refer to them, is printed on the endsheets. Complete bibliographic citations to the titles indexed follow this introduction.

Editorial Practices

All names in an indexed work are included in *BGMI*. There is no need to consult the work itself if the name being researched is not found, since it is editorial policy to index every name in a particular book.

Many source books differ in their method of alphabetizing names; therefore, some names may have an alphabetic position in a source book different from their position in this index. Names are alphabetized in *BGMI* word-by-word, with the exception of prefixes (Del, Mc, Mac, O', Van, etc.) which are not treated as separate words.

John, Terry
John-Sandy, Rene Emanuel
Johncock, Gordon

Delasa, Jose M
De las Heras, Gonzalo
Delavigne, Casimir
De La Warr, Earl

Names appear in *BGMI* exactly as they are listed in the source books; no attempt has been made to determine whether names with similar spellings and dates refer to the same individual. With a file consisting of millions of names, it is not possible to edit each name thoroughly and still publish on a timely basis. Therefore, several listings for the same individual may sometimes be found:

Bellman, Richard 1920- *ConAu 12NR*
Bellman, Richard 1920-1984 *ConAu 112*
Bellman, Richard E 1920- *WhoAm 84*
Bellman, Richard Ernest 1920- *WhoFrS 84*

Despite the variations in the form of the name, it is apparent that the same person is referred to in the above citations. The existence of such variations can be of importance to anyone attempting to determine biographical details about an individual.

In a very few cases, extremely long names have been shortened because of typesetting limitations. For example: Robertson, Alexander Thomas Parke Anthony Cecil would be shortened to:

Robertson, Alexander Thomas Parke A

It is believed that such editing will not affect the usefulness of individual entries.

Research Aids

Researchers will need to look under all possible listings for a name, especially in the cases of:

1. Names with prefixes or suffixes:

Angeles, Victoria De Los
De Los Angeles, Victoria
Los Angeles, Victoria De

2. Compound surnames which may be entered in sources under either part of the surname:

Garcia Lorca, Federico
Lorca, Federico Garcia

Benary-Isbert, Margot
Isbert, Margot Benary-

3. Chinese names which may be entered in sources in direct or inverted order:

Chiang, Kai-Shek
Kai-Shek, Chiang

Or which may be listed by the Pinyin spelling:

Hsiang, Chung-Hua
Xiang, Zhonghua

4. Names transliterated in the sources from non-Roman alphabets:

Amelko, Nikolai Nikolayevich
Amelko, Nikolay Nikolayevich
Amel'ko, Nikolay Nikolayevich

5. Pseudonyms, noms de plume, and stage names:

Clemens, Samuel Langhorne
Twain, Mark

Crosby, Bing
Crosby, Harry Lillis

6. Names which may be entered in the sources both under the full name and either initials or part of the name:

Eliot, T S
Eliot, Thomas Stearns

Welles, George Orson
Welles, Orson

All cross-references appearing in indexed publications have been retained in *BGMI*, but in the form of regular citations, e.g., *Morris, Julian SEE West, Morris* would appear in *BGMI* as *Morris, Julian* followed by the source code. No additional cross-references have been added.

Suggestions Are Welcome

Additional sources will be indexed in future publications as their availability and usefulness become known. The editor welcomes suggestions for additional works which could be indexed, or any other comments and suggestions.

Please see the chart on the next page for publication information on *BGMI* in its hardcover, microfiche, and on-line formats.

BGMI Corresponding Formats

The data base used to create *BGMI* and its updates is also available in a microfiche edition called *Bio-Base* and on-line through DIALOG Information Services, Inc., as *Biography Master Index (BMI).* The chart below outlines the relationships, in existing and future publications, between the *BGMI* hardcover annual updates and cumulations, and the microfiche and on-line formats.

<table>
<tr><th>YEAR OF PUBLICATION</th><th colspan="2">HARDCOVER</th><th>MICROFICHE</th><th>ON-LINE</th></tr>
<tr><td>1980-81</td><td colspan="2">Biography and Genealogy Master Index, 2nd ed.</td><td>Bio-Base, 2nd ed. (Superseded by 1984 Master Cumulation)</td><td rowspan="16">Entire data base is in DIALOG BMI File 287 (updated annually)</td></tr>
<tr><td>1982</td><td>BGMI 1981-82 Supplement</td><td rowspan="4">BGMI 1981-85 Cumulation</td><td></td></tr>
<tr><td>1983</td><td>BGMI 1983 Supplement</td><td>Bio-Base 1983 Supplement (Superseded by 1984 Master Cumulation)</td></tr>
<tr><td>1984</td><td>BGMI 1984 Supplement</td><td>Bio-Base 1984 Master Cumulation</td></tr>
<tr><td>1985</td><td>BGMI 1985</td><td>Bio-Base 1985</td></tr>
<tr><td>1986</td><td>BGMI 1986</td><td rowspan="5">BGMI 1986-90 Cumulation</td><td>Bio-Base 1985-86</td></tr>
<tr><td>1987</td><td>BGMI 1987</td><td>Bio-Base 1985-87</td></tr>
<tr><td>1988</td><td>BGMI 1988</td><td>Bio-Base 1985-88</td></tr>
<tr><td>1989</td><td>BGMI 1989</td><td>Bio-Base 1985-89</td></tr>
<tr><td>1990</td><td>BGMI 1990</td><td>Bio-Base 1990 Master Cumulation (Supersedes all previous editions)</td></tr>
<tr><td>1991</td><td>BGMI 1991</td><td rowspan="5">BGMI 1991-95 Cumulation</td><td>Bio-Base 1991</td></tr>
<tr><td>1992</td><td>BGMI 1992</td><td>Bio-Base 1991-92</td></tr>
<tr><td>1993</td><td>BGMI 1993</td><td>Bio-Base 1991-93</td></tr>
<tr><td>1994</td><td>BGMI 1994</td><td>Bio-Base 1991-94</td></tr>
<tr><td>1995</td><td>BGMI 1995</td><td>Bio-Base 1995 Master Cumulation</td></tr>
</table>

Bibliographic Key to Source Codes

Code	*Book Indexed*
AmLegL	*American Legislative Leaders, 1850-1910.* Edited by Charles F. Ritter and Jon L. Wakelyn. New York: Greenwood Press, 1989.
AnObit	*The Annual Obituary.* Chicago: St. James Press, 1990. ***AnObit 1988*** — *1988,* edited by Patricia Burgess, 1990. ***AnObit 1989*** — *1989,* edited by Deborah Andrews, 1990. Use thc "Alphabetical Index of Entrants" in each volume to locate biographies.
ArtLatA	*Art in Latin America: The Modern Era, 1820-1980.* By Dawn Ades. New Haven, Conn.: Yale University Press, 1989. Biographies are found in the Biographies Section which begins on page 338.
Au&Arts	*Authors & Artists for Young Adults.* Detroit: Gale Research, 1990-1991. ***Au&Arts 5*** — Volume 5, 1990 ***Au&Arts 6*** — Volume 6, 1991
AuBYP 90	*Authors of Books for Young People.* Third edition. By Martha E. Ward, et al. Metuchen, N.J.: Scarecrow Press, 1990.
Ballpl 90	*The Ballplayers: Baseball's Ultimate Biographical Reference.* Edited by Mike Shatzkin. New York: William Morrow and Co., 1990.
BestSel 90	*Bestsellers 90: Books and Authors in the News.* Detroit: Gale Research, 1991. ***BestSel 90-3*** — Issue 3; 1991 ***BestSel 90-4*** — Issue 4; 1991
BiDEWW	*A Biographical Dictionary of English Women Writers, 1580-1720.* By Maureen Bell, George Parfitt, and Simon Shepherd. Boston: G.K. Hall & Co., 1990.
BiDFrPL	*Biographical Dictionary of French Political Leaders since 1870.* Edited by David S. Bell, Douglas Johnson, and Peter Morris. New York: Simon & Schuster, 1990.
BiDWomA	*A Biographical Dictionary of Women Artists in Europe and America since 1850.* By Penny Dunford. Philadelphia: University of Pennsylvania Press, 1989.

BiDrAPA 89 *Biographical Directory: Fellows and Members of the American Psychiatric Association, 1989.* Washington, D.C.: American Psychiatric Association, 1989. Distributed by American Psychiatric Press, Washington, D.C.

BiDrUSE 89 *Biographical Directory of the United States Executive Branch, 1774-1989.* Edited by Robert Sobel. New York: Greenwood Press, 1990.

BioAmW *Biographies of American Women.* An annotated bibliography. By Patricia E. Sweeney. Santa Barbara, Calif.: ABC-Clio, 1990.

BioIn 16 *Biography Index.* A cumulative index to biographical material in books and magazines. Volume 16: September 1988-August 1990. New York: H.W. Wilson Co., 1990.

BlkAmsC *Black Americans in Congress, 1870-1989.* By Bruce A. Ragsdale and Joel D. Treese. Washington: U.S. Government Printing Office, 1990.

ChlLR *Children's Literature Review.* Excerpts from reviews, criticism, and commentary on books for children and young people. Detroit: Gale Research, 1990-1991.

ChlLR 21	Volume 21, 1990
ChlLR 22	Volume 22, 1991
ChlLR 23	Volume 23, 1991

ClMLC *Classical and Medieval Literature Criticism.* Excerpts from criticism of the works of world authors from classical antiquity through the fourteenth century, from the first appraisals to current evaluations. Detroit: Gale Research, 1991.

ClMLC 5	Volume 5, 1991
ClMLC 6	Volume 6, 1991

ConAmBL *Contemporary American Business Leaders.* A biographical dictionary. By John N. Ingham and Lynne B. Feldman. New York: Greenwood Press, 1990

Use the Index to locate biographies.

ConAu *Contemporary Authors.* A bio-bibliographical guide to current writers in fiction, general nonfiction, poetry, journalism, drama, motion pictures, television, and other fields. Detroit: Gale Research, 1990-1991.

ConAu 129	Volume 129, 1990
ConAu 130	Volume 130, 1990
ConAu 131	Volume 131, 1991
ConAu 132	Volume 132, 1991

ConAu AS *Contemporary Authors, Autobiography Series.* Detroit: Gale Research, 1990-1991.

ConAu 12AS	Volume 12, 1990
ConAu 13AS	Volume 13, 1991

ConAu NR *Contemporary Authors, New Revision Series.* A bio-bibliographical guide to current writers in fiction, general nonfiction, poetry, journalism, drama, motion pictures, television, and other fields. Detroit: Gale Research, 1990-1991.

ConAu 30NR	Volume 30, 1990
ConAu 31NR	Volume 31, 1990
ConAu 32NR	Volume 32, 1991
ConAu 33NR	Volume 33, 1991

ConDes 90 *Contemporary Designers.* Second edition. Edited by Colin Naylor. Chicago: St. James Press, 1990.

ConLC *Contemporary Literary Criticism.* Excerpts from criticism of the works of today's novelists, poets, playwrights, short story writers, scriptwriters, and other creative writers. Detroit: Gale Research, 1990-1991.

ConLC 59	Volume 59: Yearbook 1989; 1990
ConLC 60	Volume 60, 1990
ConLC 61	Volume 61, 1990
ConLC 62	Volume 62, 1991
ConLC 63	Volume 63, 1991
ConLC 64	Volume 64, 1991

Use the "Cumulative Author Index" to locate entries in the Yearbook volume.

ConMus *Contemporary Musicians: Profiles of the People in Music.* Detroit: Gale Research, 1991.

ConMus 4	Volume 4, 1991
ConMus 5	Volume 5, 1991

ConTFT 8 *Contemporary Theatre, Film, and Television.* A biographical guide featuring performers, directors, writers, producers, designers, managers, choreographers, technicians, composers, executives, dancers, and critics in the United States and Great Britain. Volume 8. Detroit: Gale Research, 1990.

CurBio 90 *Current Biography Yearbook, 1990.* Edited by Charles Moritz. New York: H.W. Wilson Co., 1991.

The Obituaries section, indicated in this index by the code *N,* begins on page 643.

DcAfAmP *Dictionary of Afro-American Performers.* 78 RPM and cylinder recordings of opera, choral music, and song, c. 1900-1949. By Patricia Turner. New York: Garland Publishing, 1990.

DcCanB 12 *Dictionary of Canadian Biography. Volume XII: 1891 to 1900.* Edited by Francess G. Halpenny. Toronto: University of Toronto Press, 1990.

DcLB *Dictionary of Literary Biography.* Detroit: Gale Research, 1990-1991.

DcLB 92	Volume 92: *Canadian Writers, 1890-1920.* Edited by W. H. New, 1990.
DcLB 93	Volume 93: *British Romantic Poets, 1789-1832.* First Series. Edited by John R. Greenfield, 1990.
DcLB 94	Volume 94: *German Writers in the Age of Goethe: Sturm und Drang to Classicism.* Edited by James Hardin and Christoph E. Schweitzer, 1990.
DcLB 95	Volume 95: *Eighteenth-Century British Poets.* First series. Edited by John Sitter, 1990.
DcLB 96	Volume 96: *British Romantic Poets, 1789-1832.* Second series. Edited by John R. Greenfield, 1990.
DcLB 97	Volume 97: *German Writers from the*

Enlightenment to Sturm und Drang, 1720-1764. Edited by James Hardin and Christoph E. Schweitzer, 1990.

DcLB 98	Volume 98: *Modern British Essayists.* First series. Edited by Robert Beum, 1990.
DcLB 99	Volume 99: *Canadian Writers before 1890.* Edited by W. H. New, 1990.
DcLB 100	Volume 100: *Modern British Essayists.* Second series. Edited by Robert Beum, 1990.
DcLB 101	Volume 101: *British Prose Writers, 1660-1800.* First series. Edited by Donald T. Siebert, 1991.
DcLB 102	Volume 102: *American Short-Story Writers, 1910-1945.* Second series. Edited by Bobby Ellen Kimbel, 1991.
DcLB 103	Volume 103: *American Literary Biographers.* First series. Edited by Steven Serafin, 1991.
DcLB 104	Volume 104: *British Prose Writers, 1660-1800.* Second series. Edited by Donald T. Siebert, 1991.
DcLB 105	Volume 105: *American Poets since World War II.* Second series. Edited by R.S. Gwynn, 1991.

DcLB DS8 *Dictionary of Literary Biography, Documentary Series: An Illustrated Chronicle.* Volume 8, The Black Aesthetic Movement. Edited by Jeffrey Louis Decker. Detroit: Gale Research, 1991.

Use the "Cumulative Index" to locate entries.

DcLB Y90 *Dictionary of Literary Biography, Yearbook: 1990.* Detroit: Gale Research, 1991.

DcLB Y90	The Nobel Prize entry begins on page 3.
DcLB Y90N	The Obituaries section begins on page 206.

DcNaB 1981 *Dictionary of National Biography, 1981-1985.* With an index covering the years 1901-1985 in one alphabetical series. Edited by Lord Blake and C.S. Nicholls. Oxford: Oxford University Press, 1990.

DcScanL *Dictionary of Scandinavian Literature.* Edited by Virpi Zuck. New York: Greenwood Press, 1990.

DcScB S2 *Dictionary of Scientific Biography.* Supplement II, vol. 17-18. Edited by Frederic L. Holmes. New York: Charles Scribner's Sons, 1990.

Volume 16, an index, contains no biographies.

DrBlPA 90 *Directory of Blacks in the Performing Arts.* Second edition. By Edward Mapp. Metuchen, N.J.: Scarecrow Press, 1990.

EarBlAP *Early Black American Playwrights and Dramatic Writers.* A biographical directory and catalog of plays, films, and broadcasting scripts. By Bernard L. Peterson, Jr. New York: Greenwood Press, 1990.

EncABHB *Encyclopedia of American Business History and Biography.* New York: Facts on File, 1989, 1990.

EncABHB 4	*The Automobile Industry, 1896-1920.* Edited by George S. May, 1990.
EncABHB 5	*The Automobile Industry, 1920-1980.* Edited by George S. May, 1989.
EncABHB 6	*Banking and Finance to 1913.* Edited by Larry Schweikart, 1990.
EncABHB 7	*Banking and Finance, 1913-1989.* Edited by Larry Schweikart, 1990.

For some volumes, use the index to locate biographies.

EncACom *The Encyclopedia of American Comics.* Edited by Ron Goulart. New York: Facts on File, 1990.

EncAL *Encyclopedia of the American Left.* Edited by Mari Jo Buhle, Paul Buhle, and Dan Georgakas. Garland Reference Library of the Social Sciences, vol. 50. New York: Garland Publishing, 1990.

Cross-references appear before other entries with similar surnames.

EncCRAm *The Encyclopedia of Colonial and Revolutionary America.* Edited by John Mack Faragher. New York: Facts on File, 1990.

EncCoWW *An Encyclopedia of Continental Women Writers.* Two volumes. Edited by Katharina M. Wilson. Garland Reference Library of the Humanities, vol. 698. New York: Garland Publishing, 1991.

EncJap *Encyclopedia of Japan: Japanese History and Culture, from Abacus to Zori.* By Dorothy Perkins. New York: Facts on File, 1991.

EncO&P 3 *Encyclopedia of Occultism & Parapsychology.* A compendium of information on the occult sciences, magic, demonology, superstitions, spiritism, mysticism, metaphysics, psychical science, and parapsychology, with biographical and bibliographical notes and comprehensive indexes. Third edition. Two volumes. Edited by Leslie Shepard. Detroit: Gale Research, 1991.

EncPaPR 91 *The Encyclopedia of Parapsychology and Psychical Research.* By Arthur S. Berger and Joyce Berger. New York: Paragon House, 1991.

EncPR&S 89 *The Encyclopedia of Pop, Rock & Soul.* Revised edition. By Irwin Stambler. New York: St. Martin's Press, 1989.

EuWr *European Writers: The Twentieth Century.* Edited by George Stade. New York: Charles Scribner's Sons, 1990 .

EuWr 12	Volume 12, 1990
EuWr 13	Volume 13, 1990

Use the "List of Subjects" at the front of each volume to locate biographies.

FemiCLE *The Feminist Companion to Literature in English.* Women writers from the Middle Ages to the Present. By Virginia Blain, Patricia Clements, and Isobel Grundy. New Haven, Conn.: Yale University Press, 1990.

HarlReB *Harlem Renaissance and Beyond.* Literary biographies of 100 black women writers, 1900-1945. By Lorraine Elena Roses and Ruth Elizabeth Randolph. Boston: G. K. Hall & Co., 1990.

HispWr 90 *Hispanic Writers.* A selection of sketches from *Contemporary Authors.* Detroit: Gale Research, 1991.

IntDcAA 90 *International Dictionary of Art and Artists: Artists.* Edited by James Vinson. Chicago: St. James Press, 1990.

IntWWM 90 *International Who's Who in Music and Musicians' Directory.* 12th edition, 1990-1991. Cambridge: International Who's Who in Music, 1990. Distributed by Taylor and Francis International Publication Services, Bristol, Pa.

IntvSpW *Interviews with Spanish Writers.* By Marie-Lise Gazarian Gautier. Elmwood Park, Ill.: Dalkey Archive Press, 1991.

LiHiK *A Literary History of Kentucky.* By William S. Ward. Knoxville, Tenn.: University of Tennessee Press, 1988.

Use the Index to locate biographies.

LitC *Literature Criticism from 1400 to 1800.* Excerpts from criticism of the works of fifteenth-, sixteenth-, seventeenth-, and eighteenth-century novelists, poets, playwrights, philosophers, and other creative writers, from the first published critical appraisals to current evaluations. Detroit: Gale Research, 1990-1991.

LitC 13	Volume 13, 1990
LitC 14	Volume 14, 1991
LitC 15	Volume 15, 1991

MajTwCW *Major 20th-Century Writers.* A selection of sketches from *Contemporary Authors.* Four volumes. Detroit: Gale Research, 1991.

ModArCr 1 *Modern Arts Criticism.* A biographical and critical guide to painters, sculptors, photographers, and architects from the beginning of the modern era to the present. Vol. 1. Detroit: Gale Research, 1991.

MusmAFA *Museum of American Folk Art Encyclopedia of Twentieth-Century American Folk Art and Artists.* By Chuck and Jan Rosenak. New York: Abbeville Press, 1990.

NewAgE 90 *New Age Encyclopedia.* A guide to the beliefs, concepts, terms, people, and organizations that make up the New Global Movement toward spritual development, health and healing, higher consciousness, and related subjects. First edition. Detroit: Gale Research, 1990.

NewAgMG *The New Age Music Guide.* Profiles and recordings of 500 top New Age musicians. By Patti Jean Birosik. New York: Collier Books, Macmillan Publishing Co., 1989.

NewYTBS 90 *The New York Times Biographical Service.* A compilation of current biographical information of general interest. Volume 21, Numbers 1-12. Ann Arbor, Mich.: University Microfilms International, 1990.

Use the annual Index to locate biographies.

News — *Newsmakers: The People behind Today's Headlines.* Detroit: Gale Research, 1990-1991.

News 90-3	90, Issue 3; 1990
News 90	90 Cumulation; 1990
News 91-1	91, Issue 1; 1990
News 91-2	91, Issue 2; 1991

Use the "Cumulative Newsmaker Index" to locate entries in each quarterly edition. Biographies in each quarterly issue can also be located in the annual cumulation.

NinCLC — *Nineteenth-Century Literature Criticism.* Excerpts from criticism of the works of novelists, poets, playwrights, short story writers, philosophers, and other creative writers who died between 1800 and 1899, from the first published critical appraisals to current evaluations. Detroit: Gale Research, 1990-1991.

NinCLC 27	Volume 27, 1990
NinCLC 29	Volume 29, 1991
NinCLC 30	Volume 30, 1991

Volume 28 contains no biographies.

NotWoAT — *Notable Women in the American Theatre: A Biographical Dictionary.* Edited by Alice M. Robinson, Vera Mowry Roberts, and Milly S. Barranger. New York: Greenwood Press, 1989.

ODwPR 91 — *O'Dwyer's Directory of Public Relations Executives, 1991.* Seventh edition. Edited by Jack O'Dwyer. New York: J.R. O'Dwyer Co., 1990.

OxCCanT — *The Oxford Companion to Canadian Theatre.* Edited by Eugene Benson and L.W. Conolly. Toronto: Oxford University Press, 1989.

OxCPMus — *The Oxford Companion to Popular Music.* By Peter Gammond. Oxford: Oxford University Press, 1991.

PenDiDA 89 — *The Penguin Dictionary of Decorative Arts.* Revised edition. By John Fleming and Hugh Honour. London: Viking, 1989.

PenDiMP — *The Penguin Dictionary of Musical Performers.* A biographical guide to significant interpreters of classical music - singers, solo instrumentalists, conductors, orchestras, and string quartets - ranging from the seventeenth century to the present day. By Arthur Jacobs. London: Viking, 1990.

Biographies located in the "Index of Composers," indicated in this index by the code *A,* begin on page 239.

PoeCrit — *Poetry Criticism.* Excerpts from criticism of the works of the most significant and widely studied poets of world literature. Detroit: Gale Research, 1991.

PoeCrit 1	Volume 1, 1991
PoeCrit 2	Volume 2, 1991

PolLCME — *Political Leaders of the Contemporary Middle East and North Africa.* A biographical dictionary. Edited by Bernard Reich. New York: Greenwood Press, 1990.

RGTwCSF *Reader's Guide to Twentieth-Century Science Fiction.* Compiled and edited by Marilyn P. Fletcher. Chicago: American Library Association, 1989.

ShSCr *Short Story Criticism.* Excerpts from criticism of the works of short fiction writers. Detroit: Gale Research, 1990-1991.

ShSCr 6	Volume 6, 1990
ShSCr 7	Volume 7, 1991

SmATA *Something about the Author.* Facts and pictures about authors and illustrators of books for young people. Detroit: Gale Research, 1990-1991.

SmATA 60	Volume 60, 1990
SmATA 61	Volume 61, 1990
SmATA 62	Volume 62, 1990
SmATA 63	Volume 63, 1991
SmATA 64	Volume 64, 1991

SmATA AS *Something about the Author, Autobiography Series.* Detroit: Gale Research, 1991.

SmATA 11AS	Volume 11, 1991
SmATA 12AS	Volume 12, 1991

SmATA X This code refers to pseudonym entries which appear only as cross-references in the cumulative index to *Something about the Author.*

SpyFic *Spy Fiction: A Connoisseur's Guide.* By Donald McCormick and Katy Fletcher. New York: Facts on File, 1990.

St&PR 91 *Standard & Poor's Register of Corporations, Directors and Executives, 1991.* New York: Standard & Poor's Corp., 1991.

St&PR 91	Volume 2: *Directors and Executives.*
St&PR 91N	Obituary section begins on page 901 of Volume 3.

TwCCr&M 91 *Twentieth-Century Crime and Mystery Writers.* Third edition. Edited by Lesley Henderson. Chicago: St. James Press, 1991.

The "Nineteenth-Century Writers" section, indicated in this index by the code *A,* begins on page 1121. The "Foreign-Language Writers" section, indicated in this index by the code *B,* begins on page 1129.

TwCLC *Twentieth-Century Literary Criticism.* Excerpts from criticism of the works of novelists, poets, playwrights, short story writers, and other creative writers who died between 1900 and 1960, from the first published critical appraisals to current evaluations. Detroit: Gale Research, 1991.

TwCLC 37	Volume 37, 1991
TwCLC 39	Volume 39, 1991
TwCLC 40	Volume 40, 1991

Volume 38 contains no biographies.

WhNaAH *Who Was Who in Native American History.* Indians and non-Indians from early contacts through 1900. By Carl Waldman. New York: Facts on File, 1990.

WhoAm 90 *Who's Who in America.* 46th edition, 1990-1991. Two volumes. Wilmette, Ill.: Marquis Who's Who, 1990.

WhoAmA 91 *Who's Who in American Art.* 19th edition, 1991-1992. New Providence, N.J.: R.R. Bowker, 1990.

The Necrology, indicated in this index by the code *N,* begins on page 1387.

WhoAmW 91 *Who's Who of American Women.* 17th edition, 1991-1992. Wilmette, Ill.: Marquis Who's Who, 1991.

WhoE 91 *Who's Who in the East.* 23rd edition, 1991-1992. Wilmette, Ill.: Marquis Who's Who, 1990.

WhoEmL 91 *Who's Who of Emerging Leaders in America.* Third edition, 1991-1992. Wilmette, Ill.: Marquis Who's Who, 1991.

WhoHisp 91 *Who's Who among Hispanic Americans, 1991-92.* First edition. Detroit: Gale Research, 1991.

The Obituaries, indicated in this index by the code *N,* begin on page 423.

WhoNeCM *Who's Who in New Country Music.* By Andrew Vaughan. New York: St. Martin's Press, 1989.

The Introduction, indicated in this index by the code *A,* begins on page 7. The "UK Country" section, indicated in this index by the code *B,* begins on page 115. The "Classic Country" section, indicated in this index by the code *C,* begins on page 119.

WhoSSW 91 *Who's Who in the South and Southwest.* 22nd edition, 1991-1992. Wilmette, Ill.: Marquis Who's Who, 1990.

WhoWor 91 *Who's Who in the World.* 10th edition, 1991-1992. Wilmette, Ill.: Marquis Who's Who, 1990.

WhoWrEP 89 *Who's Who in Writers, Editors & Poets.* United States & Canada, 1989-1990. Third edition. Edited by Curt Johnson. Highland Park, Ill.: December Press, 1989.

WomArch *Women in Architecture.* A contemporary perspective. By Clare Lorenz. New York: Rizzoli International Publications, 1990.

WomFie *Women in the Field.* America's pioneering women naturalists. By Marcia Myers Bonta. College Station, Tex.: Texas A & M University Press, 1991.

Use the Index to locate biographies.

WomWR *Women Who Ruled.* By Guida M. Jackson. Santa Barbara, Calif.: ABC-Clio, 1990.

WorAlBi *The World Almanac Biographical Dictionary.* By the editors of *The World Almanac.* New York: World Almanac, 1990.

WorAu 1980 *World Authors, 1980-1985.* Edited by Vineta Colby. Wilson Authors Series. New York: H.W. Wilson Co., 1991.

WrPh *Writers and Philosophers.* A sourcebook of philosophical influences on literature. By Edmund J. Thomas and Eugene G. Miller. New York: Greenwood Press, 1990.

The "Profiles of Philosophers" section, indicated in this index by the code *P,* begins on page 215.

BIOGRAPHY AND GENEALOGY MASTER INDEX 1992

A

A., Miss *EncPaPR 91*
A., Mrs. *EncPaPR 91*
A B, Orlando 1946- *WhoHisp 91*
A. E. 1867-1935 *BioIn 16*
a-g *EncCoWW*
A.P. *EncCoWW*
A.Z.I.N.S.O. *EncCoWW*
Aab, R.T. 1949- *St&PR 91*
Aaberg, Philip *NewAgMG*
Aaby, Andee Alesia 1955- *WhoSSW 91*
Aach, Allyn Jay 1933- *St&PR 91*
Aach, Herb 1923-1985 *WhoAmA 91N*
Aadahl, Jorg 1937- *WhoAm 90*
Aadland, Beverly *BioIn 16*
Aagaard, Earla Gardner *BiDrAPA 89*
Aagaard, George Nelson 1913- *WhoAm 90*
Aagaard, Stanley Anderson, II 1932- *WhoE 91*
Aagard, Todd Allen 1961- *WhoEmL 91*
Aagesen, Carl Arthur 1940- *BiDrAPA 89*
Aakalu, Geetha N 1949- *BiDrAPA 89*
Aaker, David A 1938- *ConAu 31NR*
Aaker, David Allen *WhoAm 90*
Aakesson, Lars-Olof 1948- *WhoWor 91*
Aakjaer, Jeppe 1866-1930 *DcScanL*
Aal, Katharyn Machan 1952- *WhoWrEP 89*
Aalseth, Jack E. 1932- *St&PR 91*
Aalseth, Jack Eldon 1932- *WhoAm 90, WhoSSW 91, WhoWor 91*
Aalto, Alvar 1898-1976 *BioIn 16, ConDes 90*
Aalto, Hugo Alvar 1898-1976 *WorAlBi*
Aalto, Hugo Alvar Henrik 1898-1976 *PenDiDA 89*
Aalund, Suzy 1932- *WhoAmA 91*
Aamodt, Roger Louis 1941- *WhoAm 90*
Aandahl, Fredrick 1919- *WhoE 91*
Aanderud, Stephen Allen 1948- *St&PR 91*
Aanstoos, Christopher Michael 1952- *WhoSSW 91*
Aanstoos, James Duffy 1951- *WhoSSW 91*
Aaquist Johansen, Svend 1948- *IntWWM 90*
Aardema, Verna 1911- *AuBYP 90*
Aare, Juhan *BioIn 16*
Aarestad, James Harrison 1924- *WhoE 91*
Aarestrup, Emil 1800-1856 *DcScanL*
Aarnio, Eero 1932- *ConDes 90*
Aaron, Allen Harold 1932- *WhoAm 90*
Aaron, Andrew Lewis 1953- *WhoEmL 91*
Aaron, Anna 1931- *SmATA X*
Aaron, Arnold 1930- *St&PR 91*
Aaron, Arthur Myron 1957- *WhoEmL 91*
Aaron, Benjamin 1915- *WhoAm 90*
Aaron, Bertram Donald 1922- *WhoE 91, WhoWor 91*
Aaron, Betsy 1938- *WhoAm 90*
Aaron, Chester 1923- *AuBYP 90, BioIn 16, SmATA 12AS [port]*
Aaron, Chloe Wellingham 1938- *WhoAmW 91*
Aaron, Daniel 1912- *WhoAm 90*
Aaron, David *SpyFic*
Aaron, Evalyn Keisler *WhoAmA 91*
Aaron, Evalyn Wilhelmina *WhoE 91*
Aaron, Friedlieb Leslie 1936- *WhoE 91*
Aaron, Hank 1934- *Ballpl 90 [port], BioIn 16*
Aaron, Harold *BioIn 16*
Aaron, Harry J *BiDrAPA 89*
Aaron, Henry 1934- *WhoAm 90, WorAlBi*
Aaron, Henry 1936- *ConAu 129*
Aaron, Henry Jacob 1936- *WhoAm 90, WhoE 91*
Aaron, Howard Berton 1939- *St&PR 91*
Aaron, Ira Edward 1919- *WhoAm 90*
Aaron, Jesse J. 1887-1979 *MusmAFA*
Aaron, M. Robert 1922- *WhoAm 90*
Aaron, Marcus, II 1929- *WhoAm 90*
Aaron, Merik Roy 1947- *WhoE 91*
Aaron, Neal C. 1940- *St&PR 91*
Aaron, Patricia J. 1947- *St&PR 91*
Aaron, Paul *BioIn 16*
Aaron, Richard *ODwPR 91*
Aaron, Richard James 1930- *St&PR 91*
Aaron, Robert Steven 1943- *BiDrAPA 89*
Aaron, Roy H. 1929- *St&PR 91*
Aaron, Roy Henry 1929- *WhoAm 90*
Aaron, Ruth *BiDrAPA 89*
Aaron, Shirley Mae 1935- *WhoAmW 91*
Aaron, Tommie 1939-1984 *Ballpl 90*
Aaron, Truman Elwood 1930- *St&PR 91*
Aarons, Edward S 1916-1975 *TwCCr&M 91*
Aarons, Edward Sidney 1916-1975 *SpyFic*
Aarons, George 1896-1980 *WhoAmA 91N*
Aarons, Lawrence *BioIn 16*
Aarons, Shelley Fox 1951- *BiDrAPA 89*
Aarons, Z Alexander 1918- *BiDrAPA 89*
Aarons-Holder, Charmaine Michele 1959- *WhoEmL 91*
Aaronson, Allen G. 1926- *St&PR 91*
Aaronson, Arthur Lee 1946- *WhoEmL 91*
Aaronson, Brenda Caryl 1938- *WhoAmW 91, WhoE 91*
Aaronson, David Ernest 1940- *WhoAm 90*
Aaronson, Herbert G 1927- *BiDrAPA 89*
Aaronson, Herbert Gerald 1927- *WhoE 91*
Aaronson, Howard Arnold, Jr. 1935- *St&PR 91*
Aaronson, Hubert Irving 1924- *WhoAm 90*
Aaronson, Irving 1895-1963 *OxCPMus*
Aaronson, Lawrence 1941- *St&PR 91*
Aaronson, Marc Arnold *BioIn 16*
Aaronson, Robert H. 1955- *St&PR 91*
Aaronson, Robert Jay 1942- *WhoAm 90*
Aaronson, Scott Tyler *BiDrAPA 89*
Aaronson, Stephen F. 1938- *St&PR 91*
Aaronson, Stuart J. 1944- *St&PR 91*
Aaronson, Victor Stephen 1941- *St&PR 91*
Aarsleff, Hans *WhoAm 90*
Aase, Don 1954- *Ballpl 90*
Aasen, Ivar Andreas 1813-1896 *DcScanL*
Aasen, Lawrence Obert 1922- *WhoAm 90, WhoE 91*
Aasen, Terry 1954- *WhoSSW 91*
Aaseng, Nathan 1953- *SmATA 12AS [port]*
Aaseng, Nathan 1956- *BioIn 16*
Aaslestad, Halvor Gunerius 1937- *WhoE 91*
Aastrup, Rondi Suzanne 1955- *WhoWrEP 89*
Abad, Carlos 1957- *WhoWor 91*
Abad, Gloria E Joco 1928- *BiDrAPA 89*
Abad, Lilia Sales *BiDrAPA 89*
Abad, Pacita 1946- *WhoAmA 91*
Abad, Rainerio Sion 1936- *WhoWor 91*
Abad, Raul Melo 1940- *WhoE 91*
Abad, Rosario Dalida 1936- *WhoAmW 91, WhoSSW 91*
Abad, Vicente 1937- *BiDrAPA 89*
Abad-Rico, Juan Manuel 1945- *WhoWor 91*
Abadi, Fritzie *WhoAmA 91*
Abadi, Fritzie 1915- *WhoAm 90*
Abadie, Francis Wade, Jr. 1953- *WhoSSW 91*
Abadie, Jean M. 1919- *WhoWor 91*
Abadie, Jeannette *EncO&P 3*
Abadie, Lloyd Joseph 1929- *St&PR 91*
Abadie, Marie-Jeanne 1933- *WhoE 91*
Abadie, Robelynn Hood 1950- *WhoEmL 91*
Abady, Samuel Aaron 1954- *WhoEmL 91*
Abajian, Henry Krikor 1909- *St&PR 91, WhoWor 91*
Abajian, Vincent V. 1922- *St&PR 91*
Abajian, Wendy Elisse 1955- *WhoAmW 91*
Abakanowicz, Magdalena *BioIn 16*
Abakanowicz, Magdalena 1930- *BiDWomA, WhoWor 91*
Abal Khail, Muhammad-Ali 1935- *WhoWor 91*
Abalkin, Leonid 1930- *WhoWor 91*
Aballi, Arturo Jose, Jr. 1944- *WhoHisp 91*
Abalos, Rosario M 1944- *BiDrAPA 89*
Aban, Jeffrey S. Derick Christopher 1954- *WhoWor 91*
Abany, Albert Charles 1921- *WhoAmA 91*
Abaquesne, Masseot *PenDiDA 89*
Abara, Candace DeVooght 1950- *WhoAmW 91*
Abaray, Raymond F. 1932- *St&PR 91*
Abarbanel, Judith Edna 1956- *WhoAmW 91, WhoEmL 91*
Abarbanell, Gayola Havens 1939- *WhoAmW 91, WhoWor 91*
Abarbanell, Lina 1880-1963 *OxCPMus*
Abarca de Bolea, Pedro Pablo 1718-1798 *BioIn 16*
Abare, Marion L. 1927- *ODwPR 91*
Abas, Maximilian 1934- *WhoWor 91*
Abas, Piet 1946- *WhoWor 91*
Abashidze, Irakliy Vissarionovich 1909- *WhoWor 91*
Abastillas, Benjamin F *BiDrAPA 89*
Abate, Frank J. 1928- *WhoE 91*
Abate, M. Andrew 1936- *St&PR 91*
Abayakoon, Cyrus D. F. 1912- *EncO&P 3*
Abazinge, Michael Dennis 1956- *WhoSSW 91*
ABBA *EncPR&S 89, OxCPMus*
Abba, Marta 1900-1988 *AnObit 1988, BioIn 16*
Abbadie, Michel 1951- *WhoWor 91*
Abbado, Claudio *BioIn 16*
Abbado, Claudio 1933- *IntWWM 90, PenDiMP, WhoAm 90, WhoWor 91, WorAlBi*
Abbado, Marcello 1926- *IntWWM 90, PenDiMP*
Abbagnaro, Louis Anthony 1942- *WhoE 91*
Abbas, Sheik *BioIn 16*
Abbas, Elizabeth Keutgen 1947- *WhoAmW 91*
Abbas, Ferhat 1899-1985 *PolLCME*
Abbas, Mahmoud Fouad 1931- *BiDrAPA 89*
Abbasi, Mohammad Bukhsh 1947- *WhoWor 91*
Abbasi, Tariq Afzal 1946- *BiDrAPA 89, WhoWor 91*
Abbassian, Mehrdad 1959- *BiDrAPA 89*
Abbate, Niccolo dell' 1509?-1571? *IntDcAA 90*
Abbate, Paul J. 1919- *WhoAm 90*
Abbate, Paul S 1884-1972 *WhoAmA 91N*
Abbati, Giuseppe 1836-1868 *BioIn 16*
Abbaticchio, Ed 1877-1957 *Ballpl 90*
Abbe, Charles L. 1928- *St&PR 91*
Abbe, Cleveland 1838-1916 *WorAlBi*
Abbe, Colman 1932- *WhoE 91*
Abbe, Elfriede Martha *WhoAm 90, WhoAmA 91*
Abbe, George Bancroft 1911- *WhoWrEP 89*
Abbell, Samuel 1925-1969 *WhoAmA 91N*
Abbema, Louise 1858-1927 *BiDWomA*
Abben, Peer 1916- *WhoAm 90*
Abbene, Michael 1936- *St&PR 91*
Abberley, John J. 1916- *WhoAm 90*
Abbert, Martin F 1936- *BiDrAPA 89*
Abbett, George W. 1900- *St&PR 91*
Abbett, J. Conrad 1927- *St&PR 91*
Abbett, Leon 1836-1894 *AmLegL*
Abbett, Robert Kennedy 1926- *WhoAmA 91*
Abbey, Arthur Newton 1935- *WhoAm 90*
Abbey, Edward 1927- *WhoWrEP 89*
Abbey, Edward 1927-1989 *AnObit 1989, BioIn 16, ConLC 59 [port], WorAu 1980 [port]*
Abbey, G. Marshall 1933- *St&PR 91*
Abbey, George Marshall 1933- *WhoAm 90*
Abbey, James Blades 1949- *WhoEmL 91*
Abbey, Kieran *TwCCr&M 91*
Abbey, Nancy Carroll 1939- *WhoAm 90*
Abbey, Richard S. 1950- *St&PR 91*
Abbey, Scott Gerson 1951- *WhoAm 90*
Abbey, Susan Elizabeth 1955- *BiDrAPA 89*
Abbey, Wallace W. *ODwPR 91*
Abbing, Justine *EncCoWW*
Abbo, Gordon Eugene 1948- *BiDrAPA 89*
Abbot, Edith *WhoAmA 91N*
Abbot, Eleanor Hallowell 1872-1958 *FemiCLE*
Abbot, Nicholas *BioIn 16*
Abbot, Quincy Sewall 1932- *WhoAm 90*
Abbot, William Wright 1922- *WhoAm 90*
Abbot, Willis John 1863-1934 *BioIn 16*
Abbott & Costello *Ballpl 90*
Abbott, Alvin Arthur 1928- *WhoE 91*
Abbott, Barbara Diane 1959- *WhoAmW 91*
Abbott, Barry A. 1950- *WhoEmL 91*
Abbott, Bellamy Priest 1913- *WhoSSW 91*
Abbott, Benjamin Edward, Jr. 1928- *WhoWor 91*
Abbott, Berenice 1898- *BioAmW, BioIn 16, WhoAm 90, WorAlBi*
Abbott, Betty Jane 1931- *WhoAmW 91*
Abbott, Brian C. 1941- *ODwPR 91*
Abbott, Bud 1895-1974 *WorAlBi*
Abbott, Carl John 1944- *WhoAm 90*
Abbott, Charles Favour, Jr. 1937- *WhoWor 91*
Abbott, Charles Homer 1909- *WhoAm 90*
Abbott, Charles Warren 1930- *WhoSSW 91*
Abbott, David Henry 1936- *WhoAm 90*
Abbott, David P 1863-1934 *EncO&P 3*
Abbott, David T. 1948- *WhoSSW 91*
Abbott, David Warren 1948- *BiDrAPA 89*
Abbott, Deyuos C., Jr. 1936- *St&PR 91*
Abbott, Diane *BioIn 16*
Abbott, Douglas Eugene 1934- *WhoAm 90*
Abbott, Dwayne Lamont 1959- *WhoEmL 91*

Abbott, Edith 1876-1957 *BioIn 16*
Abbott, Edward Leroy 1930- *St&PR 91, WhoAm 90, WhoSSW 91*
Abbott, Edwin Hunt 1941- *WhoAm 90*
Abbott, Emma 1850-1891 *BioAmW*
Abbott, Eric Symes 1906-1983 *DcNaB 1981*
Abbott, Ernest Monroe 1931- *WhoSSW 91*
Abbott, Forrest A. 1921- *St&PR 91*
Abbott, Frances Elizabeth Dowdle 1924- *WhoAmW 91*
Abbott, Frank Harry 1919- *WhoAm 90*
Abbott, Gayle Elizabeth 1954- *WhoEmL 91, WhoSSW 91*
Abbott, George 1887- *OxCPMus, WorAlBi*
Abbott, George Lindell 1941- *WhoE 91*
Abbott, Glenn 1951- *Ballpl 90*
Abbott, Grace 1878-1939 *BioIn 16, WorAlBi*
Abbott, Gregory *DrBlPA 90*
Abbott, Gregory B. 1948- *St&PR 91*
Abbott, Herschel Lee, Jr. 1941- *WhoAm 90*
Abbott, Isabella Aiona 1919- *WhoAm 90*
Abbott, Jacquelyn Meng 1951- *WhoEmL 91*
Abbott, James Ayre 1928- *WhoAm 90*
Abbott, James C. *BioIn 16*
Abbott, James Edward 1959- *WhoEmL 91*
Abbott, Jim *BioIn 16*
Abbott, Jim 1967- *Ballpl 90*
Abbott, Job 1845-1896 *DcCanB 12*
Abbott, John Adams 1902- *BiDrAPA 89*
Abbott, John B., Jr. 1956- *WhoWrEP 89*
Abbott, John Evans *WhoAmA 91N*
Abbott, John Joseph Caldwell 1821-1893 *DcCanB 12*
Abbott, John Sheldon 1926- *WhoAm 90*
Abbott, Joseph C. 1929- *St&PR 91*
Abbott, Keith George 1944- *WhoWrEP 89*
Abbott, Kenneth Wayne 1950- *WhoSSW 91, WhoWrEP 89*
Abbott, Laurence Frederick 1950- *WhoAm 90*
Abbott, Lee Kittredge 1947- *WhoWrEP 89*
Abbott, Lyman 1835-1922 *BioIn 16*
Abbott, Margaret *BiDEWW, FemiCLE*
Abbott, Mark Steven 1959- *WhoE 91*
Abbott, Mary Ann 1955- *WhoEmL 91*
Abbott, Mary Elaine 1922- *WhoAmW 91, WhoWor 91*
Abbott, Maude E. 1869-1940 *BioIn 16*
Abbott, Maxwell Todd 1946- *St&PR 91*
Abbott, Melanie Beth 1951- *WhoAmW 91*
Abbott, Muriel Macpherson *WhoAmW 91*
Abbott, Neil Gow Gratwick 1939- *WhoE 91*
Abbott, Philip 1924- *WhoAm 90*
Abbott, Preston Sargent 1922- *WhoAm 90*
Abbott, R Tucker 1919- *SmATA 61 [port]*
Abbott, Ralph E. 1940- *St&PR 91*
Abbott, Richard Conant 1946- *WhoEmL 91*
Abbott, Robert Alvin 1929- *WhoWrEP 89*
Abbott, Robert Carl 1955- *WhoEmL 91*
Abbott, Robert Dean 1946- *WhoAm 90, WhoEmL 91*
Abbott, Robert Lavell 1945- *WhoEmL 91*
Abbott, Robert S. 1868-1940 *BioIn 16*
Abbott, Robert Tucker 1919- *AuBYP 90, WhoAm 90, WhoWrEP 89*
Abbott, Rohn Dunseth 1943- *St&PR 91*
Abbott, Rosalie Boucher 1947- *WhoAmW 91*
Abbott, Sarah *AuBYP 90*
Abbott, Shelley 1954- *WhoAmW 91*
Abbott, Spencer 1877-1951 *Ballpl 90*
Abbott, Stanley E 1926- *BiDrAPA 89*
Abbott, Stanley Eugene 1942- *WhoAm 90*
Abbott, Steven Anthony 1949- *WhoEmL 91*
Abbott, Steven R. 1947- *St&PR 91*
Abbott, Susan Alicia 1947- *WhoAmW 91*
Abbott, Thomas Benjamin *WhoAm 90*
Abbott, Thomas C. 1926- *ODwPR 91*
Abbott, Vicky Lynn 1951- *WhoSSW 91*
Abbott, William Thomas 1938- *WhoSSW 91*
Abbott, William Wallace 1931- *St&PR 91*
Abbott, Wilton Robert 1916- *WhoAm 90*
Abbott, Woodrow Acton 1919- *WhoAm 90, WhoWor 91*
Abbott, Zane Allen, Jr. 1964- *WhoEmL 91*
Abbou, Pierre 1955- *WhoWor 91*
Abboud, A. Robert 1929- *BioIn 16, St&PR 91*
Abboud, Alfred Robert 1929- *WhoAm 90, WhoSSW 91*
Abboud, Francois Mitry 1931- *WhoAm 90*
Abboud, Ghassan Jason 1955- *WhoE 91*
Abboud, John Matthew 1942- *St&PR 91*
Abboud, Joseph 1950- *BioIn 16*
Abbrecht, Peter Herman 1930- *WhoAm 90*
Abbrederis, Dale Edward 1957- *WhoEmL 91*
Abbreschcia, Joseph Leonard 1936- *WhoAmA 91*
Abbruzzese, Carlo Enrico 1923- *WhoWor 91*
Abbruzzese, John Anthony, Jr. 1928- *WhoE 91*
Abbs, Peter Francis 1942- *WhoWor 91*
Abd Al-Aziz Ibn Saud 1881-1953 *PolLCME*
Abdalian, Arbak Arshak 1920- *WhoAm 90*
Abdalla, Lawrence Hamadi 1954- *WhoEmL 91*
Abdallah 1882-1951 *BioIn 16*
Abdallah Al-Salim Al-Sabah 1895-1965 *PolLCME*
Abdallah, Mahmoud M. 1948- *St&PR 91*
Abdel-Ghany, Mohamed 1940- *WhoAm 90*
Abdel-Hamid, Tarek Kamal 1950- *WhoEmL 91*
Abdel Kader, Hamdy Abdel Aziz 1933- *WhoWor 91*
Abdel-Khalik, Ahmed Rashad 1940- *WhoAm 90*
Abdel-Khalik, Said Ibrahim 1948- *WhoAm 90*
Abdel Kuddous, Ihsan *NewYTBS 90*
Abdel-Latif, A. Ismail 1944- *WhoE 91*
Abdel Meguid, Ahmed Esmat 1923- *WhoWor 91*
Abdel-Quddous, Ihsan 1920?-1990 *ConAu 130*
Abdel-Rahim, Gamal 1924- *IntWWM 90*
Abdel-Rahman, Aisha *WhoWor 91*
Abdela, Angelo Solomon 1942- *St&PR 91, WhoAm 90*
Abdelazys *EncO&P 3*
Abdelhak, Sherif Samy 1946- *WhoAm 90*
Abdelhamid, Mohamed Salah 1944- *St&PR 91*
Abdell, Douglas 1947- *WhoAmA 91*
Abdella, Joseph James 1935- *St&PR 91*
Abdellah, Faye Glenn 1919- *WhoAm 90, WhoAmW 91*
Abdelmalek, Ezzat Tadros *BiDrAPA 89*
Abdelnour, Frederick C. *BioIn 16*
Abdelnour, Ziad Khalil 1961- *WhoE 91, WhoEmL 91*
Abdelrahman, Talaat Ahmad Mohammad 1940- *WhoE 91*
Abderholden, Susan 1954- *WhoAmW 91*
Abdnor, James 1923- *WhoAm 90*
Abdo, Beverly Virginia 1954- *WhoAmW 91*
Abdo, E.J. 1912- *St&PR 91*
Abdo, Joseph T. 1920- *St&PR 91*
Abdo, Lynda Lee 1955- *WhoEmL 91*
Abdoo, Angela Fontana 1941- *WhoAmW 91*
Abdou, Richard A. 1944- *St&PR 91*
Abdou, Fathy Amin 1934- *BiDrAPA 89*
Abdou, Ikram Escandar 1948- *WhoSSW 91*
Abdou, Nabih I. 1934- *WhoAm 90*
Abdul Latif *EncPaPR 91*
Abdul, Paula *BioIn 16*
Abdul, Paula 1962- *News 90 [port], -90-3 [port]*
Abdul, Paula 1963?- *WorAlBi*
Abdul, Raoul 1929- *BioIn 16, DrBlPA 90*
Abdul-Ghani, Abdul-Aziz 1939- *WhoWor 91*
Abdul-Hadi, Mahdi 1944- *WhoWor 91*
Abdul Halim Mu'adzam Shah, Ibni 1927- *WhoWor 91*
Abdul-Jabbar, Kareem 1947- *BioIn 16, WhoAm 90, WorAlBi*
Abdul-Malik, Ahmed 1927- *IntWWM 90*
Abduljaami, John 1941- *MusmAFA*
Abdulla, Amina *BiDrAPA 89*
Abdulla, Elizabeth Carver 1941- *WhoSSW 91*
Abdullah Badawi 1939- *WhoWor 91*
Abdullah Bin Mohd Salleh, Tan Sri 1926- *WhoWor 91*
Abdullah Ibn Hussein 1882-1951 *PolLCME*
Abdullah Ibrahim *BioIn 16*
Abdullah, King of Jordan 1882-1951 *BioIn 16*
Abdullah, Edythe Mahasin 1953- *WhoSSW 91*
Abdullah, Mena 1930- *FemiCLE*
Abdullah, Syed *BiDrAPA 89*
Abdullah, Syed 1928- *WhoE 91*
Abdullah, Syed Mohammad *WhoSSW 91*
Abdurahman, Abdullah *BioIn 16*
Abdus Salam 1926- *BioIn 16*
Abdy, Maria 1797?-1867 *FemiCLE*
Abe Kobo 1924- *EncJap*
Abe Masahiro 1819-1857 *EncJap*
Abe, George Y *BiDrAPA 89*
Abe, Kobo 1924- *BioIn 16, MajTwCW, WhoWor 91*
Abe, Margherita C 1944- *BiDrAPA 89*
Abe, Shintaro 1924- *WhoWor 91*
Abe, Yuzuru 1916-1990 *BioIn 16*
Abed, Ramona Panaque 1926- *BiDrAPA 89*
Abedi, Jafar Mehdi 1946- *WhoWor 91*
Abegg, Elisabeth 1882- *BioIn 16*
Abegg, Martin G. 1925- *WhoAm 90*
Abegg, Sharon 1960- *BiDrAPA 89*
Abegglen, Ricki Lee 1960- *WhoEmL 91*
Abejuela, Reynaldo R *BiDrAPA 89*
Abejuro, Romeo Molo *BiDrAPA 89*
Abel, Alan *BioIn 16*
Abel, Allan Bernard 1924- *WhoAm 90*
Abel, Andrew Bruce 1952- *WhoE 91*
Abel, Arend Jesse 1960- *WhoEmL 91*
Abel, Brent Maxwell 1916- *WhoAm 90*
Abel, Christian Ferdinand 1682-1761 *PenDiMP*
Abel, Colin Anthony 1959- *WhoWor 91*
Abel, David 1922- *BiDrAPA 89*
Abel, David Robert 1960- *BiDrAPA 89*
Abel, Elie *BioIn 16*
Abel, Elie 1920- *WhoAm 90*
Abel, Ernest Lawrence 1943- *WhoWrEP 89*
Abel, Florence Catherine Harris 1941- *WhoAmW 91*
Abel, Francis Lee 1931- *WhoAm 90*
Abel, Fred Herman 1936- *WhoE 91*
Abel, Frederick Augustus 1827-1902 *WorAlBi*
Abel, Gene Gordon 1939- *BiDrAPA 89*
Abel, Gene Paul 1941- *WhoWor 91*
Abel, Georgie Lee *BioIn 16*
Abel, Harold 1926- *WhoAm 90*
Abel, Harry A. 1945- *WhoSSW 91*
Abel, I. W. 1908-1987 *BioIn 16, WorAlBi*
Abel, Iorwith Wilbur 1908-1987 *BioIn 16*
Abel, James Joseph 1946- *St&PR 91*
Abel, John 1947- *St&PR 91*
Abel, Mark Martin 1960- *St&PR 91*
Abel, Michael L. 1952- *WhoEmL 91, WhoWor 91*
Abel, Myer 1904- *WhoAmA 91N*
Abel, Nancy S. *St&PR 91*
Abel, Ray 1914- *WhoAmA 91*
Abel, Reuben 1911- *WhoAm 90*
Abel, Richard 1941- *ConAu 129*
Abel, Richard Bruce 1947- *WhoEmL 91*
Abel, Richard L. 1941- *ConAu 131*
Abel, Robert, Jr. 1943- *WhoAm 90, WhoWor 91*
Abel, Robert Allen 1958- *WhoEmL 91*
Abel, Robert Berger 1926- *WhoAm 90*
Abel, Robert Halsall 1941- *WhoWrEP 89*
Abel, Rudolf 1902?-1971 *WorAlBi*
Abel, Rudolph 1936- *St&PR 91*
Abel, Willard Edward 1906- *WhoAm 90*
Abel, William Luther 1942- *St&PR 91*
Abel-Christian, Stacey Lynn 1960- *WhoEmL 91*
Abel-Horowitz, H Jay 1949- *BiDrAPA 89*
Abela Fitzpatrick, Joseph 1945- *WhoWor 91*
Abelairas, Ariel Jorge 1949- *WhoSSW 91*
Abelard, Pierre 1079?-1142 *WorAlBi*
Abele, Henry Byrne *BiDrAPA 89*
Abele, Homer E. 1916- *WhoAm 90, WhoWor 91*
Abele, Robert Christopher 1958- *WhoEmL 91*
Abeles, Charles Calvert 1929- *WhoAm 90*
Abeles, Francine *WhoAmW 91*
Abeles, James David 1916- *WhoAm 90*
Abeles, Joseph Charles 1915- *St&PR 91, WhoAm 90*
Abeles, Kelly Ann 1961- *WhoEmL 91*
Abeles, Kim Victoria 1952- *WhoAmA 91*
Abeles, Norman 1928- *WhoAm 90*
Abeles, Robert H. *BioIn 16*
Abeles, Robert Heinz 1926- *WhoAm 90*
Abeles, Sigmund 1934- *WhoAmA 91*
Abeles, Sigmund M. 1934- *WhoAm 90, WhoE 91*
Abeles, Walter *BiDrAPA 89*
Abelin, Ernst Leo 1933- *BiDrAPA 89*
Abelin, Graciela E *BiDrAPA 89*
Abelita, Gil 1950- *BiDrAPA 89*
Abelite, Jahnis John 1950- *WhoEmL 91*
Abell, Creed W. *WhoAm 90*
Abell, David Robert 1934- *WhoAm 90*
Abell, Erwin Marshall 1962- *WhoSSW 91*
Abell, Ferdinand A. 1833-1913 *Ballpl 90*
Abell, George 1904-1989 *AnObit 1989*
Abell, Jerrold J. 1934- *St&PR 91*
Abell, Kjeld 1901-1961 *DcScanL*
Abell, Lawrence Carlisle 1941- *WhoAm 90*
Abell, Millicent Demmin 1934- *WhoAm 90, WhoAmW 91*
Abell, Murray Richardson 1920- *WhoAm 90*
Abell, Paul Irving 1923- *WhoAm 90*
Abell, Richard Bender 1943- *WhoAm 90, WhoE 91*
Abell, Richard G *BiDrAPA 89*
Abell, Richard Gurley 1904- *WhoE 91*
Abell, Thomas Henry 1909- *WhoAm 90*
Abell, Walter Halsey 1897-1956 *WhoAmA 91N*
Abell, William A 1935- *BiDrAPA 89*
Abell, William Frederick 1947- *St&PR 91*
Abella, Marisela Carlota 1943- *WhoAmW 91*
Abeloff, Abram Joseph 1900- *WhoAm 90*
Abelov, Stephen L. 1923- *St&PR 91*
Abelov, Stephen Lawrence 1923- *WhoAm 90, WhoWor 91*
Abels, Bruce Arthur 1953- *WhoEmL 91*
Abels, Harriette Sheffer 1926- *BioIn 16*
Abels, Joann Carla 1952- *WhoEmL 91*
Abels, Mark E. 1951- *ODwPR 91*
Abelshauser, Werner Ludwig 1944- *WhoWor 91*
Abelson, Alan 1925- *WhoAm 90*
Abelson, Ann 1918- *SmATA X*
Abelson, Harold H. 1904-1989 *BioIn 16*
Abelson, Herbert Traub 1941- *WhoAm 90*
Abelson, Jack Irwin 1946- *St&PR 91*
Abelson, James Lawrence 1952- *BiDrAPA 89*
Abelson, John Norman 1938- *WhoAm 90*
Abelson, Kassel Elijah 1924- *BioIn 16*
Abelson, Max Moss 1912- *BiDrAPA 89*
Abelson, Philip Hauge 1913- *WhoAm 90*
Abelson, Raziel Alter 1921- *WhoAm 90*
Abelson, Robert Paul 1928- *WhoAm 90*
Abelt, Ralph W. 1929- *St&PR 91*
Abelt, Ralph William 1929- *WhoAm 90*
Abely, Joseph F. 1929- *St&PR 91*
Aben-Ragel 4--?- *EncO&P 3*
Abend, Sander M 1932- *BiDrAPA 89*
Abend, Sheldon 1929- *WhoWrEP 89*
Abendana, Isaac *BioIn 16*
Abendana, Jacob *BioIn 16*
Abendroth, Hermann 1883-1956 *PenDiMP*
Abendroth, Jo Jewell 1954- *WhoEmL 91*
Abenoja, Febe Agumo 1937- *WhoWor 91*
Aber, Al 1927- *Ballpl 90*
Aber, Geoffrey Michael 1928- *WhoWor 91*
Aber, Ita 1932- *WhoAmA 91*
Aber, John David 1949- *WhoE 91*
Aber, Marvin 1936- *St&PR 91*
Aber, Stanley Irwin 1939- *WhoE 91*
Aber, William Thomas 1935- *St&PR 91*
Aber-Count, Alice Lawson 1916- *IntWWM 90*
Aberbach, Joel D 1940- *WhoWrEP 89*
Aberbach, Robert Joseph 1939- *WhoE 91*
Aberconway, Charles Melville McLaren 1913- *WhoWor 91*
Abercrombie, Beverly *WhoE 91*
Abercrombie, George Forbes 1935- *WhoWor 91*
Abercrombie, James 1706-1781 *WorAlBi*
Abercrombie, John Ralph Alexander Giles 1949- *IntWWM 90*
Abercrombie, Josephine *BioIn 16*
Abercrombie, Stanley 1935- *WhoAm 90*
Abercrombie, Virginia Townsend 1927- *WhoAmW 91*
Abercromby, Ralph 1734-1801 *WorAlBi*
Abere, Andrew Evan 1961- *WhoAm 90, WhoEmL 91*
Abergavenny, Frances *BiDEWW, FemiCLE*
Aberle, Charles D. 1929- *St&PR 91*
Aberle, David Friend 1918- *WhoAm 90*
Aberle, George Frederick 1929- *WhoE 91*
Abernathy, Alexander Guion 1947- *WhoSSW 91*
Abernathy, Barbara Eubanks 1963- *WhoAmW 91, WhoSSW 91*
Abernathy, Bobby Franklin 1933- *St&PR 91*
Abernathy, Charles C., Jr. 1934- *St&PR 91*
Abernathy, Frederick H. 1930- *WhoAm 90*
Abernathy, George Ernest 1931- *St&PR 91*
Abernathy, Jack Harvey 1911- *WhoAm 90*
Abernathy, James L. *ODwPR 91*
Abernathy, James Logan 1941- *WhoAm 90, WhoWor 91*
Abernathy, John Daniel 1937- *WhoAm 90*
Abernathy, Joseph Duncan 1944- *WhoAm 90*
Abernathy, Kathleen *BiDrAPA 89*
Abernathy, M. Glenn 1921-1990 *BioIn 16*
Abernathy, M Glenn 1921-1990 *ConAu 131*
Abernathy, Mabra Glenn 1921- *WhoAm 90*
Abernathy, Mabra Glenn 1921-1990 *BioIn 16*
Abernathy, Ralph 1926-1990 *CurBio 90N, News 90, -90-3, WorAlBi*
Abernathy, Ralph D. *BioIn 16*
Abernathy, Ralph David 1926- *WhoAm 90*
Abernathy, Ralph David 1926-1990 *ConAu 131, NewYTBS 90 [port]*
Abernathy, Robert L. 1931- *St&PR 91*
Abernathy, Robert Noel 1952- *WhoEmL 91*
Abernathy, Robert Shields 1923- *WhoAm 90*
Abernathy, Stewart Ray 1968- *WhoSSW 91*
Abernathy, Ted 1933- *Ballpl 90, BioIn 16*
Abernathy, Vicki Marie 1949- *WhoAmW 91*
Abernathy, Will Kendall 1870- *AmLegL*
Abernathy, William R. 1925- *St&PR 91*
Abernathy-Baldwin, Judith Ann 1942- *WhoAmA 91*
Abernethy, Avery Mark 1962- *WhoSSW 91*

Abernethy, David Beaven 1937- *WhoAm 90*
Abernethy, David Ford 1958- *WhoEmL 91*
Abernethy, Deborah Benson 1953- *WhoSSW 91*
Abernethy, George Lawrence 1910- *WhoAm 90*
Abernethy, James Arthur 1920- *St&PR 91*
Abernethy, Joseph Williams 1948- *WhoSSW 91*
Abernethy, Ronald Bruce 1948- *St&PR 91*
Abernethy, Virginia Deane 1934- *WhoAmW 91*
Abersfeller, Heinz Andrew 1920- *WhoAm 90*
Aberson, John Francis 1929- *St&PR 91*
Aberson, Leslie Donald 1936- *WhoAm 90*
Abess, John F 1946- *BiDrAPA 89*
Abess, Leonard, Jr. *BioIn 16*
Abetti, Pier Antonio 1921- *WhoAm 90*
Abetz, Otto 1903-1958 *BioIn 16*
Abeyesundere, Nihal Anton Aelian 1932- *WhoWor 91*
Abeyratne, Ruwantissa Indranath Ramya 1951- *WhoWor 91*
Abeyta, Frank *WhoHisp 91*
Abgarian, Robert 1928- *St&PR 91*
Abhau, William Conrad 1912- *WhoAm 90*
Abhyanker, Vimal Vasant 1938- *BiDrAPA 89*
Abi-Ali, Ricky Salim 1940- *WhoWor 91*
Abi-Dargham, Anissa *BiDrAPA 89*
Abichandani, Chandrap *BiDrAPA 89*
Abichandani, Lachman Kalacha *BiDrAPA 89*
Abid, Ann B 1942- *WhoAmA 91*
Abid, Nicholas Albert *BiDrAPA 89*
Abila, Enedina Vejil 1939- *WhoHisp 91*
Abildgaard, Nikolai Abraham 1743-1809 *PenDiDA 89*
Abildskov, J. A. 1923- *WhoAm 90*
Abilheira, Richard B. 1949- *WhoEmL 91*
Abir, Adi 1950- *WhoWor 91*
Abisch, Leo 1925- *WhoWor 91*
Abisch, Roslyn Kroop *AuBYP 90*
Abisch, Roz 1927- *AuBYP 90*
Abisellan, Georgina A *BiDrAPA 89*
Abish, Cecile *WhoAm 90, WhoAmA 91*
Abitanta, Jane N. *WhoAmW 91*
Abitz, James H. 1945- *St&PR 91*
Abitz, Kenneth G. 1952- *St&PR 91*
Abkari, Shashikala *BiDrAPA 89*
Abkowitz, Martin Aaron 1918- *WhoAm 90*
Abkowitz, Stanley 1927- *St&PR 91*
Abla, Vern W. 1943- *St&PR 91*
Ablack, Cecile 1954- *ODwPR 91*
Ablahat, Newton Andre 1914- *St&PR 91*
Ablan, Francis Adiarte 1928- *WhoWor 91*
Ablao, Arsenio Banez 1927- *BiDrAPA 89*
Ablard, Charles David *WhoAm 90*
Able, David *BioIn 16*
Able, Stephen Smith 1949- *BiDrAPA 89*
Able, W. Walter 1932- *St&PR 91*
Abler, David Gerard 1960- *WhoE 91*
Abler, Ronald Francis 1939- *WhoE 91*
Ables, Jo Angela 1950- *WhoAmW 91*
Ables, Murray French 1932- *BiDrAPA 89*
Ables, Paul 1925- *St&PR 91*
Ables, Willis Scott 1943- *WhoSSW 91*
Ablin, George, Jr. *BiDrAPA 89*
Ablin, Jack Alan 1958- *WhoE 91*
Ablin, Richard Joel 1940- *WhoAm 90, WhoE 91*
Ablon, Arnold Norman 1921- *WhoSSW 91, WhoWor 91*
Ablon, Benjamin Manuel 1929- *WhoSSW 91*
Ablon, Carl S. 1918- *St&PR 91*
Ablon, Ralph E. 1916- *St&PR 91, WhoAm 90, WhoE 91*
Ablon, Steven Luria 1941- *BiDrAPA 89*
Ablow, Joseph 1928- *WhoAmA 91*
Ablow, Keith Russell 1961- *BiDrAPA 89, WhoE 91*
Ablow, Roselyn Karol *WhoAmA 91*
Abnee, A. Victor 1923- *WhoAm 90*
Abney, Bobbie Jean 1933- *WhoAmW 91*
Abney, Frederick Sherwood 1919- *WhoAm 90*
Abney, Ray Chandler 1947- *BiDrAPA 89, WhoE 91*
Abo, Ronald Kent 1946- *WhoEmL 91*
Abodaher, David J. 1919- *AuBYP 90*
Aboff, Sheldon Jay 1947- *St&PR 91, WhoAm 90, WhoE 91, WhoWor 91*
Abolafia, Yossi 1944- *BioIn 16, SmATA 60*
Abolins, Maris Arvids 1938- *WhoAm 90*
Abood, Leo George 1922- *WhoAm 90*
Abood, Richard R. 1948- *WhoEmL 91*
Abood, Robert George 1961- *WhoEmL 91*
Aboody, Albert Victor 1947- *WhoAm 90*
Aborn, Carlene Mello 1932- *WhoAmW 91, WhoSSW 91*
Aborn, Foster L. 1934- *St&PR 91*
Aborn, Foster Litchfield 1934- *WhoE 91*
Aboshamaa, Kamal Nasr 1946- *WhoE 91*
Abou Ghazala, Mohammad Abdel-Halim 1930- *WhoWor 91*
Abou Haidar, Said N *BiDrAPA 89*
Abou-Ryhan *EncO&P 3*
Abou Saif, Laila *BioIn 16*
Abou-Taleb, Hossam Y S *BiDrAPA 89*
Abouchar, John W. 1929- *St&PR 91*
Aboussie, Marilyn 1948- *WhoEmL 91*
Abouzeid, George A. 1931- *St&PR 91*
Abplanalp, Glen Harold 1914- *St&PR 91, WhoAm 90*
Abracheff, Ivan 1903-1960 *WhoAmA 91N*
Abragam, Anatole 1914- *WhoWor 91*
Abraham *BioIn 16, WorAlBi*
Abraham *WhNaAH*
Abraham the Jew 1362?-1460? *EncO&P 3*
Abraham, Abe Samuel *BiDrAPA 89*
Abraham, Alan Rockwell 1931- *WhoAm 90, WhoE 91*
Abraham, Andrew 1958- *WhoEmL 91*
Abraham, Carl Joel 1937- *WhoE 91, WhoWor 91*
Abraham, Carol Jeanne 1949- *WhoAmA 91*
Abraham, Claude 1931- *WhoWor 91*
Abraham, David 1946- *ConAu 129*
Abraham, Edward Penley 1913- *WhoWor 91*
Abraham, Eileen Mary 1949- *WhoEmL 91*
Abraham, F. Murray *BioIn 16*
Abraham, F. Murray 1939- *WhoAm 90, WorAlBi*
Abraham, Gail Deana 1945- *WhoAmW 91*
Abraham, George 1918- *WhoAm 90*
Abraham, George G. 1906- *WhoAm 90*
Abraham, Gerald 1904-1988 *AnObit 1988, BioIn 16*
Abraham, Gerald M 1945- *BiDrAPA 89*
Abraham, Gerald Morris 1916- *BiDrAPA 89*
Abraham, Henry David 1942- *BiDrAPA 89, WhoE 91*
Abraham, Henry Julian 1921- *WhoAm 90*
Abraham, Irene 1946- *WhoAmW 91*
Abraham, Jacob A. 1948- *WhoAm 90*
Abraham, John A. *St&PR 91*
Abraham, Joy 1946- *BiDrAPA 89*
Abraham, Katharine Gail 1954- *WhoE 91*
Abraham, Laurie 1957- *WhoEmL 91*
Abraham, Lawrence Dagger 1949- *WhoSSW 91*
Abraham, Louis, III 1953- *WhoSSW 91*
Abraham, Mohanraj 1944- *WhoWor 91*
Abraham, Nathan Samuel 1946- *WhoEmL 91*
Abraham, Nicholas Albert 1941- *WhoE 91*
Abraham, Patricia Sisson 1954- *WhoSSW 91*
Abraham, Paul 1892-1960 *OxCPMus*
Abraham, Richard Kenneth 1955- *WhoEmL 91*
Abraham, Rita Betty 1951- *WhoEmL 91*
Abraham, Robert 1938- *St&PR 91*
Abraham, Robert E. 1952- *St&PR 91*
Abraham, S. Clifford 1956- *WhoAm 90*
Abraham, Samathanam N *BiDrAPA 89*
Abraham, Seth Gabriel *BioIn 16*
Abraham, Stephen Henry 1958- *WhoEmL 91*
Abraham, Susan Gail *BiDrAPA 89*
Abraham, Thundathil O *BiDrAPA 89*
Abraham, Victor Elias, Jr. 1935- *WhoHisp 91*
Abraham, Willard *BioIn 16*
Abraham, Willard 1916- *WhoAm 90*
Abrahams, Allen E. 1926- *WhoSSW 91*
Abrahams, Athol Denis 1946- *WhoAm 90*
Abrahams, Doris Caroline 1901?-1982? *ConAu 129, DcNaB 1981*
Abrahams, Elaine 1926- *WhoSSW 91*
Abrahams, Glen D. 1953- *St&PR 91*
Abrahams, Israel 1858-1924 *BioIn 16*
Abrahams, Joel Peter 1944- *WhoSSW 91*
Abrahams, John Hambleton 1913- *St&PR 91, WhoAm 90*
Abrahams, Joseph 1916- *BiDrAPA 89*
Abrahams, Lawrence M 1934- *BiDrAPA 89*
Abrahams, Lloyd Alan 1952- *WhoEmL 91*
Abrahams, Mark Nathan 1953- *WhoSSW 91*
Abrahams, Marshall Alan 1947- *St&PR 91*
Abrahams, Maurice 1883-1931 *OxCPMus*
Abrahams, Peggy *ODwPR 91*
Abrahams, Peter 1919- *MajTwCW*
Abrahams, Richard L. 1929- *St&PR 91*
Abrahams, Robert David 1905- *AuBYP 90, WhoAm 90*
Abrahams, Sidney Cyril 1924- *WhoWor 91*
Abrahams, Vivian Cecil 1927- *WhoAm 90*
Abrahams, William Miller 1919- *WhoAm 90, WhoWor 91, WhoWrEP 89*
Abrahamsen, Catherine Ellen 1950- *WhoEmL 91*
Abrahamsen, Dana F. 1956- *WhoEmL 91*
Abrahamsen, David *BiDrAPA 89*
Abrahamsen, David 1903- *WhoAm 90*
Abrahamsen, Hans 1952- *IntWWM 90*
Abrahamsen, Samuel 1917- *WhoAm 90*
Abrahamson, A. Craig 1954- *WhoEmL 91*
Abrahamson, Barry 1933- *WhoAm 90*
Abrahamson, Barry B. 1933- *St&PR 91*
Abrahamson, Dale Raymond 1949- *WhoSSW 91*
Abrahamson, Irving 1925- *ConAu 129*
Abrahamson, James Leonard 1937- *WhoSSW 91*
Abrahamson, Jeffery Alan 1958- *WhoE 91*
Abrahamson, John E. 1961- *St&PR 91*
Abrahamson, Lark Anne 1952- *WhoEmL 91*
Abrahamson, Ronald G. 1947- *St&PR 91*
Abrahamson, Shirley Schlanger 1933- *WhoAm 90, WhoAmW 91*
Abrahamson, Susan Marie 1953- *WhoWor 91*
Abrahamsson, Katarina Irene 1962- *WhoWor 91*
Abraira, Rosa M E 1938- *BiDrAPA 89*
Abram, Arlene N. 1942- *WhoAmW 91*
Abram, Blanche Schwartz 1925- *IntWWM 90*
Abram, Jill Denise 1958- *BiDrAPA 89*
Abram, Jonathan Adam 1955- *WhoSSW 91*
Abram, Jonathan Lynwood 1956- *WhoE 91*
Abram, Marian Christine 1958- *WhoAmW 91, WhoEmL 91*
Abram, Morris Berthold 1918- *WhoAm 90*
Abram, Prudence Beatty 1942- *WhoAm 90, WhoAmW 91*
Abramczuk, Tomasz 1954- *WhoWor 91*
Abramenkov, Andrey *PenDiMP*
Abramis, David Joseph 1955- *WhoEmL 91*
Abramoff, Peter 1927- *WhoAm 90*
Abramovic, Anthony Mark 1948- *St&PR 91*
Abramovich, Serge 1956- *BiDrAPA 89*
Abramovich, Teodora *BiDrAPA 89*
Abramovitz *AuBYP 90*
Abramovitz, Max 1908- *WhoAm 90, WhoE 91, WhoWor 91*
Abramovitz, Moses 1912- *WhoAm 90*
Abramovsky, Abraham 1946- *WhoEmL 91*
Abramow-Newerly, Jaroslaw 1933- *WhoWor 91*
Abramowicz, Alfred L. 1919- *WhoAm 90*
Abramowicz, Helen Kaufman *BiDrAPA 89*
Abramowicz, Janet *WhoAmA 91*
Abramowitz, Ann Jacoff 1948- *WhoAmW 91*
Abramowitz, Ava J. 1948- *WhoEmL 91*
Abramowitz, Harold *BiDrAPA 89*
Abramowitz, Herman 1880-1947 *BioIn 16*
Abramowitz, Howard D. *BioIn 16*
Abramowitz, Jerrold 1953- *WhoEmL 91*
Abramowitz, Jonathan 1947- *WhoEmL 91, WhoSSW 91*
Abramowitz, Morton I. 1933- *WhoAm 90*
Abramowitz, Sharone Ann 1956- *BiDrAPA 89*
Abramowski, Robert John 1950- *St&PR 91*
Abrams, A Leonard *BiDrAPA 89*
Abrams, Al 1904-1977 *Ballpl 90*
Abrams, Alan Michael 1936- *St&PR 91*
Abrams, Albert 1863-1924 *EncO&P 3*
Abrams, Alfred L *BiDrAPA 89*
Abrams, Allan Stanley 1937- *BiDrAPA 89*
Abrams, Anne 1953- *WhoAmW 91*
Abrams, Arnold Louis 1927- *BiDrAPA 89*
Abrams, Barbara Esme Kessler 1927- *WhoAmW 91*
Abrams, Bernard 1920- *St&PR 91*
Abrams, Bernard W. 1925- *St&PR 91*
Abrams, Bernard William 1925- *WhoAm 90*
Abrams, Beth Phyllis 1960- *BiDrAPA 89*
Abrams, Burton M. 1923- *St&PR 91*
Abrams, Cal 1924- *Ballpl 90, BioIn 16*
Abrams, Charles L. 1932- *St&PR 91*
Abrams, Cheryl 1955- *WhoAmW 91*
Abrams, Creighton W. 1914-1974 *WorAlBi*
Abrams, Creighton Williams 1914-1974 *BioIn 16*
Abrams, Deborah *BioIn 16*
Abrams, Diane Kobisher 1954- *WhoAmW 91*
Abrams, Douglas Breen 1954- *WhoEmL 91*
Abrams, Edith Lillian *WhoAmA 91*
Abrams, Edward M. 1927- *St&PR 91*
Abrams, Edward Marvin 1927- *WhoAm 90*
Abrams, Ellen *ODwPR 91*
Abrams, Elliott *BioIn 16*
Abrams, Elliott 1948- *WhoAm 90, WhoEmL 91*
Abrams, Eugene Bernard 1919- *WhoAm 90*
Abrams, Gerald David 1932- *WhoAm 90*
Abrams, Harold Eugene 1933- *WhoAm 90*
Abrams, Harry N 1905-1979 *WhoAmA 91N*
Abrams, Herbert E 1921- *WhoAmA 91, WhoE 91*
Abrams, Herbert Kerman 1913- *WhoAm 90*
Abrams, Herbert LeRoy 1920- *WhoAm 90*
Abrams, Howard Edward *BiDrAPA 89*
Abrams, Irwin 1914- *WhoAm 90*
Abrams, Jane Eldora 1940- *WhoAmA 91*
Abrams, Jay Harrison 1948- *St&PR 91*
Abrams, Jerome Brian 1956- *WhoEmL 91*
Abrams, Joseph 1936- *St&PR 91, WhoAm 90*
Abrams, Joyce Diana 1945- *WhoAmA 91*
Abrams, Jules Clinton 1927- *WhoAm 90*
Abrams, Karen 1960- *WhoEmL 91*
Abrams, Kym *BioIn 16*
Abrams, Lawrence F. *BioIn 16*
Abrams, Lee *BioIn 16*
Abrams, Leigh J. 1942- *St&PR 91*
Abrams, Leigh Jeffrey 1942- *WhoAm 90*
Abrams, Leonard I. 1916- *St&PR 91*
Abrams, Linda *ODwPR 91*
Abrams, Linsey 1951- *WhoWrEP 89*
Abrams, Lloyd Raymond 1953- *WhoEmL 91*
Abrams, Lori 1959- *WhoAmW 91*
Abrams, M. H. 1912- *BioIn 16*
Abrams, M.H. 1912- *ConAu 33NR*
Abrams, Mathis *BiDrAPA 89*
Abrams, Meyer Howard 1912- *BioIn 16, WhoAm 90*
Abrams, Michael *BioIn 16*
Abrams, Milton Ross 1942- *WhoE 91*
Abrams, Morris *BioIn 16*
Abrams, Muhal Richard 1930- *WhoAm 90*
Abrams, Norman 1933- *WhoAm 90*
Abrams, Ouida Thompson 1946- *WhoAmW 91*
Abrams, Pamela *BioIn 16*
Abrams, Paul Gordon 1948- *WhoEmL 91*
Abrams, Philip 1933?-1981 *ConAu 129*
Abrams, Richard 1937- *BiDrAPA 89*
Abrams, Richard Brill 1931- *WhoAm 90*
Abrams, Richard Lee 1941- *WhoAm 90*
Abrams, Richard M. 1948- *WhoE 91*
Abrams, Richard Martin 1932- *WhoAm 90*
Abrams, Richard S *BiDrAPA 89*
Abrams, Robert 1938- *WhoAm 90, WhoE 91*
Abrams, Robert Allen 1937- *WhoAm 90, WhoE 91*
Abrams, Robert Clark *BiDrAPA 89*
Abrams, Robert Herman 1932- *St&PR 91*
Abrams, Roberta Busky 1937- *WhoAm 90, WhoAmW 91*
Abrams, Roy 1943- *St&PR 91*
Abrams, Rubin 1921- *St&PR 91*
Abrams, Ruth *WhoAmA 91N*
Abrams, Ruth Ida 1930- *WhoAm 90, WhoAmW 91, WhoE 91*
Abrams, Samuel *BiDrAPA 89*
Abrams, Samuel K. 1913- *WhoAm 90*
Abrams, Sheri Hope 1952- *WhoE 91*
Abrams, Shirley Ann 1945- *WhoEmL 91*
Abrams, Sol Bernard 1925- *St&PR 91*
Abrams, Stanley David 1940- *WhoE 91*
Abrams, Stephen Irwin 1938- *EncO&P 3*
Abrams, Steven L 1940- *BiDrAPA 89*
Abrams, Stuart 1941- *WhoE 91*
Abrams, Susan Elizabeth 1945- *WhoAm 90*
Abrams, Talbert *NewYTBS 90*
Abrams, Talbert 1895- *WhoAm 90*
Abrams, Vivien 1946- *WhoAmA 91*
Abrams, Warren Elliott 1928- *WhoAm 90*
Abrams, William Bernard 1922- *WhoAm 90, WhoWor 91*
Abrams, William Michael 1953- *WhoE 91*
Abrams Sacks, Julie Barnett 1960- *WhoAmW 91*
Abramski, Stanley F 1943- *BiDrAPA 89*
Abramson, Andrew Edward 1924- *St&PR 91*
Abramson, Arnold Ernest 1914- *WhoAm 90*
Abramson, Arthur Seymour 1925- *WhoAm 90*
Abramson, Bernard 1926- *BiDrAPA 89*
Abramson, Bruce S. 1936- *WhoE 91*
Abramson, Burton Ivan 1931- *BiDrAPA 89*
Abramson, David Irvin 1905- *WhoAm 90*
Abramson, Earl 1934- *St&PR 91*
Abramson, Elaine Sandra 1942- *WhoAmA 91*
Abramson, Hanley Norman 1940- *WhoAm 90*
Abramson, Henry M 1935- *BiDrAPA 89*
Abramson, Hyman Norman 1926- *St&PR 91, WhoAm 90*
Abramson, Ira 1930- *St&PR 91*
Abramson, Irwin Barry 1939- *St&PR 91, WhoE 91*
Abramson, Israel Jack 1960- *BiDrAPA 89*
Abramson, Jean Margaret 1926- *IntWWM 90*
Abramson, Jerry 1946- *WhoSSW 91*
Abramson, Lawrence 1946- *St&PR 91*
Abramson, Leonard 1932- *St&PR 91*
Abramson, Lowell E. 1928- *St&PR 91*

Abramson, Marc F 1936- *BiDrAPA 89*
Abramson, Mark Chad 1956- *WhoEmL 91*
Abramson, Mark Joseph 1949- *WhoEmL 91*
Abramson, Marsha A. 1950- *St&PR 91*
Abramson, Martin 1921- *WhoAm 90, WhoWrEP 89*
Abramson, Maxwell 1935- *WhoAm 90*
Abramson, Morrie K. 1934- *St&PR 91*
Abramson, Morrie Kaplan 1934- *WhoAm 90*
Abramson, Norman 1939- *WhoAm 90*
Abramson, Patty 1944- *ODwPR 91*
Abramson, Paul Robert 1937- *WhoAm 90*
Abramson, Robert J. 1921- *St&PR 91*
Abramson, Robert Joseph 1921- *WhoAm 90*
Abramson, Roberta B. 1937- *WhoAmW 91*
Abramson, Rochelle Susan 1953- *WhoAmW 91*
Abramson, Ronald David 1940- *BiDrAPA 89*
Abramson, Stephen Davis 1945- *St&PR 91*
Abramson, Ted Jerome 1928- *WhoE 91*
Abramson, William E 1935- *BiDrAPA 89*
Abramson, William Edward 1935- *WhoE 91*
Abrantes, Laure Junot, duchesse d' 1784-1838 *BioIn 16*
Abrantes, Laure Saint-Martin Perman J d' 1784-1838 *EncCoWW*
Abrasha *BioIn 16*
Abrashkin, Raymond 1911-1960 *AuBYP 90, BioIn 16*
Abravanel, Allan Ray 1947- *WhoEmL 91*
Abravanel, Maurice 1903- *BioIn 16, IntWWM 90, PenDiMP, WhoAm 90*
Abreu, Alba Maria *BiDrAPA 89*
Abreu, Eduardo 1949- *PenDiMP*
Abreu, Elizabeth F. 1953- *WhoSSW 91*
Abreu, Francisco P. 1831-1879 *AmLegL*
Abreu, Gregorio Benito 1928- *WhoWor 91*
Abreu, Jose Domingos Vistulo 1926- *WhoWor 91*
Abreu, Judith Ann *WhoAmW 91*
Abreu, Luis Alberto 1956- *WhoEmL 91*
Abreu, M. Albert 1927- *St&PR 91*
Abreu, Roberto Daniel 1937- *WhoHisp 91*
Abreu, Sergio 1948- *PenDiMP*
Abreu, Sue Hudson 1956- *WhoAmW 91*
Abreu de la Mota, Francisco Julio 1955- *WhoE 91*
Abrew, Frederick H. 1937- *WhoAm 90*
Abriel, Albert G 1912- *BiDrAPA 89*
Abright, Arthur Reese 1947- *BiDrAPA 89*
Abrikosov, Aleksey Alekseyevich 1928- *WhoWor 91*
Abril, Ben 1923- *WhoAmA 91*
Abril, Jorge L. 1934- *WhoHisp 91*
Abromitis, Joseph Peter 1926- *St&PR 91*
Abromowitz, Leslie Mira *BiDrAPA 89*
Abroms, Eugene M 1933- *BiDrAPA 89*
Abromson, I. Joel 1938- *St&PR 91*
Abron, Neal R. 1933- *St&PR 91*
a'Brook, Michael Ferrahs 1933- *BiDrAPA 89*
Abs, Hermann J. 1901- *WhoWor 91*
Absalom, Roger Neil Lewis 1929- *ConAu 31NR*
Abse, David Wilfred *BiDrAPA 89*
Absher, Janet S. 1955- *WhoEmL 91*
Abshier, H.A., Jr. 1931- *St&PR 91*
Abshier, Shirley Ann 1936- *WhoAmW 91*
Abshire, Alvis John 1942- *WhoSSW 91*
Abshire, David Manker 1926- *WhoAm 90, WhoWor 91*
Abshire, Richard Brian 1952- *St&PR 91*
Absolon, Karel B. 1926- *WhoWrEP 89*
Absolon, William 1751-1815 *PenDiDA 89*
Abston, Dunbar, Jr. 1931- *St&PR 91, WhoAm 90*
Abt, Clark C. 1929- *St&PR 91, WhoWrEP 89*
Abt, Clark Claus 1929- *WhoAm 90*
Abt, Jeffrey 1949- *WhoAm 90*
Abt, Ralph Edwin 1960- *WhoEmL 91*
Abt, Renee Judith *BiDrAPA 89*
Abt, Sylvia Hedy 1957- *WhoAmW 91, WhoEmL 91, WhoWor 91*
Abts, Gwyneth Hartmann 1923- *WhoAmW 91*
Abts, H.W. 1918- *St&PR 91*
Abts, Henry William 1918- *WhoAm 90*
Abu Bakr 573?-634 *WorAlBi*
Abu Hassan Bin Omar 1940- *WhoWor 91*
Abu Jihad *BioIn 16*
Abu Nidal *BioIn 16*
Abu Yazid al-Bestami 801?-874 *EncO&P 3*
Abu Bakar, Jaafar 1946- *WhoWor 91*
Abu Haligia, Mansoor Moosa Essa 1957- *WhoWor 91*
Abu-Lisan, Mustafa Abdelrauf 1947- *WhoWor 91*
Abu-Lughod, Janet Lippman 1928- *WhoAm 90*
Abu Salim, Mohammed Ibrahim 1927- *WhoWor 91*
Abu-Soud, Tawfiq Sufyan 1958- *WhoWor 91*
Abu Suud, Khaled *BioIn 16*
Abu Zayyad, Ray S. *WhoAm 90*
Abubakar, Siddiq, III 1903-1988 *AnObit 1988*
Abuchowski, Abraham 1948- *St&PR 91*
Abud, Danilo S *BiDrAPA 89*
Abugov, Aleksandr 1913- *BioIn 16*
Abularach, Rodolfo Marco 1933- *WhoAmA 91*
Abularach, Rodolfo Marco Antonio 1933- *WhoAm 90*
Abuls, Larissa Klavins 1962- *WhoAmW 91*
Abumrad, Naji 1945- *WhoAm 90*
Abuna Tekle Haimanot *BioIn 16*
Abusch, Sidney 1941- *St&PR 91*
Abushadi, Mohamed Mahmoud 1913- *WhoWor 91*
Abusharif, Ibrahim Naseem 1958- *WhoWrEP 89*
Abut, Charles C. 1944- *WhoAm 90*
Abuza, Susan 1945- *St&PR 91*
Abuzinada, Abdulaziz Hamid 1940- *WhoWor 91*
Abuzzahab, Faruk Said 1932- *WhoAm 90*
Abuzzahab, Faruk Said, Sr. 1932- *BiDrAPA 89*
Abyholm, Frank Ellof 1939- *WhoWor 91*
Abzug, Bella *BioIn 16*
Abzug, Bella 1920- *WorAlBi*
Abzug, Bella Savitzky 1920- *WhoAm 90*
Abzug, Robert Henry 1945- *WhoWrEP 89*
AC/DC *ConMus 4 [port], EncPR&S 89*
Acampora, Anthony Salvator 1946- *WhoAm 90*
Acampora, Louis V. 1913- *St&PR 91*
Acampora, Ralph Joseph 1941- *St&PR 91, WhoAm 90, WhoWor 91*
Acar, Joseph 1926- *St&PR 91*
Acar, Yalcin Bekir 1951- *WhoSSW 91*
Acaros, Nicholas Kyprianos 1929- *WhoWor 91*
Accampo, Anthony David 1959- *WhoSSW 91*
Accardi, Carla 1924- *BiDWomA*
Accardi, Michael Vincent 1947- *St&PR 91*
Accardi, Susan Joan 1949- *BiDrAPA 89*
Accardo, Salvatore 1941- *PenDiMP*
Accardo, Salvatore Francis 1937- *WhoWor 91*
Accarino, Joseph Henry 1949- *St&PR 91*
Accas, Gene A. 1926- *St&PR 91*
Accetta, Suzanne Rusconi 1953- *WhoAmA 91*
Accettola, Albert Bernard 1918- *WhoAm 90, WhoE 91*
Accettola, Albert Bernard, Jr. 1945- *WhoE 91*
Accettura, Guy 1919- *WhoAm 90*
Acciacca, Jess Jack 1935- *St&PR 91*
Acconci, Vito 1940- *BioIn 16, WhoAm 90, WhoAmA 91*
Accordino, Frank Joseph 1946- *WhoAm 90, WhoEmL 91*
Accordino, Margaret Spillane 1948- *WhoAmW 91*
Accorsi, Ernest William, Jr. 1941- *WhoAm 90*
Accuosti, William V. 1934- *St&PR 91*
Accurso, Catherine Josephine 1955- *WhoAmW 91*
Ace, Drexel Maurice, Jr. 1950- *WhoE 91, WhoEmL 91*
Aceituno, Andres Avelino *BiDrAPA 89*
Acenas, Antoinette D *BiDrAPA 89*
Acerboni, Marcello 1940- *WhoWor 91*
Acerra, Andrew Jeri 1916- *WhoSSW 91*
Acerra, Angelo Thomas 1925- *WhoAm 90*
Acerra, Michele 1937- *St&PR 91, WhoAm 90*
Acers, Maurice Wilson 1907- *St&PR 91*
Aceto, Benjamin T. 1951- *St&PR 91*
Aceto, Vincent John 1932- *WhoE 91, WhoWor 91*
Acevedo, Carlos F 1941- *BiDrAPA 89*
Acevedo, Domingo Elio 1936- *WhoE 91*
Acevedo, George L. 1955- *WhoHisp 91*
Acevedo, Hector Luis 1947- *WhoSSW 91*
Acevedo, Jorge Terrazas 1914- *WhoHisp 91*
Acevedo, Jose Enrique 1939- *WhoHisp 91*
Acevedo, Julio Eduardo 1931- *WhoHisp 91*
Acevedo, Ralph Angel 1950- *WhoHisp 91*
Acevedo-Borges, Douglas 1952- *WhoWor 91*
Acevedo Diaz, Eduardo 1851-1921 *BioIn 16*
Acevedo Peralta, Ricardo de Jesus 1941- *WhoWor 91*
Aceves, Jose *WhoHisp 91*
Acey, Thomas M. 1946- *St&PR 91*
Ach, Roger Workum, II 1943- *St&PR 91*
Achad, Frater 1886-1950 *EncO&P 3*
Achar, Sudha *BiDrAPA 89*
Acharya, Kalpana R *BiDrAPA 89*
Acharya, Malini Govind *BiDrAPA 89*
Acharya, Sagri Vasudeva 1943- *WhoE 91*
Achbar, Francine 1946- *WhoAmW 91*
Achebe, Chinua 1930- *BioIn 16, MajTwCW, WhoWor 91, WorAlBi*
Acheik ibn Oumar *WhoWor 91*
Achen, Norman Charles 1942- *St&PR 91*
Achenbach, Jan Drewes 1935- *WhoAm 90*
Achenbaum, Alvin A. *BioIn 16*
Achenbaum, Alvin A. 1925- *St&PR 91*
Achenbaum, Alvin Allen 1925- *WhoAm 90*
Achenbaum, Warren D. 1934- *St&PR 91*
Achepohl, Keith Anden 1934- *WhoAmA 91*
Acheson, Allen Morrow 1926- *St&PR 91, WhoAm 90*
Acheson, Anne Crawford 1882-1962 *BiDWomA*
Acheson, David C 1921- *ConAu 132*
Acheson, David Campion 1921- *WhoAm 90*
Acheson, Dean 1893-1971 *BioIn 16*
Acheson, Dean G. 1893-1971 *WorAlBi*
Acheson, Dean Gooderham 1893-1971 *BiDrUSE 89*
Acheson, James *WhoAm 90*
Acheson, James C. 1936- *St&PR 91*
Acheson, Louis Kruzan, Jr. 1926- *WhoAm 90*
Acheson, Patricia Castles 1924- *AuBYP 90*
Acheson, Roy Malcolm 1921- *WhoAm 90*
Achille-Fould, Georges 1868-1951 *BiDWomA*
Achilles, Jackson T. 1951- *BiDrAPA 89*
Achin, Milos Kosta 1915- *WhoE 91*
Achinstein, Asher 1900- *WhoAm 90*
Achinstein, Peter Jacob 1935- *WhoAm 90*
Achitoff, Louis *BioIn 16*
Achleitner, Paul Michael 1956- *WhoE 91*
Achmet *EncO&P 3*
Achor, Leonard Bruce *BiDrAPA 89*
Achor, Louis Joseph 1948- *WhoSSW 91*
Achord, James Lee 1931- *WhoSSW 91*
Achord, Thaddeus C 1941- *BiDrAPA 89*
Achorn, Robert Comey 1922- *WhoAm 90*
Achte, Kalle A 1928- *BiDrAPA 89*
Achtemeier, Gary Lynn 1943- *WhoAm 90*
Achtenberg, Joel Franklin 1946- *WhoEmL 91*
Achtenhagen, Frank 1939- *WhoWor 91*
Achterberg, Charles Richard 1939- *St&PR 91*
Achterberg, Thomas Dale 1952- *WhoSSW 91*
Achterman, James William 1945- *WhoEmL 91*
Achtermann, Marvin Dale 1945- *WhoEmL 91*
Achtert, Walter Scott 1943- *WhoAm 90, WhoWrEP 89*
Achtman, Carol 1941- *BiDrAPA 89*
Achtziger, Harold LeRoy 1934- *St&PR 91*
Achucarro, Joaquin 1932- *BioIn 16*
Achucarro, Joaquin 1936- *PenDiMP*
Acier, Michel-Victor 1736-1795 *PenDiDA 89*
Acitelli, Linda Katherine 1951- *WhoAmW 91*
Acito, Daniel Joseph 1918- *WhoAm 90*
Ackdoe, Emmit F *BiDrAPA 89*
Ackell, Edmund Ferris 1925- *WhoAm 90, WhoSSW 91*
Ackelson, Rolland D. 1926- *St&PR 91*
Acker, Albert Harold 1941- *St&PR 91*
Acker, Arthur Malcolm 1930- *WhoAm 90*
Acker, Charles R. 1912- *St&PR 91*
Acker, David De Peyster 1921- *WhoAm 90*
Acker, Dieter 1940- *IntWWM 90*
Acker, Donald M. 1955- *St&PR 91*
Acker, Duane Calvin 1931- *WhoAm 90*
Acker, Francois-Paul 1721- *PenDiDA 89*
Acker, Frederick George 1934- *WhoAm 90*
Acker, Helen *AuBYP 90*
Acker, Jim 1958- *Ballpl 90*
Acker, Jon A. 1945- *St&PR 91*
Acker, Kathy 1948- *FemiCLE*
Acker, Martin Herbert 1921- *WhoAm 90*
Acker, Nathaniel Hull 1927- *WhoAm 90*
Acker, Paul Arthur 1952- *St&PR 91*
Acker, Richard William 1940- *WhoSSW 91*
Acker, Robert Flint 1920- *WhoAm 90*
Acker, Robert Wayne 1949- *St&PR 91*
Acker, Ronald Walter 1956- *WhoE 91*
Acker, Tom 1930- *Ballpl 90*
Acker, Virginia Margaret 1946- *WhoAmW 91*
Acker, W. L. 1937- *WhoSSW 91*
Acker, William Marsh, Jr. 1927- *WhoAm 90*
Acker-Gherardino, Ernest 1924- *WhoAmA 91*
Ackerley, Barry *WhoAm 90*
Ackerley, Chris 1947- *ConAu 129*
Ackerley, J. R. 1896-1967 *BioIn 16*
Ackerley, Joe Randolph 1896-1967 *BioIn 16*
Ackerley, Mary Beth 1956- *BiDrAPA 89*
Ackerly, Donna Marie 1957- *WhoEmL 91*
Ackerly, Howard F. 1928- *St&PR 91*
Ackerly, Robert Nelson, Jr. 1944- *BiDrAPA 89*
Ackerly, Robert Saunders, Jr. 1929- *WhoAm 90*
Ackerly, Wendy Saunders 1960- *WhoAmW 91, WhoEmL 91*
Ackerly, William C 1928- *BiDrAPA 89*
Ackerman, Albert J *BiDrAPA 89*
Ackerman, Allan Douglas 1947- *WhoEmL 91*
Ackerman, Anne *BioIn 16*
Ackerman, Arthur F. 1903-1989 *BioIn 16*
Ackerman, Baer Max 1953- *BiDrAPA 89*
Ackerman, Bettye Louise 1928- *WhoAm 90*
Ackerman, Bruce Arnold 1943- *WhoAm 90*
Ackerman, Carl William 1890-1970 *BioIn 16*
Ackerman, Caroline Iverson 1918- *WhoE 91*
Ackerman, David Paul 1949- *WhoEmL 91*
Ackerman, Diana Felicia 1947- *WhoAmW 91*
Ackerman, Diane 1948- *ConAu 31NR, WhoWrEP 89*
Ackerman, Don E. 1933- *St&PR 91*
Ackerman, Don Eugene 1933- *WhoAm 90, WhoSSW 91*
Ackerman, Duane F. *BioIn 16*
Ackerman, Eugene 1920- *WhoAm 90*
Ackerman, Frank Edward 1933- *WhoAmA 91N*
Ackerman, Gary L. 1942- *WhoAm 90, WhoE 91*
Ackerman, George S. 1920- *St&PR 91*
Ackerman, Gerald Martin 1928- *WhoAm 90, WhoAmA 91*
Ackerman, H. Don 1926- *St&PR 91*
Ackerman, Harold A. 1928- *WhoAm 90*
Ackerman, Harry S. 1912- *WhoAm 90*
Ackerman, Helen Page 1912- *WhoAm 90*
Ackerman, Henry Sweets 1942- *WhoAm 90*
Ackerman, Herbert 1929- *St&PR 91*
Ackerman, Herbert 1930- *St&PR 91*
Ackerman, Jack Rossin 1931- *WhoAm 90*
Ackerman, Jacqueline Kay 1943- *WhoAmW 91*
Ackerman, James F. 1924- *St&PR 91*
Ackerman, James Nils 1912- *WhoAm 90*
Ackerman, James S. 1919- *BioIn 16, WhoAmA 91*
Ackerman, James Sloss 1919- *WhoAm 90*
Ackerman, John A. 1937- *St&PR 91*
Ackerman, John Cyril *WhoAm 90*
Ackerman, John Cyril 1937- *St&PR 91*
Ackerman, John Edward 1939- *WhoWor 91*
Ackerman, John Henry 1925- *WhoAm 90*
Ackerman, John Michael *BiDrAPA 89*
Ackerman, John Tryon 1941- *St&PR 91, WhoAm 90*
Ackerman, Jolene Kay 1952- *WhoAmW 91*
Ackerman, Joseph J. H. 1949- *WhoAm 90*
Ackerman, Karen *AuBYP 90*
Ackerman, Katherine *BiDrAPA 89*
Ackerman, Kenneth Benjamin 1932- *WhoAm 90*
Ackerman, L.C. 1917- *St&PR 91*
Ackerman, Larry Leonard 1938- *BiDrAPA 89*
Ackerman, LaVerne Jean 1945- *WhoEmL 91*
Ackerman, Lennis Campbell 1917- *WhoAm 90*
Ackerman, Linda Helman Picow 1942- *WhoSSW 91*
Ackerman, Lisa Marilyn 1960- *WhoE 91*
Ackerman, Louise Magaw 1904- *WhoAmW 91*
Ackerman, Marshall 1925- *WhoAm 90*
Ackerman, Melvin 1937- *WhoAm 90*
Ackerman, Mona Riklis 1946- *WhoAmW 91*
Ackerman, Neil Richard 1943- *WhoAm 90*
Ackerman, Noreen Carol 1944- *WhoWrEP 89*
Ackerman, Ora Ray 1931- *WhoAm 90, WhoSSW 91*
Ackerman, Otto 1909-1960 *PenDiMP*
Ackerman, Paul Henry 1936- *BiDrAPA 89*
Ackerman, Philip Charles 1944- *St&PR 91, WhoAm 90*
Ackerman, Ray B. 1922- *St&PR 91*
Ackerman, Raymond Basil 1922- *WhoAm 90*
Ackerman, Raymond E *BiDrAPA 89*
Ackerman, Robert Adolph 1928- *WhoSSW 91*
Ackerman, Robert Alan 1951- *WhoEmL 91*
Ackerman, Robert O. 1946- *St&PR 91*
Ackerman, Robert Paul 1948- *WhoAm 90*
Ackerman, Robert W. 1938- *St&PR 91*
Ackerman, Robert Wallace 1938- *WhoWor 91*
Ackerman, Roger G. 1938- *St&PR 91*

Ackerman, Ronald Harry 1947- *WhoSSW 91*
Ackerman, Roy Alan 1951- *St&PR 91*, *WhoEmL 91*
Ackerman, Rudy Schlegel 1933- *WhoAmA 91*
Ackerman, Samuel 1917- *St&PR 91*
Ackerman, Sandra J. 1957- *WhoAmW 91*
Ackerman, Sanford Selig 1932- *WhoAm 90*, *WhoE 91*
Ackerman, Scott Fulton 1944- *WhoSSW 91*
Ackerman, Sigurd H *BiDrAPA 89*
Ackerman, Stephanie C. *St&PR 91*
Ackerman, Susan Yoder 1945- *BioIn 16*
Ackerman, Tedd H 1957- *BiDrAPA 89*
Ackerman, Wesley Ardmore 1921- *WhoAm 90*
Ackerman, Will *BioIn 16*
Ackerman, William *NewAgMG*
Ackermann, John Joseph 1889-1950 *WhoAmA 91N*
Ackermann, Louise 1813-1890 *EncCoWW*
Ackermann, Marsha Ellen 1950- *WhoEmL 91*
Ackermann, Norbert Joseph, Jr. 1942- *WhoSSW 91*
Ackermark, Peter *PenDiDA 89*
Ackerson, Duane Wright, Jr. *WhoWrEP 89*
Ackerson, Jeffrey Townsend 1944- *WhoE 91*
Ackerson, Lynn M. 1957- *WhoAmW 91*
Ackerson, Nels John 1944- *WhoE 91*
Ackerstein, Giora 1938- *WhoWor 91*
Acklam, Jon Neil 1947- *WhoEmL 91*
Ackland, Joss 1928- *BioIn 16*
Ackland, Valentine *BioIn 16*
Ackland, Valentine 1906-1968 *FemiCLE*
Ackles, Janice Vogel *WhoAmW 91*, *WhoWor 91*
Ackles, Robert 1952- *St&PR 91*
Ackley, Danielle Renee 1970- *WhoWrEP 89*
Ackley, Dean Ralph *BiDrAPA 89*
Ackley, Diane Denise 1951- *WhoEmL 91*
Ackley, Gardner 1915- *WhoAm 90*
Ackley, John Brian 1948- *WhoSSW 91*
Ackley, Kenneth E. 1938- *St&PR 91*
Ackley, Marie *WhoWrEP 89*
Ackley, Peggy Jo 1955- *BioIn 16*
Ackley, Richard Alan 1945- *St&PR 91*
Acklie, Duane William 1931- *St&PR 91*
Acklie, Phyllis Ann 1933- *St&PR 91*
Ackman, David Matthew 1961- *BiDrAPA 89*
Ackman, Milton Roy 1932- *WhoAm 90*
Ackmann, Lowell Eugene 1923- *WhoAm 90*
Ackoff, Russell L 1919- *ConAu 32NR*
Ackoff, Russell Lincoln 1919- *WhoAm 90*
Ackourey, Paul Philip 1958- *WhoEmL 91*
Ackrill, Marion 1957- *IntWWM 90*
Ackroyd, Alan Wile *BiDrAPA 89*
Ackroyd, Henry James, III 1958- *WhoE 91*
Ackroyd, Peter 1949- *WhoWor 91*, *WorAu 1980 [port]*
Ackroyd, Peter R 1917- *ConAu 31NR*
Ackte, Aino 1876-1944 *PenDiMP*
Acland, Sarah 1940- *BiDrAPA 89*
Acle, Eduardo R 1928- *BiDrAPA 89*
Acobe, Fernando 1941- *WhoHisp 91*
Acomb, Dan T. 1956- *St&PR 91*
Aconcio, Jacques *EncO&P 3*
Acontius, Jacobus 1500?-1566? *EncO&P 3*
Acord, Craig Paul 1948- *WhoSSW 91*
Acord-Skelton, Barbara Burrows 1928- *WhoAmW 91*
Acosta, Able 1930- *WhoHisp 91*
Acosta, Adolovni P. 1946- *IntWWM 90*
Acosta, Alirio 1933- *WhoHisp 91*
Acosta, Antonio A. 1929- *WhoHisp 91*, *WhoWor 91*
Acosta, Armando *BioIn 16*
Acosta, Armando Joel 1956- *WhoHisp 91*
Acosta, Camilo Luis *BiDrAPA 89*
Acosta, Carlos Alberto 1957- *WhoHisp 91*
Acosta, Carlos Julis 1939- *WhoHisp 91*
Acosta, Cy 1946- *Ballpl 90*
Acosta, Edesa 1962- *WhoSSW 91*
Acosta, Estrella P *BiDrAPA 89*
Acosta, Frank Xavier 1945- *WhoWor 91*
Acosta, Ivan Mariano 1943- *WhoHisp 91*
Acosta, Jose 1891- *Ballpl 90*
Acosta, Joseph 1921- *WhoHisp 91*
Acosta, Joseph de 1540-1600 *BioIn 16*
Acosta, Juana Maria 1952- *WhoSSW 91*
Acosta, Julio Bernard 1927- *WhoAm 90*
Acosta, Lucy 1960- *WhoHisp 91*
Acosta, Lucy G. 1926- *WhoHisp 91*
Acosta, Manuel Gregorio 1921- *BioIn 16*, *WhoAmA 91*, *WhoHisp 91*
Acosta, Oscar *BioIn 16*
Acosta, Oscar Zeta 1935?- *ConAu 131*, *HispWr 90*
Acosta, Raymond Luis 1925- *WhoAm 90*, *WhoSSW 91*
Acosta, Ricardo A. 1945- *WhoHisp 91*
Acosta, Robert J. 1939- *BioIn 16*
Acosta, Ursula 1933- *WhoSSW 91*
Acosta De Hernandez, Daisy M *BiDrAPA 89*
Acosta-Lespier, Luis 1939- *WhoHisp 91*
Acosta-Rua, Maria Victoria 1939- *BiDrAPA 89*
Acquaotta, Henry Francis 1926- *St&PR 91*
Acquavella, Demian *BioIn 16*, *NewYTBS 90*
Acquavella, William *NewYTBS 90 [port]*
Acquaviva, Ellen Long 1945- *St&PR 91*
Acquaviva, Joseph 1956- *BiDrAPA 89*
Acquaviva, Nicholas 1951- *St&PR 91*
Acra, Jose A 1937- *BiDrAPA 89*
Acre, Stephen *TwCCr&M 91*
Acree, Elaine Strong 1954- *WhoAmW 91*
Acree, Elick Henry 1935- *WhoSSW 91*
Acree, Glennis Earl 1942- *WhoSSW 91*
Acree, Robert Edwin 1928- *WhoSSW 91*
Acri, Robert James 1948- *St&PR 91*
Acs, Gabriel Alexander 1956- *WhoEmL 91*
Acton, Arlo C 1933- *WhoAmA 91*
Acton, Charles 1914- *IntWWM 90*
Acton, Constance Foster 1947- *WhoEmL 91*
Acton, David 1933- *WhoAm 90*
Acton, David Lawrence 1949- *WhoWor 91*
Acton, Eliza 1799-1859 *BioIn 16*
Acton, John Emerich 1834-1902 *WorAlBi*
Acton, John Emerich Edward Dalberg 1834-1902 *BioIn 16*
Acton, Norman 1918- *WhoAm 90*
Acton, Peter Neville 1952- *WhoWor 91*
Acton, William 1813-1875 *BioIn 16*
Acton, William Anthony 1910- *WhoWor 91*
Acuff, A. Marshall, Jr. 1939- *St&PR 91*
Acuff, John Edgar 1940- *WhoSSW 91*
Acuff, Robert Vann 1952- *WhoSSW 91*
Acuff, Roy 1903- *BioIn 16*, *OxCPMus*, *WhoNeCM C [port]*, *WorAlBi*
Acuff, Roy Claxton 1903- *WhoAm 90*
Acuff, Thomas Aldrich 1936- *WhoWor 91*
Acuna, Conrad Santos, Sr. 1946- *WhoHisp 91*
Acuna, Felipe 1932- *BiDrAPA 89*
Acuna, Rodolfo *ConAu 131*, *HispWr 90*
Acuna, Rodolfo 1932- *BioIn 16*, *WhoHisp 91*
Acuna, Rodolfo F 1932- *ConAu 131*, *HispWr 90*
Acuna, Rosario de 1851-1923 *EncCoWW*
Acuna, Rudy *ConAu 131*, *HispWr 90*
Aczel, Janos Dezso 1924- *WhoAm 90*
Aczel, Susan Kende 1927- *WhoAmW 91*
Aczel, Tamas 1921- *WhoWrEP 89*
Aczel, Thomas 1930- *WhoAm 90*
Ada *WomWR*
Ada, Christen *EncCoWW*
Ada, Joseph Franklin 1943- *WhoWor 91*
Adachi, Agnes Magdalene 1918- *WhoAmW 91*
Adaikan, Ganesan Periannan 1944- *WhoWor 91*
Adair, Adam *BioIn 16*
Adair, Allan 1897-1988 *AnObit 1988*
Adair, Allen Raymond 1945- *WhoSSW 91*
Adair, Charles E. 1947- *WhoAm 90*
Adair, Charles Norman 1941- *WhoE 91*
Adair, Charles Robert, Jr. 1914- *WhoAm 90*
Adair, Charles Valloyd 1923- *WhoAm 90*
Adair, Charles W. 1923- *St&PR 91*
Adair, Charles Watkins 1923- *WhoAm 90*
Adair, Clark Hazen *BiDrAPA 89*
Adair, Dale Keith *BiDrAPA 89*
Adair, Dale Keith 1959- *WhoEmL 91*
Adair, Dianna Lynn 1950- *WhoWor 91*
Adair, Ian 1942- *BioIn 16*
Adair, Jack Richard 1944- *BiDrAPA 89*
Adair, James *WhNaAH*
Adair, James 1709?-1783? *EncCRAm*
Adair, James 1909- *IntWWM 90*
Adair, Janice K. *BioIn 16*
Adair, Jeffrey R. 1953- *ODwPR 91*
Adair, Jerry 1936-1987 *Ballpl 90*
Adair, John Douglas, Jr. 1943- *St&PR 91*
Adair, Mary Roberts 1933- *WhoE 91*
Adair, Maureen Lenore *BiDrAPA 89*
Adair, Red 1915- *BioIn 16*, *WhoAm 90*
Adair, Robert Charles 1952- *St&PR 91*
Adair, Robert Kemp 1924- *WhoAm 90*
Adair, Tony 1953- *St&PR 91*
Adair, Wendy Hilty 1949- *WhoSSW 91*
Adair, William Benjamin, Jr. 1951- *WhoEmL 91*
Adair, Yvonne 1946- *WhoAmW 91*
Adal 1947- *WhoHisp 91*
Adalbert *EncO&P 3*
Adalbert, Leo Joseph 1961- *WhoE 91*
Adalsteinn, Kristmundsson *DcScanL*
Adam, L'Abbe *EncO&P 3*
Adam, Adolphe 1803-1856 *OxCPMus*
Adam, Alan B *BiDrAPA 89*
Adam, Balkozar Seifeld *BiDrAPA 89*
Adam, Claus *PenDiMP*
Adam, Cornel 1915- *WhoAm 90*
Adam, Diona *BiDrAPA 89*
Adam, Gary Lee 1946- *WhoEmL 91*, *WhoWor 91*
Adam, George F., Jr. 1946- *WhoAm 90*
Adam, Gerold Helge 1933- *WhoWor 91*
Adam, Graeme Mercer 1839-1912 *DcLB 99*
Adam, Hans Christian 1948- *ConAu 131*
Adam, J. Marc 1938- *St&PR 91*
Adam, James Vernon 1948- *St&PR 91*
Adam, Jean 1710-1765 *BioIn 16*
Adam, John *BioIn 16*
Adam, John, Jr. 1914- *St&PR 91*, *WhoAm 90*
Adam, John C 1918- *BiDrAPA 89*
Adam, Judy Z. 1955- *St&PR 91*
Adam, Juliette 1836-1936 *EncCoWW*
Adam, Ken 1921- *ConDes 90*
Adam, LaVern Lester 1943- *WhoWor 91*
Adam, Lucie *ODwPR 91*
Adam, Mary Lou 1933- *St&PR 91*
Adam, Orval Michael 1930- *St&PR 91*, *WhoAm 90*
Adam, Patrick 1955- *WhoWor 91*
Adam, Paul James 1934- *WhoAm 90*
Adam, Robert 1728-1792 *PenDiDA 89*, *WorAlBi*
Adam, Robert B. 1918- *St&PR 91*
Adam, Ruth 1907-1977 *FemiCLE*
Adam, Stephen Ferenc 1929- *WhoAm 90*
Adam, Theo 1926- *IntWWM 90*, *PenDiMP*
Adam, Thomas Lorenzo 1946- *WhoEmL 91*
Adam, Thomas R. *NewYTBS 90*
Adam, Waldemar 1937- *WhoWor 91*
Adam, William Atkinson 1920- *WhoWor 91*
Adam, Z. Alfred 1928- *St&PR 91*
Adam Smith, Janet 1905- *SmATA 63*
Adama, Hein R.H. 1944- *WhoWor 91*
Adamakos, Arthur Louis 1956- *WhoE 91*
Adamantius *BioIn 16*, *EncO&P 3*
Adamany, David Walter 1936- *WhoAm 90*, *WhoWor 91*
Adamany, Richard C. 1952- *St&PR 91*
Adamberger, Valentin 1743-1804 *PenDiMP*
Adamchek, Janice Lynn 1949- *WhoAmW 91*
Adamczak, Eugeniusz 1935- *WhoWor 91*
Adamczyk, Edmond David 1957- *WhoSSW 91*
Adamczyk, Joachim Josef 1926- *St&PR 91*
Adame, Leonard 1947- *ConAu 131*, *HispWr 90*, *WhoHisp 91*
Adamec, Joseph V. 1935- *WhoE 91*
Adamec, Ladislav 1926- *WhoWor 91*
Adamec, Michele Marie *BiDrAPA 89*
Adamenko, Victor G. *EncPaPR 91*
Adames, Maria 1941- *WhoHisp 91*
Adames Palma, Abdiel Jose 1938- *WhoWor 91*
Adamez, Alma Carrales 1958- *WhoHisp 91*
Adami-Charney, Anne Sybell 1949- *WhoEmL 91*
Adamian, Gerald *BiDrAPA 89*
Adamian, Gregory Harry 1926- *WhoAm 90*, *WhoE 91*
Adamian, Haig J. 1923- *St&PR 91*
Adamides, Odysseus, Jr. *BiDrAPA 89*
Adamitis, Donald M. 1944- *St&PR 91*
Adamkiewicz, Vincent Witold 1924- *WhoAm 90*
Adamko, Joseph Michael 1932- *St&PR 91*
Adamo, Ido 1929- *BiDrAPA 89*
Adamo, James Darryl *BiDrAPA 89*
Adamo, Joseph F. 1946- *St&PR 91*
Adamo, Marilyn Hank 1953- *WhoAmW 91*
Adamo, Ralph 1948- *WhoWrEP 89*
Adamo, Salvatore 1943- *OxCPMus*
Adamoli, David Robert 1940- *St&PR 91*
Adamov, Arthur 1908-1970 *MajTwCW*
Adamovich, Shirley Gray 1927- *WhoAm 90*, *WhoAmW 91*
Adamowicz, Irena 1910-1963 *BioIn 16*
Adams, A. John 1931- *ODwPR 91*
Adams, A. John Bertrand 1931- *WhoAm 90*, *WhoWor 91*
Adams, Abigail *BioIn 16*
Adams, Abigail 1744-1818 *BioAmW*, *BioIn 16*, *EncCRAm [port]*, *FemiCLE*, *WorAlBi*
Adams, Ace 1912- *Ballpl 90*
Adams, Aden Cornelius 1939- *St&PR 91*
Adams, Agnes Louise 1897- *BioIn 16*
Adams, Albert Willie, Jr. 1948- *WhoAm 90*
Adams, Alfred Gray 1946- *WhoSSW 91*
Adams, Alfred Hugh 1928- *WhoAm 90*
Adams, Algalee Pool 1919- *WhoAm 90*
Adams, Alice *BiDEWW*
Adams, Alice 1926- *BioIn 16*, *MajTwCW*, *WhoAm 90*, *WhoAmW 91*, *WhoWrEP 89*, *WorAlBi*, *WorAu 1980 [port]*
Adams, Alice 1930- *WhoAmA 91*
Adams, Alice Patricia 1930- *WhoAm 90*, *WhoAmW 91*
Adams, Alton W. 1946- *St&PR 91*
Adams, Alvin Philip 1905- *WhoAm 90*
Adams, Alvin Philip, Jr. 1942- *WhoAm 90*
Adams, Amy Brown 1950- *WhoSSW 91*
Adams, Andrew Joseph 1909- *WhoAm 90*
Adams, Andrew Stanford 1922- *WhoAm 90*
Adams, Andy *TwCCr&M 91*
Adams, Ann 1948- *ODwPR 91*
Adams, Ann Elizabeth 1948- *WhoAmW 91*
Adams, Anna 1926- *FemiCLE*
Adams, Anna Christie 1952- *WhoWrEP 89*
Adams, Anne *WhoWrEP 89*
Adams, Ansel 1902-1984 *BioIn 16*, *ModArCr 1 [port]*, *WorAlBi*
Adams, Ansel Easton 1902-1984 *WhoAmA 91N*
Adams, Arlin Marvin 1921- *WhoAm 90*
Adams, Arthur Eugene 1917- *WhoAm 90*
Adams, Arthur Gray 1935- *WhoWrEP 89*
Adams, Arthur Harvey 1915- *WhoAm 90*
Adams, Arthur Raymond 1909- *St&PR 91*
Adams, Arvil Van 1943- *WhoE 91*
Adams, Aubrey *BioIn 16*
Adams, Audrey Lee 1952- *WhoAmW 91*
Adams, Augustus E. 1931- *St&PR 91*
Adams, Aundrea Jasmine Kaye 1954- *WhoSSW 91*
Adams, Austin Alfred 1943- *St&PR 91*
Adams, Babe 1882-1968 *Ballpl 90 [port]*
Adams, Barbara Helen 1932- *WhoAmW 91*
Adams, Barbara Johnston 1943- *SmATA 60 [port]*
Adams, Barton Knight 1932- *BiDrAPA 89*
Adams, Beejay 1920- *WhoAmW 91*
Adams, Benjamin *PenDiDA 89*
Adams, Bernard Schroder 1928- *WhoAm 90*
Adams, Bertha Jane 1837?-1912 *FemiCLE*
Adams, Bett Yates 1942- *WhoSSW 91*
Adams, Betty Virginia 1925- *WhoAmW 91*
Adams, Beverly Josephine 1951- *WhoAmW 91*, *WhoEmL 91*
Adams, Bobbi 1939- *WhoAmA 91*
Adams, Bobby 1921- *Ballpl 90*
Adams, Bradway B. 1956- *St&PR 91*
Adams, Bradway Burke 1956- *WhoEmL 91*
Adams, Brock 1927- *WhoAm 90*, *WhoWor 91*
Adams, Brockman 1927- *BiDrUSE 89*
Adams, Brooke *BioIn 16*
Adams, Brooke 1949- *WhoAm 90*
Adams, Brooks 1848-1927 *BioIn 16*, *WorAlBi*
Adams, Bruce 1936- *WhoE 91*
Adams, Bruce 1952- *St&PR 91*
Adams, Bruce E. 1947- *St&PR 91*
Adams, Bryan *BioIn 16*
Adams, Buel Thomas 1933- *WhoAm 90*
Adams, Buster 1915- *Ballpl 90*
Adams, Byron 1955- *IntWWM 90*
Adams, Carl Morgan, Jr. 1940- *WhoSSW 91*
Adams, Carol Ann Jacobs 1946- *WhoAmW 91*
Adams, Caroline Jeanette H. 1951- *WhoAmW 91*, *WhoEmL 91*
Adams, Carolyn 1943- *DrBIPA 90*
Adams, Cary Meredith 1948- *WhoAm 90*, *WhoEmL 91*
Adams, Casey *ConTFT 8*
Adams, Catherine Ann 1960- *WhoSSW 91*
Adams, Celeste Marie 1947- *WhoAmA 91*
Adams, Charles A 1947- *BiDrAPA 89*
Adams, Charles Edwards, Jr. 1939- *WhoSSW 91*
Adams, Charles F. 1910- *St&PR 91*
Adams, Charles Francis 1807-1886 *BioIn 16*
Adams, Charles Francis 1835-1915 *BioIn 16*
Adams, Charles Francis 1866-1954 *BiDrUSE 89*
Adams, Charles Francis 1927- *WhoAm 90*, *WhoWor 91*
Adams, Charles Henry 1918- *WhoAm 90*
Adams, Charles Jairus 1917- *WhoAm 90*
Adams, Charles Lynford 1929- *WhoAm 90*
Adams, Charles Preston 1942- *St&PR 91*
Adams, Charles Wally 1934- *St&PR 91*
Adams, Charlotte 1899- *AuBYP 90*
Adams, Christine B L 1949- *BiDrAPA 89*
Adams, Christine Hanson 1950- *WhoEmL 91*
Adams, Christopher Bertlin 1939- *WhoWor 91*
Adams, Christopher M *BiDrAPA 89*
Adams, Christopher Steve, Jr. 1930- *WhoAm 90*
Adams, Cleve F 1895-1949 *TwCCr&M 91*
Adams, Cliff 1923- *OxCPMus*
Adams, Clifford Emerson *WhoWor 91*
Adams, Clinton 1918- *WhoAm 90*, *WhoAmA 91*
Adams, Clyde *BiDrAPA 89*
Adams, Conrad Robert, II 1942- *St&PR 91*

Adams, Constance Althea 1953- *WhoWrEP 89*
Adams, Courtney Sherbrooke 1929- *IntWWM 90*
Adams, Curtis L V *BiDrAPA 89*
Adams, Cynthia D. 1946- *WhoAm 90, WhoAmW 91*
Adams, Cyrus Eugene 1949- *BiDrAPA 89*
Adams, Dan Lynn 1947- *WhoEmL 91, WhoSSW 91*
Adams, Daniel Clifford 1956- *IntWWM 90*
Adams, Daniel Fenton 1922- *WhoAm 90*
Adams, Daniel Lee 1936- *WhoAm 90*
Adams, Daniel T. *BioIn 16*
Adams, David Bachrach 1939- *WhoAm 90*
Adams, David Gray 1961- *WhoSSW 91*
Adams, David Huntington 1942- *WhoSSW 91*
Adams, David John 1949- *WhoEmL 91*
Adams, David L. 1956- *St&PR 91*
Adams, Dean 1957- *WhoE 91, WhoEmL 91*
Adams, Deborah 1956- *WhoWrEP 89*
Adams, Deborah Lynn 1953- *WhoEmL 91*
Adams, Dee Briane 1942- *WhoSSW 91*
Adams, Dennis Paul 1948- *WhoAmA 91*
Adams, Diane Loretta 1948- *WhoE 91, WhoEmL 91*
Adams, Don 1927- *WorAlBi*
Adams, Donald 1928- *IntWWM 90*
Adams, Donald Edward 1951- *WhoE 91*
Adams, Donald Jeremy *BiDrAPA 89*
Adams, Donald Kendrick 1925- *WhoAm 90*
Adams, Doris Jo 1926- *St&PR 91*
Adams, Douglas 1952- *ConLC 60 [port], WorAlBi*
Adams, Douglas Fletcher 1937- *St&PR 91, WhoAm 90*
Adams, Douglas Noel 1952- *RGTwCSF*
Adams, Douglass Franklin 1935- *WhoAm 90*
Adams, E.C. 1930- *St&PR 91*
Adams, Earl William, Jr. 1937- *WhoAm 90*
Adams, Eaton, Jr. 1930- *St&PR 91*
Adams, Edgar J. 1866- *AmLegL*
Adams, Edie 1929- *WorAlBi*
Adams, Edmund John 1938- *WhoAm 90*
Adams, Edward Beverle 1939- *WhoAm 90*
Adams, Edward C 1919- *BiDrAPA 89*
Adams, Edward Thomas 1933- *WhoAm 90*
Adams, Edwin Melville 1914- *WhoAm 90*
Adams, Egbert Harrison 1899- *St&PR 91*
Adams, Elaine Parker 1940- *WhoSSW 91*
Adams, Eleanor *BioIn 16*
Adams, Elie Maynard 1919- *WhoAm 90, WhoWrEP 89*
Adams, Elizabeth Laura 1909- *HarlReB*
Adams, Elizabeth M *BiDrAPA 89*
Adams, Ellen *WhoWrEP 89*
Adams, Ellwood William, Jr. 1917- *WhoSSW 91*
Adams, Ephraim Douglass 1865-1930 *BioIn 16*
Adams, Eva Garza 1943- *WhoHisp 91*
Adams, Evangeline Smith 1872?-1932 *EncO&P 3*
Adams, Everett Merle 1920- *WhoAm 90*
Adams, F. Gerard 1929- *WhoAm 90*
Adams, Fay *WhoAm 90, WhoWrEP 89*
Adams, Faye Litsey 1945- *WhoAmW 91*
Adams, Florence 1932- *SmATA 61 [port]*
Adams, Floyd N. 1942- *St&PR 91*
Adams, Frances Grant, II 1955- *WhoAmW 91*
Adams, Francis Donald 1943- *WhoWor 91*
Adams, Francis W. H. 1904-1990 *BioIn 16, NewYTBS 90*
Adams, Frank H. 1935- *St&PR 91*
Adams, Frank M. *BioIn 16, NewYTBS 90*
Adams, Frank Robert 1947- *WhoEmL 91*
Adams, Franklin P. 1881-1960 *Ballpl 90, BioIn 16*
Adams, Franklin V. 1947- *St&PR 91*
Adams, Freddy 1938- *WhoWor 91*
Adams, Freeman H 1911- *BiDrAPA 89*
Adams, Gail Hayes 1944- *WhoAm 90*
Adams, Gary Dennis 1961- *WhoE 91*
Adams, Gene D. 1933- *St&PR 91*
Adams, George Bell 1930- *WhoAm 90*
Adams, George Graydon 1909- *St&PR 91*
Adams, George H N 1936- *BiDrAPA 89*
Adams, George Harold 1926- *WhoE 91*
Adams, George J. 1934- *St&PR 91*
Adams, George Leslie 1942- *BiDrAPA 89*
Adams, George R. 1936- *St&PR 91*
Adams, George Rollie 1941- *WhoE 91*
Adams, George William 1948- *WhoEmL 91*
Adams, Gerald Robert 1946- *WhoEmL 91*
Adams, Gerry *BioIn 16*
Adams, Glenda 1939- *FemiCLE*
Adams, Glenn 1947- *Ballpl 90*
Adams, Glenn T. 1919- *St&PR 91*
Adams, Grantley Herbert 1898-1971 *BioIn 16*
Adams, Gregory Burke 1948- *WhoSSW 91*
Adams, Gunilla Marie 1960- *WhoAmW 91*
Adams, Hal 1947-1990 *BioIn 16*
Adams, Hall, Jr. 1933- *WhoAm 90*
Adams, Hannah 1755-1831 *FemiCLE*
Adams, Harold 1923- *TwCCr&M 91*
Adams, Harold B 1923- *WhoWrEP 89*
Adams, Harold Lynn 1939- *WhoAm 90*
Adams, Harriet 1892-1982 *FemiCLE*
Adams, Hazard Simeon 1926- *WhoAm 90*
Adams, Hazel Greenlee Redfearn 1905- *WhoAmW 91, WhoSSW 91*
Adams, Helene Clay 1961- *ODwPR 91, WhoAmW 91*
Adams, Henry 1838-1918 *BioIn 16*
Adams, Henry 1949- *ConAu 132, WhoAmA 91*
Adams, Henry Brooks 1838-1918 *WorAlBi*
Adams, Henry Philip 1951- *WhoEmL 91*
Adams, Herbert 1874-1958? *TwCCr&M 91*
Adams, Herbert Richards 1932- *WhoAm 90*
Adams, Homer Mat, III 1937- *WhoWor 91*
Adams, Howard *BioIn 16*
Adams, Howard Glen 1940- *WhoAm 90*
Adams, J. Mack 1933- *WhoE 91*
Adams, J. Randy 1956- *St&PR 91*
Adams, Jack 1952- *WhoEmL 91*
Adams, Jack Ashton 1922- *WhoAm 90*
Adams, James A. 1927- *St&PR 91*
Adams, James Allen 1954- *WhoEmL 91*
Adams, James Blackburn 1926- *WhoAm 90*
Adams, James E. 1944- *St&PR 91, WhoAm 90*
Adams, James Edgar *BiDrAPA 89*
Adams, James Erwin 1944- *BiDrAPA 89*
Adams, James Frederick 1927- *WhoAm 90*
Adams, James G., Jr. 1954- *WhoEmL 91*
Adams, James John 1948- *BiDrAPA 89*
Adams, James Louis 1928- *WhoAm 90*
Adams, James Luther 1901- *BioIn 16, WhoAm 90*
Adams, James Lyn 1950- *WhoWrEP 89*
Adams, James Marshall, III 1945- *St&PR 91*
Adams, James Mills 1936- *WhoAm 90, WhoE 91*
Adams, James Norman 1932- *WhoAm 90*
Adams, James R. 1939- *WhoAm 90*
Adams, James Richard 1941- *WhoWrEP 89*
Adams, James Robert 1946- *WhoEmL 91*
Adams, James Thomas 1930- *WhoAm 90*
Adams, James Wilson 1928- *WhoSSW 91*
Adams, Jane F. 1957- *St&PR 91*
Adams, Jay H 1937- *WhoAmA 91*
Adams, Jean 1710-1765 *FemiCLE*
Adams, Jean Ruth 1928- *WhoAmW 91*
Adams, Jeanette 1955- *WhoAmW 91*
Adams, Jeffrey T. *ODwPR 91*
Adams, Jennifer A. 1952- *WhoEmL 91*
Adams, Jerry L. 1946- *WhoSSW 91*
Adams, Jill Elaine 1952- *WhoEmL 91*
Adams, Jim Walter 1928- *WhoSSW 91*
Adams, Jimmie Vick 1936- *WhoAm 90*
Adams, Joanna Z. *ConAu 32NR*
Adams, Joe 1922- *DrBlPA 90*
Adams, Joe C. 1936- *ODwPR 91*
Adams, Joe D. 1933- *St&PR 91*
Adams, Joe W. 1920- *St&PR 91*
Adams, Joey 1911- *WhoAm 90*
Adams, John *BioIn 16, NewAgMG*
Adams, John 1735-1826 *BiDrUSE 89, BioIn 16, EncCRAm, WorAlBi*
Adams, John 1947- *IntWWM 90, PenDiMP A*
Adams, John Allan Stewart 1926- *WhoAm 90*
Adams, John B. 1947- *St&PR 91, WhoAm 90*
Adams, John Bertram 1920-1984 *DcNaB 1981*
Adams, John Bodkin 1899-1983 *DcNaB 1981*
Adams, John Buchanan, Jr. 1948- *WhoAm 90*
Adams, John C. *WhNaAH*
Adams, John C. 1917- *St&PR 91*
Adams, John David Vessot 1934- *WhoAm 90*
Adams, John Eric 1963- *WhoEmL 91*
Adams, John Evi 1937- *BiDrAPA 89*
Adams, John F. 1919-1989 *BioIn 16*
Adams, John Francis, Jr. 1936- *WhoAm 90, WhoE 91*
Adams, John Frank 1930-1989 *BioIn 16*
Adams, John Hamilton 1936- *WhoAm 90*
Adams, John Hanly 1918- *WhoAm 90*
Adams, John Hubert 1943- *St&PR 91*
Adams, John Hurst 1929- *WhoAm 90*
Adams, John Joseph 1957- *WhoEmL 91*
Adams, John Laurence 1943- *WhoE 91*
Adams, John Lewis *WhoAm 90*
Adams, John M. 1950- *WhoSSW 91*
Adams, John Marshall 1930- *WhoAm 90*
Adams, John Martin *BiDrAPA 89*
Adams, John Michael Geoffrey Manningham 1931-1985 *BioIn 16, DcNaB 1981*
Adams, John Q, III 1938- *EncO&P 3*
Adams, John Quincy 1767-1848 *BiDrUSE 89, BioIn 16*
Adams, John Quincy 1769-1848 *WorAlBi*
Adams, John Quincy 1938- *WhoAm 90, WhoE 91*
Adams, John Quincy 1942- *WhoE 91*
Adams, John Quincy, III 1945- *WhoAm 90*
Adams, John R. 1900- *WhoAm 90*
Adams, John Richard 1918- *BiDrAPA 89, WhoAm 90*
Adams, John Robert 1938- *WhoAm 90*
Adams, John Stephen 1938- *WhoAm 90*
Adams, John Wayne 1947- *WhoEmL 91*
Adams, John William 1924- *St&PR 91*
Adams, Johnnie L. 1944- *St&PR 91*
Adams, Joseph A. 1960- *St&PR 91*
Adams, Joseph Elkan 1913- *WhoAm 90*
Adams, Joseph John 1940- *St&PR 91*
Adams, Joseph John 1945- *WhoEmL 91*
Adams, Joseph Peter 1907- *WhoAm 90, WhoWor 91*
Adams, Joseph W. 1924- *St&PR 91*
Adams, Joyce Carol 1946- *WhoE 91*
Adams, Joyce Marilyn 1934- *WhoAmW 91*
Adams, Judith Ann 1948- *WhoEmL 91*
Adams, Julius J. *BioIn 16*
Adams, Julius J. 1901?-1989 *ConAu 130*
Adams, Jura *BiDrAPA 89*
Adams, Justus C. 1841-1904 *AmLegL*
Adams, Kathleen Margaret 1952- *WhoAmW 91, WhoE 91*
Adams, Kathy Ross *WhoSSW 91*
Adams, Kaye Hall 1943- *WhoAmW 91*
Adams, Kenneth Francis 1946- *St&PR 91, WhoAm 90*
Adams, Kenneth R. 1941- *St&PR 91*
Adams, Kenneth Stanley, Jr. 1923- *St&PR 91, WhoAm 90, WhoSSW 91*
Adams, L. *PenDiDA 89*
Adams, Lamar Taft 1938- *WhoSSW 91*
Adams, Lane Webster 1915- *WhoWor 91*
Adams, Larry Edward 1945- *WhoSSW 91*
Adams, Laura Lee 1956- *WhoAmW 91*
Adams, Lawrence Charles 1948- *WhoEmL 91*
Adams, Leason Heberling 1887-1969 *DcScB S2*
Adams, Lee 1924- *OxCPMus*
Adams, Lee S. 1949- *St&PR 91*
Adams, Lee Stephen 1949- *WhoAm 90, WhoEmL 91*
Adams, Leon David 1905- *WhoAm 90*
Adams, Leonard F 1938- *BiDrAPA 89*
Adams, Leonard Joseph 1954- *WhoEmL 91*
Adams, Leonie 1899-1988 *BioIn 16, FemiCLE*
Adams, Leslie 1932- *IntWWM 90*
Adams, Leslie Bunn, Jr. 1932- *WhoAm 90, WhoSSW 91*
Adams, Levi 1802? 1832 *DcLB 99*
Adams, Linda Sharon *BiDrAPA 89*
Adams, Louisa Catherine 1775-1852 *BioIn 16*
Adams, Louisa J. 1775-1852 *BioAmW*
Adams, Lowell G 1935- *WhoAmA 91*
Adams, Lynn *BioIn 16*
Adams, Margaret Ann 1935- *WhoAmW 91*
Adams, Margaret Bernice 1936- *WhoAm 90*
Adams, Margaret Boroughs *WhoAmA 91N*
Adams, Margaret Diane 1937- *WhoAmW 91*
Adams, Margery Jane 1932- *WhoAmW 91*
Adams, Marion 1843-1885 *BioAmW*
Adams, Marjorie E. 1947- *St&PR 91*
Adams, Mark 1925- *WhoAm 90, WhoAmA 91*
Adams, Mark Kevin 1950- *St&PR 91*
Adams, Mark R. 1961- *St&PR 91*
Adams, Martha R B *BiDrAPA 89*
Adams, Mary *BiDEWW*
Adams, Mary Electa 1823-1898 *DcCanB 12*
Adams, Mary Grace Agnes 1898-1984 *DcNaB 1981*
Adams, Mason 1919- *WhoAm 90*
Adams, Maude 1872-1953 *BioAmW, BioIn 16, NotWoAT, WorAlBi*
Adams, Maureen Kay 1948- *WhoAmW 91*
Adams, Mel 1916- *ODwPR 91*
Adams, Michael *BioIn 16, ODwPR 91*
Adams, Michael August *WhoWor 91*
Adams, Michael B. 1943- *St&PR 91*
Adams, Michael F. 1948- *WhoAm 90*
Adams, Michael John 1958- *WhoE 91*
Adams, Michael L. 1948- *WhoEmL 91*
Adams, Michael Ross 1957- *WhoEmL 91*
Adams, Michael Thomas 1948- *WhoAm 90*
Adams, Michael Thomas 1965- *WhoSSW 91*
Adams, Mike 1935- *WhoWor 91*
Adams, Mildred E. 1931- *WhoE 91*
Adams, Milton S 1937- *BiDrAPA 89*
Adams, Moses Sawin *AmLegL*
Adams, Moulton Lee 1922-1971 *WhoAmA 91N*
Adams, Myrna D. 1940- *St&PR 91*
Adams, N.Q. 1925- *St&PR 91*
Adams, Nancy Ann 1932- *WhoSSW 91*
Adams, Neal 1941- *EncACom*
Adams, Neal Howard 1949- *BiDrAPA 89*
Adams, Nicholas 1952- *St&PR 91*
Adams, Noah *BioIn 16*
Adams, Noreen V. 1942- *St&PR 91*
Adams, Norman J. 1933- *St&PR 91*
Adams, Norman Joseph 1930- *WhoWor 91*
Adams, O. Edwin 1934- *St&PR 91*
Adams, Oscar William, Jr. 1925- *WhoAm 90*
Adams, P Evans 1924- *BiDrAPA 89*
Adams, Pat 1928- *WhoAm 90, WhoAmA 91*
Adams, Paul Ancil 1937- *WhoAm 90*
Adams, Paul G. 1945- *St&PR 91*
Adams, Paul L 1924- *BiDrAPA 89*
Adams, Paul Winfrey 1913- *WhoAm 90, WhoWor 91*
Adams, Payton F. 1930- *WhoAm 90, WhoSSW 91*
Adams, Pepper 1930-1986 *OxCPMus*
Adams, Perry Ronald 1921- *WhoAm 90*
Adams, Peter David 1937- *WhoE 91*
Adams, Peter Frederick *WhoAm 90*
Adams, Peter George 1949- *WhoWor 91*
Adams, Peter Sayles 1953- *WhoEmL 91*
Adams, Peter Webster 1939- *St&PR 91*
Adams, Phelps Haviland 1902- *WhoAm 90*
Adams, Philip 1905- *WhoAm 90, WhoWor 91*
Adams, R.L. 1933- *St&PR 91*
Adams, Ralph E. *BioIn 16*
Adams, Ralph E. 1935- *St&PR 91*
Adams, Ralph Edwin 1930- *WhoAm 90*
Adams, Ralph Wyatt, Sr. 1915- *WhoAm 90, WhoWor 91*
Adams, Ranald Trevor, Jr. 1925- *WhoAm 90*
Adams, Randall Dale *BioIn 16*
Adams, Randall David 1958- *WhoSSW 91*
Adams, Ray Harris 1945- *WhoEmL 91*
Adams, Raymond Edward 1933- *WhoAm 90*
Adams, Richard 1920- *AuBYP 90, MajTwCW*
Adams, Richard Crittenden 1945- *WhoEmL 91*
Adams, Richard Donald 1909- *WhoAm 90*
Adams, Richard George 1920- *WhoAm 90, WhoWor 91*
Adams, Richard Gregg 1932- *St&PR 91*
Adams, Richard Newbold 1924- *WhoAm 90*
Adams, Richard Towsley 1921- *WhoAm 90*
Adams, Richard Willey 1926- *St&PR 91*
Adams, Robert 1910- *DrBlPA 90*
Adams, Robert D. 1941- *St&PR 91*
Adams, Robert Earl 1932- *BiDrAPA 89*
Adams, Robert Edward 1941- *WhoAm 90*
Adams, Robert Francis 1947- *St&PR 91*
Adams, Robert Franklin 1907- *WhoAm 90*
Adams, Robert H. *ODwPR 91*
Adams, Robert H 1937- *WhoWrEP 89*
Adams, Robert Henry 1937- *BiDrAPA 89*
Adams, Robert Hickman 1937- *WhoAm 90, WhoAmA 91*
Adams, Robert Hugo 1943- *WhoAm 90*
Adams, Robert J. 1932- *St&PR 91*
Adams, Robert James 1922- *St&PR 91*
Adams, Robert M. 1923- *St&PR 91*
Adams, Robert McCormick 1926- *WhoAm 90, WhoAmA 91, WhoE 91*
Adams, Robert R *BiDrAPA 89*
Adams, Robert R. 1924- *St&PR 91*
Adams, Robert Richard 1965- *WhoHisp 91*
Adams, Robert Vincent 1931- *WhoAm 90*
Adams, Robert W, Jr. 1920- *BiDrAPA 89*
Adams, Robert Waugh, Jr. 1936- *WhoAm 90*
Adams, Rodger *St&PR 91*
Adams, Roger 1889-1971 *BioIn 16*
Adams, Roger Anthony 1934- *St&PR 91*
Adams, Ronald Roy *St&PR 91*
Adams, Rose Ann 1952- *WhoAmW 91*
Adams, Roy 1933- *St&PR 91*
Adams, Roy M. 1940- *WhoAm 90*
Adams, Russell Baird 1910- *WhoAm 90*
Adams, Ruth *BiDrAPA 89*
Adams, Ruth Joyce *AuBYP 90*
Adams, Ruth Salzman 1923- *WhoAm 90*
Adams, Samuel 1722-1803 *BioIn 16, EncCRAm [port], WorAlBi*
Adams, Samuel A. 1934-1988 *BioIn 16*
Adams, Samuel Clifford, Jr. 1920- *WhoAm 90*

Adams, Samuel Hopkins 1871-1958 *AuBYP 90, BioIn 16*
Adams, Samuel Louis 1927- *WhoAm 90*
Adams, Sandra Ann 1948- *WhoE 91*
Adams, Sarah 1805-1848 *FemiCLE*
Adams, Sarah Flower 1805-1848 *BioIn 16*
Adams, Sarah Virginia 1955- *WhoAmW 91*
Adams, Scott Leslie 1955- *WhoEmL 91*
Adams, Seibert 1934- *St&PR 91*
Adams, Sherman 1899-1986 *WorAlBi*
Adams, Shirley Jo 1959- *St&PR 91*
Adams, Sparky 1894-1989 *Ballpl 90*
Adams, Stanley 1907- *WhoAm 90*
Adams, Stephen 1884-1913 *OxCPMus*
Adams, Stephen 1939- *WhoAm 90*
Adams, Stephen M. *WhoAm 90, WhoE 91*
Adams, Stephen Shawn 1961- *WhoEmL 91*
Adams, Steve *WhoSSW 91*
Adams, Steven Lee 1957- *WhoWor 91*
Adams, Susan B. 1950- *WhoAm 90*
Adams, Suzanne 1872-1953 *PenDiMP*
Adams, Terri Rosenblatt 1951- *WhoEmL 91*
Adams, Thelma Michelle 1959- *WhoE 91*
Adams, Theodore Adolphus, Jr. 1929- *St&PR 91, WhoSSW 91*
Adams, Thomas Boylston 1910- *WhoAm 90*
Adams, Thomas Brooks 1919- *WhoAm 90*
Adams, Thomas Gerald 1938- *WhoAm 90*
Adams, Thomas Merritt 1935- *WhoAm 90*
Adams, Thomas Randolph 1921- *WhoAm 90*
Adams, Thomas Stanley 1948- *St&PR 91*
Adams, Thomas Tilley 1929- *WhoE 91, WhoWor 91*
Adams, Thomas Walton 1947- *WhoEmL 91, WhoWor 91*
Adams, Timothy D. 1959- *St&PR 91*
Adams, Timothy Journay 1948- *WhoEmL 91*
Adams, Timothy Raymond 1951- *WhoEmL 91*
Adams, Tom 1931-1985 *BioIn 16*
Adams, Vergil 1926- *St&PR 91*
Adams, Veronica Wadewitz 1951- *WhoAm 90*
Adams, Victoria Eleanor 1941- *WhoAmW 91, WhoWor 91*
Adams, Virginia Marie 1929- *WhoAmW 91*
Adams, W. Andrew 1945- *WhoAm 90*
Adams, W. Earl *St&PR 91*
Adams, W.G. 1934- *St&PR 91*
Adams, Walter 1922- *WhoAm 90*
Adams, Walter Sydney 1876-1956 *WorAlBi*
Adams, Warren Sanford, II 1910- *WhoAm 90*
Adams, Wayman 1885-1959 *WhoAmA 91N*
Adams, Wayne Verdun 1945- *WhoAm 90*
Adams, Wayne W. *ODwPR 91*
Adams, Welles V. 1924- *St&PR 91*
Adams, Weston 1938- *WhoAm 90, WhoWor 91*
Adams, William *PenDiDA 89*
Adams, William 1564-1620 *EncJap, WorAlBi*
Adams, William 1748-1831 *PenDiDA 89*
Adams, William 1772-1829 *PenDiDA 89*
Adams, William 1798-1865 *PenDiDA 89*
Adams, William Alfred 1960- *WhoEmL 91*
Adams, William C. 1940- *ODwPR 91*
Adams, William Duval 1917- *St&PR 91*
Adams, William Gillette 1939- *WhoAm 90*
Adams, William Hensley 1929- *WhoAm 90, WhoWor 91*
Adams, William Hester, III 1926- *WhoAm 90*
Adams, William Howard *ConAu 129*
Adams, William J. 1941- *St&PR 91*
Adams, William Jack 1929- *St&PR 91*
Adams, William Jackson, Jr. 1908- *WhoAm 90*
Adams, William James 1948- *WhoE 91*
Adams, William John, Jr. 1917- *WhoAm 90*
Adams, William Johnston 1934- *WhoAm 90*
Adams, William LeRoy 1929- *St&PR 91, WhoAm 90, WhoSSW 91*
Adams, William Mansfield 1932- *WhoAm 90*
Adams, William R *BiDrAPA 89, BioIn 16*
Adams, William Richard 1923- *WhoAm 90*
Adams, William Roger 1935- *WhoAm 90*
Adams, William Taylor 1957- *WhoWrEP 89*
Adams, William V. *St&PR 91*
Adams, William Valere 1948- *WhoEmL 91*
Adams, William W. 1934- *St&PR 91*
Adams, William Wade 1956- *WhoSSW 91*
Adams, William Wells 1937- *WhoE 91*
Adams, William White 1934- *WhoAm 90, WhoE 91*
Adams, William Wright *BiDrAPA 89*
Adams, William Yewdale 1927- *WhoAm 90*
Adams-Ender, Clara *BioIn 16*
Adams-Ender, Clara Leach 1939- *WhoAm 90, WhoAmW 91*
Adams-Esquivel, Henry E. 1940- *WhoHisp 91*
Adams-Jacobson, Nancy 1952- *WhoWrEP 89*
Adams-Roberts, Irose Fernella 1945- *WhoAmW 91*
Adams-Slone, Rita Diane 1949- *WhoAmW 91*
Adams-Staskin, Irene D. 1928- *St&PR 91*
Adamski, George 1891-1965 *EncO&P 3*
Adamski, Thomas Joseph 1947- *St&PR 91*
Adamski, Thomas Robert *BiDrAPA 89*
Adamsky, Robert Stephen 1947- *St&PR 91*
Adamson, Albert Scott, Jr. 1947- *WhoEmL 91*
Adamson, Arthur Wilson 1919- *WhoAm 90*
Adamson, Carl Theodore, Jr. 1951- *St&PR 91*
Adamson, Dan Klinglesmith 1939- *WhoAm 90, WhoSSW 91*
Adamson, Dorothy Marie 1920- *WhoAmW 91*
Adamson, Edward *BioIn 16*
Adamson, Eve 1940?- *BioIn 16, NotWoAT*
Adamson, Gary Bror 1934- *St&PR 91*
Adamson, Gary M. 1936- *St&PR 91*
Adamson, Gary Milton 1936- *WhoAm 90*
Adamson, Geoffrey David 1946- *WhoAm 90, WhoEmL 91, WhoWor 91*
Adamson, George *BioIn 16*
Adamson, George 1906-1989 *AnObit 1989, ConAu 129, News 90, SmATA 63*
Adamson, Harold 1906-1980 *OxCPMus*
Adamson, J. Douglas *BioIn 16*
Adamson, Jack 1923- *St&PR 91*
Adamson, Jane N. 1931- *WhoAmW 91*
Adamson, Jerome D, Jr 1944- *WhoAmA 91*
Adamson, Joe 1945- *WhoWrEP 89*
Adamson, John 1867-1950 *DcLB 98 [port]*
Adamson, John William 1936- *WhoAm 90*
Adamson, Joy 1910-1980 *BioIn 16, MajTwCW*
Adamson, Linny J 1952- *WhoAmA 91*
Adamson, Louise *BioIn 16*
Adamson, Mary Anne 1954- *WhoAmW 91*
Adamson, Oscar Charles, II 1924- *WhoAm 90*
Adamson, Rhonda Lee 1957- *WhoEmL 91*
Adamson, Richard Todd 1954- *BiDrAPA 89*
Adamson, Robert K *BiDrAPA 89*
Adamson, Scott 1946- *St&PR 91*
Adamson, Terrence Burdett 1946- *WhoAm 90*
Adamson, Thomas Charles, Jr. 1924- *WhoAm 90*
Adamsons, Uldis 1945- *WhoE 91, WhoWor 91*
Adamsson, Nils Tommy 1945- *WhoWor 91*
Adamy, George E 1932- *WhoAmA 91, WhoE 91*
Adan, Federico *BiDrAPA 89*
Adan, Suzanne Rae 1946- *WhoAmA 91*
Adanalian, Charles Ronald 1939- *St&PR 91*
Adanti, Michael J. *WhoAm 90*
Adanti-Joy, Patricia *ODwPR 91*
Adar, Uri 1928- *St&PR 91*
Adare, Lord 1841-1926 *EncO&P 3*
Adare, J. Robert 1927- *St&PR 91*
Adario 1650?-1701 *WhNaAH*
Adaskin, Frances James *IntWWM 90*
Adaskin, Murray 1906- *WhoAm 90*
Adato, Beverly Zweig 1955- *WhoEmL 91*
Adato, Perry Miller *WhoAm 90*
Adatto, Carl P 1917- *BiDrAPA 89*
Adawi, Ibrahim Hasan 1930- *WhoAm 90*
Adawi, Nadia Sharon 1958- *WhoAmW 91*
Adcock, Albert 1929- *St&PR 91*
Adcock, Betty 1938- *DcLB 105 [port]*
Adcock, C J 1904- *EncO&P 3*
Adcock, David Filmore 1938- *WhoAm 90*
Adcock, David Shaw 1960- *WhoSSW 91*
Adcock, David William 1958- *St&PR 91*
Adcock, Elizabeth Sharp 1938- *WhoWrEP 89*
Adcock, Fleur *BioIn 16*
Adcock, Fleur 1934- *FemiCLE*
Adcock, J. Michael 1949- *St&PR 91*
Adcock, James Luther 1943- *WhoSSW 91*
Adcock, Joe 1927- *Ballpl 90*
Adcock, Louie Norman, Jr. 1930- *WhoAm 90*
Adcock, Stephen Randall 1954- *WhoSSW 91*
Adcock, William Elton 1931- *St&PR 91*
Adcock, Willis Alfred 1922- *WhoAm 90*
Adcox, Gerald Wayne, Jr. 1955- *St&PR 91*
Adcox, Stephen Irvin 1946- *WhoAm 90, WhoEmL 91*
Adda-Guppi *WomWR*
Addabbo, Philip J. 1946- *St&PR 91*
Addae, Gina A. *BiDrAPA 89*
Addagoppe *WomWR*
Addams, Charles 1912-1988 *AnObit 1988, BioIn 16, WhoAmA 91N, WorAlBi*
Addams, Jane 1860-1935 *BioAmW, BioIn 16, WorAlBi*
Addams, Janice *ODwPR 91*
Addante, Linda Ann 1952- *BiDrAPA 89*
Addante, Steven M. 1956- *St&PR 91*
Addario, Dominick *BiDrAPA 89*
Addelson, Kathryn Pyne 1932- *WhoAmW 91, WhoWrEP 89*
Addenbrook, William J. 1938- *St&PR 91*
Addeo, John A. 1948- *St&PR 91, WhoAm 90*
Adderley, Cannonball 1928-1975 *OxCPMus, WorAlBi*
Adderley, Cannonball 1928-1989 *BioIn 16*
Adderley, Julian Edwin 1928-1975 *DrBlPA 90*
Adderley, Nat 1931- *BioIn 16, DrBlPA 90*
Adderley, Terence E. 1933- *St&PR 91*
Addes, George F. *NewYTBS 90*
Addes, Ira Samuel 1949- *BiDrAPA 89*
Addesso, Dominic James 1953- *St&PR 91*
Addicott, Warren Oliver 1930- *WhoAm 90*
Addie, Bob 1911-1982 *Ballpl 90*
Addie, Pauline Betz 1919?- *AuBYP 90*
Addington, Betty Jane 1945- *St&PR 91*
Addington, Bruce 1953- *St&PR 91*
Addington, Jacqueline S. 1941- *WhoSSW 91*
Addington, James H. 1938- *St&PR 91*
Addington, Kathy *St&PR 91*
Addington, L. H. 1894-1956 *Ballpl 90*
Addington, Larry *St&PR 91*
Addington, Raymond Joseph *WhoAm 90*
Addington, Robert *St&PR 91*
Addinsell, Richard 1904-1977 *OxCPMus*
Addis, Bob 1925- *Ballpl 90*
Addis, Harold Earl 1930- *St&PR 91*
Addis, James McKim 1934- *WhoAm 90*
Addis, Karen K. 1964- *WhoAmW 91*
Addis, Laird Clark, Jr. 1937- *WhoAm 90*
Addis, Lauane Cleo 1956- *St&PR 91, WhoEmL 91*
Addis, Richard Barton 1929- *WhoWor 91*
Addis, Sara Allen 1930- *WhoAmW 91, WhoWor 91*
Addison, Adele 1925- *BioIn 16, DrBlPA 90, IntWWM 90*
Addison, Byron Kent 1937- *WhoAmA 91*
Addison, Charles Henry 1941- *St&PR 91*
Addison, Chauncey *WhoAmA 91*
Addison, David Dunham 1941- *WhoSSW 91*
Addison, Edward L. 1930- *St&PR 91, WhoAm 90, WhoSSW 91*
Addison, Era Scott 1933- *WhoWrEP 89*
Addison, Ferguson 1922- *St&PR 91*
Addison, Harry Metcalf 1938- *WhoAm 90*
Addison, Herbert John 1932- *WhoAm 90*
Addison, James Clyde, Jr. 1947- *WhoSSW 91*
Addison, John 1920- *OxCPMus*
Addison, John Mervyn 1920- *IntWWM 90*
Addison, Joseph 1672-1719 *DcLB 101 [port], WorAlBi*
Addison, Mary Jane *WhoAmW 91*
Addison, Stephen Oliver, Jr. 1954- *WhoSSW 91*
Addison, Walter John 1926- *WhoAm 90*
Addison, William Oscar 1950- *WhoE 91*
Addison, Winnifred Allen 1934- *WhoAm 90*
Addiss, Stephen 1935- *IntWWM 90, WhoAm 90*
Addlestone, Nathan S. 1913- *St&PR 91*
Addlestone, Nathan Sidney 1913- *WhoAm 90*
Addleton, David Franklin 1954- *WhoEmL 91, WhoSSW 91*
Addonizio, Gerard C 1953- *BiDrAPA 89*
Addonizio, Joseph C. 1930-1989 *BioIn 16*
Adducci, Anthony J. 1937- *St&PR 91*
Adducci, Joseph Edward 1934- *WhoAm 90*
Adduci, Liane M. 1959- *ODwPR 91*
Adduci, Vincent James 1920- *WhoAm 90*
Addy, Alva Leroy 1936- *WhoAm 90*
Addy, Emmet 1908- *St&PR 91*
Addy, Frederick S. 1932- *St&PR 91*
Addy, Frederick Seale 1932- *WhoAm 90*
Addy, George Arthur 1915- *WhoAm 90*
Addy, Jo Alison Phears 1951- *WhoAmW 91*
Addy, John Kelly 1949- *WhoEmL 91*
Addy, Lowell David 1951- *WhoEmL 91*
Addy, Michael V. *WhoAm 90*
Addy, Obo *NewAgMG*
Addy, Rudolph Obo 1947- *BiDrAPA 89*
Addy, Wesley 1913- *ConTFT 8*
Ade, George 1866-1944 *BioIn 16, OxCPMus, WorAlBi*
Ade, Ginny *WhoWrEP 89*
Ade, James L. 1932- *WhoSSW 91*
Ade, Sunny King *DrBlPA 90*
Adeane, Michael Edward 1910-1984 *DcNaB 1981*
Adebimpe, Victor R 1945- *BiDrAPA 89*
Adebimpe, Victor Rotimi 1945- *WhoE 91*
Adebonojo, Festus O. 1931- *WhoAm 90*
Adedeji, Adebayo 1930- *WhoWor 91*
Adee, Alvey Augustus 1842-1924 *BioIn 16*
Adee, Bernard E. 1934- *St&PR 91*
Adegbite, Samson G *BiDrAPA 89*
Adegbite, Samson G. 1952- *WhoE 91*
Adegbola, Sikiru Kolawole 1949- *WhoEmL 91*
Adel, Arthur 1908- *WhoAm 90*
Adel-Sabzevari, Anoushhirvan *BiDrAPA 89*
Adela 1062?-1137 *WomWR*
Adelaide 931-999 *WomWR*
Adelaide of Salona *WomWR*
Adelaide of Savona *WomWR*
Adelaja, Olukayode 1936- *BiDrAPA 89*
Adelberg, Arthur William 1951- *St&PR 91, WhoEmL 91*
Adelberg, Doris *AuBYP 90*
Adelberg, Edward Allen 1920- *WhoAm 90*
Adele *WomWR*
Adelekan, Patricia Ann 1942- *WhoAmW 91*
Adelgren, Kermit Edward 1931- *St&PR 91*
Adelhardt, Andrew J. 1935- *St&PR 91*
Adeli, Hojjat 1950- *WhoAm 90, WhoEmL 91, WhoWor 91*
Adelis, Nancy C. 1953- *WhoAmW 91*
Adelizzi, Robert F. 1935- *St&PR 91*
Adelizzi, Robert Frederick 1935- *WhoAm 90*
Adell, Hirsch 1931- *WhoAm 90*
Adelman, Bunny 1935- *WhoAmA 91*
Adelman, Daniel William 1955- *WhoEmL 91*
Adelman, David Isaac 1964- *WhoSSW 91*
Adelman, Deborah Susan 1953- *WhoEmL 91*
Adelman, Dorothy McClintock *WhoAmA 91*
Adelman, Frank L 1917- *BiDrAPA 89*
Adelman, Graham L. *St&PR 91*
Adelman, Graham Lewis 1949- *WhoAm 90*
Adelman, Harold Frank *BiDrAPA 89*
Adelman, Herbert Bernard 1928- *St&PR 91*
Adelman, Irma Glicman 1930- *WhoAm 90*
Adelman, Jonathan Reuben 1948- *WhoEmL 91*
Adelman, Kenneth L. *BioIn 16*
Adelman, Michael L. 1952- *St&PR 91*
Adelman, Richard Charles 1940- *WhoAm 90*
Adelman, Rick 1946- *WhoAm 90*
Adelman, Robert Bardwell 1952- *WhoEmL 91*
Adelman, Robert Paul 1930- *WhoAm 90*
Adelman, Robert Wharton 1954- *St&PR 91*
Adelman, Saul Joseph 1944- *WhoSSW 91*
Adelman, Solomon *BiDrAPA 89*
Adelman, Stanley Joseph 1942- *WhoAm 90*
Adelman, Stanley R. 1925- *St&PR 91*
Adelman, Steven Alan *BiDrAPA 89*
Adelman, Steven Allen 1945- *WhoAm 90*
Adelman, Steven Herbert 1945- *WhoAm 90*
Adelman, William John 1932- *WhoAm 90*
Adelmann, Dorothy Schullian *BioIn 16*
Adelmann, Frederick Joseph 1915- *WhoAm 90*
Adelmann, Howard Bernhardt 1898-1988 *BioIn 16*
Adelmann, Penelope Owens *WhoAmW 91, WhoE 91, WhoWor 91*
Adelo, A. Samuel 1923- *WhoHisp 91*
Adels, Robert Mitchell 1948- *WhoAm 90*
Adelsheim, Mark Simon 1952- *WhoEmL 91*
Adelsheim, Steven N. 1957- *BiDrAPA 89*
Adelsman, Jean 1944- *WhoAmW 91*
Adelson, Alexander M. 1934- *WhoE 91, WhoWor 91*
Adelson, Edward Ralph *BiDrAPA 89*
Adelson, Howard Laurence 1925- *WhoAm 90*
Adelson, Irwin Philip 1936- *BiDrAPA 89*
Adelson, Lawrence Seth 1950- *WhoEmL 91*
Adelson, Leone 1908- *AuBYP 90*
Adelson, Lori Michelle *BiDrAPA 89*
Adelson, Marcia *BiDrAPA 89*
Adelson, Mark Hirsch 1960- *WhoEmL 91*
Adelson, Merv *BioIn 16*
Adelson, Merv 1929- *St&PR 91*
Adelson, Mervyn Lee 1929- *WhoAm 90*
Adelson, Sheldon G. *BioIn 16*
Adelstein, Stanford Mark 1931- *St&PR 91*
Adelstein, Stanley James 1928- *WhoAm 90*
Adelung, Johann Christoph 1732-1806 *EncO&P 3*
Aden, Alonzo J 1906-1963 *WhoAmA 91N*

Aden, Arthur Laverne 1924- *WhoAm 90*
Aden, Robert Clark 1927- *WhoSSW 91*
Adenauer, Konrad 1876-1967 *WorAlBi*
Adenbaum, Robert W. 1928- *St&PR 91*
Adenis, Jacques Andre Marie 1926- *WhoWor 91*
Ader, Joseph Daniel 1947- *WhoSSW 91*
Ader, Richard 1942- *St&PR 91*
Ader, Richard Alan 1951- *WhoAm 90*
Aderhold, John Edward 1925- *St&PR 91*
Aderton, Jane Reynolds 1913- *WhoAm 90*
Adewusi, Olukemi Iyabode 1956- *WhoAmW 91*
Adey, Kathleen Yvonne 1954- *WhoSSW 91*
Adey, Lionel 1925- *ConAu 132*
Adey, Michael T. 1947- *WhoE 91*
Adey, Robert Paul 1947- *WhoSSW 91*
Adey, W. Ross 1922- *WhoAm 90*
Adeyeye, Christianah Mojisola 1951- *WhoAmW 91*
Adh-Dhib, Muhammad *BioIn 16*
Adhemar, Jean 1908-1987 *BioIn 16*
Adhikari, Ambika P. 1952- *WhoEmL 91*
Adhin, Herman Sookdew 1933- *WhoWor 91*
Adhvaryu, Hareendra G 1937- *BiDrAPA 89*
Adhvaryu, Jaykrishna Hargovinddas 1932- *WhoWor 91*
Adickes, David 1927- *WhoAmA 91*
Adickes, H Frederick, Jr. 1929- *BiDrAPA 89*
Adie, Nora Susan 1953- *WhoAmW 91*
Adiel, Ray 1927- *St&PR 91*
Adiele, Nkwachkwu Moses 1951- *WhoSSW 91*
Adik, Stephen Peter 1943- *St&PR 91, WhoAm 90*
Adikes, Park T. 1931- *St&PR 91*
Adikes, Robert Kirk 1939- *St&PR 91*
Adiletta, Debra Jean Olson 1959- *WhoAmW 91, WhoEmL 91*
Adiletta, Joseph George 1920- *St&PR 91*
Adiletti, John Carmine 1944- *WhoSSW 91*
Adilman, Philip Harvey *BiDrAPA 89*
Adimando, Carmine F. 1944- *St&PR 91*
Adin, Michael 1933- *St&PR 91*
Adin, Nancy Edith 1938- *WhoAmW 91*
Adinoff, Bryon Harlen 1953- *BiDrAPA 89*
Adirim, Aaron 1946- *WhoWor 91*
Adiseshiah, Malcolm Sathianathan 1910- *WhoWor 91*
Adisman, Irwin Kenneth 1919- *WhoAm 90*
Adison, Shirley J. 1948- *WhoEmL 91*
Adjamah, Kokouvi Michel 1942- *WhoWor 91*
Adjani, Isabelle *BioIn 16*
Adjani, Isabelle 1955- *News 91-1 [port], WhoWor 91*
Adjani, Isabelle 1958- *CurBio 90 [port]*
Adkins, Alan Jeffrey 1948- *BiDrAPA 89*
Adkins, Anthony 1949- *IntWWM 90*
Adkins, Arthur William Hope 1929- *WhoAm 90*
Adkins, Barbara L. 1946- *WhoSSW 91, WhoWor 91*
Adkins, Ben Frank 1938- *WhoWor 91*
Adkins, Betty A. 1934- *WhoAmW 91*
Adkins, Bradley W. 1937- *St&PR 91*
Adkins, Cecil D. 1932- *IntWWM 90*
Adkins, Charles F *BiDrAPA 89*
Adkins, Craig Ivan 1963- *WhoEmL 91*
Adkins, David Paul 1951- *WhoE 91*
Adkins, Edward Cleland 1926- *WhoAm 90*
Adkins, Gerald Don 1954- *WhoSSW 91*
Adkins, Grady 1897-1966 *Ballpl 90*
Adkins, Gregory D. 1941- *WhoAm 90*
Adkins, Harvey John 1948- *WhoSSW 91*
Adkins, Homer Martin 1890-1964 *BioIn 16*
Adkins, Howard Eugene 1912- *WhoAm 90*
Adkins, Jan 1944- *AuBYP 90*
Adkins, Janet *BioIn 16*
Adkins, Jess T. *BioIn 16*
Adkins, John Earl, Jr. 1937- *WhoAm 90*
Adkins, John Nathaniel 1911- *WhoAm 90*
Adkins, Luther Pryor 1926- *St&PR 91*
Adkins, M. Douglas 1936- *WhoAm 90*
Adkins, Milton R. 1928- *WhoSSW 91*
Adkins, Rosanne Brown 1944- *WhoAmW 91*
Adkins, Roy Allen 1952- *WhoEmL 91*
Adkins, Terri Lynn 1957- *WhoAmW 91*
Adkins, Terry R 1953- *WhoAmA 91*
Adkins, Vincent K. 1957- *WhoE 91*
Adkins, Walter L. 1937- *St&PR 91*
Adkins, William Edward 1945- *WhoSSW 91*
Adkins, William H., II 1925- *WhoAm 90, WhoE 91*
Adkins-Hunt, Kathy L. 1962- *WhoEmL 91*
Adkins-Regan, Elizabeth Kocher 1945- *WhoAmW 91, WhoE 91*
Adkinson, Brian Lee 1959- *WhoEmL 91*
Adkinson, D. O. *AmLegL*
Adkinson, David Keith 1949- *St&PR 91*
Adkinson, James Allen 1944- *WhoSSW 91*
Adkison, Kathleen *WhoAmA 91*
Adkisson, Perry Lee 1929- *WhoAm 90, WhoSSW 91*
Adlai, Richard S. 1942- *St&PR 91*
Adlam, Derek Leslie 1938- *IntWWM 90*
Adland, Marvin Leon 1919- *BiDrAPA 89*
Adland, Peter Friend 1949- *BiDrAPA 89*
Adler, Aaron 1914- *WhoAm 90*
Adler, Abe *WhoAmA 91*
Adler, Abraham 1952- *WhoE 91*
Adler, Alexandra 1901- *BiDrAPA 89*
Adler, Alfred F. 1870-1937 *WorAlBi*
Adler, Allan Jack 1940- *BiDrAPA 89*
Adler, Benjamin *NewYTBS 90*
Adler, Benjamin 1903-1990 *BioIn 16*
Adler, Bill, Jr. 1956- *WhoEmL 91*
Adler, C. Mack 1920- *St&PR 91*
Adler, C. S. 1932- *BioIn 16*
Adler, C S 1932- *SmATA 63 [port], WhoWrEP 89*
Adler, Carol Ellen 1938- *WhoWrEP 89*
Adler, Carole 1932- *AuBYP 90*
Adler, Carole S. 1932- *BioIn 16*
Adler, Charles Elliot 1952- *BiDrAPA 89*
Adler, Charles S 1941- *BiDrAPA 89*
Adler, Charles Spencer 1941- *WhoAm 90, WhoWor 91*
Adler, Claire B. *BioIn 16*
Adler, Cyrus 1863-1940 *BioIn 16, WorAlBi*
Adler, Daniel Joseph 1954- *WhoEmL 91*
Adler, Dankmar 1844-1900 *BioIn 16*
Adler, David *BioIn 16*
Adler, David A. 1947- *BioIn 16, WhoWrEP 89*
Adler, David Avram 1947- *BiDrAPA 89, WhoE 91*
Adler, David Leon 1929- *St&PR 91*
Adler, David N *BiDrAPA 89*
Adler, David Neil 1955- *WhoEmL 91*
Adler, Dwain Robert 1955- *WhoEmL 91, WhoSSW 91*
Adler, Edward I. 1954- *ODwPR 91*
Adler, Edward Jerome 1932- *St&PR 91*
Adler, Erwin Ellery 1941- *WhoAm 90, WhoWor 91*
Adler, Felix 1851-1933 *WorAlBi*
Adler, Fred Peter 1925- *WhoAm 90*
Adler, Freda Schaffer 1934- *WhoAm 90*
Adler, Frederick R. 1925- *St&PR 91*
Adler, Frederick Richard 1925- *WhoAm 90*
Adler, Gerald 1924- *WhoAm 90*
Adler, Gerald 1930- *BiDrAPA 89*
Adler, Hans Gunther 1910-1988 *BioIn 16*
Adler, Harry 1906- *BiDrAPA 89*
Adler, Herbert M 1929- *BiDrAPA 89*
Adler, Herbert Morris 1929- *WhoE 91*
Adler, Hope *ODwPR 91*
Adler, Howard, Jr. 1925- *WhoAm 90*
Adler, Howard Bruce 1951- *WhoAm 90*
Adler, Irving 1913- *AuBYP 90, WhoE 91*
Adler, Isidore *NewYTBS 90*
Adler, Isidore 1916-1990 *BioIn 16*
Adler, Isidore 1925?-1990 *ConAu 131*
Adler, Jack Philip 1953- *WhoEmL 91*
Adler, Jacob P 1855-1926 *BioIn 16*
Adler, Jacques Henri 1916- *St&PR 91*
Adler, James Barron 1932- *WhoAm 90*
Adler, James R. 1950- *WhoEmL 91*
Adler, James Richard 1938- *St&PR 91*
Adler, Jane Eve 1944- *WhoAmW 91*
Adler, Jeffrey Alan 1952- *WhoEmL 91*
Adler, Jeffrey William 1962- *WhoEmL 91*
Adler, Jerome K. 1931- *St&PR 91*
Adler, Jerry *BioIn 16*
Adler, John Stanley 1948- *WhoEmL 91*
Adler, Julian 1917- *St&PR 91*
Adler, Julius 1930- *WhoAm 90*
Adler, Julius Ochs 1892-1955 *WorAlBi*
Adler, Justin H 1907- *BiDrAPA 89*
Adler, Karl 1957- *BiDrAPA 89*
Adler, Karl Paul 1939- *WhoAm 90*
Adler, Kenneth A. 1934- *St&PR 91*
Adler, Kenneth E *BiDrAPA 89*
Adler, Kenneth Harold 1947- *BiDrAPA 89*
Adler, Kraig 1940- *WhoAm 90*
Adler, Kurt 1905-1988 *AnObit 1988*
Adler, Kurt 1907- *BiDrAPA 89*
Adler, Kurt Alfred *BiDrAPA 89*
Adler, Kurt Alfred 1905- *WhoE 91*
Adler, Kurt Herbert 1905-1988 *BioIn 16, PenDiMP*
Adler, Kurt S. 1921- *St&PR 91*
Adler, Larry 1914- *IntWWM 90, OxCPMus, PenDiMP*
Adler, Larry 1938- *WhoAm 90*
Adler, Laszlo 1932- *WhoAm 90*
Adler, Laurel Ann 1948- *WhoWor 91*
Adler, Lawrence *BioIn 16*
Adler, Lawrence 1923- *WhoAm 90*
Adler, Lawrence E 1950- *BiDrAPA 89*
Adler, Lawrence Warren 1949- *BiDrAPA 89*
Adler, Lee 1926- *WhoAm 90*
Adler, Lee 1934- *WhoAmA 91*
Adler, Lee Paul 1956- *WhoEmL 91*
Adler, Lenard A *BiDrAPA 89*
Adler, Leonore Loeb 1921- *WhoAm 90, WhoAmW 91, WhoE 91, WhoWor 91*
Adler, Luther 1903- *WorAlBi*
Adler, Margot Susanna 1946- *WhoWrEP 89*
Adler, Marion *BioIn 16*
Adler, Mark 1955- *WhoEmL 91*
Adler, Martin 1934- *St&PR 91*
Adler, Marvin H. 1947- *St&PR 91*
Adler, Michael F. 1936- *St&PR 91*
Adler, Michael M. *WhoSSW 91*
Adler, Michael Richard 1945- *St&PR 91*
Adler, Michael S. 1943- *WhoAm 90*
Adler, Milton Leon 1926- *WhoWor 91*
Adler, Morris 1906-1966 *BioIn 16*
Adler, Mortimer J. 1902- *ConAu 33NR, MajTwCW*
Adler, Mortimer Jerome 1902- *WhoAm 90*
Adler, Myril 1920- *WhoAmA 91*
Adler, Myron 1924- *St&PR 91*
Adler, Nathan 1741-1800 *BioIn 16*
Adler, Nathan Marcus 1803-1890 *BioIn 16*
Adler, Norman Abner 1909-1989 *BioIn 16*
Adler, Patricia Ann 1951- *WhoEmL 91*
Adler, Peggy *AuBYP 90*
Adler, Peter Herman *NewYTBS 90*
Adler, Peter Herman 1899- *IntWWM 90, PenDiMP*
Adler, Philip *BioIn 16*
Adler, Philip 1925- *WhoAm 90*
Adler, Renata 1938- *MajTwCW, WhoAm 90, WhoWrEP 89, WorAu 1980 [port]*
Adler, Richard 1921- *OxCPMus, WhoAm 90*
Adler, Richard 1931- *ODwPR 91*
Adler, Richard Brooks *NewYTBS 90*
Adler, Richard Brooks 1922-1990 *BioIn 16*
Adler, Richard H 1939- *BiDrAPA 89*
Adler, Richard J. *St&PR 91*
Adler, Richard Seth 1958- *BiDrAPA 89, WhoE 91*
Adler, Robert 1913- *WhoAm 90*
Adler, Robert 1930- *WhoAmA 91*
Adler, Robert Jerome 1931- *WhoAm 90*
Adler, Robert M. 1953- *St&PR 91*
Adler, Roger Elliott 1942- *BiDrAPA 89*
Adler, Ruth 1915-1968 *AuBYP 90*
Adler, Ruth G. *St&PR 91*
Adler, Samuel 1898-1979 *WhoAmA 91N*
Adler, Samuel 1928- *IntWWM 90*
Adler, Samuel Elliot 1949- *BiDrAPA 89*
Adler, Samuel Hans 1928- *WhoAm 90*
Adler, Samuel I. 1924- *St&PR 91*
Adler, Samuel Irwin 1924- *WhoAm 90*
Adler, Sharon Swetz 1960- *WhoAmW 91*
Adler, Sherman 1928- *WhoE 91*
Adler, Sidney 1914- *BiDrAPA 89*
Adler, Sidney W. 1952- *WhoEmL 91*
Adler, Sol 1925- *WhoWrEP 89*
Adler, Stella *BioIn 16*
Adler, Stella 1902- *NotWoAT*
Adler, Stephen Fred 1930- *WhoAm 90*
Adler, Stephen Louis 1939- *WhoAm 90*
Adler, Theodore W. 1906- *St&PR 91*
Adler, Thomas W. 1929- *St&PR 91*
Adler, Verda Virginia 1956- *WhoE 91*
Adler, Warren 1927- *SpyFic*
Adler, William F. 1944- *St&PR 91*
Adler, Wolfe N 1933- *BiDrAPA 89*
Adler-Karlsson, Gunnar 1933- *WhoWor 91*
Adlerstein, Jo Anne Chernev 1947- *WhoEmL 91*
Adlestein, Joseph 1920- *BiDrAPA 89*
Adlman, Monroe 1925- *St&PR 91*
Adlmann, Jan Ernst 1936- *WhoAm 90*
Adloff, Virginia Thompson *NewYTBS 90*
Adloff, Virginia Thompson 1903-1990 *ConAu 130*
Adlon, Percy *BioIn 16*
Adlon, Percy 1935- *ConTFT 8*
Adlova, Vera 1919- *EncCoWW*
Adlow, Dorothy *WhoAmA 91N*
Admire, Sharman Lynne 1952- *WhoAmW 91*
Adney, Robert William 1955- *WhoEmL 91*
Adni, Daniel 1951- *IntWWM 90, PenDiMP*
Adnot, John 1950- *WhoSSW 91*
Adnrushkiw, Roman Ihor 1937- *WhoE 91*
Adodo, Yaovi 1942- *WhoWor 91*
Adoff, Arnold 1935- *AuBYP 90, BioIn 16*
Adoff, Arnold, Mrs. *WhoAmW 91*
Adolfi, Anthony J. 1931- *ODwPR 91*
Adolfo 1933- *BioIn 16, ConDes 90, WhoAm 90, WhoHisp 91, WhoWor 91*
Adolph, Mary Rosenquist 1949- *WhoAmW 91*
Adolph, Robert J. 1927- *WhoAm 90*
Adolphe, Enide *BiDrAPA 89*
Adolphi, Ronald Lee 1946- *WhoE 91, WhoWor 91*
Adolphs, Hans-Dieter 1942- *WhoWor 91*
Adolphus, Stephen Harris 1939- *WhoE 91*
Adom, Edwin Akuete 1939- *BiDrAPA 89*
Adom, Edwin Nii Amalai 1941- *WhoE 91*
Adomian, George 1922- *WhoAm 90, WhoSSW 91*
Adonizio, Ann Marie Catherine 1945- *WhoE 91*
Adonizio, Bernadine E 1948- *BiDrAPA 89*
Adorjan, Carol 1934- *ConAu 31NR*
Adorjan, Carol Madden 1934- *WhoWrEP 89*
Adorjan, Julius Joe 1938- *WhoAm 90*
Adorno, Theodor W. 1903-1969 *BioIn 16*
Adouette *WhNaAH*
Adoum, Jorge Enrique 1926- *HispWr 90*
Adragna, Mary Phyllis *BiDrAPA 89*
Adreon, Beatrice Marie Rice 1929- *WhoAmW 91*
Adreon, Harry Barnes 1929- *WhoAm 90*
Adri *WhoAm 90, WhoAmW 91*
Adriaenssens, Paul Joannes 1952- *IntWWM 90*
Adrian 1903-1959 *BioIn 16*
Adrian, Barbara 1931- *WhoAm 90, WhoAmA 91*
Adrian, Charles Raymond 1922- *WhoAm 90*
Adrian, David J. *ODwPR 91*
Adrian, Donna Jean 1940- *WhoAm 90*
Adrian, Edgar Douglas 1889-1977 *WorAlBi*
Adrian, Gary Alan 1951- *WhoEmL 91*
Adrian, Jane *BioIn 16*
Adrian, Mary *AuBYP 90*
Adrian, Max 1903-1973 *OxCPMus*
Adrian, Robert Mac 1954- *WhoEmL 91*
Adrian, William Bryan, Jr. 1937- *WhoAm 90*
Adriani, John 1907-1988 *BioIn 16*
Adrianopoli, Barbara Catherine 1943- *WhoAmW 91*
Adrianov, Oleg Sergeevitch 1923- *WhoWor 91*
Adrien, Daniel Omer 1942- *St&PR 91*
Adrine-Robinson, Kenyette 1951- *WhoEmL 91*
Adsett, C Alex *BiDrAPA 89*
Adshead, Mary 1904- *BiDWomA*
Adtkinson, D. O. *AmLegL*
Adubato, Richie *WhoAm 90*
Adubato, Susan Ann 1954- *WhoAmW 91*
Adubifa, Oludotun Akinyinka 1940- *WhoWor 91*
Aduddle, Larry Steven 1946- *WhoEmL 91*
Aduja, Peter Aquino 1920- *WhoAm 90*
Adulyadej, Bhumibol *BioIn 16*
Advani, Gul B 1938- *BiDrAPA 89*
Advani, Gulu Nanik 1953- *WhoEmL 91*
Advani, Mohan T 1934- *BiDrAPA 89*
Advincula, Marietta Magsaysay 1939- *WhoWor 91*
Ady, Cecilia Mary 1881-1958 *BioIn 16*
Ady, Julia Mary Cartwright 1851-1924 *BioIn 16*
Ady, Robert M. *St&PR 91*
Adzer, Laise *BioIn 16*
Adzigian, David John 1940- *WhoSSW 91*
AE 1867-1935 *EncO&P 3*
Aebel, Charles F. 1946- *St&PR 91*
Aebersold, Robert Neil 1935- *WhoAm 90, WhoE 91*
Aebi, Ernst *BioIn 16*
Aebi, Ernst Walter 1938- *WhoAmA 91*
Aebi, Tania *BioIn 16*
Aebischer, Delmer Wayne 1933- *IntWWM 90*
Aeby, Urs 1940- *St&PR 91*
Aegeri, Karl von *PenDiDA 89*
Aegerter, Ernest 1906- *WhoAm 90*
Aegerter, Michel Andre 1939- *WhoWor 91*
Aegerter, Paul Alan, Jr. 1956- *WhoSSW 91*
Aegidius, Carl Christian 1944- *WhoWor 91*
Aehegma, Aelbert Clark *WhoWrEP 89*
Aehlert, Barbara June 1956- *WhoAmW 91*
Aein, Joseph Morris 1936- *WhoAm 90*
Aeken, Hieronymus van *BioIn 16*
Aelders, Etta Palm d' 1743-1795? *EncCoWW*
Aelfgifu of Northumbria *WomWR*
Aelfwyn *WomWR*
Aelmis, Jan *PenDiDA 89*
Aelst, Pieter van *PenDiDA 89*
Aenou-Koutouzi, Marianna *EncCoWW*
Aeoliah *NewAgMG*
Aeolian Quartet *PenDiMP*
Aeolus *NewAgMG*
Aeppel, Glyn Ferguson 1958- *WhoWor 91*
Aerosmith *EncPR&S 89*
Aertsen, Pieter 1509-1575 *IntDcAA 90*
Aertsens, Henri Paul 1940- *WhoWor 91*
Aery, Shaila Rosalie 1938- *WhoAmW 91*
Aeschbach, Heinz 1946- *BiDrAPA 89*
Aeschbach, Walter 1946- *BiDrAPA 89*
Aeschbacher, Niklaus 1917- *IntWWM 90*
Aeschliman, Barbara Leigh *BiDrAPA 89*
Aeschylus 525?BC-456BC *WorAlBi*
Aesop 620?BC-560?BC *SmATA 64 [port], WorAlBi*
Aethelflaed *WomWR*
Aevermann, Richard R. 1946- *St&PR 91*
Afanas'ev, Mitrofan Michaelovich 1900-1988 *BioIn 16*
Afanas'ev, Yuri *BioIn 16*

Afanasiyev, Georgiy Dmitriyevich 1906- *WhoWor 91*
Afdahl, Daniel K. 1946- *St&PR 91*
Affandi 1910-1990 *BioIn 16*
Affatato, Joseph Frank 1952- *WhoWor 91*
Affaticati, Giuseppe Eugenio 1932- *WhoWor 91*
Affel, Giffin P. 1949- *St&PR 91*
Affelder, Lewis J. 1914- *St&PR 91*
Affeldt, John Ellsworth 1918- *WhoAm 90*
Affeldt, Thomas Michael 1946- *WhoEmL 91*
Affholder, Robert Wilson 1935- *St&PR 91*
Affinito, Lilyan Helen 1931- *St&PR 91*
Affleck, James Gelston 1923- *St&PR 91*
Affleck, Marilyn 1932- *WhoAm 90*
Affleck, Raymond Tait 1922-1989 *BioIn 16*
Affleck, Thomas 1740-1795 *PenDiDA 89*
Affler, Manuel *St&PR 91*
Afflerbach, Roy C., II 1945- *WhoE 91*
Affourtit, Daniel J. 1936- *St&PR 91*
Affronti, Lewis Francis 1928- *WhoAm 90*
Afgan, Naim Hamdija 1929- *WhoWor 91*
Afield, Walter Edward 1935- *WhoAm 90*
Afifi, Abdelmonem A. 1939- *WhoAm 90*
Aflak, Michel 1910-1989 *BioIn 16*
Aflaq, Michel 1910-1989 *PolLCME*
Aflatooni, Saeed 1936- *BiDrAPA 89*
Afman, Frans *BioIn 16*
Afnan, Ali-Mohammad Masoud 1957- *WhoWor 91*
Afonsky, Nicholas 1892-1943 *EncACom*
Afrah, Hussein Kulmie 1920- *WhoWor 91*
Africa, Birdie *BioIn 16*
Africa, Bruce 1941- *BiDrAPA 89*
Africk, Jack 1928- *St&PR 91, WhoAm 90*
Africk, Joel Jay 1956- *WhoEmL 91*
Afridi, Aijaz M.K. 1933- *WhoAm 90*
Afridi, Mohammed Arif 1939- *BiDrAPA 89*
Afridi, Parveen Niaz *BiDrAPA 89*
Afridi, Parveen Niaz 1944- *WhoAmW 91*
Afroz, Syed Mansoor 1955- *BiDrAPA 89*
Afsary, Cyrus *BioIn 16*
Afsary, Cyrus 1940- *WhoAmA 91*
Afshar, Amir Aslan 1922- *WhoWor 91*
Afshar, Farhad 1941- *WhoWor 91*
Aftalion, Albert 1874-1956 *BioIn 16*
Aftalion, Belinde 1921- *WhoAmW 91*
Aftanski, J. Alan 1948- *WhoEmL 91*
Aftergut, David 1953- *BiDrAPA 89*
Afterman, Allan B. 1944- *WhoWor 91*
Afterman, Joseph *BiDrAPA 89*
Afton, William E 1918- *BiDrAPA 89*
Aftoora, Albert Bruce 1939- *St&PR 91*
Aftoora, Patricia J. 1940- *St&PR 91*
Aftuck, Rodney D. 1955- *WhoSSW 91*
Afua Koba *WomWR*
Afxentiou, Afxentis Costa 1932- *WhoWor 91*
Afzal, Sayed Mohammad Javed 1952- *WhoEmL 91*
Afzali, Abdi 1955- *WhoEmL 91*
Afzali, Mansour 1949- *WhoWor 91*
Aga Khan, Karim, IV 1936- *WhoWor 91*
Aga Khan, Sadruddin 1933- *WhoWor 91*
Aga Khan, Yasmin *BioIn 16*
Aga-Oglu, Mehmet 1896-1948 *WhoAmA 91N*
Agaarwal, Uma Nandan 1944- *St&PR 91*
Agabian, Nina Martha 1945- *WhoAm 90*
Agadi, Venkappa M. 1932- *WhoWor 91*
Agaiby, Nagwa Nashed *BiDrAPA 89*
Agallianos, Dennis D 1923- *BiDrAPA 89*
Agam, Yaacov *WhoWor 91*
Aganbegian, Abel Gezevich *BioIn 16*
Aganoor Pompilj, Vittoria 1855-1910 *EncCoWW*
Agar, Eileen 1899- *BiDWomA*
Agar, Eunice Jane 1934- *WhoAmA 91*
Agar, Herbert 1897-1980 *BioIn 16*
Agar, John 1921- *BioIn 16, ConTFT 8*
Agar, John Russell, Jr. 1949- *WhoE 91*
Agard, Claire Nadya 1958- *WhoE 91*
Agard, David L. 1941- *IntWWM 90*
Agard, Emma Estornel *WhoAmW 91*
Agardy, Franklin J. 1933- *St&PR 91*
Agarwal, Arun Kumar 1944- *WhoSSW 91*
Agarwal, Ashok Kumar 1949- *WhoE 91*
Agarwal, Ashok Kumar 1950- *WhoWor 91*
Agarwal, Chouth Mal 1924- *WhoWor 91*
Agarwal, Constance Snyder 1943- *WhoAmW 91*
Agarwal, Dinesh 1955- *WhoEmL 91*
Agarwal, Gyan Chand 1940- *WhoAm 90*
Agarwal, Jagdish Prasad 1939- *St&PR 91*
Agarwal, Jugal Kishore 1947- *WhoEmL 91*
Agarwal, Kamala *BiDrAPA 89*
Agarwal, Rajiv 1956- *WhoWor 91*
Agarwal, Ramesh C *BiDrAPA 89*
Agarwal, Ramesh Chandra 1946- *WhoAm 90*
Agarwal, Ramesh Kumar 1947- *WhoEmL 91*
Agarwal, Satish Kumar 1938- *WhoE 91*
Agarwal, Uma *BiDrAPA 89*
Agarwala, Om Prakash 1942- *WhoE 91*
Agarwala, Rakesh 1952- *WhoEmL 91*
Agassi, Andre *BioIn 16*
Agassi, Andre 1970- *News 90 [port]*
Agassi, Joseph 1927- *WhoWor 91*
Agassiz, Elizabeth Cary 1822-1907 *BioAmW*
Agassiz, Louis 1807-1873 *BioIn 16, WorAlBi*
Agata, Burton C. 1928- *WhoAm 90*
Agate, James 1877-1947 *BioIn 16*
Agate, Robert M. 1936- *St&PR 91*
Agatep, Rodolfo Arellano 1940- *WhoE 91*
Agather, Victor N. 1912- *St&PR 91*
Agay, Karola 1927- *IntWWM 90*
Agbabian, Mihran Siragan 1923- *WhoAm 90*
Agbayewa, M Oluwafemi 1950- *BiDrAPA 89*
Agbetsiafa, Douglas Kofi *WhoWor 91*
Agboruche, William 1954- *WhoEmL 91*
Agee, Bob R. 1938- *WhoAm 90*
Agee, Candida Fink *BiDrAPA 89*
Agee, Earleen Heiner 1933- *WhoSSW 91*
Agee, James 1909-1955 *BioIn 16*
Agee, Joel *BioIn 16*
Agee, Mark L. 1956- *WhoEmL 91*
Agee, Mary Cunningham 1951- *WhoEmL 91*
Agee, Nelle Hulme 1940- *WhoAmW 91*
Agee, Philip 1935- *BioIn 16*
Agee, Thomas Anderson 1943- *St&PR 91*
Agee, Tommie 1942- *Ballpl 90*
Agee, Warren Kendall 1916- *WhoAm 90*
Agee, William C 1936- *WhoAmA 91*
Agee, William M. 1938- *St&PR 91, WhoAm 90*
Agee, William McReynolds *BioIn 16*
Agee, William Revelie 1931- *WhoE 91*
Ageloff, Lester 1927- *St&PR 91*
Ager, Eric Eduard 1940- *WhoWor 91*
Ager, Harvey Gerald *BiDrAPA 89*
Ager, Laurence Mitchell 1904- *IntWWM 90*
Ager, Law L *BiDrAPA 89*
Ager, Mary Ann Linz *BiDrAPA 89*
Ager, Milton 1893-1979 *BioIn 16, OxCPMus*
Ager, Stephanie 1946- *ODwPR 91*
Ager, Steven Allen 1941- *BiDrAPA 89*
Ager, Waldemar 1869-1941 *BioIn 16*
Agersborg, Helmer Pareli K. 1928- *WhoAm 90*
Agerwala, Tilak Krishna Mahesh 1950- *WhoAm 90*
Agganis, Harry 1930-1955 *Ballpl 90*
Aggarwal, Ajay Kumar 1959- *WhoSSW 91*
Aggarwal, Jagdishkumar Keshoram 1936- *WhoAm 90*
Aggarwal, Kumud *BiDrAPA 89*
Aggarwal, Shiv Shankar *BiDrAPA 89*
Aggarwal, Sundar Lal 1922- *WhoAm 90*
Aggarwal, Uma Nandan 1944- *St&PR 91, WhoAm 90*
Agger, Carolyn E. 1909- *St&PR 91, WhoAm 90, WhoAmW 91*
Agger, James H. 1936- *WhoAm 90*
Agger, James Harrington 1936- *St&PR 91*
Aggrey, Orison Rudolph 1926- *WhoAm 90*
Agha, Babar 1954- *WhoWor 91*
Agha, Ildiko S 1944- *BiDrAPA 89*
Agha, Jalal 1945- *WhoWor 91*
Agha, Mehemed Fehmy 1896-1978 *BioIn 16, ConDes 90*
Agha, Riaz Mahmood 1927- *St&PR 91*
Aghajanian, George Kevork 1932- *WhoAm 90*
Agharkar, Ujwala Shireesh 1961- *BiDrAPA 89*
Aghazadeh, Fereydoun 1948- *WhoSSW 91*
Aghill, Gordon *ConAu 130, MajTwCW*
Aghiorgoussis, Maximos Demetrios 1935- *WhoAm 90*
Aghoian, Sherry Lynne 1962- *WhoE 91*
Agi, Fuat 1940- *St&PR 91*
Agin, Frank C. 1929- *St&PR 91*
Aginian, Richard Dicran 1941- *St&PR 91*
Agins, Carol Ruth 1947- *WhoAmW 91*
Agins, Richard Howard 1943- *St&PR 91*
Agins, Theodore C. 1908-1989 *BioIn 16*
Agisheva, Nina *BioIn 16*
Agisim, Frederick Alan 1952- *BiDrAPA 89*
Agisim, Philip 1919- *WhoAm 90*
Agius, J.G. 1929- *St&PR 91*
Agius, Marcus Ambrose Paul 1946- *WhoAm 90*
Agle, David Patton 1933- *BiDrAPA 89*
Agle, Nan Hayden 1905- *AuBYP 90*
Agler, Charles F 1932- *BiDrAPA 89*
Agles, Charles Richard 1942- *St&PR 91*
Aglialoro, John J. 1943- *St&PR 91*
Aglialoro, John Joseph 1943- *WhoAm 90*
Aglietti, Hugo L. 1916- *St&PR 91*
Aglinsky, William 1951- *St&PR 91*
Aglio, James J. 1952- *St&PR 91*
Agnar, Thordarson *DcScanL*
Agnelli, Giovanni *BioIn 16*
Agnelli, Giovanni 1921- *WhoWor 91*
Agnelli, Umberto 1934- *WhoWor 91*
Agnello, Highland Mary 1964- *WhoAmW 91*
Agnello, Joseph 1938- *St&PR 91*
Agnes B. *BioIn 16*
Agnes B 1941- *ConDes 90*
Agnes de Nevers *WomWR*
Agnes of Dunbar *WomWR*
Agnes of Poitou 1024?- *WomWR*
Agness de Dampierre *WomWR*
Agnew, Allen Francis 1918- *WhoAm 90*
Agnew, Arthur Vincent 1932- *St&PR 91*
Agnew, Charles D. 1926- *St&PR 91*
Agnew, Dan F. 1944- *St&PR 91*
Agnew, F.E., III 1934- *St&PR 91*
Agnew, Franklin Ernest, III 1934- *WhoAm 90*
Agnew, Harold Melvin 1921- *WhoAm 90*
Agnew, Jack 1935- *ODwPR 91*
Agnew, James Blanchard 1915- *WhoAm 90*
Agnew, James Kemper 1939- *WhoAm 90*
Agnew, Jeanne LeCaine 1917- *WhoSSW 91*
Agnew, Jim 1945- *WhoWrEP 89*
Agnew, Miriam Nelwyn 1901- *WhoAmW 91*
Agnew, Patrick James 1942- *St&PR 91*
Agnew, Paul C *BiDrAPA 89*
Agnew, Paul C. 1923-1989 *BioIn 16*
Agnew, Peter Tomlin 1948- *WhoE 91, WhoEmL 91, WhoWor 91*
Agnew, Robert W. 1942- *St&PR 91*
Agnew, Rudolph Ion Joseph 1934- *WhoAm 90*
Agnew, Sam 1887-1951 *Ballpl 90*
Agnew, Seth Marshall 1921?-1967 *AuBYP 90*
Agnew, Spiro 1918- *BioIn 16, WorAlBi*
Agnew, Spiro Theodore 1918- *BiDrUSE 89*
Agnew, Theodore Lee, Jr. 1916- *WhoAm 90*
Agnew, Timothy Parsons 1954- *WhoEmL 91*
Agni, Aruna S *BiDrAPA 89*
Agnich, Richard John 1943- *St&PR 91, WhoAm 90*
Agnihotri, Krishna Venktesh 1946- *St&PR 91*
Agnihotri, Newal K. 1941- *WhoWrEP 89*
Agnihotri, Shashindra 1950- *WhoWor 91*
Agno, John G. 1940- *WhoAm 90*
Agnon, S Y 1888-1970 *MajTwCW*
Agnon, S. Y. 1888-1970 *WorAlBi*
Agnon, Shmuel Yosef 1888-1970 *BioIn 16*
Agnone, Anthony Michael 1941- *WhoE 91*
Agnos, Art *BioIn 16*
Agnos, Arthur Christ 1938- *WhoAm 90*
Agocs, Stephen F. 1928- *St&PR 91*
Agogino, George Allen 1920- *WhoAm 90, WhoWor 91*
Agoglia, John 1937- *BioIn 16*
Agol, Izrail' Iosifovich 1891-1937 *DcScB S2*
Agonafer, Dereje 1950- *WhoE 91*
Agonia, Barbara Ann 1934- *WhoWrEP 89*
Agoos, Herbert M 1915- *WhoAmA 91*
Agopoff, Agop Minass *WhoAmA 91N*
Agosin, Manuel Rodolpho 1943- *WhoWor 91*
Agosin, Marjorie 1955- *BioIn 16, ConAu 131, HispWr 90*
Agosin, Moises Kankolsky 1922- *WhoAm 90*
Agosin, Roberto Tomas 1948- *BiDrAPA 89*
Agosta, Karin Engstrom 1936- *WhoAm 90*
Agosta, Vito 1923- *WhoAm 90, WhoE 91*
Agosta, William Carleton 1933- *WhoAm 90*
Agosti, Frank Emanuel 1936- *St&PR 91*
Agostinelli, Richard J. 1941- *St&PR 91*
Agostinelli, Robert Francesco 1953- *WhoAm 90*
Agostini, Federico *PenDiMP*
Agostini, Peter 1913- *WhoAmA 91*
Agostini, Richard Joseph 1939- *St&PR 91*
Agostino, Joan *WhoWrEP 89*
Agostino, Veneziano 1490?-1540 *PenDiDA 89*
Agosto, Jose A 1961- *BiDrAPA 89*
Agosto, Juan 1958- *Ballpl 90*
Agoston, Thomas Charles 1957- *WhoEmL 91*
Agoult, Countess d' *EncCoWW*
Agoult, Marie, countess d' 1805-1876 *EncCoWW*
Agpaoa, Tony 1939- *EncO&P 3*
Agrait, Fernando E. *WhoAm 90*
Agrama, Frank *BioIn 16*
Agran, Larry *BioIn 16*
Agranoff, Bernard William 1926- *WhoAm 90*
Agras, William Stewart 1929- *WhoAm 90*
Agrawal, Bimalkumar R *BiDrAPA 89*
Agrawal, Dharma Prakash 1945- *WhoAm 90, WhoSSW 91*
Agrawal, Giridhari Lal 1937- *WhoE 91*
Agrawal, Harish Chandra *WhoAm 90*
Agrawal, Jagdish C. 1938- *WhoSSW 91*
Agrawal, Krishna Chandra 1937- *WhoAm 90*
Agrawal, Paramjit K *BiDrAPA 89*
Agrawal, Piyush C. 1936- *WhoSSW 91*
Agrawal, Prema 1936- *BiDrAPA 89*
Agrawal, Radheshyam B 1947- *BiDrAPA 89*
Agrawal, Sudha *BiDrAPA 89*
Agrawal, Vishwani Deo 1943- *WhoAm 90*
Agraz-Guerena, Jorge *WhoHisp 91*
Agre, Karl 1932- *St&PR 91*
Agre, Rodger S *BiDrAPA 89*
Agreda, Victor Hugo 1953- *WhoHisp 91*
Agrell, Alfhild 1849-1923 *EncCoWW*
Agren, P. Arlen 1936- *St&PR 91*
Agres, Stuart J. 1945- *St&PR 91, WhoAm 90*
Agres, Theodore Joel 1949- *WhoE 91*
Agress, Lynne Joy 1941- *WhoAmW 91*
Agress, M. Clifford *WhoE 91*
Agrest, Diana *WomArch*
Agresti, Jack Joseph 1937- *St&PR 91*
Agresti, Mark G *BiDrAPA 89*
Agresti, Michael L. 1942- *St&PR 91*
Agresti, Paul A. *St&PR 91*
Agresti, Virginia Mary 1932- *WhoAmW 91*
Agria, John Joseph 1938- *WhoE 91*
Agricola 1490-1555 *EncO&P 3*
Agricola, Georgius 1494-1555 *WorAlBi*
Agrin, Alfred *BiDrAPA 89*
Agrin, Gloria 1923-1988 *BioIn 16*
Agrippa von Nettesheim, Henry Cornelius 1486-1535 *EncO&P 3*
Agron, Joseph 1960- *St&PR 91*
Agrons, Laura Melohn 1957- *WhoEmL 91*
Agrusa, Lisa *BioIn 16*
Agsar, Vasant Baboorao 1945- *WhoWor 91*
Aguado, Dionisio 1784-1849 *PenDiMP*
Aguayo, Marquis de 1677-1734 *EncCRAm*
Aguayo, Albert J. *WhoAm 90*
Aguayo, Luis 1959- *Ballpl 90*
Aguayo, Luis Antonio Ferre 1904- *BioIn 16*
Aguayo, Miguel Mancera 1932- *WhoWor 91*
Aguayo, Patricia 1962- *WhoHisp 91*
Agud, Roger 1926- *WhoE 91*
Agudelo Botero, Orlando 1946- *WhoHisp 91*
Ague, Claudio 1937- *WhoWor 91*
Aguero, Bidal 1949- *WhoHisp 91*
Aguero Rocha, Fernando 1917?- *BioIn 16*
Agueros, Jack 1934- *WhoHisp 91*
Aguiar, Adam Martin 1929- *WhoAm 90, WhoE 91*
Aguiar, Yvette M. 1959- *WhoHisp 91*
Aguiar-Velez, Deborah 1955- *WhoHisp 91*
Aguiari, Lucrezia 1743-1783 *PenDiMP*
Aguila, Gumersindo, Jr. 1959- *WhoEmL 91*
Aguila, Pancho 1945- *HispWr 90*
Aguilar, Carlos A. 1943- *WhoHisp 91*
Aguilar, Carolyn Dexter 1948- *WhoAmW 91*
Aguilar, Eduardo E., Sr. 1940- *WhoHisp 91*
Aguilar, Ernest I. J. *WhoHisp 91*
Aguilar, Francis Joseph 1932- *WhoAm 90*
Aguilar, Gale Ramon 1932- *St&PR 91*
Aguilar, George A. 1930- *WhoHisp 91*
Aguilar, George Albert 1930- *St&PR 91*
Aguilar, Grace 1816-1847 *BioIn 16, FemiCLE*
Aguilar, Humberto Juan 1952- *WhoEmL 91, WhoSSW 91*
Aguilar, Ingrid Maria 1958- *WhoAmW 91*
Aguilar, Irma G. 1947- *WhoHisp 91*
Aguilar, Isabel 1936- *WhoAmW 91*
Aguilar, John L. 1934- *WhoHisp 91*
Aguilar, Juan David 1957- *WhoWor 91*
Aguilar, Karen 1952- *WhoHisp 91*
Aguilar, Maria P *BiDrAPA 89*
Aguilar, Mario Roberto 1952- *WhoHisp 91*
Aguilar, Octavio M. 1931- *WhoHisp 91*
Aguilar, Pat L. 1950- *WhoHisp 91*
Aguilar, Ricardo *HispWr 90*
Aguilar, Richard 1955- *WhoHisp 91*
Aguilar, Robert *WhoHisp 91*
Aguilar, Robert P. *WhoHisp 91*
Aguilar, Robert P. 1931- *WhoAm 90*
Aguilar, Rodolfo Jesus 1936- *WhoHisp 91*
Aguilar, Santiago J *BiDrAPA 89*
Aguilar Cardona, Antonio 1944- *WhoWor 91*
Aguilar Melantzon, Ricardo 1947- *HispWr 90, WhoHisp 91*
Aguilera, Augusto 1915- *BiDrAPA 89*
Aguilera, Bruce Allen 1948- *St&PR 91*
Aguilera, Donna Conant *WhoAm 90*
Aguilera, Elisa J. *WhoHisp 91*
Aguilera, L.C. 1949- *St&PR 91*
Aguilera, Rick 1961- *Ballpl 90, WhoHisp 91*
Aguilera, Salvador, Jr. 1955- *WhoHisp 91*
Aguilera-Jones, Linda Irma 1955- *WhoAmW 91*

Aguilera Malta, Demetrio 1909-1981 *HispWr 90*
Aguillon, Pablo R., Jr. 1945- *WhoHisp 91*
Aguilo-Seara, Miguel R *BiDrAPA 89*
Aguilu, Dalila E *BiDrAPA 89*
Aguina, Mary Elizabeth 1954- *WhoHisp 91*
Aguinaldo, Jorge Tansingco 1952- *WhoWor 91*
Aguinaldo, Rodolfo *BioIn 16*
Aguinsky, Lorenzo 1934- *WhoSSW 91*
Aguinsky, Richard Daniel 1958- *WhoWor 91*
Aguirre, Alfredo Aurelio 1956- *BiDrAPA 89*
Aguirre, Carlos Ernesto 1943- *St&PR 91*
Aguirre, Edmundo Soto 1926- *WhoHisp 91*
Aguirre, Edward *WhoHisp 91*
Aguirre, Francisca 1930- *EncCoWW*
Aguirre, Gabriel E. 1935- *St&PR 91*
Aguirre, Gabriel Eloy 1935- *WhoHisp 91*
Aguirre, Hank 1932- *Ballpl 90*
Aguirre, Henry John 1931- *WhoHisp 91*
Aguirre, Jesse 1944- *St&PR 91*
Aguirre, Jesse 1945- *WhoHisp 91*
Aguirre, Jimmie 1953- *WhoEmL 91*
Aguirre, Mark Anthony 1959- *WhoAm 90*
Aguirre, Michael Jules 1949- *WhoHisp 91*
Aguirre, Raul Ernesto 1955- *WhoHisp 91*
Aguirre, Robert 1964- *WhoEmL 91*
Aguirre, Roberto E *BiDrAPA 89*
Aguirre Cerda, Pedro 1878-1941 *BioIn 16*
Aguirre-Hauchbaum, Salvador F *BiDrAPA 89*
Aguirre Ramirez, Gonzalo *WhoWor 91*
Aguirre-Sacasa, Francisco 1944- *WhoAm 90*
Agujari, Lucrezia 1743-1783 *PenDiMP*
Agular, Steve G *BiDrAPA 89*
Agus, Jacob Bernard 1911-1986 *BioIn 16*
Agus, Zalman S. 1941- *WhoAm 90*
Agusta, Benjamin J. 1931- *WhoAm 90*
Agusta, Corrado *BioIn 16*
Agustin I, Emperor of Mexico 1783-1824 *BioIn 16*
Agustini, Delmira 1886-1914 *BioIn 16, HispWr 90*
Ah-Yoong, Georges 1949- *St&PR 91*
Ahaddian, Soheil *BiDrAPA 89*
Aharon, Paul 1945- *WhoSSW 91*
Ahart, Jan F. 1941- *St&PR 91*
Ahart, Jan Fredrick 1941- *WhoAm 90*
Ahart, Wayne Eugene 1940- *St&PR 91*
Ahasueris, King of Persia *BioIn 16*
Ahatsistari *WhNaAH*
Ahearn, Donald Patrick 1929- *WhoE 91*
A'hearn, Francis William 1932- *St&PR 91*
Ahearn, James 1931- *WhoAm 90*
Ahearn, Jo Ann 1948- *WhoAmW 91*
A'Hearn, Joan M. 1937- *WhoWrEP 89*
Ahearn, Joanne Theresa 1957- *WhoAmW 91*
Ahearn, John 1951- *WhoAmA 91*
Ahearn, John Francis, Jr. 1921- *WhoAm 90*
Ahearn, John Stephen 1944- *WhoE 91*
Ahearn, Patricia Jean 1936- *WhoAmW 91*
Ahearn, William Barry 1950- *WhoSSW 91*
Ahearn, William J. *ODwPR 91*
Ahearne, John Francis 1934- *WhoAm 90, WhoE 91*
Ahern, Donald Hugh 1928- *St&PR 91*
Ahern, Eugene 1896-1960 *WhoAmA 91N*
Ahern, F. Gregory 1951- *St&PR 91*
Ahern, Francis Thomas 1953- *WhoE 91*
Ahern, Geary Edward *BiDrAPA 89*
Ahern, Gene 1895-1960 *EncACom*
Ahern, John Joseph 1942- *WhoAm 90*
Ahern, Margaret Ann 1931- *WhoAmW 91*
Ahern, Patrick V. 1919- *WhoAm 90*
Ahern, Peter Lawrence 1947- *WhoEmL 91, WhoSSW 91*
Ahern, Thomas Francis 1947- *WhoWrEP 89*
Aherne, Brian 1902- *WorAlBi*
Ahhotep *WomWR*
Ahidjo, Ahmadou 1924-1989 *AnObit 1989, BioIn 16*
Ahl, Adolf Johannes 1933- *WhoWor 91*
Ahl, Alwynelle Self 1941- *WhoAm 90*
Ahl, David Howard 1939- *WhoAm 90*
Ahl, Frederick Michael 1941- *ConAu 30NR*
Ahl, Henry C *WhoAmA 91*
Ahl, Henry Curtis 1905- *WhoE 91*
Ahl, Marian Antoinette 1952- *WhoSSW 91*
Ahl, Richard A. 1948- *St&PR 91*
Ahl, Roger John 1963- *WhoWor 91*
Ahlander, Leslie Judd *WhoAmA 91*
Ahlberg, Allan 1938- *AuBYP 90*
Ahlberg, Daniel Berton 1945- *WhoEmL 91*
Ahlberg, Goran Lars 1942- *WhoWor 91*
Ahlberg, James George 1951- *WhoEmL 91*
Ahlberg, Janet 1944- *AuBYP 90*
Ahlberg, John Harold 1927- *WhoAm 90*
Ahlberg, Per Nnils Inge 1938- *WhoWor 91*
Ahlbrand, Russell L. 1924- *St&PR 91*
Ahlem, Lloyd Harold 1929- *WhoAm 90*
Ahlen, John William, III 1947- *WhoAm 90*
Ahlenius, William Matheson 1934- *WhoAm 90*
Ahlers, B. Orwin 1926- *WhoE 91*
Ahlers, Carl Theodor Joachim 1942- *St&PR 91*
Ahlers, Eleanor Emily 1911- *WhoAm 90*
Ahlers, Guenter 1934- *WhoAm 90*
Ahlers, Kenneth George 1958- *St&PR 91*
Ahlers, Rolf Willi 1936- *WhoAm 90*
Ahlersmeyer, Matthieu 1896-1979 *PenDiMP*
Ahlert, Fred 1892-1953 *BioIn 16*
Ahlert, Fred E. 1892-1953 *OxCPMus*
Ahlert, Robert Christian 1932- *WhoAm 90*
Ahles, Scott R 1951- *BiDrAPA 89*
Ahlfeld, William J. 1922- *ODwPR 91*
Ahlfeld, William Joseph 1922- *WhoE 91*
Ahlgren, Carl J. 1924- *St&PR 91*
Ahlgren, Ernst *DcScanL*
Ahlgren, Gilbert Harold 1913- *WhoAm 90*
Ahlgren, Roy B 1927- *WhoAmA 91*
Ahlgren, Torsten Lennart Siguard 1941- *WhoWor 91*
Ahlin, Gunnel Maria 1918- *EncCoWW*
Ahlin, Lars 1915- *DcScanL*
Ahlmann, Lis 1894-1979 *ConDes 90*
Ahlschier, Joseph Bailey 1928- *WhoAm 90*
Ahlschwede, Arthur Martin 1914- *WhoAm 90*
Ahlsted, David R 1943- *WhoAmA 91*
Ahlstone, Arthur 1933- *St&PR 91*
Ahlstrand, George Scott 1958- *WhoEmL 91*
Ahlstroem, G W 1918- *WhoWrEP 89*
Ahlstrom, Bert Tavelli, Jr. 1945- *WhoEmL 91*
Ahlstrom, Bjorn 1933- *WhoAm 90, WhoE 91*
Ahlstrom, David 1927- *IntWWM 90*
Ahlstrom, Michael Joseph 1953- *WhoEmL 91, WhoSSW 91*
Ahlstrom, Patrick Carlton 1945- *WhoEmL 91*
Ahlstrom, Richard Mather 1934- *WhoAm 90*
Ahlstrom, Richard Ward 1924- *St&PR 91*
Ahlstrom, Ronald Gustin 1922- *WhoAm 90, WhoAmA 91*
Ahlstrom, Timothy P. 1938- *St&PR 91*
Ahlstrom, Tom 1943- *ConDes 90*
Ahlstrom, William F. 1944- *WhoE 91*
Ahluvalia, Jasjit T. 1938- *St&PR 91, WhoE 91*
Ahluwalia, Bira 1944- *St&PR 91*
Ahluwalia, Madhu Bala 1948- *BiDrAPA 89*
Ahluwalia, Montek Singh 1943- *WhoWor 91*
Ahluwalia, Satwant 1945- *BiDrAPA 89*
Ahluwalia, Trevinder *BiDrAPA 89*
Ahluwalia, Yoglackshan K *BiDrAPA 89*
Ahmad ibn Sirin *EncO&P 3*
Ahmad Rithaudeen bin Ismail 1932- *WhoWor 91*
Ahmad Shah Ibni Al-Marhum Sultan Abu B 1930- *WhoWor 91*
Ahmad, Ambreen Altaf *BiDrAPA 89*
Ahmad, Anwar 1945- *WhoEmL 91*
Ahmad, Aqeeb *BiDrAPA 89*
Ahmad, Bashir *BiDrAPA 89*
Ahmad, Eqbal 1931- *WhoAm 90*
Ahmad, Kabir Uddin 1934- *WhoE 91*
Ahmad, M. Abraham 1953- *WhoE 91*
Ahmad, Mirza Muzaffar 1913- *WhoE 91*
Ahmad, Munawar 1948- *BiDrAPA 89*
Ahmad, Munawwar 1938- *WhoWor 91*
Ahmad, Naseer 1937- *WhoWor 91*
Ahmad, Rhona Beth *BiDrAPA 89*
Ahmad, Saleem M *BiDrAPA 89*
Ahmad, Salih 'Ubayd *WhoWor 91*
Ahmad, Shafi 1931- *BiDrAPA 89*
Ahmad, Shair 1935- *WhoAm 90*
Ahmad, Sheikh Nasir 1919- *WhoWor 91*
Ahmad, Sohail Ijaz 1950- *BiDrAPA 89*
Ahmad, Sohail Pervez 1945- *WhoWor 91*
Ahmad, Suleiman M. 1943- *WhoWor 91*
Ahmad, Syed Mashooq 1944- *BiDrAPA 89*
Ahmad, Syed Nisar *BiDrAPA 89*
Ahmadi, Manocher 1940- *BiDrAPA 89*
Ahmann, John Stanley 1921- *WhoAm 90*
Ahmann, Mathew Hall 1931- *WhoAm 90*
Ahmed, Abdulraouf Osman 1947- *WhoWor 91*
Ahmed, Ali 1934- *BiDrAPA 89, WhoE 91*
Ahmed, Anis 1931- *WhoWor 91*
Ahmed, Batul Anees 1950- *BiDrAPA 89*
Ahmed, Durre-Sameen 1949- *WhoWor 91*
Ahmed, Ghiasuddin 1933- *WhoWor 91*
Ahmed, Ilyas *BiDrAPA 89*
Ahmed, Iqbal 1951- *BiDrAPA 89, WhoE 91*
Ahmed, Javed 1960- *WhoE 91*
Ahmed, Khaled 1943- *WhoWor 91*
Ahmed, Khalil 1934- *WhoAm 90*
Ahmed, Mahmoud M 1954- *BiDrAPA 89*
Ahmed, Mohammed B 1935- *BiDrAPA 89*
Ahmed, Moudud 1940- *WhoWor 91*
Ahmed, Paul Iqbal 1933- *WhoE 91*
Ahmed, Qazi Zafar 1940- *WhoWor 91*
Ahmed, Saad Attia 1950- *WhoEmL 91*
Ahmed, Saeed Ud Din 1950- *WhoWor 91*
Ahmed, Samir El-Sebae 1946- *WhoWor 91*
Ahmed, Syed 1951- *BiDrAPA 89*
Ahmed, William *BioIn 16*
Ahmose-Nofretari *WomWR*
Ahn, Byung Hwan *BiDrAPA 89*
Ahn, Dae Hyun *BioIn 16*
Ahn, Don C 1937- *WhoAmA 91*
Ahn, Gregory B *BiDrAPA 89*
Ahn, Junghyo 1941- *BioIn 16*
Ahn, Sangwoo 1938- *St&PR 91*
Ahna, Heinrich de *PenDiMP*
Ahna, Pauline de 1863-1950 *PenDiMP*
Ahnell, Edward Eric, III 1963- *WhoE 91*
Ahneman, Patricia Mae, Jr. 1951- *WhoAmW 91*
Ahner, David Hurley 1943- *BiDrAPA 89*
Ahner, David James 1950- *St&PR 91*
Ahnert, W. Peter 1944- *St&PR 91*
Ahnsjo, Claes-Haakan 1942- *PenDiMP*
Ahnsjo, Claes Haakon 1942- *IntWWM 90*
Ahnstrom, Doris N. 1915- *AuBYP 90*
Aho, Juhani 1861-1921 *DcScanL*
Aho, Kalevi 1949- *IntWWM 90*
Aho, Kathleen Gail 1960- *WhoWrEP 89*
Aho, Paul Edward 1953- *WhoEmL 91*
Ahola, Joanne *BiDrAPA 89*
Ahonen, Roy R. 1926- *St&PR 91*
Ahonen, Vaino Axel 1933- *St&PR 91*
Ahrari, M. E. 1945- *WhoEmL 91, WhoSSW 91*
Ahren, Bo Arthur 1952- *WhoWor 91*
Ahrenberg, Johan Jakob 1847-1914 *DcScanL*
Ahrendt, Christine *WhoAmA 91*
Ahrendt, Eric *ODwPR 91*
Ahrendt, Karl F. 1904- *IntWWM 90*
Ahrendt, Mary E 1940- *WhoAmA 91*
Ahrens, Dale Elmer 1949- *WhoEmL 91*
Ahrens, Edward Hamblin, Jr. 1915- *WhoAm 90*
Ahrens, Franklin Alfred 1936- *WhoAm 90*
Ahrens, Gilbert Pomeroy 1938- *St&PR 91, WhoWor 91*
Ahrens, Hanno 1954- *BioIn 16*
Ahrens, Henry William 1918- *WhoE 91*
Ahrens, Kathleen Kay 1951- *WhoAmW 91, WhoEmL 91, WhoWor 91*
Ahrens, Kent *WhoAm 90, WhoAmA 91*
Ahrens, Mary Ann Painovich 1942- *WhoAmW 91*
Ahrens, Michael 1949- *WhoWor 91*
Ahrens, Paul C. 1952- *St&PR 91*
Ahrens, Paul Wesley 1939- *St&PR 91*
Ahrens, Rolland William 1933- *WhoSSW 91*
Ahrens, Rudiger 1939- *WhoWor 91*
Ahrens, Thomas H. 1919- *WhoAm 90*
Ahrens, William Henry 1925- *WhoAm 90, WhoWor 91*
Ahrensdorf, Robert Edgar 1916- *St&PR 91*
Ahrensfeld, Thomas Frederick 1923- *WhoAm 90*
Ahrold, Kyle Warren 1949- *WhoAm 90*
Ahrold, Robbin *ODwPR 91*
Ahroni, Jessie Helen 1948- *WhoEmL 91*
Ahronovitch, Yuri 1932- *PenDiMP*
Ahronovitch, Yuri 1933- *IntWWM 90*
Ahsan, Aitzaz *WhoWor 91*
Ahsanuddin, Khaja M 1936- *BiDrAPA 89*
Ahtes, James O. 1932- *ODwPR 91*
Ahti, Keijo Aatos 1935- *WhoWor 91*
Ahtiala, Pekka 1935- *WhoWor 91*
Ahuja, Jagdish Chand 1927- *WhoAm 90*
Ahuja, Manju 1961- *WhoAmW 91*
Ahuja, Pradeep 1950- *WhoWor 91*
Ahysen, Harry Joseph 1928- *WhoAmA 91*
Ai 1947- *ConAu 13AS [port]*
Ai Ch'ing 1910- *WorAu 1980 [port]*
Ai Qing 1910- *WorAu 1980 [port]*
Ai, Steven C. 1953- *St&PR 91*
Aibel, Howard James 1929- *St&PR 91, WhoAm 90*
Aich, Robert Louis 1953- *WhoEmL 91*
Aichele, Michael James 1948- *WhoSSW 91*
Aicher, Otl 1922- *ConDes 90*
Aicher, Richard Edward 1950- *St&PR 91*
Aichi, Kazuo 1937- *BioIn 16*
Aichinger, Ilse 1921- *EncCoWW*
Aickman, Robert 1914-1981 *WorAu 1980 [port]*
Aida, Ichiro 1932- *WhoWor 91*
Aida, Usuke *PenDiDA 89*
Aidekman, Alex *NewYTBS 90*
Aidekman, Alex 1915- *BioIn 16*
Aidinoff, M. Bernard 1929- *St&PR 91*
Aidinoff, Merton Bernard 1929- *WhoAm 90, WhoWor 91*
Aidlen, Jerome 1935-1986 *WhoAmA 91N*
Aidman, Charles *WhoAm 90*
Aidoo, Ama Ata 1942- *FemiCLE*
Aidt, Glenn E. 1940- *St&PR 91*
Aiello, Barbara 1947- *WhoAmW 91*
Aiello, Danny *BioIn 16, NewYTBS 90 [port]*
Aiello, Danny 1933- *News 90 [port], WorAlBi*
Aiello, Edward A. 1945- *WhoE 91*
Aiello, Edward J. 1963- *WhoE 91*
Aiello, Gennaro C. 1953- *WhoE 91, WhoEmL 91*
Aiello, Ray 1946- *St&PR 91*
Aiello, Robert *BioIn 16*
Aiello, Robert J. 1937- *ODwPR 91*
Aiello, Robert James 1937- *St&PR 91*
Aiello, Stephen *ODwPR 91*
Aiello-Contessa, Angela M. 1954- *WhoAmW 91*
Aig, Dennis Ira 1950- *WhoEmL 91*
Aigen, Betsy Paula 1938- *WhoAmW 91*
Aigen, Irving 1930- *St&PR 91*
Aigen, Jeffrey 1960- *St&PR 91*
Aiginger, Johannes 1937- *WhoWor 91*
Aigner, Dennis John 1937- *WhoAm 90*
Aigner, Lucien 1901- *WhoAmA 91*
Aihara, Cornellia 1926- *WhoWrEP 89*
Aihara, Herman 1920- *WhoWrEP 89*
Aikawa, Jerry Kazuo 1921- *WhoAm 90*
Aikawa, Masamichi 1931- *WhoAm 90*
Aiken, Beverly 1934- *MusmAFA*
Aiken, Charles 1872-1965 *WhoAmA 91N*
Aiken, Charles Moffatt 1934- *WhoSSW 91*
Aiken, Conrad 1889-1973 *AuBYP 90, BioIn 16, DcLB 102 [port], MajTwCW, WorAlBi, WrPh*
Aiken, Howard Hathaway 1900-1973 *WorAlBi*
Aiken, Jefferson Kirksey, Jr. 1941- *WhoSSW 91*
Aiken, Joan 1924- *AuBYP 90, BioIn 16, FemiCLE, MajTwCW, TwCCr&M 91*
Aiken, Lawrence James 1944- *WhoE 91*
Aiken, Lewis Roscoe, Jr. 1931- *WhoAm 90*
Aiken, Linda Harman 1943- *WhoAm 90, WhoAmW 91*
Aiken, Michael Thomas 1932- *WhoAm 90*
Aiken, Peter Haynes 1959- *WhoSSW 91*
Aiken, Richard Chalon *BiDrAPA 89*
Aiken, Robert McCutchen 1930- *WhoAm 90*
Aiken, Robert Morris, Jr. 1942- *St&PR 91*
Aiken, Scott *ODwPR 91*
Aiken, Ta-coumba T. *BioIn 16*
Aiken, William 1934- *WhoAm 90*
Aiken, William A 1934- *WhoAmA 91*
Aiken, William Eric 1935- *WhoE 91*
Aiken, William Minor 1932- *WhoWrEP 89*
Aiken, William Strauss, Jr. 1920- *WhoAm 90*
Aikens, Charlotte A. 1868-1949 *BioIn 16*
Aikens, Clyde Melvin 1938- *WhoAm 90*
Aikens, Joan Deacon 1928- *WhoAm 90*
Aikens, Martha Brunette 1949- *WhoAmW 91*
Aikens, Tom Pitt *ConAu 131*
Aikens, Willie 1954- *Ballpl 90*
Aikin, Lucy 1781-1864 *BioIn 16, FemiCLE*
Aikin, Warren *St&PR 91*
Aikins, Carroll 1888-1967 *OxCCanT*
Aikins, William Thomas 1827-1897 *DcCanB 12*
Aikman, Albert Edward 1922- *WhoSSW 91, WhoWor 91*
Aikman, Elflora Anna 1929- *WhoAmW 91*
Aikman, John Rae 1931- *St&PR 91*
Aikman, Ralph Coleman 1944- *WhoE 91*
Aikman, Robert E. 1932- *St&PR 91*
Aikman, Troy *BioIn 16*
Aikman, William Henry 1927- *St&PR 91*
Ailes, Roger 1940- *BioIn 16*
Ailes, Roger Eugene 1940- *WhoAm 90*
Ailes, Walter A. 1942- *St&PR 91*
Ailey, Alvin *BioIn 16*
Ailey, Alvin 1931-1989 *AnObit 1989, CurBio 90N, DrBlPA 90, News 90, WorAlBi*
Ailion, Bruce David 1957- *WhoEmL 91*
Aillaud, Charlotte *BioIn 16*
Aillaud, Emile 1902-1988 *BioIn 16*
Aillon, Gonzalo A 1940- *BiDrAPA 89*
Aillon, Gonzalo Alberto 1940- *WhoSSW 91*
Aillon, Julio Garret 1925- *WhoWor 91*
Ailloni-Charas, Dan 1930- *WhoAm 90, WhoWor 91*
Ailloni-Charas, Miriam Clara 1935- *WhoAmW 91, WhoE 91*
Aills, James Thomas *BiDrAPA 89*
Ailor, Earl Starnes 1920- *WhoSSW 91*
Aimbez, Gil 1940- *ConDes 90*
Aimee, Anouk 1932- *WorAlBi*
Aimee, Joyce 1930- *WhoAmW 91*
Ain, Maxine *BiDrAPA 89*
Ain, Sanford King 1947- *WhoE 91, WhoEmL 91*
Ainbender, David Lawrence 1959- *WhoEmL 91*
Ainbinder, Alfred J *BiDrAPA 89*
Ainbinder, Martin I 1935- *BiDrAPA 89*
Aine, Veli Valo 1919- *WhoWor 91*
Ainge, Danny *BioIn 16*
Ainge, Danny 1959- *Ballpl 90*

Ainley, Alison Claire 1963- *WhoWor 91*
Ainsbury, Ray *ConAu 31NR*
Ainsbury, Roy *ConAu 31NR*
Ainscough, Julie 1957- *IntWWM 90*
Ainsley, Alix *ConAu 30NR*
Ainsley, Sam 1950- *BiDWomA*
Ainslie, George 1944- *BiDrAPA 89*
Ainslie, Hew 1792-1878 *LiHiK*
Ainslie, John D *BiDrAPA 89*
Ainslie, Michael Lewis 1943- *WhoAm 90*
Ainslie, Tom *WhoWrEP 89*
Ainsmith, Eddie 1892-1981 *Ballpl 90*
Ainsworth, Catherine Harris 1910- *BioIn 16*, *WhoWrEP 89*
Ainsworth, Clifford F., Jr. 1942- *WhoE 91*
Ainsworth, David A. 1950- *WhoE 91*
Ainsworth, Don Ray 1953- *WhoSSW 91*
Ainsworth, Gary Michael 1942- *BiDrAPA 89*
Ainsworth, Kenneth George 1923- *WhoE 91*
Ainsworth, Mary D. Salter 1913- *BioIn 16*
Ainsworth, Mary Dinsmore Salter 1913- *WhoAm 90*
Ainsworth, Oscar Richard 1922- *WhoAm 90*
Ainsworth, Patricia 1947- *BiDrAPA 89*
Ainsworth, Ray *ConAu 31NR*
Ainsworth, Roy *ConAu 31NR*
Ainsworth, Thomas Clayton 1942- *St&PR 91*
Ainsworth, Walter S. 1928- *St&PR 91*
Ainsworth, William Harrison 1805-1882 *BioIn 16*
Ainsworthy, Roy *ConAu 31NR*
Airamo, Martti Mauno 1927- *WhoWor 91*
Aird, A. Marie 1934- *St&PR 91*
Aird, Catherine 1930- *TwCCr&M 91*
Aird, Eric Ronald 1936- *St&PR 91*
Aird, Jack A. 1924- *St&PR 91*
Aird, John Black 1923- *WhoAm 90*, *WhoWor 91*
Aird, Richard L. 1949- *St&PR 91*
Aird, Steven Douglas 1952- *WhoEmL 91*
Airen, Mahendra Singh 1944- *BiDrAPA 89*
Aires, Randolf H. 1935- *WhoAm 90*
Aires, Randolf Hess 1935- *St&PR 91*
Airhart, Judith Moss 1947- *WhoAmW 91*
Airington, Harold L. 1927- *WhoAm 90*, *WhoSSW 91*
Airola, Paavo *WhoAmA 91N*
Airth, Miskit 1939- *WhoAm 90*
Airto 1941- *BioIn 16*
Airut *EncCoWW*
Airy, Anna 1882-1964 *BiDWomA*
Aisenberg, Alan C. 1926- *WhoE 91*
Aisenberg, Irwin Morton 1925- *WhoAm 90*
Aisenberg, Sol 1928- *WhoAm 90*
Aisenbrey, Stuart K. 1942- *St&PR 91*
Aisenbrey, Stuart Keith 1942- *WhoAm 90*
Aisenstein, Clara *BiDrAPA 89*
Aisner, Joseph 1944- *WhoAm 90*
Aissa Koli *WomWR*
Aisse *EncCoWW*
Aissen, Michael Israel 1921- *WhoAm 90*
Aistars, John 1938- *WhoAmA 91*
Aistrop, Jack Bentley 1916- *AuBYP 90*
Aita, Carolyn Rubin 1943- *WhoAmW 91*
Aita, John A 1914- *BiDrAPA 89*
Aita, John Fordyce *BiDrAPA 89*
Aita, Mary Majella 1958- *WhoAmW 91*
Aitay, Victor *IntWWM 90*, *WhoAm 90*
Aitcheson, Gary E. 1944- *BiDrAPA 89*
Aitcheson, Robert Day 1946- *WhoEmL 91*
Aitchison, Beatrice 1908- *WhoAmW 91*, *WhoWor 91*
Aithal, S. Krishnamoorthy 1938- *WhoWor 91*
Aitken, Amy 1952- *BioIn 16*
Aitken, Diane Legner 1938- *WhoAmW 91*
Aitken, Greig Dwight Walker 1948- *WhoSSW 91*
Aitken, Hugh 1924- *IntWWM 90*
Aitken, Hugh George Jeffrey 1922- *WhoAm 90*
Aitken, Molly Bennett 1944- *WhoAmW 91*
Aitken, Philip M. 1902- *St&PR 91*
Aitken, Robert 1917- *ConAu 130*
Aitken, Robert 1939- *IntWWM 90*
Aitken, Rosemary Theresa 1946- *WhoEmL 91*
Aitken, Thomas Dean 1939- *WhoAm 90*
Aitken, William Nelson 1926- *St&PR 91*
Aitkin, W. Roy 1932- *WhoAm 90*
Aitmatov, Chingiz *BioIn 16*
Aitmatov, Chingiz 1928- *MajTwCW*
Aitmatov, Chingiz Torekulovich 1928- *WhoWor 91*
Aittokoski, Margaretha Marina 1934- *WhoWor 91*
Aiuto, Beverly Bradley 1938- *WhoAmW 91*
Aiuto, Russell 1934- *WhoAm 90*
Aiuvalasit, Anthony George, Jr. 1949- *WhoAm 90*
Aivazian, Garabed H 1912- *BiDrAPA 89*
Aiyangar, Srinivasa Ramanujan 1887-1920 *BioIn 16*
Aizawa, Takashi 1946- *WhoWor 91*
Aizenberg, Roberto 1928- *ArtLatA*
Aizu, Izumi 1952- *WhoWor 91*
Ajans, Z A *BiDrAPA 89*
Ajawara, Augustus Chiedozie 1953- *WhoEmL 91*
Ajax, Henry Adam 1940- *WhoSSW 91*
Ajax, Tom R. 1949- *St&PR 91*
Ajay, Abe 1919- *WhoAm 90*, *WhoAmA 91*
Ajaye, Franklin 1949- *DrBlPA 90*
Ajayi, Lawrence Olatunde 1949- *WhoWor 91*
Ajayi, Oladejo Oyeleke 1942- *WhoWor 91*
Ajayi, William Olufemi 1945- *WhoWor 91*
Ajbani, Prabodh D. 1949- *St&PR 91*
Ajemian, Anahid *PenDiMP*
Ajemian, Robert Myron 1925- *WhoAm 90*
Ajemian, Warren Haig 1919- *St&PR 91*
Ajigbotafe, Christopher I *BiDrAPA 89*
Ajlouny, Joseph Saeed, Jr. 1958- *WhoEmL 91*
Ajmone-Marsan, Guido 1947- *IntWWM 90*, *PenDiMP*
Ajootian, Khosrov 1891-1958 *WhoAmA 91N*
Ajrawat, Sukhveen K *BiDrAPA 89*
Ajroldi, Paolo *BioIn 16*
Ajzen, Daniel 1950- *WhoHisp 91*
Ajzenberg-Selove, Fay 1926- *WhoAm 90*, *WhoAmW 91*
Ak, Dogan 1928- *WhoE 91*
Akabas, Sheila Helene 1931- *WhoE 91*
Akacich, Richelle Dee 1958- *WhoAmW 91*
Akaha, Tsuneo 1949- *WhoEmL 91*
Akaishi, Tadashi 1925- *WhoAm 90*
Akaka, Daniel Kahikina 1924- *WhoAm 90*
Akaka, Jeffrey 1953- *BiDrAPA 89*
Akalaitis, JoAnne *BioIn 16*
Akalaitis, JoAnne 1937- *NotWoAT*
Akamu, Nina 1955- *WhoAmA 91*
Akao, Bin 1899-1990 *BioIn 16*
Akaoka, Ieo 1928- *WhoWor 91*
Akaraguian, Haiganoush 1923- *St&PR 91*
Akaruru, Inatio *WhoWor 91*
Akas, Thomas C. 1930- *ODwPR 91*
Akasaki, Toshiro 1925- *WhoAm 90*
Akashah, Mary Scoboria 1949- *WhoWrEP 89*
Akashi, Jiro 1920- *St&PR 91*
Akashi, Yasushi 1931- *WhoWor 91*
Akashi, Yoji 1928- *WhoWor 91*
Akasofu, Syun-Ichi 1930- *WhoAm 90*
Akass, John Ewart 1933-1990 *ConAu 131*
Akass, Jon *ConAu 131*
Akawie, Thomas Frank 1935- *WhoAmA 91*
Akay, Emin 1938- *WhoWor 91*
Akaydin, Mehmet Saban *BiDrAPA 89*
Akbar, Emperor of Hindustan 1542-1605 *BioIn 16*
Akbar, Mohammad Zia 1945- *WhoWor 91*
Akbar, Raja Muhammad 1949- *BiDrAPA 89*
Akbarally, Tyeab 1957- *WhoWor 91*
Akbiyik, M. Aydin 1935- *WhoWor 91*
Akbulut, Yildirim 1935- *WhoWor 91*
Akcasu, Ahmet Ziyaeddin 1924- *WhoAm 90*
Ake, Catherine Ann 1949- *WhoE 91*
Ake, John Notley 1941- *WhoAm 90*
Ake, Mary Katherine 1930- *WhoAmW 91*
Ake, Simeon 1932- *WhoWor 91*
Akeley, Delia 1875-1970 *BioAmW*
Akeley, Robert N 1930- *BiDrAPA 89*
Aken, Harold E., Jr. 1929- *St&PR 91*
Akenhead, Linda Casselman 1955- *WhoSSW 91*
Akenson, Donald Harman 1941- *WhoAm 90*, *WhoWrEP 89*
Aker, G. Colburn 1944- *ODwPR 91*
Aker, Jack 1940- *Ballpl 90 [port]*
Aker, Walter William 1918- *St&PR 91*
Akera, Tai 1932- *WhoAm 90*
Akerberg, Ake 1917- *BiDrAPA 89*
Akerblom, Mats 1933- *WhoWor 91*
Akerkar, Shobha Anand 1941- *WhoAmW 91*
Akerlof, Carl William 1938- *WhoAm 90*
Akerlow, Charles W. 1940- *St&PR 91*
Akerman, Amos Tappan 1821-1880 *BiDrUSE 89*
Akerman, Chantal *BioIn 16*
Akerman, John *PenDiDA 89*
Akerman, Joseph Lax, Jr. 1950- *WhoEmL 91*
Akerman, Nathaniel Howard 1947- *WhoE 91*
Akers, Adela 1933- *WhoAmA 91*
Akers, Brock Cordt 1956- *WhoEmL 91*
Akers, CathayAnne Marie 1952- *WhoAmW 91*
Akers, Charles David 1948- *WhoEmL 91*
Akers, Floyd *AuBYP 90*, *MajTwCW*
Akers, Gary 1951- *WhoAmA 91*
Akers, James Michael 1961- *WhoSSW 91*
Akers, John F. *St&PR 91*
Akers, John F. 1934- *BioIn 16*, *WorAlBi*
Akers, John Fellows 1934- *WhoAm 90*, *WhoE 91*, *WhoWor 91*
Akers, Karen *BioIn 16*
Akers, Larry S. 1949- *St&PR 91*
Akers, M.F. 1939- *St&PR 91*
Akers, Monte Edward 1950- *WhoEmL 91*
Akers, Ottie Clay 1949- *WhoE 91*
Akers, Sharon Lynn 1956- *WhoEmL 91*
Akers, Sheldon Buckingham, Jr. 1926- *WhoAm 90*
Akers, Suzanne Selberg 1947- *WhoEmL 91*
Akers, Tom, Jr. 1919- *WhoAm 90*
Akers, William Walter 1922- *WhoAm 90*
Akerson, Alan W. *ODwPR 91*, *WhoAm 90*
Akerson, Daniel Francis 1948- *St&PR 91*
Akerson, Louise *BioIn 16*
Akerstedt, Allan Nils 1950- *WhoWor 91*
Akert, Konrad Hans 1919- *WhoWor 91*
Akeson, Bertil Johan 1934- *WhoWor 91*
Akeson, Wayne Henry 1928- *WhoAm 90*
Akesson, Anders Gustav 1951- *WhoWor 91*
Akesson, Norman Berndt 1914- *WhoAm 90*
Akesson, Sonja 1926-1977 *DcScanL*
Akhenaton, King of Egypt *BioIn 16*
Akhiezer, Naum Il'ich 1901-1980 *DcScB S2*
Akhmadulina, Bella Akhatovna 1937- *EncCoWW*
Akhmatova, Anna 1888-1966 *MajTwCW*, *PoeCrit 2 [port]*, *WorAlBi*
Akhmatova, Anna 1889-1966 *ConLC 64 [port]*, *EncCoWW*
Akhmatova, Anna Andreevna 1889-1966 *BioIn 16*
Akhromeyev, Sergei 1923- *BioIn 16*
Akhtar, Abdul Hafeez 1940- *WhoWor 91*
Akhtar, Masud 1943- *WhoWor 91*
Akhtar, Nadeema 1954- *BiDrAPA 89*
Akhtar, Salim 1933- *BiDrAPA 89*
Akhtar, Salman *BiDrAPA 89*
Akhtar, Shaheda B 1949- *BiDrAPA 89*
Akhtar, Shamim *WhoWor 91*
Akhter, Mohammad Nasir 1944- *WhoAm 90*
Akhund, Iqbal 1924- *WhoWor 91*
Akhurst, Harold Weldon 1913- *St&PR 91*
Akhvlediani, Elena Dmitrievna 1901- *BiDWomA*
Aki, Keiiti 1930- *WhoAm 90*
Akiba ben Joseph 50?-132 *EncO&P 3*
Akiba, Hiroya 1945- *WhoWor 91*
Akihito, Emperor 1933- *EncJap*
Akihito, Emperor of Japan *BioIn 16*
Akihito, Emperor of Japan 1933- *NewYTBS 90 [port]*, *News 90 [port]*
Akil, Mayada 1958- *BiDrAPA 89*
Akimoto, Eiichi 1943- *WhoWor 91*
Akimoto, Haruo 1906- *BiDrAPA 89*
Akin, Bobby *BioIn 16*
Akin, Gwen 1950- *WhoAmA 91*
Akin, Hikmet 1948- *WhoWor 91*
Akin, John G. 1911- *St&PR 91*
Akin, Judith Blevins *BiDrAPA 89*
Akin, Mary Jane 1948- *WhoEmL 91*
Akin, Nyla Maudean 1945- *WhoAmW 91*
Akin, Phil *BioIn 16*
Akin, Ralph Hardie, Jr. 1938- *WhoWor 91*
Akin, Richard Ellis 1945- *St&PR 91*
Akin, Robert M. *BioIn 16*
Akin, Robert M., Jr. 1904- *St&PR 91*
Akin, Saim B *BiDrAPA 89*
Akin, Wallace Elmus 1923- *WhoAm 90*
Akin, Warren 1811-1877 *AmLegL*
Akina, Eleanore G 1921- *BiDrAPA 89*
Akina, Joseph Apukai *AmLegL*
Akinaka, Asa Masayoshi 1938- *WhoAm 90*
Akinc, Umit 1944- *WhoSSW 91*
Akinkugbe, Oladipo Olujimi 1933- *WhoWor 91*
Akins, Claude 1918- *WorAlBi*
Akins, Future Renee 1950- *WhoAmA 91*
Akins, George Charles 1917- *WhoWor 91*
Akins, Jerry Wayne 1943- *St&PR 91*
Akins, Keith B *BiDrAPA 89*
Akins, Richard Nevin *BiDrAPA 89*
Akins, Thomas Beamish 1809-1891 *DcCanB 12*
Akins, Zane Vernon 1940- *WhoAm 90*, *WhoE 91*
Akins, Zoe 1886-1958 *BioIn 16*, *FemiCLE*, *NotWoAT*, *WorAlBi*
Akipa *WhNaAH*
Akiskal, Hagop Souren 1944- *BiDrAPA 89*
Akiyama Saneyuki 1868-1918 *EncJap*
Akiyama, Carol Lynn 1946- *WhoEmL 91*
Akiyama, Kazuo *AuBYP 90*
Akiyama, Kazuyoshi 1941- *IntWWM 90*, *WhoAm 90*, *WhoE 91*
Akiyama, Masayuki 1930- *WhoWor 91*
Akiyoshi Toshiko 1929- *EncJap*
Akiyoshi, Toshiko 1929- *BioIn 16*, *WhoAm 90*
Akl, Aida F. 1957- *WhoWrEP 89*
Aklonis, John Joseph 1940- *WhoAm 90*
Akman, Jeffrey Scott 1956- *BiDrAPA 89*, *WhoE 91*
Akman, Sevil *BiDrAPA 89*
Akmatov, Tashtanbek Akmatovich 1938- *WhoWor 91*
Akolkar, Vasant Vinayak 1911- *EncPaPR 91*
Akomer, Argon 1925- *BiDrAPA 89*
Akos, Francis 1922- *IntWWM 90*, *WhoAm 90*
Akoto, Yaw 1952- *WhoEmL 91*
Akre, Charles Thomas, Jr. 1942- *St&PR 91*
Akre, Steven Heetland 1952- *WhoEmL 91*
Akridge, Paul Bai 1952- *WhoWor 91*
Akritidis, Constantinos Basil 1938- *WhoWor 91*
Aksakof, Alexander N. 1832-1903 *EncO&P 3*
Aksakoff, Alexander Nikolajewitsch 1832-1903 *EncPaPR 91*
Akselrad, David Martin 1959- *WhoEmL 91*
Akselrod, Pavel Borisovich 1850-1928 *BioIn 16*
Akselrod, Yulia *BioIn 16*
Aksen, Gerald 1930- *WhoAm 90*
Aksen, Howard Stephen 1936- *WhoAm 90*
Aksenov, Vasilii Pavlovich 1932- *BioIn 16*
Aksin, Mustafa 1931- *WhoWor 91*
Aksoy, Atilla Cezmi 1949- *WhoWor 91*
Akst, Barbara Blattner 1955- *WhoAmW 91*
Akst, Harry 1894-1963 *BioIn 16*, *OxCPMus*
Akston, James *WhoAmA 91N*
Aksu, Engin Gungor *BiDrAPA 89*
Aksu, Errol Michael 1961- *BiDrAPA 89*
Aksyonov, Vassily 1932- *BioIn 16*, *CurBio 90 [port]*
Aksyonov, Vassily Pavlovich 1932- *WhoAm 90*, *WhoWrEP 89*
Aktug, Bulent K 1931- *BiDrAPA 89*
Akubue, Innocent Emeka 1957- *WhoWor 91*
Akuna, Janis Cindy 1950- *WhoAmW 91*
Akurgal, Ekrem 1911- *ConAu 130*
Akutagawa Ryunosuke 1892-1927 *EncJap*
Akutagawa, Donald 1923- *WhoAm 90*
Akylas, Triantaphyllos R. 1955- *WhoE 91*
Al B. Sure *BioIn 16*
Al-Abed, Ibrahim Abdul-Rahman 1941- *WhoWor 91*
Al-Afghani, Sayyid Jamal ad-Din 1838-1897 *BioIn 16*
Al-Alawi, Ahmad ibn Mustafa 1869-1934 *BioIn 16*
Al-Ali, Saleh Ali 1955- *WhoWor 91*
Al-Amiri, Fatina *BiDrAPA 89*
Al-Amri, Saad Saeed 1953- *WhoWor 91*
Al-Ansari, Essam Adel *BiDrAPA 89*
Al-Arashi, Abdul Karim *WhoWor 91*
Al-Arrayed, Jalil Ebrahim 1933- *WhoWor 91*
Al-Asadi, Ghada O *BiDrAPA 89*
Al-Ashtal, Abdalla Saleh 1940- *WhoWor 91*
Al-Attas, Syed Muhammad al-Naquib 1931- *WhoWor 91*
Al-Attiyah, Abdulla bin Khalifa *WhoWor 91*
Al-Baid, Ali Salim *WhoWor 91*
Al-Banna, Hassan 1906-1949 *BioIn 16*
Al-Basha, Imad Musa 1954- *BiDrAPA 89*
Al-Chalabi, Hatem Rasheed 1942- *BiDrAPA 89*, *WhoE 91*
Al-Chalabi, Issam Abdulraheem 1942- *WhoWor 91*
Al-Chalabi, Margery Lee 1939- *WhoAmW 91*, *WhoWor 91*
Al-Dhahir, Mohammad Wassil 1924- *WhoWor 91*
Al-Faqih, Asad Mansur 1909-1989 *BioIn 16*
Al-Faruqi, Lamya' 1927-1986 *BioIn 16*
Al-Faruqi, Lois Ibsen 1927-1986 *BioIn 16*
Al-Fayed, Mohamed 1933- *BioIn 16*
Al-Fishawi, Sabet Girgis 1930- *WhoWor 91*
Al-Ghussein, Jaweed *BioIn 16*
Al-Hafeez, Humza 1931- *WhoAm 90*, *WhoWor 91*
Al-Hammad, Mohammed Abdulla 1940- *WhoWor 91*
Al-Hammami, Rafik Ismail 1947- *WhoWor 91*
Al-Hosri, Mohammad Salem *BiDrAPA 89*
Al-Husayni, Amin *BioIn 16*
Al-Husseini, Amin *BioIn 16*
Al-Iryani, Abdul Karim 1935- *WhoWor 91*
Al-Jamali, Mohammed Fadhel 1903- *BioIn 16*
Al-Kabbani, Samir 1954- *WhoSSW 91*
Al-Kaderi, Nazem *BioIn 16*
Al-Kadhi, Isam Nouri 1933- *WhoWor 91*
Al-Kawari, Hamad Abdelaziz 1948- *WhoAm 90*, *WhoWor 91*
al-Khadim, Sa'd *ConAu 131*
Al-Khalifa, Hamad Ibn Isa 1950- *WhoWor 91*
Al-Khalifa, Isa Ibn Salman 1933- *WhoWor 91*

Al-Khalifa, Khalifa ibn Salman 1935- *WhoWor 91*
Al-Khalifa, Muhammad Bin Mubarak 1935- *WhoWor 91*
Al-Khalifa, Muhammad ibn Khalifa bin H. 1937- *WhoWor 91*
Al-Kharafi, Jassim Mohamed 1940- *WhoWor 91*
Al-Kharafi, Mohammed *BioIn 16*
Al-Khateeb, Rabaa Abdulhameed 1952- *WhoWor 91*
Al-Khayyal, Faiz Abdullah 1949- *WhoSSW 91*
Al-Mahmoud, Ahmed Abdulla Zaid 1953- *WhoAm 90*
Al-Maktoum, Ahmad Bin Saeed 1958- *WhoWor 91*
Al-Maktum, Hamdan bin Rashid 1945- *WhoWor 91*
Al-Maktum, Maktum ibn Rashid 1940- *WhoWor 91*
Al-Maktum, Muhammad ibn Rashid 1946- *WhoWor 91*
Al-Maktum, Rashid ibn Said 1914- *WhoWor 91*
Al-Mansour, Khalid Abdullah 1936- *WhoWor 91*
Al-Maraghi, Mustafa 1881-1945 *BioIn 16*
Al-Masri, Ahmad Fathi 1932- *WhoWor 91*
Al-Masri, Munib *BioIn 16*
Al-Mateen, Cheryl Singleton *BiDrAPA 89*
Al-Mateen, Cheryl Singleton 1959- *WhoEmL 91*
Al Mohanny, Ahmed 1934- *WhoWor 91*
Al-Mualla, Rashid bin Ahmad 1930- *WhoWor 91*
Al-Mufti, Jenan *BiDrAPA 89*
Al-Nahayan, Hamdan ibn Muhammad 1930- *WhoWor 91*
Al-Nahayan, Zayid ibn Sultan 1918- *WhoWor 91*
Al-Naimi, Taha 1942- *WhoWor 91*
Al-Najjar, Mufid Bahnam 1938- *BiDrAPA 89*
Al-Naser, Mohammed Hamad 1952- *WhoWor 91*
Al-Nuami, Humaid ibn Rashid 1930- *WhoWor 91*
Al-Qasimi, Saqr ibn Muhammad 1920- *WhoWor 91*
Al-Qassimi, Sultan Bin Mohammed 1939- *WhoWor 91*
Al Radi, Abbad Mohammed Salim 1944- *WhoWor 91*
Al-Rahim, Basil Mehdi 1953- *WhoE 91, WhoEmL 91*
Al-Rqobah, Homoud Abdulla 1951- *WhoWor 91*
Al-Sabah, Abdullah al-Salem 1895-1965 *BioIn 16*
Al-Sabah, Ali al-Khalifa al-Athbi 1945- *WhoWor 91*
Al-Sabah, Jaber al-Ahmad al-Jaber 1926- *BioIn 16*
Al-Sabah, Jabir Al-Ahmad Al-Jabir 1926- *WhoWor 91*
Al-Sabah, Nawwaf Al-Ahmad al-Jabir *WhoWor 91*
Al-Sabah, Sabah al-Ahmad al-Jabir 1929- *WhoWor 91*
Al-Sabah, Sa'd al-Abdallah al-Salim *WhoWor 91*
Al-Sabah, Salem Abdulaziz Al Saud 1951- *WhoWor 91*
Al-Sabah, Salem Sabah 1937- *WhoWor 91*
Al-Sabah, Saud Nasir 1944- *WhoAm 90, WhoWor 91*
Al-Said, Sayyed Fahad Bin Mahmoud 1944- *WhoWor 91*
Al-Said, Sayyed Faher Bin Taimur 1928- *WhoWor 91*
Al-Saigh, Nassir Mohammad 1942- *WhoWor 91*
Al-Saigh, Zeki Yehya 1945- *WhoSSW 91*
Al Salami, Mohamed Abdullah Sultan 1960- *WhoWor 91*
Al-Sari, Ahmad Mohammad 1947- *WhoWor 91*
Al-Saud, Muhammad Ibn Abdul Aziz 1910-1988 *BioIn 16*
Al-Sayyari, Hamad Saud *WhoWor 91*
Al-Shakar, Karim Ebrahim 1945- *WhoWor 91*
Al-Shaker, Abdullah Jassim *BioIn 16*
Al-Sharhan, Yacoub Saleh 1959- *WhoWor 91*
Al Sharouni, Youssef 1924- *ConAu 131*
Al-Sharqi, Hamad ibn Muhammad 1949- *WhoWor 91*
Al-Shawa, Rashad *BioIn 16*
Al-Shewaihy, Mohammed Ali 1933- *WhoWor 91*
Al-Solaim, Soliman Abdul-Aziz *WhoWor 91*
Al-Suwaidi, Salem Mohammed 1956- *WhoEmL 91*
Al-Thani, Abdul Aziz Bin Khalifa 1948- *WhoWor 91*
Al-Thani, Abdulla bin Khalifa *WhoWor 91*
Al-Thani, Hamad Bin Khalifa 1949- *WhoWor 91*
Al-Thani, Hamad Bin Suham 1940- *WhoWor 91*
Al-Thani, Khalifa Bin Hamad 1932- *WhoWor 91*
Al-Turaihi, Mohammed Said 1957- *WhoWor 91*
Al-Wazir, Khalil *BioIn 16*
Al Yasiri, Kahtan Abbass 1939- *WhoAm 90*
Al-Zamil, Faisal Saleh 1955- *WhoEmL 91, WhoWor 91*
Al-Zein, Nabil 1944- *WhoWor 91*
Al-Zubaidi, Amer Aziz 1945- *WhoEmL 91, WhoSSW 91*
Alabau, Magali 1945- *WhoHisp 91*
Alabdulrazzaq, Abdul Mohsin Yousof 1934- *WhoWor 91*
Alacaklioglu, Haluk 1956- *WhoWor 91*
Alacseal, Virgili *EncCoWW*
Aladjem, Silvio 1928- *WhoAm 90*
Alafouzo, Antonia 1952- *WhoAmW 91, WhoE 91, WhoEmL 91*
Alahouzos, John, Jr. 1948- *WhoEmL 91*
Ala'i, Cyrus 1929- *WhoWor 91*
Alaia, Azzedine *BioIn 16*
Alaie, Belinda Jean 1954- *WhoE 91, WhoEmL 91*
Alaimo, Anthony A. 1920- *WhoAm 90, WhoSSW 91*
Alaimo, Anthony Louis 1954- *WhoE 91*
Alain 1868-1951 *BiDFrPL*
Alain of Lille 1128?-1203 *EncO&P 3*
Alain, Jehan 1911-1940 *PenDiMP*
Alain, Marie-Claire 1926- *IntWWM 90, PenDiMP*
Alain-Fournier 1886-1914 *BioIn 16*
Alaini, Mohsin Ahmed 1932- *WhoAm 90*
Alaix, Emperatriz 1949- *WhoHisp 91*
Alajalov, Constantin 1900-1987 *BioIn 16*
Alakszay, Elizabeth Maria 1963- *WhoAmW 91*
Alala, Joseph Basil, Jr. 1933- *WhoAm 90*
Alalou 1902- *BiDWomA*
Alalou-Jonquieres, Tatiana 1902- *BiDWomA*
Alam, Abrar 1948- *WhoWor 91*
Alam, Akhter-Ul 1939- *WhoWor 91*
Alam, Juan Shamsul 1946- *WhoHisp 91*
Alam, Mohammad Shahid 1950- *WhoE 91*
Alaman, Lucas 1792-1853 *BioIn 16*
Alameda, George Kevin 1955- *WhoEmL 91*
Alamia, Louis Joseph 1948- *BiDrAPA 89*
Alamo, Rafael 1952- *WhoHisp 91*
Alan, Jay 1907-1965 *WhoAmA 91N*
Alandt, Franklin D. 1932- *St&PR 91*
Alanis, Joan Marti *WhoWor 91*
Alanis, Roy 1939- *St&PR 91*
Alaniz, Arnoldo Rene 1957- *WhoHisp 91*
Alaniz, Johnny Segura 1929- *WhoHisp 91*
Alaniz, Joseph J. 1956- *WhoHisp 91*
Alaniz, Robert Manuel 1957- *WhoHisp 91*
Alaniz, Salvador, Sr. *WhoHisp 91*
Alanko, Matti Lauri Juhani 1935- *WhoWor 91*
Alanne, Lasse Kari 1946- *WhoWor 91*
Alaoglu, Ann E *BiDrAPA 89*
Alaoui, Moulay Ahmed 1919- *WhoWor 91*
Alappatt, Jose Lonappan *BiDrAPA 89*
Alarcon, Arthur Lawrence 1925- *WhoAm 90, WhoHisp 91*
Alarcon, Francisco X. 1954- *WhoHisp 91*
Alarcon, Graciela Solis 1942- *WhoHisp 91*
Alarcon, Guillermo Gerardo 1960- *WhoHisp 91*
Alarcon, Hernando De 1500?- *EncCRAm*
Alarcon, Jose 1937- *BiDrAPA 89*
Alarcon, Justo S. 1930- *WhoHisp 91*
Alarcon, Pedro Antonio de 1833-1891 *BioIn 16*
Alarcon, Raul, Jr. *WhoHisp 91*
Alarcon, Renato D. 1942- *WhoHisp 91*
Alarcon, Renato Daniel 1942- *BiDrAPA 89*
Alarcon, Ricardo *BioIn 16*
Alarcon, Terry Quentin 1948- *WhoEmL 91, WhoSSW 91*
Alaric 370?-410 *WorAlBi*
Alarid, Albert Joseph 1948- *WhoEmL 91*
Alarid, Albert Joseph, III 1948- *WhoHisp 91*
Alarid, Jake Ignacio 1934- *WhoHisp 91*
Alarid, Michael *WhoHisp 91*
Alarie, Pierrette 1921- *IntWWM 90, PenDiMP*
Alarie, Yves C. 1939- *WhoAm 90*
Alary, Francois *EncO&P 3*
Alas, Leopoldo 1852-1901 *BioIn 16, ConAu 131, HispWr 90*
Alas y Urena, Leopoldo 1852-1901 *HispWr 90*
Alastair, Kyle *WhoWor 91*
Alatalo, Frances E. 1917- *WhoAmW 91*
Alatas, Ali 1932- *WhoWor 91*
Alatis, James Efstathios 1926- *WhoAm 90*
Alaton, Kalef *BioIn 16*
Alatorre, Richard 1943- *WhoHisp 91*
Alatur, Tengiz M A 1928- *BiDrAPA 89*
Alaupovic, Alexandra V 1921- *WhoAmA 91*
Alaupovic, Alexandra Vrbanic 1921- *WhoAmW 91*
Alavi, Najmuddin Ahmed 1949- *WhoSSW 91*
Alawi, Ahmad ibn Mustafa al- 1869-1934 *BioIn 16*
Alazraki, Jaime 1934- *WhoAm 90, WhoHisp 91, WhoWrEP 89*
Alba, duque de 1507-1582 *BioIn 16*
Alba, Camilo Benjamin 1956- *WhoWor 91*
Alba, Jose J *BiDrAPA 89*
Alba, Ray *WhoHisp 91*
Alba, Ray 1918- *St&PR 91*
Alba-Buffill, Elio 1930- *WhoHisp 91*
Albacete, Manuel Joseph 1939- *WhoAm 90*
Albach, Carl Rudolph 1907- *WhoAm 90*
Albahary, Robert S 1925- *BiDrAPA 89*
Albala, A Ari 1947- *BiDrAPA 89*
Albala, Leila *AuBYP 90*
Albam, Manny 1922- *OxCPMus*
Alban Berg Quartet *PenDiMP*
Alban, Charles E. 1924- *St&PR 91*
Alban, James Carlton, Jr. 1917- *St&PR 91*
Alban, Roger C. 1948- *St&PR 91*
Alban, Roger Charles 1948- *WhoWor 91*
Albane, P. *EncCoWW*
Albanese, Antonio 1927- *WhoWor 91*
Albanese, Charles C. 1937- *St&PR 91*
Albanese, Eda 1901- *St&PR 91*
Albanese, Ellen Louise 1949- *WhoAmW 91*
Albanese, Helen G *BiDrAPA 89*
Albanese, John Charles 1925- *St&PR 91*
Albanese, Lee R. 1926- *St&PR 91*
Albanese, Licia 1913- *IntWWM 90, PenDiMP, WhoAm 90, WorAlBi*
Albanese, Mark Joseph *BiDrAPA 89*
Albanese, Thomas 1957- *St&PR 91*
Albanesi, Enrico Peter 1938- *St&PR 91*
Albanesi, Roberto *WhoWor 91*
Albaneze, David Thomas 1952- *WhoSSW 91*
Albani, Emma 1847-1930 *PenDiMP*
Albano, Domenico Bruno 1943- *St&PR 91*
Albano, James Gennaro 1941- *WhoE 91*
Albano, James R. *BioIn 16*
Albano, Jill 1959- *WhoEmL 91*
Albano, Patrick Louis 1947- *WhoAmA 91*
Albans, Nick *BioIn 16*
Albany, Joe 1924-1988 *OxCPMus*
Albarado, Bill Joe 1946- *WhoSSW 91*
Albarella, Joan Katherine 1944- *WhoWrEP 89*
Albarelli, Dean *BioIn 16*
Albarosa, Nino 1933- *IntWWM 90*
Albas, Jose Maria Escriva de Balaguer 1902-1975 *BioIn 16*
Albaugh, Fred William 1913- *WhoAm 90*
Albaugh, Judson 1925- *BiDrAPA 89*
Albaugh, Mary Anne *BiDrAPA 89*
Albaum, Jean Stirling 1932- *WhoAmW 91*
Albea, Emmette Harvey, Jr. 1944- *WhoSSW 91*
Albea, John Morgan *BiDrAPA 89*
Albeck, Joseph Henry 1946- *BiDrAPA 89, WhoE 91*
Albeck, Stan 1931- *WhoAm 90*
Albeda, Willem Frederick 1925- *WhoWor 91*
Albee, Arden Leroy 1928- *WhoAm 90*
Albee, Daniel Joe 1953- *BiDrAPA 89*
Albee, Donald Edward 1950- *St&PR 91*
Albee, Edward 1928- *BioIn 16, MajTwCW, WorAlBi, WrPh*
Albee, Edward Franklin 1928- *WhoAm 90, WhoE 91, WhoWor 91, WhoWrEP 89*
Albee, Percy F 1885-1959 *WhoAmA 91N*
Albemarle, Elizabeth, Duchess of 1654-1734 *BiDEWW*
Albenda, David 1936- *WhoAm 90*
Albeniz, Isaac 1860-1909 *BioIn 16, PenDiMP A*
Alber, Howard 1911- *WhoE 91*
Alber, Stephen A. 1945- *WhoEmL 91*
Alberda, Linda Kresge 1956- *WhoEmL 91*
Alberda Vanekenstein, Peter C.W. 1940- *St&PR 91*
Alberdi, Juan Bautista 1810-1884 *BioIn 16*
Alberding, Richard C. 1931- *WhoAm 90*
Alberg, Mildred Freed 1921- *WhoAm 90*
Alberg, Stephen Barry 1941- *BiDrAPA 89*
Alberg, Tom Austin 1940- *WhoAm 90*
Alberga, Alta W *WhoAmA 91*
Alberga, Alta Wheat *WhoAmW 91*
Alberger, William Relph 1945- *WhoAm 90*
Albergo, Horace 1932- *St&PR 91*
Albergo, Horace Maurice 1932- *WhoE 91*
Albergo, Paul Francis 1960- *WhoE 91*
Alberici, Gabriel J. 1909- *St&PR 91, WhoAm 90*
Alberman, John *PenDiMP*
Alberni Quartet *PenDiMP*
Alberoni, Francesco 1929- *ConAu 130*
Alberoni, Giulio 1664-1752 *BioIn 16*
Albers, Anni 1899- *BiDWomA, ConDes 90, WhoAm 90, WhoAmA 91, WhoE 91*
Albers, Charles E. 1940- *St&PR 91*
Albers, Charles Edgar 1940- *WhoAm 90*
Albers, Donald J. 1925- *St&PR 91*
Albers, Fern B. 1951- *St&PR 91*
Albers, Fern Beth 1951- *WhoEmL 91*
Albers, Gerd 1919- *WhoWor 91*
Albers, Glennon Alvin 1951- *St&PR 91*
Albers, Hermann G. *BioIn 16*
Albers, Jo-Ann Huff 1938- *WhoAmW 91*
Albers, John Richard 1931- *St&PR 91, WhoAm 90, WhoSSW 91*
Albers, Josef 1888-1976 *BioIn 16, IntDcAA 90, WhoAmA 91N*
Albers, Kenneth F.X. 1927- *St&PR 91*
Albers, Lawrence James 1961- *BiDrAPA 89*
Albers, Rick M. 1954- *WhoEmL 91*
Albers, William M. 1927- *St&PR 91*
Albers-Schonberg, Joyce Marie 1943- *St&PR 91*
Albersheim, Gerhard 1902- *IntWWM 90*
Albersheim, Peter 1934- *WhoAm 90*
Alberson, Robert 1951- *St&PR 91*
Alberson, Robert Monroe 1951- *WhoSSW 91*
Albert, Duke of York 1895-1952 *BioIn 16*
Albert of Cologne 1206?-1280 *EncO&P 3*
Albert, of Saxe-Coburg-Gotha 1819-1861 *WorAlBi*
Albert, Prince Consort of Victoria 1819-1861 *BioIn 16*
Albert, Prince of Monaco 1958- *BioIn 16*
Albert, Abraham Adrian 1905-1972 *DcScB S2*
Albert, Alfred Gerhardt 1920- *WhoAm 90*
Albert, Burton, Jr. 1936- *WhoWrEP 89*
Albert, Calvin 1918- *WhoAmA 91*
Albert, Carl 1908- *ConAu 132, WorAlBi*
Albert, Charles Thompson 1930- *WhoAm 90*
Albert, Christian E. *BioIn 16*
Albert, Conrad Preston 1946- *St&PR 91*
Albert, Daniel Myron 1936- *WhoAm 90*
Albert, David H. 1950- *WhoWrEP 89*
Albert, Deborah Gail Freifeld 1961- *WhoWor 91*
Albert, Don 1908-1986 *BioIn 16*
Albert, Eddie 1908- *ConTFT 8 [port], OxCPMus, WhoAm 90, WorAlBi*
Albert, Edward 1951- *WhoAm 90*
Albert, Edward Frank 1936- *IntWWM 90*
Albert, Eugen d' 1864-1932 *BioIn 16*
Albert, Eugene d' 1864-1932 *PenDiMP*
Albert, Frank Augustine 1938- *WhoSSW 91*
Albert, Garett J. 1943- *WhoAm 90*
Albert, Gary Harwood *BiDrAPA 89*
Albert, Gerald 1917- *WhoE 91, WhoWor 91*
Albert, Gerald 1925- *St&PR 91, WhoAm 90, WhoE 91*
Albert, Hans 1921- *WhoWor 91*
Albert, Harold S 1920- *BiDrAPA 89*
Albert, Harold William 1949- *WhoEmL 91*
Albert, Harry Francis 1935- *WhoE 91*
Albert, Helen Mary 1953- *WhoAmW 91*
Albert, Jade 1951- *BioIn 16*
Albert, Jean-Marie 1938- *BiDrAPA 89*
Albert, Joel Stuart 1943- *BiDrAPA 89*
Albert, John 1942- *WhoE 91*
Albert, Josef 1826-1886 *BioIn 16*
Albert, Karl Vernon 1957- *WhoSSW 91*
Albert, Kathy Swift 1961- *WhoAmW 91*
Albert, Kevin K. 1952- *St&PR 91*
Albert, Kim Thomas 1953- *St&PR 91*
Albert, Leslie *BiDrAPA 89*
Albert, Lois Eldora Wilson 1938- *WhoAm 90*
Albert, Marv *BioIn 16*
Albert, Marv 1943- *WhoAm 90*
Albert, Marvin 1924- *TwCCr&M 91*
Albert, Marvin H. *AuBYP 90*
Albert, Marvin H 1924- *ConAu 30NR*
Albert, Mary Day 1926- *WhoAmW 91*
Albert, Maurice Gabriel 1939- *WhoWor 91*
Albert, Michael P. 1940- *St&PR 91*
Albert, Morton Barry *BiDrAPA 89*
Albert, Neale M. 1937- *WhoAm 90*
Albert, Paul Monroe, Jr. 1943- *WhoAm 90*
Albert, Robert Alan 1933- *WhoAm 90*
Albert, Robert Bertrand 1932- *St&PR 91, WhoAm 90*
Albert, Robert Hartman 1924- *St&PR 91*
Albert, Robert V. 1956- *WhoE 91*
Albert, Roger Charles 1944- *WhoAm 90*
Albert, Ross Alan 1958- *WhoEmL 91*
Albert, Roy Ernest 1924- *WhoAm 90*
Albert, Samuel Harry *BiDrAPA 89*
Albert, Sherwin O., Jr. 1950- *WhoE 91*
Albert, Sidney G. *BioIn 16*
Albert, Stephen 1941- *IntWWM 90*
Albert, Stephen Joel 1941- *WhoAm 90*
Albert, Stephen W. 1952- *St&PR 91*

Albert, Susan Wittig 1940- *WhoAm 90*
Albert, Theodore Merton 1927- *WhoE 91*
Albert, William Eastwood 1951- *St&PR 91*
Albert i Paradis, Caterina 1869-1966 *EncCoWW*
Albert-Nelson, Ilene 1955- *WhoE 91, WhoEmL 91*
Alberta, Baronesa *EncCoWW*
Albertalli, Stephen L. 1929- *St&PR 91*
Albertazzi, Mario 1920- *WhoAmA 91, WhoE 91*
Albertelli, Guy Leo 1950- *WhoEmL 91*
Albertelli, Lawrence 1946- *St&PR 91*
Alberthal, Lester M. *St&PR 91*
Alberthal, Lester M., Jr. 1944- *WhoAm 90, WhoSSW 91*
Alberti, Don Wesley 1950- *WhoAmA 91*
Alberti, Leon Battista 1404-1472 *WorAlBi*
Alberti, Peter William 1934- *WhoAm 90*
Alberti, Rafael 1902- *IntvSpW [port]*
Albertini, Gerald Francis 1950- *WhoEmL 91*
Albertini, Ralph Stephen 1948- *BiDrAPA 89*
Albertini, Stephen A. *ODwPR 91*
Albertini, William O. 1943- *St&PR 91*
Albertolli, Giocondo 1742-1839 *PenDiDA 89*
Alberton, Paul Gregory *BiDrAPA 89*
Alberts, Gary R. 1941- *St&PR 91*
Alberts, Irwin N. *WhoAm 90, WhoE 91*
Alberts, Marion Edward 1923- *WhoAm 90*
Alberts, Mary Elizabeth 1957- *WhoAmW 91*
Alberts, Robert *BiDrAPA 89*
Alberts, Robert C. 1907- *WhoAm 90, WhoWor 91*
Alberts, Robert J. 1952- *St&PR 91*
Alberts, Sylvia 1928- *MusmAFA*
Albertson, Bill *BioIn 16*
Albertson, Bradley LeRoy 1955- *WhoWor 91*
Albertson, Charles H. 1946- *St&PR 91*
Albertson, Dean 1920- *WhoAm 90*
Albertson, Dean 1920-1989 *BioIn 16*
Albertson, Fred Woodward 1908- *WhoAm 90, WhoWor 91*
Albertson, Jack 1910-1981 *WorAlBi*
Albertson, Lillie *BioIn 16*
Albertson, Michael Owen 1946- *WhoE 91*
Albertson, Paul Allen, Jr. 1932- *St&PR 91*
Albertson, Robert Bernard 1946- *WhoE 91*
Albertson, Robert Brooke 1859-1919 *AmLegL*
Albertson, Robert Paul 1952- *WhoWor 91*
Albertson, Susan L. 1929- *WhoAmW 91*
Albertus Magnus 1206?-1280 *EncO&P 3*
Albertus Magnus, Saint 1193?-1280 *WorAlBi*
Alberty, Robert Arnold 1921- *WhoAm 90*
Albertyn, Dorothy *ConAu 30NR*
Albery, Donald 1914-1988 *AnObit 1988, BioIn 16*
Albetta, Victor F. 1943- *St&PR 91*
Albi, Dominic 1921- *St&PR 91*
Albi, Emilio 1945- *WhoWor 91*
Albiach, Anne-Marie 1937- *EncCoWW*
Albigerius *EncO&P 3*
Albin, David L 1937- *BiDrAPA 89*
Albin, Edgar A 1908- *WhoAmA 91*
Albin, George L. 1942- *St&PR 91*
Albin, Joan Elizabeth 1948- *WhoEmL 91*
Albin, Leslie *BioIn 16*
Albin, Leslie Diane 1954- *WhoE 91*
Albin, Majorie Ann 1930- *WhoAmW 91*
Albin, Randy Clark 1957- *WhoEmL 91*
Albin, William Francis, III 1947- *WhoE 91*
Albini, Franco 1905-1977 *ConDes 90*
Albini, Franco 1905-1978 *PenDiDA 89*
Albini, Walter 1941-1983 *ConDes 90*
Albino, George Robert 1929- *WhoAm 90*
Albino, Pamela E. 1963- *WhoAmW 91*
Albino, Robert N. 1954- *St&PR 91*
Albino, Vito 1957- *WhoWor 91*
Albinski, Nan Bowman 1934- *WhoWor 91*
Albiston, Alfred Joseph 1929- *St&PR 91*
Albitz, William E. 1934- *St&PR 91*
Albizu Campos, Pedro 1891-1965 *BioIn 16*
Albo, Richard Gerald 1946- *St&PR 91*
Albon, E. D. *EncCoWW*
Alboni, Marietta 1823-1894 *PenDiMP*
Albores Garcia, Victor A *BiDrAPA 89*
Alborg-Dominguez, Miguel 1946- *WhoWor 91*
Albornoz, Aurora de 1926- *EncCoWW*
Albornoz-Ruiz, Jose 1933- *BiDrAPA 89*
Alborough, Jez 1959- *ConAu 131*
Albosta, Richard Francis 1936- *St&PR 91, WhoAm 90*
Alboszta, Maria Helena 1940- *BiDrAPA 89*
Albrand, Martha 1914-1981 *SpyFic, TwCCr&M 91*
Albrecht, Anthony W. 1930- *St&PR 91*
Albrecht, Arthur John 1931- *WhoAm 90*
Albrecht, Carolina *ODwPR 91*
Albrecht, Charles Frank, Jr. 1939- *St&PR 91*
Albrecht, Donald James 1951- *WhoAm 90*
Albrecht, Dorothy Richter 1938- *WhoSSW 91*
Albrecht, Duane Taylor 1927- *WhoAm 90*
Albrecht, Edward Daniel 1937- *St&PR 91, WhoAm 90*
Albrecht, Ernst Carl Julius 1930- *WhoWor 91*
Albrecht, Felix Robert 1926- *WhoAm 90*
Albrecht, Fred I. 1917- *St&PR 91*
Albrecht, Frederick Ivan 1917- *WhoAm 90*
Albrecht, Frederick Steven 1949- *WhoAm 90*
Albrecht, Georgene Lee 1941- *WhoAmW 91*
Albrecht, Gerd 1935- *IntWWM 90, PenDiMP*
Albrecht, Harold William 1942- *St&PR 91*
Albrecht, Herbert Hermann 1939- *WhoWor 91*
Albrecht, Irving Augustine 1954- *WhoEmL 91*
Albrecht, Jane Katherine 1952- *WhoAmW 91*
Albrecht, Janette Sun *BiDrAPA 89*
Albrecht, Johanne Sophie Dorothea 1757-1840 *EncCoWW*
Albrecht, John Conrad 1939- *WhoWor 91*
Albrecht, Kay Montgomery 1949- *WhoSSW 91*
Albrecht, Mary Dickson 1930- *WhoAmA 91*
Albrecht, Maureen Ann 1952- *WhoEmL 91*
Albrecht, Paul 1951- *WhoWor 91*
Albrecht, Paul Abraham 1922- *WhoAm 90*
Albrecht, Peggy Stoddard 1919- *WhoWrEP 89*
Albrecht, Richard Raymond 1932- *St&PR 91, WhoAm 90*
Albrecht, Robert Downing 1931- *WhoE 91*
Albrecht, Ronald Frank 1937- *WhoAm 90*
Albrecht, Ronald Lewis 1935- *WhoE 91*
Albrecht, Ronald Norman 1952- *IntWWM 90*
Albrecht, Sterling Jean 1937- *WhoAm 90*
Albrecht, Susan Ann 1953- *WhoE 91*
Albrecht, Suzanne Alice *BiDrAPA 89*
Albrecht, Theodore John 1945- *IntWWM 90*
Albrecht, Timothy Edward 1950- *WhoSSW 91*
Albrecht, Vern Eugene 1928- *St&PR 91*
Albrecht, William Price, Jr. 1935- *WhoAm 90*
Albrektsen, Helge Normann 1950- *WhoWor 91*
Albret, Jeanne d' 1528-1572 *EncCoWW*
Albright, Adam Emory 1862-1957 *WhoAmA 91N*
Albright, Alan David 1956- *WhoEmL 91*
Albright, Archie E. 1920- *St&PR 91*
Albright, Archie Earl, Jr. 1920- *WhoAm 90*
Albright, Barbara Joy 1955- *WhoAm 90, WhoAmW 91*
Albright, Barbara Lynn 1949- *WhoAmW 91*
Albright, Carl Wayne 1944- *St&PR 91*
Albright, Carl Wayne, Jr. 1944- *WhoAm 90*
Albright, Charles Lloyd, Jr. 1920- *WhoAm 90*
Albright, Chip 1953- *WhoEmL 91*
Albright, David Foxwell 1932- *WhoAm 90, WhoWor 91*
Albright, David Wesley *BiDrAPA 89*
Albright, Dorothy Jane 1945- *WhoEmL 91, WhoWor 91*
Albright, Fred Ronald 1944- *WhoAm 90*
Albright, Fuller 1900-1969 *DcScB S2*
Albright, George Franklin 1916- *WhoAm 90*
Albright, Glen Patrick 1956- *WhoWrEP 89*
Albright, Harry Wesley, Jr. 1925- *WhoAm 90*
Albright, Henry J *WhoAmA 91N*
Albright, Horace Marden *BioIn 16*
Albright, Hugh Norton 1928- *WhoAm 90*
Albright, Ivan Le Lorraine 1897-1983 *WhoAmA 91N*
Albright, Jack Lawrence 1930- *WhoAm 90*
Albright, James Michael 1940- *WhoE 91*
Albright, Jerry Wallace 1936- *St&PR 91*
Albright, John Rupp 1937- *WhoAm 90*
Albright, Joseph William 1954- *WhoEmL 91*
Albright, Justin W. 1908- *WhoAm 90*
Albright, Laurie Jo 1952- *WhoEmL 91*
Albright, Lois 1904- *WhoAm 90*
Albright, Lovelia Fried 1934- *WhoAmW 91, WhoE 91*
Albright, Lyle Frederick 1921- *WhoAm 90*
Albright, Madeleine 1937- *WhoAmW 91*
Albright, Madeleine Korbel 1937- *BioIn 16*
Albright, Malvin Marr 1897- *WhoAmA 91*
Albright, Maureen Terese 1961- *WhoAmW 91*
Albright, Nancy Eggelhof 1940- *WhoWrEP 89*
Albright, Nancy Elizabeth 1938- *WhoAmW 91*
Albright, Paul Herman 1948- *WhoE 91*
Albright, Phyllistean Hardrick 1956- *WhoAmW 91*
Albright, Raymond Jacob 1929- *WhoAm 90*
Albright, Richard Sheldon, II 1951- *WhoE 91*
Albright, Susie Kathleen 1908-1988 *BioIn 16*
Albright, Thomas 1935- *WhoAmA 91N*
Albright, Townsend Shaul 1942- *WhoAm 90*
Albright, Warren Edward 1937- *St&PR 91, WhoAm 90*
Albright, William 1944- *IntWWM 90*
Albright-Saad, Michelle Louise 1961- *WhoAmW 91*
Albrittain, James Sydney 1948- *WhoE 91*
Albritton, Claude Carroll, Jr. 1913- *WhoAm 90*
Albritton, Dondi Ortiz 1957- *WhoEmL 91, WhoWor 91*
Albritton, Paul Howard, Jr. 1943- *St&PR 91*
Albritton, Robert Sanford 1914- *WhoAm 90*
Albritton, Sarah Carlyle 1960- *WhoSSW 91*
Albritton, William Harold, III 1936- *WhoAm 90*
Albritton, William Hoyle 1942- *WhoE 91*
Albritton, William Leonard 1941- *WhoAm 90*
Albrizzi, Isabella Teotochi 1763-1836 *EncCoWW*
Albro, Harley Marcus 1932- *St&PR 91*
Albu, Florenta 1934- *EncCoWW*
Albucher, Ronald Craig *BiDrAPA 89*
Albumazar 805-885 *EncO&P 3*
Albuquerque, Lita 1946- *WhoAm 90, WhoAmA 91*
Alburger, James Reid 1950- *WhoEmL 91*
Alburger, Mary Anne 1943- *WhoWor 91*
Albury, Vic 1947- *Ballpl 90*
Albyn, Richard Keith 1927- *WhoAm 90*
Alcala, Luis A., Jr. 1943- *WhoHisp 91*
Alcala, Santo 1952- *Ballpl 90*
Alcala Zamora y Torres, Niceto 1877-1949 *BioIn 16*
Alcalay, Adolph Haim 1908- *St&PR 91*
Alcalay, Albert S. 1917- *WhoAm 90, WhoAmA 91*
Alcalde, Renato Ragudo 1947- *BiDrAPA 89*
Alcantar, Joe *WhoHisp 91*
Alcantara, Filemon O *BiDrAPA 89*
Alcantara, Theo 1941- *IntWWM 90, WhoAm 90*
Alcantara-Medel, Flordeliza 1944- *WhoAmW 91*
Alcaraz, Ernest C. 1935- *WhoSSW 91*
Alcaraz Figueroa, Estanislao 1918- *WhoAm 90*
Alcaraz Lozano, Federico Nestor 1931- *WhoWor 91*
Alcarez, Robert F. 1947- *St&PR 91*
Alcayaga, Lucila Godoy *ConAu 131, HispWr 90, MajTwCW*
Alcayaga, Lucila Godoy 1889-1957 *BioIn 16*
Alce, Jean *BiDrAPA 89*
Alcerro-Castro, Ramon 1918- *BiDrAPA 89*
Alchesay *WhNaAH*
Alchian, Armen Albert 1914- *WhoAm 90*
Alchindus *EncO&P 3*
Alchise *WhNaAH*
Alcibiades 450?BC-404BC *BioIn 16*
Alcindor, Lew 1947- *BioIn 16*
Alcindor, Lewis Ferdinand 1947- *WhoAm 90*
Alcipe *EncCoWW*
Alcocer, Alberto *BioIn 16*
Alcock, Alfred John 1938- *WhoAm 90*
Alcock, Charles Benjamin 1923- *WhoAm 90*
Alcock, David 1954- *St&PR 91*
Alcock, Garland Shaw *BiDrAPA 89*
Alcock, Gudrun 1908- *BioIn 16*
Alcock, Mary 1742?-1798 *FemiCLE*
Alcock, Sue Ellyn 1959- *WhoEmL 91*
Alcock, Vivien 1924- *AuBYP 90, BioIn 16*
Alcock, Walter 1861-1947 *PenDiMP*
Alcon, Sonja Lee de Bey Ryan 1937- *WhoAmW 91*
Alcopley, L 1910- *WhoAmA 91*
Alcorn, Charles S. 1954- *St&PR 91*
Alcorn, David S. 1923- *St&PR 91*
Alcorn, David Stewart 1923- *WhoAm 90*
Alcorn, Gordon Dee 1907- *WhoAm 90*
Alcorn, Howard Wells 1901- *WhoAm 90*
Alcorn, Joseph Nichols, III 1941- *WhoAm 90*
Alcorn, Robert W 1944- *BiDrAPA 89*
Alcorn, Samuel 1927- *St&PR 91*
Alcorn, Stephen 1958- *BioIn 16*
Alcosser, Sandra B. 1944- *WhoWrEP 89*
Alcott, Abigail 1800-1877 *BioAmW*
Alcott, Amos Bronson 1799-1888 *BioIn 16, WorAlBi*
Alcott, Amy Strum 1956- *WhoAm 90, WhoAmW 91*
Alcott, James Arthur 1930- *St&PR 91, WhoAm 90*
Alcott, Louisa May 1832-1888 *AuBYP 90, BioAmW, BioIn 16, FemiCLE, WorAlBi*
Alcott, Mark Howard 1939- *WhoAm 90*
Alcott, May 1840-1879 *BiDWomA*
Alcouloumre, Henry I. 1926- *ODwPR 91*
Alcox, Michael Thomas 1947- *St&PR 91*
Alcox, Patrick Joseph 1946- *WhoEmL 91*
Alcozer, Romalda Francesca 1950- *WhoAmW 91, WhoEmL 91*
Alcuin 735-804 *BioIn 16*
Alda, Alan *BioIn 16*
Alda, Alan 1936- *WhoAm 90, WorAlBi*
Alda, Frances 1883-1952 *PenDiMP*
Alda, Robert 1914- *OxCPMus*
Alda, Robert 1914-1986 *WorAlBi*
Aldag, Ramon John 1945- *WhoAm 90*
Aldag, Richard Jeffrey 1955- *WhoEmL 91*
Aldan, Daisy 1923- *WhoWrEP 89*
Aldana, Carl 1936- *WhoAmA 91*
Aldape, Alina Alicia Catalina Elizabeth 1952- *WhoEmL 91*
Aldave, Barbara Bader 1938- *WhoAm 90, WhoAmW 91*
Alday, Amelia Burog *BiDrAPA 89*
Alday, Luis Eduardo 1938- *WhoWor 91*
Aldea, Patricia 1947- *WhoAm 90, WhoAmW 91, WhoEmL 91*
Aldecoa, Josefina Rodriguez 1926- *EncCoWW*
Aldeen, Norris A. 1917- *St&PR 91*
Aldegrever, Heinrich 1502-1555? *PenDiDA 89*
Alden, Douglas William 1912- *WhoAm 90*
Alden, Elizabeth Joan 1953- *St&PR 91*
Alden, Gary Wade 1951- *WhoAmA 91*
Alden, Ingemar Bengt 1943- *WhoWor 91*
Alden, Isabella 1841-1930 *FemiCLE*
Alden, Jack *AuBYP 90*
Alden, John 1599?-1687 *BioIn 16, EncCRAm, WorAlBi*
Alden, John 1903- *BiDrAPA 89*
Alden, John Edgar 1941- *St&PR 91*
Alden, John M. *BioIn 16*
Alden, John Ramon 1945- *St&PR 91*
Alden, Judith Abato 1946- *WhoE 91*
Alden, Meredith 1950- *BiDrAPA 89*
Alden, Paulette Bates 1947- *BioIn 16*
Alden, Priscilla *BioIn 16*
Alden, Priscilla 1602- *EncCRAm*
Alden, Richard *WhoAmA 91*
Alden, Richard 1942- *WhoE 91*
Alden, Richard John *BiDrAPA 89*
Alden, Richard M. 1945- *St&PR 91*
Alden, Vernon Roger 1923- *St&PR 91, WhoAm 90*
Alder, Berni Julian 1925- *WhoAm 90*
Alder, Gail Cecelia 1944- *WhoAmW 91*
Alder, Kurt 1902-1958 *WorAlBi*
Alder, Mary Ann *WhoAmA 91N*
Alder, Richard Welsley 1939- *St&PR 91*
Alder, William Confer *BiDrAPA 89*
Alderdice, John Thomas 1955- *WhoWor 91*
Alderdice, Paul W. 1953- *St&PR 91*
Alderete, Joseph F 1920- *BiDrAPA 89*
Alderete, Joseph Frank 1920- *WhoSSW 91, WhoWor 91*
Alderfer, Clayton Paul 1940- *WhoAm 90*
Alderman, Bissell 1912- *WhoAm 90*
Alderman, Brian Robert 1938- *WhoWor 91*
Alderman, Charles Wayne 1950- *WhoEmL 91, WhoSSW 91*
Alderman, Clifford Lindsey 1902- *AuBYP 90*
Alderman, Eugene Wayne 1936- *WhoSSW 91*
Alderman, John Perry 1935- *WhoAm 90*
Alderman, John Richard 1947- *WhoEmL 91*
Alderman, Katharine McFarland Ansley 1895-1987 *BioIn 16*
Alderman, Michael Harris 1936- *WhoAm 90*
Alderman, Michael James 1952- *WhoEmL 91*
Alderman, Minnis Amelia 1928- *WhoAmW 91*
Alderman, Myles Harris 1936- *St&PR 91*
Alderman, Ray Sumner, Jr. 1947- *WhoSSW 91*
Alderman, Silvia Morell 1952- *WhoEmL 91*
Alderman, Walter A., Jr. 1945- *St&PR 91*
Alderman, Walter Arthur, Jr. 1945- *WhoE 91, WhoEmL 91*
Aldershof, Kent Leroy 1936- *St&PR 91*
Alderson, Creed F., Jr. 1933- *St&PR 91*
Alderson, Creed Flanary, Jr. 1933- *WhoSSW 91*
Alderson, J.W., Jr. 1906- *St&PR 91*

Alderson, Jack C. 1930- *St&PR 91*
Alderson, Jerry Dennis, Jr. 1928- *WhoSSW 91*
Alderson, Karen Ann 1947- *WhoAmW 91*
Alderson, Margaret Northrop 1936- *WhoAmW 91, WhoSSW 91*
Alderson, Martha J. 1942- *WhoAmW 91*
Alderson, Richard Lynn 1947- *WhoAm 90*
Alderson, Sandy *BioIn 16*
Alderson, Sue Ann 1940- *BioIn 16*
Alderson, William Thomas 1926- *WhoAm 90, WhoSSW 91*
Alderton, Harvey R 1927- *BiDrAPA 89*
Alderton, Susan Edith 1952- *St&PR 91, WhoAm 90, WhoAmW 91*
Aldhizer, Carthon Evans 1922- *WhoE 91*
Aldi, Andrew Vincent 1947- *St&PR 91*
Aldin, Peter *BiDrAPA 89*
Aldin, Peter 1932- *WhoE 91*
Alding, Peter *TwCCr&M 91*
Aldinger, William F. 1947- *St&PR 91*
Aldington, Richard 1892-1962 *BioIn 16, DcLB 100 [port]*
Aldis, Dorothy 1896-1966 *AuBYP 90*
Aldis, Henry 1913- *WhoWor 91*
Aldisert, Ruggero John 1919- *WhoAm 90*
Aldiss, Brian 1925- *WorAlBi*
Aldiss, Brian W 1925- *MajTwCW, RGTwCSF*
Aldiss, Brian Wilson 1925- *WhoAm 90, WhoWor 91*
Aldissi, Mahmoud Ali Yousef 1952- *WhoEmL 91*
Aldo-Benson, Marlene Ann 1939- *WhoAmW 91*
Aldon, Adair *AuBYP 90*
Aldon, Howard *ConAu 129*
Aldoroty, Neil *BiDrAPA 89*
Aldous, Joan *WhoAm 90*
Aldovrandi-Marescotti, Carlo *PenDiDA 89*
Aldred, Jeffrey Kent 1943- *St&PR 91*
Aldredge, Theoni *BioIn 16*
Aldredge, Theoni 1932- *ConDes 90*
Aldredge, Theoni Vachlioti 1932- *NotWoAT*
Aldredge, Theoni Vachliotis 1932- *WhoAm 90, WhoAmW 91, WhoE 91*
Aldrete, Joaquin Salcedo 1936- *WhoHisp 91*
Aldrete, Mike 1961- *Ballpl 90*
Aldrich, Alexander 1928- *WhoAm 90*
Aldrich, Alfred Proctor 1814-1897 *AmLegL*
Aldrich, Ann *MajTwCW*
Aldrich, Ann 1927- *SmATA X [port], WhoAm 90, WhoAmW 91*
Aldrich, Bailey 1907- *WhoAm 90*
Aldrich, Bess 1881-1954 *FemiCLE*
Aldrich, C. Elbert 1923- *WhoSSW 91*
Aldrich, C Knight 1914- *BiDrAPA 89*
Aldrich, Carole Ann 1944- *WhoAm 90*
Aldrich, Clarence Knight 1914- *WhoAm 90*
Aldrich, Clifford W. 1948- *St&PR 91*
Aldrich, Clifton Henry 1940- *WhoSSW 91*
Aldrich, Daniel G. *NewYTBS 90*
Aldrich, Daniel G. 1918-1990 *BioIn 16*
Aldrich, David Beals 1931- *WhoAm 90*
Aldrich, David Lawrence 1948- *WhoEmL 91, WhoWor 91*
Aldrich, Edgar 1848-1921 *AmLegL*
Aldrich, Edward Adams 1964- *BioIn 16*
Aldrich, Frank Nathan 1923- *WhoAm 90, WhoE 91, WhoWor 91*
Aldrich, Franklin Dalton 1929- *WhoAm 90*
Aldrich, George E. 1946- *St&PR 91*
Aldrich, Gilbert Eugene 1933- *St&PR 91*
Aldrich, Hulbert S. 1907- *St&PR 91*
Aldrich, Janet Alice 1960- *WhoAmW 91*
Aldrich, Jeffrey William 1942- *St&PR 91*
Aldrich, John Herbert 1947- *WhoAm 90*
Aldrich, Karen Bailey 1959- *WhoAmW 91*
Aldrich, Larry *WhoAmA 91*
Aldrich, Larry 1948- *ODwPR 91*
Aldrich, Lynne Merrill 1946- *WhoAmW 91*
Aldrich, Michael Ray 1942- *WhoWor 91*
Aldrich, Mildred 1853-1928 *FemiCLE*
Aldrich, Nancy Armstrong 1925- *WhoAmW 91, WhoE 91*
Aldrich, Nancy Welz 1939- *WhoAmW 91*
Aldrich, Nelson W. 1841-1915 *EncABHB 6 [port]*
Aldrich, Nelson W., Jr. *BioIn 16*
Aldrich, Nelson Wilmarth 1841-1915 *AmLegL*
Aldrich, Patricia Anne Richardson 1926- *WhoAm 90, WhoAmW 91*
Aldrich, Richard John 1925- *WhoAm 90*
Aldrich, Richard Orth 1921- *WhoAm 90*
Aldrich, Robert 1918-1983 *BioIn 16*
Aldrich, Robert A *BiDrAPA 89*
Aldrich, Robert Adams 1924- *WhoAm 90*
Aldrich, Robert Anderson 1917- *WhoAm 90*
Aldrich, Roland W., Jr. 1944- *St&PR 91*
Aldrich, Roland Walter, Jr. 1944- *WhoE 91*
Aldrich, Ronnie 1916- *OxCPMus*
Aldrich, Thomas Albert 1923- *St&PR 91, WhoAm 90*
Aldrich, Thomas L. 1936- *St&PR 91*
Aldrich, Virgil Charles 1903- *WhoAm 90*
Aldrich, William Rolland 1959- *WhoEmL 91*
Aldrich, William Thomas, Jr. *BiDrAPA 89*
Aldrich, Winthrop Williams 1885-1974 *BioIn 16*
Aldridge, Alan 1943- *ConDes 90*
Aldridge, Alfred Owen 1915- *WhoAm 90*
Aldridge, Anne Caroline Frances 1955- *IntWWM 90*
Aldridge, Arleen Rash 1949- *WhoHisp 91*
Aldridge, Charles Ray 1946- *WhoEmL 91*
Aldridge, Danny Wayne 1947- *WhoSSW 91*
Aldridge, Diana D. 1951- *ODwPR 91*
Aldridge, Edward C., Jr. 1938- *WhoAm 90*
Aldridge, Freemon LeVonier, II 1956- *WhoSSW 91*
Aldridge, Gordon James 1916- *WhoAm 90*
Aldridge, Ira 1807-1867 *DrBIPA 90, EarBIAP*
Aldridge, James R. 1930- *St&PR 91*
Aldridge, James Richard 1949- *WhoEmL 91*
Aldridge, John Arthur Malcolm 1905-1983 *DcNaB 1981*
Aldridge, John W. *BioIn 16*
Aldridge, John Watson 1922- *WhoAm 90, WhoWrEP 89*
Aldridge, John William 1923- *WhoAm 90*
Aldridge, John William 1924- *St&PR 91*
Aldridge, Josephine Haskell *AuBYP 90*
Aldridge, Kenneth William 1955- *WhoSSW 91*
Aldridge, Mary Hennen Dellinger 1919- *WhoAm 90*
Aldridge, Melvin Dayne 1941- *WhoAm 90*
Aldridge, Myron Anthony 1953- *WhoE 91*
Aldridge, Ray 1948- *WhoWrEP 89*
Aldridge, Richard C., Jr. 1925- *St&PR 91*
Aldridge, Robert Bruce 1939- *St&PR 91*
Aldridge, Robert Lee 1945- *WhoEmL 91*
Aldridge, Roger Merle 1946- *WhoEmL 91*
Aldridge, Rosemary Robinson 1962- *WhoAmW 91*
Aldridge, Sidney A. 1940- *St&PR 91*
Aldridge, Susanna *BiDEWW*
Aldridge, Vic 1893-1973 *Ballpl 90*
Aldrin, Buzz *BioIn 16*
Aldrin, Buzz 1930- *WhoAm 90*
Aldrin, Edwin E. *BioIn 16*
Aldrin, Edwin E., Jr. 1930- *WorAlBi*
Alduino, Joseph P. *BioIn 16*
Aldulescu, Radu 1922- *PenDiMP*
Aldunate, Wilson Ferreira *BioIn 16*
Aldwinckle, Eric 1909-1980 *WhoAmA 91N*
Aldworth, Thomas Patrick 1947- *WhoSSW 91*
Ale Ruiz, Rafael 1960- *WhoWor 91*
Alea, Tomas Gutierrez *BioIn 16*
Aleandri, Emelise Francesca *WhoAmW 91*
Aleandro, Norma *WhoHisp 91*
Alebua, Ezekiel 1947- *WhoWor 91*
Alechinsky, Pierre 1927- *BioIn 16, ModArCr 1 [port]*
Aledort, Paul Jeffrey 1954- *WhoEmL 91*
Aledort, Stewart L *BiDrAPA 89*
Aleem, Asaf *BiDrAPA 89*
Alef, John H. 1924- *St&PR 91*
Alegi, August Paul 1943- *St&PR 91*
Alegi, Peter Claude 1935- *WhoAm 90*
Alegria, Ciro 1909-1967 *BioIn 16, ConAu 131, HispWr 90*
Alegria, Claribel *BioIn 16*
Alegria, Claribel 1924- *ConAu 131, HispWr 90*
Alegria, Fernando 1918- *BioIn 16, ConAu 32NR, HispWr 90, WhoHisp 91*
Alegria, Isabel L. 1951- *WhoHisp 91*
Alegria, Ricardo E 1921- *ConAu 32NR, HispWr 90*
Alegria-Ortega, Idsa E. 1945- *WhoHisp 91*
Aleichem, Sholem 1859-1916 *BioIn 16*
Aleichem, Sholom 1859-1916 *WorAlBi*
Aleixandre, Vicente 1898-1984 *BioIn 16, HispWr 90, MajTwCW*
Aleixandre Y Merlo, Vicente 1898-1984 *WorAlBi*
Alejandro, Carlos F Diaz *ConAu 131, HispWr 90*
Alejandro, Carlos Frederico Diaz- 1937-1985 *BioIn 16*
Alejandro, Esteban 1911- *WhoHisp 91*
Alejo, Francisco Javier 1941- *WhoAm 90*
Alejos, Marlene M *BiDrAPA 89*
Alejos Soriano, Vincent 1949- *WhoWor 91*
Alekhine, Alexander 1892-1946 *BioIn 16*
Alekman, Stanley Lawrence 1938- *WhoAm 90*
Aleksander, Bernardo 1935- *BiDrAPA 89*
Aleksandr I, Emperor of Russia 1777-1825 *BioIn 16*
Aleksandrov, A. *EncCoWW*
Aleksandrov, Aleksandr Pavlovich 1943- *BioIn 16*
Aleksandrov, Anatoliy Petrovich 1903- *WhoWor 91*
Aleksandrov, Mikhail Stepanovich 1863-1933 *BioIn 16*
Aleksandrov, Pavel Sergeevich 1896-1982 *DcScB S2*
Alekseeva, Lidiia 1909- *EncCoWW*
Aleksic, Branko 1951- *WhoWor 91*
Aleksy, Patriarch of Russia *BioIn 16*
Aleksy, Ronald James 1947- *WhoEmL 91, WhoWrEP 89*
Alem, Leandro N. 1842-1896 *BioIn 16*
Aleman, Hector E. 1936- *WhoHisp 91*
Aleman, John Stephen 1935- *St&PR 91*
Aleman, Mindy Robin 1950- *WhoAmW 91*
Aleman, Narciso L. 1946- *WhoHisp 91*
Aleman, Victor 1946- *WhoHisp 91*
Aleman Valdez, Miguel 1903-1983 *BioIn 16*
Alemann, Eduardo Armando 1922- *IntWWM 90*
Alemany, Jose Sadoc 1814-1888 *BioIn 16*
Alemar, Evelyn T. 1943- *WhoHisp 91*
Alemar, Jose David 1949- *WhoSSW 91*
Alembert, Jean Le Rond d' 1717-1783 *BioIn 16*
Alencar, Jose Martiniano de 1829-1877 *BioIn 16*
Alenier, Karren LaLonde 1947- *WhoEmL 91, WhoWrEP 89*
Alenov, Lydia 1948- *SmATA 61 [port]*
Aleo, Joseph John 1925- *WhoAm 90*
Aler, John 1949- *IntWWM 90, PenDiMP*
Aleramo, Sibilla 1876-1960 *EncCoWW*
Alers, Juan M. 1943- *WhoHisp 91*
Ales, Beverly Gloria 1928- *WhoWrEP 89*
Alesana, Tofilau Eti 1924- *WhoWor 91*
Aleschus, Justine Lawrence 1925- *WhoAmW 91*
Aleshire, Richard Joe 1947- *WhoEmL 91*
Alesia, Patrick L. 1948- *St&PR 91*
Alesia, Patrick Lawrence 1948- *WhoAm 90*
Alesina, Alberto *BioIn 16*
Alesker, Eugenya *BiDrAPA 89*
Alessandri Palma, Arturo 1868-1950 *BioIn 16*
Alessandri Rodriguez, Jorge 1896-1986 *BioIn 16*
Alessandrini, Walter *St&PR 91*
Alessandroni, Hugo Vincent 1908-1989 *BioIn 16*
Alessandroni, Venan Joseph 1915- *WhoAm 90*
Alessi, George Anthony 1926- *WhoE 91*
Alessi, Larry Edward 1942- *BiDrAPA 89*
Alessi, Norman Emil 1950- *BiDrAPA 89*
Alessi, Robert Frank *BiDrAPA 89*
Alessio, Debra Ann 1957- *WhoAmW 91*
Alevizos, Susan B. 1936- *WhoAm 90*
Alevizos, Theodore G. 1926- *WhoAm 90*
Alevras, John S. 1929- *St&PR 91*
Alewine, James William 1930- *WhoSSW 91*
Alex, Gary Benninger 1941- *WhoAm 90*
Alex, Robert John 1947- *St&PR 91*
Alex, Spero Manuel 1957- *WhoEmL 91*
Alexander *WhNaAH*
Alexander ab Alexandro 1461?-1523 *EncO&P 3*
Alexander I, Emperor of Russia 1777-1825 *BioIn 16*
Alexander, Mrs. 1825-1902 *BioIn 16, FemiCLE*
Alexander Nevsky 1220?-1263 *WorAlBi*
Alexander of Tralles *EncO&P 3*
Alexander, the Great 356BC-323BC *BioIn 16*
Alexander The Great 356BC-323BC *WorAlBi*
Alexander the Paphlagonian *EncO&P 3*
Alexander, Alec Peter 1923- *WhoAm 90*
Alexander, Allen D. 1940- *St&PR 91*
Alexander, Alvin Melvin 1943- *WhoE 91*
Alexander, Andrew Lamar 1940- *WhoAm 90*
Alexander, Andrew Lamar, Jr. *NewYTBS 90 [port]*
Alexander, Anna 1913- *AuBYP 90*
Alexander, Anne *AuBYP 90*
Alexander, Annie Montague 1867-1950 *WomFie [port]*
Alexander, Arthur Albert *BioIn 16*
Alexander, Arthur Frank 1948- *WhoSSW 91*
Alexander, Barbara Leah Shapiro 1943- *WhoAmW 91*
Alexander, Barbara Toll 1948- *WhoAmW 91*
Alexander, Benjamin Bates 1920- *St&PR 91*
Alexander, Benjamin Harold 1921- *WhoAm 90*
Alexander, Beverly Moore 1947- *WhoAmW 91*
Alexander, Bill 1910- *ConAu 130*
Alexander, Bob Gene 1933- *St&PR 91*
Alexander, Bruce D. 1943- *St&PR 91*
Alexander, Bruce Donald 1943- *WhoAm 90*
Alexander, Bruce Kirby 1948- *WhoEmL 91*
Alexander, Carl Albert 1928- *WhoAm 90, WhoWor 91*
Alexander, Carlos 1915- *IntWWM 90*
Alexander, Caroline 1956- *ConAu 132*
Alexander, Cecil Frances 1818-1895 *FemiCLE*
Alexander, Charles H. 1942- *WhoSSW 91*
Alexander, Charles Michael 1952- *WhoEmL 91*
Alexander, Charles P *BiDrAPA 89*
Alexander, Charles Thomas 1928- *WhoAm 90*
Alexander, Charlotte Anne *WhoWrEP 89*
Alexander, Cheryl Dyer 1953- *St&PR 91*
Alexander, Cheryl Lee 1946- *WhoWor 91*
Alexander, Christina Lillian 1942- *WhoE 91*
Alexander, Christine 1893-1975 *WhoAmA 91N*
Alexander, Clifford L. *BioIn 16*
Alexander, Clifford L., Jr. 1933- *WhoAm 90*
Alexander, Constantine 1941- *WhoAm 90*
Alexander, Dale 1903-1979 *Ballpl 90*
Alexander, Daniel Saunders 1953- *WhoE 91*
Alexander, Dave Almon 1915- *WhoSSW 91*
Alexander, David 1907-1973 *AuBYP 90, LiHiK, TwCCr&M 91*
Alexander, David Cleon, III 1941- *WhoWor 91*
Alexander, Deborah Radford 1953- *WhoSSW 91*
Alexander, Denton Eugene 1917- *WhoAm 90*
Alexander, Diana Valdez 1963- *WhoHisp 91*
Alexander, Diane *WhoWrEP 89*
Alexander, Diane Marie 1945- *WhoAmW 91, WhoSSW 91*
Alexander, Dietrich Biemann, Jr. 1902- *WhoSSW 91, WhoWor 91*
Alexander, Donald Crichton 1921- *WhoAm 90*
Alexander, Donald Lee 1948- *WhoSSW 91*
Alexander, Donna *ConAu 131*
Alexander, Doyle 1950- *Ballpl 90*
Alexander, Drury Blakeley 1924- *WhoAm 90*
Alexander, Duane Frederick 1940- *WhoAm 90*
Alexander, E. Curtis 1941- *WhoWrEP 89*
Alexander, Earle Fitzroy *BiDrAPA 89*
Alexander, Earle Straughan, Jr. 1931- *WhoAm 90*
Alexander, Eben, Jr. 1913- *WhoAm 90*
Alexander, Edmund Brooke 1937- *WhoAmA 91*
Alexander, Edna M. DeVeaux *WhoAmW 91*
Alexander, Edward Porter 1835-1910 *BioIn 16*
Alexander, Edward Russell 1928- *WhoAm 90*
Alexander, Edward Ryckman, Jr. 1932- *St&PR 91*
Alexander, Elaine Harriett 1949- *WhoAmW 91*
Alexander, Ellin Dribber 1955- *WhoAmW 91*
Alexander, Elmer 1922-1988 *BioIn 16*
Alexander, Erika *BioIn 16*
Alexander, Ethel Skyles 1925- *WhoAmW 91*
Alexander, Eugene Morton 1926- *WhoE 91*
Alexander, F. O. 1897- *EncACom*
Alexander, Fernande Gardner 1910- *WhoE 91*
Alexander, Floyce 1938- *WhoWrEP 89*
Alexander, Francesca 1837-1917 *BiDWomA, BioAmW*
Alexander, Frank C. 1933- *WhoAm 90*
Alexander, Frank Lyon 1939- *St&PR 91, WhoAm 90*
Alexander, Frank P 1853- *AmLegL*
Alexander, Frank Scott 1943- *WhoWrEP 89*
Alexander, Fred Calvin, Jr. 1931- *WhoAm 90*
Alexander, Frederick Matthias 1869-1955 *NewAgE 90*
Alexander, Fritz W., II 1926- *WhoAm 90, WhoE 91*
Alexander, Gary 1953- *Ballpl 90*
Alexander, George 1858-1918 *BioIn 16*
Alexander, George Gambrell 1926- *WhoAm 90*
Alexander, George Jonathon 1931- *WhoAm 90*

Alexander, George L. Jr. 1926- *BiDrAPA 89*

Alexander, George Martin 1950- *WhoWor 91*

Alexander, Gertrude *BiDrAPA 89*

Alexander, Gideon 1932- *WhoWor 91*

Alexander, Gloria Janice 1941- *WhoSSW 91*

Alexander, Grover Cleveland 1887-1950 *Ballpl 90 [port], WorAlBi*

Alexander, H G *ConAu 129*

Alexander, H. Heath 1954- *WhoEmL 91*

Alexander, Haim 1915- *IntWWM 90*

Alexander, Harold 1891-1969 *WorAlBi*

Alexander, Harold 1940- *WhoAm 90*

Alexander, Harold Campbell 1920- *WhoSSW 91, WhoWor 91*

Alexander, Harold Edwin, Jr. 1949- *BiDrAPA 89*

Alexander, Harry 1953- *WhoEmL 91*

Alexander, Hattie Elizabeth 1901-1968 *BioIn 16*

Alexander, Helen 1654?-1729 *FemiCLE*

Alexander, Henry Clay 1902-1969 *BioIn 16*

Alexander, Herbert E. 1927- *WhoAm 90*

Alexander, Herbert W. 1910-1988 *BioIn 16*

Alexander, Hezekiah 1728-1801 *BioIn 16*

Alexander, Horace G. 1889-1989 *ConAu 129*

Alexander, Horace Gundry 1889-1989 *BioIn 16*

Alexander, Hugh *BioIn 16*

Alexander, Hughie 1917- *Ballpl 90*

Alexander, Ingrid *BioIn 16*

Alexander, James 1691-1756 *EncCRAm*

Alexander, James Crew 1942- *WhoE 91*

Alexander, James Eckert 1913- *WhoAm 90*

Alexander, James Edwin 1930- *WhoWor 91*

Alexander, James L. 1924- *St&PR 91*

Alexander, James Marshall, Jr. 1921- *WhoAm 90*

Alexander, James Maurice 1937- *BiDrAPA 89*

Alexander, James Morton 1924- *St&PR 91*

Alexander, James Patrick 1944- *WhoSSW 91*

Alexander, James Sidney 1958- *BiDrAPA 89*

Alexander, James Wesley 1934- *WhoAm 90*

Alexander, Jane *BioIn 16*

Alexander, Jane 1939- *NotWoAT, WhoAm 90, WhoAmW 91, WhoWor 91, WorAlBi*

Alexander, Janet *AuBYP 90*

Alexander, Jason *BioIn 16*

Alexander, Jason 1959- *ConTFT 8, WhoAm 90*

Alexander, Jeff *NewYTBS 90*

Alexander, Jeff 1910-1989 *BioIn 16*

Alexander, Jeffrey Scott 1959- *WhoEmL 91*

Alexander, Jeri Jo 1948- *WhoSSW 91*

Alexander, Jocelyn Anne Arundel 1930- *AuBYP 90*

Alexander, John *NewYTBS 90 [port]*

Alexander, John 1923- *IntWWM 90*

Alexander, John B. 1927- *St&PR 91*

Alexander, John Charles 1943- *WhoAm 90*

Alexander, John David, Jr. 1932- *WhoAm 90*

Alexander, John E 1945- *WhoAmA 91*

Alexander, John J. 1940- *WhoAm 90*

Alexander, John Macmillan, Jr. 1931- *WhoAm 90*

Alexander, John Noel 1941- *WhoSSW 91*

Alexander, John Thorndike 1940- *WhoAm 90*

Alexander, John Wesley 1919-1990 *BioIn 16*

Alexander, John William 1949- *WhoEmL 91*

Alexander, John William, Jr. 1933- *St&PR 91*

Alexander, Jonathan 1947- *WhoAm 90, WhoE 91, WhoEmL 91*

Alexander, Josef 1907- *IntWWM 90*

Alexander, Joseph Kunkle, Jr. 1940- *WhoAm 90*

Alexander, Joshua Willis 1852-1936 *AmLegL, BiDrUSE 89*

Alexander, Joyce Mary 1927- *WhoAmW 91*

Alexander, Judd Harris 1925- *St&PR 91, WhoAm 90, WhoSSW 91*

Alexander, Judith 1932- *WhoAmA 91*

Alexander, Judith Ann 1940- *WhoAm 90, WhoAmW 91*

Alexander, Julie *BioIn 16*

Alexander, Keith *BioIn 16*

Alexander, Kenneth Edward 1947- *WhoSSW 91*

Alexander, Kenneth Lewis 1924- *WhoAm 90, WhoAmA 91*

Alexander, Kobi 1952- *St&PR 91*

Alexander, Kyle *BioIn 16*

Alexander, Lamar *BioIn 16*

Alexander, Lamar 1940- *News 91-2 [port]*

Alexander, Lawrence Dennis 1934- *WhoAm 90*

Alexander, Leckie Frederick 1929- *WhoAm 90*

Alexander, Leeland Neill 1945- *WhoSSW 91*

Alexander, Leni 1924- *IntWWM 90*

Alexander, Lewis M. 1900-1945 *EarBlAP*

Alexander, Lewis McElwain 1921- *WhoAm 90*

Alexander, Lincoln MacCauley 1922- *WhoAm 90, WhoE 91*

Alexander, Linda Annette 1948- *WhoSSW 91*

Alexander, Linda Diane 1953- *WhoAmW 91*

Alexander, Linda Dianne 1942- *WhoSSW 91*

Alexander, Linda Marie 1955- *WhoEmL 91*

Alexander, Lloyd *BioIn 16*

Alexander, Lloyd 1924- *MajTwCW*

Alexander, Lloyd Chudley 1924- *AuBYP 90, WhoAm 90, WhoWrEP 89*

Alexander, Lois K. *BioIn 16*

Alexander, Louis 1917- *WhoSSW 91*

Alexander, Lynn 1938- *WhoAm 90, WhoAmW 91*

Alexander, Lynne 1958- *WhoAmW 91*

Alexander, Madelyn M. 1953- *WhoAmW 91*

Alexander, Marcia 1933- *BiDrAPA 89*

Alexander, Margaret Ames 1916- *WhoAmA 91*

Alexander, Margo Nickle 1947- *St&PR 91*

Alexander, Martha 1920- *AuBYP 90*

Alexander, Martin 1930- *WhoAm 90*

Alexander, Mary Blackwell 1928- *WhoSSW 91*

Alexander, Mary E. 1947- *WhoAmW 91*

Alexander, Mary Louise 1926- *WhoAmW 91, WhoSSW 91, WhoWor 91*

Alexander, Mary Louise 1950- *WhoAmW 91*

Alexander, Mary Spratt Provoost 1677-1734 *EncCRAm*

Alexander, Maurice Myron 1917- *WhoAm 90, WhoE 91*

Alexander, Melton Lee 1927- *WhoAm 90*

Alexander, Melvin Taylor 1949- *WhoE 91*

Alexander, Michael Lee 1959- *WhoAm 90, WhoEmL 91, WhoSSW 91*

Alexander, Miles Jordan 1931- *WhoAm 90*

Alexander, Molly Mary Bushong 1958- *WhoAmW 91*

Alexander, Myrl Early 1909- *WhoAm 90*

Alexander, Nicholas Anthony 1938- *WhoE 91*

Alexander, Norman D., Jr. 1930- *St&PR 91*

Alexander, Norman E. 1914- *St&PR 91, WhoAm 90, WhoE 91*

Alexander, Norman J. 1909- *St&PR 91*

Alexander, Norman James 1909- *WhoAm 90*

Alexander, Pamela 1948- *WhoWrEP 89*

Alexander, Patricia Darcy 1955- *WhoAmW 91, WhoEmL 91*

Alexander, Patricia Ross 1955- *WhoAmW 91*

Alexander, Patrick Byron 1950- *WhoAm 90*

Alexander, Patrick Lynch 1955- *WhoSSW 91*

Alexander, Patti *BioIn 16*

Alexander, Paul Evan *BiDrAPA 89*

Alexander, Peter 1939- *WhoAmA 91*

Alexander, Peter Albert 1942- *WhoAm 90*

Alexander, Peter Marquis 1945- *IntWWM 90*

Alexander, Philip B *BiDrAPA 89*

Alexander, Phillip Ross 1936- *St&PR 91*

Alexander, Quentin 1919- *WhoAm 90*

Alexander, Ralph 1946- *BiDrAPA 89*

Alexander, Ralph William, Jr. 1941- *WhoAm 90*

Alexander, Raymond 1929- *St&PR 91*

Alexander, Raymond Jackson, Jr. 1928- *St&PR 91*

Alexander, Renee Rafaela 1932- *WhoAmW 91*

Alexander, Richard 1944- *WhoWor 91*

Alexander, Richard B. 1920- *St&PR 91*

Alexander, Richard Douglas 1947- *WhoE 91*

Alexander, Robert Clifton 1957- *BiDrAPA 89, WhoEmL 91*

Alexander, Robert David 1927- *St&PR 91*

Alexander, Robert Earl 1939- *WhoAm 90*

Alexander, Robert Evans 1907- *WhoAm 90*

Alexander, Robert Jackson 1918- *WhoAm 90, WhoWor 91*

Alexander, Robert McNeill 1934- *WhoWor 91*

Alexander, Robert Raymond 1951- *BiDrAPA 89*

Alexander, Robert Seymour 1923- *WhoAmA 91*

Alexander, Robert William 1924- *WhoWor 91*

Alexander, Roberta *BioIn 16*

Alexander, Roberta 1949- *IntWWM 90, PenDiMP*

Alexander, Ronald Clifford 1949- *WhoE 91*

Alexander, Rosemary Elizabeth 1926- *WhoAm 90*

Alexander, Roy 1928- *ODwPR 91*

Alexander, Roy 1930- *WhoAm 90*

Alexander, S. Allan 1951- *WhoSSW 91*

Alexander, Sadie Tanner Mosell *BioIn 16*

Alexander, Samuel Allen, Jr. 1938- *WhoE 91, WhoWor 91*

Alexander, Samuel Craighead 1930- *WhoAm 90*

Alexander, Samuel P. *WhoHisp 91*

Alexander, Sander Peter 1929- *WhoAm 90*

Alexander, Saunders P *BiDrAPA 89*

Alexander, Saundra Weisband 1944- *WhoE 91*

Alexander, Scott Emerson 1949- *St&PR 91*

Alexander, Shana 1925- *WhoAm 90, WhoAmW 91, WhoWrEP 89, WorAlBi*

Alexander, Sheila M. *BioIn 16*

Alexander, Sherry A. 1943- *WhoAmW 91*

Alexander, Shirley Jean *BiDrAPA 89*

Alexander, Stacy Ann 1959- *WhoAmW 91*

Alexander, Stanford J. 1928- *St&PR 91*

Alexander, Stanley Warren 1933- *WhoSSW 91*

Alexander, Stanton Malone 1941- *WhoSSW 91*

Alexander, Stephanie *ODwPR 91*

Alexander, Steve 1947- *WhoWrEP 89*

Alexander, Sue 1933- *BioIn 16*

Alexander, Terry James 1946- *St&PR 91*

Alexander, Theodore Martin 1909- *WhoAm 90*

Alexander, Theron *WhoAm 90*

Alexander, Thomas Benjamin 1918- *WhoAm 90*

Alexander, Thomas F. 1951- *WhoWrEP 89*

Alexander, Vance T 1904- *BiDrAPA 89*

Alexander, Vera 1932- *WhoAm 90, WhoAmW 91*

Alexander, Victor Theodore 1956- *WhoWor 91*

Alexander, Vikky M 1959- *WhoAmA 91*

Alexander, Welborn Excell, Jr. 1941- *WhoAm 90*

Alexander, William *DrBIPA 90*

Alexander, William 1726-1783 *EncCRAm*

Alexander, William B., Jr. 1937- *St&PR 91*

Alexander, William Brooks 1921- *WhoAm 90*

Alexander, William C. 1935-1988 *BioIn 16*

Alexander, William Carter 1937- *WhoSSW 91*

Alexander, William D., III 1911- *WhoAm 90*

Alexander, William H. 1941- *St&PR 91*

Alexander, William Henry 1902- *WhoAm 90*

Alexander, William Henry 1930- *WhoAm 90*

Alexander, William Herbert 1941- *WhoAm 90*

Alexander, William Louis, Jr. 1961- *WhoEmL 91*

Alexander, William Major, Jr. 1928- *St&PR 91*

Alexander, William O. 1924- *St&PR 91*

Alexander, William Olin 1939- *WhoAm 90*

Alexander, William Polk, III 1947- *WhoEmL 91*

Alexander, William Powell 1934- *WhoAm 90*

Alexander, William Vincent 1936- *St&PR 91*

Alexander, William Vollie, Jr. 1934- *WhoAm 90, WhoSSW 91*

Alexander, Wilma Jean 1938- *WhoAmW 91*

Alexander, Zenon L. 1943- *St&PR 91*

Alexander-Greene, Grace George 1918- *WhoAmA 91*

Alexander-Grinalds, Julia C. 1947- *WhoEmL 91*

Alexander-Guerra, Lycia Lucia *BiDrAPA 89*

Alexander-Guerra, Lycia Lucia 1955- *WhoE 91*

Alexander-Williams, Vynessa 1957- *WhoEmL 91*

Alexanderson, Alvin 1947- *St&PR 91*

Alexanderson, Ernst F. 1878-1975 *WorAlBi*

Alexanderson, Gerald Lee 1933- *WhoAm 90*

Alexanderwicz, Melvin John *BiDrAPA 89*

Alexandra *EncCoWW*

Alexandra *WomWR*

Alexandra 1872-1918 *WomWR [port]*

Alexandre 1922- *BioIn 16*

Alexandre, Gerard-Eugene 1930- *WhoWor 91*

Alexandre, Gilbert Fernand A.E. 1944- *WhoWor 91*

Alexandre, Judith Lee 1944- *WhoAmW 91*

Alexandre, Leah *WhoWrEP 89*

Alexandre du Portal, Luc Jean 1941- *WhoWor 91*

Alexandroff, Pavel Sergeevich 1896-1982 *DcScB S2*

Alexandrou, Ares *BioIn 16*

Alexandrov, Yaroslav *PenDiMP*

Alexanian, Diran 1881?-1954 *PenDiMP*

Alexanian, Raymond 1932- *WhoAm 90*

Alexanian, Vahan Dikran 1931- *WhoSSW 91*

Alexeev, Dimitri 1947- *IntWWM 90*

Alexeev, Dmitry 1947- *PenDiMP*

Alexeff, Alexander 1934- *St&PR 91*

Alexeff, Igor 1931- *WhoAm 90, WhoSSW 91*

Alexenberg, Mel 1937- *WhoAmA 91*

Alexeyev, Dmitry 1947- *PenDiMP*

Alexeyev, Eduard Y. 1937- *IntWWM 90*

Alexich, Milton P. 1930- *St&PR 91*

Alexick, David Francis 1942- *WhoAmA 91*

Alexiou, Elle 1898?- *EncCoWW*

Alexiou, Elli *EncCoWW*

Alexiou, James 1932- *St&PR 91*

Alexiou, Margaret Beatrice 1939- *WhoAm 90*

Alexiou, Marina S. 1940- *WhoE 91*

Alexis, Jody Rae 1940- *WhoWor 91*

Alexis, Kim *BioIn 16*

Alexis, Marcus 1932- *St&PR 91*

Alexopoulos, George S 1946- *BiDrAPA 89*

Alexopoulos, Helene *BioIn 16, WhoAm 90*

Alexopoulos, Nicolaos George 1942- *WhoAm 90*

Alexsovich, George 1946- *WhoAm 90*

Alexy, Dale Stewart *BioIn 16*

Alexy, R. James 1940- *WhoAm 90*

Alexy, Robert Werner 1945- *WhoWor 91*

Alexy, Walter Karl 1935- *WhoWor 91*

Aley, Charles R. 1956- *WhoEmL 91*

Aley, Paul Nathaniel 1944- *St&PR 91*

Alf, Martha Joanne 1930- *WhoAmA 91*

Alfandari, Jean-Pierre 1934- *WhoWor 91*

Alfange, Dean 1899?-1989 *BioIn 16*

Alfange, Dean, Jr. 1930- *WhoAm 90*

Alfano, Blaise Francis 1923- *WhoAm 90*

Alfano, Charles Thomas, Sr. 1920- *WhoAm 90*

Alfano, Franco 1876-1954 *PenDiMPA*

Alfano, Joseph M. 1946- *St&PR 91*

Alfano, Michael Charles 1947- *St&PR 91, WhoAm 90, WhoEmL 91*

Alfarabi 870?-950 *EncO&P 3*

Alfaro, Armando Joffroy, Jr. 1950- *WhoHisp 91*

Alfaro, Carlos, Jr. 1964- *WhoWor 91*

Alfaro, Eloy 1842-1912 *BioIn 16*

Alfaro, Felix Benjamin 1939- *WhoWor 91*

Alfaro, Ricardo J. 1882-1971 *BioIn 16*

Alferez, Faust 1930- *St&PR 91*

Alfero, Veronica *BiDrAPA 89*

Alfers, Gerald Junior 1931- *WhoAm 90*

Alfheim, Roar Lemcke 1935- *WhoWor 91*

Alfidi, Ralph Joseph 1932- *WhoAm 90*

Alfie, Salomon 1953- *BiDrAPA 89*

Alfieri, Frank Thomas 1930- *WhoAm 90*

Alfieri, John Joseph 1917- *WhoAm 90*

Alfiero, Sal *BioIn 16*

Alfiero, Sal H. 1937- *St&PR 91*

Alfiero, Salvatore Harry 1937- *WhoAm 90*

Alfin-Slater, Roslyn Berniece 1916- *WhoAm 90*

Alfonsin, Raul *BioIn 16*

Alfonsin, Raul Ricardo 1927- *WhoWor 91*

Alfonso 1881-1953 *BioIn 16*

Alfonso 1902- *BioIn 16*

Alfonso XII, King of Spain 1857-1885 *BioIn 16*

Alfonso XIII, King of Spain 1886-1941 *BioIn 16*

Alfonso, Alfredo Zayas y 1861-1934 *BioIn 16*

Alfonso, Antonio Escolar 1943- *WhoAm 90*

Alfonso, Carlos Juan 1955- *WhoSSW 91*

Alfonso, Eduardo 1952- *WhoSSW 91*

Alfonso, Elisa J. 1955- *WhoHisp 91*

Alfonso, Gabriel M 1922- *BiDrAPA 89*

Alfonso, Imelda Carlos *BiDrAPA 89*

Alfonso, Kristian *BioIn 16, WhoHisp 91*

Alfonso, Robert John 1928- *WhoAm 90*

Alfonso, Rosanne Brunello 1960- *WhoAmW 91, WhoEmL 91, WhoWor 91*

Alfonzo, Carlos 1950- *WhoHisp 91*

Alford, Albert H. 1862-1927 *AmLegL*

Alford, B.W. 1957- *St&PR 91*

Alford, Bobby Ray 1932- *WhoAm 90*

Alford, Brad Alan 1953- *WhoE 91*

Alford, C Fred 1947- *ConAu 131*

Alford, Donald E. 1926- St&PR 91
Alford, Fred F., Jr. 1931- St&PR 91
Alford, Gloria K 1928- WhoAmA 91
Alford, Harry 1883-1939 OxCPMus
Alford, J. Keith 1941- St&PR 91, WhoAm 90
Alford, Jack Leland 1920- WhoAm 90
Alford, James Allen 1922- BiDrAPA 89
Alford, Joan Franz 1940- WhoAmW 91
Alford, John W. 1912- St&PR 91
Alford, John William 1912- WhoAm 90
Alford, Kenneth J. 1881-1945 OxCPMus
Alford, Kenneth W. 1938- St&PR 91
Alford, Lionel Devon 1925- St&PR 91
Alford, Lore 1838-1900 AmLegL
Alford, Mary Ann 1954- WhoEmL 91
Alford, Neill Herbert, Jr. 1919- WhoAm 90, WhoWor 91
Alford, Newell G., Jr. WhoAm 90
Alford, Olita M. 1907- St&PR 91
Alford, Paul Legare 1930- WhoAm 90
Alford, Philip John 1953- St&PR 91
Alford, Richard Dana 1951- WhoSSW 91
Alford, Robert E. 1926- St&PR 91
Alford, Robert Ross 1928- WhoAm 90
Alford, Robert Wilfrid, Jr. 1955- WhoEmL 91, WhoSSW 91
Alford, Thomas Earl 1935- WhoAm 90
Alford, Thomas Wildcat 1860-1938 WhNaAH
Alford, Walter Helion 1938- St&PR 91, WhoAm 90
Alford, William Parker 1927- WhoAm 90
Alford-McIntosh, Sara S BiDrAPA 89
Alfred The Great 849-899 WorAlBi
Alfred, Dewitt C, Jr. 1937- BiDrAPA 89
Alfred, Karl Sverre 1917- WhoAm 90
Alfred, Lindbergh Davis 1948- WhoEmL 91
Alfred, Stephen Jay 1934- WhoAm 90
Alfred, William 1922- WhoAm 90, WhoWrEP 89
Alfreds, Joe WhoWrEP 89
Alfredson, Jens WhoWrEP 89
Alfring, James G. 1913- St&PR 91
Alfrink, Bernard 1900-1987 BioIn 16
Alfs, Matthew Gerd 1956- WhoWrEP 89
Alfsen, John Martin WhoAmA 91N
Alfven, Hannes Olof Gosta 1908- WhoAm 90, WhoWor 91
Alfven, Inger 1940- DcScanL
Algabid, Hamid WhoWor 91
Algaier, Robert J 1953- BiDrAPA 89
Algardi, Alessandro 1598-1654 IntDcAA 90, PenDiDA 89
Algarin, Miguel 1941- BioIn 16
Algaze, Joshua BiDrAPA 89
Algazi, Jacques E. 1934- WhoWor 91
Alger, Chadwick Fairfax 1924- WhoAm 90
Alger, Derek S. WhoWrEP 89
Alger, Fred M. 1934- St&PR 91
Alger, Horatio, Jr. 1832-1899 WorAlBi
Alger, Ian E BiDrAPA 89
Alger, Leclaire Gowans 1898-1969 AuBYP 90
Alger, Martin Joseph 1944- St&PR 91
Alger, R. Kennedy 1947- St&PR 91
Alger, Russell Alexander 1836-1905 BiDrUSE 89
Algino, Joseph Michael, II 1954- WhoEmL 91
Algra, Ronald James 1949- WhoEmL 91
Algren, Nelson 1909-1981 BioIn 16, EncAL, MajTwCW, WorAlBi
Alhadeff, Benjamin Jay 1948- St&PR 91
Alhadeff, Charles D. 1909- St&PR 91
Alhadeff, David Albert 1923- WhoAm 90
Alhadeff, Leslie H. 1955- WhoSSW 91
Alhadeff, Leslie Haco BiDrAPA 89
Alhadeff, Morris Jerome 1914- WhoAm 90
Alheit, Dieter 1931- WhoWor 91
Alhilali, Neda 1938- WhoAmA 91
Ali Hassan Mwinyi BioIn 16
Ali, Abul Hasan S BiDrAPA 89
Ali, Agha Shahid 1949- WhoWrEP 89
Ali, Alan Hassan 1953- BiDrAPA 89
Ali, Fatima Z 1954- BiDrAPA 89
Ali, Grace Lucy Moore 1952- WhoEmL 91
Ali, Gregory F. 1956- St&PR 91
Ali, H. A. Mukti 1923- WhoWor 91
Ali, Karen Sani 1956- WhoAmW 91, WhoE 91
Ali, Khalilah BioIn 16
Ali, May May BioIn 16
Ali, Mehdi BioIn 16
Ali, Mehdi Raza 1944- St&PR 91
Ali, Mohammad Sarwat 1934- WhoWor 91
Ali, Mohammed Mubbasher 1957- WhoWor 91
Ali, Mostafa Abdul Muneim 1957- WhoEmL 91
Ali, Muhammad 1942- BioIn 16, WhoAm 90, WorAlBi
Ali, Nighat Z. BiDrAPA 89
Ali, Owais Aslam 1958- WhoWor 91
Ali, Patty Marie 1963- WhoAmW 91
Ali, Perveen Khan 1957- WhoAmW 91
Ali, Rafath 1944- St&PR 91
Ali, Rashied 1933- DrBlPA 90
Ali, Sajid 1950- BiDrAPA 89
Ali, Salim BioIn 16
Ali, Salim 1896-1987 ConAu 132
Ali, Salim Rubay 1934-1978 PolLCME
Ali, Shaffideen Z 1942- BiDrAPA 89
Ali, Syed Irfan 1948- BiDrAPA 89, WhoEmL 91
Ali-Khan, Mir Iftekhar 1955- BiDrAPA 89
Alia, Ramiz 1925- WhoWor 91
Alianak, Hrant 1950- OxCCanT
Aliano, David BiDrAPA 89
Alias, Aikarakudy G BiDrAPA 89
Aliber, James A. 1925- WhoAm 90
Aliber, Robert Z. 1930- WhoAm 90
Aliberti, Lucia 1957- IntWWM 90
Alibrandi, Joseph F. 1928- St&PR 91
Alibrandi, Joseph Francis 1928- WhoAm 90
Alibrandi, Pasquale Antonio 1930- WhoAm 90
Alice 1106?- WomWR
Alice Cooper BioIn 16
Alice Mary Victoria Augusta Pauline 1883-1981 DcNaB 1981
Alice, Mary 1941- DrBlPA 90, WhoAmW 91
Alicea, Jose 1928- WhoAmA 91
Alicea, Victor Gabriel 1938- WhoHisp 91
Alicea-Berrios, Ingrid BiDrAPA 89
Alicea-Colon, Carlos N. 1961- WhoSSW 91
Alich, Agnes Amelia 1932- WhoAmW 91
Alich, John Arthur, Jr. 1942- St&PR 91
Alick, Nafe Joe 1936- St&PR 91, WhoAm 90
Alick, Richard WhoAm 90
Alidon, Gildegardo P 1940- BiDrAPA 89
Alie, Arthur Henry 1939- St&PR 91, WhoAm 90
Aliengena, Tony BioIn 16
Aliesan, Jody 1943- WhoWrEP 89
Alig, Frank Douglas Stalnaker 1921- WhoWor 91
Alig, Vincent B BiDrAPA 89
Aligada, Reynaldo Antoine BiDrAPA 89
Aliger, Margarita 1915- EncCoWW
Alights-on-the-Cloud WhNaAH
Alijani, Bohloul 1946- WhoWor 91
Alikakos, Louis Chris 1923- BiDrAPA 89
Alikhan, Inayat Mir BiDrAPA 89
Alikhanov, Abram Isaakovich 1904-1970 DcScB S2
Aliki AuBYP 90, ConAu 30NR, WhoAmA 91
Alikonis, James Justin BiDrAPA 89
Alim, Marilyn Pryce 1941- WhoAmW 91
Alimanestianu, Mihai BioIn 16
Alimansky, Burt 1943- WhoE 91
Alimaras, Gus 1958- WhoEmL 91
Alimario, Teresita E BiDrAPA 89
Alimchandani, Guloo Mohan 1953- WhoWor 91
Alimena, Jim 1952- St&PR 91
Alin, Robert David 1952- St&PR 91
Alina, Walter Paul 1931- St&PR 91
Alinder, James Gilbert 1941- WhoAm 90, WhoAmA 91
Alinder, Mary Street 1946- WhoAmA 91
Aline, Countess of Romanones BioIn 16
Aline Sitoe 1920?-1944 WomWR
Alinsky, Saul BioIn 16
Alinsky, Saul 1909-1972 WorAlBi
Alinsky, Saul David 1909-1972 EncAL
Alio, Ivan Stamenitov 1921- WhoAm 90
Aliprandi, Giambattista 1942- St&PR 91
Aliseda, Jose Luis, Jr. 1956- WhoHisp 91
Alisky, Marvin Howard 1923- WhoAm 90
Alison, Barley BioIn 16
Alison, Barley 1920-1989 AnObit 1989
Alison, Francis 1705-1779 EncCRAm
Alison, Paul Nordell 1950- WhoEmL 91
Alito, Samuel Anthony, Jr. 1950- WhoAm 90
Alivizatos, Gerasimos Dionysios 1952- WhoWor 91
Alix of Vergy WomWR
Alix, Jacquelyn J. 1940- WhoE 91
Alizai, Azam 1931- St&PR 91
Aljian, James D. 1932- St&PR 91
Aljian, James Donovan 1932- WhoAm 90
Alkalay-Gut, Karen 1945- ConAu 129, WhoWor 91, WhoWrEP 89
Alkali, Zaynab 1950- FemiCLE
Alkan, Charles Henri Valentin 1813-1888 BioIn 16
Alkan, Valentin 1813-1888 PenDiMP A
Alkar, Y M BiDrAPA 89
Alkema, Evert Albert 1939- WhoWor 91
Alker, George 1929- WhoAm 90
Alker, Hayward Rose, Jr. 1937- WhoAm 90
Alkhoury, Raja S. 1961- WhoSSW 91
Alkin, Elizabeth BiDEWW
Alkire, Edward Arthur 1953- St&PR 91
Alkire, Richard Charles 1955- WhoEmL 91
Alkire, Richard Collin 1941- WhoAm 90
Alkis-Alchimavicius, Jaras 1929- WhoWor 91
Alkon, Ellen Skillen 1936- WhoAm 90
Alkon, Paul Kent WhoAm 90
Allaby, Stanley Reynolds 1931- WhoAm 90
Alladice, Darryl BioIn 16
Allain, Emery Edgar 1922- WhoAm 90
Allain, Leon Gregory 1924- WhoSSW 91
Allain-Targe, Francois Henri Rene 1832-1902 BiDFrPL
Allaire, Paul Arthur 1938- St&PR 91, WhoAm 90, WhoE 91
Allais, Maurice 1911- BioIn 16, WhoWor 91, WorAlBi
Allalouf, Sam ODwPR 91
Allam, Mark Whittier 1908- WhoAm 90
Allamong, Betty D. 1935- WhoAm 90
Allan, Andrew 1907-1974 OxCCanT
Allan, Andrew Thomas BiDrAPA 89
Allan, Barry David 1935- WhoAm 90
Allan, Blandford M E BiDrAPA 89
Allan, Donald Aspinwall 1922- WhoAm 90
Allan, Douglas Wayne 1945- WhoEmL 91
Allan, Edward R 1931- BiDrAPA 89
Allan, Harry Thain 1928- WhoAm 90
Allan, Hugh James Pearson 1928- WhoAm 90
Allan, John 1746-1805 EncCRAm
Allan, John Dykes 1925- St&PR 91, WhoAm 90
Allan, John Malcolm, Jr. 1955- WhoEmL 91
Allan, Laura NewAgMG
Allan, Lois 1905-1989 AnObit 1989
Allan, Mabel Esther 1915- AuBYP 90, BioIn 16, SmATA 11AS [port]
Allan, Martha 1895-1942 OxCCanT
Allan, Peggy BioIn 16
Allan, Peter 1935- ODwPR 91
Allan, Ralph T. Mackinnon 1942- St&PR 91
Allan, Ralph Thomas Mackinnon 1942- WhoAm 90
Allan, Richard van PenDiMP
Allan, Roger D. 1933- ODwPR 91
Allan, Ronald C. 1937- St&PR 91
Allan, Rupert Mortimer, Jr. 1912- WhoAm 90
Allan, Stanley Nance 1921- WhoAm 90
Allan, Ted 1916- OxCCanT
Allan, Walter Scott 1913- WhoAm 90
Allan, William BioIn 16
Allan, William George 1936- WhoAmA 91
Allan, William Laird BiDrAPA 89
Allan, William Norman 1925- St&PR 91
Allan, Yvonne Leticia 1927- WhoAmW 91
Allanach, Elaine Jacqueline 1954- WhoAmW 91, WhoEmL 91
Allanbrook, Douglas 1921- IntWWM 90
Alland, Alexander, Jr. 1931- WhoWor 91
Allansmith, Mathea Reuter 1930- WhoAm 90, WhoAmW 91
Allanson, Andy 1961- Ballpl 90
Allanson, Bruce D. 1930- St&PR 91
Allanson, Patrick Robt 1912- BiDrAPA 89
Allara, Pamela Edwards 1943- WhoAmA 91
Allard, Ann Helmuth 1950- WhoEmL 91
Allard, Brenda Jo 1954- WhoAmW 91
Allard, David Henry 1929- WhoAm 90
Allard, Dean Conrad 1933- WhoAm 90
Allard, Edward Tiernan, III 1945- WhoWor 91
Allard, Harry 1928- BioIn 16
Allard, Harry, Jr. 1928- AuBYP 90
Allard, James E. 1942- St&PR 91
Allard, James Edward 1942- WhoAm 90
Allard, Jean 1924- St&PR 91, WhoAm 90, WhoAmW 91
Allard, Jeffrey Thomas 1938- WhoWor 91
Allard, Judith Louise 1945- WhoE 91
Allard, Leon D. 1938- WhoAm 90
Allard, Linda BioIn 16
Allard, Lisa Anne BiDrAPA 89
Allard, Marvel June WhoAmW 91
Allard, Nicholas Leo 1929- St&PR 91, WhoAm 90
Allard, Richard C. 1945- St&PR 91
Allard, Robert Wayne 1919- WhoAm 90
Allard, Roger P. 1945- St&PR 91
Allard, Ronald A. 1946- St&PR 91
Allard, Thurman J. 1959- WhoEmL 91
Allard, William Kenneth 1941- WhoAm 90, WhoSSW 91
Allardice, John McCarrell 1940- WhoE 91
Allardt, Erik 1925- ConAu 30NR
Allardt, Erik Anders 1925- WhoWor 91
Allardt, Linda 1926- WhoWrEP 89
Allardyce, Dale H. 1949- St&PR 91
Allardyce, Fred A. 1941- St&PR 91
Allardyce, Paula TwCCr&M 91
Allart, Jean Claude 1944- WhoWor 91
Allason, Rupert 1951- ConAu 132
Allaster, Kingsley G. 1930- St&PR 91
Allatini, Rose 1890?-1980? FemiCLE
Allawala, Shamim Ahmed 1938- WhoWor 91
Allbee, Sandra Moll 1947- WhoEmL 91
Allbery, Debra L. 1957- WhoWrEP 89
Allbeury, Ted 1917- TwCCr&M 91
Allbeury, Theodore Edward Le Bouthillier 1917- SpyFic
Allbright, Bruce G. 1928- St&PR 91
Allbright, Bruce Galloway 1928- WhoAm 90
Allbright, Karan Elizabeth 1948- WhoAmW 91, WhoEmL 91
Allbritton, Barbara B. 1937- St&PR 91
Allbritton, Cliff 1931- WhoSSW 91
Allbritton, Elwyn James 1937- St&PR 91
Allbritton, Joe L. BioIn 16
Allbritton, Joe L. 1924- St&PR 91
Allbritton, Joe Lewis 1924- WhoAm 90, WhoE 91
Allchin, Theodore Adam BiDrAPA 89
Allcock, Harry Melvin, Jr. 1932- St&PR 91, WhoAm 90
Allcock, Harry Rex 1932- WhoAm 90, WhoE 91
Allday, Martin Lewis 1926- WhoAm 90
Alldis, John 1929- IntWWM 90, PenDiMP
Alldredge, Alice Louise 1949- WhoAmW 91
Alldredge, Ernest George 1938- St&PR 91
Alldredge, Leroy Romney 1917- WhoAm 90
Alldredge, Robert Louis 1922- WhoWor 91
Alldredge, William 1940- St&PR 91
Alldritt, Virgil Everett 1954- WhoEmL 91
Allee, David Jepson 1931- WhoAm 90
Allee, Nancy Jane WhoSSW 91
Allee, Warder Clyde 1885-1955 DcScB S2
Allegaert, Burr 1934- St&PR 91
Allegra, Peter Alexander 1953- WhoEmL 91
Allegra-Calzolari, Marisa Ida BiDrAPA 89
Allegranti, Maddalena 1754-1801? PenDiMP
Allegretti, Albert P. 1954- St&PR 91
Allegretti, Joseph Benedict 1938- WhoAm 90
Allegretti, Joseph Nicholas 1937- St&PR 91
Allegretto, Michael 1944- TwCCr&M 91
Allegretto, Neil P. 1940- St&PR 91
Allegri Quartet PenDiMP
Allegro EncCoWW
Allegro, John 1923- EncO&P 3
Allegro, John Marco 1923-1988 BioIn 16
Allegrucci, Donald Lee 1936- WhoAm 90
Alleine, Theodosia BiDEWW
Alleine, Theodosia FemiCLE
Alleman, Aurelia Rushton 1928- WhoAmW 91
Allemandi, Umberto 1938- BioIn 16, WhoWor 91
Allemane, Jean 1843-1935 BiDFrPL
Allemann, Sabina WhoAm 90
Allen, Adam AuBYP 90
Allen, Adela Artola WhoHisp 91
Allen, Adrienne Lynn 1950- WhoAmW 91
Allen, Albert John BiDrAPA 89
Allen, Alex B. WhoWrEP 89
Allen, Alfred Keys 1914- WhoAm 90
Allen, Alfred Reginald BioIn 16
Allen, Alice 1943- ODwPR 91
Allen, Alice Catherine Towsley 1924- WhoAm 90, WhoAmW 91
Allen, Allyn AuBYP 90
Allen, Amanda White 1947- WhoSSW 91
Allen, Andree Mariller 1945- BiDrAPA 89
Allen, Andrew Raymond 1933- St&PR 91
Allen, Andrew V. 1941- St&PR 91
Allen, Anita Louise 1964- WhoAmW 91
Allen, Ann Elizabeth BiDrAPA 89
Allen, Anna Foster 1901- WhoAm 90
Allen, Anna Jean 1955- WhoAmW 91, WhoEmL 91
Allen, Anna Marie 1955- WhoEmL 91
Allen, Anne Hymee 1932- WhoE 91
Allen, Anthony Campbell 1925- IntWWM 90
Allen, Arly Harrison 1938- St&PR 91
Allen, Arnold 1920- BiDrAPA 89
Allen, Arnold Raymond 1932- St&PR 91
Allen, Arthur BioIn 16
Allen, Arthur Clinton, III 1944- St&PR 91
Allen, Arthur D WhoAmA 91N
Allen, Arthur Hamilton 1928- St&PR 91
Allen, B. Marc WhoE 91
Allen, Barbara Ann 1956- WhoAmW 91, WhoEmL 91
Allen, Barry M. ODwPR 91
Allen, Beatrice 1917- WhoAmW 91, WhoE 91
Allen, Belle St&PR 91, WhoAm 90
Allen, Ben WhoWrEP 89
Allen, Bernard Lee 1937- WhoSSW 91
Allen, Bernie 1939- Ballpl 90
Allen, Beth Elaine 1952- WhoAm 90
Allen, Betsy AuBYP 90
Allen, Betty DrBlPA 90, WhoAm 90
Allen, Betty 1930- BioIn 16, CurBio 90 [port], IntWWM 90
Allen, Betty Jeanne 1929- WhoAmW 91

Allen, Betty Rea 1937- WhoAmW 91, WhoSSW 91
Allen, Blair H. 1933- WhoWrEP 89
Allen, Bob 1913-1989 BioIn 16
Allen, Bob 1937- Ballpl 90
Allen, Bonnie Lynn 1957- WhoWor 91
Allen, Bruce Templeton 1938- WhoAm 90
Allen, Bruce Wayne 1953- WhoAmA 91
Allen, Buck 1925- WhoWrEP 89
Allen, Burnie B. 1952- St&PR 91
Allen, Byron BioIn 16
Allen, Byron 1961- DrBlPA 90
Allen, Byron Gilchrist 1901-1988 BioIn 16
Allen, Caffilene 1951- WhoSSW 91
Allen, Carl Monroe, Jr. 1954- WhoSSW 91
Allen, Carolyn J. 1935- St&PR 91
Allen, Carolyn Sessions 1939- WhoWrEP 89
Allen, Catherine B 1942- ConAu 129
Allen, Catherine MacDonald 1949- WhoAmA 91
Allen, Ceylon BioIn 16
Allen, Chad BioIn 16
Allen, Charles Crawford, II 1948- WhoSSW 91
Allen, Charles Curtis 1886-1950 WhoAmA 91N
Allen, Charles Earnest 1940- St&PR 91
Allen, Charles Eugene 1939- WhoAm 90
Allen, Charles H., Jr. 1914- St&PR 91
Allen, Charles Joseph, II 1917- WhoAm 90
Allen, Charles Leffler 1959- WhoSSW 91
Allen, Charles Mengel 1916- WhoAm 90
Allen, Charles Richard 1926- WhoAm 90
Allen, Charles Robert 1911- WhoAm 90
Allen, Charles Upton 1953- WhoSSW 91
Allen, Charles William 1912- WhoAm 90
Allen, Charles William 1932- WhoAm 90
Allen, Charlie Joe 1939- WhoSSW 91
Allen, Charlotte Hale 1928- ConAu 130
Allen, Charlotte Vale 1941- ConAu 30NR
Allen, Christina Marie 1964- WhoAmW 91
Allen, Christina Ruth 1961- WhoAmW 91
Allen, Clarence Canning 1897-1989 WhoAmA 91N
Allen, Clarence Reginald, Jr. 1945- WhoEmL 91
Allen, Clarence Richard 1949- WhoEmL 91
Allen, Clarence Roderic 1925- WhoAm 90
Allen, Claxton Edmonds, III 1944- WhoE 91, WhoWor 91
Allen, Clay ConAu 31NR
Allen, Clifton Brown 1932- St&PR 91
Allen, Clive Victor 1935- St&PR 91, WhoAm 90
Allen, Constance Olleen Webb 1923- WhoAmA 91
Allen, Corey 1934- ConTFT 8
Allen, Crawford Leonard 1952- WhoEmL 91
Allen, Cyrus McCracken 1817-1883 AmLegL
Allen, Dale 1938- St&PR 91
Allen, Daniel E. 1935- St&PR 91
Allen, Darina 1948- WhoWor 91
Allen, Darryl Frank 1943- St&PR 91, WhoAm 90
Allen, Davia M. 1945- WhoSSW 91
Allen, David 1942- WhoE 91
Allen, David 1960- St&PR 91
Allen, David Christian 1949- WhoEmL 91
Allen, David Christopher 1933- WhoE 91
Allen, David Donald 1931- St&PR 91, WhoAm 90
Allen, David Dudley 1925- WhoWrEP 89
Allen, David F 1943- BiDrAPA 89
Allen, David Henry 1938- BiDrAPA 89
Allen, David James 1935- WhoAm 90, WhoWor 91
Allen, David Mark 1949- BiDrAPA 89
Allen, David Rayvern 1938- ConAu 129
Allen, David Robert 1956- WhoEmL 91
Allen, David Russell 1940- WhoE 91
Allen, David Russell 1942- WhoAm 90
Allen, David W 1922- BiDrAPA 89
Allen, David Woodroffe 1944- WhoE 91
Allen, Debbie BioIn 16, WhoAm 90
Allen, Debbie 1950- DrBlPA 90
Allen, Debbie 1953- WorAlBi
Allen, Deborah 1954- WhoAm 90
Allen, Debra Janiece 1953- WhoAmW 91
Allen, Dee Dee BioIn 16
Allen, Delmas James 1937- WhoAm 90, WhoSSW 91
Allen, Denise BioIn 16
Allen, Denny 1939- WhoSSW 91
Allen, Dick BioIn 16
Allen, Dick 1942- Ballpl 90 [port]
Allen, Diogenes 1932- WhoAm 90
Allen, Don Lee 1934- WhoAm 90
Allen, Donald Clinton 1931- WhoAm 90
Allen, Donald Vail 1928- WhoAm 90, WhoWor 91
Allen, Donald Wayne 1960- WhoEmL 91, WhoSSW 91
Allen, Douglas Leslie 1924- St&PR 91, WhoAm 90
Allen, Duane BioIn 16
Allen, Duane David 1943- WhoAm 90
Allen, Durward Leon 1910- WhoAm 90
Allen, Dwight W. 1946- St&PR 91
Allen, Earl T., Jr. 1919- St&PR 91
Allen, Edda Lynne 1932- WhoAmA 91
Allen, Edward 1948- ConLC 59 [port]
Allen, Edward A 1943- BiDrAPA 89
Allen, Edward D 1923- ConAu 31NR
Allen, Edward Hathaway 1948- WhoSSW 91
Allen, Edward Lawrence 1913-1989 ConAu 130
Allen, Edward Warren 1928- BiDrAPA 89
Allen, Elbert Enrico 1921- WhoAm 90
Allen, Elisha Hunt 1804-1883 BioIn 16
Allen, Elizabeth 1931- BiDrAPA 89
Allen, Elizabeth 1934- ConTFT 8
Allen, Elizabeth Akers 1832-1911 FemiCLE
Allen, Elizabeth Ann 1954- WhoEmL 91
Allen, Elizabeth Maresca 1958- WhoAmW 91
Allen, Ellen Louise 1939- WhoAmW 91
Allen, Ernest Mason 1904- WhoAm 90
Allen, Ethan 1738-1789 EncCRAm [port], WorAlBi
Allen, Ethan 1904- Ballpl 90
Allen, Ethan 1907- St&PR 91
Allen, Eugene 1928- BiDrAPA 89
Allen, Eugene J., Jr. 1950- St&PR 91
Allen, Eugene Murray 1916- WhoAm 90
Allen, Eugene Thomas 1864-1964 DcScB S2
Allen, Faye Gibson BiDrAPA 89
Allen, Florence E. 1884-1966 BioAmW
Allen, Frances Elizabeth 1932- WhoAm 90, WhoAmW 91
Allen, Frances Michael 1939- WhoAmW 91
Allen, Frances Ruth 1929- WhoSSW 91
Allen, Francis Alfred 1919- WhoAm 90
Allen, Francis P., Jr. 1914- St&PR 91
Allen, Frank 1889-1933 Ballpl 90
Allen, Frank 1916- IntWWM 90
Allen, Frank Carroll 1913- WhoAm 90
Allen, Frank Richard 1922- St&PR 91
Allen, Franklin Glenn 1925- WhoAm 90
Allen, Fred 1894-1956 BioIn 16, OxCPMus, WorAlBi
Allen, Fred Cary 1917- WhoAm 90
Allen, Fred E. 1938- St&PR 91, WhoAm 90
Allen, Frederic W. 1926- WhoAm 90, WhoE 91
Allen, G C 1900-1982 ConAu 32NR
Allen, Garland Edward 1936- WhoAm 90
Allen, Gary Curtiss 1939- WhoSSW 91
Allen, Gary James 1948- St&PR 91, WhoAm 90
Allen, Gary Joe 1946- WhoEmL 91
Allen, Gay Wilson 1903- DcLB 103 [port], WhoAm 90
Allen, Geoffrey 1928- WhoWor 91
Allen, George 1808-1876 BioIn 16
Allen, George 1902-1989 AnObit 1989
Allen, George David, Jr. 1961- WhoSSW 91
Allen, George Howard 1914- WhoAm 90
Allen, George James 1944- WhoAm 90
Allen, George Sewell 1942- WhoAm 90
Allen, George Venable 1903-1970 BioIn 16
Allen, George Whitaker 1928- WhoWor 91
Allen, Gerald Campbell Forrest 1923- WhoWor 91
Allen, Geri BioIn 16
Allen, Gilbert Bruce 1951- WhoWrEP 89
Allen, Gina WhoAm 90, WhoAmW 91
Allen, Gloria B. 1926- St&PR 91
Allen, Grace 1906-1964 BioAmW
Allen, Gracie 1906?-1964 BioIn 16, WorAlBi
Allen, Grant 1848-1899 BioIn 16, DcLB 92 [port]
Allen, Gregory Bryce 1950- WhoEmL 91
Allen, H Alton BiDrAPA 89
Allen, H.L., Jr. 1941- St&PR 91
Allen, Hank 1940- Ballpl 90
Allen, Hannah BiDEWW, FemiCLE
Allen, Harlan G. 1942- St&PR 91
Allen, Harold 1912- WhoAmA 91
Allen, Harold G. 1911- WhoAm 90
Allen, Harry Clay, Jr. 1920- WhoAm 90
Allen, Harry Franklin 1956- WhoEmL 91
Allen, Harry R. 1937- BiDrAPA 89
Allen, Harry William 1930- St&PR 91
Allen, Heath Ledward 1927- WhoAm 90
Allen, Henry 1908-1967 OxCPMus
Allen, Henry Clay 1838-1889 AmLegL
Allen, Henry D, Jr. BiDrAPA 89
Allen, Henry Muriel 1952- WhoWrEP 89
Allen, Henry W. 1912- BioIn 16
Allen, Henry Wilson AuBYP 90
Allen, Herbert 1907- WhoAm 90, WhoSSW 91
Allen, Herbert 1908- WhoAm 90
Allen, Herbert Ellis 1939- WhoAm 90
Allen, Herbert Martin BiDrAPA 89
Allen, Homer J. 1923- St&PR 91
Allen, Howard BioIn 16
Allen, Howard P. 1925- St&PR 91
Allen, Howard Pfeiffer 1925- WhoAm 90
Allen, India BioIn 16
Allen, Irving M 1939- BiDrAPA 89
Allen, Irwin WhoAm 90
Allen, Ivan, Jr. 1911- St&PR 91, WhoAm 90
Allen, Ivy M. 1932- IntWWM 90
Allen, J. Everett 1903- St&PR 91
Allen, J Scott 1938- BiDrAPA 89
Allen, Jack 1914- WhoAm 90
Allen, James 1864-1912 EncO&P 3
Allen, James Albert 1930- WhoAm 90
Allen, James B. 1912- St&PR 91
Allen, James Dennis 1941- WhoE 91
Allen, James Douglas 1958- WhoSSW 91
Allen, James Frederick 1950- WhoAm 90
Allen, James Harrill 1906- WhoAm 90
Allen, James Lane 1849-1925 LiHiK
Allen, James Lane 1904- St&PR 91
Allen, James Lee 1957- WhoEmL 91
Allen, James Lovic, Jr. 1929- WhoAm 90, WhoWrEP 89
Allen, James P. 1949- St&PR 91
Allen, James R. 1925- WhoAm 90
Allen, James Richard 1956- WhoEmL 91
Allen, James Ross 1935- BiDrAPA 89, WhoAm 90
Allen, James Wentworth 1938- St&PR 91
Allen, James William, Jr. 1944- St&PR 91
Allen, Jane Addams WhoAmA 91
Allen, Jane Mengel 1888-1952 WhoAmA 91N
Allen, Jay Presson 1922- WhoAm 90
Allen, Jean Curry 1923- WhoAm 90
Allen, Jean William 1923- St&PR 91
Allen, Jeannie Renee 1963- WhoSSW 91
Allen, Jeffrey Michael 1948- WhoAm 90, WhoEmL 91, WhoWor 91
Allen, Jeffrey Rodgers 1953- WhoEmL 91
Allen, Jere Hardy 1944- WhoAmA 91
Allen, Jeri 1947- WhoAmW 91
Allen, Jerry Clark 1939- St&PR 91
Allen, Jerry Linn 1942- St&PR 91
Allen, Jesse 1936- WhoAmA 91
Allen, Jesse Owen, III 1938- WhoSSW 91, WhoWor 91
Allen, Jessie Lee 1923- WhoAmW 91
Allen, Joan 1956- WhoAm 90, WhoAmW 91
Allen, Joan S. 1945- ODwPR 91
Allen, Joe Bailey, III 1951- WhoEmL 91
Allen, Joel Asaph 1838-1921 DcScB S2
Allen, Joel V BiDrAPA 89
Allen, John B. 1941- St&PR 91
Allen, John Campbell 1817-1898 DcCanB 12
Allen, John E BiDrAPA 89
Allen, John Earling St&PR 91
Allen, John Edward 1911- St&PR 91
Allen, John Edward 1950- WhoEmL 91
Allen, John Eliot 1908- WhoAm 90
Allen, John F. 1944- St&PR 91
Allen, John Frank 1908- WhoWor 91
Allen, John J. 1936- St&PR 91
Allen, John Logan 1941- WhoAm 90
Allen, John Loyd 1931- WhoAm 90
Allen, John Owen 1935- St&PR 91
Allen, John Thomas, Jr. 1935- WhoSSW 91, WhoWor 91
Allen, John Trevett, Jr. 1939- WhoAm 90, WhoWor 91
Allen, John W. 1923- St&PR 91
Allen, John Warner BiDrAPA 89
Allen, Johnny 1905-1959 Ballpl 90
Allen, Jon Rockne 1942- WhoWor 91
Allen, Jonelle 1944- DrBlPA 90
Allen, Jordan ConAu 129, -31NR
Allen, Joseph ODwPR 91
Allen, Joseph C. 1949- ODwPR 91
Allen, Joseph Doorley, III 1945- WhoEmL 91
Allen, Joseph Dulles 1945- WhoEmL 91
Allen, Joseph Garrott 1912- WhoAm 90, WhoWor 91
Allen, Joseph Henry 1916- WhoAm 90
Allen, Joseph Jethro BiDrAPA 89
Allen, Joseph P. 1937- WhoAm 90
Allen, Joseph W. BioIn 16
Allen, Joyce Smith 1939- WhoAmW 91
Allen, Judith 1938- WhoE 91
Allen, Judith Ruth 1943- WhoAmW 91
Allen, Julia H. 1951- WhoAmW 91
Allen, Julia Roberta BiDrAPA 89
Allen, Julian Myrick, Jr. 1956- WhoEmL 91, WhoSSW 91, WhoWor 91
Allen, Junius 1898-1962 WhoAmA 91N
Allen, Kaola 1952- WhoAmA 91
Allen, Karen BioIn 16
Allen, Karen Alfstad 1942- WhoAmW 91
Allen, Karen Jane 1951- WhoAm 90
Allen, Kellie Jeanne 1963- WhoAmW 91
Allen, Kenneth D. 1939- St&PR 91
Allen, Kenneth Dale 1939- WhoAm 90
Allen, Kenneth H. ODwPR 91
Allen, Kenneth J. WhoAm 90
Allen, Kenneth S. 1913- BioIn 16
Allen, Kenneth S. 1913-1981 ConAu 32NR
Allen, Kirsten BioIn 16
Allen, L David 1940- ConAu 130
Allen, L. Nash, Jr. 1944- St&PR 91
Allen, Larry Eugene 1948- WhoEmL 91
Allen, Laura Jean BioIn 16
Allen, Laurence T BiDrAPA 89
Allen, Laurie Catherine 1948- WhoAm 90
Allen, Lawrence A. WhoAm 90
Allen, Lawrence David, Jr. 1952- WhoEmL 91
Allen, Layman Edward 1927- WhoAm 90
Allen, Leatrice Delorice 1948- WhoAmW 91
Allen, Lee 1915-1969 AuBYP 90, Ballpl 90
Allen, Lee H. 1924- St&PR 91
Allen, Lee Harrison 1924- WhoAm 90
Allen, Lee Norcross 1926- WhoAm 90, WhoSSW 91
Allen, Leilani Eleanor 1949- WhoAmW 91
Allen, Lemuel 1839- AmLegL
Allen, Lenora 1948- BiDrAPA 89
Allen, Leon Arthur, Jr. 1933- WhoAm 90
Allen, Lew, Jr. 1925- WhoAm 90
Allen, Lewis, Jr. 1925- WhoSSW 91
Allen, Lillian 1951- FemiCLE
Allen, Lloyd 1950- Ballpl 90
Allen, Loretta B WhoAmA 91
Allen, Louis Alexander 1917- St&PR 91, WhoAm 90, WhoWor 91
Allen, Louis La Boiteaux 1925- St&PR 91
Allen, Louise 1910- WhoAmW 91
Allen, Louise Crawford 1903- WhoAmW 91
Allen, Lowell Archibald 1926- St&PR 91
Allen, Lunelle Spencer 1931- WhoAmW 91
Allen, Lyle McDowell 1922-1989 BioIn 16
Allen, Lyle Wallace 1924- WhoAm 90
Allen, Malcolm Dennis 1951- WhoWor 91
Allen, Marcus BioIn 16, NewAgMG
Allen, Marcus 1960- WhoAm 90, WorAlBi
Allen, Margo 1894-1988 WhoAmA 91N
Allen, Maria Georgina Quevedo WhoAmW 91
Allen, Marie Louise AuBYP 90
Allen, Marilyn Myers Pool 1934- WhoAmW 91
Allen, Marion 1862-1941 BiDWomA
Allen, Mark Gerard 1958- WhoE 91
Allen, Mark Hill 1956- WhoEmL 91
Allen, Mark R. 1953- St&PR 91
Allen, Martha BiDEWW
Allen, Martha Leslie 1948- WhoWrEP 89
Allen, Martin G 1939- BiDrAPA 89
Allen, Martin Joseph, Jr. 1936- St&PR 91
Allen, Martin R. 1955- St&PR 91
Allen, Martin Steven 1947- WhoEmL 91
Allen, Mary Catherine Mitchell WhoAmW 91
Allen, Mary H 1932- BiDrAPA 89
Allen, Mary Kathryn 1953- WhoAmW 91, WhoEmL 91
Allen, Mary Stockbridge 1869-1949 WhoAmA 91N
Allen, Maryon Pittman 1925- WhoAm 90, WhoAmW 91, WhoSSW 91
Allen, Matthew Arnold 1930- WhoAm 90
Allen, Maurice Bartelle, Jr. 1926- WhoAm 90
Allen, Maury 1932- Ballpl 90, BioIn 16
Allen, Mel BioIn 16
Allen, Mel 1913- AuBYP 90, Ballpl 90, WorAlBi
Allen, Melba Till 1933-1989 BioIn 16
Allen, Merle Maeser, Jr. 1932- WhoAm 90
Allen, Merritt Parmelee 1892-1954 AuBYP 90
Allen, Michael G. 1950- St&PR 91
Allen, Michael Glynne 1938- WhoAm 90
Allen, Michael Hall 1954- BiDrAPA 89
Allen, Michael Joseph 1962- WhoE 91
Allen, Michael L. 1948- St&PR 91
Allen, Michael Lewis 1937- WhoAm 90
Allen, Michelle JoAnne 1960- WhoAmW 91
Allen, Mildred Mesch WhoHisp 91
Allen, Moira Anderson 1959- WhoEmL 91
Allen, Murray E. 1931- St&PR 91
Allen, Nancy Kachelriess 1951- WhoEmL 91
Allen, Nancy Schuster 1948- WhoAm 90, WhoAmA 91
Allen, Neil 1948- Ballpl 90
Allen, Neil Hutchins 1950- WhoEmL 91
Allen, Newt 1901-1988 Ballpl 90
Allen, Newton Perkins 1922- WhoAm 90, WhoSSW 91
Allen, Nicholas Eugene 1907- WhoAm 90
Allen, Noble Curtis 1954- WhoEmL 91, WhoSSW 91
Allen, Noel Lee 1947- WhoEmL 91
Allen, Olive BioIn 16
Allen, Olive Marie 1949- WhoAmW 91
Allen, Oscar C BiDrAPA 89
Allen, Pamela AuBYP 90, BioIn 16
Allen, Patricia J. 1940- St&PR 91
Allen, Patricia J. 1941- WhoAmW 91

Allen, Patricia Jean 1940- WhoAmW 91
Allen, Patrick David 1955- WhoEmL 91
Allen, Patrick Joseph 1948- WhoEmL 91
Allen, Paul WhoAm 90
Allen, Paul Alfred 1948- WhoEmL 91
Allen, Paul Howard 1954- WhoE 91, WhoEmL 91
Allen, Paul James 1955- WhoEmL 91
Allen, Paul Steven 1956- WhoSSW 91
Allen, Paula Gina 1953- WhoAmW 91
Allen, Paula Gunn 1939- FemiCLE
Allen, Paula Karen 1962- WhoE 91
Allen, Pauline Virginia 1909- WhoAmW 91, WhoWor 91
Allen, Peter BioIn 16
Allen, Peter Ackerman 1940- WhoAm 90
Allen, Phil R. 1926- St&PR 91
Allen, Philip Maxwell 1946- WhoEmL 91
Allen, Philip W. 1951- St&PR 91
Allen, Phillip Richard 1939- WhoAm 90
Allen, Phillip Stephen 1952- WhoE 91, WhoEmL 91, WhoWor 91
Allen, Phylicia Ayers- BioIn 16
Allen, Prudence 1945- BiDrAPA 89
Allen, R Michael BiDrAPA 89
Allen, Ralph 1926- WhoAmA 91
Allen, Ralph D. 1941- St&PR 91
Allen, Ralph Dean 1941- WhoAm 90
Allen, Ralph Gilmore 1934- WhoAm 90
Allen, Randy BioIn 16
Allen, Randy Lee 1946- WhoAmW 91, WhoE 91, WhoWor 91
Allen, Raye Virginia 1929- WhoAmW 91
Allen, Raymond Ralph 1931- St&PR 91
Allen, Red 1900-1967 WorAlBi
Allen, Red 1908-1967 BioIn 16
Allen, Regina Ward 1959- WhoEmL 91
Allen, Rex Whitaker 1914- WhoAm 90
Allen, Richard BioIn 16
Allen, Richard 1760-1831 BioIn 16
Allen, Richard A. 1932- St&PR 91
Allen, Richard Alcoke 1932- WhoE 91
Allen, Richard Blose 1919- WhoAm 90
Allen, Richard C. 1926- WhoAm 90
Allen, Richard Chester 1926- WhoWrEP 89
Allen, Richard Duane 1942- St&PR 91
Allen, Richard Edward, Jr. 1949- WhoSSW 91
Allen, Richard Garrett 1923- WhoAm 90
Allen, Richard J. AuBYP 90
Allen, Richard M. St&PR 91
Allen, Richard R. 1940- St&PR 91
Allen, Richard Stanley 1939- WhoAm 90, WhoWrEP 89
Allen, Richard V. BioIn 16
Allen, Richard Vincent 1936- WhoAm 90, WhoWor 91
Allen, Riley Harris 1884-1966 BioIn 16
Allen, Robert 1744-1835 PenDiDA 89
Allen, Robert C. 1924- St&PR 91
Allen, Robert Carroll 1950- WhoSSW 91
Allen, Robert Dee 1928- WhoAm 90
Allen, Robert E. BioIn 16
Allen, Robert Edwin 1942- BiDrAPA 89
Allen, Robert English 1945- WhoEmL 91
Allen, Robert Eugene 1935- WhoAm 90, WhoE 91, WhoWor 91
Allen, Robert Eugene Barton 1940- WhoWor 91
Allen, Robert Francis 1938- WhoAm 90
Allen, Robert Harold 1928- St&PR 91, WhoSSW 91
Allen, Robert Hugh 1924- WhoAm 90
Allen, Robert Jefferson 1940- WhoSSW 91
Allen, Robert Nelson, Jr. 1956- WhoEmL 91
Allen, Robert T 1956- BiDrAPA 89
Allen, Robert Willard 1931- St&PR 91
Allen, Robert Willard 1943- WhoAm 90
Allen, Roberta WhoWrEP 89
Allen, Roberta 1945- WhoAmA 91
Allen, Roberta L. 1945- WhoAm 90
Allen, Rocelia J. 1924- WhoE 91
Allen, Rodney F. 1938- WhoSSW 91
Allen, Roger Harrington 1952- WhoSSW 91
Allen, Roger Preston 1944- St&PR 91
Allen, Roland ConAu 31NR, MajTwCW
Allen, Roland 1869-1947 BioIn 16
Allen, Ronald John 1940- WhoAm 90
Allen, Ronald Roger, Jr. 1955- WhoEmL 91
Allen, Ronald Royce 1930- ConAu 32NR, WhoAm 90
Allen, Ronald W. 1941- BioIn 16, St&PR 91, WhoAm 90, WhoSSW 91
Allen, Ronnie BioIn 16
Allen, Roy Kevin 1941- St&PR 91
Allen, Russell Lee 1944- St&PR 91
Allen, Sally Lyman 1926- WhoAm 90, WhoAmW 91
Allen, Sally Vance 1940- WhoAmW 91
Allen, Sam WhoWrEP 89
Allen, Sam P. 1931- ODwPR 91
Allen, Samuel E. 1936-1987 BioIn 16
Allen, Samuel J. 1920- St&PR 91
Allen, Samuel Ward King 1842-1919 AmLegL
Allen, Samuel Washington 1917- WhoAm 90
Allen, Sandra ODwPR 91
Allen, Sarah Frances 1943- WhoAmW 91
Allen, Scott Edward 1962- WhoE 91
Allen, Sharman 1949- BiDrAPA 89
Allen, Sharon Amerine 1942- WhoAmW 91
Allen, Sheila Hill 1935- WhoAmW 91
Allen, Stanley Lee 1957- WhoEmL 91
Allen, Stanley M. 1940- St&PR 91
Allen, Stephen Andrew 1941- WhoE 91
Allen, Stephen Dean 1943- WhoWor 91
Allen, Stephen Michael 1951- BiDrAPA 89
Allen, Stephen Valentine Patrick William 1921- WhoAm 90
Allen, Steve 1921- AuBYP 90, BioIn 16, WorAlBi
Allen, Stuart 1943- WhoE 91, WhoWor 91
Allen, Sture 1928- WhoWor 91
Allen, Susan Au WhoEmL 91
Allen, Susan Phillips 1963- WhoAmW 91
Allen, Tami Marie 1967- WhoWrEP 89
Allen, Tandy M. 1935- St&PR 91
Allen, Terry 1943- BioIn 16, WhoNeCM [port]
Allen, Theodore John 1960- WhoE 91
Allen, Theodore R. 1926- St&PR 91
Allen, Theresa Ohotnicky 1948- WhoAmW 91
Allen, Thomas 1944- BioIn 16, IntWWM 90, PenDiMP
Allen, Thomas Cox BioIn 16
Allen, Thomas Draper 1926- WhoAm 90
Allen, Thomas E. 1919- WhoE 91
Allen, Thomas Ernest 1936- BiDrAPA 89, WhoE 91
Allen, Thomas John 1931- WhoAm 90
Allen, Thomas Nelson 1938- WhoSSW 91
Allen, Thomas Oscar 1914- WhoAm 90
Allen, Thomas S. 1954- St&PR 91
Allen, Timothy Andrew 1955- WhoAm 90
Allen, Timothy Charles 1954- WhoEmL 91
Allen, Tina BioIn 16
Allen, Toby 1941- WhoAm 90
Allen, Tom, Jr 1927- WhoAmA 91
Allen, Toni K. 1940- WhoAm 90
Allen, Vicki Thomas 1955- WhoSSW 91
Allen, Vicky 1957- WhoAmW 91, WhoEmL 91
Allen, Viola 1867?-1948 BioIn 16, NotWoAT
Allen, Virginia Ann 1953- WhoAmW 91, WhoE 91
Allen, Vivien Gore 1940- WhoAmW 91
Allen, W.P. 1921- St&PR 91
Allen, Wade W. 1912- St&PR 91
Allen, Walter Ernest 1911- BioIn 16
Allen, Wells Preston, Jr. 1921- WhoAm 90
Allen, Wilbur Coleman 1925- WhoSSW 91
Allen, William 1704-1780 EncCRAm
Allen, William A. 1944- St&PR 91
Allen, William B 1860- AmLegL
Allen, William Cecil 1919- WhoAm 90
Allen, William Dale 1938- WhoAm 90
Allen, William Dean 1950- WhoWrEP 89
Allen, William Duncan 1906- IntWWM 90
Allen, William E. 1932- St&PR 91
Allen, William F., Jr. 1919- St&PR 91
Allen, William Frederick, Jr. 1919- WhoAm 90
Allen, William H., Jr. 1935- St&PR 91
Allen, William Hand 1952- WhoE 91
Allen, William Harley 1946- St&PR 91
Allen, William Hayes 1926- WhoAm 90
Allen, William J 1945- WhoAmA 91
Allen, William L. 1943- St&PR 91
Allen, William Richard 1924- WhoAm 90
Allen, William Richard, Jr. 1940- St&PR 91, WhoSSW 91
Allen, William Riley 1953- WhoEmL 91
Allen, William Sheridan 1932- WhoAm 90
Allen, William Stephen 1912- WhoAm 90
Allen, Woody BioIn 16
Allen, Woody 1935- ConTFT 8 [port], MajTwCW, WhoAm 90, WhoE 91, WorAlBi
Allen, Yorke 1915-1989 BioIn 16
Allen-Langdon, Barbara 1958- WhoWrEP 89
Allen-Morano, Susan Elizabeth 1947- WhoAmW 91
Allen-Noble, Rosie Elizabeth 1938- WhoE 91
Allen-Reussow, Laurell Lee 1962- WhoSSW 91
Allen-Taylor, Jesse Douglas BioIn 16
Allenby, Edmund 1861-1936 WorAlBi
Allenby, Steven J. 1954- St&PR 91
Allende, Isabel BioIn 16
Allende, Isabel 1942- ConAu 130, HispWr 90, MajTwCW, WorAu 1980 [port]
Allende, Octavio, Jr. 1930- St&PR 91
Allende Gossens, Salvador 1908-1973 BioIn 16, WorAlBi
Allender, John Roland 1950- WhoEmL 91
Allender, Julie Ann 1950- WhoAmW 91
Allender, Nancy G. 1957- WhoAmW 91
Allender, Patrick W. 1946- St&PR 91, WhoAm 90
Allendorf, Donald A. 1934- St&PR 91
Allenson, Alexandra Chryssomallis 1956- WhoAmW 91
Allenson, Gary 1955- Ballpl 90
Allenstein, Leland Carl 1925- WhoAm 90
Allensworth, Dorothy Alice 1907- WhoAmW 91
Allentuck, Marcia Epstein 1928- WhoAmA 91, WhoAmW 91
Aller, Eleanor PenDiMP
Aller, Lawrence Hugh 1913- WhoAm 90
Aller, Margo Friedel 1938- WhoAmW 91
Aller, Richard F. 1931- St&PR 91
Aller, Richard Francis 1931- WhoAm 90
Aller, Robert Lundeen 1934- St&PR 91, WhoAm 90
Aller, Wayne Kendall 1933- WhoAm 90
Allerhand, Adam 1937- WhoAm 90
Allerheiligen, Sandra Renee 1953- WhoSSW 91
Allers, Franz 1905- IntWWM 90, WhoAm 90
Allers, George Frederick, Jr. 1962- WhoE 91
Allers, Marlene Elaine 1931- WhoAmW 91
Allerton, Isaac 1586?-1659? EncCRAm
Allerton, John Stephen 1926- WhoAm 90
Allerton, Mary AuBYP 90
Allerton, Michael John 1935- WhoAm 90
Allerton, Samuel W. 1828-1914 WorAlBi
Allerton, William S 1925- BiDrAPA 89
Allery, Kenneth Edward 1925- WhoAm 90
Alles, Herman 1922- St&PR 91
Alletzhauser, Albert Joseph 1960- WhoWor 91
Alleva, Paula Savino 1924- WhoE 91
Allewaert, Jack R. WhoAm 90
Alley, A. Kenneth 1943- St&PR 91
Alley, Barrett Le Quatte 1934- WhoSSW 91
Alley, Connie Ann 1963- WhoSSW 91
Alley, D.D. St&PR 91N
Alley, Gene 1940- Ballpl 90
Alley, Henry Melton 1945- WhoWrEP 89
Alley, James Pinckney, Jr. 1942- WhoSSW 91
Alley, Kirstie BioIn 16, WhoAm 90
Alley, Kirstie 1955- News 90 [port], -90-3 [port], WorAlBi
Alley, Michael James 1956- St&PR 91
Alley, Nancy Patricia 1957- WhoAmW 91
Alley, Patricia Merryman 1943- WhoAmW 91
Alley, Patricia Passmore 1950- WhoE 91
Alley, Ralph L. 1951- St&PR 91
Alley, Rewi 1897-1987 BioIn 16
Alley, Richard Kenneth 1931- St&PR 91
Alley, Robert Sutherland 1932- WhoSSW 91
Alley, Wayne Edward 1932- WhoAm 90
Alley, William J. 1929- BioIn 16, St&PR 91
Alley, William Jack 1929- WhoAm 90, WhoE 91, WhoWor 91
Alleyne, Barbara Christina 1936- WhoAmW 91
Alleyne, John BioIn 16
Alleyne, John 1861-1933 EncO&P 3
Alleyne, Mervyn 1933- ConAu 130
Allf, Nancy Lee 1957- WhoAmW 91
Allfrey, Katherine AuBYP 90
Allfrey, Phyllis 1915- FemiCLE
Allgeier, Edward J. 1934- St&PR 91
Allgood, Charles Henry 1923- WhoAmA 91
Allgood, Edward PenDiDA 89
Allgood, Jimmy Eugene 1955- WhoEmL 91, WhoWor 91
Allgood, John PenDiDA 89
Allgood, Myralyn Frizzelle 1939- WhoSSW 91
Allgood, Thomas PenDiDA 89
Allgood, Thomas Bowden 1949- WhoSSW 91
Allgyer, Robert Earl 1944- WhoAm 90, WhoWor 91
Alli, Aino Sophia 1879- BiDWomA
Alli, Al 1933- St&PR 91
Alli, Richard James, Sr. 1932- WhoWor 91
Allibone, T E 1903- ConAu 131
Allies, Donna Marie Kitun 1946- WhoAmW 91
Alligator 1795?- WhNaAH
Alliger, Jeremy David 1952- WhoEmL 91, WhoWor 91
Alligood, Bob 1932- WhoAm 90
Alligood, David Lamar 1934- St&PR 91
Alligood, Paul St&PR 91
Allik, Michael 1935- WhoAm 90
Alliker, Stanford Arnold 1946- WhoE 91
Allilueva, Svetlana 1926- WhoWrEP 89
Allin, John Maury 1921- WhoAm 90
Allin, Lawrence Carroll 1932- WhoE 91, WhoWor 91
Allin, Norman 1884-1973 PenDiMP
Allin, Patrick Joseph 1951- St&PR 91
Allin, Thomas Banbury 1949- St&PR 91, WhoWor 91
Alline, Anna Lowell 1864-1934 BioIn 16
Alline, Henry 1748-1784 DcLB 99
Alling, Charles Booth, Jr. 1921- WhoAm 90
Alling, Clarence 1933- WhoAmA 91
Alling, Frederic A 1930- BiDrAPA 89
Alling, Janet D 1939- WhoAmA 91
Alling, Norman Larrabee 1930- WhoAm 90, WhoE 91
Alling, Stearly 1935- BiDrAPA 89
Allinger, Norman Louis 1928- WhoAm 90
Allingham, Cedric EncO&P 3
Allingham, Dennis John 1950- St&PR 91, WhoEmL 91
Allingham, Helen 1848-1926 BiDWomA
Allingham, John Paul 1944- WhoAm 90
Allingham, Margery 1904-1966 BioIn 16, FemiCLE, MajTwCW, TwCCr&M 91, WorAlBi
Allingham, William 1824-1889 BioIn 16
Allington, Gloria Jean Ham 1945- WhoAmW 91, WhoEmL 91, WhoSSW 91
Allington, Richard L 1947- ConAu 30NR
Allington, Robert William 1935- St&PR 91
Allinson, A. Edward 1934- WhoAm 90
Allinson, Deborah Louise 1950- WhoEmL 91
Allinson, Edward A. 1934- St&PR 91
Allinson, Elihu E 1924- BiDrAPA 89
Allinson, Gary Dean 1942- WhoAm 90
Allio, David Franklin 1955- WhoEmL 91
Allio, Robert John 1931- WhoAm 90
Alliot-Lugaz, Colette 1947- PenDiMP
Allis, Horace B 1814- AmLegL
Allis, Lyle M BiDrAPA 89
Allish, Richard Eugene, Jr. 1958- WhoEmL 91
Allison, A. Reid 1957- St&PR 91
Allison, Abraham Kykendal 1810-1893 AmLegL
Allison, Adrienne Amelia 1940- WhoE 91
Allison, Albert Ray, III 1960- WhoSSW 91
Allison, Alden Gary 1956- WhoWrEP 89
Allison, Anne Elizabeth 1954- WhoAmW 91
Allison, B. R. 1915- WhoAm 90
Allison, Beryl 1936- WhoWor 91
Allison, Beverly A. 1942- IntWWM 90
Allison, Bob AuBYP 90
Allison, Bob 1934- Ballpl 90
Allison, Bobby 1937- WorAlBi
Allison, Bonnie J. WhoAmW 91
Allison, Charles W. 1940- St&PR 91
Allison, Christopher FitzSimons 1927- WhoAm 90, WhoSSW 91
Allison, David Neal 1957- WhoEmL 91
Allison, Donald G. 1950- WhoAm 90, WhoWor 91
Allison, Dwight Leonard, Jr. 1929- WhoAm 90
Allison, Edgar Lee, III 1960- WhoSSW 91
Allison, Elisabeth 1946- St&PR 91
Allison, Fran BioIn 16, WorAlBi
Allison, Fran 1907-1989 AnObit 1989
Allison, Fred, Jr. 1922- WhoAm 90
Allison, Fred F 1919- BiDrAPA 89
Allison, Genevieve J. 1939- WhoSSW 91
Allison, George H 1921- BiDrAPA 89
Allison, George Lloyd 1931- St&PR 91
Allison, Grace 1946- WhoEmL 91
Allison, Graham Tillett, Jr. 1940- WhoAm 90
Allison, Harrison Clarke 1917- WhoWrEP 89
Allison, Harry V. 1934- St&PR 91
Allison, Herbert Monroe, Jr. 1943- St&PR 91, WhoAm 90
Allison, Hughes EarBlAP
Allison, Jack H. St&PR 91
Allison, James 1955- ODwPR 91
Allison, James B 1933- BiDrAPA 89
Allison, James Claybrooke, II 1942- WhoAm 90
Allison, James Ralph 1930- WhoAm 90
Allison, James Richard, Jr. 1924- WhoAm 90
Allison, Jane Shawver 1938- WhoAmW 91
Allison, Janet Noel BiDrAPA 89
Allison, Janine BiDrAPA 89
Allison, Joe Marion 1924- WhoSSW 91
Allison, John Andrew, IV 1948- St&PR 91, WhoSSW 91
Allison, John Moore 1905-1978 BioIn 16
Allison, John R. 1913- WhoAm 90
Allison, John Robert 1948- WhoAm 90, WhoSSW 91
Allison, John T. 1950- St&PR 91, WhoEmL 91
Allison, Jonathan 1916- WhoE 91
Allison, Joy Elaine 1953- WhoEmL 91
Allison, Karen Anne 1958- WhoAmW 91
Allison, Karl 1948-1990 NewYTBS 90
Allison, Laird Burl 1917- WhoWor 91
Allison, Larry Edward 1946- St&PR 91

Allison, Latham Lee 1933- St&PR 91, WhoAm 90
Allison, Lew 1935- ODwPR 91
Allison, Linda Merz 1951- St&PR 91
Allison, Loyette E. 1946- WhoAmW 91
Allison, Lydia W 1880-1959 EncO&P 3
Allison, Lydia Winterhalter 1880-1959 EncPaPR 91
Allison, Melissa Lynn 1961- WhoAmW 91
Allison, Michael PenDiDA 89
Allison, Mose 1927- OxCPMus
Allison, Oliver Claude 1908-1989 ConAu 129
Allison, Pamela Susan 1950- WhoAmW 91
Allison, Ralph B 1931- BiDrAPA 89
Allison, Rand AuBYP 90
Allison, Richard Clark 1924- WhoAm 90
Allison, Richard Dale 1957- WhoEmL 91
Allison, Robert Arthur 1937- WhoAm 90
Allison, Robert Harry 1952- WhoEmL 91
Allison, Robert J., Jr. 1939- St&PR 91
Allison, Robert James, Jr. 1939- WhoAm 90
Allison, Rufus K. 1918- St&PR 91
Allison, Samuel King 1900-1965 DcScB S2
Allison, Scott ODwPR 91
Allison, Stacy BioIn 16
Allison, Stacy Marie 1958- WhoAmW 91
Allison, Stephen Galender 1952- WhoEmL 91, WhoSSW 91, WhoWor 91
Allison, Susan Katherine 1955- WhoAmW 91
Allison, Terry Elizabeth 1956- WhoSSW 91
Allison, Thomas H BiDrAPA 89
Allison, William James 1927- St&PR 91
Allison, William Whitaker 1933- St&PR 91
Allison, Young E. 1853-1932 LiHiK
Allister, Jean Maria 1932- IntWWM 90
Allix, John Hereward 1922- WhoWrEP 89
Allman Brothers, The EncPR&S 89
Allman Brothers Band OxCPMus
Allman, Charles Bradie 1950- St&PR 91
Allman, Douglas P. BioIn 16
Allman, Duane 1946-1971 EncPR&S 89, OxCPMus, WorAlBi
Allman, Edward Lee 1926- St&PR 91
Allman, Gregg 1947- EncPR&S 89, OxCPMus, WorAlBi
Allman, John 1935- WhoWrEP 89
Allman, Linden Andrea 1958- WhoEmL 91
Allman, Margo 1933- WhoAmA 91
Allman, Margo Hutz 1933- WhoE 91
Allman, William Berthold 1927- WhoE 91, WhoWor 91
Allman-Ward, Michele Ann 1950- WhoAm 90, WhoE 91, WhoWor 91
Allmand, Linda Faith 1937- WhoAm 90, WhoAmW 91, WhoSSW 91
Allmand, W. Warren 1932- WhoAm 90
Allmendinger, Paul Florin 1922- WhoAm 90
Allmightey, Jon 1963- WhoSSW 91
Allmon, Sandra Rae 1942- WhoAmW 91
Allmond, Frances Irene 1931- WhoAmW 91
Allner, Walter 1909- ConDes 90
Allner, Walter H 1909- WhoAmA 91
Allner, Walter Heinz 1909- WhoAm 90
Allnutt, Gillian 1949- FemiCLE
Allnutt, Robert F. 1935- St&PR 91
Allnutt, Robert Frederick 1935- WhoAm 90
Allocca, John Anthony 1948- WhoWor 91
Allocca, Michael A. 1934- St&PR 91
Alloggiamento, Nancy Thomas 1937- WhoAm 90
Allora, Ralph Anthony 1946- St&PR 91
Allott, Gordon 1907-1989 BioIn 16
Allott, Kenneth 1912-1973 ConAu 129
Allotta, Joseph John 1947- WhoEmL 91
Allouba, Naela Hassan 1928- WhoWor 91
Allouez, Claude Jean 1622-1689 EncCRAm, WhNaAH
Allouis, Jean Francois 1951- WhoWor 91
Alloway, Anne Maureen Schubert 1954- WhoAmW 91, WhoWor 91
Alloway, Lawrence 1926-1990 BioIn 16, NewYTBS 90 [port]
Alloway, Lawrence 1927-1990 WhoAmA 91N
Alloway, Robert Malcombe 1944- WhoE 91
Alloy, Stephen Lyle 1947- BiDrAPA 89
Allphin, Helen Louise 1946- WhoAmW 91
Allport, William Wilkens 1944- WhoAm 90
Allread, Neal Martin 1949- St&PR 91
Allred, Albert Louis 1931- WhoAm 90
Allred, Barry Lee 1947- St&PR 91
Allred, Christine A. 1940- St&PR 91
Allred, Evan Leigh 1929- WhoAm 90, WhoWor 91
Allred, Forrest Carlson 1955- WhoEmL 91
Allred, George Burton 1914- St&PR 91
Allred, Ivan D., Jr. St&PR 91
Allred, John Burton 1956- WhoSSW 91
Allred, John Caldwell 1926- WhoAm 90
Allred, Michael Sylvester 1945- WhoAm 90
Allred, Rita Reed 1935- WhoAmW 91
Allred, William David 1933- WhoSSW 91
Allred, Winston G. 1942- St&PR 91
Allrich, M Louise Barco 1947- WhoAmA 91
Alls, Willard Jess 1938- WhoSSW 91
Allsbrook, Linwood Robert BiDrAPA 89
Allshouse, Merle Frederick 1935- WhoAm 90
Allsop, Jim D. 1948- St&PR 91
Allsop, Kenneth Lee 1939- St&PR 91
Allsop, Richard Edward 1940- WhoWor 91
Allsopp, James Edward, Jr. 1929- St&PR 91
Allsopp, Thomas 1918- WhoAm 90
Allston, Washington 1779-1843 WorAlBi
Allston Stiles, Carol Lynn 1961- WhoE 91
Allsup, Judith Ann 1959- WhoAmW 91
Allswang, John Myers 1937- WhoAm 90
Allswede, Ralph Dahl 1939- St&PR 91
Alltmont, Jack Marks 1947- WhoEmL 91
Allton, Judith A. Schroeder 1948- WhoEmL 91
Alltop, Jane Elizabeth 1963- WhoAmW 91
Alluaud, Francois PenDiDA 89
Allumbaugh, James 1941- WhoAmA 91
Allwarden, Joseph Christopher 1930- St&PR 91
Allwell, Stephen S 1906- WhoAmA 91N
Allwine, Lawrence PenDiDA 89
Allwood, Ralph 1950- IntWWM 90
Allyn, Angela 1961- WhoEmL 91
Allyn, Barbara WhoWrEP 89
Allyn, David E 1955- BiDrAPA 89
Allyn, Jerome B. 1937- St&PR 91
Allyn, Jerri WhoAmA 91
Allyn, William F. 1935- St&PR 91
Allyn, William Finch 1935- WhoAm 90
Allyson, June 1917- OxCPMus, WorAlBi
Alm, Alvin Leroy 1937- WhoAm 90
Alm, James 1937- WhoAm 90
Alm, John R. 1946- St&PR 91
Alm, Richard Sanford 1921- WhoAm 90
Alma, Peter ConAu 130
Alma-Tadema, Anna 1865-1943 BiDWomA
Alma-Tadema, Laura Theresa 1852-1909 BiDWomA
Almada, Manuel 1912- WhoWrEP 89
Almada, Mel 1913-1988 Ballpl 90
Almader, Minnie 1957- WhoHisp 91
Almagia, Edoardo Achille 1928- WhoWor 91
Almagro, Guillermo Ausejo 1921- WhoSSW 91
Almaguer, Henry, Jr. 1947- WhoHisp 91
Almaguer, Imara Arredondo 1953- WhoHisp 91
Almaguer, Tomas 1948- WhoHisp 91
Alman, Emily Arnow 1922- WhoAmW 91
Alman, Richard D. St&PR 91
Almanac Singers OxCPMus
Almand, J. D. 1917- WhoWrEP 89
Almand, James Frederick 1948- WhoEmL 91
Almanqour, Nasser Al-Hamad 1927- WhoWor 91
Almansa Pastor, Angel F. 1934- WhoWor 91
Almansi, Renato J 1909- BiDrAPA 89
Almansi, Renato Joseph 1909- WhoE 91
Almaraz, Carlos 1941-1989 BioIn 16, WhoHisp 91N
Almario, Justo NewAgMG
Almasi, George Stanley WhoAm 90
Almazan, James A. 1935- WhoHisp 91
Almdale, James 1952- St&PR 91
Almeda, Boris Raoul 1936- WhoWor 91
Almedingen, E. M. 1898-1971 AuBYP 90
Almeida, Antonio WhoHisp 91
Almeida, Antonio de 1928- PenDiMP
Almeida, Antonio Jacques De 1928- IntWWM 90
Almeida, Carlos E, Jr. BiDrAPA 89
Almeida, Damien C. 1927- St&PR 91
Almeida, John G. 1953- St&PR 91
Almeida, Jose BiDrAPA 89
Almeida, Jose Agustin 1933- WhoSSW 91, WhoWor 91
Almeida, Jose Miguel Ramos 1930- WhoWor 91
Almeida, Joseph John 1930- St&PR 91
Almeida, Laurindo 1917- IntWWM 90, OxCPMus, WhoAm 90
Almeida, Paul 1948- St&PR 91
Almeida, Paulo Roberto 1949- WhoWor 91
Almeida, Victoria Martin 1951- WhoAmW 91, WhoE 91
Almeida de Portugal, Leonor de 1750-1839 EncCoWW
Almeida Merino, Adalberto 1916- WhoAm 90
Almeleh, Jack 1943- BiDrAPA 89
Almen, Louis Theodore 1925- WhoAm 90, WhoWor 91
Almen, Lowell Gordon 1941- WhoAm 90, WhoWrEP 89
Almenara, Juan Ramon 1933- WhoHisp 91
Almendarez, Bob 1952- WhoHisp 91
Almendros, Nestor BioIn 16
Almendros, Nestor 1930- WhoAm 90
Almer, Eugene R BiDrAPA 89
Almeraz, Ricardo 1940- WhoHisp 91
Almering, Mireille Francoise 1960- WhoWor 91
Almers, Wolfhard 1943- WhoAm 90
Almgren, Beverly Stewart 1935- WhoE 91
Almgren, Frederick Justin, Jr. 1933- WhoAm 90
Almgren, Herbert Philip 1916- WhoAm 90
Almgren, Knut Mats Axel 1940- WhoWor 91
Almgren, Vera J. 1910- St&PR 91
Almighty Voice DcCanB 12
Almirall, Valenti 1841-1904 BioIn 16
Almirante, Giorgio 1914-1988 AnObit 1988, BioIn 16
Almlie, Linda Lee 1945- WhoAmW 91
Almoayed, Tawfeeq Abdulrahman 1948- WhoWor 91
Almoayyed, Farouk Yousuf 1944- WhoWor 91
Almodovar, Pedro BioIn 16, NewYTBS 90
Almodovar, Pedro 1949- WhoWor 91
Almodovar, Pedro 1951- CurBio 90 [port]
Almon, Bill 1952- Ballpl 90
Almon, James E. 1932- St&PR 91
Almon, Leroy, Sr. 1938- MusmAFA
Almon, Reneau Pearson 1937- WhoAm 90
Almond, Barbara R 1938- BiDrAPA 89
Almond, Carl Herman 1926- WhoAm 90
Almond, David R. 1940- St&PR 91
Almond, Gabriel Abraham 1911- WhoAm 90
Almond, Giles Kevin 1956- WhoSSW 91
Almond, Greenbrier D 1948- BiDrAPA 89
Almond, Joan 1934- WhoAmW 91, WhoSSW 91
Almond, Linda Stevens BioIn 16
Almond, Mable Minor 1947- WhoSSW 91
Almond, Paul 1931- WhoAm 90, WhoAmA 91
Almond, Richard J 1938- BiDrAPA 89
Almonte, Rosa ConAu 31NR
Almony, Robert Allen, Jr. 1945- WhoAm 90
Almore, Mary G. 1932- WhoAmW 91
Almquist, Don 1929- WhoAm 90
Almquist, Donald John 1933- WhoAm 90
Almquist, Mary Rebecca 1958- WhoWrEP 89
Almquist, Sharon Kristina 1962- WhoWrEP 89
Almqvist, Carl Jonas Love 1793-1866 DcScanL
Alms, Paul Robert 1936- St&PR 91
Almunia, Miguel Tomas BiDrAPA 89
Almy, Earle Vaughn, Jr. 1930- WhoWor 91
Almy, Frank Atwood 1900-1956 WhoAmA 91N
Almy, Marion Marable 1946- WhoAmW 91
Almy, Max 1948- WhoAmA 91
Almy, Thomas Pattison 1915- WhoAm 90
Alnaes, Finn 1932- DcScanL
Alnes, Ellis Stephen 1926- WhoAm 90
Aloff, Mindy 1947- WhoAm 90
Alofsin, Herman 1898-1989 BioIn 16
Alogna, John A. 1943- St&PR 91
Alogna, John Joseph 1923- St&PR 91
Aloia, Roland Craig 1943- WhoWor 91
Alois, Edward J. 1960- St&PR 91
Aloisi, A. Pierre 1937- WhoWor 91
Aloisio, Arthur O. 1934- WhoE 91
Alomair, Omair Abdul Aziz 1941- WhoWor 91
Alomar, Carlos NewAgMG
Alomar, Roberto 1968- Ballpl 90, WhoHisp 91
Alomar, Sandy 1943- Ballpl 90, WhoHisp 91
Alomar, Sandy, Jr. 1966- WhoHisp 91
Aloneftis, Andreas 1945- WhoWor 91
Alongi, Frank 1929- St&PR 91
Alonso, Alicia 1921- WhoWor 91, WorAlBi
Alonso, Antonio Enrique 1924- WhoWor 91
Alonso, Carmen Maria 1952- BiDrAPA 89
Alonso, Damaso NewYTBS 90
Alonso, Damaso 1898-1990 BioIn 16, ConAu 130, -131, HispWr 90
Alonso, Danilo WhoHisp 91
Alonso, Magaly I BiDrAPA 89
Alonso, Manrique Domingo 1910- WhoHisp 91
Alonso, Maria Conchita BioIn 16, WhoHisp 91
Alonso, Maria Rosa 1910- EncCoWW
Alonso, Miguel Angel 1930- WhoHisp 91
Alonso, Nicolas Salmeron y BioIn 16
Alonso, Raoul O 1932- BiDrAPA 89
Alonso, William 1933- WhoAm 90
Alonso-Fernandez, Jose Ramon 1946- WhoWor 91
Alonso Garcia, Manuel Jose 1939- WhoWor 91
Alonso L. Inarra, Javier 1950- WhoWor 91
Alonso-Mendoza, Emilio 1954- WhoHisp 91
Alonso-Santiago, Ramon BiDrAPA 89
Alonte, Reynaldo D 1931- BiDrAPA 89
Alonzo, Cecil DrBlPA 90
Alonzo, John A. 1934- BioIn 16
Alonzo, Juan A. 1936- WhoHisp 91
Alonzo, Leoncio O BiDrAPA 89
Alonzo, Luis BiDrAPA 89
Alonzo, Maria Cristina M BiDrAPA 89
Alonzo, Martin Vincent 1931- St&PR 91, WhoAm 90
Alonzo, Ralph Edward 1950- WhoHisp 91
Alonzo, Richard Lawrence 1939- St&PR 91
Alonzo, Ronald 1942- St&PR 91
Aloot, Mariano Daniel 1947- WhoEmL 91
Alopaeus, Marianne 1918- EncCoWW
Alorna, Marquesa de EncCoWW
Alos, Concha 1922- EncCoWW
Alost, Robert Allen 1935- WhoAm 90, WhoSSW 91
Alotto, Anthony Lee 1950- WhoEmL 91
Alou, Felipe 1935- Ballpl 90
Alou, Felipe Rojas 1935- WhoHisp 91
Alou, Jesus 1942- Ballpl 90
Alou, Jesus Maria Rojas 1942- WhoHisp 91
Alou, Matty 1938- Ballpl 90, WhoHisp 91
Alouf, Francois E BiDrAPA 89
Alp, Necati-Mehmet 1924- BiDrAPA 89
Alpa, Guido Peter 1947- WhoWor 91
Alpan, Sadrettin H. 1924- WhoWor 91
Alpaugh, Harland Ellsworth, Jr. 1943- WhoE 91
Alpen, Edward Lewis 1922- WhoAm 90
Alpen-Whiteside, Dale 1942- WhoAmA 91
Alpenheim, Ilse von 1927- IntWWM 90
Alper, Albert 1912- WhoAm 90
Alper, Anne Elizabeth 1942- WhoAm 90
Alper, Frank 1930- NewAgE 90
Alper, Harvey Martin 1946- WhoEmL 91
Alper, Howard 1941- WhoAm 90
Alper, Hyman 1921- St&PR 91
Alper, Jerome 1897-1989 BioIn 16
Alper, Jerome Milton 1914- WhoAm 90
Alper, Joel Richard 1938- WhoAm 90
Alper, Jonathan Louis 1950- WhoAm 90
Alper, Keith Michael 1962- WhoEmL 91
Alper, Merlin Lionel 1932- St&PR 91, WhoAm 90
Alper, Seymour Lewis 1915- St&PR 91
Alper Kramer, Lorraine 1949- WhoAmW 91
Alperin, Aron BioIn 16
Alperin, Barry J. 1940- St&PR 91
Alperin, George 1927- St&PR 91
Alperin, Goldie Green 1905- WhoAmW 91, WhoWor 91
Alperin, Irwin Ephraim 1925- WhoE 91, WhoWor 91
Alperin, Richard Martin 1946- WhoE 91, WhoWor 91
Alperin, Stanley I. 1931- WhoWor 91
Alperman, Whitey 1879-1942 Ballpl 90
Alpern, Andrew 1938- WhoAm 90
Alpern, Barbara Bellman 1947- WhoAm 90
Alpern, Frederick P 1940- BiDrAPA 89
Alpern, Linda Lee Wevodau 1949- WhoAmW 91, WhoEmL 91
Alpern, Lynne Shapiro 1944- WhoWrEP 89
Alpern, Mathew 1920- WhoAm 90
Alpern, Mildred 1931- WhoAmW 91
Alpern, Robert Jay 1940- BiDrAPA 89
Alperovitz, Gar 1936- WhoAm 90, WhoWrEP 89
Alpers, David Hershel 1935- WhoAm 90
Alpers, Edward Alter 1941- WhoAm 90
Alpers, Helmut A. 1930- St&PR 91
Alpers, Robert W. 1931- St&PR 91
Alpert, A. Sidney 1938- St&PR 91
Alpert, Ann Sharon 1938- WhoWor 91
Alpert, Arnold Lewis 1935- St&PR 91
Alpert, Benjamin 1910- St&PR 91
Alpert, Bill 1934- WhoAmA 91
Alpert, Caroline Evelyn 1926- WhoE 91
Alpert, Daniel 1917- WhoAm 90
Alpert, Daniel 1952- WhoEmL 91
Alpert, Ettarae Lipsy 1932- WhoE 91
Alpert, George 1898-1988 BioIn 16
Alpert, George 1922- WhoAmA 91
Alpert, Harry A. 1913- St&PR 91
Alpert, Herb BioIn 16
Alpert, Herb 1935- EncPR&S 89, WhoAm 90, WorAlBi
Alpert, Herb 1937- OxCPMus
Alpert, Herbert S. 1918- St&PR 91
Alpert, Herman S BiDrAPA 89
Alpert, Hollis 1916- WhoAm 90, WhoWrEP 89

Alpert, James Donald 1947- *BiDrAPA 89*
Alpert, Janet A. 1946- *St&PR 91*
Alpert, Janet Anne 1946- *WhoEmL 91*
Alpert, Joel Jacobs 1930- *WhoAm 90*
Alpert, Jonathan Louis 1945- *WhoSSW 91*
Alpert, Joseph M. 1938- *St&PR 91*
Alpert, Joseph Stephen 1942- *WhoAm 90*
Alpert, Marc S. 1944- *St&PR 91*
Alpert, Marco Moser 1947- *WhoEmL 91*
Alpert, Mark Ira 1942- *WhoAm 90*
Alpert, Michael C 1943- *BiDrAPA 89*
Alpert, Michael Edward 1942- *WhoAm 90*
Alpert, Norman 1921- *WhoAm 90*
Alpert, Norman Joseph 1931- *WhoAm 90*
Alpert, Richard *NewAgE 90*
Alpert, Richard 1931- *EncO&P 3*
Alpert, Richard Henry 1947- *WhoAmA 91*
Alpert, Seymour 1918- *WhoAm 90*
Alpert, Shell R. 1931- *WhoE 91*
Alpert, Warren 1920- *St&PR 91, WhoAm 90, WhoWor 91*
Alpert, Wesley S. 1926- *St&PR 91*
Alpert, William Titlar 1949- *WhoE 91*
Alphabet, Dr. *WhoWrEP 89*
Alpher, Ralph Asher 1921- *WhoAm 90*
Alphin, Elaine Marie 1955- *WhoWrEP 89*
Alphonsa, Mother *BioIn 16*
Alphonso, Mervyn Lyttleton 1941- *St&PR 91*
Alpiar, Hal 1941- *WhoE 91*
Alpiser, Joanne Duncan 1957- *WhoEmL 91*
Alprin, Brian Dean 1954- *WhoEmL 91*
Alps, Glen Earl 1914- *WhoAm 90, WhoAmA 91*
Alquilar, Maria 1935- *WhoAmA 91*
Alquilar, Maria 1938- *WhoAmW 91*
Alquist, Lewis 1946- *WhoAmA 91*
Alquizola, Teresito Tito 1936- *BiDrAPA 89*
Alreck, Pamela Lynn 1950- *WhoEmL 91*
Alrich, Alexis 1955- *IntWWM 90*
Alrich, William Morris 1917- *WhoE 91*
Alroy, David 1147?- *EncO&P 3*
Alroy, Yoram Adam 1954- *WhoSSW 91*
Alruy, David 1147?- *EncO&P 3*
Als, Joanne Davida *BiDrAPA 89*
Alsafi, Mohammed Hussein 1960- *WhoWor 91*
Alsaker, Robert John 1945- *WhoEmL 91*
Alsap, John T. 1832-1886 *AmLegL*
Alsberg, Dietrich Anselm 1917- *WhoAm 90*
Alscher, Ruth Grene 1943- *WhoAmW 91*
Alschuler, Al 1934- *WhoWrEP 89*
Alsdorf, James W. *NewYTBS 90*
Alsdorf, James W. 1913-1990 *BioIn 16*
Alsentzer, Gerald G. 1947- *St&PR 91*
Alsgaard, Hartley Charles *BiDrAPA 89*
Alsina, Margaret Lowenthal *BioIn 16*
Alsobrook, Bob Fox 1940- *St&PR 91*
Alsobrook, Henry Bernis, Jr. 1930- *WhoAm 90, WhoWor 91*
Alsobrook, Rosalyn Rutledge 1952- *WhoWrEP 89*
Alsop, Donald Douglas 1927- *WhoAm 90*
Alsop, John DeKoven 1915- *St&PR 91*
Alsop, Joseph 1910-1989 *AnObit 1989, BioIn 16, ConAu 129*
Alsop, Joseph, Jr. 1910-1989 *WorAlBi*
Alsop, Reese Fell *AuBYP 90*
Alsop, Stewart 1914-1974 *BioIn 16, WorAlBi*
Alspach, Bruce W 1922- *BiDrAPA 89*
Alspach, Philip Halliday 1923- *WhoAm 90*
Alspaugh, Nancy *BioIn 16*
Alspaugh, Robert Eugene 1933- *St&PR 91*
Alspaugh, Robert Odo *WhoAm 90*
Alspaugh, Robert Odo 1912- *St&PR 91*
Alspaw, Dalton E. 1940- *St&PR 91*
Alstadt, Donald Martin 1921- *WhoAm 90*
Alstat, Philip R. 1894-1976 *BioIn 16*
Alsted, Birgitte 1942- *IntWWM 90*
Alston, Archer Sills 1918- *WhoSSW 91*
Alston, Bettye Jo 1938- *WhoAmW 91*
Alston, Charles Henry 1907-1977 *WhoAmA 91N*
Alston, Cheryl Ann 1946- *WhoAmW 91*
Alston, Clifford 1910- *WhoSSW 91*
Alston, Doris Faye 1934- *WhoAmW 91*
Alston, Francine Ann-Catherine 1962- *WhoAmW 91*
Alston, J M 1901?-1990 *ConAu 131*
Alston, James A 1913- *BiDrAPA 89*
Alston, Jan M. 1955- *St&PR 91*
Alston, Joanie Deloris 1955- *WhoAmW 91*
Alston, JoAnn 1950- *WhoAmW 91*
Alston, John F. 1944- *BiDrAPA 89*
Alston, John M. 1928- *St&PR 91*
Alston, Lawrence Leighton 1952- *WhoEmL 91, WhoSSW 91*
Alston, Leila Joyce 1956- *WhoAmW 91*
Alston, Lela 1942- *WhoAmW 91*
Alston, Mary Elizabeth 1953- *WhoWrEP 89*
Alston, Philip Henry 1911-1988 *BioIn 16*
Alston, Richard John William 1948- *WhoWor 91*
Alston, Robert Merritt 1949- *WhoEmL 91*
Alston, Robin 1933- *ConAu 131*
Alston, Walt 1911-1984 *Ballpl 90 [port]*
Alston, Walter 1911-1984 *BioIn 16, WorAlBi*
Alston, William Payne 1921- *WhoAm 90*
Alsworth, Frances Wilkerson 1927- *WhoSSW 91*
Alt, Carol *BioIn 16*
Alt, Christopher Boyden 1948- *WhoEmL 91*
Alt, Daniel Mark 1949- *St&PR 91*
Alt, Dottie Kay Hinkle 1943- *WhoAmW 91*
Alt, James Edward 1946- *WhoAm 90*
Alt, Jane Eileen Stoner 1956- *WhoAmW 91*
Alt, Louis Albert 1948- *WhoE 91*
Alt, Walter Louis 1926- *St&PR 91*
Alt, Willis E. 1944- *St&PR 91*
Alt, Winston Drew 1946- *BiDrAPA 89*
Alta 1942- *FemiCLE, WhoWrEP 89*
Alta, Lina Maria 1961- *WhoAmW 91*
Altabe, Joan Augusta Berg 1935- *WhoAm 90*
Altaker, Lawrence L 1937- *BiDrAPA 89*
Altamirano, Ben D. 1930- *WhoHisp 91*
Altamirano, Salvador H. 1947- *WhoHisp 91*
Altamura, Michael Victor 1923- *WhoWor 91*
Altan, Taylan 1938- *WhoAm 90*
Altani, Ipolit 1846-1919 *PenDiMP*
Altbach, Philip 1941- *WhoAm 90*
Altchuler, Steven I. 1951- *BiDrAPA 89*
Altdorfer, Albrecht 1480?-1538 *IntDcAA 90, PenDiDA 89, WorAlBi*
Altekruse, Joan Morrissey 1928- *WhoAm 90*
Altekruse, Philip D *BiDrAPA 89*
Altemus, Linda 1951- *WhoAmW 91*
Altemus, Margaret 1956- *BiDrAPA 89, WhoE 91*
Alten, Felix Charles 1928- *St&PR 91*
Alten, Fred 1871-1945 *MusmAFA*
Alten, Jerry *WhoAmA 91*
Alten, Jerry 1931- *WhoE 91*
Altena, Maarten *BioIn 16*
Altenau, Alan Giles 1938- *WhoAm 90, WhoWor 91*
Altenau, Richard Dale 1960- *St&PR 91*
Altenbaumer, Larry F. 1948- *St&PR 91*
Altenberg, Barry M 1935- *BiDrAPA 89*
Altenberg, Henry Edward 1925- *BiDrAPA 89*
Altenbernd, August Lynn 1918- *WhoAm 90*
Altenbernd, Nicholas 1946- *IntWWM 90*
Altenburger, Christian 1957- *IntWWM 90*
Altenhaus, Amy Louise 1950- *WhoAmW 91*
Alter, Brian Reid 1956- *St&PR 91*
Alter, Carol Lynn *BiDrAPA 89*
Alter, David 1923- *WhoAm 90*
Alter, David Emmet, Jr. 1921- *WhoAm 90*
Alter, Dennis Ira 1951- *St&PR 91*
Alter, Edward T. 1941- *WhoAm 90*
Alter, Eleanor Breitel 1938- *WhoAm 90, WhoAmW 91*
Alter, Eleanor Reed 1908- *WhoAmW 91*
Alter, Gerald L. 1910- *WhoWor 91*
Alter, Harvey 1932- *WhoAm 90*
Alter, Jean Victor 1925- *WhoAm 90*
Alter, Jonathan Hammerman 1957- *ConAu 129, WhoAm 90*
Alter, Judith 1938- *ConAu 31NR*
Alter, Judith Anne 1938- *WhoSSW 91*
Alter, Judith MacBain 1938- *BioIn 16*
Alter, Judy *ConAu 31NR*
Alter, Louis 1902-1980 *OxCPMus*
Alter, Lynne 1953- *WhoAmW 91, WhoEmL 91*
Alter, Marc Fred 1955- *WhoE 91*
Alter, Milton 1929- *WhoAm 90*
Alter, Nelson T. 1926- *St&PR 91*
Alter, Nelson Tobias 1926- *WhoSSW 91*
Alter, Norman B. 1935- *St&PR 91*
Alter, Robert 1935- *WorAu 1980 [port]*
Alter, Robert B. 1935- *WhoAm 90*
Alter, Robert Edmond 1925-1965 *AuBYP 90*
Alter, Shirley Jacobs 1929- *St&PR 91, WhoAmW 91*
Alter, Tom *BioIn 16*
Alter, Victor 1890-1942? *BioIn 16*
Alterio, Phillip 1938- *St&PR 91*
Alterman, Caroline McAlpine 1954- *WhoSSW 91*
Alterman, Dean N. 1960- *WhoEmL 91*
Alterman, Irwin Michael 1941- *WhoAm 90*
Altermann, Tony 1940- *WhoAmA 91*
Altermatt, Paul Barry 1930- *WhoAm 90*
Alterovitz, Samuel Adar 1939- *WhoWor 91*
Alters, Dennis Brian *BiDrAPA 89*
Alterwain, Paulo Fabrykant *BiDrAPA 89*
Altesman, Richard Ira *BiDrAPA 89*
Altfas, Jules R *BiDrAPA 89*
Altfeld, Merwin Richard 1913- *WhoAmA 91*
Altfeld, Theodore Sandford 1943- *St&PR 91*
Altgilbers, Larry Lee 1945- *WhoSSW 91*
Althans, John H., Jr. 1935- *St&PR 91*
Althaus, Barbara Donalson 1937- *WhoAmW 91*
Althaus, David Steven 1945- *St&PR 91, WhoEmL 91, WhoSSW 91, WhoWor 91*
Althaver, Lambert E. 1931- *St&PR 91*
Althaver, Lambert Ewing 1931- *WhoAm 90*
Altheimer, Alan J. 1903- *St&PR 91, WhoAm 90*
Altheimer, Jerome H. 1924- *St&PR 91*
Althen, Wayne W. 1937- *St&PR 91*
Alther, Jack R. 1926- *St&PR 91*
Alther, Lisa 1944- *ConAu 30NR, FemiCLE, MajTwCW*
Altherr, Rainer 1947- *WhoWor 91*
Althof, Timothy D. 1948- *St&PR 91*
Althoff, Catherine L. 1956- *St&PR 91*
Althoff, Gordon 1948- *St&PR 91*
Altholz, Thomas I. 1950- *St&PR 91*
Althorp, Charles Edward Maurice Spencer *BioIn 16*
Althotas *EncO&P 3*
Althouse, Ernest E. 1904- *WhoAm 90*
Althouse, Frances Yvonne Seay 1965- *WhoAmW 91*
Althouse, Gary Carl 1963- *WhoSSW 91*
Althusser, L. *ConAu 131, -132*
Althusser, Louis *BioIn 16*
Althusser, Louis 1918- *ConAu 131*
Althusser, Louis 1918-1990 *ConAu 132, NewYTBS 90*
Altier, Theodore J. 1921- *St&PR 91*
Altier, William John 1935- *WhoE 91, WhoWor 91*
Altieri, Earl R. 1930- *St&PR 91*
Altieri, Gregory Joseph 1955- *WhoSSW 91*
Altieri, James V. 1909-1988 *BioIn 16*
Altieri, Joseph J 1956- *BiDrAPA 89*
Altieri, Maria Rita 1957- *WhoEmL 91*
Altieri, Peter Louis 1955- *WhoEmL 91*
Altimari, Frank X. 1928- *WhoAm 90*
Altinok, Tevfik 1943- *WhoWor 91*
Altizer, Barbara Walters 1948- *WhoEmL 91*
Altizer, Dave 1876-1964 *Ballpl 90*
Altizer, Thomas J. J. *BioIn 16*
Altizer, Thomas Jonathan Jackson 1927- *WhoAm 90*
Altland, Marilou 1955- *WhoEmL 91*
Altman, Abby *BiDrAPA 89*
Altman, Adele Rosenhain 1924- *WhoAmW 91, WhoWor 91*
Altman, Allan 1929- *WhoE 91*
Altman, Allen Burchard 1942- *WhoE 91*
Altman, Arnold David 1917- *WhoAm 90*
Altman, Barbara Jean Friedman 1947- *WhoEmL 91*
Altman, Bernard Richard *St&PR 91*
Altman, David Bruce 1945- *BiDrAPA 89*
Altman, David R. 1952- *ODwPR 91*
Altman, David Ronald 1944- *WhoE 91*
Altman, Edward Ira 1941- *WhoAm 90, WhoWrEP 89*
Altman, Edwin N. *BioIn 16*
Altman, Elaine Ruthe 1943- *WhoE 91*
Altman, Ellen 1936- *WhoAm 90, WhoAmW 91*
Altman, Emily Sally *BiDrAPA 89*
Altman, Ernest V *BiDrAPA 89*
Altman, Franc Collier 1926- *St&PR 91*
Altman, Gene 1941- *BiDrAPA 89*
Altman, George 1933- *Ballpl 90*
Altman, Harold 1924- *WhoAmA 91*
Altman, Henry G 1926- *BiDrAPA 89*
Altman, Herb *BioIn 16*
Altman, Irwin 1930- *WhoAm 90, WhoWrEP 89*
Altman, Jane Callahan 1949- *WhoAmW 91*
Altman, Janice Mary 1938- *WhoAmW 91*
Altman, Jerold H 1933- *BiDrAPA 89*
Altman, John Joseph 1951- *St&PR 91*
Altman, Jonathan *BioIn 16, ODwPR 91*
Altman, Joseph 1925- *WhoAm 90*
Altman, Kathyrn *BioIn 16*
Altman, Kenneth L. 1952- *ODwPR 91*
Altman, Laurence 1933- *St&PR 91*
Altman, Lawrence Gene 1952- *WhoE 91, WhoEmL 91*
Altman, Lawrence Kimball 1937- *WhoAm 90*
Altman, Leo Sidney 1911- *WhoAm 90*
Altman, Leon L *BiDrAPA 89*
Altman, Linda Jacobs 1943- *ConAu 30NR*
Altman, Lorin Jay 1946- *St&PR 91*
Altman, Louis *BiDrAPA 89*
Altman, Lyle D. 1930- *St&PR 91*
Altman, Martin S. 1949- *St&PR 91*
Altman, Mary Ann 1930- *WhoAm 90*
Altman, Michael A 1939- *BiDrAPA 89*
Altman, Milton Hubert 1917- *WhoAm 90*
Altman, Nathaniel 1948- *WhoWrEP 89*
Altman, Norman Eugene 1919- *St&PR 91*
Altman, Norman Jon 1957- *St&PR 91*
Altman, Norman W *BiDrAPA 89*
Altman, Philip Lawrence 1924- *WhoE 91*
Altman, Randy Allan 1954- *WhoE 91*
Altman, Richard L. 1946- *WhoE 91*
Altman, Robert 1925- *BioIn 16, WorAlBi*
Altman, Robert B. 1925- *WhoAm 90*
Altman, Robert Lee 1935- *WhoAm 90*
Altman, Robert Michael *BiDrAPA 89*
Altman, Robin M. 1958- *WhoEmL 91*
Altman, Rodney Stephen *BiDrAPA 89*
Altman, Roman *BiDrAPA 89*
Altman, Roy Peter 1934- *WhoAm 90, WhoE 91*
Altman, Ruth B. 1933- *WhoAmW 91*
Altman, Sharon Lee *BiDrAPA 89*
Altman, Sidney *WorAlBi*
Altman, Sidney 1939- *WhoAm 90, WhoE 91, WhoWor 91*
Altman, Sidney I 1928- *BiDrAPA 89*
Altman, Steven 1945- *WhoSSW 91*
Altman, Steven C. 1947- *St&PR 91*
Altman, Stuart Harold 1937- *WhoAm 90*
Altman, Tom 1958- *WhoSSW 91*
Altman, Wendell Thomas 1952- *WhoSSW 91*
Altman, William Kean 1944- *WhoSSW 91, WhoWor 91*
Altman-Fischer, Linda Susan 1955- *BiDrAPA 89, WhoE 91*
Altmann, Alexander 1906-1987 *BioIn 16*
Altmann, Anthony Frederick 1955- *WhoAm 90, WhoE 91*
Altmann, Esther Nesbin 1910- *WhoAmW 91*
Altmann, Henry S 1946- *WhoAmA 91*
Altmann, Johann Gottlieb *PenDiDA 89*
Altmann, Kenneth 1933- *St&PR 91*
Altmann, Michael Stewart 1952- *WhoE 91*
Altmann, Stuart Allen 1930- *WhoAm 90*
Altmansberger, Richard Alan 1944- *BiDrAPA 89*
Altmayer, Jay P 1915- *WhoAmA 91*
Altmeyer, Jeannine 1948- *IntWWM 90, PenDiMP*
Altmeyer, John W. 1959- *St&PR 91*
Altmeyer, Theodor Daniel 1931- *IntWWM 90*
Altmiller, Jeanne Elizabeth 1960- *WhoAmW 91*
Altner, Peter Christian 1932- *WhoAm 90*
Altobelli, Joe 1932- *Ballpl 90*
Altobelli, Peter Michael 1954- *WhoE 91*
Altobello, Daniel Joseph 1941- *St&PR 91, WhoAm 90*
Altobello, Mildred Frances 1953- *WhoAmW 91, WhoSSW 91*
Altom, Rhoda Lynn 1957- *WhoEmL 91*
Altom, William H. 1925- *St&PR 91*
Alton, Ann Leslie 1945- *WhoAmW 91, WhoEmL 91, WhoWor 91*
Alton, Bruce Taylor 1939- *WhoAm 90*
Alton, David C. 1930- *St&PR 91*
Alton, Elaine Vivian 1925- *WhoAm 90*
Alton, Howard Robert, Jr. 1927- *St&PR 91*
Alton, John G. 1954- *WhoWrEP 89*
Alton, Margaret Ann 1943- *WhoAmW 91*
Altrocchi, Sally Archer 1960- *WhoAmW 91*
Altrock, Nick 1876-1965 *Ballpl 90*
Altrock, Richard Charles 1940- *WhoAm 90*
Altschaeffl, Adolph George 1930- *WhoAm 90*
Altscher, Stanley Gary 1952- *St&PR 91*
Altschuh, Gregory William 1946- *WhoEmL 91*
Altschul, Aaron Mayer 1914- *WhoAm 90*
Altschul, Alfred S. 1939- *St&PR 91*
Altschul, Alfred Samuel 1939- *WhoAm 90*
Altschul, Arthur G. 1920- *St&PR 91, WhoAmA 91*
Altschul, Arthur Goodhart 1920- *WhoAm 90*
Altschul, B J 1948- *ODwPR 91*
Altschul, BJ 1948- *WhoAmW 91, WhoEmL 91*
Altschul, David Edwin 1947- *WhoEmL 91*
Altschul, James Sloan 1960- *WhoE 91*
Altschul, Joel Henry 1948- *WhoEmL 91*
Altschul, Sol 1922- *BiDrAPA 89*
Altschuler, David Edward 1952- *WhoEmL 91*
Altschuler, Milton 1929- *BiDrAPA 89*
Altschuler, Modest 1873-1963 *PenDiMP*
Altschuler, Stephen 1932- *St&PR 91*
Altsheler, Joseph A. 1862-1919 *AuBYP 90*
Altsheler, Joseph Alexander 1862-1919 *LiHiK*
Altshul, Victor Anthony 1935- *BiDrAPA 89*
Altshuler, Alan Anthony 1936- *WhoAm 90*
Altshuler, Bernard 1919- *WhoE 91*
Altshuler, Harry *BioIn 16*
Altshuler, Harry 1913?-1990 *ConAu 131*
Altshuler, J. 1939- *St&PR 91*

Altshuler, Kenneth Z 1929- *BiDrAPA 89, WhoAm 90, WhoSSW 91*
Altshuler, Lanny Stephen 1948- *WhoSSW 91*
Altshuler, Lori Lynn 1957- *BiDrAPA 89*
Altshuler, Nathan 1925- *WhoAm 90*
Altstadt, Manfred 1950- *St&PR 91*
Altstiel, Thomas B. 1952- *WhoEmL 91*
Altuch, Peter Mark 1952- *WhoEmL 91*
Altura, Burton Myron 1936- *WhoAm 90, WhoWor 91*
Altvater, Arthur William, Jr. 1942- *St&PR 91*
Altvater, Donald 1921- *St&PR 91*
Altvater, Thomas Steffen 1945- *WhoE 91*
Altweger, John 1919-1990 *BioIn 16*
Altwegg, Raffaele 1938- *IntWWM 90*
Altwerger, Libby 1921- *WhoAmA 91*
Aluise, Timothy John 1956- *WhoEmL 91*
Alumbaugh, deLyn Ross 1950- *WhoEmL 91*
Alurista *ConAu 32NR, HispWr 90*
Alurista 1947- *BioIn 16, WhoAm 90, WhoHisp 91*
Alushin, Michael Stephen 1947- *WhoEmL 91*
Alusik, George 1935- *Ballpl 90*
Alutto, Joseph Anthony 1924- *St&PR 91*
Alutto, Joseph Anthony 1941- *WhoAm 90, WhoE 91*
Alva, Juan 1936- *WhoSSW 91*
Alva, Luigi 1927- *PenDiMP*
Alva Castro, Luis Juan *WhoWor 91*
Alvarado, Blanca *WhoHisp 91*
Alvarado, Carlos S. 1955- *EncPaPR 91*
Alvarado, Caroline R. 1954- *WhoAmW 91*
Alvarado, Elvia *BioIn 16*
Alvarado, Esteban P. 1962- *WhoHisp 91*
Alvarado, Jose Antonio 1951- *WhoEmL 91, WhoHisp 91*
Alvarado, Juan Bautista 1809-1882 *BioIn 16*
Alvarado, Juan Velasco 1910-1977 *BioIn 16*
Alvarado, Luis 1949- *Ballpl 90*
Alvarado, Marilu 1938- *IntWWM 90*
Alvarado, Pedro De 1485?-1541 *WorAlBi*
Alvarado, Raul, Jr. 1946- *WhoHisp 91*
Alvarado, Ricardo R. 1927- *St&PR 91*
Alvarado, Ricardo Raphael 1927- *WhoAm 90, WhoHisp 91*
Alvarado, Richard A. 1943- *WhoHisp 91*
Alvarado, Richard A., Sr. 1943- *St&PR 91*
Alvarado, Ruben B. 1941- *WhoHisp 91*
Alvarado, Susan E. 1954- *WhoHisp 91*
Alvarado, Yolanda H. 1943- *WhoHisp 91*
Alvarado, Yolanda Hernandez 1943- *WhoAmW 91*
Alvarado-Juarez, Francisco 1950- *WhoAmA 91*
Alvare, Carlos A 1948- *BiDrAPA 89*
Alvares, Eduardo 1940- *IntWWM 90*
Alvares, Joe 1935- *St&PR 91*
Alvarez, A. 1929- *ConAu 33NR*
Alvarez, Aileen 1960- *WhoE 91*
Alvarez, Alberto *BiDrAPA 89*
Alvarez, Alejandro Rodriguez 1903-1965 *ConAu 131, HispWr 90*
Alvarez, Anne Maino 1941- *WhoHisp 91*
Alvarez, Antonia V. 1951- *WhoHisp 91*
Alvarez, Avelino 1934- *WhoHisp 91*
Alvarez, Barry 1947- *WhoHisp 91*
Alvarez, Candida 1955- *WhoAmA 91*
Alvarez, Carlos 1936- *WhoSSW 91*
Alvarez, Carmen Hilda 1952- *WhoEmL 91*
Alvarez, Cecil 1935- *St&PR 91*
Alvarez, Cecilia, and Emese de Murcia *WomArch*
Alvarez, Cesar L. *WhoHisp 91*
Alvarez, Danny 1949- *WhoEmL 91*
Alvarez, Eduardo Jorge 1945- *WhoHisp 91*
Alvarez, Eduardo T. 1930- *WhoHisp 91*
Alvarez, Enrique 1940- *BiDrAPA 89*
Alvarez, Everett 1937- *BioIn 16*
Alvarez, Everett, Jr. 1937- *WhoHisp 91*
Alvarez, F. Dennis 1945- *WhoHisp 91*
Alvarez, Felix Augusto 1954- *WhoHisp 91*
Alvarez, Ferdinand Chat, Jr. 1944- *WhoHisp 91*
Alvarez, Flavio E *BiDrAPA 89*
Alvarez, Francia 1949- *WhoAmW 91*
Alvarez, Francisco Alvarez 1957- *WhoHisp 91*
Alvarez, Francisco Sanchez 1928-1980 *BioIn 16*
Alvarez, Frank D. *WhoHisp 91*
Alvarez, Fred T. 1937- *WhoHisp 91*
Alvarez, Gregorio 1925- *BioIn 16*
Alvarez, Hector Justo 1938- *WhoHisp 91*
Alvarez, Hortensia W *BiDrAPA 89*
Alvarez, Javier P. 1951- *WhoHisp 91*
Alvarez, Jeronimo *WhoHisp 91*
Alvarez, John *MajTwCW*
Alvarez, Jon Hugh 1954- *WhoEmL 91*
Alvarez, Jorge 1936- *WhoHisp 91*
Alvarez, Jorge Montt 1846?-1922 *BioIn 16*
Alvarez, Jose 1940- *WhoSSW 91*
Alvarez, Jose 1944- *WhoHisp 91*
Alvarez, Jose 1956- *Ballpl 90*
Alvarez, Jose Armando 1949- *WhoSSW 91*
Alvarez, Jose Florencio 1948- *WhoEmL 91, WhoSSW 91*
Alvarez, Jose O. 1947- *WhoHisp 91*
Alvarez, Juan Holquin 1944- *WhoHisp 91*
Alvarez, Juan Rafael 1956- *WhoHisp 91*
Alvarez, Leonardo 1938- *St&PR 91*
Alvarez, Lizette Ann 1964- *WhoHisp 91*
Alvarez, Louis Lefcourt 1955- *WhoEmL 91*
Alvarez, Luis 1911-1988 *AnObit 1988*
Alvarez, Luis Alfonso *BiDrAPA 89*
Alvarez, Luis Echeverria *BioIn 16*
Alvarez, Luis W. *BioIn 16*
Alvarez, Luis W. 1911-1988 *WorAlBi*
Alvarez, Lynne *ConAu 131, HispWr 90*
Alvarez, Manuel 1794-1856 *BioIn 16*
Alvarez, Manuel Antonio, Sr. 1933- *WhoHisp 91*
Alvarez, Maria Cecilia 1952- *WhoAmW 91*
Alvarez, Maria Elena 1947- *WhoHisp 91*
Alvarez, Mario 1937- *WhoHisp 91*
Alvarez, Martin *WhoHisp 91*
Alvarez, Mercedes *WhoAmW 91*
Alvarez, Michael John 1949- *WhoHisp 91*
Alvarez, Miguel A S 1944- *BiDrAPA 89*
Alvarez, Paul H. 1942- *ODwPR 91, St&PR 91*
Alvarez, Paul Hubert 1942- *WhoAm 90*
Alvarez, Praxedes Eduardo 1958- *WhoHisp 91*
Alvarez, Raymond P. *WhoWrEP 89*
Alvarez, Reinaldo G 1936- *BiDrAPA 89*
Alvarez, Richard G. *WhoHisp 91*
Alvarez, Robert Smyth 1912- *WhoAm 90*
Alvarez, Rodolfo 1936- *WhoAm 90, WhoHisp 91*
Alvarez, Roman *WhoHisp 91*
Alvarez, Ronald Julian 1935- *WhoHisp 91*
Alvarez, Santiago 1919- *BioIn 16*
Alvarez, Sarah Lynn 1953- *WhoHisp 91*
Alvarez, Stephen Walter 1952- *WhoHisp 91*
Alvarez, Steven Grant 1955- *WhoHisp 91*
Alvarez, Thomas 1948- *WhoEmL 91*
Alvarez, Walter 1940- *WhoAm 90*
Alvarez, William A *BiDrAPA 89*
Alvarez-Altman, Grace de Jesus 1926- *WhoHisp 91*
Alvarez Bischoff, Ana Maria 1953- *WhoHisp 91*
Alvarez Bravo, Manuel 1902- *ArtLatA*
Alvarez-Breckenridge, Carmen 1951- *WhoHisp 91*
Alvarez-Cervela, Jose Maria 1922- *WhoAmA 91*
Alvarez Del Castillo, Enrique 1923- *WhoWor 91*
Alvarez de Toledo, Luisa Isabel 1936- *EncCoWW*
Alvarez-Ghersi, Juan F *BiDrAPA 89*
Alvarez-Gonzalez, Jose Julian 1952- *WhoHisp 91*
Alvarez-Martinez, Rosario 1949- *IntWWM 90*
Alvarez-Mullin, Angeles A *BiDrAPA 89*
Alvarez Murena, Hector Alberto 1923- *HispWr 90*
Alvarez-Pont, Victor 1949- *WhoHisp 91*
Alvarez-Recio, Emilio 1938- *St&PR 91*
Alvarez-Recio, Emilio, Jr. 1938- *WhoHisp 91*
Alvarez-Recio, Emilio De La Torre 1938- *WhoE 91*
Alvarez Rendueles, Jose Ramon 1940- *WhoWor 91*
Alvarez-Santori, Jose 1917- *St&PR 91*
Alvarez-Sharpe, Maria Elena 1954- *WhoHisp 91*
Alvarez y Mendizabal, Juan 1790?-1853 *BioIn 16*
Alvarino, Angeles 1916- *WhoAm 90*
Alvarino De Leira, Angeles 1916- *WhoAm 90*
Alvaro, Anthony Joseph 1945- *St&PR 91*
Alvaro, Filipe Nunes 1945- *WhoWor 91*
Alvary, Lorenzo 1909- *IntWWM 90, WhoAm 90*
Alvear, Cecilia Estela *WhoHisp 91*
Alverio, Daisy M. 1958- *WhoHisp 91*
Alverio-Girot, Carmen Enid 1960- *WhoAmW 91*
Alverio-Nieves, Carmen Socorro 1958- *WhoAmW 91*
Alverno, Luca A *BiDrAPA 89*
Alverson, Ben Earl 1940- *WhoSSW 91*
Alverson, Fred Dwight 1955- *WhoEmL 91*
Alverson, Joy Ferguson 1954- *WhoEmL 91*
Alverson, William H. 1933- *WhoAm 90*
Alves, Carlos Pereira 1942- *WhoWor 91*
Alves, Castro 1847-1871 *BioIn 16*
Alves, Dorothy Louise 1929- *WhoAmW 91*
Alves, Herbert A. 1933- *St&PR 91*
Alves, Joaquim Paredes 1922- *WhoWor 91*
Alves, Joseph Thomas 1921- *WhoE 91*
Alves, Juliet 1887-1947 *LiHiK*
Alvey, Doris May Giordano 1945- *WhoAmW 91, WhoEmL 91*
Alvey, Joseph Earl, Jr. 1937- *WhoSSW 91, WhoWor 91*
Alvi, Zahoor Mohem 1942- *WhoAm 90*
Alvin, Dave *EncPR&S 89*
Alvine, Carol Christine 1942- *WhoAmW 91, WhoSSW 91*
Alvine, Robert 1938- *WhoAm 90, WhoE 91, WhoWor 91*
Alvine, William, Sr. 1922- *WhoSSW 91*
Alvino, Gloria Dora 1931- *WhoE 91*
Alvis, Max 1938- *Ballpl 90, BioIn 16*
Alvis, William Truett 1951- *WhoE 91*
Alviso, Edward F. 1963- *WhoHisp 91*
Alvord, Joel Barnes 1938- *St&PR 91, WhoAm 90*
Alvord, Muriel *WhoAmA 91N*
Alvord, Susan B. 1942- *WhoAmW 91*
Alvord, Thomas Gold 1810-1897 *AmLegL*
Alwaleed bin Talal Al Saud, Prince 1954- *BioIn 16*
Alwin, Karl *PenDiMP*
Alwine, Janet Darlene 1952- *WhoAmW 91*
Alwis, Kantha D 1939- *BiDrAPA 89*
Alworth, Lance 1940- *WorAlBi*
Alwyn, Kenneth 1925- *PenDiMP*
Alwyn, Kenneth 1928- *IntWWM 90*
Alwyn, William 1905-1985 *OxCPMus*
Alyea, Brant 1940- *Ballpl 90*
Alzado, Lyle 1949- *ConTFT 8*
Alzado, Lyle Martin 1949- *WhoAm 90*
Alzaga, Florinda 1930- *WhoHisp 91*
Alzaibag, Muayed Abdullah 1951- *WhoWor 91*
Alzamora, Elio F *BiDrAPA 89*
Am, Magnar 1952- *IntWWM 90*
Amabile, Anthony A. 1934- *WhoWrEP 89*
Amabile, John Louis 1934- *WhoAm 90, WhoE 91*
Amabile, Phyllis Esther *BiDrAPA 89*
Amabile, Ralph J., Jr. 1928- *St&PR 91*
Amacher, Joan Marsh 1926- *WhoAmW 91*
Amacher, Richard C. 1943- *WhoAm 90*
Amacher, Richard Earl 1917- *WhoAm 90*
Amadei, Deborah Lisa 1952- *WhoE 91, WhoEmL 91*
Amadeo, King of Spain 1845-1890 *BioIn 16*
Amadeo, Jose H. 1928- *WhoAm 90*
Amadeo, Marco *BiDrAPA 89*
Amadeus *EncO&P 3*
Amadeus Quartet *PenDiMP*
Amadi, Elechi 1934- *WorAu 1980 [port]*
Amadio, Bari Ann 1949- *WhoAmW 91, WhoE 91, WhoEmL 91, WhoWor 91*
Amadio, Ernest Richard 1944- *St&PR 91*
Amadio, John 1884-1964 *PenDiMP*
Amado, Henry 1951- *BiDrAPA 89*
Amado, Jorge 1912- *BioIn 16, MajTwCW, WhoWor 91, WorAlBi*
Amado, Patricia Ann 1960- *WhoEmL 91*
Amado, Ralph David 1932- *WhoAm 90*
Amador, Jose M 1923- *BiDrAPA 89*
Amador, Luis V. *BioIn 16*
Amador, Luis Valentine 1920- *WhoHisp 91*
Amador, Michael George Sanchez 1936- *WhoHisp 91*
Amador, Victor John 1928- *St&PR 91*
Amador Guerrero, Manuel 1833-1909 *BioIn 16*
Amador Pinero, Efrain 1947- *IntWWM 90*
Amadou, Robert 1924- *EncO&P 3, EncPaPR 91*
Amaker, Alit Leigh 1965- *WhoAmW 91*
Amaker, Julius Fletcher *BiDrAPA 89*
Amakudari *NewAgMG*
Amaldi, Edoardo 1908-1989 *AnObit 1989, BioIn 16*
Amalfitano, Joey 1934- *Ballpl 90*
Amalfitano, John Michael 1950- *St&PR 91*
Amalia, Verfasserin der *EncCoWW*
Amaliksen, Arne S. 1938- *St&PR 91*
Amalsuntha 498-535 *WomWR [port]*
Amalswinthe 498-535 *WomWR [port]*
Aman, Alfred Charles, Jr. 1945- *WhoAm 90*
Aman, George B. 1943- *St&PR 91*
Aman, George Matthias, III 1930- *WhoAm 90*
Aman, Joseph Patrick 1957- *WhoEmL 91*
Aman, Mary Lenore 1964- *WhoEmL 91*
Aman, Mohammed Mohammed 1940- *WhoAm 90*
Aman, Reinhold Albert 1936- *WhoAm 90, WhoWrEP 89*
Amanat, Ebrahim *BiDrAPA 89*
Amandolia, Cynthia Lorene 1963- *WhoAmW 91*
Amaning, Kwadwo Owusu 1956- *WhoSSW 91*
Amanishakhete *WomWR*
Amann, Charles Albert 1926- *WhoAm 90*
Amann, Cynthia Clair 1948- *WhoAmW 91*
Amann, David William 1958- *WhoEmL 91*
Amann, Henry J. 1950- *ODwPR 91*
Amann, Michael Paul 1949- *St&PR 91*
Amann, Peter Henry 1927- *WhoAm 90*
Amano, Taka 1950- *WhoAmA 91*
Amantea, Rebecca Anne 1955- *WhoAmW 91*
Amanuddin, Syed 1934- *WhoWrEP 89*
Amar Quartet *PenDiMP*
Amar, Licco *PenDiMP*
Amar, Romesh Chandra *BiDrAPA 89*
Amara, Lucine 1927- *IntWWM 90, WhoAm 90, WhoAmW 91*
Amaral, Donald J. 1952- *St&PR 91*
Amaral, Jesus Eduardo 1927- *WhoAm 90*
Amaral, Tarsila do 1886-1973 *ArtLatA*
Amaranto, Ernesto Ayque 1940- *BiDrAPA 89*
Amarel, Saul 1928- *WhoAm 90*
Amargos, Gerardo M 1921- *BiDrAPA 89*
Amari, Robert Francis 1955- *WhoEmL 91*
Amari, Shun-ichi 1936- *WhoWor 91*
Amarilios, John Alexander 1958- *WhoEmL 91*
Amaro, Hortensia *WhoHisp 91*
Amaro, Ismael de Sousa 1942- *WhoWor 91*
Amaro, Ruben 1936- *Ballpl 90*
Amarotico, Joseph Anthony 1931- *WhoAmA 91N*
Amash, Charles Elias 1932- *St&PR 91*
Amason, Alvin Eli 1948- *WhoAmA 91*
Amason, Mary Susan 1952- *WhoSSW 91*
Amat, Nuria 1950- *EncCoWW*
Amat, Oriol Salas 1957- *WhoWor 91*
Amata, Anthony J. 1951- *St&PR 91*
Amatangelo, Nicholas S. 1935- *WhoWor 91*
Amateis, Edmond Romulus 1897-1981 *WhoAmA 91N*
Amati, Orlanda *IntWWM 90*
Amatniek, Sara 1922- *WhoAmA 91*
Amato, Albert Louis, Jr. 1948- *St&PR 91*
Amato, Camille Jean 1942- *WhoAmW 91*
Amato, Christine Coffin 1951- *WhoAmW 91*
Amato, Elinor Barbara d' *IntWWM 90*
Amato, Emanuel 1924- *BiDrAPA 89*
Amato, Gary N. 1951- *St&PR 91*
Amato, Guiliano 1938- *WhoWor 91*
Amato, Isabella Antonia 1942- *WhoAm 90*
Amato, Jose F 1931- *BiDrAPA 89*
Amato, Larry 1953- *WhoAm 90*
Amato, Michele 1945- *WhoAmA 91*
Amato, Paul H. 1939- *St&PR 91*
Amato, Paula Ann 1962- *WhoAmW 91*
Amato, Robert Louis 1948- *WhoE 91*
Amato, Rosalie 1920- *WhoE 91*
Amato, Rosemarie Helen 1950- *WhoAmW 91, WhoEmL 91*
Amato, Thomas Gabriel 1945- *St&PR 91, WhoAm 90*
Amato, Vincent Vito 1929- *WhoAm 90*
Amatori, Michael Louis 1951- *WhoEmL 91*
Amaya, Armando 1935- *WhoAmA 91*
Amaya, Jorge 1954- *WhoHisp 91*
Amaya, Leland Hubert 1923- *St&PR 91*
Amaya, Marcelino *BiDrAPA 89*
Amaya, Maria Alvarez 1955- *WhoHisp 91*
Amaya, Naohiro 1925- *WhoWor 91*
Amazeen, Paul Gerard 1939- *St&PR 91*
Amazing Randi, The *EncO&P 3*
Amazon, Elizabeth Gannon 1912- *WhoAmW 91*
Ambach, Dwight Russell 1931- *WhoAm 90*
Ambach, Gordon Mac Kay 1934- *WhoAm 90*
Ambache, Diana Bella 1948- *IntWWM 90*
Ambasz, Emilio 1943- *ConDes 90, WhoAm 90, WhoHisp 91, WhoWor 91*
Ambedkar, Bhimrao Ramji 1892-1956 *BioIn 16*
Amber, Douglas George 1956- *WhoEmL 91*
Amber, McLain Quinn 1962- *WhoEmL 91*
Amber, Rich 1949- *WhoEmL 91*
Ambereen, D. 1966- *St&PR 91*
Amberg, Adolf 1874-1913 *PenDiDA 89*
Amberg, John W. 1931- *St&PR 91*
Amberg, Richard Hiller, Jr. 1942- *St&PR 91, WhoAm 90, WhoSSW 91*
Amberg, Thomas Law 1948- *WhoAm 90*
Amberson, Grace D 1894-1957 *WhoAmA 91N*
Amberson, James Burns, III *BiDrAPA 89*
Ambhoj and Devakant *NewAgMG*
Ambielli, Adam Frederick 1937- *St&PR 91*
Ambielli, Robert John 1951- *WhoE 91, WhoEmL 91*
Amblat, Joao 1941- *WhoWor 91*
Ambler, David Samuel 1954- *WhoEmL 91, WhoSSW 91, WhoWor 91*
Ambler, Eric 1909- *BioIn 16, MajTwCW, SpyFic, TwCCr&M 91, WhoAm 90, WhoWor 91, WorAlBi*
Ambler, Ernest 1923- *WhoAm 90*
Ambler, John Doss 1934- *WhoAm 90, WhoWor 91*
Ambler, Thomas Wilson 1953- *WhoEmL 91*
Ambler, Wayne 1915- *Ballpl 90*

Amboian, John Peter 1931- *St&PR 91, WhoAm 90*
Amborski, Dale John 1948- *St&PR 91*
Amborski, Leonard Edward 1921- *WhoE 91*
Ambrister, John Charles 1944- *St&PR 91*
Ambroe, Mary Ellen 1945- *WhoEmL 91*
Ambroggio, Luis Alberto 1945- *WhoHisp 91*
Ambrogio, John P. 1934- *WhoE 91*
Ambros, Mario D 1925- *BiDrAPA 89*
Ambrose, Amy Christine 1963- *WhoAmW 91*
Ambrose, Bert 1897-1971 *OxCPMus*
Ambrose, Charles Clarke 1924- *WhoAm 90*
Ambrose, Charles Edward 1922- *WhoAmA 91*
Ambrose, Charles Stuart 1951- *WhoSSW 91*
Ambrose, Daniel *BioIn 16*
Ambrose, Daniel Michael 1955- *WhoE 91*
Ambrose, Donald Eric 1947- *WhoEmL 91*
Ambrose, Ed 1913- *MusmAFA*
Ambrose, James McLean 1943- *WhoWor 91*
Ambrose, James Richard 1922- *WhoAm 90*
Ambrose, Jay *BioIn 16*
Ambrose, Joseph V., Jr. 1929- *St&PR 91*
Ambrose, Joseph Vincent, Jr. 1929- *WhoAm 90*
Ambrose, Mark David 1949- *BiDrAPA 89*
Ambrose, Morris Jay 1944- *WhoAm 90*
Ambrose, Myles Joseph 1926- *WhoAm 90*
Ambrose, Phillip Ishmael 1962- *WhoSSW 91*
Ambrose, Richard Edgar 1945- *WhoSSW 91*
Ambrose, Samuel Sheridan, Jr. 1923- *WhoAm 90*
Ambrose, Thomas C. 1932- *ODwPR 91*
Ambrose, Tommy W. 1926- *WhoAm 90*
Ambrosetti, Alfredo 1931- *WhoWor 91*
Ambrosi, Gustinus 1893-1975 *BioIn 16*
Ambrosini, Paul John 1950- *BiDrAPA 89, WhoE 91*
Ambrosino, Barbara Jean *BiDrAPA 89*
Ambrosino, Carmen Felice 1948- *WhoWor 91*
Ambrosino, Ralph Thomas, Jr. 1940- *WhoAm 90*
Ambrosino, Salvatore V *BiDrAPA 89*
Ambrosio, Francesco Vittorio 1932- *WhoAm 90*
Ambrosio, Giorgio 1924- *BiDrAPA 89*
Ambroziak, Shirley Ann 1953- *WhoAmW 91, WhoEmL 91*
Ambrozic, Aloysius Matthew 1930- *WhoAm 90*
Ambrus, Clara Maria 1924- *WhoAm 90*
Ambrus, Julian L. 1924- *WhoAm 90*
Ambrusko, John Stephen 1913- *WhoSSW 91*
Ambruster, John R. 1931- *St&PR 91*
Ambruz, John F. 1955- *St&PR 91*
Ambuhl, Frank Jerrold 1925- *WhoWor 91*
Amcher, Jeannie Webb 1953- *WhoAmW 91*
Amchin, Jess David *BiDrAPA 89*
Amdahl, Byrdelle John 1934- *WhoAm 90*
Amdahl, Douglas Kenneth 1919- *WhoAm 90*
Amdahl, Gene Myron 1922- *St&PR 91, WhoAm 90*
Amdall, William J. 1953- *St&PR 91*
Amdall, William John 1953- *WhoAm 90*
Amdur, Deborah Lynne *BiDrAPA 89*
Amdur, James A. 1936- *St&PR 91*
Amdur, James Austin 1936- *WhoAm 90*
Amdur, Mark Alan 1944- *BiDrAPA 89*
Amdur, Nikki 1950- *AuBYP 90*
Amdur Small, Catherine Richardson 1963- *WhoE 91*
Amdursky, Loren Jaye 1959- *BiDrAPA 89*
Amdursky, Robert S. 1937-1990 *BioIn 16*
Amdursky, Robert Sidney *NewYTBS 90 [port]*
Amdursky, Robert Sidney 1937- *WhoAm 90*
Ameche, Alan 1933-1988 *BioIn 16*
Ameche, Don *BioIn 16*
Ameche, Don 1908- *OxCPMus, WhoAm 90, WorAlBi*
Ameduri, Ardow Richard, Jr. 1942- *BiDrAPA 89*
Ameen, Christine Applin 1953- *WhoAmW 91*
Ameen, June Delia 1955- *WhoAmW 91*
Ameen, Lane 1923- *BiDrAPA 89*
Ameen, Louis J.E. 1929- *WhoWor 91*
Ameen, Mark Joseph 1958- *WhoWrEP 89*
Ameling, Elly 1934- *PenDiMP*
Ameling, Elly 1938- *IntWWM 90, WhoAm 90, WhoWor 91*
Amelio, Gilbert Frank 1943- *WhoAm 90*
Ameller, Andre 1912- *IntWWM 90*
Amelung, Donald Eugene 1957- *St&PR 91*
Amelung, Johann Friedrich *PenDiDA 89*
Amemiya, Takeshi 1935- *WhoAm 90*
Amen, Daniel Gregory 1954- *BiDrAPA 89*
Amen, Irving 1918- *WhoAm 90, WhoAmA 91, WhoWor 91*
Amen, John Douglas 1947- *St&PR 91*
Amen, Paul D. 1934- *St&PR 91*
Amen, Robert A. 1937- *ODwPR 91*
Amen, Robert Anthony 1937- *WhoE 91*
Amend, A.L. 1916- *St&PR 91*
Amend, Eugene Michael 1950- *WhoAmA 91*
Amend, William John Conrad, Jr. 1941- *WhoAm 90*
Amende, Lynn Meridith 1959- *WhoAmW 91*
Amendt, Marilyn Joan 1928- *WhoAmW 91*
Amenhotep IV, King of Egypt *BioIn 16*
Amenoff, Gregory 1948- *WhoAmA 91*
Ament, Aaron 1937- *BiDrAPA 89*
Ament, Mark Steven 1951- *WhoEmL 91, WhoSSW 91*
Ament, Richard 1919- *WhoAm 90*
Amenta, Caroline 1928- *WhoAmW 91*
Amenta, Michael Joseph 1933- *WhoAm 90, WhoE 91*
Amenta, Peter Sebastian 1927- *WhoAm 90, WhoWor 91*
Amer, M. A. 1944-1989 *BioIn 16*
Amer, Magid Hashim 1941- *WhoWor 91*
Amerasinghe, Chittharanjan Felix 1933- *WhoE 91, WhoWor 91*
America *OxCPMus*
American Gramaphone *NewAgMG*
American Horse 1840-1908 *WhNaAH [port]*
American Horse 1860?-1876 *WhNaAH*
Americus, Robert Lear 1950- *St&PR 91*
Amerikaner, Steven Albert 1947- *WhoEmL 91*
Amerine, Anne Follette 1950- *WhoAmW 91, WhoEmL 91*
Amerine, Maynard Andrew 1911- *WhoAm 90*
Amerine, Terry Lee 1964- *WhoEmL 91*
Ameringer, Charles D. 1926- *WhoAm 90*
Ameringer, Oscar 1870-1943 *EncAL*
Amerisov, Alexander *BioIn 16*
Amerlan *NewAgMG*
Amerlan, Michael *NewAgMG*
Amerman, John Ellis 1944- *WhoAm 90*
Amerman, John W. 1932- *St&PR 91, WhoAm 90*
Amerman, Lockhart 1911-1969 *AuBYP 90*
Amernick, Ann Silverberg 1943- *WhoAmW 91*
Amery, Diane *WhoWrEP 89*
Amery, Leopold Charles Maurice Stennett 1873-1955 *BioIn 16*
Ames, A. Gary *St&PR 91*
Ames, A. Gary 1944- *WhoAm 90*
Ames, Adelbert 1880-1955 *BioIn 16*
Ames, Adelbert, III 1921- *WhoAm 90*
Ames, Alfred Campbell 1916- *WhoAm 90*
Ames, Arthur Forbes 1906-1975 *WhoAmA 91N*
Ames, Arthur Hazen 1929- *St&PR 91*
Ames, Arthur R., Jr. 1917- *St&PR 91*
Ames, B. Charles *BioIn 16*
Ames, Barbara Frances 1936- *WhoAm 90, WhoAmW 91*
Ames, Bruce Nathan 1928- *WhoAm 90*
Ames, Charles O. 1926- *St&PR 91*
Ames, Christopher Norman 1953- *WhoE 91*
Ames, Craig L. 1944- *WhoAm 90*
Ames, Damaris 1944- *St&PR 91, WhoAm 90, WhoAmW 91*
Ames, David Anthony 1941- *BiDrAPA 89*
Ames, David J. 1945- *St&PR 91*
Ames, Delano 1906- *TwCCr&M 91*
Ames, Donald Paul 1922- *St&PR 91, WhoAm 90, WhoWor 91*
Ames, Donna 1960- *BiDrAPA 89*
Ames, Ed 1927- *WorAlBi*
Ames, Evelyn *NewYTBS 90*
Ames, Evelyn 1908-1990 *ConAu 130, SmATA 64*
Ames, Evelyn Perkins 1908-1990 *BioIn 16*
Ames, Fisher 1758-1808 *BioIn 16*
Ames, Fisher 1905- *WhoAm 90*
Ames, Frank Anthony 1942- *WhoAm 90*
Ames, George Joseph 1917- *WhoAm 90*
Ames, George Ronald 1939- *St&PR 91*
Ames, Gerald 1906- *AuBYP 90*
Ames, Henry Peck, III 1954- *WhoSSW 91*
Ames, James B. 1911- *St&PR 91*
Ames, James Barr 1911- *WhoAm 90*
Ames, Jimmy Ray 1951- *WhoSSW 91*
Ames, John Lewis 1912- *WhoWor 91*
Ames, Kathleen Marie 1966- *WhoAmW 91*
Ames, Kathryn Ann Eckstam 1956- *WhoEmL 91*
Ames, Lee J. 1921- *BioIn 16*
Ames, Lee Judah 1921- *AuBYP 90, WhoAmA 91*
Ames, Leon 1903- *WorAlBi*
Ames, Leslie *ConAu 32NR*
Ames, Lincoln 1932- *St&PR 91*
Ames, Louise Bates 1908- *WhoAm 90, WhoAmW 91*
Ames, Marc L. 1943- *WhoE 91*
Ames, Marshall Howard 1944- *St&PR 91*
Ames, Mary Clemmer 1839-1884 *BioIn 16*
Ames, Marybeth 1951- *WhoEmL 91*
Ames, Michael Allen 1944- *St&PR 91*
Ames, Michael E. 1822-1861 *AmLegL*
Ames, Michael McClean 1933- *WhoAm 90*
Ames, Mildred 1919- *BioIn 16*
Ames, Milton Benjamin, Jr. 1913- *WhoAm 90*
Ames, Noel *AuBYP 90*
Ames, Oakes 1931- *WhoAm 90*
Ames, Oliver Filley 1920- *St&PR 91*
Ames, Patricia Yvonne 1946- *WhoEmL 91*
Ames, Patrick W. 1954- *WhoWrEP 89*
Ames, Polly Scribner 1908- *WhoAmA 91*
Ames, Red 1882-1936 *Ballpl 90 [port]*
Ames, Richard Scott 1954- *St&PR 91*
Ames, Robert 1941- *WhoAm 90*
Ames, Robert Arthur 1925- *WhoAm 90*
Ames, Robert Forbes 1930- *WhoAm 90*
Ames, Robert S. 1919- *St&PR 91*
Ames, Robert San 1919- *WhoAm 90*
Ames, Sandra Patience 1947- *WhoAmW 91, WhoEmL 91*
Ames, Stephen C. 1938- *St&PR 91*
Ames, Steven Edmund 1940- *WhoWrEP 89*
Ames, Steven Reede 1951- *WhoE 91, WhoEmL 91*
Ames, Trey *BioIn 16*
Ames, William Clark 1950- *WhoWor 91*
Ames, William Francis 1926- *WhoAm 90*
Ames, William H. 1944- *St&PR 91*
Ames, William Harold 1944- *WhoAm 90*
Ames, William L. 1952- *WhoE 91*
Amestoy, Jay *ODwPR 91*
Amestoy, Jeffrey Lee 1946- *WhoAm 90, WhoE 91*
Amethyst *WhoWrEP 89*
Amey, David Edward 1947- *WhoWrEP 89*
Amey, Lorne James 1940- *WhoAm 90*
Amey, Rae 1947- *WhoAmW 91, WhoEmL 91*
Amey, William Greenville 1918- *WhoAm 90*
Amezcua, Consuelo Gonzalez *BioIn 16*
Amezquita, Jesusa Maria 1958- *WhoHisp 91*
Amfahr, Donald F. 1929- *St&PR 91*
Amfiteatrov, Daniele 1901-1983 *OxCPMus*
Amfitheatrof, Daniele 1901-1983 *OxCPMus*
Amft, Robert 1916- *WhoAmA 91*
Amghar, Alain 1952- *WhoWor 91*
Amgott, Madeline 1931- *WhoAmW 91*
Amherst, Jeffrey 1717-1797 *EncCRAm, WhNaAH, WorAlBi*
Amiano, Fred A. 1945- *St&PR 91*
Amicarelli, Debra Lee 1957- *WhoAmW 91*
Amice, Carol Rizzardi 1955- *WhoWrEP 89*
Amichai, Yehuda 1924- *MajTwCW, WorAlBi*
Amici Quartet *PenDiMP*
Amicis, Anna Lucia De *PenDiMP*
Amick, Lawrence D *BiDrAPA 89*
Amick, Leticia Cleotilde 1965- *WhoEmL 91*
Amick, Martin Sherman 1951- *WhoEmL 91*
Amick, Roger *BiDrAPA 89*
Amick, Steven Hammond 1947- *WhoEmL 91*
Amico, David Michael 1951- *WhoAmA 91*
Amico, Gina Maria 1936- *WhoE 91*
Amico, Jacqueline Marie 1961- *BiDrAPA 89*
Amico, Richard Joseph 1953- *WhoEmL 91*
Amidei, L. Neal 1933- *ODwPR 91*
Amidei, Lester A., Jr. 1944- *St&PR 91*
Amidon, Charles John 1952- *St&PR 91*
Amidon, Richard B. 1916- *WhoE 91, WhoWor 91*
Amidon, Roger Lyman 1938- *WhoAm 90*
Amidon, Stephen 1959- *ConAu 132*
Amiel, Barbara *WhoAm 90*
Amiel, Karen Baggett 1950- *WhoEmL 91*
Amiel, Madeleine *BiDrAPA 89*
Amiel, Michael Joseph 1955- *BiDrAPA 89*
Amies, Hardy *BioIn 16*
Amies, Hardy 1909- *ConAu 129*
Amiet, Cuno 1868-1961 *BioIn 16*
Amigoni, Jacopo 1675?-1752 *IntDcAA 90*
Amin, Ashokkumar A *BiDrAPA 89*
Amin, Ashokkumar I *BiDrAPA 89*
Amin, Aurora Mabel *BiDrAPA 89*
Amin, Chandrakant F *BiDrAPA 89*
Amin, Farooq 1955- *BiDrAPA 89*
Amin, Idi 1925- *BioIn 16*
Amin, Jamillah Maarij 1947- *WhoAmW 91*
Amin, Muhammad 1945- *WhoSSW 91*
Amin, Prakash 1958- *BiDrAPA 89*
Amin, Ramesh *BiDrAPA 89*
Amin, Samir 1931- *WhoWor 91*
Amin, Saroja R *BiDrAPA 89*
Amin, Sayed Amanuddin 1932- *WhoWor 91*
Amin, Smarhar Mahendraprasad *BiDrAPA 89*
Amin Dada, Idi 1925?- *WorAlBi*
Amina *WomWR*
Amini, Bijan Khajehnouri 1943- *WhoSSW 91, WhoWor 91*
Aminian, Houshang 1942- *BiDrAPA 89*
Amino, Leo 1911- *WhoAmA 91*
Amino, Leo 1911-1989 *WhoAmA 91N*
Aminoff, Judith 1947- *WhoAmA 91*
Aminoff, Judith Gayle 1947- *WhoWor 91*
Aminu, Jubril *WhoWor 91*
Aminullah, Sayed Muhammad 1931- *WhoWor 91*
Amiotte, Donald Paul 1946- *WhoE 91*
Amir-Moez, Ali Reza 1919- *WhoWor 91*
Amiri, Afsaneh 1962- *WhoEmL 91*
Amiri, Aman F. 1951- *St&PR 91*
Amiri, Tami Mina *BiDrAPA 89*
Amirikian, Arsham 1899- *WhoAm 90*
Amirkhanian, Charles 1945- *IntWWM 90*
Amirouche, Farid M. L. 1954- *WhoEmL 91*
Amirthalingam, Vanchi 1929- *WhoWor 91*
Amirtharajah, Appiah 1940- *WhoSSW 91*
Amis, Edward Stephen, Jr. 1941- *WhoAm 90*
Amis, Kingsley 1922- *BioIn 16, DcLB 100 [port], MajTwCW, WhoAm 90*
Amis, Kingsley William 1922- *SpyFic*
Amis, Martin *BioIn 16, NewYTBS 90*
Amis, Martin 1949- *BestSel 90-3 [port], ConLC 62 [port], CurBio 90 [port], WorAu 1980 [port]*
Amis, Suzy *BioIn 16*
Amis, William B. 1937- *St&PR 91*
Amisano, Joseph 1917- *WhoAm 90*
Amish, Keith Warren 1923- *WhoAm 90*
Amistad, Glenn Repiedad 1955- *WhoWor 91*
Amitay, Noach 1930- *WhoAm 90*
Amitin, Sigmund A 1933- *BiDrAPA 89*
Amitrano, Sergio 1939- *St&PR 91*
Amjad, Afsari *BiDrAPA 89*
Amjad Ali Khan, Ustad 1945- *IntWWM 90*
Amjadi, Darius H 1934- *BiDrAPA 89*
Amlicke, Thos. R. 1936- *St&PR 91*
Amling, Frederick 1926- *WhoAm 90*
Ammaducci, Bruno 1935- *IntWWM 90*
Amman, Robert J. 1938- *WhoAm 90*
Ammanati, Bartolommeo 1511-1592 *IntDcAA 90*
Ammann, Lillian Ann Nicholson 1946- *WhoSSW 91*
Ammann, William R. 1941- *St&PR 91*
Ammannati, Giovanni *PenDiDA 89*
Ammar, K.A., Jr. 1933- *St&PR 91*
Ammar, Najeeb A., Jr. 1946- *St&PR 91*
Ammar, Raymond George 1932- *WhoAm 90, WhoWor 91*
Ammar, Richard Frederick 1938- *St&PR 91*
Ammarell, John S. 1920- *St&PR 91*
Ammarell, John Samuel 1920- *WhoAm 90*
Ammen, Helen Joanne 1944- *WhoAmW 91*
Ammer, Donald Scott 1962- *WhoWrEP 89*
Ammer, Stephen D. *St&PR 91*
Ammerman, Craig L. 1948- *WhoE 91*
Ammerman, Jay Neil 1945- *WhoEmL 91*
Ammerman, Richard Gene *BiDrAPA 89*
Ammerman, Robert Ray 1927- *WhoAm 90*
Ammidon, Hoyt 1909-1988 *BioIn 16*
Ammirati, Ralph *WhoAm 90*
Ammon, Caroline Linda 1965- *WhoAmW 91*
Ammon, Gunter K *BiDrAPA 89*
Ammon, Harry 1917- *WhoAm 90*
Ammon, Henry J. 1934- *St&PR 91*
Ammon, Hermann Philipp Theodor 1933- *WhoWor 91*
Ammon, James E. 1935- *WhoAm 90*
Ammon, James Edward 1935- *St&PR 91*
Ammon, Kenneth George 1951- *WhoSSW 91*
Ammons, A. R. 1926- *BioIn 16*
Ammons, A R 1926- *MajTwCW*
Ammons, Albert 1907-1949 *BioIn 16*
Ammons, Albert C. 1907-1949 *OxCPMus*
Ammons, Archie Randolph 1926- *WhoAm 90, WhoWrEP 89*
Ammons, Benjamin G. 1935- *St&PR 91*
Ammons, Edsel Albert 1924- *WhoAm 90*
Ammons, Elias Milton 1860-1925 *AmLegL*
Ammons, Gene 1925-1974 *BioIn 16*
Ammons, Robert Allen 1941- *WhoE 91*
Ammons, Robert Bruce 1920- *WhoAm 90*
Ammons, Roger L. 1950- *WhoEmL 91*
Amneus, D. A. 1919- *WhoAmW 91*
Amoako, Nana 1953- *WhoEmL 91*
Amobi, Ifediora Chimezie 1960- *WhoE 91*
Amochaev, Tania 1949- *St&PR 91*
Amodie, Janet S. 1955- *WhoEmL 91*
Amole, Warren Ralph, III 1950- *St&PR 91*

Amolochitis, George 1951- WhoWor 91
Amon, Aline 1928- AuBYP 90
Amon, Arthur Howard, Jr. 1927- WhoAm 90
Amon, William Frederick, Jr. 1922- WhoAm 90
Amon Parisi, Cristina Hortensia 1956- WhoE 91
Amond, Chester D. 1926- St&PR 91
Amonett, Thomas N. 1943- WhoAm 90
Amonson, Johanne Leslie 1949- WhoEmL 91
Amor, Alexander Geopano 1928- WhoWor 91
Amor, Anne Clark 1933- ConAu 31NR
Amor, Anthony Roger 1945- St&PR 91
Amora, Aderito S. Vieira 1941- WhoWor 91
Amore, Joseph Robert 1944- St&PR 91, WhoSSW 91
Amore, Michael Joseph 1947- WhoE 91
Amori, Geraldine Heller 1951- WhoE 91
Amorim, Enrique 1900-1960 HispWr 90
Amorim, Paulo Ernesto Carvalho 1946- WhoWor 91
Amornmarn, Rumpa 1946- WhoEmL 91, WhoSSW 91
Amornpimol, Suma 1964- WhoWor 91
Amoros, Amparo 194-?- EncCoWW
Amoros, Sandy 1930- Ballpl 90, BioIn 16
Amoroso, Emmanuel Ciprian 1901-1982 DcNaB 1981
Amoroso, Linda Marie 1951- WhoE 91
Amoroso, Marie Dorothy 1924- WhoAmW 91, WhoE 91, WhoWor 91
Amort, John Alexander 1926- St&PR 91
Amory, Charles Reginald, Jr. 1940- St&PR 91
Amory, Claudia WhoAmA 91
Amory, Cleveland 1917- WhoAm 90, WhoWrEP 89
Amory, Daniel 1946- WhoEmL 91
Amory, Derick Heathcoat 1899-1981 DcNaB 1981
Amory, Jan BioIn 16
Amory, Mark 1941- BioIn 16
Amory, Robert 1915-1989 BioIn 16
Amory, Robert F. 1945- St&PR 91
Amory, Thomas Carhart 1933- WhoAm 90
Amos, Alan TwCCr&M 91
Amos, Alan Scott 1956- WhoEmL 91
Amos, Betty Ann 1948- WhoAmW 91
Amos, Betty Giles 1941- WhoSSW 91
Amos, Carolyn Sue 1945- WhoSSW 91
Amos, Charles Weldon 1922- St&PR 91
Amos, Daniel Paul 1951- St&PR 91, WhoAm 90
Amos, Dennis B. 1923- WhoAm 90
Amos, Emma 1938- WhoAmA 91
Amos, James H., Jr. 1946- ConAu 132
Amos, James Lysle 1929- WhoAm 90
Amos, Janet 1945- OxCCanT
Amos, Janice Rae 1953- WhoEmL 91
Amos, Joan Marie 1935- WhoAmW 91, WhoWor 91
Amos, John 1939- DrBlPA 90
Amos, John Beverly BioIn 16, St&PR 91N
Amos, John Beverly 1924- WhoAm 90, WhoSSW 91
Amos, Paul Shelby 1926- WhoAm 90
Amos, Timothy Franklin 1955- WhoEmL 91
Amos, Wallace, Jr. 1936- ConAmBL
Amos, William LaFayette, Jr. 1944- WhoSSW 91
Amos, Wray McMichael 1925- St&PR 91
Amos, Wray McMichael, Jr. 1958- St&PR 91
Amoss, Berthe 1925- WhoAmA 91
Amoss, W. James, Jr. 1924- WhoAm 90
Amoss, Walter James, Jr. 1924- St&PR 91
Amoss, William Hamilton 1936- WhoE 91
Amotz, Dahn Ben- BioIn 16
Amoyal, Pierre 1949- IntWWM 90, PenDiMP
Amparado, Keith D. 1952- WhoE 91, WhoEmL 91
Amparo, Acelita Dy BiDrAPA 89
Amparo, Adonis C BiDrAPA 89
Ampel, Leon Louis 1936- WhoAm 90
Amper, Leslie Ruth 1954- IntWWM 90, WhoEmL 91
Ampere, Andre Marie 1775-1836 BioIn 16, WorAlBi
Amplo, William Joseph 1968- WhoEmL 91
Ampola, Massimo Filippo 1944- WhoWor 91
Ampudia, Peter Albert 1964- BiDrAPA 89
Amr, Asad Tamer 1941- WhoSSW 91
Amram, David 1930- IntWWM 90
Amram, David Werner 1930- WhoAm 90
Amram, Philip W. BioIn 16
Amram, Philip Werner NewYTBS 90
Amram, Philip Werner 1900-1990 ConAu 131
Amrein, Peter Josef 1941- WhoWor 91
Amrein, Yost Ursus Lucius 1918- WhoAm 90
Amrhein, Leo Francis, Jr. 1944- BiDrAPA 89
Amrhine, Karen 1950- ODwPR 91
Amrhyn, O. C. BioIn 16
Amrine, Danny Andrew 1951- WhoEmL 91
Amrine, Frank B., Jr. 1920- St&PR 91
Amrouche, Fadhma A. M. 1882?-1967 BioIn 16
Amrung, Suchakorn A 1945- BiDrAPA 89
Amsden, Floyd T 1913- WhoAmA 91N
Amsden, Ted Thomas 1950- WhoEmL 91
Amsel, Abram 1922- WhoAm 90
Amsel, Bram Jules 1949- WhoWor 91
Amsel, Harold BiDrAPA 89
Amsel, Larry Victor 1953- BiDrAPA 89
Amsel, Robert Gary 1957- WhoEmL 91
Amsellem, David 1946- BiDrAPA 89
Amspaugh, Jerry L. 1931- St&PR 91
Amspoker, James Mack 1926- WhoAm 90
Amstadter, Laurence 1922- St&PR 91
Amstadter, Robert L 1932- BiDrAPA 89
Amster, Bruce Joel 1948- WhoAm 90
Amster, Harvey Jerome 1928- WhoAm 90
Amster, Linda Evelyn 1938- WhoAm 90, WhoAmW 91
Amster, Sally WhoAmA 91N
Amsterdam, Anthony Guy 1935- WhoAm 90
Amsterdam, Jane BioIn 16
Amsterdam, Jane Ellen 1951- WhoAm 90
Amsterdam, Jay David 1949- BiDrAPA 89
Amsterdam, Morey 1914- WorAlBi
Amstrong, Frank Harris 1921- WhoE 91
Amstutz, Arnold Everet 1936- St&PR 91
Amstutz, Daniel Gordon 1932- WhoAm 90
Amstutz, Gary Paul 1955- WhoEmL 91
Amstutz, Harold Emerson 1919- WhoAm 90
Amstutz, Larry Warren BiDrAPA 89
Amthor, Carl Burleigh 1934- St&PR 91
Amtmann, James S. 1947- St&PR 91
Amtoft-Nielsen, Joan Theresa 1940- WhoAmW 91
Amua-Sekyi, E.T. 1957- St&PR 91
Amundrud, Lawrence 1954- IntWWM 90
Amundsen, James Edward 1961- WhoWor 91
Amundsen, Joanne Elaine 1954- WhoEmL 91
Amundsen, Roald 1872-1928 BioIn 16, WorAlBi
Amundson, Clyde Howard 1927- WhoAm 90
Amundson, Duane Melvin 1925- WhoAm 90
Amundson, Gary Robert 1949- St&PR 91
Amundson, John Melvin, Jr. 1926- WhoAm 90
Amundson, Neal Russell 1916- WhoAm 90
Amundson, Patricia W. 1957- St&PR 91
Amussen, Gretchen Duke 1952- WhoE 91
Amussen, Theodore S. 1915-1988 BioIn 16
Amy, Brian Winford 1952- WhoSSW 91
Amy, Gilbert 1936- IntWWM 90, PenDiMP, -A
Amy, Jonathan Weekes 1923- WhoAm 90
Amylon, Michael David 1950- WhoAm 90
Amyot, Arthur Antoine 1937- WhoAm 90
Amyot, Edmond Nazaire 1948- BiDrAPA 89
Amyot, Guillaume 1843-1896 DcCanB 12
Amyot, Leopold Henri 1930- WhoAm 90
Amyotte, Sherry Jo 1956- WhoAmW 91
Amyx, Barry Clinton 1951- BiDrAPA 89
Amyx, Darrell Arlynn 1911- WhoAm 90
Amyx, Leon Kirkman 1908- WhoAmA 91
An, Pham Xuan BioIn 16
An, Zhimin 1924- WhoWor 91
Ana-Alicia WhoHisp 91
Ana-Alicia 1956- ConTFT 8 [port]
Anable, Anne Currier Steinert WhoAmW 91
Anable, Wayne Ruey BiDrAPA 89
Anacker, George E. 1923- St&PR 91
Anacker, John William 1960- WhoAmA 91
Anacker, R. David 1935- WhoAm 90
Anacreon 572?BC- WorAlBi
Anagnost, Alexander Themis 1945- WhoEmL 91
Anagnost, Catherine Cook 1919- WhoAmW 91
Anagnost, Maria Athena 1943- WhoAmW 91, WhoWor 91
Anagnostake, Loula EncCoWW
Anagnostaki, Loula 1935?- EncCoWW
Anagnostakis, Manolis 1925- WorAu 1980 [port]
Anagnoste, Berta BiDrAPA 89
Anagnoste, Vivian Gabriela 1929- WhoAmW 91
Anagnostis, Randy St&PR 91
Anagnostopoulos, Constantine E. 1922- St&PR 91
Anagnostopoulos, Constantine Efthymios 1940- WhoAm 90
Anagnostopoulos, Constantine Emmanuel 1922- WhoAm 90, WhoWor 91
Anagnou, Nicholas P. 1947- WhoWor 91
Anahid BioIn 16
Anand, Man Mohan BiDrAPA 89
Anand, Mulk Raj 1905- ConAu 32NR, MajTwCW
Anand, Nirupma BiDrAPA 89
Anand, Saroja BiDrAPA 89
Anand, Suresh Chandra 1931- WhoAm 90, WhoWor 91
Anand, Vandana BiDrAPA 89
Anand, Yogindra Nath 1939- WhoWor 91
Ananda NewAgMG
Ananda Metteya 1872-1947 EncO&P 3
Anandam, Kamala 1929- WhoAmW 91
Anandamayi Ma, Sri 1896- EncO&P 3
Anandamurti, Shri EncO&P 3
Anandu, Venkata Subbiah 1935- WhoSSW 91
Anania, Michael Angelo 1939- WhoWrEP 89
Ananth, Jambur V 1932- BiDrAPA 89
Ananthanarayanan, Venkataraman 1936- WhoSSW 91
Anantharam, Venkat 1960- WhoE 91
Anaporte-Easton, Jean Boehlke 1942- WhoWrEP 89
Anargirou, Pauline 1958- WhoE 91
Anargyros, Spero 1915- WhoAm 90, WhoAmA 91
Anas, David BioIn 16
Anas, Demetra Economos 1960- WhoEmL 91
Anast, David George 1955- WhoEmL 91
Anastas, Terrence Joseph 1958- WhoEmL 91
Anastasescu, Anda 1949- IntWWM 90
Anastasi, Anne 1908- WhoAm 90, WhoAmW 91
Anastasi, William 1933- WhoAmA 91
Anastasi, William Joseph 1933- WhoE 91
Anastasio, James 1930- St&PR 91, WhoAm 90
Anastasio, Louis N. 1944- St&PR 91
Anastasio, Roger Michael BiDrAPA 89
Anastasoff, Dennis James 1951- WhoE 91
Anastole, Dorothy Jean 1932- WhoAmW 91
Anastos, George 1920- WhoAm 90
Anastos, Milton Vasil 1909- WhoAm 90
Anastos, Peter BioIn 16
Anastos, Peter G. 1948- WhoAm 90
Anastos, Rosemary Park 1907- WhoAm 90
Anatolitissa EncCoWW
Anawati, Joseph Soliman 1941- WhoWor 91
Anaxagoras 500?BC-428BC WorAlBi
Anaximander 611BC-547BC WorAlBi
Anaya, Baltazar G 1930- BiDrAPA 89
Anaya, George, Jr. 1964- WhoHisp 91
Anaya, Herbert Ernesto BioIn 16
Anaya, Richard Alfred, Jr. 1932- WhoAm 90
Anaya, Rudolfo A. BioIn 16
Anaya, Rudolfo A 1937- ConAu 32NR, HispWr 90, MajTwCW, WhoHisp 91, WhoWrEP 89
Anaya, Tobias 1908-1988 MusmAFA
Anaya, Toney BioIn 16
Anaya, Toney 1941- WhoHisp 91
Anazagasty, Anita Dolores 1944- WhoWrEP 89
Anazagasty, Maria Louisa 1950- WhoAmW 91
Anbar, Michael 1927- WhoAm 90
Anbinder, Paul 1940- WhoAmA 91, WhoE 91
Anbunathan, Sneha Pradan 1953- BiDrAPA 89
Ancel, Steven Harlan 1937- WhoAm 90
Ancelet, Barry Jean 1951- ConAu 131, WhoEmL 91
Ancell, Nathan S. 1908- St&PR 91
Ancerl, Karel 1908-1973 PenDiMP
Ances, I. George 1935- WhoAm 90
Ancetti, Carlo Guido 1933- WhoWor 91
Anchel, Edward 1939- St&PR 91
Anchel, Marjorie 1910- WhoE 91
Ancher, Anna Kirstine 1859-1935 BiDWomA
Ancheta, Bart D. 1927- St&PR 91
Anciaux, Jean 1930- WhoWor 91
Ancient Future NewAgMG
Ancier, Garth BioIn 16
Ancil, Cynthia Ann 1945- WhoWor 91
Ancira, Ernesto, Jr. WhoHisp 91
Ancira, Robert BiDrAPA 89
Ancizar-Sordo, Jorge 1908- WhoWor 91
Anckarsvard, Karin Inez Maria 1915-1969 AuBYP 90
Ancker, Clinton James, Jr. 1919- WhoAm 90
Ancker-Johnson, Betsy 1927- St&PR 91, WhoAm 90, WhoAmW 91
Anckner, Joseph Edward 1932- St&PR 91
Anclien, Jeffrey J. 1961- St&PR 91
Ancliffe, Charles 1880-1952 OxCPMus
Ancog, Romulo S BiDrAPA 89
Ancoli-Israel, Sonia 1951- WhoEmL 91
Ancona, Barry 1948- WhoAm 90
Ancona, George 1929- AuBYP 90, BioIn 16
Ancona, George Ephraim 1929- WhoAm 90
Ancona, Joseph I. 1924- St&PR 91
Ancona, Michael Joseph 1948- St&PR 91
Ancona, Sam A. 1922- St&PR 91
Ancona, Vito d' 1825-1884 BioIn 16
Ancrum, Cheryl Denise 1958- WhoAmW 91
Ancy, Richard A. 1936- St&PR 91
Anda, Geza 1921-1976 PenDiMP
Andal, Marian WhoWrEP 89
Andaloro, John Joseph 1956- WhoEmL 91
Andell, Nancy 1953- WhoAmA 91
Andelman, David ODwPR 91
Andelson, Robert Vernon 1931- WhoAm 90
Andelson, Sherman L. 1925- St&PR 91
Andenaes, Johannes 1912- ConAu 129
Ander, Stig Lennart 1917- WhoWor 91
Andera, Katherine Anne 1949- WhoEmL 91
Anderberg, Lorraine Jensen 1939- St&PR 91
Anderberg, Roy Anthony 1921- WhoWor 91
Anderberg, Russell Frank, III 1938- St&PR 91
Anderdon, Jane BiDEWW
Anderdon, Mary 1635- BiDEWW
Anderegg, George Francis, Jr. 1937- WhoAm 90
Anderegg, John Swift, Jr. 1924- St&PR 91
Anderegg, Karen BioIn 16
Anderegg, Karen Klok WhoAm 90
Anderegg, Karen Klok 1940- WhoWrEP 89
Anderer, Jeanmarie 1956- BiDrAPA 89
Anderer, Joseph H. BioIn 16
Anderer, Joseph Henry 1924- WhoAm 90
Anderhalter, Oliver Frank 1922- WhoAm 90
Anderholm, Spencer F. 1933- St&PR 91
Anderl, Stephen 1910- WhoWor 91
Anderluh, John Russell 1934- WhoAm 90
Anderman, Arthur BioIn 16
Anderman, Sigmund 1941- St&PR 91
Anders, Barbara Lynne Gainey IntWWM 90
Anders, Catherine 1953- St&PR 91
Anders, David BioIn 16
Anders, Edward 1926- WhoAm 90
Anders, Gerald R. 1943- IntWWM 90
Anders, Howard G. 1943- St&PR 91
Anders, Jeanne WhoWrEP 89
Anders, Laura E. ODwPR 91
Anders, Mark Leslie 1955- WhoEmL 91
Anders, Micheal Fred 1954- IntWWM 90
Anders, Peter 1908-1954 PenDiMP
Anders, Thomas F 1936- BiDrAPA 89
Anders, William Alison 1933- St&PR 91, WhoAm 90
Anders, Wolfhart Hermann 1941- WhoWor 91
Andersch, Alfred 1914-1980 MajTwCW
Andersdatter, Karla M. 1938- WhoWrEP 89
Andersen, Andreas Storrs 1908-1974 WhoAmA 91N
Andersen, Anne Elaine BiDrAPA 89
Andersen, Anthony L. 1935- WhoAm 90
Andersen, Arnold E 1943- BiDrAPA 89
Andersen, Arnold M. 1916- St&PR 91
Andersen, Arthur J. 1929- St&PR 91
Andersen, Astrid Hjertenaes 1915-1985 DcScanL
Andersen, Benny Allan 1929- DcScanL
Andersen, Bill Byron 1936- WhoAm 90
Andersen, Burton Robert 1932- WhoAm 90
Andersen, Carolyn Annette Perez 1948- WhoEmL 91
Andersen, Carsten Steen 1943- St&PR 91
Andersen, Cay M. BioIn 16
Andersen, Christopher P 1949- ConAu 31NR
Andersen, Dale Gordon 1933- WhoAm 90
Andersen, Dana Kimball 1946- WhoWor 91
Andersen, Daniel Johannes 1909- WhoAm 90, WhoE 91
Andersen, David BioIn 16
Andersen, David 1843-1901 PenDiDA 89
Andersen, David C. 1948- ODwPR 91
Andersen, David Lance 1953- St&PR 91
Andersen, David Lee 1951- WhoEmL 91
Andersen, David R L 1957- WhoAmA 91
Andersen, Donald Edward 1923- WhoAm 90
Andersen, Doris Evelyn 1923- WhoAm 90, WhoAmW 91, WhoWor 91
Andersen, Elmer L. 1909- St&PR 91
Andersen, Elmer Lee 1909- WhoAm 90
Andersen, Ernest Christopher 1909- WhoWor 91

Andersen, Frank Angelius 1953- *WhoWor 91*
Andersen, Frank N. *St&PR 91*
Andersen, Gabriele *BioIn 16*
Andersen, Gordon Walter 1934- *St&PR 91*
Andersen, Gunner 1948- *WhoWor 91*
Andersen, Hans 1955- *WhoWor 91*
Andersen, Hans Christian 1805-1875 *AuBYP 90, BioIn 16, DcScanL, ShSCr 6 [port], WorAlBi*
Andersen, Hans Christian 1941- *WhoAm 90*
Andersen, Harold R. 1945- *St&PR 91*
Andersen, Harold Wayne 1923- *WhoAm 90*
Andersen, Henning 1934- *WhoAm 90*
Andersen, Ib Steen 1954- *WhoAm 90, WhoE 91*
Andersen, James A. 1924- *WhoAm 90*
Andersen, Janet Linda 1947- *WhoE 91*
Andersen, John Theodore *BiDrAPA 89*
Andersen, Juel 1923- *WhoWrEP 89*
Andersen, Karen Louise 1951- *WhoAmW 91*
Andersen, Karl Georg 1924- *WhoWor 91*
Andersen, Karsten 1920- *IntWWM 90*
Andersen, Kathleen 1951- *BiDrAPA 89*
Andersen, Kenneth A. 1934- *St&PR 91*
Andersen, Kenneth Benjamin 1905- *WhoAm 90*
Andersen, Kenneth Eldon 1933- *WhoAm 90*
Andersen, Kenneth Kaae 1934- *WhoAm 90*
Andersen, Kent Tucker 1942- *WhoAm 90, WhoE 91, WhoWor 91*
Andersen, Kurt 1954- *WhoWrEP 89*
Andersen, Laird Bryce 1928- *WhoAm 90*
Andersen, Lale 1910-1972 *OxCPMus*
Andersen, Larry *BioIn 16*
Andersen, Larry 1953- *Ballpl 90*
Andersen, Lee Dixon 1952- *WhoEmL 91*
Andersen, Leif 1925- *WhoAmA 91*
Andersen, M. Rita *St&PR 91*
Andersen, Marianne Singer *WhoAmW 91, WhoE 91*
Andersen, Mark Gerald 1959- *WhoEmL 91*
Andersen, Martin *DcScanL*
Andersen, Mary Schwartz 1953- *WhoEmL 91*
Andersen, Mogens 1916- *WhoWor 91*
Andersen, Morten *BioIn 16*
Andersen, Paul Kent 1948- *WhoWor 91*
Andersen, Richard 1946- *WhoWrEP 89*
Andersen, Richard Esten 1957- *WhoE 91, WhoEmL 91, WhoWor 91*
Andersen, Robert Allen 1936- *WhoAm 90*
Andersen, Robert David 1945- *WhoEmL 91*
Andersen, Ronald Max 1939- *WhoAm 90*
Andersen, Roy B. *St&PR 91*
Andersen, Sharon L. 1947- *WhoSSW 91*
Andersen, Sheree Hilton 1954- *WhoEmL 91*
Andersen, Shirley Anne 1942- *WhoAmW 91*
Andersen, Steve Richard 1946- *WhoSSW 91*
Andersen, Steven Mark 1945- *WhoEmL 91, WhoWor 91*
Andersen, Stig Karl Gustav 1946- *WhoWor 91*
Andersen, Svein 1946- *St&PR 91*
Andersen, Svein Erik Tondel 1950- *WhoWor 91*
Andersen, Tage 1927- *WhoWor 91*
Andersen, Ted *AuBYP 90*
Andersen, Thomas Edward 1952- *St&PR 91*
Andersen, Tryggve 1866-1920 *DcScanL*
Andersen, Vagn 1929- *St&PR 91, WhoAm 90, WhoWor 91*
Andersen, Vita 1944- *EncCoWW*
Andersen, Wayne Vesti 1930- *WhoAmA 91*
Andersen, Yvonne 1932- *AuBYP 90*
Andersland, Orlando Baldwin 1929- *WhoAm 90*
Anderson, A. Elaine 1950- *St&PR 91*
Anderson, Adele Konkel 1949- *WhoEmL 91*
Anderson, Agnes M. 1900- *WhoAmW 91*
Anderson, Al 1942- *ODwPR 91*
Anderson, Alan E. *St&PR 91*
Anderson, Alan L. *St&PR 91*
Anderson, Alan Marshall 1955- *WhoEmL 91*
Anderson, Alan Stewert 1948- *WhoE 91*
Anderson, Albert Esten 1921- *St&PR 91, WhoAm 90*
Anderson, Albert M., Jr. 1935- *St&PR 91*
Anderson, Alden 1867-1944 *AmLegL*
Anderson, Alden M. 1939- *WhoAm 90*
Anderson, Aldon J. 1917- *WhoAm 90*
Anderson, Alexander Cunninghame 1939- *IntWWM 90*
Anderson, Alexandra C. 1942- *WhoAm 90, WhoAmA 91, WhoWrEP 89*
Anderson, Alfred *EarBlAP*
Anderson, Alfred Lamar 1942- *IntWWM 90*
Anderson, Alfred Oliver 1928- *WhoE 91, WhoWor 91*
Anderson, Alice Jane 1947- *WhoEmL 91*
Anderson, Alison Grey 1943- *WhoAm 90*
Anderson, Allamay Eudoris 1933- *WhoAmW 91, WhoE 91*
Anderson, Allan 1964- *Ballpl 90*
Anderson, Allan A *BiDrAPA 89*
Anderson, Allan Crosby 1932- *WhoAm 90*
Anderson, Allan George 1923- *WhoSSW 91*
Anderson, Amos Robert 1920- *St&PR 91*
Anderson, Andre Nelson 1964- *WhoSSW 91*
Anderson, Andrew Edwin 1940- *St&PR 91*
Anderson, Andrew Herbert 1928- *WhoAm 90*
Anderson, Ann 1952- *WhoAmW 91*
Anderson, Anna R. 1948- *St&PR 91*
Anderson, Anne Elizabeth *BiDrAPA 89*
Anderson, Anne Victoria 1958- *WhoAmW 91*
Anderson, Annelise Graebner 1938- *WhoAm 90, WhoAmW 91*
Anderson, Annethea Elizabeth 1932- *WhoWrEP 89*
Anderson, Annette Grace 1936- *WhoE 91*
Anderson, Ansel Cochran 1933- *WhoAm 90*
Anderson, Armour Axil 1920- *St&PR 91*
Anderson, Arnold Herbert 1915- *WhoAm 90*
Anderson, Arnold Stuart 1934- *St&PR 91, WhoAm 90*
Anderson, Arthur A 1926- *BiDrAPA 89*
Anderson, Arthur Allan 1939- *WhoAm 90*
Anderson, Arthur G., Jr. 1918- *WhoAm 90*
Anderson, Arthur Irvin 1951- *WhoAm 90*
Anderson, Arthur N. 1912- *WhoAm 90*
Anderson, Arthur Roland 1910- *WhoAm 90*
Anderson, Arthur Salzner 1923- *WhoAm 90*
Anderson, Arthur W. 1938- *St&PR 91*
Anderson, Aubrey Lee 1940- *WhoAm 90*
Anderson, Austin Gilman 1942- *St&PR 91*
Anderson, Austin Gothard 1931- *WhoAm 90*
Anderson, B.J. 1928- *St&PR 91*
Anderson, Barbara A. 1948- *WhoAmW 91*
Anderson, Barbara Gallatin *BioIn 16*
Anderson, Barbara Louise 1951- *WhoAmW 91*
Anderson, Barbara Tunnell 1894-1974 *LiHiK*
Anderson, Barry Stanley 1942- *WhoWor 91*
Anderson, Benard Harold 1935- *WhoAm 90*
Anderson, Benita *BiDrAPA 89*
Anderson, Bernard R. 1926- *St&PR 91*
Anderson, Beth 1950- *WhoE 91, WhoEmL 91*
Anderson, Bette B. *ODwPR 91*
Anderson, Beverly Dawn 1958 *WhoAmW 91*
Anderson, Bill 1937- *BioIn 16*
Anderson, Blair Richard 1953- *WhoSSW 91*
Anderson, Bob 1932- *WhoWor 91*
Anderson, Bob 1935- *Ballpl 90*
Anderson, Brad J 1924- *WhoAmA 91*
Anderson, Bradford William 1956- *WhoWor 91*
Anderson, Bradley Jay 1924- *WhoAm 90*
Anderson, Brady 1964- *Ballpl 90*
Anderson, Brenda Shore 1958- *WhoAmW 91*
Anderson, Brian E. 1944- *WhoWrEP 89*
Anderson, Brian Thomas 1957- *WhoEmL 91*
Anderson, Brierly W. 1932- *St&PR 91*
Anderson, Brocke *WhoWrEP 89*
Anderson, Brooke 1939- *St&PR 91*
Anderson, Bruce A 1948- *WhoAmA 91*
Anderson, Bruce Carl 1941- *WhoAm 90*
Anderson, Bruce James 1940- *WhoAmA 91*
Anderson, Bruce Kenneth 1943- *WhoE 91*
Anderson, Bruce Morgan 1941- *WhoE 91, WhoWor 91*
Anderson, Bruce Murray 1929- *WhoAm 90*
Anderson, Bruce N 1939- *BiDrAPA 89*
Anderson, Bruce Stanley 1952- *WhoEmL 91*
Anderson, Bud 1956- *Ballpl 90*
Anderson, Buist Murfee 1904- *WhoAm 90*
Anderson, Byron Edward 1954- *WhoEmL 91*
Anderson, C. A. 1954- *WhoE 91*
Anderson, C. Farley *MajTwCW*
Anderson, C.H. *St&PR 91*
Anderson, C. Leonard 1946- *WhoEmL 91*
Anderson, C Leroy *BiDrAPA 89*
Anderson, C. Merton 1927- *St&PR 91*
Anderson, Camilla M *BiDrAPA 89*
Anderson, Carl *DrBIPA 90*
Anderson, Carl 1865-1948 *EncACom*
Anderson, Carl B. 1922- *St&PR 91*
Anderson, Carl D. 1905- *WorAlBi*
Anderson, Carl David 1905- *WhoAm 90, WhoWor 91*
Anderson, Carl Edward 1950- *St&PR 91*
Anderson, Carl Elving 1933- *BiDrAPA 89*
Anderson, Carl Elving 1953- *WhoE 91*
Anderson, Carl H. 1938- *St&PR 91*
Anderson, Carl Lennart 1919- *WhoSSW 91*
Anderson, Carl R. 1932- *St&PR 91*
Anderson, Carl Thomas 1865-1948 *WhoAmA 91N*
Anderson, Carla Lee 1930- *WhoAmW 91*
Anderson, Carol Ann 1961- *WhoAmW 91*
Anderson, Carol Boyles 1953- *WhoEmL 91*
Anderson, Carol Joyce 1935- *WhoAmW 91*
Anderson, Carol June 1942- *WhoAmW 91*
Anderson, Carol Lynn 1952- *WhoAmW 91*
Anderson, Carol McMillan 1938- *WhoAmW 91*
Anderson, Carol Patricia 1946- *WhoAmW 91*
Anderson, Carol Pauline 1962- *BiDrAPA 89*
Anderson, Carol Ruth 1946- *WhoE 91*
Anderson, Carole Ann 1938- *WhoAm 90, WhoAmW 91*
Anderson, Carole Lewis 1944- *WhoAm 90, WhoAmW 91*
Anderson, Carolyn Jennings 1913- *WhoAm 90*
Anderson, Carolyn Joyce 1947- *WhoEmL 91*
Anderson, Carolyn Marie 1955- *WhoAmW 91*
Anderson, Carson Anthony 1951- *WhoEmL 91*
Anderson, Cat 1916-1981 *OxCPMus*
Anderson, Catherine A. 1946- *St&PR 91*
Anderson, Catherine Agnes 1946- *WhoAmW 91, WhoEmL 91*
Anderson, Charlene Marie 1952- *WhoAmW 91*
Anderson, Charles A. 1902-1990 *BioIn 16*
Anderson, Charles Albert 1932- *WhoAm 90*
Anderson, Charles Alfred *BioIn 16*
Anderson, Charles Arnold 1907- *WhoAm 90*
Anderson, Charles Arthur 1917- *WhoAm 90*
Anderson, Charles Bernard 1938- *WhoAm 90*
Anderson, Charles D. 1931- *St&PR 91*
Anderson, Charles L 1914- *BiDrAPA 89*
Anderson, Charles Leroy *BiDrAPA 89*
Anderson, Charles Lester 1960- *WhoEmL 91*
Anderson, Charles McKenna 1933- *St&PR 91*
Anderson, Charles R. S. 1927- *WhoAm 90*
Anderson, Charles Ralph Seibold 1927- *St&PR 91*
Anderson, Charles Roberts 1902- *WhoAm 90*
Anderson, Charles Ross 1937- *WhoWor 91*
Anderson, Charles S. *St&PR 91*
Anderson, Charles S. 1930- *WhoAm 90*
Anderson, Cheryl *WhoAmW 91*
Anderson, Cheryl Kay 1961- *WhoAmW 91*
Anderson, Chester 1932- *ConAu 131*
Anderson, Chester Grant 1923- *WhoAm 90*
Anderson, Christine Pidgeon 1955- *WhoEmL 91*
Anderson, Christine Ruth Minton 1951- *WhoAmW 91*
Anderson, Christopher James 1950- *WhoEmL 91*
Anderson, Clarence William 1891-1971 *AuBYP 90*
Anderson, Claudia 1949- *IntWWM 90*
Anderson, Clifford I. 1937- *St&PR 91*
Anderson, Clifford Thomas 1959- *WhoSSW 91*
Anderson, Clinton Presba 1895-1975 *BiDrUSE 89*
Anderson, Clyde Eugene 1923- *St&PR 91*
Anderson, Court 1942- *St&PR 91*
Anderson, Craig 1938- *Ballpl 90*
Anderson, Craig Alan 1955- *WhoEmL 91*
Anderson, Craig Barry 1942- *WhoAm 90*
Anderson, Craig Earl 1941- *WhoAm 90*
Anderson, Craig Edgar 1947- *WhoEmL 91*
Anderson, Craig Lester 1950- *St&PR 91*
Anderson, Cromwell Adair 1926- *WhoAm 90*
Anderson, Curtiss Martin 1928- *WhoAm 90, WhoWrEP 89*
Anderson, Cynthia Ann 1964- *WhoAmW 91*
Anderson, Cynthia Finkbeiner Sjoberg 1949- *WhoAmW 91*
Anderson, Cynthia Gay 1945- *WhoAmW 91*
Anderson, Cynthia Harvey 1950- *WhoE 91*
Anderson, D. Kent 1941- *St&PR 91*
Anderson, Dale *BiDrAPA 89, WhoWrEP 89*
Anderson, Dale 1933- *WhoAm 90*
Anderson, Dale Arden 1936- *WhoAm 90, WhoSSW 91*
Anderson, Dale Kenneth 1922- *WhoAm 90*
Anderson, Dan Charles 1945- *St&PR 91*
Anderson, Dana L. *St&PR 91*
Anderson, Daniel H 1930- *BiDrAPA 89*
Anderson, Daniel Odin 1941- *WhoAm 90*
Anderson, Danita Ruth 1956- *WhoEmL 91*
Anderson, Daphne 1919- *ConAu 130*
Anderson, Darel Burton 1927- *WhoAm 90*
Anderson, Darlene Y. 1953- *WhoEmL 91*
Anderson, Darrel James 1950- *WhoEmL 91*
Anderson, Darrell Edward 1932- *WhoAm 90*
Anderson, Darrell Glenn *BiDrAPA 89*
Anderson, Darryl Kent 1941- *WhoAm 90, WhoSSW 91*
Anderson, Daryl 1951- *WhoAm 90*
Anderson, Dave 1929- *SmATA X [port]*
Anderson, Dave 1960- *Ballpl 90*
Anderson, David 1935- *WhoAmA 91*
Anderson, David 1937- *WhoAm 90, WhoWor 91*
Anderson, David 1952- *ConAu 130*
Anderson, David B. 1942- *St&PR 91*
Anderson, David Boyd 1942- *WhoAm 90*
Anderson, David C 1931- *WhoAmA 91*
Anderson, David Charles 1931- *WhoWrEP 89*
Anderson, David Charles 1955- *ODwPR 91, WhoEmL 91*
Anderson, David Daniel 1924- *WhoAm 90, WhoWor 91*
Anderson, David E. 1926- *St&PR 91*
Anderson, David Eugene *BiDrAPA 89*
Anderson, David George 1951- *WhoEmL 91*
Anderson, David Gilroy 1930- *WhoAm 90, WhoE 91*
Anderson, David Harold, Jr. 1948- *St&PR 91*
Anderson, David Hugh Tweed 1931- *WhoWor 91*
Anderson, David James 1939- *WhoAm 90*
Anderson, David John *BiDrAPA 89*
Anderson, David John 1943- *St&PR 91*
Anderson, David Langley 1944- *WhoE 91*
Anderson, David Laron 1955- *St&PR 91*
Anderson, David Lawrence 1948- *WhoAm 90, WhoE 91, WhoEmL 91*
Anderson, David Lee 1953- *WhoEmL 91*
Anderson, David Lloyd 1935- *WhoAm 90*
Anderson, David Martin 1930- *WhoE 91*
Anderson, David Paul 1946- *WhoAmA 91*
Anderson, David Poole 1929- *SmATA 60 [port], WhoAm 90, WhoWrEP 89*
Anderson, David Prewitt 1934- *WhoAm 90*
Anderson, David Ralph 1946- *WhoEmL 91*
Anderson, David Robert 1951- *WhoE 91*
Anderson, David Sidney 1954- *WhoEmL 91*
Anderson, David Trevor 1938- *WhoAm 90*
Anderson, David Turpeau 1942- *WhoAm 90*
Anderson, Davin Charles 1955- *WhoEmL 91, WhoWor 91*
Anderson, Dawn Renee 1962- *WhoAmW 91*
Anderson, Dean *St&PR 91*
Anderson, Dean Herbert 1950- *WhoEmL 91*
Anderson, Dean William 1946- *WhoAm 90*
Anderson, Debbie Ann 1955- *WhoAmW 91*
Anderson, Debra *WhoAm 90*
Anderson, Decatur Curran 1816-1890 *AmLegL*
Anderson, Della Louise 1946- *WhoE 91*
Anderson, Delores Faye 1936- *WhoAmW 91*
Anderson, Denice Anna 1947- *WhoAmW 91*
Anderson, Denise *BioIn 16*
Anderson, Dennis A *BiDrAPA 89*
Anderson, Dennis Alan 1953- *WhoE 91*
Anderson, Derek H. 1940- *St&PR 91*
Anderson, Diana Dawn 1959- *WhoEmL 91*
Anderson, Don Lynn 1933- *WhoAm 90*
Anderson, Donald 1943- *St&PR 91*
Anderson, Donald Bernard 1919- *WhoAm 90*
Anderson, Donald Edward 1931- *WhoAm 90*
Anderson, Donald George 1930- *WhoAm 90*

Anderson, Donald Gordon Marcus 1937- *WhoAm 90*
Anderson, Donald Keith 1931- *WhoAm 90*
Anderson, Donald Kennedy, Jr. 1922- *WhoAm 90*
Anderson, Donald Lee 1945- *BiDrAPA 89*
Anderson, Donald Meredith 1928- *WhoAm 90*
Anderson, Donald Milton *WhoAm 90*
Anderson, Donald Morgan 1930- *WhoAm 90, WhoE 91, WhoWor 91*
Anderson, Donald Myers *WhoAmA 91*
Anderson, Donald Paul 1930- *WhoAm 90*
Anderson, Donald R. 1935- *St&PR 91*
Anderson, Donald S. 1913- *St&PR 91*
Anderson, Donald S. 1947- *ODwPR 91*
Anderson, Donald Thomas 1931- *WhoWor 91*
Anderson, Donna Kay 1935- *WhoAm 90*
Anderson, Donna Sue Wagnon 1956- *WhoAmW 91*
Anderson, Doris Ehlinger 1926- *WhoAmW 91*
Anderson, Dorothy L *BiDrAPA 89*
Anderson, Dorrine Ann Petersen 1923- *WhoAmW 91, WhoWor 91*
Anderson, Doug 1954- *WhoAmA 91*
Anderson, Douglas Alan 1945- *WhoSSW 91*
Anderson, Douglas Arthur 1947- *WhoEmL 91*
Anderson, Douglas Burtman 1947- *BiDrAPA 89*
Anderson, Douglas Glenn 1963- *WhoSSW 91*
Anderson, Douglas McDougall 1918- *WhoAm 90*
Anderson, Douglas Poole 1939- *WhoSSW 91*
Anderson, Douglas Richard 1938- *WhoAm 90, WhoSSW 91*
Anderson, Douglas Scranton Hesley 1929- *WhoE 91*
Anderson, Douglas William 1943- *WhoAm 90*
Anderson, Douglas Williams 1932- *WhoE 91, WhoWor 91*
Anderson, Duwayne Marlo 1927- *WhoAm 90*
Anderson, Dwayne Richard 1956- *WhoEmL 91*
Anderson, E. Karl 1931- *WhoAm 90*
Anderson, E. Van 1944- *St&PR 91*
Anderson, Earl Milton, Jr. 1925- *St&PR 91*
Anderson, Eddie 1905-1977 *DrBlPA 90, OxCPMus*
Anderson, Edgar 1897-1969 *DcScB S2*
Anderson, Edgar 1920- *ConAu 30NR*
Anderson, Edith Helen 1927- *WhoAm 90, WhoAmW 91*
Anderson, Edna 1922- *WhoAmW 91*
Anderson, Edward *BioIn 16*
Anderson, Edward 1906-1969 *BioIn 16*
Anderson, Edward Allan *BiDrAPA 89*
Anderson, Edwina Haycraft 1926- *WhoSSW 91*
Anderson, Edwyna 1930- *WhoAmW 91*
Anderson, Eileen E. 1931- *St&PR 91*
Anderson, Einar Wulfsberg 1942- *IntWWM 90*
Anderson, Electa Allen 1963- *WhoSSW 91*
Anderson, Elisabeth Madge Kehrer *WhoAmW 91*
Anderson, Elizabeth Carmal 1925- *WhoAmW 91*
Anderson, Elizabeth Garrett 1836-1917 *BioIn 16*
Anderson, Elizabeth Maltby 1917- *St&PR 91*
Anderson, Elliott Van 1944- *WhoAm 90*
Anderson, Ellis Bernard 1926- *WhoAm 90*
Anderson, Elmer Ebert 1922- *WhoAm 90*
Anderson, Elmer Ray, Jr. 1954- *WhoEmL 91*
Anderson, Elsie Miners 1931- *WhoSSW 91*
Anderson, Eric 1935- *WhoWor 91*
Anderson, Eric Edward 1951- *WhoEmL 91*
Anderson, Eric Hall 1936- *WhoE 91*
Anderson, Eric Leonard 1950- *WhoE 91*
Anderson, Eric Severin 1943- *WhoSSW 91*
Anderson, Eric Thomas 1960- *WhoSSW 91*
Anderson, Eric William 1923- *WhoAm 90*
Anderson, Ernest *DrBlPA 90*
Anderson, Ernest Washington 1922- *WhoAm 90*
Anderson, Eskil 1913- *St&PR 91*
Anderson, Esther *DrBlPA 90*
Anderson, Ethel 1883-1958 *FemiCLE*
Anderson, Ethel Avara *WhoAmW 91*
Anderson, Ethel Todd *AuBYP 90*
Anderson, Eugene A. 1908- *St&PR 91*
Anderson, Eugene Karl 1935- *St&PR 91*
Anderson, Eva Klauber 1935- *WhoAmW 91*
Anderson, Evalyn Ruth 1931- *WhoAmW 91*
Anderson, Evelyn Ruth 1928- *IntWWM 90*
Anderson, F. Allan 1944- *St&PR 91*
Anderson, Fletcher Neal 1930- *WhoAm 90*
Anderson, Floyd Owen 1948- *BiDrAPA 89*
Anderson, Forrest H. 1913-1989 *BioIn 16*
Anderson, Frances Swem 1913- *WhoAmW 91, WhoWor 91*
Anderson, Frank Russell 1923- *WhoWrEP 89*
Anderson, Frank Wayne 1949- *WhoSSW 91*
Anderson, Fred 1885-1957 *Ballpl 90*
Anderson, Frederick Irving 1877-1947 *TwCCr&M 91*
Anderson, Frederick Randolph, Jr. 1941- *WhoAm 90*
Anderson, G. Norman 1932- *WhoAm 90, WhoWor 91*
Anderson, Gail Fisk *BiDrAPA 89*
Anderson, Garland 1886-1939 *EarBlAP*
Anderson, Garland 1887?-1939 *DrBlPA 90*
Anderson, Gary Dean 1947- *WhoAm 90, WhoE 91*
Anderson, Gary F. 1953- *St&PR 91*
Anderson, Gary William 1951- *WhoE 91, WhoEmL 91*
Anderson, Gay Raymond 1938- *BiDrAPA 89*
Anderson, Gene Randall 1940- *St&PR 91*
Anderson, Geoffrey Allen 1947- *WhoAm 90*
Anderson, George 1889-1962 *Ballpl 90*
Anderson, George Edward 1938- *WhoWor 91*
Anderson, George Eli 1946- *St&PR 91*
Anderson, George Frederick *PenDiMP*
Anderson, George Frederick 1914- *WhoAm 90*
Anderson, George Harding 1931- *WhoAm 90*
Anderson, George Joseph 1960- *WhoEmL 91*
Anderson, George Lee 1934- *WhoAm 90*
Anderson, George Ross, Jr. 1929- *WhoAm 90, WhoSSW 91*
Anderson, George W. 1934- *WhoAm 90*
Anderson, Georgia Rae 1954- *WhoAmW 91*
Anderson, Gerald A *BiDrAPA 89*
Anderson, Gerald Benton 1925- *WhoSSW 91*
Anderson, Gerald E. 1931- *St&PR 91*
Anderson, Gerald Edwin 1931- *WhoAm 90, WhoE 91*
Anderson, Gerald Leslie 1940- *St&PR 91, WhoAm 90, WhoSSW 91*
Anderson, Geraldine Louise 1941- *WhoAmW 91*
Anderson, Gerard Fenton 1951- *WhoE 91*
Anderson, Gilbert John, Sr. 1905- *St&PR 91*
Anderson, Gilbert W. 1928- *St&PR 91*
Anderson, Gillian Bunshaft 1943- *IntWWM 90*
Anderson, Girard F. 1932- *St&PR 91, WhoSSW 91*
Anderson, Glen Keith 1955- *WhoSSW 91, WhoWor 91*
Anderson, Glenn *BioIn 16*
Anderson, Glenn E. 1914- *St&PR 91*
Anderson, Glenn Elwood 1914- *WhoAm 90*
Anderson, Glenn M. *BioIn 16*
Anderson, Glenn Malcolm *WhoAm 90*
Anderson, Gordon Benjamin 1927- *St&PR 91*
Anderson, Gordon Louis 1947- *WhoE 91*
Anderson, Gregory Joseph 1944- *WhoAm 90*
Anderson, Gregory Reid 1959- *WhoSSW 91*
Anderson, Gregory Stephen 1956- *WhoEmL 91*
Anderson, Grover D. 1942- *St&PR 91*
Anderson, Gunnar Donald 1927- *WhoAmA 91*
Anderson, Guy Irving 1906- *WhoAm 90, WhoAmA 91*
Anderson, H. Richard 1953- *WhoEmL 91*
Anderson, Hampton G., III 1932- *St&PR 91*
Anderson, Harold Albert 1908- *WhoAm 90*
Anderson, Harrison Clarke 1932- *WhoAm 90*
Anderson, Harry 1931- *Ballpl 90*
Anderson, Harry 1952?- *BioIn 16, WorAlBi*
Anderson, Harry Frederick, Jr. 1927- *WhoAm 90*
Anderson, Harry J *BiDrAPA 89*
Anderson, Helen I *BiDrAPA 89*
Anderson, Helen Sharp 1916- *WhoSSW 91*
Anderson, Henry Warren 1956- *WhoEmL 91, WhoSSW 91*
Anderson, Herbert H. 1920- *WhoAm 90*
Anderson, Herbert Henry 1918- *WhoSSW 91*
Anderson, Herbert Lawrence *BioIn 16*
Anderson, Herman 1944- *WhoSSW 91*
Anderson, Herschel Vincent 1932- *WhoAm 90*
Anderson, Howard 1913-1986 *BioIn 16*
Anderson, Howard Benjamin 1903- *WhoAmA 91N*
Anderson, Howard Palmer 1915- *WhoSSW 91*
Anderson, Hugh George 1932- *WhoAm 90*
Anderson, Hugh R. *WhoAm 90*
Anderson, Hurst Robins 1904-1989 *BioIn 16*
Anderson, Ian 1947- *BioIn 16, WorAlBi*
Anderson, Iris Anita 1930- *WhoAmW 91*
Anderson, Irma Louise 1941- *WhoWrEP 89*
Anderson, Irving Edward, Jr. 1946- *WhoEmL 91, WhoWor 91*
Anderson, Ivan Delos 1915- *WhoAm 90, WhoAmA 91*
Anderson, Ivan Verner, Jr. 1939- *WhoSSW 91*
Anderson, Ivie 1904-1949 *DrBlPA 90*
Anderson, Ivie 1905-1949 *OxCPMus*
Anderson, J. Denton 1908- *St&PR 91*
Anderson, J. Robert 1936- *St&PR 91*
Anderson, J. Thomas 1931- *St&PR 91*
Anderson, J. Trent 1939- *WhoWor 91*
Anderson, Jack 1922- *WorAlBi*
Anderson, Jack A. 1938- *St&PR 91*
Anderson, Jack G. 1922- *St&PR 91*
Anderson, Jack L. 1936- *St&PR 91*
Anderson, Jack Northman 1922- *WhoAm 90, WhoWrEP 89*
Anderson, Jack Oland 1921- *WhoAm 90*
Anderson, Jack Roy 1925- *WhoAm 90, WhoWor 91*
Anderson, Jack Warren 1935- *WhoWrEP 89*
Anderson, James *TwCCr&M 91*
Anderson, James Arthur 1935- *St&PR 91, WhoAm 90*
Anderson, James Brent 1950- *WhoE 91, WhoEmL 91, WhoWor 91*
Anderson, James Burton 1943- *WhoE 91*
Anderson, James C.H. 1931- *St&PR 91*
Anderson, James Carroll 1950- *WhoEmL 91*
Anderson, James Doig 1940- *WhoE 91*
Anderson, James Donald 1952- *WhoEmL 91*
Anderson, James E 1933- *WhoWrEP 89*
Anderson, James Everett 1943- *WhoE 91*
Anderson, James Francis, Jr. 1954- *WhoEmL 91*
Anderson, James Frederick 1927- *WhoAm 90*
Anderson, James George 1936- *WhoAm 90*
Anderson, James Gerard 1944- *WhoAm 90*
Anderson, James H. *St&PR 91*
Anderson, James Henry 1926- *WhoAm 90*
Anderson, James Keith 1924- *WhoAm 90*
Anderson, James Kenneth 1936- *St&PR 91*
Anderson, James L. 1933- *BioIn 16*
Anderson, James M. *BiDrAPA 89*
Anderson, James Michael 1948- *WhoSSW 91*
Anderson, James Milton 1941- *St&PR 91, WhoAm 90*
Anderson, James Mitchell 1937- *St&PR 91*
Anderson, James Noel 1951- *WhoEmL 91*
Anderson, James P. *BioIn 16*
Anderson, James P 1929- *WhoAmA 91*
Anderson, James Patrick *BiDrAPA 89*
Anderson, James R. 1953- *St&PR 91*
Anderson, James Richard 1941- *WhoAm 90*
Anderson, James S. 1940- *St&PR 91*
Anderson, James Taylor 1936- *IntWWM 90*
Anderson, James Thomas 1939- *St&PR 91, WhoAm 90*
Anderson, James William 1918- *St&PR 91*
Anderson, Jane C 1939- *BiDrAPA 89*
Anderson, Jane Louise Blair 1948- *WhoAmW 91, WhoE 91*
Anderson, Jane Virginia *BiDrAPA 89*
Anderson, Janelle Marie 1954- *WhoAmW 91*
Anderson, Janet Alm 1952- *WhoAmW 91, WhoEmL 91, WhoWor 91*
Anderson, Janet Isabelle 1950- *WhoE 91*
Anderson, Janet Kathleen 1950- *WhoAmW 91*
Anderson, Janet Stettbacher 1936- *WhoAmW 91*
Anderson, Janice Linn 1943- *WhoAmW 91, WhoSSW 91, WhoWor 91*
Anderson, Jean 1931- *AuBYP 90, ConAu 31NR*
Anderson, Jean Blanche 1940- *WhoWrEP 89*
Anderson, Jean Jensen 1932- *WhoAmW 91*
Anderson, Jean Lorraine 1945- *WhoAmW 91, WhoEmL 91*
Anderson, Jeanne S 1924- *BiDrAPA 89*
Anderson, Jeannie Ellen 1959- *WhoAmW 91*
Anderson, Jeffery Stuart 1949- *WhoE 91*
Anderson, Jennifer Kennedy *BiDrAPA 89*
Anderson, Jeremy H. 1935-1987 *BioIn 16*
Anderson, Jeremy Radcliffe 1921-1982 *WhoAmA 91N*
Anderson, Jerry Allen 1947- *WhoE 91, WhoWor 91*
Anderson, Jerry Lee 1941- *IntWWM 90*
Anderson, Jerry Maynard 1933- *WhoAm 90*
Anderson, Jerry William, Jr. 1926- *WhoWor 91*
Anderson, Jessica *FemiCLE*
Anderson, Jessica 1917- *WorAu 1980 [port]*
Anderson, Jim 1957- *Ballpl 90*
Anderson, Jo *BioIn 16*
Anderson, Joan Wellin Freed 1945- *WhoAmW 91*
Anderson, Joan Wester 1938- *WhoWrEP 89*
Anderson, Joann Morgan 1933- *WhoAmW 91*
Anderson, Joel A. *St&PR 91*
Anderson, John *WhoNeCM [port]*
Anderson, John 1873-1949 *Ballpl 90*
Anderson, John 1956?- *ConMus 5*
Anderson, John A. 1938- *St&PR 91*
Anderson, John Ansel 1903- *WhoAm 90*
Anderson, John Arthur 1924- *St&PR 91*
Anderson, John Bailey 1945- *WhoAm 90*
Anderson, John Bayard 1922- *WhoAm 90*
Anderson, John Bethune 1943- *WhoE 91*
Anderson, John C. 1958- *St&PR 91*
Anderson, John Calvin 1952- *WhoEmL 91, WhoWor 91*
Anderson, John Charles 1954- *WhoWrEP 89*
Anderson, John David 1926- *WhoAm 90*
Anderson, John David 1963- *WhoSSW 91*
Anderson, John David, Jr. 1937- *WhoAm 90*
Anderson, John Edward *BioIn 16*
Anderson, John Edward 1917- *WhoAm 90*
Anderson, John Edward 1927- *WhoAm 90*
Anderson, John Fergus Scott 1934- *WhoSSW 91*
Anderson, John Firth 1928- *WhoAm 90*
Anderson, John Freeman 1945- *WhoEmL 91*
Anderson, John Gaston 1922- *WhoAm 90*
Anderson, John Harvey, Jr. 1949- *WhoEmL 91*
Anderson, John Henderson 1929- *WhoSSW 91*
Anderson, John Kerby 1951- *WhoSSW 91, WhoWrEP 89*
Anderson, John L. 1927- *St&PR 91*
Anderson, John Lawrence 1953- *BiDrAPA 89*
Anderson, John Leonard 1945- *WhoAm 90*
Anderson, John Lonzo 1905- *AuBYP 90*
Anderson, John M. 1943- *St&PR 91*
Anderson, John MacKenzie 1938- *WhoAm 90, WhoWor 91*
Anderson, John Mueller 1914- *WhoAm 90*
Anderson, John Murray 1886-1954 *OxCCanT, OxCPMus*
Anderson, John Murray 1926- *WhoAm 90*
Anderson, John Richard 1931- *WhoAm 90*
Anderson, John Robert 1928- *WhoAm 90*
Anderson, John Robert 1936- *WhoAm 90*
Anderson, John Robert 1947- *WhoAm 90*
Anderson, John S 1928- *WhoAmA 91*
Anderson, John Thomas 1930- *WhoAm 90*
Anderson, John Weir 1928- *WhoAm 90*
Anderson, John Wesley 1941- *BiDrAPA 89*
Anderson, John Whiting 1934- *WhoAm 90*
Anderson, Jolene Slover *WhoAmW 91, WhoWor 91*
Anderson, Jon 1940- *WhoWrEP 89*
Anderson, Jon G. 1951- *St&PR 91*
Anderson, Jon Mac 1937- *WhoAm 90*
Anderson, Jon Stephen 1936- *WhoAm 90*
Anderson, Jon Tobin Kildruff 1942- *WhoE 91*
Anderson, Jon Wilson 1946- *WhoE 91*
Anderson, Jonpatrick Schuyler 1951- *WhoWor 91*
Anderson, Joseph Andrew, Jr. 1921- *WhoAm 90*
Anderson, Joseph Crook *BioIn 16, NewYTBS 90*
Anderson, Joseph Nelson 1948- *WhoEmL 91*
Anderson, Joseph Norman 1926- *WhoAm 90*
Anderson, Judith 1898- *BioIn 16, NotWoAT, WorAlBi*
Anderson, Judith Helena 1940- *WhoAm 90*
Anderson, Julie *BioIn 16*
Anderson, Julie Alm 1953- *WhoAmW 91, WhoE 91*
Anderson, Julie Kay 1961- *WhoEmL 91*
Anderson, Julius H *BiDrAPA 89*

Anderson, June BioIn 16, IntWWM 90, WhoAm 90, WhoAmW 91
Anderson, June 1950- PenDiMP
Anderson, Karen 1945- WhoAmW 91
Anderson, Karen L. 1948- WhoWrEP 89
Anderson, Karl Herbert 1929- St&PR 91
Anderson, Karl Richard 1917- WhoWor 91
Anderson, Katherine Doster 1932- WhoAmW 91
Anderson, Kathleen Gay 1950- WhoEmL 91
Anderson, Kathryn Boyd 1934- WhoAmW 91
Anderson, Kathryn Mae 1959- WhoEmL 91
Anderson, Keith 1917- WhoAm 90
Anderson, Keith E. 1936- St&PR 91
Anderson, Kenneth 1957- WhoSSW 91
Anderson, Kenneth Charles 1947- WhoEmL 91
Anderson, Kenneth Edmund 1950- WhoAmA 91
Anderson, Kenneth Eugene 1944- WhoWor 91
Anderson, Kenneth L 1939- WhoAmA 91
Anderson, Kenneth Norman 1921- WhoAm 90, WhoWor 91
Anderson, Kenneth Oscar 1917- WhoWor 91
Anderson, Kenneth Ward 1931- WhoSSW 91
Anderson, Kenny BioIn 16
Anderson, Kent Taylor 1953- WhoAm 90
Anderson, Kent Thomas 1942- St&PR 91
Anderson, Kent Victor 1935- St&PR 91
Anderson, Kerrii B. 1957- St&PR 91
Anderson, Kevin BioIn 16
Anderson, Kevin 1912- BioIn 16
Anderson, Kevin Roger 1957- WhoEmL 91
Anderson, Kim Cox 1958- WhoAmW 91
Anderson, Kimberly Muriel 1960- WhoEmL 91
Anderson, Kinsey A. 1926- WhoAm 90
Anderson, Kirk S. 1937- St&PR 91
Anderson, Kristian St&PR 91
Anderson, Kurt BioIn 16
Anderson, Kurt A. 1941- St&PR 91
Anderson, Kym 1950- WhoWor 91
Anderson, Larry ODwPR 91
Anderson, Larry Robert 1960- WhoSSW 91
Anderson, Laura Lorenz 1948- WhoAmW 91
Anderson, Laurence Alexis 1940- WhoAm 90
Anderson, Laurie 1947- BiDWomA, ConTFT 8, IntWWM 90, WhoAm 90, WhoAmA 91, WhoE 91
Anderson, LaVerne Eric 1922- WhoAm 90
Anderson, Lawrence Bernhart 1906- WhoAm 90
Anderson, Lawrence Keith 1935- WhoAm 90
Anderson, Lawrence Leslie, Jr. 1930- WhoAm 90
Anderson, Lawrence Richard 1942- WhoAm 90
Anderson, Lee Ann 1959- St&PR 91
Anderson, Lee Stratton 1925- WhoAm 90, WhoSSW 91
Anderson, LeMoyne W. 1923- WhoAm 90
Anderson, Lennart 1928- WhoAm 90, WhoAmA 91
Anderson, Leo E. 1902- WhoAm 90
Anderson, Leo R BiDrAPA 89
Anderson, Leonard Gustave 1919- WhoAm 90
Anderson, Leonard Mark 1963- IntWWM 90
Anderson, Leone Castell 1923- BioIn 16
Anderson, Leroy 1908-1975 OxCPMus
Anderson, Leslie Brian 1948- WhoE 91
Anderson, Leslie J. 1949- ODwPR 91
Anderson, Lewis Daniel 1930- WhoAm 90
Anderson, Linda Kay 1957- WhoEmL 91
Anderson, Linda Lea Penny 1943- WhoAmW 91
Anderson, Linda Lee 1957- WhoAmW 91
Anderson, Linda Marie 1949- WhoAmW 91
Anderson, Linda Sue 1948- WhoAmW 91
Anderson, Lindsay 1923- BioIn 16
Anderson, Lindsay Gordon 1923- WhoWor 91
Anderson, Lisa ODwPR 91
Anderson, Lisa Renee 1954- WhoAmW 91
Anderson, Lloyd L. 1933- St&PR 91
Anderson, Lloyd Lee 1933- WhoAm 90, WhoWor 91
Anderson, Lloyd Vincent 1943- WhoWor 91
Anderson, Logan B. St&PR 91
Anderson, Lois Ann 1937- WhoAmW 91
Anderson, Lois Ann 1952- WhoE 91
Anderson, Loni BioIn 16
Anderson, Loni 1946- WorAlBi
Anderson, Lorna 1962- IntWWM 90
Anderson, Lorraine Marie WhoAmW 91
Anderson, Louie BioIn 16
Anderson, Louis Wilmer, Jr. 1933- WhoAm 90
Anderson, Louise Eleanor 1934- WhoAmW 91
Anderson, Louise Goings 1930- WhoAmW 91
Anderson, Lowell Carlton 1937- St&PR 91, WhoAm 90
Anderson, Lucinda Kay 1941- WhoAmW 91, WhoSSW 91
Anderson, Lucy 1797-1878 PenDiMP
Anderson, Lucy Margarita 1940- WhoAmW 91
Anderson, Lyle Arthur 1931- WhoAm 90
Anderson, Lynn BioIn 16
Anderson, Lynn 1947- WhoAm 90
Anderson, M. Augusta ODwPR 91
Anderson, Maggie 1948- WhoWrEP 89
Anderson, Marcia BioIn 16
Anderson, Margaret 1886-1973 FemiCLE
Anderson, Margaret 1920- EncO&P 3
Anderson, Margaret L. 1920-1986 EncPaPR 91
Anderson, Margaret Lavinia 1941- WhoAmW 91
Anderson, Margaret Lynn 1950- WhoEmL 91
Anderson, Margaret M BiDrAPA 89
Anderson, Margaret Pomeroy 1943- WhoAmA 91
Anderson, Margaret Rose BiDrAPA 89
Anderson, Margaret Steel 1869-1921 LiHiK
Anderson, Marian 1902- BioAmW, BioIn 16, DcAfAmP, DrBIPA 90, IntWWM 90, OxCPMus, PenDiMP, WhoAm 90, WhoAmW 91, WorAlBi
Anderson, Marie Barbara 1934- WhoWrEP 89
Anderson, Marilyn June 1935- WhoAmW 91
Anderson, Marilyn Nelle 1942- WhoWor 91
Anderson, Marion Cornelius 1926- WhoAm 90
Anderson, Marjo Elizabeth 1954- WhoE 91
Anderson, Mark Reid 1951- WhoSSW 91
Anderson, Mark Robert 1948- WhoAmA 91
Anderson, Mark Robert 1951- WhoEmL 91
Anderson, Marna Kline 1945- WhoE 91
Anderson, Marquard John 1920- St&PR 91
Anderson, Marshall Lee 1918- St&PR 91
Anderson, Martha Alene 1945- WhoAmW 91
Anderson, Martha Gail 1951- WhoAmW 91
Anderson, Martha Jean 1946- WhoAmW 91
Anderson, Martin Carl 1936- WhoAm 90
Anderson, Martin H.F. 1949- St&PR 91
Anderson, Marty BioIn 16
Anderson, Mary 1859-1940 BioIn 16, LiHiK, NotWoAT
Anderson, Mary 1873-1964 BioAmW
Anderson, Mary 1929- BioIn 16
Anderson, Mary 1939- AuBYP 90
Anderson, Mary Jane 1930- WhoAmW 91, WhoWrEP 89
Anderson, Mary Jane 1935- WhoAm 90
Anderson, Mary Leigh 1956- WhoAmW 91
Anderson, Mary Lou 1949- WhoAmW 91
Anderson, Mary Rose Scanlan 1950- WhoWor 91
Anderson, Mary Virginia 1949- WhoEmL 91
Anderson, Maryann Jane 1935- WhoAmW 91
Anderson, Maud 1903- WhoAmW 91
Anderson, Mauritz Gunnar 1918- WhoE 91
Anderson, Max Elliot 1946- WhoEmL 91
Anderson, Maxine Karen BiDrAPA 89
Anderson, Maxwell 1888-1959 BioIn 16, OxCPMus, WorAlBi
Anderson, Maxwell L 1956- WhoAmA 91
Anderson, Megan Bothwell 1944- WhoAmW 91
Anderson, Mel 1928- WhoAm 90
Anderson, Mel 1952- St&PR 91
Anderson, Mel, Jr. 1932- ODwPR 91
Anderson, Melissa Eva 1959- WhoAmW 91
Anderson, Melvern 1929- St&PR 91
Anderson, Michael 1920- ConTFT 8
Anderson, Michael David 1958- St&PR 91
Anderson, Michael George 1951- WhoEmL 91
Anderson, Michael Harold BiDrAPA 89
Anderson, Michael James 1943- WhoWrEP 89
Anderson, Michael Joseph 1920- WhoAm 90
Anderson, Michael Kent 1956- WhoSSW 91
Anderson, Michael L. 1958- WhoAm 90, WhoEmL 91
Anderson, Michael Larsen 1941- WhoAmW 91
Anderson, Michael Robert 1953- WhoEmL 91, WhoWor 91
Anderson, Michael Steven 1954- WhoEmL 91
Anderson, Michael Thomas 1950- WhoE 91
Anderson, Michael William 1954- St&PR 91
Anderson, Michael William 1955- WhoEmL 91
Anderson, Michelle BioIn 16
Anderson, Mike 1951- Ballpl 90
Anderson, Milada Filko 1922- St&PR 91, WhoAmW 91
Anderson, Milton H. 1911- St&PR 91
Anderson, Milton H 1919- BiDrAPA 89
Anderson, Milton Henry 1919- WhoAm 90
Anderson, Milton Webster BiDrAPA 89
Anderson, Minton M. NewYTBS 90
Anderson, Mo Imozelle 1937- WhoAmW 91
Anderson, Moira 1938- OxCPMus
Anderson, Murphy 1926- EncACom
Anderson, Myrtle DrBIPA 90
Anderson, N. Christian, III 1950- WhoAm 90
Anderson, Nancy WhoAmW 91
Anderson, Nancy Katherine 1948- WhoEmL 91
Anderson, Neal BioIn 16
Anderson, Ned, Sr. 1943- WhoAm 90
Anderson, Neil AuBYP 90
Anderson, Neil 1945- WhoSSW 91
Anderson, Nils, Jr. 1914- WhoAm 90, WhoWor 91
Anderson, Nina Kaye 1953- WhoAmW 91
Anderson, Nina Louise BiDrAPA 89
Anderson, Norman Dean 1928- WhoSSW 91
Anderson, Norman J. 1931- St&PR 91
Anderson, Norman S BiDrAPA 89
Anderson, O. J. 1957- WorAlBi
Anderson, Odin Waldemar 1914- WhoAm 90
Anderson, Oliver Duncan 1940- WhoAm 90
Anderson, Oliver R. 1932- St&PR 91
Anderson, Ollie Ballpl 90
Anderson, Olof V. 1912- St&PR 91
Anderson, Ora Sterling 1931- WhoE 91
Anderson, Orley H. 1929- St&PR 91
Anderson, Orson Lamar 1924- WhoAm 90
Anderson, Orvil Roger 1937- WhoAm 90
Anderson, Owen Raymond 1919- WhoAm 90
Anderson, Pamela Jo 1951- WhoEmL 91
Anderson, Pamela Jo 1955- WhoAmW 91, WhoEmL 91
Anderson, Pamela Sue 1959- WhoEmL 91
Anderson, Patricia Alice 1952- WhoAmW 91
Anderson, Patricia Jean 1945- WhoEmL 91
Anderson, Patrick Lee 1959- WhoEmL 91
Anderson, Patrick Michael 1953- WhoEmL 91, WhoWor 91
Anderson, Paul BioIn 16
Anderson, Paul Dale 1944- WhoWrEP 89
Anderson, Paul Dean 1946- BiDrAPA 89
Anderson, Paul Edward 1921- WhoAm 90
Anderson, Paul F. 1938- St&PR 91
Anderson, Paul Gene 1943- WhoAm 90
Anderson, Paul Irving 1935- WhoAm 90
Anderson, Paul Julius BiDrAPA 89
Anderson, Paul Maurice 1926- WhoAm 90
Anderson, Paul Milton 1945- WhoAm 90
Anderson, Paul Nathaniel 1937- WhoWor 91
Anderson, Paul Nathaniel, III 1952- WhoEmL 91
Anderson, Paul Nathaniel, Jr. 1923- St&PR 91
Anderson, Paul S BiDrAPA 89
Anderson, Paula Jean 1948- WhoSSW 91
Anderson, Paula Lee 1953- WhoAmW 91
Anderson, Paulette D BiDrAPA 89
Anderson, Peer L. 1944- St&PR 91
Anderson, Peggy Perry AuBYP 90
Anderson, Peter Irving 1950- WhoE 91
Anderson, Peter Joseph 1951- WhoEmL 91
Anderson, Peter MacArthur 1937- WhoAm 90
Anderson, Phil BioIn 16
Anderson, Philip Alden 1948- WhoEmL 91
Anderson, Philip Bradly 1954- BiDrAPA 89
Anderson, Philip Sidney 1935- WhoAm 90
Anderson, Philip W. 1923- WorAlBi
Anderson, Philip Warren 1923- WhoAm 90, WhoE 91, WhoWor 91
Anderson, Phillip Doak 1923- St&PR 91
Anderson, Porter 1953- WhoEmL 91
Anderson, Poul 1926- Au&Arts 5 [port], AuBYP 90, MajTwCW, RGTwCSF
Anderson, Poul William 1926- WhoAm 90, WhoWrEP 89, WorAlBi
Anderson, Quentin 1912- WhoAm 90
Anderson, R. Duane 1942- St&PR 91
Anderson, R. Quintus 1930- St&PR 91, WhoAm 90, WhoE 91, WhoWor 91
Anderson, Rachael Keller 1938- WhoAm 90
Anderson, Ralph Alexander 1923-1990 BioIn 16
Anderson, Ralph Alexander, Jr. 1923- WhoAm 90
Anderson, Ralph F. 1914- St&PR 91
Anderson, Ralph Robert 1932- WhoAm 90
Anderson, Ralph Tobias 1956- St&PR 91
Anderson, Ranaka Kay 1960- WhoAmW 91
Anderson, Randall Keith 1952- WhoE 91, WhoWor 91
Anderson, Ray BioIn 16
Anderson, Raymond Hartwell, Jr. 1932- WhoWor 91
Anderson, Raymond T. 1932- St&PR 91
Anderson, Reg A. 1937- St&PR 91
Anderson, Regina 1901- EarBIAP
Anderson, Reid Bryce 1949- WhoAm 90
Anderson, Reuben V. 1942- WhoAm 90
Anderson, Rex Herbert 1920- WhoAm 90, WhoWor 91
Anderson, Richard A. WhoSSW 91
Anderson, Richard A. 1929- St&PR 91
Anderson, Richard Carl 1928- WhoAm 90
Anderson, Richard Carl 1932- St&PR 91
Anderson, Richard Clough 1788-1826 BioIn 16
Anderson, Richard Dean 1950- ConTFT 8 [port]
Anderson, Richard Dean 1953- WorAlBi
Anderson, Richard Edmund 1938- WhoAm 90
Anderson, Richard Ernest 1926- WhoWor 91
Anderson, Richard Gene 1930- St&PR 91
Anderson, Richard H 1921- BiDrAPA 89
Anderson, Richard H 1940- BiDrAPA 89
Anderson, Richard Harold 1950- BiDrAPA 89
Anderson, Richard J. 1927- St&PR 91
Anderson, Richard John 1943- St&PR 91
Anderson, Richard Kim 1956- WhoEmL 91
Anderson, Richard L. 1944- ODwPR 91
Anderson, Richard Loree 1915- WhoAm 90
Anderson, Richard Louis 1927- WhoAm 90
Anderson, Richard Marc 1949- WhoSSW 91
Anderson, Richard Norman 1926- WhoAm 90
Anderson, Richard O 1934- BiDrAPA 89
Anderson, Richard Powell 1934- WhoAm 90
Anderson, Richard R. 1941- St&PR 91
Anderson, Richard W 1919- BiDrAPA 89
Anderson, Richard William 1919- WhoAm 90
Anderson, Rick 1956- Ballpl 90
Anderson, Rick Gary 1941- WhoAm 90
Anderson, Robbie Jo 1952- WhoAmW 91
Anderson, Robbin Colyer 1914- WhoAm 90
Anderson, Robert BioIn 16
Anderson, Robert 1803-1896 DcCanB 12
Anderson, Robert 1917- ConAu 32NR
Anderson, Robert 1920- St&PR 91, WhoAm 90
Anderson, Robert 1948- WhoSSW 91
Anderson, Robert Alexander 1946- WhoAmA 91, WhoEmL 91
Anderson, Robert Andrew 1934- BiDrAPA 89
Anderson, Robert B. 1910- St&PR 91
Anderson, Robert B. 1910-1989 AnObit 1989
Anderson, Robert Banks, Jr. 1935- WhoSSW 91
Anderson, Robert Bennett 1924- St&PR 91
Anderson, Robert Bernard 1910-1989 BiDrUSE 89
Anderson, Robert Bernerd 1910-1989 BioIn 16
Anderson, Robert Bruce 1956- WhoEmL 91
Anderson, Robert Buehn 1926- WhoAm 90
Anderson, Robert C BiDrAPA 89
Anderson, Robert C 1930-1990 ConAu 130
Anderson, Robert D 1936- BiDrAPA 89
Anderson, Robert David 1927- IntWWM 90
Anderson, Robert Davis 1934- St&PR 91
Anderson, Robert Douglas 1939- WhoSSW 91
Anderson, Robert E. 1919- St&PR 91
Anderson, Robert E 1934- BiDrAPA 89
Anderson, Robert E., III 1934- St&PR 91
Anderson, Robert Edward BioIn 16
Anderson, Robert F. 1921- St&PR 91

Anderson, Robert Galen 1931- *WhoSSW 91*
Anderson, Robert Gene 1939- *St&PR 91*
Anderson, Robert Gregg 1928- *WhoAm 90*
Anderson, Robert Helms 1939- *WhoAm 90*
Anderson, Robert Henry 1918- *WhoAm 90*
Anderson, Robert K. 1935- *WhoAm 90*
Anderson, Robert Kenneth 1935- *St&PR 91*
Anderson, Robert Lanier, III 1936- *WhoAm 90*
Anderson, Robert Marshall 1933- *WhoAm 90*
Anderson, Robert Morris, Jr. 1939- *WhoAm 90*
Anderson, Robert Norton 1937- *St&PR 91*
Anderson, Robert O. 1917- *St&PR 91*
Anderson, Robert Orville 1917- *BioIn 16, WhoAm 90*
Anderson, Robert Raymond 1945- *WhoAmA 91*
Anderson, Robert Theodore 1934- *IntWWM 90, WhoAm 90*
Anderson, Robert Thomas *BiDrAPA 89*
Anderson, Robert W 1929- *BiDrAPA 89*
Anderson, Robert Woodruff 1917- *WhoAm 90*
Anderson, Roberta Joan *WhoAmW 91*
Anderson, Robin *BioIn 16*
Anderson, Robin Melody 1955- *WhoE 91*
Anderson, Rodger I 1943- *EncO&P 3*
Anderson, Roger E. 1921- *St&PR 91, WhoAm 90*
Anderson, Roger Ivan 1943- *EncPaPR 91*
Anderson, Rolph Ely 1936- *WhoAm 90*
Anderson, Ron *BioIn 16*
Anderson, Ron Joe 1946- *WhoAm 90, WhoSSW 91*
Anderson, Ronald A. 1946- *St&PR 91*
Anderson, Ronald C. 1942- *St&PR 91*
Anderson, Ronald Dale 1932- *St&PR 91*
Anderson, Ronald Dean *WhoAm 90*
Anderson, Ronald Delaine 1937- *WhoAm 90*
Anderson, Ronald Earl 1948- *WhoSSW 91*
Anderson, Ronald R. 1942- *St&PR 91*
Anderson, Ronni 1947- *WhoAmW 91*
Anderson, Rosalind Coogan 1937- *WhoAmW 91*
Anderson, Roscoe Odell Dale 1913- *WhoWor 91*
Anderson, Ross Barrett 1951- *WhoE 91, WhoWor 91*
Anderson, Ross Cornelius 1951- *WhoAmA 91*
Anderson, Roy *ODwPR 91*
Anderson, Roy, III 1957- *St&PR 91*
Anderson, Roy, Jr. 1929- *St&PR 91*
Anderson, Roy Arnold 1920- *St&PR 91, WhoAm 90*
Anderson, Roy Everett 1918- *WhoE 91*
Anderson, Roy H. 1938- *St&PR 91*
Anderson, Roy Kenneth 1952- *WhoSSW 91*
Anderson, Roy R. 1920- *St&PR 91*
Anderson, Roy Ryden 1920- *WhoAm 90*
Anderson, Roy W. *BioIn 16*
Anderson, Royal J. 1914- *WhoWor 91*
Anderson, Rudolph J., Jr. 1924- *WhoAm 90*
Anderson, Russell Karl, Jr. 1943- *WhoE 91*
Anderson, Ruth *NewAgMG*
Anderson, Ruth Irene 1919- *AuBYP 90*
Anderson, S. J. *BioIn 16*
Anderson, S. William, III 1938- *St&PR 91*
Anderson, Sally Claire Danos 1960- *WhoEmL 91*
Anderson, Sally J 1942- *WhoAmA 91*
Anderson, Samuel Armistead, III 1933- *WhoAm 90*
Anderson, Samuel T D 1922- *BiDrAPA 89*
Anderson, Sandra Lenore 1964- *WhoE 91*
Anderson, Sandra Wood 1949- *WhoAmW 91*
Anderson, Sarah Pia 1952- *WhoWor 91*
Anderson, Scott Charles 1951- *WhoEmL 91*
Anderson, Seawright W *BiDrAPA 89*
Anderson, Sharon 1950- *St&PR 91*
Anderson, Sharon Anne *WhoAmW 91*
Anderson, Sharon Denise 1953- *WhoAmW 91*
Anderson, Sharon Kay 1955- *WhoE 91*
Anderson, Sherry *ODwPR 91*
Anderson, Sherwood 1876-1941 *BioIn 16, MajTwCW, WorAlBi*
Anderson, Sidney Lamar 1947- *WhoEmL 91*
Anderson, Sophie 1823-1898? *BiDWomA*
Anderson, Sparky *BioIn 16*
Anderson, Sparky 1934- *Ballpl 90 [port], WhoAm 90*
Anderson, Stanford Owen 1934- *WhoAm 90*
Anderson, Stanley Warner 1920- *St&PR 91*
Anderson, Stanton Dean 1940- *WhoAm 90*
Anderson, Stefan S. 1934- *St&PR 91*
Anderson, Stefan Stolen 1934- *WhoAm 90*
Anderson, Stephen Donald 1958- *BiDrAPA 89*
Anderson, Stephen Francis 1950- *WhoEmL 91*
Anderson, Stephen Gerard 1966- *WhoE 91*
Anderson, Stephen Hale 1932- *WhoAm 90*
Anderson, Stephen N. 1939- *ODwPR 91*
Anderson, Stephen Peter 1951- *WhoEmL 91*
Anderson, Stephen Thomas *St&PR 91*
Anderson, Stephen Warde 1953- *MusmAFA*
Anderson, Steven Goodwin 1939- *WhoSSW 91*
Anderson, Steven Jay 1950- *WhoSSW 91*
Anderson, Stewart A *BiDrAPA 89*
Anderson, Stuart LeRoy 1912- *WhoAm 90*
Anderson, Suellen 1950- *WhoEmL 91*
Anderson, Susan *BioIn 16*
Anderson, Susan Holliday 1944- *WhoWor 91*
Anderson, Susan Lou 1947- *WhoAm 90*
Anderson, Susan M. *BioIn 16*
Anderson, Susan May 1950- *BiDrAPA 89*
Anderson, Susan Renita 1958- *WhoAmW 91*
Anderson, Susan Scruggs *BiDrAPA 89*
Anderson, Susan Stuebing 1951- *WhoAm 90*
Anderson, Swan F. 1879-1963 *WorAlBi*
Anderson, Sydney 1927- *WhoAm 90*
Anderson, Sylvia 1938- *IntWWM 90*
Anderson, T. J., Jr. 1928- *IntWWM 90*
Anderson, Tad Stephen 1955- *WhoEmL 91*
Anderson, Taura Linda Colleen 1951- *WhoAmW 91*
Anderson, Ted G. 1930- *St&PR 91*
Anderson, Terri Ann 1949- *WhoEmL 91*
Anderson, Terry *BioIn 16*
Anderson, Terry Lee 1947- *WhoE 91*
Anderson, Terry Lynn 1957- *WhoWrEP 89*
Anderson, Terry Marlene 1954- *WhoAmW 91*
Anderson, Thelma Deane 1920- *WhoWrEP 89*
Anderson, Theodore A *BiDrAPA 89*
Anderson, Theodore C. *BioIn 16*
Anderson, Theodore I 1931- *BiDrAPA 89*
Anderson, Theodore Wilbur 1918- *WhoAm 90*
Anderson, Theresa Lee 1963- *WhoAmW 91*
Anderson, Thomas 1906- *DrBIPA 90*
Anderson, Thomas Dunaway 1912- *WhoAm 90*
Anderson, Thomas Ernest 1945- *WhoEmL 91*
Anderson, Thomas Foxen 1911- *WhoAm 90*
Anderson, Thomas Harold 1924- *WhoAm 90*
Anderson, Thomas J. *St&PR 91*
Anderson, Thomas J. 1910- *WhoAm 90*
Anderson, Thomas J. 1945- *St&PR 91*
Anderson, Thomas Jefferson, Jr. 1928- *WhoAm 90*
Anderson, Thomas Kemp, Jr. 1926- *WhoAm 90*
Anderson, Thomas Norman 1949- *WhoSSW 91*
Anderson, Thomas Patrick 1934- *WhoAm 90*
Anderson, Thomas Peter 1948- *WhoEmL 91*
Anderson, Thomas R 1934- *BiDrAPA 89*
Anderson, Thomas Ralph 1938- *WhoAm 90*
Anderson, Thomas Robert 1954- *WhoEmL 91*
Anderson, Timothy Christopher 1950- *WhoAm 90*
Anderson, Tom Troy 1962- *WhoEmL 91*
Anderson, Tommy 1932- *St&PR 91*
Anderson, Tony 1947- *WhoE 91*
Anderson, Totton James 1909- *WhoAm 90*
Anderson, Tracey Allen 1957- *WhoEmL 91*
Anderson, Troy 1948- *BioIn 16, WhoAmA 91*
Anderson, Valborg 1911-1990 *BioIn 16*
Anderson, Valerie Lee 1955- *WhoE 91*
Anderson, Veda Leone 1932- *WhoAmW 91*
Anderson, Vernon Russell 1931- *WhoAm 90*
Anderson, Victor Elving 1921- *WhoAm 90*
Anderson, Victor O. 1913- *St&PR 91*
Anderson, W. Alden, Jr. 1929- *St&PR 91*
Anderson, W. French 1936- *BioIn 16*
Anderson, Wallace Ervin 1913- *WhoAm 90*
Anderson, Walter Dixon 1932- *WhoAm 90*
Anderson, Walter E 1923- *BiDrAPA 89*
Anderson, Walter Faust 1950- *BiDrAPA 89*
Anderson, Walter Herman 1944- *WhoAm 90, WhoE 91*
Anderson, Walter Lee 1950- *St&PR 91*
Anderson, Ward Lyman 1929- *St&PR 91*
Anderson, Warren DeWitt 1920- *IntWWM 90*
Anderson, Warren Harold 1925- *WhoAmA 91*
Anderson, Warren Lee, II 1952- *WhoEmL 91*
Anderson, Warren M. 1915- *BioIn 16*
Anderson, Warren M. 1921- *St&PR 91*
Anderson, Warren Mattice 1915- *WhoAm 90*
Anderson, Wayne *BioIn 16*
Anderson, Wendell William, Jr. 1925- *St&PR 91*
Anderson, Willam Craig 1946- *WhoEmL 91*
Anderson, William, Jr. 1939- *WhoAm 90*
Anderson, William Alan 1952- *WhoSSW 91*
Anderson, William Augustus 1942- *WhoWor 91*
Anderson, William Banks, Jr. 1931- *WhoAm 90*
Anderson, William Bert 1938- *WhoE 91*
Anderson, William Blair *BiDrAPA 89*
Anderson, William Brady, Jr. 1945- *WhoSSW 91*
Anderson, William Carl 1943- *WhoAm 90*
Anderson, William Carl 1958- *WhoEmL 91*
Anderson, William D. 1944- *St&PR 91*
Anderson, William Edward 1922- *WhoAm 90*
Anderson, William Edward 1943- *St&PR 91*
Anderson, William H., II 1937- *St&PR 91*
Anderson, William Harold 1919- *WhoWor 91*
Anderson, William Heartly 1930- *WhoAm 90*
Anderson, William Henry 1940- *BiDrAPA 89, WhoAm 90, WhoE 91, WhoWor 91*
Anderson, William Hopple 1926- *WhoAm 90*
Anderson, William R. 1939- *St&PR 91*
Anderson, William Robert 1921- *WhoAm 90*
Anderson, William Scovil 1927- *WhoAm 90*
Anderson, William Thomas 1936- *WhoAmA 91*
Anderson, William Wells *St&PR 91N*
Anderson, Winslow 1917- *WhoAmA 91*
Anderson, Wyatt Wheaton 1939- *WhoAm 90*
Anderson-Baer, Linda 1949- *IntWWM 90*
Anderson-Harper, Heidi Milia 1955- *WhoSSW 91*
Anderson Imbert, Enrique 1910- *BioIn 16, HispWr 90, WhoAm 90*
Anderson Olivo, Margaret Ellen 1941- *WhoAmW 91*
Anderson-Tidwell, Mary Ellen 1940- *WhoAmW 91*
Andersons, Edgars *ConAu 30NR*
Andersons, Maris 1937- *St&PR 91*
Anderssen, Laila 1941- *IntWWM 90*
Andersson, Albin Bertil 1928- *WhoWor 91*
Andersson, Alf Lennart 1935- *WhoWor 91*
Andersson, Allen Arvid 1944- *WhoAm 90*
Andersson, Arja Tellervo 1955- *WhoWor 91*
Andersson, Arthur *BioIn 16*
Andersson, Barbro Linnea 1933- *WhoAmW 91*
Andersson, Bibi 1935- *WhoWor 91, WorAlBi*
Andersson, Billie Venturatos 1947- *WhoAmW 91*
Andersson, Bo Ingvar 1929- *WhoWor 91*
Andersson, Claes 1937- *DcScanL*
Andersson, Craig Remington 1937- *WhoAm 90*
Andersson, Dan 1888-1920 *DcScanL*
Andersson, Hans Jan-Erik 1940- *WhoWor 91*
Andersson, Harriet 1932- *ConTFT 8*
Andersson, Jan Otto 1943- *WhoWor 91*
Andersson, Johanna Elizabeth 1941- *WhoWor 91*
Andersson, Leif Per Roland 1923- *WhoWor 91*
Andersson, Ola S. 1944- *St&PR 91*
Andersson, Rolf Gosta 1944- *WhoWor 91*
Andersson, Sten 1923- *WhoWor 91*
Andersson, Torbjorn SvenErik 1950- *WhoWor 91*
Andersson, W. Paul 1946- *WhoEmL 91*
Andert, Jeffrey Norman 1950- *WhoWor 91*
Andert, Nancy Ann 1963- *WhoEmL 91*
Anderton, Charles Harold 1957- *WhoEmL 91*
Anderton, Cindy *BioIn 16*
Anderton, James Franklin, IV 1943- *St&PR 91*
Anderton, Steve *BioIn 16*
Anderzhon, Mamie Louise 1906-1988 *BioIn 16*
Andes, Charles L. 1930- *St&PR 91*
Andes, Charles Lovett 1930- *WhoAm 90*
Andes, Joan Keenen 1930- *WhoAmW 91*
Andeweg, Johannes 1930- *BiDrAPA 89*
Andewelt, Roger B. *WhoAm 90*
Andia, Ernesto *BiDrAPA 89*
Andino, Julio 1919- *St&PR 91*
Andino, Tiburcio Carias *BioIn 16*
Andis, Matthew G. 1908- *St&PR 91*
Andlauer, Edgar L. 1923- *St&PR 91*
Andlauer, Edgar Louis 1923- *WhoAm 90*
Andlauer, Lynn Anne 1959- *WhoEmL 91*
Andler, Donald Andrew 1938- *WhoAm 90*
Ando, Albert K. 1929- *WhoAm 90*
Ando, Motoo 1934- *WhoWor 91*
Ando, Tadao 1941- *BioIn 16*
Ando, Takao 1934- *WhoWor 91*
Andolf, Ellika Margareta 1949- *WhoWor 91*
Andolsek, Charles Merrick 1947- *WhoAm 90*
Andolsek, Ludwig J. 1910- *WhoAm 90*
Andolsen, Alan Anthony 1943- *WhoE 91*
Andolshek, Richard Anders 1952- *WhoWor 91*
Andonian, Archie Arsavir Takfor 1950- *WhoEmL 91*
Andorfer, Donald Joseph 1937- *WhoAm 90*
Andorka, Frank Henry 1946- *WhoEmL 91*
Andorn, Anne Cramer 1947- *BiDrAPA 89*
Andrachuk, Brenda *BioIn 16*
Andrade, Mme. *EncO&P 3*
Andrade, Alfredo Rolando 1932- *WhoHisp 91*
Andrade, Augusto A. 1952- *WhoHisp 91*
Andrade, Bruno 1947- *WhoAmA 91*
Andrade, C. Roberto 1925- *St&PR 91, WhoHisp 91*
Andrade, Carlos Drummond de *BioIn 16, ConAu 132*
Andrade, Dorothy M. 1931- *St&PR 91*
Andrade, Edna *WhoAm 90*
Andrade, Edna 1917- *BioIn 16*
Andrade, Edna Wright 1917- *WhoAmA 91*
Andrade, James Clyde 1953- *WhoHisp 91*
Andrade, Jorge 1951- *St&PR 91, WhoHisp 91*
Andrade, Jorge Carrera *HispWr 90*
Andrade, Jose Eduardo 1942- *St&PR 91*
Andrade, Juan, Jr. 1947- *WhoHisp 91*
Andrade, Levine *PenDiMP*
Andrade, Luiz Carlos De Souza *ODwPR 91*
Andrade, Mario de 1893-1945 *BioIn 16*
Andrade, Mario de 1928-1990 *BioIn 16*
Andrade, Mary Juana 1943- *WhoHisp 91*
Andrade, Naleen N *BiDrAPA 89*
Andrade, Ronald Philip 1947- *WhoWor 91*
Andrade, Stephen Paul 1952- *WhoEmL 91*
Andrae, Theodore E., III 1933- *St&PR 91*
Andrakovich, Felix *BiDrAPA 89*
Andras, Kenneth Bertram 1909- *St&PR 91*
Andrasick, James Stephen 1944- *St&PR 91, WhoAm 90*
Andrasik, Stephen Samuel 1961- *WhoEmL 91*
Andrasovan, Tibor 1917- *IntWWM 90*
Andrassy, Timothy Francis 1948- *WhoAm 90*
Andre, Brother 1845-1937 *BioIn 16*
Andre Leo 1824-1900 *EncCoWW*
Andre the Giant *BioIn 16*
Andre, Alexis 1832-1893 *DcCanB 12*
Andre, Arlee *BioIn 16*
Andre, Calvin G. 1948- *St&PR 91*
Andre, Carl 1935- *BioIn 16, WhoAm 90, WhoAmA 91, WhoWor 91*
Andre, Franz 1893-1975 *PenDiMP*
Andre, Frederic N. 1933- *WhoAm 90*
Andre, Harvie 1940- *WhoAm 90, WhoE 91*
Andre, Herman William 1938- *St&PR 91*
Andre, John 1750-1780 *WorAlBi*
Andre, John 1751-1780 *EncCRAm*
Andre, Joseph 1908-1973 *BioIn 16*
Andre, Kenneth B., Jr. 1933- *St&PR 91*
Andre, Louis Joseph Nicolas 1838-1913 *BiDFrPL*
Andre, Marion 1920- *OxCCanT*
Andre, Maurice 1933- *PenDiMP*
Andre, Michael 1946- *ConAu 13AS [port], WhoWrEP 89*
Andre, Oscar Jules 1900- *WhoAm 90*
Andre, Paul Dean 1928- *WhoAm 90, WhoWrEP 89*
Andre, Pierre *BiDrAPA 89*
Andre, Rae 1946- *WhoE 91*
Andre, Richard A. 1950- *St&PR 91*
Andre De La Porte, Charles Arnout 1935- *WhoAm 90*
Andre de La Porte, Freerk 1961- *WhoWor 91*
Andrea del Castagno 1419?-1457? *IntDcAA 90*
Andrea del Sarto 1486-1530 *IntDcAA 90*
Andrea Del Sarto 1486-1531 *WorAlBi*
Andrea, Elma Williams *WhoAmW 91*
Andrea, Frank A.D., Jr. 1926- *St&PR 91*

Andrea, Frederick Wilhelm, III 1952- *WhoSSW 91*
Andrea, Mario Iacobucci 1917- *WhoE 91*
Andreach, Marianne 1958- *WhoE 91*
Andreae, Elisabeth Aloysia 1902- *EncCoWW*
Andreae, Illa *EncCoWW*
Andreae, Marc Edouard 1939- *IntWWM 90*
Andreae, Otto A. 1913- *St&PR 91*
Andreae, Volkmar 1879-1962 *PenDiMP*
Andreae, Wayne A. 1912- *St&PR 91*
Andreani, Jacques 1929- *WhoWor 91*
Andreano, Ralph Louis 1929- *WhoAm 90*
Andreanszky, Gabor Lipto Szentandrasi 1942- *WhoWor 91*
Andreas, Bruce Frederick 1925- *WhoAm 90*
Andreas, David Lowell 1949- *St&PR 91, WhoAm 90*
Andreas, Dwayne O. *BioIn 16*
Andreas, Dwayne O. 1918- *St&PR 91*
Andreas, Dwayne Orville 1918- *WhoAm 90, WhoWor 91*
Andreas, Glen Allen 1943- *St&PR 91*
Andreas, Glenn Allen, Jr. 1943- *WhoAm 90*
Andreas, Lowell W. 1922- *St&PR 91*
Andreas, Michael Dwayne 1948- *St&PR 91, WhoAm 90*
Andreas, Ray A. 1944- *St&PR 91*
Andreas-Salome, Lou 1861-1937 *BioIn 16, EncCoWW*
Andreasen, Charles Peter 1930- *WhoE 91*
Andreasen, George F. 1934-1989 *BioIn 16*
Andreasen, George Fredrick 1934- *WhoAm 90*
Andreasen, Nancy Coover *BiDrAPA 89, WhoAm 90, WhoAmW 91*
Andreasen, Stephanie Han 1964- *WhoEmL 91*
Andreason, George Edward 1932- *WhoSSW 91, WhoWor 91*
Andreason, John C. 1924- *St&PR 91*
Andreason, John Christian 1924- *WhoAm 90*
Andreassen, Karl *AuBYP 90*
Andreassen, Poul 1928- *St&PR 91*
Andreaus, Ronald E. 1941- *St&PR 91*
Andrecic, Marguerite Marie 1958- *WhoAmW 91*
Andreeff, Nickolas P. 1931- *St&PR 91*
Andreen, Per Johan Christoph 1952- *WhoWor 91*
Andreen-Salkin-Penn, Aviva Louise 1952- *WhoAmW 91*
Andreev, Nikolai Nikolaevich 1880-1970 *DcScB S2*
Andregg, Charles Harold 1917- *WhoSSW 91*
Andrei, Michael G. *ODwPR 91*
Andrei, Stefan 1931- *WhoWor 91*
Andreini, Isabella 1562-1604 *EncCoWW*
Andreis, Henry Jerome 1931- *St&PR 91*
Andreissen, David *ConAu 30NR*
Andrejevic, Milet 1925-1989 *BioIn 16, WhoAmA 91N*
Andrejewski, Pat *WhoAmW 91*
Andrejko, Dennis Andrew 1952- *WhoE 91*
Andrejkovics, Bernard 1920- *St&PR 91*
Andrejzchick, Marsha Lorene 1954- *WhoAmW 91*
Andren, Henry E A *BiDrAPA 89*
Andren, Tord 1936- *WhoWor 91*
Andreoff, Christopher Andon 1947- *WhoEmL 91, WhoWor 91*
Andreoli, Giorgio 1465?-1553? *PenDiDA 89*
Andreoli, Giovanni *PenDiDA 89*
Andreoli, Kathleen Gainor 1935- *WhoAm 90, WhoAmW 91*
Andreoli, Salimbene *PenDiDA 89*
Andreoli, Thomas Eugene 1935- *WhoAm 90*
Andreoli, Ubaldo *PenDiDA 89*
Andreoli, Vincenzo *PenDiDA 89*
Andreoni, Aurelio I.P. 1912- *St&PR 91*
Andreoni, Carlo *PenDiDA 89*
Andreoni, Giovanni *PenDiDA 89*
Andreopoulos, Spyros George 1929- *WhoWor 91*
Andreotti, Eugene R. 1924- *St&PR 91*
Andreotti, Giulio 1919- *WhoWor 91, WorAlBi*
Andreozzi, Louis Joseph 1959- *WhoEmL 91*
Andrepont, James A. 1946- *St&PR 91*
Andres, Alexander Francis 1942- *WhoWor 91*
Andres, Elena *EncCoWW*
Andres, F. William 1906- *St&PR 91*
Andres, Francis D 1935- *BiDrAPA 89*
Andres, Frederick William 1906- *WhoAm 90, WhoWor 91*
Andres, Glenn Merle 1941- *WhoAmA 91*
Andres, Marian Gail 1944- *WhoAmW 91*
Andres, Reubin 1923- *WhoAm 90*
Andres, Robert P. 1930- *St&PR 91*
Andres, Ronald Paul 1938- *WhoAm 90*
Andres, Stephen Michael 1945- *St&PR 91*
Andres, Valentino W, Jr. 1935- *BiDrAPA 89*
Andres, William A. 1926- *St&PR 91*
Andresakes, George J. 1913- *St&PR 91*
Andresen, Finn O. 1932- *St&PR 91*
Andresen, Jeffry J 1939- *BiDrAPA 89*
Andresen, John David 1936- *St&PR 91*
Andresen, Linda Skeen 1951- *WhoEmL 91*
Andresen, Malcolm 1917- *WhoE 91*
Andresen, Rolf S. 1935- *St&PR 91*
Andresen, Sven Erik 1938- *WhoWor 91*
Andresier, Rose 1942- *IntWWM 90*
Andreson, Charles Jeremiah 1947- *WhoE 91*
Andreson, Laura F 1902- *WhoAmA 91*
Andress, Carl O'Neil 1931- *WhoSSW 91*
Andress, Charlotte Frances 1910- *WhoAmW 91*
Andress, Hal Gregory 1948- *WhoEmL 91*
Andress, James Gillis 1939- *St&PR 91*
Andress, Lesley *TwCCr&M 91*
Andress, Peter 1931- *St&PR 91*
Andress, Samuel Coe 1906- *WhoAm 90*
Andress, Ursula *BioIn 16*
Andress, Ursula 1936- *WorAlBi*
Andress, Vern Randolph 1935- *WhoAm 90*
Andretti, Mario *BioIn 16*
Andretti, Mario 1940- *WhoAm 90, WhoWor 91, WorAlBi*
Andretti, Michael *BioIn 16*
Andreuzzi, Denis 1931- *St&PR 91, WhoAm 90*
Andrew, Prince 1960- *BioIn 16*
Andrew, Barbara Jean 1948- *WhoEmL 91*
Andrew, Catherine Blansfield 1954- *WhoAmW 91*
Andrew, Clyde M. 1909- *St&PR 91*
Andrew, David Neville 1934- *WhoAmA 91*
Andrew, Edward Raymond 1921- *WhoAm 90*
Andrew, Fred William 1927- *St&PR 91*
Andrew, Gordon G. 1950- *ODwPR 91*
Andrew, Gwen 1922- *WhoAm 90*
Andrew, Herbert Allen 1940- *St&PR 91*
Andrew, James Robert 1954- *St&PR 91*
Andrew, Jane Hayes 1947- *WhoAm 90, WhoAmW 91*
Andrew, John E. 1931- *St&PR 91*
Andrew, John Henry 1936- *WhoAm 90*
Andrew, Kenneth L. 1919- *WhoAm 90*
Andrew, Leo 1957- *ConTFT 8 [port]*
Andrew, Lloyd B. 1923- *St&PR 91*
Andrew, Lucius Archibald David, III 1938- *WhoAm 90*
Andrew, Ludmilla 1939- *IntWWM 90*
Andrew, Raymond Arthur 1936- *St&PR 91*
Andrew, Raymond Hall *BiDrAPA 89*
Andrew, Robert Jay 1943- *BiDrAPA 89*
Andrew, Robert Lynal 1944- *WhoAm 90*
Andrew, William Patrick 1947- *WhoE 91*
Andrewes, Christopher 1896-1988 *AnObit 1988, BioIn 16*
Andrewes, Richard Michael 1943- *IntWWM 90*
Andrews Sisters *OxCPMus*
Andrews Sisters, The *WorAlBi*
Andrews, A A *ConAu 31NR*
Andrews, Anthony 1948- *WhoAm 90*
Andrews, Archie Moulton 1919- *WhoAm 90*
Andrews, Audrey *St&PR 91*
Andrews, Audrey Elaine 1961- *WhoAmW 91*
Andrews, Benjamin Koo *BioIn 16*
Andrews, Benny 1930- *BioIn 16, WhoAmA 91*
Andrews, Bernard W. *WhoAm 90*
Andrews, Bernard W. 1941- *St&PR 91*
Andrews, Billy F. 1932- *WhoWrEP 89*
Andrews, Billy Franklin 1932- *WhoAm 90, WhoSSW 91, WhoWor 91*
Andrews, Bob Lee 1930- *St&PR 91*
Andrews, Bolivar Coleman 1937- *WhoAm 90*
Andrews, Brooke 1941- *WhoAmW 91*
Andrews, C. F. 1871-1940 *BioIn 16*
Andrews, Carolyn Fraser 1951- *WhoAmW 91*
Andrews, Cecelia *WhoAmW 91*
Andrews, Cecily Isabel Fairfield 1892-1983 *BioIn 16*
Andrews, Charleen Kohl 1925- *WhoAmA 91*
Andrews, Charles Freer 1871-1940 *BioIn 16*
Andrews, Charles Rolland 1930- *WhoAm 90*
Andrews, Chonta Teane 1962- *WhoAmW 91*
Andrews, Chris 1960- *St&PR 91*
Andrews, Clara Padilla *WhoHisp 91*
Andrews, Clarence Adelbert 1912- *WhoAm 90*
Andrews, Colin Mark 1956- *IntWWM 90*
Andrews, Collins Adams, III 1946- *WhoAm 90*
Andrews, Craig S. *ODwPR 91*
Andrews, Cushman Loring 1940- *St&PR 91*
Andrews, Dana 1909- *WorAlBi*
Andrews, David Frank, III 1951- *WhoEmL 91*
Andrews, David Henry 1933- *WhoAm 90*
Andrews, David Stanley 1947- *St&PR 91*
Andrews, Dayton Taylor 1927- *St&PR 91*
Andrews, Deborah Ellen *BiDrAPA 89*
Andrews, Donald L. 1946- *St&PR 91*
Andrews, Dwain C. 1929- *St&PR 91*
Andrews, E. Lee 1935- *St&PR 91*
Andrews, Edson James, Jr. 1940- *WhoSSW 91*
Andrews, Edwin Joseph 1941- *WhoAm 90*
Andrews, Eleanor Lattimore *AuBYP 90*
Andrews, Eliza 1840-1931 *FemiCLE*
Andrews, Elizabeth 1628?-1718 *BiDEWW*
Andrews, Elmer 1948- *ConAu 132*
Andrews, Elton V. *MajTwCW*
Andrews, Ernest Carroll 1926- *WhoSSW 91*
Andrews, Frank M. 1884-1943 *WorAlBi*
Andrews, Frank Meredith 1935- *WhoAm 90*
Andrews, Fred Charles 1924- *WhoAm 90*
Andrews, Frederick *BioIn 16*
Andrews, Frederick Franck 1938- *WhoAm 90*
Andrews, Frederick Newcomb 1914- *WhoAm 90*
Andrews, Gary Blaylock 1946- *WhoSSW 91*
Andrews, Gary Ritchie *BiDrAPA 89*
Andrews, George Amil 1939- *St&PR 91*
Andrews, George Eyre 1938- *WhoAm 90, WhoE 91*
Andrews, Gerald Bruce 1937- *St&PR 91*
Andrews, Glenn 1909- *WhoAm 90*
Andrews, Gloria Maxine 1927- *WhoAmW 91*
Andrews, Gordon Clark 1941- *St&PR 91, WhoAm 90*
Andrews, Harold J. 1928- *St&PR 91*
Andrews, Harold P. 1932- *St&PR 91*
Andrews, Harry 1911-1989 *AnObit 1989, BioIn 16*
Andrews, Harvey Wellington 1928- *WhoSSW 91*
Andrews, Heber J. 1935- *WhoWrEP 89*
Andrews, Henry Nathaniel, Jr. 1910- *WhoAm 90*
Andrews, Holdt 1946- *WhoEmL 91*
Andrews, Howard Frederick 1944-1988 *BioIn 16*
Andrews, Inez *DrBIPA 90*
Andrews, Israel DeWolf 1813-1871 *BioIn 16*
Andrews, Ivy 1907-1970 *Ballpl 90*
Andrews, J. David 1933- *WhoAm 90*
Andrews, J. Floyd *BioIn 16*
Andrews, Jack B. 1936- *St&PR 91*
Andrews, James Edgar 1928- *WhoAm 90*
Andrews, James J. 1942- *St&PR 91*
Andrews, James R. 1936- *ConAu 129*
Andrews, James Seldon 1959- *WhoSSW 91*
Andrews, James Sydney 1934- *AuBYP 90*
Andrews, James V., Jr. 1930- *WhoSSW 91*
Andrews, James Whitmore, Jr. 1950- *WhoEmL 91*
Andrews, Jan 1942- *BioIn 16*
Andrews, Jean 1923- *WhoAmW 91*
Andrews, Joel *NewAgMG*
Andrews, John *WhoWrEP 89*
Andrews, John Frank 1930- *WhoAm 90*
Andrews, John Frank 1942- *WhoAm 90, WhoWor 91*
Andrews, John Hamilton 1933- *WhoWor 91*
Andrews, John Hobart McLean 1926- *WhoAm 90*
Andrews, John Nolan 1928- *St&PR 91*
Andrews, John Stewart 1919- *WhoAm 90*
Andrews, Julie *AuBYP 90, BioIn 16*
Andrews, Julie 1935- *ConMus 4 [port], OxCPMus, WhoAm 90, WhoAmW 91, WhoWor 91, WorAlBi*
Andrews, Katherine Dane 1966- *WhoWor 91*
Andrews, Keith 1920-1989 *BioIn 16*
Andrews, Keith Hilton 1945- *WhoEmL 91*
Andrews, Kenneth Karlton 1953- *BiDrAPA 89*
Andrews, Kenneth Richmond 1916- *WhoAm 90*
Andrews, Kim 1939- *WhoAmA 91*
Andrews, Laverne 1915-1967 *OxCPMus, WorAlBi*
Andrews, Lavone D. 1912- *WhoAm 90*
Andrews, Lawrence *WhoAmA 91*
Andrews, Lee M. 1952- *St&PR 91*
Andrews, Lewis Marshall 1946- *WhoE 91*
Andrews, Lynn V. *ConAu 129, NewAgE 90*
Andrews, M. DeWayne 1944- *WhoSSW 91*
Andrews, Marcia Stephanie 1947- *WhoWrEP 89*
Andrews, Margery Mag 1932- *WhoAmW 91*
Andrews, Mari 1955- *WhoAmA 91*
Andrews, Mark 1926- *WhoAm 90*
Andrews, Mark E. 1950- *St&PR 91*
Andrews, Mark Edwin 1903- *WhoAm 90*
Andrews, Mary *EncO&P 3*
Andrews, Mary 1860-1936 *FemiCLE*
Andrews, Mary Anita 1931- *WhoWrEP 89*
Andrews, Mary Ann 1928- *WhoAmW 91*
Andrews, Mary Ella 1935- *WhoAmW 91*
Andrews, Mary Gibson Duffy 1949- *WhoAmW 91*
Andrews, Mary R. Shipman 1865?-1936 *LiHiK*
Andrews, Mason Cooke 1919- *WhoAm 90*
Andrews, Maxine 1918- *OxCPMus, WorAlBi*
Andrews, Maxine Ramseur *WhoSSW 91*
Andrews, Michael Allen 1944- *WhoAm 90, WhoSSW 91*
Andrews, Michael Curtis 1949- *WhoWor 91*
Andrews, Michael Duane 1944- *WhoWrEP 89*
Andrews, Michael Frank 1916- *WhoAmA 91*
Andrews, Michael J. 1947- *St&PR 91*
Andrews, Michael Paul 1948- *WhoE 91*
Andrews, Mike 1943- *Ballpl 90*
Andrews, N. L. 1823- *AmLegL*
Andrews, Nancy *BioIn 16*
Andrews, Nancy 1924-1989 *ConTFT 8*
Andrews, Nate 1913- *Ballpl 90*
Andrews, Oliver, Jr. 1917- *WhoAm 90*
Andrews, Patricia Amanda 1939- *WhoE 91*
Andrews, Patti 1920- *OxCPMus*
Andrews, Patty 1920- *WorAlBi*
Andrews, Peggy A. 1951- *St&PR 91*
Andrews, Peter Bruce 1937- *WhoE 91*
Andrews, R. Bruce 1940- *St&PR 91*
Andrews, Raymond 1934- *WhoWrEP 89*
Andrews, Raymond Douglas 1953- *WhoEmL 91*
Andrews, Regina M. 1901- *EarBlAP*
Andrews, Regina M. Anderson 1901- *HarlReB*
Andrews, Richard John 1954- *WhoEmL 91*
Andrews, Richard L. 1937- *WhoSSW 91*
Andrews, Richard L 1947- *BiDrAPA 89*
Andrews, Richard Lamar 1937- *St&PR 91*
Andrews, Richard Nigel Lyon 1944- *WhoAm 90*
Andrews, Richard Otis 1949- *WhoAm 90*
Andrews, Richard Vincent 1932- *WhoAm 90*
Andrews, Rob 1952- *Ballpl 90*
Andrews, Robert Frederick 1927- *WhoAm 90*
Andrews, Robert Parker 1923- *WhoSSW 91*
Andrews, Robert Ross 1947- *WhoEmL 91*
Andrews, Robert V. *ODwPR 91*
Andrews, Robin Michael 1942- *St&PR 91*
Andrews, Ronald Allen 1940- *WhoAm 90, WhoE 91*
Andrews, Rowena 1944- *ODwPR 91*
Andrews, Roy Chapman 1884-1960 *AuBYP 90, BioIn 16, WorAlBi*
Andrews, Sharyn Moore 1957- *St&PR 91*
Andrews, Sherman Giles 1930- *St&PR 91*
Andrews, Stafford Elmore 1928- *WhoSSW 91*
Andrews, Stephen *BioIn 16*
Andrews, Steven James 1940- *WhoSSW 91*
Andrews, Susan Beth 1948- *WhoEmL 91*
Andrews, Susan Dalton 1946- *WhoAmW 91*
Andrews, Susan Lynn 1962- *WhoAmW 91, WhoWor 91*
Andrews, Sybil 1898- *WhoAmA 91*
Andrews, Sylvia Joyce 1959- *WhoAmW 91*
Andrews, T. Coleman 1925-1989 *BioIn 16*
Andrews, Teddy *BioIn 16*
Andrews, Terri Dean 1963- *WhoAmW 91*
Andrews, Theodora Anne 1921- *WhoAmW 91*
Andrews, Thomas James 1954- *BiDrAPA 89*
Andrews, Thomas Michael 1951- *WhoSSW 91*
Andrews, Thomas P. 1928- *St&PR 91*
Andrews, Tina *DrBIPA 90*
Andrews, V. C. *BioIn 16*
Andrews, V C *MajTwCW*
Andrews, Victoria Leslie 1949- *WhoAmW 91*
Andrews, Virginia C. *BioIn 16*
Andrews, Willard Douglas 1926- *WhoAm 90, WhoWor 91*
Andrews, William *BioIn 16*
Andrews, William Cooke 1924- *WhoAm 90*
Andrews, William Dixson 1948- *WhoEmL 91*

Andrews, William Dorey 1931- WhoAm 90
Andrews, William E. 1943- St&PR 91
Andrews, William Eugene 1943- WhoAm 90
Andrews, William Frederick 1931- St&PR 91, WhoAm 90
Andrews, William George 1930- WhoAm 90
Andrews, William H. 1958- St&PR 91
Andrews, William Henry 1929- WhoSSW 91, WhoWor 91
Andrews, William Hinton, Jr. 1958- WhoSSW 91
Andrews, William Leake 1946- WhoAm 90
Andrews, William Pernell 1947- WhoE 91
Andrews, William T., Mrs. 1901- EarBlAP
Andrews, William Taylor 1924- WhoE 91
Andrews, Wolcott BioIn 16
Andrews-Wilkerson, Miron Ann 1942- WhoAmW 91
Andrews Zeichner, Robin Dawn 1962- WhoEmL 91
Andrewson, Dale E. 1947- St&PR 91
Andreychek, Timothy Sergius 1948- WhoEmL 91
Andreychuk, John Patrick 1950- St&PR 91
Andreyev, Leonid 1871-1919 WrPh
Andrezel, Pierre MajTwCW
Andrezel, Pierre 1885-1962 BioIn 16
Andrezeski, Anthony 1947- WhoE 91
Andri, Emmy K BiDrAPA 89
Andrial, Raul Hernan 1959- St&PR 91
Andriamahazo, Gilles 1919-1989 BioIn 16
Andrianarivo, Tantely Rene 1954- WhoWor 91
Andriani, Marino N. 1947- St&PR 91, WhoAm 90
Andrianne, Rene Eugene Joseph 1928- WhoWor 91
Andriate, Gary Anthony 1953- St&PR 91
Andric, Ivo 1892-1975 MajTwCW, WorAlBi
Andrica, John D. 1946- St&PR 91
Andrick, Annita Arlene 1949- WhoAmW 91
Andrie, Stanley John 1933- St&PR 91
Andries, Dorothy Delacoma 1937- WhoWrEP 89
Andries, Frans PenDiDA 89
Andries, Guido PenDiDA 89
Andries, Jasper PenDiDA 89
Andries, Joris PenDiDA 89
Andries, Lucas PenDiDA 89
Andriessen, Frans H. J. J. 1929- WhoWor 91
Andriessen, Jacobus Eije 1928- WhoWor 91
Andriessen, Jurriaan 1925- IntWWM 90
Andriessen, Louis 1939- IntWWM 90
Andrieu, Raymond Charles 1948- WhoWor 91
Andrieu, Rene Gabriel 1920- BiDFrPL
Andringa, Calvin Bruce 1941- WhoAm 90
Andringa, Hans Jan 1946- WhoSSW 91
Andriola, Alfred 1912-1983 EncACom
Andriola, Rocco F. 1958- WhoEmL 91
Andriole, Stephen John 1949- WhoAm 90
Andriolo, Mario, Jr. BioIn 16
Andriotakis, Tina Marie 1958- WhoEmL 91
Andrisani, Paul Joseph 1946- WhoEmL 91
Andrist, Ralph K. 1914- AuBYP 90
Andritsch, Marianne Feldman 1954- WhoEmL 91
Andriulli, Gerardo BiDrAPA 89
Andriulli, Robert 1948- WhoAmA 91
Andrix, George 1932- IntWWM 90
Andrle, Terese Eileen BiDrAPA 89
Androla, Ron 1954- WhoWrEP 89
Andronescu, Serban 1924- WhoE 91
Andronico, Bill James 1957- St&PR 91
Andronico, Demetra 1920- St&PR 91
Andronico, John F. 1922- St&PR 91
Andropov, Yuri BioIn 16
Andros, Edmund 1637-1714 EncCRAm, WhNaAH
Andros, Hazel LaVerne 1939- WhoAmW 91
Andros, Helen Mary WhoWor 91
Andros, Stephen John 1955- WhoEmL 91
Androsch, Hannes 1938- WhoWor 91
Androski, Michael Alan 1949- WhoEmL 91
Androutsellis-Theotokis, Paul 1939- WhoWor 91
Androvar ConAu 131, HispWr 90
Andrulonis, Paul Anthony 1946- BiDrAPA 89
Andrus, Cecil D 1931- BiDrUSE 89
Andrus, Cecil Dale 1931- WhoAm 90, WhoWor 91
Andrus, David Clifford 1953- WhoEmL 91
Andrus, Gerald L. 1904- St&PR 91
Andrus, Gerald Louis 1904- WhoAm 90
Andrus, James Francis 1953- WhoEmL 91
Andrus, James Roman 1907- WhoAmA 91
Andrus, John C 1953- BiDrAPA 89
Andrus, John Stebbins 1927- WhoE 91
Andrus, Leonard C. 1933- St&PR 91
Andrus, Lloyd Loyl 1945- St&PR 91
Andrus, Miriam Jay Wurts 1909- WhoWor 91
Andrus, Peter F 1943- BiDrAPA 89
Andrus, Peter Frederick 1943- WhoE 91
Andrus, Reed S BiDrAPA 89
Andrus, Thomas R., Jr. 1951- WhoSSW 91
Andrus, Wayne Burton 1935- BiDrAPA 89
Andruskevich, Thomas Anthony 1951- St&PR 91, WhoAm 90, WhoE 91
Andruszka, Walter A. 1923- St&PR 91
Andruzzi, Ellen Adamson 1917- WhoAmW 91
Andry, Keith Anthony 1960- WhoAmA 91
Andrzejak-Andre, Marilyn Kathleen 1960- WhoEmL 91, WhoSSW 91
Andrzejewski, Julie 1945- ConAu 129
Andrzejewski, Margaret Rusek 1953- WhoWrEP 89
Andrzejewski, Robert Joseph 1953- WhoE 91
Andujar, Joaquin 1952- Ballpl 90, WhoHisp 91
Andujar, Manuel Jose 1943- WhoWor 91
Andujar, Rafael 1946- WhoEmL 91
Anekstein, Carol Beth 1955- BiDrAPA 89
Anenias, Sancho C 1932- BiDrAPA 89
Anerousis, John Peter 1949- WhoEmL 91
Aneson, Sophie Diane BiDrAPA 89
Anestos, Harry Peter 1917- WhoE 91
Anewalt, Thomas C. 1953- WhoEmL 91
Aney, John Franken 1961- BiDrAPA 89
Aneziris, Charilaos N 1961- WhoE 91
Anfindsen, Cyrus Peter 1934- St&PR 91
Anfinsen, Christian B. 1916- WorAlBi
Anfinsen, Christian Boehmer 1916- WhoAm 90, WhoE 91, WhoWor 91
Anfinson, A.A. 1923- St&PR 91
Anfinson, Thomas Elmer 1941- WhoAm 90
Anfinson, Verna A. 1929- St&PR 91
Anfousse, Ginette 1944- BioIn 16
Ang, Alfredo Hua-Sing 1930- WhoAm 90
Ang, B.C. St&PR 91
Ang, Jessy E A BiDrAPA 89
Ang, Ke Bing Cua 1950- WhoWor 91
Ang, Lolita O 1946- BiDrAPA 89
Ang, Luis C BiDrAPA 89
Anga WomWR
Angalet, Gwendoline Bain 1947- WhoAmW 91
Angara, Prasad BiDrAPA 89
Angarita, Isaias Medina 1897-1953 BioIn 16
Angarola, Robert Thomas 1945- WhoAm 90
Angas, Richard IntWWM 90
Ange, Constance E BiDrAPA 89
Angebranndt, Betsy Jo White 1931- IntWWM 90
Angel, Albert David 1937- St&PR 91
Angel, Allen Robert 1942- WhoE 91
Angel, Arthur Ronald 1948- WhoAm 90
Angel, Aubie 1935- WhoAm 90
Angel, Benjamin J. 1936- St&PR 91
Angel, Dennis 1947- WhoEmL 91
Angel, Frank BioIn 16
Angel, Frank, Jr. 1914- WhoHisp 91
Angel, Frank Philip 1953- WhoEmL 91
Angel, Grover LaMarr 1909- WhoAm 90
Angel, Heather 1941- BioIn 16
Angel, J. Lawrence 1915-1986 BioIn 16
Angel, J. Steven 1949- St&PR 91
Angel, Jack E. 1938- St&PR 91
Angel, Jack Easton 1938- WhoWor 91
Angel, James Burrill 1829-1916 WorAlBi
Angel, James Roger Prior 1941- WhoAm 90
Angel, James Terrance 1945- WhoAm 90
Angel, Joe WhoHisp 91
Angel, John 1881-1960 WhoAmA 91N
Angel, John Lawrence 1915-1986 BioIn 16
Angel, Leonard 1945- OxCCanT
Angel, Marie 1923- BioIn 16
Angel, Mary Margaret 1949- WhoSSW 91
Angel, Michelle Robin 1963- WhoAmW 91
Angel, Milton Israel 1921- St&PR 91
Angel, Ralph Michael 1951- WhoWrEP 89
Angel, Rodney Alan 1947- WhoSSW 91
Angel, Steven Michael 1950- WhoEmL 91, WhoWor 91
Angel-Shaffer, Arlene Beth 1951- WhoEmL 91
Angela da Foligno 1248?-1309 EncCoWW
Angela Merici, Saint 1474-1540 WorAlBi
Angelake-Rooke, Katerina EncCoWW
Angelaki-Rooke, Katerina EncCoWW
Angelakos, Diogenes James 1919- WhoAm 90
Angelakos, Evangelos Theodorou 1929- WhoAm 90, WhoE 91
Angelastro, Jane Ellen 1942- WhoAmW 91
Angele, Alfred Robert 1940- WhoWor 91
Angeles, Victoria de Los PenDiMP
Angeli, Gerry 1946- St&PR 91
Angelica, Mother 1923- BioIn 16
Angelicchio, David John 1951- St&PR 91
Angelicchio, Domenic Louis 1944- St&PR 91
Angelich, Anton P. R. 1950- WhoEmL 91
Angelich, Mark S. St&PR 91
Angelich, Samuel Michael 1924- St&PR 91
Angelici, Robert J. 1937- WhoAm 90
Angelico, Fra 1400?-1455 IntDcAA 90, WorAlBi
Angelico, Halma 1880-1952 EncCoWW
Angelilli, Frank George 1948- St&PR 91
Angelillo, Lori Ann 1963- WhoAmW 91
Angelin, Bo Anders 1949- WhoWor 91
Angelini, Carl A. 1935- St&PR 91
Angelini, Daniel Joseph 1956- WhoE 91
Angelini, John Michael 1921- WhoAmA 91
Angelini, Louis Anthony 1935- IntWWM 90
Angelini, Sherry Laraine 1945- WhoAmW 91
Angelini, Valerio Brigante Colonna BioIn 16
Angell, Betty Ruth Johnson 1943- WhoAmW 91
Angell, Charles T. 1941- St&PR 91
Angell, J. Steven 1949- St&PR 91
Angell, James Browne 1924- WhoAm 90
Angell, James Burrill 1829-1916 BioIn 16
Angell, James Rowland 1869-1949 BioIn 16
Angell, John William 1920- WhoSSW 91
Angell, Joseph, III 1816?-1891? PenDiDA 89
Angell, Judie 1937- BioIn 16
Angell, Karol 1950- WhoAmW 91
Angell, Lynn Elizabeth 1960- WhoEmL 91
Angell, Norman Rockefeller 1944- St&PR 91
Angell, Norman Thomas 1874-1967 WorAlBi
Angell, Richard Bradshaw 1918- WhoAm 90
Angell, Richard Henry BiDrAPA 89
Angell, Roger 1920- WhoAm 90, WhoWrEP 89
Angell, Roger 1921- Ballpl 90
Angell, Rosalind J. ODwPR 91
Angell, Tony 1940- WhoAmA 91
Angell, Valentine Chauncey 1941- WhoWrEP 89
Angell, Walter F 1941- BiDrAPA 89
Angell, Wayne D. 1939- WhoAm 90, WhoWor 91
Angelle, Paul J. 1937- St&PR 91
Angelo, Alfred Anthony 1935- WhoE 91
Angelo, Charles A BiDrAPA 89
Angelo, Domenick Michael 1925-1976 WhoAmA 91N
Angelo, E Joanne BiDrAPA 89
Angelo, Emidio 1903- WhoAmA 91
Angelo, Gayle-Jean 1951- WhoWor 91
Angelo, John Patrick 1957- WhoEmL 91
Angelo, Margaret Ida 1960- WhoAmW 91, WhoE 91
Angelo, Peter Gregory 1947- WhoE 91
Angelo, Richard John 1940- St&PR 91
Angelo, Ronald John 1952- WhoEmL 91
Angelo, Sandra Ann 1952- WhoEmL 91
Angelo, Valenti 1897- AuBYP 90
Angeloch, Robert 1922- WhoAmA 91
Angeloch, Robert Henry 1922- WhoE 91
Angeloff, Dann V. 1935- St&PR 91, WhoAm 90, WhoWor 91
Angelone, A.C. 1939- St&PR 91
Angelone, Catherine 1946- WhoAmW 91
Angeloni, Gianni Antonio 1947- WhoWor 91
Angelopoulos, Angelos George 1952- WhoWor 91
Angelopoulos, Thodoros 1935- BioIn 16
Angelos, Peter BioIn 16
Angelou, Maya BioIn 16
Angelou, Maya 1928- ConLC 64 [port], DrBlPA 90, FemiCLE, MajTwCW, NotWoAT, WhoAm 90, WhoWrEP 89
Angelozzi, Nicholas J. 1942- St&PR 91
Angenieux, Bernard Edouard 1937- WhoWor 91
Anger, Allan Wolcott 1931- WhoE 91
Anger, Darol NewAgMG
Anger, Jane BiDEWW, BioIn 16, FemiCLE
Anger, Kenneth 1930- EncO&P 3
Anger, Kenneth 1932- WhoWrEP 89
Anger, Roland Andre 1929- WhoWor 91
Angerdal, Lars Goran 1937- IntWWM 90
Angerer, Paul 1927- IntWWM 90
Angermair, Christoph 1580?-1633 PenDiDA 89
Angermueller, Hans H. 1924- WhoAm 90, WhoE 91, WhoWor 91
Angermuller, Rudolph Kurt 1940- IntWWM 90
Angert, Ashley Joel 1942- BiDrAPA 89
Angevine, Eric Neil 1949- WhoSSW 91
Angevine, George Braud 1918- WhoAm 90
Angevine, Richard ODwPR 91
Anghaie, Samim 1949- WhoAm 90
Anghelaki-Rooke, Katerina 1939- EncCoWW
Anghinetti, Joseph Richard 1936- St&PR 91
Angier, Bradford AuBYP 90
Angino, Ernest Edward 1932- WhoAm 90
Angioli, Renata Maria 1962- WhoEmL 91
Angiolillo, Amedeo 1949- WhoE 91
Angione, Howard Francis 1940- WhoAm 90
Angiuoli, Ralph 1936- St&PR 91, WhoAm 90
Anglada, Maria Angels 1930- EncCoWW
Angle, Edward H. 1855-1930 WorAlBi
Angle, John Charles 1923- St&PR 91, WhoAm 90, WhoE 91
Angle, John Edwin 1931- WhoAm 90
Angle, Richard W. 1941- St&PR 91
Angle, Roger R. 1938- WhoWrEP 89
Anglemire, Kenneth Norton WhoAm 90
Anglemyer, Grant M. 1946- St&PR 91
Anglesey, Zoe R. 1941- WhoWrEP 89
Anglewicz, David James 1947- St&PR 91
Anglieri EncO&P 3
Angliker, Colin C J 1937- BiDrAPA 89
Anglin, Betty Lockhart 1937- WhoAmA 91
Anglin, Larry Michael 1947- WhoEmL 91
Anglin, Linda McCluney 1929- WhoSSW 91
Anglin, Margaret 1876-1958 BioIn 16, NotWoAT, OxCCanT
Anglin, Michael Williams 1946- WhoEmL 91
Anglin, Richard D. 1933- St&PR 91
Anglin, Richard Lee, Jr. 1945- WhoEmL 91
Anglin, Richard R. 1938- St&PR 91
Anglin, Timothy Warren 1822-1896 DcCanB 12
Anglund, Joan Walsh 1926- AuBYP 90
Angoff, Allan 1910- EncO&P 3, EncPaPR 91
Angoff, Marion Brenda 1939- WhoWrEP 89
Angoli, Nancy Elderkin 1949- WhoAmW 91
Angotti, Antonio Mario 1958- WhoEmL 91
Angotti, Arthur A. 1944- St&PR 91
Angotti, Catherine Marie 1946- WhoEmL 91
Angotti, Rocky 1958- WhoSSW 91
Angres, Daniel Herbert BiDrAPA 89
Angres, Erwin BiDrAPA 89
Angrisani, Frank 1950- St&PR 91
Angst, Carl L. 1921- WhoAm 90
Angst, Jules 1926- BiDrAPA 89
Angstadt, Debra Jordan 1960- WhoAmW 91
Angstadt, Diane 1959- BiDrAPA 89
Angstadt, L Jean 1931- EncO&P 3
Angster, John David 1952- St&PR 91
Angstman, Clifford W. 1952- St&PR 91
Angstrom, Anders Jonas 1814-1874 WorAlBi
Angstrom, Wayne Raymond 1939- WhoAm 90, WhoWor 91
Anguiano, Lupe 1929- WhoAmW 91, WhoHisp 91
Anguiano, Raul 1915- WhoAmA 91, WhoWor 91
Anguiano Valdez, Raul 1915- BioIn 16
Anguisciola, Sofonisba 1527?-1625 BioIn 16
Anguizola, Gustavo Antonio 1928- WhoAm 90, WhoWor 91
Angulo, Chappie 1928- WhoAmA 91
Angulo, Charles Bonin 1943- WhoE 91, WhoWor 91
Angulo, Gerard Antonio 1956- WhoAm 90, WhoEmL 91
Angulo, Lawrence George 1948- WhoEmL 91
Angulo, Manuel R. 1917- St&PR 91
Angulo, Manuel Rafael 1917- WhoAm 90
Angulo, Ramiro 1938- WhoHisp 91
Angulo, Vivian B BiDrAPA 89
Angulo Iniguez, Diego 1901-1986 BioIn 16
Angus, Bruce 1906- St&PR 91
Angus, Catherine LaVerne 1950- WhoAmW 91
Angus, Fay 1929- ConAu 33NR
Angus, John Cotton 1934- WhoAm 90
Angus, Leslie R 1904- BiDrAPA 89
Angus, Marlene Ann 1947- WhoAmW 91
Angus, William Arthur, III 1946- St&PR 91
Angus, William Arthur, Jr. 1923- WhoE 91
Angwin, Maria Louisa 1849-1898 DcCanB 12
Anhalt, Herbert S BiDrAPA 89
Anhalt, Istvan 1919- IntWWM 90
Anhava, Tuomas 1927- DcScanL
Anielewicz, Mordecai 1919-1943 BioIn 16
Aniello, Carol M. 1944- St&PR 91
Anievas, Agustin 1934- IntWWM 90, PenDiMP
Anikeeff, Anthony Hotchkiss 1952- WhoEmL 91

Aniline, Orm *BiDrAPA 89*
Animals, The *EncPR&S 89*
Aniolek, David Francis 1961- *WhoE 91*
Anis, Syed Qaiser 1949- *WhoWor 91*
Anise-Levine, Zahra Musa 1947- *WhoEmL 91*
Aniskovich, Paul Peter, Jr. 1936- *St&PR 91, WhoAm 90*
Anisman, Martin Jay 1942- *WhoAm 90*
Anisoglu, Rahsan 1920- *BiDrAPA 89*
Anixter, Alan B. 1920- *WhoAm 90*
Anixter, James R. 1944- *WhoAm 90*
Anixter, William L *BiDrAPA 89*
Anjard, Ronald Paul, Sr 1935- *WhoAm 90*
Anka, Paul 1941- *EncPR&S 89, OxCPMus, WhoAm 90, WorAlBi*
Anka, Phyllis Catherine 1933- *WhoAmW 91*
Ankele, Felix 1916- *WhoSSW 91*
Ankenbrandt, Helen *BiDrAPA 89*
Ankeny, DeWalt Hosmer, Jr. 1932- *WhoAm 90*
Anker, Jack *St&PR 91*
Anker, Jeffrey *BiDrAPA 89*
Anker, Nini Roll 1873-1942 *EncCoWW*
Anker, Peter L. 1935- *St&PR 91*
Anker, Peter Louis 1935- *WhoAm 90, WhoE 91*
Anker, Robert Alvin 1941- *WhoAm 90*
Anker, Suzanne C 1946- *WhoAmA 91*
Ankerman, William Lewis 1947- *WhoEmL 91*
Ankrum, Joan *WhoAmA 91*
Ankrum, L. Doyle 1928- *St&PR 91*
Ankrum, William Dean 1930- *St&PR 91*
Ankum, Johan Albert 1930- *WhoWor 91*
Anlyan, William George 1925- *WhoAm 90*
Anmar, Frank *TwCCr&M 91*
Ann-Margret 1941- *BioIn 16, WhoAm 90, WorAlBi*
Anna 1693-1740 *WomWR*
Anna Amalia, Duchess of Saxe-Weimar 1739-1807 *BioIn 16*
Anna Amalie, Princess of Prussia 1723-1787 *BioIn 16*
Anna Anachoutlou *WomWR*
Anna Dalassena *WomWR*
Anna Ivanovna, Empress of Russia 1693-1740 *BioIn 16*
Anna Leopoldovna 1718-1746 *WomWR*
Anna Livia 1955- *FemiCLE*
Anna of Savoy *WomWR*
Anna Palaeologina *WomWR*
Anna Palaeologina-Cantacuzena *WomWR*
Anna, Karl Edward 1932- *St&PR 91*
Annable, Weldon Grant 1937- *WhoAm 90, WhoE 91*
Annalett, Diane Smith *BiDrAPA 89*
Annan, Douglas Bruce 1917- *WhoAm 90*
Annan, Noel Gilroy 1916- *BioIn 16*
Annand, James Earle 1929- *WhoAm 90*
Annaud, Jean-Jacques 1943- *WhoWor 91*
Annawan *WhNaAH*
Anne *WhNaAH*
Anne 1477-1514 *WomWR*
Anne 1665-1714 *WomWR [port]*
Anne Boleyn, Queen 1507-1536 *BioIn 16*
Anne d'Autriche 1601-1666 *WomWR*
Anne de Beaujeu *EncCoWW*
Anne de France 1461-1522 *EncCoWW*
Anne, Empress of Russia 1693-1740 *BioIn 16*
Anne Marie Louise d'Orleans *WomWR*
Anne of Austria 1601-1666 *WomWR*
Anne of Denmark, Queen 1574-1619 *BiDEWW*
Anne of England *WomWR*
Anne of France 1461-1522 *WomWR*
Anne, Princess 1950- *BioIn 16, WhoWor 91*
Anne, Queen of England 1665-1714 *BiDEWW*
Anne, Queen of Great Britain 1665-1714 *BioIn 16*
Anne, Clair *WhoWrEP 89*
Annear, Gwynneth 1939- *IntWWM 90*
Annear, Laurence I. 1949- *St&PR 91*
Annee, Paul A. *WhoAm 90*
Anneken, William B. 1933- *WhoAm 90*
Anneken, William Bernard 1933- *St&PR 91*
Annenberg, Barnet 1931- *St&PR 91*
Annenberg, Sophia Morris 1910- *St&PR 91*
Annenberg, Ted M. 1927- *St&PR 91*
Annenberg, Ted Max 1927- *WhoAm 90*
Annenberg, Walter H. 1908- *BioIn 16, WhoAm 90*
Annes, Shari *ODwPR 91*
Annese, Betsy J. *ODwPR 91*
Annese, Domenico 1919- *WhoAm 90*
Annesley, Thomas Michael 1953- *WhoEmL 91*
Annesley, William H., Jr. 1925- *WhoAm 90*
Annessi, Jane *BioIn 16*
Annessi, Jean Ludeman 1958- *WhoAmW 91*
Annestrand, Stig Alvar 1933- *WhoAm 90, WhoWor 91*
Annett, Bruce James, Jr. 1952- *WhoWrEP 89*
Annett, Cora *AuBYP 90*
Annetta, Catherine 1951- *WhoAmW 91*
Annetti, Robert J. 1936- *St&PR 91*
Annexy Rexach, Rafael Julio 1942- *WhoSSW 91*
Annibali, Domenico 1705?-1779? *PenDiMP*
Annibali, Joseph Andrew *BiDrAPA 89*
Annigoni, Pietro 1910-1988 *AnObit 1988, BioIn 16*
Anning, Mary 1799-1847 *BioIn 16*
Annis, Francesca 1944- *ConTFT 8*
Annis, Helen M 1935- *BiDrAPA 89*
Annis, Martin 1922- *St&PR 91*
Annis, Norman L 1931- *WhoAmA 91*
Annis, Robert Lyndon 1949- *IntWWM 90, WhoEmL 91*
Annitto, William J *BiDrAPA 89*
Annius de Viterbo 1432-1502 *EncO&P 3*
Annixter, Jane *AuBYP 90*
Annixter, Paul *AuBYP 90*
Anno, James Nelson 1934- *WhoAm 90, WhoWor 91*
Annot 1894-1981 *BiDWomA*
Anns, Arlene Eiserman *WhoAmW 91*
Anns, Philip Harold 1925- *St&PR 91, WhoAm 90*
Annunziata, Frank 1942- *WhoE 91*
Annunziata, Kimberly J. 1955- *WhoAmW 91*
Annunziata, Michael S 1941- *BiDrAPA 89*
Annunziata, Patrick *BioIn 16*
Annunziato, Vincent Robert 1965- *WhoEmL 91*
Annunzio, Frank 1915- *WhoAm 90*
Annus, John Augustus 1935- *WhoAm 90, WhoAmA 91*
Ano, Nelita R *BiDrAPA 89*
Anodea Judith *NewAgE 90*
Anokye, Akua Duku 1948- *WhoAmW 91*
Anolik, Boris *BiDrAPA 89*
Anon, Julian Louis 1954- *WhoEmL 91*
Anosa, Nellie Tejero *BiDrAPA 89*
Anosov, Nikolay Pavlovich *PenDiMP*
Anouilh, Jean 1910- *WorAlBi*
Anouilh, Jean 1910-1987 *BioIn 16, ConAu 32NR, EuWr 13, MajTwCW*
Anreiter von Zirnfeld, Anton 1725?-1801 *PenDiDA 89*
Anreiter von Zirnfeld, Johann Karl W. 1702?-1747 *PenDiDA 89*
Anrig, Gregory Richard 1931- *WhoAm 90*
Ansari, Ayaz Akhtar 1954- *WhoWor 91*
Ansari, Mary Blanche 1939- *WhoAmW 91*
Ansari, Megill Shakir 1957- *WhoEmL 91*
Ansari, Mohammad B *BiDrAPA 89*
Ansary, Cyrus A. 1933- *WhoAm 90*
Ansary, Hassan J. 1949- *St&PR 91, WhoAm 90*
Ansbach, Elizabeth Berkeley Craven 1750-1828 *BioIn 16*
Ansbach, Robert J. 1938- *St&PR 91*
Ansbacher, Charles Alexander 1942- *WhoAm 90*
Ansbacher, Jessie *WhoAmA 91N*
Ansbacher, Lewis 1928- *WhoAm 90*
Ansbacher, Max George 1935- *WhoE 91*
Ansbacher, Rudi 1934- *WhoAm 90*
Anscher, Bernard 1922- *WhoAm 90, WhoSSW 91*
Anscher, Marcia Daniel *St&PR 91*
Anschuetz, Lou John 1952- *WhoEmL 91*
Anschuetz, Norbert Lee 1915- *WhoAm 90*
Anscombe, Elizabeth *ConAu 129*
Anscombe, G E M 1919- *ConAu 129*
Anscombe, Roderick John 1947- *BiDrAPA 89*
Ansel, Howard Carl 1933- *WhoAm 90*
Anselen, Jaime *BiDrAPA 89*
Ansell, Edward Orin 1926- *WhoAm 90*
Ansell, George Stephen 1934- *WhoAm 90*
Ansell, John 1874-1948 *OxCPMus*
Ansell, Joseph Paul 1949- *WhoAmA 91*
Ansell, Julian S. 1922- *WhoAm 90*
Ansell, Leonard 1923- *ODwPR 91*
Ansell, Marylee 1936- *WhoAmW 91*
Ansell, Rod *BioIn 16*
Ansell, Ruth Elizabeth 1956- *WhoEmL 91*
Anselm de Parma *EncO&P 3*
Anselme, Jean-Pierre Louis Marie 1936- *WhoAm 90*
Anselmi, Alessandro *BioIn 16*
Anselmini, Jean-Pierre 1940- *WhoAm 90, WhoWor 91*
Anselmo, Peter Edward 1946- *St&PR 91*
Anselmo, Rene *BioIn 16, NewYTBS 90 [port]*
Ansen, Alan Joseph 1922- *WhoWor 91*
Ansermet, Ernest 1883-1969 *PenDiMP, WorAlBi*
Ansfield, Joseph 1932- *BiDrAPA 89*
Anshaw, Carol 1946- *WhoAm 90, WhoAmW 91*
Anshell, Joseph G. 1946- *St&PR 91*
Anshen, Melvin 1912- *WhoAm 90*
Anshen, Ruth Nanda *BioIn 16*
Anshin, Roman Norman 1934- *BiDrAPA 89*
Ansin, Ronald M. 1934- *St&PR 91*
Ansingh, Lizzy 1875-1959 *BiDWomA*
Ansink, Bernard Jan Johannes 1931- *WhoWor 91*
Ansley, Addie 1933- *St&PR 91*
Ansley, Campbell Wallace, Jr. 1921- *WhoSSW 91*
Ansley, David George 1956- *WhoEmL 91*
Ansley, Shepard Bryan 1939- *WhoSSW 91*
Anslow, David Reese 1948- *WhoEmL 91*
Ansnick, Joseph Michael 1945- *WhoEmL 91*
Anson, Abraham 1912- *WhoWrEP 89*
Anson, Adrian 1851-1922 *WorAlBi*
Anson, Cap 1851-1897 *Ballpl 90 [port]*
Anson, Cap 1852-1922 *BioIn 16*
Anson, F. Martin 1942- *St&PR 91*
Anson, Fred Colvig 1933- *WhoAm 90*
Anson, Joseph Bruce 1945- *WhoEmL 91*
Anson, Lesia 1946- *WhoAmA 91*
Anson, Robert Sam 1945- *BioIn 16*
Anson-Weber, Joan E. 1927- *WhoWrEP 89*
Anspach, Elizabeth 1750-1828 *FemiCLE*
Anspach, Ernst 1913- *WhoAm 90, WhoAmA 91, WhoE 91*
Anspach, Eugene J. *BioIn 16*
Anspach, Herbert Kephart 1926- *WhoAm 90*
Anspach, Kenneth Gordon 1952- *WhoEmL 91*
Anspaugh, David 1946- *ConTFT 8*
Ansseau, Marc Michel 1951- *BiDrAPA 89*
Anstaet, Herbert B. 1902-1989 *BioIn 16*
Anstatt, Peter Jan 1942- *WhoAm 90, WhoE 91*
Anstee, Margaret Joan 1926- *WhoWor 91*
Anstei, Olga Nikolaevna 1912-1985 *EncCoWW*
Anstett, Louis Charles *BiDrAPA 89*
Anstett, Robert Emory 1933- *WhoWrEP 89*
Anstey, Edgar 1907-1987 *BioIn 16*
Anstine, Mary K. 1940- *St&PR 91*
Anstreicher, Kurt *BiDrAPA 89*
Anstrom, Decker *BioIn 16*
Ansuperomin *EncO&P 3*
Ant, Adam 195-?- *EncPR&S 89*
Antaky, Donald E. *St&PR 91*
Antal, Kimberly Joan 1959- *WhoAmW 91*
Antal, Michael Jerry, Jr. 1947- *WhoEmL 91*
Antalis, Angelo John *BiDrAPA 89*
Antall, Jozsef *WhoWor 91*
Antall, Jozsef, Jr. 1932- *CurBio 90 [port]*
Antanaitis, Cynthia Emily 1954- *WhoAmW 91, WhoEmL 91*
Antaya, Kenneth Francis 1947- *St&PR 91*
Antczak, John R. *St&PR 91*
Antell, Joan Lee 1934- *WhoE 91*
Antelline, Fred F. 1910- *St&PR 91*
Antelman, Goldie Gisele *BiDrAPA 89*
Antenberg, Bruce Franklin 1938- *St&PR 91*
Antes, Ernie Charles 1934- *St&PR 91*
Antes, Harry W. 1930- *St&PR 91*
Antes, Horst 1936- *WhoWor 91*
Anthes, John A., Jr. 1949- *St&PR 91*
Anthoine, Mo *BioIn 16*
Anthoine, Robert 1921- *WhoAm 90*
Anthonisen, George Rioch 1936- *WhoAmA 91, WhoE 91*
Anthony and the Imperials *EncPR&S 89*
Anthony, Bishop 1935- *WhoAm 90*
Anthony Peter, His Beatitude 1907- *WhoWor 91*
Anthony, St. *EncO&P 3*
Anthony, Amy Ellen 1955- *WhoAmA 91*
Anthony, Beryl, Jr. *BioIn 16*
Anthony, Beryl Franklin, Jr. 1938- *WhoAm 90, WhoSSW 91*
Anthony, Betty Arlene 1926- *WhoAmW 91*
Anthony, Bonnie Rubin *BiDrAPA 89*
Anthony, Burton C. 1932- *St&PR 91*
Anthony, Carolyn Additon 1949- *WhoEmL 91*
Anthony, Charles 1929- *IntWWM 90*
Anthony, Clary 1924- *St&PR 91*
Anthony, David Vincent 1929- *WhoAm 90*
Anthony, Dean Wade 1948- *WhoSSW 91*
Anthony, Donald Barrett 1948- *St&PR 91, WhoAm 90, WhoEmL 91, WhoSSW 91*
Anthony, Donald Charles 1926- *WhoAm 90*
Anthony, Donald Harold 1950- *WhoEmL 91*
Anthony, Edward 1895-1971 *AuBYP 90*
Anthony, Edward Lovell, II 1921- *WhoAm 90*
Anthony, Edward Mason 1922- *WhoAm 90*
Anthony, Elaine Margaret 1932- *WhoAmW 91*
Anthony, Elwyn James *BiDrAPA 89*
Anthony, Ethan 1950- *WhoE 91, WhoEmL 91*
Anthony, Evelyn 1928- *SpyFic, TwCCr&M 91*
Anthony, Fred Paul 1935- *WhoE 91*
Anthony, Gordon *ConAu 129*
Anthony, Grace Louise *BiDrAPA 89*
Anthony, Gretchen Wilhelmina Hauser 1936- *WhoSSW 91*
Anthony, Guy M. 1915- *St&PR 91*
Anthony, Harry Antoniades 1922- *WhoAm 90, WhoWor 91*
Anthony, Henry S *AmLegL*
Anthony, J. Marshall 1944- *St&PR 91*
Anthony, Jacqueline 1966- *WhoAmW 91*
Anthony, James Kermit *BiDrAPA 89*
Anthony, James Raymond 1922- *IntWWM 90*
Anthony, Jane Marie 1950- *WhoE 91*
Anthony, Joe L. 1951- *St&PR 91*
Anthony, John *ConAu 33NR, MajTwCW*
Anthony, John Edward 1932- *St&PR 91*
Anthony, John T. *St&PR 91*
Anthony, Joseph 1960- *WhoWrEP 89*
Anthony, Joseph Harry 1949- *WhoEmL 91*
Anthony, Julian Danford, Jr. 1935- *WhoAm 90*
Anthony, Kara Lee 1965- *WhoAmW 91*
Anthony, Lawrence Kenneth 1934- *WhoAmA 91*
Anthony, Lysette *BioIn 16*
Anthony, Michael 1932- *WorAu 1980*
Anthony, Patrick Allan 1954- *WhoEmL 91*
Anthony, Paul Barrie 1934- *WhoE 91*
Anthony, Perry 1940- *St&PR 91, WhoAm 90*
Anthony, Peter *MajTwCW*
Anthony, Peter 1958- *WhoAmA 91*
Anthony, Piers 1934- *MajTwCW, RGTwCSF*
Anthony, Ray 1922- *OxCPMus*
Anthony, Richard E. 1946- *St&PR 91*
Anthony, Richard W. 1930- *ODwPR 91*
Anthony, Robert Armstrong 1931- *WhoAm 90*
Anthony, Robert Holland 1948- *WhoAm 90, WhoSSW 91*
Anthony, Robert Hugh, Jr. 1954- *WhoSSW 91*
Anthony, Robert Newton 1916- *WhoAm 90*
Anthony, Robert Newton, Jr. *BiDrAPA 89*
Anthony, Ronald T. 1939- *St&PR 91*
Anthony, Rowland Barney 1918- *St&PR 91*
Anthony, Sara 1954- *WhoAmW 91*
Anthony, Sharon Arnold 1965- *WhoAmW 91*
Anthony, Stephen Hopkins 1937- *WhoAm 90*
Anthony, Susan *ODwPR 91*
Anthony, Susan B. 1820-1906 *BioAmW, FemiCLE, WorAlBi*
Anthony, Susan Brownell 1820-1906 *BioIn 16*
Anthony, Susan Brownwell 1820-1906 *EncPaPR 91*
Anthony, Thomas Dale 1952- *WhoEmL 91*
Anthony, Thomas Nile 1935- *WhoSSW 91*
Anthony, Virginia Quinn Bausch 1943- *WhoAm 90*
Anthony, Webster D 1838- *AmLegL*
Anthony, William *BioIn 16*
Anthony, William Graham 1934- *WhoAm 90, WhoAmA 91*
Anthony, William Philip 1943- *WhoSSW 91*
Anthony, William Ross 1924- *St&PR 91*
Anthony-Perez, Bobbie Murphy 1923- *WhoWor 91*
Anthony Podruh, Anton Julius 1918- *WhoSSW 91*
Antic, Michael 1963- *WhoEmL 91*
Antignani, Bonnie Provenzano 1952- *WhoWrEP 89*
Antigonus, King of Macedonia 382BC-301BC *BioIn 16*
Antila, V. Anna *WhoWrEP 89*
Antilla, Susan 1954- *WhoAm 90, WhoAmW 91, WhoEmL 91*
Antin, Anthony Lenard 1923- *WhoE 91*
Antin, David 1932- *WhoAm 90, WhoWrEP 89*
Antin, David A 1932- *WhoAmA 91*
Antin, Eleanor 1935- *BiDWomA, WhoAm 90, WhoAmA 91, WhoAmW 91*
Antin, Mary 1881-1949 *FemiCLE*
Antin, Todd Mitchell *BiDrAPA 89*
Antinori, Dennis J. 1948- *St&PR 91*
Antinozzi, Mary Lou *WhoAmW 91*
Antioco, John F. *BioIn 16*
Antion, David Stephen 1961- *WhoEmL 91*
Antioquia, Clarence 1940- *St&PR 91*
Antipa, Gregory Alexis 1941- *WhoAm 90*
Antipov, Vladimir *BioIn 16*
Antisdel, James Richard *BiDrAPA 89*
Antisthenes 444?BC-370?BC *WorAlBi*
Antle, Charles Edward 1930- *WhoAm 90*
Antler, Morton 1928- *WhoAm 90*
Antley, Chris 1966?- *BioIn 16*

Antliff, John Cooper 1929- *St&PR 91*
Antman, Lori Linette 1960- *WhoAmW 91, WhoEmL 91*
Antman, Stuart Sheldon 1939- *WhoAm 90, WhoE 91*
Antoci, Mario 1934- *WhoAm 90, WhoWor 91*
Antoine, Bernadette 1940- *IntWWM 90*
Antoine, Florence Sheila 1941- *WhoAmW 91*
Antoine, Gloria Ann 1953- *WhoEmL 91*
Antoine, Greta Jane 1934- *WhoAmW 91*
Antoine, Louis Bernard 1950- *BiDrAPA 89*
Antoine, Marc *MajTwCW*
Antoine, Robert *BiDrAPA 89*
Antoine, Robert Francis 1927- *St&PR 91*
Antokoletz, Elliott 1942- *ConAu 129*
Antokoletz, Elliott Maxim 1942- *IntWWM 90*
Antoku, Emperor *EncJap*
Antol, Joseph James 1947- *WhoAmA 91*
Antoli Guarch, Miguel 1934- *WhoWor 91*
Anton, Blanca R 1933- *BiDrAPA 89*
Anton, Bruce Norman 1951- *St&PR 91, WhoEmL 91, WhoWor 91*
Anton, Catherine Gayle 1945- *WhoAmW 91*
Anton, Cheryl Lynn 1953- *WhoAmW 91*
Anton, Constance A *BiDrAPA 89*
Anton, David Michael 1911- *WhoAm 90*
Anton, Frank A. 1949- *WhoAm 90*
Anton, Frank Robert 1920- *WhoAm 90*
Anton, Frederick W., III 1934- *St&PR 91*
Anton, George Louis 1923- *WhoAm 90*
Anton, Harvey 1923- *St&PR 91, WhoE 91, WhoWor 91*
Anton, John M. 1947- *WhoEmL 91*
Anton, Manuel P 1932- *BiDrAPA 89*
Anton, Mark J. 1926- *WhoAm 90, WhoE 91*
Anton, Nicholas Guy 1906- *WhoAm 90, WhoWor 91*
Anton, Raymond F, Jr. 1951- *BiDrAPA 89*
Anton, Richard Henry 1946- *WhoEmL 91*
Anton, Thomas 1931- *St&PR 91, WhoAm 90, WhoWor 91*
Anton, Thomas Julius 1934- *WhoAm 90*
Anton, William *WhoHisp 91*
Anton, William Lloyd 1938- *St&PR 91*
Antonacci, Anthony Eugene 1949- *WhoWor 91*
Antonacci, Diana Jo 1957- *BiDrAPA 89*
Antonacci, Lori 1947- *WhoAmW 91, WhoE 91*
Antonakos, Stephen 1926- *WhoAm 90, WhoAmA 91*
Antonazzi, Frank Joseph, Jr. 1950- *WhoWrEP 89*
Antonazzo, Nicholas Orlando 1937- *St&PR 91, WhoAm 90*
Antoncich, Betty 1913- *AuBYP 90*
Antone, Karen Ann 1947- *WhoAmW 91*
Antone, Nahil Peter 1952- *WhoEmL 91, WhoWor 91*
Antonell, Walter John 1934- *St&PR 91, WhoAm 90*
Antonelli, Amy Solit 1941- *IntWWM 90*
Antonelli, Bautista *BioIn 16*
Antonelli, Ferdinando Giuseppe 1896- *WhoWor 91*
Antonelli, John William 1917- *St&PR 91*
Antonelli, Johnny 1930- *Ballpl 90*
Antonelli, Luciano 1935- *WhoWor 91*
Antonelli, Pattie Ellen 1953- *WhoEmL 91*
Antonelli, Romano 1923- *BiDrAPA 89*
Antonellis, Charlene Adele 1948- *WhoEmL 91*
Antonellis, Domenic M. 1940- *St&PR 91*
Antonello da Messina 1430?-1479 *IntDcAA 90*
Antonescu, Ion 1882-1946 *BioIn 16, WorAlBi*
Antonescu, Mihai 1907-1946 *BioIn 16*
Antoniacci, Cesare Robert *BiDrAPA 89*
Antoniades, Harry Nicholas 1923- *WhoAm 90*
Antonibon, Giovanni Battista *PenDiDA 89*
Antonich, John Julius 1933- *St&PR 91*
Antonini, Joseph *BioIn 16*
Antonini, Joseph 1941- *News 91-2*
Antonini, Joseph E. 1941- *St&PR 91, WhoAm 90*
Antonini, Luigi 1883-1968 *BioIn 16*
Antonini, Marion Hugh 1930- *WhoAm 90*
Antonini, Michael Joseph 1946- *WhoEmL 91*
Antonini, Richard Lee 1942- *St&PR 91, WhoAm 90*
Antoninus, Brother 1912- *WhoAm 90, WhoWor 91*
Antoninus, Marcus Aurelius 121-180 *WrPh P*
Antonio, Corazon Garcia *BiDrAPA 89*
Antonio, Douglas John 1955- *WhoEmL 91, WhoWor 91*
Antonio, Johnson 1931- *MusmAFA*
Antonio, Juan *NewYTBS 90*
Antonio, Juan 1783?-1863 *WhNaAH*
Antonio, Juan 1945-1990 *BioIn 16, WhoHisp 91N*
Antonio, Julio 1889-1919 *BioIn 16*
Antonio, Lou 1934- *ConTFT 8*
Antonio, Marlene Joan 1936- *WhoAmW 91*
Antonio, Susan Riccio 1963- *WhoE 91*
Antonioli, Jean-Francois Marc 1959- *IntWWM 90*
Antonioli, Robert *St&PR 91*
Antonioni, Michelangelo *BioIn 16*
Antonioni, Michelangelo 1912- *WorAlBi*
Antoniou, Andreas 1938- *WhoAm 90*
Antoniou, Lucy D. 1929- *WhoAmW 91*
Antoniou, Panagiotis Ayis 1950- *WhoE 91*
Antoniou, Theodore 1935- *IntWWM 90, PenDiMP A*
Antonius, Marcus 83?BC-30BC *BioIn 16*
Antonoff, Gary L. 1936- *WhoAm 90*
Antonoff, Steven Ross 1948- *WhoAm 90, WhoEmL 91*
Antonov-Ovseenko, Vladimir A. 1884-1939 *BioIn 16*
Antonova, Irina Aleksandrovna 1922- *BioIn 16*
Antonovici, Constantin 1911- *WhoAmA 91*
Antonow, Joseph P. 1915- *St&PR 91*
Antonowich, Alexander 1919- *IntWWM 90*
Antonowicz, Joseph L 1956- *BiDrAPA 89*
Antonsen, Elmer Harold 1929- *WhoAm 90*
Antonsen, John Edward *BiDrAPA 89*
Antonson, Joan Margaret 1951- *WhoEmL 91*
Antonucci, Tammy K. 1958- *WhoEmL 91*
Antonuccio, Joseph Albert 1932- *WhoAm 90*
Antony, Marc 82?BC-30BC *WorAlBi*
Antony, Peter 1926- *TwCCr&M 91*
Antos, John Jeffrey 1949- *WhoSSW 91*
Antos, Kenneth Martin 1943- *St&PR 91*
Antosh, Natalie Jean 1964- *WhoAmW 91*
Antosiewicz, Linda A. 1952- *St&PR 91*
Antosz, Henry *BioIn 16*
Antosz, Raymond Martin 1938- *St&PR 91*
Antoun, Annette Agnes 1927- *WhoE 91*
Antoun, M. Lawreace 1927- *WhoAmW 91, WhoE 91*
Antreasian, Garo Zareh 1922- *WhoAm 90, WhoAmA 91*
Antrim, Craig Keith 1942- *WhoAmA 91*
Antrim, Robert Wayne 1932- *WhoAm 90*
Antrobus, C. L. 1846-1919 *FemiCLE*
Antsaklis, Aristides 1946- *WhoWor 91*
Antschel, Paul 1920-1970 *ConAu 33NR, MajTwCW*
Anttila, Arjo Eeronpoika 1932- *WhoWor 91*
Antunes, Jorge 1942- *IntWWM 90*
Antupit, Samuel Nathaniel 1932- *WhoAm 90*
Antwerpen, Fortuna *BiDrAPA 89*
Antz, Tracy N. 1960- *WhoEmL 91*
Antzelevitch, Charles 1951- *WhoEmL 91*
Anuar, Hedwig Elizabeth 1928- *WhoWor 91*
Anucha, Chibuike Enyereibe 1961- *WhoEmL 91*
Anudeva *NewAgMG*
Anugama *NewAgMG*
Anula *WomWR*
Anuswith, Christopher Edwin 1951- *WhoSSW 91*
Anuszkiewicz, Richard Joseph 1930- *WhoAmA 91*
Anuta, Michael Joseph 1901- *WhoWor 91*
Anutta, Lucile Jamison 1943- *WhoSSW 91*
Anvari, Morteza 1931- *WhoAm 90*
Anvaripour, M. A. 1935- *WhoAm 90*
Anwar, Imran 1962- *St&PR 91*
Anwar, Pervaiz 1947- *St&PR 91*
Anwar, Syed Hashmath 1956- *BiDrAPA 89*
Anwar, Usman 1968- *St&PR 91*
Anwar, Zakira Khatoon 1939- *BiDrAPA 89*
Anway, Randall Robert 1958- *WhoE 91*
Anwyll, Jean *ODwPR 91*
Anya, Innocent Okwudili 1954- *BiDrAPA 89*
Anyaeto, Callistus Chijioke 1962- *WhoWrEP 89*
Anyamani, Sutin 1939- *WhoWor 91*
Anyanwu, Chukwukre 1943- *WhoE 91*
Anyanwu, Timothy Uwadiegwu 1949- *WhoWor 91*
Anyte *EncCoWW*
Anz, Reg Dean 1942- *WhoWor 91*
Anza, Juan Baptista De 1735-1788 *EncCRAm*
Anza, Juan Bautista De 1735-1788 *WhNaAH*
Anzaghi, Davide 1936- *IntWWM 90*
Anzai, Neal 1955- *BiDrAPA 89*
Anzalone, Carmen James 1927- *St&PR 91*
Anzalone, William Francis 1951- *WhoEmL 91*
Anzel, Sanford Harold 1929- *WhoAm 90*
Anzia, Daniel Joseph *BiDrAPA 89*
Anziani, Carmen *BiDrAPA 89*
Anzini, Ann Elizabeth Urban 1962- *WhoE 91*
Anzovino, Robert Dominic 1945- *St&PR 91*
Anzuini, Henry G. 1930- *St&PR 91*
Aoki, Chieko N. *BioIn 16*
Aoki, Hiroyoshi *BioIn 16*
Aoki, Junjiro 1910- *WhoWor 91*
Aoki, Masaki 1934- *WhoWor 91*
Aoki, Masamitsu 1945- *WhoWor 91*
Aoki, Rocky 1940- *News 90 [port]*
Aoley, Prakash Vithalrao 1947- *WhoWor 91*
Aona, Gretchen Mann 1933- *WhoAmW 91*
Aouita, Said *BioIn 16*
Aouita, Said 1960- *CurBio 90 [port]*
Aoun, Michel *BioIn 16*
Aoun, Michel 1935- *CurBio 90 [port]*
Aoyama, Fujio 1933- *WhoWor 91*
Aoyama, Hiroyuki 1932- *WhoWor 91*
Apache Kid 1865?-1894? *WhNaAH*
Apacible, Mariano, Jr. *BiDrAPA 89*
Apagyi, Maria 1941- *IntWWM 90*
Aparacio, Luis 1934- *Ballpl 90 [port]*
Aparicio, Frances R. 1955- *WhoHisp 91*
Aparicio, Jaime 1955- *WhoWor 91*
Aparicio, Luis Ernesto Montiel 1934- *WhoHisp 91*
Aparisi y Guijarro, Antonio 1815-1872 *BioIn 16*
Apatoff, Michael John 1955- *WhoAm 90*
Apel, Barbara Jean 1935- *WhoAmA 91*
Apel, Harry M. 1931- *St&PR 91*
Apel, John Paul 1932- *St&PR 91*
Apel, John Ralph 1930- *WhoAm 90*
Apel, Myrna L. 1942- *WhoAmW 91*
Apel, Steven Gary 1956- *WhoE 91*
Apel, Willi 1893-1988 *BioIn 16*
Apelian, Virginia 1934- *WhoE 91*
Apelt, Colin James 1931- *WhoWor 91*
Apen, Gregory John 1945- *St&PR 91*
Apen, John Robert 1937- *St&PR 91*
Apenbrink, Edwin John 1946- *WhoEmL 91*
Apengeter von Sassenlant, Hans *PenDiDA 89*
Aperghis, Georges 1945- *IntWWM 90*
Apesos, Steve 1953- *ODwPR 91*
Apetz, Edward L. 1946- *WhoE 91*
Apfel, Kalman 1907-1988 *BioIn 16*
Apfel, Necia 1930- *WhoWrEP 89*
Apfel, Necia H. 1930- *BioIn 16*
Apfel, Robert Edmund 1943- *WhoAm 90*
Apfel, Roberta Joyce 1938- *BiDrAPA 89*
Apfelberg, Herbert Jack 1909- *BiDrAPA 89*
Apfeldorf, William Jay *BiDrAPA 89*
Apfelschnitt, Carl 1948-1990 *BioIn 16, NewYTBS 90*
Apffel, Phillip R 1916- *BiDrAPA 89*
Apgar, Arthur Frederick 1939- *St&PR 91*
Apgar, B. Jean 1936- *WhoAmW 91*
Apgar, Clifford Marshall 1936- *St&PR 91*
Apgar, Frank Alan 1949- *WhoEmL 91*
Apgar, Jean E 1949- *WhoAmA 91*
Apgar, Mahlon *BioIn 16*
Apgar, Mahlon, IV 1941- *WhoE 91*
Apgar, Nicolas Adam 1918- *WhoAmA 91*
Apgar, Phillip E. 1953- *St&PR 91*
Apgar, Virginia 1909-1974 *BioIn 16*
Aphelion *BioIn 16*
Api-kai-ees 1864?-1897 *DcCanB 12*
Apibunyopas, Krisak 1945- *WhoEmL 91*
Apikuni 1859-1947 *BioIn 16*
Apirion, David 1935- *WhoAm 90*
Apitz, Renate 19--?- *EncCoWW*
Apivor, Denis 1916- *IntWWM 90*
Apjohn, Nelson George 1956- *WhoEmL 91*
Apkarian, Harry 1922- *St&PR 91*
Apking, Anne Marie 1960- *WhoAmW 91*
Aplan, Frank Fulton 1923- *WhoAm 90*
Aplan, Peter Donaghue 1957- *WhoE 91*
Apodaca, Bob 1950- *Ballpl 90*
Apodaca, Clara R. 1934- *WhoHisp 91*
Apodaca, Dennis Ray 1956- *WhoHisp 91*
Apodaca, Ed C. 1941- *WhoHisp 91*
Apodaca, Frank B. 1962- *WhoHisp 91*
Apodaca, Jerry 1934- *BioIn 16, WhoHisp 91*
Apodaca, Rudy S 1939- *ConAu 131, HispWr 90*
Apodaca, Rudy Samuel 1939- *WhoWrEP 89*
Apodaca, Victor, Jr. *WhoHisp 91*
Apolinar 1928- *ArtLatA*
Apolito, Arnaldo 1927- *BiDrAPA 89*
Apollinaire, Guillaume 1880-1918 *BioIn 16, WorAlBi*
Apollonia 1959?- *DrBlPA 90*
Apollonius of Rhodes 295?BC-215?BC *WorAlBi*
Apollonius of Tyana *EncO&P 3*
Apolonio, Domingo G *BiDrAPA 89*
Apolonio, Gloria Cruz V *BiDrAPA 89*
Apone, Carl Anthony 1923- *WhoAm 90*
Aponte, Antonio 1957- *WhoHisp 91*
Aponte, Luis 1922- *WhoHisp 91*
Aponte, Luis 1953- *Ballpl 90*
Aponte, Mari Carmen 1946- *WhoHisp 91*
Aponte, Miriam *BiDrAPA 89*
Aponte, Philip 1936- *WhoHisp 91*
Aponte, Wayne Lionel *BioIn 16*
Aponte De Rodriguez, Elba G 1938- *BiDrAPA 89*
Aponte-Hernandez, Nestor S. 1948- *WhoHisp 91*
Aponte-Ledee, Rafael 1938- *IntWWM 90*
Aponte Martinez, Luis 1922- *WhoAm 90, WhoWor 91*
Aportela, Sinesio Z 1929- *BiDrAPA 89*
Apostle, Donald T 1941- *BiDrAPA 89*
Apostle, Hippocrates G. *NewYTBS 90*
Apostle, Hippocrates George 1910- *WhoAm 90*
Apostle, James A. 1956- *St&PR 91*
Apostol, Alma Alingod 1938- *BiDrAPA 89*
Apostolakis, James John 1942- *WhoAm 90*
Apostoleris, Nicholas Harry 1960- *WhoE 91*
Apostolopoulos, Steve 1961- *WhoE 91*
Apostolopoulos, Theodore 1941- *WhoWor 91*
Apostolos, Paul Michael 1936- *WhoE 91*
Apostolos-Cappadona, Diane 1948- *ConAu 30NR*
App, James Leonard 1936- *WhoSSW 91*
App, Timothy 1947- *WhoAmA 91*
Appalaraju, Gunasekar V. 1958- *WhoE 91*
Appalaraju, Ramakanth Venkataramana 1960- *WhoE 91*
Appeau, Antoine 1930- *WhoWor 91*
Appel, Alfred 1906- *St&PR 91, WhoAm 90*
Appel, Alfred, Jr. 1934- *WhoWrEP 89*
Appel, Andrew 1951- *IntWWM 90*
Appel, Antoinette Ruth 1943- *WhoAm 90*
Appel, Barbara Cole- *BioIn 16*
Appel, Barry 1931- *WhoAm 90*
Appel, Bernard Sidney 1932- *WhoAm 90*
Appel, Celia *BioIn 16*
Appel, Cheri 1901- *BiDrAPA 89*
Appel, Clare Rostan *NewYTBS 90*
Appel, Daniel *BiDrAPA 89*
Appel, David *AuBYP 90*
Appel, Eric A 1945- *WhoAmA 91*
Appel, Eric Michael 1960- *WhoEmL 91*
Appel, Garry Richard 1952- *WhoEmL 91*
Appel, John J. 1921- *WhoAm 90*
Appel, John W 1911- *BiDrAPA 89*
Appel, Karel 1921- *BioIn 16, IntDcAA 90, WhoAmA 91*
Appel, Karel Christian 1921- *WhoAm 90, WhoWor 91*
Appel, Keith Kenneth 1934- *WhoAmA 91*
Appel, Kenneth I. 1932- *WhoAm 90*
Appel, Kenneth Mark 1949- *WhoE 91*
Appel, Marcia Faye 1950- *WhoWrEP 89*
Appel, Marsha Ceil 1953- *WhoAmW 91*
Appel, Martin Eliot 1948- *WhoE 91, WhoEmL 91*
Appel, Michael 1949- *WhoE 91*
Appel, Michael R. 1938- *St&PR 91*
Appel, Michael Robert 1938- *WhoAm 90*
Appel, Nina S. 1936- *WhoAm 90, WhoAmW 91*
Appel, Norman 1924- *St&PR 91*
Appel, Norman 1945- *WhoAm 90, WhoE 91, WhoEmL 91, WhoWor 91*
Appel, Phyllis A 1938- *BiDrAPA 89*
Appel, Rena Lee *BiDrAPA 89*
Appel, Robert Eugene 1958- *WhoE 91, WhoEmL 91*
Appel, Samuel David *BiDrAPA 89*
Appel, Susanne S *BiDrAPA 89*
Appel, Thelma 1940- *WhoAmA 91, WhoE 91*
Appel, Theodore Julius 1936- *St&PR 91*
Appel, U.J. 1917- *St&PR 91*
Appel, Virginia Barr 1955- *WhoAmW 91*
Appel, Wallace Henry 1925- *WhoAm 90*
Appel, William Frank 1924- *WhoAm 90*
Appelbaum, Alan 1936- *WhoAm 90*
Appelbaum, Ann Halsell 1924- *BiDrAPA 89*
Appelbaum, Jacob Gregory 1945- *WhoSSW 91*
Appelbaum, Joel Alan 1941- *WhoAm 90*
Appelbaum, Judith Pilpel 1939- *WhoAmW 91*
Appelbaum, Kenneth L *BiDrAPA 89*
Appelbaum, Kurt *BioIn 16*
Appelbaum, Laurie Robbins 1952- *BiDrAPA 89*
Appelbaum, Michael Arthur 1945- *WhoAm 90*
Appelbaum, Murray Clark 1935- *St&PR 91*
Appelbaum, Paul Stuart 1951- *BiDrAPA 89, WhoE 91*
Appelbaum, Stanley 1931- *St&PR 91*
Appelbaum, Stephen *BioIn 16*
Appelberg, Carl 1930- *WhoWor 91*
Appeldorn, Francis R. 1935- *St&PR 91, WhoAm 90*
Appelgren, Curt 1945- *IntWWM 90*
Appelhof, Ruth A 1945- *WhoAmA 91*
Appell, Don *BioIn 16, NewYTBS 90*

Appell, Don 1917?-1990 *ConAu 131*
Appell, Gail Peck 1939- *WhoAmW 91*
Appell, Kathleen Marie 1943- *WhoAmW 91, WhoSSW 91*
Appell, Lawrence 1949- *St&PR 91*
Appelman, Evan Hugh 1935- *WhoAm 90*
Appelson, Herbert J 1937- *WhoAmA 91*
Appelson, Wallace Bertrand 1930- *WhoAm 90*
Appenzeller, Stan *ODwPR 91*
Apperson, Bernard James 1956- *WhoEmL 91, WhoSSW 91, WhoWor 91*
Apperson, Edgar 1869-1959 *EncABHB 4 [port]*
Apperson, Elmer 1861-1920 *EncABHB 4 [port]*
Apperson, Jack A. 1934- *St&PR 91*
Apperson, Jack Alfonso 1934- *WhoAm 90*
Apperson, Jean 1934- *WhoAmW 91*
Apperson, Polly Merrill 1910- *WhoE 91*
Appert, Donald Lawrence 1953- *IntWWM 90*
Appert, Edward Carl 1944- *St&PR 91*
Appert, Peter P. 1955- *St&PR 91*
Appia, Adolphe 1862-1928 *BioIn 16*
Appia, Edmond 1894-1961 *PenDiMP*
Appiah, Joe 1918-1990 *NewYTBS 90 [port]*
Appignani, Louis Joseph 1933- *St&PR 91*
Appignani, Peter Lawrence 1951- *WhoE 91*
Appl, Franklin John 1937- *WhoSSW 91*
Appl, Fredric Carl 1932- *WhoAm 90*
Applbaum, Ronald Lee 1943- *WhoAm 90*
Apple, B. Nixon 1924- *St&PR 91, WhoAm 90*
Apple, Billy R. 1938- *St&PR 91*
Apple, Cass P. 1940- *St&PR 91*
Apple, Daina Dravnieks 1944- *WhoAmW 91, WhoWor 91*
Apple, David Joseph 1941- *WhoAm 90*
Apple, F. Dean 1935- *St&PR 91*
Apple, Jacki *WhoAmA 91*
Apple, Jacki 1941- *WhoWrEP 89*
Apple, John B. 1935- *St&PR 91*
Apple, John Boyd 1935- *WhoAm 90*
Apple, Leslie Mark 1949- *St&PR 91*
Apple, Margot *SmATA 64*
Apple, Martin Allen 1938- *WhoWor 91*
Apple, Mary Florence 1950- *WhoEmL 91*
Apple, Max *BioIn 16*
Apple, Max 1941- *WorAu 1980 [port]*
Apple, Max Isaac 1941- *WhoAm 90*
Apple, Raymond Walter, Jr. 1934- *WhoAm 90, WhoE 91*
Apple, Robah Warren, Jr. 1955- *WhoEmL 91*
Apple, Roger W. 1956- *WhoEmL 91*
Apple, Steven Anthony 1954- *WhoEmL 91*
Apple, William Marlan 1929- *WhoWrEP 89*
Apple, Willis Wade 1951- *St&PR 91, WhoEmL 91*
Applebaum, Edward 1937- *WhoAm 90*
Applebaum, Edward Leon 1940- *WhoAm 90*
Applebaum, Edward Nathan 1951- *BiDrAPA 89*
Applebaum, Eugene 1936- *St&PR 91*
Applebaum, Harvey Milton 1937- *WhoAm 90*
Applebaum, Louis 1918- *IntWWM 90, WhoAm 90*
Applebaum, Louis 1936- *St&PR 91*
Applebaum, Michael Joel *BiDrAPA 89*
Applebaum, Michael Murray 1958- *WhoEmL 91*
Applebaum, Seymour 1930- *BiDrAPA 89*
Applebaum, Stuart S. 1949- *WhoAm 90*
Applebee, Arthur N 1946- *ConAu 31NR*
Applebee, William Kemp 1948- *WhoSSW 91*
Appleberry, James Bruce 1938- *WhoAm 90*
Applebroog, Ida *BioIn 16*
Applebroog, Ida 1929- *WhoAmA 91*
Appleby, Daniel Bart 1954- *WhoAmA 91*
Appleby, David John 1923-1988 *BioIn 16*
Appleby, James R., Jr. 1945- *St&PR 91*
Appleby, John 1920- *BiDrAPA 89*
Appleby, John Winfred 1922- *St&PR 91*
Appleby, Joyce Oldham 1929- *WhoAm 90*
Appleby, Marjory Lu 1930- *WhoAmW 91, WhoE 91*
Appleby, Robert Houston 1931- *WhoSSW 91*
Appleby, William Franklin, Sr. 1928- *WhoSSW 91*
Applefeld, Laurie Sue 1953- *WhoEmL 91*
Appleford, G Burton 1915- *BiDrAPA 89*
Applegarth, Adrienne P 1926- *BiDrAPA 89*
Applegarth, Paul Vollmer 1946- *WhoE 91*
Applegarth, Virginia Bevington 1953- *WhoAmW 91*
Applegate, Arthur Lowrie 1914- *St&PR 91*
Applegate, Christina *BioIn 16*
Applegate, Colleen 1963-1984 *BioIn 16*
Applegate, Debra Annette 1962- *WhoWrEP 89*
Applegate, Douglas 1928- *WhoAm 90*
Applegate, Edward Timothy 1934- *St&PR 91*
Applegate, Henry M., III 1947- *St&PR 91*
Applegate, Jeffrey *BioIn 16*
Applegate, Malcolm W. 1936- *WhoAm 90*
Applegate, Mary Sollinger 1961- *WhoAmW 91*
Applegate, Paul Dean 1946- *WhoSSW 91*
Applegate, Steven C. 1948- *St&PR 91*
Appleman, David Earl 1943- *WhoAmA 91*
Appleman, Howard C. 1927- *St&PR 91*
Appleman, M. Michael 1933- *WhoAm 90*
Appleman, Mark J. *BioIn 16*
Appleman, Philip 1926- *WhoAm 90, WhoWrEP 89*
Appleman, Stratton L. 1906- *St&PR 91*
Appleman, Todd *ODwPR 91*
Appleman, Wilber *BioIn 16*
Appleman-Vassil, Nanci 1953- *WhoEmL 91*
Applequist, Jon Barr 1932- *WhoAm 90*
Applequist, Virgil H. 1947- *St&PR 91*
Appleseed, Johnny 1774-1845 *BioIn 16*
Appleton, Arthur Ivar 1915- *WhoAm 90*
Appleton, Daniel Randolph, Jr. 1942- *WhoE 91, WhoWor 91*
Appleton, Donald 1894-1989 *BioIn 16*
Appleton, Edward V. 1892-1965 *WorAlBi*
Appleton, Edward Victor 1892-1965 *BioIn 16*
Appleton, Gordon 1947- *IntWWM 90*
Appleton, Herbert Morison 1922- *St&PR 91*
Appleton, James Edward 1947- *WhoE 91*
Appleton, James Robert 1937- *WhoAm 90*
Appleton, John 1935- *St&PR 91*
Appleton, Jon 1939- *IntWWM 90*
Appleton, Joseph Hayne 1927- *WhoAm 90*
Appleton, Kathleen Barr *BiDrAPA 89*
Appleton, Lawrence *MajTwCW*
Appleton, Myra 1934- *WhoAm 90, WhoAmW 91*
Appleton, Pete 1904-1974 *Ballpl 90*
Appleton, R. O., Jr. 1945- *WhoAm 90, WhoEmL 91*
Appleton, Robert *BioIn 16*
Appleton, Robert Wayne 1953- *WhoE 91*
Appleton, Susan Frelich 1948- *WhoAm 90*
Appleton, William S 1934- *BiDrAPA 89*
Applewhite, James 1935- *DcLB 105 [port]*
Applewhite, James William 1935- *WhoWrEP 89*
Appley, Lawrence A. 1904- *St&PR 91, WhoAm 90*
Appley, Mortimer Herbert 1921- *WhoAm 90*
Appleyard, David Frank 1939- *WhoAm 90*
Appleyard, Milton Herbert 1929- *WhoAm 90*
Applin, Thomas Leo *BiDrAPA 89*
Appling, Luke 1909- *Ballpl 90 [port]*
Apprill, Earl John 1941- *St&PR 91*
Apreleva, Elena 1846-1923 *EncCoWW*
April Wine *EncPR&S 89*
April, Gary Charles 1940- *WhoSSW 91*
April, Lori Sue 1959- *WhoEmL 91*
April, Rand Scott 1951- *WhoEmL 91*
Aprille, Thomas Joseph, Jr. 1943- *WhoAm 90*
Aprison, Morris Herman 1923- *WhoAm 90*
Apruzzi, Gene *St&PR 91*
Apruzzi, Gene 1934- *WhoAm 90*
Apsler, Alfred 1907- *AuBYP 90*
Apstein, Theodore 1918- *ConAu 131*
Apt, Charles 1933- *WhoAmA 91*
Apt, Harold H. 1928- *St&PR 91*
Apt, Leonard 1922- *WhoAm 90*
Apte, Sue-Ellen Ilene 1956- *WhoSSW 91*
Aptekar, Ken 1950- *WhoAmA 91*
Apter, David Ernest 1924- *WhoAm 90*
Apter, J. Scott 1947- *St&PR 91*
Apter, Jeffrey Trevor 1950- *BiDrAPA 89, WhoE 91*
Apter, Marc 1944- *ODwPR 91*
Apter, Nathaniel 1913- *BiDrAPA 89*
Aptheker, Herbert 1915- *EncAL, WhoAm 90*
Aptidon, Hassan Gouled 1916- *WhoWor 91*
Aptowitz, Frederick *BiDrAPA 89*
Aptowitzer, Willi Zeev 1918- *WhoWor 91*
Apuleius, Lucius 123?- *WorAlBi*
Apumatec *WomWR*
Apuron, Anthony Sablan 1945- *WhoAm 90, WhoEmL 91*
Apurvo *NewAgMG*
Apuzzi, Joseph James 1935- *WhoE 91*
Apuzzo, William J. 1942- *WhoSSW 91*
Apyan, Roseanne Lucille 1949- *WhoAmW 91*
Aqazadeh-Khoi, Qolam Reza *WhoWor 91*
Aquila, Francis Joseph 1957- *WhoE 91*
Aquila, Vincent Salvador 1963- *WhoSSW 91*
Aquilera, Bruce A. 1948- *St&PR 91*
Aquilina, Benjamin 1943- *St&PR 91*
Aquiline, Judith 1947- *WhoAmW 91*
Aquilino, Daniel 1924- *WhoAm 90*
Aquilino, Paul Philip 1941- *St&PR 91*
Aquilino, Thomas Joseph, Jr. 1939- *WhoAm 90*
Aquinas, Thomas 1224-1274 *WrPh P*
Aquinas, Thomas 1225?-1274 *BioIn 16, EncO&P 3*
Aquino, Benigno S. *BioIn 16*
Aquino, Corazon *BioIn 16*
Aquino, Corazon Cojuangco *NewYTBS 90 [port]*
Aquino, Corazon Cojuangco 1933- *WhoWor 91*
Aquino, Edmundo 1939- *WhoAmA 91*
Aquino, Felix John 1952- *WhoEmL 91*
Aquino, Humberto 1947- *WhoAmA 91, WhoHisp 91*
Aquino, John Goddard 1960- *WhoEmL 91*
Aquino, John Thomas 1949- *WhoEmL 91*
Aquino, Luis 1965- *Ballpl 90*
Aquino, Luis Hernandez *HispWr 90*
Aquino, Maria Corazon 1933- *WomWR [port]*
Aquino-Caro, Evelyn B 1937- *BiDrAPA 89*
Ar Bras, Dan *NewAgMG*
Ara, Ugo *PenDiMP*
Arabia, Joseph V. 1942- *St&PR 91*
Arabian, John K. 1943- *St&PR 91*
Arabie, Phipps 1948- *WhoAm 90*
Arad, Atar *PenDiMP*
Arad, Ron 1951- *BioIn 16, PenDiDA 89*
Arader, W. Graham, III *BioIn 16*
Arader, Walter Graham, III 1950- *WhoE 91*
Aradillos, Nancy Glime 1962- *WhoAmW 91*
Arado, Joseph Edwin 1929- *St&PR 91*
Arafat, Yasir 1929- *BioIn 16, WorAlBi*
Arafat, Yasser 1929- *PolLCME*
Arafeh, Mehadin Kamel *BiDrAPA 89*
Aragall, Giacomo 1939- *IntWWM 90, PenDiMP*
Aragno, Michel 1942- *WhoWor 91*
Aragon 1897-1982 *BioIn 16*
Aragon, Bill John 1946- *WhoHisp 91*
Aragon, Carla Y. 1955- *WhoHisp 91*
Aragon, Enrique O. 1879-1950 *EncPaPR 91*
Aragon, Gloria Tamayo 1918- *WhoWor 91*
Aragon, Jacob Joseph 1901- *St&PR 91*
Aragon, John A. 1930- *BioIn 16, WhoHisp 91*
Aragon, Joseph William 1941- *St&PR 91*
Aragon, Louis 1897- *WorAlBi*
Aragon, Louis 1897-1982 *BioIn 16, MajTwCW*
Aragon, Louis-Marie 1897-1982 *BiDFrPL*
Aragon, Luis Cardoza y *HispWr 90*
Aragon, Manny *WhoHisp 91*
Aragon, Robert Joseph 1935- *St&PR 91*
Aragon, Ruben Victor 1949- *St&PR 91*
Aragona, Tullia d' 1510?-1570? *EncCoWW*
Aragones, John Negre *BiDrAPA 89*
Aragones, Sergio 1937- *BioIn 16*
Arai, Hakuseki 1657-1725 *BioIn 16*
Arai, Junichi 1932- *ConDes 90*
Arai, Shinji 1940- *WhoAm 90*
Arain, Ataur Rahman 1940- *WhoWor 91*
Araiza, Francisco 1950- *IntWWM 90, PenDiMP, WhoWor 91*
Arak, Gladys 1943- *BiDrAPA 89*
Arakawa 1936- *WhoAmA 91*
Arakawa, Kasumi 1926- *WhoAm 90, WhoWor 91*
Arakawa, Toshimasa 1950- *WhoSSW 91*
Araki, Huzihiro 1932- *WhoWor 91*
Araki, Shunichi 1942- *WhoWor 91*
Araki, Yoshiro *BioIn 16*
Aram, Zeev *BioIn 16*
Arambourg, Camille Louis Joseph 1885-1969 *DcScB S2*
Arambula, Michael Ray *BiDrAPA 89*
Aramburu, Albert 1934- *WhoHisp 91*
Aramburu, Jennifer Travers 1964- *WhoAmW 91*
Aramburu, Juan Carlos 1912- *WhoWor 91*
Aramburu, Pedro Eugenio 1903-1970 *BioIn 16*
Aramian, S. Sue 1932- *St&PR 91*
Aramony, William 1927- *WhoAm 90*
Arams, Frank Robert 1925- *WhoAm 90*
Aran, Fernando Santiago 1957- *WhoEmL 91*
Arana, Albert 1946- *WhoEmL 91, WhoSSW 91, WhoWor 91*
Arana, George W *BiDrAPA 89*
Arana, Jose Domingo 1939- *BiDrAPA 89*
Arana, Jose Luis 1943- *WhoWor 91*
Arana, Kimberly Ann 1957- *WhoEmL 91*
Arana, Therese A. 1945- *St&PR 91*
Arana Goiri, Sabino de 1865-1903 *BioIn 16*
Aranas, Maria Elena Lizares 1937- *WhoAmW 91*
Aranbarri, Ricardo 1959- *WhoHisp 91*
Arancia, Louis John 1928- *WhoE 91*
Arand, Frederick Francis 1954- *WhoEmL 91*
Aranda, Benjamin, III 1940- *WhoHisp 91*
Aranda, Charles 1931- *WhoWrEP 89*
Aranda, Miguel Angel 1939- *WhoAm 90, WhoSSW 91, WhoWor 91*
Araneda, Constance Elizabeth 1933- *WhoE 91*
Araneo, Barbara Ann 1948- *WhoAmW 91*
Araneta, Myrna Roberta Hipolito 1949- *WhoAmW 91*
Arango, Denise 1965- *WhoE 91*
Arango, J. A. *WhoHisp 91*
Arango, Jorge Sanin 1916- *WhoAm 90*
Arango, Ricardo *BiDrAPA 89*
Aranha, Oswaldo 1894-1960 *BioIn 16*
Aranha, Ray 1939- *DrBlPA 90*
Arani, Ardy A. 1954- *WhoEmL 91*
Arano, Ramon 1939- *Ballpl 90*
Aranow, Peter Jones 1946- *St&PR 91*
Aranow, Robert B *BiDrAPA 89*
Aranow, Robert Bittman 1954- *WhoE 91*
Aranow, Ruth Lee Horowitz 1929- *WhoAmW 91*
Aranson, Michael J. 1944- *WhoE 91*
Aranson, Robert 1953- *WhoE 91*
Arant, Eugene Wesley 1920- *WhoAm 90, WhoWor 91*
Arant, Patricia M. 1930- *WhoAm 90, WhoAmW 91*
Aranyi, Jelly d' 1893-1966 *PenDiMP*
Aranyi de Hunyadvar, Jelly d' 1893-1966 *PenDiMP*
Araoz, Daniel Leon 1930- *WhoAm 90*
Arapoglou, Christopher Theodore 1955- *St&PR 91*
Arapooish 1790?-1834 *WhNaAH*
Arapoosh 1790?-1834 *WhNaAH*
Arapov, Boris Aleksandrovich 1905- *WhoWor 91*
Arapov, Boris Alexandrovich 1905- *IntWWM 90*
Araquistain, Paul A. 1927- *St&PR 91*
Arasanayagam, Jean 1934- *FemiCLE*
Araskog, Rand V. *BioIn 16*
Araskog, Rand Vincent 1931- *St&PR 91, WhoAm 90, WhoE 91, WhoWor 91*
Arason, Steingrimur *AuBYP 90*
Arasteh, Abdal-Reza 1927- *WhoAm 90*
Arat, Metin 1928- *BiDrAPA 89*
Araton, Beth Albert 1958- *ODwPR 91*
Arauco, Ingrid Colette 1957- *IntWWM 90*
Araujo, Doris Martens *BiDrAPA 89*
Araujo, Jess J., Sr. 1947- *WhoHisp 91*
Araujo, Jose Emilio Goncalves 1922- *WhoWor 91*
Araujo, Julius C. 1926- *WhoHisp 91*
Araujo, Paulo Cabral 1922- *WhoWor 91*
Araujo Porto Alegre, Manuel de 1806-1879 *ArtLatA*
Aravosis, George D. *BioIn 16*
Arax, Christine 1961- *WhoWrEP 89*
Arazan, Virginia 1924- *BiDrAPA 89*
Arb, Tim K. 1938- *St&PR 91*
Arbaleste de la Borde, Charlotte 1548-1606 *EncCoWW*
Arban, Jean-Baptiste 1825-1889 *PenDiMP*
Arbatov, Georgi A. *BioIn 16*
Arbatov, Georgiy Arkadyevich 1923- *WhoWor 91*
Arbaugh, Charles H. 1943- *St&PR 91*
Arbaugh, Scott Johann *BiDrAPA 89*
Arbegast, James L. 1932- *St&PR 91*
Arbeit, Robert David 1947- *WhoE 91*
Arbeiter, Jean S. 1937- *AuBYP 90*
Arbell, Mordechai 1929- *WhoWor 91*
Arbenz Guzman, Jacobo 1913-1971 *BioIn 16*
Arber, Werner 1929- *WhoAm 90, WhoWor 91, WorAlBi*
Arbesfeld, Douglas *ODwPR 91*
Arbesu Fraga, Jose Antonio 1940- *NewYTBS 90 [port]*
Arbib, Michael Anthony 1940- *WhoAm 90*
Arbit, Beryl Ellen 1949- *WhoEmL 91*
Arbit, Harvey Marvin 1947- *WhoEmL 91*
Arbit, Terry Steven 1958- *WhoEmL 91*
Arbiter, Nathaniel 1911- *WhoAm 90*
Arbitman, Kahren J 1948- *WhoAmA 91*
Arblay, Frances Burney d' 1752-1840 *BioIn 16*
Arbogast, Oliver Wendell, Jr. 1954- *WhoEmL 91*
Arbogast, Richard C 1942- *BiDrAPA 89*
Arbogast, Robert Ernest 1946- *St&PR 91*
Arbogast, Zollie O., Jr. 1929- *WhoAm 90*
Arboleda, Evelyn Duran 1948- *BiDrAPA 89*
Arboleda-Florez, Julio E 1939- *BiDrAPA 89*
Arboleya, Carlos Jose 1929- *WhoHisp 91*
Arbon, Georgene Kay 1949- *WhoEmL 91*
Arbos, Enrique Fernandez 1863-1939 *PenDiMP*
Arbour, Al 1932- *WorAlBi*
Arbour, Alger 1932- *WhoAm 90, WhoE 91*
Arbour, Claude Marc 1961- *BiDrAPA 89*
Arbour, Harold Cyril 1939- *WhoAm 90*
Arbtin, Keith Emil 1947- *WhoWor 91*

Arbuckle, Fatty 1887-1933 *WorAlBi*
Arbuckle, James Ernest 1939- *St&PR 91*
Arbuckle, Scott G. 1931- *St&PR 91, WhoAm 90*
Arbulu, Agustin 1928- *WhoHisp 91*
Arbulu, Agustin Victor 1949- *WhoHisp 91*
Arbury, Andrew Stephen, III 1953- *WhoEmL 91*
Arbus, Diane 1923-1971 *BioAmW, ModArCr 1 [port], WorAlBi*
Arbuse, David I 1900- *BiDrAPA 89*
Arbuse, David I. 1900-1990 *BioIn 16*
Arbuthnot, John 1667-1735 *DcLB 101 [port]*
Arbuthnot, May Hill 1884-1969 *AuBYP 90*
Arbuthnot, Peter Ivan 1948- *WhoSSW 91*
Arcan, Petru P 1933- *BiDrAPA 89*
Arcand, Denys 1941- *CurBio 90 [port]*
Arcara, James Paul 1934- *WhoAm 90, WhoE 91*
Arcari, Mario *BioIn 16*
Arcari, Ralph Donato 1943- *WhoAm 90*
Arcaro, Eddie 1916- *BioIn 16, WorAlBi*
Arcaro, Harold Conrad, Jr. 1935- *WhoAm 90*
Arce, A Anthony 1923- *BiDrAPA 89*
Arce, A. Anthony 1923- *WhoAm 90*
Arce, Jaime Ardiles- *BioIn 16*
Arce, Jaime Barrios Perez de *BioIn 16*
Arce, Jose Antonio 1948- *WhoHisp 91*
Arce, Manuel Jose 1783?-1847 *BioIn 16*
Arce, Miguel Luis 1951- *WhoHisp 91*
Arce, Phillip William 1937- *WhoAm 90*
Arce, Ramon *St&PR 91*
Arce-Cacho, Eric Amaury 1940- *WhoWor 91*
Arce-Larreta, Jorge J. 1939- *WhoHisp 91*
Arcella, Lisa 1961- *WhoWrEP 89*
Arceneaux, George, Jr. 1928- *WhoAm 90, WhoSSW 91*
Arceneaux, Jean *ConAu 131*
Arceneaux, Martin Thomas 1951- *WhoEmL 91*
Arceneaux, William 1941- *WhoAm 90*
Arcesi, Beverly Ann 1959- *WhoSSW 91*
Arch, Charles E. *BioIn 16*
Arch, Michael Alexis 1951- *WhoEmL 91*
Archabal, Nina Marchetti 1940- *WhoAm 90, WhoAmW 91*
Archambault, Andre 1949- *St&PR 91*
Archambault, Bennett *St&PR 91, WhoAm 90*
Archambault, Francis X., Jr. 1944- *WhoAm 90*
Archambault, J.K. 1938- *St&PR 91*
Archambault, John *BioIn 16*
Archambault, John Kenehan 1938- *WhoAm 90*
Archambault, Joseph-Sergius 1871-1950 *OxCCanT*
Archambault, Louis 1915- *WhoAm 90, WhoAmA 91*
Archambault, Lynn *St&PR 91*
Archambault, Robert Joseph 1940- *WhoE 91*
Archambeau, Felicien d' *PenDiMP*
Archambeau, Iwan d' *PenDiMP*
Archambeau, John Orin 1925- *WhoAm 90*
Archambeau, Leo Bruce 1932- *St&PR 91*
Archambeau, Lurley John 1944- *BiDrAPA 89*
Archambeau, Robert *BioIn 16*
Archambo, Peter *PenDiDA 89*
Archangel, Cesar Santos 1926- *BiDrAPA 89*
Archbold, Douglas P. 1944- *St&PR 91*
Archbold, John D. *BioIn 16*
Archbold, Phil Carlos 1936- *WhoE 91*
Archbold, Rodolfo Lesandro 1954- *WhoE 91*
Archer, Anne *BioIn 16*
Archer, Anne 1950- *WorAlBi*
Archer, Arthur Elliott 1943- *WhoAm 90*
Archer, Bruce 1922- *ConDes 90*
Archer, Carl Marion 1920- *WhoSSW 91, WhoWor 91*
Archer, Claudette Cheryl 1951- *WhoAmW 91*
Archer, Cynthia 1953- *WhoAmA 91*
Archer, Danna Kay 1948- *WhoEmL 91*
Archer, David Horace 1928- *WhoAm 90*
Archer, Dennis *ConAu 31NR*
Archer, Dennis Wayne 1942- *WhoAm 90*
Archer, Dewey Dale, Jr. *BiDrAPA 89*
Archer, Dorothy Bryant 1919- *WhoAmA 91N*
Archer, Ellen M. 1946- *WhoAmW 91*
Archer, Evangeline 1947- *BiDrAPA 89*
Archer, Frederick Scott 1813-1857 *BioIn 16*
Archer, Glenn LeRoy, Jr. 1929- *WhoAm 90*
Archer, Harry 1888-1960 *OxCPMus*
Archer, Herbert Winslow *MajTwCW*
Archer, Hugh *AmLegL*
Archer, Ira Fletcher 1940- *WhoSSW 91*
Archer, James Elson 1922- *WhoAm 90*
Archer, Jeffrey 1940- *BioIn 16, NewYTBS 90 [port], WorAlBi*
Archer, Jeffrey Howard 1940- *WhoWor 91*
Archer, Jimmy 1883-1958 *Ballpl 90*
Archer, Jules *BioIn 16*
Archer, Jules 1915- *AuBYP 90, WhoWrEP 89*
Archer, Kathleen Frances 1955- *WhoAmW 91*
Archer, Kenneth Davidson 1940- *WhoAm 90*
Archer, Lee *MajTwCW*
Archer, Leonard C. 1911-1974 *EarBlAP*
Archer, Leonie 1955- *ConAu 132*
Archer, Marian Phyllis 1927- *WhoAm 90*
Archer, Mary Jane 1949- *WhoAmW 91, WhoEmL 91*
Archer, Mary Jane 1950- *WhoAmW 91, WhoEmL 91*
Archer, Myrtle Lilly 1926- *WhoWrEP 89*
Archer, Nuala Miriam 1955- *WhoSSW 91, WhoWrEP 89*
Archer, O.R. 1904- *St&PR 91*
Archer, Osceola 1890?-1983 *DrBlPA 90*
Archer, R.M. 1951- *St&PR 91*
Archer, Richard Donald 1947- *IntWWM 90*
Archer, Richard Earl 1945- *WhoEmL 91*
Archer, Richard Joseph 1922- *WhoAm 90*
Archer, Robyn 1948- *FemiCLE*
Archer, Ronald Dean 1932- *WhoAm 90*
Archer, Stephen Hunt 1928- *WhoAm 90*
Archer, Stephen Murphy 1934- *WhoAm 90*
Archer, Sydney 1917- *WhoAm 90*
Archer, Teri Lynn 1965- *WhoAmW 91*
Archer, Thomas Charles 1940- *St&PR 91*
Archer, Violet Balestreri 1913- *IntWWM 90*
Archer, Vivian Thomas 1939- *WhoE 91*
Archer, William 1820-1874 *EncPaPR 91*
Archer, William 1856-1924 *BioIn 16*
Archer, William Reynolds, Jr. 1928- *WhoAm 90, WhoSSW 91*
Archey, Lisa Ann 1957- *WhoAmW 91*
Archibald, Adams George 1814-1892 *DcCanB 12*
Archibald, Claudia Jane 1939- *WhoAmW 91*
Archibald, Edith Jessie 1854-1936 *FemiCLE*
Archibald, Fred John 1922- *WhoE 91*
Archibald, Glenn Orlando 1956- *BiDrAPA 89*
Archibald, Herbert C *BiDrAPA 89*
Archibald, Joseph 1898-1986 *AuBYP 90*
Archibald, Joseph S. 1898-1986 *BioIn 16*
Archibald, Kenneth Warren 1914- *St&PR 91*
Archibald, Margaret Helen 1949- *IntWWM 90*
Archibald, Michael Montbatton 1947- *WhoWor 91*
Archibald, Nolan D. *BioIn 16*
Archibald, Nolan D. 1943- *St&PR 91, WhoAm 90, WhoE 91*
Archibald, Rae William 1941- *St&PR 91*
Archibald, Reginald Mac Gregor 1910- *WhoAm 90*
Archibald, Russell D. 1924- *St&PR 91*
Archibald, Thomas 1936- *WhoSSW 91*
Archibald, Thomas William 1937- *St&PR 91, WhoAm 90*
Archibald, W. Douglas M. 1941- *St&PR 91*
Archie, David Esden 1925- *St&PR 91*
Archie, James Lee 1924- *WhoAm 90*
Archie, Victoria Esther 1960- *WhoAmW 91*
Archilei, Vittoria 1550-1620? *PenDiMP*
Archimedes *BioIn 16*
Archimedes 287?BC-212?BC *WorAlBi*
Archinto Marconi, Rosellina 1935- *WhoWor 91*
Archip, Ticu Sevastia 1891-1965 *EncCoWW*
Archipenko, Alexander 1880-1964 *IntDcAA 90*
Archipenko, Alexander 1887-1964 *BioIn 16, WhoAmA 91N*
Archuleta, Adelmo E. *WhoHisp 91*
Archuleta, Celestino E. *WhoHisp 91*
Archuleta, Diego 1814-1884 *BioIn 16*
Archuleta, Felipe Benito 1910- *MusmAFA*
Archuleta, Isaac Rivera 1933- *WhoHisp 91*
Archuleta, Leroy Ramon 1949- *MusmAFA*
Arcia, Jose 1943- *Ballpl 90*
Arcidy, Louis M. 1954- *St&PR 91*
Arciello, Michael Joseph 1934- *St&PR 91*
Arcieri, Sandy Lee 1955- *WhoAmW 91*
Arciero, Jean Mary 1932- *WhoAmW 91*
Arcilesi, Richard William 1934- *St&PR 91*
Arcilesi, Vincent J 1932- *WhoAmA 91*
Arcilesi, Vincent Jasper 1932- *WhoAm 90*
Arcimboldo, Giuseppe 1527?-1593 *BioIn 16*
Arcinas, Teresita R 1933- *BiDrAPA 89*
Arciniaga, Robert *WhoHisp 91*
Arciniega, Ricardo Jesus 1939- *WhoHisp 91*
Arciniega, Tomas A. 1937- *BioIn 16, WhoHisp 91*
Arciniega, Tomas Abel 1937- *WhoAm 90*
Arciniegas, German 1900- *BioIn 16, HispWr 90*
Arcomano, Cathryn *WhoAmA 91*
Arconti, Richard David 1952- *WhoEmL 91*
Arcos, Cresencio S. 1943- *WhoWor 91*
Arcos, Cresencio S., Jr. 1943- *WhoHisp 91*
Arcuni, Orestes Joseph 1943- *BiDrAPA 89*
Arcuri, Leonard Philip 1947- *WhoE 91*
Arcuri, Mary Anne 1947- *WhoEmL 91*
Arcuri, Michael A *BiDrAPA 89*
Arcuri, Vincent, Jr. 1939- *WhoE 91*
Ard, Charles Walter 1932- *St&PR 91*
Ard, Harold Jacob 1940- *WhoAm 90*
Ard, Max Wayne 1958- *BiDrAPA 89*
Ard, Saradell 1920- *WhoAmA 91*
Ard, William 1922-1960 *TwCCr&M 91*
Ardali, Cahit *BiDrAPA 89*
Ardans, Alexander Andrew 1941- *WhoAm 90*
Arday, Donald K. 1955- *WhoEmL 91*
Ardekani, Ahmad Beheshti *BiDrAPA 89*
Arden, Allyn 1941- *St&PR 91*
Arden, Bruce Wesley 1927- *WhoAm 90*
Arden, Elizabeth 1878-1966 *BioIn 16, WorAlBi*
Arden, Elizabeth 1884-1966 *BioAmW*
Arden, Eugene 1923- *WhoAm 90*
Arden, Eve 1912- *WorAlBi*
Arden, Eve 1912?-1990 *NewYTBS 90 [port], News 91-2*
Arden, John *BioIn 16*
Arden, John 1930- *ConAu 31NR, MajTwCW, WhoWor 91*
Arden, Sherry W. 1930- *WhoAm 90, WhoAmW 91, WhoE 91*
Arden, William *TwCCr&M 91, WhoWrEP 89*
Arden, William 1924- *BioIn 16*
Arden-Griffith, Paul 1952- *IntWWM 90*
Ardern, John 1945- *WhoWor 91*
Ardery, Philip Pendleton 1914- *WhoAm 90*
Ardia, Stephen Vincent 1941- *St&PR 91, WhoAm 90*
Ardies, Tom 1931- *SpyFic, TwCCr&M 91*
Ardiles-Arce, Jaime *BioIn 16*
Ardinger, Richard Kirk 1953- *WhoWrEP 89*
Ardis, Janita Marguerite *BiDrAPA 89*
Ardis, Mark Burkett 1929- *BiDrAPA 89*
Ardison, Linda Gail 1940- *WhoAmW 91*
Arditi, Andrea *PenDiDA 89*
Arditi, Isak 1924- *St&PR 91*
Arditi, Luigi 1822-1903 *PenDiMP*
Arditi, Ralph Vincent 1927- *St&PR 91*
Arditti Quartet *PenDiMP*
Arditti, Fred D. 1939- *WhoAm 90, WhoWor 91*
Arditti, Irvine *PenDiMP*
Arditti, Sol J. 1928- *St&PR 91*
Ardizzone, Edward 1900-1979 *AuBYP 90, WhoAmA 91N*
Ardleigh, Joseph D. 1914-1988 *BioIn 16*
Ardley, Gavin 1915- *ConAu 129*
Ardley, Neil Richard 1937- *IntWWM 90*
Ardoin, John Louis 1935- *WhoAm 90*
Ardoin, Jolene Ann 1954- *WhoSSW 91*
Ardolino, Emile *WhoAm 90*
Ardon, Marjorie S 1939- *BiDrAPA 89*
Ardov, E. *EncCoWW*
Ardrey, R. Leigh 1937- *St&PR 91*
Ardrey, Rushton Leigh, Jr. 1937- *WhoAm 90*
Ardrey, William J. 1936- *ODwPR 91*
Ardrey, William James, IV 1965- *WhoE 91*
Arduini, Lewis Charles, III 1939- *WhoE 91*
Ardussi, W. Philip 1934- *St&PR 91*
Are, Lisa Darryl 1950- *WhoEmL 91*
Area, Ronald Gilbert 1945- *WhoSSW 91*
Areddy, Joseph M. 1933- *ODwPR 91*
Areddy, Joseph Michael 1933- *St&PR 91*
Areeda, Phillip 1930- *WhoAm 90*
Areen, Gordon E. 1918- *WhoAm 90*
Areen, Judith Carol 1944- *WhoAm 90*
Areglado, Nancy 1946- *WhoAmW 91*
Aregood, Richard Lloyd 1942- *WhoAm 90*
Arekapudi, Vijayalakshmi 1948- *WhoEmL 91, WhoWor 91*
Arel, Bulent 1918- *IntWWM 90*
Arel, Maurice Louis 1937- *St&PR 91*
Arellanes, Audrey Spencer 1920- *WhoAmA 91*
Arellanes, Frank 1882-1918 *Ballpl 90*
Arellano, Albert E. *WhoHisp 91*
Arellano, C. Rolando 1945- *WhoHisp 91*
Arellano, Diana Ramirez de *HispWr 90*
Arellano, George R. 1933- *WhoHisp 91*
Arellano, Ignacio 1928- *WhoAm 90*
Arellano, Javier 1956- *WhoHisp 91*
Arellano, Jose M. 1944- *WhoHisp 91*
Arellano, Oswaldo Lopez 1921- *BioIn 16*
Arellano, Rafael W Ramirez de *HispWr 90*
Arellano Mejia, Rodrigo 1952- *WhoWor 91*
Arem, Lawrence Jay 1950- *WhoEmL 91*
Arena, Alan Joseph 1950- *WhoWor 91*
Arena, Albert A. 1929- *WhoE 91*
Arena, Angelo Richard 1928- *St&PR 91*
Arena, Charles John 1953- *WhoEmL 91*
Arena, J. Sylvester 1961- *WhoEmL 91*
Arena, Jay M. 1909- *WhoAm 90*
Arena, John I. 1929-1989 *BioIn 16*
Arena, M. Scott 1946- *St&PR 91, WhoAm 90, WhoEmL 91*
Arena, Nick F. 1939- *St&PR 91*
Arena, Nick Frank 1939- *WhoAm 90*
Arena, Roberta J. 1948- *St&PR 91*
Arenal, Concepcion 1820-1893 *EncCoWW*
Arenal, Julie *WhoAm 90*
Arenal, Julie 1942- *WhoHisp 91*
Arenal de Garcia Carrasco, Concepcion 1820-1893 *BioIn 16*
Arenas, Fernando George, Jr. 1937- *WhoHisp 91*
Arenas, Reinaldo 1943- *BioIn 16, HispWr 90, WhoHisp 91*
Arenas, Reinaldo 1943-1990 *NewYTBS 90 [port]*
Arenberg, Julius Theodore, Jr. 1923- *WhoAm 90*
Arenberg, Paul M. 1931- *St&PR 91*
Arenberg, William Donald 1930- *St&PR 91*
Arencibia, Raul Antonio 1955- *WhoEmL 91*
Arend, John Tim 1940- *St&PR 91*
Arend, Servatius *PenDiDA 89*
Arend, William W. 1934- *St&PR 91*
Arendall, Beverly S. 1928- *St&PR 91*
Arendall, Charles Baker, Jr. 1915- *WhoAm 90, WhoWor 91*
Arendrup, Edith 1846- *BiDWomA*
Arends, Ronald George 1945- *WhoAm 90*
Arends, Stuart 1950- *WhoAmA 91*
Arendt, Gernot 1962- *WhoWor 91*
Arendt, Hannah *BioIn 16*
Arendt, Hannah 1906-1975 *FemiCLE, MajTwCW, WorAlBi, WrPh P*
Arendt, Hannah 1906-1986 *EncCoWW*
Arendt, Kathleen Elizabeth 1963- *WhoE 91*
Arendt, William F. 1920- *ODwPR 91*
Arenowitz, Albert Harold 1925- *BiDrAPA 89, WhoAm 90, WhoWor 91*
Arens, Juho 1946- *St&PR 91*
Arens, Moshe *BioIn 16*
Arens, Nicholas Herman 1937- *WhoE 91, WhoWor 91*
Arens, Stephen Richard 1951- *WhoEmL 91*
Arens, Steven Carlton 1955- *WhoEmL 91*
Arensberg, Chas. C. 1913- *St&PR 91*
Arensdorf, Alfred M 1940- *BiDrAPA 89*
Arensman, Craig Louis 1955- *WhoEmL 91*
Arenson, Barbara Levine 1947- *WhoEmL 91*
Arenson, Edwin Walker 1950- *WhoEmL 91*
Arenson, Gregory K. 1949- *WhoEmL 91*
Arenson, Karen Wattel 1949- *WhoAm 90, WhoAmW 91*
Arenson, Richard S *BiDrAPA 89*
Arent, Albert E. 1911- *St&PR 91*
Arent, Albert Ezra 1911- *WhoAm 90*
Arent, Marvin L. 1917- *St&PR 91*
Arent, Richard Joseph 1963- *WhoEmL 91*
Arent, Servatius *PenDiDA 89*
Arenth, Linda Magnusson 1932- *WhoAmW 91*
Arentzen, Glenda *BioIn 16*
Areskine, Margaret *BiDEWW*
Areskog, Donald Clinton 1926- *WhoE 91*
Arestie, Edward Alan 1952- *St&PR 91*
Aresty, Esther Bradford *WhoAmW 91*
Aresty, Jeffrey 1951- *WhoEmL 91*
Arevalo, Henrietta Martinez 1949- *WhoHisp 91*
Arevalo, Jorge Enrique 1940- *WhoHisp 91*
Arevalo, Juan Jose 1904- *BioIn 16*
Arevalo, Mila Roxas *BiDrAPA 89*
Arevalo, Vinicio Cerezo *BioIn 16*
Arevalo Bermejo, Juan Jose 1904-1990 *NewYTBS 90 [port]*
Arevalo Martinez, Rafael 1884-1975 *HispWr 90*
Arevian, Sarkis Toros *BiDrAPA 89*
Arey, Linda Lugenia 1944- *WhoAm 90*
Arey, Patrick Kane 1947- *WhoEmL 91*
Arey, Robert Jackson, Jr. 1952- *St&PR 91, WhoSSW 91*
Arfa, Kenneth Scott *BiDrAPA 89*
Arfa, Milton 1920- *WhoAm 90*
Arfe, Enrique de 1470?-1545? *PenDiDA 89*
Arfe y Villafane, Juan de 1535-1603 *PenDiDA 89*
Arfeen, Sultan Ul 1941- *WhoWor 91*
Arffa, Sharon Mary 1954- *WhoAmW 91*
Arffa, Stanley H. 1923- *St&PR 91*
Arfield, George *ODwPR 91*
Arfin, Ronald R. 1953- *St&PR 91*
Arfons, Craig *BioIn 16*
Arft, Hank 1922- *Ballpl 90*
Arft, Larry Norman 1946- *WhoEmL 91*
Argall, Charles G *WhoAmA 91N*

Argall, Samuel EncCRAm
Argana, Luis Maria 1932- WhoWor 91
Arganbright, A.D. 1930- St&PR 91
Arganbright, A. Dean 1930- WhoAm 90
Argenson, Marc-Antoine-Rene d' 1722-1787 BioIn 16
Argent EncPR&S 89
Argenta, Ataulfo 1913-1958 PenDiMP
Argenta, Craig Jon 1952- WhoEmL 91
Argenta, Nancy 1957- IntWWM 90
Argenta Maza, Ataulfo 1913-1958 PenDiMP
Argenti, Paul Anthony 1953- WhoE 91
Argentieri, Federigo 1953- WhoWor 91
Argentieri, Mary Ellen BioIn 16
Argentine, Peter Dominic 1948- St&PR 91
Argento, Dario 1940- ConTFT 8
Argento, Dominick 1927- IntWWM 90, PenDiMP A
Argento, Liborio John 1958- WhoEmL 91
Argenziano, Carmen 1943- ConTFT 8 [port]
Argerich, Martha BioIn 16
Argerich, Martha 1941- IntWWM 90, PenDiMP
Argersinger, Marnie Hayes 1922- WhoAmW 91
Argersinger, William John, Jr. 1918- WhoAm 90
Argirion, Michael 1940- WhoAm 90
Argiz, Antonio L. 1952- WhoHisp 91
Argo, Betty Earnest 1934- WhoAmW 91
Argo, Dorothy Peck WhoSSW 91
Argo, Neil BioIn 16
Argo, Rebecca White BiDrAPA 89
Argo, William Alexander 1923- St&PR 91
Argo, William Frank 1951- WhoE 91
Argon, Ali Suphi 1930- WhoAm 90
Argow, Keith Angevin 1936- WhoAm 90
Argroves, Kenneth W. 1947- St&PR 91
Argue, Douglas WhoAmA 91
Argue, John Clifford 1932- WhoAm 90
Argue, Lowell Francis 1938- St&PR 91
Arguedas, Jose Maria BioIn 16
Arguedas, Jose Maria 1911-1969 HispWr 90
Arguelles, Ivan 1939- WhoWrEP 89
Arguelles, John A. 1927- WhoAm 90
Arguelles, Jose NewAgE 90
Arguello, Alexis 1952- WhoHisp 91
Arguello, Fares J BiDrAPA 89
Arguello, Robert J. T., Sr. 1932- WhoHisp 91
Arguello, Roberto Jose 1955- WhoHisp 91
Argueta, Manlio 1936- ConAu 131, HispWr 90
Arguijo, Conrad V. WhoHisp 91
Argun, Fatima Hatice 1959- WhoAmW 91
Argy, John 1944- BiDrAPA 89
Argyelan, Michael Charles St&PR 91
Argyilan, Kristi Ann 1958- WhoAmW 91
Argyll, Duchess of BiDWomA
Argyll, Margaret Campbell, Duchess of BioIn 16
Argyres, Petros Nicholaos 1927- WhoAm 90
Argyriadou, Chryssoula EncCoWW
Argyros, George 1937- Ballpl 90
Ariadne BiDEWW, BioIn 16, FemiCLE
Ariail, Edward Denton 1958- WhoEmL 91
Arial, David B. 1942- St&PR 91
Arial, Jean Claude 1958- WhoEmL 91
Arian, Rahim 1931- St&PR 91
Ariano, Marjorie Ann 1951- WhoAmW 91
Arians, Bruce BioIn 16
Arias, Alejandro Antonio 1959- WhoHisp 91
Arias, Armando Antonio, Jr. 1953- WhoHisp 91
Arias, Arnulfo 1901-1988 AnObit 1988
Arias, David 1929- WhoAm 90
Arias, Horacio BiDrAPA 89
Arias, Irwin Monroe 1926- WhoAm 90
Arias, Javier S. R. 1938- WhoWor 91
Arias, Miguel Agustin BiDrAPA 89
Arias, Rafael 1937- WhoHisp 91
Arias, Ramon H. WhoHisp 91
Arias, Roberto 1918-1989 AnObit 1989
Arias, Roberto E. 1918-1989 BioIn 16
Arias, Ron 1941- BioIn 16, ConAu 131, HispWr 90
Arias, Ronald F. 1941- WhoHisp 91
Arias, Victor R., Jr. 1936- WhoHisp 91
Arias Calderon, Ricardo WhoWor 91
Arias Madrid, Arnulfo BioIn 16
Arias Madrid, Harmodio 1886-1962 BioIn 16
Arias-Misson, Alain 1939- WhoAmA 91
Arias-Misson, Alain August 1939- WhoE 91, WhoWrEP 89
Arias-Misson, Nela 1925- WhoAmA 91
Arias Navarro, Carlos 1908-1989 BioIn 16, CurBio 90N
Arias Sanchez, Oscar BioIn 16
Arias Sanchez, Oscar 1941- HispWr 90, WhoWor 91, WorAlBi
Aricha, Amos SpyFic
Arico, Margaret Mary 1952- WhoAmW 91
Aridjis, Homero 1940- ConAu 131, HispWr 90
Arie, Elie 1938- WhoWor 91
Arie, Raphael 1920-1988 PenDiMP
Arieff, Alex Joseph 1908- BiDrAPA 89
Ariel EncCoWW
Aries, Philippe 1914-1984 WorAu 1980
Ariet, Mario 1939- WhoSSW 91
Arieti, James Alexander 1948- WhoSSW 91
Arif, Iftikhar Husain 1943- WhoWor 91
Arifin, Houtman Zainal 1950- WhoWor 91
Arigo, Jose 1918-1971 EncO&P 3, EncPaPR 91
Arigoni, Duilio 1928- WhoWor 91
Arikawa, Hiroo 1926- WhoWor 91
Arikian, Alan Jay BiDrAPA 89
Arimond, Joseph K. 1948- ODwPR 91
Aring, Charles Dair 1904- BiDrAPA 89
Arino, Miguel Angel 1959- WhoWor 91
Arinsburg, Larry 1947- WhoE 91
Arinze, Francis 1932- WhoWor 91
Ariosto, Ludovico 1474-1533 WorAlBi
Aris, Rutherford 1929- WhoAm 90
Aris, Stanley Joseph 1940- WhoAm 90
Aris, Theodoor Willebrord 1940- WhoWor 91
Arisco, Joseph 1956- BiDrAPA 89
Arisman, Marshall 1938- BioIn 16
Arismendi, Rodney 1913-1989 ConAu 130
Arison, Micky 1949- WhoAm 90, WhoSSW 91
Arison, Ted BioIn 16
Arison, Ted 1924- News 90 [port], -90-3 [port], WhoAm 90, WhoSSW 91, WhoWor 91
Arison, Zipora 1947- BiDrAPA 89
Ariss, Herbert Joshua 1918- WhoAm 90, WhoAmA 91
Ariss, Margot 1929- WhoAmA 91
Aristaeus EncO&P 3
Aristide, Jean-Bertrand BioIn 16
Aristide, Jean-Bertrand 1953- NewYTBS 90 [port]
Aristide, Samuel James, Jr. 1928- WhoE 91
Aristigueta, Narciso BiDrAPA 89
Aristodomou, Chrystoforos 1927- WhoWor 91
Aristophanes 450?BC-385?BC WorAlBi
Aristotelous, Panayiotis Meletiou 1939- WhoWor 91
Aristotle 384BC-322BC BioIn 16, EncPaPR 91, WorAlBi, WrPh P
Ariturk, Haluk 1949- St&PR 91
Ariyoshi, George Ryoichi 1926- WhoAm 90
Ariyoshi, Rita Clare 1939- WhoWrEP 89
Ariyoshi, Sawako 1931-1984 WorAu 1980 [port]
Ariza, Cesar Augusto BiDrAPA 89
Ariza, Guaroa D J BiDrAPA 89
Arizpe, Lourdes 1946- WhoWor 91
Ark, Connie Eileen 1951- WhoWrEP 89
Arkadyev, N. ConAu 129
Arkell, John A. 1962- St&PR 91
Arkell, Robert B. 1931- St&PR 91
Arkema, Paul Harold 1940- BiDrAPA 89
Arkenstone, David NewAgMG
Arkham, Gerald WhoWrEP 89
Arkhipova, Irina 1925- PenDiMP
Arkhipova, Irina Konstantinova 1925- IntWWM 90
Arkhurst, Joyce 1921- AuBYP 90, BioIn 16
Arkilic, Galip Mehmet 1920- WhoAm 90
Arkin, Alan 1934- BioIn 16, WorAlBi
Arkin, Alan Wolf 1934- WhoAm 90
Arkin, David 1906- AuBYP 90
Arkin, Frances 1904- BiDrAPA 89
Arkin, Joseph 1922- WhoWrEP 89
Arkin, Joseph 1923- WhoE 91, WhoWor 91
Arkin, L. Jules WhoSSW 91
Arkin, Michael 1955- St&PR 91
Arkin, Michael Barry 1941- WhoAm 90
Arkin, Robert David 1954- WhoEmL 91, WhoSSW 91
Arkin, Stanley Herbert 1932- WhoSSW 91
Arkin, William Morris 1956- WhoAm 90
Arking, Lucille Musser 1936- WhoWor 91
Arking, Richard 1945- BiDrAPA 89
Arkins, Matt BioIn 16
Arkles, Barry 1947- St&PR 91
Arko, Nancy Agnes 1950- BiDrAPA 89
Arkoff, Samuel Z. 1918- BioIn 16, WhoAm 90
Arkoosh, Fred G. 1914- St&PR 91
Arkoosh, Fred G., Jr. 1945- St&PR 91
Arkow, Stan David 1952- BiDrAPA 89
Arkowitz, Martin Arthur 1935- WhoAm 90
Arkus, Allen Sol 1946- WhoSSW 91
Arkus, Jane C. 1929- St&PR 91
Arkus, Jane Callomon 1929- WhoAmW 91
Arkus, Leon A 1915- WhoAmA 91
Arkus, Leon Anthony 1915- WhoAm 90
Arkus-Duntov, Zora BioIn 16
Arkuss, Neil Philip 1945- WhoAm 90
Arkwright, Richard 1732-1792 WorAlBi
Arky, Ronald Alfred 1929- WhoAm 90
Arlant, Pedro Alberto 1945- WhoWor 91
Arle, G. H. Henrik 1948- WhoWor 91
Arlea, Michael Nicholas 1944- St&PR 91
Arledge, Charles Stone 1935- St&PR 91, WhoAm 90
Arledge, Patricia O'Brien 1934- WhoAmW 91
Arledge, Roone BioIn 16
Arledge, Roone 1931- WhoAm 90, WhoE 91
Arlen, Gary O'Hara 1945- WhoWrEP 89
Arlen, Harold 1905-1986 BioIn 16, OxCPMus, WorAlBi
Arlen, Harold W 1930- BiDrAPA 89
Arlen, Jennifer Hall 1959- WhoAmW 91, WhoEmL 91
Arlen, Michael J. 1930- WhoAm 90, WhoWor 91, WhoWrEP 89
Arlen, Monroe S 1931- BiDrAPA 89
Arlett, Buzz 1899-1964 Ballpl 90
Arley, Niels Henrik 1911- WhoWor 91
Arlidge, John Walter 1933- St&PR 91
Arlin, Harold Ballpl 90
Arlin, Steve 1945- Ballpl 90
Arling, Bryan Jeremy 1944- WhoE 91
Arlinghaus, Bruce Edward 1950- WhoWor 91
Arlinghaus, Edward James 1925- WhoWor 91
Arlinghaus, Kimberly Ann BiDrAPA 89
Arlinghaus, Sandra Judith Lach 1943- WhoAmW 91
Arlington, William David 1944- WhoSSW 91
Arlis, Anthony T. 1930- St&PR 91
Arlis, Chrissie P. 1932- St&PR 91
Arliss, George 1868-1946 WorAlBi
Arlook, Theodore David 1910- WhoWor 91
Arlow, Arnie BioIn 16
Arlow, Arnold Jack 1933- WhoAm 90
Arlow, Jacob A 1912- BiDrAPA 89, WhoAm 90, WhoE 91
Arlow, Robert 1934- ODwPR 91
Arlow, Seth Martin 1946- WhoEmL 91
Arlt, Roberto 1900-1942 BioIn 16, ConAu 131, HispWr 90
Arlt, William H 1868- WhoAmA 91N
Arm, Edward Solomon 1936- BiDrAPA 89
Armacost, George H. 1905-1990 BioIn 16
Armacost, John Cooper 1936- WhoAm 90
Armacost, Michael Hayden 1937- WhoAm 90, WhoWor 91
Armacost, Peter Hayden 1935- WhoAm 90
Armacost, Samuel Henry 1939- EncABHB 7 [port] St&PR 91
Armada, Cris Delarosa BiDrAPA 89
Armagost, Elsa Gafvert WhoAmW 91, WhoWor 91
Armah, Avi Kwei 1939- MajTwCW
Armah, Ayi Kwei 1939- WhoWrEP 89
Armajani, Siah 1939- BioIn 16, WhoAmA 91
Armaly, Joseph W. 1936- St&PR 91
Armaly, Mansour Farid 1927- WhoAm 90
Arman 1928- BioIn 16, WhoAmA 91
Arman, Ara 1930- WhoAm 90
Arman, Edward W 1929- BiDrAPA 89
Arman, Theodore W. 1922- St&PR 91
Armand, Camille EncCoWW
Armand, Inessa BioIn 16
Armand, Octavio Rafael 1946- ConAu 131, HispWr 90
Armand, Richard Maurius 1938- WhoWor 91
Armandt, Sven-Ake 1939- WhoWor 91
Armani, Giorgio BioIn 16
Armani, Giorgio 1934- ConDes 90, News 91-2 [port], WhoAm 90, WhoWor 91
Armannsson, Armann Orn 1944- WhoWor 91
Armanski, Gerhard 1942- WhoWor 91
Armantrout, Rae 1947- WhoWrEP 89
Armas, Carlos Castillo 1914-1957 BioIn 16
Armas, Tony 1953- Ballpl 90, WhoHisp 91
Armas Portela, Andres 1954- WhoWor 91
Armatis, Leo R. 1937- ODwPR 91, St&PR 91
Armato, David N. 1961- WhoE 91
Armato, Peter 1953- WhoEmL 91
Armatrading, Joan 1950- ConMus 4 [port], DrBlPA 90, EncPR&S 89, OxCPMus, WhoAm 90
Armbrecht, Edward C., Jr. 1932- St&PR 91
Armbrecht, William H. 1908- WhoAm 90
Armbrecht, William Henry, III 1929- WhoAm 90
Armbrecht, Wm. H. 1908- St&PR 91
Armellino, Michael Ralph 1940- WhoAm 90
Armen, Harry 1940- WhoE 91
Armen, Jacob BioIn 16
Armen, Robert William 1943- St&PR 91
Armendariz, David Esteban 1950- WhoHisp 91
Armendariz, Debra M. 1960- WhoHisp 91
Armendariz, Guadalupe M. 1943- WhoHisp 91
Armendariz, Lorenzo 1957- WhoHisp 91
Armendariz, Victor Manuel 1945- WhoHisp 91
Armentano, Anthony John, Jr. 1946- BiDrAPA 89
Armentano, Marie Elena 1949- BiDrAPA 89
Armenteros, Jorge Luis 1961- BiDrAPA 89
Armenti, Joseph Rocco 1950- WhoE 91, WhoEmL 91, WhoWor 91
Armento, Donald Francis 1956- WhoEmL 91
Armentrout, Peter Bruce 1953- WhoEmL 91
Armentrout, Steven Alexander 1933- WhoAm 90
Armer, Laura Adams 1874-1963 AuBYP 90
Armer, Sondra Schecter 1944- WhoWrEP 89
Armero, Juan Manuel BiDrAPA 89
Armes, Tommy 1948- WhoEmL 91
Armetta, Joseph James 1943- St&PR 91
Armey, Richard Keith 1940- WhoAm 90, WhoSSW 91
Armgard, Beatrix Wilhelmina 1938- BioIn 16
Armiger, Bernadette 1915-1979 BioIn 16
Armiger, George D. 1945- St&PR 91
Armijo WhNaAH
Armijo, Alan B. 1951- WhoHisp 91
Armijo, David C. 1916- WhoHisp 91
Armijo, Dennis 1940- WhoHisp 91
Armijo, Jacqulyn Doris 1938- WhoAmW 91
Armijo, John Joe 1954- WhoHisp 91
Armijo, Manuel 1792-1853 BioIn 16
Armijo, Salvador 1823-1879 BioIn 16
Arminana, Ruben 1947- WhoEmL 91, WhoHisp 91
Armington, Caroline Helena 1875-1939 BiDWomA
Armington, James Hervey 1827-1906 AmLegL
Armington, John Howard 1913- St&PR 91
Armington, R Q 1907- ConAu 131
Arminio, Alphonse P. 1942- St&PR 91
Arminius, Jacobus 1560-1609 BioIn 16
Armistead, Charles W 1920- BiDrAPA 89
Armistead, George Clayton 1916-1990 BioIn 16
Armistead, John Irving 1949- WhoEmL 91
Armistead, Katherine Kelly 1926- WhoAmW 91
Armistead, Lew 1945- ODwPR 91
Armistead, Moss William, III 1915- WhoAm 90
Armistead, Russell Eugene, Jr. 1946- WhoEmL 91
Armistead, Willis William 1916- WhoAm 90
Armitage, Arthur Llewellyn 1916-1984 DcNaB 1981
Armitage, Barri June 1937- WhoWrEP 89
Armitage, David T BiDrAPA 89
Armitage, Frank ConTFT 8
Armitage, George Faulkner 1849-1937 BioIn 16
Armitage, Karole BioIn 16
Armitage, Karole 1954- WhoAm 90
Armitage, Kenneth Barclay 1925- WhoAm 90
Armitage, Richard 1918- WhoAm 90
Armitage, Robert Allen 1948- WhoEmL 91
Armitage, Ronda 1943- BioIn 16
Armitage, Thomas Watson BioIn 16
Armknecht, Paul Anthony 1945- WhoE 91
Armocida, Patricia Anne 1956- WhoAmW 91
Armold, Judith Ann 1945- WhoEmL 91
Armon, Michael William 1953- St&PR 91
Armon, Norma 1937- WhoWor 91
Armon-Jones, Claire April 1953- WhoWor 91
Armondo, Angelo Anthony 1948- WhoEmL 91
Armor, David J. 1938- WhoAm 90
Armor, James Burton 1926- WhoAm 90
Armour, Agatha 1846-1891 FemiCLE
Armour, Bill 1869-1922 Ballpl 90
Armour, David Edward Ponton 1921- WhoAm 90
Armour, James A. 1943- St&PR 91
Armour, James Lott 1938- WhoAm 90
Armour, John ConAu 31NR
Armour, Laurance Hearne, Jr. 1923- WhoAm 90
Armour, Lawrence 1935- St&PR 91
Armour, Lawrence A. 1935- ODwPR 91
Armour, Lawrence Frederick 1920- St&PR 91
Armour, Mary Nicol Neill 1902- BiDWomA
Armour, Maya Lynne 1959- WhoEmL 91

Armour, Norman 1887-1982 *BioIn 16*
Armour, Norman E. 1928- *St&PR 91*
Armour, Philip D. 1832-1901 *WorAlBi*
Armour, R.J. *St&PR 91*
Armour, Rebecca Agatha 1845-1891 *DcCanB 12*
Armour, Richard 1906-1989 *AuBYP 90, ConAu 32NR, SmATA 61, WorAlBi*
Armour, Richard Willard 1906-1989 *BioIn 16*
Armour, Walter B. 1929- *St&PR 91*
Armpriester, Ginger Gail 1948- *WhoE 91*
Arms, Brewster Lee 1925- *WhoAm 90*
Arms, Johnson *ConAu 31NR*
Arms, Margaret Irene 1948- *WhoAmW 91*
Armsby, Henry Prentiss 1853-1921 *BioIn 16*
Armstead, Clark A. 1932- *St&PR 91*
Armstrong, A. Rodman 1927- *St&PR 91*
Armstrong, Alexander 1818-1899 *DcCanB 12*
Armstrong, Alexandra 1939- *WhoAm 90*
Armstrong, Alfreda J. 1939- *WhoE 91*
Armstrong, Alice Catt *WhoWrEP 89*
Armstrong, Anne Legendre 1927- *BioIn 16, WhoAm 90, WhoAmW 91*
Armstrong, Bill Howard 1926- *WhoAmA 91*
Armstrong, Brenda Estelle 1949- *WhoAm 90*
Armstrong, C. Michael 1938- *WhoAm 90*
Armstrong, Carl Hines 1926- *WhoAm 90*
Armstrong, Carol *WhoAmA 91*
Armstrong, Charlotte 1905-1969 *FemiCLE, TwCCr&M 91*
Armstrong, Christopher Paul 1955- *WhoWor 91*
Armstrong, Clara Julia Evershed 1911- *WhoAmW 91*
Armstrong, Claresa F M 1916- *BiDrAPA 89*
Armstrong, Craig Evan 1962- *WhoE 91*
Armstrong, Craig Stephen 1947- *WhoE 91*
Armstrong, Curtis 1953- *ConTFT 8 [port]*
Armstrong, Curtis Edward 1946- *WhoWor 91*
Armstrong, D M 1926- *ConAu 31NR*
Armstrong, Daniel McMullen *BioIn 16*
Armstrong, Daniel Wayne 1949- *WhoAm 90, WhoEmL 91*
Armstrong, Darlene L. 1949- *WhoAmW 91*
Armstrong, David Anthony 1930- *WhoAm 90*
Armstrong, David Ballard 1940- *St&PR 91*
Armstrong, David Ligon 1927- *BiDrAPA 89*
Armstrong, Deanna Frances 1962- *WhoAmW 91*
Armstrong, Deanna L 1957- *BiDrAPA 89*
Armstrong, Denise Grace *WhoAmW 91, WhoE 91, WhoWor 91*
Armstrong, Dickwin Dill 1934- *WhoAm 90*
Armstrong, Donald B. 1915-1990 *BioIn 16*
Armstrong, Donald Edward, Jr. 1950- *WhoSSW 91*
Armstrong, Edward Ambler 1858-1932 *AmLegL*
Armstrong, Edward Bradford, Jr. 1928- *WhoE 91*
Armstrong, Edward W. 1921- *St&PR 91*
Armstrong, Edwin H. 1890-1954 *WorAlBi*
Armstrong, Edwin Richard 1921- *WhoAm 90*
Armstrong, Eugene M. 1918- *St&PR 91*
Armstrong, Francis K., Jr. 1849- *AmLegL*
Armstrong, Fredric Michael 1942- *St&PR 91, WhoAm 90*
Armstrong, Gary Alan 1947- *WhoSSW 91*
Armstrong, Gary Edward 1952- *WhoEmL 91*
Armstrong, Gary L. 1943- *St&PR 91*
Armstrong, Gene Lee 1922- *WhoAm 90, WhoWor 91*
Armstrong, Gene Lee 1939- *WhoSSW 91*
Armstrong, Geoffrey 1928- *WhoAmA 91*
Armstrong, Gerald S. *WhoE 91*
Armstrong, Gibson E. 1943- *WhoE 91*
Armstrong, Gillian *BioIn 16*
Armstrong, Grant 1907- *WhoAm 90*
Armstrong, Greg L. 1960- *St&PR 91*
Armstrong, Gregory Timon 1933- *WhoAm 90*
Armstrong, Harry 1879-1951 *OxCPMus*
Armstrong, Henry 1912- *WorAlBi*
Armstrong, Henry 1912-1988 *AnObit 1988, BioIn 16*
Armstrong, Henry Clay 1840-1900 *AmLegL*
Armstrong, Henry Conner 1925- *WhoAm 90*
Armstrong, Herbert Stoker 1915- *WhoAm 90*
Armstrong, Jack 1965- *Ballpl 90*
Armstrong, Jack Gilliland 1929- *WhoAm 90*
Armstrong, James 1924- *WhoAm 90*
Armstrong, James Franklin *WhoAm 90*
Armstrong, James Isbell 1919- *St&PR 91*
Armstrong, James R., Sr. 1929- *St&PR 91*
Armstrong, James Sinclair 1915- *WhoAm 90*
Armstrong, James W. 1926- *St&PR 91*
Armstrong, James Wray 1950- *WhoE 91*
Armstrong, Jan Robert 1953- *WhoEmL 91*
Armstrong, Jane Ann 1951- *WhoSSW 91*
Armstrong, Jane Botsford *WhoAm 90, WhoAmW 91*
Armstrong, Jane Botsford 1921- *WhoAmA 91*
Armstrong, Janet True *BiDrAPA 89*
Armstrong, Jared George 1926- *IntWWM 90*
Armstrong, Joanna 1915- *WhoAmW 91*
Armstrong, Joanne Marie 1956- *WhoAmW 91*
Armstrong, John 1758-1843 *BiDrUSE 89, BioIn 16, EncCRAm*
Armstrong, John A. 1934- *BioIn 16*
Armstrong, John Alexander 1922- *WhoAm 90*
Armstrong, John Allan 1934- *WhoAm 90*
Armstrong, John Archibald 1917- *WhoAm 90*
Armstrong, John Belmer 1838?-1892 *DcCanB 12*
Armstrong, John Chace 1918- *WhoAm 90*
Armstrong, John D 1917- *BiDrAPA 89*
Armstrong, John Dale 1918- *WhoAm 90*
Armstrong, John Gordon 1952- *IntWWM 90*
Armstrong, John Kenaston 1929- *WhoE 91*
Armstrong, John Kremer 1934- *WhoE 91, WhoWor 91*
Armstrong, John M. 1943- *St&PR 91*
Armstrong, John Michael 1944- *St&PR 91*
Armstrong, Joyce *BioIn 16*
Armstrong, Karan *BioIn 16*
Armstrong, Karan 1941- *IntWWM 90, PenDiMP*
Armstrong, Lance *BioIn 16*
Armstrong, Laura Quirk 1952- *ODwPR 91*
Armstrong, Leonard Otho 1921- *St&PR 91*
Armstrong, Lil 1898-1971 *DrBlPA 90, OxCPMus*
Armstrong, Lina Helen 1923- *WhoE 91*
Armstrong, Lloyd, Jr. 1940- *WhoAm 90*
Armstrong, Louis 1900-1971 *BioIn 16, ConMus 4 [port], WorAlBi*
Armstrong, Louis 1901-1971 *DrBlPA 90, OxCPMus*
Armstrong, Louise *AuBYP 90*
Armstrong, Marian Louise 1929- *WhoAmW 91*
Armstrong, Martha 1935- *WhoAmA 91*
Armstrong, Martha Susan 1954- *WhoSSW 91*
Armstrong, Mary Vaughn 1934- *WhoWrEP 89*
Armstrong, Mary W. 1936- *St&PR 91*
Armstrong, Mike 1954- *Ballpl 90*
Armstrong, Moses Kimball 1832-1906 *AmLegL*
Armstrong, Nancy L. 1948- *WhoAmW 91*
Armstrong, Neal Earl 1941- *WhoAm 90*
Armstrong, Neil 1930- *BioIn 16*
Armstrong, Neil A. 1930- *WhoAm 90, WhoWor 91, WorAlBi*
Armstrong, Neill 1926- *WhoAm 90*
Armstrong, Nelson William, Jr. 1941- *St&PR 91, WhoAm 90*
Armstrong, Nolen L 1917- *BiDrAPA 89*
Armstrong, Oliver Wendell 1919- *WhoAm 90, WhoWor 91*
Armstrong, Orville A. 1929- *WhoAm 90*
Armstrong, Pamela Ann 1948- *WhoAmW 91*
Armstrong, Pamela Gayle 1945- *WhoAmW 91*
Armstrong, Patricia Kay 1936- *WhoWrEP 89*
Armstrong, Peter M. 1954- *St&PR 91*
Armstrong, R. G. 1917- *ConTFT 8*
Armstrong, Ralph Hudson *BiDrAPA 89*
Armstrong, Richard *IntWWM 90*
Armstrong, Richard 1903- *AuBYP 90*
Armstrong, Richard 1943- *PenDiMP*
Armstrong, Richard A. 1935- *WhoAm 90*
Armstrong, Richard Alford 1929- *WhoAm 90*
Armstrong, Richard Burke 1924- *WhoAm 90, WhoWor 91*
Armstrong, Richard L. 1944- *St&PR 91*
Armstrong, Richard Lee 1937- *WhoAm 90*
Armstrong, Richard Q. *St&PR 91*
Armstrong, Richard Robert 1951- *WhoSSW 91*
Armstrong, Richard Stoll 1924- *WhoAm 90*
Armstrong, Robert Arnold 1928- *WhoAm 90*
Armstrong, Robert Baker 1914- *WhoAm 90*
Armstrong, Robert F. 1942- *St&PR 91*
Armstrong, Robert Harris 1931- *WhoAm 90*
Armstrong, Robert L. *BioIn 16*
Armstrong, Robert M. *St&PR 91*
Armstrong, Robert Sitgreaves 1956- *WhoEmL 91*
Armstrong, Robert Stevenson, Jr. 1954- *WhoEmL 91*
Armstrong, Robert Weeks, III 1949- *St&PR 91*
Armstrong, Robin Louis 1935- *WhoAm 90*
Armstrong, Rodney 1923- *WhoAm 90*
Armstrong, Roger Joseph 1917- *WhoAmA 91*
Armstrong, Rosemary 1951- *WhoSSW 91*
Armstrong, Russell 1916- *St&PR 91*
Armstrong, Sarah Elizabeth 1943- *BiDrAPA 89*
Armstrong, Scott Chester *BiDrAPA 89*
Armstrong, Sebert Ray 1935- *St&PR 91*
Armstrong, Sheila 1942- *IntWWM 90, PenDiMP*
Armstrong, Sue 1942- *WhoAmW 91*
Armstrong, Synetta Silverstein Anderson 1953- *WhoAmW 91*
Armstrong, Theodore M. 1939- *St&PR 91*
Armstrong, Theodore Morelock 1939- *WhoAm 90*
Armstrong, Thomas Field 1947- *WhoSSW 91*
Armstrong, Thomas Henry 1829-1890 *AmLegL*
Armstrong, Thomas K. 1954- *St&PR 91*
Armstrong, Thomas Newton, III 1932- *WhoAm 90, WhoAmA 91, WhoWor 91*
Armstrong, Thomas R. 1944- *St&PR 91*
Armstrong, Timothy Joseph 1945- *WhoWor 91*
Armstrong, Viola Gibson 1910- *WhoAmW 91*
Armstrong, W.D. 1932- *St&PR 91*
Armstrong, W. James 1929- *St&PR 91*
Armstrong, Walter Preston, Jr. 1916- *WhoAm 90, WhoSSW 91, WhoWor 91*
Armstrong, Walter William 1928- *St&PR 91, WhoAm 90*
Armstrong, Warren Bruce 1933- *WhoAm 90*
Armstrong, William *BioIn 16*
Armstrong, William Harold 1954- *WhoSSW 91*
Armstrong, William Henry 1943- *WhoAm 90*
Armstrong, William Howard 1914- *AuBYP 90, WhoAm 90*
Armstrong, William L. 1937- *WhoAm 90, WhoWor 91*
Armstrong, William Warren 1935- *WhoAm 90*
Armstrong, Willis Coburn 1912- *WhoE 91*
Armstrong, Zebedee, Jr. 1911- *MusmAFA*
Armstrong-Jones, Antony Charles Robert 1930- *WhoWor 91*
Armstrong-Jones, David Albert Charles 1961- *BioIn 16*
Armstrong Leiper, George 1924- *WhoWor 91*
Armstrong-Poppelbaum, Sylvia Finch 1939- *WhoAmW 91*
Armuth, Douglas 1924- *St&PR 91*
Army, Thomas F. 1930- *St&PR 91*
Arn, Kenneth Dale 1921- *WhoAm 90, WhoWor 91*
Arnaboldi, Joseph Paul 1920- *WhoE 91*
Arnaboldi, Leo Peter, III 1959- *WhoEmL 91*
Arnaboldi, Nicole Sinek 1958- *WhoE 91*
Arnaldus de Villanova 1235?-1311 *EncO&P 3*
Arnall, Ellis Gibbs 1907- *St&PR 91, WhoAm 90*
Arnason, Barry Gilbert Wyatt 1933- *WhoAm 90*
Arnason, H Harvard 1909-1986 *WhoAmA 91N*
Arnaud, Claude Donald, Jr. 1929- *WhoAm 90*
Arnauld, Celine 1895-1952 *EncCoWW*
Arnauld, Serge 1944- *IntWWM 90*
Arnault, Bernard *BioIn 16*
Arnault, Bernard Jean 1949- *WhoWor 91*
Arnault, Ronald J. 1943- *WhoAm 90*
Arnaz, Desi 1917-1986 *BioIn 16, ConAmBL, WorAlBi*
Arnaz, Desi, Jr. 1953- *WorAlBi*
Arnaz, Lucie 1951- *WhoHisp 91, WorAlBi*
Arnaz, Lucie Desiree 1951- *WhoAm 90*
Arnaz Y De Acha, Desiderio Alberto, III 1917-1986 *ConAmBL*
Arnberg, Robert Lewis 1945- *WhoAm 90, WhoE 91, WhoEmL 91*
Arndt, Angelica 1937- *WhoWor 91*
Arndt, C. C. *WhoWrEP 89*
Arndt, Carmen Gloria 1942- *WhoAmW 91*
Arndt, Dianne Joy 1939- *WhoAmW 91, WhoWor 91*
Arndt, Felix 1889-1918 *OxCPMus*
Arndt, Fred W. 1923- *St&PR 91*
Arndt, George W 1925- *BiDrAPA 89*
Arndt, Gunther 1907-1976 *PenDiMP*
Arndt, Hans Joachim *BiDrAPA 89*
Arndt, Heinz Wolfgang 1915- *WhoWor 91*
Arndt, Helmut 1911- *WhoWor 91*
Arndt, Isabelle Owen *BiDrAPA 89*
Arndt, Jack M. 1931- *St&PR 91*
Arndt, James *BiDrAPA 89*
Arndt, Jim *BioIn 16*
Arndt, Joan Marie 1945- *WhoAmW 91, WhoEmL 91*
Arndt, Karl John Richard 1903- *WhoWrEP 89*
Arndt, Kenneth Alfred 1936- *WhoAm 90*
Arndt, Kenneth Eugene 1933- *WhoAm 90*
Arndt, Mary Ellen 1943- *WhoAmW 91*
Arndt, Nancy Yvonne 1938- *WhoAmW 91*
Arndt, Paul Wilhelm, Jr. 1934- *St&PR 91*
Arndt, Richard T. 1928- *WhoAm 90*
Arndt, Robert H. 1942- *St&PR 91*
Arndt, Roger Edward Anthony 1935- *WhoAm 90*
Arndt, Rolf Werner 1932- *WhoWor 91*
Arndt, Stephen Allen 1949- *WhoEmL 91*
Arndt, Ursula *BioIn 16*
Arndt, Walter Werner 1916- *WhoAm 90*
Arne, Gary R. 1957- *St&PR 91*
Arne, Marshall C. 1930- *St&PR 91*
Arne, Thomas 1710-1778 *PenDiMP A*
Arnebeck, William Clifford 1940- *St&PR 91*
Arnell, Gordon E. 1935- *St&PR 91*
Arnell, Peter *BioIn 16*
Arnell, Richard Anthony 1938- *WhoAm 90, WhoWor 91*
Arnell, Richard Anthony Sayer 1917- *IntWWM 90*
Arnell, Walter James William 1924- *WhoAm 90, WhoWor 91*
Arner, Robert David 1943- *WhoWrEP 89*
Arner, Sivar 1901- *DcScanL*
Arnesen, Borghild 1872-1950 *BiDWomA*
Arnesen, Deborah Arnie 1953- *WhoAmW 91*
Arnesen, Eric Andrew 1950- *St&PR 91*
Arnesen, Finn 1932- *WhoWor 91*
Arnesen, Richard B 1929- *BiDrAPA 89*
Arneson, Arne Jon 1943- *IntWWM 90*
Arneson, Dora Williams 1947- *WhoAmW 91*
Arneson, Genevieve A. 1922- *BiDrAPA 89*
Arneson, George Stephen 1925- *WhoAm 90*
Arneson, James Herman 1952- *WhoEmL 91*
Arneson, Janet *ODwPR 91*
Arneson, Jay Clair 1936- *St&PR 91*
Arneson, Mark A. 1915- *St&PR 91*
Arneson, Robert 1930- *BioIn 16, WhoAmA 91*
Arneson, Robert Carston 1930- *WhoAm 90*
Arneson, Wendell H 1946- *WhoAmA 91*
Arness, James *BioIn 16*
Arness, James 1923- *WorAlBi*
Arnest, Bernard 1917-1986 *WhoAmA 91N*
Arnestad, Finn 1915- *IntWWM 90*
Arnet, Neil Steven *BiDrAPA 89*
Arnetoli, Graziano 1938- *WhoWor 91*
Arnetova, Renata 1936- *IntWWM 90*
Arnett, Bradis 1927- *St&PR 91*
Arnett, C. E. *WhoAm 90*
Arnett, Carroll 1927- *WhoWrEP 89*
Arnett, Carroll D. 1946- *WhoEmL 91*
Arnett, Dianne Mix 1957- *WhoSSW 91*
Arnett, Donald L *BiDrAPA 89*
Arnett, Edward McCollin 1922- *WhoAm 90*
Arnett, Foster Deaver 1920- *WhoAm 90, WhoWor 91*
Arnett, Gerald Alan 1962- *WhoSSW 91*
Arnett, Harold Edward 1931- *WhoAm 90*
Arnett, James E. 1951- *St&PR 91*
Arnett, James Edward 1912- *WhoWor 91*
Arnett, James Edward, II 1955- *WhoSSW 91*
Arnett, James William 1949- *WhoAm 90*
Arnett, Janice E. 1942- *WhoAmW 91*
Arnett, Lonnie A. 1946- *St&PR 91*
Arnett, Marion Lee, Jr. 1948- *WhoSSW 91*
Arnett, Norman Jeffrey 1953- *WhoEmL 91*
Arnett, Penelope Pratt 1948- *WhoSSW 91*
Arnett, Warren Grant 1923- *WhoAm 90*
Arnette, Jeannetta *BioIn 16*
Arnette, Robert *MajTwCW*
Arney, David Christopher 1949- *WhoE 91*
Arney, James *TwCCr&M 91*
Arney, Karla Jean 1960- *WhoAmW 91*
Arney, William G 1920- *BiDrAPA 89*
Arney, William Ray 1950- *WhoEmL 91*
Arnez, Nancy Levi 1928- *WhoAm 90*
Arnheim, Gus 1897-1955 *OxCPMus*
Arnheim, Rudolf *BioIn 16*
Arnheim, Rudolf 1904- *WhoAm 90, WhoAmA 91, WorAu 1980 [port]*
Arnhoff, Franklyn Nathaniel 1926- *WhoAm 90*
Arnhold, Henry H. 1921- *St&PR 91*
Arnholm, Ronald Fisher 1939- *WhoAmA 91*
Arnicar, Dolph James 1955- *BiDrAPA 89*
Arnim, Bettina von 1785-1859 *BioIn 16*

Arnim, Bettina von 1940- *BiDWomA*
Arnim, Bettine von 1785-1859 *EncCoWW*
Arning, Bill A 1960- *WhoAmA 91*
Arning, Eddie 1898- *MusmAFA*
Arning, Holger K. 1931- *St&PR 91*
Arning, John F. 1925- *St&PR 91*
Arning, John Fredrick 1925- *WhoAm 90*
Arnink, Donna Jean 1946- *WhoWrEP 89*
Arno, Peter 1904-1968 *WhoAmA 91N, WorAlBi*
Arnof, Ian 1939- *WhoAm 90, WhoSSW 91*
Arnoff, E. Leonard 1922- *WhoAm 90*
Arnoff, Judith Unger 1946- *WhoEmL 91*
Arnold, A James 1939- *ConAu 132*
Arnold, Adolf Wilhelm 1926- *WhoE 91*
Arnold, Alexander Abab 1833-1915 *AmLegL*
Arnold, Alice Marie 1958- *WhoE 91*
Arnold, Allen J. 1934- *St&PR 91*
Arnold, Anthony *BioIn 16*
Arnold, Armin Herbert 1931- *WhoWrEP 89*
Arnold, Arthur L 1925- *BiDrAPA 89*
Arnold, Barbara Eileen 1927- *WhoAmW 91*
Arnold, Barbara Jean 1950- *WhoEmL 91*
Arnold, Ben 1955- *IntWWM 90*
Arnold, Benedict 1741-1801 *EncCRAm [port], WorAlBi*
Arnold, Bob 1952- *WhoWrEP 89*
Arnold, Bruce Allen 1954- *WhoE 91*
Arnold, Bruce Robert 1955- *WhoE 91*
Arnold, Carole Anne Walcutt 1954- *WhoAmW 91*
Arnold, Caroline 1944- *AuBYP 90, BioIn 16*
Arnold, Cecil Benjamin 1927- *WhoSSW 91*
Arnold, Charles Burle, Jr. 1934- *WhoAm 90*
Arnold, Charles Parker 1933- *St&PR 91*
Arnold, Charles Randy 1949- *WhoSSW 91*
Arnold, Christine Annette 1966- *WhoAmW 91*
Arnold, Connie Jean *WhoEmL 91*
Arnold, Craig Glen 1949- *WhoWrEP 89*
Arnold, Cynthia Jean 1942- *WhoAmW 91*
Arnold, Daniel Calmes 1930- *WhoAm 90*
Arnold, Daryl 1924- *WhoWor 91*
Arnold, David Burton 1939- *St&PR 91, WhoAm 90*
Arnold, David Charles 1943- *IntWWM 90*
Arnold, David P. 1942- *St&PR 91*
Arnold, David Paul 1942- *WhoWor 91*
Arnold, David Walker 1936- *St&PR 91, WhoAm 90*
Arnold, Deborah Ann 1957- *WhoSSW 91*
Arnold, Dianne E. 1944- *St&PR 91*
Arnold, Dianne Ekberg 1944- *WhoAm 90*
Arnold, Dorothy Cavanee 1922- *WhoAmW 91*
Arnold, Dorothy Jean *BiDrAPA 89*
Arnold, Douglas Norman 1954- *WhoE 91*
Arnold, Douglas Ray 1948- *St&PR 91*
Arnold, Doyle Louis 1948- *St&PR 91*
Arnold, Duane Wade-Hampton 1953- *WhoWor 91*
Arnold, Eddy 1918- *OxCPMus, WhoAm 90, WorAlBi*
Arnold, Eddy William 1951- *WhoEmL 91*
Arnold, Edgar Frank, Jr. 1925- *WhoWrEP 89*
Arnold, Edward 1890-1956 *WorAlBi*
Arnold, Edward Henry 1939- *St&PR 91, WhoAm 90*
Arnold, Edwin Roy 1962- *WhoEmL 91*
Arnold, Elizabeth *BiDEWW*
Arnold, Elizabeth Appleby 1966- *WhoEmL 91*
Arnold, Elliott 1912-1980 *AuBYP 90*
Arnold, Elting 1912-1988 *BioIn 16*
Arnold, Emily *AuBYP 90, WhoWrEP 89*
Arnold, Emily 1939- *BioIn 16*
Arnold, Eric H. *AuBYP 90*
Arnold, Ethel M. 1866-1930 *FemiCLE*
Arnold, Eugene, Jr. 1922- *St&PR 91*
Arnold, Eve 1913- *ConAu 31NR*
Arnold, Everett John *St&PR 91N*
Arnold, Florence *BioIn 16*
Arnold, Florence M 1900- *WhoAmA 91*
Arnold, Frederick J. 1931- *St&PR 91*
Arnold, Frederick James 1908- *IntWWM 90*
Arnold, G. Dewey, Jr. 1925- *WhoAm 90*
Arnold, G. S. *WhoAm 90*
Arnold, Gary Howard 1942- *WhoAm 90, WhoWrEP 89*
Arnold, Gary Stephen 1954- *WhoWor 91*
Arnold, Gene G. *WhoAm 90*
Arnold, George John 1942- *St&PR 91*
Arnold, George Lawrence 1942- *WhoAm 90*
Arnold, Hans 1935- *WhoWor 91*
Arnold, Harold W. 1930- *St&PR 91*
Arnold, Harry Bartley 1912- *WhoAm 90*
Arnold, Harry Loren, Jr. 1912- *WhoAm 90*
Arnold, Helen 1958- *IntWWM 90*
Arnold, Henri *WhoAm 90*
Arnold, Henry 1886-1950 *WorAlBi*
Arnold, Henry Harley 1886-1950 *BioIn 16*
Arnold, Herbert Anton 1935- *WhoAm 90*
Arnold, Hugh R. 1943- *St&PR 91*
Arnold, Jack *WhoAmA 91*
Arnold, Jackie Smith 1932- *WhoWrEP 89*
Arnold, James E. 1943- *ODwPR 91*
Arnold, James Ellsworth 1956- *WhoEmL 91*
Arnold, James L. 1946- *St&PR 91*
Arnold, James Leonard 1946- *WhoEmL 91*
Arnold, James Richard 1923- *WhoAm 90*
Arnold, James Romer 1933- *St&PR 91*
Arnold, James Walter 1931- *St&PR 91*
Arnold, Janet Nina 1933- *WhoAmW 91*
Arnold, Jasper Henry, III 1944- *WhoAm 90*
Arnold, Jean Ann 1948- *WhoAmW 91*
Arnold, Jeanne 1931- *ConTFT 8 [port]*
Arnold, Jeanne Gosselin 1917- *WhoAmW 91, WhoE 91*
Arnold, Jeffrey Robert 1946- *St&PR 91*
Arnold, Jill Marie 1958- *WhoSSW 91*
Arnold, Joan Dean 1944- *WhoAmW 91*
Arnold, Joanne Easley 1930- *WhoAmW 91*
Arnold, Joe Roger 1942- *St&PR 91*
Arnold, John Dirk 1950- *WhoEmL 91*
Arnold, John Fox 1937- *WhoAm 90*
Arnold, John P. 1946- *WhoE 91*
Arnold, John Phillip 1944- *IntWWM 90*
Arnold, John Q. 1944- *St&PR 91*
Arnold, John Robert 1923- *St&PR 91*
Arnold, Joseph B 1943- *BiDrAPA 89*
Arnold, Joseph H *ConAu 30NR*
Arnold, Joshua David 1951- *WhoEmL 91*
Arnold, Juli Ann 1963- *WhoEmL 91*
Arnold, Junius Harold, Jr. 1926- *St&PR 91*
Arnold, Kathleen Spelts 1941- *WhoAmW 91*
Arnold, Kenneth James 1927- *WhoAm 90*
Arnold, Kenneth Lloyd 1944- *WhoAm 90*
Arnold, Kenneth Mark 1951- *WhoE 91*
Arnold, Kerttu Havola 1938- *WhoAmW 91*
Arnold, L Eugene 1936- *BiDrAPA 89*
Arnold, Landis Stevens 1960- *WhoEmL 91*
Arnold, Larrie W *BiDrAPA 89*
Arnold, Leonard J. 1947- *WhoWor 91*
Arnold, Leslie Bisger 1956- *WhoAmW 91*
Arnold, Leslie Kingsland 1938- *WhoE 91*
Arnold, Lewis Tracy 1933- *St&PR 91*
Arnold, Linda Gayle 1947- *WhoEmL 91*
Arnold, Lorna Jean 1945- *WhoEmL 91, WhoSSW 91*
Arnold, Lynn Ellis 1934- *WhoAm 90, WhoWor 91*
Arnold, Madelyn M. 1948- *ConAu 129*
Arnold, Malcolm 1921- *OxCPMus, PenDiMP A*
Arnold, Malcolm Henry 1921- *IntWWM 90*
Arnold, Margaret Long 1914- *WhoAm 90*
Arnold, Margaret S. 1760-1804 *BioAmW*
Arnold, Margot *WhoWrEP 89*
Arnold, Martha G. *St&PR 91*
Arnold, Martin 1929- *WhoAm 90*
Arnold, Mary Bertucio 1924- *WhoAmW 91*
Arnold, Mary Pamela 1949- *WhoAmW 91*
Arnold, Matthew 1822-1888 *BioIn 16, NinCLC 29 [port], WorAlBi, WrPh*
Arnold, Matthew Charles 1927- *St&PR 91, WhoAm 90*
Arnold, Mercia Elayne 1962- *WhoE 91*
Arnold, Mildred Maxine Berry 1936- *WhoAmW 91*
Arnold, Morris Fairchild 1915- *WhoAm 90*
Arnold, Morris Sheppard 1941- *WhoAm 90, WhoSSW 91*
Arnold, Nancy Lee 1950- *WhoAmW 91*
Arnold, Neil David 1948- *St&PR 91, WhoAm 90*
Arnold, Olinda Dias 1945- *WhoAmW 91*
Arnold, Paul Beaver 1918- *WhoAm 90, WhoAmA 91*
Arnold, Peter Gordon 1943- *WhoE 91*
Arnold, Philip Mills 1911- *WhoAm 90, WhoWor 91*
Arnold, Phyllis H. 1948- *St&PR 91*
Arnold, Ralph *AuBYP 90*
Arnold, Ralph L. 1951- *St&PR 91*
Arnold, Ralph Moffett 1928- *WhoAm 90, WhoAmA 91*
Arnold, Richard Earle 1921- *WhoAm 90*
Arnold, Richard K. 1923- *ODwPR 91*
Arnold, Richard Keith 1913- *WhoAm 90*
Arnold, Richard L. 1931- *St&PR 91*
Arnold, Richard M *BiDrAPA 89*
Arnold, Richard R 1923- *WhoAmA 91*
Arnold, Richard Sheppard 1936- *WhoAm 90, WhoSSW 91*
Arnold, Richard Walker 1947- *WhoAm 90*
Arnold, Robert Don 1939- *WhoSSW 91*
Arnold, Robert Edwin 1948- *WhoEmL 91*
Arnold, Robert H. 1917- *St&PR 91*
Arnold, Robert Lloyd 1940- *WhoAmA 91*
Arnold, Robert Lloyd 1952- *WhoEmL 91*
Arnold, Robert M. *ODwPR 91*
Arnold, Robert Morris 1928- *WhoAm 90*
Arnold, Robert Moses 1948- *WhoAm 90*
Arnold, Robert W. 1933- *St&PR 91*
Arnold, Rocky Richard 1948- *WhoEmL 91*
Arnold, Ron *BioIn 16*
Arnold, Ron L. 1930- *ODwPR 91*
Arnold, Ron R. 1942- *St&PR 91*
Arnold, Rose Mary 1935- *WhoAmW 91*
Arnold, Samuel C. 1937- *St&PR 91*
Arnold, Scott Gregory 1961- *WhoEmL 91*
Arnold, Sheila 1929- *WhoAmW 91, WhoWor 91*
Arnold, Stanley Norman 1915- *WhoAm 90*
Arnold, Stanley Richard 1932- *WhoAm 90*
Arnold, Steven E. 1958- *BiDrAPA 89*
Arnold, Susan 1951- *BioIn 16*
Arnold, Susan Bird 1951- *WhoAmW 91*
Arnold, Tedd *AuBYP 90*
Arnold, Terrell E. 1925- *ConAu 130*
Arnold, Terrence Eugene 1955- *WhoEmL 91*
Arnold, Thomas 1795-1842 *BioIn 16, WorAlBi*
Arnold, Timothy James 1958- *IntWWM 90*
Arnold, Tom *BioIn 16*
Arnold, Udo 1940- *WhoWor 91*
Arnold, Val *BioIn 16*
Arnold, Valerie Denise 1956- *WhoAmW 91*
Arnold, Walter Martin 1906- *WhoAm 90*
Arnold, William Brenton *BiDrAPA 89*
Arnold, William Edwin 1938- *WhoE 91*
Arnold, William George 1926- *St&PR 91*
Arnold, William Henry 1932- *BiDrAPA 89*
Arnold, William Howard 1931- *WhoAm 90*
Arnold, William Lee 1952- *WhoEmL 91*
Arnold, William Noble *BiDrAPA 89*
Arnold, William P. 1946- *St&PR 91*
Arnold, William Strang 1921- *WhoAm 90*
Arnold-Harris, Susan Ann 1951- *WhoEmL 91*
Arnoldi, Charles Arthur 1946- *WhoAm 90, WhoAmA 91*
Arnoldi, Harold 1924- *IntWWM 90*
Arnoldi, Per 1941- *BioIn 16*
Arnoldi, Robert A. 1921- *WhoE 91*
Arnoldy, Julie *AuBYP 90*
Arnoldy, Roman F. 1911- *WhoSSW 91*
Arnon, Dan 1938- *BiDrAPA 89*
Arnon, Daniel Israel 1910- *WhoAm 90*
Arnon, Meir 1951- *WhoWor 91*
Arnon, Michael 1925- *St&PR 91*
Arnond, J. Harold 1900- *WhoE 91*
Arnoni, Yoram 1928- *WhoSSW 91*
Arnosky, James Edward 1946- *ConAu 32NR*
Arnosky, Jim *ConAu 32NR*
Arnosky, Jim 1946- *AuBYP 90*
Arnot, David Sheldon 1930- *St&PR 91, WhoAm 90*
Arnot, Robert 1487-1566 *BioIn 16*
Arnot, Robert E 1916- *BiDrAPA 89*
Arnot, Robert Eugene 1916- *WhoE 91*
Arnot, Susan Eileen 1957- *WhoAmW 91*
Arnott, C.G. 1939- *St&PR 91*
Arnott, Eric John 1929- *WhoWor 91*
Arnott, Howard Joseph 1928- *WhoAm 90*
Arnott, J. Michael *St&PR 91*
Arnott, Peter Douglas 1931- *WhoE 91*
Arnott, R. Jackson 1938- *St&PR 91*
Arnott, Randall Glenn 1953- *WhoE 91*
Arnott, Robert Douglas 1954- *WhoAm 90*
Arnott, Struther 1934- *WhoAm 90*
Arnould, Richard Julius 1941- *WhoAm 90*
Arnould, Sophie 1740-1802 *PenDiMP*
Arnoult, Sophie 1740-1802 *PenDiMP*
Arnoux, Francois *EncO&P 3*
Arnoux, Joseph-Francois-Leon *PenDiDA 89*
Arnov, Boris, Jr. 1926- *AuBYP 90*
Arnove, Robert Frederick *WhoAm 90*
Arnovich, Morrie 1910-1959 *Ballpl 90*
Arnovitz, Benton Mayer 1942- *WhoAm 90, WhoWrEP 89*
Arnow, Aron J 1908- *BiDrAPA 89*
Arnow, Harriette 1908-1986 *BioAmW, FemiCLE*
Arnow, Harriette Louisa Simpson 1908-1986 *BioIn 16*
Arnow, Harriette Simpson 1908-1986 *LiHiK, MajTwCW*
Arnow, Leslie Earle 1909- *WhoAm 90*
Arnow, Winston Eugene 1911- *WhoAm 90*
Arns, David H. 1950- *ODwPR 91*
Arns, Paulo Evaristo 1921- *WhoWor 91*
Arnsan, Daniel Carlton 1946- *WhoEmL 91*
Arnsdorf, Dennis Abraham 1953- *WhoEmL 91*
Arnsdorf, Morton Frank 1940- *WhoAm 90, WhoWor 91*
Arnsdorff, Ursula K 1911- *BiDrAPA 89*
Arnson, Alan Norton 1935- *BiDrAPA 89*
Arnson, Joshua Daniel 1963- *WhoE 91*
Arnspiger, Curt Edward 1956- *WhoEmL 91*
Arnstein, Arnold 1898-1989 *BioIn 16*
Arnstein, Daphne Barritt-Vane *BioIn 16, NewYTBS 90*
Arnstein, Margaret Gene 1904-1972 *BioIn 16*
Arnstein, Robert Leo 1919- *BiDrAPA 89*
Arnstein, Sherry Phyllis *WhoAm 90, WhoAmW 91*
Arnstein, Walter Leonard 1930- *WhoAm 90*
Arnt, Charles *NewYTBS 90*
Arnthorsson, Valur 1935- *WhoWor 91*
Arntsen, Henry 1932- *WhoWor 91*
Arntson, Judith Christine 1938- *WhoAmW 91*
Arntson, Peter Andrew 1938- *WhoAm 90, WhoSSW 91*
Arntzen, Charles Joel 1941- *WhoAm 90*
Arnuphis *EncO&P 3*
Arnwine, Don Lee 1932- *WhoAm 90*
Arnwine, William Carrol 1929- *WhoAm 90*
Arny, Deane Cedric 1917- *WhoAm 90*
Arny, William Frederick Milton 1813-1881 *BioIn 16*
Aro, Mary *BioIn 16*
Aroesty, Sidney Albert 1946- *St&PR 91*
Aroesty, Steven Mitchell 1961- *WhoEmL 91*
Arogyaswamy, Bernard Anthony 1945- *WhoE 91*
Arola, Burton Charles 1953- *St&PR 91*
Aromaa, Jukka *BioIn 16*
Aron, Alan Milford 1933- *WhoE 91*
Aron, Jaime 1943- *WhoWor 91*
Aron, Jean-Paul *BioIn 16*
Aron, Mark G. 1943- *WhoAm 90*
Aron, Mark Gidell 1943- *St&PR 91*
Aron, Paul H. 1921- *St&PR 91*
Aron, Peter H 1942- *BiDrAPA 89*
Aron, Raymond 1905-1983 *BioIn 16*
Aron, Raymond Claude Ferdinand 1905-1983 *BiDFrPL*
Aron, Stephen C 1940- *BiDrAPA 89*
Aron, Susan Marlene 1956- *WhoE 91*
Aronberg, Ronald Jerry 1932- *St&PR 91*
Arone, Anne 1959- *St&PR 91*
Aronek, George 1927- *St&PR 91*
Aroni, Samuel 1927- *WhoAm 90*
Aronin, Irene C. 1951- *St&PR 91*
Aronin, Lewis Richard 1919- *WhoE 91*
Aronin, Patricia Anne 1948- *WhoAm 90*
Aronne-Amestoy, Lida Beatriz 1940- *WhoAmW 91*
Aronoff, Bille Louis 1914- *WhoAm 90*
Aronoff, Craig Ellis 1951- *WhoSSW 91*
Aronoff, Gerald M 1944- *BiDrAPA 89*
Aronoff, Mark H. 1949- *WhoAm 90*
Aronoff, Michael S 1940- *BiDrAPA 89*
Aronoff, Michael Stephen 1940- *WhoE 91*
Aronoff, Stuart Bertram 1932- *St&PR 91*
Aronow, Edward 1945- *WhoE 91, WhoEmL 91, WhoWor 91*
Aronow, Jani 1957- *ODwPR 91*
Aronow, Jani Allison 1957- *WhoE 91*
Aronow, Les 1937- *ODwPR 91*
Aronow, Paul 1935- *BiDrAPA 89*
Aronow, Richard Avery 1953- *WhoEmL 91*
Aronowitz, Cecil 1916-1978 *PenDiMP*
Aronowitz, Jack Leon 1940- *St&PR 91*
Aronowitz, Marvin 1924- *St&PR 91, WhoAm 90, WhoSSW 91*
Aronowitz, Stanley 1933- *ConAu 131*
Arons, Annette *BioIn 16*
Arons, Barbara M *BiDrAPA 89*
Arons, Elissa Beron 1945- *WhoE 91*
Arons, Elissa L B 1945- *BiDrAPA 89*
Arons, Ernest *BiDrAPA 89*
Arons, Irving J. 1935- *WhoE 91*
Arons, Jonathan 1943- *WhoAm 90*
Arons, Mark David 1958- *WhoEmL 91*
Arons, Martin 1934- *BiDrAPA 89*
Arons, Michael Eugene 1939- *WhoAm 90*
Arons, Michael James 1942- *BiDrAPA 89*
Aronson, Alan A. 1947- *St&PR 91*
Aronson, Angelica S. W. *BiDrAPA 89*
Aronson, Arnold P. 1943- *WhoWrEP 89*
Aronson, Arthur H. 1935- *St&PR 91*
Aronson, Arthur Lawrence 1933- *WhoAm 90*
Aronson, Bernard *BioIn 16*
Aronson, Boris 1898-1980 *ConDes 90*
Aronson, Boris 1900-1980 *WhoAmA 91N*
Aronson, Carl Edward 1936- *WhoAm 90*
Aronson, Carol Lena 1941- *WhoE 91*
Aronson, Dana *ODwPR 91*
Aronson, David 1894-1988 *BioIn 16*
Aronson, David 1912- *WhoAm 90*
Aronson, David 1923- *WhoAm 90, WhoAmA 91*
Aronson, Deborah Jan 1955- *WhoAmW 91*
Aronson, Donald Eric 1934- *WhoAm 90*
Aronson, Edgar David 1934- *WhoAm 90*
Aronson, Esther Leah 1941- *WhoAmW 91*
Aronson, Frederick Rupp 1953- *WhoEmL 91*
Aronson, Georgianna B *WhoAmA 91*
Aronson, Gerald 1922- *BiDrAPA 89*
Aronson, Helene Ella *BiDrAPA 89*
Aronson, Herbert 1923- *WhoE 91*

Aronson, Hillel S. 1931- *St&PR 91*
Aronson, Howard Isaac 1936- *WhoAm 90*
Aronson, Irene Hilde 1918- *WhoAmA 91*
Aronson, James *EncAL*
Aronson, James 1915-1988 *BioIn 16*
Aronson, Jason 1928- *BiDrAPA 89, WhoE 91*
Aronson, Jay Richard 1937- *WhoAm 90*
Aronson, Leon 1935- *WhoWor 91*
Aronson, Louis V., II 1923- *St&PR 91*
Aronson, Louis Vincent, II 1923- *WhoAm 90*
Aronson, Marc David *BiDrAPA 89*
Aronson, Mark Berne 1941- *WhoAm 90, WhoE 91, WhoWor 91*
Aronson, Michael Andrew 1939- *WhoAm 90, WhoWrEP 89*
Aronson, Michael Harvey *BiDrAPA 89*
Aronson, Milton Howard 1918- *WhoAm 90, WhoE 91*
Aronson, Miriam Klausner 1940- *WhoWor 91*
Aronson, Morton Jerome 1923- *BiDrAPA 89*
Aronson, Morton L *BiDrAPA 89*
Aronson, Peter Damien 1943- *WhoWor 91*
Aronson, Rebecca 1941- *WhoAmW 91*
Aronson, Richard Jay 1916- *WhoE 91*
Aronson, Richard Norman 1953- *St&PR 91*
Aronson, Robert A. 1949- *WhoEmL 91*
Aronson, Sanda 1940- *WhoAmA 91*
Aronson, Sidney Herbert 1924- *WhoAm 90*
Aronson, Stanley Maynard 1922- *WhoAm 90*
Aronson, Stephen Michael *BiDrAPA 89*
Aronson, Thomas Alan *BiDrAPA 89*
Aronson, Virginia Ruth 1931- *WhoAmW 91*
Aronsson, Herbert A. 1929- *St&PR 91*
Aronstam, Neil Lee 1945- *WhoAm 90*
Aronstein, Martin Joseph 1925- *WhoAm 90*
Aroon, Javali B 1947- *BiDrAPA 89*
Arora, G.K. Jim 1941- *St&PR 91*
Arora, Jasbir Singh 1943- *WhoAm 90*
Arora, Raj *BiDrAPA 89*
Arora, Rajesh *BiDrAPA 89*
Arora, Shirley Lease 1930- *WhoAm 90*
Arora, Sudesh Kumar 1939- *St&PR 91*
Arora, Veena Walia 1944- *BiDrAPA 89*
Aros, Arnold Robert 1947- *St&PR 91*
Arouh, Jeffrey Alan 1945- *WhoAm 90*
Arova, Sonia 1928- *WhoAmW 91, WhoSSW 91*
Arowesty, Jill 1964- *WhoAmW 91*
Arozarena, Marcelino 1912- *HispWr 90*
Arp, Hans 1887-1966 *BioIn 16, IntDcAA 90, WorAlBi*
Arp, Jean 1887-1966 *BioIn 16, ModArCr 1 [port]*
Arp, Marilyn LaDean 1940- *WhoAmW 91*
Arp, S. *BiDWomA*
Arpaia, Lello *BioIn 16*
Arpante, Stephen John 1935- *St&PR 91*
Arpeika 1765?-1860 *WhNaAH*
Arpel, Adrien *BioIn 16*
Arpel, Adrien 1941- *WhoAm 90*
Arpel, John David 1949- *WhoWor 91*
Arpin, David Allen 1950- *St&PR 91*
Arpin, Gary Quintin 1944- *WhoE 91*
Arpin, Paul 1925- *St&PR 91*
Arpin, Peter 1957- *St&PR 91*
Arpino, Gerald Peter 1928- *WhoAm 90, WhoE 91*
Arquette, Lois *AuBYP 90*
Arquette, Rosanna *BioIn 16*
Arquette, Rosanna 1959- *WorAlBi*
Arquilla, George, Jr. 1921- *St&PR 91*
Arquilla, Robert 1926- *WhoAm 90*
Arquimbau, Rosa Maria 1910- *EncCoWW*
Arrabal, Fernando 1932- *IntvSpW [port], WhoWor 91, WrPh*
Arraj, Alfred Albert 1906- *WhoAm 90*
Arranaga, Christopher Lee 1960- *WhoHisp 91*
Arranaga, Robert *WhoHisp 91*
Arrasmith, J. W. 1850- *AmLegL*
Arrathoon, Siran 1915- *St&PR 91*
Arrathoon, Tigran 1909- *St&PR 91*
Arrau, Claudio 1903- *BioIn 16, IntWWM 90, PenDiMP, WhoAm 90, WhoWor 91, WorAlBi*
Arre, Helen *ConAu 130*
Arrebo, Anders Christensen 1587-1637 *DcScanL*
Arredondo, David E *BiDrAPA 89*
Arredondo, David Ernest 1953- *WhoE 91*
Arredondo, Jo Marie 1940- *WhoHisp 91*
Arredondo, Lorenzo 1941- *WhoHisp 91*
Arredondo, Mario 1925- *BiDrAPA 89*
Arredondo, Patricia Maria 1945- *WhoHisp 91*
Arredondo, Rudy, Sr. 1942- *WhoHisp 91*
Arreguin, Alfredo *BioIn 16*
Arreguin, Alfredo Mendoza 1935- *WhoHisp 91*
Arreguin, Arturo B. 1937- *WhoHisp 91*
Arreguin, Esteban Jose 1958- *WhoEmL 91*
Arrendale, Thomas A. *St&PR 91*
Arrendale, William Lee *St&PR 91N*
Arreola, Daniel David 1950- *WhoHisp 91*
Arreola, John Bradley 1935- *WhoSSW 91*
Arreola, Juan Jose 1918- *BioIn 16, ConAu 131, HispWr 90*
Arreola, Mona Jean 1940- *WhoAmW 91*
Arreola, Philip 1940- *WhoHisp 91*
Arretteig, Ann Joyce 1938- *BiDrAPA 89*
Arrhenius, Svante A. 1859-1927 *WorAlBi*
Arrhenius, Svante August 1859-1927 *BioIn 16*
Arriaga, Julian de *BioIn 16*
Arrieta, Jose Agustin 1802-1874 *ArtLatA*
Arrieta, Ruben O. 1935- *WhoHisp 91*
Arrieta-Walden, Frances Damaris 1958- *WhoHisp 91*
Arrigan, Nicholas Joseph 1941- *St&PR 91*
Arrighi, Pascal Laurent 1921- *BiDFrPL*
Arrighi de Casanova, Jean-Francois 1949- *WhoWor 91*
Arrigo, Jerry 1941- *Ballpl 90*
Arrigo, Joseph D. 1923- *St&PR 91*
Arrigoni, Giampiera 1944- *WhoWor 91*
Arrillaga, Josefina 1933- *WhoWor 91*
Arrindell, Clement Athelston 1931- *WhoWor 91*
Arrington, Carolyn Ruth 1942- *WhoAmW 91*
Arrington, Charles Hammond, Jr. 1920- *WhoAm 90*
Arrington, Doris Banowsky 1933- *WhoAmW 91*
Arrington, Dorothy Anita Collins 1922- *WhoAmW 91, WhoSSW 91*
Arrington, Gerald Lynn 1955- *WhoE 91*
Arrington, Harriet Ann 1924- *WhoAmW 91*
Arrington, James S. 1930- *St&PR 91*
Arrington, John Leslie, Jr. 1931- *WhoAm 90, WhoSSW 91, WhoWor 91*
Arrington, Katherine Clark Pendleton 1876- *BioIn 16*
Arrington, Lawrence Edward 1953- *WhoEmL 91, WhoSSW 91*
Arrington, Leonard J. *BioIn 16*
Arrington, Leonard J 1917- *ConAu 30NR*
Arrington, Leonard James 1917- *WhoAm 90*
Arrington, Lloyd Madison, Jr. 1947- *WhoE 91*
Arrington, Melvin Slay, Jr. 1949- *WhoSSW 91*
Arrington, Michael Browne 1943- *WhoAm 90*
Arrington, Pamela Gray 1953- *WhoAmW 91*
Arrington, Richard *BioIn 16*
Arrington, Richard 1934- *WhoAm 90, WhoSSW 91*
Arrington, Tracy Lynn 1966- *WhoSSW 91*
Arriola, Carlos L. 1946- *WhoHisp 91*
Arriola, David Bruce 1950- *WhoAm 90*
Arriola, Gus *BioIn 16*
Arriola, Gus 1917- *ConAu 129, EncACom*
Arriola, Gustavo Montano 1917- *WhoHisp 91*
Arriola, Helen Dolores 1943- *WhoHisp 91*
Arriola, Jose *WhoHisp 91*
Arriola, Pepito *EncO&P 3*
Arrison, Clement R. 1930- *St&PR 91, WhoAm 90*
Arrivi, Francisco 1915- *BioIn 16*
Arrizurieta, Jorge L. 1965- *WhoSSW 91*
Arrocha, Eduardo Ernesto 1952- *WhoWor 91*
Arrojo, Rosemary 1950- *WhoWor 91*
Arrol, John 1923- *St&PR 91, WhoAm 90*
Arron, Henck Alphonsus Eugene 1936- *BioIn 16, WhoWor 91*
Arron, Judith Hagerty 1942- *WhoE 91*
Arronte, Albert Ray 1944- *WhoHisp 91*
Arrott, Anthony Schuyler 1928- *WhoAm 90*
Arrott, William 1925- *ODwPR 91*
Arrouet, Dennis 1937- *St&PR 91, WhoAm 90*
Arrow, Dennis Wayne 1949- *WhoSSW 91*
Arrow, Kenneth Joseph 1921- *WhoAm 90, WhoWor 91*
Arrow Yasko, Amy 1957- *WhoAmW 91*
Arrowood, Lisa Gayle 1956- *WhoEmL 91*
Arrowsmith, Marian Campbell 1943- *WhoAmW 91*
Arrowsmith, Pat 1930- *FemiCLE*
Arrowsmith, Peter Dean 1934- *St&PR 91*
Arrowsmith, William Ayres 1924- *WhoAm 90, WhoWrEP 89*
Arroyo, Andrea 1962- *WhoHisp 91*
Arroyo, Antonio Maria 1928- *WhoWor 91*
Arroyo, Antonio Perez 1950- *WhoHisp 91*
Arroyo, Carlos 1954- *WhoHisp 91*
Arroyo, Fernando 1952- *Ballpl 90*
Arroyo, Frank V., Sr. 1926- *WhoHisp 91*
Arroyo, Jose Antonio 1931- *WhoHisp 91*
Arroyo, Lourdes Maria 1953- *WhoHisp 91*
Arroyo, Luis 1927- *Ballpl 90*
Arroyo, Martina *WhoAm 90, WhoAmW 91, WhoHisp 91*
Arroyo, Martina 1936- *IntWWM 90, PenDiMP*
Arroyo, Martina 1940- *BioIn 16, WorAlBi*
Arroyo, Melissa Juanita 1949- *WhoHisp 91*
Arroyo, Richard *ODwPR 91*
Arroyo, Ruy D. *BiDrAPA 89*
Arroyo, William *BiDrAPA 89*
Arroyo del Rio, Carlos Alberto 1893-1969 *BioIn 16*
Arroyo-Rivera, Lillian M. *BiDrAPA 89*
Arroyo San Martin, Enrique 1942- *WhoWor 91*
Arroyos, Alexander Garcia, Sr. 1936- *WhoHisp 91*
Arruda, John B. 1934- *St&PR 91*
Arrue, Salvador Salazar 1899-1975 *BioIn 16*
Arrufat, Anton B. 1935- *HispWr 90*
Arsaga, Russell Francis 1951- *WhoSSW 91*
Arsem, Alvan Donald 1923- *WhoAm 90*
Arsenault, Jacques 1915- *St&PR 91*
Arsenault, Joseph-Octave 1828-1897 *DcCanB 12*
Arsenault, Kate Whitman 1922- *WhoAmA 91*
Arsenault, Leona Marie 1954- *WhoAmW 91*
Arseneault, Edmond John 1927- *St&PR 91*
Arseneault, Gerard Armand 1933- *St&PR 91*
Arshad, Mohammad *BiDrAPA 89*
Arshad, Muhammad Kaleem 1955- *BiDrAPA 89*
Arsht, S. Samuel 1910- *St&PR 91*
Arsinde *WomWR*
Arsinoe II 316?BC-270BC *WomWR*
Arst, Lee N. 1946- *St&PR 91*
Arstark, Lester D. 1924- *WhoE 91*
Art, Henry Warren 1944- *WhoAm 90*
Artal, Michal *BiDrAPA 89*
Artam, Michael T. *St&PR 91N*
Artaud, Antonin 1896-1948 *BioIn 16*
Arteaga, Gertrudis Gomez de Avellaneda 1814-1873 *BioIn 16*
Arteaga, Leonardo E. 1943- *WhoHisp 91*
Arteche 1934- *WhoAmA 91*
Artel, Jorge 1909- *HispWr 90*
Artemiou, Artemis L. 1961- *WhoWor 91*
Artemis, Maria 1945- *WhoAmA 91*
Artemisia I *WomWR*
Artemisia II *WomWR [port]*
Artemisia, Queen of Halicarnassus *BioIn 16*
Artephius *EncO&P 3*
Arterbery, Vivian J. 1937- *St&PR 91*
Arterburn, Katherine Greer 1962- *WhoAmW 91*
Arterburn, Stephen Forrest 1953- *St&PR 91, WhoAm 90*
Arters, Linda B. 1951- *ODwPR 91*
Arters, Linda Bromley 1951- *WhoAmW 91*
Artevelde, Jacob van 1290?-1345 *BioIn 16*
Artevelde, Philip van 1340?-1382 *BioIn 16*
Arth, Clare Elizabeth *BiDrAPA 89*
Arth, Lawrence Joseph 1943- *St&PR 91*
Arthaud, John C. 1939- *St&PR 91*
Arthos, John 1908- *WhoAm 90*
Arthur, King *EncO&P 3*
Arthur, Anthony Henry 1934- *St&PR 91*
Arthur, Beatrice 1923- *WorAlBi*
Arthur, Beatrice 1926- *WhoAm 90*
Arthur, Brenda Kay 1951- *WhoAmW 91*
Arthur, Charles Burton 1911- *WhoSSW 91*
Arthur, Chester Alan 1829-1886 *WorAlBi*
Arthur, Chester Alan 1830-1886 *BiDrUSE 89, BioIn 16*
Arthur, Donna Carole 1942- *WhoWrEP 89*
Arthur, Edna M. A. 1928- *IntWWM 90*
Arthur, Elizabeth 1953- *WhoWrEP 89*
Arthur, Elizabeth Aldrich 1923- *WhoWrEP 89*
Arthur, Elizabeth Evans 1954- *St&PR 91*
Arthur, Ellen Lewis Herndon 1837-1880 *BioIn 16*
Arthur, Gary David 1950- *WhoEmL 91*
Arthur, Gary Kenneth 1944- *BiDrAPA 89*
Arthur, George *ConAu 131*
Arthur, George Roland 1925- *WhoAm 90, WhoE 91*
Arthur, Greer Martin 1935- *WhoAm 90*
Arthur, Jacquelyn D. 1949- *WhoAmW 91*
Arthur, James Greig 1944- *WhoAm 90*
Arthur, James Harrison, Jr. 1938- *WhoSSW 91*
Arthur, Jean 1905- *BioIn 16, WorAlBi*
Arthur, John M *BiDrAPA 89*
Arthur, John M. 1922- *St&PR 91*
Arthur, John Morrison 1922- *WhoAm 90*
Arthur, Julia 1869-1950 *OxCCanT [port]*
Arthur, Lloyd 1930- *WhoAm 90*
Arthur, Michael Elbert 1952- *WhoEmL 91*
Arthur, Michael W. 1939- *St&PR 91*
Arthur, Nan Kene 1954- *WhoEmL 91*
Arthur, Paul Keith 1931- *WhoAm 90*
Arthur, Ransom J *BiDrAPA 89*
Arthur, Robert 1909-1969 *AuBYP 90*
Arthur, Robert Henry 1935- *WhoSSW 91*
Arthur, Robert Thomas 1952- *WhoSSW 91*
Arthur, Ruth Mabel 1905-1979 *AuBYP 90*
Arthur, Susan *ODwPR 91*
Arthur, Thomas Hahn 1937- *WhoSSW 91*
Arthur, Wallace Russell 1954- *BiDrAPA 89*
Arthur, Warren Dupree, IV 1948- *WhoSSW 91*
Arthur, William Bolling 1914- *WhoAm 90*
Arthur, William Brian 1946- *WhoAm 90*
Arthur, William Edgar 1929- *WhoAm 90*
Arthur-Mensah, Theophilus 1952- *BiDrAPA 89*
Arthurs, Alberta Bean 1932- *WhoAmW 91*
Arthurs, Eugene Gerard 1947- *St&PR 91*
Arthurs, Harry William 1935- *WhoAm 90*
Arthursdotter, Karin Emilia 1926- *WhoWor 91*
Arthus, Nicolas Maurice 1862-1945 *DcScB S2*
Artigas, Jose Gervasio 1764-1850 *BioIn 16*
Artigas, Jose Llorenz 1892- *PenDiDA 89*
Artigliere, Anthony 1961- *St&PR 91*
Artigues, Jean Marie 1934- *WhoWor 91*
Artigues, Marta Pessarrodona 1941- *EncCoWW*
Artiles, Antonio G. *St&PR 91*
Artimez, John Edward, Jr. 1956- *WhoEmL 91*
Artinian, Artine 1907- *WhoAm 90, WhoAmA 91*
Artis, Edward Allen 1945- *WhoWor 91*
Artis, John Burl 1946- *WhoEmL 91*
Artis, William Ellisworth 1914-1977 *WhoAmA 91N*
Artiss, Kenneth L *BiDrAPA 89*
Artman, Florence Jean 1937- *WhoAmW 91*
Artman, Samuel Raleigh 1866-1930 *AmLegL*
Artner, Alan Gustav 1947- *WhoAm 90*
Arton, Gavin Rendell 1950- *St&PR 91*
Arton, Patrick D. O. *ODwPR 91*
Artot, Desiree 1835-1907 *PenDiMP*
Artrip, Mary Len Monday 1955- *WhoSSW 91*
Artrip, William James, III 1950- *WhoSSW 91*
Arts, Herwig 1935- *ConAu 32NR*
Artschwager, Richard 1923- *BioIn 16, CurBio 90 [port]*
Artschwager, Richard 1924- *WhoAm 90*
Artschwager, Richard Ernst 1923- *WhoAmA 91*
Artsybashev, Boris *AuBYP 90*
Artucio, Hernan 1929- *WhoWor 91*
Artushenia, Marilyn Joanne 1950- *WhoE 91*
Artuso, Michael Joseph 1960- *WhoEmL 91*
Artwohl, Paul J. 1953- *St&PR 91*
Artymowska, Krystyna J 1923- *BiDrAPA 89*
Artyomov, Vyacheslav 1940- *IntWWM 90*
Artz, Arlene Betty 1922- *St&PR 91*
Artz, Frederick B 1894-1983 *WhoAmA 91N*
Artz, Frederick James 1949- *WhoEmL 91*
Artz, Kenneth Buckley 1928- *WhoAm 90*
Artz, Milton 1916- *St&PR 91*
Artz, Richard Thomas 1953- *St&PR 91*
Artz, Susan C. 1955- *St&PR 91*
Artzbybasheff, Boris 1899-1965 *WhoAmA 91N*
Artzi, Zvi 1951- *WhoWor 91*
Artzt, Alice Josephine 1943- *IntWWM 90*
Artzt, Edwin Lewis *BioIn 16*
Artzt, Edwin Lewis 1930- *St&PR 91, WhoAm 90*
Artzybasheff, Boris 1899-1965 *AuBYP 90*
Aruca, Francisco G. 1940- *WhoHisp 91*
Aruffo, A. James 1932- *St&PR 91*
Aruffo, John Ford *BiDrAPA 89*
Aruffo, Roy N 1931- *BiDrAPA 89*
Aruhn, Britt Marie 1943- *IntWWM 90*
Arum, Barbara 1937- *WhoAmA 91*
Arum, Robert 1931- *WhoAm 90*
Arumugham, Bagyalakshmi 1945- *BiDrAPA 89*
Arundale, George Sydney 1878-1945 *EncO&P 3*
Arundel, Anne, Countess of 1577?-1630? *BiDEWW*
Arundel, Arthur Windsor 1928- *St&PR 91, WhoAm 90, WhoSSW 91*
Arundel, Honor 1919-1973 *AuBYP 90*
Arundel, Ian Bresson 1914- *WhoAm 90, WhoWor 91*
Arundel, Jocelyn *AuBYP 90*
Arundell, Dennis 1898-1988 *AnObit 1988*
Arundell, Dorothy *BiDEWW*
Arundell, Mary *BiDEWW*
Arundell, Victor Charles 1931- *WhoWor 91*
Arup, Ove 1895-1988 *AnObit 1988*
Arup, Ove Nyquist 1895-1988 *BioIn 16*

Arva *EncCoWW*
Arvanetes, Gregory L. 1935- *St&PR 91*
Arvanigian, Gregory G. 1961- *St&PR 91*
Arvanitaki, Angelique *BioIn 16*
Arvanites, Peter Thomas 1963- *WhoE 91*
Arvanitis, Cyril Steven 1926- *WhoE 91*
Arvantinos, S.C. 1938- *St&PR 91*
Arvay, Lisa A. 1960- *WhoAmW 91*
Arvay, Nancy Joan 1952- *WhoAmW 91, WhoEmL 91, WhoWor 91*
Arveson, William Barnes 1934- *WhoAm 90*
Arvidson, Philip R. 1938- *St&PR 91*
Arvidson, Randall Anthony 1960- *WhoEmL 91*
Arvidson, Raymond Ernst 1948- *WhoAm 90*
Arvin, Charles Stanford 1931- *WhoWor 91*
Arvin, Irmgard Pinckernell 1923- *WhoAmA 91*
Arvin, Lawrence P. 1942- *St&PR 91*
Arvin, Newton 1900-1963 *DcLB 103 [port]*
Arvizu, John Henry 1945- *WhoHisp 91*
Arvizu, Robert E. 1943- *WhoHisp 91*
Arvonen, Faith Lynn 1956- *WhoEmL 91*
Arvystas, Michael Geciauskas 1942- *WhoWor 91*
Arway, Joseph William, Jr. 1943- *WhoAm 90*
Arwood, Donald Eugene 1955- *WhoEmL 91*
Arwood, Jana Michel 1958- *BiDrAPA 89*
Ary, T S 1925- *WhoAm 90, WhoE 91*
Aryan, Izzedin *BioIn 16*
Arye, Leonora E 1931- *WhoAmA 91*
Arzac, Adriana Maria 1947- *WhoHisp 91*
Arzbaecher, Robert Charles 1931- *WhoAm 90*
Arzberger, William Albers 1924- *St&PR 91*
Arze, Jose Antonio 1904-1955 *BioIn 16*
Arze, Walter Guevara 1911- *BioIn 16*
Arzhak, Nikolai 1925-1988 *BioIn 16*
Arzonetti, Walter Charles 1938- *WhoE 91*
Arzoumanian, Linda Lee 1942- *WhoAmW 91*
Arzoumanidis, Gregory G. 1936- *WhoAm 90*
Arzt, Frank J. 1937- *WhoAm 90*
Arzt, Max 1897-1975 *BioIn 16*
Arzt, William Charles 1951- *WhoEmL 91*
Asa *WomWR*
Asa, Cheryl Suzanne 1945- *WhoAmW 91*
Asaad, Ghazi 1950- *BiDrAPA 89*
Asada, Toshi 1919- *WhoWor 91*
Asadi, Asad 1946- *WhoEmL 91, WhoWor 91*
Asaff, Glenn W. 1950- *St&PR 91*
Asahina, Robert James 1950- *WhoEmL 91*
Asai, Hitohisa 1931- *WhoSSW 91*
Asai-Sato, Carol Yuki 1951- *WhoAmW 91*
Asaka, Sunao 1923- *IntWWM 90*
Asakawa, Takako 1939- *WhoAm 90*
Asakura, Gabriel Bun-ichi 1935- *WhoWor 91*
Asalone, Anthony J. 1933- *St&PR 91*
Asam, Cosmas Damian 1686-1739 *PenDiDA 89*
Asam, Egid Quirinus 1692-1750 *PenDiDA 89*
Asam, J Kuhio 1952- *BiDrAPA 89*
Asam, Michael Evans 1948- *WhoEmL 91*
Asamoah, Obed Yao 1936- *WhoWor 91*
Asana, Jehangir Jamasji 1890-1954 *EncO&P 3*
Asante, Molefi K 1942- *WhoWrEP 89*
Asanuma Inejiro 1898-1960 *EncJap*
Asanuma, Hiroshi 1926- *WhoAm 90*
Asao, Naohiro 1931- *WhoWor 91*
Asatiani, Liana *BioIn 16*
Asay, Riley Elliott 1951- *WhoSSW 91*
Asazuma, Fumiki 1931- *WhoWor 91*
Asbed, Mona H. 1935- *WhoAmW 91*
Asbell, Bernard 1923- *WhoAm 90, WhoWrEP 89*
Asbell, Fred Thomas 1948- *WhoAm 90*
Asberg, Marie 1938- *WhoWor 91*
Asberry, Bobbie Jo 1934- *WhoAmW 91*
Asbjornson, Ronald Anton 1938- *St&PR 91*
Asbury, Arthur Knight 1928- *WhoAm 90*
Asbury, Francis 1745-1816 *EncCRAm, WorAlBi*
Asbury, Jo-Ellen 1956- *WhoAmW 91, WhoSSW 91*
Asbury, Larry Wayne 1947- *St&PR 91, WhoAm 90*
Asbury, Samuel Jennings, IV 1956- *WhoSSW 91*
Ascalon, David 1945- *WhoE 91*
Ascani, Paolo 1957- *WhoEmL 91, WhoWor 91*
Ascanio, Montiano *WhoHisp 91*
Ascasubi, Hilario 1807-1875 *BioIn 16*
Ascenio, Diego C. *WhoHisp 91*
Asch, Adrienne *BioIn 16*
Asch, Arthur L. 1941- *St&PR 91*
Asch, Arthur Louis 1941- *WhoAm 90*
Asch, Charlotte Endres 1930- *WhoAmW 91*
Asch, Donald Richard 1944- *WhoE 91*
Asch, Frank *BioIn 16*
Asch, Frank 1946- *AuBYP 90*
Asch, Jane Elizabeth 1953- *BiDrAPA 89*
Asch, Moses 1905-1986 *BioIn 16*
Asch, Nolan E. 1949- *St&PR 91*
Asch, Ricardo Hector 1947- *WhoAm 90*
Asch, Sholem 1880-1957 *WorAlBi*
Asch, Stuart S *BiDrAPA 89*
Aschaffenburg, Walter 1927- *IntWWM 90*
Aschaffenburg, Walter Eugene 1927- *WhoAm 90*
Aschauer, Charles Joseph, Jr. 1928- *WhoAm 90*
Aschauer, Mary Ann 1947- *WhoEmL 91*
Asche, David E. 1937- *St&PR 91*
Asche, Oscar 1871-1936 *OxCPMus*
Aschenbrenner, Frank Aloysious 1924- *WhoWor 91*
Aschenbrenner, Karl 1911-1988 *BioIn 16*
Ascher, Barbara Lazear 1946?- *ConAu 130*
Ascher, Bernard 1933- *WhoE 91*
Ascher, Eduard 1915- *BiDrAPA 89*
Ascher, Harold E. 1935- *WhoE 91*
Ascher, Iris Susan 1942- *BiDrAPA 89*
Ascher, James John 1928- *WhoWor 91*
Ascher, John A *BiDrAPA 89*
Ascher, Leo 1880-1942 *OxCPMus*
Ascher, Mark Louis 1953- *WhoEmL 91*
Ascher, Mary *WhoAmA 91N*
Ascher, Rebecca *BioIn 16*
Ascher, Robert 1931- *WhoAm 90*
Ascher, Robert C 1924- *BiDrAPA 89*
Ascher, Steven Peter 1955- *WhoEmL 91*
Ascher-Nash, Franzi 1910- *WhoAmW 91, WhoE 91, WhoWor 91*
Ascherman, Lee Ian 1956- *BiDrAPA 89*
Aschheim, Emil *BiDrAPA 89*
Aschheim, Joseph 1930- *WhoAm 90*
Aschheim, Lydie *BiDrAPA 89*
Aschinger, Eric Dean 1947- *St&PR 91*
Aschinger, Gerhard Adolf 1943- *WhoWor 91*
Aschinger, Keith Lee, Sr. 1943- *St&PR 91*
Aschinger, Zdena Anna 1923- *St&PR 91*
Aschoff, Jurgen Christoff 1938- *WhoWor 91*
Aschoff, Lorraine Marie 1950- *WhoAmW 91, WhoE 91, WhoEmL 91*
Aschoff, Thorpe Brewster 1935- *WhoE 91*
Aschwanden, Richard Josef 1927- *WhoWrEP 89*
Ascian 1943- *WhoAmA 91*
Ascian, Kythe 1943- *WhoAm 90*
Ascione, Alfred M. *BioIn 16*
Ascione, Joseph Anthony 1952- *WhoEmL 91*
Ascolese, Michael J. 1946- *ODwPR 91*
Ascolese, Michael John 1946- *WhoE 91*
Ascoli, Bernard d' *PenDiMP*
Ascoli, Marion Rosenwald *NewYTBS 90 [port]*
Ascoli, Max 1898- *WorAlBi*
Ascone, Teresa Palmer 1945- *WhoAmW 91*
Aseer, Ghulam Nabi 1940- *WhoWor 91*
Aselage, Susan Seabury 1954- *St&PR 91, WhoAmW 91*
Asell, Lars-Ake 1946- *WhoWor 91*
Asen, Shel F. 1937- *WhoAm 90*
Asen, Sheldon F. 1937- *St&PR 91*
Asenbryl, Oldrich *BioIn 16*
Asencio, Diego C. 1931- *WhoAm 90*
Aseniero, Mary Anne Rodis *BiDrAPA 89*
Asenjo, Florencio Gonzalez 1926- *WhoHisp 91*
Asfoury, Zakaria Mohammed 1921- *WhoWor 91*
Asgrimsson, Halldor 1947- *WhoWor 91*
Ash Ra Tempel *NewAgMG*
Ash, Arlene Sandra 1946- *WhoAmW 91*
Ash, Beryl W. 1919- *St&PR 91*
Ash, David Charles 1951- *St&PR 91*
Ash, Eric Duane 1959- *WhoSSW 91*
Ash, Ernest M. 1916- *St&PR 91, WhoE 91*
Ash, Fayola 1926- *IntWWM 90*
Ash, Gilbert 1717-1785 *PenDiDA 89*
Ash, Gregory Lee 1952- *St&PR 91*
Ash, Hiram Newton 1934- *WhoE 91*
Ash, J. Marshall 1940- *WhoAm 90*
Ash, James Lee, Jr. 1945- *WhoAm 90*
Ash, Kenneth H M 1937- *BiDrAPA 89*
Ash, Major McKinley, Jr. 1921- *WhoAm 90, WhoWor 91*
Ash, Mary Kay *BioIn 16, St&PR 91*
Ash, Mary Kay 19--?- *WorAlBi*
Ash, Mary Kay 1915?- *ConAmBL*
Ash, Mary Kay Wagner *WhoAm 90, WhoAmW 91*
Ash, Michael Edward 1937- *WhoE 91*
Ash, Mildred *BiDrAPA 89*
Ash, Patricia Eleanore 1944- *WhoAmW 91*
Ash, Paul J. 1929- *St&PR 91*
Ash, Peter 1947- *BiDrAPA 89*
Ash, Philip 1917- *WhoAm 90, WhoWor 91*
Ash, Robert Lafayette 1941- *WhoSSW 91*
Ash, Robert Lee 1954- *St&PR 91*
Ash, Robert W. *WhoWrEP 89*
Ash, Robert William 1926- *St&PR 91*
Ash, Rodney Beryl 1946- *St&PR 91*
Ash, Roy Lawrence 1918- *WhoAm 90*
Ash, Sharon Kaye 1943- *WhoAmW 91*
Ash-Shara, Farouk 1938- *WhoWor 91*
Ashabranner, Brent 1921- *Au&Arts 6 [port]*
Ashabranner, Brent K. 1921- *BioIn 16*
Ashadawi, Ahmed Ali 1939- *WhoWor 91*
Ashai, Riffat Shafqet *BiDrAPA 89*
Ashamalla, Medhat G 1942- *BiDrAPA 89*
Ashamalla, Medhat Guirguis 1942- *WhoAm 90*
Ashanti, Baron James 1950- *WhoWrEP 89*
Ashbaugh, Dennis John 1946- *WhoAmA 91*
Ashbee, C. R. 1863-1942 *BioIn 16*
Ashbee, Charles Robert 1863-1942 *BioIn 16, PenDiDA 89*
Ashbery, John *BioIn 16*
Ashbery, John 1927- *MajTwCW*
Ashbery, John Lawrence 1927- *WhoAm 90, WhoAmA 91, WhoE 91, WhoWor 91, WhoWrEP 89*
Ashbey, Dwight R, Jr. 1921- *BiDrAPA 89*
Ashbridge, Elizabeth 1713-1755 *FemiCLE*
Ashbrook, Beulah Mae 1934- *WhoAmW 91, WhoSSW 91*
Ashbrook, James B 1925- *ConAu 31NR*
Ashbrook, James Barbour 1925- *WhoAm 90*
Ashbrook, Tammy Jane 1959- *WhoEmL 91*
Ashbrook, William Sinclair, Jr. 1922- *WhoWor 91*
Ashburn, Anderson 1919- *WhoAm 90*
Ashburn, Richie 1927- *Ballpl 90 [port]*
Ashby, Alan 1951- *Ballpl 90*
Ashby, B R 1939- *BiDrAPA 89*
Ashby, Carl 1914- *WhoAmA 91*
Ashby, Carl Crittenden, III 1946- *WhoSSW 91*
Ashby, Carter *ConAu 31NR*
Ashby, Christi Ann 1955- *WhoAmW 91*
Ashby, Christofer *NewAgMG*
Ashby, Cliff 1919- *BioIn 16*
Ashby, Denise Stewart 1941- *WhoAmW 91*
Ashby, Donald Wayne, Jr. 1926- *WhoAm 90*
Ashby, Dorothy Loraine 1939- *WhoSSW 91*
Ashby, Eugene Christopher 1930- *WhoAm 90*
Ashby, Gary 1943- *St&PR 91*
Ashby, Hal *BioIn 16*
Ashby, Hal 1930?-1988 *AnObit 1988*
Ashby, Harold R. 1940- *St&PR 91*
Ashby, Howard Bennett *BiDrAPA 89*
Ashby, Hugh Clinton 1934- *St&PR 91, WhoAm 90*
Ashby, Jack L. *NewYTBS 90*
Ashby, Jack L. 1911-1990 *BioIn 16*
Ashby, John Edmund, Jr. 1936- *WhoSSW 91, WhoWor 91*
Ashby, John Forsythe 1929- *WhoAm 90*
Ashby, Linda Sue 1946- *WhoAmW 91*
Ashby, Lynn Cox 1938- *WhoAm 90*
Ashby, Margery Irene Corbett 1882-1981 *DcNaB 1981*
Ashby, Mark A 1955- *BiDrAPA 89*
Ashby, Norma Rae Beatty 1935- *WhoAmW 91*
Ashby, Patricia F. 1927- *WhoSSW 91*
Ashby, Richard J. 1944- *St&PR 91*
Ashby, Richard James, Jr. 1944- *WhoAm 90*
Ashby, Robert Howe 1930-1975 *EncPaPR 91*
Ashby, Robert S. *St&PR 91N*
Ashby, Robert Scott 1959- *WhoSSW 91*
Ashby, Roger A. 1940- *St&PR 91*
Ashby, Roger Arthur 1940- *WhoAm 90*
Ashby, Rosemary Gillespy 1940- *WhoAmW 91*
Ashby, Steven 1904-1980 *MusmAFA*
Ashby, Steven James 1948- *WhoSSW 91*
Ashby, Thomas Todd 1954- *WhoE 91*
Ashby, William M. 1889- *EarBlAP*
Ashby, Winifred 1879-1975 *BioIn 16*
Ashcom, John M. 1945- *WhoEmL 91*
Ashcraft, David Lee 1946- *St&PR 91*
Ashcraft, Eve 1963- *WhoAmA 91*
Ashcraft, Frances Brett 1965- *WhoSSW 91*
Ashcraft, James Harold, Jr. 1957- *WhoSSW 91*
Ashcraft, Johnny Herbert 1940- *St&PR 91*
Ashcraft, Patricia Rogers 1944- *WhoSSW 91*
Ashcraft, Susan Collins 1954- *WhoEmL 91*
Ashcroft, John David 1942- *WhoAm 90, WhoWor 91*
Ashcroft, Neil William 1938- *WhoAm 90*
Ashcroft, Peggy 1907- *BioIn 16, WhoWor 91*
Ashcroft, Shelley Alane 1953- *WhoWrEP 89*
Ashdjian, Vilma 1954- *WhoEmL 91*
Ashdown, Clifford *TwCCr&M 91*
Ashdown, Ellen Abernethy 1945- *WhoWrEP 89*
Ashdown, Jeremy John 1941- *WhoWor 91*
Ashdown, Marie Matranga *WhoAm 90, WhoAmW 91, WhoE 91, WhoWor 91*
Ashdown, Paddy *BioIn 16*
Ashe, A.J. 1924- *St&PR 91*
Ashe, Arthur *BioIn 16*
Ashe, Arthur 1943- *WorAlBi*
Ashe, Arthur James, III 1940- *WhoAm 90*
Ashe, Arthur Robert, Jr. 1943- *WhoAm 90, WhoE 91*
Ashe, Bernard Flemming 1936- *WhoE 91, WhoWor 91*
Ashe, Charlotte Janet Rosamund 1953- *IntWWM 90*
Ashe, David 1952- *St&PR 91*
Ashe, Douglas *TwCCr&M 91*
Ashe, Edward David 1813?-1895 *DcCanB 12*
Ashe, Geoffrey 1923- *ConAu 31NR*
Ashe, Gordon *MajTwCW, TwCCr&M 91*
Ashe, James Neely, Jr. 1951- *WhoEmL 91*
Ashe, John Baptist 1720-1781 *EncCRAm*
Ashe, Mary Ann *TwCCr&M 91*
Ashe, Mary Ann 1907-1988 *SmATA X*
Ashe, Maude Llewellyn 1908- *WhoAmW 91*
Ashe, Sharon J. 1950- *WhoAmW 91*
Ashe, Victor Henderson 1945- *WhoAm 90, WhoSSW 91*
Ashe, William J. 1920- *St&PR 91*
Asheim, Lester Eugene 1914- *WhoAm 90*
Ashen, Frank Z. 1944- *St&PR 91*
Ashenberg, Wayne R. 1947- *St&PR 91*
Ashenfelter, David Louis 1948- *WhoAm 90*
Ashenfelter, Jayne Eberly 1955- *St&PR 91*
Ashenfelter, Orley Clark 1942- *WhoAm 90*
Asher, Aaron 1929- *WhoAm 90*
Asher, Betty Turner *WhoAm 90*
Asher, Dale L. 1933- *St&PR 91*
Asher, Don *BioIn 16*
Asher, Duffey Ann 1959- *WhoWor 91*
Asher, Dustin T. 1942- *WhoWrEP 89*
Asher, Elise *WhoAmA 91*
Asher, Frederick 1915- *St&PR 91, WhoAm 90*
Asher, Frederick M 1941- *WhoAmA 91*
Asher, Garland Parker 1944- *WhoAm 90*
Asher, Gary Harry 1944- *WhoE 91*
Asher, Harvey 1939- *BiDrAPA 89*
Asher, James Leonard 1947- *WhoEmL 91*
Asher, Jane 1946- *ConTFT 8 [port]*
Asher, Jerome M. 1922- *St&PR 91*
Asher, Joseph *BioIn 16*
Asher, Kamlesh 1953- *WhoEmL 91*
Asher, Lila Oliver *WhoAmA 91*
Asher, Lila Oliver 1921- *WhoAm 90*
Asher, M. Richard 1932- *St&PR 91*
Asher, Martin Richard 1932- *WhoAm 90*
Asher, Michael 1943- *WhoAmA 91*
Asher, Mukul Govindji 1943- *WhoWor 91*
Asher, Robert D. 1927- *St&PR 91*
Asher, Robin Wendy 1960- *BiDrAPA 89*
Asher, Sandra Darlene 1948- *WhoEmL 91*
Asher, Sandra Fenichel 1942- *WhoWrEP 89*
Asher, Sandy 1942- *BioIn 16*
Asher, Steven Alan 1947- *WhoEmL 91*
Asher, Thomas M. 1926- *St&PR 91*
Asher, Timothy Alan 1960- *WhoEmL 91*
Asher, W. Russell 1942- *St&PR 91*
Asher, William M *BiDrAPA 89*
Asheroff, Stephen Carl 1946- *St&PR 91*
Ashfield, Patience 1627-1708 *BiDEWW*
Ashford & Simpson *EncPR&S 89*
Ashford, Anita Rhea 1950- *WhoAmW 91*
Ashford, Carolyn *St&PR 91*
Ashford, Clinton Rutledge 1925- *WhoAm 90*
Ashford, Daisy 1881-1972 *BioIn 16, FemiCLE*
Ashford, Douglas Elliott 1928- *WhoAm 90*
Ashford, Emmett 1914-1980 *Ballpl 90*
Ashford, Evelyn *BioIn 16, WhoAm 90, WhoAmW 91*
Ashford, Evelyn 1957- *WorAlBi*
Ashford, James Knox 1937- *St&PR 91, WhoAm 90*
Ashford, Janet Isaacs 1949- *WhoEmL 91*
Ashford, Jeffrey *AuBYP 90, TwCCr&M 91*
Ashford, John Wesson, Jr. 1948- *BiDrAPA 89*
Ashford, Marguerite Kamehaokalani 1953- *WhoEmL 91*
Ashford, Mary Jane 1948- *WhoWrEP 89*
Ashford, Nicholas *BioIn 16*
Ashford, Nicholas *NewYTBS 90*
Ashford, Nicholas 1943- *DrBlPA 90*
Ashford, Nicholas 1943?-1990 *ConAu 130*
Ashford, Nickolas 1942- *BioIn 16, EncPR&S 89*
Ashford, Patricia Bowden 1945- *WhoSSW 91*

Ashford, Rosalind Mary 1954- *WhoAmW 91, WhoEmL 91*
Ashford, Susan Jane 1954- *WhoAmW 91*
Ashford, Theodore H. 1937- *St&PR 91*
Ashford, Tucker 1954- *Ballpl 90*
Ashforth, Alden 1933- *IntWWM 90, WhoAm 90*
Ashforth, Henry Adams 1901- *St&PR 91*
Ashgriz, Nasser 1957- *WhoE 91, WhoEmL 91*
Ashhurst, Anna Wayne 1933- *WhoWor 91*
Ashihara, Yoshinobu 1918- *ConAu 129, WhoWor 91*
Ashikaga Takauji 1305-1358 *EncJap*
Ashikaga Yoshiaki *EncJap*
Ashikaga Yoshimasa 1436-1490 *EncJap*
Ashikaga Yoshimitsu 1358-1408 *EncJap*
Ashikaga Yoshinori *EncJap*
Ashikawa, Satoru 1945- *WhoWor 91*
Ashin, Mark 1917- *WhoAm 90*
Ashington-Pickett, Michael Derek 1931- *WhoSSW 91*
Ashinoff, Susan Jane 1949- *WhoAmW 91*
Ashiya, Nobukazu 1929- *WhoWor 91*
Ashjian, Mesrob 1941- *WhoAm 90*
Ashkar, Fu'ad 1930- *BiDrAPA 89*
Ashkenazi, Elliott Uriel 1941- *WhoE 91*
Ashkenazi, Isaac 1953- *St&PR 91*
Ashkenazi, Joshua *BioIn 16*
Ashkenazi, Zebi Hirsch 1660?-1718 *BioIn 16*
Ashkenazy, Vladimir *BioIn 16*
Ashkenazy, Vladimir 1937- *IntWWM 90, PenDiMP, WorAlBi*
Ashkenazy, Vladimir Davidovich 1937- *WhoAm 90, WhoWor 91*
Ashkenazy, Vovka 1961- *IntWWM 90*
Ashkin, Roberta Ellen 1953- *WhoAmW 91*
Ashkin, Ronald Evan 1957- *St&PR 91, WhoEmL 91, WhoWor 91*
Ashkinaze, Carole Lynne 1945- *WhoAm 90, WhoAmW 91*
Ashkinazy, Larry Robert 1952- *WhoE 91, WhoEmL 91, WhoWor 91*
Ashlandonian *WhoWrEP 89*
Ashleigh, E Alexandra 1949- *BiDrAPA 89*
Ashler, Philip Frederic 1914- *WhoAm 90, WhoSSW 91, WhoWor 91*
Ashley, Amber Kim 1959- *WhoAmW 91*
Ashley, Austin S. 1916- *St&PR 91*
Ashley, Bernard 1926- *BioIn 16*
Ashley, Bernard 1935- *BioIn 16*
Ashley, Camilla Bloom 1942- *BiDrAPA 89*
Ashley, Darlene Joy 1945- *WhoAmW 91*
Ashley, Diana Gaye 1948- *WhoAmW 91*
Ashley, Douglas Daniels *IntWWM 90*
Ashley, Edward Everett 1906- *WhoWor 91*
Ashley, Eliza Jane *BioIn 16*
Ashley, Elizabeth 1939- *ConTFT 8, WorAlBi*
Ashley, Elizabeth 1941- *WhoAm 90*
Ashley, Elizabeth Ann 1950- *WhoSSW 91, WhoWor 91*
Ashley, Fletcher 1926- *WhoAm 90*
Ashley, Frank *BiDrAPA 89, ODwPR 91*
Ashley, Frank 1941- *DrBIPA 90*
Ashley, Frank P. 1917- *St&PR 91*
Ashley, George Edward 1919- *WhoAm 90*
Ashley, Holt 1923- *WhoAm 90*
Ashley, James MacGregor 1941- *WhoSSW 91*
Ashley, James Wheeler 1923- *WhoAm 90*
Ashley, Janelle Coleman 1941- *WhoAm 90*
Ashley, John 1934- *BioIn 16*
Ashley, John Thomas 1943- *WhoAm 90*
Ashley, Joyce *BiDrAPA 89*
Ashley, Kathy Littlefield 1945- *WhoAmW 91, WhoEmL 91*
Ashley, Kenneth Bryan 1960- *BiDrAPA 89*
Ashley, Laura *BioIn 16*
Ashley, Laura 1925-1985 *ConDes 90, DcNaB 1981*
Ashley, Lawrence A., Jr. 1929- *St&PR 91*
Ashley, Lawrence Atwell, Jr. 1929- *WhoAm 90*
Ashley, Len Robert 1952- *WhoEmL 91*
Ashley, LeNora M *BiDrAPA 89*
Ashley, Merrill *WhoAm 90, WhoAmW 91, WhoE 91*
Ashley, Michael 1948- *ConAu 30NR*
Ashley, Milton M 1922- *BiDrAPA 89*
Ashley, Ona C. 1954- *WhoEmL 91*
Ashley, Patricia L *BiDrAPA 89*
Ashley, Paula Claire 1939- *WhoAmW 91*
Ashley, Robert 1930- *IntWWM 90*
Ashley, Robert Edward 1930- *BiDrAPA 89*
Ashley, Robert Paul, Jr. 1915- *AuBYP 90, WhoAm 90*
Ashley, Rosalind Minor 1923- *WhoAmW 91, WhoWrEP 89*
Ashley, Sharon Anita 1948- *WhoAmW 91*
Ashley, Sheila Starr 1941- *WhoAmW 91*
Ashley, Simon K. *WhoWrEP 89*
Ashley, Velma Dolphin 1910- *BioIn 16*
Ashley, Virginia Lynn *BiDrAPA 89*
Ashley, Walter Edward 1923- *WhoE 91*
Ashley, William Henry 1778?-1838 *WhNaAH*
Ashley-Cameron, Sylvia Elaine 1955- *WhoEmL 91*
Ashley-Tinney, Lori Jean 1960- *WhoAmW 91*
Ashlock, Donna *BioIn 16*
Ashlock, Ken *WhoAm 90*
Ashlock, Robert B. 1930- *WhoSSW 91*
Ashman, Glen Edward 1956- *WhoEmL 91*
Ashman, Harry W. *St&PR 91*
Ashman, Howard 1950- *ConAu 131*
Ashman, John David 1948- *WhoE 91*
Ashman, Michael Nathan 1940- *WhoE 91*
Ashman, Raymond Donald 1923- *St&PR 91*
Ashman, Stephen Neil 1948- *St&PR 91*
Ashman, Stuart 1927- *BiDrAPA 89*
Ashmead, Gordon *AuBYP 90*
Ashment, Arvil L. 1947- *St&PR 91*
Ashmole, Bernard 1894-1988 *AnObit 1988, BioIn 16*
Ashmore, Charles Wayne 1938- *WhoSSW 91*
Ashmore, Harry S. *BioIn 16*
Ashmore, Harry Scott 1916- *WhoAm 90*
Ashmore, James Loyd 1951- *WhoEmL 91*
Ashmore, Robert T. 1904-1989 *BioIn 16*
Ashmore, William Thomas, Jr. 1912- *St&PR 91, WhoSSW 91*
Ashmun, Clifford S., Jr. 1923- *St&PR 91*
Ashmun, John B. 1923- *St&PR 91*
Ashmus, Keith Allen 1949- *WhoAm 90*
Ashner, Marvin 1936- *St&PR 91*
Ashokkumar, Komarla R 1954- *BiDrAPA 89*
Ashpes, Philip 1938- *St&PR 91*
Ashraf, Syed Javed 1940- *WhoWor 91*
Ashton, Adam Keller *BiDrAPA 89*
Ashton, Betsy Finley 1944- *WhoAmW 91, WhoE 91, WhoWor 91*
Ashton, C. Earl 1944- *St&PR 91*
Ashton, David John 1921- *WhoAm 90*
Ashton, Dore *WhoAm 90, WhoAmA 91, WhoAmW 91, WhoWrEP 89*
Ashton, Dore 1928- *ConAu 30NR, WorAu 1980 [port]*
Ashton, Edward Joseph 1941- *St&PR 91*
Ashton, Elizabeth *BiDEWW*
Ashton, Ethel V *WhoAmA 91N*
Ashton, Frederic 1906- *WorAlBi*
Ashton, Frederick 1904-1988 *AnObit 1988, BioIn 16*
Ashton, Geoffrey Cyril 1925- *WhoAm 90*
Ashton, George 1923-1987 *BioIn 16*
Ashton, Harris John 1932- *St&PR 91, WhoAm 90*
Ashton, Helen 1891-1958 *FemiCLE*
Ashton, John Howard 1938- *IntWWM 90*
Ashton, John K., Jr. 1927- *WhoE 91*
Ashton, Larry James 1941- *St&PR 91*
Ashton, Lillian Ruth 1944- *WhoAmW 91*
Ashton, M. Anthony 1935- *St&PR 91*
Ashton, Mal Stanhope 1878-1976 *WhoAmA 91N*
Ashton, Mary Madonna *WhoAm 90, WhoAmW 91*
Ashton, Nancy Lynn 1950- *WhoEmL 91*
Ashton, Neil K. 1944- *St&PR 91*
Ashton, Norman Henry 1913- *WhoWor 91*
Ashton, P. J. 1935- *WhoAm 90*
Ashton, Peter Jack 1935- *St&PR 91*
Ashton, Peter Kent 1954- *WhoE 91*
Ashton, Peter Shaw 1934- *WhoAm 90*
Ashton, Philip T. 1934- *St&PR 91*
Ashton, Price Richard 1917- *WhoWor 91*
Ashton, Rick James 1945- *WhoAm 90*
Ashton, Robert W. 1937- *St&PR 91, WhoAm 90*
Ashton, Robin G. 1949- *WhoWrEP 89*
Ashton, Stewart Leslie 1920- *St&PR 91*
Ashton, Thomas Walsh 1929- *WhoWor 91*
Ashton, Vincent J. *BioIn 16*
Ashton, Winifred 1887-1965 *BioIn 16*
Ashton-Warner, Sylvia 1908-1984 *BioIn 16, FemiCLE, MajTwCW*
Ashurst, Henry Fountain 1874-1962 *AmLegL*
Ashurst, Merrill 1815?-1869 *AmLegL*
Ashwill, Terry M. 1944- *St&PR 91*
Ashworth, Brent Ferrin 1949- *St&PR 91, WhoWor 91*
Ashworth, Denise Marchant 1917- *WhoSSW 91*
Ashworth, Elinor Gene 1942- *WhoAmW 91, WhoSSW 91*
Ashworth, Jeffrey Todd 1964- *WhoEmL 91*
Ashworth, John Charles 1949- *WhoWor 91*
Ashworth, John Lawrence 1934- *WhoAm 90*
Ashworth, John M. *BioIn 16*
Ashworth, Kenneth Hayden 1932- *WhoAm 90*
Ashworth, Maynard Richard 1894- *WhoAm 90*
Ashworth, Phyllis Corbett 1952- *WhoAmW 91*
Ashworth, Richard G. 1926- *St&PR 91*
Ashworth, Richard Goodspeed 1926- *WhoAm 90*
Ashworth, Ronald Broughton 1945- *WhoAm 90*
Ashworth, Valerie Grace 1956- *IntWWM 90*
Ashworth, Willis Louis 1945- *WhoWor 91*
Ashy, Doug Elias 1930- *St&PR 91*
Ashy, Steve M. 1953- *St&PR 91*
Asic, Miroslav 1956- *WhoWor 91*
Asihene, Emmanuel V 1937- *WhoAmA 91*
Asija, Satya Pal 1942- *WhoWor 91*
Asimakopoulos, John L. 1948- *St&PR 91*
Asimakopulos, Athanasios 1930- *WhoAm 90*
Asimov, Isaac 1920- *AuBYP 90, BioIn 16, MajTwCW, RGTwCSF, TwCCr&M 91, WhoAm 90, WhoWor 91, WhoWrEP 89, WorAlBi*
Asimov, Janet Jeppson 1926- *WhoE 91*
Asimov, Stanley 1929- *St&PR 91, WhoAm 90, WhoE 91*
Asimus, Daniel Marion 1946- *BiDrAPA 89*
Asin, Alfredo Quispez *ConAu 131, HispWr 90*
Asin, Cesar Quispez *ConAu 131, HispWr 90*
Asinor, Freddie Andrew 1955- *WhoSSW 91*
Asip, Patricia Victoria *WhoHisp 91*
Asjer, Garland Parker 1944- *St&PR 91*
Ask, Chris *BioIn 16*
Aska, Warabe 1944- *BioIn 16*
Askanas-Engel, Valerie 1937- *WhoAm 90*
Askari, Hasan 1945- *WhoWor 91*
Askarov, Tendik *BioIn 16*
Askegaard, Lewis David 1947- *WhoSSW 91*
Askeland, Calvin Keith 1954- *St&PR 91*
Askenase, Stefan 1896-1985 *PenDiMP*
Askenazy, Mischa 1888-1961 *WhoAmA 91N*
Askevold, David 1940- *WhoAmA 91*
Askew, Anne 1520-1546 *FemiCLE*
Askew, Anne 1521-1546 *BioIn 16*
Askew, Jonathan Stephen 1950- *WhoEmL 91*
Askew, Juanita M. 1936- *WhoE 91*
Askew, Laurin Barker, Jr. 1942- *St&PR 91*
Askew, Linda Lee *BiDrAPA 89*
Askew, Mary Frances 1921- *WhoSSW 91*
Askew, Pamela *WhoAmA 91*
Askew, Reubin O'Donovan 1928- *WhoAm 90, WhoSSW 91*
Askew, Richard *PenDiDA 89*
Askew, Thomas A 1931- *ConAu 130*
Askew, William E. 1949- *St&PR 91*
Askey, Arthur 1900-1982 *OxCPMus*
Askey, Arthur Bowden 1900-1982 *DcNaB 1981*
Askey, Richard Allen 1933- *WhoAm 90*
Askin, Jacalyn Ann 1954- *WhoAmW 91*
Askin, Leon 1907- *WhoAm 90, WhoWor 91*
Askin, Richard Henry, Jr. 1947- *WhoAm 90*
Askin, Seymour R. *BioIn 16*
Askin, Simon 1910- *St&PR 91*
Askin, Walter Miller 1929- *WhoAm 90, WhoAmA 91*
Askin, William D. 1924- *ODwPR 91*
Askinazi, Clifford *BiDrAPA 89*
Askine, Ruth Parse 1936- *WhoAmW 91*
Askins, Arthur James 1944- *WhoE 91, WhoWor 91*
Askins, Nancy Paulsen 1948- *WhoAmW 91, WhoEmL 91*
Askins, Wallace Boyd 1930- *St&PR 91, WhoAm 90*
Askman, Tom K 1941- *WhoAmA 91*
Askoldov, Alexander 1932- *BioIn 16*
Aslam, Mohammad 1945- *WhoWor 91*
Aslan, N. J. 1912-1988 *BioIn 16*
Aslanian, Azed Ozzie 1918- *St&PR 91*
Aslanian, Jacob Raphael 1945- *BiDrAPA 89*
Aslanides, Peter Constantine 1940- *WhoAm 90*
Asleep at the Wheel *ConMus 5 [port], WhoNeCM [port]*
Asleson, Ruth Ann 1926- *WhoAmW 91*
Aslet, Clive 1955- *ConAu 32NR*
Aslin, M. M. 1947- *WhoAm 90*
Aslin, Malcolm M. 1947- *St&PR 91*
Asling, Clarence Willet 1913- *WhoAm 90*
Aslund, Christer 1942- *WhoWor 91*
Asmann, Paul Thomas 1964- *WhoE 91*
Asmann, Robert W. 1933- *St&PR 91*
Asmar, Alice *WhoAmA 91*
Asmar, Laila Michelle 1957- *WhoSSW 91*
Asmodi, Herbert 1923- *WhoWor 91*
Asmundson, Robert Mark 1950- *WhoEmL 91*
Asmus, John Fredrich 1937- *WhoAm 90*
Asmussen, Svend 1916- *OxCPMus*
Asner, Edward *BioIn 16*
Asner, Edward 1929- *WhoAm 90, WorAlBi*
Asner, Marie A. 1941- *IntWWM 90*
Asnes, Daniel Paul 1941- *BiDrAPA 89*
Asnes, Marvin A. 1928- *St&PR 91*
Asnis, Gregory Mark *BiDrAPA 89*
Asnis, Martin 1928- *BiDrAPA 89, WhoE 91*
Asoka 273BC-232?BC *WorAlBi*
Asoma, Tadashi 1923- *WhoAmA 91*
Asomaning, Susan Adwoa *WhoAmW 91*
Asonevich, Walter Jozef 1950- *WhoSSW 91*
Asonsky, George *WhoAm 90*
Asp, William George 1943- *WhoAm 90*
Aspatore, George Alfred 1949- *WhoEmL 91*
Aspaturian, Vernon Varaztat 1922- *WhoAm 90*
Aspazija 1865-1943 *EncCoWW*
Aspbury, Herbert F. 1944- *St&PR 91*
Aspe Armella, Pedro 1950- *WhoWor 91*
Aspel, Bennett David 1937- *BiDrAPA 89*
Aspell, James Fitzgerald 1961- *WhoEmL 91*
Aspen, Janet Elizabeth 1958- *WhoEmL 91*
Aspenstrom, Karl Werner 1918- *DcScanL*
Asper, Israel Harold 1932- *WhoAm 90*
Asper, Vernon Lowell 1956- *WhoSSW 91*
Aspero, Benedict Vincent 1940- *WhoAm 90*
Aspetti, Tiziano 1565-1607 *PenDiDA 89*
Aspholm, Wilford Thomas 1913- *St&PR 91*
Aspin, Les 1938- *WhoAm 90, WorAlBi*
Aspinall, John *BioIn 16*
Aspinall, Keith Wilton 1953- *WhoAm 90*
Aspinall, Mara Glickman *WhoAmW 91*
Aspinet *WhNaAH*
Aspinwall, Leonard H. 1906- *St&PR 91*
Aspiotou, Koula 1946- *WhoWor 91*
Aspis, Harold B. 1954- *St&PR 91*
Aspland, George J. 1915-1989 *BioIn 16*
Aspland, Joseph Robert 1928- *WhoAm 90*
Asplen, Ellen Richardson 1943- *WhoE 91*
Asplen, William Purnell, Jr. 1941- *WhoE 91*
Asplin, Edward W. 1922- *St&PR 91*
Asplin, Edward William 1922- *WhoAm 90*
Asplund, Bronwyn Lorraine 1947- *WhoAmW 91*
Asplund, Clifford Martin 1936- *St&PR 91*
Asplund, Doris Elaine 1931- *WhoAmW 91*
Asplund, Erik Gunnar 1885-1940 *PenDiDA 89*
Asplundh, Barr E. 1927- *St&PR 91*
Asprey, Robert Brown 1923- *WhoWor 91*
Asprey, Winifred Alice 1917- *WhoAm 90*
Aspromonte, Bob 1938- *Ballpl 90*
Aspromonte, Ken 1931- *Ballpl 90*
Aspuru, Carlos M. 1936- *WhoHisp 91*
Aspy, Jane Catherine 1935- *WhoAmW 91*
Asquith, Brian 1930- *ConDes 90*
Asquith, Cynthia 1887-1960 *FemiCLE*
Asquith, Cynthia Mary Evelyn Charteris 1887-1960 *BioIn 16*
Asquith, Herbert Henry 1852-1928 *WorAlBi*
Asquith, Margot 1864-1945 *BioIn 16*
Asquith, Philip Ernest 1940- *St&PR 91*
Asrican, Dorothy C 1903- *BiDrAPA 89*
Asriel, Andre 1922- *IntWWM 90*
Assacumbuit *WhNaAH*
Assad, Albert Joseph 1915- *St&PR 91*
Assad, David A. 1950- *St&PR 91*
Assad, Hafez *BioIn 16*
Assad, Hafez Al- 1928- *WorAlBi*
Assad, Hafez Al- 1930- *PolLCME*
Assad, Hafiz 1928- *WhoWor 91*
Assad, Mounir Hassan 1953- *WhoWor 91*
Assad, Rif'at al- 1937- *WhoWor 91*
Assael, Henry 1935- *WhoAm 90*
Assael, Michael 1949- *WhoE 91, WhoEmL 91*
Assaf, Ali Youssef 1947- *WhoSSW 91*
Assaf, Emile Joseph 1927- *St&PR 91*
Assaf, Francis Beshara 1945- *WhoSSW 91*
Assaf, Ronald George 1935- *St&PR 91*
Assagioli, Roberto 1888-1974 *EncO&P 3, NewAgE 90*
Assailly, Alain Jean Joseph 1909- *EncO&P 3*
Assall, Friedrich W. *WhNaAH*
Assaratt, Prapatt 1939- *WhoWor 91*
Asscher, Abraham 1880-1950 *BioIn 16*
Assefa, Liban 1932- *WhoWor 91*
Asselin, Anna 1954- *WhoAmW 91*
Asselin, David C 1921- *BiDrAPA 89*
Asselin, Dean Regis 1915- *BiDrAPA 89*
Asselin, Jacques J.A. 1929- *WhoWor 91*
Asselin, John Thomas 1951- *WhoEmL 91*
Asselin, Olivar 1874-1937 *DcLB 92 [port]*
Asselineau, Roger Maurice 1915- *WhoWor 91*
Asselstine, Brian 1953- *Ballpl 90*
Asselta, Carolyn Ann 1945- *WhoEmL 91*
Assenmacher, Ivan Andre 1927- *WhoWor 91*
Assenmacher, Paul 1960- *Ballpl 90*
Assensoh, Akwasi B. 1946- *WhoWrEP 89*
Asseo, Lee A. 1938- *St&PR 91*

Asseo, Roger Robert 1931- *WhoWor 91*
Asseo, Yosef Dov 1956- *WhoEmL 91*
Assereto, Oreste 1940- *WhoWor 91*
Assheton, Ralph 1901-1984 *DcNaB 1981*
Assink, Anne Hoekstra 1948- *WhoEmL 91*
Assiri, Abdul-Reda Ali 1946- *WhoWor 91*
Association, The *EncPR&S 89*
Assour, Jacques M. 1932- *St&PR 91*
Assousa, George Elias 1936- *WhoAm 90, WhoWor 91*
Assue, Clare Melba 1922- *BiDrAPA 89*
Ast, Eileen Roper 1946- *WhoEmL 91*
Asta, August F. 1931- *St&PR 91*
Asta, Patricia Ellen 1945- *WhoAmW 91*
Astaire, Adele 1898-1981 *OxCPMus, WorAlBi*
Astaire, Fred *BioIn 16*
Astaire, Fred 1899-1987 *OxCPMus, WorAlBi*
Astarita, Susan Gallagher 1941- *WhoAmW 91*
Astaurov, Boris L'Vovich 1904-1974 *DcScB S2*
Astbury, John 1686-1743 *PenDiDA 89*
Aste, George James 1939- *St&PR 91*
Astell, Mary 1666-1731 *BiDEWW, BioIn 16, FemiCLE*
Asterino, Pamela J. *ODwPR 91*
Asthalter, Jack Horace 1914- *WhoE 91*
Astheimer, David Levengood 1951- *St&PR 91*
Asti, Alison Louise 1954- *WhoEmL 91*
Asti, Sergio 1926- *ConDes 90*
Astier de la Vigerie, Emmanuel d' 1900-1969 *BiDFrPL*
Astigueta, Fernando D *BiDrAPA 89*
Astill, Joanne Lynn 1960- *BiDrAPA 89*
Astill, Kenneth Norman 1923- *WhoAm 90, WhoE 91*
Astill, Norma Di Lauro *WhoAmW 91*
Astin, Alexander William 1932- *WhoAm 90*
Astin, John 1930- *WorAlBi*
Astin, Patty Duke *ConAu 130*
Astle, Thora Myrlene 1913- *WhoWrEP 89*
Astley, Eugene Roy 1926- *St&PR 91*
Astley, Neil 1953- *ConAu 132*
Astley, Neil Philip 1953- *WhoWor 91*
Astley, Richard Parker *St&PR 91N*
Astley, Rick *BioIn 16*
Astley, Rick 1966?- *ConMus 5 [port]*
Astley, Robert Murray 1944- *St&PR 91*
Astley, Thea *BioIn 16*
Astley, Thea 1925- *FemiCLE, WorAu 1980 [port]*
Astley, Thorne M. *WhoWrEP 89*
Astley-Bell, Rita Duis *WhoAmA 91*
Astman, Barbara Ann 1950- *WhoAmA 91*
Aston, Francis W. 1877-1945 *WorAlBi*
Aston, Gertrude *BiDEWW*
Aston, Harry Gordon 1927- *WhoSSW 91*
Aston, James William 1911- *St&PR 91*
Aston, Jay *BioIn 16*
Aston, Joseph L. 1937- *St&PR 91*
Aston, Judith *NewAgE 90*
Aston, Katherine 1619?-1658 *FemiCLE*
Aston, Mary *BiDEWW*
Aston, Michael *BioIn 16*
Aston, Miriam *WhoAmA 91*
Aston, Miriam Elizabeth 1947- *WhoSSW 91*
Aston, Peter George 1938- *IntWWM 90*
Aston, Robert D. 1927- *St&PR 91*
Aston, Sheree Jean 1954- *WhoAmW 91*
Astor, Brooke *BioIn 16, WhoAm 90*
Astor, Caroline Webster Schermerhorn 1830-1908 *BioIn 16*
Astor, Frank Charles 1927- *WhoHisp 91*
Astor, Fred G. 1951- *St&PR 91*
Astor, John Jacob 1763-1848 *BioIn 16, EncABHB 6 [port], WhNaAH, WorAlBi*
Astor, Josef 1959- *BioIn 16*
Astor, Mary 1906-1987 *WorAlBi*
Astor, Nancy 1879-1964 *BioAmW, WorAlBi*
Astor, Nancy Witcher Langhorne 1879-1964 *BioIn 16*
Astor, Susan Irene 1946- *WhoWrEP 89*
Astor, Vincent, Mrs. *WhoWrEP 89*
Astorga, Alicia Albacete 1947- *WhoHisp 91*
Astorga, Nora *BioIn 16*
Astorga, Nora 1949-1988 *AnObit 1988*
Astorga-Switzer, Cecilia J. 1952- *BiDrAPA 89*
Astori, Antonia *PenDiDA 89*
Astorino, Louis Don 1946- *WhoAm 90*
Astrachan, Boris M 1931- *BiDrAPA 89*
Astrachan, John Mann 1928- *BiDrAPA 89, WhoE 91*
Astrada, Carlos A *BiDrAPA 89*
Astrand, Hans 1925- *IntWWM 90*
Astrauskas, Vitautas Stasevich 1930- *WhoWor 91*
Astrin, Marvin H. 1925- *WhoAm 90*
Astro, Richard Bruce 1941- *WhoAm 90*
Astrom, Kathleen *ODwPR 91*
Astroth, Joe 1922- *Ballpl 90*
Astrove, Charles S 1941- *BiDrAPA 89*
Astruc, Alexandre 1923- *BioIn 16*
Astrue, Michael James 1956- *WhoAm 90*
Astry, Diana 1679-1716 *BiDEWW*
Astuguevielle, Christian *BioIn 16*
Asturias, Miguel Angel *BioIn 16*
Asturias, Miguel Angel 1899-1974 *ConAu 32NR, HispWr 90, MajTwCW, WorAlBi*
Astuto, Philip Louis 1923- *WhoAm 90*
Astwood, William Peter 1940- *WhoE 91*
Asumaa, Michael Walfred 1942- *WhoSSW 91*
Asuncion, Perla Queyquep 1936- *WhoAmW 91*
Asuni, Tolani *BiDrAPA 89*
Asunsolo, Elizabeth V *BiDrAPA 89*
Aswad, Betsy 1939- *WhoAmW 91, WhoE 91, WhoWor 91*
Aswad, Richard Nejm 1936- *WhoE 91*
Asylmuratova, Altynai *BioIn 16*
Aszyk-Krol, Urszula 1944- *WhoWor 91*
Atack, Douglas 1923- *WhoAm 90*
Atahan, Berna Fatos 1964- *WhoWor 91*
Atal, Bishnu Saroop 1933- *WhoAm 90*
Atala, Katherine Dawson *BiDrAPA 89*
Atam-Alibeckoff, Galib-Bey 1923- *St&PR 91*
Atamian, Dickran *BioIn 16*
Atamian, Elliott L. 1919- *St&PR 91*
Atamian, Susan 1950- *WhoAmW 91, WhoEmL 91*
Atanasoff, John V. *BioIn 16*
Atanasoff, John Vincent 1903- *WhoAm 90*
Atanassov, Anton Alexandrov 1942- *WhoWor 91*
Atares, Carlos Saura *ConAu 131*
Atash, Farhad 1954- *WhoEmL 91*
Ataturk, Kemal 1881-1938 *BioIn 16, WorAlBi*
Atcheson, John Donald 1917- *BiDrAPA 89*
Atcheson, Richard W. 1948- *WhoSSW 91*
Atchinson, Gregory Mac 1957- *WhoSSW 91*
Atchison, Beth Elaine *BiDrAPA 89*
Atchison, Joseph E. 1914- *St&PR 91*
Atchison, Richard Calvin 1932- *WhoAm 90*
Atchity, Kenneth J. 1944- *WhoWrEP 89*
Atchley, Dana Winslow, Jr. 1917- *WhoAm 90*
Atchley, Daniel Gene 1942- *WhoSSW 91*
Atchley, John Adams *BiDrAPA 89*
Atchley, Patricia Provenza 1960- *WhoSSW 91*
Atchley, William Reid 1942- *WhoAm 90*
Atema, Thomas Roy 1948- *WhoE 91*
Atencia, Maria Victoria 1931- *EncCoWW*
Atencio, Alonzo C. 1929- *BioIn 16*
Atencio, Alonzo Cristobal 1929- *WhoHisp 91*
Atencio, Denise L. 1953- *WhoHisp 91*
Ater, William Clement 1940- *St&PR 91*
Ates, J. Robert 1945- *WhoEmL 91, WhoSSW 91, WhoWor 91*
Ates, Kenneth 1955- *WhoE 91*
Atget, Eugene 1856-1927 *BioIn 16*
Atha, Stuart Kimball, Jr. 1925- *WhoAm 90*
Athaliah *WomWR [port]*
Athanas, Anthony *BioIn 16*
Athanason-Dymersky, Nickie Ann 1954- *WhoEmL 91*
Athanassoulas, Sotirios 1936- *WhoAm 90*
Athar, Zillur Rahman *BiDrAPA 89*
Athas, Elaine Joanna *WhoAmW 91*
Athas, Gus J. 1936- *St&PR 91*
Atheling, William *MajTwCW*
Atheling, William, Jr. *MajTwCW*
Athenais *BioIn 16*
Athens, Andrew A. *WhoAm 90*
Atherly, Jerome S. *AmLegL*
Atherton, Alexander Simpson 1913- *WhoAm 90*
Atherton, Alfred Leroy 1921- *BioIn 16*
Atherton, Alfred Leroy, Jr. 1921- *WhoAm 90*
Atherton, Charles Henry 1932- *WhoAm 90*
Atherton, David 1944- *IntWWM 90, PenDiMP*
Atherton, David Reed 1952- *WhoEmL 91*
Atherton, Denise Lynn 1964- *WhoAmW 91*
Atherton, Gertrude 1857-1948 *BioAmW, FemiCLE*
Atherton, J Carlton 1900-1964 *WhoAmA 91N*
Atherton, James 1943- *IntWWM 90*
Atherton, James Dale 1935- *WhoAm 90*
Atherton, James Kenneth Ward 1927- *WhoAm 90*
Atherton, Joan 1948- *IntWWM 90*
Atherton, John 1900-1952 *WhoAmA 91N*
Atherton, Keith 1959- *Ballpl 90*
Atherton, Leonard James Archibald 1941- *IntWWM 90*
Atherton, Lucius *MajTwCW*
Atherton, Neil Pierce 1924- *St&PR 91*
Atherton, Robert 1910- *IntWWM 90*
Atherton, Selwyn I. 1929- *WhoAm 90*
Atherton, Virginia Elizabeth Gravenor 1941- *IntWWM 90*
Atherton, William 1947- *WhoEmL 91*
Athes-Perrelet, Louise 1865?- *BiDWomA*
Athey, George Richard *BiDrAPA 89*
Athey, Mary Frances 1944- *WhoE 91*
Athey, Paul Rothgeb 1944- *St&PR 91*
Athey, Robert Marsh 1937- *WhoAm 90*
Athlone, Countess of 1883-1981 *DcNaB 1981*
Athon, Bobbie Lee 1954- *WhoEmL 91*
Athos, Ethel Papageorge 1922- *WhoE 91*
Athreya, Mrityunjay 1941- *WhoWor 91*
Atia, Abdel Kader Mohamed 1938- *WhoWor 91*
Atieh, Michael Gerard 1953- *WhoEmL 91*
Atigh, Stephanie Anne 1951- *WhoAmW 91*
Atil, Esin 1938- *ConAu 32NR*
Atilgan, Timur Faik 1943- *WhoE 91*
Atinc, Ethem 1948- *WhoWor 91*
Atirnomis 1938- *WhoAmA 91N*
Atisanoe, Salevaa *BioIn 16*
Atiyah, Michael Francis 1929- *WhoWor 91*
Atiyeh, George Nicholas 1923- *WhoAm 90, WhoE 91*
Atiyeh, Victor George 1923- *WhoAm 90*
Atkeson, Ray *NewYTBS 90*
Atkeson, Ray 1907-1990 *BioIn 16*
Atkeson, Roy A. 1907-1990 *ConAu 131*
Atkeson, Timothy Breed 1927- *WhoAm 90*
Atkey, Philip *TwCCr&M 91*
Atkin, Edmond 1707-1761 *WhNaAH*
Atkin, Edmund 1707-1761 *EncCRAm*
Atkin, Gerald Clifford 1936- *St&PR 91*
Atkin, J. Myron 1927- *WhoAm 90*
Atkin, James Blakesley 1930- *WhoAm 90*
Atkin, Jerry Clayton 1949- *St&PR 91*
Atkin, Joseph Raymond 1945- *St&PR 91*
Atkin, Louis Phillip 1951- *WhoEmL 91, WhoWor 91*
Atkin, Sidney Joseph 1934- *St&PR 91*
Atkin, William Walter 1947- *St&PR 91*
Atkind, Leon *BioIn 16*
Atkins, Albert H *WhoAmA 91N*
Atkins, Anna 1799-1871 *FemiCLE*
Atkins, Arleen Gail 1951- *WhoSSW 91*
Atkins, Bill 1943- *WhoAmA 91*
Atkins, Bruce Lawrence 1951- *WhoEmL 91*
Atkins, Candi 1946- *WhoAmW 91*
Atkins, Carl Clyde 1914- *WhoAm 90*
Atkins, Charles Gilmore 1939- *WhoWor 91*
Atkins, Chester Burton 1924- *WhoAm 90*
Atkins, Chester Greenough 1948- *WhoAm 90, WhoE 91*
Atkins, Chet *WhoNeCM C [port]*
Atkins, Chet 1924- *BioIn 16, ConMus 5 [port], OxCPMus, WorAlBi*
Atkins, Cholly *BioIn 16*
Atkins, Christopher 1954- *ODwPR 91*
Atkins, Craig Starbuck 1903-1990 *BioIn 16*
Atkins, Dale Morrell 1922- *WhoAm 90*
Atkins, Daphne Lanette 1961- *BiDrAPA 89*
Atkins, David Alexander 1960- *BiDrAPA 89*
Atkins, DeBorah Kaye 1958- *WhoAmW 91*
Atkins, Diane *BioIn 16*
Atkins, George L. 1941- *St&PR 91*
Atkins, George W.P., Jr. 1938- *St&PR 91*
Atkins, Gordon Lee 1937- *WhoAmA 91*
Atkins, Hannah D. *WhoAm 90, WhoAmW 91, WhoSSW 91*
Atkins, Howard Ian 1951- *WhoAm 90*
Atkins, James H. 1929- *St&PR 91*
Atkins, James Howard 1931- *WhoAm 90*
Atkins, Jerilyn Horne 1954- *WhoEmL 91*
Atkins, Jerry Charles *BiDrAPA 89*
Atkins, Joe T. 1928- *St&PR 91*
Atkins, John 1938- *WhoWor 91*
Atkins, John Gordon 1933- *IntWWM 90*
Atkins, Joseph P. 1940- *WhoAm 90*
Atkins, Junius *BiDrAPA 89*
Atkins, Kay Roberta 1939- *WhoAmW 91*
Atkins, Leslie 1954- *WhoEmL 91*
Atkins, Martin *BioIn 16*
Atkins, Michelle Blaine 1953- *WhoAmW 91, WhoEmL 91*
Atkins, Norman B 1922- *BiDrAPA 89*
Atkins, Pervis *DrBIPA 90*
Atkins, Richard Bart 1951- *WhoE 91, WhoEmL 91, WhoWor 91*
Atkins, Richard G. *WhoAm 90, WhoE 91*
Atkins, Richard L. 1926- *WhoAm 90*
Atkins, Richard N 1948- *BiDrAPA 89*
Atkins, Richard Norman 1948- *WhoE 91*
Atkins, Robert Emmett, Jr. 1936- *St&PR 91, WhoAm 90*
Atkins, Robert Michael 1953- *BiDrAPA 89, WhoE 91*
Atkins, Robert W *BiDrAPA 89*
Atkins, Ronald Raymond 1933- *WhoAm 90*
Atkins, Rosalie Marks 1921- *WhoAmA 91*
Atkins, Russell 1926- *WhoWrEP 89*
Atkins, Sally Anne 1959- *WhoAmW 91*
Atkins, Samuel James, III 1944- *St&PR 91*
Atkins, Spencer Bert 1951- *WhoEmL 91*
Atkins, Stephen Robert 1946- *BiDrAPA 89*
Atkins, Stuart 1914- *WhoAm 90*
Atkins, Theodore William 1938- *St&PR 91*
Atkins, Thomas Jay 1943- *WhoWor 91*
Atkins, Thomas Lee 1921- *WhoWor 91*
Atkins, Victor B. 1927- *St&PR 91*
Atkins, Victor Kennicott, Jr. 1945- *WhoAm 90*
Atkins, Victor Michael 1933- *WhoWor 91*
Atkins, William Allen 1934- *WhoE 91*
Atkins, William Derrick 1947- *WhoSSW 91*
Atkins, William Reed, Jr. 1959- *WhoEmL 91*
Atkinson, Allen *BioIn 16*
Atkinson, Allen 1953?-1987 *SmATA 60*
Atkinson, Ann Lennette 1949- *WhoE 91*
Atkinson, Arlis 1945- *WhoSSW 91*
Atkinson, Arthur Sheridan 1918- *St&PR 91*
Atkinson, B. Richard 1926- *ODwPR 91*
Atkinson, Basil Eric 1926- *St&PR 91*
Atkinson, Bill 1916- *WhoAm 90*
Atkinson, Brooks 1894-1984 *WorAlBi*
Atkinson, Bryan Herbert 1940- *St&PR 91*
Atkinson, Charles M. 1941- *IntWWM 90*
Atkinson, Charles Ora 1944- *WhoWrEP 89*
Atkinson, Connie Zeanah 1950- *WhoSSW 91*
Atkinson, Conrad 1940- *WhoAmA 91*
Atkinson, Daniel Edward 1921- *WhoAm 90*
Atkinson, David Skillman 1921- *WhoAm 90*
Atkinson, Dawson Ross 1953- *WhoSSW 91*
Atkinson, Denis S *BiDrAPA 89*
Atkinson, Denis Stuart, Jr. *BiDrAPA 89*
Atkinson, Dewey Franklin 1930- *WhoSSW 91*
Atkinson, Edward Arthur 1948- *St&PR 91*
Atkinson, Elizabeth *BiDEWW, FemiCLE*
Atkinson, Elizabeth Ann 1957- *WhoEmL 91*
Atkinson, Emma Willsher 1826?-1900 *FemiCLE*
Atkinson, Eric Newton 1928- *WhoAmA 91*
Atkinson, Eugene D. 1944- *WhoAm 90*
Atkinson, Frederick Griswold 1904- *WhoAm 90*
Atkinson, Frederick Stuart 1944- *WhoE 91*
Atkinson, Gordon 1930- *WhoAm 90*
Atkinson, Harold Witherspoon 1914- *WhoSSW 91, WhoWor 91*
Atkinson, Henry 1782-1842 *WhNaAH*
Atkinson, Holly Gail 1952- *WhoAm 90, WhoE 91*
Atkinson, Howard Phillip 1954- *WhoSSW 91*
Atkinson, James Peter 1947- *WhoEmL 91*
Atkinson, Jeff *BioIn 16*
Atkinson, Jeff John Frederick 1948- *WhoEmL 91*
Atkinson, John Bond 1950- *WhoEmL 91*
Atkinson, John Morgan 1870-1934 *AmLegL*
Atkinson, John Pepper 1942- *WhoSSW 91*
Atkinson, John T. 1948- *St&PR 91*
Atkinson, Joseph H, Jr. 1945- *BiDrAPA 89*
Atkinson, Joseph William 1940- *St&PR 91*
Atkinson, Larry Gordon 1951- *WhoEmL 91*
Atkinson, Lawrence Rush, IV 1952- *WhoAm 90, WhoE 91*
Atkinson, Leslie Jane 1951- *WhoAmA 91*
Atkinson, Lloyd C. 1942- *St&PR 91*
Atkinson, Louisa 1834-1872 *FemiCLE*
Atkinson, Lucy Jo 1931- *WhoWrEP 89*
Atkinson, Lynn Ann 1954- *WhoSSW 91*
Atkinson, Margaret Fleming *AuBYP 90*
Atkinson, Mark Edward 1954- *WhoE 91*
Atkinson, Mayme Green 1925- *St&PR 91*
Atkinson, Michael 1925- *WhoWor 91*
Atkinson, Nancy Jane 1952- *WhoAmW 91*
Atkinson, Nancy Lou Sheppeard 1940- *WhoSSW 91*
Atkinson, Neville Thomas 1932- *IntWWM 90*
Atkinson, Oriana Torrey MacIlveen 1894-1989 *BioIn 16*
Atkinson, Paul Phillip 1924- *WhoSSW 91, WhoWor 91*
Atkinson, Ray N. 1929- *St&PR 91, WhoAm 90*
Atkinson, Regina Elizabeth 1952- *WhoAmW 91*
Atkinson, Richard C. *BioIn 16*
Atkinson, Richard Chatham 1929- *WhoAm 90, WhoWor 91*
Atkinson, Richard Collier 1942- *St&PR 91*
Atkinson, Richard Henry 1952- *WhoWor 91*
Atkinson, Rick *BioIn 16*

Atkinson, Robert Poland 1927- WhoAm 90, WhoSSW 91
Atkinson, Roland M 1936- BiDrAPA 89
Atkinson, Rupert Leigh 1938- WhoWor 91
Atkinson, Russell Welsh 1947- St&PR 91
Atkinson, Shannon Marlow 1962- WhoAmW 91
Atkinson, Sheridan Earle 1945- WhoEmL 91, WhoWor 91
Atkinson, Stella ODwPR 91
Atkinson, Stephen Richard 1953- BiDrAPA 89
Atkinson, Steven Douglas 1947- WhoEmL 91
Atkinson, Steven James 1950- St&PR 91
Atkinson, Sue G. 1940- ODwPR 91
Atkinson, Thomas Emory 1853-1923 AmLegL
Atkinson, Thomas Joseph, Sr. 1935- WhoSSW 91
Atkinson, Tracy 1928- WhoAm 90, WhoAmA 91
Atkinson, William Edward 1939- WhoAm 90
Atkinson, William Lee 1953- WhoEmL 91
Atkinson, William McKinley 1936- WhoSSW 91
Atkinson, William Yates 1854-1899 AmLegL
Atkisson, Curtis T., Jr. 1933- St&PR 91
Atkisson, Curtis Trumbull, Jr. 1933- WhoAm 90
Atkisson, Debra Lynn 1961- BiDrAPA 89
Atl, Dr ArtLatA
Atlan, Paul 1942- WhoWor 91
Atlantov, Vladimir 1939- IntWWM 90, PenDiMP
Atlas, Allan Jay 1952- WhoSSW 91
Atlas, Allan W. 1943- IntWWM 90
Atlas, Charles 1893-1972 BioIn 16
Atlas, David 1924- WhoAm 90
Atlas, Elena 1934- WhoE 91
Atlas, James Robert 1949- WhoAm 90, WhoWrEP 89
Atlas, Jay David 1945- WhoEmL 91
Atlas, Nava 1955- WhoAmA 91
Atlas, Randall I. 1953- WhoSSW 91
Atlas, Scott Jerome 1950- WhoEmL 91
Atlas, Yeheskel 1913-1942 BioIn 16
Atlee, Debbie Gayle 1955- WhoAmW 91, WhoEmL 91
Atlee, Emilie Des 1915- WhoAmA 91
Atlee, Frank V. 1940- WhoAm 90
Atlee, Philip 1915- SpyFic, TwCCr&M 91
Atlee, William A. 1914- WhoE 91
Atlow, Bernard N. 1928- WhoE 91
Atluri, Satya Nadham 1945- WhoAm 90, WhoWor 91
Atluru, Sitaramaiah 1936- St&PR 91
Atma WhoWrEP 89
Atmer, ThomasNils 1930- WhoWor 91
Atnip, Deborah Kay 1960- WhoAmW 91
Atnip, Michael Grant 1948- St&PR 91
Atnipp, Douglas Clay 1959- WhoEmL 91
Atobe, Yasuzo 1926- WhoAm 90
Atoki, Christopher Adesanmi 1934- WhoWor 91
Atoman, Daniel BiDrAPA 89
Aton, Mary Fredericka Lawhon 1930- WhoAmW 91
Ator, Donald Wilbur 1930- WhoSSW 91
Ator, Paul 1927- WhoSSW 91
Atotarho WhNaAH [port]
Atotarhoh WhNaAH [port]
Atoynatan, Tanash H 1920- BiDrAPA 89
Atran, Scott 1952- WhoWor 91
Atrat, James Ray 1957- St&PR 91
Atre-Vaidya, Nutan 1957- BiDrAPA 89
Atreya, Bhikhan Lal 1897- EncO&P 3
Atreya, Bhikhan Lal 1897-1967 EncPaPR 91
Atreya, Sushil Kumar 1946- WhoAm 90
Atri, Padmini B BiDrAPA 89
Atsidi Sani WhNaAH
Atsumi, Toyo 1935- WhoWor 91
Atta, Morris Minoru 1956- WhoEmL 91
Attacullaculla 1700?-1778? WhNaAH
Attakullakulla 1700?-1778? WhNaAH
Attal, Charles Alfred, III 1959- WhoEmL 91
Attal, Gene 1947- WhoEmL 91, WhoSSW 91, WhoWor 91
Attali, Jacques Jose 1944- BiDFrPL
Attalli, Georget Yves 1943- WhoWor 91
Attanasio, John Baptist 1954- WhoEmL 91
Attanasio, Virginia 1958- WhoE 91
Attara, Raquel B BiDrAPA 89
Attard, Adelaide 1930- WhoAmW 91
Attard, Janet 1944- WhoWrEP 89
Attardi, Charles, Jr. 1942- St&PR 91
Attardo, Lewis Charles 1950- WhoEmL 91, WhoWor 91
Attardo, Michael J. 1941- St&PR 91
Attas, Haydar Abu Bakr al- 1939- WhoWor 91
Attaway, David Henry 1938- WhoE 91
Attaway, John Allen 1930- WhoSSW 91
Attaway, Julian J. St&PR 91
Attaway, Le Roy Banks, Jr. 1937- WhoWrEP 89
Attaway, LeRoy Banks 1937- WhoAm 90
Attaway, Nancy Hilliard 1954- WhoAmW 91
Attaway, Robert A. 1926- St&PR 91
Attaway, Ruth DrBIPA 90
Atteberry, William D. 1920- St&PR 91
Atteberry, William Duane 1920- WhoAm 90
Atteberry-Luckinbill, Clara DeAnn 1937- WhoSSW 91
Attebury, Janice Marie 1954- WhoAmW 91
Attee, Joyce Valerie Jungclas 1926- WhoAmW 91
Attenborough, David 1926- ConAu 30NR
Attenborough, Richard BioIn 16
Attenborough, Richard 1923- ConTFT 8 [port], WhoWor 91, WorAlBi
Attenborough, Suzanne 1958- WhoE 91
Attenweiler, Andrew James 1927- St&PR 91
Atterbom, Per Daniel Amadeus 1790-1855 DcScanL
Atterbury, Lee Richard 1948- WhoEmL 91
Atterbury, Thomas J. 1931- St&PR 91
Attermeier, Fredric Joseph 1946- WhoSSW 91
Atthowe, Jean Fausett 1931- WhoWrEP 89
Attia, Claire William 1951- BiDrAPA 89
Attia, Evelyn 1960- BiDrAPA 89
Atticus MajTwCW
Attie, Dotty 1938- WhoAmA 91, WhoAmW 91
Attie, Oliver Moses 1965- WhoE 91
Attieh, Bassam Wahab 1936- WhoWor 91
Attila, King of the Huns 406?-453 WorAlBi
Attinello, John Salvatore 1920- WhoAm 90
Attinger, Ernst Otto 1922- WhoAm 90
Attix, Frank Herbert 1925- WhoAm 90
Attiyeh, Richard Eugene 1937- WhoAm 90
Attlee, Clement 1883-1967 WorAlBi
Attles, Joseph E 1903- DrBIPA 90
Attman, Patricia C BiDrAPA 89
Attoe, Wayne Osborne 1940- WhoSSW 91
Attra, Harvey David 1931- WhoWor 91
Attridge, Daniel F. 1954- WhoEmL 91
Attridge, George N. 1928- St&PR 91
Attridge, Richard Byron 1933- WhoAm 90
Attucks, Crispus 1723?-1770 EncCRAm, WhNaAH, WorAlBi
Attwell, Emilie 1959- BiDrAPA 89
Attwell, Kirby 1935- St&PR 91, WhoAm 90
Attwood, Cynthia Lou 1946- WhoAmW 91
Attwood, Elspeth Mary Beatrice 1957- IntWWM 90
Attwood, James A. BioIn 16
Attwood, James Albert 1927- St&PR 91
Attwood, James Albert, Jr. 1958- WhoE 91
Attwood, Madge Louise 1928- WhoAmW 91
Attwood, William 1919-1989 AnObit 1989, BioIn 16
Atwal, Nasib K 1944- BiDrAPA 89
Atwal, Satnam S BiDrAPA 89
Atwater, Caleb 1778-1867 WhNaAH
Atwater, Edward S. 1945- St&PR 91
Atwater, Franklin S. 1916- St&PR 91
Atwater, Franklin Simpson 1916- WhoAm 90
Atwater, Harvey Leroy 1951- BioIn 16
Atwater, Horace Brewster, Jr. 1931- St&PR 91, WhoAm 90
Atwater, James David 1928- WhoAm 90
Atwater, John Spencer 1913- WhoAm 90
Atwater, Lee 1951- BioIn 16, WorAlBi
Atwater, Marshall Anderson 1940- WhoE 91
Atwater, Montgomery Meigs 1904- AuBYP 90
Atwater, N. William 1934- WhoAm 90, WhoE 91
Atwater, Neil William 1934- St&PR 91
Atwater, Richard Merlin 1946- WhoWrEP 89
Atwater, Richard Tupper 1892-1948 BioIn 16
Atwater, Tanya Maria 1942- WhoAm 90, WhoAmW 91
Atwater, Verne Stafford 1920- WhoAm 90
Atwell, Allen 1925- WhoAmA 91
Atwell, Anthony E BiDrAPA 89
Atwell, Charles McHugh 1939- St&PR 91
Atwell, Constance Woodruff 1942- WhoAmW 91
Atwell, Herbert 1937- WhoWor 91
Atwell, Robert Herron 1931- WhoAm 90
Atwell, Robert James 1919- WhoAm 90
Atwell, Toby 1924- Ballpl 90
Atwell, Winifred 1914-1983 OxCPMus
Atwell-Holler, Rita Irene 1941- WhoWrEP 89
Atwill, William Henry 1932- WhoSSW 91
Atwood, Ann 1913- AuBYP 90
Atwood, Ann Margaret 1913- WhoAm 90
Atwood, Bill 1911- Ballpl 90
Atwood, Brian BioIn 16
Atwood, Bruce Gilbert 1937- St&PR 91
Atwood, Charles Henry 1952- WhoSSW 91
Atwood, Clare 1866-1962 BiDWomA
Atwood, Diana Field 1946- WhoAmW 91
Atwood, Donald J. BioIn 16
Atwood, Donald Jesse 1924- St&PR 91
Atwood, Donald Jesse, Jr. 1924- WhoAm 90
Atwood, Donald Keith 1933- WhoSSW 91
Atwood, Edward Charles, Jr. 1922- WhoAm 90
Atwood, Eric Brian 1958- BiDrAPA 89
Atwood, Genevieve 1946- WhoAmW 91
Atwood, Harold Leslie 1937- WhoAm 90
Atwood, Horace, Jr. 1918- St&PR 91
Atwood, James R. 1944- WhoAm 90
Atwood, Jeffrey B. 1948- WhoWrEP 89
Atwood, John Brian 1942- WhoAm 90
Atwood, Kelly Palmer 1946- WhoEmL 91
Atwood, Kenneth Ward, Jr. 1922- WhoAm 90
Atwood, Linda 1946- WhoAmW 91
Atwood, Margaret 1939- BioIn 16, ConAu 33NR, FemiCLE, MajTwCW
Atwood, Margaret Eleanor 1939- WhoAm 90, WhoAmW 91, WhoWrEP 89
Atwood, Margaret Jane 1952- WhoEmL 91
Atwood, Mary Ann 1817-1910 EncO&P 3
Atwood, Mary Sanford 1935- WhoAmW 91, WhoWor 91
Atwood, Peter J. 1965- WhoWrEP 89
Atwood, Raymond Percival, Jr. 1952- WhoEmL 91
Atwood, Robert Bruce 1907- WhoAm 90
Atwood, Roslyn Irene 1945- WhoEmL 91
Atwood, Sue C 1934- BiDrAPA 89
Atwood, Thomas Donald 1940- St&PR 91
Atwood, Wallace Walter 1872-1949 DcScB S2
Atwood, William 1927- WhoAm 90
Atwood, William Makepeace 1927- St&PR 91
Atwood, William Robert 1927- St&PR 91
Atwood Pinardi, Brenda 1941- WhoAmA 91, WhoE 91
Atzberger, Frank J. 1937- St&PR 91
Atzmon, Moshe 1931- IntWWM 90, PenDiMP
Au, Alice Man-Jing WhoAmW 91
Au, Alice Miu-Hing 1958- WhoE 91
Au, Auser Kee-Wah 1948- WhoWor 91
Au, Joanlin 1953- WomArch [port]
Au, Kenneth Wai Kit 1944- WhoSSW 91
Au, Leo Yuin 1949- St&PR 91
Au, Susan Neubauer BiDrAPA 89
Au, Tung 1923- WhoAm 90
Au, William August, III 1949- WhoE 91
Au, Winnie Wai-Yu WhoE 91
Aub, A. Edgar, Jr. 1928- St&PR 91
Aub, Deborah Thrasher 1953- WhoAmW 91
Aube, Randy Alan 1957- WhoEmL 91
Auber, Daniel Francois Esprit 1782-1871 PenDiMP A
Auberjonois, Rene 1940- ConTFT 8 [port]
Auberjonois, Rene Murat 1940- WhoAm 90
Auberjunois, Rene 1940- WorAlBi
Auberry, Horace 1931- St&PR 91
Aubert, Eric Louis 1921- IntWWM 90
Aubert, George EncO&P 3
Aubert, Isabella BiDEWW
Aubert, Jacques 1947- St&PR 91
Aubert, Julie-Marie EncCoWW
Aubert, Laurent 1949- IntWWM 90
Aubert, Pierre 1927- WhoWor 91
Aubert, Richard J, Jr. 1949- BiDrAPA 89
Aubert de Gaspe, Philippe-Ignace-F 1814-1841 DcLB 99
Aubert de Gaspe, Philippe-Joseph 1786-1871 DcLB 99 [port]
Aubigne, Agrippa d' 1552-1630 BioIn 16
Aubigny, Julie d' PenDiMP
Aubigny, Pierre d' MajTwCW
Aubin, Barbara 1928- WhoAmA 91
Aubin, Bruce R. 1931- St&PR 91
Aubin, Denis 1951- St&PR 91
Aubin, Gary Paul 1945- WhoE 91
Aubin, Napoleon 1812-1890 DcLB 99 [port]
Aubin, Penelope 1679-1731 BiDEWW
Aubin, Penelope 1685- BioIn 16
Aubin, Penelope 1685?-1731 FemiCLE
Aubin, Thomas William 1953- St&PR 91, WhoAm 90
Aubin, William Mark 1929- WhoE 91
Aubke, Friedhelm 1932- WhoAm 90
Aubock, Carl 1925- ConDes 90
Aubourg, Michel 19?1- EncO&P 3
Aubrecht, Richard Albert 1944- St&PR 91
Aubrey, Crispin 1946- ConAu 129
Aubrey, Gertrude Marion 1921- St&PR 91
Aubrey, John 1626-1697 BioIn 16
Aubrey, Roger Frederick 1929- WhoAm 90
Aubrey-Smith, Peter Robert 1944- WhoE 91
Aubry, Eugene Edwards 1935- WhoAm 90
Aubry, Lloyd Walter 1924- St&PR 91
Aubry, Michele Christine 1951- WhoAmW 91
Aubry, Vicki A. 1953- WhoAmW 91
Aubuchon, Penny Amelia 1952- WhoAmW 91
Aubuchon, William Edward, Jr. 1916- St&PR 91
Auburn, Norman Paul 1905- WhoAm 90
Aubut, Marcel 1948- WhoAm 90, WhoE 91
Aucello, Mae D. ODwPR 91
Auch, Stephen Edward 1930- St&PR 91
Auch, Walter E. 1921- St&PR 91
Auch, Walter Edward 1921- WhoAm 90
Auchincloss, Douglas, Mrs. BioIn 16
Auchincloss, Elizabeth 1951- BiDrAPA 89
Auchincloss, Janet BioIn 16
Auchincloss, Kenneth 1937- WhoAm 90
Auchincloss, Louis BioIn 16
Auchincloss, Louis 1917- MajTwCW, WorAlBi
Auchincloss, Louis Stanton 1917- WhoAm 90, WhoE 91, WhoWor 91, WhoWrEP 89
Auchincloss, Samuel Sloan, Jr. 1942- WhoE 91
Auchincloss, Sarah Sedgwick 1949- BiDrAPA 89, WhoE 91
Auchinleck, Claude John Eyre 1884-1981 BioIn 16, DcNaB 1981
Auchterlonie, Domingo 1942- IntWWM 90
Auchy, Lynda Goho 1942- WhoAmW 91
Auckland, James Craig 1948- WhoSSW 91
Auclair, Jacques Lucien 1923- WhoAm 90
Auclair, Michel 1950- St&PR 91
Auclair, Robert A. 1937- St&PR 91
Auclair, Sue 1949- WhoEmL 91
Auclert, Marie-Anne-Hubertine 1848-1914 EncCoWW
Aucoin, John Hubert 1943- St&PR 91
Aucoin, Kevyn BioIn 16
AuCoin, Les 1942- WhoAm 90
Aucott, George W. 1934- WhoWor 91
Aucott, George William 1934- St&PR 91
Audemars, Pierre 1909-1989 TwCCr&M 91
Auden, W. H. 1907-1973 BioIn 16
Auden, W H 1907-1973 MajTwCW
Auden, W. H. 1907-1973 PoeCrit 1 [port], WorAlBi
Auden, W H 1907-1973 WrPh
Auden, Wystan Hugh 1907-1973 BioIn 16
Audet, Armand Albert 1934- St&PR 91
Audet, Henri 1918- WhoAm 90
Audet, Leonard 1932- WhoAm 90
Audet, Paul Andre 1923- WhoAm 90
Audet, Pierre 1932- St&PR 91
Audet, Rene 1920- WhoAm 90
Audett, Theophilus Bernard 1905- WhoWor 91
Audette, Anna Held WhoAmA 91
Audia, Christina 1941- WhoAm 90
Audifret-Pasquier, Edmond Armand G. d' 1823-1905 BiDFrPL
Audino, Diane Mary 1961- St&PR 91
Audland, Anne 1627-1705 BiDEWW, FemiCLE
Audley, Eleanor BiDEWW
Audley, Eleanor 1598?-1652 BioIn 16
Audley, Lucy BiDEWW
Audlin, David John, Jr. 1957- WhoEmL 91
Audoux, Marguerite 1863-1937 EncCoWW
Audran, Claude, III 1658-1734 PenDiDA 89
Audran, Edmond 1842-1901 OxCPMus
Audran, Stephane 1932- ConTFT 8
Audretsch, David Bruce 1954- WhoWor 91
Audretsch, Hubertus Anton Hermann 1938- WhoWor 91
Audry, Colette NewYTBS 90
Audubon, John James 1785-1851 BioIn 16, WorAlBi
Audubon, Lucy G. 1788-1874 BioAmW
Auel, Jean M 1936- BestSel 90-4 [port], WhoWrEP 89, WorAlBi
Auer, Alfons 1915- WhoWor 91
Auer, Edward T BiDrAPA 89
Auer, Edward Thomas 1919- WhoAm 90
Auer, James Edward 1941- WhoSSW 91
Auer, James Matthew 1928- WhoAm 90, WhoAmA 91
Auer, John 1937- St&PR 91
Auer, Leopold 1845-1930 PenDiMP
Auer, Peter Louis 1928- WhoAm 90
Auer, Ruth Thompson 1928- WhoAmW 91
Auer, Wilma Tucker 1918- WhoE 91
Auerbach, Alan Jeffrey 1951- WhoAm 90, WhoE 91
Auerbach, Arnold 1917- BioIn 16, ConAu 131
Auerbach, Arthur H 1928- BiDrAPA 89

Auerbach, Beatrice Fox 1887-1968 *ConAmBL*
Auerbach, Boris 1931- *St&PR 91, WhoAm 90*
Auerbach, Bradford Carlton 1957- *WhoEmL 91*
Auerbach, Carl Abraham 1915- *WhoAm 90*
Auerbach, Daniel B 1943- *BiDrAPA 89*
Auerbach, Daniel Jonathan 1942- *WhoAm 90*
Auerbach, David A. 1943- *St&PR 91*
Auerbach, Earl 1922- *St&PR 91*
Auerbach, Eric David *BiDrAPA 89*
Auerbach, Ernest Sigmund 1936- *WhoAm 90, WhoE 91*
Auerbach, Frank 1931- *WhoWor 91*
Auerbach, Frank H. 1931- *BioIn 16*
Auerbach, George 1923- *ODwPR 91*
Auerbach, Isaac L. 1921- *St&PR 91, WhoAm 90*
Auerbach, Jonathan Keith 1949- *BiDrAPA 89*
Auerbach, Joseph 1916- *WhoAm 90*
Auerbach, Marjorie 1932- *AuBYP 90*
Auerbach, Marshall Jay 1932- *WhoAm 90, WhoWor 91*
Auerbach, Michael Howard 1943- *WhoE 91*
Auerbach, Nina Joan 1943- *WhoAmW 91*
Auerbach, Norman E. 1920- *St&PR 91*
Auerbach, Philip 1926- *St&PR 91*
Auerbach, Red *ConAu 131*
Auerbach, Red 1917- *BioIn 16, WhoAm 90, WhoE 91*
Auerbach, Rick 1950- *Ballpl 90*
Auerbach, Seymour 1929- *WhoAm 90, WhoE 91*
Auerbach, Sheryl Lynn 1952- *WhoEmL 91*
Auerbach, Stanley Irving 1921- *WhoAm 90*
Auerbach, Stuart Charles 1935- *WhoAm 90, WhoE 91*
Auerbach, William 1914- *WhoAm 90*
Auerbach-Levy, William 1889-1964 *WhoAmA 91N*
Auerback, Alfred 1915- *BiDrAPA 89, WhoAm 90*
Auerback, Sandra Jean 1946- *WhoAmW 91, WhoEmL 91*
Auerswald, Edgar H *BiDrAPA 89*
Auerswald, Heinz 1908- *BioIn 16*
Auf der Maur, Nick 1942- *ConAu 129*
Aufdembrink, Ray Lynn 1942- *St&PR 91*
Aufdenkamp, Jo Ann 1926- *WhoAmW 91*
Aufderhaar-King, Susan 1951- *WhoAmW 91*
Aufderheide, May 1888-1972 *OxCPMus*
Auffant, James Robert 1949- *WhoHisp 91*
Auffant, Rafael 1947- *BiDrAPA 89*
Auffenwerth, Anna Elisabeth 1696- *PenDiDA 89*
Auffenwerth, Johann *PenDiDA 89*
Auffenwerth, Sabina 1706- *PenDiDA 89*
Aufhauser, Alfred 1910- *St&PR 91*
Aufox, Jerry M. *WhoAm 90*
Aufox, Jerry M. 1942- *St&PR 91*
Aufranc, Otto 1909-1990 *BioIn 16*
Aufraser, Reynold Marc 1949- *WhoE 91*
Aufses, Arthur Harold, Jr. 1926- *WhoAm 90*
Aufzien, Alan L. *WhoAm 90, WhoE 91*
Aug, Robert G *BiDrAPA 89*
Aug, Stephen M. 1936- *WhoE 91*
Augarten, Stan 1952- *WhoEmL 91*
Augat, Ernest H. 1906- *St&PR 91*
Augelli, John Pat 1921- *WhoAm 90*
Augello, William Joseph 1926- *WhoAm 90*
Augenblick, Harry A. 1926- *St&PR 91*
Augenfeld, Lorraine P. 1942- *WhoAmW 91*
Augenstein, Bruno W. 1923- *WhoAm 90*
Auger, Arleen *BioIn 16*
Auger, Arleen 1939- *IntWWM 90, PenDiMP, WhoAm 90*
Auger, David J. *WhoAm 90*
Auger, Harvey Joseph, Jr. 1947- *St&PR 91*
Augerson, Scott William 1949- *WhoWrEP 89*
Aughuet, Michel 1944- *WhoWor 91*
Augsburger, Aaron Donald 1925- *WhoAm 90*
Augspurger, Ann Marie 1964- *WhoAmW 91*
Augspurger, Terrence Lee 1951- *BiDrAPA 89*
Augstein, Rudolf 1923- *WhoWor 91*
Auguis, Lourdes Degracia 1940- *WhoWor 91*
August *EncCoWW*
August, Burton 1920- *BiDrAPA 89*
August, Don 1963- *Ballpl 90*
August, Harry E *BiDrAPA 89*
August, Jeremy 1952- *BiDrAPA 89*
August, Joan Frieda 1948- *WhoAmW 91*
August, Katherine 1948- *WhoEmL 91*
August, R. Diedrich 1947- *ODwPR 91*
August, Raymond William 1936- *WhoE 91*
August, Robert Olin 1921- *WhoAm 90*
August, Robert Werner 1952- *St&PR 91*
August, Rudolf 1926- *WhoAm 90*
Augusta, Cristobal de *PenDiDA 89*
Auguste Le Breton 1913- *WhoWor 91*
Auguste, Macdonald 1948- *St&PR 91*
Auguste, Robert-Joseph 1723?-1805 *PenDiDA 89*
Augusthy, Roy K 1942- *BiDrAPA 89*
Augustin, Marc Dominique 1959- *WhoWor 91*
Augustin, Ruzindana 1947- *WhoWor 91*
Augustin, Sally Jean 1959- *WhoAmW 91*
Augustine of Canterbury, Saint *WorAlBi*
Augustine of Hippo, Saint 354-430 *WorAlBi*
Augustine, Saint *BioIn 16*
Augustine, Saint 354-430 *ClMLC 6 [port], EncPaPR 91, WrPh P*
Augustine, Daniel Gerald 1946- *St&PR 91*
Augustine, James Robert 1946- *WhoSSW 91*
Augustine, Jane 1931- *WhoE 91, WhoWrEP 89*
Augustine, Jeffrey B. 1953- *St&PR 91*
Augustine, Jerome Samuel 1928- *WhoE 91, WhoWor 91*
Augustine, Jerry 1952- *Ballpl 90*
Augustine, Norman R. *BioIn 16*
Augustine, Norman Ralph 1935- *WhoAm 90, WhoE 91*
Augustine, Richard John 1946- *St&PR 91*
Augusto, Antonio C. 1937- *WhoHisp 91*
Augustus, Emperor of Rome 63BC-14AD *BioIn 16*
Augustus, Gaius Julius Caesar Octavianus 63BC-14AD *WorAlBi*
Augustyn, Frank Joseph 1953- *WhoAm 90*
Augustyn, Frederick John, Jr. 1951- *WhoE 91, WhoEmL 91*
Augustyn, Noel James 1946- *WhoE 91, WhoEmL 91*
Auh, Chule Hwan 1930- *BiDrAPA 89*
Auh, Yang John 1934- *WhoWor 91*
Aujla, Sarbjit S *BiDrAPA 89*
Auker, Eldon 1910- *Ballpl 90*
Aukland, Duncan Dayton 1954- *WhoEmL 91*
Aukrust, Olav 1883-1929 *DcScanL*
Aulakh, Sukhinderpal S 1953- *BiDrAPA 89*
Aulbach, George Louis 1925- *St&PR 91, WhoSSW 91*
Aulby, Mike *BioIn 16*
Auld, Bertram Alexander 1922- *WhoAm 90*
Auld, Bruce 1954- *WhoEmL 91*
Auld, David Vinson 1907- *WhoAm 90*
Auld, Dennis Brian 1944- *St&PR 91*
Auld, Elizabeth B 1934- *BiDrAPA 89*
Auld, Frank 1923- *WhoAm 90*
Auld, Georgie *NewYTBS 90*
Auld, Georgie 1919-1990 *BioIn 16*
Auld, Ian *BioIn 16*
Auld, John Phillips 1916- *St&PR 91*
Auld, Linda Sue 1945- *WhoEmL 91*
Auldridge, Mike 1938- *ConMus 4*
Aulenbach, William Craig 1951- *WhoEmL 91*
Aulenti, Anthony Russell 1950- *St&PR 91*
Aulenti, Gae *BioIn 16, WomArch*
Aulenti, Gae 1927- *ConDes 90*
Auler, Angela Cruz 1949- *WhoAmW 91*
Auler, Susan Teeple 1945- *WhoSSW 91*
Aulert, Robert Henry, Jr. 1951- *WhoEmL 91*
Auletta, Patrick Vincent 1950- *St&PR 91*
Auletta, Richard C. 1937- *ODwPR 91, St&PR 91*
Auletta-Anzilotti, Lori Lynn 1959- *WhoAmW 91*
Aulette, Judy Root 1948- *WhoSSW 91*
Auletto, Leonard T. 1941- *St&PR 91*
Aulich, James 1952- *ConAu 132*
Auliczek, Dominicus 1734-1804 *PenDiDA 89*
Aulin, Arvid Yrjo 1929- *WhoWor 91*
Aulisi, Joseph G. *ConTFT 8*
Aulisio, Joseph P. 1910-1973 *MusmAFA*
Aull, Elizabeth Berryman 1951- *WhoEmL 91*
Aull, James Stroud 1931- *WhoSSW 91*
Aull, Jeffrey Lee 1949- *St&PR 91*
Aulnoy, Baronne d' 1650?-1705 *EncCoWW*
Aulnoy, Marie-Catherine 1649-1705 *FemiCLE*
Aulson, Philip Joseph 1924- *St&PR 91*
Ault, Charles C *BiDrAPA 89*
Ault, Charles Rollin 1923- *WhoAm 90*
Ault, Doug 1950- *Ballpl 90*
Ault, Ethyl Lorita 1939- *WhoAmW 91*
Ault, Frank H. 1944- *St&PR 91*
Ault, George *WhoAmA 91N*
Ault, George C. 1891-1948 *BioIn 16*
Ault, George Copeland 1891-1948 *WhoAmA 91N*
Ault, Hugh Joseph 1940- *WhoAm 90*
Ault, James Mase 1918- *WhoAm 90*
Ault, James William 1926- *WhoAm 90*
Ault, John Brady 1951- *WhoEmL 91*
Ault, John L. 1946- *St&PR 91*
Ault, Lawrence Eugene 1948- *WhoEmL 91*
Ault, Lee A., III 1936- *St&PR 91, WhoAm 90*
Ault, Linda Cae 1954- *WhoAmW 91*
Ault, Phillip Halliday 1914- *AuBYP 90*
Ault, Thomas Jefferson, III 1911- *WhoAm 90, WhoWor 91*
Ault, William *PenDiDA 89*
Aultman, Donnald Boyd 1954- *St&PR 91*
Aultman, Mims Crowell 1928- *WhoE 91*
Aultman, Roy Douglas, Sr. 1935- *WhoSSW 91*
Aultman, William W. 1924- *St&PR 91*
Auluck, Harinder S. 1944- *BiDrAPA 89*
Auman, Delbert A. 1926- *St&PR 91*
Aumann, Robert John 1930- *WhoWor 91*
Aument, George Clair 1923- *St&PR 91*
Aumiller, G.E. 1937- *St&PR 91*
Aumonier, Frederic *PenDiDA 89*
Aumont, Jean-Pierre 1911- *WhoAm 90, WorAlBi*
Aun, Lim Chien 1948- *WhoWor 91*
Aune, Jon Brian 1939- *St&PR 91*
Auneuil, Comtesse d' 16--?-17--? *EncCoWW*
Aung San Suu Kyi *BioIn 16*
Aung-Bwint, Cherry 1932- *BiDrAPA 89*
Aungkhin, Bob 1938- *BiDrAPA 89*
Aungst, Brian James 1954- *WhoE 91*
Aungst, Clarence William 1926- *WhoAm 90*
Aunon, Jorge Ignacio 1942- *WhoHisp 91*
Auping, Michael G. 1949- *WhoAm 90*
Auping, Michael Graham 1949- *WhoAmA 91*
Aupperle, Peter Mark *BiDrAPA 89*
Aura Pokou *WomWR*
Aura, William *NewAgMG*
Auran, David B 1932- *BiDrAPA 89*
Aurand, Charles Henry, Jr. 1932- *IntWWM 90, WhoAm 90*
Aurand, Robert Elwin 1946- *WhoSSW 91*
Aurandt, Paul 1948- *ConAu 129*
Aurangzeb 1618-1707 *WorAlBi*
Aurangzeb, Emperor of Hindustan 1618-1707 *BioIn 16*
Auray, Delbert L. 1930- *St&PR 91*
Aurbach, Gerald Donald 1927- *WhoAm 90*
Aurbach, Herbert Alexander 1924- *WhoAm 90*
Aureli, Giles 1926- *WhoAm 90*
Aurelio, Richard 1928- *ODwPR 91*
Aurelio, Richard 1929- *St&PR 91*
Aurell, John Karl 1935- *WhoAm 90*
Aurell, Tage 1895-1976 *DcScanL*
Auriach, Albert Noel Henri 1923- *WhoWor 91*
Auric, Georges 1899-1983 *OxCPMus, PenDiMP A*
Auric, Robert 1941- *BiDrAPA 89*
Aurichio, Joseph Louis 1931- *WhoAm 90*
Auriema, Carlos 1925- *St&PR 91*
Auriema, Robert C. 1925- *St&PR 91*
Auriemma, Donald Joseph 1942- *St&PR 91*
Auriemma, Louis Francis 1937- *St&PR 91, WhoE 91*
Auriemmo, Frank Joseph, Jr. 1942- *St&PR 91*
Aurin, Robert James 1943- *WhoAm 90, WhoWor 91*
Auriol, Jules Vincent 1884-1966 *BiDFrPL*
Auritt, Robert David 1951- *St&PR 91*
Aurner, Robert Ray 1898- *WhoAm 90*
Aurner, Robert Ray, II 1937- *WhoE 91*
Aurobindo, Sri 1872-1950 *BioIn 16, EncO&P 3, NewAgE 90*
Aurrecoechea, Rafael 1962- *WhoHisp 91*
Ausanka, John Joseph, III 1943- *St&PR 91*
Ausby, Ellsworth Augustus 1942- *WhoAmA 91*
Ausefski, James A. 1949- *St&PR 91*
Auser, Wallace Van Cortlandt, III 1950- *WhoEmL 91*
Ausere, Joe Morris 1929- *St&PR 91, WhoAm 90*
Ausfahl, William Friend 1940- *St&PR 91, WhoAm 90*
Auskaps, Aina Marija 1921- *WhoAmW 91*
Auslander, Edgar Denis 1964- *WhoE 91*
Auslander, Rose 1901- *EncCoWW*
Ausley, Geneva Gardner 1933- *WhoE 91*
Ausman, Robert K. 1933- *St&PR 91, WhoAm 90*
Ausmus, James T. 1937- *St&PR 91*
Auspitz, Norman Eugene 1946- *WhoSSW 91*
Ausprich, Harry *WhoAm 90*
Ausseil, Jean 1925- *WhoWor 91*
Ausserer, Roy Louis 1922- *St&PR 91*
Aussure, Pierre 1952- *WhoWor 91*
Aust, Anthony Ivall 1942- *WhoE 91*
Aust, Gerald Aldric 1950- *St&PR 91*
Aust, Joe Bradley 1926- *WhoAm 90*
Aust, Mary Catherine Cowan 1946- *WhoSSW 91*
Aust, Steven Douglas 1938- *WhoAm 90*
Austad, Carol C 1944- *BiDrAPA 89*
Austad, David Brian 1960- *St&PR 91*
Austad, Mark E. 1917-1988 *BioIn 16*
Austad, Oscar Melvin 1922- *St&PR 91*
Austad, Vigdis 1954- *WhoE 91*
Austein, Sidney *BiDrAPA 89*
Austein, Sidney 1936- *WhoE 91*
Austell, Edward Callaway 1937- *St&PR 91, WhoAm 90*
Austen, Alice 1866-1952 *BioAmW*
Austen, Burton Gustave *BiDrAPA 89*
Austen, George 1941- *St&PR 91*
Austen, Hallie Iglehart 1947- *WhoEmL 91*
Austen, Jane 1775-1817 *BioIn 16, FemiCLE, WorAlBi*
Austen, Karl Frank 1928- *WhoAm 90*
Austen, Katherine 1628-1683 *FemiCLE*
Austen, Katherine 1629-1683 *BiDEWW*
Austen, William Gerald 1930- *WhoAm 90, WhoWor 91*
Austen, William John 1920- *WhoWor 91*
Auster, Andrew Howard 1950- *IntWWM 90*
Auster, Clark C. 1924- *St&PR 91*
Auster, Kenneth 1953- *St&PR 91*
Auster, Lawrence Scott 1947- *St&PR 91*
Auster, Paul 1947- *BioIn 16, TwCCr&M 91, WhoWrEP 89, WorAu 1980 [port]*
Auster, Rosalie Joan *BiDrAPA 89*
Auster, Simon L 1932- *BiDrAPA 89*
Auster, Stanley *BioIn 16*
Austerlade, Evald K. 1932- *St&PR 91*
Austerlitz, Carl Frederick 1939- *WhoSSW 91*
Austerlitz, Robert Paul 1923- *WhoAm 90*
Austern, Linda Phyllis 1957- *IntWWM 90*
Austi, Donna *ODwPR 91*
Austill, Allen 1927- *WhoAm 90*
Austill, Bridget 1637-1693 *BiDEWW*
Austin, Ada Mary 1926- *WhoAmW 91*
Austin, Andrea Korzenik 1963- *WhoSSW 91*
Austin, Andrew Lance 1944- *WhoSSW 91*
Austin, Anne Lucippa 1891-1986 *BioIn 16*
Austin, Arthur C. *BioIn 16*
Austin, Arthur Donald, II 1932- *WhoAm 90*
Austin, Barbara Jean *WhoAmA 91*
Austin, Berit Synnove 1938- *WhoAmW 91*
Austin, Carol *BioIn 16*
Austin, Cathy Kiselyak 1954- *WhoEmL 91*
Austin, Charles A., III 1934- *St&PR 91*
Austin, Charles Edwin 1928- *WhoAm 90*
Austin, Charles John 1934- *WhoAm 90*
Austin, Charles Marshall 1941- *WhoE 91*
Austin, Charles Thomas 1932- *St&PR 91*
Austin, Charles Vincent 1931- *St&PR 91, WhoAm 90, WhoWor 91*
Austin, Charolette Price 1958- *WhoAmW 91*
Austin, Cheryl Lynne 1955- *WhoAmW 91*
Austin, Chris *WhoNeCM [port]*
Austin, Dan 1929- *WhoSSW 91*
Austin, Daniel Lynn 1952- *WhoEmL 91*
Austin, Daniel William 1949- *WhoEmL 91*
Austin, Darrel 1907- *WhoAm 90, WhoAmA 91*
Austin, David George 1951- *WhoEmL 91*
Austin, David Mayo 1923- *WhoAm 90*
Austin, Deborah Ruth 1953- *WhoEmL 91*
Austin, Denise *BioIn 16*
Austin, Donald Stafford 1922- *WhoAm 90*
Austin, Doris Browning 1942- *WhoE 91*
Austin, Dorothy Mayover 1931- *WhoAmW 91*
Austin, Dwight Warren 1940- *St&PR 91*
Austin, Edwin W. 1938- *St&PR 91*
Austin, Eileen Rita 1933- *WhoAmW 91*
Austin, Elizabeth 1907- *AuBYP 90*
Austin, Elsie *EarBlAP*
Austin, Eric Stuart 1957- *St&PR 91*
Austin, Francis M., Jr. 1928- *WhoAm 90*
Austin, Frank Holm 1952- *WhoSSW 91*
Austin, Fred C. 1926- *St&PR 91*
Austin, Frederic 1872-1952 *PenDiMP*
Austin, Gabriel Christopher 1935- *WhoAm 90*
Austin, Gene 1900-1972 *OxCPMus*
Austin, George Kenneth, Jr. 1931- *St&PR 91*
Austin, Gerald Grant 1937- *WhoAm 90, WhoSSW 91*
Austin, Gerald J. *BioIn 16*
Austin, Grace Baliunas 1940- *WhoAmW 91, WhoE 91*
Austin, Gregory Alan 1945- *St&PR 91*
Austin, Harry George, III 1958- *St&PR 91*
Austin, Harry Gregory 1936- *WhoAm 90*
Austin, Harry Guiden 1917- *WhoAm 90*
Austin, Harvey *BioIn 16*
Austin, Herbert 1866-1941 *WorAlBi*
Austin, Ian George 1951- *St&PR 91*
Austin, Irma Caroline 1941- *WhoAmW 91*
Austin, Jack Spencer 1936- *WhoSSW 91*
Austin, Jacob 1932- *WhoAm 90*

Austin, James *BioIn 16*
Austin, James 1813-1897 *DcCanB 12*
Austin, James E. 1942- *St&PR 91*
Austin, James Henry 1925- *WhoAm 90*
Austin, James William 1906- *WhoAm 90*
Austin, Jane 1831-1894 *FemiCLE*
Austin, Jerry L. 1932- *St&PR 91*
Austin, Jesse *PenDiDA 89*
Austin, Jesse Hinnant, III 1954- *WhoSSW 91*
Austin, Jimmy 1879-1965 *Ballpl 90*
Austin, Jo-Anne 1925- *WhoAmA 91N*
Austin, Joan Donna 1931- *St&PR 91*
Austin, Joann Clark 1939- *WhoAmW 91*
Austin, John David 1936- *WhoAm 90*
Austin, John Norman 1937- *WhoAm 90*
Austin, John Page 1914- *WhoAm 90*
Austin, John Robert 1951- *WhoEmL 91*
Austin, John Teufel 1925- *St&PR 91*
Austin, Karen M. N. 1955- *WhoAmW 91*
Austin, Larry 1930- *IntWWM 90*
Austin, Lawrence E *BiDrAPA 89*
Austin, Leland M., Jr. 1943- *St&PR 91*
Austin, Linda Smith 1951- *BiDrAPA 89*
Austin, Lois Ann Loehr 1939- *WhoAmW 91*
Austin, Lucille Carroll 1950- *WhoE 91, WhoEmL 91*
Austin, Margot *AuBYP 90*
Austin, Margot *NewYTBS 90*
Austin, Margot 1909?-1990 *ConAu 132*
Austin, Marilyn J. 1940- *St&PR 91*
Austin, Marshall Edward 1957- *WhoE 91, WhoEmL 91*
Austin, Marshall M. *St&PR 91N*
Austin, Mary 1868-1934 *FemiCLE*
Austin, Mary Hunter 1868-1934 *BioAmW, BioIn 16*
Austin, Michael Charles 1955- *WhoE 91, WhoEmL 91, WhoWrEP 89*
Austin, Michael F. 1944- *ODwPR 91*
Austin, Nancy *BioIn 16*
Austin, Nancy Elizabeth 1953- *WhoWrEP 89*
Austin, Norman K. 1953- *WhoEmL 91*
Austin, Oliver L. 1903-1988 *BioIn 16*
Austin, Oliver Luther, Jr. 1903- *AuBYP 90*
Austin, Page Insley 1942- *WhoAmW 91*
Austin, Pat 1937- *WhoAmA 91*
Austin, Patricia *WhoWrEP 89*
Austin, Patti *BioIn 16*
Austin, Phil 1910- *WhoAmA 91*
Austin, Philip Edward 1942- *WhoAm 90*
Austin, Philip Robert 1955- *WhoEmL 91*
Austin, Phylis Ann 1943- *WhoWrEP 89*
Austin, Ralph Leroy 1929- *WhoWor 91*
Austin, Ralph Steven 1949- *BiDrAPA 89*
Austin, Randolph Lee 1940- *WhoAm 90*
Austin, Raymond Darrel 1953- *WhoEmL 91*
Austin, Rhea Cochran 1938- *WhoAmW 91*
Austin, Rhonda Toni 1956- *WhoAmW 91*
Austin, Richard 1903-1989 *AnObit 1989*
Austin, Richard Henry 1913- *WhoAm 90*
Austin, Richard R. 1926- *St&PR 91*
Austin, Richard Stephen 1933- *WhoE 91*
Austin, Richard William 1931- *WhoAm 90*
Austin, Rick 1946- *Ballpl 90*
Austin, Robert C. 1919- *St&PR 91*
Austin, Robert C. 1947- *ODwPR 91*
Austin, Robert Clarke 1931- *WhoAm 90*
Austin, Robert Eugene, Jr. 1937- *WhoAm 90, WhoSSW 91, WhoWor 91*
Austin, Robert Farias 1948- *WhoSSW 91*
Austin, Robert Fredric 1950- *WhoSSW 91*
Austin, Robert G *BiDrAPA 89*
Austin, Robert Lee 1918- *St&PR 91*
Austin, Robert M. 1938- *St&PR 91*
Austin, Sam *Ballpl 90*
Austin, Sam M. 1933- *WhoAm 90*
Austin, Sarah 1793-1867 *FemiCLE*
Austin, Spencer Peter 1909- *WhoAm 90*
Austin, Stephen 1793-1836 *WorAlBi*
Austin, Stephen Jerome 1939- *St&PR 91*
Austin, Susan Rebecca 1945- *WhoE 91*
Austin, T. Louis, Jr. 1919- *WhoAm 90*
Austin, Terri Louise 1952- *WhoSSW 91*
Austin, Thomas Noell 1916- *St&PR 91*
Austin, Tracy 1962- *BioIn 16, WorAlBi*
Austin, Van O *BiDrAPA 89*
Austin, Wally *ODwPR 91*
Austin, Warren Robinson 1877-1962 *BioIn 16*
Austin, Wendy Page 1961- *WhoAmW 91, WhoE 91*
Austin, William *WhoSSW 91*
Austin, William King 1946- *BiDrAPA 89*
Austin, William Lamont 1915- *WhoAm 90*
Austin, William Weaver 1920- *IntWWM 90, WhoAm 90*
Austin, William Winter 1945- *WhoEmL 91*
Austin-Lucas, Barbara Etta 1951- *WhoAmW 91*
Austin-Nuhfer, Olive H *WhoAmA 91*
Austing, Lawrence B. 1925- *St&PR 91*
Auston, David Henry 1940- *WhoAm 90*
Austral, Florence 1894-1968 *PenDiMP*
Austria, Antonia 1955- *BiDrAPA 89*
Austria, David Mijares *BiDrAPA 89*
Austrian, Mark Louis 1945- *WhoE 91*
Austrian, Neil R. 1940- *St&PR 91*
Austrian, Robert 1916- *WhoAm 90*
Austrian, Susan E 1957- *BiDrAPA 89*
Ausubel, David Paul 1918- *BiDrAPA 89*
Ausubel, Marvin Victor 1927- *WhoAm 90*
Ausubel, Sheva 1896-1957 *WhoAmA 91N*
Auten, David Charles 1938- *WhoAm 90, WhoWor 91*
Auten, John Harold 1922- *WhoAm 90*
Auten, Paul W. 1953- *St&PR 91*
Autera, Michael E. *BioIn 16*
Autera, Michael E. 1938- *St&PR 91*
Autera, Michael Edward 1938- *WhoAm 90*
Autere, Eeva *DcScanL*
Auteri, Rose Mary Patti 1928- *WhoE 91*
Auteuil, Daniel 1950- *ConTFT 8*
Auth, Robert R 1926- *WhoAmA 91*
Auth, Susan Handler 1939- *WhoAmA 91*
Auth, Tony 1942- *BioIn 16, WhoAm 90, WhoE 91*
Auth, Tony, Jr 1942- *WhoAmA 91*
Author of An Everyday Tale *EncCoWW*
Autin, A. Anthony, Jr. 1938- *St&PR 91*
Autin, Ernest Anthony, II 1957- *WhoAm 90, WhoEmL 91*
Autio, Dudley Arne 1932- *BiDrAPA 89*
Autio, Rudy 1926- *PenDiDA 89, WhoAmA 91*
Autolitano, Astrid 1938- *WhoHisp 91*
Autori, Franco *NewYTBS 90*
Autorino, Anne Turnbull 1914- *WhoAmW 91*
Autorino, Anthony D. 1938- *St&PR 91*
Autrey, Frank Eugene 1924- *St&PR 91*
Autrey, Pamela Sanders 1945- *WhoAmW 91*
Autry, Carolyn 1940- *WhoAm 90, WhoAmA 91*
Autry, Gene 1907- *BioIn 16, EncACom, OxCPMus, WhoAm 90, WorAlBi*
Autry, Gwynne Wheeler 1933- *WhoAmW 91*
Autry, Howard Winton 1930- *St&PR 91*
Autry, James Arthur 1933- *WhoAm 90*
Autry, James L. 1830-1862 *AmLegL*
Autry, Jimmy Martin 1955- *WhoEmL 91*
Autry, Joseph Henry, III 1943- *BiDrAPA 89*
Autry, Lana Mathis 1947- *WhoSSW 91*
Autry, Larry Frank 1959- *WhoSSW 91*
Autry, Niles Patterson 1937- *St&PR 91*
Auvera, Johann Wolfgang van der 1708-1756 *PenDiDA 89*
Auvil, John S. 1911- *St&PR 91*
Auvil, Kenneth William 1925- *WhoAmA 91*
Auw, Dorothy Babette 1935- *WhoAmW 91*
Auwarter, Franklin Paul 1934- *WhoAm 90*
Auwers, Stanley John 1923- *WhoAm 90*
Auxier, Gary *ODwPR 91*
Auxier, Sylvia Trent 1900-1969 *LiHiK*
Auxietre, Camille-Georges 1922- *WhoWor 91*
Au-Yeung, Hang Stephen 1953- *WhoEmL 91*
Ava, Beth *BioIn 16*
Avakian, Alexandra 1960- *BioIn 16*
Avakian, Anahid Manoushak 1957- *WhoE 91*
Avakian, John *WhoAmA 91*
Avakoff, Joseph Carnegie 1936- *WhoWor 91*
Avalle-Arce, Juan Bautista 1927- *WhoAm 90*
Avalle-Arce, Juan Bautista de 1927- *ConAu 32NR, HispWr 90*
Avallone, John V. 1947- *St&PR 91*
Avallone, Michael 1924- *TwCCr&M 91*
Avallone, Michael Angelo 1924- *WhoAm 90*
Avallone, Michael Angelo, Jr. 1924- *SpyFic*
Avalon, Arthur 1865-1936 *EncO&P 3*
Avalon, Frankie 1940- *ConMus 5 [port], EncPR&S 89, OxCPMus, WorAlBi*
Avalone, Ronnie 1922- *WhoSSW 91*
Avalos, Andy Anthony 1956- *WhoHisp 91*
Avalos, Juan A *BiDrAPA 89*
Avalos-Bevan, Beatrice 1935- *WhoWor 91*
Avance, Gayland T. 1953- *St&PR 91*
Avant, David Alonzo, Jr. 1919- *WhoAm 90, WhoSSW 91*
Avant, Grady, Jr. 1932- *WhoAm 90*
Avant, Robert Frank 1937- *WhoAm 90*
Avanzado-Macaraeg, Leby Bae *BiDrAPA 89*
Avarius *ConAu 131*
Avasia, Maya 1942- *WhoWor 91*
Avasthi, Ram Bandhu 1941- *WhoWor 91*
Avati, Mario 1921- *BioIn 16*
Avazian, Richard William 1937- *St&PR 91*
Avchen, Malvin 1934- *St&PR 91*
Avdeyeva, Larissa 1925- *PenDiMP*
Avdiev, M. Rita *WhoWor 91*
Avdoian, Richard John 1951- *WhoEmL 91*
Ave, John Robert 1932- *St&PR 91, WhoAm 90, WhoE 91*
Aved, Barry 1943- *WhoAm 90*
Avedis, Hikmet *ConAu 132*
Avedis, Howard *ConAu 132*
Avedisian, Archie Harry 1928- *WhoE 91*
Avedisian, Armen G. 1926- *WhoAm 90*
Avedisian, Edward 1936- *WhoAm 90, WhoAmA 91*
Avedissian, Gevork *BioIn 16*
Avedon, Barry 1941- *WhoAmA 91*
Avedon, Richard *BioIn 16*
Avedon, Richard 1923- *WhoAm 90, WhoAmA 91, WhoE 91*
Avelar, Carl Louis 1937- *St&PR 91*
Aveline, Mark Oxenford 1941- *WhoWor 91*
Aveling, Eleanor Marx 1855-1898 *BioIn 16*
Aveling, Hugh *ConAu 131*
Aveling, J C H 1917- *ConAu 131*
Aveling, Valda 1920- *IntWWM 90*
Avelino, Jose Francisco *BioIn 16*
Avelino, Kim H. *ODwPR 91*
Avella, Arthur N 1923- *BiDrAPA 89*
Avella, William Ronald 1936- *WhoAm 90*
Avellaneda, Marco Marcelo 1955- *WhoE 91*
Avellano, Albert *TwCCr&M 91*
Avelli, Francesco Xanto *PenDiDA 89*
Avellis-Abrams, Rosemary Marisa 1945- *St&PR 91*
Aven, Manuel 1924- *WhoE 91*
Avenali, Peter 1918- *St&PR 91*
Avenar *EncO&P 3*
Avendano, Fausto 1941- *ConAu 131, HispWr 90, WhoHisp 91*
Aveni, Anthony Francis 1938- *WhoAm 90*
Avenick, Karen Reinhardt 1946- *WhoEmL 91*
Avenirov, Alexander G *BiDrAPA 89*
Average White Band *EncPR&S 89*
Average White Band, The *OxCPMus*
Averbach, Irwin J 1927- *BiDrAPA 89*
Averbeck, Karen Marie 1961- *WhoAmW 91*
Averbook, Beryl David 1920- *WhoWor 91*
Averbuch, Gerald 1921- *St&PR 91*
Averbuch, Gloria 1951- *BioIn 16*
Averbuch, Ilan 1953- *WhoAmA 91*
Averbuch, Philip Fred 1941- *WhoSSW 91*
Averch, Harvey Allan 1935- *WhoAm 90*
Averell, Lois Hathaway 1917- *WhoAmW 91*
Averett-Short, Geneva Evelyn 1938- *WhoE 91*
Averill, Earl 1902-1983 *Ballpl 90 [port]*
Averill, Earl 1931- *Ballpl 90*
Averill, Esther Holden 1902- *AuBYP 90*
Averill, James H 1947- *ConAu 129*
Averill, James Reed 1935- *WhoAm 90, WhoE 91*
Averill, Lawrence Herman, Jr. 1940- *WhoSSW 91*
Averill, Lloyd James, Jr. 1923- *WhoAm 90*
Averill, Robert Guyer *WhoSSW 91*
Averill, Stuart Carson 1924- *BiDrAPA 89*
Averill, Thomas Fox 1949- *WhoWrEP 89*
Averino, Olga *BioIn 16*
Averitt, George Robert 1931- *St&PR 91*
Averitt, George Ronald 1949- *WhoEmL 91*
Averitt, Gerald Eastep 1943- *St&PR 91*
Averitt, Richard Garland, III 1945- *WhoEmL 91*
Averitt, Robert C. 1903- *St&PR 91*
Averoff, Evangelos 1910-1990 *NewYTBS 90*
Averoff-Tositsas, Evangelos 1910-1990 *CurBio 90N*
Averoff-Tossizza, Evangelos 1910-1990 *BioIn 16*
Averroes 1126-1198 *EncO&P 3, WorAlBi*
Avers, Charlotte J. 1926-1990 *BioIn 16, ConAu 131*
Avers, Jeffrey Paul 1954- *WhoSSW 91*
Avers, Max R. 1945- *WhoSSW 91*
Aversa, Andre Anthony 1934- *WhoAm 90*
Aversa, Dolores Sejda 1932- *WhoAmW 91, WhoE 91, WhoWor 91*
Aversa, Guido Antonio *BiDrAPA 89*
Aversenti, Candida Covino 1952- *St&PR 91*
Aversenti, Edmund V., Jr. 1944- *St&PR 91*
Avery, Al *AuBYP 90*
Avery, Bruce C. 1940- *St&PR 91*
Avery, Bruce Edward 1949- *WhoEmL 91*
Avery, Byllye Y. *BioIn 16*
Avery, Cameron Scott 1938- *WhoAm 90*
Avery, Cheryl Brown 1959- *WhoWrEP 89*
Avery, Christine Ann 1951- *WhoAmW 91*
Avery, Colin R. 1942- *St&PR 91*
Avery, David H 1946- *BiDrAPA 89*
Avery, David Wayne 1953- *WhoSSW 91*
Avery, Donald Hills 1937- *WhoAm 90, WhoWor 91*
Avery, Elizabeth *FemiCLE*
Avery, Elizabeth 1595-1677 *BiDEWW*
Avery, Frances 1910- *WhoAmA 91*
Avery, Frederick Fifield 1930- *WhoAm 90*
Avery, Gillian Elise 1926- *AuBYP 90*
Avery, Gordon Bennett 1931- *WhoAm 90*
Avery, Helen Palmer 1910- *WhoWrEP 89*
Avery, Irwin *BiDrAPA 89*
Avery, Jack Alexander 1928- *St&PR 91*
Avery, James Knuckey 1921- *WhoAm 90*
Avery, James Robert 1940- *St&PR 91*
Avery, James Stephen 1923- *WhoAm 90*
Avery, James Thomas, III 1945- *WhoEmL 91*
Avery, Jeanne 1931- *WhoE 91*
Avery, John E. 1941- *St&PR 91*
Avery, John Edwin 1928- *WhoE 91*
Avery, John T. 1931- *St&PR 91*
Avery, Julia May 1917- *WhoAmW 91*
Avery, Kenneth Arnold 1926- *WhoSSW 91*
Avery, Kenneth Austin 1953- *WhoWrEP 89*
Avery, Lee Ann 1957- *WhoAmW 91, WhoEmL 91*
Avery, Lynn *AuBYP 90*
Avery, Margaret *ConTFT 8, DrBlPA 90*
Avery, Margaret 1951- *WhoAmW 91*
Avery, Mary Ellen 1927- *WhoAm 90, WhoAmW 91*
Avery, Michael Aaron 1944- *WhoAm 90*
Avery, Milton 1893-1965 *BioIn 16, WhoAmA 91N*
Avery, Myrtilla *WhoAmA 91N*
Avery, Nathan M. 1934- *St&PR 91*
Avery, Neil Francis 1953- *WhoWrEP 89*
Avery, Nicholas C 1933- *BiDrAPA 89*
Avery, Ralph Hillyer 1906-1976 *WhoAmA 91N*
Avery, Richard *ConAu 31NR*
Avery, Robert David 1953- *WhoSSW 91*
Avery, Sally Michel 1905- *BioIn 16*
Avery, Sherrie L. 1943- *WhoAmW 91*
Avery, Susan Paula 1960- *WhoAmW 91*
Avery, Valeen Tippetts 1936- *ConAu 129*
Avery, William H. 1905- *St&PR 91*
Avery, William Henry 1911- *WhoAm 90*
Avery, William Herbert 1905- *WhoAm 90*
Avery, William Hinckley 1912- *WhoAm 90*
Avery, William J. 1940- *St&PR 91*
Avery, William Joseph 1940- *WhoAm 90, WhoE 91*
Avery, William P. 1918- *WhoWrEP 89*
Averyt, Gayle O. 1933- *St&PR 91*
Averyt, Gayle Owen 1933- *WhoAm 90*
Avgerakis, George Harris 1949- *WhoEmL 91*
Avgerinos, Cecily Terese 1945- *WhoWrEP 89*
Avgiris, Catherine 1959- *St&PR 91*
Avi 1937- *BioIn 16*
Aviado, Domingo M. 1924- *WhoAm 90*
Avian, Bob 1937- *WhoAm 90*
Avicenna 980-1037 *EncO&P 3, WorAlBi*
Avidom, Manahem 1908- *IntWWM 90*
Avigad, Nachman 1905- *ConAu 129*
Avila, Albert Enrique 1958- *WhoSSW 91*
Avila, Bobby 1924- *Ballpl 90*
Avila, Carlos Francisco 1925- *WhoHisp 91*
Avila, Charles 1945- *ConAu 129*
Avila, David A. 1953- *WhoHisp 91*
Avila, Edgar V. 1949- *St&PR 91*
Avila, Eli Narciso 1959- *WhoHisp 91*
Avila, Elza S. 1931- *WhoHisp 91*
Avila, Humberto Nuno 1954- *WhoHisp 91*
Avila, Joaquin G. 1948- *BioIn 16, WhoHisp 91*
Avila, Juan Antonio 1948- *BiDrAPA 89*
Avila, Juan Manuel 1948- *BiDrAPA 89*
Avila, Juan Marcos 1959- *WhoHisp 91*
Avila, Karole Samantha 1953- *BiDrAPA 89*
Avila, Lorna Arenas *BiDrAPA 89*
Avila, Maria V *BiDrAPA 89*
Avila, Missy *BioIn 16*
Avila, Pablo 1949- *WhoHisp 91*
Avila, Rafael 1941- *ConAu 132*
Avila, Rafael Urbano 1930- *WhoHisp 91*
Avila, Ralph 1957- *WhoHisp 91*
Avila, Vernon L. 1941- *WhoHisp 91*
Avila, William Thaddeus 1954- *WhoEmL 91, WhoSSW 91*
Avila Camacho, Manuel 1897-1955 *BioIn 16*
Avildsen, Edward B. 1929- *St&PR 91*
Avildsen, John G. *BioIn 16*
Avildsen, John Guilbert 1935- *WhoAm 90*
Aviles, Alice Alers 1934- *WhoE 91*
Aviles, Juan 1905- *WhoHisp 91*
Aviles, Rick *BioIn 16*
Aviles, Rosemarie 1957- *WhoHisp 91*
Aviles-Roig, Carlos A *BiDrAPA 89*
Aviles-Roig, Francisco 1943- *BiDrAPA 89*
Avillion, Dianne Faith 1954- *WhoSSW 91*
Avina, Philip Indalecio 1940- *WhoWor 91*
Avina-Rhodes, Nina Alvarado 1944- *WhoAmW 91*
Avineri, Shlomo 1933- *WhoWor 91*
Avino-Barracato, Kathleen 1956- *WhoAmW 91*
Avinoff, Andrey 1884-1948 *WhoAmA 91N*
Avioli, James P. 1938- *St&PR 91*
Avioli, Louis Vincent 1931- *WhoAm 90*
Avirett, John Williams, II 1902- *WhoAm 90*
Avirgan, Anthony Lance 1944- *ConAu 31NR*

Avirgan, Tony *ConAu 31NR*
Avis, John Boyd 1875-1944 *AmLegL*
Avis, Kenneth Edward 1918- *WhoSSW 91*
Avison, David 1937- *WhoAm 90, WhoAmA 91*
Avison, Margaret 1918- *FemiCLE, MajTwCW*
Avisse, Jean 1723-1796? *PenDiDA 89*
Avisseau, Charles-Jean 1796-1861 *PenDiDA 89*
Avitabile, John 1942- *ODwPR 91*
Avitan, Isaac 1950- *WhoEmL 91*
Avksent'ev, Nikolai Dmitrievich 1878-1943 *BioIn 16*
Avlon-Daphnis, Helen Basilea 1932- *WhoAmA 91*
Avner, L.L. 1915- *St&PR 91*
Avner, Louis Leonard 1915- *WhoAm 90*
Avni, Tzvi Jacob 1927- *IntWWM 90*
Avni, Yoram *BioIn 16*
Avogadro, Amadeo 1776-1856 *WorAlBi*
Avoglio, Christina Maria *PenDiMP*
Avolio, John F. 1940- *WhoE 91*
Avolio, Wendy Freedman 1953- *WhoEmL 91*
Avon Comedy Four *OxCPMus*
Avon, Anthony Eden, Earl of 1897-1977 *BioIn 16*
Avondoglio, Leo 1913- *St&PR 91*
Avorgbedor, Daniel Kodzo 1952- *IntWWM 90*
Avraham, Regina 1935- *WhoAmW 91*
Avram, Henriette D. 1919- *BioIn 16*
Avram, Henriette Davidson 1919- *WhoAm 90, WhoAmW 91*
Avrashow, Wayne 1950- *St&PR 91*
Avrett, John Glenn 1929- *WhoAm 90*
Avrick, Stuart J. 1934- *St&PR 91*
Avril, Franck Thierry Olivier 1953- *IntWWM 90*
Avril, John G. 1930- *St&PR 91*
Avril, Prosper *BioIn 16*
Avril, Thomas B. 1925- *St&PR 91*
Avrit, Richard Calvin 1932- *WhoAm 90*
Avrunin, Charlene Pattishall 1946- *WhoAmW 91*
Avrunin, George Sam'l 1952- *WhoE 91*
Avry, Dominique *EncCoWW*
Avshalomov, David 1946- *WhoEmL 91*
Avshalomov, Jacob 1919- *IntWWM 90*
Awa, Ngozi Mary 1956- *WhoEmL 91*
Awa-Bajas, Teresita Y *BiDrAPA 89*
Awad, Eric Adrian *BiDrAPA 89*
Awad, Joseph F. 1929- *ODwPR 91*
Awad, Lily *BiDrAPA 89*
Awad, Mubarak E. *BioIn 16*
Awad, Shahrzad H. 1952- *WhoAmW 91*
Awais, George Musa 1929- *WhoAm 90, WhoWor 91*
Awakessien, Herbert Simon 1957- *WhoWor 91*
Awalt, Elizabeth Grace 1956- *WhoAmA 91*
Awalt, Marilene Kay 1942- *WhoSSW 91*
Awashonks *WhNaAH*
Awasthi, Rajendra Kumar 1940- *WhoWor 91*
Awasthi, Sangeeta S *BiDrAPA 89*
Awasthi, Sheodulare Prasad 1937- *WhoWor 91*
Awazu, Kiyoshi 1929- *ConDes 90*
Awazu, Shoji 1933- *WhoWor 91*
Awde, Franklin M. 1919- *St&PR 91*
Awdry, W. V. 1911- *ChlLR 23 [port]*
Aweida, Jesse Issa 1931- *WhoAm 90*
Awerbuch, Shimon 1946- *WhoE 91*
Awes, Lorraine E 1922- *BiDrAPA 89*
Awojoodu, Samson Olalekan 1955- *WhoE 91*
Awoonor, Kofi Nyidevu 1935- *ConAu 13AS [port], WhoWor 91*
Awramik, Stanley Michael 1946- *WhoEmL 91*
Awramtchuk-Klim, Iya *BiDrAPA 89*
Awret, Irene 1921- *ConAu 131*
Awura Pokou *WomWR*
Awwa, Bassam 1952- *BiDrAPA 89*
Ax, Emanuel *BioIn 16*
Ax, Emanuel 1949- *IntWWM 90, PenDiMP, WhoAm 90, WhoWor 91*
Ax, Peter 1959- *WhoEmL 91*
Ax, Torsten Karl Johan 1928- *WhoWor 91*
Ax, Wolfram Karl 1944- *WhoWor 91*
Axam, John Arthur 1930- *WhoAm 90*
Axe, John Randolph 1938- *WhoAm 90*
Axel, Bernard 1946- *WhoSSW 91, WhoWor 91*
Axel, Gabriel *BioIn 16*
Axel, John Werner 1941- *St&PR 91, WhoAm 90*
Axel, Marc 1945- *WhoSSW 91*
Axel, Richard 1946- *WhoAm 90*
Axel, Robert Jay 1946- *WhoE 91*
Axelrad, Allan David 1943- *BiDrAPA 89*
Axelrad, Charles Steven 1949- *WhoE 91*
Axelrad, Irving Irmas 1915- *WhoAm 90*
Axelrad, James Alan 1950- *St&PR 91*
Axelrod, Barry Leon 1947- *WhoEmL 91*
Axelrod, Charles Paul 1941- *WhoAm 90*
Axelrod, Daniel Isaac 1910- *WhoAm 90*
Axelrod, David 1935- *WhoAm 90*
Axelrod, David Bruce 1943- *WhoWrEP 89*
Axelrod, Herbert Richard 1927- *WhoWor 91*
Axelrod, Howard S 1923- *BiDrAPA 89*
Axelrod, Jerome 1945- *WhoWrEP 89*
Axelrod, Jonathan Gans 1946- *WhoAm 90*
Axelrod, Julius 1912- *WhoAm 90, WhoE 91, WhoWor 91, WorAlBi*
Axelrod, Leah Joy 1929- *WhoAmW 91*
Axelrod, Leonard 1950- *WhoEmL 91*
Axelrod, Mark Richard 1946- *WhoWrEP 89*
Axelrod, Marvin F. 1927- *St&PR 91*
Axelrod, Michael Dan 1951- *WhoSSW 91*
Axelrod, Miriam *WhoAmA 91*
Axelrod, Norman Nathan 1934- *WhoAm 90, WhoE 91, WhoWor 91*
Axelrod, Robert Marshall 1943- *WhoAm 90*
Axelrod, Stephen Lee 1951- *WhoWor 91*
Axelrod, Susan Ellen 1948- *WhoAmW 91*
Axelrod, Sylvia Levine 1925- *BiDrAPA 89*
Axelrod, Valija M. 1944- *WhoAmW 91*
Axelrod, William B. 1910- *St&PR 91*
Axelroth, Lynn Robin 1954- *WhoEmL 91*
Axelsen, Richard H. 1933- *St&PR 91*
Axelson, Alan Arthur 1941- *BiDrAPA 89*
Axelson, Carl Mark 1948- *WhoEmL 91*
Axelson, Charles Frederic 1917- *WhoAm 90*
Axelson, David Brian *BiDrAPA 89*
Axelson, Joseph Allen 1927- *WhoAm 90, WhoWor 91*
Axelson, Kenneth S. 1922- *St&PR 91*
Axelson, Teresa Elaine 1947- *St&PR 91*
Axelsson, Ake 1932- *ConDes 90*
Axelsson, Alf Gustav-Adolf 1929- *WhoWor 91*
Axelsson, Gudjon 1935- *WhoWor 91*
Axerlis, Stella 1944- *IntWWM 90*
Axford, Clinton B. 1898-1988 *BioIn 16*
Axford, D.W. 1920- *St&PR 91*
Axford, Roy Arthur 1928- *WhoAm 90, WhoWor 91*
Axford, Warren Scott 1956- *WhoE 91*
Axilrod, Stephen H. 1926- *St&PR 91*
Axilrod, Stephen Harvey 1926- *WhoAm 90*
Axinn, Donald Everett 1929- *WhoAm 90, WhoWrEP 89*
Axinn, George Harold 1926- *WhoAm 90*
Axinn, Sidney 1923- *WhoE 91*
Axis Sally 1900-1988 *BioIn 16*
Axler, Joel Lee *BiDrAPA 89*
Axley, Linda Deanne 1950- *WhoSSW 91*
Axline, Robert Paul 1935- *WhoE 91*
Axline, Stanton Gerald 1935- *St&PR 91*
Axlund, Richard C. 1941- *St&PR 91*
Axt, Harry S. 1935- *St&PR 91*
Axtell, James Lewis 1941- *WhoAm 90*
Axtell, John David 1934- *WhoAm 90*
Axtell, Lucy Deborah *BiDrAPA 89*
Axthelm, Pete 1943- *WhoWrEP 89*
Axtmann, Robert Clark 1925- *WhoAm 90*
Axton, David *MajTwCW, TwCCr&M 91*
Axton, Hoyt 1938- *WorAlBi*
Axton, William Fitch *WhoSSW 91*
Axworthy, Thomas Sydney 1947- *WhoAm 90*
Aya 1965- *BioIn 16*
Aya, Roderick Honeyman 1916- *WhoE 91, WhoWor 91*
Ayad, Boulos Ayad 1928- *WhoAm 90*
Ayad, Joseph Magdy 1926- *WhoSSW 91*
Ayal, Jacob Wilhelmus 1925- *IntWWM 90*
Ayala, Alberto Andres *BiDrAPA 89*
Ayala, Arthur Angel 1934- *WhoHisp 91, WhoWor 91*
Ayala, Benny 1951- *Ballpl 90*
Ayala, Bernardo Lozano 1938- *WhoHisp 91*
Ayala, Francisco Jose 1934- *WhoAm 90*
Ayala, Gonzalo F. 1949- *WhoHisp 91*
Ayala, Gustavo Lopez 1968- *WhoWor 91*
Ayala, Jaime 1939- *BiDrAPA 89*
Ayala, John Louis 1943- *WhoHisp 91*
Ayala, Manuel 1959- *WhoHisp 91*
Ayala, Marta Stiefel 1937- *WhoHisp 91*
Ayala, Ramon Perez de 1880-1962 *BioIn 16*
Ayala, Reynaldo 1934- *WhoHisp 91*
Ayala, Ruben S. 1922- *WhoHisp 91*
Ayala-Lasso, Jose 1932- *WhoWor 91*
Ayano, Katsutoshi 1949- *WhoWor 91*
Ayars, Albert Lee 1917- *WhoAm 90*
Ayars, James Sterling 1898- *AuBYP 90*
Ayars, Rebecca Caudill *AuBYP 90*
Ayaso, Manuel 1934- *WhoAm 90, WhoAmA 91*
Aybar, Romeo 1930- *WhoAm 90*
Aycinena, Juan Jose de 1792?-1865 *BioIn 16*
Ayckbourn, Alan 1939- *BioIn 16, ConAu 31NR, MajTwCW, NewYTBS 90 [port], WhoWor 91, WorAlBi*
Aycock, Alice *BioIn 16*
Aycock, Alice 1946- *WhoAm 90, WhoAmA 91*
Aycock, Alice Frances 1946- *BiDWomA*
Aycock, Don Milton 1951- *WhoWrEP 89*
Aycock, Edwin Norton 1929- *St&PR 91*
Aycock, Helen Phillips 1938- *WhoSSW 91*
Aycock, Hugh David 1930- *St&PR 91, WhoAm 90, WhoSSW 91*
Aycock, Jean Elizabeth 1953- *BiDrAPA 89*
Aycock, Jesse N. 1907- *St&PR 91*
Aycock, Pamela Gayle 1961- *WhoAmW 91*
Aycock, Phillip D *BiDrAPA 89*
Aycock, William Brantley 1915- *WhoAm 90*
Aycrigg, John B *BiDrAPA 89*
Ayd, Frank J, Jr. 1920- *BiDrAPA 89*
Aydelott, Madison P., III 1954- *WhoEmL 91*
Aydelotte, Myrtle Kitchell 1917- *WhoAm 90, WhoAmW 91*
Aydelotte, William Osgood 1910- *WhoAm 90, WhoWrEP 89*
Aydin, Ulvi I. 1960- *WhoWor 91*
Aydy, Catherine *WorAu 1980*
Ayer, A. J. 1910-1989 *BioIn 16*
Ayer, A J 1910-1989 *ConAu 129*
Ayer, A.L., Jr. 1925- *St&PR 91*
Ayer, Alfred 1910-1989 *AnObit 1989*
Ayer, Alfred Jules 1910-1989 *BioIn 16*
Ayer, Anne 1917- *WhoWrEP 89*
Ayer, Donald Belton 1949- *WhoAm 90*
Ayer, Francis W. 1848-1923 *WorAlBi*
Ayer, Harriet 1849-1903 *WorAlBi*
Ayer, Harriet H. 1849-1903 *BioAmW*
Ayer, Jane Davis 1952- *WhoEmL 91*
Ayer, Kristin Vander Meer 1951- *WhoAmW 91, WhoE 91*
Ayer, Nat D. 1887-1952 *OxCPMus*
Ayer, William Alfred 1932- *WhoAm 90*
Ayers, A. Merrill 1946- *WhoEmL 91*
Ayers, Anne Louise 1948- *WhoEmL 91*
Ayers, Carlos R. 1932- *WhoAm 90*
Ayers, Carol Lee 1929- *WhoAmA 91*
Ayers, Doc 1890-1968 *Ballpl 90*
Ayers, Donald Walter 1933- *St&PR 91, WhoAm 90*
Ayers, Emory Daniel 1928- *WhoAm 90*
Ayers, George Edward Lewis 1938- *WhoAm 90, WhoE 91*
Ayers, Harry Brandt 1935- *WhoAm 90, WhoWor 91*
Ayers, Herbert D. 1908-1988 *BioIn 16*
Ayers, Hester Merwin 1902-1975 *WhoAmA 91N*
Ayers, James Edson 1932- *St&PR 91, WhoAm 90*
Ayers, James Lee 1919- *WhoWor 91*
Ayers, James Wilber 1928- *WhoWrEP 89*
Ayers, Jeffrey David 1960- *WhoEmL 91, WhoWor 91*
Ayers, Jennie Lee 1941- *St&PR 91*
Ayers, John Franklin, III 1953- *WhoE 91*
Ayers, Joseph Williams 1904- *WhoWor 91*
Ayers, Oscar Lee 1927- *St&PR 91*
Ayers, Patricia Ann 1958- *WhoAmW 91*
Ayers, Ralston E. 1932- *St&PR 91*
Ayers, Randall Wayne 1954- *WhoEmL 91*
Ayers, Rendall P. 1937- *ODwPR 91*
Ayers, Richard H. 1942- *St&PR 91, WhoAm 90*
Ayers, Richard Winston 1910- *WhoAm 90*
Ayers, Ronald Marvin 1947- *WhoSSW 91*
Ayers, Russell Cameron 1914- *WhoSSW 91*
Ayers, Scott N. 1944- *St&PR 91*
Ayers, Tim W. 1945- *WhoE 91*
Ayers, W. Floyd 1938- *St&PR 91*
Ayers, William Borden 1952- *St&PR 91*
Ayers, William McClean 1950- *WhoE 91*
Ayers-Allen, Phylicia *BioIn 16*
Aygen, Sumer 1938- *BiDrAPA 89*
Ayik, Sakir 1947- *WhoSSW 91*
Aykanian, Ara 1928- *St&PR 91*
Aykoler, Medih 1923- *BiDrAPA 89*
Aykroyd, Dan *BioIn 16*
Aykroyd, Daniel Edward 1952- *WhoAm 90*
Ayler, Albert *BioIn 16*
Ayler, Albert 1936-1970 *OxCPMus*
Ayler, Ethel 1934?- *DrBlPA 90*
Aylesworth, Jim 1943- *WhoWrEP 89*
Aylesworth, Thomas Gibbons 1927- *AuBYP 90, WhoAm 90, WhoWrEP 89*
Aylesworth, William Andrew 1942- *St&PR 91*
Ayling, John R. 1943- *St&PR 91*
Ayling, Robert *BioIn 16*
Ayllon, Lucas Vasquez De 1475?-1526 *EncCRAm*
Aylon, Helene *WhoAmA 91*
Aylor, Ronald Lee 1950- *WhoSSW 91*
Aylor, Sarah Brown *BiDrAPA 89*
Ayloush, Cynthia Marie 1950- *WhoAmW 91*
Aylsworth, Clark 1920- *St&PR 91*
Aylward, Florence 1862-1950 *OxCPMus*
Aylward, Gladys 1902-1970 *BioIn 16*
Aylward, James Francis 1942- *WhoE 91*
Aylward, Ronald Lee 1930- *St&PR 91, WhoAm 90*
Aylward, Thomas James, Jr. 1923- *WhoAm 90*
Aylward, William J 1875-1958 *WhoAmA 91N*
Aylwin, Patricio 1918- *CurBio 90 [port], WhoWor 91*
Aylwin, Susan 1946- *WhoWor 91*
Ayme, Marcel 1902-1967 *EuWr 12*
Aymerich, Adrian J. 1937- *St&PR 91*
Aymerich, Angela Figuera 1902- *EncCoWW*
Aymond, Gregory Ray 1956- *WhoEmL 91*
Ayo, Donald Joseph 1934- *WhoSSW 91*
Ayo, Felix 1933- *PenDiMP*
Ayoob, Richard Joseph 1953- *WhoEmL 91*
Ayotte, Elizabeth Ann 1952- *WhoAmW 91*
Ayoub, Christine Williams 1922- *WhoAmW 91, WhoE 91*
Ayoub, Linda Marie 1964- *WhoAmW 91*
Ayoub, Mahmoud Amin 1942- *WhoAm 90*
Ayoub, Victor Ferris 1923- *WhoWor 91*
Ayoung, Judith M. 1965- *WhoAmW 91*
Ayrault, Evelyn West 1922- *WhoAmW 91*
Ayre, John Randolph 1938- *St&PR 91*
Ayre, Robert Hugh 1900- *AuBYP 90*
Ayrer, James 1924- *St&PR 91*
Ayres, Ed 1941- *WhoWrEP 89*
Ayres, Frances Lynch 1950- *WhoSSW 91*
Ayres, Gillian 1930- *BiDWomA*
Ayres, James Marx 1922- *WhoAm 90*
Ayres, Janice Ruth 1930- *WhoAmW 91, WhoWor 91*
Ayres, Jeffrey Peabody 1952- *WhoEmL 91*
Ayres, Jeremiah Johnston 1932- *St&PR 91*
Ayres, John Cecil 1919- *WhoAm 90*
Ayres, John Samuel 1914- *St&PR 91, WhoAm 90*
Ayres, Julia Spencer 1931- *WhoAmA 91*
Ayres, Larry Marshall 1939- *WhoAmA 91*
Ayres, Lew 1908- *WorAlBi*
Ayres, Linda L 1947- *WhoAmA 91, WhoAmW 91*
Ayres, Lyman S. 1908- *St&PR 91*
Ayres, Mary Ellen 1924- *WhoAm 90*
Ayres, Paul *TwCCr&M 91*
Ayres, Ray Morris 1928- *WhoSSW 91*
Ayres, Robert B. 1928- *St&PR 91*
Ayres, Robert Moss, Jr. 1926- *WhoAm 90*
Ayres, Robert Underwood 1932- *WhoAm 90*
Ayres, Ruby M. 1883-1955 *BioIn 16*
Ayres, Ruby Mildred 1883-1955 *FemiCLE*
Ayres, Russell William, Jr. 1926- *WhoAm 90*
Ayres, Samuel, III 1919- *WhoAm 90*
Ayres, Stephen McClintock 1929- *WhoAm 90, WhoWor 91*
Ayres, Steven B. 1952- *St&PR 91*
Ayres, Steven Douglas 1948- *WhoSSW 91*
Ayres, Ted Dean 1947- *WhoEmL 91*
Ayres, Terrell C. 1932- *St&PR 91*
Ayres, Thomas Almond 1816?-1858 *BioIn 16*
Ayres, William H 1932- *BiDrAPA 89*
Ayromlooi, Cyrus *BiDrAPA 89*
Ayrton, Hertha 1854-1923 *DcScB S2*
Ayrton, J. Calder 1838-1884 *FemiCLE*
Ayrton, Norman Walter 1924- *IntWWM 90*
Ayscough, Florence 1875-1942 *FemiCLE*
Ayton, W A 1816-1909 *EncO&P 3*
Ayub, Zahid Hussain 1954- *WhoEmL 91*
Ayupova, Zhanna *BioIn 16*
Ayuso-Gutierrez, Jose L *BiDrAPA 89*
Ayyala, Murty S R 1954- *BiDrAPA 89*
Ayyala, Sarma S.V.S. 1940- *St&PR 91*
Ayyaswamy, Vatsala *BiDrAPA 89*
Azaceta, Luis Cruz 1942- *WhoAmA 91, WhoE 91, WhoHisp 91*
Azad, Abdul Kalam 1888-1958 *BioIn 16*
Azad, Firoozeh M *BiDrAPA 89*
Azadovskii, Mark Konstantinovich 1888-1954 *BioIn 16*
Azaid *ConAu 131*
Azaid 1908-1990 *BioIn 16*
Azalais d'Altier *EncCoWW*
Azalais de Porcairages 1140?- *EncCoWW*
Azam, Mohd Zaki 1931- *WhoWor 91*
Azama-Edwards, Gwendolyn Joyce 1949- *WhoAmW 91*
Azana, Manuel 1880-1940 *BioIn 16*
Azar, Henry Amin 1927- *WhoAm 90*
Azar, Jimmy 1936- *St&PR 91*
Azar, Kathryne K *BiDrAPA 89*
Azar, Richard Thomas 1954- *WhoE 91, WhoEmL 91*
Azara, Nancy 1940- *BiDWomA*
Azara, Nancy J 1939- *WhoAmA 91*
Azarch, Tanya Sednew 1951- *St&PR 91*
Azarian, Mardiros 1929- *WhoE 91*
Azarian, Martin Vartan 1927- *WhoAm 90*
Azarmedukht *WomWR*
Azarnoff, Daniel Lester 1926- *St&PR 91, WhoAm 90*
Azaroff, Leonid Vladimirovitch 1926- *WhoAm 90*
Azarya, Victor 1946- *ConAu 129*

Azbill, Russell Darrell 1965- *WhoSSW 91*
Azcarate, Carlos Leonel 1943- *BiDrAPA 89*
Azcarraga Milmo, Emilio *WhoAm 90*
Azcona Hoyo, Jose *BioIn 16*
Azcona Hoyo, Jose Simon 1927- *WhoWor 91*
Azcue, Joe 1939- *Ballpl 90*
Azcuenaga, Mary L. 1945- *WhoHisp 91*
Azcuenaga, Mary Laurie 1945- *WhoAm 90, WhoAmW 91*
Azcuy, Orlando Diaz- *BioIn 16*
Azen, Elaine T. 1931- *ODwPR 91*
Azevedo, Aluisio 1857-1913 *BioIn 16*
Azevedo, Belmiro de *BioIn 16*
Azevedo Oliveira, Maria Deodata 1924- *WhoWor 91*
Azfar, Kamal Uddin 1938- *WhoWor 91*
Azim, Abdus Sattar 1938- *WhoE 91*
Azim, Hassan F A 1932- *BiDrAPA 89*
Azima, Farhad 1941- *WhoAm 90*
Azimuth *NewAgMG*
Azis, Iwan Jaya 1953- *WhoWor 91*
Aziz, Abdul 1939- *WhoWor 91*
Aziz, Ali Darius *BiDrAPA 89*
Aziz, Muhammed Shahid 1947- *BiDrAPA 89*
Aziz, Nabil Adly *BiDrAPA 89*
Aziz, Nadim Mahmoud 1954- *WhoSSW 91*
Aziz, Omar Ibn 1960- *WhoSSW 91*
Aziz, Sardar Akhtar *BiDrAPA 89*
Aziz, Tariq *NewYTBS 90 [port]*
Aziz, Tariq Mikhayl 1936- *WhoWor 91*
Aziz, Ungku Abdul 1922- *WhoWor 91*
Azizbekov, Meshadi Azim-bek-ogly 1876-1918 *BioIn 16*
Azkoul, Karim 1915- *WhoWor 91*
Azlan Muhibbuddin Shah Yussuff Izzuddin 1928- *WhoWor 91*
Azlin, Denise Roxane 1962- *WhoAmW 91*
Aznavour, Charles 1924- *OxCPMus, WhoWor 91, WorAlBi*
Azneer, J. Leonard 1921- *WhoAm 90*
Aznoian, Nicholas David 1929- *St&PR 91*
Azocar, Patricio 1918- *CurBio 90 [port]*
Azoff, Edward Arthur 1945- *WhoSSW 91*
Azon, Glenn 1956- *WhoHisp 91*
Azorin *HispWr 90*
Azpeitia, Alfonso G. 1922- *WhoE 91*
Azpeitia, Lynne Marie 1951- *WhoAmW 91*
Azrael, Judith Anne 1938- *WhoWrEP 89*
Azrin, Nathan Harold 1930- *WhoAm 90*
Azua, Ernest R. 1941- *WhoHisp 91*
Azuela, Arturo 1938- *ConAu 131, HispWr 90*
Azuela, Mariano 1873-1952 *BioIn 16, ConAu 131, HispWr 90, MajTwCW*
Azuma *NewAgMG*
Azuma, Atsuko 1936- *WhoWor 91*
Azuma, Atsuko 1939- *IntWWM 90*
Azuma, Nagato 1956- *EncPaPR 91*
Azuma, Norio 1928- *WhoAm 90, WhoAmA 91*
Azuma, Takamitsu 1933- *WhoWor 91*
Azure, Leo Lawrence 1939- *St&PR 91*
Azymuth *NewAgMG*
Azzalina, Charles Samuel 1932- *St&PR 91*
Azzam, Rasheed M.A. 1945- *WhoSSW 91*
Azzam, Roshdi A 1934- *BiDrAPA 89*
Azzara, Michael William 1947- *WhoAm 90*
Azzato, Louis E. 1930- *St&PR 91*
Azzato, Louis Enrico 1930- *WhoAm 90, WhoE 91*
Azzi, Jennifer *BioIn 16*
Azziz, Ricardo 1958- *WhoHisp 91*
Azzolina, Joseph *BioIn 16*

B

B., Agnes *BioIn 16*
B, M *BiDEWW*
B, Rosemarie *WhoAmA 91*
B-52's *ConMus 4 [port]*
B-52's, The *EncPR&S 89*
B.V.R.B. *PenDiDA 89*
Ba Jin *BioIn 16*
Ba Jin 1904- *WhoWor 91*
Ba, Mariama 1929-1981 *FemiCLE*
BAAAs, Madame de *EncCoWW*
Baab, David Francis 1962- *WhoEmL 91, WhoSSW 91*
Baack, John Edward 1936- *St&PR 91, WhoAm 90*
Baader, Andreas 1943-1977 *BioIn 16*
Baak, William W 1932- *BiDrAPA 89*
Baake, Charles C. 1921- *St&PR 91*
Baaklini, Diane King 1958- *BiDrAPA 89*
Baal Shem Tov 1700?-1760 *EncO&P 3*
Ba'al-Shem-Tov 1700?-1760 *WorAlBi*
Baang, Young-Min 1948- *WhoWor 91*
Baar, J Mark *BiDrAPA 89*
Baar, James A. 1929- *ODwPR 91, WhoAm 90, WhoE 91*
Baarda, Tjitze 1932- *WhoWor 91*
Baars, Aalbert Jan 1943- *WhoWor 91*
Baars, Bruce Terry 1952- *WhoEmL 91*
Baartman, John L., III 1930- *St&PR 91*
Baas, Era Dawn 1956- *WhoAmW 91*
Baas, Jacquelynn 1948- *WhoAm 90, WhoAmA 91, WhoAmW 91*
Baatz, Stan M. 1952- *St&PR 91*
Bab 1819-1850 *EncO&P 3*
Baba Ram Dass *NewAgE 90*
Baba, Ahmed Ould *WhoWor 91*
Baba, Isamu 1923- *WhoWor 91*
Baba, Jason Nobuo 1957- *WhoEmL 91*
Baba, Marietta Lynn 1949- *WhoAmW 91, WhoEmL 91*
Babai, Massood Reza 1939- *BiDrAPA 89*
Babak, Renata 1939- *IntWWM 90*
Babangida, Ibrahim *WhoWor 91*
Babangida, Ibrahim 1941- *CurBio 90 [port]*
Babaoglu, Rehim 1946- *WhoEmL 91, WhoSSW 91*
Babaoka, Marian L. 1960- *St&PR 91*
Babar, Raza Ali 1947- *WhoEmL 91*
Babashoff, Diane L. 1944- *St&PR 91*
Babatunde, Obba *DrBIPA 90*
Babauta, Juan Nekai 1953- *WhoEmL 91, WhoWor 91*
Babb, Albert Leslie 1925- *WhoAm 90*
Babb, Barbara Caroline 1933- *WhoAmW 91*
Babb, Charles Keith 1952- *WhoEmL 91*
Babb, Charlie 1873-1954 *Ballpl 90*
Babb, Emerson M. *BioIn 16*
Babb, Frank Edward 1932- *WhoAm 90*
Babb, Harold 1926- *WhoAm 90*
Babb, James G., Jr. *BioIn 16*
Babb, Judith Ann 1949- *WhoSSW 91*
Babb, Julius Wistar, III 1946- *WhoAm 90*
Babb, Kristen *BioIn 16*
Babb, Lawrence A. *WhoAm 90*
Babb, Marion Standahl 1918- *WhoAmW 91*
Babb, Marva Tew 1951- *WhoAmW 91, WhoSSW 91*
Babb, Melissa Marek 1960- *WhoE 91*
Babb, Ralph W. 1949- *St&PR 91*
Babb, Ralph Wheeler, Jr. 1949- *WhoAm 90*
Babb, Sanora 1907- *WhoWrEP 89*
Babb, Stuart Virginia *BiDrAPA 89*
Babb, Wylie Sherrill 1940- *WhoAm 90*
Babbage, Charles 1792-1871 *BioIn 16, WorAlBi*
Babbage, Joan Dorothy 1926- *WhoAmW 91, WhoE 91*
Babbel, David Frederick 1949- *WhoE 91*
Babbie, Earl 1938- *WhoWrEP 89*
Babbis, Eleanor *AuBYP 90*
Babbitt, Bruce E. *BioIn 16*
Babbitt, Bruce Edward 1938- *WhoAm 90*
Babbitt, Donald Patrick 1922- *WhoWor 91*
Babbitt, Hattie *BioIn 16*
Babbitt, Irving 1865-1933 *BioIn 16, WorAlBi*
Babbitt, James E. 1948- *St&PR 91*
Babbitt, Kathy Jean 1950- *WhoEmL 91*
Babbitt, Milton 1916- *BioIn 16, IntWWM 90*
Babbitt, Milton Byron 1916- *WhoAm 90*
Babbitt, Natalie *BioIn 16*
Babbitt, Natalie 1932- *AuBYP 90*
Babbitt, Samuel Fisher 1929- *WhoAm 90*
Babbs, Donald Max 1939- *WhoSSW 91*
Babby, Ellen Reisman 1950- *WhoAm 90*
Babchuk, Nicholas 1922- *WhoAm 90*
Babcock, Barbara Allen 1938- *WhoAm 90*
Babcock, Brenda C. *ODwPR 91*
Babcock, Brenda Lynn 1960- *WhoE 91*
Babcock, Charles Luther 1924- *WhoAm 90*
Babcock, Elaine Louise 1925- *WhoE 91*
Babcock, Elisha *BioIn 16*
Babcock, Ernest Brown 1877-1954 *DcScB S2*
Babcock, Fred C. 1913- *St&PR 91*
Babcock, George F. 1948- *WhoEmL 91*
Babcock, Henry H 1913- *BiDrAPA 89*
Babcock, Horace Welcome 1912- *WhoAm 90*
Babcock, J. Paul 1941- *St&PR 91*
Babcock, Jack Emerson 1915- *WhoAm 90*
Babcock, Jacqueline Eileen 1948- *WhoAmW 91*
Babcock, James F. 1933- *St&PR 91*
Babcock, Janice Beatrice 1942- *WhoAmW 91, WhoWor 91*
Babcock, Judith Ann 1956- *WhoEmL 91*
Babcock, Leverett Wright 1840-1906 *AmLegL*
Babcock, Lewis Thornton 1943- *WhoAm 90*
Babcock, Lyndon Ross, Jr. 1934- *WhoAm 90*
Babcock, Madolyn Evelyn 1924- *WhoAmW 91*
Babcock, Mary Ellen *BiDrAPA 89*
Babcock, Michael Joseph 1941- *WhoAm 90*
Babcock, Nellie Jo 1951- *WhoAmW 91*
Babcock, Peter H. 1949- *WhoAm 90*
Babcock, Richard *BioIn 16*
Babcock, Richard Felt 1917- *WhoAm 90*
Babcock, Richard Felt, Jr. 1947- *WhoE 91*
Babcock, Sherra Walls 1948- *WhoEmL 91*
Babcock, Stephen Lee 1939- *WhoAm 90*
Babcock, Theodore A. 1954- *St&PR 91*
Babcock, Warner King 1951- *WhoEmL 91*
Babcock, Wendell Keith 1925- *WhoWor 91*
Babcock, William E. 1939- *St&PR 91*
Babcook, Douglas Robert 1927- *St&PR 91*
Babel, Dietrich 1930- *WhoWor 91*
Babel', I. 1894-1941 *BioIn 16*
Babel', Isaac 1894-1941 *BioIn 16, NewYTBS 90 [port], WorAlBi*
Baber, Alice 1928-1982 *WhoAmA 91N*
Baber, Bradford John 1959- *WhoEmL 91*
Baber, Charles B, III *BiDrAPA 89*
Baber, Harriet Erica 1950- *WhoEmL 91*
Baber, Riaz A *BiDrAPA 89*
Baber, Robert Henry 1950- *WhoWrEP 89*
Baber, Rodney Derrick 1949- *WhoSSW 91*
Baber, Wilbur H., Jr. 1926- *WhoSSW 91, WhoWor 91*
Babette *BioIn 16*
Babetti, Donna Marie 1953- *WhoAmW 91*
Babeuf, Francois Noel 1760-1797 *BioIn 16*
Babeuf, Gracchus 1760-1797 *BioIn 16*
Babiak, Taras 1951- *BiDrAPA 89*
Babiarz, John Edward 1915- *WhoAm 90*
Babiarz, Joseph F. 1927- *St&PR 91*
Babic, Michael Walter 1951- *WhoEmL 91*
Babich, Adam 1955- *WhoEmL 91*
Babich, Joanne Marie 1951- *WhoAmW 91*
Babich, Johnny 1913- *Ballpl 90*
Babich, Michael Wayne 1945- *WhoSSW 91*
Babich, Nicholas 1930- *St&PR 91*
Babigian, Haroutun *BiDrAPA 89*
Babiiha, Thaddeo Kitasimbwa 1945- *WhoSSW 91*
Babij, Mark John 1956- *WhoEmL 91*
Babij, Tadeusz Michal 1933- *WhoSSW 91*
Babik, Paul B. 1947- *St&PR 91*
Babikian, George Haig 1927- *St&PR 91*
Babikian, Hrair M 1930- *BiDrAPA 89*
Babil, Simon 1945- *St&PR 91*
Babilonia, Tai *BioIn 16*
Babin, Claude Hunter 1924- *WhoAm 90*
Babin, Claude Hunter, Jr. 1952- *WhoEmL 91, WhoSSW 91*
Babin, Joseph Gordon *BiDrAPA 89*
Babin, Mara L. 1950- *St&PR 91*
Babin, Maria Teresa 1910- *HispWr 90*
Babin, Victor 1908-1972 *PenDiMP*
Babin, W. Edward 1935- *St&PR 91*
Babine, Alexis Vasil'evich 1866-1930 *BioIn 16*
Babineau, G Raymond 1937- *BiDrAPA 89*
Babinec, George Frederick 1957- *WhoEmL 91*
Babington, Anthony 1920- *BioIn 16*
Babington Smith, Constance 1912- *ConAu 131*
Babiniec, Dennis Henry 1956- *WhoEmL 91*
Babinski, Joseph Stephen *BiDrAPA 89*
Babinski, Ludwig 1909- *IntWWM 90*
Babish, Richard Constantine 1918- *WhoE 91*
Babish, Timothy James 1951- *WhoWor 91*
Babits, John Joseph 1927- *St&PR 91*
Babiuch, Jacqueline Marie 1964- *WhoAmW 91*
Babler, Wayne E. 1915- *WhoAm 90*
Babler, Wayne Elroy, Jr. 1942- *WhoAm 90*
Babock, Ronald Pringle 1936- *St&PR 91*
Baboian, Robert 1934- *WhoE 91*
Babson, Arthur C. 1909- *St&PR 91*
Babson, Arthur Clifford 1909- *WhoAm 90*
Babson, David Leveau 1911- *WhoAm 90*
Babson, Donald Paul 1924- *St&PR 91*
Babson, Irving K. 1936- *WhoAm 90, WhoWor 91*
Babson, Marian *TwCCr&M 91*
Babson, Nicholas C. 1946- *St&PR 91*
Babson, Stanley M., Jr. 1925- *St&PR 91*
Babson, Susan Averill 1924- *St&PR 91*
Babthorpe, Grace 1573-1635 *BiDEWW*
Babu, Sajja L Prasad 1942- *BiDrAPA 89*
Babula, William 1943- *WhoAm 90, WhoWrEP 89*
Babur, Emperor of Hindustan 1483-1530 *BioIn 16*
Babut, Robert Bruce 1955- *WhoEmL 91*
Baca, Bernal C. 1952- *WhoHisp 91*
Baca, Elfego 1865-1949 *BioIn 16*
Baca, Ezequiel Cabeza de 1864-1917 *BioIn 16*
Baca, Fernando E. Cabeza de 1937- *BioIn 16*
Baca, Fernie 1939- *WhoHisp 91*
Baca, George Mark 1954- *BiDrAPA 89*
Baca, Gloria Yvonne 1957- *WhoHisp 91*
Baca, Guy A. 1936- *WhoHisp 91*
Baca, Jimmy Santiago 1952- *ConAu 131, HispWr 90, WhoHisp 91*
Baca, Jose Santiago *ConAu 131, HispWr 90*
Baca, Joseph F. 1936- *WhoHisp 91*
Baca, Joseph Francis 1936- *WhoAm 90*
Baca, Lee F., Jr. 1944- *WhoHisp 91*
Baca, Linda Todd 1946- *WhoEmL 91*
Baca, Mimi 1938- *ODwPR 91*
Baca, Polly B. 1941- *WhoHisp 91*
Baca, Roman Antonio 1833-1889 *AmLegL*
Baca, Roman Liberato 1864-1935 *AmLegL*
Baca, Rowena Joyce *WhoHisp 91*
Baca, Ruben Albert 1936- *WhoHisp 91*
Baca, Sacramento Henry, Jr. 1938- *WhoHisp 91*
Baca, Samuel Valdez 1949- *WhoHisp 91*
Baca, Ted Paul 1941- *WhoHisp 91*
Baca, Virginia G. 1933- *WhoHisp 91*
Baca-Barragan, Polly 1941- *BioIn 16*
Baca Zinn, Maxine 1942- *BioIn 16, WhoHisp 91*
Bacak, Velma Anne 1954- *BiDrAPA 89*
Bacal, Howard A *BiDrAPA 89*
Bacall, Cortland B. 1919- *St&PR 91*
Bacall, Lauren *BioIn 16*
Bacall, Lauren 1924- *BioAmW, WhoAm 90, WorAlBi*
Bacani, Nicanor-Guglielmo Vila 1947- *WhoEmL 91*
Baccarella, Flavia *WhoAmA 91*
Baccari, John Patrick 1960- *WhoEmL 91*
Baccaloni, Salvatore 1900-1969 *PenDiMP*
Bacchetti, J. Thomas 1942- *WhoSSW 91*
Baccigaluppi, John David 1961- *WhoEmL 91*
Baccigaluppi, Roger J. 1934- *St&PR 91*
Baccigaluppi, Roger John 1934- *WhoAm 90*
Baccin, Giovanni Maria *PenDiDA 89*
Baccini, Laurance Ellis 1945- *WhoWor 91*
Baccio d'Agnolo, Bartolomeo Baglioni 1462-1543 *PenDiDA 89*
Baccouche, Hedi 1930- *WhoWor 91*
Baccus, Lloyd Tevis 1939- *BiDrAPA 89*
Baccus, Shirley Pohl 1929- *WhoAmW 91*
Bacdayan, Carolyn Bakke 1936- *WhoAmW 91*
Bace, Edward J. 1952- *St&PR 91*
Bace, Edward Jan, Jr. 1952- *WhoE 91*
Bach, Aino Gustavovna 1901-1976? *BiDWomA*

Bach, Alice 1942- AuBYP 90
Bach, Arthur James 1929- WhoAm 90
Bach, Carl Philipp Emanuel 1714-1788 BioIn 16, PenDiMP A, WorAlBi
Bach, Charles L. Moyne, Jr. 1952- WhoE 91
Bach, Claudia Stewart 1956- WhoAmW 91
Bach, Daryl Gene 1936- St&PR 91
Bach, David Sebastian 1946- IntWWM 90
Bach, Dianne E. 1952- ODwPR 91
Bach, Dirk 1939- WhoAmA 91
Bach, Dirk Palmer 1939- WhoE 91
Bach, Edward 1886-1936 EncO&P 3, NewAgE 90
Bach, Elizabeth Marie 1952- WhoEmL 91
Bach, Erik 1946- IntWWM 90
Bach, George Leland 1915- WhoAm 90
Bach, Gerhard P. 1943- WhoWor 91
Bach, Gideon 1940- WhoWor 91
Bach, Jan Morris 1937- IntWWM 90, WhoAm 90
Bach, Jerome M 1933- BiDrAPA 89
Bach, Johann Christian 1735-1782 PenDiMP A, WorAlBi
Bach, Johann Sebastian 1685-1750 BioIn 16, PenDiMP A, WorAlBi
Bach, Kenneth Wayne 1933- St&PR 91
Bach, Laurence 1947- WhoAmA 91
Bach, Marcus 1906- WhoAm 90, WhoWrEP 89
Bach, Muriel Dunkleman 1918- WhoAmW 91
Bach, Orville Euing, Jr. 1946- WhoSSW 91
Bach, Otto Karl 1909- WhoAmA 91
Bach, Penelope Caroline 1946- WhoEmL 91
Bach, Perry Bernard 1939- BiDrAPA 89
Bach, Peter E. 1935- St&PR 91
Bach, Richard 1935- EncPaPR 91
Bach, Richard 1936- EncO&P 3, MajTwCW, NewAgE 90
Bach, Richard D. 1934- WhoAm 90
Bach, Richard F 1887-1968 WhoAmA 91N
Bach, Robert 1917-1989 BioIn 16
Bach, Robert Bourree 1923- WhoE 91
Bach, Steve Crawford 1921- WhoAm 90, WhoWor 91
Bach, William G 1936- BiDrAPA 89
Bach-Limand, Aino Gustavovna 1901-1976? BiDWomA
Bach-Stewart, Gwendolyn Faye 1945- WhoEmL 91
Bach-y-Rita, George 1936- BiDrAPA 89
Bach-y-Rita, Paul 1934- WhoAm 90
Bach-Zelewski, Erich 1899-1972 BioIn 16
Bachand, Andre 1917- St&PR 91
Bacharach, Burt 1928- EncPR&S 89, OxCPMus
Bacharach, Burt 1929- WhoAm 90, WorAlBi
Bacharach, Melvin Lewis 1924- WhoAm 90
Bacharach, Richard BiDrAPA 89
Bachardy, Don 1934- WhoAmA 91
Bachauer, Gina 1913-1976 BioIn 16, PenDiMP
Bache, Benjamin Franklin 1769-1798 BioIn 16
Bache, Ellyn 1942- ConAu 129, WhoWrEP 89
Bache, Harold L. 1894-1968 WorAlBi
Bache, Theodore Stephen 1936- St&PR 91, WhoE 91
Bachelder, Joseph D. BioIn 16
Bachelder, Joseph Elmer, III 1932- WhoAm 90
Bachelier, Jean-Jacques 1724-1805 PenDiDA 89
Bachelor, Herbert James 1944- WhoAm 90
Bachem-Alent, Rose Marie WhoAm 90, WhoWrEP 89
Bachenheimer, Klaus G. 1926- WhoAm 90
Bachenheimer, Steven I. 1942- St&PR 91
Bacher, Ingrid 1930- EncCoWW
Bacher, Judith St. George 1946- WhoAm 90, WhoE 91
Bacher, Norman M 1926- BiDrAPA 89
Bacher, Rosalie Wride 1925- WhoAmW 91, WhoWor 91
Bachert, Hildegard Gina 1921- WhoAmA 91, WhoE 91
Bachhuber, Carl Nelson 1943- St&PR 91
Bachhuber, Theodore Joseph 1913- St&PR 91
Bachicha, Joseph Alfred WhoWor 91
Bachik, Mark 1955- WhoEmL 91
Bachinski, Walter Joseph 1939- WhoAmA 91
Bachleda, Kathleen Margaret 1948- WhoAmW 91
Bachman, Bonnie Jean 1950- WhoEmL 91
Bachman, Brian Richard 1945- WhoEmL 91
Bachman, Carol Christine 1959- WhoAmW 91
Bachman, Charles William 1924- St&PR 91
Bachman, David Christian 1934- WhoAm 90
Bachman, Gary Eugene 1951- WhoEmL 91
Bachman, George 1933- WhoAm 90
Bachman, Gilbert 1926- St&PR 91
Bachman, Henry L. 1930- St&PR 91
Bachman, James Edward 1947- St&PR 91, WhoAm 90
Bachman, Jean Collom 1935- WhoAmW 91
Bachman, John Andrew, Jr. 1926- WhoSSW 91
Bachman, Karen ODwPR 91
Bachman, Lawrence William 1923- St&PR 91
Bachman, Lee William 1947- St&PR 91
Bachman, Leonard 1925- WhoAm 90
Bachman, Nathan Dulaney, IV 1935- WhoAm 90
Bachman, Ralph Walter 1944- WhoAm 90
Bachman, Richard ConAu 30NR, ConTFT 8, MajTwCW, WorAu 1980
Bachman, Richard 1947- BioIn 16
Bachman, Stanley Frederick 1924- St&PR 91
Bachman, Vernon Emil 1937- St&PR 91
Bachman, Walter Crawford 1911- WhoAm 90
Bachman-Turner Overdrive EncPR&S 89, OxCPMus
Bachmann, Albert Edward 1917- WhoSSW 91
Bachmann, Ann Marie 1961- WhoE 91
Bachmann, Bill 1946- WhoEmL 91, WhoSSW 91, WhoWor 91
Bachmann, Donald M. BioIn 16, NewYTBS 90
Bachmann, Ingeborg 1926-1973 EncCoWW, WorAlBi
Bachmann, John W. 1938- St&PR 91
Bachmann, John William 1938- WhoAm 90
Bachmann, Konrad 1939- WhoWor 91
Bachmann, Luise 1903- EncCoWW
Bachmann, Manfred 1928- WhoWor 91
Bachmann, Mark Edward 1948- St&PR 91
Bachmann, Rhonda 1952- IntWWM 90
Bachmann, Richard A. 1944- St&PR 91
Bachmann, Richard Arthur 1944- WhoAm 90
Bachmann, William Vincent 1913- WhoWor 91
Bachmann-Geiser, Brigitte 1941- IntWWM 90
Bachmeyer, Robert Wesley 1915- WhoAm 90
Bachner, Donald J. 1930- St&PR 91
Bachner, John Philip 1944- WhoE 91
Bachner, Margaret G. BioIn 16
Bachop, William G. 1928- St&PR 91
Bachrach, Bradford K. 1910- WhoAm 90
Bachrach, Charles Lewis 1946- WhoAm 90
Bachrach, David Arthur 1952- WhoEmL 91
Bachrach, Eve Elizabeth 1951- WhoAmW 91, WhoEmL 91
Bachrach, Harry BioIn 16
Bachrach, Howard L. 1920- WhoAm 90
Bachrach, Ira Nathaniel 1938- WhoAm 90
Bachrach, L. Fabian, Jr. 1917- St&PR 91
Bachrach, Leona L 1931- BiDrAPA 89
Bachrach, Louis F., III 1950- St&PR 91
Bachrach, Louis Fabian, III 1950- WhoEmL 91
Bachrach, Louis Fabian, Jr. 1917- WhoAm 90
Bachrach, Nancy 1948- WhoAm 90, WhoAmW 91
Bachrach, Robert D. 1954- St&PR 91
Bachrach, Robert Lee 1926- St&PR 91
Bachstein, Harry Samuel 1943- WhoWor 91
Bachstein, James Michael BiDrAPA 89
Bachtell, Clifton M. 1937- St&PR 91
Bachtold, Thomas Eugene 1935- WhoWor 91
Bachur, Nicholas Robert, Sr. 1933- WhoAm 90
Bachus, Benson Floyd 1917- WhoWor 91
Bachus, Ernest Wayne 1946- WhoEmL 91
Bachus, Larry Glenn 1948- WhoSSW 91
Bachus, Walter Otis 1926- WhoAm 90
Bachynski, Morrel Paul 1930- WhoAm 90
Baciewicz, Gloria Jean BiDrAPA 89
Baciewicz, Gloria Jean 1952- WhoAmW 91
Bacigalupa, Andrea 1923- WhoAmA 91
Bacigalupo, Charles Anthony 1934- St&PR 91
Bacigalupo, Massimo Andrea 1947- WhoWor 91
Bacigalupo, Thomas 1944- WhoE 91
Bacik, Carl Stephen 1925- St&PR 91
Bacin, William Fredric 1923- IntWWM 90
Bacino, Joseph Nicholas 1930- St&PR 91
Back, Edward William, Jr. St&PR 91
Back, George 1939- St&PR 91
Back, Howard 1927- ODwPR 91
Back, John Joseph BiDrAPA 89
Back, Sven-Erik 1919- IntWWM 90
Backas, James Jacob 1926- WhoAm 90
Backberg, Bruce Allen 1948- St&PR 91
Backe, John David 1932- St&PR 91, WhoAm 90
Backe, John Elliott 1960- WhoE 91, WhoEmL 91
Backe, Pamela Renee 1955- WhoEmL 91
Backeland, Gerald H. 1945- St&PR 91
Backenroth, Gunnel Anne Maj 1951- WhoWor 91
Backenstoss, Henry Brightbill 1912- WhoE 91
Backer, David F. 1940- St&PR 91
Backer, Gert Otto 1933- St&PR 91
Backer, Harriet 1845-1932 BiDWomA
Backer, Laszlo 1931- WhoWor 91
Backer, Marjorie K. St&PR 91
Backer, Matthias Henry, Jr. 1926- WhoAm 90
Backer, Morris 1927- St&PR 91
Backer, Terry BioIn 16
Backer, Todd Gilbert 1960- WhoEmL 91
Backer, W. Dale 1946- St&PR 91
Backer, William Earnest 1922- St&PR 91
Backer, William Montague 1926- St&PR 91, WhoAm 90, WhoE 91
Backers-Hoyle, Angela Cherie 1958- WhoAmW 91
Backes, Clarus D. BioIn 16
Backes, Paul Gilbert 1952- WhoAm 90
Backes, Susan Elizabeth 1947- BiDrAPA 89
Backes, Wilfied 1943- St&PR 91
Backhaus, Juergen Georg 1950- WhoWor 91
Backhaus, Patricia Dawn 1959- IntWWM 90
Backhaus, Wilhelm 1884-1969 PenDiMP
Backhouse, Ian William 1953- WhoWor 91
Backhouse, Margaret 1818-1885? BiDWomA
Backhus, James Robert 1957- St&PR 91
Backinoff, Irving 1925- St&PR 91
Backis, Robert Joseph 1949- WhoWor 91
Backlund, Larry Robert 1945- WhoEmL 91
Backlund, Ralph Theodore 1918- WhoAm 90, WhoWrEP 89
Backlund, Winifred 1946- WhoE 91
Backman, Alan Gregory 1950- WhoE 91
Backman, Gerald Stephen 1938- WhoAm 90
Backman, Grace Straim BioIn 16
Backman, Jean Adele 1931- WhoAmW 91
Backman, John Herbert BiDrAPA 89
Backman, Wally 1959- Ballpl 90
Backman, William D., Jr. 1931- St&PR 91
Backman, William Lewis 1947- WhoSSW 91
Backon, Joshua 1950- WhoWor 91
Backon, Mitchell 1928- St&PR 91
Backos, Catherine Athas 1943- WhoE 91
Backrass, Erwin 1922- BiDrAPA 89
Backscheider, Frank Andrew 1930- St&PR 91
Backster, Cleve EncO&P 3
Backster, Cleve 1924- EncPaPR 91
Backstrom-Bouayad, Camilla Pauline 1960- WhoAmW 91
Backup, Clifford E BiDrAPA 89
Backus, Ann Swift Newell 1941- WhoAmW 91
Backus, Charles Edward 1937- WhoAm 90
Backus, Dana Converse 1907-1989 BioIn 16
Backus, Frank Ira 1936- BiDrAPA 89
Backus, G. Richard 1935- St&PR 91
Backus, George Edward 1930- WhoAm 90
Backus, Isaac 1724-1806 BioIn 16, EncCRAm
Backus, James Edward 1928- WhoSSW 91
Backus, James Gilmore 1913-1989 ConAu 129, SmATA 63
Backus, Jim BioIn 16, ConAu 129
Backus, Jim 1913-1989 AnObit 1989, News 90, SmATA X, WorAlBi
Backus, Joe Tom BiDrAPA 89
Backus, John 1924- WhoAm 90
Backus, John King 1925- WhoAm 90
Backus, Myron Port 1908-1988 BioIn 16
Backus, Richard Grant, II 1949- WhoSSW 91
Backus, Standish, Jr 1910-1989 WhoAmA 91N
Backus, Varda Peller 1931- BiDrAPA 89
Bacmeister, Erwin 1935- BiDrAPA 89
Bacon, Alice Mabel 1858-1918 FemiCLE
Bacon, Ann 1528-1610 BiDEWW, FemiCLE
Bacon, Anne Cooke 1528?-1610 BioIn 16
Bacon, Augustus Octavius 1839-1914 AmLegL
Bacon, Barbara McNutt 1946- WhoWor 91
Bacon, Brett Kermit 1947- WhoAm 90
Bacon, C. Everett 1890-1989 BioIn 16
Bacon, Carolyn Louise 1945- WhoEmL 91
Bacon, Darwin Dee 1947- WhoE 91
Bacon, David Walter 1935- WhoAm 90
Bacon, Delia Salter 1811-1859 BioAmW, FemiCLE
Bacon, Denis F. 1929- St&PR 91
Bacon, Denise IntWWM 90
Bacon, Dennis Ray 1957- WhoEmL 91
Bacon, Donald Conrad 1935- WhoAm 90, WhoWrEP 89
Bacon, Donna L. 1951- St&PR 91
Bacon, Edgar 1903-1989 BioIn 16
Bacon, Edmund Castell 1903-1982 DcNaB 1981
Bacon, Edmund Norwood 1910- WhoAm 90
Bacon, Edward Michael, Jr. 1930- St&PR 91
Bacon, Ernst NewYTBS 90
Bacon, Ernst 1898- IntWWM 90
Bacon, Ernst 1898-1990 BioIn 16, ConAu 131
Bacon, Francis 1561-1626 WorAlBi, WrPh P
Bacon, Francis 1909- BioIn 16, IntDcAA 90, WhoWor 91, WorAlBi
Bacon, Francis Warner 1920- St&PR 91
Bacon, Frank 1864-1922 BioIn 16
Bacon, George A., Jr. 1929- St&PR 91
Bacon, George Edgar 1932- WhoAm 90
Bacon, George Hughes 1935- WhoE 91
Bacon, Georgeanna Muirson Woolsey 1833-1906 BioIn 16
Bacon, Glenn A 1921- BiDrAPA 89
Bacon, Helen Hazard 1919- WhoAm 90
Bacon, Howard Arthur 1929- St&PR 91
Bacon, Hugh Macrae BiDrAPA 89
Bacon, James Edmund 1931- St&PR 91, WhoAm 90, WhoE 91
Bacon, James Thomas 1957- WhoEmL 91
Bacon, Janice Lynne 1954- WhoEmL 91
Bacon, Joan Chase 1925- BioIn 16
Bacon, John 1740-1799 BioIn 16
Bacon, John A., Jr. 1927- St&PR 91
Bacon, John Joseph 1928- WhoAm 90
Bacon, John O. 1950- St&PR 91
Bacon, John Stille 1935- St&PR 91
Bacon, Josephine Dodge Daskam 1876-1961 BioIn 16
Bacon, Kathleen 1954- WhoAmW 91
Bacon, Kevin 1958- WhoAm 90
Bacon, Larry Stephen 1946- St&PR 91
Bacon, Leonard Anthony 1931- WhoWor 91
Bacon, Louis Albert 1921- WhoAm 90
Bacon, Lucinda S. 1943- ODwPR 91
Bacon, Martha Brantley 1938- WhoAmW 91
Bacon, Martha Sherman 1917-1981 AuBYP 90
Bacon, Nancy Marie 1946- St&PR 91
Bacon, Nathaniel 1647-1676 WhNaAH, WorAlBi
Bacon, Neil F. 1956- St&PR 91
Bacon, Patrick Desmond BiDrAPA 89
Bacon, Paul 1913- AuBYP 90
Bacon, Paula WhoAmW 91
Bacon, Peggy 1895- BiDWomA
Bacon, Peggy 1895-1987 BioIn 16, WhoAmA 91N
Bacon, Phillip 1922- WhoAm 90, WhoWor 91, WhoWrEP 89
Bacon, Ralph 1934- IntWWM 90
Bacon, Robert 1860-1919 BiDrUSE 89, BioIn 16
Bacon, Robert C. 1940- St&PR 91
Bacon, Robert John, Jr. BiDrAPA 89
Bacon, Roger 1214-1294? EncO&P 3, WorAlBi
Bacon, Sylvia 1931- WhoE 91
Bacon, Tony ODwPR 91
Bacon, Vicky Lee 1950- WhoEmL 91
Bacon, Virginia Murray BioIn 16
Bacon, Wallace Alger 1914- WhoAm 90, WhoWrEP 89
Bacon, William Francis 1956- WhoEmL 91, WhoWor 91
Bacon, William T., Jr. 1923- St&PR 91
Bacon-Taggart, Jill Ann 1964- WhoE 91
Bacot, Henry Parrott 1941- WhoAmA 91
Bacot, J. Carter BioIn 16
Bacot, John Carter 1933- St&PR 91, WhoAm 90, WhoE 91
Bacot, Marie 1942- WhoSSW 91
Bacque, Angela 1957- WhoAmW 91
Bacque, Harvey G. 1943- WhoWor 91
Bacque, Odon Lessley, Jr. 1944- WhoSSW 91
Bacquier, Gabriel IntWWM 90
Bacquier, Gabriel 1924- PenDiMP, WhoWor 91
Bacsik, Mike 1952- Ballpl 90
Bacstrom, Sigismond 1750?-1805 EncO&P 3
Baczek, Peter Gerard 1945- WhoAmA 91
Baczewski, Fred 1926-1976 Ballpl 90
Bada Shanren 1624?-1705? BioIn 16
Bada, Anthony Dominic 1929- St&PR 91
Badal, Daniel Walter 1912- BiDrAPA 89, WhoAm 90
Badalamenti, Anthony 1940- WhoWor 91

Badalamenti, Anthony Francis 1943- WhoE 91
Badalamenti, Fred 1935- WhoAmA 91
Badalamenti, Margret 1959- WhoAmW 91
Badami, Andrea 1913- MusmAFA
Badanes, Jerome 1937- ConLC 59 [port]
Badanes, Menke WhoWrEP 89
Badar, Jehangir WhoWor 91
Badaracco, Cheryl Kay 1962- WhoAmW 91, WhoSSW 91
Badaracco, Mary Anne 1948- BiDrAPA 89
Badash, Lawrence 1934- WhoAm 90
Badawi, Mohsen Maher 1956- WhoWor 91
Badawi, Raouf Fabmy BiDrAPA 89
Badayos, Alicia P BiDrAPA 89
Badcock, Wogan S., Jr. 1932- St&PR 91
Badcock, Wogan Stanhope, Jr. 1932- WhoSSW 91
Baddeley, D. Jeffery 1938- St&PR 91
Baddeley, Hermione 1906-1986 OxCPMus
Baddigam, Konda Reddi BiDrAPA 89
Baddiley, James 1918- WhoWor 91
Baddish, Andy ODwPR 91
Baddish, Laura ODwPR 91
Baddour, Anne Bridge 1930- WhoAmW 91, WhoWor 91
Baddour, Paul M. 1944- WhoSSW 91
Baddour, Raymond Frederick 1925- WhoAm 90
Bade, Harry A. BioIn 16
Bade, Robert Alan 1946- St&PR 91
Bade, Tom 1946- WhoEmL 91
Bade, William Frederic 1871-1936 BioIn 16
Badeer, Henry Sarkis 1915- WhoAm 90
Badel, Julie 1946- WhoAm 90, WhoEmL 91
Bademian, Leon 1932- St&PR 91
Baden, Conrad 1908- IntWWM 90
Baden, Michael M. 1934- WhoAm 90, WhoE 91, WhoWor 91
Baden, Robert Charles 1942- WhoAm 90
Baden, Sophie Louise Charlotte 1740-1824 EncCoWW
Baden, Thomas Arthur 1929- WhoAm 90
Baden-Powell, Robert Stephenson Smyth 1857-1941 WorAlBi
Baden-Powell of Gilwell, Baron 1857-1941 BioIn 16
Bader, Albert Xavier, Jr. 1932- WhoAm 90, WhoE 91
Bader, Alfred R. 1924- St&PR 91
Bader, Alfred Robert 1924- WhoAm 90
Bader, Andrea Elizabeth 1955- WhoEmL 91
Bader, Barbara AuBYP 90
Bader, Cal Joseph, Jr. 1950- WhoE 91
Bader, Douglas 1910-1982 BioIn 16
Bader, Douglas Robert Steuart 1910-1982 DcNaB 1981
Bader, Franz 1903- WhoAmA 91, WhoE 91
Bader, Fredric George 1947- St&PR 91
Bader, Gregory Dennis 1950- St&PR 91
Bader, Harry Frederick 1924- WhoE 91
Bader, Izaak Walton 1922- WhoWor 91
Bader, John Merwin 1919- WhoAm 90
Bader, Joseph Francis 1939- St&PR 91
Bader, Martin St&PR 91
Bader, Michael Haley 1929- WhoAm 90
Bader, Richard E. 1932-1989 BioIn 16
Bader, Richard Eugene WhoAm 90
Bader, Robert Smith 1925- WhoAm 90
Bader, Talat Abdelaziz 1948- WhoWor 91
Bader, Walter M. 1911- St&PR 91
Bader, William Banks 1931- WhoAm 90
Badertscher, David Glen 1935- WhoAm 90
Badertscher, Donald 1934- St&PR 91
Badertscher, Nancy Lee 1955- WhoAmW 91
Badesch, Roger ODwPR 91
Badessa, Robert C. 1948- St&PR 91
Badet, Bernard Francois 1949- WhoWor 91
Badet, Jean Francois 1952- WhoWor 91
Badetti, Rolando Emilio 1947- WhoWor 91
Badgeley, C. Dale NewYTBS 90
Badger, Alison Mary 1935- WhoAmW 91
Badger, Charles H. 1917- St&PR 91, WhoAm 90
Badger, David Harry 1931- WhoWor 91
Badger, David Russell 1947- WhoEmL 91
Badger, Eugene Carroll 1928- WhoSSW 91
Badger, Gail Frances 1952- WhoE 91
Badger, George Edmund 1795-1866 BiDrUSE 89
Badger, James Winifred 1941- WhoSSW 91
Badger, John A. BioIn 16
Badger, Lois G. 1944- WhoAmW 91
Badger, Mildred Rita 1939- St&PR 91
Badger, Richard McLean 1896-1974 DcScB S2
Badger, Thomas Mark 1945- WhoSSW 91
Badger, Timothy C. 1949- St&PR 91
Badgerow, John Nicholas 1951- WhoEmL 91
Badgett, Lee Douglas 1939- WhoAm 90
Badgley, John Roy 1922- WhoWor 91
Badgley, Marie Minor Curry 1926- WhoAmW 91
Badgley, Theodore McBride 1925- BiDrAPA 89, WhoAm 90
Badgley, William S. 1930- St&PR 91
Badgro, Red 1902- Ballpl 90
Badham, John 1939- ConTFT 8 [port]
Badham, John MacDonald 1939- WhoAm 90
Badham, Robert E. 1929- WhoAm 90
Badhiwala, Shamji P 1956- BiDrAPA 89
Badia-Batalla, Francesc 1923- WhoWor 91
Badiali, Carla 1907- BiDWomA
Badian, Ernst 1925- WhoAm 90
Badian, Maya 1939- IntWWM 90
Badias, Maria Elena 1959- WhoHisp 91
Badie, Ronald Peter 1942- St&PR 91, WhoAm 90
Badikian, Arthur V 1944- BiDrAPA 89
Badilla, Gloria Ann 1961- WhoEmL 91
Badillo, Diane 1946- WhoEmL 91
Badillo, Herman 1929- WhoHisp 91
Badillo-Sciortino, Olga Esther 1941- WhoWrEP 89
Badini, Aldo Anthony 1958- WhoEmL 91
Badinski, Nikolai I. 1937- IntWWM 90
Badinter, Robert 1928- BiDFrPL
Badlam, Stephen 1751-1815 PenDiDA 89
Badler, Mitchell M. ODwPR 91
Badler, Richard D. 1951- ODwPR 91
Badman, John, III 1944- St&PR 91, WhoAm 90, WhoE 91
Badner, Mino 1940-1978 WhoAmA 91N
Bado-Santana, Eduardo 1950- WhoHisp 91
Badoglio, Pietro 1871-1956 BioIn 16
Badon, Calvin L. 1935- St&PR 91
Badonnel, Marie-Claude Helene Marquerite 1939- WhoAmW 91
Badoux, Dick Marius 1929- WhoWor 91
Badovinich, Roberta Lynn 1952- WhoAmW 91
Badr, Gamal Moursi 1924- WhoE 91
Badran, Mudaar Mohamad 1934- WhoWor 91
Badran, Rasem 1945- BioIn 16
Badrawy, Galal Akasha BiDrAPA 89
Badruddin, Gitaujali 1961-1977 FemiCLE
Badstuebner, Hans Alexander 1916- WhoWor 91
Badtke, Donald J. 1936- St&PR 91
Badtke, Sandra Ann 1938- WhoAmW 91
Badura-Skoda, Eva 1929- IntWWM 90
Badura-Skoda, Paul 1927- IntWWM 90, PenDiMP, WhoAm 90
Badwi, Abby F. 1946- St&PR 91
Bae, Kun Chae 1934- St&PR 91
Bae, Myoung Hwa St&PR 91
Bae, Sung Ho 1947- WhoEmL 91
Bae, Sung Nam 1944- WhoWor 91
Bae, Young Hoon BiDrAPA 89
Baebler, Drew Charles 1960- WhoEmL 91
Baechel, Charles William, II 1952- WhoE 91
Baechle, James Joseph 1932- St&PR 91, WhoAm 90
Baechle, Susan Jean Parks 1946- WhoEmL 91
Baechler, Donald 1956- WhoAmA 91
Baechler, Jean 1937- ConAu 30NR
Baechtold, Robert Louis 1937- WhoAm 90
Baeck, Leo 1873-1956 BioIn 16
Baeder, Donald L. 1925- St&PR 91
Baeder, Donald Lee 1925- WhoAm 90
Baeder, John 1938- WhoAmA 91
Baehr, Hans Guenther 1933- WhoWor 91
Baehr, Juergen 1940- WhoWor 91
Baehr, Theodore 1946- WhoSSW 91
Baehr, Timothy James 1943- WhoWrEP 89
Baek, Se-Min 1943- WhoWor 91
Baekeland, Frederick BiDrAPA 89
Baekeland, Leo H. 1863-1944 WorAlBi
Baekeland, Leo Hendrik 1863-1944 BioIn 16
Baekey, Anita Susemihl 1927- IntWWM 90
Baena, Robert Bob 1930- WhoE 91
Baena Soares, Joao Clemente 1931- WhoWor 91
Baender, Margaret Woodruff 1921- WhoAmW 91, WhoWor 91, WhoWrEP 89
Baens, Aida S 1946- BiDrAPA 89
Baer, Abel 1893-1976 OxCPMus
Baer, Albert M. 1905- St&PR 91
Baer, Albert Max 1905- WhoAm 90
Baer, Andrew Rudolf 1946- WhoAm 90
Baer, Barbara 1936- WhoAmW 91
Baer, Ben Kayser 1926- WhoAm 90
Baer, Benjamin Franklin 1918- WhoAm 90
Baer, Bernard Allan 1925- WhoSSW 91
Baer, Bugs 1876-1969 Ballpl 90
Baer, Carol F. ODwPR 91
Baer, Daniel H. 1929- ODwPR 91
Baer, David, Jr. 1905- St&PR 91, WhoWor 91
Baer, Donald M. WhoAm 90
Baer, Donald Ray 1947- WhoEmL 91
Baer, Edna BioIn 16
Baer, Emil 1917- St&PR 91
Baer, Eric 1932- WhoAm 90
Baer, Frances Dorothea WhoAmW 91, WhoE 91
Baer, Frederic L 1911- BiDrAPA 89
Baer, Frederick Eugene 1924- St&PR 91
Baer, George F. 1842-1914 WorAlBi
Baer, George Martin 1936- WhoAm 90
Baer, Gregor 1958- WhoE 91
Baer, Henry 1930- WhoAm 90
Baer, Hilde 1917- St&PR 91
Baer, J. Arthur, II 1921- St&PR 91
Baer, James Edward 1952- WhoEmL 91
Baer, Jane Frances 1963- WhoSSW 91
Baer, Jay William 1956- BiDrAPA 89
Baer, Jo 1929- WhoAmA 91
Baer, John Metz 1908- WhoWor 91
Baer, John Richard Frederick 1941- WhoAm 90, WhoWor 91
Baer, Jon Alan 1945- WhoE 91
Baer, Joseph Albert 1929- St&PR 91
Baer, Joseph Winslow 1917- WhoAm 90
Baer, Karl Gunter 1941- BiDrAPA 89
Baer, Karla B. 1935- St&PR 91
Baer, Kenneth A. 1946- St&PR 91
Baer, Kenneth Peter 1930- WhoAm 90
Baer, Leopold S. 1926- St&PR 91
Baer, Luke 1950- WhoEmL 91, WhoWor 91
Baer, Marcie M. 1933- WhoWrEP 89
Baer, Martha Lynn 1939- WhoAm 90
Baer, Michael Alan 1943- WhoAm 90
Baer, Morley BioIn 16
Baer, Morley 1916- WhoAmA 91
Baer, Norbert Sebastian 1938- WhoAm 90, WhoAmA 91
Baer, Ralph August 1933- St&PR 91, WhoAm 90
Baer, Richard BioIn 16
Baer, Richard Kenyth 1952- BiDrAPA 89
Baer, Richard Myron 1928- WhoWor 91
Baer, Robert J. 1937- WhoAm 90
Baer, Robert Jacob 1924- WhoAm 90
Baer, Robert Joseph 1937- St&PR 91
Baer, Roland C., Jr. 1937- St&PR 91
Baer, Rudolf Lewis 1910- WhoAm 90, WhoWor 91
Baer, Stephen H. 1925- ODwPR 91
Baer, Steve H. 1949- St&PR 91
Baer, Thomas James 1927- WhoAm 90
Baer, Thomas S. 1942- St&PR 91
Baer, Walter S., III 1937- WhoAm 90
Baer, Werner 1931- WhoAm 90
Baer, William Harold 1947- WhoEmL 91
Baer-Kaupert, Friedrich-Wilhelm 1930- WhoWor 91
Baerdt, Claes Fransen 1628?-1691? PenDiDA 89
Baerg, Richard Henry 1937- WhoAm 90, WhoWor 91
Baerlecken, Marta 1909- WhoWor 91
Baermann, Donna Lee Roth 1939- WhoAmW 91
Baermann, Robert Paul 1929- St&PR 91
Baernstein, Albert, II 1941- WhoAm 90
Baert, Andre E 1941- BiDrAPA 89
Baervoets, Raymond 1930- IntWWM 90
Baerwald, John Edward 1925- WhoAm 90, WhoWor 91
Baerwald, Richard 1867-1929 EncPaPR 91
Baesel, Stuart Oliver 1925- WhoAm 90
Baetens, Jan 1957- WhoWor 91
Baetzhold, Howard George 1923- WhoAm 90
Baeumer, Max Lorenz WhoAm 90, WhoWrEP 89
Baeurle, Charles Andrew 1942- St&PR 91
Baey, Lian Peck 1931- WhoWor 91
Baeyer, Adolf Johann Von 1835-1917 WorAlBi
Baez, Albert Vinicio 1912- WhoHisp 91
Baez, Buenaventura 1810-1884 BioIn 16
Baez, Carmen Aponte 1957- WhoEmL 91
Baez, Cecilio 1862-1941 BioIn 16
Baez, Joan BioIn 16
Baez, Joan 1941- HispWr 90, OxCPMus, WorAlBi
Baez, Joan Chandos 1941- IntWWM 90, WhoAm 90, WhoAmW 91, WhoHisp 91
Baez, Luis Antonio 1948- WhoHisp 91
Baez, Manuel 1941- WhoSSW 91
Baez, Rafael Marino 1935- BiDrAPA 89
Baeza, Daniel Michael 1952- WhoE 91
Baeza, Mario 1951- BioIn 16
Baezconde-Garbanati, Lourdes A. 1955- WhoHisp 91
Baffes, Thomas Gus 1923- WhoAm 90
Baffeti, Ronald H. ODwPR 91
Baffi, Paolo 1911-1989 BioIn 16
Baffin, William 1584?-1622 EncCRAm, WorAlBi
Bafford, E. Donald 1929- St&PR 91
Bafile, Corrado 1903- WhoWor 91
Bagadia, Vrajlal N 1922- BiDrAPA 89
Bagai, Eric Paul 1940- WhoWrEP 89
Bagarazzi, James Michael 1951- WhoEmL 91
Bagataj, Vinko 1932- WhoWor 91
Bagatelle, Hugh Grant 1948- St&PR 91
Bagaza, Jean-Baptiste 1946- WhoWor 91
Bagby, Albert Morris BioIn 16
Bagby, Arthur Pendleton 1794-1858 BioIn 16
Bagby, Daniel Gordon 1941- WhoSSW 91
Bagby, Frederick Lair, Jr. 1920- WhoAm 90
Bagby, George TwCCr&M 91
Bagby, Jim, Jr. 1916-1988 Ballpl 90
Bagby, Jim, Sr. 1887-1954 Ballpl 90
Bagby, William Rardin 1910- WhoSSW 91, WhoWor 91
Bagdan, Gloria 1929- WhoAmW 91, WhoE 91, WhoWor 91
Bagdazian, Richard William 1955- WhoEmL 91
Bagdikian, Ben Haig 1920- WhoAm 90, WhoWrEP 89
Bagdonas, John Louis 1950- St&PR 91
Bagehot, Walter 1826-1877 BioIn 16, WorAlBi
Bagenal, Alison Mary 1927- IntWWM 90
Bageris, John 1924- WhoAm 90, WhoAmA 91
Bagg, Kirk Joseph 1959- WhoEmL 91
Bagg, Robert Ely 1935- WhoAm 90
Baggaley, Philip Andrew 1952- St&PR 91
Baggally, W. W. EncO&P 3
Baggally, William Wortley EncPaPR 91
Baggarly, Alva Larry 1943- WhoSSW 91
Bagge, Carl Elmer 1927- WhoAm 90
Bagge, Marla Jean 1952- WhoEmL 91
Bagge, Richard Wayne 1945- BiDrAPA 89
Bagger, Hope S. BioIn 16
Bagger, Jerel Vernon 1949- WhoEmL 91
Bagger, Richard Hartvig 1960- WhoEmL 91
Baggesen, Jens 1764-1826 DcScanL
Baggett, Byrd B. 1949- St&PR 91
Baggett, Clint Allen 1950- WhoSSW 91
Baggett, David Amon 1930- WhoSSW 91
Baggett, James Camp, Jr. 1942- BiDrAPA 89
Baggett, Jeanie Shaddix 1952- St&PR 91
Baggett, Robert Joseph, Jr. 1920- St&PR 91
Baggett, W. Mike 1946- WhoEmL 91
Baggett, William Carter, Jr 1946- WhoAmA 91
Baggio, Sebastiano 1913- WhoWor 91
Baggott, Clifford Deveney 1948- St&PR 91
Baggott, George E. 1942- St&PR 91
Baggott, George Theodore 1909- St&PR 91
Baggott, John Wayne 1918- St&PR 91
Baggs, Arthur Eugene PenDiDA 89
Baggs, Fred Taylor 1925- St&PR 91
Baggs, Wilbur James 1919- WhoWor 91
Bagheri, Abbas S BiDrAPA 89
Bagheri, Shahla BiDrAPA 89
Baghio'o, Jean-Louis 1910- WorAu 1980
Bagin, Bruce Albert 1940- WhoE 91
Bagin, Douglas H. 1948- St&PR 91
Bagin, Richard D. 1948- ODwPR 91
Baginski, Gerard Henry 1951- WhoEmL 91, WhoWor 91
Baglan, Charles E., Jr. 1951- WhoEmL 91
Bagley, Ben 1933- OxCPMus
Bagley, Brian G. 1934- WhoE 91, WhoWor 91
Bagley, Carla Lynn 1937- IntWWM 90
Bagley, Charles, III 1922- BiDrAPA 89
Bagley, Charles Michael 1956- WhoEmL 91
Bagley, Colleen 1954- WhoAmW 91, WhoWor 91
Bagley, Constance Elizabeth 1952- WhoAmW 91
Bagley, Desmond 1923-1983 SpyFic, TwCCr&M 91
Bagley, Edwin E. 1857-1922 OxCPMus
Bagley, Gailian Dean, Jr. 1945- St&PR 91
Bagley, H. Prescott, II 1927- St&PR 91
Bagley, James Maher 1954- WhoEmL 91
Bagley, James Paul 1942- St&PR 91
Bagley, James W. St&PR 91
Bagley, Mary Carol 1958- WhoAmW 91, WhoWor 91
Bagley, Mary H. 1949- St&PR 91
Bagley, Michael 1947- ConAu 129
Bagley, Robert Waller 1921- WhoSSW 91
Bagley, Thomas Steven 1952- WhoEmL 91
Bagley, William Chandler 1874-1946 BioIn 16
Bagley, William Thompson 1928- WhoAm 90
Bagli, Vincent Joseph 1925- WhoE 91
Baglio, Vincent Paul 1960- WhoE 91
Bagliore, Virginia 1931- WhoAmW 91
Bagnal, Charles W., Jr. 1957- WhoE 91
Bagnal, Kimberly Baughman 1949- WhoWrEP 89

Bagnall, Oscar 1893- EncO&P 3
Bagnall, Roger Shaler 1947- WhoAm 90
Bagnall, Walter Thomas 1923- St&PR 91
Bagnard, William L. 1923- St&PR 91
Bagnell, L. H. St&PR 91
Bagneris, Renee Michelle Wing 1949- WhoEmL 91
Bagneris, Vernal DrBlPA 90
Bagneschi, Michael T. 1942- St&PR 91
Bagney, Elizabeth 1924- WhoWor 91
Bagnold, Enid BioIn 16
Bagnold, Enid 1889-1981 AuBYP 90, FemiCLE, WorAlBi
Bagnold, Enid Algerine 1889-1981 DcNaB 1981
Bagnold, Ralph NewYTBS 90
Bagnold, Ralph A. 1896-1990 BioIn 16
Bagnold, Ralph Alger 1896-1990 ConAu 131
Bagnoli, Vincent James, Jr. 1952- WhoAm 90
Bagoon, Robert 1923- St&PR 91
Bagot, Walter M. 1935- St&PR 91
Bagot, William A. 1935- St&PR 91
Bagration, Pyotr 1765-1812 WorAlBi
Bagri, Kashi S BiDrAPA 89
Bagri, Sushil BiDrAPA 89
Bagryana, Yelisaveta EncCoWW
Bagshaw, Joseph Charles 1943- WhoAm 90
Bagshaw, Malcolm A. 1925- WhoAm 90
Bagshawe, Kenneth Dawson 1925- WhoWor 91
Bagwell, Billy McArthur 1936- WhoSSW 91
Bagwell, Clarence L. 1942- St&PR 91
Bagwell, Debra Ruth 1961- IntWWM 90
Bagwell, H Roberts 1938- BiDrAPA 89
Bagwell, J. C., III 1946- WhoEmL 91
Bagwell, Joe Wheeler 1926- St&PR 91
Bagwell, Mary Kate 1962- WhoSSW 91
Bagwell, William Francis, Jr. 1923- ConAu 31NR
Bagwill, John W., Jr. 1930- St&PR 91
Bagwill, John Williams, Jr. 1930- WhoE 91
Bahadue, George Paul 1954- WhoSSW 91
Bahadur, Chance 1942- St&PR 91, WhoAm 90
Bahalim, Abdul Latif 1940- WhoWor 91
Bahan, Roland Aloysius, Jr. 1930- WhoSSW 91
Bahar, Ezekiel 1933- WhoAm 90
Bahash, Robert Joseph 1945- St&PR 91
Bahat, Ari BioIn 16
Bahbah, Bishara Assad 1958- WhoE 91
Bahcall, John Norris 1934- WhoAm 90
Bahcall, Neta Assaf 1942- WhoAmW 91
Bahl, John C. 1943- St&PR 91
Bahl, John Charles 1943- WhoSSW 91
Bahl, Om Parkash 1927- WhoAm 90
Bahler, John BioIn 16
Bahler, Tom BioIn 16
Bahlman, Dudley Ward Rhodes 1923- WhoAm 90
Bahlman, William Thorne, Jr. 1920- WhoAm 90
Bahlmann, David William 1939- WhoAm 90
Bahlo, Peter 1959- WhoEmL 91
Bahls, Gene Charles 1929- WhoAm 90, WhoWor 91
Bahls, Jane Easter 1954- WhoWrEP 89
Bahls, Steven Carl 1954- St&PR 91, WhoEmL 91
Bahm, Archie John 1907- WhoAm 90
Bahmer, Robert H. NewYTBS 90
Bahmer, Robert H. 1904-1990 BioIn 16
Bahn, Charles Frederick, Jr. 1954- WhoEmL 91
Bahnassi, Amjad 1959- BiDrAPA 89
Bahnassi, Mohamad Amjad 1959- WhoE 91
Bahner, Carl Tabb 1908- WhoSSW 91
Bahner, Sue WhoAmW 91
Bahner, Thomas Maxfield 1933- WhoAm 90
Bahnik, Roger L. 1944- St&PR 91
Bahnini, M'Hamed 1914- WhoWor 91
Bahniuk, Eugene 1926- WhoAm 90
Bahniuk, Frank Theodore 1937- St&PR 91, WhoAm 90
Bahnsen, Stan 1944- Ballpl 90
Bahnson, Henry Theodore 1920- WhoAm 90
Bahou, Kamil Emil BiDrAPA 89
Bahr, Alice Harrison 1946- WhoE 91
Bahr, Carman Bloedow 1931- WhoSSW 91
Bahr, Ed 1919- Ballpl 90
Bahr, Edward Richard 1941- IntWWM 90
Bahr, Ehrhard 1932- WhoAm 90
Bahr, Howard Miner 1938- WhoAm 90
Bahr, Klaus 1929- St&PR 91
Bahr, Laren S. 1944- WhoWrEP 89
Bahr, Lauren S. 1944- WhoAm 90
Bahr, Mark A. 1952- WhoAm 90
Bahr, Neil E. 1925- St&PR 91
Bahr, Paulo Roberto 1948- BiDrAPA 89
Bahr, Raymond Alfred 1930- St&PR 91
Bahr, Therese PenDiMP
Bahr-Mildenburg, Anna 1872-1947 PenDiMP
Bahrani, Khosrow BiDrAPA 89
Bahrani, Mustafa David 1927- St&PR 91
Bahrawy, Ibrahim BiDrAPA 89
Bahrawy, Lisa de Serbine 1929- WhoAmW 91
Bahre, Everett T. 1936- St&PR 91
Bahrenburg, D. Claeys 1947- St&PR 91, WhoAm 90, WhoE 91
Bahrenburg, Rolf W. 1922- St&PR 91
Bahti, Tom 1926-1972 BioIn 16
Bahuguna, Bulbul BiDrAPA 89
Bahuguna, Sunderlal BioIn 16
Bai WomWR
Bai Jieming ConAu 131
Bai Shuxiang 1939- BioIn 16
Bai, Xiqing 1904- WhoWor 91
Bai-Lan, Dschu EncCoWW
Bai-yi, Xu WhoWor 91
Baia, Joseph 1931- St&PR 91
Baian EncO&P 3
Baianus EncO&P 3
Baiardi, John Charles 1918- WhoAm 90
Baiardi, John Joseph 1942- BiDrAPA 89
Baida, Peter 1950- WhoE 91
Baier, Edward John 1925- WhoAm 90, WhoE 91
Baier, Ellen P. 1948- WhoAmW 91
Baier, Frederick William, Jr. 1945- St&PR 91
Baier, John Leonard 1943- WhoSSW 91
Baier, Sue BioIn 16
Baig, Mirza Sadat Ali BiDrAPA 89
Baig, Saleem 1938- WhoWor 91
Baigent, Julia Marie 1958- WhoEmL 91
Baigi, Marla Jean 1959- WhoAmW 91
Baik, Hyo Whi 1942- WhoAm 90
Bail, Bernard W 1920- BiDrAPA 89
Bail, Joe Paul 1925- WhoAm 90
Bailar, Barbara Ann 1935- WhoAm 90, WhoAmW 91, WhoHisp 91
Bailar, Benjamin Franklin 1934- St&PR 91, WhoAm 90
Bailar, John Christian, III 1932- WhoAm 90
Bailar, John Christian, Jr. 1904- WhoAm 90
Bailas, Maria M BiDrAPA 89
Bailer, Albert John 1939- St&PR 91
Bailer, Bonnie Lynn 1946- WhoE 91
Bailes, Anthony James 1947- IntWWM 90
Bailes, Gordon Lee 1946- WhoSSW 91
Bailes, Kendall E. BioIn 16
Bailes, Randall Powell 1950- WhoEmL 91
Bailes, Robert Lee 1932- St&PR 91
Bailes, Scott 1961- Ballpl 90
Bailey, Abigail Abbot 1746-1815 BioIn 16
Bailey, Alan James 1947- St&PR 91
Bailey, Alice 1880-1949 NewAgE 90
Bailey, Alice A 1880-1949 EncO&P 3
Bailey, Alvin Riley, Jr. 1954- WhoEmL 91
Bailey, Amos Purnell 1918- WhoAm 90, WhoWor 91
Bailey, Ann ODwPR 91
Bailey, Annette Lee 1950- WhoAmW 91, WhoEmL 91
Bailey, Anthony 1933- WorAu 1980 [port]
Bailey, Anthony William 1943- IntWWM 90
Bailey, Barbara Ann 1928- WhoAmA 91
Bailey, Barry D. 1954- St&PR 91
Bailey, Barry Stone 1952- WhoAmA 91
Bailey, Bernadine Freeman 1901- AuBYP 90
Bailey, Bernard Allen 1918- St&PR 91
Bailey, Beverly Ann 1965- WhoAmW 91
Bailey, Bill DrBlPA 90
Bailey, Bill 1889-1926 Ballpl 90
Bailey, Bob 1942- Ballpl 90
Bailey, Brad Duane 1958- WhoEmL 91
Bailey, Brian Mercer 1952- WhoE 91
Bailey, Bruce H 1932- BiDrAPA 89
Bailey, Bruce Stewart 1936- St&PR 91
Bailey, Calvin Dean 1955- WhoEmL 91
Bailey, Carl BioIn 16, NewYTBS 90
Bailey, Carl Edward 1894-1948 BioIn 16
Bailey, Carl Franklin 1930- WhoSSW 91
Bailey, Carmine Michael 1958- WhoSSW 91
Bailey, Carolyn Sherwin 1875-1961 AuBYP 90
Bailey, Cecil Cabaniss 1901- WhoAm 90
Bailey, Cecil Dewitt 1921- WhoAm 90, WhoWor 91
Bailey, Charles EncO&P 3
Bailey, Charles 1870-1947 EncPaPR 91
Bailey, Charles Ed BiDrAPA 89
Bailey, Charles F. 1946- St&PR 91
Bailey, Charles-James Nice 1926- WhoWor 91
Bailey, Charles Lyle 1934- WhoAm 90
Bailey, Charles S. 1924- St&PR 91
Bailey, Charles Stanley 1949- WhoAm 90
Bailey, Charles Waldo, II 1929- WhoAm 90, WhoWrEP 89
Bailey, Clark T 1932-1978 WhoAmA 91N
Bailey, Clayton George 1939- WhoAmA 91
Bailey, Coley L. 1950- St&PR 91, WhoAm 90
Bailey, Dana Kavanagh 1916- WhoAm 90
Bailey, Daniel Allen 1953- WhoEmL 91
Bailey, David 1938- BioIn 16
Bailey, David Clifton 1939- WhoSSW 91
Bailey, David John 1944- St&PR 91
Bailey, David Michael 1951- WhoSSW 91
Bailey, David Nelson 1945- WhoAm 90
Bailey, David Roy Shackleton 1917- WhoAm 90
Bailey, David Thomas 1946- WhoAm 90
Bailey, Deborah Mitchell 1964- WhoAmW 91
Bailey, Debra Sue 1953- WhoAmW 91
Bailey, Deena Tamara 1947- WhoAmW 91
Bailey, Derek 1930- IntWWM 90, WhoWor 91
Bailey, Diana Marion 1951- WhoEmL 91
Bailey, Diane WhoWrEP 89
Bailey, Don M. 1946- St&PR 91
Bailey, Don Matthew 1946- WhoEmL 91
Bailey, Donna Jean 1951- WhoSSW 91
Bailey, Dudley 1918- WhoAm 90
Bailey, E Duff BiDrAPA 89
Bailey, Ed 1931- Ballpl 90
Bailey, Edd H. 1904-1988 BioIn 16
Bailey, Edward G. Beau, II 1960- WhoSSW 91
Bailey, Edward Joseph 1932- WhoAm 90
Bailey, Elizabeth Ellery 1938- WhoAm 90, WhoAmW 91, WhoE 91
Bailey, Eunice Delores 1928- WhoAmW 91
Bailey, Exine Margaret Anderson 1922- WhoAm 90
Bailey, F. Lee 1933- WorAlBi
Bailey, Flora AuBYP 90
Bailey, Florence Merriam 1863-1948 WomFie [port]
Bailey, Frances Anne Lockridge 1927- WhoAmW 91
Bailey, Frank 1907- St&PR 91
Bailey, Frank Henry 1946- WhoEmL 91
Bailey, Fred Arthur 1947- ConAu 129
Bailey, Fred Coolidge 1925- WhoAm 90
Bailey, Frederick Eugene, Jr. 1927- WhoAm 90
Bailey, Gary Bernard 1954- WhoSSW 91
Bailey, Genie Lark BiDrAPA 89
Bailey, George A., Jr. 1925- St&PR 91
Bailey, George C., Jr. 1944- WhoSSW 91
Bailey, George Paul 1961- WhoEmL 91
Bailey, George W. 1941- BiDrAPA 89
Bailey, Glenn E. 1954- St&PR 91
Bailey, Glenn W. 1925- St&PR 91
Bailey, Glenn Waldemar 1925- WhoAm 90, WhoE 91
Bailey, Greg 1954- WhoWrEP 89
Bailey, Gregory Wayne 1952- WhoSSW 91
Bailey, Guy Vernie 1929- WhoSSW 91
Bailey, Gwen 1930- St&PR 91
Bailey, H C 1878-1961 TwCCr&M 91
Bailey, Harold Stevens, Jr. 1922- WhoAm 90
Bailey, Harriet 1875-1953 BioIn 16
Bailey, Harry Augustine, Jr. 1932- WhoAm 90
Bailey, Harry Bell, III 1957- WhoEmL 91
Bailey, Harvey A. 1937- St&PR 91
Bailey, Helen McShane 1916- WhoAm 90
Bailey, Henry John, III 1916- WhoAm 90
Bailey, Herbert Smith, Jr. 1921- WhoAm 90
Bailey, Herman Tracy 1922- WhoAm 90
Bailey, Hilary 1936- FemiCLE
Bailey, Horace C. 1914- St&PR 91
Bailey, Howard 1958- Ballpl 90
Bailey, Howard Hoffman 1929- WhoE 91
Bailey, Hugh Coleman 1929- WhoAm 90, WhoSSW 91
Bailey, Ida BioIn 16
Bailey, Irving Widmer, II 1941- St&PR 91, WhoAm 90, WhoSSW 91
Bailey, J. Hugh 1936- St&PR 91
Bailey, Jackson Holbrook 1925- WhoWrEP 89
Bailey, Jacob 1731-1808 DcLB 99
Bailey, James 1946- WhoAm 90
Bailey, James A. 1933- ODwPR 91
Bailey, James Curtis 1936- WhoSSW 91
Bailey, James Hinton, Jr. 1946- St&PR 91
Bailey, James M 1916- BiDrAPA 89
Bailey, James Martin 1929- WhoAm 90, WhoWrEP 89
Bailey, Janet Adalind 1960- WhoEmL 91
Bailey, Janet Dee 1946- WhoE 91, WhoEmL 91
Bailey, Janet Lee 1953- WhoAmW 91
Bailey, Jann L M 1952- WhoAmA 91
Bailey, Jerald Thomas, Jr. 1961- WhoSSW 91
Bailey, Jerry Lynn 1948- WhoEmL 91
Bailey, Joe Edward 1954- WhoSSW 91
Bailey, Joel Furness 1913- WhoAm 90
Bailey, John AuBYP 90
Bailey, John 1940- BioIn 16
Bailey, John C. 1941- St&PR 91
Bailey, John Frederick 1945- WhoEmL 91
Bailey, John J. ODwPR 91
Bailey, John Martin 1928- WhoAm 90
Bailey, John Maxwell 1927- WhoAm 90
Bailey, John Michael BiDrAPA 89
Bailey, John Milton 1925- WhoAm 90
Bailey, John N. 1935- ODwPR 91
Bailey, John Provine BioIn 16
Bailey, John Stuart 1933- WhoWor 91
Bailey, John T. 1926- ODwPR 91
Bailey, John Temple BiDrAPA 89
Bailey, John Turner 1926- WhoAm 90
Bailey, Johnny BioIn 16
Bailey, Joselyn Elizabeth WhoAmW 91
Bailey, Joy Hafner 1928- WhoAmW 91
Bailey, Joyce Mae BiDrAPA 89
Bailey, Judith Irene 1946- WhoE 91
Bailey, K. Ronald 1947- WhoEmL 91
Bailey, Kathrine E. 1922- WhoWrEP 89
Bailey, Kathy Clark 1956- WhoEmL 91
Bailey, Keith Anthony 1934- WhoWor 91
Bailey, Keith E. 1942- St&PR 91, WhoAm 90, WhoSSW 91
Bailey, Kenneth Kyle 1923- WhoAm 90
Bailey, Kristen 1952- WhoAmW 91, WhoEmL 91
Bailey, L. H. 1858-1954 BioIn 16
Bailey, L. Storm 1931- St&PR 91
Bailey, Larrie 1934- WhoAm 90
Bailey, Larry Dayton 1937- St&PR 91
Bailey, Lawrence Randolph 1918- St&PR 91
Bailey, Lawrence Randolph, Jr. 1949- WhoEmL 91
Bailey, Lee Edwin 1952- St&PR 91
Bailey, Lena WhoAm 90
Bailey, Leonard L. BioIn 16
Bailey, Leonard Lee 1942- WhoAm 90
Bailey, Liberty Hyde 1820-1912 BioIn 16
Bailey, Liberty Hyde 1858-1954 BioIn 16, WorAlBi
Bailey, Lilian PenDiMP
Bailey, Linda Anne 1960- WhoAmW 91
Bailey, Linda Dodson 1952- WhoAm 90
Bailey, Lona M. 1928- WhoAmW 91
Bailey, Lonnie Gene 1939- WhoAm 90
Bailey, Louie Lee 1946- WhoSSW 91
Bailey, Louise Slagle 1930- WhoWrEP 89
Bailey, Lynn Gordon 1936- St&PR 91
Bailey, Major Windsor, II 1961- WhoWor 91
Bailey, Marcia Mead 1947- WhoAmA 91
Bailey, Mark 1961- Ballpl 90
Bailey, Mary 1792-1873 FemiCLE
Bailey, Mary 1931- WhoAmW 91
Bailey, Mary Beatrice 1933- WhoAmW 91
Bailey, Mary Etta 1947- WhoSSW 91
Bailey, Michael Keith 1956- WhoSSW 91
Bailey, Michael Robert 1947- WhoE 91
Bailey, Mildred BioIn 16
Bailey, Mildred 1907-1951 OxCPMus
Bailey, Moreen Deloris 1957- WhoAmW 91
Bailey, Nancy Joyce 1942- WhoE 91
Bailey, Natalie D. ODwPR 91
Bailey, Neill E. 1873-1956 AmLegL
Bailey, Norman IntWWM 90
Bailey, Norman 1933- PenDiMP
Bailey, Norman Stanley 1933- IntWWM 90
Bailey, Norman Thomas John 1923- WhoWor 91
Bailey, Orville Taylor 1909- WhoAm 90
Bailey, Oscar 1925- WhoAmA 91
Bailey, Palmer Kent 1947- WhoEmL 91
Bailey, Patricia Price 1937- WhoAmW 91
Bailey, Paul E. 1947- St&PR 91
Bailey, Paul Fredrick 1954- WhoEmL 91
Bailey, Pearl 1918- DrBlPA 90, WhoAm 90, WorAlBi
Bailey, Pearl 1918-1990 BioIn 16, ConAu 132, ConMus 5 [port], CurBio 90N, NewYTBS 90 [port], News 91-1, OxCPMus
Bailey, Percy William, Jr. BiDrAPA 89
Bailey, Peter Geoffrey 1940- St&PR 91
Bailey, Philip 1951- EncPR&S 89
Bailey, Philip Sigmon 1916- WhoAm 90
Bailey, Philip Sigmon, Jr. 1943- WhoAm 90
Bailey, Phillip Bruce 1955- WhoEmL 91
Bailey, Ray 1913-1975 EncACom
Bailey, Ray H. 1949- St&PR 91
Bailey, Ray Vernon 1913- WhoWor 91
Bailey, Raymond James 1940- St&PR 91
Bailey, Reeve Maclaren 1911- WhoAm 90
Bailey, Reubena Winona 1926- WhoWrEP 89
Bailey, Richard Allin 1949- St&PR 91
Bailey, Richard B. 1926- St&PR 91
Bailey, Richard Briggs 1926- WhoAm 90
Bailey, Richard H 1940- WhoAmA 91
Bailey, Richard Weld 1939- WhoAm 90
Bailey, Richard Williams 1933- WhoWor 91
Bailey, Ricky E. 1959- WhoEmL 91
Bailey, Robert, Jr. 1945- WhoEmL 91

Bailey, Robert Allen 1954- *BiDrAPA 89, WhoSSW 91*
Bailey, Robert D. 1953- *WhoEmL 91, WhoWor 91*
Bailey, Robert David 1939- *St&PR 91*
Bailey, Robert Duke 1944- *WhoSSW 91*
Bailey, Robert Elliott 1932- *WhoAm 90, WhoSSW 91*
Bailey, Robert Fred 1932- *St&PR 91*
Bailey, Robert George 1943- *WhoE 91*
Bailey, Robert Greg 1954- *WhoEmL 91*
Bailey, Robert L. 1937- *St&PR 91*
Bailey, Robert Marland 1930- *St&PR 91*
Bailey, Robert Marshall 1954- *WhoEmL 91*
Bailey, Robert Mike 1947- *WhoSSW 91*
Bailey, Robert Mikell 1955- *WhoEmL 91*
Bailey, Robert Short 1931- *WhoAm 90*
Bailey, Robert Sterling 1930- *St&PR 91*
Bailey, Robert W 1943- *WhoWrEP 89*
Bailey, Robert William 1944- *WhoAm 90*
Bailey, Robert William 1951- *WhoE 91*
Bailey, Robin Lynn *BiDrAPA 89*
Bailey, Roderick F. 1934- *St&PR 91*
Bailey, Rodney N. 1944- *St&PR 91*
Bailey, Ronald E. 1937- *WhoAm 90*
Bailey, Ronald E. 1944- *St&PR 91*
Bailey, Ronald Wade 1935- *WhoAm 90*
Bailey, Ruth Hill 1916- *WhoWor 91*
Bailey, Ryburn Hancock 1929- *St&PR 91*
Bailey, Sammy *BioIn 16*
Bailey, Samuel 1791-1870 *BioIn 16*
Bailey, Scott A. 1947- *St&PR 91*
Bailey, Scott Arthur 1947- *WhoEmL 91*
Bailey, Sherry Keith 1950- *WhoEmL 91*
Bailey, Steven George 1957- *WhoEmL 91*
Bailey, Sturges Williams 1919- *WhoAm 90*
Bailey, Sue *BiDrAPA 89*
Bailey, Susan Carol 1954- *WhoAmW 91, WhoEmL 91*
Bailey, Sydney D 1916- *ConAu 31NR*
Bailey, Tania 1927- *WhoAmW 91*
Bailey, Temple 1869?-1953 *FemiCLE*
Bailey, Thomas Andrew 1902-1983 *BioIn 16*
Bailey, Thomas D. 1945- *St&PR 91*
Bailey, Thomas Edward 1947- *WhoSSW 91*
Bailey, Timothy Gordon 1950- *WhoEmL 91*
Bailey, Victor *BioIn 16*
Bailey, Virginia Ellen *WhoAmA 91*
Bailey, Walter *BioIn 16*
Bailey, Wes *BioIn 16*
Bailey, Wilford Sherrill 1921- *WhoAm 90*
Bailey, Willia Jewel 1949- *WhoSSW 91*
Bailey, William 1930- *WhoAmA 91*
Bailey, William Henry 1949- *WhoSSW 91*
Bailey, William John 1921-1989 *BioIn 16*
Bailey, William O. 1926- *St&PR 91, WhoAm 90*
Bailey, William Scherer 1948- *WhoEmL 91*
Bailey, William W. 1941- *St&PR 91*
Bailey, Willoughby James 1933- *WhoWor 91*
Bailey, Worth 1908-1980 *WhoAmA 91N*
Bailey, Zan Tamar *WhoSSW 91*
Bailey, Zelda Chapman 1949- *WhoEmL 91*
Baileys, Charles Neal 1948- *St&PR 91*
Baileys, Steven Jeffery 1954- *St&PR 91*
Bailin, David *WhoAmA 91*
Bailin, Hella 1915- *WhoAmA 91*
Bailin, Lionel J. 1928- *WhoAm 90*
Bailin, Toby 1941- *St&PR 91*
Bailine, Samuel H 1939- *BiDrAPA 89*
Bailitz, Ronald E. 1941- *St&PR 91*
Baillairge, Louis De Gonzague 1808-1896 *DcCanB 12*
Baillargeon, Jacques Guy *BiDrAPA 89*
Baillargeon, Victor Paul 1958- *WhoSSW 91*
Baillen, Claude *ConAu 33NR*
Baillie And The Boys *WhoNeCM [port]*
Baillie, Alexander Charles, Jr. 1939- *WhoAm 90*
Baillie, C.D. 1918- *St&PR 91*
Baillie, Charles Douglas 1918- *WhoAm 90*
Baillie, Donald Macpherson 1887-1954 *BioIn 16*
Baillie, Grisell 1665-1746 *FemiCLE*
Baillie, Grissel 1665-1746 *BiDEWW*
Baillie, Grizel Hume 1665-1746 *BioIn 16*
Baillie, Hugh 1890-1966 *BioIn 16*
Baillie, Isobel 1895-1983 *DcNaB 1981, PenDiMP*
Baillie, Joanna 1762-1851 *BioIn 16, DcLB 93 [port], FemiCLE*
Baillie, John 1886-1960 *BioIn 16*
Baillie, Mary Helen 1926- *WhoAmW 91, WhoWor 91*
Baillie, Priscilla Woods 1935- *WhoAmW 91*
Baillie Scott, Mackay Hugh 1865-1945 *PenDiDA 89*
Baillie Strong, Stuart 1943- *WhoWor 91*
Bailliet, Betty Humphries 1945- *WhoEmL 91*
Bailliet, Esther Rebeca *BiDrAPA 89*
Bailliet, Marcelo C *BiDrAPA 89*
Baillieul, John Brouard 1945- *WhoE 91*
Baillif, Ernest Allen 1925- *WhoAm 90*
Baillio, O. Dallas, Jr. 1940- *WhoAm 90, WhoSSW 91*
Baillon, Austin John 1927- *WhoWor 91*
Baillot, Philippe Adriano 1955- *WhoWor 91*
Baillot, Pierre 1941- *WhoWor 91*
Baillou, Jean 1924- *WhoWor 91*
Bailly, Alice 1872-1938 *BiDWomA*
Bailly, Henri-Claude A. 1946- *St&PR 91*
Bailly, Henri-Claude Albert 1946- *WhoAm 90*
Bailly, Louis *PenDiMP*
Bailly, Richard L. 1934- *St&PR 91*
Bailly-Blanchard, Arthur 1855-1925 *BioIn 16*
Bailon, Gilbert Herculano 1959- *WhoHisp 91*
Bailor, Bob 1951- *Ballpl 90*
Bailor, Mike Eugene 1952- *St&PR 91*
Baily, Alfred Ewing 1925- *WhoE 91*
Baily, Bernard 1920- *EncACom*
Baily, Douglas Boyd 1937- *WhoAm 90*
Baily, Edward Hodge *PenDiDA 89*
Baily, George D. 1950- *St&PR 91*
Baily, Jack H. 1924- *St&PR 91*
Baily, Nathan A. 1920- *St&PR 91*
Baily, Nathan Ariel 1920- *WhoAm 90*
Bailyn, Bernard 1922- *WhoAm 90*
Bailyn, Lotte 1930- *WhoAmW 91*
Bailyn, Ronald E 1954- *BiDrAPA 89*
Bailys, David M. 1961- *St&PR 91*
Baim, Dean Vernon 1949- *WhoWor 91*
Baima, Margaret A 1923- *BiDrAPA 89*
Baiman, Gail 1938- *WhoAmW 91, WhoSSW 91*
Bain, Barbara 1932- *BioIn 16*
Bain, Bruce Alan 1957- *WhoSSW 91*
Bain, Bruce Kahrs 1931- *St&PR 91*
Bain, C. Jackson 1944- *ODwPR 91*
Bain, Clinton Dwight 1960- *WhoSSW 91*
Bain, Conrad 1923- *WorAlBi*
Bain, Conrad Stafford 1923- *WhoAm 90*
Bain, Deborah L. 1958- *WhoSSW 91*
Bain, Donald Knight 1935- *WhoAm 90*
Bain, Donald R. 1937- *St&PR 91*
Bain, Douglas Cogburn, Jr. 1940- *WhoSSW 91*
Bain, Douglas Gilman 1926- *St&PR 91*
Bain, Duncan *BioIn 16*
Bain, Edward Ustick *AuBYP 90*
Bain, Francis 1842-1894 *DcCanB 12*
Bain, George Sayers *BioIn 16*
Bain, George Sayers 1939- *ConAu 132*
Bain, Geri Rhonda 1951- *WhoWrEP 89*
Bain, Irving 1927- *St&PR 91*
Bain, James Arthur 1918- *WhoAm 90*
Bain, Jane E 1934- *BiDrAPA 89*
Bain, John D., III 1940- *St&PR 91*
Bain, John Harper 1940- *St&PR 91*
Bain, Kenneth 1923- *ConAu 130*
Bain, Larry Ray 1946- *WhoEmL 91*
Bain, Lawrence David 1950- *WhoAm 90, WhoWor 91*
Bain, Lilian Pherne 1873- *WhoAmA 91N*
Bain, Linda Valerie 1947- *WhoAmW 91*
Bain, Lorne Donald 1941- *St&PR 91*
Bain, Pierre *PenDiDA 89*
Bain, Richard Anthony 1942- *St&PR 91*
Bain, Robert Addison 1932- *WhoAm 90, WhoWrEP 89*
Bain, Sherwood E. 1922- *St&PR 91*
Bain, Travis Whitsett, II 1934- *WhoAm 90*
Bain, W.D., Jr. 1925- *St&PR 91*
Bain, Wilfred Connell 1908- *IntWWM 90*
Bain, Wilfred Conwell 1908- *WhoAm 90*
Bain, William Donald, Jr. 1925- *WhoAm 90*
Bain, William E. *BioIn 16*
Bain, William Herbert 1927- *WhoWor 91*
Bain, William J., Jr. 1930- *St&PR 91*
Bain, William James, Jr. 1930- *WhoAm 90*
Bain, William W., Jr. *BioIn 16*
Bainbridge, Beryl 1933- *BioIn 16, ConLC 62 [port], FemiCLE, MajTwCW*
Bainbridge, Beryl 1934- *WhoWor 91*
Bainbridge, Cyril 1928- *ConAu 129*
Bainbridge, Dona Bardelli 1953- *WhoAmW 91*
Bainbridge, Elizabeth 1936- *IntWWM 90*
Bainbridge, Frederick Freeman, III 1927- *WhoAm 90*
Bainbridge, Harry M. *BioIn 16*
Bainbridge, Helen King *BioIn 16*
Bainbridge, John 1913- *WhoAm 90, WhoWrEP 89*
Bainbridge, Kenneth Tompkins 1904- *WhoAm 90*
Bainbridge, Russell Benjamin, Jr. 1945- *WhoSSW 91, WhoWor 91*
Bainbridge, Simon Jeremy 1952- *IntWWM 90*
Baine, James Everitt 1941- *St&PR 91, WhoSSW 91*
Bainer, Philip La Vern 1931- *WhoAm 90*
Baines, David Elliot 1946- *WhoSSW 91*
Baines, Edward 1933- *St&PR 91*
Baines, Harold 1959- *Ballpl 90*
Baines, Harold Douglass 1959- *WhoAm 90*
Bains, David Paul 1950- *WhoEmL 91*
Bains, Harrison Mackellar, Jr. 1943- *St&PR 91, WhoAm 90*
Bains, Lee Edmundson 1912- *WhoAm 90, WhoWor 91*
Bains, Leslie Elizabeth 1943- *WhoAm 90*
Bains, Louis W 1930- *BiDrAPA 89*
Bainter, Fay 1892-1968 *WorAlBi*
Bainter, Patricia Ann 1961- *WhoAmW 91*
Bainton, Donald J. 1931- *St&PR 91, WhoAm 90, WhoWor 91*
Bainton, Dorothy Ford 1933- *WhoAm 90, WhoAmW 91*
Bainton, J. Joseph *BioIn 16*
Bainton, John Joseph 1947- *WhoE 91*
Bainton, John William *BioIn 16*
Bainum, Peter Montgomery 1938- *WhoAm 90*
Bainum, Stewart 1919- *St&PR 91, WhoAm 90*
Bainum, Stewart, Jr. 1946- *St&PR 91*
Bainum, Stewart William, Jr. 1946- *WhoAm 90, WhoE 91*
Baio, Scott 1961- *WorAlBi*
Baione, Luke 1921-1989 *BioIn 16*
Bair, Bruce Macklem 1943- *St&PR 91*
Bair, Byron Dee 1956- *BiDrAPA 89*
Bair, Clifford Edwin 1907- *IntWWM 90*
Bair, Deirdre *BioIn 16*
Bair, Deirdre 1935- *BestSel 90-4 [port]*
Bair, Doug 1949- *Ballpl 90*
Bair, Edward Jay 1922- *WhoAm 90*
Bair, Frieda Augusta 1904- *WhoAmW 91*
Bair, Howard S. 1946- *St&PR 91*
Bair, Howard Vernon 1918- *BiDrAPA 89*
Bair, Jeffrey Glenn 1950- *WhoEmL 91*
Bair, Myrna Lynn 1940- *WhoAmW 91*
Bair, Robert Rippel 1925- *WhoAm 90*
Bair, Royden Stanley 1924- *WhoAm 90, WhoSSW 91*
Bair, Sheldon Eugene 1954- *IntWWM 90*
Bair, Stuart Alan 1947- *BiDrAPA 89*
Bair, William Alois 1931- *WhoE 91*
Bair, William J. 1924- *WhoAm 90*
Bair, William L 1930- *BiDrAPA 89*
Baird, Alan C. 1951- *WhoEmL 91*
Baird, Barbara Lillian 1952- *WhoEmL 91*
Baird, Bil 1904-1987 *BioIn 16*
Baird, Bill *BioIn 16*
Baird, Brent D. 1939- *St&PR 91*
Baird, Catherine Merena 1944- *IntWWM 90*
Baird, Charles F. 1922- *St&PR 91*
Baird, Charles Fitz 1922- *WhoAm 90, WhoWor 91*
Baird, Clifton Eugene 1919- *St&PR 91*
Baird, Dale William 1941- *WhoSSW 91*
Baird, David G., Jr. 1924- *St&PR 91*
Baird, Donn A. 1941- *St&PR 91*
Baird, Doug 1891-1967 *Ballpl 90*
Baird, Douglas James 1962- *WhoE 91*
Baird, Dugald Euan 1937- *St&PR 91, WhoAm 90, WhoE 91*
Baird, Edward Rouzie, Jr. 1936- *WhoAm 90*
Baird, Eva-Lee *AuBYP 90*
Baird, Gordon Prentiss 1950- *WhoAm 90*
Baird, Haynes Wallace 1943- *WhoWor 91*
Baird, James Abington 1926- *WhoAm 90*
Baird, James Kern 1941- *WhoSSW 91*
Baird, James L. 1917- *St&PR 91*
Baird, Jeanne Armentrout 1939- *WhoSSW 91*
Baird, John Absalom, Jr. 1918- *WhoAm 90, WhoE 91, WhoWor 91*
Baird, John L. 1888-1946 *WorAlBi*
Baird, John Northcote 1940- *St&PR 91*
Baird, John Wyllys 1915- *St&PR 91*
Baird, Joni Elaine 1948- *WhoEmL 91*
Baird, Joseph Armstrong, Jr. 1922- *WhoAm 90, WhoAmA 91*
Baird, Joseph Arthur 1922- *WhoAm 90*
Baird, Joseph Bedent, Jr. *BiDrAPA 89*
Baird, Keim L 1934- *BiDrAPA 89*
Baird, Kenneth David 1939- *St&PR 91*
Baird, Leona Mae 1937- *St&PR 91*
Baird, Lisa Morrison 1954- *WhoEmL 91*
Baird, Lourdes G. 1935- *WhoHisp 91*
Baird, Mary Louise 1947- *WhoE 91*
Baird, Mary Stevens *BioIn 16*
Baird, Mellon Campbell, Jr. 1931- *WhoAm 90, WhoSSW 91*
Baird, Michael 1945- *WhoSSW 91*
Baird, Nancy Disher 1935- *ConAu 32NR*
Baird, Nat T. 1935- *WhoSSW 91*
Baird, Pamela Jo 1948- *WhoAmW 91, WhoEmL 91*
Baird, Patricia Ann *WhoAm 90*
Baird, Richard L. 1924- *St&PR 91*
Baird, Richard S. 1951- *St&PR 91*
Baird, Robert A. *St&PR 91*
Baird, Robert B. 1923- *St&PR 91*
Baird, Robert Dahlen 1933- *WhoAm 90*
Baird, Robert Malcolm 1937- *WhoAm 90*
Baird, Roger Allen 1914- *WhoAm 90*
Baird, Russell Miller 1916- *WhoAm 90*
Baird, Spencer Fullerton 1823-1887 *WhNaAH*
Baird, Stanley 1924- *St&PR 91*
Baird, Steven *BioIn 16*
Baird, Stuart G. 1927- *ODwPR 91*
Baird, Terry 1946- *St&PR 91*
Baird, Thomas 1923- *WhoWrEP 89*
Baird, Thomas 1923-1990 *ConAu 131, SmATA 64*
Baird, Thomas P. 1923- *AuBYP 90*
Baird, Thomas P. 1923-1990 *BioIn 16*
Baird, William David 1939- *WhoAm 90*
Baird, William McKenzie 1944- *WhoAm 90*
Baird, William Miller 1849- *AmLegL*
Baird, William Robb 1924- *WhoSSW 91*
Baird, William Stanley 1935- *St&PR 91*
Baird, William Teel 1819?-1897 *DcCanB 12*
Baireuther, James 1946- *St&PR 91*
Bairstow, Frances Kanevsky 1920- *WhoAmW 91*
Bairstow, Richard Raymond 1917- *WhoWor 91*
Bais, Janie 1956- *WhoSSW 91*
Baisch, Wister S. 1926- *St&PR 91*
Baisden, Charles Robert 1939- *WhoSSW 91*
Baisden, Eleanor Marguerite 1935- *WhoAmW 91*
Baish, Richard O. *St&PR 91*
Baisley, James M. 1932- *St&PR 91*
Baisley, James Mahoney 1932- *WhoAm 90*
Baisley, Robert William 1923- *WhoAm 90*
Baitinger, Utz G. 1938- *WhoWor 91*
Baity, John Cooley 1933- *WhoAm 90*
Baizan, Gabriel *WhoHisp 91*
Baize, Deborah Ann 1963- *WhoAmW 91*
Baizer, Eric Wyatt 1950- *WhoWrEP 89*
Baizerman, Saul 1889-1957 *WhoAmA 91N*
Bajackson, Richard Alan 1947- *WhoE 91*
Bajaj, Rahul Kamalnayan 1938- *WhoWor 91*
Bajamunde, Lupicino *BiDrAPA 89*
Bajjaly, Floyd L 1928- *BiDrAPA 89*
Bajor, George F 1933- *BiDrAPA 89*
Bajorinas, Eugene A. 1960- *WhoSSW 91*
Bajorunas, Daiva Regina 1946- *WhoEmL 91*
Bajt, Aleksander 1921- *WhoWor 91*
Bajwa, Jagdeep Kaur 1950- *BiDrAPA 89*
Bajwa, LaCretia Yvonne 1948- *WhoAmW 91*
Bajwa, Waheed K 1957- *BiDrAPA 89*
Bak, Brafford Blair 1951- *WhoEmL 91*
Bak, Mary Magnuson 1953- *WhoEmL 91*
Bak, Sunny 1958- *WhoAmW 91*
Baka, Jeremy *ODwPR 91*
Bakac, Andreja 1946- *WhoAmW 91*
Bakal, Carl 1918- *WhoAm 90, WhoWrEP 89*
Bakal, Dennis A. 1944- *St&PR 91*
Bakal, Sid 1920- *ODwPR 91*
Bakalar, John S. 1948- *St&PR 91*
Bakalar, John Stephen 1948- *WhoAm 90*
Bakaly, Charles George, Jr. 1927- *WhoAm 90*
Bakamis, Gretchen K. 1954- *ODwPR 91*
Bakane, John L. 1951- *St&PR 91*
Bakanowsky, Louis J 1930- *WhoAmA 91*
Bakanowsky, Louis Joseph 1930- *WhoAm 90*
Bakatin, Vadim 1937- *BioIn 16*
Bakatin, Vadim Viktorovich 1937- *WhoWor 91*
Bakaty, Mike 1936- *WhoAmA 91*
Bakay, Louis 1917- *WhoAm 90*
Bakay, Roy Arpad Earle 1949- *WhoAm 90*
Bakeless, John Edwin 1894-1978 *AuBYP 90*
Bakeless, Katherine Little *AuBYP 90*
Bakeman, Carol Ann 1934- *WhoAmW 91*
Baken, Emerson Donley 1902- *St&PR 91*
Baker, A. Vicki *WhoAmW 91*
Baker, Adolph 1917- *WhoAm 90*
Baker, Alan L. 1929- *St&PR 91*
Baker, Albert I. 1946- *St&PR 91*
Baker, Alison Ruth 1962- *IntWWM 90*
Baker, Alma Nicoll *BioIn 16*
Baker, Althea Ross 1949- *WhoAmW 91*
Baker, Alton Fletcher, Jr. 1919- *St&PR 91, WhoWrEP 89*
Baker, Alton Wesley 1912- *WhoAm 90, WhoWor 91*
Baker, Andrew Hartill 1948- *WhoAm 90*
Baker, Anita *BioIn 16*
Baker, Anita 1958- *DrBlPA 90, WhoAm 90, WhoAmW 91, WorAlBi*
Baker, Anita Diane 1955- *WhoAmW 91, WhoEmL 91, WhoSSW 91*
Baker, Asa *TwCCr&M 91*
Baker, Augusta 1911- *BioIn 16*
Baker, Ava Jean 1947- *WhoEmL 91*
Baker, Avery D. 1935- *St&PR 91*
Baker, B. Lea *ODwPR 91*
Baker, Barbara *AuBYP 90*
Baker, Barbara Ann 1948- *WhoEmL 91*

Baker, Barbara Kay 1953- *St&PR 91*
Baker, Belle 1895-1957 *OxCPMus*
Baker, Benjamin Oswald 1917- *WhoAm 90*
Baker, Bernard Robert, II 1915- *St&PR 91, WhoAm 90*
Baker, Bert O. 1918- *St&PR 91*
Baker, Betty *BioIn 16*
Baker, Betty 1928-1987 *BioIn 16*
Baker, Betty Lou 1928-1987 *AuBYP 90*
Baker, Betty Louise 1937- *WhoAmW 91*
Baker, Brian Dean 1963- *WhoSSW 91*
Baker, Bruce E. 1934- *St&PR 91*
Baker, Bruce Edward 1937- *WhoE 91, WhoWor 91*
Baker, Bruce F. 1930- *St&PR 91*
Baker, Bruce J. 1954- *WhoEmL 91*
Baker, Burke, Jr. 1914- *WhoAm 90*
Baker, Byron N. *St&PR 91*
Baker, C. Russell 1926- *St&PR 91*
Baker, C.W. 1930- *St&PR 91*
Baker, Cameron 1937- *WhoAm 90, WhoWor 91*
Baker, Candace L. 1953- *WhoEmL 91*
Baker, Carl Joseph 1950- *WhoE 91*
Baker, Carl Leroy 1943- *WhoAm 90*
Baker, Carleton Harold 1930- *WhoAm 90*
Baker, Carlos 1909-1987 *DcLB 103 [port]*
Baker, Carolyn Croom 1946- *WhoWrEP 89*
Baker, Carri Lynn 1962- *WhoAmW 91*
Baker, Carroll *BioIn 16*
Baker, Carroll 1931- *ConTFT 8 [port], WhoAm 90, WorAlBi*
Baker, Cecil Lamar 1944- *St&PR 91*
Baker, Charles A. 1932- *St&PR 91*
Baker, Charles B. 1933- *St&PR 91*
Baker, Charles D. 1928- *St&PR 91*
Baker, Charles DeWitt 1932- *WhoAm 90*
Baker, Charles Douglas, Jr. 1948- *WhoSSW 91*
Baker, Charles Duane 1928- *WhoAm 90*
Baker, Charles E. 1946- *WhoE 91, WhoEmL 91, WhoWor 91*
Baker, Charles Edwin 1902-1971 *WhoAmA 91N*
Baker, Charles Gary 1946- *WhoEmL 91*
Baker, Charles Ray 1932- *WhoSSW 91*
Baker, Charlotte 1910- *AuBYP 90*
Baker, Cheryl Louise 1948- *WhoAmW 91*
Baker, Chester Bird 1918- *WhoAm 90*
Baker, Chet *BioIn 16*
Baker, Chet 1929-1988 *AnObit 1988, OxCPMus*
Baker, Clarence Albert, Sr. 1919- *WhoWor 91*
Baker, Clifford Howard 1932- *WhoWor 91*
Baker, Connie L. 1948- *WhoAmW 91*
Baker, Cornelia Draves 1929- *WhoAmA 91, WhoE 91*
Baker, Cyril *IntWWM 90*
Baker, Dale Edwin 1946- *WhoAm 90*
Baker, Dana 1949- *WhoSSW 91*
Baker, Daniel Neil 1948- *WhoAm 90, WhoEmL 91*
Baker, Daniel Richard 1932- *WhoSSW 91*
Baker, Darryl Ellis 1952- *WhoEmL 91*
Baker, David 1931- *IntWWM 90*
Baker, David A. 1915- *St&PR 91*
Baker, David Alan 1957- *WhoWrEP 89*
Baker, David B., Jr. 1927- *St&PR 91*
Baker, David Hiram 1939- *WhoAm 90*
Baker, David Keith 1926-1988 *BioIn 16*
Baker, David R. 1932- *St&PR 91*
Baker, David Ray *BiDrAPA 89*
Baker, David Remember 1932- *WhoAm 90*
Baker, David S. 1937- *WhoAm 90*
Baker, David Scott 1946- *WhoEmL 91*
Baker, Deborah Ann 1956- *WhoEmL 91*
Baker, Deborah Warrington 1949- *WhoAmW 91*
Baker, Del 1892-1973 *Ballpl 90*
Baker, Delbert Wayne 1953- *WhoAm 90*
Baker, Dennis Wayne 1946- *WhoAm 90, WhoEmL 91*
Baker, Dewleen Gay 1947- *BiDrAPA 89*
Baker, Dexter F. 1927- *St&PR 91*
Baker, Dexter Farrington 1927- *WhoAm 90*
Baker, Diane 1932- *WhoAm 90*
Baker, Diane 1938?- *BioIn 16*
Baker, Dina Gustin *WhoAmA 91*
Baker, Don 1960- *WhoEmL 91*
Baker, Don Forrest 1947- *WhoEmL 91*
Baker, Don G. 1934- *WhoAm 90*
Baker, Don James 1946- *WhoEmL 91*
Baker, Don M. 1932- *WhoSSW 91*
Baker, Don Marion 1932- *St&PR 91*
Baker, Don R. 1948- *WhoEmL 91*
Baker, Donald 1929- *WhoAm 90*
Baker, Donald A. 1927- *St&PR 91*
Baker, Donald Adrian 1936- *WhoE 91*
Baker, Donald James 1937- *WhoAm 90*
Baker, Donald Parks 1932- *WhoAm 90*
Baker, Donald Scott 1939- *St&PR 91, WhoAm 90*
Baker, Donald Whitelaw 1923- *WhoWrEP 89*
Baker, Donna Kashulines 1952- *WhoEmL 91*
Baker, Dorothy *BioIn 16*
Baker, Dorothy 1907-1968 *FemiCLE*
Baker, Dorothy M 1911- *BiDrAPA 89*
Baker, Douglas M. 1922- *EncO&P 3*
Baker, Douglas M. 1935- *St&PR 91*
Baker, Dreama Gail 1948- *WhoSSW 91, WhoWor 91*
Baker, Durward A 1931- *BiDrAPA 89*
Baker, Dusty 1949- *Ballpl 90 [port]*
Baker, Earl Homer 1946- *WhoSSW 91*
Baker, Earl Russel, II 1950- *WhoSSW 91*
Baker, Edward George 1908- *WhoSSW 91, WhoWor 91*
Baker, Edward Kevin 1948- *WhoSSW 91*
Baker, Edward L. 1946- *WhoAm 90*
Baker, Edward Martin 1941- *WhoAm 90*
Baker, Edwin M. 1923- *St&PR 91*
Baker, Edwin Moody 1923- *WhoAm 90*
Baker, Edwin Robert 1930- *St&PR 91*
Baker, Edwin Stuart 1944- *WhoWor 91*
Baker, Elbert Hall, II 1910- *WhoWrEP 89*
Baker, Eleanor Jeanette 1920- *St&PR 91*
Baker, Elgan Louis 1949- *WhoAm 90*
Baker, Eliott Goodman 1952- *WhoEmL 91*
Baker, Elizabeth C *WhoAmA 91*
Baker, Elizabeth Calhoun *WhoAm 90, WhoWrEP 89*
Baker, Ella 1859-1888 *FemiCLE*
Baker, Ella 1903-1986 *BioIn 16, EncAL*
Baker, Ellen Harte 1944- *WhoAmW 91*
Baker, Ellen Shulman 1953- *WhoAmW 91*
Baker, Elmer Elias, Jr. 1922- *WhoAm 90*
Baker, Elsa J. *BioIn 16*
Baker, Emily L. 1961- *ODwPR 91*
Baker, Eric Edward 1933- *WhoAm 90*
Baker, Ernest 1912- *IntWWM 90*
Baker, Ernest Beasley, Jr. 1926- *WhoAm 90*
Baker, Eugene Ames 1928- *WhoAmA 91N*
Baker, Eugene H. *BioIn 16*
Baker, Evalyn Irene 1947- *WhoEmL 91*
Baker, F M 1942- *BiDrAPA 89*
Baker, Faith Mero 1941- *WhoAmW 91*
Baker, Floyd 1916- *Ballpl 90*
Baker, Floyd Wilmer 1927- *WhoAm 90*
Baker, Francis E., Jr. 1929- *St&PR 91*
Baker, Frank 1886-1963 *Ballpl 90 [port]*
Baker, Frank C. 1944- *St&PR 91*
Baker, Fred Greentree 1950- *WhoEmL 91*
Baker, Frederick Cecil 1941- *WhoAm 90, WhoE 91*
Baker, Frederick John 1941- *WhoAm 90*
Baker, Frederick Milton, Jr. 1949- *WhoEmL 91*
Baker, Frederick Waller 1949- *WhoWrEP 89*
Baker, Frederick William 1928- *WhoWor 91*
Baker, G. Derwood 1899-1989 *BioIn 16*
Baker, G. P. *ConAu 130*
Baker, Gail Verleen 1952- *WhoWrEP 89*
Baker, Gary N. 1946- *St&PR 91*
Baker, Gary Roger 1944- *WhoSSW 91*
Baker, Gene 1925- *Ballpl 90*
Baker, Geoffrey Hewett 1949- *WhoWor 91*
Baker, George 1885-1976 *OxCPMus, PenDiMP*
Baker, George 1915-1975 *EncACom*
Baker, George Allen, Jr. 1932- *WhoAm 90*
Baker, George Chisholm 1918- *WhoAm 90*
Baker, George F. 1840-1931 *EncABHB 6 [port]*
Baker, George Gillespie 1910-1984 *DcNaB 1981*
Baker, George P 1931- *WhoAmA 91*
Baker, George Pierce 1866-1935 *WorAlBi*
Baker, George Stanley 1950- *WhoE 91*
Baker, George William 1928- *St&PR 91*
Baker, George William 1953- *WhoSSW 91*
Baker, Gerry Lynne *ODwPR 91*
Baker, Gilbert Jens 1946- *WhoWor 91*
Baker, Ginger *BioIn 16, EncPR&S 89*
Baker, Ginger 1939- *WorAlBi*
Baker, Gladys Corvera 1950- *WhoHisp 91*
Baker, Gordon 1938- *ConAu 130*
Baker, Gordon Newton 1954- *WhoWor 91*
Baker, Grace *BiDrAPA 89*
Baker, Gwendolyn C. *BioIn 16*
Baker, Gwendolyn Calvert 1931- *WhoAmW 91*
Baker, Harold Cecil 1954- *WhoEmL 91, WhoWor 91*
Baker, Helen Doyle Peil 1943- *WhoAmW 91*
Baker, Helen Hicks 1950- *WhoAmW 91*
Baker, Henry 1890-1990 *BioIn 16, NewYTBS 90 [port]*
Baker, Henry 1952- *WhoEmL 91*
Baker, Henry John, Jr. 1935- *WhoAm 90*
Baker, Henry S., Jr. 1926- *St&PR 91, WhoAm 90*
Baker, Herbert 1924- *WhoAm 90*
Baker, Herbert George 1920- *WhoAm 90*
Baker, Herman 1926- *WhoAm 90*
Baker, Hollis MacLure 1916- *WhoAm 90*
Baker, Horace W. 1914- *St&PR 91*
Baker, Houston A. *BioIn 16*
Baker, Houston Alfred, Jr. 1943- *WhoAm 90*
Baker, Howard, Jr. 1925- *WorAlBi*
Baker, Howard Allen 1914- *WhoSSW 91*
Baker, Howard H. 1925- *BioIn 16*
Baker, Howard S *BiDrAPA 89*
Baker, Howard Wilson 1905-1990 *ConAu 132*
Baker, Ida Kathryn 1968- *WhoSSW 91*
Baker, Ira Lee 1915- *WhoAm 90, WhoWor 91*
Baker, Isaac M., Jr. 1913- *St&PR 91*
Baker, Israel 1921- *IntWWM 90*
Baker, J. A. 1944- *WhoE 91*
Baker, J. Richard 1931- *WhoAm 90*
Baker, Jack Sherman 1920- *WhoAm 90*
Baker, Jackson Arnold 1938- *WhoAm 90*
Baker, James A. 1942- *St&PR 91*
Baker, James A., III *BioIn 16, NewYTBS 90 [port]*
Baker, James A., III 1930- *News 91-2 [port], WorAlBi*
Baker, James Addison, III 1930- *BiDrUSE 89, WhoAm 90, WhoE 91, WhoWor 91*
Baker, James Barnes 1933- *WhoAm 90*
Baker, James Donald 1943- *WhoSSW 91*
Baker, James Donald 1956- *BiDrAPA 89*
Baker, James E *BiDrAPA 89*
Baker, James Edward 1930- *WhoAm 90*
Baker, James Edward Sproul 1912- *WhoAm 90, WhoWor 91*
Baker, James Edyrn 1951- *WhoEmL 91*
Baker, James Estes 1935- *WhoAm 90*
Baker, James Eugene 1951- *WhoEmL 91*
Baker, James Gilbert 1914- *WhoAm 90*
Baker, James Guy *BiDrAPA 89*
Baker, James Jay 1953- *WhoEmL 91*
Baker, James Johnston 1926- *St&PR 91*
Baker, James K. 1931- *St&PR 91*
Baker, James Kendrick 1931- *WhoAm 90*
Baker, James Louis *BiDrAPA 89*
Baker, James Marion 1861-1940 *BioIn 16*
Baker, James Patrick 1934- *St&PR 91*
Baker, James Porter 1931- *WhoAm 90*
Baker, James Webb 1926- *WhoSSW 91*
Baker, Jan Eliese 1958- *WhoAmW 91*
Baker, Jane Elaine 1923- *WhoAmW 91*
Baker, Janet 1933- *PenDiMP*
Baker, Janet Abbott 1921- *IntWWM 90*
Baker, Janet Abbott 1933- *WhoWor 91*
Baker, Janet Lenz 1943- *WhoAmW 91*
Baker, Jean Harvey 1933- *WhoAm 90, WhoAmW 91*
Baker, Jean Mary 1944- *WhoAmW 91*
Baker, Jeanette Sledge 1947- *WhoAmW 91, WhoEmL 91*
Baker, Jeanne M. 1928- *WhoSSW 91*
Baker, Jeannette L *BiDrAPA 89*
Baker, Jeannine Ann 1949- *WhoWrEP 89*
Baker, Jeffrey Stephen 1947- *WhoEmL 91*
Baker, Jill Withrow 1942- *WhoAmA 91*
Baker, Joanne Evelyn 1933- *WhoAmW 91, WhoE 91, WhoWor 91*
Baker, Joanne Helen 1944- *WhoE 91*
Baker, Joe 1946- *WhoAmA 91*
Baker, Joe Benny 1948- *WhoSSW 91*
Baker, John Alexander 1927- *WhoAm 90*
Baker, John Alexander 1957- *BiDrAPA 89*
Baker, John C. 1930- *St&PR 91*
Baker, John Cooper 1947- *WhoE 91*
Baker, John Daniel 1948- *St&PR 91*
Baker, John Daniel, II 1948- *WhoAm 90*
Baker, John Edward 1940- *St&PR 91*
Baker, John Fleetwood 1901-1985 *DcNaB 1981*
Baker, John Frank 1963- *WhoEmL 91*
Baker, John Franklin 1918- *WhoAm 90*
Baker, John Gatch 1946- *WhoEmL 91*
Baker, John Herbert, Jr. *BiDrAPA 89*
Baker, John L. 1928- *St&PR 91*
Baker, John Lee 1928- *WhoAm 90, WhoWor 91*
Baker, John Milnes 1932- *WhoAm 90*
Baker, John R. 1926- *St&PR 91*
Baker, John Russell 1926- *WhoAm 90*
Baker, John Stevenson 1931- *WhoWor 91*
Baker, John T. *WhoAm 90*
Baker, Joseph Edward 1917- *WhoWrEP 89*
Baker, Joseph John 1952- *St&PR 91*
Baker, Joseph Lee 1943- *St&PR 91*
Baker, Joseph Preston 1946- *St&PR 91*
Baker, Josephine 1906-1975 *BioAmW, BioIn 16, DrBlPA 90, OxCPMus, WorAlBi*
Baker, Josephine L. Redenius 1920- *WhoE 91, WhoSSW 91, WhoWor 91*
Baker, Joy Lynn 1954- *WhoSSW 91, WhoWor 91*
Baker, Joyce *BiDrAPA 89*
Baker, Judith Karen 1945- *St&PR 91*
Baker, Judith Minnix 1946- *WhoSSW 91*
Baker, Justine Clara 1939- *WhoAmW 91*
Baker, Katherine June 1932- *WhoAmW 91, WhoSSW 91*
Baker, Kathryn Ware 1942- *WhoSSW 91*
Baker, Kathy *BioIn 16*
Baker, Kathy 1950- *ConTFT 8*
Baker, Kathy Whitton *ConTFT 8*
Baker, Keith Michael 1938- *WhoAm 90*
Baker, Kelly Shane 1962- *WhoEmL 91*
Baker, Kendall L. 1942- *WhoAm 90*
Baker, Kenneth 1934- *WhoWor 91*
Baker, Kenneth 1946- *WhoAmA 91*
Baker, Kenneth Albert 1946- *WhoAm 90*
Baker, Kenny 1912- *OxCPMus*
Baker, Kenny 1921- *OxCPMus*
Baker, Kenny 1934- *ConTFT 8*
Baker, Kent Alfred 1948- *WhoEmL 91, WhoWor 91*
Baker, Kerry Allen 1949- *WhoEmL 91, WhoSSW 91, WhoWor 91*
Baker, Kimberly S. 1964- *WhoEmL 91*
Baker, Kristin *BioIn 16*
Baker, Kristine A W *BiDrAPA 89*
Baker, Larry Alan 1967- *WhoEmL 91*
Baker, Laura Ann 1955- *WhoEmL 91*
Baker, Laura Nelson 1911- *AuBYP 90*
Baker, Laurence C. 1946- *St&PR 91*
Baker, Laurence Howard 1943- *WhoAm 90*
Baker, LaVern 1928- *OxCPMus*
Baker, Lawrence Colby, Jr. 1935- *WhoAm 90*
Baker, Lawrence D 1942- *BiDrAPA 89*
Baker, Lee Edward 1924- *WhoAm 90*
Baker, Lee W. 1919- *ODwPR 91*
Baker, Lenox Dial 1902- *WhoAm 90*
Baker, Lenox Dial, Jr. 1941- *WhoAm 90*
Baker, Leonard Ava 1921- *WhoSSW 91*
Baker, Leonard Morton 1934- *WhoAm 90*
Baker, Leslie Mayo 1942- *St&PR 91*
Baker, Lester 1930- *WhoAm 90*
Baker, Lewis *ConAu 129*
Baker, Lewis T, III 1953- *ConAu 129*
Baker, Lillian 1921- *WhoAmW 91, WhoWor 91*
Baker, Linda Ann 1949- *WhoAmW 91*
Baker, Linda Leslie 1948- *WhoAmW 91, WhoEmL 91*
Baker, Liva 1930- *AuBYP 90*
Baker, Loran Ellis 1831-1899 *DcCanB 12*
Baker, Lori Ann 1957- *WhoAmW 91*
Baker, Lori Kay 1958- *WhoAmW 91*
Baker, Lorraine 1935- *WhoAmW 91*
Baker, Louis Coombs Weller 1921- *WhoE 91*
Baker, Louis W. 1931- *St&PR 91*
Baker, Louisa Alice 1858-1926 *FemiCLE*
Baker, Lynn Sandra 1948- *BiDrAPA 89*
Baker, Lynne Rudder 1944- *WhoAm 90*
Baker, M. Gerald 1939- *St&PR 91*
Baker, Madeline Ruth 1963- *WhoAmW 91*
Baker, Margaret Ann 1955- *WhoAmW 91*
Baker, Margaret Joyce 1918- *AuBYP 90*
Baker, Margery 1948- *St&PR 91*
Baker, Margery Claire 1948- *WhoAm 90*
Baker, Marian Gray 1931- *WhoAmW 91*
Baker, Mark Allen 1957- *WhoE 91*
Baker, Mark Early 1953- *WhoSSW 91*
Baker, Mark William 1948- *St&PR 91*
Baker, Martha *BioIn 16*
Baker, Marvin Duane 1937- *St&PR 91*
Baker, Mary 1649?-1743? *BiDEWW*
Baker, Mary Alice 1937- *WhoSSW 91*
Baker, Mary Elizabeth 1923- *AuBYP 90*
Baker, Mary Jordan *WhoAmW 91*
Baker, Mary Lou 1935- *WhoE 91*
Baker, Max Alden 1939- *BiDrAPA 89*
Baker, Melvin C. 1920- *WhoAm 90*
Baker, Merl 1924- *WhoAm 90*
Baker, Merrily Dean *BioIn 16*
Baker, Michael Harry 1916- *WhoAm 90*
Baker, Milton 1908- *St&PR 91*
Baker, Milton G., Mrs. *WhoSSW 91*
Baker, Morton H. 1930- *St&PR 91*
Baker, Nathaniel Bradley 1818-1876 *AmLegL*
Baker, Nell Williams 1934- *WhoAmW 91*
Baker, Nevin S. 1922- *St&PR 91*
Baker, Newell A. 1926- *St&PR 91*
Baker, Newton Diehl 1871-1937 *BiDrUSE 89*
Baker, Niamh 1934- *WhoWor 91*
Baker, Nicholson 1957- *ConLC 61 [port]*
Baker, Nina Brown 1888-1957 *AuBYP 90*
Baker, Norma Jean 1926-1962 *ConAu 129*
Baker, Norman Henderson 1917- *WhoAm 90*
Baker, Norman Lee 1926- *WhoE 91*
Baker, Norman Robert 1937- *WhoAm 90*
Baker, Olaf 187-?- *ConAu 129*
Baker, Ophelia V 1932- *BiDrAPA 89*
Baker, Pamela Carolyn 1957- *WhoSSW 91*
Baker, Patricia Alice 1940- *WhoAmW 91*
Baker, Patricia Marie 1961- *WhoAmW 91*
Baker, Patricia O. 1956- *St&PR 91*
Baker, Paul, Jr. 1921- *WhoAm 90*
Baker, Paul Alan 1955- *WhoWrEP 89*
Baker, Paul L *BiDrAPA 89*
Baker, Paul M. 1950- *St&PR 91*
Baker, Paul Raymond 1927- *WhoAm 90*
Baker, Paul Thornell 1927- *WhoAm 90*
Baker, Pauline Halpern 1941- *WhoE 91*

Baker, Peter Harrison 1952- *WhoE 91*
Baker, Phil 1896-1963 *OxCPMus*
Baker, Philip Benton 1934- *St&PR 91*
Baker, Philip Douglas 1922- *WhoAm 90*
Baker, Philip John Noel- 1889-1982 *DcNaB 1981*
Baker, Priscilla Rand 1937- *WhoE 91*
Baker, R. Palmer, Jr. 1918- *WhoAm 90*
Baker, R. Robinson 1928- *WhoAm 90*
Baker, Rachel M 1930- *BiDrAPA 89*
Baker, Rachel Mininberg 1904-1978 *AuBYP 90*
Baker, Ralph *BiDrAPA 89*
Baker, Ralph Bernard 1932- *WhoAmA 91N*
Baker, Ralph K 1936- *BiDrAPA 89*
Baker, Ray Stannard 1870-1946 *BioIn 16*
Baker, Raymond R.J. 1938- *St&PR 91*
Baker, Rebecca Louise 1951- *WhoSSW 91*
Baker, Rex Gavin, Jr. 1920- *WhoAm 90*
Baker, Richard A. 1953- *ODwPR 91*
Baker, Richard Brown 1912- *WhoAm 90, WhoAmA 91, WhoE 91*
Baker, Richard Douglas James 1925- *IntWWM 90*
Baker, Richard E. 1939- *St&PR 91*
Baker, Richard Eugene 1939- *WhoAm 90*
Baker, Richard Freligh 1910- *WhoAm 90*
Baker, Richard Graves 1938- *WhoAm 90*
Baker, Richard Hill 1936- *BiDrAPA 89*
Baker, Richard Hugh 1948- *WhoAm 90, WhoSSW 91*
Baker, Richard Joint 1931- *St&PR 91*
Baker, Richard Kenneth George 1941- *WhoWor 91*
Baker, Richard M. 1945- *St&PR 91*
Baker, Richard Southworth 1929- *WhoAm 90, WhoWor 91*
Baker, Richard Wheeler, Jr. 1916- *WhoAm 90*
Baker, Robert *BioIn 16*
Baker, Robert 1940- *WhoAm 90*
Baker, Robert Allen, Jr. 1921- *WhoAm 90*
Baker, Robert Andrew 1925- *WhoAm 90*
Baker, Robert E. 1930- *St&PR 91*
Baker, Robert Edward 1930- *WhoAm 90*
Baker, Robert Eric 1959- *WhoSSW 91*
Baker, Robert Ernest, Jr. 1916- *WhoAm 90*
Baker, Robert F., Jr. *ODwPR 91*
Baker, Robert Frank 1936- *WhoAm 90*
Baker, Robert Hart 1954- *WhoAm 90, WhoEmL 91, WhoWor 91*
Baker, Robert Hunt 1943- *WhoSSW 91*
Baker, Robert I. 1940- *St&PR 91*
Baker, Robert J 1930- *BiDrAPA 89*
Baker, Robert John 1944- *WhoAm 90*
Baker, Robert Lawrance 1928- *WhoE 91*
Baker, Robert Lee, III 1949- *WhoSSW 91*
Baker, Robert Leon 1920- *WhoWrEP 89*
Baker, Robert Leon 1925- *WhoAm 90*
Baker, Robert M. L., Jr. 1930- *WhoAm 90*
Baker, Robert Maurice 1928- *St&PR 91*
Baker, Robert Stephen *BiDrAPA 89*
Baker, Robert Stevens 1916- *WhoAm 90*
Baker, Robert Thomas 1932- *WhoAm 90*
Baker, Robert William 1924- *WhoAm 90*
Baker, Robert Winfield 1958- *BiDrAPA 89*
Baker, Robert Woodward 1944- *St&PR 91, WhoAm 90*
Baker, Robin Rose 1959- *WhoAmW 91*
Baker, Rodney Lee 1950- *WhoEmL 91*
Baker, Roland Charles 1938- *WhoE 91*
Baker, Roland Jerald 1938- *WhoAm 90*
Baker, Rollin Harold 1916- *WhoAm 90*
Baker, Ronald Dale 1932- *WhoAm 90*
Baker, Ronald James 1924- *WhoAm 90*
Baker, Ronald Lee 1937- *WhoAm 90*
Baker, Ronald Phillip 1942- *WhoWor 91*
Baker, Ronald R. 1943- *St&PR 91*
Baker, Ronald Ray 1943- *WhoAm 90*
Baker, Ronald Seymour 1949- *WhoEmL 91*
Baker, Russell 1925- *BioIn 16, MajTwCW, WorAlBi*
Baker, Russell Tremaine, Jr. 1942- *WhoAm 90*
Baker, Russell Wayne 1925- *WhoAm 90, WhoWrEP 89*
Baker, Sally 1932- *WhoWor 91*
Baker, Samm Sinclair 1909- *WhoWrEP 89*
Baker, Samuel White 1821-1893 *WorAlBi*
Baker, Saul P. 1925- *St&PR 91*
Baker, Saul Phillip 1924- *WhoAm 90, WhoWor 91*
Baker, Sharon 1938- *WhoWrEP 89*
Baker, Sheila Ann 1944- *WhoAmW 91*
Baker, Sheldon S. 1936- *WhoAm 90*
Baker, Sheridan 1918- *WhoAm 90, WhoWrEP 89*
Baker, Sherman Nelson 1919- *St&PR 91*
Baker, Sherry *BioIn 16*
Baker, Simon 1924- *WhoSSW 91*
Baker, Stanley Eugene 1944- *WhoSSW 91*
Baker, Stephen 1923- *WhoAm 90*
Baker, Stephen Anthony 1953- *St&PR 91*
Baker, Stephen Gregory 1955- *St&PR 91*
Baker, Stephen R *BiDrAPA 89*
Baker, Steve 1956- *Ballpl 90*
Baker, Steve L. 1946- *WhoSSW 91*
Baker, Steven Howard *BiDrAPA 89*
Baker, Steven Jeffery 1959- *WhoEmL 91*
Baker, Stewart L, Jr. 1920- *BiDrAPA 89*
Baker, Stuart David 1935- *WhoAm 90, WhoE 91*
Baker, Susan Beggs 1939- *WhoSSW 91*
Baker, Susan Himber 1943- *WhoAmW 91*
Baker, Susan P. 1930- *WhoAm 90, WhoAmW 91, WhoE 91*
Baker, Suzanne *BioIn 16*
Baker, Suzanne Schneider 1947- *WhoEmL 91*
Baker, T. Harri 1933- *WhoSSW 91*
Baker, Teresa Lynn 1958- *WhoAmW 91*
Baker, Terry John 1943- *WhoSSW 91*
Baker, Thomas 1933- *WhoE 91*
Baker, Thomas, Jr. 1859-1916 *AmLegL*
Baker, Thomas Edgar 1931- *St&PR 91, WhoAm 90*
Baker, Thomas Edward 1923- *WhoAm 90*
Baker, Thomas Eugene 1953- *WhoEmL 91*
Baker, Thomas J. 1945- *St&PR 91*
Baker, Thomas John 1939- *WhoE 91*
Baker, Thomas L. 1943- *WhoSSW 91*
Baker, Thomas Lyle 1945- *St&PR 91*
Baker, Thomas Wayne 1946- *WhoEmL 91*
Baker, Thompson Simkins 1905- *St&PR 91, WhoAm 90, WhoSSW 91*
Baker, Timothy Danforth 1925- *WhoAm 90, WhoE 91*
Baker, Timothy James 1951- *St&PR 91*
Baker, Timothy John 1948- *WhoE 91*
Baker, Tina Patrice Higgins 1959- *WhoSSW 91*
Baker, Vance *BiDrAPA 89*
Baker, Veronica *BioIn 16*
Baker, Victoria Jean 1955- *WhoAmW 91*
Baker, Victoria Kathleen 1958- *WhoE 91*
Baker, W. Howard 1944- *WhoSSW 91*
Baker, Walter C. 1867-1955 *EncABHB 4 [port]*
Baker, Walter E. 1936- *St&PR 91, WhoAm 90*
Baker, Walter Louis 1924- *WhoAm 90, WhoWor 91*
Baker, Warren Joseph 1938- *WhoAm 90*
Baker, Warren W. 1931- *St&PR 91*
Baker, Wayne Delmas 1932- *St&PR 91*
Baker, Wilfred Edmund 1924- *WhoSSW 91*
Baker, William C. 1891- *AuBYP 90*
Baker, William C. 1939- *St&PR 91*
Baker, William Costello, Jr. 1959- *WhoEmL 91*
Baker, William Dunlap 1932- *WhoAm 90*
Baker, William E 1944- *ODwPR 91*
Baker, William Franklin 1942- *WhoAm 90*
Baker, William Garrett, Jr. 1933- *WhoAm 90*
Baker, William George 1935- *WhoAm 90*
Baker, William J. 1932- *St&PR 91*
Baker, William Kaufman 1919- *WhoAm 90*
Baker, William Oliver 1915- *WhoAm 90*
Baker, William Parr 1946- *WhoAm 90, WhoE 91*
Baker, William Radcliffe 1946- *WhoWrEP 89*
Baker, William Steven 1947- *BiDrAPA 89*
Baker, William Thompson, Jr. 1944- *WhoAm 90, WhoE 91*
Baker, William Wallace 1921- *WhoAm 90*
Baker, William Wendell 1956- *WhoE 91*
Baker, Winda Louise 1952- *WhoAmW 91, WhoSSW 91*
Baker, Winthrop Patterson, Jr. 1931- *WhoAm 90, WhoWor 91*
Baker Holliday, Karen 1948- *WhoAmW 91*
Baker Knoll, Catherine *WhoAmW 91, WhoE 91*
Baker-Lievanos, Nina Gillson 1950- *WhoAmW 91, WhoEmL 91, WhoWor 91*
Baker-Upton, Debbie Ann 1960- *WhoSSW 91*
Bakes, Annie *BioIn 16*
Bakes, Philip John, Jr. 1946- *WhoAm 90, WhoSSW 91*
Bakes, Robert Eldon 1932- *WhoAm 90*
Bakewell, Benjamin *PenDiDA 89*
Bakewell, John Palmer *PenDiDA 89*
Bakewell, Robert *PenDiDA 89*
Bakewell, William E, Jr. 1923- *BiDrAPA 89*
Bakhai, Yogesh D 1956- *BiDrAPA 89*
Bakhru, Ashok N. 1942- *St&PR 91*
Bakhru, Ashok Naraindas 1942- *WhoAm 90*
Bakhtin, M. M. 1895-1975 *BioIn 16*
Bakhtin, Mikhail Mikhailovich 1895-1975 *BioIn 16, WorAu 1980*
Bakian, Victor Benon 1938- *St&PR 91*
Bakka, Egil Sigmund 1943- *IntWWM 90*
Bakke, Bruce B. *ODwPR 91*
Bakke, Duwayne Allan 1939- *St&PR 91*
Bakke, Jill Hance 1936- *WhoWrEP 89*
Bakke, Jill Merie 1936- *WhoAmW 91*
Bakke, Karen Lee 1942- *WhoAmA 91*
Bakke, Larry Hubert 1932- *WhoAmA 91*
Bakke, M. Russell 1945- *WhoEmL 91*
Bakken, A. Christopher, Jr. 1931- *St&PR 91*
Bakken, Bruce Michael 1953- *WhoEmL 91*
Bakken, Dick 1941- *WhoWrEP 89*
Bakken, Douglas Adair 1939- *WhoAm 90*
Bakken, Earl Elmer 1924- *WhoAm 90*
Bakken, Gary Maynard 1945- *WhoEmL 91*
Bakken, Haakon 1932- *WhoAmA 91*
Bakken, Timothy C. 1957- *WhoEmL 91*
Bakkensen, Laurie Jean 1956- *WhoAmW 91*
Bakker, Cornelis B *BiDrAPA 89*
Bakker, Cornelis B. 1929- *WhoAm 90*
Bakker, Has N. 1947- *St&PR 91*
Bakker, James 1940- *WorAlBi*
Bakker, Jim *BioIn 16*
Bakker, Jonathan Bushnell 1945- *WhoEmL 91*
Bakker, Kornelis 1931- *WhoWor 91*
Bakker, Tammy *BioIn 16*
Bakker, Thomas Gordon 1947- *WhoAm 90, WhoEmL 91*
Bakker, Willem Frederik 1934- *WhoWor 91*
Bakko, Orville Edwin 1919- *WhoAm 90*
Baklanoff, Eric N 1925- *ConAu 30NR*
Baklanoff, Eric Nicholas 1925- *WhoAm 90*
Baklanoff, Joy Driskell 1953- *WhoAmW 91*
Bakman, Patrick T. *NewYTBS 90*
Bakony, Hedwig C *BiDrAPA 89*
Bakos, Edward R *BiDrAPA 89*
Bakos, John A. 1932- *St&PR 91*
Bakos, Thomas Leslie 1945- *St&PR 91*
Bakota, Jerald A. 1937- *St&PR 91*
Bakoyannis, Pavlos *BioIn 16*
Bakri, M. Hani Abdul Kader 1960- *WhoWor 91*
Bakros, Lee Ann 1963- *WhoAmW 91*
Bakrow, William John 1924- *WhoAm 90*
Baksa, Robert Frank 1938- *IntWWM 90*
Bakshi, Jayant 1950- *WhoWor 91*
Bakshi, Ralph *BioIn 16, WhoAm 90*
Bakunin, Mikhail 1814-1876 *WorAlBi*
Bakunin, Mikhail Aleksandrovich 1814-1876 *BioIn 16*
Bakwa *WomWR*
Bakwin, Edward Morris 1928- *St&PR 91, WhoAm 90*
Baky, Laszlo 1889-1946 *BioIn 16*
Bal, Rajeev Gopal 1952- *St&PR 91*
Balaban, Alvin Bernard 1924- *BiDrAPA 89*
Balaban, Bob *BioIn 16*
Balaban, Diane 1935- *WhoAmA 91*
Balaban, Donald Eugene 1932- *St&PR 91*
Balaban, Edward Lee 1949- *BiDrAPA 89*
Balaban, Joseph George 1940- *WhoE 91*
Balaban, Julie 1956- *BiDrAPA 89*
Balaban, Robert J *BiDrAPA 89*
Balabanian, David Mark 1938- *WhoAm 90*
Balabanian, Norman 1922- *WhoAm 90*
Balacek, Thomas Vincent, Jr. 1961- *WhoEmL 91, WhoWor 91*
Balachandra, Devalalpura Mahadevaiah 1936- *WhoWor 91*
Balachandran, Bala Venkataraman 1937- *WhoAm 90, WhoWor 91*
Balachandran, Kashi Ramamurthi 1941- *WhoE 91*
Balada, Leonardo 1933- *IntWWM 90, WhoAm 90*
Balado, Manuel *WhoHisp 91*
Balado, Raul Fontela 1938- *WhoWor 91*
Balafonte, Shari *BioIn 16*
Balague Domenech, Jose Carlos 1939- *WhoWor 91*
Balaguer, Joaquin 1907- *BioIn 16, WhoWor 91*
Balaguer, Joaquin 1950- *WhoHisp 91*
Balahtsis, Jack 1938- *St&PR 91*
Balahutrak, Lydia Bodnar 1951- *WhoAmA 91*
Balakian, Anna 1916- *ConAu 129, WhoAm 90*
Balakian, Nona Hilda *WhoAm 90*
Balakian, Peter 1951- *WhoWrEP 89*
Balakirev, Mily Alexeyevich 1837-1910 *PenDiMP A*
Balakrishnan, Govind *BiDrAPA 89*
Balakrishnan, Ramaswami 1943- *BioIn 16*
Balan, Jerry 1948- *St&PR 91*
Balan, Visvanathan *BiDrAPA 89*
Balance, Jerrald Clark 1944- *WhoAmA 91*
Balanchine, George 1904-1983 *BioIn 16, WorAlBi*
Balanchivadze, Andrei 1906- *IntWWM 90*
Balanda, Mikuin Leliel 1939- *WhoWor 91*
Balanis, Constantine Apostle 1938- *WhoAm 90*
Balanky, Michael Fredrick 1957- *WhoSSW 91*
Balarac, Norbert Rene Felix 1946- *WhoWor 91*
Balaram, Prabha 1952- *WhoWor 91*
Balas, Anna 1950- *BiDrAPA 89*
Balas, Charles 1945- *St&PR 91*
Balas, Egon 1922- *WhoAm 90*
Balas, Iolanda 1936- *BioIn 16*
Balas, Irene 1928- *WhoAmA 91*
Balasa, Joseph John 1932- *St&PR 91*
Balashov, Alexander *PenDiMP*
Balasko, Yves 1945- *WhoWor 91*
Balassa, Bela 1928- *WhoAm 90*
Balassa, Bela A. *BioIn 16*
Balassa, Leslie L. 1903- *St&PR 91*
Balassa, Leslie Ladislaus 1903- *WhoE 91*
Balassa, Sandor 1935- *IntWWM 90*
Balasubramaniam, Kunjithapatham 1939- *WhoWor 91*
Balasubramanian, Krishnaswami 1932- *BiDrAPA 89*
Balasubramanian, V 1940- *BiDrAPA 89*
Balavender, Richard Joseph 1944- *St&PR 91*
Balay, Felicie 1940- *WhoAmA 91*
Balay, Robert Elmore 1930- *WhoAm 90*
Balaz, Beverly Ann 1949- *WhoE 91*
Balaz, Jack C. 1924- *St&PR 91*
Balazs, Bela 1884-1949 *BioIn 16*
Balazs, Cecilia Anne 1943- *WhoE 91*
Balazs, Endre Alexander 1920- *WhoAm 90*
Balazs, Mary E. Webber 1939- *WhoSSW 91*
Balazs, Mary W. 1939- *WhoWrEP 89*
Balbach, Anatol B. 1927- *St&PR 91*
Balbach, Stanley Byron 1919- *WhoAm 90*
Balbes, Michael S. 1937- *St&PR 91*
Balbilla *EncCoWW*
Balbilla, Julia *EncCoWW*
Balbin, Julius Yul 1917- *WhoE 91*
Balbin, Ricardo 1904-1981 *BioIn 16*
Balbirer, Andrew Gordon 1954- *WhoAm 90*
Balbo, Italo 1896-1940 *WorAlBi*
Balboa, Carol 1940- *IntWWM 90*
Balboa, Richard Mario 1936- *WhoHisp 91*
Balboa, Vasco Nunez de 1475-1519 *BioIn 16, EncCRAm [port], WorAlBi*
Balbona, Jose L 1931- *BiDrAPA 89*
Balboni, Robert Michael 1954- *WhoE 91*
Balboni, Steve 1957- *Ballpl 90*
Balbuena, Bernardo de 1561?-1627 *BioIn 16*
Balbus *MajTwCW*
Balcanoff, Eugene J *BiDrAPA 89*
Balcar, Gerald Pierce 1932- *St&PR 91*
Balcazar, Carlos 1931- *BiDrAPA 89*
Balcer, Anne Elaine 1953- *WhoE 91*
Balcer, Charles Louis 1921- *WhoAm 90*
Balcer, Charlotte Marie 1960- *BiDrAPA 89*
Balcer, Rene Chenevert 1954- *WhoEmL 91*
Balcer, Yves Michel 1946- *WhoE 91*
Balcerzak, Marion John 1933- *WhoAm 90*
Balcerzak, Stanley Paul 1930- *WhoAm 90*
Balch, Charles M. 1942- *WhoAm 90*
Balch, Clyde Wilkinson 1917- *WhoAm 90*
Balch, Emily G. 1867-1961 *BioAmW*
Balch, Emily Greene 1867-1961 *BioIn 16, WorAlBi*
Balch, Glenn 1902- *AuBYP 90, WhoWrEP 89*
Balch, Glenn 1902-1989 *SmATA 11AS [port]*
Balch, Glenn McClain, Jr. 1937- *WhoAm 90*
Balch, John A. 1935- *St&PR 91*
Balch, John Wayne 1947- *WhoE 91*
Balch, Richard K. 1952- *St&PR 91*
Balch, Samuel Eason 1919- *WhoAm 90, WhoWor 91*
Balchen, Bernt 1899-1973 *WorAlBi*
Balchin, I. David 1940- *St&PR 91*
Balchunas, Gerard Andrew 1955- *WhoE 91*
Balciar, Gerald George 1942- *WhoAmA 91*
Balco, George Joseph 1940- *St&PR 91*
Balcoin, Marie *EncO&P 3*
Balcom, Gloria Darleen 1939- *WhoAmW 91*
Balcom, Jean Elizabeth 1915- *WhoAmW 91*
Balcon, Jonathan Michael H. 1931- *WhoWor 91*
Baldacci, Robert Eugene, Jr. 1952- *WhoE 91*
Baldanza, Deb *WhoWrEP 89*
Baldassano, Corinne Leslie 1950- *WhoAmW 91*
Baldassari, Fred J. 1932- *St&PR 91*
Baldassarre, Joseph Anthony 1950- *IntWWM 90*
Baldassarre, Vito Antonio 1934- *WhoWor 91*
Baldauf, Mark Edward 1957- *WhoE 91*
Baldauf, Richard John 1920- *WhoAm 90*
Baldemor, Anita Baisas *BiDrAPA 89*

Balderacchi, Arthur Eugene 1937- WhoAmA 91
Baldermann, Ingo Herbert 1929- WhoWor 91
Balderson, S. Clark 1948- St&PR 91
Balderston, Jean Merrill 1936- WhoWrEP 89
Balderston, Thomas William 1941- WhoSSW 91
Balderston, William, III 1927- St&PR 91, WhoAm 90
Baldeschi-Balleani, Aurelio BioIn 16
Baldeschwieler, John Dickson 1933- WhoAm 90, WhoWor 91
Baldessari, John 1931- BioIn 16
Baldessari, John Anthony 1931- WhoAm 90, WhoAmA 91
Baldessari, Luciano 1896-1982 BioIn 16
Baldessarini, Ross J 1937- BiDrAPA 89
Baldi, Angelo C. 1942- WhoSSW 91
Baldi, Virgil B. 1928- St&PR 91
Baldin, Lionel Siluan 1907- WhoAm 90
Baldinger, Allan Lee 1945- WhoEmL 91
Baldino, Jennifer 1969- WhoAmW 91
Baldino, Lisa ODwPR 91
Baldino, Nicholas G. WhoAm 90
Baldino, Nicholas G. 1924- St&PR 91
Baldinucci, Filippo 1625-1696 BioIn 16
Baldisseri, Marie Rosanne 1955- WhoAmW 91
Baldocchi, Linda Joyce 1961- WhoSSW 91
Baldock, Bobby Ray 1936- WhoAm 90
Baldomir, Alfredo 1884-1948 BioIn 16
Baldon, Cleo 1927- WhoWor 91
Baldonado, Michael WhoHisp 91
Baldoni, Lauren Patricia 1958- WhoEmL 91
Baldorioty de Castro, Ramon 1822-1889 BioIn 16
Baldridge, Anita Carol 1956- WhoAmW 91
Baldridge, Charlene 1934- WhoWrEP 89
Baldridge, Deborah Marsh 1947- WhoSSW 91
Baldridge, Malcolm 1922-1987 BiDrUSE 89
Baldridge, Mark S 1946- WhoAmA 91
Baldridge, Robert Crary 1921- WhoAm 90
Baldridge, Terry Jayne 1954- WhoSSW 91
Baldrige, Letitia BioIn 16, ODwPR 91, WhoAm 90, WhoAmW 91, WhoE 91
Baldry, John 1940?- EncPR&S 89
Baldschun, Jack 1936- Ballpl 90
Balducci Family BioIn 16
Balducci, Carolyn 1946- AuBYP 90
Balducci, Louis BioIn 16
Balducci, Maria BioIn 16
Balducci, Richard Joseph 1942- WhoE 91
Baldung, Hans 1484?-1545 IntDcAA 90
Baldursson, Thor NewAgMG
Baldwin, Abraham 1754-1807 BioIn 16
Baldwin, Alec BioIn 16
Baldwin, Alexander Rae, III 1958- WhoAm 90
Baldwin, Ann T. 1944- St&PR 91
Baldwin, Anne 1938- AuBYP 90
Baldwin, Arthur Dwight, Jr. 1938- WhoAm 90
Baldwin, Arthur H. AuBYP 90
Baldwin, Arthur L. 1945- WhoE 91
Baldwin, Austin 1807-1886 AmLegL
Baldwin, Bates AuBYP 90
Baldwin, Benjamin Armistead, Jr. 1943- WhoAm 90
Baldwin, Billy ConAu 129
Baldwin, Calvin Benham, Jr. 1925- WhoAm 90
Baldwin, Charlene Marie 1946- WhoEmL 91
Baldwin, Charles Henry 1942- WhoE 91
Baldwin, Christina 1946- ConAu 31NR
Baldwin, Chuck Howard 1961- WhoSSW 91
Baldwin, Craig Martin 1945- St&PR 91
Baldwin, Cynthia Ann 1951- WhoEmL 91
Baldwin, Dalton 1931- IntWWM 90, PenDiMP
Baldwin, Dave 1938- Ballpl 90
Baldwin, David H. 1924- St&PR 91
Baldwin, David Kendrick 1937- St&PR 91
Baldwin, David Rawson 1923- WhoAm 90
Baldwin, David Shepard 1921- WhoAm 90
Baldwin, Deborah 1949- WhoAmW 91
Baldwin, Debra Jo 1956- WhoAmW 91
Baldwin, Deidra B. 1945- WhoWrEP 89
Baldwin, DeWitt Clair, Jr. 1922- WhoAm 90, WhoWor 91
Baldwin, Dick WhoWrEP 89
Baldwin, Dorothy Leila 1948- WhoE 91
Baldwin, Douglas V. 1939- St&PR 91
Baldwin, Edith Ann 1949- WhoE 91
Baldwin, Edward 1756-1836 BioIn 16
Baldwin, Edward R 1935- WhoWrEP 89
Baldwin, Everett N. 1932- St&PR 91
Baldwin, Everett Newton 1932- WhoAm 90
Baldwin, Faith 1893-1978 FemiCLE
Baldwin, Francis Gregory 1956- St&PR 91
Baldwin, Frank Bruce, III 1939- WhoAm 90
Baldwin, Frank Dwight 1842-1923 WhNaAH
Baldwin, Gary Eual 1937- St&PR 91
Baldwin, Gary Lee 1943- WhoAm 90
Baldwin, Garza, Jr. 1921- St&PR 91, WhoAm 90
Baldwin, George Curriden 1917- WhoAm 90
Baldwin, Gordo AuBYP 90
Baldwin, Gordon Brewster 1929- WhoAm 90, WhoWor 91
Baldwin, Gordon C. 1908- AuBYP 90
Baldwin, Gregory Alan 1946- WhoEmL 91
Baldwin, Gustave B., III 1942- St&PR 91
Baldwin, H. Furlong 1932- St&PR 91
Baldwin, Harold Fletcher 1923- WhoAmA 91
Baldwin, Harry, II WhoAmA 91N
Baldwin, Henry Furlong 1932- WhoAm 90
Baldwin, Irene S. 1939- WhoAmW 91
Baldwin, James 1841-1925 AuBYP 90
Baldwin, James 1924-1987 BioIn 16, DrBlPA 90, MajTwCW, WorAlBi
Baldwin, James J. 1937- St&PR 91
Baldwin, James Patric 1954- WhoEmL 91
Baldwin, James Ray 1935- St&PR 91
Baldwin, James William 1923- WhoAm 90
Baldwin, Janet DeLage 1933- St&PR 91
Baldwin, Janice Murphy 1926- WhoAmW 91
Baldwin, Janice Renee BiDrAPA 89
Baldwin, Jeffrey Kenton 1954- WhoEmL 91
Baldwin, Jeffrey William 1958- WhoEmL 91
Baldwin, John 1922-1987 WhoAmA 91N
Baldwin, John Ashby, Jr. 1933- WhoAm 90
Baldwin, John Brown 1820-1873 AmLegL
Baldwin, John Charles 1948- WhoAm 90, WhoWor 91
Baldwin, John D 1930- BiDrAPA 89
Baldwin, John Edwin 1937- WhoAm 90
Baldwin, John Lucian 1926- St&PR 91
Baldwin, John Wesley 1929- WhoAm 90
Baldwin, Kathleen Cooper 1944- BiDrAPA 89
Baldwin, Kathren St&PR 91
Baldwin, Kenneth Price 1926- St&PR 91
Baldwin, Kim Stacy 1959- WhoAmW 91
Baldwin, Lady 1859-1937 Ballpl 90
Baldwin, Lee G., Jr. 1922- St&PR 91
Baldwin, Leona B. 1934- WhoAmW 91
Baldwin, Louisa 1845-1925 FemiCLE
Baldwin, Lucian E. 1925- St&PR 91
Baldwin, Lynne J. 1946- St&PR 91
Baldwin, Margaret Morgan 1952- WhoSSW 91
Baldwin, Marie BiDrAPA 89
Baldwin, Mark 1865-1929 Ballpl 90
Baldwin, Mark Patrick 1950- St&PR 91
Baldwin, Martha Martin 1941- WhoSSW 91
Baldwin, Max Russell, Jr. 1964- WhoEmL 91
Baldwin, Melvin Dana, II 1941- St&PR 91
Baldwin, Muriel Frances WhoAmA 91N
Baldwin, Nancy Chen 1950- WhoAmW 91
Baldwin, Neil 1947- ConAu 130
Baldwin, Oliver Hazard Perry BioIn 16
Baldwin, Peter Arthur 1932- WhoAm 90
Baldwin, Phillip Benjamin 1924- WhoAm 90
Baldwin, Ralph Belknap 1912- St&PR 91
Baldwin, Rhoda Louise 1927- St&PR 91
Baldwin, Richard Duane BiDrAPA 89
Baldwin, Richard Wood 1920- WhoAmA 91
Baldwin, Rick 1953- Ballpl 90
Baldwin, Robert C. 1905-1988 BioIn 16
Baldwin, Robert C. 1934- St&PR 91
Baldwin, Robert Davidson 1937- St&PR 91
Baldwin, Robert Edward 1924- WhoAm 90
Baldwin, Robert Frederick, Jr. 1939- WhoAm 90
Baldwin, Robert George 1927- WhoAm 90
Baldwin, Robert Hayes Burns BioIn 16
Baldwin, Robert Lesh 1927- WhoAm 90
Baldwin, Robert Martin 1924- St&PR 91
Baldwin, Robert McCuller 1954- WhoEmL 91
Baldwin, Roderick George 1946- St&PR 91
Baldwin, Roger 1928- WhoE 91
Baldwin, Roger M. 1953- St&PR 91
Baldwin, Roger N. 1884-1981 WorAlBi
Baldwin, Ronald Kent 1947- St&PR 91
Baldwin, Russell W 1933- WhoAmA 91
Baldwin, Scott BioIn 16
Baldwin, Stan 1929- SmATA 62 [port]
Baldwin, Stephen BioIn 16
Baldwin, Susan L. 1949- ODwPR 91
Baldwin, Thomas 1753-1825 BioIn 16
Baldwin, Velma Neville Wilson 1918- WhoAmW 91, WhoE 91
Baldwin, Wayne Jay 1948- St&PR 91
Baldwin, Wendy Harmer 1945- WhoAmW 91
Baldwin, William, Jr. 1903-1983 ConAu 129
Baldwin, William A. 1949- WhoHisp 91
Baldwin, William David 1939- WhoAm 90
Baldwin, William Henry 1827-1894 DcCanB 12
Baldwin, William Howard 1916- WhoAm 90
Baldwin, William Lee 1928- WhoAm 90
Baldwin, William Russell 1926- WhoAm 90
Baldwyn, Rodney Clifford 1927- IntWWM 90
Baleela, Moustafa 1941- WhoWor 91
Balegno, Sergio 1953- WhoEmL 91
Balek, Thomas J. 1954- St&PR 91
Balenciaga BioIn 16
Balenciaga, Cristobal 1895-1972 ConDes 90, WorAlBi
Balent, Andrew BioIn 16
Balent, Andrew 1934- IntWWM 90
Balenti, Joyce G. 1951- WhoAmW 91
Balentine, Donald C. 1943- St&PR 91
Balentine, Phil H. 1928- St&PR 91
Balentine, Robert Chapman 1934- WhoSSW 91
Baler, Blanche K 1924- BiDrAPA 89
Bales, Carol Ann 1940- BioIn 16
Bales, J 1946- WhoAmA 91
Bales, Jack ConAu 30NR
Bales, James E 1951- ConAu 30NR
Bales, Jewel 1911- WhoAmA 91
Bales, John Thompson 1941- WhoE 91
Bales, Keith Stuart 1946- WhoWor 91
Bales, Kent Roslyn 1936- WhoAm 90
Bales, Lidia BiDrAPA 89
Bales, Richard 1915- IntWWM 90
Bales, Richard Henry Horner 1915- WhoAm 90
Bales, Robert Freed 1916- WhoAm 90
Bales, Ronald C. 1938- WhoAm 90
Bales, Royal Eugene 1934- WhoAm 90
Bales, Susan Morgan Lee 1945- WhoAmW 91
Bales, Thomas Oren, Jr. 1948- WhoSSW 91
Bales, Velma Jean Reckling 1927- WhoWrEP 89
Bales, William NewYTBS 90
Bales, William Baxter 1935- St&PR 91
Bales-Courte, Joy Diane 1958- WhoEmL 91
Balestiero, Peter John 1943- St&PR 91
Balestreri, Ted BioIn 16
Balestrero, Gregory 1947- WhoAm 90, WhoSSW 91
Balestrino, Claudio 1923- WhoWor 91
Balet, Elizabeth Virtue 1948- WhoE 91
Balet, Jan Bernard 1913- AuBYP 90
Balewa, Eshe 1939- WhoAmW 91
Baley, Geneve WhoWrEP 89
Baley, Thomas Richard 1948- WhoEmL 91
Balfe, Harry 1922- WhoE 91
Balfe, Michael William 1808-1870 BioIn 16, PenDiMPA
Balfort, Neil ConAu 32NR
Balfour, Lord 1897-1988 AnObit 1988
Balfour, Arthur 1848-1930 WorAlBi
Balfour, Arthur James 1848-1903 EncPaPR 91
Balfour, Arthur James 1848-1930 BioIn 16, EncO&P 3
Balfour, Clara 1808-1878 FemiCLE
Balfour, Douglas James 1952- WhoEmL 91
Balfour, Gerald William 1853-1945 EncO&P 3, EncPaPR 91
Balfour, Henry Hallowell, Jr. 1940- WhoAm 90, WhoWor 91
Balfour, Katharine BioIn 16, NewYTBS 90
Balfour, Mary 1755?-1820? FemiCLE
Balfour, Reginald James 1928- WhoAm 90
Balfour, Robert William 1954- St&PR 91
Balfour, St. Clair 1910- St&PR 91
Balfour, Victoria 1954- ConAu 129
Balfour, William Douglas 1851-1896 DcCanB 12
Balfour, William Mayo 1914- WhoAm 90
Balgord, James R. 1941- St&PR 91
Bali, Domkat Yah 1940- WhoWor 91
Balian, Harry 1958- WhoE 91
Balian, Lorna 1929- AuBYP 90
Balich, George T. WhoAm 90
Balick, Helen Shaffer WhoAmW 91
Balick, Steven Jeffrey 1956- WhoEmL 91
Balicki, Boguslaw 1937- ConDes 90
Balicki, Mikolaj W. BioIn 16
Baliga, Bantval Jayant 1948- WhoAm 90
Baliga, Ravindranath 1949- BiDrAPA 89
Balikov, Harold BiDrAPA 89
Balikov, Henry R. 1946- WhoWor 91
Baliles, Gerald L. 1940- WhoAm 90, WhoSSW 91, WhoWor 91
Balin, Ina NewYTBS 90 [port]
Balin, Marty 1942- WhoAm 90
Balinski, Michel Louis 1933- WhoWor 91
Balinsky, David 1944- St&PR 91
Balinsky, Edward 1929- St&PR 91
Balinson, Norman V BiDrAPA 89
Baliotis, Stephen St&PR 91
Balis, Charles Edward 1935- St&PR 91
Balis, George S. 1947- St&PR 91
Balis, George U 1929- BiDrAPA 89
Balis, Moses Earl 1921- WhoAm 90
Balistreri, Virginia M. 1947- ODwPR 91
Bality, Irene Milvius 1925- St&PR 91
Baliunas, Sallie Louise 1953- WhoAm 90, WhoAmW 91, WhoEmL 91
Balius, Louis Merrill 1936- St&PR 91
Balk, Alfred William 1930- WhoAm 90, WhoWrEP 89
Balk, Fairuza BioIn 16
Balk, Kenneth 1934- WhoAm 90
Balk, Melvin W. 1943- St&PR 91
Balka, Sigmund Ronell 1935- WhoE 91, WhoWor 91
Balkcom, Carol Ann 1952- WhoAmW 91, WhoEmL 91
Balke, Victor H. 1931- WhoAm 90
Balkey, Rita 1922- ConAu 30NR
Balkin, Ruth Goldring 1951- WhoAmW 91, WhoEmL 91
Balkin, Seymour David 1920- St&PR 91
Balkind, Alvin Louis 1921- WhoAm 90, WhoAmA 91
Balkis WomWR
Balkman, James H. 1936- St&PR 91
Balko, Gregg Brian 1951- WhoEmL 91
Balkoski, Victoria BiDrAPA 89
Balkoura, Athanasia BiDrAPA 89
Balkus-Knight, Joan Claire 1933- WhoAmW 91
Balkwill, Bryan Havell 1922- IntWWM 90
Ball, Andrew Justin 1949- WhoWor 91
Ball, Angela 1952- WhoWrEP 89
Ball, Anne H. 1939- WhoAmW 91
Ball, Armand Baer 1930- WhoAm 90
Ball, Ben Calhoun, Jr. 1928- WhoE 91
Ball, Blair Evan 1954- WhoEmL 91, WhoSSW 91, WhoWor 91
Ball, Brad BioIn 16
Ball, Brian F. 1945- St&PR 91
Ball, Carol Maskaleris 1956- ODwPR 91
Ball, Carroll Raybourne 1925- WhoAm 90
Ball, Charles Elihue 1924- WhoAm 90
Ball, Charles Thomas 1962- WhoEmL 91
Ball, Christina F 1952- BiDrAPA 89
Ball, Corinne BioIn 16
Ball, Darrell Wayne 1960- WhoEmL 91
Ball, David George 1936- St&PR 91
Ball, David Standish WhoAm 90
Ball, Desmond John 1947- WhoWor 91
Ball, Dianne Mitchell WhoAmA 91
Ball, Donald Edward 1949- WhoEmL 91
Ball, Donald Lewis 1922- WhoAm 90
Ball, Donald Lincoln 1932- St&PR 91
Ball, Donald Ray, Jr. 1956- St&PR 91
Ball, Douglas Schelling 1920- WhoAm 90
Ball, Edward H., Jr. 1923- St&PR 91
Ball, Elissa Mary 1954- BiDrAPA 89
Ball, Elizabeth Pierce 1959- WhoAmW 91
Ball, Eric 1903-1989 AnObit 1989, OxCPMus
Ball, Ernest 1878-1927 WorAlBi
Ball, Ernest R. 1878-1927 OxCPMus
Ball, Eugene Hugh 1921- BiDrAPA 89
Ball, Frances Louise 1924- WhoAmW 91
Ball, Frank Jervey 1919- WhoAm 90
Ball, Fred Shelton 1932- WhoAm 90
Ball, George Carl 1921- WhoAm 90
Ball, George L. WhoAm 90, WhoE 91
Ball, George W. BioIn 16
Ball, George Wildman 1909- WhoAm 90, WhoWrEP 89
Ball, Gordon 1948- St&PR 91
Ball, H. Stuart 1943- St&PR 91
Ball, Hannah 1734-1792 FemiCLE
Ball, Henry PenDiDA 89
Ball, Henry A. 1915- St&PR 91
Ball, Hiram P. St&PR 91
Ball, Howard 1937- WhoAm 90
Ball, Howard Guy 1930- WhoAm 90
Ball, Howard Lee 1929- WhoE 91
Ball, Ivern Imogene 1926- WhoWrEP 89
Ball, James Allan 1943- WhoE 91, WhoSSW 91
Ball, James Atward, III 1941- ODwPR 91
Ball, James P. 1950- St&PR 91
Ball, James Peter 1950- WhoSSW 91
Ball, James Robert 1944- St&PR 91
Ball, Jess Carl 1941- St&PR 91
Ball, Joe Dale 1949- WhoSSW 91, WhoWor 91
Ball, John 1911- AuBYP 90
Ball, John 1911-1988 AnObit 1988, TwCCr&M 91
Ball, John Charles 1949- WhoEmL 91
Ball, John Dudley 1911- WorAlBi
Ball, John Dudley 1911-1988 BioIn 16
Ball, John Fleming 1930- WhoAm 90
Ball, John H. 1919- St&PR 91
Ball, John Hanstein 1919- WhoAm 90
Ball, John K. 1958- St&PR 91
Ball, John Paul 1946- WhoAm 90
Ball, John Robert 1944- WhoAm 90

Ball, John W. 1925- St&PR 91
Ball, Joseph W 1932- BiDrAPA 89
Ball, Joyce 1932- WhoAm 90
Ball, K. 1932- St&PR 91
Ball, Kay Evans 1952- WhoEmL 91
Ball, Kenny 1930- OxCPMus
Ball, Larry Russell 1946- WhoSSW 91
Ball, Laurence Joseph 1945- WhoSSW 91
Ball, Leonard F. 1939- St&PR 91
Ball, Lewis Edwin, II 1931- St&PR 91, WhoAm 90
Ball, Lillian 1955- WhoAmA 91
Ball, Linda Suzanne 1951- WhoAmW 91
Ball, Lorraine 1956- WhoSSW 91
Ball, Louis Oliver 1929- IntWWM 90
Ball, Lucille 1911-1989 AnObit 1989, BioAmW, BioIn 16, ConTFT 8 [port], OxCPMus, WorAlBi
Ball, Lyle V 1909- WhoAmA 91
Ball, M. Isabel 1929- WhoAmW 91
Ball, Maria-Elena 1940- WhoAmW 91
Ball, Markham 1934- WhoAm 90
Ball, Markley 1959- WhoEmL 91
Ball, Mattie 1888- BioIn 16
Ball, Mavis Maxine 1921- WhoAmW 91
Ball, Michael 1946- IntWWM 90
Ball, Michael Lee 1946- St&PR 91
Ball, Neal 1881-1957 Ballpl 90
Ball, Nelson T. 1924- St&PR 91
Ball, Nicole 1948- ConAu 31NR
Ball, Owen Keith, Jr. 1950- WhoEmL 91
Ball, Patricia Ann 1941- WhoAmW 91
Ball, Patrick NewAgMG
Ball, Phil deCateesby 1864-1933 Ballpl 90
Ball, Philip L. 1934- St&PR 91
Ball, Randall Eugene 1956- WhoSSW 91
Ball, Rex Martin 1934- St&PR 91
Ball, Richard Woodruff 1946- St&PR 91
Ball, Robert H. 1944- St&PR 91
Ball, Robert Hamilton 1902-1988 BioIn 16
Ball, Robert L. 1946- St&PR 91
Ball, Robert M. 1914- WhoAm 90, WhoWrEP 89
Ball, Robert Michael 1952- WhoAm 90
Ball, Roberta R 1940- BiDrAPA 89
Ball, Roger C. St&PR 91
Ball, Roger T. St&PR 91
Ball, Ronald Edward 1946- WhoEmL 91
Ball, Sheri Beth 1963- WhoAmW 91
Ball, Stuart 1956- ConAu 130
Ball, Susan K 1943- BiDrAPA 89
Ball, Susan Kay 1959- WhoAmW 91
Ball, Susan L 1947- WhoAmA 91
Ball, Susan Lee 1947- WhoAm 90, WhoAmW 91
Ball, Susan Lucille 1961- WhoAmW 91
Ball, Theresa Kilgore 1951- WhoSSW 91
Ball, Thomas F 1924- BiDrAPA 89
Ball, Thomas J. 1936- St&PR 91
Ball, Walter N 1930- WhoAmA 91
Ball, Wes T. 1956- WhoEmL 91
Ball, William PenDiDA 89
Ball, William Amos 1932- St&PR 91
Ball, William Austin 1948- WhoE 91
Ball, William Bentley 1916- WhoAm 90
Ball, William Ernest 1930- WhoAm 90
Ball, William Kenneth 1927- WhoAm 90
Ball, William Lee 1959- WhoEmL 91
Ball, William Lockhart, III 1948- WhoAm 90
Ball, Zachary AuBYP 90
Balla, Giacomo 1871-1958 IntDcAA 90, PenDiDA 89
Balla, Wesley G. 1955- WhoE 91
Balladur, Edouard 1929- BiDFrPL
Ballagas, Emilio BioIn 16
Ballah, Lennox F. 1929- WhoWor 91
Ballal, Sunil Chandra 1947- BiDrAPA 89
Ballam, Joseph 1917- WhoAm 90
Ballam, Samuel Humes, Jr. 1919- WhoAm 90
Ballance, Robert Michael 1957- WhoEmL 91
Ballanfant, Kathleen Gamber 1945- WhoAmW 91
Ballanfant, Lee 1895- Ballpl 90
Ballantine, Christopher John 1942- IntWWM 90
Ballantine, Ian 1916- WhoAm 90, WhoWrEP 89, WorAlBi
Ballantine, Ian Keith 1916- ConAmBL
Ballantine, James C. 1941- St&PR 91
Ballantine, Morley Cowles 1925- WhoAm 90, WhoAmW 91
Ballantine, William Thomas 1945- St&PR 91
Ballantyne, Catherine Turk 1912- WhoAmA 91
Ballantyne, Dorothy Dunning 1910- WhoAmW 91
Ballantyne, Lowyd W. R. 1923-1989 BioIn 16
Ballantyne, Richard L. 1939- WhoAm 90
Ballantyne, Richard Lee 1939- St&PR 91
Ballantyne, Robert Jadwin 1925- WhoAm 90
Ballantyne, Robert Michael 1825-1894 DcCanB 12
Ballantyne, Sara BioIn 16
Ballantyne, W.G. 1942- St&PR 91
Ballard, Betty Ruth Wesley 1924- WhoAmW 91
Ballard, Bruce Laine 1939- BiDrAPA 89
Ballard, Burnie William 1950- WhoEmL 91
Ballard, Carlos Raymond, Jr. 1926- St&PR 91
Ballard, Carlos Raymond, Sr. 1907- St&PR 91
Ballard, Carroll 1937- ConTFT 8
Ballard, Charles Alan St&PR 91, WhoAm 90
Ballard, Charles Lee 1933- WhoSSW 91
Ballard, Charlotte BioIn 16
Ballard, Claude BioIn 16
Ballard, Claude Mark, Jr. 1929- WhoAm 90
Ballard, David Eugene 1949- WhoAm 90
Ballard, Debbi Ann 1949- WhoEmL 91
Ballard, Del, Jr. BioIn 16
Ballard, Donald A BiDrAPA 89
Ballard, Edna Anne Wheeler NewAgE 90
Ballard, Edward Brooks 1906- WhoAm 90
Ballard, Edward Goodwin 1910- ConAu 30NR, WhoWrEP 89
Ballard, Edward L. BioIn 16
Ballard, Emmett Jessee, II 1950- WhoEmL 91
Ballard, Eugene Henry 1934- WhoAm 90
Ballard, Frederick Armstrong 1907- WhoAm 90
Ballard, Glenda Day 1943- WhoAmW 91
Ballard, Guy W 1878-1939 EncO&P 3
Ballard, Guy Warren 1878-1939 NewAgE 90
Ballard, Hank 1936- EncPR&S 89
Ballard, Harold BioIn 16
Ballard, Harold 1903-1990 NewYTBS 90 [port]
Ballard, J. G. 1930- BioIn 16
Ballard, J G 1930- MajTwCW
Ballard, J. G. 1930- RGTwCSF
Ballard, James Graham NewYTBS 90 [port]
Ballard, James Henry Curtis 1934- WhoSSW 91
Ballard, Jeff 1963- Ballpl 90
Ballard, John Houston 1944- St&PR 91
Ballard, John Stuart 1922- WhoAm 90
Ballard, John W., Jr. 1922- St&PR 91
Ballard, John William, Jr. 1922- WhoAm 90
Ballard, K. G. TwCCr&M 91
Ballard, Larry Coleman 1935- St&PR 91, WhoAm 90
Ballard, Linda Burdick 1958- WhoAmW 91
Ballard, Lockett Ford, Jr 1946- WhoAmA 91
Ballard, Louis Wayne 1931- WhoAm 90
Ballard, Lowell Clyne 1904-1988 BioIn 16
Ballard, Lowell Douglas 1933- WhoE 91, WhoWor 91
Ballard, Lucien BioIn 16
Ballard, Lucien 1908-1988 AnObit 1988
Ballard, Lucinda 1906- NotWoAT
Ballard, Lucinda 1908?- BioIn 16
Ballard, Marguerite Louisa Candler 1920- WhoAmW 91
Ballard, Marshall 1942- St&PR 91
Ballard, Martha Moore 1735-1812 BioIn 16
Ballard, Marvin K 1938- BiDrAPA 89
Ballard, Mary Beth 1954- WhoEmL 91
Ballard, Mary Melinda 1957- WhoAm 90, WhoAmW 91
Ballard, Melinda M. 1951- ODwPR 91
Ballard, Melinda Mary 1956- WhoAm 90
Ballard, Michael Eugene 1953- WhoEmL 91
Ballard, Michael P. 1950- St&PR 91
Ballard, Mignon Franklin 1934- BioIn 16, SmATA 64
Ballard, P. D. TwCCr&M 91
Ballard, Paul Eugene, Jr. 1951- WhoSSW 91
Ballard, Phillip Ault, Jr. BiDrAPA 89
Ballard, Richard Alan 1946- St&PR 91
Ballard, Robert Duane 1942- WhoAm 90
Ballard, Ronald Michael 1958- WhoEmL 91
Ballard, Sallie Gethers 1938- WhoSSW 91
Ballard, Stanley Sumner 1908- WhoAm 90
Ballard, Theresa Marie 1962- WhoEmL 91
Ballard, Thomas Hickok 1941- WhoAm 90, WhoSSW 91
Ballard, Thomas William 1950- WhoSSW 91
Ballard, Walter BioIn 16
Ballard, William Hedges 1951- WhoSSW 91
Ballard, Willis Todhunter 1903-1980 TwCCr&M 91
Ballard, Yolanda BioIn 16
Ballard-Sell, Susan Elizabeth 1956- WhoAmW 91
Balleani, Aurelio Baldeschi- BioIn 16
Ballek, Ann Warburton ODwPR 91
Ballek, Ladislav 1941- WhoWor 91
Ballem, John Bishop 1925- WhoAm 90
Ballen, Ada Sara 1951- WhoE 91
Ballen, John W. 1959- St&PR 91
Ballen, Philip Henry BiDrAPA 89
Ballen, Robert Gerald 1956- WhoEmL 91
Ballen, Samuel Bernard 1922- St&PR 91
Ballengee, Bert 1924- St&PR 91
Ballengee, James M. 1923- St&PR 91
Ballengee, James McMorrow 1923- WhoAm 90
Ballengee, James R. 1935- St&PR 91
Ballengee, Jerry Hunter 1937- St&PR 91
Ballengee, John M. 1950- St&PR 91
Ballenger, David Louis 1944- St&PR 91
Ballenger, James Caudell 1944- BiDrAPA 89
Ballenger, John George 1931- St&PR 91, WhoE 91
Ballenger, Thomas Cass 1926- St&PR 91, WhoAm 90, WhoSSW 91
Ballenger, William Leighton 1934- ODwPR 91
Ballentine, Henry Vern 1955- WhoSSW 91
Ballentine, J. Gregory 1948- WhoAm 90
Ballentine, James Macallan, Jr. 1933- St&PR 91
Ballentine, Lee Kenney 1954- WhoWrEP 89
Ballentine, Ralph Edwin, II BiDrAPA 89
Ballentine, Richard O. 1936- St&PR 91
Ballentine, Rudolph M. 1941- WhoWrEP 89
Baller, James 1947- WhoEmL 91
Baller, Jay 1960- Ballpl 90
Balles, John Joseph 1921- WhoAm 90
Ballester, Frank 1908- St&PR 91
Ballester, Jose Felix 1944- St&PR 91
Ballestero, Manuel 1937- WhoHisp 91
Ballesteros, David 1933- WhoHisp 91
Ballesteros, Hugo 1923- WhoHisp 91
Ballesteros, Juventino Ray, Jr. 1953- WhoEmL 91, WhoSSW 91, WhoWor 91
Ballesteros, Mario Alberto 1952- WhoHisp 91
Ballesteros, Mercedes 1913- EncCoWW
Ballesteros, Seve BioIn 16
Ballesteros, Severiano 1957- WhoWor 91
Ballestrero, Anastasio Alberto 1913- WhoWor 91
Ballew, Anthony Robert 1952- WhoEmL 91
Ballew, Charles William 1931- WhoAm 90
Ballew, David Wayne 1940- WhoAm 90
Ballew, Doris Evelyn 1938- WhoAmW 91
Ballew, Jeffery Allen 1955- St&PR 91
Ballew, Mary Augusta 1951- WhoAmW 91
Ballew, Nellie Hester 1914- WhoAmW 91
Balley, Murray 1933- St&PR 91
Balleza, Phillip Bersoza BiDrAPA 89
Ballhaus, Michael 1935- BioIn 16
Ballhaus, William Francis 1918- WhoAm 90
Ballhaus, William Francis, Jr. 1945- WhoAm 90, WhoEmL 91
Ballich, Nicholas L, Jr. 1913- BiDrAPA 89
Balliet, Jeniffer Dee BiDrAPA 89
Balliet, Marvin Joseph 1957- WhoEmL 91
Balliett, Gene 1931- WhoAm 90
Balliett, Pierre Boucher 1934- St&PR 91
Balliett, Whitney 1926- ConAu 30NR, WhoAm 90, WhoWrEP 89
Ballif, Claude 1924- IntWWM 90
Ballin, Claude, I 1615?-1678 PenDiDA 89
Ballin, Claude, II 1661-1754 PenDiDA 89
Ballin, Gene 1919- St&PR 91
Ballin, Hugo 1879-1956 WhoAmA 91N
Ballin, Mogens 1871-1914 PenDiDA 89
Ballin, William Christopher 1927- WhoAm 90, WhoWor 91
Ballina, Rafael A. Penalver BioIn 16
Ballina, Robin Regina 1951- BiDrAPA 89
Ballinger, Bill S. 1912-1980 TwCCr&M 91
Ballinger, Charles Kenneth 1950- WhoEmL 91
Ballinger, Ed 1869-1966 Ballpl 90
Ballinger, Harry Russell 1892- WhoAm 90
Ballinger, James K 1949- WhoAmA 91
Ballinger, Janet Lynn 1948- WhoEmL 91
Ballinger, Malcolm George 1947- St&PR 91
Ballinger, Michael C. ODwPR 91
Ballinger, Richard Achilles 1858-1922 BiDrUSE 89
Ballinger, Walter Francis 1925- WhoAm 90
Ballinger, William Sanborn 1912-1980 SpyFic
Ballis, Richard Paul 1940- St&PR 91
Ballista, Antonio 1936- IntWWM 90, PenDiMP
Ballman, Donald K. 1910-1989 BioIn 16
Ballmer, Ray Wayne 1926- WhoAm 90
Ballmer, Walter 1923- ConDes 90
Ballmeyer, William Henry 1946- St&PR 91
Ballner-Bear, Lisabeth Geiser 1950- WhoEmL 91
Ballocq, E. J. 1873-1949 BioIn 16
Ballon, Edward Mahler 1925- WhoAm 90
Ballon, Lawrence Marc 1947- BiDrAPA 89
Ballon, Robert J 1919- WhoWrEP 89
Ballot, Alissa E. 1955- WhoEmL 91
Ballot, Bryan Allen BiDrAPA 89
Ballots, Joan Hessdorfer 1932- WhoE 91
Ballou, Adin 1803-1890 EncO&P 3
Ballou, Anne MacDougall WhoAmA 91
Ballou, Carol Bryan BiDrAPA 89
Ballou, Earline 1935- WhoSSW 91
Ballou, Kathy Deanne Taylor 1951- WhoAmW 91, WhoEmL 91, WhoWor 91
Ballou, Kenneth Walter 1930- WhoAm 90
Ballou, Sullivan 1829-1861 AmLegL
Ballou, Win 1897-1963 Ballpl 90
Balloun, Joseph Le 1941- WhoSSW 91
Ballowe, James 1933- WhoAm 90
Balluck, Don BioIn 16
Balluff, John Joseph 1910- WhoWor 91
Ballweber, Hettie Lou 1944- WhoAmW 91
Ballwieser, Wolfgang Karl 1948- WhoWor 91
Bally, Laurent Marie Joseph 1943- WhoWor 91
Balmaceda, Jose Manuel 1840-1891 BioIn 16
Balmaceda, Margarita S 1933- WhoAmA 91
Balmain, Keith George 1933- WhoAm 90
Balmain, Pierre 1914-1982 ConDes 90, WorAlBi
Balmaseda, Elizabeth R. 1959- WhoHisp 91
Balme, David 1912-1989 AnObit 1989
Balme, Louis 1951- WhoWor 91
Balmer, Edwin 1883-1959 TwCCr&M 91
Balmer, James Walter 1948- WhoAm 90
Balmer, Thomas Ancil 1952- WhoEmL 91
Balmes, Edward James 1953- St&PR 91
Balmori, Diana 1936- WhoE 91
Balodis, Frances Mae 1949- IntWWM 90
Baloff, Nicholas 1937- WhoAm 90
Balog, Betty Enocksen 1932- WhoWrEP 89
Balog, James 1928- St&PR 91, WhoAm 90
Balog, James Dennis 1952- WhoAm 90
Balog, John F 1934- BiDrAPA 89
Balog, Linda Marie 1946- WhoAmW 91
Balogh, Connie Lee 1949- WhoWor 91
Balogh, Endre 1954- IntWWM 90
Balogh, Erno 1897-1989 BioIn 16
Balogh, Julius Geza 1932- St&PR 91
Balogh, Michael L 1955- BiDrAPA 89
Balogh, Olga Mitana 1917- IntWWM 90
Balogh, Roger John 1954- BiDrAPA 89
Balogh, Stephen 1924- St&PR 91
Balogh, Thomas 1905-1985 DcNaB 1981
Balon, Richard 1951- BiDrAPA 89
Balose, Charles A. 1946- St&PR 91
Balossi, John 1931- WhoAmA 91
Baloun, John Charles 1934- St&PR 91, WhoAm 90
Balovlenkov, Elena BioIn 16
Balovlenkov, Yuri BioIn 16
Balow, Irving Henry 1927- WhoAm 90
Balows, Albert 1921- WhoAm 90
Baloy, Rolando A BiDrAPA 89
Baloyra, Enrique Antonio 1942- WhoAm 90, WhoHisp 91
Balph, Gail Elizabeth 1957- ODwPR 91
Balph, Martha Hatch 1943- WhoAmW 91
Balsam, Artur 1906- IntWWM 90, PenDiMP
Balsam, Gerald James BiDrAPA 89
Balsam, Martin 1919- WorAlBi
Balsam, Martin Henry 1919- WhoAm 90
Balsan, Consuelo V. 1877-1964 BioAmW
Balsan, Consuelo Vanderbilt 1877-1964 BioIn 16
Balsborg, Kaj 1937- WhoWor 91
Balseiro, Jose Agustin 1900- BioIn 16, HispWr 90
Balser, Elnora Marie 1952- WhoEmL 91
Balser, Paul Fisher 1942- WhoE 91
Balsiger, David Wayne 1945- WhoAm 90, WhoWrEP 89
Balsiger, John Richard 1932- St&PR 91
Balslev, Lisbeth 1945- IntWWM 90
Balsley, Howard Lloyd 1913- WhoAm 90, WhoWor 91
Balsley, James F. 1939- St&PR 91
Balsley, John Gerald 1944- WhoAmA 91
Balsley, Philip Elwood 1939- WhoAm 90
Balson, Paul Michael BiDrAPA 89
Balster, Gary Allen 1958- BiDrAPA 89
Balta, Victor A 1949- BiDrAPA 89
Baltake, Joe 1945- WhoAm 90, WhoWor 91
Baltakis, Paul Antanas 1925- WhoAm 90
Baltayan, Ara M. 1920- WhoE 91
Baltazar, Josephina Cifra BiDrAPA 89
Baltazzi, Evan Serge 1921- WhoAm 90
Baltensperger, Ernst 1942- WhoWor 91
Balter, Andrew Lloyd BiDrAPA 89
Balter, Frances Sunstein WhoAmW 91, WhoE 91
Balter, James Jonathan 1966- WhoE 91

Balter, Leon 1936- *BiDrAPA 89*
Balter, Leslie Marvin 1920- *WhoE 91*
Balter, Marie *BioIn 16*
Balter, Stuart M. *St&PR 91*
Balterman, Harry 1919- *St&PR 91*
Baltermants, Dmitri 1912-1990 *NewYTBS 90*
Baltes, Kenneth John 1936- *St&PR 91*
Baltes, Mark Edward *BioIn 16*
Baltes, Paul B. 1939- *WhoWor 91*
Balth, Carel 1939- *WhoWor 91*
Balthasar, Hans Urs von *ConAu 130*
Balthasar, Hans Urs von 1905-1988 *BioIn 16*
Balthazard, Mark Joseph 1957- *WhoEmL 91*
Balthazor, Albert, Jr. 1925- *WhoWor 91*
Balthild *WomWR*
Balthrop, Carmen 1954?- *DrBIPA 90*
Balthus 1908- *BioIn 16*
Baltimore, Lords of *EncCRAm*
Baltimore, David 1938- *BioIn 16, WhoAm 90, WhoE 91, WhoWor 91, WorAlBi*
Baltimore, Gertrude 1909-1988 *BioIn 16*
Baltis, Russell V., Jr. 1928- *St&PR 91*
Baltodano, Guiselle 1944- *WhoHisp 91*
Balton, Allen R. 1908- *St&PR 91*
Baltsa, Agnes 1944- *IntWWM 90, PenDiMP*
Baltuch, Leigh 1954- *BiDrAPA 89*
Baltus, Jean Francois 1667-1743 *EncO&P 3*
Baltz, Lewis 1945- *WhoAmA 91*
Baltz, Timothy Stephen 1957- *BiDrAPA 89*
Baltzell, Edward Digby 1915- *WhoAm 90*
Baltzell, Jean P. *BioIn 16*
Baltzer, Kimberly Lenore 1964- *WhoAmW 91*
Baltzer, Rebecca A. 1940- *IntWWM 90*
Baltzly, Alexander 1892-1989 *BioIn 16*
Baluni, Alice 1945- *WhoEmL 91*
Baluyot, Agustina A 1939- *BiDrAPA 89*
Baluyot, Cherita Costales 1947- *St&PR 91*
Balverde-Sanchez, Laura *BioIn 16*
Baly, Denis 1913-1987 *BioIn 16*
Balyeat, Kent Windsor 1925-1983 *BioIn 16*
Balyo, John Gabriel 1920- *WhoAm 90*
Balz, Daniel John 1946- *WhoAm 90*
Balz, Douglas Charles 1943- *WhoAm 90*
Balz, Frank Joseph 1950- *WhoE 91*
Balzac, Audrey FloBelle Adrian 1928- *WhoAmW 91, WhoE 91*
Balzac, Edme-Pierre *PenDiDA 89*
Balzac, Honore De 1799-1850 *WorAlBi*
Balzac, Jean-Francois *PenDiDA 89*
Balzani, Vincenzo 1936- *WhoWor 91*
Balzar-Koppe, Elfriede 1904- *PenDiDA 89*
Balzarett, Joseph R *BiDrAPA 89*
Balzekas, Stanley, Jr. 1924- *WhoAm 90*
Balzer, Daniel Lee 1937- *WhoE 91*
Balzer, Joel Adam 1962- *WhoE 91*
Baizhiser, Richard E. *BioIn 16*
Balzhiser, Richard Earl 1932- *WhoAm 90*
Balzotti, Linda Marie 1961- *WhoEmL 91*
Bam, Foster 1927- *WhoAm 90, WhoE 91, WhoWor 91*
Bamace, Angela 1900-1976 *BioIn 16*
Bamashmus, Abdalla Mohamed *BiDrAPA 89*
Bambace, Felix S 1906- *BiDrAPA 89*
Bambacus, John Nicholas 1945- *WhoE 91*
Bambara, A John *BiDrAPA 89*
Bambara, Toni Cade 1931- *FemiCLE*
Bambara, Toni Cade 1939- *Au&Arts 5 [port], MajTwCW*
Bambenek, John Charles, III *BiDrAPA 89*
Bamber, Margaret Mary 1953- *WhoAmW 91*
Bamberg, David 1904-1974 *BioIn 16*
Bamberg, Robert Douglas 1928- *WhoAm 90*
Bamberger, Carl 1902- *IntWWM 90*
Bamberger, Charles 1944- *WhoHisp 91*
Bamberger, David 1940- *IntWWM 90, WhoAm 90*
Bamberger, David Harned 1942- *WhoAm 90*
Bamberger, Elizabeth 1889- *BioIn 16*
Bamberger, Fred Hans 1898- *WhoE 91*
Bamberger, Gabrielle 1938- *WhoAmW 91*
Bamberger, George 1925- *Ballpl 90*
Bamberger, Gerald Francis 1920- *WhoAm 90*
Bamberger, J. David 1928- *St&PR 91, WhoAm 90*
Bamberger, Julia Kathryn 1960- *WhoAmW 91, WhoE 91*
Bamberger, Louis 1855-1944 *WorAlBi*
Bamberger, Michael Albert 1936- *WhoAm 90*
Bamberger, Robert J 1926- *BiDrAPA 89*
Bambic, Robert M. 1954- *WhoE 91*
Bambola, Vincent J. 1942- *St&PR 91*
Bambrick, James Alan 1946- *St&PR 91*
Bambrick, James Joseph 1917- *WhoWor 91*
Bambrick, Susan Caroline 1941- *WhoWor 91*
Bambrick, William H. *BioIn 16*
Bambrick, Winifred 1892?-1969 *FemiCLE*
Bambury, Joseph Anthony, Jr. 1932- *St&PR 91*
Bamdad, Jalil *BiDrAPA 89*
Bame, Samuel Jarvis, Jr. 1924- *WhoAm 90*
Bamert, Matthias 1942- *IntWWM 90, PenDiMP*
Bamford, Carol Marie 1948- *WhoEmL 91*
Bamford, Clement Henry 1912- *WhoWor 91*
Bamford, Edward G. 1932- *St&PR 91*
Bamford, Thomas Bennett 1928- *WhoE 91*
Bamford, Thomas Horst 1940- *St&PR 91*
Bamforth, Stuart Shoosmith 1926- *WhoAm 90*
Bamji, Dinshaw D *BiDrAPA 89*
Bamman, Robert H. 1921- *St&PR 91*
Bammel, Brian Paul 1943- *St&PR 91*
Bammes, Christina Lodell *BiDrAPA 89*
Bampi, Richard 1896-1965 *PenDiDA 89*
Bampoe, Isaac Godwin *BiDrAPA 89*
Bampton, Betsy Ann 1937- *WhoSSW 91*
Bampton, James William 1909- *WhoAm 90*
Bampton, Rose *BioIn 16*
Bampton, Rose E. *IntWWM 90*
Ban, Edward David 1949- *WhoEmL 91*
Ban, Joseph D 1926- *WhoWrEP 89*
Ban, Thomas A *BiDrAPA 89*
Ban, Zsofia Marcella 1957- *WhoWor 91*
Banaag, Cornelio G, Jr. *BiDrAPA 89*
Banach, Richard E. 1946- *St&PR 91*
Banach, Stefan 1892-1945 *BioIn 16*
Banados, Patricio *BioIn 16*
Banal, Vicente Heraldo 1938- *WhoWor 91*
Banales, Frank 1945- *WhoHisp 91*
Banales, Irma 1956- *WhoHisp 91*
Banana, Anna 1940- *WhoAmA 91*
Banana, Canaan Sodindo 1936- *WhoWor 91*
Banas, Anne 1948- *WhoAmA 91*
Banas, Richard Frederick 1948- *WhoEmL 91*
Banas, Ronald John 1936- *St&PR 91*
Banas, Stanley R. 1927- *St&PR 91*
Banas, William R *BiDrAPA 89*
Banash, Malinda E. 1959- *ODwPR 91*
Banashek, Mary-Ellen 1951- *WhoAmW 91*
Banasik, Robert Casmer 1942- *WhoWor 91*
Banasz, Walter Ronald 1943- *WhoE 91*
Banaszynski, Jacqueline Marie 1952- *WhoAm 90*
Banat, D R 1920- *SmATA X [port]*
Banazak, Deborah A. 1957- *BiDrAPA 89*
Banchoff, Thomas Francis 1938- *WhoAm 90*
Banchs, Enrique J. 1888-1968 *HispWr 90*
Bancquart, Marie-Claire 1932- *EncCoWW*
Bancroft, Alexander Clerihew 1938- *WhoAm 90*
Bancroft, Anne 1931- *BioAmW, BioIn 16, NotWoAT, WhoAm 90, WhoAmW 91, WorAlBi*
Bancroft, Arthur M. 1923- *St&PR 91*
Bancroft, Barbara *BioIn 16*
Bancroft, Bruce Richard 1940- *WhoAm 90*
Bancroft, Dave 1891-1972 *Ballpl 90 [port]*
Bancroft, Edgar Addison 1857-1925 *BioIn 16*
Bancroft, Edith D *BiDrAPA 89*
Bancroft, Edward 1744-1821 *EncCRAm*
Bancroft, Elizabeth Abercrombie 1947- *WhoAmW 91*
Bancroft, Frank C. 1846-1921 *Ballpl 90*
Bancroft, George 1800-1891 *BiDrUSE 89, BioIn 16, WorAlBi*
Bancroft, George Michael 1942- *WhoAm 90*
Bancroft, Griffing 1907- *AuBYP 90*
Bancroft, Hubert Howe 1832-1918 *WhNaAH*
Bancroft, James Ramsey 1919- *WhoAm 90*
Bancroft, Joseph C. 1900- *St&PR 91*
Bancroft, Laura *MajTwCW*
Bancroft, Levi Horace 1860-1948 *AmLegL*
Bancroft, Margaret Armstrong 1938- *WhoAmW 91*
Bancroft, Paul, III 1930- *St&PR 91, WhoAm 90, WhoE 91, WhoWor 91*
Bancroft, Ronald Mann 1943- *St&PR 91, WhoAm 90*
Bancroft, Squire 1841-1926 *BioIn 16*
Band, The *EncPR&S 89, OxCPMus*
Band, David 1942- *WhoAm 90, WhoWor 91*
Band, David Marc *BiDrAPA 89*
Band, David Moshe 1947- *WhoAmA 91*
Band, Jeffrey D. 1948- *WhoEmL 91*
Band, Raymond I 1924- *BiDrAPA 89*
Band, Stanley Irving 1930- *St&PR 91*
Banda, Marianne 1964- *WhoAmW 91*
Banda, Ngwazi Kamuzu 1906- *WhoWor 91*
Bandaranaike, S.W.R.D. 1899-1959 *BioIn 16*
Bandaranaike, Sirimavo 1916- *BioIn 16*
Bandaranaike, Sirimavo Ratevatte Dias 1916- *WomWR*
Bandaranaike, Solomon West Ridgeway Dias 1899-1959 *BioIn 16*
Bandeen, Robert Angus 1930- *St&PR 91, WhoAm 90*
Bandeen, William Reid 1926- *WhoAm 90*
Bandeian, John Jacob 1912- *WhoWor 91*
Bandeira, Manuel 1886-1968 *BioIn 16*
Bandel, Betty 1912- *BioIn 16*
Bandel, Lennon Raymond 1906- *WhoAmA 91*
Bandel, Manville H. 1930- *St&PR 91*
Bandelier, Adolph Francis Alphonse 1840-1914 *WhNaAH*
Bander, Carol Jean 1945- *WhoAmW 91*
Bander, Edward Julius 1923- *WhoE 91*
Bander, Martin Stanley 1928- *WhoE 91*
Bander, Myron 1937- *WhoAm 90*
Bander, Norman Robert *WhoSSW 91*
Bander, Peter 1930- *EncO&P 3*
Bander, Robert Nelson 1944- *WhoSSW 91*
Bander, Stephen *BioIn 16*
Bander, Thomas Samuel 1924- *WhoWor 91*
Bandera, Cesareo 1934- *WhoAm 90*
Bandera, Stefan 1909-1959 *BioIn 16*
Bandes, Chester 1930- *St&PR 91*
Bandettini, Teresa Landucci 1763-1836 *EncCoWW*
Bandiere, Richard C. 1943- *St&PR 91*
Bandiere, Richard Charles 1943- *WhoAm 90*
Bandieri, Leo P. 1929- *St&PR 91*
Bandini, Juan 1800-1859 *BioIn 16*
Bandini, Pietro *BioIn 16*
Bandla, Hanumaiah *BiDrAPA 89*
Bandle, Donald F 1920- *BiDrAPA 89*
Bandler, Bernard 1904- *BiDrAPA 89, WhoE 91*
Bandler, Faith 1918- *FemiCLE*
Bandler, John William 1941- *WhoAm 90*
Bandler, Michael Louis 1938- *St&PR 91, WhoAm 90*
Bandler, Ned Wendell 1929- *St&PR 91*
Bandler, Richard *BioIn 16*
Bandlow, Betty R 1931- *BiDrAPA 89*
Bando, Chris 1956- *Ballpl 90*
Bando, Sal 1944- *Ballpl 90 [port]*
Bando, Yoshichika 1934- *WhoWor 91*
Bandow, Douglas Leighton 1957- *WhoAm 90, WhoWor 91, WhoWrEP 89*
Bandrowski, James Francis 1948- *WhoEmL 91*
Bandrowski, Jeffrey A. 1942- *St&PR 91*
Bandt, Rosalie Edith 1951- *IntWWM 90*
Banducci, Enrico *BioIn 16*
Bandukwala, Quresh Z 1953- *BiDrAPA 89*
Bandura, Albert 1925- *BioIn 16, WhoAm 90*
Bandurski, Bruce Lord 1940- *WhoWor 91*
Bandy, Gary 1944- *WhoAmA 91*
Bandy, Jo Etta 1956- *St&PR 91*
Bandy, Lisa *ODwPR 91*
Bandy, Mary Lea 1943- *WhoAm 90, WhoAmA 91, WhoAmW 91*
Bandy, Orville Lee 1917-1973 *DcScB S2*
Bandy, Ron F 1936- *WhoAmA 91*
Bandy, W T 1903-1989 *ConAu 129*
Bandy, William T. 1903-1989 *BioIn 16*
Bane, Charles Arthur 1913- *WhoAm 90*
Bane, Eddie 1952- *Ballpl 90*
Bane, Madelyn Richardson 1942- *WhoAmW 91*
Bane, Margo Ewing 1949- *WhoAmW 91*
Bane, Marilyn A. 1943- *St&PR 91*
Bane, McDonald 1928- *WhoAmA 91*
Banegas, Marta Emilia *BiDrAPA 89*
Banerdt, Dawn Marie 1964- *WhoAmW 91*
Banerjee 1939- *WhoAm 90, WhoAmA 91, WhoE 91, WhoWor 91*
Banerjee, Amitava 1936- *WhoWor 91*
Banerjee, Arup Kumar 1936- *WhoWor 91*
Banerjee, Bela *BioIn 16*
Banerjee, Kamala Ranjan *BiDrAPA 89*
Banerjee, Nitaidas 1936- *WhoWor 91*
Banerjee, Samarendranath 1932- *WhoAm 90, WhoWor 91*
Banerji, Anandanath 1956- *WhoWor 91*
Banerji, Kalyan Sanjibon 1939- *WhoWor 91*
Banerji, Ranan Bihari 1928- *WhoAm 90*
Banerji, S. K. 1913- *BioIn 16*
Banerji, Shishir Kumar 1913- *BioIn 16*
Banes, Daniel 1918- *WhoAm 90, WhoWrEP 89*
Banet, Charles Henry 1922- *WhoAm 90*
Banet, Maurice H. 1937- *St&PR 91*
Baney, John Edward 1934- *St&PR 91, WhoAm 90*
Baney, Ralph Ramoutar 1929- *WhoAmA 91*
Baney, Richard Neil 1937- *WhoSSW 91*
Baney, Vera 1930- *WhoAmA 91*
Banez, Colita R 1941- *BiDrAPA 89*
Banfalvy, Bela *PenDiMP*
Banfer, Franklin Arthur, II 1959- *WhoEmL 91*
Banfi, Baffo *NewAgMG*
Banfield, Bever-Leigh *DrBIPA 90*
Banfield, Carolyn E. 1934- *WhoE 91*
Banfield, Edward Christie 1916- *WhoAm 90*
Banfield, Joanne 1954- *WhoAmW 91, WhoEmL 91*
Banfield, Stephen David 1951- *IntWWM 90*
Banford, David 1947- *St&PR 91*
Bang, Betsy 1912- *BioIn 16*
Bang, Carmen D. *WhoSSW 91*
Bang, Ed 1880-1968 *Ballpl 90*
Bang, Herman 1857-1912 *DcScanL*
Bang, Hieronymus 1553-1630 *PenDiDA 89*
Bang, John Charles 1948- *St&PR 91*
Bang, Molly Garrett 1943- *AuBYP 90*
Bang, Sherrie *ODwPR 91*
Bangara, Suresh *BiDrAPA 89*
Bangaru, Babu Rajendra Prasad 1947- *WhoEmL 91*
Bangaru, Rajyasri *BiDrAPA 89*
Bangasser, Elizabeth 1956- *WhoAmW 91*
Bangdiwala, Ishver Surchand 1922- *WhoAm 90*
Bangdiwala, Shrikant Ishver 1954- *WhoSSW 91*
Bange, Raymond Fabian 1939- *WhoWor 91*
Bangel, Edward W. 1942- *St&PR 91*
Bangert, Colette Stuebe 1934- *WhoAmA 91*
Bangert, Richard Elmer 1920- *WhoAm 90*
Bangerter, Darrell Howell 1935- *St&PR 91*
Bangerter, Lee R. 1944- *St&PR 91*
Bangerter, Norman Howard 1933- *WhoAm 90, WhoWor 91*
Bangham, Robert Arthur 1942- *WhoWor 91*
Banghart, Rick D. 1957- *WhoEmL 91*
Bangles, The *EncPR&S 89*
Bango, Francisco Jose 1948- *WhoSSW 91*
Bangou, Henri 1922- *BioIn 16*
Bangs Sisters *EncO&P 3*
Bangs, Carol Jane 1949- *WhoWrEP 89*
Bangs, Frank Kendrick 1914- *WhoAm 90*
Bangs, Jeremy Dupertuis 1946- *WhoE 91*
Bangs, John Kendrick 1920- *WhoAm 90*
Bangs, John Wesley, III 1941- *WhoWor 91*
Bangs, Lizzie *EncO&P 3, EncPaPR 91*
Bangs, Mark Edward *BiDrAPA 89*
Bangs, May *EncO&P 3, EncPaPR 91*
Bangs, Nelson A. 1952- *St&PR 91*
Bangs, Will Johnston 1923- *WhoAm 90*
Bangser, Henry Maimin 1930- *St&PR 91*
Bangura, Abdul Karim 1953- *WhoE 91*
Banham, Reyner *BioIn 16*
Banham, Reyner 1922-1988 *AnObit 1988*
Banholzer, Frank J. 1929- *St&PR 91*
Bani-Sadr, Abu al-Hasan *BioIn 16*
Baniak, Sheila Mary 1953- *WhoEmL 91, WhoWor 91*
Banis, William J. *BioIn 16*
Banister, Harold Bertram 1951- *WhoAm 90*
Banister, James H., Jr. 1930- *St&PR 91*
Banister, John 1734-1788 *EncCRAm*
Banister, Judith 1943- *WhoAmW 91*
Banister, Richard Albert 1948- *WhoE 91*
Banister, Ronald Kitchener 1917- *WhoAm 90*
Banister, Zilphia P. G. 1794-1874 *BioAmW*
Banitt, Peter Frederick 1962- *WhoEmL 91*
Banjo, Ladipo Ayodeji 1934- *WhoWor 91*
Bank, Arnold 1931-1989 *BioIn 16*
Bank, Jacques 1943- *IntWWM 90*
Bank, Jonathan F. 1943- *WhoAm 90*
Bank, Joseph 1938- *St&PR 91*
Bank, Malvin E. 1930- *WhoAm 90*
Bank, Ralph 1919- *St&PR 91*
Bank, Robert Louis 1948- *BiDrAPA 89*
Bank, Ronald 1906- *St&PR 91*
Bank, Steven Barry 1939- *WhoAm 90*
Bank, William Julius 1913- *WhoWor 91*
Bankaitis-Davis, Bunki *BioIn 16*
Bankard, Robert Roy 1937- *St&PR 91*
Banker, Clarice Emery 1947- *WhoSSW 91*
Banker, Cynthia Anne 1949- *WhoAmW 91*
Banker, Dave Vinodkumar 1943- *WhoSSW 91*
Banker, David Wayne 1959- *WhoEmL 91*
Banker, Edward Keith 1925- *St&PR 91*
Banker, Frederick William 1925- *St&PR 91*
Banker, Gilbert Stephen 1931- *WhoAm 90*
Banker, James R. 1938- *ConAu 132*
Banker, Joel I. 1927- *St&PR 91*
Bankert, Joseph Edward 1949- *WhoEmL 91*
Bankert, Pamela Beryl 1954- *WhoAmW 91*
Bankett, Paula R. 1959- *WhoAmW 91*
Bankhead, Dan 1920-1976 *Ballpl 90*

Bankhead, Sam 1910-1976 *Ballpl 90*
Bankhead, Scott 1963- *Ballpl 90*
Bankhead, Tallulah 1902-1968 *BioIn 16*
Bankhead, Tallulah 1903-1968 *BioAmW, WorAlBi*
Bankhead, Tallulah Brockman 1902-1968 *NotWoAT*
Bankier, Robert G 1926- *BiDrAPA 89*
Bankier, William 1928- *TwCCr&M 91*
Bankl, Hans Egmont 1940- *WhoWor 91*
Bankoff, Seymour George 1921- *WhoAm 90*
Bankowski, Mary Theresa 1931- *WhoAmW 91*
Banks, A L *ConAu 129*
Banks, A Leslie *ConAu 129*
Banks, Albert Victor, Jr. 1956- *WhoAm 90, WhoE 91, WhoEmL 91*
Banks, Allan R 1948- *WhoAmA 91*
Banks, Amy Elizabeth *BiDrAPA 89*
Banks, Anne Johnson 1924- *WhoAmA 91*
Banks, Annie Ashleigh 1957- *WhoAmW 91*
Banks, Arthur Leslie 1904-1989 *ConAu 129*
Banks, Arthur Sparrow 1926- *WhoAm 90*
Banks, Audrey C. *WhoAmW 91*
Banks, Bettie Sheppard 1933- *WhoAmW 91*
Banks, C. Vernon 1937- *St&PR 91*
Banks, Carolyn *WhoWrEP 89*
Banks, Cecil James 1947- *WhoAm 90*
Banks, David Charles 1938- *WhoWor 91*
Banks, David R. 1937- *St&PR 91*
Banks, David Russell 1937- *WhoAm 90*
Banks, Dean 1941- *St&PR 91*
Banks, Dennns Craig 1948- *St&PR 91*
Banks, Elizabeth 1870-1938 *FemiCLE*
Banks, Elmore Sherwood 1866-1936 *AmLegL*
Banks, Ephraim 1918- *WhoAm 90*
Banks, Ernie *BioIn 16*
Banks, Ernie 1931- *Ballpl 90 [port], WorAlBi*
Banks, George, Jr. 1958- *WhoEmL 91*
Banks, Hannah *BiDEWW*
Banks, Harold Ralph 1954- *WhoSSW 91*
Banks, Henry H. 1921- *WhoAm 90*
Banks, Henry Stephen 1920- *WhoE 91*
Banks, Hugh C. *NewYTBS 90*
Banks, Isabella 1821-1897 *FemiCLE*
Banks, Isabella Varley 1821-1897 *BioIn 16*
Banks, J.E. 1908- *St&PR 91*
Banks, Jacob William 1918- *St&PR 91*
Banks, Jacquelin LaVern 1939- *WhoE 91*
Banks, James A. 1828- *AmLegL*
Banks, James A 1941- *ConAu 32NR*
Banks, James Albert 1941- *WhoAm 90*
Banks, James B. 1951- *St&PR 91*
Banks, James Barber 1951- *WhoAm 90, WhoEmL 91*
Banks, James Paul 1941- *St&PR 91*
Banks, John Houston 1911- *WhoAm 90*
Banks, John L. 1949- *St&PR 91*
Banks, John Willard 1912-1988 *MusmAFA*
Banks, Jonathan *BioIn 16*
Banks, Joni Wheeler 1957- *WhoAmW 91, WhoSSW 91*
Banks, Joseph 1743-1820 *BioIn 16*
Banks, Joseph Eugene 1908- *WhoAm 90*
Banks, Karen Whitaker 1957- *WhoSSW 91*
Banks, Kenneth A. *BioIn 16*
Banks, Leslie J. 1953- *St&PR 91*
Banks, Lisa Jean 1956- *WhoAmW 91, WhoEmL 91, WhoWor 91*
Banks, Lloyd J. 1923- *St&PR 91*
Banks, Lynne Reid 1929- *AuBYP 90, BioIn 16*
Banks, Marcia Abbott 1958- *WhoEmL 91*
Banks, Margaret Amelia 1928- *WhoAmW 91*
Banks, Margaret Downie 1950- *IntWWM 90*
Banks, Marjorie Elaine 1945- *WhoEmL 91*
Banks, Mitchell Ford *BiDrAPA 89*
Banks, Nancy Houston 1850?-1934 *LiHiK*
Banks, Nathaniel 1816-1894 *WorAlBi*
Banks, Nathaniel Prentice, Jr. 1816-1894 *AmLegL*
Banks, Paula A. 1950- *WhoAmW 91*
Banks, Peter Morgan 1937- *WhoAm 90*
Banks, Philip Francis 1933- *St&PR 91*
Banks, Raymond Charles 1963- *WhoEmL 91*
Banks, Rela 1933- *WhoAm 90, WhoE 91*
Banks, Robert C. 1930- *St&PR 91*
Banks, Robert J. 1928- *WhoAm 90*
Banks, Robert Sherwood 1934- *St&PR 91, WhoAm 90*
Banks, Robert Thomas 1931- *WhoSSW 91*
Banks, Roland Fitzgerald, Jr. 1932- *WhoAm 90*
Banks, Russell 1919- *St&PR 91, WhoAm 90, WhoE 91, WhoWor 91*
Banks, Russell 1940- *BioIn 16, WorAu 1980 [port]*
Banks, Samuel Lee 1931- *WhoE 91*
Banks, Sheila *ODwPR 91*
Banks, Theodore Lee 1951- *WhoEmL 91*
Banks, Thomas 1735-1805 *BioIn 16*
Banks, Virginia 1920-1985 *WhoAmA 91N*
Banks-Tarr, Sharon Elizabeth 1950- *WhoAmW 91, WhoEmL 91*
Bankson, Douglas 1920- *ConAu 31NR*
Bankson, Douglas Henneck 1920- *WhoWrEP 89*
Bankston, Archie M. 1937- *St&PR 91*
Bankston, Archie Moore, Jr. 1937- *WhoAm 90*
Bankston, Gene Clifton 1924- *WhoAm 90*
Bankston, Gordon *BioIn 16*
Bankston, James William 1931- *St&PR 91*
Bann, Kathleen Winters 1957- *WhoAmW 91*
Banna, Hassan al- 1906-1949 *BioIn 16*
Banna, Sabri Khalil Al- 1937- *PolLCME*
Bannan, Bernard Jerome 1920- *St&PR 91*
Bannan, Charles F. 1915- *St&PR 91*
Bannard, Walter Darby 1934- *WhoAm 90, WhoAmA 91*
Bannasch, Gerald John *BiDrAPA 89*
Bannat, Edward George 1947- *WhoE 91*
Banneker, Benjamin 1731-1806 *BioIn 16, EncCRAm, WorAlBi*
Bannen, Carol Ann 1951- *WhoEmL 91*
Bannenberg, Jon *BioIn 16*
Banner, Abraham Leo 1929- *WhoE 91*
Banner, Bob 1921- *WhoAm 90*
Banner, Robert L. 1924- *St&PR 91*
Banner, Stephen Edward 1938- *WhoAm 90*
Banner, Vicki M. *ODwPR 91*
Banner, William Augustus 1915- *WhoAm 90*
Bannerman, Anne 1765-1829 *FemiCLE*
Bannerman, Helen 1862?-1946 *BioIn 16, ChlLR 21 [port], FemiCLE*
Bannerman, Margaret 1896-1976 *OxCCanT*
Bannerman, Martha G. 1943- *St&PR 91*
Bannerot, Karin Sofia 1960- *WhoE 91*
Bannes, Stephen William 1958- *WhoEmL 91*
Bannigan, Thomas Aloysius 1953- *St&PR 91*
Banning, Beatrice Harper 1885- *WhoAmA 91N*
Banning, Elizabeth 1908- *WhoAm 90*
Banning, Frederica Mabel 1951- *WhoE 91*
Banning, Jack, Jr 1939- *WhoAmA 91*
Banning, Margaret 1891-1982 *FemiCLE*
Banning, William Benjamin 1953- *WhoEmL 91*
Bannister, Alan 1951- *Ballpl 90*
Bannister, Candida Cleve 1957- *WhoAmW 91*
Bannister, Daniel R. 1930- *St&PR 91, WhoSSW 91*
Bannister, Edward Mitchell 1828-1901 *WhoAmA 91N*
Bannister, Floyd 1955- *Ballpl 90*
Bannister, Geoffrey 1945- *WhoAm 90*
Bannister, John Howard 1944- *WhoSSW 91*
Bannister, Lawrence 1945- *WhoSSW 91*
Bannister, Pat *AuBYP 90*
Bannister, Pati 1929- *WhoAmA 91*
Bannister, Patricia Brown *WhoAmA 91*
Bannister, Robert Corwin, Jr. 1935- *WhoAm 90*
Bannister, Roger 1929- *BioIn 16, WorAlBi*
Bannister, Roger Gilbert 1929- *WhoWor 91*
Banno, John A. 1940- *St&PR 91*
Bannon, Laura May *AuBYP 90*
Bannwarth, Horst Otto 1944- *WhoWor 91*
Banny, Jean Konan 1929- *WhoWor 91*
Banocy-Payne, Margaret Theresa 1949- *WhoSSW 91*
Banonis, Barbara Ann Cuccioli 1947- *WhoAmW 91, WhoEmL 91*
Banos, J. Luis 1918- *St&PR 91*
Banos, Jose Luis 1918- *WhoWor 91*
Banovic, Zlatko Josip 1951- *WhoWor 91*
Banowetz, Joseph Murray 1934- *WhoWor 91*
Banquen Lama 1937-1989 *BioIn 16*
Banquer, Cleve Stephen 1947- *St&PR 91*
Bansak, Stephen A., Jr. 1939- *WhoAm 90*
Bansal, Harinder K 1957- *BiDrAPA 89*
Bansal, Krishan K 1947- *BiDrAPA 89*
Bansal, Raj Kumari *BiDrAPA 89*
Bansal, Raul 1957- *St&PR 91*
Banschick, Mark Robert *BiDrAPA 89*
Banse, Karl 1929- *WhoAm 90*
Banse, Robert Lee 1927- *St&PR 91, WhoAm 90*
Bansemer, Roger 1948- *BioIn 16*
Bansemer, Roger L 1948- *WhoAmA 91*
Bansil, Rakesh Kumar *BiDrAPA 89*
Banta, Henry David 1938- *WhoAm 90*
Banta, Jack 1925- *Ballpl 90*
Banta, Lawrence Estel 1954- *BiDrAPA 89*
Banta, Merle Henry 1932- *St&PR 91*
Banta, Michelle Marie 1954- *BiDrAPA 89*
Banta, Richard Glenn 1947- *BiDrAPA 89*
Banta, Robert R. 1942- *St&PR 91*
Bantel, Linda Mae 1943- *WhoAmW 91*
Bantey, Bill 1928- *ODwPR 91, WhoE 91*
Banti, Anna 1895-1985 *EncCoWW*
Banti, Joan Riera 1925- *WhoWor 91*
Banting, Frederick G. 1891-1941 *WorAlBi*
Banting, Keith G. 1947- *ConAu 129*
Bantle, Louis Francis 1928- *St&PR 91, WhoAm 90, WhoE 91*
Bantly, Thomas W 1952- *BiDrAPA 89*
Bantock, Granville 1868-1946 *PenDiMP, -A*
Banton, Michael Roman 1958- *BiDrAPA 89*
Bantry, Bryan 1956- *WhoE 91, WhoEmL 91, WhoWor 91*
Bantum, Otis *BioIn 16*
Banuelos, Rodrigo 1954- *WhoHisp 91*
Banuelos, Romana Acosta 1925- *BioIn 16, WhoHisp 91*
Banus, Maria 1914- *EncCoWW*
Banvard, Kris 1957- *WhoEmL 91*
Banville, James Patrick 1941- *WhoWor 91*
Banville, John *NewYTBS 90 [port]*
Banville, John 1945- *WhoWor 91*
Banwart, George Junior 1926- *WhoAm 90*
Banyacski, Stephen 1936- *St&PR 91*
Banyai, Geraldine Lepera 1940- *St&PR 91*
Banyai, Geraldline L. 1940- *WhoAmW 91*
Banyard, Alfred Lothian 1908- *WhoAm 90*
Banyas, Jeffrey Brian 1959- *WhoSSW 91*
Banys, Peter *BiDrAPA 89*
Banz, George 1928- *WhoAmA 91*
Banzer, Jerry Lee 1938- *St&PR 91*
Banzer Suarez, Hugo 1926- *BioIn 16*
Banzhaf, Clayton Harris 1917- *WhoAm 90*
Banzhaf, Donald 1942- *BiDrAPA 89*
Banzhaf, John F., III 1940- *WhoAm 90*
Bao Tong *BioIn 16*
Bapat, Kalyani C. 1957- *WhoE 91*
Bapat, Vijay Narayan 1940- *BiDrAPA 89*
Bapst, Georges-Michel *PenDiDA 89*
Bapst, Germain *PenDiDA 89*
Baptie, T.J. *ODwPR 91*
Baptist, Allwyn J. 1943- *WhoAm 90*
Baptist, Sylvia Evelyn 1944- *WhoAmW 91, WhoWor 91*
Baptista, Mariano 1832-1907 *BioIn 16*
Baptiste, Idella Lou 1952- *WhoAmW 91*
Baptiste, Nancy Ellen 1946- *WhoAmW 91*
Baquero, Marco 1948- *BiDrAPA 89*
Baquet, Dean Paul 1956- *WhoAm 90*
Baquet, Rene Philippe 1951- *WhoEmL 91*
Bar, Catherine de 1614-1698 *EncCoWW*
Bar, Christian Friedrich-Wilhelm von 1952- *WhoWor 91*
Bar, Olaf 1957- *IntWWM 90, PenDiMP*
Bar, Peter Rudolf 1950- *WhoWor 91*
Bar-El, Raphael 1943- *WhoWor 91*
Bar-Illan, David 1930- *IntWWM 90, PenDiMP*
Bar-Levav, Leora Pnina *BiDrAPA 89*
Bar-Ness, Yeheskel 1932- *WhoE 91*
Bar-on, Miriam Elizabeth 1955- *WhoSSW 91*
Bar-Ziv, Haim Emanuel 1937- *St&PR 91*
Bara, Theda 1890-1955 *WorAlBi*
Baraban, Jack 1919- *St&PR 91*
Baraban, Jay Matthew *BiDrAPA 89*
Barabas, Sari 1918- *IntWWM 90, PenDiMP*
Barabas, Silvio 1920- *WhoAm 90*
Barabas, Tom *NewAgMG*
Barabaschi, Sergio 1930- *WhoWor 91*
Barabba, Vincent Pasquale 1934- *WhoAm 90*
Barabino, William Albert 1932- *WhoE 91*
Barabtarlo, Jack *BiDrAPA 89*
Barac, Bosko Anton 1930- *WhoWor 91*
Barach, Philip G. 1930- *St&PR 91*
Barad, Jill Elikann 1951- *St&PR 91, WhoAm 90, WhoAmW 91*
Baraduc, Hyppolite 1850-1902 *EncO&P 3, EncPaPR 91*
Baraga, Frederic 1797-1868 *WhNaAH*
Barager, Wendy Ayrian 1949- *WhoEmL 91*
Baragona, Freddie James, Jr. 1952- *WhoSSW 91*
Baragwanath, Albert Kingsmill 1917- *WhoAm 90*
Barahal, Hyman S 1905- *BiDrAPA 89*
Barahal, Hyman Samuel 1905- *WhoAm 90*
Barahona-Fernandes, H J *BiDrAPA 89*
Barajas, Charles 1944- *WhoHisp 91*
Barajas, Richard 1953- *WhoHisp 91*
Barak, Shlomo 1938- *St&PR 91*
Baraka, Amiri 1934- *BioIn 16, DcLB DS8 [port], DrBIPA 90, MajTwCW, WhoAm 90*
Baraka, Imamu Amiri 1934- *BioIn 16 WorAlBi*
Barakat, Frederick Emil 1939- *WhoSSW 91*
Barakat, Samir F. 1954- *WhoAm 90*
Baraket, Edmund S., Jr. 1947- *WhoE 91*
Baral, Vicki *BioIn 16*
Barald, Katharine Francesca 1945- *WhoEmL 91*
Barall, Bertram *BiDrAPA 89*
Barall, Milton 1911- *WhoAm 90*
Baran, Carolyn Jones 1942- *WhoAmW 91*
Baran, E. J. 1936- *WhoAm 90*
Baran, Edward John 1936- *St&PR 91*
Baran, Irving D *BiDrAPA 89*
Baran, Josh 1950- *ODwPR 91*
Baran, Paul 1910-1964 *EncAL*
Baran, William Lee 1943- *WhoSSW 91*
Baranauckas, Carla May 1955- *WhoAmW 91*
Barancik, Charles 1928- *St&PR 91*
Baranco, Gregory *BioIn 16*
Baranczak, Stanislaw *WhoAm 90*
Baranczak, Stanislaw 1946- *WhoWrEP 89*
Barande, Eric Cyril 1955- *WhoWor 91*
Barandes, Robert 1947- *WhoAm 90*
Barange, Charles 1897-1985 *BiDFrPL*
Baranick, Wilfred John 1927- *St&PR 91*
Baranik, Rudolf 1920- *WhoAm 90, WhoAmA 91*
Baranishyn, Peter 1944- *St&PR 91*
Barankin, Tatyana 1951- *BiDrAPA 89*
Baranof, Alexander Andreyevich 1747-1819 *WhNaAH*
Baranoff, Mort 1923-1978 *WhoAmA 91N*
Baranoff, Susan Lyn 1957- *WhoEmL 91*
Baranov, Aleksandr Andreevich 1747-1819 *WhNaAH*
Baranovsky, Max Gregory 1944- *BiDrAPA 89*
Baranow, Joan Marie 1958- *WhoWrEP 89*
Baranowski, Carl 1957- *WhoEmL 91*
Baranowski, Edward Alfred 1938- *WhoSSW 91*
Baranowski, Edwin Michael 1947- *WhoEmL 91*
Baranowski, Frank Paul 1921- *WhoAm 90*
Baranowski, Hermann 1884-1940 *BioIn 16*
Baranowski, Irene T. 1927- *St&PR 91*
Baranowski, Janice Carlson Henske 1952- *WhoSSW 91*
Baranowski, Leslie Boleslaw 1912- *St&PR 91*
Baranowski, Thomas Joseph, Jr. 1955- *WhoSSW 91*
Baranowski, Tom 1946- *WhoSSW 91*
Baranski, Christine 1952- *WhoAm 90, WhoAmW 91*
Baranski, Dennis Anthony 1950- *St&PR 91*
Baranski, Joan Sullivan 1933- *WhoAm 90, WhoAmW 91*
Baranski, Lawrence Anthony 1955- *WhoEmL 91*
Barany, James Walter 1930- *WhoAm 90, WhoWor 91*
Barany, Kate 1929- *WhoAmW 91*
Baras, Karen Jean *BiDrAPA 89*
Barasch, Alan Sidney 1951- *BiDrAPA 89*
Barasch, Clarence Sylvan 1912- *WhoAm 90*
Barasch, Mal Livingston 1929- *WhoAm 90*
Barasch, Violette Kasica 1954- *WhoE 91*
Barash, Anthony Harlan 1943- *WhoAm 90*
Barash, Bernard *BiDrAPA 89*
Barash, Carol Lynn 1958- *WhoE 91*
Barash, Harvey Alan *BiDrAPA 89*
Barash, Paul George 1942- *WhoAm 90*
Barassi, Dario 1940- *WhoWor 91*
Barasz, Efraim 1892-1943 *BioIn 16*
Barati, George 1913- *IntWWM 90*
Baratka, Thomas Edward 1946- *St&PR 91*
Baratka, William G. 1934- *St&PR 91*
Baratotti, Galerana *EncCoWW*
Baratta, Anthony J., Jr. 1943- *St&PR 91*
Baratta, Anthony Joseph, Jr. 1943- *WhoAm 90*
Baratta, Evelyn N. *ODwPR 91*
Baratta, Pamela Amelia 1960- *WhoAmW 91*
Baratta, Philip A, Jr. 1926- *BiDrAPA 89*
Baratta, Salvatore Peter 1935- *St&PR 91*
Baratz, Morton Sachs 1923- *WhoAm 90*
Barayon, Ramon Sender *ConAu 130, HispWr 90*
Barazani, Morris 1924- *WhoAmA 91*
Barazone, Mounque 1948- *WhoEmL 91*
Barba, Carlos 1935- *WhoHisp 91*
Barba, Enrique M. 1909-1988 *BioIn 16*
Barba, Estrella G 1941- *BiDrAPA 89*
Barba, Frank Peter 1932- *WhoE 91*
Barba, Harry 1922- *WhoAm 90, WhoWrEP 89*
Barba, J. Brendan 1941- *St&PR 91*
Barba, Ralph N. *WhoHisp 91*
Barba, Raymond Felix 1923- *WhoHisp 91*
Barbachano, Fernando G. R. 1926- *WhoWor 91*
Barbagallo, Antonio 1949- *WhoWor 91*
Barbagallo, Ronald Mark 1959- *WhoE 91*
Barbagelata, Robert Dominic 1925- *WhoAm 90*
Barbakoff, Paul 1931- *St&PR 91*
Barban, Arnold Melvin 1932- *WhoAm 90*

Barbanel, Charles J *BiDrAPA 89*
Barbanell, Maurice 1902-1981 *EncO&P 3, EncPaPR 91*
Barbanell, Robert Louis 1930- *St&PR 91, WhoAm 90*
Barbano, Frances Elizabeth 1944- *WhoWrEP 89*
Barbanti, Amedeo A 1921- *BiDrAPA 89*
Barbar, Anne *BiDEWW*
Barbara, Dominick A 1914- *BiDrAPA 89*
Barbara, Mark Joseph 1955- *BiDrAPA 89*
Barbara, Maurice Edward 1933- *St&PR 91*
Barbare, Walter 1891-1965 *Ballpl 90*
Barbaree, George Ralph 1925- *WhoAm 90*
Barbaro, Ronald Delano 1933- *WhoSSW 91*
Barbarosh, Milton Harvey 1955- *WhoEmL 91, WhoSSW 91*
Barbarossa, Theodore C *WhoAmA 91*
Barbaroux, Paula Elizabeth 1961- *WhoSSW 91*
Barbarow, Thomas Steven 1951- *WhoWor 91*
Barbarowicz, Robert Paul 1946- *WhoAm 90*
Barbasetti Di Prun, Adalberto 1940- *WhoE 91*
Barbash, Fred 1945- *WhoAm 90*
Barbash, Jack 1910- *WhoAm 90*
Barbash, Joseph 1921- *WhoAm 90*
Barbatelli, Ettore, Sr. 1923- *St&PR 91*
Barbatelli, Lovedy P. 1925- *St&PR 91*
Barbato, Gene A. 1935- *St&PR 91*
Barbato, Joseph Allen 1944- *WhoWrEP 89*
Barbato, Lewis *BiDrAPA 89*
Barbauld, Anna Laetitia 1743-1825 *FemiCLE*
Barbauld, Anna Letitia Aikin 1743-1825 *BioIn 16*
Barbe, Betty Catherine 1930- *WhoAmW 91, WhoWor 91*
Barbe, David Franklin 1939- *WhoAm 90*
Barbe, Henri 1902-1966 *BiDFrPL*
Barbe, Walter Burke 1926- *WhoAm 90, WhoWor 91*
Barbeau, Francois 1935- *OxCCanT [port]*
Barbeau, Jacques Jean 1938- *WhoWor 91*
Barbeau, Jean 1945- *OxCCanT [port]*
Barbeau, Marcel 1925- *WhoAmA 91*
Barbeau, Marius 1883-1969 *DcLB 92 [port]*
Barbeau, Susanne 1950- *WhoAmW 91*
Barbedienne, Ferdinand 1810-1892 *PenDiDA 89*
Barbee, George E. L. 1943- *WhoE 91, WhoWor 91*
Barbee, Gwen 1948- *WhoSSW 91*
Barbee, H. Randoloph, Jr. 1940- *WhoSSW 91*
Barbee, James Gray, IV *BiDrAPA 89*
Barbee, Jeanette H. 1934- *St&PR 91*
Barbee, Joe Ed 1934- *WhoWor 91*
Barbee, Lloyd Augustus 1925- *WhoAm 90*
Barbee, Rob 1940- *WhoAmA 91*
Barbee, Robert Thomas 1921- *WhoAmA 91*
Barbee, Victor *BioIn 16*
Barbee, Victor 1954- *WhoE 91*
Barbee, William Arthur 1947- *WhoSSW 91*
Barbee, William Henry, Jr. 1937- *WhoAm 90, WhoE 91*
Barbeito, Nelson 1946- *WhoHisp 91*
Barbellion, W. N. P. 1889-1919 *BioIn 16*
Barber, Albert Alcide 1929- *WhoAm 90*
Barber, Andrew B. 1909- *St&PR 91*
Barber, Andrew Bollons 1909- *WhoAm 90*
Barber, Ann Marie Teresa 1965- *WhoE 91*
Barber, Anthony John 1929- *WhoWor 91*
Barber, Arthur Whiting 1926- *WhoAm 90*
Barber, Ben Bernard Andrew 1944- *WhoAm 90*
Barber, Benjamin R. 1939- *ConAu 32NR, WhoWrEP 89*
Barber, Bruce Alistair 1950- *WhoAmA 91*
Barber, Charles Edward 1939- *St&PR 91, WhoSSW 91, WhoWor 91*
Barber, Charles F. 1917- *St&PR 91*
Barber, Charles Finch 1917- *WhoAm 90, WhoE 91*
Barber, Charles Turner 1941- *WhoWor 91*
Barber, Charles W. *WhoSSW 91*
Barber, Chris 1930- *OxCPMus*
Barber, Clarence Lyle 1917- *WhoAm 90*
Barber, Cynthia 1939- *WhoAmA 91*
Barber, D. Robert 1920- *St&PR 91*
Barber, Deborah E. 1939- *St&PR 91*
Barber, Donald B. 1906- *St&PR 91*
Barber, Donald L. 1953- *St&PR 91*
Barber, Donn Paul 1934- *St&PR 91*
Barber, Earl Eugene 1939- *WhoWor 91*
Barber, Edmund Amaral, Jr. 1916- *WhoE 91*
Barber, Edward John 1916-1989 *BioIn 16*
Barber, Edwin Barnard 1927- *St&PR 91*
Barber, Edwin Ford 1932- *St&PR 91*
Barber, Gerald E. 1946- *St&PR 91*
Barber, Graham 1948- *IntWWM 90*
Barber, Gregory Paul 1948- *St&PR 91*
Barber, Hugh Remegius Kilroe 1918- *WhoAm 90*
Barber, Jack Willard *BiDrAPA 89*
Barber, Jacqueline Renee 1956- *WhoAmW 91*
Barber, James Alden 1934- *WhoE 91*
Barber, James Arthur 1936- *St&PR 91*
Barber, James David 1930- *WhoAm 90*
Barber, James Laurance 1951- *St&PR 91*
Barber, Janice Ann 1947- *WhoEmL 91*
Barber, Jeffrey Wilson 1953- *St&PR 91, WhoEmL 91*
Barber, Jerry Randel 1940- *WhoAm 90*
Barber, Joan K 1925- *BiDrAPA 89*
Barber, Joel Allen 1809-1881 *AmLegL*
Barber, John 1898-1965 *WhoAmA 91N*
Barber, John Anthony 1941- *St&PR 91*
Barber, John Ernest, Jr. 1950- *WhoSSW 91*
Barber, John Merrell 1935- *WhoAm 90*
Barber, Kathryn Lee 1962- *WhoAmW 91*
Barber, Kenneth W. 1952- *WhoE 91*
Barber, Kim Michelle 1964- *WhoAmW 91*
Barber, Langdon Laws 1922- *St&PR 91*
Barber, Larry L. 1939- *St&PR 91*
Barber, Lloyd Ingram 1932- *WhoAm 90*
Barber, Margaret D 1905- *BiDrAPA 89*
Barber, Margaret Fairless 1869-1901 *BioIn 16*
Barber, Marsha 1946- *WhoAmW 91*
Barber, Mary 1690?-1757 *FemiCLE*
Barber, Mary Pamela 1947- *WhoAmW 91*
Barber, Melanie Margaret Cecilia 1958- *WhoE 91, WhoEmL 91*
Barber, Monty Clyde 1931- *St&PR 91*
Barber, Muriel V *WhoAmA 91N*
Barber, Orion Metcalf, II 1935- *WhoAm 90*
Barber, Patricia Louise 1953- *WhoAmW 91*
Barber, Patrick George 1942- *WhoSSW 91*
Barber, Perry Oscar, Jr. 1938- *WhoAm 90, WhoE 91*
Barber, Peter Pitts 1941- *WhoSSW 91*
Barber, Philip Judd 1951- *WhoAmA 91*
Barber, Phillip R. 1935- *St&PR 91*
Barber, Phillip Robert, III 1959- *WhoEmL 91*
Barber, Polly 1803-1898 *DcCanB 12*
Barber, Red 1908- *Ballpl 90 [port], WorAlBi*
Barber, Richard 1941- *ConAu 32NR*
Barber, Robert Allen 1942- *St&PR 91*
Barber, Robert Charles 1936- *WhoAm 90*
Barber, Robert E. 1932- *St&PR 91*
Barber, Robert Latimer 1946- *WhoEmL 91*
Barber, Ronald *WhoAmA 91*
Barber, Rupert T. 1903- *St&PR 91*
Barber, Russell Brooks Butler 1934- *WhoAm 90*
Barber, Russell Jeffrey 1950- *WhoEmL 91*
Barber, Sam 1943- *WhoAmA 91*
Barber, Samuel 1910-1981 *BioIn 16, PenDiMPA, WorAlBi*
Barber, Stanley Arthur 1921- *WhoAm 90*
Barber, Stephan Allen 1950- *WhoEmL 91*
Barber, Steve 1939- *Ballpl 90*
Barber, Susan 1954- *WhoAmW 91*
Barber, Thomas King 1923- *WhoAm 90*
Barber, Thomas Ward 1956- *WhoE 91*
Barber, Turner 1893-1968 *Ballpl 90*
Barber, Virginia *BioIn 16*
Barber, William Henry *WhoSSW 91*
Barber, William Joseph 1925- *WhoAm 90*
Barbera, Anthony Thomas 1955- *WhoE 91*
Barbera, Augusto Antonio 1938- *WhoWor 91*
Barbera, Carmen 1927- *EncCoWW*
Barbera, Joe *WhoAmA 91*
Barbera, Joe 1911- *BioIn 16*
Barbera, Joseph *WhoAm 90*
Barbera, Joseph 1911- *ConTFT 8*
Barbera, Michael Anthony 1952- *WhoEmL 91*
Barbera, Rodney R. 1953- *St&PR 91*
Barberi, Robert Obed 1945- *St&PR 91, WhoAm 90*
Barberie, Michael E 1945- *BiDrAPA 89*
Barberie, Richard C. 1939- *St&PR 91*
Barberio, Diane Elizabeth 1945- *WhoWrEP 89*
Barberio, Dominic Vito 1956- *BiDrAPA 89*
Barberis, Dorothy Watkeys 1918- *WhoAmA 91*
Barberis, Juan C 1920- *SmATA 61*
Barbero, Giulio John 1923- *WhoAm 90*
Barbero, Jesus 1953- *WhoWor 91*
Barbero, Mary Beth 1965- *WhoAmW 91*
Barbero, Robert J. 1929- *St&PR 91*
Barbero, Teresa *EncCoWW*
Barbero, Victoria Anielski 1942- *WhoAmW 91*
Barbet, Jean *PenDiDA 89*
Barbetta, Maria Ann 1956- *WhoAmW 91*
Barbette, Jay *TwCCr&M 91*
Barbey, Adelaide 1948- *WhoWor 91*
Barbey, Daniel E. 1889-1969 *BioIn 16*
Barbey, Grace Holmes *NewYTBS 90*
Barbey, Grace Holmes 1907-1990 *BioIn 16*
Barbi, Alessio 1948- *WhoWor 91*
Barbi, Josef Walter 1949- *WhoEmL 91, WhoWor 91*
Barbie, Klaus *BioIn 16*
Barbie, Klaus 1913- *WorAlBi*
Barbieri, Anthony G. *BioIn 16*
Barbieri, Christopher George 1941- *WhoAm 90*
Barbieri, Fedora 1920- *IntWWM 90, PenDiMP*
Barbieri, Francisco Asenjo 1823-1894 *OxCPMus*
Barbieri, Joseph Peter 1923- *WhoAm 90*
Barbieri, Lee Allan 1947- *WhoSSW 91*
Barbieri, Margaret Elizabeth 1947- *WhoWor 91*
Barbieri, Mary Kay *BioIn 16*
Barbieri, Norma Beatriz *BiDrAPA 89*
Barbieri, Richard *NewAgMG*
Barbieri, Rocco A. 1936- *WhoAm 90*
Barbieri, Rocco Anthony 1936- *St&PR 91*
Barbirolli, Evelyn 1911- *IntWWM 90*
Barbirolli, John 1899-1970 *PenDiMP, WorAlBi*
Barbizet, A. *PenDiDA 89*
Barbo, Dorothy Marie 1932- *WhoAmW 91*
Barboncita 1820?-1871 *WhNaAH*
Barbone, Stephen Gerard 1934- *WhoE 91*
Barbor, John Howard 1952- *WhoEmL 91*
Barbosa, Jose Celso 1857-1921 *BioIn 16*
Barbosa, Romulo Xavier 1928- *WhoWor 91*
Barbosa, Rosa Lillian *BiDrAPA 89*
Barbosa, Ruy 1849-1923 *BioIn 16*
Barbour, Anita Estelle 1958- *WhoAmW 91*
Barbour, Arthur J 1926- *WhoAmA 91*
Barbour, Billy Michael 1953- *WhoSSW 91*
Barbour, Charlene 1949- *WhoAmW 91, WhoSSW 91*
Barbour, David A. *WhoAm 90*
Barbour, Delta Rae 1937- *WhoAmW 91*
Barbour, Hugh Revell 1929- *WhoAm 90*
Barbour, Ian Graeme 1923- *WhoAm 90*
Barbour, J. Pius *BioIn 16*
Barbour, James 1775-1842 *BiDrUSE 89, BioIn 16*
Barbour, James Keith 1948- *WhoWor 91*
Barbour, Joseph Lane 1846-1915 *AmLegL*
Barbour, Karen 1956- *SmATA 63 [port]*
Barbour, Michael George 1942- *WhoAm 90*
Barbour, Ralph Henry 1870-1944 *AuBYP 90*
Barbour, Richard Randolph 1957- *WhoEmL 91*
Barbour, Robert Charles 1935- *St&PR 91*
Barbour, Ross Edwin 1928- *WhoAm 90*
Barbour, Sue Jennifer 1950- *WhoAmW 91*
Barbour, Thomas D. 1928- *St&PR 91*
Barbour, Walworth 1908-1982 *BioIn 16*
Barbour, William Ernest, Jr. 1909- *WhoAm 90*
Barbour, William Rinehart, Jr. 1922- *WhoAm 90*
Barbour, Williams H., Jr. 1941- *WhoAm 90*
Barbouti, Ihsan *BioIn 16*
Barboza, Anthony 1944- *WhoAmA 91*
Barboza, Gloria 1951- *WhoAmW 91, WhoEmL 91*
Barboza, Michael J. 1945- *St&PR 91*
Barbry, William Henry, III 1943- *WhoSSW 91*
Barbu, Ion 1895-1961 *WrPh*
Barbusse, Henri 1873-1935 *BiDFrPL*
Barbusse, Henri 1874-1935 *BioIn 16*
Barbuti, Joseph F. 1935- *St&PR 91*
Barbuti, Ray *BioIn 16*
Barbuto, Joseph 1947- *BiDrAPA 89, WhoE 91*
Barca, Frances Erskine Inglis Calderon d 1804-1882 *BioIn 16*
Barca, George Gino 1937- *WhoAm 90, WhoWor 91*
Barca, James Joseph 1944- *WhoSSW 91*
Barca, Kathleen 1946- *WhoAmW 91, WhoEmL 91*
Barcella, Ernest Lawrence, Jr. 1945- *WhoEmL 91*
Barcelo, Carlos Romero 1932- *BioIn 16*
Barcelo, Gertrudis 1800-1852 *BioIn 16*
Barcelo, John James, III 1940- *WhoAm 90*
Barcelona, Ricardo Go 1955- *WhoWor 91*
Barcenas, Camilo Gustavo 1944- *WhoWor 91*
Barcenilla, Lisa Misterio *BiDrAPA 89*
Barch, Karen Martin 1954- *WhoEmL 91*
Barch, Michael Mackie 1944- *WhoAm 90, WhoE 91*
Barch, Robert Louis 1941- *St&PR 91*
Barchas, Jack D 1935- *BiDrAPA 89*
Barchas, Rebecca Elise 1949- *BiDrAPA 89*
Barchers, Charles William 1929- *St&PR 91*
Barchers, Suzanne Inez 1946- *WhoEmL 91*
Barchet, Stephen 1932- *WhoAm 90*
Barchha, Ramnik G 1936- *BiDrAPA 89*
Barchi, Robert Lawrence 1946- *WhoAm 90*
Barchie-McIntyre, Janet Louise 1952- *WhoAmW 91*
Barchiesi, Alessandro 1925- *BiDrAPA 89*
Barchilon, Jose *BiDrAPA 89*
Barci, Robert John 1954- *WhoWrEP 89*
Barcic, Joseph, Jr. 1946- *St&PR 91*
Barckert, Lee 1946- *St&PR 91*
Barckley, Robert Eugene 1922- *WhoAm 90*
Barclay, Bennett *TwCCr&M 91*
Barclay, Bill *MajTwCW*
Barclay, Billy Oral 1942- *BiDrAPA 89*
Barclay, Carl Archie 1922- *WhoSSW 91*
Barclay, Caryl Ann Morris 1945- *WhoEmL 91*
Barclay, Curt 1931- *Ballpl 90*
Barclay, Florence 1862-1920 *FemiCLE*
Barclay, George 1876-1909 *Ballpl 90*
Barclay, Gregory *BiDrAPA 89*
Barclay, Hugh Douglas 1932- *WhoAm 90*
Barclay, James Edward 1941- *WhoAm 90*
Barclay, James Ralph 1926- *WhoAm 90*
Barclay, James Turner 1807-1874 *BioIn 16*
Barclay, John Allen 1951- *WhoEmL 91*
Barclay, Joseph Boimah *WhoWor 91*
Barclay, Joseph Johnson 1933- *St&PR 91*
Barclay, Judith Shaffer 1942- *WhoE 91*
Barclay, Lawson Eugene 1945- *WhoEmL 91*
Barclay, Mark Alan 1950- *St&PR 91*
Barclay, Richard Laurence 1951- *St&PR 91*
Barclay, Ronald David 1934- *WhoAm 90*
Barclay, Thomas Laird 1925- *WhoWor 91*
Barclay, William A *BiDrAPA 89*
Barclay, William Ewert *MajTwCW*
Barclift, William C. 1949- *St&PR 91*
Barclift, William C., III 1949- *WhoAm 90*
Barco, Virgilio 1921- *WhoWor 91*
Barco Vargas, Virgilio *BioIn 16*
Barco Vargas, Virgilio 1921- *CurBio 90 [port]*
Barcus, Benjamin Franklin 1960- *WhoWor 91*
Barcus, Gilbert Martin 1937- *WhoE 91, WhoWor 91*
Barcus, James Edgar 1938- *WhoAm 90, WhoWrEP 89*
Barcus, James Roy *BioIn 16*
Barcus, Mary Evelyn 1938- *WhoAmW 91*
Barcynska, Helene 1894-1964 *FemiCLE*
Barczak, Bernard Gerard 1947- *WhoE 91, WhoEmL 91*
Barczyk, John A. 1947- *St&PR 91*
Barczynski, Joerg 1940- *WhoWor 91*
Bard, Allen Joseph 1933- *WhoAm 90*
Bard, Bernard 1927- *WhoE 91*
Bard, Gayle *WhoAmA 91*
Bard, George 1926- *St&PR 91*
Bard, Joellen 1942- *WhoAmA 91*
Bard, John 1716-1799 *EncCRAm*
Bard, John Franklin 1941- *WhoAm 90*
Bard, Jonathan D. *ODwPR 91*
Bard, Nelson P. 1908- *St&PR 91*
Bard, Nicholas Van 1955- *St&PR 91*
Bard, Richard Alan 1945- *WhoEmL 91*
Bard, Richard H. 1947- *WhoAm 90*
Bard, Susan M. 1954- *WhoWrEP 89*
Bard, Susan Martha 1954- *WhoEmL 91*
Bard, Theodore 1923- *St&PR 91*
Bard, Wilkie 1874-1944 *OxCPMus*
Barda, Jean Francis 1940- *WhoWor 91*
Bardach, Joan Lucile 1919- *WhoAm 90*
Bardach, Neil Max 1948- *St&PR 91*
Bardach, Sheldon Gilbert 1937- *WhoAm 90*
Bardack, Paul Roitman 1953- *WhoAm 90*
Bardacke, Paul Gregory 1944- *WhoAm 90*
Bardagy, Robert A. 1939- *St&PR 91, WhoAm 90*
Bardasano, Carlos Raul 1945- *WhoWor 91*
Bardasz, Ewa Alice 1943- *WhoAm 90*
Bardawil, Anita Aiken 1931- *WhoAmW 91*
Bardazzi, Peter 1943- *WhoAmA 91, WhoE 91*
Bardeche, Maurice 1907- *BiDFrPL*
Bardeck, Walter Peter 1910- *WhoWrEP 89*
Bardeen, John 1908- *BioIn 16, WhoAm 90, WhoWor 91, WorAlBi*
Bardell, Eunice Ruth 1915- *WhoAmW 91*
Barden, George Richard 1935- *St&PR 91*
Barden, Janice Kindler *WhoAmW 91, WhoSSW 91*
Barden, Karl Alvin 1940- *WhoWor 91*
Barden, Kenneth Eugene 1955- *WhoEmL 91*
Barden, Mitchell Seth *BiDrAPA 89*
Barden, Royston 1962- *WhoWor 91*
Barden, William Charles 1952- *St&PR 91*
Barden, Yakov 1929- *BiDrAPA 89*
Bardens, Pete *NewAgMG*
Bardenwerper, Walter William 1951- *WhoEmL 91*
Bardet, Gaston Alexis 1907-1989 *BioIn 16*
Bardill, Donald Ray 1934- *WhoAm 90*
Bardin, Christian Andre 1939- *St&PR 91*

Bardin, Clyde Wayne 1934- *WhoAm 90*
Bardin, David J. 1933- *WhoAm 90*
Bardin, Irwin B. 1943- *WhoE 91*
Bardin, Jesse Redwin 1923- *WhoAmA 91*
Bardin, John Franklin 1916-1981 *TwCCr&M 91*
Bardin, Michael D. 1942- *ODwPR 91*
Bardin, Rodney Norman, II 1957- *WhoEmL 91*
Bardin, W. Earl 1927- *St&PR 91*
Bardinelli, Anthony J 1937- *BiDrAPA 89*
Bardinon, Pierre 1931- *BioIn 16*
Bardis, Panos Demetrios 1924- *WhoAm 90*
Bardo, Charles J. 1938- *St&PR 91*
Bardo, John William 1948- *WhoAm 90*
Bardoliwalla, Dinshaw Framroze 1945- *WhoE 91*
Bardolph, Richard 1915- *WhoAm 90*
Bardon, Daniel Russell 1947- *St&PR 91*
Bardon, Edward J 1933- *BiDrAPA 89*
Bardon, Jack Irving 1925- *WhoAm 90*
Bardon, Marcel 1927- *WhoAm 90*
Bardos, Denes Istvan 1938- *WhoAm 90*
Bardos, Thomas Joseph 1915- *WhoAm 90*
Bardos-Feltoronyi, Nicolas 1935- *WhoWor 91*
Bardot, Brigitte *BioIn 16*
Bardot, Brigitte 1934- *WhoWor 91*, *WorAlBi*
Bardsley, Elizabeth Skeats 1931- *WhoAmW 91*
Bardsley, John Edward *BiDrAPA 89*
Bardsley, Richard Geoffrey 1928- *St&PR 91*
Bardwell, Richard Paul 1936- *St&PR 91*
Bardwell, William 1915- *IntWWM 90*
Bardwick, Judith Marcia 1933- *WhoAm 90*
Bardwil, James J. 1949- *ODwPR 91*
Bardwil, Joseph A. 1928- *St&PR 91*
Bardwil, Joseph Anthony 1928- *WhoAm 90*, *WhoE 91*
Bardy, Linda L. 1955- *WhoE 91*
Bardyguine, Patricia Wilde 1928- *WhoAm 90*, *WhoAmW 91*, *WhoE 91*
Bare, Bruce 1914- *WhoAm 90*
Bare, Joseph Edward, Jr. 1923- *WhoAm 90*
Bare, Joseph Lee 1941- *WhoSSW 91*
Bare, Ray 1949- *Ballpl 90*
Bare, Robert Joseph 1935- *WhoAm 90*
Barefoot, Donald L. 1954- *St&PR 91*
Barefoot, John Roy, Jr. 1918- *St&PR 91*
Barefoot, Paul D. 1943- *ODwPR 91*
Bareis, Donna Lynn 1954- *WhoE 91*
Bareiss, Erwin Hans 1922- *WhoAm 90*
Bareiss, Philip C 1949- *WhoAmA 91*
Bareiss, Walter 1919- *WhoAmA 91*
Barel, Phyllis Barbara 1947- *St&PR 91*
Barela, Arturo Madrid- 1939- *BioIn 16*
Barela, Casimiro 1847-1920 *BioIn 16*
Barela, Esmerlindo Jaramillo 1948- *WhoEmL 91*
Barela, Patrocinio 1908-1964 *BioIn 16*
Barenberg, Ernest John 1929- *WhoWor 91*
Barenberg, Paul A 1925- *BiDrAPA 89*
Barenberg, Russ *NewAgMG*
Barenboim, Daniel *BioIn 16*
Barenboim, Daniel 1932- *WorAlBi*
Barenboim, Daniel 1942- *IntWWM 90*, *PenDiMP*, *WhoAm 90*, *WhoWor 91*
Barends, Arne 1968- *WhoWor 91*
Barendsen, Gerrit Willem 1927- *WhoWor 91*
Barenfeld, Michael 1943- *St&PR 91*
Barenfeld, Steven Jan 1956- *WhoE 91*
Barenholtz, Benjamin 1912- *BiDrAPA 89*
Barenholtz, Bernard 1914-1989 *SmATA 64*
Barenholtz, Bernard M. *BioIn 16*
Barenholtz, Bernard M. 1914- *St&PR 91*
Barenis, Pat Peaster 1951- *WhoEmL 91*
Barenklau, Keith Edward 1931- *WhoSSW 91*
Barents, Willem 1550?-1597 *WorAlBi*
Barere, Simon 1896-1951 *PenDiMP*
Bares, Allen Ray 1936- *WhoSSW 91*
Bares, Fioravante Antonio 1931- *WhoE 91*
Bares, William G. 1941- *WhoAm 90*
Baretich, John Francis 1954- *St&PR 91*
Baretski, Charles Allan 1918- *WhoE 91*, *WhoWor 91*
Baretz, Roger M 1930- *BiDrAPA 89*
Bareuther, Ernst Ellis 1910- *WhoAm 90*
Barfield, Jesse 1959- *Ballpl 90*
Barfield, Kenny Dale 1947- *WhoSSW 91*
Barfield, Larry M. 1948- *St&PR 91*
Barfield, Richard Donald 1947- *WhoSSW 91*
Barfield, Robert F. 1933- *WhoAm 90*
Barfield, Shirley Rosalis 1940- *WhoAmW 91*
Barfield, Stewart Bayne 1957- *WhoEmL 91*
Barfield, Thomas Harwell 1917- *WhoAm 90*
Barfield, Walter Michael 1953- *WhoSSW 91*
Barfod, Gustav 1919- *WhoWor 91*
Barfod, Niels Michael 1948- *WhoWor 91*
Barfoot, Clyde 1891-1971 *Ballpl 90*
Barfoot, Fisher L. 1929- *St&PR 91*
Barfoot, Joan 1946- *FemiCLE*
Barford, George, IV 1940- *WhoAm 90*
Barford, Philip Trevelyan 1925- *IntWWM 90*
Barford, R.M. 1929- *St&PR 91*
Barford, Ralph MacKenzie 1929- *WhoAm 90*
Barg, Bernard B. 1926- *St&PR 91*
Barg, Gale Ann 1952- *WhoE 91*
Barg, Jankiel *BiDrAPA 89*
Bargainer, Paul V. 1954- *WhoSSW 91*
Bargamian, Nancy C. 1950- *WhoAmW 91*
Bargar, Gary W. 1947-1985 *SmATA 63 [port]*
Bargar, Robert S. 1919- *St&PR 91*
Bargar, Robert Sellstrom 1919- *WhoAm 90*
Barge, Daniel Bythewood 1922- *St&PR 91*
Barge, Daniel Bythewood, Jr. 1922- *WhoAm 90*
Bargellini, Pier Luigi 1914- *WhoAm 90*
Bargen, Karl *NewYTBS 90*
Bargeon, Herbert Alexander, Jr. 1934- *WhoSSW 91*, *WhoWor 91*
Barger, Abraham Clifford 1917- *WhoAm 90*
Barger, Cecil Edwin 1917- *WhoAm 90*
Barger, Cy 1885-1964 *Ballpl 90*
Barger, Darlene J. 1954- *WhoAmW 91*
Barger, Donald G. 1943- *St&PR 91*
Barger, Donald Gordon, Jr. 1943- *WhoAm 90*
Barger, Harold *BioIn 16*
Barger, J.P. 1927- *St&PR 91*
Barger, James Daniel 1917- *WhoAm 90*
Barger, James Edwin 1934- *WhoAm 90*
Barger, Lilian Calles 1955- *WhoSSW 91*
Barger, Melvin D. 1925- *ODwPR 91*
Barger, Paul Wendell 1940- *WhoSSW 91*
Barger, R. Vincent 1942- *St&PR 91*
Barger, Richard Wilson 1934- *WhoAm 90*
Barger, Richards D. 1928- *St&PR 91*
Barger, Robert Vincent 1942- *WhoAm 90*
Barger, Vernon Duane 1938- *WhoAm 90*
Barger, William C 1904- *BiDrAPA 89*
Barger, William James 1944- *WhoAm 90*
Barget, Mark Kevin 1958- *WhoE 91*
Barglow, Peter 1931- *BiDrAPA 89*
Bargmann, Valentine 1908-1989 *BioIn 16*
Bargmeyer, Alan K. 1941- *St&PR 91*
Barham, A. Caludette Vail 1953- *WhoAmW 91*
Barham, Allan *EncPaPR 91*
Barham, Charles Dewey, Jr. 1930- *St&PR 91*, *WhoAm 90*
Barham, Charles Middleton 1726-1813 *BioIn 16*
Barham, Edmund 1950- *IntWWM 90*
Barham, Francis L 1935- *BiDrAPA 89*
Barham, Jesse Walter 1924- *WhoWor 91*
Barham, John 1942- *IntWWM 90*
Barham, Mack Elwin 1924- *WhoAm 90*
Barham, Mel A. 1937- *St&PR 91*
Barham, Patte *WhoAmW 91*
Barham, Richard Wendell 1923- *WhoAm 90*
Barham, Thomas Alan 1954- *WhoE 91*
Barhyte, Donald J. 1937- *St&PR 91*
Bari, Ihsan-Ul 1941- *WhoSSW 91*
Bari, Lynn 1913-1989 *AnObit 1989*, *BioIn 16*
Bari, Mohammed Abdul *BiDrAPA 89*
Baribeau, Michel 1931- *St&PR 91*
Baribeau, Simon 1928- *St&PR 91*
Barich, Dewey Frederick 1911- *WhoAm 90*
Baridon, Philip Clarke 1946- *WhoE 91*
Barie, Philip Steven 1953- *WhoEmL 91*
Barienbrock, Ronald Charles 1947- *St&PR 91*
Bariff, Martin Louis 1944- *WhoWor 91*
Barik, Audhakar 1949- *WhoSSW 91*
Barikin, Viktor *BioIn 16*
Baril, Carlo Joseph 1938- *BiDrAPA 89*
Baril, Marie-Claire 1963- *BiDrAPA 89*
Baril, Nancy Ann 1952- *WhoAmW 91*
Barilan, Amiram *St&PR 91*
Barile, Frank D. 1933- *St&PR 91*
Barili, Antonio 1453-1516 *PenDiDA 89*
Barilich, Thomas Anthony 1955- *WhoEmL 91*, *WhoWor 91*
Baring, Arnulf Martin 1932- *WhoWor 91*
Baringer, George R *BiDrAPA 89*
Baringer, John Lee 1921-1989 *BioIn 16*
Baringer, Richard E 1921-1980 *WhoAmA 91N*
Bario, Patricia Yaroch 1932- *WhoE 91*
Barisano, Joseph *WhoWrEP 89*
Barish, Evelyn 1935- *ConAu 132*
Barish, Jonas Alexander 1922- *WhoAm 90*
Barish, Julian I *BiDrAPA 89*
Barish, Julian I. 1917- *WhoE 91*
Barish, Matthew 1907- *AuBYP 90*
Baritz, Loren 1928- *WhoAm 90*
Barjacoba, Pedro 1934- *WhoHisp 91*
Barjansky, Alexander 1883-1961 *PenDiMP*
Bark, Nigel Martyn 1941- *BiDrAPA 89*
Barka, Tibor 1926- *WhoAm 90*
Barkai, Joseph 1953- *WhoSSW 91*
Barkalow, Mary Elizabeth *BiDrAPA 89*
Barkan, Alexander E. 1909-1990 *NewYTBS 90 [port]*
Barkan, Joel David 1941- *WhoAm 90*
Barkan, John Martin, Jr. 1945- *WhoEmL 91*
Barkan, Leonard 1926- *St&PR 91*
Barkan, Philip 1925- *WhoAm 90*
Barkas, J.L. *ConAu 30NR*
Barkas, Janet *ConAu 30NR*
Barkauskas, Vytautas Pranas Marius 1931- *IntWWM 90*
Barke, Allen *BioIn 16*
Barkel, Kathleen *EncO&P 3*
Barkelew, Ann H. *ODwPR 91*
Barkeley, Norman A. 1930- *St&PR 91*
Barkemeijer de Wit, Jeanne Sandra 1955- *WhoAmW 91*
Barker, A. L. 1919- *BioIn 16*
Barker, A W 1930- *ConAu 32NR*
Barker, Al C 1941- *WhoAmA 91*
Barker, Albert Charles 1941- *WhoE 91*
Barker, Albert Winslow 1874-1947 *WhoAmA 91N*
Barker, Allan Leslie 1947- *WhoSSW 91*
Barker, Andrew 1943- *ConAu 130*
Barker, Anita Joyce 1947- *St&PR 91*
Barker, Anne Elizabeth Latimer 1964- *WhoAmW 91*
Barker, Audrey Lillian 1919- *BioIn 16*
Barker, Barbara 1938- *WhoAmW 91*
Barker, Barbara Ann 1943- *WhoAmW 91*
Barker, Barry W. 1943- *WhoWrEP 89*
Barker, Benjamin *PenDiDA 89*
Barker, Betty Lou Starr 1929- *WhoAmW 91*
Barker, Bruce Allen 1952- *WhoSSW 91*
Barker, C. Austin 1911- *St&PR 91*
Barker, C. Kelly Ann Murri 1951- *WhoAmW 91*
Barker, Calvin LaRue 1930- *WhoSSW 91*
Barker, Celeste Arlette 1947- *WhoAmW 91*, *WhoEmL 91*, *WhoWor 91*
Barker, Charles Holt 1942- *BiDrAPA 89*
Barker, Charles P 1915- *BiDrAPA 89*
Barker, Cicely Mary 1895-1973 *BioIn 16*
Barker, Clarence Austin 1911- *WhoAm 90*
Barker, Clayton Robert, III 1957- *WhoE 91*, *WhoEmL 91*
Barker, Clive *BioIn 16*
Barker, Clive 1952- *BestSel 90-3 [port]*, *ConAu 129*, *MajTwCW*
Barker, Clyde Frederick 1932- *WhoAm 90*, *WhoWor 91*
Barker, Colin George 1939- *WhoSSW 91*
Barker, Cynthia Raechel 1959- *WhoAmW 91*
Barker, Daniel Stephen 1934- *WhoAm 90*
Barker, Danny 1909- *OxCPMus*
Barker, David A. 1940- *St&PR 91*
Barker, David Bertram 1946- *WhoEmL 91*
Barker, Dennis 1929- *ConAu 32NR*
Barker, Donald P 1931- *BiDrAPA 89*
Barker, Douglas Wayne 1952- *St&PR 91*
Barker, Dudley *TwCCr&M 91*
Barker, Edith Ellen 1954- *WhoSSW 91*
Barker, Edwin Bogue 1954- *IntWWM 90*, *WhoAm 90*
Barker, Elizabeth B 1930- *BiDrAPA 89*
Barker, Elliott Speer 1886-1988 *BioIn 16*
Barker, Elsa *EncO&P 3*
Barker, Emmett Wilson, Jr. 1937- *WhoAm 90*
Barker, Eva B. 1932- *WhoAmW 91*
Barker, Felix 1917- *ConAu 130*
Barker, Frank H. 1930- *St&PR 91*
Barker, Frederick Henry, Jr. 1953- *WhoEmL 91*
Barker, Gail Austing 1955- *BiDrAPA 89*
Barker, Garry G. 1943- *WhoWrEP 89*
Barker, George Arthur 1812-1876 *OxCPMus*
Barker, George Granville 1913- *MajTwCW*
Barker, George Jerome 1842-1912 *AmLegL*
Barker, Gray 1925- *EncO&P 3*
Barker, Gregory Kimball 1946- *WhoEmL 91*
Barker, Gregson Leard 1918- *WhoAm 90*
Barker, Harold Grant 1917- *WhoAm 90*, *WhoE 91*
Barker, Harold Kenneth 1922- *WhoAm 90*
Barker, Harold M 1920- *BiDrAPA 89*
Barker, Horace Albert 1907- *WhoAm 90*
Barker, Hugh Alton 1925- *St&PR 91*
Barker, Jaime *BiDrAPA 89*
Barker, James 1946- *WhoWrEP 89*
Barker, James Cecil 1948- *St&PR 91*, *WhoSSW 91*
Barker, James Monroe, IV 1936- *St&PR 91*
Barker, James Rex 1935- *St&PR 91*, *WhoAm 90*
Barker, Jane 1652-1727? *BioIn 16*, *FemiCLE*
Barker, Jane 1660-1723 *BiDEWW*
Barker, Jane Ellen 1935- *WhoAmW 91*
Barker, John E. 1947- *St&PR 91*
Barker, Joyce 1937- *IntWWM 90*
Barker, Judy 1941- *WhoAmW 91*
Barker, Karen Jean *WhoAmW 91*
Barker, Kate 1872-1935 *WorAlBi*
Barker, Keith Rene 1928- *WhoWor 91*
Barker, Kenneth Neil 1937- *WhoAm 90*
Barker, Larry Lee 1941- *WhoAm 90*, *WhoWor 91*
Barker, Laurenn Russell 1945- *WhoAmW 91*
Barker, Lee Charles 1952- *WhoE 91*
Barker, Len 1955- *Ballpl 90*
Barker, Leslie P. 1901-1990 *BioIn 16*
Barker, Lewis 1818-1885 *AmLegL*
Barker, Linda Gail 1948- *WhoAmW 91*
Barker, Linda Weir 1942- *WhoSSW 91*
Barker, Llyle James, Jr. 1932- *WhoAm 90*
Barker, Mary *BiDEWW*
Barker, Mary Anne 1831-1911 *FemiCLE*
Barker, Mary K. 1921- *WhoAmW 91*
Barker, Mary Lew 1940- *WhoSSW 91*
Barker, Muhammad Abd-al-Rahman 1929- *WhoAm 90*
Barker, Nancy *BioIn 16*
Barker, Nancy Lepard 1936- *WhoAm 90*
Barker, Nicholas *BioIn 16*
Barker, Noelle 1928- *IntWWM 90*
Barker, Norman, Jr. 1922- *St&PR 91*, *WhoAm 90*
Barker, Pat 1943- *FemiCLE*
Barker, Paul 1914- *St&PR 91*
Barker, Paul Alan 1956- *IntWWM 90*
Barker, Philip George 1944- *WhoWor 91*
Barker, R. Mildred *BioIn 16*, *NewYTBS 90*
Barker, Richard Alexander 1947- *WhoWor 91*
Barker, Richard Gordon 1937- *WhoAm 90*
Barker, Richard L. 1934- *St&PR 91*
Barker, Robert 1928- *St&PR 91*, *WhoAm 90*
Barker, Robert John 1941- *St&PR 91*
Barker, Robert Rankin 1915- *WhoE 91*
Barker, Robert William *WhoAm 90*
Barker, Roger Garlock *NewYTBS 90*
Barker, Ronald C. 1927- *St&PR 91*
Barker, Ronald Eugene 1947- *St&PR 91*
Barker, Samuel Booth 1912- *WhoAm 90*, *WhoSSW 91*, *WhoWor 91*
Barker, Sarah Evans 1943- *WhoAm 90*, *WhoAmW 91*
Barker, Simon Andrew 1956- *WhoWor 91*
Barker, Stanley Anthony 1956- *WhoWrEP 89*
Barker, Stephen Francis 1927- *WhoAm 90*
Barker, Stephen R. 1955- *St&PR 91*
Barker, Steven Richard 1950- *WhoSSW 91*
Barker, Ted Alan 1947- *St&PR 91*
Barker, Teresa Lynn 1954- *WhoAmW 91*
Barker, Thomas Carl 1931- *WhoAm 90*
Barker, Thomas Edward 1940- *BiDrAPA 89*
Barker, Thomas Watson, Jr. 1944- *St&PR 91*, *WhoAm 90*
Barker, Virgil 1890-1964 *WhoAmA 91N*
Barker, W. Gardner *NewYTBS 90*
Barker, Walter Lee 1928- *WhoAm 90*
Barker, Walter William, Jr. 1921- *WhoAm 90*, *WhoAmA 91*
Barker, Warren J *BiDrAPA 89*
Barker, Will 1913-1983 *AuBYP 90*
Barker, William 1817?-1894 *DcCanB 12*
Barker, William Alfred 1919- *WhoAm 90*
Barker, William Benjamin 1947- *St&PR 91*
Barker, William Clinton 1950- *St&PR 91*
Barker, William Daniel 1926- *WhoAm 90*, *WhoWor 91*
Barker, William Griffith, Jr. 1933- *St&PR 91*
Barker, William Henry 1946- *WhoE 91*
Barker, William Shirmer, II 1934- *WhoE 91*
Barker, Winona Clinton 1938- *WhoAm 90*
Barkett, Henry Richard Frank 1958- *WhoEmL 91*
Barkett, Rosemary 1939- *WhoAm 90*, *WhoAmW 91*
Barkey, W. Jim *St&PR 91*
Barkhamer, Josephine Rita 1949- *WhoWrEP 89*
Barkhorn, Henry C., III 1949- *St&PR 91*
Barkhorn, Henry Charles, III 1949- *WhoE 91*
Barkhorn, Jean Cook 1931- *WhoAm 90*, *WhoWrEP 89*
Barkhouse, Joyce C. 1913- *BioIn 16*
Barkhuus, Arne 1906- *WhoAm 90*
Barkin, Amy Claire 1947- *WhoE 91*
Barkin, Ben 1915- *WhoAm 90*
Barkin, Carol *AuBYP 90*

Barkin, Carol 1944- BioIn 16
Barkin, Elaine R. 1932- IntWWM 90
Barkin, Ellen BioIn 16
Barkin, Ellen 1955- WhoAm 90
Barkin, Jeffrey S BiDrAPA 89
Barkin, Jeffrey Samuel 1962- WhoE 91
Barkin, Joshua Aaron 1918-1982 BioIn 16
Barkin, Kay Anita Frohlich 1952- WhoEmL 91
Barkin, Leonard BiDrAPA 89
Barkin, Martin 1936- WhoAm 90
Barkin, Marvin E. 1933- WhoAm 90
Barkin, Robert Allan 1939- WhoAm 90
Barkin, Solomon 1907- WhoAm 90
Barkin-Leeds, Temme 1940- WhoSSW 91
Barklage, Nancy Elizabeth BiDrAPA 89
Barkley, Alben W. 1877-1956 WorAlBi
Barkley, Alben William 1877-1956 BiDrUSE 89
Barkley, Barry R. 1943- St&PR 91
Barkley, Brian Evan 1945- WhoAm 90
Barkley, Charles BioIn 16
Barkley, Charles 1963- WorAlBi
Barkley, Charles Wade 1963- WhoAm 90
Barkley, Henry Brock, Jr. 1927- WhoSSW 91, WhoWor 91
Barkley, Kenneth Ray 1940- St&PR 91
Barkley, Miriam Corn 1952- WhoAmW 91
Barkley, Raymond E. 1927- St&PR 91
Barkley, Richard Clark 1932- WhoAm 90, WhoWor 91
Barkley, Rufus C., Jr. 1930- St&PR 91
Barkley, Tamminy WhoWrEP 89
Barkley, William Donald 1941- WhoAm 90
Barkman, Jon Albert 1947- WhoE 91, WhoEmL 91
Barko, Randall S. 1951- St&PR 91
Barkofske, Francis Lee 1939- WhoAm 90
Barkopoulos, Paul Nicholas 1953- BiDrAPA 89
Barkow, Robert F. 1942- St&PR 91
Barks, Carl 1901- EncACom
Barks, William Harold 1942- WhoSSW 91
Barksdale, Arthur Sydnor, III 1951- St&PR 91
Barksdale, C. Bruce, Jr. 1931- St&PR 91
Barksdale, Chandlee Murphy 1942- WhoAmW 91
Barksdale, Clarence C. 1932- St&PR 91
Barksdale, Clarence Caulfield 1932- WhoAm 90
Barksdale, Hiram Collier 1921- WhoAm 90
Barksdale, James Love 1943- St&PR 91, WhoAm 90, WhoSSW 91
Barksdale, Lena AuBYP 90
Barksdale, Milton Kendall, Jr. 1945- WhoSSW 91
Barksdale, Phillip Dunlap, Jr. 1935- St&PR 91
Barksdale, Richard 1915- BioIn 16
Barksdale, Richard Dillon 1938- WhoAm 90
Barksdale, Richard Kenneth 1915- WhoAm 90
Barksdale, Shirley BioIn 16
Barksdale, Stephen Webb BiDrAPA 89
Barksdale, Thomas G. 1937- St&PR 91
Barksdale, Vernon Cosby BiDrAPA 89
Barksdale, William E. 1931- St&PR 91
Barkus, Mariona Marcia 1948- WhoAmA 91
Barkwell, Donald D. 1930- St&PR 91
Barkwill, Linda Klobasa 1947- WhoEmL 91
Barlach, Ernst PenDiDA 89
Barlach, Ernst 1870-1938 BioIn 16, IntDcAA 90, ModArCr 1 [port]
Barlage, Harry E. 1941- St&PR 91
Barlament, Robert John 1928- St&PR 91
Barlar, Rebecca Nance 1950- WhoEmL 91
Barlas, Julie Sandall 1944- WhoAm 90
Barlett, Donald L. 1936- WhoAm 90, WhoE 91
Barlett, James Edward 1944- WhoAm 90
Barletta, Joseph Francis 1936- WhoAm 90, WhoWrEP 89
Barletta, Robert T. 1946- St&PR 91
Barley, Albert Lawrence 1942- St&PR 91
Barley, Barbara Ann 1954- WhoEmL 91
Barley, Doris Faye 1936- WhoSSW 91
Barley, Gilbert R. ODwPR 91
Barley, John Alvin 1940- WhoSSW 91
Barley, Kathryn Myers 1954- WhoEmL 91
Barley, Leonard V., Jr. 1946- BiDrAPA 89
Barley, Nena Stewart 1958- WhoAmW 91
Barley, Nigel BioIn 16
Barley, Robert Eugene 1930- St&PR 91
Barlick, Al 1915- Ballpl 90 [port]
Barlieb, Earl Frederick 1947- WhoWor 91
Barlinska, Izabela 1955- WhoWor 91
Barloga, Viola H 1890- WhoAmA 91N
Barlow, A. William 1906- WhoWor 91
Barlow, Alvin Wellington 1961- WhoEmL 91
Barlow, Anne Louise 1925- WhoAm 90
Barlow, August Ralph, Jr. 1934- WhoE 91, WhoWor 91
Barlow, Bob 1934- BioIn 16
Barlow, Carl Morton 1925- WhoE 91
Barlow, Catherine C BiDrAPA 89
Barlow, Charles Beach 1926- St&PR 91
Barlow, Charles Franklin 1923- WhoAm 90
Barlow, Clark W. 1938- St&PR 91
Barlow, Conrad R. 1920- St&PR 91
Barlow, Curtis Hudson 1948- St&PR 91
Barlow, Deborah Lunn 1958- WhoAmA 91
Barlow, DeWitt D. 1946- St&PR 91
Barlow, Florence PenDiDA 89
Barlow, Frank 1911- ConAu 30NR
Barlow, Frank John 1914- St&PR 91, WhoAm 90
Barlow, Fred EncPaPR 91
Barlow, Genevieve 1910- AuBYP 90
Barlow, Hannah PenDiDA 89
Barlow, Harold 1899-1989 AnObit 1989
Barlow, Harold 1915- IntWWM 90
Barlow, Ian Dean BiDrAPA 89
Barlow, James Craig 1946- WhoEmL 91
Barlow, Jane 1857-1917 FemiCLE
Barlow, Joel 1754-1812 BioIn 16
Barlow, Joel 1908- WhoAm 90
Barlow, Joel William 1942- WhoAm 90
Barlow, John David, Jr. 1935- St&PR 91
Barlow, Kenneth James 1932- WhoAm 90
Barlow, Kent Michael 1935- St&PR 91
Barlow, Laurie Patricia Hildebrand 1952- WhoEmL 91
Barlow, Leo 1952- St&PR 91
Barlow, Lolete Falck 1932- WhoWrEP 89
Barlow, Mark, Jr. 1925- WhoAm 90
Barlow, Michael 1940- IntWWM 90
Barlow, Mike 1948- Ballpl 90
Barlow, Nathan B. 1939- St&PR 91
Barlow, Oliver B. 1960- St&PR 91
Barlow, Richard Gordon 1945- WhoEmL 91
Barlow, Roger AuBYP 90
Barlow, Tani E. 1950- ConAu 130
Barlow, Walter Greenwood 1917- WhoAm 90, WhoE 91
Barlow, Wayne 1912- IntWWM 90
Barlow, William Edward 1917- WhoAm 90, WhoWrEP 89
Barlow, William Pusey, Jr. 1934- WhoAm 90
Barmann, Lawrence Francis 1932- WhoAm 90
Barme, Geremie 1954- ConAu 131
Barmmer, Russell G., II 1941- ODwPR 91
Barmore, Gregory T. 1941- BioIn 16
Barmore, Gregory Terhune 1941- St&PR 91
Barmore, Kenneth R. 1917- St&PR 91
Barna, Douglas Peter 1945- WhoE 91
Barna, Gary Stanley 1940- St&PR 91
Barna, Peter 1943- St&PR 91, WhoAm 90
Barna, Richard A. 1948- St&PR 91
Barnabas Ip, Seng Chi 1948- WhoWor 91
Barnaby, Ralph Stanton 1893- AuBYP 90
Barnacle, Nora 1884-1951 BioIn 16
Barnaku, Frank Richardson, Jr. 1943- WhoSSW 91
Barnao, Jack TwCCr&M 91
Barnard, Anne 1750-1825 FemiCLE
Barnard, Anne 1750-1826 BioIn 16
Barnard, Aubrey D. 1936- St&PR 91
Barnard, Barbara Nell 1929- WhoSSW 91
Barnard, Bonnie Marie 1957- WhoAmW 91
Barnard, Carl Alvin 1946- WhoEmL 91
Barnard, Charlene ODwPR 91
Barnard, Charles Francis 1928- St&PR 91
Barnard, Charles N. BioIn 16
Barnard, Charles Nelson 1924- WhoAm 90, WhoWrEP 89
Barnard, Charles Preston, Sr. 1928- St&PR 91
Barnard, Charlotte 1830-1869 FemiCLE, OxCPMus
Barnard, Chris 1950- St&PR 91
Barnard, Christiaan BioIn 16
Barnard, Christiaan N. 1922- WorAlBi
Barnard, Christiaan Neethling 1922- WhoWor 91
Barnard, D.R. 1932- St&PR 91
Barnard, Dafferlin J. BiDrAPA 89
Barnard, Daniel Dewey 1797-1861 BioIn 16
Barnard, Donald Edward 1939- St&PR 91
Barnard, Donald Roy 1946- WhoWor 91
Barnard, Douglas Craig 1958- WhoEmL 91
Barnard, Druie Douglas, Jr. 1922- WhoAm 90, WhoSSW 91
Barnard, Edouard-Andre 1835-1898 DcCanB 12
Barnard, Edward PenDiDA 89
Barnard, Edward Emerson 1857-1923 BioIn 16
Barnard, Elaine Patricia 1930- WhoAmW 91
Barnard, Ernest S. Ballpl 90
Barnard, Frederick 1809-1889 WorAlBi
Barnard, G. Dene 1932- IntWWM 90
Barnard, George W 1928- BiDrAPA 89
Barnard, Howard Clive 1884-1985 DcNaB 1981
Barnard, James A. 1929- St&PR 91
Barnard, John William BiDrAPA 89
Barnard, Kathleen Rainwater 1927- WhoAmW 91, WhoWor 91
Barnard, Kathryn Elaine 1938- WhoAmW 91
Barnard, Kurt 1927- WhoAm 90
Barnard, Marjorie 1897-1987 FemiCLE
Barnard, Michael Dana 1946- WhoAm 90
Barnard, Neal Dana 1953- BiDrAPA 89
Barnard, Robert 1936- TwCCr&M 91
Barnard, Rollin Dwight 1922- WhoAm 90
Barnard, Rosalyn Mynette 1961- WhoAmW 91
Barnard, Ruth I BiDrAPA 89
Barnard, Sandra Kay 1941- WhoAmW 91
Barnard, Scott Henry 1943- WhoAm 90
Barnard, Seph 1956- WhoEmL 91, WhoWor 91
Barnard, Sheri WhoAmW 91
Barnard, Susan Muller 1935- WhoAm 90
Barnard, Thomas Elliot 1941- WhoWor 91
Barnard, Thomas H. 1939- WhoAm 90
Barnard, Timpoochee WhNaAH
Barnard, Trevor 1938- IntWWM 90
Barnard, W Winston 1922- BiDrAPA 89
Barnard, Walther M. 1937- WhoAm 90
Barnard, William Calvert 1914- WhoAm 90
Barnard, William M 1949- BiDrAPA 89
Barnardo, Thomas John 1845-1905 BioIn 16
Barnat, Rhonda Katz 1952- WhoAmW 91
Barnathan, Julius 1927- St&PR 91, WhoAm 90
Barnaud, Nicholas EncO&P 3
Barnave, Antonie Pierre Joseph Marie 1761-1793 BioIn 16
Barncord, Ronald L. 1947- St&PR 91
Barnden, Robert John 1946- WhoWor 91
Barnds, John Edward 1932- St&PR 91
Barndt, Walter Dewey, Jr. 1928- WhoE 91
Barne, Kitty 1883-1957 AuBYP 90
Barne, Marion Catherine AuBYP 90
Barnea, Uri N. 1943- IntWWM 90
Barnebey, Kenneth Alan 1931- WhoAm 90
Barneby, Rupert C. BioIn 16
Barner, Brett Lee 1963- WhoSSW 91
Barner, Bruce Monroe 1951- WhoEmL 91, WhoWor 91
Barnert, Cyril, III BiDrAPA 89
Barnes, A. James 1942- WhoAm 90
Barnes, Alan Jay 1941- BiDrAPA 89
Barnes, Alan Watson 1925-1987 BioIn 16
Barnes, Albert Francis 1934- WhoE 91
Barnes, Allan Randall 1946- WhoEmL 91
Barnes, Alvin F. 1929- St&PR 91
Barnes, Andre LaMont 1957- WhoSSW 91
Barnes, Andrew Earl 1939- St&PR 91, WhoAm 90, WhoSSW 91, WhoWrEP 89
Barneo, Anna Sue 1935- WhoSSW 91
Barnes, Annette Casey BiDrAPA 89
Barnes, Audrey Bryant 1930- WhoAmW 91
Barnes, B. Jack 1934- WhoAm 90
Barnes, Barbara Green 1938- WhoSSW 91
Barnes, Ben 1956- IntWWM 90
Barnes, Ben Frank 1938- WhoSSW 91
Barnes, Benjamin Shields, Jr. 1919- WhoAm 90
Barnes, Bernard Ellis 1931- WhoSSW 91
Barnes, Bruce Herbert 1931- WhoE 91
Barnes, Burton V 1930- ConAu 130
Barnes, Byron E. 1927- St&PR 91
Barnes, Calvin K. 1929- St&PR 91
Barnes, Carlyle F. 1924- St&PR 91
Barnes, Carlyle Fuller 1924- WhoAm 90
Barnes, Carmen Dee 1912- FemiCLE
Barnes, Carole D 1935- WhoAmA 91
Barnes, Carolyn S. Machalec 1957- WhoEmL 91
Barnes, Cassius McDonald 1845-1925 AmLegL
Barnes, Cathy Lynn 1952- WhoAmW 91
Barnes, Charles Andrew 1921- WhoAm 90
Barnes, Charles D. 1935- WhoAm 90
Barnes, Charles David 1935- St&PR 91
Barnes, Charlotte Sanford 1818-1863 FemiCLE
Barnes, Christopher E. 1953- St&PR 91
Barnes, Christopher J 1942- ConAu 132
Barnes, Christopher John 1942- IntWWM 90
Barnes, Christopher Richard 1940- WhoAm 90
Barnes, Clarence W. 1938- St&PR 91
Barnes, Cliff 1940- WhoAmA 91
Barnes, Clifton Odell 1928- St&PR 91
Barnes, Clive Alexander 1927- WhoAm 90
Barnes, Constance Ingalls 1903- WhoAmW 91
Barnes, Corinne Ann 1928- WhoAmW 91
Barnes, Craig Martin 1949- WhoEmL 91, WhoSSW 91
Barnes, Craig W. 1945- St&PR 91
Barnes, Curt 1943- WhoAmA 91
Barnes, Cynthia Ann 1949- WhoEmL 91
Barnes, Cynthia Darnell BiDrAPA 89
Barnes, Daniel Walter 1953- WhoSSW 91, WhoWor 91
Barnes, David Robert, Jr. 1952- WhoEmL 91
Barnes, Deborah Dickson 1944- WhoAmW 91
Barnes, Denis Tat 1929- WhoAmW 91
Barnes, Dick 1932- WhoWrEP 89
Barnes, Djuna 1892-1982 BioAmW, BioIn 16, FemiCLE, MajTwCW, NotWoAT, WorAlBi
Barnes, Donald Gayle 1940- WhoAm 90
Barnes, Donald Michael 1943- WhoAm 90
Barnes, Donald Winfree 1943- WhoAm 90
Barnes, Douglas Charles 1935- WhoSSW 91
Barnes, Douglas J. 1936- St&PR 91
Barnes, Douglass M. 1941- ODwPR 91, St&PR 91
Barnes, Duncan 1935- WhoAm 90
Barnes, Edward Larrabee 1915- WhoAm 90, WhoAmA 91
Barnes, Eric Wollencott 1907- AuBYP 90
Barnes, Francis F 1923- BiDrAPA 89
Barnes, Frank Stephenson 1932- WhoAm 90
Barnes, Fred 1885-1938 OxCPMus
Barnes, Frederick Walter, Jr. 1909- WhoAm 90
Barnes, Gene ODwPR 91
Barnes, Gene 1926- WhoWor 91
Barnes, George Elton 1900- WhoAm 90
Barnes, George William 1927- WhoAm 90
Barnes, Germaine Emma 1948- WhoAmW 91
Barnes, H.M. St&PR 91
Barnes, Harry G., Jr. 1926- WhoAm 90
Barnes, Hazel Estella 1915- WhoAm 90
Barnes, Helen Cross 1945- WhoAmW 91
Barnes, Howard G. 1913- WhoAm 90
Barnes, Howard Turner 1873-1950 DcScB S2
Barnes, Hubert Lloyd 1928- WhoAm 90
Barnes, Isabel Janet 1936- WhoAm 90, WhoAmW 91
Barnes, J Robert 1942- BiDrAPA 89
Barnes, Jack Whittier 1940- WhoAm 90
Barnes, James Arthur 1954- St&PR 91
Barnes, James Byron 1942- WhoAm 90
Barnes, James E. 1934- St&PR 91, WhoAm 90, WhoSSW 91
Barnes, James John 1931- WhoAm 90
Barnes, James Keith BiDrAPA 89
Barnes, James McGregor 1953- St&PR 91
Barnes, James Milton 1923- WhoAm 90
Barnes, James R. 1938- St&PR 91
Barnes, James Thomas, Jr. 1940- WhoSSW 91
Barnes, Jane Ellen 1943- WhoWrEP 89
Barnes, Jean 1923- WhoSSW 91
Barnes, Jean Fredenburgh 1923- WhoAmW 91
Barnes, Jeff BioIn 16
Barnes, Jerry Neal 1933- WhoWrEP 89
Barnes, Jesse 1892-1961 Ballpl 90
Barnes, Jhane Elizabeth 1954- WhoAm 90, WhoAmW 91
Barnes, Jill 1953- WhoWrEP 89
Barnes, Jim Weaver 1933- WhoWrEP 89
Barnes, Jo Ann 1935- WhoAmW 91
Barnes, Joanna 1934- WhoAm 90
Barnes, John Andrew 1960- WhoAm 90
Barnes, John E. 1935- St&PR 91
Barnes, John Fayette 1930- WhoAm 90
Barnes, John Gilbert Presslie 1937- WhoWor 91
Barnes, John Joseph 1924- St&PR 91
Barnes, John Lawrence 1947- WhoAm 90, WhoWor 91
Barnes, John M. 1924- St&PR 91
Barnes, John R. 1944- St&PR 91
Barnes, John Wadsworth 1920- WhoE 91
Barnes, Jonathan A. 1946- St&PR 91
Barnes, Joy Chappell 1950- WhoEmL 91
Barnes, Judith Anne 1948- WhoAmW 91
Barnes, Julia O'Teala 1937- WhoAmW 91
Barnes, Julian BioIn 16, TwCCr&M 91
Barnes, Julian 1946- WorAu 1980 [port]
Barnes, Karen Geddes 1940- WhoSSW 91
Barnes, Kate Miller 1953- WhoAmW 91, WhoEmL 91
Barnes, Keith Allen 1940- St&PR 91
Barnes, Kitt 1946- WhoAmA 91
Barnes, L.V. 1912- St&PR 91
Barnes, Leo 1910- WhoAm 90
Barnes, Linda ConAu 132
Barnes, Linda 1949- TwCCr&M 91
Barnes, Linda Baxter 1943- WhoSSW 91
Barnes, Linda J. 1949- ConAu 132
Barnes, Linda Joyce 1949- WhoAmW 91
Barnes, Lorna Elaine 1958- WhoAmW 91
Barnes, Louie Burton, III 1948- WhoAm 90, WhoEmL 91, WhoSSW 91

Barnes, Lucinda Ann 1951- *WhoAmA 91*
Barnes, Mae 1907- *DrBlPA 90*
Barnes, Maggie Lue Shifflett 1931- *WhoAmW 91*
Barnes, Margaret 1886-1967 *FemiCLE*
Barnes, Margaret Anderson *WhoAmW 91*
Barnes, Margaret Ayer 1886-1967 *BioAmW*
Barnes, Margaret Marie 1954- *WhoEmL 91*
Barnes, Margo 1947- *WhoAmA 91*
Barnes, Margo L. 1955- *ODwPR 91*
Barnes, Marianne Ruth *BiDrAPA 89*
Barnes, Marjorie *DrBlPA 90*
Barnes, Mark 1960- *WhoEmL 91*
Barnes, Mark James 1957- *WhoAm 90, WhoEmL 91*
Barnes, Marshall Hayes, II 1937- *WhoWor 91*
Barnes, Martin E. 1948- *St&PR 91*
Barnes, Martin McRae 1920- *WhoAm 90*
Barnes, Mary Catherine Banning 1954- *WhoAmW 91*
Barnes, Mary Jane 1913- *WhoWrEP 89*
Barnes, Michael 1934- *BioIn 16*
Barnes, Michael Darr 1943- *WhoAm 90*
Barnes, Michael Edwin *BiDrAPA 89*
Barnes, Milford Edwin, Jr. 1918- *BiDrAPA 89*
Barnes, Milton 1931- *IntWWM 90*
Barnes, Molly 1936- *WhoAmA 91*
Barnes, N. Kurt 1947- *ODwPR 91*
Barnes, Nancy Carol 1953- *WhoWrEP 89*
Barnes, Norman Frank 1939- *WhoE 91*
Barnes, Norman John 1916- *IntWWM 90*
Barnes, Pancho 1901-1975 *BioIn 16*
Barnes, Patricia Jane 1944- *BiDrAPA 89*
Barnes, Paul *BioIn 16*
Barnes, Paul D 1929- *BiDrAPA 89*
Barnes, Paul McClung 1914- *WhoAm 90*
Barnes, Paula Carolyn 1952- *WhoSSW 91*
Barnes, Peter 1931- *ConAu 33NR, ConAu 12AS [port], MajTwCW*
Barnes, Philippa Kay 1956- *WhoWor 91*
Barnes, Phyllis Lundy 1950- *WhoAmW 91*
Barnes, Ramon Murray 1940- *WhoE 91*
Barnes, Randy *BioIn 16*
Barnes, Randy Morgan 1955- *WhoSSW 91*
Barnes, Red 1903-1959 *Ballpl 90*
Barnes, Richard George 1922- *WhoAm 90*
Barnes, Richard Gordon 1932- *WhoAm 90, WhoWrEP 89*
Barnes, Richard Jeremy 1937- *WhoWor 91*
Barnes, Robert Allan 1927- *St&PR 91*
Barnes, Robert C. 1927- *St&PR 91*
Barnes, Robert E. 1927- *St&PR 91, WhoAm 90*
Barnes, Robert E. 1933- *WhoAm 90*
Barnes, Robert F 1946- *BiDrAPA 89*
Barnes, Robert G., Jr. 1929- *St&PR 91*
Barnes, Robert Goodwin 1914- *WhoAm 90, WhoWrEP 89*
Barnes, Robert H 1921- *BiDrAPA 89*
Barnes, Robert M 1934- *WhoAmA 91*
Barnes, Robert Marshall 1923- *WhoAm 90*
Barnes, Robert Merton 1934- *WhoAm 90*
Barnes, Rosemary Lois 1946- *WhoEmL 91*
Barnes, Ross 1850-1915 *Ballpl 90*
Barnes, Roswell P. 1901-1990 *NewYTBS 90 [port]*
Barnes, Roy James 1937- *BiDrAPA 89*
Barnes, Roy V. *ODwPR 91*
Barnes, Russell Hanlon 1959- *WhoEmL 91*
Barnes, Russell Miller 1927- *St&PR 91*
Barnes, S. Arlene 1934- *WhoAmW 91*
Barnes, Samuel Henry 1931- *WhoAm 90*
Barnes, Samuel Lee 1941- *St&PR 91*
Barnes, Sandra S. 1943- *St&PR 91*
Barnes, Sandra Sue 1943- *WhoAm 90, WhoAmW 91, WhoWor 91*
Barnes, Scott Andrew 1963- *WhoSSW 91*
Barnes, Scott Wright 1945- *St&PR 91*
Barnes, Sharon Eurich 1942- *WhoAmW 91*
Barnes, Simon 1951- *ConAu 130*
Barnes, Stephen Paul 1957- *WhoEmL 91*
Barnes, Steven Lee 1950- *WhoEmL 91*
Barnes, Susan Kelly *BioIn 16*
Barnes, Thomas Joseph 1930- *WhoAm 90*
Barnes, Thomas Vance 1956- *WhoSSW 91*
Barnes, Timothy Lee 1951- *WhoEmL 91*
Barnes, V. Lee 1936- *St&PR 91*
Barnes, Vera Lewis 1936- *WhoAmW 91*
Barnes, Virgil 1897-1958 *Ballpl 90*
Barnes, Virgil Everett, II 1935- *WhoAm 90*
Barnes, Waddell 1925- *WhoAm 90*
Barnes, Wade 1917- *WhoWrEP 89*
Barnes, Wallace 1926- *St&PR 91, WhoAm 90*
Barnes, Wallace Ray 1928- *WhoAm 90*
Barnes, Walter Carlyle, Jr. 1922- *WhoSSW 91*
Barnes, Walter S. 1860- *Ballpl 90*
Barnes, Wendell Wright, Jr. 1950- *WhoEmL 91*
Barnes, Wesley Edward 1937- *WhoAm 90*
Barnes, Will C. 1858-1936 *BioIn 16*
Barnes, William, III *St&PR 91N*
Barnes, William Arthur, III 1938- *WhoAm 90*
Barnes, William Douglas 1953- *WhoEmL 91*
Barnes, William E. *BioIn 16*
Barnes, William E. 1911- *St&PR 91*
Barnes, William M. 1925- *St&PR 91*
Barnes, William Oliver, Jr. 1922- *WhoAm 90*
Barnes, Willie R. 1931- *WhoWor 91*
Barnes, Wilson King 1907- *WhoAm 90*
Barnes, Z.E. 1921- *St&PR 91*
Barnes, Zane Edison 1921- *WhoAm 90*
Barnes, Zelma *BioIn 16*
Barnes-Miller, Dorothy Louise 1945- *WhoAmW 91*
Barness, Amnon Shemaya 1924- *WhoAm 90*
Barness, Lewis Abraham 1921- *WhoAm 90*
Barnet, Ann Birnbaum 1930- *WhoAmW 91*
Barnet, Charlie 1913- *BioIn 16, OxCPMus*
Barnet, John H. 1935- *St&PR 91*
Barnet, Richard Jackson 1929- *WhoAm 90, WhoWrEP 89*
Barnet, Robert Joseph 1929- *WhoAm 90*
Barnet, Sylvan 1926- *WhoAm 90*
Barnet, Will 1911- *WhoAm 90, WhoAmA 91*
Barnetson, William Denholm 1917-1981 *DcNaB 1981*
Barnett, Alison Karen 1946- *BiDrAPA 89*
Barnett, Allen Marshall 1940- *WhoE 91*
Barnett, Arden Davis *BiDrAPA 89*
Barnett, Arthur Doak 1921- *WhoAm 90*
Barnett, Barney 1945- *Ballpl 90*
Barnett, Barry Howard 1954- *WhoEmL 91*
Barnett, Benjamin Lewis, Jr. 1926- *WhoAm 90*
Barnett, Bennie Everson 1926- *St&PR 91*
Barnett, Bernard 1920- *WhoAm 90*
Barnett, Bertha LaMyrtle 1941- *WhoSSW 91*
Barnett, Bill Marvin 1931- *WhoAm 90, WhoWrEP 89*
Barnett, Billy J. 1931- *WhoSSW 91*
Barnett, Bruce Philip 1949- *St&PR 91*
Barnett, Burton 1933- *St&PR 91*
Barnett, Carol Edith 1949- *IntWWM 90*
Barnett, Charles 1958- *WhoE 91*
Barnett, Charles Edward 1915- *St&PR 91*
Barnett, Charlie 1954?- *DrBlPA 90*
Barnett, Christopher Morgan 1955- *WhoEmL 91*
Barnett, Claire Margaret *BiDrAPA 89*
Barnett, Crawford Fannin, Jr. 1938- *WhoSSW 91*
Barnett, Dana Golden 1941- *St&PR 91*
Barnett, David J 1946- *WhoAmA 91*
Barnett, David Leon 1922- *WhoWrEP 89*
Barnett, Don 1929- *St&PR 91*
Barnett, Dwight Lee 1944- *St&PR 91*
Barnett, Earl D *WhoAmA 91*
Barnett, Edith A. *FemiCLE*
Barnett, Edward William 1933- *WhoAm 90*
Barnett, Edward Willis 1922-1987 *WhoAmA 91N*
Barnett, Elizabeth 1954- *WhoAmW 91*
Barnett, Elizabeth Hale 1940- *WhoAmW 91*
Barnett, Emily 1947- *WhoAmA 91*
Barnett, Eugene Victor 1932- *WhoAm 90*
Barnett, Evelyn Snead 1861-1921 *LiHiK*
Barnett, Florence Lloyd-Jones 1913- *WhoAm 90, WhoAmW 91*
Barnett, Franklin DeWees 1935- *WhoSSW 91*
Barnett, Frederic 1951- *WhoE 91*
Barnett, George Leonard 1915- *WhoAm 90*
Barnett, Glenn Ellis 1945- *WhoEmL 91*
Barnett, Helmut 1946- *WhoAmA 91*
Barnett, Henry Lewis 1914- *WhoAm 90*
Barnett, Herbert P 1910-1972 *WhoAmA 91N*
Barnett, Hollis 1939- *St&PR 91*
Barnett, Holly Billings 1956- *WhoEmL 91*
Barnett, Holly L. 1956- *ODwPR 91*
Barnett, Howard Albert 1920- *WhoAm 90*
Barnett, Howard Gentry, Jr. 1950- *WhoAm 90*
Barnett, Hoyt Robinson 1943- *St&PR 91*
Barnett, J. Paul *BioIn 16*
Barnett, Jacalyn F. 1952- *WhoAmW 91*
Barnett, James Wallace 1930- *WhoAm 90*
Barnett, Jane Ayne 1950- *WhoAmW 91*
Barnett, Joanne 1954- *WhoEmL 91*
Barnett, Joel 1923- *ConAu 129*
Barnett, John Vincent 1912- *WhoAm 90*
Barnett, John W. 1924- *St&PR 91*
Barnett, Jonathan 1937- *WhoAm 90, WhoE 91*
Barnett, Joseph 1926-1988 *BioIn 16*
Barnett, Karl Fredrick 1927- *St&PR 91*
Barnett, Keith *BiDrAPA 89*
Barnett, Ken *ConTFT 8*
Barnett, L. David *AuBYP 90*
Barnett, Leah Kenote 1934- *WhoE 91*
Barnett, Lena Sue 1959- *WhoAmW 91*
Barnett, Leo 1925- *AuBYP 90*
Barnett, Leroy Elliot 1936- *WhoSSW 91*
Barnett, Lester Alfred 1915- *WhoAm 90*
Barnett, Lynn Laree 1954- *BiDrAPA 89*
Barnett, M. Robert 1916- *WhoAm 90*
Barnett, Margaret Edwina 1949- *WhoAmW 91*
Barnett, Margaret Mary 1936- *St&PR 91*
Barnett, Marguerite Ross 1942- *WhoAm 90*
Barnett, Marie *WhoAmW 91*
Barnett, Marilyn 1934- *WhoAmW 91*
Barnett, Mark 1957- *WhoE 91*
Barnett, Martha Walters 1947- *WhoAm 90*
Barnett, Mary Louise 1941- *WhoAmW 91*
Barnett, Michael Stanley *BiDrAPA 89*
Barnett, Moneta 1922-1976 *BioIn 16*
Barnett, Ola Wilma 1940- *WhoAmW 91*
Barnett, Pam *BioIn 16*
Barnett, Patricia Ann 1956- *WhoAmW 91*
Barnett, Peter John 1944- *WhoE 91*
Barnett, Peter Ralph 1951- *WhoSSW 91*
Barnett, Philip 1937- *St&PR 91*
Barnett, Preston Baker 1946- *St&PR 91*
Barnett, R. David 1926- *WhoSSW 91*
Barnett, Ralph Lipsey 1933- *WhoAm 90*
Barnett, Rebecca Lynn 1957- *WhoEmL 91, WhoWor 91*
Barnett, Rex M. 1934- *St&PR 91*
Barnett, Richard Allen 1949- *WhoSSW 91*
Barnett, Richard Blair 1927- *WhoAm 90*
Barnett, Richard Chambers 1932- *WhoAm 90*
Barnett, Richard Meyer 1934- *St&PR 91*
Barnett, Robert Bruce 1946- *WhoEmL 91*
Barnett, Robert Don 1929- *St&PR 91*
Barnett, Robert Glenn 1933- *WhoAm 90*
Barnett, Robert L. 1940- *WhoAm 90*
Barnett, Robert Warren 1911- *WhoAm 90*
Barnett, Rosalea 1946- *WhoAmW 91*
Barnett, Rosalind C. 1937- *ConAu 129*
Barnett, Ross Robert 1898-1987 *BioIn 16*
Barnett, Steve 1941- *ODwPR 91*
Barnett, Steven Dale 1947- *St&PR 91*
Barnett, Stuart Alan 1942- *St&PR 91*
Barnett, Susanne La Mar 1946- *WhoEmL 91*
Barnett, Theresa Ann 1952- *WhoEmL 91*
Barnett, Thomas Buchanan 1919- *WhoAm 90*
Barnett, Thomas Glen 1946- *St&PR 91*
Barnett, Thomas W 1950- *BiDrAPA 89*
Barnett, Trevor N. 1948- *St&PR 91*
Barnett, Vincent MacDowell, Jr. 1913- *WhoAm 90*
Barnett, Virginia Rich 1934- *WhoAmW 91*
Barnett, Vivian Endicott 1944- *WhoAm 90, WhoAmA 91, WhoAmW 91, WhoE 91, WhoWor 91*
Barnett, Walter Michael 1903- *WhoAm 90*
Barnett, William Arnold 1941- *WhoAm 90*
Barnett, William D., Jr. 1943- *St&PR 91*
Barnett-Reyes, Saundra *BiDrAPA 89*
Barnett Scharf, Lauren Ileene 1956- *WhoWrEP 89*
Barnett-Walker, Alison Karen 1946- *WhoE 91*
Barnette, C. Joseph 1941- *St&PR 91*
Barnette, Charles R. 1945- *ODwPR 91*
Barnette, Charles Robert 1945- *WhoSSW 91*
Barnette, Curtis H. 1935- *St&PR 91*
Barnette, Curtis Handley 1935- *WhoAm 90*
Barnette, David Allen 1952- *WhoEmL 91*
Barnette, Dennis Arthur 1941- *WhoAm 90*
Barnette, Henlee H 1911- *ConAu 31NR*
Barnette, James *BioIn 16*
Barnette, Marge C. 1944- *WhoAmW 91*
Barnette, Sharon Mildred 1951- *WhoAmW 91*
Barnevik, Percy *BioIn 16*
Barnevik, Percy Nils 1941- *WhoAm 90, WhoWor 91*
Barnewall, Gordon Gouverneur 1924- *WhoAm 90*
Barney, Alice Pike 1857-1931 *BiDWomA*
Barney, C. Lynn 1943- *St&PR 91*
Barney, Carlton Elliott 1946- *St&PR 91*
Barney, Carol Ross 1949- *WhoEmL 91*
Barney, Charles Lester 1925- *WhoAm 90*
Barney, Charles Richard 1935- *WhoAm 90*
Barney, Christine Anne 1959- *BiDrAPA 89*
Barney, Debora Alter *BiDrAPA 89*
Barney, Duane R. 1956- *WhoEmL 91*
Barney, Harry *ConAu 30NR*
Barney, James Earl 1926- *WhoE 91*
Barney, John A. 1929- *WhoE 91*
Barney, John Charles 1939- *WhoAm 90*
Barney, Lawrence Davis 1906-1989 *BioIn 16*
Barney, Maginal Wright *WhoAmA 91N*
Barney, Michael Eugene 1947- *WhoSSW 91*
Barney, Natalie C. 1876-1972 *BioAmW*
Barney, Natalie Clifford *BioIn 16*
Barney, Natalie Clifford 1876-1972 *EncCoWW, FemiCLE*
Barney, Rex 1924- *Ballpl 90, BioIn 16*
Barney, Robert John 1952- *WhoSSW 91*
Barney, Robert L. *WhoAm 90*
Barney, Robert L. 1936- *St&PR 91*
Barney, Thomas McNamee 1938- *WhoAm 90*
Barney, William Joshua, Jr. 1911- *WhoAm 90*
Barney, Wm. Joshua, Jr. 1911- *St&PR 91*
Barnhard, Albert A. *St&PR 91N*
Barnhard, Ronald Harris 1948- *St&PR 91*
Barnhard, Sherwood A. 1921- *St&PR 91*
Barnhard, Sherwood Arthur 1921- *WhoE 91, WhoWor 91*
Barnhardt, J.C. *St&PR 91N*
Barnhardt, James Harper 1913- *St&PR 91*
Barnhardt, Robert Alexander 1937- *WhoAm 90*
Barnhardt, Sadler Hayes 1948- *St&PR 91*
Barnhardt, T. M. 1932- *St&PR 91*
Barnhardt, Zeb Elonzo, Jr. 1941- *WhoAm 90*
Barnhart, Beverly Jean 1954- *WhoAmW 91*
Barnhart, Charles Elmer 1923- *WhoAm 90*
Barnhart, Clarence L. 1900- *WorAlBi*
Barnhart, Clarence Lewis 1900- *BioIn 16, WhoAm 90, WhoWrEP 89*
Barnhart, Clyde 1895-1980 *Ballpl 90*
Barnhart, David Brown 1956- *WhoEmL 91*
Barnhart, David Knox 1941- *WhoWrEP 89*
Barnhart, Dorothy Kohrs 1933- *WhoAmW 91*
Barnhart, Elizabeth Anne 1955- *WhoAmW 91*
Barnhart, James Howard 1938- *WhoE 91*
Barnhart, James Paul 1941- *St&PR 91*
Barnhart, Jo Anne B. 1950- *WhoAmW 91*
Barnhart, Mary Ann 1930- *WhoSSW 91*
Barnhart, Noah Chisholm *BioIn 16*
Barnhart, Stephen Ray 1956- *WhoEmL 91*
Barnhill, Barbara Anne 1942- *WhoSSW 91*
Barnhill, Cecile Taylor *WhoSSW 91*
Barnhill, Charles Joseph, Jr. 1943- *WhoAm 90*
Barnhill, Charles L. 1934- *St&PR 91*
Barnhill, Claude A 1931- *BiDrAPA 89*
Barnhill, David 1914-1983 *Ballpl 90*
Barnhill, David Stan 1949- *WhoEmL 91*
Barnhill, Georgia Brady 1944- *WhoAmA 91, WhoE 91*
Barnhill, Howard Eugene 1923- *St&PR 91, WhoAm 90*
Barnhill, John *ODwPR 91*
Barnhill, John Herschel 1947- *WhoSSW 91*
Barnhill, John W., Jr. 1936- *St&PR 91*
Barnhill, John Warren 1959- *BiDrAPA 89, WhoEmL 91*
Barnhill, Larry Jarrett, Jr. 1949- *BiDrAPA 89*
Barnhill, Raymond L. 1950- *WhoE 91*
Barnhill, Robert Edward, Jr. 1947- *St&PR 91*
Barnhill, Stephen Fuller 1948- *WhoSSW 91*
Barnholdt, Terry Joseph 1954- *WhoEmL 91*
Barnhouse, Paul E. 1926- *St&PR 91*
Barnhouse, Ruth Tiffany 1923- *BiDrAPA 89*
Barnidge, Mary Shen 1948- *WhoWrEP 89*
Barnidge, Thomas Howard 1948- *WhoAm 90*
Barnie, Bill 1853-1900 *Ballpl 90*
Barnoff, Sharon Holloway 1952- *WhoAmW 91*
Barnothy, Jeno Michael 1904- *WhoAm 90*
Barnouw, Adriaan Jacob 1877-1968 *AuBYP 90*
Barnouw, Erik 1908- *WhoAm 90, WhoWrEP 89*
Barns, Doretha Mae Clayton 1917- *WhoAmW 91, WhoWor 91*
Barns, William Derrick 1917- *WhoAm 90, WhoWor 91*
Barns-Graham, Wilhemina 1912- *BiDWomA*
Barnshaw, H Douglas 1936- *BiDrAPA 89*
Barnsley, Edward 1900-1987 *BioIn 16*
Barnsley, Edwin *PenDiDA 89*
Barnsley, Ernest *PenDiDA 89*
Barnsley, Sidney *PenDiDA 89*
Barnstead, William A. 1919- *St&PR 91*
Barnstone, Howard 1923-1987 *BioIn 16*
Barnstone, Willis 1927- *WhoAm 90, WhoWrEP 89*
Barnthouse, William Joseph 1948- *WhoEmL 91*
Barnum, Anna Maria 1943- *WhoAmW 91*
Barnum, Barbara J. 1937- *St&PR 91*
Barnum, Daniel Boone 1938- *WhoSSW 91*
Barnum, Donald G. 1931- *St&PR 91*
Barnum, H. James *BioIn 16*

Barnum, Howard James, Jr. 1922- *St&PR 91*
Barnum, Jay Hyde 1888?-1962 *AuBYP 90*
Barnum, John Wallace 1928- *WhoAm 90*
Barnum, Nan Martin 1951- *WhoEmL 91*
Barnum, Otis Ray 1951- *WhoWor 91*
Barnum, P. T. 1810-1891 *BioIn 16, WorAlBi*
Barnum, Phineas Taylor 1810-1891 *BioIn 16, OxCPMus*
Barnum, Richard W 1947- *BiDrAPA 89*
Barnum, Robert L. *BioIn 16*
Barnum, Robert T. 1945- *St&PR 91*
Barnum, Thomas Grossenbach 1932- *St&PR 91*
Barnum, William Douglas 1946- *WhoE 91, WhoEmL 91, WhoWor 91*
Barnum, William J. Jr. *BiDrAPA 89*
Barnum, William Laird 1916- *WhoAm 90*
Barnum, William Milo 1927- *WhoAm 90, WhoWor 91*
Barnwell, Charles Brison, Jr. 1942- *WhoSSW 91*
Barnwell, D. Robinson 1915- *AuBYP 90*
Barnwell, Franklin Hershel 1937- *WhoAm 90*
Barnwell, George Morgan, Jr. 1939- *WhoSSW 91*
Barnwell, John L 1922- *WhoAmA 91*
Barnwell, Michele R. *BioIn 16*
Barnwell, Sarah *BiDEWW*
Barnwell, Thomas Pinkney, III 1943- *WhoAm 90*
Baro, Robert Aristides 1948- *WhoHisp 91*
Baro, Walter Z *BiDrAPA 89*
Barocas, Susan Honey 1952- *WhoEmL 91*
Barocci, Nancy *BioIn 16*
Barocci, Robert Louis 1942- *WhoAm 90*
Baroch, Jerome Paul, Jr. 1942- *WhoAm 90*
Baroda, Dawna Michele 1967- *St&PR 91*
Baroda, Marcia Ann 1935- *St&PR 91*
Baroda, Richard J. 1936- *St&PR 91*
Baroff, George Stanley 1924- *WhoAm 90*
Baroff, Leonard 1925- *St&PR 91*
Baroff, Lynn Elliott 1949- *WhoEmL 91*
Baroja, Pio 1872-1956 *BioIn 16, WrPh*
Baroja y Nessi, Pio 1872-1956 *BioIn 16*
Barojas, Salome 1957- *Ballpl 90*
Barolini, Helen 1925- *WhoAmW 91, WhoWrEP 89*
Barolsky, Paul 1941- *WhoAm 90*
Baron 1926- *WhoAmA 91*
Baron di Novara 1940- *WhoWor 91*
Baron, Abraham 1922- *St&PR 91*
Baron, Allen A. 1941- *St&PR 91*
Baron, Alma Fay S. 1923- *WhoAm 90*
Baron, Arthur 1952- *WhoSSW 91*
Baron, Carol Kitzes *WhoE 91*
Baron, Carolyn 1940- *WhoAm 90, WhoWrEP 89*
Baron, Charles Hillel 1936- *WhoAm 90*
Baron, David *ConAu 33NR, MajTwCW*
Baron, David A 1953- *BiDrAPA 89*
Baron, David Harris 1959- *BiDrAPA 89*
Baron, Deborah 1887-1956 *EncCoWW*
Baron, Deborah Jo 1956- *WhoE 91*
Baron, Franklin Andrew Merrifield 1923- *WhoWor 91*
Baron, Frederick David 1947- *WhoAm 90*
Baron, George C. 1910- *St&PR 91*
Baron, Gino Victor 1948- *WhoWor 91*
Baron, Gregory *PenDiMP*
Baron, Gregory John 1938- *IntWWM 90*
Baron, Hans 1900-1988 *BioIn 16*
Baron, Howard N. 1922- *St&PR 91*
Baron, Ira Saul 1948- *WhoSSW 91*
Baron, Jason Dennis 1942- *BiDrAPA 89*
Baron, Jeffrey 1942- *WhoAm 90*
Baron, Jeffrey Allen 1963- *WhoSSW 91*
Baron, Jessica Ruth 1945- *WhoAmW 91*
Baron, Joel R. 1938- *St&PR 91*
Baron, John Anthony 1945- *WhoE 91*
Baron, John Herschel 1936- *IntWWM 90*
Baron, Judson Richard 1924- *WhoAm 90*
Baron, Laura Ann 1962- *WhoAmW 91, WhoEmL 91*
Baron, Linda Ann 1943- *WhoAmW 91*
Baron, Marilyn *BiDrAPA 89*
Baron, Martin Raymond 1922- *WhoAm 90*
Baron, Mary Kelley 1944- *WhoWrEP 89*
Baron, Maureen 1930- *St&PR 91*
Baron, Maureen Walsh 1930- *WhoAm 90*
Baron, Melvin Leon 1927- *WhoAm 90*
Baron, Miron 1947- *BiDrAPA 89*
Baron, Nancy *AuBYP 90*
Baron, Naomi Susan 1946- *WhoAmW 91*
Baron, Othello *ConAu 32NR*
Baron, Paul B. 1921- *St&PR 91*
Baron, Paul Dulaney 1944- *WhoSSW 91*
Baron, Robert Adelor 1922- *WhoE 91*
Baron, Robert Alan 1943- *WhoAm 90*
Baron, Robert Bruce 1940- *BiDrAPA 89*
Baron, Ronald B 1933- *BiDrAPA 89*
Baron, Ronald H. 1950- *St&PR 91*
Baron, Ronald Stephen 1943- *WhoE 91*
Baron, Salo 1895-1989 *AnObit 1989*
Baron, Salo W 1895-1989 *ConAu 130*
Baron, Salo Wittmayer 1895-1989 *BioIn 16*
Baron, Samuel 1925- *WhoAm 90*
Baron, Samuel 1928- *WhoAm 90*
Baron, Samuel Haskell 1921- *WhoAm 90*
Baron, Seymour 1923- *St&PR 91, WhoAm 90*
Baron, Sheldon 1934- *WhoAm 90*
Baron, Ted *ODwPR 91*
Baron, Theodore 1928- *WhoE 91*
Baron, Virginia Olsen 1931- *AuBYP 90*
Baron-Hall, Daria *AuBYP 90*
Barondes, Samuel Herbert 1933- *BiDrAPA 89, WhoAm 90*
Barondess, Jeremiah Abraham 1924- *WhoAm 90*
Barone, Anthony A. 1949- *St&PR 91*
Barone, Anthony Angelo 1949- *WhoAm 90*
Barone, Anthony L. 1945- *St&PR 91*
Barone, Anthony Thomas 1940- *WhoE 91*
Barone, Bruce M. 1949- *WhoAm 90*
Barone, Bruce Michael 1949- *St&PR 91*
Barone, Dennis 1955- *WhoWrEP 89*
Barone, Donald Anthony 1948- *WhoE 91, WhoEmL 91*
Barone, Elizabeth Ann 1962- *WhoSSW 91*
Barone, Enrico 1859-1924 *BioIn 16*
Barone, Frederick Edward 1945- *St&PR 91*
Barone, James George 1947- *St&PR 91*
Barone, John *St&PR 91*
Barone, John Anthony 1924- *WhoAm 90*
Barone, Mark F. 1952- *WhoE 91*
Barone, Michael *St&PR 91*
Barone, Michael D. 1944- *WhoAm 90*
Barone, Mike *ConAu 30NR, TwCCr&M 91*
Barone, Robert Austin 1942- *St&PR 91*
Barone, Robert Paul 1937- *St&PR 91, WhoAm 90*
Barone, Rose Marie Pace 1920- *WhoAm 90, WhoAmW 91, WhoWor 91, WhoWrEP 89*
Barone, Salvatore V. 1934- *St&PR 91*
Barone, Sherry Joy 1960- *WhoEmL 91*
Barone, Stephen Salvatore 1922- *WhoAm 90*
Barone-Khan, Francesca M 1940- *BiDrAPA 89*
Baroni, Catarina *PenDiMP*
Baroni, Geno *BioIn 16*
Baroni, Karen Marie 1957- *WhoAmW 91*
Baroni, Leonora 1611-1670 *PenDiMP*
Baroni, Mario 1934- *IntWWM 90*
Baronner, Robert Francis 1926- *St&PR 91*
Baronoff, William *WhoAm 90*
Barons, Christopher Macon 1953- *WhoEmL 91*
Barons, Richard Irwin 1946- *WhoAmA 91*
Baroody, Michael Elias 1946- *WhoAm 90*
Baroody, Michael Norman, Jr. 1950- *WhoE 91*
Barooshian, Martin 1929- *WhoAmA 91*
Barosa, Jose Pedro 1956- *WhoWor 91*
Baroudy, Bahige Mourad 1950- *WhoEmL 91, WhoWor 91*
Baroudi, Victor *St&PR 91*
Barous, John T. 1933- *St&PR 91*
Barousse, J. Kurt 1960- *St&PR 91*
Barovier, Angelo *PenDiDA 89*
Barovier, Angelo 1927- *PenDiDA 89*
Barovier, Antonio 1822-1896 *PenDiDA 89*
Barovier, Benedetto 1857-1930 *PenDiDA 89*
Barovier, Benvenuto 1855-1932 *PenDiDA 89*
Barovier, Ercole 1889- *PenDiDA 89*
Barovier, Giovanni *PenDiDA 89*
Barovier, Giovanni 1839-1908 *PenDiDA 89*
Barovier, Giuseppe 1836-1942 *PenDiDA 89*
Barovier, Maria *PenDiDA 89*
Barovier, Marino *PenDiDA 89*
Barowitz, Elliott 1936- *WhoAmA 91, WhoE 91*
Barowsky, Andrew Phillip 1950- *St&PR 91*
Barowsky, Harris White 1949- *WhoEmL 91*
Barozzi, Alva Coplon 1937- *WhoE 91*
Barpal, I. R. 1940- *St&PR 91*
Barpal, Isaac Ruben 1940- *WhoAm 90*
Barquin, Ramon Carlos 1942- *WhoE 91*
Barquist, G. Sheldon *St&PR 91*
Barquist, Walter Eric 1943- *BiDrAPA 89*
Barr, Albert J. 1947- *ODwPR 91*
Barr, Alfred Hamilton 1902-1981 *BioIn 16*
Barr, Alfred Hamilton, Jr 1902-1981 *WhoAmA 91N*
Barr, Alfred Lowell 1933- *WhoAm 90*
Barr, Allan 1890-1959 *WhoAmA 91N*
Barr, Amelia 1831-1919 *FemiCLE*
Barr, Andrew 1961- *ConAu 130*
Barr, Andy *BioIn 16*
Barr, Bonnie Belle 1937- *WhoE 91*
Barr, Burt 1938- *WhoAmA 91*
Barr, Charles Francis 1950- *St&PR 91*
Barr, Charles Joseph Gore 1940- *WhoAm 90*
Barr, Daniel Wayne 1952- *WhoEmL 91*
Barr, Danny *BioIn 16*
Barr, Dave *BioIn 16*
Barr, David Charles 1950- *WhoAm 90*
Barr, David John 1939- *WhoAm 90, WhoAmA 91*
Barr, Dojna Galich *BiDrAPA 89*
Barr, Donald 1921- *AuBYP 90*
Barr, Donald J. *WhoAm 90*
Barr, Donald Joseph 1935- *St&PR 91*
Barr, Donald M. 1948- *St&PR 91*
Barr, Donald Roy 1938- *WhoAm 90*
Barr, Frederick Reichert, Jr. 1956- *WhoEmL 91*
Barr, Gary Keith 1945- *St&PR 91*
Barr, George 1897-1974 *Ballpl 90*
Barr, George 1907- *AuBYP 90*
Barr, Ginger 1947- *WhoAmW 91*
Barr, Gregory Philip 1949- *WhoE 91*
Barr, H. Buford *ODwPR 91*
Barr, Harvey Stephen 1941- *WhoE 91*
Barr, Howard Raymond 1910- *WhoAm 90*
Barr, Irwin Robert 1920- *WhoAm 90*
Barr, J. James 1941- *St&PR 91*
Barr, Jacob Dexter 1944- *WhoAm 90*
Barr, James 1924- *WhoWor 91*
Barr, James David 1943- *St&PR 91*
Barr, James Houston, III 1941- *WhoSSW 91*
Barr, James Milton 1936- *WhoAm 90*
Barr, Jene 1900-1985 *AuBYP 90*
Barr, Jesse *BioIn 16*
Barr, Jim 1948- *Ballpl 90*
Barr, John *WhoSSW 91*
Barr, John Baldwin 1932- *WhoAm 90*
Barr, John Hanson 1938- *St&PR 91*
Barr, John Robert 1936- *WhoAm 90*
Barr, John W. 1943- *WhoAm 90*
Barr, John W., III 1921- *St&PR 91*
Barr, John Z. 1949- *St&PR 91*
Barr, Joseph W. 1918- *St&PR 91*
Barr, Joseph Walker 1918- *BiDrUSE 89, WhoAm 90, WhoWor 91*
Barr, Joseph Williston 1949- *WhoAm 90*
Barr, Kenneth J. 1926- *St&PR 91*
Barr, Kenneth John 1926- *WhoAm 90*
Barr, Laurence James 1935- *St&PR 91*
Barr, Linda Carole 1961- *BiDrAPA 89*
Barr, Lloyd 1929- *WhoAm 90*
Barr, Martin *PenDiDA 89*
Barr, Martin 1925- *WhoAm 90*
Barr, Mary Louise *BiDrAPA 89*
Barr, Michael Blanton 1948- *WhoE 91*
Barr, Michael Charles 1947- *WhoE 91*
Barr, Murray L 1908- *ConAu 130*
Barr, Murray Llewellyn 1908- *WhoAm 90*
Barr, Norman 1908- *WhoAmA 91*
Barr, Norman I 1936- *BiDrAPA 89*
Barr, Pamela S. *ODwPR 91*
Barr, Pat 1934- *ConAu 30NR*
Barr, Ralph Ivan 1946- *BiDrAPA 89, WhoSSW 91*
Barr, Ray D. 1929- *St&PR 91*
Barr, Raymond Arthur 1932- *IntWWM 90*
Barr, Richard 1917-1989 *AnObit 1989, BioIn 16*
Barr, Richard C. 1934- *St&PR 91*
Barr, Richard Stuart 1943- *WhoSSW 91*
Barr, Robert 1831-1897 *DcCanB 12*
Barr, Robert 1850-1912 *DcLB 92 [port], TwCCr&M 91*
Barr, Robert Alfred, Jr. 1934- *WhoAm 90*
Barr, Robert Dale 1939- *WhoAm 90*
Barr, Robin Noel 1940- *IntWWM 90*
Barr, Robin Reed *BiDrAPA 89*
Barr, Roger 1921- *WhoAmA 91*
Barr, Roger Coke 1942- *WhoSSW 91*
Barr, Roger Moore 1934- *WhoE 91*
Barr, Roger Terry 1921- *WhoAm 90*
Barr, Rosalie M Corigliano 1932- *BiDrAPA 89*
Barr, Roseanne *BioIn 16*
Barr, Roseanne 1952- *ConTFT 8 [port], WorAlBi*
Barr, Roseanne 1953- *WhoAm 90*
Barr, Sanford Lee 1952- *WhoEmL 91*
Barr, Sarah Louise 1963- *WhoAmW 91, WhoE 91*
Barr, Shirley 1936- *ODwPR 91*
Barr, Shirley Ann 1946- *WhoAm 90, WhoEmL 91*
Barr, Steve *BioIn 16*
Barr, Thomas A. 1927- *St&PR 91*
Barr, Thomas D. 1949- *St&PR 91*
Barr, Thomas Delbert 1931- *WhoAm 90*
Barr, Timothy Patrick 1960- *WhoE 91, WhoEmL 91*
Barr, Tina 1955- *WhoWrEP 89*
Barr, Vilmae *ODwPR 91*
Barr, Wallace R. 1946- *St&PR 91*
Barr, William Pelham 1950- *NewYTBS 90 [port], WhoAm 90*
Barr-Sharrar, Beryl *WhoAmA 91*
Barra, Joseph Alfred 1928- *St&PR 91*
Barrabe, Louis 1895-1961 *DcScB S2*
Barrack, Richard M. 1940- *St&PR 91*
Barrack, William S., Jr. 1929- *St&PR 91*
Barrack, William Sample, Jr. 1929- *WhoAm 90*
Barraclough, Geoffrey 1908-1984 *DcNaB 1981*
Barraclough, June 1930- *ConAu 132*
Barraclough, Robert John 1941- *WhoSSW 91*
Barraclough, William George 1935- *WhoAm 90*
Barradas, Carlos Helio Barata T. 1927- *WhoWor 91*
Barradas, Rafael 1890-1929 *ArtLatA*
Barragan, Frank, Jr. 1918- *St&PR 91*
Barragan, Linda Diane 1950- *WhoAmW 91*
Barragan, Luis 1902-1988 *BioIn 16*
Barragan, Lydia Marie *BioIn 16*
Barragan, Miguel F. *WhoHisp 91*
Barragan, Polly Baca- 1941- *BioIn 16*
Barragan Munoz, Fernando 1941- *WhoWor 91*
Barral, Carlos *BioIn 16*
Barral, Carlos 1928-1989 *AnObit 1989, ConAu 130*
Barram, David *St&PR 91*
Barranco, Robert George 1940- *St&PR 91*
Barrand, Anthony Grant 1945- *IntWWM 90, WhoE 91*
Barranger, Milly Hilliard Slater 1937- *NotWoAT*
Barranger, Milly S. 1937- *BioIn 16*
Barrantes Lingan, Alfonso 1928- *BioIn 16*
Barranti, Robert *WhoAm 90*
Barraque, Jean 1928-1973 *BioIn 16*
Barratt, Cynthia Louise 1953- *WhoAm 90, WhoAmW 91, WhoSSW 91*
Barratt, Donald C. 1937- *St&PR 91*
Barratt, Eric George 1938- *WhoWor 91*
Barratt, Ernest Stoelting 1925- *WhoAm 90*
Barratt, George 1927- *St&PR 91*
Barratt, Raymond William 1920- *WhoAm 90*
Barraud, Henry 1900- *IntWWM 90*
Barraza, Rosaleo N. 1947- *WhoHisp 91*
Barre, Bart A. 1937- *St&PR 91*
Barre, Fred D. 1943- *St&PR 91*
Barre, H. Walter 1948- *St&PR 91*
Barre, Isaac 1726-1802 *EncCRAm*
Barre, Loren D. 1925- *St&PR 91*
Barre, Raymond *BioIn 16*
Barre, Raymond 1924- *WhoWor 91, WorAlBi*
Barre, Raymond Octave Joseph 1924- *BiDFrPL*
Barre, Stephen Alan 1938- *St&PR 91*
Barre, William Michael 1949- *WhoEmL 91*
Barreau, Herve Albert 1929- *WhoWor 91*
Barreda, Antonio 1942- *WhoHisp 91*
Barreda, Jose Pardo y 1864-1947 *BioIn 16*
Barreira, Paul Joseph *BiDrAPA 89*
Barreiro, Alvaro 1936- *ConAu 131*
Barreiro, Jay 1932- *St&PR 91*
Barrelet, Charles Edouard 1934- *St&PR 91*
Barrell, Bernard 1919- *IntWWM 90*
Barrell, Bill 1932- *WhoAmA 91*
Barrell, Harry Daniel 1941- *St&PR 91*
Barrell, Howard *BioIn 16*
Barrell, Joyce Howard 1917- *IntWWM 90*
Barrell, Maria *FemiCLE*
Barrell, P. *FemiCLE*
Barrell, Rex A. 1921- *ConAu 129*
Barren, Bruce Willard 1942- *WhoAm 90, WhoWor 91*
Barreno de Farias Martin, Maria Isabel 1939- *EncCoWW*
Barrer, Lester A. 1923- *St&PR 91*
Barrer, Mary Burgess 1936- *WhoSSW 91*
Barrer, Roger Aaron 1926- *St&PR 91*
Barrera, Elvira Puig 1943- *WhoAmW 91, WhoSSW 91, WhoWor 91*
Barrera, Felix N. 1936- *WhoHisp 91*
Barrera, Giulia 1942- *IntWWM 90*
Barrera, Jorge Aurelio 1938- *BiDrAPA 89*
Barrera, Manuel, Jr. 1943- *WhoHisp 91*
Barrera, Mario 1939- *WhoHisp 91*
Barrera, Ralph A. 1959- *WhoHisp 91*
Barrera, Ruben Rivera 1939- *WhoWor 91*
Barreras, Lourdes *BiDrAPA 89*
Barrere, Jamie Newton 1946- *WhoEmL 91, WhoSSW 91*
Barreres, Domingo 1941- *WhoAm 90, WhoAmA 91*
Barres, Carmen Isabel 1961- *WhoAmW 91*
Barres, Maurice 1862-1923 *BiDFrPL*
Barresi, Mariana 1962- *WhoE 91*
Barreto, Afonso Henrique de Lima 1881-1922 *BioIn 16*
Barreto, Eduardo 1957- *BiDrAPA 89*
Barreto, Kathleen Anne 1954- *WhoAmW 91, WhoEmL 91, WhoWor 91*
Barrett, A. M., Jr. 1921- *St&PR 91*
Barrett, Alan Hildreth 1927- *WhoAm 90*
Barrett, Allen M., Jr. *ODwPR 91*
Barrett, Andrew *BioIn 16*
Barrett, Andrew Delgado 1926- *WhoSSW 91*
Barrett, Andrew S. *St&PR 91*

Barrett, Anthony G. M. 1952- WhoAm 90
Barrett, Arthur J., Jr. 1910- WhoAm 90
Barrett, Arthur Paul 1930- St&PR 91
Barrett, Barbara McConnell 1950- WhoAm 90, WhoEmL 91
Barrett, Beatrice Helene 1928- WhoAmW 91
Barrett, Benjamin Smith 1920- WhoSSW 91
Barrett, Bernard Morris, Jr. 1944- WhoWor 91
Barrett, Bill 1900-1951 Ballpl 90
Barrett, Bill 1934- WhoAm 90, WhoAmA 91
Barrett, Bruce Alan 1950- WhoEmL 91
Barrett, Bruce Richard 1939- WhoAm 90
Barrett, Catherine Glass 1952- WhoEmL 91
Barrett, Charles 1871-1939 Ballpl 90
Barrett, Charles Clayton 1918- WhoAm 90
Barrett, Charles E. 1931- St&PR 91
Barrett, Charles M. St&PR 91N
Barrett, Charles Marion 1913- WhoAm 90
Barrett, Charles N. 1913-1989 BioIn 16
Barrett, Charles Sanborn 1902- WhoAm 90
Barrett, Clyde Jackson 1942- WhoSSW 91
Barrett, Cody 1947- WhoE 91
Barrett, Colleen C. 1944- St&PR 91
Barrett, David BioIn 16
Barrett, David Eugene 1955- WhoEmL 91, WhoSSW 91
Barrett, David Owen 1954- BiDrAPA 89
Barrett, Dean M. ODwPR 91
Barrett, Diana Herran 1944- WhoAmW 91
Barrett, Dick 1906-1966 Ballpl 90
Barrett, Edward 1910-1989 AnObit 1989
Barrett, Edward W. 1910-1989 BioIn 16, ConAu 130, CurBio 90N
Barrett, Edythe Hart 1915- WhoAmW 91
Barrett, Eleanor B BiDrAPA 89
Barrett, Elizabeth Ann Manhart 1934- WhoAmW 91
Barrett, Elizabeth Anne 1961- WhoAmW 91
Barrett, Evelyn Carol 1928- WhoE 91
Barrett, Frank 1913- Ballpl 90
Barrett, Frank J. 1932- St&PR 91
Barrett, Frank Joseph 1932- WhoAm 90
Barrett, Frederick Charles 1949- WhoEmL 91
Barrett, Gerald Francis 1936- St&PR 91
Barrett, Gregory R. 1947- St&PR 91
Barrett, H Stanford 1909-1970 WhoAmA 91N
Barrett, Harold C., Jr. 1924- St&PR 91
Barrett, Harold Francis, Jr. 1919- WhoWrEP 89
Barrett, Helen Hunt 1943- WhoAmW 91, WhoSSW 91
Barrett, Herbert 1910- WhoAm 90
Barrett, Izadore 1926- WhoAm 90
Barrett, J. Patrick 1937- St&PR 91
Barrett, James E. 1922- WhoAm 90
Barrett, James E 1934- BiDrAPA 89
Barrett, James Emmett 1923- WhoE 91
Barrett, James Lee 1929- WhoWrEP 89
Barrett, James M. BioIn 16
Barrett, James P. 1936- WhoAm 90
Barrett, James Thomas 1927- WhoAm 90
Barrett, Jane Hayes 1947- WhoAm 90
Barrett, Jessica 1952- WhoAmW 91, WhoEmL 91
Barrett, Jimmy 1875-1921 Ballpl 90
Barrett, Joan 1950- St&PR 91
Barrett, John 1866-1938 BioIn 16
Barrett, John Eugene, Jr. 1949- WhoE 91
Barrett, John F. WhoAm 90
Barrett, John James, Jr. 1948- WhoEmL 91
Barrett, John Richard 1926- WhoSSW 91, WhoWor 91
Barrett, Johnny 1915-1974 Ballpl 90
Barrett, Joseph M. 1934- St&PR 91
Barrett, Joseph Michael 1934- WhoAm 90
Barrett, Judi 1941- BioIn 16
Barrett, Judith 1941- AuBYP 90
Barrett, June Bivins 1950- WhoAmW 91
Barrett, Karen Anne 1961- WhoE 91
Barrett, Karen Moore 1950- WhoEmL 91
Barrett, Laurence Irwin 1935- WhoE 91
Barrett, Lee Ann 1952- WhoAmW 91
Barrett, Leni Mancuso WhoAmA 91
Barrett, Lida Kittrell 1927- WhoAm 90, WhoAmW 91
Barrett, Linda L. 1948- WhoAmW 91
Barrett, Loretta Anne 1941- WhoAm 90, WhoAmW 91
Barrett, Lyle Eugene 1942- WhoSSW 91
Barrett, Lyn WhoWrEP 89
Barrett, Lynn S. 1943- ODwPR 91
Barrett, Marty 1958- Ballpl 90
Barrett, Michael Henry 1932- WhoAm 90
Barrett, Michael J. 1946- St&PR 91
Barrett, Michael John 1954- WhoEmL 91, WhoSSW 91, WhoWor 91
Barrett, Minna Sara 1948- WhoEmL 91
Barrett, Nancy Smith 1942- WhoE 91
Barrett, Norma Sutton 1951- WhoSSW 91
Barrett, O'Neill, Jr. 1929- WhoAm 90
Barrett, Patricia Louise 1947- WhoAmW 91
Barrett, Patrick J. 1928- St&PR 91
Barrett, Paul H. 1917-1987 BioIn 16
Barrett, Paulette S. 1937- ODwPR 91
Barrett, Paulette Singer 1937- WhoAm 90, WhoAmW 91
Barrett, Raymond James 1924- WhoAm 90
Barrett, Raymond V. 1947- St&PR 91
Barrett, Red 1915- Ballpl 90
Barrett, Richard David 1931- WhoAm 90
Barrett, Richard Hewins 1949- WhoEmL 91
Barrett, Richard M 1943- BiDrAPA 89
Barrett, Robert Dumas 1903- WhoAmA 91N
Barrett, Robert Edward 1931- BiDrAPA 89
Barrett, Robert James, III 1944- WhoAm 90
Barrett, Robert John, Jr. 1917- WhoAm 90
Barrett, Robert Mason 1960- WhoEmL 91
Barrett, Robert South, IV 1927- WhoAm 90, WhoWor 91
Barrett, Roger F. 1929- St&PR 91
Barrett, Roger Watson 1915- WhoAm 90
Barrett, Roland George 1944- St&PR 91
Barrett, Ron 1937- BioIn 16
Barrett, Ronald Eugene 1923- St&PR 91
Barrett, Ronald William 1949- WhoEmL 91
Barrett, Roy Carmen 1929- St&PR 91
Barrett, Samuel Cassell 1911- WhoAm 90
Barrett, Sharon Nelson 1952- BiDrAPA 89
Barrett, Stephen D. ODwPR 91
Barrett, Stephen D. 1941- St&PR 91
Barrett, Stephen Jeremy 1931- WhoWor 91
Barrett, Thom Hans 1930- St&PR 91
Barrett, Thomas R 1927- WhoAmA 91
Barrett, Thomas Weeks 1902-1947 WhoAmA 91N
Barrett, Timothy John 1948- St&PR 91
Barrett, Tom Hans 1930- WhoAm 90
Barrett, Tony R. 1939- St&PR 91
Barrett, William C. 1913- WhoAm 90
Barrett, William E. BioIn 16
Barrett, William Emerson 1858-1906 AmLegL
Barrett, William Fletcher 1844-1925 EncO&P 3, EncPaPR 91
Barrett, William Hale 1929- St&PR 91
Barrett, William Irwin, Jr. 1923- WhoSSW 91
Barrett, William Joel 1939- WhoE 91
Barrett, William O 1945- WhoAmA 91
Barrett, William Owen 1945- WhoAm 90
Barrett, William Thomas 1931- St&PR 91
Barrett, William W BiDrAPA 89
Barrett-Connor, Elizabeth L. 1935- WhoAmW 91
Barrett-Stafford, Susan Christine 1960- WhoAmW 91, WhoWor 91
Barrett-Weber, Patricia Ann 1953- WhoAmW 91
Barretta, Anthony John 1941- St&PR 91
Barretta, Jolie Ann 1954- WhoAmW 91
Barrette, Raymond 1950- St&PR 91
Barrette, Sarah Catharine 1936- WhoAmW 91, WhoWor 91
Barretto, Dennis 1915- St&PR 91
Barretto, Gene M. 1929- St&PR 91
Barretto, John J. St&PR 91
Barretton, Grandall ConAu 130
Barri, Joseph Paul 1946- St&PR 91
Barri, Odoardo 1884-1920 OxCPMus
Barricelli, Jane Margaret 1941- WhoE 91
Barricelli, Jean-Pierre 1924- WhoWrEP 89
Barrick, Augusta Irene 1903- WhoAmW 91
Barrick, William Henry 1916- WhoAm 90
Barrickman, Les BiDrAPA 89
Barrie, Barbara 1931- WorAlBi
Barrie, David Scott 1952- WhoEmL 91
Barrie, Dennis Ray 1947- WhoAmA 91
Barrie, Douglas S. 1933- St&PR 91
Barrie, Erwin S 1886-1983 WhoAmA 91N
Barrie, George 1943- St&PR 91
Barrie, Gordon BiDrAPA 89
Barrie, J. M. 1860-1937 BioIn 16, WorAlBi
Barrie, James Matthew 1860-1937 BioIn 16
Barrie, John Paul 1947- WhoEmL 91
Barrie, Mohammed S. 1952- WhoE 91
Barrie, Pauline 1954- BiDWomA
Barrie, Robert 1927- WhoAm 90
Barrie, Scott 1946- ConDes 90
Barrientos, Gonzalo 1941- WhoHisp 91
Barrientos, Julian WhoHisp 91
Barrientos, Maria 1883-1946 PenDiMP
Barrientos, Raul Ernesto 1942- WhoHisp 91
Barrientos, Robert John 1953- WhoEmL 91
Barrientos Ortuno, Rene 1919-1969 BioIn 16
Barrier, George Edgar 1928- WhoE 91
Barrier, John Wayne 1949- WhoEmL 91, WhoSSW 91
Barriere, Francoise Regine Cecile 1944- IntWWM 90
Barriere, Jean-Baptiste Marie 1958- IntWWM 90
Barrilleaux, Christopher Nissen 1954- WhoSSW 91
Barrineau-Welsh, Robin BiDrAPA 89
Barringer, Anthony Rene 1925- WhoAm 90
Barringer, Bob BioIn 16
Barringer, Daniel Moreau 1806-1873 BioIn 16
Barringer, Daniel Moreau 1900- AuBYP 90
Barringer, Joanne McCoy 1946- WhoSSW 91
Barringer, John Paul 1903- WhoAm 90, WhoE 91
Barringer, Margaret Chew 1946- WhoEmL 91
Barringer, Paul Brandon 1930- St&PR 91
Barringer, Paul Brandon, II 1930- WhoAm 90, WhoSSW 91
Barringer, Philip E. 1916- WhoAm 90
Barringer, Thad J 1927- BiDrAPA 89
Barringer, Thad Jones, Jr. 1952- BiDrAPA 89
Barrington, Bruce David 1942- WhoSSW 91
Barrington, Emilie 1840-1933 FemiCLE
Barrington, James Stephen 1952- WhoSSW 91
Barrington, Judith M. 1944- WhoWrEP 89
Barrington, Mary Rose 1926- EncPaPR 91
Barrington, Michael MajTwCW
Barrington, Rodney Craig 1953- WhoEmL 91
Barrington, Rutland 1853-1922 OxCPMus
Barrington-Carlson, Sharyn Marie 1946- WhoEmL 91
Barrington-Ward, Simon 1930- BioIn 16
Barrio, Guilmo 1939- WhoHisp 91
Barrio, Jorge Raul 1941- WhoAm 90
Barrio, Raymond 1921- BioIn 16, ConAu 32NR, HispWr 90, WhoAm 90, WhoAmA 91, WhoHisp 91, WhoWrEP 89
Barrio-Garay, Jose Luis 1932- WhoAmA 91
Barrionuevo, Juan Carlos BiDrAPA 89
Barrios, Agustin 1885-1944 PenDiMP
Barrios, Benny Perez 1925- WhoAmA 91
Barrios, Digby Wayne 1937- WhoAm 90
Barrios, Eduardo 1884-1963 BioIn 16, HispWr 90
Barrios, Francisco 1953-1982 Ballpl 90
Barrios, Gonzalo 1902- BioIn 16
Barrios, John Anthony 1969- WhoEmL 91
Barrios, Justo Rufino 1835-1885 BioIn 16
Barrios, Olga Cruz 1945- BiDrAPA 89
Barrios, Pilar E. 1889- HispWr 90
Barrios, Zulma X. 1943- WhoHisp 91
Barrios Perez de Arce, Jaime BioIn 16
Barrios Tassano, Luis WhoWor 91
Barris, George AuBYP 90
Barris, George 1925- BioIn 16
Barris, Harry 1905-1962 BioIn 16, OxCPMus
Barris, Madeleine BiDrAPA 89
Barriskill, Maudanne Kidd 1932- WhoAmW 91
Barritt, Clay F 1925- BiDrAPA 89
Barritt, Evelyn Ruth Berryman 1929- WhoAm 90
Barritt, Lester S. 1933- St&PR 91
Barritt, Paul 1953- IntWWM 90
Barrnett, R Joffree 1950- BiDrAPA 89
Barrnett, Russell Joffree 1920-1989 BioIn 16
Barro, Mary Helen 1938- WhoHisp 91
Barro, Robert Joseph 1944- WhoAm 90
Barrocas, Alberto 1923- St&PR 91
Barroero, Louis Francis 1920- St&PR 91
Barrol, Grady AuBYP 90
Barron, Alistair O BiDrAPA 89
Barron, Almen Leo 1926- WhoAm 90
Barron, Antioco R BiDrAPA 89
Barron, Barbara Jane 1959- WhoEmL 91
Barron, Barbara Marilyn 1937- WhoAmW 91
Barron, Bernie Garcia 1956- WhoHisp 91
Barron, Bill 1927-1989 BioIn 16
Barron, Bruce N. 1955- St&PR 91
Barron, Caroline 1958- WhoEmL 91
Barron, Charles E. 1928- St&PR 91
Barron, Charles Elliott 1928- WhoAm 90
Barron, Charles Henson, Jr. 1937- WhoSSW 91
Barron, Charles Irwin 1916- WhoAm 90
Barron, Charles Thomas 1950- BiDrAPA 89, WhoE 91
Barron, Clemente 1943- WhoHisp 91
Barron, David W BiDrAPA 89
Barron, Dennis H. 1940- St&PR 91, WhoAm 90
Barron, Donald H. 1905- WhoAm 90
Barron, Donald Ray 1947- St&PR 91
Barron, Edward L. 1935- St&PR 91
Barron, Eliot B 1935- BiDrAPA 89
Barron, Eugene D. 1958- WhoE 91
Barron, Francis Patrick 1951- WhoEmL 91
Barron, Gary A. 1944- St&PR 91
Barron, Grover Cleveland, III 1948- WhoEmL 91
Barron, Harold Sheldon 1936- WhoAm 90
Barron, Henry Danforth 1833-1882 AmLegL
Barron, Howard Robert 1930- WhoAm 90
Barron, Ilona Eleanor 1929- WhoAmW 91
Barron, James Turman 1954- WhoE 91
Barron, Janice Marie 1966- WhoAmW 91
Barron, Jerome Aure 1933- WhoAm 90
Barron, John Field 1952- St&PR 91
Barron, John Marshall 1912- WhoSSW 91
Barron, Kevin Delgado 1929- WhoAm 90
Barron, Laura Rowe WhoAmW 91
Barron, Lisbeth Rae 1962- WhoEmL 91
Barron, Louis NewYTBS 90
Barron, Louis 1919- WhoAm 90
Barron, Louis 1920- IntWWM 90
Barron, Mel St&PR 91
Barron, Milton Leon 1918- WhoAm 90
Barron, Patrick Kenneth 1945- WhoSSW 91
Barron, Peggy Pennisi 1958- WhoAmW 91
Barron, Pepe 1937- WhoHisp 91
Barron, Randall DeWayne 1929- WhoAm 90
Barron, Randall Franklin 1936- WhoSSW 91
Barron, Ray 1925- WhoWrEP 89
Barron, Reginald BioIn 16
Barron, Robert A. 1933- St&PR 91
Barron, Roberta 1940- WhoAmW 91
Barron, Ros 1933- WhoAm 90, WhoAmA 91
Barron, Ruth A BiDrAPA 89
Barron, Stanley Perry BiDrAPA 89
Barron, Susan 1940- WhoAmW 91
Barron, Susan Hood 1942- WhoSSW 91
Barron, Thomas 1949- WhoE 91
Barron, Tom 1949- WhoAmA 91
Barrone, Gerald D. 1931- St&PR 91
Barronton, Deward Neal 1937- St&PR 91
Barros, Henry 1960- WhoHisp 91
Barros, Jose Cunha 1945- WhoWor 91
Barros Luco, Ramon 1835-1919 BioIn 16
Barroso, Sergio Fernandez 1946- IntWWM 90
Barrow, Bernard Elliott 1927- WhoAm 90
Barrow, Betty Harris 1950- St&PR 91
Barrow, Charles Herbert 1930- St&PR 91, WhoAm 90
Barrow, Charles Wallace 1921- WhoAm 90
Barrow, Clyde 1909-1934 WorAlBi
Barrow, Deborah BiDEWW
Barrow, Digby Paul Gordon 1956- IntWWM 90
Barrow, Dunstan 1945- WhoWor 91
Barrow, Ed 1868-1953 Ballpl 90 [port]
Barrow, Errol W. 1920-1987 BioIn 16
Barrow, Frank Pearson, Jr. 1928- WhoAm 90
Barrow, Geoffrey W S 1924- ConAu 30NR
Barrow, George Terrell 1909- WhoAm 90
Barrow, Gregory Stephen BiDrAPA 89
Barrow, Isaac 1630-1677 BioIn 16
Barrow, John 1931- IntWWM 90
Barrow, Kal 1933- WhoE 91
Barrow, Keith BioIn 16
Barrow, Lionel Ceon, Jr. 1926- WhoAm 90
Barrow, Mary ODwPR 91
Barrow, Robert Earl 1930- WhoAm 90
Barrow, Robert Guy 1936- St&PR 91
Barrow, Stephen A. 1934- St&PR 91
Barrow, Thomas Davies 1924- St&PR 91, WhoAm 90, WhoWor 91
Barrow, Thomas Francis 1938- WhoAm 90, WhoAmA 91
Barrow, Willie T. BioIn 16
Barrow, Wylie Winfield 1935- St&PR 91
Barrows, Anita 1947- ConAu 31NR
Barrows, Augustus R. 1838- AmLegL
Barrows, Diana BioIn 16
Barrows, Frank Clemence 1946- WhoSSW 91
Barrows, Ira George 1945- WhoE 91
Barrows, Jordan Edward 1939- St&PR 91
Barrows, Leland Conley 1942- WhoWor 91
Barrows, Marjorie 1892?-1983 AuBYP 90
Barrows, Robert Guy 1926- WhoWor 91
Barrows, Stanley BioIn 16
Barry, Alan S 1948- BiDrAPA 89
Barry, Alfred E. 1935- St&PR 91
Barry, Allan Ronald 1945- WhoEmL 91, WhoSSW 91, WhoWor 91
Barry, Anne Elizabeth Jackson 1928- WhoAmW 91
Barry, Anne Meredith 1932- WhoAmA 91
Barry, Anthony F. BioIn 16
Barry, Archana BiDrAPA 89
Barry, Arthur J. NewYTBS 90
Barry, Arthur J. 1909-1990 BioIn 16
Barry, Ben WhoWrEP 89
Barry, Betty Lynn 1946- WhoAmW 91

Barry, Bonnie B. 1940- WhoAmW 91
Barry, Bridget 1959- WhoAmW 91
Barry, Carole Joyce 1933- BiDrAPA 89
Barry, Charles 1795-1860 BioIn 16
Barry, Colman James 1921- WhoAm 90
Barry, Dan 1923- EncACom
Barry, Daniel F. 1946- St&PR 91
Barry, Daniel Leo 1951- St&PR 91
Barry, Daniel Mark 1966- WhoE 91
Barry, Daniel Patrick 1947- St&PR 91
Barry, Dave BioIn 16, NewYTBS 90 [port], WhoAm 90, WhoSSW 91
Barry, Dave 1947?- ConAu 129, News 91-2 [port]
Barry, Dave 1948- BestSel 90-4 [port]
Barry, David WhoE 91
Barry, David A. 1946- St&PR 91
Barry, David E. 1925- St&PR 91
Barry, David F. 1854-1934 WhNaAH
Barry, David John BiDrAPA 89
Barry, David L. 1936- St&PR 91
Barry, David Richard 1935- St&PR 91
Barry, Desmond Thomas, Jr. 1945- WhoAm 90, WhoE 91
Barry, Diane D. 1956- ODwPR 91
Barry, Donald H. 1938- St&PR 91
Barry, Donald J., Jr. 1946- St&PR 91
Barry, Donald Lee 1953- WhoEmL 91, WhoWor 91
Barry, Donald Thomas 1927- WhoE 91
Barry, E. J. 1933- St&PR 91
Barry, Edward William 1937- St&PR 91, WhoAm 90, WhoWrEP 89
Barry, Elizabeth Lottes 1958- WhoAmW 91
Barry, Ellen M. 1953- WhoAmW 91
Barry, Francis J. St&PR 91N
Barry, Francis Julian, Jr. 1949- WhoAm 90, WhoEmL 91
Barry, Franklyn Stanley, Jr. 1939- St&PR 91
Barry, Fred 1887-1964 OxCCanT [port]
Barry, Gene BioIn 16
Barry, Gene 1919- WhoAm 90
Barry, Gene 1922- WorAlBi
Barry, George J BiDrAPA 89
Barry, Gerald 1952- PenDiMP A
Barry, Gerald Anthony 1952- IntWWM 90
Barry, Gregory Steven 1959- WhoE 91
Barry, Henry M. 1929- ODwPR 91
Barry, Herbert, III 1930- WhoAm 90, WhoWor 91
Barry, J. Edward 1912- St&PR 91
Barry, Jack 1887-1961 Ballpl 90
Barry, Jack 1918-1984 BioIn 16
Barry, Jacquelyn ODwPR 91
Barry, James 1741-1806 IntDcAA 90
Barry, James B. 1930- St&PR 91
Barry, James C. 1941- St&PR 91
Barry, James Potvin 1918- WhoWor 91
Barry, James Russell 1960- WhoEmL 91
Barry, Jan 1943- WhoWrEP 89
Barry, Janet Cecilia 1944- WhoAmW 91
Barry, Joan 1953- WhoAmW 91
Barry, Joanne S. 1955- ODwPR 91, WhoE 91
Barry, Joel Mark 1950- St&PR 91
Barry, John 1745-1803 EncCRAm, WorAlBi
Barry, John 1933- OxCPMus
Barry, John Abbott 1948- WhoWrEP 89
Barry, John Eduard 1959- WhoEmL 91
Barry, John Emmet 1953- WhoEmL 91
Barry, John H. 1931- St&PR 91
Barry, John Joseph, III BiDrAPA 89
Barry, John Kevin 1925- WhoAm 90
Barry, John Reagan 1921- WhoSSW 91
Barry, John Stephen 1924- St&PR 91
Barry, Joseph Amber 1917- WhoWor 91
Barry, Joseph B. 1757- PenDiDA 89
Barry, Joseph B. 1759?-1838 BioIn 16
Barry, Joyce Alice 1932- WhoAmW 91
Barry, Katharina Watzen 1936- AuBYP 90
Barry, Kathleen 1941- ConAu 129
Barry, Kim 1969- WhoEmL 91
Barry, Lei 1941- WhoAmW 91
Barry, Leo H. BioIn 16
Barry, Leroy M 1913- BiDrAPA 89
Barry, Lynda BioIn 16
Barry, Marilyn White 1936- WhoAmW 91, WhoE 91
Barry, Marion 1936- BioIn 16, News 91-1 [port]
Barry, Marion Shepilov, Jr. 1936- WhoAm 90, WhoE 91, WhoWor 91
Barry, Mary Alice 1928- St&PR 91, WhoAm 90, WhoAmW 91
Barry, Maryanne Trump 1937- WhoAm 90, WhoAmW 91
Barry, Maurice J 1919- BiDrAPA 89
Barry, Michaela Marie 1960- WhoEmL 91
Barry, Mike TwCCr&M 91
Barry, Mimi Neal WhoWrEP 89
Barry, N. Niles 1919- St&PR 91
Barry, Pamela Jane 1944- WhoAmW 91
Barry, Patricia Dowling 1941- WhoE 91
Barry, Patricia Pound 1941- WhoAmW 91
Barry, Patrick J. ODwPR 91
Barry, Peter E. 1927- St&PR 91
Barry, Philip 1896-1949 WorAlBi
Barry, Philip Semple 1923- WhoAm 90
Barry, Richard A. 1934- ODwPR 91
Barry, Richard Arthur 1945- WhoAm 90, WhoSSW 91
Barry, Richard Francis 1917- WhoAm 90
Barry, Richard Francis, III 1943- WhoAm 90, WhoSSW 91, WhoWrEP 89
Barry, Rick 1944- WhoAm 90, WorAlBi
Barry, Robert E 1931- WhoAmA 91
Barry, Robert Everett 1931- AuBYP 90, WhoE 91
Barry, Robert F. BioIn 16
Barry, Robert R. 1915-1988 BioIn 16
Barry, Robert Thomas 1936- WhoAmA 91
Barry, Roger Graham 1935- WhoAm 90
Barry, Ronald 1950- WhoEmL 91
Barry, Ronald M BiDrAPA 89
Barry, Scott BioIn 16
Barry, Seymour EncACom
Barry, Seymour 1928- WhoAm 90
Barry, Shad 1876-1936 Ballpl 90
Barry, Susan Brown 1944- WhoAmW 91, WhoWor 91
Barry, Teresa Trupiano 1950- WhoAmW 91
Barry, Theodore J BiDrAPA 89
Barry, Thomas Anthony 1918- WhoE 91
Barry, Thomas Corcoran 1944- WhoAm 90
Barry, Thomas Hubert 1918- WhoWor 91
Barry, Thomas Joseph 1955- WhoEmL 91
Barry, Thomas K. 1945- St&PR 91
Barry, Thomas Michael 1949- St&PR 91, WhoE 91
Barry, Timothy Francis 1951- WhoAm 90
Barry, Tina S. 1956- ODwPR 91
Barry, Virginia C 1948- BiDrAPA 89
Barry, Walter Richard, Jr. 1933- St&PR 91, WhoAm 90
Barry, William Edward 1957- WhoEmL 91
Barry, William Garrett, III 1955- WhoAm 90
Barry, William H. 1918- St&PR 91
Barry, William James 1927- St&PR 91
Barry, William Taylor 1785-1835 BiDrUSE 89
Barry, William Taylor Sullivan 1821-1868 AmLegL
Barrymore, Drew BioIn 16
Barrymore, Drew 1975- WorAlBi
Barrymore, Ethel 1879-1959 BioIn 16, NotWoAT, WorAlBi
Barrymore, John 1882-1942 BioIn 16, WorAlBi
Barrymore, Lionel 1878-1954 WorAlBi
Barsa, John Joseph BiDrAPA 89
Barsa, Michael S. 1944- St&PR 91
Barsalona, Frank Samuel 1938- WhoAm 90, WhoE 91, WhoWor 91
Barsalou, Joseph 1822-1897 DcCanB 12
Barsan, Richard Emil 1945- WhoEmL 91, WhoWor 91
Barsan, Robert Blake 1948- WhoWor 91
Barsano, Ron 1945- WhoAmA 91
Barsanti, John Richard, Jr. 1928- WhoAm 90
Barsanti, Robert Randolph 1932- St&PR 91
Barsch, Wulf Erich 1943- WhoAmA 91
Barschall, Henry Herman 1915- WhoAm 90
Barschel, Hans J 1912- WhoAmA 91
Barselou, Paul Edgar 1922- WhoAm 90
Barsh, Gregory Scott 1961- WhoE 91
Barshack, Scott BiDrAPA 89
Barshafsky, Beverly Ann 1963- WhoSSW 91
Barshai, Rudolf 1924- IntWWM 90, PenDiMP
Barshai, Rudolf Borisovich 1924- WhoAm 90, WhoWor 91
Barshop, Mark N. 1953- St&PR 91
Barshop, Samuel Edwin 1929- St&PR 91, WhoAm 90
Barsi, Judith BioIn 16
Barsi, Louis Michael 1941- WhoE 91, WhoWor 91
Barske, Bodo 1938- WhoAm 90
Barsky, Arthur Joseph, III 1943- BiDrAPA 89, WhoE 91
Barsky, Bernard St&PR 91
Barsky, David L. 1943- St&PR 91
Barsky, Stephen Frank 1942- WhoE 91
Barsman, Jack 1931- BiDrAPA 89
Barsness, Richard Webster 1935- WhoAm 90
Barsom, George K., Jr. 1926- WhoSSW 91
Barsom, George Martin 1940- St&PR 91
Barson, Michael 1951- ConAu 129
Barsook, Beverly Jean 1945- WhoEmL 91
Barsotti, Roger 1901- OxCPMus
Barsoum, Camelia K. St&PR 91
Barsoum, Marlene BiDrAPA 89
Barss, Mary Brooke BiDrAPA 89
Barst, Haskell 1907-1990 BioIn 16
Barstow, Amos Chafee 1813-1894 AmLegL
Barstow, George 1825?-1883 AmLegL
Barstow, Josephine 1940- PenDiMP
Barstow, Josephine Clare 1940- IntWWM 90
Barstow, Roland J. 1919- St&PR 91, WhoAm 90
Bart, Harm 1942- WhoWor 91
Bart, Lionel 1930- IntWWM 90, OxCPMus, WhoWor 91
Bart, Polly Turner 1944- WhoAmW 91
Bart, Randall Kerr 1952- WhoEmL 91
Bart, Walter John, Jr. 1943- St&PR 91
Barta, Dorothy Elaine 1924- WhoAmA 91
Barta, Frank R BiDrAPA 89
Barta, Frank Rudolph, Sr. 1913- WhoAm 90, WhoWor 91
Barta, Fredrick Michael 1949- WhoEmL 91
Barta, James Omer 1931- WhoAm 90
Barta, John David 1946- BiDrAPA 89
Barta, Michael 1954- IntWWM 90
Barta, Patrick Ernest BiDrAPA 89
Barta, Thomas James 1940- St&PR 91
Bartak, Gary J. 1953- WhoEmL 91
Bartalini, C. Richard 1931- WhoAm 90
Barteau, John 1928- St&PR 91
Barteau, John Frank 1928- WhoAm 90
Barteau, Mary Alice 1963- WhoEmL 91
Barteaux, John W BiDrAPA 89
Bartecek, Adolf BiDrAPA 89
Bartee, Dyrel Patrick 1958- BiDrAPA 89, WhoE 91
Bartee, Ted Ray 1938- WhoSSW 91
Bartee, Thomas Creson 1926- WhoAm 90
Bartek, Gordon Luke 1925- WhoWor 91
Bartek, Ronald 1953- WhoSSW 91
Bartek, Tom 1932- WhoAmA 91
Bartek, Victoria Jean 1945- WhoEmL 91
Bartel, Alice J. 1946- WhoE 91
Bartel, Fred Frank 1917- WhoAm 90
Bartel, Lavon Lee 1951- WhoAmW 91
Bartel, Pauline C. 1952- WhoWrEP 89
Bartel, Richard Joseph 1950- WhoEmL 91, WhoSSW 91
Bartel, Roger Francis 1951- WhoEmL 91
Bartel, Tina Slemmer 1954- WhoAmW 91
Barteld, John T. 1946- St&PR 91
Bartelds, Robert Willem 1947- WhoWor 91
Bartelink, Bernard G. M. 1929- IntWWM 90
Bartell, Bruce 1932- St&PR 91
Bartell, Charles 1916- WhoSSW 91
Bartell, Dick 1907- Ballpl 90 [port]
Bartell, Gary Dennis BiDrAPA 89
Bartell, George D. St&PR 91
Bartell, George H., Jr. St&PR 91
Bartell, Gerald Aaron 1914- St&PR 91, WhoAm 90
Bartell, James E. 1942- St&PR 91
Bartell, Jeffrey Bruce 1943- WhoAm 90
Bartell, Lawrence Sims 1923- WhoAm 90
Bartell, Nancy Kramer 1941- WhoAmW 91
Bartelmay, Dale Nevin 1926- St&PR 91
Bartels, Ann-Marie 1954- ODwPR 91
Bartels, Christine 1961- WhoE 91
Bartels, Donald Hoyt 1948- WhoEmL 91
Bartels, Donald James 1956- WhoEmL 91
Bartels, John Ries 1897- WhoAm 90
Bartels, Juergen E. 1940- St&PR 91
Bartels, Louis J. 1927- St&PR 91
Bartels, Mary Garber 1956- BiDrAPA 89
Bartels, Millard 1905- WhoAm 90
Bartels, Stanley Leonard 1927- WhoAm 90
Bartels, Stephen James BiDrAPA 89
Bartels Wilkinson, Jami Elizabeth 1941- WhoAmW 91
Bartelstone, Rona Sue 1951- WhoAmW 91
Bartelstone, Steven David 1947- WhoAm 90
Bartelstone, Ted Henry 1950- WhoEmL 91
Bartelt, Doris Ann 1955- WhoAmW 91
Bartelt, Wilbert Bruce 1936- St&PR 91
Barten, Anton Peter 1930- WhoWor 91
Barten, Gunter 1941- WhoWor 91
Barten, Harvey H 1933- BiDrAPA 89
Bartenstein, Louis 1946- St&PR 91
Barter, Barbara Ann 1934- WhoAmW 91
Barter, James T 1930- BiDrAPA 89
Barter, John W. 1946- St&PR 91
Barter, John William, III 1946- WhoAm 90
Barter, Judith A 1951- WhoAmA 91
Barter, Robert Henry 1913- WhoAm 90
Barter, Ruby Sunshine WhoAmW 91
Bartevian, Arsho BiDrAPA 89
Barth, Alan 1906-1979 BioIn 16
Barth, Alfred W. 1903-1988 BioIn 16
Barth, Brenda Jean BiDrAPA 89
Barth, Charles John 1942- WhoAmA 91
Barth, Daniel Stephen 1954- WhoEmL 91
Barth, David K. 1943- St&PR 91
Barth, David Keck 1943- WhoAm 90
Barth, Diana WhoWrEP 89
Barth, Edna 1914-1980 AuBYP 90
Barth, Elaine Marie BiDrAPA 89
Barth, Elmer Ernest 1922- WhoAm 90
Barth, Frances 1946- WhoAmA 91
Barth, Frances D. 1946- WhoAm 90, WhoE 91
Barth, Ilene Joan 1944- WhoAm 90
Barth, Jack Alexander 1946- WhoAmA 91
Barth, James Richard 1943- WhoAm 90
Barth, Jim BioIn 16
Barth, John BioIn 16
Barth, John 1930- MajTwCW, WorAlBi, WrPh
Barth, John M. 1946- St&PR 91
Barth, John Robert 1931- WhoAm 90
Barth, John Simmons 1930- WhoAm 90, WhoWor 91, WhoWrEP 89
Barth, Karl 1886-1968 BioIn 16, WorAlBi
Barth, Katrine 1947- ODwPR 91
Barth, Laurie BioIn 16
Barth, Mark Harold 1951- WhoEmL 91
Barth, Max 1907- WhoAm 90
Barth, Michael Carl 1941- WhoAm 90, WhoE 91
Barth, R L 1947- WhoWrEP 89
Barth, Richard 1931- St&PR 91, WhoAm 90, WhoE 91
Barth, Richard 1943- TwCCr&M 91
Barth, Robert W. WhoAm 90
Barth, Roger Vincent 1938- WhoWor 91
Barth, Rolf Frederick 1937- WhoAm 90
Barth, Sandra Lynne 1956- WhoEmL 91
Barth, Stephen Joseph 1948- St&PR 91
Barth-Wehrenalp, Gerhard 1920- WhoAm 90
Bartha, Denes 1908- IntWWM 90
Barthe, Georges-Isidore 1834-1900 DcCanB 12
Barthe, John R. 1924- St&PR 91
Barthe, Joseph-Guillaume 1816-1893 DcCanB 12
Barthe, Richmond 1901-1989 BioIn 16, WhoAmA 91N
Barthel, Cheryl Ann 1961- WhoAmW 91
Barthel, F. Ernest 1933- St&PR 91, WhoAm 90
Barthel, Hazel Phoebe 1933- WhoAmW 91
Barthel, Oliver E 1877-1969 EncABHB 4 [port]
Barthel, Richard Paul 1944- BiDrAPA 89
Barthelemy, Sidney John 1942- WhoAm 90, WhoSSW 91
Barthelmas, Ned Kelton 1927- WhoAm 90, WhoWor 91
Barthelme, Donald BioIn 16
Barthelme, Donald 1907- WhoAm 90
Barthelme, Donald 1931- WhoWrEP 89
Barthelme, Donald 1931-1989 AnObit 1989, AuBYP 90, ConAu 129, ConLC 59 [port], MajTwCW, SmATA 62, WorAlBi
Barthelme, Frederick 1943- WorAu 1980 [port]
Barthelmes, William Harold 1946- St&PR 91
Barthelmess, Karl Theodore 1940- St&PR 91
Barthes, Roland 1915-1980 ConAu 130, EuWr 13, MajTwCW
Barthmare, Lynn Barbara 1951- WhoAmW 91
Barthold, Clementine B. 1921- WhoAmW 91
Barthold, Lauren Swayne 1965- WhoSSW 91
Barthold, Lionel Olav 1926- WhoAm 90
Bartholdson, John Robert 1944- St&PR 91, WhoAm 90
Bartholemew, Linda Curry 1948- St&PR 91
Bartholet, Elizabeth Ives WhoAmA 91
Bartholomae, Richard C. 1925- St&PR 91
Bartholomay, William C. 1928- WhoAm 90, WhoSSW 91
Bartholomay, William Conrad 1928- St&PR 91
Bartholomeusz, Dennis 1930- ConAu 130
Bartholomew, Alice Jean 1941- WhoAmW 91
Bartholomew, Allan Camp 1915- WhoAm 90
Bartholomew, Amy Lee BiDrAPA 89
Bartholomew, Anita 1949- WhoAmW 91, WhoE 91
Bartholomew, Anne Charlotte 1800-1862 BiDWomA
Bartholomew, Arthur Peck, Jr. 1918- WhoAm 90
Bartholomew, Byron Simpson 1927- St&PR 91
Bartholomew, Cheryl Gibbons 1943- WhoAmW 91
Bartholomew, Donald Dekle 1929- WhoWor 91
Bartholomew, Eric 1926-1984 DcNaB 1981
Bartholomew, Frank H. 1898-1985 BioIn 16
Bartholomew, Freddie 1924- WorAlBi

Bartholomew, Gary Alan 1956- *WhoEmL 91*
Bartholomew, Gene Carroll 1934- *St&PR 91*
Bartholomew, George Adelbert 1919- *WhoAm 90*
Bartholomew, Gilbert Alfred 1922- *WhoAm 90*
Bartholomew, Harland 1889-1989 *BioIn 16*
Bartholomew, James 1950- *ConAu 132*
Bartholomew, James J. 1934- *St&PR 91*
Bartholomew, Lloyd Gibson 1921- *WhoAm 90*
Bartholomew, Lynn Michele 1949- *WhoAmW 91*
Bartholomew, Orland 1899-1957 *BioIn 16*
Bartholomew, Reginald 1936- *WhoWor 91*
Bartholomew, William Lee 1950- *WhoEmL 91, WhoWor 91*
Bartholomy, John Martin 1935- *WhoAm 90*
Bartholow, George W 1930- *BiDrAPA 89*
Barthou, Jean Louis 1862-1934 *BiDFrPL*
Barthwell, David Anthony 1952- *BiDrAPA 89*
Bartilucci, Andrew Joseph 1922- *WhoAm 90*
Bartine, Errol Wiley 1931- *St&PR 91*
Bartirome, Tony 1932- *Ballpl 90*
Bartizal, Robert George 1932- *WhoAm 90*
Bartkoski, Michael John, Jr. 1945- *WhoEmL 91*
Bartkowech, Raymond A. 1950- *WhoWrEP 89*
Bartkowski, William Patrick 1951- *St&PR 91*
Bartkus, John Gregory 1960- *WhoSSW 91*
Bartkus, Richard Anthony 1931- *WhoAm 90*
Bartl, Hans Adolf 1933- *WhoWor 91*
Bartl, James F. 1940- *St&PR 91*
Bartlam, John *PenDiDA 89*
Bartle, Annette Gruber *WhoAmW 91, WhoE 91, WhoWor 91*
Bartle, Dorothy Budd 1924- *WhoAmA 91*
Bartle, Graham Alfred Reginald 1928- *IntWWM 90*
Bartle, Harvey, Jr. 1909- *BiDrAPA 89*
Bartle, Marla Jo 1964- *WhoAmW 91*
Bartle, Robert Gardner 1927- *WhoAm 90*
Bartle, Stuart Hall 1924- *BiDrAPA 89, WhoE 91*
Bartle, Thomas *ODwPR 91*
Bartlemay, Susan Elaine 1946- *WhoEmL 91*
Bartlett, Albert Allen 1923- *WhoAm 90*
Bartlett, Alex 1937- *WhoAm 90*
Bartlett, Allen Lyman, Jr. 1929- *WhoAm 90*
Bartlett, Arthur Eugene 1933- *WhoAm 90, WhoWor 91*
Bartlett, Bonnie *WhoAmW 91*
Bartlett, Boyd C. 1925- *WhoAm 90*
Bartlett, Bruce Allen 1948- *WhoWrEP 89*
Bartlett, Bruce L. 1944- *St&PR 91*
Bartlett, Bruce Reeves 1951- *WhoAm 90*
Bartlett, Byron Allan 1940- *WhoWrEP 89*
Bartlett, Byron Robert 1952- *WhoE 91*
Bartlett, C. Scott, Jr. 1933- *St&PR 91*
Bartlett, Charles Leffingwell 1921- *WhoAm 90*
Bartlett, Christopher E 1944- *WhoAmA 91*
Bartlett, Clifford Adams, Jr. 1937- *WhoAm 90, WhoE 91, WhoWor 91*
Bartlett, Clifford Alfred James 1939- *IntWWM 90*
Bartlett, Cody Blake 1939- *WhoAm 90*
Bartlett, Colleen Elizabeth 1963- *WhoE 91*
Bartlett, Connie Suzanne 1953- *WhoEmL 91*
Bartlett, Craig Scott, Jr. 1933- *WhoAm 90*
Bartlett, Dana 1882-1957 *WhoAmA 91N*
Bartlett, David *BioIn 16*
Bartlett, David Farnham 1938- *WhoAm 90*
Bartlett, David Loomis 1941- *St&PR 91*
Bartlett, Dede Thompson 1943- *St&PR 91, WhoAm 90*
Bartlett, Desmond William 1931- *WhoAm 90*
Bartlett, Diane Sue 1947- *WhoAmW 91*
Bartlett, Dwight Kellogg 1931- *St&PR 91*
Bartlett, Edmund 1910- *St&PR 91*
Bartlett, Edward W 1939- *BiDrAPA 89*
Bartlett, Elizabeth *WhoWrEP 89*
Bartlett, Elizabeth 1924- *FemiCLE*
Bartlett, Elizabeth Susan 1927- *WhoAm 90, WhoE 91*
Bartlett, Ethel 1900-1978 *PenDiMP*
Bartlett, F Lewis 1914- *BiDrAPA 89*
Bartlett, Fred Stewart 1905-1988 *WhoAmA 91N*
Bartlett, Gene E. 1910-1989 *BioIn 16, ConAu 130*
Bartlett, George W. 1920- *St&PR 91*
Bartlett, Glenna M. 1932- *St&PR 91*
Bartlett, Gregg Edward 1962- *WhoSSW 91*
Bartlett, Hall 1929- *WhoAm 90, WhoWor 91*
Bartlett, Helen Buck 1959- *WhoWrEP 89*
Bartlett, Ian James 1934- *IntWWM 90*
Bartlett, Jacqueline Anne *BiDrAPA 89*
Bartlett, James Lowell, III 1945- *WhoAm 90, WhoEmL 91*
Bartlett, James Richard, III 1960- *WhoSSW 91*
Bartlett, James Theodore 1937- *St&PR 91*
Bartlett, James W 1926- *BiDrAPA 89*
Bartlett, James Williams 1926- *WhoAm 90*
Bartlett, James Wilson, III 1946- *WhoEmL 91*
Bartlett, Janell Alison 1965- *WhoAmW 91*
Bartlett, Janeth Marie 1946- *WhoAmW 91, WhoEmL 91*
Bartlett, Jeffrey Warner 1943- *St&PR 91*
Bartlett, Jennifer 1941- *BiDWomA, BioIn 16*
Bartlett, Jennifer Losch 1941- *WhoAm 90, WhoAmA 91, WhoAmW 91*
Bartlett, Joe Michael 1955- *WhoSSW 91*
Bartlett, John 1820-1905 *WorAlBi*
Bartlett, John Allen 1861-1933 *EncO&P 3*
Bartlett, John Bruen 1941- *St&PR 91*
Bartlett, John Cook 1947- *BiDrAPA 89*
Bartlett, John Louis 1929- *St&PR 91*
Bartlett, John Russell 1805-1886 *WhNaAH*
Bartlett, John Scott 1950- *WhoSSW 91*
Bartlett, John W *BiDrAPA 89*
Bartlett, Joseph Jackson 1834-1893 *BioIn 16*
Bartlett, Joseph T., Jr. 1936- *St&PR 91*
Bartlett, Joseph Warren 1933- *WhoAm 90*
Bartlett, Josiah 1729-1795 *EncCRAm, WorAlBi*
Bartlett, Kathleen *ConAu 31NR*
Bartlett, Larry Lee 1954- *WhoEmL 91*
Bartlett, Lee Anthony 1950- *WhoWrEP 89*
Bartlett, Leonard Lee 1930- *WhoAm 90*
Bartlett, Linda Gail 1943- *WhoE 91*
Bartlett, Lynn Conant 1921- *WhoAm 90, WhoWrEP 89*
Bartlett, Marshall 1925- *St&PR 91*
Bartlett, Neil 1932- *BioIn 16, WhoAm 90*
Bartlett, Paul D., Jr. 1919- *St&PR 91*
Bartlett, Paul Dana, Jr. 1919- *WhoAm 90*
Bartlett, Paul Doughty 1907- *WhoAm 90*
Bartlett, Peter Barry 1934- *St&PR 91*
Bartlett, Richard C. 1935- *St&PR 91*
Bartlett, Richard James 1926- *WhoAm 90*
Bartlett, Richard W. 1939- *St&PR 91*
Bartlett, Ricky Alan 1955- *WhoE 91*
Bartlett, Robert A. 1917- *St&PR 91*
Bartlett, Robert Abram 1875-1946 *WorAlBi*
Bartlett, Robert Addison, Jr. 1945- *St&PR 91*
Bartlett, Robert Perry, Jr. 1938- *WhoAm 90*
Bartlett, Robert V 1953- *WhoWrEP 89*
Bartlett, Robert Watkins 1933- *WhoAm 90*
Bartlett, Robert Webster 1922-1979 *WhoAmA 91N*
Bartlett, Samuel B. 1935- *St&PR 91*
Bartlett, Scott *NewYTBS 90*
Bartlett, Scott 1943-1990 *WhoAmA 91N*
Bartlett, Shirley Mae Anne 1933- *WhoAmW 91, WhoWor 91*
Bartlett, Steve 1947- *WhoAm 90, WhoSSW 91*
Bartlett, Steven James 1945- *WhoWrEP 89*
Bartlett, Steven Thade 1962- *WhoEmL 91*
Bartlett, Thomas Alva 1930- *WhoAm 90*
Bartlett, Thomas Eastman, Jr. 1948- *WhoEmL 91*
Bartlett, Vernon 1894-1983 *DcNaB 1981*
Bartlett, Walter E. 1928- *St&PR 91, WhoAm 90, WhoWor 91*
Bartlett, William McGillivray 1932- *WhoAm 90*
Bartlett Diaz, Manuel 1936- *WhoWor 91*
Bartlette, Donald Lloyd 1939- *WhoWor 91*
Bartley, Burnett Graham, Jr. 1924- *St&PR 91, WhoAm 90*
Bartley, David Anthony 1946- *St&PR 91, WhoEmL 91*
Bartley, Donald F 1921- *BiDrAPA 89*
Bartley, Harry B., Jr. *WhoSSW 91*
Bartley, Mary Lou Ruf 1940- *WhoAmW 91, WhoE 91*
Bartley, Michael Alan *BiDrAPA 89*
Bartley, Robert LeRoy 1937- *WhoAm 90, WhoE 91, WhoWrEP 89*
Bartley, Robert Paul 1926- *WhoE 91, WhoWor 91*
Bartley, S. Howard 1901-1988 *BioIn 16*
Bartley, Samuel Howard 1901-1988 *BioIn 16*
Bartley, Shirley Kay 1955- *WhoAmW 91*
Bartley, William Warren 1934-1990 *BioIn 16*
Bartley, William Warren, III 1934- *WhoAm 90, WhoWor 91*
Bartlik, Barbara D 1954- *BiDrAPA 89*
Bartling, John B., Jr. 1957- *St&PR 91*
Bartling, Kim K. 1958- *St&PR 91*
Bartling, Peter R. 1942- *St&PR 91*
Bartling, Phyllis McGinness 1927- *WhoAmW 91*
Bartling, Theodore Charles 1922- *WhoAm 90*
Bartlo, Sam D. 1919- *WhoAm 90*
Bartlom, John Alexander 1951- *St&PR 91*
Bartman, Jeffrey 1951- *WhoWrEP 89*
Bartmess, Geary, III 1948- *WhoEmL 91*
Bartner, Bernard I. 1926- *St&PR 91*
Bartner, Martin 1930- *WhoAm 90*
Bartnett, Edmond P. *BioIn 16*
Bartnett, Robert Elliott 1929- *WhoSSW 91*
Bartnick, Harry William 1950- *WhoAmA 91*
Bartnicki, Stanley Thomas 1933- *WhoWor 91*
Bartnicki-Garcia, Salomon 1935- *WhoAm 90*
Bartnikas, Ray 1936- *WhoAm 90*
Bartnoff, Judith 1949- *WhoAm 90*
Barto, J.V. 1935- *St&PR 91*
Barto, Tzimon 1963- *IntWWM 90*
Bartocha, Bodo 1928- *WhoAm 90*
Bartoe, Otto Edwin, Jr. 1927- *WhoAm 90*
Bartok Quartet *PenDiMP*
Bartok, Bela 1881-1945 *BioIn 16, PenDiMP A, WorAlBi*
Bartok, William 1930- *WhoAm 90*
Bartol, Ernest Thomas 1946- *WhoE 91, WhoWor 91*
Bartol, George E., III *BioIn 16*
Bartol, Julio R. 1939- *St&PR 91*
Bartolacci, Guido J. 1929- *St&PR 91*
Bartolacci, Guido Jamess 1929- *WhoAm 90*
Bartolacci, Raymond Anthony 1923- *St&PR 91*
Bartoletti, Bruno 1926- *IntWWM 90, PenDiMP, WhoAm 90, WhoWor 91*
Bartolf, Philip S. 1949- *St&PR 91*
Bartoli, Carlo 1931- *ConDes 90*
Bartoli, Henry E. 1946- *St&PR 91*
Bartolini, Anthony Louis 1931- *WhoAm 90*
Bartolini, Bruce Anthony 1950- *WhoE 91*
Bartolini, Lando 1937- *IntWWM 90*
Bartolini, Nicholas Phillip 1936- *WhoWor 91*
Bartolini, Robert A. 1942- *BioIn 16*
Bartolino, John Bruce 1944- *WhoE 91*
Bartolo, Adolph Marion 1929- *St&PR 91*
Bartolo, Anthony Joseph 1934- *WhoWor 91*
Bartolo, Domenico di 1400-1445 *BioIn 16*
Bartolo, Donna M. 1941- *WhoAmW 91*
Bartolome, Numeriano 1945- *WhoWor 91*
Bartolomei, Felix R. 1939- *WhoSSW 91*
Bartolomeo, Richard Nicholas 1935- *St&PR 91*
Bartolommeo, Fra 1475-1517 *IntDcAA 90, WorAlBi*
Bartolone, Frank Joseph 1931- *St&PR 91*
Bartolotta, Anthony J. 1929- *St&PR 91*
Bartolucci, Giampiero 1933- *BiDrAPA 89*
Bartolucci, Luis A. 1946- *WhoHisp 91*
Bartolucci, Luis Alberto 1946- *WhoSSW 91*
Barton, Alan R. 1925- *St&PR 91*
Barton, Alexander James 1924- *WhoWor 91*
Barton, Allen Hoisington 1924- *WhoAm 90, WhoE 91*
Barton, Barbara Ann 1954- *WhoAmW 91*
Barton, Ben 1900-1989 *BioIn 16*
Barton, Benny M. 1952- *WhoSSW 91*
Barton, Bernard 1784-1849 *DcLB 96 [port]*
Barton, Bernard Alan, Jr. 1948- *WhoSSW 91*
Barton, Blake Douglas 1960- *BiDrAPA 89*
Barton, Bob 1941- *Ballpl 90*
Barton, Brett *WhoWrEP 89*
Barton, Brigid Anne 1943- *WhoAmW 91*
Barton, Brooke Millon 1954- *BiDrAPA 89*
Barton, Bruce 1886-1967 *BioIn 16, WorAlBi*
Barton, Bruce Glenn 1952- *WhoEmL 91*
Barton, Byron 1930- *AuBYP 90*
Barton, C. Robert 1926- *St&PR 91, WhoAm 90*
Barton, Carl P. 1916- *WhoAm 90*
Barton, Charles Andrews, Jr. 1916- *WhoWor 91*
Barton, Charles Compton *BiDrAPA 89*
Barton, Charles D, Jr. *BiDrAPA 89*
Barton, Charles Dennis, Jr. 1963- *WhoEmL 91*
Barton, Clara 1821-1912 *BioIn 16, FemiCLE, WorAlBi*
Barton, Clara H. 1821-1912 *BioAmW*
Barton, Colleen 1923- *WhoWrEP 89*
Barton, Cynthia *ODwPR 91*
Barton, Cynthia Kathleen 1958- *WhoAmW 91*
Barton, David 1936- *BiDrAPA 89*
Barton, David Knox 1927- *WhoAm 90*
Barton, Derek H. R. 1918- *WorAlBi*
Barton, Derek Harold Richard 1918- *WhoAm 90, WhoWor 91*
Barton, Edwin S., Jr. 1909- *St&PR 91*
Barton, Ellen Louise 1946- *WhoAmW 91*
Barton, Enos M. 1842-1916 *WorAlBi*
Barton, Erle *ConAu 32NR*
Barton, Evan Mansfield 1903- *WhoAm 90*
Barton, Fred Delano *BiDrAPA 89*
Barton, Frederick Durrie 1949- *WhoE 91*
Barton, Fredrick Preston 1948- *WhoWrEP 89*
Barton, Gail M 1937- *BiDrAPA 89*
Barton, Gail Melinda 1937- *WhoE 91*
Barton, Gary F. 1944- *ODwPR 91*
Barton, Georgie Read *WhoAmA 91*
Barton, Gerald Gaylord 1931- *St&PR 91*
Barton, Gerald Lee 1934- *St&PR 91, WhoAm 90*
Barton, Glenys 1944- *BiDWomA*
Barton, Graham G. 1928- *St&PR 91*
Barton, Greg *BioIn 16*
Barton, Gregory Edward 1961- *WhoEmL 91*
Barton, Helen B *BiDrAPA 89*
Barton, Jacqueline K. 1952- *WhoAm 90, WhoAmW 91*
Barton, James *PenDiMP*
Barton, James Cary 1940- *WhoSSW 91, WhoWor 91*
Barton, James Levi 1855-1936 *BioIn 16*
Barton, James Miller 1942- *WhoAm 90*
Barton, James T. *WhoAm 90*
Barton, Jay 1922- *WhoAm 90*
Barton, Jean Marie 1945- *WhoAmW 91*
Barton, Jerry O'Donnell 1947- *WhoE 91*
Barton, Jo Ann 1949- *WhoAmW 91*
Barton, Joe Linus 1949- *WhoAm 90, WhoSSW 91*
Barton, John Bernard Adie 1928- *WhoWor 91*
Barton, John Frederick 1932- *WhoE 91*
Barton, John Laing 1938- *BiDrAPA 89*
Barton, John Murray 1921- *WhoAmA 91*
Barton, John Selby 1918- *WhoAm 90*
Barton, Justin R. 1942- *St&PR 91*
Barton, Kenneth Rogers 1931- *St&PR 91*
Barton, Larry David 1947- *WhoEmL 91*
Barton, Lee *ConAu 32NR*
Barton, Lewis 1940- *WhoE 91, WhoWor 91*
Barton, Louis Anthony 1956- *BiDrAPA 89*
Barton, Lucy 1891-1979 *BioIn 16*
Barton, Lucy Adalade 1891-1979 *NotWoAT*
Barton, Marie Tidwell 1937- *WhoAmW 91*
Barton, Meta Packard 1928- *WhoAmW 91*
Barton, Nelda Ann Lambert 1929- *WhoAm 90, WhoAmW 91, WhoSSW 91*
Barton, Pat *WhoWrEP 89*
Barton, Pat 1928- *BioIn 16*
Barton, Patsy Sue 1931- *St&PR 91*
Barton, Phylliş Settecase 1934- *WhoAmA 91*
Barton, R.H. 1935- *St&PR 91*
Barton, Ralph 1891-1931 *BioIn 16*
Barton, Ralph G. 1940- *St&PR 91*
Barton, Raymond Oscar, III 1949- *WhoSSW 91*
Barton, Rhea Marie *BiDrAPA 89*
Barton, Robert H. 1933- *St&PR 91*
Barton, Robert James 1942- *St&PR 91*
Barton, Robert Wayne 1948- *WhoEmL 91*
Barton, Roger 1947- *WhoWrEP 89*
Barton, Rose Maynard 1856-1929 *BiDWomA*
Barton, Russell W *BiDrAPA 89*
Barton, Russell William 1923- *WhoAm 90, WhoWor 91*
Barton, Ruth Ann 1941- *WhoWrEP 89*
Barton, Stanley 1927- *WhoAm 90*
Barton, Stanley Faulkner 1927- *St&PR 91*
Barton, Stephen Nye 1946- *BiDrAPA 89*
Barton, Thomas Frank, Sr. 1905- *WhoWrEP 89*
Barton, Thomas H. 1924- *St&PR 91*
Barton, Thomas Jackson 1940- *WhoAm 90*
Barton, Thomas Pennant 1803-1869 *BioIn 16*
Barton, Troyce Dell 1940- *WhoSSW 91*
Barton, Walter E 1906- *BiDrAPA 89*
Barton, Walter Earl 1906- *WhoE 91*
Barton, Wendell Lewis 1932- *St&PR 91*
Barton, Willene *BioIn 16*
Barton, William Arnold 1948- *WhoWor 91*
Barton, William Blackburn 1899- *WhoAm 90*
Barton, William Clyde, Jr. 1931- *St&PR 91*
Barton, William E. 1861-1930 *LiHiK*
Barton, William Russell 1925- *WhoAm 90*
Barton-Hass, Lorraine Dorothea *BiDrAPA 89*
Bartonico, Antonio Sablad 1953- *BiDrAPA 89*
Bartoo, Kenneth Gary 1940- *WhoE 91*
Bartos, Jerry Garland 1933- *WhoSSW 91*

Bartos, Leonard Francis 1947- WhoSSW 91
Bartos, Michael Richard 1947- BiDrAPA 89
Bartosic, Florian 1926- WhoAm 90
Bartoszek, Joseph Edward 1952- WhoE 91
Bartoszewski, Wladyslaw 1922- BioIn 16
Bartov, Hanoch 1926- ConAu 129
Bartow, Jerome Edward 1930- St&PR 91
Bartow, Stuart Allen, Jr. 1951- WhoWrEP 89
Bartram, George ConAu 129
Bartram, John 1699-1777 EncCRAm
Bartram, Maynard Cleveland 1926- St&PR 91
Bartram, Maynard Cleveland, Jr. 1926- WhoAm 90
Bartram, Ralph Herbert 1929- WhoAm 90, WhoWor 91
Bartram, William 1739-1823 BioIn 16, WhNaAH
Bartsch, David A. 1951- St&PR 91
Bartsch, Donald Kenneth 1929- St&PR 91
Bartsch, Susanne BioIn 16
Bartsch, William Henry 1933- WhoWor 91
Bartscherer, Joseph 1954- WhoAmA 91
Bartschi, Werner 1950- IntWWM 90
Bartscht, Heri Bert 1919- WhoAm 90
Bartter, Martha Ann 1932- WhoWrEP 89
Bartucci, Janet E. 1952- ODwPR 91
Bartucci, Robert John BiDrAPA 89
Bartula, Ray A. 1940- St&PR 91
Bartunek, James Scott BiDrAPA 89
Bartunek, Kenneth Steven 1965- WhoEmL 91
Bartunek, Robert Richard 1914- WhoAm 90
Bartunek, Robert Richard, Jr. 1946- WhoEmL 91
Bartus, Raymond Thomas 1947- WhoAm 90
Bartusiak, Marcia 1950- ConAu 129
Bartusis, Mary Ann 1930- BiDrAPA 89
Barty, Peter Frederick 1934- WhoSSW 91
Barty, Warren 1941- WhoSSW 91
Bartynski, Cynthia Lynn 1958- WhoE 91
Bartz, Debra Ann 1960- WhoEmL 91
Bartz, Freeman Edwin 1930- St&PR 91
Bartz, James Ross 1942- WhoAmA 91
Bartz, Jerzy 1936- IntWWM 90
Bartz, Jim NewAgMG
Bartz, John K BiDrAPA 89
Bartz, Mary Russo WhoAmW 91
Bartzatt, Ronald Lee 1953- WhoEmL 91
Bartzokis, George 1956- BiDrAPA 89
Bartzokis, Spiro C. 1952- St&PR 91
Barua, Khanindra 1951- WhoWor 91
Barucci, Piero BioIn 16
Baruch, Anne WhoAmA 91
Baruch, Bernard M. 1870-1965 WorAlBi
Baruch, Bernard Mannes 1870-1965 BioIn 16
Baruch, Eduard 1907- St&PR 91, WhoAm 90, WhoWor 91
Baruch, Grace K. BioIn 16
Baruch, Jack 1939- BiDrAPA 89
Baruch, John Alfred 1926- St&PR 91, WhoE 91
Baruch, Jordan Jay 1923- WhoAm 90
Baruch, Joseph BiDrAPA 89
Baruch, Monica Lobo-Filho 1954- WhoAmW 91
Baruch, Ralph M. 1923- WhoAm 90
Baruch, Ruth-Marion Evelyn 1922- WhoAmA 91
Baruh, Haim 1954- WhoE 91
Baruk, Henri 1897- BiDrAPA 89
Barusch, Lawrence Roos 1949- WhoEmL 91
Barut, Asim Orhan 1926- WhoAm 90
Barvinok, Hanna EncCoWW
Barvoets, Brooks R. 1927- St&PR 91
Barvoets, Ernest 1957- St&PR 91
Barwell, Basil B. 1915- St&PR 91
Barwick, B.J., Jr. St&PR 91
Barwick, Grace 1618?-1701 BiDEWW
Barwick, John O., III 1949- St&PR 91
Barwick, John Samuel 1962- WhoE 91
Barwick, Pamela Jean 1957- WhoAmW 91
Barwick, Robert Charles 1930- St&PR 91
Barwick, Steven 1921- IntWWM 90
Barwick, Steven James 1947- St&PR 91
Barwick-Snell, Katherine Lane 1955- WhoAmW 91
Barwinski, Richard Conrad 1951- WhoEmL 91
Barwise, Tom BioIn 16
Barwood, Hal ConAu 129
Barwood, Lee WhoWrEP 89
Bary, Etienne de 1962- WhoWor 91
Barye, Antoine-Louis 1795-1875 IntDcAA 90
Barylli, Walter 1921- IntWWM 90
Baryshnikov, Mikhail 1948- BioIn 16, WhoAm 90, WhoE 91, WhoWor 91, WorAlBi
Barz, Diane 1943- WhoAmW 91
Barz, Patricia 1953- WhoAmW 91
Barza, Sidney 1920- BiDrAPA 89
Barzach, Michele 1943- BiDFrPL
Barzd, Vera M BiDrAPA 89
Barzilay, Isaac Eisenstein 1915- WhoAm 90
Barzilay, Zvi 1946- St&PR 91
Barzin, Leon 1900- IntWWM 90, PenDiMP
Barzman, Anita Josefa BiDrAPA 89
Barzman, Ben BioIn 16
Barzman, Ben 1912- ConAu 132
Barzun, Jacques 1907- IntWWM 90, WhoAm 90, WhoAmA 91, WhoWor 91, WhoWrEP 89
Barzun, Kathleen A BiDrAPA 89
Barzune, Dolores 1939- WhoHisp 91
Bas, Rutger EncCoWW
Basa, Angela 1952- WhoE 91
Basa, Soledad R 1943- BiDrAPA 89
Basalla, John Louis 1954- WhoEmL 91
Basanez, Edward Samuel 1930- WhoSSW 91
Basar, Tamer 1946- WhoAm 90
Basara, Stanley Eugene BioIn 16
Basaraba, Jacqueline Marie 1952- WhoEmL 91
Basart, Ann Phillips 1931- WhoWrEP 89
Basart, John Philip 1938- WhoAm 90
Basbas, Monte G. 1921- WhoE 91
Basch, Avraham Alvin 1931- WhoWor 91
Basch, Gail Marie 1960- BiDrAPA 89
Basch, Joseph Martin 1920- St&PR 91
Basch, Michael Franz BiDrAPA 89, ConAu 130
Basch, Paul Frederick 1933- WhoAm 90
Basch, Richard Vennard 1945- WhoE 91, WhoEmL 91, WhoWor 91
Basch, Samuel H BiDrAPA 89
Baschenis, Evaristo 1617-1677 IntDcAA 90
Bascher, Christophe Jacques Marcel 1948- WhoWor 91
Bascom, Earl W 1906- WhoAmA 91
Bascom, Florence 1862-1945 BioIn 16
Bascom, George Nicholas WhNaAH
Bascom, John G. 1943- St&PR 91, WhoAm 90
Bascom, Perry Bagnall 1924- WhoAm 90
Bascom, Willard BioIn 16
Bascom, Willard Newell 1916- WhoAm 90
Bascug, Yvonne Leonor BiDrAPA 89
Basden, Barbara Holz 1940- WhoAmW 91
Basdeo, Sahadeo 1945- WhoWor 91
Base, Graeme AuBYP 90
Base, Graeme 1958- BioIn 16, ChILR 22 [port]
Base, Richard G. 1945- St&PR 91
Base, Romulo Alegarbes 1947- WhoWor 91
Base, Steven W. 1944- St&PR 91
Base, Thomas Sidney 1948- WhoSSW 91
Basecqz, Guy M 1937- BiDrAPA 89
Basefsky, Stuart Mark 1949- WhoEmL 91
Basehart, Richard 1914-1984 WorAlBi
Basel, Arthur R 1928- BiDrAPA 89
Basel, Frances Rita 1933- WhoAmW 91, WhoWor 91
Baselitz, Georg 1938- WhoWor 91
Baselt, Franz Bernhard Bernd 1934- IntWWM 90
Baseman, Alan Howard 1953- WhoSSW 91
Baseman, Robert Lynn 1932- St&PR 91, WhoAm 90
Baser, Robert Earl 1946- WhoSSW 91
Baserga, Renato Luigi 1925- WhoAm 90
Basevi, James 1890- ConDes 90
Basford, Emory S. BioIn 16
Basford, James O. 1931- St&PR 91
Basford, Robert Eugene 1923- WhoAm 90
Basgall, Monty 1922- Ballpl 90
Bash, Charles Dayton 1949- WhoEmL 91
Bash, Frank Ness 1937- WhoAm 90
Bash, James Francis 1925- WhoAm 90
Bash, Nicholas P 1914- BiDrAPA 89
Bash, Philip Edwin 1921- WhoAm 90
Bash, Yigal Amir 1938- WhoAm 90
Basham, Jimmye Kay 1958- WhoSSW 91
Basham, Lloyd M. 1947- St&PR 91
Basham, Lloyd Moman 1947- WhoEmL 91
Basham, Michael Alan 1957- WhoEmL 91
Basham, Nancy Milcarsky 1963- WhoSSW 91
Basham, Nancy W. 1944- St&PR 91
Basham-Tooker, Janet Brooks 1919- WhoAmW 91
Bashant, Floyd Thomas St&PR 91
Bashara, George N. St&PR 91
Bashaw, Thomas P. 1843- AmLegL
Bashe, Elinor Diane 1958- WhoAmW 91
Bashe, Gilbert G. 1954- ODwPR 91
Bashe, Gilbert Gregg 1954- WhoEmL 91, WhoWor 91
Bashe, Lawrence Douglas 1944- St&PR 91
Basheda, Randall Steven 1958- St&PR 91
Bashevis, Isaac MajTwCW
Bashevkin, Albert 1907- St&PR 91
Bashevkin, Irving 1924- St&PR 91
Bashevkin, Robert 1930- St&PR 91
Bashford, Eric Rainer 1959- WhoEmL 91
Bashford, Robert Alonzo BiDrAPA 89
Bashford, Wilkes BioIn 16
Bashinsky, Sloan Young, II 1942- WhoWrEP 89
Bashir, Mir 1907- EncO&P 3
Bashir, Nazrat 1956- WhoWor 91
Bashir, Umar Hasan Ahmad al- WhoWor 91
Bashkin, Edmund A BiDrAPA 89
Bashkin, Lloyd Scott 1951- WhoE 91, WhoEmL 91, WhoWor 91
Bashkirov, Dmitri 1931- IntWWM 90
Bashkirtseff, Maria Constantinova 1858-1884 EncCoWW
Bashkirtseff, Marie 1858-1884 BiDWomA
Bashkirtseff, Marie 1859?-1884 NinCLC 27 [port]
Bashkow, Theodore Robert 1921- WhoAm 90
Bashline, Donald Theodore 1948- WhoE 91
Bashline, Terry Lee Morgan 1953- WhoE 91, WhoWor 91
Bashmakov, Pyotr EncCRAm
Bashmet, Yuri 1953- IntWWM 90, PenDiMP
Basho 1644-1694 BioIn 16, EncJap
Basho, Robbie NewAgMG
Bashor, John W 1926- WhoAmA 91
Bashor, Ronald Leslie 1949- WhoEmL 91, WhoSSW 91
Bashore, Charles Eicker 1914- St&PR 91
Bashore, George Willis 1934- WhoAm 90
Bashore, Helen L. 1921- St&PR 91
Bashwiner 1944- WhoSSW 91
Bashwiner, Steven Lacelle 1941- WhoAm 90, WhoWor 91
Basia BioIn 16
Basia 1959?- ConMus 5 [port]
Basich, Vladimir Walter 1934- St&PR 91
Basichis, Gordon Allen 1947- WhoWor 91
Basie, Count 1904-1984 BioIn 16, DrBIPA 90, OxCPMus, WorAlBi
Basie, William 1904-1984 BioIn 16
Basil EncO&P 3
Basil, Douglas Constantine 1923- WhoAm 90, WhoWrEP 89
Basil, Frank E. BioIn 16
Basil, Marvin B. 1934- St&PR 91
Basil, Stephen Joseph 1950- WhoSSW 91
Basil, Toni BioIn 16
Basile, Abigail Julia Ellen Herron 1915- WhoAmW 91
Basile, Andreana 1580?-1640? PenDiMP
Basile, Antoine E. 1938- WhoE 91
Basile, Carol Ann 1953- WhoAmW 91
Basile, Ernesto 1857-1932 PenDiDA 89
Basile, Mary Knight 1920- WhoAmW 91
Basile, Michael E. 1923- St&PR 91
Basile, Neal F. 1944- St&PR 91
Basile, Neal Fahr 1944- WhoE 91
Basile, Paul Louis, Jr. 1945- WhoAm 90, WhoEmL 91, WhoWor 91
Basile, Richard Emanuel 1921- WhoAm 90
Basili, Renzo S 1930- BiDrAPA 89
Basili, Robert Andrew 1934- St&PR 91
Basilico, Claudio 1936- WhoAm 90
Basilio, Mary Louise 1937- WhoAmW 91
Basinger, Cheryl Kathryn R. 1955- WhoAmW 91
Basinger, Kim BioIn 16
Basinger, Kim 1953- CurBio 90 [port], WhoAm 90, WhoAmW 91, WorAlBi
Basinger, Malcolm D. 1929- St&PR 91
Basinger, Robert 1931- St&PR 91
Basinger, Thomas Preston 1947- St&PR 91
Basinskas, Justinas 1923- IntWWM 90
Basinski, Eddie 1922- Ballpl 90
Basinski, Zbigniew Stanislaw 1928- WhoAm 90
Basista, Kenneth 1952- WhoAmA 91
Basista, Michael Paul 1952- WhoE 91
Basiszta, Martin Winston 1943- WhoAm 90
Basit, Mohammad A 1937- BiDrAPA 89
Basius, Francis L. 1931- St&PR 91
Baska, James Louis 1927- St&PR 91, WhoAm 90
Baskaran, Thanesseri S BiDrAPA 89
Baskervill, Jane Gibbs 1955- WhoWrEP 89
Baskerville, Charles 1896- WhoAmA 91
Baskerville, Charles Alexander 1928- WhoAm 90
Baskerville, John 1706-1775 PenDiDA 89
Baskett, James 1904-1948 DrBIPA 90
Baskett, Kathleen Thomas BiDrAPA 89
Baskett, Sarah J BiDrAPA 89
Baskett, Thomas Sebree 1916- WhoAm 90
Baskette, Floyd Kenneth, Jr. 1940- WhoAm 90
Baskin, Barbara H 1929- WhoWrEP 89
Baskin, Charles Richard 1926- WhoSSW 91
Baskin, David Stuart 1952- WhoAm 90
Baskin, Fred 1941- WhoSSW 91
Baskin, Herbert Bernard 1933- WhoAm 90, WhoWor 91
Baskin, Jerry M. 1944- St&PR 91
Baskin, Jonathan ODwPR 91
Baskin, Leland Burleson 1952- WhoAm 90
Baskin, Leonard 1922- WhoAm 90, WhoAmA 91
Baskin, Robert E. 1952- ODwPR 91
Baskin, Roberta BioIn 16
Baskin, Ronald Joseph 1935- WhoAm 90
Baskin, T Grady 1923- BiDrAPA 89
Baskin, Tery L. 1953- WhoEmL 91
Baskin, Yvonne Cecile 1948- WhoEmL 91
Baskind, Barry St&PR 91
Baskind, Stanley Marvin 1930- St&PR 91
Baskinger, Patricia JoAnne 1949- WhoAmW 91
Baskwill, Geoffrey Randall 1920- WhoAm 90
Basler, Floyd Joseph 1914- St&PR 91
Basler, Roy P 1906-1989 ConAu 130
Basler, Thomas G. 1940- WhoAm 90
Basler, Warren BioIn 16
Basler, Wayne G. 1930- St&PR 91
Basler, Wayne Gordon 1930- WhoAm 90, WhoSSW 91
Basler, William L. 1944- St&PR 91
Basmaci, Kevork BiDrAPA 89
Basmajian, John Varoujan 1921- WhoAm 90
Basmeson, Gustavo Adolfo 1952- WhoHisp 91
Basnett, Lord 1924-1989 AnObit 1989
Basnett, David 1924-1989 BioIn 16
Basnett, Frank Ray 1946- WhoEmL 91, WhoSSW 91
Basnett, Patricia Moreland 1953- WhoAmW 91
Basolo, Fred 1920- WhoAm 90
Bason, George R. 1919- ODwPR 91
Bason, Lillian 1913- AuBYP 90
Basore, Joe Neff 1927- St&PR 91
Basos, William 1932- St&PR 91
Basosi, Riccardo 1947- WhoWor 91
Basov, Nikolai Gennadievich 1922- WhoWor 91, WorAlBi
Basque, Norman F. 1923- St&PR 91
Basquette, Lina BioIn 16
Basquiat, Jean-Michel 1960-1988 BioIn 16
Basquiat, Jean Michel 1961-1988 WhoAmA 91N
Basquin, Kit 1941- WhoAmA 91
Basra, Devinder Singh 1942- WhoWor 91
Basrai, Imtiaz Siraj 1953- BiDrAPA 89
Bass, Adrienne Paula 1951- WhoAmW 91
Bass, Albert Sidney, Jr. 1947- WhoSSW 91
Bass, Anne BioIn 16
Bass, Arthur Charles 1932- WhoAm 90
Bass, Barbara DeJong 1946- WhoAm 90
Bass, Barry C 1938- BiDrAPA 89
Bass, Bernard Morris 1925- WhoAm 90
Bass, Bob WhoAm 90
Bass, Charles Wesley 1947- St&PR 91
Bass, David Jason 1954- WhoEmL 91
Bass, David Loren 1943- WhoAmA 91
Bass, Deborah Livingston 1956- WhoWrEP 89
Bass, Dorothy Elizabeth 1931- WhoWrEP 89
Bass, E. Warner 1941- WhoSSW 91
Bass, Eloise 1935- WhoWrEP 89
Bass, Elsa Adler BioIn 16
Bass, Frank Thomas, Jr. 1946- WhoSSW 91
Bass, G. Allen 1943- WhoAm 90
Bass, Gene 1934- St&PR 91
Bass, George 1921- St&PR 91
Bass, George Fletcher 1932- WhoAm 90
Bass, George Houston NewYTBS 90
Bass, Gordon Michael 1948- WhoSSW 91
Bass, Harold Neal 1939- WhoAm 90
Bass, Herbert 1929- St&PR 91
Bass, Howard Hudson 1937- WhoSSW 91
Bass, Hyman 1932- WhoAm 90
Bass, James Orin 1910- WhoAm 90
Bass, Jerome Lewis 1947- BiDrAPA 89
Bass, Jerry S. 1937- St&PR 91
Bass, Joel 1942- WhoAmA 91
Bass, Joel Leonard 1942- WhoAm 90
Bass, Johanna WhoAmA 91N
Bass, John 1891-1978 WhoAmA 91N
Bass, John David 1955- WhoEmL 91
Bass, John F. 1946- St&PR 91
Bass, John Fred 1941- WhoAm 90
Bass, Jonathan N 1951- BiDrAPA 89
Bass, Jordan Tully 1925- St&PR 91
Bass, Judy 1946- WhoAmA 91
Bass, Judy Marsha 1946- WhoSSW 91
Bass, Kevin 1959- Ballpl 90
Bass, Kingsley B., Jr. MajTwCW
Bass, Leonard Hodges 1931- St&PR 91
Bass, Lewis 1947- WhoEmL 91
Bass, Linda Sue 1949- WhoSSW 91
Bass, Marshall B. 1926- St&PR 91
Bass, Mary Anna 1930- WhoAmW 91
Bass, Maudelle BioIn 16
Bass, Max S. 1928- St&PR 91
Bass, Max S. 1940- WhoAm 90

Bass, Michele Diane 1950- *WhoAmW 91*
Bass, Milton Ralph 1923- *WhoWrEP 89*
Bass, Nancy Agnes 1937- *WhoAmW 91*
Bass, Neil F. 1931- *St&PR 91*
Bass, Nelson Estupinan *HispWr 90*
Bass, Norm 1939- *Ballpl 90*
Bass, Norman Herbert 1936- *WhoAm 90*
Bass, Pamela Jean 1949- *WhoSSW 91*
Bass, Paul 1928- *WhoAm 90*
Bass, Perry Richardson 1914- *WhoAm 90*
Bass, Richard Carey 1944- *St&PR 91*
Bass, Richard S 1938- *BiDrAPA 89*
Bass, Robert M. *BioIn 16*
Bass, Robert Muse 1948- *WhoAm 90*
Bass, Robert O. 1934- *St&PR 91*
Bass, Robert Olin 1917- *WhoAm 90*
Bass, Ronald *WhoAm 90*
Bass, Ruth 1938- *WhoAmA 91*
Bass, Sampson H., Jr. 1929- *St&PR 91*
Bass, Saul 1920- *ConDes 90*
Bass, Shailer L. 1906-1988 *BioIn 16*
Bass, Stevan Keith 1953- *WhoEmL 91*
Bass, William Lang 1927- *BiDrAPA 89*
Bass, William M 1928- *ConAu 31NR*
Bass, William Marvin, III 1928- *WhoAm 90*
Bass, William Scott 1937- *BiDrAPA 89*
Bass, Zelig Leonard 1925- *St&PR 91*
Bass-Wilson, Amy 1957- *WhoEmL 91*
Bassabi, Souleymane Karim 1941- *WhoWor 91*
Bassam, Bertha *BioIn 16*
Bassan, Jacobo 1932- *WhoWor 91*
Bassanelli, Anthony Gerard *BiDrAPA 89*
Bassani, Giorgio 1916- *ConAu 33NR, MajTwCW*
Bassani, Giuseppe 1937- *WhoAm 90*
Bassano, Jacopo 1510?-1592 *IntDcAA 90*
Bassantin, James *EncO&P 3*
Bassat Coen, Luis 1941- *WhoWor 91*
Basse, Arno 1916- *St&PR 91*
Bassen, Cecile R *BiDrAPA 89*
Bassen, Cecile Ruth 1952- *WhoE 91*
Bassermann, Peter Paul 1949- *St&PR 91*
Basset, Gene 1927- *WhoAmA 91*
Basset, Mary 1522?-1572 *FemiCLE*
Bassett, Alan Brownsey 1947- *WhoSSW 91*
Bassett, Alice Cook 1925- *WhoAmW 91*
Bassett, Anne Susan *BiDrAPA 89*
Bassett, Barbara Wies 1939- *WhoAm 90*
Bassett, Barry David 1942- *WhoE 91*
Bassett, C. David 1936- *St&PR 91*
Bassett, Carol Hoffer 1931- *WhoE 91*
Bassett, Charles Andrew Loockerman 1924- *WhoAm 90*
Bassett, Charles Columbus 1934- *St&PR 91*
Bassett, Charles Walker 1932- *WhoAm 90, WhoE 91*
Bassett, David West *BiDrAPA 89*
Bassett, Ebenezer Don Carlos 1833-1908 *BioIn 16*
Bassett, Edward Powers 1929- *WhoAm 90*
Bassett, Elizabeth Ewing 1937- *WhoAm 90, WhoWrEP 89*
Bassett, Gary Lee 1946- *BiDrAPA 89*
Bassett, Gerald D. 1940- *St&PR 91*
Bassett, Glen Earl 1926- *St&PR 91*
Bassett, Harry H. 1875-1926 *WorAlBi*
Bassett, Harry Hood 1917- *St&PR 91, WhoAm 90*
Bassett, Harry Hoxie 1875-1926 *EncABHB 5 [port]*
Bassett, James H. 1929- *WhoAm 90*
Bassett, Jean Williams 1926- *WhoE 91*
Bassett, Jeni 1959- *SmATA 64 [port]*
Bassett, Joel Eric 1944- *WhoAm 90*
Bassett, John Gibbs 1948- *WhoEmL 91*
Bassett, John Keith *AuBYP 90*
Bassett, John T. *BioIn 16*
Bassett, John White Hughes 1915- *St&PR 91, WhoAm 90*
Bassett, Joseph H. 1920- *St&PR 91*
Bassett, Katalin J. 1952- *BiDrAPA 89*
Bassett, Kimberly Taber *WhoE 91*
Bassett, Kimbrough Stone 1931- *WhoWor 91*
Bassett, Lawrence C 1931- *WhoE 91*
Bassett, Leland K. 1945- *ODwPR 91*
Bassett, Leland Kinsey 1945- *WhoWor 91*
Bassett, Leslie Raymond 1923- *IntWWM 90, WhoAm 90*
Bassett, Linda 1950?- *ConTFT 8*
Bassett, Lisa *AuBYP 90*
Bassett, Lisa 1958- *SmATA 61 [port]*
Bassett, Lonnie A. *BioIn 16*
Bassett, Michael Edward Rainton 1938- *WhoWor 91*
Bassett, Paul Edward 1923- *St&PR 91*
Bassett, Ralph Edward 1944- *WhoAm 90*
Bassett, Richard 1745-1815 *BioIn 16*
Bassett, Robert Cochem 1911- *WhoAm 90, WhoWor 91*
Bassett, Scott Gregory 1956- *WhoEmL 91*
Bassett, Tina *WhoAmW 91*
Bassett, Tina 1945- *ODwPR 91*
Bassett, Vivienne London *WhoE 91*
Bassett, William Akers 1931- *WhoAm 90*
Bassett, William H. 1922- *St&PR 91*
Bassett, Woodson William, Jr. 1926- *WhoAm 90*
Bassette, Alfred 1845-1937 *BioIn 16*
Bassetti, Fred Forde 1917- *WhoAm 90*
Bassey, Shirley 1937- *DrBIPA 90, EncPR&S 89, OxCPMus, WorAlBi*
Bassford, Paul Stanley *BiDrAPA 89*
Bassham, Genevieve Prieto 1939- *WhoHisp 91*
Bassi, Luigi 1766-1825 *PenDiMP*
Bassi Verati, Laura Maria Caterina 1711-1778 *EncCoWW*
Bassin, Joan 1938- *WhoAmA 91*
Bassin, Joan Clara 1938- *WhoE 91*
Bassin, Jules 1914- *WhoAm 90*
Bassin, Milton G. 1923- *WhoE 91*
Bassin, Robert Harris 1938- *WhoAm 90*
Bassingthwaighte, James Bucklin 1929- *WhoAm 90*
Bassingthwaighte, M. E. 1958- *BiDrAPA 89*
Bassion, Susan *WhoSSW 91*
Bassiouni, M. Cherif 1937- *WhoAm 90, WhoWor 91*
Bassiouni, Zaki 1943- *WhoSSW 91*
Bassiri, Reza G 1935- *BiDrAPA 89*
Bassler, Johnny 1895-1979 *Ballpl 90*
Bassler, Robert Covey 1935- *WhoAm 90*
Bassman, Bruce Conlin 1949- *St&PR 91*
Bassman, Robert Stuart 1947- *WhoAm 90, WhoEmL 91*
Bassnett, Peter James 1933- *WhoAm 90*
Basso, Deborah Anne *BiDrAPA 89*
Basso, Joseph Nicholas 1961- *WhoEmL 91*
Basso, Karen Nelson 1952- *WhoEmL 91*
Basso, Keith H 1940- *ConAu 131*
Basso, Keith Hamilton 1940- *WhoAm 90*
Basso, Leonardo Fernando Cruz 1950- *WhoWor 91*
Basso, Robert Anthony 1948- *St&PR 91*
Basso, Ronald Joseph 1932- *St&PR 91*
Bassoff, Evelyn Silten 1944- *WhoAmW 91*
Bassot, Jacques 1924- *WhoWor 91*
Bassuk, Allen I. 1946- *St&PR 91*
Bassuk, Ellen Linda *BiDrAPA 89*
Bassuk, Ellen Linda 1945- *WhoE 91*
Bassuk, Richard 1941- *St&PR 91, WhoAm 90*
Bast, James Louis 1936- *St&PR 91, WhoAm 90, WhoE 91*
Bast, Karin Dorathe Anderson 1945- *WhoEmL 91*
Bast, Robert Clinton, Jr. 1943- *WhoAm 90*
Bast, Robert Lower 1925- *St&PR 91*
Bastable, Diane Marie 1950- *WhoEmL 91*
Bastani, Jehangir Boman *BiDrAPA 89*
Bastarache, Julie Rico 1957- *WhoHisp 91*
Bastardina, La *PenDiMP*
Bastedo, Eleanor Maday 1937- *WhoAmW 91*
Bastedo, Philip Russell 1939- *WhoE 91*
Bastedo, Ralph Walter 1953- *WhoAm 90*
Bastedo, Wayne Webster 1948- *WhoE 91, WhoEmL 91, WhoWor 91*
Bastedo, William G., Jr. 1960- *WhoSSW 91*
Bastek, Deborah Ann 1953- *WhoEmL 91*
Basten, Fred E *WhoWrEP 89*
Basten, Karl Albert 1939- *WhoWor 91*
Bastiaanse, Gerard C. 1935- *WhoAm 90*
Bastian, Andrew Bart 1961- *St&PR 91*
Bastian, Carolyn Fisher 1932- *St&PR 91*
Bastian, Debora Laine 1951- *WhoAmW 91*
Bastian, Donald Noel 1925- *WhoAm 90*
Bastian, Harry *EncO&P 3*
Bastian, James H. 1956- *St&PR 91*
Bastian, James Harold 1927- *WhoAm 90, WhoWor 91*
Bastian, Jon Arnold 1949- *WhoEmL 91*
Bastian, Linda 1940- *WhoAmA 91*
Bastian, Lisa Ann 1958- *WhoWrEP 89*
Bastian, R. Richard 1946- *St&PR 91*
Bastian, Robert Edward 1937- *WhoE 91*
Bastianini, Ettore 1922-1967 *PenDiMP*
Bastias, John Costis 1936- *WhoWor 91*
Bastiat, Frederic 1801-1850 *BioIn 16*
Bastida, Daniel 1954- *WhoWor 91*
Bastidos, Hugo A. *WhoHisp 91*
Bastien, Christopher Paul 1958- *WhoEmL 91*
Bastien, Jean-Luc 1939- *OxCCanT*
Bastien, Jean Raymond *BiDrAPA 89*
Bastien, Jean Raymond 1949- *WhoE 91*
Bastien, Joseph William 1935- *WhoSSW 91*
Bastiks, Edward *BiDrAPA 89*
Bastin, Gary Charles 1950- *WhoSSW 91*
Bastin, Jules 1933- *IntWWM 90, PenDiMP*
Bastin, Kathy Louise 1953- *WhoAmW 91, WhoEmL 91*
Bastinelli, Alexander Richard 1950- *WhoE 91*
Bastis, Thomas E. 1928- *St&PR 91*
Bastoky, Bruce Michael 1953- *WhoEmL 91, WhoWor 91*
Bastoky, Linda Rae 1949- *WhoAmW 91*
Baston, Elvira 1944- *WhoHisp 91*
Baston, S.C. 1924- *St&PR 91*
Bastos, Armando de Lemos 1931- *WhoWor 91*
Bastos, Augusto Antonio Roa *BioIn 16*
Bastos, Augusto Roa *ConAu 131, HispWr 90*
Bastow, Susan Lynell 1959- *WhoAmW 91*
Bastron, Robert A. 1926- *St&PR 91*
Bastwick, Susanna *BiDEWW*
Bastyr, Douglas W. 1928- *St&PR 91*
Basu, Asish Ranjan 1944- *WhoAm 90*
Basu, Asit Prakas 1937- *WhoAm 90*
Basu, Rajat Subhra *WhoAm 90*
Basu, Romen 1923- *ConAu 30NR*
Basu, Tapendu Kumar 1944- *WhoWrEP 89*
Basuray, Rita 1953- *WhoE 91*
Baswell, Cathy D. 1945- *WhoSSW 91*
Basye, Paul Edmond 1901- *WhoAm 90*
Baszile, Janet Dean 1939- *St&PR 91*
Baszto, Theodore Francis, Jr. 1954- *WhoSSW 91*
Bat-Miriam, Yocheved 1901-1980 *EncCoWW*
Bata, George L. 1924- *WhoAm 90*
Bata, Rudolph Andrew, Jr. 1947- *WhoEmL 91*
Batacan, George A *BiDrAPA 89*
Batacheldor, Kenneth 1921-1988 *EncPaPR 91*
Batagol, Bruce Phillip 1941- *BiDrAPA 89*
Bataille, Dr. *EncO&P 3*
Bataille, Nicolas *PenDiDA 89*
Batal, Abdulrahman Misbah 1931- *WhoWor 91*
Batal, Joseph S. 1936- *St&PR 91*
Batalden, Paul Bennett 1941- *WhoAm 90*
Batalian, Sonia 1963- *WhoE 91*
Batalla, Pedro Ramon 1950- *WhoE 91*
Batarse, Anthony Abraham, Jr. 1933- *WhoHisp 91*
Batastini, Ralph Charles 1929- *St&PR 91, WhoAm 90*
Batbon, Bruce 1960- *St&PR 91*
Batch, Emil 1880-1926 *Ballpl 90*
Batchelder, A.R. 1910- *St&PR 91*
Batchelder, Alice M. 1944- *WhoAmW 91*
Batchelder, Anne Stuart 1920- *WhoWor 91*
Batchelder, Ardern R. 1910- *WhoAm 90*
Batchelder, David *BioIn 16*
Batchelder, James Kendricks 1842-1925 *AmLegL*
Batchelder, Joan S. 1944- *St&PR 91*
Batchelder, John Thomas Hutchins 1956- *WhoEmL 91*
Batchelder, Kenneth Thomas 1932- *St&PR 91*
Batchelder, Samuel Lawrence, Jr. 1932- *WhoAm 90*
Batcheller, George Sherman 1837-1908 *BioIn 16*
Batcheller, Thomas Joseph 1946- *St&PR 91*
Batchelor, Andrew Goolden Grant 1951- *WhoWor 91*
Batchelor, Anthony John 1944- *WhoAmA 91*
Batchelor, Barrington de Vere 1928- *WhoAm 90*
Batchelor, Betsey Ann 1952- *WhoAmA 91*
Batchelor, Celia Tunstall Ashe 1947- *WhoAmW 91*
Batchelor, Clarence Daniel 1888-1977 *WhoAmA 91N*
Batchelor, James Kent 1934- *WhoAm 90*
Batchelor, John Ellsworth 1947- *WhoSSW 91*
Batchelor, Joseph Brooklyn, Jr. 1922- *WhoSSW 91*
Batchelor, Reg *ConAu 31NR*
Batchman, John Clifford 1944- *WhoWor 91*
Batcho, Ronald Frank 1947- *WhoEmL 91*
Batdorf, Samuel Burbridge 1914- *WhoAm 90*
Bate, Charles Thomas 1932- *WhoAm 90*
Bate, Eugene R. 1949- *St&PR 91*
Bate, Geoffrey 1929- *WhoAm 90*
Bate, Jennifer Lucy 1944- *IntWWM 90*
Bate, Judith Ellen 1934- *WhoAmW 91, WhoWor 91*
Bate, Marilyn Anne 1939- *WhoAmW 91*
Bate, Norman Arthur 1916- *AuBYP 90*
Bate, Norman Arthur 1916-1980 *WhoAmA 91N*
Bate, Richard H. 1928- *St&PR 91*
Bate, Robert T. *BioIn 16*
Bate, Robert Thomas 1931- *WhoSSW 91*
Bate, Walter Jackson 1918- *BioIn 16, DcLB 103 [port], WhoAm 90, WhoWrEP 89*
Bate-Smith, E. C. 1900-1989 *BioIn 16*
Bateman, Alan Lawrence 1946- *BiDrAPA 89*
Bateman, Alan Mara 1889-1971 *DcScB S2*
Bateman, Dottye Jane Spencer *WhoWor 91*
Bateman, Dupuy, Jr. 1904- *WhoAm 90*
Bateman, Durward Franklin 1934- *WhoAm 90*
Bateman, Ellen Douglas 1844-1936 *BioIn 16, NotWoAT*
Bateman, F. Ellis, Jr. 1942- *WhoSSW 91*
Bateman, Frank Elliot 1927- *WhoE 91*
Bateman, Fred Willom 1916- *WhoAm 90*
Bateman, Giles Hirst Litton 1944- *WhoAm 90*
Bateman, Herbert Harvell 1928- *WhoAm 90, WhoSSW 91*
Bateman, Hester *PenDiDA 89*
Bateman, Hugh Elton 1937- *WhoSSW 91*
Bateman, Iris Hendrix 1940- *WhoAmW 91*
Bateman, Isabel Emilie 1854-1934 *BioIn 16, NotWoAT*
Bateman, Jason *BioIn 16*
Bateman, John 1942- *Ballpl 90*
Bateman, John Edwards 1931- *BiDrAPA 89*
Bateman, John H. 1934- *St&PR 91*
Bateman, John Jay 1931- *WhoAm 90*
Bateman, John Roger 1927- *WhoAm 90*
Bateman, Justine *BioIn 16*
Bateman, Justine 1966- *WhoAmW 91*
Bateman, Kate Josephine 1842?-1917 *BioIn 16, NotWoAT*
Bateman, Paul Trevier 1919- *WhoAm 90*
Bateman, Paul William 1957- *WhoAm 90, WhoEmL 91*
Bateman, Phoebe 1675- *BiDEWW*
Bateman, Ray, Jr. *BioIn 16*
Bateman, Rebecca Anne 1945- *WhoE 91*
Bateman, Robert 1842-1922 *BioIn 16*
Bateman, Robert James 1945- *WhoE 91*
Bateman, Robert McLellan 1930- *WhoAm 90, WhoAmA 91*
Bateman, Ronald C 1947- *WhoAmA 91*
Bateman, S.F. 1940- *St&PR 91*
Bateman, Samuel M. 1930- *St&PR 91*
Bateman, Sandra E. 1944- *ODwPR 91*
Bateman, Sharon L. 1949- *ODwPR 91*
Bateman, Sharon Louise 1949- *WhoEmL 91*
Bateman, Sidney Frances 1823-1881 *BioIn 16*
Bateman, Sidney Frances Cowell 1823-1881 *NotWoAT*
Bateman, Susanna *BiDEWW*
Bateman, Veda Mae 1921- *WhoAmW 91*
Bateman, Virginia Frances 1853-1940 *BioIn 16, NotWoAT*
Bateman, William Maxwell 1920- *WhoAm 90*
Bateman-Lumb, Cynthia Annie *IntWWM 90*
Batemans, The *NotWoAT*
Baten'kov, Gavrila Stepanovich 1793-1863 *BioIn 16*
Bates, Al R. 1931- *WhoSSW 91*
Bates, Alan 1934- *WhoAm 90, WhoWor 91, WorAlBi*
Bates, Alan Blair 1955- *WhoSSW 91*
Bates, Albert Kealiinui 1947- *WhoEmL 91*
Bates, Artie Ann *BioIn 16*
Bates, B.A., Jr. 1925- *St&PR 91*
Bates, Barbara J. Neuner 1927- *WhoAmW 91, WhoE 91*
Bates, Barbara Jeanne *WhoAmW 91*
Bates, Baron Kent 1934- *St&PR 91, WhoAm 90*
Bates, Betty *ConAu 32NR*
Bates, Beverly Bailey 1938- *WhoSSW 91*
Bates, Blanche 1873-1941 *BioIn 16, NotWoAT*
Bates, Bruce Alan 1958- *WhoEmL 91*
Bates, Bruce B. 1931- *St&PR 91*
Bates, Carol 1895- *WhoAmA 91N*
Bates, Charles Carpenter 1918- *WhoAm 90*
Bates, Charles Laurance 1924- *St&PR 91*
Bates, Charles Turner 1932- *St&PR 91, WhoAm 90*
Bates, Charles W. 1910- *St&PR 91*
Bates, Clarence Edward, Jr. 1946- *WhoEmL 91*
Bates, Daisy *BioIn 16*
Bates, Daniel M. 1951- *St&PR 91*
Bates, Darrell 1913-1989 *ConAu 129*
Bates, David 1952- *BioIn 16, WhoAmA 91*
Bates, David Martin 1934- *WhoAm 90*
Bates, David Mayfield 1946- *WhoSSW 91*
Bates, David Quentin, Jr. 1951- *WhoAm 90*
Bates, David Robert 1916- *WhoWor 91*
Bates, David T. 1947- *St&PR 91*
Bates, David Vincent 1922- *WhoAm 90*
Bates, David Wynn, Sr. 1935- *St&PR 91*
Bates, Don *ODwPR 91*
Bates, Don F. 1939- *WhoE 91*
Bates, Donald Vincent 1936- *St&PR 91*
Bates, Donnette Marie 1949- *WhoEmL 91*
Bates, Duane A. 1940- *IntWWM 90*
Bates, Dwight Lee 1943- *WhoWor 91*
Bates, Edgar H. 1905-1990 *BioIn 16*
Bates, Edward 1793-1869 *BiDrUSE 89*
Bates, Edward Brill 1919- *WhoAm 90*
Bates, Elizabeth 1921- *ConAu 32NR*

Bates, Frank 1934- St&PR 91
Bates, George Edmonds 1933- WhoAm 90
Bates, George Handy 1845- AmLegL
Bates, George William 1940- WhoAm 90
Bates, Gerald Earl 1933- WhoAm 90
Bates, Gladys Edgerly 1896- WhoAm 90, WhoAmA 91
Bates, Griffin M. Jr. BiDrAPA 89
Bates, H E 1905-1974 MajTwCW
Bates, H. Jack EarBlAP
Bates, Harold Martin 1928- WhoWor 91
Bates, Harry Clark, III BiDrAPA 89
Bates, Henry Walter 1825-1892 BioIn 16
Bates, Hudson H BiDrAPA 89
Bates, James Earl 1923- WhoAm 90, WhoE 91, WhoWor 91
Bates, James Leonard 1919- WhoAm 90
Bates, Jim 1941- WhoAm 90
Bates, John 1935- ConDes 90
Bates, John Bertram 1914- WhoAm 90
Bates, John Burnham 1918- WhoAm 90
Bates, John Cecil, Jr. 1936- WhoAm 90
Bates, John Lewis 1859-1946 AmLegL
Bates, John Walter 1939- WhoSSW 91
Bates, Johnny 1882-1949 Ballpl 90
Bates, Joseph Henry 1933- WhoAm 90
Bates, Katharine Lee BioIn 16
Bates, Katharine Lee 1859-1929 BioAmW, FemiCLE
Bates, Kenneth 1895-1973 WhoAmA 91N
Bates, Kenneth F. 1904- BioIn 16
Bates, Kenneth Francis 1904- WhoAmA 91
Bates, Kenneth Scott, Jr. 1943- WhoE 91
Bates, Lana WhoAmW 91
Bates, Laura Mae 1933- WhoWrEP 89
Bates, Lawrence Fulcher 1954- WhoEmL 91
Bates, Leo James 1944- WhoAmA 91, WhoE 91
Bates, Leslie Fleetwood 1897-1978 DcScB S2
Bates, Lucious Christopher 1901-1980 BioIn 16
Bates, Lura Wheeler 1932- WhoAmW 91
Bates, Mariette J. 1950- WhoAmW 91
Bates, Marion Virginia 1919- WhoAmW 91
Bates, Mark Roger 1956- WhoEmL 91
Bates, Marston 1906-1974 DcScB S2
Bates, Mary Ellen 1954- WhoAmW 91
Bates, Mary Jane Bean 1945- WhoE 91
Bates, Mary L. 1930- St&PR 91
Bates, Mary Louise 1930- WhoAmW 91
Bates, Mary Lynn Dovith 1947- WhoEmL 91
Bates, Maxwell Bennett 1906-1980 WhoAmA 91N
Bates, Michael John 1950- WhoE 91
Bates, Patricia Stamper 1947- WhoEmL 91, WhoSSW 91
Bates, Peg Leg 1907- DrBlPA 90
Bates, Peter L. 1952- IntWWM 90
Bates, Philip K., Jr. 1931- St&PR 91
Bates, Philip S. 1954- St&PR 91
Bates, Ralph Samuel 1906- WhoE 91, WhoWor 91
Bates, Rex James 1923- St&PR 91
Bates, Rhonda Barber 1962- WhoAmW 91
Bates, Richard F. 1923- St&PR 91
Bates, Richard Mather 1932- WhoAm 90
Bates, Robert Dale, Sr. 1941- St&PR 91
Bates, Robert Ernest 1940- WhoWor 91
Bates, Robert Hinrichs 1942- WhoSSW 91
Bates, Robert M. 1933- St&PR 91
Bates, Robert William 1961- WhoEmL 91
Bates, Rodney Lin 1946- WhoEmL 91
Bates, Ruby Lee 1940- WhoAmW 91
Bates, Samuel P 1929- ODwPR 91
Bates, Scott 1923- WhoWrEP 89
Bates, Susan B. 1956- ODwPR 91
Bates, Susan Viola 1951- WhoAmW 91, WhoEmL 91, WhoWor 91
Bates, Terry Bryan 1959- WhoEmL 91
Bates, Thomas William 1937- St&PR 91
Bates, Valentino Travis 1955- WhoSSW 91
Bates, Walter Alan 1925- WhoAm 90
Bates, William, III 1949- WhoEmL 91
Bates, William H. 1921- St&PR 91
Bates, William Horatio 1881-1931 NewAgE 90
Bateson, Marion 1935- WhoWor 91
Bateson, Mary 1865-1906 BioIn 16
Bateson, Mary Catherine 1939- WhoAm 90, WhoAmW 91
Bateson, William 1861-1926 BioIn 16
Batey, Amanda 1950- WhoAmW 91
Batey, David McGill 1914- WhoSSW 91
Batey, Peter William James 1948- WhoWor 91
Batey, Sharyn Rebecca 1946- WhoSSW 91
Batey, Thomas Elliott 1931- St&PR 91
Bath, Clifford O., Jr. 1930- St&PR 91
Bath, David A. 1947- St&PR 91
Bath, Hubert 1883-1945 OxCPMus
Bath, Joanne McMath 1935- WhoAmW 91
Bathel, Darryl Donald 1949- WhoEmL 91
Batherman, Muriel 1926- AuBYP 90
Bathija, Jagdish T BiDrAPA 89
Bathon, Edward G.A. 1933- St&PR 91
Bathon, Edward Gregory Anthony 1933- WhoAm 90
Bathon, Thomas Neil 1961- WhoEmL 91
Bathori, Jane 1877-1970 PenDiMP
Bathurst, Anne 1638?-1696? FemiCLE
Bathurst, Anne 1656?-1682 BiDEWW
Bathurst, Elizabeth 1655?-1685 BiDEWW, FemiCLE
Bathurst, Grace 1634-1703 BiDEWW
Batignani, Laurie A. 1953- WhoAmW 91
Batin, Christopher Michael 1955- WhoWrEP 89
Batinkoff, Randall BioIn 16
Batista, Alberto Victor 1963- WhoHisp 91
Batista, April Adelaide 1949- WhoWor 91
Batista, Emily Johnson 1954- WhoE 91
Batista, Juan E. 1936- WhoHisp 91
Batista, Kenneth 1952- WhoAmA 91
Batista, Leon Felix 1964- WhoHisp 91
Batista, Melchor Ignacio 1944- WhoHisp 91
Batista, Santiago 1931- WhoHisp 91
Batista-Wales, Maria Carmen 1960- WhoHisp 91
Batista y Zaldivar, Fulgencio 1901-1973 BioIn 16, WorAlBi
Batiste, Curt G BiDrAPA 89
Batiste, Robert Joseph 1950- WhoEmL 91
Batiuchok, John Richard BiDrAPA 89
Batiuk, Thomas Martin 1947- WhoAm 90
Batiuk, Tom 1947- EncACom
Batiz, Enrique 1942- IntWWM 90
Batizy, Gusztav 1918- BiDrAPA 89
Batjer, Cameron McVicar 1919- WhoAm 90
Batkiewicz, Raymond J. 1952- St&PR 91
Batkin, Sanford Lewis 1923- St&PR 91
Batkis, Marcelo Fernando BiDrAPA 89
Batko, Blaise Joseph 1961- WhoAmA 91
Batla, Raymond John, Jr. 1947- WhoWor 91
Batlin, Alfred Robert 1930- WhoWrEP 89
Batlin, Robert Alfred 1930- WhoAm 90
Batlle Berres, Luis 1897-1964 BioIn 16
Batlle y Ordonez, Jose 1856-1929 BioIn 16
Batmasian, Marta Tersakian 1949- WhoEmL 91
Batmonh, Jambyn 1926- WhoWor 91
Batoff, Steven Irving 1951- WhoEmL 91
Batoff, William Warren 1935- WhoAm 90
Baton, Charles PenDiMP
Baton, Henri PenDiMP
Batoni, Pompeo 1708-1787 IntDcAA 90
Bator, Francis Michel 1925- WhoAm 90, WhoE 91
Bator, James M. 1942- St&PR 91
Bator, Jane Crawford 1953- ODwPR 91
Bator, Paul 1929-1989 BioIn 16
Batori, Ron 1941- ODwPR 91
Bators, Stiv BioIn 16, NewYTBS 90
Batorski, Judith Ann 1949- WhoAmW 91, WhoE 91, WhoEmL 91
Batory, Anne Heineman 1946- WhoEmL 91
Batory, Ronald Louis 1930- WhoAm 90, WhoEmL 91
Batra, Ashok K.J. 1940- St&PR 91
Batra, Krishan K BiDrAPA 89
Batra, Ranjit Ratan 1943- WhoWor 91
Batra, Raveendra N 1943- ConAu 31NR
Batra, Ravi ConAu 31NR
Batra, Ravi 1943- WhoSSW 91
Batsa, Kofi 1931- WhoWor 91
Batsakis, John George 1929- WhoAm 90
Batschkus, Friedrich Karl 1943- WhoWor 91
Batson, Alice Kiper 1929- WhoSSW 91
Batson, Blair Everett 1920- WhoAm 90
Batson, C Daniel 1943- ConAu 129
Batson, David Warren 1956- WhoEmL 91
Batson, Flora BioIn 16
Batson, Jackie David 1931- WhoSSW 91
Batson, John Allen 1955- WhoSSW 91
Batson, Larry Floyd 1930- WhoAm 90, WhoWrEP 89
Batson, Lawrence Franklin 1951- St&PR 91
Batson, Leonora Little 1936- WhoE 91
Batson, Pascal Gayle BiDrAPA 89
Batson, Pascal Gayle BioIn 16
Batson, Randolph 1916- WhoAm 90
Batson, Richard Neal 1941- WhoAm 90, WhoSSW 91
Batson, Robert Grover 1950- WhoSSW 91
Batson, Ronald M 1952- BiDrAPA 89
Batson, Stephen Wesley 1946- WhoEmL 91, WhoSSW 91
Batson, Susan 1944?- DrBlPA 90
Batt, Allen Edward 1949- WhoEmL 91, WhoWrEP 89
Batt, Charles Andrew BiDrAPA 89
Batt, David M. 1948- St&PR 91
Batt, Jurgen Otto Helmut 1933- WhoWor 91
Batt, Lourie T. 1927- St&PR 91
Batt, Miles Girard 1933- WhoAmA 91
Batt, Nick 1952- WhoEmL 91
Batt, Roberta S BiDrAPA 89
Batt, Ronald Elmer 1933- WhoE 91, WhoWor 91
Batta, Edward J. 1937- St&PR 91
Battaglia, Adolfo 1930- WhoWor 91
Battaglia, Anthony Sylvester 1927- WhoAm 90
Battaglia, Aurelius 1910- BioIn 16
Battaglia, Frederick Camillo 1932- WhoAm 90
Battaglia, John BiDrAPA 89
Battaglia, Joseph Paul 1950- WhoE 91
Battaglia, Michael Salvatore 1944- WhoAm 90
Battaglia, Pasquale M 1905-1959 WhoAmA 91N
Battaglini, Frank Paul 1944- WhoE 91
Battaglini, Linda Jackson 1950- WhoAmW 91
Battaile, Joseph C BiDrAPA 89
Battaile, Najiba A H BiDrAPA 89
Battalino, Barbara 1945- BiDrAPA 89
Battam, Thomas 1810?-1864 PenDiDA 89
Battat, Emile A. 1938- WhoE 91, WhoWor 91
Batte, Gerald L 1934- BiDrAPA 89
Batteast, Robert V. 1931- St&PR 91
Battegay, Raymond 1927- WhoWor 91
Battei, Antonio 1949- WhoWor 91
Battel, Giovanni Umberto 1956- IntWWM 90
Battelle, Beverly Kay 1951- WhoEmL 91
Battelle, Kenneth Everette 1927- WhoAm 90
Batten, Alan Henry 1933- WhoAm 90
Batten, Charles Francis 1942- WhoSSW 91
Batten, Dallas Sanford 1951- WhoE 91
Batten, Edith Mary 1905-1985 DcNaB 1981
Batten, Frank 1927- St&PR 91, WhoAm 90, WhoSSW 91, WhoWrEP 89
Batten, James Knox 1936- St&PR 91, WhoAm 90, WhoSSW 91, WhoWrEP 89
Batten, James William 1919- WhoSSW 91, WhoWor 91
Batten, Joan BiDEWW
Batten, John H. 1912-1989 BioIn 16
Batten, Mary 1937- AuBYP 90
Batten, Michael Ellsworth 1940- St&PR 91, WhoAm 90
Batten, Roger Lyman 1923- WhoAm 90
Batten, W. Howard 1929- St&PR 91
Batten, William Milfred 1909- WhoAm 90
Battenberg, Louis Francis, Prince of 1900-1979 BioIn 16
Battenfield, Betty Lee 1926- WhoSSW 91
Battenfield, Jackie 1950- WhoAmA 91
Battenhouse, Roy Wesley 1912- WhoAm 90
Battenson, J. Robert 1937- St&PR 91
Batterberry, Ariane Ruskin AuBYP 90
Batterberry, Michael Carver 1932- AuBYP 90
Batterman, Boris William 1930- WhoAm 90
Batterman, Steven Charles 1937- WhoAm 90, WhoE 91
Battern, Timothy Hill 1950- WhoEmL 91
Battersby, Alan Rushton 1925- WhoWor 91
Battersby, Barbara Ann 1960- WhoSSW 91
Battersby, Christine 1946- ConAu 132
Battersby, Harold Ronald 1922- WhoAm 90
Battersby, James Lyons, Jr. 1936- WhoAm 90
Battersby, Mark Edwin 1941- WhoE 91
Batterson, James Robert 1962- BiDrAPA 89
Batterson, Steven L. 1950- WhoSSW 91
Battesti, Christine Denise 1960- WhoWor 91
Battestin, Martin Carey 1930- WhoAm 90
Battey, Charles W. 1932- WhoAm 90
Battey, Charles Wheaton 1932- St&PR 91
Battey, Earl 1935- Ballpl 90
Battey, Robert Anderson 1954- IntWWM 90
Battey, Thomas C. 1828-1897 WhNaAH
Battey, William R., Jr. 1953- St&PR 91
Batthyany, Lajos 1806-1849 BioIn 16
Battier, Henrietta 1751?-1813 FemiCLE
Battilana, Raymond E. 1937- St&PR 91
Battin, B. Norris 1936- St&PR 91
Battin, B W 1941- ConAu 30NR
Battin, Buck ConAu 30NR
Battin, James Franklin 1925- WhoAm 90
Battin, Patricia M. BioIn 16
Battin, Patricia Meyer 1929- WhoAm 90, WhoAmW 91
Battin, Richard Horace 1925- WhoAm 90
Battin, Wendy J 1953- WhoWrEP 89
Batting, Robert Davidson 1941- WhoAm 90
Battino, Rubin 1931- WhoAm 90
Battison, John Henry 1915- WhoAm 90
Battison, William James 1949- St&PR 91
Battista da Montefeltro 1383-1450 EncCoWW
Battista da Varano 1458-1524 EncCoWW
Battista, Charles Ernest 1951- WhoEmL 91
Battista, David Mark 1958- BiDrAPA 89
Battista, Elizabeth Ann St&PR 91
Battista, Giampiero 1942- WhoWor 91
Battista, Helen Keffer St&PR 91
Battista, Matthew J. 1933- St&PR 91
Battista, Orlando Aloysius 1917- St&PR 91, WhoAm 90
Battista, Robert James 1939- WhoAm 90
Battista, Vito P. NewYTBS 90 [port]
Battista, Vito P. 1908-1990 BioIn 16
Battista, William Keffer St&PR 91
Battistello, Marc J. 1942- St&PR 91
Battisti, Frank L. 1931- IntWWM 90
Battisti, Paul Oreste 1922- WhoAm 90
Battisti, Salvatore C. 1903- St&PR 91
Battistini, Mattia 1856-1928 BioIn 16, PenDiMP
Battistini, Noe 1936- WhoWor 91
Battjes, Kenneth John 1923- St&PR 91
Battle, Allen Overton, Jr. 1927- WhoAm 90
Battle, Barbara L. Brown WhoAmW 91
Battle, Beverly Lynn 1943- WhoAmW 91
Battle, Calvin William 1942- St&PR 91
Battle, Edward G. 1931- St&PR 91
Battle, Edward Gene 1931- WhoAm 90
Battle, Emery Alford, Jr. 1947- WhoSSW 91
Battle, Emily Anne 1934- WhoAmW 91, WhoSSW 91
Battle, Hinton DrBlPA 90
Battle, J. A., Mrs. 1916- WhoSSW 91
Battle, Jean Allen 1914- WhoAm 90, WhoWor 91, WhoWrEP 89
Battle, Joe David 1958- WhoEmL 91
Battle, John S., Jr. 1919- St&PR 91
Battle, Kathleen BioIn 16, DrBlPA 90, WorAlBi
Battle, Kathleen 1948- IntWWM 90, PenDiMP
Battle, Kathleen Deanna WhoAm 90, WhoAmW 91, WhoWor 91
Battle, Lucius Durham 1918- BioIn 16, WhoAm 90
Battle, Lucius Winston, Jr. 1934- WhoSSW 91, WhoWor 91
Battle, Lucy Troxell 1916- WhoAmW 91, WhoSSW 91, WhoWor 91
Battle, Thomas Peyton 1942- St&PR 91, WhoAm 90
Battle, Turner Charles, III 1926- WhoE 91, WhoWor 91
Battle, William R. 1924- St&PR 91
Battle, William Rainey 1924- WhoAm 90
Battle, William Robert 1927- WhoAm 90, WhoWrEP 89
Battleman, Murray 1936- St&PR 91
Battles, Edith 1921- AuBYP 90, WhoWrEP 89
Battles, May Fairy 1946- WhoAmW 91
Battles, Roxy Edith 1921- WhoAmW 91
Battles, William Melvin BiDrAPA 89
Battoclette, Augusta Rose 1929- WhoAmW 91
Battocletti, Joseph Henry 1925- WhoAm 90
Batton, Kenneth Duff 1942- WhoSSW 91
Batton, Monica Kim 1956- WhoE 91, WhoEmL 91, WhoWor 91
Batton, Steven Thomas 1951- BiDrAPA 89
Batton, Theodore BioIn 16
Battram, Richard L. 1934- WhoAm 90
Batts, Matt 1921- Ballpl 90
Batts, Michael Stanley 1929- WhoAm 90, WhoWrEP 89
Batts, Patrick 1948- ODwPR 91
Batts, Thomas EncCRAm
Batts, Warren L. 1932- St&PR 91
Batts, Warren Leighton 1932- WhoAm 90
Batty, H. Andrew, Jr. 1947- St&PR 91
Baty, Daniel R. 1943- St&PR 91
Baty, Vicki Louise 1948- WhoWrEP 89
Batzel, Roger Elwood 1921- WhoAm 90
Batzer, Gabrielle Bemis BiDrAPA 89
Batzer, R. Kirk 1915- WhoAm 90
Batzer, Wayne Bemis BiDrAPA 89
Batzli, George Oliver 1936- WhoAm 90
Batzold, Joan R. 1953- WhoE 91
Baublitz, Frederick Ulrich 1915- WhoSSW 91
Baublys, Petras BioIn 16
Baucam, Darwin Darryl 1953- WhoSSW 91
Bauch, Thomas Jay 1943- St&PR 91, WhoAm 90
Bauch, William H. 1961- WhoEmL 91
Bauchart MajTwCW
Bauchman, Robert W. 1920- St&PR 91
Bauchman, Robert Worthington 1949- WhoSSW 91
Bauchwitz, Maria-Helena BiDrAPA 89

Bauck, Jeanna Maria Charlotta 1846-1925 *BiDWomA*
Bauckham, James Arthur 1936- *St&PR 91*
Baucom, Bill L. 1933- *St&PR 91*
Baucom, Sidney G. 1930- *St&PR 91*
Baucom, Sidney George 1930- *WhoAm 90*
Baucum, Charles W 1939- *BiDrAPA 89*
Baucum, William Emmett, Jr. 1945- *WhoSSW 91*
Baucus, Max S. 1941- *WhoAm 90, WhoWor 91*
Baudains, Linton 1931- *St&PR 91*
Baudelaire, Charles 1821-1867 *BioIn 16, NinCLC 29 [port], PoeCrit 1 [port], WorAlBi*
Bauder, John Frank 1943- *WhoSSW 91*
Baudez, Louis Rene 1912- *WhoWor 91*
Baudhuin, Donald Joseph 1949- *St&PR 91*
Baudier, Julian Gerald, Sr. 1919- *St&PR 91*
Baudis, Dominique Pierre Jean Albert 1947- *BiDFrPL*
Baudo, Serge 1927- *IntWWM 90, PenDiMP, WhoWor 91*
Baudonivia 6--?- *EncCoWW*
Baudouin 1930- *WorAlBi*
Baudouin I 1930- *WhoWor 91*
Baudouin I, King of the Belgians 1930- *BioIn 16*
Baudouin, Jacques-Rene 1943- *WhoWor 91*
Baudouin, Patrick 1946- *WhoWor 91*
Baudouine, Charles A. 1808- *PenDiDA 89*
Baudrillard, Jean 1929- *ConLC 60 [port]*
Baudry, Francis D 1931- *BiDrAPA 89*
Baudry, Francois 1791-1859 *PenDiDA 89*
Baudy, Romona Theresa 1947- *WhoAmW 91*
Baue, Arthur Edward 1929- *WhoAm 90*
Bauer, Adam *PenDiDA 89*
Bauer, Anne Claudia *BiDrAPA 89*
Bauer, Arthur James 1947- *WhoEmL 91*
Bauer, August Robert, Jr. 1928- *WhoAm 90, WhoWor 91*
Bauer, Barbara A. 1944- *ODwPR 91*
Bauer, Barbara Gae 1958- *WhoAmW 91*
Bauer, Beaver *BioIn 16*
Bauer, Brian *BioIn 16*
Bauer, Brian H. 1947- *St&PR 91*
Bauer, Carl Maria *PenDiDA 89*
Bauer, Carl W. 1933- *St&PR 91*
Bauer, Caroline Feller *WhoAmW 91*
Bauer, Caroline Feller 1935- *AuBYP 90, BioIn 16*
Bauer, Catherine Marie 1954- *WhoAmW 91*
Bauer, Charles T. 1919- *St&PR 91*
Bauer, Cynthia Mary 1955- *WhoEmL 91*
Bauer, Dale Robert 1928- *St&PR 91, WhoAm 90, WhoE 91*
Bauer, Daniel George 1960- *WhoE 91, WhoEmL 91*
Bauer, David 1924-1988 *BioIn 16*
Bauer, David E. 1929- *St&PR 91*
Bauer, Debra Rosenthal 1952- *WhoEmL 91*
Bauer, Douglas F. 1942- *St&PR 91, WhoAm 90*
Bauer, Drew J. 1957- *WhoEmL 91*
Bauer, Eberhard 1944- *EncPaPR 91*
Bauer, Edward Ewing 1917- *St&PR 91*
Bauer, Edward G., Jr. 1928- *St&PR 91*
Bauer, Elaine Louise 1949- *WhoAm 90*
Bauer, Elizabeth A. 1964- *St&PR 91*
Bauer, Elizabeth Kelley 1920- *WhoAmW 91*
Bauer, Ernest 1927- *WhoE 91*
Bauer, Esther May 1943- *WhoSSW 91*
Bauer, Felice 1887-1960 *BioIn 16*
Bauer, Francis C *BiDrAPA 89*
Bauer, Fred C. 1927- *St&PR 91*
Bauer, Frederick Christian 1927- *WhoAm 90*
Bauer, Gary L. *BioIn 16*
Bauer, Gary Lee 1946- *WhoAm 90*
Bauer, Georg 1490-1555 *EncO&P 3*
Bauer, George E. 1920- *St&PR 91*
Bauer, George Victor 1932- *St&PR 91*
Bauer, Gerd Walter 1948- *WhoWor 91*
Bauer, Gordon P. 1938- *St&PR 91*
Bauer, Grant Winans 1913- *WhoE 91*
Bauer, Gunther Erwin A. 1936- *WhoAm 90*
Bauer, Hank 1922- *Ballpl 90*
Bauer, Harold 1873-1951 *BioIn 16, PenDiMP*
Bauer, Henry Hermann 1931- *WhoAm 90, WhoSSW 91*
Bauer, Herbert 1910- *BiDrAPA 89*
Bauer, Ilona 1936- *WhoAmW 91*
Bauer, Irving L *BiDrAPA 89*
Bauer, James August 1933- *WhoSSW 91*
Bauer, James P. 1945- *St&PR 91*
Bauer, Jean-Francois 1955- *St&PR 91*
Bauer, Jeffrey Patrick 1949- *WhoEmL 91*
Bauer, Jerome Leo, Jr. 1938- *WhoWor 91*
Bauer, Jerry 1948- *WhoEmL 91*
Bauer, John R. 1932- *St&PR 91*
Bauer, Joseph Peter 1945- *WhoEmL 91*
Bauer, Judy Marie 1947- *WhoAmW 91*
Bauer, Larry Alan 1954- *WhoEmL 91*
Bauer, Lawrence Michael 1950- *WhoEmL 91*
Bauer, Linda Marie 1944- *WhoE 91*
Bauer, Lois Marlene 1931- *WhoAmW 91*
Bauer, Malcolm Clair 1914- *WhoWrEP 89*
Bauer, Mark S 1954- *BiDrAPA 89*
Bauer, Marty *BioIn 16*
Bauer, Max William 1957- *WhoEmL 91*
Bauer, Michael D. 1948- *St&PR 91*
Bauer, Michael John 1951- *St&PR 91*
Bauer, Nancy *ODwPR 91*
Bauer, Nancy Elaine 1953- *WhoAmW 91, WhoE 91, WhoWor 91*
Bauer, Otto Frank 1931- *WhoAm 90*
Bauer, Paul David 1943- *St&PR 91, WhoAm 90*
Bauer, Philip Lane 1941- *WhoAm 90, WhoWor 91*
Bauer, Ralph Glenn 1925- *WhoAm 90*
Bauer, Randall Richard 1949- *WhoEmL 91*
Bauer, Raymond Gale 1934- *WhoE 91, WhoWor 91*
Bauer, Raymond Jack 1948- *WhoSSW 91*
Bauer, Raymond W. 1915- *St&PR 91*
Bauer, Rhonda Leah 1959- *WhoEmL 91*
Bauer, Richard Carlton 1944- *WhoAm 90, WhoE 91*
Bauer, Richard Frank 1930- *WhoAm 90*
Bauer, Richard J. 1938- *St&PR 91*
Bauer, Robert Albert 1910- *WhoAm 90*
Bauer, Robin David 1959- *St&PR 91*
Bauer, Rocky *ConTFT 8*
Bauer, Roger 1918- *WhoWor 91*
Bauer, Roger Duane 1932- *WhoAm 90*
Bauer, Ronald Lee 1937- *WhoE 91*
Bauer, Rudolph 1939- *WhoWor 91*
Bauer, Ruth Kruse 1956- *WhoAmA 91*
Bauer, Ruth Warfield 1936- *WhoE 91*
Bauer, Stephen F 1930- *BiDrAPA 89*
Bauer, Steven 1956- *ConTFT 8, WhoHisp 91*
Bauer, Steven Albert 1948- *WhoWrEP 89*
Bauer, Steven E. *WhoAm 90*
Bauer, Steven Michael 1949- *WhoEmL 91*
Bauer, Theodore James 1909- *WhoAm 90*
Bauer, Victor John 1935- *WhoAm 90*
Bauer, W. Neil 1946- *St&PR 91*
Bauer, Walter B. 1916- *St&PR 91*
Bauer, William 1926- *BiDrAPA 89*
Bauer, William Cecil 1916- *St&PR 91*
Bauer, William Joseph 1926- *WhoAm 90*
Bauer-Patitz, D. *WhoWrEP 89*
Bauer-Stumpf, Jo 1873-1964 *BiDWomA*
Bauer-Theussl, Franz 1928- *IntWWM 90*
Bauerlein, Dudley Lawrence, Jr. 1946- *St&PR 91*
Bauerly, Ronald John 1953- *WhoEmL 91*
Bauermann, Julius Frank 1932- *St&PR 91*
Bauermeister, Martin *BiDrAPA 89*
Bauermeister, Mary Hilde Ruth 1934- *BiDWomA*
Bauers, Russ 1914- *Ballpl 90*
Bauersfeld, Carl Frederick 1916- *WhoAm 90*
Baues, Hans-Joachim 1943- *WhoWor 91*
Bauge, Cynthia Wise 1943- *WhoAmW 91*
Baugh, Charles Milton 1931- *WhoAm 90*
Baugh, Charles R. 1950- *St&PR 91*
Baugh, Coy Franklin *St&PR 91*
Baugh, Elaine Dorothy 1953- *WhoEmL 91*
Baugh, James Edward 1941- *WhoAm 90*
Baugh, John Frank 1916- *St&PR 91, WhoAm 90*
Baugh, John Vincent 1952- *BiDrAPA 89*
Baugh, Linda Sue 1945- *WhoEmL 91*
Baugh, Lynda Louise 1962- *WhoAmW 91*
Baugh, Samuel 1914- *WorAlBi*
Baugh, Terry *ODwPR 91*
Baugh, Thomas Calvin 1956- *WhoSSW 91*
Baughan, Blanche 1870-1958 *FemiCLE*
Baugher, John Oliver 1937- *St&PR 91*
Baugher, Peter V. 1948- *WhoAm 90, WhoEmL 91*
Baugher, Tara Lou Auxt 1953- *WhoEmL 91*
Baughman, Bruce Alfred 1949- *WhoSSW 91*
Baughman, Bruce Prentiss 1948- *WhoSSW 91*
Baughman, David 1949- *St&PR 91*
Baughman, Donald LeRoy, Jr. 1958- *WhoEmL 91*
Baughman, Dorothy 1940- *SmATA 61 [port]*
Baughman, Earle W., Jr. 1937- *BiDrAPA 89*
Baughman, Fred Hubbard 1926- *WhoAm 90*
Baughman, George Fechtig 1915- *WhoAm 90*
Baughman, J. Ross 1953- *WhoAm 90, WhoWrEP 89*
Baughman, James Porter 1936- *WhoE 91*
Baughman, Kathy 1949- *ODwPR 91*
Baughman, L.E. 1923- *St&PR 91*
Baughman, Leonora Knoblock 1956- *WhoEmL 91*
Baughman, Ray Edward 1925- *WhoWrEP 89*
Baughman, Robert Patrick 1938- *WhoAm 90, WhoWor 91*
Baughn, Robert Elroy 1940- *WhoSSW 91*
Baughn, Steven Peyton 1947- *WhoE 91*
Baughn, William Hubert 1918- *WhoAm 90*
Bauguess, Milton Vaughn 1943- *WhoSSW 91*
Bauhoff, Eugen Peter 1946- *WhoWor 91*
Baujan, Robert Raymond 1930- *St&PR 91*
Baukhage, Hilmar Robert 1889-1976 *BioIn 16*
Bauknecht, Gert Friedrich 1938- *WhoWor 91*
Bauknecht, John Waltner 1930- *St&PR 91*
Bauknight, Clarence Brock 1936- *St&PR 91, WhoAm 90, WhoSSW 91*
Baukol, Elsie Sata 1925- *WhoAmW 91*
Baukol, Ronald Oliver 1937- *WhoAm 90*
Baulard, Valerie Joyce 1939- *IntWWM 90*
Bauld, Alison Margaret 1944- *IntWWM 90*
Bauleke, Howard Paul 1959- *WhoEmL 91*
Bauley, Thomas Kelly 1954- *WhoEmL 91*
Baulieu, Etienne-Emile *BioIn 16*
Baulieu, Etienne-Emile 1926- *News 90 [port], WhoWor 91*
Baum, Alan Stuart 1955- *WhoEmL 91*
Baum, Arthur H. 1916- *St&PR 91*
Baum, Barbara Jean 1944- *BiDrAPA 89*
Baum, Bernard 1924- *St&PR 91*
Baum, Bernard Helmut 1926- *WhoAm 90*
Baum, Bernard Rene 1937- *WhoAm 90*
Baum, Betty *AuBYP 90*
Baum, Carl Edward 1940- *WhoAm 90, WhoWor 91*
Baum, Charles C. 1942- *St&PR 91*
Baum, David Barry 1934- *WhoAm 90*
Baum, David Roy 1946- *WhoAm 90*
Baum, Dwight C. 1912- *St&PR 91*
Baum, Dwight Crouse 1912- *WhoAm 90*
Baum, Eileen *BioIn 16*
Baum, Elaine Joan Eisele 1948- *WhoAmW 91*
Baum, Eleanor 1940- *WhoAm 90*
Baum, Eric B. 1923- *St&PR 91*
Baum, Hank *WhoAmA 91*
Baum, Helmut 1909- *BiDrAPA 89*
Baum, Herbert Mark 1951- *WhoE 91*
Baum, Herbert Merrill 1936- *St&PR 91, WhoAm 90, WhoE 91*
Baum, Jaime S. *ODwPR 91*
Baum, Jayne H 1954- *WhoAmA 91*
Baum, Jeanne Ann 1937- *WhoAmW 91*
Baum, Jeffrey David 1952- *WhoEmL 91*
Baum, Jerome Barry 1946- *St&PR 91*
Baum, John 1927- *WhoAm 90*
Baum, Jonathan R. 1961- *St&PR 91*
Baum, Joseph Herman 1927- *WhoE 91*
Baum, Jules Leonard 1931- *WhoAm 90*
Baum, Karl 1907- *WhoWor 91*
Baum, Kenneth R. 1948- *St&PR 91*
Baum, Kurt 1908- *IntWWM 90*
Baum, Kurt 1908-1989 *BioIn 16, CurBio 90N*
Baum, L Frank 1856-1919 *MajTwCW*
Baum, L. Frank 1856-1919 *WorAlBi*
Baum, Lester *BioIn 16*
Baum, Louis 1948- *BioIn 16, SmATA 64*
Baum, Louis F. *MajTwCW*
Baum, Lyman Frank 1856-1919 *AuBYP 90*
Baum, Marilyn Ruth 1939- *WhoAmA 91*
Baum, Matthew C. 1931- *St&PR 91*
Baum, Melissa Layton 1968- *WhoAmW 91*
Baum, Michael Ernest 1951- *WhoWor 91*
Baum, Michael Scott 1952- *WhoE 91*
Baum, Neil F. 1942- *St&PR 91*
Baum, Nic *BioIn 16*
Baum, Patricia *AuBYP 90*
Baum, Peter Alan 1947- *WhoEmL 91*
Baum, Ralph Augustus 1932- *St&PR 91*
Baum, Richard Theodore 1919- *WhoAm 90, WhoE 91, WhoWor 91*
Baum, Sara Hoffman *WhoAmW 91*
Baum, Selma 1924- *WhoAmW 91*
Baum, Seymour A. 1908- *St&PR 91*
Baum, Siegmund Jacob 1920- *WhoAm 90*
Baum, Stanley 1929- *WhoAm 90*
Baum, Stefi Alison 1958- *WhoWor 91*
Baum, Stephen H. 1941- *St&PR 91*
Baum, Sumner G. 1931- *St&PR 91*
Baum, Theodore *BiDrAPA 89*
Baum, Vicki 1888-1960 *EncCoWW*
Baum, Werner A. 1923- *WhoAm 90*
Baum, William Alvin 1924- *WhoAm 90*
Baum, William Wakefield 1926- *WhoAm 90, WhoWor 91*
Bauman, Anna *BiDrAPA 89*
Bauman, Arnold 1914- *WhoAm 90*
Bauman, Arnold 1914-1989 *BioIn 16*
Bauman, Charles Joseph 1924- *St&PR 91*
Bauman, Clarence 1928- *ConAu 32NR*
Bauman, Dale Elton 1942- *WhoAm 90*
Bauman, Earl William 1916- *WhoWor 91*
Bauman, Frederick Carl 1952- *WhoEmL 91*
Bauman, Gene *BiDrAPA 89*
Bauman, George Duncan 1912- *WhoAm 90, WhoWrEP 89*
Bauman, Gus Bloch 1949- *WhoEmL 91*
Bauman, Guy C. 1951-1990 *BioIn 16*
Bauman, Guy Caesar *NewYTBS 90*
Bauman, Howard Eugene 1925- *St&PR 91*
Bauman, Jerome Alan 1931- *WhoAm 90*
Bauman, Joe 1922- *Ballpl 90*
Bauman, John Duane 1930- *WhoAm 90*
Bauman, John E., Jr. 1933- *WhoAm 90*
Bauman, Jon Ward 1939- *IntWWM 90*
Bauman, Jonathan Hugh 1948- *BiDrAPA 89, WhoE 91*
Bauman, Karl Ianovich 1892-1937 *BioIn 16*
Bauman, Karl R. 1902?-1989 *ConAu 130*
Bauman, Le Roy 1925- *St&PR 91*
Bauman, Louis William 1932- *St&PR 91*
Bauman, Martin H 1936- *BiDrAPA 89*
Bauman, Merritt Richard 1923- *St&PR 91*
Bauman, Nansi 1954- *WhoWor 91*
Bauman, Raquel 1948- *WhoHisp 91*
Bauman, Richard 1940- *WhoAm 90*
Bauman, Richard Arnold 1924- *WhoAm 90*
Bauman, Robert P. 1931- *St&PR 91*
Bauman, Robert Patten 1931- *WhoAm 90, WhoE 91*
Bauman, Robert Warren, Jr. 1953- *WhoSSW 91*
Bauman, Roger Frederick, Jr. 1963- *WhoE 91*
Bauman, Sherry 1946- *BiDrAPA 89*
Bauman, Susan Joan Mayer 1945- *WhoEmL 91*
Bauman, Walter Ollendorff 1915- *St&PR 91*
Bauman, William Winter 1961- *WhoEmL 91*
Bauman-Bork, Marci Denise *BiDrAPA 89*
Baumann, Albert J *BiDrAPA 89*
Baumann, Angela Lauria 1945- *WhoAmW 91*
Baumann, Barbara Johnson 1957- *WhoAmW 91*
Baumann, Daniel E. 1937- *St&PR 91, WhoAm 90*
Baumann, E. *BiDWomA*
Baumann, Edward Robert 1921- *WhoAm 90*
Baumann, Elwood D. *AuBYP 90*
Baumann, Eugene Heinz 1950- *WhoWor 91*
Baumann, Felix Martin Andreas 1937- *WhoWor 91*
Baumann, Francois 1945- *WhoWor 91*
Baumann, Frank 1933- *Ballpl 90*
Baumann, Frank Edward 1941- *WhoSSW 91*
Baumann, Fred William 1945- *WhoEmL 91*
Baumann, Frederick William, Jr. 1945- *St&PR 91*
Baumann, Gary Joseph 1949- *WhoAm 90*
Baumann, Gerhart 1920- *WhoWor 91*
Baumann, Gregory William 1947- *WhoEmL 91*
Baumann, H.D. *St&PR 91*
Baumann, Hans 1914- *BioIn 16*
Baumann, Hans Theodor 1924- *ConDes 90*
Baumann, Harry A., Jr. 1926- *St&PR 91*
Baumann, Hermann 1934- *PenDiMP*
Baumann, Janet Anne 1938- *WhoAmW 91*
Baumann, John 1948- *WhoSSW 91*
Baumann, John M., Jr. 1960- *WhoEmL 91*
Baumann, Jurgen 1922- *WhoWor 91*
Baumann, Kathy *ODwPR 91*
Baumann, Lillian Rose 1939- *WhoAmW 91*
Baumann, Mark J. 1957- *IntWWM 90*
Baumann, Nancy Ruth 1935- *WhoSSW 91*
Baumann, Peter *NewAgMG*
Baumann, Phillip Allen 1949- *WhoEmL 91*
Baumann, Richard Gordon 1938- *WhoAm 90*
Baumann, Robert J. 1940- *WhoSSW 91*
Baumann, Roxanne Lee 1953- *WhoEmL 91*
Baumann, Stanley J. 1931- *WhoSSW 91*
Baumann, Susan B 1959- *BiDrAPA 89*
Baumann, Walter Melvin 1936- *WhoSSW 91*
Baumbach, Alice Thompson *WhoAmW 91*
Baumbach, Dick *ODwPR 91*
Baumbach, Donna Jean 1948- *WhoSSW 91*
Baumbach, Harold 1904- *WhoAm 90*
Baumbach, Harold 1905- *WhoAmA 91*
Baumbach, Jonathan 1933- *BioIn 16, MajTwCW, WhoWrEP 89*
Baumbacher, Gordon David 1944- *BiDrAPA 89*
Baumbartner, Bernhard 1948- *WhoWor 91*
Baumberger, David Lee 1955- *WhoEmL 91*

Baumberger, Martha Kail 1913- *WhoAmW 91*
Baumecker, Peter 1927- *BiDrAPA 89*
Baumeister, Alfred J. 1927- *St&PR 91*
Baumeister, Donald E. 1950- *WhoEmL 91*
Baumel, Abraham 1926- *WhoE 91*
Baumel, C. Phillip *BioIn 16*
Baumel, Herbert 1919- *WhoWor 91*
Baumel, Jacques 1918- *BiDFrPL*
Baumel, Joan Patricia French 1930- *WhoAmW 91*
Baumel, Judith 1956- *WhoAm 90, WhoAmW 91*
Baumel, Lee Nat *BiDrAPA 89*
Baumel, Rey *WhoSSW 91*
Baumer, Beverly Belle 1926- *WhoAmW 91*
Baumer, Gertrud 1873-1954 *EncCoWW*
Baumer, Robert John *BiDrAPA 89*
Baumer, William Henry 1909-1989 *BioIn 16*
Baumfeld, Rudi *BioIn 16*
Baumfree, Isabella *BioIn 16*
Baumgaertel, Hermann Detlef 1932- *WhoWor 91*
Baumgardner, Barbara Ann 1937- *WhoAmW 91*
Baumgardner, Dennis *St&PR 91*
Baumgardner, Dwight Ernest 1923- *St&PR 91*
Baumgardner, George 1891-1970 *Ballpl 90*
Baumgardner, James Lewis 1938- *WhoAm 90*
Baumgardner, John Dwane 1940- *St&PR 91, WhoAm 90*
Baumgardner, Kandy Diane 1946- *WhoAmW 91*
Baumgardner, Karen T. 1953- *WhoAmW 91*
Baumgardner, Roger Leroy 1942- *St&PR 91*
Baumgardner, Russell Howard 1918- *St&PR 91*
Baumgardner, T. Miesse 1904- *St&PR 91*
Baumgardt, Arden C. 1941- *St&PR 91*
Baumgardt, Billy Ray 1933- *WhoAm 90*
Baumgart, Norbert K. 1931- *WhoAm 90*
Baumgart, Winfried Eckhart 1938- *WhoWor 91*
Baumgartel, Howard J., Jr. 1920- *WhoAm 90*
Baumgarten, Barbara Dee 1955- *WhoAmW 91*
Baumgarten, David A. 1951- *St&PR 91*
Baumgarten, Harvey Jay 1939- *St&PR 91*
Baumgarten, Herbert J. 1935- *St&PR 91*
Baumgarten, Herbert Joseph 1935- *WhoAm 90*
Baumgarten, Joseph Russell 1928- *WhoAm 90*
Baumgarten, Lee A. 1918- *St&PR 91*
Baumgarten, Marc Todd 1961- *WhoEmL 91*
Baumgarten, Marion Betor 1960- *WhoEmL 91*
Baumgarten, Paul Anthony 1934- *WhoAm 90*
Baumgarten, Roger H. 1960- *ODwPR 91*
Baumgarten, Ronald Neal 1942- *WhoWor 91*
Baumgarten, Ross 1955- *Ballpl 90*
Baumgarten, Sidney 1933- *WhoAm 90*
Baumgartner, Allan Rodney 1938- *WhoWor 91*
Baumgartner, Anton Edward 1948- *WhoEmL 91, WhoWor 91*
Baumgartner, Bruce *BioIn 16*
Baumgartner, Daniel Benton 1944- *WhoWrEP 89*
Baumgartner, Donald W. 1930- *St&PR 91*
Baumgartner, Eileen Mary *WhoAmW 91*
Baumgartner, Frederic Joseph 1945- *WhoSSW 91*
Baumgartner, Gregory R. *BiDrAPA 89*
Baumgartner, James Earl 1943- *WhoAm 90*
Baumgartner, John H. 1936- *WhoAm 90*
Baumgartner, Leona 1902- *WhoAm 90, WhoAmW 91*
Baumgartner, Lynn F *BiDrAPA 89*
Baumgartner, Nancy Helen 1956- *WhoEmL 91*
Baumgartner, Paul August 1934- *WhoWor 91*
Baumgartner, Richard Lysle 1933- *BiDrAPA 89*
Baumgartner, Robert A. 1947- *St&PR 91*
Baumgartner, Robert V. 1956- *St&PR 91*
Baumgartner, Rudolf 1917- *IntWWM 90, PenDiMP*
Baumgartner, Ruth Gabriele 1954- *IntWWM 90*
Baumgartner, Stan 1894-1955 *Ballpl 90*
Baumgartner, Ulrich 1580-1652 *PenDiDA 89*
Baumgartner, Vito H. 1940- *St&PR 91*
Baumgartner, Warren W 1894-1963 *WhoAmA 91N*
Baumgold, Charles 1912- *St&PR 91*
Baumhart, Raymond Charles 1923- *WhoAm 90*
Baumhauer, Joseph *PenDiDA 89*
Baumheckel, David Allen 1952- *St&PR 91*
Baumhefner, Clarence Herman 1912- *WhoAm 90*
Baumholtz, Frankie 1918- *Ballpl 90*
Baumholtz, Laurie Ann 1961- *WhoAmW 91*
Bauminger, Heshek 1919-1943 *BioIn 16*
Bauml, Albert *PenDiDA 89*
Bauml, Franz Heinrich 1926- *WhoAm 90*
Baumm, N Craig 1933- *BiDrAPA 89*
Baumoel, Joseph 1928- *St&PR 91*
Baumol, William Jack 1922- *WhoAm 90, WhoE 91*
Baumrin, Bernard Stefan Herbert 1934- *WhoAm 90*
Baumrin, Judith Marti 1935- *WhoE 91*
Baumrind, Diana 1927- *WhoAm 90*
Baumrind, Rosalyn Muriel 1933- *WhoE 91*
Baumruck, Scott Alan 1952- *WhoEmL 91*
Baumwell, Clyde Stuart 1948- *WhoE 91*
Baumwoll, Joel Phillip 1940- *St&PR 91*
Baumzweiger-Bauer, William E *BiDrAPA 89*
Baur, Alfred K 1913- *BiDrAPA 89*
Baur, Andre 1904-1943 *BioIn 16*
Baur, Dale Alan 1954- *WhoEmL 91*
Baur, Erwin 1875-1933 *DcScB S2*
Baur, Eugene James, Jr. 1958- *WhoSSW 91*
Baur, Frank *BioIn 16*
Baur, Hans 1897- *BioIn 16*
Baur, James Gerard 1940- *St&PR 91*
Baur, Matthias *PenDiDA 89*
Baur, Philip J., Jr. 1930- *St&PR 91*
Baur, Stephen 1922- *St&PR 91*
Baur, Tassilo *BioIn 16*
Baur, Werner Heinz 1931- *WhoAm 90*
Baur, Xaver 1947- *WhoWor 91*
Baurer, Frederic M 1957- *BiDrAPA 89*
Baurer, Frederic Martin 1957- *WhoE 91*
Baurgeois, Douglas 1951- *WhoAmA 91*
Baurs-Krey, Detlev H. U. 1943- *WhoE 91, WhoWor 91*
Baus, John Villars 1927- *WhoAm 90*
Bausch, James John 1936- *WhoAm 90, WhoE 91, WhoWor 91*
Bausch, Pina *BioIn 16*
Bausch, Richard Carl 1945- *WhoWrEP 89*
Bausch, Thomas A. 1938- *WhoAm 90*
Bausch-Davenson, Wendy H. 1943- *WhoAmW 91*
Bause, Richard Marshall 1925- *St&PR 91*
Bausek, Gerald 1944- *BiDrAPA 89*
Bausek, Victoria Lynne 1955- *WhoAmW 91*
Bausher, Verne Charles *WhoE 91*
Bausman, Dennis Charles 1949- *WhoAm 90*
Bausman, S. David 1946- *St&PR 91*
Baustian, Robert Frederick 1921- *WhoAm 90*
Baut, Eugene R. *BioIn 16*
Bauta, Ed 1935- *Ballpl 90*
Bautch, Thomas A. 1949- *St&PR 91*
Baute, Joseph A. 1928- *St&PR 91*
Bauter, Robert Theodore 1929- *St&PR 91*
Bautista, Angela Melinda 1964- *WhoAmW 91*
Bautista, Basilio Nery 1935- *WhoE 91, WhoWor 91*
Bautista, Carol Stoney 1949- *WhoAmW 91*
Bautista, Florosa Aguinaldo 1928- *WhoWor 91*
Bautista, Jose 1964- *Ballpl 90*
Bautista, L Judith *BiDrAPA 89*
Bautista, Liberato de la Cruz 1959- *WhoWor 91*
Bautista, Luis C. 1947- *WhoEmL 91*
Bautista, Manuel Francisco 1941- *BiDrAPA 89*
Bautista, Pilar 1958- *WhoHisp 91*
Bautista, Renato Go 1934- *WhoAm 90*
Bautz, Laura Patricia 1940- *WhoAmW 91*
Bauumgartner, Michael Lee 1957- *WhoSSW 91*
Bauza, Ramon E. *St&PR 91*
Bava, Mario 1914- *ConTFT 8*
Bavadra, Timoci *BioIn 16*
Bavadra, Timoci 1934-1989 *AnObit 1989*
Bavasi, Buzzie *BioIn 16*
Bavasi, Peter 1942- *St&PR 91*
Bavasi, Peter Joseph 1942- *WhoAm 90*
Bavicchi, John 1922- *IntWWM 90*
Baviello, Michael Angelo, Jr. 1951- *WhoEmL 91*
Bavier, Frances *BioIn 16*
Bavinger, Eugene Allen 1919- *WhoAmA 91*
Bavly, Dan 1929- *ConAu 130*
Bavoso, William David 1946- *WhoEmL 91*
Bavota, Michael Francis 1952- *WhoE 91, WhoWrEP 89*
Bavuso, Margaret 1948- *WhoAmW 91*
Bawazer, Abbas A *BiDrAPA 89*
Bawden, David George 1949- *BiDrAPA 89*
Bawden, Edward 1903-1989 *AnObit 1989, ConDes 90*
Bawden, Frederick Charles 1908-1972 *DcScB S2*
Bawden, Garth Lawry 1939- *WhoAm 90*
Bawden, Harry Reginald 1921- *IntWWM 90*
Bawden, Nina 1925- *AuBYP 90, BioIn 16, FemiCLE*
Bawden, Rupert 1958- *IntWWM 90*
Bawerk, Eugen von Bohm- 1851-1914 *BioIn 16*
Bawly, Dan *ConAu 130*
Bawtinhimer, Gary George 1952- *BiDrAPA 89*
Bawtree, Michael 1937- *OxCCanT*
Bax, Arnold 1883-1953 *BioIn 16, PenDiMP A*
Bax, Clifford 1886-1962 *DcLB 100 [port]*
Bax, Roger *TwCCr&M 91*
Baxendell, Peter 1925- *WhoAm 90, WhoWor 91*
Baxi, Shreyas 1958- *BiDrAPA 89*
Baxley, Barbara *NewYTBS 90 [port]*
Baxley, Barbara 1927-1990 *BioIn 16*
Baxley, Kathryn Wise 1927- *WhoAmW 91*
Baxley, Robert S. 1950- *BiDrAPA 89*
Baxley, William Clegg 1948- *St&PR 91*
Baxt, Barbara Stefanie 1949- *WhoAmW 91*
Baxt, George 1923- *TwCCr&M 91*
Baxt, Victor J. 1917- *St&PR 91*
Baxter, Alfred Xavier 1925- *St&PR 91*
Baxter, Anne 1923-1985 *WorAlBi*
Baxter, Annie 1816-1905 *FemiCLE*
Baxter, Arthur Pearce 1943- *St&PR 91, WhoAm 90, WhoSSW 91*
Baxter, Betty Carpenter 1937- *WhoAmW 91, WhoSSW 91*
Baxter, Bonnie Jean 1946- *WhoAmA 91*
Baxter, Brian Lee 1948- *St&PR 91*
Baxter, Bruce Osborne 1945- *WhoE 91*
Baxter, Carla Louise Chaney 1955- *WhoAmW 91, WhoEmL 91*
Baxter, Carol Cairns 1940- *WhoAmW 91*
Baxter, Cecil William, Jr. 1923- *WhoAm 90*
Baxter, Charles D. 1926- *St&PR 91*
Baxter, Cleveland Anthony 1956- *WhoE 91*
Baxter, Craig 1929- *WhoE 91*
Baxter, Daniel Minort 1872-1938 *EarBlAP*
Baxter, Donald 1925- *St&PR 91*
Baxter, Donald William 1926- *WhoAm 90*
Baxter, Douglas W 1949- *WhoAmA 91*
Baxter, Douglas Wayne 1949- *WhoE 91*
Baxter, Duby Yvonne 1953- *WhoAmW 91*
Baxter, Elaine 1933- *WhoAm 90, WhoAmW 91*
Baxter, Elisha 1827-1899 *BioIn 16*
Baxter, Frank 1853- *AmLegL*
Baxter, Frank Edward 1936- *WhoAm 90*
Baxter, Frederica Boatwright 1941- *St&PR 91*
Baxter, Gene Kenneth 1939- *WhoWor 91*
Baxter, Gordon 1923- *BioIn 16*
Baxter, Gregory Stephen 1948- *WhoEmL 91*
Baxter, Gregory Wayne 1948- *WhoSSW 91*
Baxter, Harry Stevens 1915- *WhoAm 90*
Baxter, James Albert 1926- *BiDrAPA 89*
Baxter, James Edward 1949- *St&PR 91*
Baxter, James George 1948- *St&PR 91*
Baxter, James William, III 1931- *WhoAm 90, WhoWor 91*
Baxter, Janet Schwartz 1947- *WhoAmW 91*
Baxter, Jerrel Clyde 1955- *WhoEmL 91*
Baxter, Joan 1927- *WhoSSW 91*
Baxter, Joe E., Sr. 1924- *St&PR 91*
Baxter, John 1819-1886 *AmLegL*
Baxter, John Darling 1940- *WhoAm 90*
Baxter, John Lincoln, Jr. 1920- *WhoAm 90*
Baxter, Karen Grimsley 1949- *WhoWrEP 89*
Baxter, Kathy Land 1951- *WhoEmL 91*
Baxter, LeRoy Everette 1932- *IntWWM 90*
Baxter, Les 1922- *OxCPMus*
Baxter, Lewis Rhea, Jr. 1952- *BiDrAPA 89*
Baxter, Lori DeAnne 1963- *WhoAmW 91*
Baxter, Lowell D 1925- *BiDrAPA 89*
Baxter, Margaret 1636-1681 *BiDEWW*
Baxter, Mark E. 1953- *ODwPR 91*
Baxter, Mary Abigail 1956- *WhoAmW 91*
Baxter, Maurice Glen 1920- *WhoAm 90*
Baxter, Meredith *BioIn 16*
Baxter, Michael John 1944- *WhoAm 90, WhoWrEP 89*
Baxter, Michael St. Patrick 1955- *WhoE 91*
Baxter, Millie McLean 1926- *WhoAmW 91*
Baxter, Nevins D. 1941- *St&PR 91*
Baxter, Paul George 1938- *St&PR 91*
Baxter, Paula Adell 1954- *WhoAmA 91*
Baxter, Phil 1896-1972 *OxCPMus*
Baxter, Prudence 1950- *BiDrAPA 89*
Baxter, Ralph F. 1925- *St&PR 91*
Baxter, Ralph Felix 1925- *WhoAm 90*
Baxter, Reginald Robert 1925- *WhoAm 90*
Baxter, Richard L. 1934- *St&PR 91*
Baxter, Robert Dale 1953- *WhoEmL 91*
Baxter, Robert Ferris 1938- *BiDrAPA 89*
Baxter, Robert Hampton, III 1931- *WhoAm 90*
Baxter, Robert Henry 1940- *WhoE 91*
Baxter, Robert Scott 1952- *WhoEmL 91*
Baxter, Rodd M. 1950- *St&PR 91*
Baxter, Ruth Sackett 1928- *WhoAmW 91*
Baxter, Seymour 1931- *BiDrAPA 89*
Baxter, Stephen Bartow 1929- *WhoAm 90*
Baxter, Thomas 1782-1821 *PenDiDA 89*
Baxter, Thomas C. 1932- *St&PR 91*
Baxter, Valerie 1899-1989 *SmATA X*
Baxter, Victoria Lynn 1948- *WhoAmW 91*
Baxter, Violet *WhoAmA 91*
Baxter, William Alexander 1929- *St&PR 91*
Baxter, William Francis 1929- *WhoAm 90*
Baxter, William MacNeil 1923- *WhoAm 90*
Baxter-Birney, Meredith 1947- *WhoAm 90, WhoAmW 91, WorAlBi*
Bay City Rollers *OxCPMus*
Bay, Alfred P *BiDrAPA 89*
Bay, Alfred Paul 1910- *WhoAm 90*
Bay, Austin 1951- *ConAu 131*
Bay, Catherine Marie *WhoAmW 91*
Bay, Christian *NewYTBS 90*
Bay, Christian 1921-1990 *BioIn 16, ConAu 131*
Bay, Harry 1878-1952 *Ballpl 90*
Bay, Howard 1912-1986 *ConDes 90*
Bay, Josephine H. 1900- *WorAlBi*
Bay, Juan 1892- *ArtLatA*
Bay, Paul Norman 1935- *St&PR 91*
Bay, Peter *BioIn 16*
Bay, Richard Anthony 1948- *WhoEmL 91*
Bay, Scot Nelson 1960- *BiDrAPA 89*
Bayan, Ali *BioIn 16*
Bayan, Lauren *BioIn 16*
Bayar, Demirtas Celal 1931- *WhoE 91*
Bayard, Alton Ernest, III 1952- *WhoEmL 91*
Bayard, Charles *PenDiDA 89*
Bayard, Edward Quint *BiDrAPA 89*
Bayard, Jean 1923- *WhoWrEP 89*
Bayard, John Bubenheim 1738-1807 *EncCRAm*
Bayard, Thomas Francis 1828-1898 *BiDrUSE 89, BioIn 16*
Bayardi, Elizabeth Audrey 1948- *WhoEmL 91*
Bayardo, J Fernando 1941- *BiDrAPA 89*
Baybars, Ilker 1947- *WhoWor 91*
Baybayan, Ronald Alan 1946- *WhoEmL 91*
Baycura, David Peter 1953- *WhoSSW 91*
Bayda, Edward Dmytro 1931- *WhoAm 90*
Baye, Nathalie 1948- *ConTFT 8*
Bayefsky, Aba 1923- *WhoAmA 91*
Bayer, Albert Norman 1960- *BiDrAPA 89*
Bayer, Arlyne *WhoAmA 91*
Bayer, Carol Lynn 1954- *BiDrAPA 89*
Bayer, Cary Stuart 1953- *WhoWrEP 89*
Bayer, D. Lucille *St&PR 91*
Bayer, Darryl Lee 1944- *WhoAmW 91*
Bayer, Gary Richard 1941- *WhoAm 90*
Bayer, Gudrun 1945- *WhoSSW 91*
Bayer, Henry Frederick 1925- *St&PR 91*
Bayer, Herbert 1900- *WhoAmA 91N*
Bayer, Herbert 1900-1985 *ConDes 90*
Bayer, Herbert Eugene 1921- *St&PR 91*
Bayer, Ian Douglas 1939- *St&PR 91*
Bayer, J.C. *PenDiDA 89*
Bayer, Jeffrey Joshua 1942- *WhoAmA 91*
Bayer, Jules M. *St&PR 91*
Bayer, Margret Helene Janssen 1931- *WhoAmW 91*
Bayer, Peter Brandon *BioIn 16*
Bayer, Raymond H. 1938- *St&PR 91*
Bayer, Richard Stewart 1951- *WhoWor 91*
Bayer, Svend *PenDiDA 89*
Bayer, Thomas Steele, Jr. 1938- *WhoSSW 91*
Bayer, Timothy Lee 1948- *BiDrAPA 89*
Bayer, Walter A. 1920- *St&PR 91*
Bayer, William *BioIn 16*
Bayers, Hazel Joyce 1947- *WhoAmW 91*
Bayerschmidt, Carl Frank 1905-1989 *BioIn 16*
Bayes, Nora 1880-1928 *BioIn 16, NotWoAT, OxCPMus*
Bayes, Paul Eugene 1944- *WhoSSW 91*
Bayes, Ronald Homer 1932- *WhoWrEP 89*
Bayes, Thomas 1702-1761 *BioIn 16*
Bayfield, E. G. *FemiCLE*
Bayfield, Fanny Amelia *DcCanB 12*
Bayford, Frank Raymond 1941- *IntWWM 90*
Bayh, Birch 1928- *WorAlBi*
Bayh, Birch Evans, Jr. 1928- *WhoAm 90*
Bayh, Evan 1955- *WhoAm 90*
Bayi, Filbert 1953- *WorAlBi*
Bayko, Emil Thomas 1947- *WhoSSW 91, WhoWor 91*

Bayle, Francois 1932- *IntWWM 90*
Baylen, Joseph Oscar 1920- *WhoAm 90*
Baylen, Kenneth Bruce 1946- *WhoEmL 91*
Bayler, Lavon Ann Burrichter 1933- *WhoWrEP 89*
Bayles, Deborah Leigh 1953- *WhoAmW 91*
Bayles, Janis Rylo Golon 1946- *WhoAmW 91*
Bayles, Librada C. 1936- *WhoAmW 91*
Bayles, Samuel Heagan 1910- *WhoAm 90, WhoWor 91*
Bayles, Spencer *BiDrAPA 89*
Bayles, William Fred 1938- *St&PR 91*
Bayless, Charles Edward 1942- *St&PR 91*
Bayless, Charles F. 1942- *St&PR 91*
Bayless, Raymond 1920- *EncPaPR 91, WhoAmA 91*
Bayless, Steve Allen 1944- *St&PR 91*
Bayless, Theodore Morris 1931- *WhoAm 90, WhoE 91*
Bayley, Charles Calvert 1907- *WhoWrEP 89*
Bayley, Christopher T. 1938- *St&PR 91, WhoAm 90*
Bayley, Iris *BioIn 16*
Bayley, Molly Gilbert 1944- *WhoAm 90, WhoAmW 91*
Bayley, Nicola 1949- *BioIn 16*
Bayley, Robert E. 1926- *St&PR 91*
Bayley, Ronald E. 1952- *St&PR 91*
Bayley, Ted Dwight 1937- *WhoSSW 91*
Baylies, Francis 1783-1852 *BioIn 16*
Baylin, George Jay 1911-1988 *BioIn 16*
Baylin, Sharon Bloodsworth 1946- *WhoE 91*
Baylinson, A S 1882-1950 *WhoAmA 91N*
Baylis, Carl Emmet 1943- *WhoE 91*
Baylis, R.H. 1937- *St&PR 91*
Baylis, Robert Montague 1938- *St&PR 91*
Bayliss, Colin Ernest 1944- *St&PR 91*
Bayliss, David 1938- *WhoWor 91*
Bayliss, E Virginia *BiDrAPA 89*
Bayliss, George 1931- *WhoAmA 91*
Bayliss, George Vincent 1931- *WhoAm 90*
Bayliss, James Milward 1949- *BiDrAPA 89*
Bayliss, John M.H. 1940- *St&PR 91*
Bayliss, John William 1934- *WhoWor 91*
Bayliss, Larry D. 1940- *St&PR 91*
Bayliss, Larry Dale 1940- *WhoAm 90*
Bayliss, Malcolm B. 1928- *WhoAm 90*
Bayliss, Thomas Andrews, III 1944- *WhoSSW 91*
Bayliss, William M. 1860-1924 *WorAlBi*
Baylor, Byrd 1924- *AuBYP 90*
Baylor, David Anton 1949- *St&PR 91*
Baylor, Don 1949- *Ballpl 90 [port], BioIn 16*
Baylor, Elgin 1934- *WorAlBi*
Baylor, Elgin Gay 1934- *WhoAm 90*
Baylor, Frances 1848-1920 *FemiCLE*
Baylor, H. Murray 1913- *IntWWM 90, WhoWrEP 89*
Baylor, Hugh Murray 1913- *WhoAm 90*
Baylor, John Patrick 1952- *WhoSSW 91*
Baylos, Zelma U *WhoAmA 91N*
Bayly, Ada Ellen 1857-1903 *BioIn 16*
Bayly, John Henry, Jr. 1944- *WhoAm 90*
Bayly, Mary *BiDEWW*
Bayly, Melvyn Arthur, Jr. 1945- *WhoEmL 91*
Bayly, Rachel Rima 1963- *WhoE 91*
Bayly, Thomas Haynes 1797-1839 *OxCPMus*
Baym, Gordon Alan 1935- *WhoAm 90*
Baym, Nina 1936- *ConAu 32NR, WhoAm 90, WhoAmW 91*
Baymiller, Lynda Doern 1943- *WhoAmW 91*
Baynard, Ed 1940- *WhoAmA 91*
Baynard, Ernest Cornish, III 1944- *WhoAm 90*
Baynard, Mildred Moyer 1902- *WhoSSW 91*
Bayne, Adele Wehman 1916- *WhoAmW 91, WhoE 91, WhoWor 91*
Bayne, Bill 1899-1981 *Ballpl 90*
Bayne, David Cowan 1918- *WhoAm 90*
Bayne, David Lee, Sr. 1931- *St&PR 91*
Bayne, Donald Storm 1949- *WhoEmL 91*
Bayne, James Wilmer 1925- *WhoAm 90*
Bayne, Nicholas 1937- *ConAu 130*
Bayne, Russ C. 1938- *St&PR 91*
Bayne, William Henry, Jr. 1912- *WhoWor 91*
Baynes, Curtis Edward 1951- *WhoSSW 91*
Baynes, Lacy G. 1933- *St&PR 91*
Baynes, Pauline 1922- *BioIn 16*
Baynes, Richard C. 1924- *St&PR 91*
Baynes, Thomas Edward, Jr. 1940- *WhoAm 90*
Baynton, Barbara 1857-1929 *FemiCLE*
Bayol, Irene Sledge 1933- *WhoAmW 91, WhoWor 91*
Bayon, Maurice Marcel 1909- *St&PR 91*
Bayraktar, Ali Ulvi 1955- *WhoWor 91*
Bays, David Arque 1937- *St&PR 91*
Bays, Edric Hill 1949- *WhoWrEP 89*
Bays, Eric 1932- *WhoAm 90*
Bays, Karl *BioIn 16*
Bays, Karl D. *St&PR 91N*
Bays, L Jerald *BiDrAPA 89*
Bays, Robert Earl 1921- *IntWWM 90*
Bayshore, Charles Alexander 1919- *WhoSSW 91*
Bayus, Brian Edward 1945- *St&PR 91*
Bayusik, Robert Edward 1927- *WhoE 91*
Bayzik, Barbara A. 1948- *WhoAmW 91*
Baz, Tom 1933- *St&PR 91*
Bazan, Ciro Alegria 1909-1967 *BioIn 16*
Bazan, Emilia Pardo 1851-1921 *EncCoWW*
Bazan, Emilia Pardo 1852-1921 *BioIn 16*
Bazan, Jose Luis 1946- *WhoHisp 91*
Bazant, Zdenek Pavel 1937- *WhoAm 90*
Bazany, LeRoy Francis 1932- *St&PR 91, WhoAm 90*
Bazarova, Roza Atamuradovna 1933- *WhoWor 91*
Bazdorf, Theodore Alan 1939- *St&PR 91*
Bazela, Jean Ann 1947- *WhoAmW 91, WhoEmL 91*
Bazeley, Ailwyn Geoffrey 1906-1989 *BioIn 16*
Bazell, Arthur H 1924- *BiDrAPA 89*
Bazell, Robert Joseph 1945- *WhoAm 90*
Bazelon, David L 1909- *BiDrAPA 89*
Bazelon, David Lionel 1909- *WhoAm 90*
Bazelon, Eileen Amy 1944- *BiDrAPA 89*
Bazelon, Irwin 1922- *IntWWM 90*
Bazemore, Jack G. 1935- *St&PR 91*
Bazemore, James Robert 1963- *WhoSSW 91*
Bazemore, Thomas Clifford 1922- *WhoAm 90*
Bazer, Angie 1928- *WhoAmW 91*
Bazer-Schwartz, Jeannine *WhoAm 90*
Bazerman, Charles 1945- *WhoE 91*
Bazerman, Steven Howard 1940- *WhoAm 90, WhoE 91, WhoWor 91*
Bazie, Mary Ida 1953- *WhoAmW 91*
Bazigian, Anita Kizirian *WhoAmW 91*
Bazik, Edna Frances 1946- *WhoEmL 91*
Bazille, Jean-Frederic 1841-1870 *BioIn 16*
Bazin, Albert Jeil 1904- *St&PR 91*
Bazin, Germain *NewYTBS 90*
Bazin, Germain 1901-1990 *BioIn 16, ConAu 131, CurBio 90N*
Bazin, Nancy Topping 1934- *WhoSSW 91*
Bazinet, Jack Charles 1951- *WhoE 91*
Bazini, Salomon *BiDrAPA 89*
Baziotes, William 1912-1963 *WhoAmA 91N*
Bazozowski, Lester 1952- *St&PR 91*
Bazzano, Edie 1938- *WhoAmW 91, WhoE 91*
Bazzarre, John T. 1930- *St&PR 91*
Bazzarre, John Thomas 1930- *WhoSSW 91*
Bazzaz, Fakhri A. 1933- *WhoAm 90*
Bazzoui, Widad 1929- *BiDrAPA 89*
BB *ConAu 132*
Bcinskaite-Buciene, Salomeja 1904-1945 *EncCoWW*
Be Bop Deluxe *EncPR&S 89*
Beabout, Douglas Howard 1950- *WhoEmL 91*
Beach Boys, The *EncPR&S 89, OxCPMus, WorAlBi*
Beach, Amy Marcy Cheney 1867-1944 *BioIn 16*
Beach, Arthur Thomas 1920- *St&PR 91*
Beach, Barbara Eileen 1944- *WhoAmW 91*
Beach, Cecil Prentice 1927- *WhoAm 90, WhoSSW 91*
Beach, Charles Addison 1945- *WhoEmL 91*
Beach, Charles Arthur 1953- *St&PR 91*
Beach, David Louis 1939- *St&PR 91*
Beach, David Williams 1938- *IntWWM 90*
Beach, Donn *BioIn 16*
Beach, Dwight Edward, Jr. 1937- *St&PR 91*
Beach, Edward Latimer 1918- *WhoE 91*
Beach, Elizabeth C *BiDrAPA 89*
Beach, Frank Ambrose 1911-1988 *BioIn 16*
Beach, Gary S. 1954- *St&PR 91*
Beach, H. H. A., Mrs. 1867-1944 *BioIn 16*
Beach, James David, Jr. 1935- *St&PR 91*
Beach, John Arthur 1932- *WhoAm 90, WhoE 91*
Beach, Kenneth H 1912- *BiDrAPA 89*
Beach, Kevin L. 1948- *St&PR 91*
Beach, Lani Leroy 1944- *WhoAm 90*
Beach, Lee Roy 1936- *WhoAm 90*
Beach, Lisa Ann 1964- *WhoAmW 91*
Beach, Margaret Gastaldi 1915- *WhoAmW 91*
Beach, Mary Filbin *BioIn 16*
Beach, Michele Raymonde 1961- *WhoE 91*
Beach, Morrison Howard 1917- *WhoAm 90*
Beach, Moses Yale 1800-1868 *BioIn 16*
Beach, Pennie 1945- *St&PR 91*
Beach, Robert E. 1952- *St&PR 91*
Beach, Robert Oliver, II 1932- *WhoAm 90*
Beach, Robert Preston 1916- *WhoE 91*
Beach, Stewart Taft 1899-1979 *AuBYP 90*
Beach, Sylvia *BioIn 16*
Beach, Sylvia 1887-1962 *FemiCLE*
Beach, Sylvia W. 1887-1962 *BioAmW*
Beach, Thomas Billis 1841-1894 *DcCanB 12*
Beach, Walter Alden 1924- *St&PR 91*
Beach, Warren 1914- *WhoAmA 91*
Beach, William B, Jr. 1921- *BiDrAPA 89*
Beach, William Roeder 1938- *St&PR 91*
Beacha, R. 1926- *St&PR 91*
Beacham, Stephanie *BioIn 16*
Beachell, Henry Monroe 1906- *WhoWor 91*
Beacher, Abraham I *BiDrAPA 89*
Beachler, Edwin Harry, III 1940- *WhoWor 91*
Beachley, Donovan R., Jr. 1925- *St&PR 91*
Beachley, Michael Charles 1940- *WhoAm 90, WhoWor 91*
Beachley, Norman Henry 1933- *WhoAm 90*
Beachman, Ronald *BiDrAPA 89*
Beachy, Natalie A *BiDrAPA 89*
Beachy, Philip Arden 1958- *WhoE 91*
Beacock, E. Stanley 1921- *WhoAm 90*
Beacom, Vincent Edward 1929- *St&PR 91*
Beaconsfield, Benjamin Disraeli, Earl of 1804-1881 *BioIn 16*
Beacroft, Percival Thomas 1935- *WhoSSW 91*
Beaderstadt, Andrea Anglin 1949- *WhoAmW 91*
Beadle, Alfred Newman 1927- *WhoAm 90*
Beadle, Erastus Flavel 1821-1894 *WorAlBi*
Beadle, George 1903-1989 *AnObit 1989*
Beadle, George W. 1903- *WorAlBi*
Beadle, George W. 1903-1989 *BioIn 16*
Beadle, J. Grant 1932- *St&PR 91*
Beadle, John Grant 1932- *WhoAm 90*
Beadle, Robert Sheldon 1949- *St&PR 91*
Beadle, Sandy J. 1948- *WhoEmL 91*
Beadles, Glenn Harris, Jr. 1948- *WhoSSW 91*
Beadles, Larry J. 1941- *St&PR 91*
Beadleston, William L 1938- *WhoAmA 91*
Beadsmoore, Michael David 1947- *St&PR 91*
Beagle, Gary J. 1945- *St&PR 91*
Beagle, Peter S 1939- *SmATA 60 [port]*
Beagle, Peter Soyer 1939- *WhoAm 90, WhoWrEP 89*
Beagle, Robert M. 1926- *St&PR 91*
Beagley, Karen Grace 1957- *WhoEmL 91*
Beagrie, George Simpson 1925- *WhoAm 90*
Beahan, Kermit 1918-1989 *BioIn 16*
Beahan, Laurence T 1930- *BiDrAPA 89*
Beahler, John Leroy 1930- *WhoAm 90*
Beahrs, John Oakley 1940- *BiDrAPA 89*
Beahrs, Oliver Howard 1914- *WhoAm 90*
Beaini, Joseph Elias 1960- *WhoSSW 91*
Beaird, Betty *WhoAm 90*
Beaird, Byron Lynn 1936- *WhoSSW 91*
Beaird, Charles T. 1922- *St&PR 91, WhoAm 90*
Beaird, Eric Thomas 1954- *WhoE 91*
Beaird, J. Pat, Jr. 1936- *St&PR 91*
Beaird, James R. *St&PR 91*
Beaird, James Ralph 1925- *WhoAm 90*
Beak, Gene 1914- *St&PR 91*
Beak, Peter Andrew 1936- *WhoAm 90*
Beake, John *WhoAm 90*
Beakes, John Herbert, Jr. 1943- *WhoE 91*
Beakley, George Carroll, Jr. 1922- *WhoAm 90*
Beakley, Robert Paul 1946- *WhoEmL 91*
Beal, Bob 1949- *ConAu 130*
Beal, Bruce Curtis 1950- *WhoEmL 91*
Beal, Dallas Knight 1926- *WhoAm 90, WhoE 91*
Beal, Daniel M *BiDrAPA 89*
Beal, E Clifford *BiDrAPA 89*
Beal, Edward W 1940- *BiDrAPA 89*
Beal, Edward Wescott 1940- *WhoE 91*
Beal, Frank Bradley 1946- *St&PR 91*
Beal, Frederick James 1954- *WhoEmL 91*
Beal, George Melvin 1917- *WhoAm 90*
Beal, George W. 1940- *St&PR 91*
Beal, Graham William John 1947- *WhoAmA 91*
Beal, Ilene *WhoAm 90*
Beal, Ilene 1946- *St&PR 91*
Beal, Jack 1931- *BioIn 16, WhoAm 90, WhoAmA 91*
Beal, Jeff *BioIn 16, NewAgMG*
Beal, John 1909- *WhoAm 90*
Beal, John Franklin 1932- *St&PR 91*
Beal, John M. 1915- *WhoAm 90*
Beal, Jules 1953- *St&PR 91*
Beal, Leigh Coulter *ODwPR 91*
Beal, Mack 1924- *WhoAmA 91*
Beal, Merrill David 1926- *WhoAm 90*
Beal, Michael McNulty 1959- *WhoEmL 91*
Beal, Myron Clarence 1920- *WhoAm 90*
Beal, Pamela K.M. 1956- *St&PR 91*
Beal, Reynolds 1867-1951 *WhoAmA 91N*
Beal, Richard Lowell 1945- *St&PR 91*
Beal, Robert Joseph 1936- *St&PR 91*
Beal, Robert Lawrence 1941- *WhoAm 90, WhoE 91, WhoWor 91*
Beal, Roy Wilson 1918- *St&PR 91*
Beal, S. Maxwell 1932- *St&PR 91*
Beal, Scott Andrew 1960- *St&PR 91*
Beal, Susan Ruth 1940- *WhoAmW 91*
Beal, Winnona Marie 1938- *WhoWrEP 89*
Beale, Arthur C 1940- *WhoAmA 91*
Beale, Barbara Edwards 1951- *WhoAmW 91*
Beale, Betty *WhoAm 90*
Beale, Christopher William 1947- *St&PR 91, WhoAm 90*
Beale, Dorothea 1831-1906 *BioIn 16*
Beale, Edward Fitzgerald 1822-1893 *BioIn 16, WhNaAH*
Beale, Estela A *BiDrAPA 89*
Beale, Georgia Robison 1905- *WhoAmW 91, WhoE 91*
Beale, Guy R., Jr. 1924- *St&PR 91*
Beale, Irene Alleman 1920- *WhoWrEP 89*
Beale, J. Burkhardt 1955- *WhoEmL 91*
Beale, James Haden 1961- *WhoE 91*
Beale, Mary 1632-1697 *BiDEWW*
Beale, Michelle *ODwPR 91*
Beale, Paul 1933- *ConAu 130*
Beale, Peter 1943- *St&PR 91*
Beale, Rhonda Joyce R *BiDrAPA 89*
Beale, Samuel E., III 1950- *WhoSSW 91*
Beale, Susan M. 1948- *St&PR 91*
Beale, Truxtun 1856-1936 *BioIn 16*
Beale, Virginia Davis 1936- *WhoAmW 91*
Beale, Walter Michael 1955- *WhoEmL 91*
Bealer, Alex 1921-1980 *AuBYP 90*
Bealer, Barbara Jane 1949- *WhoEmL 91*
Bealer, George Persson 1944- *ConAu 32NR*
Beales, Char *BioIn 16*
Beales, James Alfred Geaves, III 1923- *WhoE 91*
Bealey, Laura Ann 1934- *WhoSSW 91*
Bealieu, Elphege Alphonse 1930- *St&PR 91*
Bealka, Richard J *BiDrAPA 89*
Beall, Bobby D 1931- *BiDrAPA 89*
Beall, Burtch W., Jr. 1925- *WhoAm 90*
Beall, Charles C., Jr. 1935- *St&PR 91*
Beall, Dennis Ray 1929- *WhoAm 90, WhoAmA 91*
Beall, Donald R. 1938- *St&PR 91*
Beall, Donald Ray 1938- *WhoAm 90, WhoWor 91*
Beall, George 1937- *WhoAm 90*
Beall, Ingrid Lillehei 1926- *WhoAm 90, WhoAmW 91*
Beall, J Harvey, Jr. 1930- *BiDrAPA 89*
Beall, James Howard 1945- *WhoE 91, WhoWor 91*
Beall, Joanna 1935- *WhoAmA 91*
Beall, Joanna May 1935- *WhoAmW 91*
Beall, Kenneth Sutter, Jr. 1938- *WhoSSW 91*
Beall, Lee M. 1933- *IntWWM 90*
Beall, Lester Thomas 1902-1969 *WhoAmA 91N*
Beall, Richard Olin 1931- *St&PR 91*
Beall, Robert Joseph 1943- *WhoAm 90*
Beall, Robert Matthews, II 1943- *WhoAm 90*
Beall, Royce Milton 1926- *St&PR 91*
Beall, Samuel E., III 1950- *WhoAm 90*
Beallor, Fran 1957- *WhoAmA 91, WhoE 91*
Bealmer, William 1919- *WhoAmA 91*
Beals, Carleton 1893-1979 *AuBYP 90*
Beals, Clem Kip, III 1949- *WhoEmL 91*
Beals, Cynthia Louise 1957- *WhoEmL 91*
Beals, Edward Wesley 1933- *IntWWM 90*
Beals, Jeffrey A. 1947- *St&PR 91*
Beals, Jennifer 1963- *DrBIPA 90*
Beals, Jessie Tarbox 1870-1942 *BioAmW*
Beals, Kenneth Albert 1946- *WhoEmL 91*
Beals, Kimberly Faye 1957- *WhoE 91*
Beals, Loren Alan 1933- *WhoAm 90, WhoWor 91*
Beals, Mark Graden 1936- *WhoAm 90, WhoWor 91*
Beals, Ralph 1929- *St&PR 91*
Beals, Ralph Everett 1936- *WhoAm 90, WhoE 91*
Beals, Sharon Kathleen Key 1958- *WhoAmW 91, WhoSSW 91*
Beals, Vaughn Leroy, Jr. 1928- *St&PR 91, WhoAm 90*
Beam, Beverly J. 1941- *WhoAmW 91*
Beam, Beverly Jane 1941- *St&PR 91*
Beam, Clarence Arlen 1930- *WhoAm 90*
Beam, Frank Letts 1942- *WhoWor 91*
Beam, Jacob Dyneley 1908- *BioIn 16*
Beam, John M., Jr. 1947- *St&PR 91*
Beam, Margaret Anne Ridgeway 1948- *WhoEmL 91*
Beam, Mary Todd 1931- *WhoAmA 91*
Beam, Michael Newton 1942- *St&PR 91*
Beam, Philip Conway 1910- *WhoAmA 91, WhoE 91*

Beam, Raymond Robert, Jr. 1946- *WhoEmL 91*
Beam, Robert Thompson 1919- *WhoAm 90*
Beam, Steven Gerald 1956- *WhoSSW 91*
Beam, Teresa Lynn 1957- *WhoEmL 91*
Beam, Walter Raleigh 1928- *WhoAm 90*
Beam, William Lawrence 1935- *St&PR 91*
Beam, William T. 1936- *St&PR 91*
Beaman, Ann Thomson 1933- *WhoAmW 91*
Beaman, E. O. 1837?-1876 *BioIn 16*
Beaman, George B 1905- *BiDrAPA 89*
Beaman, Janice Ellen 1961- *WhoAmW 91*
Beaman, Joyce Proctor 1931- *WhoWrEP 89*
Beaman, Kenneth Dale 1953- *WhoEmL 91*
Beaman, Libby *BioIn 16*
Beaman, Margarine Gaynell *WhoAmW 91*
Beaman, Richard Bancroft 1909- *WhoAm 90*
Beaman, Robert H. 1947- *St&PR 91*
Beament, Harold 1898- *WhoAmA 91N*
Beament, Thomas Harold 1941- *WhoAm 90*
Beament, Tib 1941- *WhoAmA 91*
Beamer, John Harden *BiDrAPA 89*
Beamer, Robert Lewis 1933- *WhoSSW 91*
Beamer-Patton, June Elizabeth 1944- *WhoAmW 91*
Beamguard, Elizabeth Parks *WhoAmW 91*
Beamish, James Robert 1936- *St&PR 91*
Beamish, Silvia Katharine 1928- *IntWWM 90*
Beamish, T. Robert 1937- *St&PR 91*
Beams, Mary Ann 1939- *WhoAmW 91*
Bean, Alan *BioIn 16*
Bean, Alan LaVern 1932- *WhoAm 90, WhoWor 91*
Bean, Atherton 1910- *WhoAm 90*
Bean, Belve 1905-1988 *Ballpl 90*
Bean, Bennett 1941- *BioIn 16, WhoAmA 91*
Bean, Bourne 1920- *St&PR 91*
Bean, Bruce William 1945- *St&PR 91*
Bean, Bruce Winfield 1941- *WhoAm 90*
Bean, Charles Palmer 1923- *WhoAm 90*
Bean, Claire S. 1952- *St&PR 91*
Bean, Clifford A. 1929- *St&PR 91*
Bean, Curtis B. *WhoAm 90*
Bean, David W 1936- *BiDrAPA 89*
Bean, Delcie D. 1942- *St&PR 91*
Bean, Donald W. 1935- *St&PR 91*
Bean, Elizabeth Harriman 1923- *WhoAm 90*
Bean, Ethelle Susannah 1952- *WhoEmL 91*
Bean, Frank Dawson 1942- *WhoAm 90*
Bean, Gary 1949- *WhoSSW 91*
Bean, Gregory Richard 1950- *St&PR 91*
Bean, Hugh 1929- *PenDiMP*
Bean, Hugh Cecil 1929- *IntWWM 90*
Bean, J Ronald 1936- *BiDrAPA 89*
Bean, Jacob 1923- *WhoAm 90, WhoE 91*
Bean, James W. 1941- *St&PR 91*
Bean, James W., Jr. 1947- *St&PR 91*
Bean, Joan Nona 1929- *WhoAmW 91*
Bean, Joan P. 1933- *WhoAm 90*
Bean, Joe Currie, Jr. 1934- *WhoSSW 91*
Bean, Jonathan Spangler 1963- *WhoSSW 91*
Bean, Kenneth F 1934- *BiDrAPA 89*
Bean, Marvin Day 1921- *WhoWor 91*
Bean, Maurice Darrow 1928- *WhoAm 90*
Bean, Nancy Ann Morgan 1936- *WhoAmW 91*
Bean, Normal *ConAu 132, MajTwCW*
Bean, Orson *BioIn 16*
Bean, Orson 1928- *WhoAm 90*
Bean, Richard A. 1950- *St&PR 91*
Bean, Roy 1825?-1903 *WorAlBi*
Bean, Roy H. 1943- *St&PR 91*
Bean, Russell Owen 1948- *WhoSSW 91*
Bean, Theo B. 1926- *St&PR 91*
Bean, William Bennett 1909-1989 *BioIn 16*
Bean-Bayog, Margaret *BiDrAPA 89*
Beanblossom, Robert Lee 1936- *WhoSSW 91*
Beane, Elizabeth A *BiDrAPA 89*
Beane, Jerry Lynn 1944- *WhoAm 90*
Beane, Lois Velleda 1938- *WhoAmW 91*
Beane, Robert Lowell 1956- *WhoEmL 91*
Beans-Clark, Patricia *BioIn 16*
Beanstock, Sam 1907- *BiDrAPA 89*
Bear Hunter *WhNaAH*
Bear, The Mama *WhoWrEP 89*
Bear, Ann 1937- *WhoWrEP 89*
Bear, Charles Benson 1919- *WhoAm 90*
Bear, Dinah 1951- *WhoAmW 91*
Bear, Donald 1905-1952 *WhoAmA 91N*
Bear, Frederick Thomas 1937- *WhoSSW 91*
Bear, G. *WhoWrEP 89*
Bear, Gregory Dale 1951- *WhoAm 90*
Bear, Jeffrey Warren 1945- *WhoEmL 91*
Bear, Jon H. 1934- *St&PR 91*
Bear, Larry Alan 1928- *WhoAm 90, WhoE 91, WhoWor 91*
Bear, Marcelle L 1917- *WhoAmA 91*
Bear, Mary Qualey 1941- *WhoSSW 91*
Bear, Stephen E. *BioIn 16*
Bear, Sun 1929- *WhoWrEP 89*
Bear, William Forrest 1927- *WhoAm 90*
Bearak, Corey Becker 1955- *WhoE 91, WhoWor 91*
Bearce, Jeana Dale *WhoAm 90, WhoE 91*
Bearce, Jeana Dale 1929- *WhoAmA 91*
Beard, A.D. *St&PR 91*
Beard, Ann Southard 1948- *WhoAmW 91*
Beard, Bruce H *BiDrAPA 89*
Beard, C. Randolph 1931- *St&PR 91*
Beard, Charles A. 1874-1948 *WorAlBi*
Beard, Charles Austin 1874-1948 *BioIn 16*
Beard, Charles Irvin 1916- *WhoAm 90*
Beard, Charles Julian 1943- *WhoAm 90*
Beard, Charles Lawrence 1947- *WhoE 91*
Beard, Charles Walter 1932- *WhoAm 90*
Beard, Christopher Harold 1949- *WhoSSW 91*
Beard, Cynthia Aldridge 1953- *WhoAmW 91*
Beard, Dan 1850-1941 *WorAlBi*
Beard, Daniel Carter 1859-1941 *AuBYP 90*
Beard, Daniel Paul 1948- *WhoEmL 91*
Beard, Dave 1959- *Ballpl 90*
Beard, David Breed 1922- *WhoAm 90*
Beard, E. Lee *BioIn 16*
Beard, Elizabeth Letitia 1932- *WhoAm 90*
Beard, Ellis Mabry 1925- *St&PR 91*
Beard, Eugene P. *St&PR 91*
Beard, Frederick K. 1941- *St&PR 91*
Beard, Geoffrey 1929- *ConAu 130*
Beard, George Breckenridge 1924- *WhoAm 90*
Beard, Helen 1931- *ConAu 32NR*
Beard, Howard Leo 1937- *St&PR 91*
Beard, James 1903-1985 *BioIn 16, WorAlBi*
Beard, James F 1919-1989 *ConAu 130*
Beard, James Franklin 1919-1989 *BioIn 16*
Beard, John 1717?-1791 *PenDiMP*
Beard, John Edwards 1932- *St&PR 91*
Beard, Leo Roy 1917- *WhoAm 90*
Beard, Marion L Patterson *WhoAmA 91N*
Beard, Marlene Denise 1960- *WhoE 91*
Beard, Mary 1876-1946 *BioIn 16*
Beard, Mary 1876-1958 *FemiCLE*
Beard, Mary Ritter 1876-1958 *BioAmW, BioIn 16*
Beard, Matthew 1925-1981 *DrBlPA 90*
Beard, Michael Kenneth 1941- *WhoE 91*
Beard, Mike 1950- *Ballpl 90*
Beard, Nancy Marie 1955- *WhoAmW 91*
Beard, Paul 1901- *IntWWM 90*
Beard, Paul 1901-1989 *AnObit 1989*
Beard, Paul 1906- *EncPaPR 91*
Beard, Percy *BioIn 16*
Beard, Richard Elliott 1928- *WhoAmA 91*
Beard, Richard Leonard 1909- *WhoAm 90*
Beard, Robert Gruber 1927- *St&PR 91*
Beard, Robert Jean 1929- *St&PR 91*
Beard, Rodney Rau 1911- *WhoAm 90*
Beard, Stephen Ross 1950- *WhoEmL 91*
Beard, Thomas D. 1934- *St&PR 91*
Beard, Thomas Rex 1934- *WhoAm 90*
Beard, Walker Rankin 1946- *St&PR 91*
Beard, William David 1923- *St&PR 91*
Beard, William Jennings 1926- *St&PR 91*
Beard, William Kelly *NewYTBS 90*
Beard, William Kelly 1898-1990 *BioIn 16*
Beard, William M. 1928- *St&PR 91, WhoAm 90*
Beard, Winston *ConTFT 8*
Beardall, Dennis K. 1953- *St&PR 91*
Beardall, James C. 1939- *St&PR 91*
Bearden, David Christopher 1959- *WhoSSW 91*
Bearden, Donn Robert 1933- *St&PR 91*
Bearden, Dwight Lee 1952- *BiDrAPA 89*
Bearden, Fred Burnette, Jr. 1923- *WhoSSW 91*
Bearden, Gene 1920- *Ballpl 90*
Bearden, James Hudson 1933- *WhoAm 90*
Bearden, James William 1947- *St&PR 91*
Bearden, John T. *AmLegL*
Bearden, Joseph Marion 1948- *WhoEmL 91*
Bearden, Nancy Carpenter 1958- *WhoWrEP 89*
Bearden, Romare 1914-1988 *BioIn 16, ModArCr 1 [port]*
Beardmore, Harvey Ernest 1921- *WhoAm 90*
Beardslee, Bethany 1927- *IntWWM 90*
Beardslee, Daniel Bain 1960- *WhoEmL 91*
Beardslee, Robert Lewis 1868-1926 *AmLegL*
Beardslee, William Armitage 1916- *WhoAm 90*
Beardslee, William Rigby 1945- *BiDrAPA 89*
Beardsley, Alberta 1946- *WhoAmW 91*
Beardsley, Aubrey 1872-1898 *BioIn 16, WorAlBi*
Beardsley, Barbara H 1945- *WhoAmA 91*
Beardsley, Charles William 1939- *WhoE 91*
Beardsley, George Peter 1940- *WhoAm 90*
Beardsley, Harrison T. 1922- *ODwPR 91*
Beardsley, Jeanne Margaret 1940- *WhoAmW 91*
Beardsley, John R. 1937- *ODwPR 91*
Beardsley, Joseph Warren 1821-1868 *AmLegL*
Beardsley, Karen 1957- *BioIn 16*
Beardsley, Lehman Franklin 1923- *St&PR 91*
Beardsley, Michael Leigh 1951- *St&PR 91*
Beardsley, Monroe C. 1915-1985 *BioIn 16*
Beardsley, Robert Eugene 1923- *WhoAm 90*
Beardsley, Theodore Sterling, Jr. 1930- *WhoAm 90, WhoE 91, WhoWor 91*
Beardwood, Bruce A. 1936- *St&PR 91*
Beardwood, Bruce Allan 1936- *WhoAm 90*
Beare, Charles Albert *EncO&P 3*
Beare, Christopher Thomas 1950- *WhoWor 91*
Beare, Gary 1952- *Ballpl 90*
Beare, Gene Kerwin 1915- *St&PR 91, WhoAm 90*
Beare, Nikki 1928- *ODwPR 91*
Beare, Steven Douglas 1944- *WhoE 91*
Beare-Rogers, Joyce Louise 1927- *WhoAm 90*
Bearelly, Manoher Rao *BiDrAPA 89*
Beares, Paul Richard 1946- *St&PR 91*
Bearg, David Warren 1948- *WhoEmL 91*
Bearg, Martin Lee 1952- *WhoE 91, WhoEmL 91*
Bearley, William Leon 1938- *WhoWor 91*
Bearman, Toni Carbo 1942- *WhoAm 90, WhoAmW 91*
Bearn, Alexander Gordon 1923- *WhoAm 90*
Bearn, Margaret Slocum 1924- *WhoAmW 91*
Bearnarth, Larry 1941- *Ballpl 90, BioIn 16*
Bearns, Robert *NewAgMG*
Bear's Heart 1851-1882 *WhNaAH*
Bearsch, Jack Max 1927- *St&PR 91*
Bearse, Amanda *BioIn 16, ConTFT 8*
Bearss, Russell L. 1925- *St&PR 91*
Beart, Emmanuelle *BioIn 16*
Bearup, Dennis Ray 1953- *St&PR 91*
Bearwald, Jean Haynes 1924- *WhoAmW 91, WhoWor 91*
Beary, John Francis, III 1946- *WhoAm 90*
Beary, Shirley Fogelsanger 1928- *IntWWM 90*
Beascoechea, German 1943- *WhoWor 91*
Beasley, Barbara Starin 1955- *WhoAmW 91*
Beasley, Bea Cassandra 1942- *WhoAmW 91*
Beasley, Bruce 1939- *WhoAmA 91*
Beasley, Bruce Miller 1939- *WhoAm 90*
Beasley, C. Elizabeth 1952- *BiDrAPA 89*
Beasley, Cecil Ackmond, Jr. 1912- *WhoAm 90, WhoE 91*
Beasley, Charles Merritt, Jr. *BiDrAPA 89*
Beasley, Charles Merritt, Jr. 1950- *WhoEmL 91*
Beasley, Cloyd Orris, Jr. 1933- *WhoSSW 91*
Beasley, Conger, Jr. 1940- *WhoWrEP 89*
Beasley, David Lewis 1955- *St&PR 91*
Beasley, Debra Kay 1954- *WhoAmW 91*
Beasley, Delilah Leontium 1871-1931 *HarlReB [port]*
Beasley, Ernest William, Jr. 1924- *WhoSSW 91*
Beasley, G.E. 1945- *St&PR 91*
Beasley, George Garland 1932- *WhoAm 90*
Beasley, Georgia Mae 1948- *WhoSSW 91*
Beasley, Ica Chester 1943- *WhoSSW 91*
Beasley, James Wallace, Jr. 1943- *St&PR 91*
Beasley, Jerry L. 1944- *WhoAm 90*
Beasley, Jim Sanders 1936- *WhoAm 90*
Beasley, John C. 1942- *St&PR 91*
Beasley, John H. 1943- *St&PR 91*
Beasley, Kim Allen 1952- *WhoSSW 91*
Beasley, Lawrence H. 1946- *St&PR 91*
Beasley, Mary Catherine 1922- *WhoAmW 91*
Beasley, Mary Sharman 1944- *WhoSSW 91*
Beasley, Maurine Hoffman 1936- *WhoAmW 91, WhoE 91*
Beasley, Michael Jeffrey 1959- *WhoSSW 91*
Beasley, Oscar H. 1925- *St&PR 91*
Beasley, Phoebe *BioIn 16*
Beasley, Rita J. *BioIn 16*
Beasley, Robert Harlin, Jr. *BiDrAPA 89*
Beasley, Robert Palmer *WhoAm 90*
Beasley, Robert Scott 1949- *WhoE 91*
Beasley, Ronald Rex 1925- *WhoSSW 91*
Beasley, Ronald W. 1946- *St&PR 91*
Beasley, William Howard, III *BioIn 16*
Beasley, William Howard, III *NewYTBS 90 [port]*
Beasley, William Howard, III 1946- *St&PR 91, WhoAm 90*
Beasley, William R. 1941- *WhoSSW 91*
Beasley, William Rex 1934- *WhoAm 90, WhoSSW 91*
Beason, Amos T. 1940- *St&PR 91*
Beason, Donald Ray 1943- *WhoAmA 91*
Beason, James Douglas 1953- *WhoEmL 91*
Beason, Robert Gayle 1927- *WhoAm 90, WhoWrEP 89*
Beath, Betty 1932- *IntWWM 90*
Beathard, Bobby *BioIn 16*
Beatie, Russel Harrison, Jr. 1938- *WhoE 91*
Beatles, The *EncPR&S 89, OxCPMus*
Beatly, Jeffrey G. 1958- *St&PR 91*
Beatman, Leslie Harvey *St&PR 91*
Beato, Felice *BioIn 16*
Beato, Maritza 1949- *WhoAmW 91, WhoHisp 91*
Beaton, Cecil 1904-1980 *WorAlBi*
Beaton, Gary Steven 1953- *WhoE 91*
Beaton, Michael Steve 1950- *WhoSSW 91*
Beaton, Roy Howard 1916- *WhoAm 90, WhoWor 91*
Beaton-Simmons, Karen 1944- *WhoAmW 91*
Beatrice *WomWR*
Beatrice *WomWR*
Beatrice Mary Victoria Feodore 1857-1944 *BiDWomA*
Beatrice, Princess of York 1988- *BioIn 16*
Beatrix de Bourgogne *WomWR*
Beatrix, Her Majesty 1938- *WhoWor 91*
Beatrix, Queen of the Netherlands 1938- *BioIn 16*
Beatrix Wilhelmina Armgard 1938- *WomWR*
Beattie, Allan Leslie 1926- *St&PR 91*
Beattie, Ann 1947- *BioAmW, ConLC 63 [port], FemiCLE, MajTwCW, WhoAm 90, WhoWrEP 89, WorAlBi*
Beattie, Bonita Lynn 1949- *WhoEmL 91*
Beattie, David Stuart 1924- *WhoWor 91*
Beattie, Diana Scott 1934- *WhoAm 90*
Beattie, Donald A. 1929- *WhoAm 90*
Beattie, Edward James 1918- *WhoAm 90, WhoE 91, WhoWor 91*
Beattie, George 1919- *WhoAmA 91*
Beattie, Henry C. 1921- *St&PR 91*
Beattie, Herbert 1926- *IntWWM 90*
Beattie, Janet Holtzman 1927- *WhoAm 90*
Beattie, Jim 1954- *Ballpl 90*
Beattie, John *EncO&P 3*
Beattie, John 1915-1990 *ConAu 131*
Beattie, Melody *BioIn 16*
Beattie, Melody 1948- *BestSel 90-4 [port]*
Beattie, Melody Lynn 1948- *WhoWrEP 89*
Beattie, Nora Maureen 1925- *WhoAm 90*
Beattie, Pamela Marie Pash 1944- *WhoAmW 91*
Beattie, Paul H. *BioIn 16*
Beattie, Richard Irwin 1939- *WhoE 91*
Beattie, Susan 1940-1989 *BioIn 16*
Beattie, Ted Arthur 1945- *WhoAm 90*
Beattie, William C. *BioIn 16*
Beattie, William Graham, Jr. 1937- *WhoE 91*
Beatty, Alan Edwin 1933- *St&PR 91*
Beatty, Bessie 1886-1947 *BioIn 16*
Beatty, Carolyn Ann 1942- *WhoAmW 91*
Beatty, Curtis Marvin 1951- *St&PR 91*
Beatty, David 1871-1936 *BioIn 16*
Beatty, Douglas C *BiDrAPA 89*
Beatty, Elwood T. 1810?-1883 *AmLegL*
Beatty, Frances 1940- *WhoAmW 91*
Beatty, Frances Fielding Lewis 1948- *WhoAmA 91, WhoEmL 91*
Beatty, Garry Hamilton 1935- *WhoAm 90*
Beatty, Henry Perrin 1950- *WhoAm 90, WhoE 91, WhoWor 91*
Beatty, Hetty Burlingame 1907-1971 *AuBYP 90*
Beatty, Jack J. 1945- *WhoAm 90, WhoWrEP 89*
Beatty, Jerome, Jr. 1918- *AuBYP 90*
Beatty, Jerry Alfred 1947- *WhoE 91*
Beatty, John *AuBYP 90*
Beatty, John Cabeen, Jr. 1919- *WhoAm 90*
Beatty, John Lee 1948- *WhoAm 90*
Beatty, Karen L. 1948- *WhoAmW 91*
Beatty, Kenneth Orion, Jr. 1913- *WhoAm 90*
Beatty, Lorne Alan 1955- *St&PR 91*
Beatty, Mark W. 1953- *WhoEmL 91*
Beatty, Michael L. 1947- *WhoAm 90, WhoSSW 91*
Beatty, Michael Lance 1947- *St&PR 91*
Beatty, Ned 1937- *WhoAm 90, WorAlBi*
Beatty, Patricia Jean *WhoAm 90, WhoWrEP 89*
Beatty, Patricia Robbins 1922- *AuBYP 90*
Beatty, Richard C. 1945- *St&PR 91*
Beatty, Richard Paul 1953- *WhoE 91*
Beatty, Richard S. 1934- *St&PR 91*
Beatty, Richard Scott 1959- *St&PR 91*
Beatty, Richard Scrivener 1934- *WhoAm 90*
Beatty, Robert D. 1926- *St&PR 91*
Beatty, Stephen Earl 1951- *St&PR 91*

Beatty, Talley *DrBlPA 90*
Beatty, Tina Marie 1955- *WhoAmW 91*
Beatty, Warren 1937- *BioIn 16, WhoAm 90*
Beatty, Warren 1938- *WorAlBi*
Beatty, Wilbur C. 1942- *WhoE 91*
Beatty, William 1835-1898 *DcCanB 12*
Beatty, William Coombs 1946- *BiDrAPA 89*
Beatty, William Louis 1925- *WhoAm 90*
Beatty-deSana, Jeanne Warren 1920- *WhoSSW 91*
Beatus, Ben Louis, Jr. 1936- *BiDrAPA 89*
Beaty, Bill G. 1930- *St&PR 91*
Beaty, David Alvin 1948- *WhoEmL 91*
Beaty, Harry Nelson 1932- *WhoAm 90*
Beaty, James 1798-1892 *DcCanB 12*
Beaty, James Dillon, Jr. 1953- *WhoE 91*
Beaty, John Franklin *BiDrAPA 89*
Beaty, John Yocum 1884- *AuBYP 90*
Beaty, Orren, Jr. 1919- *WhoAm 90*
Beaty, Sandra Diane 1951- *WhoSSW 91*
Beaty, Shirley MacLean *ConAu 32NR*
Beaty, William T, II 1923- *BiDrAPA 89*
Beaubien, Carlos 1800-1864 *BioIn 16*
Beaubien, David James 1934- *St&PR 91, WhoAm 90*
Beaubien, Jacques Felix *BiDrAPA 89*
Beaubien, Michael *BioIn 16*
Beaubrun, Jean Edouard *BiDrAPA 89*
Beaubrun, Michael H 1924- *BiDrAPA 89*
Beaucage, Serge Laurent 1951- *WhoE 91*
Beauchamp, Aubrey *BioIn 16*
Beauchamp, Bernard D. 1931- *St&PR 91*
Beauchamp, David Fitzgerald 1940- *WhoAm 90*
Beauchamp, Gary Fay 1951- *WhoEmL 91, WhoSSW 91*
Beauchamp, George 1933- *WhoAmA 91*
Beauchamp, Jacques 1948- *St&PR 91, WhoAm 90*
Beauchamp, James Harry 1942- *WhoSSW 91*
Beauchamp, Jim 1939- *Ballpl 90*
Beauchamp, John Herndon 1911- *St&PR 91*
Beauchamp, Lucille Marie 1922- *WhoAmW 91*
Beauchamp, Mark Thomas 1951- *WhoEmL 91*
Beauchamp, Patrick Lowell 1933- *St&PR 91*
Beauchamp, Pierre 1943- *WhoAm 90*
Beauchamp, Robert 1923- *WhoAmA 91*
Beauchamp, Ronald Andrew 1938- *WhoAm 90*
Beauchemin, Francine Lahaie 1951- *WhoAmW 91*
Beauchemin, Nathalie *BiDrAPA 89*
Beauchemin, Neree 1850-1931 *DcLB 92*
Beauchemin, Susan-Marie 1950- *WhoEmL 91*
Beauchemin, Yves 1941- *BioIn 16, ConAu 129*
Beauclair, Linda *BiDrAPA 89*
Beauclerc, Amelia *FemiCLE*
Beaudet, Eugene Charles 1924- *WhoWrEP 89*
Beaudet, Margaret K. 1927- *St&PR 91*
Beaudett, Malcolm S 1956- *BiDrAPA 89*
Beaudin, James A. 1944- *St&PR 91*
Beaudine, Frank Richard 1923- *WhoAm 90*
Beaudoin, Andre Eugene 1920- *WhoAmA 91*
Beaudoin, Bernard J. 1940- *St&PR 91*
Beaudoin, Carol Ann 1949- *WhoAmW 91*
Beaudoin, Claude L. 1933- *St&PR 91*
Beaudoin, Gerald-Armand 1929- *WhoAm 90*
Beaudoin, James Ronald 1942- *BiDrAPA 89*
Beaudoin, Laurent *BioIn 16*
Beaudoin, Laurent 1938- *St&PR 91, WhoAm 90*
Beaudoin, Robert Lawrence 1933- *WhoWor 91*
Beaudouin, Mark T. 1955- *St&PR 91*
Beaudreau, David Eugene 1929- *WhoAm 90*
Beaudry, Jacques 1929- *IntWWM 90*
Beaudry, Janis Stonier 1956- *WhoEmL 91*
Beaudry, Louise Francine *BiDrAPA 89*
Beaudry-Anstreicher, Agathe *BiDrAPA 89*
Beaudway, James E. 1916- *St&PR 91*
Beaufait, Frederick William 1936- *WhoAm 90*
Beauford, Richard Micheal 1953- *St&PR 91*
Beaufort, Duke of 1900-1984 *DcNaB 1981*
Beaufort, D. A. 1739-1821 *BioIn 16*
Beaufort, Daniel Augustus 1739-1821 *BioIn 16*
Beaufort, John David 1912- *WhoAm 90, WhoWrEP 89*
Beaugrand, Honore 1848-1906 *DcLB 99 [port]*
Beauharnais, Marie 1737-1813 *EncCoWW*
Beaulac, Willard L. *NewYTBS 90*
Beaulac, Willard L 1899-1990 *ConAu 132, CurBio 90N*
Beaulac, Willard Leon 1899-1990 *BioIn 16*
Beaulieu, Elphege Alphonse 1930- *St&PR 91*
Beaulieu, Jacques Alexandre 1932- *WhoAm 90*
Beaulieu, Jean Paul 1952- *St&PR 91*
Beaulieu, Lionel Joseph 1950- *WhoEmL 91*
Beaulieu, Philippine Leroy- *BioIn 16*
Beaulieu, Richard 1952- *St&PR 91*
Beaulieu, Roger L. 1924- *St&PR 91*
Beaulieu, Roger Louis 1924- *WhoAm 90*
Beaulieu, Serge *BiDrAPA 89*
Beaulne, Guy 1921- *OxCCanT [port]*
Beaulnes, Aurele 1928- *WhoAm 90*
Beauman, E Bentley 1891-1989 *ConAu 129*
Beaumarchais, Pierre Augustin Caron de 1732-1799 *BioIn 16*
Beaumarchais, Pierre Augustin De 1732-1799 *WorAlBi*
Beaumarchais, Pierre Augustine Caron De 1732-1799 *EncCRAm*
Beaumont, Adrian 1937- *IntWWM 90*
Beaumont, Agnes 1652-1720 *BiDEWW, FemiCLE*
Beaumont, Edward Arthur 1951- *WhoEmL 91*
Beaumont, Francis 1584-1616 *BioIn 16, WorAlBi*
Beaumont, George Howland 1753-1827 *BioIn 16*
Beaumont, Gerald Paul 1943- *WhoSSW 91*
Beaumont, Germaine 1890-1983 *EncCoWW*
Beaumont, Ginger 1876-1956 *Ballpl 90*
Beaumont, Graham *BiDrAPA 89*
Beaumont, Hugh 1908-1973 *BioIn 16*
Beaumont, Jeanne-Marie Le Prince de 1711-1780 *EncCoWW*
Beaumont, John *EncO&P 3*
Beaumont, Mona *WhoAmA 91, WhoAmW 91, WhoWor 91*
Beaumont, Neil 1936- *St&PR 91*
Beaumont, Pamela Jo 1944- *WhoAm 90*
Beaumont, Ralph Harrison *BiDrAPA 89*
Beaumont, Richard Austin 1925- *WhoAm 90*
Beaumont, Robert George 1930- *St&PR 91*
Beaumont, Roger Alban 1935- *WhoSSW 91*
Beaumont, Waleran de 1104-1166 *BioIn 16*
Beaumont, William 1785-1853 *BioIn 16, WorAlBi*
Beaupain, Elaine Shapiro 1949- *WhoAmW 91, WhoE 91*
Beaupre, Andre P. *ODwPR 91*
Beaupre, Arthur Matthias 1853-1919 *BioIn 16*
Beaupre, Vicki Louise 1953- *WhoAmW 91*
Beauregard, Avery Justin 1946- *WhoE 91*
Beauregard, Charles R. 1919- *St&PR 91*
Beauregard, Pierre 1818-1893 *WorAlBi*
Beauregard, Robert Alden 1926- *St&PR 91*
Beausejour, Pierre A. 1946- *BiDrAPA 89*
Beausey, Maureen McArdle 1951- *WhoAmW 91*
Beausoleil, Doris Mae 1932- *WhoAmW 91, WhoE 91*
Beausoleil, Jean du Chatelot, Baron de 1576?-1643 *EncO&P 3*
Beauvais, Edward R. 1936- *St&PR 91, WhoAm 90*
Beauvais, Laura Lynn 1957- *WhoAmW 91*
Beauvau, Marie-Francoise Catherine de 1711-1786 *EncCoWW*
Beauvoir, Simone Bernard de 1908-1986 *BiDFrPL*
Beauvoir, Simone de 1908-1986 *EncCoWW, FemiCLE, MajTwCW, WorAlBi, WrPh*
Beaux, Cecilia 1855-1942 *BiDWomA*
Beaux, Cecilia 1863?-1942 *BioIn 16*
Beaven, Barba H *BiDrAPA 89*
Beaven, Freda Margaret 1923- *IntWWM 90*
Beaven, John Lewis 1930- *WhoWor 91*
Beaven, Peter Jamieson 1925- *WhoWor 91*
Beaven, Peter Richard 1954- *IntWWM 90*
Beaven, Robert Pendelton 1917- *St&PR 91*
Beaven, Winton Henry 1915- *WhoAm 90*
Beaver and Krause *NewAgMG*
Beaver, Allan 1937- *WhoAm 90, WhoE 91*
Beaver, Bonnie Veryle 1944- *WhoAm 90*
Beaver, Donavon F. 1935- *St&PR 91*
Beaver, Frank Eugene 1938- *WhoAm 90*
Beaver, Howard Oscar, Jr. 1925- *St&PR 91, WhoAm 90*
Beaver, Jack 1900-1963 *OxCPMus*
Beaver, James Scott 1950- *WhoSSW 91*
Beaver, Jeffrey Thorp 1937- *St&PR 91*
Beaver, Joseph H. 1933- *St&PR 91*
Beaver, Joseph Harley, Jr. 1945- *WhoSSW 91*
Beaver, Kerry Eugene 1963- *WhoSSW 91*
Beaver, Lester Albert 1923- *St&PR 91*
Beaver, Paul Chester 1905- *WhoAm 90*
Beaver, R. Pierce 1906-1987 *BioIn 16*
Beaver, Robert Lynn 1961- *WhoSSW 91*
Beaver, Robert Pierce 1906-1987 *BioIn 16*
Beaver, Stanley Henry 1907-1984 *DcNaB 1981*
Beaver, Thomas, Jr. 1923- *St&PR 91*
Beaver, William Henry 1940- *WhoAm 90*
Beaver, William Lee, Jr. 1917- *WhoWor 91*
Beaverbrook, Lord 1879-1964 *WorAlBi*
Beavers, Alvin Herman 1913- *WhoAm 90*
Beavers, Dorothy Anne Johnson 1927- *WhoE 91*
Beavers, Ellington McHenry 1916- *WhoAm 90*
Beavers, Gerald Reinhardt 1940- *WhoSSW 91*
Beavers, Louise 1902-1962 *DrBlPA 90*
Beavers, Patsy A. 1937- *WhoAmW 91*
Beavers, Robert Franklin 1933- *St&PR 91*
Beavers, Robert M., Jr. *BioIn 16*
Beavers, Roy L. 1930- *WhoSSW 91*
Beavers, Susan Jane 1945- *WhoAmW 91*
Beavers, William R 1929- *BiDrAPA 89*
Beaverson, Roger E. *St&PR 91*
Beaverson, Wayne A. 1924- *St&PR 91*
Beavoir, Simone de 1908-1986 *BioIn 16*
Beazer, Richard *St&PR 91*
Beazley, Brett Sherman 1939- *WhoSSW 91*
Beazley, Hamilton Scott 1943- *WhoAm 90*
Beazley, Johnny 1918- *Ballpl 90*
Beazley, Johnny 1918-1990 *BioIn 16*
Beazley, Kim Christian 1948- *WhoWor 91*
Beazley, William Henry, Jr. 1931- *St&PR 91*
Beban, Gary Joseph 1946- *WhoAm 90*
Bebbington, John 1925- *St&PR 91*
Bebbington, Warren Arthur 1952- *IntWWM 90, WhoWor 91*
Bebchick, Leonard Norman 1932- *WhoWor 91*
Bebchuk, William 1934- *BiDrAPA 89*
Bebee, Gary Richard 1946- *WhoEmL 91*
Bebee, Jim R. 1951- *St&PR 91*
Bebel, August 1840-1913 *BioIn 16*
Beber, Jorge Heriberto 1954- *BiDrAPA 89*
Beber, Robert H. 1933- *WhoAm 90*
Bebon, Robert E. 1943- *WhoE 91*
Bebout, Eli Daniel 1946- *St&PR 91*
Bebout, William Roach, Sr. 1955- *WhoSSW 91*
Becaud, Gilbert 1927- *OxCPMus*
Beccafumi 1486?-1551? *IntDcAA 90*
Beccali, Luigi *NewYTBS 90*
Beccari, Arrigo *BioIn 16*
Beccari, Nancy Hall Hiers *WhoAmW 91*
Beccatelli, Theresa Cecilia 1949- *WhoE 91*
Becchetti, Frederick Daniel, Jr. 1943- *WhoAm 90*
Beccue, Diana Lynn 1955- *WhoEmL 91*
Becerra, Abel 1936- *WhoHisp 91*
Becerra, Felipe Edgardo 1958- *WhoHisp 91*
Becerra, Francisco 1932- *WhoHisp 91*
Becerra, Francisco J., Jr. 1961- *WhoHisp 91*
Becerril, Francisco 1500?-1573 *PenDiDA 89*
Bech, Douglas York 1945- *WhoSSW 91*
Bech, Inge V. 1912- *WhoWor 91*
Bechara, Jose A., Jr. 1944- *WhoHisp 91*
Bechaud, Robert L. 1943- *St&PR 91*
Becher, Edmund Theodore 1904- *WhoWor 91*
Becher, Elaine Marie *BiDrAPA 89*
Becher, Harold T 1934- *BiDrAPA 89*
Becher, Kurt 1909- *BioIn 16*
Becher, N.E.H. 1932- *St&PR 91*
Becher, Nancy Ann Klopp 1931- *WhoAmW 91*
Becher, Paul Ronald 1934- *WhoAm 90, WhoWrEP 89*
Becher, Sheldon Herbert 1929- *St&PR 91*
Becher, William Don 1929- *WhoAm 90*
Becherer, Deborah Zorn 1958- *WhoAmW 91, WhoEmL 91*
Becherer, Hans Walter 1935- *St&PR 91, WhoAm 90*
Bechert, Heinz Helmut 1932- *WhoWor 91*
Bechet, Sidney *BioIn 16*
Bechet, Sidney 1897-1959 *DrBlPA 90, OxCPMus, WorAlBi*
Bechi, Gino 1913- *IntWWM 90*
Bechily, Maria Concepcion 1949- *WhoHisp 91*
Bechler, Edwin Christopher 1913- *St&PR 91*
Bechler, Richard Wells 1938- *St&PR 91*
Bechly, Paul Lorin 1958- *WhoEmL 91*
Bechor, Isac I *BiDrAPA 89*
Bechstein, Ludwig 1801-1860 *AuBYP 90*
Becht, Edward F. 1930- *St&PR 91*
Becht, Hermann 1939- *IntWWM 90*
Becht, Richard Paul 1933- *St&PR 91*
Bechtel, H. Robert 1949- *St&PR 91*
Bechtel, John Frederick 1914- *WhoSSW 91*
Bechtel, Laura Meadows 1963- *WhoSSW 91*
Bechtel, Philipp Karl Heinrich 1935- *WhoWor 91*
Bechtel, Riley *WhoAm 90*
Bechtel, Robert C. 1924- *St&PR 91*
Bechtel, Ronald W. 1903- *St&PR 91*
Bechtel, Stephen 1900-1989 *AnObit 1989*
Bechtel, Stephen D., Jr. 1925- *St&PR 91*
Bechtel, Stephen Davison 1900-1989 *BioIn 16*
Bechtel, Stephen Davison, Jr. 1925- *WhoAm 90, WhoWor 91*
Bechtel, Warren R. 1936- *ODwPR 91*
Bechtholdt, Henry W. 1933- *WhoAm 90*
Bechtle, C Ronald 1924- *WhoAmA 91*
Bechtle, Louis Charles 1927- *WhoAm 90*
Bechtle, Robert Alan 1932- *WhoAm 90, WhoAmA 91*
Bechtol, William Milton 1931- *WhoAm 90*
Bechtold, Donald William 1954- *BiDrAPA 89*
Bechtold, Grace *BioIn 16*
Bechtold, Kimball John 1947- *WhoE 91*
Bechtold, Susan Hatfield 1948- *WhoSSW 91*
Becich, Raymond Brice 1945- *WhoE 91*
Beck, Aaron T 1921- *BiDrAPA 89*
Beck, Aaron Temkin 1921- *WhoAm 90*
Beck, Abe Jack 1914- *WhoAm 90*
Beck, Adrian Robert 1932- *WhoAm 90*
Beck, Alan M 1942- *WhoWrEP 89*
Beck, Albert 1928- *St&PR 91, WhoAm 90*
Beck, Allen Earl 1937- *IntWWM 90*
Beck, Anatole 1930- *WhoAm 90*
Beck, Andrew James 1948- *WhoE 91, WhoEmL 91, WhoWor 91*
Beck, Anna Nadine 1922- *WhoAmW 91*
Beck, Art *WhoWrEP 89*
Beck, Audrey 1954- *WhoAmW 91*
Beck, B. Michael 1961- *WhoWor 91*
Beck, Beatrix 1914- *EncCoWW*
Beck, Bethany Ann 1948- *St&PR 91*
Beck, Boom-Boom 1904-1987 *Ballpl 90*
Beck, Brenda Faye 1952- *WhoAmW 91*
Beck, Brent Allen 1958- *WhoEmL 91*
Beck, Bruce *ODwPR 91*
Beck, Burt *BioIn 16, NewYTBS 90*
Beck, C. C. 1910-1989 *AnObit 1989, BioIn 16, EncACom [port], WorAlBi*
Beck, Carl A. 1917- *St&PR 91*
Beck, Charles E 1921- *BiDrAPA 89*
Beck, Charles W., Jr. *St&PR 91*
Beck, Christopher Alan 1953- *WhoEmL 91*
Beck, Clyde 1902- *Ballpl 90*
Beck, Conrad 1901- *IntWWM 90*
Beck, Curt Werner 1927- *WhoAm 90*
Beck, Cynthia A.S. 1949- *WhoAmW 91*
Beck, Daniel Edward 1960- *WhoSSW 91*
Beck, Daniel James 1948- *WhoEmL 91*
Beck, David A. 1953- *St&PR 91*
Beck, David C. 1942- *St&PR 91*
Beck, Donald R., Jr. 1955- *St&PR 91*
Beck, Doreen 1935- *WhoAmA 91, WhoE 91*
Beck, Doris Jean *WhoAmW 91*
Beck, Dorothy Amelia 1928- *WhoE 91*
Beck, Dorothy Fahs *WhoAmW 91, WhoE 91*
Beck, Earl Ray 1916- *WhoAm 90, WhoSSW 91*
Beck, Edward Henry, III 1950- *WhoEmL 91*
Beck, Edward W. 1944- *St&PR 91*
Beck, Edward William 1944- *WhoAm 90*
Beck, Eileen M. 1941- *St&PR 91*
Beck, Elizabeth *ODwPR 91*
Beck, Ellen Hackett 1961- *ODwPR 91*
Beck, Emil *BioIn 16*
Beck, Eric Robert 1934- *WhoWor 91*
Beck, Eugen Alexander 1933- *WhoWor 91*
Beck, Felix M. 1926- *St&PR 91*
Beck, Frances Josephine Mottey 1918- *WhoWor 91*
Beck, Frances Patricia *WhoE 91*
Beck, Fred 1886-1962 *Ballpl 90*
Beck, Frederick Allan 1946- *IntWWM 90*
Beck, George Eugene 1926- *St&PR 91*
Beck, George L. 1937- *St&PR 91*
Beck, George Preston 1930- *WhoSSW 91, WhoWor 91*
Beck, George William 1921- *WhoAm 90*
Beck, H. Thomas *WhoAm 90*
Beck, Hanno 1923- *WhoWor 91*
Beck, Harry *ConAu 31NR*
Beck, Heinrich 1929- *WhoWor 91*
Beck, Henry Lawrence 1923- *St&PR 91*
Beck, Henry M., Jr. 1951- *WhoEmL 91*
Beck, Howard Fred 1928- *St&PR 91*
Beck, Hubert Park 1907-1989 *BioIn 16*
Beck, Irwin Y. 1924- *St&PR 91*
Beck, Isabel 1898-1990 *BioIn 16*
Beck, J. Edward, Jr. 1948- *St&PR 91*
Beck, James 1930- *WhoAmA 91*
Beck, James Beck 1930- *WhoWrEP 89*
Beck, James C *BiDrAPA 89*
Beck, James Carl 1939- *St&PR 91*
Beck, James H. 1925- *St&PR 91*
Beck, James P. 1941- *St&PR 91*
Beck, Jan Scott 1955- *WhoEmL 91*

Beck, Jay Vern 1912- WhoAm 90
Beck, Jeff 1944- ConMus 4 [port], EncPR&S 89
Beck, Jeffrey C. BioIn 16
Beck, Jeffrey Haines 1949- WhoEmL 91
Beck, Joan Wagner 1923- WhoAm 90, WhoAmW 91, WhoWrEP 89
Beck, Joe BioIn 16
Beck, Joe Eugene 1947- WhoSSW 91
Beck, John Albert 1925- WhoAm 90
Beck, John Christian 1924- WhoAm 90
Beck, John LeRoy 1947- WhoEmL 91
Beck, John Paul BiDrAPA 89
Beck, Joseph James 1946- WhoEmL 91
Beck, K. K. TwCCr&M 91
Beck, Keith Lindell 1946- WhoEmL 91
Beck, Leah 1919- BiDrAPA 89
Beck, Lily Adams FemiCLE
Beck, Lily Yallourakis 1929- WhoE 91
Beck, Lisa 1928- BioIn 16
Beck, Livia Grunwald BiDrAPA 89
Beck, Livia Grunwald 1947- WhoE 91
Beck, Lonnie Lee 1942- WhoAmA 91
Beck, Lowell Richard 1934- WhoAm 90
Beck, Mae Lucille 1936- WhoAmW 91
Beck, Manfred Herman Josef 1943- WhoE 91
Beck, Margaret BiDEWW
Beck, Margit WhoAmA 91, WhoAmW 91
Beck, Marilyn Mohr 1928- WhoAm 90, WhoAmW 91
Beck, Marjorie Ruth 1956- WhoE 91, WhoEmL 91
Beck, Marshall G. 1944- St&PR 91
Beck, Martha 1900- IntWWM 90
Beck, Martha Ann 1938- WhoAmA 91
Beck, Martin BioIn 16
Beck, Martin L. BioIn 16
Beck, Mary Berenice 1890-1960 BioIn 16
Beck, Mary L. 1924- ConAu 131
Beck, Mortimer D 1937- BiDrAPA 89
Beck, Myrwood A. 1910- St&PR 91
Beck, Noelle BioIn 16
Beck, Norman Saul 1922- St&PR 91
Beck, Paul Adams 1908- WhoAm 90
Beck, Paul Allen 1944- WhoAm 90
Beck, Philip Rodney BiDrAPA 89
Beck, R. Albert 1919- St&PR 91
Beck, Raymond Edward 1939- WhoE 91
Beck, Rea B BiDrAPA 89
Beck, Robert Alfred 1920- WhoAm 90
Beck, Robert Arthur 1925- WhoAm 90
Beck, Robert Beryl 1935- WhoSSW 91
Beck, Robert Charles 1951- WhoE 91
Beck, Robert Holmes 1918- WhoAm 90
Beck, Robert Louis 1938- WhoAm 90
Beck, Robert N. BioIn 16
Beck, Robert Nelson 1924- WhoWrEP 89
Beck, Robert Randall 1940- St&PR 91
Beck, Robert W BiDrAPA 89
Beck, Roger D. 1936- St&PR 91
Beck, Roger Seaton 1921- WhoE 91
Beck, Roland Peter 1931- WhoAm 90
Beck, Ronnie Lee 1954- WhoSSW 91
Beck, Rosemarie 1924- WhoAm 90
Beck, Roy Howard BioIn 16
Beck, Sarah BiDEWW
Beck, Simone Simca 1904- WhoWor 91
Beck, Stanley Clifton 1929- WhoAm 90
Beck, Stanley Dwight 1919- WhoAm 90
Beck, Stephen Craig 1946- BiDrAPA 89
Beck, Stuart BioIn 16
Beck, Sydney 1906- IntWWM 90
Beck, Theresa 1953- WhoAmA 91
Beck, Thomas Edwin 1946- WhoEmL 91
Beck, Thomas Russell 1949- WhoAm 90
Beck, Timothy Daniel 1953- WhoEmL 91, WhoWor 91
Beck, William Harold, Jr. 1928- WhoSSW 91
Beck, William Lynn 1943- WhoE 91
Beck, William Samson 1923- WhoAm 90
Beckedorff, David Lawrence 1940- WhoAm 90
Beckel, Charles Leroy 1928- WhoAm 90
Beckel, George Louis 1932- St&PR 91
Beckelheimer, Christine Elizabeth C. 1916- WhoAmW 91, WhoSSW 91
Beckemeyer, Nancy Scott 1953- WhoEmL 91, WhoSSW 91
Beckemeyer, W.H. 1946- St&PR 91
Becken, Bradford Albert 1924- WhoAm 90
Becken, Garold Wallace 1953- WhoEmL 91
Beckenbach, W.S. 1912- St&PR 91
Beckenbach, William Charles 1937- St&PR 91
Beckenstein, Myron 1938- WhoAm 90, WhoWrEP 89
Becker, Allen Edward 1948- WhoE 91
Becker, Alvin 1930- BiDrAPA 89
Becker, Alvin Gerald 1938- St&PR 91
Becker, Anne W BiDrAPA 89
Becker, Arthur Frank 1905- St&PR 91
Becker, Beals 1886-1943 Ballpl 90
Becker, Benjamin J 1912- BiDrAPA 89
Becker, Beril 1901- AuBYP 90
Becker, Bernard William, Jr. 1926- St&PR 91
Becker, Betsy 1939- WhoAmW 91, WhoE 91, WhoWor 91
Becker, Bettie 1918- WhoAmA 91
Becker, Bettie Geraldine 1918- WhoAmW 91
Becker, Boris BioIn 16
Becker, Boris 1967- WhoAm 90, WhoWor 91, WorAlBi
Becker, Brandon 1954- WhoEmL 91
Becker, Bruce Carl, II 1948- WhoEmL 91
Becker, Carl E. 1938- St&PR 91
Becker, Carol Ann 1949- WhoAmW 91
Becker, Craig Stevens 1952- WhoEmL 91
Becker, Daniel Francis 1955- BiDrAPA 89
Becker, Daniel Franklin BiDrAPA 89
Becker, Daniel Frome 1955- WhoEmL 91
Becker, David 1937- WhoAmA 91
Becker, David Alan 1964- St&PR 91, WhoEmL 91
Becker, David Bruce 1953- WhoWor 91
Becker, David Leigh 1960- WhoEmL 91
Becker, David Mandel 1935- WhoAm 90
Becker, David Manning 1949- WhoEmL 91
Becker, Deborah R. 1960- ODwPR 91
Becker, Don C. 1933- St&PR 91
Becker, Don Crandall 1933- WhoAm 90
Becker, Donald Eugene 1923- WhoAm 90
Becker, Donna Marie 1942- WhoAmW 91
Becker, Douglas Wesley 1950- WhoSSW 91
Becker, Dwight Lowell 1918- WhoAm 90
Becker, E. Allen 1938- St&PR 91
Becker, Edward A. 1938- WhoSSW 91, WhoWor 91
Becker, Edward Roy 1933- WhoAm 90
Becker, Edwin Demuth 1930- WhoAm 90
Becker, Edwin F. 1946- St&PR 91
Becker, Edwin H. 1910- St&PR 91
Becker, Elaine Wellman 1942- WhoE 91
Becker, Elizabeth BioIn 16
Becker, Eric David BiDrAPA 89
Becker, Eric Jay 1960- WhoE 91
Becker, Erich Peter 1939- St&PR 91, WhoAm 90
Becker, Eugene BiDrAPA 89
Becker, Frank W. 1931- St&PR 91
Becker, Fred Reinhardt, Jr. 1949- WhoEmL 91
Becker, Frederick Fenimore 1931- WhoAm 90, WhoSSW 91
Becker, G. Ted 1944- St&PR 91
Becker, Gary Michael 1958- WhoEmL 91
Becker, Gary Stanley 1930- WhoAm 90
Becker, George A. ODwPR 91
Becker, George J 1908-1989 ConAu 130
Becker, George J. 1916- St&PR 91
Becker, George Joseph 1908- WhoWrEP 89
Becker, George Joseph 1908-1989 BioIn 16
Becker, George Raymond 1931- St&PR 91, WhoAm 90
Becker, Gerhard 1938- WhoWor 91
Becker, Glenn Edward 1948- St&PR 91
Becker, Gunther 1924- IntWWM 90
Becker, H. Merrill, Jr. 1938- St&PR 91
Becker, Hans Richard 1936- WhoWor 91
Becker, Hayward Charles 1924- WhoAm 90
Becker, Heber W, Jr. 1935- BiDrAPA 89
Becker, Heinz 1922- IntWWM 90
Becker, Herman Eli 1910- WhoSSW 91
Becker, Herman F. 1907-1985 BioIn 16
Becker, Howard Edward 1954- St&PR 91
Becker, Howard Saul 1928- BioIn 16
Becker, Hugh Alwyn, Jr. 1948- WhoSSW 91
Becker, Hugo 1863-1941 PenDiMP
Becker, Isidore A. 1926- WhoAm 90, WhoWor 91
Becker, Ivan 1948- WhoEmL 91
Becker, Jamee BioIn 16
Becker, James Elias 1944- BiDrAPA 89
Becker, James W. 1942- St&PR 91
Becker, Jean 1833-1884 PenDiMP
Becker, Jerry 1929- St&PR 91
Becker, Jill B. 1952- WhoEmL 91
Becker, Joachim BioIn 16
Becker, Joel Mark 1945- St&PR 91
Becker, Johanna Lucille 1921- WhoAmA 91
Becker, John 1943- St&PR 91
Becker, John A. 1942- St&PR 91
Becker, John Leonard 1901- AuBYP 90
Becker, Joseph 1923- WhoAm 90
Becker, Joseph Scott 1950- WhoE 91
Becker, Joshua A. 1932- WhoAm 90
Becker, Julie A. Taylor 1961- WhoAmW 91
Becker, Julius 1919- St&PR 91
Becker, Jurek 1937- BioIn 16, WorAu 1980 [port]
Becker, Jurgen 1932- WhoWor 91
Becker, Karl Martin 1943- WhoAm 90
Becker, Kenneth Arthur 1946- WhoEmL 91
Becker, Kenneth Melvin 1948- WhoEmL 91
Becker, Kenneth Richard 1947- WhoEmL 91
Becker, Larry Wayne 1946- WhoEmL 91
Becker, Lawrence M. 1955- St&PR 91
Becker, Lee Howard BiDrAPA 89
Becker, Leon BioIn 16
Becker, Leon Henry 1928- St&PR 91
Becker, Leslaw Edward 1946- WhoWor 91
Becker, Lydia 1827-1890 FemiCLE
Becker, Lydia Ernestine 1827-1890 BioIn 16
Becker, Magdalene Neuenschwander 1915- WhoAmW 91
Becker, Marie G. 1955- WhoHisp 91
Becker, Marie Grace 1926- St&PR 91
Becker, Marilyn R. BioIn 16
Becker, Marshall Hilford 1940- WhoAm 90
Becker, Marvin Burton 1922- WhoAm 90
Becker, Marvin Oren 1930- St&PR 91
Becker, Mary Louise WhoAm 90, WhoAmW 91, WhoE 91, WhoWor 91
Becker, Max 1906- St&PR 91
Becker, Michael Lewis 1940- WhoAm 90
Becker, Michael M. BioIn 16
Becker, Michael Wynne 1937- St&PR 91
Becker, Nancy Scott BiDrAPA 89
Becker, Naomi WhoAmA 91N
Becker, Natalie Harriton WhoE 91
Becker, Natalie Rose WhoAmA 91
Becker, Norman H. 1937- St&PR 91
Becker, Olga Agatha 1909- WhoAmW 91
Becker, Paul Albert 1939- WhoWor 91
Becker, Paul Irwin 1930- WhoE 91
Becker, Paula Modersohn- 1876-1907 BioIn 16
Becker, Philip L 1912- BiDrAPA 89
Becker, Philip Michael 1952- BiDrAPA 89
Becker, Quinn Henderson 1930- WhoAm 90
Becker, Ralph Edward 1931- St&PR 91, WhoE 91
Becker, Ralph Elihu 1907- WhoAm 90
Becker, Ralph Elihu, Jr. 1952- WhoEmL 91
Becker, Randall B. 1942- St&PR 91
Becker, Randall Biehl 1942- WhoAm 90
Becker, Raymond J. 1905- St&PR 91
Becker, Rena BiDrAPA 89
Becker, Rex Louis 1913- WhoAm 90
Becker, Richard Charles 1931- WhoAm 90
Becker, Richard J. 1925- St&PR 91
Becker, Richard Stanley 1934- WhoAm 90
Becker, Robert 1954- St&PR 91
Becker, Robert A. 1920- WhoAm 90, WhoE 91
Becker, Robert B. 1949- St&PR 91
Becker, Robert C. 1941- St&PR 91
Becker, Robert Cappel 1941- WhoAm 90
Becker, Robert Clarence 1927- WhoAm 90
Becker, Robert E 1934- BiDrAPA 89
Becker, Robert Edward, III 1963- WhoE 91
Becker, Robert Eugene 1929- St&PR 91
Becker, Robert Eugene 1933- WhoAm 90
Becker, Robert Jerome 1922- WhoAm 90
Becker, Robert Joseph 1946- WhoEmL 91, WhoWor 91
Becker, Robert O 1923- EncO&P 3
Becker, Robert Otto 1923- WhoAm 90
Becker, Robert Richard 1923- WhoAm 90
Becker, Ronald Ivan 1942- St&PR 91
Becker, Ronald Leonard 1950- WhoE 91
Becker, Samuel 1903- WhoAm 90
Becker, Samuel Leo 1923- WhoAm 90
Becker, Samuella R. 1954- ODwPR 91
Becker, Sandra Neiman Hammer 1947- WhoEmL 91
Becker, Stanley R. BioIn 16
Becker, Stephen Edward 1948- WhoE 91
Becker, Stephen William 1955- WhoEmL 91
Becker, Steven Allen WhoE 91
Becker, Susan Kaplan 1948- WhoAmW 91
Becker, Suzette Toledano 1955- WhoEmL 91
Becker, Suzy 1962- WhoE 91
Becker, Ted E 1922- BiDrAPA 89
Becker, Theo Redman 1921- WhoE 91
Becker, Thomas Richard 1939- St&PR 91
Becker, Ulrich 1930- WhoWor 91
Becker, Walter Edward 1935- St&PR 91
Becker, Wesley Clemence 1928- WhoAm 90
Becker, Wilhelm 1947- WhoWor 91
Becker, William Clifford 1948- St&PR 91
Becker, William Henry 1909- WhoAm 90
Becker, William Watters 1943- WhoAm 90
Becker, Wolf-Dieter 1922- WhoWor 91
Becker-Carus, Christian 1936- WhoWor 91
Becker-Glauch, Irmgard 1914- IntWWM 90
Becker-Lewke, Laura Virginia 1955- WhoEmL 91
Becker-Roukas, Helane Renee 1957- WhoE 91, WhoEmL 91
Beckerdite, A.D. 1926- St&PR 91
Beckerman, Bernard 1921- WhoWrEP 89
Beckerman, Murray 1924- St&PR 91
Beckerman, Nancy Greyson WhoAmA 91
Beckerman, Nancy Greyson 1943- WhoE 91
Beckermann, Carol 1946- WhoSSW 91
Beckers, Carl L.A. 1907- St&PR 91
Beckers, William K. BioIn 16
Beckert, Glenn 1940- Ballpl 90
Beckert, John Francis 1940- St&PR 91
Becket, George C. 1901-1990 BioIn 16
Becket, Henry S A ConAu 31NR
Beckett, Alexandra 1954- BiDrAPA 89
Beckett, Eugene Francis 1929- WhoE 91
Beckett, Grace 1912- WhoAmW 91
Beckett, Henry S.A. WhoWrEP 89
Beckett, J. Overton 1927- St&PR 91
Beckett, John Angus 1916- WhoAm 90
Beckett, John Douglas 1938- St&PR 91, WhoAm 90
Beckett, John R. 1918- St&PR 91
Beckett, Samuel 1906-1989 AnObit 1989, BioIn 16, ConAu 130, -33NR, ConLC 59 [port], CurBio 90N, DcLB Y90N [port], MajTwCW, News 90, WorAlBi, WrPh
Beckett, Stewart Winfield, III 1957- WhoEmL 91
Beckett, Susan Kay 1948- WhoAmW 91
Beckett, Theodore Charles 1929- WhoAm 90, WhoWor 91
Beckett, Theodore Cornwall 1952- WhoEmL 91, WhoWor 91
Beckett, Thomas L. 1953- WhoWrEP 89
Beckett, William Wade 1928- WhoAm 90
Beckey, Samuel Scott 1958- WhoE 91
Beckey, Sylvia Louise 1946- WhoAm 90, WhoAmW 91, WhoE 91, WhoEmL 91
Beckfeld, William Francis 1933- St&PR 91
Beckford, Ernest Raul 1958- WhoEmL 91
Beckford, William 1760-1844 BioIn 16
Beckham, Edgar Frederick 1933- WhoAm 90
Beckham, Gaynelle Mathews 1944- WhoAmW 91
Beckham, Howard Richard, Jr. 1955- WhoSSW 91
Beckham, James Charles 1953- WhoEmL 91
Beckham, John Crepps Wickliffe 1869-1940 AmLegL
Beckham, Paul Dearmin 1943- St&PR 91
Beckham, Richard F. 1936- St&PR 91
Beckham, Stephen Andrew 1959- WhoSSW 91
Beckham, William Arthur 1927- WhoAm 90
Beckham, William J., Jr. 1941- ODwPR 91
Beckham-Burnett, Susan Gay 1956- WhoAmW 91
Beckhard, Arthur J. AuBYP 90
Beckhard, Herbert 1926- WhoAm 90
Beckhardt, Robert Michael 1948- BiDrAPA 89
Beckius, Larry V. 1934- St&PR 91
Beckjord, Jon Erik 1951- WhoEmL 91
Becklake, Margaret Rigsby 1922- WhoAm 90
Beckler, David Zander 1918- WhoAm 90
Beckley, Bill 1946- WhoAmA 91
Beckley, Donald K. 1916- WhoAm 90
Beckley, Frederick William 1874-1943 AmLegL
Beckley, Jake 1867-1918 Ballpl 90 [port]
Beckley, Jay Charles 1928- St&PR 91
Beckley, John Luther 1913- St&PR 91
Beckley, Michael John 1942- WhoAm 90
Beckley, Richard D. 1935- St&PR 91
Beckley, Robert Howard 1920- WhoSSW 91
Beckman, Arnold Orville 1900- BioIn 16, St&PR 91, WhoAm 90
Beckman, Arthur Herman 1930- St&PR 91
Beckman, Delores 1914- BioIn 16
Beckman, Dennis Donald 1952- WhoEmL 91
Beckman, Donald 1932- WhoAm 90, WhoE 91
Beckman, E. Mark 1935-1989 BioIn 16
Beckman, Ericka 1951- WhoAmA 91, WhoE 91
Beckman, Frank Samuel 1921- WhoE 91
Beckman, Gail McKnight 1938- WhoAm 90
Beckman, Hester Finke WhoE 91
Beckman, Irving C. 1908- St&PR 91
Beckman, James Wallace Bim 1936- WhoWor 91
Beckman, Jean Catherine 1951- WhoAmW 91
Beckman, John BioIn 16
Beckman, John 1898?-1989 ConTFT 8
Beckman, John Stephen 1936- WhoAm 90
Beckman, Joseph Alfred 1937- WhoSSW 91
Beckman, Judith 1951- WhoAmW 91
Beckman, Judith Kalb 1940- WhoAmW 91, WhoE 91, WhoWor 91

Beckman, Kenneth Oren 1948- WhoEmL 91
Beckman, Kenneth W. 1918- St&PR 91
Beckman, Martin J. 1940- St&PR 91
Beckman, Mort M. 1944- WhoSSW 91
Beckman, Penny Elizabeth 1949- WhoAmW 91
Beckman, Pierina Elizabeth 1958- WhoSSW 91
Beckman, Robert 1949- St&PR 91
Beckman, Stan 1931- BioIn 16
Beckman, Vincent H. 1915- St&PR 91
Beckman, William BioIn 16
Beckmann, Bill 1907- Ballpl 90
Beckmann, Emma 1888- BioIn 16
Beckmann, George M. 1926- WhoAm 90
Beckmann, John 1960- WhoAmA 91
Beckmann, Jon Michael 1936- WhoAm 90
Beckmann, Judith 1935- IntWWM 90
Beckmann, Max 1884-1950 IntDcAA 90 [port], WorAlBi
Beckmann, Michele Lillian 1957- WhoAmW 91
Beckmann, Petr 1924- WhoAm 90
Beckmann, Robert Bader 1918- WhoAm 90
Beckmeyer, Harold Edward 1920- St&PR 91
Beckmeyer, Henry Ernest 1939- WhoWor 91
Becknell, Patricia Ann 1950- WhoEmL 91
Becknell, William 1787?-1856 BioIn 16
Becknell, William 1796?-1865 WorAlBi
Beckner, Donald Lee 1939- WhoAm 90
Beckner, Morton Orvan 1928- WhoAm 90
Beckon, Weir Emil 1938- St&PR 91
Becksford, Dennis 1955- St&PR 91
Beckson, Mace 1959- BiDrAPA 89
Beckstead, Richard L. 1929- St&PR 91
Beckstead, Robert Dale 1959- WhoWrEP 89
Beckstrom, John Michael Smith 1952- WhoSSW 91
Becktell, William E. 1933- St&PR 91
Beckum, Leonard Charles 1937- WhoAm 90
Beckwith, Barbara Jean 1948- WhoAmW 91
Beckwith, Catherine S. 1958- WhoAmW 91
Beckwith, Charles Emilio 1917- WhoAm 90
Beckwith, Charles Gates 1921- WhoAm 90
Beckwith, Christopher I. 1945- WhoWrEP 89
Beckwith, David WhoAm 90
Beckwith, David R. 1956- ODwPR 91
Beckwith, Don L. 1946- St&PR 91
Beckwith, Elizabeth BiDEWW
Beckwith, Hannah 1667- BiDEWW
Beckwith, Henry Hopkins 1935- St&PR 91, WhoAm 90, WhoSSW 91, WhoWor 91
Beckwith, Herbert L. 1903- WhoAm 90, WhoWor 91
Beckwith, James 1907- WhoAmA 91N
Beckwith, James S., III 1932- St&PR 91
Beckwith, Jim 1800?-1866? WhNaAH
Beckwith, Joe 1955- Ballpl 90
Beckwith, John 1902-1956 Ballpl 90
Beckwith, John 1927- IntWWM 90, WhoAm 90
Beckwith, John Charles 1941- St&PR 91
Beckwith, Jonathan Roger 1935- WhoAm 90
Beckwith, Lewis Daniel 1948- WhoEmL 91
Beckwith, Merle Ray 1942- WhoWrEP 89
Beckwith, Rodney Fisk 1935- St&PR 91, WhoE 91, WhoWor 91
Beckwith, Samuel PenDiDA 89
Beckwith, William Hunter 1896- WhoAm 90
Beckwith, William L. 1926- St&PR 91
Beckwitt, Morris C 1906- BiDrAPA 89
Beckworth, John Barney 1958- WhoEmL 91
Beckwourth, James Pierson 1800?-1866? WhNaAH
Becnel, Philip Alfred, III 1942- WhoSSW 91
Becofsky, Arthur Luke 1950- WhoAm 90
Becquer, Gustavo Adolfo 1836-1870 BioIn 16
Becquer, Julio 1931- Ballpl 90
Becquerel, Antoine Henri 1852-1908 WorAlBi
Becquerel, Jean Antoine Edmond Marie 1878-1953 DcScB S2
Becraft, Frank Joseph 1943- St&PR 91, WhoAm 90
Bectel, Maurice Quinn 1935- WhoE 91
Becton, A. James 1936- St&PR 91
Becton, Henry Prentiss, Jr. 1943- WhoAm 90, WhoE 91
Becton, Julius Wesley, Jr. 1926- WhoAm 90
BecVar, Bruce NewAgMG
Beda, Bruce A. 1940- St&PR 91
Bedacht, Max EncAL
Bedacier-Durand, Catherine 1650?-1714 EncCoWW
Bedard, Joel 1953- BiDrAPA 89
Bedard, Mark D. 1956- St&PR 91
Bedard, Mylene BiDrAPA 89
Bedard, Patrick Joseph 1941- WhoAm 90, WhoWrEP 89
Bedard, Peter C. 1945- ODwPR 91
Bedard, Pierre-Michel 1955- IntWWM 90
Bedard, R. Richard 1943- St&PR 91
Bedard, Raymond R. 1954- St&PR 91
Bedarf, George Eugene 1951- WhoE 91
Bedaske, Angela Margaret 1961- WhoAmW 91, WhoE 91, WhoWor 91
Bedau, Hugo Adam 1926- WhoAm 90
Beddall, Thomas Henry 1922- WhoAm 90
Beddingfield, John Jefferson BiDrAPA 89
Beddoe-Stephens, Clive 1943- St&PR 91
Beddoes, Thomas Lovell 1803-1849 DcLB 96 [port]
Beddome, John Macdonald 1930- WhoAm 90
Beddow, David P. 1943- St&PR 91, WhoAm 90
Beddow, Jack W. 1921- St&PR 91
Beddow, John Warren 1952- WhoEmL 91
Beddow, Margery BioIn 16
Beddow, Thomas John 1914- WhoAm 90
Bede, the Venerable 672?-735 WorAlBi
Bede, Jim BioIn 16
Bede, Sylvesta WhoWrEP 89
Bedeaux, Linda Lu 1956- WhoWrEP 89
Bedeian, Arthur George 1946- WhoAm 90
Bedelia, Bonnie 1948- WhoAm 90, WorAlBi
Bedell, Alan Nichols 1954- BiDrAPA 89
Bedell, Catherine May WhoAm 90, WhoAmW 91
Bedell, David Thorpe 1938- BiDrAPA 89
Bedell, Doris Elizabeth 1938- WhoE 91
Bedell, George Chester 1928- WhoAm 90
Bedell, George Noble 1922- WhoAm 90
Bedell, Graysanne L. St&PR 91
Bedell, John J. 1934- St&PR 91
Bedell, Melody Joy Hammond 1956- IntWWM 90
Bedell, Ralph Clarion 1904- WhoAm 90, WhoWor 91
Bedell, Rowland Holbrook Smith 1934-1990 BioIn 16
Bedell, Thomas Walter 1950- St&PR 91
Bedell, William 1571-1642 BioIn 16
Bedenbaugh, Ameliann BiDrAPA 89
Bedenko, D Mitchell 1936- BiDrAPA 89
Bedenko, Dimitri Mitchell 1936- WhoE 91
Bederka, John Matthew 1928- St&PR 91
Bederson, Benjamin 1921- WhoAm 90
Bedeschini, Francesco PenDiDA 89
Bedewi, Elizabeth M. 1937- St&PR 91
Bedford, Amy Aldrich 1912- St&PR 91
Bedford, Anthony John 1943- WhoWor 91
Bedford, Brian 1935- WhoAm 90
Bedford, Clay Patrick, Sr. 1903- WhoAm 90
Bedford, Daniel Ross 1945- WhoEmL 91
Bedford, David 1937- IntWWM 90, PenDiMP A
Bedford, Donald J. BioIn 16
Bedford, Frances Murray IntWWM 90
Bedford, Francis 1816-1894 BioIn 16
Bedford, Gunning 1747-1812 BioIn 16
Bedford, Harry 1873-1939 OxCPMus
Bedford, J.J. 1950- St&PR 91
Bedford, Jean 1946- FemiCLE
Bedford, John Michael 1932- WhoAm 90
Bedford, John Russell, Duke of 1710-1771 BioIn 16
Bedford, Kenneth ConAu 31NR
Bedford, Madeleine Alann Peckham 1910- WhoAmW 91, WhoSSW 91
Bedford, Michael 1949- IntWWM 90
Bedford, Norman C. 1915- St&PR 91
Bedford, Norton Moore 1916- WhoAm 90
Bedford, Steuart 1939- PenDiMP
Bedford, Steuart John Rudolf 1939- IntWWM 90
Bedford, Sybille BioIn 16
Bedford, Sybille 1911- CurBio 90 [port], FemiCLE
Bedford, Virginia Mary 1951- WhoAmW 91
Bedford, William Purdy, Jr. 1944- WhoSSW 91
Bedi, Ashok R 1948- BiDrAPA 89
Bedi, Ashok Ramprakash 1948- WhoEmL 91
Bedi, Gopal Krishan 1945- BiDrAPA 89
Bedi, Joyce Elizabeth 1954- WhoE 91
Bedi, Sarjivan Singh 1934- WhoWor 91
Bedics, Lynn Fay 1947- WhoAmW 91
Bedient, Hugh 1889-1965 Ballpl 90
Bedingfield, Jack L. 1935- St&PR 91
Bedingfield, Robert E. BioIn 16
Bedini, Silvio A. 1917- WhoAm 90, WhoWrEP 89
Bedke, Ernest Alford 1934- WhoAm 90
Bedke, Kathryn Lynn 1951- WhoAmW 91
Bedlin, Dorothy Roberta 1951- WhoAmW 91
Bednall, Ian Lindsay IntWWM 90
Bednar, Carolyn Diane 1953- WhoAmW 91, WhoEmL 91
Bednar, Charles Sokol 1930- WhoAm 90
Bednar, James Edmund 1911- WhoAm 90
Bednar, Marlene Ann BiDrAPA 89
Bednar, Michael John 1942- WhoSSW 91
Bednar, Rudy Gerard 1951- WhoWor 91
Bednar, Tomi Michelle 1959- WhoEmL 91
Bednarek, Alexander Robert 1933- WhoAm 90
Bednarek, Jana Maria 1934- WhoAmW 91, WhoWor 91
Bednarski, Dennis A. 1947- St&PR 91
Bednarski, Theodore Mark 1942- WhoAm 90
Bednarz, Gene Marion 1925- St&PR 91
Bednarz, James Cary 1953- WhoE 91
Bednarz, Susan Clare 1955- WhoAmW 91, WhoEmL 91
Bednorz, J. Georg 1950- WhoAm 90, WhoWor 91
Bedol, Alan P. 1925- St&PR 91
Bedol, Marshall Theodore 1925- St&PR 91
Bedoukian, Kerop 1907-1981 BioIn 16
Bedoya, Alberto St&PR 91
Bedoya, Consuelo WhoHisp 91
Bedoya, Jaime BiDrAPA 89
Bedoya, Roberto Eligio 1951- WhoHisp 91
Bedoya Reyes, Luis 1919- BioIn 16
Bedregal de Conitzer, Yolanda 1918- WhoWor 91
Bedregal Gutierrez, Guillermo WhoWor 91
Bedrich, Curtis Allen 1942- St&PR 91
Bedrij, Orest 1933- St&PR 91
Bedrij, Orest, Jr. 1958- St&PR 91
Bedrij, Orest J. 1933- WhoE 91
Bedrin, David Paul BiDrAPA 89
Bedrosian, Edward 1922- WhoAm 90
Bedrosian, Edward Robert 1932- St&PR 91, WhoAm 90
Bedrosian, Samuel Der 1921- WhoAm 90
Bedrosian, Steve 1957- Ballpl 90, WhoAm 90
Bedrossian, Peter Stephen 1926- WhoWor 91
Bedsole, Ann Smith 1930- WhoAmW 91, WhoSSW 91
Bedson, Samuel Lawrence 1842-1891 DcCanB 12
Bedsworth, Gary Jay 1939- WhoSSW 91
Bedsworth, O. Diane 1942- WhoAmW 91
Bedway, Mariann Louise WhoAmW 91
Bedwell, Theodore Cleveland, Jr. 1909- WhoAm 90
Bedwell, William 1561?-1632 BioIn 16
Bedwell, William L 1916- BiDrAPA 89
Bee Gees, The EncPR&S 89, OxCPMus, WorAlBi
Bee, Clair Francis 1900-1983 AuBYP 90
Bee, Hamilton Proleau 1822-1877 AmLegL
Bee, Kevin Michael 1964- WhoE 91
Bee, Mary Rice 1933- WhoE 91
Bee, Robert Norman 1925- WhoAm 90
Beebe, Burdetta Faye 1920- AuBYP 90
Beebe, Cora Prifold 1937- WhoAm 90
Beebe, Curt 1936- BiDrAPA 89
Beebe, Diane Marie 1961- WhoAmW 91
Beebe, F. Lisa 1952- WhoWrEP 89
Beebe, Fred 1880-1957 Ballpl 90
Beebe, George H. NewYTBS 90
Beebe, George H. 1910-1990 BioIn 16
Beebe, Helen Hulick BioIn 16
Beebe, Herman K. BioIn 16
Beebe, Jack H. 1942- St&PR 91
Beebe, John E. 1923- St&PR 91
Beebe, John Eldridge 1923- WhoAm 90
Beebe, John Eliott, III 1939- BiDrAPA 89
Beebe, Joseph E. 1944- St&PR 91
Beebe, Leo Clair 1917- St&PR 91, WhoAm 90
Beebe, Lucius Morris 1902-1966 BioIn 16
Beebe, Mary Livingstone 1940- WhoAmA 91
Beebe, Mike 1946- WhoSSW 91
Beebe, Raymond Mark 1942- St&PR 91, WhoAm 90
Beebe, Richard Townsend 1902- WhoAm 90
Beebe, Robert H 1924- BiDrAPA 89
Beebe, Steven Arnold 1950- WhoSSW 91
Beebe, Susan Kay 1956- WhoEmL 91
Beebe, William 1877-1962 WorAlBi
Beebe, William Andrews 1935- WhoAm 90
Beebee, Alex M 1950- BiDrAPA 89
Beeber, Alan Roger 1946- BiDrAPA 89, WhoE 91
Beeby, Kenneth Jack 1936- St&PR 91, WhoAm 90
Beeby, Nell Viola 1896-1957 BioIn 16
Beeby, Thomas H. WhoAm 90
Beece, Debby BioIn 16
Beech, E. Martin 1950- WhoEmL 91
Beech, Gould BioIn 16
Beech, Johnny Gale 1954- WhoSSW 91
Beech, Keyes 1913- WhoE 91
Beech, Keyes 1913-1990 BioIn 16, ConAu 130, NewYTBS 90
Beech, Linda AuBYP 90
Beech, Olive Ann 1903- St&PR 91, WorAlBi
Beech, Olive Ann Mellor 1903- WhoAm 90
Beech, Thomas Foster 1939- WhoSSW 91
Beech, Walter H. 1891-1950 WorAlBi
Beech, Webb AuBYP 90
Beecham, Clayton Tremain 1907- WhoAm 90, WhoWor 91
Beecham, Paul Everett 1938- BiDrAPA 89
Beecham, Thomas 1879-1961 PenDiMP, WorAlBi
Beechcroft, William WhoWrEP 89
Beechcroft, William 1924- SpyFic
Beecher, Catharine 1800-1878 FemiCLE, NinCLC 30 [port]
Beecher, Catharine E. 1800-1878 BioAmW
Beecher, Catharine Esther 1800-1878 BioIn 16, WorAlBi
Beecher, Earl William 1947- St&PR 91
Beecher, Frederick H. 1841-1868 WhNaAH
Beecher, Graciela F. 1927- WhoHisp 91
Beecher, Henry Ward 1813-1887 BioIn 16, WorAlBi
Beecher, Lee Hewitt 1939- BiDrAPA 89
Beecher, Lyman 1775-1863 WorAlBi
Beecher, Robert William 1931- WhoAm 90
Beecher, Thomas Wylie 1958- WhoEmL 91
Beecher, William John 1914- WhoAm 90
Beecher, William Manuel 1933- WhoE 91
Beechey, Gwilym Edward 1938- IntWWM 90
Beeching, Charles Train, Jr. 1930- WhoAm 90
Beeching, Richard 1913-1985 DcNaB 1981
Beechler, Carol Dawn 1954- WhoSSW 91
Beechler, Sylvia Hart 1926- WhoAmW 91
Beecroft, Geoffrey Halls 1921- St&PR 91
Beecroft, Jack C. 1927- St&PR 91
Beecroft, John William Richard 1902-1966 AuBYP 90
Beecroft, William Thomas 1954- BiDrAPA 89
Beed, David James 1945- St&PR 91
Beeder, David Charles 1930- WhoE 91
Beeding, Francis SpyFic
Beeding, Francis 1885-1944 TwCCr&M 91
Beeding, Francis 1898-1951 TwCCr&M 91
Beedle, Dennis Dean BiDrAPA 89
Beedle, Lynn Simpson 1917- WhoAm 90
Beedles, William LeRoy 1948- WhoAm 90
Beeferman, Harvey L. 1942- St&PR 91
Beeghly, James Hugh L 1950- BiDrAPA 89
Beeghly, R. Thornton 1912- St&PR 91
Beehler, Bruce McPherson 1951- WhoE 91
Beehler, Michael Thomas 1950- WhoEmL 91
Beek, Barton 1924- St&PR 91
Beek, Jan Bontjes van 1899-1969 PenDiDA 89
Beekman, Carol ODwPR 91
Beekman, Philip Emmet 1931- St&PR 91
Beekman, William Bedloe 1949- WhoEmL 91
Beeks, Graydon Fisher, Jr. 1948- WhoEmL 91
Beeks, Michele Lynn 1953- WhoEmL 91
Beeks, Steven 1956- St&PR 91
Beeksma, B. R. BioIn 16
Beel, Robert Wayne 1952- St&PR 91
Beeler, Barbara Louise 1963- WhoAmW 91
Beeler, George BioIn 16
Beeler, Janet 1937- SmATA X [port]
Beeler, Joe 1931- WhoAmA 91
Beeler, Myrton Freeman 1922- WhoWrEP 89
Beeler, Nelson Frederick 1910- AuBYP 90
Beeler, Thomas J. 1933- St&PR 91
Beeler, Thomas Joseph 1933- WhoAm 90
Beeler, Thomas Taylor, III 1944- WhoAm 90, WhoE 91, WhoWrEP 89
Beeler, Warren Jennings 1932- WhoSSW 91
Beeley, Robert Alfred 1938- St&PR 91
Beelke, Ralph G 1917- WhoAmA 91N
Beels, Clemens C 1930- BiDrAPA 89
Beem, Jack Darrel 1931- WhoAm 90
Beem, Jane A. 1934- WhoWrEP 89
Beem, Jane Arlyne 1934- WhoAmW 91
Beem, John Kelly 1942- WhoAm 90, WhoWor 91
Beem, Randy Rae 1943- BiDrAPA 89
Beeman, John William 1940- St&PR 91
Beeman, Josiah Horton 1935- WhoE 91
Beeman, Keith R. 1915- St&PR 91
Beeman, Malinda 1949- WhoAmA 91
Beeman, Richard E. 1945- St&PR 91, WhoAm 90, WhoEmL 91
Beeman, Richard R. 1942- WhoAm 90

Beemon, Karen Louise 1947- *WhoE 91*
Beemsterboer, Cornelis Petrus 1939- *WhoWor 91*
Been, Harold 1939- *BiDrAPA 89*
Beene, Fred 1942- *Ballpl 90*
Beene, Geoffrey *BioIn 16*
Beene, Geoffrey 1927- *ConDes 90, WhoAm 90, WhoWor 91*
Beene, Geraldine Wallis 1931- *WhoAmW 91*
Beenen, Richard 1953- *WhoAmA 91*
Beeners, Wilbert John 1921- *WhoAm 90*
Beenstock, Raymond 1930- *St&PR 91*
Beeny, Robert Eugene 1927- *St&PR 91*
Beer, A.E. 1932- *St&PR 91*
Beer, Alan Earl 1937- *WhoAm 90*
Beer, Alice Stewart 1912- *WhoAmW 91*
Beer, Andrew Eilers 1932- *WhoAm 90*
Beer, Barrett Lynn 1936- *WhoAm 90*
Beer, Clara Louise Johnson 1918- *WhoAm 90*
Beer, Gillian Patricia 1935- *WhoWor 91*
Beer, Hans 1932- *WhoWor 91*
Beer, Jakob Liebmann 1791-1864 *BioIn 16*
Beer, Janos Miklos 1923- *WhoAm 90*
Beer, Jeanette Mary Ayres *WhoAm 90, WhoAmW 91*
Beer, Joseph Ernest 1959- *WhoEmL 91*
Beer, Kenneth E. *BioIn 16*
Beer, Kenneth John 1932- *WhoAmA 91*
Beer, Michael 1926- *WhoAm 90*
Beer, Murray L. 1928- *St&PR 91*
Beer, Otto F. 1910- *WhoWor 91*
Beer, Patricia *BioIn 16*
Beer, Patricia 1924- *FemiCLE*
Beer, Peter Hill 1928- *WhoAm 90, WhoSSW 91*
Beer, Reinhard 1935- *WhoAm 90*
Beer, Samuel Hutchison 1911- *ConAu 31NR*
Beer, Susan R. 1938- *ODwPR 91*
Beer, Timothy Brian 1959- *WhoEmL 91*
Beer, William Reed 1943- *ConAu 31NR*
Beerbohm, Max 1872-1956 *BioIn 16, DcLB 100 [port], WorAlBi*
Beerbower, Cynthia Gibson 1949- *WhoAmW 91*
Beere, Carole Ann 1944- *WhoAmW 91*
Beerel, Annabel Constance 1953- *WhoWor 91*
Beerer, Larry D. 1955- *WhoEmL 91*
Beering, Steven Claus 1932- *WhoAm 90, WhoWor 91*
Beerman, Bernard Marvin 1936- *WhoAm 90, WhoWor 91*
Beerman, Burton 1943- *IntWWM 90*
Beerman, Herbert 1926- *WhoAmA 91*
Beerman, Herman 1901- *WhoAm 90, WhoWrEP 89*
Beerman, Herman M *BiDrAPA 89*
Beerman, Miriam *WhoAmA 91, WhoE 91*
Beermann, Allen J. 1940- *WhoAm 90*
Beernaerts, Euphrosine 1831-1901 *BiDWomA*
Beernink, Darrell Wayne 1937- *WhoAm 90*
Beers, Anne Cole *WhoE 91*
Beers, Charlotte L. 1935- *WhoAm 90, WhoAmW 91*
Beers, Deborah Yardley 1954- *IntWWM 90*
Beers, Donald Osborne 1949- *WhoEmL 91*
Beers, Franklin Arthur 1919- *WhoAm 90, WhoWor 91*
Beers, George St. Clair 1933- *WhoSSW 91*
Beers, John William 1937- *St&PR 91*
Beers, Lonna Jane 1950- *WhoSSW 91*
Beers, Steven C. 1945- *St&PR 91*
Beers, Victor Gilbert 1928- *WhoAm 90, WhoWrEP 89*
Beers, William George 1841-1900 *DcCanB 12*
Beers, William O. 1914- *WhoAm 90*
Beerup, Robert Dale 1949- *WhoEmL 91*
Beery, Arthur O 1930- *WhoAmA 91*
Beery, Donald Thomas 1960- *WhoSSW 91*
Beery, Edwin N. 1910-1989 *BioIn 16*
Beery, Fred Jerome 1955- *WhoEmL 91*
Beery, Noah, Jr. 1916- *WorAlBi*
Beery, Roger Lewis, II 1957- *WhoEmL 91, WhoSSW 91, WhoWor 91*
Beery, Wallace 1889-1949 *WorAlBi*
Beery, Warren Gordon 1925- *WhoAm 90*
Beese, Hedda *BioIn 16*
Beese, Jane V. 1943- *St&PR 91*
Beesemyer, Fritz Timothy 1952- *WhoAm 90*
Beesley, Horace Brent 1946- *WhoAm 90*
Beesley, Kenneth Horace 1926- *WhoAm 90*
Beesley, Linda Holland 1951- *WhoEmL 91*
Beesley, Robert David 1935- *St&PR 91*
Beeson, Beth Ann 1951- *WhoSSW 91*
Beeson, Brant Robert 1951- *WhoEmL 91*
Beeson, Dorothy Patton 1921- *WhoAmW 91*
Beeson, George H. 1943- *St&PR 91*
Beeson, Jack Hamilton 1921- *IntWWM 90, WhoAm 90*
Beeson, John *WhNaAH*
Beeson, Montel Eileen 1939- *WhoAmW 91*
Beeson, Paul Bruce 1908- *WhoAm 90*
Beeson, W. Malcolm 1911-1988 *BioIn 16*
Beeson, William B. 1927- *St&PR 91*
Beeson, William Malcolm 1911-1988 *BioIn 16*
Beeston, Paul *WhoAm 90*
Beeth, Howard 1942- *WhoSSW 91*
Beetham, Stanley Williams 1933- *St&PR 91, WhoAm 90, WhoE 91, WhoWor 91*
Beethoven Quartet *PenDiMP*
Beethoven, Ludwig van 1770-1827 *BioIn 16, PenDiMP A, WorAlBi*
Beetler, Dianne Lynn 1951- *WhoWrEP 89*
Beeton, Alfred Merle 1927- *WhoAm 90*
Beeton, Isabella Mary Mayson 1836-1865 *BioIn 16*
Beets, Freeman Haley 1919- *WhoAm 90*
Beets, Latin Renee 1959- *WhoSSW 91*
Beetz, Carl Hugo 1911-1974 *WhoAmA 91N*
Beetz, Jean 1927- *WhoAm 90*
Beevers, Harry 1924- *WhoAm 90*
Beevor, Antony 1946- *ConAu 129*
Beezer, Robert Renaut 1928- *WhoAm 90*
Beffort, Anne 1880-1966 *EncCoWW*
Befoure, Jeannine Marie 1923- *WhoAmW 91, WhoWor 91*
Beg, M. Rashid 1949- *WhoE 91*
Beg, Mirza Abdul Baqi 1934-1990 *BioIn 16*
Beg, Nuzhat Rais *BiDrAPA 89*
Beg, Raihana Rizvi 1934- *BiDrAPA 89*
Bega, Melchiorre 1898-1976 *ConDes 90*
Begam, Robert George 1928- *WhoAm 90, WhoWor 91*
Begando, Joseph Sheridan 1921- *WhoAm 90*
Begas, Luise 1850- *BiDWomA*
Begas-Parmentier, Luise 1850- *BiDWomA*
Begbie, Matthew Baillie 1819-1894 *DcCanB 12*
Begel, Thomas M. 1942- *WhoAm 90*
Begell, William 1928- *WhoAm 90, WhoWrEP 89*
Begelman, Lee Reynolds *BioIn 16*
Begelman, Mitchell C. *WhoAm 90*
Beger, John David 1954- *WhoEmL 91*
Beger, Rudolf 1946- *WhoWor 91*
Begg, Alexander 1839-1897 *DcCanB 12*
Begg, Heather 1932- *IntWWM 90*
Begg, John Alfred 1903-1974 *WhoAmA 91N*
Begg, Karin Elisabet 1939- *WhoE 91*
Begg, Kathleen Mikel *WhoAmW 91*
Beggiani, Seely 1935- *WhoE 91*
Beggs, David Walker 1929- *WhoE 91*
Beggs, Harry Mark 1941- *WhoWor 91*
Beggs, James Montgomery 1926- *BioIn 16, WhoAm 90, WhoE 91*
Beggs, Joe 1910-1983 *Ballpl 90*
Beggs, Thomas Montague 1899-1990 *WhoAmA 91N*
Beggs, Veronica Doloures 1948- *WhoWor 91*
Beggs-Uema, Marck Lewis 1958- *WhoWrEP 89*
Beghe, Renato 1933- *WhoAm 90*
Beghini, Victor Gene 1934- *St&PR 91, WhoAm 90*
Begien, Martin 1928- *St&PR 91*
Begin, Bruce Hudson 1944- *WhoE 91*
Begin, Menachem 1913- *BioIn 16, PolLCME, WhoWor 91, WorAlBi*
Begin, Raymond F. 1939- *St&PR 91*
Begin, Robert 1925- *St&PR 91, WhoAm 90*
Begin, Roger Normand 1952- *WhoAm 90, WhoE 91*
Begin, Simon *BiDrAPA 89*
Beginin, Igor 1931- *WhoAmA 91*
Beglarian, Grant 1927- *IntWWM 90, WhoAm 90*
Begleiter, Alvin Leon 1933- *St&PR 91*
Begleiter, Martin David 1945- *WhoEmL 91*
Begley, Ed, Jr. 1949- *WhoAm 90, WorAlBi*
Begley, Evelyn Maria 1953- *WhoE 91, WhoEmL 91*
Begley, J 1947- *WhoAmA 91*
Begley, Kathleen A 1948- *WhoAmW 91*
Begley, Kevin Robert 1958- *St&PR 91*
Begley, Kim 1955- *IntWWM 90*
Begley, Louis 1933- *WhoAm 90*
Begley, Patrick Anthony 1932- *St&PR 91*
Begley, Robert William 1930- *St&PR 91*
Begley, Wayne E 1937- *WhoAmA 91*
Begley-Rotte, Kathryn E. 1956- *St&PR 91*
Begner, Edith *BioIn 16*
Begner, Edith 1918-1989 *ConAu 129*
Begnis, Giuseppe De *PenDiMP*
Begnis, Giuseppina Ronzi De *PenDiMP*
Bego, Jean *St&PR 91*
Begon, Elisabeth 1696-1755 *DcLB 99 [port]*
Begos, Jane Du Pree 1930- *WhoE 91*
Begov, Lucie *BioIn 16*
Begovic, Dijana *BiDrAPA 89*
Begovic, Miroslav Miodrag 1956- *WhoSSW 91*
Begovich, Michael 1959- *WhoEmL 91*
Begovich, Nicholas Anthony 1921- *WhoAm 90*
Begtrup, Robert Oscar 1942- *BiDrAPA 89*
Begue, John Samuel 1937- *St&PR 91*
Begue, Pierre-Charles 1939- *WhoWor 91*
Beguin, Bernard Auguste 1923- *WhoWor 91*
Beguin, Fred Paul 1909- *WhoAm 90*
Beguin, Hubert 1932- *WhoWor 91*
Beguin, Nancy Ellyn 1943- *WhoAmW 91*
Begun, Benson Harris 1932- *St&PR 91*
Begun, David Lawrence *BiDrAPA 89*
Begun, Norman W. 1942- *ODwPR 91*
Begun, Semi J. 1905- *St&PR 91*
Begun, Semi Joseph 1905- *WhoAm 90*
Beha, James J. 1916- *St&PR 91*
Beha, James Joseph 1916- *WhoAm 90*
Beha, Ralph Werner 1950- *WhoEmL 91*
Beham, Hans Sebald 1500-1550 *PenDiDA 89*
Behan, Brendan *BioIn 16*
Behan, Brendan 1923-1964 *ConAu 33NR, MajTwCW, WorAlBi*
Behan, Dominic 1928?-1989 *ConAu 129*
Behan, Edmund J. 1929- *St&PR 91*
Behan, Edmund Joseph 1929- *WhoAm 90*
Behan, Lawrence G *BiDrAPA 89*
Behan, Michael John 1946- *St&PR 91*
Behan, Robert C *BiDrAPA 89*
Behan, Robert F. 1933- *St&PR 91*
Behar, David 1951- *BiDrAPA 89*
Behar, Diane Susan 1952- *WhoAmW 91*
Behar, Leon Isidore 1956- *WhoEmL 91*
Behar, Lonny Jay 1958- *BiDrAPA 89*
Behar, Michael Stephan 1953- *BiDrAPA 89*
Beharriell, Frederick John 1918- *WhoAm 90*
Behbehani, Abbas M. 1925- *WhoAm 90*
Behham, John F. 1921- *St&PR 91*
Behl, Wolfgang 1918- *WhoAm 90, WhoAmA 91*
Behlen, Charles William 1949- *WhoWrEP 89*
Behlen, Herbert Peter 1909- *WhoAm 90*
Behler, Diana Ipsen 1938- *WhoAm 90*
Behling, Charles Frederick 1940- *WhoAm 90*
Behling, Dorothy Clara 1930- *WhoAmW 91, WhoWor 91*
Behling, George Rogers 1938- *St&PR 91*
Behling, J. Haigler 1931- *St&PR 91*
Behling, Mary Katherine 1954- *BiDrAPA 89*
Behlke, Charles Edward 1926- *WhoAm 90*
Behlmer, Rudy H., Jr. 1926- *WhoWor 91*
Behm, Brian Scott 1954- *WhoEmL 91*
Behm, Cynthia Joan 1962- *WhoAmW 91*
Behm, Edward L 1933- *St&PR 91*
Behm, Forrest E. 1919- *St&PR 91*
Behm, Forrest Edwin 1919- *WhoAm 90*
Behm, Richard H. 1948- *WhoWrEP 89*
Behm, Ronald Thomas 1938- *St&PR 91*
Behmer, Elsie A. 1943- *ODwPR 91*
Behmer, Elsie Ann 1943- *WhoAmW 91*
Behn, Aphra 1640?-1689? *BiDEWW, BioIn 16, FemiCLE, WorAlBi*
Behn, Arthur E. 1924- *St&PR 91*
Behn, Erik Jenserik 1936- *WhoWor 91*
Behn, Harry *BioIn 16*
Behn, Harry 1898-1973 *AuBYP 90*
Behn, Noel 1928- *ConAu 129, SpyFic, TwCCr&M 91*
Behn, Robert Dietrich 1941- *WhoWrEP 89*
Behn, Sally A. 1928- *St&PR 91*
Behn, Sosthenes 1882-1957 *WorAlBi*
Behne, Noel David 1936- *St&PR 91*
Behne, Thomas David 1931- *St&PR 91*
Behner, Janice Rose 1938- *WhoAmW 91*
Behney, Charles Augustus, Jr. 1929- *WhoWor 91*
Behnke, Bruce I. 1944- *St&PR 91*
Behnke, Carl Gilbert 1945- *St&PR 91, WhoAm 90, WhoEmL 91*
Behnke, Ernst-August 1943- *WhoWor 91*
Behnke, Harlan James 1929- *St&PR 91*
Behnke, James Ralph 1943- *St&PR 91*
Behnke, Leigh 1946- *WhoAmA 91, WhoE 91*
Behnke, Marylou 1950- *WhoAmW 91*
Behnke, Roy Herbert 1921- *WhoAm 90*
Behnke, Wallace Blanchard, Jr. 1926- *WhoAm 90, WhoSSW 91*
Behnke, William Alfred 1924- *WhoAm 90*
Behnke, William Charles, Jr. 1950- *WhoSSW 91*
Behr, Bruce Charles 1948- *BiDrAPA 89*
Behr, Edward Samuel 1926- *WhoWor 91*
Behr, Guenter Adolf 1938- *WhoWor 91*
Behr, Ira Steven 1953- *WhoEmL 91*
Behr, Jack Gardiner 1948- *WhoEmL 91*
Behr, Joseph Louis 1926- *St&PR 91*
Behr, Melissa Joan 1954- *WhoAmW 91*
Behr, Ralph Steven 1951- *St&PR 91*
Behr, Raymond Anthony 1948- *BiDrAPA 89, WhoE 91*
Behr, Richard Alan 1933- *St&PR 91*
Behr, Richard Henry 1942- *WhoAm 90, WhoE 91*
Behr, Shirley Kaye 1953- *WhoEmL 91*
Behrakis, George D. 1934- *St&PR 91*
Behre, Louis J. 1929- *ODwPR 91*
Behrenbeck, Julia Gage 1956- *WhoEmL 91*
Behrenbruch, William David 1946- *WhoEmL 91*
Behrend, Donald Fraser 1931- *WhoAm 90*
Behrend, Jeanne 1911-1988 *BioIn 16*
Behrend, Rona Ann 1959- *WhoAmW 91*
Behrend, Siegfried 1933- *IntWWM 90, PenDiMP*
Behrend, William Louis 1923- *WhoAm 90, WhoWor 91*
Behrends, Cynthia Joan 1961- *WhoAmW 91*
Behrends, Robert Williams 1947- *BiDrAPA 89*
Behrends, Wolfgang *BioIn 16*
Behrends, Wolfgang 1926- *WhoWor 91*
Behrendt, Bill Lee 1958- *WhoEmL 91*
Behrendt, David Frogner 1935- *WhoAm 90, WhoWrEP 89*
Behrendt, John Charles 1932- *WhoAm 90*
Behrendt, John Thomas 1945- *WhoAm 90, WhoEmL 91, WhoWor 91*
Behrendt, Lore *WhoE 91*
Behrendt, Theresa Elmore 1949- *WhoAm 90*
Behrens, Albert Paul 1934- *St&PR 91*
Behrens, Alfred J. 1915- *WhoAm 90*
Behrens, Berel Lyn 1940- *WhoAm 90, WhoAmW 91*
Behrens, Hildegard *BioIn 16, WorAlBi*
Behrens, Hildegard 1937- *IntWWM 90, PenDiMP, WhoAm 90, WhoWor 91*
Behrens, Jean Marie 1950- *WhoEmL 91*
Behrens, Jeffrey Marc 1951- *WhoSSW 91*
Behrens, June York 1925- *AuBYP 90*
Behrens, Laura Suzanne 1956- *WhoEmL 91*
Behrens, Mary Snyder 1957- *WhoAmA 91*
Behrens, Peter 1869-1940 *PenDiDA 89*
Behrens, Peter G. 1927- *St&PR 91*
Behrens, Richard John 1946- *WhoSSW 91*
Behrens, Robert H. 1923- *WhoAm 90*
Behrens, Roy R 1946- *WhoAmA 91*
Behrens, Rudolph 1953- *WhoE 91*
Behrens, Wayne C. 1956- *St&PR 91*
Behrens, William Blade 1956- *WhoSSW 91*
Behrens, William Carl 1951- *WhoSSW 91*
Behrensmeyer, J.H. 1957- *St&PR 91*
Behrhorst, Carroll 1922-1990 *BioIn 16*
Behrhorst, Lee D. 1941- *St&PR 91*
Behring, Emil A. Von 1854-1917 *WorAlBi*
Behring, Kenneth E. 1928- *WhoAm 90*
Behringer, Scott Martin 1952- *WhoEmL 91*
Behringer, Thomas Edward, Jr. 1930- *St&PR 91*
Behrle, Franklin Charles 1922- *WhoAm 90*
Behrman, Beatrice *NewYTBS 90 [port]*
Behrman, Carol H 1925- *WhoWrEP 89*
Behrman, Daniel 1923- *WhoWrEP 89*
Behrman, Daniel 1923-1990 *BioIn 16, ConAu 131*
Behrman, Daniel S *NewYTBS 90*
Behrman, David *NewAgMG*
Behrman, Edward 1926- *St&PR 91*
Behrman, Edward Joseph 1930- *WhoAm 90*
Behrman, Hank 1921- *Ballpl 90*
Behrman, Harold Richard 1939- *WhoAm 90*
Behrman, Jack N 1922- *ConAu 30NR*
Behrman, Jack Newton 1922- *WhoAm 90*
Behrman, James Milton 1917- *BiDrAPA 89*
Behrman, Jere Richard 1940- *WhoAm 90*
Behrman, Myron M. 1906- *WhoSSW 91*
Behrman, Richard Elliot 1931- *WhoAm 90*
Behrmann, Arthur E 1953- *BiDrAPA 89*
Behrmann, Joan Metzner *WhoAmW 91*
Behrmann, John Reynolds 1935- *St&PR 91*
Behrmann, Thomas William *BiDrAPA 89*
Behrns, Robert S *BiDrAPA 89*
Behrstock, Julian Robert 1916- *WhoAm 90*
Behuniak, Peter, Jr. 1950- *WhoE 91, WhoEmL 91*
Beichley, Ruthanne 1946- *St&PR 91*
Beichman, Arnold 1913- *ConAu 31NR, WhoAm 90*
Beichman, Janine 1942- *WhoWor 91*
Beickel, Sharon Lynne 1943- *WhoAmW 91*
Beidel, Hyun Sook 1935- *WhoWrEP 89*
Beidel, Sturla 1949- *WhoWor 91*
Beidelman, T O 1931- *ConAu 129*

Beider, Andrew Michael 1951- WhoEmL 91
Beiderbecke, Bix 1903-1931 BioIn 16, OxCPMus, WorAlBi
Beidler, George A. 1944- St&PR 91
Beidler, J. Roger ODwPR 91
Beidler, Peter Grant 1940- WhoAm 90
Beidler, Sheppard 1918- St&PR 91
Beier, B. J. 1956- WhoAmW 91
Beier, Dorothea EncCoWW
Beier, Eric Henry 1945- St&PR 91
Beier, Karl A. 1947- St&PR 91
Beier, Thomas E. 1945- St&PR 91
Beierle, James Michael 1949- St&PR 91
Beierwaltes, William Henry 1916- WhoAm 90, WhoWor 91
Beigbeder, Jean-Michel 1938- St&PR 91, WhoWor 91
Beigel, Allan 1940- BiDrAPA 89, WhoAm 90
Beigel, Jerome 1912- WhoSSW 91
Beighey, Lawrence Jerome 1938- St&PR 91, WhoAm 90
Beighle, Douglas Paul 1932- St&PR 91, WhoAm 90
Beighley, Ruthanne 1946- St&PR 91
Beightol, Michael ODwPR 91
Beights, Nancy Craik 1951- WhoAmW 91
Beigie, Carl Emerson 1940- WhoAm 90
Beigl, William 1950- WhoWor 91
Beigler, Jerome S 1916- BiDrAPA 89
Beikman, Dennis Wayne 1940- St&PR 91
Beil, Barry Jay 1947- St&PR 91
Beil, Charles A WhoAmA 91N
Beil, Gerhard 1926- WhoWor 91
Beil, Marshall Howard 1946- WhoE 91
Beil, Ralph Edwin 1927- St&PR 91
Beil, Sheldon L. 1928- St&PR 91
Beilby, Margaret Glenn 1949- WhoAmW 91
Beilby, Mary 1749-1797 PenDiDA 89
Beilby, Ralph 1743-1817 PenDiDA 89
Beilby, William 1740-1819 PenDiDA 89
Beilenson, Anthony Charles 1932- WhoAm 90
Beilenson, Laurence W. 1899-1988 BioIn 16
Beiler, Edna 1923- SmATA 61 [port]
Beiles, Herbert Noel 1939- St&PR 91
Beilig, Richard Henry 1930- St&PR 91
Beilin, Howard WhoAmA 91
Beiling-Sheerer, Christine Lynn 1963- WhoAmW 91
Beilke, James Ernest 1929- WhoAm 90
Beilke, Marlan 1940- WhoWrEP 89
Beilman, Laurence E. 1931- St&PR 91
Beilman, Mary Louise St&PR 91
Beim, David Odell 1940- WhoAm 90
Beim, Norman WhoAm 90, WhoWrEP 89
Beims, Kari 1960- WhoEmL 91
Bein, Robert H. BiDrAPA 89
Bein, Ward E BiDrAPA 89
Beinecke, Candace Krugman 1946- WhoAmW 91
Beinecke, Frederick William 1943- WhoAm 90
Beinecke, Joy Dewey BioIn 16
Beinecke, Walter St&PR 91
Beinecke, William S. 1914- WhoAm 90
Beineke, J Frederick BiDrAPA 89
Beineke, Lowell Wayne 1939- WhoAm 90
Beineke, Thomas Andrew 1939- WhoE 91
Beinfield, Lynn Adrian 1949- BiDrAPA 89
Beinhocker, Gilbert David 1932- WhoE 91, WhoWor 91
Beinker, Dale J. 1931- St&PR 91
Beinner, Michael D. 1937- ODwPR 91
Beinstein, Arnold Robert 1920- St&PR 91
Beinum, Eduard van PenDiMP
Beique, Pierre 1910- IntWWM 90
Beirer, Hans 1911- IntWWM 90
Beirne, Kenneth Joseph 1946- WhoAm 90
Beirne, Martin Douglas 1944- WhoSSW 91
Beirne, Paul Roe 1961- WhoEmL 91
Beirne, Thomas Joseph 1951- St&PR 91
Beisang, Arthur A. 1932- St&PR 91
Beise, S. Clark 1898-1989 BioIn 16
Beiseigel, Shirley-Ann 1927- WhoAmW 91
Beiseker, Thomas C. 1920- St&PR 91
Beisel, Daniel Cunningham 1916- WhoAm 90
Beiser, Arthur 1931- AuBYP 90
Beiser, Ernest M 1911- BiDrAPA 89
Beiser, Gerald J. 1930- WhoAm 90
Beiser, Gerald Jay 1930- St&PR 91
Beiser, Helen R 1914- BiDrAPA 89
Beiser, Helen Ruth 1914- WhoAmW 91
Beiser, Kathryn H. ODwPR 91
Beiser, Morton 1936- BiDrAPA 89
Beisler, Henry, Jr. 1920- St&PR 91
Beisler, Peter C. 1942- St&PR 91
Beisman, James Joseph 1933- St&PR 91
Beisner, Monika BioIn 16
Beispiel, Harriette Judith 1934- WhoAmW 91
Beissel, Henry 1929- OxCCanT
Beisser, Arnold R. BioIn 16
Beisser, Arnold R 1925- BiDrAPA 89
Beisser, Judith Kay 1946- WhoAmW 91
Beisswenger, Harry Louis, Jr. 1935- WhoE 91
Beistline, Earl Hoover 1916- WhoAm 90
Beiswinger, George L. 1924- ODwPR 91
Beiswinger, George Lawrence 1924- WhoE 91
Beiswinger, Virginia Graves 1928- WhoAmW 91
Beitel-Smutny, Donna L BiDrAPA 89
Beitenman, Edward T 1927- BiDrAPA 89
Beiting, John Morgan 1938- St&PR 91
Beitins, Inese Zinta 1937- WhoAmW 91
Beitler, J. Paul BioIn 16
Beitler, Stanley Samuel 1924- AuBYP 90
Beitlerin EncCoWW
Beitman, Bernard David 1942- BiDrAPA 89
Beito, G.A. 1933- St&PR 91
Beittel, Adam D. BioIn 16
Beittel, Daniel C 1928- BiDrAPA 89
Beittenmiller, J.G. 1959- St&PR 91
Beitzel, George B. 1928- St&PR 91, WhoAm 90
Beitzel, Harald Matthias 1941- WhoWor 91
Beitzel, J.E. 1939- St&PR 91
Beizer, Richard L. 1942- WhoAm 90
Beizer, Samuel 1931- WhoE 91
Beja, Morris 1935- WhoAm 90
Bejarano, Carmen 1944- WhoHisp 91
Bejarano, Luis Enrique 1917- WhoE 91
Bejart, Maurice 1928- WorAlBi
Bejart, Maurice Jean 1927- WhoWor 91
Bejczy, Antal Karoly 1930- WhoAm 90
Bejerot, Nils 1921-1988 BioIn 16
Bejma, Ollie 1907- Ballpl 90
Bejnar, Thaddeus Putnam 1948- WhoEmL 91
Bejot, Francis Edwin 1934- St&PR 91
Bek, Adeline Ann WhoWor 91
Bekaert, Geert Albrecht 1928- WhoWor 91
Bekaert, Stefaan 1930- WhoWor 91
Bekassy de Bekas, Stefan Peter Adam 1947- WhoWor 91
Bekavac, Nancy Yavor 1947- WhoAm 90
Bekefi, George 1925- WhoAm 90
Bekenstein, Susan 1952- WhoAmW 91
Beker, Gisela WhoAmA 91
Beker, Johan Christiaan WhoAm 90
Bekes, Carolyn Ethel 1947- WhoAmW 91
Bekesy, Georg Von 1899-1972 DcScB S2
Bekey, George Albert 1928- WhoAm 90
Bekhrad, Fereshteh 1946- WhoAmW 91
Bekir, Nagwa Esmat 1944- WhoWor 91
Bekke, Hans Albertus Geruardus Naria 1940- WhoWor 91
Bekkedahl, Brad Douglas 1957- WhoEmL 91, WhoWor 91
Bekkum, Owen D. 1924- WhoAm 90, WhoWor 91
Bekman, Paul D. 1946- WhoEmL 91
Bekoff, Oscar 1917- WhoSSW 91
Bekritsky, Bruce Robert 1946- WhoEmL 91
Bel, Bernard 1949- IntWWM 90
Bel, Ernest Fred 1936- WhoSSW 91
Bel, Juan Manuel 1958- BiDrAPA 89
Bel Air, Roger 1946- WhoWrEP 89
Bel Geddes, Barbara 1922- BioIn 16, NotWoAT, WhoAm 90, WhoAmW 91, WorAlBi
Bel Geddes, Joan 1916- WhoAm 90, WhoWrEP 89
Bel Geddes, Norman 1893-1958 PenDiDA 89, WhoAmA 91N
Belack, James Paul 1933- St&PR 91
Belafonte, Gina BioIn 16
Belafonte, Harry BioIn 16
Belafonte, Harry 1927- DrBlPA 90, OxCPMus, WhoAm 90, WhoWor 91, WorAlBi
Belafonte, Shari 1954- DrBlPA 90
Belag, Andrea 1951- WhoAmA 91
Belaga, Marshall E 1947- BiDrAPA 89
Belaiche, Raymond Bernard 1943- WhoWor 91
Belak, Edmund R., Jr. 1947- ODwPR 91
Belan, William Wells 1950- WhoEmL 91
Belaney, William Louis 1926- St&PR 91
Belanger, A. Douglas 1953- St&PR 91
Belanger, Arthur Cyril 1925- St&PR 91
Belanger, Francine 1959- St&PR 91
Belanger, Francois-Joseph 1744-1818 PenDiDA 89
Belanger, Gerard 1940- WhoAm 90
Belanger, Horace 1836-1892 DcCanB 12
Belanger, Mark 1944- Ballpl 90
Belanger, Michel Ferdinand 1929- WhoE 91
Belanger, Pierre Rolland 1937- WhoAm 90
Belanger, Rich 1952- ODwPR 91
Belanger, Sandra Emily 1944- WhoAmW 91
Belanger, Wayne Jean 1957- WhoE 91
Belanger, William Joseph 1925- WhoAm 90
Belar, Karl 1895-1931 DcScB S2
Belardi, James Richard 1957- St&PR 91
Belardi, Wayne 1930- Ballpl 90
Belasco, Andrea Laurie 1951- BiDrAPA 89
Belasco, David 1853-1931 BioIn 16, EncPaPR 91, WorAlBi
Belasco, Leon 1902-1988 BioIn 16
Belasco, Marvin Sam 1945- WhoSSW 91
Belasco, Simon 1918- WhoAm 90
Belashova, Ekaterina Fedorovna 1906- BiDWomA
Belasky, Michael Bruce 1945- St&PR 91
Belau, Jane Carol Gullickson 1934- WhoAmW 91
Belau, Jane Gullickson 1934- St&PR 91
Belaunde Terry, Fernando 1912- BioIn 16
Belaustegui, Leon 1926- St&PR 91
Belavic, Andrew Michael 1925- St&PR 91
Belawich, Lee Bruno St&PR 91N
Belbas, Dean 1932- St&PR 91
Belbeck, Kenneth George 1928- St&PR 91
Belcastro, Frank A. 1936- St&PR 91
Belcastro, Patrick Frank 1920- WhoAm 90
Belcer, Roy C. 1927- St&PR 91
Belceva, Mar Ivanova 1868-1937 EncCoWW
Belch, J. Edwin 1833- AmLegL
Belcher, Alice Ann 1960- WhoAmW 91
Belcher, Benjamin Moore 1912-1988 BioIn 16
Belcher, Brent 1949- St&PR 91
Belcher, Dennis Irl 1951- WhoEmL 91
Belcher, Diana Steinbach 1952- WhoEmL 91
Belcher, Donald David 1938- St&PR 91
Belcher, Donald W. 1922- St&PR 91
Belcher, Edward L. 1926- St&PR 91
Belcher, Forrest Renfrow 1922- WhoSSW 91, WhoWor 91
Belcher, George 1941- WhoAmA 91
Belcher, Grace Daley 1902- WhoWrEP 89
Belcher, Hilda 1881-1963 WhoAmA 91N
Belcher, Jennifer Marion 1944- WhoAmW 91
Belcher, John Arthur 1956- WhoEmL 91
Belcher, John Cheslow 1920- WhoAm 90
Belcher, Joseph John 1918- St&PR 91
Belcher, La Jeune 1960- WhoAmW 91, WhoEmL 91
Belcher, Louis David 1939- WhoAm 90
Belcher, Nancy Foote 1921- WhoWor 91
Belcher, Samuel 1814-1886 AmLegL
Belcher, Sandra 1950- WhoE 91
Belcher, Taylor Garrison 1920-1990 BioIn 16
Belcher, Thomas Lamar, Jr. 1948- WhoSSW 91
Belcher, Tim 1961- Ballpl 90
Belcher, Wendy 1962- ConAu 130
Belcher, William Alvis 1918- WhoSSW 91
Belcher, William Walter, Jr. 1943- WhoWor 91
Belcheva 1893- EncCoWW
Belcourt, Emile 1934- IntWWM 90
Beldegreen, Karen J. 1950- St&PR 91
Belden, Allan D 1936- BiDrAPA 89
Belden, Arthur B. 1945- St&PR 91
Belden, Catherine Ellen 1941- WhoSSW 91
Belden, Daniel M. 1944- St&PR 91
Belden, David Leigh 1935- WhoAm 90, WhoE 91
Belden, Herbert L. 1923- St&PR 91
Belden, Jack BioIn 16
Belden, Jeffrey Lynn 1952- St&PR 91
Belden, Louis de Keyser 1926- WhoWor 91
Belden, Sanford Adams 1942- WhoAm 90
Belden, Shirley AuBYP 90
Belden, Simeon 1830- AmLegL
Belden, Stephen Frederic 1954- WhoEmL 91
Belden, Wilanne Schneider 1925- BioIn 16, WhoWrEP 89
Belden, William H., Jr. 1942- St&PR 91
Belden, William Hinchliffe 1914- St&PR 91
Belding, Eser Uzun 1951- WhoE 91
Belding, Jeffrey Harwood 1943- WhoAm 90
Belding, Meric W. 1922- St&PR 91
Belding, Stephen T. 1952- St&PR 91
Beldner, Richard Steven 1942- St&PR 91
Beldock, D.T. 1934- St&PR 91
Beldock, Donald Travis 1934- WhoAm 90
Beldock, Myron 1929- WhoAm 90
Beldon, Heather ODwPR 91
Beldon, Sanford T. 1932- WhoAm 90, WhoWrEP 89
Beldone, Phil MajTwCW
Beldotti, Pat Julio 1934- WhoE 91
Belegundu, Ashok Dhondu 1956- WhoE 91
Belen, Frederick Christopher 1913- WhoAm 90
Belen, Nenita C BiDrAPA 89
Belenke, Burton 1926- St&PR 91
Belenky, Gregory 1945- BiDrAPA 89
Beleno ConAu 131, HispWr 90, MajTwCW
Belenson, Allen George 1935- St&PR 91
Beleson, Robert Brian 1950- WhoEmL 91, WhoWor 91
Beless, Rosemary June 1947- WhoEmL 91
Belet, Jacques H. 1948- St&PR 91
Belet, Jacques Henry, III 1948- WhoAm 90
Beletz, Elaine Ethel 1944- WhoAmW 91, WhoE 91
Belew, Adrian 1950?- ConMus 5 [port]
Belew, David Lee 1931- St&PR 91, WhoAm 90
Belew, David Owen, Jr. 1920- WhoSSW 91
Belew, John Seymour 1920- WhoAm 90
Belfer, Myron Lowell 1939- BiDrAPA 89
Belfi, John Robert 1934- WhoWor 91
Belfield, Judith Ann 1946- WhoWrEP 89
Belfiglio, Edward E. 1938- St&PR 91
Belfiglio, Valentine John 1934- WhoSSW 91
Belfiore-Greco, Maddalena WhoE 91
Belflower, Joseph Nevin 1932- St&PR 91
Belford, Gary Cinney 1948- St&PR 91
Belford, Jeffrey Bryon 1947- St&PR 91
Belford, Lee Archer 1913-1988 BioIn 16
Belford, Roz 1929- WhoSSW 91
Belfort-Chalat, Jacqueline 1930- WhoAmA 91, WhoE 91
Belfrage, Cedric H. NewYTBS 90
Belfrage, Cedric H. 1904-1990 ConAu 132
Belfrage, Erik Jean Christian 1946- WhoWor 91
Belfus, Isaac Lou 1925- St&PR 91
Belgard, Tildon Kurt BiDrAPA 89
Belgin, Harvey Harry 1912- WhoSSW 91
Belgrader, Andrei BioIn 16
Belgrave, Cynthia 1926- DrBlPA 90
Belgrave, Joyce Mary Cynthia 1935- WhoAmW 91
Belian, Garabed WhoAmA 91
Belian, Isabelle WhoAmA 91
Belica, Marina Elena 1959- WhoE 91
Belica, Paul M. 1946- St&PR 91
Belich, John Patrick 1938- WhoAm 90
Belicic, Andrew BiDrAPA 89
Beligratis, Steven D. 1931- St&PR 91
Beliles, Karen Elizabeth BiDrAPA 89
Belille, Ronald 1947- WhoEmL 91
Belin, David William 1928- WhoAm 90, WhoWor 91
Belin, Gaspard d'Andelot 1918- WhoAm 90
Belin, J.C. 1914- St&PR 91
Belin, Jacob Chapman 1914- WhoAm 90, WhoSSW 91
Belin, Jean Albert 1610-1677 EncO&P 3
Belin, Rene Joseph Jean-Baptiste 1898-1977 BiDFrPL
Belina, Maria WhoAmW 91
Belinfante, Alexander Erik Ernst 1944- WhoE 91
Belinfante, Geoffrey Warren 1947- WhoEmL 91
Belinfante, Johan Gijsbertus Frederik 1940- WhoSSW 91
Beling, Gregory N. 1945- St&PR 91
Beling, Helen 1914- WhoAm 90, WhoAmA 91
Beling, Willard A. 1919- WhoAm 90
Belinger, Arthur 1944- WhoSSW 91
Belinger, Harry R. 1927- ODwPR 91
Belinger, Harry Robert 1927- St&PR 91, WhoAm 90
Belinkoff, Irving L. 1928- St&PR 91
Belinkoff, Julius BiDrAPA 89
Belinsky, Bo 1936- Ballpl 90
Belinsky, Vissarion Grigoryevich 1811-1848 BioIn 16
Belinson, Louis BiDrAPA 89
Belis, Annie IntWWM 90
Belisarius 505?-565 WorAlBi
Belisle, Gilles 1923- WhoAm 90
Belisle, Leo G BiDrAPA 89
Belisle, Mavis BioIn 16
Belissary, Karen 1959- WhoAmW 91
Belitsky, Melvin J. 1946- St&PR 91
Belitsky, Richard 1950- BiDrAPA 89
Belitt, Ben 1911- WhoAm 90, WhoWrEP 89
Belitz, Martin Jerome 1937- St&PR 91
Beliveau, Daniele 1951- St&PR 91
Beliveau, Jean 1931- WorAlBi
Beliveau, Juliette 1890-1975 OxCCanT
Beliveau, L.C. 1917- St&PR 91
Beliveau-Jones, Marguerite Anita 1944- WhoAmW 91
Belizario, Evangelina M BiDrAPA 89
Beljan, John Richard 1930- WhoAm 90, WhoWor 91
Belk, Audrey Marie Walters 1938- WhoAmW 91
Belk, Colleen G. Webb 1929- WhoWrEP 89
Belk, Donna Below 1945- WhoSSW 91
Belk, Henry EncO&P 3
Belk, Irwin 1922- WhoAm 90
Belk, John Blanton 1925- WhoAm 90
Belk, John M. 1920- St&PR 91
Belk, Lowell Warner 1937- St&PR 91
Belk, Thomas M. 1925- St&PR 91

Belk, Thomas Milburn 1925- *WhoAm 90*
Belk, William Herbert 1937- *WhoSSW 91*
Belkhouche, Boumediene 1950- *WhoSSW 91*
Belkin, Alan Ivor 1951- *IntWWM 90*
Belkin, Boris 1948- *IntWWM 90, PenDiMP*
Belkin, Boris David 1948- *WhoAm 90*
Belkin, Jack Howard *BiDrAPA 89*
Belkin, Janet Ehrenreich 1938- *WhoAmW 91*
Belkin, Maurice H. *BioIn 16*
Belkin, Nathan Leon 1926- *St&PR 91*
Belkin, Riva 1925- *BiDrAPA 89*
Belkin, Stanley 1936- *St&PR 91*
Belknap, Bonnie *BioIn 16*
Belknap, John Cortsould 1946- *WhoAm 90*
Belknap, Morris B *WhoAmA 91N*
Belknap, Norton 1925- *WhoAm 90*
Belknap, Robert Lamont 1929- *WhoAm 90*
Belknap, William Worth 1829-1890 *BiDrUSE 89*
Bell, Acton 1820-1849 *BioIn 16*
Bell, Adele Lanford 1949- *WhoSSW 91*
Bell, Alan Robert 1952- *WhoE 91*
Bell, Alan Russell 1939- *St&PR 91*
Bell, Alan W. 1919- *ODwPR 91*
Bell, Alberta S. 1944- *WhoAmW 91*
Bell, Alexander Graham 1847-1922 *BioIn 16, WorAlBi*
Bell, Alistair Macready 1913- *WhoAmA 91*
Bell, Andrew 1753-1832 *WorAlBi*
Bell, Andrew Michael 1946- *WhoE 91*
Bell, Anita I *BiDrAPA 89*
Bell, Anita Jayne Wise 1961- *WhoAmW 91*
Bell, Ann 1951- *WhoAmW 91*
Bell, Anne Murray *BiDrAPA 89*
Bell, Araminta Hobbs 1941- *WhoAmW 91*
Bell, Arthur 1926- *WhoWor 91*
Bell, Barbara Gail 1938- *WhoAmW 91*
Bell, Battle, III 1945- *WhoSSW 91*
Bell, Beau 1907-1977 *Ballpl 90*
Bell, Bradley John 1952- *St&PR 91*
Bell, Brenda Estelle 1944- *WhoAmW 91*
Bell, Brian Dutcher 1937- *St&PR 91*
Bell, Bryan 1918- *WhoSSW 91, WhoWor 91*
Bell, Buddy *BioIn 16*
Bell, Buddy 1951- *Ballpl 90 [port]*
Bell, Buddy F.E. 1938- *St&PR 91*
Bell, Carl *BioIn 16*
Bell, Carl Compton *BiDrAPA 89*
Bell, Carl Compton 1947- *WhoEmL 91*
Bell, Carl Kennedy 1924- *WhoAm 90*
Bell, Carleton L. 1928- *St&PR 91*
Bell, Carol Willsey 1939- *WhoAmW 91*
Bell, Carolyn Shaw 1920- *WhoAm 90, WhoAmW 91*
Bell, Charles Anderson 1925- *St&PR 91*
Bell, Charles Davis 1923- *St&PR 91*
Bell, Charles E *BiDrAPA 89*
Bell, Charles Eugene, Jr. 1932- *WhoWor 91*
Bell, Charles G 1916- *ConAu 12AS [port]*
Bell, Charles Greenleaf 1916- *WhoWrEP 89*
Bell, Charles H. 1927- *St&PR 91*
Bell, Charles Henry 1823-1893 *AmLegL*
Bell, Charles Lee *BiDrAPA 89*
Bell, Charles Ray 1941- *WhoAm 90*
Bell, Charles Robert, Jr. 1930- *WhoAm 90*
Bell, Charles S 1935- *WhoAmA 91*
Bell, Charlotte Dorothy 1931- *WhoWrEP 89*
Bell, Cheryl Jane 1946- *WhoAm 90*
Bell, Chester Gordon 1934- *WhoAm 90*
Bell, Claire Ippolito 1950- *WhoE 91*
Bell, Clarence Deshong 1914- *WhoE 91*
Bell, Clarence Elmo 1912- *WhoSSW 91*
Bell, Claude K. *BioIn 16*
Bell, Clive 1881-1964 *MajTwCW*
Bell, Coca 1924- *WhoAmA 91*
Bell, Colin 1938- *ConAu 32NR*
Bell, Colin W. 1903-1988 *BioIn 16*
Bell, Cool Papa 1903- *Ballpl 90 [port]*
Bell, Cornelius 1946- *WhoE 91*
Bell, Craig Wilson 1950- *WhoEmL 91*
Bell, Currer 1816-1855 *BioIn 16*
Bell, Cynthia Sue 1959- *WhoAmW 91*
Bell, Daniel *BioIn 16*
Bell, Daniel 1919- *WhoAm 90*
Bell, Daniel L., Jr. 1929- *St&PR 91*
Bell, Daniel Long, Jr. 1929- *WhoAm 90*
Bell, Darla Dee 1946- *WhoEmL 91*
Bell, David A. 1942- *St&PR 91*
Bell, David Arthur 1943- *WhoAm 90*
Bell, David Julian 1951- *WhoEmL 91*
Bell, Deborah 1686-1738 *BiDEWW*
Bell, Deborah 1689?-1738 *FemiCLE*
Bell, Deborah Marie 1955- *WhoAmW 91*
Bell, Delen Craig 1945- *WhoEmL 91*
Bell, Dennis Arthur 1934- *St&PR 91*
Bell, Dennis Lee 1949- *WhoSSW 91*
Bell, Dennis Philip 1948- *WhoAm 90*
Bell, Derek *BioIn 16*
Bell, Derek 1921- *IntWWM 90*
Bell, Derrick Albert 1930- *WhoAm 90*
Bell, Donald Allen 1938- *WhoAmA 91*
Bell, Donald Atkinson 1941- *WhoWor 91*
Bell, Donald Curtis 1931- *BiDrAPA 89*
Bell, Donald Munro 1934- *IntWWM 90*
Bell, Dorothy Franklin 1927- *WhoAmW 91*
Bell, Douglas McCall 1955- *WhoEmL 91*
Bell, Dozier 1957- *WhoAmA 91*
Bell, E. John 1937- *St&PR 91*
Bell, Eddie *BioIn 16*
Bell, Edward 1929-1988 *BioIn 16*
Bell, Edward, Jr. 1939- *St&PR 91*
Bell, Edward Francis 1930- *St&PR 91, WhoAm 90*
Bell, Edward Price 1869-1943 *BioIn 16*
Bell, Edwin Lewis, II 1926- *WhoE 91*
Bell, Eileen Eberenz 1936- *WhoAmW 91*
Bell, Eldrin *WhoSSW 91*
Bell, Elise Stone *WhoWrEP 89*
Bell, Elizabeth 1928- *IntWWM 90*
Bell, Ella *BioIn 16*
Bell, Ellis 1818-1848 *BioIn 16*
Bell, Enid 1904- *BiDWomA*
Bell, Eric 1963- *Ballpl 90*
Bell, Ernest Lorne, III 1926- *WhoAm 90*
Bell, Eugene 1918- *St&PR 91*
Bell, Frances Louise 1926- *WhoAmW 91*
Bell, Frank A. 1935- *St&PR 91*
Bell, Frank Joseph, III 1955- *WhoE 91, WhoEmL 91*
Bell, Frank Ouray, Jr. 1940- *WhoAm 90*
Bell, Frank S., Jr. 1937- *St&PR 91*
Bell, Frederic 1928- *AuBYP 90*
Bell, Fredric J. 1941- *St&PR 91*
Bell, Gary *BioIn 16*
Bell, Gary 1936- *Ballpl 90*
Bell, Gawain 1909- *ConAu 131*
Bell, Geo Robert 1912- *St&PR 91*
Bell, George *BioIn 16*
Bell, George 1874-1941 *Ballpl 90*
Bell, George 1959- *Ballpl 90, WhoHisp 91, WorAlBi*
Bell, George Antonio 1959- *WhoAm 90*
Bell, George De Benneville 1924- *St&PR 91, WhoAm 90*
Bell, George Edwin 1923- *WhoAm 90*
Bell, George Irving 1926- *WhoAm 90*
Bell, George Stuart 1945- *BiDrAPA 89*
Bell, Gerald 1924- *St&PR 91*
Bell, Gertrude 1868-1926 *FemiCLE*
Bell, Gertrude 1911- *AuBYP 90*
Bell, Gertrude Margaret Lowthian 1868-1926 *BioIn 16*
Bell, Griffin B 1918- *BiDrUSE 89*
Bell, Gus 1928- *Ballpl 90*
Bell, H Craig 1912- *BiDrAPA 89*
Bell, H. Darline 1942- *WhoSSW 91*
Bell, Haney Hardy, III 1944- *WhoAm 90*
Bell, Hannah Boyd *ODwPR 91*
Bell, Harold Grover, Jr. 1945- *WhoSSW 91*
Bell, Harrison B. 1925- *WhoWrEP 89*
Bell, Harrison Bancroft 1925- *WhoAm 90*
Bell, Harry Edward 1947- *WhoEmL 91*
Bell, Harry Fullerton, Jr. 1954- *WhoEmL 91*
Bell, Harry Satcher 1927- *WhoSSW 91*
Bell, Helen Choate 1830-1918 *BioAmW*
Bell, Henry, Jr. 1940- *WhoE 91*
Bell, Henry Marsh, Jr. 1928- *St&PR 91, WhoAm 90, WhoSSW 91*
Bell, Herbert Aubrey Frederick 1921- *WhoAm 90*
Bell, Hi 1897-1949 *Ballpl 90*
Bell, Howard Earl 1934- *St&PR 91, WhoAm 90*
Bell, Hubert T. *BioIn 16*
Bell, Hugh H. 1941- *St&PR 91*
Bell, Iris Roberta 1950- *BiDrAPA 89, WhoAmW 91*
Bell, Irving 1912- *WhoE 91*
Bell, Isaac 1846-1889 *BioIn 16*
Bell, J. A. Gordon 1929- *WhoAm 90, WhoE 91*
Bell, J. Frank 1938- *St&PR 91*
Bell, Jack William 1946- *St&PR 91*
Bell, Jacqueline S. 1941- *St&PR 91*
Bell, James A. 1947- *WhoSSW 91*
Bell, James Adrian 1917- *WhoAm 90, WhoWrEP 89*
Bell, James Brugler 1932- *WhoAm 90*
Bell, James D. 1937- *St&PR 91*
Bell, James E. 1940- *St&PR 91*
Bell, James Frederick 1914- *WhoAm 90*
Bell, James Frederick 1922- *WhoAm 90*
Bell, James M *BiDrAPA 89, WhoAmA 91*
Bell, James M. 1943- *WhoSSW 91*
Bell, James M., Sr. 1928- *WhoSSW 91*
Bell, James Milton 1921- *WhoAm 90, WhoE 91, WhoWor 91*
Bell, James T. 1921- *St&PR 91*
Bell, Jane Matlack 1949- *WhoWrEP 89*
Bell, Janet *AuBYP 90*
Bell, Jay 1965- *Ballpl 90*
Bell, Jeanne 1944?- *DrBIPA 90*
Bell, Jeanne Viner 1923- *WhoAmW 91*
Bell, Jerry *WhoAm 90*
Bell, Jerry 1947- *Ballpl 90*
Bell, Jewel Hairston *NewYTBS 90*
Bell, John 1797-1869 *BiDrUSE 89*
Bell, John 1928- *BioIn 16*
Bell, John Atherton *BioIn 16*
Bell, John Boyle, Jr. 1933- *St&PR 91*
Bell, John Frantz 1914- *WhoAm 90*
Bell, John Kim *BioIn 16*
Bell, John Lewis 1942- *WhoAm 90*
Bell, John Lewis, Jr. 1942- *St&PR 91*
Bell, John Milton 1922- *WhoAm 90*
Bell, John N. 1931- *St&PR 91*
Bell, John Oscar 1912- *WhoAm 90*
Bell, John Peay 1916- *BiDrAPA 89*
Bell, John R., II *ODwPR 91*
Bell, John Richard 1959- *WhoE 91*
Bell, John Stewart *NewYTBS 90*
Bell, John Stewart 1928- *WhoWor 91*
Bell, John William 1946- *WhoEmL 91*
Bell, John Wright 1925- *WhoWor 91*
Bell, Jon Andrew 1950- *BiDrAPA 89*
Bell, Jonathan Robert 1947- *WhoAm 90*
Bell, Joseph A. 1936- *St&PR 91*
Bell, Joseph L *BiDrAPA 89*
Bell, Joseph N. 1921- *AuBYP 90*
Bell, Josephine 1897-1987 *TwCCr&M 91*
Bell, Joshua 1967- *IntWWM 90*
Bell, Katherine Valois 1930- *WhoAmW 91*
Bell, Kathryn Leise 1942- *WhoAmA 91*
Bell, Katie Roberson 1936- *WhoAm 90*
Bell, Kelly Denny 1958- *WhoWrEP 89*
Bell, Kenneth John 1930- *WhoAm 90*
Bell, Kensil 1907- *AuBYP 90*
Bell, Kevin 1955- *Ballpl 90*
Bell, Kimberly Diane 1960- *WhoEmL 91*
Bell, Larry Prentice 1950- *WhoEmL 91*
Bell, Larry Stuart 1939- *WhoAm 90, WhoAmA 91*
Bell, Lauralee *BioIn 16*
Bell, Laurie 1952- *WhoEmL 91*
Bell, Lawrence Miller 1927- *St&PR 91*
Bell, Lee Phillip *WhoAm 90, WhoWor 91*
Bell, Leo, Jr. 1948- *WhoEmL 91*
Bell, Les 1901- *Ballpl 90*
Bell, Lilah Mae 1908- *WhoAmW 91*
Bell, Lilian A 1943- *WhoAmA 91*
Bell, Linda Crawford 1948- *WhoAmW 91*
Bell, Linda Flounders 1952- *WhoWrEP 89*
Bell, Linda L. *ODwPR 91*
Bell, Linda Odum *BiDrAPA 89*
Bell, Linda R. 1949- *WhoEmL 91*
Bell, Louise H. 1959- *WhoEmL 91*
Bell, Mabel 1859-1923 *BioAmW*
Bell, Madison Smartt 1957- *WhoWrEP 89*
Bell, Margaret Couvillon 1943- *St&PR 91*
Bell, Margaret E J 1937- *BiDrAPA 89*
Bell, Margaret Elizabeth 1898- *AuBYP 90*
Bell, Marion Wayne 1933- *WhoAm 90*
Bell, Marja-Liisa Sanelma 1930- *WhoWor 91*
Bell, Mark Gerald 1950- *WhoEmL 91*
Bell, Martin Allen 1951- *WhoAm 90*
Bell, Marvin 1937- *ConAu 33NR, MajTwCW*
Bell, Marvin H. *WhoAm 90*
Bell, Mary 1907- *WhoWor 91*
Bell, Mary Catherine 1946- *WhoAmA 91*
Bell, Mary Catlett 1924- *WhoAmW 91*
Bell, Mary E. Beniteau 1937- *WhoSSW 91*
Bell, Maxine Toolson 1931- *WhoAmW 91*
Bell, Merton I. 1935- *St&PR 91*
Bell, Michael Henry *BiDrAPA 89*
Bell, Michael Steven 1946- *WhoAmA 91, WhoWrEP 89*
Bell, Mildred Bailey 1928- *WhoAmW 91, WhoSSW 91*
Bell, Morris L. 1924- *St&PR 91*
Bell, Neill 1946- *BioIn 16*
Bell, Norman Brooke 1920- *St&PR 91*
Bell, Norman Howard 1931- *WhoAm 90*
Bell, Ovid H. 1917- *St&PR 91*
Bell, P. Jackson 1941- *St&PR 91, WhoAm 90*
Bell, Patricia Ann 1957- *WhoSSW 91*
Bell, Patricia Jimerson 1931- *WhoAmW 91*
Bell, Patricia Lauderdale 1930- *WhoAmW 91*
Bell, Paul David 1955- *WhoEmL 91*
Bell, Pearl Thomazena 1936- *WhoAmW 91*
Bell, Peggy Kirk *BioIn 16*
Bell, Peter Mayo 1934- *WhoAm 90, WhoE 91*
Bell, Philip A. 1808-1889 *BioIn 16*
Bell, Philip Michael 1942- *WhoAmA 91*
Bell, Philip Wilkes 1924- *WhoAm 90*
Bell, Phillip Michael 1942- *WhoAm 90*
Bell, Quentin *BioIn 16*
Bell, R Murray *WhoAmA 91*
Bell, Randall 1943- *WhoSSW 91*
Bell, Randall William 1938- *WhoAm 90*
Bell, Reaver Garland *WhoAmW 91, WhoWor 91*
Bell, Regina Jean *WhoAmW 91*
Bell, Richard 1920- *WhoAm 90*
Bell, Richard E. 1934- *St&PR 91*
Bell, Richard Eugene 1934- *WhoAm 90*
Bell, Richard G. 1947- *St&PR 91, WhoEmL 91*
Bell, Richard Harding, II 1946- *WhoEmL 91*
Bell, Richard V. 1922- *St&PR 91*
Bell, Robert *St&PR 91*
Bell, Robert 1732?-1784 *EncCRAm*
Bell, Robert 1808-1894 *DcCanB 12*
Bell, Robert Arnold 1950- *WhoE 91*
Bell, Robert Austin 1933- *St&PR 91, WhoAm 90*
Bell, Robert Brooks 1953- *WhoEmL 91*
Bell, Robert Cecil 1951- *WhoWor 91*
Bell, Robert Collins 1912- *WhoE 91, WhoWor 91*
Bell, Robert E. 1947- *St&PR 91*
Bell, Robert Edward 1918- *WhoAm 90*
Bell, Robert Eugene 1914- *WhoAm 90*
Bell, Robert L. 1919- *St&PR 91*
Bell, Robert Lawrence 1919- *WhoE 91*
Bell, Robert Lewis 1951- *WhoEmL 91*
Bell, Robert M 1901- *BiDrAPA 89*
Bell, Robert Maurice 1944- *WhoAm 90*
Bell, Robert Paul 1918- *WhoAm 90*
Bell, Robert Vaughn 1924- *BioIn 16*
Bell, Robin *ConAu 130*
Bell, Robin Ellen *BiDrAPA 89*
Bell, Robin V. *BioIn 16*
Bell, Robinette N 1930- *BiDrAPA 89*
Bell, Ronald 1937- *St&PR 91*
Bell, Ronald Lee 1955- *WhoEmL 91*
Bell, Roseanne 1946- *WhoAmW 91, WhoSSW 91*
Bell, Samuel H. 1925- *WhoAm 90*
Bell, Sharon Kaye 1943- *WhoAmW 91*
Bell, Sharon Teresa Echerd 1950- *WhoAmW 91*
Bell, Sidney 1929- *WhoSSW 91*
Bell, Stanley R. 1946- *St&PR 91*
Bell, Stanton Paul 1933- *WhoSSW 91*
Bell, Stephen 1946- *St&PR 91*
Bell, Stephen M. 1948- *St&PR 91*
Bell, Stephen Scott 1935- *WhoAm 90*
Bell, Steven 1943- *WhoSSW 91*
Bell, Stewart Lynn 1945- *WhoEmL 91*
Bell, Stoughton 1923- *WhoAm 90, WhoWor 91*
Bell, Stuart John 1944- *St&PR 91*
Bell, Susan Jane 1946- *WhoAmW 91*
Bell, Susanna *BiDEWW*
Bell, Taylor Harvey Aylesworth 1940- *WhoAm 90*
Bell, Teja *NewAgMG*
Bell, Terrel Howard *BioIn 16*
Bell, Terrel Howard 1921- *BiDrUSE 89, WhoAm 90*
Bell, Thelma 1896- *AuBYP 90*
Bell, Thelma, and Corydon Whitten Bell *AuBYP 90*
Bell, Theodore Augustus 1946- *WhoAm 90*
Bell, Thom 1941- *OxCPMus*
Bell, Thomas *St&PR 91*
Bell, Thomas D., Jr. 1949- *St&PR 91*
Bell, Thomas Devereaux, Jr. 1949- *WhoAm 90*
Bell, Thomas E *BiDrAPA 89*
Bell, Thomas E. 1943- *St&PR 91*
Bell, Thomas J. *AmLegL*
Bell, Thomas Reid 1923- *WhoAm 90*
Bell, Thomas Rowe 1928- *St&PR 91, WhoAm 90*
Bell, Thornton *ConAu 32NR*
Bell, Timothy Harwell 1949- *WhoEmL 91*
Bell, Tom *BioIn 16*
Bell, Travers J. *BioIn 16*
Bell, Trevor 1930- *WhoAmA 91*
Bell, Vanessa 1879-1961 *BiDWomA, BioIn 16*
Bell, Vanessa Regina 1955- *WhoAmW 91, WhoEmL 91*
Bell, Vera *FemiCLE*
Bell, Verle Leonard 1949- *BiDrAPA 89*
Bell, Victor Altmark, Jr. 1942- *St&PR 91, WhoAm 90*
Bell, Victor Leroy 1935- *WhoWrEP 89*
Bell, Vincent G., Jr. 1925- *St&PR 91*
Bell, W. Douglas 1921- *St&PR 91*
Bell, W. James 1929- *WhoAm 90*
Bell, W L D *MajTwCW*
Bell, Walter 1915- *St&PR 91, WhoAm 90*
Bell, Walter Alfred 1943- *WhoSSW 91*
Bell, Walter Douglas 1921- *WhoAm 90*
Bell, Warren *BioIn 16*
Bell, Wayne Steven 1954- *WhoEmL 91, WhoWor 91*
Bell, Wendell 1924- *WhoAm 90*
Bell, Wendell Dean 1939- *BiDrAPA 89*
Bell, Whitfield Jenks, Jr. 1914- *WhoAm 90*
Bell, Willard Renwick, Jr. 1927- *St&PR 91*
Bell, William *PenDiDA 89*
Bell, William E. 1926- *St&PR 91*
Bell, William Henry, Jr. 1918- *St&PR 91, WhoAm 90*
Bell, William Jack 1915- *WhoAm 90*
Bell, William James 1929- *St&PR 91*
Bell, William Joseph 1927- *WhoWrEP 89*
Bell, William M. 1935- *St&PR 91*
Bell, William Mathew 1955- *WhoEmL 91*

Bell, William T. 1919- *St&PR 91*
Bell, William Wallis, Jr. 1946- *WhoSSW 91*
Bell Burnell, Susan Jocelyn 1943- *BioIn 16*
Bell-Hanson, Karen Sue 1958- *WhoAmW 91*
Bell-Taylor, Ava Patrice *BiDrAPA 89*
Bell-Teneketzis, Barbara 1947- *WhoWrEP 89*
Bella, Salvatore Joseph 1919- *WhoAm 90*
Bella, Stefano della *PenDiDA 89*
Bellace, Janice Rose 1949- *WhoE 91*
Bellack, Alan Scott 1944- *WhoAm 90*
Bellack, Dan *ODwPR 91*
Bellacosa, Joseph W. 1937- *WhoE 91*
Bellah, Kenneth David 1955- *WhoEmL 91*
Bellah, Robert Neelly 1927- *WhoAm 90*
Bellairs, George 1902-1982 *TwCCr&M 91*
Bellak, Leopold 1916- *BiDrAPA 89, WhoAm 90*
Bellak, Richard Charles 1945- *WhoEmL 91*
Bellamah, Joseph Louis 1914- *IntWWM 90*
Bellamy, Angela Robinson 1952- *WhoWor 91*
Bellamy, Atwood C *MajTwCW*
Bellamy, Calvin Edward 1942- *WhoAm 90*
Bellamy, David Parham 1944- *WhoE 91*
Bellamy, Edward 1850-1898 *BioIn 16, EncAL, WorAlBi*
Bellamy, George Anne 1731?-1788 *BioIn 16*
Bellamy, James Carl 1926- *WhoAm 90*
Bellamy, Jeanne 1911- *WhoAmW 91*
Bellamy, Joe David 1941- *WhoAm 90, WhoE 91, WhoWrEP 89*
Bellamy, Madge *NewYTBS 90*
Bellamy, Madge 1900-1990 *BioIn 16*
Bellamy, Markita Moore 1958- *WhoAmW 91*
Bellamy, Ralph 1904- *WorAlBi*
Bellamy, Ralph Rexford 1904- *WhoAm 90*
Bellamy, Richard 1927- *WhoAmA 91*
Bellamy, Ronald Roy 1948- *WhoE 91, WhoEmL 91*
Bellamy, Russell Milton 1901- *WhoSSW 91*
Bellamy, William A 1910- *BiDrAPA 89*
Bellanca, Giuseppe Mario 1886-1960 *BioIn 16*
Bellando, Lila Rae 1940- *St&PR 91*
Bellange, Alexandre-Louis *PenDiDA 89*
Bellange, Alexandre-Louis 1799-1863 *PenDiDA 89*
Bellange, Louis-Francois *PenDiDA 89*
Bellange, Louis-Francois 1759-1827 *PenDiDA 89*
Bellange, Pierre-Antoine 1758-1827 *PenDiDA 89*
Bellanger, Serge Rene 1933- *WhoAm 90, WhoE 91, WhoWor 91*
Bellante, Donald J. 1945- *St&PR 91, WhoEmL 91*
Bellanti, John A. 1932- *St&PR 91*
Bellantoni, Joseph J. 1945- *St&PR 91*
Bellantoni, Maureen Blanchfield 1949- *St&PR 91, WhoAmW 91, WhoE 91, WhoEmL 91*
Bellar, Will F. 1933- *St&PR 91*
Bellard, James Ernest 1955- *BiDrAPA 89*
Bellas, Albert C. 1942- *St&PR 91*
Bellas, Albert Constantine 1942- *WhoAm 90, WhoWor 91*
Bellas, Demetrius G. 1928- *St&PR 91*
Bellatti, Lawrence Lee 1944- *WhoAm 90*
Bellavance, Joseph Arthur 1939- *St&PR 91*
Bellavance, Roland 1957- *St&PR 91*
Bellavance, Thomas Eugene 1934- *WhoE 91*
Belle, Anna *WhoAmA 91*
Belle, John Leighton 1932- *WhoAm 90*
Belle, Nancy Krome 1944- *WhoAmW 91*
Belle, Norman M. 1939- *St&PR 91*
Belle Isle, Albert Pierre 1943- *WhoAm 90*
Belle-Isle, David Richard 1950- *WhoSSW 91*
Belleau, Narcisse-Fortunat 1808-1894 *DcCanB 12*
Belleau, Thomas 1930- *BiDrAPA 89*
Bellecci, John Salvador 1923- *WhoAm 90*
Bellefleur, Cherryl *BioIn 16*
Bellefroid, Marthe 1901-1979 *EncCoWW*
Bellegarde, Jules 1946- *St&PR 91*
Bellego, Herve M. 1947- *St&PR 91*
Bellego, Herve Melaine 1947- *WhoEmL 91*
Bellem, Robert Leslie 1902-1968 *TwCCr&M 91*
Bellemare, David John 1960- *WhoE 91, WhoEmL 91*
Bellenchia, Al *ODwPR 91*
Bellenger, Dominic Aidan 1950- *WhoWor 91*
Bellens, Roel 1951- *WhoWor 91*
Bellentani, Stefano 1954- *WhoWor 91*
Beller, Gary A. 1938- *WhoE 91*
Beller, George Allan 1940- *WhoAm 90*
Beller, Gerald Stephen 1935- *WhoWor 91*
Beller, Kathleen *BioIn 16*
Beller, Martin Leonard 1924- *WhoAm 90, WhoWor 91*
Beller, Ronald E. 1935- *WhoSSW 91*
Beller, Suha A 1928- *BiDrAPA 89*
Bellerby, Frances 1899-1975 *FemiCLE*
Belleri, Marguerite *BioIn 16*
Bellermann, Peter Robert Wilhelm 1939- *WhoE 91*
Bellerose, Arthur Louis 1944- *St&PR 91*
Bellerose, Joseph-Hyacinthe 1820-1899 *DcCanB 12*
Bellerose, Richard J. 1941- *St&PR 91*
Belles, Anita Louise 1948- *WhoAmW 91, WhoEmL 91, WhoWor 91*
Bellessa, James Lloyd, Jr. 1946- *St&PR 91*
Belleville, Anna Caroline 1808-1880 *BioIn 16*
Belleville, Philip Frederick 1934- *WhoAm 90*
Bellezza, Leonard, Jr. 1947- *St&PR 91*
Bellezza, Richard Alan 1948- *WhoSSW 91*
Bellezza, Vincenzo 1888-1964 *PenDiMP*
Belli, Arcangelo 1933- *WhoWor 91*
Belli, Carlos German 1927- *ConAu 131, HispWr 90*
Belli, Claudio 1928- *ODwPR 91*
Belli, Melvin Louron 1907- *WhoWrEP 89*
Belli, Melvin M. 1907- *WorAlBi*
Belli, Melvin Mouron 1907- *WhoAm 90*
Belli, Remo *BioIn 16*
Belli, Valerio 1460-1546 *PenDiDA 89*
Belli, Vincenzo 1710-1787 *PenDiDA 89*
Belliard, Rafael 1961- *Ballpl 90*
Bellido, Ricardo L. 1953- *WhoHisp 91*
Bellin, Anne 1957- *WhoAmW 91*
Bellin, Carolyn Catherine 1953- *WhoEmL 91*
Bellin, Christina Paolozzi *BioIn 16*
Bellin, Evan Hillel *BiDrAPA 89*
Bellin, Marvin L 1929- *BiDrAPA 89*
Bellin, Matthew E. 1956- *St&PR 91*
Bellin, Milton R *WhoAmA 91*
Bellincioni, Gemma 1864-1950 *PenDiMP*
Bellinfante, Bruno 1929- *BiDrAPA 89*
Belling, Donald William 1956- *St&PR 91*
Belling, Susan 1943- *IntWWM 90*
Bellinger, George M. 1932- *St&PR 91*
Bellinger, Gretchen 1946- *ConDes 90*
Bellinger, John Bellinger, Jr. 1926- *WhoE 91, WhoWor 91*
Bellinger, John D. *St&PR 91N*
Bellinger, Louisa *WhoAmA 91N*
Bellinger, Sidney B *BiDrAPA 89*
Bellingham, Brenda 1931- *BioIn 16*
Bellingham, John *PenDiDA 89*
Bellingham, Sydney Robert 1808-1900 *DcCanB 12*
Bellingham-Smith, Elinor 1906-1988 *BiDWomA*
Bellini, Gentile 1429-1507? *IntDcAA 90, WorAlBi*
Bellini, Giovanni 1430?-1516 *IntDcAA 90, WorAlBi*
Bellini, Jacopo 1400?-1470? *WorAlBi*
Bellini, Jacopo 1400?-1471 *IntDcAA 90*
Bellini, Mario *PenDiDA 89*
Bellini, Mario 1935- *ConDes 90*
Bellini, Vincenzo 1801-1835 *PenDiMP A, WorAlBi*
Bellink, Alan A. 1948- *WhoEmL 91*
Bellino, Carmine 1905-1990 *BioIn 16*
Bellino, Carmine S. *NewYTBS 90 [port]*
Bellino, Robert Angelo 1930- *St&PR 91*
Bellino, Robert John *BiDrAPA 89*
Bellino, Vincent J. 1943- *St&PR 91*
Bellis, Arthur Albert 1928- *WhoWor 91*
Bellis, David R. 1931- *St&PR 91*
Bellis, Frank A., Jr. 1953- *St&PR 91*
Bellis, John M 1922- *BiDrAPA 89*
Bellis, John Marvin 1922- *WhoE 91*
Bellis, Kirk 1951- *BiDrAPA 89*
Bellis, Milton B. *ODwPR 91*
Bellis, Warren Tarleton 1923- *IntWWM 90*
Bellisario, Earl J. 1949- *St&PR 91*
Bellisario, Marisa *BioIn 16*
Bellisario, Marisa 1938?-1988 *AnObit 1988*
Bellison, Simeon 1883-1953 *PenDiMP*
Belliston, Angus Henry 1932- *St&PR 91*
Bellizia, Pieta Cohen *ODwPR 91*
Bellizzi, John J. 1919- *WhoE 91, WhoWor 91*
Bellm, Charles Newton 1912- *St&PR 91*
Bellm, Peggy Ann *WhoAmW 91*
Bellman, Carl Michael 1740-1795 *DcScanL*
Bellman, Joan Y. 1952- *WhoAmW 91*
Bellmer, Hans 1902-1975 *WhoAmA 91N*
Bellmon, Henry Louis 1921- *WhoAm 90, WhoSSW 91, WhoWor 91*
Bello, Andres 1781-1865 *BioIn 16*
Bello, Carmelita Angela 1955- *WhoAmW 91*
Bello, Doris M. 1948- *WhoHisp 91*
Bello, George Ernest 1935- *St&PR 91*
Bello, Harry Antonio 1942- *St&PR 91*
Bello, J. Rafael 1951- *WhoEmL 91*
Bello, Judith Hippler *WhoE 91*
Bello, Louis A. 1926- *St&PR 91*
Bello, Mohammed 1930- *WhoWor 91*
Bello, Roberto 1933- *WhoHisp 91*
Bello, Shere Capparella 1956- *WhoAmW 91, WhoEmL 91*
Bello-Reuss, Elsa Noemi 1939- *WhoAmW 91*
Bello Ruiz, Rafael 1926- *WhoAm 90*
Belloc, Hilaire 1870-1953 *DcLB 100 [port]*
Belloc, Jeanne *EncO&P 3*
Belloc, Joseph Hilaire Pierre 1870-1953 *AuBYP 90*
Belloc, Marc Henri 1922- *WhoWor 91*
Bellocchi, Natale H. 1926- *WhoAm 90*
Bellocchio, Marco *BioIn 16*
Bellocq, Louise *EncCoWW*
Belloit, Nicholas George 1950- *WhoSSW 91*
Bellomo, Gaspare M. 1930- *St&PR 91*
Bellomo, Salvatore 1959- *WhoEmL 91*
Bellonci, Christopher *BiDrAPA 89*
Bellonci, Maria 1902- *EncCoWW*
Belloni, Robert Clinton 1919- *WhoAm 90*
Bellos, David 1945- *WhoWor 91*
Bellosio, Eugenio 1847-1927 *PenDiDA 89*
Bellot-Rosado, Francisco 1941- *WhoWor 91*
Bellotti, Francis Xavier 1923- *WhoAm 90*
Bellotti, Grace *BiDrAPA 89*
Bellotti, Lawrence F. 1933- *St&PR 91*
Bellovin, Barry Lawrence 1957- *WhoEmL 91*
Bellovin, Evan Scott 1964- *St&PR 91*
Bellovin, Jonas 1914- *St&PR 91*
Bellovin, Michael Keith 1961- *St&PR 91*
Bellovin, Sheldon 1940- *St&PR 91*
Bellow, Alexandra 1935- *WhoAm 90*
Bellow, Donald Grant 1931- *WhoAm 90*
Bellow, Saul *BioIn 16*
Bellow, Saul 1915- *ConLC 63 [port], MajTwCW, WhoAm 90, WhoWor 91, WhoWrEP 89, WorAlBi, WrPh*
Bellows, Ann C. *ODwPR 91*
Bellows, Bambi Kim 1963- *WhoAmW 91*
Bellows, Carole Kamin 1935- *WhoAmW 91*
Bellows, Cathy *AuBYP 90*
Bellows, Charles Sanger 1915- *WhoAm 90*
Bellows, Cheryl Elaine 1950- *St&PR 91*
Bellows, George 1882-1925 *BioIn 16, IntDcAA 90*
Bellows, George Wesley 1882-1925 *WorAlBi*
Bellows, H. Arthur, Jr. 1938- *St&PR 91*
Bellows, Howard Arthur, Jr. 1938- *WhoAm 90*
Bellows, Jean Farley 1940- *WhoE 91*
Bellows, John 1906- *WhoAm 90*
Bellows, Paul Felton 1946- *WhoEmL 91, WhoSSW 91*
Bellows, Randall Trueblood 1946- *WhoAm 90*
Bellows, Thomas J 1935- *ConAu 31NR*
Bellows, Thomas John 1935- *WhoAm 90*
Bellows, William *ODwPR 91*
Bellows-Blakely, David S 1951- *BiDrAPA 89*
Bellringer, Stephen Terrence 1946- *WhoAm 90*
Bellrose, Frank Chapman *BioIn 16*
Bellson, Louis 1924- *BioIn 16, OxCPMus*
Bellson, Louis Paul 1924- *WhoAm 90*
Bellugi, Piero 1924- *IntWWM 90, PenDiMP*
Belluomini, Frank Stephen 1934- *WhoAm 90*
Bellus, Ronald Joseph 1951- *WhoEmL 91*
Belluschi, Anthony C. 1941- *WhoWor 91*
Belluschi, Pietro 1899- *WhoAm 90*
Bellush, Bernard 1917- *ConAu 132*
Bellville, Charles George 1947- *BiDrAPA 89*
Bellville, Cheryl Walsh 1944- *BioIn 16*
Bellville, John Kyper *BiDrAPA 89*
Bellville, Tara Marie *BiDrAPA 89*
Bellville, Titus P *BiDrAPA 89*
Bellwoar, John Elmer 1919- *St&PR 91*
Bellwood, Sherman Jean 1917- *WhoAm 90*
Bellwood, Wesley E. 1923- *St&PR 91*
Belmaker, Robert Henry 1947- *BiDrAPA 89*
Belman, A. Barry 1938- *WhoAm 90*
Belman, Murray Joel 1935- *WhoAm 90*
Belmar, Warren 1942- *WhoE 91*
Belmares, Hector 1938- *WhoWor 91*
Belmer, Charles Miller, Jr. 1949- *WhoEmL 91*
Belmondo, Jean-Paul 1933- *WhoWor 91, WorAlBi*
Belmont, Alejandro F. 1943- *WhoWor 91*
Belmont, Alva *BioIn 16*
Belmont, August 1813-1890 *EncABHB 6 [port]*
Belmont, August 1816-1890 *BioIn 16*
Belmont, August 1853-1924 *WorAlBi*
Belmont, August 1908- *WhoAm 90*
Belmont, Elisabeth 1956- *WhoAmW 91*
Belmont, Herman S 1920- *BiDrAPA 89*
Belmont, Ira Jean 1885-1964 *WhoAmA 91N*
Belmont, Jim 1924- *St&PR 91*
Belmont, Oliver Hazard Perry 1858-1908 *BioIn 16*
Belmont, Perry 1851-1947 *BioIn 16*
Belmont, Vincent 1923- *St&PR 91*
Belmonte, Kathleen Ann 1961- *WhoAmW 91*
Belmonte, Maria A G *BiDrAPA 89*
Belnap, David Foster 1922- *WhoAm 90, WhoWrEP 89*
Belnap, Michael Gary 1953- *WhoEmL 91*
Belnap, Norma Lee Madsen 1927- *IntWWM 90, WhoAm 90*
Belnap, Norman B 1927- *BiDrAPA 89*
Belnap, Nuel Dinsmore, Jr. 1930- *WhoAm 90*
Belnap, Wilford Dean 1926- *BiDrAPA 89*
Belnick, Ben 1920- *St&PR 91*
Belnick, Mark Alan 1946- *WhoEmL 91*
Belo, Fernando 1933- *ConAu 131*
Beloe, Robert 1905-1984 *DcNaB 1981*
Beloff, Fae Claire 1937- *WhoAmW 91*
Beloff, John 1920- *EncO&P 3, EncPaPR 91*
Belohlav, James Anthony 1946- *WhoEmL 91*
Belohlavek, Jiri 1946- *IntWWM 90, WhoWor 91*
Beloiu, Nicolae 1927- *IntWWM 90*
Belok, Michael Victor 1923- *WhoAm 90*
Belon, Philippe-Etienne 1949- *WhoWor 91*
Belonga, Bianca *BioIn 16*
Beloof, Robert Lawrence 1923- *WhoAm 90, WhoWrEP 89*
Belot, Thomas G. 1950- *St&PR 91*
Belote, Kendall F. 1943- *St&PR 91*
Belotti, R.T. 1917- *St&PR 91*
Belousov, Boris Mikhaylovich 1934- *WhoWor 91*
Belov, Nikolai Vasil'evich 1891-1982 *DcScB S2*
Belovanoff, Olga 1932- *WhoAmW 91*
Belove, Edward J. 1950- *St&PR 91*
Beloyianis, Jim *BioIn 16*
Belozerskii, Andrei Nikolaevich 1905-1972 *DcScB S2*
Belpaire, Maria Elisa 1853-1948 *EncCoWW*
Belpre, Pura 1899-1982 *AuBYP 90*
Belsasso, Guido 1935- *BiDrAPA 89*
Belser, Edgar Heinz 1931- *WhoWor 91*
Belser, James Burkey 1947- *WhoE 91*
Belsevica, Vizma 1931- *EncCoWW*
Belsha, Leslie Beeks, Jr. 1934- *St&PR 91*
Belshaw, Cyril Shirley 1921- *WhoAm 90*
Belshaw, George Phelps Mellick 1928- *WhoAm 90*
Belshaw, Gordon Charles 1925- *St&PR 91*
Belshaw, Jack William 1932- *St&PR 91*
Belshaw, Thomas E. 1920- *St&PR 91*
Belsito, Donald Vincent 1950- *WhoE 91*
Belsito, Linda Jo 1957- *WhoAmW 91*
Belsito, Luke Richard 1946- *St&PR 91*
Belskis, David 1954- *WhoEmL 91*
Belsky, Alberte M. 1926- *St&PR 91*
Belsky, Jerome 1917- *St&PR 91*
Belsky, Judith E 1937- *BiDrAPA 89*
Belsky, Martin A. 1930- *St&PR 91*
Belsky, Martin Henry 1944- *WhoAm 90, WhoE 91, WhoWor 91*
Belsley, David Alan 1939- *WhoE 91*
Belsly, John Robert 1930- *St&PR 91*
Belson, James Anthony 1931- *WhoE 91*
Belson, Jan Verona 1942- *St&PR 91*
Belson, Walter W. 1902-1989 *BioIn 16*
Belstead, Lord 1932- *WhoWor 91*
Belsterling, Jean Innes 1928- *WhoAmW 91*
Belt, Audrey Evon 1948- *WhoAmW 91, WhoEmL 91, WhoWor 91*
Belt, Bill A. 1935- *WhoSSW 91*
Belt, Bradley Deck 1958- *WhoEmL 91*
Belt, Brian 1945- *WhoEmL 91*
Belt, Donald Clifford 1947- *St&PR 91*
Belt, Donald E. 1924- *St&PR 91*
Belt, Edward Scudder 1933- *WhoAm 90, WhoE 91*
Belt, Guillermo 1905-1989 *BioIn 16*
Belt, Larry 1939- *IntWWM 90*
Belt, Larry Reynolds 1932- *St&PR 91*
Beltaire, Beverly 1926- *ODwPR 91*
Beltaire, Beverly Ann 1926- *WhoAm 90*
Beltangady, Shamal S 1947- *BiDrAPA 89*
Belteau, Kenneth Raymond 1946- *WhoEmL 91*
Belter, Edgar William 1929- *WhoWor 91*
Belter, John Henry 1804-1863 *BioIn 16, PenDiDA 89*
Belth, Joseph Morton 1929- *WhoAm 90*
Belth, Nathan C. *BioIn 16*
Belthoff, Richard Charles, Jr. 1958- *WhoEmL 91*
Belting, Natalia Maree 1915- *AuBYP 90*
Belton, Betty Rose 1934- *WhoWrEP 89*
Belton, Ian *PenDiMP*
Belton, Jennifer H. *BioIn 16*
Belton, John Thomas 1947- *WhoEmL 91*

Belton, Kepka Hochman WhoWrEP 89
Belton, Ronald Wayne 1943- WhoSSW 91
Beltrame, James Michael 1943- St&PR 91
Beltrame, Joseph Robert 1943- St&PR 91
Beltrametti, Franco 1937- ConAu 13AS [port]
Beltrami, Edouard BiDrAPA 89
Beltrami, Marie BioIn 16
Beltrami, Pier Angelo 1950- WhoE 91
Beltramini, Antonio U BiDrAPA 89
Beltran, Alberto 1923- ArtLatA
Beltran, Armando 1949- WhoHisp 91
Beltran, Celestino Martinez 1945- WhoHisp 91
Beltran, Eufrocino N 1931- BiDrAPA 89
Beltran, Eusebius Joseph 1934- WhoAm 90, WhoSSW 91
Beltran, Felix 1938- ConDes 90, WhoAmA 91
Beltran, Lourdes Luz 1961- WhoHisp 91
Beltran, Mario Alberto 1952- WhoHisp 91
Beltran, Michael R. 1940- St&PR 91
Beltran, Romulo Garcia BiDrAPA 89
Beltrane, Sheryl Ann 1945- WhoAmW 91, WhoSSW 91
Beltrao, Alexandre Fontana 1924- WhoWor 91
Beltz, Charles Robert 1913- WhoAm 90
Beltz, Herbert Allison 1926- WhoAm 90
Beltz, William Albert 1929- St&PR 91, WhoAm 90, WhoWrEP 89
Beltzer, Herman M. 1927- St&PR 91
Beltzer, Herman Martin 1927- WhoAm 90
Beltzman, David Gary BiDrAPA 89
Beltzner, Gail Ann 1950- WhoAmW 91, WhoE 91, WhoEmL 91, WhoWor 91
Belue, Buck BioIn 16
Belushi, James 1954- WorAlBi
Belushi, Jim BioIn 16
Belushi, John 1949-1982 BioIn 16, WorAlBi
Belville, Barbara Ann 1957- WhoEmL 91
Belville, Scott Robert 1952- WhoAmA 91
Bely, Andrey 1880-1934 WrPh
Belyea, Robert C. 1925- St&PR 91
Belz, Carl Irvin 1937- WhoAmA 91, WhoE 91
Belz, Irving 1937- BiDrAPA 89
Belz, Stephen Robert 1953- St&PR 91
Belzberg, Brent Stanley 1951- WhoAm 90
Belzberg, Samuel 1928- St&PR 91, WhoAm 90
Belzberg, William 1932- WhoAm 90
Belzer, Alan 1932- St&PR 91, WhoAm 90, WhoE 91
Belzer, Burton E. 1926- St&PR 91
Belzer, Ellen J. 1951- WhoAmW 91
Belzer, John D. 1951- St&PR 91
Belzile, Gabriel BiDrAPA 89
Belzoni, Giovanni Battista 1778-1823 BioIn 16
Belzu, Manuel Isidoro 1809-1865 BioIn 16
Beman, Deane Randolph 1938- WhoAm 90
Beman, Lynn Susan 1942- WhoAmA 91
Bemananjara, Jean Andrianaribone 1943- WhoWor 91
Bembenek, Alan Roger 1960- WhoEmL 91
Bemberg, Gerald Francis 1945- St&PR 91
Bembo, Illuminata 1410?-1496 EncCoWW
Bemelmans, Ludwig 1898-1962 AuBYP 90, WorAlBi
Bemelmans, Ludwig 1898-1963 WhoAmA 91N
Bement, Arden Lee, Jr. 1932- WhoAm 90
Bemis, Charles E BiDrAPA 89
Bemis, Claudia Claire 1956- BiDrAPA 89
Bemis, F. Gregg, Jr. 1928- St&PR 91
Bemis, Hal L. 1912- St&PR 91
Bemis, Hal Lawall 1912- WhoE 91, WhoWor 91
Bemis, Harry 1874-1947 Ballpl 90
Bemis, Lawrence Preston 1930- WhoE 91
Bemis, Michael B. 1947- St&PR 91, WhoAm 90
Bemis, Nancy Lynne 1952- WhoE 91
Bemis, Royce Edwin 1941- WhoSSW 91
Bemis, Samuel Flagg 1891-1973 BioIn 16
Bemis, Thomas Bruce 1953- WhoEmL 91
Bemis, Waldo Edmund WhoAmA 91N
Bemister, John 1815-1892 DcCanB 12
Bemmann, Guenter 1927- WhoWor 91
Bemmann, Kathryn C 1931- BiDrAPA 89
Bemporad, Jules R 1937- BiDrAPA 89
Ben, Joan 1967- WhoEmL 91
Ben, Max 1926- WhoSSW 91
Ben Abdallah, Moncef 1946- WhoWor 91
Ben Ali, Zine Al-Abidine 1936- WhoWor 91
Ben Ali, Zine El Abidine 1936- PolLCME
Ben-Ami, Yitshaq 1913- ConAu 130
Ben Amor, Ismail 1937- WhoWor 91
Ben-Amotz, Dahn BioIn 16
Ben-Amotz, Dan 1923?-1989 ConAu 130
Ben-Asher, Daniel Lawrence 1946- WhoE 91, WhoEmL 91
Ben Ayed, Abdelahed 1938- WhoWor 91
Ben Bella, Ahmed 1918- PolLCME
Ben Daniel, David Jacob 1931- WhoAm 90
Ben-David, Ron 1946- St&PR 91
Ben-Gal, Joseph 1951- St&PR 91
Ben-Gurion, David 1886-1973 BioIn 16, PolLCME, WorAlBi
Ben-Haim, Paul 1897-1984 BioIn 16, PenDiMP A
Ben-Haim, Tsipi 1951- WhoAmA 91
Ben-Haim, Zigi 1945- WhoAmA 91
Ben-Israel, Shabtai WhoWrEP 89
Ben-Menachem, Yoram 1934- WhoAm 90
Ben-Moshe, Baoz 1946- St&PR 91
Ben-Naftali, Abraham 1935- WhoWor 91
Ben-Or, Nelly IntWWM 90
Ben Salah, Ahmed BioIn 16
Ben-Shir, Rya Helen 1955- WhoEmL 91
Ben-Tovim, Atarah 1940- PenDiMP
Ben Tre, Howard B 1949- WhoAmA 91
Ben Yahia, Habib 1938- WhoAm 90
Ben-Yohanan, Asher 1929- IntWWM 90
Ben-Zvi, Phillip N. 1942- St&PR 91
Ben-Zvi, Phillip Norman 1942- WhoAm 90
Benacerraf, Baruj 1920- WhoAm 90, WhoE 91, WhoWor 91, WorAlBi
Benacerraf, Paul 1931- WhoAm 90
Benach, Henry 1917- St&PR 91
Benach, Sharon Ann 1944- WhoAmW 91
Benacin, Philippe 1958- St&PR 91
Benackova, Gabriela BioIn 16
Benackova, Gabriela 1944- IntWWM 90
Benackova, Gabriela 1947- PenDiMP
Benade, Arthur H. 1925-1987 BioIn 16
Benade, Leo Edward 1916- WhoAm 90
Benado, Nissim BiDrAPA 89
Benagh, Jim 1937- AuBYP 90
Benak, James Donald 1954- WhoEmL 91, WhoWor 91
Benaksas-Schwartz, Elaine Julie 1959- WhoAmW 91
Benamati, Dennis Charles 1948- WhoEmL 91
Benanav, Gary G. 1945- St&PR 91
Benard, Andre Pierre Jacques 1922- WhoWor 91
Benard, Bruce Raymond 1949- WhoEmL 91, WhoSSW 91
Benardete, Mair Jose 1895-1989 BioIn 16
Benaresh, Ehsanollah 1934- WhoE 91
Benario, Herbert William 1929- WhoAm 90, WhoSSW 91
Benaron, Tully 1909- BiDrAPA 89
Benaroya, Haym 1954- WhoE 91
Benarroche, Cesar Luis 1948- BiDrAPA 89
Benary-Isbert, Margot 1889-1979 AuBYP 90
Benatar, Leo 1930- St&PR 91, WhoAm 90, WhoSSW 91
Benatar, Pat 1953?- EncPR&S 89, WhoAm 90, WhoAmW 91
Benatar, Solomon Robert 1942- WhoWor 91
Benatzky, Ralph 1884-1957 OxCPMus
Benaud, Richard 1930- ConAu 131
Benaud, Richie ConAu 131
Benavante Y Martinez, Jacinto 1866-1954 WorAlBi
Benavente, Jacinto 1866-1954 ConAu 131, HispWr 90, MajTwCW
Benavente y Martinez, Jacinto MajTwCW
Benavente y Martinez, Jacinto 1866-1954 HispWr 90
Benavidas, Alonso De WhNaAH
Benavides, Alonso EncCRAm
Benavides, Alonzo de WhNaAH
Benavides, George Henry 1944- WhoHisp 91
Benavides, Jaime Miguel 1923- WhoSSW 91, WhoWor 91
Benavides, Julie Maria 1952- WhoAmW 91
Benavides, Norma WhoHisp 91
Benavides, Oscar R. 1876-1945 BioIn 16
Benavides, Patrick R. 1953- St&PR 91
Benavides, Placido 1836-1919 BioIn 16
Benavides, Roger J. 1950- St&PR 91
Benavides, Santos 1823-1891 BioIn 16
Benavides, Steven Mel 1963- WhoHisp 91
Benavidez, Frank Gregory 1927- WhoHisp 91
Benavidez, Jose Modesto 1941- WhoHisp 91
Benavidez, Michael D. 1959- WhoHisp 91
Benavidez, Roy Perez 1935- WhoHisp 91
Benavidez, Thomas R. WhoHisp 91
Benbassat, Mario 1933- WhoWor 91
BenBassett, Jane Schumer 1961- WhoEmL 91
Benberry, Cuesta Ray 1923- WhoAmW 91
Benbow, Camilla Persson 1956- WhoAmW 91, WhoEmL 91
Benbow, Charles Clarence 1929- WhoAm 90, WhoWrEP 89
Benbow, John 1653-1702 BioIn 16
Benbow, John Robert 1931- WhoAm 90
Benbow, Sam H 1930- BiDrAPA 89
Benbow, Terence Howard 1929- WhoE 91
Benbow, William E. 1930- St&PR 91
Benca, Ruth Myra 1954- BiDrAPA 89
Bence, Kenneth C. 1928- St&PR 91
Bence, Kevin James 1961- St&PR 91
Bench, Dan A. 1934- St&PR 91
Bench, Johnny 1947- Ballpl 90 [port], WorAlBi
Bench, Johnny Lee 1947- WhoAm 90
Benchley, Belle Jennings 1882-1973 BioIn 16
Benchley, Nathaniel Goddard 1915-1981 AuBYP 90
Benchley, Peter 1940- MajTwCW
Benchley, Peter Bradford 1940- WhoAm 90, WhoWrEP 89
Benchley, Robert 1889-1945 BioIn 16, WorAlBi
Benchoff, J. Martin 1927- St&PR 91
Benchoff, James Martin 1927- WhoAm 90
Bencini, Sara Haltiwanger 1926- WhoAmW 91
Bencivenga, Ernest V. 1918- St&PR 91
Bencivenga, Marylou A. 1943- WhoE 91
Bencke, Ronald L. 1940- St&PR 91
Benckenstein, John Henry 1903- WhoSSW 91, WhoWor 91
Benckgraff, Johann PenDiDA 89
Bencks, Rodney N. 1934- St&PR 91
Bencze, Eva Ivanyos 1932- WhoAmW 91
Benczene Mezo, Judit 1933- IntWWM 90
Benczik, Terry Ann 1957- WhoAmW 91, WhoEmL 91
Benda, Carl Thomas 1937- St&PR 91
Benda, Julien 1867-1956 BiDFrPL, BioIn 16
Benda, Marilyn Virginia 1935- WhoAmW 91
Benda, W T 1891-1948 WhoAmA 91N
Bendah, David BioIn 16
Bendale, Ulhas Yashwant 1950- BiDrAPA 89
Bendall, Mildred 1891-1977 BiDWomA
Bendavid, Joseph 1930- St&PR 91
Bende, Andras V. 1938- St&PR 91
Bendel, Peggy R. 1943- ODwPR 91
Bendelius, Albert 1913- St&PR 91
Bendelius, Arthur George 1936- WhoAm 90, WhoWor 91
Bendell, Marilyn 1921- BioIn 16, WhoAmA 91
Benden, William Joseph 1933- WhoE 91
Bender, Chief 1883-1954 Ballpl 90 [port]
Bender, Albert K. EncO&P 3
Bender, Bernd Harald 1919- WhoWor 91
Bender, Betty Barbee 1932- WhoAmW 91
Bender, Betty Wion 1925- WhoAm 90, WhoAmW 91
Bender, Beverly Sterl 1918- WhoAmA 91
Bender, Bill 1919- WhoAmA 91
Bender, Bruce Dean 1951- WhoEmL 91
Bender, Bruce F. 1949- St&PR 91
Bender, Byron Wilbur 1929- WhoAm 90
Bender, Carl Martin 1943- WhoAm 90
Bender, Charles A. 1937- St&PR 91
Bender, Charles C. 1936- St&PR 91
Bender, Charles Christian 1936- WhoAm 90
Bender, Charles William 1933- WhoAm 90
Bender, Chris A. 1950- St&PR 91
Bender, David BiDrAPA 89, ODwPR 91
Bender, David R. 1942- BioIn 16
Bender, David Ray 1942- WhoAm 90
Bender, Denise Margaret 1960- WhoAmW 91
Bender, Diane Louise Wolf 1955- WhoAmW 91, WhoWor 91
Bender, Douglas Ray 1953- WhoSSW 91
Bender, Edward C. 1937- St&PR 91
Bender, Eileen Teper 1935- WhoAmW 91
Bender, Eleanor M. 1941- WhoWrEP 89
Bender, Elizabeth Melchert 1960- WhoAmW 91
Bender, Estelle P BiDrAPA 89
Bender, Esther Louise 1942- WhoWrEP 89
Bender, Gary Nedrow 1940- WhoAm 90
Bender, Gary William 1948- WhoE 91
Bender, Gerald Joseph 1937- IntWWM 90
Bender, Graham I. 1939- St&PR 91
Bender, Hans 1907- EncO&P 3, EncPaPR 91
Bender, Harold 1910- St&PR 91
Bender, Henry Elias 1938- WhoWor 91
Bender, Howard BioIn 16
Bender, James David 1957- WhoSSW 91
Bender, James Frederick 1905- WhoAm 90
Bender, James Martin BiDrAPA 89
Bender, Jay Mitchell 1935- St&PR 91
Bender, Joel Charles 1939- WhoWor 91
Bender, John Charles 1940- WhoAm 90
Bender, John Henry, Jr. 1931- WhoSSW 91, WhoWor 91
Bender, Katie ODwPR 91
Bender, Kenneth Ray 1926- WhoAm 90
Bender, Lauretta 1897-1987 BioIn 16
Bender, Linda ODwPR 91
Bender, Linda Arlene 1951- WhoEmL 91
Bender, Louis W. 1927- ConAu 32NR
Bender, Michael Keith 1947- WhoSSW 91
Bender, Miles D. 1937- St&PR 91
Bender, Miles Dennis 1937- WhoSSW 91, WhoWor 91
Bender, Nathan J BiDrAPA 89
Bender, Paul 1875-1947 PenDiMP
Bender, Phoebe Powell 1933- WhoAmW 91
Bender, Richard 1930- WhoAm 90
Bender, Ross Thomas 1929- WhoAm 90
Bender, Stephen H BiDrAPA 89
Bender, Steven N. ODwPR 91
Bender, Theodore J., III 1947- St&PR 91
Bender, Thomas 1944- WhoAm 90, WhoWrEP 89
Bender, Thomas Richard 1939- WhoAm 90
Bender, Virginia Best 1945- WhoAmW 91, WhoEmL 91, WhoWor 91
Bender, Wanda Marie 1958- WhoAmW 91
Bender, Welcome William 1915- WhoAm 90
Benderly, Beryl Lieff 1943- ConAu 30NR
Benderson, Bruce 1952- WhoWrEP 89
Bendetsen, Karl Robin 1907-1989 BioIn 16
Bendetson, Robert Rome 1951- St&PR 91
Bendheim, C.H. 1917- St&PR 91
Bendheim, Otto L BiDrAPA 89
Bendick, Jeanne 1919- AuBYP 90
Bendick, Marc, Jr. 1946- WhoE 91
Bendick, Robert Louis 1917- AuBYP 90
Bendick, Robert Louis, Jr. 1946- WhoAm 90
Bendig, Judith Joan 1955- WhoAmW 91
Bendig, William Charles 1927- WhoAm 90
Bendikas, Omar Jurgis 1927- St&PR 91
Bendiner, Robert 1909- BioIn 16, WhoAm 90, WhoWrEP 89
Bendit, Daniel Cohn- BioIn 16
Bendit, Emile Abraham 1943- BiDrAPA 89, WhoE 91
Bendit, L J 1898-1974 EncO&P 3
Bendit, Phoebe Daphne 1891- EncO&P 3
Benditt, Theodore Matthew 1940- WhoAm 90
Bendix, Reinhard BioIn 16
Bendix, Richard C. 1948- St&PR 91
Bendix, Vincent 1881-1945 EncABHB 4, WorAlBi
Bendix, William E. 1935- St&PR 91
Bendix, William Emanuel 1935- WhoAm 90
Bendixen, Arturo 1950- WhoHisp 91
Bendixen, Ethel Tolena WhoAmW 91
Bendixen, Fanny 1820?-1899 DcCanB 12
Bendixen, Henrik Holt 1923- WhoAm 90
Bendjedid Chadli BioIn 16
Bendjedid, Chadli 1925- PolLCME
Bendjedid, Chadli 1929- WhoWor 91
Bendjou WomWR
Bendor, Daniel Edmond BiDrAPA 89
Bendorf, Ronald Lee 1937- BiDrAPA 89
Bendorz, Johanes Georg 1950- WorAlBi
Bendowski, Joseph Adam 1943- St&PR 91
Bendt, Norma June 1955- WhoAmW 91
Bendure, Raymond L. 1943- WhoE 91
Bendzin, Leonard John 1925- St&PR 91
Bene, Adriana Ferrarese Del PenDiMP
Benecki, Walter T. 1939- St&PR 91
Benedek, Elissa P 1936- BiDrAPA 89
Benedek, George Bernard 1928- WhoAm 90
Benedek, Melinda 1951- St&PR 91
Benedek, William Clark 1957- WhoEmL 91
Benedet, Maria Gertrude BiDrAPA 89
Benedetta 1897-1977 BiDWomA
Benedetti, Charles BiDrAPA 89
Benedetti, David J. St&PR 91
Benedetti, Dean BioIn 16
Benedetti, Joseph C. 1942- St&PR 91
Benedetti, Joseph Carmelo 1942- WhoAm 90
Benedetti, Mario 1920- BioIn 16, HispWr 90
Benedetti, Rene PenDiMP
Benedetti, Richard 1949- St&PR 91
Benedetti, Thomas Joseph 1947- WhoAm 90
Benedetti Michelangeli, Arturo 1920- PenDiMP
Benedetto da Maiano PenDiDA 89
Benedetto da Maiano 1442-1497 IntDcAA 90
Benedetto, Maestro PenDiDA 89
Benedetto, Antonio di HispWr 90
Benedetto, Donna A. 1962- WhoWrEP 89
Benedetto, Giuliana 1949- WhoWor 91
Benedetto, Lorraine Ann 1949- WhoAmW 91, WhoE 91, WhoEmL 91
Benedetto, Lynda Elizabeth 1943- WhoAmW 91
Benedetto, M. William 1941- St&PR 91, WhoE 91
Benedetto, Nancy Beth 1959- WhoE 91
Benedetto, Peter P. 1930- St&PR 91
Benedetto, Salvatore A. 1937- St&PR 91
Benedick, Dale Raymond 1941- WhoSSW 91
Benedick, Richard Elliot 1935- WhoAm 90

Benedict IX 1021?-1054? *EncO&P 3*
Benedict XIV 1678-1758 *EncPaPR 91*
Benedict, Mrs *EncO&P 3*
Benedict, Saint *BioIn 16*
Benedict, Saint 480-547 *WorAlBi*
Benedict, Saint, of Nursia *BioIn 16*
Benedict, Andrew Bell, Jr. 1914- *St&PR 91*
Benedict, Bruce 1955- *Ballpl 90, BioIn 16*
Benedict, Bruce Whitlock 1937- *St&PR 91*
Benedict, Burton 1923- *WhoAm 90*
Benedict, Clyde 1927- *St&PR 91*
Benedict, Debbie Sweeney 1952- *WhoAmW 91*
Benedict, Donwayne 1933- *St&PR 91*
Benedict, Dorothy Catherine 1931- *WhoE 91*
Benedict, Edward E. *BioIn 16*
Benedict, Elinor Divine 1931- *WhoAmW 91, WhoWrEP 89*
Benedict, Elizabeth 1954- *ConAu 131*
Benedict, Ellen Maring 1931- *WhoAmW 91*
Benedict, Francis E. 1939- *St&PR 91*
Benedict, Fred K. 1923- *St&PR 91*
Benedict, Fredric Allen 1914- *WhoAm 90*
Benedict, Helen Elizabeth 1946- *WhoAm 90*
Benedict, Jack R. 1931- *St&PR 91*
Benedict, Jim *BioIn 16*
Benedict, John G. *NewYTBS 90*
Benedict, Julius 1804-1885 *PenDiMP A*
Benedict, Linda Sherk 1945- *WhoE 91, WhoEmL 91*
Benedict, Manson 1907- *WhoAm 90*
Benedict, Mark J 1951- *WhoSSW 91*
Benedict, Mary Wilson Holt-Smith *BioIn 16*
Benedict, Paul C. 1943- *St&PR 91*
Benedict, Peter Folger 1943- *St&PR 91*
Benedict, Philip 1949- *ConAu 130*
Benedict, Pinckney 1964- *BioIn 16*
Benedict, Rex 1920- *AuBYP 90*
Benedict, Robert C. 1938- *St&PR 91*
Benedict, Ruth *EncJap*
Benedict, Ruth 1887-1948 *BioIn 16, FemiCLE, WorAlBi*
Benedict, Ruth F. 1887-1948 *BioAmW*
Benedict, Salli M. Kawennotakie 1954- *WhoAm 90*
Benedict-Jones, Linda L 1947- *WhoAmA 91*
Benedictsson, Victoria 1850-1888 *DcScanL*
Benedictus, David 1938- *BioIn 16*
Benedik, Kenneth Joseph 1946- *WhoSSW 91*
Benedikt Sveinbjarnarson *DcScanL*
Benedikt, Bozidar D. 1938- *WhoWor 91*
Benedikt, Michael 1935- *WhoAm 90, WhoAmA 91, WhoE 91, WhoWrEP 89, WorAu 1980 [port]*
Benediktsson, Einar 1864-1940 *DcScanL*
Benediktsson, Jakob 1907- *WhoWor 91*
Benedit, Luis 1937- *ArtLatA*
Benedosso, Anthony Nechols 1949- *WhoEmL 91*
Benefiel, Billy Joe 1949- *WhoSSW 91*
Benefiel-Ertter, Annette Marie 1962- *WhoAmW 91*
Benefield, James Dewey, Jr. 1931- *St&PR 91*
Benegal, Shyam *BioIn 16*
Beneke, Everett Smith 1918- *WhoAm 90*
Beneke, Tex 1914- *OxCPMus*
Beneke, Walter 1923- *HispWr 90*
Benelbas, Leon Amram 1952- *WhoWor 91*
Benelli, Ugo 1935- *IntWWM 90*
Beneman, Guillaume *PenDiDA 89*
Benemerito, Maria Luisa *BiDrAPA 89*
Benensohn, Howard S 1940- *BiDrAPA 89*
Benenson, Alan Keith 1947- *BiDrAPA 89*
Benenson, Claire Berger *WhoE 91*
Benenson, David Maurice 1927- *WhoAm 90*
Benenson, Edward Hartley 1914- *WhoAm 90, WhoAmA 91, WhoWor 91*
Benenson, James, Jr. 1936- *St&PR 91, WhoAm 90*
Benenson, Lawrence A. *AuBYP 90*
Benenson, Mark Keith 1929- *WhoAm 90*
Benenson, Walter 1936- *WhoAm 90*
Benepe, Andrew *BioIn 16*
Benepe, James L. Jr. *BiDrAPA 89*
Benequit, Maryjane Grace 1926- *St&PR 91*
Beneria, Lourdes 1937- *WhoE 91*
Benerito, Ruth Rogan 1916- *WhoAm 90*
Benerofe, Stanley 1933- *St&PR 91*
Benes, Barton Lidice 1942- *WhoAmA 91*
Benes, Eduard 1884-1948 *WorAlBi*
Benes, Edvard 1884-1948 *BioIn 16*
Benes, Jiri 1928- *IntWWM 90*
Benes, Juraj 1940- *IntWWM 90*
Benes, Marcia Elizabeth 1949- *WhoAmW 91*
Benes, Patricia Ellen 1950- *WhoE 91*
Benes, Susan Carleton 1948- *WhoWor 91*
Benesch, Katherine 1946- *WhoEmL 91*
Benesch, Otto 1896-1964 *WhoAmA 91N*
Benesch, Ruth Erica 1925- *WhoAm 90*
Benesch, William Milton 1922- *WhoAm 90*
Benesh, Bruce Leonard *BiDrAPA 89*
Benesi, Betty-Ann B. 1952- *WhoAmW 91*
Benesova, Bo'ena 1873-1936 *EncCoWW*
Benestad, Finn 1929- *IntWWM 90*
Benet, Juan 1928- *IntvSpW [port]*
Benet, Laura 1884-1979 *AuBYP 90, FemiCLE*
Benet, Leslie Zachary 1937- *WhoAm 90*
Benet, Peter *BiDrAPA 89*
Benet, Stephen Vincent 1898-1943 *AuBYP 90, DcLB 102 [port], WorAlBi*
Benet, Sula 1906-1982 *AuBYP 90*
Benet, Thomas Carr 1926- *WhoAm 90, WhoWrEP 89*
Benet, William Rose 1886-1950 *WorAlBi*
Benetti, Federico Jose 1947- *WhoWor 91*
Beneventano, Thomas C. *BioIn 16*
Benevento, Francis O. 1942- *St&PR 91*
Beneyto Cunyat, Maria 1925- *EncCoWW*
Benezet, Anthony 1713-1784 *EncCRAm*
Benezet, Louis Tomlinson 1915- *WhoAm 90, WhoWor 91*
Benezra, E Eliot 1922- *BiDrAPA 89*
Benezra, Jeffrey C 1946- *BiDrAPA 89*
Benezra, Joseph Michael *BiDrAPA 89*
Benezra, Neal 1953- *WhoAm 90*
Benezra, Raymond Leon 1930- *St&PR 91*
Benfari, Robert Charles 1929- *WhoE 91*
Benfatti, Irene 1948- *WhoE 91*
Benfer, David William 1946- *WhoAm 90*
Benfey, Otto Theodor 1925- *WhoAm 90, WhoWrEP 89*
Benfield, Ann Kolb 1946- *WhoSSW 91*
Benfield, David William 1941- *WhoE 91, WhoWor 91*
Benfield, Derek 1926- *ConAu 30NR*
Benfield, Edward Stanley, II 1953- *BiDrAPA 89*
Benfield, James H. 1953- *St&PR 91*
Benfield, John Richard 1931- *WhoAm 90*
Benfield, Marion Wilson, Jr. 1932- *WhoAm 90*
Benfield, Thomas Charles *BiDrAPA 89*
Benforado, David M. 1925- *WhoAm 90*
Benford, Elizabeth B 1918- *BiDrAPA 89*
Benford, Gregory 1941- *RGTwCSF*
Benford, Gregory Albert 1941- *WhoAm 90, WhoWrEP 89*
Benford, Harry Bell 1917- *WhoAm 90*
Benford, Tim *ODwPR 91*
Bengali, Sakina H *BiDrAPA 89*
Benge, Christine J. H. 1951- *WhoAmW 91*
Benge, Douglas R. 1948- *St&PR 91*
Benge, Mary Cecelia Riley 1952- *WhoEmL 91*
Benge, Phillip James 1949- *WhoWor 91*
Benge, Ray 1902- *Ballpl 90*
Bengelloun, Ali 1927- *WhoWor 91*
Bengelsdorf, Herbert 1925- *BiDrAPA 89*
Bengelsdorf, Peter A. 1946- *St&PR 91*
Bengelsdorf, Rosalind 1916-1979 *BiDWomA*
Benger, Elizabeth Ogilvy 1778-1827 *FemiCLE*
Benghiat, Russell Alan 1948- *WhoEmL 91*
Benghozi, Tawfik M *BiDrAPA 89*
Bengisu, Turan 1922- *BiDrAPA 89*
Benglis, Lynda 1941- *BiDWomA, WhoAm 90, WhoAmA 91, WhoE 91*
Bengmark, Stig 1929- *WhoWor 91*
Bengoechea, Shane Orin 1956- *WhoEmL 91*
Bengough, Benny 1898-1968 *Ballpl 90*
Bengston, Billy Al *BioIn 16*
Bengston, Billy Al 1934- *WhoAm 90, WhoAmA 91*
Bengston, Clarence William 1921- *WhoAm 90*
Bengtson, Bruce D. 1938- *WhoAm 90*
Bengtson, Clifton David 1944- *St&PR 91*
Bengtson, Esther G. 1927- *WhoAmW 91*
Bengtson, Goran 1934- *WhoWor 91*
Bengtson, J.N. 1945- *St&PR 91*
Bengtson, Karl Wayne 1955- *WhoEmL 91*
Bengtson, Kathleen Ann 1949- *WhoAmW 91*
Bengtson, Roger Dean 1941- *WhoAm 90*
Bengtson, Vern LeRoy 1941- *WhoAm 90*
Bengtsson, Erling Blondal *IntWWM 90*
Bengtsson, Frans G. 1894-1954 *DcScanL*
Bengtsson, Ingemund 1919- *WhoWor 91*
Bengtsson, Ingmar 1920- *IntWWM 90*
Bengtsson, John-Ebbe 1933- *WhoWor 91*
Bengtz, Ture 1907-1973 *WhoAmA 91N*
Benhabib, Seyla 1950- *WhoWor 91*
Benham, David Blair 1918- *St&PR 91, WhoAm 90*
Benham, Douglas Neal 1956- *WhoSSW 91*
Benham, Helen Wheaton 1941- *IntWWM 90*
Benham, Isabel Hamilton 1909- *WhoAmW 91, WhoE 91*
Benham, James Mason 1935- *WhoAm 90*
Benham, Leslie 1922- *BioIn 16*
Benham, Lois 1924- *BioIn 16*
Benham, Mary Lile 1914- *BioIn 16*
Benham, Neil Roger 1936- *St&PR 91*
Benham, Pamela J 1947- *WhoAmA 91*
Benham, Robert Charles 1913- *WhoAmA 91*
Benham, Robert S. 1938- *St&PR 91*
Benham, Webster Lance 1949- *St&PR 91*
Benhard, F. Gordon 1934- *St&PR 91*
Benhart, Gary Len 1949- *WhoEmL 91*
Beni, Gerardo 1946- *WhoAm 90, WhoEmL 91*
Beni, John Joseph 1932- *WhoAm 90*
Benicewicz, Brian Chester 1954- *WhoEmL 91*
Benidt, Bruce *ODwPR 91*
Benigno, Thomas Daniel 1954- *WhoEmL 91*
Beninati, Francis Anthony 1947- *WhoEmL 91*
Benincasa, Louis 1927- *St&PR 91*
Benington, George Beaubien 1959- *WhoWrEP 89*
Benini 1941- *WhoAmA 91*
Benini, Paolo *PenDiDA 89*
Beniquez, Juan 1950- *Ballpl 90*
Benirschke, Kurt 1924- *WhoAm 90*
Benirschke, Rolf *BioIn 16*
Benisek, John Paul 1935- *St&PR 91*
Benish, George A. 1921- *St&PR 91*
Benislawska, Konstancja 1747-1806 *EncCoWW*
Benison, John E. 1926- *St&PR 91*
Benison, Peter 1950- *WhoEmL 91*
Benitez, Daniel 1940- *WhoHisp 91*
Benitez, Fernando 1911- *HispWr 90*
Benitez, Jellybean *BioIn 16*
Benitez, John Griswold 1957- *WhoEmL 91, WhoSSW 91, WhoWor 91*
Benitez, Jose Luis *BiDrAPA 89*
Benitez, Jose Rafael 1949- *WhoHisp 91*
Benitez, Juan Antonio 1949- *WhoAm 90*
Benitez, Margarita *WhoAm 90*
Benitez, Mario Antonio 1926- *WhoAm 90*
Benitez, Maurice Manuel 1928- *WhoAm 90*
Benitez, Raul 1958- *BiDrAPA 89*
Benitez, Robert J. *WhoHisp 91*
Benitez, Shirley Ann 1943- *WhoAmW 91*
Benitez-Hodge, Grissel Minerva 1950- *WhoHisp 91*
Benito, Roberto Patricio 1941- *WhoWor 91*
Benito-Alonso, Miguel Angel 1946- *WhoWor 91*
Benjamin, Adelaide Wisdom 1932- *WhoAmW 91, WhoSSW 91, WhoWor 91*
Benjamin, Albert, III 1904- *WhoAm 90*
Benjamin, Alfred David 1848-1900 *DcCanB 12*
Benjamin, Alice 1936- *WhoAmA 91*
Benjamin, Arthur 1893-1960 *PenDiMP A*
Benjamin, Arthur 1961- *BioIn 16*
Benjamin, Bennie 1907- *DrBIPA 90, OxCPMus*
Benjamin, Bennie 1907-1989 *BioIn 16*
Benjamin, Betsy Sterling *BioIn 16*
Benjamin, Bezaleel Solomon 1938- *WhoAm 90*
Benjamin, Burton *BioIn 16*
Benjamin, Charles Thomas 1921- *WhoE 91*
Benjamin, Clarence B. 1907- *St&PR 91*
Benjamin, Colin Henry 1936- *St&PR 91*
Benjamin, David *WhoWrEP 89*
Benjamin, David Joel, III 1947- *WhoAm 90*
Benjamin, David Marshall 1946- *WhoE 91*
Benjamin, Edward A. 1938- *WhoAm 90*
Benjamin, Edward Alan 1938- *St&PR 91*
Benjamin, Edward Bernard, Jr. 1923- *WhoAm 90, WhoSSW 91*
Benjamin, Eric 1952- *BiDrAPA 89*
Benjamin, Ernst 1937- *WhoAm 90*
Benjamin, G.P. 1930- *St&PR 91*
Benjamin, George 1960- *IntWWM 90*
Benjamin, George David 1933- *St&PR 91, WhoE 91*
Benjamin, George S. 1935- *St&PR 91*
Benjamin, Harry 1885-1986 *BioIn 16*
Benjamin, Harvey E. 1941- *WhoAm 90*
Benjamin, Herbert *EncAL*
Benjamin, Herbert S 1922- *BiDrAPA 89*
Benjamin, James Cover 1952- *St&PR 91, WhoAm 90, WhoEmL 91*
Benjamin, James Gilbert 1949- *WhoEmL 91*
Benjamin, James Leo 1941- *St&PR 91*
Benjamin, Janice Yukon 1951- *WhoEmL 91*
Benjamin, Jeffrey 1945- *WhoAm 90*
Benjamin, Jeffrey Royce 1954- *WhoAm 90*
Benjamin, Joe 1919-1974 *BioIn 16*
Benjamin, John 1945- *BiDrAPA 89*
Benjamin, Joseph Isaiah 1938- *BiDrAPA 89*
Benjamin, Joseph Wilmer, Jr. 1929- *WhoWrEP 89*
Benjamin, Judah Philip 1811-1884 *BioIn 16*
Benjamin, Karl Stanley 1925- *WhoAm 90, WhoAmA 91*
Benjamin, Lisa Carol 1959- *WhoAmW 91*
Benjamin, Lloyd 1956- *BiDrAPA 89*
Benjamin, Lloyd William, III 1944- *WhoAmA 91*
Benjamin, Lois *MajTwCW*
Benjamin, Lorna Smith 1934- *WhoAm 90*
Benjamin, Louis 1926- *St&PR 91*
Benjamin, Louis Kuhn 1954- *WhoSSW 91*
Benjamin, Ludy Thompson, Jr. 1945- *WhoSSW 91*
Benjamin, Mary A. *BioIn 16*
Benjamin, Mary Lynn 1942- *WhoWrEP 89*
Benjamin, Nora *AuBYP 90*
Benjamin, Nora 1899-1988 *BioIn 16*
Benjamin, Park 1809-1864 *BioIn 16*
Benjamin, Paul *DrBIPA 90, TwCCr&M 91*
Benjamin, R.O. 1926- *St&PR 91*
Benjamin, Richard 1938- *WhoAm 90, WorAlBi*
Benjamin, Richard Walter 1935- *WhoSSW 91*
Benjamin, Robba Lee 1947- *WhoAmW 91*
Benjamin, Robert 1948- *BiDrAPA 89*
Benjamin, Robert John 1938- *St&PR 91*
Benjamin, Robert L. *ODwPR 91*
Benjamin, Robert L. 1923- *WhoWrEP 89*
Benjamin, Robert Lewis 1923- *St&PR 91*
Benjamin, Robert Spiers 1917- *WhoAm 90, WhoWor 91, WhoWrEP 89*
Benjamin, Ruth *WhoWrEP 89*
Benjamin, S. Rodgers 1926- *St&PR 91*
Benjamin, Samuel Greene Wheeler 1837-1914 *BioIn 16*
Benjamin, Sheldon *BiDrAPA 89*
Benjamin, Stan 1914- *Ballpl 90*
Benjamin, Susan Pietrzyk 1948- *WhoAmW 91*
Benjamin, Theodore Simon 1926- *WhoAm 90*
Benjamin, Thomas Edward 1940- *IntWWM 90*
Benjamin, Walter 1892-1940 *BioIn 16, TwCLC 39 [port]*
Benjamin, William P *BiDrAPA 89*
Benjamin, William Philip 1922- *WhoE 91*
Benjamine, Elbert *NewAgE 90*
Benjenk, Munir Peter 1924- *WhoWor 91*
Benjey, William G. *St&PR 91*
Benkard, James W. B. 1937- *WhoAm 90*
Benke, Paul Arthur 1921- *WhoAm 90*
Benke, Robin Paul 1953- *WhoEmL 91*
Benke, Sandra Rae Jones 1954- *IntWWM 90*
Benkei *EncJap*
Benkendorf, Bert *ODwPR 91*
Benker, George Arthur 1904- *St&PR 91*
Benkert, Marianne *BiDrAPA 89*
Benkert, William M. *BioIn 16*
Benko, Elaine Terretta 1944- *WhoAmW 91*
Benko, Ralph J. 1952- *WhoEmL 91*
Benkovic, Stephen James 1938- *WhoAm 90*
Benkovich, James F. 1945- *ODwPR 91*
Benkovitz, Carmen Mary 1940- *WhoAmW 91*
Benkow, Josef 1924- *WhoWor 91*
Benktzon, Maria 1946- *ConDes 90*
Benlifer, Ginger Engel 1949- *WhoAmW 91*
Benmbarek, Jilani 1947- *WhoWor 91*
Benmosche, Robert H. 1944- *St&PR 91*
Benn, Alexander 1918- *WhoAm 90, WhoE 91*
Benn, Anthony Neil Wedgwood 1925- *ConAu 131*
Benn, Ben 1884-1983 *WhoAmA 91N*
Benn, Douglas Frank 1936- *WhoWor 91*
Benn, Gottfried 1886-1956 *BioIn 16, WorAlBi*
Benn, Jim *BioIn 16*
Benn, June *ConAu 132*
Benn, June Wedgwood *ConAu 132*
Benn, Niles S. 1945- *WhoWor 91*
Benn, S I *ConAu 129*
Benn, Sally Ann 1956- *WhoAmW 91*
Benn, Stanley 1939-1989 *BioIn 16*
Benn, Stanley I 1920-1986 *ConAu 129*
Benn, Tony *ConAu 131*
Benn, Tony 1925- *BioIn 16*
Bennack, Frank Anthony, Jr. 1933- *WhoAm 90*
Bennard, George 1873-1958 *OxCPMus*
Bennardo, S.A. 1951- *St&PR 91*
Benne, Kenneth Dean 1908- *WhoAm 90, WhoWor 91*
Benner, Bruce 1927- *St&PR 91*
Benner, Carol Ann 1948- *WhoE 91*
Benner, Colin Keith 1944- *WhoAm 90*
Benner, Dorothy Spurlock 1938- *WhoAmW 91*
Benner, Howard J. 1945- *ODwPR 91*
Benner, James E. 1939- *St&PR 91*
Benner, Randall Ray 1952- *WhoSSW 91*
Benner, Richard Edward, Jr. 1932- *WhoAm 90*

Bennert, Arthur James 1926- *St&PR 91, WhoAm 90*
Bennet, Dorcas *BiDEWW*
Bennet, Douglas Joseph, Jr. 1938- *WhoAm 90*
Bennet, Eric Roland 1956- *WhoWor 91*
Bennet, Gladys May *BiDrAPA 89*
Bennet, Hiram Pitt 1826-1914 *AmLegL*
Bennet, Wilhelm Rutger Arvid 1951- *WhoWor 91*
Bennetsen, W. J. *WhoAm 90*
Bennett, A.R. 1926- *St&PR 91*
Bennett, Abram E *BiDrAPA 89*
Bennett, Alan 1934- *BioIn 16, ConTFT 8, MajTwCW, NewYTBS 90*
Bennett, Alan C. 1924- *St&PR 91*
Bennett, Alan Jerome 1941- *St&PR 91, WhoAm 90*
Bennett, Albert Farrell 1944- *WhoAm 90*
Bennett, Alden S. 1919- *St&PR 91*
Bennett, Alexander Elliot 1940- *WhoAm 90*
Bennett, Allan 1872-1923 *EncO&P 3*
Bennett, Allan Robert 1930- *WhoAm 90*
Bennett, Amanda Anne 1956- *WhoAmW 91, WhoE 91*
Bennett, Amy Spear 1949- *WhoAmW 91*
Bennett, Andrew Jackson *BioIn 16*
Bennett, Anna Elizabeth 1914- *WhoWrEP 89*
Bennett, Anna Maria *BioIn 16*
Bennett, Anna Maria 1750?-1808 *FemiCLE*
Bennett, Anne McGrew *BioIn 16*
Bennett, Arlene Parsons 1933- *BiDrAPA 89*
Bennett, Arnold 1867-1931 *BioIn 16, DcLB 98 [port], WorAlBi*
Bennett, Aurora Jorge *BiDrAPA 89*
Bennett, Austin W *BiDrAPA 89*
Bennett, Barbara 1952- *WhoEmL 91, WhoSSW 91*
Bennett, Barbara Esther 1953- *WhoAmW 91*
Bennett, Barry Steven 1953- *St&PR 91*
Bennett, Ben *BioIn 16*
Bennett, Benjamin James *BiDrAPA 89*
Bennett, Bernice Spitz *WhoWrEP 89*
Bennett, Bettie McKinney 1951- *WhoEmL 91*
Bennett, Betty T. *WhoAm 90*
Bennett, Bobbie Jean 1940- *WhoSSW 91*
Bennett, Bradford Carl 1953- *WhoEmL 91*
Bennett, Brian Timothy 1951- *WhoE 91*
Bennett, Brian Timothy 1962- *WhoE 91*
Bennett, Bruce David 1948- *WhoEmL 91*
Bennett, Bruce Harry 1941- *WhoWor 91*
Bennett, Bruce Scott 1958- *WhoEmL 91*
Bennett, Bruce W. 1930- *St&PR 91*
Bennett, Bruce W., Jr. 1930- *WhoAm 90*
Bennett, Bryce H., Jr. 1953- *WhoEmL 91*
Bennett, C. Leonard 1939- *WhoAm 90*
Bennett, Carl 1920- *WhoAm 90*
Bennett, Carl Edward 1918- *WhoWrEP 89*
Bennett, Carl McGhie 1933- *WhoWor 91*
Bennett, Carol Elizabeth 1951- *WhoAmW 91, WhoEmL 91*
Bennett, Carol Weaver 1944- *WhoSSW 91*
Bennett, Carolyn Linda 1950- *WhoWrEP 89*
Bennett, Catherine Cecilia 1958- *WhoAmW 91*
Bennett, Catherine June 1950- *WhoAmW 91*
Bennett, Cedric Eugene 1926- *WhoWor 91*
Bennett, Celestine C. T. 1932- *WhoAmW 91*
Bennett, Charles Alan 1947- *WhoEmL 91*
Bennett, Charles Andrew 1943- *WhoE 91*
Bennett, Charles Edward 1910- *WhoAm 90, WhoSSW 91*
Bennett, Charles Franklin, Jr. 1926- *WhoAm 90*
Bennett, Charles Leo 1920- *WhoAm 90*
Bennett, Charles Randolph *BioIn 16*
Bennett, Charles Turner 1932- *WhoAm 90*
Bennett, Charles Wilfred, Jr. 1947- *WhoSSW 91*
Bennett, Charlie 1854-1927 *Ballpl 90*
Bennett, Christine Lora 1948- *WhoAmW 91*
Bennett, Claire Richardson 1928- *WhoAm 90*
Bennett, Clarence Henry 1946- *WhoWor 91*
Bennett, Connie Sue 1955- *WhoAmW 91*
Bennett, Constance 1904-1965 *WorAlBi*
Bennett, Cornelius *BioIn 16*
Bennett, Craig W. 1959- *WhoSSW 91*
Bennett, Dale L. 1936- *St&PR 91*
Bennett, Dale T. 1930- *St&PR 91*
Bennett, Darlene B. 1930- *St&PR 91*
Bennett, Dave 1930- *WhoSSW 91*
Bennett, David McAlpine 1954- *WhoEmL 91, WhoSSW 91*
Bennett, David Spencer 1935- *WhoWor 91*
Bennett, Deborah Elizabeth 1958- *WhoE 91*
Bennett, Deborah R. 1941- *WhoAmW 91*
Bennett, Denman T. 1925- *St&PR 91*
Bennett, Dennis 1939- *Ballpl 90*
Bennett, Dollie *BioIn 16*
Bennett, Don Bemco 1916- *WhoAmA 91*
Bennett, Donald Dean 1937- *St&PR 91*
Bennett, Donald Emerson *St&PR 91N*
Bennett, Dorothea 1929- *WhoAm 90*
Bennett, Douglas Carleton 1946- *WhoAm 90*
Bennett, Douglas Marshall 1947- *WhoWor 91*
Bennett, Douglas P. 1948- *St&PR 91*
Bennett, Dwight 1945- *IntWWM 90*
Bennett, E.L. 1929- *St&PR 91*
Bennett, Edmund Taylor 1932- *St&PR 91*
Bennett, Edward Blair, Jr. 1936- *St&PR 91, WhoAm 90*
Bennett, Edward Henry 1917- *WhoE 91*
Bennett, Edward Herbert, Jr. 1915- *WhoAm 90*
Bennett, Edward J., Jr. 1932- *St&PR 91*
Bennett, Edward James 1941- *WhoWor 91*
Bennett, Edward Joseph 1945- *WhoSSW 91*
Bennett, Edward Moore 1927- *WhoAm 90*
Bennett, Edward Nevill 1936- *WhoAm 90*
Bennett, Edward Virdell, Jr. 1947- *WhoEmL 91*
Bennett, Edwin 1818-1905 *PenDiDA 89*
Bennett, ElDean 1928- *WhoAm 90*
Bennett, Elinor 1943- *IntWWM 90*
Bennett, Elizabeth *MajTwCW*
Bennett, Elizabeth Deare *ConAu 131*
Bennett, Elmer F. 1917-1989 *BioIn 16*
Bennett, Elsie Margaret 1919- *WhoAmW 91*
Bennett, Enoch Arnold 1867-1931 *BioIn 16*
Bennett, Ernest 1868-1947 *EncO&P 3*
Bennett, Eve *AuBYP 90*
Bennett, Fran 1935- *DrBlPA 90*
Bennett, Frank Cantelo, Jr. 1930- *WhoAm 90, WhoWor 91*
Bennett, Fred Alus 1939- *St&PR 91*
Bennett, Fred Lawrence 1939- *WhoAm 90*
Bennett, Frederick Elwood 1934- *St&PR 91*
Bennett, G. Delmar 1915- *St&PR 91*
Bennett, G. Kirk, Jr. 1955- *St&PR 91*
Bennett, Gary Lee 1940- *WhoAm 90, WhoWrEP 89*
Bennett, Gary Paul 1941- *St&PR 91*
Bennett, Geoffrey W. *St&PR 91*
Bennett, George F. 1911- *St&PR 91*
Bennett, George F., Jr. 1941- *St&PR 91*
Bennett, George Frederick 1911- *WhoAm 90*
Bennett, George O. 1958- *St&PR 91*
Bennett, Georgette 1946- *St&PR 91, WhoE 91*
Bennett, Gladys Jenkins 1929- *WhoWrEP 89*
Bennett, Gordon C 1935- *ConAu 31NR*
Bennett, Gordon Clowe 1922- *WhoWrEP 89*
Bennett, Grover Bryce 1921- *WhoAm 90*
Bennett, Gwendolyn B. 1902- *BioAmW*
Bennett, Gwendolyn B. 1902-1981 *FemiCLE, HarlReB [port]*
Bennett, Hal 1930- *BioIn 16, ConAu 13AS [port]*
Bennett, Harold Clark 1924- *WhoAm 90*
Bennett, Harriet Cook 1945- *WhoSSW 91*
Bennett, Harry 1895- *WhoAm 90*
Bennett, Harry Daniel 1955- *WhoWor 91*
Bennett, Harry Herbert 1892-1979 *EncABHB 5 [port]*
Bennett, Harry Louis 1923- *WhoAm 90*
Bennett, Harve 1930- *BioIn 16, ConTFT 8 [port], WhoAm 90*
Bennett, Harvey Lee 1950- *WhoSSW 91*
Bennett, Helen Donele 1948- *WhoAmW 91*
Bennett, Henry James 1942- *St&PR 91*
Bennett, Herschel 1896-1964 *Ballpl 90*
Bennett, Hywel 1944- *WhoWor 91*
Bennett, Irving 1923- *WhoAm 90, WhoWrEP 89*
Bennett, Irwin Kenneth 1947- *BiDrAPA 89*
Bennett, Ivan F 1919- *BiDrAPA 89*
Bennett, Ivan Frank 1919- *WhoAm 90, WhoWor 91*
Bennett, Ivan L., Jr. *NewYTBS 90 [port]*
Bennett, Ivan Loveridge, Jr. 1922- *WhoAm 90*
Bennett, J G 1897-1974 *EncO&P 3*
Bennett, J M *BiDrAPA 89*
Bennett, Jack Arthur Walter 1911-1981 *DcNaB 1981*
Bennett, Jack Franklin 1924- *St&PR 91, WhoAm 90*
Bennett, Jack Olen 1914- *WhoWor 91*
Bennett, Jacqueline Beekman 1946- *WhoEmL 91, WhoWor 91*
Bennett, James Austin 1915- *WhoAm 90, WhoWor 91*
Bennett, James Brown, III 1940- *St&PR 91*
Bennett, James D. *BioIn 16*
Bennett, James Edward 1925- *WhoAm 90*
Bennett, James G. 1927- *ODwPR 91*
Bennett, James Gerald, Jr. 1959- *WhoSSW 91*
Bennett, James Gordon 1795-1872 *BioIn 16*
Bennett, James Gordon 1841-1918 *BioIn 16*
Bennett, James Gordon, Jr. 1841-1918 *WorAlBi*
Bennett, James Jefferson 1920- *WhoAm 90*
Bennett, James Marvin 1939- *WhoE 91*
Bennett, James Patrick 1957- *WhoSSW 91*
Bennett, James Stark 1947- *WhoAm 90*
Bennett, James T. 1942- *WhoAm 90*
Bennett, James Thurston 1945- *WhoSSW 91*
Bennett, Jamie 1948- *WhoAmA 91*
Bennett, Janet Welch *BiDrAPA 89*
Bennett, Jarratt Graham 1935- *WhoSSW 91*
Bennett, Jay 1912- *AuBYP 90, BioIn 16*
Bennett, Jay I. 1925- *St&PR 91*
Bennett, Jean Louise McPherson 1930- *WhoAm 90*
Bennett, Jeffrey Richard 1948- *WhoE 91*
Bennett, Jennie Marie 1950- *WhoSSW 91*
Bennett, Jerome 1922- *WhoAm 90*
Bennett, Jim 1921- *WhoAm 90*
Bennett, Joan 1910- *WhoAm 90, WorAlBi*
Bennett, Joan 1910-1990 *NewYTBS 90 [port], News 91-2*
Bennett, Joan S. 1941- *ConAu 132*
Bennett, Joanne B. 1931- *WhoAmW 91*
Bennett, Joe Claude 1933- *WhoAm 90*
Bennett, Joel H. 1936- *St&PR 91*
Bennett, John *TwCCr&M 91*
Bennett, John 1840-1907 *PenDiDA 89*
Bennett, John A. 1943- *St&PR 91*
Bennett, John Campbell White 1948- *WhoEmL 91*
Bennett, John Frederic 1920- *WhoAm 90, WhoWrEP 89*
Bennett, John J. 1938- *WhoWrEP 89*
Bennett, John Joseph 1923- *WhoAm 90*
Bennett, John M 1942- *WhoAmA 91, WhoWrEP 89*
Bennett, John Morrison 1933- *WhoAm 90*
Bennett, John Norman, II *BiDrAPA 89*
Bennett, John R. 1922- *St&PR 91*
Bennett, John Richard 1952- *WhoEmL 91*
Bennett, John Roscoe 1922- *WhoAm 90*
Bennett, John Rutherfoord, V 1955- *WhoAm 90*
Bennett, John Townsend, Jr. 1939- *WhoE 91*
Bennett, Joseph 1932- *ODwPR 91*
Bennett, Joseph P. 1929- *St&PR 91*
Bennett, Kathleen McManus 1948- *WhoAmW 91*
Bennett, Keith Michael 1942- *IntWWM 90*
Bennett, Kenneth A 1935- *ConAu 131*
Bennett, Kenneth Alan 1935- *WhoAm 90*
Bennett, LaFell Dickinson 1954- *WhoEmL 91*
Bennett, Laura 1953- *ODwPR 91*
Bennett, Lawrence Allen 1923- *WhoAm 90*
Bennett, Lawrence Herman 1930- *WhoAm 90*
Bennett, Lerone 1928- *BioIn 16*
Bennett, Lerone, Jr. 1928- *WhoAm 90, WhoWrEP 89*
Bennett, Lewis Tilton, Jr. 1940- *WhoWor 91*
Bennett, Libbie Ann *WhoWrEP 89*
Bennett, Lillian F *BiDrAPA 89*
Bennett, Linda Griffin 1952- *WhoSSW 91*
Bennett, Lois 1933- *WhoAmW 91*
Bennett, Louis 1849-1918 *AmLegL*
Bennett, Louis Deerfoot 1830-1896 *WhNaAH*
Bennett, Louis Lowell 1909- *WhoAm 90*
Bennett, Louise 1919- *FemiCLE*
Bennett, Lowell Howard 1913- *WhoSSW 91, WhoWor 91*
Bennett, Lynne Dee 1953- *WhoAmW 91*
Bennett, M. Julie 1962- *St&PR 91*
Bennett, Maisha B. Hamilton 1948- *WhoAmW 91*
Bennett, Marcus C. 1936- *St&PR 91*
Bennett, Margaret Ethel Booker 1923- *WhoAmW 91, WhoWor 91*
Bennett, Margaret Theresa 1950- *WhoEmL 91*
Bennett, Margot 1912-1980 *TwCCr&M 91*
Bennett, Marion Tinsley 1914- *WhoAm 90*
Bennett, Marshall Alton, Jr. 1955- *WhoEmL 91*
Bennett, Marshall Goodloe, Jr. 1943- *WhoSSW 91*
Bennett, Marsi Ann 1960- *WhoAmW 91*
Bennett, Mary 1918- *WhoAmW 91*
Bennett, Max Edwin 1934- *WhoAm 90*
Bennett, Michael *BioIn 16*
Bennett, Michael 1955- *WhoSSW 91*
Bennett, Michael Isaiah 1945- *BiDrAPA 89*
Bennett, Michael J. 1934- *St&PR 91*
Bennett, Michael John 1934- *WhoAm 90, WhoE 91*
Bennett, Michael Vander Laan 1931- *WhoAm 90*
Bennett, Michele Marlene 1964- *WhoAmW 91*
Bennett, Mildred R. 1909-1989 *BioIn 16, ConAu 130*
Bennett, Miriam Frances 1928- *WhoAm 90*
Bennett, Mona B 1941- *BiDrAPA 89*
Bennett, Monty Clare 1938- *St&PR 91*
Bennett, Myrna Lea 1942- *WhoWor 91*
Bennett, Nicholas C. *St&PR 91*
Bennett, Noall John 1941- *St&PR 91*
Bennett, Norman E. 1917- *WhoAm 90, WhoWrEP 89*
Bennett, Otes 1921- *St&PR 91*
Bennett, Otes, Jr. 1921- *WhoAm 90*
Bennett, Pamela McHardy 1947- *WhoAmW 91*
Bennett, Pat *BioIn 16*
Bennett, Patricia Ann Work 1947- *WhoWrEP 89*
Bennett, Paul 1921- *WhoWrEP 89*
Bennett, Paul Lester 1946- *WhoEmL 91*
Bennett, Peter Brian 1931- *WhoAm 90*
Bennett, Peter Dunne 1933- *WhoAm 90*
Bennett, Peter G *BiDrAPA 89*
Bennett, Phil E. 1953- *St&PR 91*
Bennett, Philomene Dosek 1935- *WhoAmA 91*
Bennett, Phyllis Redmon 1944- *WhoAmW 91*
Bennett, Pinto *WhoNeCM [port]*
Bennett, Rachel *AuBYP 90*
Bennett, Rainey 1907- *WhoAmA 91*
Bennett, Ralph Stephen 1940- *St&PR 91*
Bennett, Randall Clarence 1947- *WhoSSW 91*
Bennett, Ransom, Jr. 1923- *St&PR 91*
Bennett, Raymond J 1907- *BiDrAPA 89*
Bennett, Reynold 1918- *WhoAm 90*
Bennett, Richard Clark 1941- *WhoE 91, WhoWor 91*
Bennett, Richard Douglas 1948- *WhoEmL 91*
Bennett, Richard E. 1933- *St&PR 91*
Bennett, Richard Earle 1919- *WhoAm 90*
Bennett, Richard Edward 1954- *WhoEmL 91*
Bennett, Richard Edwin 1943- *WhoSSW 91*
Bennett, Richard Henry 1939- *St&PR 91*
Bennett, Richard Joseph 1917- *WhoAm 90*
Bennett, Richard Rodney 1936- *BioIn 16, IntWWM 90, OxCPMus, PenDiMP A*
Bennett, Richard T. 1945- *St&PR 91*
Bennett, Richard Thomas 1930- *WhoAm 90*
Bennett, Rita 1951- *St&PR 91*
Bennett, Robert 1952- *WhoEmL 91*
Bennett, Robert A. *BioIn 16*
Bennett, Robert A. 1927- *WhoE 91*
Bennett, Robert Alvin 1947- *WhoEmL 91*
Bennett, Robert David *BiDrAPA 89*
Bennett, Robert Earl, Jr. 1952- *WhoSSW 91*
Bennett, Robert Eugene *BiDrAPA 89*
Bennett, Robert Frederick 1927- *WhoAm 90*
Bennett, Robert Harris *BiDrAPA 89*
Bennett, Robert J. 1941- *St&PR 91*
Bennett, Robert John 1941- *St&PR 91, WhoAm 90*
Bennett, Robert LeRoy 1937- *WhoE 91*
Bennett, Robert Louis 1925- *WhoWor 91*
Bennett, Robert Menzies 1926- *WhoAm 90, WhoSSW 91*
Bennett, Robert Putnam 1932- *WhoSSW 91*
Bennett, Robert Royce 1926- *WhoAm 90*
Bennett, Robert Russell 1894-1981 *OxCPMus*
Bennett, Robert Stephen 1939- *NewYTBS 90 [port]*
Bennett, Roger Edman 1955- *WhoSSW 91*
Bennett, Ron Stephan 1953- *WhoEmL 91*
Bennett, Ronald Lee 1942- *St&PR 91*
Bennett, Ronald Thomas 1944- *WhoAm 90*
Bennett, Roy 1912-1989 *BioIn 16*
Bennett, Roy F. 1928- *St&PR 91*
Bennett, Russell Odbert 1915- *WhoAm 90*
Bennett, Ruth M 1899-1960 *WhoAmA 91N*
Bennett, Saul *ODwPR 91*
Bennett, Saul 1936- *WhoAm 90*
Bennett, Scott Lawrence 1949- *St&PR 91*
Bennett, Sharon Kay 1947- *WhoSSW 91*
Bennett, Shelley M. 1947- *ConAu 131*
Bennett, Stephanie Mitchell 1941- *WhoAmW 91, WhoE 91*
Bennett, Stephen *ODwPR 91*
Bennett, Stephen L 1928- *BiDrAPA 89*
Bennett, Stephen Sydney 1945- *IntWWM 90*
Bennett, Steven Carroll 1952- *WhoEmL 91*

Bennett, Steven Fredrick 1959- WhoWor 91
Bennett, Susan Carroll 1953- WhoAmW 91
Bennett, Thomas A. St&PR 91
Bennett, Thomas Albert 1949- WhoSSW 91
Bennett, Thomas B., III 1947- St&PR 91
Bennett, Thomas E. 1929- WhoAm 90
Bennett, Thomas Edward 1929- St&PR 91
Bennett, Thomas Joseph 1954- St&PR 91
Bennett, Thomas LeRoy, Jr. 1942- WhoAm 90
Bennett, Thomas Peter 1937- WhoAm 90, WhoSSW 91
Bennett, Thomas T 1922- BiDrAPA 89
Bennett, Thomas William 1954- WhoWor 91
Bennett, Tony 1926- OxCPMus, WhoAm 90, WorAlBi
Bennett, Ward 1917- ConDes 90
Bennett, William PenDiDA 89, WhoAm 90
Bennett, William 1943- News 90 [port], WorAlBi
Bennett, William A. BioIn 16
Bennett, William C. ODwPR 91
Bennett, William E. 1946- St&PR 91
Bennett, William Frederick 1937- WhoE 91
Bennett, William Gordon 1924- WhoAm 90
Bennett, William J. 1943- WorAlBi
Bennett, William John 1943- BiDrUSE 89, BioIn 16, WhoAm 90, WhoE 91
Bennett, William L., Jr. 1921- WhoSSW 91
Bennett, William Michael 1938- WhoAm 90
Bennett, William Ralph, Jr. 1930- WhoAm 90, WhoE 91, WhoWor 91
Bennett, William Sterndale 1816-1875 BioIn 16, PenDiMP A
Bennett, William Tapley 1917- BioIn 16
Bennett, William Tapley, Jr. 1917- WhoWor 91
Bennett, William Thomas 1926- WhoAm 90
Bennett, Winfield Scott, III 1946- WhoSSW 91
Bennett, Winslow Wood 1925- WhoAm 90
Bennett-Brown, Mary 1958- St&PR 91
Bennett-Kastor, Tina L. 1954- WhoAmW 91
Bennetts, Debra L. 1951- ODwPR 91
Bennetts, Michael Peter 1949- BiDrAPA 89
Benney, Douglas Mabley 1922- WhoE 91, WhoWor 91
Benney, Robert WhoAmA 91
Benney, Robert 1904- WhoAm 90
Bennie, R.T. 1933- St&PR 91
Bennighof, James Malcolm 1957- IntWWM 90
Bennigsen-Foerder, Rudolf von 1926-1989 BioIn 16
Benning, Arthur E. 1929- St&PR 91
Benning, George Louis 1924- WhoAm 90
Benning, John Alan 1934- St&PR 91
Benning, Joseph Francis, Jr. 1922- WhoE 91
Benninger, Edward Charles, Jr. 1942- St&PR 91
Benninger, Fred 1917- St&PR 91, WhoAm 90
Benninghoff, William Shiffer 1918- WhoAm 90
Benningsen, Lilian 1924- IntWWM 90
Bennington, Leslie Orville, Jr. 1946- WhoEmL 91
Bennington, Neville Lynne 1906- WhoAm 90
Bennington, Ronald Kent 1936- WhoAm 90
Bennington, Timothy R. 1944- St&PR 91
Bennington, William J. 1939- ODwPR 91
Bennington, William Jay 1939- St&PR 91, WhoAm 90
Bennion, Douglas Noel 1935- WhoAm 90
Bennis, Robert E. BioIn 16
Bennis, Warren G. BioIn 16
Bennis, Warren Gameliel 1925- WhoAm 90, WhoWor 91
Bennison, Allan Parnell 1918- WhoSSW 91
Bennison, William D. 1944- St&PR 91
Bennon, Saul 1914- WhoAm 90
Benny, Jack 1894-1974 BioIn 16, WorAlBi
Benny, Jeffrey Allan 1956- St&PR 91
Benny, Sandra 1944- WhoAmA 91
Beno, Candice Lynn 1951- WhoAmW 91, WhoEmL 91
Benois, Nadia 1896-1975 BiDWomA
Benoist, Charles Augustin 1861-1936 BiDFrPL
Benoit, Andre 1938- St&PR 91
Benoit, Charles Francis 1958- WhoSSW 91
Benoit, David BioIn 16
Benoit, Diane BiDrAPA 89
Benoit, Donald Anthony 1936- WhoWor 91
Benoit, Elise BiDrAPA 89
Benoit, Harvey 1933- ODwPR 91
Benoit, Henri PenDiMP
Benoit, Henri Charles 1921- WhoWor 91
Benoit, Jacques 1941- BioIn 16
Benoit, Joan BioIn 16
Benoit, Joyce Difford 1945- WhoSSW 91
Benoit, Leroy James 1913- WhoAm 90
Benoit, Marie 1895- BioIn 16
Benoit, Marilyn B BiDrAPA 89
Benoit, Nancy Louise 1944- WhoAmW 91
Benoit, Normand George 1949- WhoEmL 91
Benoit, Olivier-David 1837-1897 DcCanB 12
Benoit, Pierre 1906-1987 BioIn 16
Benoit, R.E. 1947- St&PR 91
Benoit, Raymond Robert 1942- WhoSSW 91
Benoit, Rigaud 1911-1986 ArtLatA
Benoliel, Bernard 1943- IntWWM 90
Benoliel, P.A. 1932- St&PR 91
Benovitz, Larry Paul BiDrAPA 89
Benrud, Audrey Elaine 1927- WhoAmW 91
Bensadoun, Andre 1931- WhoAm 90
Bensaid, Julien 1933- WhoWor 91
Bensch, Klaus George 1928- WhoAm 90
Bensch, Leonard Ernest 1946- St&PR 91
Benscheidt, Steven Eugene 1954- WhoEmL 91
Benscher, Walter 1923- St&PR 91
Benschip, Gary John 1947- WhoEmL 91
Benschneider, Donald 1940- WhoAm 90
Benschoter, Reba Ann 1930- WhoAmW 91
Bensco, Charles J 1894-1960 WhoAmA 91N
Benscuter, Thomas Donald 1950- St&PR 91
Bensel, Carolyn Kirkbride 1941- WhoAmW 91
Bensen, Annette Wolf 1938- WhoWor 91
Bensen, Robert George 1929- St&PR 91
Bensen, Roger D. 1935- St&PR 91
Bensenhaver, Charles Brook 1960- BiDrAPA 89
Benser, Caroline Coker Cepin IntWWM 90
Benser, Frank Leroy 1945- WhoEmL 91
Benser, Suzanne Kerstin 1960- BiDrAPA 89
Benshoof, Terrence James 1946- WhoEmL 91
Bensignor, Paulette 1948- WhoAmA 91, WhoE 91
Bensimon, Gilles BioIn 16
Bensimon, Helen Frank 1941- WhoAmW 91
Bensimon, Patrick Nathan Jacques 1962- WhoWor 91
Bensimon, Rachel 1933- St&PR 91
Bensinger, David August 1926- WhoAm 90
Bensinger, Peter Benjamin 1936- WhoAm 90
Bensink, John Robert 1948- WhoWrEP 89
Benskina, Princess Orelia WhoAmW 91, WhoE 91
Bensko, John 1949- WhoWrEP 89
Bensley, Edward Horton 1906- WhoAm 90
Bensman, Charles J. 1933- WhoAm 90, WhoSSW 91
Bensmida, Hassen 1954- WhoEmL 91
Benso, William Eldon 1937- St&PR 91
Benson, A C 1862-1925 DcLB 98 [port]
Benson, Andrew Alm 1917- WhoAm 90
Benson, Andrew B. 1940- St&PR 91
Benson, Ann M. 1930- WhoSSW 91
Benson, Ben 1915-1959 TwCCr&M 91
Benson, Betty Jones 1928- WhoAmW 91, WhoSSW 91
Benson, Bradley Duane 1959- WhoEmL 91
Benson, Brian Joseph 1941- WhoSSW 91
Benson, Bruce B. 1922-1990 BioIn 16
Benson, Carville Dickinson 1872-1929 AmLegL
Benson, Charles Scott 1922- WhoAm 90
Benson, Clara Mays 1932- WhoWrEP 89
Benson, Clifford George 1946- IntWWM 90
Benson, Corby Jay BiDrAPA 89
Benson, David F. 1949- St&PR 91
Benson, David Samuel 1944- BiDrAPA 89
Benson, David William 1931- WhoAm 90
Benson, Debra A. 1953- WhoAmW 91
Benson, Dennis N. 1943- St&PR 91
Benson, Diane BioIn 16
Benson, Donald E. 1930- St&PR 91
Benson, Donald Erick 1930- WhoAm 90
Benson, Donald Ray 1937- St&PR 91
Benson, Douglas Jay 1961- WhoE 91
Benson, E. F. BioIn 16
Benson, E F 1867-1940 EncO&P 3
Benson, Earl Charles 1939- IntWWM 90
Benson, Edward J BiDrAPA 89
Benson, Edward Louis 1936- St&PR 91
Benson, Edwin Welburn, Jr. 1945- WhoSSW 91
Benson, Egbert 1746-1833 BioIn 16
Benson, Elaine K G 1924- WhoAmA 91
Benson, Elaine K. G. 1924- WhoAmW 91, WhoE 91
Benson, Elizabeth Polk 1924- WhoAmA 91
Benson, Emanuel M 1904-1971 WhoAmA 91N
Benson, Ezra Taft BioIn 16
Benson, Ezra Taft 1899- BiDrUSE 89, WhoAm 90
Benson, Francis M. 1958- WhoEmL 91
Benson, Francis Post 1927- WhoE 91
Benson, Frank W 1862-1951 WhoAmA 91N
Benson, Gene 1913- Ballpl 90
Benson, George BioIn 16
Benson, George 1943- DrBlPA 90, EncPR&S 89, WhoAm 90
Benson, George Charles Sumner 1908- WhoAm 90
Benson, George Leonard 1934- WhoE 91
Benson, George Stuart 1898- WhoAm 90
Benson, Gregory Vincent 1954- St&PR 91
Benson, Harold Philip 1949- WhoSSW 91
Benson, Henry L. 1854-1921 AmLegL
Benson, I. John 1946- St&PR 91
Benson, J. Jeffrey 1957- WhoEmL 91
Benson, Jack M. 1933- St&PR 91
Benson, James 1925- WhoAm 90
Benson, James Albert 1930- St&PR 91
Benson, James Bracken 1945- WhoEmL 91
Benson, James Carl 1935- WhoAm 90
Benson, James DeWayne 1925- WhoAm 90
Benson, James E BiDrAPA 89
Benson, James O. 1933- St&PR 91
Benson, Jan Elizabeth 1955- IntWWM 90
Benson, Janet Elizabeth 1954- WhoEmL 91
Benson, Jared 1821-1894 AmLegL
Benson, Jerry S. 1932- St&PR 91
Benson, Joan IntWWM 90
Benson, Joan Louise 1951- WhoSSW 91
Benson, John 1920- St&PR 91
Benson, John 1945- ConAu 131
Benson, John Alexander, Jr. 1921- WhoAm 90
Benson, John Irving 1947- BiDrAPA 89
Benson, John P 1865-1947 WhoAmA 91N
Benson, John R 1929- BiDrAPA 89
Benson, John Schuler 1927- St&PR 91
Benson, Jon G. St&PR 91
Benson, Judith Anne 1951- WhoWor 91
Benson, Judith K. 1950- St&PR 91
Benson, Julie Morton 1937- St&PR 91
Benson, Kathleen 1947- SmATA 62
Benson, Kenneth Peter 1927- St&PR 91, WhoAm 90
Benson, Kenneth S. 1937- St&PR 91
Benson, Kenneth Samuel 1937- WhoAm 90
Benson, Kenneth Victor 1929- WhoAm 90
Benson, Kim Derrick 1954- WhoAmW 91, WhoWrEP 89
Benson, Larry Dean 1929- WhoWrEP 89
Benson, Lenni Beth 1958- WhoEmL 91
Benson, Lenore J. WhoAm 90, WhoAmW 91
Benson, Leo, III 1938- St&PR 91
Benson, Lucy Peters Wilson 1927- WhoAm 90, WhoAmW 91
Benson, Lucy Wilson 1927- St&PR 91
Benson, Lyle Charles 1949- WhoSSW 91
Benson, Lyman 1909- ConAu 32NR
Benson, M Christina 1948- BiDrAPA 89
Benson, Mabel 1605?-1692 BiDEWW
Benson, Mark James 1955- St&PR 91
Benson, Martha J 1928- WhoAmA 91
Benson, Matthew T. 1957- WhoWrEP 89
Benson, Michaela Chasser 1948- WhoAmW 91
Benson, Mildred W. AuBYP 90
Benson, Morton 1924- WhoAm 90, WhoWor 91
Benson, Nancy Jane 1953- WhoEmL 91
Benson, Nannette I. 1954- St&PR 91
Benson, Nettie Lee 1905- WhoAm 90
Benson, Nils E. 1923- St&PR 91
Benson, Patricia A. 1958- St&PR 91
Benson, Paul Richard 1953- BiDrAPA 89
Benson, Peter Allen 1950- St&PR 91
Benson, Ray BioIn 16
Benson, Raymond Ellis 1924- WhoE 91
Benson, Richard A. 1943- St&PR 91
Benson, Richard Edward 1936- St&PR 91
Benson, Robby 1955- WorAlBi
Benson, Robby 1956- ConTFT 8 [port]
Benson, Robert Clinton, Jr. 1946- WhoE 91, WhoWor 91
Benson, Robert Elliott 1916- WhoAm 90
Benson, Robert Eugene 1940- WhoAm 90
Benson, Robert L. 1942- WhoAm 90
Benson, Robert Scott 1943- BiDrAPA 89
Benson, Robert Slater 1942- St&PR 91, WhoAm 90
Benson, Ronald Edward 1936- WhoSSW 91
Benson, Ronald M 1938- BiDrAPA 89
Benson, Rosemary McLean 1955- WhoSSW 91
Benson, Sally 1900-1972 FemiCLE
Benson, Samuel George BiDrAPA 89
Benson, Sidney William 1918- WhoAm 90
Benson, Stella 1892-1933 BioIn 16, FemiCLE
Benson, Steve 1949- WhoWrEP 89
Benson, Susan 1942- OxCCanT [port]
Benson, Susan M. 1957- WhoAmW 91
Benson, Theodora 1906-1968 FemiCLE
Benson, Thomas Avery 1953- St&PR 91
Benson, Thomas Quentin 1943- WhoAm 90
Benson, Tom 1927- WhoAm 90
Benson, Tom Erlin 1937- St&PR 91
Benson, W. A. S. 1854-1924 BioIn 16
Benson, Warren Frank 1924- IntWWM 90, WhoAm 90
Benson, William Arthur Smith 1854-1924 BioIn 16, PenDiDA 89
Benson, William Edward 1919- WhoAm 90
Benson, William Edward 1923- WhoSSW 91
Benson, William Frank 1945- WhoSSW 91
Benson, William H BiDrAPA 89
Benson, William Henry 1936- St&PR 91
Benson, William Jeffrey 1922- St&PR 91
Bensonhaver, Charles L BiDrAPA 89
Benstead, Horace Melville, Jr. 1927- St&PR 91
Benstock, Gerald M. 1930- St&PR 91
Benston, George James 1932- WhoAm 90
Bensusan, Pierre NewAgMG
Bensussen, Estelle Esther 1926- WhoAmW 91
Bent, Alan Edward 1939- WhoAm 90
Bent, Charles 1799-1847 WhNaAH
Bent, Charlie WhNaAH
Bent, Devin 1940- WhoSSW 91
Bent, Gardner L. 1923- St&PR 91
Bent, George 1843-1918 WhNaAH
Bent, Gordon 1920- St&PR 91
Bent, Henry Albert 1926- WhoAm 90
Bent, Ian David 1938- IntWWM 90
Bent, Jan Brigham 1939- WhoAmW 91
Bent, Margaret 1903- BiDWomA
Bent, Michael William 1951- WhoEmL 91, WhoWor 91
Bent, Robert Demo 1928- WhoAm 90
Bent, Sandra Diane 1941- WhoE 91
Bent, William NewAgMG
Bent, William 1809-1869 BioIn 16, WhNaAH
Bentall, H. Clark 1915- St&PR 91
Bentall, Robert Gilmour 1922- St&PR 91
Bentall, Shirley Franklyn 1926- WhoAm 90, WhoAmW 91
Bentcover, Bruce Jay 1954- WhoAm 90
Bente, Kathleen Ellen 1957- WhoEmL 91
Bente, Wolfgang 1927- WhoWor 91
Benteen, Frederick W. 1834-1898 WhNaAH
Bentel, Dwight 1909- WhoAm 90, WhoWor 91
Bentel, Frederick Richard 1928- WhoAm 90
Bentel, Maria-Luise Ramona Azzarone 1928- WhoAm 90, WhoAmW 91
Bentel, Pearl Bucklen 1901- AuBYP 90
Bentele, Raymond F. 1936- WhoAm 90
Bentele, Raymond Frank 1936- St&PR 91
Benter, George H. 1942- St&PR 91
Benthall, Deedra 1946- WhoSSW 91
Bentham, George Wesley 1944- St&PR 91
Bentham, Jeremy 1748-1832 BioIn 16, WorAlBi
Bentin, Emmanuel Antoine 1951- WhoWor 91
Bentin, Michael BioIn 16
Bentinck-Smith, William 1914- WhoAm 90
Bentivoglio, Mirella 1922- BiDWomA
Bentley, Andrew 1952- IntWWM 90
Bentley, Antoinette Cozell 1937- St&PR 91, WhoAm 90, WhoAmW 91
Bentley, Beth Singer 1921- WhoAmW 91
Bentley, Carol Jane 1945- WhoAmW 91
Bentley, Carolyn E. 1923- St&PR 91
Bentley, Catherine FemiCLE
Bentley, Charles Fred 1914- WhoAm 90
Bentley, Charles Raymond 1929- WhoAm 90
Bentley, Charles W., Sr. 1915- St&PR 91
Bentley, Cheryl L. 1950- St&PR 91
Bentley, Clarence Edward 1921- WhoAm 90
Bentley, Claude 1915- WhoAm 90, WhoAmA 91
Bentley, Danny L. 1958- St&PR 91
Bentley, David Michael 1959- WhoEmL 91
Bentley, Dewey Jordan 1933- WhoSSW 91
Bentley, E C 1875-1956 TwCCr&M 91
Bentley, Earl Wilson, Jr. 1920- St&PR 91
Bentley, Edward Nelson 1948- WhoEmL 91

Bentley, Elizabeth 1767-1839 *FemiCLE*
Bentley, Eric 1916- *WhoAm 90, WhoWrEP 89*
Bentley, Fred Douglas, Sr. 1926- *WhoSSW 91, WhoWor 91*
Bentley, G. Firman 1934- *St&PR 91*
Bentley, Geoffrey Kingsley 1935- *WhoE 91*
Bentley, Gerald Eades 1901- *WhoAm 90*
Bentley, Gordon W. 1946- *St&PR 91*
Bentley, Helen Delich *WhoAm 90, WhoAmW 91, WhoE 91*
Bentley, Hershel Paul, Jr. 1928- *WhoAm 90*
Bentley, J.P. 1918- *St&PR 91*
Bentley, Jack 1895-1969 *Ballpl 90, BioIn 16*
Bentley, James Daniel 1945- *WhoAm 90*
Bentley, James Luther 1937- *WhoAm 90*
Bentley, James Robert 1942- *WhoSSW 91*
Bentley, Joanne 1928- *ConAu 130*
Bentley, John Joseph 1934- *St&PR 91*
Bentley, Judith 1945- *WhoWrEP 89*
Bentley, Julia 1958- *St&PR 91*
Bentley, Keith 1946- *IntWWM 90*
Bentley, Kenneth Chessar 1935- *WhoAm 90*
Bentley, Kenton Earl 1927- *WhoAm 90*
Bentley, Lionel *PenDiMP*
Bentley, Lisa Jane 1936- *WhoAmW 91*
Bentley, Lloyd Kenneth 1935- *BiDrAPA 89*
Bentley, Lois Elinor Dempsey 1936- *WhoSSW 91*
Bentley, Magdalene Augustine *BiDEWW*
Bentley, Norma Elizabeth 1916- *WhoAmW 91*
Bentley, Orville George 1918- *WhoAm 90*
Bentley, Peter 1915- *St&PR 91, WhoAm 90*
Bentley, Peter John Gerald 1930- *WhoAm 90*
Bentley, Peter John Hilton 1934- *WhoAm 90*
Bentley, Phyllis 1894-1977 *BioIn 16, FemiCLE*
Bentley, Robert Clyde 1926- *WhoWor 91*
Bentley, Sean Singer 1954- *WhoWrEP 89*
Bentley, Sharon Ruth 1947- *WhoAmW 91*
Bentley, Stephen Linwood 1940- *WhoSSW 91*
Bentley, Susan M 1947- *BiDrAPA 89*
Bentley, Thomas H., Jr. 1923- *St&PR 91*
Bentley, Thomas Roy 1931- *WhoAm 90*
Bentley, Tim Edward 1953- *WhoSSW 91*
Bentley, W Perry 1880- *EncO&P 3*
Bentley, William Elbert 1941- *St&PR 91*
Bentley, William H. 1931- *St&PR 91*
Bently, Donald E. 1924- *St&PR 91*
Bently, Donald Emery 1924- *WhoWor 91*
Benton, Allen Haydon 1921- *WhoAm 90*
Benton, Andrew Keith 1952- *WhoEmL 91*
Benton, Arnold J 1932- *BiDrAPA 89*
Benton, Auburn Edgar 1926- *WhoAm 90*
Benton, Bradley Keith 1957- *WhoEmL 91*
Benton, Brian Theodore *BiDrAPA 89*
Benton, Brook 1931-1988 *AnObit 1988, BioIn 16, DrBlPA 90*
Benton, Curtis D., Jr. *BioIn 16*
Benton, David Charles 1954- *WhoE 91*
Benton, Deane W 1914- *BiDrAPA 89*
Benton, Deborah Sally 1958- *WhoEmL 91*
Benton, Donald Stewart 1924- *WhoE 91, WhoWor 91*
Benton, Edward Henry 1950- *WhoE 91, WhoEmL 91*
Benton, Edward M. 1906- *St&PR 91*
Benton, Edward M. 1906-1988 *BioIn 16*
Benton, Edward Wayne *BiDrAPA 89*
Benton, Elizabeth Laquetta 1936- *WhoAmW 91*
Benton, Faye Louise 1939- *WhoAmW 91*
Benton, Fletcher 1931- *WhoAm 90, WhoAmA 91*
Benton, Gene Ray 1933- *St&PR 91*
Benton, George Stock 1917- *WhoAm 90*
Benton, Geraldine Ann 1960- *WhoAmW 91*
Benton, Hugh Arthur 1929- *WhoAm 90*
Benton, Jack Mitchell 1941- *St&PR 91*
Benton, Jean Elizabeth 1943- *WhoAmW 91*
Benton, Jesse Wilson, Jr. *St&PR 91N*
Benton, Jesse Wilson, Jr. 1921- *WhoAm 90*
Benton, Jim *BioIn 16*
Benton, John F. 1931-1988 *BioIn 16*
Benton, John L. *TwCCr&M 91*
Benton, Kay Myers 1940- *WhoE 91*
Benton, Kenneth Carter 1909- *SpyFic*
Benton, Lyn L. 1950- *WhoEmL 91*
Benton, Margaret Peake *WhoAmA 91N*
Benton, Nicholas *BioIn 16*
Benton, Nicholas 1926- *WhoE 91*
Benton, Odell *WhoSSW 91*
Benton, Owen D *BiDrAPA 89*
Benton, Peggie 1906- *ConAu 31NR*
Benton, Philip E. *BioIn 16*
Benton, Philip Eglin, Jr. 1928- *St&PR 91, WhoAm 90*
Benton, Randall Keith 1952- *St&PR 91*
Benton, Raymond S. *BioIn 16*
Benton, Robert *BioIn 16*
Benton, Robert Austin, Jr. 1921- *WhoAm 90*
Benton, Robert Dean 1929- *WhoAm 90*
Benton, Sandra Gunderson 1945- *WhoEmL 91*
Benton, Suzanne E 1936- *WhoAmA 91*
Benton, Thomas Hart 1782-1858 *EncABHB 6 [port], WorAlBi*
Benton, Thomas Hart 1889-1975 *BioIn 16, IntDcAA 90, WhoAmA 91N, WorAlBi*
Benton, Timothy Thomas 1948- *WhoEmL 91*
Benton, Will *ConAu 31NR*
Benton, William 1900-1973 *WhoAmA 91N*
Benton, William L. 1941- *St&PR 91*
Benton, William Pettigrew 1923- *WhoAm 90*
Benton-Borghi, Beatrice Hope 1946- *WhoAmW 91, WhoEmL 91*
Bentoy, Mirtala *WhoAmA 91*
Bentsen, B Steven 1957- *BiDrAPA 89*
Bentsen, Beryl Ann *BioIn 16*
Bentsen, Calvin *BioIn 16*
Bentsen, Harry Richard 1932- *St&PR 91*
Bentsen, Kenneth Edward 1926- *WhoAm 90*
Bentsen, Lloyd *BioIn 16*
Bentsen, Lloyd *BioIn 16*
Bentsen, Lloyd 1921- *WhoAm 90, WhoSSW 91, WhoWor 91*
Bentsen, Lloyd, Jr. 1921- *WorAlBi*
Bentz, Alfred Theodor 1897-1964 *DcScB S2*
Bentz, Dale Monroe 1919- *WhoAm 90*
Bentz, Edward Joseph, Jr. 1945- *WhoEmL 91*
Bentz, Frederick Jacob 1922- *WhoAm 90*
Bentz, Harry Donald 1931- *WhoAmA 91*
Bentz, Henry William 1930- *St&PR 91*
Bentz, John *WhoAmA 91N*
Bentz, John W. 1959- *ODwPR 91*
Bentzel, Todd Harold 1957- *WhoEmL 91*
Bentzen, Janet Rose 1934- *WhoAmW 91*
Bentzin, Charles Gilbert 1932- *WhoAm 90*
Bentzon, Niels Viggo 1919- *IntWWM 90*
Bentzon, Therese *EncCoWW*
Benua, Richard Squier 1921- *WhoAm 90*
Benua, Thomas Ray, Jr. 1945- *WhoAm 90*
Benucci, Francesco 1745?-1824 *PenDiMP*
Benveniste, Asa 1925-1990 *ConAu 131, -33NR*
Benveniste, Jacob 1921- *WhoAm 90*
Benvenisti, Meron *BioIn 16*
Benvenuti, Robert Peter 1934- *BiDrAPA 89*
Benvenuto, di Giovanni 1436-1518? *BioIn 16*
Benvenuto, Elaine E. 1943- *ODwPR 91*
Benvenuto, Elio 1914- *WhoAmA 91*
Benvenuto, Sergio, Sr. 1930- *WhoHisp 91*
Benvenuto, Virginia Alison 1959- *WhoHisp 91*
Benway, Alfred J. 1939- *St&PR 91*
Benway, Joseph Calise 1949- *WhoAm 90*
Beny, Roloff *ConAu 32NR*
Beny, Roloff 1924- *WhoAmA 91N*
Beny, Wilfred Roy 1924-1984 *ConAu 32NR*
Benya, Rosemarie Ann 1942- *WhoAmW 91*
Benyamina, Mohamed 1949- *WhoWor 91*
Benyamini, Daniel *PenDiMP*
Benyei, Candace Reed 1946- *WhoAmW 91*
Benyesh-Melnick, Matilda *BiDrAPA 89*
Benyo, Alison Shallcross 1961- *WhoAmW 91*
Benyo, Richard Stephen 1946- *WhoAm 90, WhoWor 91, WhoWrEP 89*
Benz, Allen 1945- *WhoEmL 91*
Benz, Barry A. 1955- *WhoEmL 91*
Benz, Carl Friedrich 1844-1929 *BioIn 16*
Benz, Edward John 1923- *WhoAm 90*
Benz, George Albert 1926- *WhoAm 90*
Benz, Gregory Paul 1953- *WhoEmL 91*
Benz, Harry R. 1937- *St&PR 91, WhoAm 90*
Benz, Joe 1886-1957 *Ballpl 90*
Benz, Karl Friedrich 1844-1929 *WorAlBi*
Benz, Lee R *WhoAmA 91N*
Benz, Linda Lou 1957- *WhoEmL 91*
Benz, Paul A. 1938- *St&PR 91*
Benzer, Seymour 1921- *WhoAm 90, WhoWor 91*
Benzi, Roberto 1937- *IntWWM 90, PenDiMP*
Benzie, Bruce John 1942- *WhoSSW 91*
Benziger, J. Bruno *BioIn 16*
Benziger, Peter Hamilton 1926- *WhoAm 90*
Benzing, Cynthia Dell 1951- *WhoE 91*
Benzing, David Warren 1953- *WhoEmL 91*
Benzing, Louis Henry 1926- *St&PR 91*
Benzing, Walter C. *St&PR 91N*
Benzinger, Raymond Burdette 1938- *WhoAm 90, WhoWor 91*
Benzinger, Todd 1963- *Ballpl 90*
Benzle, Curtis Munhall 1949- *WhoAmA 91, WhoEmL 91, WhoWor 91*
Benzle, Susan 1950- *WhoEmL 91*
Benzon, Honorio Tabal 1946- *WhoEmL 91*
Beobachterin *EncCoWW*
Beohm, Richard Thomas 1943- *WhoSSW 91*
Beozzo, Sylvester Anthony 1952- *WhoEmL 91*
Bepler, Stephen Edward 1942- *St&PR 91*
Bera, Regina Helen 1938- *WhoE 91*
Bera, Victoire-Leodile *EncCoWW*
Beracha, Barry Harris 1942- *St&PR 91, WhoAm 90*
Berain, Jean 1637-1711 *PenDiDA 89*
Beral, Harold 1939- *St&PR 91*
Berall, Frank Stewart 1929- *WhoAm 90, WhoE 91, WhoWor 91*
Beran, Andrew Nast 1958- *WhoEmL 91*
Beran, Bohumil F *BiDrAPA 89*
Beran, Denis Carl 1935- *WhoE 91*
Beran, Robert Lynn 1943- *WhoSSW 91*
Beran, Rudolf Jaroslav Vaclav 1943- *WhoAm 90*
Beranbaum, Rose Levy *BioIn 16*
Berande *EncO&P 3*
Beranek, Bruce Frank 1938- *St&PR 91*
Beranek, Leo Leroy 1914- *WhoAm 90*
Beranger, Pierre-Jean De 1780-1857 *WorAlBi*
Berard, Andre 1940- *St&PR 91, WhoAm 90*
Berard, Armand 1904-1989 *BioIn 16*
Berard, Christian 1902-1949 *BioIn 16*
Berard, John 1952- *ODwPR 91*
Berard, Louis J 1958- *BiDrAPA 89*
Berard, Paul Michael 1946- *WhoEmL 91*
Berard, William Burnet 1921- *St&PR 91*
Berardelli, Dandolo *BiDrAPA 89*
Berardelli, Francis Mario 1930- *St&PR 91*
Berardi, John Francis 1943- *WhoAm 90*
Berardi, Michael Anthony, Jr. 1959- *WhoE 91*
Berardi, Ronald Stephen 1943- *WhoE 91, WhoWor 91*
Berardino, Johnny 1917- *Ballpl 90*
Berardino, Thomas Joseph 1940- *St&PR 91*
Beras Rojas, Octavio Antonio 1906- *WhoWor 91*
Beratis, Stavroula 1942- *BiDrAPA 89*
Beraud, Jean 1899-1965 *OxCCanT*
Beraud, Marthe *EncO&P 3, EncPaPR 91*
Berbano, Victoria P. 1946- *WhoAmW 91*
Berbary, Maurice Shehadeh 1923- *WhoAm 90, WhoSSW 91, WhoWor 91*
Berberet, Lou 1929- *Ballpl 90, BioIn 16*
Berberian, Cathy 1925-1983 *PenDiMP*
Berberian, Paul Anthony 1945- *WhoSSW 91*
Berberich, L Robert 1936- *BiDrAPA 89*
Berberich, Raymond W. 1947- *St&PR 91*
Berberich, William Dorris 1937- *WhoAm 90*
Berberova, Nina 1901- *EncCoWW*
Berbie, Jane 1934- *IntWWM 90, PenDiMP*
Berbrich, Joan D. 1925- *WhoWrEP 89*
Berc, Kenneth Myles 1942- *BiDrAPA 89*
Bercaw, John Edward 1944- *WhoAm 90*
Bercel, Danielle Suzanne 1951- *WhoAmW 91*
Bercel, Nicholas A *BiDrAPA 89*
Berch, Bettina 1950- *ConAu 129*
Berche, Stephane Jacques 1944- *WhoWor 91*
Berchem, Claes 1620-1683 *IntDcAA 90*
Berchem, Douglas M. 1951- *St&PR 91*
Berchem, Steven P. 1958- *ODwPR 91*
Berchem, Theodor 1935- *WhoWor 91*
Berchenko, Frank 1911- *BiDrAPA 89*
Bercher, Thomas *BioIn 16*
Berchert, Henry J. *St&PR 91*
Berchin, Holly Ann 1953- *WhoAmW 91*
Berchtold, Gladys B. 1922- *St&PR 91*
Berchuck, Ivy Schiff 1933- *WhoE 91*
Berck, Martin Gans 1928- *WhoWrEP 89*
Bercka, Heinrich Wolf *PenDiDA 89*
Berckheyde, Gerrit 1638-1698 *IntDcAA 90*
Berckman, Evelyn 1900-1978 *TwCCr&M 91*
Bercovitch, Hanna Margareta 1934- *WhoAm 90, WhoWrEP 89*
Bercovitch, Sacvan 1933- *WhoAm 90*
Bercowetz, Bonnie Shane 1947- *WhoAmW 91*
Bercowetz, Cynthia Susan 1930- *WhoAmW 91*
Bercq, Alexis Claude 1960- *WhoEmL 91*
Berczeller, Emery 1920- *BiDrAPA 89*
Berczi, Andrew Stephen 1934- *WhoAm 90*
Berczynska-Kus, Elisabeth 1940- *IntWWM 90*
Berd, Morris 1914- *WhoAmA 91*
Berdahl, Paul Hilland 1945- *WhoEmL 91*
Berdahl, Richard A. 1943- *St&PR 91*
Berdahl, Robert Max 1937- *WhoAm 90*
Berdanier, Carolyn Dawson 1936- *WhoAmW 91*
Berdela, Edmund Zenon 1925- *St&PR 91*
Berdich, Alla 1940- *BiDrAPA 89*
Berdick, Edward Lee 1952- *WhoAm 90, WhoSSW 91*
Berdy, Jack *BioIn 16*
Berdyaev, Nikolai 1874-1948 *WorAlBi*
Bere, James Frederick 1922- *St&PR 91, WhoAm 90*
Berebitsky, Michael Jay 1948- *WhoEmL 91*
Beregovoy, Pierre Eugene *BioIn 16*
Beregovoy, Pierre Eugene 1925- *BiDFrPL*
Bereiter, Susan Roberta 1962- *WhoAmW 91, WhoE 91*
Berek, Peter 1940- *WhoAm 90*
Berelson, Bernard 1912-1979 *BioIn 16*
Beren, Joel S. 1957- *St&PR 91*
Beren, Stanley O 1920- *WhoAmA 91*
Berenato, Anthony F. 1922- *St&PR 91*
Berenato, Anthony Francis 1922- *WhoE 91*
Berenato, Mark Anthony 1958- *WhoE 91*
Berenbaum, Isidore L *BiDrAPA 89*
Berenberg, Danny Bob 1944- *WhoWor 91*
Berenblum, Eduardo Guido 1955- *WhoWor 91*
Berenbom, Loren David 1953- *WhoEmL 91*
Berend, Ivan T. 1930- *WhoWor 91*
Berend, Robert W. 1931- *St&PR 91*
Berend, Robert William 1931- *WhoAm 90*
Berenda, Ruth W. *WhoAmW 91*
Berendes, Heinz Werner 1925- *WhoAm 90*
Berendes, M. Benedicta 1927- *IntWWM 90*
Berendes, Margret F 1921- *BiDrAPA 89*
Berendi, S Alexander 1943- *BiDrAPA 89*
Berends, Polly Berrien *BioIn 16*
Berendsen, Raymond George *BiDrAPA 89*
Berendt, H C 1911- *EncO&P 3*
Berendt, Heinz C. 1911- *EncPaPR 91*
Berendt, Joachim Ernst 1922- *ConAu 30NR*
Berendt, Rob 1952- *WhoAm 90*
Berendzen, Richard E. *BioIn 16*
Berendzen, Richard Earl 1938- *WhoAm 90, WhoE 91*
Berengaria *WomWR*
Berenger, Tom 1950- *WorAlBi*
Berengo-Gardin, Gianni 1930- *WhoWor 91*
Berenguer, Juan 1954- *Ballpl 90*
Berenguer, Juan Bautista 1954- *WhoHisp 91*
Berenguer y Fuste, Damaso 1873-1953 *BioIn 16*
Berenholtz, Jim *NewAgMG*
Berenice *WomWR*
Berenice III *WomWR*
Berenice IV *WomWR*
Berens, Mark Harry 1928- *WhoAm 90*
Berens, Rodney Bristol 1945- *WhoAm 90*
Berensohn, Roger 1933- *WhoHisp 91*
Berenson, Bernard 1865-1959 *BioIn 16, WhoAmA 91N*
Berenson, Berry *BioIn 16*
Berenson, David James *BiDrAPA 89*
Berenson, F M 1929- *ConAu 129*
Berenson, Gerald Sanders 1922- *WhoAm 90*
Berenson, Jeffrey Lee 1950- *WhoAm 90*
Berenson, Marisa 1942- *BioIn 16*
Berenson, Marvin H 1926- *BiDrAPA 89*
Berenson, Robert Leonard 1939- *St&PR 91, WhoAm 90*
Berenson, William Keith 1954- *WhoSSW 91*
Berenstain, Jan 1923- *BioIn 16, SmATA 64 [port]*
Berenstain, Janice *AuBYP 90*
Berenstain, Stan 1923- *BioIn 16, SmATA 64 [port]*
Berenstain, Stanley 1923- *AuBYP 90*
Berenstein, Alejandro 1947- *WhoAm 90*
Berent, Irving *BiDrAPA 89*
Berent, Janet Lee 1960- *WhoAmW 91*
Berent, Philip Joseph 1941- *BiDrAPA 89*
Berentsen, Fern Florence 1927- *WhoAmW 91*
Berentsen, Kurtis George 1953- *WhoEmL 91*
Berenyi, Bruce 1954- *Ballpl 90*
Berenyi, G. Alex 1931- *St&PR 91*
Berenzweig, Jack Charles 1942- *WhoWor 91*
Bereolos, Demetrius Theodore 1954- *WhoEmL 91*
Beres, David *BiDrAPA 89*
Beres, Kenneth David 1931- *WhoE 91*
Beres, Mary Elizabeth 1942- *WhoSSW 91*
Beres, Michael John 1950- *WhoEmL 91*
Beresford, Anne 1929- *BioIn 16, FemiCLE*
Beresford, Bruce *BioIn 16*
Beresford, Bruce 1940- *WhoAm 90, WhoWor 91*
Beresford, Bruce Scovill 1937- *WhoE 91*

Beresford, Dennis Robert 1938- WhoWor 91
Beresford, Elizabeth WhoWrEP 89
Beresford, Hugh 1925- IntWWM 90
Beresford, Marian Sweeny 1939- WhoAmW 91
Beresford, Spencer Moxon 1918- WhoAm 90
Beresford, Thomas P 1946- BiDrAPA 89
Beresford-Hill, Paul Vincent 1949- WhoE 91, WhoWor 91
Beresford-Howe, Constance 1922- FemiCLE
Beresford-Howe, Constance Elizabeth 1922- WhoWrEP 89
Beresin, Eugene Victor 1950- BiDrAPA 89, WhoE 91
Bereston, Eugene Sydney 1914- WhoAm 90, WhoE 91, WhoWor 91
Beretta, Anne-Marie 1935- ConDes 90
Bereuter, Douglas K. BioIn 16
Bereuter, Douglas Kent 1939- WhoAm 90
Berey, Lewis A. 1944- St&PR 91
Berez, Ernest S. 1925- St&PR 91, WhoAm 90
Berez, Mark 1953- St&PR 91
Berezdivin, Robert 1945- WhoE 91
Berezin, Alexandre 1927- WhoWor 91
Berezin, Evelyn 1925- St&PR 91
Berezin, Martin A BiDrAPA 89
Berezin, Martin Arthur 1912- WhoE 91
Berezin, Robert Alan BiDrAPA 89
Berezin, Tanya BioIn 16
Bereznoff, Gregory Michael 1951- WhoEmL 91
Berezov, David A. 1952- St&PR 91
Berg Quartet PenDiMP
Berg, A. Scott BioIn 16
Berg, Abby Marvin 1928- WhoWrEP 89
Berg, Alan S. 1930- St&PR 91
Berg, Alban 1885-1935 PenDiMP A, WorAlBi
Berg, Alton Evert 1918- St&PR 91
Berg, Andrew Scott BioIn 16
Berg, Anton 1917- WhoWor 91
Berg, Arthur Z 1931- BiDrAPA 89
Berg, Barbara J. 1958- WhoAmW 91
Berg, Bjorn 1923- BioIn 16
Berg, Bruce Jeffrey BiDrAPA 89
Berg, Bruce Jeffrey 1956- WhoE 91
Berg, Bruce L 1952- BiDrAPA 89
Berg, Carolyn Nourse 1938- WhoAmW 91
Berg, Chris M. 1939- St&PR 91
Berg, Christa 1940- WhoWor 91
Berg, Christine Dorothy 1954- WhoE 91
Berg, Constance Demuth BioIn 16
Berg, Danny 1922- St&PR 91
Berg, David 1920- EncACom, WhoAm 90, WhoWrEP 89
Berg, Debra Kay 1954- WhoEmL 91
Berg, Dennis G. 1944- St&PR 91
Berg, Donald Crowley 1955- WhoEmL 91
Berg, Ericson 1942- St&PR 91, WhoAm 90
Berg, Esther Cosner 1906- St&PR 91
Berg, Eugene P. 1913- St&PR 91
Berg, Eugene Paulsen 1913- WhoAm 90
Berg, F. Steven 1935- St&PR 91
Berg, Finn Alarik 1944- WhoWor 91
Berg, Floyd BioIn 16
Berg, Fred Jay 1955- WhoE 91, WhoEmL 91
Berg, Gerald J. 1926- St&PR 91
Berg, Gertrude 1899-1966 BioIn 16, NotWoAT, WorAlBi
Berg, Gordon Hercher 1937- WhoE 91
Berg, Herman 1938- St&PR 91
Berg, Howard C. 1934- WhoAm 90
Berg, Howard Stephen 1949- WhoEmL 91
Berg, Ian J. 1941- St&PR 91
Berg, Irving D BiDrAPA 89
Berg, Irwin August 1913- WhoAm 90
Berg, Ivar Elis, Jr. 1929- WhoE 91
Berg, James L. 1940- St&PR 91
Berg, Janet Marie 1948- BiDrAPA 89
Berg, Jean Horton 1913- AuBYP 90, WhoWrEP 89
Berg, Jean Horton Lutz 1913- WhoAm 90, WhoAmW 91, WhoE 91
Berg, Jean Scholl 1950- WhoAmW 91
Berg, Jeffrey Spencer 1947- WhoAm 90
Berg, Jeffrey Tucker 1957- WhoSSW 91
Berg, John BioIn 16
Berg, John Richard 1932- WhoAm 90
Berg, Judith Leah 1929- BiDrAPA 89
Berg, Karen Eleanor 1943- WhoAmW 91
Berg, Lee Michael 1948- WhoSSW 91
Berg, Leonard 1927- WhoAm 90
Berg, Linda Lee 1955- WhoAmW 91
Berg, Lloyd 1914- WhoAm 90
Berg, Lloyd Olin 1953- WhoEmL 91
Berg, Lorine McComis 1919- WhoAmW 91
Berg, Louis Leslie 1919- WhoWor 91
Berg, Marie Majella 1916- WhoAm 90, WhoAmW 91, WhoSSW 91
Berg, Mary C 1926- BiDrAPA 89
Berg, Menachem S. 1944- WhoWor 91
Berg, Mitchell Lee 1951- WhoSSW 91
Berg, Moe 1902-1972 Ballpl 90
Berg, Mona Lea 1935- WhoAmA 91
Berg, Naomi Louise 1951- WhoAmW 91
Berg, Nate BioIn 16
Berg, Norbert R. BioIn 16
Berg, Norbert Raymond 1932- St&PR 91
Berg, Norman A. 1937- St&PR 91
Berg, Norman Alf 1918- WhoAm 90
Berg, Norman Asplund 1930- WhoAm 90
Berg, Patricia Elene 1943- WhoE 91
Berg, Patty 1918- WorAlBi
Berg, Paul 1926- WhoAm 90, WhoWor 91, WorAlBi
Berg, Peter 1949- BioIn 16
Berg, Phil 1902- WhoAmA 91N
Berg, Raisa 1913- BioIn 16
Berg, Ralph 1941- BioIn 16
Berg, Rebecca Anne 1957- WhoEmL 91
Berg, Robert Bradford 1919- St&PR 91
Berg, Robert D.W. 1927- St&PR 91
Berg, Robert J. 1949- St&PR 91
Berg, Robert Lewis 1918- WhoAm 90
Berg, Robert Raymond 1924- WhoAm 90
Berg, Robert Warren, Jr. 1954- WhoSSW 91
Berg, Roland 1943- WhoWor 91
Berg, Ron 1952- BioIn 16
Berg, Ronald M. 1945- St&PR 91
Berg, Roy Torgny 1927- WhoAm 90
Berg, Seymour 1921- BiDrAPA 89
Berg, Siri WhoAmA 91
Berg, Siri 1921- WhoE 91
Berg, Stanton Oneal 1928- WhoWor 91
Berg, Stephen 1936- ODwPR 91
Berg, Thomas 1914- St&PR 91, WhoAm 90
Berg, Thomas Sidney 1952- WhoEmL 91
Berg, Tom 1943- WhoAmA 91
Berg, W. Robert 1932- St&PR 91
Berg, Warren Carrol 1938- St&PR 91
Berg, William 1931- St&PR 91
Berg, William James 1942- WhoAm 90
Bergami, Frank G. 1939- St&PR 91
Bergamo, Anthony BioIn 16
Bergamo, Anthony 1946- St&PR 91
Bergan, Hans R. 1937- WhoSSW 91
Bergan, John Jerome 1927- WhoAm 90
Bergantini, Piero PenDiDA 89
Berganza, Teresa 1935- IntWWM 90, PenDiMP, WhoAm 90, WhoWor 91
Berganza Vargas, Teresa 1935- PenDiMP
Bergau, Frank Conrad 1926- WhoSSW 91
Bergaust, Erik 1925-1978 AuBYP 90, ConAu 32NR
Bergaust, Paul Richard 1955- WhoE 91
Bergavenny, Frances BiDEWW
Bergbauer, Patricia Anne 1949- WhoAmW 91
Berge, Carol WhoAm 90, WhoWrEP 89
Berge, Carol 1928- FemiCLE
Berge, Dorothy Alphena 1923- WhoAmA 91
Berge, Henry 1908- WhoAmA 91
Berge, Jerome D. 1948- St&PR 91
Berge, Kenneth George 1926- WhoAm 90
Berge, Paul Morton 1937- St&PR 91, WhoAm 90
Berge, Pierre BioIn 16
Berge, Pierre 1930- CurBio 90 [port]
Berge, Robert Allen 1952- WhoEmL 91
Bergel, Erich 1930- PenDiMP
Bergel, Richard 1935- St&PR 91, WhoAm 90
Bergelt, Philip Robert, Sr. 1940- WhoSSW 91
Bergeman, Carl T. 1937- St&PR 91
Bergeman, George William 1946- WhoSSW 91
Bergen, Bill 1873-1943 Ballpl 90
Bergen, Bruce Harry 1955- WhoEmL 91
Bergen, Candice BioIn 16
Bergen, Candice 1946- News 90 [port], WhoAm 90, WhoAmW 91, WorAlBi
Bergen, D Thomas 1930- WhoAmA 91
Bergen, D. Thomas 1930- WhoE 91, WhoWor 91
Bergen, Daniel C. 1942- St&PR 91
Bergen, Daniel Patrick 1935- WhoAm 90
Bergen, Edgar 1903-1978 WorAlBi
Bergen, Edgar John 1903-1978 EncPaPR 91
Bergen, G. S. Peter 1936- WhoAm 90
Bergen, Harold A. 1927- ODwPR 91, St&PR 91
Bergen, James J. 1847-1923 AmLegL
Bergen, John D. 1943- ODwPR 91
Bergen, John Donald 1942- WhoAm 90
Bergen, Kenneth William 1911- WhoAm 90
Bergen, Polly WhoAm 90
Bergen, Polly 1930- WorAlBi
Bergen, Sidney L 1922- WhoAmA 91
Bergen, Stanley Silvers, Jr. 1929- WhoAm 90
Bergen, Werner Gerhard 1943- WhoAm 90
Bergendahl, Goran Henrik 1940- WhoWor 91
Bergendahl, Waldemar 1933- WhoWor 91
Bergendi, Pierre-Noel 1934- WhoWor 91
Bergendoff, Conrad John Immanuel 1895- WhoAm 90
Bergendorf, Harold William 1935- St&PR 91
Bergendorff, Frederick L. 1944- WhoAm 90
Bergengruen, Werner 1892-1964 BioIn 16
Bergenn, James Walter 1954- WhoEmL 91
Berger, Abraham 1903-1989 BioIn 16
Berger, Alf-Jorg 1941- WhoWor 91
Berger, Allan S 1931- BiDrAPA 89
Berger, Allan Sidney 1931- WhoE 91
Berger, Amy H. 1942- WhoWrEP 89
Berger, Andrew 1944- WhoE 91
Berger, Andrew L. 1946- WhoAm 90
Berger, Anita Hazel 1930- WhoE 91
Berger, Arnold Lester 1916- WhoE 91
Berger, Arthur S. 1945- EncO&P 3
Berger, Arthur Seymour 1920- EncPaPR 91
Berger, Arthur Victor 1912- IntWWM 90, WhoAm 90
Berger, Audrey Marilyn 1955- WhoAmW 91
Berger, Barbara 1945- BioIn 16
Berger, Barbara A. 1958- WhoAmW 91
Berger, Barry G. 1928- St&PR 91
Berger, Bennett M. BioIn 16
Berger, Bennett Maurice 1926- WhoAm 90
Berger, Bernard Ben 1912- WhoAm 90
Berger, Beverly Jane 1939- WhoAmW 91
Berger, Boze 1910- Ballpl 90
Berger, Brigitte 1928- ConAu 131
Berger, Bruce 1938- ConAu 30NR
Berger, Bruce 1944- WhoAm 90
Berger, Bruce R 1952- BiDrAPA 89
Berger, Carl BiDrAPA 89
Berger, Carl Frederick 1936- WhoAm 90
Berger, Charles J 1938- BiDrAPA 89
Berger, Christine Lee 1956- WhoAmW 91
Berger, Curtis Jay 1926- WhoAm 90
Berger, Dana Jill 1950- WhoE 91
Berger, David 1912- WhoAm 90, WhoWor 91
Berger, David G. 1941- ConAu 129
Berger, Diane Klein 1946- WhoWor 91
Berger, Dirk Marc 1943- BiDrAPA 89
Berger, Doris E 1929- BiDrAPA 89
Berger, Douglas Marc 1958- BiDrAPA 89
Berger, Edmond Louis 1939- WhoAm 90
Berger, Elizabeth Ann 1955- WhoAmW 91
Berger, Elizabeth C 1948- BiDrAPA 89
Berger, Ellen 1955- WhoAmW 91
Berger, Eric 1906- WhoAm 90, WhoWrEP 89
Berger, Eric Hoadley 1944- BiDrAPA 89
Berger, Erna 1900- IntWWM 90, PenDiMP
Berger, Eugene L. 1916- St&PR 91
Berger, Francine Ellis 1949- WhoAmW 91
Berger, Frank Milan 1913- WhoAm 90, WhoE 91
Berger, Frank Stanley 1936- WhoAm 90, WhoE 91
Berger, Fred 1925- ODwPR 91
Berger, Fred Keith 1947- BiDrAPA 89
Berger, Fredericka AuBYP 90
Berger, Fredericka 1932- ConAu 131
Berger, George 1936- WhoE 91
Berger, Gordon Mark 1942- WhoAm 90
Berger, Gregory Alan 1954- WhoEmL 91
Berger, Gustav A 1920- WhoAmA 91
Berger, Gustav Adolphe 1920- WhoAm 90
Berger, Harold 1925- WhoAm 90, WhoE 91, WhoWor 91
Berger, Harold 1926- WhoAm 90
Berger, Harold Phillip 1947- WhoEmL 91
Berger, Harvey James 1950- WhoAm 90, WhoE 91
Berger, Harvey L. 1938- St&PR 91
Berger, Harvey Robert 1927- WhoE 91
Berger, Heinie 1882-1954 Ballpl 90
Berger, Henry BiDrAPA 89
Berger, Henry 1947- WhoE 91
Berger, Henry Grant BiDrAPA 89
Berger, Herbert 1909- WhoAm 90
Berger, Howard S 1941- BiDrAPA 89
Berger, Howard Stephen 1941- WhoE 91
Berger, Howard Steven 1952- WhoE 91
Berger, Irving L 1913- BiDrAPA 89
Berger, Isidore Marvin 1919- WhoE 91
Berger, Ivan Bennett 1939- WhoWrEP 89
Berger, J. Walter 1947- St&PR 91
Berger, Jack C 1923- BiDrAPA 89
Berger, James Charles 1941- WhoE 91, WhoWor 91
Berger, Jason 1924- WhoAmA 91
Berger, Jay BioIn 16
Berger, Jay S. 1955- WhoSSW 91
Berger, Jeffrey Allen 1958- BiDrAPA 89
Berger, Jerry Allen 1943- WhoAmA 91
Berger, John Peter 1926- WhoWor 91
Berger, Joseph WhoAm 90
Berger, Joseph 1941- BiDrAPA 89
Berger, Joseph Herman 1904- St&PR 91
Berger, Karol 1947- IntWWM 90
Berger, Kathleen Kammerer 1958- WhoAmW 91
Berger, Kay 1939- WhoAm 90, WhoAmW 91
Berger, Kay S. 1939- ODwPR 91
Berger, Kenneth James Edward 1951- WhoWor 91
Berger, Kenneth Walter 1924- WhoAm 90
Berger, Larry F 1951- BiDrAPA 89
Berger, Laszlo BioIn 16
Berger, Lawrence Douglas 1947- WhoEmL 91
Berger, Lawrence Howard 1947- WhoEmL 91
Berger, Leo 1907- St&PR 91
Berger, Louis 1914- St&PR 91
Berger, Luc 1933- WhoAm 90
Berger, Marcel 1927- WhoWor 91
Berger, Mark D 1929- BiDrAPA 89
Berger, Matthew Adam BiDrAPA 89
Berger, Maureen 1941- WhoAmW 91
Berger, Maurice 1927- WhoWor 91
Berger, Maurice 1956- WhoAmA 91, WhoE 91
Berger, Meir 1937- BiDrAPA 89
Berger, Melvin H. 1927- AuBYP 90
Berger, Michael L 1943- ConAu 32NR
Berger, Miles 1930- St&PR 91
Berger, Milton M BiDrAPA 89
Berger, Miriam Roskin 1934- WhoAmW 91, WhoE 91, WhoWor 91
Berger, Morton 1935-1988 BioIn 16
Berger, Murray H. 1924- St&PR 91
Berger, Murry P. 1926- WhoAm 90
Berger, Natalie Stelle 1950- WhoAmW 91
Berger, Norman L. 1917- St&PR 91
Berger, Oscar 1901- WhoAm 90, WhoAmA 91, WhoE 91, WhoWor 91
Berger, Otto PenDiMP
Berger, Pat WhoAmA 91
Berger, Patricia Wilson 1926- WhoAm 90
Berger, Paul Eric 1948- WhoAm 90, WhoAmA 91
Berger, Peter Ludwig 1929- WhoAm 90
Berger, Phil 1942- AuBYP 90, SmATA 62 [port]
Berger, Philip Alan BiDrAPA 89
Berger, Philip Jeffrey 1943- WhoAm 90
Berger, Raoul 1901- WhoAm 90
Berger, Raydelle H. 1923- St&PR 91
Berger, Raymond H. 1931- St&PR 91
Berger, Richard L. 1947- St&PR 91
Berger, Richard Lee 1935- WhoAm 90
Berger, Rick E. 1952- EncPaPR 91
Berger, Robert Bertram 1924- WhoAm 90
Berger, Robert H BiDrAPA 89
Berger, Robert J. 1946- St&PR 91
Berger, Robert Lewis 1925- WhoAm 90
Berger, Robert Michael 1942- WhoAm 90
Berger, Robert Oscar, III 1951- WhoE 91
Berger, Robert S. 1917- St&PR 91
Berger, Roman 1930- IntWWM 90
Berger, Ron Ariel 1948- St&PR 91
Berger, Samuel David 1911-1980 BioIn 16
Berger, Samuel Martin 1938- BiDrAPA 89
Berger, Sandra Beth 1939- WhoE 91
Berger, Sandra Christine Q 1948- WhoAmA 91
Berger, Sanford Jason 1926- WhoAm 90
Berger, Scott Andrew BiDrAPA 89
Berger, Senta 1941- BioIn 16
Berger, Seymour Maurice 1928- WhoAm 90
Berger, Seymour P. 1923- St&PR 91
Berger, Spencer S. 1913- St&PR 91
Berger, Steven H. 1947- BiDrAPA 89
Berger, Steven John 1957- WhoEmL 91
Berger, Steven R. 1945- WhoEmL 91
Berger, Suzanne 1939- WhoAm 90
Berger, Thomas 1924- BioIn 16, MajTwCW
Berger, Thomas Jan 1952- WhoAm 90
Berger, Thomas Louis 1924- WhoAm 90, WhoWrEP 89
Berger, Ulrich 1919- WhoWor 91
Berger, Valery A BiDrAPA 89
Berger, Victor L. 1860-1929 EncAL
Berger, Wally 1905-1988 Ballpl 90 [port], BioIn 16
Berger, Wilhelm Georg 1929- WhoWor 91
Berger, William Ernest 1918- WhoAm 90
Berger, William Merriam Bart 1925- St&PR 91
Berger-Homan, Anje 1945- WhoAmW 91
Berger-Tuna, Helmut 1942- IntWWM 90
Bergerbest, Nathan Steven 1957- WhoEmL 91
Bergere, C. Wendell 1945- St&PR 91
Bergere, Clifford Wendell, Jr. 1945- WhoAm 90
Bergere, Lee ConTFT 8
Bergere, Thea AuBYP 90
Bergeron, Andre Louis 1922- BiDFrPL
Bergeron, Charles E. 1945- St&PR 91
Bergeron, Clifton George 1925- WhoAm 90
Bergeron, Danielle BiDrAPA 89
Bergeron, David F. 1957- St&PR 91
Bergeron, Francis A. 1935- St&PR 91
Bergeron, J. Donald 1944- St&PR 91
Bergeron, Jan Paul 1937- St&PR 91

Bergeron, Kathleen Yvonne 1953- WhoWrEP 89
Bergeron, Michel 1946- WhoE 91
Bergeron, Paul James 1954- WhoEmL 91
Bergeron, Peter L. St&PR 91
Bergeron, R. Thomas 1931- WhoAm 90
Bergeron, Richard BiDrAPA 89
Bergeron, Richard F BiDrAPA 89
Bergeron, Victor Jules 1902-1984 AuBYP 90
Bergeron, William Noah, II BiDrAPA 89
Bergerson, David Raymond 1939- St&PR 91
Bergerson, Kenneth E. 1933- St&PR 91
Bergery, Gaston Frank 1892-1974 BiDFrPL
Berges, David M. 1950- WhoEmL 91
Berges, Emily Trafford 1937- ConAu 132
Berges, Marshall William WhoAm 90, WhoWrEP 89
Bergesch, Louis William 1927- WhoAm 90
Bergesen, Robert Nelson 1937- St&PR 91
Bergeson, Marian WhoAmW 91
Bergeson, Scott 1938- WhoAm 90
Bergethon, Kaare Roald 1918- WhoAm 90
Bergevin, Yvon J. 1942- St&PR 91
Bergevin, Yvon Joseph 1942- WhoAm 90
Bergevine, George John 1948- WhoE 91
Bergfield, Gene Raymond 1951- WhoSSW 91
Berggol'ts, Ol'ga 1910-1975 EncCoWW
Berggren, Anna M. 1929- WhoWor 91
Berggren, Glenn Merritt 1928- St&PR 91
Berggren, Jean Reddell 1941- BiDrAPA 89
Berggren, Ronald Bernard 1931- WhoAm 90, WhoWor 91
Berggren, Thage BioIn 16
Berggren, Thommy 1937- WhoWor 91
Berggren, William Alfred 1931- WhoAm 90
Berggren Lowe, Margareteva Ruth 1919- WhoWrEP 89
Berggruen, Heinz 1914- BioIn 16
Berggruen, John Henry 1943- WhoAmA 91
Bergh, Andrew G. 1950- St&PR 91
Bergh, Arpad Albert 1930- WhoAm 90
Bergh, Kjell 1945- St&PR 91
Bergh, Sven-Erik 1912- WhoWor 91
Berghash, Mark W 1935- WhoAmA 91
Bergheim, Jerome F 1938- BiDrAPA 89
Bergheim, Laura Ann 1962- WhoE 91
Berghel, Victoria Smouse 1952- WhoEmL 91
Bergher, Moises BiDrAPA 89
Berghman, Donald Howard BiDrAPA 89
Berghmans, Jean-Pierre 1949- WhoWor 91
Berghof, Herbert 1909-1990 NewYTBS 90 [port]
Berghoff, Carlyn BioIn 16
Berghoff, Paul Johannes 1943- WhoSSW 91
Berghold, Joseph Philip 1938- St&PR 91, WhoAm 90
Bergholm, Ernst Tauno Herman 1935- WhoWor 91
Bergholz, Eleanor BioIn 16
Bergholz, Richard Cady 1917- WhoAm 90
Bergholz, Warren Ernest, Jr. 1945- WhoEmL 91
Berghorn, Forrest Jay 1932- WhoAm 90
Berghout, Phia 1909- PenDiMP
Berghuis, Peter Lange 1951- WhoEmL 91
Berghuis, Thomas G. 1945- St&PR 91
Bergia, Fred L. 1940- St&PR 91
Bergier, Jacques 1912-1978 EncO&P 3
Bergier, Jean-Francois 1931- WhoWor 91
Bergin, Daniel Timothy 1930- St&PR 91, WhoAm 90
Bergin, Darby 1826-1896 DcCanB 12
Bergin, John Francis 1924- St&PR 91, WhoAm 90
Bergin, Robert Allen 1938- WhoSSW 91
Bergin, Thomas Goddard 1904-1987 BioIn 16
Bergius, Friedrich 1884-1949 WorAlBi
Bergius, Friedrich Karl Rudolph 1884-1949 BioIn 16
Bergklint, Karl Gustaf 1955- WhoSSW 91
Bergl, Nancy 1959- WhoWrEP 89
Bergland, Bob Selmer 1928- BiDrUSE 89
Bergland, Martha 1945- ConAu 130
Berglas, Eitan 1934- WhoWor 91
Berglas, Steven 1950- WhoE 91
Bergleitner, George Charles, Jr. 1935- WhoAm 90, WhoE 91, WhoWor 91
Bergles, Arthur Edward 1935- WhoAm 90
Berglin, Brian P. 1950- St&PR 91
Berglin, Eva Elisabet 1947- WhoWor 91
Berglin, Linda 1944- WhoAmW 91
Berglund, Brita 1909- WhoWor 91
Berglund, Carl Neil 1938- WhoAm 90
Berglund, David Craver 1925- WhoWor 91
Berglund, Erik NewAgMG
Berglund, Joel 1903- PenDiMP
Berglund, Mabel M. 1908- St&PR 91
Berglund, Paavo 1929- PenDiMP
Berglund, Paavo Allan Engelbert 1929- WhoWor 91
Berglund, Paavo Allan Englebert 1929- IntWWM 90
Berglund, Robin G. 1945- St&PR 91
Berglund, Stig Anders 1934- WhoWor 91
Bergman, A. Barrie 1942- St&PR 91
Bergman, Alan WhoAm 90
Bergman, Allan H. 1934- St&PR 91
Bergman, Anna-Eva 1909-1987 BiDWomA
Bergman, Barrie 1942- WhoAm 90
Bergman, Benjamin S. 1921- St&PR 91
Bergman, Bernard Allen 1945- BiDrAPA 89
Bergman, Bo 1869-1967 DcScanL
Bergman, Bruce John BioIn 16
Bergman, Bruce John 1941- St&PR 91
Bergman, Carl A. 1921- St&PR 91
Bergman, Charles Cabe 1933- WhoAm 90
Bergman, Clifford Irvin 1937- St&PR 91
Bergman, Dani L. 1949- WhoEmL 91
Bergman, Dann Wayne 1953- WhoEmL 91
Bergman, Dave 1953- Ballpl 90
Bergman, David 1950- WhoWrEP 89
Bergman, David B 1942- BiDrAPA 89
Bergman, David Marc 1948- St&PR 91
Bergman, Elliot J. 1926- St&PR 91
Bergman, Eric Charles 1947- BiDrAPA 89
Bergman, Erik 1911- IntWWM 90
Bergman, Garrett Edward 1946- WhoE 91
Bergman, George Mark 1943- WhoAm 90
Bergman, Hans Otto Mauritz 1938- WhoWor 91
Bergman, Harlan Wayne 1932- St&PR 91
Bergman, Harold John 1935- St&PR 91
Bergman, Harry St&PR 91
Bergman, Harry 1912- WhoAm 90, WhoWor 91
Bergman, Harry Richard 1914- St&PR 91
Bergman, Heidi Suzanne 1958- IntWWM 90, WhoEmL 91
Bergman, Hermas John 1926- WhoAm 90
Bergman, Hjalmar Fredrik Elgerus 1883-1931 DcScanL
Bergman, Ingmar 1918- BioIn 16, ConAu 33NR, WhoAm 90, WhoWor 91, WorAlBi
Bergman, Ingmar Ernst 1918- DcScanL
Bergman, Ingrid 1915-1982 ConAu 132, WorAlBi
Bergman, Ira M 1959- BiDrAPA 89
Bergman, Janet Louise Marx 1920- IntWWM 90
Bergman, Jerry Alan 1945- ODwPR 91
Bergman, Klaus 1931- St&PR 91, WhoAm 90, WhoE 91
Bergman, Laurence Richard 1956- St&PR 91
Bergman, Lee ODwPR 91
Bergman, Lewis 1918-1988 BioIn 16
Bergman, Marilyn Keith 1929- WhoAm 90
Bergman, Mark Steven 1956- WhoE 91, WhoEmL 91
Bergman, Mats Olof A. 1947- WhoWor 91
Bergman, Monica BioIn 16
Bergman, Murray 1902- BiDrAPA 89
Bergman, Nancy Palm 1938- WhoAm 90
Bergman, Richard Isaac 1934- WhoE 91
Bergman, Robert Edward 1944- St&PR 91
Bergman, Robert George 1942- WhoAm 90
Bergman, Robert L. 1935- St&PR 91
Bergman, Robert L 1938- BiDrAPA 89
Bergman, Robert P 1945- WhoAmA 91
Bergman, Robert Paul 1945- WhoAm 90, WhoE 91
Bergman, Robert Scribner 1934- WhoWor 91
Bergman, Samuel Hugo 1883- EncO&P 3
Bergman, Sidney H 1933- BiDrAPA 89
Bergman, Stefan 1895-1977 DcScB S2
Bergman, Trish 1953- WhoAmW 91
Bergman, W. Dieter 1920- IntWWM 90
Bergman, Yolanda BioIn 16
Bergmann, Arthur M. 1927- WhoE 91, WhoWor 91
Bergmann, Barbara Rose 1927- WhoAm 90, WhoAmW 91, WhoE 91
Bergmann, Carl K. 1929- St&PR 91
Bergmann, Donald Gerald 1949- WhoEmL 91
Bergmann, Fred Heinz 1928- WhoAm 90
Bergmann, Fredrick Louis 1916- WhoAm 90
Bergmann, Richard Ronald 1935- WhoAm 90
Bergmann, Richard Willis 1937- St&PR 91
Bergmann, Walter BioIn 16
Bergner, Amos 1935- St&PR 91
Bergner, Cathy L. 1951- WhoAmW 91
Bergner, Heinz 1936- WhoWor 91
Bergner, Jane Cohen 1943- WhoAmW 91
Bergner, William Joseph 1948- WhoEmL 91
Bergold, Harry Earl, Jr. 1931- WhoAm 90
Bergold, Orm 1925- WhoWor 91
Bergomi, Joseph G. 1933- St&PR 91
Bergonia, Raymond David 1951- WhoAm 90, WhoEmL 91
Bergonzi, Carlo 1924- IntWWM 90, PenDiMP, WhoAm 90
Bergonzi, Franklyn Michael 1945- St&PR 91
Bergquist, Bruce Orville 1948- St&PR 91
Bergquist, David W. 1941- St&PR 91
Bergquist, Gloria ODwPR 91
Bergquist, Gordon Neil 1932- WhoAm 90
Bergquist, Harold B. 1937- St&PR 91
Bergquist, Ingvar Sone BioIn 16
Bergquist, Nils Robert 1939- WhoWor 91
Bergquist, Robert Louis 1931- WhoSSW 91
Bergreen, Laurence 1950- BestSel 90-4 [port]
Bergreen, Stanley W BiDrAPA 89
Bergs, Joseph Theodore 1958- BiDrAPA 89
Bergseth, Robert Reid 1945- WhoEmL 91
Bergsland, Katherine Smith 1934- St&PR 91
Bergsland, Thomas Grant 1933- St&PR 91
Bergsma, Alan Stuart 1944- BiDrAPA 89
Bergsma, Daniel 1909- WhoAm 90
Bergsma, Syb 1936- WhoWor 91
Bergsma, William Laurence 1921- IntWWM 90, WhoAm 90
Bergsmark, Edwin Martin 1941- St&PR 91, WhoAm 90
Bergsoe, Clara 1837-1905 EncCoWW
Bergson, Abram 1914- WhoAm 90
Bergson, Henri 1859-1941 EncO&P 3, WorAlBi, WrPh P
Bergson, Henri-Louis 1859-1941 EncPaPR 91
Bergson, Lisa Marie 1950- St&PR 91
Bergson, Maria WhoAm 90
Bergsson, Gurdbergur 1932- DcScanL
Bergstein, Harry Benjamin 1916- WhoAm 90
Bergsteiner, Harald 1944- WhoWor 91
Bergsteinsson, Paul 1942- St&PR 91
Bergsten, C. Fred 1941- WhoAm 90
Bergstra, Jan Aldert 1951- WhoWor 91
Bergstrand, Wilton Everet 1909- WhoAm 90
Bergstresser, Paul Richard 1941- WhoSSW 91
Bergstrom, Albion Andrew 1947- WhoE 91
Bergstrom, Betty Howard 1931- WhoAmW 91
Bergstrom, Dean Ernest 1926- St&PR 91
Bergstrom, Dedric Waldemar 1919- WhoAm 90
Bergstrom, Edith Harrod WhoAmA 91
Bergstrom, George Frederick 1950- WhoEmL 91
Bergstrom, Helen Marie 1930- WhoAmW 91
Bergstrom, Ingvar Erik 1913- WhoWor 91
Bergstrom, James D 1933- WhoAm 90
Bergstrom, James David 1933- St&PR 91
Bergstrom, John J. 1925- St&PR 91
Bergstrom, John Jacob 1925- WhoAm 90
Bergstrom, K. Sune 1916 WorAlBi
Bergstrom, K. Sune D. 1916- WhoAm 90, WhoWor 91
Bergstrom, Lorie Ann BiDrAPA 89
Bergstrom, Richard Norman 1921- WhoAm 90
Bergstrom, Robert William 1918- WhoAm 90, WhoWor 91
Bergstrom, Rolf Olof Bernhard 1934- WhoWor 91
Bergstrom, Roy E. 1935- St&PR 91
Bergstrom, Stig Magnus 1935- WhoAm 90
Bergstrom, Villy Abel 1938- WhoWor 91
Bergstrom-Nielsen, Carl 1951- IntWWM 90
Bergtraum, Howard Michael 1946- WhoEmL 91
Bergum, Steven John 1945- St&PR 91
Berguson, Robert Jenkins 1944- WhoAmA 91
Berhang, Mattie WhoAmA 91, WhoE 91
Berhard, Richard J, Mrs WhoAmA 91N
Beria, Lavrenti BioIn 16
Beria, Lavrenti 1899-1953 WorAlBi
Berick, James H. 1933- St&PR 91
Berick, James Herschel 1933- WhoAm 90
Berie-Henault, Mary Beth BioIn 16
Berigan, Bunny 1908-1942 BioIn 16, OxCPMus
Berigan, Bunny 1909-1942 WorAlBi
Berigan, Patrick Tierney 1956- WhoEmL 91
Berigan, Rory Ann 1954- WhoSSW 91
Berigard of Pisa 1578?-1664 EncO&P 3
Berin, Barnet N. BioIn 16
Berin, Harvey BioIn 16
Bering, Carol Gretchen 1938- WhoAmW 91
Bering, Edgar Andrew, III 1946- WhoEmL 91
Bering, Vitus Jonassen 1681-1741 EncCRAm, WhNaAH, WorAlBi
Beringer, Oscar 1844-1922 PenDiMP
Beringer, Robert McGinnis 1957- WhoEmL 91
Beringer, Stuart M. 1923- St&PR 91
Beringer, Stuart Marshall 1923- WhoAm 90
Beringer, William Ernst 1928- St&PR 91, WhoAm 90, WhoSSW 91
Beringhaus, Oscar Edmund 1874-1952 BioIn 16
Berini, Bianca 1928- IntWWM 90
Berio, Luciano 1925- IntWWM 90, PenDiMP A, WhoAm 90, WhoWor 91
Beriosova, Svetlana 1932- WorAlBi
Beriot, Charles-Auguste de 1802-1870 PenDiMP
Berisavljevic, Slobodanka 1942- WhoWor 91
Berish, Barry M. 1932- St&PR 91
Beriss, Michael S. 1964- WhoE 91
Beristain Ipina, Antonio 1924- WhoWor 91
Berk, Alan 1940- St&PR 91
Berk, Alan S. 1934- WhoAm 90
Berk, Alexander WhoAm 90
Berk, Allen Joel 1940- WhoAm 90
Berk, Ann E. WhoAmW 91
Berk, Arthur BiDrAPA 89
Berk, Bradford Charles 1953- WhoSSW 91
Berk, Burton Benjamin 1930- WhoWor 91
Berk, Carole Doull 1950- WhoEmL 91
Berk, Jack Edward WhoAm 90
Berk, James Edward 1945- St&PR 91
Berk, James Lawrence, II 1960- WhoE 91
Berk, Joseph BiDrAPA 89
Berk, Kerry M. 1953- WhoAmW 91
Berk, Morton Emmett 1913- WhoAm 90
Berk, Norland F 1937- BiDrAPA 89
Berk, Paul David 1938- WhoAm 90
Berk, Peggy Faith 1951- WhoAmW 91, WhoE 91, WhoEmL 91
Berk, Richard Charles 1948- WhoSSW 91
Berk, Steven Lee 1949- WhoAm 90, WhoWor 91
Berk, Theodore G. 1938- ODwPR 91
Berk, William Stewart 1957- WhoEmL 91
Berka, Dusan 1945- St&PR 91
Berka, Marianne Guthrie 1944- WhoAmW 91
Berkal, Allen Brian BiDrAPA 89
Berkarda, Bulent 1932- WhoWor 91
Berkau, Gunther 1924- WhoWor 91
Berkbigler, Marsha Lee 1950- WhoAmW 91
Berke, Anita Diamant WhoAmW 91
Berke, Deborah 1954- BioIn 16
Berke, Erwin M. 1917- St&PR 91
Berke, Ivan H. 1943- St&PR 91
Berke, Judie 1938- WhoAmW 91
Berke, Jules 1926- WhoAm 90
Berke, Michael 1939- St&PR 91, WhoE 91
Berke, Pamela Sue 1959- WhoAmW 91
Berke, Raoul Ben 1940- BiDrAPA 89
Berke, Rena F. BioIn 16
Berke, Ronald Alan 1940- St&PR 91
Berke, Steven Leigh 1954- WhoE 91, WhoEmL 91
Berke, Yvette Nancy 1961- WhoAmW 91
Berkel, Charles John 1925- St&PR 91
Berkeley, Anthony 1893-1970 WorAlBi
Berkeley, Anthony 1893-1971 TwCCr&M 91
Berkeley, Ballard 1904-1988 AnObit 1988
Berkeley, Bernard 1923- St&PR 91
Berkeley, Betty Life 1924- WhoAmW 91
Berkeley, Eliza 1734-1800 FemiCLE
Berkeley, Frances 1634-1695? EncCRAm
Berkeley, Francis Lewis, Jr. 1911- WhoSSW 91
Berkeley, Frederick D. 1928- St&PR 91
Berkeley, George 1685-1753 DcLB 101 [port], EncCRAm, WorAlBi, WrPh P
Berkeley, Lennox 1903- PenDiMP A
Berkeley, Lennox 1903-1989 AnObit 1989, BioIn 16
Berkeley, Marvin H. 1922- WhoAm 90
Berkeley, Michael 1948- IntWWM 90, PenDiMP A
Berkeley, Norborne, Jr. 1922- St&PR 91
Berkeley, Pamela BioIn 16
Berkeley, Thomas 1352-1417 BioIn 16
Berkeley, William 1606-1677 BioIn 16, EncCRAm, WhNaAH
Berkelhammer, Gerald 1931- WhoE 91
Berkelhammer, Robert Bruce 1949- WhoEmL 91
Berkell, Arthur 1943- WhoE 91
Berken, Gilbert H 1937- BiDrAPA 89
Berken, Mitchell Lloyd 1937- St&PR 91
Berkenbile, Glen Lee 1922- WhoSSW 91
Berkenes, Joyce Marie Poore 1953- WhoAmW 91, WhoEmL 91, WhoWor 91
Berkenkamp, Fred Julius 1925- WhoAm 90
Berkenkamp, John 1936- St&PR 91
Berkery, Michael John 1945- WhoAm 90
Berkes, Howard 1954- WhoAm 90

Berkes, Kalman 1952- *IntWWM 90*
Berkes, Leslie John 1946- *WhoEmL 91*
Berkey, Barbara Ann 1943- *WhoAmW 91*
Berkey, Barry Robert 1935- *BiDrAPA 89*
Berkey, Richard L 1938- *BiDrAPA 89*
Berkhan, Sharon Lee 1954- *WhoAmW 91*
Berkhemer-Credaire, Betsy *ODwPR 91*
Berkhemer-Credaire, Betsy 1947- *WhoAm 90*
Berkin, Jeffrey Jack 1957- *WhoEmL 91*
Berkin, Rona *St&PR 91*
Berkland, James Omer 1930- *WhoWor 91*
Berkley, Charles *BioIn 16*
Berkley, E.B. 1923- *St&PR 91*
Berkley, Erma Van Meter 1922- *WhoAmW 91*
Berkley, Eugene Bertram 1923- *WhoAm 90*
Berkley, Florence Pfullmann 1953- *WhoAmW 91*
Berkley, Herbert Ronald 1933- *St&PR 91*
Berkley, John Lee 1948- *WhoE 91*
Berkley, Peter Lee 1939- *WhoAm 90*
Berkley, Richard Bruce 1941- *BiDrAPA 89*
Berkley, Richard L. *WhoAm 90*
Berkley, Robert Lee 1946- *St&PR 91*
Berkley, Stephen Mark 1944- *WhoAm 90*
Berkley, William R. 1945- *BioIn 16*, *St&PR 91*
Berkman, Aaron 1900- *WhoAmA 91*
Berkman, Alexander *EncAL*
Berkman, Alexander 1870-1936 *BioIn 16*
Berkman, Claire Fleet 1942- *WhoAmW 91*
Berkman, Gerald R. 1949- *St&PR 91*
Berkman, Harold W 1926- *WhoWrEP 89*
Berkman, Harold William 1926- *WhoAm 90*, *WhoSSW 91*
Berkman, Irwin J 1925- *BiDrAPA 89*
Berkman, Jack M. 1946- *ODwPR 91*
Berkman, Jack Neville 1905- *St&PR 91*, *WhoAm 90*
Berkman, Jerome 1931- *WhoWor 91*
Berkman, Joyce Eleanor Avrech 1937- *WhoAmW 91*
Berkman, Kathy Hope G 1946- *BiDrAPA 89*
Berkman, Lillian *WhoAm 90*, *WhoAmA 91*, *WhoWor 91*
Berkman, Louis 1909- *St&PR 91*
Berkman, Marshall L. 1936- *WhoAm 90*
Berkman, Marshall Lee 1936- *St&PR 91*
Berkman, Michael G. 1917- *WhoAm 90*
Berkman, Morland Edward 1931- *St&PR 91*
Berkman, Neil G. 1949- *ODwPR 91*
Berkman, Seymour J. 1925- *St&PR 91*
Berkman, William Roger 1928- *WhoAm 90*
Berkner, Lloyd Viel 1905-1967 *DcScB S2*
Berkness, Brad John 1961- *WhoEmL 91*
Berko, Ferenc 1916- *WhoAm 90*, *WhoAmA 91*
Berko, Stephan 1924- *WhoAm 90*
Berkoff, Charles Edward 1932- *WhoAm 90*
Berkoff, Steven *BioIn 16*
Berkon, Martin 1932- *WhoAmA 91*, *WhoE 91*
Berkovitch, Boris S. 1921- *WhoAm 90*
Berkovits, Annette Rochelle 1943- *WhoAmW 91*
Berkovitz, Irving H *BiDrAPA 89*
Berkovitz, Roslyn A. 1942- *WhoAmW 91*
Berkovitz, Stanley 1943- *St&PR 91*
Berkow, Albert J. 1923- *St&PR 91*
Berkow, Ira Harvey 1940- *WhoAm 90*, *WhoE 91*, *WhoWrEP 89*
Berkow, Michael 1955- *WhoEmL 91*
Berkower, Lary R 1937- *BiDrAPA 89*
Berkowitz, Alan Lee 1958- *BiDrAPA 89*
Berkowitz, Bernard 1936- *BiDrAPA 89*
Berkowitz, Bernard Joseph 1945- *WhoE 91*
Berkowitz, Bernard Solomon 1930- *WhoAm 90*
Berkowitz, David 1953- *WorAlBi*
Berkowitz, David Alan 1944- *BiDrAPA 89*
Berkowitz, David Benjamin 1962- *WhoE 91*
Berkowitz, David Victor 1943- *BiDrAPA 89*
Berkowitz, Donald Allen 1948- *St&PR 91*
Berkowitz, Ellen Kay 1950- *BiDrAPA 89*
Berkowitz, Emily Sue 1954- *WhoAmW 91*
Berkowitz, Eric Neal 1949- *WhoEmL 91*
Berkowitz, Freda Pastor 1910- *AuBYP 90*
Berkowitz, Henry 1933- *WhoAmA 91*
Berkowitz, Herbert Mattis 1947- *WhoEmL 91*
Berkowitz, Howard L 1948- *BiDrAPA 89*
Berkowitz, J. 1928- *St&PR 91*
Berkowitz, Jay Kenneth *BiDrAPA 89*
Berkowitz, Jill *BiDrAPA 89*
Berkowitz, Joan B. 1931- *St&PR 91*
Berkowitz, Kenneth Paul 1942- *WhoE 91*
Berkowitz, Leon 1919-1987 *BioIn 16*
Berkowitz, Leonard 1926- *BioIn 16*
Berkowitz, Leonard Irving 1916- *WhoSSW 91*
Berkowitz, Leonard M. 1921- *St&PR 91*
Berkowitz, Marvin 1938- *ConAu 30NR*
Berkowitz, Michael H. 1942- *St&PR 91*
Berkowitz, Michael Harold 1942- *WhoAm 90*
Berkowitz, Monroe 1919- *ConAu 130*
Berkowitz, Mortimer, Jr. 1915- *St&PR 91*
Berkowitz, Morton I 1930- *BiDrAPA 89*
Berkowitz, Murray Richard 1952- *WhoSSW 91*
Berkowitz, Phil 1930- *St&PR 91*
Berkowitz, Ralph Steven 1949- *WhoSSW 91*
Berkowitz, Richard Alan 1951- *WhoSSW 91*
Berkowitz, Robert 1941- *BiDrAPA 89*
Berkowitz, Robert Howard 1922- *St&PR 91*
Berkowitz, Robert Louis 1959- *BiDrAPA 89*
Berkowitz, Roger M 1944- *WhoAmA 91*
Berkowitz, Steve *WhoE 91*
Berkowitz, Steven Jay *BiDrAPA 89*
Berkowitz, Steven Paul 1940- *St&PR 91*
Berkowitz, Teri Marla 1966- *WhoE 91*
Berkowitz, Terry *WhoAmA 91*
Berkshire Traveller *BioIn 16*
Berkshire, Gerald Lynn 1951- *WhoEmL 91*
Berkson, Bill 1939- *WhoAmA 91*
Berkson, Jacob Benjamin 1925- *WhoE 91*
Berkson, Marshall H. 1925- *St&PR 91*
Berkson, Myron E 1923- *BiDrAPA 89*
Berkson, Richard Paul 1936- *BiDrAPA 89*
Berkson, Robert Gary 1939- *WhoWor 91*
Berkus, Barry A. *BioIn 16*
Berkus, David William 1941- *WhoWor 91*
Berkvist, Robert John 1932- *WhoAm 90*
Berkwits, Gloria K *BiDrAPA 89*
Berkwitt, George Joseph 1921- *WhoAm 90*, *WhoWrEP 89*
Berl, Alfred *BiDrAPA 89*
Berl, Christine 1943- *IntWWM 90*
Berl, John David 1927- *St&PR 91*
Berl, Soll 1918- *BiDrAPA 89*
Berl, Warren Harry 1920- *St&PR 91*
Berla, Peter A. *St&PR 91N*
Berla, Peter Amzi 1930-1989 *BioIn 16*
Berlacher, Phyllis O'Brien 1958- *WhoAmW 91*, *WhoEmL 91*
Berlage, Gai Ingham 1943- *WhoAm 90*, *WhoAmW 91*, *WhoE 91*, *WhoWor 91*
Berlage, Hendrikus Petrus 1856-1934 *PenDiDA 89*
Berland *DcCanB 12*
Berland, Abel E. 1915- *St&PR 91*
Berland, Abel Edward 1915- *WhoAm 90*
Berland, James Fred 1943- *WhoAm 90*
Berland, Karen Ina 1947- *WhoAmW 91*
Berlandier, Jean Louis 1805?-1851 *WhNaAH*
Berlanga, Carlos *BiDrAPA 89*
Berlanga Marti, Luis Garcia 1921- *BioIn 16*
Berlant, Anthony 1941- *WhoAm 90*
Berlant, Jeffrey Lionel 1945- *BiDrAPA 89*
Berlant, Tony 1941- *WhoAmA 91*
Berlau, Ruth 1906- *BioIn 16*
Berle, Adolf Augustus 1895-1971 *BioIn 16*
Berle, Milton *BioIn 16*
Berle, Milton 1908- *OxCPMus*, *WhoAm 90*, *WorAlBi*
Berle, Peter A. A. 1937- *BioIn 16*
Berle, Peter Adolf Augustus 1937- *WhoAm 90*
Berleant, Arnold 1932- *WhoAm 90*
Berlekamp, Elwyn Ralph 1940- *WhoAm 90*
Berlepsch, Emilie 1755?-1830 *EncCoWW*
Berl[illegible]**s**, James John 1957- *WhoWrEP 89*
Berlet, Nancy Weir 1949- *WhoE 91*
Berley, David Richard 1942- *WhoWor 91*
Berlie, Elizabeth Marie 1966- *WhoEmL 91*
Berliet, Paul 1918- *WhoWor 91*
Berlik, Leonard J. 1947- *St&PR 91*
Berlin, Alan D. 1939- *St&PR 91*
Berlin, Alan Daniel 1939- *WhoAm 90*, *WhoE 91*, *WhoWor 91*
Berlin, Barry Neil 1954- *WhoEmL 91*
Berlin, Beatrice 1922- *BioIn 16*
Berlin, Beatrice Winn 1922- *WhoAmA 91*
Berlin, Bruce Atkisson 1920- *St&PR 91*
Berlin, Caren Ann 1959- *WhoE 91*
Berlin, Charles S 1947- *BiDrAPA 89*
Berlin, Charles Seder 1947- *WhoE 91*
Berlin, Daniel 1920- *St&PR 91*
Berlin, David Nelson 1949- *St&PR 91*
Berlin, Doris A 1919- *BiDrAPA 89*
Berlin, Edward Perry, Jr. 1928- *St&PR 91*
Berlin, Ellin 1903-1988 *BioIn 16*
Berlin, Emily 1947- *WhoAmW 91*
Berlin, Frank 1922- *St&PR 91*
Berlin, Fred S *BiDrAPA 89*
Berlin, Fred Saul 1941- *WhoAm 90*
Berlin, Ira 1941- *WhoAm 90*, *WhoWrEP 89*
Berlin, Irving 1888-1989 *AnObit 1989*, *BioIn 16*, *ConAu 129*, *ConTFT 8*, *News 90*, *OxCPMus*, *WorAlBi*
Berlin, Irving N 1917- *BiDrAPA 89*
Berlin, Isaiah *BioIn 16*
Berlin, Isaiah 1909- *WhoWor 91*
Berlin, Jenny de Jesus 1947- *WhoHisp 91*
Berlin, Jerome Clifford 1942- *WhoSSW 91*, *WhoWor 91*
Berlin, Jon Scott 1950- *BiDrAPA 89*
Berlin, Kenneth Darrell 1933- *WhoAm 90*
Berlin, Lawrence Henry 1924- *WhoE 91*
Berlin, Lorna Chumley 1938- *WhoAmW 91*
Berlin, Martin Henry 1934- *St&PR 91*
Berlin, Meredith Rise 1955- *WhoAmW 91*, *WhoE 91*, *WhoEmL 91*, *WhoWor 91*
Berlin, Overton Brent 1936- *WhoAm 90*
Berlin, Richard L. 1915- *St&PR 91*
Berlin, Richard Marc 1950- *BiDrAPA 89*
Berlin, Robert Joel *BiDrAPA 89*
Berlin, Rudy Cerry 1928- *WhoSSW 91*
Berlin, Stanton Henry 1934- *WhoAm 90*
Berlin, Steven R. 1944- *St&PR 91*
Berlincourt, Marjorie Alkins 1928- *WhoAmW 91*
Berlind, Bruce Peter 1926- *WhoAm 90*
Berlind, Jeffrey P. 1939- *St&PR 91*
Berlind, Robert 1938- *WhoAmA 91*
Berlind, Robert Elliot 1938- *WhoE 91*
Berlind, Roger S. 1930- *St&PR 91*
Berlind, Roger Stuart 1930- *WhoAm 90*
Berline, James H. 1946- *WhoAm 90*
Berliner, Allen Irwin 1947- *WhoAm 90*
Berliner, Debra *ODwPR 91*
Berliner, Don 1930- *WhoWrEP 89*
Berliner, Emile 1851-1929 *WorAlBi*
Berliner, Ernst 1915- *WhoAm 90*
Berliner, Hans Jack 1929- *WhoAm 90*
Berliner, Henry Adler, Jr. 1934- *St&PR 91*
Berliner, Herman Albert 1944- *WhoE 91*
Berliner, Joseph Scholom 1921- *WhoAm 90*
Berliner, M. Harold 1929- *St&PR 91*
Berliner, Michael Alan 1954- *St&PR 91*
Berliner, Neil Evan 1955- *BiDrAPA 89*
Berliner, Patricia Mary 1946- *WhoAmW 91*
Berliner, Robert William 1915- *WhoAm 90*
Berliner, Ruth Shirley 1928- *WhoAmW 91*
Berliner, William Michael 1923- *WhoAm 90*, *WhoE 91*, *WhoWor 91*
Berlinerblau, Michele M *BiDrAPA 89*
Berlinger, Bernard Ernst 1908- *St&PR 91*
Berlinger, Joseph W. 1933- *St&PR 91*
Berlinger, Joseph William 1933- *WhoWor 91*
Berlinger, Warren 1937- *WhoAm 90*
Berlinger, William G., Jr. 1916- *St&PR 91*
Berlinghof, Charles Overton 1930- *St&PR 91*
Berlinski, Edward C. 1942- *St&PR 91*
Berlinski, Herman 1910- *IntWWM 90*
Berlinski, Milton R. 1956- *WhoE 91*
Berlinsky, Valentin *PenDiMP*
Berlioz, Georges Louis 1943- *WhoWor 91*
Berlioz, Hector 1803-1869 *BioIn 16*, *PenDiMP A*, *WorAlBi*
Berlioz, Louis Hector 1803-1869 *BioIn 16*
Berlis, Douglas A. 1920- *St&PR 91*
Berliss, Herman 1948- *BiDrAPA 89*
Berlitz, Charles 1914- *EncO&P 3*
Berlitz, Charles Frambach 1914- *WhoWrEP 89*
Berlow, Robert Alan 1947- *St&PR 91*, *WhoAm 90*
Berlowe, Jay B 1926- *BiDrAPA 89*
Berlowe, Phyllis H. *ODwPR 91*
Berlowitz, Yocheved Julia 1950- *BiDrAPA 89*
Berlowitz Tarrant, Laurence 1934- *WhoAm 90*
Berlusconi, Silvio *BioIn 16*
Berly, Jack 1903-1977 *Ballpl 90*
Berly, Joel Anderson, III 1956- *WhoEmL 91*
Berly, Madeleine 1896-1953 *BiDWomA*
Berlye, Milton K 1915- *ConAu 31NR*
Berlyn, Sheldon 1929- *WhoAmA 91*
Berlyne, Geoffrey Merton 1931- *WhoWor 91*
Bermak, Gordon E 1927- *BiDrAPA 89*
Berman, Aaron 1922- *WhoAmA 91*
Berman, Abraham *St&PR 91*
Berman, Adolf Abraham 1906-1978 *BioIn 16*
Berman, Alan 1925- *WhoAm 90*
Berman, Allan 1940- *WhoAm 90*
Berman, Allan Bertrand 1931- *WhoE 91*
Berman, Andrew 1959- *St&PR 91*
Berman, Ann Muriel 1951- *WhoWrEP 89*
Berman, Ariane R. 1937- *WhoAm 90*, *WhoAmA 91*
Berman, Arthur Jerome 1928- *WhoE 91*
Berman, Arthur Malcolm 1935- *WhoAm 90*
Berman, Barbara Sandra 1938- *WhoAmW 91*, *WhoE 91*
Berman, Barnett 1922- *WhoAm 90*
Berman, Barry Bruce 1948- *BiDrAPA 89*
Berman, Barry I. 1942- *St&PR 91*
Berman, Bennett I. 1918- *WhoAm 90*
Berman, Bennett Irwin 1918- *St&PR 91*
Berman, Bernard 1920- *WhoAmA 91*
Berman, Bernard Alvin 1924- *WhoAm 90*
Berman, Bob 1899-1988 *BioIn 16*
Berman, Brad Laurence 1957- *WhoEmL 91*
Berman, Carol Wendy *BiDrAPA 89*
Berman, Chris 1955- *Ballpl 90*
Berman, Claire 1936- *WhoWrEP 89*
Berman, Daniel Lewis 1934- *WhoAm 90*, *WhoWor 91*
Berman, Daniel Micah 1957- *WhoEmL 91*
Berman, Daniel S. 1921- *WhoE 91*
Berman, David 1934- *WhoAm 90*
Berman, Douglas C. *WhoE 91*
Berman, Edgar Frank 1915- *WhoWrEP 89*
Berman, Edward Henry 1940- *WhoSSW 91*
Berman, Eileen 1930- *WhoE 91*
Berman, Eleanore 1928- *WhoAmA 91*
Berman, Ellen M 1944- *BiDrAPA 89*
Berman, Ellen Mercil Trew 1946- *WhoAmA 91*
Berman, Elvina *BiDrAPA 89*
Berman, Erwin David *BiDrAPA 89*
Berman, Eugene 1899-1972 *WhoAmA 91N*
Berman, Fred J 1926- *WhoAmA 91*
Berman, Fred Jean 1926- *WhoAm 90*
Berman, Frederic Sanford 1927- *WhoE 91*
Berman, Graham 1934- *BiDrAPA 89*
Berman, Greta W *WhoAmA 91*
Berman, H. Lawrence 1937- *St&PR 91*
Berman, Harvey Michael 1953- *BiDrAPA 89*
Berman, Helen Miriam 1943- *WhoAmW 91*
Berman, Herbert Lawrence 1920- *WhoAm 90*
Berman, Howard Allen 1949- *WhoEmL 91*
Berman, Howard Lawrence 1941- *WhoAm 90*
Berman, Jacob Henry 1956- *BiDrAPA 89*
Berman, Jane M 1914- *BiDrAPA 89*
Berman, Janis Gail 1946- *WhoAm 90*
Berman, Jay Arnold 1950- *St&PR 91*
Berman, Jay Harris 1958- *WhoEmL 91*
Berman, Jay Michael 1952- *WhoEmL 91*
Berman, Jenifer M. 1940- *WhoAmW 91*
Berman, Joel Arthur 1932- *WhoE 91*
Berman, Jonathan D 1949- *BiDrAPA 89*
Berman, Joshua Mordecai 1938- *WhoAm 90*
Berman, Kenneth Everett 1932- *St&PR 91*
Berman, Kenneth Kurt 1906- *BiDrAPA 89*
Berman, Lawrence J. 1927- *St&PR 91*
Berman, Layne Alan 1956- *WhoSSW 91*
Berman, Lazar 1930- *BioIn 16*, *IntWWM 90*, *PenDiMP*, *WhoAm 90*, *WhoWor 91*
Berman, Leo H 1916- *BiDrAPA 89*
Berman, Leon E A 1930- *BiDrAPA 89*
Berman, Lewis Paul 1937- *WhoAm 90*
Berman, Linda Fran 1952- *WhoAmW 91*
Berman, Lisa Myra 1960- *WhoAmW 91*
Berman, Lori Beth 1958- *WhoE 91*
Berman, Louise Marguerite 1928- *WhoAm 90*
Berman, Lynne Moskowitz 1940- *WhoE 91*
Berman, Marcelo Samuel 1945- *WhoWor 91*
Berman, Mark Edward 1945- *St&PR 91*
Berman, Mark Niles 1952- *WhoEmL 91*
Berman, Marlene Oscar 1939- *WhoAm 90*, *WhoAmW 91*
Berman, Marshall Fox 1939- *WhoAm 90*
Berman, Marshall Howard 1940- *WhoAm 90*
Berman, Martin Samuel 1933- *WhoE 91*
Berman, Mary Etta *BiDrAPA 89*
Berman, Merrill Ian 1936- *BiDrAPA 89*
Berman, Michael David 1948- *WhoEmL 91*
Berman, Milton 1924- *WhoAm 90*
Berman, Mira 1928- *WhoAm 90*, *WhoAmW 91*
Berman, Miriam Naomi 1929- *WhoE 91*
Berman, Mona S. 1925- *WhoAmW 91*
Berman, Morris A. *ODwPR 91*
Berman, Muriel Mallin *WhoAm 90*
Berman, Muriel Mallin 1924- *WhoAmA 91*
Berman, Myron 1928- *BioIn 16*
Berman, Myron J. *St&PR 91*
Berman, Neil Sheldon 1933- *WhoAm 90*
Berman, Noel B. 1932- *St&PR 91*
Berman, Pamela Jill 1947- *WhoAmW 91*
Berman, Pamela Joy 1962- *WhoE 91*
Berman, Patricia Karatsis 1953- *WhoAmW 91*
Berman, Perry A 1937- *BiDrAPA 89*
Berman, Philip I. 1915- *WhoAm 90*, *WhoAmA 91*, *WhoE 91*
Berman, Phyllis *BioIn 16*
Berman, Ralph Henry *BiDrAPA 89*
Berman, Richard Angel 1945- *WhoAm 90*
Berman, Richard Miles 1943- *WhoAm 90*
Berman, Robert Howard 1944- *St&PR 91*
Berman, Robert I. 1938- *St&PR 91*

Berman, Robert S. 1932- *WhoAm 90*
Berman, Robert Samuel 1953- *St&PR 91*
Berman, Ronald Charles 1949- *WhoWor 91*
Berman, Ronald Stanley 1930- *WhoWrEP 89*
Berman, Samuel 1923- *St&PR 91*
Berman, Sandra Rita 1938- *WhoE 91*
Berman, Sanford 1933- *BioIn 16, WhoWrEP 89*
Berman, Scott Irwin 1958- *BiDrAPA 89*
Berman, Scott Mitchell 1957- *WhoEmL 91*
Berman, Sheldon S 1941- *BiDrAPA 89*
Berman, Shelley 1926- *WorAlBi*
Berman, Sheryl Hope 1957- *WhoAmW 91*
Berman, Sidney 1908- *BiDrAPA 89, WhoAm 90*
Berman, Sidney 1919- *BiDrAPA 89, WhoE 91*
Berman, Siegrid Visconti 1944- *WhoAmW 91*
Berman, Simeon Moses 1935- *WhoAm 90*
Berman, Stanley G. 1934- *St&PR 91*
Berman, Steve William 1954- *WhoEmL 91*
Berman, Steven H. 1952- *St&PR 91*
Berman, Stuart M. 1923- *St&PR 91*
Berman, Todd Robert 1957- *WhoEmL 91, WhoWor 91*
Berman, Vivian 1928- *WhoAmA 91*
Berman, William Howard 1936- *St&PR 91*
Berman, Zeke *WhoAmA 91*
Bermann, George Alan 1945- *WhoAm 90*
Bermann, Leslie Kay 1966- *WhoEmL 91*
Bermann, Nancy Stewart 1957- *WhoAmW 91, WhoEmL 91*
Bermann, Sylvia N 1922- *BiDrAPA 89*
Bermant, Chaim 1929- *ConAu 31NR*
Bermant, Charles Mark 1954- *WhoWrEP 89*
Bermant, David *BioIn 16*
Bermant, David W 1919- *WhoAmA 91*
Bermant, George Wilson 1926- *WhoAm 90*
Bermanzohn, Paul Carl 1949- *BiDrAPA 89*
Bermas, Stephen 1925- *St&PR 91, WhoAm 90*
Bermejo, Bartolome 1450?-1498? *IntDcAA 90*
Bermello, Willy *WhoHisp 91*
Bermeo, Nancy 1951- *ConAu 131*
Bermes, Robert Joel 1932- *WhoWor 91*
Bermingham, Ann 1948- *WhoAmA 91*
Bermingham, Debra Pandell 1953- *WhoAmA 91*
Bermingham, John C 1920- *WhoAmA 91*
Bermingham, John Thomas 1932- *St&PR 91*
Bermingham, Peter *WhoAm 90*
Bermingham, Peter 1937- *WhoAmA 91*
Bermingham, Richard P. 1939- *St&PR 91, WhoAm 90*
Bermon, Maurice 1944- *BiDrAPA 89*
Bermon, Michael F. 1944- *St&PR 91*
Bermond, Pierre Georges 1922- *WhoWor 91*
Bermont, Richard Barry 1939- *WhoSSW 91*
Bermudez, Diana *WhoHisp 91*
Bermudez, Eduardo *WhoHisp 91*
Bermudez, Egberto 1954- *IntWWM 90*
Bermudez, Eugenia M *WhoAmA 91*
Bermudez, Eugenia M. 1932- *WhoAm 90*
Bermudez, Francisco Morales 1921- *BioIn 16*
Bermudez, Jose Ygnacio 1922- *WhoAmA 91*
Bermudez, Juan 1941- *WhoHisp 91*
Bermudez, Luis A 1953- *WhoAmA 91*
Bermudez Colom, Helcias Daniel 1947- *WhoHisp 91*
Bern, Howard Alan 1920- *WhoAm 90*
Bern, Ronald L. 1936- *St&PR 91*
Bern, Ronald Lawrence 1936- *WhoAm 90*
Bern Heimer, Richard 1907-1958 *WhoAmA 91N*
Berna, Paul 1910- *AuBYP 90*
Bernabe, Mary Susan 1961- *WhoEmL 91*
Bernabei, Joanne Yvonne *BiDrAPA 89*
Bernabela, Josephine E. Walker 1954- *WhoAmW 91*
Bernabo, Marcello 1948- *WhoWor 91*
Bernac, Pierre 1899-1979 *PenDiMP*
Bernacchi, Richard Lloyd 1938- *WhoAm 90*
Bernadet, Paul 1930- *St&PR 91*
Bernadette *ConAu 31NR*
Bernadette, Saint 1844-1879 *EncPaPR 91, WorAlBi*
Bernadotte, Folke 1895-1948 *BioIn 16*
Bernadotte, Sigvard 1907- *ConDes 90*
Bernal, Harriet Jean 1931- *WhoAmW 91*
Bernal, Igancio 1910- *WhoWor 91*
Bernal, Ileana *BiDrAPA 89*
Bernal, Jesus Rodriguez 1953- *WhoHisp 91*
Bernal, John Desmond 1901-1971 *BioIn 16*
Bernal, Louis Carlos 1941- *WhoAmA 91*
Bernal, Margarita Solano 1954- *WhoHisp 91*
Bernal, Martha E. 1931- *WhoHisp 91*
Bernal, Vicente J. 1888-1915 *HispWr 90*
Bernal Vargas, Jorge 1929- *WhoAm 90*
Bernal Y Del Rio, Victor 1917- *BiDrAPA 89*
Bernanke, Ben Shalom 1953- *WhoAm 90*
Bernanos, Georges 1888-1948 *BioIn 16, ConAu 130*
Bernard, Alexander 1952- *WhoEmL 91, WhoWor 91*
Bernard, Andre 1946- *IntWWM 90*
Bernard, Andre 1956- *ConAu 132*
Bernard, April *ConLC 59 [port]*
Bernard, April 1956- *ConAu 131*
Bernard, Benoit 1958- *WhoWor 91*
Bernard, Catherine 1662-1712 *EncCoWW*
Bernard, Cathy S. 1949- *WhoAmW 91, WhoEmL 91*
Bernard, Charles Keith 1938- *WhoAm 90*
Bernard, Christine Charlotte 1938- *WhoSSW 91*
Bernard, David A. 1945- *WhoE 91*
Bernard, David Edwin 1913- *WhoAmA 91*
Bernard, David George 1921- *WhoAm 90*
Bernard, David Kane 1956- *WhoWrEP 89*
Bernard, Donald Ray 1932- *WhoSSW 91, WhoWor 91*
Bernard, Dwight 1952- *Ballpl 90*
Bernard, Ed 1939- *DrBlPA 90*
Bernard, Eddie Nolan 1946- *WhoAm 90*
Bernard, Emile Nachemja 1920- *St&PR 91*
Bernard, Eric *BioIn 16*
Bernard, Felix 1897-1944 *OxCPMus*
Bernard, Glen Richard 1955- *WhoEmL 91*
Bernard, H. Russell 1940- *WhoAm 90*
Bernard, Harry 1898-1979 *DcLB 92*
Bernard, Henriette Rosine 1844-1923 *BiDWomA*
Bernard, Hewitt 1825-1893 *DcCanB 12*
Bernard, Jack A. 1947- *WhoEmL 91*
Bernard, Jacqueline 1921-1983 *AuBYP 90*
Bernard, James Donald 1938- *WhoSSW 91*
Bernard, James Harvey, Jr. 1951- *WhoEmL 91*
Bernard, James M. 1951- *St&PR 91*
Bernard, James W. *BioIn 16*
Bernard, James William 1937- *St&PR 91, WhoAm 90*
Bernard, Jason *DrBlPA 90*
Bernard, Jason 1938- *ConTFT 8*
Bernard, Jerry Wayne 1937- *WhoSSW 91*
Bernard, Jessie Shirley 1903- *BioIn 16*
Bernard, Jonathan Walter 1951- *IntWWM 90*
Bernard, Jules Frank 1920- *St&PR 91*
Bernard, Kenneth 1930- *WhoAm 90, WhoWrEP 89*
Bernard, Kenneth John 1958- *WhoEmL 91*
Bernard, Lola Diane 1928- *WhoAm 90, WhoAmW 91*
Bernard, Louis 1937- *St&PR 91*
Bernard, Louis Joseph 1925- *WhoAm 90*
Bernard, Louise Isaacson 1926- *WhoSSW 91*
Bernard, Lowell Francis 1931- *WhoAm 90*
Bernard, Mary Elizabeth *WhoAmW 91*
Bernard, Michael Mark 1926- *WhoAm 90*
Bernard, Myron Jules 1930- *St&PR 91*
Bernard, Nancy S. 1934- *WhoAmW 91*
Bernard, Norman P. 1945- *St&PR 91*
Bernard, Otis 1930- *WhoAm 90*
Bernard, Pierre 1875-1955 *EncO&P 3, NewAgE 90*
Bernard, Richard Lawson 1926- *WhoAm 90*
Bernard, Robert *WhoWrEP 89*
Bernard, Robert A. 1952- *St&PR 91*
Bernard, Robert Andrew 1952- *WhoSSW 91*
Bernard, Robert John 1922- *WhoAm 90*
Bernard, Ronald Allan 1953- *WhoE 91*
Bernard, Ronald C. 1943- *St&PR 91*
Bernard, Sam 1863-1927 *OxCPMus*
Bernard, Sharon Elaine 1943- *WhoAmW 91*
Bernard, Steven F. 1947- *St&PR 91*
Bernard, Theos 1908-1947 *EncO&P 3*
Bernard, Viola W 1907- *BiDrAPA 89*
Bernard, William Bekker 1914- *WhoSSW 91*
Bernard, William Herbert 1955- *WhoEmL 91*
Bernardes, Artur da Silva 1875-1955 *BioIn 16*
Bernardet, Georges 1913-1989 *BioIn 16*
Bernardez, Romulo Catris 1935- *St&PR 91*
Bernardez, Teresa 1931- *BiDrAPA 89, WhoAmW 91, WhoHisp 91*
Bernardi, Francesco *PenDiMP*
Bernardi, Giorgio 1929- *WhoWor 91*
Bernardi, Giovanni Desiderio 1496-1553 *PenDiDA 89*
Bernardi, James Edward 1946- *WhoWor 91*
Bernardi, John Lawrence, Jr. 1944- *WhoE 91*
Bernardi, Mario 1930- *IntWWM 90, WhoAm 90*
Bernardi, Richard B. *St&PR 91*
Bernardin, Amor Samson *BiDrAPA 89*
Bernardin, George Flynn 1933- *St&PR 91*
Bernardin, James Irwin 1929- *St&PR 91, WhoAm 90*
Bernardin, Joseph L. *BioIn 16*
Bernardin, Joseph Louis 1928- *WhoAm 90, WhoWor 91*
Bernardini, Alfredo 1961- *IntWWM 90*
Bernardini, Allen J. 1938- *St&PR 91*
Bernardini, Dario Frank 1954- *WhoE 91*
Bernardini, Isa 1943- *WhoAmW 91*
Bernardini, Orestes 1880-1957 *WhoAmA 91N*
Bernardini, Richard Albert 1951- *WhoE 91*
Bernardino, Elizabeth V 1955- *BiDrAPA 89*
Bernardino, Minerva 1907- *WhoAmW 91*
Bernardo, Charles Michael 1937- *WhoAm 90*
Bernardo, Diosdado L. *BiDrAPA 89*
Bernardo, Elma Zapanta 1936- *BiDrAPA 89*
Bernardo, Everett *WhoHisp 91*
Bernardo, Jose Raul 1938- *WhoHisp 91*
Bernardo, Raymond Francis 1917- *WhoE 91*
Bernardo, Stephanie *ConAu 30NR*
Bernards, Solomon Schnair 1914- *WhoAm 90*
Bernarducci, Frank *BioIn 16*
Bernas, Denise Mary 1943- *WhoAmW 91*
Bernas, Lilian Helen 1948- *WhoAmW 91, WhoEmL 91*
Bernas, Richard 1950- *IntWWM 90*
Bernat, Mary K. 1958- *St&PR 91*
Bernatchez, Jean-Pierre 1941- *BiDrAPA 89*
Bernathova, Eva 1922- *IntWWM 90*
Bernatowicz, Frank Allen 1954- *WhoWor 91*
Bernau, George 1945- *SpyFic*
Bernau, Simon John 1937- *WhoAm 90*
Bernauer, Carol Candice 1956- *WhoEmL 91*
Bernay, Betti *WhoAmA 91*
Bernay, Betti 1926- *WhoAm 90, WhoAmW 91*
Bernay, Laura Jane *BiDrAPA 89*
Bernays, Anne 1930- *WhoWrEP 89*
Bernays, Anne Fleischman 1930- *WhoAm 90*
Bernays, Edward L. 1891- *BioIn 16, WhoAm 90, WhoE 91*
Bernays, Elizabeth Anna 1940- *WhoAm 90, WhoAmW 91*
Bernays, Minna 1865-1941 *BioIn 16*
Bernays, Paul Isaac 1888-1977 *DcScB S2*
Bernazard, Tony 1956- *Ballpl 90*
Bernazzani, Odette *BiDrAPA 89*
Bernbach, John Lincoln 1944- *St&PR 91, WhoAm 90*
Bernbach, Paul 1945- *WhoAm 90*
Bernbach, William 1911-1982 *ConAmBL, WorAlBi*
Bernberg, Arthur 1943- *St&PR 91*
Bernberg, Bruce Arthur 1943- *WhoAm 90*
Bernd, David LeMoine 1949- *WhoAm 90*
Bernd, James D. *WhoSSW 91*
Bernd, James D. 1933- *St&PR 91*
Bernd, John Jeffery *BioIn 16*
Bernds, Edward *BioIn 16*
Berndt, Cynthia Jean 1957- *WhoEmL 91*
Berndt, Jerry W 1943- *WhoAmA 91*
Berndt, John Edward 1940- *St&PR 91*
Berndt, Joyce L. 1929- *St&PR 91*
Berndt, Kim Lawrence 1956- *WhoEmL 91*
Berndt, Richard E. 1930- *St&PR 91*
Berndt, Scott D. 1951- *St&PR 91*
Berndt, Walter 1899-1979 *EncACom*
Berndt, Walter 1900-1979 *WhoAmA 91N*
Berne, Bruce J. 1940- *WhoAm 90*
Berne, Eric 1910-1970 *MajTwCW*
Berne, Joel Edward *BiDrAPA 89*
Berne, Karin *WhoWrEP 89*
Berne, Max L. 1921- *St&PR 91*
Berne, Robert Matthew 1918- *WhoAm 90*
Berne, Stanley 1923- *WhoWrEP 89*
Berneburg, James Albert 1925- *St&PR 91*
Berneche, Jerry Douglas 1932- *WhoAmA 91*
Bernecker, Larry O. 1948- *St&PR 91*
Bernee, Andrea Lorel 1960- *WhoEmL 91*
Bernell, Sue 1942- *WhoWrEP 89*
Bernens, Donald L. 1929- *St&PR 91*
Berner, Arthur Samuel 1943- *St&PR 91*
Berner, Ernst Peter 1924- *BiDrAPA 89*
Berner, G. Gary 1948- *St&PR 91*
Berner, Gerhard G *BiDrAPA 89*
Berner, Leo De Witte, Jr. 1922- *WhoAm 90*
Berner, Norman Arthur 1910- *WhoAm 90*
Berner, Robert Arbuckle 1935- *WhoAm 90*
Berner, Robert Frank 1917- *WhoAm 90*
Berner, Robert K. 1928- *ODwPR 91*
Berner, Robert Lee, Jr. 1931- *WhoAm 90*
Berner, Stephen Paul 1934- *St&PR 91*
Berner, T. Roland *St&PR 91N*
Berner, T. Roland *NewYTBS 90 [port]*
Berner, T. Roland 1910-1990 *BioIn 16*
Berner, Thomas Franklyn 1954- *WhoEmL 91*
Berners, Juliana *FemiCLE*
Bernert, Lawrence A, Jr. 1935- *BiDrAPA 89*
Bernert, Peter H. 1945- *WhoWor 91*
Bernet, Frank E. 1918- *St&PR 91*
Bernet, Robert G. 1926- *St&PR 91*
Bernet, William *BiDrAPA 89*
Bernett, Carole Marie 1943- *WhoAmW 91*
Berney, Arnold E. 1943- *St&PR 91*
Berney, Bertram S 1884- *WhoAmA 91N*
Berney, Betty Lou 1932- *WhoWrEP 89*
Berney, Isabel McPhee 1941- *WhoAmW 91*
Berney, Jerome Dennis 1946- *BiDrAPA 89*
Berney, Joseph H. 1932- *St&PR 91*
Berney, Joseph Henry 1932- *WhoAm 90*
Berney, Ruth Virginia *BiDrAPA 89*
Berney, S.R. 1938- *St&PR 91*
Bernfeld, Jerrold Saul 1957- *WhoSSW 91*
Bernfeld, Jules E. 1917- *St&PR 91*
Bernfeld, Peter Harry William 1912- *WhoAm 90*
Bernfield, Audrey Anne 1937- *WhoAmW 91*
Bernfield, Merton Ronald 1938- *WhoAm 90*
Bernhagen, Lillian Flickinger 1916- *WhoAm 90, WhoWor 91*
Bernhard 1911- *WhoWor 91*
Bernhard, Alexander Alfred 1936- *WhoAm 90*
Bernhard, Arnold 1901- *WhoWrEP 89*
Bernhard, Berl 1929- *WhoAm 90*
Bernhard, Bill 1871-1949 *Ballpl 90*
Bernhard, Brian Ahrens 1946- *WhoEmL 91*
Bernhard, Brigitte 1953- *IntWWM 90*
Bernhard, Charles Weber, Jr. 1951- *WhoEmL 91*
Bernhard, Herbert Ashley 1927- *WhoAm 90*
Bernhard, Janet K. 1904- *St&PR 91*
Bernhard, Jon Casper 1961- *WhoEmL 91*
Bernhard, Lucian 1883-1972 *ConDes 90*
Bernhard, Manfred Eugen 1917- *WhoE 91*
Bernhard, Richard Harold 1933- *WhoSSW 91*
Bernhard, Robert Arthur 1928- *St&PR 91, WhoAm 90*
Bernhard, Ruth 1905- *BioIn 16, WhoAmA 91*
Bernhard, Sandra *BioIn 16*
Bernhard, Sandra 1955- *CurBio 90 [port]*
Bernhard, Thomas *BioIn 16*
Bernhard, Thomas 1931-1989 *AnObit 1989, ConAu 32NR, ConLC 61 [port], MajTwCW*
Bernhard, William Francis 1924- *WhoAm 90*
Bernhardsen, Bris *AuBYP 90*
Bernhardsen, Christian 1923- *AuBYP 90*
Bernhardson, Ivy Schutz 1951- *St&PR 91, WhoEmL 91*
Bernhardt, Arthur Dieter 1937- *WhoAm 90, WhoE 91, WhoWor 91*
Bernhardt, Donald John 1937- *WhoE 91*
Bernhardt, Donna Beth 1945- *WhoAmW 91*
Bernhardt, George Alexander 1943- *St&PR 91*
Bernhardt, Gregory Ralph 1948- *WhoEmL 91*
Bernhardt, Herbert Nelson *WhoAm 90, WhoE 91*
Bernhardt, Jay 1943- *St&PR 91*
Bernhardt, John Bowman 1929- *St&PR 91, WhoAm 90*
Bernhardt, John C. 1906- *St&PR 91*
Bernhardt, Juan 1953- *Ballpl 90*
Bernhardt, Karen Lee 1955- *WhoAmW 91*
Bernhardt, Leon Louis 1948- *BiDrAPA 89*
Bernhardt, Marcia Brenda 1938- *WhoSSW 91*
Bernhardt, Martin Russell 1954- *WhoEmL 91*
Bernhardt, Melvin *WhoAm 90*
Bernhardt, Richard Bruce 1961- *WhoEmL 91*
Bernhardt, Sarah 1844-1923 *BiDWomA, BioIn 16, WorAlBi*
Bernhardt, William Gene 1960- *WhoEmL 91*
Bernhart, John Thomas 1930- *St&PR 91*
Bernheim, Frederick 1905- *WhoAm 90*
Bernheim, Heather Stanchfield Peterson *WhoAmW 91*
Bernheim, Joyce Mary 1952- *WhoEmL 91*
Bernheim, Stephanie Hammerschlag *WhoAmA 91*
Bernheimer, Martin 1936- *IntWWM 90, WhoAm 90*
Bernheimer, Walter S., II 1940- *St&PR 91*

Bernheisel, Donald Paul 1945- *St&PR 91*
Bernholz, Bonnie L. 1951- *ODwPR 91*
Berni, Antonio 1905-1981 *ArtLatA*
Bernick, Carol Lavin 1952- *St&PR 91*
Bernick, Carol M. 1952- *St&PR 91*
Bernick, Howard B. 1952- *St&PR 91*
Bernick, Howard Barry 1952- *WhoAm 90*
Bernick, Randal N. 1958- *St&PR 91*
Bernick, Raymond I 1937- *BiDrAPA 89*
Bernie, Ben 1891-1943 *OxCPMus*
Bernie, Bruce Jeremy 1948- *WhoEmL 91*
Bernier, Alexis 1956- *ConAu 130*
Bernier, George Matthew, Jr. 1934- *WhoAm 90*
Bernier, Jean 1936- *WhoAm 90*
Bernier, John Rodrigue 1945- *St&PR 91*
Bernier, Olivier 1941- *ConAu 30NR*
Bernier, Rick 1956- *BiDrAPA 89*
Bernier, Rosamond *BioIn 16*
Berniere, Jacques Jean 1937- *WhoWor 91*
Bernikow, Louise 1940- *BioIn 16*, *ConAu 132*
Berning, John Regis 1930- *St&PR 91*
Berning, Randall Karl 1950- *WhoEmL 91*
Berninger, Lori Dobbs 1961- *WhoEmL 91*
Berninger, Virginia Wise 1946- *WhoAmW 91*
Berninghaus, Oscar E 1874-1952 *WhoAmA 91N*
Berninghaus, Oscar Edmund 1874-1952 *BioIn 16*
Bernini, Gian Lorenzo 1598-1680 *IntDcAA 90*, *PenDiDA 89*
Bernini, Giorgio Vittorio 1928- *WhoWor 91*
Bernini, Giovanni Lorenzo 1598-1680 *WorAlBi*
Bernis, Francisco 1946- *WhoWor 91*
Bernitz, Ulf 1936- *WhoWor 91*
Bernkrant, M.C. 1927- *St&PR 91*
Bernlohr, Robert William 1933- *WhoAm 90*
Bernoff, John *NewAgMG*
Bernosky, Herman George 1921- *WhoE 91*, *WhoWor 91*
Bernotas, Ralph Joseph 1927- *WhoAm 90*
Bernoulli, Daniel 1700-1782 *BioIn 16*, *WorAlBi*
Berns, Alan Samuel *BiDrAPA 89*
Berns, Ben 1936- *BioIn 16*
Berns, Ellen Marsha Schimmel 1948- *WhoEmL 91*
Berns, Eugene H. 1936- *St&PR 91*
Berns, Herman Jerome 1907- *WhoWor 91*
Berns, Joseph J. 1946- *St&PR 91*
Berns, Kenneth Ira 1938- *WhoAm 90*
Berns, Martin Allen 1936- *WhoSSW 91*
Berns, Pamela Kari 1947- *WhoAmA 91*
Berns, Robert S 1911- *BiDrAPA 89*
Berns, Walter Fred 1919- *WhoAm 90*
Bernsen, Corbin *BioIn 16*
Bernsen, Corbin 1954- *WorAlBi*
Bernsen, Corbin 1955- *News 90 [port]*
Bernson, Lionel A 1930- *BiDrAPA 89*
Bernson, Marcella S 1952- *BiDrAPA 89*
Bernstam, Mikhail S. 1943- *ConAu 130*
Bernstein, Abraham *NewYTBS 90*
Bernstein, Abraham 1918- *WhoE 91*
Bernstein, Abraham 1918-1990 *BioIn 16*
Bernstein, Aimee Susan 1949- *WhoAmW 91*, *WhoEmL 91*
Bernstein, Alan Barry 1947- *WhoAm 90*
Bernstein, Alfred *BioIn 16*
Bernstein, Alfred S. 1914- *St&PR 91*
Bernstein, Aline 1881-1955 *BioIn 16*
Bernstein, Aline F. 1881-1955 *BioAmW*
Bernstein, Aline Frankau 1880-1955 *NotWoAT*
Bernstein, Anne E H 1937- *BiDrAPA 89*
Bernstein, Anne Elayne 1937- *WhoE 91*
Bernstein, Arthur Dan 1926- *St&PR 91*
Bernstein, Arthur J. 1947- *WhoSSW 91*
Bernstein, Barbara Jane 1961- *WhoAmW 91*
Bernstein, Basil G *BiDrAPA 89*
Bernstein, Benedict J 1910- *BiDrAPA 89*
Bernstein, Benjamin D 1907- *WhoAmA 91*
Bernstein, Bernard *NewYTBS 90*
Bernstein, Bernard 1908-1990 *BioIn 16*
Bernstein, Bernard 1929- *St&PR 91*, *WhoAm 90*
Bernstein, Beth Anne *BiDrAPA 89*
Bernstein, Betsy Bennett 1950- *WhoEmL 91*
Bernstein, Bettina *BiDrAPA 89*
Bernstein, Burt 1937- *St&PR 91*
Bernstein, Burton 1932- *WhoWrEP 89*
Bernstein, Carl *BioIn 16*
Bernstein, Carl 1944- *WhoAm 90*, *WhoWrEP 89*, *WorAlBi*
Bernstein, Carol Ann 1947- *BiDrAPA 89*, *WhoAmW 91*, *WhoE 91*
Bernstein, Caryl Salomon 1933- *St&PR 91*, *WhoAm 90*, *WhoAmW 91*, *WhoE 91*
Bernstein, Charles 1950- *ConAu 129*, *WhoE 91*, *WhoWrEP 89*
Bernstein, Charles Marc 1952- *WhoEmL 91*
Bernstein, Craig Steven 1962- *WhoEmL 91*
Bernstein, Daniel Harris 1956- *WhoSSW 91*
Bernstein, Daniel Lewis 1937- *WhoAm 90*
Bernstein, David H. 1935- *St&PR 91*
Bernstein, David M *BiDrAPA 89*
Bernstein, Dennis Alan 1958- *WhoE 91*
Bernstein, Donald Chester 1942- *WhoAm 90*
Bernstein, Dorothy M. 1919- *BiDrAPA 89*
Bernstein, Douglas Lon 1958- *WhoEmL 91*
Bernstein, Eduard *BioIn 16*
Bernstein, Edward I 1917- *WhoAmA 91*
Bernstein, Edwin S. 1930- *WhoAm 90*
Bernstein, Elliot 1923- *St&PR 91*
Bernstein, Elliot Louis 1934- *WhoAm 90*
Bernstein, Elmer 1922- *IntWWM 90*, *OxCPMus*, *WhoAm 90*, *WorAlBi*
Bernstein, Emil Steven 1946- *St&PR 91*, *WhoAm 90*
Bernstein, Eric Martin 1957- *WhoEmL 91*
Bernstein, Esther 1921- *St&PR 91*
Bernstein, Eugene Felix 1930- *WhoAm 90*
Bernstein, Eugene Merle 1931- *WhoAm 90*
Bernstein, Eva 1871-1958 *WhoAmA 91N*
Bernstein, Eva Gould 1918- *WhoAmW 91*
Bernstein, Frances B. 1932-1989 *BioIn 16*
Bernstein, George L. 1932- *WhoAm 90*, *WhoE 91*
Bernstein, Gerald 1917- *WhoAmA 91*
Bernstein, Gerda Meyer *WhoAmA 91*
Bernstein, H. Bruce 1943- *WhoAm 90*
Bernstein, Harold Lintz 1921- *St&PR 91*
Bernstein, Harris Joshua 1948- *WhoEmL 91*
Bernstein, Haskell E *BiDrAPA 89*
Bernstein, Herbert J. 1944- *WhoWrEP 89*
Bernstein, Herman 1876-1935 *BioIn 16*
Bernstein, Hilda 1915- *ConAu 130*
Bernstein, I. Leonard 1924- *WhoAm 90*
Bernstein, I. Melvin 1938- *WhoAm 90*
Bernstein, Ira Borah 1924- *WhoAm 90*
Bernstein, Irving 1921- *WhoAm 90*, *WhoE 91*
Bernstein, Irving C 1918- *BiDrAPA 89*
Bernstein, Irwin Frederick 1933- *St&PR 91*
Bernstein, Isadore Abraham 1919- *WhoAm 90*
Bernstein, Isidor *BiDrAPA 89*
Bernstein, Jacqueline Wolf *BioIn 16*
Bernstein, Jane 1949- *WhoWrEP 89*
Bernstein, Jane Agar 1947- *IntWWM 90*
Bernstein, Janet O 1942- *BiDrAPA 89*
Bernstein, Jay 1927- *WhoAm 90*
Bernstein, Jean *BioIn 16*
Bernstein, Jeffrey P 1952- *BiDrAPA 89*
Bernstein, Jeremy 1929- *WorAu 1980*
Bernstein, Jerrold G 1941- *BiDrAPA 89*
Bernstein, Jerry Daniel 1949- *WhoEmL 91*
Bernstein, Jonathan E. 1944- *St&PR 91*
Bernstein, Joseph 1930- *WhoSSW 91*, *WhoWor 91*
Bernstein, Judith 1942- *WhoAmA 91*
Bernstein, Kenneth Alan 1956- *WhoEmL 91*
Bernstein, Kenny *BioIn 16*
Bernstein, Laurel 1945- *WhoAmW 91*
Bernstein, Lawrence 1940- *WhoE 91*
Bernstein, Lawrence F. 1939- *IntWWM 90*
Bernstein, Lawrence H 1945- *BiDrAPA 89*
Bernstein, Lawson F 1957- *BiDrAPA 89*
Bernstein, Leonard 1918- *IntWWM 90*, *PenDiMP*, *-A*, *WorAlBi*
Bernstein, Leonard 1918-1990 *BioIn 16*, *ConAu 132*, *CurBio 90N*, *NewYTBS 90 [port]*, *News 91-1*, *OxCPMus*, *WhoAm 90*, *WhoE 91*, *WhoWor 91*
Bernstein, Lester 1920- *WhoAm 90*
Bernstein, Lori Ann 1961- *WhoAmW 91*
Bernstein, Louis 1927- *WhoAm 90*
Bernstein, Mark David 1949- *BiDrAPA 89*
Bernstein, Mark Henry *BiDrAPA 89*
Bernstein, Martin L. 1941- *St&PR 91*
Bernstein, Marver H. *NewYTBS 90 [port]*
Bernstein, Marver H. 1919-1990 *BioIn 16*
Bernstein, Mashey Maurice 1946- *WhoWrEP 89*
Bernstein, Merton Clay 1923- *WhoAm 90*
Bernstein, Michael Howard 1943- *St&PR 91*
Bernstein, Michael J 1954- *BiDrAPA 89*
Bernstein, Michael Joel 1938- *WhoSSW 91*
Bernstein, Morey 1919- *EncO&P 3*
Bernstein, Myron Elliott 1938- *St&PR 91*
Bernstein, Nathan K 1908- *BiDrAPA 89*
Bernstein, Nathaniel 1911- *BiDrAPA 89*
Bernstein, Neil S. 1938- *St&PR 91*
Bernstein, Norman Ralph 1927- *BiDrAPA 89*, *WhoAm 90*
Bernstein, Patricia Robin 1956- *WhoAmW 91*
Bernstein, Paul 1927- *WhoAm 90*
Bernstein, Paul Murray 1929- *WhoAm 90*, *WhoE 91*
Bernstein, Ralph 1921- *AuBYP 90*
Bernstein, Ralph 1933- *WhoAm 90*
Bernstein, Raymond *BioIn 16*
Bernstein, Richard *BioIn 16*
Bernstein, Richard 1928- *St&PR 91*
Bernstein, Richard A. 1946- *St&PR 91*, *WhoAm 90*
Bernstein, Richard Alan 1943- *BiDrAPA 89*
Bernstein, Richard B. *NewYTBS 90*
Bernstein, Richard Barry 1923-1990 *BioIn 16*
Bernstein, Richard K. *BioIn 16*
Bernstein, Richard Mark 1957- *WhoE 91*
Bernstein, Robert *BioIn 16*
Bernstein, Robert 1920- *WhoAm 90*
Bernstein, Robert Alan 1958- *WhoEmL 91*
Bernstein, Robert I. 1927- *St&PR 91*
Bernstein, Robert Jay 1948- *WhoEmL 91*
Bernstein, Robert L. 1923- *BioIn 16*
Bernstein, Robert Louis 1923- *WhoAm 90*, *WhoWrEP 89*
Bernstein, Sam *BioIn 16*
Bernstein, Saralinda 1951- *WhoAmA 91*
Bernstein, Sidney 1938- *WhoAm 90*
Bernstein, Sidney Ralph 1907- *WhoAm 90*, *WhoWrEP 89*
Bernstein, Sol 1927- *WhoAm 90*, *WhoWor 91*
Bernstein, Stanley 1921- *BiDrAPA 89*
Bernstein, Stephen Bruce 1939- *BiDrAPA 89*
Bernstein, Stephen L. 1933- *St&PR 91*
Bernstein, Stephen Michael 1941- *WhoE 91*, *WhoWor 91*
Bernstein, Steven 1957- *St&PR 91*
Bernstein, Stuart Paul 1932- *BiDrAPA 89*
Bernstein, Susan Powell 1938- *WhoAm 90*
Bernstein, Sylvia *BioIn 16*, *WhoAm 90*
Bernstein, Sylvia 1914-1990 *WhoAmA 91N*
Bernstein, Theodore 1926- *WhoAm 90*
Bernstein, Theresa *WhoAmA 91*
Bernstein, Theresa 1886- *BiDWomA*
Bernstein, Theresa 1896- *BioIn 16*
Bernstein, Thomas Paul 1937- *WhoAm 90*
Bernstein, William 1933- *St&PR 91*, *WhoAm 90*
Bernstein, William E 1934- *BiDrAPA 89*
Bernstein, William G *BiDrAPA 89*
Bernstein, William Joseph 1945- *WhoAmA 91*
Bernstein, Zalman C. 1926- *St&PR 91*
Bernstorf, Elaine Denise *IntWWM 90*
Bernstorf, Steven Wesley 1953- *WhoSSW 91*
Bernstorff, Johann Heinrich, Graf von 1862-1939 *BioIn 16*
Bernt, Benno Anthony 1931- *WhoAm 90*
Bernt Hazzard, Charlotte Irene 1953- *WhoAmW 91*, *WhoEmL 91*
Bernthal, David Gary 1950- *WhoEmL 91*
Bernthal, Frederick Michael 1943- *WhoAm 90*
Bernthal, Frederick W. 1928- *St&PR 91*
Bernthal, Harold George 1928- *WhoAm 90*
Bernthal, Russell Lee 1957- *WhoEmL 91*
Berntsen, Bjarne T. 1935- *St&PR 91*
Bernucca, Louis F. 1938- *St&PR 91*
Bernuth, Ernest Patrick, Jr. 1939- *WhoWrEP 89*
Bernward of Hildesheim, St *PenDiDA 89*
Berny, Laure de 1777-1836 *EncCoWW*
Bernzott, Michael Roy *BiDrAPA 89*
Bero, Marilyn Procino 1937- *WhoAmW 91*
Bero, Ronald Arthur 1935- *St&PR 91*, *WhoAm 90*
Bero, William Burke 1932- *St&PR 91*
Beroff, Michel 1950- *IntWWM 90*, *PenDiMP*
Berolzheimer, Karl 1932- *WhoAm 90*
Beron, Gail Laskey 1943- *WhoAmW 91*, *WhoWor 91*
Beroth, Leon *EncACom*
Beroza, Kenneth Walter *BiDrAPA 89*
Berquez, Gerard Paul 1945- *WhoWor 91*
Berquist, George W. 1932- *St&PR 91*
Berra, Dale 1956- *Ballpl 90*
Berra, P. Bruce 1935- *WhoAm 90*
Berra, Robert Louis 1924- *St&PR 91*, *WhoAm 90*
Berra, Yogi 1925- *Ballpl 90 [port]*, *BioIn 16*, *WorAlBi*
Berrada, Mohammed 1944- *WhoWor 91*
Berre, Andre Dieudonne 1940- *WhoWor 91*
Berres, Frances Brandes *WhoWor 91*
Berres, Luis Batlle 1897-1964 *BioIn 16*
Berres, Ray 1908- *Ballpl 90*
Berresford, Susan Vail 1943- *WhoAm 90*
Berresford, Virginia 1902- *WhoAmA 91*
Berreth, David Scott 1949- *WhoAmA 91*
Berreth, Richard A. 1936- *St&PR 91*
Berrettini, Wade Hayhurst 1951- *BiDrAPA 89*
Berrey, Bedford Hudson, Jr. 1950- *WhoE 91*
Berrey, Robert Forrest 1939- *St&PR 91*, *WhoAm 90*
Berrg, Robert James 1949- *St&PR 91*
Berri, Claude *BioIn 16*
Berri, Claude 1934- *ConTFT 8*, *WhoWor 91*
Berri, Nabih *BioIn 16*
Berriault, Gina 1926- *ConAu 129*
Berridge, Edward 1843?-1923 *EncO&P 3*
Berridge, Elizabeth 1921- *BioIn 16*
Berridge, George B. 1928- *St&PR 91*
Berridge, George Bradford 1928- *WhoAm 90*
Berrie, Russell 1933- *WhoAm 90*
Berrien, James S. *BioIn 16*
Berrien, James S. 1952- *St&PR 91*
Berrien, James Stuart 1952- *WhoAm 90*
Berrien, John MacPherson 1781-1856 *BiDrUSE 89*
Berrier, Ronald G. 1943- *St&PR 91*
Berrigan, A. John 1943- *St&PR 91*
Berrigan, Daniel *BioIn 16*
Berrigan, Daniel 1921- *WhoWrEP 89*
Berrigan, Philip 1923- *BioIn 16*
Berrill, Jacquelyn 1905- *AuBYP 90*
Berrill, Norman John 1903- *WhoAm 90*
Berrill, Simon Philip 1953- *WhoWor 91*
Berriman, W. Thomas 1930- *St&PR 91*
Berring, Robert Charles, Jr. 1949- *WhoEmL 91*
Berrios, Elsa I. *WhoAm 90*
Berrios, Joseph 1952- *WhoHisp 91*
Berrios, L. Enrique Aguilar 1957- *WhoWor 91*
Berriozabal, Manuel Phillip 1931- *WhoHisp 91*
Berriozabal, Maria Antonietta 1941- *WhoHisp 91*
Berrisford, Judith Mary 1921- *AuBYP 90*
Berritt, Harold Edward 1936- *St&PR 91*
Berruguete, Alonso 1487?-1561 *IntDcAA 90*
Berruguete, Pedro 1450?-1503 *IntDcAA 90*
Berry, Abner Winston 1902-1987 *EncAL*
Berry, Ambrose *St&PR 91*
Berry, Ann Roper 1934- *WhoAmW 91*
Berry, Bill 1943- *WhoE 91*
Berry, Brewton 1901- *WhoAm 90*
Berry, Brian Joe Lobley 1934- *WhoAm 90*
Berry, Bruce *BioIn 16*
Berry, Buford Preston 1935- *WhoAm 90*, *WhoSSW 91*
Berry, Burton Yost 1901-1985 *BioIn 16*
Berry, C.S. 1910- *St&PR 91*
Berry, Campbell Polson 1834-1901 *AmLegL*
Berry, Carlos E 1955- *BiDrAPA 89*
Berry, Carmen *BioIn 16*
Berry, Carolyn 1930- *WhoAmA 91*
Berry, Catherine 1813-1891 *EncO&P 3*
Berry, Charles Gordon 1950- *WhoEmL 91*
Berry, Charles Oscar 1907- *WhoAm 90*
Berry, Charlie 1902-1972 *Ballpl 90*
Berry, Chuck 1926- *BioIn 16*, *DrBIPA 90*, *EncPR&S 89*, *OxCPMus*, *WhoAm 90*, *WorAlBi*
Berry, Cornelia Tate 1944- *WhoSSW 91*
Berry, Cynthia *BiDrAPA 89*
Berry, Cynthia K. *ODwPR 91*
Berry, David Holmes 1951- *WhoEmL 91*
Berry, David Jerome 1951- *WhoE 91*
Berry, David Lawton 1926- *St&PR 91*
Berry, David Michael 1951- *WhoAm 90*
Berry, Dean Frank 1932- *WhoWor 91*
Berry, Dean Lester 1935- *WhoAm 90*
Berry, Deanne L. 1962- *ODwPR 91*
Berry, Debra L. 1949- *WhoAmW 91*
Berry, Don H. 1931- *St&PR 91*
Berry, Don Michael 1941- *St&PR 91*
Berry, Donald Kent 1953- *WhoSSW 91*
Berry, Donald Reese 1953- *WhoEmL 91*
Berry, Dorothy *BiDEWW*
Berry, Doyle G. 1930- *St&PR 91*
Berry, Edna Janet 1917- *WhoAm 90*
Berry, Edward C. 1927- *St&PR 91*
Berry, Erick *AuBYP 90*
Berry, Frank N. 1930- *St&PR 91*
Berry, Fred Clifton, Jr. 1931- *WhoAm 90*, *WhoE 91*
Berry, Frederick E. 1949- *WhoE 91*
Berry, George *EncO&P 3*
Berry, George A., III 1918- *St&PR 91*
Berry, George B. 1936- *St&PR 91*
Berry, George Joseph 1930- *BiDrAPA 89*
Berry, Glenn 1929- *WhoAmA 91*
Berry, Guy Curtis 1935- *WhoAm 90*
Berry, Harold James 1913- *St&PR 91*
Berry, Henry Arnold, Jr. 1945- *WhoWrEP 89*
Berry, Henry G. 1936- *St&PR 91*
Berry, James *BioIn 16*
Berry, James 1841-1913 *BioIn 16*
Berry, James 1925- *ChILR 22 [port]*
Berry, James 1932- *AuBYP 90*
Berry, James D., III 1938- *WhoAm 90*
Berry, James Frederick 1927- *WhoAm 90*
Berry, James Henderson 1841-1913 *AmLegL*
Berry, James R. 1913- *St&PR 91*

Berry, Janis Marie 1949- *WhoEmL 91*
Berry, Jay 1928- *WhoWor 91*
Berry, Jim *WhoSSW 91*
Berry, Joan Ann 1939- *WhoE 91*
Berry, Joan Elizabeth 1956- *WhoEmL 91*
Berry, Joe 1904-1958 *Ballpl 90*
Berry, Joe Wilkes 1938- *WhoAm 90*
Berry, John *WhoWrEP 89*
Berry, John Charles 1938- *WhoWor 91*
Berry, John F. 1943- *St&PR 91*
Berry, John Nichols, III 1933- *WhoAm 90, WhoWrEP 89*
Berry, John Stevens 1938- *ConAu 132*
Berry, John Summerfield 1822-1901 *AmLegL*
Berry, John Widdup 1939- *WhoAm 90*
Berry, John Willard 1947- *WhoAm 90*
Berry, John William 1922- *St&PR 91, WhoAm 90*
Berry, Jonas *MajTwCW*
Berry, Joseph J. 1946- *St&PR 91*
Berry, Joy Wilt 1944- *BioIn 16*
Berry, Joyce Charlotte 1937- *WhoAm 90, WhoWrEP 89*
Berry, Joyce T. *WhoAmW 91*
Berry, Julianne Elward 1946- *WhoAmW 91*
Berry, Karen Waldrip *BiDrAPA 89*
Berry, Kathleen Ann 1961- *WhoEmL 91*
Berry, Keehn W., Jr. 1922- *WhoSSW 91*
Berry, Ken 1933- *ConTFT 8, WorAlBi*
Berry, Ken 1941- *Ballpl 90*
Berry, Lemuel, Jr. 1946- *IntWWM 90, WhoEmL 91, WhoSSW 91*
Berry, Leonidas H. *BioIn 16*
Berry, Leonidas Harris 1902- *WhoAm 90*
Berry, Linden Farrar 1944- *WhoWrEP 89*
Berry, Lisette Moraillon 1940- *WhoE 91*
Berry, Marie Braun 1913- *WhoAmW 91*
Berry, Martha M. 1866-1942 *BioAmW*
Berry, Mary 1763-1852 *BioIn 16, FemiCLE*
Berry, Mary Frances 1938- *WhoAm 90*
Berry, Max 1926- *St&PR 91*
Berry, Michael Francis 1945- *WhoSSW 91*
Berry, Michael James 1947- *WhoAm 90, WhoWor 91*
Berry, Nancy Michaels 1928- *WhoAm 90*
Berry, Neil 1922- *Ballpl 90*
Berry, Nelson Scott 1942- *St&PR 91*
Berry, Norma Jean 1946- *WhoAmW 91*
Berry, Norman *BioIn 16*
Berry, Peter DuPre 1943- *WhoSSW 91*
Berry, Philippa Jane 1955- *WhoWor 91*
Berry, Phillip Reid 1950- *WhoEmL 91, WhoWor 91*
Berry, Phillip S. 1937- *BioIn 16*
Berry, Phillip Samuel 1937- *WhoWor 91*
Berry, Priscilla 1946- *WhoSSW 91*
Berry, Ralph *ODwPR 91*
Berry, Ralph Lincoln, III *BiDrAPA 89*
Berry, Ravi B 1945- *BiDrAPA 89*
Berry, Ray 1933- *WorAlBi*
Berry, Raymond Rodney 1928- *St&PR 91*
Berry, Reginald V 1906- *BiDrAPA 89*
Berry, Richard *BioIn 16*
Berry, Richard C. 1928- *St&PR 91*
Berry, Richard Cameron 1927- *WhoSSW 91*
Berry, Richard Chisholm 1928- *WhoAm 90, WhoE 91*
Berry, Richard Douglas 1926- *WhoAm 90*
Berry, Richard Emerson 1933- *WhoAm 90*
Berry, Richard Lewis 1946- *WhoAm 90, WhoWrEP 89*
Berry, Richard Stephen 1931- *WhoAm 90*
Berry, Ricky *BioIn 16*
Berry, Robert Bass 1948- *WhoEmL 91, WhoSSW 91*
Berry, Robert H. 1944- *St&PR 91*
Berry, Robert John 1947- *WhoE 91, WhoEmL 91*
Berry, Robert K. 1942- *ODwPR 91*
Berry, Robert Vaughan 1933- *St&PR 91, WhoAm 90*
Berry, Robert Worth 1926- *WhoAm 90, WhoWor 91*
Berry, Roberta Marie 1955- *WhoEmL 91*
Berry, Roger Julian 1935- *WhoWor 91*
Berry, Ronald Neil 1931- *BiDrAPA 89*
Berry, Ruth Emmert 1930- *WhoSSW 91*
Berry, Ruth H. *ODwPR 91*
Berry, Shirley Nichols 1930- *WhoAmW 91*
Berry, Sidney Bryan 1926- *WhoAm 90*
Berry, Stephen Gardner 1951- *WhoEmL 91*
Berry, Susan Michele 1953- *WhoSSW 91*
Berry, Thomas *BioIn 16*
Berry, Thomas Clayton 1948- *WhoWor 91*
Berry, Thomas Ernest 1947- *WhoEmL 91*
Berry, Thomas Joseph 1925- *WhoAm 90*
Berry, Thomas Robert 1931- *WhoAm 90*
Berry, Timothy Brooks 1948- *St&PR 91*
Berry, Todd Andrew 1951- *WhoEmL 91*
Berry, Tom *St&PR 91*
Berry, Vickie Lee 1954- *WhoAmW 91*
Berry, Virgil J. 1928- *St&PR 91*
Berry, Virgil Jennings, Jr. 1928- *WhoAm 90*
Berry, W. Christopher 1949- *WhoAm 90*
Berry, W. H. 1872-1951 *OxCPMus*
Berry, Wallace 1928- *IntWWM 90*
Berry, Wallace Taft 1928- *WhoAm 90*
Berry, Wallace Thomas 1927- *IntWWM 90*
Berry, Walter 1929- *IntWWM 90, PenDiMP, WhoAm 90*
Berry, Walter Van Rensselaer 1859-1927 *BioIn 16*
Berry, Warren O. 1924- *WhoE 91*
Berry, Wayne Martin 1941- *WhoSSW 91*
Berry, Wendell 1934- *LiHiK, WhoAm 90, WhoWrEP 89*
Berry, William Augustus 1933- *WhoAmA 91*
Berry, William Benjamin Newell 1931- *WhoAm 90*
Berry, William David 1926- *AuBYP 90*
Berry, William David 1926-1979 *WhoAmA 91N*
Berry, William James, III 1950- *WhoSSW 91*
Berry, William Lee 1935- *WhoAm 90*
Berry, William Martin 1920- *St&PR 91*
Berry, William Russell 1953- *WhoSSW 91*
Berry, William S. 1941- *St&PR 91*
Berry, William W. 1932- *St&PR 91*
Berry, William Wells 1917- *WhoAm 90, WhoSSW 91*
Berry, William Willis 1932- *WhoAm 90, WhoSSW 91*
Berry Caban, Cristobal Santiago 1953- *WhoEmL 91, WhoSSW 91*
Berry-Teichner, Gail W 1939- *BiDrAPA 89*
Berryer, Jacqueline *BiDrAPA 89*
Berryessa, Richard Greaves 1947- *WhoEmL 91*
Berryhill, Damon 1963- *Ballpl 90*
Berryhill, Dennis G. 1947- *St&PR 91*
Berryhill, Henry Lee, Jr. 1921- *WhoAm 90*
Berryhill, Leroy Kenneth 1929- *BiDrAPA 89*
Berryman, Clifford K. 1869-1949 *BioIn 16*
Berryman, Clifford Kennedy 1869-1949 *WhoAmA 91N*
Berryman, David Homer 1952- *St&PR 91*
Berryman, James Thomas 1902-1971 *BioIn 16*
Berryman, John 1914-1972 *BioIn 16, ConLC 62 [port], MajTwCW, WorAlBi*
Berryman, Richard Byron 1932- *WhoAm 90*
Berryman, Rose Warren 1940- *WhoWor 91*
Berryman, Sally Helyn *BiDrAPA 89*
Berryman, Treva Griffith 1952- *WhoSSW 91*
Bers, Donald Martin 1953- *WhoEmL 91*
Bers, Lipman 1914- *WhoAm 90*
Bersadsky, Leona *BiDrAPA 89*
Bersani, Ferdinando 1942- *EncPaPR 91*
Berscheid, Ellen S. 1936- *WhoAm 90, WhoAmW 91*
Berschin, Walter 1937- *WhoWor 91*
Berschling, Chester M 1933- *BiDrAPA 89*
Bersentes, Natsika J 1931- *WhoAmA 91*
Bersh, Philip Joseph 1921- *WhoAm 90*
Bershad, David L 1942- *WhoAmA 91*
Bershad, Jack R. 1930- *St&PR 91, WhoAm 90*
Bershad, Karen Frances 1948- *WhoSSW 91*
Bershadsky, Luba 1916- *ConAu 131*
Bersia, John Cesar 1956- *WhoWor 91*
Bersianik, Louky 1930- *BioIn 16, FemiCLE*
Bersin, Kaethe Zemach- 1958- *BioIn 16*
Bersoff, Donald Neil 1939- *WhoAm 90*
Berson, Bella Zevitovsky 1925- *WhoAm 90*
Berson, Deane Shore 1943- *BiDrAPA 89*
Berson, Eliot Lawrence 1937- *WhoAm 90*
Berson, Harold E 1924- *BiDrAPA 89*
Berson, Harold Eugene 1924- *WhoE 91*
Berson, Iola Portia 1952- *WhoAmW 91*
Berson, Jerome Abraham 1924- *WhoAm 90*
Berson, Joan Semel *BiDrAPA 89*
Berson, Sidney Harry 1924- *WhoE 91*
Berssenbrugge, Mei-Mei 1947- *WhoWrEP 89*
Berst, Barb Jo 1957- *WhoWrEP 89*
Berst, John *BioIn 16*
Berstein, Irving Aaron 1926- *WhoE 91, WhoWor 91*
Berstein, Robert Louis 1923- *St&PR 91*
Bersticker, Albert C. *BioIn 16*
Bersticker, Albert Charles 1934- *St&PR 91, WhoAm 90*
Bert, Carol Lois 1938- *WhoAmW 91*
Bert, Charles Wesley 1929- *WhoAm 90, WhoSSW 91*
Bert, Clara Virginia 1929- *WhoAmW 91, WhoSSW 91, WhoWor 91*
Bert, Eleanor Lucille 1939- *WhoAmW 91*
Berta, Joseph Michel 1940- *IntWWM 90*
Berta, Ray Joseph 1933- *St&PR 91*
Berta, Robert Michael 1955- *WhoE 91*
Berta, Vince 1958- *St&PR 91*
Bertain, George Joseph, Jr. 1929- *WhoAm 90, WhoWor 91*
Bertaina, Frank 1944- *Ballpl 90*
Bertan, Howard S. 1935- *St&PR 91*
Bertaux, Helene 1825-1909 *BiDWomA*
Bertch, Robert B. 1952- *St&PR 91*
Berte, Dennis James 1950- *St&PR 91*
Berte, Heinrich 1858-1924 *OxCPMus*
Berte, Neal Richard 1940- *WhoAm 90*
Berteau, David John 1949- *WhoAm 90*
Bertel, Charles G. 1926- *St&PR 91*
Berteling, Jan 1945- *WhoWor 91*
Bertell, Dick 1935- *Ballpl 90*
Bertelle, Jeanne T. 1947- *WhoAmW 91, WhoEmL 91*
Bertellotti, Christopher Paul 1950- *WhoEmL 91*
Bertellotti, Edward A. 1952- *St&PR 91*
Bertels, Thomas More, Sister *BioIn 16*
Bertels, William Charles 1951- *WhoEmL 91*
Bertelsen, Christian Cameron 1943- *St&PR 91*
Bertelsen, Cynthia Diane 1960- *WhoAmW 91*
Bertelsen, Thomas Elwood, Jr. 1940- *WhoAm 90*
Bertelsman, William Odis 1936- *WhoAm 90*
Bertelsmann-Kadalie, Rhoda 1953- *BioIn 16*
Bertelson, Amy Dayle 1952- *WhoAmW 91*
Bertelson, Kenneth P 1936- *BiDrAPA 89*
Bertenshaw, Bobbi Cherrelle 1961- *WhoEmL 91*
Bertenshaw, William Howard, III 1930- *WhoE 91*
Bertez, Bruno Jacques 1944- *WhoWor 91*
Bertges, John C. 1925- *WhoAm 90*
Bertha of Willich *EncCoWW*
Berthelot, Hector 1842-1895 *DcCanB 12*
Berthelot, John 1930- *St&PR 91*
Berthelot, Pierre Eugene Marcellin 1827-1907 *WorAlBi*
Berthelsdorf, Siegfried 1911- *WhoAm 90, WhoWor 91*
Berthelsdorf, Siegfried R 1911- *BiDrAPA 89*
Berthelsen, John Robert 1954- *WhoEmL 91*
Berthelsen, Jorgen Gymoese 1945- *WhoWor 91*
Berthet, Jacques Maurice 1926- *WhoWor 91*
Berthet, Philippe R. 1926- *St&PR 91*
Berthevin, Pierre *PenDiDA 89*
Berthiaume, Marc Andre 1956- *WhoEmL 91*
Berthiaume, Terry J. 1953- *St&PR 91*
Berthiaume, Wayne Henry 1955- *WhoE 91*
Berthoff, Ann E 1924- *ConAu 129*
Berthoff, Rowland Tappan 1921- *WhoAm 90*
Berthoff, Warner Bement 1925- *WhoAm 90*
Berthold, Bonnie Madeline 1950- *WhoAmW 91*
Berthold, Dennis Alfred 1942- *WhoSSW 91*
Berthold, Fred, Jr. 1922- *WhoAm 90*
Berthold, James K. 1938- *St&PR 91*
Berthold, John William, III 1945- *WhoEmL 91*
Berthold, Norbert 1952- *WhoWor 91*
Berthold, Richard M 1946- *ConAu 131*
Berthold, Werner Horst Erich 1923- *WhoWor 91*
Bertholet, Marc Bernard 1956- *WhoE 91*
Bertholf, Neilson Allan, Jr. 1933- *WhoAm 90*
Berthon, George Theodore 1806-1892 *DcCanB 12*
Berthon, Rene Max 1914- *WhoWor 91*
Berthot, Jake 1939- *WhoAmA 91, WhoE 91*
Berthoud, Edward L. 1828- *AmLegL*
Berti, Luciano 1922- *WhoWor 91*
Bertie, Mary 1655-1709 *BiDEWW*
Bertig, Darrick Lee 1962- *WhoE 91*
Bertig, Mordecai 1877-1942 *BioIn 16*
Bertiger, Karen Lee 1954- *WhoAmW 91, WhoEmL 91*
Bertilsson, Gote Olof 1935- *WhoWor 91*
Bertin, John Joseph 1938- *WhoAm 90*
Bertinelli, Valerie 1960?- *BioIn 16, WorAlBi*
Bertini, Gary 1927- *IntWWM 90, PenDiMP, WhoWor 91*
Bertini, Mary Ann Comen 1941- *WhoE 91*
Bertini, Robert, Jr. *ODwPR 91*
Bertino, Joseph Rocco 1930- *WhoAm 90*
Bertken, Sister 1427-1514 *EncCoWW*
Bertland, Linda Harpring 1940- *WhoE 91*
Bertles, John F., Jr. 1959- *IntWWM 90*
Bertles, John Francis 1925- *WhoAm 90*
Bertman, Richard Jay 1934- *WhoAm 90*
Bertman, Stephen 1937- *WhoAmA 91*
Bertmar, Lars 1945- *WhoWor 91*
Bertness, Steven Lowell 1960- *WhoEmL 91*
Berto, Gene *WhoWrEP 89*
Berto, Juliet *BioIn 16*
Bertoch, Ronald Henry 1929- *St&PR 91*
Bertoia, Harry 1915-1978 *ConDes 90, PenDiDA 89, WhoAmA 91N*
Bertoia, Reno 1935- *Ballpl 90, BioIn 16*
Bertoia, Val 1949- *WhoAmA 91*
Bertol, Roland *AuBYP 90*
Bertola, Mariana 1868- *BioIn 16*
Bertolami, John Francis 1944- *WhoE 91*
Bertolami, Peter Joseph 1937- *WhoE 91*
Bertoldi, Alberto Manuel 1938- *BiDrAPA 89*
Bertoldo, Joseph Ramon 1950- *WhoEmL 91*
Bertoli, Barbara *BioIn 16*
Bertoli, Julius Karr 1920- *IntWWM 90*
Bertoli, Paolo 1908- *WhoWor 91*
Bertoli Cividino, Franca 1959- *IntWWM 90*
Bertolini, Andrea *PenDiDA 89*
Bertolini, Fernando 1925- *WhoWor 91*
Bertolini, Henry 1921- *St&PR 91*
Bertolini, Petro *PenDiDA 89*
Bertolino, James D. 1942- *WhoWrEP 89*
Bertolino, Mario Ercole 1934- *IntWWM 90*
Bertolino, Rosaleen 1956- *WhoWrEP 89*
Bertolli, Eugene Emil 1923- *WhoAm 90, WhoAmA 91*
Bertolli, Lisa Marie 1958- *WhoE 91*
Bertolucci, Bernardo *BioIn 16*
Bertolucci, Bernardo 1941- *WhoAm 90, WhoWor 91*
Bertolucci, Giuseppe *PenDiDA 89*
Bertolucci, Kenneth John 1956- *WhoEmL 91*
Berton, Lee 1931- *WhoAm 90*
Berton, Pierre 1920- *WhoAm 90, WhoWrEP 89*
Bertoncini, Gene *BioIn 16*
Bertoni, Christina 1945- *WhoAmA 91*
Bertoni, Dante H 1926- *WhoAmA 91*
Bertoni, Henry Louis 1938- *WhoAm 90*
Bertos, Rigas Nicholas 1929- *WhoAm 90*
Bertouille, Robert William 1930- *St&PR 91, WhoSSW 91*
Bertozzini, Terenzio *PenDiDA 89*
Bertram, Master 1340?-1414? *IntDcAA 90*
Bertram, Amy Ann 1960- *WhoAmW 91*
Bertram, Frederic Amos 1937- *WhoAm 90*
Bertram, George Hope 1847-1900 *DcCanB 12*
Bertram, Gwendolyn Seibert 1958- *WhoAmW 91*
Bertram, H. Neal 1941- *WhoAm 90*
Bertram, Lynn D 1958- *BiDrAPA 89*
Bertram, Manya M. *WhoWor 91*
Bertram, Noel *ConAu 32NR*
Bertram, Paul Frederick 1926- *St&PR 91*
Bertram, Philip William 1954- *WhoAm 90*
Bertram, Robert Whitcomb 1948- *WhoE 91*
Bertramson, B. Rodney 1914- *WhoAm 90*
Bertran de Born 1140?-1215 *ClMLC 5 [port]*
Bertran, Ross Frederick 1952- *WhoEmL 91*
Bertran Armand, Beatriz A. 1958- *WhoSSW 91*
Bertrana, Aurora 1899-1974 *EncCoWW*
Bertrand, Alvin L 1918- *ConAu 30NR*
Bertrand, Annabel Hodges 1915- *WhoAmW 91*
Bertrand, Bettina Lee 1958- *WhoEmL 91*
Bertrand, Carie Lynn 1964- *WhoAmW 91*
Bertrand, Charles 1824-1896 *DcCanB 12*
Bertrand, Danyelle *BiDrAPA 89*
Bertrand, Donald Ernest 1946- *WhoEmL 91*
Bertrand, Estelle *BiDrAPA 89*
Bertrand, Frederic H. 1936- *St&PR 91*
Bertrand, Frederic Howard 1936- *WhoAm 90*
Bertrand, Gabrielle 1923- *WhoAmW 91*
Bertrand, George Robinson 1940- *WhoE 91*
Bertrand, Mary Ellen 1955- *WhoAmW 91*
Bertrand, Robert Norman 1954- *WhoAm 90*
Bertrand, Sandra 1943- *ConAu 130*
Bertrand, Scott Richard 1954- *WhoSSW 91*
Bertrand, Watson Clark 1931- *WhoAm 90*
Bertrand, William Ellis 1944- *WhoAm 90*
Bertsch, Frank Henry 1925- *St&PR 91, WhoAm 90*
Bertsch, Frederick Charles, III 1942- *WhoAm 90*
Bertsch, James L. 1943- *St&PR 91*
Bertsch, John P. 1940- *WhoAm 90*
Bertsch, Robert Joseph 1948- *WhoEmL 91*
Bertsche, Bernard B. 1942- *St&PR 91*
Bertschie, George 1953- *St&PR 91*
Bertschinger, Kurt Arnold *BiDrAPA 89*
Bertschmann, Peter W. 1935- *St&PR 91*

Bertuol, Bernard Pierre 1948- *WhoAm 90*
Berty, John Jeffry 1953- *WhoEmL 91*
Berube, Jacques B. 1941- *WhoAm 90*
Berube, Margery Stanwood 1943- *WhoAmW 91*
Berube, Yves 1940- *WhoWor 91*
Beruh, Joseph 1924-1989 *BioIn 16*, *ConTFT 8*
Berumen, Julio *BioIn 16*
Berv, Douglas Allen 1948- *BiDrAPA 89*
Berv, Kenneth R *BiDrAPA 89*
Berwald, Helen Dorothy 1925- *WhoAm 90*
Berwaldt, Carl P. 1956- *St&PR 91*
Berwick, Virginia G. 1939- *St&PR 91*
Berwind, C. Graham, Jr. 1928- *St&PR 91*
Berwish, Neil Justin *BiDrAPA 89*
Berzelius, Jons Jakob 1779-1848 *BioIn 16*, *WorAlBi*
Berzeviczy-Pallavicini, Federico von 1909-1989 *BioIn 16*
Berzins, Erna Marija 1914- *WhoAmW 91*, *WhoWor 91*
Berzok, Robert M. 1944- *ODwPR 91*
Berzok, Robert Martin 1944- *WhoE 91*
Berzon, Bernard L. 1913-1989 *BioIn 16*
Berzon, Betty 1928- *WhoAmW 91*
Berzon, Faye Clark 1926- *WhoAmW 91*
Besancenez, Richard Peter 1929- *WhoSSW 91*
Besancon, Alain J. 1932- *ConAu 130*
Besant, Annie 1847-1933 *BioIn 16*, *EncO&P 3*, *EncPaPR 91*, *FemiCLE*, *NewAgE 90*, *WorAlBi*
Besant, Derek Michael 1950- *WhoAmA 91*
Besant, Larry Xon 1935- *WhoAm 90*
Besch, Anthony John Elwyn 1924- *IntWWM 90*
Besch, Emerson Louis 1928- *WhoAm 90*
Besch, Everett Dickman 1924- *WhoAm 90*
Besch, Henry Roland, Jr. 1942- *WhoAm 90*
Besch, Mark Ernst 1951- *WhoSSW 91*
Beschel, Robert Paine, Jr. 1957- *WhoE 91*
Bescher, Bob 1884-1942 *Ballpl 90*
Beschle, Donald L. 1951- *WhoEmL 91*
Besen, Aaron Jay 1958- *WhoEmL 91*
Besen, Jane Phyllis Triptow 1921- *WhoAmW 91*
Besen, Stanley Martin 1937- *WhoAm 90*
Besenhard, Jurgen Otto 1944- *WhoWor 91*
Beser, Jacques 1950- *WhoEmL 91*
Beshar, Christine 1929- *WhoAm 90*, *WhoAmW 91*
Beshar, Robert Peter 1928- *WhoAm 90*, *WhoE 91*
Beshara, Dennis Lee 1944- *BiDrAPA 89*
Beshara, Edmund *BiDrAPA 89*
Besharov, Douglas John 1945- *WhoE 91*
Beshear, Steven L. 1944- *WhoAm 90*
Beshears, C.O. 1926- *St&PR 91*
Beshears, Charles Daniel 1917- *WhoAm 90*
Beshears, Lydia Jean 1945- *WhoAmW 91*
Besicovitch, Abram Samoilovitch 1891-1970 *DcScB S2*
Besing, Ray Gilbert 1934- *WhoAm 90*
Besinnet, Ada M *EncO&P 3*
Beskind, Harry 1932- *BiDrAPA 89*
Beskow, Elsa 1874-1953 *AuBYP 90*
Besl, Alfred B. 1924- *St&PR 91*
Besley, Richard N 1937- *BiDrAPA 89*
Besnard, Thomas Pope 1806?-1878 *OxCCanT*
Besner, Bram 1932- *St&PR 91*
Besner, J Jacques 1919- *WhoAmA 91*
Besner, Lance A 1961- *BiDrAPA 89*
Besner, Lance Alan 1961- *WhoE 91*
Besnier, Nicolas *PenDiDA 89*
Besnoff, Larry 1951- *WhoEmL 91*
Besonen, Joanne Frances 1946- *WhoAmW 91*
Besore, George Raleigh, Jr. 1924- *WhoSSW 91*
Besoyan, Rick 1924-1970 *OxCPMus*
Besozzi, Paul Charles 1947- *WhoE 91*
Bespalov, Yuri Aleksandrovich 1939- *WhoWor 91*
Bess, Barbara E 1939- *BiDrAPA 89*
Bess, Charles Wayne 1958- *WhoEmL 91*
Bess, Clayton *ConAu 129*
Bess, Clayton 1944- *BioIn 16*, *SmATA X [port]*
Bess, Douglas R *BiDrAPA 89*
Bess, Harold Leon 1924- *WhoE 91*, *WhoWor 91*
Bess, Paul William 1949- *WhoSSW 91*
Bess, Robert Wade 1958- *WhoWrEP 89*
Bessa-Luis, Augustina 1923?- *EncCoWW*
Besse, Georges N. *BioIn 16*
Besse, Herman 1911-1972 *Ballpl 90*
Besse, Philippe Lucien 1931- *WhoWor 91*
Besse, Ralph Moore 1905- *WhoAm 90*
Besse, Robert Gale 1923- *WhoWor 91*
Besse, Ronald Duncan 1938- *WhoAm 90*
Besseghini, Victoria H *BiDrAPA 89*
Bessel, Friedrich Wilhelm 1784-1846 *WorAlBi*
Besseling, Charles Reinier Johannes 1920- *IntWWM 90*
Bessell, Iris Karen 1948- *WhoAmW 91*
Bessell, Ted *BioIn 16*
Bessemans, Joseph Francois Antoine A 1888- *EncO&P 3*
Bessemer, Conrad M. 1951- *WhoE 91*
Bessemer, Henry 1813-1898 *WorAlBi*
Bessent, Don 1931- *Ballpl 90*
Bessent, Malcolm 1945- *EncPaPR 91*
Bessenyey, Francis B. 1925- *St&PR 91*, *WhoE 91*
Besser, Amy Helene 1956- *WhoEmL 91*
Besser, Arne Charles 1935- *WhoAmA 91*
Besser, Howard Russell 1941- *WhoAm 90*
Besser, Joe 1907-1988 *BioIn 16*
Besser, John Edward 1942- *St&PR 91*, *WhoAm 90*
Besses o' th' Barn *OxCPMus*
Bessette, Joseph Thomas 1925- *WhoAm 90*
Bessette, Linda *ODwPR 91*
Bessette, Richard Pierre 1948- *St&PR 91*
Bessette, Robert Felix, Jr. *BiDrAPA 89*
Bessey, B. Thomas 1936- *St&PR 91*
Bessey, Edward Cushing 1934- *St&PR 91*, *WhoAm 90*
Bessey, William Higgins 1913- *WhoAm 90*
Bessho, Takehiko *Ballpl 90*
Bessie, Alvah Cecil 1904-1985 *BioIn 16*
Bessie, Cornelia *BioIn 16*
Bessie, Simon Michael *BioIn 16*
Bessie, Simon Michael 1916- *WhoAm 90*
Bessinger, Jess Balsor, Jr. 1921- *WhoAm 90*
Bessire, Henry Edmond 1935- *St&PR 91*
Bessler, Stephen Craig 1951- *WhoEmL 91*
Bessman, Samuel Paul 1921- *WhoAm 90*
Bessmertnova, Natalia 1941- *BioIn 16*
Bessmertnova, Natalya Igorevna 1941- *WhoWor 91*
Bessmertnykh, Aleksandr A. *NewYTBS 90*
Besso, Marc Joseph 1931- *St&PR 91*
Besso, Michelangelo 1873-1955 *BioIn 16*
Besso, W. James 1935- *St&PR 91*
Bessom, Malcolm Eugene 1940- *WhoWrEP 89*
Besson, Frank Schaeffer, III 1936- *St&PR 91*
Besson, Michel Louis 1934- *St&PR 91*, *WhoAm 90*, *WhoE 91*
Bessor, Bryan W. 1955- *St&PR 91*
Bessor, Joyce M. 1931- *St&PR 91*
Bessor, William D. 1927- *St&PR 91*
Best, Allena Champlin 1892- *AuBYP 90*
Best, Angela Pizza *BiDrAPA 89*
Best, Charles Herbert 1899-1978 *DcScB S2*
Best, Diana Ramsbottom 1962- *WhoAmW 91*
Best, Edgar Everett 1904- *WhoE 91*
Best, Elizabeth Allaire 1956- *WhoAmW 91*
Best, Eugene Crawford, Jr. 1939- *WhoAm 90*
Best, Franklin Luther, Jr. 1945- *WhoE 91*
Best, Frederick Napier 1943- *WhoSSW 91*
Best, Herbert 1894- *AuBYP 90*
Best, Jacob Hilmer, Jr. 1937- *WhoAm 90*
Best, Jane Evans 1926- *WhoE 91*
Best, Janis Lea *BiDrAPA 89*
Best, Janna Luebkemann 1960- *WhoEmL 91*
Best, Jay Arthur 1933- *St&PR 91*
Best, Joel Gordon 1946- *WhoAm 90*
Best, John, Jr. 1932- *St&PR 91*
Best, Judah 1932- *WhoAm 90*
Best, Karl 1959- *Ballpl 90*
Best, Kathleen Francis 1946- *WhoEmL 91*
Best, Kimberly Renee 1955- *BiDrAPA 89*
Best, Laurence John 1950- *WhoE 91*
Best, Mary Sue 1930- *WhoWrEP 89*
Best, Matthew 1957- *IntWWM 90*
Best, Michael K. 1936- *St&PR 91*
Best, Patricia Marie 1953- *WhoAmW 91*
Best, Paul Wesley, Jr. *BiDrAPA 89*
Best, Peter 1925- *WhoWor 91*
Best, Philip Ernest 1938- *WhoE 91*
Best, Raymond Merle 1938- *St&PR 91*
Best, Richard Allen, Jr. 1957- *WhoWor 91*
Best, Richard Lundelius 1923- *WhoAm 90*
Best, Robert Mulvane 1922- *St&PR 91*, *WhoAm 90*
Best, Robert Wayne 1946- *St&PR 91*, *WhoAm 90*, *WhoSSW 91*
Best, Robert Worth 1922- *St&PR 91*
Best, Roger *PenDiMP*
Best, Roger 1938- *IntWWM 90*
Best, Roger Norman 1949- *WhoEmL 91*, *WhoWor 91*
Best, Ronald 1936- *St&PR 91*
Best, Steven R *BiDrAPA 89*
Best, Thirza Louise 1934- *WhoE 91*
Best, W T 1826-1897 *PenDiMP*
Best, Wayne Allison, Jr. 1927- *WhoSSW 91*
Best, Werner 1903- *BioIn 16*
Best, William Andrew, III 1961- *WhoE 91*
Best, Willie 1915-1962 *DrBIPA 90*
Best, Wilma Ann 1946- *St&PR 91*
Best, Winfield Judson 1919- *WhoAm 90*, *WhoWrEP 89*
Bestall, Alfred Edmeades 1892-1986 *BioIn 16*
Bestard, Jose M. 1943- *WhoHisp 91*
Bestdorf, Ellen Bell 1915- *WhoAmW 91*
Beste, Harold E. *NewYTBS 90*
Bestehorn, Ute Wiltrud 1930- *WhoAmW 91*, *WhoWor 91*
Besten, Robert Bruce 1929- *St&PR 91*
Besteni, Barbara Amnerys 1958- *WhoEmL 91*, *WhoWor 91*
Bester, Alfred 1913- *RGTwCSF*
Bester, Alfred 1913-1987 *BioIn 16*, *MajTwCW*, *WorAu 1980 [port]*
Bester, Hester 1945- *WhoAmW 91*
Bester, Tim 1944- *WhoWor 91*
Besterly, Robert John 1931- *St&PR 91*
Besterman, Theodore 1904-1976 *EncO&P 3*
Besterman, Theodore Deodatus Nathaniel 1904-1976 *EncPaPR 91*
Besthoff, Anthony Warren 1935- *St&PR 91*
Besthoff, Sydney J., III *WhoAm 90*, *WhoSSW 91*
Bestimt, William Joseph 1945- *WhoSSW 91*
Bestler, Gerald M. 1929- *St&PR 91*
Bestler, Gerald Milton 1929- *WhoAm 90*, *WhoWor 91*
Beston, Rose Marie 1937- *WhoAm 90*, *WhoAmW 91*, *WhoE 91*
Bestor, Charles Lemon 1924- *IntWWM 90*, *WhoAm 90*
Bestwick, David M. 1933- *St&PR 91*
Bestwick, Warren William 1922- *WhoAm 90*
Besuden, Heinrich Walter Karl 1924- *WhoWor 91*
Beszterczey, Akos C 1944- *BiDrAPA 89*
Beszterczey, Akos Csaba 1944- *WhoE 91*
Beszterczey, Lesley Margaret 1945- *St&PR 91*, *WhoAmW 91*
Betancourt, Amaury P. 1917- *St&PR 91*
Betancourt, Antonio Miguel *BiDrAPA 89*
Betancourt, Antonio Miguel 1949- *WhoSSW 91*
Betancourt, Jeanne 1941- *BioIn 16*, *ConAu 31NR*
Betancourt, John 1950- *WhoHisp 91*
Betancourt, Jorge *BiDrAPA 89*
Betancourt, Jose Luis 1956- *WhoHisp 91*
Betancourt, Mary Aliece 1938- *WhoE 91*
Betancourt, Romulo 1908-1981 *BioIn 16*, *WorAlBi*
Betancur, Belisario *BioIn 16*
Betancur, Belisario 1923- *WhoWor 91*
Betanova 1954- *ConDes 90*
Betanzos, Louis 1936- *St&PR 91*, *WhoAm 90*, *WhoHisp 91*
Betanzos, Ramon James 1933- *WhoHisp 91*
Betanzos-Palacios, Odon 1926- *WhoHisp 91*
Betchek, James L. 1930- *St&PR 91*
Betcher, Albert Maxwell 1911- *WhoAm 90*
Betcher, Robert William *BiDrAPA 89*
Betchkal, James Joseph 1936- *WhoWrEP 89*
Betchkal, James Joseph 1936-1989 *WhoAm 90*
Bete, Channing Lindquist, Jr. 1936- *St&PR 91*
Beteille, Andre 1934- *ConAu 130*
Betenbaugh, Gordon Murray 1941- *IntWWM 90*
Betensky, Rose Hart *WhoAmA 91*
Betger, Evgenii Karlovich *BioIn 16*
Betham, Mary Matilda 1776-1852 *FemiCLE*
Betham-Edwards, Matilda 1836-1919 *BioIn 16*, *FemiCLE*
Bethancourt, T. Ernesto *BioIn 16*
Bethania, Maria *BioIn 16*
Bethe, Hans A. 1906- *WorAlBi*
Bethe, Hans Albrecht 1906- *WhoAm 90*, *WhoE 91*, *WhoWor 91*
Bethea, Charles 1933- *WhoE 91*
Bethea, J. D. *ConAu 130*
Bethea, James D. 1933?-1990 *ConAu 130*
Bethea, James Stephen, III 1938- *WhoSSW 91*
Bethea, Joseph Benjamin 1932- *WhoAm 90*
Bethea, Louise Huffman 1947- *WhoSSW 91*
Bethea-Shields, Karen Louise 1949- *WhoEmL 91*, *WhoSSW 91*
Bethel, C.A. *WhoWrEP 89*
Bethel, David Lee 1944- *BiDrAPA 89*
Bethel, Dell 1929- *BioIn 16*
Bethel, James William 1937- *BiDrAPA 89*
Bethel, Jeanne Anita 1942- *WhoAmW 91*
Bethel, Mark Leslie 1950- *WhoE 91*
Bethel, Michael R. 1943- *St&PR 91*
Bethell, John E. *IntWWM 90*
Bethell, Ursula 1874-1945 *FemiCLE*
Bethers, Ray 1902- *AuBYP 90*
Bethiea, R. Steven 1947- *St&PR 91*
Bethke, Dale L. 1928- *St&PR 91*
Bethke, William M. 1947- *WhoE 91*
Bethke, William Milford 1947- *St&PR 91*
Bethlen, Francis Rhedey 1925- *WhoE 91*
Bethlen, Kata 1700-1759 *EncCoWW*
Bethlen, T. D. *MajTwCW*
Bethmann, Siegfried 1915- *IntWWM 90*
Bethray, Adrian Joseph 1947- *St&PR 91*, *WhoE 91*
Bethune, David R. 1940- *St&PR 91*
Bethune, David Ross 1940- *WhoAm 90*, *WhoE 91*
Bethune, Joanna G. 1770-1860 *BioAmW*
Bethune, John Johnson 1956- *WhoEmL 91*
Bethune, Mary 1875-1955 *FemiCLE*
Bethune, Mary Jane McLeod 1875-1955 *BioIn 16*
Bethune, Mary McLeod 1875-1955 *BioAmW*, *WorAlBi*
Bethune, Norman *BioIn 16*
Bethune, Norman 1822-1892 *DcCanB 12*
Bethune, Robert Henry 1836-1895 *DcCanB 12*
Bethune, Thomas Greene 1849-1908 *BioIn 16*
Bethune, Zina 1950- *WhoAmW 91*
Beti, Mongo *MajTwCW*
Betitia *EncCoWW*
Betjeman, John 1906-1984 *BioIn 16*, *ConAu 33NR*, *DcNaB 1981*, *MajTwCW*, *WorAlBi*
Betker, Rick Girard 1954- *St&PR 91*
Betley, Leonard John 1933- *WhoAm 90*
Beto, George John 1916- *WhoAm 90*, *WhoSSW 91*
Beton, John A. 1950- *St&PR 91*
Beton, John Allen 1950- *WhoEmL 91*
Betros, Joanne 1959- *WhoAmW 91*
Betrosoff, Pamela Anne 1950- *WhoAmW 91*
Betsch, Madeline *WhoAm 90*, *WhoAmW 91*
Betson, Laurence O. 1944- *St&PR 91*
Bett, Arlene Marcy 1962- *WhoAmW 91*
Bettega, Paulo Roberto 1947- *BiDrAPA 89*
Bettelheim, Bruno *BioIn 16*
Bettelheim, Bruno 1903-1990 *ConAu 131*, *CurBio 90N*, *MajTwCW*, *NewYTBS 90 [port]*, *News 90*, *-90-3*
Betten, Paul Robert 1946- *WhoEmL 91*
Bettenbender, John I. *BioIn 16*
Bettencourt, Jose Fernando Silva C. 1938- *WhoWor 91*
Bettencourt, Larry 1905-1978 *Ballpl 90*
Bettendorf, James Bernard 1933- *WhoWor 91*
Bettenhausen, Elizabeth Ann 1942- *WhoAm 90*
Better Days *EncPR&S 89*
Better, Cathy Drinkwater 1952- *WhoE 91*
Better, William Joel 1951- *WhoEmL 91*
Betteridge, Don *TwCCr&M 91*
Betteridge, Frances Carpenter 1921- *WhoAmW 91*
Betteridge, Lois Etherington 1928- *WhoAmA 91*
Betterley, George Morgan 1921- *WhoE 91*
Betters, Thomas H. 1950- *St&PR 91*
Bettersworth, John Knox 1909- *WhoAm 90*, *WhoWrEP 89*
Bettes, Jerry Lee 1932- *St&PR 91*
Bettes, Richard S., III 1951- *St&PR 91*
Bettey, J H 1932- *ConAu 130*
Betti, Adolfo *PenDiMP*
Betti, Franco Gino 1932- *WhoAm 90*
Betti, John A. 1931- *WhoAm 90*
Betti, Laura 1934- *ConTFT 8 [port]*
Betti van der Noot, Dino Alfredo 1936- *WhoWor 91*
Bettig, Laura Jean 1956- *WhoEmL 91*
Bettignies, Jean-Maximilian-Joseph de *PenDiDA 89*
Bettilyon, Mark M. 1958- *WhoEmL 91*
Bettin, Janene Edna 1943- *WhoAmW 91*
Bettina *AuBYP 90*
Bettinger, Fred J. 1934- *ODwPR 91*
Bettinger, K.B. 1953- *St&PR 91*
Bettinghaus, Erwin Paul 1930- *WhoAm 90*
Bettinson, Brenda 1929- *WhoAmA 91*
Bettio, Francesca Giuseppina 1950- *WhoWor 91*
Bettis, Barry Phillip 1954- *WhoEmL 91*
Bettisi, Leonardo *PenDiDA 89*
Bettison, James *WhoAmA 91*
Bettleheim, Bruno 1903- *WhoWrEP 89*
Bettleheim, Bruno 1903-1990 *WorAlBi*
Bettman, Gary Bruce 1952- *WhoAm 90*
Bettman, James Ross 1943- *WhoAm 90*, *WhoSSW 91*
Bettmann, Frank Adam, Jr. 1955- *WhoEmL 91*
Bettmann, Otto Ludwig 1903- *BioIn 16*, *WhoAm 90*, *WhoAmA 91*
Betto, Kaoru 1920- *Ballpl 90*
Bettris, Jone *BiDEWW*
Betts, Ann Brantly 1947- *WhoAmW 91*
Betts, Austin Wortham 1912- *WhoAm 90*
Betts, Barbara Lang 1926- *WhoWor 91*
Betts, Bert A. 1923- *WhoAm 90*, *WhoWor 91*

Betts, David Sheridan 1936- *WhoE 91*
Betts, Dicky 1943- *WhoAm 90*
Betts, Doris June Waugh 1932- *WhoAm 90, WhoAmW 91, WhoWrEP 89*
Betts, Edward Howard 1920- *WhoAmA 91*
Betts, Huck 1897-1987 *Ballpl 90*
Betts, James William, Jr. 1923- *WhoWor 91*
Betts, John M.C. 1912- *St&PR 91*
Betts, Kathleen Vanetta 1955- *WhoE 91*
Betts, Kay *ODwPR 91*
Betts, Kirk Howard 1951- *WhoEmL 91*
Betts, Louis 1873-1961 *WhoAmA 91N*
Betts, Mary Avis 1959- *WhoAmW 91*
Betts, Mary E.W. 1824-1854 *LiHiK*
Betts, Robert B. 1922-1989 *BioIn 16*
Betts, Stanley 1924- *St&PR 91*
Betts, Susan Jeannette 1955- *WhoAmW 91*
Betts, Ted 1953- *WhoWrEP 89*
Betts, Thomas *PenDiDA 89*
Betts, Wilmer C 1925- *BiDrAPA 89*
Betty, Maurice Moore- *BioIn 16*
Betz, Allen David 1937- *St&PR 91*
Betz, Andrew John 1938- *St&PR 91*
Betz, Augustin E. A. 1920- *WhoWor 91*
Betz, Betty 1920- *AuBYP 90*
Betz, Brian Richard 1932- *WhoE 91*
Betz, Charles W. 1922- *WhoAm 90*
Betz, Donald 1945- *WhoEmL 91*
Betz, Eberhard Ludwig 1926- *WhoWor 91*
Betz, Ebon Elbert 1914- *WhoE 91*
Betz, Edward Bergan 1934- *St&PR 91*
Betz, Eugene William 1921- *WhoAm 90*
Betz, Fredric James 1934- *St&PR 91*
Betz, Hans D. 1940- *EncPaPR 91*
Betz, Hans Dieter 1931- *WhoAm 90*
Betz, Mary-Etta Doris 1947- *WhoEmL 91*
Betz, Otto Wilhelm 1917- *WhoWor 91*
Betzag, Fred Charles 1941- *St&PR 91*
Betzel, Bruno 1894-1965 *Ballpl 90*
Betzinez, Jason 1860-1960 *WhNaAH*
Beu, Marjorie Janet 1921- *WhoAmW 91*
Beube, Frank Edward 1904- *WhoE 91, WhoWor 91*
Beuchel, Patrick Thomas 1959- *WhoEmL 91*
Beuchert, Edward William 1937- *WhoAm 90*
Beuck, Jules Edward 1950- *WhoEmL 91*
Beudert, Mark 1951- *IntWWM 90*
Beuerlein, Juliana 1921- *WhoAm 90, WhoAmW 91*
Beugelmans, Daniel Boris 1949- *BiDrAPA 89*
Beugen, Joan Beth 1943- *WhoAmW 91*
Beugnot, Bernard Andre Henri 1932- *WhoAm 90*
Beukelman, Douglas D. 1955- *St&PR 91*
Beukema, Marenus James *BiDrAPA 89*
Beukenkamp, Cornelius F J *BiDrAPA 89*
Beuker, Friedhelm Maria 1932- *WhoWor 91*
Beumee, John K. 1925- *St&PR 91*
Beumer, Richard E. 1938- *St&PR 91*
Beumer, Richard Eugene 1938- *WhoAm 90*
Beurdeley, Louis-Auguste-Alfred 1808-1882 *PenDiDA 89*
Beurdeley, Michel 1911- *ConAu 30NR*
Beury-Saurel, Amelie 1848-1924 *BiDWomA*
Beuschold, George 1942- *WhoE 91*
Beute, William H 1943- *BiDrAPA 89*
Beutelspacher, Albrecht Friedrich 1950- *WhoWor 91*
Beuter, Richard William 1942- *WhoAm 90*
Beuth, Philip R. 1932- *St&PR 91*
Beuthner, Hertha *BioIn 16*
Beutler, Abigail Elaine 1930- *WhoAmW 91*
Beutler, Arthur Julius 1924- *WhoWor 91*
Beutler, Ernest 1928- *WhoAm 90*
Beutler, Frederick Joseph 1926- *WhoAm 90*
Beutler, Margarete 1876-1949 *EncCoWW*
Beutlerin, Magdalena *EncCoWW*
Beutner, Roger Earl 1930- *St&PR 91*
Beuttenmuller, Rudolf William 1953- *WhoSSW 91*
Beuve-Mery, Hubert 1902-1989 *AnObit 1989, BiDFrPL, BioIn 16, ConAu 129*
Beuys, Joseph 1921-1986 *BioIn 16*
Bevack, Patrick W. 1946- *St&PR 91*
Bevacqua, J. *St&PR 91*
Bevacqua, Kurt 1947- *Ballpl 90*
Bevan, Aneurin 1897-1960 *BioIn 16*
Bevan, Charles *PenDiDA 89*
Bevan, Charles Albert, Jr. 1944- *WhoAm 90*
Bevan, Clifford James 1934- *IntWWM 90*
Bevan, David Richard 1941- *WhoAm 90*
Bevan, Donald Edward 1921- *WhoAm 90*
Bevan, Maurice Guy Smalman 1921- *IntWWM 90*
Bevan, Richard Gary 1943- *St&PR 91*
Bevan, Robert 1865-1925 *BioIn 16*
Bevan, Robert Lewis 1928- *WhoAm 90, WhoWor 91*
Bevan, Robert Palmer 1945- *BiDrAPA 89*
Bevan, Robert Stanley 1926- *St&PR 91*
Bevan, William 1922- *WhoAm 90*
Bevans, Duane Arlo 1945- *BiDrAPA 89*
Bevans, Margaret *AuBYP 90*
Bevans, Michael H. *AuBYP 90*
Bevcic, Mirko *WhoWor 91*
Bevel, Christine MacDonald 1944- *WhoAmW 91*
Bevel, James Luther 1936- *BioIn 16*
Beven, Gary Edward *BiDrAPA 89*
Bevenour, R.J. 1929- *St&PR 91*
Bevens, Bill 1916- *Ballpl 90*
Bever, Christopher T 1919- *BiDrAPA 89*
Bever, Christopher Theodore 1919- *WhoE 91*
Bever, Robert Lynn 1953- *WhoEmL 91*
Bever, Thomas Gordon 1939- *WhoAm 90*
Bever, Timothy Michael 1953- *WhoEmL 91*
Beveridge, Albert Jeremiah 1862-1927 *BioIn 16*
Beveridge, Albert Jeremiah, III 1935- *WhoAm 90, WhoE 91*
Beveridge, George David, Jr. 1922- *WhoWrEP 89*
Beveridge, James MacDonald Richardson 1912- *WhoAm 90*
Beveridge, Karl J 1945- *WhoAmA 91*
Beveridge, Terrance James 1945- *WhoAm 90*
Beverina, Francis Felice 1936- *WhoSSW 91*
Beverland, Wanda Lou 1941- *WhoAmW 91*
Beverley, Elizabeth *FemiCLE*
Beverley, Jane Taylor 1918- *WhoAmW 91, WhoWor 91*
Beverley, John Gray, Jr. 1935- *WhoE 91*
Beverley, P.S. 1940- *St&PR 91*
Beverley, Robert 1673?-1722 *EncCRAm*
Beverley, Thomas Anthony 1940- *WhoWor 91*
Beverley, Trazana 1945- *ConTFT 8, DrBlPA 90*
Beverlos, Cornelis van 1922- *BioIn 16*
Beverly, Creigs C. 1942- *WhoAm 90*
Beverly, Frankie *BioIn 16*
Beverly, Patty Libby 1954- *WhoAmW 91*
Beverly, Thomas More 1958- *WhoEmL 91*
Bevers, Jonathan Hugh 1953- *BiDrAPA 89*
Beversdorf, Anne Elizabeth 1949- *WhoAmW 91*
Bevevino, James William 1939- *St&PR 91*
Bevier, Deborah L. 1951- *St&PR 91*
Bevier, Isabel 1860-1942 *BioAmW*
Bevier, James Hasbrouck 1924- *WhoE 91, WhoWor 91*
Bevier, Richard Charles 1929- *St&PR 91*
Bevignani, Enrico 1841-1903 *PenDiMP*
Bevil, J. Marshall 1947- *IntWWM 90*
Bevil, Jack Marshall 1947- *WhoSSW 91*
Bevilacqua, Aldo Romano *BiDrAPA 89*
Bevilacqua, Anthony J. 1923- *WhoAm 90, WhoE 91*
Bevilacqua, Joseph A. 1918-1989 *BioIn 16*
Bevill, Evangeline Stonecipher 1928- *WhoWrEP 89*
Bevill, Tom 1921- *WhoAm 90, WhoSSW 91*
Bevin, Ernest 1881-1951 *WorAlBi*
Bevinetto, Tony *BioIn 16*
Bevington, David Martin 1931- *WhoAm 90, WhoWrEP 89*
Bevington, E. Milton 1928- *St&PR 91*
Bevington, Edmund Milton 1928- *WhoAm 90*
Bevington, Helen S. 1906- *WhoWrEP 89*
Bevington, L. S. 1845-1895? *FemiCLE*
Bevington, Louisa Sarah 1845- *BioIn 16*
Bevington, Mariette De Coriolis 1925- *WhoAmW 91*
Bevington, Paula Lawton 1937- *St&PR 91*
Bevins, Karl Alten 1915- *IntWWM 90*
Bevis, Benjamin W. 1926- *St&PR 91*
Bevis, George E. 1913- *St&PR 91*
Bevis, Herman W. 1909-1989 *BioIn 16*
Bevis, J. Wayne 1934- *St&PR 91*
Bevis, James Wayne 1934- *WhoAm 90*
Bevis, Joseph C. 1910-1990 *BioIn 16, NewYTBS 90*
Bevis, Patricia Ann 1955- *WhoAmW 91*
Bevlin, Marjorie Elliott 1917- *WhoAmA 91*
Bewick, John Arters 1937- *WhoAm 90*
Bewkes, Eugene Garrett, Jr. 1926- *WhoAm 90*
Bewley, Christina 1924- *ConAu 129*
Bewley, John Derek 1943- *WhoAm 90*
Bewley, Truman Fassett 1941- *WhoAm 90*
Bexon, Roger 1926- *St&PR 91*
Bextermiller, Theresa Marie 1960- *WhoAmW 91, WhoE 91, WhoWor 91*
Bey, Douglas R, Jr. 1938- *BiDrAPA 89*
Bey, Gwendolyn Konigsberg 1954- *WhoE 91*
Bey, La Rocque *DrBlPA 90*
Bey, Marki 1946?- *DrBlPA 90*
Bey, Pilaff 1868-1952 *BioIn 16*
Bey, Stanley Stuart 1937- *St&PR 91*
Beyda, Daniel 1953- *WhoEmL 91*
Beyens, Michel Yvon 1932- *St&PR 91*
Beyer, Aaron Jay 1946- *WhoEmL 91*
Beyer, Alan L. 1944- *St&PR 91*
Beyer, Alvin, Jr. *BiDrAPA 89*
Beyer, Andrew *BioIn 16*
Beyer, Barbara L. 1947- *St&PR 91*
Beyer, Barbara Lynn 1947- *WhoAmW 91*
Beyer, Brenda Reed 1955- *WhoSSW 91*
Beyer, Bud *BioIn 16*
Beyer, Charlotte Bishop 1947- *WhoAmW 91, WhoEmL 91*
Beyer, Clara *NewYTBS 90*
Beyer, Daniel G. 1954- *WhoEmL 91*
Beyer, David H *BiDrAPA 89*
Beyer, David Henry, Jr. 1948- *BiDrAPA 89*
Beyer, Ferdinand Augustine 1930- *St&PR 91*
Beyer, Frank Michael 1928- *IntWWM 90*
Beyer, Glenn, Jr. 1950- *WhoSSW 91*
Beyer, Gordon Robert 1930- *WhoAm 90*
Beyer, Heidi Beryl 1964- *WhoAmW 91*
Beyer, Henri-Paul-Auguste *PenDiDA 89*
Beyer, Herbert Albert 1923- *St&PR 91*
Beyer, Jacquelyn L. 1924- *WhoAmW 91*
Beyer, Jeffrey C. 1954- *St&PR 91*
Beyer, Johann Christian Wilhelm 1725-1806 *PenDiDA 89*
Beyer, John Rolland *BiDrAPA 89*
Beyer, John Treacy 1943- *St&PR 91*
Beyer, Karen Ann 1942- *WhoAmW 91*
Beyer, Karl Henry, Jr. 1914- *WhoAm 90*
Beyer, Klaus Dietrich 1937- *WhoE 91*
Beyer, Kurt Gerhard 1931- *WhoWor 91*
Beyer, Lawrence Gerald 1933- *St&PR 91*
Beyer, Marie Elena O'Neill 1945- *WhoEmL 91*
Beyer, Mary Irene 1962- *WhoEmL 91*
Beyer, Morten S. 1921- *St&PR 91*
Beyer, Morten Sternoff 1921- *WhoAm 90*
Beyer, Norma Warren 1926- *WhoAmW 91*
Beyer, Robert Thomas 1920- *WhoAm 90*
Beyer, Sonya von Zitzewitz 1931- *WhoAmW 91*
Beyer, Steven J 1951- *WhoAmA 91*
Beyer, Stuart Edward 1924- *WhoE 91*
Beyer, Suzanne 1928- *WhoAmW 91, WhoE 91*
Beyer, Troy 1964?- *DrBlPA 90*
Beyer, Wayne Herman 1956- *WhoEmL 91*
Beyer-Mears, Annette 1941- *WhoAmW 91, WhoWor 91*
Beyerchen, Alan Duane 1945- *WhoEmL 91*
Beyerle, Jean-Louis de *PenDiDA 89*
Beyerlein, Douglas Craig 1950- *WhoEmL 91*
Beyerlein, Fred Gordon 1947- *St&PR 91, WhoAm 90*
Beyers, Patricia Joan *WhoAmW 91*
Beyers, William Bjorn 1940- *WhoAm 90*
Beyersdorf, Marguerite Mulloy 1922- *WhoAmW 91*
Beyette, B. Donald Leslie 1945- *St&PR 91*
Beyl, Ernest 1928- *ODwPR 91*
Beyle, Hank *ConAu 130*
Beylerian, Haroton Arthur 1950- *WhoE 91*
Beyman, Jonathan Eric 1955- *WhoE 91*
Beynen, Gijsbertus Koolemans 1935- *WhoWor 91*
Beynon, David J. 1932- *St&PR 91*
Beynon, Ira D. *St&PR 91N*
Beyreis, James Robert 1944- *St&PR 91*
Beyrer, Mary K. *BioIn 16*
Beyster, John Robert 1924- *St&PR 91, WhoAm 90*
Beytagh, Francis Xavier, Jr. 1935- *WhoAm 90*
Beytagh-Maldonado, Guillermo Jose 1957- *WhoHisp 91*
Beytelman, Mayor *BiDrAPA 89*
Bezahler, Donald J. 1932- *St&PR 91*
Bezahler, Donald Jay 1932- *WhoAm 90*
Bezahler, Harvey B 1930- *BiDrAPA 89*
Bezahler, Harvey Bernard 1930- *WhoE 91*
Bezaire, Helen Darline 1937- *WhoAmW 91*
Bezar, Gilbert Edward 1930- *WhoAm 90*
Bezark, Richard Samuel 1922- *St&PR 91*
Bezdek, Hugo Frank 1936- *WhoAm 90*
Bezdek, Patrick T *BiDrAPA 89*
Bezdicek, Albert J. 1929- *St&PR 91*
Bezencon, Jacqueline 1924- *BioIn 16*
Bezeredi, Tibor 1930- *BiDrAPA 89*
Bezic, Sandra *BioIn 16*
Bezik, Cynthia Burns 1953- *WhoAmW 91*
Bezirganian, George 1928- *BiDrAPA 89*
Bezirganian, John Bernard *BiDrAPA 89*
Bezmen, Pamir 1936- *WhoWor 91*
Bezou, Henry Charles 1913- *WhoAm 90*
Bezrodny, Igor *PenDiMP*
Bezucha, Vlastimil 1928- *EncO&P 3*
Bezzola, Eugenio Luis 1926- *WhoWor 91*
Bezzone, Albert Paul 1931- *WhoAm 90*
Bgoya, Walter 1942- *WhoWor 91*
Bhagat, Dhanraj 1917- *WhoWor 91*
Bhagat, Surinder Kumar 1935- *WhoAm 90*
Bhagwan Shree Rajneesh 1931-1990 *NewYTBS 90 [port]*
Bhajan, Yogi 1929- *NewAgE 90*
Bhaktivedanta, Swami Prabhupada 1896-1977 *EncO&P 3*
Bhalla, Ajit Singh 1939- *WhoWor 91*
Bhalla, Ravinder Nath *BiDrAPA 89*
Bhalodkar, Narendra Chandrakant 1948- *WhoAm 90*
Bhama, Savitri R *BiDrAPA 89*
Bhan, Chand Kishan 1943- *BiDrAPA 89*
Bhana, Mahomed S 1943- *BiDrAPA 89*
Bhandari, Adarsh Kumar 1946- *WhoWor 91*
Bhandari, Arvind 1950- *WhoAm 90*
Bhandari, Chitra *BiDrAPA 89*
Bhandari, Suman 1955- *WhoWor 91*
Bhandarkar, Dilip Ramaraya 1949- *WhoE 91*
Bhangoo, Surjeet Kaur *BiDrAPA 89*
Bhanot, Veena Kumari *BiDrAPA 89*
Bhapkar, Vasant P. 1931- *WhoSSW 91*
Bharadwaj, Tapobroto 1935- *WhoWor 91*
Bharati, Agehananda 1923- *EncO&P 3, WhoAm 90, WhoWrEP 89*
Bharati, Ralph 1945- *BiDrAPA 89*
Bharati, Saroja *WhoAmW 91*
Bharatiya, Pat 1942- *St&PR 91*
Bharatiya, Purabi 1945- *BiDrAPA 89*
Bhardwaj, Yogi R. 1952- *WhoEmL 91*
Bhargava, Anju Page 1956- *WhoE 91*
Bhargava, Pradeep 1943- *St&PR 91*
Bhargava, Pushpa Mittra 1928- *WhoWor 91*
Bharvaney, Tahilram Rochiram 1930- *WhoWor 91*
Bhashani, Maulani Abdul Hamid 1883-1976 *BioIn 16*
Bhaskaran, Krishnaswamy 1924- *BiDrAPA 89*
Bhaskaran, Vatsala 1955- *BiDrAPA 89*
Bhasker, Kedar Nath *BiDrAPA 89*
Bhat, Chandrahas V *BiDrAPA 89*
Bhat, Rita 1963- *WhoE 91*
Bhatara, Vinod Sagar 1945- *BiDrAPA 89*
Bhateja, Renu *BiDrAPA 89*
Bhati, Om P *BiDrAPA 89*
Bhatia, Amin *NewAgMG*
Bhatia, Anil Kumar 1945- *WhoWor 91*
Bhatia, Dil Mohan Singh 1939- *WhoSSW 91*
Bhatia, Gopal 1945- *WhoWor 91*
Bhatia, Jeet 1945- *St&PR 91*
Bhatia, June 1919- *BioIn 16*
Bhatia, Madhu *BiDrAPA 89*
Bhatia, Malini Prakash *BiDrAPA 89*
Bhatia, Maya C 1942- *BiDrAPA 89*
Bhatia, Peter K. 1953- *WhoAm 90*
Bhatia, Shashi Kanta 1946- *BiDrAPA 89*
Bhatia, Subhash C 1945- *BiDrAPA 89*
Bhatia, Subhash Chander 1945- *WhoEmL 91*
Bhatiya, Savji L 1948- *BiDrAPA 89*
Bhatla, Manmohan N. 1939- *St&PR 91*
Bhatla, Rajiv *BiDrAPA 89*
Bhatnagar, Shanti Swarupa 1894-1955 *BioIn 16*
Bhatnagar, Vinod K *BiDrAPA 89*
Bhatt, Ashok Natver 1952- *BiDrAPA 89*
Bhatt, Jagdish J 1939- *ConAu 31NR*
Bhatt, Prakash C. 1947- *St&PR 91*
Bhatt, Pravin J 1945- *BiDrAPA 89*
Bhatt, Satish Someshwar *BiDrAPA 89*
Bhatt, Sharad H *BiDrAPA 89*
Bhatt, Usha Prafulla *BiDrAPA 89*
Bhattacharjee, Swapan Kumar 1942- *WhoSSW 91*
Bhattacharya, Bhabani 1906- *WorAu 1980 [port]*
Bhattacharya, Bhabani 1906-1988 *AnObit 1988*
Bhattacharya, Pradeep Kumar 1945- *WhoSSW 91*
Bhattacharya, Purna 1946- *St&PR 91*
Bhattacharya, Subhransu Sekhar 1941- *WhoWor 91*
Bhattacharya, Syamal Kanti 1949- *WhoEmL 91, WhoWor 91*
Bhattacharya-Chatterjee, Malaya 1946- *WhoAmW 91*
Bhattacharyya, Arati M 1941- *BiDrAPA 89*
Bhattacharyya, Gargi *BiDrAPA 89*
Bhattacharyya, Gouri Kanta 1940- *WhoAm 90*
Bhattacharyya, Santosh Kumar 1927- *WhoWor 91*
Bhattacherjee, Parimal 1937- *WhoSSW 91*
Bhattarai, Krishna Prasad *WhoWor 91*
Bhatti, Mohammad Akram *BiDrAPA 89*
Bhatti, Tajammul H 1937- *BiDrAPA 89*
Bhatty, Mansukh M 1950- *BiDrAPA 89*
Bhatty, Ravji Mohanlal *BiDrAPA 89*
Bhavaraju, Murty Parabrahma 1940- *WhoAm 90*

Bhave, Pramod Raghunath 1932- *WhoWor 91*
Bhavsar, Munishvar Kantilal 1950- *WhoWor 91*
Bhavsar, Natvar Prahladji 1934- *WhoAm 90, WhoAmA 91*
Bhavsar, Raman N 1933- *BiDrAPA 89*
Bhaya Nair, Rukmini 1952- *WhoWor 91*
Bhayani, Kiran Lilachand 1944- *WhoWor 91*
Bhella, Harbans 1943-1989 *BioIn 16*
Bhichai Rattakul 1926- *WhoWor 91*
Bhide, Amar 1955- *ConAu 130*
Bhide, Anupam Keshav 1960- *WhoE 91*
Bhojak, Madan Mohan 1946- *BiDrAPA 89*
Bhojwani, Mohan *BiDrAPA 89*
Bhoothalingom, Easwara *BiDrAPA 89*
Bhore, Jayawant Narayan 1915- *BiDrAPA 89*
Bhumibol Adulyadej, His Majesty 1927- *WhoWor 91*
Bhumibol Adulyadej, King of Thailand *BioIn 16*
Bhumitra, Marina D'Souza *BiDrAPA 89*
Bhushan, Insook *BioIn 16*
Bhutta, Omar I 1945- *BiDrAPA 89*
Bhutto, Benazir *BioIn 16*
Bhutto, Benazir 1953- *ConAu 131, WhoWor 91, WomWR [port], WorAlBi*
Bhutto, Zulfikar Ali 1928-1979 *BioIn 16*
Bhuva, Bharat Laxmidas 1960- *WhoSSW 91*
Bhuyan, Elly 1942- *BiDrAPA 89*
Bhuyan, Ruprekha 1954- *BiDrAPA 89*
Biafora, Joseph R. *WhoAm 90*
Biafora, Joseph R. 1920- *St&PR 91*
Biafora, Rosanne 1962- *WhoAmW 91*
Biaggi, Cristina Shelley 1937- *WhoAmW 91, WhoWor 91*
Biaggi, Hector Roberto 1960- *BiDrAPA 89*
Biaggi, Mario 1917- *BioIn 16*
Biagi, Richard Charles 1925- *WhoAm 90*
Biagi, Shirley 1944- *ConAu 32NR*
Biagioni, Gloria M. 1928- *St&PR 91*
Biagiotti, Laura 1943- *ConDes 90, WhoWor 91*
Biago, Anthony Joseph 1938- *WhoWor 91*
Bial, Morrison David 1917- *SmATA 62*
Bial, Raymond Steven 1948- *WhoWrEP 89*
Biala, Harvey 1936- *BiDrAPA 89*
Biala, Janice 1903- *WhoAmA 91*
Bialas, Gunther 1907- *IntWWM 90*
Bialas, Paul Anthony 1949- *WhoEmL 91*
Biale, Renae *ODwPR 91*
Bialer, Philip Aaron *BiDrAPA 89*
Bialer, Seweryn 1926- *WhoAm 90*
Bialick, David W. 1942- *St&PR 91*
Bialik, Mayim *BioIn 16*
Bialk, Elisa *ConAu 131*
Bialk, Elisa 1912-1990 *BioIn 16, AuBYP 90 CurBio 90N*
Bialkin, Kenneth J. 1929- *St&PR 91*
Bialkin, Kenneth Jules 1929- *WhoAm 90*
Bialkowski, Grzegorz *BioIn 16*
Bialla, Rowley 1914- *WhoE 91*
Bialo, Walter 1917- *St&PR 91*
Bialobroda, Anna 1946- *WhoAmA 91*
Bialos, Donald S 1940- *BiDrAPA 89*
Bialostocki, Jan 1921-1988 *BioIn 16*
Bialow, Linda Gordon 1940- *WhoAmW 91*
Bialy, Linda Lee 1947- *WhoE 91*
Bianca *WomWR*
Bianca Maria *WomWR*
Bianca, Andrew Michael 1956- *WhoEmL 91*
Biancalana, Buddy 1960- *Ballpl 90*
Biancardi, Peter A. 1933- *St&PR 91*
Biancheri, John Joseph 1930- *St&PR 91*
Bianchetta, Peter Jay 1955- *WhoSSW 91*
Bianchi, Al *BioIn 16, NewYTBS 90 [port]*
Bianchi, Alfred 1932- *WhoAm 90, WhoE 91*
Bianchi, Angelo 1892-1970 *DcScB S2*
Bianchi, Bettie S. 1931- *St&PR 91*
Bianchi, Carmine Paul 1927- *WhoAm 90*
Bianchi, Charles Paul 1945- *WhoEmL 91*
Bianchi, Donald Ernest 1933- *WhoAm 90*
Bianchi, Doreen Elizabeth 1947- *WhoEmL 91*
Bianchi, Edgardo C *BiDrAPA 89*
Bianchi, James A. 1954- *ODwPR 91*
Bianchi, John *BioIn 16*
Bianchi, Laurie Ann 1964- *WhoAmW 91*
Bianchi, Lino 1920- *IntWWM 90*
Bianchi, Michael Carl 1958- *WhoEmL 91*
Bianchi, Michael D *BiDrAPA 89*
Bianchi, P. Benigno *EncO&P 3*
Bianchi, Pietro 1953- *IntWWM 90*
Bianchi, Robert N. 1944- *St&PR 91*
Bianchine, Joseph R. 1929- *St&PR 91*
Bianchini, Peter Albert 1963- *St&PR 91*
Bianco, Anthony Christopher *BiDrAPA 89*
Bianco, Fernando Jose 1944- *BiDrAPA 89*
Bianco, Hugh *BioIn 16*
Bianco, Joan 1954- *WhoAmW 91*
Bianco, Joseph Paul, Jr. 1936- *WhoAm 90*
Bianco, Margery 1881-1944 *AuBYP 90*
Bianco, Pamela 1906- *AuBYP 90*
Bianco, Peter 1963- *WhoE 91*
Biancolli, Louis 1907- *WhoWrEP 89*
Bianconi, Lorenzo Gennaro 1946- *IntWWM 90*
Biancotti, Peter Joel 1943- *St&PR 91*
Biangasso, Joseph John *BiDrAPA 89*
Bianki, Vitali *AuBYP 90*
Biardo, John Charles 1950- *WhoWrEP 89*
Biarelle, Johann Adolph *PenDiDA 89*
Biarelle, Paul Amadeus *PenDiDA 89*
Bias, Dana G. 1959- *WhoEmL 91*
Bias, Len 1963-1986 *BioIn 16*
Biasca, Rodolfo Eduardo 1944- *WhoWor 91*
Biasi, Gino P. 1931- *St&PR 91*
Biassey, Earle Lambert *BiDrAPA 89*
Bibaud, Adele 1854-1941 *DcLB 92*
Bibaud, Michel 1782-1857 *DcLB 99 [port]*
Bibaud, Richard Edgar 1937- *St&PR 91*
Bibb, Daniel Roland 1951- *WhoSSW 91*
Bibb, George Mortimer 1776-1859 *BiDrUSE 89*
Bibb, Leon 1926?- *DrBIPA 90*
Bibb, Mary Hoyt 1944- *BiDrAPA 89*
Bibb, Richard Clark 1938- *BiDrAPA 89*
Bibb, Richard E 1933- *BiDrAPA 89*
Bibb, Richard T. 1925- *St&PR 91*
Bibb, Thomas Zachary 1922- *St&PR 91*
Bibbo, Marluce 1939- *WhoAm 90*
Bibbs, Karol Lee 1935- *WhoE 91*
Bibbs, Lona Carol 1948- *WhoEmL 91*
Bibby, Douglas Martin 1946- *St&PR 91*
Bibby, Jim 1944- *Ballpl 90*
Bibby, Violet 1908- *AuBYP 90*
Bibeault, Donald B. *St&PR 91*
Bibel, Debra Jan 1945- *WhoAmW 91, WhoEmL 91*
Bibelnieks, Yanis 1946- *ODwPR 91*
Biber, Deborah 1953- *ODwPR 91*
Biber, Susanne 1952- *WhoWor 91*
Bibergal, Hillel 1945- *St&PR 91*
Biberian, Gilbert Emanuel 1944- *IntWWM 90*
Biberman, Edward 1904-1986 *WhoAmA 91N*
Biberman, Herbert J. 1900-1971 *BioIn 16*
Biberman, Lucien Morton 1919- *WhoAm 90*
Biberstein, Ernst Ludwig 1922- *WhoAm 90*
Biberstein, Marek *BioIn 16*
Bibile, Kavinda Ranil 1948- *WhoWor 91*
Bible, Alan 1909-1988 *BioIn 16*
Bible, Carl Raymond, Jr. 1958- *WhoSSW 91*
Bible, Charles 1937- *BioIn 16*
Bible, Douglas Spencer 1946- *WhoSSW 91*
Bible, Frances 1927- *IntWWM 90*
Bible, Francis Lillian *WhoAm 90*
Bible, Henry Harold 1952- *BiDrAPA 89*
Bibler, Joseph W. 1924- *St&PR 91*
Biblowitz, Jesse 1920- *WhoAm 90*
Biblowitz, Joshua 1920- *St&PR 91*
Biblowitz, Max 1907- *WhoAm 90*
Bibo, Bobette *ConAu 31NR*
Bibo, Solomon *BioIn 16*
Bicat, Tony 1945- *ConAu 130*
Bice, Clare 1909-1976 *AuBYP 90, WhoAmA 91N*
Bice, Debra Louise 1953- *WhoEmL 91*
Bice, Michael David 1956- *WhoEmL 91, WhoSSW 91*
Bice, Scott Haas 1943- *WhoAm 90*
Bice, Sue Ellen 1952- *WhoAmW 91*
Bicerano, Jozef 1952- *WhoEmL 91*
Bicester, Vivian Hugh Smith 1867-1956 *BioIn 16*
Bich, Marcel 1914- *WorAlBi*
Bicha, Karel Denis 1937- *WhoAm 90*
Bichachi, Olga Victoria 1952- *WhoHisp 91*
Bichalho Oswald, Henrique Carlos 1918-1965 *ArtLatA*
Bichara, Victor Sidhom 1924- *BiDrAPA 89*
Bichelonne, Jean 1904-1945 *BiDFrPL*
Bicher, George A. 1929- *St&PR 91*
Bichsel, Dean E. 1938- *St&PR 91*
Bichsel, Terrence Earl 1949- *St&PR 91*
Bick, Cort L. 1941- *St&PR 91*
Bick, David Greer 1953- *WhoAm 90, WhoEmL 91, WhoWor 91*
Bick, Frank C. 1927- *St&PR 91*
Bick, Ilsa Joy *BiDrAPA 89*
Bick, John William, III *BiDrAPA 89*
Bick, Katherine Livingstone 1932- *WhoAm 90, WhoAmW 91, WhoE 91*
Bick, Michael S 1943- *BiDrAPA 89*
Bick, Peter Anthony 1953- *BiDrAPA 89*
Bick, Robert Steven 1961- *WhoEmL 91, WhoWor 91*
Bickart, Theodore Albert 1935- *WhoAm 90*
Bickel, Dietrich 1932- *WhoWor 91*
Bickel, Gordon 1944- *St&PR 91*
Bickel, Henry Joseph 1929- *WhoAm 90*
Bickel, Herbert Jacob, Jr. 1930- *WhoAm 90*
Bickel, Peter John 1940- *WhoAm 90*
Bickel, Stephen Douglas 1939- *St&PR 91, WhoAm 90, WhoSSW 91*
Bickel, William Jon 1955- *WhoWrEP 89*
Bickelhaupt, Ethan Edwin 1952- *BiDrAPA 89*
Bickelhaupt, Herbert Ernst 1924- *St&PR 91*
Bicker, Daniel Wayne 1953- *WhoEmL 91*
Bickerdyke, Mary 1817-1901 *BioAmW*
Bickerdyke, Mary Ann Ball 1817-1901 *BioIn 16*
Bickerman, Hylan A. 1913- *WhoE 91*
Bickers, David Rinsey 1941- *WhoAm 90*
Bickerstaff, Bernie Lavelle 1944- *WhoAm 90*
Bickerstaff, David L. 1956- *St&PR 91*
Bickerstaff, David Lee 1956- *WhoSSW 91*
Bickerstaff, George W. 1955- *St&PR 91*
Bickerstaff, Robert 1932- *IntWWM 90*
Bickert, Robert H. 1939- *St&PR 91*
Bickerton, John Thorburn 1930- *WhoAm 90*
Bicket, Nancy Brown 1945- *WhoAmW 91*
Bickett, Robert Winston 1948- *WhoAm 90*
Bickett, Thomas J. 1939- *WhoE 91*
Bickford, Andrew Thomas 1952- *St&PR 91, WhoAm 90*
Bickford, Carol Jean 1948- *WhoAmW 91*
Bickford, Charles 1889-1967 *WorAlBi*
Bickford, Clarence E., Jr. 1935- *St&PR 91*
Bickford, Drucilla 1925- *WhoAmW 91*
Bickford, Gail Holmgren 1930- *WhoAmW 91, WhoE 91*
Bickford, George 1901- *WhoAmA 91*
Bickford, George P. 1901- *St&PR 91*
Bickford, George Percival 1901- *WhoAm 90*
Bickford, James Gordon 1928- *St&PR 91, WhoAm 90*
Bickford, John Van Buren 1934- *St&PR 91, WhoAm 90*
Bickford, Karin *St&PR 91*
Bickford, Maggie 1944- *WhoE 91*
Bickford, Nathaniel Judson 1940- *St&PR 91*
Bickford, Sharon Sue 1962- *WhoAmW 91*
Bickford, Vern 1920-1960 *Ballpl 90*
Bickham, Ben William 1929- *WhoSSW 91*
Bickham, Charles Edward, Jr. 1918- *WhoWor 91*
Bickham, Dudley Wayne 1935- *BiDrAPA 89*
Bickham, Jack M 1930- *WhoWrEP 89*
Bickham, Jack Miles 1930- *SpyFic*
Bickle, Thomas Anthony 1940- *WhoWor 91*
Bickley, Benjamin *PenDiDA 89*
Bickley, Gary Steven 1953- *WhoAmA 91*
Bickling, Dorothy Inez 1939- *WhoAmW 91*
Bickman, Leonard 1941- *BioIn 16*
Bickmore, J. Grant 1916- *WhoAm 90*
Bickmore, Roger Grant 1942- *St&PR 91*
Bicknell, Basil Cedric 1930- *WhoWor 91*
Bicknell, Charles F. 1840- *AmLegL*
Bicknell, David 1906-1988 *AnObit 1988*
Bicknell, Gene *BioIn 16*
Bicknell, John Nathan 1925- *BiDrAPA 89*
Bicknell, Joseph McCall 1933- *WhoAm 90*
Bickner, Bruce Pierce 1943- *St&PR 91, WhoAm 90*
Bicks, David Peter 1933- *WhoAm 90*
Bicks, Robert Alan 1927- *WhoAm 90*
Bicofsky, David Marc 1947- *WhoE 91*
Bicole, Baiba 1931- *EncCoWW*
Bicouvaris, Mary Vassilikou *BioIn 16*
Bida, Franco Luigi 1940- *WhoWor 91*
Bidart de Satulsky, Gay-Darlene *WhoHisp 91*
Bidault, Georges Augustin 1899-1983 *BiDFrPL*
Biddick, Bradley D. 1947- *St&PR 91*
Biddick, Roger Dean 1923- *St&PR 91*
Biddick-Liepins, Diane Kay 1954- *WhoAmW 91*
Biddinger, Paul Williams 1953- *WhoAm 90*
Biddington, William Robert 1925- *WhoAm 90*
Biddix, Fred Thomas 1960- *WhoSSW 91*
Biddix, Sharon Yvonne 1947- *WhoAmW 91*
Biddle, Albert G. W. 1930- *WhoAm 90, WhoE 91, WhoWor 91*
Biddle, Anthony Joseph Drexel 1896-1961 *BioIn 16*
Biddle, Anthony Joseph Drexel, III 1948- *WhoEmL 91*
Biddle, Bruce Jesse 1928- *WhoAm 90*
Biddle, Daniel R. *WhoAm 90*
Biddle, Flora Miller *WhoAm 90*
Biddle, Francis Beverley 1886-1968 *BiDrUSE 89*
Biddle, Gary James 1938- *St&PR 91*
Biddle, George 1885-1973 *WhoAmA 91N*
Biddle, Hester 1629-1696 *BiDEWW, FemiCLE*
Biddle, James 1783-1848 *BioIn 16*
Biddle, James 1929- *WhoAmA 91*
Biddle, John 1615-1662 *WorAlBi*
Biddle, Livingston Ludlow, Jr. 1918- *WhoAm 90, WhoAmA 91, WhoWor 91, WhoWrEP 89*
Biddle, Nicholas 1786-1844 *EncABHB 6 [port], WorAlBi*
Biddle, Samuel *AmLegL*
Biddle, Stanton Fields 1943- *WhoAm 90*
Biddle, Wayne Thomas 1924- *St&PR 91*
Biddlecome, Jack Eugene 1927- *St&PR 91*
Biddlestone, W Robert 1923- *BiDrAPA 89*
Biddy, Earl Kevin 1950- *WhoSSW 91*
Biddy, Fred Douglas 1932- *WhoSSW 91*
Biddy, Ralph Leo 1932- *BiDrAPA 89*
Bidelman, Wayne D. 1947- *St&PR 91*
Bidelman, William Pendry 1918- *WhoAm 90*
Bidelspach, David Allen 1961- *WhoSSW 91*
Biden, Joseph R. *BioIn 16*
Biden, Joseph R., Jr. 1942- *WorAlBi*
Biden, Joseph Robinette, Jr. 1942- *WhoAm 90, WhoE 91, WhoWor 91*
Bident, Pierre 1964- *WhoWor 91*
Biderman, Charles Israel 1946- *WhoEmL 91*
Biderman, Mark Charles 1945- *WhoAm 90*
Bidez, Martha Warren 1957- *WhoSSW 91*
Bidinger, Lawrence Paul 1946- *WhoEmL 91*
Bidlack, Benjamin Alden 1804-1849 *BioIn 16*
Bidlack, Jerald Dean 1935- *St&PR 91, WhoAm 90*
Bidlack, Russell Eugene 1920- *WhoAm 90*
Bidlo, Mike 1953- *WhoAmA 91*
Bidstrup, G. Peter 1930- *WhoAm 90*
Bidwell, Bennett E. 1927- *WhoAm 90*
Bidwell, Charles Edward 1932- *WhoAm 90*
Bidwell, Donald 1930- *St&PR 91*
Bidwell, Jacalyn 1946- *WhoAmW 91*
Bidwell, James Kerry 1947- *WhoEmL 91*
Bidwell, James Truman, Jr. 1934- *WhoAm 90, WhoE 91*
Bidwell, Robert E G 1932- *BiDrAPA 89*
Bidwell, Robert Ernest 1926- *WhoE 91, WhoWor 91*
Bidwell, Roger Grafton Shelford 1927- *WhoAm 90*
Bidwell, Thomas J. 1833- *AmLegL*
Bidwell, Thomas L. 1932- *St&PR 91*
Bidwell, Watson 1904- *WhoAmA 91N*
Biebel, Curt Fred, Jr. 1947- *WhoEmL 91*
Biebel, Franklin M 1908-1966 *WhoAmA 91N*
Bieber, Elinore Maria Korow 1934- *WhoAmA 91*
Bieber, Eric Bruce 1954- *ODwPR 91*
Bieber, Irving 1908- *BiDrAPA 89*
Bieber, James Richard 1942- *BiDrAPA 89*
Bieber, Margarete 1880-1978 *WhoAmA 91N*
Bieber, Owen *BioIn 16*
Bieber, Owen Frederick 1929- *EncABHB 5 [port]*
Bieber, Paul D. *St&PR 91*
Bieber, Robert Morton 1940- *WhoE 91*
Bieber-Meek, Susan Kay 1951- *WhoEmL 91*
Biebow, Hans 1902-1947 *BioIn 16*
Biebuyck, Daniel P 1925- *ConAu 30NR*
Biebuyck, Daniel Prosper 1925- *WhoAm 90*
Biebuyck, Julien Francois 1935- *WhoAm 90*
Biechler, George E. 1950- *ODwPR 91*
Biechler, George Eugene 1950- *WhoE 91*
Bieck, Gary L. 1947- *St&PR 91*
Bieck, Louis F., Jr. 1944- *St&PR 91*
Bied, Dan 1925- *WhoWrEP 89*
Biedenharn, Eric C., Jr. 1950- *St&PR 91*
Biedenharn, Lawrence C., Jr. 1922- *WhoAm 90, WhoSSW 91*
Biederman, Barron Zachary 1930- *WhoAm 90*
Biederman, Barry 1930- *ODwPR 91*
Biederman, Charles 1906- *WhoAmA 91*
Biederman, Charles Joseph 1906- *WhoAm 90*
Biederman, Donald Ellis 1934- *WhoAm 90, WhoWor 91*
Biederman, James Mark 1947- *WhoAmA 91*
Biederman, Joseph 1947- *BiDrAPA 89*
Biederman, Les *Ballpl 90*
Biederman, Ronald R. 1938- *WhoAm 90*
Biedermann, Armin Werner 1924- *St&PR 91*
Biedermann, Carlos Jorge 1954- *WhoWor 91*
Biederwolf, Robert I. 1928- *IntWWM 90*
Biediger, George Edward 1949- *WhoSSW 91*
Biedinger, Henry Jacob 1929- *St&PR 91*
Biedrzycki, Sherry Lynn *BioIn 16*
Bieganowski, Arthur Chester *BiDrAPA 89*
Biegel, Eileen Mae 1937- *WhoAmW 91*
Biegel, Paul 1925- *ConAu 32NR*

Biegel, Paul 1930- *St&PR 91*
Biegelman, Eugene Michael *BiDrAPA 89*
Biegen, Arnold Irwin 1933- *WhoAm 90*
Biegen, Elaine Ruth 1939- *WhoE 91*
Biegler, Antonius Michael 1945- *St&PR 91*
Biegler, David W. 1946- *WhoSSW 91*
Biegler, David Wayne 1946- *St&PR 91*
Biegler, Walter Joe 1942- *St&PR 91*
Biehl, Charlotte Dorothea 1731-1788 *EncCoWW*
Biehl, Dallis Derrick 1938- *WhoSSW 91*
Biehl, Elizabeth Ann 1964- *WhoEmL 91*
Biehl, Kathy Anne 1956- *WhoEmL 91*
Biehl, Kurt Edward 1960- *BiDrAPA 89*
Biehl, Mark David 1937- *BiDrAPA 89*
Biehl, Michael M. 1951- *WhoEmL 91*
Biehl, Robert John 1950- *St&PR 91*
Biehl, Robert Thomas 1952- *WhoE 91*
Biehl, Vicki 1956- *WhoWrEP 89*
Biehle, Karen Jean 1959- *WhoAmW 91*
Biehler, Rod W. 1947- *WhoEmL 91*
Biehler, Steven G. *St&PR 91*
Biehn, Michael 1957- *ConTFT 8*
Bieiris de Romans *EncCoWW*
Biekkola, Lee Raymond 1947- *St&PR 91*
Biel, George Everett 1949- *WhoEmL 91*
Biel, Jack Harold 1943- *WhoSSW 91*
Biel, Jacquelyn 1945- *WhoEmL 91*
Biel, Lindsey 1959- *WhoEmL 91*
Biela, Edward John, Jr. 1953- *WhoSSW 91*
Bielak, Robert Stanley 1946- *WhoEmL 91*
Bielawski, Barbara A. 1960- *WhoAmW 91*
Bielawski, Elizabeth Anne 1950- *WhoAmW 91*
Bielawski, Ludwik Augustyn 1929- *IntWWM 90*
Bielawski, Teresa Antonina *BiDrAPA 89*
Biele, Anthony R. 1943- *St&PR 91*
Biele, Flora Herman *BiDrAPA 89*
Bielecki, David Lee 1943- *WhoE 91*
Bielecki, Mike 1959- *Ballpl 90*
Bielecki, Paul Michael 1947- *WhoE 91, WhoEmL 91*
Bielecky, Andrew Roman, III 1937- *St&PR 91*
Bielefeld, Joan Leidy *BiDrAPA 89*
Bielefeldt, Catherine C. *WhoAmW 91*
Bielenberg, Douglas O. 1929- *St&PR 91*
Bielenberg, John David 1957- *WhoEmL 91*
Bielenstein, Hans Henrik August 1920- *WhoAm 90*
Bieler, Andre Charles 1896- *WhoAmA 91*
Bieler, Charles Linford 1935- *WhoAm 90*
Bieler, Ted Andre 1938- *WhoAmA 91*
Bieliauskas, Vytautas Joseph 1920- *WhoAm 90*
Bielinski, Bruce Walter *BiDrAPA 89*
Bielinski, Donald E. 1949- *St&PR 91*
Bielke, Patricia Anne 1949- *WhoEmL 91*
Bielkus, Algimantas V 1922- *BiDrAPA 89*
Bielman, Kenneth D. 1924- *St&PR 91*
Bielory, Abraham Melvin 1946- *WhoE 91, WhoEmL 91, WhoWor 91*
Bielory, Leonard 1954- *WhoEmL 91*
Bielowsky, Sol 1925- *St&PR 91*
Bielski, Donald Joseph 1959- *WhoEmL 91*
Bielski, Robert John 1947- *BiDrAPA 89*
Bielski, Tuvia 1906-1987 *BioIn 16*
Bielss, Otto William, Jr. 1933- *WhoSSW 91*
Bieluch, Philip James 1955- *WhoE 91, WhoEmL 91*
Biely, George Gordon *BiDrAPA 89*
Biemann, Dominik 1800-1857 *PenDiDA 89*
Biemann, Klaus 1926- *WhoAm 90*
Biemeck, Bruce J. 1949- *St&PR 91*
Biemiller, Carl Ludwig 1912-1979 *AuBYP 90*
Bien, Frederic Vincent 1961- *WhoE 91*
Bien, Joseph Julius 1936- *ConAu 31NR, WhoAm 90*
Bien, Michael W. 1955- *WhoEmL 91*
Bien, Peter Adolph 1930- *WhoAm 90, WhoWrEP 89*
Bien, Robert Lowell 1923- *St&PR 91*
Bien, Zeungnam 1943- *WhoWor 91*
Bieneck, Bjorn 1943- *St&PR 91*
Bienefeld, David Gerald 1953- *BiDrAPA 89*
Bienema, Kristine K. 1962- *WhoAmW 91*
Bienen, Leigh Buchanan 1938- *WhoWrEP 89*
Bienenfeld, David Gerald 1953- *WhoEmL 91*
Bienenfeld, Jerome 1923- *St&PR 91*
Bienenfeld, Marvin S. 1932- *St&PR 91*
Bienenstock, Arthur Irwin 1935- *WhoAm 90*
Bienenstock, Audrie Marie *BiDrAPA 89*
Bienenstock, Bruce 1945- *BiDrAPA 89*
Bienenstock, John 1936- *WhoAm 90*
Biener, Robert 1925- *BiDrAPA 89*
Bienert, Walter B. 1931- *St&PR 91*
Bienfait, Aline 1941- *BiDWomA*
Bieniawski, Zdzislaw Tadeusz 1936- *WhoAm 90*
Biennais, Martin-Guillaume 1764-1843 *PenDiDA 89*
Bienville, Sieur De 1680-1768 *WorAlBi*
Bienville, Jean-B Le Moyne, Sieur de 1680-1767 *EncCRAm*
Bienville, Jean Baptiste Le M., Sieur De 1680-1768 *WhNaAH*
Bienz, Darrel Rudolph 1926- *WhoAm 90*
Bier, Barry 1945- *St&PR 91*
Bier, Carol Manson 1947- *WhoEmL 91*
Bier, Martin M *BiDrAPA 89*
Bier, Rob 1949- *WhoEmL 91*
Bierbauer, Lou 1865-1926 *Ballpl 90*
Bierbaum, Dennis Robert 1937- *St&PR 91*
Bierbaum, Edward *St&PR 91*
Bierbaum, J. Armin 1924- *WhoAm 90*
Bierbaum, Janith Marie 1927- *WhoAmW 91*
Bierbaum, Otto Julius 1865-1910 *BioIn 16*
Bierbaum, Paul Martin, Jr. 1946- *WhoEmL 91*
Bierbaum, Philip James 1942- *WhoAm 90*
Bierbaum, Robert 1912- *St&PR 91*
Bierbrier, Doreen 1946- *WhoWrEP 89*
Bierce, Ambrose 1842-1914? *BioIn 16, WorAlBi*
Bierce, Carol Anne Hoover 1954- *WhoAmW 91*
Bierce, Harley Ross 1941- *St&PR 91*
Bierce, William B. 1949- *WhoEmL 91*
Biercuk, Jeffrey A. 1945- *St&PR 91*
Bierdeman, Louise J. 1949- *St&PR 91*
Bierds, Linda Louise 1945- *WhoWrEP 89*
Bierdz, Thom *BioIn 16*
Bierer, Lee S. 1954- *ODwPR 91*
Bierer, Linda Margret *BiDrAPA 89*
Bierfreund, Sigmund 1620-1702 *PenDiDA 89*
Bierhoff, Hans Werner 1948- *WhoWor 91*
Bierhorst, John W. 1936- *AuBYP 90*
Bieri, Jacqueline Elizabeth 1962- *WhoAmW 91*
Bieri, Michael D *BiDrAPA 89*
Bierig, Jack R. 1947- *WhoEmL 91*
Bierig, Jeffrey D. *ODwPR 91*
Biering-Sorensen, Fin 1948- *WhoWor 91*
Bieringa, Luitjen Hendrik 1942- *WhoWor 91*
Bieringer, Walter H. 1899- *WhoAm 90*
Bierkamt, Robert 1945- *St&PR 91*
Bierley, John Charles 1936- *WhoAm 90*
Bierley, Paul Edmund 1926- *IntWWM 90, WhoAm 90*
Bierlin, Thelma Pauline 1927- *St&PR 91*
Bierly, Edward J 1920- *WhoAmA 91*
Bierly, Eugene Wendell 1931- *WhoAm 90*
Bierman, Carl A. 1914- *St&PR 91*
Bierman, Charles Warren 1924- *WhoAm 90*
Bierman, Dick 1943- *EncPaPR 91*
Bierman, Edwin Lawrence 1930- *WhoAm 90*
Bierman, Everett Eugene 1924- *WhoWor 91*
Bierman, George William 1925- *WhoAm 90*
Bierman, Harold, Jr. 1924- *WhoAm 90*
Bierman, Irene A *WhoAmA 91*
Bierman, Jane Carl 1919- *St&PR 91*
Bierman, Joseph S 1927- *BiDrAPA 89*
Bierman, Judith Ann 1950- *WhoEmL 91*
Bierman, Rebecca Sue *BiDrAPA 89*
Bierman, Samuel 1902-1978 *WhoAmA 91N*
Biermann, Aenne Sternefeld 1898-1933 *BioIn 16*
Biermann, Charles H. 1930- *St&PR 91*
Biernacki, Halina T. *WhoE 91*
Biernacki-Poray, Wlad Otton 1924- *St&PR 91*
Biernat, Lillian M. Nahumenuk 1931- *WhoE 91, WhoWor 91*
Biernoff, Michael P 1946- *BiDrAPA 89*
Bierschbach, Raymond Anton 1933- *WhoAm 90*
Bierstadt, Albert 1830-1902 *BioIn 16, IntDcAA 90, WhNaAH, WorAlBi*
Bierstedt, Peter Richard 1943- *WhoAm 90*
Bierstedt, Robert 1913- *WhoAm 90, WhoWrEP 89*
Biersteker, Melvin C. 1950- *St&PR 91*
Bierut, Michael *BioIn 16*
Bierwirth, John C. 1924- *St&PR 91*
Bierwirth, John Cocks 1924- *WhoAm 90*
Bierwirth, Warren Moise 1950- *WhoWor 91*
Bierylo, John I. 1941- *St&PR 91*
Bies, Barbara Agnes 1962- *WhoAmW 91*
Bies, Susan Schmidt 1947- *St&PR 91, WhoAm 90, WhoAmW 91*
Biesanz, Mavis Hiltunen 1919- *BioIn 16*
Biese, Leo Paul 1932- *WhoAm 90*
Biesecker, James Robert 1950- *WhoE 91*
Biesecker, Norma Jean 1939- *WhoE 91*
Biesel, David Barrie 1931- *WhoE 91*
Biesel, Diane Jane 1934- *WhoAmW 91*
Biesele, John Julius 1918- *WhoAm 90, WhoWor 91*
Biesemeier, John Allen 1946- *WhoAm 90*
Biesenbach, Ginn M. 1924- *St&PR 91*
Bieser, Harold Leslie 1928- *St&PR 91*
Biess, Barbara Dziedzic 1963- *WhoAmW 91*
Biester, Edward George, Jr. 1931- *WhoAm 90*
Biesterfeld, Craig Stewart 1953- *WhoEmL 91*
Biesterfeld, Wolfgang Heinrich 1940- *WhoWor 91*
Bieter, Thomas G 1939- *BiDrAPA 89*
Bietz, Ralph L. R. 1953- *WhoSSW 91*
Biever, Angela Mary 1953- *WhoEmL 91*
Biever, John Albert *BiDrAPA 89*
Biever, Robert Henry 1931- *St&PR 91*
Biever-Mondavi, Margrit *BioIn 16*
Biewen, Robert L. 1936- *WhoWrEP 89*
Biewener, Kelly Ann 1957- *WhoAmW 91, WhoEmL 91*
Bifano, George M 1942- *BiDrAPA 89*
Biferie, Dan, Jr 1950- *WhoAmA 91*
Biffi, Giacomo 1928- *WhoWor 91*
Biffle, Richard Lee, III 1949- *WhoEmL 91*
Big Bear 1825-1888 *WhNaAH [port]*
Big Bopper, The *EncPR&S 89*
Big Bow 1830?-1900? *WhNaAH*
Big Brother and the Holding Company *EncPR&S 89*
Big Eagle 1827-1906 *WhNaAH*
Big Elk 1772?-1846 *WhNaAH*
Big Foot 1825?-1890 *WhNaAH*
Big Hawk Chief 1850?- *WhNaAH*
Big Jim 1834-1900 *WhNaAH*
Big Tree 1847?-1929 *WhNaAH*
Big Warrior *WhNaAH*
Big White *WhNaAH*
Big, Susan Nagy 1946- *WhoAmW 91*
Bigaouette, Laura Ann 1960- *WhoE 91, WhoEmL 91*
Bigard, Barney 1906-1980 *BioIn 16, OxCPMus*
Bigaud, Wilson 1931- *ArtLatA*
Bigback, Bonnie Dee Woodward 1950- *WhoAmW 91*
Bigbee, Carson 1895-1964 *Ballpl 90*
Bigbie, Charles Roy, III 1959- *WhoEmL 91, WhoSSW 91*
Bigbie, John Taylor 1923- *WhoAm 90*
Bigda, John Paul 1938- *St&PR 91*
Bigda, Rudolph A. 1916- *WhoSSW 91*
Bigeleisen, Jacob 1919- *WhoAm 90*
Bigelow, Anita 1946- *WhoAmA 91*
Bigelow, Beverly 1947- *WhoAmW 91*
Bigelow, Charles Cross 1928- *WhoAm 90*
Bigelow, David Skinner, III 1931- *WhoWor 91*
Bigelow, Donald Nevius 1918- *WhoAm 90, WhoE 91*
Bigelow, E. Thayer, Jr. 1941- *St&PR 91*
Bigelow, Erastus B. 1814-1879 *WorAlBi*
Bigelow, Eugene Thayer, Jr. 1941- *WhoAm 90*
Bigelow, G. B. *AmLegL*
Bigelow, Gayle *BiDrAPA 89*
Bigelow, Howard E. 1923-1987 *BioIn 16*
Bigelow, Jane 1933- *WhoE 91*
Bigelow, John 1817-1911 *BioIn 16*
Bigelow, John B. *BioIn 16*
Bigelow, Jonathan Lehr 1950- *WhoEmL 91*
Bigelow, Kathryn *BioIn 16*
Bigelow, Kathryn 1952?- *News 90 [port]*
Bigelow, Llewellyn B 1936- *BiDrAPA 89*
Bigelow, Lynne Thayer 1942- *WhoAmW 91*
Bigelow, Margaret Elizabeth Barr 1923- *WhoAmW 91*
Bigelow, Martha Mitchell 1921- *WhoAm 90, WhoAmW 91*
Bigelow, Newton J T *BiDrAPA 89*
Bigelow, Page Elizabeth 1948- *WhoAmW 91, WhoEmL 91*
Bigelow, Richard A. 1931- *St&PR 91*
Bigelow, Robert Clayton 1940- *WhoAmA 91*
Bigelow, Robert O. 1926- *St&PR 91*
Bigelow, Robert P. 1927- *WhoAm 90*
Bigelow, Timothy L. 1939- *ODwPR 91*
Bigelow, William R. 1928- *WhoAm 90*
Bigelow Burton, Mary D. *WhoWor 91*
Bigelow-Lourie, Anne Edwige 1946- *WhoAmW 91*
Bigg, John Herbert 1930- *IntWWM 90*
Biggar, James McCrea 1928- *St&PR 91, WhoAm 90*
Biggar, John R. 1944- *St&PR 91*
Biggar, Robert McCrea 1932- *St&PR 91*
Biggart, Eleanor Marie 1926- *WhoWrEP 89*
Bigger, B. Frank 1942- *St&PR 91*
Bigger, Hester 1919- *WhoAmW 91*
Bigger, John P. 1934- *St&PR 91, WhoAm 90*
Bigger, John Thomas, Jr. 1935- *WhoAm 90*
Bigger, Joseph M. *AmLegL*
Bigger, Margaret Goldsborough 1939- *WhoWrEP 89*
Bigger, Michael D 1937- *WhoAmA 91*
Bigger, Richard Andrew, Jr. 1937- *WhoSSW 91*
Biggers, Ann Peeples 1943- *WhoWrEP 89*
Biggers, Earl Derr 1884-1933 *TwCCr&M 91, WorAlBi*
Biggers, Emory Melvin 1951- *WhoE 91*
Biggers, John Thomas 1924- *WhoAmA 91*
Biggers, Neal Brooks, Jr. 1935- *WhoSSW 91*
Biggers, W.J. 1928- *St&PR 91*
Biggers, William Henry 1934- *BiDrAPA 89*
Biggers, William Joseph 1928- *WhoAm 90, WhoSSW 91, WhoWor 91*
Biggerstaff, Marilyn Anne 1946- *WhoEmL 91*
Biggerstaff, Myra 1905- *WhoAmA 91*
Biggins, Charles Clyde 1935- *St&PR 91*
Biggins, Cloice Henry *BiDrAPA 89*
Biggins, Franklin N. 1946- *WhoEmL 91*
Biggins, James J. 1928- *St&PR 91*
Biggio, Craig *BioIn 16*
Biggio, Craig 1965- *Ballpl 90*
Biggle, Lloyd, Jr. 1923- *RGTwCSF*
Biggott, Robert B. 1952- *St&PR 91*
Biggs, Arthur Edward 1930- *WhoAm 90*
Biggs, Barton Michael 1932- *WhoAm 90*
Biggs, Clinton A. 1911- *St&PR 91*
Biggs, David H. 1945- *St&PR 91*
Biggs, Donald Anthony 1936- *WhoAm 90*
Biggs, E. Glenn 1933- *St&PR 91*
Biggs, E Power 1906-1977 *PenDiMP*
Biggs, E. Power 1906-1977 *WorAlBi*
Biggs, Edmund Logan 1938- *WhoE 91, WhoWor 91*
Biggs, Electra Waggoner 1916- *WhoAm 90, WhoSSW 91*
Biggs, Fowler A 1917- *BiDrAPA 89*
Biggs, Frederick William 1927- *WhoWor 91*
Biggs, Gary Damian 1948- *St&PR 91*
Biggs, Gordon Brian 1959- *WhoSSW 91*
Biggs, Hugh Lawry 1904- *WhoAm 90*
Biggs, J. O. 1925- *WhoAm 90*
Biggs, Jackson T *BiDrAPA 89*
Biggs, James Pearson 1940- *St&PR 91*
Biggs, Jane Ewart- *BioIn 16*
Biggs, Janet 1959- *WhoAmA 91*
Biggs, Jeremy Hunt 1935- *St&PR 91, WhoE 91*
Biggs, Jerry Armand 1940- *BiDrAPA 89*
Biggs, John H. 1936- *St&PR 91*
Biggs, John Herron 1936- *WhoAm 90, WhoE 91*
Biggs, John Thomas *BiDrAPA 89*
Biggs, Lawrence Raymond, Jr. 1959- *WhoSSW 91*
Biggs, Margaret Key 1933- *WhoWrEP 89*
Biggs, Mark McCampbell 1954- *WhoEmL 91*
Biggs, Mary 1944- *WhoWrEP 89*
Biggs, Murchison Bolton 1954- *St&PR 91*
Biggs, Paul Joseph 1952- *WhoEmL 91*
Biggs, Rittie Jean 1942- *WhoAmW 91*
Biggs, Robert Dale 1934- *WhoAm 90*
Biggs, Ronald 1929- *BioIn 16*
Biggs, Sewell C. 1823-1889 *AmLegL*
Biggs, Shirley A. 1937- *WhoE 91*
Biggs, Susan Leah 1952- *WhoSSW 91*
Biggs, Thomas Jones 1912- *WhoAm 90*
Biggs, Thomas Wylie 1950- *WhoEmL 91*
Biggs, Tina Cornelius 1957- *WhoAmW 91*
Biggs, Wellington Allen 1923- *WhoAm 90, WhoWrEP 89*
Biggs-Davison, John 1918-1988 *AnObit 1988*
Biggy, Mary Virginia 1924- *WhoAm 90, WhoAmW 91, WhoE 91, WhoWor 91*
Bigham, James E. 1951- *WhoEmL 91*
Bigham, James John 1937- *St&PR 91*
Bigham, Thomas J. 1911-1990 *BioIn 16*
Bigham, Wanda Durrett *WhoAm 90, WhoAmW 91*
Bighley, Mark Steven 1954- *WhoSSW 91*
Bigi, Leonardo Antonio 1942- *WhoWor 91*
Bigler, Bernard Philip 1952- *WhoE 91*
Bigler, David Alan 1936- *St&PR 91*
Bigler, Eddie Lee 1953- *WhoSSW 91*
Bigler, Harold Edwin, Jr. 1931- *WhoAm 90*
Bigler, Harold S. 1926- *St&PR 91*
Bigler, John 1805-1871 *AmLegL*
Bigler, M. Jayn 1958- *WhoWrEP 89*
Bigler, William Eugene, Jr. 1935- *St&PR 91*
Bigley, Nancy Jane 1932- *WhoAm 90*
Bigley, Roger *PenDiMP*
Bigley, William Joseph, Jr. 1924- *WhoAm 90, WhoE 91*
Biglieri, Edward George 1925- *WhoAm 90*
Bigman, Anton W. 1929- *WhoE 91*
Bigman, Orin L. 1954- *BiDrAPA 89*
Bignami, Mauro 1944- *WhoWor 91*
Bigois *EncO&P 3*
Bigongiari, Mary Julia 1945- *WhoAmW 91, WhoWor 91*
Bigot, Alexandre 1862-1927 *PenDiDA 89*
Bigot, Eugene 1888-1965 *PenDiMP*

Bigot, Jean-Michel Roger 1935- *WhoWor 91*
Bigot, Marie 1786-1820 *PenDiMP*
Bigotis *EncO&P 3*
Bigsby, Helene Hathaway Robinson 1878-1950 *Ballpl 90*
Biguenet, John Joseph 1949- *WhoWrEP 89*
Bigus, Lawrence Weaver 1955- *WhoEmL 91*
Bigwood, Gerald Frank 1924- *BiDrAPA 89*
Bigwood, Robert Maurice 1918- *St&PR 91*
Bihari, Bernard *BiDrAPA 89*
Bihari, Bernard 1931- *WhoE 91*
Bihary, David Joseph 1947- *WhoE 91*
Bihary, Joyce *WhoAmW 91*
Bihary, Kristen M. 1953- *ODwPR 91*
Bihldorff, John Pearson 1945- *WhoAm 90*
Bihlmeyer, Larry Lee 1946- *WhoSSW 91*
Bihr, James Elwood 1927- *WhoAm 90*
Biilmann, Einar Christian Saxtorph 1873-1946 *BioIn 16*
Biittner, Larry 1946- *Ballpl 90*
Bijker, Eco Wiebe 1924- *WhoWor 91*
Bijlani, Judith Ann 1949- *WhoAmW 91*
Bijlani, Subash Khanchand 1942- *WhoWor 91*
Bijlsma, Anner *PenDiMP*
Bijns, Anna 1493-1575 *EncCoWW*
Bijou, Sidney William 1908- *WhoAm 90*
Bijur, Peter I. *WhoAm 90, WhoWor 91*
Bijur, Peter I. 1942- *St&PR 91*
Bikadoroff, Serge 1934- *BiDrAPA 89*
Bikales, Norman Allen 1935- *WhoAm 90, WhoE 91*
Bikales, Victor W *BiDrAPA 89*
Bike, William Stanley 1957- *WhoWrEP 89*
Bikel, Theodore 1924- *IntWWM 90, WhoAm 90, WorAlBi*
Bikkembergs, Dirk *BioIn 16*
Biklen, Paul 1915- *WhoAm 90*
Biko, Stephen 1946-1977 *BioIn 16*
Bilal, Ali Mustafa 1938- *WhoWor 91*
Bilandic, Michael A. 1923- *WhoAm 90*
Bilanluk, Larissa Tetiana 1941- *WhoAmW 91*
Bilaniuk, Olexa Myron 1926- *WhoAm 90*
Bilardello, Dann 1959- *Ballpl 90*
Bilawsky, Mark A. 1947- *St&PR 91*
Bilbao, Francisco 1823-1865 *BioIn 16*
Bilbao, Francisco Ernesto 1933- *WhoHisp 91*
Bilberry, Debra Sue 1954- *WhoEmL 91*
Bilbow, James Robert 1923- *WhoE 91*
Bilbray, Fred Richard 1939- *St&PR 91*
Bilbray, James Hubert 1938- *WhoAm 90*
Bilby, Richard Mansfield 1931- *WhoAm 90*
Bilderbach, Joe 1938- *St&PR 91*
Bilderback, Willis Peter *BioIn 16*
Bildersee, Robert Alan 1942- *WhoAm 90*
Bildner, James Lebson 1954- *WhoE 91*
Bildner, Stuart 1950- *St&PR 91*
Bile, Abdi *BioIn 16*
Bilello, John Charles 1938- *WhoAm 90*
Bilello, John H. *WhoAm 90*
Bilenky, William Stephen 1945- *WhoSSW 91*
Biles, John Alexander 1923- *WhoAm 90*
Biles, John D. *AmLegL*
Biles, Marilyn Marta 1935- *WhoAmW 91*
Biles, Murray Robert 1931- *St&PR 91*
Biles, Robert Erle 1942- *WhoSSW 91*
Biles, William Roger 1950- *WhoSSW 91*
Bilezikjian, John Haig 1948- *WhoEmL 91*
Bilfield, Jennifer Frances 1965- *WhoE 91*
Bilgen, Albert William 1927- *WhoAm 90*
Bilger, David Victor 1945- *IntWWM 90, WhoEmL 91*
Bilger, Jeffrey M. 1960- *St&PR 91*
Bilger, Paul Cameron 1927- *St&PR 91*
Bilgutay, Sabahattin *BiDrAPA 89*
Bilhardt, Diane Marie 1952- *WhoE 91*
Bilhartz, John Francis 1921- *WhoSSW 91*
Bilheimer, Robert William 1956- *WhoE 91*
Bilhorn, William W. 1930- *WhoAm 90*
Bilibin, Ivan 1876-1942 *SmATA 61 [port]*
Bilich, John M. 1935- *St&PR 91*
Bilimoria, Minoo Manekshah 1932- *WhoWor 91*
Bilimoria, Pheroza Jimmy 1951- *WhoWor 91*
Bilinkas, Edward W. *BioIn 16*
Bilinska, Anna 1857-1893 *BiDWomA [port]*
Bilinska-Bohdanowicz, Anna 1857-1893 *BiDWomA [port]*
Bilinski, John Nestor 1947- *WhoEmL 91*
Bilinski, Raynold J. 1946- *WhoE 91*
Bilinsky, Yaroslav 1932- *WhoAm 90, WhoWor 91*
Bilirakis, Michael 1930- *WhoAm 90, WhoSSW 91*
Bilivert, Jacopo 1550-1603 *PenDiDA 89*
Biliverti, Jacopo 1550-1603 *PenDiDA 89*
Biliyar, Vedavyasa B 1957- *BiDrAPA 89*
Bilk, Acker 1929- *OxCPMus*
Bilk, Bernard Stanley 1929- *IntWWM 90*
Bilka, Paul Joseph 1919- *WhoAm 90*
Bilker, Iris June 1927- *BiDrAPA 89*
Bilker, Mindy Sue 1952- *WhoAmW 91*
Bilkey, Beverly Yvonne 1926- *WhoAmW 91*
Bilko, Steve 1928-1978 *Ballpl 90*
Bill, Aydin Zekai *BiDrAPA 89*
Bill, Buffalo 1846-1917 *BioIn 16*
Bill, G. Dana 1926- *St&PR 91*
Bill, Ingraham Ebenezer 1805-1891 *DcCanB 12*
Bill, J Brent 1951- *WhoWrEP 89*
Bill, Max 1908- *BioIn 16, ConDes 90, PenDiDA 89, WhoWor 91*
Bill, Robert O *BiDrAPA 89*
Bill, Sharon Lynn 1946- *WhoAmW 91*
Bill, Tony *BioIn 16*
Bill, Tony 1940- *WhoAm 90*
Billam, Rosemary 1952- *SmATA 61*
Billante, Samuel J. 1942- *St&PR 91*
Billard, Jean 1933- *WhoWor 91*
Billau, Robin Louise 1951- *WhoAmW 91*
Billcliffe, Roger 1946- *ConAu 132*
Bille, Donald Allen 1943- *WhoE 91*
Bille, Jean-Georges 1931- *WhoWor 91*
Bille, S. Corinna 1912-1979 *EncCoWW*
Billeci, Andre George 1933- *WhoAmA 91*
Billen, Thomas Raymond 1945- *St&PR 91*
Biller Family *PenDiDA 89*
Biller, Albrecht 1663-1720 *PenDiDA 89*
Biller, Carmen George 1953- *WhoEmL 91*
Biller, Charles Mayo 1926- *BiDrAPA 89*
Biller, Frank Joseph 1953- *St&PR 91*
Biller, Henry Burt 1940- *WhoAm 90*
Biller, Hugh Frederick 1934- *WhoAm 90*
Biller, Joel Wilson 1929- *WhoAm 90*
Biller, Johann Jacob *PenDiDA 89*
Biller, Johann Ludwig 1656-1746 *PenDiDA 89*
Biller, Johann Ludwig 1692-1746 *PenDiDA 89*
Biller, Johannes 1696-1745 *PenDiDA 89*
Biller, Morris 1915- *WhoAm 90, WhoE 91*
Biller, Pamela Manno 1954- *WhoAmW 91*
Billerbeck, Margarethe 1945- *WhoWor 91*
Billeres, Rene 1910- *BiDFrPL*
Billes, D.G. 1938- *St&PR 91*
Billes, I. V. 1919- *WhoAm 90*
Billet, Sanford Louis 1926- *BiDrAPA 89*
Billetdoux, Raphaele 1951- *EncCoWW*
Billgert, Stig Nils 1928- *WhoWor 91*
Billharz, Constance Ellen Clark 1921- *WhoAmW 91*
Billia, Darlene A. 1948- *WhoAmW 91*
Billian, Cathey R *WhoAmA 91, WhoE 91*
Billian, Virginia L 1939- *BiDrAPA 89*
Billias, George Athan 1919- *WhoAm 90, WhoE 91*
Billick, Stephen Bates 1947- *BiDrAPA 89*
Billie, L. Clark 1938- *St&PR 91*
Billig, Arnold *BioIn 16*
Billig, Erwin H. 1927- *WhoAm 90*
Billig, Frederick Stucky 1933- *WhoE 91*
Billig, Nathan 1941- *BiDrAPA 89*
Billig, Otto 1910- *BiDrAPA 89, ConAu 129*
Billig, Thomas Clifford 1930- *WhoAm 90*
Billik, Eugene 1927- *St&PR 91*
Billing, Grant D. 1951- *St&PR 91*
Billing, Terence N. *ODwPR 91*
Billingham, Jack 1943- *Ballpl 90*
Billingham, Rupert Everett 1921- *WhoAm 90*
Billinghurst, Guillermo 1851-1915 *BioIn 16*
Billings, Bruce Hadley 1915- *WhoAm 90*
Billings, Charlene W. *AuBYP 90*
Billings, Charles Edgar 1929- *WhoAm 90*
Billings, Charles Kelso, Jr. 1947- *BiDrAPA 89*
Billings, Cynthia Anne 1933- *WhoAmW 91*
Billings, David Alan 1945- *St&PR 91*
Billings, David S. 1942- *St&PR 91*
Billings, Dick 1942- *Ballpl 90*
Billings, Edward Robert 1913- *WhoAm 90*
Billings, Edwin C. 1933- *St&PR 91*
Billings, Franklin Swift, Jr. 1922- *WhoAm 90, WhoE 91*
Billings, Harold Wayne 1931- *WhoAm 90, WhoWrEP 89*
Billings, Henry 1901-1987 *WhoAmA 91N*
Billings, Karen S. 1943- *St&PR 91*
Billings, Luanne *BioIn 16*
Billings, Marland Pratt 1902- *WhoAm 90*
Billings, Martin Hewett *WhoE 91*
Billings, Patricia Ann Collins 1946- *WhoAmW 91*
Billings, Peggy Marie 1928- *WhoAmW 91*
Billings, Peter Watson 1917- *St&PR 91*
Billings, Suzanne Chung-A-On 1963- *WhoAmW 91*
Billings, Thomas Neal 1931- *WhoWor 91*
Billings, William 1746-1800 *BioIn 16, EncCRAm*
Billings, William Dwight 1910- *WhoAm 90*
Billings, William Howard 1921- *WhoAm 90*
Billingslea, Charles 1914-1989 *BioIn 16*
Billingsley, Bill Brian 1948- *WhoSSW 91*
Billingsley, Charles E. 1933- *St&PR 91*
Billingsley, David Lewis, Jr. 1957- *WhoSSW 91*
Billingsley, James Ray 1927- *St&PR 91, WhoAm 90*
Billingsley, John C. 1941- *St&PR 91*
Billingsley, Ray *BioIn 16*
Billingsley, Robert Earl, Jr. 1954- *BiDrAPA 89*
Billingsley, Robert Thaine 1954- *WhoEmL 91*
Billingsley, Thad Hoffman 1941- *BiDrAPA 89*
Billingsley, Weyland Dee, Jr. 1946- *WhoSSW 91*
Billingsley, William 1758-1828 *PenDiDA 89*
Billingsley, William Franklin, III 1958- *WhoSSW 91*
Billington, Barry E. 1940- *WhoSSW 91*
Billington, David Perkins 1927- *WhoAm 90*
Billington, Deborah Gail 1949- *WhoAmW 91*
Billington, Elizabeth 1765-1818 *PenDiMP*
Billington, Elizabeth T. *BioIn 16*
Billington, James 1929- *News 90 [port], -90-3 [port]*
Billington, James H. 1929- *BioIn 16, ConAu 132, WorAlBi*
Billington, James Hadley 1929- *WhoAm 90, WhoE 91, WhoWor 91*
Billington, Rachel 1942- *WorAu 1980 [port]*
Billington, Steven Miles 1952- *WhoEmL 91*
Billington, Wilbur T. 1922- *WhoAm 90*
Billington, William Howard, Jr. 1924- *St&PR 91, WhoAm 90*
Billinsky, John Milton, Jr. 1947- *BiDrAPA 89*
Billinsley, Charles Edward 1933- *St&PR 91*
Billinton, Roy 1935- *WhoAm 90*
Billiter, William Overton, Jr. 1934- *WhoAm 90, WhoWrEP 89*
Billman, Irwin Edward 1940- *WhoAm 90, WhoWor 91, WhoWrEP 89*
Billmeyer, Fred Wallace, Jr. 1919- *WhoAm 90*
Billmeyer, Kurt Conrad 1955- *St&PR 91*
Billmire, Karen Leigh *BiDrAPA 89*
Billmyer, John Edward 1912- *WhoAmA 91*
Billot, G. P. *EncO&P 3*
Billout, Guy *BioIn 16*
Billoux, Francois 1903-1976 *BiDFrPL*
Billow, Marvin L. 1929- *St&PR 91*
Billowitz, Aaron T 1940- *BiDrAPA 89*
Bills, Daniel G. 1924- *St&PR 91*
Bills, John T., Mrs. 1911- *WhoAmW 91*
Bills, Lyndra Jewell *BiDrAPA 89*
Bills, Marvin Lee *BiDrAPA 89*
Bills, Mitchell 1950- *WhoAmA 91*
Bills, Robert Howard 1944- *WhoAm 90*
Bills, Scott Laurence 1948- *WhoSSW 91*
Bills, Sheryl Jean 1945- *WhoWrEP 89*
Billups, Charles Edward 1929- *St&PR 91*
Billups, Clinton Ford, Jr. 1947- *WhoEmL 91*
Billups, Norman Fredrick 1934- *WhoAm 90*
Billy Boy *BioIn 16*
Billy, the Kid *BioIn 16*
Billy The Kid 1859-1881 *WorAlBi*
Billy, Dennis Joseph 1953- *WhoWor 91*
Bilodeau, Alain 1950- *St&PR 91*
Bilodeau, Louis E. 1952- *St&PR 91*
Bilodeau, Steven Jules 1958- *St&PR 91*
Bilodeaux, Caitlin *BioIn 16*
Bilolikar, Suresh 1943- *BiDrAPA 89*
Bilotta, Diane Briley 1953- *WhoAmW 91*
Bilotta, Jeffrey Joseph 1950- *WhoE 91*
Bilotti, Eugene 1949- *St&PR 91*
Bilotti, Michael Joseph 1941- *St&PR 91, WhoAm 90*
Bilotti, Salvatore F 1879-1953 *WhoAmA 91N*
Bilous, Priscilla Haley *WhoAmA 91*
Bilow, Alison Leigh 1960- *WhoAmW 91*
Bilow, Steven Craig 1960- *WhoEmL 91*
Bilowit, David Solomon 1921- *WhoSSW 91*
Bilozerchev, Dmitri *BioIn 16*
Bilpuch, Edward George 1927- *WhoAm 90, WhoWor 91*
Bilsing, David Charles 1933- *St&PR 91, WhoAm 90*
Bilski, Peter 1918- *WhoWor 91*
Bilsky, Earl 1928- *St&PR 91*
Bilsky, Manuel 1910- *WhoAm 90*
Bilson, F. Barry 1953- *St&PR 91*
Bilstein, Robert *BioIn 16*
Biltcliffe, George Henry 1935- *St&PR 91*
Bilton, Stuart Douglas 1946- *St&PR 91*
Bilton, William George 1944- *WhoSSW 91*
Biltonen, Rodney Lincoln 1937- *WhoAm 90*
Biltz, Stuart James 1946- *WhoEmL 91*
Bilyea, M.E. 1947- *St&PR 91*
Bilyi, Mikhail Ulianovich *WhoWor 91*
Bilzerian, Paul A. *BioIn 16*
Biman, Dominik *PenDiDA 89*
Bimba, Anthony 1894-1982 *EncAL*
Bimberg, Dieter Herbert 1942- *WhoWor 91*
Bimberg, Siegfried Wolfgang 1927- *IntWWM 90*
Bimblick, Warren N. 1954- *ODwPR 91*
Bimmerle, John Francis 1912- *BiDrAPA 89*
Bimrose, Arthur Sylvanus, Jr 1912- *WhoAmA 91*
Bimson, Carl Alfred 1900- *WhoAm 90*
Bimson, Earl L. 1921- *St&PR 91*
Bimson, Walter Reed 1892-1980 *EncABHB 7 [port]*
Bimstein, Irving I. 1926- *St&PR 91*
Bimstein, Ronnie 1956- *St&PR 91*
Bina, Cyrus 1946- *WhoE 91*
Bina, Gian Carlo 1935- *WhoWor 91*
Bina, Shashi 1943- *BiDrAPA 89*
Binai, Paul Freye 1932- *WhoAmA 91, WhoE 91*
Binaisa, Godfrey *BioIn 16*
Biname, Charles 1949- *WhoEmL 91*
Binau, Donald C. 1927- *St&PR 91*
Binazzi, Lapo 1943- *BioIn 16*
Binbasgil, Seda 1959- *WhoWor 91*
Bincer, Adam Marian 1930- *WhoAm 90*
Bincer, Wanda Lawendel *BiDrAPA 89*
Binch, James Gardner 1947- *WhoEmL 91*
Binchy, Maeve 1940- *FemiCLE*
Bindel, William Eugene 1963- *WhoSSW 91*
Bindelglas, Paul Melvin *BiDrAPA 89*
Bindell, Anna F. 1918- *St&PR 91*
Bindenga, Andre Jacobus 1941- *WhoWor 91*
Binder, Amy 1955- *ODwPR 91*
Binder, Amy Finn 1955- *WhoAm 90, WhoAmW 91*
Binder, Carroll 1896-1956 *BioIn 16*
Binder, David Brian 1949- *BiDrAPA 89*
Binder, David Franklin 1935- *WhoAm 90, WhoE 91, WhoWor 91*
Binder, David George 1936- *St&PR 91*
Binder, David Otto 1960- *WhoE 91*
Binder, Eando *AuBYP 90*
Binder, Elizabeth Ann 1957- *WhoAmW 91*
Binder, Erwin 1934- *WhoAmA 91*
Binder, Frederick Moore 1920- *WhoAm 90*
Binder, Frederick William 1926- *St&PR 91*
Binder, Gerald Samuel 1924- *St&PR 91*
Binder, Harold J 1910- *BiDrAPA 89*
Binder, Hartmut 1937- *WhoWor 91*
Binder, J. Morris 1939- *St&PR 91*
Binder, James Kauffman 1920- *WhoWor 91*
Binder, Jerry Lee 1946- *WhoSSW 91*
Binder, Joseph 1898-1972 *ConDes 90*
Binder, Leonard James 1926- *WhoAm 90, WhoWor 91*
Binder, Lois F Q *BiDrAPA 89*
Binder, Lucy S. 1937- *St&PR 91*
Binder, Lucy Simpson 1937- *WhoAm 90*
Binder, Martin R. 1918- *St&PR 91*
Binder, Mildred Katherine 1918- *WhoAmW 91*
Binder, Mitchell Barry 1955- *St&PR 91*
Binder, Otto 1911-1974 *EncACom*
Binder, Otto Oscar 1911-1974 *AuBYP 90*
Binder, Paul *BioIn 16*
Binder, Renee Leslie *BiDrAPA 89*
Binder, Richard Allen 1937- *WhoE 91*
Binderman, Melvin David 1940- *WhoE 91*
Bindesboll, Thorvald 1846-1908 *PenDiDA 89*
Binding, Rudolf Georg 1867-1938 *BioIn 16*
Bindler, Donald E. 1939- *ODwPR 91, St&PR 91*
Bindler, Franci Sara 1946- *WhoSSW 91*
Bindley, William Edward 1940- *St&PR 91, WhoAm 90*
Bindra, Satish Chander 1934- *WhoWor 91*
Bindseil, Edwin R. 1930- *St&PR 91*
Bindseil, Reinhart Werner Martin 1935- *WhoWor 91*
Bineau, Roger E. 1956- *St&PR 91*
Biner, Margaret Lavin 1952- *WhoAmW 91, WhoE 91*
Binet, Alfred 1857-1911 *WorAlBi*
Binet, Luc Desire 1951- *WhoWor 91*
Binford, Alfred G. 1960- *WhoE 91*
Binford, Chapman H 1900-1990 *ConAu 130*
Binford, Chapman Hunter 1900- *WhoAm 90*
Binford, Charles A *BiDrAPA 89*
Binford, Lewis R 1930- *ConAu 131*
Binford, Robert Bailey 1935- *BiDrAPA 89*
Binford, Ruth 1925- *St&PR 91*
Binford, Susan E. *ODwPR 91*
Binford, Valorie Ydette 1964- *WhoAmW 91*
Bing, Alexander 1878-1959 *WhoAmA 91N*
Bing, Dave 1943- *WorAlBi*

Bing, Eric Gordon *BiDrAPA 89*
Bing, Howard Monroe 1940- *St&PR 91*
Bing, J. Edward 1935- *ODwPR 91*
Bing, J.H. *PenDiDA 89*
Bing, M.H. *PenDiDA 89*
Bing, Richard *BioIn 16*
Bing, Roland Edward, Jr. 1921- *WhoAm 90, WhoSSW 91*
Bing, Rudolf 1902- *BioIn 16, NewYTBS 90 [port]*
Bing, Rudolph 1902- *WorAlBi*
Bing, Samuel 1838-1905 *PenDiDA 89*
Bingaman, Jeff 1943- *WhoAm 90, WhoWor 91*
Bingaman, Steven West 1956- *WhoE 91*
Bingcang, Cornelia *BiDrAPA 89*
Binge, Ronald 1910-1979 *OxCPMus*
Bingeman, Jonas Byron 1925- *WhoAm 90*
Bingen, Hildegard von 1098-1179 *BioIn 16*
Binger, Charles M 1930- *BiDrAPA 89*
Binger, Eugene Thomas 1923- *St&PR 91*
Binger, Wilson Valentine 1917- *WhoAm 90*
Bingham family *BioIn 16*
Bingham, Alice 1936- *WhoAmA 91*
Bingham, Barbara 1957- *ODwPR 91*
Bingham, Barbara Gilmour 1957- *WhoE 91*
Bingham, Barry 1906-1988 *BioIn 16*
Bingham, Charles Tiffany, Jr. 1933- *WhoAm 90*
Bingham, Charles W. 1933- *St&PR 91*
Bingham, Christopher 1937- *WhoAm 90*
Bingham, David *BioIn 16*
Bingham, Edward *PenDiDA 89*
Bingham, Edward F. 1921- *St&PR 91*
Bingham, Eula 1929- *WhoAm 90, WhoAmW 91*
Bingham, George Barry 1906- *BioIn 16*
Bingham, George Barry, Jr. 1933- *WhoAm 90, WhoSSW 91*
Bingham, George Caleb 1811-1879 *IntDcAA 90, WorAlBi*
Bingham, George Walter Chandler 1925- *WhoWor 91*
Bingham, H. Raymond 1945- *WhoAm 90*
Bingham, Harry Hobart 1931- *WhoAm 90*
Bingham, Harry Payne, Mrs *WhoAmA 91*
Bingham, Henry J. *St&PR 91*
Bingham, Hiram 1875-1956 *WorAlBi*
Bingham, Hiram A. 1935- *WhoWrEP 89*
Bingham, James Hugh 1946- *St&PR 91*
Bingham, James Monroe 1828-1885 *AmLegL*
Bingham, Jinsie Scott 1935- *WhoAmW 91*
Bingham, John 1908-1988 *AnObit 1988, TwCCr&M 91*
Bingham, John A. 1815-1900 *BioIn 16*
Bingham, John Michael Ward 1908-1988 *SpyFic*
Bingham, Judith 1952- *IntWWM 90*
Bingham, Jules 1921- *WhoE 91*
Bingham, June 1919- *WhoE 91*
Bingham, Kathleen S. 1939- *St&PR 91*
Bingham, Lois A 1913- *WhoAmA 91*
Bingham, Paul M. 1942- *St&PR 91*
Bingham, Richard *BiDrAPA 89*
Bingham, Robert E. 1948- *St&PR 91*
Bingham, Robert Worth 1871-1937 *BioIn 16*
Bingham, Roy Everett 1901- *BiDrAPA 89*
Bingham, Sallie *BioIn 16*
Bingham, Sallie 1937- *FemiCLE, LiHiK, WhoWrEP 89*
Bingham, Susan Adams Hulsman 1944- *IntWWM 90*
Bingham, Walter D. 1921- *WhoAm 90*
Bingham, William Allen 1962- *WhoE 91*
Bingham, William Floyd 1938- *BiDrAPA 89*
Bingle, Donald J. 1954- *WhoEmL 91*
Bingley, Leo Jullian, Jr. 1936- *WhoAm 90*
Bingman, Craig Charles 1953- *WhoEmL 91*
Bingman, Richard Thomas 1923- *St&PR 91*
Bingo-Duggins, Karen Leiko 1942- *WhoAmW 91*
Bini, Carlo 1947- *IntWWM 90*
Bini, Dante Natale 1932- *WhoWor 91*
Biniek, Joseph Paul 1922- *WhoWrEP 89*
Binion, Beatrice Marie 1958- *WhoAmW 91, WhoWor 91*
Binion, Benny *BioIn 16*
Binion, Linda Diane 1948- *WhoAmW 91*
Binion, Rudolph 1927- *WhoAm 90*
Binion, Willie Clayte, Jr. 1912- *WhoAm 90*
Binkerd, Gordon Ware 1916- *WhoAm 90*
Binkert, Alvin John 1910- *WhoAm 90*
Binkert, Christopher C. 1949- *St&PR 91*
Binkhorst, Sonja 1922- *BiDrAPA 89*
Binkiene, Sofija 1902-1984 *BioIn 16*
Binkley, Barry D. *BiDrAPA 89*
Binkley, James Arthur 1930- *St&PR 91*
Binkley, Janet Ramage 1930- *WhoAmW 91, WhoWrEP 89*
Binkley, Olin Trivette 1908- *WhoAm 90*
Binkley, Ronald Howard 1958- *WhoEmL 91*
Binkley, Thomas Eden 1931- *IntWWM 90*
Binkley, Timothy 1943- *WhoAm 90*
Binkow, Michael Jay 1958- *St&PR 91*
Binkowski, Edward Stephan 1948- *WhoE 91*
Binkowski, Kathleen 1950- *WhoE 91*
Binkowski, Norbert James *BiDrAPA 89*
Binks, George 1914- *Ballpl 90*
Binks, Rebecca Anne 1955- *WhoAmW 91*
Binks, Ronald C 1934- *WhoAmA 91*
Binn, Moreton I. 1936- *St&PR 91*
Binnette, Owens Joseph 1930- *St&PR 91*
Binnie, Alan G. 1906- *St&PR 91*
Binnie, Frances Sue 1954- *WhoAmW 91*
Binnig, Gerd 1947- *WorAlBi*
Binnig, Gerd Karl 1947- *WhoAm 90, WhoWor 91*
Binning, Bertram Charles 1909-1976 *WhoAmA 91N*
Binning, Bette Finese 1927- *WhoWor 91*
Binning, John Harlan 1923- *St&PR 91*
Binnion, John Edward 1918- *WhoAm 90*
Binns, Charles Fergus 1857-1934 *PenDiDA 89*
Binns, Edward 1916-1990 *NewYTBS 90 [port]*
Binns, Grace *BiDEWW*
Binns, James Edward 1931- *WhoAm 90*
Binns, James Hazlett, Jr. 1945- *WhoAm 90*
Binns, James W. 1946- *WhoAm 90*
Binns, James Walter 1946- *St&PR 91*
Binns, Malcolm 1936- *IntWWM 90*
Binns, Ruth Anne *BioIn 16*
Binns, W. Gordon, Jr. *BioIn 16*
Binns, Walter Gordon, Jr. 1929- *WhoAm 90, WhoE 91, WhoWor 91*
Binowitz, Charles 1905- *St&PR 91*
Binsfeld, Connie Berube 1924- *WhoAmW 91*
Binski, Sigurd R 1921- *EncO&P 3*
Binstock, Robert Henry 1935- *WhoAm 90, WhoWrEP 89*
Binswanger, Frank G., Jr. 1928- *St&PR 91, WhoAm 90*
Binswanger, Frank G., Sr. 1902- *St&PR 91*
Binswanger, John K. 1932- *St&PR 91*
Bintliff, David C. 1901- *St&PR 91*
Bintz, Joan Heiderer 1931- *St&PR 91*
Bintz, John Carl 1931- *St&PR 91*
Binus, Gregory K *BiDrAPA 89*
Binwal, Jagdish Chandra 1939- *WhoWor 91*
Binyon, Hal O., III 1940- *St&PR 91*
Binzen, Bill *AuBYP 90*
Binzen, Peter Husted 1922- *WhoAm 90, WhoWrEP 89*
Binzenbach, Georg 1955- *IntWWM 90*
Binzley, Richard F *BiDrAPA 89*
Biobaku, Saburi Oladeni 1918- *WhoWor 91*
Bioko, Cristino Seriche *WhoWor 91*
Biolchini, Robert Fredrick 1939- *WhoSSW 91*
Biondi, Dick *BioIn 16*
Biondi, Frank J., Jr. 1945- *WhoAm 90, WhoE 91*
Biondi, Giovanni 1950- *BiDrAPA 89*
Biondi, Lawrence 1938- *WhoAm 90*
Biondi, Manfred Anthony 1924- *WhoAm 90*
Biondi, Matt *BioIn 16*
Biondi, Matt 1965- *WorAlBi*
Biondi, Richard Glenn 1943- *WhoSSW 91*
Biondillo, Philip 1947- *WhoEmL 91, WhoSSW 91*
Biondo, Andre Nicholas 1960- *WhoEmL 91*
Biondo, Dino Dominick 1958- *WhoEmL 91, WhoWor 91*
Biondo, Michael Thomas 1928- *WhoAm 90*
Biorck, Gunnar Carl Wilhelm 1916- *WhoWor 91*
Bioy Casares, Adolfo 1914- *BioIn 16, HispWr 90, MajTwCW*
Bippus, David Paul 1949- *WhoAm 90*
Bippus, Leon Dale 1936- *WhoSSW 91*
Bippus, Sunny *BioIn 16*
Bir, Michelle Marie 1965- *WhoAmW 91*
Biraben, Pierre 1945- *WhoE 91*
Biram, Geraldine Louise 1923- *WhoAmW 91*
Birashk, Kambiz *BiDrAPA 89*
Birbaum, Joseph Louis 1939- *St&PR 91*
Birch, Bryan 1937- *St&PR 91*
Birch, David Geoffrey 1949- *WhoSSW 91*
Birch, Eric Norman 1942- *St&PR 91*
Birch, Grace Morgan 1925- *WhoAmW 91, WhoE 91, WhoWor 91*
Birch, Jack Willard 1915- *WhoAm 90*
Birch, John *WorAlBi*
Birch, John 1931- *ODwPR 91*
Birch, John Paul 1939- *St&PR 91*
Birch, Louis Charles 1918- *WhoWor 91*
Birch, Mary Lynn 1945- *WhoEmL 91*
Birch, Murray Patrick 1953- *WhoAm 90*
Birch, Nigel 1906-1981 *DcNaB 1981*
Birch, Norman John 1930- *St&PR 91*
Birch, Stephen 1872-1940 *WorAlBi*
Birch, Thomas Carl 1952- *WhoAm 90*
Birch, Thomas Howard 1875-1929 *BioIn 16*
Birch, Thomas Lee 1945- *WhoE 91*
Birch, William Charles 1932- *St&PR 91*
Birch, William Dunham, Jr. 1940- *WhoE 91*
Birch, Willie M 1942- *WhoAmA 91*
Birch-Pfeiffer, Charlotte Johanna 1799-1868 *EncCoWW*
Birchak, James Robert 1939- *WhoSSW 91*
Birchak, Michael Joseph 1954- *WhoEmL 91*
Birchall, Ellen Frances 1920- *BiDrAPA 89*
Birchall, Frederick Thomas 1871-1955 *BioIn 16*
Bircham, Deric Neale 1934- *WhoWor 91*
Birchansky, Bonnie-Lee *BiDrAPA 89*
Birchansky, Leo 1887-1949 *WhoAmA 91N*
Birchard, Kendon Thomas 1938- *St&PR 91*
Birchard, Kenneth King 1939- *BiDrAPA 89*
Birchby, Kenneth L. 1915- *St&PR 91*
Birchby, Kenneth Lee 1915- *WhoAm 90*
Birchem, Regina 1938- *WhoAmW 91*
Birchenough, Mabel 1860-1936 *FemiCLE*
Bircher, Andrea Ursula 1928- *WhoSSW 91*
Bircher, Edgar Allen 1934- *St&PR 91, WhoAm 90*
Bircher-Benner, Max *NewAgE 90*
Birchfield, James H. *ODwPR 91*
Birchfield, John Kermit, Jr. 1940- *St&PR 91, WhoAm 90*
Birchfield, Mary Eva 1909- *WhoAmW 91*
Birck, Michael John 1938- *WhoAm 90*
Birckbichler, Richard Dean 1948- *St&PR 91, WhoAm 90, WhoEmL 91*
Birckett, Anna Belle *WhoAmA 91*
Bird Woman 1786-1884 *BioIn 16*
Bird, Agnes Thornton 1921- *WhoAm 90, WhoWor 91*
Bird, Bessie Calhoun 1906?- *HarlReB*
Bird, Brian Rigg *BiDrAPA 89*
Bird, C. *MajTwCW*
Bird, Caroline 1915- *WhoAm 90, WhoWor 91, WhoWrEP 89*
Bird, Charles Russell 1954- *WhoE 91*
Bird, Claudia Storm 1954- *St&PR 91*
Bird, Cordwainer *MajTwCW*
Bird, David Jacobs 1954- *WhoEmL 91*
Bird, Donna Clarice 1950- *WhoE 91*
Bird, Doug 1950- *Ballpl 90*
Bird, E. J. 1911- *BioIn 16*
Bird, Eddie *BioIn 16*
Bird, Edward Dennis 1926- *WhoAm 90*
Bird, Etta G 1916- *BiDrAPA 89*
Bird, Francis 1667-1731 *BioIn 16*
Bird, Francis Marion 1902- *WhoAm 90, WhoSSW 91*
Bird, George Richmond 1925- *WhoAm 90*
Bird, Harrie Waldo 1917- *BiDrAPA 89*
Bird, Harrie Waldo, Jr. 1917- *WhoAm 90*
Bird, Hector Ramon 1939- *WhoHisp 91*
Bird, Isabel 1942- *WhoWor 91*
Bird, Isabella 1831-1904 *FemiCLE*
Bird, Isabella L. 1831-1904 *BioIn 16*
Bird, Ivan Frank *BiDrAPA 89*
Bird, J Malcolm 1886- *EncO&P 3*
Bird, Jacqueline Faye 1954- *WhoAmW 91*
Bird, James 1798?-1892 *DcCanB 12*
Bird, James Malcolm 1886- *EncPaPR 91*
Bird, James T. 1949- *St&PR 91*
Bird, Joanne Lynne 1954- *WhoAmW 91*
Bird, John 1941- *ConAu 130*
Bird, John Adams 1937- *WhoAm 90*
Bird, John Alexander 1910- *WhoAm 90*
Bird, John L. 1928- *ODwPR 91*
Bird, John Malcolm 1931- *WhoAm 90*
Bird, John William Clyde 1932- *WhoAm 90*
Bird, Jon Arthur 1939- *St&PR 91*
Bird, Junius Bouton 1907-1982 *BioIn 16*
Bird, L. Raymond 1914- *WhoE 91*
Bird, Larry *BioIn 16*
Bird, Larry 1956- *News 90 [port], -90-3 [port], WorAlBi*
Bird, Larry Joe 1956- *WhoAm 90, WhoE 91*
Bird, Lee C *BiDrAPA 89*
Bird, Lester 1938- *WhoWor 91*
Bird, Luis Jesus *BiDrAPA 89*
Bird, M. Kendall *St&PR 91N*
Bird, Margaret Helena 1954- *WhoE 91*
Bird, Margaret N 1918- *BiDrAPA 89*
Bird, Martha A 1957- *BiDrAPA 89*
Bird, Mary Lynne Miller 1934- *WhoAm 90*
Bird, Matthew Alexius 1957- *WhoEmL 91*
Bird, Patricia Amy 1941- *WhoWrEP 89*
Bird, Patricia Clare 1946- *WhoE 91*
Bird, Peter 1951- *WhoAm 90*
Bird, Peter G. 1944- *St&PR 91*
Bird, R. Curtman 1957- *St&PR 91*
Bird, Ralph G. 1933- *St&PR 91*
Bird, Ralph Gordon 1933- *WhoAm 90*
Bird, Richard *BioIn 16*
Bird, Robert Byron 1924- *WhoAm 90, WhoWrEP 89*
Bird, Robert E. 1929- *St&PR 91*
Bird, Robert Hutchins 1932- *St&PR 91*
Bird, Robert Montgomery 1803-1854 *LiHiK*
Bird, Robert Wilson 1918- *WhoAm 90*
Bird, Rose Elizabeth 1936- *WhoAm 90, WhoAmW 91, WorAlBi*
Bird, Samuel R. *BioIn 16*
Bird, Sarah Ann *WhoWrEP 89*
Bird, Seymour E *BiDrAPA 89*
Bird, Suzanne *BiDrAPA 89*
Bird, Thomas Edward 1935- *WhoE 91*
Bird, Traveller *AuBYP 90*
Bird, Vere Cornwall 1909- *BioIn 16*
Bird, Vere Cornwall, Sr. 1909- *WhoWor 91*
Bird, Wendell Raleigh 1954- *WhoEmL 91, WhoSSW 91, WhoWor 91*
Bird, William 1888-1963 *BioIn 16*
Bird-Porto, Patricia Anne 1952- *WhoAmW 91*
Birdie Africa *BioIn 16*
Birdman, Jerome M. 1930- *WhoAm 90, WhoE 91*
Birdsall, Arthur Anthony 1947- *WhoEmL 91*
Birdsall, Blair 1907- *WhoAm 90*
Birdsall, Byron 1937- *WhoAmA 91*
Birdsall, Charles Kennedy 1925- *WhoAm 90*
Birdsall, Jane Elaine 1947- *WhoAmW 91*
Birdsall, Jesse *BioIn 16*
Birdsall, Norton Philo 1910- *WhoE 91*
Birdsall, William Forest 1937- *WhoAm 90*
Birdsell, Regina Sullivan 1946- *WhoAmW 91*
Birdsell, Sandra 1942- *ConAu 130, FemiCLE*
Birdsey, Anna Campas 1949- *WhoAmW 91*
Birdseye, Clarence 1886-1956 *WorAlBi*
Birdseye, Joseph Warren 1831- *AmLegL*
Birdsong, Alta Marie 1934- *WhoAmW 91*
Birdsong, George Yancy 1939- *St&PR 91, WhoAm 90*
Birdsong, McLemore, Jr. 1943- *St&PR 91*
Birdsong, William Herbert, Jr. 1918- *WhoAm 90*
Birdsong, William M., Jr. 1934- *St&PR 91*
Birdwell, Carolyn Campbell 1947- *WhoAmW 91*
Birdwell, Donald Wayne 1952- *St&PR 91*
Birdwell, Randall Patrick 1956- *WhoSSW 91*
Birdwell, Roy Dean 1937- *St&PR 91*
Birdwhistell, Ray L. 1918- *WhoAm 90*
Birdzell, Samuel Henry 1916- *WhoAm 90*
Bireline, George Lee 1923- *WhoAmA 91*
Birely, William Cramer 1919- *WhoAm 90*
Biren, Matthew Bennett 1948- *WhoEmL 91*
Biren, Paula Sarah *BiDrAPA 89*
Birenbaum, Cynthia *WhoAmA 91*
Birenbaum, David Elias 1937- *WhoAm 90, WhoE 91*
Birenbaum, William M. 1923- *WhoAm 90*
Birendra Bir Bikram Shah Dev 1945- *WhoWor 91*
Birendra Bir Bikram Shah Deva 1945- *BioIn 16*
Bires, Dennis Eugene 1954- *WhoEmL 91*
Bires, Jerry 1950- *ODwPR 91*
Biret, Idil 1941- *PenDiMP*
Birge, Phillip L. 1939- *St&PR 91*
Birge, Raymond T 1887- *EncO&P 3*
Birge, Raymond Thayer 1887-1980 *DcScB S2*
Birge, Robert Richards 1946- *WhoAm 90, WhoWor 91*
Birge, Robert Walsh 1924- *WhoAm 90*
Birgeneau, Robert Joseph 1942- *WhoAm 90*
Birger, Daniel M 1936- *BiDrAPA 89*
Birgitta, Saint 1303?-1373 *DcScanL*
Birgmajer, Fani 1950- *WhoWor 91*
Biringer, Paul Peter 1924- *WhoAm 90*
Birinyi, Laszlo, Jr. *BioIn 16*
Birish, George James 1928- *St&PR 91*
Birk, Ann Climo 1943- *BiDrAPA 89*
Birk, Bernhard William 1926- *St&PR 91*
Birk, Carl Lee *BiDrAPA 89*
Birk, Carol Jean 1935- *St&PR 91*
Birk, Jim *WhoAm 90*
Birk, John R. 1951- *St&PR 91, WhoAm 90, WhoE 91, WhoEmL 91*
Birk, Robert Eugene 1926- *WhoAm 90, WhoWor 91*
Birk, Roger Emil 1930- *St&PR 91, WhoAm 90*
Birk, Sharon Anastasia 1937- *WhoAm 90*
Birk, Timothy Edward 1951- *WhoEmL 91*
Birkbeck, Mike 1961- *Ballpl 90*
Birkelbach, Albert Ottmar 1927- *WhoAm 90*
Birkelo, Ralph J. 1929- *St&PR 91*
Birkelund, John P. 1930- *St&PR 91*
Birkelund, John Peter 1930- *WhoAm 90*

Birkemeier, Susan Gail 1947- *WhoAmW 91*
Birken, Dolan *TwCCr&M 91*
Birkenhauer, Candace Ludwig 1947- *WhoAmW 91*
Birkenhauer, Josef August Christoph 1929- *WhoWor 91*
Birkenhead, Frederick E. Smith, Earl of 1872-1930 *BioIn 16*
Birkenhead, Susan 1935- *BioIn 16*
Birkenhead, Thomas Bruce 1931- *WhoAm 90, WhoWor 91*
Birkenmeier, Gary Francis 1946- *WhoSSW 91*
Birkenruth, Harry H. 1931- *St&PR 91*
Birkenstock, James Warren 1912- *WhoAm 90*
Birkerts, Gunnar 1925- *WhoAm 90*
Birkett, David Peter 1934- *BiDrAPA 89*
Birkett, John Hooper 1925- *WhoAm 90*
Birkett, Maria Grace Liggiera 1956- *WhoAmW 91*
Birkhead, Anne *BiDEWW*
Birkhead, Guthrie Sweeney, Jr. 1920- *WhoAm 90*
Birkhoff, Deborah Lorraine 1959- *WhoAmW 91*
Birkhoff, Garrett 1911- *WhoAm 90*
Birkhoff, Robert D. 1925- *WhoAm 90*
Birkholm, Michael Peter 1952- *St&PR 91*
Birkholtz, Susan *ODwPR 91*
Birkholz, E. Terry 1937- *St&PR 91*
Birkholz, Gabriella S. *ODwPR 91*
Birkholz, Gabriella Sonja 1938- *WhoAmW 91, WhoWor 91*
Birkholz, Raymond J. 1936- *St&PR 91*
Birkholz, Raymond James 1936- *WhoAm 90*
Birkin, Morton 1919- *WhoAmA 91N*
Birkinbine, John, II 1930- *WhoAm 90, WhoWor 91*
Birkins, R. Parker 1926- *St&PR 91*
Birkins, Rodney Mann 1930- *St&PR 91, WhoSSW 91*
Birkland, Robert M. 1951- *St&PR 91*
Birkle, Alexander *BiDrAPA 89*
Birkmaier, Robert David 1955- *WhoEmL 91*
Birkner, Edward Charles 1920- *WhoE 91*
Birkner, Hans-Joachim 1931- *WhoWor 91*
Birkofer, Ralph 1908-1971 *Ballpl 90*
Birks, Drummond 1919- *St&PR 91*
Birks, George Drummond 1919- *WhoAm 90*
Birks, H. Jonathan 1945- *St&PR 91*
Birks, Neil 1935- *WhoAm 90*
Birks, Ronald *PenDiMP*
Birky, John Edward 1934- *St&PR 91, WhoAm 90*
Birley, Anthony 1937- *ConAu 129*
Birley, Anthony R. *ConAu 129*
Birley, Robert 1903-1982 *DcNaB 1981*
Birmaher, Boris *BiDrAPA 89*
Birmaher, Boris 1952- *WhoE 91*
Birman, Joseph Leon 1927- *WhoAm 90*
Birmelin, A Robert 1933- *WhoAmA 91*
Birmelin, August Robert 1933- *WhoAm 90*
Birmingham, Bascom Wayne 1925- *WhoAm 90*
Birmingham, Fletcher Ansil 1956- *WhoEmL 91*
Birmingham, Joe 1884-1946 *Ballpl 90*
Birmingham, John James 1939- *St&PR 91*
Birmingham, Richard Gregory 1929- *WhoAm 90, WhoE 91*
Birmingham, Richard Joseph 1953- *WhoEmL 91*
Birmingham, Stephen 1931- *WhoAm 90, WhoWrEP 89*
Birmingham, Stephen 1932?- *WorAu 1980 [port]*
Birmingham, William Joseph 1923- *WhoWor 91*
Birn, Donald S. 1937- *ConAu 132*
Birn, Raymond Francis 1935- *WhoAm 90*
Birnbach, Gerald Marshall 1931- *St&PR 91*
Birnbach, Lisa *BioIn 16*
Birnbach, Seymour 1920-1989 *BioIn 16*
Birnbaum, Allan S. 1937- *St&PR 91*
Birnbaum, Burton H. 1942- *St&PR 91*
Birnbaum, David 1940- *WhoE 91*
Birnbaum, Eleazar 1929- *WhoAm 90, WhoWrEP 89*
Birnbaum, Gisele Blankstein *BioIn 16*
Birnbaum, Henrik 1925- *WhoAm 90*
Birnbaum, Henry 1917- *WhoAm 90*
Birnbaum, Howard Kent 1932- *WhoAm 90*
Birnbaum, Jacob *BiDrAPA 89*
Birnbaum, Jane *ODwPR 91*
Birnbaum, Joan Welker 1923- *WhoAmW 91*
Birnbaum, Joel Samuel 1937- *WhoAm 90*
Birnbaum, Max 1919- *St&PR 91*
Birnbaum, Morton *BiDrAPA 89*
Birnbaum, Philip 1904-1988 *BioIn 16*
Birnbaum, Robert 1936- *WhoAm 90*
Birnbaum, Robert J. 1953- *BiDrAPA 89*
Birnbaum, Robert Jack 1927- *WhoAm 90*
Birnbaum, Robert Jay 1930- *WhoE 91*
Birnbaum, Sheila L. 1940- *WhoAmW 91*
Birnbaum, Solomon 1891-1989 *BioIn 16*
Birnbaum, Solomon Asher 1891-1989 *ConAu 130*
Birnbaum, Stephen 1937- *ConAu 129*
Birnbaum, Stephen Norman 1937- *WhoAm 90, WhoWrEP 89*
Birnbaum, Steve *ConAu 129*
Birnbaum, Zygmunt William 1903- *WhoAm 90*
Birnberg, Howard Gene 1950- *WhoEmL 91*
Birnberg, Jack 1937- *WhoE 91*
Birnberg, Nathan Norman 1950- *BiDrAPA 89*
Birne, Cindy Frank 1956- *WhoSSW 91*
Birney, Arthur A. 1927- *St&PR 91*
Birney, David *BioIn 16*
Birney, David Bell, IV *WhoAm 90*
Birney, David Edwin *WhoAm 90*
Birney, Earle 1904- *MajTwCW, OxCCanT, WhoWrEP 89*
Birney, Margaret Linda Hamilton 1954- *WhoEmL 91*
Birney, Meredith Baxter *BioIn 16*
Birney, Robert Charles 1925- *WhoAm 90*
Birnhak, Sam 1950- *St&PR 91*
Birnhak, Sandra Jean 1945- *WhoAmW 91, WhoE 91, WhoEmL 91, WhoWor 91*
Birnholz, Jack 1931- *St&PR 91*
Birnholz, Jason Cordell 1942- *WhoAm 90*
Birnie, Janice Dorothy 1940- *WhoAmW 91*
Birnkrant, Harold *BiDrAPA 89*
Birnkrant, Henry Joseph 1955- *WhoEmL 91*
Birnkrant, Jeanne Ann *WhoAmW 91*
Birns, Mark Theodore 1949- *WhoAm 90, WhoE 91*
Biro, Bruce-Michael 1950- *WhoEmL 91, WhoSSW 91*
Biro, Charles 1911-1972 *EncACom*
Biro, Edith Varga- 1927-1986 *BioIn 16*
Biro, Joan S. 1955- *St&PR 91*
Biro, Laszlo 1929- *WhoAm 90*
Biro, Mihaly 1886-1948 *BioIn 16*
Biro, Nicholas G. 1929- *ODwPR 91*
Biro, Sari 1912-1990 *NewYTBS 90*
Birochak, Edward, Jr. 1955- *BiDrAPA 89*
Biron, Christine Anne 1951- *WhoAmW 91*
Biros, Dennis Gerald *BiDrAPA 89*
Biros, Lorraine 1946- *WhoAmW 91*
Birrell, Anne *ConAu 130*
Birrell, Augustine 1850-1933 *DcLB 98 [port]*
Birrell, George Andrew 1921- *WhoAm 90*
Birrell, Robert Warren 1930- *St&PR 91*
Birren, Faber 1900-1988 *BioIn 16*
Birren, James Emmett 1918- *WhoAm 90*
Birren, Jeffrey Emmett 1951- *WhoEmL 91*
Birrenkott, Pete S. 1948- *St&PR 91*
Birrer, Babe 1928- *Ballpl 90*
Birrer, Richard Bruce 1953- *WhoE 91*
Birschtein, Barbara Ann *WhoAmW 91*
Birsh, Andrew Seth 1956- *WhoE 91*
Birsh, Arthur Thomas 1932- *WhoAm 90, WhoWrEP 89*
Birsic, Dorothy Ann 1961- *WhoAmW 91*
Birsner, Eleanor Patricia 1928- *WhoAmW 91*
Birstein, Ann *WhoWrEP 89*
Birstein, Seymour Joseph 1927- *WhoE 91*
Birt, Carol Marie *BiDrAPA 89*
Birt, Diane Feickert 1949- *WhoEmL 91*
Birtcher, Wendy Catharine 1962- *WhoAmW 91*
Birtel, Frank Thomas 1932- *WhoAm 90*
Birtles, Dora 1903- *FemiCLE*
Birtsas, Tim 1960- *Ballpl 90*
Birtwistle, Donald B. 1920- *St&PR 91*
Birtwistle, Harrison 1934- *IntWWM 90, PenDiMPA*
Birx, H. James 1941- *WhoAm 90, WhoE 91, WhoWor 91*
Biryukova, Aleksandra 1929- *WhoWor 91*
Biryukova, Aleksandra P. 1929- *BioIn 16*
Bisarnsin, Tanongsak 1948- *WhoSSW 91*
Bisbee, David Wise 1950- *WhoEmL 91*
Bisbee, Gerald E. 1942- *St&PR 91*
Bisbee, Gerald Elftman, Jr. 1942- *WhoE 91*
Bisbee, J.E. 1935- *St&PR 91*
Bisbee, Royal Daniel, Jr. 1923- *WhoAm 90*
Bisby, Mark Ainley 1946- *WhoAm 90*
Biscaccianti, Elisa 1824-1896 *BioIn 16*
Biscar, Jeanette *EncO&P 3*
Biscardi, Chester 1948- *IntWWM 90, WhoAm 90*
Bisceglio, Anthony F. 1947- *St&PR 91*
Bisch, John J. 1928- *St&PR 91*
Bischak, Cynthia D. 1956- *WhoAmW 91*
Bischel, George W 1927- *BiDrAPA 89*
Bischel, John David 1933- *BiDrAPA 89*
Bischof, Harrington 1935- *St&PR 91*
Bischof, Merriem Lanova *WhoAmW 91*
Bischof, Rainer 1947- *IntWWM 90*
Bischoff, Carol Louise *WhoAmW 91*
Bischoff, David Canby 1930- *WhoAm 90*
Bischoff, Elmer 1916- *WhoAm 90, WhoAmA 91*
Bischoff, Frederic John 1939- *St&PR 91*
Bischoff, Ilse Marthe 1903- *AuBYP 90*
Bischoff, James R. 1936- *St&PR 91*
Bischoff, Joyce Arlene 1938- *WhoAmW 91*
Bischoff, Julia Bristol 1909-1970 *AuBYP 90*
Bischoff, Kenneth Bruce 1936- *WhoAm 90*
Bischoff, Marilyn Brett 1930- *WhoE 91*
Bischoff, Robert H. 1920- *St&PR 91*
Bischoff, Susan Ann 1951- *WhoAm 90*
Bischoff, Timothy Alan *BiDrAPA 89*
Bischoff, Wendy Winona 1960- *WhoAmW 91*
Bischoff, Werner W. 1928- *St&PR 91*
Bischoff, William Eugene 1939- *WhoE 91*
Bisco, Michael John 1930- *BiDrAPA 89*
Bisco, Sharon Diane *BiDrAPA 89*
Bisdorff, Georgette 1944- *EncCoWW*
Bisel, Harry Ferree 1918- *WhoAm 90*
Bisenius, Charles J. 1931- *St&PR 91*
Bisgaard, Hans Peter 1954- *WhoSSW 91*
Bisgard, Gerald Edwin 1937- *WhoAm 90*
Bisgard, James Dewey 1898-1975 *WhoAmA 91N*
Bisgard, Sharon Kay 1939- *WhoAmW 91*
Bisgyer, Barbara G 1933- *WhoAmA 91*
Bisgyer, Jay Lewis 1927- *BiDrAPA 89*
Bish, James Herring 1931- *St&PR 91*
Bish, Katherine Kaye 1958- *WhoAmW 91*
Bish, Milan David 1929- *WhoAm 90*
Bish, Ronald E. 1928- *St&PR 91*
Bishaf, Morris 1926- *St&PR 91*
Bishar, John Joseph, Jr. 1950- *WhoAm 90*
Bishara, Angele 1948- *WhoSSW 91*
Bishara, Samir Edward 1935- *WhoAm 90*
Bishea, P. Maurice 1931- *ODwPR 91*
Bisher, James Furman 1918- *WhoAm 90, WhoSSW 91, WhoWrEP 89*
Bishop, Albert Bentley 1929- *WhoAm 90*
Bishop, Albert Jeffry 1931- *St&PR 91*
Bishop, Alice June 1955- *WhoAmW 91*
Bishop, Andrew Charles 1956- *BiDrAPA 89*
Bishop, Anna 1810-1884 *PenDiMP*
Bishop, Anne *BiDEWW*
Bishop, Anne 1912- *WhoWrEP 89*
Bishop, Anne Hughes 1935- *WhoSSW 91*
Bishop, Avery Alvin 1913- *WhoAm 90*
Bishop, B. H. *WhoAm 90*
Bishop, Barbara Evelyn 1940- *WhoAmW 91*
Bishop, Barbara Lee 1938- *WhoAmA 91*
Bishop, Barbara N. *WhoAmW 91*
Bishop, Barney Tipton, III 1951- *WhoSSW 91*
Bishop, Ben 1923- *WhoAmA 91*
Bishop, Betty Josephine 1947- *WhoAmW 91, WhoWor 91*
Bishop, Beverly Petterson 1922- *WhoAmW 91*
Bishop, Billy 1894-1956 *BioIn 16*
Bishop, Bruce Howard 1928- *St&PR 91*
Bishop, Bruce Taylor 1951- *WhoSSW 91*
Bishop, Bryan Edwards 1945- *WhoEmL 91*
Bishop, Budd Harris 1936- *WhoAm 90, WhoAmA 91, WhoSSW 91*
Bishop, C. Diane 1943- *WhoAm 90, WhoAmW 91*
Bishop, Calvin Thomas 1929- *WhoAm 90*
Bishop, Carolyn Louise 1946- *WhoAmW 91*
Bishop, Charles Edwin 1921- *WhoAm 90*
Bishop, Charles Johnson 1920- *WhoAm 90*
Bishop, Charles Joseph 1941- *St&PR 91, WhoAm 90*
Bishop, Charlie 1924- *Ballpl 90*
Bishop, Claire *AuBYP 90, FemiCLE*
Bishop, Claude Titus 1925- *WhoAm 90*
Bishop, Clay Massey, Jr. 1953- *WhoEmL 91*
Bishop, Connie Bossons 1953- *WhoAmW 91*
Bishop, Curtis 1912-1967 *AuBYP 90*
Bishop, Dan R. 1933- *ODwPR 91*
Bishop, David 1928-1989 *BioIn 16*
Bishop, David Fulton 1937- *WhoAm 90*
Bishop, David Lee 1948- *WhoE 91*
Bishop, Di *BioIn 16*
Bishop, Diane Marie 1958- *WhoAmW 91*
Bishop, Donald S. 1932- *St&PR 91*
Bishop, Duane S *BiDrAPA 89*
Bishop, E. William 1939- *St&PR 91*
Bishop, Edwin Lyman 1930- *WhoSSW 91*
Bishop, Eliza H. 1920- *WhoAmW 91*
Bishop, Elizabeth 1911-1979 *AuBYP 90, BioAmW, BioIn 16, FemiCLE, MajTwCW*
Bishop, Elizabeth Shreve 1951- *WhoEmL 91*
Bishop, Elvin 1942- *EncPR&S 89*
Bishop, Emmett Rucker, Jr. 1946- *BiDrAPA 89*
Bishop, Ernest Eugene 1930- *St&PR 91*
Bishop, Ernest Eugene, Jr. 1930- *WhoSSW 91*
Bishop, Eugene E. *WhoAm 90*
Bishop, Francis Earl 1920- *BiDrAPA 89*
Bishop, Frank E 1945- *BiDrAPA 89*
Bishop, Gene H. 1930- *St&PR 91*
Bishop, Gene Herbert 1930- *WhoAm 90, WhoSSW 91*
Bishop, George Albert 1932- *BiDrAPA 89*
Bishop, George Franklin 1942- *WhoAm 90*
Bishop, Gloria Stenson 1937- *WhoAm 90*
Bishop, Gordon Bruce 1938- *WhoAm 90, WhoE 91*
Bishop, Grace *AuBYP 90*
Bishop, Gregory Floyd 1959- *BiDrAPA 89*
Bishop, Harold Ezra 1923- *WhoSSW 91*
Bishop, Harry Craden 1921- *WhoAm 90*
Bishop, Hazel Gladys 1906- *WorAlBi*
Bishop, Hedy Manon 1960- *WhoAmW 91*
Bishop, Henry Rowley 1786-1855 *BioIn 16*
Bishop, Henry S. 1942- *St&PR 91*
Bishop, Homer G. *BioIn 16, NewYTBS 90 [port]*
Bishop, Howard Stuart 1938- *WhoE 91*
Bishop, Isabel 1902- *BiDWomA*
Bishop, Isabel 1902-1988 *BioIn 16*
Bishop, Isabella Lucy Bird 1831-1904 *BioIn 16*
Bishop, J. Michael 1936- *WorAlBi*
Bishop, J. Richard 1952- *St&PR 91*
Bishop, Jack *AuBYP 90*
Bishop, Jacqueline K 1955- *WhoAmA 91*
Bishop, James *St&PR 91*
Bishop, James 1927- *WhoAmA 91*
Bishop, James C., Jr. 1936- *St&PR 91*
Bishop, James Francis 1937- *WhoE 91*
Bishop, James Keough 1938- *WhoAm 90, WhoWor 91*
Bishop, James Oliver, Jr. 1942- *WhoSSW 91*
Bishop, Jeffrey Britton 1949- *WhoAmA 91*
Bishop, Jemma Won-Ja 1944- *WhoE 91*
Bishop, Jerold 1936- *WhoAmA 91*
Bishop, Jim 1907- *WorAlBi*
Bishop, Jim B. 1944- *St&PR 91*
Bishop, Joey 1918- *WhoAm 90, WorAlBi*
Bishop, John *BioIn 16*
Bishop, John F. 1924- *St&PR 91*
Bishop, John J. 1950- *St&PR 91*
Bishop, John M. 1945- *St&PR 91*
Bishop, John Michael 1936- *WhoAm 90, WhoWor 91*
Bishop, John Russell 1947- *WhoEmL 91*
Bishop, Jonathan P 1927- *ConAu 129*
Bishop, Joyce Ann 1935- *WhoAmW 91*
Bishop, Kathryn Elizabeth 1945- *WhoAmW 91, WhoEmL 91*
Bishop, Keith Bryan 1957- *WhoAm 90*
Bishop, Larry A. 1936- *ODwPR 91*
Bishop, Larry Alan 1936- *St&PR 91*
Bishop, Leigh Carlton 1952- *BiDrAPA 89*
Bishop, Leo Kenneth 1911- *WhoAm 90*
Bishop, Lon A. 1942- *St&PR 91*
Bishop, Lon Alfred 1942- *WhoE 91*
Bishop, Louise Williams 1933- *WhoAmW 91*
Bishop, Luther Doyle 1921- *WhoAm 90*
Bishop, Margaret 1920- *WhoAmW 91*
Bishop, Marjorie Cutler *WhoAmA 91*
Bishop, Martin *ConAu 31NR*
Bishop, Mary *WhoAm 90*
Bishop, Mary Chambers 1955- *WhoE 91, WhoEmL 91*
Bishop, Mary McFayden 1915- *BiDrAPA 89*
Bishop, Mary Robinson 1922- *WhoAmW 91*
Bishop, Maurice *BioIn 16*
Bishop, Max 1899-1962 *Ballpl 90 [port]*
Bishop, Michael E. 1938- *ODwPR 91*
Bishop, Michael Joseph 1951- *WhoEmL 91*
Bishop, Michael Mason 1960- *WhoEmL 91*
Bishop, Oliver Richard 1928- *WhoWor 91*
Bishop, Patrick 1952- *ConAu 132*
Bishop, Paul Edward 1940- *WhoAm 90*
Bishop, Peg *BioIn 16*
Bishop, Peter 1932- *St&PR 91*
Bishop, Peter Orlebar 1917- *WhoWor 91*
Bishop, Pike *WhoWrEP 89*
Bishop, R. E. 1903-1989 *AnObit 1989*
Bishop, Raymond Holmes, Jr. 1925- *WhoAm 90*
Bishop, Richard Evett 1897-1975 *WhoAmA 91N*
Bishop, Robert 1938- *WhoAm 90, WhoE 91*
Bishop, Robert C. 1943- *St&PR 91*
Bishop, Robert Calvin 1943- *WhoAm 90*
Bishop, Robert Charles *BioIn 16*
Bishop, Robert Charles 1929- *WhoWor 91*
Bishop, Robert Charles 1938- *WhoAmA 91*
Bishop, Robert D. *St&PR 91*
Bishop, Robert Joseph 1954- *BiDrAPA 89*
Bishop, Robert Lyle 1916- *WhoAm 90*
Bishop, Robert Milton 1921- *WhoAm 90*
Bishop, Robert Vance 1949- *WhoSSW 91*

Bishop, Robert Welch 1955- *WhoEmL 91*
Bishop, Robert Whitsitt 1949- *WhoEmL 91, WhoWor 91*
Bishop, Robert Willis 1943- *St&PR 91*
Bishop, Ron *BioIn 16*
Bishop, Ronald 1903-1989 *BioIn 16*
Bishop, Ronald E. *WhoAm 90*
Bishop, Roy Lovitt 1939- *WhoAm 90*
Bishop, Ruth Ann 1942- *WhoAmW 91*
Bishop, Sarah 1901- *BiDrAPA 89*
Bishop, Sid Glenwood 1923- *WhoSSW 91*
Bishop, Sidney W. 1926- *St&PR 91*
Bishop, Sidney Willard 1926- *WhoAm 90*
Bishop, Stephen 1952- *WhoAm 90*
Bishop, Stephen John 1951- *BiDrAPA 89*
Bishop, Stephen Richard 1953- *WhoWrEP 89*
Bishop, Sue 1953- *WhoAmW 91*
Bishop, Sue Marquis 1939- *WhoSSW 91*
Bishop, Susan Katharine 1946- *WhoAmW 91, WhoWor 91*
Bishop, Terrell P., Jr. *BiDrAPA 89*
Bishop, Thomas Burke, Jr. 1951- *WhoEmL 91*
Bishop, Thomas R. 1948- *St&PR 91*
Bishop, Thomas Ray 1925- *WhoSSW 91*
Bishop, Thomas Walter 1929- *WhoAm 90*
Bishop, Timothy Neal 1947- *WhoSSW 91*
Bishop, Vernon Richard 1937- *St&PR 91*
Bishop, Virginia Wakeman 1927- *WhoAmW 91, WhoWor 91*
Bishop, Wallis Dilworth 1927- *WhoE 91*
Bishop, Walter L. 1925- *St&PR 91*
Bishop, Warner Bader 1918- *WhoAm 90*
Bishop, Washington Irving 1856-1889 *EncPaPR 91*
Bishop, Wayne Staton 1937- *WhoAm 90*
Bishop, Wendy S. 1953- *WhoWrEP 89*
Bishop, William A. 1894-1956 *BioIn 16*
Bishop, William Hardy 1935- *St&PR 91*
Bishop, William John 1956- *St&PR 91*
Bishop, William Peter 1940- *WhoAm 90*
Bishop, William T. *WhoSSW 91*
Bishop, William W., Jr. *BioIn 16*
Bishop, William Wade 1939- *WhoAm 90*
Bishop, Z. C. 1815- *AmLegL*
Bishop-Kovacevich, Stephen 1940- *IntWWM 90, PenDiMP*
Bishop-Prasanna, Timothy *NewAgMG*
Bishopric, Karl 1925- *WhoAm 90*
Bishopric, Susan 1946- *ODwPR 91*
Bishopric, Welsford Farrell 1928- *WhoSSW 91*
Bishow, Howard 1929- *WhoAm 90*
Bisiewicz, Alan Walter 1951- *WhoEmL 91*
Bisk, Anatole 1919- *WhoWor 91*
Biskey, Dean Freeman 1940- *WhoSSW 91*
Biskin, Miriam Marcia Newell 1920- *WhoWrEP 89*
Bismarck, Mona, Grafin von 1897-1983 *BioIn 16*
Bismarck, Otto, Furst von 1815-1898 *BioIn 16*
Bismarck, Otto Von 1815-1898 *WorAlBi*
Bisno, Alan Lester 1936- *WhoSSW 91*
Bisno, Alison Peck 1955- *WhoAm 90, WhoEmL 91*
Bisnow, Mark 1952- *ConAu 130*
Bisoglio, Val 1926- *ConTFT 8*
Bispham, David 1857-1921 *PenDiMP*
Bisping, Bruce Henry 1953- *WhoAm 90*
Bispo, Antonio Alexandre 1949- *IntWWM 90, WhoWor 91*
Bisquerra, Jose 1927- *BiDrAPA 89*
Biss, Terry Joel 1948- *WhoE 91*
Bissada, Nabil Kaddis 1938- *WhoWor 91*
Bissaillon, Francis Philip 1948- *St&PR 91*
Bisschop-Robertson, Suze 1857-1922 *BiDWomA*
Bissell, Betty Dickson 1932- *WhoAmW 91*
Bissell, Charles Overman 1908- *WhoAm 90, WhoAmA 91*
Bissell, Eleanor Amoret 1960- *WhoAmW 91*
Bissell, Emily Perkins 1861-1948 *WorAlBi*
Bissell, George Arthur 1927- *WhoAm 90*
Bissell, George H. 1821-1884 *WorAlBi*
Bissell, George P., Jr. *St&PR 91N*
Bissell, James Dougal, III 1951- *WhoEmL 91*
Bissell, Janet Smitheran 1950- *WhoE 91*
Bissell, Jean Galloway *NewYTBS 90*
Bissell, Jean Galloway 1936-1990 *BioIn 16*
Bissell, John Howard 1935- *St&PR 91, WhoAm 90*
Bissell, John W. 1940- *WhoAm 90*
Bissell, John Wm. 1929- *St&PR 91*
Bissell, LeClair 1928- *WhoWrEP 89*
Bissell, Patricia *BioIn 16*
Bissell, Patrick *BioIn 16*
Bissell, Phil 1926- *WhoAm 90, WhoAmA 91, WhoE 91*
Bissell, Richard Etter 1946- *WhoAm 90*
Bissell, Richard M. 1862-1941 *WorAlBi*
Bissell, Richard Mervin, Jr. 1909- *WhoAm 90*
Bissell, Sumner F. 1928- *St&PR 91*
Bissell, William Gerald *BiDrAPA 89*
Bissell, Wilson Shannon 1847-1903 *BiDrUSE 89*
Bisselle, Morgan Fitch 1908- *WhoAm 90*
Bissen, Gregory John 1953- *WhoEmL 91*
Bisset, Andrew David 1947- *BiDrAPA 89*
Bisset, Andrew Walzer 1919- *WhoAm 90*
Bisset, Davies W., Jr. 1930- *St&PR 91*
Bisset, Jacqueline *BioIn 16*
Bisset, Jacqueline 1946- *WhoAm 90*
Bissett, Alexander Forbes 1933- *St&PR 91*
Bissett, Barbara Anne 1950- *WhoAmW 91, WhoEmL 91, WhoWor 91*
bissett, bill 1939- *MajTwCW*
Bissett, Del Weston 1948- *WhoSSW 91*
Bissett, Jacqueline 1946- *WorAlBi*
Bissetta, Bruno George 1934- *St&PR 91*
Bissette, Samuel Delk 1921- *WhoAmA 91, WhoSSW 91*
Bissette, Winston Louis, Jr. 1943- *WhoAm 90*
Bissex, Janice Newell 1959- *WhoAmW 91*
Bissinger, Frederick Lewis 1911- *WhoAm 90*
Bissinger, Harry Gerard 1954- *WhoAm 90*
Bissland, Mary Lou 1935- *WhoAmW 91*
Bissmeyer, Albert J. 1945- *St&PR 91*
Bisson, Andre 1929- *WhoAm 90, WhoE 91, WhoWor 91*
Bisson, Claude 1931- *WhoAm 90*
Bisson, Edmond Emile 1916- *WhoAm 90*
Bisson, Francis R *BiDrAPA 89*
Bisson, Juliette *EncO&P 3*
Bisson, T. A. 1900-1979 *BioIn 16*
Bisson, Thomas Arthur 1900-1979 *BioIn 16*
Bissonette, D.P. 1939- *St&PR 91*
Bissonette, Del 1899-1972 *Ballpl 90*
Bissonette, Florentina B. *BiDrAPA 89*
Bissonette, Raymond Peter 1939- *WhoE 91*
Bissonette, William Theadore, Sr. 1942- *WhoSSW 91*
Bissonnette, Gerald W *BiDrAPA 89*
Bissonnette, Larry 1957- *MusmAFA*
Bissonnette, Lynne B *BiDrAPA 89*
Bissoondath, Neil 1955- *BioIn 16*
Bistline, Stephen 1921- *WhoAm 90*
Bistoni, Francesco 1943- *WhoWor 91*
Bistram, Gregory Mark 1951- *WhoEmL 91*
Biswas, Asit Kumar 1939- *WhoWor 91*
Biswas, Minati *BiDrAPA 89*
Biswas, Sutapa 1962- *BiDWomA*
Biswell, C. David 1936- *St&PR 91*
Biszick, Doris Anna Maria 1963- *WhoAmW 91*
Bita, Lili 1935- *WhoWrEP 89*
Bitar, Adib Husni 1947- *BiDrAPA 89*
Bitar, Salah Al-Din 1912-1980 *PolLCME*
Bitar, Thomas J. 1932- *St&PR 91*
Bitetti, Ernesto 1943- *PenDiMP*
Bithell, Thomas C. 1946- *St&PR 91*
Bither, David L. *ODwPR 91*
Bither, Richard A. 1946- *St&PR 91*
Bithorn, Hi 1916-1952 *Ballpl 90*
Bitker, Marjorie M 1901-1990 *ConAu 132*
Bitko, Sheldon 1927- *St&PR 91*
Bitler, Cathy Fitzpatrick 1958 *WhoAmW 91*
Bitler, Harold Paul 1942- *St&PR 91*
Bitman, Harold Lloyd 1921- *BiDrAPA 89*
Bitner, Gary E. 1953- *ODwPR 91*
Bitner, Harry 1916- *WhoAm 90*
Bitner, John Howard 1940- *WhoAm 90*
Bitner, John William 1948- *St&PR 91, WhoE 91*
Bitner, William Lawrence, III 1931- *St&PR 91, WhoAm 90*
Bito, Janos Ferenc 1936- *WhoWor 91*
Bitomsky, Brigitte *BioIn 16*
Bitomsky, Hartmut *BioIn 16*
Bitondo, Domenic 1925- *WhoAm 90*
Bitonti, James Anthony 1930- *WhoAm 90*
Bittel, Lester Robert 1918- *WhoWrEP 89*
Bittel, Muriel Helene *WhoAmW 91*
Bittel, Patricia Thomas 1951- *WhoEmL 91*
Bitten, Mary Josephine 1942- *WhoAmW 91*
Bittenbender, Brad James 1948- *WhoEmL 91, WhoWor 91*
Bitter, Edwin Ward 1930- *St&PR 91*
Bitter, Gary G 1940- *ConAu 31NR*
Bitter, Gehart Leonard 1921- *WhoAm 90*
Bitter, Harold Hugo 1922- *St&PR 91*
Bitter, John 1909- *WhoAm 90*
Bitter, John Leonard, Jr. 1932- *WhoSSW 91*
Bitter, Mark Joseph 1958- *St&PR 91*
Bitterman, Morton Edward 1921- *WhoAm 90*
Bittiger, Jeff 1962- *Ballpl 90*
Bittikofer, Frederick C *BiDrAPA 89*
Bitting, George Capen 1935- *WhoSSW 91*
Bittinger, Allen Walter 1953- *St&PR 91*
Bittke, Brian E. 1937- *St&PR 91*
Bittke, Brian Edmund 1937- *WhoAm 90*
Bittker, Thomas Eliot 1940- *BiDrAPA 89*
Bittle, Bonnie Jean 1950- *WhoSSW 91*
Bittle, Robert Merle 1937- *BiDrAPA 89*
Bittleman, Arnold I 1933- *WhoAmA 91N*
Bittleman, Dolores Dembus 1931- *WhoAmA 91*
Bittlinger, Arnold 1928- *ConAu 31NR*
Bittman, Betsy Jo *BiDrAPA 89*
Bittman, William Omar 1931- *WhoAm 90*
Bittmann, Susan Wilkins 1946- *WhoAmW 91*
Bittner, Egon 1921- *WhoAm 90*
Bittner, George Russell 1928- *St&PR 91*
Bittner, Hans Oskar 1905- *WhoAmA 91*
Bittner, Harlan Fletcher 1951- *WhoEmL 91*
Bittner, John Robert 1943- *WhoAm 90*
Bittner, Katherine Louise 1960- *WhoAmW 91*
Bittner, Mary Ellen 1947- *WhoAmW 91*
Bittner, Stephen Jon 1947- *BiDrAPA 89*
Bitton, Davis 1930- *ConAu 31NR*
Bitton, Livia Elvira *ConAu 130*
Bitton-Jackson, Livia *ConAu 130*
Bitton Jackson, Livia E 1931- *ConAu 130*
Bittone, Richard Edward 1929- *St&PR 91*
Bittrich, Gustav 1937- *IntWWM 90, WhoE 91*
Bitts, Todd Michael 1946- *WhoAm 90*
Bitz, Gerald M. 1935- *St&PR 91*
Bitzer, Donald Lester 1934- *WhoAm 90*
Biuckians, Edward 1937- *BiDrAPA 89*
Biumo, Guiseppe Panza di *BioIn 16*
Biunno, Fred 1947- *St&PR 91*
Biurrun Salanueva, Francisco Javier 1946- *WhoWor 91*
Bivens, Constance Ann 1938- *WhoAmW 91*
Bivens, Donald Wayne 1952- *WhoEmL 91*
Bivens, Gordon Ellsworth 1927- *WhoAm 90*
Bivens, Lynette 1952- *WhoAmW 91*
Bivins, C. Benny 1956- *WhoEmL 91*
Bivins, Daniel Eugene 1932- *WhoSSW 91*
Bivona, Riccardo Alfredo Carlo 1951- *WhoE 91*
Bix, Helen Helman 1935- *WhoAmW 91*
Bixby, Allan Barton 1936- *St&PR 91*
Bixby, Bill 1934- *WorAlBi*
Bixby, Edward K. 1935- *St&PR 91*
Bixby, Frank Lyman 1928- *WhoAm 90*
Bixby, Harold Glenn 1903- *WhoAm 90*
Bixby, J.E. 1922- *St&PR 91*
Bixby, Jerome 1923- *BioIn 16*
Bixby, Joseph Nathan 1950- *WhoEmL 91*
Bixby, Katherine Costlow 1920- *WhoAmW 91*
Bixby, R. Burdell 1914- *WhoAm 90, WhoWor 91*
Bixby, R. Phillip 1953- *St&PR 91*
Bixby, Richard W. 1936- *St&PR 91*
Bixby, Robert Jay 1952- *WhoWrEP 89*
Bixby, Tom 1947- *WhoEmL 91*
Bixby, Walter E. 1932- *WhoAm 90*
Bixby, Walter Edwin 1932- *St&PR 91*
Bixby, William 1920-1986 *BioIn 16*
Bixby, William Courtney 1920-1986 *AuBYP 90*
Bixenstine, Kim Fenton 1958- *WhoEmL 91*
Bixler, Andrew Loy M. 1909- *WhoSSW 91*
Bixler, David 1929- *WhoAm 90*
Bixler, George W., Jr. 1940- *BiDrAPA 89*
Bixler, Gloria Anne 1934- *BiDrAPA 89*
Bixler, Howard *WhoWrEP 89*
Bixler, Lois Jane 1958- *WhoAmW 91*
Bixler, Paul 1899- *WhoWrEP 89*
Bixler, Robert Howard 1937- *WhoE 91*
Bixler, Roland M. 1913- *St&PR 91*
Bixler, William Elwell 1947- *St&PR 91*
Biya, Paul 1933- *WhoWor 91*
Biyani, Babulal Champalal 1925- *WhoWor 91*
Biyidi, Alexandre 1932- *MajTwCW*
Bizar, Irving 1932- *WhoAm 90, WhoE 91*
Bizet, Georges 1838-1875 *PenDiMP A, WorAlBi*
Bizic, Peter, Jr. 1937- *WhoSSW 91*
Bizily, Dale Francis 1945- *St&PR 91*
Bizimungu, Casimir 1951- *WhoWor 91*
Bizoe, Raymond D. 1936- *St&PR 91*
Bizub, Johanna Catherine 1957- *WhoAmW 91, WhoEmL 91*
Bizzell, Bobby Gene 1940- *WhoAm 90*
Bizzi, Emilio 1933- *WhoAm 90*
Bizzoco, Daniel Joseph 1953- *WhoE 91*
Bizzoco, Francis Anthony 1947- *WhoE 91*
Bjarkman, Peter C 1941- *ConAu 130*
Bjarnason, Bjorn 1944- *WhoWor 91*
Bjarnason, Gudmundur 1944- *WhoWor 91*
Bjarni Thorarensen *DcScanL*
Bjelfvenstam, Nils Erik 1896- *EncO&P 3*
Bjerg, Nils 1933- *St&PR 91*
Bjerknes, Jacob 1897-1975 *WorAlBi*
Bjerknes, Jacob Aall Bonnevie 1897-1975 *DcScB S2*
Bjerknes, Michael Leif 1956- *WhoAm 90*
Bjerknes, Vilhelm 1862-1951 *BioIn 16*
Bjerneld, Hakan 1947- *WhoWor 91*
Bjerregaard, William James *BiDrAPA 89*
Bjoner, Ingrid 1927- *PenDiMP*
Bjoner, Ingrid 1928- *IntWWM 90*
Bjontegard, Arthur Martin, Jr. 1938- *St&PR 91, WhoAm 90*
Bjoraker, Walter Thomas 1920- *WhoAm 90*
Bjorck, AndersPer-Arne 1944- *WhoWor 91*
Bjorge, Gary J 1940- *ConAu 130*
Bjorgum, Jan Sigmund 1939- *WhoWor 91*
Bjorhovde, Reidar 1941- *WhoE 91*
Bjorhus, Kari 1958- *ODwPR 91*
Bjork, Carl Kenneth, Jr. 1956- *WhoEmL 91*
Bjork, Christina 1938- *ChlLR 22 [port]*
Bjork, Darla Ann 1939- *BiDrAPA 89*
Bjork, Gordon Carl 1935- *WhoAm 90*
Bjork, Janeen *BioIn 16*
Bjork, Philip Reese 1940- *WhoAm 90*
Bjork, Robert Allen 1939- *WhoAm 90*
Bjork, Robert David, Jr. 1946- *WhoEmL 91, WhoWor 91*
Bjork, Robert William 1926- *St&PR 91*
Bjorkhem, John 1910-1963 *EncO&P 3*
Bjorkholm, John Ernst 1939- *WhoAm 90*
Bjorklund, Anders Gunnar 1935- *WhoWor 91*
Bjorklund, Frederick 1913- *WhoAm 90*
Bjorklund, Harold P. 1940- *St&PR 91*
Bjorklund, J Harman *BiDrAPA 89*
Bjorklund, Janet Vinsen 1947- *WhoEmL 91, WhoWor 91*
Bjorklund, Karna L. *AuBYP 90*
Bjorklund, Lee 1940- *WhoAmA 91*
Bjorklund, Mark *BioIn 16*
Bjorkman, Arlene Doris 1947- *WhoEmL 91*
Bjorkman, Olle Erik 1933- *WhoAm 90*
Bjorksten, Johan 1907- *St&PR 91*
Bjorksten, Oliver James W *BiDrAPA 89*
Bjorling, Gunnar 1887-1960 *DcScanL*
Bjorling, Jussi 1911-1960 *BioIn 16, PenDiMP, WorAlBi*
Bjorling, Rolf 1928- *IntWWM 90, PenDiMP*
Bjorling, Sigurd 1907-1983 *PenDiMP*
Bjorn, Acton 1910- *ConDes 90*
Bjorndahl, David Lee 1927- *St&PR 91*
Bjorndal, Earl Martin 1951- *St&PR 91*
Bjorneboe, Jens Ingvald 1920-1976 *DcScanL*
Bjornfot, Bror Oscar 1933- *WhoWor 91*
Bjornsen, Louise Cathrine Elisabeth 1824-1899 *EncCoWW*
Bjornson, Bjornstjerne 1832-1910 *TwCLC 37 [port], WorAlBi*
Bjornson, Bjornstjerne Martinius 1832-1910 *DcScanL*
Bjornson, Carroll Norman 1929- *WhoE 91, WhoWor 91*
Bjornson, Edward Lee 1931- *St&PR 91*
Bjornson, Jon 1932- *BiDrAPA 89*
Bjornson, Maria *BioIn 16, WhoAmW 91*
Bjornsson, Arnold Bruce 1931- *St&PR 91*
Bjornsson, Sigurdur 1942- *WhoWor 91*
Bjornstad, Harry *BiDrAPA 89*
Bjornvig, Thorkid Strange 1918- *WhoWor 91*
Bjornvig, Thorkild 1918- *DcScanL*
Bjorquist, Karin 1927 *ConDes 90*
Bjurman, George Andrew 1948- *St&PR 91*
Bjurman, George D. 1906- *St&PR 91*
Bjurstrom, Per Gunnar 1928- *WhoWor 91*
Blaas, Wolfgang Rudolf 1947- *WhoWor 91*
Blaaubder, James William 1938- *St&PR 91*
Blaauw, Russell Wayne 1944- *WhoWor 91*
Blach, Harold B., Jr. 1931- *St&PR 91*
Blacharsh, Jill June *BiDrAPA 89*
Blache, Klaus Michael 1951- *WhoEmL 91*
Blacher, Boris 1903-1975 *PenDiMP A*
Blacher, Deanna 1940- *IntWWM 90*
Blacher, Richard S 1924- *BiDrAPA 89*
Blacher, Richard Stanley 1924- *WhoE 91*
Blachford, Peter Carl Howard 1949- *WhoAm 90*
Blachly, Jack Lee 1942- *St&PR 91, WhoAm 90, WhoSSW 91, WhoWor 91*
Blachman, Nelson Merle 1923- *WhoAm 90*
Blachut, Beno 1913-1985 *PenDiMP*
Blachut, Teodor Josef 1915- *WhoAm 90*
Blacik, Stephen Mark 1951- *WhoWrEP 89*
Black Bear *WhNaAH*
Black Beaver 1806-1880 *WhNaAH*
Black Dyke Mills Band *OxCPMus*
Black Elk 1863-1950 *WhNaAH*
Black Flag *EncPR&S 89*
Black Hawk 1767-1838 *WhNaAH [port], WorAlBi*
Black Hoof *WhNaAH*
Black Jim *WhNaAH*
Black Kettle *WhNaAH*
Black Kettle 1803?-1868 *WhNaAH*
Black Partridge *WhNaAH*
Black Patti *DrBlPA 90*
Black Patti 1870-1933 *BioIn 16*
Black Sabbath *EncPR&S 89*
Black Swan 1809-1876 *DcAfAmP*
Black Wood Ashes *DcCanB 12*

Black, Alexander 1914- *WhoAm 90, WhoWor 91*
Black, Alexander Chisholm 1954- *WhoEmL 91*
Black, Allen Decatur 1942- *WhoAm 90*
Black, April Marie 1961- *WhoAmW 91*
Black, Arthur Geiger 1948- *WhoEmL 91*
Black, Arthur Leo 1922- *WhoAm 90*
Black, Arthur O. 1920- *St&PR 91*
Black, Barbara Aronstein 1933- *WhoAm 90*
Black, Barbara Ellen 1938- *WhoE 91*
Black, Barry Martin 1946- *St&PR 91*
Black, Barton Tyler 1953- *St&PR 91, WhoEmL 91*
Black, Benjamin F. 1908- *St&PR 91*
Black, Billy Charleston 1937- *WhoAm 90*
Black, Bobby Gene 1937- *BiDrAPA 89*
Black, Boyd C. 1926- *St&PR 91*
Black, Bradford 1936- *St&PR 91*
Black, Brady Forrest 1908- *WhoAm 90, WhoWrEP 89*
Black, Bruce 1953- *BiDrAPA 89*
Black, Bud 1957- *Ballpl 90*
Black, Calvin *BioIn 16*
Black, Calvin 1903-1972 *MusmAFA*
Black, Carl Clifton, II 1955- *WhoSSW 91*
Black, Cathleen *BioIn 16*
Black, Cathleen P. 1944- *St&PR 91*
Black, Cathleen Prunty 1944- *WhoAm 90, WhoAmW 91, WhoWrEP 89*
Black, Charles 1928- *ConAu 132*
Black, Charles 1947- *NewYTBS 90 [port]*
Black, Charles Allen 1916- *WhoAm 90*
Black, Charles Alvin 1920- *WhoAm 90*
Black, Charles Robert 1935- *WhoAm 90*
Black, Cilla 1943- *OxCPMus*
Black, Claire Alexander 1953- *WhoEmL 91*
Black, Clanton Candler, Jr. 1931- *WhoAm 90*
Black, Clementina 1853-1922 *BioIn 16*
Black, Clementina 1855-1923 *FemiCLE*
Black, Clint *BioIn 16*
Black, Clint 1962- *ConMus 5 [port]*
Black, Clinton V 1918- *ConAu 30NR*
Black, Clyde Joseph, III 1945- *St&PR 91*
Black, Cobey 1922- *WhoAmW 91, WhoWor 91*
Black, Conrad M. *BioIn 16*
Black, Conrad Moffat 1944- *St&PR 91, WhoAm 90*
Black, Craig McKnight 1923- *St&PR 91*
Black, Creed Carter 1925- *St&PR 91, WhoAm 90, WhoWrEP 89*
Black, Curtis Doersam 1951- *WhoEmL 91*
Black, Cynthia Joy *BiDrAPA 89*
Black, Cyril Edwin 1915-1989 *BioIn 16, ConAu 129*
Black, Daniel Hugh 1947- *WhoEmL 91, WhoSSW 91, WhoWor 91*
Black, Daniel James 1931- *St&PR 91*
Black, Danny Earl 1944- *WhoSSW 91*
Black, David *BioIn 16*
Black, David 1945- *WhoAm 90, WhoWor 91*
Black, David A. 1949- *St&PR 91*
Black, David Evans 1928- *WhoAmA 91*
Black, David Luther 1934- *WhoE 91*
Black, David Phillip 1935- *BiDrAPA 89*
Black, David R. 1952- *St&PR 91*
Black, David Randall 1947- *WhoEmL 91*
Black, David Scott 1961- *WhoEmL 91*
Black, David Statler 1928- *WhoAm 90*
Black, Dawn 1943- *WhoAmW 91*
Black, Don 1916-1959 *Ballpl 90*
Black, Donald Bruce 1932- *WhoAm 90*
Black, Donald Chain 1935- *WhoWrEP 89*
Black, Donald E. 1942- *St&PR 91*
Black, Donald W 1956- *BiDrAPA 89*
Black, Dorothy 1914- *ConAu 30NR*
Black, Douglas D. 1961- *WhoEmL 91*
Black, Edward *BiDrAPA 89*
Black, Eileen Mary 1944- *WhoAmW 91*
Black, Eleanor Simms 1872-1949 *WhoAmA 91N*
Black, Elinor G. *BioIn 16*
Black, Ellen *ODwPR 91*
Black, Emilie Annabelle 1919- *WhoAm 90*
Black, Erroll Vic 1945- *WhoEmL 91*
Black, Eugene Charlton 1927- *WhoAm 90*
Black, Forrest Edward 1941- *WhoSSW 91*
Black, Francene W 1945- *BiDrAPA 89*
Black, Frances Patterson 1949- *WhoAmW 91*
Black, Frederick Evan 1944- *WhoWor 91*
Black, Gavin 1913- *TwCCr&M 91*
Black, George 1920- *WhoAm 90*
Black, George Frederick 1947- *WhoSSW 91*
Black, George Lawrence, Jr. 1932- *WhoSSW 91*
Black, George Malcolm *WhoAm 90*
Black, Georgia *BioIn 16*
Black, Hans Peter 1953- *WhoE 91*
Black, Harold S. 1898-1983 *BioIn 16*
Black, Harry George 1933- *WhoWrEP 89*
Black, Hillel Moses 1929- *WhoAm 90, WhoWrEP 89*
Black, Howard 1947- *WhoEmL 91*
Black, Hugo 1886-1971 *WorAlBi*
Black, Hugo LaFayette 1886-1971 *BioIn 16*
Black, Hugo LaFayette, Jr. *BioIn 16*
Black, Hugo Lafayette, Jr. 1922- *WhoAm 90*
Black, Ira B. *WhoAm 90*
Black, Irma Simonton 1906-1972 *AuBYP 90*
Black, Irvin R. 1918- *St&PR 91*
Black, James 1823-1893 *WorAlBi*
Black, James 1924- *WhoWor 91*
Black, James Allen, Jr. 1951- *WhoSSW 91*
Black, James Coke *BiDrAPA 89*
Black, James F. 1945- *St&PR 91*
Black, James Frederick 1953- *WhoEmL 91*
Black, James Isaac, III 1951- *WhoEmL 91*
Black, James N. *BioIn 16*
Black, James R. 1943- *St&PR 91*
Black, James Sinclair 1940- *WhoAm 90*
Black, James Thompson 1925- *St&PR 91*
Black, James W. 1924- *WorAlBi*
Black, James Whyte 1924- *BioIn 16*
Black, James William, Jr. 1936- *BiDrAPA 89*
Black, Janice Karen 1946- *St&PR 91*
Black, Janice T. 1946- *St&PR 91*
Black, Jarrett C 1930- *BiDrAPA 89*
Black, Jean Belcher *EarBIAP*
Black, Jeremiah Sullivan 1810-1883 *BiDrUSE 89, BioIn 16*
Black, Jesse M., Jr. 1942- *St&PR 91*
Black, Joe 1924- *Ballpl 90*
Black, Joe 1945- *St&PR 91*
Black, John D. 1919- *St&PR 91*
Black, John Logan *BiDrAPA 89*
Black, John Richard 1923- *BiDrAPA 89*
Black, John Thomas *BiDrAPA 89*
Black, John Wilson 1906-1987 *BioIn 16*
Black, John Woodland 1925- *WhoAm 90*
Black, Joseph 1924- *WhoAm 90*
Black, Joseph Lee 1938- *BiDrAPA 89*
Black, Judy A. *ODwPR 91*
Black, Karen 1942- *BioIn 16, WorAlBi*
Black, Kathleen 1908-1984 *BioIn 16*
Black, Kaylene Slay 1945- *WhoAmW 91*
Black, Kelly *BioIn 16*
Black, Kelly Hunter 1960- *WhoAmW 91*
Black, Kelly Marie 1960- *WhoAmW 91*
Black, Kenneth, Jr. 1925- *WhoAm 90*
Black, Kent M. 1939- *St&PR 91*
Black, Kent March 1939- *WhoAm 90, WhoSSW 91*
Black, Kirby Samuel 1954- *WhoEmL 91*
Black, Kitty *ConAu 30NR*
Black, L.K. 1930- *St&PR 91*
Black, Larry 1943- *WhoSSW 91*
Black, Larry 1949- *WhoSSW 91*
Black, Larry David 1949- *WhoAm 90*
Black, Laverne Nelson *BiDrAPA 89*
Black, Lawrence Richard 1949- *WhoE 91*
Black, Leon David, Jr. 1926- *WhoSSW 91*
Black, Leonard J. 1919- *WhoAm 90*
Black, Lionel 1910-1980 *TwCCr&M 91*
Black, Lisa *ODwPR 91*
Black, Lisa 1934- *WhoAmA 91*
Black, Lois Mae 1931- *WhoAm 90*
Black, Lydia T. 1925- *WhoAm 90*
Black, Lynda Kay 1959- *WhoAmW 91*
Black, Maggie *ConAu 32NR*
Black, Malcolm 1928- *OxCCanT*
Black, Malcolm Charles Lamont 1928- *WhoAm 90*
Black, Mansell *TwCCr&M 91*
Black, Margaret K 1921- *ConAu 32NR*
Black, Martha Susan Lowe 1945- *WhoAmW 91*
Black, Mary Ann 1953- *WhoSSW 91*
Black, Mary Childs *WhoAmA 91*
Black, Mary McCune 1915- *WhoAmA 91*
Black, Maureen 1937- *WhoAmW 91*
Black, Max 1909-1988 *BioIn 16*
Black, Michael 1928- *ConAu 131*
Black, Michael R. 1960- *WhoEmL 91*
Black, Minnie 1899- *MusmAFA [port]*
Black, Misha 1910-1977 *ConDes 90*
Black, Naomi Ruth 1957- *WhoAmW 91, WhoE 91*
Black, Natalie A. 1949- *St&PR 91*
Black, Noel Anthony 1937- *WhoAm 90*
Black, Norman M., III *St&PR 91*
Black, Norman William 1931- *WhoAm 90, WhoSSW 91*
Black, Page Morton *WhoAmW 91, WhoE 91, WhoWor 91*
Black, Patti Carr 1934- *WhoAm 90, WhoAmW 91*
Black, Paul Henry 1930- *WhoAm 90*
Black, Paul Stephen 1953- *WhoSSW 91*
Black, Paul William 1934- *WhoSSW 91*
Black, Percy 1922- *WhoAm 90*
Black, Perry 1930- *WhoAm 90*
Black, R D Collison 1922- *ConAu 131*
Black, Ralph 1919-1989 *BioIn 16*
Black, Randall L *BiDrAPA 89*
Black, Raymond Charles 1938- *WhoE 91*
Black, Richard Bruce 1933- *WhoAm 90, WhoE 91*
Black, Richard Eugene 1934- *WhoSSW 91*
Black, Richard R 1932- *WhoAmA 91*
Black, Robert *ConAu 131*
Black, Robert Alan 1944- *WhoSSW 91*
Black, Robert Bliss 1944- *St&PR 91*
Black, Robert Coleman 1934- *WhoAm 90*
Black, Robert E. *St&PR 91*
Black, Robert Frederick 1920- *WhoAm 90*
Black, Robert G. 1929- *ODwPR 91*
Black, Robert Irvin 1923- *St&PR 91*
Black, Robert James 1955- *WhoEmL 91*
Black, Robert Lincoln 1930- *WhoAm 90*
Black, Robert P. 1927- *St&PR 91*
Black, Robert Perry 1927- *WhoAm 90*
Black, Rosalie Jean 1938- *WhoAmW 91*
Black, Ruby 1913-1980 *MusmAFA*
Black, Samuel 1937- *BiDrAPA 89*
Black, Samuel Baer *BiDrAPA 89*
Black, Samuel Harold 1930- *WhoAm 90*
Black, Samuel MacArthur 1942- *WhoSSW 91*
Black, Samuel Matthew 1933- *WhoSSW 91*
Black, Samuel P., Jr. 1902- *St&PR 91*
Black, Samuel Paul West 1916- *WhoAm 90*
Black, Sandra Kay 1942- *WhoWrEP 89*
Black, Sandra Rose 1950- *WhoEmL 91*
Black, Sarah Colleen 1961- *WhoAmW 91*
Black, Shirley Renee 1960- *WhoAmW 91*
Black, Shirley Sharp 1940- *St&PR 91*
Black, Shirley T. *BioAmW*
Black, Shirley Temple 1928- *BioIn 16, WhoAm 90, WhoAmW 91, WhoWor 91*
Black, Stan A. 1937- *St&PR 91*
Black, Stanley 1913- *IntWWM 90, OxCPMus, PenDiMP*
Black, Stanley Warren, III 1939- *ConAu 31NR*
Black, Stephen Franklin 1944- *WhoAm 90*
Black, Steven D. 1952- *St&PR 91*
Black, Stuart M. 1926- *St&PR 91*
Black, Susan 1953- *ODwPR 91*
Black, Susan Faye 1937- *WhoSSW 91*
Black, Susan Harrell 1943- *WhoAm 90, WhoAmW 91*
Black, Suzanne Alexandra 1958- *WhoAmW 91*
Black, Sydney Doree 1915- *WhoE 91*
Black, Terrance 1944- *St&PR 91*
Black, Theodore Halsey 1928- *St&PR 91, WhoAm 90, WhoE 91*
Black, Theodore Michael 1919- *WhoAm 90, WhoWrEP 89*
Black, Thomas Donald 1920- *WhoAm 90*
Black, W.G. 1927- *St&PR 91*
Black, Walter Evan, Jr. 1926- *WhoAm 90, WhoE 91*
Black, Walter Kerrigan 1915- *WhoAm 90*
Black, Wendell H 1919-1972 *WhoAmA 91N*
Black, William Alan 1953- *St&PR 91*
Black, William David 1952- *IntWWM 90*
Black, William Earl 1951- *WhoEmL 91*
Black, William Edward 1947- *WhoSSW 91*
Black, William Gordon 1927- *WhoAm 90*
Black, William Grant 1920- *WhoAm 90*
Black, William H., Jr. 1919- *St&PR 91*
Black, William Harman, II 1925- *St&PR 91*
Black, William R. 1926- *St&PR 91*
Black, William S. 1919- *St&PR 91*
Black, Winifred 1863-1936 *BioIn 16*
Black-Keefer, Sharon Kay 1949- *WhoAmW 91, WhoEmL 91, WhoWor 91*
Black-Rhodes, Diana Karen 1953- *WhoAmW 91*
Blackadar, Alfred Kimball 1920- *WhoAm 90*
Blackadder, Elizabeth 1931- *BiDWomA*
Blackall, Eric A. 1914-1989 *BioIn 16*
Blackall, Eric Albert 1914-1989 *ConAu 130*
Blackall, Frederick Steele, III 1925- *WhoE 91*
Blackaller, Tom *BioIn 16*
Blackaller, Tom 1940-1989 *AnObit 1989*
Blackberry, Sarah *BiDEWW*
Blackborow, Sarah *FemiCLE*
Blackborow, Sarah *BiDEWW*
Blackbourn, David 1949- *ConAu 132*
Blackburn, Amy Clements 1948- *WhoSSW 91*
Blackburn, Archie B *BiDrAPA 89*
Blackburn, Barbara Ann 1942- *WhoWrEP 89*
Blackburn, Bonnie J. 1939- *IntWWM 90*
Blackburn, Bonnie S. 1949- *St&PR 91*
Blackburn, Catherine Elaine 1953- *WhoAmW 91, WhoEmL 91, WhoSSW 91, WhoWor 91*
Blackburn, Charles Lee 1928- *St&PR 91, WhoSSW 91*
Blackburn, Claire *ConAu 30NR*
Blackburn, D. Joann 1941- *St&PR 91*
Blackburn, David Alan 1944- *St&PR 91*
Blackburn, Donald F. 1927- *St&PR 91*
Blackburn, Ed M 1940- *WhoAmA 91*
Blackburn, Edith H. *AuBYP 90*
Blackburn, Edward J. 1923- *St&PR 91*
Blackburn, Edward Jack 1931- *St&PR 91*
Blackburn, Elizabeth Helen 1948- *WhoAmW 91*
Blackburn, Helen 1842-1903 *BioIn 16, FemiCLE*
Blackburn, Henry Webster, Jr. 1925- *WhoAm 90*
Blackburn, Howard *BioIn 16*
Blackburn, Jack Bailey 1922- *WhoAm 90*
Blackburn, Jack L. 1917- *St&PR 91*
Blackburn, James H *BiDrAPA 89*
Blackburn, James Ross, Jr. 1930- *WhoAm 90, WhoWor 91*
Blackburn, Jeffrey Joe 1954- *WhoSSW 91*
Blackburn, Jeffrey R. 1952- *St&PR 91*
Blackburn, Jemima 1823-1909 *BiDWomA, BioIn 16*
Blackburn, John 1923- *TwCCr&M 91*
Blackburn, John Fenwick 1923- *SpyFic*
Blackburn, John Glenn, Jr. 1941- *WhoSSW 91*
Blackburn, John H. 1942- *St&PR 91*
Blackburn, John Lewis 1913- *WhoAm 90*
Blackburn, John Oliver 1929- *WhoAm 90*
Blackburn, Kenneth Floyd 1926- *St&PR 91*
Blackburn, Lenora Whitmire 1904- *WhoAmA 91*
Blackburn, Linda Z 1941- *WhoAmA 91*
Blackburn, Loren Hayner 1929- *WhoAmA 91*
Blackburn, Marsh Hanly 1929- *St&PR 91*
Blackburn, Martha Grace 1944- *WhoAm 90, WhoAmW 91*
Blackburn, Michael James 1957- *WhoSSW 91*
Blackburn, Mitchell Derek 1961- *WhoEmL 91*
Blackburn, Morris 1902-1979 *WhoAmA 91N*
Blackburn, Norman *BioIn 16, NewYTBS 90*
Blackburn, Norman 1904?-1990 *ConAu 131*
Blackburn, Olivia *IntWWM 90*
Blackburn, Paul Pritchard 1937- *WhoAm 90*
Blackburn, Richard S. 1927- *St&PR 91*
Blackburn, Richard Wallace 1942- *St&PR 91, WhoAm 90*
Blackburn, Robert Barnett 1930- *St&PR 91*
Blackburn, Robert L. 1960- *WhoSSW 91*
Blackburn, Robert McGrady 1919- *WhoAm 90*
Blackburn, Roger Lloyd 1946- *WhoEmL 91*
Blackburn, Ron 1935- *Ballpl 90*
Blackburn, Steven Peter 1952- *WhoEmL 91*
Blackburn, Terry Michael 1951- *WhoEmL 91*
Blackburn, Theresa N *BiDrAPA 89*
Blackburn, Thomas C 1936- *WhoWrEP 89*
Blackburn, Thomas Harold 1932- *WhoAm 90*
Blackburn, Thomas Irven 1949- *WhoEmL 91*
Blackburn, Tom 1912- *BioIn 16*
Blackburn, Ulric 1926- *WhoE 91*
Blackburn, William Martin 1939- *WhoAm 90*
Blackburne, Anne *BiDEWW*
Blackburne, E. Owens 1848?-1894 *FemiCLE*
Blackburne, Lena 1886-1968 *Ballpl 90*
Blackburne, Rebecka 1661- *BiDEWW*
Blacken, John Dale 1930- *WhoAm 90, WhoWor 91*
Blacker, Deborah Lynne *BiDrAPA 89*
Blacker, Harriet 1940- *WhoAm 90, WhoAmW 91, WhoWrEP 89*
Blacker, Ian T. 1954- *WhoEmL 91*
Blacker, Kate 1955- *BiDWomA*
Blacker, Kay Hill 1930- *BiDrAPA 89*
Blackerby, Charles Julien 1932- *WhoAm 90*
Blackert, John Edward 1933- *St&PR 91*
Blackert, Virginia Rose 1948- *WhoAmW 91, WhoE 91*
Blacketer, James Richard 1931- *WhoAmA 91*
Blackett, Mary *FemiCLE*
Blackett, Patrick M. S. *BioIn 16*
Blackett, Patrick M. S. 1897-1974 *WorAlBi*
Blackett, Stanley E. 1938- *St&PR 91*
Blackey, Edwin Arthur, Jr. 1927- *WhoE 91*
Blackey, Mary Madlyn *WhoAmA 91, WhoE 91*
Blackfan, Cyrus Linton 1935- *WhoWor 91*
Blackfield, Cecilia Malik 1915- *WhoAmW 91*
Blackfoot 1795?-1877 *WhNaAH*
Blackford, Leo Price 1951- *St&PR 91*

Blackford, Robert Newton 1937- *St&PR 91, WhoAm 90, WhoSSW 91*
Blackford, Staige D. 1931- *WhoWrEP 89*
Blackham, Ann Rosemary 1927- *WhoAmW 91, WhoE 91*
Blackham, Joyce 1934- *IntWWM 90*
Blackhurst, Eric Paul 1961- *WhoEmL 91*
Blackie, Gordon Neil 1954- *WhoWor 91*
Blackie, Penelope Jane 1944- *WhoWor 91*
Blackie, William 1906- *ConAmBL*
Blackin, Jack M. 1942- *St&PR 91*
Blacking, John Anthony Randoll 1928- *IntWWM 90*
Blackington, Frank H., II *WhoAm 90*
Blackinton, Charles Harry 1937- *BiDrAPA 89, WhoE 91*
Blackledge, Kenneth Allen 1950- *St&PR 91*
Blackler, Antonie William Charles 1931- *WhoAm 90*
Blackler, Sharon Renda 1947- *WhoAmW 91*
Blacklidge, James B. 1943- *St&PR 91*
Blacklidge, Melodie Gayle *BiDrAPA 89*
Blacklidge, Raymond Mark 1960- *WhoWor 91*
Blacklidge, Richard Henry 1914- *WhoWrEP 89*
Blacklidge, Virginia Y 1931- *BiDrAPA 89*
Blacklin, Malcolm *ConAu 31NR*
Blacklock, Charles B. 1924- *St&PR 91*
Blacklow, Robert Stanley 1934- *WhoAm 90*
Blackman, Audrey 1907-1990? *ConAu 132*
Blackman, Benjamin 1925- *BiDrAPA 89*
Blackman, Bruce Elliott 1950- *BiDrAPA 89*
Blackman, Cindy *BioIn 16*
Blackman, Darrell *St&PR 91*
Blackman, David Ira 1951- *WhoEmL 91*
Blackman, Dorman R. 1935- *St&PR 91*
Blackman, Dorothy Loyte 1935- *WhoWrEP 89*
Blackman, George Raymond 1960- *WhoEmL 91*
Blackman, Ghita Waucheta 1932- *WhoAmW 91*
Blackman, Honor 1926- *BioIn 16*
Blackman, James Ray 1942- *St&PR 91*
Blackman, James Timothy 1951- *WhoEmL 91*
Blackman, Jeanne A. 1943- *WhoAmW 91*
Blackman, Jerome Scott *BiDrAPA 89*
Blackman, John Calhoun, IV 1944- *WhoSSW 91*
Blackman, John M. 1942- *St&PR 91*
Blackman, Karen Selin *BiDrAPA 89*
Blackman, Kenneth Robert 1941- *WhoAm 90*
Blackman, Lionel Hart *BiDrAPA 89*
Blackman, Murray Ivan 1945- *WhoEmL 91*
Blackman, Patricia Ann 1946- *WhoEmL 91*
Blackman, Paul Charles 1941- *St&PR 91, WhoAm 90*
Blackman, Percy C. 1907- *St&PR 91*
Blackman, Raymond V. B. 1910-1989 *BioIn 16*
Blackman, Richard Gus, Jr. 1948- *WhoSSW 91*
Blackman, Robert Irwin 1928- *WhoAm 90*
Blackman, Steven Theodore 1945- *St&PR 91*
Blackman, Sue Anne Batey 1948- *ConAu 132*
Blackman, Thomas Patrick 1951- *WhoAmA 91*
Blackman, Vernon Harold 1929- *WhoAm 90*
Blackman, Victor *BioIn 16*
Blackmar, Charles Blakey 1922- *WhoAm 90*
Blackmer, David L. *ODwPR 91*
Blackmer, Donald Laurence Morton 1929- *WhoAm 90*
Blackmer, Mary Louise 1909- *BiDrAPA 89*
Blackmer, Richard H. 1929- *St&PR 91*
Blackmon, Antonia A. *WhoWrEP 89*
Blackmon, Cleretta Arizana 1939- *WhoAm 90*
Blackmon, Frederick L. 1952- *St&PR 91*
Blackmon, James Donald 1941- *WhoSSW 91*
Blackmon, Joyce McAnulty 1937- *St&PR 91*
Blackmon, Lawrence George 1919- *WhoAm 90*
Blackmon, Michael James 1946- *WhoEmL 91*
Blackmon, Wayne Douglas 1952- *BiDrAPA 89*
Blackmon, William J. 1921- *MusmAFA*
Blackmore, Denis Louis 1943- *WhoE 91*
Blackmore, Michael Adams 1954- *BiDrAPA 89*
Blackmore, R. D. 1825-1900 *BioIn 16*
Blackmore, R.D. 1939- *St&PR 91*
Blackmore, Richard Doddridge 1825-1900 *BioIn 16*
Blackmore, Ritchie *EncPR&S 89*
Blackmore, Susan J. *EncO&P 3*
Blackmore, Susan Jane 1951- *EncPaPR 91*
Blackmun, Barbara Winston 1928- *WhoAmA 91*
Blackmun, Harry A. *BioIn 16*
Blackmun, Harry A. 1908- *WorAlBi*
Blackmun, Harry Andrew 1908- *WhoAm 90, WhoE 91, WhoWor 91*
Blackmur, R. P. 1904-1965 *BioIn 16*
Blackmur, Richard P. 1904-1965 *BioIn 16*
Blackner, Boyd Atkins 1933- *WhoAm 90*
Blackshear, A. T., Jr. 1942- *WhoAm 90*
Blackshear, Helen F. 1911- *WhoAmW 91*
Blackshear, Helen Friedman 1911- *WhoWrEP 89*
Blackshear, Margaret Ruth Bonham *WhoAmW 91*
Blackshear, Thomas R. *BioIn 16*
Blacksmith, Sara *WhoWrEP 89*
Blacksnake 1760?-1859 *WhNaAH*
Blackson, Benjamin Franklin 1933- *WhoE 91*
Blackson, David Lynn 1931- *St&PR 91*
Blacksten-Plantz, Anna Marie 1948- *WhoAmW 91*
Blackstock, Charity *TwCCr&M 91*
Blackstock, James Fielding 1947- *WhoEmL 91*
Blackstock, Jerry Byron 1945- *WhoAm 90, WhoEmL 91, WhoSSW 91*
Blackstock, Lee *TwCCr&M 91*
Blackstock, LeRoy 1914- *WhoAm 90, WhoWor 91*
Blackstock, Virginia Lee Lowman 1917- *WhoAmW 91, WhoSSW 91*
Blackstone, George Arthur 1922- *WhoAm 90*
Blackstone, Harriet 1864-1939 *BiDWomA*
Blackstone, Harry 1885-1965 *BioIn 16*
Blackstone, Harry 1934- *BioIn 16*
Blackstone, Harry Bouton, Jr. 1934- *WhoAm 90*
Blackstone, John Homer, Jr. 1948- *WhoSSW 91*
Blackstone, Mike *BioIn 16*
Blackstone, Patricia Clark 1952- *WhoSSW 91*
Blackstone, R. Loring 1926- *St&PR 91*
Blackstone, Richmond Loring 1926- *WhoAm 90*
Blackstone, Sandra Lee *WhoAm 90, WhoAmW 91*
Blackstone, William 1596-1675 *EncCRAm*
Blackstone, William 1723-1780 *WorAlBi*
Blackton, Charles Stuart 1913- *WhoAm 90*
Blacktree, Barbara *WhoWrEP 89*
Blackwelder, Alice Nash 1928- *WhoSSW 91*
Blackwelder, John Norris 1936- *St&PR 91*
Blackwelder, Ron Forest 1941- *WhoAm 90*
Blackwell, Albert T., Jr. *WhoE 91*
Blackwell, Alice Stone 1857-1950 *FemiCLE*
Blackwell, Anna *EncO&P 3*
Blackwell, Anna Derby 1932- *WhoAmW 91*
Blackwell, Antoinette 1815-1921 *FemiCLE*
Blackwell, Antoinette B. 1825-1921 *BioAmW*
Blackwell, Antoinette Brown 1825-1921 *WorAlBi*
Blackwell, Antoinette Lynn 1960- *WhoAmW 91*
Blackwell, Barry 1934- *BiDrAPA 89*
Blackwell, Basil Henry 1889-1984 *DcNaB 1981*
Blackwell, Bernard Constanstine 1940- *WhoE 91*
Blackwell, Bill *BioIn 16*
Blackwell, Cecil 1924- *WhoSSW 91*
Blackwell, Chris *BioIn 16*
Blackwell, Dan P. 1952- *WhoEmL 91*
Blackwell, David Eric 1945- *WhoSSW 91*
Blackwell, David H. 1919- *WhoAm 90*
Blackwell, David Jefferson 1927- *WhoAm 90*
Blackwell, Douglas L. 1933- *St&PR 91*
Blackwell, Earl 1913- *WhoAm 90, WhoWor 91, WhoWrEP 89*
Blackwell, Ed *BioIn 16*
Blackwell, Elizabeth 1821-1910 *BioAmW, BioIn 16, WorAlBi*
Blackwell, Ewell 1922- *Ballpl 90, BioIn 16*
Blackwell, Gus Ray 1955- *WhoSSW 91*
Blackwell, Henry Barlow, II 1928- *WhoAm 90*
Blackwell, Henry Browne 1825-1909 *WorAlBi*
Blackwell, James Augusta, Jr. 1940- *WhoAm 90*
Blackwell, James Madison, IV 1931- *WhoE 91*
Blackwell, James Robert 1936- *WhoSSW 91*
Blackwell, Jeffrey David 1943- *St&PR 91*
Blackwell, John 1942- *WhoAm 90*
Blackwell, John 1945- *WhoEmL 91*
Blackwell, John Norman 1948- *WhoWor 91*
Blackwell, John Wesley 1941- *WhoAm 90*
Blackwell, Judith Ellen 1956- *WhoAmW 91*
Blackwell, Kim Lois 1959- *WhoE 91*
Blackwell, Lelia Elisabeth 1955- *WhoEmL 91*
Blackwell, Linda Christine 1953- *WhoWrEP 89*
Blackwell, Lucy White 1912- *WhoAmW 91*
Blackwell, Mary Ann 1932- *WhoAmW 91*
Blackwell, Menefee Davis 1916- *WhoAm 90*
Blackwell, Milford *BiDrAPA 89*
Blackwell, Nigel Stirling 1947- *St&PR 91*
Blackwell, Otis 1931- *OxCPMus*
Blackwell, Paul Eugene 1941- *WhoE 91*
Blackwell, Richard Manning 1940- *St&PR 91, WhoAm 90*
Blackwell, Ronald Eugene 1933- *WhoAm 90*
Blackwell, Saundra Cochran 1946- *WhoEmL 91*
Blackwell, Stanley Michael 1951- *WhoEmL 91*
Blackwell, Terry Glenn 1947- *WhoSSW 91*
Blackwell, Thomas F. 1961- *WhoEmL 91*
Blackwell, Tim 1952- *Ballpl 90*
Blackwell, Tom 1938- *WhoAmA 91*
Blackwell, William Allen 1920- *WhoAm 90*
Blackwell, William Ernest 1932- *St&PR 91, WhoAm 90, WhoSSW 91*
Blackwood, Algernon 1869-1951 *EncO&P 3, TwCCr&M 91*
Blackwood, Arthur Leonard 1932- *WhoSSW 91*
Blackwood, Caroline 1931- *ConAu 32NR, FemiCLE, MajTwCW*
Blackwood, David 1941- *WhoAmA 91*
Blackwood, Easley 1933- *IntWWM 90*
Blackwood, Lois Anne 1949- *WhoAmW 91*
Blackwood, Robert Adair, Jr. 1948- *BiDrAPA 89*
Blackwood, Russell Thorn, III 1928- *WhoAm 90*
Blackwood, William Jonathan 1953- *WhoE 91*
Blacque, Taurean *BioIn 16, ConTFT 8, DrBlPA 90, WhoAm 90*
Blade, Alexander *ConAu 130, MajTwCW*
Blade, Martin Alan 1947- *St&PR 91*
Blade, Melinda Kim 1952- *WhoAmW 91, WhoEmL 91*
Blade, Werner *BiDrAPA 89*
Blades, A.T. 1908- *St&PR 91*
Blades, Ann 1947- *WhoWrEP 89*
Blades, Barbara Oakey 1951- *WhoAmW 91*
Blades, Brian 1955- *St&PR 91*
Blades, Carol Brady 1947- *ODwPR 91*
Blades, Herbert William 1908- *WhoAm 90*
Blades, James 1901- *IntWWM 90, PenDiMP*
Blades, Jane M. 1953- *WhoAmW 91*
Blades, John Donaldson 1936- *WhoWrEP 89*
Blades, Ray 1896-1979 *Ballpl 90*
Blades, Ruben *BioIn 16*
Blades, Ruben 1948- *ConAu 131, HispWr 90, WhoAm 90, WhoHisp 91*
Blades, Steven Paul 1951- *WhoWor 91*
Blados, Walter Roman 1931- *WhoSSW 91*
Bladsoe, Gary Owen 1947- *WhoSSW 91*
Blaedel, Walter John 1916- *WhoAm 90*
Blaeholder, George 1904-1947 *Ballpl 90*
Blaes, Peter Viggo *BiDrAPA 89*
Blaesi, Mary Virginia 1953- *WhoAmW 91*
Blaess, Donna Adele 1948- *WhoAmW 91, WhoSSW 91*
Blagden, Allen 1938- *WhoAmA 91*
Blagden, Isa 1816?-1873 *FemiCLE*
Blagden, Thomas P 1911- *WhoAmA 91*
Blager, Florence Berman *WhoAmW 91*
Blagg, Christopher Robin 1931- *WhoAm 90*
Blagge, Margaret 1652-1678 *BiDEWW*
Blaha, Ivo 1936- *IntWWM 90*
Blaha, Margaret Wirth 1909- *WhoAmW 91*
Blaha, Verle Dennis 1929- *St&PR 91*
Blahd, William Henry 1921- *WhoAm 90*
Blahetka, Russell Ernest 1952- *WhoEmL 91*
Blahous, Charles Paul 1935- *St&PR 91*
Blahove, Marcos 1928- *WhoAmA 91*
Blahun, George 1921- *WhoSSW 91*
Blahut, Richard Edward 1937- *WhoAm 90*
Blahut, Stephen George 1952- *WhoSSW 91*
Blai, Bertha *WhoAmA 91*
Blai, Boris 1898-1985 *WhoAmA 91N*
Blaich, Robert I 1930- *ConDes 90*
Blaik, Earl Henry 1897-1989 *BioIn 16*
Blaik, Red 1897-1989 *BioIn 16*
Blaik, Robert Elliot 1942- *BiDrAPA 89*
Blaikie, Thomas 1750-1838 *BioIn 16*
Blain, Alexander, III 1918- *WhoAm 90*
Blain, Mary Vrzak 1950- *St&PR 91*
Blain, Ray 1893-1989 *BioIn 16*
Blaine, Anita M. 1866-1954 *BioAmW*
Blaine, Armin Al 1923- *WhoE 91*
Blaine, Charles G. 1925- *St&PR 91*
Blaine, Charles Gillespie 1925- *WhoAm 90*
Blaine, David Bradley 1946- *St&PR 91*
Blaine, Davis Robert 1943- *WhoAm 90*
Blaine, Dorman 1939- *St&PR 91*
Blaine, Dorothea Constance Ragette 1930- *WhoAmW 91*
Blaine, Graham Burt, Jr. 1918- *BiDrAPA 89*
Blaine, Jack David 1943- *BiDrAPA 89*
Blaine, James G. 1830-1893 *WorAlBi*
Blaine, James Gillespie 1830-1893 *AmLegL, BiDrUSE 89, BioIn 16*
Blaine, John *AuBYP 90, ConAu 131*
Blaine, John 1914-1990 *BioIn 16*
Blaine, Kathleen Elaine 1953- *WhoAmW 91*
Blaine, Margery Kay 1937- *AuBYP 90*
Blaine, Matthew Frederick 1947- *WhoAmA 91*
Blaine, Nell 1922- *BiDWomA, WhoAmA 91*
Blaine, Nell Walden 1922- *WhoAm 90*
Blaine, William D. 1929- *St&PR 91*
Blaine, William McKinley, Jr. 1931- *St&PR 91*
Blair, Alan J. 1924- *St&PR 91*
Blair, Alistair *BioIn 16*
Blair, Alvin Francis 1931- *St&PR 91*
Blair, Andrew Lane, Jr. 1946- *WhoAm 90*
Blair, Andrew Ronald 1937- *WhoAm 90*
Blair, Anne Meem Peachy 1914- *WhoE 91*
Blair, Barbara Anne 1926- *WhoAmW 91, WhoSSW 91*
Blair, Barbara D. 1938- *St&PR 91*
Blair, Becky Westmoreland 1958- *WhoSSW 91*
Blair, Betty Stepp 1947- *WhoAmW 91*
Blair, Bonnie *BioIn 16*
Blair, Bowen 1918- *St&PR 91, WhoAm 90*
Blair, Calvin Patton 1924- *WhoAm 90*
Blair, Carl Raymond 1932- *WhoAmA 91*
Blair, Carol Lynn 1951- *BiDrAPA 89*
Blair, Charles Lee 1954- *BiDrAPA 89, WhoE 91*
Blair, Charles Melvin 1910- *WhoAm 90*
Blair, Charles Michael 1942- *WhoSSW 91*
Blair, Christopher David 1944- *St&PR 91*
Blair, Claude 1922- *BioIn 16*
Blair, Clay Drewry 1925- *WhoWrEP 89*
Blair, Clyde Edmon 1950- *WhoEmL 91*
Blair, Craig John 1943- *St&PR 91, WhoAm 90*
Blair, Damian J. W. 1957- *WhoWor 91*
Blair, Dana Miller 1957- *WhoAmW 91*
Blair, David Fairlie 1955- *WhoWor 91*
Blair, Dennis 1954- *Ballpl 90*
Blair, Dennis Earl 1947- *WhoEmL 91*
Blair, Diana 1947- *WhoWrEP 89*
Blair, Diane Divers 1938- *WhoSSW 91*
Blair, Dike 1952- *WhoAmA 91*
Blair, Donald R. 1928- *WhoAm 90*
Blair, Donald Robert 1928- *St&PR 91*
Blair, Dorothy Lillian 1890-1989 *BioIn 16*
Blair, Earl F. 1943- *St&PR 91*
Blair, Earl Henry 1951- *WhoSSW 91*
Blair, Edward Joseph 1944- *St&PR 91*
Blair, Edward McCormick 1915- *St&PR 91, WhoAm 90*
Blair, Elaine Judith 1957- *WhoAmW 91*
Blair, Elizabeth Tyree 1947- *WhoEmL 91, WhoSSW 91, WhoWor 91*
Blair, Eric 1903-1950 *ConAu 132, MajTwCW*
Blair, Etcyl Howell 1922- *WhoAm 90*
Blair, Footsie 1900-1982 *Ballpl 90*
Blair, Francis Preston 1791-1876 *BioIn 16*
Blair, Fred Edward 1933- *WhoAm 90*
Blair, Frederick David 1946- *WhoEmL 91, WhoWor 91*
Blair, George Arthur, II *BiDrAPA 89*
Blair, George Simms 1924- *WhoAm 90*
Blair, Glenn Myers 1908- *WhoAm 90*
Blair, Gloria Christine 1946- *WhoEmL 91*
Blair, Graham Kerin 1951- *WhoWor 91*
Blair, Harry Armon 1937- *WhoSSW 91*
Blair, Helen 1910- *WhoAmA 91*
Blair, Hunter *AuBYP 90*
Blair, Jack R. 1942- *St&PR 91*
Blair, James 1655-1743 *EncCRAm, WorAlBi*
Blair, James 1945- *IntWWM 90*
Blair, James Burton 1935- *WhoSSW 91*
Blair, James M. 1944- *St&PR 91*
Blair, James Pease 1931- *WhoAm 90*
Blair, James Robert, Jr. 1913- *BiDrAPA 89*
Blair, James Walter, Jr. 1936- *WhoAm 90*
Blair, Jane Coleman 1928- *WhoAmW 91*
Blair, John 1732-1800 *BioIn 16*

Blair, John 1929- *WhoAm 90*
Blair, John H. *BioIn 16*
Blair, John Norman 1926- *St&PR 91*
Blair, John Orlando, Jr. 1941- *St&PR 91*
Blair, John R. 1946- *St&PR 91*
Blair, John Thomas 1951- *WhoSSW 91*
Blair, Joseph Andrew 1946- *WhoAm 90*
Blair, Joseph Edward, Jr. 1931- *St&PR 91*
Blair, Kathie Lynn 1951- *WhoAmW 91, WhoEmL 91*
Blair, Kerrie Jane 1956- *WhoEmL 91*
Blair, Lachlan Ferguson 1919- *WhoAm 90*
Blair, Laurel Manenti *ODwPR 91*
Blair, Lee Everett 1911- *WhoAmA 91*
Blair, Leon Borden 1917- *WhoAm 90*
Blair, Lucille *AuBYP 90*
Blair, Mardian John 1931- *WhoAm 90*
Blair, Marie Lenore 1931- *WhoAmW 91*
Blair, Mary Ellen 1921- *WhoAmW 91*
Blair, Mattie D. *WhoAmW 91*
Blair, Montgomery 1813-1883 *BiDrUSE 89*
Blair, Patricia Jean 1939- *WhoAmW 91*
Blair, Paul 1944- *Ballpl 90*
Blair, Paul Alex 1951- *WhoSSW 91*
Blair, Philip Joseph 1955- *WhoEmL 91*
Blair, Prentice Randol 1928- *St&PR 91*
Blair, R. Cary 1939- *St&PR 91*
Blair, R. Gregory 1947- *St&PR 91*
Blair, Richard Albert *BiDrAPA 89*
Blair, Robert 1933- *WhoAm 90*
Blair, Robert Allen 1946- *WhoWor 91*
Blair, Robert J. 1950- *ODwPR 91*
Blair, Robert Noel 1912- *WhoAm 90, WhoAmA 91, WhoE 91*
Blair, Roy Thomas 1946- *St&PR 91*
Blair, Ruth Van Ness 1912- *AuBYP 90*
Blair, S. Robert 1929- *St&PR 91*
Blair, Samuel Davidson 1927- *WhoAm 90*
Blair, Samuel Rufus 1932- *WhoWrEP 89*
Blair, Sidney Martin 1932- *BiDrAPA 89*
Blair, Sidney Robert 1929- *WhoAm 90*
Blair, Steven Noel 1939- *WhoAm 90, WhoSSW 91*
Blair, Stewart D. *BioIn 16*
Blair, Stewart D. 1949- *St&PR 91*
Blair, Stewart D. 1950- *WhoAm 90*
Blair, Streeter *WhoAmA 91N*
Blair, Thomas Edward 1946- *WhoEmL 91*
Blair, Thomas Michael 1957- *WhoEmL 91*
Blair, Thomas S. 1922- *St&PR 91, WhoAm 90*
Blair, Tony 1953- *WhoWor 91*
Blair, Virginia Ann 1925- *WhoAmW 91*
Blair, W Arthur 1921- *BiDrAPA 89*
Blair, Walter 1883-1948 *Ballpl 90*
Blair, Walter 1900- *AuBYP 90*
Blair, Walter B *BiDrAPA 89*
Blair, Watson Bayard 1954- *WhoEmL 91*
Blair, William Draper, Jr. 1927- *WhoAm 90*
Blair, William F *BiDrAPA 89*
Blair, William Granger 1925- *WhoAm 90*
Blair, William McCormick 1916- *BioIn 16*
Blair, William McCormick, Jr. 1916- *WhoAm 90*
Blair, William Richardson 1908- *WhoAm 90*
Blair, William Sutherland 1917- *WhoAm 90*
Blair, William Travis 1925- *WhoAm 90*
Blair-Larsen, Susan Margaret 1950- *WhoAmW 91*
Blais, Allison Schau 1943- *WhoAmW 91*
Blais, Madeleine Helena 1949- *WhoWrEP 89*
Blais, Marie-Claire 1939- *FemiCLE, MajTwCW, OxCCanT*
Blais, Norman J. 1929- *St&PR 91*
Blais, Pierre 1948- *WhoAm 90, WhoE 91*
Blais, Richard Leo 1927- *WhoE 91*
Blais, Roger Nathaniel 1944- *WhoSSW 91, WhoWor 91*
Blaisdell, Anne *TwCCr&M 91*
Blaisdell, Bruce 1945- *St&PR 91*
Blaisdell, Donald C. *BioIn 16*
Blaisdell, Frank F. *BioIn 16*
Blaisdell, Frank Ferron *St&PR 91N*
Blaisdell, Jack D. 1933- *St&PR 91*
Blaisdell, Thomas Charles 1895-1988 *BioIn 16*
Blaise, Clark, Mrs. *WhoAmW 91*
Blaise, Clark Lee 1940- *WhoWrEP 89*
Blaise, Marion 1955- *EncCoWW*
Blaithwaite, Mary *BiDEWW*
Blaivas, Alex Simon *BiDrAPA 89*
Blaize, Herbert *BioIn 16*
Blaize, Samuel Allen 1946- *St&PR 91*
Blake, Sheriff 1899-1982 *Ballpl 90*
Blake, Alan C. 1952- *St&PR 91*
Blake, Amanda 1929-1989 *AnObit 1989, BioIn 16, WorAlBi*
Blake, Ann Beth 1944- *WhoAmW 91*
Blake, Buckeye 1946- *BioIn 16*
Blake, Bud 1918- *EncACom, WhoAm 90*
Blake, Carl LeRoy 1951- *IntWWM 90*
Blake, Carlton Hugh 1934- *BiDrAPA 89*
Blake, Charles *BioIn 16*
Blake, Christopher Robert 1951- *WhoEmL 91*
Blake, Daniel Jackson *BiDrAPA 89*
Blake, Daniel Robert 1927- *St&PR 91*
Blake, Darlene Evelyn 1947- *WhoAmW 91, WhoEmL 91, WhoWor 91*
Blake, David 1936- *PenDiMP A*
Blake, David Gordon 1946- *WhoE 91, WhoEmL 91, WhoWor 91*
Blake, David Leonard 1936- *IntWWM 90*
Blake, Donald George 1929- *St&PR 91*
Blake, Donald H. 1935- *ODwPR 91*
Blake, Elias, Jr. 1929- *WhoAm 90*
Blake, Elizabeth *EncO&P 3*
Blake, Emily Jane *BiDrAPA 89*
Blake, Ernie *BioIn 16*
Blake, Eubie 1883-1983 *BioIn 16, DrBlPA 90, OxCPMus*
Blake, Eugene Carson 1906-1985 *WorAlBi*
Blake, Florence Guinness 1907-1983 *BioIn 16*
Blake, Fordyce Turner, III 1943- *St&PR 91*
Blake, Gary Boman 1947- *WhoEmL 91, WhoWor 91*
Blake, George Rowell 1945- *St&PR 91, WhoAm 90*
Blake, George Rowland 1918- *WhoAm 90, WhoWor 91*
Blake, Gerald Rutherford 1939- *WhoAm 90*
Blake, Gilbert Easton 1953- *WhoEmL 91*
Blake, Gwyn Adams 1927- *St&PR 91*
Blake, Henry William 1923- *BiDrAPA 89*
Blake, Howard 1938- *IntWWM 90*
Blake, Irene Elvin 1947- *WhoAmW 91*
Blake, Jack E. 1934- *ODwPR 91*
Blake, James Frederick, Jr. 1933- *WhoSSW 91*
Blake, Jane 1933- *WhoAmA 91*
Blake, Jane Salley 1937- *WhoAmA 91, WhoAmW 91, WhoWrEP 89*
Blake, Joan Johnston Wallman 1930- *WhoAmW 91*
Blake, John Ballard 1922- *WhoAm 90, WhoWrEP 89*
Blake, John Clemens 1945- *WhoAmA 91*
Blake, John Edward 1933- *St&PR 91*
Blake, John Francis 1922- *WhoAm 90*
Blake, John Freeman 1950- *WhoEmL 91, WhoWor 91*
Blake, John Herman 1934- *WhoAm 90*
Blake, John Paul *BiDrAPA 89*
Blake, Jonathan Daniels 1946- *St&PR 91*
Blake, Josh 1975- *ConTFT 8*
Blake, Judith 1926- *WhoAm 90*
Blake, Jules 1924- *St&PR 91, WhoAm 90*
Blake, Kevin E. 1958- *WhoEmL 91*
Blake, Lamont Vincent 1913- *WhoAm 90, WhoE 91*
Blake, Larry Jay 1930- *WhoAm 90*
Blake, Laura 1959- *WhoAmW 91*
Blake, Leo B 1887-1976 *WhoAmA 91N*
Blake, Leonard W. *BioIn 16*
Blake, Leroy Carl 1935- *WhoE 91*
Blake, Lesley Margaret 1953- *BiDrAPA 89*
Blake, Lillie 1833-1913 *FemiCLE*
Blake, Lillie D. 1833-1913 *BioAmW*
Blake, Margaret *ConAu 132*
Blake, Margaret Tate 1927- *WhoAmW 91*
Blake, Maxwell 1877-1959 *BioIn 16*
Blake, Michael James 1956- *WhoEmL 91*
Blake, Naomi 1924- *BiDWomA*
Blake, Nicholas *MajTwCW*
Blake, Nicholas 1904-1972 *TwCCr&M 91*
Blake, Norman Perkins 1941- *St&PR 91*
Blake, Norman Perkins, Jr. 1941- *WhoAm 90*
Blake, Patricia Dawn 1966- *WhoSSW 91*
Blake, Patrick *TwCCr&M 91*
Blake, Peter Jost 1920- *WhoAm 90, WhoAmA 91*
Blake, Priscilla Ann 1952- *WhoAmA 91*
Blake, Quentin 1932- *BioIn 16*
Blake, Ran 1935- *BioIn 16, WhoAm 90*
Blake, Ray Edward, III 1947- *St&PR 91*
Blake, Renee *WhoWrEP 89*
Blake, Richard Allan 1945- *WhoWrEP 89*
Blake, Richard Charles 1938- *WhoAm 90*
Blake, Robert 1598-1657 *BioIn 16*
Blake, Robert 1933- *WorAlBi*
Blake, Robert Frederick 1915- *WhoE 91*
Blake, Robert Rogers 1918- *BioIn 16, WhoAm 90*
Blake, Robert W 1930- *ConAu 31NR*
Blake, Robert Wallace 1921- *WhoAm 90*
Blake, Rockwell *BioIn 16*
Blake, Rockwell 1951- *IntWWM 90*
Blake, Sexton *TwCCr&M 91*
Blake, Sophia Louisa Jex- 1840-1912 *BioIn 16*
Blake, Stewart Prestley 1914- *WhoAm 90*
Blake, Thomas Clinton 1927- *St&PR 91*
Blake, Thomas E. 1938- *St&PR 91*
Blake, Thomas Hughes 1950- *WhoSSW 91*
Blake, Trudi Odella 1921- *WhoAmW 91*
Blake, Veronica Elizabeth 1953- *WhoWrEP 89*
Blake, Victor Harold 1935- *St&PR 91*
Blake, Vincent Patrick 1932- *St&PR 91, WhoAm 90*
Blake, Wendon *WhoAmA 91*
Blake, William 1757-1827 *AuBYP 90, BioIn 16, DcLB 93 [port], EncO&P 3, EncPaPR 91, IntDcAA 90, WorAlBi, WrPh*
Blake, William Ernest, Jr. 1930- *WhoSSW 91*
Blake, William George 1949- *WhoEmL 91*
Blake, William Henry 1913- *WhoAm 90*
Blake, William P. 1941- *St&PR 91*
Blake, William Rufus 1802-1863 *OxCCanT*
Blakeley, Charles P. 1834-1889 *AmLegL*
Blakeley, David 1944- *WhoWor 91*
Blakeley, Linda 1941- *WhoAmW 91*
Blakelock, Ralph Albert 1847-1919 *BioIn 16, WhNaAH*
Blakelock, Robert Edward 1934- *St&PR 91*
Blakely, Alexander 1829- *AmLegL*
Blakely, Diane *WhoSSW 91*
Blakely, Don *DrBlPA 90*
Blakely, Edward James 1938- *WhoAm 90*
Blakely, George C 1951- *WhoAmA 91*
Blakely, James Russell 1935- *WhoE 91*
Blakely, Leonard Morrell 1946- *WhoSSW 91*
Blakely, Mary Kay *BioIn 16*
Blakely, Mary Kay 1948- *ConAu 131*
Blakely, Maurilia Ortiz 1928- *WhoHisp 91*
Blakely, Robert John 1915- *WhoAm 90, WhoWrEP 89*
Blakely, Susan *ODwPR 91*
Blakely, T.T., Jr. 1937- *St&PR 91*
Blakely-Scott, Sandra Gail 1949- *WhoAmW 91*
Blakeman, Beth Renee 1951- *WhoWrEP 89*
Blakeman, D.G. 1932- *St&PR 91*
Blakeman, Jeffrey Allen 1963- *St&PR 91*
Blakeman, Marie Barbara 1917- *St&PR 91*
Blakeman, Royal Edwin 1923- *WhoAm 90*
Blakeman, Thomas Ledyard *BioIn 16*
Blakeman Lenz, Virginia 1949- *IntWWM 90*
Blakemore, Claude Coulehan 1909- *WhoAm 90*
Blakemore, Colin Brian 1944- *WhoWor 91*
Blakemore, Sally Gay 1947- *WhoAmW 91*
Blakemore, Steven Michael 1954- *St&PR 91*
Blakemore, William Barnett, III 1944- *WhoAm 90*
Blakeney, Allan Emrys 1925- *WhoAm 90*
Blakeney, Rae *WhoAmA 91*
Blakeney, Roger Neal 1939- *WhoWor 91*
Blakeney, Tom A., Jr. 1929- *St&PR 91*
Blakeney, Whiteford Carlyle, Jr. 1944- *WhoSSW 91*
Blakenham, Viscount 1911-1982 *DcNaB 1981*
Blaker, Charles William 1918- *WhoWrEP 89*
Blakeslee, Alton Lauren 1913- *WhoAm 90, WhoWrEP 89*
Blakeslee, Arthur Leopold, III 1927- *WhoAm 90*
Blakeslee, Edward Eaton 1921- *WhoAm 90*
Blakeslee, Howard Walter 1880-1952 *BioIn 16*
Blakeslee, Leroy Lawrence 1935- *WhoAm 90*
Blakeslee, Mary *BioIn 16*
Blakeslee, Robert Norman, Jr. 1953- *WhoE 91*
Blakeslee, Sandra 1943- *ConAu 131*
Blakeslee, Sarah 1912- *WhoAmA 91*
Blakeslee, Susan Singleton 1959- *WhoE 91*
Blakeslee, Tammy Lynne 1961- *WhoAmW 91*
Blakesley, Christopher Lee 1945- *WhoEmL 91*
Blakesley, Stephen J. 1940- *WhoSSW 91*
Blakeslley, David M. 1944- *St&PR 91*
Blakewood, Jim *BioIn 16*
Blakey, Art *BioIn 16*
Blakey, Art *NewYTBS 90 [port]*
Blakey, Art 1919- *DrBlPA 90, WhoAm 90, WorAlBi*
Blakey, Art 1919-1990 *News 91-1, OxCPMus*
Blakey, Hubert H 1924- *BiDrAPA 89*
Blakey, Robert Coleman 1948- *WhoSSW 91*
Blakey, Robert E 1936- *BiDrAPA 89*
Blakey, Tom *St&PR 91*
Blakey, William Arthur 1943- *WhoE 91*
Blakkan, Jan Marie *BiDrAPA 89*
Blakley, Benjamin Spencer, III 1952- *WhoE 91, WhoEmL 91, WhoWor 91*
Blakley, George Robert, Jr. 1932- *WhoAm 90*
Blakley, John Clyde 1955- *WhoEmL 91*
Blakney, Hurley *St&PR 91*
Blakney-Richards, Bettye Ruth 1939- *WhoAmW 91*
Blalock, Alfred 1899-1964 *BioIn 16*
Blalock, Hubert M. 1926- *BioIn 16*
Blalock, Hubert Morse, Jr. 1926- *WhoAm 90*
Blalock, Marion Gale 1948- *WhoEmL 91*
Blalock, Terry Lynn 1964- *WhoSSW 91*
Blalock, Wallace Davis 1931- *St&PR 91*
Blaman, Anna *EncCoWW*
Blamey, Richard Lyle 1941- *St&PR 91*
Blamey, Thomas Albert 1884-1951 *BioIn 16*
Blamire, Susanna 1747-1794 *BioIn 16, FemiCLE*
Blan, Ollie Lionel, Jr. 1931- *WhoAm 90*
Blanc, Alan Howard 1943- *BiDrAPA 89*
Blanc, Ernest 1923- *PenDiMP*
Blanc, Ernest Marius Victor 1923- *IntWWM 90*
Blanc, Esther S. 1913- *ConAu 131*
Blanc, Jean-Marc 1947- *WhoWor 91*
Blanc, Jonny 1939- *IntWWM 90*
Blanc, Linda Gay *ODwPR 91*
Blanc, Louis 1811-1882 *WorAlBi*
Blanc, Louis Jean Joseph 1811-1882 *BiDFrPL*
Blanc, Marie-Therese de Solms 1840-1907 *EncCoWW*
Blanc, Martin D. 1925- *St&PR 91*
Blanc, Mel *BioIn 16*
Blanc, Mel 1908-1989 *AnObit 1989, ConTFT 8, SmATA 64, WorAlBi*
Blanc, Peter 1912- *WhoAm 90, WhoAmA 91*
Blanc, Roger David 1945- *WhoEmL 91*
Blanca, Dona *WomWR*
Blanca, Queen of Navarre 1385?-1441 *BioIn 16*
Blancart Kubber, Teresa *WhoHisp 91*
Blancato, William Alfred 1957- *WhoEmL 91*
Blanch, Arnold 1896-1968 *WhoAmA 91N*
Blanch, Francis J. 1939- *St&PR 91*
Blanch, Stuart Yarworth 1918- *WhoWor 91*
Blanchard, Alan Franklin 1939- *WhoAm 90*
Blanchard, Arthur Bailly- 1855-1925 *BioIn 16*
Blanchard, Carol 1918- *WhoAmA 91N*
Blanchard, Carol Kline 1937- *WhoAmW 91*
Blanchard, Charles H. 1937- *St&PR 91*
Blanchard, Craig A. 1942- *St&PR 91*
Blanchard, David Andrew 1958- *WhoSSW 91*
Blanchard, David Beresford 1943- *WhoAm 90*
Blanchard, David Lawrence 1931- *WhoE 91*
Blanchard, Doc 1924- *BioIn 16*
Blanchard, Duane Everett 1938- *St&PR 91*
Blanchard, Elwood P. 1931- *St&PR 91*
Blanchard, George Samuel 1920- *WhoAm 90*
Blanchard, James *BioIn 16*
Blanchard, James Hubert 1941- *WhoAm 90*
Blanchard, James Humphreys 1931- *St&PR 91*
Blanchard, James J. 1942- *WhoAm 90, WhoWor 91*
Blanchard, Jerry Clifton 1950- *WhoSSW 91*
Blanchard, Johnny 1933- *Ballpl 90*
Blanchard, Joseph Bateman 1946- *St&PR 91*
Blanchard, Joseph Procter 1945- *WhoEmL 91*
Blanchard, Joyce Ruth 1949- *WhoWrEP 89*
Blanchard, Kenneth E. 1940- *St&PR 91*
Blanchard, Kirk F. 1949- *St&PR 91*
Blanchard, Lawrence E., Jr. 1921- *St&PR 91*
Blanchard, Lawrence Eley, Jr. 1921- *WhoAm 90*
Blanchard, Maria 1881-1932 *BiDWomA*
Blanchard, Martin Glenn 1946- *St&PR 91*
Blanchard, Mary Ellen *BioIn 16*
Blanchard, Norman H. 1930- *St&PR 91*
Blanchard, Norman Harris 1930- *WhoE 91*
Blanchard, Paula L. 1944- *ODwPR 91*
Blanchard, Paula Lynn 1949- *WhoSSW 91*
Blanchard, Richard Emile 1928- *WhoSSW 91*
Blanchard, Richard F. 1920- *St&PR 91*
Blanchard, Richard F. 1933- *St&PR 91*
Blanchard, Robert Johnstone Weir 1934- *WhoAm 90*
Blanchard, Robert T. 1944- *St&PR 91*
Blanchard, Robert Treat 1937- *WhoAm 90*
Blanchard, Townsend Eugene 1931- *St&PR 91, WhoAm 90*
Blanchard, William Clifford 1933- *St&PR 91*

Blanchard Wildman, Suzanne 1940- WhoWor 91
Blanche of Castile 1188-1252 WomWR [port]
Blanche, Ernest Evred 1912- WhoE 91
Blanche, Jacques-Emile 1861-1942 BioIn 16
Blanche, Robert V BiDrAPA 89
Blanchet, Bertrand 1932- WhoAm 90
Blanchette, Carleen BiDrAPA 89
Blanchette, Craig BioIn 16
Blanchette, James Edward 1924- BiDrAPA 89, WhoWor 91
Blanchette, Jeanne E. Maxant 1944- WhoAmW 91
Blanchette, Oliva 1929- WhoAm 90
Blanchette, Rita T. Billings 1913- WhoWrEP 89
Blanchette, Robert Wilfred 1932- WhoAm 90
Blanchfield, Florence Aby 1882-1971 BioIn 16
Blanchfield, Howard James 1896-1957 WhoAmA 91N
Blanchfield, James Edward 1945- St&PR 91
Blanchfield, Kevin J. 1955- St&PR 91
Blanchflower, David Graham 1952- WhoWor 91
Blanchot, Pierre-Marcel Robert 1955- St&PR 91
Blanck, James Edward 1958- WhoSSW 91
Blancke, W. Wendell 1908-1971 BioIn 16
Blanckenburg, Christian Friedrich von 1744-1796 DcLB 94 [port]
Blanckenhagen, Peter Heinrich von 1909-1990 BioIn 16
Blanco, Anna 1955- WhoEmL 91
Blanco, Antonio BioIn 16
Blanco, Antonio F BiDrAPA 89
Blanco, Antonio Guzman 1828-1899 BioIn 16
Blanco, Bruce M. 1949- St&PR 91
Blanco, Dianne Hayes 1947- St&PR 91
Blanco, Emilio 1921- BiDrAPA 89
Blanco, Humberto Jose BiDrAPA 89
Blanco, Jorge Luis 1928- St&PR 91
Blanco, Josefa Joan-Juana 1954- WhoAmW 91
Blanco, Julio C. 1931- WhoHisp 91
Blanco, Lenora BioIn 16
Blanco, Melanie Lynn 1968- WhoSSW 91
Blanco, Otilio Ulate 1891?-1973 BioIn 16
Blanco, Ray Stephen 1955- WhoE 91, WhoHisp 91
Blanco, Richard L 1926- SmATA 63
Blanco, Sylvia 1943- WhoAmA 91
Blanco, Victor 1936- WhoAm 90
Blanco, Yolanda Maria 1954- WhoHisp 91
Blanco Fombona, Rufino 1874-1944 BioIn 16, HispWr 90
Blanco Galdos, Hugo 1934- BioIn 16
Blanco-Sibila, Aixa Flora BiDrAPA 89
Blancornelas, Jesus BioIn 16
Blancos, Roberto WhoWrEP 89
Bland, A. Lee 1932- ODwPR 91
Bland, Alexander ConAu 129
Bland, Arnold Gene 1927- St&PR 91
Bland, Beatrice 1864?-1951 BiDWomA
Bland, Bobby 1930- DrBIPA 90, EncPR&S 89, OxCPMus
Bland, Charles PenDiMP
Bland, Edith 1858-1924 AuBYP 90
Bland, Edward EncCRAm
Bland, Edward Albert 1930- WhoAm 90
Bland, Edward Franklin 1901- WhoAm 90
Bland, Elizabeth BiDEWW
Bland, Eveline Mae 1939- WhoAmW 91
Bland, Frederick Aves 1945- WhoE 91
Bland, Henry Flesher 1818-1898 DcCanB 12
Bland, Irma J BiDrAPA 89
Bland, James A 1854-1911 DrBIPA 90, OxCPMus
Bland, James Allen 1854-1911 DcAfAmP
Bland, James Garland BiDrAPA 89
Bland, James Henry BiDrAPA 89
Bland, Jeanette E BiDrAPA 89
Bland, John 1911- BioIn 16
Bland, John Hannam 1930- WhoWor 91
Bland, Maria Theresa 1769-1838 PenDiMP
Bland, Peter George 1937- St&PR 91, WhoE 91
Bland, Raymond Steven BiDrAPA 89
Bland, Richard 1710-1776 EncCRAm
Bland, Richard C. 1922- St&PR 91
Bland, Richard P. 1835-1899 EncABHB 6 [port]
Bland, Robert E. 1943- St&PR 91
Bland, Roger Caudwell 1937- BiDrAPA 89
Bland, Thomas A. WhNaAH
Bland, Thomas Richard, Jr. 1955- WhoEmL 91
Bland, Walter Phillip BiDrAPA 89
Bland, William W. 1907- St&PR 91
Blanda, George 1927- WorAlBi
Blandau, Richard Julius 1911- WhoAm 90
Blandford, Donald Joseph 1938- WhoAm 90, WhoSSW 91
Blandford, Donald W. 1946- St&PR 91
Blandford, Gregory McAdoo 1962- WhoSSW 91
Blandford, Jeremy Richard 1943- IntWWM 90
Blandford, Percy William 1912- AuBYP 90
Blandford, Roger David 1949- WhoAm 90
Blandford, Susannah BiDEWW
Blandford, Teresa J. St&PR 91
Blandiana, Ana 1942- EncCoWW
Blandin, Bill St&PR 91
Blandin, Nanette Marie 1948- WhoAmW 91, WhoE 91, WhoEmL 91
Blanding, Don 1894-1957 WhoAmA 91N
Blanding, Fred 1888-1950 Ballpl 90
Blanding, Sandra Ann 1951- WhoEmL 91
Blandy, John Peter 1927- WhoWor 91
Blandy, Richard John 1938- WhoWor 91
Blane, Howard Thomas 1926- WhoE 91
Blane, Ralph 1914- OxCPMus
Blanes, Juan Manuel 1830-1901 ArtLatA
Blaney, Carole Ann 1946- WhoAmW 91, WhoEmL 91, WhoWor 91
Blaney, Connie Gayle 1955- WhoAmW 91
Blaney, Elizabeth Charlotte 1954- WhoAmW 91
Blaney, Geoffrey 1948- WhoEmL 91
Blaney, Harry Clay NewYTBS 90
Blaney, James Bernard 1961- WhoEmL 91
Blaney, Nancee Lou 1951- WhoAmW 91
Blanford, Anthony Lee BiDrAPA 89
Blanford, Charles 1841- AmLegL
Blanford, John William 1940- St&PR 91
Blangsted, Else BioIn 16
Blank, Allan 1925- IntWWM 90
Blank, Alvin Robert 1944- BiDrAPA 89
Blank, Andrew Russell 1945- WhoEmL 91, WhoSSW 91, WhoWor 91
Blank, Arthur M. 1942- WhoSSW 91
Blank, Arthur Saxton, Jr. 1936- BiDrAPA 89, WhoE 91
Blank, Benjamin 1929- St&PR 91, WhoAm 90
Blank, Blanche Davis WhoAm 90
Blank, Carroll Joseph 1942- St&PR 91
Blank, Charles Eugene 1929- WhoAm 90
Blank, Clair 1915-1965 SmATA X [port]
Blank, Clarissa Mabel 1915-1965 SmATA 62 [port]
Blank, Cynthia Fisher 1925- WhoAm 90
Blank, David 1943- St&PR 91
Blank, Dennis Ray 1942- St&PR 91
Blank, Franklin 1921- WhoWrEP 89
Blank, H Robert 1914- BiDrAPA 89
Blank, H. Robert 1914- WhoE 91
Blank, Harvey 1918- WhoAm 90
Blank, Howard David 1931- St&PR 91
Blank, Howard E. 1909- St&PR 91
Blank, Irwin Maurice 1925- WhoE 91
Blank, Jack Maurice 1930- St&PR 91
Blank, Jeremy Brendon St&PR 91
Blank, John Edward BiDrAPA 89
Blank, Jonas LeMoyne 1921- WhoAm 90
Blank, Jonathan William 1960- WhoSSW 91
Blank, Karen 1950- BiDrAPA 89
Blank, Leo Joseph 1917- St&PR 91
Blank, Leon William 1932- St&PR 91
Blank, Les BioIn 16
Blank, Les 1935- ConAu 131
Blank, Marion Sue 1933- WhoAm 90
Blank, Martin J. St&PR 91
Blank, Melody Hollen 1956- WhoE 91
Blank, Melvin E. 1944- St&PR 91
Blank, Naomi Ruth 1959- WhoEmL 91
Blank, Peaches Gunter 1951- WhoSSW 91
Blank, Peter Joseph 1933- St&PR 91
Blank, Philip B. 1934-1989 BioIn 16
Blank, Rebecca Margaret 1955- WhoE 91
Blank, Robert Gerhard 1942- St&PR 91
Blank, Robert Henry 1943- WhoAm 90
Blank, Rolf 1937- ODwPR 91
Blank, Ronald J 1948- BiDrAPA 89
Blank, Ronald M. 1947- St&PR 91
Blank, Roneen 1957- BiDrAPA 89
Blank, Sheldon H. 1896-1989 BioIn 16
Blank, Susan Berman 1958- BiDrAPA 89
Blank, Thomas Craig 1956- WhoEmL 91
Blank, Wanda WhoWrEP 89
Blankart, Charles Beat 1942- WhoWor 91
Blanke, Gail ODwPR 91
Blanke, Gail Ann 1941- WhoAmW 91
Blanke, Jordan Matthew 1954- WhoSSW 91
Blankemeier, John Louis 1953- BiDrAPA 89
Blankemeyer, Gary C. 1955- WhoSSW 91
Blankenbaker, Ronald Gail 1941- WhoAm 90
Blankenbaker, Virginia Murphy 1933- WhoAmW 91
Blankenburg, Heinz Horst 1931- IntWWM 90
Blankenburg, Judith B. 1933- WhoSSW 91
Blankenheim, Toni 1921- IntWWM 90
Blankenheimer, Bernard 1920- WhoAm 90
Blankenhorn, David Henry 1924- WhoAm 90
Blankenship, Asa L. 1926- St&PR 91
Blankenship, Barbara Stewart 1949- WhoSSW 91
Blankenship, Brantle E BiDrAPA 89
Blankenship, David Bruce 1949- St&PR 91
Blankenship, David L. 1951- St&PR 91
Blankenship, David Lynn 1951- WhoEmL 91
Blankenship, Edward G. 1943- WhoAm 90, WhoWor 91
Blankenship, Gilmer L. 1945- WhoAm 90
Blankenship, J. Randall 1953- WhoWrEP 89
Blankenship, James L. 1943- ODwPR 91
Blankenship, John L. 1948- WhoWrEP 89
Blankenship, Letha Pearl 1966- WhoAmW 91
Blankenship, Marie 1925- St&PR 91
Blankenship, Nancy Carol 1946- WhoAmW 91
Blankenship, Raymond Earl 1956- WhoEmL 91
Blankenship, Richard Eugene 1948- WhoEmL 91, WhoSSW 91
Blankenship, Robert Taylor 1953- WhoSSW 91
Blankenship, Ted 1901-1945 Ballpl 90
Blankenship, Terry Lee 1945- WhoSSW 91
Blankenship, Wanda B. 1939- St&PR 91
Blanker, Charles H. 1951- St&PR 91
Blankers, Donald J. 1939- St&PR 91
Blankers-Koen, Fanny 1918- BioIn 16
Blankert, Albert 1940- WhoWor 91
Blankerts, Beth Ann 1954- WhoAmW 91
Blankfein, Jules 1900-1989 BioIn 16
Blankfeld, Howard Martin 1941- BiDrAPA 89
Blankinship, Henry Massie 1942- WhoSSW 91, WhoWor 91
Blankinship, Kathleen Flo 1947- WhoAmW 91
Blankinship, Rex 1902- BiDrAPA 89
Blankley, Walter Elwood 1935- St&PR 91, WhoAm 90
Blankman, Howard M. 1925- ODwPR 91
Blankmeyer, Bonnie Lou 1937- WhoAmW 91
Blankmeyer, Robert H. 1946- St&PR 91
Blanks, Larvell 1950- Ballpl 90
Blanksteen, Merrill B. 1953- St&PR 91
Blankstein, Charles Sidney 1936- WhoSSW 91
Blann, Jerry Michael 1948- St&PR 91
Blannbekin, Agnes EncCoWW
Blanqui, Louis Auguste 1805-1881 BiDFrPL
Blanshard, Richard 1817-1894 DcCanB 12
Blanshei, Sarah Rubin 1938- WhoAm 90
Blanson, Vincent Price 1959- WhoEmL 91
Blanton, Barbara 1937- WhoAmW 91
Blanton, Catherine 1907- AuBYP 90
Blanton, Charles Brooker, Jr. 1959- WhoSSW 91
Blanton, Cy 1908-1945 Ballpl 90
Blanton, Edward Lee, Jr. 1931- WhoAm 90
Blanton, Fred, Jr. 1919- WhoSSW 91
Blanton, Gerald W BiDrAPA 89
Blanton, Hoover Clarence 1925- WhoAm 90, WhoSSW 91, WhoWor 91
Blanton, Jack Christopher 1935- WhoAm 90
Blanton, Jack S. 1927- St&PR 91
Blanton, Jack Sawtelle, Jr. 1953- St&PR 91
Blanton, James C. 1930- St&PR 91
Blanton, Jeremy 1939- WhoAm 90
Blanton, Jesse William 1923- St&PR 91
Blanton, Jimmy 1918-1942 BioIn 16, OxCPMus
Blanton, Jimmy 1921?-1942 WorAlBi
Blanton, John Arthur 1928- WhoWor 91
Blanton, Joseph Dan BiDrAPA 89
Blanton, Lawton Walter 1914- WhoE 91
Blanton, Patricia Louise 1941- WhoAmW 91
Blanton, Raymond 1950- St&PR 91
Blanton, Robert D'Alden 1943- WhoAm 90
Blanton, W. C. 1946- WhoEmL 91
Blanton-Flowers, Catherine Elizabeth 1958- BiDrAPA 89
Blaquier, Nelly Arrieta de BioIn 16
Blaquier, Nelly Arrieta de 1931- WhoWor 91
Blasch, Robert Edward 1931- IntWWM 90, WhoSSW 91
Blaschke, Gottfried Otmar 1937- WhoWor 91
Blasco, Alfred Joseph 1904- WhoAm 90
Blasco Ibanez, Vicente 1867-1928 BioIn 16, ConAu 131, HispWr 90, MajTwCW
Blase, Karl Oskar 1925- ConDes 90
Blase, Marvin 1941- BiDrAPA 89
Blase, Sharon Plahy WhoE 91
Blase, William Thomas 1949- WhoEmL 91
Blasek, William Edward, III 1952- WhoE 91
Blaser, Cathy B. 1950- WhoWrEP 89
Blaser, Richard John 1946- St&PR 91
Blaser, Stephen Jeffery WhoWor 91
Blasi, Alberto 1931- WhoAm 90
Blasier, John W. 1932- St&PR 91
Blasingame, Barbara Pyle 1941- St&PR 91
Blasingame, Benjamin Paul 1918- WhoAm 90
Blasingame, David Thomas 1947- WhoEmL 91
Blasingame, Don 1932- Ballpl 90
Blasingame, Francis James Levi 1907- WhoAm 90
Blasingame, Tom BioIn 16
Blasingame, Wade 1943- Ballpl 90
Blasius, Donald C. 1929- St&PR 91
Blasius, Donald Charles 1929- WhoAm 90
Blask, Christopher Ernst 1965- WhoSSW 91
Blaska, Gregory WhoAm 90
Blaskie, Henry Peter, Jr. 1934- St&PR 91
Blaskiewicz, John A. 1948- St&PR 91
Blasko, Janice Marie 1958- WhoAmW 91
Blasko, Leonard 1939- St&PR 91
Blasor, Scott Ellis 1949- St&PR 91
Blasquez, Jaime 1930- BiDrAPA 89
Blass, Bill 1922- ConDes 90, WhoAm 90, WorAlBi
Blass, Gerhard Alois 1916- WhoAm 90, WhoWor 91, WhoWrEP 89
Blass, John Paul 1937- WhoAm 90
Blass, Jolan Wirth 1901- BiDrAPA 89
Blass, Marcus Gabriel 1950- WhoEmL 91
Blass, Noland, Jr. 1920- WhoAm 90
Blass, Paul Joseph 1943- St&PR 91
Blass, Steve 1944- Ballpl 90
Blass, Walter Paul 1930- WhoE 91
Blass, William Errol 1937- WhoSSW 91
Blasse, Pierre PenDiDA 89
Blassel, Jean-Francois Paul 1956- WhoWor 91
Blasser, Jacob Cweiber 1930- BiDrAPA 89
Blassingame, Gary Joe 1955- WhoEmL 91, WhoSSW 91, WhoWor 91
Blassingame, Lurton 1904-1988 BioIn 16
Blassingame, Wyatt Rainey 1909-1985 AuBYP 90
Blasters, The EncPR&S 89
Blaszak, Michael William 1953- WhoEmL 91
Blaszczak, Dru Joseph 1953- WhoSSW 91
Blaszczenski, Jessie H BiDrAPA 89
Blaszczynski, Carol J. ODwPR 91
Blaszkowski, Thomas Paul 1934- WhoAm 90
Blatch, Harriot Stanton 1856-1939 EncAL
Blatch, Mari Ann Rhodes 1941- St&PR 91
Blatchford, Richard Milford 1798-1875 BioIn 16
Blatchford, Robert 1851-1943 EncO&P 3
Blate, Samuel Robert 1944- WhoWrEP 89
Blatecky, Alan Rudolph 1946- WhoSSW 91
Blatherwick, Gerald D. 1936- St&PR 91, WhoAm 90
Blatman, Holly M BiDrAPA 89
Blatner, Adam 1937- BiDrAPA 89
Blatner, Barbara Ann 1949- WhoWrEP 89
Blatner, Sherry Diane 1947- WhoAmW 91
Blatnick, Jeff 1957?- BioIn 16
Blatt, Allison Quensen 1962- WhoAmW 91
Blatt, Beverly Faye 1944- WhoAmW 91
Blatt, Burton 1927-1985 BioIn 16
Blatt, Jerry BioIn 16
Blatt, Kenneth Saul 1946- BiDrAPA 89
Blatt, Lee N. 1928- St&PR 91
Blatt, Leslie Alan 1944- WhoE 91
Blatt, Lola St&PR 91
Blatt, Melanie Judith 1946- WhoAmW 91
Blatt, Morton Bernard 1923- WhoWor 91
Blatt, Nancie M. 1938- WhoAmW 91
Blatt, Neil A. 1954- St&PR 91
Blatt, Richard Lee 1940- WhoAm 90
Blatt, Ronald W 1930- BiDrAPA 89
Blatt, Sidney I. 1921- St&PR 91
Blatt, Sidney Jules 1928- WhoAm 90, WhoE 91
Blatt, Solomon, Jr. 1921- WhoSSW 91
Blattberg, Robert Charles 1942- WhoAm 90
Blatter, Alfred 1937- IntWWM 90
Blatter, Frank E. 1939- St&PR 91
Blatter, Frank Edward 1939- WhoAm 90
Blatter, William B. 1934- St&PR 91
Blattman, H. Eugene 1936- St&PR 91
Blattner, Buddy 1920- Ballpl 90
Blattner, Christopher J. 1943- St&PR 91
Blattner, David Jones, Jr. 1938- WhoAm 90
Blattner, Jeffrey Hirsh 1954- WhoEmL 91
Blattner, Joseph Lorne, Jr. 1945- St&PR 91
Blattner, Meera McCuaig 1930- WhoAmW 91, WhoWor 91
Blattner, Robert Henry 1906- WhoAmA 91

Blattner, Stephen Christian 1941- St&PR 91
Blatty, William Peter BioIn 16
Blatty, William Peter 1928- WhoAm 90, WhoWrEP 89
Blatz, Durand B. 1918- St&PR 91
Blatz, Karen Ellen BiDrAPA 89
Blatz, Laurie Lynn 1962- WhoEmL 91
Blatz, Linda Jeanne 1950- WhoAmW 91, WhoE 91, WhoEmL 91
Blatz, Susan L. 1954- WhoE 91
Blau, Barry 1927- St&PR 91, WhoAm 90
Blau, Charles William 1943- WhoAm 90
Blau, David 1926- BiDrAPA 89
Blau, Francine Dee 1946- WhoAm 90, WhoEmL 91
Blau, Harvey Ronald 1935- WhoAm 90, WhoSSW 91
Blau, Helen Margaret 1948- WhoAmW 91
Blau, Jeffrey Alan 1951- WhoEmL 91
Blau, Joel Michael 1959- WhoEmL 91
Blau, Monte 1926- WhoAm 90
Blau, Peter Michael 1918- WhoAm 90
Blau, Stanley M. 1937- St&PR 91
Blau, Stanley Marvin 1937- WhoAm 90
Blau, Stephen Perry 1942- BiDrAPA 89
Blau, Theodore Hertzl 1928- WhoAm 90
Blau, Tina 1845-1916 BioIn 16
Blau, Victoria Jewel 1944- WhoAmW 91
Blauel, Renate BioIn 16
Blauer, Charles L. 1929- St&PR 91
Blauer, Maurice 1921- St&PR 91
Blaufox, Morton Donald 1934- WhoAm 90
Blaug, Mark 1927- WhoWor 91
Blaugdone, Barbara 1609-1704 BiDEWW
Blaugdone, Barbara 1609?-1705 FemiCLE
Blaugrund, Clifford Earl 1945- St&PR 91
Blaugrund, Howard Joseph 1909- St&PR 91
Blaugrund, Lee S. 1947- St&PR 91
Blaukopf, Herta 1924- ConAu 131
Blauner, Bob 1929- WhoAm 90
Blauner, Jeanne Alison 1954- WhoE 91
Blauner, Laurie Ann 1953- WhoWrEP 89
Blauser, Jeff 1965- Ballpl 90
Blaustein, Al 1924- WhoAmA 91
Blaustein, Alan Scott 1953- BiDrAPA 89
Blaustein, Albert Paul 1921- WhoAm 90, WhoWor 91
Blaustein, Alvin Bernard BiDrAPA 89
Blaustein, Alvin Bernard 1925- WhoE 91
Blaustein, Mel Ira 1942- BiDrAPA 89
Blaustein, Milton Jack BiDrAPA 89
Blaustein, Morton K. WhoAm 90, WhoE 91
Blaustein, Morton K. NewYTBS 90
Blaustein, Morton K. 1926- St&PR 91
Blaustein, Richard BioIn 16
Blauvelt, Brian Mourrie 1956- WhoEmL 91, WhoSSW 91
Blauvelt, Gerrit John 1941- BiDrAPA 89
Blauvelt, John Clifford 1920- WhoAm 90
Blauvelt, Melinda 1949- WhoAmW 91
Blauvelt, Pete Wayne 1955- WhoE 91
Blauvelt, Ralph 1942- WhoWrEP 89
Blauvelt, Randal R. 1954- ODwPR 91
Blauvelt, Robert Ward BioIn 16
Blavatsky, H. P. 1831-1891 BioIn 16
Blavatsky, Helena 1831-1891 WorAlBi
Blavatsky, Helena Petrovna 1831-1891 EncPaPR 91, NewAgE 90
Blavatsky, Helene Petrovna 1831-1891 BioIn 16, EncO&P 3
Blaxter, Kenneth Lyon 1919- WhoWor 91
Blaya, Joaquin F. WhoHisp 91
Blaya, Marcelo Perez BiDrAPA 89
Blaydes, Sophia Boyatzies 1933- WhoAm 90
Blaydon, Colin Campbell 1940- WhoAm 90, WhoE 91
Blaylock, Denny Alan 1946- St&PR 91
Blaylock, Jerry Douglas 1943- BiDrAPA 89
Blaylock, Mabry Gene 1927- WhoSSW 91
Blaylock, Marv 1929- Ballpl 90
Blaylock, Ted BioIn 16
Blaylock, Thomas C. 1914- St&PR 91
Blayney, William Alvin 1917-1986 MusmAFA
Blayton, Betty 1937- WhoAmA 91
Blayton-Taylor, Betty 1937- WhoE 91
Blaz, Ben 1928- WhoAm 90
Blazar, Sheldon Marvin 1931- WhoAm 90, WhoE 91
Blaze, Marci 1955- ODwPR 91
Blazeje, Zbigniew 1942- WhoAmA 91
Blazek, Doris Defibaugh 1943- WhoAm 90
Blazek, Douglas David 1941- WhoWrEP 89
Blazek, Frank E. St&PR 91
Blazek, John William, Jr. 1952- WhoEmL 91
Blazek, Joseph Lawrence 1957- WhoWrEP 89
Blazek, Mary Carol BiDrAPA 89
Blazek, Wayne Joseph 1950- WhoE 91, WhoEmL 91
Blazekovic, Zdravko 1956- IntWWM 90
Blazer, Dan German 1944- WhoSSW 91
Blazer, Dan German, II 1944- BiDrAPA 89
Blazer, Dennis Wayne 1947- St&PR 91
Blazewicz, Marcin 1953- IntWWM 90
Blazey, Lawrence Edwin 1902- WhoAmA 91
Blazey, Mark Lee 1948- WhoE 91, WhoEmL 91
Blazina, Janice Fay 1953- WhoEmL 91
Blazon, Denise G. 1952- WhoAmW 91
Blazquez, Carlos Humberto 1926- WhoSSW 91
Blazy, Diane Edith 1952- WhoEmL 91
Blazzard, Norse Novar 1937- WhoAm 90
Blea, Irene Isabel 1946- WhoHisp 91
Bleach, Bruce R 1950- WhoAmA 91
Bleakley, Marjorie Sue 1921- WhoSSW 91
Bleakley, Peter Kimberley 1936- WhoAm 90
Bleam, Donna Lees 1944- WhoAmW 91, WhoSSW 91
Bleau, Barbara Lee WhoSSW 91
Blech Quartet PenDiMP
Blech, David BioIn 16
Blech, Harry 1910- IntWWM 90, PenDiMP
Blech, Isaac BioIn 16
Blech, Leo 1871-1958 PenDiMP
Blech, Marion Rose 1931- IntWWM 90
Blecha, Karl 1933- WhoWor 91
Blecher, Anthony Foster 1945- St&PR 91, WhoEmL 91
Blecher, Franklin Hugh 1929- WhoAm 90
Blecher, Melvin 1922- WhoAm 90
Blecher, Steven Donald 1942- St&PR 91
Blecher-Sass, Hope Sara 1962- WhoE 91
Blechman, R. O. 1930- WhoAm 90
Blechman, R O 1930- WhoAmA 91
Bleck, Phyllis Claire 1936- WhoAmW 91
Bleck, Robert George 1944- BiDrAPA 89
Bleck, Virginia Eleanore 1929- WhoAmW 91
Bleck-Muschler, Catherine Mary 1956- WhoAmW 91
Blecker, Alla BiDrAPA 89
Blecker, Naomi Perle 1956- WhoAmW 91
Bleckner, Edward, Jr. 1933- St&PR 91, WhoSSW 91
Bleckner, Ross 1949- BioIn 16, WhoAmA 91
Bleckstein, Ted Craig 1953- WhoEmL 91
Bledsoe, Elsa Andresen BioIn 16
Bledsoe, Garry Paul 1947- St&PR 91
Bledsoe, Gilbert H. 1940- St&PR 91
Bledsoe, Jane Kathryn 1937- WhoAm 90, WhoAmA 91, WhoAmW 91, WhoSSW 91
Bledsoe, Janeva Leigh 1949- WhoEmL 91
Bledsoe, Jules 1898-1943 DrBlPA 90, OxCPMus
Bledsoe, Julius C 1898-1943 DcAfAmP
Bledsoe, June Elizabeth Jaycox 1958- WhoSSW 91
Bledsoe, Ralph Champion 1933- WhoAm 90
Bledsoe, Tempestt BioIn 16
Bledsoe, Tempestt 1973- DrBlPA 90, WorAlBi
Bledsoe, Walter Arthur, Jr. 1916- St&PR 91
Bledsoe, Woodrow Wilson 1921- WhoAm 90
Bleeck, Oliver TwCCr&M 91
Bleecker, Ann Eliza 1752-1783 FemiCLE
Bleecker, Ruth Hall BioIn 16
Bleehen, Norman Montague 1930- WhoWor 91
Bleeke, Joel Allen 1953- WhoEmL 91
Bleetstein, Gary 1953- St&PR 91
Blefary, Curt 1943- Ballpl 90
Blegen, Judith 1941- IntWWM 90, PenDiMP
Blegvad, Lenore 1926- ConAu 31NR
Blehert, Dean 1942- WhoWrEP 89
Blei, Gary 1940- St&PR 91
Blei, Hermann 1929- WhoWor 91
Blei, Peter 1949- St&PR 91
Bleiberg, Efrain BiDrAPA 89
Bleiberg, Gertrude Tiefenbrun WhoAmA 91
Bleiberg, Robert Marvin 1924- WhoAm 90, WhoWrEP 89
Bleich, David Lloyd 1943- WhoAm 90
Bleich, Jack Benton BiDrAPA 89
Bleicher, Marc A. BiDrAPA 89
Bleicher, Samuel Abram 1942- WhoE 91
Bleicher, Sheldon Joseph 1931- WhoAm 90, WhoE 91, WhoWor 91
Bleichrodt, Robert Paul 1952- WhoWor 91
Bleicken, Benjamin David 1964- WhoSSW 91
Bleicken, Jochen Ferdinand 1926- WhoWor 91
Bleidner, Roger Crozier 1929- WhoE 91
Bleidt, Barry Anthony 1951- WhoSSW 91
Bleidt, Beverly Jean 1948- WhoAmW 91
Bleier, Henry Robert 1948- BiDrAPA 89
Bleier, Richard M. NewYTBS 90
Bleier, Ruth 1923-1988 BioIn 16
Bleifeld, Stanley 1924- WhoAmA 91
Bleimann, Karl Richard 1934- St&PR 91
Bleiweiss, Herbert Irving 1931- WhoAm 90, WhoWrEP 89
Bleiweiss, Irene 1960- WhoEmL 91
Bleiweiss, Robert Morton 1934- WhoAm 90
Bleksley, Arthur Edward Herbert 1908- EncO&P 3
Bleksley, Arthur Edward Herbert 1908-1984 EncPaPR 91
Bleman, Daniel Ben 1950- BiDrAPA 89
Blemaster, Norman Lee 1940- St&PR 91
Bleming, Jone BiDEWW
Blenden, Donald Covey 1929- WhoAm 90
Blenderman, Ronald J. 1927- St&PR 91
Blendon, Robert Jay 1942- WhoAm 90
Blendy, Michael M. 1946- St&PR 91
Blenis, Barry G. 1943- St&PR 91
Blenkarn, Donald BioIn 16
Blenko, Richard Deakin 1953- St&PR 91
Blenko, Walter John, Jr. 1926- WhoE 91, WhoWor 91
Blenko, William H., Jr. 1921- St&PR 91
Blenner, Serge NewAgMG
Blennerhassett, Margaret Agnew 1773?-1842 DcLB 99 [port]
Blenod, Barthelemy de PenDiDA 89
Bleriot, Louis 1872-1936 WorAlBi
Blesch, Christopher John 1958- WhoEmL 91
Blesch, Larie Frances 1958- WhoSSW 91
Blesch, Robert William 1959- WhoEmL 91
Bleser, Clarence Peter 1915- St&PR 91
Bleser, Joseph G. 1945- WhoAm 90
Bleser, Katherine Alice 1942- WhoAmA 91
Bleser, Peter Leo St&PR 91N
Blesh, Rudi 1899-1985 OxCPMus
Bless, Franklyn Rothe 1926- St&PR 91
Bless, Robert Charles 1927- WhoAm 90
Blessed Virgin Mary, Saint BioIn 16
Blessed, Brian 1937- ConTFT 8
Blessen, Karen WhoAm 90, WhoAmW 91, WhoSSW 91
Blessing, Beth Brownlow 1944- BiDrAPA 89
Blessing, Donald Carl 1955- WhoEmL 91
Blessing, Edward Warfield 1936- WhoSSW 91
Blessing, Gene S. 1939- St&PR 91
Blessing, Mark Frederick 1963- WhoSSW 91
Blessing, Scott Francis 1957- WhoE 91
Blessing-Moore, Joann Catherine 1946- WhoAmW 91
Blessington, Countess of 1789-1849 BioIn 16, FemiCLE
Blessington, Francis C 1942- ConAu 130
Blest Gana, Alberto 1830-1920 BioIn 16
Blethen, David Lawrence 1959- WhoE 91
Blethen, Harold Tyler, III 1945- WhoSSW 91
Blethen, William Kingsley, Jr. 1945- St&PR 91
Bletter, Rosemarie Haag 1941- WhoAmW 91
Bleuler, Manfred E 1903- BiDrAPA 89
Bleveans, John 1938- WhoAm 90, WhoWor 91
Blevins, Bradley Edward 1960- WhoEmL 91
Blevins, Charlie R. 1921- St&PR 91
Blevins, Clifford Lyle 1952- WhoE 91
Blevins, Florence Evelyn 1933- WhoAmW 91
Blevins, Gary Lynn 1941- WhoAm 90
Blevins, James Ray 1949- WhoEmL 91
Blevins, James Richard 1934- WhoAmA 91
Blevins, James V. 1912- St&PR 91
Blevins, James Wesley BiDrAPA 89
Blevins, Jeffrey Alexander 1955- WhoEmL 91
Blevins, Jeffrey Reeves 1963- WhoSSW 91
Blevins, Jerry R. 1946- St&PR 91
Blevins, Kathleen Suessdorf 1945- WhoEmL 91
Blevins, Kimberly Ann 1964- WhoAmW 91
Blevins, Lee Dudley 1951- St&PR 91
Blevins, Linda R. 1958- St&PR 91
Blevins, Mark Carlton 1953- WhoEmL 91
Blevins, William Edward 1927- St&PR 91, WhoAm 90
Blewer, Julia McGuire BioIn 16
Blewett, Duncan Bassett 1920- EncO&P 3
Blewett, Jean 1862-1934 FemiCLE
Blewett, John Paul 1910- WhoAm 90
Blewett, Patrick B. 1928- WhoAm 90
Blewett, Robert Noall 1915- WhoAm 90
Blewett, Stephen Douglas 1942- WhoWrEP 89
Blewitt, George Augustine 1937- WhoAm 90
Blewitt, Joan McGuiness 1952- WhoAmW 91
Blewitt, Jonathan 1782-1853 OxCPMus
Blewitt, Richard F. 1947- ODwPR 91
Blewitt, Richard Francis 1947- WhoE 91
Blewitt, Wayne L. 1931- St&PR 91
Bley, Carla BioIn 16
Bley, Elmer O. 1936- St&PR 91
Bley, Paul BioIn 16
Bleyer, Archie 1909-1989 BioIn 16
Bleyer, John Francis 1936- WhoE 91
Bleyl, Katherine Lorraine 1949- WhoEmL 91
Bleyle, John Allen 1944- St&PR 91
Bleymaier, Joseph Sylvester 1915- WhoAm 90
Bleyman, Lea Kanner 1936- WhoAmW 91
Bleyzer, Gedaly 1929- BiDrAPA 89
Bleyzer, Vladimir D BiDrAPA 89
Bleznick, Donald William 1924- WhoAm 90
Blezzard, Judith Helen 1944- IntWWM 90
Blicher, Bert 1943- St&PR 91, WhoAm 90
Blicher, Steen Steensen 1782-1848 DcScanL
Blick, Ambler Montquire 1947- WhoE 91
Blickens, Robert P. 1948- St&PR 91
Blickenstaff, Bradley Smith 1929- St&PR 91
Blicksilver, Edith 1926- WhoSSW 91
Blickwede, Donald Johnson 1920- WhoAm 90
Blide, Todd David Foster 1959- WhoEmL 91
Blieberg, Helene Andrea 1955- WhoEmL 91
Blier, Bernard 1916-1989 AnObit 1989, BioIn 16, ConTFT 8
Blier, Bernard Benedict 1917- WhoE 91
Blier, Bertrand BioIn 16
Blier, Bertrand 1939- ConTFT 8
Blier, Pierre 1957- BiDrAPA 89
Blietz, Kenneth W. 1933- St&PR 91
Bligh, William 1754-1817 BioIn 16, WorAlBi
Blight, Rose ConAu 33NR, MajTwCW
Blijk, J. van den PenDiDA 89
Bliley, John Earle 1919- St&PR 91
Bliley, Mark A. 1958- St&PR 91
Bliley, Thomas Jerome, Jr. 1932- WhoAm 90, WhoSSW 91
Blim, Richard Don 1927- WhoAm 90
Blin-Stoyle, Roger John 1924- WhoWor 91
Blind Faith EncPR&S 89
Blind Lemon DrBlPA 90
Blind Tom 1849-1908 BioIn 16
Blind, Mathilde 1841-1896 BioIn 16, FemiCLE
Blind, Tom 1849-1908 DrBlPA 90
Blind, William Charles 1911- St&PR 91, WhoAm 90
Blinde, Gene A. 1944- St&PR 91
Blinder, Abe Lionel 1909- WhoAm 90
Blinder, Alan S 1945- ConAu 32NR
Blinder, Alan Stuart 1945- WhoE 91
Blinder, Barton Jerome 1938- BiDrAPA 89
Blinder, James F. 1934- St&PR 91
Blinder, Mark Fisher 1948- St&PR 91
Blinder, Martin BiDrAPA 89
Blinder, Martin S. 1946- BioIn 16, St&PR 91, WhoAm 90, WhoAmA 91, WhoEmL 91
Blinder, Richard Lewis 1935- WhoAm 90
Blinder, Seymour Michael 1932- WhoAm 90
Blinderman, Barry Robert 1952- WhoAmA 91
Blindt, David A. 1953- WhoEmL 91
Blinka, Gary Lane 1941- St&PR 91
Blinken, Donald 1925- WhoAm 90
Blinken, Robert J. 1929- St&PR 91
Blinken, Robert James 1929- WhoAm 90
Blinkhof, Jan 1940- IntWWM 90
Blinks, John Rogers 1931- WhoAm 90
Blinn, Clara BioIn 16
Blinn, Keith W. BioIn 16
Blinn, Keith Wayne 1917-1990 ConAu 131
Blinn, Lorena Virginia 1939- WhoAmW 91
Blinn, Stephen M. 1947- St&PR 91
Blinn, William Frederick 1937- WhoAm 90
Blish, James 1921-1975 MajTwCW, RGTwCSF, WorAlBi
Blish, Nelson Adrian 1945- WhoEmL 91
Bliss, Arthur 1891-1975 BioIn 16, PenDiMP A
Bliss, Barbara E BiDrAPA 89
Bliss, Cathy BioIn 16
Bliss, Corinne Demas 1947- WhoWrEP 89
Bliss, Cornelius Newton 1833-1911 BiDrUSE 89
Bliss, Daniel Howard 1961- WhoEmL 91, WhoWor 91
Bliss, David C. 1937- St&PR 91
Bliss, Dorothy Crandall 1916- WhoAmW 91
Bliss, Edward 1912- BioIn 16
Bliss, Edwin C 1923- ConAu 131
Bliss, Eliot 1903- FemiCLE
Bliss, Eugene L 1918- BiDrAPA 89

Bliss, G.R. 1931- *St&PR 91*
Bliss, George *BioIn 16*
Bliss, George, Jr. 1793-1873 *AmLegL*
Bliss, James C. 1933- *St&PR 91*
Bliss, Jeffrey Ross 1953- *WhoEmL 91*
Bliss, Jerry Evan 1949- *WhoEmL 91*
Bliss, John S. 1943- *ODwPR 91*
Bliss, Josephine *BioIn 16*
Bliss, Michael 1941- *ConAu 31NR*
Bliss, Michael Bruce 1948- *WhoEmL 91*
Bliss, Reginald *MajTwCW*
Bliss, Richard Donald 1947- *WhoEmL 91*
Bliss, Richard Earle, Jr. 1952- *WhoSSW 91*
Bliss, Robert Earl 1939- *St&PR 91*
Bliss, Robert Harms 1940- *WhoAm 90*
Bliss, Robert Woods 1875-1962 *BioIn 16, WhoAmA 91N*
Bliss, Robert Woods, Mrs *WhoAmA 91N*
Bliss, Roland Boyd 1934- *St&PR 91*
Bliss, Ronald Gene 1942- *WhoWrEP 89*
Bliss, Shirley Anne 1923- *St&PR 91*
Bliss, Sidney H. 1947- *St&PR 91*
Bliss, Stanley Michael 1939- *St&PR 91*
Bliss, Tamara Colleen 1952- *WhoAmW 91*
Bliss, Tasker Howard 1853-1930 *BioIn 16*
Bliss, Valerie Elizabeth 1964- *WhoAmW 91*
Bliss, William E. 1936- *St&PR 91*
Bliss, William Stanley, Jr. 1932- *WhoAm 90*
Blissard, Thomasina 1925- *BiDrAPA 89*
Blissenbach, Kenneth William 1942- *BiDrAPA 89*
Blissert, Julie Harrison 1954- *WhoAmW 91*
Blissett, William Frank 1921- *WhoAm 90*
Blissitt, Patricia Ann 1953- *WhoAmW 91, WhoEmL 91, WhoSSW 91, WhoWor 91*
Blitch, James Bedford, Jr. *BiDrAPA 89*
Blitch, James Buchanan 1923- *WhoAm 90*
Blitch, Ronald Buchanan 1953- *WhoSSW 91*
Blitman, Bruce Alan 1956- *WhoEmL 91*
Blitman, Howard Norton 1926- *WhoAm 90*
Blitman, Judy *BiDrAPA 89*
Blitshteyn, Mark 1950- *St&PR 91*
Blitz, Daniel 1920- *WhoE 91*
Blitz, Gerard 1912-1990 *BioIn 16, NewYTBS 90*
Blitz, Judith *BiDrAPA 89*
Blitz, Marvin Barry *BiDrAPA 89*
Blitz, Peggy Sanderfur 1940- *WhoAmW 91*
Blitz, Stephen M. 1941- *WhoAm 90*
Blitzer, Andrew 1946- *WhoAm 90, WhoEmL 91*
Blitzer, Charles 1927- *BioIn 16, WhoAm 90*
Blitzer, Charles Robert 1944- *WhoE 91*
Blitzer, David Mayers 1948- *St&PR 91*
Blitzer, John Ritchie *BiDrAPA 89*
Blitzstein, Marc *BioIn 16*
Blitzstein, Marc 1905-1964 *EncAL, OxCPMus*
Bliukher, Vasilii Konstantinovich 1889-1938 *BioIn 16*
Bliven, A. Robert 1925- *St&PR 91*
Bliven, Bruce, Jr. 1889-1977 *AuBYP 90*
Bliven, Bruce, Jr. 1916- *WhoAm 90, WhoE 91, WhoWor 91, WhoWrEP 89*
Bliven, Naomi 1925- *WhoAm 90*
Bliwas, Crain Henry 1947- *BiDrAPA 89*
Bliwas, James Charles 1946- *WhoEmL 91*
Bliwas, Ronald Lee 1942- *WhoAm 90*
Blix, Hans Martin 1928- *WhoWor 91*
Blix, Susanne 1949- *BiDrAPA 89*
Blixen, Karen *DcScanL*
Blixen, Karen 1885-1962 *BioIn 16, MajTwCW*
Blixen-Finecke, Karen Christence Dinesen *EncCoWW*
Bliznakov, Emile George 1926- *WhoAm 90*
Bliznakov, Milka Tcherneva 1927- *WhoAm 90, WhoAmW 91*
Blizzard, Alan 1939- *WhoAm 90, WhoAmA 91*
Blizzard, Georgia 1919- *MusmAFA*
Blizzard, Robert M. 1924- *WhoAm 90*
Blizzard, Victoria *BiDrAPA 89*
Blizzard, William D., Jr. 1944- *St&PR 91*
Blizzard, William DeVan, Jr. 1944- *WhoSSW 91*
Blobaum Berman, Colleen Ann 1950- *WhoEmL 91*
Blobel, Gunter 1936- *WhoAm 90*
Blobel, Hans-Georg 1929- *WhoWor 91*
Blobel, Paul 1894-1951 *BioIn 16*
Bloch, Alan L. 1930- *St&PR 91*
Bloch, Alan Neil 1932- *WhoAm 90*
Bloch, Albert 1882-1961 *WhoAmA 91N*
Bloch, Alfred M *BiDrAPA 89*
Bloch, Andrea Lynn 1952- *WhoAmW 91*
Bloch, Antoine 1938- *WhoWor 91*
Bloch, Arthur H 1948- *BiDrAPA 89*
Bloch, Barbara Joyce 1925- *WhoAmW 91, WhoWrEP 89*
Bloch, Clifford Alan 1953- *WhoEmL 91*
Bloch, Daniel Morry *BiDrAPA 89*
Bloch, Donald Alan 1922- *BiDrAPA 89*
Bloch, Douglas George 1949- *WhoWrEP 89*
Bloch, E. Maurice *WhoAm 90*
Bloch, E Maurice *WhoAmA 91N*
Bloch, Edward 1932- *ODwPR 91*
Bloch, Erich *BioIn 16*
Bloch, Erich 1925- *WhoAm 90*
Bloch, Ernest 1880-1959 *PenDiMP A*
Bloch, Ernest 1921- *WhoAm 90*
Bloch, Ernest, II 1938- *ODwPR 91*
Bloch, Ernst 1885-1977 *BioIn 16*
Bloch, Felix 1905-1983 *BioIn 16, WorAlBi*
Bloch, Felix 1935- *NewYTBS 90 [port]*
Bloch, Felix S. *BioIn 16*
Bloch, Gordon Bakoulis *BioIn 16*
Bloch, Gottfried R *BiDrAPA 89*
Bloch, H Spencer 1937- *BiDrAPA 89*
Bloch, Henry Wollman 1922- *BioIn 16, ConAmBL, St&PR 91*
Bloch, Howard M. 1927- *St&PR 91*
Bloch, Ivan S. *St&PR 91*
Bloch, J. Thomas 1938- *St&PR 91*
Bloch, Jeff 1959- *ConAu 130*
Bloch, Jonathan Michael 1952- *WhoWor 91*
Bloch, Joseph 1917- *IntWWM 90*
Bloch, Julia Chang 1942- *WhoAm 90, WhoAmW 91, WhoE 91*
Bloch, Julius 1888-1966 *WhoAmA 91N*
Bloch, Konrad 1912- *WorAlBi*
Bloch, Konrad Emil 1912- *WhoAm 90, WhoE 91, WhoWor 91*
Bloch, Kurt Julius 1929- *WhoAm 90*
Bloch, Lester Bernard 1930- *St&PR 91*
Bloch, Marc 1886-1944 *BioIn 16*
Bloch, Marie Halun 1910- *AuBYP 90*
Bloch, Martin B. 1935- *St&PR 91, WhoAm 90*
Bloch, Michel Georges 1948- *WhoWor 91*
Bloch, Milton Joseph 1937- *WhoAm 90, WhoAmA 91*
Bloch, Moise B. 1907- *St&PR 91*
Bloch, Paul 1939- *WhoAm 90*
Bloch, Rene M. 1923- *WhoWor 91*
Bloch, Richard A 1926- *ConAmBL*
Bloch, Richard Isaac 1943- *WhoAm 90*
Bloch, Robert 1917- *RGTwCSF, TwCCr&M 91*
Bloch, Robert Albert 1917- *WhoAm 90, WhoWrEP 89*
Bloch, Robert W. 1928- *ODwPR 91*
Bloch, Sheldon F *BiDrAPA 89*
Bloch, Silvia M A 1955- *BiDrAPA 89*
Bloch, Thomas M. 1954- *St&PR 91*
Bloch, Thomas Morton 1954- *WhoAm 90*
Bloch-Laine, Francois 1912- *BiDFrPL*
Bloch-Wresinski, Margot *BioIn 16*
Blocher, Kenyon Raymond 1937- *St&PR 91*
Blocher, Robert Moulton 1933- *St&PR 91*
Blocher, Thomas Anthony 1948- *BiDrAPA 89*
Blochman, Lawrence G 1900-1975 *TwCCr&M 91*
Block, Adolph 1906-1978 *WhoAmA 91N*
Block, Adriaen *EncCRAm*
Block, Alan Jay 1938- *WhoAm 90*
Block, Alexander 1881-1953 *BioIn 16*
Block, Allan 1923- *ConAu 31NR*
Block, Allan James 1954- *WhoEmL 91*
Block, Alvin V. 1926- *St&PR 91*
Block, Amanda Roth 1912- *WhoAm 90, WhoAmA 91*
Block, Andrew 1879-1969 *MusmAFA*
Block, Arnold 1927- *St&PR 91*
Block, Arnold S *BiDrAPA 89*
Block, Bartley C. 1933- *WhoE 91*
Block, Bruce 1938- *BiDrAPA 89*
Block, Charles L *BiDrAPA 89*
Block, Curt *ODwPR 91*
Block, Curtis 1938- *St&PR 91*
Block, Cy 1919- *Ballpl 90, BioIn 16*
Block, David Alan *BiDrAPA 89*
Block, Dennis Jeffery 1942- *WhoAm 90*
Block, Diane Zuern 1946- *WhoAmW 91*
Block, Donald 1936- *St&PR 91*
Block, Donald Grove 1953- *WhoE 91*
Block, Dorothy 1904- *WhoAmA 91*
Block, Douglas C. 1953- *St&PR 91*
Block, Edward M. *ODwPR 91*
Block, Edward Martel 1927- *WhoAm 90*
Block, Elise Robin *BiDrAPA 89*
Block, Elliott 1945- *WhoEmL 91*
Block, Emil Nathaniel, Jr. 1930- *WhoAm 90*
Block, Eric 1942- *WhoAm 90*
Block, Francesca 1962- *ConAu 131*
Block, Franklin Lee 1936- *WhoSSW 91*
Block, Gay 1942- *WhoAmA 91*
Block, Gene R. 1937- *St&PR 91*
Block, Geoffrey 1948- *IntWWM 90*
Block, George Edward 1926- *WhoAm 90*
Block, Harvey 1924- *St&PR 91*
Block, Haskell Mayer 1923- *WhoAm 90*
Block, Herbert Lawrence 1909- *BioIn 16, WhoAm 90, WhoE 91, WorAlBi*
Block, Isaac Edward 1924- *WhoAm 90, WhoWor 91*
Block, James P. 1930- *St&PR 91*
Block, Janet *ODwPR 91*
Block, Janet Leven *WhoAmW 91*
Block, Janet Lou 1937- *WhoWrEP 89*
Block, Jeanne Taylor *BioIn 16*
Block, Jerome D. 1948- *WhoHisp 91*
Block, John Douglas 1948- *St&PR 91, WhoAm 90*
Block, John Robinson 1954- *St&PR 91*
Block, John Rusling 1935- *BiDrUSE 89, WhoAm 90*
Block, Jon Marshall *BiDrAPA 89*
Block, Joseph 1934- *ODwPR 91*
Block, Joseph Douglas 1919- *WhoAm 90*
Block, Joseph K. 1955- *St&PR 91*
Block, Jules Richard 1930- *WhoAm 90*
Block, Julian 1934- *WhoWrEP 89*
Block, Kenneth L. 1920- *St&PR 91*
Block, Larry 1942- *ConTFT 8*
Block, Lawrence 1938- *TwCCr&M 91, WhoAm 90, WhoWrEP 89*
Block, Leonard Nathan 1911- *WhoAm 90*
Block, Leslie C. 1945- *St&PR 91*
Block, Lisa Mendel *BiDrAPA 89*
Block, Louis Stuart 1947- *WhoSSW 91*
Block, Lynne Wood 1943- *WhoAmW 91*
Block, Marvin A. 1903-1989 *BioIn 16*
Block, Maurine 1914- *WhoAmW 91*
Block, Max *BioIn 16*
Block, Melvin August 1921- *WhoAm 90*
Block, Michael Kent 1942- *WhoAm 90, WhoWor 91*
Block, Michael S. 1945- *St&PR 91*
Block, Mickey *BioIn 16*
Block, Murray Harold 1924- *WhoAm 90*
Block, Myrna 1946- *St&PR 91*
Block, Myron W. 1947- *St&PR 91*
Block, Nancy Thoms *BiDrAPA 89*
Block, Ned 1942- *WhoAm 90*
Block, Nelson Richard 1951- *WhoEmL 91*
Block, Pamela Jo 1947- *WhoAmW 91, WhoEmL 91*
Block, Peter *BioIn 16*
Block, Ralph A. 1936- *St&PR 91*
Block, Richard Earl 1931- *WhoAm 90*
Block, Richard Raphael 1938- *WhoE 91, WhoWor 91*
Block, Robert *BioIn 16*
Block, Robert Charles 1929- *WhoAm 90*
Block, Robert Jackson 1922- *WhoAm 90, WhoWor 91*
Block, Robert Michael 1947- *WhoEmL 91*
Block, Ruth 1930- *WhoAm 90*
Block, Ruth S. 1930- *St&PR 91*
Block, S. Lester 1917- *WhoAm 90*
Block, Seymour H 1947- *BiDrAPA 89*
Block, Stanley H 1937- *BiDrAPA 89*
Block, Stanley L *BiDrAPA 89*
Block, Stanley Marlin 1922- *WhoAm 90*
Block, Steven D. 1952- *IntWWM 90*
Block, Susan Dale 1952- *BiDrAPA 89*
Block, Virginia Schaffer 1946- *WhoAmA 91*
Block, Walter 1941- *WhoWrEP 89*
Block, William 1915- *St&PR 91, WhoAm 90*
Block, William Karl, Jr. 1944- *WhoAm 90*
Block, William Kenneth 1950- *WhoE 91*
Block, Zenas 1916- *WhoAm 90*
Blocker, Kent Robert 1946- *WhoSSW 91*
Blocker, Robert Lewis 1946- *WhoAm 90, WhoSSW 91*
Blockley, John 1800-1882 *OxCPMus*
Blockley, Lance Sinclair 1956- *St&PR 91*
Blocksma, Mary *AuBYP 90*
Blocksma, Mary 1942- *ConAu 130, WhoWrEP 89*
Blocksom, Rita Verlene Haynes 1952- *WhoAmW 91*
Blodgett, A L Nelson 1919- *BiDrAPA 89*
Blodgett, Anne Washington 1940- *WhoAm 90, WhoAmA 91*
Blodgett, Barbara *BioIn 16*
Blodgett, David Richard 1957- *WhoSSW 91*
Blodgett, Edmund Walton 1908- *WhoAmA 91N*
Blodgett, Forrest Clinton 1927- *WhoWor 91*
Blodgett, Frank Caleb 1927- *St&PR 91, WhoAm 90*
Blodgett, George Winslow 1888- *WhoAmA 91N*
Blodgett, John Talbott *BiDrAPA 89*
Blodgett, Katharine *BioIn 16*
Blodgett, Mark Wentworth 1957- *WhoEmL 91*
Blodgett, Omer William 1917- *WhoAm 90*
Blodgett, Stephen Russell 1957- *WhoEmL 91*
Blodgett, Vernon L., Jr. 1946- *St&PR 91*
Blodgett, Warren Terrell 1923- *WhoAm 90*
Blodgett, William A. 1937- *ODwPR 91*
Blodgett, William Arthur 1937- *WhoAm 90*
Blodgett, William Winthrop, IV 1942- *WhoAm 90*
Blodig, John L 1926- *BiDrAPA 89*
Bloebaum, William Douglas, Jr. 1939- *St&PR 91*
Bloede, Kirk Jonathan 1961- *WhoE 91*
Bloede, Merle Huie 1921- *WhoE 91*
Bloede, Victor Carl 1917- *WhoAm 90*
Bloede, Victor Gustav 1920- *WhoAm 90, WhoWor 91*
Bloedel, Joan Stuart Ross 1942- *WhoAmA 91*
Bloedel, Lawrence Hotch Kiss 1902-1976 *WhoAmA 91N*
Bloem, James H. 1950- *St&PR 91*
Bloem, Marion 1952- *EncCoWW*
Bloembergen, Nicolaas 1920- *WhoAm 90, WhoE 91, WhoWor 91, WorAlBi*
Bloemendal, Hans 1923- *WhoWor 91*
Bloemer, Rosemary Celeste 1930- *WhoAmW 91, WhoWor 91*
Bloemers, Henri Petrus Johan 1936- *WhoWor 91*
Bloemsma, Marco Paul 1924- *WhoWor 91*
Bloes, Richard K 1951- *WhoAmA 91*
Bloesch, Maureen Lee 1942- *WhoAmW 91*
Blofeld, John 1913- *EncO&P 3*
Blofeld, John Eaton Calthorpe 1913- *BioIn 16*
Blogna, Charles 1928- *St&PR 91*
Blohm, Douglas L. 1953- *St&PR 91*
Blohm, Tomas *BioIn 16*
Blois, Marsden S 1919- *ConAu 132*
Blois, Marsden S. 1919-1988 *BioIn 16*
Blois Montes de Souza, Roberto 1950- *WhoWor 91*
Bloise, Linda Elizabeth 1948- *WhoAmW 91*
Blok, Aleksandr 1880-1921 *WorAlBi*
Blokhin, Nikolai Nikolaevitch 1912- *WhoWor 91*
Bloland, Paul Anson 1923- *WhoAm 90*
Blom, Daniel C. 1919- *St&PR 91*
Blom, Daniel Charles 1919- *WhoAm 90*
Blom, Donald, Jr. 1944- *St&PR 91*
Blom, Gaston Eugene 1920- *BiDrAPA 89, WhoE 91*
Blom, Graham Edward 1954- *WhoWor 91*
Blom, Jack 1927- *St&PR 91*
Blom, Jan *ConAu 129*
Blom, Nicole Jan 1958- *WhoAm 90, WhoE 91, WhoEmL 91*
Blom, Richard Frederick 1932- *WhoE 91*
Blomberg, Erik 1894-1965 *DcScanL*
Blomberg, Ron 1948- *Ballpl 90, BioIn 16*
Blomberg, Werner von 1878-1946 *BioIn 16*
Blomdahl, Karl-Birger 1916-1968 *PenDiMP A*
Blomdahl, Sonja 1952- *WhoAmA 91*
Blome, Anthony E. 1935- *St&PR 91*
Blomeyer, Wolfgang 1934- *WhoWor 91*
Blomfield, Richard Best 1919- *WhoAm 90*
Blomgren, Bruce Holmes 1945- *WhoAm 90, WhoSSW 91*
Blomgren, Ronald Walter 1934- *WhoE 91*
Blomgren, Sharon Lorraine *BiDrAPA 89*
Blomjous, A. T. *BiDWomA*
Blomme, Kay Lynn 1959- *WhoAmW 91*
Blommer, Henry 1906- *St&PR 91*
Blomquist, Bernard L. 1926- *St&PR 91*
Blomquist, Brian L. *BioIn 16*
Blomquist, Carl Gunnar 1931- *WhoAm 90*
Blomquist, David Wels 1956- *WhoE 91*
Blomquist, Glenda L H *BiDrAPA 89*
Blomquist, Richard Frederick 1912- *WhoAm 90*
Blomquist, Richard T. 1952- *St&PR 91*
Blomquist, Robert Oscar 1930- *St&PR 91, WhoAm 90*
Blomquist, Susan Gail 1953- *WhoAmW 91*
Blomstedt, Dona Linder 1937- *WhoSSW 91*
Blomstedt, Herbert 1927- *PenDiMP*
Blomstedt, Herbert Thorson 1927- *IntWWM 90, WhoAm 90, WhoWor 91*
Blomstedt, Robert Kent 1931- *WhoAm 90*
Blomstrom, Bruce A. 1937- *St&PR 91*
Blond, Anthony *BioIn 16*
Blond, Maurice *BioIn 16*
Blondal, Patricia 1926-1959 *FemiCLE*
Blondek, John 1943- *St&PR 91*
Blondel, Marc 1938- *BiDFrPL*
Blondell, Joan 1909-1979 *WorAlBi*
Blonder, Lloyd 1939- *St&PR 91*
Blondie *EncPR&S 89*
Blondin, Antoine 1922- *WhoWor 91*
Blondin, Charles *DcCanB 12*
Blondin, Ethel 1951- *WhoAmW 91*
Blondot, Francois 1942- *WhoWor 91*
Blonston, Gary Lee 1942- *WhoAm 90*
Blood, Sweat and Tears *EncPR&S 89, OxCPMus*
Blood, Sweat & Tears *WorAlBi*
Blood, Archer Kent 1923- *WhoAm 90*
Blood, Arthur M 1922- *BiDrAPA 89*
Blood, Benjamin Donald 1914- *WhoSSW 91*
Blood, Edward Linford 1945- *St&PR 91, WhoAm 90, WhoEmL 91*
Blood, Karen A. 1959- *WhoAmW 91*

Blood, Matthew *TwCCr&M 91*
Blood, Opal Sue 1939- *WhoWrEP 89*
Blood, Robert Justus 1931- *WhoE 91, WhoWor 91*
Blood, Thomas 1618?-1680 *BioIn 16*
Bloodgood, Charles Froeb 1952- *WhoSSW 91*
Bloodgood, Clifford 1894-1957 *Ballpl 90*
Bloodgood, John Dudley 1931- *WhoAm 90*
Bloodworth, Albert William 1935- *WhoAm 90, WhoWor 91*
Bloodworth, Albert William Franklin 1935- *WhoSSW 91*
Bloodworth, Donald A. 1956- *St&PR 91*
Bloodworth, J. M. Bartow, Jr. 1925- *WhoAm 90*
Bloodworth, Jimmy 1917- *Ballpl 90*
Bloodworth, Ronald C 1938- *BiDrAPA 89*
Bloodworth, Ronald Coleman 1938- *WhoSSW 91*
Bloodworth, Smaro George 1948- *WhoSSW 91*
Bloody Fellow *WhNaAH*
Bloody Knife 1840?-1876 *WhNaAH*
Bloom, A. William 1923- *St&PR 91*
Bloom, Alan 1945- *St&PR 91, WhoAm 90*
Bloom, Allan 1930- *ConAu 131, WhoAm 90*
Bloom, Allan David *BioIn 16*
Bloom, Allen 1930- *WorAlBi*
Bloom, Allen J. 1935- *St&PR 91*
Bloom, Anne R. 1959- *WhoSSW 91*
Bloom, Arnold Sanford 1942- *WhoAm 90*
Bloom, Barbara 1951- *WhoAmA 91*
Bloom, Barbara L. 1939- *WhoAmW 91*
Bloom, Barry Malcolm 1928- *St&PR 91, WhoAm 90*
Bloom, Benjamin Harris 1946- *WhoE 91*
Bloom, Bernard 1912- *St&PR 91*
Bloom, Bruce Jay 1935- *WhoE 91*
Bloom, Bryan Scott 1955- *WhoEmL 91*
Bloom, C. Creighton 1928- *St&PR 91*
Bloom, C. Hugh 1933- *St&PR 91*
Bloom, Claire 1931- *WhoAmW 91, WorAlBi*
Bloom, Claudia *ODwPR 91*
Bloom, Clive 1953- *ConAu 131*
Bloom, David Edward 1938- *WhoE 91*
Bloom, David Myron 1928- *WhoSSW 91*
Bloom, David Peter *BioIn 16*
Bloom, David Ronald 1943- *WhoE 91*
Bloom, Don *BioIn 16*
Bloom, Donald 1931- *St&PR 91*
Bloom, Donald S 1932- *WhoAmA 91*
Bloom, Donald Stanley 1932- *WhoE 91*
Bloom, Edith Salvin 1917- *WhoAmA 91*
Bloom, Edward Alan 1914- *WhoAm 90, WhoWrEP 89*
Bloom, Edwin John, Jr. 1931- *WhoE 91*
Bloom, Eugene Charles 1933- *WhoSSW 91, WhoWor 91*
Bloom, Floyd E. 1936- *BiDrAPA 89*
Bloom, Floyd Elliott 1936- *WhoAm 90*
Bloom, Frank 1937- *WhoAm 90*
Bloom, Frank R. 1946- *St&PR 91*
Bloom, Fred Abraham 1944- *BiDrAPA 89*
Bloom, Harold *AuBYP 90*
Bloom, Harold 1930- *BioIn 16, WhoAm 90, WhoWrEP 89*
Bloom, Herbert 1930- *WhoAm 90, WhoWrEP 89*
Bloom, Hyman 1913- *WhoAm 90, WhoAmA 91*
Bloom, Hyman 1952- *BiDrAPA 89*
Bloom, James Edward 1941- *WhoWor 91*
Bloom, Jane Ira 1955- *WhoEmL 91*
Bloom, Janet K. *WhoWrEP 89*
Bloom, Joel Barnet 1940- *WhoE 91*
Bloom, Joel N. 1925- *St&PR 91, WhoAm 90*
Bloom, John Porter 1924- *WhoAm 90*
Bloom, Joseph D 1938- *BiDrAPA 89*
Bloom, Kathryn Ruth *ODwPR 91, WhoE 91*
Bloom, Lary Roger 1943- *WhoAm 90, WhoWrEP 89*
Bloom, Lawrence M *BiDrAPA 89*
Bloom, Lawrence Stephen 1930- *St&PR 91, WhoAm 90*
Bloom, Lee B B *BiDrAPA 89*
Bloom, Lee Hurley 1919- *WhoAm 90*
Bloom, Lloyd *BioIn 16*
Bloom, Lynda 1956- *St&PR 91*
Bloom, Lynn Marie Zimmerman 1934- *WhoWrEP 89*
Bloom, Man *BioIn 16*
Bloom, Martha 1951- *WhoAmA 91*
Bloom, Martin J. 1930- *St&PR 91*
Bloom, Max *NewYTBS 90*
Bloom, Michael Eugene 1947- *WhoWor 91*
Bloom, Michael Jay 1958- *WhoEmL 91, WhoWor 91*
Bloom, Murray Teigh 1916- *WhoAm 90*
Bloom, Myer 1928- *WhoAm 90*
Bloom, Naomi *BiDrAPA 89*
Bloom, Olga *BioIn 16*
Bloom, Olive Zoe 1933- *WhoAmW 91*
Bloom, Pauline *WhoWrEP 89*
Bloom, Peter Brower 1936- *BiDrAPA 89, WhoE 91*
Bloom, Peter Herbert 1949- *IntWWM 90, WhoEmL 91*
Bloom, Robert 1908- *BioIn 16*
Bloom, Robert M. 1923- *St&PR 91*
Bloom, Robert Wayne 1952- *BiDrAPA 89*
Bloom, Rodney M. 1933- *St&PR 91*
Bloom, Rodney Merlin 1933- *WhoAm 90*
Bloom, Ruth Elsa 1954- *WhoE 91*
Bloom, Sandra Lynn 1948- *BiDrAPA 89*
Bloom, Sherman 1934- *WhoAm 90*
Bloom, Shirley Gordon 1944- *St&PR 91*
Bloom, Stephen Earl 1941- *WhoE 91*
Bloom, Stephen Edward 1955- *WhoEmL 91, WhoSSW 91*
Bloom, Stephen I. 1945- *WhoSSW 91*
Bloom, Stephen Joel 1936- *WhoAm 90*
Bloom, Stuart Ian 1953- *WhoSSW 91*
Bloom, Susan *ODwPR 91*
Bloom, Susan 1951- *WhoAmW 91*
Bloom, Tony *BioIn 16*
Bloom, Valerie 1956- *FemiCLE*
Bloom, Victor 1931- *BiDrAPA 89*
Bloom, William A, Jr. *BiDrAPA 89*
Bloom, William J. *St&PR 91*
Bloom, William John 1949- *St&PR 91*
Bloomberg, Mary Beth 1947- *WhoEmL 91*
Bloomberg, Robert Joseph 1947- *WhoEmL 91*
Bloomberg, Sanford 1924- *BiDrAPA 89*
Bloomberg, Warner, Jr. 1926- *WhoAm 90*
Bloome, Enid P. 1925- *AuBYP 90*
Bloomer, Amelia 1818-1894 *WorAlBi*
Bloomer, Amelia Jenks 1818-1894 *BioAmW, FemiCLE*
Bloomer, Elizabeth Mary 1962- *WhoAmW 91*
Bloomer, Harold Franklin, Jr. 1933- *WhoE 91*
Bloomer, Jack 1935- *St&PR 91*
Bloomer, Margaret *DcCanB 12*
Bloomfield, Arthur Irving 1914- *WhoAm 90*
Bloomfield, Arthur John 1931- *IntWWM 90, WhoAm 90*
Bloomfield, Clara Derber 1942- *WhoAm 90*
Bloomfield, Daniel Kermit 1926- *WhoAm 90*
Bloomfield, Fannie *PenDiMP*
Bloomfield, Georgetta Snyder 1952- *WhoAmW 91*
Bloomfield, Harold H 1944- *BiDrAPA 89*
Bloomfield, Keith Martin 1951- *WhoEmL 91*
Bloomfield, Lincoln Palmer 1920- *WhoAm 90*
Bloomfield, Lisa Diane 1951- *WhoAmA 91*
Bloomfield, Maxwell Herron, III 1931- *WhoAm 90, WhoE 91*
Bloomfield, Maxwell I *BiDrAPA 89*
Bloomfield, Mike 1942-1981 *EncPR&S 89*
Bloomfield, Morton Wilfred 1913-1987 *BioIn 16*
Bloomfield, Peter 1946- *WhoSSW 91*
Bloomfield, Robert 1766-1823 *DcLB 93 [port]*
Bloomfield, Robert Russell, Jr. 1955- *WhoE 91*
Bloomfield, Ronald James 1948- *WhoEmL 91*
Bloomfield, Serena Lurie 1953- *WhoAmW 91*
Bloomfield, Steven Jay 1950- *WhoEmL 91*
Bloomfield, Suzanne 1934- *WhoAmA 91*
Bloomfield, Theodore 1923- *IntWWM 90*
Bloomfield, Victor Alfred 1938- *WhoAm 90*
Bloomfield, William Mendel 1948- *WhoEmL 91*
Bloomgarden, Judith Mary 1942- *WhoAmA 91*
Bloomgarden, Kathleen Finn 1949- *WhoAm 90, WhoAmW 91*
Bloomgarden, Kathy 1949- *ODwPR 91*
Bloomgarden, Robert Evan 1942- *BiDrAPA 89*
Bloomingdale, Irma Asiel *BioIn 16*
Bloomingdale, Joseph B. 1842-1904 *WorAlBi*
Bloomingdale, Kerry Lewis *BiDrAPA 89*
Bloomingdale, Lewis Morgan *BiDrAPA 89*
Bloomingdale, Teresa 1930- *WhoWrEP 89*
Bloomquist, Al 1921- *ODwPR 91*
Bloomquist, Aldrich Carl 1921- *St&PR 91*
Bloomquist, Carol Lynn 1953- *BiDrAPA 89*
Bloomquist, E. Glynn, Jr. 1954- *St&PR 91*
Bloomquist, Eunice I. 1940- *WhoAmW 91*
Bloomquist, John Hayes 1946- *WhoEmL 91*
Bloomquist, Kenneth Gene 1931- *WhoAm 90*
Bloor, Ella Reeve 1862-1951 *EncAL*
Bloor, Ian Thomas 1940- *WhoWor 91*
Bloor, Robert *PenDiDA 89*
Bloor, William Spencer 1918- *WhoAm 90*
Bloostein, Allan Jerome 1929- *St&PR 91*
Blore, Chuck *BioIn 16*
Blos, Joan W. 1928- *AuBYP 90, SmATA 11AS [port], WhoAm 90, WhoAmW 91, WhoWrEP 89*
Blos, Peter, Jr. 1929- *BiDrAPA 89*
Blos, Peter W 1908-1986 *WhoAmA 91N*
Blose, Irvin Leroy 1920- *BiDrAPA 89*
Bloskas, John D. 1928- *WhoSSW 91*
Blosl, Thomas Louis 1934- *St&PR 91*
Blosser, Henry Gabriel 1928- *WhoAm 90*
Blosser, Henry L. 1952- *WhoEmL 91*
Blosser, Merrill 1892-1983 *EncACom*
Blosser, Nicholas 1958- *WhoAmA 91*
Blosser, Patricia Ellen 1931- *WhoAm 90, WhoAmW 91*
Blosser-Rainey, Priscilla *BioIn 16*
Blossman, Alfred Rhody, Jr. 1931- *WhoAm 90*
Blossom, Beth *ODwPR 91*
Blossom, Beth 1926- *WhoAmW 91, WhoWrEP 89*
Blossom, Henry 1866-1919 *OxCPMus*
Blotcky, Mark Joel 1946- *BiDrAPA 89*
Blotkamp, Carel Hendrik 1945- *WhoWor 91*
Blotner, Adrian Brian 1957- *BiDrAPA 89*
Blotner, Joseph Leo 1923- *WhoAm 90*
Blotner, Linda Solow 1947- *IntWWM 90*
Blotner, Norman David 1918- *WhoAm 90*
Blotnick-Pender, Vivian S 1944- *BiDrAPA 89*
Blouch, G.B. 1946- *St&PR 91*
Blouch, Susan Elizabeth 1947- *WhoEmL 91*
Blouch, Timothy Craig 1954- *WhoEmL 91*
Blouet, Brian Walter 1936- *ConAu 32NR*
Blouet, Olwyn M 1948- *ConAu 130*
Blough, Donald S. 1929- *WhoAm 90*
Blough, Douglas Duane 1949- *WhoEmL 91*
Blough, Freeman, Jr. 1946- *WhoE 91*
Blough, Glenn Orlando 1907- *AuBYP 90, WhoAm 90, WhoWrEP 89*
Blough, Roger M. 1904-1985 *WorAlBi*
Blough, Roy 1901- *WhoAm 90, WhoE 91*
Blough, William LeRoy 1946- *WhoEmL 91*
Blouin, Francis Joseph 1910- *WhoE 91*
Blouin, Francis Xavier, Jr. 1946- *WhoEmL 91*
Blouin, Maurice F. 1905- *St&PR 91*
Blouin, Paul 1925- *OxCCanT*
Blount, Amie *BiDEWW*
Blount, Ben B., Jr. 1939- *St&PR 91*
Blount, C.B. 1925- *St&PR 91*
Blount, Charles *BioIn 16*
Blount, Dan S. 1928- *St&PR 91*
Blount, David Laurence 1954- *WhoEmL 91*
Blount, Don H. 1929- *WhoAm 90*
Blount, Donald Binion 1948- *WhoSSW 91*
Blount, Evelyn 1942- *WhoAmW 91*
Blount, Gary Lester *BiDrAPA 89*
Blount, James Henderson 1837-1903 *BioIn 16*
Blount, Luther Hammond 1916- *St&PR 91*
Blount, Mel *BioIn 16*
Blount, Michael Eugene 1949- *WhoAm 90*
Blount, Robert Arthur 1949- *WhoEmL 91*
Blount, Robert Grier 1938- *St&PR 91*
Blount, Robert Haddock 1922- *WhoAm 90*
Blount, Roy, Jr. 1941- *MajTwCW*
Blount, Sam *BioIn 16*
Blount, Stanley Freeman 1929- *WhoAm 90*
Blount, Terry Jacob 1943- *St&PR 91*
Blount, William 1749-1800 *BioIn 16, EncCRAm*
Blount, William Allan 1954- *WhoAm 90*
Blount, William H. 1922- *St&PR 91*
Blount, William Houston 1922- *WhoAm 90, WhoSSW 91*
Blount, Winton Malcolm 1921- *BiDrUSE 89, BioIn 16, St&PR 91*
Blount, Winton Malcolm, III 1943- *WhoAm 90*
Blount, Winton Malcolm, Jr. 1921- *WhoAm 90, WhoSSW 91*
Bloustein, Bruce Robert 1948- *St&PR 91*
Bloustein, Edward J. 1925-1989 *BioIn 16, CurBio 90N*
Bloustein, Jean *BioIn 16*
Bloustein, Peter Edward 1937- *WhoSSW 91*
Bloustein, Ruth Ellen Steinman 1923-1988 *BioIn 16*
Blout, Bart Boyd 1943- *St&PR 91*
Blout, Elkan Rogers 1919- *WhoAm 90*
Blow, Anne *BiDEWW*
Blow, David Dale 1944- *WhoSSW 91*
Blow, David Mervyn 1931- *WhoWor 91*
Blow, Garth W. 1911- *St&PR 91*
Blow, Henry Taylor 1817-1875 *BioIn 16*
Blow, Kurtis 1959- *DrBlPA 90*
Blow, Michael *AuBYP 90*
Blow, Michael 1930- *ConAu 130*
Blow, Sandra 1925- *BiDWomA*
Blower, Bruce Gregory 1937- *WhoWor 91*
Blower, David Harrison 1901-1976 *WhoAmA 91N*
Blower, Elizabeth 1757?-1816? *FemiCLE*
Blowers, J. Garrett 1941- *ODwPR 91*
Blowfield, Ian Stuart 1947- *WhoWor 91*
Bloxham, Arnall 1881?- *EncO&P 3*
Bloxham, Eleanor Joan Earle 1957- *WhoAmW 91*
Bloxom, David Leon 1950- *St&PR 91*
Blozis, Jolene McCoy 1941- *WhoWrEP 89*
Blucher, Walter H. *BioIn 16*
Blucher Von Wahlstatt, Gebhard Leberecht 1742-1819 *WorAlBi*
Bluck, Alan Stuart 1952- *WhoWor 91*
Blucker, Linda Sue *BiDrAPA 89*
Bludman, Sidney Arnold 1927- *WhoAm 90*
Bludworth, Charles E, Jr. 1930- *BiDrAPA 89*
Blue Jacket *WhNaAH*
Blue Oyster Cult *EncPR&S 89*
Blue, Anthony Dias *BioIn 16*
Blue, Ben 1901-1975 *WorAlBi*
Blue, Catherine Anne 1957- *WhoAmW 91*
Blue, Charles Toomey 1952- *WhoSSW 91*
Blue, Elmer 1925- *St&PR 91*
Blue, James N. 1935- *St&PR 91*
Blue, Lu 1897-1958 *Ballpl 90*
Blue, Monte Lynn 1945- *WhoEmL 91*
Blue, Patt 1945- *WhoAmA 91*
Blue, Percie *WhoWrEP 89*
Blue, Robert D 1898-1989 *CurBio 90N*
Blue, Robert Donald 1898-1989 *BioIn 16*
Blue, Robert Lee 1920- *WhoWor 91*
Blue, Rose 1931- *AuBYP 90, WhoAmW 91*
Blue, Shanda Genevieve Hansma 1948- *WhoAmW 91*
Blue, Vida *BioIn 16*
Blue, Vida 1949- *Ballpl 90 [port], WorAlBi*
Blue, Warren Grant 1926- *St&PR 91*
Blue, William *BioIn 16*
Blue, William Lacy 1914- *WhoE 91*
Bluebello, James Joseph 1926- *St&PR 91*
Bluebond, Sheri Ann 1961- *WhoEmL 91*
Bluefarb, Samuel Mitchell 1912- *WhoAm 90*
Bluege, Ossie 1900- *Ballpl 90*
Bluejacket, Jim 1887-1947 *Ballpl 90*
Bluemke, David W. 1953- *St&PR 91*
Bluemke, John Albert, Jr. 1949- *St&PR 91*
Bluemle, Lewis William, Jr. 1921- *WhoAm 90*
Bluemle, Robert Louis 1933- *WhoAm 90*
Blues Project, The *EncPR&S 89*
Bluestein, Abram Isaac 1948- *St&PR 91*
Bluestein, Daniel Thomas 1943- *WhoWrEP 89*
Bluestein, Edwin A., Jr. 1930- *WhoAm 90*
Bluestein, Herman W. 1947- *St&PR 91*
Bluestein, Joan S. 1920- *St&PR 91*
Bluestein, Judith A. 1948- *St&PR 91*
Bluestein, Judith Ann 1948- *WhoAmW 91*
Bluestein, Louis L *BiDrAPA 89*
Bluestein, Paul H. 1923- *St&PR 91*
Bluestein, Paul Harold 1923- *WhoAm 90*
Bluestein, Venus Weller 1933- *WhoAm 90, WhoAmW 91*
Bluestone, Andrew Lavoott 1951- *WhoEmL 91*
Bluestone, Harvey 1920- *BiDrAPA 89*
Bluestone, Hugh Lawrence 1948- *WhoAm 90, WhoEmL 91*
Bluestone, Naomi Ruth *BiDrAPA 89*
Bluett, Thomas Byron, Sr. 1931- *WhoWor 91*
Blueweiss, Herbert *BioIn 16*
Bluford, Guion S. *BioIn 16*
Bluford, Guion Stewart, Jr. 1942- *WhoAm 90*
Bluhm, Barbara Jean 1925- *WhoAm 90*
Bluhm, Heinz 1907- *WhoAm 90*
Bluhm, Leslie 1940- *St&PR 91*
Bluhm, Norman 1920- *WhoAm 90*
Bluhm, Norman 1921- *WhoAmA 91*
Bluhm, William Theodore 1923- *WhoAm 90*
Bluitt, Karen 1957- *WhoAmW 91*
Blum, Abraham 1905-1943 *BioIn 16*
Blum, Alexandra Lynne 1956- *WhoAmW 91*
Blum, Andrea 1950- *WhoAmA 91*
Blum, Arthur 1926- *WhoAm 90*
Blum, Barbara Davis 1939- *WhoAm 90, WhoAmW 91*
Blum, Barbara Meddock 1938- *WhoAmW 91*
Blum, Caryn Elizabeth 1959- *WhoAmW 91*
Blum, David 1920- *St&PR 91*
Blum, David Lawrence 1962- *WhoEmL 91*
Blum, Donald R. 1931- *St&PR 91*
Blum, Eva Tansky 1949- *WhoEmL 91*
Blum, Fred Andrew 1939- *WhoAm 90*
Blum, Geoffrey Carl 1951- *WhoWrEP 89*
Blum, Gerald H. 1926- *St&PR 91*
Blum, Gerald Henry 1926- *WhoAm 90*
Blum, Gerald Myron 1932- *BiDrAPA 89*
Blum, Gerald S. 1932- *St&PR 91*
Blum, Gerald Saul 1922- *WhoAm 90*
Blum, Harold Philip 1929- *BiDrAPA 89*
Blum, Heinz Egon 1920- *WhoE 91*

Blum, Helaine Dorothy WhoAmA 91
Blum, Howard Robert 1951- WhoE 91
Blum, Jacob Joseph 1926- WhoAm 90
Blum, Jan BioIn 16
Blum, Jeffrey Stuart 1947- WhoEmL 91
Blum, Jerome 1913- WhoAm 90
Blum, Joan Kurley 1926- WhoAmW 91
Blum, Joel A 1942- BiDrAPA 89
Blum, John A. 1915- St&PR 91
Blum, John Alan 1933- WhoAm 90
Blum, John Curtis 1915- WhoAm 90
Blum, John Leo 1917- WhoAm 90
Blum, John Morton 1921- WhoAm 90
Blum, Joseph 1919- WhoE 91
Blum, Joseph F. 1934- WhoE 91
Blum, June 1939- WhoAmA 91
Blum, Klara 1904- EncCoWW
Blum, Klaus-Uwe 1927- WhoWor 91
Blum, Lawrence David 1955- BiDrAPA 89
Blum, Lawrence Philip 1917- WhoAm 90
Blum, Leon 1872-1950 BiDFrPL, BioIn 16
Blum, Lester 1906-1989 BioIn 16
Blum, Manuel 1938- WhoAm 90
Blum, Marc Paul 1942- St&PR 91
Blum, Mark 1950- ConTFT 8
Blum, Mark J. 1953- St&PR 91
Blum, Martin H 1932- BiDrAPA 89
Blum, Michael A. 1944- St&PR 91
Blum, Michael Stephen 1939- WhoAm 90
Blum, Nancy K. WhoAmW 91
Blum, Paula Louise 1959- WhoAmW 91
Blum, Peter 1950- WhoEmL 91
Blum, Peter J. BioIn 16
Blum, Philip 1928- St&PR 91
Blum, R.J. 1946- St&PR 91
Blum, Reinhard 1933- WhoWor 91
Blum, Richard C. BioIn 16
Blum, Richard Hosmer Adams 1927- WhoAm 90
Blum, Richard I. 1953- WhoEmL 91
Blum, Richard Steven 1938- WhoE 91
Blum, Robert Allan 1938- BiDrAPA 89, WhoE 91
Blum, Robert Edward 1899- WhoAm 90, WhoWor 91
Blum, Seymour 1916- St&PR 91
Blum, Seymour L. 1925- WhoAm 90
Blum, Steven B. 1951- WhoEmL 91
Blum, Virgil C. NewYTBS 90
Blum, Virgil C. 1913-1990 BioIn 16
Blum, Walter J. 1918- WhoAm 90
Blum, William Lee 1920- WhoAm 90
Blum-Goldstein, Susan Ruth 1963- WhoAmW 91
Blumberg, Adele Rosenberg 1916- WhoAmW 91
Blumberg, Alyse Neiburg 1946- WhoAmW 91, WhoEmL 91
Blumberg, Arnold G. 1920-1989 BioIn 16
Blumberg, Avrom Aaron 1928- WhoAm 90
Blumberg, Barbara Griffiths 1920- WhoAmA 91
Blumberg, Barbara Marilyn 1936- WhoAmW 91
Blumberg, Barbara Salmanson 1927- WhoAmW 91, WhoE 91, WhoWor 91
Blumberg, Baruch Samuel 1925- WhoAm 90, WhoE 91, WhoWor 91
Blumberg, David 1925- St&PR 91, WhoAm 90
Blumberg, David M. 1911-1989 BioIn 16
Blumberg, Donald D. 1929- St&PR 91
Blumberg, Edward J. 1908- St&PR 91
Blumberg, Edward Robert 1951- WhoSSW 91, WhoWor 91
Blumberg, Gerald 1911- WhoAm 90
Blumberg, Grace Ganz 1940- WhoAm 90, WhoAmW 91
Blumberg, Herbert K. 1925- St&PR 91
Blumberg, Herbert Kurt 1925- WhoAm 90
Blumberg, Jerome J. 1905- St&PR 91
Blumberg, Joel Myron 1940- WhoE 91
Blumberg, Julia Baum WhoAmW 91
Blumberg, Leda BioIn 16
Blumberg, Leda 1956- WhoWrEP 89
Blumberg, Marc Helman BiDrAPA 89
Blumberg, Marvin E. 1926- St&PR 91
Blumberg, Michael S. 1926- St&PR 91
Blumberg, Michael Zangwill 1945- WhoSSW 91
Blumberg, Nancy Fern 1946- WhoEmL 91
Blumberg, Nathan Bernard 1922- WhoWrEP 89
Blumberg, Nathaniel Bernard 1922- WhoAm 90
Blumberg, Neil Howard 1951- BiDrAPA 89, WhoE 91
Blumberg, Peter S. 1944- St&PR 91
Blumberg, Philip Flayderman 1957- WhoSSW 91, WhoWor 91
Blumberg, Phillip Irvin 1919- WhoAm 90
Blumberg, Rena Joy 1934- WhoAmW 91
Blumberg, Rhoda 1917- BioIn 16, ChlLR 21 [port]
Blumberg, Rhoda L 1926- ConAu 30NR
Blumberg, Richard Winston 1914- WhoAm 90
Blumberg, Robert H. 1939- St&PR 91
Blumberg, Ron WhoAmA 91
Blumberg, Stephen 1944- St&PR 91
Blumberg, Walter B. 1911- St&PR 91
Blumberg, Yuli 1894-1964 WhoAmA 91N
Blume, Clinton W. 1957- WhoEmL 91
Blume, Clinton W., Jr. 1934- St&PR 91
Blume, Elizabeth Renee 1953- WhoAmW 91
Blume, Helmut 1914- IntWWM 90
Blume, Horst Karl 1927- WhoE 91
Blume, Jack Paul 1915- WhoAm 90
Blume, John August 1909- WhoAm 90
Blume, Judy BioIn 16
Blume, Judy 1938- AuBYP 90, FemiCLE, MajTwCW, WorAlBi
Blume, Judy Sussman 1938- WhoAm 90, WhoAmW 91, WhoWrEP 89
Blume, Kathryn Alice 1947- WhoEmL 91
Blume, Lawrence Dayton 1948- WhoE 91
Blume, Mark Gregory 1962- WhoEmL 91
Blume, Marshall Edward 1941- WhoAm 90
Blume, Martin 1932- WhoAm 90
Blume, Myron R. 1931- St&PR 91
Blume, Peter 1906- BioIn 16, WhoAm 90, WhoAmA 91, WhoE 91
Blume, Peter Frederick 1946- WhoAm 90, WhoE 91
Blume, Sheila B 1934- BiDrAPA 89
Blume, Sheila Bierman 1934- WhoAmW 91
Blume, Stephen Craig 1948- WhoEmL 91
Blume, Walter Manley 1958- WhoEmL 91
Blumel, Joseph Carlton 1928- WhoAm 90
Blumenberg, Robert Murray 1934- WhoE 91
Blumenfeld, Alfred Morton 1919- WhoAm 90
Blumenfeld, Anita 1933- WhoAmW 91
Blumenfeld, Erwin 1897-1969 BioIn 16
Blumenfeld, Esther Richter 1936- WhoSSW 91
Blumenfeld, Hans 1892-1988 BioIn 16
Blumenfeld, Harold 1923- IntWWM 90
Blumenfeld, Helaine BioIn 16
Blumenfeld, Jeffry A. 1952- ODwPR 91
Blumenfeld, Jeffry Alan 1952- WhoEmL 91
Blumenfeld, M. Joseph 1904-1988 BioIn 16
Blumenfeld, Michael ODwPR 91
Blumenfeld, Michael Joseph 1946- WhoAm 90
Blumenfeld, Samuel 1926- BiDrAPA 89, WhoE 91
Blumenfeld, Seth David 1940- St&PR 91, WhoAm 90
Blumenfeld, Sharna Faye 1934- WhoAmW 91
Blumenfield, Helaine 1940?- BiDWomA
Blumenfield, Michael 1938- BiDrAPA 89
Blumenkrantz, Jeff 1965- ConTFT 8 [port]
Blumenreich, Patricia Estela BiDrAPA 89
Blumenreich, Patricia Estela 1954- WhoEmL 91, WhoSSW 91
Blumenschein, Ernest Leonard 1874-1960 WhoAmA 91N
Blumenschein, Mary Greene 1869-1958 WhoAmA 91N
Blumenson, Martin 1918- WhoWrEP 89
Blumenstock, David Albert 1927- WhoAm 90
Blumental, Felicja 1915- PenDiMP
Blumenthal, Aaron H. 1908-1982 BioIn 16
Blumenthal, Andre 1904-1989 BioIn 16
Blumenthal, Andrea Kathryn 1943- WhoE 91
Blumenthal, Barbara Anne 1949- WhoAmW 91
Blumenthal, Barry Howard 1955- BiDrAPA 89
Blumenthal, Carol 1951- WhoEmL 91
Blumenthal, Ellen Gravitz 1947- BiDrAPA 89
Blumenthal, Fritz 1913- WhoAm 90, WhoAmA 91
Blumenthal, Gerald Paul 1945- WhoE 91
Blumenthal, Harold Jay 1926- WhoAm 90
Blumenthal, Herman 1915- St&PR 91
Blumenthal, Herman Bertram 1916- WhoAm 90
Blumenthal, Howard J. 1952- WhoEmL 91
Blumenthal, Irving Jack 1910- BiDrAPA 89, WhoE 91
Blumenthal, Isidor 1909- St&PR 91
Blumenthal, Jack 1919- St&PR 91
Blumenthal, Jerome Barry BiDrAPA 89
Blumenthal, John 1949- ConAu 129
Blumenthal, John Frederick 1949- WhoEmL 91
Blumenthal, Joseph NewYTBS 90 [port]
Blumenthal, Kurt Douglas 1944- St&PR 91
Blumenthal, Lyn 1948-1988 BioIn 16
Blumenthal, Margaret M 1905- WhoAmA 91
Blumenthal, Michael 1935- WhoWor 91
Blumenthal, Mortimer J 1921- BiDrAPA 89
Blumenthal, Robert S. 1928- St&PR 91
Blumenthal, Ronnie 1944- WhoAmW 91
Blumenthal, Stanley Len 1946- WhoWrEP 89
Blumenthal, Steven 1948- WhoEmL 91, WhoSSW 91, WhoWor 91
Blumenthal, Susan Jane 1952- BiDrAPA 89, WhoAmW 91, WhoE 91
Blumenthal, Sydney C., Jr. 1916- St&PR 91
Blumenthal, Terry Dale 1954- WhoSSW 91
Blumenthal, W. Michael BioIn 16
Blumenthal, W Michael 1926- ConAmBL
Blumenthal, W. Michael 1926- St&PR 91, WhoAm 90, WhoE 91
Blumenthal, Werner Michael 1926- BiDrUSE 89
Blumenthal-Weiss, Ilse 1899-1987 EncCoWW
Blumer, Anne M. 1956- WhoAmW 91
Blumer, Dietrich P 1929- BiDrAPA 89
Blumer, Frederick Elwin 1933- WhoAm 90
Blumer, James William 1924- St&PR 91
Blumer, Thomas William 1954- WhoEmL 91
Blumhardt, Rodney S. 1935- St&PR 91
Blummer, Kathleen Ann 1945- WhoEmL 91
Blumofe, Robert Fulton WhoAm 90
Blumrich, Josef Franz 1913- WhoWor 91
Blumrich, Stephen 1941- WhoAmA 91
Blumrosen, Ruth Gerber 1927- WhoE 91, WhoWor 91
Blumstein, Alex BiDrAPA 89
Blumstein, Alfred 1930- WhoAm 90
Blumstein, James Franklin 1945- WhoAm 90
Blumstein, Jerome 1930- St&PR 91
Blumstein, Sheila Ellen 1944- WhoAm 90
Blumstein, William A. 1948- WhoAm 90
Blumstein-Elder, Renee 1957- WhoAmW 91
Blunck, Hans Friedrich 1888-1961 BioIn 16
Blundall, Joan BioIn 16
Blundell, Gordon Lane, Jr. 1954- BiDrAPA 89
Blundell, William Edward 1934- WhoAm 90
Blundell, William R.C. 1927- St&PR 91
Blundell, William Richard Charles 1927- WhoAm 90, WhoWor 91
Blunden, Anna E. 1829-1915 BiDWomA
Blunden, Caroline 1948- ConAu 132
Blunden, Edmund 1896-1974 DcLB 100 [port], MajTwCW
Blundon, Jill M. 1953- St&PR 91
Blundy, David BioIn 16
Blundy, David 1945-1989 AnObit 1989
Blunier, Doris E. 1952- St&PR 91
Blunk, Dan Isbell 1947- BiDrAPA 89
Blunk, Forrest Stewart 1913- WhoAm 90
Blunk, Nancy M. St&PR 91
Blunt, Anthony 1907-1983 BioIn 16
Blunt, Anthony Frederick 1907-1983 DcNaB 1981
Blunt, Charles William 1951- WhoWor 91
Blunt, James Gilpatrick 1826-1881 WhNaAH
Blunt, Lynn Waldo 1937- BiDrAPA 89
Blunt, Marcus 1947- IntWWM 90
Blunt, Roger Reckling 1930- St&PR 91
Blunt, Roy D. 1950- WhoAm 90
Blunt, William David 1924- St&PR 91
Blurton, Keith Frederick 1940- WhoSSW 91
Blust, John Louis 1944- St&PR 91
Blustein, Joseph Edward 1936- BiDrAPA 89
Bluteau, L.M. 1927- St&PR 91
Bluth, B. J. 1934- WhoAm 90
Bluth, Dewey C. 1922- St&PR 91
Blutig, Eduard ConAu 30NR
Blutstein, Harvey M. 1927- WhoE 91
Blutter, Joan Wernick 1929- WhoAm 90
Bluvas, William J. 1943- St&PR 91
Bly, Carol McLean 1930- WhoWrEP 89
Bly, David Alan 1953- WhoEmL 91
Bly, Herbert Arthur 1929- St&PR 91
Bly, Lloyd George 1947- St&PR 91
Bly, Mark John 1949- WhoWrEP 89
Bly, Nellie 1865-1922 BioAmW
Bly, Nellie 1867-1922 BioIn 16, WorAlBi
Bly, Robert 1926- MajTwCW, WorAlBi
Bly, Robert Elwood 1926- WhoAm 90, WhoWrEP 89
Bly, Robert W. 1957- BioIn 16
Bly, Stephen Arthur 1944- WhoWrEP 89
Bly-Fulton, Margaret Anne 1942- WhoSSW 91
Blydenburgh, John Carl 1938- WhoAm 90
Blyholder, George Donald 1931- WhoAm 90, WhoSSW 91
Blyleven, Bert BioIn 16
Blyleven, Bert 1951- Ballpl 90 [port], WorAlBi
Blyn, Charlotte L BiDrAPA 89
Blyn, George 1919- WhoE 91
Blyn, Stefany 1953- WhoE 91
Blystone, F. Lynn 1935- St&PR 91
Blystone, Jane Marie 1951- WhoWrEP 89
Blystone, Robert Vernon 1943- WhoSSW 91
Blyth, Alan 1929- IntWWM 90
Blyth, Ann 1928- WorAlBi
Blyth, Ann Marie 1949- WhoAmW 91, WhoWor 91
Blyth, John William 1909- WhoAm 90
Blyth, Michael Leslie 1950- WhoAm 90
Blyth, Myrna Greenstein 1939- St&PR 91, WhoAm 90, WhoAmW 91, WhoE 91, WhoWrEP 89
Blyth, Sam BioIn 16
Blythe, Angela D. 1960- WhoAmW 91
Blythe, Arthur BioIn 16
Blythe, Domini BioIn 16
Blythe, Domini 1947- OxCCanT
Blythe, Gus BioIn 16
Blythe, James Edwin 1929- WhoAm 90
Blythe, Joseph John 1947- WhoEmL 91
Blythe, Marguerite M. 1947- BiDrAPA 89
Blythe, Mary Susan 1945- WhoEmL 91
Blythe, Robert Allen 1944- St&PR 91
Blythe, Robert Richard 1949- WhoEmL 91
Blythe, Ronald R. 1948- St&PR 91
Blythe, William Brevard 1928- WhoAm 90
Blyton, Carey 1932- IntWWM 90
Blyton, Enid 1897-1968 BioIn 16, ConAu 33NR, FemiCLE
Blyton, Enid Mary 1897-1968 AuBYP 90
Blyveis, Barry 1939- WhoAm 90
Blyzka, Mike 1928- Ballpl 90
Bo and Peep EncO&P 3
Bo Yibo 1908- WhoWor 91
Bo, Kristie Lee 1954- WhoEmL 91
Boada Vilallonga, Claudio 1920- WhoWor 91
Boaden, Lucille Ann 1945- WhoAmW 91, WhoEmL 91
Boadicea, Queen BioIn 16
Boag, Thomas J 1922- BiDrAPA 89
Boag, Thomas Johnson 1922- WhoAm 90
Boak, Joseph Gordon 1942- WhoE 91
Boak, Ruth Alice 1906- WhoAm 90
Boake, Capel 1899-1944 FemiCLE
Boal, Bernard Harvey 1937- WhoWor 91
Boal, Dean 1931- WhoAm 90
Boal, Jan List 1930- WhoSSW 91
Boal, Peter Cadbury 1965- WhoAm 90
Boal, Pierre de Lagarde 1895-1966 BioIn 16
Boal, Sara Metzner 1896-1979 WhoAmA 91N
Boalt, Gunnar Rudolf 1910- WhoWor 91
Boam, Jeffrey BioIn 16
Boam, Jeffrey David 1949- WhoEmL 91
Boan, Bobby Jack 1945- WhoAm 90
Boand, Charles Wilbur 1908- WhoWor 91
Board, Dwight Vernon 1944- WhoAm 90
Board, Francis A BiDrAPA 89
Board, Frederick Allen 1941- St&PR 91
Board, Howard E. 1943- St&PR 91
Board, Joseph Breckinridge, Jr. 1931- WhoAm 90
Board, Thomas P 1914- BiDrAPA 89
Board, Warren Lee 1942- WhoAm 90, WhoSSW 91
Boardman, Barrington 1933- ConAu 130
Boardman, Brigid M 1931- ConAu 129
Boardman, Edwin Welstead 1936- WhoSSW 91
Boardman, Eleanor 1898- BioIn 16
Boardman, Eugene Powers 1910-1987 BioIn 16
Boardman, Eunice 1926- WhoAm 90, WhoAmW 91
Boardman, Fon Wyman, Jr. 1911- WhoE 91
Boardman, Gwenn R 1924- SmATA X
Boardman, Harold F. 1939- St&PR 91
Boardman, Harold Frederick, Jr. 1939- WhoE 91, WhoWor 91
Boardman, Harriet L BiDrAPA 89
Boardman, John Michael 1938- WhoAm 90, WhoE 91
Boardman, Linda I. 1948- WhoSSW 91
Boardman, Mabel Thorp 1860-1946 BioIn 16
Boardman, Mark Seymour 1958- WhoEmL 91
Boardman, Michael Neil 1942- WhoE 91
Boardman, Myron L. BioIn 16
Boardman, Nell WhoAmA 91N
Boardman, Pauline BioIn 16
Boardman, Richard Stanton 1923- WhoAm 90
Boardman, Robert Emmett 1932- St&PR 91
Boardman, Rosanne Virginia 1946- WhoAmW 91, WhoEmL 91, WhoWor 91
Boardman, Samantha BioIn 16
Boardman, Samuel H. BioIn 16
Boardman, Serena BioIn 16
Boardman, Seymour 1921- WhoAm 90, WhoAmA 91, WhoE 91

Boardman, Thomas Gray 1919- WhoWor 91
Boardman, Thomas L. 1919-1990 BioIn 16
Boardman, Thomas Leslie 1919-1990 ConAu 131
Boardman, William Penniman 1941- St&PR 91, WhoAm 90
Boarman, Gerald Jude 1940- WhoE 91
Boarman, Patrick Madigan 1922- WhoAm 90
Boarman, William Dale 1949- St&PR 91
Boas, Anne Berta BiDrAPA 89
Boas, Frank 1930- WhoWor 91
Boas, Franz 1858-1942 WhNaAH, WorAlBi
Boas, Herbert A., Jr. 1917- St&PR 91
Boas, Ralph Philip, Jr. 1912- WhoAm 90
Boas, Robert Sanford 1923- WhoAm 90
Boas, Roger 1921- WhoAm 90
Boasberg, Howard 1934- ODwPR 91
Boasberg, Leonard W. 1923- WhoAm 90
Boast, Keith Edwin 1940- St&PR 91
Boast, Warren Benefield 1909- WhoAm 90
Boateng, Adwoa Achia 1955- WhoAmW 91
Boateng, Paul BioIn 16
Boates, Christopher Reid 1950- WhoEmL 91
Boatman, Bonny E. 1950- St&PR 91
Boatman, Ralph Henry, Jr. 1921- WhoAm 90
Boatner, Edward 1898-1981 DrBlPA 90
Boatner, Edward Hammond 1898-1981 DcAfAmP
Boatner, Joseph BioIn 16
Boatner, Roy Alton 1941- WhoSSW 91
Boatright, Ann Long 1947- WhoAmW 91, WhoEmL 91
Boatright, Dale 1952- WhoSSW 91
Boatright, James Francis 1933- WhoAm 90
Boatright, Joanna Morson 1958- WhoEmL 91, WhoWor 91
Boatright, Joyce Murray 1945- WhoEmL 91
Boatwright, Charlotte Jeanne 1937- WhoAmW 91
Boatwright, H. Lee, III 1933- St&PR 91
Boatwright, Helen 1916- IntWWM 90
Boatwright, Howard 1918- IntWWM 90
Boatwright, James 1933-1988 BioIn 16
Boatwright, John T. 1934- St&PR 91
Boatwright, Martha Helen 1940- BiDrAPA 89
Boatwright, McHenry 1928- DrBlPA 90, IntWWM 90
Boatwright, Purvis James, Jr. 1927- WhoAm 90
Boatwright, Ronald G. 1959- St&PR 91
Boatwright, William Heard 1933- St&PR 91
Boaz, Daniel York 1959- WhoEmL 91
Boaz, David Douglas 1953- WhoAm 90
Boaz, Doniella 1934- WhoAmW 91
Boaz, Stephen Scott 1948- WhoEmL 91
Boazman, Franklin Meador 1939- WhoSSW 91, WhoWor 91
Bob & Bob WhoAmA 91
Bob, Indiana WhoWrEP 89
Bob, Sharon Helene 1949- WhoEmL 91
Boba, Denise Anne 1961- WhoEmL 91
Boba, Imre 1919- WhoAm 90
Bobak, Bruno Joseph 1923- WhoAmA 91
Boban, Kathleen 1962- WhoAmW 91
Bobb, Harold Daniel 1952- WhoWor 91
Bobb, Richard A. 1937- St&PR 91
Bobb, Richard M. 1938- St&PR 91
Bobba, Sharda BiDrAPA 89
Bobbitt, Finley Marvin, Jr. 1931- St&PR 91
Bobbitt, Francis S 1916- BiDrAPA 89
Bobbitt, Gary Lee 1951- WhoEmL 91
Bobbitt, Helen Davis 1913- WhoAmW 91
Bobbitt, James McCue 1930- WhoAm 90
Bobbitt, Nancy Marie 1951- WhoSSW 91
Bobbitt, Philip Chase 1948- WhoAm 90
Bobbitt, Phillip Lamar 1948- WhoEmL 91
Bobco, Richard Phillip 1929- WhoAm 90
Bobco, William David, Jr. 1946- WhoEmL 91
Bobe, Henry Dale 1952- St&PR 91
Bober, Bernard R. 1934- St&PR 91
Bober, Harold Lewis 1936- St&PR 91
Bober, Harry 1915-1988 BioIn 16
Bober, John Franklin 1952- BiDrAPA 89
Bober, Kenneth Frank 1948- St&PR 91
Bober, Lawrence H. 1924- St&PR 91
Bober, Lawrence Harold 1924- WhoAm 90
Boberg, Anna Katarina PenDiDA 89
Boberg, James Odell 1959- WhoEmL 91
Boberg, Richard Wayne 1948- WhoAm 90
Bobette ConAu 129, MajTwCW
Bobick, Bruce 1941- WhoAmA 91
Bobinchuck, William R. 1927- St&PR 91
Bobins, Norman BioIn 16
Bobins, Norman R. WhoAm 90
Bobinski, George Sylvan 1929- WhoAm 90
Bobinski, Stanislaw 1882-1937 BioIn 16
Bobis, Arthur H. 1936- St&PR 91
Bobisud, Larry Eugene 1940- WhoAm 90
Bobleter, Lowell Stanley 1902-1973 WhoAmA 91N
Bobo, Donald Arthur 1918- WhoAm 90
Bobo, Jack C. 1940- St&PR 91
Bobo, Jack Edward 1924- WhoAm 90
Bobo, James Robert 1923- WhoAm 90
Bobo, Len Davis 1949- WhoSSW 91
Bobo, Leslie Joyner 1958- WhoEmL 91
Bobo, Leslie Renee 1963- WhoSSW 91
Boboc, Nicolae 1920- IntWWM 90
Bobon, Jean Joseph BiDrAPA 89
Bobon, Jean Joseph 1912- WhoWor 91
Bobonis De Miranda, Maria T BiDrAPA 89
Bobosky, W. Brand 1939- St&PR 91
Bobrin, Lawrence Joel 1947- BiDrAPA 89
Bobrin, Yale Robert 1935- BiDrAPA 89, WhoE 91
Bobritsky, Vladimir 1898- BioIn 16
Bobroff, Geoffrey Hunter 1944- St&PR 91
Bobroff, Harold 1920- WhoAm 90
Bobrow, Alvan Lee 1949- St&PR 91, WhoEmL 91
Bobrow, Davis Bernard 1936- WhoAm 90
Bobrow, Henry Bernard 1924- WhoE 91
Bobrowicz, Yvonne P 1928- WhoAmA 91
Bobrowski, Johannes 1917-1965 ConAu 33NR, WorAlBi
Bobruff, Arthur BiDrAPA 89
Bobruff, Carole Marks 1935- WhoE 91
Bobruff, Martha R BiDrAPA 89
Bobst, Mary Elizabeth Stevens BioIn 16
Bobula, Edward Michael 1915- St&PR 91
Bobzien, H. J. 1935- WhoAm 90
Bocage, Anne-Marie Fiquet du 1710-1802 EncCoWW
Bocage, Ronald Joseph 1946- St&PR 91
Bocanegra, Ubaldo, Jr. BiDrAPA 89
Bocca, Julio BioIn 16
Boccabella, John 1941- Ballpl 90
Boccaccio, Giovanni 1313-1375 WorAlBi
Boccardi, Louis D. 1937- St&PR 91
Boccardi, Louis Donald 1937- WhoAm 90, WhoE 91
Bocchino, Robert Louis 1936- WhoE 91
Bocci, Marilyn Kathleen 1949- WhoAmW 91
Bocci, Raymond BioIn 16
Boccia, Ann Marie 1958- WhoAmW 91
Boccia, Edward Eugene 1921- WhoAmA 91
Boccia, Maria Liboria 1953- WhoAmW 91
Boccio, Barbara Ann 1958- WhoAmW 91
Boccio, Karen Corinne 1954- WhoWrEP 89
Boccioni, Umberto 1882-1916 IntDcAA 90
Boccitto, Elio WhoAm 90, WhoE 91, WhoWor 91
Boccone, Andrew A. St&PR 91
Boccuzzi, Nancy Kowa 1945- WhoAmW 91
Bocell, James Russell 1921- St&PR 91
Boch, Francois PenDiDA 89
Boch, Jean-Francois PenDiDA 89
Boch, William PenDiDA 89
Bochco, Steve 1943- WhoAm 90
Bochco, Steven BioIn 16
Bocher, Main Rousseau 1890- BioIn 16
Bochero, Peter 1898-1960 MusmAFA
Bochicchio-Ausura, Jill Arden 1951- WhoAmW 91, WhoEmL 91
Bochkarev, Bela 1933- BiDrAPA 89
Bochnak, Mary Louise 1951- WhoEmL 91
Bochner, Alfred BiDrAPA 89
Bochner, Hart BioIn 16
Bochner, Mel 1940- BioIn 16, WhoAmA 91
Bochner, Salomon 1899-1982 DcScB S2
Bochow, Carl Evans 1928- St&PR 91
Bochsa, Robert-Nicolas-Charles 1789-1856 PenDiMP
Bochte, Bruce 1950- Ballpl 90
Bochy, Bruce 1955- Ballpl 90
Bock, Carolyn Ann 1942- WhoAmW 91
Bock, D. Joleen 1925- BioIn 16
Bock, Edward John 1916- WhoAm 90
Bock, Gisela 1942- WhoWor 91
Bock, Gordon Honold 1952- WhoWrEP 89
Bock, Hal 1939- Ballpl 90
Bock, Irmgard 1937- WhoWor 91
Bock, J. Kathryn 1948- WhoAmW 91
Bock, Jacques 1932- St&PR 91
Bock, James Whitney 1944- St&PR 91
Bock, Jay Lawrence 1950- WhoE 91
Bock, Jeffrey William 1950- WhoEmL 91
Bock, Jerry 1928- OxCPMus, WhoAm 90, WorAlBi
Bock, John Louis 1945- WhoSSW 91
Bock, Joseph Reto 1929- St&PR 91
Bock, Lee 1927- ODwPR 91
Bock, Peter Vilhelm 1930- WhoWor 91
Bock, Richard A. 1963- ODwPR 91
Bock, Richard Arthur 1938- WhoE 91
Bock, Robert Howard 1932- WhoAm 90
Bock, Robert J. St&PR 91
Bock, Robert M. 1923- WhoAm 90
Bock, Russell Samuel 1905- WhoAm 90, WhoWrEP 89
Bock, Walter Joseph 1933- WhoAm 90
Bock, William Richard, Jr. 1939- St&PR 91
Bock, William Sauts-Netamux'we 1939- WhoAmA 91
Bock-Brett, Linda C. ODwPR 91
Bockar, Joyce Ann 1941- BiDrAPA 89
Bockart, Richard L. 1934- St&PR 91
Bocke, John J. 1947- St&PR 91
Bockelman, John Richard 1925- WhoAm 90, WhoWor 91
Bocker, Hans Jurgen 1939- WhoWor 91
Bockerstette, Joseph A. 1957- WhoAm 90, WhoEmL 91
Bockewitz, Aleta June 1945- WhoAmW 91
Bockewitz, Wilma Gertrude WhoAmW 91
Bockey, Pamela Sue 1952- WhoAmW 91
Bockhoff, Frank James 1928- WhoAm 90
Bockhop, Clarence William 1921- WhoAm 90
Bockhorn, Robert K. 1935- St&PR 91
Bockian, Donna Marie 1946- WhoAmW 91
Bockian, Herbert H 1927- BiDrAPA 89
Bockian, James Bernard 1936- WhoE 91, WhoWor 91
Bocking, Alfred Hermann 1944- WhoWor 91
Bocklett, Mary Byrne BioIn 16
Bocklin, Arnold 1827-1910 IntDcAA 90
Bockman, Eddie 1920- Ballpl 90
Bockmann, Rick Daniel 1955- WhoE 91
Bockner, Andrew C 1943- BiDrAPA 89
Bockoven, John Sanbourne 1915- BiDrAPA 89
Bockstaele, Paul Pieter 1920- WhoWor 91
Bockstahler, Harold W. 1906-1987 BioIn 16
Bockstanz, Douglas L. 1941- St&PR 91
Bockstein, Herbert 1943- WhoAm 90
Bockstruck, Arnold Herbert 1927- St&PR 91
Bockus, C. Barry 1934- St&PR 91, WhoSSW 91
Bockus, Harry N., Jr. 1926- St&PR 91
Bockus, Randy 1960- Ballpl 90
Bocobo, Christian Reyes 1954- WhoWor 91
Bocour, Leonard 1910- WhoAmA 91
Bocskor, Catherine Esther 1949- WhoE 91
Bocuse, Paul 1926- BioIn 16, WhoWor 91, WorAlBi
Boczko, Miklos Lajos 1929- WhoE 91
Boda, Veronica Constance 1952- WhoAmW 91, WhoEmL 91
Bodaan, Harry Jacobus 1951- WhoAm 90
Bodai Daruma EncJap
Bodalski, Richard A. 1939- St&PR 91
Bodani, Amrit S 1950- BiDrAPA 89
Bodansky, David 1924- WhoAm 90
Bodanszky, Miklos 1915- WhoAm 90
Bodanza, Joseph Frank 1947- St&PR 91
Bodanzky, Artur 1877-1939 PenDiMP
Bodart, William Roger 1931- St&PR 91
Bodart-Talbot, Joni 1947- WhoWrEP 89
Bodary, Walter David 1922- St&PR 91
Bodde, William, Jr. 1931- WhoAm 90, WhoE 91
Boddeker, Edward William, III 1929- WhoSSW 91
Bodden, Jane Ellen 1948- WhoSSW 91
Bodden, John M. 1930- St&PR 91
Bodden, William Michael 1929- WhoAm 90
Boddicker, Mike 1957- Ballpl 90
Boddie, Benjamin F. 1925- ODwPR 91, WhoSSW 91
Boddie, Don O'Mar 1944- WhoWor 91
Boddie, Grace Collins 1917- St&PR 91
Boddie, Reginald Alonzo 1959- WhoEmL 91
Boddie, William Willis 1945- WhoEmL 91
Boddiger, George Cyrus 1917- WhoAm 90
Boddington, Craig Thornton 1952- WhoAm 90, WhoWrEP 89
Bode, Barbara 1940- WhoAm 90
Bode, Boyd Henry 1873-1953 BioIn 16
Bode, Carl 1911- WhoAm 90, WhoWrEP 89
Bode, Hannelore 1941- IntWWM 90
Bode, Henry Joseph 1934- St&PR 91
Bode, Janet 1943- SmATA 60
Bode, Lori Monney 1950- WhoEmL 91
Bode, Margaret Ann ODwPR 91
Bode, Richard A. 1931- St&PR 91
Bode, Richard Albert 1931- WhoAm 90
Bode, Robert W. 1912- WhoAm 90
Bode, Robert William 1912- WhoAmA 91
Bode, Roy Evan 1948- WhoAm 90
Bodecker, N. M. BioIn 16
Bodeen, DeWitt 1908-1988 BioIn 16
Bodeen, George H. 1924- St&PR 91
Bodega Y Quadra, Juan Francisco De La 1743-1794 EncCRAm
Bodek, Gordon S. 1920- St&PR 91
Bodek, Norman 1932- WhoWrEP 89
Bodeker, Robert Allen 1936- St&PR 91
Bodell, Gerald H. 1939- St&PR 91
Bodell, Mark B. 1952- St&PR 91
Bodell, Michael James 1949- St&PR 91
Bodelsen, Anders 1937- DcScanL
Bodely, Elizabeth BiDEWW
Bodem, Dennis Richard 1937- WhoAm 90, WhoAmA 91
Boden, Constantin Robert 1936- St&PR 91
Boden, Hilda AuBYP 90
Boden, William David 1941- St&PR 91
Bodenbender, Douglas 1945- St&PR 91
Bodenham, Hilda 1901- AuBYP 90
Bodenheimer, Henry Charles, Jr. 1950- WhoE 91
Bodenheimer, Max 1928- WhoE 91
Bodenhoefer, Hans J. 1941- WhoWor 91
Bodenmann, John 1936- St&PR 91
Bodensiek, Herbert K. 1927- St&PR 91
Bodenstein, Christel Elisabeth BiDrAPA 89
Bodenstein, Ira 1954- WhoEmL 91
Bodenstein, Nancy Miller St&PR 91
Bodenstein, Robert Q. 1936- St&PR 91
Bodensteiner, Carol A. 1948- ODwPR 91
Bodereau, Xavier Jacques 1951- WhoWor 91
Bodet, Jaime Torres HispWr 90, MajTwCW
Bodet, Jaime Torres 1902-1974 BioIn 16
Bodett, Tom BioIn 16
Bodewitz, Hendrik Wilhelm 1939- WhoWor 91
Bodey, Gerald Paul 1934- WhoAm 90
Bodey, Richard Allen 1930- WhoWrEP 89
Bodge, Clifford A. 1935- St&PR 91
Bodger, Howard Stanton 1921- St&PR 91
Bodhi Dharma EncJap
Bodian, David 1910- WhoAm 90
Bodian, Nat G. 1921- WhoAm 90
Bodichon, Barbara 1827-1891 BiDWomA, FemiCLE
Bodichon, Barbara Leigh Smith 1827-1891 BioIn 16
Bodie, Idella Fallaw 1925- WhoWrEP 89
Bodie, Ping 1887-1961 Ballpl 90
Bodiford, Charlene 1953- WhoEmL 91
Bodiford, David Wayne 1955- St&PR 91
Bodily, David Martin 1933- WhoAm 90
Bodimer, Robert Lyman 1946- WhoSSW 91
Bodin, Jean 1529-1596 EncO&P 3
Bodin, Paul 1910- WhoAmA 91, WhoE 91
Bodine, Charlene Louise 1942- WhoAmW 91
Bodine, Della L. 1951- WhoAmW 91
Bodine, Edward F. 1921- St&PR 91
Bodine, Helen WhoAmA 91N
Bodine, James Forney 1921- WhoAm 90
Bodine, John J BiDrAPA 89
Bodine, Laurence 1950- WhoAm 90, WhoEmL 91
Bodine, Michelle Dawn 1964- WhoAmW 91
Bodine, Paul J., Jr. 1924- St&PR 91
Bodine, Ralph E. 1942- WhoAm 90
Bodine, Richard P. 1926- St&PR 91
Bodine, Robert J. 1924- St&PR 91
Bodine, Sarah Elliott 1930- WhoAmW 91
Bodine, Willis Ramsey, Jr. 1935- WhoSSW 91
Bodinson, Holt 1941- WhoWor 91
Bodker, Cecil 1927- ChlLR 23 [port], DcScanL, EncCoWW
Bodker, John Reardon St&PR 91N
Bodkin, Amy Maud 1875-1967 BioIn 16
Bodkin, Henry Grattan, Jr. 1921- WhoAm 90
Bodkin, J. Alexander 1956- BiDrAPA 89
Bodkin, Lawrence Edward 1927- WhoSSW 91, WhoWor 91
Bodkin, Ruby Pate 1926- WhoAmW 91, WhoSSW 91, WhoWor 91
Bodley, Harley Ryan, Jr. 1936- WhoAm 90
Bodley Scott, Ronald 1906-1982 DcNaB 1981
Bodman, Helene Dunn 1936- WhoAmW 91
Bodman, Richard Stockwell 1938- WhoAm 90
Bodman, Roger A. 1952- St&PR 91
Bodman, Samuel W., III 1938- WhoAm 90, WhoE 91
Bodmer, Arnold Rudolph 1929- WhoAm 90, WhoWor 91
Bodmer, Johann Jakob 1698-1783 DcLB 97 [port]
Bodmer, Karl 1809-1893 WhNaAH [port]
Bodmer, Martin 1899-1971 BioIn 16
Bodmer, Sylvia 1902-1989 AnObit 1989
Bodmershof, Imma von 1895-1982 EncCoWW
Bodnar, Donald George 1941- WhoSSW 91
Bodnar, Paul Zoltan 1950- WhoE 91
Bodnar, Peter 1928- WhoAmA 91
Bodnarskii, Bogdan Stepanovich BioIn 16
Bodner, Emanuel 1947- WhoSSW 91
Bodner, John, Jr. 1927- WhoAm 90
Bodner, M. Gayle 1963- WhoAmW 91

Bodner, William R, Jr. 1937- *BiDrAPA 89*
Bodo, Murray 1937- *WhoWrEP 89*
Bodo, Sandor 1920- *WhoAmA 91*
Bodoni, Philip P. 1952- *St&PR 91*
Bodony, Stephen Gerald 1947- *WhoEmL 91*
Bodor, Nicholas S. 1939- *St&PR 91*
Bodor, Nicholas Stephen 1939- *WhoAm 90*
Bodson, Marc 1957- *WhoE 91*
Bodsworth, Charles Frederick 1918- *WhoAm 90*
Bodt, Brian Schofield- *BioIn 16*
Bodvarsson, Gudmundur 1904-1974 *DcScanL*
Bodway, Craig Alan 1959- *WhoEmL 91*
Bodwell, David Edward 1939- *St&PR 91*
Bodwell, Russell S. 1921- *St&PR 91*
Bodzy, Glen Alan 1952- *St&PR 91*
Boe, Alf 1927- *WhoWor 91*
Boe, Anne Carol 1946- *WhoAmW 91*
Boe, Archie R. 1921-1989 *BioIn 16*
Boe, David Stephen 1936- *WhoAm 90*
Boe, Eugene H. 1937- *St&PR 91*
Boe, Jason 1929-1990 *BioIn 16*
Boe, Myron Timothy 1948- *WhoEmL 91, WhoSSW 91, WhoWor 91*
Boe, Nils Andreas 1913- *WhoAm 90*
Boe, Roy Asbjorn 1919- *WhoAmA 91N*
Boe, Thomas Daniel 1960- *WhoEmL 91*
Boebel, Carl Paul 1931- *St&PR 91*
Boecher, Otto Hermann Konrad 1935- *WhoWor 91*
Boechler, Paul M. 1958- *St&PR 91*
Boeck, Harald Christian Anando von Hamm 1925- *WhoWor 91*
Boeck, Phil H. 1948- *St&PR 91*
Boeckel, Tony 1892-1924 *Ballpl 90*
Boeckman, Charles 1920- *AuBYP 90*
Boeckman, Robert Kenneth, Jr. 1944- *WhoAm 90*
Boeckmann-Ross, LaVerne 1949- *WhoAmW 91*
Boeckner, Robert G. 1941- *St&PR 91*
Boeddeker, Timothy Mark 1948- *WhoEmL 91*
Boedecker, Anne L. 1951- *WhoAmW 91*
Boedecker, Erin Elaine 1959- *WhoAmW 91*
Boedeker, Alice Vernelle 1921- *WhoAm 90*
Boedeker, Harold W. 1913- *St&PR 91*
Boegehold, Betty Virginia 1913-1985 *AuBYP 90*
Boegen, Anne S. *BioIn 16*
Boegner, Dieter K.H. 1932- *St&PR 91*
Boegner, Mary Elizabeth Blanche 1925- *WhoAmW 91*
Boehk, Paul E. 1931- *St&PR 91*
Boehl, Kenneth Frank 1954- *WhoAm 90*
Boehle, William Randall 1919- *WhoAm 90*
Boehler, George 1892-1958 *Ballpl 90*
Boehler, Hans 1884-1961 *WhoAmA 91N*
Boehlert, Robert James *St&PR 91N*
Boehlert, Sherwood Louis 1936- *WhoAm 90, WhoE 91*
Boehling, Joe 1891-1941 *Ballpl 90*
Boehlke, Christine 1946- *ODwPR 91*
Boehm, Arthur Bruce, Jr. 1931- *St&PR 91*
Boehm, David Alfred 1914- *WhoAm 90*
Boehm, Edward Marshall *PenDiDA 89*
Boehm, Eric H. *St&PR 91*
Boehm, Eric Hartzell 1918- *WhoAm 90, WhoWor 91*
Boehm, Felix Hans 1924- *WhoAm 90*
Boehm, Gottfried Karl 1942- *WhoWor 91*
Boehm, Gunther 1946- *WhoWor 91*
Boehm, Inge P. *St&PR 91*
Boehm, John Francis 1926- *St&PR 91, WhoAm 90, WhoSSW 91*
Boehm, Josef Franz 1944- *St&PR 91*
Boehm, Klaus Juergen 1949- *St&PR 91*
Boehm, Margaret Stitt 1944- *WhoAmW 91*
Boehm, Richard Harry 1928- *St&PR 91*
Boehm, Richard Joseph 1924- *WhoE 91*
Boehm, Richard Wood 1926- *WhoAm 90*
Boehm, Robert Foty 1940- *WhoAm 90*
Boehm, Ronald James 1953- *St&PR 91*
Boehm, Steven Bruce 1954- *WhoEmL 91*
Boehm, Thomas Edward 1946- *St&PR 91*
Boehm, Walter E F *BiDrAPA 89*
Boehm, Werner William 1913- *WhoAm 90*
Boehm, William J. 1936- *St&PR 91*
Boehm, Wolfgang 1928- *WhoWor 91*
Boehme, Artur 1937- *WhoWor 91*
Boehme, Gerard Herbert 1954- *WhoEmL 91*
Boehme, Hilary C. 1935- *St&PR 91*
Boehme, Jakob 1575-1624 *EncO&P 3, EncPaPR 91, WorAlBi*
Boehme, Ronald Edward 1937- *WhoWor 91*
Boehme, Sarah Elizabeth 1948- *WhoAmW 91*
Boehme, Vernon P. 1953- *St&PR 91*
Boehmer, Darryl W. *St&PR 91*
Boehmer, Raquel Davenport 1938- *WhoAmW 91*
Boehmer, Ronald Glenn 1947- *WhoEmL 91*
Boehmler, E. William 1940- *St&PR 91, WhoAm 90*
Boehmler, William John 1938- *BiDrAPA 89*
Boehne, Edward G. 1940- *St&PR 91*
Boehne, Edward George 1940- *WhoAm 90*
Boehne, Patricia Jeanne 1940- *WhoWrEP 89*
Boehnen, David Leo 1946- *St&PR 91, WhoEmL 91*
Boehner, Leonard Bruce 1930- *WhoE 91*
Boehning, Joseph Frederick 1931- *WhoAm 90*
Boehnlein, James 1954- *BiDrAPA 89*
Boehs, Kenneth Robert 1947- *St&PR 91*
Boeing, Marcia Delano Comley 1946- *WhoAmW 91*
Boek, Walter Erwin 1923- *WhoE 91*
Boeke, Duffy *BioIn 16*
Boeke, Eugene H., Jr. 1925- *WhoAm 90*
Boeke, Norbert Henry 1940- *WhoWor 91*
Boeke, Robert William 1925- *St&PR 91*
Boekelheide, Priscilla Day *BiDrAPA 89*
Boekelheide, Virgil Carl 1919- *WhoAm 90*
Boekenheide, Russell W. 1930- *St&PR 91*
Boekenheide, Russell William 1930- *WhoAm 90*
Boeker, Egbert 1937- *WhoWor 91*
Boeker, Paul Harold 1938- *WhoAm 90*
Boekf, Eugene H., Jr. 1925- *St&PR 91*
Boekhout, Robert Stanley 1937- *St&PR 91*
Boelen, Jacob 1657-1729 *PenDiDA 89*
Boelens, Simon Wigger 1957- *WhoWor 91*
Boelens, Theodore Martin 1943- *WhoSSW 91*
Boell, Edgar John 1906- *WhoAm 90*
Boell, Heinrich 1917-1985 *MajTwCW*
Boelter, Joseph Anthony 1943- *WhoE 91*
Boelts, Kenneth J. 1935- *St&PR 91*
Boelzner, Gordon 1937- *WhoE 91*
Boemer, Lois E. 1934- *WhoAmW 91*
Boemi, A. Andrew 1915- *St&PR 91, WhoAm 90, WhoWor 91*
Boemi, Andrew Anthony 1944- *St&PR 91*
Boen, Bradley N 1936- *BiDrAPA 89*
Boendermaker, Johannes Pieter 1925- *WhoWor 91*
Boenders, Frans Frederik Louis 1942- *WhoWor 91*
Boenning, Henry Dorr, Jr. 1914- *WhoAm 90*
Boentje, John D., Jr. 1916- *St&PR 91*
Boer, F. Peter 1941- *WhoAm 90*
Boerhaave, Hermann 1668-1738 *BioIn 16*
Boeri, Cini 1924- *ConDes 90*
Boeri, Renato Raimondo 1922- *WhoWor 91*
Boerner, Eugene S. 1893-1966 *BioIn 16*
Boerner, H. L. 1937- *ODwPR 91*
Boerner, Herman F, Jr. *BiDrAPA 89*
Boerner, Jo M. 1944- *WhoAmW 91, WhoSSW 91*
Boerner, John M. 1934- *St&PR 91*
Boerner, Joseph C., Jr. 1927- *St&PR 91*
Boerner, Peter 1926- *WhoAm 90*
Boerrigter, Glenn Charles 1932- *WhoAm 90*
Boers, Terry John 1950- *WhoAm 90*
Boersch-Supan, Axel H. 1954- *WhoWor 91*
Boersma, Diana Lurie 1956- *WhoEmL 91*
Boersma, Johannes Sipko 1935- *WhoWor 91*
Boersma, Mark A. 1950- *St&PR 91*
Boerstler, Barry L. 1947- *St&PR 91*
Boerstler, Barry Lee 1947- *WhoEmL 91*
Boerstler, Richard William 1923- *WhoWrEP 89*
Boertje, Stanley Benjamin 1930- *WhoSSW 91*
Boertlein, Paul L. 1948- *ODwPR 91*
Boes, Francis Xavier 1939- *St&PR 91*
Boes, Gunter Karl-Heinz 1930- *WhoWor 91*
Boes, Lawrence William 1935- *WhoAm 90, WhoE 91*
Boesak, Allan Aubrey 1946- *BioIn 16, WhoWor 91*
Boesch, Christian 1941- *IntWWM 90*
Boesch, Ernest Eduard 1916- *WhoWor 91*
Boesch, Francis Theodore 1936- *WhoAm 90*
Boesch, Karen Renee *BiDrAPA 89*
Boesch, Lawrence Michael 1951- *WhoEmL 91*
Boesche, Fenelon 1910- *St&PR 91*
Boeschen, Carol Alice 1945- *WhoEmL 91*
Boeschenstein, Bernice 1906-1951 *WhoAmA 91N*
Boeschenstein, Peter Bernhard 1931- *WhoWor 91*
Boeschenstein, William Wade 1925- *WhoAm 90*
Boeschenstein, Wm. W. 1925- *St&PR 91*
Boese, Alvin William 1910-1986 *WhoAmA 91N*
Boese, Gilbert Karyle 1937- *WhoAm 90*
Boese, James Stephen 1940- *St&PR 91, WhoAm 90*
Boese, Robert Alan 1934- *WhoAm 90*
Boese, Ursula 1928- *IntWWM 90*
Boese, Virginia Ellen 1907- *WhoWor 91*
Boesel, Elizabeth Parks 1962- *WhoAmW 91*
Boesel, Kenneth S. 1912- *St&PR 91*
Boesel, Milton Charles, Jr. 1928- *WhoAm 90, WhoWor 91*
Boesen, John F. 1918- *St&PR 91*
Boesen, John Michael 1946- *WhoEmL 91*
Boesen, Melvin Peter 1931- *St&PR 91*
Boesen, Ulla Birgitte 1929- *WhoWor 91*
Boesen, Victor 1908- *AuBYP 90*
Boesenberg, Charles M. 1948- *St&PR 91*
Boeser, William F. *St&PR 91*
Boeshaar, Patricia Chikotas 1947- *WhoEmL 91*
Boeshe, Barbara Louise *WhoE 91*
Boesing, Martha *FemiCLE*
Boesing, Martha 1936- *BioIn 16*
Boesing, Martha Gross 1936- *NotWoAT*
Boesinger, Richard M. 1942- *St&PR 91*
Boeske, Adele Claire 1947- *WhoAmW 91*
Boesky, Dale 1930- *BiDrAPA 89*
Boesky, Ivan F. *BioIn 16*
Boesky, Ivan F. 1937- *EncABHB 7 [port]*
Boesky, S.J. 1956- *St&PR 91*
Boesler, Cynthia Sue 1960- *WhoEmL 91*
Boesler, Klaus-Achim 1931- *WhoWor 91*
Boesmans, Phillipe 1936- *IntWWM 90*
Boesten, Hubert Karl 1937- *BiDrAPA 89*
Boethius, Anicius Manlius Severinus 480?-524 *WrPh P*
Boetig, Donna Byrnes 1950- *WhoWrEP 89*
Boetsch, Urs 1943- *WhoWor 91*
Boettcher, Bryan Clair 1956- *WhoEmL 91*
Boettcher, Diane Ruth 1957- *WhoSSW 91*
Boettcher, Donald Albert 1928- *St&PR 91*
Boettcher, Harold Paul 1923- *WhoAm 90*
Boettcher, Norbe Birosel 1932- *WhoAmW 91*
Boettcher, Richard Stanley 1928- *St&PR 91*
Boettcher, Robert Richard, II 1944- *WhoSSW 91*
Boettcher, Siegfried Bruno 1928- *WhoWor 91*
Boettcher, Thomas D. 1944- *ConAu 129*
Boettcher, Wilfried 1929- *IntWWM 90*
Boettcher, Wolfgang *PenDiMP*
Boettger, Otto Werner 1923- *WhoWor 91*
Boettger, Susan Doris 1952- *WhoAmW 91*
Boettger, William F. 1945- *WhoEmL 91*
Boeve, Edgar Gene 1929- *WhoAmA 91*
Boeve, Gerald Lee 1936- *WhoSSW 91*
Boever, Joe 1960- *Ballpl 90*
Boff, Kenneth Richard 1947- *WhoEmL 91*
Boff, Leonardo *BioIn 16*
Boffa, Louis A. 1948- *St&PR 91*
Boffeli, Todd Joseph 1962- *BiDrAPA 89*
Boffi, Bryan Vincent *BiDrAPA 89*
Boffman, James 1929-1988 *BioIn 16*
Bofill, Rano Solidum 1942- *WhoSSW 91*
Bofill, Ricardo 1939- *BioIn 16, WhoWor 91*
Bofinger, Pamela Lynn 1964- *WhoAmW 91*
Bogaard, Johannes 1891-1974 *BioIn 16*
Bogaard, William Joseph 1938- *St&PR 91, WhoAm 90*
Bogaczyk, Stanley J. 1942- *St&PR 91*
Bogado, Pablo Raul *BiDrAPA 89*
Bogaert, Thomas 1597-1652? *PenDiDA 89*
Bogage, Alan Richard 1953- *WhoE 91*
Bogan, Elizabeth Chapin 1944- *WhoAm 90*
Bogan, Kathleen May 1947- *WhoAmW 91*
Bogan, Louise 1897-1970 *AuBYP 90, BioAmW, ConAu 33NR, FemiCLE, MajTwCW*
Bogan, Mary Flair 1948- *WhoAmW 91*
Bogan, Neil Earnest 1945- *WhoSSW 91*
Bogan, Ralph A.L., Jr. 1922- *St&PR 91*
Bogan, Ralph A. L., Jr. 1922- *WhoAm 90*
Bogani, Tina Marie 1962- *WhoEmL 91*
Bogard, Bernard John *BiDrAPA 89*
Bogard, Bruce Nils 1942- *WhoE 91*
Bogard, Carole Christine *WhoAm 90*
Bogard, George Albert 1948- *WhoEmL 91*
Bogard, Harry Gene 1932- *St&PR 91*
Bogard, William J *BiDrAPA 89*
Bogarde, Dirk 1920- *WorAlBi*
Bogardus, Carl Robert, Jr. 1933- *WhoAm 90*
Bogardus, John A., Jr. 1927- *St&PR 91*
Bogardus, Raymond B. 1946- *St&PR 91*
Bogardus, Sarah Emily Ray 1920- *WhoAmW 91*
Bogarin, Rafael 1946- *WhoAmA 91*
Bogart, Adrian Thomas, III 1959- *WhoE 91*
Bogart, Charles Henry 1940- *WhoSSW 91*
Bogart, George A 1933- *WhoAmA 91*
Bogart, Grace Elizabeth 1923- *WhoE 91*
Bogart, Homer Gordon 1922- *St&PR 91, WhoAm 90*
Bogart, Humphrey 1899-1957 *BioIn 16, WorAlBi*
Bogart, James Willoughby 1946- *St&PR 91*
Bogart, Jeffrey D. 1942- *ODwPR 91*
Bogart, Jeffrey David 1942- *WhoE 91*
Bogart, John-Paul 1952- *IntWWM 90*
Bogart, Judith Saunders 1936- *WhoAmW 91*
Bogart, Keith Charles 1936- *WhoWor 91*
Bogart, Larry Frank 1938- *BiDrAPA 89*
Bogart, Leo *BioIn 16*
Bogart, Michele Helene 1952- *WhoAmA 91*
Bogart, Paul 1919- *WhoAm 90*
Bogart, Peter T. 1937- *St&PR 91*
Bogart, Richard Jerome 1929- *WhoAmA 91*
Bogart, Robert B. 1944- *WhoAm 90, WhoWor 91*
Bogart, Susan Alexander 1959- *WhoAmW 91*
Bogart, Vincent LaVaughn 1922- *WhoWor 91*
Bogart, W. Humphrey 1944- *St&PR 91*
Bogart, Wanda Lee 1939- *WhoAmW 91, WhoWor 91*
Bogart, William Harry 1931- *WhoWor 91*
Bogash, Richard 1922- *WhoAm 90*
Bogash, Richard R. 1948- *WhoE 91, WhoEmL 91*
Bogatay, Lynne Marie 1955- *WhoAmW 91*
Bogaty, Lisa Bradford 1952- *WhoAmW 91*
Bogavelli, Vijayalaxmi *BiDrAPA 89*
Bogdahn, Joseph R. 1962- *WhoSSW 91*
Bogdan, Carolyn Louetta 1941- *WhoAmW 91*
Bogdan, Corneliu *NewYTBS 90*
Bogdan, Corneliu 1921-1990 *BioIn 16*
Bogdan, Donald Fred 1929- *BiDrAPA 89*
Bogdan, Linda Wilson *BioIn 16*
Bogdan, Michael 1946- *WhoWor 91*
Bogdan, Victor Michael 1933- *WhoAm 90*
Bogdaniak, Roman Coronado 1954- *WhoEmL 91*
Bogdanich, Walt 1950- *WhoAm 90, WhoE 91*
Bogdanoff, John Lee 1916- *WhoAm 90*
Bogdanoff, Leonard 1930- *WhoAm 90*
Bogdanoff, Phyllis Sweed 1931- *WhoAmW 91*
Bogdanoff Eisenberg, Cindy Ann 1954- *WhoSSW 91*
Bogdanov, Aleksei Alekseevich 1907-1971 *DcScB S2*
Bogdanov, Michael 1938- *ConAu 129*
Bogdanovic, Bogomir 1923- *WhoAmA 91*
Bogdanovich, Peter 1939- *BioIn 16, WhoAm 90, WhoWor 91, WorAlBi*
Bogdasarian, John Robert 1944- *WhoAm 90*
Bogden, John Dennis 1945- *WhoE 91*
Bogdon, Eugene C. 1925- *St&PR 91*
Bogdon, Glendon Joseph 1935- *WhoWor 91*
Bogdonoff, Morton David 1925- *WhoAm 90*
Bogdonoff, Seymour Moses 1921- *WhoAm 90*
Bogdonoff Feit, Lisa Carol *BiDrAPA 89*
Boge, Herbert E. 1921- *St&PR 91*
Boge, Kari 1950- *EncCoWW*
Bogedain, Carol Sienski 1952- *WhoAmW 91*
Bogen, Constance *AuBYP 90*
Bogen, Don 1949- *WhoWrEP 89*
Bogen, Laurel Ann 1950- *WhoWrEP 89*
Bogen, Mark David 1959- *WhoEmL 91*
Bogen, Steven *BiDrAPA 89*
Bogenstadt, Ludwig Von *WhoWrEP 89*
Boger, Dan Calvin 1946- *WhoEmL 91*
Boger, David Sprott *BiDrAPA 89*
Boger, Gail Green Parsons 1914- *WhoAm 90*
Boger, Lawrence Leroy 1923- *WhoAm 90*
Boger, William Pierce, III 1945- *WhoEmL 91, WhoWor 91*
Bogert, George Taylor 1920- *WhoAm 90*
Bogert, Ivan Lathrop 1918- *WhoAm 90*
Bogert, Jeremiah Milbank 1941- *St&PR 91*
Bogert, Joan N. 1934- *St&PR 91*
Bogert, John Allen 1945- *St&PR 91*
Bogert, John Rogers 1924- *St&PR 91*
Bogert, Jonathan 1941- *WhoAm 90*
Bogert, Richard D. 1933- *St&PR 91*
Bogese, Charles Everette 1950- *St&PR 91*
Bogetic, Zeljko 1960- *WhoE 91*
Boggeri, Antonio 1900- *ConDes 90*
Boggess, Dusty 1904-1968 *Ballpl 90*
Boggess, Gary Thomas 1952- *WhoEmL 91*
Boggess, Jerry R. 1944- *St&PR 91*
Boggess, Robert E. 1929- *St&PR 91*
Boggess, Thomas Phillip, III 1921- *WhoWor 91*
Boggess, William Talbot 1940- *St&PR 91*
Boggiano, William E *BiDrAPA 89*
Boggild, Johannes 1920- *WhoWor 91*
Boggs, Angela Rosalie 1947- *WhoAmW 91*
Boggs, Billie *BioIn 16*

Boggs, Corinne 1916- *WorAlBi*
Boggs, Corinne Claiborne 1916- *WhoAm 90, WhoAmW 91, WhoSSW 91*
Boggs, Danny Julian 1944- *WhoAm 90*
Boggs, Debbie-Sue 1956- *WhoAmW 91*
Boggs, Deirdre Poste 1950- *WhoSSW 91*
Boggs, Duane Gary 1945- *WhoE 91*
Boggs, Elizabeth M 1913- *BiDrAPA 89*
Boggs, Elizabeth Monroe 1913- *WhoAmW 91*
Boggs, Franklin 1914- *WhoAmA 91*
Boggs, Jack Aaron 1935- *WhoAm 90*
Boggs, James Ernest 1921- *WhoAm 90*
Boggs, Jean Sutherland 1922- *WhoAmA 91*
Boggs, John C. 1825-1909 *BioIn 16*
Boggs, Joseph Dodridge 1921- *WhoAm 90, WhoWor 91*
Boggs, Josiah Clendennen 1927- *St&PR 91*
Boggs, Judith Susan 1946- *WhoEmL 91*
Boggs, Marcus Livingstone, Jr. 1947- *WhoWrEP 89*
Boggs, Martha Ann 1928- *WhoSSW 91*
Boggs, Mayo Mae 1942- *WhoAmA 91*
Boggs, Phil *NewYTBS 90 [port]*
Boggs, Ralph Steele 1901- *AuBYP 90*
Boggs, Ralph Stuart 1917- *WhoAm 90*
Boggs, Robert Newell 1930- *WhoAm 90, WhoWrEP 89*
Boggs, Sam, Jr. 1928- *WhoAm 90*
Boggs, Thomas Hale, Jr. 1940- *WhoAm 90*
Boggs, Tommy 1955- *Ballpl 90*
Boggs, Wade *BioIn 16*
Boggs, Wade 1958- *Ballpl 90 [port], CurBio 90 [port], WorAlBi*
Boggs, Wade Anthony 1958- *WhoAm 90*
Boggs, William B. *St&PR 91*
Boggs, William Dixon 1933- *WhoAm 90*
Boghaert, Jan *PenDiDA 89*
Boghosian, Paula der 1933- *WhoAmW 91*
Boghosian, Varujan 1926- *WhoAmA 91*
Boghosian, Varujan Yegan 1926- *WhoAm 90*
Boghosian, Vorton B. 1924- *St&PR 91*
Boghossian, P.O., III 1955- *St&PR 91*
Bogianckino, Massimo 1922- *IntWWM 90*
Bogicevic, Bogic *WhoWor 91*
Bogie, Duane C. *BioIn 16*
Bogin, Abba 1925- *IntWWM 90, WhoE 91*
Bogle, Chester Vernon 1924- *St&PR 91*
Bogle, Hugh Andrew 1909- *WhoAm 90*
Bogle, John C. 1929- *St&PR 91*
Bogle, John Clifton 1929- *WhoAm 90, WhoE 91*
Bogle, Jon 1940- *WhoAmA 91*
Bogle, Jon Robert 1940- *WhoE 91*
Bogle, Michael MacLaine 1944- *WhoWor 91*
Bogle, Paul 1822-1865 *BioIn 16*
Bogle, Robert Angell, Jr. 1937- *St&PR 91*
Bognar, Dorothy McAdoo 1944- *IntWWM 90*
Bogner, Inge *BiDrAPA 89*
Bogner, M. Eugene 1946- *St&PR 91*
Bogner, Margaret Ann 1947- *WhoAmW 91*
Bogniard, David Scott 1942- *WhoSSW 91*
Bognon, Pierre Desire 1940- *St&PR 91*
Bogoch, Elenore S *BiDrAPA 89*
Bogoch, Samuel *BiDrAPA 89*
Bogomolny, Richard Joseph 1935- *St&PR 91*
Bogomolny, Robert Lee 1938- *St&PR 91, WhoAm 90*
Bogorad, Lawrence 1921- *WhoAm 90*
Bogorad, Samuel Nathaniel 1917- *WhoAm 90*
Bogosian, Eric *BioIn 16*
Bogosian, Eric 1953- *News 90 [port]*
Bogost, Bruce Richard 1932- *BiDrAPA 89*
Bograd, Gerald David *BiDrAPA 89*
Bograd, Larry 1953- *AuBYP 90, BioIn 16*
Bograd, Michele Louise 1952- *WhoAmW 91*
Bogren, Hugo Gunnar 1933- *WhoAm 90*
Bogrow, Michael Arthur *BiDrAPA 89*
Bogstahl, Deborah Marcelle 1950- *WhoAmW 91*
Bogue, Allan G. 1921- *WhoAm 90*
Bogue, Bruce 1924- *WhoWor 91*
Bogue, Carrie Anne 1952- *WhoAmW 91*
Bogue, Ernest Grady 1935- *WhoAm 90, WhoSSW 91*
Bogue, Lucille Maxfield 1911- *WhoWrEP 89*
Bogue, Merwyn 1908- *BioIn 16, ConAu 131*
Bogue, Philip Roberts 1924- *WhoAm 90*
Boguet, Henri 1550?-1619 *EncO&P 3*
Bogun, Maceptaw 1917- *MusmAFA [port]*
Bogus, Carl Thomas 1948- *WhoEmL 91*
Bogus, Charley 1850?-1880 *WhNaAH*
Bogusky, Alf 1947- *WhoAm 90*
Boguslaw, Robert 1919- *ConAu 132, WhoAm 90*
Boguslawski, Alexander Prus 1951- *WhoSSW 91*
Boguslawski, Edward 1940- *IntWWM 90*
Boguszewska, Helena 1883-1978 *EncCoWW*
Bogutz, Jerome E. 1935- *WhoAm 90*
Bogutz, Jerome Edwin 1935- *WhoWor 91*
Bogy, David Beauregard 1936- *WhoAm 90*
Bogyi, Antonia Maria *BiDrAPA 89*
Boh, Ivan 1930- *WhoAm 90*
Boh, Robert Henry 1930- *St&PR 91*
Bohac, Josef 1929- *IntWWM 90*
Bohamed, Gary M. 1960- *St&PR 91*
Bohan, Edmund *IntWWM 90*
Bohan, John E. 1931- *St&PR 91*
Bohan, Marc 1926- *ConDes 90, WhoWor 91*
Bohan, Ruth L 1946- *WhoAmA 91*
Bohan, Stephen John 1957- *WhoEmL 91*
Bohan, Thomas E. *WhoAm 90*
Bohana, Roy 1938- *IntWWM 90*
Bohanan, David John 1946- *WhoE 91, WhoEmL 91*
Bohannan, Paul James 1920- *WhoAm 90*
Bohannon, Barbara Jean 1943- *WhoE 91*
Bohannon, David D. 1898- *WhoAm 90*
Bohannon, Raymond Lawrence 1954- *WhoWor 91*
Bohannon, Richard F 1923- *BiDrAPA 89*
Bohannon, Richard Leland 1907- *WhoAm 90*
Bohannon, Shari Ann 1946- *WhoAmW 91*
Bohannon, Versie Darnell 1931- *WhoAmW 91*
Bohanon, Luther L. 1902- *WhoAm 90, WhoSSW 91*
Bohart, James Arthur 1942- *IntWWM 90*
Bohata, Emil Anton 1918- *WhoWor 91*
Bohdanowicz, A. *BiDWomA*
Bohem, Endre *BioIn 16*
Bohem, Endre 1901?-1990 *ConAu 131*
Bohemian Quartet *PenDiMP*
Bohen, Barbara E 1941- *WhoAmA 91*
Bohi, Douglas Ray 1939- *WhoE 91*
Bohl, Michael E. 1956- *St&PR 91*
Bohl, Robert Daniel 1948- *WhoEmL 91*
Bohl, Robert Walter 1925- *WhoAm 90*
Bohl de Faber y Larrea, Cecilia *EncCoWW*
Bohland, Gustav 1897-1959 *WhoAmA 91N*
Bohlander, Robert F. 1934- *St&PR 91*
Bohle, Bruce William 1918- *WhoAm 90, WhoWrEP 89*
Bohle, Daniel James 1946- *WhoEmL 91*
Bohle, Sue *ODwPR 91*
Bohle, Sue 1943- *WhoAmW 91*
Bohlen, Charles E. 1904-1974 *BioIn 16, WorAlBi*
Bohlen, Christopher Wayne 1949- *WhoEmL 91*
Bohlen, Jeanne Louise 1938- *WhoE 91*
Bohlen, Nina 1931- *BioIn 16, WhoAm 90, WhoAmA 91*
Bohlen, Richard William 1935- *WhoAm 90*
Bohlender, Hugh Darrow 1951- *WhoEmL 91*
Bohler, Joseph Stephen 1938- *WhoAmA 91*
Bohler, Tyrus Augustus 1947- *WhoSSW 91*
Bohler, Wallace H. 1927- *St&PR 91*
Bohley, Peter Hans Joachim 1932- *WhoWor 91*
Bohlin, Bruce Gordon 1948- *St&PR 91*
Bohlin, Daniel James 1949- *WhoEmL 91*
Bohlin, Jonas 1953- *ConDes 90*
Bohlin, Peter Quarfordt 1937- *WhoAm 90*
Bohlin, R. Paul 1936- *WhoE 91*
Bohlke, Gary Lee 1941- *WhoE 91*
Bohlken, Deborah Kay 1952- *WhoAmW 91, WhoSSW 91*
Bohlmann, Daniel Robert 1948- *WhoEmL 91, WhoWor 91*
Bohlmann, Paul F. 1925- *St&PR 91*
Bohlmann, Ralph Arthur 1932- *WhoAm 90*
Bohls, Sally Ruth 1956- *WhoAmW 91*
Bohm, August 1812-1890 *PenDiDA 89*
Bohm, Denis M. 1939- *St&PR 91*
Bohm, Gottfried 1920- *WhoWor 91*
Bohm, Hans 1937- *WhoWor 91*
Bohm, Henry Victor 1929- *WhoAm 90*
Bohm, Howard Allen 1943- *WhoSSW 91*
Bohm, Joel Lawrence 1942- *St&PR 91*
Bohm, Karl 1894-1981 *PenDiMP, WorAlBi*
Bohm, Ludwig 1947- *IntWWM 90*
Bohm, Michael Neil 1952- *WhoE 91*
Bohm, Ralph Arthur *BiDrAPA 89*
Bohm, Werner 1939- *St&PR 91*
Bohm-Bawerk, Eugen von 1851-1914 *BioIn 16*
Bohman, Andrew Clive 1933- *IntWWM 90*
Bohme, Carl Wilhelm *PenDiDA 89*
Bohme, Diethard Kurt 1941- *WhoAm 90*
Bohme, Kurt 1908- *IntWWM 90*
Bohmer, David Alan 1947- *WhoAm 90*
Bohmer, John *BioIn 16*
Bohmer, William T. 1947- *St&PR 91*
Bohmfalk, George Lee 1947- *WhoSSW 91*
Bohmius, Jean *EncO&P 3*
Bohmont, Dale Wendell 1922- *WhoAm 90*
Bohn, Barbara Ann 1943- *WhoSSW 91*
Bohn, Charlotte Galitz 1930- *WhoAmW 91, WhoWor 91*
Bohn, Cheryl Metcalfe 1955- *WhoEmL 91*
Bohn, Henry Edmond 1937- *WhoSSW 91*
Bohn, John A., Jr. 1937- *St&PR 91*
Bohn, John Augustus, Jr. 1937- *WhoAm 90*
Bohn, Karen M. 1953- *St&PR 91*
Bohn, Marie Hannah *BiDrAPA 89*
Bohn, Paul Bradley 1957- *BiDrAPA 89*
Bohn, Peter N. 1919- *St&PR 91*
Bohn, Ralph Carl 1930- *WhoAm 90*
Bohn, Sarah A 1956- *WhoAmW 91*
Bohn, Sherman Elwood 1927- *WhoAm 90*
Bohn, Virginia Elizabeth 1960- *WhoEmL 91*
Bohne, Carl John, Jr. 1916- *WhoAm 90*
Bohne, Matthew P. 1965- *WhoSSW 91*
Bohne, Mildred Thompson 1917- *WhoAmW 91*
Bohne, Sammy 1896-1977 *Ballpl 90*
Bohne, Steven Michael 1953- *WhoEmL 91*
Bohnen, Blythe 1940- *WhoAmA 91*
Bohnen, Eli Aaron 1909- *BioIn 16*
Bohnenkamp, Jeffry Joseph 1955- *WhoEmL 91*
Bohnenkamp, Leslie George 1943- *WhoAmA 91*
Bohner, Charles 1927- *SmATA 62 [port]*
Bohner, Charles Henry 1927- *WhoAm 90*
Bohnert, Herbert 1890-1967 *WhoAmA 91N*
Bohnert, Michael J *BiDrAPA 89*
Bohnert, Peggy Ann *BiDrAPA 89*
Bohnert, Philip Joseph *BiDrAPA 89*
Bohnert, Thom 1948- *WhoAmA 91*
Bohnet, Richard Herbert 1941- *St&PR 91*
Bohnett, William H. *St&PR 91*
Bohnhoff, William John 1938- *St&PR 91*
Bohning, Elizabeth Edrop 1915- *WhoAm 90*
Bohning, Gerry 1934- *WhoSSW 91*
Bohnke, Emil *PenDiMP*
Bohnn, Jules Henry 1935- *BiDrAPA 89*
Bohnsack, M. Gregory 1950- *St&PR 91*
Bohnslav, Edward, IV 1959- *WhoSSW 91*
Bohny, Robert William 1939- *St&PR 91*
Bohon, Scott Alan *BiDrAPA 89*
Bohonak, Noni Elizabeth 1942- *WhoSSW 91*
Bohorfoush, Joseph George 1907- *WhoSSW 91, WhoWor 91*
Bohoskey, Bernice Fleming 1918- *WhoAmW 91, WhoWor 91*
Bohr, Aage Niels 1922- *WhoAm 90, WhoWor 91, WorAlBi*
Bohr, Christian Harald Lauritz Peter E 1855-1911 *DcScB S2*
Bohr, Mary Jo *ODwPR 91*
Bohr, Niels 1885-1962 *WorAlBi*
Bohr, Niels Henrik David 1885-1962 *BioIn 16*
Bohr, Vernon C 1924- *BiDrAPA 89*
Bohren, Michael Oscar 1947- *WhoEmL 91*
Bohrer, Betty 1962- *WhoAmW 91*
Bohrer, Bruce Brickner 1951- *WhoEmL 91*
Bohrer, Catherine Ann 1962- *WhoEmL 91*
Bohrer, Michael Steven 1945- *St&PR 91*
Bohrer, Priscilla Jeannette 1922- *WhoE 91*
Bohrnstedt, George William 1938- *WhoAm 90*
Bohrod, Aaron 1907- *WhoAm 90, WhoAmA 91*
Bohrod, John R 1932- *BiDrAPA 89*
Bohrofen, Eldon LaVern 1941- *WhoAm 90*
Bohs, G. Lee 1959- *St&PR 91*
Boht, Jean 1936- *ConTFT 8 [port]*
Bohunicky, Debra Ann 1954- *WhoAmW 91*
Boiardi, Hector *BioIn 16*
Boiarski, Philip S. 1945- *WhoWrEP 89*
Boice, Ann Kelley 1932- *WhoAmW 91*
Boice, Craig Kendall 1952- *WhoE 91, WhoEmL 91, WhoWor 91*
Boice, John Kyle 1961- *WhoSSW 91*
Boice, Stephen Crosby 1951- *St&PR 91*
Boie, Heinrich Christian 1744-1806 *DcLB 94 [port]*
Boies, Earl B. 1904- *St&PR 91*
Boies, Wilber H. 1944- *WhoAm 90*
Boigon, Brian Joseph 1955- *WhoAmA 91*
Boigon, Helen W 1921- *BiDrAPA 89*
Boike, Edward Joseph 1923- *St&PR 91*
Boilanger, Mitzi Lu 1953- *WhoEmL 91*
Boileau, Leo Victor 1944- *St&PR 91*
Boileau, Oliver Clark 1927- *St&PR 91*
Boileau, Pierre 1906- *TwCCr&M 91B*
Boileau, Pierre, and Thomas Narcejac *TwCCr&M 91B*
Boileau-Despreaux, Nicolas 1636?-1711 *WorAlBi*
Boiles, John W. 1945- *St&PR 91*
Boilini, James John 1949- *WhoSSW 91*
Boillot, Paul Raymond W. 1961- *WhoEmL 91*
Boily, Jeffrey O. 1955- *St&PR 91*
Boily, Marcel *BiDrAPA 89*
Boiman, Donna Rae 1946- *WhoAmW 91, WhoEmL 91, WhoWor 91*
Boime, Albert Isaac 1933- *WhoAm 90*
Boineau, Cynthia Kaliher 1953- *WhoSSW 91*
Boineau, Elizabeth Lloyd 1956- *WhoAmW 91*
Boineau, Franklin Girard 1943- *WhoAm 90*
Boinest, William Calhoun 1933- *St&PR 91*
Boirac, Emile 1851-1917 *EncO&P 3, EncPaPR 91*
Boire, Richard Larry 1952- *WhoEmL 91*
Bois, Pierre 1924- *WhoAm 90*
Bois, Rob Du 1934- *IntWWM 90*
Boisclair, Bruce 1952- *Ballpl 90*
Boisclair, Joan 1956- *WhoWrEP 89*
Boise, Audrey Lorraine 1933- *WhoAmW 91, WhoE 91*
Boiseau, Joseph Eugene 1944- *St&PR 91*
Boisfontaine, Curtis Rich 1929- *WhoAm 90*
Boisonnault, Jean 1939- *St&PR 91*
Boissard, Janine *BioIn 16*
Boisse, Joseph Adonias 1937- *WhoAm 90*
Boisseau, Jerry Philip 1939- *WhoE 91*
Boisson, Robert Richard 1946- *St&PR 91*
Boisture, W.W., Jr. 1944- *St&PR 91*
Boisvert, Denis Ernest 1955- *BiDrAPA 89*
Boisvert, Ellen A. 1963- *WhoE 91*
Boitano, Brian *BioIn 16*
Boitano, Brian 1963- *WorAlBi*
Boitel, Ana Maria 1952- *WhoAmW 91*
Boiter, Donald Harry 1935- *St&PR 91*
Boito, Arrigo 1842-1918 *BioIn 16, PenDiMP A, WorAlBi*
Boivie, Jorgen G. 1939- *WhoWor 91*
Boivin, Claude 1934- *St&PR 91, WhoAm 90*
Boixados, Maria Dolores 192-?- *EncCoWW*
Boizot, Louis-Simon 1743-1809 *PenDiDA 89*
Bojangles *DrBlPA 90*
Bojar, Samuel 1915- *BiDrAPA 89*
Bojarski, Edmund Anthony 1924- *WhoSSW 91*
Bojarski, Jeanne Frances 1951- *WhoAmW 91*
Bojaxhiu, Agnes Gonxha 1910- *WhoWor 91*
Bojer, Johan 1872-1959 *DcScanL*
Bojesen, Kaj *PenDiDA 89*
Bojrab, Steven L 1953- *BiDrAPA 89*
Bojtar, Endre 1940- *WhoWor 91*
Bojtos, Peter 1949- *St&PR 91*
Bok, Alexander Toland 1959- *WhoEmL 91*
Bok, Bart J 1906-1983 *ConAu 30NR*
Bok, Dean 1939- *WhoAm 90*
Bok, Derek 1930- *WhoAm 90, WhoE 91, WhoWor 91*
Bok, Derek C. 1930- *WorAlBi*
Bok, Derek Curtis *BioIn 16*
Bok, Edward William 1863-1930 *BioIn 16*
Bok, Joan T. 1929- *St&PR 91*
Bok, Joan Toland 1929- *WhoAm 90*
Bok, John Fairfield 1930- *WhoAm 90*
Bok, Sissela *BioIn 16*
Bok, Sissela 1934- *WhoAm 90, WhoAmW 91, WorAu 1980 [port]*
Bok, Sissela Ann 1934- *ConAu 32NR*
Bok, W Eduard *BiDrAPA 89*
Bokaie, Michael 1950- *WhoWor 91*
Bokan, John A 1948- *BiDrAPA 89*
Bokanowski, Helene *BioIn 16*
Bokat, Peter Akulin *BiDrAPA 89*
Bokat, Stephen Arthur 1946- *WhoEmL 91*
Boke, Norman Hill 1913- *WhoAm 90*
Bokelmann, Gary Wayne 1949- *WhoEmL 91*
Boker, George H. 1823-1890 *BioIn 16*
Bokes, Vladimir 1946- *IntWWM 90*
Bokhari, Habib 1948- *St&PR 91*
Boklund-Lagopoulou, Karin Margareta 1948- *WhoWor 91*
Boknecht, Louis H. 1941- *St&PR 91*
Bokor, Judith Marie 1958- *IntWWM 90*
Bokovoy, R.D. 1943- *St&PR 91*
Bokros, Paul 1928- *WhoAm 90*
Boksay, Istvan J E 1940- *BiDrAPA 89*
Boksenberg, Alexander 1936- *WhoWor 91*
Bokser, Ben Zion 1907-1984 *BioIn 16*
Bokser, Lewis 1904- *WhoE 91, WhoWor 91*
Bokulic, Christine Ann 1965- *WhoAmW 91*
Bol, Jan Willem 1951- *WhoEmL 91*
Bola, Marybeth Marx 1959- *WhoAmW 91*
Bolac, M. L. *WhoSSW 91*
Bolaffi, Janice Lerner 1933- *WhoAmW 91*
Bolaffio, Vitorrio 1883-1931 *BioIn 16*
Bolaji, Rotimi Michael 1952- *WhoEmL 91, WhoWor 91*
Bolan, Kim Mary *BiDrAPA 89*
Bolan, Marc *EncPR&S 89*
Bolan, Marc 1947-1977 *OxCPMus*
Bolan, Robert 1941- *St&PR 91*
Bolan, Robert S. 1941- *WhoAm 90*
Bolan, Thomas A. 1924- *St&PR 91*

Bolan, Thomas Anthony 1924- WhoAm 90, WhoWor 91
Boland, Annie 1951- BiDrAPA 89
Boland, Bernie 1892-1973 Ballpl 90
Boland, Bridget 1913- FemiCLE
Boland, Bridget 1913-1988 AnObit 1988
Boland, Christopher Thomas, II 1915- WhoAm 90, WhoE 91
Boland, Eavan 1944- FemiCLE
Boland, Edward P. 1911- WhoE 91
Boland, Ellen Clark 1955- WhoEmL 91
Boland, Gerald Lee 1946- WhoE 91, WhoEmL 91, WhoWor 91
Boland, Gregory Harold 1953- BiDrAPA 89
Boland, Howard Leland 1955- BiDrAPA 89
Boland, Iris Anne 1931- St&PR 91
Boland, Jack Edward, IV 1942- St&PR 91
Boland, Janet Lang 1924- WhoAm 90, WhoAmW 91
Boland, John Dempsie BiDrAPA 89
Boland, John Francis, Jr. 1915- WhoAm 90
Boland, John Joseph, Jr. 1920- St&PR 91
Boland, Mark Sheridan 1955- WhoE 91, WhoWor 91
Boland, Marty WhoWrEP 89
Boland, Mary 1880?-1965 NotWoAT
Boland, Mary 1885?-1965 BioIn 16
Boland, Raymond J. 1932- WhoAm 90
Boland, Robert James 1937- St&PR 91
Boland, Robert Joseph BiDrAPA 89
Boland, Thomas Edwin 1934- St&PR 91, WhoAm 90
Boland, Tom 1929- St&PR 91
Boland-Robillard, Virginia Anne 1958- WhoEmL 91
Bolande, Robert Paul 1926- WhoAm 90
Bolander, Glen S. 1946- St&PR 91
Bolander, Glen S., Jr. 1946- WhoEmL 91
Bolanos, Magtangol Hilario 1930- WhoWor 91
Bolanos-Tiongson, Nora BiDrAPA 89
Bolanovich, Lester John 1925- BiDrAPA 89
Bolar, Larry D. 1936- St&PR 91
Bolas, Gerald Douglas 1949- WhoAm 90, WhoAmA 91
Bolasini, Alfredo 1947- BiDrAPA 89
Bolce, Donn W. 1928- St&PR 91
Bolch, Carl Edward, Jr. 1943- St&PR 91, WhoAm 90, WhoSSW 91
Bolcik, Charles Gabriel 1932- WhoE 91
Bolcom, William BioIn 16
Bolcom, William 1938- CurBio 90 [port], OxCPMus
Bolcom, William E. 1938- WorAlBi
Bolcom, William Elden 1938- IntWWM 90, WhoAm 90
Bold, Alan Norman 1943- ConAu 30NR
Bold, Frances Ann 1930- WhoAm 90
Bold, John W. 1930- ODwPR 91
Bold, Mary Ellender 1952- WhoAmW 91
Bold, Russell Clinton 1921- St&PR 91
Bolda, Peter G. 1930- St&PR 91
Bolden, Bernadine J. 1938- WhoSSW 91
Bolden, Buddy 1868-1931 DrBlPA 90, WorAlBi
Bolden, Charles 1877-1931 OxCPMus
Bolden, Johnna A. 1964- WhoEmL 91
Bolden, Leo F. 1938- St&PR 91
Bolden, R.D. 1941- St&PR 91
Bolden, Rosamond 1938- WhoAmW 91
Bolden, Theodore Edward 1920- WhoAm 90, WhoE 91
Bolding, Deborah Marlene 1954- WhoSSW 91
Bolding, James Tarpley, Jr. 1933- WhoSSW 91
Boldizsar, Ivan 1912-1988 BioIn 16
Boldosser, Nancy Shilay 1957- WhoE 91
Boldrey, Edwin B. 1906-1988 BioIn 16
Boldridge, David William 1954- WhoSSW 91
Boldrin, Laurie-Anne 1964- WhoAmW 91
Boldry, Joseph Stuart, Jr. 1956- WhoEmL 91
Boldt, Charles Martin 1950- WhoAm 90
Boldt, Dennise M. 1951- WhoAmW 91
Boldt, Donald Bernard 1934- St&PR 91
Boldt, Heinz 1923- WhoWor 91
Boldt, James Robert 1951- St&PR 91
Boldt, Oscar Charles 1924- St&PR 91, WhoAm 90
Boldt, Peter 1927- WhoWor 91
Boldt, Waldemar H 1908- BiDrAPA 89
Bolduc, Donald Raymond 1946- St&PR 91
Bolduc, Ernest Joseph 1924- WhoAm 90
Bolduc, J. Paul R. 1939- St&PR 91
Bolduc, James Philip 1949- WhoAm 90
Bolduc, Jerome M. 1929- St&PR 91
Bolduc, Joseph Patrick 1943- St&PR 91
Bolduc, Gerald J. St&PR 91
Bole, Giles G., Jr. 1928- WhoAm 90
Bolea, Pedro Pablo Abarca de 1718-1798 BioIn 16
Bolebruch, Lori Ann 1957- WhoAmW 91
Boleck WhNaAH
Bolek WhNaAH
Boleman, Ray Judson, Jr. 1944- WhoAm 90
Bolen, Amos Alonzo 1909- WhoAm 90
Bolen, Bob 1926- WhoAm 90, WhoSSW 91
Bolen, Charles Warren 1923- IntWWM 90, WhoAm 90
Bolen, David B. 1923- WhoAm 90, WhoWor 91
Bolen, Edward Snow 1938- WhoSSW 91
Bolen, Eric George 1937- WhoSSW 91
Bolen, Jean Shinoda 1936- BiDrAPA 89
Bolen, Jennifer Diane BiDrAPA 89
Bolen, John E 1953- WhoAmA 91
Bolen, Lynne N 1954- WhoAmA 91
Bolen, Terry Lee 1945- WhoEmL 91, WhoSSW 91
Bolen, Waldo Emerson, Jr. 1931- St&PR 91
Bolender, Carroll Herdus 1919- WhoAm 90
Bolender, David Francis 1932- WhoAm 90
Bolender, James Henry 1937- St&PR 91
Bolender, Todd 1919- WhoAm 90
Bolene, Margaret Rosalie Steele 1923- WhoAmW 91
Boler, John Alfred 1942- WhoAmA 91
Boles, Alan E. 1906-1989 BioIn 16
Boles, Donald Michael 1951- WhoEmL 91
Boles, Gary Thomas 1945- WhoSSW 91
Boles, Janet Kay 1944- WhoAmW 91
Boles, John 1900-1969 OxCPMus
Boles, John Culson 1953- WhoSSW 91
Boles, Roger 1928- WhoAm 90
Bolet, Jorge 1914- BioIn 16, IntWWM 90, PenDiMP, WhoHisp 91
Bolet, Jorge 1914-1990 NewYTBS 90
Boley, Bruno Adrian 1924- WhoAm 90, WhoE 91
Boley, Dennis Lynn 1951- WhoSSW 91
Boley, Donna Jean 1935- WhoAmW 91
Boley, Eugene Conlee 1928- St&PR 91
Boley, Forrest Irving 1925- WhoAm 90
Boley, Jacqueline 1954- WhoAmW 91
Boley, Joe 1896-1962 Ballpl 90
Boley, Theresa Maria 1951- WhoEmL 91
Boley Bolaffio, Rita WhoAmW 91, WhoWor 91
Boleyn, Anne BioIn 16
Boleyn, Anne 1507?-1536 WorAlBi
Bolgar, Robert Andrew 1959- BiDrAPA 89
Bolge, George S WhoAmA 91
Bolger, Brenna 1942- ODwPR 91
Bolger, David P. 1957- St&PR 91
Bolger, Francine Jo 1956- WhoAmW 91
Bolger, James Brendan 1935- WhoWor 91
Bolger, Jim 1932- Ballpl 90
Bolger, Justin Christopher 1929- St&PR 91
Bolger, Mary Kenealy 1949- WhoEmL 91
Bolger, Ray 1904- OxCPMus
Bolger, Ray 1904-1987 BioIn 16, WorAlBi
Bolger, Richard John 1929- WhoE 91
Bolger, Robert Joseph 1922- WhoSSW 91
Bolger, Thomas Edward 1927- WhoE 91
Bolger, William F. BioIn 16
Bolgiano, Ralph, Jr. 1922- WhoAm 90
Boli, Sarah Collins 1958- WhoAmW 91, WhoEmL 91
Bolian, George C. II 1930- BiDrAPA 89
Bolian, George Clement 1930- WhoAm 90
Bolick, Ernest Bernard, Jr. 1933- WhoSSW 91
Bolie, Victor Wayne 1924- WhoAm 90, WhoWor 91
Bolin, Alpha E., Jr. 1927- St&PR 91
Bolin, Bertil Axel 1923- WhoWor 91
Bolin, Bobby 1939- Ballpl 90
Bolin, Charles William 1926- St&PR 91
Bolin, Jerry Doyle 1944- WhoSSW 91
Bolin, Jewel N. 1926- St&PR 91
Bolin, John H., Jr. 1926- St&PR 91
Bolin, John Richard 1938- St&PR 91
Bolin, Kenneth O'Neal 1951- WhoSSW 91
Bolin, Per Eric 1933- WhoWor 91
Bolin, Richard Reuel 1925- BiDrAPA 89
Bolin, Shirley Judith 1928- St&PR 91
Bolin, Vernon Spencer 1913- WhoWor 91
Bolin, William Harvey 1922- WhoAm 90
Bolinao, Engracia I BiDrAPA 89
Bolinder, Robert Donald 1931- St&PR 91, WhoAm 90
Boling, Beth A. 1960- WhoAmW 91, WhoSSW 91
Boling, Carole Jean 1943- WhoAmW 91
Boling, David Gordon 1937- WhoSSW 91
Boling, Edward Joseph 1922- WhoAm 90, WhoSSW 91, WhoWor 91
Boling, Harold Edward 1939- WhoWor 91
Boling, James Mark BiDrAPA 89
Boling, Jewell 1907- WhoAmW 91, WhoSSW 91, WhoWor 91
Boling, Joseph Edward 1942- WhoE 91, WhoWor 91
Boling, Judy Atwood 1921- WhoAmW 91
Boling, Kathleen Mary 1950- WhoAmW 91
Boling, Lenore A BiDrAPA 89
Boling, Mark Edward 1954- WhoSSW 91
Bolingbroke, Henry St. John 1678-1751 WorAlBi
Bolingbroke, Henry St. John, Viscount 1678-1751 DcLB 101 [port]
Bolingbroke, Robert A. 1938- St&PR 91, WhoAm 90
Bolinger, Becky Lynn 1959- WhoAmW 91
Bolinger, Bonnie Lou 1938- WhoAmW 91
Bolinger, Corbin Eugene 1929- St&PR 91
Bolinger, George James 1950- St&PR 91
Bolinger, John C., Jr. 1922- St&PR 91, WhoAm 90
Bolinger, John Mccallie BiDrAPA 89
Bolinger, Robert Stevens 1936- St&PR 91, WhoAm 90
Bolinger, Terry Dean 1947- WhoSSW 91
Bolino, John Vincent 1941- WhoAm 90
Bolinsky, Joseph Abraham 1917- WhoAmA 91
Bolitho, Louise Greer 1927- WhoAmW 91
Bolivar, Joanne BioIn 16
Bolivar, Simon 1783-1830 BioIn 16, WorAlBi
Bolker, Ethan David 1938- WhoE 91
Bolker, Henry Irving 1926- WhoAm 90
Bolkiah, Muda Hassanal 1946- BioIn 16
Bolks, Ervin Jay 1941- WhoAm 90
Boll, Charles Raymond 1920- WhoAm 90
Boll, Heinrich MajTwCW
Boll, Heinrich 1917-1985 BioIn 16, EuWr 13, WorAlBi
Boll, Robert Francis BiDrAPA 89
Bolla, William Joseph 1947- WhoE 91
Bolle, Donald Martin 1933- WhoAm 90
Bolle, Frank 1924- EncACom
Bolle, James Dougan 1931- WhoE 91
Bollen, Peter Douglas 1948- WhoWrEP 89
Bollen, Roger 1941- WhoAm 90
Bollenbach, Stephen Frasier 1942- St&PR 91, WhoAm 90
Bollenbeck, Georg 1947- WhoWor 91
Boller, Margaret Mary 1956- WhoEmL 91
Boller, Raymond J. 1916-1989 BioIn 16
Boller, Ronald Cecil 1939- WhoAm 90
Bollerer, Fred L. St&PR 91
Bollerman, James Michael 1954- St&PR 91
Bolles, Blair 1911-1990 BioIn 16, ConAu 130
Bolles, E. Blair NewYTBS 90
Bolles, John W. 1945- St&PR 91
Bolles, Peter Piper 1937- St&PR 91
Bolles, Richard Nelson 1927- WhoAm 90
Bollet, Alfred Jay 1926- WhoAm 90
Bollettieri, Nick BioIn 16
Bollheimer, Denise 1950- WhoEmL 91
Bollich, Elridge Nicholas 1941- WhoSSW 91
Bollier, Gary L. 1952- WhoEmL 91
Bolliger, Erwin 1929- WhoWor 91
Bollimpalli, Rao G. 1938- St&PR 91
Bollin, William Robert 1949- St&PR 91
Bolline, Peter E. 1948- St&PR 91
Bolling, Blair 1791-1839 BioIn 16
Bolling, Claude BioIn 16
Bolling, Frank BioIn 16
Bolling, Frank 1931- Ballpl 90
Bolling, John Randolph 1935- St&PR 91
Bolling, Landrum Rymer 1913- WhoAm 90
Bolling, Milt 1930- Ballpl 90
Bolling, Richard Norman 1926- St&PR 91
Bolling, Roger 1926- St&PR 91
Bollinger, Don M. 1914- St&PR 91
Bollinger, Don Mills 1914- WhoAm 90
Bollinger, John Gustave 1935- WhoAm 90
Bollinger, Lee Carroll 1946- WhoAm 90
Bollinger, Lowell Moyer 1923- WhoAm 90
Bollinger, Pamela Beemer 1947- WhoAmW 91
Bollinger, Ralph Randal 1944- WhoAm 90
Bollinger, Sheryl Lea 1957- St&PR 91
Bollinger, Taree 1949- WhoWrEP 89
Bollinger, Thomas Richard 1943- St&PR 91
Bollman, Mark Brooks, Jr. 1925- St&PR 91, WhoAm 90
Bollmann, Henry P. 1935- St&PR 91
Bollmann, Juergen 1943- St&PR 91
Bollom, Daniel Arthur 1936- St&PR 91
Bollon, Arthur Peter 1942- WhoAm 90
Bollum, Frederick James 1927- WhoAm 90
Bolman, Lee Garrison 1941- WhoE 91
Bolman, William M 1929- BiDrAPA 89
Bolmann, Andrew R 1938- BiDrAPA 89
Bolmarcich, Francisco Jose Orlich 1907-1969 BioIn 16
Bolmarcich, Virginia Devlin 1944- WhoAmW 91
Bolmer, John Edwin, II 1958- WhoEmL 91
Bolnick, Bruce Robert 1947- WhoE 91
Bolnick, Howard Jeffrey 1945- WhoAm 90, WhoEmL 91
Bolo, Peter Michael BiDrAPA 89
Bolocan, Hyam 1922- BiDrAPA 89
Bologna, Calogero Antonio 1957- WhoEmL 91
Bologna, Joanne Denise 1961- WhoAmW 91
Bologna, Joseph 1938- WhoAm 90
Bologna, T.A. 1948- St&PR 91
Bolognesi, Dani Paul 1941- WhoAm 90
Bolomey, Roger Henry 1918- WhoAm 90, WhoAmA 91
Bolon, Andrew J 1822?-1855 WhNaAH
Bolooki, Hooshang 1937- WhoAm 90
Bolotin, Irving 1932- St&PR 91
Bolotin, Lora M. WhoAmW 91
Bolotine, Leonid 1901-1988 BioIn 16
Bolotow, Norman Jay 1936- WhoE 91
Bolotowsky, Andrew Ilyitch 1949- WhoEmL 91, WhoWor 91
Bolotowsky, Ilya 1907-1981 WhoAmA 91N
Boloyan, Myron B. 1957- WhoSSW 91
Bolsen, Barbara Ann 1950- WhoAmW 91
Bolsky, Abraham S. 1922- St&PR 91
Bolstad, Ralph Arthur BiDrAPA 89
Bolster, Archie Milburn 1933- WhoAm 90
Bolster, Arthur Stanley, Jr. 1922- WhoAm 90
Bolster, Jacqueline Neben WhoAmW 91
Bolster, Stephen Clark 1951- WhoSSW 91
Bolster, William Lawrence 1943- WhoAm 90
Bolsterli, Margaret Jones 1931- WhoAm 90
Bolt, Alan BioIn 16
Bolt, Bruce Alan 1930- WhoAm 90
Bolt, Carol 1941- BioIn 16, FemiCLE, OxCCanT
Bolt, Charles Murphy 1930- St&PR 91
Bolt, David Bruce 1954- WhoEmL 91
Bolt, David Ernest 1921- WhoWor 91
Bolt, Katherine Heym 1944- WhoAmW 91
Bolt, M. Ronald 1948- St&PR 91
Bolt, Paul Boudewyn Edward 1943- WhoWor 91
Bolt, Richard Henry 1911- WhoAm 90, WhoWor 91
Bolt, Robert BioIn 16
Bolt, Robert 1924- MajTwCW
Bolt, Robert E. 1919- St&PR 91
Bolt, Robert Louis 1953- WhoEmL 91
Bolt, Robert Oxton 1924- WhoWor 91
Bolt, Ron 1938- WhoAmA 91
Bolt, Stephen Richard 1955- WhoSSW 91
Bolt, Thomas Alvin Waldrep 1956- WhoSSW 91
Bolt, William Frank BiDrAPA 89
Bolt, William J., Jr. St&PR 91N
Boltanski, Christian 1944- WhoWor 91
Boltax-Stern, Sandra BiDrAPA 89
Bolte, Brown 1908- St&PR 91, WhoAm 90, WhoWor 91
Bolte, Candice Regina 1948- WhoAmW 91
Bolte, Charles Guy 1920- WhoWrEP 89
Bolte, Charles Lawrence 1895-1989 BioIn 16
Bolte, MaryAnn Priscilla 1953- BiDrAPA 89
Bolten, John, Jr. 1920- St&PR 91
Bolter, Delano W BiDrAPA 89
Bolter, Eugene Paul 1932- WhoE 91
Bolter, Sidney 1924- BiDrAPA 89
Bolthouse, William J. 1940- St&PR 91
Boltinoff, Henry 1914- EncACom
Bolton, Barbara Diane 1950- WhoAmW 91
Bolton, Brian J. 1938- St&PR 91
Bolton, Carole 1926- AuBYP 90
Bolton, Charles Thomas 1943- WhoAm 90
Bolton, Cliff 1907-1979 Ballpl 90
Bolton, David BioIn 16
Bolton, David J. 1929- St&PR 91
Bolton, David Robert 1946- BiDrAPA 89
Bolton, Earl Clinton 1919- WhoAm 90
Bolton, Elizabeth ConAu 32NR
Bolton, Elsie B. St&PR 91
Bolton, Eric BioIn 16
Bolton, Evelyn AuBYP 90
Bolton, Evelyn 1928- SmATA X [port]
Bolton, Frances P. 1885-1977 BioAmW
Bolton, Frances Payne 1885-1977 EncPaPR 91
Bolton, Frances Payne Bingham 1885-1977 BioIn 16
Bolton, Gambier EncO&P 3
Bolton, Gene Thomas 1942- St&PR 91
Bolton, George W. 1841- AmLegL
Bolton, Guy 1884-1979 OxCPMus
Bolton, Harold C. 1932- St&PR 91
Bolton, Harvey Verndale 1938- St&PR 91
Bolton, Ivy May 1879- AuBYP 90
Bolton, James R. 1945- St&PR 91
Bolton, Jan E. 1945- St&PR 91
Bolton, John Robert 1948- WhoAm 90
Bolton, John Roger 1950- WhoAm 90
Bolton, John W. St&PR 91N
Bolton, Kenneth Albert 1941- WhoE 91
Bolton, Martha O. 1951- WhoAmW 91, WhoEmL 91, WhoWor 91
Bolton, Mary Jane 1934- WhoAmW 91
Bolton, Melvin 1938- SpyFic
Bolton, Michael BioIn 16
Bolton, Michael 1955?- ConMus 4 [port]
Bolton, Michael G. 1949- St&PR 91

Bolton, Richard 1956- *WhoAmA 91*
Bolton, Robert H. 1908- *St&PR 91*
Bolton, Robert Harvey 1908- *WhoAm 90, WhoSSW 91*
Bolton, Roger Edwin 1938- *WhoAm 90, WhoE 91*
Bolton, Roger Park 1934- *WhoSSW 91*
Bolton, Sara 1841-1916 *FemiCLE*
Bolton, Sarah T. 1820-1893 *LiHiK*
Bolton, Sarah Tittle 1814-1893 *FemiCLE*
Bolton, Tom 1962- *Ballpl 90*
Bolton, William Elvin, III 1946- *St&PR 91*
Bolton, William J. 1937- *St&PR 91*
Bolton, William Michael *BiDrAPA 89*
Bolton-Smith, Carlile, Jr. 1937- *St&PR 91, WhoAm 90*
Bolton-Smith, Robin Lee 1941- *WhoAmA 91*
Boltuck, Richard Dale 1955- *WhoE 91*
Boltwood, Bertram Borden 1870-1927 *BioIn 16*
Boltz, Carol Hofmann 1934- *WhoAmW 91*
Boltz, Gerald Edmund 1931- *WhoAm 90*
Boltz, Mary Ann 1923- *WhoAm 90, WhoAmW 91, WhoWor 91*
Boltz, Ronald R. 1945- *St&PR 91*
Bolusky, Eric Bruce 1949- *WhoEmL 91*
Bolvig, C.P. 1929- *St&PR 91*
Bolwell, Edward John 1886-1956 *BioIn 16*
Bolwell, H.J. 1925- *St&PR 91*
Bolwig, Tom G 1937- *BiDrAPA 89*
Bolyard, Brent Lee *BiDrAPA 89*
Bolyard, Gary M. 1935- *St&PR 91*
Bolz, Harriett *IntWWM 90*
Bolz, Henry H. *BioIn 16*
Bolz, Ray Emil 1918- *WhoAm 90*
Bolz, Sanford Hegleman 1915- *WhoAm 90*
Bolze, Dorene *BioIn 16*
Boman, Axel Enoch *PenDiDA 89*
Boman, Eric *BioIn 16*
Boman, Fred Hjalmar 1943- *WhoWor 91*
Boman, John Harris, Jr. 1910- *WhoAm 90*
Boman, Michael Leonard 1952- *WhoEmL 91*
Boman, Primavera Roxan 1946- *WhoEmL 91*
Bomar, Clifton Patrick, Jr. 1942- *St&PR 91*
Bomar, Kenneth A. *ODwPR 91*
Bomar, Samuel G. 1945- *St&PR 91*
Bomazeen 1675?-1724 *WhNaAH*
Bomba, I. M. *BioIn 16*
Bomba, Margaret Ann 1947- *WhoAmW 91*
Bomback, Mark 1953- *Ballpl 90*
Bombal, Maria Luisa 1910-1980 *BioIn 16, HispWr 90, WorAu 1980 [port]*
Bombardier, J. R. Andre 1942- *St&PR 91*
Bombart, Philip 1945- *St&PR 91*
Bombaugh, Karl Jacob 1922- *WhoWor 91*
Bombazine 1675?-1724 *WhNaAH*
Bombeck, Erma *BioIn 16*
Bombeck, Erma 1927- *MajTwCW, WorAlBi*
Bombeck, Erma Louise 1927- *WhoAm 90, WhoAmW 91, WhoWrEP 89*
Bombei, Gary V. 1941- *St&PR 91*
Bombela, Rose Mary 1950- *WhoHisp 91*
Bomberg, David 1890-1957 *BioIn 16*
Bomberg, Thomas James 1928- *WhoAm 90*
Bomberger, David Richard, Jr. 1948- *WhoAm 90*
Bomberger, Glen R. 1937- *WhoAm 90*
Bomberger, John Henry Augustus 1929- *WhoE 91*
Bomberger, Roy Landis 1926- *WhoE 91*
Bomberger, Russell Branson 1934- *WhoAm 90*
Bomberger, Samuel W. 1927- *St&PR 91*
Bombino, Isabel Pinera 1954- *WhoEmL 91*
Bomgaars, Mona Ruth 1939- *WhoAmW 91*
Bomgardner, William Earl 1925- *WhoAm 90*
Bomhard, Allan Robert 1943- *WhoE 91*
Bommarito, Peter 1915-1989 *BioIn 16*
Bommelaer, Alain 1947- *WhoAm 90*
Bommer, Gerhard 1946- *WhoWor 91*
Bompart, Bill Earl 1933- *WhoSSW 91*
Bompey, Stuart Howard 1940- *WhoWor 91*
Bomstein, Alan Charles 1945- *WhoSSW 91*
Bomzer, David J. 1961- *WhoEmL 91*
Bon, Henri 1885- *EncO&P 3*
Bon, Maarten 1933- *IntWWM 90*
Bon Jovi, Jon *BioIn 16, EncPR&S 89*
Bon Jovi, Jon 1962- *CurBio 90 [port], WhoAm 90*
Bona of Savoy *WomWR*
Bona, Frederick E. 1939- *ODwPR 91, St&PR 91*
Bona, Frederick Emil 1939- *WhoE 91*
Bona, Jerry Lloyd 1945- *WhoE 91*
Bona, Joseph R 1960- *BiDrAPA 89*
Bona, Nicholas 1931- *BiDrAPA 89*
Bonaca, Paul Luciano 1941- *St&PR 91*
Bonacci, Donald Nicholas 1929- *St&PR 91, WhoAm 90*
Bonacci, Eugene Charles 1939- *St&PR 91*
Bonacci, John Carl 1935- *WhoE 91*
Bonaccorsi, Maria Teresa *BiDrAPA 89*
Bonaccorso, Anthony 1929- *WhoSSW 91*
Bonaccorso, Edward Chester 1943- *WhoE 91*
Bonaccorso, Rosemary Galambos 1961- *WhoE 91*
Bonacorda, James Joseph 1952- *WhoE 91*
Bonacorsi, Gregory James 1955- *WhoE 91, WhoEmL 91*
Bonacorsi, Larry Joseph 1948- *WhoEmL 91*
Bonadeo, Alfredo Angelo 1928- *WhoAm 90*
Bonaduce, Danny *BioIn 16*
Bonafe, Eddie *BioIn 16*
Bonaguide, John M. 1935- *St&PR 91*
Bonaguidi, Orland 1914- *St&PR 91*
Bonaldi, Jane Gayle 1942- *WhoAmW 91*
Bonan, A Ferdinand 1918- *BiDrAPA 89*
Bonan, Seon Pierre 1917- *WhoAm 90*
Bonang, Gerard Hok-gie 1935- *WhoWor 91*
Bonanni, Laudamia 1909- *EncCoWW*
Bonanno, Raymond J. 1940- *St&PR 91*
Bonanno di Linguaglossa, Giuseppe 1940- *WhoWor 91*
Bonapart, Alan David 1930- *WhoAm 90*
Bonaparte *WomWR*
Bonaparte, Charles Joseph 1851-1921 *BiDrUSE 89*
Bonaparte, Elisabeth P. 1785-1879 *BioAmW*
Bonaparte, Joseph 1768-1844 *BioIn 16*
Bonaparte, Louis-Napoleon 1808-1873 *BioIn 16*
Bonaparte, Napoleon 1769-1821 *BioIn 16*
Bonaparte, Norton Nathaniel, Jr. 1953- *WhoE 91*
Bonaparte, Tony Hillary 1939- *WhoAm 90*
Bonapfel, Paul Walter 1951- *WhoEmL 91*
Bonar, Linda Louise 1949- *WhoAmW 91*
Bonar, Lucian George 1934 *WhoAm 90*
Bonardi, Leo E. *ODwPR 91*
Bonaros, Thomas P. 1941- *St&PR 91*
Bonaskiewich, Sharon Jane 1956- *WhoEmL 91*
Bonastia, Peter Joseph 1938- *St&PR 91*
Bonati, Guido *EncO&P 3*
Bonatti, Gertrude Clare 1925- *WhoWor 91*
Bonatus, Guido *EncO&P 3*
Bonatz, Kurt Mandle 1963- *WhoSSW 91*
Bonauro, Tom *BioIn 16*
Bonaventura, Leo Mark 1945- *WhoWor 91*
Bonaventura, Mario di 1924- *IntWWM 90*
Bonaventure, Saint 1217?-1274 *WrPh P*
Bonaventure, Jacques 1955- *St&PR 91*
Bonavia, David 1940-1988 *BioIn 16*
Bonavitz, Gerald Ralph 1910- *St&PR 91*
Bonazinga, Marie T. 1948- *St&PR 91*
Bonazinga, Marie Therese 1948- *WhoAmW 91, WhoE 91*
Bonazzi, Elaine 1936- *IntWWM 90*
Bonazzi, Elaine Claire *WhoAm 90*
Bonazzo, Anthony Henry, II 1957- *WhoE 91*
Bonch-Bruevich, Mikhail Dmitrievich 1870-1956 *BioIn 16*
Bonch-Bruevich, Vladimir Dmitrievich 1873-1955 *BioIn 16*
Boncher, Mary 1946- *WhoAmW 91*
Bonci, Alessandro 1870-1940 *PenDiMP*
Boncyk-Jappinga, Elaine Marie 1960- *WhoEmL 91*
Bond, A Gordon *BiDrAPA 89*
Bond, Alan *BioIn 16, WhoWor 91*
Bond, Aline Blakely 1940- *WhoAmW 91*
Bond, Alma H 1923- *ConAu 130*
Bond, Amanda Odessa 1942- *WhoAmW 91, WhoE 91, WhoWor 91*
Bond, Arthur Chalmer 1917- *WhoAm 90*
Bond, Arthur D., Jr. 1933- *St&PR 91*
Bond, Audrey Mae 1932- *WhoAmW 91*
Bond, B J *ConAu 129*
Bond, Bruce 1939- *SmATA 61 [port]*
Bond, Bruce R. 1946- *St&PR 91*
Bond, C. LaNoel 1940- *WhoSSW 91*
Bond, Calhoun 1921- *WhoAm 90*
Bond, Carrie Jacobs 1862-1946 *OxCPMus*
Bond, Cathy Louise Elizabe 1952- *WhoAmW 91*
Bond, Charles C., Jr. 1923- *St&PR 91*
Bond, Charles Dailey 1932- *WhoE 91*
Bond, Charles Eugene 1930- *WhoAm 90*
Bond, Charles H., Sr. 1944- *St&PR 91*
Bond, Christopher Samuel 1939- *WhoAm 90, WhoWor 91*
Bond, Cornelius Combs, Jr. 1933- *WhoAm 90*
Bond, Dan Murray 1937- *St&PR 91*
Bond, Edward 1934- *MajTwCW, WhoWor 91*
Bond, Edward Anthony 1957- *St&PR 91*
Bond, Elaine R. 1935- *St&PR 91, WhoAm 90*
Bond, Elisabeth 1945- *FemiCLE*
Bond, Elizabeth Hunt 1953- *WhoAmW 91*
Bond, Epperson Ellis 1923- *WhoAm 90*
Bond, Erika 1914- *BioIn 16*
Bond, Felicia 1954- *BioIn 16*
Bond, Floyd Alden 1913- *WhoAm 90*
Bond, Frederick Bligh 1864-1945 *EncO&P 3, EncPaPR 91*
Bond, Frederick Edwin 1920- *WhoAm 90*
Bond, Frederick W. *EarBlAP*
Bond, George Cline 1920- *WhoAm 90*
Bond, Harold Herant 1939- *WhoWrEP 89*
Bond, Horace Mann *BioIn 16*
Bond, James 1900-1989 *AnObit 1989, BioIn 16*
Bond, James, III *BioIn 16*
Bond, James Joseph 1937- *St&PR 91*
Bond, Janice Sachiko 1941- *WhoAmW 91*
Bond, Jean Carey *AuBYP 90, BioIn 16*
Bond, Jessie 1853-1942 *OxCPMus*
Bond, Jim L. *WhoAm 90*
Bond, Julian *BioIn 16*
Bond, Julian 1940- *WhoAm 90, WorAlBi*
Bond, Lewis 1839-1878 *AmLegL*
Bond, Lewis H *ConAu 31NR*
Bond, Lewis H. 1921- *St&PR 91*
Bond, Linda Christine 1962- *BiDrAPA 89*
Bond, Lora 1917- *WhoAmW 91*
Bond, Louis J. 1959- *St&PR 91*
Bond, Marc Douglas 1954- *WhoEmL 91*
Bond, Marvin Andrew 1949- *WhoE 91*
Bond, Mary Lou 1936- *WhoAmW 91*
Bond, Michael 1926- *AuBYP 90, BioIn 16*
Bond, Michael Peter 1946- *BiDrAPA 89*
Bond, Milton Wallace 1918- *MusmAFA*
Bond, Morris Lindsay 1936- *St&PR 91*
Bond, Nancy 1945- *AuBYP 90*
Bond, Nelson Leighton, Jr. 1935- *WhoE 91*
Bond, Niles Woodbridge 1916- *WhoAm 90*
Bond, Oriel Edmund 1911- *WhoAmA 91*
Bond, Paterson *BioIn 16*
Bond, Peter Danford 1940- *WhoAm 90*
Bond, Preston Donnell 1934- *WhoE 91*
Bond, Raleigh Verne *BioIn 16*
Bond, Richard Agustin 1954- *WhoSSW 91*
Bond, Richard C. 1909-1989 *BioIn 16*
Bond, Richard Norman 1950- *WhoAm 90*
Bond, Richard O. 1946- *St&PR 91*
Bond, Richard Randolph 1927- *WhoAm 90*
Bond, Robert 1928- *IntWWM 90*
Bond, Roland S 1898- *WhoAmA 91N*
Bond, Ronald Richard 1958- *WhoEmL 91*
Bond, Ruskin 1934- *ConAu 31NR*
Bond, Sarah Ann 1955- *WhoAmW 91*
Bond, Stanley John 1943- *St&PR 91*
Bond, Thomas 1713-1784 *EncCRAm*
Bond, Thomas 1913- *WhoAm 90, WhoWor 91*
Bond, Thomas Cannon 1942- *BiDrAPA 89*
Bond, Thomas Jefferson, Jr. 1936- *WhoE 91*
Bond, Tommy 1856-1941 *Ballpl 90*
Bond, Victoria 1945- *IntWWM 90*
Bond, Victoria Ellen 1945- *WhoAm 90, WhoAmW 91, WhoSSW 91*
Bond, Virginia F. 1919- *WhoWrEP 89*
Bond, Walt 1937-1967 *Ballpl 90*
Bond, Walter Pearson 1942- *St&PR 91*
Bond, Ward 1903-1960 *WorAlBi*
Bond, William Edward 1943- *St&PR 91*
Bond, William Henry 1915- *WhoAm 90*
Bond, Winkler D *BiDrAPA 89*
Bond-Upson, Deborah Gwendolyn 1949- *WhoEmL 91*
Bondalapati, Sivaji B *BiDrAPA 89*
Bondar, Roberta Lynn 1945- *WhoAmW 91*
Bondarchuk, Sergei *BioIn 16*
Bondarchuk, Sergey Fedorovich 1920- *WhoWor 91*
Bondareff, William 1930- *BiDrAPA 89, WhoAm 90*
Bondarew, Beverly Ann 1949- *WhoAmW 91*
Bondarowicz, John Frank 1961- *WhoEmL 91*
Bonde, James R. 1932- *St&PR 91*
Bonde, John Richard *BiDrAPA 89*
Bonde, Olaf Carl 1927- *St&PR 91, WhoAm 90*
Bonder, Daniel L. 1953- *St&PR 91*
Bondestam, Anna 1907- *DcScanL*
Bondevik, Kjell Magne *WhoWor 91*
Bondi, A.M. 1913- *St&PR 91*
Bondi, Bert Roger 1945- *WhoEmL 91*
Bondi, Enrico 1933- *WhoWor 91*
Bondi, Hermann 1919- *WhoWor 91*
Bondi, James Oliver 1949- *WhoSSW 91*
Bondi, Joseph Charles, Jr. 1936- *WhoAm 90, WhoSSW 91*
Bondi, Kathleen 1952- *WhoAmW 91*
Bondi, Nikki C. 1950- *WhoAmW 91*
Bondi, Richard John 1951- *WhoSSW 91*
Bondin, Ray Anthony 1956- *WhoWor 91*
Bondinell, Stephanie 1948- *WhoAmW 91, WhoEmL 91, WhoSSW 91, WhoWor 91*
Bondini, Caterina *PenDiMP*
Bondoc, Eduardo C 1956- *BiDrAPA 89*
Bondol, Jean de *PenDiDA 89*
Bondolf, Jean de *PenDiDA 89*
Bondroff, Ben F. 1942- *St&PR 91*
Bonds, Barry 1964- *Ballpl 90*
Bonds, Bobby 1946- *Ballpl 90 [port]*
Bonds, Frank Lanier 1930- *St&PR 91*
Bonds, Gary U. S. 1939- *EncPR&S 89*
Bonds, Jean Fulton *WhoAmW 91*
Bonds, John D. 1941- *St&PR 91*
Bonds, Margaret 1913-1972 *DrBlPA 90*
Bonds, Margaret Allison 1913-1972 *DcAfAmP*
Bonds, Parris Afton *BioIn 16*
Bonds, Suzanne M. 1950- *St&PR 91*
Bonds, Thyra Verle 1927- *WhoAmW 91*
Bonds, William Kenneth 1929- *WhoAm 90*
Bondurant, Byron Lee 1925- *WhoAm 90*
Bondurant, David William 1948- *WhoEmL 91*
Bondurant, Emmet Jopling, II 1937- *WhoAm 90*
Bondurant, Kathleen Alice 1958- *IntWWM 90*
Bondurant, Leo Horace 1935- *WhoSSW 91*
Bondurant, Stuart 1929- *WhoAm 90*
Bondurant, William W, III 1936- *BiDrAPA 89*
Bondus, Thom B. 1953- *St&PR 91*
Bondy, Eugene L., Jr. 1920- *St&PR 91*
Bondy, James D. 1933- *St&PR 91*
Bondy, Lee Allan 1925- *St&PR 91*
Bondy, Martin 1929- *St&PR 91*
Bondy, Neal Dennis 1942- *WhoSSW 91*
Bondy, Peter J. 1944- *St&PR 91*
Bondy, Philip Kramer 1917- *WhoAm 90*
Bondy, Robert Earl 1895-1990 *BioIn 16*
Bondy, Sebastian Salazar *HispWr 90*
Bone, B.C. 1928- *St&PR 91*
Bone, Brenda Kay 1960- *WhoWrEP 89*
Bone, Bruce Charles 1928- *WhoAm 90*
Bone, David Earl *BiDrAPA 89*
Bone, Diane Elizabeth Baker 1955- *WhoEmL 91*
Bone, Hugh Alvin, Jr. 1909- *WhoAm 90*
Bone, James R., Jr. 1942- *St&PR 91*
Bone, Janet Witmeyer 1930- *WhoAmW 91*
Bone, Jere Hepler 1934- *WhoSSW 91*
Bone, John *ODwPR 91*
Bone, Larry Earl 1932-1989 *BioIn 16*
Bone, Phyllis Mary 1896-1927 *BiDWomA*
Bone, Robert 1943- *WhoSSW 91*
Bone, Robin 1947- *IntWWM 90*
Bone, Roger Conley 1941- *WhoAm 90*
Bone, Stanley 1948- *BiDrAPA 89*
Bonebrake, Alan Ray 1954- *WhoWor 91*
Bonee, John Leon, III 1947- *WhoE 91*
Bonekeosh *DcCanB 12*
Bonell, Carlos 1949- *PenDiMP*
Bonell, Carlos Antonio 1949- *IntWWM 90*
Bonella, John J. 1934- *St&PR 91*
Bonelli, Norma Lee 1945- *WhoEmL 91*
Bonelli, Robert Allen 1950- *St&PR 91*
Bonenberger, Larry David 1936- *St&PR 91*
Boner, Donald Leslie 1944- *WhoWor 91*
Boner, Vera Winifred Breland 1928- *WhoSSW 91*
Boner, William H. 1945- *WhoSSW 91*
Bonerz, Peter 1938- *WhoAm 90*
Bonese, Kathryn F 1946- *BiDrAPA 89*
Bonesio, Woodrow Michael 1943- *WhoAm 90*
Bonestell, Chesley *BioIn 16*
Bonet, Frank Joseph 1937- *WhoAm 90*
Bonet, Jose 1955- *WhoWor 91*
Bonet, Lisa *BioIn 16*
Bonet, Lisa 1967- *DrBlPA 90, WorAlBi*
Bonet-Ayendez, Miguel A *BiDrAPA 89*
Bonete, Salvacion R *BiDrAPA 89*
Bonett, Emery *TwCCr&M 91*
Bonett, John *TwCCr&M 91*
Bonetti, Antoni Robert 1952- *IntWWM 90*
Bonetti, Gabriele Francesco 1961- *WhoWor 91*
Bonetti, Kay Jacqueline 1940- *WhoWrEP 89*
Bonetti, Mattia *BioIn 16*
Bonetto, Frank J. 1950- *St&PR 91*
Bonetto, Rodolfo 1929- *ConDes 90*
Bonevardi, Marcelo 1929- *WhoAmA 91*
Bonewits, P E I 1949- *EncO&P 3*
Boney, Alice *BioIn 16*
Boney, Sarah A. *ODwPR 91*
Boney, Sion A. 1923- *St&PR 91*
Boney, W.A. 1933- *St&PR 91*
Bonfante, Larissa *WhoAm 90, WhoE 91*
Bonfield, Arthur Earl 1936- *WhoAm 90*
Bonfield, Gordon Bradley 1926- *St&PR 91*
Bonfield, Gordon Bradley, Jr. 1926- *WhoAm 90*
Bonfield, William C 1947- *BiDrAPA 89*
Bonfiglio, Joel David 1958- *WhoEmL 91*
Bonfiglio, Michael 1917- *WhoAm 90*
Bonfiglio, Salvatore J. 1959- *WhoE 91*
Bonfils, Frederick Gilmer 1860-1933 *BioIn 16*
Bonfils, Helen Gertrude 1889-1972 *BioIn 16, NotWoAT*
Bonfoey, Robert D. 1924- *St&PR 91*
Bonforte, Richard James 1940- *WhoAm 90*
Bong, Keith 1961- *WhoE 91*
Bonga, George 1802?- *WhNaAH*

Bongard, Richard Harold 1949- *BiDrAPA 89*
Bongart, Sergei R *WhoAmA 91*
Bongartz, Roy *BioIn 16*
Bongartz, Walter 1946- *WhoWor 91*
Bongers, Piet Frans 1930- *WhoWor 91*
Bongiorni, Domenic Frank 1908- *WhoWor 91*
Bongiorno, Angelo 1923- *St&PR 91*
Bongiorno, Anthony Michael 1959- *WhoEmL 91*
Bongiorno, James William 1943- *WhoAm 90*
Bongiorno, John Anthony 1951- *WhoWor 91*
Bongiorno, John J. 1938- *St&PR 91*
Bongiorno, John Jacques 1938- *WhoAm 90*
Bongiorno, Joseph A *BiDrAPA 89*
Bongiorno, Joseph John, Jr. 1936- *WhoAm 90*
Bongiorno, Laurine Mack 1903-1988 *WhoAmA 91N*
Bongiorno, Margaret Rohde 1954- *WhoEmL 91*
Bongiorno, Sandra L. *WhoAmW 91, WhoWor 91*
Bongiovani, Maryanne Bozarth 1943- *WhoE 91*
Bongiovanni, Gerard Anthony 1926- *St&PR 91*
Bongiovanni, Michael 1920- *St&PR 91*
Bongiovi, Albert R. 1923- *St&PR 91*
Bongiovi, Mary Elizabeth 1959- *BiDrAPA 89*
Bongo, Albert-Bernard 1935- *WhoWor 91*
Bongo, Ali Ben *WhoWor 91*
Bongo, Martin 1940- *WhoWor 91*
Bonhag, Thomas Edward 1952- *WhoE 91, WhoEmL 91, WhoWor 91*
Bonham, Bill 1948- *Ballpl 90*
Bonham, Clifford Vernon 1921- *WhoAm 90*
Bonham, David *BioIn 16*
Bonham, Ernie 1913- *Ballpl 90*
Bonham, Frank *BioIn 16*
Bonham, Frank 1914- *AuBYP 90*
Bonham, Frank 1914-1989 *SmATA 62*
Bonham, Gaylor Matthew 1941- *WhoE 91*
Bonham, George Wolfgang 1924- *WhoAm 90, WhoWrEP 89*
Bonham, Gordon Clinton 1957- *WhoAm 90, WhoEmL 91*
Bonham, Henry Edward Eugene 1941- *BiDrAPA 89*
Bonham, James Paul 1940- *St&PR 91*
Bonham, John Stephen Henry 1936- *WhoAm 90*
Bonham, Robert G. 1918- *St&PR 91*
Bonham, Terrence James 1938- *WhoWor 91*
Bonham-Yeaman, Doria 1932- *WhoAmW 91, WhoSSW 91, WhoWor 91*
Bonheim, Frank Werner 1926- *St&PR 91*
Bonheur, Juliette 1830-1891 *BiDWomA*
Bonheur, Rosa 1822-1899 *BiDWomA, BioIn 16, IntDcAA 90, WorAlBi*
Bonhoeffer, Dietrich 1906-1945 *BioIn 16*
Bonhomme, Henri *PenDiDA 89*
Bonhomme, Leonard *PenDiDA 89*
Bonhorst, Carl William 1917- *WhoAm 90*
Bonhote, Elizabeth 1744-1818 *BioIn 16, FemiCLE*
Boni, John Anthony 1937- *WhoAm 90*
Boni, Margaret Bradford 1893?-1974 *AuBYP 90*
Boni, Miki 1938- *WhoAmW 91*
Boni, Robert Eugene 1928- *St&PR 91, WhoAm 90, WhoE 91, WhoWor 91*
Boni, William 1952- *ODwPR 91*
Bonica, John Joseph 1917- *WhoAm 90*
Bonich, Bob 1936- *St&PR 91*
Boniface VIII 1228?-1303 *EncO&P 3*
Boniface, Raymond Sesti *BiDrAPA 89*
Boniface, Thomas John 1944- *St&PR 91*
Bonifacio, Amelia Lapena *ConAu 130*
Bonifacio, Jose 1763-1838 *BioIn 16*
Bonifas, Barbara J. 1947- *WhoAmW 91*
Bonifazi, Stephen 1924- *WhoSSW 91*
Bonifield, John D. 1942- *St&PR 91*
Bonifield, William C. 1934- *WhoAm 90*
Bonilla, Bobby *BioIn 16*
Bonilla, Bobby 1963- *Ballpl 90, WhoHisp 91*
Bonilla, Frank *WhoHisp 91*
Bonilla, Gladys *WhoHisp 91*
Bonilla, Henry 1954- *WhoHisp 91*
Bonilla, Juan 1956- *Ballpl 90*
Bonilla, Julio 1957- *WhoHisp 91*
Bonilla, Manuel 1849-1913 *BioIn 16*
Bonilla, Mary Ann 1956- *WhoAmW 91*
Bonilla, Policarpo 1856-1926 *BioIn 16*
Bonilla, Ruben, Jr. *WhoHisp 91*
Bonilla, Shari Louise 1965- *WhoAmW 91*
Bonilla, Tony 1936- *WhoAm 90, WhoHisp 91*
Bonilla de Giroldi, Adela *BioIn 16*
Bonilla-Mathe, Salvador 1954- *WhoSSW 91*
Bonilla-Santiago, Gloria 1954- *WhoHisp 91*
Bonime, Walter R 1909- *BiDrAPA 89*
Bonime-Blanc, Andrea 1957- *WhoE 91, WhoEmL 91*
Bonin, Georges Robert 1930- *WhoWor 91*
Bonin, John Paul 1945- *WhoAm 90*
Bonin, Paul Joseph 1929- *WhoAm 90*
Bonina, Mary 1950- *WhoWrEP 89*
Bonine, Dan R. 1940- *St&PR 91*
Bonine, Joan Marlyn Griffen 1942- *WhoAmW 91*
Bonington, Chris *BioIn 16*
Bonington, Richard Parkes 1802-1828 *IntDcAA 90*
Bonini, Frank J. 1937- *St&PR 91*
Bonini, Victor 1934- *WhoAm 90*
Bonini, Victor L. 1934- *St&PR 91*
Bonini, Victor Louis 1958- *WhoWrEP 89*
Bonini, William Emory 1926- *WhoAm 90*
Bonino, Alfredo 1925-1981 *WhoAmA 91N*
Bonino, Fernanda 1927- *WhoAmA 91, WhoE 91*
Boninsegna, Celestina 1877-1947 *PenDiMP*
Boniol, Eddie Eugene 1931- *WhoSSW 91*
Bonior, David E. *BioIn 16*
Bonior, David Edward 1945- *WhoAm 90*
Bonis, Ferenc 1932- *IntWWM 90*
Bonis, Laszlo Joseph 1931- *WhoE 91*
Bonis Fast, Francine Dale 1951- *WhoAmW 91*
Bonisolli, Franco 1938- *IntWWM 90*
Bonistalli, Donald Raymond 1948- *St&PR 91*
Bonitati, Robert F. 1938- *ODwPR 91*
Bonitt, John E. 1948- *WhoE 91*
Bonjean, Charles Michael 1936- *WhoAm 90*
Bonk, David Thomas 1956- *WhoEmL 91*
Bonk, Sharon Catherine 1943- *WhoAmW 91*
Bonkoski, Kenneth John 1941- *St&PR 91*
Bonkoski, R.J. 1946- *St&PR 91*
Bonkovsky, Herbert Lloyd 1941- *WhoSSW 91*
Bonkowski, Ronald Lawrence 1938- *WhoAm 90*
Bonmartini, Francesco 1926- *St&PR 91*
Bonn, Ethel M *BiDrAPA 89*
Bonn, Ethel May 1925- *WhoAm 90*
Bonn, Jerrold Charles *BiDrAPA 89*
Bonn, Jerrold Charles 1937- *WhoE 91*
Bonn, Paul Douglas 1934- *St&PR 91*
Bonn, Paul Verne 1939- *WhoAm 90*
Bonnabel, David *BioIn 16*
Bonnaire, Sandrine *BioIn 16*
Bonnamour, Bernard 1940- *WhoWor 91*
Bonnar, Douglas Kershaw 1931- *WhoWor 91*
Bonnar, James King 1885-1961 *WhoAmA 91N*
Bonnar, James Millar, III *BiDrAPA 89*
Bonnard, Pierre 1867-1947 *BioIn 16, IntDcAA 90, WorAlBi*
Bonneau, Frederic Daniel 1962- *WhoEmL 91, WhoSSW 91*
Bonnechere, Francois Joseph 1937- *WhoWor 91*
Bonnefoy, Antonine *PenDiDA 89*
Bonnefoy, Yves 1923- *ConAu 33NR, MajTwCW*
Bonnefoy, Yves Jean 1923- *WhoWor 91*
Bonnell, Allen Thomas 1912- *WhoAm 90*
Bonnell, Barry 1953- *Ballpl 90*
Bonnell, Benjamin 1744-1828 *BioIn 16*
Bonnell, Dorothy 1914- *AuBYP 90*
Bonnell, Loretta Gail 1939- *WhoSSW 91*
Bonnell, R.E. 1930- *St&PR 91*
Bonnell, Victoria Eileen 1942- *WhoAmW 91*
Bonner, Alice *BioIn 16*
Bonner, Bernadette Mae 1963- *WhoAmW 91*
Bonner, Bester Davis 1938- *WhoAmW 91*
Bonner, Beverly Ann 1953- *WhoEmL 91*
Bonner, Boyd Lee 1925- *St&PR 91*
Bonner, Brigid Ann 1960- *WhoAmW 91*
Bonner, C.D. 1934- *St&PR 91*
Bonner, Carl Edward 1925- *BiDrAPA 89*
Bonner, Charles William, III 1928- *WhoAm 90*
Bonner, David C. 1946- *St&PR 91*
Bonner, David Calhoun 1946- *WhoAm 90*
Bonner, Edwin Joseph 1932- *St&PR 91*
Bonner, Elena *BioIn 16*
Bonner, Ernest Wayne 1942- *WhoSSW 91*
Bonner, Frances Jones *BiDrAPA 89*
Bonner, Francis Truesdale 1921- *WhoAm 90*
Bonner, Geraldine 1870-1930 *FemiCLE*
Bonner, Hypatia Bradlaugh 1858-1935 *BioIn 16*
Bonner, Jack *ConAu 31NR*
Bonner, Jack 1948- *ODwPR 91, WhoAm 90*
Bonner, Jack Wilbur, III 1940- *BiDrAPA 89, WhoAm 90, WhoSSW 91, WhoWor 91*
Bonner, Jocelyn Wolffe *BiDrAPA 89*
Bonner, John Arthur 1929- *WhoWor 91*
Bonner, John Tyler 1920- *WhoAm 90*
Bonner, Jonathan G *WhoAmA 91*
Bonner, Karl Heinz 1932- *WhoWor 91*
Bonner, Lewis E. 1944- *St&PR 91*
Bonner, Marita O. 1899-1971 *EarBlAP*
Bonner, Marita Odette 1898-1971 *HarlReB*
Bonner, Mary Graham 1890-1974 *AuBYP 90*
Bonner, Parker *TwCCr&M 91*
Bonner, Robert Cleve 1942- *WhoAm 90*
Bonner, Robert W. *St&PR 91*
Bonner, Robert William 1920- *WhoAm 90*
Bonner, Sherwood 1849-1883 *BioAmW, FemiCLE*
Bonner, Terry Nelsen *WhoWrEP 89*
Bonner, Thomas, Jr. 1942- *WhoWrEP 89*
Bonner, Thomas Neville 1923- *WhoAm 90*
Bonner, Thomas Perry 1958- *WhoEmL 91*
Bonner, Thomas R. 1838- *AmLegL*
Bonner, Walter Daniel, Jr. 1919- *WhoAm 90*
Bonner, Walter Joseph 1925- *WhoAm 90*
Bonner, William Neely, Jr. 1923- *WhoAm 90*
Bonner, William Russell 1942- *St&PR 91*
Bonner-Miller, Lila Morse 1899- *BiDrAPA 89*
Bonner Occomy, Marita Odette 1898-1971 *HarlReB*
Bonners, Susan 1947- *BioIn 16*
Bonnerup, Erik 1939- *WhoWor 91*
Bonnes, Charles Andrew 1941- *St&PR 91, WhoAm 90*
Bonnes, David Ralph 1930- *St&PR 91*
Bonness, Patrice Marie 1964- *WhoAmW 91*
Bonnet, Andre 1953- *WhoWor 91*
Bonnet, Beatriz Alicia 1959- *WhoAmW 91*
Bonnet, Felix A. 1955- *WhoHisp 91*
Bonnet, Georges 1889-1973 *BiDFrPL*
Bonnet, Juan Amedee 1939- *WhoAm 90*
Bonnet, Sixtine Caroline 1961- *WhoWor 91*
Bonnet, Stede *EncCRAm*
Bonnett, Kendra R. 1955- *WhoWrEP 89*
Bonnevault, Pierre *EncO&P 3*
Bonneville, Benjamin Louis Eulalie De 1796-1878 *WhNaAH*
Bonneville, Richard Briggs 1942- *St&PR 91, WhoAm 90*
Bonney, Barbara 1956- *IntWWM 90*
Bonney, Charles Stephen *BiDrAPA 89*
Bonney, Donald Ernest 1952- *WhoEmL 91*
Bonney, Hal James, Jr. 1929- *WhoAm 90*
Bonney, John Dennis 1930- *St&PR 91, WhoAm 90*
Bonney, Lores 1897- *BioIn 16*
Bonney, Samuel Robert 1943- *WhoAm 90*
Bonney, Therese 1895-1978 *WhoAmA 91N*
Bonney, Weston L. 1925- *St&PR 91*
Bonney, Weston Leonard 1925- *WhoAm 90*
Bonney, William H. *BioIn 16*
Bonney, William Lawless 1932- *WhoE 91*
Bonnie, Richard John 1936- *St&PR 91*
Bonnier, Albert 1907-1989 *BioIn 16*
Bonnier, Karl-Adam 1934- *WhoSSW 91*
Bonnier, Per Lukas Daniel 1922- *WhoWor 91*
Bonnin, Gertrude Simmons 1876-1938 *BioIn 16*
Bonnin, Gouse *PenDiDA 89*
Bonnington, Donald John *BiDrAPA 89*
Bonnivier, B. William *WhoSSW 91*
Bonniwell, George Barton 1939- *St&PR 91*
Bonniwell, Katherine *BioIn 16, WhoAm 90, WhoAmW 91*
Bonny, Oscar E. *BioIn 16*
Bonnycastle, Lawrence Christopher 1907- *WhoAm 90*
Bonnycastle, Murray C *WhoAmA 91N*
Bonnyman, George Gordon 1919- *WhoAm 90, WhoSSW 91*
Bono *BioIn 16*
Bono 1960- *WorAlBi*
Bono, Anthony Salvatore Emanuel, II 1946- *WhoEmL 91*
Bono, B. Charles, III 1948- *St&PR 91*
Bono, Chastity *BioIn 16*
Bono, Philip 1921- *WhoAm 90*
Bono, Sonny *BioIn 16*
Bono, Sonny 1935- *WorAlBi*
Bono, Sonny Salvatore 1935- *WhoAm 90*
Bono, Vincent H, Jr. *BiDrAPA 89*
Bonoma, T.V. 1946- *ConAu 33NR*
Bonomelli, Charles James 1948- *WhoWrEP 89*
Bonomi, John Gurnee 1923- *WhoAm 90*
Bonomini, Louis Peter 1929- *St&PR 91*
Bonomo, Joseph Ralph 1951- *WhoE 91, WhoEmL 91*
Bonomo, Marne Louise 1947- *WhoEmL 91*
Bonosaro, Carol Alessandra 1940- *WhoAm 90*
Bonovitz, Jay Stuart 1943- *BiDrAPA 89, WhoE 91*
Bonow, Raysa Rose 1930- *WhoAmW 91*
Bonquet, Carole *BioIn 16*
Bonsal, David F. 1939- *St&PR 91*
Bonsal, Philip Wilson 1903- *BioIn 16*
Bonsal, Richard I. 1920- *St&PR 91*
Bonsal, Richard Irving 1920- *WhoAm 90*
Bonsall, Edward H., III 1930- *St&PR 91*
Bonsall, Eric Keith 1959- *BiDrAPA 89*
Bonsanti, Giorgio 1944- *WhoWor 91*
Bonsel, Adriaan 1918- *IntWWM 90*
Bonser, Sidney H. 1924- *St&PR 91, WhoAm 90*
Bonsib, Richard E. 1931- *St&PR 91*
Bonsiepe, Gui 1934- *ConDes 90*
Bonsignore, Joseph John 1920- *WhoAm 90, WhoE 91*
Bonsignore, Michael Robert 1941- *WhoAm 90*
Bonsky, Jack Alan 1938- *WhoAm 90*
Bonsor, Brian 1926- *IntWWM 90*
Bonstead, Douglas Lyal 1947- *WhoEmL 91*
Bonstedt, Theodor 1924- *BiDrAPA 89*
Bonstein, Robert Glenn, Jr. 1953- *WhoSSW 91*
Bonstelle, Jessie 1871?-1932 *NotWoAT*
Bonstelle, Jessie 1872-1932 *BioIn 16*
Bonta, Diana Marie 1950- *WhoHisp 91*
Bonta, Ray Withers 1913- *WhoSSW 91*
Bonte, Frederick James 1922- *WhoAm 90*
Bontebal, Henk *ConAu 131*
Bontecou, Lee 1931- *BiDWomA*
Bontempo, Ann *ODwPR 91*
Bontempo, Blaine Allen 1947- *St&PR 91*
Bontempo, Salvatore A. 1909-1989 *BioIn 16*
Bontemps, Arna 1902-1973 *EarBlAP, MajTwCW*
Bontemps, Arna Wendell 1902-1973 *AuBYP 90, BioIn 16*
Bontemps, Georges 1799-1884 *PenDiDA 89*
Bontez, Maria 1933- *WhoAmW 91*
Bonting, Sjoerd Lieuwe 1924- *WhoAm 90*
Bontos, George Emmanuel 1924- *WhoSSW 91*
Bontoyan, Warren Roberts 1932- *WhoAm 90*
Bonura, Joseph 1931- *St&PR 91*
Bonura, Luke Joseph 1947- *WhoSSW 91*
Bonura, Zeke 1908-1987 *Ballpl 90*
Bonus, Robert Harold 1927- *St&PR 91*
Bonventre, Joseph Vincent 1949- *WhoAm 90, WhoE 91, WhoWor 91*
Bonventre, Vincent Martin 1948- *WhoE 91, WhoEmL 91*
Bonvillian, William Boone 1947- *WhoAm 90, WhoEmL 91*
Bonwell, Miner Welsh 1925- *St&PR 91*
Bonwick, Roy Edwin 1929- *WhoE 91*
Bony, Jean-Francois 1754-1825 *PenDiDA 89*
Bony, Jean Victor 1908- *WhoAmA 91*
Bonyhadi, Ernest 1924- *WhoAm 90*
Bonynge, Jeanne Redfield 1925- *WhoAmW 91*
Bonynge, Richard 1930- *IntWWM 90, PenDiMP, WhoAm 90, WhoWor 91*
Bonz, Bernhard 1932- *WhoWor 91*
Bonzagni, Vincent Francis 1952- *WhoSSW 91*
Bonzani, Peter Lawrence 1945- *St&PR 91*
Bonzanigo, Giuseppe Maria 1745-1820 *PenDiDA 89*
Bonzon, Paul-Jacques 1908-1978 *AuBYP 90*
Boo, Ben 1925- *WhoAm 90*
Boobyer, Don J. 1953- *WhoEmL 91*
Boochever, Robert 1917- *WhoAm 90*
Boock, H. Frank 1942- *St&PR 91*
Boocks Neff, Nancy Louise 1952- *WhoEmL 91*
Boocock, Sarane Spence 1935- *WhoAm 90*
Boocock, Stephen William 1948- *WhoEmL 91*
Boodey, Cecil Webster, Jr. 1931- *WhoAm 90*
Boodman, David M. 1923- *St&PR 91*
Boodman, David Morris 1923- *WhoAm 90*
Boodman, H Citron 1927- *WhoAmA 91*
Boodoosingh, Lal Andrew *BiDrAPA 89*
Boodoosingh, Vishnu 1952- *WhoWor 91*
Boody, Irving R., Jr. 1917- *St&PR 91*
Boog, Janet M *BiDrAPA 89*
Boogaarts, Jan 1934- *IntWWM 90*
Boogar, William F 1893-1958 *WhoAmA 91N*
Booh Booh, Jacques Roger *WhoWor 91*
Booher, Alice Ann 1941- *WhoAmW 91, WhoSSW 91*
Booher, Edward E. 1911- *WhoAm 90*
Booher, Edward E. 1911-1990 *NewYTBS 90*
Booher, Jacob Orial 1937- *WhoAm 90*
Booher, John P. 1946- *St&PR 91*

Book, Edward R. 1931- *WhoAm 90*
Book, Howard Earl 1941- *BiDrAPA 89*
Book, Jan Arvid 1915- *WhoWor 91*
Book, Jeffrey Scott 1959- *WhoSSW 91*
Book, John Kenneth 1950- *WhoEmL 91, WhoSSW 91, WhoWor 91*
Book, Jonathan D 1949- *BiDrAPA 89*
Book, Kenneth Merten 1938- *St&PR 91*
Book, Kim Fredrik 1940- *WhoWor 91*
Book, Martin Joel 1949- *BiDrAPA 89*
Book, Samuel Howard 1940- *WhoE 91*
Book, Stephen Mark 1954- *WhoSSW 91*
Bookataub, S. Joseph 1948- *St&PR 91*
Bookatz, Samuel 1910- *WhoAm 90, WhoAmA 91*
Bookbinder, Hyman Harry 1916- *WhoAm 90*
Bookbinder, Jack 1911- *WhoAmA 91*
Bookbinder, Jack 1911-1990 *WhoAm 90*
Bookchin, Murray 1921- *EncAL*
Booker T. & Priscilla *EncPR&S 89*
Booker T & the M.G.s *EncPR&S 89*
Booker T and the MGs *OxCPMus*
Booker, Betty Mae 1948- *WhoAmW 91*
Booker, Beverly Beville 1954- *WhoAmW 91*
Booker, Bodley, Jr. 1918- *St&PR 91*
Booker, Deidre Elizabeth 1965- *WhoAmW 91*
Booker, Donald Brandon 1942- *WhoSSW 91, WhoWor 91*
Booker, Greg 1960- *Ballpl 90*
Booker, James Gary 1953- *BiDrAPA 89*
Booker, John Franklin 1934- *WhoAm 90*
Booker, John William 1942- *St&PR 91*
Booker, Larry Frank 1950- *WhoEmL 91*
Booker, Lewis Thomas 1929- *WhoAm 90*
Booker, Nana Laurel 1946- *WhoAmW 91, WhoEmL 91*
Booker, Stephen B. 1957- *St&PR 91*
Bookhalter, Sophie *WhoE 91*
Bookhalter, Sophie 1910- *BiDrAPA 89*
Bookhammer, Eugene Donald 1918- *WhoAm 90*
Bookhammer, Robert Smith *BiDrAPA 89*
Bookhardt, Fred Barringer, Jr. 1934- *WhoAm 90, WhoE 91, WhoWor 91*
Bookholane, Feziwe 1928- *BioIn 16*
Bookman, Dale George 1921- *St&PR 91*
Bookman, George B. 1914- *WhoAm 90*
Bookman, John Jacob 1911-1988 *BioIn 16*
Bookman, Richard Charles 1944- *St&PR 91*
Bookman, Ron *BioIn 16*
Bookman, Steven 1952- *WhoE 91*
Booko, Chrystal *BioIn 16*
Bookout, John F., Jr. *BioIn 16*
Bookout, John Frank, Jr. 1922- *WhoAm 90, WhoWor 91*
Bookout, John Garber 1935- *St&PR 91*
Bookspan, Martin 1926- *IntWWM 90*
Bookspan, Michael Lloyd 1929- *WhoAm 90*
Bookspan, Saul Carl *BiDrAPA 89*
Bookstaver, Alexander 1911-1989 *BioIn 16*
Bookstein, Mel *BioIn 16*
Bookwalter, Richard Leroy 1942- *St&PR 91*
Bookwalter, Ronald Charles 1950- *WhoE 91*
Boole, George 1815-1864 *BioIn 16, WorAlBi*
Boolell, Satcam 1920- *WhoWor 91*
Boolos, George Stephen 1940- *WhoAm 90*
Boom, Glenn Leonard 1926- *St&PR 91*
Boomershine, Donald Eugene 1931- *WhoAm 90*
Boomgaarden, Donald Roy 1954- *IntWWM 90*
Boomtown Rats *EncPR&S 89*
Boon, Emilie *AuBYP 90*
Boon, Emilie 1958- *ConAu 131*
Boon, Franklin F L 1947- *BiDrAPA 89*
Boon, Paul Albert 1960- *WhoWor 91*
Boon, Richard John 1961- *WhoE 91*
Boondiskulchok, Rein 1952- *WhoWor 91*
Boone, Alan Lee 1945- *St&PR 91*
Boone, Andrew Justus 1953- *WhoSSW 91*
Boone, Ann Harrell *BioIn 16*
Boone, Ashley A., Jr. 1939?- *DrBlPA 90*
Boone, Banton G. 1838- *AmLegL*
Boone, Bob *BioIn 16*
Boone, Bob 1947- *Ballpl 90 [port]*
Boone, Byron V. 1908-1988 *BioIn 16*
Boone, Celia Trimble 1953- *WhoEmL 91*
Boone, Charles 1939- *IntWWM 90*
Boone, Charles S. 1953- *St&PR 91*
Boone, Charles Wyatt 1922- *St&PR 91*
Boone, Clara Lyle 1927- *IntWWM 90*
Boone, Daniel 1734-1820 *BioIn 16, EncCRAm [port], WhNaAH*
Boone, David 1871-1925 *BioIn 16*
Boone, David Earle 1933- *WhoE 91*
Boone, David Edwin 1946- *St&PR 91*
Boone, David Ridgway 1952- *WhoEmL 91*
Boone, Deborah Ann 1956- *WhoAm 90, WhoAmW 91*
Boone, Debra George 1958- *WhoAmW 91*
Boone, Diane Brown 1953- *WhoSSW 91*
Boone, Dorothy Mae 1919- *WhoAmW 91*
Boone, Douglas Larry 1945- *WhoSSW 91*
Boone, Edgar John 1930- *WhoAm 90*
Boone, Eugene Lawrence 1937- *WhoSSW 91*
Boone, Frances LaVonne 1929- *WhoAmW 91*
Boone, Franklin Delanor Roosevelt, Sr. 1942- *WhoAm 90, WhoSSW 91*
Boone, Gary W. 1947- *St&PR 91*
Boone, Gene 1962- *ConAu 33NR*
Boone, George Clark, Jr. 1934- *WhoAm 90*
Boone, Gray Davis 1938- *WhoAm 90*
Boone, Harold Thomas 1921- *WhoAm 90*
Boone, Hazel Robinson 1952- *WhoWor 91*
Boone, Howard E. 1940- *BioIn 16*
Boone, Ike 1897-1958 *Ballpl 90*
Boone, J. William 1952- *WhoEmL 91*
Boone, James Leroy, Jr. 1923- *WhoSSW 91*
Boone, James Virgil 1933- *WhoWor 91*
Boone, Janice Fowler 1945- *WhoAmW 91*
Boone, Jerry McDaniel 1942- *WhoAm 90*
Boone, Jerry Neal 1927- *WhoAm 90*
Boone, John A. 1923- *St&PR 91*
Boone, John Carter 1952- *WhoEmL 91*
Boone, John Clay 1947- *WhoEmL 91*
Boone, Joy Bale 1912- *LiHiK*
Boone, Kay Lanier 1941- *WhoAmW 91*
Boone, Kimberlie Ann 1960- *WhoAmW 91*
Boone, Lalia Phipps 1907- *WhoWrEP 89*
Boone, Larry *WhoNeCM [port]*
Boone, Laura Virginia 1956- *WhoSSW 91*
Boone, Lois Ann 1941- *St&PR 91*
Boone, Lois Ruth 1947- *WhoAmW 91*
Boone, Louis Eugene 1941- *WhoAm 90*
Boone, Luke 1890-1982 *Ballpl 90*
Boone, Marvin Lester, Sr. 1931- *WhoWor 91*
Boone, Mary *BioIn 16*
Boone, Mary 1951- *WhoAmA 91*
Boone, Mary Ann 1961- *WhoAmW 91*
Boone, Michael Mauldin 1941- *WhoAm 90*
Boone, Morell Douglas 1942- *WhoAm 90*
Boone, Oliver Kiel 1922- *WhoAm 90*
Boone, Pat 1934- *BioIn 16, OxCPMus, WorAlBi*
Boone, Ray 1923- *Ballpl 90*
Boone, Richard 1917-1981 *WorAlBi*
Boone, Richard Winston 1941- *WhoSSW 91*
Boone, Robert Edward 1933- *St&PR 91*
Boone, Sherman Gayloid 1955- *WhoE 91*
Boone, Steve *NewAgMG*
Boone, Susan Hobbs 1952- *St&PR 91*
Boone, Taylor Scott 1948- *WhoEmL 91*
Boone, Thomas Caleb 1957- *WhoEmL 91*
Boone, Walter S., Jr. 1926- *St&PR 91*
Boone, William 1938- *ODwPR 91*
Boone, William Roy 1938- *St&PR 91*
Boonin, Nicholas Philip 1950- *WhoE 91*
Boonshaft, Peter Loel 1958- *IntWWM 90*
Boonshaft-Lewis, Hope *BioIn 16*
Boonstra, Cornelis 1938- *WhoAm 90*
Boonstra, Earl Richard 1919- *WhoAm 90*
Boonstra, Mark Thomas 1957- *WhoEmL 91*
Boontje, Ab H. 1933- *WhoWor 91*
Boonyaprakob, Vanpen *BiDrAPA 89*
Boonyubol, Charuay 1935- *WhoWor 91*
Boor, Kenneth Steven 1945- *WhoEmL 91*
Boor, Myron Vernon 1942- *WhoWor 91*
Boorady, Roy *BiDrAPA 89*
Booraem, Hendrik 1886-1951 *WhoAmA 91N*
Booraem, Jonathan W. 1938- *St&PR 91*
Boord, Robert Lennis 1926- *WhoE 91*
Boorem, Mary Teresa 1955- *WhoAmW 91*
Booren, Jo Van Den 1935- *IntWWM 90*
Boorkman, Jo Anne 1947- *WhoAmW 91*
Boorman, Howard Lyon 1920- *WhoAm 90*
Boorman, John *BioIn 16*
Boorman, John 1933- *WhoAm 90*
Boorman, Margaret E. *BioIn 16*
Boorman, Philip Michael 1939- *WhoAm 90*
Boorman, Roy Slater 1936- *WhoAm 90*
Boorsch, Jean 1906- *WhoAm 90*
Boorstein, Laurence 1951- *WhoEmL 91*
Boorstein, Seymour 1932- *BiDrAPA 89*
Boorstin, Daniel J. 1914- *BioIn 16, WhoAm 90, WhoWor 91, WhoWrEP 89, WorAlBi*
Boorstin, James Ben 1934- *BiDrAPA 89*
Boos, Arthur Charles 1954- *WhoEmL 91*
Boosalis, Elsie 1913- *WhoWor 91*
Boosey, John A. 1929- *St&PR 91*
Boosey, John Arthur 1929- *WhoAm 90*
Boosler, Elayne 1952?- *BioIn 16*
Boostrom, William C. 1949- *WhoEmL 91*
Boot, Harry 1917-1983 *BioIn 16*
Boot, Henry Albert Howard 1917-1983 *DcNaB 1981*
Boote, Alfred Shepard 1929- *WhoE 91*
Boote, R. *PenDiDA 89*
Boote, T. *PenDiDA 89*
Booth, Agnes 1841?-1910 *NotWoAT*
Booth, Agnes 1846-1910 *BioIn 16*
Booth, Albert Edward, II 1942- *WhoE 91*
Booth, Andrew Donald 1918- *WhoAm 90*
Booth, Ballington 1859-1940 *WorAlBi*
Booth, Barbara Ribman 1928- *WhoAmW 91*
Booth, Beatrice Crosby 1938- *WhoAm 90*
Booth, Bill 1935- *WhoAmA 91*
Booth, Bonnie Nelson 1942- *WhoE 91, WhoWor 91*
Booth, Bramwell 1856-1929 *BioIn 16*
Booth, Brian Geddes 1936- *St&PR 91, WhoAm 90*
Booth, Cameron 1892-1980 *WhoAmA 91N*
Booth, Carole Mae 1946- *BiDrAPA 89*
Booth, Catherine Bramwell- 1883-1987 *BioIn 16*
Booth, Charles 1840-1916 *BioIn 16*
Booth, Charles Loomis, Jr. 1933- *St&PR 91, WhoAm 90*
Booth, David M. *St&PR 91*
Booth, Diane Elizabeth 1948- *WhoWrEP 89*
Booth, Dot *WhoAmA 91*
Booth, Douglas Wade 1924- *WhoAm 90, WhoSSW 91*
Booth, E.W. 1944- *St&PR 91*
Booth, Edgar Hirsch 1926- *WhoAm 90*
Booth, Edward *ConAu 132*
Booth, Edward Lee 1904- *St&PR 91*
Booth, Edwin 1833-1893 *BioIn 16, WorAlBi*
Booth, Enoch *PenDiDA 89*
Booth, Eva Selina Gore- 1870-1926 *BioIn 16*
Booth, Evangeline Cory 1865-1950 *WorAlBi*
Booth, Gary E. 1940- *St&PR 91*
Booth, Geoffrey Kemp 1947- *BiDrAPA 89*
Booth, Geoffrey Thornton 1928- *ConAu 132*
Booth, George 1926- *WhoAm 90*
Booth, George Geoffrey 1942- *WhoAm 90*
Booth, George Gough 1864-1949 *BioIn 16*
Booth, George Henry 1954- *St&PR 91*
Booth, George Warren 1917- *WhoAmA 91*
Booth, Gifford Marsden, Jr. 1913- *St&PR 91*
Booth, Glenna Greene 1928- *WhoAmW 91*
Booth, Gordon Dean, Jr. 1939- *WhoAm 90, WhoWor 91*
Booth, Gotthard 1899- *EncO&P 3*
Booth, Harold Waverly 1934- *WhoAm 90*
Booth, Heather Tobis 1945- *WhoAmW 91*
Booth, Helen Cornell 1949- *WhoSSW 91*
Booth, Henry 1838-1898 *AmLegL*
Booth, Hilda Earl Ferguson 1943- *WhoSSW 91*
Booth, Hillary Eugene 1945- *WhoSSW 91*
Booth, Israel MacAllister 1931- *WhoAm 90, WhoE 91*
Booth, J.K.B. 1922- *St&PR 91*
Booth, James Albert 1946- *WhoEmL 91*
Booth, James Rockne 1931- *St&PR 91*
Booth, Jane Schuele *WhoSSW 91*
Booth, John Andrew 1950- *BiDrAPA 89*
Booth, John Edwin 1927- *St&PR 91*
Booth, John Lord 1907- *WhoAm 90*
Booth, John Nicholls 1912- *WhoAm 90*
Booth, John Samuel, III 1944- *WhoSSW 91*
Booth, John T. 1929- *St&PR 91*
Booth, John Thomas 1929- *WhoAm 90*
Booth, John Wayne 1948- *WhoSSW 91*
Booth, John Wilkes 1838-1865 *BioIn 16, WorAlBi*
Booth, Laurence Ogden 1936- *WhoAm 90, WhoAmA 91*
Booth, Margaret 1946- *ODwPR 91*
Booth, Margaret Ann 1946- *WhoAmW 91, WhoEmL 91*
Booth, Martin 1936- *St&PR 91*
Booth, Martin B *BiDrAPA 89*
Booth, Mary *BiDEWW*
Booth, Mary Louise 1831-1889 *FemiCLE*
Booth, Maud B. 1865-1948 *BioAmW*
Booth, Mitchell B. 1927- *WhoAm 90*
Booth, Neil 1946- *St&PR 91*
Booth, Nina Mason 1884- *WhoAmA 91N*
Booth, Olive *BioIn 16*
Booth, Pat 1945?- *ConAu 130*
Booth, Patricia Vogt 1947- *WhoEmL 91*
Booth, Paul Henry Gore- 1909-1984 *DcNaB 1981*
Booth, Philip 1925- *WhoAm 90, WhoWrEP 89*
Booth, Philip 1942- *IntWWM 90*
Booth, Philip Alexander 1953- *IntWWM 90*
Booth, R.F. 1935- *St&PR 91*
Booth, Rachel Zonelle 1936- *WhoAm 90*
Booth, Ralph Harman 1873-1931 *BioIn 16*
Booth, Randolph Lee 1952- *WhoAm 90*
Booth, Richard Earl 1919- *WhoAm 90*
Booth, Robert Alan 1952- *WhoAmA 91, WhoE 91*
Booth, Robert Edmond 1917- *WhoAm 90*
Booth, Robert Harrison 1932- *WhoSSW 91*
Booth, Robert L. 1933- *St&PR 91*
Booth, Robert Paul 1952- *WhoEmL 91*
Booth, Robert V.D. 1908- *St&PR 91*
Booth, Rochelle Zide- 1938- *BioIn 16*
Booth, Roger George 1942- *WhoWor 91*
Booth, Shirley 1907- *BioIn 16, NotWoAT, WorAlBi*
Booth, Thomas M. 1931- *St&PR 91*
Booth, Tom *BioIn 16*
Booth, Tony Hood, Jr. 1948- *WhoEmL 91, WhoSSW 91*
Booth, Wallace Wray 1922- *St&PR 91*
Booth, Wayne C. *BioIn 16*
Booth, Wayne Clayson 1921- *WhoAm 90*
Booth, Webster 1902-1984 *OxCPMus*
Booth, William 1829-1912 *WorAlBi*
Booth, William Thomas 1920- *St&PR 91*
Booth, Windsor Peyton 1912-1989 *ConAu 130*
Booth Cabot, M 1942- *WhoAmA 91*
Booth-Jones, Christopher 1943- *IntWWM 90*
Boothby, Frances *BiDEWW, FemiCLE*
Boothby, Willard Sands, III 1946- *WhoEmL 91*
Boothby, William Munger 1918- *WhoAm 90*
Boothe, Clare 1903-1987 *BioIn 16*
Boothe, Dyas Power, Jr. 1910- *WhoAm 90*
Boothe, Fred D. 1948- *St&PR 91*
Boothe, Garland Cecil, Jr. 1932- *WhoE 91*
Boothe, Leon Estel 1938- *WhoAm 90, WhoSSW 91*
Boothe, Power 1945- *WhoAm 90, WhoAmA 91*
Boothe, Ray Walter 1947- *WhoSSW 91*
Boothe, Ursula Yvonne 1931- *WhoAmW 91*
Boothroyd, Basil 1910- *BioIn 16*
Boothroyd, Basil 1910-1988 *AnObit 1988*
Boothroyd, Geoffrey 1932- *WhoAm 90*
Boothroyd, Herbert J. 1928- *WhoAm 90*
Bootle, William Augustus 1902- *WhoAm 90*
Boots, John Ray 1940- *WhoSSW 91*
Boots, Sharon G. 1939- *WhoWrEP 89*
Boots, Sharon Gray 1939- *WhoAmW 91*
Bootsma, Kenneth B. *WhoAm 90*
Booty, John Everitt 1925- *WhoAm 90*
Bootz, Antoine H 1956- *WhoAmA 91*
Boova, Thomas F. 1949- *St&PR 91*
Booz, Gretchen Arlene 1933- *St&PR 91, WhoAmW 91*
Booze, Thomas Franklin 1955- *WhoEmL 91*
Boozer, Brenda 1948- *IntWWM 90*
Boozer, Howard Rai 1923- *WhoAm 90*
Boozer, John 1939- *Ballpl 90*
Boozer, Linda Shields 1944- *WhoAmW 91*
Boozer, Robert Charles 1930- *WhoAm 90, WhoSSW 91*
Boozer, Young J. 1948- *St&PR 91*
Booziotis, Bill Custas 1935- *WhoAm 90, WhoWor 91*
Bopp, Edward Sidney 1930- *WhoWor 91*
Bopp, Emery 1924- *WhoAmA 91*
Bopp, William C. 1943- *St&PR 91*
Boppe, Charles William 1948- *WhoE 91*
Boppe, Larry Eugene 1942- *St&PR 91*
Bopst, David Bruce 1937- *St&PR 91*
Boquet, Robert Wayne 1943- *St&PR 91*
Bor, Jonathan Steven 1953- *WhoAm 90*
Bora, Frank William, Jr. 1928- *WhoAm 90*
Boraczek, Walter M. 1941- *St&PR 91*
Borad, Martin B *BiDrAPA 89*
Borah, Brett A. 1950- *WhoEmL 91*
Borah, Frederic 1941- *St&PR 91*
Borah, William E. 1865-1940 *WorAlBi*
Borah, William Edgar 1865-1940 *BioIn 16*
Borai, Amr Mahmoud 1949- *WhoWor 91*
Borak, Robert Lawrence 1947- *St&PR 91*
Boral, Gora Chand *BiDrAPA 89*
Boran *WomWR*
Boran, Behice *BioIn 16*
Boranyak, Sharon Etzel 1951- *WhoAmW 91*
Boraqchin *WomWR*
Borash, Saul Hershel 1929- *BiDrAPA 89*
Boratyn, George Michael 1947- *St&PR 91*
Borax, Benjamin 1909- *WhoAmA 91*
Borax, Sigmund 1930- *St&PR 91*
Boraz, Robert Alan 1951- *WhoEmL 91, WhoWor 91*
Borbely, Antal Francis *BiDrAPA 89*
Borberg, Jytte 1917- *EncCoWW*
Borberg, Steen 1934- *WhoWor 91*
Borbon, Pedro 1946- *Ballpl 90*
Borbon y Dampierre, Alfonso de 1936-1989 *BioIn 16*
Borcea, Ciprian Sorin 1953- *WhoE 91*
Borch, Kurt Esben 1944- *WhoWor 91*
Borch, Otto Rose 1921- *WhoWor 91*
Borch, Richard Frederic 1941- *WhoAm 90*
Borchard, Franz 1943- *WhoWor 91*
Borchardt, Anne *WhoE 91*
Borchardt, Carrie Marie *BiDrAPA 89*
Borchardt, Frank A. 1935- *St&PR 91*

Borchardt, Frank Louis 1938- *WhoSSW 91*
Borchardt, Herbert H. 1906- *St&PR 91*
Borchardt, Paul Douglas 1942- *WhoSSW 91*
Borchardt, Robert L. 1938- *St&PR 91*
Borchardt, Ronald Evans 1935- *BiDrAPA 89*
Borchardt, Ronald T. 1944- *WhoAm 90*
Borchardt, Rudolf 1877-1945 *BioIn 16*
Borchelt, M.L. 1926- *St&PR 91*
Borchelt, Merle Lloyd 1926- *WhoAm 90, WhoSSW 91*
Borcherding, Breck Gerard *BiDrAPA 89*
Borchers, Elisabeth 1926- *EncCoWW*
Borchers, Jeremy James *BiDrAPA 89*
Borchers, Leon J. 1940- *St&PR 91*
Borchers, Orville William, Jr. 1946- *St&PR 91*
Borchers, Reba Jeanette 1939- *WhoAmW 91*
Borchers, Robert Reece 1936- *WhoAm 90*
Borchert, Donald Marvin 1934- *WhoAm 90*
Borchert, John R. 1919- *St&PR 91*
Borchert, John Robert 1918- *WhoAm 90*
Borchert, Manfred 1939- *WhoWor 91*
Borchetta, Michael Joseph 1965- *WhoE 91*
Borchman, Norman John 1923- *St&PR 91*
Borci, Joseph A. *St&PR 91*
Borciani, Piero *PenDiMP*
Borck, Chester E. 1913- *St&PR 91*
Borcoman, James 1926- *WhoAmA 91*
Borcoman, James Willmott 1926- *WhoAm 90*
Borcover, Alfred Seymour 1931- *WhoAm 90*
Borczon, Dennis Philip 1958- *BiDrAPA 89*
Borda, Daniel Jean 1932- *St&PR 91*
Borda, Deborah 1949- *WhoAm 90, WhoAmW 91*
Borda, Richard Joseph 1931- *WhoAm 90*
Bordaberry, Juan Maria 1928- *BioIn 16*
Bordacs, Krisztina 1956- *WhoAmW 91*
Bordador, Basilia Baluyot 1942- *BiDrAPA 89*
Bordagaray, Frenchy 1919- *Ballpl 90*
Bordallo, Madeleine Mary 1933- *WhoAm 90, WhoAmW 91*
Bordallo, Ricardo J. 1927-1990 *BioIn 16*
Bordas, Bonnie *BioIn 16*
Bordash, Vincent C. 1921- *WhoAm 90*
Borde, Emile *BiDrAPA 89*
Borde, Percival 1922-1979 *DrBlPA 90*
Bordeaux, Jean Luc 1937- *WhoAmA 91*
Bordeaux, Pierre William Harriston 1948- *WhoEmL 91, WhoSSW 91*
Bordeleau, Jean-Marc 1924- *BiDrAPA 89*
Bordeleau, Nancy Vivian 1934- *WhoAmW 91*
Bordelon, Cheryl Ann 1947- *WhoAmW 91*
Borden, Brenda Jane 1958- *WhoAmW 91*
Borden, Bruce F. 1951- *St&PR 91*
Borden, Charles A. 1912-1968 *AuBYP 90*
Borden, Craig Warren 1915- *WhoAm 90*
Borden, Doris Rita *BiDrAPA 89*
Borden, Edward Barry 1936- *WhoSSW 91*
Borden, Enid A. 1950- *WhoSSW 91*
Borden, Ernest Carleton 1939- *WhoAm 90*
Borden, Frank Kennon 1927- *St&PR 91*
Borden, Gail 1801-1874 *WorAlBi*
Borden, George Asa 1932- *WhoAm 90*
Borden, Harold Lothrop 1876-1900 *DcCanB 12*
Borden, James Howard 1928- *St&PR 91*
Borden, John Anthony 1933- *St&PR 91, WhoAm 90*
Borden, Kathleen Elizabeth Pedder 1955- *WhoAmW 91*
Borden, Lizzie *BioIn 16*
Borden, Lizzie 1860-1927 *WorAlBi*
Borden, Lizzie A. 1860-1927 *BioAmW*
Borden, Mary 1886-1968 *FemiCLE*
Borden, Nancy 1939- *WhoAmW 91*
Borden, Nicholas J *BiDrAPA 89*
Borden, Richard S. *ODwPR 91*
Borden, Sandra McClister 1946- *WhoAmW 91, WhoE 91, WhoWor 91*
Borden, Sarah *BioIn 16*
Borden, Sherrie Leann 1955- *WhoE 91*
Borden, Walter Arnold *BiDrAPA 89*
Borden, William 1887-1913 *BioIn 16*
Borden, William H. *BioIn 16*
Borden, William Vickers 1938- *WhoWrEP 89*
Bordenave, Mary Elizabeth 1957- *WhoEmL 91*
Bordenick, Stephanie Elaine 1962- *WhoE 91*
Border, James Robert 1956- *WhoEmL 91*
Borderieux, Carita 1874-1953 *EncO&P 3*
Borders, Charles E. 1925- *St&PR 91*
Borders, Daniel A *BiDrAPA 89*
Borders, Jack, Jr. 1949- *BiDrAPA 89*
Borders, John Gillespie 1946- *WhoEmL 91*
Borders, John Kenneth 1921- *St&PR 91*
Borders, Lana *BioIn 16*
Borders, Pat 1963- *Ballpl 90*
Borders, Philip Joseph *BiDrAPA 89*
Borders, Robert L. 1928- *St&PR 91*
Borders, William Alexander 1939- *WhoAm 90*
Borders, William Donald 1913- *WhoE 91*
Bordes, Adrienne 1935- *WhoAmA 91*
Bordes, Louis Rene 1926- *WhoWor 91*
Bordes, Pamella *BioIn 16*
Bordes, Peter Anthony 1927- *WhoAm 90*
Bordet, Jules-Jean-Baptiste-Vincent 1870-1961 *WorAlBi*
Bordett, Daniel Leonard 1923- *St&PR 91*
Bordett, Robert Daniel 1948- *WhoSSW 91*
Bordi, Rich 1959- *Ballpl 90*
Bordie, John George 1931- *WhoAm 90*
Bordiga, Benno 1920- *St&PR 91*
Bordiga, Jeffrey Scott 1952- *St&PR 91*
Bordin, Edward S. 1913- *WhoAm 90*
Bordin, Gelindo *BioIn 16, NewYTBS 90 [port]*
Bordini, Antonio Andrea 1945- *WhoWor 91*
Bordini, Ernest John 1957- *WhoSSW 91*
Bordner, Gregory Wilson 1959- *WhoEmL 91, WhoWor 91*
Bordnick, Barbara *BioIn 16*
Bordogna, Joseph 1933- *WhoAm 90, WhoWor 91*
Bordoni, Faustina 1700-1781 *PenDiMP*
Bordoni, Irene 1895-1953 *OxCPMus*
Bordow, Robert Alexander 1954- *WhoEmL 91*
Bordreau, Gregory G. 1948- *St&PR 91*
Borduas, Paul Emile *WhoAmA 91N*
Bordyn, James M. 1948- *St&PR 91*
Borecki, Kenneth Michael 1955- *WhoE 91, WhoEmL 91*
Borecky, Isidore 1911- *WhoAm 90*
Boreel, Wendela 1895-1974? *BiDWomA*
Boreham, Peter F. L. 1942- *WhoWor 91*
Boreham, Roland S. 1924- *St&PR 91*
Boreham, Roland Stanford, Jr. 1924- *WhoAm 90, WhoSSW 91*
Borei, Hans Georg 1914- *WhoE 91*
Borek, John Walter 1949- *WhoE 91*
Borel, Armand 1923- *WhoAm 90*
Borel, Georges Antoine 1936- *WhoWor 91*
Borel, Jacques 1925- *WhoWor 91*
Borel, James David 1951- *WhoWor 91*
Borel, Marie-Jeanne 1935- *WhoWor 91*
Borel, Rene C. 1948- *St&PR 91*
Borel, Richard Wilson 1943- *WhoE 91*
Borel, Terry Clayton 1953- *BiDrAPA 89*
Borel-Clerc, Charles 1879-1959 *OxCPMus*
Borell, Stephen J. 1923-1990 *BioIn 16*
Borelli, Carol Ann Kessler 1945- *WhoEmL 91*
Borelli, Francis Joseph 1935- *WhoAm 90*
Borelli, Frank J. 1935- *St&PR 91*
Borelli, Nelson 1930- *BiDrAPA 89*
Boreman, Mary 1631-1701 *BiDEWW*
Boreman, Zachariah 1738-1810 *PenDiDA 89*
Boren, Arthur Rodney 1916- *WhoAm 90*
Boren, Benjamin N. 1909- *WhoAm 90*
Boren, Charles Sidney 1943- *St&PR 91*
Boren, Charles W *BiDrAPA 89*
Boren, David L. *BioIn 16*
Boren, David Lyle 1941- *WhoAm 90, WhoSSW 91, WhoWor 91*
Boren, Hollis Grady 1923- *WhoAm 90*
Boren, Hugo 1943- *St&PR 91*
Boren, James Erwin 1921-1990 *WhoAmA 91N*
Boren, James Lewis, Jr. 1928- *St&PR 91*
Boren, Kenneth E. *St&PR 91*
Boren, Leland Emerson 1923- *St&PR 91*
Boren, Lynda Sue 1941- *WhoAmW 91*
Boren, Sidney 1943- *WhoAm 90*
Boren, Susan *BioIn 16*
Boren, Susan S. *WhoAmW 91*
Boren, William Meredith 1924- *St&PR 91, WhoAm 90, WhoSSW 91*
Boren-Tanis, Caryn 1953- *WhoEmL 91*
Borenstein, Abe Isaac 1957- *WhoAm 90*
Borenstein, Daniel B *BiDrAPA 89*
Borenstein, Emily Ruth 1923- *WhoWrEP 89*
Borenstein, Jeffrey A. *BiDrAPA 89*
Borenstein, Max 1920- *St&PR 91*
Borenstein, Milton Conrad 1914- *WhoAm 90, WhoE 91, WhoWor 91*
Borenstein, Morris V 1907- *BiDrAPA 89*
Borenstein, Nathaniel S. *BioIn 16*
Borenstein, Neal Marshall 1945- *BiDrAPA 89*
Borenstein, Walter 1927- *WhoE 91*
Borensztein, Eduardo Roberto 1954- *WhoE 91*
Borensztein, Liliana Letzen 1955- *BiDrAPA 89*
Borer, Edward Turner 1938- *St&PR 91, WhoE 91, WhoWor 91*
Borer, Jeffrey Stephen 1945- *WhoE 91*
Borer, Mark Steven 1954- *BiDrAPA 89, WhoE 91*
Boresi, Arthur Peter *WhoAm 90, WhoWrEP 89*
Boresi, Richard Leo 1951- *WhoEmL 91*
Boretz, Benjamin 1934- *IntWWM 90*
Boretz, Naomi *WhoAmA 91*
Borfiga, Jean Bernard 1945- *WhoWor 91*
Borg, Bjorn 1956- *BioIn 16, WhoAm 90, WhoWor 91, WorAlBi*
Borg, Charles W *EncABHB 4*
Borg, Dorothy 1902- *WhoAm 90*
Borg, Eugene Gerald, Jr. 1942- *St&PR 91*
Borg, Gavin *WhoWrEP 89*
Borg, George W *EncABHB 4*
Borg, Goran Lars 1913- *WhoWor 91*
Borg, Inga *AuBYP 90*
Borg, John *ODwPR 91*
Borg, Joseph Philip 1952- *WhoEmL 91*
Borg, Kim 1919- *IntWWM 90, PenDiMP, WhoWor 91*
Borg, Lisa *BiDrAPA 89*
Borg, Malcolm Austin 1938- *St&PR 91, WhoAm 90*
Borg, Sandra A. 1939- *St&PR 91*
Borg, Sidney Fred 1916- *WhoAm 90*
Borg, Stefan 1954- *WhoSSW 91*
Borg, Stefan Lennart 1945- *WhoWor 91*
Borg, Susan 1947- *ConAu 131*
Borg, Wayne M. 1923- *St&PR 91*
Borg Cardona, Andrew 1955- *WhoWor 91*
Borg-Evans, Michele Lee 1958- *WhoAmW 91*
Borgaonkar, Digamber Shankarrao 1932- *WhoE 91*
Borgardt, Steven Edward 1952- *St&PR 91*
Borgatta, Edgar F. 1924- *WhoAm 90*
Borgatta, Isabel Case 1922- *WhoAmA 91*
Borgatta, Robert Edward 1921- *WhoAmA 91*
Borgatti, Anthony A., Jr. 1916- *St&PR 91*
Borge, Carlos Alberto *BiDrAPA 89*
Borge, George Frank 1938- *BiDrAPA 89*
Borge, Joseph B. 1936- *St&PR 91*
Borge, Victor 1909- *BioIn 16, PenDiMP, WhoAm 90, WorAlBi*
Borgeaud, Pierre *WhoWor 91*
Borgelt, Burton Cook 1933- *St&PR 91*
Borgen, Bjorn K. 1937- *St&PR 91*
Borgen, Johan 1902-1979 *DcScanL*
Borgen, Ole Edvard 1925- *WhoWor 91*
Borgenicht, Grace 1915- *WhoAmA 91*
Borger, John Emory 1952- *WhoEmL 91*
Borger, Leslee *ODwPR 91*
Borger, Michael Hinton Ivers 1951- *WhoWor 91*
Borgerding, George N. 1928- *St&PR 91*
Borgers, Claas Eise 1945- *WhoWor 91*
Borges, Cindy Schultze *BioIn 16*
Borges, David Joseph 1955- *WhoEmL 91*
Borges, Francisco Lopes 1951- *WhoE 91*
Borges, Jacobo 1931- *ArtLatA, WhoWor 91*
Borges, Jorge Luis 1899- *WorAlBi*
Borges, Jorge Luis 1899-1986 *BioIn 16, ConAu 33NR, HispWr 90, MajTwCW, TwCCr&M 91B, WrPh*
Borges, Juan Roberto 1950- *WhoHisp 91*
Borges, Max E., Jr. 1942- *WhoHisp 91*
Borges, Peter Lopes 1958- *WhoE 91*
Borges, William, III 1948- *WhoEmL 91*
Borgese, Elisabeth Mann 1918- *WhoAm 90, WhoAmW 91*
Borgeson, Amy Louise 1953- *WhoAmW 91*
Borgeson, Donald Robert 1923- *St&PR 91*
Borgeson, Roger D. 1930- *WhoAm 90*
Borgeson, Wallace R. 1945- *St&PR 91*
Borget, Lloyd George 1913- *WhoAm 90*
Borghese, Livio M. 1938- *St&PR 91*
Borghi, Guido Rinaldo 1903-1971 *WhoAmA 91N*
Borghi, Peter T. 1950- *St&PR 91*
Borgia, Cesare 1475?-1507 *WorAlBi*
Borgia, John F. 1940- *WhoHisp 91*
Borgia, Lucrezia 1480-1519 *WorAlBi*
Borginis, Walter William, III 1955- *WhoEmL 91*
Borgioli, Dino 1891-1960 *PenDiMP*
Borgir, Tharald 1929- *IntWWM 90*
Borglum, Gutzon 1867-1941 *BioIn 16*
Borglum, Gutzon 1871-1941 *WorAlBi*
Borglum, James Lincoln De La Mothe 1912-1986 *WhoAmA 91N*
Borgman, Dean C. 1941- *St&PR 91*
Borgman, George Allan 1928- *WhoE 91*
Borgman, James Mark 1954- *WhoAm 90*
Borgman, Janet Jean 1962- *WhoEmL 91*
Borgmann, Glenn 1950- *Ballpl 90*
Borgnine, Ernest 1917- *WhoAm 90, WorAlBi*
Borgo, Ludovico 1930- *WhoAm 90*
Borgos, Denise Martha 1948- *WhoAmW 91*
Borgstahl, Kaylene Denise 1951- *WhoAmW 91*
Borgstedt, Agneta Dagmar 1931- *WhoAmW 91*
Borgstedt, Douglas 1911- *WhoAm 90*
Borgstedt, Harold Heinrich 1929- *WhoAm 90*
Borgstrom, Georg A 1912-1990 *ConAu 130*
Borgstrom, Georg Arne *NewYTBS 90*
Borgstrom, Georg Arne 1912-1990 *BioIn 16, WhoAm 90*
Borgwing, Lars Weiron 1953- *WhoE 91*
Borhani, Nemat O. 1926- *WhoAm 90*
Borhegyi, Suzanne Catherine Sims De 1926- *AuBYP 90*
Bori, Lucrezia 1887-1960 *BioIn 16, PenDiMP*
Boria, Teresa Maria *BiDrAPA 89*
Borich, Michael 1949- *WhoWrEP 89*
Borie, Adolph Edward 1809-1880 *BiDrUSE 89*
Borie, Bernard Simon, Jr. 1924- *WhoWor 91*
Borie, Deborah Anne 1949- *WhoE 91*
Boring, E. G. 1886-1968 *BioIn 16*
Boring, Edwin Garrigues 1886-1968 *BioIn 16*
Boring, John Wayne 1929- *WhoAm 90*
Boring, Marvin R. 1930- *St&PR 91*
Boring, Wayne 1916-1986 *EncACom*
Boriosi, Guido Domnick 1933- *BiDrAPA 89*
Boris III, Czar of Bulgaria 1894-1943 *BioIn 16*
Boris, Bessie *WhoAmA 91*
Boris, James R. *BioIn 16*
Boris, Robert Elliot 1947- *WhoWrEP 89*
Boris, Robert George 1940- *WhoE 91*
Boris, Ruthanna 1918- *WhoAm 90*
Boris, Walter R. 1921- *St&PR 91*
Boris, William O. 1939- *WhoAm 90*
Borish, Arnold Peter 1948- *WhoEmL 91*
Borish, Elaine *ConAu 132*
Boriskie, Helen Ann 1949- *WhoAmW 91*
Borison, Adam Bruce 1953- *WhoEmL 91*
Borison, Richard Lewis *BiDrAPA 89*
Borisy, Gary G. 1942- *WhoAm 90*
Borit, Judith *BiDrAPA 89*
Boritt, Gabor Szappanos 1940- *WhoAm 90, WhoE 91*
Borja, Isabel de 1498-1557 *EncCoWW*
Borja Cevallos, Rodrigo 1935- *BioIn 16, WhoWor 91*
Borjas, George Jesus 1950- *WhoAm 90, WhoEmL 91*
Borjon, Robert Patrick 1935- *WhoHisp 91*
Bork, Ferne *NewAgMG*
Bork, Mildred Ellen Marshall 1933- *WhoAmW 91*
Bork, Ned Lawrence, III 1955- *WhoEmL 91*
Bork, Robert H. 1927- *BioIn 16, ConAu 130, WorAlBi*
Bork, Robert Heron 1927- *WhoAm 90, WhoE 91*
Bork, Walter Albert 1927- *St&PR 91, WhoAm 90*
Borkan, Eugene L *BiDrAPA 89*
Borkan, Harold 1927- *WhoE 91*
Borkan, Lionel 1925- *St&PR 91*
Borkenstein, Donald M. 1936- *St&PR 91*
Borker, Wallace J. 1919- *St&PR 91*
Borkh, Inge 1917- *IntWWM 90, PenDiMP*
Borkhetaria, Rohit Madhavji 1950- *BiDrAPA 89*
Borko, Harold 1922- *WhoAm 90*
Borkosky, Bruce Glenn 1954- *WhoSSW 91*
Borkovitz, Henry S. 1935- *St&PR 91*
Borkowska, Anna *BioIn 16*
Borkowski, Bob 1926- *Ballpl 90*
Borkowski, Francis Thomas 1936- *WhoAm 90, WhoSSW 91*
Borkowski, John J. 1926- *St&PR 91*
Borkowski, Joseph 1938- *St&PR 91*
Borkowski, Marian 1934- *IntWWM 90*
Borkowski, Mary 1916- *MusmAFA*
Borland, Bruce Henninger 1929- *WhoWor 91*
Borland, Clifford R. 1937- *St&PR 91*
Borland, John Nelson 1929- *WhoAm 90*
Borland, Kathryn Kilby 1916- *WhoAm 90*
Borland, Kirk Robinson 1945- *St&PR 91*
Borland, Solon 1808-1864 *BioIn 16*
Borlaug, N. E. *BioIn 16*
Borlaug, Norman E. *BioIn 16*
Borlaug, Norman Ernest 1914- *WhoAm 90, WhoSSW 91, WhoWor 91*
Borle, Andre Bernard 1930- *WhoAm 90*
Borling, Peter Alexander, III 1949- *St&PR 91*
Borlongan, Ofelia Moralit *BiDrAPA 89*
Borm, Alfred Ervin 1937- *WhoSSW 91*
Borman, Arthur Charles, Jr. 1927- *St&PR 91*
Borman, C.A. 1952- *St&PR 91*
Borman, Carol Jean 1933- *WhoAmW 91*
Borman, David 1939- *BiDrAPA 89*
Borman, Earle Kirkpatrick, Jr. 1930- *St&PR 91, WhoE 91*
Borman, Frank 1928- *BioIn 16, St&PR 91, WhoAm 90, WhoWor 91, WorAlBi*
Borman, Lisa 1950- *ODwPR 91*
Borman, Lisa S. 1950- *WhoEmL 91*
Borman, Merle Douglas 1936- *St&PR 91*
Borman, Paul 1932- *St&PR 91*
Borman, Terry Reed 1949- *WhoE 91*
Bormann, Frederick Herbert 1922- *WhoAm 90*
Bormann, Martin 1900-1945 *BioIn 16*

Bormann, Ronald Murrie 1950- *WhoSSW 91*
Born, Adolf 1930- *BioIn 16*
Born, Allen 1933- *WhoAm 90, WhoE 91*
Born, Brooksley Elizabeth 1940- *WhoAm 90, WhoAmW 91*
Born, C. Allen 1933- *St&PR 91*
Born, David Pearson 1954- *WhoEmL 91*
Born, Emily Marie 1959- *WhoWrEP 89*
Born, Ethel Wolfe 1924- *WhoAmW 91*
Born, Gary Brian 1955- *WhoE 91, WhoEmL 91*
Born, Harold Joseph 1922- *WhoAm 90*
Born, Heidi von 1936- *DcScanL*
Born, James E 1934- *WhoAmA 91*
Born, Kathryn W. *St&PR 91*
Born, Richard L. *St&PR 91*
Born, Richard W. *St&PR 91*
Born, Samuel Roydon, II 1945- *WhoAm 90*
Born, Wolfgang 1893-1949 *WhoAmA 91N*
Born-Hansson, Adelheid von 1936- *EncCoWW*
Bornand, Ruth Chaloux 1901- *WhoAmW 91, WhoE 91*
Borne, Alan B. 1943- *St&PR 91*
Borne, Allen Helwick, Jr. 1959- *WhoEmL 91*
Borne, Dan S. *ODwPR 91*
Borne, Maureen *St&PR 91*
Borne, Mortimer 1902-1987 *WhoAmA 91N*
Borneman, Alice Gregory 1940- *WhoAmW 91*
Bornemann, Alfred Henry 1908- *WhoAm 90, WhoE 91*
Bornemann, David Richardson 1939- *WhoSSW 91*
Bornemisza, Hans Heinrich Thyssen- 1921- *BioIn 16*
Bornemisza, Tita Thyssen- *BioIn 16*
Borner, Irmgard D 1942- *BiDrAPA 89*
Borner, Klaus 1929- *WhoWor 91*
Bornet, Stephen Folwell 1947- *WhoAm 90, WhoE 91*
Bornet, Vaughn Davis 1917- *WhoAm 90*
Bornfriend, Lynn Alison 1960- *BiDrAPA 89*
Bornheimer, Allen Millard 1942- *WhoAm 90*
Bornhoeft, Jack Harry 1923- *St&PR 91*
Bornholdt, Laura Anna 1919- *WhoAm 90, WhoAmW 91*
Bornhorst, Joseph F. 1937- *St&PR 91*
Bornhorst, Michael Edward 1949- *WhoWor 91*
Bornhorst, Walter John 1941- *St&PR 91*
Bornmann, Carl Malcolm 1936- *WhoAm 90, WhoE 91, WhoWor 91*
Bornmann, John Albert, Jr. 1945- *WhoE 91*
Bornmann, Robert Clare 1931- *WhoSSW 91*
Bornor, Dora L. 1901- *St&PR 91*
Borns, Harold William, Jr. 1927- *WhoAm 90*
Bornscheuer, George Charles 1922- *WhoE 91*
Bornstein, Eli 1922- *WhoAm 90, WhoAmA 91*
Bornstein, George Jay 1941- *WhoAm 90*
Bornstein, Howard Russell 1955- *WhoEmL 91*
Bornstein, Irving David 1931- *BiDrAPA 89*
Bornstein, Jeffrey Victor 1950- *WhoEmL 91*
Bornstein, Joan 1946- *BiDrAPA 89*
Bornstein, Larry *BiDrAPA 89*
Bornstein, Laura Lee 1948- *WhoWor 91*
Bornstein, Lester Milton 1925- *WhoAm 90*
Bornstein, Linda Upham 1952- *WhoAmW 91*
Bornstein, Louis 1908- *St&PR 91*
Bornstein, Melvin 1933- *BiDrAPA 89*
Bornstein, Morris 1927- *WhoAm 90*
Bornstein, Myron Philip 1935- *BiDrAPA 89*
Bornstein, Paul 1934- *WhoAm 90*
Bornstein, Philipp E 1941- *BiDrAPA 89*
Bornstein, Robert Joseph 1937- *WhoE 91, WhoWor 91*
Bornstein, Robert Zucrow 1943- *St&PR 91*
Bornstein, Ruth 1927- *AuBYP 90*
Bornstein, Ruth Lercher 1927- *BioIn 16*
Bornstein, Sam 1913- *WhoAm 90*
Bornstein-Somoza, Miriam 1950- *HispWr 90*
Bornt, Dorothy Ellen 1961- *WhoAmW 91*
Borntraeger, Heather Houston 1966- *WhoSSW 91*
Borny, Walter Michael 1948- *WhoEmL 91, WhoWor 91*
Boroch, Anthony Walter 1937- *St&PR 91*
Borochoff, Charles Zachary 1921- *WhoWor 91*
Borochoff, Daniel *NewYTBS 90 [port]*
Borochoff, Ida Sloan 1922- *WhoWor 91*
Borochoff, Sloan *WhoAmA 91*
Borochov, Ber *EncAL*
Borochov, Ber 1881-1917 *BioIn 16*
Borod, Donald L. 1947- *St&PR 91*
Borodin Quartet *PenDiMP*
Borodin, Aleksandr 1833-1887 *WorAlBi*
Borodin, Aleksandr Porfir'evich 1833-1887 *BioIn 16*
Borodin, Alexander 1833-1887 *PenDiMP A*
Borodkin, Robert 1931- *BiDrAPA 89*
Boroff, Irving M. *BioIn 16*
Borofsky, Jon 1942- *WhoAmA 91*
Borok, Gerrie 1927- *WhoE 91*
Boronkay, Antal 1948- *IntWWM 90*
Boronow, John Joseph 1951- *BiDrAPA 89*
Borooah, Vani Kant 1947- *WhoWor 91*
Boros, Andrea Clare 1958- *WhoAmW 91*
Boros, Endre 1953- *WhoE 91*
Boros, Julius 1920- *WorAlBi*
Boros, Steve 1936- *Ballpl 90*
Borotra, Jean 1898- *BioIn 16*
Borovinsky, Jaime *BiDrAPA 89*
Borovoy, Roger Stuart 1935- *WhoAm 90*
Borovskii, Aleksandr Aleksandrovich 1887-1946 *BioIn 16*
Borow, Richard Henry 1935- *WhoAm 90*
Borowczyk, Walerian 1923- *BioIn 16*
Borowich, Abba Emanuel 1942- *BiDrAPA 89*
Borowiec, Stanley Paul 1955- *WhoE 91*
Borowitz, Albert 1930- *ConAu 32NR*
Borowitz, Albert Ira 1930- *WhoAm 90, WhoWrEP 89*
Borowitz, Gene Hanon 1929- *BiDrAPA 89*
Borowitz, Grace Burchman 1934- *WhoAm 90*
Borowitz, Joseph Leo 1932- *WhoAm 90*
Borowski, Gregory Allan 1947- *St&PR 91*
Borowski, Jennifer Lucile 1934- *WhoAmW 91*
Borowski, Norman Michael 1937- *St&PR 91*
Borowsky, Allen C. 1937- *St&PR 91*
Borowsky, Ben A. 1930- *WhoWrEP 89*
Borowsky, Philip 1946- *WhoAm 90, WhoWor 91*
Borowy, Hank 1916- *Ballpl 90*
Borowy, Richard 1960- *WhoEmL 91*
Borowy, Sandra Ann 1955- *WhoEmL 91*
Borque, Eliseo 1933- *WhoWor 91*
Borra, Pier C. 1940- *St&PR 91*
Borraccini, Janet Marie 1961- *WhoE 91*
Borras Carrera, Carlos Alberto 1952- *WhoWor 91*
Borrell, Anthony J. 1916- *St&PR 91*
Borrell, Anthony J., Jr. 1940- *St&PR 91*
Borrell, Gary Kent 1943- *BiDrAPA 89*
Borrell, Jerry 1952- *WhoEmL 91*
Borrell, Leo James *BiDrAPA 89*
Borrell, Paul Nicholas 1949- *WhoE 91, WhoEmL 91*
Borrelli, Alfred 1941- *WhoE 91*
Borrelli, Anthony Paul *BiDrAPA 89*
Borrelli, David J 1948- *BiDrAPA 89*
Borrelli, John Francis 1955- *WhoWor 91*
Borrelli, Joseph L. 1947- *St&PR 91*
Borrelli, Mario Alfredo 1922- *WhoWor 91*
Borrelli, Vincent Alphonse 1931- *St&PR 91*
Borren, Lars Per Gustaf Gideon 1928- *WhoWor 91*
Borrero, Andres 1958- *WhoWor 91*
Borrero, Guillermo 1940- *BiDrAPA 89*
Borrero, Victor 1950- *WhoSSW 91*
Borri, Josephe-Francois 1627-1695 *EncO&P 3*
Borriello, Edoardo 1940- *WhoWor 91*
Borris, Siegfried 1906- *IntWWM 90*
Borrmann, Werner A. 1939- *St&PR 91*
Borroff, Edith 1925- *IntWWM 90*
Borromeo, Federigo 1564-1631 *BioIn 16*
Borromini, Francesco 1599-1667 *WorAlBi*
Borror, Donald Alexander 1929- *St&PR 91*
Borror, Donald Joyce 1907-1988 *BioIn 16*
Borrow, George 1803-1881 *BioIn 16*
Borrowman, Merle L. 1920- *WhoAm 90*
Borrus, Bruce Joseph 1950- *WhoEmL 91*
Borrus, Jack 1928- *WhoE 91*
Borrus, Joseph C 1916- *BiDrAPA 89*
Borruso, Thomas C. 1944- *St&PR 91*
Borry, Carol Ann 1925- *WhoAmW 91*
Borsarello, Jacques *PenDiMP*
Borsari, George Robert, Jr. 1940- *WhoAm 90*
Borsch, Frederick Houk 1935- *WhoAm 90*
Borsch, Roman N 1932- *BiDrAPA 89*
Borschke, Bernard Gregory 1944- *St&PR 91*
Borshoff, Myra J. 1947- *ODwPR 91*
Borsick, Marlin Lester 1953- *WhoEmL 91*
Borski, Robert A. 1948- *WhoAm 90, WhoE 91*
Borsody, Benjamin Frank 1901-1988 *BioIn 16*
Borsody, Robert Peter 1937- *WhoAm 90*
Borson, Roo 1952- *FemiCLE*
Borson, Soo 1942- *BiDrAPA 89*
Borst, Donald Vincent 1936- *St&PR 91*
Borst, John, Jr. 1927- *St&PR 91, WhoAm 90*
Borst, Lyle Benjamin 1912- *WhoAm 90*
Borst, Martina 1957- *IntWWM 90*
Borst, Philip West 1928- *WhoAm 90*
Borst, Richard Allen 1941- *St&PR 91, WhoAm 90*
Borst, William Paul 1949- *WhoEmL 91*
Borst-Manning, Diane Gail 1937- *WhoAmW 91*
Borstein, Elena 1946- *WhoAmA 91*
Borstein, Michael Lawrence 1939- *St&PR 91*
Borstein, Yetta *WhoAmA 91N*
Borsting, Jack Raymond 1929- *WhoAm 90*
Borsuk, Karol 1905-1982 *DcScB S2*
Borsum, James Carl 1958- *WhoEmL 91*
Bort, Robert F 1936- *BiDrAPA 89*
Bortak, John J. 1947- *St&PR 91*
Borteck, Robert D. 1947- *WhoAm 90, WhoEmL 91*
Bortel, Robert William 1954- *WhoEmL 91*
Borten, Helen Jacobson 1930- *AuBYP 90*
Borten, William H. 1935- *WhoAm 90*
Borth, Frank *EncACom*
Borth, John Cleve 1935- *St&PR 91*
Borthwick, David Lumsden 1935- *St&PR 91*
Borthwick, J.M. 1936- *St&PR 91*
Borthwick, J S *TwCCr&M 91*
Borthwick, John David 1825-1900? *BioIn 16*
Bortin, Mortimer M. 1922- *WhoAm 90*
Bortis, William Francis, II 1946- *WhoEmL 91*
Bortkiewicz, Ladislaus von 1868-1931 *BioIn 16*
Bortman, David 1938- *WhoAm 90*
Bortman, Eli C. 1943- *St&PR 91*
Bortman, Ronald Arthur 1940- *BiDrAPA 89*
Bortner, Doyle McClean 1915- *WhoAm 90*
Bortner, Seymour R *BiDrAPA 89*
Bortner-Wandling, Deborah Ann 1949- *WhoAmW 91*
Bortnichak, Edward Arnold 1951- *WhoE 91*
Bortnichak, Paula Mcfadden *BiDrAPA 89*
Bortolan, Peter Roger 1937- *WhoE 91*
Bortolan, Rosa 1818-1892 *BiDWomA*
Bortolazzo, Julio Lawrence 1915- *WhoAm 90*
Bortoli, Mario 1927- *St&PR 91*
Bortoluzzi, Paolo 1938- *WhoWor 91*
Borton, Christopher Luke 1955- *St&PR 91*
Borton, E. H. *BioIn 16*
Borton, Elizabeth 1904- *BioIn 16*
Borton, George Robert 1922- *WhoWor 91*
Borton, Hugh 1903- *WhoAm 90*
Borton, John Carter, Jr. 1938- *WhoAm 90*
Borts, Robert Edward 1962- *WhoEmL 91*
Bortz, Paul Isaac 1937- *WhoAm 90*
Bortz, Phyllis E. 1926- *WhoAmW 91*
Bortz, Robert Henry 1949- *St&PR 91*
Boruch, Frank John *BiDrAPA 89*
Boruch, Marianne 1950- *WhoWrEP 89*
Boruchow, Lillibeth B 1937- *BiDrAPA 89*
Boruchow, Sheldon 1935- *BiDrAPA 89*
Borum, John R., Jr. *BioIn 16*
Borum, Olin Henry 1917- *WhoSSW 91*
Borum, Rodney Lee 1929- *WhoAm 90*
Borup, Eric Einar 1948- *St&PR 91*
Borup-Jorgensen, Jens Axel 1924- *IntWWM 90*
Borus, Jonathan F 1941- *BiDrAPA 89*
Borus, Jonathan Frederick 1941- *WhoE 91*
Boruszak, Melvin 1902- *St&PR 91*
Borut, Josephine 1942- *WhoAmW 91*
Borutta, William Earl 1938- *St&PR 91*
Borwein, David 1924- *WhoAm 90*
Borwick, Douglas Bruce 1952- *IntWWM 90*
Borwick, Leonard 1868-1925 *PenDiMP*
Borwick, Richard *ODwPR 91*
Borwick, Richard 1908- *WhoE 91*
Borwick, Susan Harden 1946- *IntWWM 90*
Borys, Theodor 1954- *WhoE 91*
Borysewicz, Mary Louise *WhoAmW 91, WhoWor 91*
Borzage, Frank 1895-1962 *WorAlBi*
Borzak, Donald 1932- *St&PR 91*
Borzillo, Michelle Marie 1956- *WhoEmL 91*
Borzutzky, Silvia 1946- *WhoHisp 91*
Bos, Carlo G *BiDrAPA 89*
Bos, Coenraad V 1875-1955 *PenDiMP*
Bos, Cornelis *PenDiDA 89*
Bos, Hiltjo Wiert Dirk 1943- *WhoWor 91*
Bos, Marilyn Whitney 1940- *WhoAmW 91*
Bos, Michael Yme 1944- *WhoWor 91*
Bos, Tamala J. E. *BiDrAPA 89*
Bos, Willem 1921- *WhoWor 91*
Bosa, Louis 1905-1981 *WhoAmA 91N*
Bosabalian, Luisa 1936- *IntWWM 90*
Bosan, Alonzo 1886-1959 *DrBlPA 90*
Bosanquet, N F G 1942- *ConAu 131*
Bosanquet, Nick *ConAu 131*
Bosanquet, Theodora 1880-1961 *FemiCLE*
Bosarge, Frederick Charles 1939- *WhoSSW 91*
Bosart, Eugene Halsey, III 1942- *St&PR 91*
Bosbach, Bruno 1932- *WhoWor 91*
Bosboom, Anthony J. 1923- *St&PR 91*
Bosboom-Toussaint, Anna Louisa G. 1812-1886 *EncCoWW*
Bosca, M.E. 1922- *St&PR 91*
Boscarino, Tom 1932- *WhoE 91*
Boscawen, Frances 1719-1805 *FemiCLE*
Bosch, Brian A. 1959- *WhoEmL 91*
Bosch, Clement A. 1938- *St&PR 91*
Bosch, Esias 1923- *BioIn 16*
Bosch, Gerald J. *St&PR 91*
Bosch, Guillermo L. 1949- *WhoHisp 91*
Bosch, Hieronymus *BioIn 16*
Bosch, Hieronymus 1450?-1516? *IntDcAA 90, WorAlBi*
Bosch, Jorge Jose 1925- *WhoAm 90*
Bosch, Jose Ignacio 1959- *WhoSSW 91*
Bosch, Juan 1909- *BioIn 16, HispWr 90*
Bosch, Marta Avalos *BiDrAPA 89*
Bosch, Miguel Angel *BiDrAPA 89*
Bosch, Robert H. 1937- *St&PR 91*
Bosch, Samuel Henry 1934- *WhoAm 90*
Boschan, Charlotte *BioIn 16, NewYTBS 90*
Boschen, Timothy Lee 1950- *WhoEmL 91*
Boschen, William O. 1921- *St&PR 91*
Boscher, Donald Harry 1932- *St&PR 91*
Boschi, Giuseppe 1675?-1743? *PenDiMP*
Boschi, Srdjan 1927- *WhoWor 91*
Boschma, Gerald A. 1938- *St&PR 91*
Boschma, William Joseph 1936- *St&PR 91*
Boschulte, Alfred F. *BioIn 16*
Boschulte, Joseph C *BiDrAPA 89*
Boschwitz, Rudy 1930- *WhoAm 90, WhoWor 91*
Boschy, Maurice 1921- *St&PR 91*
Boscia, Jon Andrew 1952- *St&PR 91*
Bosco, Anthony Gerard 1927- *WhoAm 90, WhoE 91*
Bosco, Anthony Joseph, Jr. 1957- *St&PR 91*
Bosco, Cassandra John 1957- *WhoE 91*
Bosco, Douglas H. 1946- *WhoAm 90*
Bosco, Henry A. 1922- *St&PR 91*
Bosco, Jay William 1951- *WhoEmL 91*
Bosco, John 1815-1888 *EncPaPR 91*
Bosco, Luigi Paolo 1929- *WhoWor 91*
Bosco, Philip Michael 1930- *WhoAm 90*
Bosco, Roseann 1950- *WhoE 91*
Boscoe, Claudia Frances 1948- *WhoE 91*
Boscole, Christopher *NewAgMG*
Bose, Ajay Kumar 1925- *WhoAm 90*
Bose, Amar Gopal 1929- *St&PR 91, WhoAm 90*
Bose, Animesh 1953- *WhoSSW 91*
Bose, Anjan 1946- *WhoEmL 91*
Bose, Hans-Jurgen Von 1953- *IntWWM 90*
Bose, Jagadis Chunder 1858-1937 *EncO&P 3*
Bose, Nirmal Kumar 1940- *WhoAm 90, WhoE 91*
Bose, Nripendra Kumar 1939- *WhoSSW 91*
Bose, Subhas Chandra 1897-1945 *BioIn 16*
Bose, Subir Kumar 1931- *WhoAm 90*
Bosel, Rainer 1944- *WhoWor 91*
Boselli, Giacomo 1744-1808 *PenDiDA 89*
Bosello, Domenico *PenDiDA 89*
Boseman, Glenn 1941- *WhoAm 90*
Bosenberg, Carola Elizabeth *BiDrAPA 89*
Boserup, Ester T. 1910- *WhoWor 91*
Bosetti, Guy C. *WhoAm 90*
Bosetti, Rick 1953- *Ballpl 90*
Bosh, Teddy George 1945- *St&PR 91*
Bosheck, Wilhelm Walther Ernst 1935- *WhoWor 91*
Boshell, Buris Raye 1926- *WhoAm 90*
Boshell, Edward Owen, Jr. 1935- *St&PR 91*
Bosher, William Cleveland, Jr. 1946- *WhoEmL 91*
Boshes, Louis D 1908- *BiDrAPA 89, WhoAm 90*
Boshes, Roger Arnold 1939- *BiDrAPA 89*
Boshier, Maureen Louise 1946- *WhoAmW 91*
Boshinski, Thomas Charles 1951- *WhoE 91*
Boshka, Wayne Phillip 1931- *St&PR 91*
Boshkoff, Douglass George 1930- *WhoAm 90*
Boshkov, Stefan Hristov 1918- *WhoAm 90*
Boshoven, Stephen John 1955- *St&PR 91*
Bosi, Robert A. 1955- *St&PR 91*
Bosiljevac, Joseph Edward 1951- *WhoEmL 91*
Bosin, Blackbear 1921-1980 *WhoAmA 91N*
Bosio, Chris 1963- *Ballpl 90*
Bosio, Lanfranco *PenDiDA 89*
Boskello, Dennis Jon 1953- *WhoE 91, WhoEmL 91*
Bosken, James Edward 1958- *St&PR 91*
Bosket, Willie, Jr. *BioIn 16*

Boskey, Bennett 1916- *WhoAm 90, WhoE 91*
Boskey, Howard M 1921- *BiDrAPA 89*
Boskin, Michael J. *BioIn 16*
Boskin, Michael Jay 1945- *WhoAm 90*
Boskind, Paul Arthur 1929- *WhoAm 90*
Boskovich, John 1956- *BioIn 16*
Boskovsky, Alfred 1913- *PenDiMP*
Boskovsky, Willi 1909- *IntWWM 90, PenDiMP*
Bosler, Charles Walter, Jr. 1949- *WhoEmL 91*
Bosley, John Scott 1943- *WhoAm 90*
Bosley, Karen Lee 1942- *WhoAmW 91*
Bosley, Thad 1956- *Ballpl 90*
Bosley, Tom 1927- *WorAlBi*
Boslow, Harold Meyer *BiDrAPA 89*
Bosmajian, Haig Aram 1928- *WhoAm 90*
Bosman, Dick 1944- *Ballpl 90*
Bosman, Paul *BioIn 16*
Bosman, Richard 1944- *WhoAmA 91*
Bosman, Robbert Jan 1955- *WhoWor 91*
Bosniak, Jacob 1887-1963 *BioIn 16*
Bosniak, Morton Arthur 1929- *WhoAm 90*
Bosomworth, Kenneth G. 1940- *St&PR 91*
Bosomworth, Mary 1700?-1763? *WhNaAH*
Bosomworth, Mary Musgrove *EncCRAm*
Bosomworth, Peter Palliser 1930- *WhoAm 90*
Bosone, Reva Beck 1898?- *BioAmW*
Bosonnet, Paul Graham 1932- *St&PR 91*
Bosque, Fernando De *EncCRAm*
Bosque, Jesus Manuel 1941- *WhoSSW 91*
Bosquet, Alain 1919- *WhoWor 91*
Bosquez, John 1943- *St&PR 91*
Bosquez, Juan Manuel 1941- *WhoHisp 91*
Boss Tweed 1823-1878 *BioIn 16*
Boss, Bradford R. 1933- *St&PR 91*
Boss, John E. *St&PR 91*
Boss, Kathleen Alice 1957- *WhoAmW 91*
Boss, Kenneth Jay 1935- *WhoAm 90*
Boss, Leonard John, Jr. 1948- *St&PR 91*
Boss, Medard 1903- *WhoWor 91*
Boss, Richard W. 1937- *WhoE 91*
Boss, Shelly Jeanne 1950- *WhoWrEP 89*
Bossano, Joseph John 1939- *WhoWor 91*
Bossard, Jean-Claude 1946- *WhoWor 91*
Bosschaert, Ambrosius 1573-1621 *IntDcAA 90*
Bosse, Abraham 1602-1676 *PenDiDA 89*
Bosse, Janet C *WhoAmA 91*
Bosse, Joseph Bernard 1950- *WhoEmL 91*
Bosse, Malcolm Joseph, Jr. 1926- *WhoAm 90*
Bosse, Peter Alan 1960- *WhoEmL 91*
Bosseau, Donald Lee 1936- *WhoAm 90*
Bosselman, Fred Paul 1934- *WhoAm 90*
Bossemeyer, William John, III 1950- *WhoE 91*
Bossen, David August 1927- *St&PR 91, WhoAm 90*
Bossen, Doris Stephens 1928- *ODwPR 91*
Bossen, Wendell John 1933- *WhoAm 90*
Bossert, Carol Jo 1956- *WhoAmW 91*
Bossert, Edythe H 1908- *WhoAmA 91*
Bossert, James P. 1953- *St&PR 91*
Bossert, Thomas John 1946- *WhoAm 90*
Bosses, Mark David 1962- *St&PR 91*
Bosshardt, Alexandra Hart 1960- *WhoEmL 91*
Bosshardt, Marcia Patricia 1960- *WhoWor 91*
Bossi *PenDiDA 89*
Bossi, Erma 1882?-1952 *BiDWomA*
Bossick, Richard Bruce 1954- *WhoSSW 91*
Bossidy, Lawrence Arthur 1935- *St&PR 91, WhoAm 90*
Bossier, Albert Louis, Jr. 1932- *St&PR 91, WhoAm 90*
Bossinger-Garwin, June Ann 1950- *WhoE 91*
Bossio, Salvatore 1928- *St&PR 91*
Bossman, David Manuel 1938- *WhoE 91*
Bossmeyer, Glenn D. 1949- *St&PR 91*
Bosson, Jack, Jr 1937- *WhoAmA 91*
Bossuyt, Edgard Alberic 1934- *WhoWor 91*
Bossy, Mike *BioIn 16*
Bossy, Mike 1957- *WorAlBi*
Bost, David Lee 1944- *St&PR 91*
Bost, Lloyd Cleveland 1920- *St&PR 91*
Bost, Paul Raymond, Jr. 1954- *WhoSSW 91*
Bost, Ralph Herman, Jr. 1954- *WhoSSW 91*
Bost, Raymond Morris 1925- *WhoAm 90*
Bost, Theda Kerby 1928- *WhoAmW 91*
Bost, Timothy R. 1947- *St&PR 91*
Bost, Tom F., Jr. 1916- *St&PR 91*
Bost, Walter L. 1927- *St&PR 91*
Bost, Wiley Eugene 1929- *St&PR 91*
Bostater, Joseph A. 1939- *St&PR 91*
Bostdorff, Richard Stanley 1942- *WhoSSW 91*
Bosted, Dorothy Stack 1953- *WhoAmW 91*
Bostek, Eva Maria 1961- *WhoAmW 91*
Bostelle, Thomas 1921- *WhoAmA 91*
Bostian, Carey Hoyt 1907- *WhoAm 90*
Bostian, David Boone, Jr. 1943- *St&PR 91, WhoWor 91*
Bostian, David William 1922- *BiDrAPA 89*
Bostian, Keith Allan 1951- *WhoAm 90*
Bostian, L Edgar 1923- *BiDrAPA 89*
Bostian, Nancy Lenora 1940- *St&PR 91*
Bostic, Earl 1913-1965 *DrBlPA 90, OxCPMus*
Bostic, Joe 1909- *DrBlPA 90*
Bostic, Joseph W. *BioIn 16*
Bostic, Mary Louise Price 1939- *WhoAmW 91*
Bostic, Stephanie Evon 1953- *WhoAmW 91*
Bostic, W. Wayne 1950- *WhoEmL 91*
Bostick, Charles Dent 1931- *WhoAm 90, WhoSSW 91*
Bostick, Robert Aaron 1941- *St&PR 91*
Bostick, William Allison 1913- *WhoAmA 91*
Bostleman, Richard Lee 1944- *WhoAm 90*
Bostock, Lyman 1950-1978 *Ballpl 90*
Bostock, Richard Matthew 1952- *WhoEmL 91*
Bostock, Roy Jackson 1940- *WhoAm 90, WhoE 91*
Boston *EncPR&S 89*
Boston Charley *WhNaAH*
Boston, Anne 1945- *ConAu 130*
Boston, Ben 1961- *WhoEmL 91*
Boston, Betty Lee 1935- *WhoSSW 91*
Boston, Billie 1939- *WhoSSW 91*
Boston, Bruce 1943- *WhoWrEP 89*
Boston, Bruce Ormand 1940- *WhoSSW 91*
Boston, Charles K. *TwCCr&M 91*
Boston, Charles Ray 1928- *WhoAm 90*
Boston, Daryl 1963- *Ballpl 90*
Boston, John A, Jr. 1924- *BiDrAPA 89*
Boston, John William 1933- *St&PR 91*
Boston, L. M. 1892-1990 *BioIn 16*
Boston, Leona 1914- *WhoAmW 91*
Boston, Lucy 1892-1990 *FemiCLE, NewYTBS 90*
Boston, Lucy Maria 1892- *AuBYP 90*
Boston, Lucy Maria 1892-1990 *BioIn 16, ConAu 131, SmATA 64*
Boston, Martha Bibee 1948- *WhoAmW 91, WhoE 91*
Boston, Raymond Jack 1927- *WhoWor 91*
Boston, Robert McCauley 1911- *WhoE 91, WhoWor 91*
Boston, W. Geoffrey 1949- *St&PR 91*
Boston, William Clayton 1934- *WhoWor 91*
Bostrom, John Andrew 1935- *BiDrAPA 89*
Bosttwick, Gerald 1924- *St&PR 91*
Bostwick, Barry *BioIn 16*
Bostwick, Barry 1945- *WhoAm 90*
Bostwick, Barry 1946- *WorAlBi*
Bostwick, Burdette Edwards 1908- *WhoWrEP 89*
Bostwick, Gerald J. 1942- *St&PR 91*
Bostwick, John Michael *BiDrAPA 89*
Bostwick, Randell A. 1922- *WhoAm 90*
Bostwick, Richard Raymond 1918- *WhoAm 90*
Bostwick, Sals 1902-1930 *EncACom*
Bostwick, Theresa Marie 1956- *WhoSSW 91*
Boswell Sisters, The *OxCPMus*
Boswell, Alfred Chester, Jr. 1947- *WhoE 91, WhoWor 91*
Boswell, Connee 1907-1976 *OxCPMus*
Boswell, Dave 1945- *Ballpl 90*
Boswell, Edwin Clair 1909- *St&PR 91*
Boswell, Gary Taggart 1937- *St&PR 91, WhoE 91*
Boswell, George Harvey 1947- *WhoEmL 91*
Boswell, George Marion, Jr. 1920- *WhoWor 91*
Boswell, Helvetia 1909-1988 *OxCPMus*
Boswell, James 1740-1795 *BioIn 16, DcLB 104 [port], WorAlBi*
Boswell, James Douglas 1942- *WhoAm 90*
Boswell, Janet L. 1948- *St&PR 91*
Boswell, Janette Pace 1929- *WhoSSW 91*
Boswell, Jeanetta 1922- *WhoWrEP 89*
Boswell, John I, Jr. *BiDrAPA 89*
Boswell, John Iverson, III 1955- *BiDrAPA 89*
Boswell, John J. 1947- *St&PR 91*
Boswell, John William 1935- *BiDrAPA 89*
Boswell, Ken 1946- *Ballpl 90*
Boswell, Linda Perot 1952- *BiDrAPA 89*
Boswell, Marion Lillard 1923- *WhoAm 90*
Boswell, Martha 1908-1958 *OxCPMus*
Boswell, Peyton, Jr 1904-1950 *WhoAmA 91N*
Boswell, Philip John 1949- *WhoAm 90*
Boswell, Rupert Dean, Jr. 1929- *WhoAm 90*
Boswell, Thomas Murray 1947- *WhoAm 90, WhoE 91*
Boswell, Thomas Wayne 1944- *WhoAm 90*
Boswell, Tom 1947- *Ballpl 90*
Boswell, Vet 1911-1988 *AnObit 1988*
Boswell, Wade Hampton *BiDrAPA 89*
Boswell, William P. 1946- *St&PR 91*
Boswell, William Paret 1946- *WhoEmL 91*
Boswell, Winthrop Palmer 1922- *WhoAmW 91, WhoWor 91*
Bosworth, Alfred 1812-1862 *AmLegL*
Bosworth, Brian *BioIn 16*
Bosworth, Bruce Leighton 1942- *WhoWor 91*
Bosworth, David 1947- *WhoWrEP 89*
Bosworth, Douglas LeRoy 1939- *WhoAm 90*
Bosworth, Frank *ConAu 31NR*
Bosworth, George Joseph, Jr. 1938- *St&PR 91*
Bosworth, J. Allan 1925- *AuBYP 90*
Bosworth, Jeffrey Willson 1948- *WhoEmL 91*
Bosworth, Mary Annsenetta 1950- *WhoAmW 91*
Bosworth, Michael Francis 1950- *WhoEmL 91*
Bosworth, Stephen Warren 1939- *WhoAm 90*
Bosworth, Thomas Lawrence 1930- *WhoAm 90*
Boszin, Andrew 1923- *WhoAmA 91*
Boszormenyi, Zoltan 1913- *BiDrAPA 89*
Boszormenyi-Nagy, Bela *NewYTBS 90*
Boszormenyi-Nagy, Bela 1912-1990 *BioIn 16*
Boszormenyi-Nagy, Ivan 1920- *BiDrAPA 89*
Bot, David Douglas *BiDrAPA 89*
Botana, Philip C. 1945- *St&PR 91*
Botein, Michael 1945- *WhoEmL 91*
Botek, Stephen T *BiDrAPA 89*
Botel, Max *St&PR 91*
Botella, Rita Ann 1951- *WhoHisp 91*
Botello, Angel 1913- *WhoAmA 91*
Botello, Angel 1913-1986 *WhoAmA 91N*
Botello, Fuensanta *BiDrAPA 89*
Botello, Timothy Eugene *BiDrAPA 89*
Boterf, Check 1934- *WhoAmA 91*
Boterf, Chester Arthur 1934- *WhoAm 90*
Botero, Fernando 1932- *ArtLatA, BioIn 16, ModArCr 1 [port], WhoAmA 91, WhoWor 91*
Botero, Gus 1954- *WhoSSW 91*
Botero, Samuel *BioIn 16*
Botero Restrepo, Oscar *WhoWor 91*
Botetourt, Norborne Berkeley, Baron De 1718?-1770 *EncCRAm*
Botez, Dan 1948- *WhoAm 90*
Both, Robert Allen 1952- *WhoEmL 91*
Both, Zoia 1956- *WhoWor 91*
Botha, C. John 1937- *St&PR 91*
Botha, Pieter W. *BioIn 16*
Botha, Pieter Willem 1916- *WhoWor 91*
Botha, Roelof Frederik 1932- *WhoWor 91*
Bothe, Brooke 1945- *St&PR 91*
Bothe, Davis Ross 1950- *WhoEmL 91*
Bothe, Walther 1891-1957 *WorAlBi*
Bothfeld, Edward Elms 1924- *St&PR 91*
Bothmann, Hans 1911-1946 *BioIn 16*
Bothmer, Bernard V. 1912- *WhoAm 90, WhoAmA 91*
Bothmer, Dietrich Felix von 1918- *WhoAm 90, WhoAmA 91*
Bothner-By, Aksel Arnold 1921- *WhoAm 90*
Bothun, Donald Dean 1947- *WhoEmL 91*
Bothwell, Chung Thi Nguyen 1949- *WhoAmW 91*
Bothwell, Dorr 1902- *WhoAm 90*
Bothwell, Jean *AuBYP 90*
Bothwell, John Charles 1926- *WhoAm 90*
Bothwell, Joseph C., Jr. 1923- *St&PR 91*
Bothwell, Joseph Conrad, Jr. 1923- *WhoAm 90*
Bothwell, Lawrence L. 1932- *WhoAm 90*
Bothwell, Linda Ann 1954- *WhoAmW 91, WhoEmL 91*
Botica, Luke F. 1950- *St&PR 91*
Botifoll, Luis J. 1908- *WhoSSW 91*
Botkin, Gregg A. 1960- *St&PR 91*
Botkin, Henry 1896-1983 *WhoAmA 91N*
Botkin, Monty Lane 1951- *WhoEmL 91, WhoSSW 91*
Botkin, Nancy Galley 1935- *WhoAmW 91*
Botkiss, Philip Henri 1959- *BiDrAPA 89*
Boto, Eza *MajTwCW*
Botsai, Elmer Eugene 1928- *WhoAm 90, WhoWor 91*
Botsch, Sharyn 1950- *WhoEmL 91*
Botsford, Amos Edwin 1804-1894 *DcCanB 12*
Botsford, Frank Terril *BioIn 16*
Botsford, George 1874-1949 *OxCPMus*
Botsford, Margaret *FemiCLE*
Botsford, Susi 1947- *WhoAmW 91*
Botshon, Ann 1942- *WhoWrEP 89*
Botstein, Leon 1946- *BioIn 16, WhoAm 90*
Bott, Andrew Charles *BiDrAPA 89*
Bott, Donald Herman 1932- *WhoE 91*
Bott, E. Joyce 1957- *WhoAmW 91*
Bott, Emily O'Neil 1922- *WhoAmW 91*
Bott, H J 1933- *WhoAmA 91*
Bott, Harold Sheldon 1933- *WhoAm 90, WhoWor 91*
Bott, John 1936- *WhoAmA 91*
Bott, Margaret Deats *WhoAmA 91*
Bott, Patricia Allen *WhoAmA 91*
Bott, Patricia Allen 1911- *WhoE 91*
Bott, Raoul 1923- *WhoAm 90*
Bott, Richard Harold 1947- *St&PR 91*
Bott, Robert P. 1924- *ODwPR 91*
Bott, Thomas 1829-1870 *PenDiDA 89*
Bott, Thomas John 1854-1932 *PenDiDA 89*
Botta, Anne 1815-1891 *FemiCLE*
Botta, Mario *BioIn 16*
Bottarelli, Carlo Emilio M. 1951- *WhoWor 91*
Bottari, George L. 1919- *WhoWrEP 89*
Bottazzi, Filippo *EncO&P 3*
Botte, Samuel F. 1950- *St&PR 91*
Bottel, Helen Alfea *WhoAm 90, WhoWrEP 89*
Bottelli, Richard 1937- *WhoAm 90, WhoE 91*
Bottelli, Richard Joseph, Jr. 1959- *WhoEmL 91*
Bottemiller, Donald Louis 1939- *St&PR 91*
Botten, Donald L. 1928- *WhoSSW 91*
Bottenberg, Joyce Harvey 1945- *WhoEmL 91*
Bottenberg, Wolfgang Heinz Otto 1930- *IntWWM 90*
Bottengruber, Ignaz *PenDiDA 89*
Botterbusch, Hope Roland 1950- *WhoEmL 91*
Bottero, Laura Ann 1961- *WhoAmW 91*
Bottero, Philippe Bernard 1940- *WhoWor 91*
Botteron, Kelly Nicole *BiDrAPA 89*
Bottesini, Giovanni 1821-1889 *PenDiMP A*
Bottge, Peggy Ann 1956- *WhoAmW 91*
Bottger, Johann Friedrich 1682-1719 *PenDiDA 89*
Bottger, Tracy Ann 1956- *WhoAmW 91*
Botti, Deborah *BiDrAPA 89*
Botticelli 1445-1510 *IntDcAA 90*
Botticelli, Allan Philip 1937- *WhoAm 90*
Botticelli, Denise Ellen 1951- *St&PR 91*
Botticelli, Sandro 1444?-1510 *BioIn 16*
Botticelli, Sandro 1445-1510 *WorAlBi*
Bottiglia, William Filbert 1912- *WhoAm 90*
Bottiglier, Janet Ellen 1952- *WhoWrEP 89*
Bottin, Rob *BioIn 16*
Bottini, David M 1945- *WhoAmA 91*
Bottini, Ernesto Enrique 1947- *WhoWor 91*
Bottino, Antonio *BiDrAPA 89*
Bottino, Carroll Ann 1938- *WhoE 91*
Bottis, Hugh P *WhoAmA 91N*
Bottlinger, Bruce Jay *BiDrAPA 89*
Bottlinger, Jane Louise *BiDrAPA 89*
Bottner, Barbara 1943- *AuBYP 90, BioIn 16*
Botto, Antony Alan 1938- *WhoE 91*
Botto, Philip F. 1931- *St&PR 91*
Bottom, Dale Coyle 1932- *WhoAm 90*
Bottome, Phyllis 1884-1963 *BioIn 16, FemiCLE*
Bottomley, Charles Gregory 1935- *WhoAm 90*
Bottomley, Colin 1933-1989 *BioIn 16*
Bottomley, Jim 1900-1959 *Ballpl 90 [port]*
Bottomley, Lois S. 1943- *St&PR 91*
Bottomley, Simon Charles 1959- *IntWWM 90*
Bottomore, Thomas Burton 1920- *WhoWor 91*
Bottoms, David 1949- *WhoWrEP 89*
Bottoms, Graham Neil 1954- *WhoWor 91*
Bottoms, Robert Garvin 1944- *WhoAm 90*
Bottoms, Timothy 1951- *WorAlBi*
Bottone, Anthony A *BiDrAPA 89*
Bottone, Bonaventura 1950- *IntWWM 90*
Bottoni, Robert J. 1923- *St&PR 91*
Bottorf, Richard Moser, Jr. 1934- *WhoAm 90*
Bottorff, Dennis C. 1944- *St&PR 91, WhoAm 90*
Bottorff, Michele Lynette Stanford 1952- *WhoAmW 91*
Bottrall, Ronald 1906-1989 *ConAu 129*
Bottrell, Ronald G. 1944- *ODwPR 91*
Bottros, Isis Wadie 1948- *BiDrAPA 89*
Botts, Ellen Alberta 1947- *WhoAmW 91*
Botts, Guy W. 1914- *St&PR 91*
Botts, Guy Warren 1914- *WhoAm 90*
Botts, Kenneth Charles 1926- *St&PR 91*
Bottum, C.E., Jr. 1927- *St&PR 91*
Botty, Kenneth John 1927- *St&PR 91, WhoAm 90, WhoE 91*
Botwin, Allison James *BiDrAPA 89*
Botwinick, Allen George 1943- *St&PR 91*
Botwinick, Edward 1935- *St&PR 91*
Botwinick, Michael *BioIn 16*
Botwinick, Michael 1943- *WhoAm 90, WhoAmA 91*
Botwinick, Moshe Lev 1953- *WhoE 91*
Botz, Wayne Ray 1957- *WhoEmL 91*

Botzow, William G.F. 1911- St&PR 91
Botzum, Thomas Joseph 1924- St&PR 91
Bou-Saada, Joseph Georges 1960- WhoE 91
Boubai, Wilfred Brass 1947- WhoWor 91
Boubelik, Henry F., Jr. 1936- St&PR 91
Boubelik, Henry Fredrick, Jr. 1936- WhoAm 90
Boucek, Robert J. 1936- St&PR 91
Bouchard, Antoine 1932- IntWWM 90
Bouchard, Arthur 1845-1896 DcCanB 12
Bouchard, Benoit BioIn 16
Bouchard, Benoit 1940- WhoE 91
Bouchard, Chislain 1941- St&PR 91
Bouchard, Jacques 1930- WhoAm 90
Bouchard, James 1823-1889 WhNaAH
Bouchard, James Chrysostom 1823-1889 BioIn 16
Bouchard, Jean Paul 1931- BiDrAPA 89
Bouchard, Leo-Paul BiDrAPA 89
Bouchard, Lois Kalb 1938- AuBYP 90
Bouchard, Lorne Holland 1913-1978 WhoAmA 91N
Bouchard, Lucien 1938- WhoAm 90, WhoE 91
Bouchard, Lynda M. 1956- WhoWrEP 89
Bouchard, Norman Roger 1948- St&PR 91
Bouchard, Paul E 1946- WhoAmA 91
Bouchard, Remi BioIn 16
Bouchard, Richard Joseph 1936- St&PR 91
Bouchard, Thomas Joseph, Jr. 1937- WhoAm 90
Bouchardeau, Huguette 1935- BiDFrPL
Bouchardon, Edme 1698-1762 IntDcAA 90
Bouche, Louis 1896-1969 WhoAmA 91N
Bouche, Rene WhoAmA 91N
Bouchee, Ed 1933- Ballpl 90
Boucher, Allen C. 1922- St&PR 91
Boucher, Anne Carey 1938- WhoAmW 91
Boucher, Anthony 1911-1968 RGTwCSF, TwCCr&M 91
Boucher, Catherine BiDrAPA 89
Boucher, Celeste Suzette 1956- WhoAmW 91
Boucher, Dorothy L. 1936- St&PR 91
Boucher, Francois 1703-1770 IntDcAA 90, PenDiDA 89, WorAlBi
Boucher, Gaetan BioIn 16
Boucher, Gene 1933- IntWWM 90
Boucher, Harold I. 1906- St&PR 91
Boucher, Henri BiDrAPA 89
Boucher, Henry Joseph 1947- WhoE 91
Boucher, Jonathan 1738-1804 EncCRAm
Boucher, Joseph Lee 1934- St&PR 91
Boucher, Joseph William 1951- WhoEmL 91
Boucher, Laurence James 1938- WhoSSW 91
Boucher, Louis Jack 1922- WhoAm 90
Boucher, Mildred Eileen 1928- WhoAmW 91
Boucher, Miriam Cherny 1954- WhoAmW 91
Boucher, Philip Poulin 1944- WhoSSW 91
Boucher, Rick 1946- WhoAm 90, WhoSSW 91
Boucher, Roberta Mary 1951- WhoAmW 91
Boucher, Roland A. 1945- St&PR 91
Boucher, Rosemarie 1940- WhoAmW 91
Boucher, Stephen G. 1946- St&PR 91
Boucher, Tania Kunsky 1927- WhoAmA 91
Boucher, Thomas W. 1955- St&PR 91
Boucher, Wayne Irving 1934- WhoAm 90
Boucher de Boucherville, Georges 1814-1894 DcLB 99 [port]
Boucher-Leif, Jeanne 1922- BiDrAPA 89
Boucherett, Jessie 1825-1905 FemiCLE
Boucheron, Andrea PenDiDA 89
Boucheron, Giambattista 1742-1815 PenDiDA 89
Boucherville, Georges De 1814-1894 DcCanB 12
Bouchet, Dominique Marie Clement 1949- WhoWor 91
Bouchez, Brent BioIn 16
Bouchez, Jean-Antoine Pierre 1937- WhoWor 91
Bouchie, L. Kirk 1958- St&PR 91
Bouchier, Ian Arthur 1932- WhoWor 91
Boucicault, Dion 1820-1890 BioIn 16
Bouck, Gabriel 1828-1904 AmLegL
Bouck, Noel Patrick 1936- WhoAmW 91
Bouckaert, Harm J G 1934- WhoAmA 91
Bouckley, Sandra Lynn 1959- WhoAmW 91
Boucolon, Maryse 1937- ConAu 30NR
Boucourechliev, Andre 1925- PenDiMP A
Boucouvalas, Marcie 1947- WhoAmW 91, WhoEmL 91
Boudakian, Max Minas 1925- WhoE 91
Boudart, Michel 1924- WhoAm 90
Boudart, Yves Henry 1948- WhoWor 91
Boudat, Marie-Louise 1909- EncCoWW
Boudens, Robrecht Maurits 1920- WhoWor 91
Boudewijns, Katharina 1520?-1603? EncCoWW
Boudewyn, Adri G. ODwPR 91
Boudicca BioIn 16
Boudicca 26?-60? WomWR [port]
Boudier-Bakker, Ina 1875-1966 EncCoWW
Boudin, Eugene 1824-1898 IntDcAA 90
Boudin, Katherine 1942- BioAmW
Boudin, Leonard 1735- PenDiDA 89
Boudin, Leonard 1912-1989 AnObit 1989
Boudin, Leonard B. 1912-1989 BioIn 16
Boudin, Louis B. 1874-1952 EncAL
Boudin, Michael 1939- WhoAm 90
Boudinot, Elias BioIn 16
Boudinot, Elias 1740-1821 BiDrUSE 89, BioIn 16, EncCRAm
Boudinot, Elias 1803?-1839 WhNaAH
Boudinot, Elias Cornelius 1835-1890 BioIn 16
Boudon, Raymond 1934- ConAu 30NR
Boudoulas, Harisios 1935- WhoAm 90
Boudreau, A. Allan 1936- WhoE 91
Boudreau, Aileen T. St&PR 91
Boudreau, Anne BiDrAPA 89
Boudreau, Donald David 1924- BiDrAPA 89
Boudreau, Edna Mae 1935- WhoWrEP 89
Boudreau, Edward Joseph, Jr. 1944- St&PR 91, WhoAm 90
Boudreau, James Lawton 1935- St&PR 91, WhoAm 90
Boudreau, Kevin Paul 1964- WhoEmL 91
Boudreau, Lou 1917- Ballpl 90 [port]
Boudreau, Marcel Leopold 1936- St&PR 91
Boudreau, Nancy Anna 1947- WhoAmW 91, WhoEmL 91
Boudreault, Eugene 1932- St&PR 91
Boudreaux, C. Kathleen 1934- St&PR 91
Boudreaux, Charles J. 1935- St&PR 91
Boudreaux, Dale Edwin 1943- WhoSSW 91
Boudreaux, Gloria Marie 1935- WhoAmW 91
Boudreaux, Jeffrey L. 1951- St&PR 91
Boudreaux, John 1946- WhoAm 90
Boudreaux, Kenneth Justin 1943- WhoAm 90, WhoSSW 91
Boudreaux, Laura Goerlitz 1955- WhoWrEP 89
Boudreaux, Robert Palmer 1922- St&PR 91
Boudreaux, Thomas Lee 1947- St&PR 91, WhoAm 90
Boudreaux, Warren Louis 1918- WhoSSW 91
Boudria, Cherylanne 1959- WhoAmW 91
Boudris, Janet Lynn 1954- St&PR 91
Boudwin, James Watson 1917- BiDrAPA 89
Boudy, Jose Sanchez- 1928- BioIn 16
Boue, Geori 1918- IntWWM 90, PenDiMP
Bouer, Judith 1942- WhoAmW 91
Bouet, J. P. Thibault NewYTBS 90
Bouffard, Rachelle Emilia BiDrAPA 89
Boufflers, Stanislas Jean, marquis de 1738-1815 BioIn 16
Bougainville, Louis Antoine De 1729-1811 WorAlBi
Bougeard, Daniel Roger A.M. 1948- WhoWor 91
Bough, Dale Eugene 1930- St&PR 91
Boughey, Thomas H. 1939- WhoAm 90
Boughner, Howard R. 1908- WhoWrEP 89
Boughner, James Fransis 1936- St&PR 91
Boughton, Deborah Pollak 1953- BiDrAPA 89
Boughton, James Kenneth 1922- WhoSSW 91
Boughton, James Murray 1944- WhoE 91
Boughton, Joe A. 1934- St&PR 91
Boughton, Leronia 1952- WhoAmW 91
Boughton, Loralee Georgia 1963- WhoAmW 91
Boughton, Rutland 1878-1960 PenDiMP A
Bougie, Jacques 1947- WhoAm 90, WhoE 91
Bougie, Roger M. 1933- St&PR 91
Bouguereau, E. BiDWomA
Bouhet, Jacques Emile 1942- WhoE 91
Bouhoutsos, Jacqueline Cotcher WhoAmW 91
Bouilhet, Henri PenDiDA 89
Bouilliant-Linet, Francis Jacques 1932- WhoSSW 91
Bouis, Nancy Ellen 1946- WhoE 91
Bouis, Thomas Oliver 1948- WhoE 91
Bouissac, Paul Antoine 1934- WhoAm 90
Bouisson, Fernand Emile Honore 1874-1959 BiDFrPL
Bouknight, Barbara Elvira 1946- WhoEmL 91
Bouknight, James Gilder 1950- BiDrAPA 89
Boukoff, Yuri 1923- PenDiMP
Boulainvilliers, Henri, comte de 1658-1722 BioIn 16
Boulais, Claude N BiDrAPA 89
Boulais, Marcel Joseph St&PR 91N
Boulanger, Debra Ann 1956- WhoAmW 91
Boulanger, Donald Richard 1944- St&PR 91, WhoAm 90
Boulanger, Georges Ernest Jean-Marie 1837-1891 BiDFrPL, BioIn 16
Boulanger, Jean Baptiste 1922- BiDrAPA 89
Boulanger, Lili 1893-1918 BioIn 16, PenDiMP
Boulanger, Linda Rose 1952- WhoEmL 91
Boulanger, Mary Janet 1950- WhoAmW 91
Boulanger, Nadia 1887-1979 PenDiMP, WorAlBi
Boulanger, Robert Norman 1933- St&PR 91
Boulanger, Rodney Edmund 1940- WhoAm 90
Boulard, Jean Baptiste 1725?-1789 PenDiDA 89
Boulard, Michel-Jacques PenDiDA 89
Boulay, Laurence 1925- IntWWM 90
Boulay, Robert A. 1953- St&PR 91
Boulbie, Judith BiDEWW, FemiCLE
Boulby, Judith FemiCLE
Boulden, Judith Ann 1948- WhoAmW 91
Bouldin, Joel Ray, Jr. 1956- St&PR 91
Bouldin, Marshall Jones, III 1923- WhoAmA 91
Bouldin, Mary Lee 1962- BiDrAPA 89
Boulding, Elise Marie 1920- WhoAm 90, WhoAmW 91
Boulding, Kenneth Ewart 1910- WhoAm 90
Boulding, Pam NewAgMG
Boulding, Philip NewAgMG
Bouldjoua, Daniel Pierre 1948- IntWWM 90
Boulet, Jean-Claude 1941- WhoWor 91
Boulet, Lionel 1919- WhoAm 90
Boulet, Susan Seddon 1941- BioIn 16
Bouley, C. Alan 1928- St&PR 91
Bouley, William L. 1945- St&PR 91
Boulez, Pierre 1925- IntWWM 90, PenDiMP, -A, WhoAm 90, WhoWor 91, WorAlBi
Boulger, Dorothea 1847-1923 FemiCLE
Boulger, Francis William 1913- WhoAm 90
Boulger, James Daniel, Jr. 1924- St&PR 91
Boulier, Rita Marie 1949- WhoEmL 91
Boulin, Paule Marie BioIn 16
Boulin, Robert 1920-1979 BiDFrPL
Boulle, Andre-Charles 1642-1732 PenDiDA 89
Boulle, Andre-Charles 1685-1745 PenDiDA 89
Boulle, Charles-Joseph 1688-1751 PenDiDA 89
Boullianne, George Emile 1931- St&PR 91
Boulmetis, Sammy BioIn 16
Bouloukos, Don Peter St&PR 91
Boulpaep, Emile Louis J. B. 1938- WhoAm 90
Boult, Adrian 1889-1983 PenDiMP, WorAlBi
Boult, Adrian Cedric 1889-1983 DcNaB 1981
Boult, Reber Fielding 1907- St&PR 91, WhoAm 90, WhoWor 91
Boultbee, J.A. 1943- St&PR 91
Boultbee, John A. 1943- WhoAm 90
Boulter, Eric Thomas 1917-1989 ConAu 129
Boulter, Nicholas John 1950- WhoWor 91
Boulting, John 1913-1985 DcNaB 1981
Boultinghouse, Beate Carola 1949- WhoAmW 91, WhoE 91
Boultinghouse, Marion Craig Bettinger 1930- WhoAm 90
Boulton, Charles Arkoll 1841-1899 DcCanB 12
Boulton, Donald Arthur 1930- WhoSSW 91
Boulton, Edwin Charles 1928- WhoAm 90
Boulton, Ian C. 1953- WhoWor 91
Boulton, Matthew 1728-1809 PenDiDA 89
Boulton, Robert George 1928- St&PR 91
Boulton, Samuel Richard 1947- St&PR 91
Boulton, Shauna Dee 1949- WhoAmW 91
Boulware, Lemuel R. BioIn 16
Boulware, Lemuel Ricketts NewYTBS 90
Boulware, Lemuel Ricketts 1895- WhoAm 90
Boulware, Richard Stark 1935- WhoWor 91
Boulware, Valerie H BiDrAPA 89
Bouma, Jack Q. 1928- St&PR 91
Bouma, John Henry 1919- BiDrAPA 89
Bouma, John Jacob 1937- WhoAm 90
Bouma, Robert Edwin 1938- WhoAm 90
Boumah, Augustin 1927- WhoWor 91
Bouman, Hendrik 1951- IntWWM 90
Boumann, Robert Lyle 1946- WhoEmL 91
Boume Papa, Rita EncCoWW
Boumediene, Houari 1927-1978 PolLCME
Boumi Papa, Rita 1906-1986 EncCoWW
Boundas, Louise Gooch WhoAmW 91
Bounds, Doris Swayze 1904- St&PR 91
Bounds, Julia-Anna Green 1946- WhoAmW 91, WhoSSW 91
Bounds, Laurence Harold 1922- WhoSSW 91
Bounds, Mary Lou 1949- WhoAmW 91, WhoSSW 91
Bounds, Nancy 1928- WhoAmW 91
Bounds, Sarah Etheline 1942- WhoAmW 91, WhoSSW 91, WhoWor 91
Boundy, David Eric 1957- WhoE 91
Boundy, Donna J. 1949- WhoWrEP 89
Boundy, Ray Harold 1903- WhoAm 90
Bouquet, Francis Lester 1926- WhoAm 90
Bouquet, Henry 1719-1765 EncCRAm, WhNaAH
Bour, Daniele 1939- SmATA 62 [port]
Bour, Ernest 1913- PenDiMP
Bour Deaux, John W. 1941- WhoSSW 91
Bouras, James Charles 1941- St&PR 91
Bourasaw, Noel V. 1944- WhoWrEP 89
Bourassa, Francois 1813-1898 DcCanB 12
Bourassa, Napoleon 1827-1916 DcLB 99 [port]
Bourassa, Robert 1933- WhoAm 90, WhoE 91
Bourbeau, Nina Marie 1957- WhoAmW 91
Bourbon, Alfonso de 1936-1989 AnObit 1989
Bourbon, Bruce Robert 1941- St&PR 91
Bourbon, Catherine de 1558-1604 EncCoWW
Bourbon-Parma, Zita von 1892-1989 BioIn 16
Bourbonnais et d'Auvergne, Duchesse de EncCoWW
Bourbonnaise, Mark BioIn 16
Bourdais de Charbonniere, Eric 1939- WhoAm 90
Bourdeau, Danielle BiDrAPA 89
Bourdeau, Paul Turgeon 1932- WhoAm 90
Bourdeau, Robert Charles 1931- WhoAmA 91
Bourdeau, Yvan J.P. 1948- St&PR 91
Bourdell, Pierre Van Parys WhoAmA 91N
Bourdelle, Emile Antoine 1861-1929 BioIn 16
Bourdieu, Pierre 1930- ConAu 130
Bourdieu, Pierre Felix 1930- WhoWor 91
Bourdin, Roger PenDiMP
Bourdin, Thomas Francis 1931- WhoWrEP 89
Bourdon, David 1934- WhoAm 90, WhoAmA 91, WhoWrEP 89
Bourdon, Joseph Henry, III 1930- St&PR 91
Bourdon, Robert Slayton 1947- WhoAmA 91
Bourelly, Jean-Paul BioIn 16
Bourg, Robert T. 1939- St&PR 91
Bourgaize, Linda Harper 1947- WhoAmW 91
Bourgaize, Robert G. WhoAm 90
Bourgault, Lise 1950- WhoAmW 91
Bourgault, Roy Francis 1920- WhoAm 90
Bourgeau, Jean-Paul Leonce 1939- WhoWor 91
Bourgelais, Donna Chamberlain 1948- WhoEmL 91
Bourgeois, Andre Marie Georges 1902- WhoAm 90
Bourgeois, Derek David 1941- IntWWM 90
Bourgeois, Ivan Marie 1942- WhoWor 91
Bourgeois, Leon Victor Auguste 1851-1925 BiDFrPL
Bourgeois, Louise BioIn 16, NewYTBS 90 [port]
Bourgeois, Louise 1911- BiDWomA, WhoAm 90, WhoAmA 91, WhoAmW 91, WhoWor 91
Bourgeois, Marc Louis BiDrAPA 89
Bourgeois, Peggy R. 1939- WhoAmW 91
Bourgeois, Robert C. ODwPR 91
Bourgery, Marc Edmond Clement 1941- WhoWor 91
Bourges, Herve 1933- WhoWor 91
Bourges-Maunoury, Maurice Jean-Marie 1914- BiDFrPL
Bourget, Alain 1953- ODwPR 91
Bourget, Dominique 1959- BiDrAPA 89
Bourget, Robert Bernard 1946- WhoE 91
Bourgin, Frank P. BioIn 16
Bourgin, Frank P. NewYTBS 90
Bourgmont, Etienne Venyard 1680?-1730? EncCRAm
Bourgoin, J.-B.-A. PenDiDA 89
Bourgraf, Elroy Edwin 1931- St&PR 91
Bourguiba, Habib 1903- PolLCME
Bourguiba, Habib Ben Ali 1903- WhoWor 91
Bourguignon, Erika Eichhorn 1924- WhoAm 90
Bourguignon, Philippe Etienne 1948- WhoEmL 91, WhoWor 91
Bourguinat, Henri Laurent 1933- WhoWor 91

Bourianoff, Gleb Gordon *BiDrAPA 89*
Bourillon-Tournay, Jeanne 1867?-1932 *BiDWomA*
Bourinot, John George 1837-1902 *DcLB 99 [port]*
Bourisk, Sheryl *ODwPR 91*
Bourjaily, Mary Jo 1953- *ODwPR 91*
Bourjaily, Vance 1922- *ConLC 62 [port], WhoAm 90, WhoWrEP 89*
Bourke, George Mitchell 1923- *St&PR 91*
Bourke, John Gregory 1846-1896 *WhNaAH*
Bourke, Richard Southwell 1822-1872 *BioIn 16*
Bourke, Vernon Joseph 1907- *WhoAm 90*
Bourke, William Oliver 1927- *St&PR 91, WhoAm 90, WhoSSW 91*
Bourke-White, Margaret 1904-1971 *BioAmW, BioIn 16*
Bourke-White, Margaret 1906?-1971 *FemiCLE, WorAlBi*
Bourland, Homer Lloyd 1922- *WhoAm 90*
Bourn, Benjamin 1755-1808 *BioIn 16*
Bourne, Alan Miles 1945- *St&PR 91*
Bourne, Bob *BioIn 16*
Bourne, Charles Percy 1931- *WhoAm 90*
Bourne, Daniel Carter 1955- *WhoWrEP 89*
Bourne, David J 1948- *BiDrAPA 89*
Bourne, Duncan Stewart 1959- *WhoEmL 91*
Bourne, Francis Stanley 1919- *WhoE 91*
Bourne, Geoffrey H. 1909-1988 *BioIn 16*
Bourne, Henry Clark, Jr. 1921- *WhoAm 90*
Bourne, James Edwin 1929- *St&PR 91*
Bourne, Kenneth Allen 1942- *St&PR 91*
Bourne, Lyle Eugene, Jr. 1932- *WhoAm 90*
Bourne, Mary Bonnie Murray 1903- *WhoAmW 91, WhoE 91, WhoWor 91*
Bourne, Miriam Anne 1931- *AuBYP 90*
Bourne, Miriam Anne 1931-1989 *ConAu 129, SmATA 63*
Bourne, Nehemiah 1611?-1691 *EncCRAm*
Bourne, Peter G 1939- *BiDrAPA 89*
Bourne, Peter Geoffrey 1939- *WhoAm 90*
Bourne, Randolph Silliman 1886-1918 *BioIn 16*
Bourne, Ronald Lynn 1953- *WhoSSW 91*
Bourne, Russell 1928- *WhoAm 90*
Bourne, Samuel G. 1916- *WhoAm 90*
Bourne, St. Clair 1943- *DrBlPA 90*
Bourne, Victoria Tyson 1952- *WhoEmL 91*
Bourne, William Hamilton 1918- *WhoAm 90*
Bourne, Willie R. 1931- *St&PR 91*
Bourne-Vanneck, Richard *BioIn 16*
Bournia-Anastos, Maximi *BiDrAPA 89*
Bournonville, August 1805-1879 *BioIn 16*
Bournonville, Auguste 1805-1879 *WorAlBi*
Bourns, Marlan E. 1920- *WhoAm 90*
Bourns, Richard T. 1934- *St&PR 91*
Bourquardez, Earl Constant 1948- *WhoSSW 91*
Bourque, Gail Frances 1951- *WhoE 91*
Bourque, Irby 1942- *St&PR 91*
Bourque, Jean-Jacques *BiDrAPA 89*
Bourque, M. Phyllis 1947- *St&PR 91*
Bourque, Michael H. 1948- *WhoE 91, WhoEmL 91*
Bourque, Philip John 1922- *WhoAm 90*
Bourque, Ray 1960- *WorAlBi*
Bourquin, Paul A. 1921- *St&PR 91*
Bourret, Robert 1933- *WhoAm 90*
Bours, William Alsop, III 1918- *WhoAm 90*
Boursicot, Bernard *BioIn 16*
Boursnell, Richard 1832-1909 *EncO&P 3*
Boury, Nissan *WhoE 91*
Bousfield, Edward Lloyd 1926- *WhoAm 90*
Bousfield, Weston Ashmore *BioIn 16*
Boush, George Mallory 1926- *WhoAm 90*
Boushie, Raymond W. 1940- *St&PR 91*
Bousquet, Ronald D. 1967- *WhoEmL 91*
Bousquet, Thomas Gourrier 1934- *WhoAm 90*
Bousquette, William C. 1936- *WhoAm 90*
Bousquette, William Charles 1936- *St&PR 91*
Boussardon, Alain Marcal 1948- *WhoWor 91*
Boussauw, Luc H.A. 1944- *St&PR 91*
Boussel, Pierre 1920- *BiDFrPL*
Boust, Susan Jane *BiDrAPA 89*
Bouteiller, Jacques Charles 1931- *WhoWor 91*
Boutelle, Ann Edwards 1943- *ConAu 131*
Boutelle, Jane Cronin 1926- *WhoAmW 91*
Boutelle, Richard S. 1898-1962 *WorAlBi*
Boutelle, Sara Holmes *ConAu 130*
Boutelle, William E 1940- *BiDrAPA 89*
Bouterin, Antoine *BioIn 16*
Bouterse, Desi *BioIn 16*
Bouterse, Desire *WhoWor 91*
Boutet, Benoit 1960- *WhoAm 90*
Bouthilet, Kirby Otteson 1948- *WhoAm 90*
Bouthillier, Yves Marie 1901-1977 *BiDFrPL*
Boutillette, Leroy Bruce, Jr. 1950- *St&PR 91*
Boutillier, Robert John 1924- *WhoAm 90*
Boutin, Andre J. 1932- *St&PR 91*
Boutin, Arlene P 1936- *BiDrAPA 89*
Boutin, Bernard Louis 1923- *WhoAm 90*
Boutin, Gilbert Robert 1920- *St&PR 91*
Boutis, Theodore T. 1923- *St&PR 91*
Boutis, Tom 1922- *WhoAmA 91*
Boutissou, Serge 1939- *WhoWor 91*
Boutmy, Emile Gaston 1835-1906 *BiDFrPL*
Bouton, Garrett *BioIn 16*
Bouton, Garrett Frank 1944- *WhoWor 91*
Bouton, Janet Laura 1943- *WhoAmW 91*
Bouton, Jim 1939- *Ballpl 90*
Boutris, Wendy Joseph 1963- *WhoAmW 91*
Boutros, Nashaat Nessim 1949- *BiDrAPA 89*
Bouts, Dierik 1400?-1475 *WorAlBi*
Bouts, Dirk 1415?-1475? *IntDcAA 90*
Boutte, David Gray 1944- *WhoE 91*
Boutwell, George Sewall 1818-1905 *BiDrUSE 89*
Boutwell, Herbert Chauncey, III 1948- *WhoSSW 91*
Boutwell, Roswell Knight 1917- *WhoAm 90*
Bouvard, Marguerite 1937- *WhoE 91*
Bouvard, Marguerite Gusman 1937- *WhoWrEP 89*
Bouve, Howard A., Jr. 1930- *St&PR 91*
Bouveng, Carl-Johan 1938- *WhoWor 91*
Bouvier, Janet Laubach 1930- *WhoE 91*
Bouvier, John Andre, Jr. 1903- *WhoAm 90*
Bouvier, Marshall Andre 1923- *WhoWor 91*
Bouville, Luc 1950- *WhoWor 91*
Bouwer, Herman 1927- *WhoAm 90*
Bouwer, John D. 1938- *St&PR 91*
Bouwsma, William James 1923- *WhoAm 90*
Bouygues, Francis Georges 1922- *WhoWor 91*
Bouyoucos, John Vinton 1926- *WhoAm 90*
Bouza, Anthony *BioIn 16*
Bouzianis, Melissa Farrah 1957- *WhoAmW 91*
Bova, Ben 1932- *BioIn 16, MajTwCW*
Bova, Benjamin William 1932- *AuBYP 90, RGTwCSF, WhoAm 90*
Bova, Joe *BioIn 16*
Bova, Joe 1941- *WhoAmA 91*
Bova, Paul Peter 1941- *St&PR 91*
Bova, Vincent Arthur, Jr. 1946- *WhoEmL 91, WhoWor 91*
Bovaird, Brendan P. 1948- *St&PR 91*
Bovaird, Brendan Peter 1948- *WhoE 91*
Bovard, Carl M. 1930- *St&PR 91*
Bovard, Oliver K. 1872-1945 *BioIn 16*
Bovarnick, Ellen 1954- *WhoAmW 91*
Bovasso, Julie 1930- *BioIn 16, FemiCLE, NotWoAT*
Bovay, Harry Elmo, Jr. 1914- *WhoAm 90, WhoWor 91*
Bovbjerg, Randall Richard 1946- *WhoE 91*
Bove, James Stephen 1948- *BiDrAPA 89*
Bove, Januar D., Jr. 1920- *WhoAm 90*
Bove, John Louis 1928- *WhoAm 90*
Bove, Richard 1920- *WhoAmA 91*
Bove, Robert Charles 1951- *WhoEmL 91*
Bovee, Eugene Cleveland 1915- *WhoAm 90*
Bovee, G. Spence 1962- *WhoEmL 91*
Bovee, Gerald N. 1939- *St&PR 91*
Bovee, Jan Merrill 1938- *St&PR 91*
Bovee, Kenneth C. 1936- *WhoAm 90*
Bovee, Ruth *ConAu 31NR*
Bovell, Carlton Rowland 1924- *WhoAm 90*
Bovender, Jack O. 1945- *St&PR 91*
Bovender, Jack Oliver, Jr. 1945- *WhoAm 90, WhoSSW 91*
Bovenizer, Bruce 1945- *St&PR 91*
Boverman, Harold 1927- *BiDrAPA 89*
Boverman, Maxwell 1917- *BiDrAPA 89*
Boveroux, Brooks 1943- *St&PR 91*
Boves, Joaquin Lorenzo 1949- *WhoE 91*
Bovet, Andre Marc 1954- *WhoWor 91*
Bovet, Daniel 1907- *WhoWor 91*
Bovet, Daniele 1907- *WorAlBi*
Bovet, David Marc 1948- *WhoE 91*
Bovet, Guy 1942- *IntWWM 90*
Bovey, Frank Alden 1918- *WhoAm 90*
Bovey, Rodney William 1934- *WhoSSW 91*
Bovey, Terry Robinson 1948- *WhoEmL 91*
Bovin, Aleksandr Yevgenevich 1930- *BioIn 16*
Bovin, Denis Alan 1947- *WhoEmL 91*
Bovingdon, George Geil 1934- *WhoWor 91*
Bovino, Charles A. 1940- *St&PR 91*
Bovino, Charles Anthony 1940- *WhoAm 90*
Bovis, John Milton 1937- *WhoSSW 91*
Bovit, R. Lionel 1927- *St&PR 91*
Bovo, Mary Jane 1946- *WhoE 91, WhoEmL 91*
Bovon, Fransois 1938- *WhoWor 91*
Bovoso, Carole Ione Lewis 1937- *WhoWrEP 89*
Bovsun, Mara *ODwPR 91*
Bow, Clara 1905-1965 *BioIn 16, WorAlBi*
Bow, Clara Gordon 1905-1965 *BioAmW*
Bow, Janice Meyers *BiDrAPA 89*
Bow, Stephen T. 1931- *St&PR 91*
Bow, Stephen Tyler, Jr. 1931- *WhoAm 90, WhoWor 91*
Bowa, Larry *BioIn 16*
Bowa, Larry 1945- *Ballpl 90 [port]*
Bowater, Marian 1924- *WhoAmA 91*
Bowdan, Newton Doran 1933- *BiDrAPA 89*
Bowden, Ann 1924- *WhoAmW 91, WhoSSW 91, WhoWor 91*
Bowden, Benjamin John 1932- *St&PR 91*
Bowden, Bobby *BioIn 16*
Bowden, Charles Edgar 1929- *St&PR 91*
Bowden, Charles Lee 1938- *BiDrAPA 89*
Bowden, David Leon 1943- *WhoSSW 91*
Bowden, Elbert Victor 1924- *WhoSSW 91*
Bowden, Henry Lumpkin 1910- *WhoAm 90*
Bowden, Hugh Kent 1933- *WhoAm 90*
Bowden, James Alvin 1948- *St&PR 91, WhoAm 90*
Bowden, Jesse Earle 1928- *WhoAm 90, WhoWrEP 89*
Bowden, Joan Chase 1925- *BioIn 16*
Bowden, Maxine 1943- *WhoAmW 91*
Bowden, Otis H., II 1928- *St&PR 91*
Bowden, Richard Keane 1952- *St&PR 91*
Bowden, Sally Ann 1943- *WhoAm 90*
Bowden, Susan 1936- *WhoWrEP 89*
Bowden, Ted 1930- *St&PR 91*
Bowden, Travis J. 1938- *St&PR 91*
Bowden, William Darsie 1920- *WhoAm 90*
Bowden, William Lukens 1922- *WhoAm 90*
Bowden, William P., Jr. 1944- *WhoAm 90*
Bowder, Jerry Lee 1928- *IntWWM 90*
Bowdich, Cary Ann 1953- *WhoE 91*
Bowdin, Harby Glenn 1951- *WhoSSW 91*
Bowditch, E. Francis *BioIn 16*
Bowditch, Frederick Wise 1921- *WhoAm 90*
Bowditch, H P 1840-1911 *EncO&P 3*
Bowditch, Henry Pickering 1840-1911 *EncPaPR 91*
Bowditch, Marian Hornsby 1921- *WhoSSW 91*
Bowditch, Nathaniel Rantoul 1932- *WhoE 91*
Bowditch, Robert Shaw 1909- *St&PR 91*
Bowdle, Donald Nelson 1935- *WhoSSW 91*
Bowdler, Anthony John 1928- *WhoAm 90*
Bowdler, Henrietta Maria 1753-1830 *FemiCLE*
Bowdoin, Harriette *WhoAmA 91N*
Bowdoin, James 1726-1790 *EncCRAm*
Bowdoin, James 1752-1811 *BioIn 16*
Bowdoin, Lesley 1962- *WhoEmL 91*
Bowdre, John Birch, Jr. 1954- *WhoEmL 91*
Bowdre, Paul Reid 1958- *WhoEmL 91, WhoSSW 91*
Bowe, Edward Louis 1946- *WhoEmL 91*
Bowe, James Joseph 1927- *St&PR 91*
Bowe, Jeffrey John 1963- *St&PR 91*
Bowe, John A. 1935- *St&PR 91*
Bowe, Peter Armistead 1956- *St&PR 91*
Bowe, Richard E. 1921- *St&PR 91*
Bowe, Richard Eugene 1921- *WhoAm 90, WhoE 91*
Bowe, Ruth Hennessey 1923- *BiDrAPA 89*
Bowe, William John 1942- *St&PR 91, WhoAm 90*
Bowen, A. Grant 1930- *St&PR 91*
Bowen, Albert Reeder 1905- *WhoAm 90*
Bowen, Asta 1955- *WhoWrEP 89*
Bowen, Barbara 1961- *WhoAmW 91*
Bowen, Barbara Cherry 1937- *WhoAm 90*
Bowen, Barbara Lynn 1945- *WhoAmW 91*
Bowen, Betty Morgan 1921- *AuBYP 90*
Bowen, Billy 1909-1982 *DrBlPA 90*
Bowen, Brett H. 1941- *St&PR 91*
Bowen, Brooks Jefferson 1949- *WhoEmL 91*
Bowen, Catherine 1897-1973 *FemiCLE*
Bowen, Charles Clark 1917- *WhoAm 90*
Bowen, Charles Hugh, Jr. 1923- *WhoAm 90*
Bowen, Charles Revelle 1926- *WhoE 91*
Bowen, Christine Lyn 1952- *WhoAmW 91*
Bowen, Clotilde Dent 1923- *BiDrAPA 89, WhoAm 90*
Bowen, Constance Lee 1952- *WhoAmA 91*
Bowen, Daniel Hampton 1850- *AmLegL*
Bowen, David 1941- *ODwPR 91*
Bowen, David Reece 1932- *WhoAm 90*
Bowen, Debra Jean 1955- *WhoAmW 91*
Bowen, Donald *BioIn 16*
Bowen, Donald Eyre 1912- *BiDrAPA 89, WhoE 91*
Bowen, Dudley Hollingsworth, Jr. 1941- *WhoAm 90, WhoSSW 91*
Bowen, Elizabeth 1899-1973 *AuBYP 90, BioIn 16, FemiCLE, MajTwCW, WorAlBi*
Bowen, Elizabeth Linville *BiDrAPA 89*
Bowen, Eva Joyce 1934- *WhoSSW 91*
Bowen, Francis 1811-1890 *BioIn 16*
Bowen, Frank Randolph 1937- *St&PR 91*
Bowen, Frank Weston, Jr. 1952- *WhoEmL 91*
Bowen, Fred Pasco, II 1958- *St&PR 91*
Bowen, Frederic Wayne 1946- *WhoEmL 91*
Bowen, Gary Lee 1953- *WhoSSW 91*
Bowen, George Hamilton, Jr. 1925- *WhoAm 90*
Bowen, George LeRoy, III 1948- *WhoSSW 91*
Bowen, Gordon Stewart 1950- *WhoEmL 91*
Bowen, Harrold Pasco 1934- *St&PR 91*
Bowen, Henry Albert 1952- *BiDrAPA 89*
Bowen, Herbert, Jr. *St&PR 91*
Bowen, Herbert Wolcott 1856-1927 *BioIn 16*
Bowen, Howard R 1908-1989 *ConAu 130*
Bowen, Ira Sprague 1898-1973 *DcScB S2*
Bowen, Irene *AuBYP 90*
Bowen, James Richard 1945- *WhoAm 90*
Bowen, James Ronald 1941- *WhoAm 90*
Bowen, James Thomas 1948- *WhoEmL 91*
Bowen, James Thomas, Jr. 1948- *WhoSSW 91*
Bowen, Jean 1927- *IntWWM 90*
Bowen, Jeffrey A. 1948- *St&PR 91*
Bowen, Jewell Ray 1934- *WhoAm 90*
Bowen, Jill Veronica 1947- *WhoWrEP 89*
Bowen, Joan Brady 1932- *WhoE 91*
Bowen, Joan Martin 1939- *WhoAmW 91*
Bowen, John *PenDiDA 89*
Bowen, John E., III 1931- *St&PR 91*
Bowen, John Hulan 1928- *WhoSSW 91*
Bowen, John J. 1948- *St&PR 91*
Bowen, John Metcalf 1933- *WhoAm 90*
Bowen, John Rhett Crosswell 1948- *WhoSSW 91*
Bowen, John Richard 1934- *St&PR 91, WhoAm 90*
Bowen, John Sheets 1927- *WhoAm 90, WhoE 91*
Bowen, John Thomas 1948- *WhoEmL 91*
Bowen, John Wesley Edward, IV 1954- *WhoEmL 91, WhoWor 91*
Bowen, Joshua David 1930- *AuBYP 90*
Bowen, Judith M *BiDrAPA 89*
Bowen, Kelley Bailey 1962- *WhoAmW 91*
Bowen, Kenneth 1932- *IntWWM 90*
Bowen, Lester Wells 1930- *WhoE 91*
Bowen, Lionel Frost *WhoWor 91*
Bowen, Lowell Reed 1931- *WhoAm 90*
Bowen, Malcolm Garry *BiDrAPA 89*
Bowen, Marcia Kay 1957- *WhoAmW 91, WhoWor 91*
Bowen, Marjorie *TwCCr&M 91*
Bowen, Marjorie 1888-1952 *FemiCLE*
Bowen, Martin C. 1943- *St&PR 91*
Bowen, Murray *BiDrAPA 89*
Bowen, Nancy Lynn 1955- *WhoAmW 91, WhoWor 91*
Bowen, Norman Wayne 1942- *St&PR 91*
Bowen, Otis R. *BioIn 16*
Bowen, Otis Ray 1918- *BiDrUSE 89*
Bowen, Patrick H. 1939- *St&PR 91*
Bowen, Patrick Harvey 1939- *WhoAm 90*
Bowen, Paul 1951- *WhoAmA 91*
Bowen, R. Brayton 1940- *St&PR 91*
Bowen, Richard Lee 1933- *WhoAm 90*
Bowen, Richard Mayo, III 1947- *WhoAm 90*
Bowen, Robert C. 1941- *WhoAm 90*
Bowen, Robert S. 1937- *St&PR 91*
Bowen, Robert Sidney 1900-1977 *AuBYP 90, BioIn 16*
Bowen, Robert Stevenson 1937- *WhoAm 90*
Bowen, Robert William 1960- *WhoE 91*
Bowen, Rudradeo C 1941- *BiDrAPA 89*
Bowen, Rufus 1947-1978 *DcScB S2*
Bowen, Ruth 1930- *BioIn 16, DrBlPA 90*
Bowen, Stephen Francis, Jr. 1932- *WhoAm 90*
Bowen, Stephen George 1944- *WhoAm 90*
Bowen, Stephen N. 1935- *ODwPR 91*
Bowen, Sue 1824-1875 *FemiCLE*
Bowen, Susan Arlene 1961- *WhoSSW 91*
Bowen, Thomas Allan 1951- *WhoEmL 91*
Bowen, Thomas E. 1932- *St&PR 91*
Bowen, Thomas Joseph, Jr. 1965- *WhoE 91*
Bowen, Timothy Dana 1956- *WhoEmL 91*
Bowen, W.J. 1922- *St&PR 91*
Bowen, W. J. 1922- *WhoSSW 91*
Bowen, Walter E. 1942- *St&PR 91*
Bowen, William Augustus 1930- *WhoAm 90*
Bowen, William Conrad 1953- *WhoEmL 91*
Bowen, William Gordon 1933- *WhoAm 90, WhoE 91, WhoWor 91*
Bowen, William H. 1933- *WhoAm 90*

Bowen, William Harvey 1923- *St&PR 91, WhoAm 90*
Bowen, William Joseph 1934- *WhoAm 90*
Bowen-Forbes, Jorge C 1937- *WhoAmA 91*
Bowens, Sam 1939- *Ballpl 90*
Bowens, William Clement 1942- *BiDrAPA 89*
Bower, Alexander 1875-1952 *WhoAmA 91N*
Bower, Allan Maxwell 1936- *WhoAm 90*
Bower, B. M. 1871-1940 *FemiCLE*
Bower, Bruce Edward 1950- *WhoEmL 91*
Bower, Bruce Lester 1933- *WhoAm 90*
Bower, Catherine Downes 1947- *ODwPR 91, WhoEmL 91*
Bower, Christopher James 1957- *WhoAm 90, WhoEmL 91*
Bower, Cindy Lou 1957- *WhoAmW 91*
Bower, Douglas William 1948- *WhoSSW 91*
Bower, E. Bruce 1941- *WhoSSW 91*
Bower, Fay Louise 1929- *WhoAmW 91*
Bower, Gary David 1940- *WhoAmA 91*
Bower, Glen L. 1949- *WhoEmL 91*
Bower, Glenn Nils 1930- *St&PR 91*
Bower, Gordon Howard 1932- *WhoAm 90*
Bower, Haywood W. 1948- *St&PR 91*
Bower, Janie Pittman 1955- *WhoSSW 91*
Bower, Jean Ramsay 1935- *WhoAm 90, WhoAmW 91*
Bower, Jean Watson 1949- *WhoE 91*
Bower, John Arnold, Jr. 1930- *WhoAm 90*
Bower, John Dykes 1905-1981 *DcNaB 1981*
Bower, John Joseph 1925- *WhoAm 90*
Bower, John R *BiDrAPA 89*
Bower, John W. 1930- *St&PR 91*
Bower, Joseph Lyon 1938- *WhoAm 90*
Bower, Kathleen Ann 1962- *WhoAmW 91*
Bower, Kenneth F. 1942- *WhoWor 91*
Bower, Leonard Ernest 1947- *WhoE 91*
Bower, Mark Victor 1953- *WhoSSW 91*
Bower, Marvin *BioIn 16*
Bower, Marvin 1903- *St&PR 91, WhoAm 90*
Bower, Marvin D. 1924- *St&PR 91, WhoAm 90*
Bower, Michael James Eills Graham 1938- *WhoWor 91*
Bower, Michael O. *ODwPR 91*
Bower, Murray 1926- *BiDrAPA 89*
Bower, Neville Courtenay 1934- *IntWWM 90*
Bower, Paul George 1933- *WhoAm 90*
Bower, Peter Thomas A. 1946- *St&PR 91*
Bower, R. Janet *WhoAmW 91*
Bower, Regina Patricia 1950- *St&PR 91*
Bower, Richard James 1939- *WhoAm 90*
Bower, Richard Stuart 1928- *WhoAm 90*
Bower, Robert Hewitt 1949- *WhoEmL 91*
Bower, Robert T 1919-1990 *ConAu 132*
Bower, Ruth Lawther 1917- *WhoSSW 91*
Bower, Sandra Irwin 1946- *WhoAmW 91*
Bower, Thomas Michael 1952- *WhoE 91*
Bower, Ursula Graham 1914-1988 *AnObit 1988*
Bower, William Russell 1930- *St&PR 91*
Bower, Willis Herman 1916- *BiDrAPA 89, WhoAm 90*
Bowerfind, Edgar Sihler, Jr. 1924- *WhoAm 90*
Bowering, George Harry 1936- *WhoAm 90, WhoWrEP 89*
Bowerman, Bryan Peter 1942- *St&PR 91*
Bowerman, C.L. 1939- *St&PR 91*
Bowerman, Colene Lynette Watkins 1963- *WhoAmW 91*
Bowerman, Donald Bradley 1934- *WhoAm 90*
Bowerman, Frank 1868-1948 *Ballpl 90*
Bowerman, Richard H. 1917- *St&PR 91*
Bowerman, Richard Henry 1917- *WhoAm 90*
Bowers, Albert *St&PR 91N*
Bowers, Albert *NewYTBS 90*
Bowers, Albert 1930- *WhoAm 90*
Bowers, Albert Davison 1941- *St&PR 91*
Bowers, Barbara A. 1938- *WhoAmW 91*
Bowers, Barbara Lee 1948- *WhoEmL 91*
Bowers, Bathsheba 1673?-1718 *FemiCLE*
Bowers, Carl Richard 1931- *St&PR 91*
Bowers, Charles E., Jr. 1928- *St&PR 91*
Bowers, Christine *BiDrAPA 89*
Bowers, Claude Gernade 1878-1958 *BioIn 16*
Bowers, Clifford A. 1951- *ODwPR 91*
Bowers, Clyde T. 1914- *St&PR 91*
Bowers, Daniel Kent 1947- *St&PR 91*
Bowers, David A. 1946- *St&PR 91*
Bowers, Douglas Edward 1947- *WhoSSW 91*
Bowers, Edward Albert 1941- *WhoSSW 91*
Bowers, Elliott Toulmin 1919- *WhoSSW 91*
Bowers, Eloise B. 1912- *WhoAmW 91*
Bowers, Emmett Wadsworth 1926- *WhoAm 90*
Bowers, Emory L. 1931- *WhoSSW 91*
Bowers, Eugene Dyer, Jr. 1944- *WhoE 91*
Bowers, Francis Robert 1920- *WhoAm 90*
Bowers, Frank Richard 1936- *BiDrAPA 89*
Bowers, Frederick Whyte 1933- *WhoE 91*
Bowers, Glenn Lee 1921- *WhoAm 90*
Bowers, Grayson Hunter 1897- *WhoE 91, WhoWor 91*
Bowers, James Kenneth 1941- *St&PR 91*
Bowers, Jane Ann 1940- *WhoAmW 91*
Bowers, Jane M. 1936- *IntWWM 90*
Bowers, Janice L. 1947- *WhoAmW 91*
Bowers, John *BioIn 16*
Bowers, John Spotswood 1955- *WhoE 91*
Bowers, John Waite 1935- *WhoAm 90*
Bowers, John Zimmerman 1913- *WhoAm 90*
Bowers, June Eleanore 1922- *WhoSSW 91*
Bowers, Kenneth L. 1937- *ODwPR 91*
Bowers, Klaus Dieter 1929- *WhoAm 90*
Bowers, Lawrence Ray 1918- *St&PR 91*
Bowers, Lee Ailes 1950- *WhoEmL 91*
Bowers, Leola Delean 1919- *WhoSSW 91*
Bowers, Linda Ann 1947- *WhoE 91*
Bowers, M. Deane 1952- *WhoAmW 91*
Bowers, Malcolm Baker, Jr. 1933- *BiDrAPA 89*
Bowers, Margaretta K *BiDrAPA 89*
Bowers, Mary Ellen Kathryn 1949- *WhoAmW 91*
Bowers, Michael Joseph 1941- *WhoAm 90, WhoSSW 91*
Bowers, Mollie Heath 1945- *WhoE 91*
Bowers, Norma Jean 1929- *WhoAmW 91*
Bowers, Patricia Eleanor Fritz 1928- *WhoAm 90, WhoAmW 91, WhoE 91*
Bowers, Patricia Newsome 1944- *WhoAmW 91, WhoWor 91*
Bowers, Paul Alan 1947- *WhoE 91*
Bowers, Paul Duane, Jr. 1931- *WhoAm 90*
Bowers, R. Todd 1956- *St&PR 91*
Bowers, Raymond Victor 1907- *WhoWor 91*
Bowers, Richard P. 1931- *St&PR 91*
Bowers, Richard Philip 1931- *WhoAm 90*
Bowers, Richard S. 1946- *St&PR 91*
Bowers, Richard Stewart, Jr. 1946- *WhoAm 90, WhoEmL 91*
Bowers, Rick Thomas 1961- *BiDrAPA 89*
Bowers, Robert Bruce 1948- *WhoAm 90*
Bowers, Robert E. 1956- *St&PR 91*
Bowers, Stanley Jacob 1912- *WhoAm 90*
Bowers, Susan Kathleen 1964- *WhoAmW 91*
Bowers, Theron Chester *BiDrAPA 89*
Bowers, Thomas Arnold 1942- *WhoSSW 91*
Bowers, Thomas R. 1940- *St&PR 91*
Bowers, William Clare 1951- *WhoE 91*
Bowers, William Frederick 1944- *St&PR 91*
Bowers, William James 1928- *St&PR 91*
Bowers, Zella Zane 1929- *WhoAmW 91*
Bowers-Broadbent, Christopher Joseph 1945- *IntWWM 90*
Bowersock, Glen Warren 1936- *WhoAm 90, WhoWor 91, WhoWrEP 89*
Bowersock, Von K. 1943- *St&PR 91*
Bowersox, Judith Jeane 1949- *WhoAmW 91*
Bowersox, Thomas H. 1941- *St&PR 91*
Bowersox, Thomas Omar 1947- *St&PR 91*
Bowery, Thomas Glenn 1921- *WhoAm 90*
Bowes, Arlene Dannenberg 1950- *WhoAmW 91*
Bowes, Arthur Stutz, Jr. 1932- *St&PR 91*
Bowes, Betty Miller *WhoAmA 91*
Bowes, David B. *ODwPR 91*
Bowes, Edward 1874-1946 *WorAlBi*
Bowes, Florence 1925- *WhoAmW 91, WhoWor 91*
Bowes, Frederick, III 1941- *WhoAm 90*
Bowes, Gregory B. 1954- *St&PR 91*
Bowes, Jerome *PenDiDA 89*
Bowes, Russell C., Jr. 1937- *St&PR 91*
Bowey, Donald F., Jr. 1933- *St&PR 91*
Bowhers, Vincent Carroll 1928- *WhoE 91*
Bowhill, Sidney Allan 1927- *WhoAm 90*
Bowie, David *BioIn 16*
Bowie, David 1947- *EncPR&S 89, OxCPMus, WhoAm 90, WorAlBi*
Bowie, David Bernard 1954- *WhoEmL 91*
Bowie, Douglas B. 1943- *St&PR 91*
Bowie, Edward John Walter 1925- *WhoAm 90*
Bowie, Effie Belle 1909- *WhoAmA 91*
Bowie, James 1796-1836 *WorAlBi*
Bowie, Lenard Connell 1937- *WhoSSW 91*
Bowie, Lester *BioIn 16*
Bowie, Norman Ernest 1942- *WhoAm 90*
Bowie, Sam *TwCCr&M 91*
Bowie, Stanley Hay Umphray 1917- *WhoWor 91*
Bowie, Timothy Jon 1963- *WhoEmL 91*
Bowie, William 1926- *WhoAmA 91*
Bowinski, Peter N. 1948- *St&PR 91*
Bowker, Albert Hosmer 1919- *WhoAm 90*
Bowker, Ann Marta 1935- *WhoAmW 91*
Bowker, Laura Lee 1957- *WhoEmL 91*
Bowker, Lee Harrington 1940- *WhoAm 90*
Bowkett, Gerald Edson 1926- *WhoAm 90, WhoWrEP 89*
Bowkett, Jane Maria 1837-1891 *BiDWomA*
Bowl 1756-1839 *WhNaAH*
Bowlby, Edward John M 1907- *BiDrAPA 89*
Bowlby, John 1907-1990 *ConAu 132, NewYTBS 90 [port]*
Bowlby, Rachel 1957- *ConAu 130*
Bowlby, Rachel Helena 1957- *WhoWor 91*
Bowlby, Richard Eric 1939- *WhoWor 91*
Bowlby, Richard Evans 1928- *St&PR 91*
Bowlds, Joseph Harold 1935- *WhoE 91*
Bowlds, Thomas Raymond 1957- *WhoSSW 91*
Bowlegs, Billy 1810?-1864 *WhNaAH*
Bowlen, Kennard L. 1928- *St&PR 91*
Bowler, Astrid 1941- *IntWWM 90*
Bowler, Brian *BioIn 16, WhoAm 90*
Bowler, David Lee 1936- *WhoSSW 91*
Bowler, Donald *BioIn 16*
Bowler, E. Joseph 1936- *St&PR 91*
Bowler, John Patrick 1959- *WhoSSW 91*
Bowler, Joseph, Jr 1928- *WhoAmA 91*
Bowler, Peter J 1944- *ConAu 129*
Bowler, W. Scane 1925- *St&PR 91*
Bowler-Reed, Sabina 1950- *WhoWor 91*
Bowles, A. Eugene 1934- *St&PR 91*
Bowles, Alan Derek 1960- *WhoE 91*
Bowles, Aubrey Russell, III 1933- *WhoAm 90*
Bowles, Barbara L. 1947- *St&PR 91*
Bowles, Barbara Landers 1947- *WhoAm 90, WhoAmW 91*
Bowles, Caroline 1787-1854 *FemiCLE*
Bowles, Cheryl Lee 1945- *WhoEmL 91*
Bowles, Chester 1901-1986 *BioIn 16, WorAlBi*
Bowles, Daniel Allan 1949- *St&PR 91*
Bowles, Deborah Ann 1949- *WhoAmW 91*
Bowles, Dorothy Stebbins *BioIn 16*
Bowles, Edmund A 1925- *ConAu 32NR*
Bowles, Edmund Addison 1925- *IntWWM 90*
Bowles, Edward L. *NewYTBS 90*
Bowles, Garett H. 1938- *IntWWM 90*
Bowles, Grover Cleveland, Jr. 1920- *WhoAm 90*
Bowles, Jane 1917-1973 *FemiCLE*
Bowles, Jane Auer 1918-1973 *BioAmW*
Bowles, Janet Payne 1882-1948 *WhoAmA 91N*
Bowles, Jay Clyde 1942- *WhoSSW 91*
Bowles, John 1916- *St&PR 91, WhoAm 90*
Bowles, Joseph C. 1939- *ODwPR 91*
Bowles, Larry David 1944- *St&PR 91*
Bowles, Lawrence Thompson 1931- *WhoAm 90*
Bowles, Margie H. *St&PR 91*
Bowles, Marianne Von Recklinghausen *WhoAmA 91*
Bowles, Martha Thomas 1952- *WhoAmW 91*
Bowles, Newton Rowell 1916- *WhoE 91*
Bowles, Norman Charles 1948- *WhoE 91*
Bowles, Patricia Mary 1950- *WhoE 91*
Bowles, Paul 1910- *BioIn 16, CurBio 90 [port], MajTwCW, WhoWrEP 89*
Bowles, Paul Frederick 1910- *IntWWM 90, WhoAm 90*
Bowles, Paul Richard 1953- *WhoEmL 91*
Bowles, Romald E. 1924- *St&PR 91*
Bowles, Samuel 1826-1878 *BioIn 16*
Bowles, Ted 1947- *St&PR 91*
Bowles, Walter Donald 1923- *WhoAm 90*
Bowles, William Augustus 1763-1805 *WhNaAH*
Bowles, William Lisle 1762-1850 *DcLB 93 [port]*
Bowles, William M. 1868-1930? *AmLegL*
Bowles, Windell William 1935- *WhoSSW 91*
Bowley, Albert John 1921- *WhoAm 90*
Bowley, Arthur Lyon 1869-1957 *BioIn 16*
Bowley, Norman W. 1951- *St&PR 91*
Bowlin, Earl 1935- *St&PR 91*
Bowlin, James Butler 1804-1874 *BioIn 16*
Bowlin, Kendall Duane 1933- *St&PR 91*
Bowlin, Mike R. 1943- *St&PR 91*
Bowling, Ann Trommershausen 1943- *WhoAmW 91*
Bowling, B.J. 1941- *St&PR 91*
Bowling, Clyde Ray 1949- *WhoAm 90*
Bowling, Daniel S., III 1955- *WhoEmL 91*
Bowling, David Samuel 1929- *WhoWor 91*
Bowling, Evelyn Burge 1931- *WhoAmW 91*
Bowling, Frank 1936- *WhoAmA 91*
Bowling, Gary *BioIn 16*
Bowling, Gary Robert 1948- *WhoAmA 91*
Bowling, Harold T. 1935- *St&PR 91*
Bowling, Irene Ruth 1957- *IntWWM 90*
Bowling, Jack 1903-1979 *WhoAmA 91N*
Bowling, James C. *ODwPR 91*
Bowling, James Chandler 1928- *WhoAm 90, WhoE 91*
Bowling, James Merle 1940- *WhoSSW 91*
Bowling, James W. *St&PR 91*
Bowling, John Robert 1943- *WhoSSW 91*
Bowling, Kathleen E. 1946- *WhoAmW 91, WhoEmL 91*
Bowling, Lance Christopher 1948- *WhoEmL 91, WhoWor 91*
Bowling, Lawson H 1924- *BiDrAPA 89*
Bowling, Nina Richardson 1956- *WhoEmL 91*
Bowling, Paul 1955- *WhoEmL 91*
Bowling, Rita Joan 1949- *WhoEmL 91*
Bowling, Robert J. 1925- *St&PR 91*
Bowling, Rod A. 1949- *St&PR 91*
Bowling, Thomas Barksdale 1932- *St&PR 91*
Bowling, William Glasgow 1902- *WhoAm 90, WhoWor 91*
Bowlly, Al 1899-1941 *OxCPMus*
Bowlt, John 1943- *WhoAmA 91*
Bowlt, John E 1943- *ConAu 130*
Bowlus, Douglas B. 1944- *St&PR 91*
Bowman, Amanda *ODwPR 91*
Bowman, Barbara Hyde 1930- *WhoAm 90*
Bowman, Barbara Sheryl 1953- *WhoAmW 91*
Bowman, Barbara Taylor 1928- *WhoAm 90*
Bowman, Beverly Ann 1958- *WhoAmW 91*
Bowman, Beverly Ann Hatfield 1946- *WhoAmW 91*
Bowman, Bob 1910-1972 *Ballpl 90*
Bowman, Bob 1931- *Ballpl 90*
Bowman, Bob 1936- *WhoWrEP 89*
Bowman, Bruce 1938- *WhoAmA 91*
Bowman, Bruce H. *St&PR 91*
Bowman, Bryan David 1954- *WhoE 91*
Bowman, Carl Byron 1913- *IntWWM 90*
Bowman, Carol Ann 1952- *WhoEmL 91*
Bowman, Charles Harwood, Jr. 1936- *WhoSSW 91*
Bowman, Clement Willis 1930- *WhoAm 90*
Bowman, Dale E. 1934- *St&PR 91*
Bowman, David A 1922- *BiDrAPA 89*
Bowman, David Bartholomew 1928- *WhoAm 90*
Bowman, David C. *WhoAm 90*
Bowman, David Wesley 1940- *St&PR 91, WhoAm 90*
Bowman, Dean Orlando 1909- *WhoAm 90*
Bowman, Deborah Anne 1957- *WhoAmW 91, WhoSSW 91*
Bowman, Don Jerry 1935- *St&PR 91*
Bowman, Donald E. 1948- *St&PR 91*
Bowman, Dorothy Louise 1927- *WhoAm 90*
Bowman, Dorothy Marie 1937- *WhoAmW 91*
Bowman, Edward Harry 1925- *WhoAm 90*
Bowman, Elizabeth Sue *BiDrAPA 89*
Bowman, Elizabeth Sue 1954- *WhoAmW 91*
Bowman, Erin Gardner 1948- *WhoAmW 91*
Bowman, Euday L. 1887-1949 *OxCPMus*
Bowman, Felson 1939- *St&PR 91*
Bowman, Francine Lorraine 1940- *WhoAmW 91*
Bowman, George Arthur, Jr. 1917- *WhoWor 91*
Bowman, George Leo 1935- *WhoAmA 91*
Bowman, Gerald L. *St&PR 91*
Bowman, Gerri M. *ODwPR 91*
Bowman, Gordon George 1922- *WhoWor 91*
Bowman, H.L. 1928- *St&PR 91*
Bowman, Harold J. 1931- *St&PR 91*
Bowman, Hazel Lois 1917- *WhoAmW 91*
Bowman, Irving Henry 1906- *WhoAm 90*
Bowman, Jacqueline Bonnie *WhoAmW 91*
Bowman, James 1941- *PenDiMP*
Bowman, James Cloyd 1880-1961 *AuBYP 90*
Bowman, James Donald 1933- *WhoAm 90*
Bowman, James Henry 1931- *WhoAm 90, WhoWrEP 89*
Bowman, James Kinsey 1933- *WhoAm 90*
Bowman, James R. 1946- *ODwPR 91*
Bowman, James S. 1934- *St&PR 91*
Bowman, James Scarboro, III 1952- *WhoSSW 91*
Bowman, James Thomas 1941- *IntWWM 90*
Bowman, Jeff Ray 1943- *WhoAmA 91*
Bowman, Jeffrey Lyn 1957- *St&PR 91*
Bowman, Joe *BioIn 16*
Bowman, Joe 1910- *Ballpl 90*
Bowman, John *AmLegL*
Bowman, John 1660?-1739 *PenDiMP*
Bowman, John 1953- *WhoAmA 91*
Bowman, John Alden 1933- *BiDrAPA 89*
Bowman, John B. 1902- *St&PR 91*
Bowman, John E. *BioIn 16*
Bowman, John Felipe 1931- *St&PR 91*
Bowman, John Maxwell 1925- *WhoAm 90*
Bowman, John Stewart 1931- *AuBYP 90*
Bowman, Joseph Searles 1920- *WhoAm 90*
Bowman, Kathleen 1942- *BioIn 16*
Bowman, Ken 1937- *WhoAmA 91*

Bowman, L. Allen 1932- *St&PR 91*
Bowman, Laird Price 1927- *WhoAm 90*
Bowman, Larry Alan 1948- *WhoEmL 91*
Bowman, Laura 1881-1957 *DrBlPA 90*
Bowman, Leah 1935- *WhoAm 90*
Bowman, Martha Alexander 1945- *WhoAm 90, WhoAmW 91*
Bowman, Martha Dietrich 1947- *WhoEmL 91*
Bowman, Marvis 1936- *WhoAmW 91*
Bowman, Mary Ann 1940- *WhoWrEP 89*
Bowman, Mary Beth 1948- *WhoEmL 91*
Bowman, Michael Douglas 1947- *WhoSSW 91*
Bowman, Michael Floyd 1953- *WhoEmL 91*
Bowman, Monroe Bengt 1901- *WhoWor 91*
Bowman, Nancy Moffett 1942- *WhoAmW 91*
Bowman, Ned David 1948- *WhoEmL 91, WhoSSW 91, WhoWor 91*
Bowman, Neil O'Kane 1948- *WhoSSW 91*
Bowman, Pasco Middleton, II 1933- *WhoAm 90*
Bowman, Patricia Ann 1949- *WhoAmW 91, WhoE 91, WhoWor 91*
Bowman, Peter William 1920- *BiDrAPA 89*
Bowman, Peyton Graham, III 1929- *WhoAm 90, WhoE 91*
Bowman, Richard 1918- *WhoAmA 91*
Bowman, Richard Carl 1926- *WhoAm 90*
Bowman, Richard Frederick 1952- *St&PR 91*
Bowman, Richard W. *ODwPR 91*
Bowman, Robert Allott 1955- *WhoAm 90*
Bowman, Robert F. 1933- *St&PR 91*
Bowman, Robert G. 1921- *St&PR 91*
Bowman, Robert Galen *BiDrAPA 89*
Bowman, Robert Gibson 1921- *WhoAm 90*
Bowman, Robert Henry 1915- *St&PR 91*
Bowman, Robert K. 1937- *St&PR 91*
Bowman, Robert L. 1933- *St&PR 91*
Bowman, Roger 1927- *Ballpl 90*
Bowman, Roger M. 1950- *St&PR 91*
Bowman, Roger Manwaring 1916- *WhoAm 90*
Bowman, Russell 1946- *BioIn 16*
Bowman, Ruth 1923- *WhoAmA 91*
Bowman, Susan A. 1956- *WhoAmW 91*
Bowman, Thea *BioIn 16, NewYTBS 90 [port]*
Bowman, Ward Simon, Jr. 1911- *WhoAm 90*
Bowman, William Pepper 1956- *WhoSSW 91*
Bowman, William Powell 1932- *WhoWor 91*
Bowman, William Scott 1933- *WhoAm 90*
Bowman-Dalton, Burdene Kathryn 1937- *WhoAmW 91*
Bowmer, Christopher Kenneth John 1946- *St&PR 91*
Bowmer, Jim Dewitt 1919- *WhoAm 90*
Bowmer, John Vance 1931- *St&PR 91*
Bown, Geraldine Mary 1948- *WhoWor 91*
Bown, Patti *IntWWM 90*
Bowne, Alan *BioIn 16*
Bowne, Alan 1945?-1989 *ConAu 130*
Bowne, Eliza 1783-1809 *FemiCLE*
Bowne, James Dehart 1940- *WhoAmA 91*
Bowne, Martha Hoke 1931- *WhoAmW 91*
Bownes, Hugh Henry 1920- *WhoAm 90*
Bowness, Alan 1928- *ConAu 130*
Bowness, Rick 1955- *WhoAm 90*
Bowns, Beverly Henry *WhoAm 90*
Bowra, Harriette *FemiCLE*
Bowring, Margaret Ann *BiDrAPA 89*
Bowron, Edgar Peters 1943- *ConAu 130, WhoAm 90, WhoAmA 91, WhoE 91*
Bowron, Richard Anderson 1924- *WhoAm 90*
Bows, Robert Alan 1949- *WhoEmL 91*
Bowser, Emilie Louise 1941- *WhoAmW 91*
Bowser, Hallowell *BioIn 16*
Bowser, Hallowell 1922?-1990 *ConAu 130*
Bowser, James William 1929- *WhoWrEP 89*
Bowsfield, Ted 1936- *Ballpl 90*
Bowsher, Charles Arthur 1931- *WhoE 91*
Bowyer, Allen Frank 1932- *WhoWor 91*
Bowyer, Charles Stuart 1934- *WhoAm 90*
Bowyer, Chaz 1926- *ConAu 33NR*
Bowyer, George C. 1944- *St&PR 91*
Bowyer, Joan Elizabeth 1944- *WhoAmW 91*
Bowyer, Worthy Lee, Jr. 1938- *St&PR 91*
Box, Barry Glenn 1958- *WhoAm 90, WhoEmL 91, WhoSSW 91*
Box, Brian Wayne 1965- *WhoEmL 91*
Box, Cloyce K. 1923- *St&PR 91*
Box, Dwain D. 1916- *WhoAm 90*
Box, Edgar *MajTwCW*
Box, Edgar 1925- *TwCCr&M 91*
Box, George Edward Pelham 1919- *WhoAm 90*
Box, George Lee 1934- *St&PR 91*
Box, Harold Charles 1925- *WhoAm 90*
Box, James C. 1931- *St&PR 91*
Box, Jerry Don 1942- *St&PR 91*
Box, Jerry W. 1938- *St&PR 91*
Box, John 1920- *ConDes 90*
Box, John Harold 1929- *WhoAm 90*
Box, Judyth Mitchell 1948- *BiDrAPA 89*
Box, Leonard Jerome 1933- *WhoE 91*
Box, Muriel 1905- *FemiCLE*
Box, Roger H. 1942- *St&PR 91*
Box, Steven 1937-1987 *BioIn 16*
Box, Thadis Wayne 1929- *WhoAm 90*
Boxall, Richard George 1936- *St&PR 91, WhoAm 90*
Boxberger, Matthew Dean 1959- *WhoEmL 91*
Boxberger, Michael Dwight 1946- *St&PR 91*
Boxdorfer, James Jay 1957- *St&PR 91*
Boxer, Arthur David 1934- *BiDrAPA 89*
Boxer, Barbara 1940- *WhoAm 90, WhoAmW 91*
Boxer, C. R. 1904- *BioIn 16*
Boxer, Charles Ralph 1904- *BioIn 16*
Boxer, Devorah *AuBYP 90*
Boxer, Gary Harris *BiDrAPA 89*
Boxer, Harry 1946- *WhoEmL 91*
Boxer, Jerome Harvey 1930- *WhoAm 90, WhoWor 91*
Boxer, Mark 1931-1988 *AnObit 1988, BioIn 16*
Boxer, Peter Alan 1951- *BiDrAPA 89*
Boxer, Robert William 1933- *WhoAm 90*
Boxer, Rubin 1927- *St&PR 91, WhoAm 90*
Boxer, Stanley 1926- *WhoAmA 91*
Boxer, Stanley Robert 1926- *WhoAm 90*
Boxerman, Deborah Ruth *BiDrAPA 89*
Boxhorn, Mark Zuerius 1612-1653 *EncO&P 3*
Boxill, Carlton 1896- *DcAfAmP*
Boxill, Edith Hillman 1926- *WhoE 91*
Boxill, Herbert John 1931- *St&PR 91*
Boxleiter, Thomas Raymond *BiDrAPA 89*
Boxler, Dorothy Bacino 1956- *WhoAmW 91*
Boxley, Jerry *BioIn 16*
Boxwell, Alexander 1853?-1923 *AmLegL*
Boxwill, Frank E. 1926- *WhoE 91, WhoWor 91*
Boxx, Rita McCord 1930- *WhoAmW 91*
Boy George *BioIn 16, EncPR&S 89*
Boy George 1961- *OxCPMus*
Boy, John Buckner 1917- *St&PR 91*
Boy-Ed, Ida 1852-1928 *EncCoWW*
Boyadjian, Haig John 1935- *WhoWor 91*
Boyadjian, Hayg 1938- *IntWWM 90*
Boyadjieff, George Ivan 1938- *St&PR 91*
Boyajian, Carole L. 1948- *WhoEmL 91*
Boyajian, Levon Z *BiDrAPA 89*
Boyan, Norman John 1922- *WhoAm 90*
Boyan, William L., Jr. 1937- *St&PR 91*
Boyanton, Janet Shafer 1954- *WhoWrEP 89*
Boyar, Lea A. 1958- *WhoAmW 91*
Boyar, Robert Lee 1935- *WhoE 91*
Boyars, Albert *St&PR 91*
Boyarsky, Benjamin William 1934- *WhoAm 90, WhoWrEP 89*
Boyarsky, Val David 1960- *WhoEmL 91*
Boyatt, Thomas David 1933- *WhoAm 90*
Boyatzis, Richard Eleftherios 1946- *WhoEmL 91*
Boyazis, James 1936- *St&PR 91*
Boyce, Allan R. 1943- *ODwPR 91*
Boyce, Clyde Alvin 1955- *St&PR 91*
Boyce, Daniel Hobbs 1953- *WhoEmL 91*
Boyce, David Edward 1938- *WhoAm 90*
Boyce, Donald Nelson 1938- *St&PR 91, WhoAm 90*
Boyce, Doreen Elizabeth 1934- *WhoAmW 91*
Boyce, Edward Wayne, Jr. 1926- *WhoAm 90*
Boyce, Emily Stewart 1933- *WhoAm 90, WhoAmW 91*
Boyce, Fred Comstock, Jr. 1900- *St&PR 91*
Boyce, Gerald G. 1925- *WhoAm 90, WhoAmA 91*
Boyce, Gerard Robert 1954- *WhoEmL 91*
Boyce, Ira F. 1910- *St&PR 91*
Boyce, James R., Sr. 1844- *AmLegL*
Boyce, Joanna Mary 1831-1861 *BiDWomA*
Boyce, Joseph Nelson 1937- *WhoAm 90*
Boyce, Peter Bradford 1936- *WhoAm 90*
Boyce, Raymond A. 1935- *ODwPR 91*
Boyce, Richard 1920- *WhoAmA 91N*
Boyce, Roger Wade 1948- *WhoAmA 91*
Boyce, Sonia 1962- *BiDWomA*
Boyce, Thomas K 1923- *BiDrAPA 89*
Boyce, Thomas Kenneth 1923- *WhoE 91*
Boyce, Timothy John 1954- *WhoEmL 91*
Boyce, Tracy Davenport 1966- *WhoAmW 91*
Boyce, Wayne 1926- *WhoWrEP 89*
Boyce, William Edward 1930- *WhoE 91*
Boyce, William G 1921- *WhoAmA 91*
Boyce, William George 1921- *WhoAm 90*
Boychuck, George 1929- *St&PR 91*
Boycks, Barbara Elizabeth 1944- *St&PR 91*
Boycott, Charles 1832-1897 *WorAlBi*
Boycott, Geoff *ConAu 131*
Boycott, Geoffrey 1940- *ConAu 131*
Boycott, Rosie 1951- *ConAu 132*
Boyd and Evans *BiDWomA*
Boyd, Alan Conduitt 1926- *WhoAm 90*
Boyd, Alan S. 1922- *St&PR 91*
Boyd, Alan Stephenson 1922- *BiDrUSE 89*
Boyd, Allie C 1941- *BiDrAPA 89*
Boyd, Amelia Malixi *BiDrAPA 89*
Boyd, Ann Fisher 1937- *St&PR 91*
Boyd, Anne Elizabeth 1946- *IntWWM 90*
Boyd, Barbara Ann 1956- *WhoAmW 91*
Boyd, Barry A 1921- *BiDrAPA 89*
Boyd, Belle 1843-1900 *BioAmW*
Boyd, Beverley Randolph 1947- *WhoEmL 91*
Boyd, Billy Matthew 1942- *WhoSSW 91*
Boyd, Billy Willard 1948- *WhoEmL 91*
Boyd, Blanche M. 1945- *BioIn 16*
Boyd, Bob 1926- *Ballpl 90, BioIn 16*
Boyd, Bobbie Marguerite 1957- *WhoAmW 91*
Boyd, Bruce B *BiDrAPA 89*
Boyd, C. Edward 1936- *St&PR 91*
Boyd, Candy Dawson 1946- *BioIn 16*
Boyd, Catherine Emma 1918- *WhoWrEP 89*
Boyd, Charles Graham 1938- *WhoAm 90*
Boyd, Charles H. 1934- *St&PR 91*
Boyd, Clarence E *BiDrAPA 89*
Boyd, Clarence Elmo 1911- *WhoAm 90, WhoSSW 91*
Boyd, Constance Dorothy 1943- *WhoAmW 91*
Boyd, Crowther M. 1908- *St&PR 91*
Boyd, Danny Douglass 1933- *WhoSSW 91*
Boyd, David Milton 1918- *WhoAm 90*
Boyd, David Parker 1957- *WhoEmL 91*
Boyd, David Preston 1943- *WhoE 91, WhoWor 91*
Boyd, David William 1941- *WhoAm 90*
Boyd, Dawn Michele 1952- *WhoAmW 91*
Boyd, Deborah Ann 1955- *WhoAmW 91*
Boyd, Donald Leroy 1935- *St&PR 91*
Boyd, E 1903-1974 *WhoAmA 91N*
Boyd, Edgar M. 1920- *St&PR 91*
Boyd, Edson 1912- *St&PR 91*
Boyd, Edward Lee 1930- *St&PR 91, WhoAm 90, WhoSSW 91*
Boyd, Edward Lee 1932- *WhoWor 91*
Boyd, Edwin Louis 1932- *St&PR 91*
Boyd, Elizabeth *FemiCLE*
Boyd, Emilie Lou 1935- *WhoSSW 91*
Boyd, Fionnuala 1944- *BiDWomA*
Boyd, Francis Virgil 1922- *WhoAm 90*
Boyd, Frank *TwCCr&M 91*
Boyd, Frank E., III 1951- *St&PR 91*
Boyd, Frank E., Jr. 1923- *St&PR 91*
Boyd, Fred 1938- *St&PR 91*
Boyd, Gary Delane 1932- *WhoAm 90*
Boyd, Gary Don 1947- *WhoSSW 91*
Boyd, George Edward 1911- *WhoAm 90*
Boyd, George Golden 1944- *St&PR 91*
Boyd, Hallam 1928- *St&PR 91*
Boyd, Harold Stephen 1963- *WhoSSW 91*
Boyd, Harry Dalton 1923- *St&PR 91, WhoAm 90*
Boyd, Herbert Reed, Jr. 1925- *WhoSSW 91*
Boyd, Howard Taney 1909- *WhoAm 90*
Boyd, Ina Helene *BiDrAPA 89*
Boyd, J. Cookman, Jr. 1906- *St&PR 91*
Boyd, James Brown 1937- *WhoAm 90*
Boyd, James Burdette 1937- *WhoSSW 91*
Boyd, James E. 1948- *St&PR 91*
Boyd, James E. 1959- *WhoEmL 91*
Boyd, James Henderson 1928- *WhoAmA 91*
Boyd, James R. 1921- *St&PR 91*
Boyd, James R. 1946- *St&PR 91*
Boyd, James Robert 1946- *WhoAm 90*
Boyd, James Truman 1927- *St&PR 91*
Boyd, Jane Elizabeth 1946- *WhoAmW 91*
Boyd, Jane Ellen 1958- *BiDrAPA 89*
Boyd, Jayne *BioIn 16*
Boyd, Jean K *BiDrAPA 89*
Boyd, Jeffrey Howard 1943- *BiDrAPA 89*
Boyd, Jerry Lee 1955- *St&PR 91*
Boyd, Jerry Wayne 1945- *WhoSSW 91*
Boyd, Joan *BioIn 16*
Boyd, Joe Dan 1934- *WhoSSW 91*
Boyd, John 1826-1893 *DcCanB 12*
Boyd, John 1917-1989 *AnObit 1989, BioIn 16*
Boyd, John David 1939- *WhoAmA 91*
Boyd, John Dominic 1916- *WhoAm 90*
Boyd, John H. *ODwPR 91*
Boyd, John Hamilton 1924- *WhoAm 90, WhoSSW 91*
Boyd, John Kent 1910- *WhoWor 91*
Boyd, John Patrick 1949- *WhoSSW 91*
Boyd, John S. 1946- *St&PR 91*
Boyd, John Smith Knox 1891-1981 *DcNaB 1981*
Boyd, John Thomas 1927- *WhoSSW 91*
Boyd, John Wells 1950- *WhoEmL 91*
Boyd, John William *BiDrAPA 89*
Boyd, Joseph A. 1921- *St&PR 91*
Boyd, Joseph Arthur, Jr. 1916- *WhoAm 90*
Boyd, Joseph Aubrey 1921- *WhoAm 90*
Boyd, Joseph David 1937- *BiDrAPA 89*
Boyd, Joseph Don 1926- *WhoAm 90*
Boyd, Joseph F. Jr. *BiDrAPA 89*
Boyd, Julius 1923- *St&PR 91*
Boyd, Karen White 1936- *WhoAmA 91*
Boyd, Kenneth Wade 1938- *WhoSSW 91*
Boyd, Lakin 1946- *WhoAmA 91*
Boyd, Landis Lee 1923- *WhoAm 90*
Boyd, Larry Chester 1958- *WhoE 91, WhoEmL 91*
Boyd, Leona Potter 1907- *WhoAmW 91*
Boyd, Lew Finch 1945- *WhoEmL 91*
Boyd, Linda Joyce 1946- *WhoAmW 91*
Boyd, Linda Smith 1961- *WhoE 91*
Boyd, Liona Maria *WhoAm 90*
Boyd, Lizi *AuBYP 90*
Boyd, Lorenz *AuBYP 90*
Boyd, Louis Jefferson 1928- *WhoAm 90*
Boyd, Louise Arner 1887-1972 *BioAmW*
Boyd, Louise Yvonne 1959- *WhoAmW 91*
Boyd, Malcolm 1923- *WhoAm 90, WhoWrEP 89, WorAlBi*
Boyd, Malcolm 1932- *IntWWM 90*
Boyd, Margaret Louise *WhoAmW 91*
Boyd, Martin 1893-1972 *BioIn 16*
Boyd, Mary Ann 1945- *WhoEmL 91*
Boyd, Mary Dexter 1913- *WhoAmW 91*
Boyd, Michael 1936- *WhoAmA 91*
Boyd, Michael Alan 1937- *St&PR 91, WhoAm 90*
Boyd, Michael Delen 1956- *St&PR 91*
Boyd, Mildred 1921- *AuBYP 90*
Boyd, Milton John 1941- *WhoAm 90*
Boyd, Morton 1936- *St&PR 91*
Boyd, Nancy *ConAu 130, MajTwCW*
Boyd, Neil 1951- *ConAu 129*
Boyd, Oil Can 1959- *Ballpl 90*
Boyd, Patsy Jean 1940- *WhoAmW 91*
Boyd, Patti *BioIn 16*
Boyd, Philip L. 1900-1989 *BioIn 16*
Boyd, Randall M. 1946- *St&PR 91*
Boyd, Rhonda Weiderspon 1958- *WhoEmL 91*
Boyd, Richard Alfred 1927- *WhoAm 90*
Boyd, Richard Hays 1929- *WhoAm 90*
Boyd, Richard Henry 1843-1922 *BioIn 16*
Boyd, Richard Leroy 1922- *St&PR 91*
Boyd, Rob *BioIn 16*
Boyd, Robert Arthur 1918- *St&PR 91*
Boyd, Robert Cotton 1938- *WhoEmL 91*
Boyd, Robert Friend 1927- *St&PR 91*
Boyd, Robert Giddings, Jr. 1940- *WhoAm 90*
Boyd, Robert Jamison 1930- *St&PR 91, WhoAm 90*
Boyd, Robert Lewis Fullarton 1922- *WhoWor 91*
Boyd, Robert Methven, Jr. 1933- *St&PR 91*
Boyd, Robert T. 1933- *St&PR 91*
Boyd, Robert Thompson 1914- *WhoE 91*
Boyd, Robert Wright, III 1945- *WhoE 91*
Boyd, Rodney 1943- *IntWWM 90*
Boyd, Rutherford *WhoAmA 91N*
Boyd, Samuel Matthew 1908- *WhoAm 90*
Boyd, Scott Hamilton *BiDrAPA 89*
Boyd, Stephanie C. *ODwPR 91*
Boyd, Stephen 1928-1977 *WorAlBi*
Boyd, Stephen Curtis 1949- *WhoEmL 91*
Boyd, Stephen Fayen 1952- *St&PR 91*
Boyd, Stephen Mather 1934- *WhoAm 90*
Boyd, Stuart Robert 1939- *WhoAm 90*
Boyd, Theophilus Bartholomew, III 1947- *WhoAm 90, WhoSSW 91, WhoWor 91*
Boyd, Thomas, III 1936- *St&PR 91*
Boyd, Thomas Marshall 1946- *WhoAm 90*
Boyd, Virginia Ann Lewis 1944- *WhoAmW 91*
Boyd, Waldo T. 1918- *AuBYP 90*
Boyd, Waymon Lewis 1933- *St&PR 91*
Boyd, Wayne Johnson *BiDrAPA 89*
Boyd, Willard L. 1927- *St&PR 91*
Boyd, Willard Lee 1927- *WhoAm 90*
Boyd, William 1895-1972 *WorAlBi*
Boyd, William 1952- *WorAu 1980 [port]*
Boyd, William, Jr. 1915- *St&PR 91, WhoAm 90*
Boyd, William B. 1924- *St&PR 91, WhoE 91*
Boyd, William Beaty 1923- *WhoAm 90*
Boyd, William Douglas, Jr. 1929- *WhoWor 91*
Boyd, William H 1933- *BiDrAPA 89*
Boyd, William Richard 1916- *WhoAm 90*
Boyd-Carpenter, John 1908- *ConAu 131*
Boyd-Foy, Mary Louise *WhoAmW 91*
Boyd-Kray, Peggy 1934- *St&PR 91*
Boyd-Leopard, Norree 1951- *WhoSSW 91*
Boyd-Meis, Betty Sue 1952- *WhoSSW 91*
Boyd Of Merton, Viscount 1904-1983 *DcNaB 1981*
Boyd Orr, John 1880-1971 *WorAlBi*
Boyd-Rochfort, Cecil Charles 1887-1983 *DcNaB 1981*
Boyda, Kenneth L. 1944- *St&PR 91*
Boydell, Brian Patrick 1917- *IntWWM 90*
Boyden, Allen Marston 1908- *WhoAm 90*

Boyden, Joel Michael 1937- *WhoAm 90, WhoWor 91*
Boyden, Robert W. 1932- *St&PR 91*
Boyden, Walter Lincoln 1932- *WhoAm 90*
Boydstun, James Allen 1940- *BiDrAPA 89*
Boye, Birgitte Cathrine 1742-1824 *EncCoWW*
Boye, Karin 1900-1941 *EncCoWW*
Boye, Karin Maria 1900-1941 *DcScanL*
Boyea, Bruce Walter 1951- *St&PR 91*
Boyer, Alan R. 1946- *St&PR 91*
Boyer, Barry C. *St&PR 91*
Boyer, Calvin James 1939- *WhoAm 90*
Boyer, Carl, III 1937- *WhoWor 91*
Boyer, Charles 1899-1978 *WorAlBi*
Boyer, Clete 1937- *Ballpl 90*
Boyer, Cloyd 1927- *Ballpl 90*
Boyer, Daniel Robert 1947- *WhoE 91*
Boyer, David Creighton 1930- *WhoAm 90*
Boyer, David Norman 1944- *BiDrAPA 89*
Boyer, David S. 1942- *St&PR 91*
Boyer, Edward *AuBYP 90*
Boyer, Eric Lee 1962- *WhoSSW 91*
Boyer, Ernest L. *BioIn 16*
Boyer, Ernest LeRoy 1928- *WhoAm 90, WhoE 91*
Boyer, Eugene C. 1943- *St&PR 91*
Boyer, Ford Sylvester 1934- *WhoWor 91*
Boyer, Francois *PenDiDA 89*
Boyer, G. G. *ConAu 130*
Boyer, Geoffrey Frederick 1945- *WhoEmL 91*
Boyer, George Edward, Jr. 1955- *WhoEmL 91*
Boyer, George T. 1928- *St&PR 91*
Boyer, Glenn G. 1924- *ConAu 130*
Boyer, Guy H. 1954- *St&PR 91*
Boyer, Henry K. 1850-1900? *AmLegL*
Boyer, Horace Clarence 1935- *IntWWM 90*
Boyer, James Keely 1924- *WhoAm 90, WhoE 91*
Boyer, James Lorenzen 1936- *WhoAm 90*
Boyer, James Rahn 1933- *St&PR 91*
Boyer, Jean Pierre 1776-1850 *BioIn 16*
Boyer, Jean-Pierre 1935- *WhoWor 91*
Boyer, John H. 1950- *St&PR 91*
Boyer, John W., Jr. 1928- *St&PR 91*
Boyer, Kaye Kittle 1942- *WhoAmW 91*
Boyer, Ken 1931-1982 *Ballpl 90 [port]*
Boyer, L Bryce *BiDrAPA 89*
Boyer, Laura Mercedes 1934- *WhoAmW 91, WhoWor 91*
Boyer, Lester Leroy, Jr. 1937- *WhoAm 90*
Boyer, Lillian Buckley 1916- *WhoAmW 91*
Boyer, Lucienne 1903-1983 *OxCPMus*
Boyer, Marcel 1943- *WhoAm 90*
Boyer, Marietta P 1932- *WhoAmA 91*
Boyer, Max Kevin 1953- *WhoEmL 91*
Boyer, Patricia K *BiDrAPA 89*
Boyer, Paul D. 1918- *WhoAm 90*
Boyer, Peter Jay 1950- *WhoEmL 91*
Boyer, Philip B. 1940- *St&PR 91*
Boyer, Philip Boyajian 1940- *WhoAm 90*
Boyer, Ralph Ludwig 1879-1952 *WhoAmA 91N*
Boyer, Raymond Foster 1910- *WhoAm 90*
Boyer, Richard Lewis 1943- *WhoSSW 91*
Boyer, Rick 1943- *TwCCr&M 91*
Boyer, Robert Allan 1934- *WhoE 91, WhoWor 91*
Boyer, Robert Allen 1916- *WhoAm 90*
Boyer, Robert Ernst 1929- *WhoAm 90*
Boyer, Robert Jay 1951- *WhoEmL 91*
Boyer, Ronald E. 1937- *St&PR 91*
Boyer, Susan Spark 1943- *WhoWrEP 89*
Boyer, Vincent Saull 1918- *WhoAm 90*
Boyer, Wilbur B., Jr. 1945- *St&PR 91*
Boyer, William H 1924- *WhoWrEP 89*
Boyer, Yves Maurice 1943- *WhoWor 91*
Boyers, Charles Frank 1942- *St&PR 91*
Boyers, John Hamilton 1944- *St&PR 91*
Boyers, Robert 1942- *WhoAm 90*
Boyerschoen, Arthur 1923- *WhoAmA 91*
Boyerschoen, Arthur, Mrs 1915- *WhoAmA 91*
Boyes, Stephen Richard 1950- *WhoSSW 91*
Boyett, Susan Archer 1952- *WhoSSW 91*
Boyette, Flip Huntus 1920- *St&PR 91*
Boyette, Ivern *WhoWrEP 89*
Boyette, Marsha Ann 1952- *WhoAmW 91*
Boyette, Purvis Elton 1937-1987 *BioIn 16*
Boyington, Gregory 1912-1988 *BioIn 16*
Boyington, Pappy 1912-1988 *BioIn 16*
Boyk, Fredric Michael 1953- *St&PR 91*
Boykan, Martin 1931- *IntWWM 90, WhoAm 90*
Boyke, Paul 1940- *St&PR 91*
Boyken, Donald Richard 1952- *WhoSSW 91*
Boykin, A. Hugh 1925- *St&PR 91*
Boykin, Charles Vincent 1943- *WhoAm 90*
Boykin, Edward McCallum 1913- *WhoAm 90*
Boykin, Frances Lewis *WhoAmW 91, WhoE 91, WhoWor 91*
Boykin, Hamilton Haight 1939- *St&PR 91*
Boykin, Hartford Edwin, Jr. 1952- *WhoWor 91*
Boykin, Joseph Floyd, Jr. 1940- *WhoAm 90*
Boykin, Lykes M. 1919- *WhoAm 90*
Boykin, Robert Eugene 1945- *WhoSSW 91*
Boykin, Robert H. 1926- *St&PR 91*
Boykin, Robert Heath 1926- *WhoAm 90*
Boykin, Robert N., Jr. 1947- *St&PR 91*
Boykin, Wilburn Tinsley, Jr. 1955- *WhoEmL 91*
Boykin, William Henry, Jr. 1938- *WhoSSW 91*
Boykin, William Johnson 1919- *St&PR 91*
Boyko, Christopher Allan 1954- *WhoEmL 91, WhoWor 91*
Boyko, Fred 1894-1951 *WhoAmA 91N*
Boyko, Gregory Andrew 1951- *St&PR 91, WhoAm 90, WhoE 91*
Boyko, Rudolph J. *BioIn 16*
Boyko, Yefim *PenDiMP*
Boylan, Brian Richard 1936- *WhoWor 91*
Boylan, D.J., Jr. 1924- *St&PR 91*
Boylan, David Ray 1922- *WhoAm 90*
Boylan, Dean M. 1926- *St&PR 91*
Boylan, Eleanor 1916- *ConAu 132*
Boylan, Elizabeth Shippee 1946- *WhoAmW 91*
Boylan, Gary Lynn 1952- *WhoEmL 91*
Boylan, Glenn Gerard 1959- *WhoSSW 91*
Boylan, Grace 1862-1935 *FemiCLE*
Boylan, James George 1937- *WhoE 91*
Boylan, Jeanne-Marie 1949- *St&PR 91*
Boylan, John Lester 1955- *WhoEmL 91*
Boylan, John Lewis 1921- *WhoAmA 91*
Boylan, John Patrick 1941- *WhoAm 90, WhoWor 91*
Boylan, Kathryn Carnes 1938- *WhoAmW 91*
Boylan, MaryAnn Harr 1949- *WhoAmW 91*
Boylan, Merle Nelson 1925- *WhoAm 90*
Boylan, Paul Charles 1939- *WhoAm 90*
Boylan, Roger Brendan 1951- *WhoWrEP 89*
Boylan, Virginia Walker 1941- *WhoAmW 91*
Boylan, William Alvin 1924- *WhoAm 90, WhoE 91, WhoWor 91*
Boyland, Joseph Francis 1931- *St&PR 91, WhoAm 90*
Boyle, Alexander Robert Mills 1937- *St&PR 91*
Boyle, Barbara Dorman 1935- *WhoAm 90, WhoAmW 91*
Boyle, Barbara Jane 1936- *WhoAmW 91*
Boyle, Barbara Merle Princelau 1923- *WhoE 91*
Boyle, Bruce James 1931- *WhoAm 90*
Boyle, Buzz 1908-1978 *Ballpl 90*
Boyle, C.R., III 1948- *St&PR 91*
Boyle, Charles Keith 1930- *WhoAm 90*
Boyle, Clyde Frank 1923- *St&PR 91*
Boyle, Daniel E. 1931- *St&PR 91*
Boyle, Daniel Edward, Jr. 1931- *WhoAm 90*
Boyle, Dennis McCord 1932- *WhoWor 91*
Boyle, Dennis O'Neil 1952- *St&PR 91*
Boyle, Desmond G *BiDrAPA 89*
Boyle, Donna Davis 1962- *WhoEmL 91*
Boyle, Edward Charles Gurney 1923-1981 *DcNaB 1981*
Boyle, Edward James, Jr. 1940- *St&PR 91*
Boyle, Edward Patrick 1912- *St&PR 91*
Boyle, Elizabeth Mary Hunt 1956- *WhoEmL 91*
Boyle, Francis Anthony 1950- *WhoEmL 91*
Boyle, Francis J. 1945- *St&PR 91*
Boyle, Francis Joseph 1945- *WhoAm 90*
Boyle, Georgia *BioIn 16*
Boyle, Gert *BioIn 16*
Boyle, Glenn Edward 1952- *WhoEmL 91*
Boyle, Harry *BioIn 16*
Boyle, Howard H. 1921- *St&PR 91*
Boyle, Ira Lee 1950- *St&PR 91*
Boyle, Ivy Roberta 1943- *BiDrAPA 89*
Boyle, J. Allan 1916- *St&PR 91*
Boyle, Jimmy 1944- *BioIn 16, ConAu 130*
Boyle, JoAnne Woodyard 1935- *WhoAmW 91*
Boyle, John David 1946- *WhoWrEP 89*
Boyle, John E. Whiteford 1915- *WhoWrEP 89*
Boyle, John L. 1934- *St&PR 91*
Boyle, John L 1950- *BiDrAPA 89*
Boyle, John Raymond 1941- *WhoAm 90*
Boyle, John William 1929- *WhoAm 90, WhoSSW 91*
Boyle, John William 1937- *St&PR 91*
Boyle, Joseph E. 1921- *St&PR 91*
Boyle, Kay 1902- *BioIn 16, FemiCLE, MajTwCW, WhoAm 90, WhoAmW 91, WhoWrEP 89*
Boyle, Kay 1903- *BioAmW*
Boyle, Keith 1930- *WhoAmA 91*
Boyle, Kevin D. 1944- *St&PR 91*
Boyle, Kevin John 1955- *WhoE 91*
Boyle, Lynnette Zellner 1952- *WhoEmL 91*
Boyle, M. Ross 1935- *WhoAm 90*
Boyle, Margaret Sidney Eaton *BioIn 16*
Boyle, Mark *ConAu 31NR, MajTwCW, St&PR 91*
Boyle, Mark 1934- *BioIn 16*
Boyle, Mary 1810-1890 *FemiCLE*
Boyle, Matthew Anthony 1944- *St&PR 91*
Boyle, Michael F. 1955- *St&PR 91*
Boyle, Neil 1931- *WhoAmA 91*
Boyle, Nina 1865?-1943 *FemiCLE*
Boyle, Patricia Jean *WhoAmW 91*
Boyle, Patrick Gerald 1928- *WhoAm 90*
Boyle, Peter 1933- *WorAlBi*
Boyle, Renee Kent 1926- *WhoAmW 91, WhoE 91*
Boyle, Richard 1694-1753 *BioIn 16*
Boyle, Richard Guy 1938- *St&PR 91, WhoAm 90*
Boyle, Richard J 1932- *ConAu 129, WhoAmA 91*
Boyle, Richard James 1943- *St&PR 91*
Boyle, Richard John 1932- *WhoAm 90*
Boyle, Robert 1627-1691 *WorAlBi*
Boyle, Robert 1910- *ConDes 90*
Boyle, Robert Patrick 1913- *WhoAm 90*
Boyle, Samuel John, IV 1948- *WhoAm 90*
Boyle, Scott Alan 1955- *St&PR 91*
Boyle, Sebastian *BioIn 16*
Boyle, Stephen P. 1940- *St&PR 91*
Boyle, Susan Jeanne 1952- *WhoAmW 91*
Boyle, Susan M. 1948- *St&PR 91*
Boyle, T. Coraghessan *BioIn 16, NewYTBS 90 [port]*
Boyle, T Coraghessan 1948- *BestSel 90-4 [port]*
Boyle, T. Coraghessan 1948- *WorAu 1980 [port]*
Boyle, Terence 1952- *WhoEmL 91*
Boyle, Terrence W. 1945- *WhoAm 90*
Boyle, Thomas Michael 1947- *WhoSSW 91*
Boyle, Willard Sterling 1924- *WhoAm 90*
Boyle, William C.H., Jr. 1953- *WhoSSW 91*
Boyle, William Charles 1936- *WhoAm 90*
Boyle, William Leo, Jr. 1933- *WhoAm 90, WhoE 91*
Boyle, William Pickard, Jr. 1933- *St&PR 91, WhoAm 90*
Boyle, William R. 1932- *WhoAm 90*
Boyle, William W. 1934- *St&PR 91*
Boylen, Michael Edward 1935- *WhoAmA 91*
Boyler, Geraldine V. *ODwPR 91*
Boyles, Beatrice C. 1915- *WhoAmW 91*
Boyles, Carol Ann Patterson 1932- *WhoSSW 91*
Boyles, David LeRoy 1949- *St&PR 91*
Boyles, Donna Lou Cochran 1935- *WhoAmW 91*
Boyles, Gary Edward 1951- *WhoEmL 91*
Boyles, Harlan Edward 1929- *WhoAm 90, WhoSSW 91*
Boyles, James Kenneth 1916- *WhoAm 90*
Boyles, Rex Wilson 1947- *WhoSSW 91*
Boyles, William Ray 1948- *St&PR 91*
Boyles-Sprenkel, Carolee Anita 1953- *WhoWrEP 89*
Boyll, David Lloyd 1940- *WhoAm 90*
Boylston, Adrian F. 1927- *St&PR 91*
Boylston, Benjamin Calvin 1932- *St&PR 91, WhoE 91*
Boylston, Helen 1895-1984 *AuBYP 90*
Boylston, Helen Dore 1895- *FemiCLE*
Boylston, John 1920- *St&PR 91*
Boylston, Robert Bentham 1822-1865 *AmLegL*
Boylston, Robert Judson 1931- *WhoSSW 91*
Boylston, William H 1935- *BiDrAPA 89*
Boylston, Zabdiel 1679-1766 *EncCRAm*
Boyman, John Edward George 1937- *WhoAm 90*
Boyne, Allan L. 1936- *St&PR 91*
Boyne, Robert D. 1930- *St&PR 91*
Boyne, Walter James 1929- *WhoAm 90, WhoSSW 91*
Boynton, Bruce Ryland 1948- *WhoSSW 91*
Boynton, Donald C. 1953- *ODwPR 91*
Boynton, Estelle P *BiDrAPA 89*
Boynton, Harry Gene 1928- *WhoSSW 91*
Boynton, Jack W 1928- *WhoAmA 91*
Boynton, James Lester 1936- *BiDrAPA 89*
Boynton, Jane Bodorff 1936- *WhoE 91*
Boynton, Jay Wayne 1945- *WhoSSW 91*
Boynton, Nancy H. 1933- *St&PR 91*
Boynton, Nat *BioIn 16*
Boynton, Richard S. 1934- *St&PR 91*
Boynton, Robert Granville 1951- *WhoEmL 91*
Boynton, Robert Merrill 1924- *WhoAm 90*
Boynton, Sandra *BioIn 16*
Boynton, Whitney Anne 1947- *BiDrAPA 89*
Boynton, Wyman Pender 1908- *WhoWor 91*
Boyo, Eugene 1926- *ODwPR 91*
Boyom, Bodie Michel Nguiffo 1940- *WhoWor 91*
Boyriven, Mariette Hartley 1940- *WhoAmW 91*
Boyse, Edward Arthur 1923- *WhoAm 90*
Boysen, Connie Jean 1958- *WhoEmL 91*
Boysen, Harry 1904- *WhoAm 90*
Boysen, Lars 1948- *WhoEmL 91*
Boysen, Melicent Pearl 1943- *WhoAmW 91*
Boyson, Emil 1897-1979 *DcScanL*
Boyt, Patrick Elmer 1940- *WhoSSW 91*
Boyter, Angela Marie 1944- *WhoAmW 91*
Boyter, Scott M. 1947- *WhoEmL 91*
Boytim, Joan Frey 1933- *WhoAmW 91*
Boytim, Thomas Edward 1948- *WhoE 91*
Boyton, Neil *AuBYP 90*
Boyvin, Rene *PenDiDA 89*
Boza, Clara Brizeida 1952- *WhoAmW 91*
Boza, Juan 1941- *WhoHisp 91*
Bozack, Michael James 1952- *WhoSSW 91*
Bozak, George Louis 1940- *St&PR 91*
Bozarth, George S. 1947- *IntWWM 90*
Bozarth, Glenn 1953- *ODwPR 91*
Bozarth, William T. 1940- *St&PR 91*
Bozay, Attila 1939- *IntWWM 90*
Bozdech, Marek Jiri 1946- *WhoAm 90*
Boze, Fred Adwell 1946- *WhoEmL 91*
Bozeman, Adda Bruemmer 1908- *WhoAm 90, WhoWor 91*
Bozeman, Carlton Michael 1957- *WhoSSW 91*
Bozeman, Frank Carmack 1933- *WhoAm 90, WhoSSW 91*
Bozeman, John M. 1835-1867 *WhNaAH*
Bozeman, Lynne Norman 1961- *WhoEmL 91*
Bozeman, Sylvia Trimble 1947- *WhoSSW 91*
Bozeman, Thomas Hunt 1958- *WhoEmL 91*
Bozer, Ali Husrev 1925- *WhoWor 91*
Bozic, Andrej 1960- *WhoWor 91*
Bozic, Dennis Ray 1956- *WhoSSW 91*
Bozicevic, Juraj 1935- *WhoWor 91*
Bozich, Anthony Thomas 1924- *WhoAm 90*
Bozigian, Howard Kirk 1951- *WhoEmL 91*
Boziwick, George E. 1954- *IntWWM 90*
Bozman, J. Robert 1938- *St&PR 91*
Boznanska, Olga 1865-1940 *BiDWomA*
Bozo, Dominique *BioIn 16*
Bozone, Billie Rae 1935- *WhoAm 90, WhoAmW 91*
Bozorgmanesh, H. 1943- *St&PR 91*
Bozorth, Louise Mathews 1943- *IntWWM 90*
Bozorth, Squire Newland 1935- *WhoAm 90, WhoE 91*
Bozsa, Deborah Ann 1953- *WhoAmW 91, WhoEmL 91*
Bozsan, Jacqueline Ann 1946- *WhoAmW 91*
Bozung, David Allen 1948- *WhoEmL 91*
Bozyk, Reizi *BioIn 16*
Bozymski, Michael Joseph 1959- *St&PR 91*
Bozza, Linda Susan 1949- *WhoWrEP 89*
Bozzano, Ernesto 1862-1943 *EncO&P 3, EncPaPR 91*
Bozzano, Georgette T. 1950- *WhoEmL 91*
Bozzay, William 1923- *St&PR 91*
Bozzelli, Andrew Joseph, Jr. 1931- *WhoE 91*
Bozzelli, John Wolf 1947- *WhoEmL 91*
Bozzetti, Louis Paul, Jr. *BiDrAPA 89*
Bozzetto, Bruno 1938- *ConDes 90*
Bozzi, Nicholas C. 1938- *St&PR 91*
Bozzini, Gary John 1950- *BiDrAPA 89*
Bozzone, Robert P. 1933- *WhoAm 90*
Bozzuto, Adam 1916- *St&PR 91*
Bozzuto, Carl Richard 1947- *WhoE 91*
Bozzuto, James C 1945- *BiDrAPA 89*
Bozzuto, Michael Adam 1956- *St&PR 91, WhoAm 90*
Bozzuto, Thomas Michael 1953- *WhoSSW 91*
Braak, Larry Edwin 1937- *BiDrAPA 89*
Braasch, Ernest R 1944- *BiDrAPA 89*
Braasch, John William 1922- *WhoAm 90*
Braasch, Judi Rae 1941- *WhoAmW 91*
Braasch, Lesley K 1945- *BiDrAPA 89*
Braasch, Robert 1944- *St&PR 91*
Braat, Jan P *BiDrAPA 89*
Braaten, Bruce D.A. 1926- *St&PR 91*
Braaten, Ellen Bussard 1942- *WhoSSW 91*
Braatz, Clayton Ross 1940- *St&PR 91*
Braatz, Gary Orlon 1959- *St&PR 91*
Braatz, Thomas Drew 1962- *WhoSSW 91*
Brabazon, Juliana *BiDEWW*
Brabec, Barbara 1937- *ConAu 32NR, WhoWrEP 89*
Brabender, Gene 1941- *Ballpl 90*
Brabham, Jack 1926- *WorAlBi*
Brabham, William G. 1875-1947 *Ballpl 90*
Brabham, William Lewis 1945- *St&PR 91*
Brabourne, John Ulick Knatchbull 1924- *WhoWor 91*
Brabson, Max LaFayette 1926- *WhoAm 90*

Brabston, Mary Elizabeth 1948- WhoEmL 91
Braby, Thomas Richard 1931- WhoSSW 91
Bracalini, Robert George 1933- St&PR 91
Braccini, Lisa Ann 1963- WhoE 91
Bracco, Frediano Vittorio 1937- WhoAm 90
Bracco, Lorraine BioIn 16
Brace, Barbara Ann 1936- WhoAmW 91
Brace, Ernest C. BioIn 16
Brace, Frederick H BiDrAPA 89
Brace, James Frederick 1945- St&PR 91
Brace, John Michael 1942- WhoWor 91
Brace, Kimball William 1951- WhoE 91
Brace, Robert Dewitt 1930- St&PR 91
Bracefield, Hilary Maxwell 1938- IntWWM 90
Bracesco, Giovanni EncO&P 3
Bracete, Juan Manuel 1951- WhoEmL 91, WhoSSW 91, WhoWor 91
Bracewell, Ronald Newbold 1921- WhoAm 90
Bracewell, William Riley 1938- WhoSSW 91
Bracey, Cookie Frances Lee 1945- WhoAmW 91
Bracey, Michael Alan 1954- WhoEmL 91
Bracey, Willie Earl 1950- WhoEmL 91
Brach, Paul Henry 1924- WhoAmA 91
Bracha, H Stefan BiDrAPA 89
Brache, Francisco A BiDrAPA 89
Bracher, Katherine 1938- WhoAmW 91
Brachet, J. 1909-1988 BioIn 16
Brachet, Jean 1909-1988 BioIn 16
Brachfeld, Rosalind Roth 1930- WhoE 91
Brachman, Irwin 1929- BiDrAPA 89
Brachman, Malcolm K. 1926- St&PR 91, WhoSSW 91
Brachman, Philip Sigmund 1927- WhoAm 90
Brachmann, Louise 1777-1822 EncCoWW
Bracho, Angel 1911- ArtLatA
Bracht, Roland 1952- IntWWM 90
Brachtenbach, Robert F. 1931- WhoAm 90
Brachtl, Susan P. 1941- St&PR 91
Brack, Gib 1908-1960 Ballpl 90
Brack, Graham 1955- WhoWor 91
Brack, O. M., Jr. 1938- WhoAm 90
Brack, Reginald Kufeld, Jr. 1937- WhoAm 90, WhoE 91
Brack, Victor 1904-1948 BioIn 16
Brack, William Dennis 1939- WhoAm 90
Bracke 1861-1955 BiDFrPL
Brackeen, JoAnne BioIn 16
Brackelmanns, Walter E BiDrAPA 89
Bracken, Beverly Walker 1942- BiDrAPA 89
Bracken, Darcia Daines 1946- WhoAm 90
Bracken, Eddie 1920- WhoAm 90, WorAlBi
Bracken, Frank A. 1934- WhoAm 90
Bracken, Gary K. 1939- St&PR 91
Bracken, George R. 1945- St&PR 91
Bracken, Harry McFarland 1926- WhoAm 90
Bracken, J. BiDWomA
Bracken, James A. 1929- St&PR 91
Bracken, Jeanne Munn 1946- WhoWrEP 89
Bracken, Kathleen Ann 1947- WhoAmW 91
Bracken, L. Anthony 1933- St&PR 91
Bracken, Louis Everett 1947- WhoE 91
Bracken, Nanette Beattie 1950- WhoEmL 91
Bracken, Peg 1918- WhoAm 90, WhoAmW 91
Brackenbury, Robert L. BioIn 16
Brackenbury, Rosalind 1942- FemiCLE
Brackenridge, H. H. 1748-1816 BioIn 16
Brackenridge, Henry Marie 1786-1871 WhNaAH
Brackenridge, Hugh Henry 1748-1816 BioIn 16, EncCRAm
Brackett, Don 1932- BioIn 16
Brackett, Douglas Lane 1938- WhoAm 90
Brackett, Gail Burger 1950- WhoAmW 91
Brackett, John Avery 1932- WhoSSW 91
Brackett, John Quincy Adams 1842-1918 AmLegL
Brackett, Leigh 1915-1978 RGTwCSF, TwCCr&M 91
Brackett, Ruth Brinker BiDrAPA 89
Brackett, Tracey Smith 1961- WhoEmL 91
Brackin, Henry B, Jr. 1924- BiDrAPA 89
Brackin, Phyllis Jean 1946- WhoSSW 91
Brackins, Barbara Florence 1935- WhoSSW 91
Brackley, Elizabeth 1626-1663 BiDEWW
Brackley, William Lowell 1919- WhoAm 90
Brackman, Raphael M. 1925- St&PR 91
Brackman, Robert 1898-1980 WhoAmA 91N
Brackmann, Albert 1871-1952 BioIn 16
Brackmann, Antoinette Elizabeth 1923- WhoAmW 91
Brackmann, Holly Jean 1947- WhoAmW 91
Brackney, William Austin 1928- St&PR 91
Brackney, William Henry 1948- WhoAm 90
Bracquemond, Joseph-Auguste 1833-1914 PenDiDA 89
Bracquemond, Marie 1841-1916 BiDWomA, BioIn 16
Bracy, Katherine Branfield 1938- WhoAmW 91
Bracy, Michael Blakeslee 1941- WhoAm 90
Brada, Donald Robert 1939- BiDrAPA 89
Bradburd, Arnold William 1924- St&PR 91
Bradburn, David Denison 1925- WhoAm 90
Bradburn, Donald BioIn 16
Bradburn, Eliza Weaver FemiCLE
Bradburn, John PenDiDA 89
Bradburn, John Kenny 1951- WhoEmL 91
Bradburn, Norman M. 1933- WhoAm 90
Bradbury, Alan Keith 1949- WhoWrEP 89
Bradbury, Bianca 1908- AuBYP 90
Bradbury, Bianca 1908-1982 BioIn 16
Bradbury, Bill J. 1932- St&PR 91
Bradbury, Curt WhoSSW 91
Bradbury, Daniel Joseph 1945- WhoAm 90
Bradbury, David E. 1946- St&PR 91
Bradbury, Edward P. MajTwCW
Bradbury, Edwin Morton 1933- WhoAm 90
Bradbury, Ellen A 1940- WhoAmA 91
Bradbury, Floyd E. 1930- St&PR 91
Bradbury, James Howard 1927- WhoWor 91
Bradbury, James Loren 1924- St&PR 91
Bradbury, John 1768-1823 WhNaAH
Bradbury, John Daniels 1941- WhoE 91
Bradbury, Kathleen Charlotte 1949- WhoAmW 91
Bradbury, Keith P. 1933- St&PR 91
Bradbury, Lorre Jo 1957- WhoAmW 91
Bradbury, Malcolm 1932- ConAu 33NR, ConLC 61 [port], MajTwCW
Bradbury, Malcolm Stanley 1932- WhoWor 91
Bradbury, Norris Edwin 1909- WhoAm 90
Bradbury, Ray 1920- ConAu 30NR, MajTwCW, RGTwCSF, SmATA 64 [port], WorAlBi
Bradbury, Ray Douglas 1920- WhoAm 90, WhoWrEP 89
Bradbury, Richard R. 1939- St&PR 91
Bradbury, Robert Milton, Jr. 1924- WhoAm 90
Bradbury, Thomas PenDiDA 89
Bradbury, Will BioIn 16
Bradbury, William S BiDrAPA 89
Braddell, Maurice 1900-1990 NewYTBS 90
Braddock, Edward 1695-1755 EncCRAm, WhNaAH, WorAlBi
Braddock, John E BiDrAPA 89
Braddock, John William 1947- WhoWor 91
Braddock, Richard S. 1941- WhoAm 90, WhoE 91, WhoWor 91
Braddock, William Haskell 1935- St&PR 91
Braddon, M. E. 1835-1915 BioIn 16
Braddon, Mary Elizabeth 1835-1915 BioIn 16, FemiCLE, TwCCr&M 91A
Braddy, Nella 1894- AuBYP 90
Brademas, John 1927- WhoAm 90, WhoE 91, WhoWor 91, WorAlBi
Braden, Anne 1924- EncAL
Braden, Anne McCarty 1924- WhoSSW 91
Braden, Berwyn Bartow 1928- WhoAm 90
Braden, Betty Jane 1943- WhoAmW 91
Braden, Betty L. 1944- WhoAmW 91
Braden, Carl 1914-1975 EncAL
Braden, Charles Hosea 1926- WhoAm 90
Braden, David Rice 1924- WhoAm 90
Braden, Dennis Ray 1949- WhoWrEP 89
Braden, Donna R. 1953- ConAu 130
Braden, Gail Edward 1948- WhoSSW 91
Braden, James Dale 1934- WhoAm 90
Braden, James Wylie, Jr. 1953- WhoEmL 91
Braden, Joan BioIn 16
Braden, Joan Kay 1934- WhoAmW 91
Braden, John A. 1945- WhoEmL 91, WhoSSW 91
Braden, John Harvey 1938- St&PR 91
Braden, K.G. 1938- St&PR 91
Braden, Robert Gaynor 1914- WhoAm 90
Braden, Roy Lee BiDrAPA 89
Braden, Samuel Edward 1914- WhoAm 90
Braden, Spruille 1894-1978 BioIn 16
Braden, Stanton Connell 1960- WhoEmL 91
Braden, Thomas Wardell 1918- WhoAm 90
Braden, Vic BioIn 16
Braden, Waldo W. 1911- WhoAm 90
Braden, William, III 1943- BiDrAPA 89
Braden, William Edward 1919- WhoWor 91
Bradesca, Donna Marie 1938- WhoAmW 91
Bradfield, Bill BioIn 16
Bradfield, C.J. 1934- St&PR 91
Bradfield, J.R. 1943- St&PR 91
Bradfield, James McComb 1917- WhoAm 90
Bradfield, Joe Lewis 1934- St&PR 91
Bradfield, John William, Sr. 1946- WhoSSW 91
Bradfield, Michael 1934- WhoAm 90
Bradfield, Roger 1924- AuBYP 90
Bradfield, William S. 1937- St&PR 91
Bradford, Adam M. D. AuBYP 90
Bradford, Alex 1927-1978 DrBIPA 90
Bradford, Amory Howe 1912- BioIn 16
Bradford, Andrea Carol 1951- BiDrAPA 89
Bradford, Andrew 1686-1742 BioIn 16
Bradford, Ann Liddell 1917- BioIn 16
Bradford, Barbara Reed 1948- WhoEmL 91
Bradford, Barbara Taylor WhoAm 90, WhoAmW 91
Bradford, Barbara Taylor 1933- ConAu 32NR, MajTwCW, WorAlBi
Bradford, Buddy 1944- Ballpl 90
Bradford, Carol Schlosnagle 1950- WhoAmW 91
Bradford, Charles Steven 1956- WhoEmL 91
Bradford, Christina 1942- WhoAm 90, WhoAmW 91
Bradford, Claude A. 1944- St&PR 91
Bradford, Cornelia Smith EncCRAm
Bradford, David Frantz 1939- WhoAm 90
Bradford, David Galen 1948- WhoEmL 91, WhoWor 91
Bradford, David Jeffrey 1952- WhoEmL 91
Bradford, Dennis Doyle 1945- St&PR 91, WhoSSW 91, WhoWor 91
Bradford, E. Edwin ODwPR 91
Bradford, Edmund James 1952- WhoE 91
Bradford, Elsa H. 1932- St&PR 91
Bradford, Ewing L. 1906- St&PR 91
Bradford, Francis Scott 1898-1961 WhoAmA 91N
Bradford, George Francis 1942- St&PR 91
Bradford, H. Eugene 1942- St&PR 91
Bradford, Hilary P. 1929- St&PR 91
Bradford, Howard 1919- WhoAm 90, WhoAmA 91
Bradford, Ira Burnham 1851-1916 AmLegL
Bradford, Jackie Edward 1941- WhoSSW 91
Bradford, James C., Jr. 1933- St&PR 91, WhoAm 90
Bradford, John 1749-1830 BioIn 16
Bradford, John Carroll 1924- WhoAm 90
Bradford, John Curtis 1931- St&PR 91
Bradford, John M. W. 1947- BiDrAPA 89
Bradford, Judson T. 1928- St&PR 91
Bradford, Karleen 1936- BioIn 16
Bradford, Larry 1951- Ballpl 90
Bradford, Larry Newell 1938- St&PR 91
Bradford, Lesley Jane BiDrAPA 89
Bradford, Louise Mathilde 1925- WhoAmW 91
Bradford, Marjorie Odell 1952- WhoWrEP 89
Bradford, Michael Lee 1942- WhoSSW 91
Bradford, Milton Douglas 1930- St&PR 91
Bradford, Orcelia Sylvia 1953- WhoAmW 91, WhoEmL 91
Bradford, Paul W. 1900-1989 BioIn 16
Bradford, Perry 1893-1970 BioIn 16, OxCPMus
Bradford, Peter Amory 1942- WhoAm 90
Bradford, Peter Corey 1935- WhoWor 91
Bradford, Ray 1954- WhoHisp 91
Bradford, Reagan Howard 1932- WhoAm 90
Bradford, Rebecca C. BioIn 16
Bradford, Richard 1932- BioIn 16
Bradford, Richard Roark 1932- WhoAm 90, WhoWrEP 89
Bradford, Robert E. ODwPR 91
Bradford, Robert Edward 1931- St&PR 91, WhoAm 90
Bradford, Robert Ernest WhoAm 90
Bradford, Roger R. 1928- St&PR 91
Bradford, Shirley Jean 1943- St&PR 91
Bradford, Thomas E. WhoAm 90
Bradford, Tutt Sloan 1917- WhoSSW 91
Bradford, Will ConAu 31NR
Bradford, William BioIn 16
Bradford, William 1588-1657 BioIn 16
Bradford, William 1590-1657 EncCRAm, WhNaAH, WorAlBi
Bradford, William 1663-1752 EncCRAm
Bradford, William 1721-1791 EncCRAm
Bradford, William 1755-1795 BiDrUSE 89
Bradford, William 1823-1892 DcCanB 12
Bradford, William Dalton 1931- WhoAm 90
Bradford, William E. 1917- St&PR 91
Bradford, William Elwood 1933- St&PR 91
Bradford Mathews, Felita Renee 1959- WhoEmL 91
Bradham, James V. 1940- St&PR 91
Bradigan, Brian Jay 1951- WhoEmL 91
Bradish, Warren Allen 1937- WhoSSW 91
Bradlaugh, Charles 1833-1891 BioIn 16, EncO&P 3
Bradlee, Benjamin 1921- WorAlBi
Bradlee, Benjamin C. 1921- BioIn 16
Bradlee, Benjamin Crowninshield 1921- WhoAm 90, WhoE 91, WhoWrEP 89
Bradlee, Dudley H., II 1915- St&PR 91
Bradler, James Edward 1935- WhoAm 90
Bradley, Alan BioIn 16
Bradley, Albert 1891-1983 EncABHB 5 [port]
Bradley, Allan P. BioIn 16
Bradley, Amelia Jane 1947- WhoE 91
Bradley, Amy Lorraine 1949- WhoAmW 91
Bradley, Arthur Harold 1936- St&PR 91
Bradley, Beth Ann 1963- WhoEmL 91
Bradley, Bill BioIn 16
Bradley, Bill 1878-1954 Ballpl 90 [port]
Bradley, Bill 1943- WhoAm 90, WhoE 91, WhoWor 91, WorAlBi
Bradley, Bonnie 1951- WhoAmW 91
Bradley, Carol Ann 1953- WhoAmW 91
Bradley, Carolyn C. ODwPR 91
Bradley, Cecil Arthur BiDrAPA 89
Bradley, Charles Ernest 1962- WhoSSW 91, WhoWor 91
Bradley, Charles J. 1935- St&PR 91
Bradley, Charles James, Jr. 1935- WhoAm 90
Bradley, Charles S. 1931- St&PR 91
Bradley, Charles William 1807-1865 BioIn 16
Bradley, Charles William 1923- WhoAm 90, WhoWor 91
Bradley, Charlotte Ann 1959- WhoAmW 91
Bradley, Clyde William, Jr. 1929- WhoSSW 91
Bradley, Concho ConAu 31NR
Bradley, D. Keith 1951- WhoEmL 91
Bradley, D. Scott 1949- St&PR 91
Bradley, David Gilbert 1916- WhoAm 90
Bradley, David Henry, Jr. 1950- WhoWrEP 89
Bradley, David P 1954- WhoAmA 91
Bradley, David Quentin 1936- St&PR 91
Bradley, David R. 1917-1988 BioIn 16
Bradley, David Rall, Jr. 1949- St&PR 91
Bradley, Diane Rose 1956- WhoAmW 91
Bradley, Don Bell, III 1945- WhoEmL 91, WhoSSW 91
Bradley, Donald Charles 1932- St&PR 91
Bradley, Dorothy 1920- WhoAmA 91
Bradley, Duane 1914- AuBYP 90
Bradley, E. Michael 1939- WhoE 91, WhoWor 91
Bradley, Earl Tillman, Jr. 1941- WhoSSW 91
Bradley, Ed BioIn 16
Bradley, Ed R 1941- DrBIPA 90
Bradley, Edna Pygatt 1925- WhoAmW 91
Bradley, Edward James, I 1946- WhoE 91, WhoEmL 91
Bradley, Edward R. 1941- WhoAm 90, WhoE 91
Bradley, Edward Thomas 1952- BiDrAPA 89
Bradley, Eileen 1948- WhoAm 90, WhoAmW 91
Bradley, Emmett Hughes 1927- St&PR 91
Bradley, Ernest Cerel 1915- WhoWor 91
Bradley, F H 1846-1924 WrPh P
Bradley, F. Joseph 1943- St&PR 91
Bradley, Florence Frances 1934- WhoWrEP 89
Bradley, Floyd Henry, III 1951- St&PR 91, WhoWor 91
Bradley, Francis Xavier 1915- WhoAm 90
Bradley, Frank L., Jr. 1924- St&PR 91
Bradley, Gary WhoAm 90
Bradley, George AmLegL
Bradley, George 1852-1931 Ballpl 90
Bradley, George H. 1932- WhoSSW 91
Bradley, George Havis 1937- WhoWor 91
Bradley, George J. 1916- St&PR 91
Bradley, George Russell 1954- WhoE 91
Bradley, Gerard W. 1927- St&PR 91
Bradley, Gilbert Francis 1920- WhoAm 90
Bradley, Gwendolyn BioIn 16, WhoAmW 91
Bradley, Gwendolyn 1952- IntWWM 90
Bradley, H Dennis 1878-1934 EncO&P 3
Bradley, Harold Cornelius 1878- BioIn 16
Bradley, Harold Whitman 1903- WhoAm 90
Bradley, Harry Lynde, Mrs WhoAmA 91N
Bradley, Hugh Edward 1928- St&PR 91
Bradley, Inez Mayo 1935- WhoAmW 91
Bradley, J.F., Jr. 1930- St&PR 91
Bradley, J. F., Jr. 1930- WhoAm 90

Bradley, J. Michael *St&PR 91*
Bradley, James 1693-1762 *WorAlBi*
Bradley, Joe Frank 1952- *BiDrAPA 89*
Bradley, John A. 1937- *St&PR 91*
Bradley, John Andrew 1930- *WhoAm 90*
Bradley, John D., Jr. 1945- *St&PR 91*
Bradley, John Edmund 1906- *WhoAm 90*
Bradley, John Francis 1960- *WhoE 91*
Bradley, John Layton 1928- *St&PR 91*
Bradley, John Miller, Jr. 1925- *WhoAm 90*
Bradley, Joseph Anderson, III 1964- *WhoSSW 91*
Bradley, Josephine B. 1949- *WhoEmL 91*
Bradley, Karen Anne *BiDrAPA 89*
Bradley, Katherine Harris 1846-1914 *BioIn 16*
Bradley, Kathy Annette 1956- *WhoEmL 91*
Bradley, Kenneth Daniel 1949- *WhoEmL 91*
Bradley, Kirk Jackson 1962- *WhoSSW 91*
Bradley, Laurel E 1952- *WhoAmA 91*
Bradley, Laurence Alan 1949- *WhoSSW 91*
Bradley, Lawrence D., Jr. 1920- *WhoAm 90*
Bradley, Lee Carrington, Jr. 1897- *WhoAm 90*
Bradley, Lester Eugene 1921- *WhoAm 90*
Bradley, Lorraine 1946- *St&PR 91*
Bradley, Lynn Pence 1962- *WhoAmW 91*
Bradley, Madeline A. 1948- *WhoSSW 91*
Bradley, Malcolm Ray 1922- *St&PR 91*
Bradley, Margot Tude 1952- *WhoEmL 91*
Bradley, Marie Lane 1940- *WhoAmW 91*
Bradley, Marilynne Gail 1938- *WhoAmW 91*
Bradley, Marion 1930- *FemiCLE*
Bradley, Marion Z. 1930- *BioAmW*
Bradley, Marion Zimmer 1930- *ConAu 31NR, MajTwCW, RGTwCSF, WhoAm 90, WhoWrEP 89*
Bradley, Mark Andrew 1955- *WhoSSW 91*
Bradley, Mark Edmund 1936- *WhoAm 90*
Bradley, Martha Washington Nutter *WhoWor 91*
Bradley, Marvin R. 1914- *WhoAm 90*
Bradley, Melvin LeRoy 1938- *WhoAm 90*
Bradley, Michael 1944- *ConAu 129*
Bradley, Michael John 1933- *WhoWor 91*
Bradley, Nolen Eugene, Jr. 1925- *WhoSSW 91, WhoWor 91*
Bradley, Norman Robert 1917- *WhoAm 90*
Bradley, Omar N. 1893-1981 *WorAlBi*
Bradley, Pat *BioIn 16*
Bradley, Pat 1951- *WorAlBi*
Bradley, Paul Anthony 1955- *WhoEmL 91*
Bradley, Paul William 1961- *WhoE 91*
Bradley, Penelope Hartford 1940- *WhoAmW 91*
Bradley, Phil 1959- *Ballpl 90*
Bradley, Philip Charles 1936- *St&PR 91*
Bradley, Ralph Allan 1923- *WhoAm 90, WhoSSW 91*
Bradley, Randall T. 1953- *St&PR 91*
Bradley, Raymond Edgar, Jr. 1932- *WhoSSW 91*
Bradley, Raymond Joseph 1920- *WhoAm 90*
Bradley, Richard Edwin 1926- *WhoAm 90*
Bradley, Richard Eugene 1933- *St&PR 91*
Bradley, Richard Staring 1928- *St&PR 91*
Bradley, Richard Thomas 1949- *BiDrAPA 89*
Bradley, Robert Franklin 1920- *WhoAm 90*
Bradley, Robert Lee 1920- *WhoAm 90*
Bradley, Ronald A. 1932- *St&PR 91*
Bradley, Ronald Calvin 1915- *WhoAm 90*
Bradley, Ronald James 1943- *WhoAm 90, WhoSSW 91*
Bradley, Sandra S. 1951- *St&PR 91*
Bradley, Scott 1960- *Ballpl 90*
Bradley, Stephen E. *ODwPR 91*
Bradley, Sterling Gaylen 1932- *WhoAm 90*
Bradley, Stuart B. 1907-1990 *WhoAm 90*
Bradley, Thomas 1917- *WhoAm 90, WorAlBi*
Bradley, Thomas Gerald 1931- *St&PR 91*
Bradley, Thomas L. 1946- *WhoEmL 91*
Bradley, Thomas Reid 1923- *St&PR 91*
Bradley, Tom 1917- *BioIn 16*
Bradley, Tom 1947- *Ballpl 90*
Bradley, Tyrone Bennett 1946- *WhoSSW 91*
Bradley, Velma Jean 1951- *WhoAmW 91*
Bradley, Wanda Louise 1953- *WhoAmW 91, WhoE 91, WhoWor 91*
Bradley, Ward R., Jr. 1929- *St&PR 91*
Bradley, Warren Aidan *BiDrAPA 89*
Bradley, Wesley Holmes 1922- *WhoAm 90*
Bradley, Will 1868-1962 *PenDiDA 89*
Bradley, Will 1912- *OxCPMus*
Bradley, Will 1912-1989 *BioIn 16*
Bradley, Will H. 1868-1962 *BioIn 16*
Bradley, William Arthur 1921- *WhoAm 90*
Bradley, William Arthur 1940- *WhoAm 90*
Bradley, William J *BiDrAPA 89*
Bradley, William J. *AmLegL*
Bradley, William John 1929- *St&PR 91*
Bradley, William Steven 1949- *WhoAmA 91*
Bradley-Mahin, Mary *WhoSSW 91*
Bradley-Rippey, Jackie 1952- *WhoAmW 91*
Bradley-Tillier, Winnie Elaine 1953- *WhoSSW 91*
Bradlow, John 1943- *St&PR 91*
Bradlow, Paul A 1920- *BiDrAPA 89*
Bradly, Brenton J. 1940- *St&PR 91*
Bradman, Bernard *BiDrAPA 89*
Bradman, Donald George 1908- *BioIn 16*
Bradmiller, Linda Louise 1953- *WhoAmW 91*
Bradmore, Sarah *BiDEWW*
Bradna, Joanne Justice 1952- *WhoEmL 91*
Bradnan, William A 1942- *BiDrAPA 89*
Brado, Michael Wayne 1958- *WhoEmL 91*
Bradrick, Roy Burton, Jr. 1953- *WhoEmL 91*
Bradshaw, Beverly Jean 1946- *WhoAmW 91*
Bradshaw, Bill *BioIn 16*
Bradshaw, Billy Dean 1940- *WhoWor 91*
Bradshaw, Buck *ConAu 31NR*
Bradshaw, C Marshall 1938- *BiDrAPA 89*
Bradshaw, Carl John 1930- *WhoAm 90, WhoWor 91*
Bradshaw, Charles Richard 1912- *St&PR 91*
Bradshaw, Christine C *BiDrAPA 89*
Bradshaw, Clark C. 1944- *St&PR 91*
Bradshaw, Conrad Allan 1922- *WhoAm 90*
Bradshaw, Cynthia Helene 1954- *WhoAmW 91, WhoEmL 91, WhoWor 91*
Bradshaw, Dove 1949- *WhoAmA 91, WhoE 91*
Bradshaw, Elizabeth Shepperd Morin 1947- *WhoEmL 91*
Bradshaw, Eugene Barry 1938- *St&PR 91*
Bradshaw, Fanny 1897?-1973 *BioIn 16*
Bradshaw, Fanny 1900-1973 *NotWoAT*
Bradshaw, George Smith 1717-1812 *PenDiDA 89*
Bradshaw, Glenn Raymond 1922- *WhoAmA 91*
Bradshaw, Howard Holt 1937- *WhoSSW 91*
Bradshaw, Hugh E., Jr. 1930- *WhoAm 90*
Bradshaw, James Edward 1940- *WhoSSW 91*
Bradshaw, James Vearl 1956- *WhoSSW 91*
Bradshaw, James W. 1935- *St&PR 91*
Bradshaw, Jerry Marcus 1946- *WhoE 91*
Bradshaw, John Pilcher, Jr. 1933- *St&PR 91*
Bradshaw, Lawrence James 1945- *WhoAmA 91*
Bradshaw, Lillian Moore 1915- *WhoAm 90, WhoAmW 91*
Bradshaw, Mark Davis 1954- *WhoEmL 91*
Bradshaw, Mary Ann Cavendish 1758?-1849 *FemiCLE*
Bradshaw, Melvin B. 1922- *St&PR 91*
Bradshaw, Murray Charles 1930- *IntWWM 90, WhoAm 90*
Bradshaw, Nanci Marie 1940- *WhoAmW 91*
Bradshaw, Paul C. 1926- *St&PR 91*
Bradshaw, Paul Stephen 1937- *St&PR 91*
Bradshaw, Penni Pearson 1954- *WhoEmL 91*
Bradshaw, Peter 1935- *WhoAm 90*
Bradshaw, R.S., Jr. 1905- *St&PR 91*
Bradshaw, Ralph Alden 1941- *WhoAm 90*
Bradshaw, Raymond Stanley, Jr. 1933- *St&PR 91*
Bradshaw, Richard Burnett 1927- *WhoAm 90*
Bradshaw, Richard John 1948- *St&PR 91, WhoAm 90*
Bradshaw, Richard Rotherwood 1916- *WhoAm 90*
Bradshaw, Robert George 1915- *WhoAmA 91*
Bradshaw, Robert Lee, Jr. 1944- *WhoSSW 91*
Bradshaw, Robert Llewellyn 1916-1978 *BioIn 16*
Bradshaw, Robert V. 1938- *WhoAm 90*
Bradshaw, Robert Walker 1929- *St&PR 91*
Bradshaw, Rod Eric 1951- *WhoSSW 91*
Bradshaw, Samuel L., Jr. 1937- *BiDrAPA 89*
Bradshaw, Terry *BioIn 16*
Bradshaw, Terry 1948- *WhoAm 90, WorAlBi*
Bradshaw, Thornton F. *BioIn 16*
Bradshaw, Tiny 1905-1958 *OxCPMus*
Bradshaw, Wayne Robert 1949- *St&PR 91*
Bradshaw, William David 1928- *WhoAm 90*
Bradsher, Charles Kilgo 1912- *WhoAm 90*
Bradsher, Henry St. Amant 1931- *WhoAm 90*
Bradstock, Glenda Woodard 1947- *WhoEmL 91*
Bradstock, Kirsten *BiDrAPA 89*
Bradstreet, Anne 1612-1672 *BioAmW, BioIn 16, FemiCLE, WorAlBi*
Bradstreet, Anne 1613-1672 *BiDEWW*
Bradstreet, Anne Dudley 1612-1672 *EncCRAm*
Bradstreet, Bernard Francis 1945- *WhoAm 90*
Bradstreet, John 1711?-1774 *EncCRAm*
Bradt, Hale Van Dorn 1930- *WhoAm 90*
Bradt, Jack Oldham *BiDrAPA 89*
Bradt, L. Jack 1928- *St&PR 91*
Bradway, William S. 1946- *St&PR 91*
Bradwell, John Joseph 1934- *WhoSSW 91*
Brady, Adelaide Burks 1926- *WhoAmW 91*
Brady, Agnes Marie 1895-1987 *BioIn 16*
Brady, Alfred R. 1937- *St&PR 91*
Brady, Alice 1892-1939 *BioIn 16, NotWoAT*
Brady, Andrew John 1955- *St&PR 91, WhoE 91*
Brady, B. 1947- *St&PR 91*
Brady, Bruce L. 1939- *St&PR 91*
Brady, Carl Franklin 1919- *St&PR 91, WhoAm 90*
Brady, Carolyn 1937- *WhoAmA 91*
Brady, Charles 1926- *WhoAmA 91*
Brady, Charles Augustus 1935- *WhoWor 91*
Brady, Charles Michael 1959- *WhoAm 90*
Brady, Christopher James 1950- *St&PR 91*
Brady, Colleen Anne 1951- *WhoEmL 91*
Brady, Dan Phillip 1952- *WhoWrEP 89*
Brady, Deborah A. 1954- *St&PR 91*
Brady, Denis B. 1947- *St&PR 91*
Brady, Don Gayle 1940- *WhoSSW 91*
Brady, Donald George 1928- *WhoAm 90*
Brady, Donna Elizabeth 1955- *WhoEmL 91*
Brady, E.H. 1927- *St&PR 91*
Brady, E James *BiDrAPA 89*
Brady, Edward G. 1930- *St&PR 91*
Brady, Edward L. 1919-1987 *BioIn 16*
Brady, Esther Wood 1905-1989 *BioIn 16*
Brady, Euell Gary 1935- *WhoSSW 91*
Brady, Francis C. 1944- *St&PR 91*
Brady, Frank Benton 1914- *WhoAm 90*
Brady, Frank R 1934- *WhoWrEP 89*
Brady, Gail Carolyn *BiDrAPA 89*
Brady, Gail P. 1945- *St&PR 91*
Brady, George M., Jr. 1922- *St&PR 91*
Brady, George Moore 1922- *WhoAm 90*
Brady, Gerald Lee 1930- *BiDrAPA 89*
Brady, Harry Albert 1925- *WhoAm 90, WhoWor 91*
Brady, Harry William 1930- *WhoE 91*
Brady, Henry Grady *WhoWrEP 89*
Brady, Holly Wheeler 1947- *WhoAmW 91, WhoWrEP 89*
Brady, Hugh 1924- *WhoAm 90*
Brady, Irene 1943- *BioIn 16*
Brady, Jack D. 1943- *St&PR 91*
Brady, Jack J. 1958- *WhoEmL 91*
Brady, James B. 1856-1917 *WorAlBi*
Brady, James Joseph 1904- *WhoAm 90*
Brady, James Joseph 1936- *WhoAm 90*
Brady, James P *BiDrAPA 89*
Brady, James S. *BioIn 16, NewYTBS 90 [port]*
Brady, James S. 1944- *WhoAm 90*
Brady, James Winston 1928- *WhoAm 90*
Brady, Jane Frances 1935- *WhoAm 90, WhoAmW 91*
Brady, Jane Mariette 1955- *WhoEmL 91*
Brady, Jean Vick 1937- *WhoAmW 91*
Brady, Jennie M. 1948- *WhoAmW 91*
Brady, Joan V *BiDrAPA 89*
Brady, John 1955- *ConAu 130*
Brady, John B. 1929- *St&PR 91*
Brady, John David, Jr. 1958- *WhoEmL 91*
Brady, John Green 1848-1918 *WhNaAH*
Brady, John Joseph, Jr. 1923- *WhoAm 90*
Brady, John Paul 1928- *BiDrAPA 89, WhoAm 90*
Brady, Joseph F. 1946- *St&PR 91*
Brady, Joseph John 1926- *WhoAm 90*
Brady, Joseph Vincent 1922- *WhoAm 90*
Brady, Kathleen 1947- *ConAu 129*
Brady, Kathleen Theresa 1952- *BiDrAPA 89*
Brady, Lawrence J. 1943- *St&PR 91*
Brady, Lawrence Peter 1940- *WhoE 91, WhoWor 91*
Brady, Linda 1950- *BiDrAPA 89*
Brady, Linda Carol 1949- *WhoAmW 91*
Brady, Luther W 1925- *WhoAmA 91*
Brady, Luther W., Jr. 1925- *WhoAm 90*
Brady, Lynn Robert 1933- *WhoAm 90*
Brady, Lynne Ellen 1946- *WhoEmL 91*
Brady, Mary Gerard 1959- *WhoWrEP 89*
Brady, Mary Lou *ODwPR 91*
Brady, Mary Therese 1959- *WhoAmW 91*
Brady, Mathew B. 1823?-1896 *BioIn 16, WorAlBi*
Brady, Maureen 1943- *WhoWrEP 89*
Brady, Maureen O'Keefe 1945- *WhoAmW 91*
Brady, Maxine L. 1941- *AuBYP 90*
Brady, Melvin Michael 1933- *WhoWor 91*
Brady, Michael Wade 1948- *WhoEmL 91*
Brady, Nancy Sammartino 1955- *WhoAmW 91*
Brady, Nicholas *ConAu 31NR*
Brady, Nicholas F. 1930- *BioIn 16*
Brady, Nicholas Frederick 1930- *BiDrUSE 89, WhoAm 90, WhoE 91, WhoWor 91*
Brady, Nyle C. 1920- *WhoAm 90*
Brady, Patrick 1933- *WhoAm 90*
Brady, Patrick E. 1941- *St&PR 91*
Brady, Philip 1916- *WhoWrEP 89*
Brady, Phillip Donley 1951- *WhoAm 90*
Brady, Priscilla Mae 1940- *WhoAmW 91*
Brady, Richard Alan 1934- *WhoAm 90*
Brady, Rita G. *AuBYP 90*
Brady, Robert D 1946- *WhoAmA 91*
Brady, Robert H. 1936- *St&PR 91*
Brady, Robert Lindsay 1946- *WhoE 91, WhoEmL 91*
Brady, Rodney Howard 1933- *St&PR 91, WhoAm 90*
Brady, Ronald 1935- *BiDrAPA 89*
Brady, Roscoe O. 1923- *WhoAm 90*
Brady, Roy Francis 1946- *WhoE 91*
Brady, Sarah *BioIn 16*
Brady, Sarah Kemp 1942- *NewYTBS 90 [port]*
Brady, Sharon Elizabeth 1963- *WhoAmW 91*
Brady, Sheila Ann 1935- *St&PR 91*
Brady, Sue Carol Pipes 1947- *WhoAmW 91*
Brady, Terence Christian 1931- *St&PR 91*
Brady, Thomas 1952- *BiDrAPA 89*
Brady, Thomas Arthur, Jr. 1946- *WhoEmL 91*
Brady, Thomas Carl 1947- *WhoE 91*
Brady, Thomas Denis 1955- *WhoEmL 91*
Brady, Thomas Michael, Jr. 1959- *WhoEmL 91*
Brady, Upton Birnie 1938- *WhoAm 90*
Brady, W. R. *BioIn 16*
Brady, Walter Michael 1935- *St&PR 91*
Brady, William H. *BioIn 16*
Brady, William John, Jr. 1946- *WhoEmL 91*
Brady, William Kim 1951- *WhoEmL 91*
Brady, William Milner 1945- *WhoWor 91*
Brady, Wray Grayson 1918- *WhoAm 90, WhoE 91*
Braeden, Eric *ConTFT 8*
Braemer, Richard Jeffrey 1941- *St&PR 91*
Braen, Bernard Benjamin 1928- *WhoAm 90*
Braendel, Gregory *BioIn 16*
Braestrup, Peter 1929- *WhoAm 90, WhoE 91*
Braeuninger, William Frederick 1938- *St&PR 91*
Braff, David Leon 1945- *BiDrAPA 89*
Braff, Howard 1952- *WhoE 91*
Braff, Mark 1955- *ODwPR 91*
Braff, Mark Russell 1955- *WhoEmL 91*
Braff, Ruby *BioIn 16*
Braffet, Bentley T. 1934- *St&PR 91*
Brafford, Ronald P. 1951- *WhoSSW 91*
Brafford, William Charles 1932- *St&PR 91, WhoAm 90*
Brafman, Carole Sue 1941- *BiDrAPA 89*
Braga, Daniel 1946- *WhoWor 91*
Braga, Djalma Aranha 1937- *BiDrAPA 89*
Braga, Linda Jean 1953- *WhoAmW 91*
Braga, Sonia *BioIn 16*
Braga Santos, Joly 1924-1988 *AnObit 1988*
Bragadini, Mark Antony *EncO&P 3*
Bragado-Spence, Ines Ana *BiDrAPA 89*
Bragan, Bobby 1917- *Ballpl 90*
Braganini, David R. 1951- *St&PR 91*
Braganza, Teodoro 1924- *BiDrAPA 89*
Bragar, Philip Frank 1925- *WhoAmA 91*
Bragaw, Richard S. 1940- *ODwPR 91*
Bragdon, Catherine Creamer 1957- *WhoAmA 91*
Bragdon, Clyde Albert, Jr. 1929- *WhoAm 90*
Bragdon, Lillian Jacot *AuBYP 90*
Bragdon, Paul Errol 1927- *WhoAm 90*
Bragdon, Robert Wright 1922- *St&PR 91, WhoE 91*
Brage, Carl Willis 1930- *WhoE 91*
Brager, Amy Rachel *BiDrAPA 89*
Brager, Walter S. 1925- *St&PR 91, WhoAm 90*
Bragg, Anna Lou Spencer 1943- *WhoAmW 91*
Bragg, Bernard 1928- *BioIn 16*
Bragg, Billy *BioIn 16*
Bragg, Braxton 1817-1876 *WorAlBi*
Bragg, Charles Fred, II 1910- *St&PR 91*
Bragg, David Gordon 1933- *WhoAm 90*
Bragg, David Kenneth 1948- *St&PR 91*
Bragg, E Ann 1935- *WhoAmA 91*

Bragg, Ellis Meredith, Jr. 1947- WhoEmL 91, WhoSSW 91
Bragg, George Lee 1932- St&PR 91, WhoAm 90, WhoSSW 91
Bragg, John Mackie 1921- WhoAm 90
Bragg, John Woodbury 1943- St&PR 91
Bragg, Melvyn 1939- BioIn 16
Bragg, Michael Ellis 1947- WhoAm 90, WhoEmL 91, WhoWor 91
Bragg, Patricia D. St&PR 91
Bragg, Robert Henry 1919- WhoAm 90
Bragg, Robert L 1916- BiDrAPA 89
Bragg, T. Steve 1945- St&PR 91
Bragg, William H. 1862-1942 WorAlBi
Bragg, William L. 1890-1971 WorAlBi
Bragger, Jeannette Danielle 1944- WhoE 91
Braggiotti, Enrico BioIn 16
Braggs, Glenn 1962- Ballpl 90
Bragin, D.H. 1944- St&PR 91
Bragin, Herman D. 1908-1989 BioIn 16
Braginton-Smith, Brian S. 1953- WhoEmL 91
Bragole, Robert A. 1936- St&PR 91
Brague, Remi 1947- WhoWor 91
Braha, Thomas I. 1947- WhoAm 90, WhoE 91, WhoEmL 91, WhoWor 91
Braham, David 1838-1905 OxCPMus
Braham, Delphine Doris 1946- WhoAmW 91, WhoEmL 91, WhoWor 91
Braham, John 1774-1856 OxCPMus, PenDiMP
Braham, Leonora 1853-1931 OxCPMus
Braham, Philip 1882-1934 OxCPMus
Braham, Randolph Lewis 1922- WhoAm 90
Brahan Seer, The EncO&P 3
Brahe, Sophie 1556?-1643 EncCoWW
Brahe, Tycho 1546-1601 BioIn 16, WorAlBi
Brahen, Leonard S 1921- BiDrAPA 89
Braheny, Kevin NewAgMG
Brahimi, Abdelhamid 1936- WhoWor 91
Brahm, Sumishta 1954- BioIn 16
Brahma, Chandra Sekhar 1941- WhoAm 90
Brahms, Caryl ConAu 129
Brahms, Caryl 1901-1982 DcNaB 1981
Brahms, Helma Sanders- 1940- BioIn 16
Brahms, Hero Heinrich 1941- WhoWor 91
Brahms, Johannes 1833-1897 BioIn 16, PenDiMP A, WorAlBi
Brahms, Thomas Walter 1945- WhoAm 90
Brahney, Carolyn Ann 1939- WhoAmW 91
Braibanti, Ralph John 1920- WhoAm 90
Braid, Frederick Donald 1946- WhoEmL 91
Braid, James 1795?-1860 EncO&P 3, WorAlBi
Braide, Robert David 1953- WhoAm 90
Braiden, Rose Margaret J 1923- WhoAmA 91
Braider, Donald 1923-1977 WhoAmA 91N
Braidley, Margaret BiDEWW
Braids, Olin Capron 1938 WhoSSW 91
Braidwood, Linda Schreiber 1909- WhoAmW 91
Braidwood, Robert J. 1907- WhoAm 90
Braig, Betty Lou 1931- WhoAmA 91
Brailey, Nigel John 1942- WhoWor 91
Braille, Louis 1809-1852 BioIn 16, WorAlBi
Brailow, Norma Lipton 1916- WhoAmW 91
Brailowsky, Alexander 1896-1976 PenDiMP
Brailsford, Frances AuBYP 90
Brailsford, June Evelyn 1939- WhoAmW 91
Braiman, Alex 1926- BiDrAPA 89
Braimer, Steven, Jr. 1944- WhoSSW 91
Brain, Aubrey 1893-1955 PenDiMP
Brain, Dave 1879-1959 Ballpl 90
Brain, Dennis 1921-1957 PenDiMP
Brain, George Bernard 1920- WhoAm 90
Brain, Joseph David 1940- WhoAm 90
Brain, Lawrence A BiDrAPA 89
Brain, Leonard 1915-1975 PenDiMP
Brainard, Asa 1841-1888 Ballpl 90
Brainard, Bradford Peabody 1957- St&PR 91
Brainard, Daniel Reed 1939- WhoSSW 91
Brainard, Edward Axdal 1931- WhoAm 90
Brainard, Ernest T. BioIn 16
Brainard, Frank Samuel 1917- St&PR 91
Brainard, James C. 1954- WhoEmL 91
Brainard, Jayne Dawson WhoAm 90, WhoSSW 91
Brainard, Joe 1942- WhoAmA 91
Brainard, Lawrence J. 1944- St&PR 91
Brainard, Owen 1924- WhoAmA 91
Brainard, Paul Henry 1928- WhoAm 90
Brainard, William Crittenden 1935- WhoAm 90
Brainbeau, J. C. WhoWrEP 89
Braine, Clinton Ellis 1920- St&PR 91
Braine, John 1922-1986 ConAu 33NR, MajTwCW
Brainead, Paul 1947- St&PR 91
Brainer, Susan Langenberg 1957- WhoEmL 91
Brainerd, David 1718-1747 BioIn 16, WhNaAH
Brainerd, Howard R. 1942- St&PR 91
Brainerd, Stanford Howard 1931- St&PR 91
Brainerd, Winthrop John 1939- WhoE 91
Brainin, Frederick 1913- WhoE 91
Brainin, Garry 1939- St&PR 91
Brainin, Norbert PenDiMP
Brainin, Norbert 1923- IntWWM 90
Brainin-Rodriguez, Laura 1951- WhoHisp 91
Braislin, Gordon S. NewYTBS 90 [port]
Braislin, Gordon S. 1901-1990 BioIn 16
Braisted, Madeline Charlotte 1936- WhoAmW 91
Brait, A.A. 1924- St&PR 91
Braiterman, Thea Gilda 1927- WhoAmW 91
Braithwaite, Eustace Adolphe 1922- WhoWor 91
Braithwaite, J. Lorne 1941- WhoAm 90
Braithwaite, Jeanine Dolan 1960- WhoE 91
Braithwaite, John James 1932- St&PR 91
Braithwaite, Keith G. 1931- St&PR 91
Braithwaite, Nicholas 1939- PenDiMP
Braithwaite, Nicholas Paul Dallon 1939- IntWWM 90
Braithwaite, Richard Bevan 1900-1990 ConAu 131
Braithwaite, Ruth Caroline 1944- WhoE 91
Braithwaite, Warwick 1896-1971 PenDiMP
Braitmayer, John Watson 1930- St&PR 91
Braitstein, Marcel 1935- WhoAmA 91
Brajer, Ilana M. 1965- WhoEmL 91
Brake, Barbara W. 1946- ODwPR 91
Brake, Barbara Whitaker 1946- WhoAmW 91
Brake, Brian 1927-1988 AnObit 1988
Brake, Brian 1928-1988 BioIn 16
Brake, Cecil Clifford 1932- WhoAm 90, WhoWor 91
Brake, Elizabeth J. 1925- WhoAmW 91
Brakefield, Ray 1935- St&PR 91
Brakel, Linda A Wimer 1950- BiDrAPA 89
Brakeley, George Archibald, III 1939- St&PR 91, WhoE 91
Brakeley, George Archibald, Jr. 1916- WhoAm 90, WhoE 91
Brakeman, Louis Freeman 1932- WhoAm 90
Brakeman, Mark Allan 1957- WhoWrEP 89
Brakensiek, Warren Niles 1946- St&PR 91
Braker, Ulrich 1735-1798 DcLB 94 [port]
Braker, William Paul 1926- WhoAm 90
Brakhage, James Stanley 1933- WhoAm 90, WhoAmA 91
Brakhage, Stan BioIn 16
Brakhan, Jutta Johannesson 1942- WhoAmW 91
Brakke, Myron Kendall 1921- WhoAm 90
Brakke, P Michael 1943- WhoAmA 91
Brakman, Steven 1957- WhoWor 91
Braley, Jean WhoAmA 91
Braley, Robert Bruce 1957- WhoWrEP 89
Braley, W. C. AmLegL
Bralla, James G. 1926- St&PR 91
Bralley, James Alexander 1952- WhoSSW 91
Bralove, Olga J BiDrAPA 89
Braly, Byron Duke 1930- WhoSSW 91
Braly, David Duane 1949- WhoEmL 91
Braly, Jack E. 1941- St&PR 91
Bram, Elizabeth 1948- WhoWrEP 89
Bram, Frederick M BiDrAPA 89
Bram, Isabelle Mary Rickey McDonough WhoAmW 91
Bram, Leon Leonard 1931- WhoAm 90, WhoE 91
Bram, Stephen Bennett 1942- St&PR 91
Bramah, Ernest 1868-1942 TwCCr&M 91
Braman, Donald ODwPR 91
Braman, Heather Ruth 1934- WhoAmW 91
Braman, Irma BioIn 16
Braman, Norman BioIn 16
Braman, Norman 1932- WhoAm 90, WhoE 91
Braman, Sandra 1951- WhoWrEP 89
Bramann, Jorn K. 1938- WhoWrEP 89
Bramante, Donato 1444-1514 WorAlBi
Bramante, Pietro Ottavio 1920- WhoAm 90
Brambila, Art Peralta 1941- WhoHisp 91
Brambilla, Marietta 1807-1875 PenDiMP
Brambilla, Teresa 1818-1895 PenDiMP
Bramble, Barry B. 1953- St&PR 91
Bramble, Harold Kenneth, Sr. 1939- WhoSSW 91
Bramble, James Henry 1930- WhoAm 90
Bramble, Percival Austin 1931- BioIn 16
Bramble, Ronald Lee 1937- WhoWor 91
Bramble, William David 1940- WhoSSW 91
Bramble, William Henry 1901- BioIn 16
Bramblett, William Thomas 1932- St&PR 91
Brame, Erv 1901-1949 Ballpl 90
Brame, Marillyn A. 1928- WhoAmW 91, WhoWor 91
Brame, Scott O. 1928- St&PR 91, WhoAm 90
Brame, William Watt, Jr. 1945- WhoEmL 91
Bramel, Jene E., II 1948- St&PR 91
Bramel, Tamara Ann 1961- WhoEmL 91
Brameld, John PenDiDA 89
Brameld, Theodore 1904-1987 BioIn 16
Brameld, William PenDiDA 89
Bramer, Herbert Smith 1929- WhoE 91
Bramer, Kurt Richard 1935- St&PR 91
Bramhall, James Litton BiDrAPA 89
Bramhall, Kib 1933- WhoAmA 91
Bramhall, Robert Richard 1927- WhoWor 91
Bramhall, Shirley Anne 1926- WhoAmW 91
Bramhall, Stuart Jeanne 1947- BiDrAPA 89
Bramlett, Betty Jane WhoAmA 91
Bramlett, Christopher Lewis 1938- WhoAm 90
Bramlett, Ernest 1921- St&PR 91
Bramlett, James Dolphus 1930- WhoWrEP 89
Bramlett, John 1941- BioIn 16
Bramlett, John W. 1949- St&PR 91
Bramlett, Joyce Fielder 1933- WhoSSW 91
Bramlett, Shirley Marie Wilhelm 1945- WhoSSW 91
Bramlett, William Andrew, Jr. 1959- WhoSSW 91
Bramley, Christopher W. 1941- St&PR 91
Bramley, Jenny Rosenthal 1910- BioIn 16
Bramma, Harry Wakefield 1936- IntWWM 90
Brammell, William Hartman 1955- WhoEmL 91
Brammer, Forest Evert 1913- WhoAm 90
Brammer, Lawrence Martin 1922- WhoAm 90
Bramnick, Lea Shapiro 1938- WhoAmW 91
Bramon, Risa BioIn 16
Brams, Joan WhoAmA 91
Brams, Marvin Robert 1937- WhoAm 90, WhoE 91
Brams, Robert Stuart 1959- WhoE 91
Brams, Steven John 1940- WhoAm 90
Bramsen, James E. 1936- St&PR 91
Bramson, Berenice Louise 1929- WhoAmW 91
Bramson, David Jay 1937- WhoAm 90
Bramson, Leon 1930- WhoAm 90
Bramson, Phyllis Halperin 1941- WhoAmA 91
Bramson, Robert Sherman 1938- WhoAm 90
Bramson, Ruth N. ODwPR 91
Bramson, Scott B. 1948- WhoAm 90
Bramson, Stewart Mark 1937- BiDrAPA 89, WhoE 91
Bramson, Thomas 1927- WhoAm 90
Bramstedt, William Frederick 1905-1988 BioIn 16
Bramston, Mary 1841-1912 FemiCLE
Bramwell BioIn 16
Bramwell, Henry 1919- WhoAm 90
Bramwell, Katharine Hone Emmet 1914- WhoE 91
Bramwell, Marvel Lynnette 1947- WhoAmW 91, WhoWor 91
Bramwell-Booth, Catherine 1883-1987 BioIn 16
Branagan, Barbara Lee ODwPR 91
Branagan, James Joseph 1943- WhoAm 90
Branagh, Kenneth BioIn 16
Branam, James Willie, Jr. 1951- BiDrAPA 89
Branaman, David Edward 1932- St&PR 91
Branan, Carolyn Benner 1953- WhoAmW 91, WhoEmL 91, WhoWor 91
Branan, John Maury 1933- WhoSSW 91
Branand, Dyanne Marie 1950- WhoAmW 91
Branca, John Gregory 1950- WhoWor 91
Branca, Ralph 1926- Ballpl 90
Branca, Ralph M. 1935- St&PR 91
Brancaforte, Benito 1934- WhoAm 90
Brancaforte, Charlotte Lang 1934- WhoAmW 91
Brancas, Louis-Leon-Felicite, Duc de 1733-1824 PenDiDA 89
Brancato, Carolyn Kay 1945- WhoE 91
Brancato, Emanuel Leonard 1914- WhoAm 90
Brancato, Leo John 1922- WhoAm 90
Brancato, Peter BiDrAPA 89
Brancato, Robin F. BioIn 16
Branch, Alejandro Leopoldo 1839-1896 AmLegL
Branch, Anna 1875-1937 FemiCLE
Branch, Barrington Heath 1940- WhoWor 91
Branch, Ben Shirley 1943- WhoAm 90, WhoE 91
Branch, Billy H. 1928- St&PR 91
Branch, C H Hardin 1908- BiDrAPA 89
Branch, Charles H. 1926- ODwPR 91
Branch, Charles Henry Hardin 1908- WhoAm 90
Branch, Charles William 1930- WhoAm 90
Branch, Connie Campbell 1947- WhoSSW 91
Branch, Cynthia Lynn 1957- WhoAmW 91
Branch, Daniel Hugh 1958- WhoEmL 91
Branch, Emmett Forest 1874-1932 AmLegL
Branch, Erica Danielle 1966- WhoAmW 91
Branch, Gary Leo 1942- WhoWor 91
Branch, John 1782-1863 BiDrUSE 89
Branch, John Ellison 1915- WhoWor 91
Branch, Judson B. 1906-1989 BioIn 16
Branch, Norman L. St&PR 91
Branch, Pamela 1902-1967 TwCCr&M 91
Branch, Robert Lee 1924- WhoAm 90
Branch, Taylor BioIn 16
Branch, Taylor 1947- ConAu 131, WhoAm 90
Branch, Thomas Broughton, III 1936- WhoAm 90, WhoWor 91
Branch, William 1927- DrBIPA 90
Branch, William Blackwell 1927- WhoAm 90
Branch, William H. 1926- St&PR 91
Branch, William Terrell 1937- WhoWor 91
Branchard, Emile 1881-1938 MusmAFA
Branchini, Frank Caesar 1951- WhoE 91
Branciforte, Joseph L. 1946- St&PR 91
Branciforte, Roberto 1933- BiDrAPA 89
Branco, Humberto de Alencar Castelo 1900-1967 BioIn 16
Branco, James J. 1951- St&PR 91
Branco, James Joseph 1951- WhoE 91, WhoEmL 91
Branco, Maria Clotilde 1954- WhoE 91
Branco, Pedro de Freitas PenDiMP
Brancomb, Lewis McAdory 1926- St&PR 91
Brancucci, Marion Schauler 1931- BiDrAPA 89
Brancusi, Constantin 1876-1957 BioIn 16, IntDcAA 90, WorAlBi
Brancusi, Petre 1928- WhoWor 91
Brand, Betsy 1954- WhoAm 90
Brand, Charles Macy 1932- WhoAm 90, WhoE 91
Brand, Christianna 1907-1988 AnObit 1988, BioIn 16, SmATA X, TwCCr&M 91
Brand, Craig R. 1947- St&PR 91
Brand, Dionne 1953- FemiCLE
Brand, Dollar BioIn 16
Brand, Donald Ayres 1940- St&PR 91
Brand, Edward Cabell 1923- WhoAm 90
Brand, Eugene Dew 1924- BiDrAPA 89
Brand, Eugene J. 1934- St&PR 91
Brand, Frank A. 1924- St&PR 91
Brand, Frank Amery 1924- WhoAm 90
Brand, George Edward, Jr. 1918- WhoAm 90
Brand, Hannah FemiCLE
Brand, Irene Beard 1929- WhoWrEP 89
Brand, James W. St&PR 91
Brand, Jesse R. 1948- St&PR 91
Brand, Joel 1906-1964 BioIn 16
Brand, John Charles 1921- WhoAm 90
Brand, Jonathan E. 1958- WhoEmL 91
Brand, Joseph Lyon 1936- WhoAm 90, WhoWor 91
Brand, Julia Marie 1925- WhoSSW 91
Brand, Leonard 1923- WhoAm 90
Brand, Leonard Roy 1941- WhoAm 90
Brand, Ludwig 1932- WhoAm 90, WhoWor 91
Brand, Marcia Ceperly 1962- WhoAmW 91
Brand, Mark 1949- ODwPR 91
Brand, Mary Lou 1934- WhoAmW 91
Brand, Max 1892-1944 BioIn 16, WorAlBi
Brand, Maxwell R BiDrAPA 89
Brand, Maxwell Richard 1916- WhoE 91
Brand, Michael Edward 1950- WhoEmL 91
Brand, Mona 1915- FemiCLE
Brand, Myles 1942- WhoAm 90
Brand, Myra Jean 1936- IntWWM 90
Brand, Natan NewYTBS 90
Brand, Oscar 1920- AuBYP 90, IntWWM 90, WhoAm 90
Brand, Paula Irene 1950- WhoE 91, WhoEmL 91
Brand, Ray Manning 1922- WhoE 91

Brand, Richard David 1945- *BiDrAPA 89*, *WhoE 91*
Brand, Robert Allyn 1920- *WhoAm 90*
Brand, Robert Joseph 1947- *WhoEmL 91*
Brand, Robert Lawrence 1938- *St&PR 91*
Brand, Robert N. 1936- *St&PR 91*
Brand, Ron 1940- *Ballpl 90*
Brand, Ronald Alvah 1952- *WhoE 91*, *WhoEmL 91*
Brand, S. Richard 1939- *St&PR 91*
Brand, Sheila V. *ODwPR 91*
Brand, Steve Aaron 1948- *WhoEmL 91*
Brand, Stewart 1938- *WhoAm 90*, *WhoWrEP 89*
Brand, Vance Devoe 1931- *WhoAm 90*
Brand, W. Calvert 1918- *St&PR 91*
Brandanger, Nancy Ann 1955- *WhoEmL 91*
Brandano, Phyllis Teresa 1952- *WhoAmW 91*
Brandau, Seawell 1903- *St&PR 91*
Brandauer, Frederick Paul 1933- *WhoAm 90*
Brandauer, Klaus Maria *BioIn 16*
Brandauer, Klaus Maria 1944- *CurBio 90 [port]*
Brandborg, Stewart Monroe 1925- *WhoAm 90*
Brandchaft, Bernard S *BiDrAPA 89*
Brandchaft-Matro, Deborah 1945- *BiDrAPA 89*
Brande, Edward Woodrow 1931- *WhoE 91*
Brandeberry, Linda M. *BioIn 16*
Brandegee, Augustus 1828-1904 *AmLegL*
Brandegee, Frank Bosworth 1864-1924 *AmLegL*
Brandegee, Kate 1844-1920 *WomFic [port]*
Brandeis, Irma *BioIn 16*
Brandeis, Irma 1906?-1990 *ConAu 130*
Brandeis, Louis D. 1856-1941 *WorAlBi*
Brandeis, Louis Dembitz 1856-1941 *BioIn 16*
Brandeis, Rudolf Benjamin 1924- *WhoWor 91*
Brandel, Donald Joseph 1940- *St&PR 91*
Brandely, Louis F. 1906- *St&PR 91*
Branden, Nathaniel *BioIn 16*
Brandenberg, Aliki Leacouras 1929- *AuBYP 90*
Brandenberg, Aliki Liacouras *WhoAmA 91*
Brandenberg, Aliki Liacouras 1929- *ConAu 30NR*
Brandenberg, Franz 1932- *AuBYP 90*, *ConAu 30NR*
Brandenberg, Pearline 1934- *WhoAmW 91*
Brandenburg, Carl Albert, Sr. 1946- *St&PR 91*
Brandenburg, Carlos Enrique 1948- *WhoHisp 91*
Brandenburg, Henry Lee 1925- *WhoWor 91*
Brandenburg, Jeffrey A. 1959- *WhoEmL 91*
Brandenburg, John Nelson 1929- *WhoAm 90*
Brandenburg, Richard George 1935- *WhoAm 90*
Brandenburg, Robert Fairchild, Jr. 1938- *WhoSSW 91*, *WhoWor 91*
Brandenburg, Roger Gene 1932- *St&PR 91*
Brandenburg, Ronald William 1954- *WhoEmL 91*
Brandenstein, Daniel Charles 1943- *WhoAm 90*
Brander, John Morran 1932- *WhoWrEP 89*
Brander, Thomas W. 1949- *St&PR 91*
Brandes, Georg 1842-1927 *DcScanL*
Brandes, George *WhoHisp 91*
Brandes, Jack Solomon 1943- *BiDrAPA 89*
Brandes, Lisa 1957- *WhoEmL 91*
Brandes, Louis Roche *BiDrAPA 89*
Brandes, Norman S *BiDrAPA 89*
Brandes, Norman Scott 1923- *WhoAm 90*
Brandes, Paula Lynne 1952- *WhoEmL 91*
Brandes, Peter, Jr. 1945- *BiDrAPA 89*
Brandes, Raymond Lawrence, Jr. 1933- *WhoE 91*
Brandes, Raymond Stewart 1924- *WhoAm 90*
Brandes, Richard David 1935- *St&PR 91*
Brandes, Roddy Arthur 1920- *WhoSSW 91*
Brandes, Stanley Howard 1942- *WhoAm 90*
Brandes, Zita Judith Miller *WhoAmW 91*
Brandes-Bowen, Ila Ann 1954- *WhoAmW 91*
Brandford, Napoleon 1952- *BioIn 16*
Brandhorst, Jim *BioIn 16*
Brandhorst, Wesley Theodore 1933- *WhoAm 90*
Brandi, Cesare 1906-1988 *BioIn 16*
Brandi, John 1943- *WhoWrEP 89*
Brandin, Alf Elvin 1912- *WhoAm 90*
Brandin, Donald N. 1921- *St&PR 91*
Brandin, Donald Nelson 1921- *WhoAm 90*
Brandin, Seymour *St&PR 91*
Branding, Elaine *ODwPR 91*
Brandis Quartet *PenDiMP*
Brandis, Marianne 1938- *BioIn 16*
Brandis, Pamela 1946- *WhoAmW 91*
Brandis, Thomas *PenDiMP*
Brandl, James H. 1948- *St&PR 91*
Brandl, James Martin 1943- *St&PR 91*
Brandl, John Edward 1937- *WhoAm 90*
Brandl, Margaret Maria 1937- *WhoWor 91*
Brandl, Robert W. 1933- *St&PR 91*
Brandman, Harry *BiDrAPA 89*
Brandman, Otto 1900-1989 *BioIn 16*
Brandmeyer, Donald Wayne 1919- *WhoWor 91*
Brandmueller, Josef 1921- *WhoWor 91*
Brandmuller, Walter 1929- *WhoWor 91*
Brandner, Bradley *BioIn 16*
Brandner, J. William 1937- *St&PR 91*, *WhoAm 90*, *WhoSSW 91*
Brando, Christian *BioIn 16*
Brando, Marlon 1924- *BioIn 16*, *WorAlBi*
Brando, Marlon, Jr. 1924- *WhoAm 90*
Brandoff, Neal Irvin 1945- *BiDrAPA 89*
Brandolini, Anita Jean 1956- *WhoAmW 91*
Brandolini, Melissa *BioIn 16*
Brandolini, Nuno *BioIn 16*
Brandolino, Joseph Anthony 1961- *WhoEmL 91*
Brandon, Belinda Bell 1947- *WhoE 91*
Brandon, Charles *BioIn 16*
Brandon, Claudia A. 1956- *St&PR 91*
Brandon, Clement Edwin 1915- *WhoAm 90*
Brandon, Curt *AuBYP 90*
Brandon, Daniel Morris, Jr. 1946- *WhoSSW 91*
Brandon, Darrell 1940- *Ballpl 90*
Brandon, Donald Wayne 1926- *WhoAm 90*
Brandon, Edward B. 1931- *St&PR 91*
Brandon, Edward Bermetz 1931- *WhoAm 90*
Brandon, George Maxwell 1931- *St&PR 91*
Brandon, Guilbert Lepage, Jr. 1946- *St&PR 91*
Brandon, Henry *BioIn 16*
Brandon, Henry 1912-1990 *BioIn 16*, *NewYTBS 90*
Brandon, Herbert A. *BioIn 16*
Brandon, Inman 1906- *WhoWor 91*
Brandon, James Gilbert 1940- *WhoE 91*
Brandon, Jay Robert 1953- *WhoEmL 91*
Brandon, Jeffrey Alan 1944- *St&PR 91*
Brandon, Joy *ODwPR 91*
Brandon, Karen Nicole 1965- *WhoAmW 91*
Brandon, Katherine Swint 1952- *WhoEmL 91*
Brandon, Liane *WhoAm 90*
Brandon, Mabel H. *ODwPR 91*
Brandon, Mark Edward 1954- *WhoEmL 91*
Brandon, Michael C. 1946- *ODwPR 91*
Brandon, Paul Stanley 1946- *WhoE 91*
Brandon, Ralph F 1931- *BiDrAPA 89*
Brandon, Reiko Mochinaga 1935- *BioIn 16*
Brandon, Robert Eugene 1920- *St&PR 91*
Brandon, Sheila *ConAu 30NR*
Brandon, Suzanne 1928- *WhoAmW 91*
Brandon, Thomas R 1939- *BiDrAPA 89*
Brandon, Warren Eugene 1916-1977 *WhoAmA 91N*
Brandon, William Henry, Jr. *BioIn 16*
Brandon-Smith, Faith Hope 1955- *WhoE 91*
Brandow, George Everett 1913- *WhoAm 90*, *WhoWor 91*
Brandow, Richard Walton 1930- *St&PR 91*
Brandram, Rosina 1846-1907 *OxCPMus*
Brandrup, Douglas Warren 1940- *WhoE 91*, *WhoWor 91*
Brands, Allen Jean 1914- *WhoAm 90*
Brands, Edgar G. 1888-1970 *Ballpl 90*
Brands, George Bernard 1925- *St&PR 91*
Brands, James Edwin 1937- *WhoAm 90*, *WhoSSW 91*
Brandstater, Lynn Bourdon 1958- *WhoAmW 91*
Brandstatter, Leo 1948- *ODwPR 91*
Brandstedter, Rodney 1944- *St&PR 91*
Brandstetter, Bruce George 1956- *WhoEmL 91*
Brandstetter, Robert Daniel 1947- *WhoE 91*
Brandt, Alvin George 1922- *WhoWrEP 89*
Brandt, Andreas 1935- *WhoWor 91*
Brandt, Andrew Curtis 1951- *WhoWrEP 89*
Brandt, Ann Sue 1950- *WhoSSW 91*
Brandt, Annelies 1947- *WhoWor 91*
Brandt, Arthur *BiDrAPA 89*
Brandt, Arthur Melvin *BiDrAPA 89*
Brandt, Blanch Marie 1937- *WhoAmW 91*
Brandt, Brenda Joyce 1961- *WhoAmW 91*
Brandt, C. Raymond 1923- *St&PR 91*
Brandt, Carl D. 1935- *St&PR 91*
Brandt, Connie Marie 1947- *WhoAmW 91*
Brandt, Daniel James *BiDrAPA 89*
Brandt, David Dean 1947- *WhoEmL 91*
Brandt, Douglas Mitchell 1956- *BiDrAPA 89*, *WhoE 91*
Brandt, Ed 1905-1944 *Ballpl 90*
Brandt, Edward Dupree, Jr. 1927- *St&PR 91*
Brandt, Edward Newman, Jr. 1933- *WhoAm 90*, *WhoSSW 91*, *WhoWrEP 89*
Brandt, Frederick Robert 1936- *WhoAmA 91*
Brandt, Frederick William 1933- *WhoAm 90*
Brandt, George W 1920- *ConAu 131*
Brandt, Grace Borgenicht *WhoAmA 91*
Brandt, Harold Oscar 1934- *St&PR 91*
Brandt, Harry 1925- *St&PR 91*, *WhoAm 90*
Brandt, Harry Andrew 1957- *BiDrAPA 89*
Brandt, Henry A 1924- *BiDrAPA 89*
Brandt, Herbert P *BiDrAPA 89*
Brandt, Hermann Wilhelm 1904-1983 *DcNaB 1981*
Brandt, Ira Kive 1923- *WhoAm 90*
Brandt, Jackie 1934- *Ballpl 90*
Brandt, James Andrew 1927- *St&PR 91*
Brandt, James Bradford 1951- *WhoWor 91*
Brandt, Jerrold Thurston, Jr. 1946- *St&PR 91*
Brandt, Joanna Dorin 1959- *BiDrAPA 89*
Brandt, John 1943- *ODwPR 91*
Brandt, John Henry 1940- *BiDrAPA 89*, *WhoE 91*
Brandt, Jorgen Gustava 1929- *DcScanL*
Brandt, Jurgen Franz Paul 1940- *WhoWor 91*
Brandt, Kathleen Weil-Garris *WhoAmA 91*
Brandt, Kathy *ODwPR 91*
Brandt, Keith D. 1934- *St&PR 91*
Brandt, Leslie F. 1919- *WhoWrEP 89*
Brandt, Louis J. 1904- *St&PR 91*
Brandt, Marianne 1842-1921 *PenDiMP*
Brandt, Marianne 1893-1980? *BiDWomA*
Brandt, Marianne 1893-1983 *ConDes 90*, *PenDiDA 89*
Brandt, Max 1930- *BiDrAPA 89*
Brandt, Philip Ronald 1942- *St&PR 91*
Brandt, Reinhard 1932- *WhoWor 91*
Brandt, Rex 1914- *WhoAmA 91*
Brandt, Rexford Elson 1914- *WhoAm 90*
Brandt, Reynier 1707-1784? *PenDiDA 89*
Brandt, Rheda Shapiro 1940- *WhoE 91*
Brandt, Richard 1927- *St&PR 91*
Brandt, Richard Booker 1910- *WhoAm 90*
Brandt, Richard Martin 1922- *WhoAm 90*
Brandt, Richard Paul 1927- *WhoAm 90*, *WhoE 91*
Brandt, Richard Paul 1961- *WhoEmL 91*
Brandt, Robert Frederic, III 1946- *WhoAm 90*
Brandt, Roger Del 1939- *WhoSSW 91*
Brandt, Ronald Lee 1947- *WhoEmL 91*
Brandt, Ronald Marvin 1946- *WhoE 91*
Brandt, Siegmund 1936- *WhoWor 91*
Brandt, Stephanie Ann 1952- *BiDrAPA 89*
Brandt, Sue R. 1916- *BioIn 16*
Brandt, Susan 1941- *St&PR 91*
Brandt, Susan Garbee 1956- *WhoAmW 91*
Brandt, Susan Lorae 1950- *WhoEmL 91*
Brandt, Tom *TwCCr&M 91*
Brandt, Truman L. 1931- *St&PR 91*
Brandt, Victor Leonard 1920- *WhoAm 90*
Brandt, Warren 1918- *WhoAm 90*, *WhoAmA 91*
Brandt, William Arthur, Jr. 1949- *WhoEmL 91*
Brandt, William E. *Ballpl 90*
Brandt, William Ellis 1933- *St&PR 91*
Brandt, Willy 1913- *BioIn 16*, *WhoWor 91*, *WorAlBi*
Brandt, Yale M. 1930- *WhoSSW 91*
Brandtjen, Henry A. 1928- *St&PR 91*
Brandtjen, Henry Albert, III 1959- *St&PR 91*
Brandveen, Antonio Isadore 1946- *WhoEmL 91*
Brandvold, Richard J. 1922- *St&PR 91*
Brandwein, Larry 1931- *WhoAm 90*
Brandwein, Steve Craig 1948- *St&PR 91*
Brandys, Kazimierz *BioIn 16*
Brandys, Kazimierz 1916- *ConLC 62 [port]*
Brandzel, Jacob Reuben 1939- *WhoAm 90*
Brane, Adolfo J *BiDrAPA 89*
Branegan, James Augustus, III 1950- *WhoAm 90*
Branfield, John 1931- *ConAu 33NR*
Branfield, John Charles 1931- *AuBYP 90*
Branflick, Robert Andrew 1948- *St&PR 91*
Branfman, Steven 1953- *WhoAmA 91*
Branges, Louis de 1932- *WhoAm 90*
Brangham, Suzanne *BioIn 16*
Brangwyn, Frank 1867-1956 *PenDiDA 89*
Branhagen, Darrel Raymond 1949- *WhoEmL 91*
Branham, David Cummins 1812-1877 *AmLegL*
Branham, Henry Ezell, Jr. 1931- *WhoSSW 91*
Branigan, George V. *St&PR 91N*
Branigan, Helen Marie 1944- *WhoAmW 91*
Branigin, William Joseph 1952- *WhoAm 90*
Brankovich, Mark J. 1922- *WhoWor 91*
Branley, Franklyn Mansfield 1915- *AuBYP 90*
Brann, Alton J. 1941- *St&PR 91*
Brann, Alton Joseph 1941- *WhoAm 90*
Brann, Donald Lewis, Jr. 1945- *WhoEmL 91*
Brann, Esther *AuBYP 90*
Brann, Lester William, Jr. 1925- *WhoAm 90*
Brann, W. C. 1855-1898 *BioIn 16*
Brann, William Cowper 1855-1898 *BioIn 16*
Brann, William Paul 1916- *WhoAm 90*
Brannan, Charles Franklin 1903- *BiDrUSE 89*
Brannan, Daniel Keith 1953- *WhoSSW 91*
Brannan, Eulie Ross 1928- *WhoAm 90*
Brannan, Harold David 1949- *WhoEmL 91*
Brannan, James Bernard, Jr. 1951- *WhoEmL 91*
Brannan, Peggy L. 1937- *WhoAmW 91*
Brannan, Ralph T. 1926- *St&PR 91*
Brannan, Robert D. 1942- *St&PR 91*
Brannan, Stephen K 1957- *BiDrAPA 89*
Brannan, William 1925- *WhoAm 90*
Brannan, William Breece 1958- *WhoE 91*, *WhoEmL 91*
Brannan, William C. 1949- *WhoEmL 91*
Brannen, Charles A. 1944- *St&PR 91*
Brannen, James Otis 1939- *BiDrAPA 89*
Brannen, Julia 1944- *ConAu 130*
Brannen, Malcolm Erskine 1946- *WhoEmL 91*
Brannen, William Thomas 1936- *St&PR 91*
Branner, Hans Christian 1903-1966 *DcScanL*
Branner, Martin 1888-1970 *EncACom*
Branner, Robert 1927-1973 *WhoAmA 91N*
Brannian, Ross Edwin 1925- *WhoSSW 91*
Brannick, Ellen Marie 1934- *WhoAmW 91*
Brannick, J.E. 1955- *St&PR 91*
Brannigan, James Edward 1927- *WhoAm 90*
Brannigan, James Hugh 1932- *St&PR 91*
Brannigan, Owen 1908-1973 *PenDiMP*
Brannon, Barbara 1957- *WhoEmL 91*
Brannon, Clifton Woodrow 1912- *WhoAm 90*
Brannon, Emma Collins *WhoSSW 91*
Brannon, Frances Joan 1935- *WhoAmW 91*
Brannon, Hezzie Raymond, Jr. 1926- *WhoAm 90*
Brannon, James L. 1945- *St&PR 91*
Brannon, Jean Marilyn *WhoWrEP 89*
Brannon, Lawrence T *BiDrAPA 89*
Brannon, Lester Travis, Jr. 1926- *WhoAm 90*
Brannon, Rachel Ann 1954- *WhoAmW 91*, *WhoSSW 91*
Brannon, Robert L. *ODwPR 91*
Brannon, Terence Carlin 1938- *St&PR 91*
Brannon, Winona Eileen 1948- *WhoAmW 91*
Branover, Herman 1931- *ConAu 130*
Bransby, Eric James 1916- *WhoAm 90*, *WhoAmA 91*
Branscom, Margaret E 1920- *BiDrAPA 89*
Branscomb, Anne Wells 1928- *WhoAm 90*, *WhoAmW 91*, *WhoWor 91*
Branscomb, Harvie, Jr. 1922- *WhoAm 90*
Branscomb, Lewis Capers, Jr. 1911- *WhoAm 90*
Branscomb, Lewis McAdory 1926- *WhoAm 90*
Branscombe, Nyla Ruth 1956- *WhoAmW 91*
Branscombe, Peter John 1929- *IntWWM 90*
Branscome, James Glenn 1946- *St&PR 91*
Branscum, Barton Anthony 1959- *BiDrAPA 89*
Branscum, Robbie *BioIn 16*
Branscum, T. Eugene 1935- *St&PR 91*
Bransdorfer, Stephen Christie 1929- *WhoAm 90*
Bransfield, Kitty 1875-1947 *Ballpl 90*
Bransfield, Robert C 1946- *BiDrAPA 89*
Bransfield, Robert Carroll 1946- *WhoE 91*
Bransford, Helen *BioIn 16*
Bransom, Paul 1885-1979 *WhoAmA 91N*
Branson, Allegra 1934- *WhoE 91*, *WhoWor 91*
Branson, Branley Allan 1929- *WhoAm 90*
Branson, Branley Allen 1929- *WhoWrEP 89*
Branson, Brenda Sullens 1961- *WhoAmW 91*

Branson, Dan Earle 1928- *WhoAm 90*
Branson, David 1909- *IntWWM 90*
Branson, H C *TwCCr&M 91*
Branson, Harley Kenneth 1942- *WhoWor 91*
Branson, Herman Russell 1914- *WhoAm 90*
Branson, James Richard 1940- *WhoWor 91*
Branson, Mary Lou 1932- *WhoAmW 91*
Branson, Perry Richard 1951- *BiDrAPA 89*
Branson, Richard *BioIn 16*
Branson, Robert Earl 1918- *WhoSSW 91*
Branstad, Terry Edward 1946- *WhoAm 90, WhoWor 91*
Branstetter, Gwendolyn H *WhoAmA 91*
Brant, Austin E., Jr. 1929- *St&PR 91*
Brant, Dawn Mary 1965- *WhoEmL 91*
Brant, Henry 1913- *WhoAm 90*
Brant, John 1794-1832 *WhNaAH*
Brant, John Getty 1946- *WhoEmL 91*
Brant, John Sidney 1939- *WhoAm 90*
Brant, Joseph 1742-1807 *EncCRAm, WhNaAH [port]*
Brant, L. Ray 1909- *St&PR 91*
Brant, Molly 1735?-1796 *WhNaAH*
Brant, Murray 1910- *St&PR 91*
Brant, Peter Reginald 1915- *St&PR 91*
Brant, Renee Tankenoff 1946- *BiDrAPA 89*
Brant, Richard Ross 1934- *St&PR 91*
Brant, Toby L. *BioIn 16*
Brant, William Morton 1937- *WhoWrEP 89*
Brantenberg, Gerd 1941- *EncCoWW*
Brantl, Charlesmarie 1929- *WhoE 91*
Brantley, B. Waddell 1921- *St&PR 91*
Brantley, Bobby Lynn, Sr. 1948- *WhoSSW 91*
Brantley, Charles F. 1933- *St&PR 91*
Brantley, Charles Kenneth *BiDrAPA 89*
Brantley, David Lehmon 1949- *St&PR 91*
Brantley, Ingrid Jean 1948- *BiDrAPA 89*
Brantley, Jeffrey Garland 1949- *BiDrAPA 89, WhoSSW 91*
Brantley, Julian Thweatt, Jr. 1945- *BiDrAPA 89*
Brantley, Kathryn C 1929- *BiDrAPA 89*
Brantley, Lee Reed 1906- *WhoAm 90*
Brantley, Marvin A 1935- *BiDrAPA 89*
Brantley, Mickey 1961- *Ballpl 90*
Brantley, Nancy Simpson 1938- *WhoSSW 91*
Brantley, Oliver Wiley 1915- *WhoAm 90*
Brantley, Willa John 1956- *WhoAmW 91*
Brantley, William 1933- *ODwPR 91*
Brantley, William Stanley 1956- *WhoEmL 91*
Brantly, William Theophilus 1816-1882 *BioIn 16*
Branton, Camile B. 1950- *WhoAmW 91*
Branton, Marlene Hughes 1940- *WhoE 91*
Branton, Tim M. *ODwPR 91*
Branton, Wiley A. 1923-1988 *BioIn 16*
Brantz, George M. 1930- *St&PR 91*
Branum, William Howell 1941- *WhoAm 90*
Branyan, Robert Lester 1930- *WhoAm 90*
Branyon, David Watterson 1949- *BiDrAPA 89*
Branz, Michael Anthony 1954- *WhoSSW 91*
Branzell, Karin 1891-1974 *PenDiMP*
Branzer, John Paul 1942- *WhoSSW 91, WhoWor 91*
Branzi, Andrea 1938- *PenDiDA 89*
Braque, Georges 1882-1963 *BioIn 16, IntDcAA 90, WorAlBi*
Brar, Ravinder Kaur *BiDrAPA 89*
Bras, Luisa A. *WhoHisp 91*
Bras, Rafael Luis 1950- *WhoAm 90*
Brasch, Jerome F. 1925- *St&PR 91*
Brasch, John Michael 1955- *WhoEmL 91*
Brasch, Walter Milton 1945- *WhoWrEP 89*
Brasco, James John 1928- *St&PR 91*
Brase, Michael J. *BiDrAPA 89*
Brasel, Jo Anne 1934- *WhoAm 90*
Brasell, Harold Keary 1922- *WhoWor 91*
Braselman, Lin Emery *WhoAmA 91*
Braseth, John E 1959- *WhoAmA 91*
Braseth, Paul *BioIn 16*
Brasfield, Charles R 1940- *BiDrAPA 89*
Brasfield, David Williamson 1956- *WhoSSW 91*
Brasfield, Evans Booker 1932- *St&PR 91, WhoAm 90*
Brasfield, James 1952- *WhoWrEP 89*
Brasfield, John Michael 1948- *WhoSSW 91*
Brash, Douglas Reid *BioIn 16*
Brashaw, Gerald L. 1941- *St&PR 91*
Brashear, David Mark 1961- *WhoEmL 91*
Brashear, David S *BiDrAPA 89*
Brashear, Diane Lee 1933- *WhoAmW 91*
Brashear, John A. 1840-1920 *BioIn 16*
Brashear, Russ 1954- *WhoSSW 91*
Brashears, Bobby Fuller 1934- *WhoAm 90*
Brashears, David Fredrick 1946- *St&PR 91*
Brashears, Kent Baker 1953- *WhoSSW 91*
Brashears, Wilford Session, Jr. 1925- *WhoSSW 91*
Brasher, Gary Vaughn 1950- *WhoEmL 91*
Brasher, James E. 1948- *St&PR 91*
Brasher, Nell *BioIn 16*
Brasher, Richard Curtis 1931- *St&PR 91*
Brashers, Charles 1930- *WhoWrEP 89*
Brashers, Gary Boyd 1947- *St&PR 91*
Brashier, Robert Steven 1954- *WhoSSW 91*
Brashler, William 1947- *WhoAm 90*
Brasic, James Robert 1948- *BiDrAPA 89, WhoE 91*
Brasil, Emanuel 1940- *ConAu 130*
Brasillach, Robert 1909-1945 *BiDFrPL*
Brasington, Steve Johnson *BiDrAPA 89*
Brasitus, Thomas *WhoAm 90*
Brasket, Curt Justin 1932- *WhoAm 90*
Brasler, Robert M. 1936- *St&PR 91*
Brasley, Amy Jordan 1956- *WhoAmW 91*
Braslow, Lawrence *BiDrAPA 89*
Brasmer, Randall Dane 1952- *WhoEmL 91*
Brassai 1899-1984 *ModArCr 1 [port]*
Brassard, Andre 1946- *OxCCanT*
Brassard, Christopher J. 1956- *WhoEmL 91*
Brassard, Dennis Joseph 1948- *WhoEmL 91*
Brasseale, Kent A. 1941- *St&PR 91*
Brasseaux, Mary Therese 1951- *WhoEmL 91*
Brassell, Roselyn Strauss 1930- *WhoAm 90, WhoAmW 91*
Brassens, Georges 1921-1981 *OxCPMus*
Brasser, Levinus Joseph 1925- *WhoWor 91*
Brassett, Leo Lieux 1923- *St&PR 91*
Brasseur, Henri-Alphonse-Lambe 1905- *WhoWor 91*
Brassey, Anna 1839-1887 *FemiCLE*
Brassie, Paul Stanley *BioIn 16*
Brassil, Jean Ella 1933- *WhoAmW 91*
Brassin, Louis 1840-1884 *BioIn 16*
Brast, Neil Barry 1945- *BiDrAPA 89*
Brasted, Kenneth Parker, II 1935- *St&PR 91*
Brasted, Robert Crocker, Jr. 1955- *BiDrAPA 89*
Brasunas, Anton de Sales 1919- *WhoAm 90*
Braswell, Albert M., Jr. 1920- *St&PR 91*
Braswell, Arnold Webb 1925- *WhoAm 90*
Braswell, James C. 1946- *St&PR 91*
Braswell, Jane La Rose 1927- *WhoE 91*
Braswell, John *BioIn 16*
Braswell, Laura Day 1958- *WhoAmW 91*
Braswell, Louis Erskine 1937- *WhoAm 90*
Braswell, Pearl Eva 1914- *WhoAmW 91*
Braswell, Robert B. *BioIn 16*
Braswell, Robert Neil 1932- *WhoAm 90*
Braswell, Stephen R. 1940- *WhoAm 90*
Brataas, Mark Gerard 1922- *St&PR 91*
Brataas, Nancy 1928- *WhoAmW 91*
Bratby, John 1928- *WhoWor 91*
Bratcher, Carla Elizabeth 1942- *WhoAmW 91*
Bratcher, Dale 1932- *WhoAmA 91*
Bratcher, Keith Glenn 1958- *WhoEmL 91*
Bratcher, Twila Langdon *WhoAmW 91*
Brathovde, James Robert 1926- *WhoAm 90*
Brathwaite, Harriet Louisa 1931- *WhoAmW 91*
Brathwaite, Jorge Alonso 1944- *St&PR 91*
Brathwaite, Mellissa Annette 1961- *WhoAmW 91, WhoE 91*
Brathwaite, Nicholas *WhoWor 91*
Bratitch, Edward Nicolas 1918- *WhoWor 91*
Bratnick, Michael 1942- *ODwPR 91*
Braton, David Allen 1951- *St&PR 91*
Bratsos, Diane 1958- *WhoAmW 91*
Bratt, Bengt Erik 1922- *WhoAm 90, WhoWor 91*
Bratt, Bertil 1932- *WhoWor 91*
Bratt, C. Griffith 1914- *WhoWor 91*
Bratt, John Albert 1938- *St&PR 91*
Bratt, Nicholas 1948- *St&PR 91, WhoE 91*
Bratt-Wijkander, Monica Elisabeth *PenDiDA 89*
Brattain, Arlene Jane Clark 1938- *WhoAmW 91, WhoWor 91*
Brattain, Harriet Jane 1951- *WhoAmW 91*
Brattain, Walter H. 1902-1987 *WorAlBi*
Brattain, Walter Houser 1902-1987 *BioIn 16*
Bratten, Craig K. 1953- *St&PR 91*
Bratteng, Elizabeth H *BiDrAPA 89*
Brattensborg, Henry Joseph 1933- *BiDrAPA 89*
Bratter, Thomas Edward 1939- *WhoE 91, WhoWor 91*
Bratthauer, Ted John 1946- *St&PR 91*
Brattin, Elvin Price 1948- *WhoEmL 91*
Brattin, Kathleen Ann 1957- *WhoAmW 91*
Brattinga, Pieter 1931- *ConDes 90*
Brattle, Thomas 1658-1713 *EncCRAm*
Bratton, Albert Grover 1934- *BiDrAPA 89*
Bratton, Christopher 1959- *WhoAmA 91*
Bratton, Conrad Christopher 1941- *WhoSSW 91*
Bratton, Howard Calvin 1922- *WhoAm 90*
Bratton, Ida Frank 1933- *WhoAmW 91, WhoSSW 91, WhoWor 91*
Bratton, James Henry, Jr. 1931- *WhoAm 90*
Bratton, John W. 1867-1947 *OxCPMus*
Bratton, Karl H. 1906- *AuBYP 90*
Bratton, Kathleen Wilson 1949- *WhoAmW 91*
Bratton, Kevin J. 1949- *St&PR 91*
Bratton, Mary Jo 1926- *WhoSSW 91*
Bratton, Priscilla Hoffman 1951- *WhoE 91*
Bratton, Robert O. 1948- *St&PR 91*
Bratton, Sue Carlton 1953- *WhoSSW 91*
Bratton, William Edward 1919- *St&PR 91*
Brattstrom, Bayard Holmes 1929- *WhoAm 90*
Brattstrom, Gudrun Birgitta 1954- *WhoWor 91*
Bratyanski, Doris Madeline 1952- *WhoAmW 91*
Brauch, Charles Peter 1937- *St&PR 91*
Brauch, Hans Gunter 1947- *WhoWor 91*
Brauch, Merry Ruth Moore 1920- *WhoAmW 91*
Braucher, Richard Harold 1936- *St&PR 91*
Brauchi, John T 1927- *BiDrAPA 89*
Brauchitsch, Heinrich Von 1881-1948 *WorAlBi*
Brauchle, Walter R. 1943- *St&PR 91*
Braucht, Carol Jean 1939- *WhoAmW 91*
Braucht, David William 1954- *WhoEmL 91*
Braucht, Stephanie Ann Sirotnak 1948- *WhoAmW 91*
Brauckmann, F. Paul 1947- *WhoSSW 91*
Braud, Bert Stephen 1959- *WhoEmL 91*
Braud, Elodie Pons *BiDrAPA 89*
Braud, Kenneth Warren 1952- *WhoSSW 91*
Braud, Samuel Philip, III 1930- *St&PR 91*
Braud, William G. 1942- *EncPaPR 91*
Braude, Abraham S. 1910- *St&PR 91*
Braude, Ann 1955- *ConAu 132*
Braude, Beatrice *BioIn 16*
Braude, Edwin S. 1927- *WhoAm 90*
Braude, Keith Z. 1962- *St&PR 91*
Braude, Kenneth Z. 1936- *St&PR 91*
Braude, Kevin Z. 1964- *St&PR 91*
Braude, Marjorie S 1924- *BiDrAPA 89*
Braude, Michael 1936- *WhoAm 90*
Braude, Robert Michael 1939- *WhoAm 90*
Braude, Stephen 1945- *EncPaPR 91*
Braude, Stuart 1936- *St&PR 91*
Braude, Theodore R. 1952- *WhoEmL 91*
Braudel, Fernand *BioIn 16*
Braudy, Dorothy *WhoAmA 91*
Braudy, Leo Beal 1941- *WhoAm 90, WhoWrEP 89*
Brauer, Connie Ann 1949- *WhoAmA 91*
Brauer, Eugene Richard 1936- *St&PR 91*
Brauer, Evan Zack 1957- *St&PR 91*
Brauer, Frank 1929- *St&PR 91*
Brauer, Fred Gunther 1932- *WhoAm 90*
Brauer, Harrol Andrew, Jr. 1920- *WhoSSW 91, WhoWor 91*
Brauer, Heinz Peter 1923- *WhoWor 91*
Brauer, Herbert Julien 1920- *St&PR 91*
Brauer, Jane Zion 1952- *WhoEmL 91*
Brauer, Jerald Carl 1921- *WhoAm 90*
Brauer, Lee David *BiDrAPA 89*
Brauer, Michael 1949- *WhoEmL 91, WhoWor 91*
Brauer, Paul H *BiDrAPA 89*
Brauer, Ralph Werner 1921- *WhoAm 90*
Brauer, Richard Dagobert 1901-1977 *DcScB S2*
Brauer, Rima Lois 1938- *BiDrAPA 89*
Brauer, William H. 1926- *St&PR 91*
Brauer, William W 1933- *BiDrAPA 89*
Brauers, Willem Karel 1924- *WhoWor 91*
Brault, Frank Michael 1937- *WhoSSW 91*
Brault, Gayle Lorain 1944- *WhoAmW 91, WhoWor 91*
Brault, Gerard Joseph 1929- *WhoAm 90*
Brauman, John I. 1937- *WhoAm 90*
Braumiller, Allen Spooner 1934- *St&PR 91, WhoAm 90*
Braun, Andrew James 1962- *WhoSSW 91*
Braun, Armand *BiDrAPA 89*
Braun, Artur 1925- *PenDiDA 89*
Braun, Beatrice S 1921- *BiDrAPA 89*
Braun, Bennett G 1940- *BiDrAPA 89*
Braun, Bonnie Sue 1947- *WhoEmL 91*
Braun, Charles Louis 1937- *WhoAm 90*
Braun, Charles R. 1933- *St&PR 91*
Braun, Charles Stuart 1941- *WhoAm 90, WhoSSW 91*
Braun, Claire S. 1931- *WhoWrEP 89*
Braun, Craig Allen 1939- *WhoE 91*
Braun, Daniel Carl 1905- *WhoAm 90*
Braun, David Adlai 1931- *WhoAm 90*
Braun, Devra Lynn 1950- *BiDrAPA 89*
Braun, Earl Edward, Jr. 1941- *WhoSSW 91*
Braun, Edmund M *BiDrAPA 89*
Braun, Erwin *PenDiDA 89*
Braun, Eunice Hockspeier *WhoAmW 91*
Braun, Eva 1912-1945 *WorAlBi*
Braun, George W. 1908- *St&PR 91*
Braun, Grant H. 1926- *St&PR 91*
Braun, Henry 1930- *WhoWrEP 89*
Braun, Hermann Erich 1942- *St&PR 91*
Braun, James Edward *BiDrAPA 89*
Braun, Jerome 1918- *St&PR 91*
Braun, Jerome Irwin 1929- *WhoAm 90, WhoWor 91*
Braun, Joseph A *BiDrAPA 89*
Braun, Judith S *BiDrAPA 89*
Braun, Karl F. 1850-1918 *WorAlBi*
Braun, Karl Ferdinand 1850-1918 *BioIn 16*
Braun, Kathryn A. 1951- *St&PR 91*
Braun, Kathy *AuBYP 90*
Braun, L. Erich 1944- *St&PR 91*
Braun, Lilian Jackson *TwCCr&M 91*
Braun, Loretta Carol 1933- *St&PR 91*
Braun, Ludwig 1926- *WhoAm 90*
Braun, Manfred 1948- *WhoWor 91*
Braun, Margaret Cunningham *BioIn 16*
Braun, Mary Ann Dorothy 1942- *WhoAmW 91*
Braun, Mary Jo 1961- *WhoEmL 91*
Braun, Mary Lucile Dekle *WhoSSW 91*
Braun, Matt 1932- *BioIn 16*
Braun, Maura Tracey 1966- *WhoEmL 91*
Braun, Max *PenDiDA 89*
Braun, Michael Alan 1949- *WhoAm 90, WhoEmL 91*
Braun, Neil S. 1952- *St&PR 91*
Braun, Norman L. 1931- *ODwPR 91, St&PR 91*
Braun, Philip Roy 1945- *WhoE 91*
Braun, Phyllis Cellini 1953- *WhoEmL 91*
Braun, Raymond E. 1946- *St&PR 91*
Braun, Richard Edward 1937- *St&PR 91*
Braun, Richard L. 1947- *St&PR 91*
Braun, Richard Lane 1917- *WhoAm 90*
Braun, Richard M. *ODwPR 91*
Braun, Robert A *BiDrAPA 89*
Braun, Robert Clare 1928- *WhoWor 91*
Braun, Robert Duncan 1939- *WhoWor 91*
Braun, Robert Neal *BiDrAPA 89*
Braun, Samuel James 1934- *BiDrAPA 89*
Braun, Saul M. *AuBYP 90*
Braun, Sheila *BioIn 16*
Braun, Sheldon Richard 1943- *WhoAm 90*
Braun, Steve 1948- *Ballpl 90*
Braun, Theodore E. D. 1933- *WhoAm 90, WhoE 91*
Braun, Thomas Henry 1943- *St&PR 91*
Braun, Timothy Charles 1957- *St&PR 91*
Braun, Victor 1935- *IntWWM 90*
Braun, Virginia Vickers 1947- *WhoAmW 91*
Braun, Walter Gustav 1917- *WhoAm 90*
Braun, Warren Lloyd 1922- *WhoAm 90, WhoWor 91*
Braun, Wernher Von 1912-1977 *AuBYP 90, WorAlBi*
Braun, William Joseph 1925- *WhoAm 90*
Braun, Zev *WhoAm 90*
Braun-Brashares, Barbara Sue 1948- *WhoAmW 91, WhoSSW 91*
Braun-O'Donnell, Shirley Ann 1940- *WhoSSW 91*
Braun-Prager, Kathe 1888-1967 *EncCoWW*
Braunberger, Pierre *NewYTBS 90*
Braunecker, James L. 1953- *St&PR 91*
Brauner, David A. 1942- *WhoE 91*
Brauner, Phyllis Ambler 1916- *WhoAmW 91*
Braunfels, Michael 1917- *IntWWM 90*
Braungart, Richard Gottfried 1935- *WhoAm 90*
Braunig, Martha J. *St&PR 91*
Brauninger, Jurgen 1956- *IntWWM 90*
Braunmuller, A R 1945- *ConAu 132*
Braunschweig, Philippe Georges 1928- *WhoWor 91*
Braunschweiger, Christian Carl 1926- *WhoAm 90*
Braunss, Guenter 1931- *WhoWor 91*
Braunstein, Barry David 1953- *WhoEmL 91*
Braunstein, Edith 1927- *WhoSSW 91*
Braunstein, Ethan Malcolm 1945- *WhoEmL 91*
Braunstein, H Terry 1942- *WhoAmA 91*
Braunstein, Lee J. 1936- *St&PR 91*
Braunstein, Mark Lloyd 1948- *St&PR 91*
Braunstein, Mark Mathew 1951- *WhoAmA 91*
Braunstein, Martin Lewis 1944- *St&PR 91*
Braunstein, Nadine Susan 1957- *WhoAmW 91*
Braunstein, Phillip 1930- *WhoAm 90*
Braunstein, Ronald Edwin 1941- *BiDrAPA 89*
Braunstein, Ruth *WhoAmA 91*
Brauntuch, Troy 1954- *WhoAmA 91*

Braunwald, Eugene 1929- *WhoAm 90, WhoE 91*
Braus, Anthony James 1946- *BiDrAPA 89*
Braus, Ira Lincoln 1951- *IntWWM 90*
Brause, Donna Carlene 1958- *WhoAmW 91*
Brauss, Helmut F. 1930- *IntWWM 90*
Brautbar, Nachman 1943- *WhoAm 90*
Brautigam, Hans Otto 1931- *WhoWor 91*
Brautigam, Kathe Lynne 1962- *WhoSSW 91*
Brautigan, Richard *BioIn 16*
Brautigan, Richard 1935-1984 *MajTwCW*
Brauweiler, Daniel Charles 1961- *WhoEmL 91*
Brauzer, Benjamin *BiDrAPA 89*
Bravaldo, Donald Henry, Jr. 1934- *St&PR 91*
Braver, Moshe 1954- *St&PR 91*
Braverman, Amiel 1926- *St&PR 91*
Braverman, Bruce 1951- *BiDrAPA 89*
Braverman, Donna 1947- *WhoAmA 91*
Braverman, Donna Caryn 1947- *WhoAmW 91, WhoEmL 91, WhoWor 91*
Braverman, Harold 1921- *St&PR 91*
Braverman, Harry *EncAL*
Braverman, Irwin Merton 1929- *WhoAm 90*
Braverman, Joseph H. *BioIn 16*
Braverman, Kate *BioIn 16*
Braverman, Leo 1915- *BiDrAPA 89*
Braverman, Lois 1950- *WhoEmL 91*
Braverman, Louise M. 1948- *WhoE 91*
Braverman, Louise Marcia 1948- *WhoAmW 91, WhoEmL 91*
Braverman, Malvin *BiDrAPA 89*
Braverman, Melvin 1927- *St&PR 91*
Braverman, Michael R. 1951- *St&PR 91*
Braverman, Michael Seth 1955- *BiDrAPA 89*
Braverman, Robert Carl 1935- *St&PR 91*
Braverman, Robert Jay 1933- *WhoAm 90*
Braverman, Sidney 1928- *St&PR 91*
Braverman, Susan Plavin 1937- *WhoAmW 91*
Braverman, Wayne Harris 1943- *BiDrAPA 89*
Bravman, Richard Edward 1955- *St&PR 91*
Bravmann, Carol Ruth 1956- *WhoEmL 91*
Bravmann, Ludwig 1925- *WhoAm 90, WhoE 91*
Bravmann, Rene A 1939- *WhoAmA 91*
Bravo, Anthony John 1938- *WhoE 91*
Bravo, Carlos Eduardo 1959- *WhoEmL 91*
Bravo, Claudio 1936- *ArtLatA*
Bravo, Facundo D. *WhoHisp 91*
Bravo, Francisco 1910- *BioIn 16*
Bravo, Francisco 1910-1990 *WhoHisp 91N*
Bravo, Libardo *BiDrAPA 89*
Bravo, Lucia Salas 1927- *BiDrAPA 89*
Bravo, Miguel Obando y *BioIn 16*
Bravo, Rose Marie 1951- *WhoAm 90, WhoAmW 91*
Bravo Murillo, Juan 1803-1873 *BioIn 16*
Bravy, Stan Boris 1946- *BiDrAPA 89*
Brawand, Kurt *BiDrAPA 89*
Brawer, Catherine Coleman 1943- *St&PR 91*
Brawer, Marc Harris 1946- *WhoEmL 91*
Brawley, Benjamin Griffith 1882-1939 *BioIn 16*
Brawley, Edward Allan 1935- *WhoE 91*
Brawley, Ernest Charles 1937- *WhoWrEP 89*
Brawley, Paul Holm 1942- *WhoWrEP 89*
Brawley, Paul Holm 1942-1988 *BioIn 16*
Brawley, Robert Julius 1937- *WhoAm 90, WhoAmA 91*
Brawley, Tawana *BioIn 16*
Brawn, Linda Curtis 1947- *WhoAmW 91, WhoE 91*
Brawn, Robert G. 1936- *St&PR 91*
Brawner, Colleen Colbert 1957- *WhoAmW 91*
Brawner, James Newton, Jr. *BiDrAPA 89*
Brawner, Lee Basil 1935- *WhoAm 90, WhoSSW 91*
Braxton, Anthony *BioIn 16*
Braxton, Carter 1736-1797 *EncCRAm*
Braxton, Garland 1900-1966 *Ballpl 90*
Braxton, Juanita Louise Harris 1960- *WhoAmW 91*
Braxton, Mary Ellen 1946- *WhoAmW 91*
Braxton, William E 1878-1932 *WhoAmA 91N*
Bray, Absalom Francis, Jr. 1918- *WhoAm 90*
Bray, Anna Eliza 1790-1883 *BioIn 16, FemiCLE*
Bray, Arthur Philip 1933- *WhoAm 90*
Bray, Barry Daniel 1946- *St&PR 91*
Bray, Bonnie Anderson 1929- *WhoAmW 91*
Bray, Carolyn Scott 1938- *WhoAmW 91*
Bray, Charles 1811-1884 *EncO&P 3*
Bray, Charles Allan 1937- *BiDrAPA 89*
Bray, Charles William, III 1933- *WhoAm 90*
Bray, Cynthia Ann 1943- *WhoAmW 91*
Bray, David Maurice 1941- *WhoAm 90*
Bray, Deborah Kurek 1956- *WhoAmW 91*
Bray, Douglas Weston *BioIn 16*
Bray, Eben Jitter 1942- *St&PR 91*
Bray, George August 1931- *WhoAm 90*
Bray, Gerard Anthony 1950- *WhoAm 90*
Bray, James Donald 1930- *BiDrAPA 89*
Bray, James L. 1936- *St&PR 91*
Bray, Janet Baltuch 1950- *WhoEmL 91*
Bray, John 1879-1978 *WhoAmA 91N*
Bray, John Joseph 1937- *St&PR 91*
Bray, John Roger 1929- *WhoWor 91*
Bray, Laurack Doyle 1949- *WhoE 91*
Bray, Michael *BioIn 16*
Bray, Oscar S. 1905- *WhoAm 90*
Bray, Paul Marshall 1943- *WhoE 91*
Bray, Philip James 1925- *WhoAm 90*
Bray, Pierce 1924- *WhoAm 90*
Bray, Randy *BioIn 16*
Bray, Richard Daniel 1945- *WhoEmL 91*
Bray, Richard Franklin 1939- *WhoSSW 91*
Bray, Robert Bruce 1924- *WhoAm 90*
Bray, Roger William 1944- *IntWWM 90*
Bray, Ronald L. 1932- *St&PR 91*
Bray, Thomas Joseph 1941- *WhoAm 90*
Bray, Thomas Lee 1914- *St&PR 91*
Bray, Wade Russell 1945- *WhoE 91*
Bray, Walter Thomas, Jr. 1959- *WhoSSW 91*
Bray, William Otis, IV 1949- *WhoEmL 91*
Braybon, Gail 1952- *ConAu 131*
Braybrooke, David 1924- *WhoAm 90, WhoWrEP 89*
Brayczewski, Bohdan 1932- *WhoWor 91*
Brayer, Menachem Mendel 1922- *WhoAm 90*
Brayman, Alan Linwood 1951- *St&PR 91*
Brayman, Harold 1900-1988 *WhoWor 91*
Braymer, Marguerite 1911- *St&PR 91*
Braymer, Marguerite Annetta 1911- *WhoAm 90*
Brayshaw, Nora De Brunner 1944- *BiDrAPA 89*
Brayson, Albert Aloysius, II 1953- *WhoE 91, WhoEmL 91*
Braythwaite, Elizabeth 1667?-1684 *BiDEWW*
Brayton, George Baily 1839- *EncABHB 4*
Brayton, John Summerfield, Jr. 1924- *St&PR 91*
Brayton, Lincoln D. 1905- *St&PR 91*
Brayton, Robert Clayton 1942- *St&PR 91*
Brayton, Rosewell, Sr. 1917- *St&PR 91*
Braz, Evandro Freitas 1943- *WhoWor 91*
Brazaitis, Thomas Joseph 1940- *WhoAm 90*
Brazauskas, Algirdas *WhoWor 91*
Brazda, Frederick Wicks 1945- *WhoSSW 91*
Brazeal, Donna Smith 1947- *WhoAmW 91, WhoEmL 91, WhoSSW 91*
Brazeal, Earl Henry, Jr. 1939- *WhoE 91*
Brazeau, Richard 1940- *St&PR 91*
Brazeau, Wendell 1910-1974 *WhoAmA 91N*
Brazee, Louise Ann 1956- *WhoAmW 91, WhoEmL 91*
Brazell, James Ervin 1926- *St&PR 91, WhoAm 90*
Brazell, John L. 1939- *St&PR 91*
Brazell, Karen 1938- *ConAu 31NR*
Brazell, Karen Woodard 1938- *WhoAm 90*
Brazell, Timothy John 1959- *WhoE 91*
Brazelton, Eugenia Louise 1919- *WhoWrEP 89*
Brazelton, Roy Dale 1941- *St&PR 91, WhoAm 90*
Brazelton, T. Berry 1918- *BioIn 16*
Brazelton, Thomas Berry 1918- *WhoAm 90*
Brazelton, William Thomas 1921- *WhoAm 90*
Brazer, Bruce Alan 1952- *St&PR 91*
Brazer, Mara Hope 1955- *WhoAmW 91*
Brazer, Marjorie Cahn 1927- *WhoWrEP 89*
Braziel, Farrell Hobbs *BiDrAPA 89*
Brazier, C.W. 1910- *St&PR 91*
Brazier, Don Roland 1921- *WhoAm 90*
Brazier, Donn Paul 1917- *WhoAm 90*
Brazier, Mary Margaret 1956- *WhoAmW 91*
Brazier, Robert George 1937- *St&PR 91*
Brazil, Angela 1869-1947 *BioIn 16, FemiCLE*
Brazil, Gino T. 1956- *WhoHisp 91*
Brazil, Harold Edmund 1920- *WhoAm 90*
Brazil, Horus V 1926- *BiDrAPA 89*
Brazil, John Russell 1946- *WhoAm 90, WhoE 91*
Brazile, Donna L. *BioIn 16*
Brazinsky, Irving 1936- *WhoE 91*
Brazle, Al 1913-1973 *Ballpl 90*
Brazys, Anthony A 1919- *BiDrAPA 89*
Brazzale, John Peter 1961- *WhoEmL 91*
Brazzel, Ronald D. 1940- *St&PR 91*
Brazzi, Rossano 1916- *WorAlBi*
Brdlik, Carola Emilie 1930- *WhoAmW 91*
Bread *EncPR&S 89*
Breadon, Sam 1876-1949 *Ballpl 90*
Bready, Richard L. 1944- *St&PR 91*
Break, George Farrington 1920- *WhoAm 90*
Breaker, Richard C. 1926- *St&PR 91*
Breakey, Jeffrey M. 1959- *WhoWrEP 89*
Breakey, William R *BiDrAPA 89*
Breakiron, Larry P. 1930- *St&PR 91*
Breakstone, Irving L *BiDrAPA 89*
Breakstone, Jay L. T. 1951- *WhoEmL 91*
Breakstone, Joshua *BioIn 16*
Breakstone, Kay 1936- *ODwPR 91*
Breakstone, Kay Louise 1936- *WhoAmW 91*
Breakstone, Myron 1919- *St&PR 91*
Breakstone, Robert Albert 1938- *WhoAm 90*
Bream, Julian 1933- *IntWWM 90, PenDiMP, WhoAm 90, WhoWor 91, WorAlBi*
Bream, Sid 1960- *Ballpl 90*
Brean, George Albert 1942- *St&PR 91*
Brean, Herbert 1907-1973 *TwCCr&M 91*
Breard, Jack Hendricks 1939- *St&PR 91*
Brearly, David 1745-1790 *BioIn 16*
Brearton, James Joseph 1950- *WhoEmL 91*
Brearton, Robert David 1949- *St&PR 91*
Breasted, James Henry 1865-1935 *WorAlBi*
Breathed, Berke *BioIn 16*
Breathed, Berke 1957- *Au&Arts 5 [port], EncACom*
Breathed, Berkeley 1957- *WhoAm 90*
Breathitt, Edward Thompson 1924- *St&PR 91*
Breathitt, Edward Thompson, Jr. 1924- *WhoAm 90*
Breault, David J. 1928- *St&PR 91*
Breault, Paul Armand 1947- *St&PR 91*
Breault, Theodore Edward 1938- *WhoE 91*
Breaux, James Albert 1934- *St&PR 91*
Breaux, John B. 1944- *BioIn 16, WhoAm 90, WhoSSW 91, WhoWor 91*
Breaux, Laura Lane 1940- *WhoAmW 91*
Breaux, Merlin Paul 1932- *WhoAm 90*
Breaux, Paul Whitney 1934-1986 *WhoSSW 91*
Breazeale, Mack A. 1930- *BioIn 16*
Breazeale, Mack Alfred 1930- *WhoAm 90*
Brebbia, John Henry 1932- *WhoAm 90*
Breber, Mike Velimir 1926- *WhoSSW 91*
Brebeuf, Jean De 1593-1649 *EncCRAm, WhNaAH*
Brebner, John P. 1924- *St&PR 91*
Brech, Donald Lewis 1935- *St&PR 91*
Brechbill, Bonnie Hellum 1954- *WhoWrEP 89*
Brechbill, Susan Reynolds 1943- *WhoAmW 91*
Brecheen, Harry 1914- *Ballpl 90 [port]*
Brecher, Arthur Seymour 1928- *WhoAm 90*
Brecher, Edward M. 1911-1989 *BioIn 16*
Brecher, Edward Moritz 1911- *WhoWrEP 89*
Brecher, Irving 1923- *WhoAm 90*
Brecher, Kenneth 1943- *WhoAm 90, WhoE 91*
Brecher, Kenneth S. *BioIn 16*
Brecher, Martin Bruce 1949- *BiDrAPA 89*
Brecher, Melvin 1924- *WhoAm 90*
Brecher, Michael 1925- *WhoAm 90, WhoWor 91*
Brecher, Samuel 1897-1982 *WhoAmA 91N*
Brechin, Susan J. Griffey 1950- *WhoWor 91*
Brechlin, Thomas W. 1934- *St&PR 91*
Brechner, Beverly L. 1936- *WhoAmW 91*
Brechner, Joseph Louis 1915- *WhoSSW 91*
Brechon, Edwin Joseph 1940- *St&PR 91*
Brecht, Bertolt 1898-1956 *BioIn 16, MajTwCW, OxCPMus, WorAlBi, WrPh*
Brecht, Blaine Richard 1958- *WhoEmL 91, WhoSSW 91*
Brecht, Donald L. 1935- *St&PR 91*
Brecht, George 1926- *WhoAmA 91*
Brecht, George F. 1940- *St&PR 91*
Brecht, James Allen *BiDrAPA 89*
Brecht, Martin Bryan 1953- *WhoEmL 91*
Brecht, Richard Domenick 1940- *WhoAm 90*
Brecht, Sally Ann 1951- *WhoAmW 91, WhoEmL 91*
Brecht, Warren Frederick 1932- *WhoAm 90*
Breck, Allen du Pont 1914- *WhoAm 90*
Breck, Howard Rolland 1912- *WhoAm 90*
Breck, John H. 1877-1965 *WorAlBi*
Breck, John Leslie 1860-1899 *BioIn 16*
Breck, Vivian *AuBYP 90*
Breckel, Alvina Hefeli 1948- *WhoAmW 91*
Breckenfeld, Vivian Gurney 1895- *AuBYP 90*
Breckenridge, Adam Carlyle 1916- *WhoAm 90*
Breckenridge, Betty Gayle 1945- *WhoAmW 91, WhoEmL 91*
Breckenridge, Bruce M 1929- *WhoAmA 91*
Breckenridge, Bryan Craig 1951- *WhoEmL 91*
Breckenridge, Donald E. 1931- *St&PR 91*
Breckenridge, Doris M *BiDrAPA 89*
Breckenridge, James D 1926-1982 *WhoAmA 91N*
Breckenridge, Klindt Duncan 1957- *WhoEmL 91*
Breckenridge, Marie Agatha 1937- *BiDrAPA 89*
Breckenridge, Neil 1944- *WhoSSW 91*
Breckenridge, Robert Jerald 1933- *St&PR 91*
Breckenridge, Robert Markley 1931- *St&PR 91*
Breckenridge, Sally A. 1958- *WhoEmL 91*
Brecker, Manfred 1927- *St&PR 91*
Breckinridge, James Bernard 1939- *WhoAm 90*
Breckinridge, John 1760-1806 *BiDrUSE 89*
Breckinridge, John Cabell 1821-1875 *BiDrUSE 89, WorAlBi*
Breckinridge, Madeline M. 1872-1920 *BioAmW*
Breckinridge, Mary 1881-1965 *BioIn 16*
Breckinridge, Mary Marvin 1905- *BioIn 16*
Breckinridge, Robert G. *AmLegL*
Breckinridge, Sophonisba Preston 1866-1948 *BioIn 16, WorAlBi*
Breckner, Deborah Jeanne 1962- *WhoEmL 91*
Breckner, William John, Jr. 1933- *WhoAm 90*
Brecknock, John 1937- *IntWWM 90*
Breckon, Donald John 1939- *WhoAm 90*
Breczinski, Michael Joseph 1953- *WhoEmL 91*
Bredahl, Janice Ann 1957- *WhoAmW 91, WhoEmL 91*
Bredahl, Rolf Ivar 1946- *WhoWor 91*
Bredahl, Svein Grude 1946- *WhoWor 91*
Breddan, Joe 1950- *WhoEmL 91*
Bredehoft, Elaine Charlson 1958- *WhoEmL 91, WhoSSW 91, WhoWor 91*
Bredel, Willi 1901-1964 *BioIn 16*
Bredemeier, Chet L. 1955- *St&PR 91*
Bredemeier, Mark David 1964- *WhoEmL 91*
Bredemeyer, Loretta Jeane 1942- *WhoWor 91*
Breden, Christiane Frederick von 1839-1901 *EncCoWW*
Bredenbeck, Rudolf 1931- *St&PR 91*
Bredenberg, Willard 1935- *BiDrAPA 89*
Bredenberg, Willard Alfred 1935- *WhoE 91*
Bredenkamp, Juergen 1939- *WhoWor 91*
Bredenkamp, Richard L. 1945- *St&PR 91*
Breder, Hans Dieter 1935- *WhoAmA 91*
Bredesen, Dorothy Louise Antil 1929- *WhoE 91*
Bredesen, Ivar 1958- *WhoWor 91*
Bredesen, Philip Norman 1943- *WhoAm 90*
Bredeson, John Patrick 1942- *St&PR 91*
Bredeweg, Judith Senkel 1941- *WhoAmW 91*
Bredfeldt, John Creighton 1947- *WhoEmL 91, WhoWor 91*
Bredhoff, Nancy 1958- *St&PR 91*
Brediceanu, Mihai 1920- *WhoWor 91*
Bredif, C. *EncO&P 3*
Bredin, Grace Louise Dolmage 1903-1988 *BioIn 16*
Bredin, John Bruce 1914- *WhoAm 90, WhoE 91*
Bredlow, Tom 1938- *WhoAmA 91*
Bredow, Marjorie Y. 1940- *St&PR 91*
Bredt, Carol 1939- *WhoAmW 91*
Bredt, Jack Bourquoin 1926- *St&PR 91*
Bree, Donald Lee 1935- *WhoSSW 91*
Bree, Germaine 1907- *WhoAm 90*
Breece, Robert William, Jr. 1942- *WhoAm 90*
Breech, Ernest R. 1897-1978 *EncABHB 5 [port]*
Breecher, Sheila Rae 1953- *WhoEmL 91*
Breed, Allen *BioIn 16*
Breed, Allen Forbes 1920- *WhoAm 90*
Breed, Arthur H., Jr. *St&PR 91N*
Breed, Charles Ayars 1927- *WhoAmA 91*
Breed, Charles H. 1873-1950 *BioIn 16*
Breed, Ebenezer Thompson 1899-1990 *BioIn 16*
Breed, Ernest Mark, III 1955- *WhoEmL 91*
Breed, Helen Illick 1925- *WhoAmW 91*
Breed, John S. *ODwPR 91*
Breed, Joseph Rosser 1943- *St&PR 91*

Breed, Michael Dallam 1951- WhoEmL 91
Breed, Nathaniel Preston 1908- WhoAm 90
Breed, Ria 1944- WhoAm 90
Breeden, Chris David 1955- WhoEmL 91
Breeden, Daniel Franklin 1936- St&PR 91
Breeden, David WhoAm 90
Breeden, Edward Lebbaeus, Jr. 1905- WhoAm 90
Breeden, Hal 1944- Ballpl 90
Breeden, Kenneth Ray 1938- WhoWor 91
Breeden, Rex Earl 1920- WhoAm 90
Breeden, Richard BioIn 16
Breeden, Richard C. WhoAm 90
Breeden, Robert Lewis 1925- WhoAm 90, WhoE 91
Breeden, Townsend Dean 1932- WhoSSW 91
Breeden, William Hall 1925- St&PR 91
Breeding, Carl Wayne 1954- WhoEmL 91
Breeding, David C. 1952- WhoSSW 91
Breeding, Marv 1934- Ballpl 90
Breeding, Robert Leroy 1926- St&PR 91
Breedlove, Cindy Lea 1944- WhoAmW 91
Breedlove, Lori Renee BiDrAPA 89
Breedlove, Paul Michael 1943- St&PR 91
Breedlove, S. Marc BioIn 16
Breedlove, Sarah 1867-1919 BioIn 16
Breedlove, William Davis 1940- St&PR 91
Breedveld, Dick 1939- St&PR 91
Breen, Ann E. 1940- WhoWrEP 89
Breen, Charles E 1940- BiDrAPA 89
Breen, David Hart 1960- WhoSSW 91
Breen, David Neil 1943- St&PR 91
Breen, F. Glenn 1912- St&PR 91, WhoAm 90
Breen, Faith Fei-Mei Lee 1951- WhoAmW 91, WhoEmL 91
Breen, Gerald Joseph 1945- St&PR 91
Breen, Hal J 1919- BiDrAPA 89
Breen, Harry Frederick, Jr 1930- WhoAmA 91
Breen, Harvey BiDrAPA 89
Breen, James Joseph 1929- St&PR 91
Breen, John Edward 1932- WhoAm 90
Breen, John Francis 1929- WhoAm 90
Breen, John Gerald 1934- St&PR 91, WhoAm 90
Breen, Jon L 1943- TwCCr&M 91
Breen, Joseph S. BioIn 16
Breen, Karen Marie 1955- BiDrAPA 89
Breen, Katherine Frances LaRochelle 1950- WhoEmL 91
Breen, Marilyn 1944- WhoAmW 91, WhoSSW 91
Breen, Michael Almon 1954- WhoE 91
Breen, Michael T. 1946- St&PR 91
Breen, Robert BioIn 16, NewYTBS 90
Breen, Rosemary Anne 1956- ODwPR 91
Breen, Thomas A. 1956- St&PR 91
Breen, Thomas John 1948- WhoAm 90
Breen, Timothy Alan 1951- WhoEmL 91
Breen, Timothy Hall 1942- WhoAm 90, WhoWrEP 89
Breen, Walter Henry 1928- WhoAm 90
Breene, Samuel A. 1915- St&PR 91
Breer, Carl 1883-1970 EncABHB 5 [port]
Breer, Robert C 1926- WhoAmA 91
Breese, Donald Edward 1930- St&PR 91
Breese, Edwin V. 1936- St&PR 91
Breese, Frank Chandler 1944- St&PR 91
Breese, Frank Chandler, III 1944- WhoAm 90
Breese, Gerald William 1912- WhoAm 90
Breese, James Roger 1930- WhoE 91
Breese, Sidney 1800-1878 AmLegL
Breeskin, Adelyn Dohme 1896-1986 WhoAmA 91N
Breetveld, Jim Patrick 1925- AuBYP 90
Breeze, Francis Verlon 1924- St&PR 91
Breeze, Grace Wilkie 1934- WhoWrEP 89
Breeze, William Hancock 1923- WhoAm 90, WhoSSW 91
Breezley, Roger L. 1938- St&PR 91
Breezley, Roger Lee 1938- WhoAm 90
Breffeilh, Louis Andrew 1913- WhoAm 90
Brega, Charles Franklin 1933- WhoAm 90
Brega, Doug BioIn 16
Bregar, Billy Lee 1951- St&PR 91
Bregar, Raymond E. 1947- St&PR 91
Bregendahl, Marie 1867-1940 EncCoWW
Breger, Dave 1908-1970 EncACom, WhoAmA 91N
Breger, Eli 1930- BiDrAPA 89
Breger, Herbert Joseph 1920- WhoWor 91
Breger, Joseph L. 1916- St&PR 91
Breger, Marshall J. 1946- WhoAm 90
Breger, William N. 1922- WhoAm 90
Breggin, Peter Roger 1936- BiDrAPA 89, WhoAm 90, WhoWrEP 89
Breghtel, Hans Coenraadt 1608-1675 PenDiDA 89
Breglio, John F. 1946- WhoAm 90
Breglio, Louis A. 1915-1989 BioIn 16
Bregman, Arthur Jay BiDrAPA 89
Bregman, Arthur Randolph 1946- WhoE 91, WhoWor 91
Bregman, Benjamin Bernard 1909- WhoAm 90
Bregman, Jacob Israel 1923- WhoAm 90
Bregman, Joel Donald BiDrAPA 89
Bregman, Larry 1922- WhoSSW 91
Bregman, Martin WhoAm 90
Bregman, Michael BioIn 16
Bregman, Norman Joseph 1944- WhoSSW 91
Bregman, Peter David 1953- WhoE 91
Bregman, Walter BioIn 16
Breguet, Abraham-Louis PenDiDA 89
Breheny, James Thomas 1929- St&PR 91
Brehm, Cheryl Ann 1950- WhoSSW 91
Brehm, Donna Jo 1957- BiDrAPA 89
Brehm, Henry ODwPR 91
Brehm, Jack Edmund 1931- St&PR 91
Brehm, John R. 1953- St&PR 91
Brehm, Juanita Rose 1947- WhoAmW 91
Brehm, Sharon S 1945- ConAu 30NR
Brehm, Sharon Stephens 1945- WhoAm 90
Brehman, Penny Ann 1947- WhoAmW 91
Brehmer-Andersson, Eva Elisabeth 1925- WhoWor 91
Brei, Fred J., Jr. 1942- WhoWor 91
Breibart, Jack 1931- WhoAm 90
Breidegam, Delight Edgar 1926- St&PR 91
Breidegam, DeLight Edgar, Jr. 1926- WhoAm 90
Breidenbach, Cherie Elizabeth 1952- WhoEmL 91, WhoWor 91
Breidenbach, David John 1957- WhoEmL 91
Breidenbach, Francis Anthony 1930- WhoAm 90
Breidenbach, Rowland William 1935- WhoAm 90
Breidenstein, Blaine Blair 1924- St&PR 91
Breidenstein, Thomas J BiDrAPA 89
Breien, Thor 1947- WhoWor 91
Breier, Alan Francis BiDrAPA 89
Breier, Gertrud BioIn 16
Breiger, Elaine WhoAmA 91
Breihan, Erwin Robert 1918- WhoAm 90
Breil, Kendall A BiDrAPA 89
Breiland, Keith Allen 1957- BiDrAPA 89
Breiland, Leslie Kent 1944- St&PR 91
Breillat, Catherine EncCoWW
Breimyer, Harold Frederick 1914- WhoAm 90
Breinburg, Petronella 1927- BioIn 16
Breindel, David S 1948- BiDrAPA 89
Breindel, Eric Marc 1955- WhoAm 90, WhoEmL 91
Breindler, Gerald 1946- St&PR 91
Breiner, James M. 1918- St&PR 91
Breiner, Rosemary 1937- WhoHisp 91
Breiner, Sander James 1925- BiDrAPA 89
Breiner, Sheldon 1936- St&PR 91
Breines, Simon 1906- WhoAm 90
Breinin, Goodwin M. 1918- WhoAm 90
Breinin, Raymond 1910- WhoAm 90, WhoAmA 91
Breining, Fred 1955- Ballpl 90
Breininger, John Francis 1949- WhoE 91
Breipohl, Walter Eugene 1953- WhoEmL 91
Breisach, Ernst WhoAm 90
Breiseth, Christopher Neri 1936- WhoAm 90, WhoE 91
Breister, Karl A 1930- BiDrAPA 89
Breit, Jeffrey Arnold 1955- WhoEmL 91
Breit, Samuel Norbert 1949- WhoWor 91
Breit, William 1933- WhoSSW 91
Breitbach, Robert Walter 1943- WhoWor 91
Breitbach, Stephanie Hannelore 1959- WhoAmW 91
Breitbart, Barbara Renee 1935- WhoWor 91
Breitbart, George J BiDrAPA 89
Breitbart, William 1951- BiDrAPA 89
Breitbarth, Gary Glen 1950- WhoE 91, WhoEmL 91
Breitbarth, Larry Allen 1963- WhoEmL 91
Breitbarth, S. Robert 1925- WhoAm 90, WhoE 91
Breitbarth, Steven Eldor 1949- WhoEmL 91
Breite, Marlies BioIn 16
Breite, Olaf BioIn 16
Breitel, Charles D. 1908- WhoAm 90
Breiten, John W. 1943- St&PR 91
Breitenbach, Edgar 1903-1977 WhoAmA 91N
Breitenbach, Lisa Maida 1956- BiDrAPA 89
Breitenbach, Mary Louise McGraw 1936- WhoAmW 91
Breitenbach, Thomas George 1947- WhoAm 90
Breitenbach, William John 1936- WhoAmA 91
Breitenbeck, Joseph M. 1914- WhoAm 90
Breitenecker, Rudiger 1929- WhoAm 90, WhoE 91
Breitenfeld, Frederick, Jr. 1931- WhoAm 90
Breitenstein, Mary Kathleen 1960- WhoSSW 91
Breitenstein, Ted 1869-1935 Ballpl 90
Breiter, Hans Charles BiDrAPA 89
Breiter, Thomas Herman 1960- WhoSSW 91
Breitfuss, Thomas K. 1924- St&PR 91
Breithaupt, David Evans 1940- WhoAm 90
Breithaupt, Erwin M 1920- WhoAmA 91
Breithaupt, Ezra Carl 1866-1897 DcCanB 12
Breithaupt, Stephen Allan 1954- WhoEmL 91
Breitinger, Johann Jakob 1701-1776 DcLB 97 [port]
Breitling, Gisela A. 1939- BiDWomA
Breitman, Alan M. 1930- St&PR 91
Breitman, George 1916-1986 EncAL
Breitman, Leo R. 1941- St&PR 91
Breitman, Richard D 1947- WhoWrEP 89
Breitman, Sara Laurie 1959- BiDrAPA 89
Breitmeyer, Jo Anne 1947- WhoAmW 91
Breitnauer, Paul J. 1939- St&PR 91
Breitner, Ann Lynne 1960- WhoE 91
Breitner, Imre E BiDrAPA 89
Breitner, John Carl S 1944- BiDrAPA 89
Breitrose, Henry S. 1936- WhoAm 90
Breitwieser, Charles John 1910- WhoAm 90
Brejaart, Jan PenDiMP
Brejcha, Vernon Lee 1942- WhoAmA 91
Breker-Cooper, Steven Mark 1947- WhoEmL 91
Brekke, Paal 1923- DcScanL
Brekke, Toril 1949- EncCoWW
Brel, Jacques 1929-1978 OxCPMus, WorAlBi
Breland, Anita Lesser 1947- WhoAmW 91
Breland, Jabe Armistead, II 1949- WhoSSW 91
Breland, Jake D. 1946- St&PR 91
Breland, Laurence Eduard, Jr. 1946- WhoSSW 91
Breland, Pascal 1811-1896 DcCanB 12
Brelis, Dean Constantine 1924- WhoE 91
Brelis, Matthew 1957- ConAu 132
Brelis, Matthew Dean Burns 1957- WhoAm 90
Brelsford, Gates Grissom 1950- St&PR 91
Brelsford, William Joseph, Jr. 1941- St&PR 91
Brem, Peter PenDiMP
Brema, Marie 1856-1925 PenDiMP
Breman, Joseph Eliot 1945- WhoAm 90
Brembeck, Winston Lamont 1912- WhoAm 90
Bremehr, Norbert A. 1927- St&PR 91
Bremen, Barry 1947- BioIn 16
Bremen, Ronald David 1950- WhoEmL 91, WhoWor 91
Bremenkamp, Victor Dale 1935- WhoE 91
Bremer, Brenda A BiDrAPA 89
Bremer, Charles A. 1944- St&PR 91
Bremer, Christine Dodge 1952- WhoAmW 91, WhoEmL 91
Bremer, Donald Duane 1934- WhoWor 91
Bremer, Elaine Ross 1950- WhoAmW 91
Bremer, Francis John 1947- WhoE 91
Bremer, Fredrika 1801-1865 DcScanL
Bremer, James Henry, Jr. 1938- WhoE 91
Bremer, John Paul 1926- WhoE 91
Bremer, Karen Ingrid 1959- WhoSSW 91
Bremer, Klaus Gustav 1931- St&PR 91
Bremer, Louis Henry, Jr. 1951- WhoSSW 91
Bremer, Marlene S WhoAmA 91
Bremigan, Nick 1945- Ballpl 90
Bremigan, Nick 1945-1989 BioIn 16
Bremkamp, Gloria Howe 1924- WhoWrEP 89
Bremm, Hazel G. Stagg BioIn 16
Bremner, James D 1932- BiDrAPA 89
Bremner, James Douglas 1932- WhoAm 90
Bremner, James Douglas 1961- BiDrAPA 89
Bremner, John McColl 1922- WhoAm 90
Bremner, Steven Scott 1950- WhoEmL 91
Bremond, Andre Serge 1934- WhoWor 91
Brems, Hans Julius 1915- WhoAm 90
Bremser, George, Jr. 1928- WhoAm 90
Bremser, Rudolph E. 1931- St&PR 91
Bren, Donald L. BioIn 16
Bren, Fernando 1942- WhoE 91
Bren, Joel 1949- St&PR 91
Brenaa, Hans 1910-1988 AnObit 1988, BioIn 16
Brence, Joel John 1945- BiDrAPA 89
Brenchley, Jean Elnora 1944- WhoAm 90, WhoAmW 91
Brende, Joel Osler 1936- BiDrAPA 89
Brendel, Albert Edward 1936- St&PR 91
Brendel, Alfred BioIn 16
Brendel, Alfred 1931- IntWWM 90, PenDiMP, WhoAm 90, WhoWor 91
Brendel, Bettina WhoAmA 91
Brendel, Erica Marie 1939- BiDrAPA 89
Brendel, Otto J 1901-1973 WhoAmA 91N
Brendel, Wolfgang 1947- IntWWM 90
Brenden, Rita Ann 1953- WhoEmL 91
Brendle, Alison Smith 1954- WhoAmW 91
Brendle, Douglas David 1928- St&PR 91, WhoAm 90
Brendle, Patricia Ruth 1955- WhoE 91
Brendlinger, Darwin Lamar 1934- WhoE 91
Brendlinger, LeRoy R. 1918- WhoAm 90
Brendon, Piers 1940- ConAu 31NR
Brendon, Rupert Timothy Rundle 1943- WhoAm 90
Brendsel, Leland C. WhoAm 90
Brendtro, Larry Kay 1940- WhoAm 90
Brendzel, Ronald I. 1949- St&PR 91
Breneman, David Clinton, II 1959- WhoEmL 91
Breneman, David Worthy 1940- WhoAm 90
Breneman, Donald Paul 1936- BiDrAPA 89
Breneman, Gerald Myers 1924- WhoAm 90
Breneman, William Calvin 1941- WhoSSW 91
Brener, Daniel Michael 1949- BiDrAPA 89
Brener, Lazard S 1912- BiDrAPA 89
Brener, Pablo BioIn 16
Brener, Rochelle 1945- WhoWrEP 89
Brener, Roland 1942- WhoAmA 91
Brener, Zidella S BiDrAPA 89
Brengel, Fred L. 1923- St&PR 91, WhoAm 90
Brengle, Thomas Alan 1952- WhoEmL 91
Brenin, Barnett E. 1935- St&PR 91
Brenin, Jules 1936- St&PR 91
Brenken, Ernst Georg BiDrAPA 89
Brenkman, Guy L. 1947- St&PR 91
Brenly, Bob 1954- Ballpl 90
Brenman, Albert 1926- St&PR 91
Brenna, Carol Diane 1959- WhoAmW 91
Brennagh, Michael C 1947- BiDrAPA 89
Brennan, Ad 1881-1962 Ballpl 90
Brennan, Barbara Taylor 1950- WhoAmW 91
Brennan, Bernard F. BioIn 16
Brennan, Bernard Francis 1938- St&PR 91
Brennan, Carroll Ann 1956- WhoAmW 91
Brennan, Charles Martin, III 1942- St&PR 91, WhoAm 90
Brennan, Ciaran Brendan 1944- WhoSSW 91, WhoWor 91
Brennan, Daniel Christopher 1954- WhoEmL 91
Brennan, Daniel Francis 1960- WhoSSW 91
Brennan, David Daniel 1938- WhoWrEP 89
Brennan, David John 1958- WhoWor 91
Brennan, Dennis AuBYP 90
Brennan, Dianne ODwPR 91
Brennan, Don 1903-1953 Ballpl 90
Brennan, Donald WhoSSW 91
Brennan, Donald P. 1940- St&PR 91
Brennan, Donna L. 1945- ODwPR 91
Brennan, Donna Lesley 1945- WhoAm 90
Brennan, Dorothea Elizabeth 1950- WhoAmW 91
Brennan, Douglas Francis 1955- WhoEmL 91
Brennan, Edward A. BioIn 16
Brennan, Edward A 1934- CurBio 90 [port], St&PR 91, WhoAm 90, WhoWor 91
Brennan, Edward James, Jr. 1941- WhoE 91
Brennan, Edward N 1929- BiDrAPA 89
Brennan, Edwin P 1931- BiDrAPA 89
Brennan, Eileen BioIn 16
Brennan, Eileen 1935- ConTFT 8, WorAlBi
Brennan, Eileen Hughes 1951- WhoAmW 91, WhoSSW 91
Brennan, Elizabeth Lane 1951- WhoEmL 91
Brennan, Eugene Robert 1935- St&PR 91
Brennan, Fanny WhoAmA 91
Brennan, Francis Edwin 1910- WhoAmA 91
Brennan, Francis M WhoAmA 91
Brennan, Francis Martin 1953- WhoWor 91
Brennan, Francis P. 1917- St&PR 91
Brennan, Francis Patrick 1917- WhoAm 90
Brennan, Francis W. 1919- WhoAm 90
Brennan, Gale 1927- BioIn 16, SmATA 64 [port]
Brennan, Harold J. 1903-1989 BioIn 16
Brennan, Henry Higginson 1932- WhoAm 90
Brennan, Herbert Joseph 1935- St&PR 91
Brennan, J.B. 1921- St&PR 91
Brennan, James Beach 1947- WhoEmL 91
Brennan, James G. 1927- WhoAm 90
Brennan, James Joseph 1936- WhoAm 90
Brennan, James Thomas 1916- WhoAm 90, WhoWor 91
Brennan, John A. 1931- St&PR 91
Brennan, John D. 1947- St&PR 91
Brennan, John E. 1928- St&PR 91
Brennan, John Edward 1928- WhoAm 90

Brennan, John Joseph 1954- WhoEmL 91
Brennan, John M. 1935- St&PR 91
Brennan, John Merritt 1935- WhoAm 90
Brennan, John Wolf 1954- IntWWM 90
Brennan, Joseph Benjamin 1903- WhoAm 90
Brennan, Joseph Edward 1934- WhoAm 90, WhoE 91
Brennan, Joseph Gerard 1910- AuBYP 90, WhoAm 90
Brennan, Joseph Payne 1918- WhoWrEP 89
Brennan, Joseph Thomas 1931- WhoE 91
Brennan, Karen 1941- WhoWrEP 89
Brennan, Kathleen Noelle 1966- WhoWrEP 89
Brennan, Kevin John 1949- WhoE 91
Brennan, Lawrence Brian 1953- WhoE 91
Brennan, Lawrence Edward 1927- WhoAm 90
Brennan, Leo Joseph, Jr. 1930- WhoAm 90
Brennan, Leo Thomas 1935- St&PR 91
Brennan, Leonard H 1927- BiDrAPA 89
Brennan, Martin Joseph 1929- St&PR 91
Brennan, Mary Maureen 1946- WhoSSW 91
Brennan, Michael Edward 1948- BiDrAPA 89
Brennan, Michael Joseph 1928- WhoAm 90
Brennan, Michael Louis 1956- WhoWor 91
Brennan, Molly BioIn 16
Brennan, Murray Frederick 1940- WhoAm 90
Brennan, Nicholas 1948- AuBYP 90
Brennan, Nizette 1950- WhoAmA 91, WhoE 91
Brennan, Noel-Anne Gerson 1948- WhoE 91
Brennan, Norma Jean 1939- WhoAmW 91
Brennan, Patricia Anne 1953- WhoAmW 91
Brennan, Patricia Violet 1961- WhoAmW 91
Brennan, Patrick Francis 1931- St&PR 91, WhoAm 90
Brennan, Patrick Thomas 1952- WhoE 91
Brennan, Paul 1934- St&PR 91
Brennan, Paul Joseph 1920- WhoAm 90, WhoWor 91
Brennan, Peter James 1911- St&PR 91
Brennan, Peter John 1931- WhoAm 90
Brennan, Peter Joseph 1918- BiDrUSE 89
Brennan, Rhonda Kay BiDrAPA 89
Brennan, Richard S. 1938- St&PR 91
Brennan, Robert Bryan 1941- WhoAm 90
Brennan, Robert F. 1947- St&PR 91
Brennan, Robert J. WhoAm 90
Brennan, Robert J. 1936- WhoE 91
Brennan, Robert Lawrence 1944- WhoAm 90
Brennan, Robert T. 1929- St&PR 91
Brennan, Robert Timothy 1959- WhoE 91
Brennan, Simon Patrick 1928- St&PR 91
Brennan, Steven Wesley 1951- WhoE 91
Brennan, T. Casey 1948- WhoEmL 91
Brennan, Terence Kelley 1952- St&PR 91
Brennan, Terrence Paul 1955- WhoEmL 91
Brennan, Thom NewAgMG
Brennan, Thomas Emmett 1929- WhoAm 90
Brennan, Thomas John 1923- WhoE 91, WhoWor 91
Brennan, Thomas M. BioIn 16
Brennan, Thomas Mark 1952- WhoEmL 91
Brennan, Thomas Paul 1928- St&PR 91
Brennan, Tim ConAu 131
Brennan, Timothy William 1951- WhoE 91
Brennan, Tom 1952- Ballpl 90
Brennan, Walter 1894-1974 WorAlBi
Brennan, Walter Joseph BiDrAPA 89
Brennan, Will ConAu 31NR
Brennan, William Bernard, Jr. 1931- WhoSSW 91
Brennan, William J. 1928- St&PR 91
Brennan, William J., Jr. BioIn 16
Brennan, William J., Jr. 1906- WorAlBi
Brennan, William John 1940- WhoE 91
Brennan, William Joseph 1928- WhoAm 90
Brennan, William Joseph 1937- St&PR 91
Brennan, William Joseph, Jr. 1906- WhoAm 90, WhoE 91
Brennan, William Philip 1936- WhoE 91
Brennan-Sparks, Jennifer Anne 1935- WhoWor 91
Brennecke, Allen Eugene 1937- WhoAm 90
Brenneman, Delbert Jay 1950- WhoEmL 91
Brenneman, Howard L. 1940- St&PR 91
Brenneman, John 1945- WhoEmL 91
Brenneman, Mary Beth 1950- WhoEmL 91
Brenneman, Mary Louise 1923- BiDrAPA 89
Brenneman, Terry Richard 1950- WhoEmL 91
Brennen, Patrick Wayne 1940- WhoAm 90
Brennen, Stephen Alfred WhoAm 90
Brenner, Alfred Ephraim 1931- WhoE 91
Brenner, Anita 1905-1974 BioIn 16
Brenner, Barbara 1925- AuBYP 90, ConAu 31NR
Brenner, Barbara Johnes 1925- WhoWrEP 89
Brenner, Barry Morton 1937- WhoAm 90
Brenner, Beverly Ann 1936- WhoAmW 91
Brenner, Charles BiDrAPA 89
Brenner, Daeg Scott 1939- WhoAm 90
Brenner, Daniel Leon 1904- WhoAm 90
Brenner, David 1944- St&PR 91
Brenner, David 1945- WhoAm 90, WorAlBi
Brenner, Donald Robert 1936- St&PR 91, WhoE 91
Brenner, Edgar H. 1930- WhoAm 90
Brenner, Edward John 1923- WhoAm 90
Brenner, Egon 1925- WhoAm 90
Brenner, Ellen 1936- WhoAm 90
Brenner, Erma 1911- WhoAm 90
Brenner, Esther Lerner 1931- WhoAmW 91
Brenner, Frank 1927- WhoAm 90
Brenner, Frank 1930- St&PR 91
Brenner, Frederic James 1936- WhoE 91
Brenner, Gail 1946- BiDrAPA 89
Brenner, Gunter 1928- WhoWor 91
Brenner, Harris 1927- BiDrAPA 89
Brenner, Henry 1914- WhoAm 90
Brenner, Howard 1929- WhoAm 90
Brenner, Howard M. 1933- WhoAm 90
Brenner, Ira BiDrAPA 89
Brenner, Janet Maybin Walker WhoWor 91
Brenner, Joseph D. 1917- St&PR 91
Brenner, Joseph Donald 1917- WhoAm 90
Brenner, Keith E. 1944- St&PR 91
Brenner, Kenneth James 1923- St&PR 91
Brenner, Laura Ennis 1953- BiDrAPA 89
Brenner, Marshall Leib 1933- WhoE 91, WhoWor 91
Brenner, Martin BiDrAPA 89
Brenner, Mary Ellen 1960- WhoAmW 91
Brenner, Myron David 1942- BiDrAPA 89
Brenner, R. Larry 1938- WhoSSW 91
Brenner, Rena Claudy WhoAmW 91
Brenner, Richard L. 1935- St&PR 91
Brenner, Robert Charles 1941- WhoWrEP 89
Brenner, Ronald 1949- BiDrAPA 89
Brenner, Ronald John 1933- St&PR 91, WhoAm 90
Brenner, Sayers Robert 1945- BiDrAPA 89
Brenner, Shore Hodge 1949- WhoAmA 91N
Brenner, Sophia Elisabet 1659-1730 EncCoWW
Brenner, Stephen Mark 1948- WhoEmL 91
Brenner, Sydney 1927- WhoWor 91
Brenner, Theodor Eduard 1942- WhoE 91, WhoWor 91
Brenner, Theodore Engelbert 1930- WhoAm 90
Brenner, Thomas Edward 1955- WhoEmL 91
Brenner, William Alan 1940- WhoE 91
Brenner, William Edward 1936- WhoAm 90
Brenner, Zev Joseph 1958- WhoE 91
Brennessel, Barbara Anne 1948- WhoAmW 91
Brennfoerder, Roxann R. 1951- St&PR 91
Brenni, Vito J 1923- ConAu 31NR
Brenno, Vonnie Mei-Lin 1950- WhoAmA 91
Brensinger, David Drew 1956- WhoEmL 91
Brenson, Theodore 1893-1959 WhoAmA 91N
Brent, Andrew J. 1918- St&PR 91
Brent, Andrew Jackson 1918- WhoAm 90, WhoSSW 91
Brent, Andrew Mason 1950- St&PR 91
Brent, Carolyn Maas 1925- WhoE 91
Brent, Charlotte 1735?-1802 PenDiMP
Brent, Daniel Franklin 1945- WhoEmL 91
Brent, David Alan BiDrAPA 89
Brent, Donita May 1939- WhoAmW 91
Brent, Frank Nevil 1934- WhoSSW 91
Brent, George 1904-1979 WorAlBi
Brent, Graham John 1954- WhoSSW 91
Brent, Ira Martin BiDrAPA 89
Brent, Jennifer Kay 1960- WhoAmW 91
Brent, John William 1944- WhoAm 90
Brent, Joleene Adalie 1920- WhoAm 90
Brent, Lana Jane Lewis- BioIn 16
Brent, Lawrence Barry 1929- WhoAm 90
Brent, Margaret 1600?-1671? WorAlBi
Brent, Margaret 1601-1671 EncCRAm
Brent, Mary Hartel 1943- WhoAmW 91
Brent, Nancy Jean 1947- WhoEmL 91
Brent, Paul Leslie 1916- WhoAm 90, WhoWor 91
Brent, Richard Howard BiDrAPA 89
Brent, Richard Peirce 1946- WhoWor 91
Brent, Robert Leonard 1927- WhoAm 90
Brent, Ruth S. BioIn 16
Brent, Ruth Stumpe 1951- WhoEmL 91
Brent, Stuart AuBYP 90
Brent, Tommy Joe 1959- WhoSSW 91
Brent, Walter Rudolf 1919- WhoAm 90
Brent, William Thomas 1926- St&PR 91
Brentano, Bernard von 1901-1964 BioIn 16
Brentano, Theodore 1854-1940 BioIn 16
Brentford, W Joynson-Hicks, Viscount 1865-1932 BioIn 16
Brentlinger, Paul S. 1927- St&PR 91
Brentlinger, Paul Smith 1927- WhoAm 90
Brentlinger, William Brock 1926- WhoAm 90
Brenton, Donald Leverett 1935- St&PR 91
Brenton, Frank Howard 1925- St&PR 91
Brenton, Howard 1942- ConAu 33NR, MajTwCW
Brenton, Michael Scott 1952- WhoEmL 91
Brenza, Robert 1936- St&PR 91
Brereton, Jane 1685-1740 FemiCLE
Bresani, Federico Fernando 1945- WhoE 91, WhoWor 91
Breschi, Karen Lee 1941- WhoAmA 91
Brescia, Anthony Joseph 1950- WhoWor 91
Brescia, Bernardo Fort- BioIn 16
Brescia, Frank Joseph 1942- WhoE 91
Brescia, James A. 1945- St&PR 91
Brescia, James Andrew 1945- WhoAm 90
Brescia, Robert Anthony BiDrAPA 89
Bresee, James Collins 1925- WhoAm 90, WhoE 91
Bresee, Paul K. 1901- St&PR 91
Bresee, Philip W. 1924- St&PR 91
Bresee, Wilmer E. 1910- St&PR 91
Breshahan, Pamela Anne 1954- WhoEmL 91
Breshears, Ronald G. St&PR 91
Breshko-Breshkovskaya, Ekaterina K 1844-1934 BioIn 16
Breshkovskaya, Ekaterina K Breshko- 1844-1934 BioIn 16
Breskman, Ellis L. 1950- St&PR 91
Breskman, Joseph S. 1917- St&PR 91
Breslau, Alan Jeffry 1926- WhoE 91
Breslau, Lawrence D 1930- BiDrAPA 89
Breslau, Louise Catherine 1856-1927 BiDWomA
Breslauer, Charles S. 1925- WhoSSW 91
Breslauer, Grace Koehler NewYTBS 90
Breslav, Marc A. 1957- ODwPR 91
Breslawsky, Marc C. 1942- WhoAm 90, WhoE 91
Breslawsky, Marc Carl 1942- St&PR 91
Bresler, Boris 1918- WhoAm 90
Bresler, Charles S. 1927- St&PR 91
Bresler, Charles Sheldon 1927- WhoE 91
Bresler, Eshel 1930- WhoWor 91
Bresler, Jack Barry 1923- WhoE 91
Bresler, Mark Irwin 1953- WhoAm 90, WhoEmL 91, WhoSSW 91
Bresler, Martin I. 1931- WhoAm 90, WhoE 91
Bresler, Robert Joel 1937- WhoE 91
Breslerman, Sabina BiDrAPA 89
Breslin, Barbara Lee 1958- WhoAmW 91
Breslin, Daniel L BiDrAPA 89
Breslin, Donald Joseph 1929- WhoE 91, WhoWor 91
Breslin, Edward Francis 1947- WhoAm 90
Breslin, Hugh Joseph, III 1955- WhoEmL 91
Breslin, James 1930- ConAu 31NR, MajTwCW
Breslin, Jimmy BioIn 16, ConAu 31NR, MajTwCW
Breslin, Jimmy 1929- WhoE 91, WhoWrEP 89, WorAlBi
Breslin, John B. 1943- ConAu 132
Breslin, John Bernard 1943- WhoE 91
Breslin, Leo Harold 1932- St&PR 91
Breslin, Marianne S BiDrAPA 89
Breslin, Mary 1936- WhoAm 90, WhoAmW 91
Breslin, Nancy A 1957- BiDrAPA 89
Breslin, Nancy Ann 1957- WhoE 91
Breslin, Patrick 1940- SpyFic
Breslin, Paul Thomas 1951- WhoE 91
Breslin, Reuben H BiDrAPA 89
Breslin, Richard D. BioIn 16
Breslin, Richard David 1937- WhoAm 90
Breslin, Wynn 1932- WhoAmA 91
Breslouf, Morris 1924- St&PR 91
Breslow, Alan David BiDrAPA 89
Breslow, Esther May Greenberg 1931- WhoAmW 91
Breslow, Jan Leslie 1943- WhoAm 90
Breslow, Jerome W. 1934- St&PR 91
Breslow, Jerome Wilfred 1934- WhoAm 90
Breslow, Jules W. 1929- St&PR 91
Breslow, Lester 1915- WhoAm 90
Breslow, Marilyn G. 1944- St&PR 91
Breslow, Michael Frank BiDrAPA 89
Breslow, Norman Edward 1941- WhoAm 90
Breslow, Richard Eric 1946- BiDrAPA 89
Breslow, Ronald Charles 1931- WhoAm 90
Breslow, Sara Rae 1950- WhoE 91
Breslow, Susan 1951- WhoE 91
Breslow, Tina ODwPR 91
Breslow, Tina 1946- WhoEmL 91
Bresnahan, Boyd K BiDrAPA 89
Bresnahan, Dave BioIn 16
Bresnahan, David Boyd BiDrAPA 89
Bresnahan, David Parsons 1930- St&PR 91
Bresnahan, James Francis 1926- WhoAm 90
Bresnahan, John 1944- St&PR 91
Bresnahan, Joseph Estill 1928- St&PR 91
Bresnahan, Maurice Joseph, III 1960- WhoEmL 91
Bresnahan, Richard Anthony 1924- WhoAm 90
Bresnahan, Roger 1879-1944 Ballpl 90 [port]
Bresnahan, Roger 1880-1944 BioIn 16
Bresnahan, William J. 1950- St&PR 91
Bresnahan, William W. 1918- St&PR 91
Bresnick, Martin 1946- IntWWM 90
Bress, Michael E. 1933- WhoAm 90
Bressack, Mitchell Leslie 1953- WhoEmL 91
Bressan, Paul Louis 1947- WhoAm 90, WhoEmL 91
Bressanelli, Jerome P. 1936- St&PR 91
Bressant, Michele Renee 1956- WhoAmW 91
Bresse, Guillaume 1833-1892 DcCanB 12
Bressen, David H. 1934- ODwPR 91
Bressi, Betty WhoAmA 91
Bressler, Barry Evan 1947- WhoEmL 91
Bressler, Bernard BiDrAPA 89
Bressler, Bernard 1928- St&PR 91, WhoAm 90, WhoE 91
Bressler, Charles 1926- IntWWM 90
Bressler, Gary David 1956- WhoEmL 91
Bressler, H.G. von PenDiDA 89
Bressler, Howard Jay 1941- St&PR 91
Bressler, Lee M. 1959- St&PR 91
Bressler, Richard M. 1930- St&PR 91
Bressler, Rube 1894-1966 Ballpl 90
Bressler, Steven L. 1951- WhoAm 90
Bressman, Arthur Y. 1928- St&PR 91
Bresson, Henri Cartier- 1908- BioIn 16
Bresson, Robert 1901- WhoWor 91
Bresson, Robert 1907- ConTFT 8
Bressoud, Ed 1932- Ballpl 90
Brest, Albert N. 1928- WhoAm 90
Brest, Joyce E BiDrAPA 89
Brest, Martin 1951- WhoAm 90
Brest, Paul 1940- WhoAm 90
Brest, Stuart BiDrAPA 89
Bresticker, Robert Baruch 1955- WhoEmL 91
Bretey, Pierre R. 1898-1988 BioIn 16
Breth, James Raymond 1929- St&PR 91
Brethen, Charles A., III 1946- St&PR 91
Brethen, Robert Herschell 1926- St&PR 91
Bretherick, John H., Jr. WhoE 91
Bretherton, Patricia Ann 1932- St&PR 91
Bretl, Paul G. 1934- St&PR 91
Bretnall, Arthur John 1911- St&PR 91
Bretnall, Arthur John, Jr. 1943- St&PR 91
Breton, Albert A. 1929- WhoAm 90
Breton, Andre 1896-1966 BioIn 16, MajTwCW, WorAlBi
Breton, Maurice John, Jr. 1952- WhoSSW 91
Breton, Roger A. 1926- St&PR 91
Breton, Serge BiDrAPA 89
Breton, Tracy Ann 1951- WhoAmW 91, WhoE 91, WhoEmL 91
Breton y Hernandez, Tomas 1850-1923 OxCPMus
Bretschneider, Ann Margery 1934- WhoAmW 91
Brett 1883-1977 FemiCLE
Brett, Annabelle 1947- WhoEmL 91
Brett, Arthur Cushman, Jr. 1928- WhoAm 90
Brett, Barbara Jeanne WhoAm 90
Brett, Charles 1941- IntWWM 90
Brett, Dorothy 1883-1977 BioIn 16
Brett, George BioIn 16
Brett, George 1953- Ballpl 90 [port], WorAlBi
Brett, George Wendell 1912- WhoAm 90
Brett, Guilford Harold 1931- St&PR 91
Brett, Jacquelyn Ann 1947- WhoAmW 91
Brett, Jan 1949- BioIn 16
Brett, Jeremy BioIn 16
Brett, Jeremy 1933- ConTFT 8
Brett, Ken 1948- Ballpl 90
Brett, Leo ConAu 32NR
Brett, Lionel 1913- ConAu 131
Brett, Lisa Farrell 1956- WhoAmW 91
Brett, Mary L. 1940- WhoAmW 91
Brett, Michael TwCCr&M 91
Brett, Peter D. 1943- WhoWrEP 89
Brett, Philip 1937- ConAu 129

Brett, Richard John 1921- *WhoWor 91*
Brett, Richard M. 1903-1989 *BioIn 16*
Brett, Robin 1935- *WhoE 91*
Brett, Rosa 1829-1882 *BiDWomA*
Brett, Simon 1945- *TwCCr&M 91*
Brett, Thomas E. 1932- *WhoE 91*
Brett, Thomas Rutherford 1931- *WhoAm 90, WhoSSW 91*
Brett, Tybe Ann 1954- *WhoEmL 91*
Brett, William Howard 1893-1989 *BioIn 16*
Brett-Elspas, Janis *ODwPR 91*
Brett-Elspas, Janis E. 1956- *WhoEmL 91*
Brett-Major, Lin 1943- *WhoAmW 91, WhoSSW 91, WhoWor 91*
Brettell, Caroline B. 1950- *WhoSSW 91*
Brettell, Richard Robson 1949- *WhoAm 90, WhoAmA 91*
Bretthauer, Erich Walter 1937- *WhoAm 90*
Bretting, Denise Ann 1950- *WhoEmL 91*
Bretting, Henry Lyman, Jr. *BioIn 16*
Brettner, Donald M. 1936- *St&PR 91*
Bretton, Barbara 1950- *WhoWrEP 89*
Bretton, Henry L. 1916- *WhoAm 90*
Bretuo, Akwasi *WhoWrEP 89*
Bretz, John W. 1943- *St&PR 91*
Bretz, Linda M. 1934- *WhoAm 90, WhoAmW 91*
Bretz, Mark *ODwPR 91*
Bretz, Ronald James 1951- *WhoEmL 91*
Bretz, Thurman Wilbur 1934- *St&PR 91*
Bretzfelder, Deborah May 1932- *WhoAm 90*
Bretzfield, Henry 1912- *WhoE 91, WhoWor 91*
Bretzlaff, Katherine Nelle 1956- *WhoAmW 91*
Breu, George 1954- *WhoEmL 91*
Breuer, Adam A. 1925- *St&PR 91*
Breuer, Bessie 1893-1975 *FemiCLE*
Breuer, Fritz *BiDrAPA 89*
Breuer, Harry 1901-1989 *BioIn 16*
Breuer, Helmut B. 1936- *St&PR 91*
Breuer, Horst 1943- *WhoWor 91*
Breuer, Josef 1932- *WhoWor 91*
Breuer, Marcel 1902-1981 *BioIn 16, ConDes 90, WorAlBi*
Breuer, Marcel Lajos 1902-1981 *PenDiDA 89*
Breuer, Marv 1914- *Ballpl 90*
Breuer, Melvin Allen 1938- *WhoAm 90*
Breuer, Menahem *PenDiMP*
Breuer, Richard Ervin 1936- *St&PR 91*
Breuer Baculis, Diana Ruth 1949- *WhoAmW 91, WhoEmL 91*
Breuker, Willem *BioIn 16*
Breul, Elisabeth 1936- *IntWWM 90*
Breunig, Richard H. 1943- *St&PR 91*
Breunig, Sharon Day 1957- *WhoSSW 91*
Breuninger, Tyrone 1939- *WhoAm 90*
Breur, Lester Mons 1939- *WhoWrEP 89*
Breval, Lucienne 1869-1935 *PenDiMP*
Brevard, Henry Clyde, Jr. 1921- *St&PR 91*
Brevard, Mary E. *ODwPR 91*
Breve, Franklin Stephen 1955- *WhoE 91*
Breverman, Harvey 1934- *WhoAm 90, WhoAmA 91*
Brevick, Lonnie L. 1946- *St&PR 91*
Brevig, Per 1936- *IntWWM 90*
Brevik, E. Lawrence 1920- *St&PR 91*
Brevik, J. Albert 1920- *WhoAm 90*
Brevik, Tor 1932- *IntWWM 90*
Brewbaker, William Styne, Jr. 1934- *St&PR 91*
Brewda, Joanne Keiran 1946- *St&PR 91*
Brewer, Albert Preston 1928- *WhoAm 90*
Brewer, Arthur Bruce 1951- *WhoSSW 91*
Brewer, B. Macon *WhoAm 90, WhoE 91*
Brewer, Bessie Marsh 1883-1952 *WhoAmA 91N*
Brewer, Brooke E. 1941- *St&PR 91*
Brewer, Bruce 1941- *PenDiMP*
Brewer, Bruce 1944- *IntWWM 90*
Brewer, Byron Eugene 1948- *WhoSSW 91*
Brewer, Carey 1927- *WhoAm 90*
Brewer, Charles Huddeston, Jr. *BiDrAPA 89*
Brewer, Charles Moulton 1931- *WhoAm 90*
Brewer, Cheryl Ann 1959- *WhoAmW 91*
Brewer, Chet 1907- *Ballpl 90*
Brewer, Curtis 1925- *WhoE 91*
Brewer, David Madison 1953- *WhoE 91, WhoEmL 91*
Brewer, David Meredith 1934- *WhoAm 90*
Brewer, Debra Catherine 1957- *WhoEmL 91*
Brewer, Don 1930- *St&PR 91*
Brewer, Earl Clifton, Jr. 1945- *WhoEmL 91*
Brewer, Edward Cage, III 1953- *WhoEmL 91, WhoSSW 91, WhoWor 91*
Brewer, Edward E. 1925- *St&PR 91*
Brewer, Emily Susan 1957- *BiDrAPA 89*
Brewer, Eric Joseph *BiDrAPA 89*
Brewer, Erin Marcia 1948- *WhoSSW 91*
Brewer, Frank L. *St&PR 91*
Brewer, Garry Dwight 1941- *WhoAm 90*
Brewer, George Eugene Francis 1909- *WhoAm 90*
Brewer, Gil *TwCCr&M 91*
Brewer, Gloria Ann 1954- *WhoAmW 91*
Brewer, Harold Martin 1948- *WhoSSW 91*
Brewer, Herbert L. 1926- *St&PR 91*
Brewer, Jack 1919- *Ballpl 90*
Brewer, Jack Richard 1934- *BiDrAPA 89*
Brewer, Jackie W. 1954- *St&PR 91*
Brewer, James T. *St&PR 91*
Brewer, James W. *St&PR 91*
Brewer, Janice Kay 1944- *WhoAmW 91*
Brewer, Jeanne Pickering 1962- *WhoAmW 91*
Brewer, Jim 1937-1987 *Ballpl 90*
Brewer, John Charles 1947- *WhoAm 90*
Brewer, John D 1951- *ConAu 131*
Brewer, John H. *St&PR 91*
Brewer, John Isaac 1903- *WhoWrEP 89*
Brewer, John Michael 1938- *WhoSSW 91*
Brewer, Joyce Marie 1949- *WhoAmW 91*
Brewer, Judy Daughtry 1945- *WhoSSW 91*
Brewer, Karen 1943- *WhoE 91*
Brewer, Kathleen Joy 1954- *WhoEmL 91*
Brewer, Kenneth Wayne 1941- *WhoWrEP 89*
Brewer, Leo 1919- *WhoAm 90*
Brewer, LeRoy Earl 1936- *WhoE 91*
Brewer, Leslie G 1945- *BiDrAPA 89, WhoAm 90*
Brewer, Madeleine Price 1942- *WhoWrEP 89*
Brewer, Marion Alyce 1949- *WhoEmL 91*
Brewer, Nancy Tomlinson 1950- *WhoEmL 91*
Brewer, Norma Jane 1928- *WhoSSW 91*
Brewer, O.D. 1919- *St&PR 91*
Brewer, O. Gordon, Jr. 1936- *St&PR 91*
Brewer, Olan 1930- *ODwPR 91*
Brewer, Oliver Gordon, Jr. 1936- *WhoAm 90*
Brewer, Oscar S. 1915- *St&PR 91*
Brewer, Pamela Walton *BiDrAPA 89*
Brewer, Richard C., Jr. *WhoSSW 91*
Brewer, Richard George 1928- *WhoAm 90*
Brewer, Richard W. 1947- *St&PR 91*
Brewer, Robert Edward 1933- *WhoWor 91*
Brewer, Robert Lee 1928- *WhoE 91*
Brewer, Roy Edward 1949- *WhoEmL 91*
Brewer, Shelby Templeton 1937- *WhoAm 90*
Brewer, Sheryl Anne 1946- *WhoEmL 91, WhoSSW 91*
Brewer, Soila Padilla 1942- *WhoHisp 91*
Brewer, Spencer *NewAgMG*
Brewer, Stanley R. 1937- *St&PR 91, WhoAm 90*
Brewer, T. Eugene 1938- *St&PR 91*
Brewer, Teresa 1931- *OxCPMus, WorAlBi*
Brewer, Terri Evelyn 1959- *WhoAmW 91*
Brewer, Thomas Bowman 1932- *WhoAm 90*
Brewer, Timothy Scot 1952- *WhoEmL 91*
Brewer, Tom 1931- *Ballpl 90*
Brewer, Virginia S *BiDrAPA 89*
Brewer, Walter Lyle 1960- *WhoEmL 91*
Brewer, William D. 1936- *St&PR 91*
Brewer, William Dixon 1936- *WhoAm 90, WhoE 91*
Brewer, William Dodd 1922- *WhoAm 90*
Brewer, William Everett 1953- *WhoEmL 91*
Brewer, William Robert, Jr. 1940- *WhoSSW 91*
Brewer, William W. 1924- *St&PR 91*
Brewer, William Wallace 1937- *WhoWor 91*
Brewer-Gizzarelli, Hilda *BiDrAPA 89*
Brewerton, Timothy David *BiDrAPA 89*
Brewerton, Timothy David 1953- *WhoSSW 91*
Brewin, Anne Margaret *BiDrAPA 89*
Brewin, Austin D. 1937- *St&PR 91*
Brewington, Marion Vernon 1902-1974 *WhoAmA 91N*
Brewis, Heather *BioIn 16*
Brewis, William Richard 1934- *WhoWor 91*
Brewster, A. *BiDWomA*
Brewster, Benjamin *AuBYP 90*
Brewster, Benjamin Harris 1816-1888 *BiDrUSE 89*
Brewster, Bernadette Heidt 1942- *WhoWrEP 89*
Brewster, Carroll Worcester 1936- *WhoAm 90, WhoE 91*
Brewster, Clark Otto 1956- *WhoEmL 91*
Brewster, David 1781-1868 *EncO&P 3*
Brewster, David Rodger 1948- *WhoWor 91*
Brewster, Elizabeth 1922- *BioIn 16, FemiCLE*
Brewster, Elizabeth Winifred 1922- *WhoAm 90, WhoAmW 91*
Brewster, Eva 1922- *ConAu 132*
Brewster, Francis Anthony 1929- *WhoAm 90*
Brewster, Gerry Leiper 1957- *WhoEmL 91*
Brewster, Henry H *BiDrAPA 89*
Brewster, James Henry 1922- *WhoAm 90*
Brewster, Joe Cephus, Jr. *BiDrAPA 89*
Brewster, Kingman 1919-1988 *AnObit 1988, BioIn 16, WorAlBi*
Brewster, Louise S. 1961- *WhoAmW 91*
Brewster, Martha 1710-1759? *FemiCLE*
Brewster, Martha Wadsworth 1710-1759? *EncCRAm*
Brewster, Michael 1946- *WhoAmA 91*
Brewster, O. H. *AmLegL*
Brewster, Olive Nesbitt 1924- *WhoAmW 91, WhoSSW 91, WhoWor 91*
Brewster, Patience 1952- *BioIn 16*
Brewster, Robert Charles 1921- *WhoAm 90*
Brewster, Robert Gene 1938- *WhoAm 90*
Brewster, Rudi Milton 1932- *WhoAm 90*
Brewster, Townsend *EarBlAP*
Brewster, Townsend Tyler 1924- *WhoWrEP 89*
Brewster, William 1567-1644 *EncCRAm, WorAlBi*
Brewster, William H. 1922- *St&PR 91*
Brewster, William S. 1917- *St&PR 91*
Brewster-Walker, Sandra JoAnn 1942- *WhoAm 90, WhoE 91*
Brewton, Patricia Morris *WhoSSW 91*
Brewton, Robin Denise 1964- *WhoSSW 91*
Brewton, Samuel Alton, Jr. 1931- *WhoSSW 91*
Brewton, Wilbur Emmanuel 1941- *WhoSSW 91*
Breyer, Allan David 1939- *St&PR 91, WhoAm 90*
Breyer, Carol Ann 1934- *WhoAmW 91*
Breyer, James William 1961- *WhoEmL 91*
Breyer, Julius P *BiDrAPA 89*
Breyer, Karl J. 1947- *St&PR 91*
Breyer, N L 1942- *ConAu 31NR*
Breyer, Norman Nathan 1921- *WhoAm 90*
Breyer, Stephen Gerald 1938- *WhoAm 90*
Breyfogle, Peter Howard 1958- *WhoEmL 91*
Breyfogle, Peter Nicholas 1935- *WhoAm 90*
Breymaier, Ann Meredith 1925- *WhoAmW 91*
Breytenbach, Breyten *BioIn 16*
Breytenbach, Breyten 1939?- *ConAu 129*
Breytspraak, John, Jr. 1929- *WhoSSW 91*
Brezack, Irving 1923- *St&PR 91*
Brezack, John Charles 1954- *St&PR 91*
Brezhnev, L. I. *ConAu 132*
Brezhnev, Leonid *ConAu 132*
Brezhnev, Leonid 1906-1982 *WorAlBi*
Brezhnev, Leonid I 1906-1982 *ConAu 132*
Brezhnev, Leonid Il'ich 1906-1982 *BioIn 16*
Brezillon, Claude Leon 1920- *WhoWor 91*
Brezillon, Olivier 1959- *WhoWor 91*
Brezina, Valorie Jane 1953- *WhoEmL 91*
Brezzo, Steven Louis *WhoAmA 91*
Brezzo, Steven Louis 1949- *WhoAm 90*
Bria, George Emil 1916- *WhoAm 90*
Brialy, Jean-Claude *BioIn 16*
Brian Boru 940?-1014 *WorAlBi*
Brian, Alexis Morgan, Jr. 1928- *WhoAm 90, WhoWor 91*
Brian, Donald 1877-1948 *OxCPMus*
Brian, Earl W. 1942- *WhoAm 90*
Brian, Havergal 1876-1972 *PenDiMP A*
Brian, James Sanford 1947- *St&PR 91, WhoEmL 91*
Brian, Mark Wendell 1956- *WhoEmL 91*
Brian, Pierre Leonce Thibaut 1930- *St&PR 91, WhoAm 90*
Brian, Richard Bruce 1947- *St&PR 91*
Brian, Robert Francis 1938- *WhoWor 91*
Brian, Sharon Lynn 1946- *WhoAmW 91*
Briancon, Jane Amanda 1964- *WhoWor 91*
Briand, Aristide 1862-1932 *BiDFrPL, WorAlBi*
Briand, Robert Louis, Jr. 1943- *St&PR 91*
Briand, Thomas *PenDiDA 89*
Briansky, Rita Prezament 1925- *WhoAmA 91*
Briant, Clyde Leonard 1948- *WhoAm 90*
Briar, George 1950- *St&PR 91*
Briati, Giuseppe 1686-1772 *PenDiDA 89*
Bricaud, Henri J. 1925- *WhoWor 91*
Briccetti, Joan Therese 1948- *WhoAm 90*
Briccetti, Thomas 1936- *IntWWM 90*
Brice, Ashbel G. *BioIn 16*
Brice, Bill Eugene 1930- *WhoAm 90*
Brice, Bruce 1942- *MusmAFA*
Brice, Carol 1918-1985 *BioIn 16, DcAfAmP, DrBlPA 90*
Brice, Cliff Verne, Jr. 1939- *St&PR 91*
Brice, Edgar Pinder 1905- *IntWWM 90*
Brice, Fanny 1891-1951 *BioAmW, BioIn 16, NotWoAT, OxCPMus, WorAlBi*
Brice, Harvey R. 1938- *St&PR 91*
Brice, Houston A., Jr. 1917- *St&PR 91*
Brice, Ivan 1954- *WhoE 91*
Brice, James John 1925- *WhoAm 90*
Brice, Janet Kay 1954- *WhoWrEP 89*
Brice, Judith A 1944- *BiDrAPA 89*
Brice, Walter Miller, III 1933- *St&PR 91*
Brice, William 1921- *WhoAmA 91*
Brice-Means, Peggy Jane 1953- *WhoWrEP 89*
Bricel, Mark Leon 1929- *WhoWor 91*
Brichford, Maynard Jay 1926- *WhoAm 90*
Brick, Barrett Lee 1954- *WhoE 91, WhoEmL 91*
Brick, Donald Bernard 1927- *WhoAm 90*
Brick, James David 1948- *WhoE 91*
Brick, John 1922-1973 *AuBYP 90*
Brick, Leroy William 1927- *St&PR 91, WhoE 91*
Brick, Robert Thomas 1950- *WhoEmL 91*
Brick, Sharon M. 1946- *WhoE 91*
Brick, Thomas G. 1935- *St&PR 91*
Brickard, Servatius 1676-1742 *PenDiDA 89*
Brickdale, Eleanor 1872-1945 *BiDWomA*
Brickel, Neil Ignatius *BiDrAPA 89*
Brickell, Charles Hennessey, Jr. 1935- *WhoAm 90, WhoWor 91*
Brickell, Edie *BioIn 16*
Brickell, Edward Ernest, Jr. 1926- *WhoAm 90*
Brickell, Fred 1906-1961 *Ballpl 90*
Brickell, Michael J.J. *St&PR 91*
Bricken, Fay *BioIn 16*
Bricker, Donald Lee 1935- *WhoAm 90*
Bricker, Dusty P. 1954- *WhoEmL 91*
Bricker, Gerald Wayne 1947- *WhoEmL 91*
Bricker, Harvey Miller 1940- *WhoAm 90*
Bricker, James 1935- *St&PR 91*
Bricker, Larry R. 1937- *St&PR 91*
Bricker, Neal S. 1927- *WhoAm 90, WhoWor 91*
Bricker, Richard E. 1934- *St&PR 91*
Bricker, Seymour Murray 1924- *WhoAm 90*
Bricker, Victoria Reifler 1940- *WhoAm 90, WhoAmW 91*
Bricker, William Rudolph 1923- *WhoAm 90*
Brickey, Iris Ann 1941- *WhoAmW 91*
Brickey, Kathleen Fitzgerald 1944- *WhoAmW 91*
Brickfield, Cyril Francis 1919- *WhoAm 90*
Brickhouse, Herman M 1906- *BiDrAPA 89*
Brickhouse, Jack *Ballpl 90*
Brickhouse, John B. 1916- *WhoAm 90*
Brickle, Lizabeth Scott 1964- *St&PR 91*
Brickley, Helen L. 1911- *St&PR 91*
Brickley, James H. 1928- *WhoAm 90*
Brickley, Richard Agar 1925- *WhoAm 90*
Brickley, Robert Larkin 1934- *St&PR 91*
Brickley, Ronald Jay 1941- *St&PR 91*
Bricklin, Dan *BioIn 16*
Bricklin, Malcolm *BioIn 16*
Bricklin, Mark Harris 1939- *WhoWrEP 89*
Bricklin, Patricia Ellen 1932- *WhoAm 90*
Brickman, Bernard 1928- *BiDrAPA 89*
Brickman, Charles Alfred 1932- *St&PR 91*
Brickman, David 1910- *St&PR 91*
Brickman, Harry Russell 1924- *BiDrAPA 89*
Brickman, J Brand 1933- *BiDrAPA 89*
Brickman, Jane Pacht 1946- *WhoAmW 91*
Brickman, Kristopher Ray 1956- *WhoEmL 91*
Brickman, Lawrence Howard 1943- *WhoE 91*
Brickman, Marshall *WhoAm 90*
Brickman, Ravelle *ODwPR 91*
Brickman, Ravelle 1936- *WhoE 91*
Brickman, Walter A. 1945- *St&PR 91*
Brickman, William W. 1913-1986 *BioIn 16*
Brickner, Gerald Bernard 1938- *WhoWor 91*
Brickner, John G 1922- *BiDrAPA 89*
Brickner, Ronald J. 1934- *St&PR 91*
Brickson, Richard Alan 1948- *St&PR 91, WhoAm 90*
Bricktop 1894-1984 *DrBlPA 90*
Brickwedde, Ferdinand Graft 1903-1989 *BioIn 16*
Brico, Antonia 1902-1989 *BioIn 16*
Bricusse, Leslie 1931- *OxCPMus*
Bridburg, Richard M *BiDrAPA 89*
Briddell, E. Talbot 1942- *St&PR 91*
Bride, C. Joseph, Jr. 1936- *ODwPR 91*
Bride, John William 1937- *WhoE 91, WhoWor 91*
Bride, Laurie *BioIn 16*
Brideau, Leo Paul 1947- *WhoEmL 91*
Bridegam, Willis Edward, Jr. 1935- *WhoAm 90, WhoWor 91*
Bridell, R.J. 1935- *St&PR 91*
Bridell-Fox, Eliza Florance 1825?-1895? *BiDWomA*
Bridenbaugh, Peter R. 1940- *St&PR 91*
Bridenbaugh, Peter Reese 1940- *WhoAm 90*
Bridenbaugh, Robert Harlan 1941- *BiDrAPA 89*
Bridenbaugh, William 1932- *St&PR 91*
Bridenstine, James Aloysius 1945- *WhoEmL 91*

Bridenstine, Louis Henry, Jr. 1940- St&PR 91
Brideweser, Jim 1927- Ballpl 90
Bridge, Ann 1889-1974 BioIn 16, FemiCLE
Bridge, Carl J BiDrAPA 89
Bridge, Carl James 1922- WhoE 91
Bridge, Edward W., Jr. St&PR 91
Bridge, Frank 1879-1941 PenDiMP A
Bridge, Herbert Marvin 1925- WhoWor 91
Bridge, Jonathan Joseph 1950- WhoEmL 91
Bridge, Peter 1925-1982 DcNaB 1981
Bridge, Peter J. 1935- WhoWrEP 89
Bridge, Raymond 1943- ConAu 32NR
Bridgeford, Gary James 1947- WhoEmL 91
Bridgeland, James Ralph, Jr. 1929- WhoAm 90
Bridgeman, Robert Craig 1951- WhoSSW 91
Bridger, Abraham A 1937- BiDrAPA 89
Bridger, Baldwin, Jr. 1928- WhoAm 90
Bridger, Barbara B. 1957- WhoAmW 91
Bridger, Carolyn Ann 1943- IntWWM 90
Bridger, James 1804-1881 WhNaAH
Bridger, Robert N. 1936- St&PR 91
Bridger, Wagner H 1928- BiDrAPA 89, WhoAm 90
Bridgers, Sue Ellen 1942- BioIn 16, WhoWrEP 89
Bridgers, William Frank 1932- WhoAm 90
Bridges, Alan Lynn WhoAm 90
Bridges, Althea 1936- IntWWM 90
Bridges, B. Ried 1927- WhoAm 90
Bridges, Barry Lewis 1959- WhoSSW 91
Bridges, Beau 1941- WhoAm 90, WorAlBi
Bridges, Beryl Clarke 1941- WhoAmW 91, WhoE 91
Bridges, Charles Walter 1943- St&PR 91
Bridges, David Manning 1936- WhoAm 90, WhoWor 91
Bridges, E. Thomas 1937- St&PR 91
Bridges, Edward Karl BiDrAPA 89
Bridges, Edwin Clifford 1945- WhoAm 90, WhoSSW 91
Bridges, Elizabeth 1887-1977 BioIn 16
Bridges, Eugene Drew 1947- BiDrAPA 89
Bridges, Fidelia 1834-1923 BiDWomA
Bridges, Harold Andrew 1946- WhoSSW 91
Bridges, Harold Lee 1932- WhoSSW 91
Bridges, Harry 1901- EncAL
Bridges, Harry 1901-1990 BioIn 16, CurBio 90N, NewYTBS 90 [port]
Bridges, Jack Edgar 1925- WhoAm 90
Bridges, James BioIn 16
Bridges, Jeff BioIn 16
Bridges, Jeff 1949- WorAlBi
Bridges, Jeff 1951- WhoAm 90
Bridges, Jerry Fletcher 1945- WhoSSW 91
Bridges, Jesse L. St&PR 91N
Bridges, Joe M. 1941- St&PR 91
Bridges, John Frederick 1949- BiDrAPA 89
Bridges, L. Michael 1950- St&PR 91
Bridges, Larry BioIn 16
Bridges, Laura S. St&PR 91
Bridges, Laurie 1921- BioIn 16
Bridges, Leon 1932- WhoE 91
Bridges, Leon Gerald 1943- WhoSSW 91
Bridges, Linda 1949- WhoAmW 91
Bridges, Lloyd WhoAm 90
Bridges, Lloyd 1913- CurBio 90 [port], WorAlBi
Bridges, Marshall 1931- Ballpl 90
Bridges, Neal Julian 1946- WhoSSW 91
Bridges, Norman Valette 1938- WhoAm 90
Bridges, Patricia Ann 1952- WhoWrEP 89
Bridges, Paul Kenneth 1931- WhoWor 91
Bridges, Robert 1844-1930 DcLB 98 [port]
Bridges, Robert Lysle 1909- St&PR 91, WhoAm 90
Bridges, Robert Seymour 1844-1930 BioIn 16
Bridges, Rocky 1927- Ballpl 90
Bridges, Rodney Wayne 1949- St&PR 91
Bridges, Russell Brian 1955- WhoEmL 91
Bridges, Todd BioIn 16
Bridges, Todd 1965- DrBlPA 90
Bridges, Tommy 1906-1968 Ballpl 90 [port]
Bridges, William Andrew 1901- AuBYP 90
Bridges, William Bruce 1934- WhoAm 90
Bridges, William D BiDrAPA 89
Bridges, William Russell, III 1958- St&PR 91
Bridget of Sweden 1303?-1373 EncCoWW
Bridget, Saint DcScanL
Bridgewater, Albert Louis 1941- WhoAm 90
Bridgewater, Bernard A., Jr. 1934- St&PR 91
Bridgewater, Bernard Adolphus, Jr. 1934- WhoAm 90
Bridgewater, Dee Dee 1950- DrBlPA 90
Bridgewater, Herbert Jeremiah, Jr. 1942- WhoAm 90
Bridgewater, Leslie 1893-1975 OxCPMus
Bridgewater, Walter Cleveland 1938- WhoWor 91
Bridgford, Hugh W. 1931- St&PR 91
Bridgforth, Robert Moore, Jr. 1918- WhoWor 91
Bridgforth, William A., Jr. 1948- WhoSSW 91
Bridgman, Elizabeth Klein WhoAmW 91
Bridgman, George Ross 1947- WhoEmL 91
Bridgman, James Campbell 1950- WhoEmL 91
Bridgman, Laura D. 1829-1889 BioAmW
Bridgman, Luther Harry 1919- WhoE 91
Bridgman, Percy Williams 1882-1961 WorAlBi
Bridgman, Richard 1927- ConAu 129
Bridgman, William L. St&PR 91
Bridgwater, Elizabeth E, Countess of BiDEWW
Bridgwater, Emmy 1902- BiDWomA
Bridson, John G. 1935- St&PR 91
Bridson, Martin Robert 1964- WhoEmL 91
Bridston, Keith Richard 1924- WhoAm 90
Bridston, Paul Joseph 1928- WhoAm 90
Bridwell, Al 1884-1969 Ballpl 90
Bridwell, Darla Renee 1963- WhoSSW 91
Bridwell, Margaret WhoWrEP 89
Bridwell, R. Kennedy 1943- St&PR 91
Bridwell, Robert Kennedy 1943- WhoAm 90
Bridwell, Robert S. 1940- WhoAm 90
Briedis, Laura Marija 1964- WhoWrEP 89
Brief, Bunny 1892-1963 Ballpl 90
Brief, Henry 1924- WhoAm 90
Brief, Todd Lyman 1953- IntWWM 90
Briefel, Robert E. 1944- St&PR 91
Briefer, Dick 1915-198-? EncACom
Briegel, Richard Carl 1944- St&PR 91
Briegel, William Eugene 1949- WhoWrEP 89
Brieger, Gert Henry 1932- WhoAm 90
Brien, Robert Louis BiDrAPA 89
Briening, Eileen Patricia 1950- WhoE 91
Brier, Helene 1924- WhoAmA 91
Brier, Howard Maxwell 1903-1969 AuBYP 90
Brier, Jack Harold 1946- WhoAm 90
Brier, Mac BioIn 16
Brier, Robert 1943- EncPaPR 91
Brier, Timothy George 1948- St&PR 91
Brierley, David 1936- SpyFic
Brierley, James Alan 1938- WhoAm 90
Brierley, John E. C. 1936- WhoAm 90
Brierley, Louise BioIn 16
Brierley, Richard Greer 1915- St&PR 91
Brierton, Cheryl L. Wootton Black 1947- WhoAmW 91, WhoEmL 91
Brierton, Robert Sylvester 1948- WhoE 91
Briess, Roger Charles 1937- WhoE 91
Briet, Marguerite 1510?-1552? EncCoWW
Briffel, Meyanne Putnam 1950- WhoAmW 91
Brigadere, Anna 1861-1933 EncCoWW
Brigance, Rebecca Elizabeth 1945- WhoAmW 91
Brigance, Thomas Franklin NewYTBS 90
Brigante Colonna Angelini, Valerio BioIn 16
Brigden, Richard N. 1939- St&PR 91
Brigden, Richard T. 1944- WhoSSW 91
Briggin, Clifford S 1937- BiDrAPA 89
Briggin, Irene F BiDrAPA 89
Briggle, Artus van PenDiDA 89
Briggle, William James 1925- WhoAm 90
Briggs, Asa 1921- WorAu 1980 [port]
Briggs, Austin WhoAmA 91N
Briggs, Austin 1909-1973 EncACom
Briggs, Barbara AuBYP 90
Briggs, Berta N 1884-1976 WhoAmA 91N
Briggs, Buttons 1875-1911 Ballpl 90
Briggs, Carole S. 1950- BioIn 16
Briggs, Charlie Irwin 1927- WhoWrEP 89
Briggs, Christopher Rawdon PenDiMP
Briggs, Clare BioIn 16
Briggs, Clare A. 1875-1930 EncACom
Briggs, Dan 1952- Ballpl 90
Briggs, Donald Rae 1930- St&PR 91
Briggs, E. Janette 1931- WhoAmW 91
Briggs, Edward Samuel 1926- WhoAm 90
Briggs, Ellis Ormsbee 1899-1976 BioIn 16
Briggs, Emily Pomona Edson 1830-1910 BioIn 16
Briggs, Ernest 1923-1984 WhoAmA 91N
Briggs, Everett Ellis 1934- WhoAm 90, WhoWor 91
Briggs, Frederick John 1932- WhoAm 90
Briggs, Gary Lewis 1951- St&PR 91
Briggs, Geoffrey Hugh 1926- WhoAm 90
Briggs, George Madison 1927- WhoE 91, WhoWor 91
Briggs, George Oliver 1926- St&PR 91
Briggs, Gerald 1932- St&PR 91
Briggs, Harold Melvin 1904- WhoAm 90
Briggs, Henry 1561-1630 WorAlBi
Briggs, Herbert Spencer 1910- WhoAm 90
Briggs, Herbert W. NewYTBS 90
Briggs, Herbert W. 1900-1990 BioIn 16
Briggs, James Frankland 1827-1905 AmLegL
Briggs, Jean Audrey 1943- WhoE 91
Briggs, Joe Bob 1959- ConAu 131
Briggs, John 1944- Ballpl 90
Briggs, John 1945- ConAu 132
Briggs, John G., Jr. NewYTBS 90
Briggs, John Gurney, Jr. 1916- WhoAm 90, WhoWrEP 89
Briggs, John P 1921- BiDrAPA 89
Briggs, John V. 1951- St&PR 91
Briggs, Johnny 1934- Ballpl 90
Briggs, Julia Whittington 1952- WhoSSW 91
Briggs, K M 1898-1980 EncO&P 3
Briggs, Kenneth R 1927- BiDrAPA 89
Briggs, Kenneth Ralph 1927- WhoE 91
Briggs, Leon R, Jr. 1922- BiDrAPA 89
Briggs, Lyman James 1874-1963 DcScB S2
Briggs, Margaret Luellen 1956- WhoEmL 91
Briggs, Marian ODwPR 91
Briggs, Mark R. 1956- St&PR 91
Briggs, Morton Winfield 1915- WhoAm 90
Briggs, Nancy BioIn 16
Briggs, Patty Ann WhoWrEP 89
Briggs, Paul W. 1912-1989 BioIn 16
Briggs, Paul W. 1922- St&PR 91
Briggs, Paul Wellington 1922- WhoAm 90
Briggs, Perle W. BioIn 16
Briggs, Peter S 1946- WhoAmA 91
Briggs, Peter Stromme 1946- WhoAm 90
Briggs, Philip 1928- St&PR 91, WhoAm 90
Briggs, Philip James 1938- WhoE 91
Briggs, Philip Terry 1934- WhoAm 90
Briggs, Robert Mabbett 1944- WhoE 91
Briggs, Robert Peter 1903- WhoAm 90
Briggs, Robert Stearns 1944- St&PR 91
Briggs, Rodney Arthur 1923- WhoAm 90
Briggs, Roger T. 1929-1989 BioIn 16
Briggs, Shirley Ann 1918- WhoAm 90
Briggs, Stanley Austin 1941- St&PR 91
Briggs, Susan Shadinger 1941- WhoAm 90
Briggs, Taylor Rastrick 1933- WhoAm 90
Briggs, Terry William 1955- WhoEmL 91
Briggs, Thomas Edward 1945- St&PR 91
Briggs, Vernon Mason, Jr. 1937- WhoAm 90
Briggs, Wallace Neal 1915- WhoAm 90
Briggs, Walter O., Sr. 1877-1952 Ballpl 90
Briggs, Ward Wright 1945- WhoSSW 91
Briggs, William Benajah 1922- WhoAm 90
Briggs, William Egbert 1925- WhoAm 90
Briggs, Winslow Russell 1928- WhoAm 90
Brigham, E. Oran 1940- St&PR 91
Brigham, Francis Gorham, Jr. 1915- St&PR 91
Brigham, H. Day, Jr. 1926- St&PR 91
Brigham, James R. 1922- St&PR 91
Brigham, James R. 1945- St&PR 91
Brigham, John Allen, Jr. 1942- WhoWor 91
Brigham, Kenneth Larry 1939- WhoAm 90
Brigham, S.T. Jack, III 1939- St&PR 91
Brigham, Samuel Townsend Jack, III 1939- WhoAm 90
Brigham, Tom 1947- ODwPR 91
Bright Eyes WhNaAH
Bright Eyes 1854-1903 BioAmW
Bright, Al 1940- WhoAmA 91
Bright, Alma Louie IntWWM 90
Bright, Barney 1927- WhoAmA 91
Bright, Betty Suida WhoAmW 91
Bright, Cecil Burlington 1919- WhoWor 91
Bright, Charles A 1908- BiDrAPA 89
Bright, Craig Bartley 1931- WhoAm 90
Bright, David Forbes 1942- WhoAm 90
Bright, David R. 1939- St&PR 91
Bright, Debra Ann 1957- WhoAmW 91
Bright, Donald Bolton 1930- WhoWor 91
Bright, Donald Lee 1928- St&PR 91
Bright, Dora 1863-1951 PenDiMP
Bright, Edgar Allen Gordon 1929- St&PR 91
Bright, Edward David 1936- St&PR 91
Bright, Elise Marie 1952- WhoSSW 91
Bright, Francis Edward 1917- St&PR 91
Bright, George Walter 1945- WhoEmL 91
Bright, Gerald 1923- St&PR 91, WhoAm 90
Bright, H. David 1934- WhoAm 90
Bright, Harold Frederick 1913- WhoAm 90
Bright, Harry 1929- Ballpl 90
Bright, Harry Andrew 1947- WhoSSW 91
Bright, Harvey R. 1920- BioIn 16, WhoAm 90
Bright, Harvey Roberts 1920- St&PR 91
Bright, Jerlene Ann 1942- WhoAmW 91
Bright, Joe EarBlAP
Bright, John BioIn 16
Bright, John 1811-1889 BioIn 16
Bright, John M 1908-1989 ConAu 129
Bright, John Willis 1932- WhoAm 90
Bright, Margaret 1918- WhoAm 90
Bright, Mary 1859-1945 BioIn 16
Bright, Myron H. 1919- WhoAm 90
Bright, Nancy Elizabeth 1944- WhoWrEP 89
Bright, Nellie Rathborne 1902-1976 HarlReB
Bright, Noble, Jr. 1931- WhoE 91
Bright, Robert 1902-1988 BioIn 16, SmATA 60, -63 [port]
Bright, Ruth Wingate Ockenden 1929- IntWWM 90
Bright, Sam Raymond 1936- St&PR 91
Bright, Simeon Miller 1925- WhoAm 90
Bright, Steven David 1966- WhoEmL 91
Bright, Thomas Lynn 1948- WhoEmL 91
Bright, Thomas Rhodes 1952- WhoE 91
Bright, Ursula 1830?-1915 BioIn 16
Bright, Willard M. 1914- St&PR 91
Bright, Willard Mead 1914- WhoAm 90
Bright, William A. 1948- St&PR 91
Bright, William Oliver 1928- WhoAm 90
Bright, William Townsend 1938- St&PR 91
Bright-Long, Lory E BiDrAPA 89
Brightbill, Lorenzo Otis, III 1936- St&PR 91
Brightbill, William Robert 1947- St&PR 91
Brightfield, Richard 1927- BioIn 16
Brightfield, Rick 1927- BioIn 16
Brightman, Deborah E. ODwPR 91
Brightman, Edgar Sheffield 1884-1953 BioIn 16
Brightman, James M. 1945- St&PR 91
Brightman, Jerome Bernard 1945- WhoEmL 91
Brightman, Joel P. 1935- St&PR 91
Brightman, Mary 1950- St&PR 91
Brightman, Robert Lloyd 1920- St&PR 91, WhoAm 90
Brightmire, Paul William 1924- WhoAm 90
Brighton, Carl Theodore 1931- WhoAm 90
Brighton, Catherine 1943- ConAu 130
Brighton, Gerald David 1920- WhoAm 90
Brighton, John Trevor 1936- WhoWor 91
Brightwell, Dennis R 1946- BiDrAPA 89
Brightwell, Walter 1919- WhoAmA 91
Brigida, Carlo Joseph 1938- St&PR 91
Brigido, Suely Ventura 1951- IntWWM 90
Brignet, Helen Paulette 1947- WhoEmL 91
Brignoni, Angel M BiDrAPA 89
Brignoni, Ruben BiDrAPA 89
Briguglio, Jonna 1962- WhoE 91
Brihat, Denis 1928- WhoWor 91
Brija-Towery, David Malcolm 1958- St&PR 91
Brijbhushan, Jamila 1918- ConAu 130
Briles, Judith 1946- WhoAmW 91
Briles, Nellie 1943- Ballpl 90
Briley, Ann M 1937- BiDrAPA 89
Briley, George Clifton 1925- St&PR 91
Briley, J.W. 1954- St&PR 91
Briley, John Marshall, Jr. 1940- WhoWrEP 89
Briley, Martha Clark 1949- St&PR 91, WhoAm 90, WhoAmW 91, WhoEmL 91
Briley, Noreen Galvin 1943- WhoE 91
Brilioth, Helge 1931- IntWWM 90, PenDiMP
Brill, A. Bertrand 1928- WhoAm 90
Brill, Alan Richard 1942- WhoAm 90
Brill, Arthur Sylvan 1927- WhoAm 90
Brill, Bonnie 1948- WhoAmW 91
Brill, David 1941- St&PR 91
Brill, Ernest 1945- WhoWrEP 89
Brill, F. Arthur 1930- WhoE 91
Brill, Fran ConTFT 8 [port]
Brill, Frank P. 1957- WhoSSW 91
Brill, Glenn 1949- WhoAmA 91
Brill, Henry NewYTBS 90 [port]
Brill, Henry 1906- BiDrAPA 89
Brill, I William BiDrAPA 89
Brill, Jeffrey A. 1943- St&PR 91
Brill, Joan Rothman 1930- IntWWM 90
Brill, Joel Victor 1956- WhoEmL 91
Brill, John J. St&PR 91
Brill, Joseph B 1929- BiDrAPA 89
Brill, Kristine R. ODwPR 91
Brill, Lawrence Lee 1954- WhoEmL 91
Brill, Lesley 1943- WhoAm 90
Brill, Mara 1956- BiDrAPA 89
Brill, Marvin Albert 1928- WhoE 91
Brill, Mary A. St&PR 91
Brill, Michael 1962- WhoE 91
Brill, Mitchell 1950- WhoE 91
Brill, Nicholas Steven 1946- WhoE 91
Brill, Norman Q 1911- BiDrAPA 89
Brill, Norman Quintus 1911- WhoAm 90
Brill, Peter L 1943- BiDrAPA 89
Brill, Ralph David 1944- WhoAm 90
Brill, Richard B. 1944- ODwPR 91
Brill, Richard J. 1939- St&PR 91
Brill, Ronald M. 1943- St&PR 91
Brill, Ronald Mitchel 1943- WhoAm 90
Brill, Winston J. BioIn 16
Brill, Winston Jonas 1939- WhoAm 90

Brill, Yvonne Claeys 1924- WhoAm 90, WhoAmW 91
Brill-Edwards, Harry Walter 1941- WhoAm 90, WhoE 91
Brill Wagner, Eileen Beth 1956- WhoE 91
Brillantes, Dorothy Ann 1950- WhoAmW 91
Brillantes, Tomas C BiDrAPA 89
Brillhart, David Winthrop 1925- WhoSSW 91
Brillhart, Jeffrey Lynn 1955- IntWWM 90
Brillheart, Jim 1903-1972 Ballpl 90
Brilliant, Barbara 1935- WhoE 91
Brilliant, Richard 1929- WhoAm 90, WhoAmA 91
Brillinger, Harold Roy BiDrAPA 89
Brillion, Steven Matthew 1959- WhoEmL 91
Brillouin, Leon Nicolas 1889-1969 DcScB S2
Briloff, Abraham Jacob 1917- WhoAm 90
Brilon, Robert J. 1960- St&PR 91
Brim, Armand Eugene 1930- WhoAm 90
Brim, Orville Gilbert, Jr. 1923- WhoAm 90
Brimacombe, James Keith 1943- WhoAm 90, WhoWor 91
Brimacombe, William Harold 1953- St&PR 91
Brimble, Alan 1930- WhoAm 90
Brimelow, Peter 1947- WhoAm 90
Brimer, Kenneth Kimbelin, Jr. 1945- WhoSSW 91
Brimhall, John Clark 1928- WhoWor 91
Brimley, Wilford 1934- WhoAm 90
Brimm, David 1952- ODwPR 91
Brimmer, Andrew Felton 1926- St&PR 91, WhoAm 90
Brimmer, Robert Alvah, II 1952- BiDrAPA 89
Brimner, Larry Dane AuBYP 90
Brims EncCRAm
Brims, John Sinclair 1933- WhoAm 90
Brin, David 1950- RGTwCSF, WhoAm 90
Brin, Foster Blake BiDrAPA 89
Brin, Myron 1923- WhoAm 90
Brin, Royal Henry, Jr. 1919- WhoAm 90, WhoSSW 91
Brinberg, Herbert Raphael 1926- WhoAm 90
Brincat, John N. 1936- St&PR 91
Brinckerhoff, Richard Charles 1931- WhoAm 90
Brinckerhoff, Robert EncACom
Brinckman, Donald W. 1931- St&PR 91
Brinckman, Donald Wesley 1931- WhoAm 90
Brincks, Cynthia Ann 1958- WhoAmW 91
Brind, Ira 1941- St&PR 91
Brinda, Wayne 1950- WhoEmL 91
Brind'Amour, Yvette 1918- OxCCanT
Brindel, Bernard 1912- IntWWM 90
Brindel, June 1919- AuBYP 90, ConAu 31NR
Brindel, June Rachuy 1919- WhoWrEP 89
Brindell, Charles R., Jr. 1949- St&PR 91
Brindisi, Nicholas S. 1952- WhoEmL 91
Brindley, Bill Tremaine 1947- WhoE 91
Brindley, Thomas M. 1952- St&PR 91
Brindus, Nicolae 1935- IntWWM 90
Brine, Dolores Randolph 1945- WhoAmW 91
Brine, John Joseph 1931- WhoAm 90
Brine, Kevin R. 1950- St&PR 91
Brinegar, Claude Stout 1926- BiDrUSE 89, St&PR 91, WhoAm 90, WhoWor 91
Brinegar, Willard C 1913- BiDrAPA 89
Brinegar, Willard Clouse 1913- WhoAm 90
Briner, Daniel G. 1946- St&PR 91
Briner, Pamela Joan 1950- WhoAmW 91
Brines, Seymour 1927- WhoE 91
Briney, Frank E. 1928- St&PR 91
Briney, Lester Stafford 1944- WhoE 91
Briney, Roger Albert 1949- WhoEmL 91
Bring, Dale Vincent 1949- WhoEmL 91
Bring, Murray 1935- WhoAm 90
Bringard, Jerry D. 1936- St&PR 91
Bringas, Clodualdo Villanueva 1922- WhoWor 91
Bringham, William Talbert, Jr. 1953- WhoAm 90
Bringhurst, Robert 1946- WhoWrEP 89, WorAu 1980 [port]
Bringle, Emmett Watson 1924- St&PR 91
Bringmann, Karl A. 1912- WhoWor 91
Bringmann, Michael 1940- WhoWor 91
Brings, Allen 1934- IntWWM 90
Brings, Lawrence Martin 1897- WhoAm 90
Brining, David Richard 1942- St&PR 91
Brink, Andre 1935- MajTwCW
Brink, Arthur M. 1943- WhoE 91
Brink, Carl William 1947- WhoEmL 91
Brink, Carol 1895-1981 FemiCLE
Brink, Carol Ryrie 1895-1981 AuBYP 90
Brink, Clark BioIn 16
Brink, David Ryrie 1919- WhoAm 90
Brink, Earl James 1936- BiDrAPA 89
Brink, Frances V. 1889-1978 BioIn 16
Brink, Frank, Jr. 1910- WhoAm 90
Brink, Gerald R. 1938- WhoSSW 91
Brink, Ingemar 1952- WhoWor 91
Brink, John W. 1945- St&PR 91
Brink, John William 1945- WhoEmL 91
Brink, Judith Kay 1947- WhoAmW 91, WhoWor 91
Brink, Marion Alice 1928- WhoAmW 91, WhoE 91
Brink, Marion Francis 1932- WhoAm 90
Brink, Peter BioIn 16
Brink, Richard Edward 1923- WhoAm 90
Brink, Thomas C. 1927- St&PR 91
Brink, William Joseph, Jr. 1916- WhoWrEP 89
Brink, William P. 1916- WhoAm 90
Brinker, Juergen 1940- St&PR 91
Brinker, Kenneth Chris 1953- WhoEmL 91
Brinker, Lynn John 1931- St&PR 91
Brinker, Nancy BioIn 16
Brinker, Robert Sawyer 1932- St&PR 91
Brinker, Ruth Marie 1922- WhoAmW 91
Brinker, Thomas Michael 1933- WhoAm 90, WhoE 91, WhoWor 91
Brinker, Wade Oberlin 1912- WhoAm 90
Brinkerhoff, Dericksen Morgan 1921- WhoAmA 91
Brinkerhoff, Drew BioIn 16
Brinkerhoff, Lorin C. 1929- WhoWor 91
Brinkerhoff, Peter John 1945- WhoE 91
Brinkerhoff, Philip Richard 1943- St&PR 91
Brinkerhoff, Robert Beveir 1925- St&PR 91
Brinkerhoff, Tom J. 1939- WhoAm 90
Brinkhaus, Armand J. 1935- WhoSSW 91
Brinkhous, Kenneth Merle 1908- WhoAm 90
Brinkley, Ben Paul 1952- BiDrAPA 89
Brinkley, Betsy Anne 1959- WhoAmW 91
Brinkley, Bill Robert 1936- WhoAm 90
Brinkley, Charles Alexander 1929- WhoAm 90
Brinkley, Christie BioIn 16
Brinkley, David 1920- WhoAm 90, WhoE 91, WhoWor 91, WorAlBi
Brinkley, Fred Sinclair, Jr. 1938- WhoAm 90
Brinkley, Jack Thomas 1930- WhoAm 90
Brinkley, James W. 1937- St&PR 91
Brinkley, John 1885-1942 WorAlBi
Brinkley, Joseph Willard 1926- WhoAm 90
Brinkley, Phyllis 1926- WhoAmW 91
Brinkley, Susan Rose 1949- WhoSSW 91
Brinkley, William Anthony 1942- WhoSSW 91
Brinkley, William Clark 1917- WhoAm 90, WhoWor 91, WhoWrEP 89
Brinkman, Carl Alexander 1932- WhoAm 90, WhoE 91
Brinkman, Ed 1941- Ballpl 90
Brinkman, Gabriel 1924- WhoAm 90
Brinkman, Herbert Charles 1926- WhoAm 90
Brinkman, Joe 1944- Ballpl 90
Brinkman, John Anthony 1934- WhoAm 90
Brinkman, Karen Elaine 1950- St&PR 91, WhoAm 90
Brinkman, Linda Eves 1947- BiDrAPA 89
Brinkman, Lloyd D. 1929- St&PR 91
Brinkman, Merlyn John 1923- St&PR 91
Brinkman, Ned Eugene 1934- St&PR 91
Brinkman, Paul Delbert 1937- WhoAm 90
Brinkman, Richard Gene 1927- WhoAm 90
Brinkman, Richard James 1930- St&PR 91
Brinkman, Robert A. 1947- St&PR 91
Brinkman, Sheila Perfect 1957- WhoEmL 91
Brinkman, William Frank 1938- WhoAm 90
Brinkmann, Bodo 1942- IntWWM 90
Brinkmann, Don WhoAm 90
Brinkmann, Heinrich W. 1898-1989 BioIn 16
Brinkmann, Karl Dwane 1957- WhoEmL 91
Brinkmann, Klaus P. 1931- St&PR 91
Brinkmann, Klaus Peter 1931- WhoE 91
Brinkmann, Robert Joseph 1950- WhoEmL 91
Brinkmann, Thomas Henry 1929- WhoAm 90
Brinkmeier, Roger Gene 1942- St&PR 91
Brinks, Kenneth J.H. 1935- St&PR 91
Brinley, Charles Edward 1940- St&PR 91
Brinley, Daniel Putnam 1879-1963 WhoAmA 91N
Brinley, Floyd John, Jr. 1930- WhoAm 90
Brinley, G. Robert 1949- St&PR 91
Brinley, Maryann B. 1949- ConAu 130
Brinner, Roger E. 1947- St&PR 91
Brinnin, John Malcolm 1916- WhoAm 90, WhoWrEP 89
Brinning, Nancy Gillespie 1927- St&PR 91, WhoAm 90
Brinsfield, S.D. 1922- St&PR 91
Brinsko, John Andrew 1929- WhoSSW 91
Brinsmade, Alan B 1925- BiDrAPA 89
Brinsmade, Alan Bruce 1925- WhoSSW 91
Brinsmade, Lyon Louis 1924- WhoAm 90
Brinsmead, H. F. 1922- BioIn 16
Brinsmead, Hesba Fay 1922- BioIn 16
Brinson, Benjamin Thomas 1948- WhoEmL 91
Brinson, Elaine Koger 1936- WhoAmW 91
Brinson, Gary P. 1943- St&PR 91
Brinson, Gary Paul 1943- WhoAm 90
Brinson, Gay Creswell, Jr. 1925- WhoAm 90, WhoWor 91
Brinson, Harold Thomas 1930- WhoAm 90
Brinson, Mark McClellan 1943- WhoSSW 91
Brinster, Barry ODwPR 91
Brinster, Ralph Lawrence 1932- WhoAm 90
Brintnall, John Robert 1953- St&PR 91
Brinton, Christine Louise 1948- WhoEmL 91
Brinton, Crane 1898-1968 WorAlBi
Brinton, Daniel Garrison 1837-1899 WhNaAH
Brinton, Margo Ann 1945- WhoSSW 91
Brinton, Reed Wollerton 1915- WhoAm 90
Brinton, Richard Kirk 1946- WhoEmL 91
Brinton, Tina Ree 1956- WhoAmW 91
Brinzo, John S. 1942- St&PR 91, WhoAm 90
Briody, John J. 1935- St&PR 91
Brion, Christopher Edward 1937- WhoAm 90
Brion, Guy ConAu 33NR
Brion, John P. 1920- ODwPR 91
Brion, Pacelli E BiDrAPA 89
Brion, Richard 1946- WhoWor 91
Briones, David F 1944- BiDrAPA 89
Briones, Luis BiDrAPA 89
Briones, Melba C 1943- BiDrAPA 89
Briones-Ramilo, Teresita C. BiDrAPA 89
Briot, Francois 1550?-1616? PenDiDA 89
Brisbane, Arthur 1864-1936 BioIn 16
Brisbane, Seward BioIn 16
Brisbane, William Henry 1806-1878 BioIn 16
Brisbin, Robert Edward 1946- WhoEmL 91
Brisbois, Richard Anthony 1952- WhoSSW 91
Brisbon, Eric Stephen 1954- St&PR 91
Brisby, Stewart Paul 1945- WhoWrEP 89
Briscar, Sandy Marie McCullers 1955- WhoSSW 91
Brisch, Carl Joseph 1915- St&PR 91
Brisch, James John 1953- St&PR 91
Brisch, Joseph George 1924- St&PR 91
Brisco, P. A. MajTwCW
Brisco, Patty MajTwCW
Brisco, Valerie 1960- WhoAm 90
Briscoe, Benjamin 1867-1945 EncABHB 4 [port]
Briscoe, Bimbo 1955- WhoEmL 91
Briscoe, C William 1940- BiDrAPA 89
Briscoe, Charles Henry 1831-1918 AmLegL
Briscoe, Elizabeth F. BioIn 16
Briscoe, Frank EncABHB 4
Briscoe, Jack Clayton 1920- WhoAm 90, WhoWor 91
Briscoe, Jill 1935- BioIn 16
Briscoe, John Frederick, Jr. 1952- WhoEmL 91
Briscoe, John Hanson 1934- WhoAm 90
Briscoe, Joyce Elizabeth 1950- WhoAmW 91
Briscoe, Keith G. 1933- WhoAm 90, WhoWor 91
Briscoe, Marianne Grier 1945- WhoEmL 91
Briscoe, Mary Louise 1937- WhoAmW 91
Briscoe, Ralph O. 1927- St&PR 91
Briscoe, Ralph Owen 1927- WhoAm 90
Briscoe, Robert John 1941- St&PR 91
Briscoe, Sophia FemiCLE
Briscoe, William C BiDrAPA 89
Briscoli, Paul Francis BiDrAPA 89
Brisebois, Marcel 1933- WhoAm 90, WhoE 91
Briseno, Alex 1950- WhoHisp 91
Brisentine, Cecilia Kay 1952- WhoAmW 91
Brisfjord, Inez Lorraine WhoE 91
Brisk, David C. 1930- St&PR 91
Briskin, Bernard 1924- St&PR 91, WhoAm 90
Briskin, Jonathan K BiDrAPA 89
Briskin, Jonathan Kalonymus 1960- WhoE 91
Briskin, Madeleine 1932- WhoWor 91
Briskman, Robert David 1932- WhoAm 90
Brisman, Heskel 1923- IntWWM 90
Brisolara, Ashton 1924- WhoAm 90
Brissenden, Alan 1932- ConAu 132
Brissenden, Arik 1926- BiDrAPA 89
Brissett, Belva BioIn 16
Brissette, Estelle Cook 1936- WhoAmW 91, WhoSSW 91
Brissette, Gregory Paul 1955- WhoSSW 91
Brissey, Ruben Marion 1923- WhoAm 90
Brissie, Eugene Field, Jr. 1949- WhoAm 90
Brissie, Lou 1924- Ballpl 90
Brissman, Bernard Gustave 1919- WhoAm 90
Brisson, Carl 1895-1958 OxCPMus
Brisson, Elsa Ramirez 1954- WhoHisp 91
Brisson, Eugene Henri 1835-1912 BiDFrPL
Brister, Bill H. 1930- WhoAm 90
Brister, Bubby BioIn 16
Brister, James Clayton 1954- BiDrAPA 89
Brister, John Tyler BioIn 16
Brister, Scott Andrew 1955- WhoEmL 91
Bristol, Arlen A. 1952- WhoEmL 91
Bristol, Betty Jane 1946- WhoE 91
Bristol, Dave 1933- Ballpl 90
Bristol, Horace BioIn 16
Bristol, Johnny DrBIPA 90
Bristol, Josephine Hart BiDrAPA 89
Bristol, Louise Fitzgerald 1935- WhoAmW 91
Bristol, Mark Lambert 1868-1939 BioIn 16
Bristol, Norman 1924- WhoAm 90
Bristol, R Curtis 1932- BiDrAPA 89
Bristol, Richard Fredrick 1925- WhoAm 90
Bristol, Sharon Lee 1942- WhoAmW 91
Bristol, Sherlock 1815-1906 BioIn 16
Bristor, Valerie Jayne 1954- WhoAmW 91
Bristow, Amelia 1783-1845? FemiCLE
Bristow, Benjamin Helm 1832-1896 BiDrUSE 89
Bristow, David Ian 1931- WhoAm 90
Bristow, Gwen 1903-1980 FemiCLE
Bristow, James Edward 1934- St&PR 91
Bristow, James Randle 1950- WhoSSW 91
Bristow, Joan AuBYP 90
Bristow, Joan Halbleib 1935- WhoAmW 91, WhoE 91
Bristow, Lonnie Robert 1930- WhoAm 90
Bristow, Matthew 1945- St&PR 91
Bristow, Opal Tusing 1921- WhoSSW 91
Bristow, Robert O'Neil 1926- WhoAm 90, WhoWor 91, WhoWrEP 89
Bristow, Samuel Wayne 1943- WhoSSW 91
Bristow, William Arthur 1937- WhoAmA 91
Bristow, William H, Jr. BiDrAPA 89
Bristow, William H., Jr. WhoE 91
Britain, Ian 1948- ConAu 130
Britain, Radie 1903- BioIn 16
Britain, Radie 1908- IntWWM 90, WhoAm 90
Brite, David Alan 1948- St&PR 91
Brite, Donald L. 1933- St&PR 91
Brite, Jane Fassett WhoAmA 91
Brite, K. Jane WhoAmW 91
Brite, Mary Alice 1930- WhoWrEP 89
Britko-Leese, Kimberly Lynn 1962- WhoAmW 91
Britnell, Olen Eugene 1943- WhoSSW 91
Brito, Aristeo 1942- HispWr 90, WhoHisp 91
Brito, Dagobert Llanos 1941- WhoAm 90, WhoSSW 91
Brito, Frank 1922- MusmAFA
Brito, John Solomon 1945- WhoHisp 91
Brito, Maria 1947- WhoAmA 91
Brito, Mercedes A. BiDrAPA 89
Brito, Neftali R BiDrAPA 89
Brito, Silvia E. 1933- WhoHisp 91
Brito e Cunha, Joao Carlos 1884-1950 BioIn 16
Britsky, Nicholas 1913- WhoAmA 91
Britt, Benjamin E 1922- BiDrAPA 89
Britt, Beverly Langley 1947- WhoSSW 91
Britt, Bill BioIn 16
Britt, Christina Lynn 1962- WhoAmW 91
Britt, David Paul 1939- WhoWor 91
Britt, David V.B. 1937- St&PR 91
Britt, Donald R. 1924- St&PR 91
Britt, Earl Thomas 1940- WhoAm 90
Britt, Elton 1917-1972 OxCPMus
Britt, Erlinda Ornelas 1939- WhoAmW 91
Britt, Georgetta Lee Culton 1932- WhoAmW 91
Britt, Gerald F. 1932- St&PR 91, WhoAm 90
Britt, Glen A. 1949- St&PR 91
Britt, Glenn Alan 1949- WhoAm 90, WhoEmL 91
Britt, Henry Middleton 1919- WhoAm 90
Britt, James Thomas 1904- WhoAm 90, WhoWor 91
Britt, Jim 1911-1981 Ballpl 90
Britt, John Roy 1937- WhoAm 90
Britt, Julia C. 1952- WhoEmL 91
Britt, Julie WhoAmW 91
Britt, Laura Anne 1961- WhoSSW 91
Britt, Leigh WhoWrEP 89

Britt, Maisha Dorrah *WhoAmW 91*
Britt, Robert Louis 1943- *WhoSSW 91*
Britt, Rodney Charles 1949- *WhoSSW 91*
Britt, Ronald Leroy 1935- *WhoWor 91*
Britt, Russell W. 1926- *St&PR 91*
Britt, Sam Glenn 1940- *WhoAmA 91*
Britt, Susan Fagen 1947- *WhoEmL 91*
Britt, Valerie Sipe 1950- *WhoSSW 91*
Britt, W. Earl 1932- *WhoAm 90, WhoSSW 91*
Brittain, Alfred 1922- *St&PR 91*
Brittain, Annie *EncO&P 3, EncPaPR 91*
Brittain, Bill *ConAu 30NR*
Brittain, Bruce Bennett 1957- *WhoSSW 91*
Brittain, Donald *BioIn 16*
Brittain, James Edward 1931- *WhoAm 90*
Brittain, John 1935- *St&PR 91*
Brittain, John A. 1937- *St&PR 91*
Brittain, Miller G *WhoAmA 91N*
Brittain, Rasa 1960- *WhoWrEP 89*
Brittain, Rex Boyd, Jr. 1937- *St&PR 91*
Brittain, Robert Dewey, III *BiDrAPA 89*
Brittain, Robert Dewey, Jr. 1925- *BiDrAPA 89*
Brittain, Ross 1951- *WhoE 91*
Brittain, Vera 1893-1970 *BioIn 16, FemiCLE, MajTwCW*
Brittain, William 1930- *ConAu 30NR, TwCCr&M 91*
Brittain, William E. 1930- *WhoWrEP 89*
Brittan, Leon 1939- *WhoWor 91*
Brittan, Patrick John 1958- *WhoEmL 91*
Britten, Benjamin 1913-1976 *BioIn 16, PenDiMP A, WorAlBi*
Britten, Emma Hardinge 1823-1899 *EncO&P 3*
Britten, Gerald Hallbeck 1930- *WhoAm 90*
Britten, Roy John 1919- *WhoAm 90*
Britten, William Harry 1921- *WhoWor 91*
Brittenham, Raymond Lee 1916- *WhoAm 90*
Britting, Paula Moore 1939- *WhoE 91*
Britting, Robert Joseph 1948- *WhoE 91*
Brittingham, Barbara Elizabeth 1945- *WhoEmL 91*
Brittingham, David Louis 1959- *WhoEmL 91*
Britton, Alice Faye 1952- *WhoAmW 91*
Britton, Alison *PenDiDA 89*
Britton, Allen Perdue 1914- *IntWWM 90*
Britton, Barbara Ann 1959- *WhoAmW 91*
Britton, Charles P., III 1939- *WhoAm 90*
Britton, Charles Price, III 1939- *St&PR 91*
Britton, Clarold Lawrence 1932- *WhoAm 90*
Britton, Daniel Robert 1949- *WhoAmA 91*
Britton, David 1945- *IntWWM 90*
Britton, David Carl 1946- *WhoEmL 91*
Britton, Dennis Anthony 1940- *BioIn 16*
Britton, Donald W. 1948- *WhoAm 90*
Britton, Donald Wayne 1948- *St&PR 91*
Britton, Edward Charles 1955- *WhoE 91*
Britton, Elizabeth Gertrude Knight 1858-1934 *WomFie*
Britton, Erwin Adelbert 1915- *WhoAm 90*
Britton, Harrell N. 1923- *St&PR 91*
Britton, Harry 1879-1958 *WhoAmA 91N*
Britton, James, II 1915-1983 *WhoAmA 91N*
Britton, James Edward 1946- *WhoEmL 91*
Britton, James N. *BioIn 16*
Britton, Janet Lorene 1947- *WhoWrEP 89*
Britton, Jim 1944- *Ballpl 90*
Britton, Joanne Hess *WhoE 91*
Britton, Joanne Marie 1950- *WhoEmL 91*
Britton, John E. 1921- *St&PR 91*
Britton, Laurence George 1951- *WhoSSW 91*
Britton, Lucy Ann Jeanne 1957- *WhoE 91*
Britton, Marguerite Ann 1937- *WhoAmW 91*
Britton, Marla Lynn 1960- *WhoAmW 91*
Britton, Melvin Creed, Jr. 1935- *WhoAm 90*
Britton, Richard L. *St&PR 91*
Britton, Richard Lindsay 1949- *WhoAm 90*
Britton, Robert A. 1946- *St&PR 91*
Britton, Robert Eugene 1924- *St&PR 91*
Britton, Scott Richard 1960- *WhoEmL 91*
Britton, Thomas C. 1919- *WhoSSW 91*
Britton, Verla Deane 1960- *WhoEmL 91*
Britton, William G. 1929- *St&PR 91*
Britton-Riley, Deborah Alexis 1953- *WhoE 91*
Britts, William Carlyle 1932- *St&PR 91*
Britvec, Kamela *BioIn 16*
Britz, Diane Edward 1952- *WhoAmW 91, WhoE 91, WhoEmL 91, WhoWor 91*
Brix, Kelley Ann 1952- *WhoE 91*
Brixen, Martin Gerald 1927- *WhoAm 90*
Brixey, Stephen S., Jr. 1936- *St&PR 91*
Brixner, Steven 1946- *BioIn 16*
Brizek, Robert *St&PR 91*
Brizendine, Louann 1952- *BiDrAPA 89*
Brizendine, Lyle W. 1952- *St&PR 91*
Brizer, David Allen 1953- *BiDrAPA 89*
Brizgys, Vincentas 1903- *BioIn 16*
Brizola, Leonel de Moura 1922- *BioIn 16*
Brizzi, Aldo 1960- *IntWWM 90*
Brizzolara, Bruce J. 1942- *St&PR 91*
Brizzolara, Charles Anthony 1929- *WhoAm 90*
Brizzolara, Marco Aurelio 1922- *St&PR 91*
Brkich, Josephine C *BiDrAPA 89*
Brlic-Ma'uranic, Ivana 1874-1938 *EncCoWW*
Bro, Harmon Hartzell 1919- *EncO&P 3*
Broaca, Johnny 1909- *Ballpl 90*
Broach, Rolland F *BiDrAPA 89*
Broad, C D 1889-1971 *EncO&P 3*
Broad, Charlie Dunbar 1887-1971 *EncPaPR 91*
Broad, David Martin 1947- *St&PR 91*
Broad, Edward M. 1921- *St&PR 91*
Broad, Eli *BioIn 16*
Broad, Eli 1933- *St&PR 91, WhoAm 90, WhoAmA 91, WhoWor 91*
Broad, Michael 1951- *WhoEmL 91*
Broadbent, Amalia Sayo Castillo 1956- *WhoAmW 91*
Broadbent, Edward *BioIn 16*
Broadbent, Edward Granville 1923- *WhoWor 91*
Broadbent, J. Streett 1942- *WhoE 91*
Broadbent, Peter Edwin, Jr. 1951- *WhoEmL 91*
Broadbent, Thomas Ray 1921- *WhoAm 90*
Broadbent, Thomas V. 1935- *St&PR 91*
Broadbent, Thomas Valentine 1935- *WhoAm 90*
Broadcorens, Yvonne Ramaut 1905- *WhoWrEP 89*
Broadd, Harry Andrew 1910- *WhoAmA 91N*
Broaddus, Charles David 1930- *St&PR 91, WhoAm 90*
Broaddus, John Alfred 1939- *St&PR 91*
Broaddus, Robert Lewis 1935- *WhoAm 90*
Broadfoot, Albert Lyle 1930- *WhoAm 90*
Broadhead, Alan John 1938- *BiDrAPA 89*
Broadhead, Daniel David 1943- *BiDrAPA 89*
Broadhead, James Lowell 1935- *St&PR 91, WhoSSW 91*
Broadhead, Lesa Rogers 1956- *WhoAmW 91*
Broadhead, Mark Hall 1958- *BiDrAPA 89*
Broadhurst, Austin 1917- *St&PR 91, WhoAm 90*
Broadhurst, Austin, Jr. 1947- *WhoEmL 91, WhoWor 91*
Broadhurst, Jerome A. 1945- *St&PR 91*
Broadhurst, Jerome Anthony 1945- *WhoAm 90*
Broadhurst, Norman Neil 1946- *WhoEmL 91*
Broadhurst, William C. 1939- *BioIn 16*
Broadhurst, William D. 1950- *St&PR 91*
Broadley, Hugh T 1922- *WhoAmA 91*
Broadstock, Brenton Thomas 1952- *IntWWM 90*
Broadus, James Matthew 1947- *WhoE 91*
Broadus, John Albert 1827-1895 *BioIn 16*
Broadus, Joseph Edward 1946- *WhoEmL 91, WhoSSW 91, WhoWor 91*
Broadus, Martha Jane 1928- *WhoSSW 91*
Broadwater, James E. 1945- *WhoAm 90, WhoE 91*
Broadwater, John Ralph, Jr. 1955- *WhoSSW 91*
Broadwater, Shirley Marie 1937- *WhoAmW 91*
Broadway, Eric Stark *BiDrAPA 89*
Broadway, Nancy Ruth 1946- *WhoAmW 91, WhoWor 91*
Broadway, Rosemary 1947- *WhoSSW 91*
Broadway, Roxanne Meyer 1951- *WhoAmW 91*
Broadwell, Martin M. *BioIn 16*
Broadwell, Milton Edward 1938- *WhoSSW 91, WhoWor 91*
Broadwin, Joseph Louis 1930- *St&PR 91, WhoAm 90*
Broady, Roger Derek 1947- *WhoWor 91*
Broas, Donald Sanford 1940- *WhoAm 90*
Brobeck, John Raymond 1914- *WhoAm 90*
Brobeck, John Thomas 1953- *IntWWM 90*
Brobeck, Stephen James 1944- *WhoAm 90*
Broberg, Jack McLane 1920- *St&PR 91*
Broberg, Pete 1950- *Ballpl 90*
Brobst, Vernon D. 1943- *St&PR 91*
Brobst, William Keplinger 1928- *WhoWrEP 89*
Broca, Laurent Antoine 1928- *WhoWor 91*
Broca, Philippe de 1933- *BioIn 16*
Brocard, Philippe Joseph *PenDiDA 89*
Brocato, Joseph Myron 1917- *WhoAm 90*
Brocchini, Ronald Gene 1929- *WhoAm 90*
Broccoli, Albert Romolo 1909- *WhoAm 90, WhoWor 91*
Broccoli, Louis Viscardo 1931- *St&PR 91*
Broce, Domiciano G, Jr. 1926- *BiDrAPA 89*
Broch, Lawrence Randolph 1955- *WhoEmL 91*
Brocheler, John 1945- *IntWWM 90*
Brocher, Tobias H 1917- *BiDrAPA 89*
Broches, Aron 1914- *WhoAm 90*
Brochstein, Samuel J. 1906- *St&PR 91*
Brochu, Andre 1942- *WhoAm 90, WhoWrEP 89*
Brochu, Lise 1945- *BiDrAPA 89*
Brochu, Michel *BiDrAPA 89*
Brock, Alice May 1941- *WhoAm 90*
Brock, Betty 1923- *AuBYP 90*
Brock, Beverly Eugenie 1950- *WhoAmW 91*
Brock, Brenda Gail 1950- *WhoAmW 91*
Brock, Charles Lawrence 1943- *WhoAm 90, WhoE 91, WhoWor 91*
Brock, Dan Willets 1937- *WhoAm 90*
Brock, David Allen 1936- *WhoAm 90, WhoE 91*
Brock, Doyle Lee, Jr. 1948- *BiDrAPA 89*
Brock, Ealy Harris 1941- *St&PR 91*
Brock, Edwin 1927- *ConAu 130*
Brock, Eleanor 1921- *ConAu 130*
Brock, Emma Lillian 1886-1974 *AuBYP 90*
Brock, Frank Edgar 1932- *St&PR 91*
Brock, Gerald W. *BioIn 16*
Brock, Gerald Wayne 1948- *WhoAm 90*
Brock, Greg 1957- *Ballpl 90*
Brock, Harry B., Jr. 1926- *St&PR 91*
Brock, Harry Blackwell, Jr. 1926- *WhoAm 90*
Brock, Hope D. *BioIn 16*
Brock, Horace Rhea 1927- *ConAu 33NR, WhoAm 90*
Brock, Irvin Pete, III *BiDrAPA 89*
Brock, Isaac 1769-1812 *WhNaAH*
Brock, James Daniel 1916- *WhoAm 90, WhoWor 91*
Brock, James Gerald 1951- *WhoSSW 91*
Brock, James Hassel 1941- *St&PR 91*
Brock, James Robert 1944- *WhoAm 90*
Brock, James Rush 1931- *WhoAm 90*
Brock, James Sidney 1913- *St&PR 91, WhoAm 90*
Brock, Jayne 1959- *WhoWrEP 89*
Brock, Jeffrey Stewart 1950- *WhoSSW 91*
Brock, Jim *BioIn 16*
Brock, John David 1944- *St&PR 91*
Brock, John Grove 1959- *WhoSSW 91*
Brock, John M. 1913- *St&PR 91*
Brock, John Malcolm, Jr. 1948- *St&PR 91*
Brock, Judith Anne 1950- *WhoAmW 91, WhoWor 91*
Brock, Karena Diane 1942- *WhoAm 90*
Brock, Katherine Middleton 1938- *WhoAmW 91*
Brock, Kathy Thomas 1945- *WhoEmL 91*
Brock, Kenneth James *BiDrAPA 89*
Brock, Lawrence Ephraim 1913- *St&PR 91*
Brock, Lonnie R. 1950- *St&PR 91*
Brock, Lonnie Rex 1950- *WhoEmL 91*
Brock, Lorena Rowan 1921- *St&PR 91*
Brock, Lou 1939- *Ballpl 90 [port], WorAlBi*
Brock, Louis Clark 1939- *WhoAm 90*
Brock, Lynmar, Jr. 1934- *St&PR 91*
Brock, Marilyn Amy 1957- *WhoEmL 91*
Brock, Mark *ODwPR 91*
Brock, Mary Anne 1932- *WhoAmW 91*
Brock, Mitchell 1927- *WhoAm 90, WhoWor 91*
Brock, Morris Milton 1929- *BiDrAPA 89*
Brock, Nancy Carol 1961- *WhoSSW 91*
Brock, Paul Warrington 1928- *WhoAm 90*
Brock, Randall J. 1943- *WhoWrEP 89*
Brock, Randolph David, III 1943- *St&PR 91*
Brock, Raymond Theodore 1927- *WhoSSW 91*
Brock, Richard Linton 1945- *WhoEmL 91*
Brock, Robert Lee 1924- *WhoAm 90*
Brock, Robert W 1936- *WhoAmA 91*
Brock, Stanton G. 1908- *St&PR 91*
Brock, Suanne 1962- *WhoSSW 91*
Brock, Thomas Dale 1926- *WhoAm 90*
Brock, Virginia *AuBYP 90*
Brock, William Allen, III 1941- *WhoAm 90*
Brock, William E. *ODwPR 91*
Brock, William Emerson 1930- *WhoAm 90, WhoWor 91*
Brock, William Emerson, III 1930- *BiDrUSE 89*
Brock, William George 1928- *WhoAm 90*
Brock-Nelson, Linda Louise 1942- *WhoWor 91*
Brocka, Bruce 1959- *WhoEmL 91*
Brockardt, John I. 1949- *St&PR 91*
Brockbank, Philip 1922-1989 *ConAu 129*
Brockbank, Thomas W *BiDrAPA 89*
Brockbank, W Reed 1923- *BiDrAPA 89*
Brockelsby, Lyle Gerald 1906- *St&PR 91*
Brockenbrough, Barry W. 1934- *St&PR 91*
Brockenbrough, Henry Watkins 1923- *WhoAm 90*
Brocker, Sandra Lee Potish 1947- *WhoAmW 91*
Brockert, Kenneth Harold 1951- *WhoSSW 91*
Brocket, Charles Ronald George Nall-Cain 1952- *BioIn 16*
Brockett, Oscar Gross 1923- *WhoAm 90, WhoWrEP 89*
Brockett, Peter Charles 1946- *WhoAm 90*
Brockett, Roger Ware 1938- *WhoAm 90, WhoE 91*
Brockhard, Douglas Lee 1947- *St&PR 91*
Brockhaus, Klaus 1933- *WhoWor 91*
Brockhaus, Robert Herold, Sr. 1940- *WhoWor 91*
Brockhaus, Wilhelm Bernhard 1923- *WhoWor 91*
Brockhaus, William Dillon 1945- *WhoWor 91*
Brockhouse, Bertram Neville 1918- *WhoAm 90*
Brockie, Donald Peter 1931- *St&PR 91*
Brockington, Donald Leslie 1929- *WhoAm 90*
Brockington, Howard Burnell 1922- *WhoE 91*
Brockless, Brian 1926- *IntWWM 90*
Brockman, Ann *BiDEWW*
Brockman, Daniel David *BioIn 16, NewYTBS 90*
Brockman, David D 1922- *BiDrAPA 89*
Brockman, Donald Charles 1942- *St&PR 91*
Brockman, Jeffrey Lloyd 1954- *WhoSSW 91*
Brockman, Katherine G *BiDrAPA 89*
Brockman, Keith W. 1944- *St&PR 91*
Brockman, Leslie Richard 1940- *WhoSSW 91*
Brockman, Lynn *ODwPR 91*
Brockman, Murray Wilson 1945- *WhoSSW 91*
Brockman, Ronald E. 1941- *St&PR 91*
Brockman, Shirley Blow 1950- *WhoSSW 91*
Brockman, Terry James 1955- *WhoEmL 91*
Brockmann, Helen Jane 1947- *WhoAmW 91*
Brockmann, S.E. 1928- *St&PR 91*
Brockmeyer, John D. *NewYTBS 90*
Brockner-Brower, Nora *BiDrAPA 89*
Brocksbank, Robert Wayne 1924- *WhoWor 91*
Brockschmidt, Henry F. 1920- *St&PR 91*
Brockunier, Craig 1956- *BiDrAPA 89*
Brockway, Lord 1888-1988 *AnObit 1988*
Brockway, Duncan 1932- *WhoAm 90*
Brockway, Fenner 1888-1988 *BioIn 16*
Brockway, George Pond 1915- *WhoAm 90*
Brockway, Laurie Sue 1956- *WhoAmW 91, WhoEmL 91*
Brockway, Lexie *ODwPR 91*
Brockway, Merrill LaMonte 1923- *WhoAm 90*
Brockway, Peter Craig 1956- *St&PR 91, WhoSSW 91*
Brockway, Stephen Swift *BiDrAPA 89*
Brockway, William Robert 1924- *WhoAm 90*
Brockwell, Charles Wilbur, Jr. 1937- *WhoAm 90*
Brockwell, John William, Jr. 1953- *WhoEmL 91*
Brod, Albert Thomas 1913- *St&PR 91*
Brod, Daniel 1959- *WhoEmL 91*
Brod, Harold J. 1912- *St&PR 91*
Brod, Irven J. 1909- *St&PR 91*
Brod, Michael L. 1945- *St&PR 91*
Brod, Morton Shlevin 1926- *WhoAm 90*
Brod, Stanford 1932- *WhoAm 90, WhoAmA 91*
Brod, Thomas Marcy 1942- *BiDrAPA 89*
Broda, Frederick Charles 1937- *St&PR 91*
Broda, Martine 1947- *EncCoWW*
Brodal, Jon Eilif 1911- *IntWWM 90*
Brodaty, Henry 1947- *BiDrAPA 89*
Brodaty, Yves Jacques 1944- *WhoWor 91*
Brodbeck, Charles Richard 1949- *WhoEmL 91*
Brodbeck, John Friedrich 1960- *WhoE 91*
Brodbeck, L. Emma 1893?-1989 *ConAu 130*
Brodbeck, Nancy Elizabeth 1962- *WhoAmW 91*
Brodbeck, Sharon Kay 1956- *WhoEmL 91*
Brodbeck, William Jan 1944- *St&PR 91*
Brodber, Erna 1940- *FemiCLE*
Brode, Howard S *BiDrAPA 89*
Brode, Marvin Jay 1931- *WhoAm 90*
Brode, Marvin M *BiDrAPA 89*
Brode, Patrick 1950- *ConAu 132*
Brode, Wallace Reed 1900-1974 *DcScB S2*
Brodecki, Joseph Michael 1946- *WhoEmL 91*
Brodeen, Carol Ann 1945- *WhoE 91*
Brodehl, Johannes 1931- *WhoWor 91*
Brodel, Vittorio *PenDiDA 89*
Brodell, Albert P. 1923- *St&PR 91*
Broden, Alexander R 1932- *BiDrAPA 89*
Broder, Aaron J. 1924- *WhoAm 90*
Broder, Bruce *BioIn 16*
Broder, Cliff 1948- *St&PR 91*

Broder, David S. BioIn 16
Broder, David Salzer 1929- WhoAm 90, WhoE 91, WhoWrEP 89
Broder, Donald S 1937- BiDrAPA 89
Broder, Jerry 1927- St&PR 91
Broder, Judith T BiDrAPA 89
Broder, Martin Ivan 1936- WhoE 91
Broder, Patricia Janis 1935- WhoAm 90, WhoAmA 91, WhoAmW 91
Broder, Samuel WhoAm 90
Broder, Samuel B 1901- BiDrAPA 89
Broderick, Anthony James 1943- WhoAm 90
Broderick, Carlfred Bartholomew 1932- WhoAm 90, WhoWor 91
Broderick, Cathy BioIn 16
Broderick, David 1942- BiDrAPA 89
Broderick, Dorothy M. 1929- AuBYP 90
Broderick, Edward Michael, III 1947- WhoEmL 91
Broderick, Ellen Jones 1921- WhoE 91
Broderick, Francis Lyons 1922- WhoAm 90
Broderick, Gerald BioIn 16
Broderick, Gertrude Catherine Creedon 1926- WhoAmW 91
Broderick, Grace Nolan WhoE 91
Broderick, Harold Christian 1925- WhoWor 91
Broderick, Helen 1891-1959 OxCPMus
Broderick, Herbert Reginald, III 1945- WhoAmA 91
Broderick, James Allen 1939- WhoAmA 91
Broderick, James Anthony 1943- St&PR 91
Broderick, John 1927-1989 AnObit 1989
Broderick, John 1935- St&PR 91
Broderick, John Caruthers 1926- WhoAm 90, WhoWrEP 89
Broderick, Laurence Paul 1923- St&PR 91
Broderick, Matthew BioIn 16
Broderick, Matthew 1962- WhoAm 90, WorAlBi
Broderick, Patricia Catherine 1947- WhoAmW 91
Broderick, Richard 1949- BioIn 16
Broderick, Richard James 1921- St&PR 91
Broderick, Robert L. 1911- St&PR 91
Broderick, Vincent Lyons 1920- WhoAm 90, WhoE 91
Broderick-Cantwell, John J BiDrAPA 89
Brodersen, Arthur James 1939- WhoAm 90
Broderson, Joe Thomas 1947- BiDrAPA 89
Broderson, Morris 1928- WhoAm 90, WhoAmA 91
Broderson, Robert 1920- WhoAmA 91
Brodetsky, Selig 1888-1954 BioIn 16
Brodeur, Alphonse Toner 1902- St&PR 91, WhoAm 90
Brodeur, Alphonse William H. 1931- WhoAm 90
Brodeur, Armand Edward 1922- WhoAm 90
Brodeur, J.H. 1932- St&PR 91
Brodeur, Jeanne Marie 1950- WhoSSW 91
Brodeur, John Anthony BiDrAPA 89
Brodeur, Ruth Wallace- 1941- BioIn 16
Brodey, Adrian 1911-1990 BioIn 16
Brodey, James F BiDrAPA 89
Brodey, Jim 1942- WhoWrEP 89
Brodey, Joshua B 1932- BiDrAPA 89
Brodhead, David Crawmer 1934- WhoAm 90, WhoE 91, WhoWor 91
Brodhead, George Milton 1904- WhoAm 90
Brodhead, Quita WhoAmA 91, WhoE 91
Brodhead, William McNulty 1941- WhoAm 90
Brodhurst, Albert Edward 1934- WhoE 91
Brodie, Agnes Hahn 1924- WhoAmA 91
Brodie, Bernard B. BioIn 16
Brodie, Bernard B. 1909-1989 AnObit 1989
Brodie, Christina Oakley 1951- WhoEmL 91
Brodie, Donald G. 1938- St&PR 91
Brodie, Donald Gibbs 1938- WhoAm 90
Brodie, Elizabeth BiDrAPA 89
Brodie, Fawn McKay 1915-1981 BioIn 16
Brodie, Gandy 1924-1975 WhoAmA 91N
Brodie, H Keith H 1939- BiDrAPA 89
Brodie, Harlow Keith Hammond 1939- WhoAm 90, WhoSSW 91, WhoWor 91
Brodie, Harold Johnston 1907-1988 BioIn 16
Brodie, Howard 1915- WhoAm 90, WhoWor 91
Brodie, Jonathan D 1938- BiDrAPA 89
Brodie, M. J. 1936- WhoAm 90
Brodie, Norman 1920- WhoAm 90
Brodie, Owen W BiDrAPA 89
Brodie, Paul 1934- IntWWM 90
Brodie, Regis Conrad 1942- WhoAmA 91
Brodie, Robert G. 1931- St&PR 91
Brodie, Steve 1868-1935 Ballpl 90
Brodie-Innes, J W 1848-1923 EncO&P 3
Brodin, Pierre Eugene 1909- AuBYP 90
Brodin-Ahlin, Katarina 1934- WhoWor 91
Brodine, Charles Edward 1925- WhoAm 90, WhoWor 91
Brodkey, Amy Catherine 1949- BiDrAPA 89, WhoE 91
Brodkey, Harold BioIn 16
Brodkey, Harold 1930- WorAu 1980 [port]
Brodkey, Harold Roy 1930- WhoAm 90
Brodkey, M. Ronald 1936- St&PR 91
Brodkey, Robert Stanley 1928- WhoAm 90
Brodkin, A. Keith 1935- St&PR 91
Brodkin, Adele Ruth Meyer 1934- WhoAmW 91
Brodkin, Alan Keith 1935- WhoAm 90, WhoE 91, WhoWor 91
Brodkin, Herbert NewYTBS 90 [port]
Brodkin, Herbert Harrison BioIn 16
Brodl, Raymond Frank 1924- WhoAm 90
Brodman, Estelle 1914- WhoAm 90, WhoAmW 91
Brodnax, Huey Wayne 1936- WhoSSW 91
Brodnax, Janis Browning 1945- WhoSSW 91
Brodnax, Margaret O'Bryan 1932- WhoAmW 91
Brodnik, Carl Joseph, Jr. 1949- WhoEmL 91
Brodovitch, Alexey 1898-1971 BioIn 16, ConDes 90
Brodovsky, Sue WhoWrEP 89
Brodowski, Dick 1932- Ballpl 90
Brodribb, Gerald 1915- ConAu 33NR
Brodrick, Lois Hunter 1920- WhoAmW 91
Brodsky Quartet PenDiMP
Brodsky, Adolph 1851-1929 PenDiMP
Brodsky, Arthur James 1946- WhoEmL 91
Brodsky, Bernard BiDrAPA 89
Brodsky, Bernard Steven 1939- St&PR 91
Brodsky, Carroll M BiDrAPA 89
Brodsky, Clifford St&PR 91
Brodsky, David M. 1943- WhoAm 90
Brodsky, Eugene V 1946- WhoAmA 91
Brodsky, Gregory BiDrAPA 89
Brodsky, Harry 1908- WhoAmA 91, WhoE 91
Brodsky, Iosif Alexandrovich 1940- MajTwCW, WhoAm 90, WhoE 91, WhoWor 91, WhoWrEP 89
Brodsky, Irving 1915- WhoE 91
Brodsky, Irwin Abel 1910- WhoAm 90
Brodsky, John Putnam 1930- WhoAm 90
Brodsky, Joseph MajTwCW
Brodsky, Joseph 1889-1947 EncAL
Brodsky, Joseph 1940- BioIn 16, WorAlBi
Brodsky, Judith Kapstein 1933- WhoAmA 91
Brodsky, Julian BioIn 16
Brodsky, Julian A. 1933- St&PR 91
Brodsky, Lewis 1942- BiDrAPA 89
Brodsky, Marc Herbert 1938- WhoAm 90
Brodsky, Norman BioIn 16
Brodsky, Philip Hyman 1942- WhoAm 90
Brodsky, Robert Fox 1925- WhoAm 90
Brodsky, Samuel 1912- WhoAm 90
Brodsky, Stan 1925- WhoAmA 91
Brodsky, Stanley 1925- WhoE 91
Brodsky, Stanley II BiDrAPA 89
Brodsky, Stuart Lee 1942- WhoE 91
Brodsky, William J. 1944- St&PR 91, WhoAm 90
Brodszky, Nicholas 1905-1958 OxCPMus
Brodt, John D. 1954- St&PR 91
Brody, Aaron Leo 1930- WhoAm 90, WhoE 91
Brody, Alan 1952- BiDrAPA 89
Brody, Alan Jeffrey 1952- WhoAm 90
Brody, Alexander 1933- St&PR 91, WhoAm 90
Brody, Alfred Walter 1920- WhoAm 90
Brody, Anita Blumstein 1935- WhoAmW 91
Brody, Arthur 1920- WhoAm 90
Brody, Arthur William 1943- WhoAmA 91
Brody, Bernard B. 1922- WhoAm 90
Brody, Blanche WhoAmA 91
Brody, Carol BioIn 16
Brody, Charles M 1917- BiDrAPA 89
Brody, Christopher W. WhoE 91
Brody, Christopher W. 1944- St&PR 91
Brody, Clark Louis 1914- WhoAm 90
Brody, David Allan 1916- WhoWor 91
Brody, David M BiDrAPA 89
Brody, David W 1957- BiDrAPA 89
Brody, Doug NewAgMG
Brody, Elaine 1923- WhoWor 91
Brody, Eugene B 1921- BiDrAPA 89, WhoAm 90
Brody, Eugene David 1931- WhoAm 90
Brody, Gerald L 1932- BiDrAPA 89
Brody, Harold 1923- WhoAm 90
Brody, Harry Philip 1952- WhoWrEP 89
Brody, J J 1929- ConAu 32NR
Brody, Jacob Allan 1931- WhoAm 90
Brody, Jacob Jerome 1929- WhoAmA 91
Brody, Jacqueline 1932- WhoAm 90, WhoAmA 91, WhoWrEP 89
Brody, James Patrick 1920- WhoAm 90
Brody, Jane E. 1941- WorAlBi
Brody, Jane Ellen 1941- WhoAm 90, WhoAmW 91, WhoE 91, WhoWrEP 89
Brody, Karen Howard 1949- BiDrAPA 89
Brody, Lynne M 1946- BiDrAPA 89
Brody, Margaret W BiDrAPA 89
Brody, Martin 1921- St&PR 91
Brody, Mary Jill 1951- WhoSSW 91
Brody, Matt NewAgMG
Brody, Matthew 1911- BiDrAPA 89
Brody, Michael 1940- BiDrAPA 89
Brody, Morris W 1908- BiDrAPA 89
Brody, Morris Wolf 1908- WhoE 91
Brody, Myron Roy 1940- WhoAmA 91
Brody, Nancy Louise 1954- WhoAmW 91, WhoE 91, WhoEmL 91, WhoSSW 91
Brody, Neville 1957- BioIn 16
Brody, Richard David 1952- WhoEmL 91
Brody, Robert 1925- St&PR 91
Brody, Ruth 1917- WhoAmA 91
Brody, Samuel 1890-1956 BioIn 16
Brody, Samuel Mandell 1926- WhoAm 90
Brody, Saul Nathaniel 1938- WhoAm 90
Brody, Stephen J. 1946- St&PR 91
Brody, Theodore Meyer 1920- WhoAm 90
Brodzinski, James Donald 1950- WhoSSW 91
Broecker, Howard William 1940- WhoAm 90
Broecker, Theodore J. 1929- St&PR 91
Broecker, Wallace S. 1931- WhoAm 90
Broederlam, Melchior 13--?-1409? IntDcAA 90
Broeffle, William C. 1931- St&PR 91
Broeg, Bob 1918- Ballpl 90, WhoAm 90
Broege, Peter Jonathan 1952- WhoEmL 91
Broege, Timothy David 1947- IntWWM 90
Broehl, Wayne Gottlieb, Jr. 1922- WhoAm 90
Broek, Henri Van Den 1936- WhoWor 91
Broekel, Rainer Lothar AuBYP 90
Broekel, Ray 1923- AuBYP 90
Broeker, John Milton 1940- WhoAm 90
Broelsch, Christoph Erich 1944- WhoAm 90
Broene, Gilbert Richard 1948- WhoEmL 91
Broening, Gerald F. 1934- St&PR 91
Broer, Carleton G., Jr. 1933- St&PR 91
Broer, Eileen Dennery 1946- St&PR 91, WhoAmW 91
Broer, Roger L 1945- WhoAmA 91
Broering, Naomi Cordero 1929- WhoAm 90
Broers, Frederic Lynn 1945- St&PR 91
Broers, Kimberly Ann 1956- WhoAmW 91
Brofeldt, Johannes DcScanL
Brofferio, Angelo EncO&P 3
Brofman, Lance Mark 1949- WhoE 91
Brofman, Robert H 1935- BiDrAPA 89
Brofman, Woody 1935- WhoAm 90
Brog, David 1933- WhoAm 90
Brogan, Darryl Keefer 1947- WhoEmL 91
Brogan, Deborah Ann BiDrAPA 89
Brogan, Howard Oakley WhoAm 90
Brogan, James F. 1941- St&PR 91
Brogan, Michael J. 1945- ODwPR 91
Brogan, Rita 1951- WhoAmW 91
Brogan, Roy Alan 1940- St&PR 91
Brogan, Thomas Edward 1919- St&PR 91
Brogan, Thomas J. BioIn 16
Brogan-Werntz, Bonnie Bailey 1941- WhoAmW 91
Brogdon, Brenda Kay 1959- WhoAmW 91
Brogdon, Byron Gilliam 1929- WhoAm 90
Brogdon, Gary Alan 1948- WhoSSW 91
Brogdon, Harold F. 1923- St&PR 91
Brogger, Suzanne 1944- DcScanL, EncCoWW
Brogger, Suzanne Preis 1944- WhoWor 91
Broggi, Michael Joseph 1942- WhoWor 91
Brogla, Martha Leone 1955- WhoEmL 91
Brogliatti, Barbara 1946- ODwPR 91
Brogliatti, Barbara Spencer 1946- WhoAm 90, WhoAmW 91
Broglie, Jacques Victor Albert, duc de 1821-1901 BiDFrPL
Broglio, Ernie 1935- Ballpl 90
Brogna, Luanne Elizabeth 1957- WhoEmL 91
Brogno, August 1935- St&PR 91
Brohamer, Jack 1950- Ballpl 90
Brohamer, Tom BioIn 16
Brohammer, Richard Frederic 1934- WhoSSW 91
Brohaugh, William Edward 1953- WhoAm 90, WhoWrEP 89
Brohm, Winfried 1932- WhoWor 91
Brohou, Jean EncO&P 3
Broich, Larry D. 1943- St&PR 91
Broida, Helen WhoWrEP 89
Broida, Theodore R. 1928- St&PR 91
Broide, Mace Irwin 1924- WhoAm 90
Broido, Arnold Peace 1920- IntWWM 90, St&PR 91, WhoAm 90
Broido, Lucy 1924- WhoAmA 91
Broihahn, Michael Allen 1948- WhoWor 91
Broiles, Rowland David 1938- WhoSSW 91
Broin, Kenneth Edwin 1924- St&PR 91
Broin, Mark Stuart 1945- St&PR 91, WhoEmL 91
Broitman, Selwyn Arthur 1931- WhoAm 90
Brokate, Brian William 1954- WhoEmL 91
Brokaw, Charles Jacob 1934- WhoAm 90
Brokaw, Clifford V., III 1928- St&PR 91
Brokaw, Clifford Vail, III 1928- WhoAm 90, WhoWor 91
Brokaw, Donald C. 1929- St&PR 91
Brokaw, James Albert, II 1951- IntWWM 90
Brokaw, Norman Robert 1927- WhoAm 90
Brokaw, R. Miriam 1917- WhoWrEP 89
Brokaw, Thomas John 1940- WhoAm 90, WhoE 91
Brokaw, Tom BioIn 16
Brokaw, Tom 1940- WorAlBi
Brokenbough, Willa Mae 1921- WhoWor 91
Broker, Karin 1950- WhoAmA 91
Brokl, Thomas Raymond 1948- WhoEmL 91
Brokmeier, Willi 1928- IntWWM 90
Brokowsky, Stuart Harvey 1948- St&PR 91
Brolin, James 1942- WorAlBi
Brolley, Maria BiDrAPA 89
Brom, Libor 1923- WhoAm 90, WhoWor 91
Bromage, William Thomas 1946- St&PR 91
Broman, Keith Leroy 1922- WhoAm 90
Broman, Robert Alan 1951- WhoAm 90
Bromberg, Alan Robert 1928- WhoAm 90, WhoSSW 91, WhoWor 91
Bromberg, Albert M 1932- BiDrAPA 89
Bromberg, Albert Marvin 1932- WhoE 91
Bromberg, Carl David 1957- WhoSSW 91
Bromberg, Craig 1958- WhoEmL 91
Bromberg, Faith 1919- WhoAmA 91
Bromberg, Frank M. St&PR 91
Bromberg, Frank Wallace, Jr. 1955- St&PR 91
Bromberg, Henri Louie, Jr. 1911- WhoAm 90
Bromberg, John E. 1946- WhoAm 90
Bromberg, Myron James 1934- WhoAm 90
Bromberg, Norbert 1906-1988 BioIn 16
Bromberg, Philip Allan 1930- WhoAm 90
Bromberg, Robert 1921- WhoAm 90
Bromberg, Robert Sheldon 1935- WhoAm 90
Bromberg, Walter 1900- BiDrAPA 89, WhoAm 90
Brombert, Victor H 1923- WorAu 1980 [port]
Brombert, Victor Henri 1923- WhoAm 90, WhoWrEP 89
Brome, Richard BioIn 16
Brome, Robert Harrison 1911- WhoAm 90
Bromeley, Robert B. 1910- St&PR 91
Bromelkamp, Michael Louis 1953- WhoEmL 91
Bromenshenk, Gail Lucille 1944- WhoAmW 91
Bromery, Randolph Wilson 1926- WhoAm 90, WhoE 91
Bromet, Evelyn June 1944- WhoAmW 91
Bromfield, Louis 1896-1956 BioIn 16, WorAlBi
Bromhal, Robert L. 1940- St&PR 91
Bromige, David M. 1933- WhoWrEP 89
Bromley, Alan ODwPR 91
Bromley, Albert W. 1911-1987 BioIn 16
Bromley, D. Allan 1926- BioIn 16
Bromley, Daniel Wood 1940- WhoAm 90
Bromley, David Allan 1926- BioIn 16, WhoAm 90
Bromley, Dudley 1948- BioIn 16
Bromley, Edward Neal 1936- St&PR 91, WhoAm 90
Bromley, Eliza FemiCLE
Bromley, James Hancock 1938- St&PR 91
Bromley, John W. 1927-1990 BioIn 16
Bromley, Michael 1948- WhoWor 91
Bromley, Richard H. 1940- St&PR 91
Bromley, Wayne Leon, Jr. 1951- St&PR 91, WhoAm 90, WhoEmL 91
Bromley, William PenDiDA 89
Bromley, Yulian Vladimirovich 1921-1990 ConAu 131
Bromm, Frederick Whittemore 1953- WhoEmL 91
Bromm, Hal 1947- WhoAmA 91
Bromm, Robert Dale 1950- WhoEmL 91
Bromm, Sarah Jean 1966- WhoAmW 91
Brommer, Gerald F 1927- WhoAmA 91, WhoWrEP 89
Brommer, Jere Joseph 1929- St&PR 91
Bromsen, Maury Austin 1919- WhoAm 90, WhoWor 91
Bromund, Cal E 1903-1979 WhoAmA 91N
Bron, Guillermo 1951- WhoHisp 91

Bron, Klaus Michael 1929- WhoAm 90
Bron, Robert Philip 1942- WhoAm 90
Bron, Walter Ernest 1930- WhoAm 90
Bronars, Joseph Charles, Jr. 1925- WhoE 91
Bronaugh, Edwin Lee 1932- WhoAm 90
Brondum, William Charles, Jr. 1919- St&PR 91
Broner, E. 1930- FemiCLE
Broner, E. M. BioIn 16
Broner, Herbert J. 1928- St&PR 91
Broner, Herbert Jordan 1928- WhoSSW 91
Broner, Mathew 1924- WhoAmA 91
Broner, Robert 1922- WhoAmA 91
Brones, Lynn A. 1954- WhoEmL 91
Bronfenbrenner, Martin 1914- BioIn 16
Bronfenbrenner, Urie 1917- BioIn 16
Bronfman Family BioIn 16
Bronfman, Charles Rosner 1931- St&PR 91, WhoAm 90, WhoE 91
Bronfman, Edgar M., Jr. BioIn 16
Bronfman, Edgar Miles 1929- St&PR 91, WhoAm 90, WhoE 91
Bronfman, Edward M. 1927- WhoAm 90
Bronfman, Peter Frederick 1929- WhoAm 90
Bronfman, Yefim 1958- BioIn 16, IntWWM 90
Brongniart, Alexandre PenDiDA 89
Bronheim, Benjamin E 1946- BiDrAPA 89
Bronheim, Harold E 1952- BiDrAPA 89, WhoE 91
Bronheim, Lester Allen 1932- BiDrAPA 89
Broniarek, Zygmunt 1925- WhoE 91
Bronis, Stephen J. 1947- WhoSSW 91
Bronk, Detlev W. 1897-1975 WorAlBi
Bronk, Detlev Wulf 1887-1975 DcScB S2
Bronk, John Ramsey 1929- WhoWor 91
Bronk, William 1918- WhoAm 90, WorAu 1980 [port]
Bronn, Leslie Joan Boyle 1948- WhoAmW 91
Bronner, Alfred BiDrAPA 89
Bronner, Edwin B 1920- WhoWrEP 89
Bronner, Edwin Blaine 1920- WhoAm 90
Bronner, Ellen Patricia 1954- WhoAmW 91
Bronner, Felix 1921- WhoAm 90
Bronner, Philip Robert BiDrAPA 89
Bronner, Stephen Eric 1949- ConAu 32NR
Bronner-Huszar, Judith BiDrAPA 89
Bronocco, Terri Lynn 1953- WhoAmW 91, WhoWor 91
Bronowski, Jacob 1908-1974 AuBYP 90, BioIn 16, WorAlBi
Bronsard, Joseph A. 1933- St&PR 91
Bronsberg-Adas, Thomas Joseph 1951- WhoEmL 91
Bronsdon, Melinda Ann 1940- WhoAmW 91
Bronski, Betty Jean 1952- WhoAmW 91
Bronski, Eugene William 1936- St&PR 91, WhoAm 90
Bronsky, Irving BiDrAPA 89
Bronson, A A 1946- WhoAmA 91
Bronson, Barbara June 1949- WhoEmL 91
Bronson, Charles WhoAm 90
Bronson, Charles 1920- BioIn 16
Bronson, Charles 1922- WorAlBi
Bronson, Claire Sekulski 1947- WhoAmW 91
Bronson, Clark Everice 1939- WhoAmA 91
Bronson, Daniel Braid 1943- St&PR 91
Bronson, Franklin H. 1932- WhoAm 90
Bronson, Frazier L. 1943- St&PR 91
Bronson, Henry D. 1935- St&PR 91
Bronson, Isaac 1760-1838 EncABHB 6 [port]
Bronson, Jill Ireland 1936-1990 ConAu 131
Bronson, Kenneth C. 1933- St&PR 91
Bronson, Kenneth Caldean 1933- WhoAm 90
Bronson, Kenneth P. 1951- St&PR 91
Bronson, Lynn AuBYP 90
Bronson, Lynwood F. 1932- IntWWM 90
Bronson, Miles 1812-1883 BioIn 16
Bronson, Millard E. 1928- St&PR 91
Bronson, Neal Barry 1948- WhoEmL 91
Bronson, Randolph Clifton 1944- WhoE 91
Bronson, Renee M. 1940- IntWWM 90
Bronson, Shael S 1921- BiDrAPA 89
Bronson, Wilfrid Swancourt 1894-1985 AuBYP 90
Bronson, William Howard, Jr. 1936- WhoAm 90, WhoSSW 91
Bronson, Wolfe WhoWrEP 89
Bronstad, Byron G. 1911- St&PR 91
Bronsteen, Peter 1954- WhoE 91
Bronstein, Aaron Jacob 1905- WhoAm 90
Bronstein, Arthur J. 1914- WhoAm 90
Bronstein, Carolyn BioIn 16
Bronstein, Gerald Morton 1927- St&PR 91
Bronstein, Glen Max 1960- WhoE 91, WhoEmL 91, WhoWor 91
Bronstein, Herman 1928- St&PR 91
Bronstein, Jeffrey Barry BiDrAPA 89
Bronstein, Leona Bartel 1932- WhoAmW 91
Bronstein, Melvin 1924- WhoE 91, WhoWor 91
Bronstein, Milton H 1924- BiDrAPA 89
Bronstein, Raphael BioIn 16
Bronstein, Toby J. 1951- WhoEmL 91
Bronston, Edythe Lee 1936- WhoAmW 91
Bronston, Walter Eshell 1927- St&PR 91
Bronstrup, C.R. 1933- St&PR 91
Bronte, Anne 1820-1849 BioIn 16, FemiCLE, WorAlBi
Bronte, Branwell 1817-1848 BioIn 16
Bronte, Charlotte 1816-1855 BioIn 16, FemiCLE, WorAlBi
Bronte, Emily 1818-1848 BioIn 16, FemiCLE, WorAlBi
Bronte, Louisa WhoWrEP 89
Bronte, Patrick Branwell 1817-1848 BioIn 16
Brontman, Manuel H BiDrAPA 89
Bronzina, Isabel Azucena 1948- WhoEmL 91
Bronzino, Il 1503-1572 WorAlBi
Bronzino, Agnolo 1503-1572 IntDcAA 90
Bronzino, Joseph Daniel 1937- WhoAm 90
Broo, Kenneth Richard 1924- St&PR 91
Broodthaers, Marcel 1924-1976 BioIn 16
Brook, Adrian Gibbs 1924- WhoAm 90
Brook, Alexander 1898-1980 WhoAmA 91N
Brook, Claire 1925- St&PR 91
Brook, David William 1936- BiDrAPA 89, WhoAm 90
Brook, Douglas Alan 1944- WhoAm 90
Brook, Gary Fred 1961- WhoEmL 91
Brook, Henry Wagner 1934- WhoAm 90, WhoWor 91
Brook, Judy 1926- BioIn 16
Brook, Marvin G 1924- BiDrAPA 89
Brook, Marx 1920- WhoAm 90
Brook, Mary 1726?-1782 FemiCLE
Brook, Michael NewAgMG
Brook, Peter 1925- BioIn 16, MajTwCW, WorAlBi
Brook, Robert Henry 1943- WhoAm 90
Brook, Scott Jonathan Bradley 1964- WhoSSW 91
Brook, Shelley Carolyn BiDrAPA 89
Brook, Susan G. 1949- WhoEmL 91
Brookbanks, Ian ODwPR 91
Brooke, Alan Francis 1883-1963 WorAlBi
Brooke, Amanda WhoWrEP 89
Brooke, Avery Rogers 1923- WhoAm 90, WhoWrEP 89
Brooke, Charlotte FemiCLE
Brooke, Charlotte 1740-1793 BioIn 16
Brooke, David Stopford 1931- WhoAm 90, WhoAmA 91
Brooke, Edward William 1919- WhoAm 90, WorAlBi
Brooke, Edward William, III 1919- BlkAmsC [port]
Brooke, Elizabeth 1601-1683 BiDEWW, FemiCLE
Brooke, Emma Frances 1845-1926 FemiCLE
Brooke, Frances 1724?-1789 BioIn 16, DcLB 99 [port], FemiCLE
Brooke, Francis John, III 1929- WhoAm 90
Brooke, Humphrey 1914-1988 AnObit 1988
Brooke, John Selwyn 1904-1978 BioIn 16
Brooke, Ken 1920-1983 BioIn 16
Brooke, Melissa BioIn 16
Brooke, Michael Howard 1938- WhoAm 90
Brooke, Patricia Cynthia 1953- WhoAmW 91
Brooke, Patrick Teal 1953- WhoEmL 91
Brooke, Pegan 1950- WhoAmA 91
Brooke, Peter Leonard 1934- WhoWor 91
Brooke, Ralph Ian 1934- WhoAm 90
Brooke, Richard, Jr. 1926- St&PR 91
Brooke, Rupert 1887-1915 BioIn 16, ConAu 132, MajTwCW
Brooke, Susan Rogers 1951- WhoEmL 91
Brooke, Thomas Herchmer 1926- St&PR 91
Brooke-Haven, P. ConAu 33NR, MajTwCW
Brooke-Rose, Christine 1923- BioIn 16, FemiCLE, WhoWor 91
Brookens, Tom 1953- Ballpl 90
Brooker, Bertram Richard 1888-1955 OxCCanT
Brooker, Eric Lionel 1927- St&PR 91
Brooker, Jewel Spears 1940- WhoSSW 91
Brooker, Lena Epps 1941- WhoSSW 91
Brooker, Marvin Adel 1903- WhoAm 90
Brooker, Patricia Lee 1956- WhoAmW 91, WhoEmL 91
Brooker, Robert E. 1905- St&PR 91
Brooker, Robert Elton 1905- WhoAm 90
Brooker, Rod 1946- ODwPR 91
Brooker, Susan Gay 1949- WhoAmW 91
Brooker, Thomas Kimball 1939- WhoAm 90
Brooker, Walter Eric 1916- WhoE 91, WhoWor 91
Brookes, Charles Erwin 1925- WhoAm 90
Brookes, Christopher 1943- OxCCanT
Brookes, Crittenden BiDrAPA 89
Brookes, Frank Julian 1949- WhoWor 91
Brookes, Martha BiDEWW
Brookes, Robert D 1913- BiDrAPA 89
Brookes, Valentine 1913- WhoAm 90
Brookes-Smith, Colin H. W. 1899-1982 EncPaPR 91
Brookfield, David Alan 1946- St&PR 91
Brookfield, Donald W. 1911- St&PR 91
Brookhart, John E. 1936- St&PR 91
Brookhart, John Mills 1913- WhoAm 90
Brookhart, Robert S. BioIn 16
Brookhuis, John G.K. 1921- St&PR 91
Brooking, E. Lynwood 1944- St&PR 91
Brooking, George Edward, Jr. 1925- WhoAm 90
Brooking, Robert 1813-1893 DcCanB 12
Brookings, Robert S. 1850-1932 WorAlBi
Brookings, Wilmot W. 1830-1905 AmLegL
Brookins, Carolyn Seman 1943- St&PR 91
Brookins, Douglas Gridley 1936- WhoAm 90, WhoWor 91
Brookins, Geraldine Kearse 1946- WhoAmW 91
Brookins, Jacob Boden 1935- WhoAmA 91
Brookins, James Robert 1942- WhoSSW 91
Brookins, Oscar Travis 1942- WhoE 91
Brookins, Phillip Johnson 1944- WhoSSW 91
Brooklere, Anna Maria WhoAmW 91, WhoSSW 91
Brooklere, Anthony John 1936- WhoSSW 91
Brookman, Anthony Raymond 1922- WhoWor 91
Brookman, Marilyn K. WhoAmW 91
Brookmeyer, Bob BioIn 16
Brookmeyer, Philip Robert 1954- WhoEmL 91
Brookner, Anita BioIn 16, WhoAm 90, WhoWor 91
Brookner, Anita 1938- FemiCLE, MajTwCW
Brookner, Eli 1931- WhoAm 90, WhoE 91
Brookner, Howard BioIn 16
Brookner, Jacalyn W 1945- WhoAmA 91, WhoE 91
Brookover, Barbara Ruth 1956- WhoAmW 91
Brookover, George David 1947- WhoWor 91
Brookover, J. Gordon 1922- St&PR 91
Brooks, Alan 1931- WhoAmA 91
Brooks, Albert BioIn 16
Brooks, Albert 1947- WhoAm 90, WorAlBi
Brooks, Andree Nicole 1937- WhoAm 90, WhoAmW 91
Brooks, Anita 1914- AuBYP 90
Brooks, Anita Helen WhoAmW 91, WhoE 91
Brooks, Anne AuBYP 90
Brooks, Anne 1938- BioIn 16
Brooks, Anne Lee 1948- WhoSSW 91
Brooks, Antoinette Marie 1940- WhoAmW 91
Brooks, Arthur T. 1917- St&PR 91
Brooks, Avery BioIn 16, DrBIPA 90
Brooks, Avery 19--?- WorAlBi
Brooks, Babert Vincent 1926- WhoAm 90
Brooks, Barbara T. 1906- St&PR 91
Brooks, Barry ODwPR 91
Brooks, Barry Charles 1932- St&PR 91
Brooks, Ben 1948- WhoWrEP 89
Brooks, Ben L. 1923- St&PR 91
Brooks, Beth Ann 1950- BiDrAPA 89
Brooks, Beth Ann 1962- WhoAmW 91
Brooks, Betsy Spurling 1944- WhoSSW 91
Brooks, Bill 1939- BioIn 16
Brooks, Bradford L. 1943- St&PR 91
Brooks, Bruce 1950- BioIn 16
Brooks, Bruce W 1948- WhoAmA 91
Brooks, Burton 1929- St&PR 91
Brooks, Carl E. 1937- St&PR 91
Brooks, Carla Jo 1956- WhoEmL 91, WhoSSW 91
Brooks, Caroline Dell Vogel 1938- WhoAmW 91
Brooks, Chandler McC. 1905-1989 BioIn 16
Brooks, Charlotte K. AuBYP 90
Brooks, Cheryll M. 1954- ODwPR 91
Brooks, Christine Ann 1953- WhoAmW 91
Brooks, Christine Brown 1950- WhoSSW 91
Brooks, Clarence 1895?- DrBIPA 90
Brooks, Claudia A. 1957- WhoAmW 91
Brooks, Claudia Marie 1952- WhoAmW 91
Brooks, Cleanth 1906- BioIn 16, ConAu 33NR, MajTwCW, WhoAm 90
Brooks, Clifton Rowland 1925- WhoHisp 91
Brooks, Conley, Jr. 1945- WhoEmL 91
Brooks, Constance Elizabeth 1946- WhoE 91
Brooks, Craig Charles 1946- St&PR 91
Brooks, D.W. 1901- St&PR 91
Brooks, Daisy WhoAmW 91
Brooks, Dana D. 1951- WhoSSW 91
Brooks, Daniel 1937- BiDrAPA 89
Brooks, David Allen 1959- WhoEmL 91
Brooks, David Barry 1934- WhoAm 90
Brooks, David Michael 1954- WhoEmL 91
Brooks, David Shaffer 1955- WhoSSW 91
Brooks, David William 1901- WhoAm 90
Brooks, Dawne Lea WhoAmW 91
Brooks, Dean K BiDrAPA 89
Brooks, Deborah J. 1952- St&PR 91
Brooks, Diana D 1950- News 90 [port], St&PR 91, WhoAm 90, WhoAmW 91
Brooks, Dick EncACom
Brooks, Don BioIn 16
Brooks, Donald 1955- WhoAm 90
Brooks, Donald A. 1941- St&PR 91
Brooks, Donna Lynne 1957- WhoAmW 91
Brooks, E. R. 1937- WhoAm 90, WhoSSW 91
Brooks, Edward Howard 1921- WhoAm 90
Brooks, Eleanor Idelle 1951- WhoEmL 91
Brooks, Ellen F BiDrAPA 89
Brooks, Eugene Mark 1922- BiDrAPA 89
Brooks, Eunice Woods 1929- WhoSSW 91
Brooks, Evans Bartlett 1900- WhoAm 90
Brooks, Forest Clyde 1947- WhoWor 91
Brooks, Francis French 1915- St&PR 91
Brooks, Frank C. 1919- St&PR 91
Brooks, Frank Pickering 1920- WhoAm 90, WhoWrEP 89
Brooks, Frederic H. 1934- WhoAm 90
Brooks, Frederic Henry 1934- St&PR 91
Brooks, Frederick Phillips, Jr. 1931- WhoAm 90
Brooks, Gary Calvin 1950- WhoE 91
Brooks, Gary Leon 1950- WhoEmL 91
Brooks, George MajTwCW
Brooks, George 1956- WhoE 91
Brooks, George Andrew 1900- WhoE 91
Brooks, George Andrew 1900-1988 BioIn 16
Brooks, George Gifford 1928- WhoAm 90
Brooks, George K, Jr. BiDrAPA 89
Brooks, George W 1920- BiDrAPA 89
Brooks, Gerald Alvin BiDrAPA 89
Brooks, Gerald R. 1936- St&PR 91
Brooks, Gladys Sinclair 1914- WhoAmW 91
Brooks, Glenn Allen 1960- WhoEmL 91
Brooks, Glenn Ellis 1931- WhoAm 90
Brooks, Glenn M. 1918- St&PR 91
Brooks, Gwendolyn BioIn 16
Brooks, Gwendolyn 1917- BioAmW, FemiCLE, MajTwCW, WhoAm 90, WhoAmW 91, WhoWrEP 89, WorAlBi
Brooks, H Allen 1925- ConAu 31NR
Brooks, H. Allen 1925- WhoAm 90
Brooks, H Allen 1925- WhoAmA 91
Brooks, Hadassah T 1937- BiDrAPA 89
Brooks, Harriet 1876-1933 BioIn 16
Brooks, Harry A WhoAmA 91
Brooks, Harry A. 1913- St&PR 91
Brooks, Harry Angelo 1913- WhoAm 90
Brooks, Harvey 1931- WhoE 91
Brooks, Helene Margaret 1942- WhoAmW 91
Brooks, Herb BioIn 16
Brooks, Herb 1937- WorAlBi
Brooks, Herbert 1924- St&PR 91
Brooks, Hervey PenDiDA 89
Brooks, Howard Owen 1959- WhoEmL 91
Brooks, Howard Zachary 1956- WhoE 91, WhoEmL 91
Brooks, Hubie 1956- Ballpl 90
Brooks, Isaac Watts 1838-1916 AmLegL
Brooks, Jack 1922- BioIn 16
Brooks, Jack Bascom 1922- WhoAm 90, WhoSSW 91
Brooks, James 1906- WhoAm 90, WhoAmA 91
Brooks, James A., III 1943- St&PR 91
Brooks, James E., Jr. 1948- WhoAm 90, WhoSSW 91
Brooks, James Elwood 1925- WhoAm 90
Brooks, James Frank 1928- BiDrAPA 89
Brooks, James Joe, III 1948- WhoSSW 91
Brooks, James L. 1940- BioIn 16, ConAu 32NR, WhoAm 90
Brooks, James Sprague 1925- WhoAm 90
Brooks, James Stephen BiDrAPA 89
Brooks, James W.F. 1948- St&PR 91
Brooks, Jane Peyser 1936- WhoAmW 91
Brooks, Janet Eileen 1957- WhoAmW 91
Brooks, Jeanne Ellen 1950- WhoAmW 91
Brooks, Jeffrey Martin 1958- St&PR 91, WhoSSW 91
Brooks, Jeffrey Paul 1960- WhoEmL 91
Brooks, Jermyn Paul 1939- WhoWor 91
Brooks, Jerome Alvin 1918- WhoSSW 91

Brooks, Jerome Bernard 1932- *WhoAm 90, WhoWor 91*
Brooks, Jerry Claude 1936- *WhoSSW 91, WhoWor 91*
Brooks, Jo 1949- *WhoEmL 91*
Brooks, Jo Anne White 1928- *WhoAmW 91*
Brooks, Joae Graham 1926- *BiDrAPA 89, WhoAm 90*
Brooks, Joan Logan 1940- *WhoAmW 91*
Brooks, John 1710?-1756? *PenDiDA 89*
Brooks, John 1920- *BioIn 16, WhoAm 90, WhoWrEP 89*
Brooks, John Bill 1929- *WhoSSW 91*
Brooks, John Edward 1923- *WhoAm 90*
Brooks, John F. 1919- *St&PR 91*
Brooks, John H. 1900- *St&PR 91*
Brooks, John H 1935- *WhoAmA 91, WhoE 91*
Brooks, John Lawrence, III 1951- *WhoEmL 91*
Brooks, John Robert 1960- *WhoEmL 91*
Brooks, John Robinson 1918- *WhoAm 90*
Brooks, John Wood 1917-1989 *BioIn 16*
Brooks, Joseph Conover 1927- *St&PR 91*
Brooks, Joseph T. *BioIn 16*
Brooks, Juanita 1898- *BioAmW, BioIn 16*
Brooks, Julie Agnes 1941- *BiDrAPA 89, WhoAmW 91*
Brooks, Keith 1923- *WhoAm 90*
Brooks, Kevin B. 1946- *St&PR 91*
Brooks, Kim W. *St&PR 91*
Brooks, Kimberly A. 1955- *WhoAmW 91*
Brooks, Leanne Ruth 1961- *WhoAmW 91*
Brooks, Leslie *BiDrAPA 89*
Brooks, Lester 1924- *AuBYP 90*
Brooks, Lewis Alexander 1931- *WhoE 91*
Brooks, Linda Grace 1945- *WhoWrEP 89*
Brooks, Linda Lockman- *BioIn 16*
Brooks, Linda Thomas 1963- *WhoEmL 91*
Brooks, Lorenzo 1942- *WhoAm 90*
Brooks, Lorimer Page 1917- *WhoAm 90*
Brooks, Louise *WhoE 91*
Brooks, Louise 1906-1985 *BioAmW, BioIn 16*
Brooks, Louise Cherry 1906- *WhoAmA 91*
Brooks, Maggie *ConAu 132*
Brooks, Margaret Ann 1951- *ConAu 132*
Brooks, Maria 1794-1845 *FemiCLE*
Brooks, Marion *EarBlAP*
Brooks, Marion A. *EarBlAP*
Brooks, Martin 1950- *WhoEmL 91*
Brooks, Mary Campbell 1964- *WhoAmW 91*
Brooks, Mary Rogers *BioIn 16*
Brooks, Maurice Edward 1922- *WhoAm 90*
Brooks, Mel *BioIn 16*
Brooks, Mel 1926- *WhoAm 90, WorAlBi*
Brooks, Mel, Mrs. 1931- *WhoAmW 91*
Brooks, Michael *NewAgMG*
Brooks, Michael Lee 1955- *WhoE 91*
Brooks, Michael Paul 1937- *WhoAm 90, WhoSSW 91*
Brooks, Naomi Williams 1937- *WhoAmW 91*
Brooks, Noah 1830-1903 *BioIn 16*
Brooks, Noel L. *BioIn 16*
Brooks, Norma 1941- *WhoSSW 91*
Brooks, Norman Herrick 1928- *WhoAm 90*
Brooks, Pamela Marie 1964- *WhoAmW 91*
Brooks, Patricia 1937- *IntWWM 90*
Brooks, Peggy 1919- *WhoAm 90*
Brooks, Peter 1938- *WhoAm 90*
Brooks, Peter 1952- *WhoEmL 91*
Brooks, Peter Newman 1931- *ConAu 131*
Brooks, Randy L. 1950- *St&PR 91*
Brooks, Renana Esther 1956- *WhoAmW 91*
Brooks, Richard 1912- *BioIn 16, WhoAm 90*
Brooks, Richard Alan 1960- *WhoSSW 91*
Brooks, Richard J. G. 1942- *IntWWM 90*
Brooks, Richard L. 1939- *St&PR 91*
Brooks, Richard M. 1928- *St&PR 91*
Brooks, Richard Mallon 1928- *WhoAm 90*
Brooks, Robert 1922- *WhoAmA 91*
Brooks, Robert Alan, Jr. 1940- *WhoAm 90*
Brooks, Robert Dale 1932- *WhoAm 90*
Brooks, Robert Elliott 1942- *BiDrAPA 89*
Brooks, Robert Franklin 1939- *WhoAm 90*
Brooks, Robert Jomax 1942- *BiDrAPA 89*
Brooks, Robert Lee 1949- *WhoEmL 91*
Brooks, Robert Leslie 1944- *WhoAm 90*
Brooks, Robert Liss 1936- *WhoAm 90*
Brooks, Robert Owen 1936- *St&PR 91*
Brooks, Robert Romano Ravi 1905- *WhoAm 90*
Brooks, Robert Vernon 1947- *WhoEmL 91*
Brooks, Robert W 1944- *BiDrAPA 89*
Brooks, Robert William 1935- *WhoAm 90*
Brooks, Roberta Delores 1933- *WhoAmW 91*
Brooks, Roger *BioIn 16*
Brooks, Roger Charles 1947- *WhoE 91*
Brooks, Roger Kay 1937- *St&PR 91, WhoAm 90*
Brooks, Roger Leon 1927- *WhoAm 90*
Brooks, Romaine 1874-1970 *BiDWomA, BioAmW*
Brooks, Roy Howard, Jr. 1923- *WhoSSW 91*
Brooks, Sam Allen 1939- *St&PR 91*
Brooks, Shelton 1886-1975 *BioIn 16, OxCPMus*
Brooks, Stephen Marion 1953- *WhoSSW 91*
Brooks, Susan Ann 1963- *WhoAmW 91*
Brooks, Terry 1944- *SmATA 60*
Brooks, Thomas 1811-1887 *PenDiDA 89*
Brooks, Thomas 1925- *AuBYP 90*
Brooks, Thomas Aloysius, III 1937- *WhoAm 90*
Brooks, Thomas Joseph, Jr. 1916- *WhoSSW 91*
Brooks, Timothy H. 1942- *WhoAm 90*
Brooks, Tonda Hoke 1947- *WhoSSW 91*
Brooks, Van Wyck 1886-1963 *BioIn 16, DcLB 103 [port], WorAlBi*
Brooks, Vera Ramey 1952- *WhoAmW 91*
Brooks, Vernon Bernard 1923- *WhoAm 90*
Brooks, Virginia K. 1953- *WhoWrEP 89*
Brooks, Wendell T 1939- *WhoAmA 91*
Brooks, William B *BiDrAPA 89*
Brooks, William Bogan, III 1956- *BiDrAPA 89*
Brooks, William C. *WhoAm 90*
Brooks, William Charles 1936- *St&PR 91*
Brooks, William Christopher 1964- *WhoSSW 91*
Brooks, William D. 1932- *St&PR 91*
Brooks, William E. 1941- *ODwPR 91*
Brooks, William James, III 1953- *WhoEmL 91*
Brooks, William Oliver 1951- *WhoSSW 91*
Brooks, William Sidney 1935- *WhoAm 90*
Brooks, Wynona C. 1937- *WhoSSW 91*
Brooks-Gunn, Jeanne 1946- *WhoAm 90*
Brooks-Hill, Frederick James 1944- *St&PR 91*
Brooks-Hill, Helen 1908- *BioIn 16*
Brooks-Warren, Annette *BiDrAPA 89*
Brooksbank, Randolph Wood 1947- *WhoE 91*
Brooksby, Wade Ford 1941- *St&PR 91*
Brookshaw, Valjean B., Jr. 1931- *St&PR 91*
Brookshaw, Valjean Bispham, Jr. 1931- *WhoSSW 91*
Brookshire, Bruce G. 1928- *WhoAm 90*
Brookshire, L. *WhoSSW 91*
Brookshire, Oscar *St&PR 91N*
Brookshire, Wiley Eugene 1929- *St&PR 91*
Brooksop, Joan *BiDEWW*
Brookstone, Arnold F. 1930- *St&PR 91, WhoAm 90*
Broom, Albert, Mrs. 1863-1939 *BioIn 16*
Broom, Gerald M. 1940- *St&PR 91*
Broom, Jacob 1752-1810 *BioIn 16*
Broom, Jim Howell *BiDrAPA 89*
Broom, John Joseph Willard 1917- *IntWWM 90*
Broom, Odell Ammon, III 1953- *WhoEmL 91*
Broom, William Wescott 1924- *WhoAm 90*
Broome, Billy Jean *WhoSSW 91*
Broome, Burton Edward 1935- *St&PR 91*
Broome, Claire Veronica 1949- *WhoAmW 91*
Broome, Douglas Ralph, Jr. 1936- *WhoE 91*
Broome, George Calvin, III 1938- *WhoAm 90*
Broome, George W *DcAfAmP*
Broome, Isaac *PenDiDA 89*
Broome, John William 1923- *WhoAm 90*
Broome, L. Elizabeth 1939- *WhoAmW 91*
Broome, Larry Glen *BiDrAPA 89*
Broome, Linton Dale 1933- *St&PR 91*
Broome, Oscar Whitfield, Jr. 1940- *WhoAm 90*
Broome, Paul W. 1932- *St&PR 91*
Broome, Paul Wallace 1932- *WhoAm 90*
Broome, Rick 1946- *WhoAmA 91*
Broome, Ruth Anne *BiDrAPA 89*
Broomes, Lloyd Rudy 1936- *BiDrAPA 89*
Broomes, Lloyda Renee *BiDrAPA 89*
Broomfield, Adolphus George 1906- *WhoAmA 91*
Broomfield, Robert Cameron 1933- *WhoAm 90*
Broomfield, William S. 1922- *WhoAm 90*
Broones, Martin 1892-1971 *OxCPMus*
Broonzy, Big Bill 1893-1958 *OxCPMus, WorAlBi*
Brooten, Gary *ODwPR 91*
Brooten, Kenneth Edward, Jr. 1942- *WhoWor 91*
Broowski, Casimir Jan 1947- *WhoSSW 91*
Brophy, Brigid 1929- *BioIn 16, FemiCLE, MajTwCW*
Brophy, Charles G. *ODwPR 91*
Brophy, Doris Anne 1961- *WhoE 91*
Brophy, Francis L. 1925- *St&PR 91*
Brophy, George Thomas 1935- *St&PR 91*
Brophy, Gerard 1953- *IntWWM 90*
Brophy, Hugh Francis 1937- *WhoE 91*
Brophy, James David, Jr. 1926- *WhoAm 90*
Brophy, James J. 1926- *St&PR 91*
Brophy, James John 1926- *WhoAm 90*
Brophy, Jere Hall 1934- *WhoAm 90*
Brophy, Jeremiah Joseph 1930- *WhoAm 90*
Brophy, Joseph Thomas 1933- *St&PR 91, WhoAm 90*
Brophy, Mary Nona 1959- *WhoAmW 91*
Brophy, Melonie C. 1954- *St&PR 91*
Brophy, Michael Haas *BiDrAPA 89*
Brophy, Theodore F. 1923- *WhoAm 90*
Brophy, Theodore Frederick 1923- *St&PR 91*
Brophy, Thomas Joseph 1935- *St&PR 91*
Brophy, Todd Randall 1954- *WhoEmL 91*
Broquet, Karen Elizabeth 1959- *BiDrAPA 89*
Brorby, Wade 1934- *WhoAm 90*
Brorsen, Barton Wade 1957- *WhoEmL 91*
Brorson, Hans Adolf 1694-1764 *DcScanL*
Brosa Quartet *PenDiMP*
Brosa, Antonio 1894-1979 *PenDiMP*
Brosa, Carol Joanne 1933- *WhoAmW 91, WhoWor 91*
Brosamer, Hans *PenDiDA 89*
Broschi, Carlo *PenDiMP*
Brose, E. Jerome 1926- *St&PR 91*
Brose, John Adolph 1950- *WhoEmL 91*
Brose, Paula Lynn 1942- *WhoAmW 91*
Brosens, Frank Peter 1957- *WhoAm 90*
Broser, Hansjoerg 1941- *St&PR 91*
Brosh, Kenneth C. 1914- *St&PR 91*
Brosh, Kenneth W. 1941- *St&PR 91*
Brosh, Stephanie D. 1964- *WhoEmL 91*
Broshar, John Gregory 1962- *WhoEmL 91*
Broshar, Robert Clare 1931- *WhoAm 90*
Brosheárs, Keith Macer 1948- *WhoWor 91*
Brosig, Michael Francis, Sr. 1950- *St&PR 91*
Brosilow, Coleman Bernard 1934- *WhoAm 90*
Brosin, Henry W 1904- *BiDrAPA 89*
Brosin, Henry Walter 1904- *WhoAm 90*
Brosious, Mary Anne 1951- *WhoEmL 91*
Brosius, Charles Orner *BiDrAPA 89*
Brosk, Jeffrey 1947- *WhoAmA 91*
Brosky, Robert E. 1940- *St&PR 91*
Brosman, Catharine Savage 1934- *WhoWrEP 89*
Brosnahan, James Jerome 1934- *WhoAm 90*
Brosnahan, Roger Paul 1935- *WhoAm 90*
Brosnahan, Timothy G. 1944- *ODwPR 91*
Brosnan, Carol Raphael Sarah 1931- *WhoAmW 91, WhoE 91*
Brosnan, James Patrick 1929- *AuBYP 90*
Brosnan, Jim 1929- *Ballpl 90*
Brosnan, Kathleen A 1925- *BiDrAPA 89*
Brosnan, Pierce *BioIn 16*
Bross, Albert L, Jr 1921- *WhoAmA 91*
Bross, Helmut Albert 1931- *WhoWor 91*
Bross, Irwin Dudley Jackson 1921- *WhoAm 90*
Bross, John Adams 1911- *WhoAm 90, WhoWor 91*
Bross, John Adams, Jr. *NewYTBS 90*
Bross, John Joseph 1939- *WhoE 91, WhoWor 91*
Bross, Robert B *BiDrAPA 89*
Bross, Steward Richard, Jr. 1922- *WhoAm 90, WhoWor 91*
Brossard, Nicole 1943- *FemiCLE*
Brosseau, Alden Wilfrid 1927- *St&PR 91*
Brosseau, Irma Finn 1930- *WhoAm 90, WhoAmW 91*
Brosseau, Jon Hubert 1945- *WhoEmL 91*
Brosseau, Lucien 1920- *WhoE 91*
Brossi, Mario 1952- *WhoE 91*
Brossman, Mark Edward 1953- *WhoEmL 91*
Brossman, Walter Robert 1920- *WhoAm 90*
Brossolette, Pierre 1903-1944 *BiDFrPL*
Brost, Gerard Robert 1949- *WhoSSW 91*
Broster, D. K. 1877-1950 *BioIn 16*
Broster, Dorothy Kathleen 1877-1950 *BioIn 16*
Broster, Eileen *IntWWM 90*
Brostoff, Alan Jay 1933- *St&PR 91*
Brostoff, Ben C. 1914- *St&PR 91*
Brostoff, Kathy Haskin *BiDrAPA 89*
Brostoff, Richard 1955- *BiDrAPA 89*
Brostowitz, James M. 1952- *St&PR 91*
Brosz, Don Gayle, Jr. 1954- *WhoEmL 91*
Broszat, Martin 1926-1989 *AnObit 1989, BioIn 16, ConAu 130*
Brot, Robert Jay 1953- *St&PR 91*
Brotbeck, George Nathan 1946- *WhoEmL 91*
Brother Andrew *BioIn 16*
Brother Antoninus *MajTwCW*
Brothers Grimm *BioIn 16*
Brothers, Anita U 1913- *BiDrAPA 89*
Brothers, Barry 1955- *WhoEmL 91*
Brothers, Barry A 1955- *WhoAmA 91*
Brothers, Clifford Ray 1930- *WhoE 91*
Brothers, Donald Irving 1922- *St&PR 91*
Brothers, Henry J., II 1957- *WhoEmL 91*
Brothers, Jack Anthony 1943- *WhoWor 91*
Brothers, Jill A. 1963- *St&PR 91*
Brothers, John Alfred 1940- *WhoAm 90*
Brothers, Joyce *BioIn 16*
Brothers, Joyce D. 1928- *WorAlBi*
Brothers, Joyce Diane *WhoAm 90, WhoAmW 91*
Brothers, Karen Elizabeth 1946- *WhoAmW 91*
Brothers, Milton J. 1926-1989 *BioIn 16*
Brotherton, Mary 1820-1910 *FemiCLE*
Brotherton, Maureen Saltzer 1959- *WhoAmW 91*
Brotherton, Naomi *WhoAmA 91*
Brotherton, T.W. 1924- *St&PR 91*
Brotherton, Thomas James 1945- *WhoSSW 91*
Brotman, Andrew William 1955- *BiDrAPA 89*
Brotman, Carl J 1945- *BiDrAPA 89*
Brotman, Herman B. *BioIn 16*
Brotman, Phyllis B. 1934- *ODwPR 91, St&PR 91*
Brotman, Phyllis Block 1934- *WhoAmW 91*
Brotman, Stanley Seymour 1924- *WhoAm 90, WhoE 91*
Brotman, Stephen L. 1944- *St&PR 91*
Brotons, Salvador 1959- *IntWWM 90*
Brott, Alexander 1915- *IntWWM 90, WhoAm 90*
Brott, Boris 1944- *IntWWM 90, PenDiMP, WhoE 91*
Brott, Denis 1950- *IntWWM 90*
Brott, Irving Deerin, Jr. 1930- *WhoAm 90*
Brott, Walter Howard 1933- *WhoAm 90, WhoWor 91*
Brotzen, Franz Richard 1915- *WhoAm 90*
Brotzman, Donald Glenn 1922- *WhoAm 90*
Brou, Elizabeth Emerson Howell 1956- *WhoSSW 91*
Brou, Martha Tucker *BiDrAPA 89*
Broucek, Francis J 1932- *BiDrAPA 89*
Broucek, William Samuel 1950- *WhoEmL 91*
Broud, Ronald L. 1936- *St&PR 91*
Broude, Norma Freedman 1941- *WhoAmA 91*
Broude, Richard Frederick 1936- *WhoAm 90*
Broudo, Joseph David 1920- *WhoAmA 91, WhoE 91*
Broudo, Robert Jeffrey 1949- *WhoE 91*
Broudy, Harry Samuel 1905- *WhoAm 90*
Broudy, Julius 1920- *WhoE 91*
Broudy, Norman Samuel *BiDrAPA 89*
Broue, Pierre 1926- *WhoWor 91*
Brough, Bruce A. 1937- *ODwPR 91*
Brough, Charles Hillman 1876-1935 *BioIn 16*
Brough, Cleopatra 1929- *BiDrAPA 89*
Brough, Donald M *BiDrAPA 89*
Brough, Gregory K. 1947- *St&PR 91*
Brough, John Albert 1946- *St&PR 91*
Brough, Karen Tanassy 1946- *WhoAmW 91*
Brough, Michael Bannon 1947- *WhoEmL 91*
Brough, Richard Burrell 1920- *WhoAmA 91*
Brough, Robert Joseph 1941- *St&PR 91*
Brough, Walter John 1925- *WhoWor 91*
Broughall, George 1861-1927 *OxCCanT*
Brougham, Doris Marie 1926- *WhoWor 91*
Brougham, Henry Peter 1778-1868 *EncPaPR 91*
Brougham, Kathryn C. 1954- *WhoEmL 91*
Brougham, Robert Powers 1943- *WhoE 91*
Broughton, Alan 1942- *St&PR 91*
Broughton, Beverly Jane 1927- *WhoAmW 91*
Broughton, Bradford Browne 1926- *WhoE 91*
Broughton, Carl L. 1910- *St&PR 91*
Broughton, Carl Louis 1910- *WhoAm 90*
Broughton, Jack 1925- *BioIn 16*
Broughton, James 1913- *ConAu 30NR, ConAu 12AS [port], WhoWrEP 89*
Broughton, James Walter 1946- *WhoEmL 91*
Broughton, Luke Dennis 1828-1898 *NewAgE 90*
Broughton, Pamela Kay 1946- *WhoWrEP 89*
Broughton, Paul Mitchell 1946- *WhoSSW 91*
Broughton, Phillip Charles 1930- *WhoAm 90*
Broughton, Rhoda 1840-1920 *BioIn 16, FemiCLE*
Broughton, Richard S. 1946- *EncPaPR 91*
Broughton, T. Alan 1936- *WhoWrEP 89*
Broughton, Thomas Wheatley *BiDrAPA 89*
Brouha, Paul 1946- *WhoE 91*
Brouhard, Mark 1956- *Ballpl 90*

Brouillard, John Charles 1948- St&PR 91
Brouillette, Albert C 1924- WhoAmA 91
Brouillette, Donald G. 1930- WhoAm 90
Brouillette, Donald George 1930- St&PR 91
Brouillette, Gary Joseph 1940- WhoAm 90
Brouillette, Gilbert T WhoAmA 91N
Brouillette, Johanne BiDrAPA 89
Brouillette, Marie-Josee 1961- BiDrAPA 89
Brouk, Joanna NewAgMG
Broumas, Olga 1949- FemiCLE, WhoWrEP 89
Broun, Elizabeth 1946- WhoAm 90, WhoAmW 91, WhoE 91
Broun, Elizabeth Gibson 1946- WhoAmA 91
Broun, Heywood 1888-1939 BioIn 16, WorAlBi
Broun, Heywood C. 1888-1939 Ballpl 90
Broun, Heywood Campbell 1888-1939 AuBYP 90
Broun, Heywood Hale 1918- BioIn 16
Broun, Kenneth Stanley 1939- WhoAm 90
Broun, Maurice 1906-1979 BioIn 16
Brountas, Paul BioIn 16
Brountas, Paul Peter 1932- WhoAm 90
Brous, Bernard 1924- St&PR 91
Brous, David G. 1957- St&PR 91
Brous, Philip 1930- WhoAm 90
Brous, Richard Pendleton 1908- St&PR 91
Brouse, Brian E. 1950- St&PR 91
Brouse, Jenny R. 1924- St&PR 91
Brouse, Robert Cornelius 1913- WhoAm 90
Brouse, Sidney M. 1922- St&PR 91
Broussard, Arthur J. St&PR 91
Broussard, Carol Madeline WhoAmW 91, WhoWor 91
Broussard, David N. 1948- St&PR 91
Broussard, Diana Morris 1959- WhoSSW 91
Broussard, Elsie Rita 1924- BiDrAPA 89, WhoE 91
Broussard, Huby J. 1927- St&PR 91
Broussard, Jay Remy 1920-1976 WhoAmA 91N
Broussard, Joseph Otto, III 1938- WhoAm 90
Broussard, Margaret Faye 1952- WhoAmW 91
Broussard, Thomas Rollins 1943- WhoAm 90
Broussard, Vernon James 1932- St&PR 91
Broussard, William Arren 1956- WhoEmL 91
Broussard, William Joseph 1934- WhoSSW 91
Broussard-Smith, Paula 1960- WhoSSW 91
Brousse DcCanB 12
Brousse, Paul 1844-1912 BioIn 16
Brousse, Paul Louis Marie 1844-1912 BiDFrPL
Brousseau, Christine Marie 1945- WhoWor 91
Brousseau, James Edward 1931- St&PR 91
Broustet, Arnaud 1960- WhoWor 91
Brouthers, Dan 1858-1932 Ballpl 90 [port]
Broutman, Lawrence Jay 1938- WhoAm 90
Brouwenstijn, Gre 1915- PenDiMP
Brouwenstyn, Gre 1915- IntWWM 90
Brouwer, Adriaen 1605?-1638 IntDcAA 90
Brouwer, Harry Josephus 1958- WhoWor 91
Brouwer, Hendrik Albertus 1886-1973 DcScB S2
Brouwer, Leo 1939- PenDiMP, -A
Brouwer, Willem Coenraad 1877-1933 PenDiDA 89
Brouwer-De Beer, Afke 1896- EncCoWW
Brovarski, Edward Joseph 1943- WhoAm 90
Brovetto, Gary 1946- WhoEmL 91
Broviak, Fred J.J. 1942- ODwPR 91
Brow, John Joseph 1938- St&PR 91
Brow, Thea 1934- SmATA 60 [port]
Browaldh, Tore 1917- WhoWor 91
Browallius, Irja Agnes 1901-1968 EncCoWW
Browde, Anatole 1925- St&PR 91, WhoAm 90
Browder, Charles Mack 1945- WhoEmL 91
Browder, Earl 1891-1973 EncAL
Browder, Earl R. 1891-1973 WorAlBi
Browder, Felix Earl 1927- WhoAm 90, WhoWor 91
Browder, Jeannette Zeno 1946- WhoAmW 91
Browder, John Glen 1943- WhoAm 90, WhoSSW 91
Browder, John Hartt 1946- St&PR 91
Browder, Olin Lorraine, Jr. 1913- WhoAm 90
Browder, Robert Paul 1921- WhoAm 90
Browder, Tamara BioIn 16
Browder, William 1934- WhoAm 90
Browdy, Alvin 1917- WhoAm 90
Brower, Bob 1960- Ballpl 90
Brower, Charles Harry 1948- WhoEmL 91
Brower, Charles Nelson 1935- WhoAm 90
Brower, Cheryl Diane 1958- WhoWrEP 89
Brower, David 1912- News 90 [port]
Brower, David A. 1952- St&PR 91
Brower, David John 1930- WhoWor 91
Brower, David Ross 1912- BioIn 16, WhoAm 90
Brower, Diane D. ODwPR 91
Brower, Edgar S. 1930- WhoAm 90
Brower, Edgar Seymour 1930- St&PR 91
Brower, Edward E., Jr. 1928- St&PR 91
Brower, Frank 1893-1960 Ballpl 90
Brower, George David 1948- WhoE 91
Brower, George R. 1940- St&PR 91
Brower, James Calvin 1914- WhoWor 91
Brower, Janet Sue 1944- WhoAmW 91
Brower, Joan Rafal ODwPR 91
Brower, Joy Daniels 1941- WhoAmW 91
Brower, Kirk Jeffery 1954- BiDrAPA 89
Brower, Martin A. 1928- ODwPR 91
Brower, Paul Gordon 1938- St&PR 91
Brower, Robert Hopkins 1923-1988 BioIn 16
Brower, Ross Belin 1949- BiDrAPA 89
Brower, Stuart L. 1945- St&PR 91
Brower, Wesley Allen 1949- St&PR 91
Brower, William L., Jr. 1944- St&PR 91
Browes, Pauline 1938- WhoAmW 91
Browin, Frances Williams 1898- AuBYP 90
Browing, Colin Arrott 1935- St&PR 91
Brown EarBIAP
Brown family BioIn 16
Brown, A. Peter 1943- IntWWM 90
Brown, A. Sue 1946- WhoAm 90
Brown, A. Worley 1928- St&PR 91
Brown, Aaron Venable 1795-1859 BiDrUSE 89
Brown, Abbott Louis 1943- WhoAm 90
Brown, Abbott S. 1955- WhoEmL 91
Brown, Ada 1889-1950 DrBIPA 90
Brown, Adrian 1960- BiDrAPA 89
Brown, Adrienne Jean 1950- WhoAmW 91
Brown, Adrienne Lois BioIn 16
Brown, Alan Charles 1948- St&PR 91
Brown, Alan Crawford 1956- WhoWor 91
Brown, Alan David 1947- BiDrAPA 89
Brown, Alan M, Jr WhoAmA 91
Brown, Alan Marshall, Jr. 1947- WhoE 91
Brown, Alan N. 1950- WhoSSW 91
Brown, Alan Philip 1955- BiDrAPA 89
Brown, Alan Stuart BiDrAPA 89
Brown, Albert Clarence 1918- WhoAm 90
Brown, Albert Jacob 1914- WhoAm 90
Brown, Albert Joseph, Jr. 1934- St&PR 91
Brown, Alexander 1764-1834 EncABHB 6 [port]
Brown, Alfred Keith 1917- St&PR 91
Brown, Alice 1856-1948 BioAmW
Brown, Alice 1857-1948 FemiCLE
Brown, Alice C. 1951- WhoSSW 91
Brown, Alice Dalton 1939- WhoAmA 91
Brown, Alice Marie 1955- WhoAmW 91
Brown, Alice Pratt 1908- WhoAmW 91
Brown, Alice Roberta 1952- WhoAmW 91
Brown, Alison A. WhoAmW 91
Brown, Alleene Presson 1927- WhoSSW 91
Brown, Allen D. 1951- St&PR 91
Brown, Allen W. 1908-1990 BioIn 16
Brown, Allyn Stephens 1916- WhoSSW 91
Brown, Alpha Estes 1952- WhoE 91
Brown, Andreas Le 1933- WhoAm 90
Brown, Andrew Beirne 1946- WhoSSW 91
Brown, Andrew Joseph 1945- WhoAm 90
Brown, Andrew W. L. BioIn 16
Brown, Anita Patti 1870?-1950 DcAfAmP
Brown, Ann Catherine 1935- WhoAm 90
Brown, Anna 1747-1810 FemiCLE
Brown, Anne 1912- DrBIPA 90
Brown, Anne 1915- BioIn 16
Brown, Anne Barbara 1949- WhoAmW 91
Brown, Anne Ensign 1937- SmATA 61 [port]
Brown, Anne Wiggins 1915- DcAfAmP
Brown, Annie Marie Vedel 1941- WhoAmW 91
Brown, Anthony B. 1922- WhoWor 91
Brown, Anthony Lamar 1950- ODwPR 91
Brown, Anthony S. 1934- St&PR 91
Brown, Archibald Haworth 1938- WhoWor 91
Brown, Archie 1911-1990 NewYTBS 90
Brown, Arlene Ann 1951- WhoAmW 91
Brown, Arlene Patricia Theresa 1953- WhoAmW 91
Brown, Arlin Edward 1945- BiDrAPA 89, WhoEmL 91
Brown, Arnold 1939- WhoSSW 91
Brown, Arnold A. 1929- St&PR 91
Brown, Arnold Lanehart, Jr. 1926- WhoAm 90
Brown, Arthur BioIn 16
Brown, Arthur 1922- WhoAm 90
Brown, Arthur 1940- St&PR 91, WhoAm 90
Brown, Arthur Edmon, Jr. 1929- WhoAm 90
Brown, Arthur J. 1911-1989 BioIn 16
Brown, Arthur Thomas 1900- WhoAm 90
Brown, Arthur Wayne 1917- WhoAm 90
Brown, Arvin 1940- ConTFT 8 [port]
Brown, Aubrey Neblett, Jr. 1908- WhoAm 90, WhoWrEP 89
Brown, Audrey Alexandra 1904- FemiCLE
Brown, Ava Colleen 1952- WhoAmW 91
Brown, B. Alex 1948- WhoEmL 91
Brown, B.R. 1932- St&PR 91
Brown, B. Warren 1933- St&PR 91
Brown, Barbara Black 1928- WhoWrEP 89
Brown, Barbara Canning BioIn 16
Brown, Barbara Gene 1938- WhoAmW 91
Brown, Barbara Jeanne 1941- WhoAm 90
Brown, Barclay 1958- WhoSSW 91
Brown, Barry Lee 1944- St&PR 91
Brown, Barry M BiDrAPA 89
Brown, Barry M. 1942- ConTFT 8
Brown, Barry Michael 1941- WhoE 91
Brown, Barry Rogers 1957- WhoSSW 91
Brown, Barton 1924- WhoAm 90
Brown, Beatrice 1917- WhoAmW 91
Brown, Bedford Philmore, Jr. 1938- WhoSSW 91
Brown, Ben Hill 1914-1989 BioIn 16
Brown, Ben Maurice 1943- BiDrAPA 89
Brown, Benjamin A. 1943- St&PR 91, WhoAm 90
Brown, Benjamin Andrew 1933- WhoAm 90
Brown, Benjamin Thomas 1948- WhoSSW 91
Brown, Benjamin Young 1948- St&PR 91, WhoSSW 91
Brown, Bennett Alexander 1929- St&PR 91, WhoAm 90, WhoSSW 91
Brown, Bernard Beau 1925- St&PR 91
Brown, Bernard E 1925- WhoWrEP 89
Brown, Bert Mahlon 1914- WhoWor 91
Brown, Bertram S 1931- BiDrAPA 89
Brown, Beth WhoWrEP 89
Brown, Bethel C. 1929- St&PR 91
Brown, Betty Ann 1949- WhoAmA 91
Brown, Betty J.H. 1929- St&PR 91
Brown, Betty Jo 1949- WhoEmL 91
Brown, Betty L. 1943- St&PR 91
Brown, Beverley 1954- FemiCLE
Brown, Beverly C. 1949- St&PR 91
Brown, Beverly Jean 1943- WhoAmW 91
Brown, Bill BioIn 16
Brown, Bill 1910-1964 AuBYP 90
Brown, Bill, and Rosalie Moore Brown AuBYP 90
Brown, Billie ODwPR 91, WhoAmW 91
Brown, Billie Augustine 1924- WhoAmW 91, WhoSSW 91, WhoWor 91
Brown, Blair BioIn 16
Brown, Blair 1948- WorAlBi
Brown, Boardwalk 1889-1977 Ballpl 90
Brown, Bob BioIn 16
Brown, Bob 1911- Ballpl 90
Brown, Bobby BioIn 16, ConMus 4 [port]
Brown, Bobby 1924- Ballpl 90, BioIn 16
Brown, Bobby 1954- Ballpl 90
Brown, Bobby Wayne 1955- WhoEmL 91
Brown, Bonnie L. 1943- St&PR 91
Brown, Bonnie Maryetta 1953- WhoEmL 91
Brown, Bradford Stearns 1931- WhoSSW 91
Brown, Bradley David 1961- WhoEmL 91
Brown, Brent W. 1942- St&PR 91
Brown, Brian 1911-1958 WhoAmA 91N
Brown, Brice Norman 1945- WhoAm 90
Brown, Britt 1927- WhoAm 90
Brown, Britt Murdock 1952- St&PR 91, WhoEmL 91, WhoWor 91
Brown, Bruce 1931- WhoAm 90
Brown, Bruce Allen 1948- WhoEmL 91
Brown, Bruce Keith, Jr. 1926- WhoE 91
Brown, Bruce Maitland 1947- WhoE 91, WhoEmL 91
Brown, Bruce Robert WhoE 91
Brown, Bruce Robert 1938- WhoAmA 91
Brown, Buster 1881-1914 Ballpl 90
Brown, Byron William, Jr. 1930- WhoAm 90
Brown, C. Harold 1931- WhoAm 90
Brown, C W WhoAmA 91
Brown, C Winston 1947- BiDrAPA 89
Brown, Calvin S. 1909-1989 BioIn 16
Brown, Cameron 1914- St&PR 91, WhoAm 90
Brown, Carl Curtis 1947- WhoSSW 91
Brown, Carlyle WhoAmA 91N
Brown, Carol A. 1950- WhoEmL 91
Brown, Carol Ann 1941- BiDrAPA 89
Brown, Carol Ann 1944- WhoAmW 91
Brown, Carol K WhoAmA 91
Brown, Carol Kapelow 1945- WhoSSW 91
Brown, Carol Robertson 1943- WhoAmW 91
Brown, Carolyn Elizabeth 1943- WhoAmW 91
Brown, Carolyn Marguerite Hutchinson 1936- WhoAmW 91
Brown, Carolyn P. 1923- WhoAm 90
Brown, Carolyn Smith 1946- WhoAmW 91
Brown, Carroll 1928- WhoAm 90
Brown, Carter 1923-1985 TwCCr&M 91
Brown, Cary Scott BiDrAPA 89
Brown, Cassie 1919-1986 BioIn 16
Brown, Cathy Franklin 1947- WhoAmW 91
Brown, Cecil 1907-1987 BioIn 16
Brown, Cee Scott 1952- WhoAmA 91
Brown, Channing Bolton, III 1958- WhoE 91
Brown, Charlene BioIn 16
Brown, Charlene Bernice 1953- WhoEmL 91
Brown, Charles DrBIPA 90
Brown, Charles Alexander 1915- WhoWor 91
Brown, Charles Brockden 1771-1810 BioIn 16
Brown, Charles C 1932- BiDrAPA 89
Brown, Charles Carter 1912- WhoAm 90
Brown, Charles Daniel 1927- WhoAm 90
Brown, Charles Earl 1919- WhoAm 90
Brown, Charles Eric 1946- WhoWor 91
Brown, Charles Eugene 1933- WhoSSW 91
Brown, Charles Foster, III 1947- St&PR 91, WhoAm 90
Brown, Charles Francis 1925- St&PR 91
Brown, Charles Freeman 1914- WhoAm 90
Brown, Charles Gailey 1950- WhoAm 90, WhoSSW 91
Brown, Charles Irving 1932- WhoWor 91
Brown, Charles L. BioIn 16
Brown, Charles L. 1921- St&PR 91
Brown, Charles Stuart 1918- WhoAm 90
Brown, Charles Winston 1932- WhoAm 90
Brown, Charlesey Whitehead 1926- WhoSSW 91
Brown, Charlina Pierce 1935- WhoAmW 91
Brown, Charline Hayes 1919- WhoWrEP 89
Brown, Charlotte WhoAmA 91
Brown, Charlotte Frances 1956- WhoAmW 91, WhoEmL 91
Brown, Charlotte Hawkins 1882-1961 HarlReB [port]
Brown, Charlotte Hawkins 1883-1961 BioIn 16
Brown, Charlotte Vestal 1942- WhoAmA 91
Brown, Charnele BioIn 16
Brown, Chelsea DrBIPA 90
Brown, Cherri Louise 1949- WhoWrEP 89
Brown, Chet 1938- St&PR 91
Brown, Chet, Jr. 1938- WhoWor 91
Brown, Chris 1961- Ballpl 90, BioIn 16
Brown, Christine WhoWrEP 89
Brown, Christine 1930- IntWWM 90
Brown, Christopher 1951- WhoAmA 91
Brown, Christopher Aldrich 1952- WhoWor 91
Brown, Christopher Roland 1943- IntWWM 90
Brown, Christy 1932-1981 ConLC 63 [port]
Brown, Claire Louise 1947- WhoAmW 91
Brown, Claude 1937- BioIn 16
Brown, Claude Kirtland WhoSSW 91
Brown, Claude L 1923- BiDrAPA 89
Brown, Claude Lamar, Jr. 1923- WhoSSW 91
Brown, Claude Posey 1917- St&PR 91
Brown, Clifford 1930-1956 BioIn 16
Brown, Clifford Edward 1947- WhoEmL 91
Brown, Clint 1903-1955 Ballpl 90
Brown, Coleman M BiDrAPA 89
Brown, Colin Wegand 1949- St&PR 91
Brown, Colleen Mary 1961- WhoAmW 91
Brown, Connell Jean 1924- WhoAm 90
Brown, Connie Yates 1947- WhoAmW 91, WhoSSW 91
Brown, Conny Ray 1947- WhoEmL 91, WhoSSW 91
Brown, Conrad 1922- AuBYP 90
Brown, Constance George WhoAmA 91
Brown, Corydon Partlow 1848-1891 DcCanB 12
Brown, Country BioIn 16
Brown, Courtney C. 1904-1990 BioIn 16, ConAu 131, NewYTBS 90
Brown, Craig Alan 1944- BiDrAPA 89
Brown, Craig D. 1951- St&PR 91
Brown, Craig Jay 1951- WhoSSW 91
Brown, Craig Jeffrey 1949- St&PR 91
Brown, Crispin R.W. 1951- St&PR 91
Brown, Dale BioIn 16
Brown, Dale 1947- ODwPR 91
Brown, Dale 1957?- ConAu 129
Brown, Dale Francis 1956- WhoEmL 91
Brown, Dale Marius 1931- WhoAm 90
Brown, Dale Susan 1954- WhoAmW 91, WhoEmL 91
Brown, Dale Weaver 1926- WhoAm 90
Brown, Dallas Coverdale, Jr. 1932- WhoAm 90
Brown, Daniel 1946- WhoAmA 91, WhoEmL 91, WhoWor 91

Brown, Daniel D. 1929- *St&PR 91*
Brown, Daniel H. 1933- *St&PR 91*
Brown, Daniel Herbert 1933- *WhoAm 90*
Brown, Darmae Judd 1952- *WhoAmW 91*
Brown, Darrell 1955- *Ballpl 90*
Brown, Darrell E. 1944- *St&PR 91*
Brown, Dave 1896- *Ballpl 90*
Brown, David *ConAu 129*
Brown, David 1916- *BioIn 16, WhoAm 90, WhoE 91, WhoWrEP 89*
Brown, David 1917- *WhoAm 90*
Brown, David 1929- *IntWWM 90*
Brown, David A 1922-1982 *ConAu 129*
Brown, David A. 1957- *St&PR 91*
Brown, David Alan 1942- *WhoAmA 91*
Brown, David Arthur 1934- *St&PR 91*
Brown, David Charles 1940- *St&PR 91*
Brown, David Charles 1947- *WhoSSW 91*
Brown, David E 1938- *ConAu 32NR*
Brown, David Edward *BiDrAPA 89*
Brown, David Edward 1936- *St&PR 91*
Brown, David Edward 1945- *WhoEmL 91*
Brown, David F. 1941- *St&PR 91*
Brown, David Fain 1941- *WhoAm 90*
Brown, David Grant 1936- *WhoAm 90*
Brown, David H. *ODwPR 91*
Brown, David J. 1948- *WhoE 91*
Brown, David Lee *WhoAmA 91*
Brown, David Lee 1937- *WhoE 91*
Brown, David Lee 1947- *WhoEmL 91*
Brown, David M. 1935- *WhoAm 90*
Brown, David Neil *BiDrAPA 89*
Brown, David Randolph 1923- *WhoAm 90*
Brown, David Rupert 1934- *WhoAm 90*
Brown, David S. 1952- *St&PR 91*
Brown, David S. J. *ODwPR 91*
Brown, David Springer 1915- *WhoAm 90*
Brown, David Taylor 1947- *St&PR 91*
Brown, David W. 1944- *St&PR 91*
Brown, David Warfield 1937- *WhoAm 90*
Brown, Deborah 1927- *BiDWomA*
Brown, Deborah Elizabeth 1952- *WhoEmL 91*
Brown, Deborah Lucretia 1956- *WhoE 91*
Brown, Deborah M.S. 1953- *WhoAmW 91*
Brown, Dee 1908- *MajTwCW*
Brown, Dee Alexander *BioIn 16*
Brown, Dee Alexander 1908- *AuBYP 90, WhoAm 90, WhoWrEP 89*
Brown, Delbert L 1932- *BiDrAPA 89*
Brown, Delmar *BioIn 16*
Brown, Deming Bronson 1919- *WhoAm 90*
Brown, Denise Scott 1931- *BioIn 16, WhoAm 90, WhoAmW 91, WhoWor 91, WomArch [port]*
Brown, Dennis A. *WhoAm 90*
Brown, Dennis D. *St&PR 91N*
Brown, Dennis Edward 1933- *WhoAm 90*
Brown, Dennis Woodfin 1953- *WhoEmL 91*
Brown, Dennison Robert 1934- *WhoAm 90*
Brown, Denny L. 1944- *St&PR 91*
Brown, Dewitt C *BiDrAPA 89*
Brown, Dewitt Wilcox 1916- *BiDrAPA 89*
Brown, Diana 1928- *WhoWrEP 89*
Brown, Diane 1947- *BioIn 16, WhoAmA 91*
Brown, Diane Robinson 1944- *WhoAmW 91*
Brown, Dick 1935-1970 *Ballpl 90*
Brown, Dolores Connor 1937- *WhoAmW 91*
Brown, Don E. 1933- *St&PR 91*
Brown, Don Irvin 1935- *St&PR 91*
Brown, Donald 1932- *WhoAm 90*
Brown, Donald Arthur 1929- *WhoAm 90*
Brown, Donald B 1939- *BiDrAPA 89*
Brown, Donald David 1931- *WhoAm 90*
Brown, Donald Douglas 1931- *WhoAm 90*
Brown, Donald L 1927- *BiDrAPA 89*
Brown, Donald Lewis 1938- *BiDrAPA 89*
Brown, Donald Richard 1925- *WhoWor 91*
Brown, Donald Robert 1925- *WhoAm 90*
Brown, Donald Robert 1945- *WhoAm 90*
Brown, Donald Warren 1939- *St&PR 91*
Brown, Donald Wesley 1953- *WhoWor 91*
Brown, Donaldson 1885-1965 *EncABHB 5 [port]*
Brown, Donna Lynn 1955- *WhoAmW 91*
Brown, Doreen Leah Hurwitz 1927- *WhoAmW 91, WhoE 91*
Brown, Doreen Monique 1955- *WhoEmL 91*
Brown, Dorothea Williams 1918- *WhoAmW 91*
Brown, Dorothy A. 1953- *WhoEmL 91*
Brown, Dorothy Jean 1927- *WhoAmW 91*
Brown, Dorothy McKenna 1938- *WhoAmW 91, WhoE 91*
Brown, Douglas Benedict 1954- *WhoEmL 91*
Brown, Douglas E. 1956- *St&PR 91*
Brown, Drenda Kay 1952- *WhoAmW 91, WhoEmL 91*
Brown, Drollene P. 1939- *BioIn 16*
Brown, Duart Vinson 1912- *WhoWrEP 89*
Brown, Dudley Earl, Jr. 1928- *WhoAm 90*
Brown, Dwight Edward 1945- *St&PR 91*
Brown, Dyann M. E. 1954- *WhoE 91*
Brown, Earl Kent 1925- *WhoAm 90*
Brown, Earle 1926- *IntWWM 90, WhoAm 90*
Brown, Earle Palmer 1922- *WhoAm 90*
Brown, Eddie 1891-1956 *Ballpl 90*
Brown, Edgar Cary 1916- *WhoAm 90, WhoE 91*
Brown, Edgar Henry, Jr. 1926- *WhoAm 90, WhoE 91*
Brown, Edith 1935- *WhoAmW 91*
Brown, Edith Rae 1942- *WhoAmA 91*
Brown, Edith Toliver 1916- *WhoAmW 91*
Brown, Edmund G. *ConAu 132*
Brown, Edmund G 1905- *ConAu 132, WorAlBi*
Brown, Edmund G., Jr. 1938- *WorAlBi*
Brown, Edmund Gerald 1905- *WhoAm 90*
Brown, Edmund Gerald 1938- *BioIn 16*
Brown, Edward 1941- *BiDrAPA 89*
Brown, Edward Evan Nelson 1960- *WhoEmL 91*
Brown, Edward G. 1947- *St&PR 91*
Brown, Edward James 1909- *WhoAm 90*
Brown, Edward James 1937- *WhoE 91, WhoWor 91*
Brown, Edward M *BiDrAPA 89*
Brown, Edward Maurice 1909- *WhoAm 90*
Brown, Edward Randolph 1933- *WhoAm 90*
Brown, Edward Stanton, III 1949- *WhoE 91, WhoEmL 91*
Brown, Edwin Geyer 1937- *WhoAm 90*
Brown, Edwin Lewis, Jr. 1903- *WhoAm 90*
Brown, Edwin Louis 1929- *WhoAm 90*
Brown, Edwin Wilson, Jr. 1926- *WhoAm 90*
Brown, Eileen Clare 1943- *WhoAmW 91*
Brown, Eleanor Frances 1908- *AuBYP 90*
Brown, Eleanor Moore 1936- *WhoAmW 91*
Brown, Eli Houston, Jr. 1875- *AmLegL*
Brown, Eli Matthew 1923- *WhoAm 90*
Brown, Elizabeth Ann 1918- *WhoAm 90*
Brown, Elizabeth Swift 1919- *St&PR 91*
Brown, Elizabeth Taylor 1930- *WhoAmW 91*
Brown, Elizabeth Wibberley *BioIn 16*
Brown, Ellen Zervos 1930- *WhoAmW 91*
Brown, Ellin *BiDEWW*
Brown, Ellis Langham 1915- *St&PR 91*
Brown, Ellsworth Howard 1943- *WhoAm 90*
Brown, Elvin J. 1922- *WhoAm 90*
Brown, Elzie Lee 1914- *WhoSSW 91*
Brown, Eric David 1953- *WhoEmL 91*
Brown, Eric Steven 1953- *WhoEmL 91*
Brown, Eric Vandyke, Jr. 1940- *WhoAm 90*
Brown, Eric Warren 1959- *WhoEmL 91*
Brown, Eric Wynn 1954- *WhoE 91*
Brown, Erika *BioIn 16*
Brown, Ernest Hugh 1943- *St&PR 91*
Brown, Esther Lucile *NewYTBS 90*
Brown, Euphemie A *BiDrAPA 89*
Brown, Everett *DrBlPA 90*
Brown, Faith A. 1948- *ODwPR 91*
Brown, Faith Gideon 1942- *WhoAmW 91*
Brown, Fayette 1943- *St&PR 91*
Brown, Firman Hewitt, Jr. 1926- *WhoAm 90*
Brown, Floyd R. 1929- *ODwPR 91*
Brown, Ford Madox 1821-1893 *BioIn 16, IntDcAA 90*
Brown, Foster Edward 1952- *St&PR 91*
Brown, Frances 1816-1879 *FemiCLE*
Brown, Frances Anne 1946- *WhoAmW 91*
Brown, Frances Barry 1939- *WhoAm 90*
Brown, Francis Cabell, Jr. 1936- *WhoAm 90*
Brown, Francis H., III 1959- *WhoEmL 91*
Brown, Francis Robert 1914- *WhoAm 90*
Brown, Francis Taylor 1925- *St&PR 91*
Brown, Frank 1935- *WhoAm 90*
Brown, Frank E. 1908-1988 *BioIn 16*
Brown, Frank W *BiDrAPA 89*
Brown, Franklin Boineau *BiDrAPA 89*
Brown, Franklin Conrad 1928- *St&PR 91*
Brown, Fred 1879-1955 *Ballpl 90*
Brown, Fred 1941- *WhoSSW 91*
Brown, Fred E. 1858- *AmLegL*
Brown, Fred E. 1913- *St&PR 91*
Brown, Fred Elmore 1913- *WhoAm 90*
Brown, Fred Emerson 1930- *WhoE 91*
Brown, Fred Grant 1953- *WhoEmL 91*
Brown, Fred I., Jr. 1923- *St&PR 91*
Brown, Fred Taylor, Jr. 1946- *WhoSSW 91*
Brown, Frederic 1906-1972 *WorAlBi*
Brown, Frederic Joseph 1934- *WhoAm 90*
Brown, Frederick 1794?-1838 *OxCCanT*
Brown, Frederick 1945- *BioIn 16*
Brown, Frederick Calvin 1924- *WhoAm 90*
Brown, Frederick Gramm 1932- *WhoAm 90*
Brown, Frederick Harold 1927- *St&PR 91, WhoE 91, WhoWor 91*
Brown, Frederick Isaac, Jr. 1923- *WhoAm 90, WhoSSW 91*
Brown, Frederick James 1927- *WhoE 91*
Brown, Frederick James 1945- *WhoAmA 91*
Brown, Frederick Lee 1940- *WhoAm 90, WhoWor 91*
Brown, Fredric 1906-1972 *TwCCr&M 91*
Brown, Freezell, Jr. 1957- *WhoEmL 91*
Brown, Frieda Farfour 1948- *WhoSSW 91*
Brown, G. Robert 1933- *St&PR 91*
Brown, Gardner Russell, Mrs. *WhoAmW 91, WhoE 91*
Brown, Gary Hugh 1941- *WhoAmA 91*
Brown, Gary Sandy 1940- *WhoAm 90*
Brown, Gates 1939- *Ballpl 90*
Brown, Gavin William 1925- *IntWWM 90*
Brown, Gay Correll 1943- *WhoSSW 91*
Brown, Gaye Robinson 1938- *WhoAmW 91*
Brown, Gene L. 1950- *St&PR 91*
Brown, Gene Monte 1926- *WhoAm 90*
Brown, Gene W. 1936- *St&PR 91, WhoAm 90*
Brown, Georg Stanford 1943- *DrBlPA 90*
Brown, George Alfred 1914-1985 *DcNaB 1981*
Brown, George Edward, Jr. 1920- *WhoAm 90*
Brown, George Franklin, Jr. 1946- *St&PR 91*
Brown, George Hay 1910- *WhoAm 90*
Brown, George King 1925- *St&PR 91*
Brown, George Leslie 1926- *St&PR 91, WhoAm 90, WhoWor 91*
Brown, George M. 1908- *St&PR 91*
Brown, George Mackay *BioIn 16*
Brown, George Mackay 1921- *MajTwCW*
Brown, George P 1920- *BiDrAPA 89*
Brown, George R. *BioIn 16*
Brown, George Richard *BiDrAPA 89*
Brown, George S. 1918-1978 *WorAlBi*
Brown, George S. 1930- *St&PR 91*
Brown, George Stephen 1945- *WhoAm 90, WhoEmL 91, WhoWor 91*
Brown, Georgia 1933- *OxCPMus*
Brown, Georgia Watts 1934- *WhoAmW 91*
Brown, Gerald Eugene 1949- *WhoEmL 91*
Brown, Gerald L 1940- *BiDrAPA 89*
Brown, Geraldine 1945- *WhoAmW 91*
Brown, Geraldine Reed 1947- *WhoAm 90, WhoAmW 91*
Brown, Gerard S. *St&PR 91*
Brown, GerryAnne 1945- *WhoAmW 91*
Brown, Giles Tyler 1916- *WhoAm 90, WhoWor 91*
Brown, Gillian *BioIn 16*
Brown, Gladys Tartt 1931- *WhoSSW 91*
Brown, Glenda Ann Walters 1937- *WhoSSW 91*
Brown, Glenda Carol 1949- *WhoAmW 91*
Brown, Glenn Halstead 1915- *WhoAm 90*
Brown, Glenn M. 1931- *St&PR 91*
Brown, Glenn Robbins, Jr. 1930- *WhoAm 90*
Brown, Glenn William, Jr. 1937- *St&PR 91*
Brown, Glenn William, Jr. 1955- *WhoE 91, WhoEmL 91, WhoWor 91*
Brown, Gloria Campos 1954- *WhoHisp 91*
Brown, Gordon *BioIn 16*
Brown, Gordon E., Jr. 1943- *WhoAm 90*
Brown, Gordon T 1924- *BiDrAPA 89*
Brown, Graham 1924- *DrBlPA 90*
Brown, Graham, Jr. *St&PR 91*
Brown, Gregg G. 1963- *WhoE 91*
Brown, Gregory M 1934- *BiDrAPA 89*
Brown, Gregory Neil 1938- *WhoAm 90*
Brown, Gregory Peninger *BiDrAPA 89*
Brown, Guy E, II 1940- *ODwPR 91*
Brown, H. William 1938- *WhoAm 90*
Brown, Hal 1924- *Ballpl 90*
Brown, Hallie Quinn 1845?-1949 *HarlReB [port]*
Brown, Hamish M 1934- *ConAu 129*
Brown, Hank 1940- *WhoAm 90*
Brown, Harold 1927- *BiDrUSE 89, WhoAm 90*
Brown, Harold J., Jr. 1940- *St&PR 91*
Brown, Harold W. 1902-1988 *BioIn 16*
Brown, Harris Robert 1950- *WhoE 91*
Brown, Harry Gunnison 1880-1975 *BioIn 16*
Brown, Harry Matthew 1921- *WhoSSW 91*
Brown, Harry Stavley 1929- *WhoSSW 91*
Brown, Hedley Arthur 1934- *WhoWor 91*
Brown, Helen, and Philip S. Brown *AuBYP 90*
Brown, Helen Bennett 1902- *WhoAmW 91*
Brown, Helen Frances 1947- *IntWWM 90*
Brown, Helen Gurley 1922- *WhoAm 90, WhoAmW 91, WhoWor 91, WhoWrEP 89, WorAlBi*
Brown, Helen I. 1908- *St&PR 91*
Brown, Helene Gurian 1929- *WhoAmW 91*
Brown, Henry Arthur, Jr. 1921- *St&PR 91*
Brown, Henry Bedinger Rust 1926- *WhoAm 90*
Brown, Henry Kirke 1814-1886 *BioIn 16*
Brown, Herbert *BioIn 16*
Brown, Herbert C. 1912- *WorAlBi*
Brown, Herbert Charles 1912- *WhoAm 90, WhoWor 91*
Brown, Herbert Graham 1923- *WhoSSW 91*
Brown, Herbert N *BiDrAPA 89*
Brown, Herbert Ross 1902-1988 *BioIn 16*
Brown, Hermione Kopp 1915- *WhoAm 90*
Brown, Hilton 1938- *WhoAmA 91*
Brown, Hobson, Jr. 1942- *WhoAm 90*
Brown, Homer Buford 1921- *St&PR 91*
Brown, Horace Ludwig 1906- *WhoWor 91*
Brown, Howard Bernard 1924- *WhoSSW 91*
Brown, Howard C. 1921- *WhoAm 90*
Brown, Howard Carter, III 1951- *WhoEmL 91*
Brown, Howard Earl 1920- *St&PR 91*
Brown, Howard Elliott 1949- *WhoSSW 91*
Brown, Howard L. 1906- *St&PR 91*
Brown, Howard M. *St&PR 91N*
Brown, Howard Mayer 1930- *IntWWM 90*
Brown, Ian Alexander 1951- *WhoEmL 91*
Brown, Idee Millicent *BiDrAPA 89*
Brown, Ike 1942- *Ballpl 90*
Brown, Iona *BioIn 16, PenDiMP*
Brown, Iona 1941- *WhoAmW 91*
Brown, Ira Bernard 1927- *WhoAm 90*
Brown, Irby *BioIn 16*
Brown, Irene Bennett 1932- *BioIn 16*
Brown, Irving 1911-1989 *AnObit 1989, BioIn 16*
Brown, Isabelle Ruth 1910- *WhoAmW 91*
Brown, J. Callaway 1928- *St&PR 91*
Brown, J. Curtis 1943- *ODwPR 91*
Brown, J. Duncan 1923- *St&PR 91*
Brown, J. E. 1940- *WhoSSW 91*
Brown, J. Kathleen *WhoWrEP 89*
Brown, J. Thomas 1935- *St&PR 91*
Brown, J.W. 1911- *St&PR 91*
Brown, J Warren 1934- *BiDrAPA 89*
Brown, Jack 1927- *WhoAm 90, WhoWrEP 89*
Brown, Jack Ainsworth 1930- *St&PR 91*
Brown, Jack B. 1924- *St&PR 91*
Brown, Jack C. 1919- *St&PR 91*
Brown, Jack Cole 1930- *WhoAm 90*
Brown, Jack Ernest 1914- *WhoAm 90*
Brown, Jack H. 1939- *WhoAm 90*
Brown, Jack Harold Upton 1918- *WhoAm 90*
Brown, Jack Ross 1926- *BiDrAPA 89*
Brown, Jack W. 1939- *St&PR 91*
Brown, Jack Wyman 1922- *WhoAm 90*
Brown, Jackie 1943- *Ballpl 90*
Brown, Jacob A. 1926- *WhoAm 90*
Brown, Jacqueline Sue 1947- *WhoEmL 91, WhoSSW 91*
Brown, James *BioIn 16, WhoAmA 91*
Brown, James 1766-1835 *BioIn 16*
Brown, James 1928- *EncPR&S 89, OxCPMus, WorAlBi*
Brown, James 1933- *DrBlPA 90*
Brown, James Andrew 1914- *WhoAm 90*
Brown, James Anthony 1932- *WhoSSW 91*
Brown, James Arthur 1943- *St&PR 91*
Brown, James Benjamin 1946- *WhoAm 90*
Brown, James Briggs 1922- *WhoAm 90*
Brown, James C N *BiDrAPA 89*
Brown, James Carrington, III 1939- *WhoWor 91*
Brown, James Creighton 1952- *WhoEmL 91*
Brown, James Curtiss 1921- *WhoSSW 91*
Brown, James Douglas 1958- *St&PR 91*
Brown, James Edward 1952- *St&PR 91*
Brown, James Elliott 1947- *WhoEmL 91*
Brown, James Frederick 1943- *St&PR 91*
Brown, James H 1923- *BiDrAPA 89*
Brown, James H., Jr. 1940- *WhoAm 90*
Brown, James Hamilton 1926- *WhoAm 90*
Brown, James Harlow 1937- *St&PR 91*
Brown, James Harvey 1936- *WhoAm 90*
Brown, James Hugh 1947- *St&PR 91*
Brown, James Isaac 1908- *WhoAm 90*
Brown, James Joseph 1928- *St&PR 91, WhoAm 90*
Brown, James Martin 1945- *WhoE 91*
Brown, James Melton 1925- *WhoAm 90*
Brown, James Michael 1957- *WhoWrEP 89*
Brown, James Monroe, III 1917- *WhoAm 90, WhoAmA 91*
Brown, James Nelson, Jr. 1929- *WhoE 91*
Brown, James Robert 1930- *WhoAm 90*
Brown, James Roy 1950- *WhoSSW 91*
Brown, James T., Jr. *ODwPR 91*
Brown, James Thompson, Jr. 1935- *WhoWor 91*
Brown, James W. 1947- *St&PR 91*
Brown, James Walter, Jr. 1945- *WhoSSW 91*
Brown, James Ward 1934- *WhoAm 90*
Brown, James William 1944- *WhoSSW 91*
Brown, Jan W. 1942- *WhoAmW 91*
Brown, Jane Martin Thornton 1951- *WhoAmW 91*
Brown, Janet 1936- *WhoAmW 91*
Brown, Janine Louise 1954- *WhoAmW 91*

Brown, Jason Walter 1938- *WhoAm 90*
Brown, Jay Marshall 1933- *WhoE 91*
Brown, Jay W. 1945- *St&PR 91*
Brown, Jay Wright 1945- *WhoAm 90*
Brown, Jean Bush 1947- *WhoAmW 91, WhoEmL 91*
Brown, Jean McBrayer 1908- *WhoWrEP 89*
Brown, Jean William 1928- *WhoAm 90*
Brown, Jeff *AuBYP 90*
Brown, Jeffrey 1946- *WhoEmL 91*
Brown, Jeffrey Barnett 1948- *BiDrAPA 89*
Brown, Jeffrey L. 1955- *WhoSSW 91*
Brown, Jennifer Jane 1959- *WhoAmW 91*
Brown, Jennifer S. H. 1940- *ConAu 130*
Brown, Jerome *BioIn 16*
Brown, Jerrold Stanley 1953- *WhoEmL 91*
Brown, Jerry 1938- *BioIn 16*
Brown, Jerry Glenn 1933- *St&PR 91, WhoAm 90*
Brown, Jerry William 1925- *WhoSSW 91*
Brown, Jim 1935- *DrBlPA 90*
Brown, Jim 1936- *BioIn 16, WorAlBi*
Brown, Jimmy 1910-1977 *Ballpl 90*
Brown, Joan *NewYTBS 90*
Brown, Joan Hudson 1935- *WhoSSW 91*
Brown, Joan Mazzaferro 1956- *WhoAmW 91*
Brown, Joanne Carlson 1953- *WhoEmL 91*
Brown, Joe Blackburn 1940- *WhoAm 90*
Brown, Joe E. 1892-1973 *WorAlBi*
Brown, Joe Lawrence, II 1942- *WhoSSW 91*
Brown, Joe Robert 1911- *WhoAm 90*
Brown, Joel Edward 1937- *WhoAm 90*
Brown, John 1736-1803 *BioIn 16*
Brown, John 1757-1837 *BioIn 16*
Brown, John 1800-1859 *BioIn 16, WorAlBi*
Brown, John 1826-1883 *EncO&P 3*
Brown, John Callaway 1928- *WhoAm 90*
Brown, John Carey 1948- *WhoEmL 91*
Brown, John Carter 1934- *WhoAm 90, WhoAmA 91, WhoE 91, WhoWor 91*
Brown, John D. *St&PR 91*
Brown, John E. 1922- *St&PR 91*
Brown, John Edward 1936- *WhoE 91*
Brown, John Edward 1939- *WhoAm 90*
Brown, John Fred 1941- *WhoSSW 91, WhoWor 91*
Brown, John Gilbert Newton 1916- *WhoWor 91*
Brown, John Hall 1910- *WhoAmA 91*
Brown, John Lawrence, Jr. 1925- *WhoAm 90*
Brown, John Lewis 1955- *WhoEmL 91*
Brown, John Lott 1924- *WhoAm 90*
Brown, John Marshall 1924- *WhoAm 90*
Brown, John Martin 1924- *St&PR 91*
Brown, John Mason 1837-1890 *EncO&P 3*
Brown, John Mason 1900-1969 *LiHiK*
Brown, John McFee 1922- *WhoAm 90*
Brown, John Newton 1803-1868 *BioIn 16*
Brown, John O. 1934- *St&PR 91, WhoAm 90*
Brown, John P. E. *BioIn 16*
Brown, John Patrick 1925- *WhoAm 90*
Brown, John Porter 1814-1872 *BioIn 16*
Brown, John Robert 1909- *WhoAm 90, WhoSSW 91*
Brown, John Robert 1935- *St&PR 91*
Brown, John Robert 1947- *WhoEmL 91, WhoWor 91*
Brown, John Terrell 1940- *St&PR 91*
Brown, John Trevor 1937- *WhoE 91*
Brown, John W. 1922- *St&PR 91*
Brown, John Wilford 1934- *St&PR 91*
Brown, John Y. 1933- *WorAlBi*
Brown, Johnny *DrBlPA 90*
Brown, Johnny Mack 1952- *WhoSSW 91*
Brown, Jonathan 1939- *ConAu 132, WhoAm 90, WhoAmA 91*
Brown, Joseph 1909- *WhoAmA 91N*
Brown, Joseph A. 1926- *WhoAm 90*
Brown, Joseph E. 1929- *BioIn 16*
Brown, Joseph G *BiDrAPA 89*
Brown, Joseph Gordon 1927- *WhoAm 90*
Brown, Joseph Simon, Jr. 1907- *WhoSSW 91*
Brown, Joseph W., Jr. 1949- *WhoAm 90*
Brown, Joseph Warner, Jr. 1949- *St&PR 91*
Brown, Joyce *BioIn 16*
Brown, Joyce Christine 1956- *WhoAmW 91*
Brown, Juanita Ora Luckett 1948- *WhoAmW 91*
Brown, Judith Arner 1947- *WhoE 91, WhoEmL 91*
Brown, Judith Gwyn 1933- *AuBYP 90, WhoAmA 91*
Brown, Judith M 1944- *ConAu 32NR*
Brown, Judith Olans 1941- *WhoAm 90*
Brown, Judy Marie 1957- *WhoAmW 91*
Brown, Julie *BioIn 16*
Brown, Julie Ann 1958- *WhoAmW 91*
Brown, Jumbo 1907-1966 *Ballpl 90*
Brown, June 1923- *WhoAm 90*
Brown, June Evelyn 1925- *WhoWor 91*
Brown, June Gibbs 1933- *WhoAm 90, WhoAmW 91*
Brown, June Gottlieb 1932- *WhoAmA 91*
Brown, June Wilcoxon 1914- *WhoAmW 91*
Brown, Karen Kay 1944- *WhoAmW 91*
Brown, Karen Susan *BiDrAPA 89*
Brown, Karl *NewYTBS 90*
Brown, Karl 1897-1990 *BioIn 16, ConAu 131*
Brown, Kathaleen Ruth 1937- *St&PR 91*
Brown, Katharine Eisenhart 1921- *WhoE 91*
Brown, Kathleen *WhoAmW 91*
Brown, Kathleen Maria 1960- *WhoEmL 91*
Brown, Kathryn Ann Smith 1926- *WhoSSW 91*
Brown, Kay 1950- *WhoAmW 91*
Brown, Keirn Clarke, Jr. 1947- *WhoE 91, WhoEmL 91*
Brown, Keith 1933- *IntWWM 90, WhoAm 90*
Brown, Keith A 1957- *BiDrAPA 89*
Brown, Keith Allen 1937- *St&PR 91*
Brown, Keith Lapham 1925- *WhoAm 90, WhoWor 91*
Brown, Kelly 1955- *St&PR 91*
Brown, Kenneth 1919- *WhoE 91*
Brown, Kenneth A. 1951- *ODwPR 91*
Brown, Kenneth Alan 1951- *WhoEmL 91*
Brown, Kenneth Allen 1950- *WhoSSW 91*
Brown, Kenneth Allen 1954- *WhoSSW 91*
Brown, Kenneth Ashley, Jr. 1946- *WhoSSW 91*
Brown, Kenneth Charles 1952- *St&PR 91, WhoAm 90, WhoE 91, WhoEmL 91*
Brown, Kenneth H. *WhoWrEP 89*
Brown, Kenneth Henry 1939- *WhoSSW 91*
Brown, Kenneth L. 1936- *WhoWor 91*
Brown, Kenneth Lloyd 1927- *WhoAm 90*
Brown, Kenneth R. 1936- *St&PR 91*
Brown, Kenneth Ray 1936- *WhoAm 90, WhoSSW 91*
Brown, Kent Louis, Jr. 1943- *WhoWrEP 89*
Brown, Kent Louis, Sr. 1916- *WhoAm 90*
Brown, Kent Robert 1945- *St&PR 91*
Brown, Kenton Allan 1944- *BiDrAPA 89*
Brown, Kevin 1965- *Ballpl 90*
Brown, Kevin Charles 1953- *WhoSSW 91*
Brown, Kevin Michael 1948- *WhoE 91, WhoEmL 91*
Brown, Kingsley M., Jr. 1924- *St&PR 91*
Brown, Korie Beth 1962- *WhoAmW 91*
Brown, Kyle Nelson 1958- *WhoEmL 91*
Brown, L. *BiDWomA*
Brown, L. Franklin 1943- *WhoSSW 91*
Brown, Lancelot 1715-1783 *WorAlBi*
Brown, LaRita Early Dawn Ma-Ka-Re 1937- *WhoAmW 91*
Brown, Larry *WhoAm 90*
Brown, Larry 1902-1972 *Ballpl 90*
Brown, Larry 1940- *Ballpl 90, WorAlBi*
Brown, Larry 1942- *WhoAmA 91*
Brown, Larry 1951- *ConAu 130*
Brown, Larry Eddie 1941- *WhoSSW 91, WhoWor 91*
Brown, Larry G. 1942- *St&PR 91*
Brown, Larry Kenneth 1951- *BiDrAPA 89*
Brown, Laura L. *ODwPR 91*
Brown, Laurence Watson 1937- *WhoE 91*
Brown, Laurene Krasny *BioIn 16*
Brown, Laurie Kristine *BiDrAPA 89*
Brown, Laurie Lizbeth 1946- *WhoEmL 91*
Brown, Laurie Mark 1923- *WhoAm 90*
Brown, Lavelle Shelly 1961- *WhoAmW 91*
Brown, Lawrence *DrBlPA 90*
Brown, Lawrence 1907-1988 *AnObit 1988, BioIn 16*
Brown, Lawrence Benjamin 1893-1972 *DcAfAmP*
Brown, Lawrence Charles 1951- *WhoEmL 91*
Brown, Lawrence Clifton, Jr. 1950- *WhoE 91*
Brown, Lawrence Haas 1934- *St&PR 91, WhoAm 90*
Brown, Lawrence Harvey 1940- *WhoSSW 91*
Brown, Lawrence Raymond, Jr. 1928- *WhoAm 90*
Brown, Lawrie 1949- *WhoAmA 91*
Brown, Leanna 1935- *WhoAmW 91, WhoE 91*
Brown, Lee Patrick 1937- *WhoAm 90, WhoE 91*
Brown, Leon 1907- *WhoAm 90*
Brown, Leon Carl 1928- *WhoAm 90*
Brown, Leon T. 1920- *St&PR 91*
Brown, Leon Willard 1921- *St&PR 91*
Brown, Leonard Bernard 1932- *St&PR 91*
Brown, Leonard Carlton 1915- *WhoAm 90*
Brown, Leonard S *BioIn 16*
Brown, Les 1912- *BioIn 16, OxCPMus, WorAlBi*
Brown, Les 1928- *WhoAm 90*
Brown, Leslie *ODwPR 91*
Brown, Leslie Ann 1961- *WhoAmW 91, WhoE 91*
Brown, Lester *ConAu 132*
Brown, Lester L. 1928- *WhoWrEP 89*
Brown, Lester R 1934- *ConAu 132*
Brown, Lester Russell 1934- *WhoAm 90*
Brown, Lew 1893-1958 *OxCPMus*
Brown, Lewis Arnold 1931- *WhoAm 90*
Brown, Lewis Frank 1929- *WhoWor 91*
Brown, Lewis J. 1932- *St&PR 91*
Brown, Lewis Nathan 1953- *WhoSSW 91, WhoWor 91*
Brown, Lida C *BiDrAPA 89*
Brown, Linda Anne 1953- *WhoAmW 91*
Brown, Linda Cockerham 1946- *WhoAmW 91, WhoEmL 91*
Brown, Linda Currene 1942- *WhoAmW 91*
Brown, Linda Lockett 1954- *WhoAmW 91*
Brown, Linda Odessa 1957- *WhoAmW 91*
Brown, Linda Ruth 1952- *WhoAmW 91*
Brown, Lisa Ann 1956- *WhoEmL 91*
Brown, Lisa Claire 1954- *WhoEmL 91*
Brown, Lizzie Pearl 1931- *WhoAmW 91*
Brown, Lloyd 1904-1974 *Ballpl 90*
Brown, Lloyd Arnold 1907-1966 *AuBYP 90*
Brown, Lloyd George 1944- *WhoWor 91*
Brown, Logan R. 1927- *St&PR 91*
Brown, Lois Heffington 1940- *WhoAmW 91*
Brown, Lorene Byron 1933- *WhoAm 90*
Brown, Loretta Ann Port 1945- *WhoAmW 91*
Brown, Lori Dawn 1961- *WhoSSW 91*
Brown, Lorraine Ann 1947- *WhoAmW 91*
Brown, Louis M. 1909- *WhoAm 90, WhoWor 91*
Brown, Louise Dona 1959- *WhoAmW 91*
Brown, Lowell Severt 1934- *WhoAm 90*
Brown, Lucinda Ann 1956- *WhoAmW 91*
Brown, Luther *BioIn 16*
Brown, Luther 1948- *WhoAm 90, WhoEmL 91*
Brown, Lynette Ralya 1926- *WhoAmW 91*
Brown, Lynn Curtis 1954- *WhoSSW 91*
Brown, M. K. *AuBYP 90*
Brown, Mabel Estle 1907- *WhoWor 91*
Brown, Mace 1909- *Ballpl 90*
Brown, Mackie Neal 1933- *WhoSSW 91*
Brown, Malcolm Ferrie, Jr. 1926- *St&PR 91*
Brown, Manuel W. *EarBlAP*
Brown, Marc Laurence 1951- *WhoEmL 91*
Brown, Marc Tolon *BioIn 16*
Brown, Marcia 1918- *BioIn 16*
Brown, Marcia J. 1918- *WhoAm 90, WhoAmW 91*
Brown, Marcia Joan 1918- *AuBYP 90*
Brown, Margaret *NewYTBS 90*
Brown, Margaret 1867- *FemiCLE*
Brown, Margaret 1910-1952 *WhoAmA 91N*
Brown, Margaret deBeers 1943- *WhoAmW 91*
Brown, Margaret Jean 1947- *WhoAmW 91*
Brown, Margaret Ree 1949- *WhoAmW 91*
Brown, Margaret Ruth Anderson 1944- *WhoAmW 91*
Brown, Margaret Walter *BioIn 16*
Brown, Margaret Wise 1910-1952 *AuBYP 90, BioIn 16*
Brown, Marie A. 1936- *WhoAmW 91*
Brown, Marie Magdalen Jenkins 1909- *WhoAmW 91*
Brown, Marilyn Branch 1944- *WhoAmW 91*
Brown, Marilyn V. *ODwPR 91*
Brown, Marion B 1913- *WhoAmA 91*
Brown, Marion Bakewell 1913- *WhoE 91*
Brown, Marion Lipscomb, Jr. 1925- *WhoAm 90*
Brown, Marion Marsh 1908- *AuBYP 90*
Brown, Mark Charles 1952- *WhoEmL 91*
Brown, Mark L. 1954- *St&PR 91*
Brown, Martha Constable 1954- *WhoEmL 91*
Brown, Martha Eugenia 1955- *BiDrAPA 89*
Brown, Marthe Erdos *BiDrAPA 89*
Brown, Martin *ODwPR 91*
Brown, Martin Howard 1953- *WhoE 91*
Brown, Martin Raymond 1954- *WhoAm 90*
Brown, Marvin 1912- *BioIn 16*
Brown, Marvin L., Jr. 1948- *ODwPR 91*
Brown, Marvin S. 1935- *St&PR 91*
Brown, Mary Eleanor 1906- *WhoAmW 91*
Brown, Mary Jo 1958- *WhoEmL 91*
Brown, Mary Oliver 1953- *WhoWrEP 89*
Brown, Mary Rachel *WhoAmA 91*
Brown, Mary Ward *BioIn 16*
Brown, Matthew 1905- *WhoAm 90*
Brown, Matthews 1952- *WhoEmL 91*
Brown, Max Arnold 1938- *WhoSSW 91*
Brown, Maxine *DrBlPA 90*
Brown, McTeer 1927- *St&PR 91*
Brown, Melanie Louise 1957- *WhoE 91*
Brown, Melissa Kern 1959- *WhoEmL 91*
Brown, Melvin F. 1935- *St&PR 91, WhoAm 90*
Brown, Merle C. 1929- *St&PR 91*
Brown, Merrill Edwin 1926- *IntWWM 90*
Brown, Merrill Mark 1952- *WhoAm 90, WhoEmL 91*
Brown, Meyer *BiDrAPA 89*
Brown, Michael 1943- *WhoAm 90*
Brown, Michael Arthur 1938- *WhoAm 90*
Brown, Michael David *BiDrAPA 89*
Brown, Michael DeWayne 1954- *WhoEmL 91*
Brown, Michael George 1951- *WhoSSW 91*
Brown, Michael Irwin 1943- *St&PR 91*
Brown, Michael Jay 1956- *St&PR 91*
Brown, Michael L. 1958- *WhoEmL 91*
Brown, Michael Lynn 1950- *WhoEmL 91*
Brown, Michael Lynn 1958- *WhoEmL 91*
Brown, Michael Richard 1959- *WhoEmL 91*
Brown, Michael Ross 1941- *WhoWor 91*
Brown, Michael S. 1941- *WorAlBi*
Brown, Michael Stephen 1942- *St&PR 91*
Brown, Michael Stephen 1948- *WhoEmL 91*
Brown, Michael Stuart 1941- *WhoAm 90, WhoSSW 91, WhoWor 91*
Brown, Michael Wayne 1955- *WhoSSW 91*
Brown, Michele Denise 1955- *WhoEmL 91*
Brown, Mickey Jackson 1946- *St&PR 91*
Brown, Mike 1959- *Ballpl 90*
Brown, Mildred *BioIn 16*
Brown, Milton O. 1929- *St&PR 91*
Brown, Milton Wolf 1911- *WhoAm 90, WhoAmA 91*
Brown, Mitchell Swift 1950- *St&PR 91*
Brown, Mollie Margaret 1931- *WhoAmW 91*
Brown, Mordecai 1876-1948 *BioIn 16*
Brown, Morgan Cornelius 1916- *WhoAm 90*
Brown, Morton B. 1941- *WhoAm 90*
Brown, Murray Allen 1945- *BiDrAPA 89*
Brown, Myra 1933- *St&PR 91*
Brown, Myra Berry 1918- *AuBYP 90*
Brown, Myrtle Irene 1915- *WhoAm 90*
Brown, Nacio Herb 1896-1964 *BioIn 16, OxCPMus*
Brown, Nancy Alice 1934- *WhoAmW 91*
Brown, Nancy Ann *WhoAm 90*
Brown, Nancy J. 1942- *WhoAmW 91*
Brown, Naomi 1954- *WhoAmW 91*
Brown, Naomi Yanagi 1920- *WhoSSW 91*
Brown, Natalia Taylor 1928- *WhoAmW 91*
Brown, Natalie Babel *BioIn 16*
Brown, Natalie Joy 1962- *WhoWrEP 89*
Brown, Neil Douglas 1943- *WhoWor 91*
Brown, Neill Smith 1810-1886 *AmLegL*
Brown, Nicholas 1932- *WhoAm 90, WhoE 91*
Brown, Norma 1911- *IntWWM 90*
Brown, Norman Donald 1935- *WhoAm 90*
Brown, Norman H. *WhoWrEP 89*
Brown, Norman James 1942- *WhoSSW 91*
Brown, Norman Wesley 1931- *St&PR 91, WhoAm 90*
Brown, Norris *BioIn 16*
Brown, Nyda Williams 1933- *BiDrAPA 89*
Brown, Olen Ray 1935- *WhoAm 90*
Brown, Olivia *BioIn 16, DrBlPA 90*
Brown, Ollie 1944- *Ballpl 90*
Brown, Ollie Dawkins 1941- *WhoAmW 91, WhoSSW 91, WhoWor 91*
Brown, Omer Forrest, II 1947- *WhoE 91*
Brown, Oral *BioIn 16*
Brown, Oscar, Jr. 1926- *DrBlPA 90*
Brown, Owsley, II 1942- *WhoAm 90, WhoSSW 91*
Brown, Pamela 1924-1989 *AnObit 1989, SmATA 61*
Brown, Pamela 1948- *FemiCLE*
Brown, Pamela Beatrice 1924- *AuBYP 90*
Brown, Pamela Joy Clark 1954- *WhoWor 91*
Brown, Pamela Wedd 1928- *WhoAmA 91*
Brown, Parker James 1954- *WhoE 91*
Brown, Patricia Ann 1929- *WhoAm 90*
Brown, Patricia Anne 1939- *WhoAmW 91*
Brown, Patricia Anne 1962- *WhoE 91*
Brown, Patricia Cochran 1955- *WhoAmW 91, WhoE 91*
Brown, Patricia Fortini 1936- *ConAu 131, WhoAmW 91*
Brown, Patricia H 1932- *BiDrAPA 89*
Brown, Patricia Irene *WhoAmW 91, WhoE 91, WhoWor 91*
Brown, Patricia Leonard 1950- *WhoEmL 91*
Brown, Patricia Mary 1945- *WhoAmW 91*
Brown, Patricia Metzger 1945- *WhoAmW 91*
Brown, Paul 1893- *AuBYP 90*
Brown, Paul 1893-1958 *WhoAmA 91N*
Brown, Paul 1908- *BioIn 16, WorAlBi*
Brown, Paul A. 1938- *WhoAm 90*
Brown, Paul Alan 1963- *WhoEmL 91*
Brown, Paul Appleton 1938- *St&PR 91*
Brown, Paul Bradley 1912- *WhoAm 90*
Brown, Paul Bradley 1954- *WhoE 91*
Brown, Paul E. *WhoAm 90*

Brown, Paul Edmondson 1915- WhoWor 91
Brown, Paul Edwin, Jr. 1951- WhoEmL 91
Brown, Paul G. 1955- St&PR 91
Brown, Paul Jeffrey 1957- BiDrAPA 89
Brown, Paul Joseph 1924- WhoAm 90
Brown, Paul M. 1938- WhoAm 90
Brown, Paul Neeley 1926- WhoAm 90, WhoSSW 91
Brown, Paul Richard 1930- WhoSSW 91
Brown, Paul Sheldon 1957- WhoSSW 91
Brown, Paul Truett 1954- WhoEmL 91
Brown, Paul W. 1915- WhoAm 90
Brown, Paula Kinney 1953- WhoAmW 91
Brown, Payton Gordon BiDrAPA 89
Brown, Peggy Ann 1934- WhoAmA 91
Brown, Peggy Sherburn 1918-1989 BioIn 16
Brown, Peter C 1940- WhoAmA 91
Brown, Peter Campbell 1913- WhoAm 90, WhoWor 91
Brown, Peter Gilbert 1940- WhoAm 90
Brown, Peter Hail 1940- WhoE 91
Brown, Peter J 1951- BiDrAPA 89
Brown, Peter M. St&PR 91
Brown, Peter Mason 1945- WhoEmL 91
Brown, Peter Megargee 1922- WhoAm 90
Brown, Peter Rawcliffe 1949- WhoEmL 91
Brown, Peter Robert WhoAm 90
Brown, Peter Thomson 1948- WhoAmA 91
Brown, Philip Henry 1952- WhoE 91
Brown, Philip N BiDrAPA 89
Brown, Phillip S. 1936- St&PR 91
Brown, Phyllis George BioIn 16
Brown, Phyllis Smiley 1943- WhoAmW 91
Brown, Preston 1936- WhoAm 90
Brown, Quincalee 1939- WhoAm 90, WhoAmW 91
Brown, R. Harper 1923- St&PR 91
Brown, R. Jess BioIn 16
Brown, R. Jess NewYTBS 90
Brown, Rachel Fuller 1898-1980 BioAmW
Brown, Ralph BioIn 16
Brown, Ralph NewYTBS 90
Brown, Ralph A. 1918- St&PR 91
Brown, Ralph Edward 1943- St&PR 91
Brown, Ralph Evan 1920- WhoAm 90
Brown, Ralph Sawyer, Jr. 1931- WhoAm 90
Brown, Randolph Graham 1942- St&PR 91
Brown, Ray 1926- BioIn 16, DrBlPA 90
Brown, Ray Kent 1924- WhoAm 90
Brown, Ray Nowlin 1951- WhoEmL 91
Brown, Ray William 1929- St&PR 91
Brown, Raymond 1908-1972? Ballpl 90
Brown, Raymond Jessie 1944- WhoSSW 91
Brown, Raymond Lloyd 1936- WhoAm 90
Brown, Raymond Lloyd, Jr. 1958- WhoEmL 91
Brown, Raymond Martin 1946- WhoEmL 91
Brown, Raymond Paul 1927- St&PR 91
Brown, Rayner 1912- IntWWM 90
Brown, Regina Margaret AuBYP 90
Brown, Reynold 1917- WhoAmA 91
Brown, Richard 1943- BioIn 16
Brown, Richard 1946- SmATA 61
Brown, Richard A. 1940- St&PR 91
Brown, Richard Arthur 1918- WhoE 91
Brown, Richard C, Jr. BiDrAPA 89
Brown, Richard Clark 1939- WhoSSW 91
Brown, Richard Dee 1938- WhoSSW 91
Brown, Richard E. 1946- ConAu 130
Brown, Richard Earl 1947- IntWWM 90
Brown, Richard F 1916-1979 WhoAmA 91N
Brown, Richard George 1923- St&PR 91
Brown, Richard H. 1947- St&PR 91
Brown, Richard Harris 1947- WhoAm 90
Brown, Richard Holbrook 1927- WhoAm 90
Brown, Richard James 1944- St&PR 91, WhoAm 90
Brown, Richard Jerome 1951- BiDrAPA 89
Brown, Richard Joseph BiDrAPA 89
Brown, Richard Laurence 1962- WhoE 91
Brown, Richard Lee 1925- WhoAm 90
Brown, Richard Lindley 1931- St&PR 91
Brown, Richard M WhoAmA 91N
Brown, Richard Malcolm, Jr. 1939- WhoAm 90
Brown, Richard Maurice 1924- WhoAm 90
Brown, Richard N. 1933- St&PR 91
Brown, Richard P., Jr. 1920- WhoAm 90
Brown, Richard Paul 1935- St&PR 91
Brown, Richard Paul 1953- BiDrAPA 89
Brown, Richard Stanley 1951- St&PR 91
Brown, Richard Thomas 1944- WhoSSW 91
Brown, Richard W 1922- BiDrAPA 89
Brown, Richard Willard 1947- WhoE 91
Brown, Rita Mae 1944- FemiCLE, MajTwCW, WhoAm 90, WhoAmW 91, WhoWrEP 89
Brown, Robert BioIn 16
Brown, Robert 1842-1895 DcCanB 12
Brown, Robert 1931- WhoAm 90
Brown, Robert 1949- WhoEmL 91
Brown, Robert A. 1930- St&PR 91
Brown, Robert Alan 1930- WhoAm 90
Brown, Robert Alan 1943- WhoAm 90
Brown, Robert Arthur 1951- WhoAm 90
Brown, Robert Carlton 1886-1959 BioIn 16
Brown, Robert Charles 1926- St&PR 91
Brown, Robert Charles 1954- WhoEmL 91
Brown, Robert Curtis 1920- WhoAm 90
Brown, Robert Daniel 1958- WhoEmL 91
Brown, Robert Darwin Bruce 1955- IntWWM 90
Brown, Robert Delford 1930- WhoAm 90, WhoAmA 91
Brown, Robert Edward 1930- WhoSSW 91
Brown, Robert Edward 1945- WhoE 91
Brown, Robert Frederick 1944- WhoSSW 91
Brown, Robert Glenn 1940- WhoAm 90
Brown, Robert Goodell 1923- St&PR 91, WhoE 91
Brown, Robert Grover 1926- WhoAm 90
Brown, Robert Harold 1921- WhoAm 90
Brown, Robert Horatio 1917- WhoAm 90
Brown, Robert Hugh 1959- WhoWrEP 89
Brown, Robert J, III BiDrAPA 89
Brown, Robert J., Jr. 1921- WhoWor 91
Brown, Robert Joseph 1929- WhoAm 90
Brown, Robert K. 1922- St&PR 91
Brown, Robert K 1942- WhoAmA 91
Brown, Robert L. 1945- St&PR 91
Brown, Robert Lee 1908- WhoAm 90
Brown, Robert Lyle 1920- WhoAm 90
Brown, Robert McAfee 1920- WhoAm 90
Brown, Robert Michael 1929- WhoAm 90
Brown, Robert Parkin, Jr. 1943- St&PR 91
Brown, Robert Richard 1937- St&PR 91
Brown, Robert S, Sr. 1931- BiDrAPA 89
Brown, Robert Stanley, Jr. 1954- BiDrAPA 89
Brown, Robert Stephen 1952- IntWWM 90
Brown, Robert T. 1936- St&PR 91
Brown, Robert U 1912- BioIn 16
Brown, Robert Utting 1912- WhoAm 90
Brown, Robert W. 1925- St&PR 91
Brown, Robert Wallace 1925- WhoAm 90
Brown, Robert Wayne 1942- WhoAm 90
Brown, Robert Weaver, Jr. 1946- St&PR 91
Brown, Robert Wells 1921- WhoAm 90
Brown, Roberta Dorr 1922- WhoAmW 91
Brown, Rodney Morgan 1949- IntWWM 90
Brown, Roger 1915- WhoSSW 91
Brown, Roger 1941- WhoAmA 91
Brown, Roger Alan 1948- WhoEmL 91
Brown, Roger Kevin BiDrAPA 89
Brown, Roger Oscar 1925- WhoAm 90
Brown, Roger S. 1927- St&PR 91
Brown, Roger W. 1929- St&PR 91
Brown, Roger William 1925- WhoAm 90
Brown, Ron BioIn 16
Brown, Ron 1941- News 90 [port], -90-3 [port]
Brown, Ron Robert 1957- WhoSSW 91
Brown, Ronald 1930- WhoE 91
Brown, Ronald 1933- WhoAm 90
Brown, Ronald A. 1935- St&PR 91
Brown, Ronald C. 1929- St&PR 91
Brown, Ronald Craig 1954- St&PR 91
Brown, Ronald Dean 1950- WhoEmL 91
Brown, Ronald Dee 1933- St&PR 91
Brown, Ronald Drayton 1927- WhoWor 91
Brown, Ronald Earl 1950- St&PR 91
Brown, Ronald Eric 1954- WhoSSW 91
Brown, Ronald G. 1938- St&PR 91
Brown, Ronald Harmon 1941- WhoAm 90
Brown, Ronald Lee 1946- WhoEmL 91
Brown, Ronald Malcolm 1938- WhoWor 91
Brown, Ronald Osborne 1941- WhoE 91, WhoWor 91
Brown, Rosalie WhoWrEP 89
Brown, Rose Elizabeth 1930- WhoSSW 91
Brown, Rosellen 1939- FemiCLE
Brown, Rosemary EncO&P 3
Brown, Rosemary Eleanor 1938- EncPaPR 91
Brown, Rowine Hayes 1913- WhoAm 90
Brown, Rowland Chauncey Widrig 1923- WhoAm 90
Brown, Roy 1879-1956 WhoAmA 91N
Brown, Roy 1921-1982 BioIn 16
Brown, Roy 1925-1981 OxCPMus
Brown, Rubye Golsby WhoAmW 91
Brown, Russell Glen BiDrAPA 89
Brown, Russell Wayne 1949- St&PR 91
Brown, Ruth BioIn 16, WhoAm 90, WhoAmW 91
Brown, Ruth 1928- DrBlPA 90, OxCPMus
Brown, Ruth Cardwell 1943- WhoAmW 91
Brown, S George BiDrAPA 89
Brown, S. Spencer N. 1920- St&PR 91
Brown, Sally Weiss BiDrAPA 89
Brown, Samuel B 1946- BiDrAPA 89
Brown, Samuel Joseph, Jr. 1941- WhoAm 90, WhoSSW 91
Brown, Samuel Preston 1913- St&PR 91, WhoAm 90
Brown, Sandra Ann 1963- WhoSSW 91
Brown, Sandra Jean 1936- St&PR 91, WhoAm 90, WhoAmW 91
Brown, Sandra L. St&PR 91
Brown, Sandra Lou 1942- WhoE 91
Brown, Sandra Louise Palmer WhoAmW 91
Brown, Sandra Marie 1958- WhoAmW 91
Brown, Sandy BioIn 16
Brown, Sara Lou 1942- WhoAmW 91
Brown, Sarah E. 1936- WhoAmW 91
Brown, Sarah Ruth 1956- WhoEmL 91
Brown, Sarah S. 1932- WhoAmW 91
Brown, Saul L 1922- BiDrAPA 89
Brown, Scott Keith 1960- WhoWrEP 89
Brown, Scott M. 1945- St&PR 91
Brown, Scott McLean 1945- WhoAm 90
Brown, Serena-Lynn 1951- BiDrAPA 89
Brown, Seymour R. 1924- WhoAm 90
Brown, Seymour William 1914- WhoAm 90
Brown, Seyom 1933- WhoAm 90
Brown, Shannon Arleen 1965- WhoAmW 91
Brown, Sharon WhoWrEP 89
Brown, Sharon Elizabeth 1960- WhoAmW 91, WhoEmL 91
Brown, Sharon Gail 1941- WhoAmW 91, WhoWor 91
Brown, Sharon Hendrickson 1944- WhoAmW 91
Brown, Sharon Lu 1954- WhoEmL 91
Brown, Sherrod Campbell 1952- WhoAm 90
Brown, Sherwin Olivier 1944- WhoWor 91
Brown, Shirley Anne 1955- WhoAmW 91
Brown, Shirley M. 1924- WhoAmW 91
Brown, Sidney DeVere 1925- WhoSSW 91
Brown, Solomon G BioIn 16
Brown, Spencer 1909- ConAu 130, WhoWrEP 89
Brown, Spencer 1909-1989 BioIn 16
Brown, Spencer, Jr. St&PR 91
Brown, Spencer Hunter 1928- WhoAm 90
Brown, Stephanie Barry 1943- St&PR 91
Brown, Stephen Bernard 1939- St&PR 91
Brown, Stephen C. 1947- St&PR 91
Brown, Stephen Ira 1938- WhoAm 90
Brown, Stephen John BiDrAPA 89
Brown, Stephen Joseph 1957- WhoEmL 91
Brown, Stephen L. BiDrAPA 89
Brown, Stephen Landesman 1938- WhoE 91
Brown, Stephen Lee 1937- St&PR 91, WhoAm 90, WhoE 91
Brown, Stephen Mainey 1945- IntWWM 90
Brown, Stephen Neal 1952- WhoEmL 91
Brown, Stephen Nicholas 1949- WhoE 91
Brown, Stephen Robert 1939- WhoAm 90
Brown, Stephen Smiley 1952- WhoEmL 91
Brown, Stephen Thomas 1947- WhoSSW 91
Brown, Stephen Wayne 1950- WhoSSW 91
Brown, Sterling 1901-1989 ConLC 59 [port]
Brown, Sterling Allen 1901-1989 AnObit 1989, BioIn 16, MajTwCW
Brown, Steven Ford 1952- WhoWrEP 89
Brown, Steven Harry 1948- WhoWor 91
Brown, Steven Leroy BiDrAPA 89
Brown, Steven Odell 1951- WhoEmL 91
Brown, Steven Ray 1952- WhoWor 91
Brown, Steven Robert 1958- WhoEmL 91
Brown, Steven Spencer 1948- WhoEmL 91
Brown, Steven Wesley 1955- WhoEmL 91
Brown, Stewart Kelvin, III 1950- WhoSSW 91
Brown, Stillman B. 1933- St&PR 91
Brown, Stratton Shartel 1923- WhoAm 90
Brown, Stuart I. 1933- WhoAm 90
Brown, Stuart L 1933- BiDrAPA 89
Brown, Stuart MacDonald, Jr. 1916- WhoAm 90
Brown, Susan Ann 1948- St&PR 91, WhoSSW 91
Brown, Susan K. ODwPR 91
Brown, Susan Rovaine 1948- BiDrAPA 89
Brown, Suzanne C. 1956- St&PR 91
Brown, Suzanne Goldman 1929- WhoAmA 91
Brown, Suzanne Wiley 1938- WhoAmW 91
Brown, Sylvia ODwPR 91
Brown, Sylvia 1946- WhoEmL 91
Brown, T. Graham WhoNeCM [port]
Brown, Tally BioIn 16
Brown, Ted BioIn 16
Brown, Ted Leon, Jr. 1956- WhoSSW 91
Brown, Teddy 1900-1946 OxCPMus
Brown, Temple Nix 1930- St&PR 91
Brown, Terence Michael 1941- WhoAm 90
Brown, Terrance A 1939- BiDrAPA 89
Brown, Terrence Charles 1949- WhoAm 90
Brown, Terry Michael 1954- BiDrAPA 89, WhoE 91
Brown, Terry Steven 1962- WhoSSW 91
Brown, Theodore Lawrence 1928- WhoAm 90
Brown, Theodore Morey 1925- WhoAm 90
Brown, Theodore Ralph 1951- WhoSSW 91
Brown, Theophilus 1919- WhoAmA 91
Brown, Thomas BiDrAPA 89
Brown, Thomas Andrew 1932- WhoAm 90
Brown, Thomas B. 1927- St&PR 91
Brown, Thomas C., Jr. 1945- WhoEmL 91
Brown, Thomas Daniel 1959- WhoSSW 91
Brown, Thomas Ellis 1946- WhoEmL 91
Brown, Thomas Huntington 1945- WhoE 91, WhoWor 91
Brown, Thomas J., Jr. WhoSSW 91
Brown, Thomas James 1949- St&PR 91
Brown, Thomas McPherson 1906-1989 BioIn 16
Brown, Thomas Neil 1951- WhoEmL 91
Brown, Thomas O. 1929- St&PR 91
Brown, Thomas Philip, III 1931- WhoAm 90
Brown, Thomas S. 1952- St&PR 91
Brown, Thomas Wilson BioIn 16
Brown, Three-Finger 1876-1948 Ballpl 90 [port]
Brown, Tim BioIn 16
Brown, Tim Charles 1950- St&PR 91
Brown, Timothy 1937- DrBlPA 90
Brown, Timothy Bruce 1960- WhoEmL 91
Brown, Timothy J. 1949- St&PR 91
Brown, Timothy Louis 1950- WhoEmL 91
Brown, Tina BioIn 16
Brown, Tina 1953- CurBio 90 [port], WhoAm 90, WhoAmW 91, WhoE 91, WhoWor 91, WorAlBi
Brown, Tom NewYTBS 90
Brown, Tom 1860-1927 Ballpl 90
Brown, Tommy 1927- Ballpl 90
Brown, Tony 1933- DrBlPA 90
Brown, Trevor Woodward 1947- IntWWM 90
Brown, Troy Anderson, Jr. 1934- St&PR 91, WhoAm 90
Brown, Val L. 1952- ODwPR 91
Brown, Valerie Anne BiDrAPA 89
Brown, Valerie Anne 1951- WhoAmW 91
Brown, Victoria Ann 1947- WhoAm 90, WhoAmW 91
Brown, Vinson 1912- AuBYP 90
Brown, Violeta V 1932- BiDrAPA 89
Brown, Virginia Lillie 1920- WhoAmW 91
Brown, Virginia Suggs 1924- BioIn 16
Brown, W. Perry 1930- St&PR 91, WhoAm 90
Brown, Wade Edward 1907- WhoWor 91
Brown, Wallace Lamar 1926- WhoSSW 91
Brown, Walston S. 1908- St&PR 91
Brown, Walston Shepard 1908- WhoAm 90
Brown, Walston Shepard, Mrs. 1919- WhoAmW 91
Brown, Walter Armin 1941- BiDrAPA 89
Brown, Walter E. 1915- St&PR 91
Brown, Walter Folger 1869-1961 BiDrUSE 89
Brown, Walter Franklin 1952- WhoEmL 91
Brown, Walter Frederick 1926- WhoWor 91
Brown, Walter Lyons 1924- WhoAm 90
Brown, Walter Taylor 1943- WhoAm 90
Brown, Walter Ward 1939- St&PR 91
Brown, Wanda Gaye 1943- WhoSSW 91
Brown, Wanda Marie 1945- WhoAmW 91
Brown, Wanda Yvette 1959- WhoAmW 91
Brown, Warren 1894- Ballpl 90
Brown, Warren Joseph 1924- WhoAm 90
Brown, Warren Ted 1951- St&PR 91
Brown, Warwick Miles 1940- WhoWor 91
Brown, Wayne F, II 1938- BiDrAPA 89
Brown, Weir Messick 1914- WhoE 91
Brown, Wendell 1902- WhoAm 90
Brown, Wendy Elaine 1956- WhoAmW 91
Brown, Wesley Ernest 1907- WhoAm 90
Brown, Wilbur Melvin 1930- BiDrAPA 89
Brown, Willard 1913- Ballpl 90
Brown, Willet Henry 1905- WhoAm 90
Brown, William BiDrAPA 89
Brown, William 1881-1952 EncO&P 3
Brown, William Andreas 1930- WhoAm 90, WhoWor 91
Brown, William Avon 1924- St&PR 91
Brown, William Clifford 1911- St&PR 91, WhoAm 90
Brown, William Ernest 1922- WhoAm 90
Brown, William Ernest 1939- WhoAm 90
Brown, William Ewart 1928- St&PR 91
Brown, William F. 1906?-1990 ConAu 131
Brown, William Ferdinand 1928- WhoAm 90
Brown, William Gardner 1942- WhoAm 90
Brown, William Harmon BioIn 16
Brown, William Hill, III 1928- WhoAm 90
Brown, William Holmes 1929- WhoAm 90

Brown, William Jones, II 1947- *St&PR 91*
Brown, William L. 1922- *St&PR 91, WhoAm 90*
Brown, William Lacy 1913- *WhoAm 90*
Brown, William Lee Lyons, Jr. 1936- *St&PR 91, WhoAm 90, WhoSSW 91*
Brown, William Louis *AuBYP 90*
Brown, William M. 1942- *St&PR 91*
Brown, William Milton 1932- *WhoAm 90*
Brown, William Montgomery 1854-1937 *EncAL*
Brown, William Newman 1922-1989 *BioIn 16*
Brown, William P. 1919- *St&PR 91*
Brown, William Paul 1919- *WhoAm 90*
Brown, William R. 1939- *WhoAm 90*
Brown, William Randall 1913- *WhoAm 90*
Brown, William Robert 1926- *WhoAm 90*
Brown, William Thacher 1947- *WhoAm 90*
Brown, William Warner, Jr. 1944- *WhoE 91*
Brown, William Wells 1814?-1884 *LiHiK*
Brown, William Wells 1815-1884 *EarBlAP*
Brown, Willie Lewis, Jr. *BioIn 16*
Brown, Willie Lewis, Jr. 1934- *WhoAm 90*
Brown, Wilson Gordon 1914- *WhoAm 90*
Brown, Winston Da Costa 1955- *WhoE 91*
Brown, Wood, III 1936- *WhoAm 90*
Brown-Buchanan, Deborah Ann 1956- *WhoAmW 91, WhoE 91*
Brown-Cochrane, Andrea Kane 1962- *WhoAmW 91*
Brown-Foster, Arnita Christine 1950- *WhoSSW 91*
Brown Michelson, Linda *WhoWrEP 89*
Brown-Mohr, Karen Lee 1953- *WhoAmW 91*
Brown-Olmstead, Amanda 1943- *WhoAm 90, WhoAmW 91*
Brown-Shev, Eleanor Upton 1924-1989 *BioIn 16*
Brownawell, Woodrow Dale 1942- *WhoE 91*
Brownback, Thomas Samuel 1946- *WhoE 91*
Browne, Alan K 1909-1988 *BioIn 16*
Browne, Aldis J., Jr. 1912- *St&PR 91*
Browne, Aldis Jerome, Jr. 1912- *WhoWor 91*
Browne, Alice Pauline 1918- *WhoWrEP 89*
Browne, Allan Roland 1900- *WhoAm 90*
Browne, Ann April 1945- *WhoAmW 91, WhoEmL 91*
Browne, Anna Therese 1958- *WhoAmW 91*
Browne, Anthony *BioIn 16*
Browne, Anthony 1946- *AuBYP 90, SmATA 61 [port]*
Browne, Barum *TwCCr&M 91*
Browne, Beverly Ann 1938- *WhoAmW 91*
Browne, Brooks Halsey 1949- *St&PR 91, WhoAm 90*
Browne, Byron 1942- *Ballpl 90*
Browne, Calvin O *BiDrAPA 89*
Browne, Cecil Thayer 1932- *WhoAm 90*
Browne, Charles E. 1931- *St&PR 91*
Browne, Charles Farrar 1834-1867 *BioIn 16*
Browne, Charles Idol 1922- *WhoAm 90*
Browne, Charlie 1948- *WhoEmL 91*
Browne, Cornelius Payne 1923- *WhoAm 90*
Browne, Diana Gayle 1924- *WhoAmW 91*
Browne, Dik 1917-1989 *AnObit 1989, BioIn 16, EncACom*
Browne, Donald Roger 1934- *WhoAm 90*
Browne, Edmond Patrick 1939- *St&PR 91*
Browne, Edmund John Phillip 1948- *WhoAm 90*
Browne, F. Sedgwick 1942- *WhoAm 90*
Browne, G. Morgan 1935- *St&PR 91*
Browne, George 1876-1920 *Ballpl 90*
Browne, George Byron 1907-1961 *WhoAmA 91N*
Browne, George H. 1851-1911 *AmLegL*
Browne, Gerald A. *TwCCr&M 91*
Browne, Gerald Michael 1943- *WhoAm 90*
Browne, H. Lee *St&PR 91*
Browne, Hablot Knight 1851-1882 *BioIn 16*
Browne, Henriette 1829-1901 *BiDWomA*
Browne, Howard 1908- *TwCCr&M 91*
Browne, J. L. *AmLegL*
Browne, Jackson *BioIn 16*
Browne, Jackson 1948- *EncPR&S 89, OxCPMus, WorAlBi*
Browne, James Clayton 1935- *WhoAm 90*
Browne, James George 1928- *WhoSSW 91*
Browne, Jeffrey Francis 1944- *WhoE 91*
Browne, Jennifer Lynn 1954- *WhoAmW 91*
Browne, Jerry 1966- *Ballpl 90*
Browne, John 1938- *BioIn 16*
Browne, John Charles 1942- *WhoAm 90*
Browne, John James 1837-1893 *DcCanB 12*
Browne, John R., Sr. 1914- *St&PR 91*
Browne, John Robinson 1914- *WhoAm 90*
Browne, Jonathan Herbert 1954- *St&PR 91*
Browne, Joseph Peter 1929- *WhoWor 91*
Browne, Joy 1950- *WhoAmW 91*
Browne, Kingsbury 1922- *WhoAm 90*
Browne, Larry Robert 1948- *WhoEmL 91*
Browne, Larry W. 1945- *St&PR 91*
Browne, Leslie 1957- *WhoAmW 91*
Browne, M. Steffy 1898-1990 *BioIn 16*
Browne, Malachy Francis *BiDrAPA 89*
Browne, Malcolm Wilde 1931- *WhoAm 90*
Browne, Marshall Gilmore 1926- *St&PR 91*
Browne, Martha *FemiCLE*
Browne, Martin Robert 1950- *St&PR 91*
Browne, Mary Anita *WhoAmW 91*
Browne, Mary T. *BioIn 16*
Browne, Melody Johnson 1954- *WhoEmL 91*
Browne, Michael Dennis 1940- *WhoAm 90, WhoWrEP 89*
Browne, Michael Leon 1946- *WhoAm 90, WhoWor 91*
Browne, Micou Farrar 1915- *St&PR 91*
Browne, Millard Child 1915- *WhoAm 90*
Browne, Missy 1961- *WhoEmL 91*
Browne, Morgan Trew 1919- *St&PR 91, WhoAm 90, WhoWrEP 89*
Browne, Ray Broadus 1922- *WhoAm 90*
Browne, Renni 1939- *WhoWrEP 89*
Browne, Robert G. 1941- *St&PR 91*
Browne, Robert M 1926- *WhoAmA 91*
Browne, Robert Michael 1923- *WhoAm 90*
Browne, Robert Span 1924- *WhoAm 90, WhoE 91*
Browne, Robert Thomas 1950- *St&PR 91*
Browne, Roscoe Lee 1925- *DrBlPA 90*
Browne, Sandra 1947- *IntWWM 90*
Browne, Sarah *BiDEWW*
Browne, Shirley Annette 1952- *WhoAmW 91, WhoSSW 91*
Browne, Shirley S. *ODwPR 91*
Browne, Sidney 1958- *WhoE 91*
Browne, Spencer I. 1949- *St&PR 91, WhoAm 90*
Browne, Stanhope Stryker 1931- *WhoAm 90*
Browne, Steven Emery 1950- *WhoEmL 91*
Browne, Syd J 1907- *WhoAmA 91*
Browne, Theodore 1910?-1979 *EarBlAP*
Browne, Thomas 1605-1682 *EncO&P 3*
Browne, Vivian E 1929- *WhoAmA 91*
Browne, Walter Shawn 1949- *WhoAm 90*
Browne, William 1737-1802 *EncCRAm*
Browne, William Bitner 1914- *WhoAm 90*
Browne, William J 1915- *BiDrAPA 89*
Browne, William Rowan 1884-1975 *DcScB S2*
Browne, William Thomas 1934- *St&PR 91*
Browne, William Washington 1849-1897 *BioIn 16*
Browne-Barnum, Michelle L *BiDrAPA 89*
Browne-Mayers, Albert N *BiDrAPA 89*
Brownell, Anna Gale 1942- *WhoAmW 91*
Brownell, Blaine Allison 1942- *WhoAm 90*
Brownell, David Wheaton 1941- *WhoAm 90, WhoWrEP 89*
Brownell, Edwin Rowland 1924- *WhoAm 90, WhoSSW 91, WhoWor 91*
Brownell, Eileen Olivia 1945- *WhoEmL 91*
Brownell, Eugene Bronson 1908- *St&PR 91*
Brownell, Gordon Lee 1922- *WhoAm 90*
Brownell, Herbert 1904- *WhoAm 90*
Brownell, Herbert, Jr. 1904- *BiDrUSE 89*
Brownell, Iverson O 1915- *BiDrAPA 89*
Brownell, Iverson Oakley 1915- *WhoSSW 91*
Brownell, James Garland 1933- *WhoWrEP 89*
Brownell, John Arnold 1924- *WhoAm 90*
Brownell, Joyce E. Tarrier 1942- *WhoWrEP 89*
Brownell, Linda L. 1951- *St&PR 91*
Brownell, Matthew Russell 1960- *WhoEmL 91*
Browner, Carole Helen 1947- *WhoEmL 91*
Browner, Francine 1945- *WhoAmW 91*
Browner, George Robert, Jr. 1932- *St&PR 91*
Browner, Julius Harvey 1930- *WhoSSW 91*
Brownett, Thelma Denyer 1924- *WhoAmA 91*
Brownfeld, Allan Charles 1939- *WhoE 91*
Brownfield, Bernard *BiDrAPA 89*
Brownfield, Charles William 1941- *WhoWor 91*
Brownfield, Katherine Annette 1956- *WhoEmL 91*
Brownfield, Thomas Allen 1943- *St&PR 91*
Brownhill, Harold *WhoAmA 91N*
Brownhill, Toni Robeck 1946- *WhoAmW 91*
Browning, Alan Dwight 1940- *St&PR 91*
Browning, Amanda Helen Hardy 1925- *WhoSSW 91*
Browning, Amy Katherine 1882-1978 *BiDWomA*
Browning, Barbara Ann 1936- *WhoSSW 91*
Browning, Bernard S. 1923- *St&PR 91*
Browning, Beverly Ann 1948- *WhoAmW 91*
Browning, Carol Anne 1936- *WhoAmW 91*
Browning, Carroll Welles 1916- *WhoAm 90*
Browning, Charles Benton 1931- *WhoAm 90*
Browning, Christopher Corwin 1956- *WhoEmL 91*
Browning, Colin A. 1935- *St&PR 91*
Browning, Colin Arrott 1935- *WhoAm 90, WhoE 91, WhoWor 91*
Browning, Colleen 1929- *WhoAmA 91*
Browning, Daniel Dwight 1921- *WhoAm 90*
Browning, David Ray 1940- *WhoSSW 91*
Browning, David Stuart 1939- *St&PR 91, WhoAm 90, WhoE 91*
Browning, Debbie Sue 1958- *WhoAmW 91*
Browning, Deborah Lea 1955- *WhoE 91, WhoEmL 91*
Browning, Dick Emerson 1950- *WhoEmL 91*
Browning, Dixie Burrus 1930- *WhoAmA 91*
Browning, Don Spencer 1934- *WhoAm 90*
Browning, Edmond Lee *WhoAm 90*
Browning, Elizabeth 1806-1861 *FemiCLE*
Browning, Elizabeth 1933- *WhoWrEP 89*
Browning, Elizabeth Barrett 1806-1861 *BioIn 16, EncPaPR 91, WorAlBi*
Browning, Francis L. 1946- *St&PR 91*
Browning, Frank William 1937- *St&PR 91*
Browning, G Wesley 1868-1951 *WhoAmA 91N*
Browning, Grayson Douglas 1929- *WhoAm 90*
Browning, Gregory Bruce 1955- *WhoSSW 91*
Browning, Guston Hassell 1926- *WhoSSW 91*
Browning, Henry Prentice 1911- *WhoAm 90*
Browning, Iben 1918- *WhoAm 90*
Browning, Ivan Harold 1891-1978 *DcAfAmP*
Browning, Jackson B. 1921- *St&PR 91*
Browning, James Alexander 1922- *WhoAm 90*
Browning, James Franklin 1923- *WhoAm 90*
Browning, Jesse Harrison 1935- *WhoWor 91*
Browning, John 1933- *IntWWM 90, PenDiMP, WhoAm 90*
Browning, John Huntington 1933- *St&PR 91*
Browning, John Victor 1945- *WhoEmL 91*
Browning, Kurt *BioIn 16*
Browning, Marilyn Crouch *BiDrAPA 89*
Browning, Michael Gorry *WhoAm 90, WhoWor 91*
Browning, Nita Sparks 1929- *WhoAmW 91*
Browning, Norma Lee 1914- *WhoAm 90*
Browning, Orville Hickman 1806-1881 *BiDrUSE 89*
Browning, Pamela 1942- *WhoWrEP 89*
Browning, Pete 1861-1905 *Ballpl 90*
Browning, Peter Crane 1941- *WhoAm 90, WhoSSW 91, WhoWor 91*
Browning, Ralph Leslie 1915- *WhoAm 90*
Browning, Reba Smith 1926- *WhoAmW 91*
Browning, Reed S. 1938- *WhoAm 90*
Browning, Reyburn Engle 1933- *St&PR 91*
Browning, Richard Edward 1955- *WhoEmL 91*
Browning, Robert 1812-1889 *BioIn 16, EncO&P 3, EncPaPR 91, PoeCrit 2 [port], WorAlBi*
Browning, Robert Marcellus 1911- *WhoAm 90*
Browning, Robert Masters 1912- *WhoAm 90*
Browning, Roderick Hanson 1925- *WhoAm 90*
Browning, Ronald C. *St&PR 91*
Browning, Ronald L. 1960- *WhoEmL 91*
Browning, Ruth Anna 1932- *WhoE 91*
Browning, Scott David 1931- *WhoE 91*
Browning, Sterry *TwCCr&M 91*
Browning, Tom 1960- *Ballpl 90*
Browning, Vivian Berniece 1923- *WhoE 91*
Browning, W Nicholson 1947- *BiDrAPA 89*
Browning, Warren W. 1927- *St&PR 91*
Browning, William E.S. 1932- *St&PR 91*
Browning, William Earle Strain 1932- *WhoAm 90*
Browning-Sletten, Melissa Ann 1947- *WhoAmW 91*
Brownjohn, J Maxwell 1929- *ConAu 129*
Brownlee, David B 1951- *ConAu 132*
Brownlee, David Jenus 1955- *WhoE 91*
Brownlee, Denis Norman 1947- *WhoWor 91*
Brownlee, Donald Eugene, II 1943- *WhoAm 90*
Brownlee, Ernest Nolan *BiDrAPA 89*
Brownlee, John 1900-1969 *PenDiMP*
Brownlee, Judith Marilyn 1940- *WhoAmW 91*
Brownlee, Marlys Kay 1940- *WhoAmW 91*
Brownlee, Paula Pimlott 1934- *WhoAm 90, WhoAmW 91*
Brownlee, Richard Smith 1918- *WhoAm 90*
Brownlee, Robert Calvin 1922- *WhoAm 90*
Brownlee, Robert James 1946- *WhoSSW 91*
Brownlee, Shannon *BioIn 16*
Brownlee, Thomas Marshall 1926- *WhoAm 90, WhoWor 91*
Brownlee, Walter D 1930- *SmATA 62*
Brownlee, William Harry 1935- *BiDrAPA 89*
Brownley, Floyd Irving, Jr. 1918- *WhoAm 90*
Brownley, John Forrest 1942- *St&PR 91, WhoAm 90*
Brownlie, Edward Carter 1937- *St&PR 91*
Brownlie, Ian 1932- *WhoWor 91*
Brownlie, Ian T. 1939- *St&PR 91*
Brownlie, Stanley Brechin 1926- *St&PR 91*
Brownlow, Donald Grey 1923- *WhoE 91, WhoWor 91*
Brownlow, Emma 1832-1905 *BiDWomA*
Brownlow, Frank Walsh 1934- *WhoAm 90*
Brownlow, Kevin *BioIn 16*
Brownlow, Marian F. 1933- *IntWWM 90*
Brownlow, Sheila Esther 1961- *WhoAmW 91*
Brownlow, William Gannaway 1805-1877 *BioIn 16*
Brownlow King, Emma 1832-1905 *BiDWomA*
Brownman, Harold Lionel 1923- *WhoAm 90*
Brownmiller, Susan *BioIn 16*
Brownmiller, Susan 1935- *MajTwCW, WhoAmW 91, WhoWrEP 89, WorAlBi*
Brownridge, Angela Mary 1944- *IntWWM 90*
Brownrigg, Judith Hamilton 1950- *WhoAmW 91, WhoEmL 91*
Brownrigg, Walter Grant 1940- *WhoAm 90*
Brownrout, Harvey Murray 1935- *WhoE 91*
Brownsberger, Carl N 1930- *BiDrAPA 89*
Brownson, Charles 1945- *WhoWrEP 89*
Brownson, Jacques Calmon 1923- *WhoAm 90*
Brownson, Orestes Augustus 1803-1876 *BioIn 16*
Brownson, William Clarence 1928- *WhoAm 90*
Brownstein, Alan P. 1944- *WhoAm 90*
Brownstein, Barbara Lavin 1931- *WhoAm 90*
Brownstein, Bernard 1910-1989 *BioIn 16*
Brownstein, Burton Erwin *BiDrAPA 89*
Brownstein, David M. 1958- *St&PR 91*
Brownstein, Edward J 1925- *BiDrAPA 89*
Brownstein, Howard Brod 1950- *WhoEmL 91*
Brownstein, Karen 1944-1989 *ConAu 130*
Brownstein, Martin Herbert 1935- *WhoAm 90, WhoWor 91*
Brownstein, Michael *BioIn 16*
Brownstein, Philip N. 1917- *St&PR 91*
Brownstein, Philip Nathan 1917- *WhoAm 90*
Brownstein, Rob 1946- *ODwPR 91*
Brownstein, Shale 1933- *BiDrAPA 89*
Brownstone, Caroline Taylor 1941- *WhoAmW 91*
Brownstone, Clyde R. 1935- *St&PR 91*
Brownstone, David M. 1928- *WhoWrEP 89*
Brownstone, David Martin 1928- *WhoE 91*
Brownstone, Desi Y 1956- *BiDrAPA 89*
Brownstone, George *BiDrAPA 89*
Brownstone, Hugh Michael 1957- *WhoE 91*
Brownstone, Paul Lotan 1923- *WhoAm 90*
Brownstone, Walter J. *BioIn 16*
Brownwood, David Owen 1935- *WhoE 91, WhoWor 91*
Browse, Nicholas 1954- *WhoE 91*
Brox, Eleanor Andrea 1959- *WhoWrEP 89*
Broxholme, John Franklin 1930- *ConAu 31NR*
Broxson, Evelyn Lipscomb 1948- *WhoEmL 91*
Broyard, Anatole *BioIn 16*
Broyard, Anatole 1920-1990 *ConAu 132, NewYTBS 90 [port]*
Broyhill, Craig Gary 1948- *St&PR 91*
Broyhill, James E. *St&PR 91N*
Broyhill, James E. 1892-1988 *BioIn 16*
Broyhill, Linda Sharon 1951- *WhoEmL 91*
Broyhill, Paul Hunt 1924- *St&PR 91*
Broyhill, Roy F. 1919- *St&PR 91*

Broyles, Charlie *BioIn 16*
Broyles, Laura Jane 1958- *WhoEmL 91*
Broyles, Nina Sue 1944- *WhoAmW 91*
Broyles, T.M. 1937- *St&PR 91*
Broyles, William Dodson, Jr. 1944- *WhoAm 90, WhoWrEP 89*
Brozek, Jiri 1955- *WhoWor 91*
Brozek, Josef 1913- *WhoAm 90*
Brozek, Richard Carl 1953- *WhoSSW 91*
Brozen, Kenneth *BioIn 16*
Brozen, Yale 1917- *WhoAm 90*
Brozman, Tina L. 1952- *WhoAmW 91*
Brozon, Charles A. 1946- *St&PR 91*
Brozovich, Matthew William 1930- *St&PR 91*
Brozovsky, Morris *BiDrAPA 89*
Brozowski, Patricia D. 1948- *ODwPR 91*
Bru, Federico Laredo 1875-1946 *BioIn 16*
Bru, Georgina-Ann Dorothea 1945- *WhoAmW 91*
Bru, Hedin 1901- *DcScanL*
Bruant, Aristide 1851-1925 *OxCPMus*
Brubach, David J. 1916- *St&PR 91*
Brubaker, Alta L. 1952- *BiDrAPA 89*
Brubaker, Beryl Mae Hartzler 1942- *WhoSSW 91*
Brubaker, Bill 1910-1978 *Ballpl 90*
Brubaker, Carl H., Jr. 1925- *WhoAm 90*
Brubaker, Carol *ConAu 131*
Brubaker, Charles William 1926- *WhoAm 90*
Brubaker, Crawford Francis, Jr. 1924- *WhoAm 90*
Brubaker, David H. 1939- *St&PR 91*
Brubaker, Donald 1935- *St&PR 91*
Brubaker, Earl J. 1922- *St&PR 91*
Brubaker, Edward Stehman 1924- *WhoWrEP 89*
Brubaker, Forest LeRoy, III 1947- *WhoEmL 91*
Brubaker, Herman Wallace, Jr. 1954- *WhoE 91*
Brubaker, Jack 1944- *WhoAmA 91*
Brubaker, James Clark 1947- *WhoEmL 91*
Brubaker, James Edward 1935- *WhoE 91*
Brubaker, James Robert 1955- *St&PR 91*
Brubaker, John D. 1930- *St&PR 91*
Brubaker, Karen Sue 1953- *WhoAmW 91, WhoWor 91*
Brubaker, Lauren Edgar 1914- *WhoAm 90*
Brubaker, Peter P. 1946- *St&PR 91*
Brubaker, R.C. 1921- *St&PR 91*
Brubaker, Robert Paul 1934- *St&PR 91, WhoAm 90*
Brubaker, Russel Verne 1948- *BiDrAPA 89*
Brubaker, Ruth 1959- *WhoEmL 91*
Brubaker, Vickie Lee 1962- *WhoAmW 91*
Brubeck, Daniel J. 1943- *ODwPR 91*
Brubeck, Dave 1920- *BioIn 16, OxCPMus, PenDiMP A, WorAlBi*
Brubeck, David Haughey 1942- *St&PR 91*
Brubeck, David Warren 1920- *IntWWM 90, WhoAm 90, WhoWor 91*
Brucato, John *BioIn 16*
Bruccoleri, Joseph J. 1947- *WhoE 91*
Bruccoli, Matthew J 1931- *DcLB 103 [port]*
Bruccoli, Matthew Joseph 1931- *WhoAm 90, WhoWrEP 89*
Bruce, Abbi Jan 1957- *WhoAmW 91*
Bruce, Ailsa 1901-1969 *WorAlBi*
Bruce, Alfred C. *BioIn 16*
Bruce, Amos Jerry, Jr. 1942- *WhoSSW 91*
Bruce, Aundray *BioIn 16*
Bruce, Billy J., Jr. 1953- *WhoEmL 91*
Bruce, Blanche Kelso 1841-1898 *BlkAmsC [port]*
Bruce, Bob 1933- *Ballpl 90*
Bruce, Carol 1919- *OxCPMus*
Bruce, Dania Gayle 1937- *WhoAmW 91*
Bruce, David K. E. 1898-1977 *BioIn 16*
Bruce, David K.E. 1898-1977 *WorAlBi*
Bruce, David Lionel 1933- *WhoAm 90*
Bruce, David R. 1925- *St&PR 91*
Bruce, Debra 1951- *WhoWrEP 89*
Bruce, Duane N. 1963- *WhoEmL 91*
Bruce, Edgar Perrin 1934- *WhoE 91*
Bruce, Elizabeth Alice 1948- *WhoAmW 91*
Bruce, Elmer Ivan, Jr. *BiDrAPA 89*
Bruce, Eric Wesley 1962- *WhoSSW 91*
Bruce, Estel Edward 1938- *WhoAm 90*
Bruce, F. F. 1910- *BioIn 16*
Bruce, Frank B. 1918- *St&PR 91*
Bruce, Frederick Fyvie 1910- *BioIn 16*
Bruce, Gail Clyde 1953- *WhoEmL 91*
Bruce, George H. 1900- *St&PR 91*
Bruce, H Addington 1874-1959 *EncO&P 3*
Bruce, Harry James 1931- *St&PR 91, WhoAm 90*
Bruce, Herbert L. *NewYTBS 90*
Bruce, Ian Waugh 1945- *WhoWor 91*
Bruce, Jack *EncPR&S 89*
Bruce, Jackson Martin, Jr. 1931- *WhoAm 90*
Bruce, James Donald 1936- *WhoAm 90*
Bruce, James Edmund 1920- *WhoAm 90*
Bruce, James Taylor 1953- *WhoE 91*
Bruce, James Walton 1938- *St&PR 91*
Bruce, James Walton, Jr. 1938- *WhoAm 90*
Bruce, John 1837-1893 *DcCanB 12*
Bruce, John Anthony 1931- *WhoWor 91*
Bruce, John Foster 1940- *WhoE 91*
Bruce, John Martin 1930- *WhoAm 90*
Bruce, Judith Winsor 1948- *WhoAmW 91*
Bruce, Kenneth A *BiDrAPA 89*
Bruce, Lawrence Everett, Jr. 1945- *WhoAm 90*
Bruce, Lenny 1925-1966 *BioIn 16*
Bruce, Lenny 1926-1966 *WorAlBi*
Bruce, Leo 1903-1979 *TwCCr&M 91*
Bruce, Leonard John 1920- *St&PR 91*
Bruce, Leslie *BioIn 16*
Bruce, Linda Faye 1946- *WhoAmW 91*
Bruce, Liza *BioIn 16*
Bruce, Louis Rooks 1906-1989 *BioIn 16*
Bruce, Margaret 1943- *IntWWM 90*
Bruce, Martha Elena Aguilar 1946- *WhoHisp 91*
Bruce, Marvin Ernest 1928- *WhoAm 90, WhoSSW 91*
Bruce, Mary *BioIn 16*
Bruce, Mary 1927- *AuBYP 90*
Bruce, Mary Beth 1956- *WhoAmW 91*
Bruce, Mary Grant 1878-1958 *FemiCLE*
Bruce, Michael C. 1946- *St&PR 91*
Bruce, Mildred Mary 1896?-1990 *ConAu 131*
Bruce, Nadine Cecile 1942- *WhoAm 90, WhoAmW 91*
Bruce, Nigel 1895-1953 *WorAlBi*
Bruce, Norman Macdonald 1941- *St&PR 91*
Bruce, Patricia Gray 1953- *WhoEmL 91*
Bruce, Peter W. 1945- *St&PR 91*
Bruce, Peter Wayne 1945- *WhoAm 90*
Bruce, R. Jeffrey 1959- *St&PR 91*
Bruce, Ralph 1916- *St&PR 91*
Bruce, Randall Alton 1954- *St&PR 91*
Bruce, Richard *EarBlAP*
Bruce, Robert 1274-1329 *BioIn 16*
Bruce, Robert B. 1931- *St&PR 91*
Bruce, Robert Cecil 1950- *WhoEmL 91*
Bruce, Robert James 1937- *WhoAm 90*
Bruce, Robert Lee 1925- *WhoE 91*
Bruce, Robert Nolan, Jr. 1930- *WhoAm 90*
Bruce, Robert Rockwell 1944- *WhoAm 90*
Bruce, Robert Vance 1923- *WhoAm 90, WhoE 91, WhoWrEP 89*
Bruce, Robert W., III 1944- *WhoAm 90*
Bruce, Scott *BioIn 16*
Bruce, Steven H. *ODwPR 91*
Bruce, Terry L. 1944- *WhoAm 90*
Bruce, Thomas Allen 1930- *WhoAm 90, WhoWor 91*
Bruce, Victor, Mrs. *BioIn 16*
Bruce, Wallace John 1932- *St&PR 91, WhoSSW 91*
Bruce, Walt *TwCCr&M 91*
Bruce, Wendy Louise 1966- *WhoAmW 91*
Bruce, William Cable 1952- *WhoEmL 91*
Bruce, William Rankin 1915- *St&PR 91*
Bruce, William Robert 1929- *WhoAm 90*
Bruce-Gardyne, Jock *ConAu 131*
Bruce-Gardyne, Jock 1930-1990 *BioIn 16*
Bruce-Gardyne, John 1930-1990 *ConAu 131*
Bruce-Novoa *ConAu 32NR, HispWr 90*
Bruce-Novoa, John David *ConAu 32NR, HispWr 90*
Bruce-Novoa, Juan 1944- *WhoHisp 91*
Bruce-Novoa, Juan D. 1944- *ConAu 32NR, HispWr 90*
Bruce-Payne, David Malcolm 1945- *IntWWM 90*
Bruch, Carol Sophie 1941- *WhoAm 90*
Bruch, Delores R. 1934- *IntWWM 90*
Bruch, Max *PenDiMP*
Bruch, Max 1838-1920 *BioIn 16, PenDiMP A*
Bruch, Thomas James 1959- *WhoE 91*
Bruch, Walter 1908- *BioIn 16*
Bruchner, Gordon W. 1932- *St&PR 91*
Bruck, Charles 1911- *PenDiMP*
Bruck, Connie Jane 1946- *WhoE 91*
Bruck, Edith 1932- *EncCoWW*
Bruck, Eva Doman 1950- *WhoEmL 91*
Bruck, Ferdinand Frederick 1921- *WhoAm 90*
Bruck, Lorraine 1921- *BioIn 16*
Bruck, Max A *BiDrAPA 89*
Bruck, Phoebe Ann Mason 1928- *WhoAm 90, WhoAmW 91*
Bruck, Stephen Desiderius 1927- *WhoAm 90*
Bruck-Lieb, Lilly 1918- *WhoAmW 91*
Bruckart, Bernice Carol 1935- *WhoAmW 91*
Bruckel, Jane *BioIn 16*
Brucken, Eleanor Elizabeth 1929- *WhoAmW 91*
Brucken, Robert Matthew 1934- *WhoAm 90*
Bruckenstein, Stanley 1927- *WhoAm 90*
Brucker, Connie 1946- *WhoAmW 91*
Brucker, David Lee 1938- *St&PR 91*
Brucker, Edmund 1912- *WhoAm 90, WhoAmA 91*
Brucker, Eric 1941- *WhoAm 90*
Brucker, Henry J. 1916- *St&PR 91*
Brucker, Janet Mary 1946- *WhoAmW 91*
Brucker, Robert Louis 1935- *St&PR 91*
Brucker, Wilber Marion 1926- *WhoAm 90*
Bruckheim, Stan 1960- *WhoEmL 91*
Bruckheimer, Jerry *BioIn 16*
Bruckman, Joanne Lynn 1938- *WhoE 91*
Bruckmann, Donald J. 1929- *St&PR 91*
Bruckmann, Donald John 1929- *WhoAm 90*
Bruckner, Andrew Michael 1932- *WhoAm 90*
Bruckner, Anton 1824-1896 *BioIn 16, PenDiMP A, WorAlBi*
Bruckner, Christine 1921- *EncCoWW*
Bruckner, D.J.R. 1933- *ConAu 132*
Bruckner, Howard Leon 1941- *WhoSSW 91*
Bruckner, Rolf 1928- *WhoWor 91*
Bruckner, William H. 1938- *WhoSSW 91*
Bruckshaw, Horace 1891-1917 *BioIn 16*
Brud, Wladyslaw S. 1939- *WhoWor 91*
Bruder, George Frederick 1938- *WhoAm 90*
Bruder, Harold Jacob 1930- *WhoAm 90, WhoAmA 91*
Bruder, Jerome Jay 1945- *WhoEmL 91*
Brudereck, Mary Ann 1923- *St&PR 91*
Brudereck, William C. 1916- *St&PR 91*
Bruderhans, Zdenek 1934- *IntWWM 90*
Bruderle, Louise Marie 1956- *WhoAmW 91*
Bruderman, Robert William 1951- *WhoSSW 91*
Brudi, Lois Jeanne 1931- *St&PR 91*
Brudi, Ronald Adair 1927- *St&PR 91*
Brudnak, Peggy Helene 1923- *WhoAmW 91*
Brudner, Harvey Jerome 1931- *WhoAm 90, WhoE 91*
Brudner, Helen Gross *WhoAm 90*
Brudnoy, David 1940- *WhoE 91*
Brudvig, Glenn Lowell 1931- *WhoAm 90*
Brueckheimer, William Rogers 1921- *WhoAm 90*
Brueckner, Keith Allan 1924- *WhoAm 90*
Brueckner, Richard Frederick 1949- *WhoAm 90*
Bruegel, Jan 1568-1625 *IntDcAA 90*
Bruegel, Pieter 1525?-1569 *IntDcAA 90, WorAlBi*
Brueggen, Frans 1934- *IntWWM 90*
Bruehl, Elisabeth Young- *BioIn 16*
Bruehl, Margaret Ellen 1935- *WhoAmW 91*
Bruel, Iris Barbara 1933- *WhoAmW 91*
Bruels, Mark Charles 1941- *WhoSSW 91*
Bruemmer, Arlon W. 1944- *St&PR 91*
Bruemmer, Fred *BioIn 16*
Bruemmer, Fred 1929- *WhoAm 90, WhoWrEP 89*
Bruemmer, Lorraine Venskunas *WhoAmW 91*
Bruen, James Terence 1939- *WhoE 91*
Bruen, John Dermot 1930- *WhoAm 90*
Bruen, Lawrence S. 1949- *St&PR 91*
Bruenderman, Katherine R. 1945- *WhoEmL 91*
Bruene, Warren Benz 1916- *WhoAm 90*
Bruenger, Leona *St&PR 91*
Bruenger, M.W. 1944- *St&PR 91*
Bruening, Deborah Sue 1954- *WhoEmL 91*
Bruening, J H 1929- *EncO&P 3*
Bruening, Michael L. 1949- *ODwPR 91*
Bruening, Richard P. 1939- *St&PR 91*
Bruening, Richard Patrick 1939- *WhoAm 90*
Bruenn, Howard Gerald 1905- *WhoAm 90*
Bruenner, Eric William 1949- *WhoEmL 91*
Bruenner, Frederick Herman 1920- *WhoAm 90*
Bruer, Jacquelyn Jean 1957- *WhoAmW 91, WhoEmL 91*
Bruers, Antonio 188-?-1954 *EncO&P 3*
Brues, Alice Mossie 1913- *WhoAm 90*
Bruesch, Simon Rulin 1914- *WhoAm 90*
Brueschke, Erich Edward 1933- *WhoAm 90*
Bruesewitz, Gail Cecelia 1956- *WhoAmW 91*
Bruesewitz, Lynn Joy 1952- *WhoAmW 91*
Bruess, Charles Edward 1938- *WhoAm 90*
Bruestle, Armin O. 1905- *St&PR 91*
Bruestle, Eric George 1953- *WhoEmL 91*
Brueton, Martin John 1944- *WhoWor 91*
Bruett, Karen Diesl 1945- *WhoAmW 91*
Bruett, Till Arthur 1938- *WhoAm 90*
Bruett, William H., Jr. 1944- *St&PR 91*
Bruett, William Huber, Jr. 1944- *WhoAm 90*
Bruevich, Mikhail Dmitrievich Bonch- 1870-1956 *BioIn 16*
Bruevich, Vladimir Dmitrievich Bonch- 1873-1955 *BioIn 16*
Bruff, Beverly Olive 1926- *WhoAmW 91*
Bruford, Bill *EncPR&S 89*
Bruggeman, Jack Anthony 1952- *St&PR 91*
Bruggeman, Terrance John 1946- *St&PR 91, WhoAm 90, WhoE 91*
Bruggemann, Werner H. F. 1936- *WhoWor 91*
Bruggemann-Breckwoldt, Antje *PenDiDA 89*
Bruggen, Carry van *EncCoWW*
Bruggen, Frans 1934- *PenDiMP*
Brugger, David John *BioIn 16*
Brugger, George Albert 1941- *WhoAm 90*
Brugger, Heidi Nack 1950- *WhoWrEP 89*
Brugger, James Raymond 1920- *WhoAm 90*
Brugger, Thomas C 1927- *BiDrAPA 89*
Bruggere, Thomas Hilby 1946- *St&PR 91*
Bruggink, Eric G. 1949- *WhoAm 90*
Brugh, Thomas B. 1939- *St&PR 91*
Brugler, John C. 1942- *St&PR 91*
Brugler, Richard K. 1928- *St&PR 91*
Brugler, Robert Lynn 1951- *WhoEmL 91*
Brugman, Til 1888-1958 *EncCoWW*
Brugmans, Henri J.F.W. 1885-1961 *EncO&P 3, EncPaPR 91*
Brugnatelli, Bruno E. 1935- *WhoE 91*
Bruguier, John 1849- *WhNaAH*
Bruha, William Anton 1930- *St&PR 91*
Bruhn, Arnold Rahn, Jr. 1941- *WhoE 91*
Bruhn, Erik 1928- *WorAlBi*
Bruhn, Hans-Juergen 1940- *WhoWor 91*
Bruhn, John Glyndon 1934- *WhoAm 90*
Bruhn, Lars Christian 1949- *WhoWor 91*
Bruhn, Marjorie Lee *BiDrAPA 89*
Bruhn, Siglind 1951- *IntWWM 90*
Bruin, John *WorAu 1980*
Bruin, Linda Lou 1938- *WhoAmW 91*
Bruiniers, Terence L. 1946- *St&PR 91*
Bruining, David Martin 1947- *St&PR 91*
Bruins, Amy Conant 1959- *WhoAmW 91*
Bruinsma, Theodore August 1921- *WhoAm 90*
Bruk, Fridrich 1937- *IntWWM 90*
Bruk, John 1930- *WhoAm 90*
Brukardt, David A. 1955- *ODwPR 91*
Bruker, Davenport Sanford 1950- *WhoSSW 91*
Bruker, Deborah Willis 1951- *WhoAmW 91*
Brulc, Lillian G *WhoAmA 91*
Brule, A. Lorraine 1925- *WhoAmW 91*
Brule, Etienne 1591-1632 *BioIn 16*
Brule, Etienne 1592?-1632? *WorAlBi*
Brule, Etienne 1592?-1633? *EncCRAm, WhNaAH*
Brule, John D. 1927- *WhoAm 90*
Brule, Michael Raoul 1953- *WhoEmL 91*
Brule, Thomas Raymond 1954- *WhoEmL 91*
Bruley, Duane Frederick 1933- *WhoAm 90, WhoWor 91*
Brull, Steven Victor 1958- *WhoWor 91*
Brullo, Robert Angelo 1948- *WhoEmL 91*
Brulls, Christian *ConAu 129, MajTwCW*
Brumaire, Jacqueline 1921- *IntWWM 90*
Brumbach, Mary Alice 1947- *WhoSSW 91*
Brumback, Charles Tiedtke 1928- *St&PR 91, WhoAm 90*
Brumback, Clarence Landen 1914- *WhoAm 90*
Brumback, Daniel C 1943- *BiDrAPA 89*
Brumback, Roger Alan 1948- *WhoEmL 91, WhoSSW 91*
Brumback, Ronald Allen 1947- *St&PR 91*
Brumback, Ronald Dean 1941- *WhoSSW 91*
Brumback-Henry, Sarah E. 1948- *WhoAmW 91*
Brumbaugh, David Lynn 1952- *WhoEmL 91*
Brumbaugh, Jana Jo 1959- *WhoEmL 91*
Brumbaugh, John Albert 1935- *WhoAm 90*
Brumbaugh, John Maynard 1927- *WhoAm 90*
Brumbaugh, John Moore 1945- *WhoEmL 91*
Brumbaugh, Robert Sherrick 1918- *WhoAm 90, WhoWrEP 89*
Brumbelow, Norman Ray 1948- *St&PR 91*
Brumber, K. Richard 1940- *St&PR 91*
Brumberg, G. David 1939- *WhoAm 90*
Brumby, Colin James 1933- *IntWWM 90*
Brumby, Donna Trotter 1955- *WhoSSW 91*
Brumby, Sewell 1952- *WhoEmL 91*
Brumder, Philip George 1920- *WhoAm 90*
Brumelle, Kenneth Coy 1945- *WhoSSW 91*
Brumen, Leon 1938- *WhoWor 91*
Brumer, Miriam 1939- *WhoAmA 91*
Brumer, Shulamith 1924- *WhoAmA 91, WhoE 91*
Brumfield, Craig Andrew 1952- *St&PR 91*
Brumfield, John Richard 1934- *WhoAm 90, WhoAmA 91*
Brumfield, Richard Manoah 1909- *WhoAm 90*
Brumgardt, John Raymond 1946- *WhoAm 90, WhoSSW 91*

Brumit, Lawrence Edward, III 1950- *WhoWor 91*
Brumley, David Lee 1949- *WhoAm 90*
Brumley, Jeanne Maria 1955- *WhoEmL 91*
Brumley, Mike 1938- *Ballpl 90*
Brumley, Robert Julian 1929- *St&PR 91*
Brumlik, Joel 1933- *WhoAm 90*
Brumlop, Elsa A *BiDrAPA 89*
Brumm, Brian A. 1954- *St&PR 91*
Brumm, James Earl 1942- *St&PR 91*
Brumm, Joseph Daniel 1916- *St&PR 91, WhoAm 90*
Brumm, Marcia Cowles 1921- *WhoAmW 91*
Brumm, Paul Michael 1947- *St&PR 91, WhoAm 90, WhoEmL 91*
Brumme, Marjorie Vivian 1917- *WhoWrEP 89*
Brummel, Audrey B. 1935- *St&PR 91*
Brummel, George 1778-1840 *WorAlBi*
Brummel, Mark Joseph 1933- *WhoAm 90, WhoWrEP 89*
Brummel, Steven William 1946- *WhoWor 91*
Brummer, Alexander 1949- *WhoWor 91*
Brummet, Richard Lee 1921- *WhoAm 90*
Brummett, Elizabeth Bayley 1939- *WhoSSW 91*
Brummett, Robert Eddie 1934- *WhoAm 90*
Brummit, Houston 1928- *BiDrAPA 89*
Brummond, David Joseph 1950- *WhoEmL 91*
Brummund, Francine Ann 1960- *WhoAmW 91*
Brumund, Loralee Ann 1949- *WhoAmW 91*
Brumwell, Robin Arnold 1944- *St&PR 91*
Brun, Herbert 1918- *IntWWM 90, WhoAm 90*
Brun, Judy Kay *WhoAmW 91*
Brun, Margaret Ann Charlene 1945- *WhoWor 91*
Brun, Sophie Christiane Friederike 1765-1835 *EncCoWW*
Brunale, Vito John 1925- *WhoAm 90, WhoE 91, WhoWor 91*
Brunansky, Tom 1960- *Ballpl 90*
Brundage, Avery 1887-1975 *WhoAmA 91N, WorAlBi*
Brundage, Harold Leroy 1931- *St&PR 91*
Brundage, Howard Denton 1923- *WhoAm 90*
Brundage, James Arthur 1929- *WhoAm 90*
Brundage, John Denton 1919-1989 *BioIn 16*
Brundage, Michael Robert 1942- *St&PR 91*
Brundage, Patricia Lounsbury 1953- *WhoAmW 91*
Brundage, Russell Archibald 1929- *WhoAm 90*
Brundage, Susan Lounsbury 1949- *WhoAmA 91*
Brundige, Linda Ann 1946- *WhoAmW 91*
Brundin, Clark L. *BioIn 16*
Brundrett, George L., Jr. 1921- *St&PR 91*
Brundrett, George Lee, Jr. 1921- *WhoAm 90*
Brundtland, Gro Harlem *BioIn 16*
Brundtland, Gro Harlem 1939- *WhoWor 91*
Brune, David Hamilton 1930- *St&PR 91, WhoAm 90, WhoSSW 91*
Brune, Hans A. 1925- *St&PR 91*
Brune, John Patrick 1964- *WhoE 91*
Brune, Kay 1941- *WhoWor 91*
Bruneau, Bill 1948- *WhoEmL 91, WhoWor 91*
Bruneau, Claude 1931- *WhoAm 90*
Bruneau, Kittie 1929- *WhoAmA 91*
Bruneaux, Debra Louise 1953- *WhoAmW 91*
Brunel, Isambard Kingdom 1806-1859 *BioIn 16*
Brunel, Olivier 1952- *WhoWor 91*
Brunel, Wilson 1920- *St&PR 91*
Brunell, Donald A., Jr. 1944- *St&PR 91*
Brunell, Jerry Albert 1926- *WhoWor 91*
Brunell, Jonathan 1955- *St&PR 91, WhoAm 90*
Brunell, Paul F. 1957- *St&PR 91*
Brunell, Philip A. 1931- *WhoAm 90*
Brunell, Richard F. 1944- *St&PR 91*
Brunell, Richard Howard 1916- *WhoAmA 91*
Brunell, Wayne Edward 1957- *BiDrAPA 89*
Brunell-Kaechele, Diane J. 1952- *WhoAmW 91*
Brunelle, John B. 1924- *St&PR 91*
Brunelle, Philip Charles 1943- *IntWWM 90*
Brunelle, Robert L. 1924- *WhoAm 90*
Brunelle, Thomas Eugene 1935- *St&PR 91*
Brunelleschi, Filippo 1377-1446 *WorAlBi*
Brunello, Giovan Battista *PenDiDA 89*
Bruner, Ann Craddock 1947- *WhoAmW 91*
Bruner, B. Lee 1935- *WhoSSW 91*
Bruner, Charlotte Hughes 1917- *WhoAm 90*
Bruner, Edward M. 1924- *WhoAm 90*
Bruner, Jerome S 1915- *WorAu 1980 [port]*
Bruner, Jerome Seymour *BioIn 16*
Bruner, Linda Pollard 1948- *WhoWor 91*
Bruner, Louise Katherine 1910- *WhoAmA 91*
Bruner, Martha *BioIn 16*
Bruner, Philip Lane 1939- *WhoAm 90, WhoWor 91*
Bruner, Richard H *BiDrAPA 89*
Bruner, Richard Wallace 1926- *AuBYP 90, WhoWrEP 89*
Bruner, Robert B. 1933- *WhoAm 90*
Bruner, Sewell A. 1943- *St&PR 91*
Bruner, Tom 1945- *WhoWor 91*
Bruner, Van Buren, Jr. *WhoAm 90, WhoE 91*
Bruner, William Evans, II 1949- *WhoEmL 91*
Bruner, William Wallace 1920- *WhoAm 90*
Brunet, Barrie K. 1925- *St&PR 91*
Brunet, Emile J *BiDrAPA 89*
Brunet, George 1935- *Ballpl 90*
Brunet, Jean Pierre 1952- *WhoWor 91*
Brunet, Patrick *BioIn 16*
Brunet, Pierre 1939- *St&PR 91*
Brunet, Randy Michael 1955- *WhoSSW 91*
Brunet, Wilfrid-Etienne 1832-1899 *DcCanB 12*
Brunett, Ruth Angela 1948- *WhoAmW 91*
Brunette, Marqua Lee 1950- *WhoAmW 91*
Brunette, Ray Leo 1929- *St&PR 91*
Brunette, Steven Edward 1949- *WhoEmL 91*
Brunetti, Antonio *PenDiMP*
Brunetti, Bennett E. 1922- *St&PR 91*
Brunetti, Carlo Enrico 1952- *WhoWor 91*
Brunetti, Frank A. 1941- *St&PR 91*
Brunetti, John A. 1924- *St&PR 91*
Brunetti, W.H. 1942- *St&PR 91*
Brunetti, Wayne Henry 1942- *WhoSSW 91*
Brunetto, T. *PenDiDA 89*
Bruney, Laura Ann 1957- *WhoAmW 91*
Brungardt, Helen Ruth 1931- *WhoAmW 91, WhoWor 91*
Brunhard, Glenn R. 1948- *St&PR 91*
Brunhart, Hans 1945- *WhoWor 91*
Brunhilde 550?- *WomWR [port]*
Brunhoff, Jean De 1899-1937 *AuBYP 90, WorAlBi*
Brunhoff, Laurent De 1925- *AuBYP 90, BioIn 16*
Bruni, John Richard 1951- *WhoWor 91*
Bruni, Kathy Dianne 1957- *WhoAmW 91*
Bruni, Riccardo *PenDiDA 89*
Bruni, Stephen Thomas 1949- *WhoAm 90, WhoE 91*
Bruni, Umberto 1914- *WhoAmA 91*
Brunichildis 550?- *WomWR [port]*
Brunie, Charles Henry 1930- *WhoAm 90, WhoWor 91*
Brunie, William H 1930- *BiDrAPA 89*
Brunig, Robert Arthur 1946- *WhoEmL 91*
Bruning, Alfred Aaron 1963- *WhoSSW 91*
Bruning, Anthony Steven 1955- *WhoEmL 91*
Bruning, Eberhard Otto 1925- *WhoWor 91*
Bruning, Heinrich Christian *PenDiDA 89*
Bruning, James Leon 1938- *WhoAm 90*
Bruning, John H. 1942- *St&PR 91*
Bruning, Nancy P 1948- *WhoWrEP 89*
Bruninga, Robert Ervin 1948- *WhoE 91*
Brunk, Kenneth A. 1946- *St&PR 91*
Brunk, Max Edwin 1914- *WhoAm 90*
Brunk, Samuel Frederick 1932- *WhoAm 90*
Brunk, William Edward 1928- *WhoAm 90*
Brunke, Scott Moore 1947- *WhoWor 91*
Brunkhorst, Jay Allen 1958- *WhoEmL 91*
Brunkus, Richard Allen 1950- *WhoAmA 91*
Brunnell, Jonathan 1955- *St&PR 91*
Brunner, Alois *BioIn 16*
Brunner, Curtis J. 1943- *St&PR 91*
Brunner, David Lee 1953- *WhoSSW 91*
Brunner, Donald L. 1934- *St&PR 91*
Brunner, Emil 1889-1966 *BioIn 16, WorAlBi*
Brunner, Endre Kopperl 1900- *WhoAm 90*
Brunner, Evelyn 1949- *IntWWM 90*
Brunner, George Matthew 1925- *WhoAm 90*
Brunner, Gordon F. 1938- *St&PR 91*
Brunner, Gordon Francis 1938- *WhoAm 90*
Brunner, Guido 1930- *WhoWor 91*
Brunner, H. Joseph 1942- *St&PR 91*
Brunner, Helen Ursula 1940- *IntWWM 90*
Brunner, James B 1957- *BiDrAPA 89*
Brunner, John 1934- *MajTwCW, RGTwCSF, WorAlBi*
Brunner, John J. 1938- *St&PR 91*
Brunner, John Wilson 1924- *WhoAm 90*
Brunner, Joseph Anthony 1943- *St&PR 91*
Brunner, Joseph Francis 1940- *WhoE 91*
Brunner, Julia 1926- *BioIn 16*
Brunner, Karl 1916-1989 *AnObit 1989, BioIn 16*
Brunner, Lawrence Jerome 1926- *St&PR 91*
Brunner, Lillian Sholtis *WhoAm 90, WhoAmW 91*
Brunner, Mary Martinez 1945- *WhoAmW 91*
Brunner, Mathias John 1922- *WhoE 91*
Brunner, Merlin A. 1924- *St&PR 91*
Brunner, Neal Herbert 1939- *St&PR 91*
Brunner, Richard Francis 1926- *St&PR 91, WhoAm 90*
Brunner, Thomas Rudolph, Jr. 1946- *WhoSSW 91*
Brunner, Thomas William 1945- *WhoEmL 91*
Brunner, Vernon Anthony 1940- *St&PR 91, WhoAm 90*
Brunning, Geoffrey David 1947- *WhoSSW 91*
Bruno, Adrian Anthony 1939- *St&PR 91*
Bruno, Angelo J. 1922- *WhoSSW 91*
Bruno, Angelo J. 1924- *St&PR 91*
Bruno, Audrei Ann 1946- *WhoAmW 91*
Bruno, Carmen Sivila *BiDrAPA 89*
Bruno, Cathy Eileen 1947- *WhoAmW 91*
Bruno, David Alfonse 1950- *WhoE 91, WhoEmL 91, WhoWor 91*
Bruno, Francesco 1939- *St&PR 91*
Bruno, Frank *BioIn 16*
Bruno, Giordano 1548-1600 *WrPh P*
Bruno, Grace Angelia 1935- *WhoAmW 91, WhoE 91*
Bruno, Harold Robinson, Jr. 1928- *WhoAm 90*
Bruno, Jean 1909- *EncO&P 3*
Bruno, Jim 1935- *St&PR 91*
Bruno, Jim N. 1946- *ODwPR 91*
Bruno, Jim Neil 1946- *WhoEmL 91*
Bruno, Joanna Mary 1944- *IntWWM 90*
Bruno, Joseph S. 1914 *WhoAm 90*
Bruno, Judyth Ann 1944- *WhoAmW 91*
Bruno, Kay *ODwPR 91*
Bruno, Kay Anderson 1941- *WhoAmW 91*
Bruno, Lisa Nancy 1962- *WhoEmL 91*
Bruno, Louis Leon *BiDrAPA 89*
Bruno, Michael 1932- *WhoWor 91*
Bruno, Paul Robert 1961- *WhoE 91*
Bruno, Phillip A *WhoAmA 91*
Bruno, Renee M. *BiDrAPA 89*
Bruno, Richard D. 1943- *St&PR 91*
Bruno, Richard McDaniel 1952- *St&PR 91*
Bruno, Ronald G. *WhoAm 90, WhoSSW 91*
Bruno, Santo M *WhoAmA 91*
Bruno, Thomas Anthony 1954- *WhoWor 91*
Bruno, Tom 1953- *Ballpl 90*
Bruno, Vicki *BioIn 16*
Bruno, Vincent J 1926- *WhoAmA 91*
Bruno, Vincent John 1926- *WhoAm 90*
Bruno, Virginia V. 1947- *St&PR 91*
Bruno, Yolanda M *BiDrAPA 89*
Brunon, Jacques Marie 1944- *WhoWor 91*
Brunot, Richard Lee 1932- *St&PR 91*
Brunow, Gordon Peter 1926- *WhoE 91, WhoWor 91*
Bruns, Billy Lee 1925- *WhoWor 91*
Bruns, Bryan Edward 1949- *BiDrAPA 89*
Bruns, Edward Albert 1941- *WhoWor 91*
Bruns, Frederick R, Jr 1913-1979 *WhoAmA 91N*
Bruns, George Henry, Jr. 1918- *St&PR 91*
Bruns, Henriette 1813- *BioIn 16*
Bruns, Henry Gerard *BioIn 16*
Bruns, Henry John Thompson 1950- *WhoE 91*
Bruns, Jerry R 1950- *BiDrAPA 89*
Bruns, Joe *ConAu 131*
Bruns, Maria Reyes 1947- *WhoAmW 91*
Bruns, Michael L. 1956- *St&PR 91*
Bruns, Nicolaus, Jr. 1926- *WhoAm 90*
Bruns, Peter John 1942- *WhoE 91*
Bruns, Robert Bruce 1920- *St&PR 91*
Bruns, Robert Eugene 1952- *WhoEmL 91*
Bruns, Ton 1944- *WhoWor 91*
Bruns, William Carl 1940- *BiDrAPA 89*
Bruns, William John, Jr. 1935- *WhoAm 90, WhoE 91*
Bruns, Wolfgang Bernard 1931- *WhoWor 91*
Brunschvicg, Cecile 1877-1946 *BiDFrPL*
Brunsdale, Anne E. 1923- *WhoAmW 91*
Brunson, Burlie Allen 1945- *WhoSSW 91*
Brunson, Dorothy E. 1938- *WhoAm 90, WhoAmW 91*
Brunson, Faith *BioIn 16*
Brunson, Garion Dennis 1949- *WhoSSW 91*
Brunson, Jack Edward 1956- *St&PR 91*
Brunson, Jack Rushing 1928- *St&PR 91*
Brunson, Joel Garrett 1923- *WhoWor 91*
Brunson, John S. 1934- *St&PR 91*
Brunson, Susan *BioIn 16*
Brunstetter, Richard W *BiDrAPA 89*
Brunsting, Keith Allen 1955- *WhoEmL 91*
Brunsting, Melody Ann 1955- *WhoWrEP 89*
Brunswick, Paul L. 1939- *St&PR 91*
Brunswick, Roger John *BiDrAPA 89*
Brunt, Charles Hal 1938- *BiDrAPA 89*
Brunt, Harry H., Jr. 1921- *BiDrAPA 89*
Brunt, Harry Herman, Jr. 1921- *WhoAm 90*
Brunt, Manly Y., Jr. 1926- *BiDrAPA 89*
Brunt, Manly Yates, Jr. 1926- *WhoAm 90, WhoWor 91*
Bruntjen, Worth 1936- *St&PR 91*
Bruntlandt, Gro Harlem 1939- *WomWR*
Brunton, George Delbert 1924- *WhoSSW 91*
Brunton, Gerald W. 1927- *St&PR 91*
Brunton, Joseph A. *BioIn 16*
Brunton, Linda Ann 1942- *WhoAmW 91*
Brunton, Marilyn *BioIn 16*
Brunton, Mary 1778-1818 *BioIn 16, FemiCLE*
Brunton, Mason Lee 1935- *St&PR 91*
Brunton, Paul 1898-1981 *EncO&P 3*
Brunton, Paul Edward 1922- *WhoAm 90*
Brupbacher, Frederick Arnold, II 1954- *WhoSSW 91*
Brus, Bernard Theodoor 1917- *WhoWor 91*
Brus, Helena Roza 1947- *WhoEmL 91*
Brusa, Elisabetta Olga Laura 1954- *IntWWM 90*
Brusca, Donald Richard 1939- *St&PR 91*
Brusca, Jack 1939- *WhoAmA 91, WhoE 91*
Brusca, Janet Rita 1950- *WhoEmL 91*
Brusca, Richard C. 1945- *WhoAm 90*
Brusca, Richard Charles 1945- *WhoEmL 91*
Brusca, Robert Andrew 1950- *WhoAm 90, WhoE 91*
Bruscantini, Sesto 1919- *IntWWM 90, PenDiMP*
Brusch, Rainer Maria 1951- *WhoWor 91*
Bruschi, Gaspero *PenDiDA 89*
Bruscke, Mark Karl 1951- *WhoE 91*
Brusco, Charles D. 1951- *WhoSSW 91*
Brusco, Lori *ODwPR 91*
Brusenhan, Robert Lee, Jr. 1931- *WhoSSW 91*
Brush, A Louise *BiDrAPA 89*
Brush, Alanson Partridge 1878-1952 *EncABHB 4 [port]*
Brush, Carey Wentworth 1920- *WhoAm 90*
Brush, Charles Francis 1849-1929 *WorAlBi*
Brush, Charles Francis 1923- *WhoAm 90*
Brush, Clinton E., III 1911- *WhoAm 90*
Brush, Craig Balcombe 1930- *WhoAm 90*
Brush, David Elden 1950- *WhoEmL 91*
Brush, Frank John, Jr. 1948- *St&PR 91*
Brush, George De Forest 1855-1941 *WhNaAH*
Brush, George W. 1921- *WhoAm 90*
Brush, Gloria Defilipps 1947- *WhoAmA 91*
Brush, John Dwight 1926- *St&PR 91, WhoE 91*
Brush, John T. 1845-1912 *Ballpl 90, BioIn 16*
Brush, Leif 1932- *WhoAmA 91*
Brush, Lucien Munson, Jr. 1929- *WhoAm 90*
Brush, Peter Norman 1944- *WhoAm 90*
Brush, Richard Frank 1930- *St&PR 91*
Brush, Richard W 1933- *BiDrAPA 89*
Brush, Robert A. 1937- *St&PR 91*
Brush, Robert Paul 1962- *WhoSSW 91*
Brush, Sally Anderson 1934- *WhoAmW 91*
Brush, Thomas Stewart 1922- *WhoE 91*
Brushwood, David Benson 1948- *WhoEmL 91*
Brushwood, John Stubbs 1920- *WhoAm 90*
Brusilov, Aleksei Alekseevich 1853-1926 *BioIn 16*
Brusilow, Anshel 1928- *IntWWM 90, WhoAm 90*
Brusilow, Saul 1927- *WhoAm 90*
Brusin, Joyce Helena 1958- *WhoWrEP 89*
Bruski, Fred John 1929- *WhoE 91*
Bruski, Paul Steven 1949- *WhoEmL 91, WhoWor 91*
Bruso, William F. *St&PR 91*
Bruson, Renato 1936- *IntWWM 90, PenDiMP*
Bruss, Katherine Vivian 1961- *WhoAmW 91*
Brussel, Benjamin B 1922- *BiDrAPA 89*
Brussel-Smith, Bernard 1914- *BioIn 16*
Brussel-Smith, Bernard 1914-1989 *WhoAmA 91N*
Brussell, Mary Sue 1961- *WhoAmW 91*
Brusstar, Warren 1952- *Ballpl 90*
Brust, David 1935- *WhoWor 91*
Brust, Norman *ODwPR 91*
Brust, Norman 1934- *St&PR 91*
Brust, Robert Gustave 1945- *WhoAmA 91*
Brust, Susan Melinda 1951- *WhoAmW 91, WhoE 91*

Brustad, Orin Daniel 1941- *WhoAm 90*
Brustad, Wesley O. 1943- *WhoAm 90*
Brustein, Abram Isaac 1946- *WhoE 91*
Brustein, Lawrence 1936- *WhoAm 90*
Brustein, Martin 1924- *St&PR 91, WhoE 91*
Brustein, Michael Labe 1949- *WhoEmL 91*
Brustein, Robert Sanford 1927- *WhoAm 90, WhoWrEP 89*
Brustlein, Daniel 1904- *WhoAmA 91*
Brustlein, Janice Tworkov *AuBYP 90*
Brustolon, Andrea 1662-1732 *PenDiDA 89*
Brusven, Arland Duane 1932- *St&PR 91*
Brutlag, Michael Lowell 1955- *WhoEmL 91*
Brutlag, Rodney Sheldon 1938- *WhoAm 90*
Bruton, Bill 1925- *BioIn 16*
Bruton, Bill 1929- *Ballpl 90*
Bruton, Eric 1915- *TwCCr&M 91*
Bruton, Eric Moore 1915- *WhoWor 91*
Bruton, Glenda Kay 1956- *WhoSSW 91*
Bruton, Henry Jackson 1921- *WhoAm 90, WhoE 91*
Bruton, James DeWitt, Jr. 1908- *WhoAm 90, WhoWor 91*
Bruton, John Macaulay 1937- *WhoWor 91*
Bruton, Robert William 1942- *WhoSSW 91*
Bruton, Shelby Glenn *BiDrAPA 89*
Brutosky, Mary Veronica *WhoAmA 91*
Brutsman, Joseph *BioIn 16*
Brutus, Dennis 1924- *BioIn 16, WorAu 1980 [port]*
Brutus, Dennis Vincent 1924- *WhoAm 90*
Brutus, Marcus Junius 85BC-42BC *WorAlBi*
Bruun, Erik 1926- *ConDes 90*
Bruun, Eywin 1937- *WhoWor 91*
Bruun, Geoffrey 1898-1988 *BioIn 16*
Bruun, Jens Ole 1947- *WhoWor 91*
Bruun, Ruth Dowling 1937- *BiDrAPA 89, WhoE 91*
Bruyas, Jacques 1635-1712 *WhNaAH*
Bruyn, Henry Bicker 1918- *WhoAm 90*
Bruyn, Michiel de 1608-1670? *PenDiDA 89*
Bruynel, Ton 1934- *IntWWM 90*
Bruynes, Cees 1932- *St&PR 91, WhoAm 90*
Bruza, Diane Marie 1958- *BiDrAPA 89*
Bruzas, Theodore E. 1935- *St&PR 91*
Bruzda, Francis Joseph 1935- *WhoAm 90*
Bruzdowicz, Joanna 1943- *IntWWM 90*
Bruzelius, Caroline Astrid 1949- *WhoAmW 91*
Bruzelius, Jan Oskar Alexander 1946- *WhoWor 91*
Bruzelius, Nils Johan Axel 1947- *WhoAm 90*
Bruzs, Boris Olgerd 1933- *St&PR 91, WhoE 91*
Bruzzese, Edoardo 1926- *WhoWor 91*
Bruzzese, Frank Joseph 1966- *WhoE 91*
Bruzzese, Philip Samuel 1933- *St&PR 91*
Bruzzone, Edward Joseph 1946- *WhoEmL 91*
Bry, Edith 1898 *WhoAmA 91*
Bry, Theodore de 1528-1598 *EncCRAm*
Bry, Vernon Arthur, Jr. *BiDrAPA 89*
Bryan, Anthony John Adrian 1923- *St&PR 91*
Bryan, April Beth 1964- *WhoAmW 91*
Bryan, Arthur Eldridge, Jr. 1924- *WhoAm 90*
Bryan, Ashley 1923- *BioIn 16*
Bryan, Barbara Allison 1954- *WhoSSW 91*
Bryan, Barry Richard 1930- *WhoAm 90*
Bryan, Billie Marie 1932- *WhoAmW 91, WhoE 91*
Bryan, Billy 1938- *Ballpl 90*
Bryan, C. D. B. *BioIn 16*
Bryan, Charles Faulkner, Jr. 1946- *WhoSSW 91*
Bryan, Christina Helen 1948- *WhoAmW 91*
Bryan, Clarice Adina 1923- *WhoAmW 91*
Bryan, Colgan Hobson 1909- *WhoAm 90*
Bryan, Courtlandt Dixon Barnes *BioIn 16*
Bryan, Courtlandt Dixon Barnes 1936- *WhoAm 90, WhoWrEP 89*
Bryan, D. Tennant 1906- *St&PR 91*
Bryan, David Barclay 1933- *St&PR 91, WhoWor 91*
Bryan, David Tennant 1906- *WhoAm 90, WhoSSW 91*
Bryan, Dora 1924- *OxCPMus*
Bryan, Earl Watkins 1941- *St&PR 91*
Bryan, Edna Eugenie 1936- *WhoAmW 91*
Bryan, Elizabeth P. 1960- *St&PR 91*
Bryan, F.S., Jr. 1938- *St&PR 91*
Bryan, G. Howard 1913- *St&PR 91*
Bryan, Gene Edward 1957- *WhoEmL 91*
Bryan, George Thomas 1930- *WhoAm 90*
Bryan, Gloria Elaine 1946- *WhoEmL 91*
Bryan, Gloria Jane 1959- *WhoAmW 91*
Bryan, Guy Morrison 1821-1901 *AmLegL*
Bryan, Harry Edwin *BiDrAPA 89*
Bryan, Henry Clark, Jr. 1930- *WhoAm 90*
Bryan, Hob 1952- *WhoSSW 91*
Bryan, J. Shepard, Jr. 1922- *St&PR 91*
Bryan, Jack L 1942- *WhoAmA 91*
Bryan, James C. 1927- *St&PR 91*
Bryan, James Edward 1906- *WhoAm 90*
Bryan, James Jaubert 1923- *WhoSSW 91*
Bryan, Jerry L. 1939- *ODwPR 91*
Bryan, John Alexander 1940- *WhoAm 90*
Bryan, John Gilbert 1932- *St&PR 91*
Bryan, John Henry 1936- *St&PR 91, WhoAm 90*
Bryan, John Henry, Jr. *BioIn 16*
Bryan, John Howard 1952- *IntWWM 90*
Bryan, John Leland 1926- *WhoAm 90*
Bryan, John Stewart, III 1938- *WhoAm 90, WhoSSW 91*
Bryan, Jonathan 1708-1788 *BioIn 16*
Bryan, Joseph 1845-1908 *BioIn 16*
Bryan, Joseph 1904- *AuBYP 90*
Bryan, Joseph, III 1904- *WhoAm 90*
Bryan, Joseph M. 1896- *St&PR 91*
Bryan, Joseph McKinley 1896- *WhoAm 90, WhoWor 91*
Bryan, Joseph McKinley, Jr. 1936- *WhoSSW 91*
Bryan, Katherine *BioIn 16*
Bryan, Katherine Byram *WhoE 91*
Bryan, Kathryn Timmins 1941- *WhoSSW 91*
Bryan, L Laramour *BiDrAPA 89*
Bryan, Laquey Phillip 1930- *St&PR 91*
Bryan, Larry J. *BioIn 16*
Bryan, Lawrence Donald, III 1943- *St&PR 91*
Bryan, Margaret *FemiCLE*
Bryan, Mary *FemiCLE*
Bryan, Mary 1838?-1913 *FemiCLE*
Bryan, Mary Ann 1929- *WhoAmW 91*
Bryan, Mildred Gott *WhoWor 91*
Bryan, Monk 1914- *WhoAm 90*
Bryan, Norman E. 1947- *WhoEmL 91*
Bryan, Paul Robey 1920- *IntWWM 90*
Bryan, Paul Robey, Jr. *WhoAm 90*
Bryan, Richard Conger 1924- *St&PR 91*
Bryan, Richard Gardner 1927- *St&PR 91*
Bryan, Richard H. *BioIn 16*
Bryan, Richard H. 1937- *WhoAm 90, WhoWor 91*
Bryan, Robert 1934- *ConTFT 8*
Bryan, Robert Armistead 1926- *WhoAm 90*
Bryan, Robert Fessler 1913- *WhoAm 90*
Bryan, Robert J. 1934- *WhoAm 90*
Bryan, Robert Russell 1943- *WhoWor 91*
Bryan, Sam Neal 1951- *WhoEmL 91*
Bryan, Sharon 1943- *WhoWrEP 89*
Bryan, Sharon M. 1959- *St&PR 91*
Bryan, Shawn William 1948- *St&PR 91*
Bryan, Thomas L. 1935- *St&PR 91*
Bryan, Thomas Lynn 1935- *WhoAm 90*
Bryan, Thornton Embry, Jr. 1927- *WhoAm 90*
Bryan, William *BioIn 16*
Bryan, William Alonzo 1938- *WhoSSW 91*
Bryan, William Jennings 1860-1925 *BiDrUSE 89, BioIn 16, WorAlBi*
Bryan, William Royal 1932- *WhoAm 90*
Bryan Brown, Peter 1921 *BiDrAPA 89*
Bryans, John Armond 1925- *WhoAmA 91*
Bryans, John Thomas 1924- *WhoAm 90*
Bryant, Alan Willard, Jr. 1940- *WhoWor 91*
Bryant, Alton Byrnes, Jr. 1929- *WhoSSW 91*
Bryant, Ann Aleace 1961- *WhoAmW 91*
Bryant, Anne Lincoln 1949- *WhoAm 90*
Bryant, Anthony W. 1930- *St&PR 91*
Bryant, Archer Goodney 1949- *WhoEmL 91*
Bryant, Arthur H. 1954- *WhoAm 90, WhoE 91*
Bryant, Arthur Herbert, II 1942- *WhoAm 90, WhoSSW 91*
Bryant, Arthur Lee 1934- *St&PR 91, WhoAm 90*
Bryant, Arthur Wynne Morgan 1899-1985 *DcNaB 1981*
Bryant, Babs Underwood 1959- *WhoSSW 91*
Bryant, Barbara Everitt 1926- *WhoAmW 91*
Bryant, Barbara Louise 1944- *WhoE 91*
Bryant, Barbara Phyfe 1943- *St&PR 91*
Bryant, Bear *BioIn 16*
Bryant, Bennie Lee 1951- *WhoSSW 91*
Bryant, Bernard E *BiDrAPA 89*
Bryant, Bertha Estelle 1927- *WhoAm 90*
Bryant, Beverly Jean 1958- *BiDrAPA 89*
Bryant, Billy Finney 1922- *WhoAm 90*
Bryant, Boudleaux 1920-1987 *OxCPMus*
Bryant, Brenda Joyce 1950- *WhoEmL 91*
Bryant, C.E., Jr. *St&PR 91*
Bryant, C Martel 1930- *BiDrAPA 89*
Bryant, Calvin Don 1948- *WhoSSW 91*
Bryant, Cameron Edward, Jr. 1934- *WhoAm 90*
Bryant, Carlton Ray 1958- *WhoSSW 91*
Bryant, Carolyn 1944- *IntWWM 90*
Bryant, Cecil Farris 1914- *WhoAm 90*
Bryant, Celia Mae Small 1913- *WhoAm 90*
Bryant, Charles Austin, IV 1946- *WhoAm 90*
Bryant, Clay 1911- *Ballpl 90*
Bryant, Clifton Dow 1932- *WhoAm 90, WhoWor 91*
Bryant, Clora *BioIn 16*
Bryant, David 1951- *WhoEmL 91*
Bryant, David Ernest 1922- *WhoWrEP 89*
Bryant, David Stuart 1948- *WhoE 91*
Bryant, Deborah Reid 1950- *WhoAmW 91, WhoE 91*
Bryant, Demetrius Edward 1956- *WhoEmL 91, WhoWor 91*
Bryant, Denis Russell 1944- *St&PR 91*
Bryant, Denise Delisle 1946- *WhoEmL 91*
Bryant, Dennis Michael 1947- *WhoEmL 91, WhoSSW 91*
Bryant, Don Estes 1917- *WhoWor 91*
Bryant, Donald Loudon 1908- *WhoAm 90, WhoWor 91*
Bryant, Donald Loyd 1919- *St&PR 91, WhoAm 90*
Bryant, Donna Louise 1946- *WhoAmW 91*
Bryant, Douglas Wallace 1913- *WhoAm 90*
Bryant, Edward Albert 1928- *WhoAmA 91*
Bryant, Edward Clark 1915- *WhoAm 90*
Bryant, Edward Kendall 1902- *WhoAm 90*
Bryant, Edward Winslow, Jr. 1945- *WhoWrEP 89*
Bryant, Etta Colish 1930- *BiDrAPA 89*
Bryant, Eva Lou 1941- *WhoAmW 91*
Bryant, Felice 1925- *OxCPMus*
Bryant, Frances Jane 1933- *WhoAmW 91*
Bryant, G. Preston 1933- *WhoWrEP 89*
Bryant, Gary David 1949- *WhoEmL 91*
Bryant, Gary Wayne 1949- *St&PR 91*
Bryant, Gay 1945- *WhoAm 90, WhoAmW 91, WhoWor 91, WhoWrEP 89*
Bryant, George Macon 1926- *WhoSSW 91*
Bryant, Gertrude Thomson *AuBYP 90*
Bryant, Gordon Stanton 1943- *WhoSSW 91*
Bryant, Harry Miller, Sr. 1921- *St&PR 91*
Bryant, Harvey Lee 1929- *St&PR 91*
Bryant, Hazel 1939-1983 *BioIn 16, DrBlPA 90, NotWoAT*
Bryant, Howard Louis 1921- *WhoSSW 91*
Bryant, Howard Sewall 1928- *St&PR 91*
Bryant, Hubert Hale 1931- *WhoAm 90*
Bryant, Ira Houston, III 1942- *WhoSSW 91*
Bryant, Jack G. 1936- *St&PR 91*
Bryant, James Montgomery 1954- *WhoSSW 91*
Bryant, James N. 1945- *WhoEmL 91*
Bryant, James Wesley 1921- *WhoAm 90*
Bryant, Jane Shank 1934- *WhoSSW 91*
Bryant, Jeannette Marie 1939- *WhoAmW 91*
Bryant, Jerry W. 1941- *St&PR 91*
Bryant, Joan Marie 1929- *WhoSSW 91*
Bryant, Joanne Catherine 1930- *WhoAmW 91*
Bryant, John 1943- *WhoSSW 91, WhoWor 91*
Bryant, John Bradbury 1947- *WhoAm 90*
Bryant, John Harold 1920- *WhoAm 90*
Bryant, John Hulon 1941- *WhoSSW 91*
Bryant, John Wiley 1947- *WhoAm 90, WhoSSW 91*
Bryant, Joseph Allen, Jr. 1919- *WhoAm 90*
Bryant, Josephine Harriet 1947- *WhoAm 90*
Bryant, Joyce 1927?- *DrBlPA 90*
Bryant, Karen Worstell 1942- *WhoAmW 91*
Bryant, Kathy Ann 1942- *WhoWrEP 89*
Bryant, Keith Lynn, Jr. 1937- *WhoAm 90*
Bryant, L. Gerald 1942- *WhoSSW 91*
Bryant, Lane 1879-1951 *WorAlBi*
Bryant, Larre 1942- *WhoWrEP 89*
Bryant, Leon O. 1923- *St&PR 91*
Bryant, Leon Odell 1923- *WhoSSW 91*
Bryant, Lester R. 1930- *WhoAm 90*
Bryant, Lina Antonetta 1960- *WhoAmW 91*
Bryant, Linda Goode 1949- *WhoAmA 91*
Bryant, Lisa Henderson *BiDrAPA 89*
Bryant, Louise 1885-1936 *EncAL*
Bryant, Louise 1890-1936 *BioIn 16*
Bryant, Louise Stevens 1890-1936 *BioAmW*
Bryant, Lynda Jean Darden 1941- *WhoAmW 91*
Bryant, Lynn Andrea 1952- *WhoEmL 91*
Bryant, Margot 1897-1988 *AnObit 1988*
Bryant, Martha J. 1949- *WhoAmW 91*
Bryant, Marvin Pierce 1925- *WhoAm 90*
Bryant, Mary Snell 1949- *WhoAmW 91*
Bryant, Matlynn 1957- *WhoEmL 91*
Bryant, Melissa Dunbar 1957- *WhoAmW 91*
Bryant, Michael Joseph 1945- *WhoSSW 91*
Bryant, Napoleon Bonaparte 1825-1902 *AmLegL*
Bryant, Olen L 1927- *WhoAmA 91*
Bryant, Oscar Sims, Jr. 1920- *WhoAm 90*
Bryant, Pamela Kaye 1953- *WhoAmW 91*
Bryant, Paul 1913-1983 *WorAlBi*
Bryant, Paul W. *BioIn 16*
Bryant, Paul William, Jr. *BioIn 16*
Bryant, Peter Jude 1960- *WhoEmL 91*
Bryant, R. Jeep *ODwPR 91*
Bryant, Richard James 1928- *St&PR 91*
Bryant, Richard L. 1952- *St&PR 91*
Bryant, Richard Todd 1952- *WhoEmL 91*
Bryant, Robert 1958- *WhoEmL 91*
Bryant, Robert Leamon 1953- *WhoAm 90*
Bryant, Robert Lee 1926- *St&PR 91*
Bryant, Robert Parker 1922- *WhoAm 90*
Bryant, Ron 1947- *Ballpl 90*
Bryant, Ronald *BioIn 16*
Bryant, Ruth A. 1924- *St&PR 91*
Bryant, Ruth Alyne 1924- *WhoAm 90, WhoAmW 91*
Bryant, Sandra Renee 1959- *WhoEmL 91*
Bryant, Steven Harry 1946- *WhoWor 91*
Bryant, Susan E. *BioIn 16*
Bryant, Susan Halperin *BiDrAPA 89*
Bryant, Sylvia Leigh 1947- *WhoWrEP 89*
Bryant, Tamara Thompson *WhoAmA 91*
Bryant, Tamera Sue 1955- *WhoWrEP 89*
Bryant, Tara Ann 1963- *WhoAmW 91*
Bryant, Thomas E *BiDrAPA 89*
Bryant, Thomas Edward 1936- *WhoAm 90*
Bryant, William Cullen 1794-1878 *BioIn 16, WorAlBi*
Bryant, William Junior 1904- *WhoAm 90, WhoSSW 91*
Bryant, Willie 1908- *OxCPMus*
Bryant, Willie 1908-1964 *DrBlPA 90*
Bryant, Winston 1938- *WhoSSW 91*
Bryars, Gavin *NewAgMG*
Bryars, Richard Gavin 1943- *IntWWM 90*
Bryars, Scott J. 1959- *St&PR 91*
Bryars, W.C. 1922- *St&PR 91*
Bryce, Eileen Ann 1953- *WhoAmA 91*
Bryce, Graham C. 1940- *St&PR 91*
Bryce, James 1838-1922 *BioIn 16*
Bryce, James W. 1880-1949 *WorAlBi*
Bryce, Mark Adams 1953- *WhoAmA 91*
Bryce, Owen 1920- *IntWWM 90*
Bryce, William Delf 1932- *WhoWor 91*
Brycelea, Clifford 1953- *WhoAmA 91*
Bryden, John Carrick McClure 1947- *IntWWM 90*
Bryden, Nathan 1957- *WhoEmL 91*
Bryden, Peter Thackeray 1952- *WhoE 91*
Bryden, William Donald, Jr. 1935- *WhoE 91*
Brydges, David Chandos 1949- *WhoAm 90*
Brydon, Donald James 1922- *WhoAm 90*
Brydon, Harold Wesley 1923- *WhoWor 91*
Brydon, Kim Marie *BiDrAPA 89*
Brydon, Roderick 1939- *IntWWM 90*
Brye, Steve 1949- *Ballpl 90*
Bryen, Stephen 1942- *WhoAm 90*
Bryer, Lawrence W *BiDrAPA 89*
Bryfonski, Dedria Anne 1947- *St&PR 91, WhoAm 90*
Bryher 1894-1983 *DcNaB 1981, FemiCLE*
Bryher, Annie Winifred Ellerman 1894 1983 *BioIn 16*
Bryja, Frank J. 1942- *St&PR 91*
Bryk, Rut 1916- *ConDes 90*
Bryk, William 1955- *WhoWrEP 89*
Bryles, Robert Samuel *BiDrAPA 89*
Brylski, James Ronald *BiDrAPA 89*
Brymer, Jack 1915- *IntWWM 90, PenDiMP*
Brymer, Robert L. 1932- *St&PR 91*
Brymn, James Tim 1881-1946 *OxCPMus*
Bryn, Tracey *BioIn 16*
Bryn-Jones, Delme 1935- *IntWWM 90*
Bryn-Julson, Phyllis 1945- *PenDiMP*
Brynelson, Floyd Arvold 1914- *St&PR 91*
Bryner, Lois Catharine 1923- *WhoAmW 91*
Brynes, Glenn Oliver 1951- *BiDrAPA 89*
Brynjolfsson, Ari 1926- *WhoWor 91*
Brynleifsson, Siglaugur 1922- *WhoWor 91*
Brynner, Yul *BioIn 16*
Brynner, Yul 1915-1985 *OxCPMus*
Brynner, Yul 1920-1985 *WorAlBi*
Bryskin, Lawrence *BiDrAPA 89*
Bryson, Allen Lee 1947- *WhoEmL 91*
Bryson, Arthur Earl, Jr. 1925- *WhoAm 90*
Bryson, Bill *BioIn 16*
Bryson, Brady Oliver 1915- *WhoAm 90*
Bryson, Bruce F *BiDrAPA 89*
Bryson, Dorothy Printup 1894- *WhoAmW 91*
Bryson, Gary S. 1943- *St&PR 91*
Bryson, Gary Spath 1943- *WhoAm 90*
Bryson, George 1813-1900 *DcCanB 12*
Bryson, George Mitchell 1940- *St&PR 91*
Bryson, George Tarry, Jr. 1929- *WhoAm 90*
Bryson, James Edward 1961- *WhoEmL 91*
Bryson, John D. 1941- *St&PR 91*
Bryson, John E. 1943- *WhoAm 90*
Bryson, Joyce 1928- *WhoAmW 91*
Bryson, Norman 1949- *BioIn 16*
Bryson, Peabo *BioIn 16*

Bryson, Peabo 1940?- DrBlPA 90
Bryson, Reid Allen 1920- WhoAm 90
Bryson, Roger 1944- IntWWM 90
Bryson, Vern Elrick 1920- WhoWor 91
Bryson-Israel, Doris Lorraine 1938- WhoE 91
Bryt, Albert 1913- BiDrAPA 89, WhoE 91
Brytczuk, Gary Albert 1947- WhoE 91
Bryzinski, Mark Francis 1953- WhoEmL 91
Brzana, Stanislaus Joseph 1917- WhoAm 90, WhoE 91
Brzeczek, Elizabeth BioIn 16
Brzeczek, Richard BioIn 16
Brzenk, Richard S. 1942- St&PR 91
Brzenk, Stanley Joseph 1933- St&PR 91
Brzeska, Henri Gaudier- 1891-1915 BioIn 16
Brzezinski, Ronald Thomas 1938- St&PR 91
Brzezinski, Tadeusz 1896-1990 BioIn 16, NewYTBS 90
Brzezinski, Zbigniew BioIn 16
Brzezinski, Zbigniew 1928- WhoAm 90, WhoE 91, WhoWor 91, WorAlBi
Brzostovski, Miguel 1932- BiDrAPA 89
Brzostowska, Janina 1907-1986 EncCoWW
Brzozowski, Richard Joseph 1932- WhoAmA 91, WhoE 91
Brzozowski, Ronald C. 1952- St&PR 91
Brzozowski, Thomas Henry 1941- BiDrAPA 89
Brzuskiewicz, John Edward 1955- WhoEmL 91
Brzustowicz, Richard John 1917- WhoAm 90
Brzustowicz, Stanislaw Henry 1919- WhoAm 90
Bstan-'dzin-rgya-mtsho 1935- BioIn 16
Bua, Nicholas John 1925- WhoAm 90
Buarque de Holanda Ferreira, Aurelio BioIn 16
Buatta, Mario 1935- BioIn 16
Buatti, Maryanne 1956- WhoAmW 91
Buba, Eugenia Z. 1951- St&PR 91
Buba, Joy Flinsch 1904- WhoAmA 91
Bubaris, Gus John 1952- WhoE 91
Bubb, Harry G. 1924- St&PR 91
Bubb, Harry Geiple 1924- WhoAm 90
Bubba, Joseph L. 1938- WhoE 91
Bubbles, John 1902-1986 DrBlPA 90
Bubbs, Roy H. 1949- St&PR 91
Bube, Richard Howard 1927- WhoAm 90
Bubeck, Roy R. 1946- St&PR 91
Bubel, Judith Ann 1942- WhoE 91
Buben, Arlene Carol 1948- WhoAmW 91
Bubenik, Patricia Jean Hadle 1947- WhoAmW 91
Bubenzer, Gary Dean 1940- WhoAm 90
Buber, Martin 1878-1965 MajTwCW, WorAlBi, WrPh P
Buber-Neumann, Margarete 1901-1989 AnObit 1989
Bubernak, Jon Paul 1935- St&PR 91
Bubert, James Fredrick 1931- St&PR 91
Bubien, Stanley C. 1946- St&PR 91
Bubier, Ellen Stewart 1962- WhoAmW 91
Bubis, Bess Rosenblum 1922- St&PR 91
Bubis, Marvin R. 1921- St&PR 91
Bubka, Sergei BioIn 16
Bubla, Jiri BioIn 16
Bubley, Esther BioIn 16
Bublis, Mary E D C BiDrAPA 89
Bublitz, Walter John, Jr. 1920- WhoAm 90
Bublys, Algimantas Vladas 1941- WhoAm 90
Bubnic, Anne Marie 1949- WhoAmW 91
Bubnoff, Serge Nikolaevich Von 1888-1957 DcScB S2
Bubnov, Andrei Sergeevich 1883-1940 BioIn 16
Bubnov, Igor D. 1931- WhoWor 91
Bubnova, Tatiana 1946- WhoWor 91
Bubolz, Gordon August 1905- St&PR 91
Bubolz, John Sever 1941- St&PR 91
Bubp, Gregory 1955- St&PR 91
Bubrick, George J. 1947- St&PR 91
Bubrick, George Joseph 1947- WhoAm 90
Buc, Nancy Lillian 1944- WhoAmW 91
Bucard, Marcel 1895-1946 BiDFrPL
Bucaro, Robert N. 1951- St&PR 91
Buccella, William Victor 1943- WhoAm 90
Buccello, Henry Louis 1920- WhoAm 90
Bucchi, Mark 1955- WhoEmL 91
Bucchieri, Peter Charles 1955- WhoEmL 91, WhoWor 91
Bucchignano, John J. 1947- St&PR 91
Bucci, Clotilde BiDrAPA 89
Bucci, Dick 1944- St&PR 91
Bucci, Elaine Theresa 1957- WhoAmW 91
Bucci, Luigi 1924- BiDrAPA 89, WhoWor 91
Bucci, Mark 1924- IntWWM 90
Bucci, Michael Thomas 1948- WhoE 91
Bucci, Raffaele PenDiDA 89
Bucci, Thomas WhoE 91
Buccieri, Charles Francis 1930- WhoE 91
Buccigross, Richard L 1946- BiDrAPA 89
Buccigrossi, David Eric 1956- WhoEmL 91
Buccino, Alphonse 1931- WhoAm 90, WhoSSW 91
Buccino, Gerald P. 1938- WhoAm 90
Buccino, Salvatore George 1933- WhoAm 90, WhoSSW 91
Buccitelli, Marcia Denise 1949- WhoAmW 91
Bucco-Riboulat, Rene 1926- WhoWor 91
Buceck, D.T. 1932- St&PR 91
Bucek, Dennis C. 1945- St&PR 91
Bucella, M. St&PR 91
Buceta, Joseph Benito 1950- WhoE 91
Buch, Bakul Chandrakant 1953- BiDrAPA 89
Buch, David Leslie 1952- BiDrAPA 89, WhoE 91
Buch, Donald Noel 1946- WhoSSW 91
Buch, Fred Newton 1937- WhoWor 91
Buch, Gary 1954- WhoAmA 91
Buch, Iver Winfeldt 1749-1811 PenDiDA 89
Buch, Kimberly Kreisler 1956- WhoAmW 91
Buch, Maximo Hartwig 1959- WhoWor 91
Buch, Piyush C BiDrAPA 89
Buch, Rene Augusto 1925- WhoHisp 91
Buch, Robert Hansen 1929- St&PR 91
Bucha, Edward Richard 1954- WhoE 91
Bucha, Paul BioIn 16
Buchai, Gregory 1945- St&PR 91
Buchakian, Robert BioIn 16
Buchakjian, Serge D. 1954- St&PR 91
Buchalter, Eric Neal BiDrAPA 89
Buchalter, Louis 1897-1944 WorAlBi
Buchalter, Martin 1932- St&PR 91
Buchalter, Robert 1940- BiDrAPA 89
Buchalter, Stuart D. 1937- St&PR 91
Buchalter, Stuart David 1937- WhoAm 90
Buchan, Alan Bradley 1936- WhoAm 90
Buchan, Anna 1878-1948 BioIn 16
Buchan, Barbara BioIn 16
Buchan, Cynthia 1960- IntWWM 90
Buchan, Douglas Charles 1936- WhoSSW 91
Buchan, James 1916- ConAu 130
Buchan, John 1875-1940 SpyFic, TwCCr&M 91
Buchan, Norman Findlay 1922-1990 ConAu 132
Buchan, Ronald Forbes 1915- WhoAm 90, WhoE 91, WhoWor 91
Buchan, Russell Paul 1947- WhoEmL 91, WhoWor 91
Buchan, Shahin BiDrAPA 89
Buchan, Stuart 1942-1987 BioIn 16
Buchan, Vivian Eileen 1911- WhoWrEP 89
Buchanan, Annette Dorothy 1923- St&PR 91
Buchanan, Barbara Neenan 1941- BiDrAPA 89
Buchanan, Bob R. 1932- St&PR 91
Buchanan, Brenda J. WhoAmW 91, WhoE 91, WhoWor 91
Buchanan, Charles Breneman 1931- St&PR 91, WhoAm 90
Buchanan, Chris Sharidan 1954- WhoSSW 91
Buchanan, Connie Doggett BiDrAPA 89
Buchanan, Daniel Harvey 1923- WhoAm 90
Buchanan, David 1944- St&PR 91
Buchanan, Dawn Ann 1960- WhoSSW 91
Buchanan, Debra Ann 1956- WhoAmW 91
Buchanan, Dennis Michael 1945- WhoAm 90
Buchanan, Dianne Jean Johnson 1948- WhoAmW 91, WhoWor 91
Buchanan, Dodds Ireton 1931- WhoAm 90
Buchanan, Dorothy IntWWM 90
Buchanan, Ed Buck 1948- WhoEmL 91
Buchanan, Edna BioIn 16, WhoAm 90, WhoAmW 91, WhoSSW 91
Buchanan, Edna 1939?- ConAu 132
Buchanan, Ellery R. 1950- St&PR 91
Buchanan, Ellery Rives 1950- WhoE 91
Buchanan, Emerson 1909-1988 BioIn 16
Buchanan, George 1904-1989 ConAu 129
Buchanan, George D. 1937- St&PR 91
Buchanan, George Francis 1924- WhoAm 90
Buchanan, Gloria Jean 1950- WhoAmW 91, WhoE 91
Buchanan, Hubert A. 1905- WhoWrEP 89
Buchanan, Isobel Wilson 1954- IntWWM 90
Buchanan, Jack 1891-1957 OxCPMus
Buchanan, Jack Willard 1923- St&PR 91
Buchanan, James 1791-1868 BiDrUSE 89, BioIn 16, WorAlBi
Buchanan, James Blythe 1933- St&PR 91
Buchanan, James David 1929- ConAu 130
Buchanan, James Junkin 1925- WhoAm 90
Buchanan, James M. 1919- WorAlBi
Buchanan, James McGill 1919- WhoAm 90, WhoSSW 91, WhoWor 91, WhoWrEP 89
Buchanan, James William, III 1948- WhoEmL 91
Buchanan, Jennifer Lee 1957- WhoAmW 91
Buchanan, Jerry 1936- WhoAmA 91
Buchanan, Jerry Major 1923- WhoWrEP 89
Buchanan, John A. 1925- St&PR 91
Buchanan, John Chalkley 1911- WhoSSW 91
Buchanan, John Dewey, Jr. 1933- WhoSSW 91
Buchanan, John Donald 1927- WhoAm 90
Buchanan, John Edward 1939- St&PR 91
Buchanan, John Edward, Jr. 1953- WhoAm 90, WhoAmA 91, WhoSSW 91
Buchanan, John Goodwin 1939- BiDrAPA 89
Buchanan, John Machlin 1917- WhoAm 90
Buchanan, John MacLennan 1931- WhoAm 90, WhoE 91
Buchanan, John R. 1929- St&PR 91
Buchanan, John Robert 1928- WhoAm 90, WhoWor 91
Buchanan, Joseph Rhodes 1814-1899 EncO&P 3
Buchanan, June BioIn 16
Buchanan, Lee Ann ODwPR 91
Buchanan, Lee Ann 1955- WhoEmL 91
Buchanan, Lisa M. 1968- WhoEmL 91
Buchanan, Lovell Lee 1949- WhoE 91
Buchanan, Maggie WhoWrEP 89
Buchanan, Michael Andrew 1928- St&PR 91
Buchanan, Patrick BioIn 16
Buchanan, Patrick 1938- WorAlBi
Buchanan, Patrick Henry 1937- BiDrAPA 89
Buchanan, Patrick Joseph 1938- WhoAm 90
Buchanan, Peggy Carr 1925- WhoAmW 91
Buchanan, Peter BioIn 16
Buchanan, Peter Townley 1934- WhoE 91
Buchanan, Phillip Hoge 1960- WhoSSW 91
Buchanan, Ray Allen 1947- WhoWrEP 89
Buchanan, Robert Alexander 1932- WhoAm 90
Buchanan, Robert Campbell 1940- St&PR 91, WhoAm 90
Buchanan, Robert E. BioIn 16
Buchanan, Robert Edgar 1919- WhoAm 90
Buchanan, Robert McLeod 1932- WhoAm 90
Buchanan, Robert Taylor 1944- WhoAm 90
Buchanan, Robert W 1944- BiDrAPA 89
Buchanan, Robert Williams BiDrAPA 89
Buchanan, Roy BioIn 16
Buchanan, Sherrie Lee Korous 1949- WhoAmW 91
Buchanan, Sidney Arnold 1932- WhoAmA 91
Buchanan, Susan Shaver 1954- WhoEmL 91
Buchanan, Susie 1947- ODwPR 91
Buchanan, Teri Bailey 1946- WhoAmW 91
Buchanan, Thomas K 1923- BiDrAPA 89
Buchanan, Thomas W. 1955- St&PR 91
Buchanan, Thompson 1877-1937 LiHiK
Buchanan, Wesley Evans 1917- WhoAm 90
Buchanan, William 1918- WhoAm 90
Buchanan, William 1930- AuBYP 90
Buchanan, William Burdett 1949- WhoSSW 91
Buchanan, William E. 1903- St&PR 91
Buchanan, William Eugene 1903- WhoAm 90
Buchanan, William Hobart, Jr. 1937- St&PR 91, WhoAm 90
Buchanan, William Insco 1853-1909 BioIn 16
Buchanan, William J. 1926- BioIn 16
Buchanan, William Walter 1927- WhoAm 90
Buchanan-Davidson, Dorothy Jean 1925- WhoAmW 91
Buchbinder, Rudolf 1946- PenDiMP, WhoWor 91
Buchbinder, Sharon Bell 1951- WhoAmW 91, WhoEmL 91
Buchdahl, Alice Jean BiDrAPA 89
Buchdahl, Gerd 1914- WhoWor 91
Buche, Dale Kuntz 1935- BiDrAPA 89
Bucheister, Patricia Louise 1942- WhoWrEP 89
Buchek, Jerry 1942- Ballpl 90
Buchek, Kathleen A. 1958- WhoWrEP 89
Buchel, Kurt Friedrich 1933- WhoWor 91
Buchele, Brentley Allen 1955- WhoEmL 91
Buchele, Wesley Fisher 1920- WhoAm 90
Buchen, Edwin Morrisey 1912- St&PR 91
Buchenroth, Stephen Richard 1948- WhoEmL 91
Bucher, Anton Heinrich 1942- WhoWor 91
Bucher, Carol Anne 1948- WhoAmW 91
Bucher, Charles Augustus 1912-1988 BioIn 16
Bucher, Francois 1927- WhoAmA 91
Bucher, G. Harold 1922- St&PR 91
Bucher, Hans R. 1936- St&PR 91
Bucher, Jan BioIn 16
Bucher, Jeffrey Martin 1933- WhoAm 90
Bucher, Jim 1911- Ballpl 90
Bucher, John M BiDrAPA 89
Bucher, Lloyd BioIn 16
Bucher, Robert Monroe 1920- WhoAm 90
Bucherre-Frazier, Veronique 1951- WhoAmW 91, WhoEmL 91, WhoWor 91
Buchert, Beth Frances 1961- WhoSSW 91
Buchert, Dennis George 1946- WhoAm 90
Buchert, Jean Ruth 1922- WhoSSW 91
Buchheister, Harriet G. BioIn 16
Buchholtz, George J BiDrAPA 89
Buchholz, Barbara B. 1949- WhoAmW 91
Buchholz, Carolyn Leigh 1955- WhoAmW 91, WhoEmL 91
Buchholz, David Louis 1936- WhoAm 90
Buchholz, Donald Alden 1929- WhoAm 90
Buchholz, Douglas N. 1949- St&PR 91
Buchholz, Horst 1933- WorAlBi
Buchholz, Jeffrey Carl 1947- WhoEmL 91
Buchholz, Kristi Michelle Atchley 1962- WhoEmL 91
Buchholz, Monica Finnigan 1961- WhoAmW 91
Buchholz, Richard F. 1930- St&PR 91
Buchholz, Robert Alan 1948- BiDrAPA 89
Buchholz, Roger John 1943- St&PR 91
Buchholz, Terri Anne 1958- WhoAmW 91
Buchholz, Werner 1922- WhoAm 90
Buchholz, William Edward 1942- St&PR 91, WhoAm 90
Buchholz, William James 1945- WhoE 91, WhoEmL 91, WhoWor 91
Buchholz-Shaw, Donna Marie 1950- WhoEmL 91
Buchi, George Hermann 1921- WhoAm 90
Buchignani, Leo Joseph 1922- WhoAm 90
Buchik, Glenda Marie BiDrAPA 89
Buchin, Irving D. 1920-1989 BioIn 16
Buchin, Stanley Ira 1931- WhoE 91, WhoWor 91
Buchinski, Anne L. 1955- BiDrAPA 89
Buchko, Michael Scott 1946- WhoEmL 91, WhoSSW 91, WhoWor 91
Buchla, Donald 1937- IntWWM 90
Buchler, Jean-Robert 1942- WhoSSW 91
Buchler, Justus 1914- WhoAm 90
Buchler, Ronald Michael 1944- St&PR 91
Buchman, Arles WhoAmA 91
Buchman, Donald L. 1939- St&PR 91
Buchman, Elwood 1923- WhoAm 90
Buchman, Helene Marcia 1950- WhoAmW 91
Buchman, James Wallace 1948- WhoAmA 91
Buchman, Joel 1938- WhoAm 90
Buchman, Kenneth William 1956- WhoEmL 91
Buchman, Louis Bernard 1949- WhoWor 91
Buchman, Marion WhoAmW 91, WhoE 91, WhoWor 91
Buchman, Mark Edward 1937- St&PR 91, WhoAm 90
Buchman, Seth Barry 1955- WhoEmL 91, WhoWor 91
Buchmann, Alan Paul 1934- WhoAm 90
Buchmeier, Michael Joseph 1948- WhoEmL 91
Buchner, Eberhard 1939- IntWWM 90
Buchner, Eduard 1860-1917 WorAlBi
Buchner, Klaus 1941- WhoWor 91
Buchner, Marvin 1929- St&PR 91
Buchner, Orville W. 1936- St&PR 91
Bucholtz, Jefferey D. NewYTBS 90
Bucholtz, Nancy Marie 1953- WhoSSW 91
Bucholz, Arthur Bruce 1953- WhoE 91
Buchome, Ferose 1922- IntWWM 90
Buchsbaum, Frank 1923- St&PR 91
Buchsbaum, Herbert J. 1934-1989 BioIn 16
Buchsbaum, Jay 1953- St&PR 91
Buchsbaum, Ralph 1907- WhoAm 90
Buchsbaum, Solomon Jan 1929- WhoAm 90
Buchwach, Buck Aaron 1921- WhoAm 90
Buchwald, Ann AuBYP 90
Buchwald, Art BioIn 16
Buchwald, Art 1925- AuBYP 90, MajTwCW, WhoAm 90, WhoE 91, WhoWor 91, WhoWrEP 89, WorAlBi
Buchwald, Caryl Edward 1937- WhoAm 90
Buchwald, Elias 1924- ODwPR 91, WhoAm 90
Buchwald, Henry 1932- WhoAm 90
Buchwald, Howard 1964- WhoAmA 91

Buchwald, James Paul 1928- *St&PR 91*
Buchwald, Jennifer Sullivan 1930- *WhoAmW 91*
Buchwald, Johann Georg *PenDiDA 89*
Buchwald, Lee E. 1958- *St&PR 91*
Buchwald, Martyn Jerel 1942- *WhoAm 90*
Buchwald, Monita *ODwPR 91*
Buchwald, Naomi Reice 1944- *WhoAmW 91*
Buchwald, Nathaniel Avrom *WhoAm 90*
Buchwald, Sara P. 1941- *WhoWrEP 89*
Bucich, Alexandra *St&PR 91*
Bucin, Nenad *WhoWor 91*
Buck *DrBIPA 90*
Buck and Bubbles *OxCPMus*
Buck, Albert R. 1946- *St&PR 91*
Buck, Alfred Andreas 1921- *WhoAm 90*
Buck, Alfred C. 1910- *St&PR 91*
Buck, Alison Jennifer 1952- *WhoAmW 91, WhoEmL 91*
Buck, Anne Marie 1939- *WhoAmW 91*
Buck, Carol Kathleen 1925- *WhoAm 90*
Buck, Carolyn Felter 1941- *St&PR 91*
Buck, Charles Ludwig, Jr. 1926- *St&PR 91*
Buck, Charles Neville 1879-1930 *LiHiK*
Buck, Charles Theodore 1936- *St&PR 91*
Buck, Christian Brevoort Zabriskie 1914- *WhoWor 91*
Buck, Cliff *BioIn 16*
Buck, David 1936-1989 *ConTFT 8*
Buck, David D., Jr. 1941- *St&PR 91*
Buck, David T. 1903- *St&PR 91*
Buck, David W 1930- *BiDrAPA 89*
Buck, David W. 1937- *St&PR 91*
Buck, Donald Tirrell 1931- *WhoE 91*
Buck, Ervin Oscar 1904- *WhoAm 90*
Buck, Gene 1885-1957 *OxCPMus*
Buck, Gerald Stephen 1946- *WhoE 91*
Buck, Gurdon Hall 1936- *WhoE 91, WhoWor 91*
Buck, Jack 1925- *Ballpl 90*
Buck, James M., Jr. 1934- *St&PR 91*
Buck, James Roy 1930- *WhoAm 90*
Buck, Jeffrey Clark 1959- *WhoEmL 91*
Buck, John 1946- *WhoAmA 91*
Buck, John Bonner 1912- *WhoAm 90*
Buck, Kathleen Ann 1948- *WhoAm 90, WhoAmW 91*
Buck, Lawrence Paul 1944- *WhoAm 90*
Buck, Lee Albert 1923- *WhoAm 90, WhoWor 91*
Buck, Lilli 1950- *WhoWrEP 89*
Buck, Lillie West Brown 1860?-1939 *BioIn 16*
Buck, Linda Dee 1946- *WhoAmW 91*
Buck, Linda Susan 1949- *WhoEmL 91*
Buck, Lorraine 1968- *WhoAmW 91*
Buck, Louise Zierdt 1919- *WhoAmW 91*
Buck, M. Alison 1951- *WhoSSW 91*
Buck, Margaret Waring 1910- *AuBYP 90*
Buck, Merle K. 1932- *St&PR 91*
Buck, Michael Anthony 1948- *St&PR 91*
Buck, Natalie Smith 1923- *WhoAmW 91*
Buck, Owen Delos *BiDrAPA 89*
Buck, Paul Herman 1899-1978 *BioIn 16*
Buck, Pearl 1892-1973 *AuBYP 90, FemiCLE, WorAlBi*
Buck, Pearl S. 1892-1973 *BioAmW, BioIn 16, DcLB 102 [port], MajTwCW*
Buck, Peter *PenDiMP*
Buck, Porge 1931- *WhoAmA 91*
Buck, R. Creighton 1920- *WhoAm 90*
Buck, Raymond E *BiDrAPA 89*
Buck, Regina S. 1897- *St&PR 91*
Buck, Richard Clay 1962- *WhoSSW 91*
Buck, Richard D 1903-1977 *WhoAmA 91N*
Buck, Robert Follette 1917- *WhoAm 90*
Buck, Robert R. 1947- *St&PR 91*
Buck, Robert Treat, Jr 1939- *WhoAmA 91, WhoE 91*
Buck, Rodney Allen 1948- *St&PR 91*
Buck, Sarah May 1964- *WhoAmW 91*
Buck, Stephen Clark 1948- *St&PR 91*
Buck, Steven Edward 1942- *St&PR 91*
Buck, Steven Louis 1949- *WhoEmL 91*
Buck, Susan Jane 1947- *WhoSSW 91*
Buck, Thomas E. *St&PR 91*
Buck, Thomas Randolph 1930- *WhoAm 90*
Buck, William Boyd 1933- *WhoAm 90*
Buck, William Franklin, Jr. 1936- *St&PR 91*
Buck, William Ray *AuBYP 90*
Buckalew, James M. 1940- *St&PR 91*
Buckalew, Judith Adele 1947- *WhoAm 90*
Buckangehela *WhNaAH*
Buckanin, Dorothy Louise 1945- *WhoE 91*
Buckaway, C. M. *ConAu 130*
Buckaway, Catherine M 1919- *ConAu 130*
Buckbee, Albert W. 1939- *St&PR 91*
Bucke, R M 1837-1902 *EncO&P 3*
Bucke, Richard Maurice 1837-1902 *DcLB 99 [port], EncPaPR 91*
Buckel, Ursula 1926- *IntWWM 90*
Buckel, Wolfgang 1940- *WhoWor 91*
Buckels, Marvin Wayne 1929- *WhoAm 90*
Buckely, Robert 1928- *St&PR 91*
Buckenberger, Al 1861-1917 *Ballpl 90*
Buckens, Jean Emile 1925- *WhoWor 91*
Buckett, Bonnie-Jean 1948- *WhoSSW 91*
Buckey, Robert V. 1925- *St&PR 91*
Buckeye, Garland 1897-1975 *Ballpl 90*
Buckham, Alfred G. 1880-1956 *BioIn 16*
Buckham, Kirk Darryl 1949- *St&PR 91*
Buckhold, William Charles 1953- *WhoEmL 91*
Buckholts, Claudia 1944- *WhoWrEP 89*
Buckholtz, Charles David *BiDrAPA 89*
Buckholtz, Eileen 1949- *BioIn 16*
Buckhout, Robert *NewYTBS 90*
Buckhout, Robert 1935- *WhoE 91*
Buckingham, Duke of *PenDiDA 89*
Buckingham, Charles H. 1950- *St&PR 91*
Buckingham, Douglas A. 1943- *St&PR 91*
Buckingham, Edwin John, III 1947- *St&PR 91, WhoEmL 91*
Buckingham, Harold Canute, Jr. 1930- *WhoAm 90*
Buckingham, Ian David 1945- *BiDrAPA 89*
Buckingham, James Allan 1949- *BiDrAPA 89*
Buckingham, Karen Webster 1956- *WhoE 91*
Buckingham, Lindsey *EncPR&S 89*
Buckingham, Lindsey 1949- *WhoAm 90*
Buckingham, Lisle Marion 1895- *WhoAm 90*
Buckingham, Richard L. 1945- *St&PR 91*
Buckingham, Richard Leroy 1945- *WhoAm 90*
Buckingham, Richard Sherwood 1932- *St&PR 91*
Buckingham, Robert Alexander *BiDrAPA 89*
Buckingham, Robert W. 1937- *St&PR 91*
Buckingham, William Forrest 1951- *WhoSSW 91*
Buckland, Ann Elizabeth 1933- *WhoAmW 91*
Buckland, Charles Smillie 1934- *WhoAm 90*
Buckland, John Wellington 1815-1872 *OxCCanT*
Buckland, Kate M *DcCanB 12*
Buckland, Michael Keeble 1941- *WhoAm 90*
Buckland, Raymond 1934- *EncO&P 3*
Buckland, Robert Dix 1950- *BiDrAPA 89*
Buckland, Roger Basil 1942- *WhoAm 90*
Buckland, Ross 1942- *St&PR 91*
Buckland, William Henry 1945- *St&PR 91, WhoAm 90*
Buckle, Frederick Tarifero 1949- *WhoAm 90*
Buckle, Ian George 1942- *WhoE 91*
Buckle, June M. 1951- *WhoAmW 91*
Buckle, Kwame, III 1940- *St&PR 91*
Bucklen, George B. 1941- *St&PR 91*
Buckler, Beatrice 1933- *WhoAm 90, WhoWrEP 89*
Buckler, Bruce 1917- *St&PR 91*
Buckler, Ernest Redmond 1908-1984 *BioIn 16*
Buckler, Leroy M. 1930- *St&PR 91*
Buckler, Phyllis L. 1922- *St&PR 91*
Buckler, Robert B. 1950- *WhoEmL 91*
Buckler, Robert Earl 1951- *BiDrAPA 89*
Buckler, Sheldon A. 1931- *St&PR 91, WhoAm 90, WhoE 91*
Buckler, William Earl *NewYTBS 90*
Buckler, William Earl 1924-1990 *BioIn 16*
Buckles, Robert Edwin 1917- *WhoAm 90*
Buckles, Robert Howard 1932- *WhoAm 90, WhoE 91*
Buckles, Thomas Edward 1952- *WhoSSW 91*
Buckles, William R. 1941- *St&PR 91*
Buckles, William Richards 1941- *WhoSSW 91*
Buckles-Deans, Delora Elizabeth 1940- *WhoAmW 91, WhoWor 91*
Bucklew, Larry L. 1942- *St&PR 91*
Bucklew, Neil S. 1940- *WhoAm 90, WhoSSW 91*
Buckley, Albert William 1921- *St&PR 91*
Buckley, Barry Thomas 1952- *WhoSSW 91*
Buckley, Betty Bob 1925- *WhoAmW 91*
Buckley, Carol Joy 1931- *WhoAmW 91*
Buckley, Charles Eugene 1945- *WhoAm 90*
Buckley, Charles P. *BioIn 16*
Buckley, D.J. 1917- *St&PR 91*
Buckley, Dana Ellen 1954- *WhoE 91*
Buckley, Daniel G. 1936- *St&PR 91*
Buckley, Edward Joseph 1920- *WhoE 91*
Buckley, Elliot Ross 1921- *WhoAm 90*
Buckley, Emerson 1916- *IntWWM 90*
Buckley, Emerson 1916-1989 *BioIn 16*
Buckley, Esther Gonzalez-Arroyo 1948- *WhoAmW 91, WhoHisp 91*
Buckley, F.C. 1921- *St&PR 91*
Buckley, Frank Wilson 1914- *WhoAm 90*
Buckley, Fred Thomas 1951- *WhoE 91*
Buckley, G.J. 1925- *St&PR 91*
Buckley, Gerard Duke 1940- *St&PR 91*
Buckley, Harry W. 1913- *St&PR 91*
Buckley, Helen Ann 1926- *WhoAmW 91*
Buckley, Hilda Mayer 1948- *WhoEmL 91*
Buckley, J. Stephen 1942- *St&PR 91*
Buckley, James Lane 1923- *WhoAm 90, WhoE 91*
Buckley, James Lord 1867?-1947 *EncO&P 3*
Buckley, James Taylor, Jr. 1939- *WhoAm 90*
Buckley, Jerome Hamilton 1917- *WhoAm 90*
Buckley, Joan Marie 1958- *WhoAmW 91*
Buckley, Joanne 1953- *WhoWrEP 89*
Buckley, John 1957- *BioIn 16*
Buckley, John Edward 1940- *St&PR 91*
Buckley, John Edward 1953- *WhoE 91*
Buckley, John Joseph, Jr. 1944- *WhoAm 90*
Buckley, John Lee, Jr. 1916- *WhoAm 90*
Buckley, John Michael 1891-1958 *WhoAmA 91N*
Buckley, John William 1932- *WhoAm 90*
Buckley, John William, Jr. *BiDrAPA 89*
Buckley, Joseph Paul 1924- *WhoAm 90*
Buckley, Joseph Paul, III 1949- *WhoAm 90*
Buckley, Kevin Joseph 1957- *WhoEmL 91*
Buckley, Lawrence Matthew 1962- *WhoSSW 91*
Buckley, Lea Marie 1952- *WhoAmW 91*
Buckley, Lee 1947- *WhoE 91*
Buckley, Lewis J. 1947- *IntWWM 90*
Buckley, Lisa Louise 1958- *WhoAmW 91*
Buckley, Lorraine Madsen 1953- *WhoAmW 91*
Buckley, Mary Elizabeth 1950- *WhoAmW 91*
Buckley, Mary L *WhoAmA 91*
Buckley, Michael Edward 1950- *WhoWor 91*
Buckley, Michael Francis 1943- *WhoE 91, WhoWor 91*
Buckley, Michael P. 1941- *WhoAm 90*
Buckley, Mike Clifford 1944- *WhoAm 90*
Buckley, Paul Charles 1943- *WhoE 91*
Buckley, Peter John 1943- *BiDrAPA 89*
Buckley, Priscilla Langford 1921- *WhoAm 90, WhoAmW 91, WhoWrEP 89*
Buckley, Rebecca Hatcher 1933- *WhoAm 90*
Buckley, Richard 1953- *IntWWM 90*
Buckley, Richard Edward 1953- *WhoAm 90*
Buckley, Robert 1928- *St&PR 91*
Buckley, Robert 1931- *St&PR 91*
Buckley, Robert David 1938- *St&PR 91*
Buckley, Robert E *BiDrAPA 89*
Buckley, Robert E. 1915- *St&PR 91*
Buckley, Robert John 1949- *WhoE 91, WhoEmL 91*
Buckley, Robert Paul 1947- *WhoE 91*
Buckley, Robert W *BiDrAPA 89*
Buckley, Roger William 1944- *WhoWor 91*
Buckley, Samuel Olliphant, III 1947- *WhoEmL 91*
Buckley, Stanley Joseph, Jr. 1957- *WhoEmL 91*
Buckley, T. Garry 1922- *WhoAm 90*
Buckley, Thomas 1933- *St&PR 91*
Buckley, Thomas Hugh 1932- *WhoAm 90*
Buckley, Thomas P. 1956- *WhoSSW 91*
Buckley, Timothy Andrew 1950- *WhoSSW 91*
Buckley, Timothy White 1948- *St&PR 91*
Buckley, Valerie Jeanne 1940- *WhoE 91*
Buckley, Virginia Laura 1929- *St&PR 91, WhoAm 90, WhoWrEP 89*
Buckley, William Elmhirst 1913- *WhoAm 90*
Buckley, William F. 1925- *BioIn 16*
Buckley, William F., Jr. 1925- *MajTwCW, TwCCr&M 91, WorAlBi*
Buckley, William Frank, Jr. 1925- *SpyFic, WhoAm 90, WhoE 91, WhoWrEP 89*
Buckley, William Harrison 1949- *WhoEmL 91*
Buckley, William Nicholas 1942- *St&PR 91*
Buckley-Jones, Maureen *ODwPR 91*
Buckley's Serenaders *OxCPMus*
Bucklin, L.N. *St&PR 91*
Bucklin, Patricia Kerr 1954- *WhoEmL 91*
Buckman, Frederick W. *WhoAm 90*
Buckman, James Edward 1944- *WhoAm 90*
Buckman, John 1922- *BiDrAPA 89*
Buckman, Mary Jeremy 1930- *WhoAm 90*
Buckman, Repha Joan 1942- *WhoWrEP 89*
Buckman, Robert H. 1937- *St&PR 91*
Buckman, Robert Henry 1937- *WhoSSW 91*
Buckman, Robert Owen *BiDrAPA 89*
Buckman, Rosina 1880-1948 *PenDiMP*
Buckman, Thomas Richard 1923- *WhoAm 90*
Buckmaster, Carl E. 1950- *St&PR 91*
Buckmaster, Deborah Lee 1953- *WhoAmW 91*
Buckmaster, Henrietta 1909-1983 *FemiCLE*
Buckmaster, Samuel A. 1817-1878 *AmLegL*
Buckmaster, Thomas L. 1956- *WhoE 91*
Buckmiller, Gary Lee 1941- *St&PR 91*
Buckmore, Alvah Clarence, Jr. 1944- *WhoAm 90*
Bucknall, Clifford Adrian 1956- *WhoWor 91*
Bucknall, Malcolm Roderick 1935- *WhoAmA 91*
Bucknam, Frank G 1923- *BiDrAPA 89*
Bucknam, James Romeo 1911- *WhoAm 90*
Bucknam, Mary Olivia 1914- *WhoAmW 91*
Bucknam, William Carlin 1953- *BiDrAPA 89*
Bucknell, Anita 1934- *WhoE 91, WhoWor 91*
Bucknell, Larry Alan 1950- *WhoEmL 91*
Buckner, Bill 1949- *Ballpl 90 [port], BioIn 16*
Buckner, Debbie Gignilliat 1955- *WhoSSW 91*
Buckner, Fred Lynn 1932- *St&PR 91, WhoAm 90, WhoE 91*
Buckner, James Lowell 1934- *WhoAm 90*
Buckner, James Roger 1945- *WhoSSW 91*
Buckner, Jan J. 1942- *St&PR 91*
Buckner, John Hugh 1919- *WhoAm 90*
Buckner, John Knowles 1936- *St&PR 91, WhoAm 90*
Buckner, Kay Lamoreux 1935- *WhoAmA 91*
Buckner, Layton Ray 1932- *St&PR 91*
Buckner, Leonard Wayne 1943- *St&PR 91*
Buckner, Linda Iverson 1950- *WhoAmW 91, WhoEmL 91, WhoWor 91*
Buckner, Milt 1915-1977 *OxCPMus*
Buckner, Paul Eugene 1933- *WhoAmA 91*
Buckner, Phillip Alfred 1942- *WhoWrEP 89*
Buckner, Reginald Tyrone 1938- *IntWWM 90*
Buckner, Richard Aylette, Jr. *AmLegL*
Buckner, Sally Beaver 1931- *WhoWrEP 89*
Buckner, Simon Bolivar 1823-1914 *WorAlBi*
Buckner, Simon Bolivar, Jr. 1886-1945 *WorAlBi*
Buckner Bright, Rose Laminack 1945- *WhoEmL 91*
Bucko, John J. 1937- *St&PR 91*
Bucko, John Joseph 1937- *WhoAm 90*
Buckongahelas *WhNaAH*
Buckrell, Herbert George 1933- *WhoAm 90*
Buckrose, J. E. 1868-1931 *FemiCLE*
Bucks, Charles A. 1927- *St&PR 91*
Bucks, Charles Alan 1927- *WhoAm 90*
Bucksbaum, Martin 1920- *St&PR 91*
Buckshey, Purushottan B *BiDrAPA 89*
Buckshon, Joseph, Jr. *St&PR 91*
Buckshon, Joseph J. *St&PR 91*
Buckstaff, George Angus 1861-1927 *AmLegL*
Buckstein, Mark Aaron 1939- *WhoAm 90*
Buckvar, Felice 1938- *WhoWrEP 89*
Buckwald, Edward 1926- *St&PR 91*
Buckwalter, Alan Roland, III 1947- *WhoE 91*
Buckwalter, Carole K *BiDrAPA 89*
Buckwalter, John M. 1931- *St&PR 91*
Buckwalter, Wayne Clark 1955- *WhoEmL 91*
Buckwheat *DrBIPA 90*
Buckwold, Irving 1936- *St&PR 91*
Bucove, Arnold David 1934- *BiDrAPA 89, WhoE 91*
Bucur, John Charles 1925- *WhoAm 90, WhoSSW 91*
Bucur, Nicholas Alan 1939- *St&PR 91*
Bucur, Nicholas Anthony, III 1950- *WhoEmL 91*
Bucur, Nicholas Anthony, Jr. 1924- *WhoAm 90*
Bucus, Uldis 1942- *St&PR 91, WhoAm 90*
Bucuzzo, Estelle Lemire 1927- *WhoAmW 91*
Bucy, J. Fred *BioIn 16*
Bucy, J. Fred 1928- *WhoAm 90*
Bucy, Paul C. 1904- *WhoAm 90*
Bucy, Richard Snowden 1935- *WhoAm 90*
Buczak, Douglas Chester 1949- *WhoEmL 91*
Buczek, Barbara Kazimiera Zofia 1940- *IntWWM 90*
Buczkowna, Barbara Kazimiera Zofia 1940- *IntWWM 90*
Buczkowski, David John 1954- *WhoEmL 91*
Buczkowski, Joseph 1927- *St&PR 91*
Buczynski-Smith, Donna Marie 1958- *WhoAmW 91, WhoSSW 91*

Buda, Hugo Walter 1927- *St&PR 91*
Buda, Martin *BiDrAPA 89*
Budacz, Ronald Richard 1946- *St&PR 91*
Budai, Livia *BioIn 16*
Budai, Livia 1949- *IntWWM 90*
Budai, Livia 1950- *WhoWor 91*
Budalur, Thyagarajan Subbanarayan 1929- *WhoAm 90, WhoSSW 91*
Budapest Quartet *PenDiMP*
Budapest, Zsuzsanna E. *EncO&P 3*
Budash, Ronald F. 1940- *St&PR 91*
Buday, George *ConAu 132*
Buday, Gyorgy 1907-1990? *ConAu 132*
Budd, Bernadette Smith 1943- *WhoAmW 91, WhoE 91*
Budd, Charles A. 1951- *St&PR 91*
Budd, Chester Francis 1933- *St&PR 91*
Budd, Edward Gowan 1870-1946 *EncABHB 4 [port]*
Budd, Edward H. 1933- *St&PR 91*
Budd, Edward Hey 1933- *WhoAm 90, WhoE 91, WhoWor 91*
Budd, Gene F. 1938- *St&PR 91, WhoAm 90*
Budd, Harold 1936- *IntWWM 90*
Budd, John F., Jr. 1923- *ODwPR 91*
Budd, John Frank, Jr. 1923- *St&PR 91*
Budd, John Henry 1908- *WhoAm 90*
Budd, John Herbert 1938- *St&PR 91*
Budd, Lillian 1897- *AuBYP 90*
Budd, Louis John 1921- *WhoAm 90*
Budd, Ralph 1879-1962 *WorAlBi*
Budd, Richard D *BiDrAPA 89*
Budd, Richard L. 1937- *St&PR 91*
Budd, Richard Wade 1934- *WhoAm 90*
Budd, Thomas 1934- *St&PR 91*
Budd, W.B. 1935- *St&PR 91*
Budd, William Karl 1955- *WhoEmL 91*
Budd, Zola *BioIn 16*
Budde, Douglas Ralph 1944- *BiDrAPA 89*
Budde, Rollo L. 1917- *St&PR 91*
Budde, Thomas E. *St&PR 91*
Budde, William R. 1950- *St&PR 91*
Buddemeier, Maurice R. 1930- *St&PR 91*
Buddemeyer, Herman 1917- *St&PR 91*
Budden, Harry Edward, Jr. 1945- *WhoSSW 91*
Budden, Julian 1924- *ConAu 130, IntWWM 90*
Buddenbohm, Harold William 1959- *WhoEmL 91*
Buddenbohn, Robert W. 1929- *St&PR 91*
Buddha *EncJap*
Buddha, Gautama 566?BC-486?BC *WorAlBi*
Buddhadasa Bhikkhu 1906- *BioIn 16*
Buddin, Don 1934- *Ballpl 90*
Budding, Anita 1929- *WhoAmW 91*
Buddington, Arthur Francis 1890-1980 *DcScB S2*
Buddington, R Wells *BiDrAPA 89*
Budelis, Joseph John 1943- *WhoE 91*
Budelov, Peter Roy 1947- *WhoEmL 91*
Buden, Rosemary Vidale 1931- *WhoAmW 91*
Budenholzer, Roland Anthony 1912- *WhoAm 90, WhoWor 91*
Budenny, Semyon 1883-1973 *WorAlBi*
Budennyi, Semen Mikhailovich 1883-1973 *BioIn 16*
Budge, Bruce Penwell 1930- *St&PR 91*
Budge, Don 1915- *WorAlBi*
Budge, Hamer Harold 1910- *WhoAm 90*
Budge, Hamilton W. 1928- *St&PR 91*
Budge, Hamilton Whithed 1928- *WhoAm 90*
Budgell, Rodger C. 1935- *St&PR 91*
Budgor, Aaron Bernard 1948- *WhoE 91*
Budhwar, Prem Kumar 1939- *WhoWor 91*
Budi, I. Nyoman 1946- *WhoWor 91*
Budi Santoso, Petrus 1933- *WhoWor 91*
Budiansky, Bernard 1925- *WhoAm 90*
Budig, Gene Arthur 1939- *WhoAm 90, WhoWor 91*
Budin, Beverly R. 1945- *WhoAmW 91*
Budin, Philip S. 1940- *St&PR 91*
Budington, William Stone 1919- *WhoAm 90*
Budish, Irving I. 1922- *St&PR 91*
Budke, Camilla Eunice 1928- *WhoAmW 91*
Budkevics, Girts Janis 1952- *WhoEmL 91*
Budman, Cathy Linda 1957- *WhoEmL 91*
Budmani, Lukrecija Bogasinovic 1710-1784 *EncCoWW*
Budner, Harvey M 1932- *BiDrAPA 89*
Budner, Lawrence Jay 1957- *BiDrAPA 89*
Budnick, Ernest Joseph 1948- *WhoE 91, WhoEmL 91, WhoWor 91*
Budnitz, Arron Edward 1949- *WhoEmL 91*
Budny, James Charles 1948- *WhoEmL 91*
Budny, Marco Michael 1954- *St&PR 91*
Budny, Patricia L. *St&PR 91*
Budny, Virginia 1944- *WhoAmA 91*
Budoff, Penny Wise 1939- *WhoAmW 91*
Budovitch, Brenda Louise 1950- *St&PR 91*
Budrakey, Susan Rakov 1948- *WhoE 91*
Budrevics, Alexander 1925- *WhoAm 90*
Budrow, Nancy Elizabeth 1936- *WhoWrEP 89*
Budrys, Algis 1931- *RGTwCSF*
Budson, Richard David 1935- *BiDrAPA 89*
Budson, Susan Behe 1943- *WhoAmW 91*
Budwick, Jeanine Elster 1948- *WhoAmW 91*
Budy, Andrea Hollander 1947- *WhoWrEP 89*
Budy, Sonia Lim 1937- *WhoE 91*
Budyak, John Joseph 1952- *St&PR 91*
Budzeika, George 1921- *WhoE 91*
Budzikiewicz, Herbert 1933- *WhoWor 91*
Budzinski, James Edward 1953- *WhoEmL 91*
Budzinski, John Edward 1953- *WhoWrEP 89*
Budzinski, Roman Joseph 1949- *WhoE 91*
Budzinsky, A. Alexander 1942- *St&PR 91*
Bue, Carl Olaf, Jr. 1922- *WhoAm 90, WhoSSW 91*
Bueche, Wendell Francis 1930- *St&PR 91, WhoAm 90*
Buechel, Donald Robert 1924- *WhoAm 90*
Buechele, Steve 1961- *Ballpl 90*
Buechlein, Daniel Mark 1938- *WhoAm 90, WhoSSW 91*
Buechler, Bradley Bruce 1948- *St&PR 91, WhoAm 90*
Buechler, C. Matthew 1933- *St&PR 91*
Buechler, Jean Ann 1945- *WhoAmW 91*
Buechler, Kurt Alan *BiDrAPA 89*
Buechler, Neal M. 1935- *WhoAm 90*
Buechler, Neal Merlyn 1935- *St&PR 91*
Buechner, Barry Lee 1944- *St&PR 91*
Buechner, Carl Frederick 1926- *WhoAm 90, WhoE 91*
Buechner, Frederick 1926- *BioIn 16, MajTwCW*
Buechner, Howard Albert 1919- *WhoAm 90*
Buechner, Jack William 1940- *WhoAm 90*
Buechner, John *WhoAm 90*
Buechner, Thomas Scharman 1926- *WhoAm 90, WhoAmA 91*
Buecker, Robert 1935- *WhoAmA 91*
Buegel, Dale Mark *BiDrAPA 89*
Buegeler, Barbara Stephanie 1945- *WhoAmW 91, WhoSSW 91*
Buehl, Louis H. 1932-1988 *BioIn 16*
Buehler, John A 1920- *BiDrAPA 89*
Buehler, Thomas Lee 1948- *WhoEmL 91*
Buehler, Winfried Gregor 1929- *WhoWor 91*
Buehlmeier, Harry Scott 1949- *WhoE 91, WhoEmL 91*
Buehner, Christian *NewAgMG*
Buehner, Heidi Renata 1958- *WhoAmW 91*
Buehner, Suzanne G. 1945- *St&PR 91*
Buehr, Walter Franklin 1897-1971 *AuBYP 90*
Buehrer, Beverley Bare 1947- *WhoWrEP 89*
Buehrig, Gordon M. *NewYTBS 90*
Buehrig, Gordon M. 1904-1990 *BioIn 16*
Buehring, E. Fred 1915- *St&PR 91*
Buehrle, Maureen Anne 1952- *WhoE 91*
Buek, Charles Welles 1911-1988 *BioIn 16*
Buel, Richard Van Wyck, Jr. 1933- *WhoAm 90*
Buell, Abel 1742-1822 *EncCRAm*
Buell, Bruce Temple 1932- *WhoAm 90*
Buell, Cynthia Louise 1944- *WhoAmW 91, WhoSSW 91*
Buell, David S 1921- *BiDrAPA 89*
Buell, Duncan Alan 1950- *WhoE 91*
Buell, Ellen Lewis *AuBYP 90, ConAu 130*
Buell, Ellen Lewis 1905-1989 *BioIn 16, SmATA X*
Buell, Erik *BioIn 16*
Buell, Frank A *BiDrAPA 89*
Buell, Frederick Henderson 1942- *WhoWrEP 89*
Buell, Harold G. *AuBYP 90*
Buell, Lawrence Ingalls 1939- *WhoAm 90*
Buell, Marjorie Henderson 1904- *EncACom*
Buell, Richard Howard 1931- *WhoSSW 91*
Buell, Temple Hoyne 1895-1990 *BioIn 16*
Buell, Thomas Allan 1931- *WhoAm 90*
Buell, Victor Paul 1914- *WhoAm 90*
Buell, William Ackerman 1925- *WhoAm 90*
Buelow, David L. 1945- *St&PR 91*
Buelow, Frederick Henry 1929- *WhoAm 90*
Buelow, Fritz 1876-1933 *Ballpl 90*
Buelow, George John 1929- *WhoAm 90*
Buelow, Robert J. 1945- *St&PR 91*
Buenaflor, Matthew Timothy 1957- *WhoSSW 91*
Buenaventura, Enrique 1925- *HispWr 90*
Buenaventura, Jaime *BiDrAPA 89*
Buenaventura, Milagros Paez *BiDrAPA 89*
Buenaventura, Milagros Paez 1943- *WhoE 91*
Buenaventura, Rafael B. 1938- *St&PR 91*
Buendia, Manuel *HispWr 90*
Buenger, Clement Lawrence 1926- *St&PR 91, WhoAm 90*
Bueno, Edgar Manuel 1938- *BiDrAPA 89*
Bueno, Emerson B *BiDrAPA 89*
Bueno, Marco Aurelio 1943- *BiDrAPA 89*
Bueno, Maria 1939- *WorAlBi*
Buer, Jutta 1943- *WhoWor 91*
Buerge, Robin Kenyon 1953- *WhoAm 90*
Buergenthal, Thomas 1934- *WhoAm 90, WhoE 91*
Buerger, Charles Alter 1938- *WhoE 91*
Buerger, David B. 1909- *St&PR 91*
Buerger, David Bernard 1909- *WhoAm 90, WhoE 91, WhoWor 91*
Buerger, E. *St&PR 91*
Buerger, Helene E 1930- *BiDrAPA 89*
Buerger, Janet E 1946- *WhoAmA 91*
Buerger, Mark Thomas 1948- *St&PR 91*
Buerger, William Thomas 1958- *WhoE 91*
Buergermeister, Hebert 1933- *St&PR 91*
Buerk, Richard K. 1934- *St&PR 91*
Buerkel-Rothfuss, Nancy Louise 1951- *WhoEmL 91*
Buerkle, Jack Vincent 1923- *WhoAm 90*
Buermann, Henry *BiDrAPA 89*
Buero Vallejo, Antonio 1916- *HispWr 90, IntvSpW [port], MajTwCW, WhoWor 91*
Buesch, Walter Ernst 1930- *WhoWor 91*
Bueschel, Richard T. 1933- *St&PR 91*
Bueschen, Anton Joslyn 1940- *WhoAm 90*
Buescher, Charles Albert, Jr. 1932- *St&PR 91*
Buescher, Edward L. 1925-1989 *BioIn 16*
Buescher, Thomas Paul 1949- *WhoEmL 91*
Buesing, Charles J. *BioIn 16*
Buesing, Karen Meyer 1953- *WhoEmL 91*
Buesinger, Ronald Ernest 1933- *St&PR 91, WhoAm 90*
Buess, Heinz 1941- *WhoWor 91*
Buesseler, John Aure 1919- *WhoAm 90*
Buesser, Anthony Carpenter 1929- *WhoAm 90, WhoWor 91*
Buesser, Frederick Gustavus, III 1941- *WhoWor 91*
Buesser, Frederick Gustavus, Jr. 1916- *WhoAm 90*
Buesst, Aylmer 1883-1970 *PenDiMP*
Buetens, Eric D. 1953- *WhoEmL 91*
Bueter, Arnold Gerhard 1917- *WhoAm 90*
Buetow, Dennis Edward 1932- *WhoAm 90*
Buetow, M. Kathleen 1929- *WhoAm 90*
Buettner, Carol Ann 1948- *WhoAmW 91*
Buettner, Deborah Anne 1957- *WhoWrEP 89*
Buettner, Gerald Hugo, Jr. 1955- *WhoEmL 91*
Buettner, James A *BiDrAPA 89*
Buettner, Michael Lewis 1957- *WhoE 91*
Buettner, Winfried Oskar 1949- *WhoWor 91*
Bufalini, David Anthony 1952- *WhoEmL 91*
Bufalino, William E. 1918-1990 *BioIn 16*
Bufalino, William E., Sr. *NewYTBS 90*
Bufano, Beniamino Benvenuto 1898-1970 *BioIn 16*
Bufano, Remo 1894-1948 *AuBYP 90*
Bufe, Mary Elizabeth 1961- *WhoEmL 91*
Bufe, Uwe Ernst 1944- *St&PR 91*
Buff, Conrad 1886-1975 *AuBYP 90, WhoAmA 91N*
Buff, Frank Paul 1924- *WhoAm 90*
Buff, Mary 1890-1970 *AuBYP 90*
Buff, Richard Cole 1947- *St&PR 91*
Buffa, Salvatore J *BiDrAPA 89*
Buffalo Bill *WhNaAH*
Buffalo Bill 1846-1917 *BioIn 16*
Buffalo Bob Smith 1917- *BioIn 16*
Buffalo Horn *WhNaAH*
Buffalo Hump *WhNaAH*
Buffalo Springfield *EncPR&S 89*
Buffalo, Harvey A., Jr. 1939- *WhoAm 90*
Buffaloe, Gregory Thomas 1956- *WhoSSW 91*
Buffalow, Oscar Thomas 1924- *St&PR 91*
Buffet, Bernard 1928- *WhoWor 91*
Buffet, Louis-Joseph 1818-1898 *BiDFrPL*
Buffet, Peter *NewAgMG*
Buffett, Jimmy 1946- *ConMus 4 [port], WhoAm 90*
Buffett, Warren E. *BioIn 16*
Buffett, Warren E. 1930- *St&PR 91*
Buffett, Warren Edward 1930- *ConAmBL, WhoAm 90, WhoWor 91*
Buffin, Carol 1957- *WhoWrEP 89*
Buffington, Audrey Virginia 1931- *WhoAmW 91*
Buffington, Dean 1940- *St&PR 91*
Buffington, Dennis Elvin 1944- *WhoAm 90*
Buffington, Gary Lee Roy 1946- *WhoE 91*
Buffington, Jack M *BiDrAPA 89*
Buffington, Ralph Meldrim 1907- *WhoAm 90*
Buffinton, Charlie 1861-1907 *Ballpl 90 [port]*
Buffkin, Beverly Edith 1961- *WhoAmW 91, WhoEmL 91*
Buffkins, Archie Lee 1934- *WhoAm 90*
Buffo, Dennis Daniel 1948- *St&PR 91*
Buffon, George-Louis Leclerc, Comte De 1707-1788 *WorAlBi*
Buffon, Georges Louis Leclerc, Comte de 1707-1788 *BioIn 16*
Buffum, C.G., Jr. *St&PR 91N*
Buffum, Charles Walbridge, Jr. 1939- *WhoE 91*
Buffum, Nancy Kay 1941- *WhoAmW 91, WhoWor 91*
Buffum, Paul 1945- *St&PR 91*
Bufkens, Roland 1936- *IntWWM 90*
Bufkin, I. David 1922- *St&PR 91*
Bufkin, Isaac David 1922- *WhoAm 90, WhoSSW 91*
Bufman, Zev 1930- *WhoAm 90*
Buford, Cathryn Hammons 1947- *WhoSSW 91*
Buford, Don 1937- *Ballpl 90*
Buford, Edwin Rucker 1935- *St&PR 91*
Buford, Evelyn Claudene Shilling 1940- *WhoAmW 91*
Buford, Floyd Moye, Jr. 1957- *WhoEmL 91, WhoSSW 91*
Buford, Howard *ODwPR 91*
Buford, John 1826-1863 *WorAlBi*
Buford, Lee O 1926- *BiDrAPA 89*
Buford, Phyllis *BioIn 16*
Buford, Robert John 1948- *WhoEmL 91*
Buford, Robert P., IV 1949- *ODwPR 91*
Buford, Robert Pegram 1925- *WhoSSW 91*
Bugaoan, Josefina G *BiDrAPA 89*
Bugarin, Felicitas C 1936- *BiDrAPA 89*
Bugatch, Beryl 1945- *WhoEmL 91*
Bugatti, Carlo 1855?-1940 *BioIn 16, PenDiDA 89*
Bugatti, Ettore 1881-1947 *PenDiDA 89*
Bugatti, Rembrandt *PenDiDA 89*
Bugatti, Siobhan *WhoWrEP 89*
Bugbee, Edwin Holmes 1820-1900 *AmLegL*
Bugbee, Emma 1888?-1981 *AuBYP 90*
Bugbee, George *ODwPR 91*
Bugbee, Helen Louise 1909- *WhoWrEP 89*
Bugbee, Myra Jane 1952- *WhoAmW 91*
Bugbee, Percy *BioIn 16*
Bugbee, Victoria Jean 1951- *WhoEmL 91*
Bugbee-Jackson, Joan 1941- *WhoAmA 91, WhoAmW 91*
Bugeja, Michael Joseph *WhoWrEP 89*
Bugey, William Donald *BiDrAPA 89*
Bugg, June Moore 1919- *WhoAmW 91*
Bugg, Randy 1951- *WhoEmL 91*
Bugg, William A. 1937- *St&PR 91*
Bugg, William Joseph, Jr. 1939- *St&PR 91, WhoSSW 91*
Bugge, Anne M. 1953- *St&PR 91*
Bugge, John Michael 1941- *WhoSSW 91*
Bugge, Kjell 1953- *WhoWor 91*
Bugge, Lawrence John 1936- *WhoAm 90*
Buggey, Lesley JoAnne 1938- *WhoWor 91*
Buggie, Frederick Denman 1929- *WhoWor 91*
Bugh, Mary Lou 1942- *WhoWrEP 89*
Bugh, Vernon G 1922- *BiDrAPA 89*
Bugher, Robert Dean 1925- *WhoAm 90*
Bughici, Dumitru 1921- *IntWWM 90*
Bugli, Ralph W. 1913- *ODwPR 91*
Bugliarello, George 1927- *WhoAm 90, WhoE 91*
Bugliosi, Ramon L. 1930- *St&PR 91*
Bugliosi, Vincent T. 1934- *WhoAm 90, WhoWrEP 89*
Bugnet, Georges 1879-1981 *DcLB 92*
Bugno, Richard J. *BioIn 16*
Buguet, Edouard *EncO&P 3*
Buhagiar, Marion 1932- *WhoAm 90, WhoWrEP 89*
Buhite, Thomas Jesse 1946- *WhoE 91*
Buhl, Bob 1928- *Ballpl 90*
Buhl, Cynthia Maureen 1952- *WhoEmL 91, WhoWor 91*
Buhl, Karl Franz 1953- *WhoEmL 91*
Buhl, Robert Carl 1931- *St&PR 91*
Buhler, Bill *BioIn 16*
Buhler, Frank H. 1926- *St&PR 91*
Buhler, Fred Carl 1933- *St&PR 91*
Buhler, James Warren 1959- *WhoE 91*
Buhler, Jill Lorie 1945- *WhoWor 91*
Buhler, Joan Elizabeth 1961- *WhoEmL 91*
Buhler, Lynn Bledsoe 1949- *WhoEmL 91*
Buhler, Robert 1916-1989 *AnObit 1989*
Buhlig, James Russell 1947- *St&PR 91*
Buhlinger, Linda Louann 1960- *WhoEmL 91*
Buhlmann, Hans 1930- *WhoWor 91*
Buhmann, Robert R. 1922- *St&PR 91*
Buhner, Byron Bevis 1950- *WhoEmL 91*
Buhner, David Allan 1948- *WhoEmL 91*
Buhner, Jay 1964- *Ballpl 90*
Buhner, John Colin 1920- *WhoAm 90*
Buhr, Gary Alan 1945- *WhoEmL 91*
Buhr, Karl-Heinz 1941- *WhoWor 91*
Buhr, Walter Heinrich Wilhelm 1938- *WhoWor 91*
Buhrmaster, Robert C. 1947- *St&PR 91*

Buhrow, Stanley E. 1952- *St&PR 91*
Buhrow, William Carl 1934- *WhoAm 90*
Buhse, Howard E. 1906- *St&PR 91*
Buhse, Howard Edward 1906- *WhoAm 90*
Buhsmer, John H. 1932- *St&PR 91*
Buhsmer, John Henry 1932- *WhoAm 90*
Bui, Huong Quoc 1924- *WhoWor 91*
Bui, Khoi Tien 1937- *WhoSSW 91, WhoWor 91*
Bui, Lan H P 1948- *BiDrAPA 89*
Bui-Quang, Hung 1948- *St&PR 91*
Buiar, Paul 1925- *ODwPR 91*
Buice, DeWayne 1957- *Ballpl 90*
Buick, David Dunbar 1854-1929 *EncABHB 4 [port]*
Buick, James Gordon 1932- *St&PR 91, WhoAm 90*
Buie, Bennett Frank 1910- *WhoAm 90, WhoWor 91*
Buie, Dan H, Jr. 1930- *BiDrAPA 89*
Buie, Donald Ray 1956- *WhoEmL 91*
Buie, Neil D 1918- *BiDrAPA 89*
Buie, Robert 1926- *BiDrAPA 89*
Buie, Stephen Eugene 1954- *BiDrAPA 89*
Buie, Thomas Edison, Jr. 1935- *BiDrAPA 89*
Buies, Arthur 1840-1901 *DcLB 99 [port]*
Buikus, William Robert *BiDrAPA 89*
Buis, John L. 1945- *St&PR 91*
Buis, Otto J. 1931- *St&PR 91*
Buisson, Ferdinand-Edouard 1841-1932 *BiDFrPL*
Buist, Jean Mackerley 1919- *WhoAmW 91*
Buist, Richardson 1921- *WhoE 91, WhoWor 91*
Buitendacht, Adriaan Johannes Hercules 1941- *WhoWor 91*
Buitenhuis, Peter Martinus 1925- *WhoAm 90*
Buiter, Mike Raymond 1955- *St&PR 91*
Buiteweg, Johannes A. 1926- *St&PR 91*
Buitrago, Rudy G. 1951- *WhoHisp 91*
Buitron, Diana M 1946- *WhoAmA 91*
Buivydaite, Elena Kutorgiene- 1888-1963 *BioIn 16*
Buja, Giuseppe Silvio 1946- *WhoWor 91*
Bujake, John Edward, Jr. 1933- *WhoAm 90, WhoSSW 91*
Bujard, Hermann 1934- *WhoWor 91*
Bujard, Robert Samuel 1932- *BiDrAPA 89*
Bujese, Arlene 1938- *WhoAmA 91*
Bujic, Bojan 1937- *IntWWM 90*
Bujnowski, Joel A 1949- *WhoAmA 91*
Bujold, Genevieve 1942- *BioIn 16, WorAlBi*
Bujones, Fernando 1955- *WhoHisp 91*
Bukantz, Samuel Charles 1911- *WhoAm 90*
Bukar, Margaret Witty 1950- *WhoAmW 91, WhoEmL 91*
Bukatman, Barry A *BiDrAPA 89*
Bukberg, Judith Berman 1948- *BiDrAPA 89*
Buker, Howard E. 1928- *ODwPR 91*
Buker, Robert Hutchinson, Sr. 1928- *WhoAm 90*
Buker, Robert L. 1947- *St&PR 91*
Buketoff, Igor 1915- *IntWWM 90*
Bukey, Erol Dervis 1926- *WhoWor 91*
Bukey, Evan Burr 1940- *ConAu 131, WhoSSW 91*
Bukhari, Nayer Saleha *BiDrAPA 89*
Bukhari, S. Haider Shah 1939- *WhoWor 91*
Bukharin, Nikolai 1888-1938 *WorAlBi*
Bukharin, Nikolai Ivanovich 1888-1938 *BioIn 16*
Buki, Virginia V. 1953- *BiDrAPA 89*
Buki, Zoltan 1929- *WhoAmA 91*
Bukley, Angelia P. 1957- *WhoAmW 91*
Bukman, Piet 1934- *WhoWor 91*
Buko, Walter Geza *BiDrAPA 89*
Bukota, George 1944- *ODwPR 91*
Bukovac, Martin John 1929- *WhoAm 90*
Bukovi, Dennis Frank 1939- *St&PR 91*
Bukovnik, Gary 1947- *WhoAmA 91*
Bukovsan, Laura Ann 1940- *WhoAmW 91*
Bukovsky, Vladimir 1942- *WhoWor 91*
Bukow, Ronald 1944- *St&PR 91*
Bukowicz, Colette Marie 1957- *WhoEmL 91*
Bukowski, Arthur Francis 1905-1989 *BioIn 16*
Bukowski, Charles 1920- *MajTwCW, WhoAm 90, WhoWrEP 89*
Bukowski, Elaine Louise 1949- *WhoAmW 91, WhoEmL 91*
Bukowski, Gary Donald 1950- *St&PR 91*
Bukry, John David 1941- *WhoAm 90, WhoWor 91*
Bukstein, Oscar Gary 1955- *BiDrAPA 89*
Bula, Raymond J. 1927- *WhoAm 90*
Bulajic, Radoslav Pavle 1935- *WhoWor 91*
Bulak, Sheila Leigh 1948- *WhoE 91*
Bulakul, Sirichai 1940- *WhoWor 91*
Bulandr, Peter J. 1960- *WhoEmL 91*
Bulat, Marijan 1945- *WhoWor 91*
Bulat, Marilyn Ellen 1926- *WhoAmW 91*
Bulbeck, Margaret Cachilla 1951- *WhoWor 91*
Bulbul *WhoWrEP 89*
Bulbulian, Arthur H. 1900- *WhoAm 90*
Bulbulkaya, Nihat M 1920- *BiDrAPA 89*
Buldak, Gerald E. 1944- *ODwPR 91*
Buleamante, Joseph F. 1942- *St&PR 91*
Bulette, John Lawrence 1936- *BiDrAPA 89*
Buley, Mary Therse 1956- *WhoAmW 91*
Bulfin, Preston Edward 1941- *WhoWor 91*
Bulfinch, Charles 1763-1844 *WorAlBi*
Bulford, Sally Farran 1939- *WhoAmW 91*
Bulgakov, Mikhail 1891-1940 *WorAlBi*
Bulganin, Nikolai 1895-1975 *WorAlBi*
Bulganin, Nikolai Aleksandrovich 1895-1975 *BioIn 16*
Bulgarelli, Christopher G 1954- *BiDrAPA 89*
Bulger, Bozeman *Ballpl 90*
Bulger, Dennis Bernard 1938- *WhoAm 90*
Bulger, John T. 1949- *St&PR 91*
Bulger, Roger James 1933- *WhoAm 90*
Bulger, Ruth Ellen 1936- *WhoAmW 91*
Bulgren, William Gerald 1937- *WhoAm 90*
Bulgrin, James G. 1941- *St&PR 91*
Bulinski, Daniel J. 1943- *St&PR 91*
Bulinski, Gregory Paul 1953- *WhoEmL 91*
Bulkeley, Christy Claire 1942- *WhoAmW 91, WhoE 91*
Bulkeley, Eliphant Adams 1803-1872 *AmLegL*
Bulkeley, Gershom 1636-1713 *BioIn 16*
Bulkeley, John Duncan 1911- *BioIn 16, WhoAm 90*
Bulkeley, John Z. 1938- *St&PR 91*
Bulkeley, Morgan G. 1837-1922 *Ballpl 90 [port]*
Bulkley, Robert Ellsworth 1921- *St&PR 91*
Bulkowski, Robert 1948- *St&PR 91*
Bulkowski, Virginia 1948- *St&PR 91*
Bull Bear *WhNaAH*
Bull Hump *WhNaAH*
Bull, Bergen Ira 1940- *St&PR 91, WhoAm 90*
Bull, Brian Stanley 1937- *WhoAm 90*
Bull, Christopher 1921- *BiDrAPA 89*
Bull, Clarence Sinclair 1895- *BioIn 16*
Bull, Clinton L. 1929- *St&PR 91*
Bull, Clinton LeRoy 1929- *WhoAm 90*
Bull, Colin Bruce Bradley 1928- *WhoAm 90*
Bull, David 1934- *WhoAm 90*
Bull, Dennis Lee 1946- *WhoSSW 91*
Bull, Donald Arthur 1944- *St&PR 91*
Bull, Fran 1938- *WhoAmA 91*
Bull, Frank James 1922- *WhoSSW 91*
Bull, George Albert 1927- *St&PR 91, WhoAm 90*
Bull, George Anthony 1929- *WhoWor 91*
Bull, Gerald *BioIn 16*
Bull, Gerald V. 1928-1990 *NewYTBS 90 [port]*
Bull, Hank *WhoAmA 91*
Bull, Henrik Helkand 1929- *WhoAm 90*
Bull, Howard I. 1940- *St&PR 91*
Bull, Inez Stewart 1920- *IntWWM 90*
Bull, James Robert 1941- *St&PR 91*
Bull, John V. R. 1939- *WhoE 91*
Bull, Katharine *BiDEWW*
Bull, Kenneth H 1940- *BiDrAPA 89*
Bull, Marshall R. 1941- *St&PR 91*
Bull, Mary Maley 1956- *WhoEmL 91*
Bull, Nicholas James D. 1952- *WhoWor 91*
Bull, Olaf 1883-1933 *DcScanL*
Bull, Ole Bornemann *WhoWor 91*
Bull, Richard S., Jr. 1926- *St&PR 91*
Bull, Richard Sutton, Jr. 1926- *WhoAm 90*
Bull, Sandy *BioIn 16*
Bull, Sara Gertrude *BiDrAPA 89*
Bull, Stephen B. *ODwPR 91*
Bull, Steven Tremaine 1956- *WhoEmL 91, WhoSSW 91*
Bull, Storm 1913- *IntWWM 90*
Bull, Thomas Albert *BiDrAPA 89*
Bull, Titus 1871- *EncO&P 3*
Bull, Titus 1871-1946 *EncPaPR 91*
Bull, William 1710-1791 *EncCRAm*
Bull, William Earnest 1933- *WhoAm 90*
Bulla, Ben F. 1920- *St&PR 91*
Bulla, Clyde Robert 1914- *AuBYP 90, BioIn 16, WhoAm 90*
Bulla, Robert Baxter 1939- *St&PR 91*
Bullard, Alan 1947- *IntWWM 90*
Bullard, Claude Earl 1920- *WhoAm 90*
Bullard, Dexter Means, Jr. 1929- *BiDrAPA 89*
Bullard, Edgar John, III 1942- *WhoAm 90, WhoAmA 91, WhoSSW 91*
Bullard, Edward Crisp 1907-1980 *DcScB S2*
Bullard, Edward Dickinson 1948- *St&PR 91, WhoEmL 91*
Bullard, Ethel Munday *IntWWM 90*
Bullard, Fred Bascom, Jr. 1934- *St&PR 91*
Bullard, George 1945- *WhoAm 90*
Bullard, George Woodrow, Jr. 1950- *WhoSSW 91*
Bullard, Helen 1902- *WhoAm 90*
Bullard, James 1951- *WhoEmL 91*
Bullard, James V. *BioIn 16*
Bullard, James Wilson 1935- *BiDrAPA 89*
Bullard, Janet 1935- *St&PR 91*
Bullard, John Kilburn 1947- *WhoE 91, WhoEmL 91*
Bullard, John Moore 1932- *WhoSSW 91*
Bullard, John Wilbur 1938- *St&PR 91*
Bullard, Judith Eve 1945- *WhoAmW 91, WhoEmL 91*
Bullard, Marcia Lynn 1952- *WhoAm 90*
Bullard, Mary Boykin 1933- *WhoAmW 91*
Bullard, Michael Ellsworth 1948- *WhoE 91*
Bullard, Mike *BioIn 16*
Bullard, Pamela 1948- *WhoE 91*
Bullard, Ray E, Jr. 1927- *BiDrAPA 89*
Bullard, Ray Elva, Jr. 1927- *WhoAm 90*
Bullard, Ricky J. 1947- *St&PR 91*
Bullard, Robert Oliver, Jr. 1943- *WhoAm 90*
Bullard, Roland Keith, II 1944- *St&PR 91*
Bullard, Sharon Welch 1943- *WhoAmW 91*
Bullard, Todd Hupp 1931- *WhoAm 90, WhoSSW 91*
Bullard, Todd Whittam 1955- *WhoSSW 91*
Bullard, Willis Clare, Jr. 1943- *WhoAm 90*
Bullen, Dana Ripley, II 1931- *WhoE 91*
Bullen, John Alfred 1946- *BiDrAPA 89*
Bullen, Keith Edward 1906-1976 *DcScB S2*
Bullen, Leigh M. 1944- *St&PR 91*
Bullen, Martha Mahon 1960- *WhoAmW 91*
Bullen, Richard Hatch 1919- *WhoAm 90*
Bullen, Voy M. *WhoAm 90*
Buller, John 1927- *IntWWM 90*
Buller, Kurt Werner 1959- *BiDrAPA 89*
Bullerjahn, Eduard Henri 1920- *WhoAm 90*
Bullhe Shah 1680?-1758? *BioIn 16*
Bullick, Margaret M. 1949- *St&PR 91*
Bulliet, C J 1883-1952 *WhoAmA 91N*
Bulliet, Richard Williams 1940- *WhoAm 90*
Bullington, James R. 1940- *WhoAm 90, WhoSSW 91*
Bullington, John Lewis 1945- *WhoEmL 91*
Bullins, Ed 1935- *DrBlPA 90, MajTwCW, WhoAm 90*
Bullins, Sandra Elaine 1955- *WhoAmW 91*
Bullis, Eugene Martin 1945- *WhoAm 90*
Bullis, Florence Evelyn 1919- *WhoAmW 91*
Bullister, Edward Theodore 1957- *WhoE 91*
Bullitt, Dorothy S. *BioIn 16*
Bullitt, William C. 1891-1967 *BioIn 16, WorAlBi*
Bullitt, William Marshall 1873-1957 *BioIn 16*
Bullmore, R. Steven 1950- *St&PR 91*
Bulloch, John Frederick Devon 1933- *WhoAm 90*
Bullock, Lord 1914- *WhoWor 91*
Bullock, Alexander Hamilton 1816-1882 *AmLegL*
Bullock, Anna Mae *WhoAmW 91*
Bullock, Charles Spencer, III 1942- *WhoAm 90*
Bullock, Chick 1908-1981 *OxCPMus*
Bullock, Christopher *BiDrAPA 89*
Bullock, David Graham 1941- *WhoWor 91*
Bullock, Donald Wayne 1947- *WhoEmL 91*
Bullock, Ellis F. 1945- *St&PR 91*
Bullock, Ellis Way, Jr. 1928- *WhoAm 90, WhoSSW 91*
Bullock, Faye Cater 1944- *WhoSSW 91*
Bullock, Francis Jeremiah 1937- *WhoAm 90*
Bullock, Frank William, Jr. 1938- *WhoAm 90, WhoSSW 91*
Bullock, Gale Jeaneane 1954- *WhoAmW 91*
Bullock, Gayle Nelson 1952- *WhoAmW 91*
Bullock, George 1738?-1818 *PenDiDA 89*
Bullock, George 1782?-1818? *BioIn 16*
Bullock, Gwendolyn A. 1930- *WhoAmW 91*
Bullock, Gwendolyn Catrina 1956- *WhoEmL 91*
Bullock, H. Ridgely 1934- *St&PR 91*
Bullock, Hugh 1898- *WhoAm 90*
Bullock, Jack Arlen 1929- *WhoSSW 91*
Bullock, James Benbow 1929- *WhoAmA 91*
Bullock, James Roeder 1915- *St&PR 91*
Bullock, Jerry Ross 1950- *St&PR 91*
Bullock, Jimmie Bruce 1940- *WhoAm 90*
Bullock, John G. 1854-1939 *BioIn 16*
Bullock, John McDonell 1932- *WhoAm 90*
Bullock, Kevin Edward 1951- *WhoWor 91*
Bullock, L. G. *AuBYP 90*
Bullock, Lyndal Marvin *WhoSSW 91*
Bullock, Marie 1941- *WhoAmW 91*
Bullock, Maurice Randolph 1913- *WhoAm 90*
Bullock, Norma Kathryn Rice 1945- *WhoAmW 91*
Bullock, Paul S. 1942- *St&PR 91*
Bullock, Peter Bradley 1934- *WhoWor 91*
Bullock, Randall Curtis 1948- *St&PR 91*
Bullock, Robert Daniel 1947- *WhoE 91*
Bullock, Samuel Carey *BiDrAPA 89*
Bullock, Theodore Holmes 1915- *WhoAm 90*
Bullock, Thomas Abbott 1922- *St&PR 91, WhoAm 90, WhoSSW 91*
Bullock, Tony Bernard 1959- *WhoSSW 91*
Bullock, W.E. 1923- *St&PR 91*
Bullock, Warren M. 1931- *St&PR 91*
Bullock, William Clapp, Jr. 1936- *St&PR 91, WhoAm 90, WhoE 91*
Bullock, William Joseph 1943- *IntWWM 90, WhoSSW 91*
Bullock, William Norris 1953- *St&PR 91*
Bullock, Wynn 1902-1975 *WhoAmA 91N*
Bullock-Webster, Llewelyn 1879-1970 *OxCCanT*
Bulloff, Aaron Harley 1948- *WhoEmL 91*
Bullough, Bonnie 1927- *WhoAm 90*
Bullough, Dale Clay 1944- *WhoSSW 91*
Bullough, John Frank 1928- *WhoAm 90*
Bullrich, Silvina 1915- *HispWr 90*
Bulls, Derald Joe 1955- *WhoEmL 91*
Bulluck, Janice Denise 1958- *WhoAmW 91*
Bullwinkel, Fred 1922- *St&PR 91*
Bulmahn, Lynn 1955- *WhoAmW 91*
Bulmahn, T. Paul 1943- *St&PR 91*
Bulman, Richard B. 1942- *St&PR 91*
Bulman, William Patrick 1925- *WhoE 91, WhoWor 91*
Bulmer, David R 1942- *BiDrAPA 89*
Bulmer, William Edgar 1934- *WhoE 91*
Bulnes, Sara Maria 1954- *WhoWrEP 89*
Bulnes Prieto, Manuel 1799-1866 *BioIn 16*
Bulosan, Carlos 1911-1956 *EncAL*
Bulot, Xavier Emile 1937- *WhoWor 91*
Bulova, Arde 1889-1958 *WorAlBi*
Bulow, Bernhard, Prince Von 1849-1929 *WorAlBi*
Bulow, Claus Von 1926- *WorAlBi*
Bulow, George M. 1949- *WhoE 91*
Bulow, Hans von 1830-1894 *BioIn 16, PenDiMP, WorAlBi*
Bulow, Harry Timothy 1951- *IntWWM 90*
Bulow-Hube, Torun 1927- *ConDes 90*
Bulson, Carolyn Jean 1928- *IntWWM 90*
Bulstrode, Cecelea *BiDEWW*
Bulstrode, Cicely 1584-1609 *FemiCLE*
Bult, Albert J. 1936- *St&PR 91*
Bultje, Ronald Alan 1953- *WhoEmL 91*
Bultman, Fritz 1919-1985 *WhoAmA 91N*
Bultman, James E. *WhoAm 90*
Bultmann, Rudolf Karl 1884-1976 *MajTwCW*
Bulwer-Lytton, Edward 1803-1873 *BioIn 16*
Bulwer-Lytton, Rosina 1802-1882 *BioIn 16*
Bulzacchelli, John 1939- *St&PR 91*
Bulzacchelli, John G. 1939- *WhoAm 90*
Bumanglag, Alejandro Guira 1950- *WhoWor 91*
Bumbeck, David A 1940- *WhoAmA 91*
Bumbery, Joseph Lawrence 1929- *WhoAm 90, WhoWor 91*
Bumbry, Al 1947- *Ballpl 90*
Bumbry, Grace *BioIn 16*
Bumbry, Grace 1937- *DrBlPA 90, IntWWM 90, PenDiMP, WorAlBi*
Bumby, Adain James 1926- *St&PR 91*
Bumby, Edward Wells 1946- *St&PR 91*
Bumby, John Edgar 1920- *St&PR 91*
Bumgardner, James Arliss 1935- *WhoAmA 91*
Bumgardner, Larry G. 1957- *WhoEmL 91*
Bumgardner, Thomas Arthur 1942- *IntWWM 90*
Bumgarner, Frank Edwin, Jr. *BiDrAPA 89*
Bumgarner, John Carson, Sr. 1908- *WhoAm 90*
Bump, Herbert Dewitt 1932- *WhoSSW 91*
Bump, Michael Dan 1949- *WhoEmL 91*
Bump, Paris Louis, Jr. 1928- *WhoWor 91*
Bump, Wilbur Neil 1929- *WhoAm 90*
Bumpas, M. Stevens 1937- *St&PR 91*
Bumpas, Stuart Maryman 1944- *WhoAm 90*
Bumpass, Eugene Robert *BiDrAPA 89*
Bumpass, Larry Lee 1942- *WhoAm 90*
Bumpers, Betty *BioIn 16*
Bumpers, Dale *BioIn 16*
Bumpers, Dale 1925- *WorAlBi*
Bumpers, Dale L. 1925- *WhoAm 90, WhoSSW 91, WhoWor 91*
Bumpers, W. Carroll 1921- *St&PR 91*
Bumpous, Earle Thomas, III 1943- *WhoSSW 91*
Bumpus, Charles H. 1938- *St&PR 91*
Bumpus, Frederick J. 1929- *St&PR 91*
Bumpus, Frederick Joseph 1929- *WhoAm 90*

Bumpus, Hermon Carey 1862-1943 *DcScB S2*
Bumpus, James N. 1934- *St&PR 91*
Bumpus, Jerry Don 1937- *WhoWrEP 89*
Bumpus, Linda Doster 1946- *WhoAmW 91*
Bumpus, Raymond Conrad 1937- *St&PR 91*
Bumstead, Susan 1963- *WhoAmW 91*
Bumsted, Joseph Howard 1930- *St&PR 91*
Bumsted, Roy R., III 1949- *ODwPR 91*
Bunbury, John Dennis 1929- *St&PR 91*
Bunbury, Selina 1802-1882 *FemiCLE*
Bunce, Donald Fairbairn MacDougal, II 1920- *WhoAm 90*
Bunce, Louis DeMott 1914-1983 *WhoAmA 91N*
Bunce, Richard Alan 1953- *WhoSSW 91*
Bunce, Stanley Chalmers 1917- *WhoAm 90*
Bunce, William Harvey *AuBYP 90*
Bunch, Bradley 1818-1894 *AmLegL*
Bunch, Doyle R., II 1946- *St&PR 91*
Bunch, Drexel R. 1944- *St&PR 91*
Bunch, Edwin Lewis 1948- *BiDrAPA 89*
Bunch, Franklin Swope 1913- *WhoAm 90*
Bunch, Gary Alan 1947- *St&PR 91*
Bunch, James Terrance 1942- *WhoAm 90*
Bunch, John Blake 1940- *WhoAm 90*
Bunch, John T. *AmLegL*
Bunch, Karen Shore 1957- *WhoAmW 91*
Bunch, Kenneth Alan 1961- *WhoEmL 91*
Bunch, Linda Lee 1962- *WhoEmL 91*
Bunch, Luann Victory 1955- *WhoAmW 91*
Bunch, Meribeth A. 1938- *IntWWM 90*
Bunch, Phillip Gene 1938- *St&PR 91*
Bunch, Thomas Willard 1939- *WhoAm 90*
Bunch, Troy Eugene 1946- *WhoSSW 91*
Bunch, Walter Edward 1955- *WhoEmL 91*
Bunch, William Franklin 1935- *IntWWM 90*
Bunche, Ralph 1904-1971 *WorAlBi*
Bunche, Ralph J. 1904-1971 *BioIn 16*
Bunche, Ruth *BioIn 16*
Buncher, Alan 1946- *WhoEmL 91*
Buncher, James Edward 1936- *St&PR 91, WhoAm 90*
Bunda, Donald William 1952- *WhoEmL 91*
Bundesen, Faye Stimers 1932- *WhoAmW 91*
Bundgaard, Thorleif 1956- *WhoWor 91*
Bundgaard-Jorgensen, Uffe 1945- *WhoWor 91*
Bundick, William Ross 1917- *WhoAm 90*
Bundrant, John Patton 1932- *WhoAm 90*
Bundschuh, George August William 1933- *St&PR 91, WhoAm 90*
Bundschuh, John J., Jr. 1932- *St&PR 91*
Bundschuh, Marjorie Gurevitz 1952- *WhoAmW 91, WhoWor 91*
Bundy, Brad Richard 1952- *BiDrAPA 89*
Bundy, Charles Alan 1930- *WhoAm 90*
Bundy, David Hollister 1947- *WhoEmL 91*
Bundy, Elizabeth Campbell 1960- *WhoAmW 91*
Bundy, Florence *EarBlAP*
Bundy, Harvey H., III 1944- *St&PR 91*
Bundy, Harvey Hollister 1916- *WhoAm 90*
Bundy, Judith Cox 1941- *WhoE 91*
Bundy, Kenneth Alvin 1910- *WhoWor 91*
Bundy, Mary L. 1925- *St&PR 91*
Bundy, McGeorge *BioIn 16*
Bundy, McGeorge 1919- *WhoAm 90, WhoWor 91*
Bundy, Michael Lyman 1947- *WhoSSW 91*
Bundy, Phil 1945- *St&PR 91*
Bundy, Robert Mayne 1932- *St&PR 91*
Bundy, Ronald Floyd 1941- *St&PR 91*
Bundy, Ted 1946-1989 *WorAlBi*
Bundy, Theodore Robert *BioIn 16*
Bundy, William Hatler, Jr. 1940- *St&PR 91*
Bundy, William P. 1917- *WorAlBi*
Bune, Karen Louise 1954- *WhoAmW 91*
Bunemann, Gerhard 1926- *WhoWor 91*
Bunge, Charles Albert 1936- *WhoAm 90*
Bunge, Joan Marie 1958- *WhoSSW 91*
Bunge, Mario Augusto 1919- *WhoWrEP 89*
Bunge, Robert John 1953- *BiDrAPA 89*
Bunge, Walter Richard 1911- *WhoAm 90*
Bungener, Johannes Hendrik 1934- *St&PR 91*
Bungert, John Jacob, III 1934- *St&PR 91*
Bungo, Michael William 1950- *WhoAm 90*
Bunim, Amos 1929- *ConAu 132*
Bunim, Mary-Ellis 1946- *WhoAm 90, WhoAmW 91*
Bunin, Ivan 1870-1953 *WorAlBi*
Bunin, Jeffrey Howard 1948- *WhoE 91, WhoEmL 91*
Bunin, Lou *BioIn 16*
Bunin, Louis 1904- *WhoAmA 91*
Bunio, Russell J. 1947- *St&PR 91*
Bunk, George Mark 1952- *WhoE 91*
Bunke, Jerome Samuel 1945- *WhoEmL 91*
Bunke, Robert Werner 1927- *St&PR 91*
Bunker, Anthony Louis 1933- *WhoSSW 91*
Bunker, Dana Emery 1923- *St&PR 91*
Bunker, Douglas A. 1962- *WhoEmL 91*
Bunker, Ellsworth 1894-1984 *BioIn 16, WorAlBi*
Bunker, Frederick William 1946- *WhoE 91*
Bunker, George 1923- *WhoAmA 91*
Bunker, James F. *WhoAm 90*
Bunker, Jim 1942- *ODwPR 91*
Bunker, John B. 1926- *St&PR 91*
Bunker, John Birkbeck 1926- *WhoAm 90*
Bunker, Theodore James 1947- *St&PR 91*
Bunker, Wally 1945- *Ballpl 90*
Bunkowski, Kenneth D. 1947- *St&PR 91*
Bunn, Anna Maria 1808-1889 *FemiCLE*
Bunn, Charles Nixon 1926- *WhoWor 91*
Bunn, David 1950- *WhoAmA 91*
Bunn, Dorothy Irons 1948- *WhoAmW 91*
Bunn, Emory Freeman 1935- *WhoAm 90*
Bunn, George 1925- *WhoAm 90*
Bunn, Joe Millard 1932- *WhoSSW 91*
Bunn, Joseph Forman, III 1921- *WhoSSW 91*
Bunn, Richard L. 1936- *St&PR 91*
Bunn, Ronald Freeze 1929- *WhoAm 90*
Bunn, Teddy 1909-1978 *OxCPMus*
Bunn, Thomas M. 1904- *St&PR 91*
Bunn, Timothy David 1946- *WhoAm 90, WhoE 91*
Bunn, W.B. 1952- *St&PR 91*
Bunn, Wallace R. 1922- *St&PR 91*
Bunn, Willard, III 1943- *St&PR 91*
Bunn, William Bernice, III 1952- *WhoAm 90*
Bunnell, Dale L. 1936- *St&PR 91*
Bunnell, Donald R. 1947- *St&PR 91*
Bunnell, Paul Joseph 1946- *WhoWrEP 89*
Bunnell, Peter C 1937- *ConAu 30NR*
Bunnell, Peter Curtis 1937- *WhoAm 90, WhoAmA 91, WhoE 91*
Bunnell, Roderick 1930- *St&PR 91*
Bunnell, Sandra Jean 1945- *WhoEmL 91*
Bunnell, Susan Lynn 1950- *BiDrAPA 89*
Bunnen, Lucinda Weil 1930- *WhoAmA 91*
Bunner, Patricia Andrea 1953- *WhoAmW 91, WhoSSW 91*
Bunner, William Keck 1949- *WhoEmL 91*
Bunnett, Joseph Frederick 1921- *WhoAm 90*
Bunney, Benjamin S *BiDrAPA 89*
Bunney, Benjamin Stephenson 1938- *WhoE 91*
Bunney, Herrick *IntWWM 90*
Bunney, William E, Jr. 1930- *BiDrAPA 89*
Bunning, Jim 1931- *Ballpl 90 [port], WhoAm 90, WhoSSW 91, WorAlBi*
Bunny, Rupert Charles Wolston 1864-1947 *BioIn 16*
Bunsen, Robert Wilhelm 1811-1899 *WorAlBi*
Bunshaft, Gordon 1909- *WhoAm 90*
Bunshaft, Gordon 1909-1990 *BioIn 16, CurBio 90N, NewYTBS 90, News 91-1*
Bunshaft, Robert S. 1918- *St&PR 91*
Bunt, Gregory Charles 1955- *BiDrAPA 89*
Bunt, Harry C. 1944- *WhoWor 91*
Bunt, James Richard 1941- *St&PR 91, WhoAm 90*
Bunt, Lynne Joy 1948- *WhoAmW 91*
Buntain, David Robert 1948- *WhoEmL 91*
Buntain, Ruth Jaeger *AuBYP 90*
Buntebardt, Klaus Paul 1940- *WhoWor 91*
Bunten, John R. 1932- *St&PR 91*
Bunten, William Daniel 1931- *St&PR 91, WhoAm 90*
Buntin, Alexander 1822-1893 *DcCanB 12*
Buntin, William Lee 1943- *St&PR 91*
Bunting, A. E. *AuBYP 90*
Bunting, A E 1928- *SmATA X [port]*
Bunting, Anne Eve 1928- *BioIn 16*
Bunting, Anne Evelyn 1928- *AuBYP 90, WhoAm 90, WhoWrEP 89*
Bunting, Bainbridge 1913-1981 *WhoAmA 91N*
Bunting, Basil *BioIn 16*
Bunting, Basil 1900-1985 *DcNaB 1981*
Bunting, Bruce Gordon 1948- *WhoEmL 91*
Bunting, Christopher Henry 1951- *WhoAm 90*
Bunting, Christopher William 1837-1896 *DcCanB 12*
Bunting, Dana Leigh 1961- *St&PR 91*
Bunting, Eve *AuBYP 90, WhoWrEP 89*
Bunting, Eve 1928- *Au&Arts 5 [port], BioIn 16, SmATA 64 [port]*
Bunting, George L., Jr. 1940- *St&PR 91*
Bunting, J. Pearce 1929- *St&PR 91*
Bunting, James F. 1906-1989 *BioIn 16*
Bunting, Joelle 1939- *BiDrAPA 89*
Bunting, John R., Jr. 1925- *St&PR 91*
Bunting, Lee 1915- *St&PR 91*
Bunting, Robert L. 1928- *St&PR 91*
Bunting, Susan Ethel 1956- *WhoAmW 91*
Bunting, William Franklin 1825-1897 *DcCanB 12*
Bunting, William Vernon 1940- *WhoAm 90*
Buntline, Ned 1823-1886 *WorAlBi*
Bunton, Clifford Allen 1920- *WhoAm 90*
Bunton, Lucius Desha, III 1924- *WhoAm 90, WhoSSW 91*
Bunton, Mildred Settle 1906- *WhoAmW 91*
Buntrock, Dean L. 1931- *St&PR 91*
Buntrock, Dean Lewis *WhoAm 90*
Buntrock, R. Dik 1938- *WhoWor 91*
Bunts, Frank 1932- *WhoAmA 91*
Bunts, Frank Emory 1932- *WhoAm 90, WhoE 91, WhoWor 91*
Buntschuh, Charles 1931- *St&PR 91*
Buntyn, Ralph E. 1941- *St&PR 91*
Bunuel, Luis 1900-1983 *ConAu 32NR, HispWr 90, WorAlBi*
Bunyan, Ellen Lackey Spotz 1921- *WhoE 91*
Bunyan, John 1628-1688 *BioIn 16, WorAlBi*
Bunyard, George B. 1929- *St&PR 91*
Bunzel, John Harvey 1924- *WhoAm 90*
Bunzel, Ruth L. *NewYTBS 90*
Bunzel, Ruth L 1898-1990 *ConAu 130*
Bunzel, Ruth Leah 1898-1990 *BioIn 16*
Bunzel, Tracy L. 1962- *WhoAmW 91*
Bunzl, Rudolph H. 1922- *St&PR 91*
Bunzl, Rudolph Hans 1922- *WhoAm 90, WhoSSW 91*
Buoch, William Thomas 1923- *WhoSSW 91*
Buoen, Victoria B. 1955- *BiDrAPA 89*
Buomberger, Peter Richard 1950- *WhoWor 91*
Buonagurio, Edgar R 1946- *WhoAmA 91*
Buonagurio, Toby Lee 1947- *WhoAmA 91*
Buonanni, Brian Francis 1945- *WhoE 91, WhoEmL 91*
Buonanno, Aldo Antonio 1947- *BiDrAPA 89*
Buonanno, Aurelio *BiDrAPA 89*
Buonanno, Joseph E. 1910- *St&PR 91*
Buonanno, Vincent J. 1943- *St&PR 91*
Buonarroti, Michel Angelo 1475-1564 *BioIn 16*
Buongiorno, Joseph A. 1939- *St&PR 91*
Buongiorno, Paul Anthony 1954- *BiDrAPA 89*
Buoniconti, Nicholas A. 1940- *WhoAm 90, WhoE 91*
Buoniconto, Pasquale 1908- *BiDrAPA 89*
Buonicore, Anthony Joseph 1950- *WhoEmL 91*
Buono, A. George 1930- *St&PR 91*
Buono, Antonio del 1900-1975 *BioIn 16*
Buono, Lisa Carol 1957- *WhoE 91*
Buono, Maureen Brady 1937- *WhoE 91*
Buono, Victor 1938-1982 *WorAlBi*
Buono-Alcaraz, Juan Luis 1946- *BiDrAPA 89*
Buontalenti, Bernardo *PenDiDA 89*
Buoymaster, Ned W. 1928- *St&PR 91*
Bupp, Chandler Meenen 1954- *WhoAmW 91*
Bupp, Steven Jerome 1959- *BiDrAPA 89*
Buquoy, Georg Franz Longueval, Count von *PenDiDA 89*
Bura, Corina 1948- *IntWWM 90*
Burachynskyj, Roxolana Maria 1943- *WhoE 91*
Burack, Elmer Howard 1927- *WhoAm 90*
Burack, Michael Leonard 1942- *WhoE 91*
Burack, Sylvia E. Kamerman 1916- *WhoWrEP 89*
Burak, Carl Stanton 1942- *BiDrAPA 89, WhoE 91*
Burak, Sergei *BioIn 16*
Burakoff, Steven James 1942- *WhoAm 90*
Burakowski, Joseph Earl 1952- *WhoE 91*
Bural, Ronald Michael 1950- *BiDrAPA 89*
Buran, Dennis Francis 1941- *St&PR 91*
Burandt, Gary *BioIn 16*
Burandt, Gary Edward 1943- *WhoAm 90, WhoWor 91*
Burandt, Jacqueline Hammett 1948- *WhoAm 90*
Buranelli, Marguerite *AuBYP 90*
Buranelli, Nan 1917- *WhoWrEP 89*
Buranello, Raymond Terrence 1950- *WhoE 91*
Burani, Sergio 1946- *WhoEmL 91*
Burani, Umberto 1928- *WhoWor 91*
Buranskas, Karen Lynn 1950- *IntWWM 90*
Buras, Brenda Allynn 1954- *WhoAmW 91, WhoEmL 91, WhoSSW 91*
Buratti, Bonnie J. 1953- *WhoAmW 91*
Burba, William H *BiDrAPA 89*
Burbach, Bill 1947- *Ballpl 90*
Burbach, Rodney Van 1942- *BiDrAPA 89*
Burbank, Elbridge Ayer 1858-1949 *WhNaAH*
Burbank, Gladys Verena 1947- *WhoEmL 91*
Burbank, James Carroll 1948- *St&PR 91*
Burbank, James Clarke 1946- *WhoWrEP 89*
Burbank, John Thorn 1939- *WhoWor 91*
Burbank, Joseph Theodore 1940- *WhoE 91*
Burbank, Luther 1849-1926 *EncPaPR 91, WorAlBi*
Burbank, Nelson Stone 1920- *St&PR 91, WhoAm 90*
Burbank, Russell King 1943- *St&PR 91*
Burbano, Alfredo Poveda *BioIn 16*
Burbea, Jacob N. 1942- *WhoE 91*
Burbey, Gene P. 1937- *St&PR 91*
Burbidge, Eleanor Margaret Peachey *WhoAm 90, WhoAmW 91*
Burbidge, Geoffrey 1925- *WhoAm 90*
Burbidge, John L. 1932- *St&PR 91*
Burbidge, Kenneth Parry, Jr. 1930- *St&PR 91*
Burbidge, Nicolas W.R. 1946- *St&PR 91*
Burbridge, Edward 1933- *DrBlPA 90*
Burbridge, Katherine Ann 1953- *WhoAmW 91, WhoEmL 91*
Burch Sisters, The *WhoNeCM*
Burch, Al 1883-1926 *Ballpl 90*
Burch, Arthur Leroy 1936- *St&PR 91*
Burch, Arthur Merritt 1935- *St&PR 91*
Burch, Cecil Reginald 1901-1983 *DcNaB 1981*
Burch, Claire R 1935- *WhoAmA 91*
Burch, Craig Alan 1954- *WhoE 91, WhoEmL 91, WhoWor 91*
Burch, D. Russell 1941- *St&PR 91*
Burch, Dannette Kathleen 1960- *WhoAmW 91*
Burch, Dean 1927- *WhoAm 90*
Burch, Dorothy *BiDEWW, FemiCLE*
Burch, Dwayne Lee 1946- *WhoSSW 91*
Burch, Earl Allen, Jr. 1947- *BiDrAPA 89*
Burch, F. Gene 1927- *St&PR 91*
Burch, Florine 1941- *St&PR 91*
Burch, Gladys 1899- *AuBYP 90*
Burch, James Leo 1942- *WhoAm 90*
Burch, John E 1909- *BiDrAPA 89*
Burch, John Thomas, Jr. 1942- *WhoAm 90*
Burch, John Walter 1925- *WhoWor 91*
Burch, Karl D. 1929- *St&PR 91*
Burch, Larry Thomas 1933- *BiDrAPA 89*
Burch, Linda Jane Cash 1950- *WhoSSW 91*
Burch, Lucius Edward, Jr. 1912- *WhoAm 90*
Burch, Lyndon Walkup 1899- *WhoAm 90*
Burch, Mariel Rae 1934- *WhoWrEP 89*
Burch, Mark Hetzel 1953- *WhoEmL 91*
Burch, Melvin Earl 1949- *St&PR 91, WhoEmL 91*
Burch, Michael I. 1941- *St&PR 91*
Burch, Michael Ira 1941- *WhoAm 90*
Burch, Paul Gilson 1954- *WhoEmL 91*
Burch, Robert Dale 1928- *WhoAm 90*
Burch, Robert J. 1943- *St&PR 91*
Burch, Robert Joseph 1925- *AuBYP 90, WhoAm 90*
Burch, Robert L. 1934- *St&PR 91*
Burch, Robert S. *St&PR 91*
Burch, Ruth Marie 1940- *WhoAmW 91*
Burch, Stephen Kenneth 1945- *WhoEmL 91*
Burch, Thaddeus Joseph, Jr. 1930- *WhoAm 90*
Burch, Thomas Robert 1945- *WhoEmL 91*
Burch, Voris Reagan 1930- *WhoAm 90*
Burch, William Richard, Jr. 1933- *WhoAm 90*
Burcham, Barbara June 1952- *WhoAmW 91*
Burcham, Carroll Franklin 1935- *WhoSSW 91*
Burcham, Eva Helen 1941- *WhoAmW 91, WhoWor 91*
Burcham, Stephen Dale 1956- *WhoEmL 91*
Burcham, Teri Rydzewski 1953- *WhoEmL 91*
Burcham, Wayne B. 1948- *WhoE 91*
Burchard, Charles 1914- *WhoAm 90*
Burchard, Ellen Williams 1913- *WhoWor 91*
Burchard, John Kenneth 1936- *WhoAm 90*
Burchard, Marshall *AuBYP 90*
Burchard, Peter Duncan 1921- *AuBYP 90, WhoAmA 91*
Burchard, Rachael C. 1921- *WhoWrEP 89*
Burchard, Roswell Beebe 1860-1931 *AmLegL*
Burchard, Sue 1937- *AuBYP 90*
Burchard, Thomas Kirk 1948- *BiDrAPA 89*
Burchardt, Clara Chavez 1932- *WhoSSW 91*
Burchell, Mary Cecilia *WhoAmW 91*
Burchell, S. C. *AuBYP 90*
Burchell, William Irvin 1934- *St&PR 91*
Burchenal, Joseph *AmLegL*
Burchenal, Joseph Holland 1912- *WhoAm 90*
Burcher, Hilda Beasley 1938- *WhoAmW 91*
Burcher, Robert Douglas, Jr. 1946- *WhoSSW 91*
Burchess, Arnold 1912- *WhoAmA 91*

Burchett, Betty Martela 1934- *WhoAmW 91*
Burchett, Debra 1955- *WhoAmA 91*
Burchett, H.L. 1956- *St&PR 91*
Burchette, Bruce Wilson 1963- *BiDrAPA 89*
Burchfiel, Burrell Clark 1934- *WhoAm 90*
Burchfield, Bruce Allen 1947- *WhoEmL 91*
Burchfield, Charles 1893-1967 *WhoAmA 91N*
Burchfield, Donald Francis 1932- *WhoSSW 91*
Burchfield, Harry *BioIn 16*
Burchfield, Harry Phineas, Jr. 1915- *WhoAm 90*
Burchfield, Jerry Lee 1947- *WhoAmA 91*
Burchfield, Susan Elizabeth 1958- *WhoAmW 91*
Burchfield, William H. 1935- *St&PR 91*, *WhoAm 90*
Burchill, Donn *St&PR 91*
Burchill, William Roberts, Jr. 1947- *WhoEmL 91*
Burchinal, Robert Nixon 1925- *St&PR 91*
Burchman, Howard Barry 1951- *WhoEmL 91*
Burchman, Leonard 1925- *WhoAm 90*
Burchuk, Robert 1957- *BiDrAPA 89*
Burchuladze, Paata 1950- *IntWWM 90*
Burchuladze, Paata 1955- *PenDiMP*
Burciaga, Cecilia Preciado de 1945- *BioIn 16*, *WhoHisp 91*
Burciaga, Jose Antonio 1940- *BioIn 16*, *ConAu 131*, *HispWr 90*, *WhoHisp 91*
Burciaga, Juan G. 1929- *WhoHisp 91*
Burciaga, Raul R 1951- *BiDrAPA 89*
Burck, Arthur Albert 1913- *WhoAm 90*
Burck, Jacob 1904-1982 *WhoAmA 91N*
Burck, James Lester 1938- *WhoSSW 91*
Burck, Neil Arthur 1957- *WhoEmL 91*
Burckhalter, Charles 1849-1923 *BioIn 16*
Burckhardt, Jacob 1818-1897 *BioIn 16*, *WorAlBi*
Burckhardt, Rudy *BioIn 16*
Burckhardt, Rudy 1914- *WhoAm 90*, *WhoAmA 91*
Burckhardt, Stephan *ODwPR 91*
Burckhardt, William A, III *BiDrAPA 89*
Burckhardt, Yvonne Helen *WhoAmA 91*
Burd, Charles Leslie 1947- *WhoEmL 91*
Burd, John Stephen 1939- *WhoAm 90*
Burd, Robert Meyer 1937- *WhoE 91*
Burd, Ronald M *BiDrAPA 89*
Burda, Bob 1938- *Ballpl 90*
Burda, Marianne Louise 1959- *WhoAmW 91*
Burda, Pavel 1942- *IntWWM 90*
Burdakin, John Howard 1922- *St&PR 91*
Burdan, Barbara R 1933- *BiDrAPA 89*
Burde, Ronald Marshall 1938- *WhoAm 90*
Burdell, Bill *WhoWrEP 89*
Burden, Alfred Lionel, Jr. 1934- *WhoSSW 91*
Burden, Carter *BioIn 16*
Burden, Carter 1941- *WhoAmA 91*
Burden, Charles Earle 1933- *WhoE 91*
Burden, Chris 1946- *BioIn 16*, *WhoAmA 91*
Burden, Earl 1927- *St&PR 91*
Burden, Geneva Louvenia 1950- *WhoSSW 91*
Burden, I. Townsend, III 1943- *St&PR 91*
Burden, James Ewers 1939- *WhoWor 91*
Burden, Jean *WhoAm 90*, *WhoAmW 91*
Burden, Jean 1914- *WhoWrEP 89*
Burden, John W., III 1937- *WhoE 91*
Burden, Laurance Treat 1940- *St&PR 91*
Burden, Nancy Caswell 1946- *WhoWrEP 89*
Burden, Ordway Partridge 1944- *WhoAm 90*, *WhoE 91*
Burden, Shirley 1908-1989 *BioIn 16*
Burden, Susan *BioIn 16*
Burden, Vijean Piazza 1947- *WhoSSW 91*
Burdeshaw, Walter Ray 1938- *IntWWM 90*
Burdeshaw, William Brooksbank 1930- *WhoE 91*, *WhoWor 91*
Burdetsky, Ben 1928- *WhoAm 90*
Burdett, Charles Albert 1942- *WhoWor 91*
Burdett, Howard William 1939- *WhoAm 90*
Burdett, Kelly 1928- *WhoAmW 91*
Burdett-Coutts, Angela Georgina 1814-1906 *BioIn 16*
Burdette, Charles M. 1932- *St&PR 91*
Burdette, Everette Clifton 1950- *St&PR 91*
Burdette, Forbes Willard 1932- *St&PR 91*
Burdette, J.R., Jr. 1948- *St&PR 91*
Burdette, Jane Elizabeth 1955- *WhoAmW 91*, *WhoEmL 91*
Burdette, Keith 1955- *WhoSSW 91*
Burdette, Lew 1926- *Ballpl 90 [port]*
Burdette, Milladeen Wicker 1952- *WhoEmL 91*
Burdette, Walter James 1915- *WhoAm 90*
Burdge, Jeffrey J. *WhoAm 90*, *WhoE 91*
Burdge, Jeffrey John 1922- *St&PR 91*
Burdge, Larry F. 1934- *St&PR 91*
Burdge, Rabel James 1937- *WhoAm 90*
Burdge, Ronald Everett 1938- *St&PR 91*
Burdi, Alphonse Rocco 1935- *WhoAm 90*
Burdi, Gianfranco *BiDrAPA 89*
Burdic, Joseph T 1923- *BiDrAPA 89*
Burdick, Allan Bernard 1920- *WhoAm 90*
Burdick, Ariane Neiman 1945- *WhoWrEP 89*
Burdick, Bruce 1933- *BioIn 16*
Burdick, Bruce Emerald 1947- *WhoEmL 91*
Burdick, Bruce M *BiDrAPA 89*
Burdick, Carol *BioIn 16*
Burdick, Carol 1928- *ConAu 132*
Burdick, Carolyn Jane 1938- *WhoAmW 91*
Burdick, Colin Alfred 1943- *WhoWor 91*
Burdick, David Malcolm 1943- *WhoE 91*
Burdick, Donald 1934- *WhoAm 90*
Burdick, Eugene Allan 1912- *WhoAm 90*
Burdick, Glenn Arthur 1932- *WhoAm 90*
Burdick, John M. 1942- *St&PR 91*
Burdick, Jonathan R. 1958- *St&PR 91*
Burdick, Lou Brum 1943- *ODwPR 91*, *WhoAm 90*
Burdick, Quentin Northrop 1908- *WhoAm 90*, *WhoWor 91*
Burdick, Richard E 1934- *BiDrAPA 89*
Burdick, Stephen Arthur 1952- *WhoSSW 91*
Burdick, Susan Kosakowsky *BioIn 16*
Burdick, Usher Lloyd 1879-1960 *AmLegL*
Burdin, Janece Frances 1950- *WhoE 91*
Burdine, Vicki Elaine *BiDrAPA 89*
Burditt, George Miller, Jr. 1922- *WhoAm 90*
Burditt, John Frederic 1918- *WhoE 91*
Burdman, Daphne Freda *BiDrAPA 89*
Burdock, Harriet 1944- *WhoAmA 91*
Burdon, Arthur P 1924- *BiDrAPA 89*
Burdon, Eric *BioIn 16*
Burdon, Eric 1941- *EncPR&S 89*, *OxCPMus*, *WorAlBi*
Burdsall, Clarice W. 1909- *WhoWrEP 89*
Burdsall, Meg Pier 1959- *WhoE 91*
Burdus, Julia Ann 1933- *St&PR 91*
Burdzik, Eberhard G 1926- *BiDrAPA 89*
Bureau, Michel Andre 1943- *WhoAm 90*
Burenga, Janis M. *ODwPR 91*
Burenga, Kenneth L. 1944- *WhoAm 90*, *WhoE 91*
Bures, Donald John 1938- *WhoAm 90*
Bures, Paul Leslie, Jr. 1933- *WhoAm 90*, *WhoSSW 91*
Buresh, Thomas Gordon 1951- *WhoEmL 91*
Buret, Marie-Therese-Charlotte 1865?-1941? *EncCoWW*
Buret, Pierre Emmanuel 1958- *WhoWor 91*
Burford, Anne McGill 1942- *WhoAm 90*, *WhoAmW 91*
Burford, Annette 1919- *WhoAmW 91*
Burford, Byron Leslie 1920- *WhoAm 90*, *WhoAmA 91*
Burford, Duncan D 1933- *BiDrAPA 89*
Burford, Frederick W. 1950- *St&PR 91*
Burford, Nathaniel Macon 1824- *AmLegL*
Burford, Robert Fitzpatrick 1923- *WhoAm 90*
Burford, Roger L. 1930- *WhoSSW 91*
Burford, Thomas Guy *BiDrAPA 89*
Burford, William E 1936- *WhoAmA 91*
Burford, William Jeffrey 1943- *WhoAm 90*
Burg, B R 1938- *ConAu 129*
Burg, Dale R 1942- *WhoWrEP 89*
Burg, Donald *ODwPR 91*
Burg, Fred Murray 1951- *WhoE 91*
Burg, Fredric David 1940- *WhoAm 90*
Burg, Gary G. 1956- *WhoEmL 91*
Burg, George P. 1948- *St&PR 91*
Burg, George Roscoe 1916- *WhoAm 90*
Burg, John Parker 1931- *WhoAm 90*
Burg, Patricia Jean 1934- *WhoAmA 91*
Burg, R.A. 1932- *St&PR 91*
Burg, Ruth Cooper 1926- *WhoAm 90*, *WhoAmW 91*
Burgan, John Sydney 1930- *WhoE 91*
Burgan, Mary Alice 1935- *WhoAm 90*
Burganger, Judith Treer *IntWWM 90*
Burgard, Harold Morgan 1929- *St&PR 91*
Burgarino, Joseph Jude *BiDrAPA 89*
Burgbacher, James Stanley 1943- *BiDrAPA 89*
Burgdoerfer, Jerry 1958- *WhoWor 91*
Burgdoerfer, Jerry J. 1935- *St&PR 91*, *WhoAm 90*
Burge, Catherine Alice 1956- *WhoEmL 91*
Burge, Christopher *WhoE 91*
Burge, David 1930- *IntWWM 90*
Burge, David Russell 1930- *WhoAm 90*
Burge, Henry Charles 1911- *WhoAm 90*
Burge, Henry H. 1934- *St&PR 91*
Burge, James D. 1934- *St&PR 91*
Burge, James Darrell 1934- *WhoAm 90*
Burge, John H. 1949- *WhoEmL 91*
Burge, John Kenneth 1926- *WhoSSW 91*
Burge, John Wesley, Jr. 1932- *St&PR 91*, *WhoAm 90*
Burge, Stewart L. *ODwPR 91*
Burge, Stuart 1918- *ConTFT 8*
Burge, William Lee 1918- *WhoAm 90*
Burgee, John Henry 1933- *WhoAm 90*
Burgen, Arnold 1922- *WhoWor 91*
Burgen, F.S. 1926- *St&PR 91*
Burgen, Frank Stanley, Jr. 1926- *WhoSSW 91*
Burgener, Francis Andre 1942- *WhoAm 90*
Burgener, Louis W. 1943- *St&PR 91*
Burger, Albert Ellis 1941- *St&PR 91*
Burger, Ambrose William 1923- *WhoAm 90*
Burger, Amy Louise 1956- *WhoAmW 91*
Burger, Carolyn S. 1940- *St&PR 91*
Burger, Chester *BioIn 16*
Burger, Chester 1921- *ODwPR 91*, *WhoAm 90*
Burger, Christer 1935- *WhoWor 91*
Burger, Denis Rene 1943- *WhoAm 90*
Burger, Edmund Ganes 1930- *WhoAm 90*
Burger, Eugene *WhoE 91*
Burger, Frances L *BiDrAPA 89*
Burger, Gary C 1943- *WhoAmA 91*
Burger, Gerald Keith 1952- *WhoAm 90*, *WhoEmL 91*
Burger, Gilles William 1958- *WhoE 91*
Burger, Gottfried August 1747-1794 *DcLB 94 [port]*
Burger, Henry G. 1923- *WhoAm 90*, *WhoWor 91*, *WhoWrEP 89*
Burger, Herbert Francis 1930- *St&PR 91*, *WhoAm 90*
Burger, Isabel Blogg 1902- *BioIn 16*, *NotWoAT*
Burger, Isabel Cuellar 1960- *WhoAmW 91*
Burger, Janette Marie 1958- *WhoAmW 91*
Burger, John H, Jr. *BiDrAPA 89*
Burger, Lane W. 1941- *St&PR 91*
Burger, Lewis Stephen 1941- *St&PR 91*, *WhoAm 90*
Burger, Lowell G. 1928- *St&PR 91*
Burger, Mary Louise *WhoAm 90*
Burger, Mikulas 1921- *WhoWor 91*
Burger, Peter 1936- *WhoWor 91*
Burger, Robert *BioIn 16*
Burger, Robert D. *BioIn 16*
Burger, Robert Dean 1924- *St&PR 91*
Burger, Robert Eugene 1931- *WhoAm 90*, *WhoWrEP 89*
Burger, Robert Mercer 1927- *WhoAm 90*
Burger, Steven Neal 1956- *WhoE 91*
Burger, Van Vechten 1905- *St&PR 91*
Burger, W Carl 1925- *WhoAmA 91*
Burger, Warren E. 1907- *BioIn 16*, *WorAlBi*
Burger, Warren Earl 1907- *WhoAm 90*
Burgert, David Lee 1959- *WhoEmL 91*
Burgert, Hans-Joachim 1928- *WhoWor 91*
Burgert, Theodore P. 1931- *ODwPR 91*
Burges, Mary Anne 1763-1813 *FemiCLE*
Burges, Mary Margaret 1921- *WhoAmW 91*
Burges, William 1827-1881 *PenDiDA 89*
Burgeson, Joyce Ann 1936- *WhoAmW 91*
Burgeson, Noreen Theresa 1953- *St&PR 91*
Burgess, Alan 1930- *St&PR 91*
Burgess, Alexander Mackinnon 1850-1898 *DcCanB 12*
Burgess, Alfred F. 1906- *St&PR 91*
Burgess, Alfred Franklin 1906- *WhoAm 90*
Burgess, Ann Baker 1942- *WhoAmW 91*
Burgess, Ann Marie 1914-1988 *SmATA X*
Burgess, Anthony *MajTwCW*
Burgess, Anthony 1917- *BioIn 16*, *ConLC 62 [port]*, *IntWWM 90*, *RGTwCSF*, *WhoWor 91*, *WorAlBi*
Burgess, Benjamin L., Jr. 1943- *WhoAm 90*
Burgess, Beth Brown 1959- *WhoSSW 91*
Burgess, Brian Robert 1951- *WhoEmL 91*, *WhoSSW 91*
Burgess, Brio 1943- *IntWWM 90*
Burgess, C Duane 1932- *BiDrAPA 89*
Burgess, Charles Orville 1932- *WhoAm 90*, *WhoWor 91*
Burgess, Colin 1840-1905 *OxCCanT*
Burgess, Craig E. 1944- *WhoWrEP 89*
Burgess, David 1948- *WhoAm 90*, *WhoE 91*, *WhoEmL 91*, *WhoWor 91*
Burgess, David Lowry 1940- *WhoAm 90*, *WhoAmA 91*
Burgess, Dean 1937- *WhoSSW 91*
Burgess, Dixie 1961- *WhoEmL 91*
Burgess, Douglas Holmes 1942- *St&PR 91*
Burgess, Edward Francis, VIII *WhoWrEP 89*
Burgess, Elizabeth Chamberlain 1877-1949 *BioIn 16*
Burgess, Elizabeth Lee Capes 1930- *IntWWM 90*
Burgess, Elwood Johnson, Jr. 1956- *WhoEmL 91*
Burgess, Ernest Edward, Jr. 1928- *WhoSSW 91*
Burgess, Eunice Lester 1935- *WhoAm 90*
Burgess, Fred A. 1911- *St&PR 91*
Burgess, Frederick Manley 1908- *WhoE 91*
Burgess, Glenn N *BiDrAPA 89*
Burgess, Gloria Jean 1953- *WhoEmL 91*
Burgess, Grayston 1932- *IntWWM 90*
Burgess, Hayden Fern 1946- *WhoWor 91*
Burgess, J Wesley 1952- *BiDrAPA 89*
Burgess, James E. 1936- *St&PR 91*
Burgess, James Edward 1936- *WhoAm 90*
Burgess, James Harland 1929- *WhoAm 90*
Burgess, James Scott 1959- *St&PR 91*
Burgess, Janet Helen 1933- *WhoAmW 91*
Burgess, Jay G. 1929- *St&PR 91*
Burgess, Jeanne Llewellyn 1923- *WhoAmW 91*
Burgess, John David 1946- *BiDrAPA 89*
Burgess, John Frank 1917- *WhoAm 90*, *WhoWor 91*
Burgess, John M. 1936- *St&PR 91*
Burgess, Joseph E 1891-1961 *WhoAmA 91N*
Burgess, Joseph James, Jr 1924- *WhoAmA 91*
Burgess, Judith Grissinger 1948- *WhoAmW 91*
Burgess, Kenneth Alexander 1918- *WhoAm 90*
Burgess, Larry Charles 1956- *St&PR 91*
Burgess, Leonard Randolph 1919- *WhoAm 90*
Burgess, Linda Suzanne 1954- *WhoAmA 91*
Burgess, Lloyd Albert 1917- *WhoAm 90*
Burgess, Madgelene Jones 1948- *WhoSSW 91*
Burgess, Malcolm Stewart 1945- *St&PR 91*
Burgess, Margaret *WhoWrEP 89*
Burgess, Marion Louise 1929- *WhoE 91*
Burgess, Martha Ames 1945- *WhoEmL 91*
Burgess, Mary Alice 1938- *WhoAm 90*
Burgess, Mary Ann 1937- *WhoAmW 91*
Burgess, Mary Elizabeth Schiding Warner 1932- *WhoWrEP 89*
Burgess, Mary Johannah 1925- *WhoAmW 91*
Burgess, Mary Ruth 1948- *WhoAmW 91*
Burgess, Mary Schiding 1932- *WhoAmW 91*
Burgess, May Ayres 1888-1953 *BioIn 16*
Burgess, Meredith Elaine 1925- *WhoSSW 91*
Burgess, Michael *AuBYP 90*, *BioIn 16*
Burgess, Michael 1914-1988 *SmATA X*
Burgess, Michael 1948- *WhoAm 90*, *WhoEmL 91*, *WhoWor 91*
Burgess, Myrtle Marie 1921- *WhoAmW 91*
Burgess, Patricia Ann 1938- *WhoAmW 91*
Burgess, Phillip M. 1963- *St&PR 91*
Burgess, Ralph K. 1926- *St&PR 91*
Burgess, Raymond Ulrich 1950- *WhoSSW 91*
Burgess, Richard B. 1943- *St&PR 91*
Burgess, Richard Ball 1943- *WhoAm 90*
Burgess, Richard Joseph 1931- *St&PR 91*
Burgess, Richard Ray 1942- *WhoAm 90*
Burgess, Robert Blundon, Jr. 1934- *WhoE 91*, *WhoWor 91*
Burgess, Robert Forrest 1927- *AuBYP 90*
Burgess, Robert Frederick, Jr. 1958- *WhoE 91*
Burgess, Robert K. 1944- *St&PR 91*, *WhoAm 90*
Burgess, Robert Kyle 1948- *WhoEmL 91*
Burgess, Robert Lester, Jr. 1949- *WhoSSW 91*
Burgess, Robert Lewis 1931- *WhoAm 90*
Burgess, Robert Ragsdale 1931- *St&PR 91*
Burgess, Robert S. 1950- *St&PR 91*
Burgess, Roger 1927- *WhoAm 90*
Burgess, Sally 1953- *IntWWM 90*
Burgess, Smoky 1927- *Ballpl 90*
Burgess, Susie Mae 1959- *WhoAmW 91*
Burgess, Suzette Carmen 1965- *WhoE 91*
Burgess, Thomas W. *St&PR 91*
Burgess, Thornton Waldo 1874-1965 *AuBYP 90*
Burgess, Trevor *TwCCr&M 91*
Burgess, Wayne T. 1942- *St&PR 91*
Burgess, Wayne Thomas 1942- *WhoAm 90*
Burgess, William H. *St&PR 91*
Burgess, William Patrick 1955- *WhoEmL 91*
Burgess Fongsam, Carole Sharon 1956- *WhoAmW 91*
Burget, Rosemarie 1957- *St&PR 91*
Burget, Vincent D. 1941- *St&PR 91*
Burgett, Dolores Mary 1935- *WhoAmW 91*
Burgett, Fern Marie 1956- *WhoEmL 91*
Burgett, William Brian 1951- *WhoAm 90*
Burggraf, Frank Bernard, Jr. 1932- *WhoAm 90*
Burggraf, Odus Roy 1929- *WhoAm 90*
Burggraf, Ray Lowell 1938- *WhoAmA 91*
Burghard, Sharon Laws 1946- *WhoWrEP 89*
Burghardt, Ann M. 1932- *St&PR 91*
Burghardt, Arthur N 1947?- *DrBlPA 90*
Burghardt, Jacob J. 1924- *St&PR 91*

Burghardt, Kurt Josef 1935- St&PR 91, WhoAm 90
Burghardt, Walter Francis, Jr. 1952- WhoEmL 91, WhoSSW 91, WhoWor 91
Burghart, James Henry 1938- WhoAm 90
Burghart, Philip 1926- St&PR 91
Burghauser, Jarmil Michael 1921- IntWWM 90
Burghley, Baron 1905-1981 DcNaB 1981
Burghoff, Gary WorAlBi
Burghoff, Gary 1943- ConTFT 8
Burghope, Maria BiDEWW
Burgie, Irving 1924- DrBlPA 90
Burgin, C. Rodgers 1899-1990 BioIn 16
Burgin, Christine BioIn 16
Burgin, E.J. 1927- St&PR 91
Burgin, E. J. 1927- WhoSSW 91
Burgin, George Hans 1930- WhoAm 90
Burgin, Richard Arlen 1944- WhoSSW 91
Burgin, Rick Allan 1963- WhoSSW 91
Burgin, Robert A., Jr. 1924- St&PR 91
Burgin, Robert Augustus 1924- WhoAm 90
Burgin, Robert Fleming, Jr. 1928- St&PR 91
Burgin, Victor 1941- BioIn 16
Burgin, Walter Hotchkiss, Jr. 1935- WhoE 91
Burgin Lister, Gabrielle 1946- IntWWM 90
Burgio, Jane WhoAm 90, WhoAmW 91, WhoE 91
Burgis, Hannah 1646-1704 BiDEWW
Burgis, William EncCRAm
Burgkmair, Hans 1473-1531? IntDcAA 90
Burglass, Milton Earl 1941- BiDrAPA 89
Burgman, Dierdre Ann 1948- WhoAmW 91, WhoE 91, WhoWor 91
Burgmeier, James Alphonse 1923- St&PR 91
Burgmeier, Tom 1943- Ballpl 90
Burgo, Janice Elizabeth 1938- WhoAmW 91
Burgon, Barre Glade 1950- WhoEmL 91
Burgon, Geoffrey 1941- PenDiMP A
Burgon, Geoffrey Alan 1941- IntWWM 90
Burgos, Carl 1917-1984 EncACom
Burgos, Dante Richard 1960- BiDrAPA 89
Burgos, Fernando 1927- WhoHisp 91
Burgos, Hector Hugo 1954- WhoSSW 91
Burgos, Hernan E BiDrAPA 89
Burgos, Joseph 1966- WhoHisp 91
Burgos, Joseph Agner, Jr. 1945- WhoHisp 91
Burgos, Julia de 1916-1953 BioIn 16
Burgos, Luis Noel 1963- WhoHisp 91
Burgos, Rafael Fruhbeck de PenDiMP
Burgos-Declet, Nilda BiDrAPA 89
Burgos Sequi, Carmen 1876-1933 EncCoWW
Burgot, Pierre EncO&P 3
Burgoyne, Alfred A. 1940- St&PR 91
Burgoyne, David S. Sr. 1923- BiDrAPA 89
Burgoyne, David Sidney, II 1947- BiDrAPA 89
Burgoyne, Edward Eynon 1918- WhoAm 90
Burgoyne, James Frederick 1936- St&PR 91
Burgoyne, John 1722-1792 EncCRAm, WhNaAH, WorAlBi
Burgoyne, Leon E. 1916- AuBYP 90
Burgoyne, Robert H 1920- BiDrAPA 89
Burgoyne, Rodney W 1934- BiDrAPA 89
Burgraff, Donna Lynn 1961- WhoSSW 91
Burgstresser, Richard Albert, Jr. 1954- WhoEmL 91
Burgues, Irving Carl 1906- WhoAmA 91
Burguieres, John B. 1922- St&PR 91
Burguieres, Philip Joseph 1943- St&PR 91, WhoAm 90, WhoSSW 91
Burgum, Bradley Joseph 1952- WhoEmL 91
Burgun, Guy I. 1941- St&PR 91
Burgun, J. Armand 1925- WhoE 91
Burgwin, George Collinson, III 1921- WhoE 91
Burhan, A. Michael 1956- St&PR 91
Burhans, Ira N. 1929- St&PR 91
Burhenne, Hans Joachim 1925- WhoAm 90, WhoWor 91
Burhoe, Brian Walter 1941- St&PR 91
Burhoe, Ralph Wendell 1911- WhoAm 90, WhoWor 91
Buria, Silvia 1940- WhoHisp 91
Burich, Virginia Mae 1948- WhoWrEP 89
Burick, Si 1909-1986 Ballpl 90
Burigana, Enus Anthony 1928- St&PR 91
Burine, Claude de 1933- EncCoWW
Burini, Sonia Montes de Oca 1935- WhoSSW 91
Burish, Ben Charles 1925- St&PR 91
Burk, A Darlene 1929- WhoAmA 91
Burk, A.R. WhoWrEP 89
Burk, Bernard Alan 1957- WhoEmL 91
Burk, Carl John 1935- WhoAm 90
Burk, Dana Prag 1960- WhoEmL 91
Burk, David Lynn 1944- St&PR 91, WhoAm 90
Burk, Dean 1904-1988 BioIn 16
Burk, Donald H BiDrAPA 89
Burk, Gary Maurice 1943- WhoE 91
Burk, Gloria Sax BiDrAPA 89
Burk, Joan Bednarz 1946- WhoSSW 91
Burk, Judy Ann 1955- BiDrAPA 89
Burk, Kathleen 1946- ConAu 130
Burk, Kenneth J. 1933- St&PR 91
Burk, Kenneth M. 1952- WhoEmL 91
Burk, Madge Bernadine 1924- WhoAmW 91
Burk, Martha Gertrude 1941- WhoAmW 91
Burk, Melvyn I. 1941- St&PR 91
Burk, Norman 1937- WhoAm 90
Burk, Sylvia Joan 1928- WhoAmW 91
Burka, Maria Karpati 1948- WhoAmW 91
Burkard, Michael 1947- ConAu 132
Burkard, Peter Hubert 1940- WhoWor 91
Burkart, Alan Ray 1930- WhoSSW 91
Burkart, Arnold Emil 1927- IntWWM 90
Burkart, Burke 1933- WhoAm 90
Burkart, Jordan Vincent 1935- St&PR 91
Burkart, Walter Mark 1921- WhoAm 90
Burkat, Leonard 1919- IntWWM 90
Burkdoll, Frank B. 1923- St&PR 91
Burke, Aedanus 1743-1802 BioIn 16, EncCRAm
Burke, Alexander James, Jr. 1931- WhoE 91
Burke, Anne 1785-1805 FemiCLE
Burke, Arnold D. 1938- St&PR 91
Burke, B. Meredith 1947- WhoAmW 91
Burke, Barbara ODwPR 91
Burke, Barbara 1860?-1941 FemiCLE
Burke, Barbara Clark 1953- WhoAmW 91
Burke, Barbara Florence 1935- WhoAmW 91
Burke, Beverly Gail 1952- WhoAmW 91
Burke, Bill WhoAmA 91
Burke, Billie 1885-1970 WorAlBi
Burke, Bobby 1907-1971 Ballpl 90
Burke, C. Kevin 1937- St&PR 91
Burke, Carol Elizabeth 1946- WhoWrEP 89
Burke, Charles Henry 1922- St&PR 91
Burke, Charles S 1954- BiDrAPA 89
Burke, Charles W. 1934- St&PR 91
Burke, Cheryl Lea 1963- WhoAmW 91
Burke, Chris BioIn 16
Burke, Chris 1965- ConTFT 8 [port]
Burke, Christine Eleanor 1948- WhoEmL 91
Burke, Christine Frances 1956- WhoAmW 91
Burke, Colleen 1943- FemiCLE
Burke, Daniel Barnett 1929- WhoAm 90, WhoE 91
Burke, Daniel Harold 1942- St&PR 91
Burke, Daniel Martin 1946- WhoWor 91
Burke, Daniel V 1942- WhoAmA 91
Burke, Daniel William 1926- WhoAm 90
Burke, David W. WhoAm 90, WhoE 91
Burke, Deborah Marie 1949- WhoE 91
Burke, Delta BioIn 16
Burke, Delta 1956- WorAlBi
Burke, Diana WhoWrEP 89
Burke, Donna B BiDrAPA 89
Burke, Donna Beisel 1938- ODwPR 91
Burke, Dorothy Joan Abel 1950- WhoE 91
Burke, E. Ainslie 1922- WhoAm 90
Burke, E Ainslie 1922- WhoAmA 91
Burke, Edgar Patrick 1944- WhoWrEP 89
Burke, Edmund 1729?-1797 BioIn 16, DcLB 104 [port], WorAlBi
Burke, Edmund Charles 1921- WhoAm 90
Burke, Edmund James, III 1949- WhoEmL 91
Burke, Edmund William 1912- WhoE 91
Burke, Edmund William 1948- St&PR 91, WhoAm 90
Burke, Edward A BiDrAPA 89
Burke, Edward Newell 1916- WhoE 91
Burke, Edward Walter, Jr. 1924- WhoSSW 91
Burke, Elizabeth H. Ferguson 1950- WhoEmL 91
Burke, Ellen Smith 1952- WhoAmW 91
Burke, Eugene F. 1926- ODwPR 91
Burke, Felton Gene 1941- WhoSSW 91
Burke, Frank Gerard 1927- WhoAm 90, WhoE 91
Burke, Frank Kaye 1932- WhoSSW 91
Burke, Franklin L. 1941- St&PR 91
Burke, Franklin Leigh 1941- WhoAm 90, WhoSSW 91
Burke, Gay Ann Wolesensky 1954- WhoEmL 91
Burke, George W BiDrAPA 89
Burke, Georgia 1878-1985 DrBlPA 90
Burke, Gerald F BiDrAPA 89
Burke, Gerald Michael 1944- St&PR 91
Burke, Gerald Thomas 1941- St&PR 91
Burke, Glenn 1952- Ballpl 90
Burke, Grace Reynolds 1925- WhoE 91
Burke, Halsey C. 1922- St&PR 91
Burke, Harry B. BiDrAPA 89
Burke, Inez M. EarBlAP
Burke, J. Grant 1943- WhoE 91
Burke, Jack Denning, Jr. 1948- BiDrAPA 89
Burke, Jack L. 1949- St&PR 91
Burke, Jacqueline Yvonne 1949- WhoAmW 91, WhoE 91, WhoEmL 91
Burke, James Donald 1939- WhoAm 90, WhoAmA 91
Burke, James E. BioIn 16
Burke, James Edward 1925- WhoE 91, WhoWor 91
Burke, James Gordon 1943- St&PR 91
Burke, James Joseph 1928- WhoAm 90
Burke, James Lee 1936- TwCCr&M 91, WhoWrEP 89
Burke, James R. 1938- St&PR 91
Burke, Jerome Clarence 1944- St&PR 91
Burke, Jimmy 1874-1942 Ballpl 90
Burke, Joanne BioIn 16
Burke, Joe 1884-1950 OxCPMus
Burke, Joel Howard 1961- St&PR 91
Burke, John 1922- TwCCr&M 91
Burke, John 1952- St&PR 91
Burke, John Arthur 1945- WhoEmL 91
Burke, John Burbidge 1949- WhoE 91
Burke, John Daniel 1947- WhoEmL 91
Burke, John David 1951- WhoWor 91
Burke, John Francis 1922- WhoAm 90, WhoE 91
Burke, John Garrett 1917- WhoAm 90
Burke, John James 1928- St&PR 91, WhoAm 90
Burke, John Miles 1938- WhoAm 90
Burke, John Philip 1954- WhoE 91
Burke, John T BioIn 16
Burke, John Thomas 1921- St&PR 91
Burke, Johnny 1908-1964 OxCPMus, WorAlBi
Burke, Joseph 1884-1950 BioIn 16
Burke, Joseph C. 1932- WhoAm 90
Burke, Joyce M. 1939- WhoAmW 91
Burke, Kathryn Bryant 1920 WhoAmW 91
Burke, Kelly Howard 1929- WhoAm 90
Burke, Kenneth 1897- BioIn 16, MajTwCW
Burke, Kerry 1942- WhoWor 91
Burke, Kevin Charles Antony 1929- WhoAm 90
Burke, Kevin Michael 1946- WhoEmL 91
Burke, Kevin Wayne BiDrAPA 89
Burke, Kevin Wayne 1956- WhoE 91
Burke, Kim Kenneth 1955- WhoEmL 91
Burke, Kirkland R. 1948- WhoEmL 91
Burke, Laurence Declan 1939- WhoWor 91
Burke, Laurence Gerard 1934- St&PR 91
Burke, Lawrence W. ODwPR 91
Burke, Lillian Walker 1917- WhoAm 90
Burke, Lucille Pennucci 1938- WhoAmW 91
Burke, Lynn AuBYP 90
Burke, Margaret Ann 1961- WhoAmW 91
Burke, Marian BioIn 16
Burke, Marjorie Hardman 1932- WhoAmW 91
Burke, Martha Jane 1852?-1903 WorAlBi
Burke, Mary BioIn 16
Burke, Mary 1959- St&PR 91
Burke, Mary Joan Thompson 1933- WhoAmW 91
Burke, Mary Thomas 1930- WhoAm 90
Burke, Mary Veronica 1945- WhoAmW 91
Burke, Michael Anthony BiDrAPA 89
Burke, Michael Donald 1944- St&PR 91, WhoAm 90
Burke, Michael Edmund 1942- WhoE 91
Burke, Michael Richard 1949- WhoEmL 91
Burke, Michael Thomas 1946- WhoSSW 91
Burke, Michelle Mary 1947- WhoAmW 91
Burke, Ned WhoWrEP 89
Burke, Noel TwCCr&M 91
Burke, Noel Ian 1939- WhoSSW 91
Burke, Patricia H. 1941- WhoAmW 91
Burke, Patrick Maurice 1946- BiDrAPA 89
Burke, Paul Bradford 1956- St&PR 91
Burke, Paul Edmund 1948- WhoE 91
Burke, Peter Arthur 1948- WhoAm 90
Burke, Peter F. 1951- ODwPR 91
Burke, Peter Frederick 1951- St&PR 91
Burke, Peter Michael 1948- WhoEmL 91
Burke, Philip George 1832- WhoWor 91
Burke, Ralph ConAu 130, MajTwCW
Burke, Raphael 1943- WhoWor 91
Burke, Raymond Daniel 1943- St&PR 91
Burke, Raymond W. WhoWrEP 89
Burke, Rebecca Lee 1951- WhoAmW 91
Burke, Redmond A. 1914- WhoAm 90
Burke, Richard J., Jr. 1940- WhoE 91
Burke, Richard Kitchens 1922- WhoAm 90
Burke, Richard Lawrence 1950- St&PR 91
Burke, Richard Sylvester 1932- WhoWor 91
Burke, Richard William 1933- WhoAm 90
Burke, Rita Hoffmann 1925- WhoE 91
Burke, Robert Dana 1954- WhoEmL 91
Burke, Robert Edward 1941- WhoAm 90
Burke, Robert Eugene 1921- WhoAm 90
Burke, Robert Harry 1945- WhoEmL 91, WhoWor 91
Burke, Robert James 1934- St&PR 91
Burke, Robert Lawrence 1916- St&PR 91
Burke, Robert O'Hara 1820-1861 BioIn 16
Burke, Roger M. 1930- St&PR 91
Burke, Rosann Margaret 1927- WhoAmW 91
Burke, Ruth 1933- WhoWrEP 89
Burke, Sean BioIn 16
Burke, Selma 1900- BioIn 16
Burke, Shawn Patrick 1958- WhoE 91
Burke, Shifty ConAu 31NR
Burke, Shirley BioIn 16
Burke, Solomon 194-?- EncPR&S 89
Burke, Stephen Richards 1938- St&PR 91
Burke, Thomas 1886-1945 TwCCr&M 91
Burke, Thomas E. 1930- ODwPR 91
Burke, Thomas Edmund 1932- WhoAm 90
Burke, Thomas F BiDrAPA 89
Burke, Thomas F. BioIn 16
Burke, Thomas Francis St&PR 91N
Burke, Thomas George 1947- WhoE 91
Burke, Thomas John 1947- WhoEmL 91, WhoWor 91
Burke, Thomas Joseph, Jr. 1941- WhoAm 90
Burke, Thomas Michael 1956- WhoEmL 91
Burke, Tim 1959- Ballpl 90, BioIn 16
Burke, Timothy Neal BiDrAPA 89
Burke, Timothy Robert BiDrAPA 89
Burke, Tom Clifton 1954- WhoEmL 91, WhoSSW 91
Burke, Virginia May 1933- WhoAmW 91
Burke, Wendy Jaye BiDrAPA 89
Burke, William A. BioIn 16
Burke, William B. BioIn 16
Burke, William James 1912- WhoAm 90
Burke, William John 1941- St&PR 91
Burke, William Joseph BiDrAPA 89
Burke, William Joseph, Jr. 1935- WhoE 91
Burke, William Lozier Munro 1906-1961 WhoAmA 91N
Burke, William Pat 1933- St&PR 91
Burke, William Temple, Jr. 1935- WhoAm 90
Burke, Yvette Marie 1965- WhoAmW 91, WhoEmL 91
Burke, Yvonne Brathwaite 1932- BlkAmsC [port]
Burke, Yvonne Watson Brathwaite 1932- WhoAm 90, WhoAmW 91
Burkee, Irvin 1918- WhoWor 91
Burkehart, Byron Cleveland 1947- St&PR 91
Burkemper, Richard John 1945- WhoE 91, WhoEmL 91
Burkemper, Ronald William 1950- WhoEmL 91
Burken, Ruth Marie 1956- WhoAmW 91, WhoEmL 91
Burker, Harry Snyvely, Jr. 1928- WhoAm 90, WhoSSW 91
Burkert, Robert Randall 1930- WhoAm 90, WhoAmA 91
Burkert, Walter 1931- WhoWor 91
Burkes, Jeffrey BioIn 16
Burkes, Leisa Jeanotta 1961- WhoAmW 91
Burkes, Lynn Joy BiDrAPA 89
Burkes, Lynn Joy 1945- WhoAmW 91, WhoE 91
Burkes, Sarah Beatrice 1948- WhoEmL 91
Burkes, William Sidney 1954- WhoEmL 91
Burket, David A. ODwPR 91
Burket, Gail Brook 1905- WhoAmW 91, WhoWor 91
Burket, George Edward, Jr. 1912- WhoAm 90
Burket, Harriet WhoAm 90, WhoWrEP 89
Burket, Richard Andrew 1925- St&PR 91
Burket, Richard E. 1928- St&PR 91
Burket, Richard Edward 1928- WhoAm 90
Burket, Roger Clair BiDrAPA 89
Burkett, Albert LeRoy 1897- WhoWor 91
Burkett, Cathy Crapps 1959- WhoAmW 91
Burkett, Charles William, IV 1961- WhoSSW 91
Burkett, David Ingram 1948- WhoEmL 91
Burkett, Deborah Ann 1951- St&PR 91
Burkett, Edward Eugene 1955- WhoEmL 91
Burkett, James Wendell 1930- St&PR 91
Burkett, Jesse 1868-1953 Ballpl 90 [port]
Burkett, Joe Wylie 1945- WhoWor 91
Burkett, John W BiDrAPA 89
Burkett, Joseph Hampton 1952- BiDrAPA 89
Burkett, Josephine Ruth 1927- WhoAmW 91
Burkett, Marvin Dan 1942- St&PR 91
Burkett, Rachelle Ann 1958- WhoSSW 91

Burkett, Randall Keith 1943- *WhoE 91*
Burkett, Randy James 1955- *WhoEmL 91*
Burkett, Robert E. 1954- *St&PR 91*
Burkett, Sam L., Jr. 1940- *St&PR 91*
Burkett, Steven Louis 1958- *WhoEmL 91*
Burkett, Thomas L. 1950- *St&PR 91*
Burkett, William A. 1913- *St&PR 91*
Burkett, William Andrew 1913- *WhoAm 90*
Burkey, Clarence L. 1928- *St&PR 91*
Burkey, J. Brent 1946- *St&PR 91*
Burkey, Jacob Brent 1946- *WhoAm 90, WhoEmL 91, WhoSSW 91*
Burkey, Lee Melville 1914- *WhoAm 90*
Burkey, Nancy A. *BiDrAPA 89*
Burkh, Dennis 1935- *IntWWM 90*
Burkhalter, Edward Hutcheson, Jr. 1949- *WhoEmL 91*
Burkhalter, Gary Allen 1955- *WhoSSW 91*
Burkhalter, James Clark 1939- *St&PR 91*
Burkhalter, Lela Merle 1947- *WhoAmW 91*
Burkhammer, Stewart Curtis 1943- *WhoE 91*
Burkhard, Michael Franz 1954- *WhoWor 91*
Burkhard, Oswald 1950- *WhoWor 91*
Burkhard, Paul 1911-1977 *OxCPMus*
Burkhardt, Andreas G. 1958- *St&PR 91*
Burkhardt, Bernhard G. 1959- *St&PR 91*
Burkhardt, Brent A. *ODwPR 91*
Burkhardt, Charles Henry 1915- *WhoE 91, WhoWor 91*
Burkhardt, Dolores Ann 1932- *WhoAmW 91*
Burkhardt, Eva G. 1930- *St&PR 91*
Burkhardt, Guenter H. 1931- *St&PR 91*
Burkhardt, Guenter M. 1963- *St&PR 91*
Burkhardt, Hans Gustav 1904- *WhoAmA 91*
Burkhardt, Lawrence, III 1932- *WhoAm 90*
Burkhardt, Peter Jon 1957- *WhoSSW 91*
Burkhardt, Richard Wellington 1918- *WhoAm 90*
Burkhardt, Robert F. 1936- *St&PR 91*
Burkhardt, Rolf 1920- *WhoWor 91*
Burkhardt, Ronald Robert 1948- *WhoEmL 91*
Burkhardt, Walter Heinrich 1928- *WhoWor 91*
Burkhart, Beverly Joanne 1947- *WhoAmW 91*
Burkhart, Bobbie Newman 1948- *WhoAmW 91*
Burkhart, Carole M. 1940- *WhoSSW 91*
Burkhart, Charles Barclay 1914- *WhoAm 90*
Burkhart, Craig Garrett 1951- *WhoAm 90*
Burkhart, D. Arthur 1956- *St&PR 91*
Burkhart, Deborah A. 1956- *WhoEmL 91*
Burkhart, Edward Allen 1959- *St&PR 91*
Burkhart, Elizabeth Flores 1935- *WhoHisp 91*
Burkhart, H. Z. *AmLegL*
Burkhart, Harold Eugene 1944- *WhoSSW 91*
Burkhart, Jo Ann Virginia 1926- *WhoWrEP 89*
Burkhart, John W. 1937- *St&PR 91*
Burkhart, Ken 1916- *Ballpl 90*
Burkhart, Linda Sue 1953- *WhoAmW 91*
Burkhart, Rinold W. 1946- *St&PR 91*
Burkhart, Robert Edward 1937- *WhoSSW 91, WhoWrEP 89*
Burkhead, Cheryl Elaine 1958- *WhoAmW 91*
Burkhead, James Gary 1941- *St&PR 91*
Burkhead, Jesse V. 1916- *WhoE 91*
Burkhead, Rebecca Rose 1959- *WhoEmL 91*
Burkholder, Donald Lyman 1927- *WhoAm 90*
Burkholder, J. Peter 1954- *IntWWM 90*
Burkholder, Joseph Mark 1956- *WhoEmL 91*
Burkholder, Mabel 1881-1973 *FemiCLE*
Burkholder, Martha Page *BiDrAPA 89*
Burkholder, Peter Miller 1933- *WhoAm 90*
Burkholder, Robert Stephen 1943- *WhoSSW 91*
Burkholder, Rosemary Rosenberger 1958- *WhoAmW 91*
Burkholder, Walter Edward 1945- *St&PR 91*
Burkholder, Wendell Eugene 1928- *WhoAm 90*
Burkholz, Herbert 1932- *SpyFic*
Burki, Fred Albert 1926- *WhoAm 90*
Burki, Patricia Delores 1945- *WhoE 91*
Burkin, Mary *WhoWrEP 89*
Burkins, John Andrew *BiDrAPA 89*
Burkins, John Andrew, Jr. 1949- *WhoE 91*
Burkitt, Denis Parsons 1911- *WhoWor 91*
Burkland, J. Bruce *ODwPR 91*
Burkle, Andrew C., Jr. 1943- *St&PR 91*
Burklund, Dale E. 1926- *St&PR 91*
Burkman, C. Herbert 1911- *St&PR 91*
Burkman, Ernest, Jr. 1929- *WhoSSW 91*
Burko, Diane 1945- *WhoAmA 91*
Burkoth, Terry Lee 1941- *St&PR 91*
Burkov, Anatoly 1972- *BioIn 16*
Burks, Andrew Charlie, Jr. 1950- *WhoSSW 91*
Burks, Arthur Walter 1915- *WhoAm 90*
Burks, Daniel Seamus 1942- *St&PR 91*
Burks, Ellis 1964- *Ballpl 90*
Burks, Frank E. 1946- *St&PR 91*
Burks, Graham Odell 1948- *St&PR 91*
Burks, Henry L *BiDrAPA 89*
Burks, Jack D. 1951- *WhoE 91*
Burks, Myrna R 1943- *WhoAmA 91*
Burks, Ramsey M. 1933- *St&PR 91*
Burks, Richard Thomas 1961- *WhoEmL 91*
Burks, Robert Ray 1953- *WhoSSW 91*
Burks, Thomas Franklin, II 1938- *WhoAm 90*
Burks, Verner Irwin 1923- *WhoAm 90*
Burks, William Burgess 1927- *WhoAm 90*
Burkstrand, C. Clayton 1934- *St&PR 91, WhoAm 90*
Burky, Howard F. 1920- *St&PR 91*
Burlage, James Edward 1934- *St&PR 91*
Burland, Brian Berkeley 1931- *AuBYP 90, WhoAm 90, WhoWor 91*
Burland, C A 1905-1983 *EncO&P 3*
Burland, Cottie Arthur 1905- *AuBYP 90*
Burland, J Alexis 1931- *BiDrAPA 89*
Burland, John Alexis 1931- *WhoE 91*
Burlant, William Jack 1928- *WhoAm 90*
Burlatskii, Fedor Mikhailovich *BioIn 16*
Burle-Marx, Roberto *BioIn 16*
Burle Marx, Roberto 1909- *ArtLatA*
Burleigh, Alvin 1842-1927 *AmLegL*
Burleigh, David Wayne 1953- *WhoE 91*
Burleigh, Harry T 1866-1949 *DrBlPA 90*
Burleigh, Henry Thacker 1866-1949 *DcAfAmP*
Burleigh, Joan Billger 1949- *WhoEmL 91*
Burleigh, Kimberly 1955- *WhoAmA 91*
Burleigh, Robert 1936- *BioIn 16*
Burleigh, William Robert 1935- *WhoAm 90*
Burles, Kenneth Thomas 1946- *WhoEmL 91*
Burleson, Albert Sidney 1863-1937 *BiDrUSE 89*
Burleson, Brant Raney 1952- *WhoEmL 91*
Burleson, Carolyn Odom 1942- *WhoAmW 91*
Burleson, Charles Trentman 1952- *WhoAmA 91*
Burleson, Claude Alfred 1924- *St&PR 91, WhoAm 90*
Burleson, Clay O. 1944- *St&PR 91*
Burleson, Karen Tripp 1955- *WhoAmW 91*
Burleson, Rick 1951- *Ballpl 90*
Burlew, John Swalm 1910- *WhoAm 90*
Burley, Alan John 1956- *WhoEmL 91*
Burley, Charles Frederick 1919- *St&PR 91*
Burley, Kathleen Mary 1942- *WhoWrEP 89*
Burley, Mark Alan 1951- *WhoEmL 91*
Burley, Nancy Tyler 1949- *WhoAmW 91*
Burley, W J 1914- *TwCCr&M 91*
Burlin, Paul 1886-1969 *WhoAmA 91N*
Burlin, Zerita G. 1921- *WhoAmW 91*
Burling, Irving Ray 1928- *St&PR 91*
Burling, James Sherman 1954- *WhoEmL 91*
Burling, Robbins 1926- *WhoAm 90*
Burlingame, Denise Onufrey 1953- *WhoAmW 91*
Burlingame, Edward Livermore 1935- *WhoAm 90*
Burlingame, Elizabeth Ann 1959- *WhoE 91*
Burlingame, Eugene Edward 1924- *St&PR 91*
Burlingame, Hal *BioIn 16*
Burlingame, James Montgomery, III 1926- *WhoSSW 91*
Burlingame, John Francis 1922- *WhoAm 90, WhoWor 91*
Burlingame, John Hunter 1933- *WhoAm 90*
Burlingame, Joseph P. 1858-1941 *AmLegL*
Burlingame, Leroy James 1929- *WhoAm 90*
Burlingame, Robert Kelley *BiDrAPA 89*
Burlingame, Roger 1889-1967 *AuBYP 90*
Burlingame, Roger Grinnell 1944- *WhoE 91*
Burlingham, Dorothy 1891-1979 *BioIn 16*
Burlington, Richard Boyle, Earl of 1694-1753 *BioIn 16*
Burlinson, Robert Francis 1939- *St&PR 91*
Burlton, Rogers C 1935- *BiDrAPA 89*
Burluik, David 1882-1967 *WhoAmA 91N*
Burm, Forrest H. 1930- *St&PR 91*
Burm, Forrest Henry 1930- *WhoAm 90*
Burman, Ben Lucien 1895-1984 *LiHiK*
Burman, Ben Lucien 1896-1984 *ConAu 32NR*
Burman, Beth Julianna 1912- *WhoAmW 91*
Burman, Daniel 1909-1989 *BioIn 16*
Burman, David John 1952- *WhoEmL 91*
Burman, DeeAnn Schaumberg 1949- *WhoEmL 91*
Burman, Diane Berger 1936- *WhoAmW 91*
Burman, Herman J. 1898-1988 *BioIn 16*
Burman, Julie Ann 1957- *WhoAmW 91*
Burman, Marsha Linkwald 1949- *WhoAmW 91, WhoEmL 91, WhoWor 91*
Burman, Marshall Lyle 1929- *St&PR 91*
Burman, Robert 1916- *St&PR 91*
Burman, Samuel Seidel 1902-1988 *BioIn 16*
Burman, Sneh Prabha *BiDrAPA 89*
Burmaster, M.R. 1934- *St&PR 91*
Burmaster, M. R. 1934- *WhoAm 90*
Burmeier, Frank *ODwPR 91*
Burmeister, Annelies 1929-1988 *AnObit 1988*
Burmeister, E.C. *St&PR 91*
Burmeister, Edwin 1939- *WhoAm 90*
Burmeister, James T. 1948- *St&PR 91*
Burmeister, John Luther 1938- *WhoAm 90, WhoE 91*
Burmeister, Jon 1933- *SpyFic*
Burmeister, Kristen Schnelle 1960- *WhoEmL 91*
Burmeister, Norman William 1939- *St&PR 91*
Burmeister, Paul Andrew 1952- *WhoE 91*
Burmeister, Tracy Lee 1942- *St&PR 91*
Burmer, Richard *NewAgMG*
Burmester, Pedro 1963- *IntWWM 90*
Burmester, Robert W. *BioIn 16*
Burmester, William Frederick 1923- *WhoWrEP 89*
Burn, Andrew David Haitly 1949- *IntWWM 90*
Burn, Charlene H 1934- *BiDrAPA 89*
Burn, Diane *BioIn 16*
Burn, Geoffrey Robert Forbes 1945- *WhoAm 90*
Burn, Ian John 1927- *WhoWor 91*
Burn, Lois Ann 1952- *WhoEmL 91*
Burn, Malcolm 1949- *WhoEmL 91*
Burn, William John 1851-1896 *DcCanB 12*
Burnam, Paul Wayne 1913- *WhoAm 90*
Burnam, Tom 1913- *WhoAm 90, WhoWor 91*
Burnap, Donald W 1941- *BiDrAPA 89*
Burnap, John B. 1918- *St&PR 91*
Burnash, Robert John Charles 1931- *WhoWor 91*
Burnat-Provins, Marguerite 1872-1952 *EncCoWW*
Burnbaum, Michael William 1949- *WhoEmL 91*
Burne-Jones, Edward 1833-1898 *IntDcAA 90, PenDiDA 89, WorAlBi*
Burne-Jones, Edward Coley 1833-1898 *BioIn 16*
Burnell, Bates Cavanaugh 1923- *WhoAm 90*
Burnell, Brian L. 1935- *St&PR 91*
Burnell, Elvin Wallace 1938- *WhoWrEP 89*
Burnell, George M 1930- *BiDrAPA 89*
Burnell, John T. *BioIn 16*
Burnell, Ransom 1831?-1880 *AmLegL*
Burnell, Susan Jocelyn Bell 1943- *BioIn 16*
Burnes, Carol Ganson 1942- *WhoWrEP 89*
Burnes, Edwin William 1924- *BiDrAPA 89*
Burnes, Fred N. 1929- *St&PR 91*
Burnes, Karen *BioIn 16*
Burnes, Kennett F. 1943- *St&PR 91*
Burnes, Kennett Farrar 1943- *WhoAm 90, WhoE 91*
Burnes, Linda Jane 1949- *WhoAmW 91*
Burness, Don 1941- *WhoWrEP 89*
Burness, Leonard 1910-1989 *BioIn 16*
Burness, Wallace B 1933- *WhoWrEP 89*
Burnet, David S 1921- *BiDrAPA 89*
Burnet, Elizabeth 1661-1709? *BiDEWW, BioIn 16, FemiCLE*
Burnet, Frank Macfarlane 1899-1985 *WorAlBi*
Burnet, George, Jr. 1924- *WhoAm 90*
Burnet, Gilbert 1643-1715 *DcLB 101 [port]*
Burnet, Jean R. 1920- *ConAu 130*
Burnet, Roger Hasted 1929- *WhoAm 90*
Burnet, William 1730-1791 *EncCRAm*
Burnett, Amy *BioIn 16*
Burnett, Anita M. 1965- *WhoSSW 91*
Burnett, Anne Berkeley Axton 1960- *WhoAmW 91*
Burnett, Anthony Thomas 1960- *BiDrAPA 89*
Burnett, Arthur Louis, Sr. 1935- *WhoAm 90*
Burnett, Barbara Ann 1927- *WhoAmA 91, WhoWor 91*
Burnett, Billie J. 1931- *St&PR 91*
Burnett, Brenda Bullock 1941- *WhoAmW 91*
Burnett, Calvin 1921- *WhoAmA 91*
Burnett, Calvin Wilks 1932- *WhoAm 90, WhoE 91*
Burnett, Carol *BioIn 16*
Burnett, Carol 1933- *ConTFT 8 [port], CurBio 90 [port], WorAlBi*
Burnett, Carol 1936- *WhoAm 90, WhoAmW 91*
Burnett, Charles *DrBlPA 90*
Burnett, Clarence Aubrey 1941- *WhoSSW 91, WhoWor 91*
Burnett, Claudia D. 1946- *St&PR 91*
Burnett, Constance 1893-1975 *AuBYP 90*
Burnett, Dan 1960- *BiDrAPA 89*
Burnett, David 1941- *WhoWor 91*
Burnett, David Alan 1946- *WhoAm 90*
Burnett, David Grant 1940- *WhoAmA 91*
Burnett, Deborah Becher 1949- *WhoAmW 91*
Burnett, Donald Lee, Jr. 1946- *WhoEmL 91*
Burnett, Durward A 1922- *BiDrAPA 89*
Burnett, Frances 1849-1924 *AuBYP 90, FemiCLE*
Burnett, Frances Eliza Hodgson 1849-1924 *NotWoAT, WorAlBi*
Burnett, Frances H. 1849-1924 *BioAmW*
Burnett, Frances Hodgson 1849-1924 *BioIn 16*
Burnett, Frederick William 1911- *St&PR 91*
Burnett, Gordon Arthur 1934- *St&PR 91*
Burnett, Gordon B 1937- *BiDrAPA 89*
Burnett, Grant A. *WhoAm 90*
Burnett, Helen *ODwPR 91*
Burnett, Henry 1927- *WhoAm 90*
Burnett, Henry Bowen *BioIn 16*
Burnett, Howard Jerome 1929- *WhoAm 90, WhoE 91*
Burnett, I. Compton- 1884-1969 *BioIn 16*
Burnett, James Randall, Jr. *BiDrAPA 89*
Burnett, James Robert 1925- *St&PR 91, WhoAm 90*
Burnett, James Rufus 1949- *WhoEmL 91*
Burnett, John Thomas 1931- *St&PR 91*
Burnett, Johnny 1904-1959 *Ballpl 90*
Burnett, Leo 1891-1971 *ConAmBL*
Burnett, Lonnie Sheldon 1927- *WhoAm 90*
Burnett, Lowell Jay 1941- *WhoAm 90*
Burnett, Lynn Barkley 1948- *WhoWor 91*
Burnett, Mark Thornton 1961- *WhoWor 91*
Burnett, Mary Parham 1956- *WhoEmL 91*
Burnett, Michele Marie 1956- *WhoEmL 91*
Burnett, Patricia Hill *WhoAmA 91*
Burnett, R. Curtis 1947- *ODwPR 91*
Burnett, Richard *BiDrAPA 89*
Burnett, Richard 1932- *PenDiMP*
Burnett, Rita Marline 1954- *WhoAmW 91*
Burnett, Robert A. 1927- *St&PR 91, WhoAm 90*
Burnett, Robert Adair 1934- *WhoAm 90*
Burnett, Robert Lawrence 1948- *WhoSSW 91*
Burnett, Robert Sherwin 1940- *St&PR 91*
Burnett, Rosa Scott 1945- *WhoSSW 91*
Burnett, Steven Wayne 1953- *WhoSSW 91*
Burnett, Susan Walk 1946- *WhoAmW 91*
Burnett, T-Bone *BioIn 16*
Burnett, W.E., Jr. 1927- *St&PR 91*
Burnett, W R 1899-1982 *TwCCr&M 91*
Burnett, William Earl, Jr. 1927- *WhoSSW 91*
Burnett-Zeisel, Hallie Southgate 1907- *WhoAm 90*
Burnette, Deborah Ann Bullock 1951- *WhoAm 90*
Burnette, Donald G. 1931- *St&PR 91*
Burnette, Donald Gray 1931- *WhoAm 90*
Burnette, Dorsey 1933-1979 *EncPR&S 89*
Burnette, Edward L. 1930- *St&PR 91*
Burnette, Guy Ellington, Jr. 1952- *WhoEmL 91*
Burnette, Ikey Scott 1960- *WhoEmL 91, WhoSSW 91, WhoWor 91*
Burnette, Joe Edward 1918- *WhoSSW 91*
Burnette, Johnny *EncPR&S 89*
Burnette, Johnny 1934-1964 *OxCPMus*
Burnette, Mary Malissa 1950- *WhoEmL 91*
Burnette, Ollen Lawrence, Jr. 1927- *WhoSSW 91*
Burnette, Ralph Edwin, Jr. 1953- *WhoEmL 91*
Burnette, Wally 1929- *Ballpl 90*
Burney, Andrea Joyce 1953- *WhoAmW 91*
Burney, Carol Lee 1963- *WhoSSW 91*
Burney, Derek *BioIn 16*
Burney, Derek H. 1939- *WhoAm 90, WhoWor 91*
Burney, Fanny 1752-1840 *BioIn 16, WorAlBi*
Burney, Frances 1752-1840 *FemiCLE*
Burney, Frank Burleson 1954- *WhoEmL 91*
Burney, Minna 1891-1958 *WhoAmA 91N*
Burney, Sarah Harriet 1772-1844 *BioIn 16, FemiCLE*
Burney, Victoria Kalgaard 1943- *WhoAmW 91*
Burnford, Sheila 1918-1984 *AuBYP 90, FemiCLE*

Burnham, Alan 1913- *WhoAm 90*
Burnham, Alfred Avery 1819-1879 *AmLegL*
Burnham, Bonnie 1947- *WhoAm 90*
Burnham, Bryson Paine 1917- *WhoAm 90*
Burnham, Cardon Vern 1927- *IntWWM 90*
Burnham, Charles *ConAu 31NR*
Burnham, Charles Wilson 1933- *WhoAm 90*
Burnham, Christine Elizabeth 1958- *St&PR 91*
Burnham, Crispin Reed 1949- *WhoWrEP 89*
Burnham, Daniel H. 1846-1912 *WorAlBi*
Burnham, Daniel Patrick 1946- *St&PR 91*, *WhoAm 90*
Burnham, David Bright 1933- *WhoAm 90*
Burnham, Donald Clemens 1915- *WhoAm 90*
Burnham, Donald L 1922- *BiDrAPA 89*
Burnham, Douglass Lawrence 1932- *St&PR 91*
Burnham, Duane L. 1942- *St&PR 91*
Burnham, Duane Lee 1942- *WhoAm 90*
Burnham, Forbes 1923-1985 *BioIn 16*
Burnham, Gregory Alan 1954- *WhoWrEP 89*
Burnham, Harold Arthur 1929- *WhoAm 90*, *WhoE 91*, *WhoWor 91*
Burnham, I.W., II 1909- *St&PR 91*
Burnham, Jack Wesley 1931- *WhoAmA 91*
Burnham, James 1905-1987 *BioIn 16*
Burnham, Jane *BioIn 16*
Burnham, Jed James 1944- *St&PR 91*, *WhoAm 90*
Burnham, John Chynoweth 1929- *WhoAm 90*
Burnham, John Robert 1938- *BiDrAPA 89*
Burnham, Lem 1947- *WhoEmL 91*
Burnham, Linden Forbes Sampson 1923-1985 *BioIn 16*
Burnham, Norma Sue 1934- *WhoSSW 91*
Burnham, Norman James 1951- *WhoEmL 91*
Burnham, Patricia White 1933- *WhoAmW 91*
Burnham, Robert Alan 1928- *WhoE 91*
Burnham, Robert C. 1915- *BiDrAPA 89*
Burnham, Robert Danner 1944- *WhoAm 90*
Burnham, Robert J. 1930- *St&PR 91*
Burnham, Sheila Kay 1955- *WhoAmW 91*, *WhoEmL 91*
Burnham, Sophy *WhoWrEP 89*
Burnham, Sophy 1936- *WhoAmW 91*
Burnham, Stephen John 1948- *WhoEmL 91*
Burnham, Steven James 1947- *WhoEmL 91*
Burnham, Virginia G.S. 1908- *St&PR 91*
Burnham, Walter Dean 1930- *WhoAm 90*
Burnieika, Joseph J., Jr. 1946- *ODwPR 91*
Burnier, Andreas *EncCoWW*
Burnim, Kalman Aaron 1928- *WhoAm 90*
Burningham, John 1936- *BioIn 16*
Burnison, Boyd Edward 1934- *WhoAm 90*, *WhoWor 91*
Burniston, Karen Sue 1939- *WhoAmW 91*
Burnley, Jack 1911- *EncACom*
Burnley, James Horace 1948- *BioIn 16*
Burnley, James Horace, IV 1948- *BiDrUSE 89*
Burno, Juanita Bundy 1935- *WhoE 91*
Burns, Aaron 1922- *ConDes 90*
Burns, Alan 1929- *WhoWrEP 89*
Burns, Alexander 1834-1900 *DcCanB 12*
Burns, Alexandra Darrow 1946- *WhoEmL 91*
Burns, Anneliese 1965- *WhoE 91*, *WhoEmL 91*
Burns, Anthony 1834-1862 *BioIn 16*
Burns, Arnold Irwin 1930- *St&PR 91*, *WhoE 91*
Burns, Arthur F. 1904-1987 *BioIn 16*, *EncABHB 7 [port]*, *WorAlBi*
Burns, Arthur Lee 1924- *WhoAm 90*, *WhoSSW 91*
Burns, Barbara Ann Mays 1951- *WhoAmW 91*
Burns, Barbara Belton 1944- *WhoAmW 91*
Burns, Barbara M. 1929- *WhoAmW 91*
Burns, Benjamin Joseph 1940- *WhoAm 90*
Burns, Beverly K. 1948- *St&PR 91*
Burns, Bill *BioIn 16*
Burns, Bill 1880-1953 *Ballpl 90*
Burns, Brian Patrick 1936- *WhoAm 90*
Burns, Brian Patrick 1962- *WhoE 91*
Burns, Britt 1959- *Ballpl 90*
Burns, Bushrod W. 1933- *St&PR 91*
Burns, Carol J. 1954- *WhoAmW 91*, *WhoEmL 91*
Burns, Carroll Dean 1932- *St&PR 91*, *WhoAm 90*
Burns, Catherine Elizabeth 1953- *WhoAmW 91*, *WhoEmL 91*
Burns, Chalmers 1906- *IntWWM 90*
Burns, Charles Patrick 1937- *WhoAm 90*
Burns, Charles Sloan 1926- *St&PR 91*
Burns, Conrad Ray 1935- *WhoAm 90*, *WhoWor 91*
Burns, Cornelius 1951- *WhoWor 91*
Burns, Dan 1925- *St&PR 91*
Burns, Dan W. 1925- *WhoAm 90*, *WhoWor 91*
Burns, Daniel B. 1932- *St&PR 91*
Burns, Daniel Hobart 1928- *WhoWor 91*
Burns, Daniel J. 1941- *St&PR 91*
Burns, Daniel K. 1956- *St&PR 91*
Burns, David *BioIn 16*
Burns, David 1902-1971 *OxCPMus*
Burns, David Alvin *BiDrAPA 89*
Burns, David Craig 1949- *WhoEmL 91*
Burns, David Dean 1942- *BiDrAPA 89*
Burns, David Harrison 1946- *WhoE 91*
Burns, David Michael 1953- *WhoSSW 91*
Burns, David Mitchell 1928- *WhoAm 90*
Burns, David Russell 1941- *BiDrAPA 89*
Burns, Deborah Denise 1953- *WhoAmW 91*
Burns, Dennis Raymond 1943- *WhoE 91*
Burns, Donald E. 1939- *St&PR 91*
Burns, Douglas Foster 1940- *St&PR 91*
Burns, Ed 1891-1955 *Ballpl 90*
Burns, Eddie Owen 1960- *WhoEmL 91*
Burns, Edward Bradford 1932- *WhoAm 90*
Burns, Edward William 1953- *WhoE 91*
Burns, Elizabeth Ann 1949- *WhoEmL 91*
Burns, Elizabeth Mary 1927- *WhoAm 90*
Burns, Ellen Bree 1923- *WhoAm 90*, *WhoAmW 91*, *WhoE 91*
Burns, Florence M 1905-1988 *SmATA 61*
Burns, G Creswell *BiDrAPA 89*
Burns, G Joan 1918- *WhoAmA 91*
Burns, Gene Alton 1925- *St&PR 91*
Burns, George 1889-1966 *Ballpl 90 [port]*
Burns, George 1893-1978 *Ballpl 90 [port]*
Burns, George 1896- *BioIn 16*, *WhoAm 90*, *WorAlBi*
Burns, George Washington 1913- *WhoAm 90*
Burns, Gerald Patrick 1940- *WhoWrEP 89*
Burns, Gerald Phillip 1918- *WhoAm 90*
Burns, Glenn Richard 1951- *WhoEmL 91*, *WhoWor 91*
Burns, Glenna Marie 1928- *WhoAmW 91*
Burns, Grant Francis 1947- *WhoEmL 91*
Burns, H. Michael 1937- *WhoAm 90*
Burns, Harlan Allen 1934- *St&PR 91*
Burns, Harmon E. 1945- *St&PR 91*
Burns, Harrison D 1946- *WhoAmA 91*
Burns, Harry A. 1943- *St&PR 91*
Burns, Heather Lee 1951- *WhoEmL 91*
Burns, Helen R *BiDrAPA 89*
Burns, Helene Barbara 1953- *WhoAmW 91*
Burns, Henry Thomas 1893-1989 *BioIn 16*
Burns, Ikuko Kawai 1936- *WhoWor 91*
Burns, Ivan Alfred 1935- *St&PR 91*, *WhoAm 90*
Burns, Jack 1907-1975 *Ballpl 90*
Burns, Jack Hancock 1920- *WhoAm 90*
Burns, Jacqueline 1927- *WhoAmW 91*
Burns, James *EncO&P 3*
Burns, James Francis 1937- *St&PR 91*
Burns, James John 1933- *WhoAm 90*
Burns, James Joseph 1929- *St&PR 91*
Burns, James MacGregor 1918- *WhoAm 90*
Burns, James W. 1929- *St&PR 91*
Burns, James William 1929- *WhoAm 90*
Burns, Jan Marie 1953- *WhoSSW 91*
Burns, Janet Claire 1961- *WhoEmL 91*
Burns, Jeff *BioIn 16*
Burns, Jeffrey Robert 1956- *WhoEmL 91*
Burns, Jere *BioIn 16*
Burns, Jerome 1919- *WhoAmA 91*
Burns, Jerry *BioIn 16*
Burns, Jerry 1927- *WhoAm 90*
Burns, Jethro 1920-1989 *AnObit 1989*
Burns, Joan Coulon 1921- *WhoAmW 91*
Burns, Joel Dennis 1951- *WhoEmL 91*
Burns, John 1904- *St&PR 91*
Burns, John Andrew 1928-1989 *BioIn 16*
Burns, John Dudley 1933- *St&PR 91*, *WhoAm 90*, *WhoSSW 91*
Burns, John Edward, III 1951- *St&PR 91*
Burns, John Joseph 1920- *WhoAm 90*
Burns, John Joseph 1924- *WhoAm 90*, *WhoWor 91*
Burns, John Joseph, Jr. 1931- *WhoAm 90*, *WhoE 91*
Burns, John Lawrence 1908- *St&PR 91*, *WhoAm 90*
Burns, John MacDougal, III 1933- *WhoAm 90*
Burns, John Michael 1946- *WhoEmL 91*
Burns, John Michael 1960- *WhoEmL 91*
Burns, John Scott 1947- *WhoAm 90*
Burns, John Terence 1943- *St&PR 91*
Burns, John Thomas 1943- *WhoSSW 91*
Burns, John Tolman 1922- *WhoAm 90*
Burns, Joseph Arthur 1941- *WhoAm 90*
Burns, Joseph Dennis 1940- *St&PR 91*
Burns, Joseph William 1908- *WhoAm 90*
Burns, Josephine 1917- *WhoAmA 91*
Burns, Julia Wilkerson *BiDrAPA 89*
Burns, Kathleen Joyce 1953- *WhoAmW 91*
Burns, Kathryn Ann 1957- *BiDrAPA 89*
Burns, Kathryn Anne 1948- *WhoWor 91*
Burns, Kathryn VanAken 1891-1987 *BioIn 16*
Burns, Kay *BioIn 16*
Burns, Keith R. 1956- *WhoEmL 91*
Burns, Kennedy Francis 1842-1895 *DcCanB 12*
Burns, Kenneth C. 1920-1989 *BioIn 16*
Burns, Kenneth Dean 1930- *WhoAm 90*
Burns, Kenneth Harold 1929- *WhoSSW 91*
Burns, Kenneth Jones, Jr. 1926- *St&PR 91*, *WhoAm 90*
Burns, Kenneth L *BiDrAPA 89*
Burns, Kerry Lee 1959- *WhoE 91*
Burns, Larry Kenneth 1947- *St&PR 91*
Burns, Latham C. 1930- *St&PR 91*
Burns, Lawrence Aloysius, Jr. 1949- *WhoEmL 91*
Burns, Lawrence R. 1927- *St&PR 91*
Burns, Lisa 1956- *ODwPR 91*
Burns, Lucy Denise 1956- *WhoAmW 91*
Burns, M. Anthony 1942- *St&PR 91*
Burns, Margaret V *BiDrAPA 89*
Burns, Marian Law 1954- *WhoAmW 91*
Burns, Mark A 1950- *WhoAmA 91*
Burns, Marsha 1945- *WhoAmA 91*
Burns, Martin L. 1933- *St&PR 91*
Burns, Marvin Gerald 1930- *WhoAm 90*, *WhoWor 91*
Burns, Mary Blum *WhoSSW 91*
Burns, Mary Elizabeth 1946- *WhoEmL 91*
Burns, Mary Frances 1949- *WhoSSW 91*
Burns, Michael Joseph 1943- *WhoAm 90*
Burns, Michael Keith 1940- *WhoE 91*
Burns, Michele 1960- *WhoAmW 91*
Burns, Mitchel Anthony 1942- *WhoAm 90*, *WhoSSW 91*
Burns, Muriel 1933- *St&PR 91*
Burns, Nancy Ann 1936- *WhoSSW 91*
Burns, Ned Hamilton 1932- *WhoAm 90*
Burns, Norma DeCamp 1940- *WhoAmW 91*
Burns, Olive Ann *NewYTBS 90*
Burns, Olive Ann 1924-1990 *ConAu 132*
Burns, Oliver B., Jr. 1930- *St&PR 91*
Burns, Oyster 1864-1928 *Ballpl 90*
Burns, Padraic 1929- *BiDrAPA 89*, *WhoAm 90*
Burns, Pat *BioIn 16*
Burns, Pat 1952- *WhoAm 90*, *WhoE 91*
Burns, Pat Ackerman Gonia 1938- *WhoAmW 91*
Burns, Patout, Jr. 1939- *WhoAm 90*
Burns, Patricia Henrietta 1934- *WhoWrEP 89*
Burns, Patti *BioIn 16*
Burns, Paul M. 1949- *St&PR 91*
Burns, Peter 1949- *WhoSSW 91*
Burns, Phyllis Ann 1935- *WhoWrEP 89*
Burns, Ralph M. 1916- *St&PR 91*
Burns, Raymond E. 1952- *St&PR 91*
Burns, Rebecca Ann 1946- *WhoE 91*
Burns, Rex 1935- *TwCCr&M 91*
Burns, Richard Dale 1955- *WhoE 91*
Burns, Richard Dean 1929- *WhoAm 90*
Burns, Richard Keith 1935- *WhoWrEP 89*
Burns, Richard Lee 1951- *BiDrAPA 89*
Burns, Richard Michael 1937- *St&PR 91*, *WhoAm 90*
Burns, Richard Ramsey 1946- *WhoEmL 91*
Burns, Robert 1759-1796 *BioIn 16*, *WorAlBi*
Burns, Robert, Jr. 1936- *WhoSSW 91*
Burns, Robert A. *ODwPR 91*
Burns, Robert Crawford 1962- *WhoSSW 91*
Burns, Robert E. *BioIn 16*
Burns, Robert Edward 1919- *WhoAm 90*, *WhoWor 91*, *WhoWrEP 89*
Burns, Robert Edward 1953- *WhoEmL 91*
Burns, Robert Francis 1928- *WhoAm 90*
Burns, Robert Henry 1929- *WhoAm 90*
Burns, Robert Ignatius 1921- *WhoAm 90*
Burns, Robert Michael 1938- *WhoWor 91*
Burns, Robert Paschal 1933- *WhoAm 90*
Burns, Robert Patrick 1947- *WhoAm 90*, *WhoEmL 91*
Burns, Robertta Jean 1949- *WhoAmW 91*
Burns, Robin *WhoAmW 91*
Burns, Robin 1953?- *News 91-2*
Burns, Roger George 1937- *WhoAm 90*
Burns, Ronald James 1937- *WhoAm 90*
Burns, Ruth Ann Mary 1944- *WhoAmW 91*
Burns, Sally Ann 1959- *WhoAmW 91*
Burns, Sharon Ryan 1957- *WhoAmW 91*
Burns, Sheila *WhoAmA 91*
Burns, Sid 1916-1979 *WhoAmA 91N*
Burns, Stan *WhoAmA 91*
Burns, Stan Z. *NewYTBS 90*
Burns, Stephen James 1939- *WhoAm 90*
Burns, Stephen John 1945- *BiDrAPA 89*
Burns, Steven Dwight 1948- *WhoEmL 91*
Burns, Stuart L 1932- *WhoWrEP 89*
Burns, Terrence Michael 1954- *WhoEmL 91*
Burns, Tex *MajTwCW*
Burns, Tex 1908-1988 *BioIn 16*
Burns, Thagrus Asher 1917- *WhoAm 90*
Burns, Thomas C. 1928- *St&PR 91*, *WhoSSW 91*
Burns, Thomas David 1921- *WhoAm 90*
Burns, Thomas G. 1940- *St&PR 91*
Burns, Thomas J. 1945- *St&PR 91*
Burns, Thomas Samuel 1945- *WhoAm 90*
Burns, Thomas Wade 1924- *WhoAm 90*
Burns, Todd 1963- *Ballpl 90*
Burns, Vicki Hill 1949- *WhoAmW 91*
Burns, Virginia Law 1925- *WhoAmW 91*, *WhoWrEP 89*
Burns, Ward 1928- *WhoAm 90*
Burns, Wayne D. *St&PR 91*
Burns, William *AmLegL*
Burns, William A. 1909- *WhoAm 90*
Burns, William Aloysius 1909- *AuBYP 90*
Burns, William Glenn 1949- *WhoEmL 91*
Burns, William Goodykoontz 1935- *WhoSSW 91*
Burns, William J. 1861-1932 *WorAlBi*
Burns, William Loomis, Jr. 1928- *St&PR 91*
Burns, William O. 1930- *St&PR 91*, *WhoAm 90*
Burns-Love, Darlene Louise 1959- *WhoAmW 91*
Burnshaw, Stanley 1906- *WhoAm 90*
Burnshide, Katherine Talbott *WhoAmA 91N*
Burnside, Ambrose 1824-1881 *WorAlBi*
Burnside, Barbara *ODwPR 91*
Burnside, Cameron 1887-1952 *WhoAmA 91N*
Burnside, Iain *IntWWM 90*
Burnside, John Charles 1952- *BiDrAPA 89*
Burnside, John Wayne 1941- *WhoAm 90*
Burnside, Madeleine Hilding 1948- *WhoAmA 91*, *WhoE 91*
Burnside, Mary Beth 1943- *WhoAm 90*
Burnside, Orvin Charles 1932- *WhoAm 90*
Burnside, Pete 1930- *Ballpl 90*
Burnside, Richard 1944- *MusmAFA*
Burnside, Waldo Howard 1928- *St&PR 91*
Burnstan, Rowland, Jr. 1931- *WhoAm 90*
Burnstein, Daniel 1946- *WhoWor 91*
Burnstein, Frances 1935- *WhoAmW 91*, *WhoE 91*
Burnstein, Jack D. 1947- *St&PR 91*
Burnstein, Michael H 1947- *BiDrAPA 89*
Burnstein, Michael Harrison 1947- *WhoEmL 91*
Burnstein, Robert Steven *BiDrAPA 89*
Burnsworth, Charles Carl 1931- *IntWWM 90*
Burnum Burnum *BioIn 16*
Buroker, Robert M. 1938- *St&PR 91*
Buros, Luella *WhoAmA 91*
Buroughs, Edward Elliott 1951- *WhoEmL 91*
Burpee, David 1893-1980 *WorAlBi*
Burpee, James Stanley 1938- *WhoAmA 91*
Burpee, Robert E. *St&PR 91*
Burpee, Washington A. 1858-1915 *WorAlBi*
Burpo, Christopher William 1946- *WhoSSW 91*
Burquest, Bret *BiDrAPA 89*
Burr, Aaron 1756-1836 *BiDrUSE 89*, *EncCRAm [port]*, *WorAlBi*
Burr, Alan Carleton 1926- *St&PR 91*
Burr, Anna Robeson 1873-1941 *FemiCLE*
Burr, Barbara Hertz 1944- *BiDrAPA 89*
Burr, Borden H., II 1937- *St&PR 91*
Burr, Carleton 1921- *St&PR 91*
Burr, Craig Lee 1945- *St&PR 91*, *WhoEmL 91*
Burr, Donald C. *BioIn 16*
Burr, Donald Calvin 1941- *ConAmBL*, *WhoE 91*
Burr, Donald D *NewYTBS 90*
Burr, Donald D. 1923-1990 *BioIn 16*
Burr, Edward B. 1923- *St&PR 91*
Burr, Edward Benjamin 1923- *WhoAm 90*
Burr, Esther 1732-1758 *FemiCLE*
Burr, Esther Edwards 1732-1758 *EncCRAm*
Burr, Francis H. 1914- *St&PR 91*
Burr, Francis Hardon 1914- *WhoAm 90*, *WhoWor 91*
Burr, Frank W. 1932- *St&PR 91*
Burr, George Oswald 1896- *BioIn 16*
Burr, Gladys *BioIn 16*
Burr, Gray 1919- *WhoWrEP 89*
Burr, Harry Lawson, III 1952- *WhoSSW 91*
Burr, Henry I. 1928- *St&PR 91*
Burr, Horace 1912- *WhoAmA 91*
Burr, James Hugh 1948- *St&PR 91*
Burr, Jeffrey Lynn 1952- *WhoEmL 91*
Burr, John C *BiDrAPA 89*
Burr, John Roy 1933- *WhoAm 90*
Burr, Laurie Diane 1953- *WhoAmW 91*
Burr, Lonnie 1943- *BioIn 16*
Burr, Michael Dean 1965- *WhoE 91*

Burr, Patricia Allyn 1950- *St&PR 91*
Burr, Raymond *BioIn 16*
Burr, Raymond 1917- *WhoAm 90, WorAlBi*
Burr, Richard Marshall 1943- *WhoE 91*
Burr, Robert 1936- *St&PR 91*
Burr, Robert Corbin *BiDrAPA 89*
Burr, Robert Lyndon 1944- *WhoAm 90*
Burr, Stanley A. 1943- *St&PR 91*
Burr, Theodosia 1783-1813 *BioAmW*
Burr, Thomas M. 1942- *St&PR 91*
Burr, Timothy Fuller 1952- *WhoSSW 91*
Burr, Winthrop Ames 1943- *BiDrAPA 89*
Burrall, John Patrick 1933- *St&PR 91*
Burrchett, Sandy Sue Curtis 1942- *WhoSSW 91*
Burrell, Abraham Lincoln, Jr. 1951- *WhoSSW 91*
Burrell, Arthur Brotherton 1902-1987 *BioIn 16*
Burrell, Barbara 1941- *WhoAm 90*
Burrell, Craig Donald 1926- *WhoAm 90, WhoWor 91*
Burrell, David Bakewell 1933- *WhoAm 90*
Burrell, Donald James 1936- *WhoWor 91*
Burrell, Jay Robert 1956- *WhoEmL 91*
Burrell, Kenneth Earl 1931- *WhoAm 90*
Burrell, Kenny *BioIn 16*
Burrell, Kenny 1931- *DrBIPA 90*
Burrell, Lizabeth Lorie 1952- *WhoEmL 91*
Burrell, Nancy Bradbury 1948- *WhoWrEP 89*
Burrell, Regina Holbrook 1936- *WhoSSW 91*
Burrell, Sidney Alexander 1917- *WhoAm 90*
Burrell, Sophia 1750?-1802 *FemiCLE*
Burrell, Stephen Clark 1942- *St&PR 91*
Burrell, Thomas J. *WhoAm 90*
Burrell, Thomas J. 1939- *ConAmBL*
Burrell, Walter, Jr. 1944- *DrBIPA 90*
Burrell, Wendy *ODwPR 91*
Burress, James Russell 1913- *WhoAm 90*
Burress, Kenneth R. 1934- *St&PR 91*
Burress, Robert C. 1938- *St&PR 91*
Burri, Alberto 1915- *BioIn 16*
Burri, Barbara Anne 1953- *WhoAmW 91*
Burri, Betty Jane 1955- *WhoEmL 91*
Burri, Rosmarie 1944- *IntWWM 90*
Burrichter, Ernst 1921- *WhoWor 91*
Burrichter, Robert 1955- *ODwPR 91*
Burridge, H.J. 1930- *St&PR 91*
Burrier, Gail Warren 1927- *WhoWor 91*
Burrill, Janice Hilary 1957- *WhoEmL 91*
Burrill, Kathleen R. F. 1924- *WhoAm 90, WhoE 91*
Burrill, Mary *BiDEWW*
Burrill, Mary 1879-1946 *EarBlAP*
Burrill, Mary 1882?-1946 *HarlReB*
Burrill, Melinda Jane 1947- *WhoEmL 91*
Burrill, William George, Jr. *WhoAm 90*
Burrington, David Edson 1931- *WhoAm 90*
Burris, Ada Mae A 1932- *BiDrAPA 89*
Burris, Andrew M. *EarBlAP*
Burris, Arthur B. 1925- *BiDrAPA 89*
Burris, B Cullen 1924- *BiDrAPA 89*
Burris, B. Cullen 1924- *WhoAm 90*
Burris, Barbara Diane 1941- *WhoE 91*
Burris, Betty Price 1942- *WhoAmW 91*
Burris, Bill Buchanan, Jr. 1957- *WhoE 91*
Burris, Boyd Lee *BiDrAPA 89*
Burris, Bruce 1955- *MusmAFA*
Burris, Conrad Timothy 1924- *WhoAm 90*
Burris, Frances White 1933- *WhoAmW 91*
Burris, Harriett Coleman 1920- *WhoAmW 91*
Burris, John Taylor 1828-1915 *AmLegL*
Burris, Johnny Clark 1953- *WhoEmL 91*
Burris, Joseph Stephen 1942- *WhoAm 90*
Burris, Kathryn Ann 1957- *WhoAmW 91*
Burris, Lauren Bayleran 1952- *WhoAmW 91*
Burris, Paul D. *St&PR 91*
Burris, Ray 1950- *Ballpl 90*
Burris, Robert E. 1937- *St&PR 91*
Burris, Robert Harza 1914- *WhoAm 90*
Burris, Shirley Kay 1940- *WhoAmW 91*
Burris, Steven Michael 1952- *WhoWor 91*
Burris, Thelma Ruth 1921- *WhoWrEP 89*
Burris, Wayne Scott 1955- *BiDrAPA 89*
Burriss, R Hal 1892- *WhoAmA 91*
Burriss, William C. 1921- *St&PR 91*
Burritt, Richard D. *BioIn 16*
Burritt, Victor S. 1943- *St&PR 91*
Burros, Marian *ConAu 30NR*
Burrough, Bryan, and John Helyar *BestSel 90-3 [port]*
Burroughs, Bonnie Leigh 1950- *WhoAmW 91*
Burroughs, Bruce Douglas 1944- *IntWWM 90*
Burroughs, Catharine *BioIn 16*
Burroughs, Charles *EarBlAP*
Burroughs, Edgar Rice 1875-1950 *ConAu 132, MajTwCW, RGTwCSF, WorAlBi*
Burroughs, Edith 1871-1916 *BiDWomA*
Burroughs, Gerald W *BiDrAPA 89*
Burroughs, Jack Eugene 1926- *WhoAm 90*
Burroughs, Jack Eugene 1946- *WhoSSW 91*
Burroughs, Jackie *BioIn 16*
Burroughs, Jackie 1941?- *OxCCanT*
Burroughs, Jeff 1951- *Ballpl 90*
Burroughs, John 1837-1921 *BioIn 16*
Burroughs, John Andrew, Jr. 1936- *WhoWor 91*
Burroughs, John Townsend 1926- *WhoWor 91*
Burroughs, Margaret T G 1917- *WhoAmA 91*
Burroughs, Margaret Taylor *AuBYP 90*
Burroughs, Margaret Taylor G. 1917- *BioIn 16*
Burroughs, Miggs 1946- *WhoE 91*
Burroughs, Nannie H. 1879-1961 *EarBlAP*
Burroughs, Nannie Helen 1878?-1961 *BioIn 16*
Burroughs, Richard Hansford, III 1946- *WhoE 91*
Burroughs, Robert Sidney 1941- *WhoE 91*
Burroughs, William Ellis 1951- *WhoE 91*
Burroughs, William S. 1914- *BioIn 16, MajTwCW*
Burroughs, William Seward 1914- *WhoWrEP 89*
Burrow, Bruce 1943- *St&PR 91*
Burrow, Claude Hoke 1947- *WhoEmL 91*
Burrow, Gerard Noel 1933- *WhoAm 90*
Burrow, Harold 1914- *St&PR 91, WhoAm 90*
Burrow, John W 1935- *ConAu 30NR*
Burrow, Terry Bruce 1943- *St&PR 91*
Burrow, William Fite, Sr. 1907- *WhoAm 90*
Burroway, Janet 1936- *AuBYP 90, BioIn 16*
Burroway, Janet G. 1936- *WhoSSW 91*
Burroway, Janet Gay 1936- *WhoWrEP 89*
Burrowes, Kelly L 1961- *BiDrAPA 89*
Burrowes, Norma *PenDiMP*
Burrowes, Norma Elizabeth 1944- *IntWWM 90*
Burrows, Abe 1910-1985 *OxCPMus, WorAlBi*
Burrows, Benjamin 1927- *WhoAm 90*
Burrows, Brenda *ODwPR 91*
Burrows, Brian William 1939- *St&PR 91, WhoAm 90*
Burrows, Cynthia Jane 1953- *WhoAmW 91*
Burrows, Dallas Frederick 1928- *WhoAm 90*
Burrows, Daniel J. 1954- *St&PR 91*
Burrows, Daniel L. *BioIn 16, NewYTBS 90*
Burrows, Debra Gabrielle 1954- *WhoAmW 91*
Burrows, Don *IntWWM 90*
Burrows, Donald Albert 1937- *WhoAm 90*
Burrows, Donald Francis, Jr. 1945- *St&PR 91*
Burrows, Donald James 1945- *IntWWM 90*
Burrows, Edward William 1928- *WhoHisp 91*
Burrows, Elizabeth MacDonald 1930- *WhoAmW 91, WhoWor 91*
Burrows, Eva *BioIn 16*
Burrows, F. Robert 1933- *St&PR 91*
Burrows, Frank F. 1901- *St&PR 91*
Burrows, Gates Wilson 1899- *WhoAm 90*
Burrows, George Baxter 1832-1909 *AmLegL*
Burrows, George F. *BioIn 16*
Burrows, Irving Louis 1927- *St&PR 91*
Burrows, James *BioIn 16*
Burrows, Jay Edward 1949- *WhoEmL 91*
Burrows, John 1941- *IntWWM 90*
Burrows, John Edward 1950- *WhoE 91*
Burrows, John W. *St&PR 91*
Burrows, Jon Hanes 1946- *WhoSSW 91*
Burrows, Kenneth David 1941- *St&PR 91*
Burrows, Lee R. 1935- *WhoAmW 91*
Burrows, Lewis 1931- *WhoAm 90*
Burrows, Michael Donald 1944- *WhoWor 91*
Burrows, Natalie *ODwPR 91*
Burrows, Pearl 1903-1960 *WhoAmA 91N*
Burrows, Robert Penn, III 1946- *WhoAm 90*
Burrows, Roger Ian 1945- *St&PR 91*
Burrows, Ronald George 1912- *St&PR 91*
Burrows, Selig S. 1913- *St&PR 91, WhoAmA 91*
Burrows, Selig Saul 1913- *WhoAm 90*
Burrows, Simon 1928- *BioIn 16*
Burrows, Skip 1954- *WhoEmL 91*
Burrows, Stephen 1942- *ConDes 90*
Burrows, Stephen J. 1952- *St&PR 91*
Burrows, Stuart 1933- *IntWWM 90, PenDiMP*
Burrows, Terry L. 1948- *St&PR 91*
Burrows, Vinie 1928- *DrBIPA 90*
Burrows, W. Don 1942- *St&PR 91*
Burrows, W.R., III 1931- *St&PR 91*
Burrows, William Claude 1925- *WhoAm 90*
Burrud, William James *NewYTBS 90*
Burrud, William James 1925- *WhoAm 90*
Burrus, C. David 1925- *St&PR 91*
Burrus, Charles Andrew, Jr. 1927- *WhoAm 90*
Burrus, Charles Sidney 1934- *WhoAm 90*
Burrus, Daniel Allen 1947- *WhoEmL 91*
Burrus, Dick 1898-1972 *Ballpl 90*
Burrus, George B. 1906-1990 *BioIn 16*
Burrus, John Newell 1920- *WhoAm 90*
Burrus, Robert L., Jr. 1934- *St&PR 91*
Burrus, Robert Lewis, Jr. 1934- *WhoAm 90*
Burruss, L. H. *BioIn 16*
Burruss, Terry Gene 1950- *WhoSSW 91*
Burry, Allen *ODwPR 91*
Burry, Gail Black 1939- *WhoAmW 91*
Burry, Judith Mesnick 1942- *WhoAmW 91*
Burry, Roy Douglas 1942- *St&PR 91*
Burry, William Charles 1911- *WhoE 91, WhoWor 91*
Bursardier *EncO&P 3*
Burse, Raymond Malcolm 1951- *WhoAm 90*
Bursey, Joan Tesarek 1943- *WhoAmW 91*
Bursey, Maurice M. 1939- *WhoAm 90*
Bursey, Rosetta 1912- *IntWWM 90*
Burshtan, Alvin 1935- *WhoAm 90*
Bursiek, Ralph David 1937- *WhoE 91*
Bursik, Carol Jean 1948- *WhoAmW 91*
Bursinger, JoEllen 1958- *WhoAmW 91*
Bursk, Edward C. *NewYTBS 90*
Bursk, Edward C. 1907-1990 *BioIn 16, ConAu 130*
Bursky, Herman Aaron 1938- *WhoAm 90*
Bursky, Oldrich *WhoWor 91*
Bursley, Kathleen A. 1954- *WhoAmW 91*
Bursma, Albert, Jr. 1937- *WhoAm 90*
Burson, Charles W. *WhoSSW 91*
Burson, Denise Elizabeth 1951- *WhoSSW 91*
Burson, Harold 1921- *ODwPR 91, St&PR 91, WhoAm 90*
Burson, Jay *BioIn 16*
Burson, Nancy 1948- *WhoAmA 91*
Burson, Scott Foster 1952- *WhoEmL 91*
Burson, William Ralph, Jr. 1938- *St&PR 91*
Burstall, John 1832?-1896 *DcCanB 12*
Burstein, Abraham 1893-1966 *BioIn 16*
Burstein, Albert H. *WhoAm 90*
Burstein, Allan Jay 1944- *BiDrAPA 89*
Burstein, Alvin Craig 1950- *BiDrAPA 89*
Burstein, Chaya M 1923- *SmATA 64*
Burstein, David 1947- *WhoEmL 91*
Burstein, Elias 1917- *WhoAm 90*
Burstein, Eric 1951- *BiDrAPA 89*
Burstein, Jack David 1945- *WhoAm 90, WhoSSW 91*
Burstein, John 1949- *BioIn 16*
Burstein, Karen Sue 1942- *WhoAmW 91, WhoE 91*
Burstein, Lucien 1922- *St&PR 91*
Burstein, Rena Benson 1926- *WhoAmW 91*
Burstein, Richard Joel 1945- *WhoAm 90*
Burstein, Samuel Z. 1935- *WhoE 91*
Burstein, Sharon *BioIn 16*
Burstein, Sharon Ann Palma 1952- *WhoAmW 91, WhoE 91, WhoEmL 91*
Burstein, Sol 1922- *WhoAm 90*
Burstein, Stephen David 1934- *WhoWor 91*
Burstein, Stuart S 1936- *BiDrAPA 89*
Bursten, Benjamin 1927- *BiDrAPA 89*
Burston, Richard Mervin 1924- *WhoWor 91*
Burstyn, Ellen 1932- *BioIn 16, NotWoAT, WhoAm 90, WhoAmW 91, WorAlBi*
Burstyn, Mike Lawrence 1945- *WhoE 91*
Bursztajn, Harold J 1950- *BiDrAPA 89*
Bursztajn, Harold Jonah 1950- *WhoE 91*
Bursztajn, Sherry 1946- *WhoAmW 91*
Bursztyn, Alberto Marcos 1952- *WhoE 91*
Bursztyn, Sylvia *BioIn 16*
Burt, Alvin Miller, III 1935- *WhoAm 90, WhoSSW 91*
Burt, Alvin Victor, Jr. 1927- *WhoAm 90*
Burt, Arthur Farlow 1946- *WhoSSW 91*
Burt, Barbara Swett 1955- *WhoAmW 91*
Burt, Benjamin *PenDiDA 89*
Burt, Christopher Murray 1933- *WhoAm 90*
Burt, Clyde Edwin *WhoAmA 91N*
Burt, Cynthia Marie Maultsby 1951- *WhoEmL 91*
Burt, Cyril 1883-1971 *EncO&P 3, EncPaPR 91*
Burt, Dan 1930- *WhoAmA 91*
Burt, David Sill 1917- *WhoAmA 91*
Burt, Don E. 1930- *St&PR 91*
Burt, Earl Daniel, Jr. 1948- *WhoEmL 91*
Burt, Francis 1926- *IntWWM 90*
Burt, James C. *BioIn 16*
Burt, James Edward, III 1937- *St&PR 91*
Burt, James Melvin 1933- *St&PR 91, WhoAm 90, WhoWor 91*
Burt, Jeffrey Amsterdam 1944- *WhoAm 90*
Burt, John 1690-1745 *PenDiDA 89*
Burt, John Harris 1918- *WhoAm 90*
Burt, Joseph Mark 1953- *BiDrAPA 89*
Burt, Linda K. 1951- *WhoAmW 91*
Burt, Margaret A. *BioIn 16*
Burt, Nathaniel 1913- *AuBYP 90, WhoWrEP 89*
Burt, Olive 1894- *AuBYP 90*
Burt, Ralph Hervey 1923- *WhoWor 91*
Burt, Richard *BioIn 16*
Burt, Richard Max 1944- *St&PR 91*
Burt, Robert Amsterdam 1939- *WhoAm 90*
Burt, Robert N. 1937- *St&PR 91*
Burt, Robert Norcross 1937- *WhoAm 90*
Burt, Samuel *PenDiDA 89*
Burt, Sharon Lou 1946- *WhoE 91*
Burt, Steven Earl 1949- *WhoWrEP 89*
Burt, Thomas Harrison 1960- *WhoSSW 91*
Burt, Vivien Kleinman 1944- *BiDrAPA 89*
Burt, Wallace Joseph, Jr. 1924- *St&PR 91*
Burt, Warren Arnold 1949- *IntWWM 90*
Burt, Wayne Vincent 1917- *WhoAm 90*
Burt, William *PenDiDA 89*
Burt-Edwards, Barbara 1945- *WhoSSW 91*
Burt-Frazier, Debra Renee 1953- *WhoEmL 91*
Burtch, Robert Lee 1925- *St&PR 91*
Burtch, Thomas Darrold 1949- *WhoEmL 91*
Burten, Katharine *BiDrAPA 89*
Burten, William *BiDrAPA 89*
Burtenshaw, Leonard John 1931- *WhoWor 91*
Burthe, Ronald Joseph, Jr. 1965- *WhoEmL 91*
Burti, Christopher Louis 1950- *WhoEmL 91*
Burtin, Margaret Irene 1939- *WhoAmW 91*
Burtin, Will 1903-1972 *ConDes 90*
Burtin, Will 1908-1972 *BioIn 16*
Burtis, Theodore Alfred 1922- *St&PR 91, WhoAm 90*
Burtle, Gary Jerome 1953- *WhoSSW 91*
Burtle, Paul Walter 1950- *WhoEmL 91, WhoWor 91*
Burtner, Vanessa June *BiDrAPA 89*
Burton, Al *WhoAm 90, WhoWor 91*
Burton, Alexander Martin Grant 1932- *WhoWrEP 89*
Burton, Alice Jean 1934- *WhoAmW 91*
Burton, Anna M *BiDrAPA 89*
Burton, Anna Marjorie 1931- *WhoAmW 91*
Burton, Anna Meister *WhoE 91*
Burton, Anne *ODwPR 91, TwCCr&M 91*
Burton, Anne M. *WhoE 91*
Burton, Arthur Henry, Jr. 1934- *WhoAm 90*
Burton, Barbara Anne 1948- *WhoAmW 91*
Burton, Barbara Richards 1933- *WhoAmW 91*
Burton, Barry Lawson 1942- *WhoWor 91*
Burton, Benjamin Theodore 1919- *WhoAm 90*
Burton, Bryce 1922- *St&PR 91*
Burton, Catharine 1668-1714 *FemiCLE*
Burton, Charlene G 1942- *BiDrAPA 89*
Burton, Charles *ODwPR 91*
Burton, Charles Arthur 1945- *WhoE 91*
Burton, Charles Edward 1946- *WhoEmL 91*
Burton, Charles Henning 1915- *WhoAm 90*
Burton, Charles Victor 1935- *WhoAm 90*
Burton, Courtney 1912- *St&PR 91*
Burton, Daniel S. 1953- *St&PR 91*
Burton, Danny Lee 1938- *WhoAm 90*
Burton, Darrell Irvin 1926- *WhoAm 90*
Burton, David Lee 1930- *WhoSSW 91*
Burton, Delmar Lee 1929- *St&PR 91, WhoAm 90*
Burton, Don E. 1950- *WhoEmL 91*
Burton, Donald Joseph 1934- *WhoAm 90*
Burton, Donna M. *WhoWrEP 89*
Burton, Dwight Lowell 1922- *WhoAm 90*
Burton, Earl Gillespie, III 1952- *WhoEmL 91*
Burton, Edward C., Jr. 1928- *St&PR 91*
Burton, Edward L., III 1933- *St&PR 91*
Burton, Edward Lewis 1935- *WhoWor 91*
Burton, Edwin T. *St&PR 91*
Burton, Elizabeth 1908- *AuBYP 90*
Burton, Ellen Irwin 1946- *WhoEmL 91*
Burton, Ellis 1936- *Ballpl 90*
Burton, Emory Gwinn 1938- *WhoAm 90*
Burton, Gary *BioIn 16*
Burton, Glenn S 1906- *BiDrAPA 89*
Burton, Glenn Willard 1910- *WhoAm 90*
Burton, Glenna C *BiDrAPA 89*
Burton, Harold H. 1888-1964 *WorAlBi*
Burton, Hester 1913- *AuBYP 90*
Burton, Humphrey McGuire 1931- *IntWWM 90*

Burton, Ian 1935- WhoAm 90
Burton, J.L. 1927- St&PR 91
Burton, Jake BioIn 16
Burton, James H. 1956- St&PR 91
Burton, James Harold 1956- WhoAm 90
Burton, Janet Ferree 1955- WhoEmL 91
Burton, John Campbell 1932- WhoAm 90
Burton, John Lane 1952- WhoEmL 91
Burton, John Reginald 1912- St&PR 91
Burton, John Routh 1917- WhoAm 90
Burton, John Scott 1955- WhoEmL 91
Burton, Joseph PenDiDA 89
Burton, Karen Poliner 1952- WhoAmW 91
Burton, Karen Ruth 1950- BiDrAPA 89
Burton, Katherine 1880-1969 FemiCLE
Burton, Katherine 1890-1969 AuBYP 90
Burton, Kathryn Curran 1941- WhoAmW 91
Burton, Keith ODwPR 91
Burton, Kenneth Lee 1948- St&PR 91
Burton, Larry 1944- St&PR 91
Burton, LeVar BioIn 16
Burton, Levar 1957- DrBIPA 90
Burton, Margaret Ann 1926- WhoAmW 91
Burton, Mary Alice 1954- WhoWrEP 89
Burton, Mary Louise Himes 1948- WhoE 91
Burton, Michael F. 1948- St&PR 91
Burton, Michael Ladd 1942- WhoAm 90
Burton, Miles TwCCr&M 91
Burton, Netta M WhoAmA 91N
Burton, Nigel Mark 1947- IntWWM 90
Burton, Parks William 1929- WhoSSW 91
Burton, Paul 1929- St&PR 91
Burton, Paul Denison 1929- St&PR 91
Burton, Paul W. ODwPR 91
Burton, Philip PenDiMP
Burton, Philip Ward 1910- WhoAm 90
Burton, Phillip 1926-1983 WorAlBi
Burton, Ralph Joseph 1911- WhoAm 90
Burton, Raymond C., Jr. 1938- St&PR 91
Burton, Raymond Charles, Jr. 1938- WhoAm 90
Burton, Richard 1925-1984 BioIn 16, DcNaB 1981, WorAlBi
Burton, Richard Francis 1821-1890 BioIn 16, WorAlBi
Burton, Richard Irving 1936- WhoAm 90, WhoWor 91
Burton, Richard Jay 1949- WhoEmL 91, WhoWor 91
Burton, Robert Eugene 1948- WhoSSW 91
Burton, Robert Gene 1938- WhoAm 90, WhoE 91
Burton, Robert George 1929- St&PR 91
Burton, Robert Jones 1946- WhoEmL 91
Burton, Robert W. 1927- St&PR 91
Burton, Robert W 1957- BiDrAPA 89
Burton, Robert William 1927- WhoAm 90
Burton, Roger Vernon 1928- WhoAm 90
Burton, Ron D. 1946- WhoAm 90, WhoEmL 91, WhoSSW 91
Burton, Roy H. 1933- St&PR 91
Burton, Ruth C 1912- BiDrAPA 89
Burton, Sala BioIn 16
Burton, Samuel Richard Manfred 1960- WhoSSW 91
Burton, Sandra ConAu 132
Burton, Sarah BiDEWW
Burton, Scot 1953- WhoEmL 91
Burton, Scott 1939-1989 BioIn 16, NewYTBS 90 [port], WhoAmA 91N
Burton, Shirley Thrasher 1935- WhoAmW 91
Burton, Sigrid 1951- WhoE 91
Burton, Steven B. 1952- WhoAm 90
Burton, Steven Bryant 1952- St&PR 91
Burton, Thomas Allen 1947- St&PR 91
Burton, Thomas P 1934- BiDrAPA 89
Burton, Tim BioIn 16, WhoAm 90
Burton, Timothy Angus 1943- BiDrAPA 89
Burton, Victor 1956- BioIn 16
Burton, Virginia Lee 1909-1968 AuBYP 90
Burton, William PenDiDA 89
Burton, William De K. 1926- St&PR 91
Burton-Bradley, Burton Gyrth BiDrAPA 89
Burton-Bradley, Burton Gyrth 1914- WhoWor 91
Burts, Stephen L. St&PR 91
Burtschy, Moe 1922- Ballpl 90
Burtsev, Vladimir L'vovich 1862-1942 BioIn 16
Burtt, Benjamin Pickering 1921- WhoAm 90
Burtt, Edwin A. 1892-1989 BioIn 16
Burtt, Edwin Arthur 1892-1989 ConAu 129
Burtt, Robert Elliott Speer 1954- WhoE 91
Burud, Sandra Lee 1948- WhoEmL 91
Burum, Stephen H. 1941- BioIn 16
Burwell, Adam Hood 1790-1849 DcLB 99
Burwell, Dudley Sale 1931- WhoAm 90
Burwell, Edward B. 1927- WhoAm 90, WhoSSW 91
Burwell, Edward Langdon, Jr. 1919- WhoAm 90
Burwell, Julie Ann 1957- WhoAmW 91
Burwell, Lawrence Barrett 1935- WhoSSW 91
Burwell, Lewis Carter, Jr. 1908-1988 WhoAm 90, WhoWor 91
Burwell, Robert Anda 1938- St&PR 91, WhoAm 90, WhoSSW 91
Burwell, Robert Lemmon, Jr. 1912- WhoAm 90
Burwell, Robin Anderson 1956- WhoEmL 91
Burwell, Stanley B. 1955- St&PR 91
Burwell, Vernon 1916- MusmAFA
Burwick, Israel Tutter 1915- St&PR 91
Burwick, Leo 1911- St&PR 91
Burwinkel, Jack 1931- St&PR 91
Bury, Anna Mae Keener BioIn 16
Bury, Charles Rugeley 1890-1968 DcScB S2
Bury, Charlotte 1775-1861 FemiCLE
Bury, Charlotte Campbell 1775-1861 BioIn 16
Bury, Dennis 1943- EncPaPR 91
Bury, Elizabeth 1644-1720 BiDEWW, FemiCLE
Bury, Jeffrey Dale 1956- St&PR 91
Bury, John 1925- ConDes 90, WhoAm 90, WhoWor 91
Bury, Mairi BioIn 16
Bury, Mary Jo Eleanor 1951- WhoEmL 91
Buryk, Michael John 1950- St&PR 91
Burzen, Don N. 1948- St&PR 91
Burzynski, Norman Stephen 1928- WhoAm 90
Burzynski, Peter Raymond 1948- WhoEmL 91, WhoSSW 91
Burzynski, Stanislaw Rajmund 1943- WhoWor 91
Bus, Roger Jay 1953- WhoEmL 91
Busa, Darwin Dante 1943- St&PR 91
Busa, Peter 1914-1983 WhoAmA 91N
Busacca, Antonino Giuseppe 1951- WhoWor 91
Busalacchi, Daniel L. 1942- St&PR 91
Busbee, George Dekle 1927- WhoAm 90
Busbee, Juliana Royster 1877-1962 WhoAmA 91N
Busbey, Douglas Earle 1948- WhoEmL 91
Busbin, O. Mell, Jr. 1937- WhoSSW 91
Busby, David 1926- WhoAm 90
Busby, David F 1926- BiDrAPA 89
Busby, David Michael 1964- WhoSSW 91
Busby, Donald W. 1937- St&PR 91
Busby, Edith AuBYP 90
Busby, Edward Oliver 1926- WhoAm 90
Busby, Gerald Lee 1935- St&PR 91
Busby, James L. 1946- St&PR 91
Busby, James Louie 1946- WhoAm 90, WhoWor 91
Busby, Jheryl WhoAm 90
Busby, Jim 1927- Ballpl 90
Busby, John Arthur, Jr. 1933- WhoAm 90
Busby, Marjorie Jean 1931- WhoAm 90
Busby, Robert Andrew 1929- St&PR 91
Busby, Robert L., III 1937- St&PR 91
Busby, Roger 1941- TwCCr&M 91
Busby, Shannon Nixon 1955- WhoAmW 91, WhoSSW 91
Busby, Stacy Dortch 1964- WhoAmW 91
Busby, Steve 1949- Ballpl 90
Busby, William Ross 1927- St&PR 91
Buscaglia, Chris J 1907- BiDrAPA 89
Buscaglia, Leo 1924- ConAu 30NR, WhoWrEP 89, WorAlBi
Buscaglia, Leo F. BioIn 16, ConAu 30NR
Buscaglia, Leonardo 1924- WhoAm 90
Buscaglia, Rocco Bartolomeo BioIn 16
Buscarini, Giancarlo 1935- WhoWor 91
Buscema, Charles Anthony 1950- BiDrAPA 89
Buscemi, Paul 1952- St&PR 91
Busch Family BioIn 16
Busch Quartet PenDiMP
Busch, Adolf 1891-1952 PenDiMP
Busch, Adolphus 1839-1913 WorAlBi
Busch, Anthony Karl 1905- BiDrAPA 89
Busch, Anthony W. 1943- St&PR 91
Busch, Arthur Allen 1954- WhoEmL 91
Busch, Arthur Winston 1926- WhoAm 90
Busch, August A., III BioIn 16
Busch, August A., III 1937- St&PR 91
Busch, August A., Jr. St&PR 91N
Busch, August Adolphus 1899-1989 BioIn 16
Busch, August Adolphus, III 1937- WhoAm 90, WhoWor 91
Busch, August Anheuser, Jr. 1899-1989 News 90
Busch, August Otto Ernst von dem 1704-1779 PenDiDA 89
Busch, Benjamin 1912-1989 BioIn 16
Busch, Billy BioIn 16
Busch, Briton Cooper 1936- WhoAm 90
Busch, Carole Ann 1945- WhoSSW 91
Busch, Charles BioIn 16
Busch, Chester C. St&PR 91
Busch, Chris William 1937- WhoAm 90
Busch, Christine 1947- WhoEmL 91
Busch, Daniel A 1947- BiDrAPA 89
Busch, David John 1946- WhoEmL 91
Busch, Eberhard 1937- WhoWor 91
Busch, Edwin 1929- St&PR 91
Busch, Fred W. 1932- St&PR 91
Busch, Frederick 1941- WhoWrEP 89
Busch, Frederick Matthew 1941- WhoAm 90
Busch, Fredric BiDrAPA 89
Busch, Fritz 1890-1951 PenDiMP
Busch, German 1904-1939 BioIn 16
Busch, Gussie 1899-1989 AnObit 1989, Ballpl 90
Busch, Harris 1923- WhoAm 90
Busch, Harry 1919- St&PR 91
Busch, Hermann 1897-1975 PenDiMP
Busch, Inez L 1927- BiDrAPA 89
Busch, J. Patrick 1923- St&PR 91
Busch, John Arthur 1951- WhoEmL 91
Busch, John F. 1919- St&PR 91
Busch, John H. 1927- St&PR 91
Busch, Joyce Ida 1934- WhoAmW 91, WhoWor 91
Busch, Karen Louise 1958- WhoAmW 91
Busch, Katie A 1949- BiDrAPA 89
Busch, Kenneth Gary 1946- BiDrAPA 89
Busch, Larry Peter 1944- St&PR 91
Busch, Lawrence Michael 1945- WhoEmL 91
Busch, Niven 1903- WhoAm 90
Busch, Peter Jonathan 1952- WhoEmL 91
Busch, Richard 1941- WhoAm 90
Busch, Rita Marie 1956- WhoAmW 91
Busch, Rita Mary 1926- WhoAmA 91
Busch, Robert A. 1947- St&PR 91
Busch, Robert Charles 1932- St&PR 91
Busch, Robert Douglas 1949- WhoEmL 91
Busch, Sayde Brenner NewYTBS 90
Busch, William Albert 1932- St&PR 91
Buschbach, Thomas Charles 1923- WhoAm 90
Busche, Eugene Marvin 1926- St&PR 91, WhoAm 90
Busche, Jeffry Francis 1953- WhoEmL 91
Busche, Louis R. 1930- St&PR 91
Buscher, Judith Gay WhoAmW 91
Buscher, Nancy 1941- WhoAmW 91
Busching, Allen E. 1932- St&PR 91
Busching, Larry Wayne 1945- WhoSSW 91
Buschke, Herman 1932- WhoAm 90
Buschkuhl, Matthias 1953- WhoWor 91
Buschman, Darwin 1956- BiDrAPA 89
Buschman, Henry William 1924- St&PR 91
Buschman, Milton H 1937- BiDrAPA 89
Buschmann, Ben S. 1929- St&PR 91
Buschmann, MaryBeth Tank 1942- WhoAmW 91
Buschmann, Siegfried 1937- St&PR 91, WhoAm 90
Busciglio, Richard 1935- WhoAm 90, WhoSSW 91
Busck, Ole Arnold 1937- WhoWor 91
Buscombe, William 1918- WhoAm 90
Busdicker, Gordon G. 1933- WhoAm 90
Buse, Raymond Leo, Jr. 1925- St&PR 91
Buse, Sharon Elaine 1951- WhoAmW 91
Buseck, Peter Robert WhoAm 90
Busel, Joel 1935- St&PR 91
Buselt, John Paul 1954- WhoEmL 91
Buser, Andres A.A. 1940- St&PR 91
Buser, Daniel S., Jr. 1934- ODwPR 91
Buser, Robert Anthony BiDrAPA 89
Buser, Sue 1949- WhoEmL 91
Busey, DeReath Irene EarBIAP
Busey, Diane Faye 1954- WhoAmW 91
Busey, Gary BioIn 16
Busey, Gary 1944- WhoAm 90, WorAlBi
Busey, James Buchanan, IV 1932- WhoAm 90
Busfield, Bernard L. Jr. BiDrAPA 89
Busfield, Timothy BioIn 16, ConTFT 8
Bush family BioIn 16
Bush, Alan 1900- IntWWM 90, PenDiMP A
Bush, Allen Julian 1932- St&PR 91
Bush, Anita 1883?-1974 DrBIPA 90
Bush, Anita Marie 1951- WhoWrEP 89
Bush, Ann Kathleen 1960- WhoAmW 91
Bush, Arthur W. 1956- St&PR 91
Bush, Barbara BioIn 16
Bush, Barbara 1925- BioIn 16
Bush, Barbara Pierce 1924- WorAlBi
Bush, Barbara Pierce 1925- WhoAm 90, WhoAmW 91, WhoE 91, WhoWor 91
Bush, Betty Jean 1938- WhoAmW 91
Bush, Beverly WhoAmA 91
Bush, Brendalee 1949- WhoEmL 91
Bush, Charles David 1947- WhoSSW 91
Bush, Charles Robert WhoAmA 91
Bush, Charles Vernon 1939- WhoAm 90
Bush, Christopher 1888?-1973 TwCCr&M 91
Bush, Clifford Kenneth 1951- WhoE 91
Bush, Daniel Anthony 1959- WhoEmL 91
Bush, David A. 1930- St&PR 91
Bush, David Frederic 1942- WhoE 91
Bush, David James 1948- St&PR 91
Bush, David Victor 1948- WhoEmL 91
Bush, Doanld P. 1931- St&PR 91
Bush, Donald John WhoAmA 91
Bush, Donie 1887-1972 Ballpl 90 [port]
Bush, Dorothy BioIn 16
Bush, Dorothy Vredenburgh 1916- WhoAm 90
Bush, Duncan Eric 1946- WhoWor 91
Bush, Edward Grady 1950- WhoSSW 91
Bush, Edward Philip, III 1953- WhoEmL 91
Bush, Edward S 1932- BiDrAPA 89
Bush, Ella Shepart 1863- WhoAmA 91N
Bush, Eric Wheler 1899-1985 DcNaB 1981
Bush, Ernest BioIn 16
Bush, F.L. 1925- St&PR 91
Bush, Fred Marshall, Jr. 1917- WhoAm 90
Bush, Frederick A. 1904-1989 BioIn 16
Bush, Frederick Morris 1949- WhoAm 90
Bush, G. Kenner 1934- St&PR 91
Bush, Geoffrey 1920- BioIn 16, IntWWM 90, PenDiMP A, WhoWor 91
Bush, George NewYTBS 90 [port]
Bush, George 1924- BioIn 16
Bush, George Franklin 1909- WhoE 91
Bush, George Herbert Walker 1924- BiDrUSE 89, WhoAm 90, WhoE 91, WhoWor 91, WorAlBi
Bush, George W. BioIn 16
Bush, George Walker 1946- St&PR 91
Bush, Gladys A. BiDrAPA 89
Bush, Gregory John 1956- St&PR 91
Bush, Guy 1901- Ballpl 90
Bush, Guy Louis 1929- WhoAm 90
Bush, Howard James 1953- WhoEmL 91
Bush, Hugh Sutton 1957- St&PR 91
Bush, Jack 1909-1977 WhoAmA 91N
Bush, Jack Eugene 1934- WhoAm 90, WhoSSW 91
Bush, James Sloan 1936- St&PR 91
Bush, Jane Darmon 1935- WhoSSW 91
Bush, Jeb BioIn 16
Bush, Joe 1892-1974 Ballpl 90 [port]
Bush, John Arthur W. 1943- St&PR 91
Bush, John B., Jr. 1933- St&PR 91
Bush, John Burchard, Jr. 1933- WhoAm 90
Bush, John Charles 1938- WhoWrEP 89
Bush, John H. 1922- St&PR 91
Bush, John Lawrence 1930- St&PR 91
Bush, John S., Jr. 1930- St&PR 91
Bush, Jonathan BioIn 16
Bush, Judy Lynn 1938- WhoAmW 91
Bush, June Lee 1942- WhoAmW 91
Bush, Karen Michaela 1947- WhoE 91
Bush, Kate 1958- OxCPMus
Bush, Kate 1959?- ConMus 4 [port]
Bush, Kathleen 1946- WhoSSW 91
Bush, Kenneth Alan 1948- WhoEmL 91
Bush, L.T. St&PR 91
Bush, Lee 1961- ODwPR 91
Bush, Lori Hermelin 1956- WhoAmW 91
Bush, Louis 1820- AmLegL
Bush, M L 1938- ConAu 132
Bush, Marjorie Ann 1925- WhoAmW 91
Bush, Martin David 1951- WhoSSW 91
Bush, Martin H. 1930- WhoAm 90, WhoAmA 91
Bush, Marvin BioIn 16
Bush, Melinda Johnson 1942- WhoE 91, WhoWor 91
Bush, Michael 1932- IntWWM 90
Bush, Michael J. 1943- St&PR 91
Bush, Neil BioIn 16
Bush, Norman 1929- WhoAm 90
Bush, Norman 1933- DrBIPA 90
Bush, Olivia 1869-1944 FemiCLE
Bush, Olivia Ward 1869-1944 EarBIAP, HarlReB
Bush, Patricia A. 1941- St&PR 91
Bush, Paul Stanley 1936- St&PR 91, WhoAm 90
Bush, Paul V. St&PR 91
Bush, Phyllis Kirk ODwPR 91
Bush, Prescott S. 1895-1972 BioIn 16
Bush, Ralph W. 1938- St&PR 91
Bush, Randy 1958- Ballpl 90
Bush, Raymond T. 1939- WhoE 91
Bush, Richard NewAgMG
Bush, Richard Clarence, III 1947- WhoE 91
Bush, Richard N. 1951- St&PR 91
Bush, Robert Benjamin 1928- St&PR 91, WhoAm 90
Bush, Robert Bradford 1953- WhoEmL 91
Bush, Robert Donald 1939- WhoAm 90
Bush, Robert P 1842-1923 AmLegL
Bush, Robert P 1919- BiDrAPA 89
Bush, Ronald L. 1946- WhoAm 90
Bush, Rosalyn Dunn 1943- WhoSSW 91
Bush, Sargent, Jr. 1937- WhoAm 90
Bush, Schuyler D. 1938- St&PR 91
Bush, Sherry ODwPR 91
Bush, Spencer Harrison 1920- WhoAm 90
Bush, Stephanie Regina 1952- WhoAmW 91
Bush, Stuart K BiDrAPA 89
Bush, Sydney C BiDrAPA 89
Bush, Vannevar 1890-1974 BioIn 16, DcScB S2, WorAlBi
Bush, W. Glenn 1937- St&PR 91
Bush, Werner Frederick 1939- St&PR 91

Bush, William 1929- ConAu 32NR
Bush, William 1954- WhoEmL 91
Bush, William Arden 1948- WhoEmL 91, WhoSSW 91, WhoWor 91
Bush, William Broughton 1911- WhoAmA 91N
Bush, William Glenn 1937- WhoAm 90
Bush, William M., Jr. 1951- St&PR 91
Bush, William Morgan, Jr. 1951- WhoSSW 91
Bush, William Paul, II 1950- St&PR 91, WhoEmL 91
Bush, William Sydney, Jr. 1950- WhoSSW 91
Bush, William Wallace 1914- St&PR 91
Bush-Banks, Olivia Ward 1869-1944 EarBlAP, HarlReB
Bush-Brown, Albert 1926- ODwPR 91, St&PR 91, WhoAm 90, WhoAmA 91
Bush-Brown, Louise 1896?-1973 AuBYP 90
Bushee, Eleanor Jane 1922- WhoAmW 91
Bushek, George J. 1945- St&PR 91
Bushell, Alan 1941- St&PR 91
Bushell, Garvin 1902- BioIn 16
Bushell, Gordon James 1946- BiDrAPA 89
Bushey, Alan Scott 1930- St&PR 91, WhoAm 90
Bushey, Bruce Lawrence BioIn 16
Bushey, Peter F., Jr. 1947- St&PR 91
Bushey, Richard Kenneth 1940- St&PR 91, WhoAm 90
Bushey, Robert Francis 1939- WhoWrEP 89
Bushinsky, Jay 1932- WhoAm 90
Bushkin, Joe BioIn 16
Bushkin, Merle J. 1935- St&PR 91
Bushkin, Merle Jerome 1935- WhoE 91
Bushman, Claudia L 1934- WhoWrEP 89
Bushman, David Franklin 1945- WhoAmA 91
Bushman, Francis X. 1883-1966 WorAlBi
Bushman, Irina Nikolaevna 1921- EncCoWW
Bushman, Joseph Charles 1954- WhoEmL 91
Bushman, Mary Laura Jones 1946- WhoEmL 91
Bushman, Richard L. 1931- BioIn 16, WhoWrEP 89
Bushman, Robert C. 1935- St&PR 91
Bushman, Robert R. 1927- St&PR 91
Bushman, Robert Roy 1927- WhoE 91
Bushmiller, Ernie 1905-1982 EncACom
Bushmiller, Ernie Paul 1905- WhoAmA 91N
Bushnell, Catharine 1950- WhoAmW 91, WhoE 91
Bushnell, Clarence William 1916- WhoAm 90
Bushnell, David 1742?-1824 EncCRAm, WorAlBi
Bushnell, George Edward, Jr. 1924- WhoAm 90
Bushnell, John 1630?-1701 BioIn 16
Bushnell, John Alden 1933- WhoAm 90, WhoE 91
Bushnell, Kenneth Wayne 1933- WhoAmA 91
Bushnell, Lowry Avon BiDrAPA 89
Bushnell, Margaret Mary 1945- WhoAmW 91
Bushno, Lila Joan 1931- WhoWrEP 89
Busho, Elizabeth Mary 1927- WhoWor 91
Bushong, Craig Patton BiDrAPA 89
Bushor, William Edward 1926- St&PR 91
Bushotter, George 1864-1892 WhNaAH
Bushuk, Nicholas Franklin 1952- WhoE 91
Bushyhead, Dennis Wolf 1826-1898 WhNaAH
Busi, Nat Peter 1929- St&PR 91
Busia, Akosua DrBIPA 90
Busick, Denzel Rex 1945- WhoEmL 91
Busico, Louis Frank 1935- St&PR 91
Businger, Joost Alois 1924- WhoAm 90
Busino, Orlando Francis 1926- WhoAm 90, WhoAmA 91
Busiri Vici, Andrea 1903-1989 BioIn 16
Buskas, Robert James 1932- St&PR 91
Busker, Gary Leon 1946- WhoEmL 91
Busker, Leroy Henry 1929- WhoAm 90
Buskey, Tom 1947- Ballpl 90
Buskirk, Elsworth Robert 1925- WhoAm 90
Buskirk, George Abraham 1829-1874 AmLegL
Buskirk, Richard Hobart 1927- WhoAm 90, WhoWor 91
Buskirk, Samuel Hamilton 1820-1879 AmLegL
Busko, William Devin 1929- St&PR 91
Buskuhl, Carl Thomas 1952- WhoEmL 91
Busler, Gary Lewis 1951- St&PR 91
Busnaina, Ahmed Ali 1953- WhoE 91
Busner, Philip H. 1927- WhoAm 90
Busoni, Ferruccio 1866-1924 BioIn 16, PenDiMP, -A
Busoni, Rafaello 1900-1962 AuBYP 90
Buss, Claude Albert 1903- WhoAm 90
Buss, Daniel Frank 1943- WhoAm 90
Buss, David M. BioIn 16
Buss, Dennis A. 1946- St&PR 91
Buss, Frances Mary 1827-1894 BioIn 16
Buss, Gerald Fredrick 1934- WhoSSW 91
Buss, Helen M. ConAu 130
Buss, J. Ronald 1940- St&PR 91
Buss, Walter Richard 1905- WhoAm 90
Buss, William Charles 1938- WhoAm 90
Bussabarger, Robert Franklin 1922- WhoAmA 91
Bussani, Francesco 1743-1807? PenDiMP
Bussani, Luca 1957- WhoWor 91
Bussard, Clarence Lease 1911- WhoAm 90
Bussard, Clifford Ernest 1959- WhoSSW 91
Bussard, Richard Earl 1934- WhoAm 90
Bussard, Robert William 1928- WhoAm 90
Busse, Alvin R. 1928- ODwPR 91
Busse, Ewald W 1917- BiDrAPA 89
Busse, Ewald William 1917- WhoAm 90
Busse, Fedor Fedorovich 1838-1896 BioIn 16
Busse, Friedrich Hermann 1936- WhoWor 91
Busse, George R. 1928- St&PR 91
Busse, Henry 1894-1955 OxCPMus
Busse, James P. 1943- St&PR 91
Busse, Janis D. 1951- St&PR 91
Busse, Janis Dianne 1951- St&PR 91
Busse, Leonard Wayne 1938- WhoAm 90
Busse, Lu Ann 1956- WhoAmW 91
Busse, Michael P. 1948- St&PR 91
Busse, Rido 1934- ConDes 90
Bussel, Lili R BiDrAPA 89
Bussell, Annette Troup 1945- WhoAmW 91
Bussell, Donald E. 1940- St&PR 91
Bussell, Robert E 1931- BiDrAPA 89
Bussell, Sally Carney 1958- WhoEmL 91
Bussewitz, M. Walter 1919- WhoE 91
Bussey, Charles David 1933- WhoAm 90, WhoWrEP 89
Bussey, George Davis 1949- BiDrAPA 89, WhoEmL 91
Bussey, Holly Jean 1954- WhoAmW 91
Bussey, Reuben Thomas, Jr. 1943- WhoSSW 91
Bussgang, Julian Jakob 1925- WhoAm 90
Bussi, Francesco 1926- IntWWM 90
Bussian, Eric Richard 1958- WhoEmL 91
Bussie, Jan R. 1938- WhoSSW 91
Bussiere, Bruce Charles 1954- WhoE 91
Bussieres, Arthur de 1877-1913 DcLB 92
Bussieres, Paul 1943- OxCCanT
Bussink, Jan Theo 1943- WhoWor 91
Busskohl, Charles Deforest 1932- St&PR 91
Busskohl, Doyle St&PR 91
Busskohl, Steve St&PR 91
Bussmann, Charles Haines 1924- WhoAm 90
Bussone, David Eben 1947- WhoAm 90, WhoSSW 91
Bussotti, Sylvano 1931- IntWWM 90, PenDiMP A
Busta, Christina 1915- EncCoWW
Busta, Paul Timothy 1952- WhoEmL 91
Bustad, Leo Kenneth 1920- WhoAm 90
Bustamante, Albert G. 1935- WhoHisp 91
Bustamante, Albert Garza 1935- WhoAm 90, WhoSSW 91
Bustamante, Anastasio 1780-1853 BioIn 16
Bustamante, Arturo 1944- WhoHisp 91
Bustamante, Bruce W. 1957- St&PR 91
Bustamante, Juan P 1942- BiDrAPA 89
Bustamante, Leonard Eliecer 1938- WhoHisp 91
Bustamante, Valentin M., Sr. 1931- WhoHisp 91
Bustamante, William Alexander 1884-1977 BioIn 16
Bustamante y Rivero, Jose Luis 1894-1989 BioIn 16
Bustamente, Jorge A. WhoAm 90
Bustani, Myrna 1937- WhoWor 91
Bustelli, Franz Anton 1723-1763 PenDiDA 89
Buster, Edmond Bate 1918- WhoAm 90, WhoWor 91
Buster, Lisa B. 1959- WhoAmW 91
Buster, William Frank 1927- WhoAm 90
Bustillo, Eloy 1951- WhoHisp 91
Bustillo, Gerardo BiDrAPA 89
Bustin, Beverly Miner 1936- WhoAmW 91, WhoE 91
Bustin, Edouard Jean 1933- WhoAm 90
Bustin, Greg 1955- ODwPR 91
Busto, Rafael Pedro 1939- WhoHisp 91
Bustonera, Erlinda G BiDrAPA 89
Bustos, F. ConAu 33NR, HispWr 90, MajTwCW
Bustos, Hermenegildo 1832-1907 ArtLatA
Bustos Domecq, H. ConAu 33NR, HispWr 90, MajTwCW
Busuttil, James Joseph 1958- WhoE 91, WhoEmL 91, WhoWor 91
Buswell, Debra Sue 1957- WhoAmW 91, WhoEmL 91
Buswell, Douglas H. 1921- St&PR 91
Buswell, James Oliver 1946- BioIn 16, IntWWM 90
Buswell, Susan Rowe 1935- WhoAmW 91
Buswell, Tracey ODwPR 91
Buswink, Anthony Allen 1940- WhoWrEP 89
Buszko, Irene J 1947- WhoAmA 91
Buszko, Irene Joan 1947- WhoE 91
Buszuwski, Mary L. 1954- St&PR 91
Buta, Mary Oprïtza 1913- WhoAmW 91
Butala, Gitaben A. BiDrAPA 89
Butch, William Louis 1932- St&PR 91, WhoSSW 91
Butchart, John Chalmers 1941- BiDrAPA 89
Butchart, Robert L. 1928- St&PR 91
Butcher, Amanda Kay 1936- WhoAmW 91
Butcher, Bernard B. 1928- St&PR 91
Butcher, Bobby Gene 1936- WhoAm 90
Butcher, Bruce Cameron 1947- WhoEmL 91
Butcher, Charles BioIn 16
Butcher, David J. 1948- ODwPR 91
Butcher, Dick 1946- St&PR 91
Butcher, Donald Franklin 1937- WhoAm 90
Butcher, Ed BioIn 16
Butcher, Edward Carl 1938- St&PR 91
Butcher, Grace 1934- WhoWrEP 89
Butcher, Harry William 1948- WhoSSW 91
Butcher, Harvey Raymond, III 1947- WhoWor 91
Butcher, Howard, III 1902- St&PR 91
Butcher, Jake BioIn 16
Butcher, James W., Jr. EarBlAP
Butcher, James Walter 1917- WhoAm 90
Butcher, John 1957- Ballpl 90
Butcher, John Kimberlin 1937- St&PR 91
Butcher, Larry Edward 1942- St&PR 91
Butcher, Mary Lou 1943- ODwPR 91
Butcher, Max 1910-1957 Ballpl 90
Butcher, Philip 1918- WhoAm 90
Butcher, Robert Gilliam, Jr. 1934- St&PR 91
Butcher, Robert K. 1910- St&PR 91
Butcher, Ronald H G 1914- BiDrAPA 89
Butcher, Russell Devereux 1938- WhoWor 91
Butcher, Samuel Henry 1850-1910 EncO&P 3
Butcher, Susan 1954- News 91-1 [port]
Butcher, Susan H. 1954- WhoAmW 91
Butcher, Thomas W. 1938- St&PR 91
Butcher, W.W. Keen 1916- St&PR 91
Butcher, Willard C. 1926- St&PR 91
Butcher, Willard Carlisle 1926- WhoAm 90, WhoE 91, WhoWor 91
Butcher, William 1951- ConAu 131
Butchkes, Sydney 1922- WhoAm 90, WhoAmA 91
Butchko, Emil Joseph 1935- St&PR 91
Butchko, Robert Edward 1946- WhoEmL 91
Butchvarov, Panayot Krustev 1933- WhoAm 90
Buteau, Michelle Diane 1952- WhoAmW 91
Butel, Janet Susan 1941- WhoAmW 91
Buten, Max 1932- St&PR 91
Butenandt, Adolf 1903- St&PR 91
Butenandt, Adolf F. J. 1903- WorAlBi
Butenandt, Adolf Friedrich Johann 1903- WhoWor 91
Butenschon, Ragnhild 1912- BiDWomA
Buter, Gordon H. 1919- St&PR 91
Buter, Gordon Henry 1919- WhoAm 90
Buter, Havery 1923- St&PR 91
Butera, Ann Michele 1958- WhoAmW 91, WhoEmL 91
Butera, Daniel G. 1909-1989 BioIn 16
Butera, Paul 1942- WhoAm 90
Butera, Sal 1952- Ballpl 90
Butera, Virginia Fabbri 1951- WhoAmA 91
Buterakos, Kathleen Ann 1951- WhoE 91
Buterbaugh, Arthur Dale 1948- WhoAm 90
Buteux, Patricia Ann 1944- St&PR 91
Buth, David Martin 1952- WhoEmL 91
Buth, Donald George 1949- WhoEmL 91
Buthelezi, Gatsha Mangosuthu 1928- BioIn 16
Buthelezi, Wellington 1895- BioIn 16
Buths, Julius 1851-1920 PenDiMP
Butigan, William Clay 1957- WhoEmL 91
Butin, Mitchell Paul BiDrAPA 89
Butina, Mary Ann 1949- WhoE 91
Butkiewicz, James Leon 1949- WhoE 91
Butkus, Dick 1942- WorAlBi
Butkus, Donald Eugene 1934- WhoSSW 91
Butler, A., Mrs. BiDEWW
Butler, A. L. 1912- IntWWM 90
Butler, A. Pickens BioIn 16
Butler, Albert L., Jr. 1918- St&PR 91
Butler, Anina Liberty St&PR 91
Butler, Anna Mabel Land 1901- HarlReB
Butler, Anne 1953- BiDrAPA 89
Butler, Anthony Wayne 1787-1849 BioIn 16
Butler, Art 1887-1984 Ballpl 90
Butler, Arthur D. 1923- WhoAm 90
Butler, Arthur William 1929- WhoWor 91
Butler, Benjamin Franklin 1795-1858 BiDrUSE 89
Butler, Benjamin Franklin 1818-1893 BioIn 16, WorAlBi
Butler, Betty Rae 1948- WhoAmW 91
Butler, Beverly 1932- BioIn 16
Butler, Beverly Kathleen 1932- AuBYP 90
Butler, Bill 1947- Ballpl 90
Butler, Brett 1957- Ballpl 90
Butler, Brian 1949- WhoE 91
Butler, Brinton Lee 1953- WhoEmL 91
Butler, Broadus Nathaniel 1920- WhoAm 90
Butler, Bruce Alan 1948- WhoAm 90
Butler, Bruce Allan 1948- St&PR 91
Butler, Bryan V. 1938- St&PR 91
Butler, Burridge Davenal 1868-1948 BioIn 16
Butler, Byron C 1918- WhoAmA 91
Butler, Candace Gayle 1951- WhoAmW 91
Butler, Carol King 1952- WhoAmW 91
Butler, Carolyn E BiDrAPA 89
Butler, Charles Dawson BioIn 16
Butler, Charles E. 1938- ODwPR 91
Butler, Charles Henry 1932- WhoE 91
Butler, Charles R., Jr. 1940- WhoAm 90
Butler, Charles Thomas 1951- WhoAm 90, WhoSSW 91
Butler, Charles William 1922- WhoAm 90
Butler, Christopher Williams 1950- WhoSSW 91
Butler, Claire Draper 1928- St&PR 91
Butler, Clifford Leroy 1926- WhoSSW 91
Butler, Cynthia Calibani 1959- WhoAmW 91
Butler, Daniel Patrick 1939- WhoE 91, WhoWor 91
Butler, David 1898- MusmAFA
Butler, David 1930- WhoAm 90
Butler, David Douglas 1945- WhoEmL 91
Butler, David Edward 1937- St&PR 91
Butler, Dean S. BioIn 16
Butler, Deborah Ann 1949- WhoAmW 91
Butler, Donald E. 1927- St&PR 91
Butler, Douglas Earle 1945- WhoEmL 91
Butler, Edgar Buell, Jr. 1945- St&PR 91
Butler, Edward Lee 1915- WhoAm 90
Butler, Edward Lee 1945- WhoE 91
Butler, Edward Scannell 1934- WhoAm 90, WhoWor 91
Butler, Elaine Ruth Marjorie Mallory 1922- WhoWor 91
Butler, Eleanor 1738?-1829 BioIn 16
Butler, Elizabeth S Thompson, Lady 1850-1933 BioIn 16
Butler, Elizabeth Southerden 1846-1933 BiDWomA
Butler, Ernest, Jr. 1928- St&PR 91
Butler, Ernest Alton 1926- St&PR 91
Butler, Eugene 1894- WhoAm 90
Butler, Eugene L. 1941- WhoAm 90
Butler, Eugene Louis 1941- St&PR 91
Butler, Eulous Sonny 1939- WhoSSW 91
Butler, Frances 1940- ConDes 90
Butler, Francesca Canales 1954- WhoSSW 91
Butler, Francis K. BiDrAPA 89
Butler, Frank Joseph 1932- St&PR 91
Butler, Fred Jay, Jr. 1929- WhoAm 90
Butler, Frederick George 1919- WhoAm 90, WhoWor 91
Butler, Fredrick Myron 1935- St&PR 91
Butler, George A. 1928- St&PR 91
Butler, George Andrews 1928- WhoAm 90, WhoE 91
Butler, George Harrison 1917- WhoAm 90
Butler, George Washington, Jr. 1944- WhoWor 91
Butler, Gloria Dean 1958- WhoAmW 91
Butler, Gordon Wesley 1953- St&PR 91
Butler, Grace Caroline 1937- WhoAmW 91
Butler, Gwen Elisabeth 1945- WhoE 91
Butler, Gwendoline TwCCr&M 91
Butler, Hal 1913- AuBYP 90
Butler, Harold C. 1940- St&PR 91
Butler, Harris Dewey, III 1955- WhoEmL 91
Butler, Harry William, Jr. 1924- WhoSSW 91
Butler, Heidi Lord 1958- WhoAmW 91
Butler, Helen J. 1931- WhoAmW 91
Butler, Hiram 1951- WhoAmA 91
Butler, Ian Douglas 1944- IntWWM 90
Butler, Ian Geoffrey 1925- WhoWor 91
Butler, Ida de Fatio 1868-1949 BioIn 16
Butler, Ira F. M. 1812-1909 AmLegL
Butler, J. Alden 1930- St&PR 91
Butler, Jack Fairchild 1933- WhoAm 90
Butler, Jacob 1817- AmLegL

Butler, James C. 1937- *St&PR 91*
Butler, James D 1945- *WhoAmA 91*
Butler, James Joseph, Jr. 1927- *St&PR 91*
Butler, James Lee 1927- *WhoAm 90*
Butler, James Neal 1951- *WhoE 91*
Butler, James Newton 1934- *WhoAm 90*
Butler, James Robert 1930- *WhoAm 90*
Butler, James Robertson, Jr. 1946- *WhoEmL 91, WhoWor 91*
Butler, Jeffrey Ernest 1922- *WhoAm 90*
Butler, Jerry 1939- *DrBlPA 90, EncPR&S 89*
Butler, Jerry 1959- *BioIn 16*
Butler, Jerry Duane 1937- *WhoAm 90*
Butler, Jerry Phillips 1941- *WhoSSW 91*
Butler, Jesse Lee 1953- *WhoE 91, WhoEmL 91*
Butler, Jimmie Leon 1935- *St&PR 91*
Butler, John *BioIn 16*
Butler, John 1728-1796 *EncCRAm, WhNaAH*
Butler, John A. 1932- *St&PR 91*
Butler, John Alden 1930- *WhoAm 90*
Butler, John Carleton 1954- *WhoEmL 91*
Butler, John Joseph 1957- *WhoEmL 91*
Butler, John L *BiDrAPA 89*
Butler, John L., Jr. 1931- *WhoWor 91*
Butler, John Marion 1934- *St&PR 91*
Butler, John Michael 1959- *WhoEmL 91*
Butler, John Musgrave 1928- *WhoAm 90*
Butler, John Paul 1935- *WhoSSW 91*
Butler, John Russ 1936- *St&PR 91*
Butler, Johnny 1894-1967 *Ballpl 90*
Butler, Jonathan 1961- *DrBlPA 90*
Butler, Jonathan Putnam 1940- *WhoAm 90*
Butler, Joseph 1901-1981 *WhoAmA 91N*
Butler, Joseph 1929- *St&PR 91*
Butler, Joseph Patrick 1957- *WhoWrEP 89*
Butler, Joseph Thomas 1932- *WhoAmA 91, WhoE 91*
Butler, Josephine 1828-1906 *FemiCLE*
Butler, Josephine Elizabeth 1828-1906 *BioIn 16*
Butler, Josiah P. 1936- *St&PR 91*
Butler, Judith Eileen 1957- *WhoEmL 91*
Butler, Karen Leigh Hayes 1950- *WhoAmW 91*
Butler, Karla 1933- *WhoAm 90*
Butler, Katharine 1898-1989 *BioIn 16*
Butler, Katharine Gorrell 1925- *WhoAm 90*
Butler, Kenneth Van 1934- *WhoAm 90*
Butler, Kent Alan 1958- *WhoEmL 91*
Butler, Leon N. 1917- *St&PR 91*
Butler, Leslie Ann 1945- *WhoAm 90, WhoAmW 91*
Butler, Leslie Richard 1940- *St&PR 91, WhoAm 90, WhoE 91*
Butler, Lewis Clark 1923- *WhoAm 90*
Butler, Linda K. 1944- *WhoSSW 91*
Butler, Linda Louise 1938- *WhoE 91*
Butler, Lindley Smith 1939- *WhoSSW 91*
Butler, Louis Peter 1953- *WhoE 91*
Butler, Luther Dale 1929- *WhoWrEP 89*
Butler, Malcolm Lee 1958- *WhoSSW 91*
Butler, Manley Caldwell 1925- *WhoAm 90, WhoSSW 91*
Butler, Margaret Kampschaefer 1924- *WhoAm 90, WhoAmW 91*
Butler, Marie Joseph 1860-1940 *BioAmW*
Butler, Marigene H 1931- *WhoAmA 91*
Butler, Marigene Harrington 1931- *WhoE 91*
Butler, Marilyn Ann 1937- *WhoAmW 91*
Butler, Marjorie P 1925- *BiDrAPA 89*
Butler, Mark *PenDiMP*
Butler, Marshall D. 1927- *St&PR 91*
Butler, Mary Anne 1946- *WhoAmW 91*
Butler, Michael 1928- *St&PR 91*
Butler, Michael A. 1956- *WhoWor 91*
Butler, Michael Francis 1935- *WhoAm 90, WhoE 91*
Butler, Michael Perry 1953- *WhoE 91*
Butler, Michelle Ann 1963- *WhoAmW 91*
Butler, Mike W. 1911- *St&PR 91*
Butler, Mildred Allen 1897- *AuBYP 90*
Butler, Mildred Anne 1858-1941 *BiDWomA*
Butler, Mitchell Danny 1950- *St&PR 91*
Butler, Nancy Elizabeth *BiDrAPA 89*
Butler, Nathan *WhoWrEP 89*
Butler, Nicholas Murray *BioIn 16*
Butler, Nicholas Murray 1862-1947 *WorAlBi*
Butler, Octavia E. *BioIn 16*
Butler, Octavia E. 1947- *FemiCLE, MajTwCW*
Butler, Octavia Estelle 1947- *WhoAmW 91, WhoEmL 91*
Butler, Owen B. 1923- *St&PR 91*
Butler, Owen Bradford 1923- *WhoAm 90*
Butler, Patricia Mary *BiDrAPA 89*
Butler, Patrick 1949- *ODwPR 91*
Butler, Patrick Harold 1949- *St&PR 91*
Butler, Paul Bascomb, Jr. 1947- *WhoEmL 91*
Butler, Paul William 1961- *WhoE 91*
Butler, Peter A. 1935- *St&PR 91*
Butler, Pierce 1744-1822 *BioIn 16*
Butler, R. A. 1902-1982 *BioIn 16*
Butler, Rab 1902-1982 *BioIn 16*
Butler, Reginald Cotterell 1913-1981 *DcNaB 1981*
Butler, Richard *TwCCr&M 91*
Butler, Richard 1743-1791 *EncCRAm*
Butler, Richard A., Jr. 1927- *St&PR 91*
Butler, Richard Austen 1902-1982 *DcNaB 1981*
Butler, Richard Bennett 1946- *WhoSSW 91*
Butler, Richard Carlton 1958- *WhoEmL 91*
Butler, Richard Colburn 1910- *WhoAm 90*
Butler, Richard Dean 1930- *WhoAm 90*
Butler, Rick Landes 1956- *WhoEmL 91*
Butler, Robert *BioIn 16*
Butler, Robert Allan 1923- *WhoAm 90*
Butler, Robert Andrews 1955- *WhoEmL 91*
Butler, Robert Francis 1935- *WhoWrEP 89*
Butler, Robert M. 1928?-1989 *ConAu 129*
Butler, Robert N 1927- *BiDrAPA 89*
Butler, Robert Neil 1927- *WhoAm 90, WhoE 91*
Butler, Robert Olen 1945- *WhoWrEP 89*
Butler, Robert Thomas 1925- *St&PR 91, WhoAm 90*
Butler, Robert William 1921- *St&PR 91*
Butler, Roger G. *BiDrAPA 89*
Butler, Ronnie 1931- *ConAu 130*
Butler, Roy Francis 1914- *WhoAm 90*
Butler, Russell 1949- *WhoEmL 91*
Butler, Russell Paul 1959- *WhoEmL 91*
Butler, Samuel 1613-1680 *DcLB 101 [port]*
Butler, Samuel 1835-1902 *BioIn 16, WorAlBi*
Butler, Samuel C. 1930- *St&PR 91*
Butler, Samuel Coles 1930- *WhoAm 90*
Butler, Sarah *FemiCLE*
Butler, Sherrill D. 1950- *St&PR 91*
Butler, Susan Lowell 1944- *ODwPR 91, WhoAm 90*
Butler, Suzanne 1919- *AuBYP 90*
Butler, Tarver H 1931- *BiDrAPA 89*
Butler, Thomas 1943- *BiDrAPA 89*
Butler, Thomas Wright 1952- *WhoEmL 91*
Butler, Tom, Jr. 1914- *St&PR 91*
Butler, Tubal Uriah Buzz 1897-1977 *BioIn 16*
Butler, V. Jack 1930- *BiDrAPA 89*
Butler, Viggo 1942- *St&PR 91*
Butler, Vincent Paul, Jr. 1929- *WhoAm 90*
Butler, Virgil H. 1938- *St&PR 91*
Butler, Walter 1752-1781 *WhNaAH*
Butler, Walter 1898- *EncO&P 3*
Butler, Wilford Arthur 1937- *WhoAm 90*
Butler, William 1929- *AuBYP 90*
Butler, William Joseph 1924- *WhoAm 90, WhoE 91*
Butler, William K. 1952- *St&PR 91*
Butler, William K., II *WhoSSW 91*
Butler, William Langdon 1939- *WhoE 91*
Butler, William McGregor 1957- *WhoSSW 91*
Butler, William Orlando 1791-1880 *LiHiK*
Butler, William T. 1936- *St&PR 91*
Butler, William Thomas 1932- *WhoAm 90*
Butler-Burnette, Cathy Delores 1960- *WhoAmW 91*
Butler of Saffron Walden, Baron 1902-1982 *BioIn 16*
Butler-Turner, Janice Ilene 1936- *WhoAmW 91*
Butlin, Philip Pearson 1938- *St&PR 91*
Butman, Grace Anna 1908- *WhoAmW 91*
Butner, Bonnie Jean 1952- *WhoAmW 91*
Butner, Charles M. 1936- *St&PR 91*
Butner, Fred Washington, Jr. 1927- *WhoAm 90*
Butner, Linda Roberta 1959- *WhoWrEP 89*
Butner, Mary Boemker 1954- *WhoAmW 91, WhoSSW 91, WhoWor 91*
Butner, Mary Boemker 1958- *WhoEmL 91*
Butor, Michel 1926- *ConAu 33NR, EuWr 13, MajTwCW, WhoWor 91, WorAlBi*
Butorac, Frank George 1927- *WhoE 91, WhoWor 91*
Butow, Robert Joseph Charles 1924- *WhoAm 90*
Butowsky, David Martin 1936- *WhoAm 90*
Butrin, JoAnn Elizabeth 1950- *WhoAmW 91*
Butrum, Carl Albert 1945- *BioIn 16*
Butschek, Felix 1932- *WhoWor 91*
Butsko, Jessica Juarez 1957- *WhoAmW 91*
Butson, Alton Thomas 1926- *WhoAm 90, WhoSSW 91*
Butson, Elizabeth 1938- *WhoAmW 91*
Butt, Atta Ullah *BiDrAPA 89*
Butt, Beatrice 1856-1918 *FemiCLE*
Butt, Clara 1872-1936 *PenDiMP*
Butt, Edward Thomas, Jr. 1947- *WhoEmL 91*
Butt, George Franklin 1928- *St&PR 91*
Butt, Harlan W 1950- *WhoAmA 91*
Butt, Howard Edward, Jr. 1927- *WhoAm 90*
Butt, Hugh Roland 1910- *WhoAm 90*
Butt, James Baseden 1929- *IntWWM 90*
Butt, Jimmy Lee 1921- *WhoAm 90*
Butt, John Baecher 1935- *WhoAm 90*
Butt, Mian Khadim Hussain 1911- *WhoWor 91*
Butt, Michael *BioIn 16*
Butt, Muhammad M 1942- *BiDrAPA 89*
Butt, Norman David 1952- *WhoEmL 91*
Butt, P. Lawrence 1941- *St&PR 91*
Butt, Peter D. 1929- *St&PR 91*
Butt, Tom *BioIn 16*
Butt, W.C. *St&PR 91*
Butta, J. Henry 1928- *St&PR 91*
Buttaci, Sal St. John 1941- *WhoWrEP 89*
Buttar, Oanghkar S *BiDrAPA 89*
Butte, Anthony Jeffrey 1951- *WhoSSW 91*
Buttel, Patricia Ann 1960- *WhoAmW 91*
Buttelerin *EncCoWW*
Buttemeyer, Wilhelm 1940- *WhoWor 91*
Buttenheim, Edgar Marion 1922- *WhoAm 90*
Buttenheim, Richard M. 1940- *ODwPR 91*
Buttenwieser, Helen Lehman 1905-1989 *BioIn 16*
Buttenwieser, Lawrence Benjamin 1932- *WhoAm 90*
Buttenwieser, Paul Arthur 1938- *BiDrAPA 89*
Butter, H.D. 1935- *St&PR 91*
Butter, Robert E. 1956- *ODwPR 91*
Butter, Tom 1952- *WhoAmA 91*
Butterbaugh, Robert Clyde 1931- *WhoAmA 91*
Butterbaugh, William T 1932- *BiDrAPA 89*
Butterbrodt, John 1929- *St&PR 91*
Butterbrodt, John Ervin 1929- *WhoAm 90*
Butterbrodt, Thomas C. 1934- *St&PR 91*
Butterfield, Alexander Porter 1926- *WhoAm 90*
Butterfield, Billy 1917-1988 *AnObit 1988, OxCPMus*
Butterfield, Bruce *ODwPR 91*
Butterfield, Bruce Scott 1949- *WhoAm 90*
Butterfield, Charles Edward, Jr. 1928- *WhoE 91*
Butterfield, Craig Irwin 1947- *WhoEmL 91*
Butterfield, David H. 1938- *St&PR 91*
Butterfield, Deborah 1949- *BiDWomA, BioIn 16*
Butterfield, Deborah Kay 1949- *WhoAmA 91*
Butterfield, Diane Marie 1950- *WhoAmW 91, WhoEmL 91*
Butterfield, F. G. *WhoAm 90*
Butterfield, Jack Arlington 1919- *WhoE 91*
Butterfield, Laura Louise 1952- *WhoAmW 91*
Butterfield, Patricia *ODwPR 91*
Butterfield, Patrick T 1945- *BiDrAPA 89*
Butterfield, Paul 1942-1987 *BioIn 16, EncPR&S 89*
Butterfield, Paul, and Better Days *EncPR&S 89*
Butterfield, Paul, Blues Band *EncPR&S 89*
Butterfield, R. Keith 1941- *St&PR 91*
Butterfield, Samuel Hale 1924- *WhoAm 90*
Butterfield, Shona Elizabeth 1946- *WhoWor 91*
Butterfield, Tommy Wayne 1952- *WhoSSW 91*
Butterfield, Virginia Ann 1951- *WhoE 91*
Butterick, George F. 1942-1988 *BioIn 16*
Butterley, Nigel Henry 1935- *IntWWM 90*
Butterman, Jay M *BiDrAPA 89*
Butterman, Mark Bennett 1954- *WhoEmL 91*
Buttermore, Bradley S. 1956- *St&PR 91*
Buttermore, Bradley Scott 1956- *WhoAm 90, WhoEmL 91*
Buttermore, David William 1946- *WhoEmL 91*
Buttermore, William Joseph 1941- *St&PR 91*
Butters, Alfred 1836- *AmLegL*
Butters, Dorothy Gilman *ConAu 30NR*
Butters, Dorothy Gilman 1923- *AuBYP 90, WhoAm 90*
Butters, Nancy Lee 1950- *WhoAmW 91*
Butters, Thomas Arden 1938- *WhoAm 90*
Butterweck, Hans Juergen 1932- *WhoWor 91*
Butterworth, Alan Randolph 1952- *WhoEmL 91*
Butterworth, Arthur 1923- *OxCPMus*
Butterworth, Arthur Eckersley 1923- *IntWWM 90*
Butterworth, Charles E. 1838- *WhoE 91*
Butterworth, David Neil 1934- *IntWWM 90*
Butterworth, Edward Livingston 1914- *St&PR 91*
Butterworth, George Warren 1942- *WhoSSW 91*
Butterworth, Ian 1930- *WhoWor 91*
Butterworth, Jane Rogers Fitch 1937- *WhoAmW 91, WhoWor 91*
Butterworth, Kenneth W. 1925- *St&PR 91*
Butterworth, Mary Peck 1686-1775 *EncCRAm*
Butterworth, Oliver *NewYTBS 90*
Butterworth, Oliver 1915- *AuBYP 90*
Butterworth, Oliver 1915-1990 *ConAu 132*
Butterworth, Paul Stewart 1953- *WhoE 91*
Butterworth, Robert A. 1942- *WhoSSW 91*
Butterworth, Robert Roman 1946- *WhoEmL 91*
Butterworth, William Edmund, III 1929- *AuBYP 90*
Buttery, Henry C. 1924- *St&PR 91*
Butti, Linda 1951- *WhoAmA 91, WhoAmW 91*
Butti, Mary Madeline 1921- *WhoAmW 91*
Buttigieg, Charles John 1942- *WhoWor 91*
Buttigieg, Ray *NewAgMG*
Buttimer, Jane Anne 1956- *WhoE 91*
Buttinger, Catharine 1951- *BiDrAPA 89*
Buttinger, Catharine Sarina Caroline 1951- *WhoAmW 91, WhoE 91*
Buttlar, Rudolph Otto 1934- *WhoAm 90*
Buttle, Edgar Allyn 1903- *WhoAm 90, WhoWor 91*
Buttle, Eugene H. 1927- *St&PR 91*
Buttler, Peter Haviland 1942- *St&PR 91*
Buttlerin *EncCoWW*
Buttner, Edgar Mott 1929- *St&PR 91*
Buttner, Jean Bernhard 1934- *St&PR 91, WhoAm 90*
Buttner, Steven G. 1948- *St&PR 91*
Buttner, W. Murray 1932- *St&PR 91*
Buttolph, David Daniels 1957- *WhoE 91*
Buttolph, Maria Lynn *BiDrAPA 89*
Button, A. Dwight 1917- *St&PR 91*
Button, Bruce Alan 1958- *St&PR 91*
Button, Charles Albert 1951- *WhoSSW 91*
Button, Daniel Evan 1917- *WhoAm 90*
Button, Dick 1929- *WorAlBi*
Button, Edward N. 1927- *St&PR 91*
Button, Jemmy 1816?-1864 *BioIn 16*
Button, Jesse H *BiDrAPA 89*
Button, John William 1928- *St&PR 91*
Button, Kenneth John 1922- *WhoAm 90*
Button, Kenneth Rodman 1946- *WhoE 91*
Button, Rena Pritsker 1925- *WhoAm 90*
Button, Richard Totten 1929- *WhoAm 90*
Button, Robert G. 1929- *ODwPR 91*
Button, Robert Ralph 1938- *St&PR 91*
Button, Thomas *EncCRAm*
Button, William Henry 1871-1944 *EncPaPR 91*
Button-Shafer, Janice 1931- *WhoAmW 91*
Buttons, Red 1919- *BioIn 16, WorAlBi*
Buttorf, Harry William 1952- *WhoEmL 91*
Buttorff, Curtis Deen 1948- *WhoEmL 91*
Buttram, J. Alan 1953- *St&PR 91*
Buttram, Jack Emerson 1932- *WhoSSW 91*
Buttram, James Alan 1953- *WhoSSW 91*
Buttram, James Walter 1926- *St&PR 91*
Buttrey, D. Roscoe 1921- *St&PR 91*
Buttrey, Donald Wayne 1935- *WhoAm 90*
Buttrey, John 1931- *IntWWM 90*
Buttrick, David Gardner 1927- *WhoSSW 91*
Buttrick, Harold 1931- *WhoE 91*
Buttrick, John Arthur 1919- *WhoAm 90*
Buttrum, David A. 1952- *St&PR 91*
Buttrum, Jack 1929- *St&PR 91*
Butts, Arnold William, Jr. 1946- *WhoSSW 91*
Butts, Brian B. *St&PR 91*
Butts, Calvin O., III *BioIn 16*
Butts, David Phillip 1932- *WhoAm 90*
Butts, George Francis 1923- *WhoAm 90*
Butts, H Daniel, III 1939- *WhoAmA 91*
Butts, Herbert Clell 1924- *WhoAm 90*
Butts, Mary 1890-1937 *FemiCLE*
Butts, Mary 1892-1937 *BioIn 16*
Butts, Michael C. 1948- *WhoSSW 91*
Butts, Pamela Denise 1965- *WhoAmW 91*
Butts, Pee Wee 1919-1973 *Ballpl 90*
Butts, Sherman R. 1938- *St&PR 91*
Butts, Virginia *ODwPR 91, WhoAm 90, WhoAmW 91*
Butts, William L. *St&PR 91*
Butynski, William 1944- *WhoE 91*
Butz, Earl Lauer 1909- *BiDrUSE 89*
Butz, Geneva Mae 1944- *WhoAmW 91*
Butz, Mary E. 1957- *WhoAmW 91*
Butz, Otto William 1923- *WhoAm 90*
Butzberger, Paul T. 1954- *St&PR 91*
Butzer, Harold Godfrey 1921- *St&PR 91*
Butzer, Karl W. 1934- *WhoAm 90*
Butzer, Stephen Carl 1945- *BiDrAPA 89*
Butzlaff Voss, Bambi Lyn 1962- *WhoAmW 91*
Butzner, John Decker, Jr. 1917- *WhoAm 90*
Butzow, G.N. 1929- *St&PR 91*
Butzow, Norman Gayle 1946- *St&PR 91*
Buuck, R. John 1935- *WhoAm 90*
Buvinger, Jan 1943- *WhoSSW 91*

Bux, Johann Baptist PenDiDA 89
Bux, Kuda 1905-1981 EncPaPR 91
Bux, William John 1946- WhoEmL 91
Buxbaum, Alexandra 1962- WhoAmW 91
Buxbaum, Frederick David 1946- WhoE 91
Buxbaum, Friedrich PenDiMP
Buxbaum, Linda Zelfman 1937- WhoAmW 91
Buxbaum, Michael 1952- BiDrAPA 89
Buxbaum, Otto 1935- WhoWor 91
Buxbaum, Richard M. 1930- WhoAm 90
Buxbaum, Robert 1939- WhoAmA 91, WhoE 91
Buxbaum, Robert S. 1929- St&PR 91
Buxtehude, Dietrich 1637-1707 BioIn 16
Buxton, A M Bailey 1909- BiDrAPA 89
Buxton, Barry Miller 1949- WhoWrEP 89
Buxton, Beatrice Watt 1943- WhoE 91
Buxton, Bertha Henry 1844-1881 FemiCLE
Buxton, C.L., II 1924- St&PR 91
Buxton, Charles Ingraham, II 1924- WhoAm 90
Buxton, Cindy 1950- ConAu 132
Buxton, Edward F 1917-1990 ConAu 132
Buxton, Ellen 1848- BioIn 16
Buxton, Elliott L. 1924- St&PR 91
Buxton, Eugene A. 1924- St&PR 91
Buxton, Joanna BioIn 16
Buxton, John 1912- ConAu 31NR
Buxton, Jorge Norman 1921- WhoAm 90
Buxton, Joseph Thomas 1938- St&PR 91
Buxton, Marilyn Philbrick 1947- WhoEmL 91
Buxton, Martin Norman 1944- BiDrAPA 89
Buxton, Rex E BiDrAPA 89
Buxton, Richard Millard 1948- WhoWor 91
Buxton, Robert Stevens 1925- WhoE 91
Buxton, Simon Campden 1943- WhoWor 91
Buxton, William D BiDrAPA 89
Buxton, Yvette Marie BiDrAPA 89
Buxton, Zane Kelly 1946- WhoEmL 91
Buya, Wallace Joseph 1925- St&PR 91, WhoAm 90
Buydens-Branchey, Laure B BiDrAPA 89
Buyers, John William Amerman 1928- St&PR 91, WhoAm 90
Buyers, William James Leslie 1937- WhoAm 90
Buyoya, Pierre 1949- WhoWor 91
Buys, Coenraad de 1761- BioIn 16
Buyse, Emile Jules 1927- WhoAm 90
Buyse, Valerie J 1949- BiDrAPA 89
Buyske, Donald Albert 1927- St&PR 91, WhoAm 90
Buysse, Daniel Joseph BiDrAPA 89
Buysse, Paul Henri 1945- WhoWor 91
Buytendorp, Albert August 1931- BiDrAPA 89
Buyukmihci, Hope Sawyer 1913- WhoE 91
Buzacott, John Alan 1937- WhoAm 90
Buzaglio, Abraham 1716-1788 PenDiDA 89
Buzaglo, Jorge David 1943- WhoWor 91
Buzaljko, Grace Wilson 1922- WhoAmW 91
Buzan, Norma Jeanne Stephens 1924- WhoWrEP 89
Buzan, Randall Douglas BiDrAPA 89
Buzard, James Albert 1927- WhoAm 90
Buzard, Rosie Marie 1943- WhoE 91
Buzbee, John W. 1932- St&PR 91
Buzbee, R. Robert 1942- St&PR 91
Buzbee, Richard Edgar 1931- WhoAm 90, WhoWrEP 89
Buzby, Russell Conwell 1934- St&PR 91
Buzea, Constanta 1941- EncCoWW
Buzen, Jeffrey P. 1943- St&PR 91
Buzhardt, John 1936- Ballpl 90
Buziak, Frank T. 1947- St&PR 91
Buzick, William A., Jr. 1920- St&PR 91
Buzick, William Alonson, Jr. 1920- WhoAm 90
Buzo, Alexander 1944- ConLC 61 [port]
Buzogany, Robert J. ODwPR 91
Buzogany, William M 1932- BiDrAPA 89
Buzunis, Constantine Dino 1958- WhoEmL 91, WhoWor 91
Buzza, Bonnie Wilson 1944- WhoAmW 91
Buzzard, John Andrew 1921- St&PR 91
Buzzard, Steven Ray 1946- WhoEmL 91
Buzzell, Barbara F. 1953- ODwPR 91
Buzzell, Robert Dow 1933- WhoAm 90
Buzzelli, Charlotte Grace 1947- WhoEmL 91
Buzzelli, Elizabeth Kane 1936- WhoWrEP 89
Buzzelli, Joseph Anthony 1907- WhoAmA 91N
Buzzi, Peter L. 1960- St&PR 91
Buzzitta, Louis V. 1931- St&PR 91
Bwint, Derek Shway 1941- St&PR 91
Byakod, Basappa G BiDrAPA 89
Byam, Marie Elizabeth 1949- WhoAmW 91, WhoEmL 91
Byam, Milton Sylvester 1922- WhoAm 90
Byam, Patti Lynn 1956- St&PR 91
Byam, Seward Groves, Jr. 1928- WhoE 91, WhoWor 91
Byard, Carole 1941- BioIn 16
Byard, Carole Marie 1941- WhoAmA 91
Byard, Jaki BioIn 16
Byars, Betsy 1928- AuBYP 90, MajTwCW
Byars, Donna WhoAmA 91
Byars, Ila Pearl 1908- WhoAmW 91
Byars, John Buford, Jr. 1928- St&PR 91
Byars, Walter Ryland, Jr. 1928- WhoAm 90
Byas, Don 1912-1972 BioIn 16
Byatt, A. S. 1936- BioIn 16
Byatt, A.S. 1936- ConAu 33NR
Byatt, A. S. 1936- FemiCLE
Byatt, A S 1936- MajTwCW
Byatt, Antonia Susan 1936- BioIn 16
Byatt, Ronald Archer Campbell 1930- WhoWor 91
Bybee, David William 1957- WhoEmL 91
Bybee, H. Malcolm 1944- WhoAm 90
Bybee, Jimmy L. 1937- St&PR 91
Bybee, O. Lynn 1937- St&PR 91
Bybee, Paul R 1931- BiDrAPA 89
Bybee, Rodger Wayne 1942- WhoAm 90
Bybee, Shannon L., Jr. 1938- St&PR 91
Bybee, Shannon Larmer, Jr. 1938- WhoAm 90
Byberg, Patricia J. 1937- St&PR 91
Bycer, Max 1925- St&PR 91
Bychkov, Semyon 1952- IntWWM 90, PenDiMP
Byck, Robert Samuel 1933- WhoAm 90
Bycraft, John Thomas, III 1936- St&PR 91
Byczek, Lloyd Vincent 1944- IntWWM 90
Bydzovsky, Viktor 1944- WhoWor 91
Bye, Arthur Edwin, Jr. 1919- WhoAm 90
Bye, James Edward 1930- WhoAm 90
Bye, Ranulph 1916- WhoAmA 91
Bye, Ranulph DeBayeux 1916- WhoAm 90
Bye, Raymond Erwin, Jr. 1944- WhoAm 90
Bye, Roseanne Marie 1946- WhoAmW 91
Bye, Rune 1947- WhoWor 91
Bye, William H. 1921- St&PR 91
Byer, Allan J. 1933- St&PR 91
Byer, Don BioIn 16
Byer, Howard N. 1930- ODwPR 91
Byer, James L. 1932- St&PR 91
Byer, Kathryn Stripling 1944- WhoWrEP 89
Byer, Louis BiDrAPA 89
Byer, Steven David 1955- WhoEmL 91
Byerley, Curt Joseph 1956- WhoE 91, WhoEmL 91
Byerley, William F 1953- BiDrAPA 89
Byerly, Bud 1920- Ballpl 90
Byerly, F. Hanes 1935- St&PR 91
Byerly, Greg 1949- ConAu 130
Byerly, Kenneth C. 1932- St&PR 91
Byerly, Leroy James BiDrAPA 89
Byerly, LeRoy James 1931- WhoE 91
Byerly, Theodore Carroll 1902-1990 WhoAm 90
Byerly, Thomas J. 1947- St&PR 91
Byerly, Wesley Grimes, Jr. 1926- WhoSSW 91
Byerly, William Jackson, III 1951- WhoEmL 91
Byerrum, Richard Uglow 1920- WhoAm 90
Byers, Alan Howard 1949- WhoWor 91
Byers, Brent Eugene 1950- WhoSSW 91
Byers, Buckley M. 1917-1989 BioIn 16
Byers, Buckley Morris 1917-1989 WhoAm 90
Byers, Charles F. 1946- ODwPR 91
Byers, Cynthia Ann 1964- WhoSSW 91
Byers, David Earl 1951- WhoEmL 91
Byers, David Stephen BiDrAPA 89
Byers, Donald 1930- BiDrAPA 89
Byers, Donna Jean 1956- WhoAmW 91
Byers, Edward A 1939-1989 ConAu 129
Byers, Fleur WhoAmA 91
Byers, Frank 1915-1984 DcNaB 1981
Byers, Frank M., Sr. St&PR 91N
Byers, George William 1923- WhoAm 90
Byers, Horace Robert 1906- WhoAm 90
Byers, Howard W. 1856- AmLegL
Byers, John Winchester 1939- WhoSSW 91
Byers, Lawrence Wallace 1916- WhoSSW 91
Byers, Lisa Louise 1955- WhoSSW 91
Byers, Michael Carl 1952- WhoEmL 91
Byers, Nina 1930- WhoAm 90
Byers, Paul Heed 1943- WhoE 91
Byers, Richard George 1937- St&PR 91
Byers, Rosemarie 1936- WhoAmW 91
Byers, Timothy Patrick 1954- WhoWrEP 89
Byers, Virginia Bullard 1928- WhoAmW 91
Byers, Walter 1922- WhoAm 90
Byers, William Sewell 1925- WhoSSW 91
Byford-Peterson, Evelyn Margaret 1944- WhoE 91
Bygate, Bruce Thom 1932- St&PR 91
Bygraves, Max 1922- OxCPMus
Byham, Carolyn Mentzer 1941- WhoAmW 91
Byington, Cyrus 1793-1868 WhNaAH
Byington, Homer Morrison, III 1934- WhoE 91
Byington, Robert Lee 1951- WhoEmL 91
Byington, S. John WhoAm 90
Byington, Sally Ruth 1935- WhoAmW 91
Byington, Spring 1893-1971 WorAlBi
Byington, Steven Charles 1945- St&PR 91
Byington, Walter Montgomery 1932- St&PR 91
Byk, Peter Henry 1928- WhoWor 91
Bykat, Alexander 1940- WhoSSW 91
Bykerk, Cecil Dale 1944- St&PR 91
Bykhovsky, Arkadi G. 1943- St&PR 91
Bykhovsky, Arkadi Gregory 1943- WhoAm 90
Bykov, Valery Alexeevich 1938- WhoWor 91
Bykowski, Anthony 1945- WhoEmL 91
Byledbal, Ronald W BiDrAPA 89
Byler, Jennifer Curtis 1958- WhoEmL 91
Byler, Robert Eugene 1933- BiDrAPA 89
Byles, Daniel William 1923- WhoAm 90
Byles, Edward IntWWM 90
Byles, Robert Valmore 1937- WhoSSW 91
Bylinsky, Gene Michael 1930- WhoAm 90, WhoWrEP 89
Bylivelt, Jacques PenDiDA 89
Bylsma, Anner 1934- IntWWM 90, PenDiMP
Bylsma, Carol Ann 1941- WhoAmW 91
Bymun, Dennis T. 1945- St&PR 91
Bynagle, Hans Edward 1946- WhoEmL 91
Byng, Douglas 1893-1987 OxCPMus
Byng, Julian, Mrs. 1870-1949 FemiCLE
Bynum, Barbara Stewart 1936- WhoAm 90, WhoAmW 91
Bynum, Cheryl Dianne 1960- WhoWrEP 89
Bynum, E Anderson 1922- WhoAmA 91
Bynum, George T., III 1951- WhoSSW 91
Bynum, Harry Lynell 1953- St&PR 91
Bynum, Jack Edward, Jr. 1929- WhoSSW 91
Bynum, James Lowell 1934- WhoSSW 91
Bynum, Randy Jon 1950- WhoEmL 91
Bynum, William Dallas 1846-1927 AmLegL
Byram, James Asberry, Jr. 1954- WhoEmL 91
Byram, John G. 1952- St&PR 91
Byram, Kelly Gene 1960- WhoSSW 91
Byram, Kim 1959- St&PR 91
Byram, Zooey Joan 1949- WhoAmW 91
Byrd Family EncCRAm
Byrd, Andrew Wayne 1954- WhoEmL 91, WhoSSW 91
Byrd, Benjamin Franklin, Jr. 1918- WhoAm 90
Byrd, Bette Jean 1928- WhoAm 90
Byrd, Bill 1907- Ballpl 90
Byrd, Charles W., Jr. 1950- WhoSSW 91
Byrd, Charlie 1925- OxCPMus, WorAlBi
Byrd, Chester Lamar 1936- St&PR 91
Byrd, D Gibson 1923- WhoAmA 91
Byrd, David ConTFT 8
Byrd, David Lamar 1922- WhoAm 90
Byrd, Deborah BioIn 16
Byrd, Donald BioIn 16
Byrd, Donald 1932- DrBIPA 90
Byrd, Frederick Ellis, Jr. 1956- WhoSSW 91
Byrd, Gary BioIn 16
Byrd, Gloria Jeanette 1945- WhoSSW 91
Byrd, Harriett Elizabeth 1926- WhoAmW 91
Byrd, Harry 1925- Ballpl 90
Byrd, Harry F., Jr. 1914- WorAlBi
Byrd, Harry Flood, Jr. 1914- WhoAm 90
Byrd, Helen M. 1930- St&PR 91
Byrd, Isaac Burlin 1925- WhoAm 90
Byrd, James Cozby, III BiDrAPA 89
Byrd, Jay WhoWrEP 89
Byrd, Jerry 1947- WhoAmA 91
Byrd, Joann Kathleen 1943- WhoAmW 91
Byrd, Jonathan Eugene 1952- WhoEmL 91
Byrd, Kathleen Mary 1949- WhoAmW 91
Byrd, Larry Donald 1936- WhoSSW 91
Byrd, Laura Jeanne 1963- WhoSSW 91
Byrd, LaVerne 1957- WhoSSW 91
Byrd, Linward Tonnett 1921- WhoAm 90
Byrd, Lloyd Garland 1923- WhoAm 90
Byrd, Marion Everton 1936- St&PR 91
Byrd, Martha Hunter 1930- WhoWrEP 89
Byrd, Mary Laager 1935- WhoAmW 91
Byrd, Max 1942- TwCCr&M 91
Byrd, Michaele Abner 1949- WhoAmW 91
Byrd, Milton Bruce 1922- WhoAm 90
Byrd, Odell Richard, Jr. WhoWrEP 89
Byrd, Otto Lee 1946- WhoEmL 91
Byrd, Pamela Ann 1948- WhoSSW 91
Byrd, Richard E. 1888-1957 WorAlBi
Byrd, Richard Edward 1931- WhoAm 90
Byrd, Richard Evelyn 1860-1925 AmLegL
Byrd, Richard Evelyn 1888-1957 BioIn 16
Byrd, Richard Evelyn, Jr. BioIn 16
Byrd, Richard Hays 1939- WhoAm 90
Byrd, Richard T. 1935- St&PR 91
Byrd, Robert C. BioIn 16
Byrd, Robert C. 1917- WorAlBi
Byrd, Robert Carlyle 1917- WhoAm 90, WhoSSW 91, WhoWor 91
Byrd, Robert Ernest 1919- St&PR 91
Byrd, Robert J. 1942- WhoWrEP 89
Byrd, Robert John 1942- WhoAmA 91
Byrd, Robert W. 1935- St&PR 91
Byrd, Sammy 1906-1981 Ballpl 90
Byrd, Sandra Judith 1960- WhoAmW 91
Byrd, Stephen Fred 1928- WhoAm 90
Byrd, Stephen Lee 1961- BiDrAPA 89
Byrd, Stephen Timothy 1957- WhoSSW 91
Byrd, Sue Gibson 1953- WhoAmW 91
Byrd, Timothy L BiDrAPA 89
Byrd, Walter R., Jr. BiDrAPA 89
Byrd, William 1543-1623 PenDiMPA
Byrd, William 1652-1704 EncCRAm
Byrd, William 1674-1744 BioIn 16, EncCRAm
Byrd, William 1729-1777 EncCRAm
Byrd-Lawler, Barbara Ann 1952- WhoAm 90, WhoEmL 91
Byrds, The EncPR&S 89, OxCPMus, WhoNeCM A, WorAlBi
Byrdy, Harold S 1936- BiDrAPA 89
Byres, Marshall Henry 1951- WhoWor 91
Byres, Terence James 1936- WhoWor 91
Byrkit, Donald Raymond 1933- WhoSSW 91
Byrn, William A., Jr. 1922- St&PR 91
Byrne, Anthony John 1939- WhoSSW 91
Byrne, Beth BioIn 16
Byrne, Bill Weyman 1929- St&PR 91
Byrne, Bobby 1884-1964 Ballpl 90
Byrne, Charles Joseph 1943- WhoAmA 91
Byrne, Daniel William 1958- WhoE 91, WhoEmL 91, WhoWor 91
Byrne, David BioIn 16
Byrne, David 1952- OxCPMus, WhoAm 90
Byrne, David Francis 1932- St&PR 91
Byrne, David Ronald 1936- WhoAm 90
Byrne, Dennis E. 1947- ODwPR 91
Byrne, Dennis Joseph 1940- St&PR 91
Byrne, Dennis William 1946- WhoEmL 91
Byrne, Donn Erwin 1931- WhoAm 90
Byrne, Dorothy E. 1947- St&PR 91
Byrne, Edith Teresa 1945- WhoEmL 91
Byrne, Edward Blake 1935- WhoAm 90
Byrne, Frank Loyola 1928- WhoAm 90
Byrne, Gary C. 1942- St&PR 91
Byrne, Gayle Elizabeth 1939- WhoAmW 91
Byrne, George Melvin 1933- WhoWor 91
Byrne, Gerard Anthony 1944- WhoE 91
Byrne, Granville Bland, III 1952- WhoSSW 91
Byrne, H. Richard 1947- St&PR 91
Byrne, James Frederick 1931- WhoAm 90
Byrne, James H. 1937- ODwPR 91
Byrne, James Joseph 1908- WhoAm 90
Byrne, James Thomas, Jr. 1939- WhoAm 90
Byrne, Jane 1934 BioIn 16
Byrne, Jane Burke 1934- BioAmW
Byrne, Jerome Camillus 1925- WhoAm 90
Byrne, Jessica Price 1952- BiDrAPA 89
Byrne, John 1950- EncACom
Byrne, John Albert-Charles 1958- WhoE 91
Byrne, John Edward 1925- WhoAm 90
Byrne, John J. 1932- St&PR 91
Byrne, John James 1920- WhoAm 90
Byrne, John Joseph, Jr. 1932- WhoAm 90
Byrne, John Lindley 1950- WhoE 91
Byrne, John Patrick 1951- WhoEmL 91
Byrne, John Vincent 1928- WhoAm 90
Byrne, Joseph 1923- WhoAm 90
Byrne, Joseph Ahern, Jr. 1953- WhoEmL 91
Byrne, Joseph J. 1946- St&PR 91
Byrne, Lori King 1960- WhoSSW 91
Byrne, Louis BiDrAPA 89
Byrne, Luis O BiDrAPA 89
Byrne, Maggie Ann BiDrAPA 89
Byrne, Mary Ann 1952- BiDrAPA 89
Byrne, Mary Assisium BioIn 16
Byrne, Michael C. 1954- St&PR 91
Byrne, Michael John 1948- WhoE 91
Byrne, Michael Joseph 1928- WhoWor 91
Byrne, Neil J. 1928- St&PR 91
Byrne, Noel Thomas 1943- WhoWor 91
Byrne, Patrick James 1949- WhoEmL 91
Byrne, Patrick Michael 1952- WhoE 91, WhoEmL 91
Byrne, Peter 1932- IntWWM 90
Byrne, Richard Hill 1915- WhoAm 90
Byrne, Robert William 1958- WhoEmL 91
Byrne, Tommy 1919- Ballpl 90, BioIn 16
Byrne, Virginia Marie 1967- WhoAmW 91
Byrnes, Arthur Francis 1917- WhoAm 90
Byrnes, Donald J. 1926- St&PR 91, WhoSSW 91
Byrnes, Edward G., Jr. 1941- St&PR 91
Byrnes, Frederick Joseph WhoWrEP 89

Byrnes, Gene *EncACom*
Byrnes, George Bartholomew 1911- *WhoAm 90*
Byrnes, James Bernard 1917- *WhoAm 90, WhoAmA 91*
Byrnes, James F. 1879-1972 *WorAlBi*
Byrnes, James Francis 1879-1972 *BiDrUSE 89, BioIn 16*
Byrnes, James J. 1941- *St&PR 91*
Byrnes, Kathleen Ann 1950- *WhoEmL 91*
Byrnes, Mary Alice 1931- *WhoAm 90*
Byrnes, Michael Francis 1957- *WhoEmL 91*
Byrnes, Milt 1916-1979 *Ballpl 90*
Byrnes, Ralph Robert 1942- *St&PR 91*
Byrnes, Raymond A. 1941- *WhoE 91*
Byrnes, Robert E. 1929- *St&PR 91*
Byrnes, Robert Francis 1917- *WhoAm 90, WhoWrEP 89*
Byrnes, Robert John, III 1948- *WhoEmL 91*
Byrnes, Robert Michael 1937- *St&PR 91*
Byrnes, Shirley May 1947- *WhoEmL 91*
Byrnes, Sondra J. 1944- *ODwPR 91*
Byrnes, Thomas C. 1948- *St&PR 91*
Byrnes, Victor Allen 1906- *WhoAm 90*
Byrnes, William Joseph 1940- *WhoWor 91*
Byrnes, William L. 1921- *St&PR 91*
Byrns, Joseph Wellington 1869-1936 *AmLegL*
Byrnside, Oscar Jehu, Jr. 1935- *WhoAm 90*
Byroade, Henry Alfred 1913- *BioIn 16*
Byrom, Fletcher L. 1918- *St&PR 91*
Byrom, Fletcher Lauman 1918- *WhoAm 90*
Byrom, Jack Edwards 1929- *WhoSSW 91*
Byrom, Jack L. 1946- *St&PR 91*
Byrom, John Foster, Jr. 1952- *WhoE 91*
Byron, Beverly Butcher 1932- *WhoAm 90, WhoAmW 91, WhoE 91*
Byron, Bill *Ballpl 90*
Byron, Catherine 1947- *FemiCLE*
Byron, Charles Anthony 1919- *WhoAmA 91*
Byron, Christopher *BioIn 16*
Byron, David Elliot 1949- *WhoEmL 91, WhoSSW 91, WhoWor 91*
Byron, Don *BioIn 16*
Byron, Frederick William, Jr. 1938- *WhoAm 90*
Byron, George Gordon 1788-1824 *BioIn 16, DcLB 96 [port], WorAlBi*
Byron, Harold J *BiDrAPA 89*
Byron, Marc Vincent 1963- *WhoE 91*
Byron, Medora Gordon *FemiCLE*
Byron, Michaea 1927- *WhoAmW 91*
Byron, Michael 1954- *WhoAmA 91*
Byron, N. Lovelace 1935- *WhoSSW 91*
Byron, Robert Sill 1931- *BiDrAPA 89*
Byron, Robert Welton 1925- *St&PR 91*
Byron, Stuart 1941- *WhoWrEP 89*
Byron, William James 1927- *WhoAm 90, WhoE 91*
Byrum, Donald Roy 1942- *WhoAmA 91*
Byrum, James Edward 1945- *St&PR 91*
Byrum, Joe B. 1946- *St&PR 91*
Byrum, Ruthven Holmes 1896- *WhoAmA 91N*
Byrum-Ellerman, Kay Frances 1942- *WhoAmW 91*
Bysiewicz, Shirley Raissi *WhoAmW 91*
Bystritsky, Alexander *BiDrAPA 89*
Bystrom, Marty 1958- *Ballpl 90*
Bystryn, Jean-Claude 1938- *WhoAm 90, WhoE 91, WhoWor 91*
Bywater, George Pilsbury 1929- *St&PR 91*
Bywater, Raymond L. 1911- *St&PR 91*
Bywater, William Harold 1920- *WhoAm 90*
Bywater, Willis McNeill 1939- *St&PR 91*
Bywaters, Candace Leah 1947- *WhoAmW 91*
Bywaters, David R. 1932- *St&PR 91*
Byyny, Richard Lee 1939- *WhoAm 90*
Bzdula, Wayne Barry 1951- *St&PR 91*
Bzezinski, Joseph Paul 1953- *WhoAm 90*
Bzura, Greg George 1937- *St&PR 91*

C

C, E *BiDEWW*
C de Baca, Celeste M. 1957- *WhoHisp 91*
C de Baca, Manuel 1853-1915 *AmLegL*
C. Rice, Eugene 1943- *BiDrAPA 89*
Caamano, Roberto 1923- *IntWWM 90*
Caan, James 1939- *WorAlBi*
Caan, James 1940- *WhoAm 90*
Cabada, Heriberto Ramon *BiDrAPA 89*
Cabaj, Robert Paul 1948- *BiDrAPA 89, WhoE 91*
Cabak, Michael R. 1933- *St&PR 91*
Cabala, John Anthony *BiDrAPA 89*
Caballe, Montserrat 1933- *IntWWM 90, PenDiMP, WhoWor 91, WorAlBi*
Caballero, Anna Marie 1954- *WhoHisp 91*
Caballero, Bernardino 1839-1912 *BioIn 16*
Caballero, Eduardo *WhoHisp 91*
Caballero, Fernan 1796-1877 *EncCoWW*
Caballero, Francisco Largo 1869-1946 *BioIn 16*
Caballero, Ivan Roberto *BiDrAPA 89*
Caballero, Manuel 1931- *ConAu 132, HispWr 90*
Caballero, Manuel Fernandez 1835-1906 *OxCPMus*
Caballero, Putsy 1927- *Ballpl 90*
Caballero, Ramiro *Ballpl 90*
Caballero, Raymond C. 1942- *WhoHisp 91*
Caballero, Servando 1942- *WhoHisp 91*
Caballero Calderon, E. *HispWr 90*
Caballero Calderon, Eduardo 1910- *HispWr 90*
Cabaltica, Melanio L *BiDrAPA 89*
Caban, Beatriz L. 1962- *WhoHisp 91*
Caban, Carlos Augusto *BiDrAPA 89*
Caban, Charles Henry 1941- *WhoSSW 91*
Caban, Luis A. 1939- *WhoHisp 91*
Cabanas, Elizabeth Ann 1948- *WhoAmW 91*
Cabanas, Humberto 1947- *WhoHisp 91*
Cabanas, Justo Jose 1936- *BiDrAPA 89*
Cabanas Thorton, Elizabeth Ann 1948- *WhoEmL 91*
Cabanes, Carolina B *BiDrAPA 89*
Cabanillas, Elba M. 1956- *WhoEmL 91*
Cabanis, Alain Marcel 1943- *WhoWor 91*
Cabanis, Jose 1922- *WhoWor 91*
Cabaniss, William Jelks, Jr. 1938- *WhoSSW 91*
Cabansag, Vicente Dacanay, Jr. 1942- *WhoWor 91*
Cabarcas, Elina 1932- *WhoWrEP 89*
Cabaret, Bernard 1938- *WhoWor 91*
Cabasso, Ike *St&PR 91*
Cabassol, Philippe Charles 1952- *WhoWor 91*
Cabat, Erni *BioIn 16*
Cabat, Rose *BioIn 16*
Cabbabe, Edmond Bechir 1947- *WhoEmL 91*
Cabbiness, Carl Owen 1940- *St&PR 91*
Cabeen, Samuel Kirkland 1931- *WhoAm 90*
Cabel, Antonio G., Jr. *BiDrAPA 89*
Cabell, Elizabeth Arlisse 1947- *WhoAmW 91*
Cabell, Enos 1949- *Ballpl 90*
Cabell, William Daniel 1908- *WhoAm 90*
Cabey, Alfred Arthur, Jr. 1935- *WhoSSW 91*
Cabeza de Baca, Ezequiel 1864-1917 *BioIn 16*
Cabeza de Baca, Fernando E. 1937- *BioIn 16*
Cabeza De Vaca, Alvar Nunez 1490?-1557? *EncCRAm*
Cabeza De Vaca, Alvar Nunez 1490?-1560? *WhNaAH, WorAlBi*
Cabezas, Omar 1951?- *ConAu 131, HispWr 90*
Cabezas, Robert Thomas 1940- *St&PR 91*
Cabezut, Alejandro 1962- *WhoHisp 91*
Cabezut-Ortiz, Delores J. 1948- *WhoHisp 91*
Cabib, Leila *BioIn 16*
Cabibbo, Salvatore V. 1931- *St&PR 91*
Cabieles, Lucy 1924- *WhoHisp 91*
Cabillonar, Margo Naomi 1941- *WhoAmW 91*
Cabiro, Richard J. 1943- *St&PR 91*
Cable, Carole Law-Gagnon 1944- *WhoAmW 91*
Cable, Charles Allen 1932- *WhoAm 90, WhoWor 91*
Cable, Dana Gerard 1943- *WhoE 91*
Cable, Donald Aubrey 1927- *WhoAm 90*
Cable, Goody *BioIn 16*
Cable, H. Edward *St&PR 91N*
Cable, Howard Reid 1920- *WhoAm 90*
Cable, Howard Wilson, Jr. 1937- *St&PR 91*
Cable, James 1920- *ConAu 33NR*
Cable, Jane Nicholson 1935- *WhoSSW 91*
Cable, John A. 1922- *St&PR 91*
Cable, John N. *WhoAm 90*
Cable, Mabel Elizabeth 1935- *WhoE 91*
Cable, Margaret *IntWWM 90*
Cable, Maxine Roth *WhoAmA 91*
Cable, Mildred *BioIn 16*
Cable, Mildred 1878-1952 *FemiCLE*
Cable, Mildred, and Francesca French *FemiCLE*
Cable, Nevyle R. 1952- *St&PR 91*
Cable, Richard Albert 1950- *WhoEmL 91*
Cabo, Federico *WhoHisp 91*
Caborn, Rod *ODwPR 91*
Cabot, Bruce 1905-1972 *WorAlBi*
Cabot, Charles C., Jr. 1930- *St&PR 91*
Cabot, Charles Codman, Jr. 1930- *WhoAm 90*
Cabot, Harold 1929- *WhoAm 90*
Cabot, Hugh 1930- *WhoAmA 91*
Cabot, Hugh, III 1930- *WhoWor 91*
Cabot, John *EncCRAm*
Cabot, John 1450-1498 *BioIn 16, WhNaAH*
Cabot, John 1450?-1499? *WorAlBi*
Cabot, John G.L. 1934- *St&PR 91*
Cabot, John G. L. 1934- *WhoAm 90, WhoE 91*
Cabot, John M. 1901-1981 *BioIn 16*
Cabot, Joseph 1921- *WhoWor 91*
Cabot, Lewis P. 1937- *St&PR 91*
Cabot, Lewis Pickering 1937- *WhoWor 91*
Cabot, Louis Wellington 1921- *WhoAm 90, WhoE 91, WhoWor 91*
Cabot, Paul Codman 1898- *WhoAm 90*
Cabot, Powell M. 1931- *St&PR 91*
Cabot, Powell Mason 1931- *WhoE 91*
Cabot, Robert Codman 1938- *WhoSSW 91*
Cabot, Samuel, III 1940- *St&PR 91*
Cabot, Sebastian 1482?-1557 *WorAlBi*
Cabot, Sebastian 1484?-1557 *EncCRAm*
Cabot, Susan 1927-1986 *BioIn 16*
Cabot, Thomas Dudley 1897- *WhoAm 90*
Cabot, Walter M. 1933- *St&PR 91*
Caboto, Giovanni 1450?-1498 *WhNaAH*
Cabral, Amilcar *BioIn 16*
Cabral, Elizabeth Barbara 1964- *WhoAmW 91*
Cabral, Judith Ann 1951- *WhoAmW 91*
Cabral, Olga Marie 1909- *WhoWrEP 89*
Cabral, Pedro Alvarez 1467?-1520 *WorAlBi*
Cabral, Siegfried J. 1934- *St&PR 91*
Cabranes, Jose A. 1940- *WhoHisp 91*
Cabranes, Jose Alberto 1940- *WhoAm 90, WhoE 91*
Cabrera, Aguilar Rafael 1954- *BiDrAPA 89*
Cabrera, Angelina *WhoHisp 91*
Cabrera, Eduardo *WhoHisp 91*
Cabrera, Fernando, Jr. *BiDrAPA 89*
Cabrera, Fernando J 1928- *BiDrAPA 89*
Cabrera, Gilda 1949- *WhoHisp 91*
Cabrera, Hector Ramon 1955- *WhoE 91*
Cabrera, James C. 1935- *St&PR 91*
Cabrera, Juan C *BiDrAPA 89*
Cabrera, Juan J. 1959- *St&PR 91*
Cabrera, Lydia 1900- *BioIn 16, HispWr 90*
Cabrera, Manuel Estrada 1857-1924 *BioIn 16*
Cabrera, Nestor L. 1957- *WhoHisp 91*
Cabrera, Orlando 1925- *BiDrAPA 89*
Cabrera, Richard Anthony 1941- *WhoHisp 91*
Cabrera, Rosa Maria 1918- *WhoHisp 91*
Cabrera-Baukus, Maria B. 1954- *WhoHisp 91*
Cabrera Infante, G. 1929- *BioIn 16, HispWr 90, MajTwCW*
Cabrera Infante, Guillermo 1929- *BioIn 16*
Cabrera-Mendez, Fabio 1943- *BiDrAPA 89*
Cabrillo, Juan Rodriguez *BioIn 16, WorAlBi*
Cabrillo, Juan Rodriguez 1500?-1543 *WhNaAH*
Cabrillo, Juan Rodriguez De 1495?-1543 *EncCRAm*
Cabrinety, Patricia Butler 1932- *WhoAmW 91, WhoE 91, WhoWrEP 89*
Cabrini, Frances Xavier 1850-1917 *BioIn 16*
Cabrini, Francis Xavier 1850-1917 *WorAlBi*
Cabugao, Roberto P., Jr. *BiDrAPA 89*
Cabus, Joseph *PenDiDA 89*
Cacace, John 1939- *St&PR 91*
Cacavio, Anne R. 1919- *St&PR 91*
Caccamise, Alfred Edward 1919- *WhoSSW 91*
Caccamise, Genevra Louise Ball 1934- *WhoAmW 91, WhoSSW 91*
Caccamo, Nicholas James 1944- *St&PR 91, WhoAm 90*
Caccamo, Pedro 1936- *WhoHisp 91*
Caccavale, Judith Lansdowne 1941- *WhoWrEP 89*
Caccavale, Kenneth Lee *BiDrAPA 89*
Caccavallo, Steven Mark 1953- *WhoEmL 91*
Cacchione, Peter V. 1897-1947 *EncAL*
Caccia, Harold Anthony 1905-1990 *NewYTBS 90 [port]*
Cacciamani, Eugene Richard, Jr. 1936- *WhoAm 90*
Cacciatore, Anthony Joseph 1943- *St&PR 91*
Cacciatore, Ronald Keith 1937- *WhoSSW 91*
Cacciatore, S. Sammy, Jr. 1942- *WhoAm 90*
Cacciavillan, Agostino 1926- *WhoAm 90*
Caccini, Francesca 1587-1640? *BioIn 16*
Caccini, Giulio 1545?-1618 *PenDiMP A*
Cacciola, Eugene John *BiDrAPA 89*
Caccioppoli, Giuseppe 1940- *BiDrAPA 89*
Cacciotti, Joseph John 1930- *St&PR 91*
Caceres, Andres Avelino 1836-1923 *BioIn 16*
Caceres, Edgardo 1948- *WhoWor 91*
Caceres, German Gustavo 1954- *WhoWor 91*
Caceres, Walter George 1927- *WhoSSW 91*
Cacharel, Jean 1932- *ConDes 90*
Cacheris, James C. 1933- *WhoAm 90*
Cachia, Pierre Jacques 1921- *WhoAm 90, WhoWrEP 89*
Cachin, Gilles Marcel 1869-1958 *BiDFrPL*
Cachules, Sotiros N. *BioIn 16*
Cacicedo, Jean Williams- *BioIn 16*
Cacicedo, Paul 1927- *WhoHisp 91*
Cacioppo, John Terrance 1951- *WhoAm 90*
Cacioppo, Joseph Michael 1951- *St&PR 91*
Cacioppo, Lisa Jane 1960- *ODwPR 91, WhoEmL 91*
Cackener, Helen Elizabeth Lewis 1926- *WhoWrEP 89*
Cacoyannis, Michael 1922- *BioIn 16, WhoWor 91*
Cadagan, Dan John, III 1949- *WhoEmL 91*
Cadaret, Greg 1962- *Ballpl 90*
Cadbury-Brown, Henry Thomas 1913- *ConDes 90*
Caddell, Cecilia Mary 1813?-1877 *FemiCLE*
Caddell, Debbie Eileen 1957- *WhoEmL 91*
Caddell, Foster 1921- *WhoAmA 91, WhoE 91, WhoWor 91*
Caddell, Harold Lewis 1934- *WhoWor 91*
Caddell, John A. 1910- *WhoAm 90*
Caddell, John A. 1930- *St&PR 91*
Cadden, James J 1939- *BiDrAPA 89*
Cadden, Thomas Scott 1923- *ConAu 131*
Cadden, Thomas W. 1933- *St&PR 91*
Cadden, Tom Scott *ConAu 131*
Cadden, Vivian Liebman 1917- *WhoAm 90*
Caddy, Edmund Harrington Homer, Jr. 1928- *WhoAm 90*
Caddy, Eileen 1917- *NewAgE 90*
Caddy, Ian Graham 1947- *IntWWM 90*
Caddy, Peter 1917- *NewAgE 90*
Cade, Alexander *ConAu 32NR*
Cade, Cheryl A. 1946- *WhoAmW 91*
Cade, Cynthia Todd 1959- *WhoEmL 91*
Cade, Frances Renee 1946- *WhoE 91*
Cade, Jack Carlton 1948- *WhoEmL 91, WhoWor 91*
Cade, John A. 1929- *WhoE 91*
Cade, Robin *TwCCr&M 91*
Cade, Toni *MajTwCW*
Cade, Walter, III *WhoE 91*
Cade, Walter, III 1936- *WhoAmA 91*
Cadell, Elizabeth 1903- *FemiCLE*
Cadell, Jessie Ellen 1844-1884 *FemiCLE*
Cademartori, Gary M. 1941- *St&PR 91*

Cadena, Alvaro 1943- St&PR 91
Cadena, Carlos C. WhoHisp 91
Cadena, Guillermo M BiDrAPA 89
Cadenas, Ricardo A. 1953- WhoHisp 91
Cadenhead, Alfred Paul 1926- WhoAm 90
Cadenhead, David James 1959- BiDrAPA 89
Cadenhead, Kristin Suzanne 1959- BiDrAPA 89
Cades, Julius Russell 1904- WhoAm 90
Cades, Stewart Russell 1942- WhoAm 90
Cadge, William Fleming 1924- WhoAm 90, WhoAmA 91
Cadgene, George H. 1919- St&PR 91
Cadick, John 1945- WhoSSW 91
Cadier, Eric Yves 1950- WhoWor 91
Cadieux, Michael Eugene 1940- WhoAmA 91
Cadieux, Pierre H. 1948- WhoAm 90, WhoE 91
Cadieux, Robert D. 1937- St&PR 91, WhoAm 90
Cadieux, Roger Joseph 1945- WhoAm 90, WhoE 91
Cadieuz, Roger Joseph 1945- BiDrAPA 89
Cadigan, Patrick Finbar 1935- St&PR 91
Cadigan, Patrick Joseph 1936- WhoAm 90
Cadigan, Richard Foster 1930- WhoE 91
Cadigan, Thomas Francis 1940- WhoAm 90
Cadigan, William Joseph 1919- WhoAm 90
Cadilla, Manuel Alberto 1912- WhoHisp 91
Cadillac, Antoine De La Mothe 1658-1730 EncCRAm
Cadillac, Antoine De La Mothe, Sieur De 1658-1730 WorAlBi
Cadillac, Antoine Laumet DeLaM, Sieur De 1658?-1730 WhNaAH
Cadillac, Louise Roman WhoAmA 91
Cadle, Dean 1920- LiHiK
Cadle, Nancy Massey 1953- WhoAmW 91
Cadle, Ray Kenneth 1906- WhoAmA 91
Cadle, Steven Howard 1946- WhoEmL 91
Cadman, Theodore Wesley 1940- WhoAm 90
Cadman, Thomas Lee 1947- St&PR 91
Cadman, Wilson K. 1927- St&PR 91
Cadman, Wilson Kennedy 1927- WhoAm 90
Cadmus, Paul 1904- WhoAm 90, WhoAmA 91
Cadoff, Jeffrey David 1961- WhoE 91
Cadogan, William J. 1948- St&PR 91
Cadore, Leon 1890-1958 Ballpl 90
Cadoret, Remi Jere 1928- BiDrAPA 89, EncO&P 3, EncPaPR 91
Cadorette, Teresa Mary BiDrAPA 89
Cadorin, Ettor 1876-1952 WhoAmA 91N
Cadot, Andrew Allinson 1945- WhoEmL 91
Cadou, Helene 1925- EncCoWW
Cadou, Peter Brosius 1931- St&PR 91
Cadranel, Samy 1939- WhoWor 91
Cadrecha, Charles William 1928- St&PR 91
Caduff, Sylvia 1937- IntWWM 90
Cadwalader, Lambert 1743-1823 BioIn 16
Cadwalader, Thomas 1707?-1799 EncCRAm
Cadwallader, A.H., III 1928- St&PR 91
Cadwallader, A.H., IV 1958- St&PR 91
Cadwallader, Douglas Stephen 1944- WhoSSW 91
Cadwallader, Estelle M. 1945- WhoE 91, WhoEmL 91
Cadwallader, Nancy Bennett 1944- WhoE 91
Cadwell, Carlton Morgan 1944- St&PR 91
Cadwell, David Robert 1934- WhoWor 91
Cadwell, Franchellie Margaret 1937- WhoAm 90
Cadwell, Jeffery James 1956- WhoEmL 91
Cadwell, Karen Lynn Delaney 1957- WhoEmL 91
Cadwell, Paul Matthew 1920- BiDrAPA 89
Cady, David Christian 1931- WhoSSW 91
Cady, Dennis Vern 1944- WhoAmA 91
Cady, Diane 1955- St&PR 91
Cady, Edwin H 1917- DcLB 103 [port]
Cady, Edwin Harrison 1917- WhoAm 90, WhoWor 91
Cady, George Leonard, Jr. 1950- WhoEmL 91
Cady, Henry Lord 1921- IntWWM 90
Cady, Howard 1914-1990 NewYTBS 90
Cady, Howard Stevenson 1914- WhoAm 90
Cady, Howard Stevenson 1914-1990 ConAu 132
Cady, Jack 1932- WhoWrEP 89
Cady, Jack A. 1932- LiHiK
Cady, John Lodge 1922- WhoAm 90
Cady, John Ramsden 1930- WhoAm 90
Cady, Louise Byron BiDrAPA 89
Cady, Lyle Edward, Jr. 1950- WhoEmL 91
Cady, Marlene L. S. BioIn 16
Cady, Nell Goodhue 1961- WhoWor 91
Cady, Samuel Lincoln 1943- WhoAmA 91
Cadzow, James Archie 1936- WhoAm 90, WhoSSW 91
Caeiro, Alberto 1888-1935 BioIn 16
Caemmerer, Alexander, Jr. 1923- BiDrAPA 89
Caen, Herb BioIn 16
Caen, Herb 1916- AuBYP 90
Caen, Jacques Philippe 1927- WhoWor 91
Caesar, Adolph 1934-1986 DrBlPA 90
Caesar, Gaius Julius 100BC-44BC WorAlBi
Caesar, George R 1929- BiDrAPA 89
Caesar, Gregory P. BiDrAPA 89
Caesar, Henry A., II 1914- WhoAm 90
Caesar, Irving 1895- OxCPMus
Caesar, Julius 100BC-44BC BioIn 16
Caesar, Julius 1558-1636 BioIn 16
Caesar, Mary 1677-1741 FemiCLE
Caesar, Neil Benjamin 1957- WhoE 91, WhoEmL 91
Caesar, Shirley BioIn 16
Caesar, Shirley 1938- WhoAmW 91
Caesar, Shirley 1939- DrBlPA 90
Caesar, Sid BioIn 16
Caesar, Sid 1922- WhoAm 90, WorAlBi
Caesar, Vance Roy 1944- WhoAm 90
Cafarchio, Louis Michael 1931- St&PR 91
Cafarella, Robert A. 1925- St&PR 91
Caffarel, Randal Cyril 1948- BiDrAPA 89, WhoSSW 91
Caffarelli 1710-1783 PenDiMP
Caffarelli, Joseph J. 1945- St&PR 91
Caffarelli, Luis Angel 1948- WhoAm 90
Caffarone, Douglas Peter 1946- St&PR 91, WhoEmL 91
Caffau, Stellio 1930- WhoWor 91
Caffee, Lorren Dale 1947- WhoEmL 91
Caffee, Marcus Pat 1948- WhoSSW 91
Cafferata, Patricia Ann 1944- WhoAmW 91
Cafferata, Roxane 1955- WhoWrEP 89
Cafferky, Ronald Edwin BiDrAPA 89
Cafferty, Pastora San Juan 1940- WhoHisp 91
Caffery, Jefferson 1886-1974 BioIn 16
Caffey, Donajean Smith WhoAmW 91
Caffey, Eugene M, Jr. 1919- BiDrAPA 89
Caffey, Horace Rouse 1929- WhoAm 90
Caffey, Kimberly Ann 1964- WhoE 91
Caffey, M. Douglas 1939- St&PR 91
Caffie, Barbara Jean 1938- WhoAmW 91
Caffieri, Jacques 1673-1755 PenDiDA 89
Caffieri, Jacques 1725-1792 PenDiDA 89
Caffieri, Philippe 1714-1774 PenDiDA 89
Caffrey, Andrew Augustine 1920- WhoAm 90, WhoE 91
Caffrey, Dennis Leo BiDrAPA 89
Caffrey, Francis David 1927- St&PR 91, WhoAm 90
Caffrey, James F BiDrAPA 89
Caffrey, Nancy AuBYP 90
Caffrey, William Joseph 1955- WhoE 91
Caffry, John William 1928- St&PR 91
Caffyn, Kathleen 1853-1926 FemiCLE
Cafiero, Eugene A. 1926- WhoAm 90
Cafiero, Louis V. ODwPR 91
Cafiero, Tom A. 1946 St&PR 91
Cafini, Regenia Dayree 1962- WhoAmW 91
Caflisch, Max 1916- ConDes 90
Cafritz, Gwendolyn BioIn 16
Cafritz, Peggy Cooper 1947- WhoAm 90, WhoEmL 91, WhoWor 91
Cafritz, Robert Conrad 1953- WhoAmA 91, WhoE 91
Cagan, Martin B. 1941- WhoAm 90
Cagan, Phillip David 1927- WhoAm 90
Cagan, Robert H. 1938- WhoAm 90
Cage, Bobby Nyle 1937- WhoAm 90
Cage, Duncan S. 1836- AmLegL
Cage, Gary Wayne 1944- St&PR 91
Cage, John BioIn 16
Cage, John 1912- IntWWM 90, PenDiMP A, WhoAm 90, WhoAmA 91
Cage, John, Jr. 1912- WorAlBi
Cage, Leo Spaulding 1934- St&PR 91
Cage, Nicholas 1965- WhoAm 90
Cage, Nicolas BioIn 16
Cage, Nicolas 1964- News 91-1 [port]
Cage, Nicolas 1965- WorAlBi
Cagenello, Donald 1930- St&PR 91
Caggia, Alfred R. 1931- St&PR 91
Caggiano, Joseph 1925- WhoAm 90
Caggiano, Michael V. 1936- St&PR 91
Caggiano, Michael Vincent 1936- WhoAm 90
Caggine, Carolyn Cassandra 1932- WhoAmW 91
Caggins, Ruth Porter 1945- WhoAmW 91, WhoEmL 91
Cagil, Necdet 1928- BiDrAPA 89
Caginalp, Gunduz 1952- WhoE 91
Cagle, Charles Wayne 1956- WhoSSW 91
Cagle, Diane Day 1946- WhoAmW 91
Cagle, Joni WhoWrEP 89
Cagle, Judy Palmer 1953- WhoSSW 91
Cagle, O Huston 1930- BiDrAPA 89
Cagle, Wesley Jackson 1930- St&PR 91
Cagle, William David 1954- WhoSSW 91
Cagle, William Dubreuil 1952- BiDrAPA 89
Cagle, William Howard, Jr. 1943- St&PR 91
Cagle, William Rea 1933- WhoAm 90
Cagli, Corrado 1910-1976 BioIn 16
Cagliostro EncO&P 3
Cagliostro, Alessandro 1743-1795 WorAlBi
Cagliostro, Alessandro Conte di 1743-1795 EncPaPR 91
Cagnat, Roland 1926- WhoWor 91
Cagney, James 1899-1986 OxCPMus, WorAlBi
Cagney, Nanette Heath 1957- WhoEmL 91
Caguiat, Carlos J. 1937- WhoHisp 91
Cahagnet, Louis-Alphonse 1805-1885 EncO&P 3
Cahagnet, Louis Alphonse 1809-1885 EncPaPR 91
Cahal, Mac Fullerton 1907- WhoAm 90
Cahalan, Donald 1912- WhoAm 90
Cahalan, James Patrick 1918- St&PR 91
Cahalan, Joseph M. 1943- ODwPR 91
Cahalan, William 1925-1990 BioIn 16
Cahall, Christina Orr- 1947- BioIn 16
Cahan, Abraham 1860-1951 BioIn 16, EncAL
Cahan, Bruce Brian 1954- WhoEmL 91
Cahan, Bruce I. 1949- WhoE 91
Cahan, Judith E. 1951- WhoEmL 91
Cahan, Leslie Daryll 1946- WhoEmL 91
Cahan, Robert B 1926- BiDrAPA 89
Cahan, Samuel G WhoAmA 91N
Cahan, William George 1914- WhoAm 90
Cahana, Alice Lok 1929- WhoAmA 91
Cahier, Jean-Charles 1772-1849? PenDiDA 89
Cahier, Phillippe 1932- WhoWor 91
Cahill, Allen J 1931- BiDrAPA 89
Cahill, Barton Joseph 1961- WhoEmL 91
Cahill, Calvin David 1956- St&PR 91
Cahill, Charles Adams, III 1930- BiDrAPA 89
Cahill, Donald R. 1930- St&PR 91
Cahill, Edward Eugene 1931- WhoSSW 91
Cahill, Edward R., Jr. 1937- St&PR 91
Cahill, George Francis, Jr. 1927- WhoAm 90
Cahill, Harry Amory 1930- WhoAm 90
Cahill, Holger 1893-1960 WhoAmA 91N
Cahill, J. Michael 1945- St&PR 91
Cahill, Jack ConAu 131
Cahill, James Francis 1926- WhoAm 90, WhoAmA 91
Cahill, James Frederick BiDrAPA 89
Cahill, John C. WhoAm 90, WhoE 91
Cahill, John Denis 1926- ConAu 131
Cahill, John Edward 1939- St&PR 91
Cahill, John J. 1932- St&PR 91
Cahill, John Michael 1947- WhoEmL 91
Cahill, Joseph T. WhoAm 90, WhoE 91
Cahill, Kevin E. 1955- St&PR 91
Cahill, Laurence James, Jr. 1924- WhoAm 90
Cahill, Lisa Sowle 1948- WhoAmW 91
Cahill, Marie 1870-1933 OxCPMus
Cahill, Martin George 1954- WhoEmL 91
Cahill, Mary-Carol WhoE 91
Cahill, Michael B. 1953- St&PR 91
Cahill, Michael Edward 1951- WhoEmL 91
Cahill, Michael John 1961- St&PR 91
Cahill, Pamela Lee 1953- WhoAmW 91
Cahill, Patricia BiDrAPA 89
Cahill, Patricia Anne 1949- WhoE 91
Cahill, Phyllis Henderson 1954- WhoAmW 91
Cahill, R.O. St&PR 91
Cahill, Ray Ballpl 90
Cahill, Richard E. 1943- St&PR 91
Cahill, Richard M. 1939- St&PR 91
Cahill, Richard Morton 1957- WhoEmL 91
Cahill, Rosalie Marie 1923- WhoAmW 91
Cahill, Teresa Mary 1944- IntWWM 90
Cahill, Thomas Andrew 1937- WhoAm 90
Cahill, Thomas E. 1935- St&PR 91
Cahill, William J., Jr. 1923- St&PR 91
Cahill, William Joseph, Jr. 1923- WhoAm 90
Cahill, William Walsh, Jr. 1927- WhoAm 90
Cahina WomWR
Cahir, John Joseph 1933- WhoAm 90
Cahir, Joseph M. 1956- St&PR 91
Cahlan, John Forest 1957- WhoEmL 91
Cahn, Abry S. 1930- St&PR 91
Cahn, Burton 1930- BiDrAPA 89
Cahn, Charles H 1921- BiDrAPA 89
Cahn, David Stephen 1940- St&PR 91, WhoAm 90
Cahn, Frank 1921- St&PR 91
Cahn, Harold A. 1916- St&PR 91
Cahn, Harold A 1922- EncO&P 3
Cahn, Ira L. BioIn 16
Cahn, John Werner 1928- WhoAm 90
Cahn, Joshua Binion 1915- WhoAm 90
Cahn, Julius Norman 1922- WhoAm 90
Cahn, Miriam 1949- BiDWomA
Cahn, Robert Wolfgang 1924- WhoWor 91
Cahn, Sammy BioIn 16
Cahn, Sammy 1913- OxCPMus, WhoAm 90
Cahn, Simon Seymour 1912- St&PR 91
Cahn, Stanley Eric Ollendorff 1939- WhoE 91
Cahn, Steven M. 1942- WhoAm 90
Cahn, Walter 1933- ConAu 129
Cahn, Walter B. WhoAm 90
Cahones, Carolyn WhoWrEP 89
Cahoon, James Preston 1926- St&PR 91
Cahoon, Jean Mitchell 1959- WhoEmL 91
Cahoon, Lawrence Bruce 1953- WhoSSW 91
Cahoon, Richard Stuart 1954- WhoEmL 91
Cahoon, Stuart N BiDrAPA 89
Cahoon, Stuart Newton 1916- WhoAm 90
Cahouet, Frank Vondell 1932- St&PR 91, WhoAm 90, WhoE 91
Cai Lam BioIn 16
Caiazza, Philip J. 1936- St&PR 91
Caiazza, Stephen S. BioIn 16, NewYTBS 90
Caiazzo, Frank Louis 1929- St&PR 91
Caiced, Jaimme D. 1926- WhoWor 91
Caicedo, Harry 1928- WhoHisp 91
Caicedo, Juana Esther 1949- WhoAmW 91, WhoE 91
Caidin, Phil BioIn 16
Cail, Earnestine Walker 1927- WhoSSW 91
Caillard, Emma Marie 1852-1927 FemiCLE
Caillaux, Joseph 1863-1944 BioIn 16
Caillaux, Joseph Pierre Marie Auguste 1863-1944 BiDFrPL
Caille, Andre 1943- St&PR 91, WhoAm 90
Caille, Yves 1942- WhoWor 91
Caillebotte, Gustave 1848-1894 BioIn 16
Cailler, Pierre 1901-1971 BioIn 16
Caillet, David Anthony 1952- WhoSSW 91
Cailletet, Louis Paul 1832-1913 WorAlBi
Caillou, Alan 1914- TwCCr&M 91
Caillouette, James Clyde 1927- WhoAm 90
Cailloux, Andre 1920- OxCCanT
Cain, Albert Clifford 1933- WhoAm 90
Cain, Arthur Homer 1913- AuBYP 90
Cain, Arthur J 1923- BiDrAPA 89
Cain, Barbara Ann 1946- WhoEmL 91
Cain, Brighton C. BioIn 16
Cain, Burton Edward 1942- WhoE 91, WhoWor 91
Cain, Byron W. 1918- St&PR 91
Cain, Charles Marshall 1934- WhoAm 90
Cain, Charlotte WhoAmA 91
Cain, Christopher ODwPR 91
Cain, Clifford Chalmers 1950- WhoEmL 91
Cain, Constance Marie 1955- WhoAmW 91
Cain, Craig J. 1923- St&PR 91
Cain, David Paul 1928- WhoAmA 91
Cain, Debra Lynn 1954- WhoAmW 91
Cain, Donald Ezell 1921- WhoAm 90
Cain, Douglas Mylchreest 1938- WhoAm 90
Cain, E. Lee 1928- WhoAm 90
Cain, Edmund Joseph 1918- WhoAm 90
Cain, Elise Gasque 1920- WhoSSW 91
Cain, Felicia T. 1957- WhoEmL 91
Cain, G. HispWr 90, MajTwCW
Cain, George 1930- St&PR 91
Cain, George Harvey 1920- WhoAm 90
Cain, Gloria C. 1950- WhoAmW 91
Cain, Gordon A. 1912- St&PR 91
Cain, Guillermo HispWr 90, MajTwCW
Cain, Herman BioIn 16
Cain, Howard M. 1926- St&PR 91
Cain, Jacques A 1921- BiDrAPA 89
Cain, James Allan 1935- WhoAm 90
Cain, James Clarence 1913- WhoAm 90
Cain, James M 1892-1977 MajTwCW, TwCCr&M 91, WorAlBi
Cain, James Marshall 1933- St&PR 91, WhoAm 90, WhoSSW 91
Cain, James Nelson 1930- WhoAm 90
Cain, Jeff NewAgMG
Cain, John 1931-1985 EncO&P 3
Cain, John S. 1934- St&PR 91
Cain, John William, Jr. BiDrAPA 89
Cain, Joseph Alexander 1920- WhoAmA 91
Cain, Kimberly June 1961- WhoAmW 91
Cain, Laverne Wallace 1937- St&PR 91
Cain, Leo Francis 1909- WhoAm 90
Cain, Les 1948- Ballpl 90
Cain, Madeline Ann 1949- WhoAmW 91
Cain, Marcena Jean Beesley 1935- WhoAmW 91
Cain, Margaret O'Leary 1946- St&PR 91
Cain, Marsha Lynn BiDrAPA 89
Cain, Michael Morrison 1949- WhoEmL 91
Cain, Michael Peter 1941- WhoAmA 91

Cain, Nancy Napier 1941- BiDrAPA 89, WhoE 91
Cain, Patricia Jean 1931- WhoAmW 91
Cain, Paul 1902-1966 TwCCr&M 91
Cain, Paul W. 1939- St&PR 91
Cain, Paul Willis 1939- WhoSSW 91
Cain, R. Wayne 1937- St&PR 91
Cain, Rhonda Maureen 1956- WhoAmW 91
Cain, Richard Edward 1939- WhoWrEP 89
Cain, Richard Harvey 1825-1887 BlkAmsC [port]
Cain, Robert Gaynor 1951- WhoEmL 91
Cain, Robert Sherwood 1947- WhoE 91
Cain, Russell Manly 1940- BiDrAPA 89, WhoE 91
Cain, Ruth WhoAmW 91
Cain, Sharon Elizabeth 1949- BiDrAPA 89
Cain, Sugar 1907-1975 Ballpl 90
Cain, Thomas A. 1930- St&PR 91
Cain, Thomas Richard 1957- WhoEmL 91
Cain, Tim J. 1958- WhoEmL 91
Cain, Victor Ralph 1934- WhoAm 90
Cain, Walter L. 1929- St&PR 91
Caine, Carol Whitacre 1925- WhoAmW 91
Caine, Conway N. 1937- St&PR 91
Caine, Edwin George 1938- BiDrAPA 89
Caine, Eric Douglas BiDrAPA 89
Caine, Franklyn A. 1950- St&PR 91
Caine, Marco 1923- WhoWor 91
Caine, Michael BioIn 16
Caine, Michael 1933?- BioIn 16, WhoAm 90, WhoWor 91, WorAlBi
Caine, Peter TwCCr&M 91
Caine, R.S. 1929- St&PR 91
Caine, Raymond W., Jr. 1932- ODwPR 91
Caine, Raymond William 1932- St&PR 91
Caine, Raymond William, Jr. 1932- WhoAm 90, WhoE 91
Caine, Shakira BioIn 16
Caine, Shulamith W. 1930- WhoWrEP 89
Caine, Stanley Paul 1940- WhoAm 90
Caine, Stephen Howard 1941- WhoWor 91
Caine, Steve 1940- ODwPR 91
Caine, W.P. 1935- St&PR 91
Caines, Jeannette AuBYP 90
Caines, Jeannette Franklin 1938- BioIn 16
Cainzos, Rogelio Miguel 1949- WhoSSW 91
Caiola, James C. 1933- St&PR 91
Caiola, Thomas Anthony 1933- WhoE 91
Caione, Paolo Lucio Maria 1946- WhoWor 91
Caird, Alice Mona 1858-1932 BioIn 16
Caird, Edward 1835-1908 BioIn 16
Caird, George Bradford 1917-1984 DcNaB 1981
Caird, Mona 1855-1932 FemiCLE
Caird, Mona Alison 1858-1932 BioIn 16
Caire, Patrice 1949- IntWWM 90
Caire, William 1946- WhoSSW 91
Cairncross, Alexander Kirkland 1911- WhoAm 90, WhoWor 91
Cairnes, John Elliot 1823-1875 BioIn 16
Cairnes, Joseph Francis 1907- WhoAm 90
Cairns, Brian Lee 1939- St&PR 91
Cairns, Christine 1959- IntWWM 90
Cairns, David Adam 1926- IntWWM 90
Cairns, Elizabeth 1685-1741 FemiCLE
Cairns, Elton James 1932- WhoAm 90
Cairns, H. Alan C. 1930- WhoAm 90
Cairns, Helen Smith 1938- WhoAm 90
Cairns, Ivan Robert 1946- St&PR 91
Cairns, James Robert 1930- WhoAm 90
Cairns, Jeffrey Peter 1954- WhoEmL 91
Cairns, John, Jr. 1923- WhoAm 90
Cairns, John J. 1927- St&PR 91
Cairns, Laura Jane 1961- WhoWrEP 89
Cairns, Laurence Howard 1949- St&PR 91
Cairns, Marion Grace Huey 1928- WhoAmW 91
Cairns, Roberta Anne Elizabeth 1945- WhoAmW 91
Cairns, Theodore LeSueur 1914- WhoAm 90
Cairns, Virginia Celia 1955- WhoEmL 91
Cairo, Armon A 1925- BiDrAPA 89, WhoE 91
Cairo, Sally J. 1944- WhoAmW 91
Cairone, David C. 1953- St&PR 91
Cairone, Regina H. 1944- St&PR 91
Caiserman-Roth, Ghitta 1923- WhoAmA 91
Cajal, Rosa Maria 1920- EncCoWW
Cajal, Santiago Ramon y 1852-1934 BioIn 16
Cajanello, duchessa di DcScanL
Cajero, Carmen WhoHisp 91
Cajiao Salas, Teresa 1927- WhoAm 90, WhoE 91
Cajigal, Joseph A. 1953- St&PR 91
Cajori, Charles F 1921- WhoAmA 91
Cajori, Charles Florian 1921- WhoAm 90
Cakert, Thomas Francis Xavier, Jr. 1947- WhoE 91
Cakmak, Ahmet Sefik 1934- WhoAm 90
Cakobau, George 1912-1989 AnObit 1989
Cala, Carlo EncO&P 3
Cala, Charles F., Jr. 1940- St&PR 91
Calabi, Bruno Marco 1914- WhoWor 91
Calabia, Dawn T. 1941- WhoAmW 91
Calabotta, Linda Carol 1953- WhoAmW 91
Calabrese, Arnold Joseph 1960- WhoEmL 91
Calabrese, Clement A. 1943- St&PR 91
Calabrese, Diane Marie 1949- WhoAmW 91, WhoE 91
Calabrese, Franco 1922- IntWWM 90
Calabrese, Gerard S. 1948- WhoAm 90
Calabrese, Guiseppe 1913- WhoWor 91
Calabrese, Joseph Richard, Jr. 1953- BiDrAPA 89
Calabrese, Michael Raphael 1956- WhoE 91, WhoEmL 91
Calabrese, P.J. 1927- St&PR 91
Calabrese, Rosalie Sue 1938- WhoAm 90
Calabresi, Guido 1932- St&PR 91, WhoAm 90
Calabresi, Massimo 1903-1988 BioIn 16
Calabretta, Alfio 1949- WhoWor 91
Calabretta, Marti Ann 1940- WhoAmW 91
Calabria, Alfred David 1947- St&PR 91, WhoSSW 91
Calabria, Daniel 1936- St&PR 91
Calabria, Rafael 1940- BiDrAPA 89
Calabro, Frank C. 1943- St&PR 91
Calabro, Jack Louis 1941- St&PR 91, WhoAm 90
Calabro, John A. 1909- St&PR 91
Calabro, Nicholas Anthony 1949- St&PR 91
Calabro, Richard Paul 1937- WhoAmA 91
Calabro, Salvatore R. 1912- St&PR 91
Calache, Michel Jean 1953- BiDrAPA 89
Calafati, Gabriel R. 1932- St&PR 91
Calafati, Gabriel Raffele 1932- WhoAm 90
Calafiore, Linda C. 1952- WhoAmW 91
Calafiura, Marie Bernadette 1946- WhoE 91
Calahan, Donald Albert 1935- WhoAm 90
Calamar, Gloria 1921- WhoAm 90, WhoAmA 91
Calamaras, Louis Basil 1908- WhoWor 91
Calamari, John Daniel 1921- WhoAm 90
Calamaro, Raymond Stuart 1944- WhoAm 90
Calame, Alexandre Emile 1913- WhoAm 90
Calame, Byron Edward 1939- WhoAm 90
Calame, Don L. 1914- WhoAm 90
Calame, Tracy Calvin 1923- St&PR 91
Calamelli, Virgiliotto PenDiDA 89
Calamity Jane BioAmW
Calamnius, Ilmari DcScanL
Calandro, Joseph John, Jr. 1930- St&PR 91
Calapai, Letterio WhoAm 90
Calapai, Letterio 1902- WhoAmA 91
Calarco, Margaret Marie 1956- WhoEmL 91
Calarco, Patricia Gillam WhoAm 90
Calarco, Vincent A. BioIn 16, St&PR 91
Calarco, Vincent Anthony 1942- WhoAm 90, WhoE 91
Calas, Carl-Eric 1924- WhoWor 91
Calas, Nicholas WhoAmA 91N
Calas, Nicolas 1907- WhoAmA 91
Calas, Nicolas 1907-1988 BioIn 16
Calasanz, Felipe R BiDrAPA 89
Calasibetta, John 1905- St&PR 91
Calasso, Roberto 1941- WhoWor 91
Calatchi, Ralph Franklin 1944- WhoSSW 91
Calautti, Thomas F. 1949- St&PR 91
Calaway, Dennis Louis 1960- WhoEmL 91, WhoSSW 91, WhoWor 91
Calaway, John Eric 1957- WhoSSW 91
Calaway, Maurice Edward 1921- WhoSSW 91
Calbick, Ian MacKinnon 1938- WhoAm 90
Calbo, Leonard J. 1941- St&PR 91
Calboli, Gualtiero Federico 1932- WhoWor 91
Calcagni, Edwin G. 1925- St&PR 91
Calcagni, John 1949- WhoAm 90
Calcagnie, Kevin Frank 1955- WhoEmL 91
Calcagno, Lawrence 1913- WhoAm 90, WhoAmA 91
Calcaterra, Charles Louis 1951- St&PR 91
Calcaterra, Edward L. 1930- St&PR 91
Calcaterra, Edward Lee 1930- WhoAm 90
Calcaterra, Lynette Grala 1948- WhoHisp 91
Calcavecchia, Mark BioIn 16
Calda, Pavel 1932- WhoE 91
Caldabaugh, Karl 1946- St&PR 91, WhoAm 90
Caldarella, Carl J. 1942- St&PR 91
Caldarelli, David Donald 1941- WhoAm 90
Caldecott, Ernest John 1922- St&PR 91
Caldecott, Moyra 1927- ConAu 30NR
Caldecott, Oliver BioIn 16
Caldecott, Randolph 1846-1886 BioIn 16
Caldecott, Richard Stanley 1924- WhoAm 90
Caldeira, Winston Ramon 1941- WhoWor 91
Caldemeyer, Ervin 1914- St&PR 91
Caldemeyer, Marjorie Janet 1952- WhoSSW 91
Calder, Alexander 1898-1976 BioIn 16, IntDcAA 90, WhoAmA 91N, WorAlBi
Calder, Bruce J. 1940- ConAu 132
Calder, Daniel Gillmore 1939- WhoAm 90
Calder, Duncan Graham, III 1942- WhoE 91
Calder, John BioIn 16
Calder, Kenneth T 1918- BiDrAPA 89
Calder, Kent Eyring 1948- WhoE 91
Calder, Nigel 1931- MajTwCW
Calder, Peter Ritchie 1906-1982 DcNaB 1981
Calder, Robert Mac 1932- WhoWor 91
Caldera, Donald L. 1935- St&PR 91
Caldera, Louis Edward 1956- WhoHisp 91
Caldera, Rafael 1916- BioIn 16
Calderaro, Leonard Joseph 1935- St&PR 91, WhoAm 90
Calderaro, Michela Alda 1950- WhoWor 91
Calderhead, William Dickson 1919- WhoAm 90
Calderin, Mayra M. BiDrAPA 89
Calderin, Roberto Antonio 1952- WhoHisp 91
Calderini, John Joseph 1935- St&PR 91
Calderon, Alberto P. 1920- WhoAm 90, WhoWor 91
Calderon, Alejandro A. 1963- WhoHisp 91
Calderon, Calixto P. 1939- WhoHisp 91
Calderon, Cesar, Jr. 1944- St&PR 91
Calderon, Cesar A., Jr. 1944- WhoHisp 91
Calderon, Charles 1950- WhoHisp 91
Calderon, Cynthia Ann 1964- WhoAmW 91
Calderon, Eduardo Caballero HispWr 90
Calderon, Gloria Q 1933- BiDrAPA 89
Calderon, Hazel G. 1938- WhoAmW 91
Calderon, Hernan 1925- WhoWor 91
Calderon, Howard St&PR 91
Calderon, Ivan 1962- Ballpl 90, WhoHisp 91
Calderon, Larry A. 1950- WhoHisp 91
Calderon, Leona R 1935- BiDrAPA 89
Calderon, Margarita Espino WhoHisp 91
Calderon, Rene BiDrAPA 89
Calderon, Rosa Margarita 1952- WhoHisp 91
Calderon, Rossie 1951- WhoHisp 91
Calderon, Stephen I. 1951- St&PR 91
Calderon, Zita Amponin BiDrAPA 89
Calderon de la Barca, Frances Erskine I 1804-1882 BioIn 16
Calderon De La Barca, Pedro 1600-1681 WorAlBi
Calderon Fournier, Rafael Angel 1949- WhoWor 91
Calderon Guardia, Rafael Angel 1900-1970 BioIn 16
Calderon Perez, Ivan 1962- Ballpl 90
Calderone, Mary S. 1904- WorAlBi
Calderone, Mary Steichen BioIn 16
Calderone, Mary Steichen 1904- WhoAm 90, WhoAmW 91
Calderone, Rocco Richard 1963- BiDrAPA 89, WhoEmL 91
Calderwood, Denis Compton 1941- WhoWor 91
Calderwood, James Albert 1941- WhoE 91, WhoWor 91
Calderwood, Laura Virginia BiDrAPA 89
Calderwood, Margaret 1715-1774 FemiCLE
Calderwood, Margaret Steuart 1715-1774 BioIn 16
Calderwood, Martin H. AmLegL
Calderwood, Stanford Matson 1920- WhoAm 90
Calderwood, William L. 1943- St&PR 91
Caldicott, Bill BioIn 16
Caldicott, Edric 1939- WhoWor 91
Caldicott, Helen BioIn 16
Caldicott, Helen 1938- MajTwCW, NewAgE 90
Caldiero, Raymond Paul 1935- St&PR 91
Caldini, Maria Pia 1931- WhoAmW 91
Caldow, June A. 1928- WhoAmW 91
Caldron, Royce Gene 1947- WhoSSW 91
Caldwell, Alethea Otti 1941- WhoAm 90, WhoAmW 91
Caldwell, Andrew Adam 1966- WhoWrEP 89
Caldwell, Anne 1867-1936 OxCPMus
Caldwell, Anne Marsh- 1791-1874 BioIn 16
Caldwell, Arline C 1924- BiDrAPA 89
Caldwell, Barbara Hart 1940- WhoAmW 91
Caldwell, Ben DrBIPA 90
Caldwell, Benjamin Hubbard, Jr 1935- WhoAmA 91
Caldwell, Bettye McDonald 1924- WhoAm 90, WhoSSW 91
Caldwell, Billy WhNaAH
Caldwell, Billy Ray 1932- WhoSSW 91, WhoWor 91
Caldwell, Carlyle G. 1914- St&PR 91, WhoAm 90
Caldwell, Carolyn Ann 1956- WhoE 91
Caldwell, Chase L. 1950- St&PR 91
Caldwell, Claud Reid 1909- WhoSSW 91
Caldwell, Courtney Lynn 1948- WhoEmL 91
Caldwell, Craig 1922- St&PR 91
Caldwell, Craig Hoskins 1951- WhoEmL 91
Caldwell, Cullen Jackson, Jr. 1933- WhoE 91
Caldwell, Daniel Ralston 1936- WhoAm 90
Caldwell, Daniel Wesley BiDrAPA 89
Caldwell, David Gates 1951- St&PR 91
Caldwell, David H 1951- ConAu 132
Caldwell, Dean Stephen 1946- St&PR 91
Caldwell, Donald R. 1946- WhoAm 90
Caldwell, Donna Mote 1962- WhoAmW 91
Caldwell, Douglas Lee 1940- BiDrAPA 89
Caldwell, E. Gerald 1928- St&PR 91
Caldwell, Earl 1905-1981 Ballpl 90
Caldwell, Edwin L. 1923- St&PR 91
Caldwell, Eleanor 1927- WhoAmA 91
Caldwell, Elizabeth BiDEWW
Caldwell, Elwood Fleming 1923- WhoAm 90
Caldwell, Erskine 1903-1987 BioIn 16, ConAu 33NR, ConLC 60 [port], MajTwCW
Caldwell, Erskine P. 1903- WorAlBi
Caldwell, Frank B., Jr. 1918- St&PR 91
Caldwell, Frank Wilson 1943- WhoSSW 91
Caldwell, Garnett Ernest 1934- WhoAm 90
Caldwell, George Bruce 1930- WhoAm 90
Caldwell, Gerald Dee 1942- WhoSSW 91
Caldwell, Grant G. 1942- St&PR 91
Caldwell, H. Allan 1944- St&PR 91
Caldwell, Hayes 1949- WhoAm 90
Caldwell, Howard Bryant 1944- WhoWor 91
Caldwell, Jack Landis 1923- St&PR 91
Caldwell, James PenDiDA 89
Caldwell, James D. 1928- St&PR 91
Caldwell, James Richard 1929- St&PR 91
Caldwell, James Richard, Jr. 1943- WhoSSW 91
Caldwell, James W. 1935- St&PR 91
Caldwell, James Wiley 1923- WhoAm 90
Caldwell, Jean Leonora 1928- WhoAmW 91
Caldwell, Jesse Burgoyne, Jr. 1917- WhoWor 91
Caldwell, Jim M. 1903- St&PR 91
Caldwell, John 1941- BioIn 16, WhoAmA 91
Caldwell, John Cope 1913- AuBYP 90
Caldwell, John David 1937- St&PR 91
Caldwell, John Gilmore 1931- St&PR 91, WhoAm 90
Caldwell, John L. 1940- WhoAm 90
Caldwell, John Thomas, Jr. 1932- WhoAm 90
Caldwell, John Tyler 1911- WhoAm 90
Caldwell, John Vernon, Jr. 1957- WhoEmL 91
Caldwell, John Warwick 1949- WhoEmL 91
Caldwell, Joyce M. 1944- WhoE 91
Caldwell, Judy Carol 1946- WhoAmW 91, WhoSSW 91
Caldwell, L.H., Jr. 1923- St&PR 91
Caldwell, L. Scott ConTFT 8
Caldwell, L Scott DrBIPA 90
Caldwell, L. Scott WhoAmW 91
Caldwell, Lynton Keith 1913- WhoAm 90
Caldwell, Marie BioIn 16
Caldwell, Marie Ellen 1954- WhoAmW 91
Caldwell, Marilyn R BiDrAPA 89
Caldwell, Martha Belle 1931- WhoAmA 91
Caldwell, Mary Alice 1949- WhoEmL 91
Caldwell, Mary Linton Pittard 1948- WhoSSW 91
Caldwell, Mary Peri 1935- WhoAmW 91, WhoSSW 91, WhoWor 91
Caldwell, Michael DeFoix 1943- WhoE 91
Caldwell, Mike 1949- Ballpl 90
Caldwell, Oliver Johnson 1904- WhoAm 90, WhoWor 91
Caldwell, P.H. 1933- St&PR 91
Caldwell, Patty Jean Grosskopf 1937- WhoAmW 91
Caldwell, Paula Day 1954- WhoAmW 91
Caldwell, Philip 1920- EncABHB 5 [port], St&PR 91, WhoAm 90
Caldwell, Ray 1888-1967 Ballpl 90
Caldwell, Richard Clark 1944- St&PR 91, WhoAm 90
Caldwell, Robert H. 1930- WhoAm 90
Caldwell, Robert Joseph 1939- St&PR 91
Caldwell, Robert S. 1941- St&PR 91

Caldwell, Ruth Margaret 1956- *WhoAmW 91*
Caldwell, Sandra Marie 1959- *WhoAmW 91*
Caldwell, Sarah 1924- *IntWWM 90, PenDiMP, WhoAmW 91, WhoE 91, WorAlBi*
Caldwell, Stratton Franklin 1926- *WhoWrEP 89*
Caldwell, Susan Hanes 1938- *WhoE 91*
Caldwell, Susan Havens 1938- *WhoAmA 91*
Caldwell, Tami 1953- *WhoAm 90*
Caldwell, Taylor 1900- *BioAmW*
Caldwell, Taylor 1900-1985 *BioIn 16, EncPaPR 91*
Caldwell, Thomas Howell, Jr. 1934- *WhoSSW 91*
Caldwell, Thomas Jones, Jr. 1923- *WhoWor 91*
Caldwell, Troy *BiDrAPA 89*
Caldwell, Walter Edward 1941- *WhoWor 91*
Caldwell, Warren Frederick 1928- *WhoAm 90*
Caldwell, Wiley N. 1927- *St&PR 91*
Caldwell, Wiley North 1927- *WhoAm 90*
Caldwell, Will M. 1925- *St&PR 91, WhoAm 90*
Caldwell, William Edward 1928- *WhoWor 91*
Caldwell, William Glen Elliot 1932- *WhoAm 90*
Caldwell, William Mackay, III 1922- *WhoWor 91*
Caldwell, William Malcolm 1934- *WhoWor 91*
Caldwell, William Stuart 1921- *WhoWor 91*
Caldwell, Zoe *BioIn 16*
Caldwell, Zoe 1933- *OxCCanT, WhoAmW 91*
Caldwell, Zoe Ada 1933- *NotWoAT*
Cale, Charles Griffin 1940- *WhoAm 90*
Cale, Edward E, Jr. *BiDrAPA 89*
Cale, Robert Allan 1940- *WhoAmA 91*
Caledonia, George E. 1941- *WhoAm 90*
Calef, George 1944- *ConAu 132*
Calef, Robert 1648-1719 *EncCRAm*
Calegory, Jade *BioIn 16*
Calek, Terry A. *ODwPR 91*
Calenberg-Gottingen, Elisabeth von 1510-1558 *EncCoWW*
Calenoff, Leonid 1923- *WhoAm 90*
Calenzani, David G. 1951- *BiDrAPA 89*
Calestino, Karen Joan 1952- *WhoAmW 91*
Calfa, Marian 1946- *WhoWor 91*
Calfee, Annette 1947- *WhoAmW 91*
Calfee, Helen France 1953- *St&PR 91*
Calfee, John B., Jr. 1945- *St&PR 91*
Calfee, John Beverly 1913- *WhoAm 90*
Calfee, Kate Hoover *BioIn 16*
Calfee, Robert Chilton 1933- *WhoAm 90*
Calfee, William Howard 1909- *WhoAm 90, WhoAmA 91, WhoE 91*
Calfee, William Lewis 1917- *WhoAm 90, WhoWor 91*
Calfo, Jason Philemon 1954- *WhoE 91*
Calgaard, Ronald Keith 1937- *WhoAm 90*
Calhern, Louis 1895-1956 *WorAlBi*
Calhoon, Barry A. 1936- *St&PR 91*
Calhoon, Donald F. 1951- *St&PR 91*
Calhoun, Alexander D. 1925- *St&PR 91*
Calhoun, Andrew Pickens 1925- *St&PR 91*
Calhoun, Aubrey Daniel 1953- *WhoSSW 91*
Calhoun, Barbara Louise 1949- *BiDrAPA 89*
Calhoun, Carol Victoria 1953- *WhoEmL 91*
Calhoun, Cathy 1961- *ODwPR 91*
Calhoun, Cheryl 1950- *WhoAmW 91*
Calhoun, Clayne Marsh 1950- *WhoEmL 91*
Calhoun, Craig 1952- *ConAu 130*
Calhoun, Daniel Fairchild 1929- *WhoAm 90*
Calhoun, David Allen 1960- *WhoE 91*
Calhoun, Donald Eugene, Jr. 1926- *WhoAm 90*
Calhoun, Evelyn Williams 1921- *WhoAmW 91, WhoWor 91*
Calhoun, Frank Wayne 1933- *WhoAm 90*
Calhoun, Fred Lee 1931- *St&PR 91*
Calhoun, Harold 1906- *WhoAm 90*
Calhoun, Harry L. 1953- *WhoWrEP 89*
Calhoun, Henry Clay, III 1932- *St&PR 91*
Calhoun, James Lawrence 1931- *St&PR 91*
Calhoun, Jeff 1958- *Ballpl 90*
Calhoun, John Alfred 1939- *WhoAm 90, WhoE 91, WhoWor 91*
Calhoun, John C 1782-1850 *BiDrUSE 89, BioIn 16, WorAlBi*
Calhoun, John C., Jr. 1917- *WhoAm 90*
Calhoun, John Caldwell 1782-1850 *WhNaAH*
Calhoun, John Cozart 1937- *WhoE 91, WhoWor 91*
Calhoun, John Franklin 1935- *WhoAm 90*
Calhoun, John H. 1899-1988 *BioIn 16*
Calhoun, John H. 1941- *St&PR 91*
Calhoun, John P. 1926- *WhoAm 90*
Calhoun, Joshua Wesley 1956- *BiDrAPA 89*
Calhoun, Kendall Russell 1948- *WhoAmW 91*
Calhoun, Larry Darryl 1937- *WhoAmA 91*
Calhoun, Lawrence Eugene 1939- *St&PR 91*
Calhoun, Lee 1933-1989 *BioIn 16*
Calhoun, Madeleine S. Abler 1961- *WhoAmW 91*
Calhoun, Martin Lewis 1961- *WhoAm 90*
Calhoun, Mary 1926- *BioIn 16*
Calhoun, Mary Diane Mason 1954- *WhoSSW 91*
Calhoun, Mary Huiskamp 1926- *AuBYP 90*
Calhoun, Monica Dodd 1953- *WhoEmL 91*
Calhoun, Noah Robert 1921- *WhoAm 90*
Calhoun, Richard James 1926- *WhoSSW 91*
Calhoun, Robert B. 1928- *St&PR 91*
Calhoun, Robert Franklin 1931- *WhoSSW 91*
Calhoun, Robert Lathan 1937- *WhoAm 90*
Calhoun, Rory 1923- *WorAlBi*
Calhoun, W Daniel 1935- *BiDrAPA 89*
Calhoun, Walter Bowman 1917- *WhoAm 90*
Calhoun, William F. 1844-1929 *AmLegL*
Calhoun, William James 1848-1916 *BioIn 16*
Calhoun-Senghor, Keith 1955- *WhoE 91, WhoEmL 91, WhoWor 91*
Cali, Joseph John 1928- *WhoAm 90*
Cali, Salvatore Joseph 1943- *St&PR 91*
Calia, Mary Elizabeth 1954- *WhoE 91*
Calia, Vincent Frank 1926- *WhoE 91*
Caliari, Paolo 1528-1588 *BioIn 16*
Calicdan, Raul Gomez 1950- *BiDrAPA 89*
Calice, Mark Allen 1947- *St&PR 91*
Caliendo, G.D. 1941- *St&PR 91*
Caliendo, G. D. 1941- *WhoAm 90*
Caliendo, James Gerard 1953- *St&PR 91*
Calienes, Armando Luis 1940- *WhoSSW 91*
Califano, Joseph A., Jr. 1931- *WorAlBi*
Califano, Joseph Anthony, Jr. 1931- *BiDrUSE 89, WhoAm 90*
Califano, Paul F 1925- *BiDrAPA 89*
Califf, Marilyn Iskiwitz 1932- *WhoAmA 91*
California Joe *WhNaAH*
California Ramblers, The *OxCPMus*
Caligari, Filippo Antonio *PenDiDA 89*
Caligiuri, Joseph Frank 1928- *St&PR 91*
Caligor, Eve *BiDrAPA 89*
Caliguiri, Richard S. *BioIn 16*
Caligula 12-41 *WorAlBi*
Calika, Omer Hursit 1918- *WhoE 91*
Calinescu, Matei 1934- *ConAu 131*
Calingaert, Michael 1933- *WhoAm 90*
Calinger, Ronald Steve 1942- *WhoAm 90*
Calinoiu, Nicolae 1926- *IntWWM 90*
Calinsky, Anne Constantin 1952- *WhoAmW 91*
Calio, Anthony John 1929- *WhoAm 90*
Calip, Roger E. 1941- *WhoWrEP 89*
Caliri, David Joseph 1929- *WhoSSW 91*
Calis, Hein Antonius 1948- *IntWWM 90*
Calise, Nicholas James 1941- *St&PR 91, WhoAm 90*
Calise, Ronald Jan 1948- *WhoAm 90*
Calisher, Hortense *BioIn 16*
Calisher, Hortense 1911- *FemiCLE, MajTwCW, WhoAm 90, WhoAmW 91, WhoWor 91, WhoWrEP 89, WorAlBi*
Calisher, Katherine Anne 1953- *St&PR 91*
Calisti, Louis J. P. 1925- *WhoAm 90*
Calitri, Joseph Constant 1924- *St&PR 91*
Calk, Richard E. 1938- *St&PR 91*
Calkin, Joy Durfee 1938- *WhoAm 90*
Calkin, Mark Maurice 1955- *WhoSSW 91*
Calkins, Benjamin 1956- *WhoEmL 91*
Calkins, Carroll Cecil 1918- *WhoAm 90*
Calkins, Charles C. 1950- *St&PR 91*
Calkins, Evan 1920- *WhoAm 90, WhoWor 91*
Calkins, Gary Nathan 1911- *WhoAm 90*
Calkins, Harlan D. 1932- *St&PR 91*
Calkins, Hugh 1924- *WhoAm 90*
Calkins, James E. 1951- *St&PR 91*
Calkins, Jerry Milan 1942- *WhoAm 90*
Calkins, JoAnn Ruby 1934- *WhoAmW 91*
Calkins, John W. 1927- *ODwPR 91*
Calkins, Judith Moritz 1942- *WhoAmW 91*
Calkins, Kevin L. 1958- *St&PR 91*
Calkins, Kingsley Mark 1917- *WhoAmA 91*
Calkins, Loring Gary 1887-1960 *WhoAmA 91N*
Calkins, Paul R. 1926- *St&PR 91*
Calkins, Richard *EncACom*
Calkins, Rita M. 1931- *St&PR 91*
Calkins, Robert C 1925- *BiDrAPA 89*
Calkins, Robert G. 1932- *ConAu 130, WhoAmA 91*
Calkins, Stephen 1950- *WhoEmL 91*
Calkins, Susannah Eby 1924- *WhoAm 90*
Calkins, Therese Maureen 1955- *WhoSSW 91*
Call, Barbara Jo 1960- *WhoEmL 91*
Call, David Lincoln 1932- *WhoAm 90*
Call, Douglas William 1942- *WhoSSW 91*
Call, Dwight Vincent 1934- *WhoWor 91*
Call, Jack Stanley 1949- *WhoWrEP 89*
Call, Jo-Anne M. 1953- *WhoE 91*
Call, John Arnold 1948- *WhoEmL 91*
Call, Justin D *BiDrAPA 89*
Call, Larry A. 1934- *St&PR 91*
Call, Laval J. 1937- *St&PR 91*
Call, Lawrence Michael 1942- *St&PR 91, WhoAm 90*
Call, Neil Judson 1933- *WhoAm 90*
Call, Osborne Jay 1940- *St&PR 91*
Call, Pamela 1943- *BiDrAPA 89*
Call, Reuel T. 1908- *St&PR 91*
Call, Richard C. 1930- *WhoAm 90*
Call, Richard W. 1924- *St&PR 91*
Call, Robert W. 1945- *St&PR 91*
Call, William A. 1938- *St&PR 91*
Callagan, Dwight A. 1917- *WhoAm 90*
Callaghan, Donald E. 1946- *WhoE 91*
Callaghan, J. Clair 1933- *WhoAm 90*
Callaghan, James *BioIn 16*
Callaghan, James 1912- *WorAlBi*
Callaghan, Leonard James 1912- *WhoWor 91*
Callaghan, Linda Y 1943- *BiDrAPA 89*
Callaghan, Marty 1900-1975 *Ballpl 90*
Callaghan, Mary Ellen 1950- *WhoAmW 91*
Callaghan, Michael Sean 1942- *St&PR 91*
Callaghan, Morley *BioIn 16*
Callaghan, Morley *NewYTBS 90 [port]*
Callaghan, Morley Edward 1903- *ConAu 33NR*
Callaghan, Morley Edward 1903-1990 *ConAu 132, MajTwCW*
Callaghan, Richard L. *St&PR 91*
Callaham, Betty Elgin 1929- *WhoAm 90, WhoAmW 91, WhoSSW 91*
Callaham, Thomas Hunter 1915- *WhoAm 90*
Callahan, Aileen *WhoAmA 91*
Callahan, Alston 1911- *WhoAm 90, WhoWor 91*
Callahan, Beverly Jean 1949- *WhoEmL 91*
Callahan, Bobbie Yolanda 1949- *WhoEmL 91*
Callahan, Brian J. *BioIn 16*
Callahan, Brian William 1938- *WhoE 91*
Callahan, Carroll Bernard 1908- *WhoAm 90*
Callahan, Charles Edmund, Jr. 1951- *WhoE 91*
Callahan, Charles V. 1946- *St&PR 91*
Callahan, Claire Wallis 1890- *AuBYP 90*
Callahan, D. W. *WhoSSW 91*
Callahan, Daniel J., III 1932- *St&PR 91*
Callahan, Daniel John 1930- *WhoAm 90*
Callahan, Daniel Joseph, III 1932- *WhoAm 90*
Callahan, Debra Jean 1958- *WhoE 91*
Callahan, Donna Marie 1948- *WhoAmW 91*
Callahan, Dorothy 1934- *AuBYP 90*
Callahan, Douglas Glen *BiDrAPA 89*
Callahan, Edward William 1930- *St&PR 91, WhoAm 90*
Callahan, Elias Richard, Jr. 1938- *WhoAm 90*
Callahan, Frank Thomas, Jr. 1928- *St&PR 91*
Callahan, Gene *NewYTBS 90*
Callahan, Gerald W. 1936- *St&PR 91*
Callahan, Gerald William 1936- *WhoAm 90*
Callahan, H. L. 1932- *WhoAm 90, WhoSSW 91*
Callahan, Harold Robert 1925- *St&PR 91*
Callahan, Harry 1912- *WhoAmA 91*
Callahan, Harry Leslie 1923- *WhoAm 90*
Callahan, Harry Morey 1912- *WhoAm 90, WhoWor 91*
Callahan, Jack 1889-1954 *EncACom*
Callahan, James E. 1942- *St&PR 91*
Callahan, James Francis, Jr. 1936- *WhoE 91*
Callahan, James Lawrence 1935- *St&PR 91*
Callahan, James Richard 1951- *WhoEmL 91*
Callahan, Jean Marie 1956- *WhoAmW 91*
Callahan, John *BioIn 16*
Callahan, John D. 1931- *WhoAm 90*
Callahan, John Joseph *BiDrAPA 89*
Callahan, John Lewis, Jr. 1933- *WhoE 91*
Callahan, John William 1947- *WhoEmL 91*
Callahan, Joseph D 1931- *BiDrAPA 89*
Callahan, Joseph Murray *WhoAm 90*
Callahan, Joseph Patrick 1945- *WhoAm 90*
Callahan, Kenneth 1905-1986 *WhoAmA 91N*
Callahan, Linda Louisa 1954- *WhoE 91*
Callahan, Marilyn Joy 1934- *WhoWor 91*
Callahan, Mary Helen 1942- *WhoE 91*
Callahan, Michael Joseph 1939- *WhoAm 90*
Callahan, Nixey 1874-1934 *Ballpl 90*
Callahan, Norman M., Jr. 1920- *St&PR 91*
Callahan, North 1908- *WhoAm 90*
Callahan, Patrick Joseph, Jr. 1942- *St&PR 91*
Callahan, Peter J. *BioIn 16*
Callahan, Philip Serna 1923- *AuBYP 90*
Callahan, Pia Laaster 1955- *WhoAmW 91, WhoE 91*
Callahan, Ralph W. 1906- *St&PR 91*
Callahan, Rebecca Lynne 1965- *WhoAmW 91*
Callahan, Richard Frederick 1952- *St&PR 91*
Callahan, Richard J. 1941- *WhoAm 90*
Callahan, Richard Jay 1959- *WhoE 91*
Callahan, Rickey Don 1956- *WhoSSW 91*
Callahan, Robert B 1929- *BiDrAPA 89*
Callahan, Robert J. 1930- *WhoE 91*
Callahan, Robert L. 1928- *St&PR 91*
Callahan, Robert Lee 1932- *St&PR 91*
Callahan, Ronald E. 1926- *St&PR 91, WhoAm 90*
Callahan, Rosemarie G *BiDrAPA 89*
Callahan, Stephen Vincent 1950- *WhoEmL 91*
Callahan, Thomas R *BiDrAPA 89*
Callahan, Vincent Francis, Jr. 1931- *WhoSSW 91*
Callahan, Walter D. 1929- *St&PR 91*
Callahan, William Anthony, Jr. *BiDrAPA 89*
Callahan, William Edward 1918- *St&PR 91*
Callahan, William F., III 1941- *St&PR 91*
Callan, Charles Vincent 1956- *WhoEmL 91*
Callan, Clair Marie 1940- *WhoAmW 91*
Callan, Columcille David 1950- *WhoE 91*
Callan, Curtis Gove, Jr. 1942- *WhoAm 90*
Callan, Edwin *BioIn 16*
Callan, James *ODwPR 91*
Callan, James Michael 1944- *St&PR 91*
Callan, James Ruskin 1932- *WhoE 91*
Callan, Jamie 1954- *BioIn 16*
Callan, John Garling 1946- *WhoWor 91*
Callan, John Patrick 1939- *BiDrAPA 89*
Callan, Joseph Patrick 1944- *WhoSSW 91*
Callan, Melinda Ann 1954- *WhoAmW 91*
Callan, Robert E. 1955- *St&PR 91*
Callanan, Anne McGuire 1958- *WhoEmL 91*
Callanan, Carol Lynn 1961- *WhoE 91*
Callanan, Joseph Alfred 1920- *WhoWrEP 89*
Callanan, Kathleen Joan 1940- *WhoAmW 91, WhoWor 91*
Callanan, Philip W. *BioIn 16*
Callanan, Thomas B. 1953- *St&PR 91*
Calland, Diana Baker 1935- *WhoAm 90*
Calland, Sabra Wetzler 1935- *BiDrAPA 89*
Callander, Bruce Douglas 1923- *WhoAm 90*
Callander, Kay Eileen Paisley 1938- *WhoAmW 91, WhoWor 91*
Callander, Robert John 1931- *WhoAm 90*
Callant, Marcel Alphonse 1919- *WhoAm 90*
Callard, Carole Crawford 1941- *WhoAmW 91*
Callard, David Jacobus 1938- *St&PR 91, WhoAm 90*
Callas, Charlie *WorAlBi*
Callas, James G. 1918- *St&PR 91*
Callas, Maria 1923-1977 *BioAmW, BioIn 16, PenDiMP, WorAlBi*
Callas, Theo *TwCCr&M 91*
Callaway, Anita Maria 1964- *WhoAmW 91*
Callaway, Ben 1927- *ConAu 131*
Callaway, Ben Anderson 1927- *WhoAm 90*
Callaway, Bernice 1923- *BioIn 16*
Callaway, Clifford Wayne 1941- *WhoE 91*
Callaway, David Henry 1912- *St&PR 91*
Callaway, David Henry, Jr. 1912- *WhoAm 90*
Callaway, Enoch, III 1924- *BiDrAPA 89*
Callaway, Fuller E., Jr. 1907- *St&PR 91*
Callaway, Fuller Earle, Jr. 1907- *WhoAm 90*
Callaway, Henry Jasper, IV 1955- *St&PR 91*
Callaway, Howard Hollis 1927- *WhoAm 90*
Callaway, Hugh G. 1885-1949 *EncO&P 3*
Callaway, James Edmund 1834-19--? *AmLegL*
Callaway, James Thorpe 1937- *WhoAm 90*
Callaway, Jasper Lamar 1911- *WhoAm 90*
Callaway, Jo Jeanne 1933- *BiDrAPA 89*
Callaway, Joseph A. 1920-1988 *BioIn 16*
Callaway, Karen Alice 1946- *WhoAm 90*

Callaway, Kathy Jean 1943- *WhoWrEP 89*
Callaway, Kenneth Hodges 1955- *WhoSSW 91*
Callaway, Mark Clayton 1956- *WhoEmL 91*
Callaway, Paul 1909- *IntWWM 90*
Callaway, Richard Earl 1951- *WhoWor 91*
Callaway, Robbie Adam 1951- *WhoE 91*
Callaway, Timothy A. 1952- *St&PR 91*
Callaway, William H. 1925- *St&PR 91*
Callbeck, Catherine 1939- *WhoAmW 91*
Callcott, Maria 1785-1842 *FemiCLE*
Calle, Carlos I. 1945- *WhoSSW 91*
Calle, Paul 1928- *WhoAmA 91*
Callea, Donna L. 1930- *St&PR 91*
Callebaut, Werner Gustaaf 1952- *WhoWor 91*
Callegan-Smith, Cherye Celeste *BiDrAPA 89*
Callegari, Filippo Antonio *PenDiDA 89*
Calleja, Amos B *BiDrAPA 89*
Calleja, Jose M 1936- *BiDrAPA 89*
Callejas, Manuel Mancia, Jr. 1933- *WhoHisp 91*
Callejas, Rafael Leonardo *WhoWor 91*
Callejo, Vicente E, Jr. *BiDrAPA 89*
Callen, Claire A. 1956- *WhoSSW 91*
Callen, Craig Randall 1950- *WhoEmL 91*
Callen, Gillian 1951- *WhoEmL 91*
Callen, Herbert Bernard 1919- *WhoAm 90*
Callen, Jeffrey Phillip 1947- *WhoAm 90*
Callen, John Holmes, Jr. 1932- *St&PR 91, WhoAm 90*
Callen, Kenneth E *BiDrAPA 89*
Callen, Lon Edward 1929- *WhoWor 91*
Callen, Robinson 1925- *St&PR 91*
Callenbach, Ernest *BioIn 16*
Callenbach, Ernest 1929- *WhoAm 90, WhoWrEP 89*
Callender, A. Keith 1946- *WhoAm 90*
Callender, Andrew *BioIn 16*
Callender, Angela Marie 1954- *BiDrAPA 89*
Callender, Bessie 1889-1951 *BiDWomA*
Callender, Clive O. *BioIn 16*
Callender, Clive Orville 1936- *WhoAm 90, WhoWor 91*
Callender, Everett *BioIn 16*
Callender, John Francis 1944- *WhoSSW 91*
Callender, John Hancock 1908- *WhoAm 90*
Callender, Norma Anne 1933- *WhoAmW 91, WhoSSW 91, WhoWor 91*
Callender, William L. 1933- *St&PR 91*
Callender, William Lacey 1933- *WhoAm 90*
Calleo, David P 1934- *ConAu 31NR*
Calleros, Charles R. 1953- *WhoHisp 91*
Callery, Mary 1903-1977 *BiDWomA, WhoAmA 91N*
Calles, Joseph Louis, Jr. 1950- *BiDrAPA 89*
Calles, Plutarco Elias 1877-1945 *BioIn 16*
Calleton, Theodore Edward 1934- *WhoAm 90*
Calley, John 1930- *WhoAm 90*
Calley, William Laws *BioIn 16*
Callicot, Theophilus C. 1826- *AmLegL*
Callicott, Burton Harry 1907- *WhoAmA 91*
Callicrates *WorAlBi*
Callicutt, Vernon Keith 1950- *WhoSSW 91*
Callies, Bennie L *BiDrAPA 89*
Callies, David Lee 1943- *WhoAm 90*
Calligan, Edward Leo 1948- *St&PR 91*
Calligan, Jeffrey Lynn 1940- *WhoSSW 91*
Calligan, William Dennis 1925- *WhoAm 90*
Calligas, Gary Lazaros 1950- *WhoEmL 91*
Calligas, Thrassos S 1950- *BiDrAPA 89*
Callihan, Clayton Arthur 1954- *WhoEmL 91*
Callihan, Collis Michael 1947- *WhoAm 90*
Callihan, James Marion 1925- *St&PR 91*
Callihan, John C. 1929- *ODwPR 91*
Callihan, John Clayton 1929- *St&PR 91*
Callin, Lynn R. 1908-1990 *BioIn 16*
Callinan, Terrence James 1956- *BiDrAPA 89*
Callis, Bruce 1939- *St&PR 91, WhoAm 90*
Callis, Chris *BioIn 16*
Callis, Clayton Fowler 1923- *WhoAm 90*
Callis, Jerry Jackson 1926- *WhoAm 90*
Callis, Robert 1920- *WhoAm 90*
Callis, Stewart James 1959- *BiDrAPA 89*
Callis, Victoria D. 1953- *WhoWrEP 89*
Callisen, Sterling A. *BioIn 16*
Callisen, Sterling A 1899-1988 *WhoAmA 91N*
Callison, Brian 1934- *ConAu 31NR*
Callison, Charles Hugh 1913- *WhoAm 90*
Callison, Charles Stuart 1939- *WhoE 91*
Callison, James W. 1928- *St&PR 91, WhoAm 90*
Callison, James William 1955- *WhoEmL 91*
Callison, Johnny 1939- *Ballpl 90, BioIn 16*
Callison, Nancy Fowler 1931- *WhoWor 91*
Callison, Scott Dale 1961- *WhoEmL 91*
Callison, Sue Ann 1957- *BiDrAPA 89*
Calliste, Gerald Carlton, Jr. 1965- *WhoE 91*
Callister, Lynn Clark Scott 1942- *WhoAmW 91*
Callister, Marion Jones 1921- *WhoAm 90*
Callister, Susan Price 1945- *WhoEmL 91*
Callmer, James Peter 1919- *WhoAm 90*
Callmeyer, Ferenc 1928- *WhoWor 91*
Callner, Bruce Warren 1948- *WhoEmL 91*
Callner, Richard 1927- *WhoAmA 91*
Callo, Joseph Francis 1929- *WhoAm 90*
Callon, Frederick Lindsey 1950- *St&PR 91*
Callon, John S. 1920- *St&PR 91*
Callot, Jacques 1592-1635 *IntDcAA 90, PenDiDA 89*
Callow, Allan Dana 1916- *WhoAm 90*
Callow, Keith McLean 1925- *WhoAm 90, WhoWor 91*
Callow, Simon 1949- *ConTFT 8*
Callow, William Grant 1921- *WhoAm 90*
Calloway, Blanche 1902-1978 *DrBlPA 90*
Calloway, Cab 1907- *BioIn 16, DrBlPA 90, OxCPMus, WorAlBi*
Calloway, Chris *DrBlPA 90*
Calloway, D. Wayne *BioIn 16*
Calloway, D. Wayne 1935- *St&PR 91, WhoAm 90, WhoE 91*
Calloway, David Leroy 1958- *WhoSSW 91*
Calloway, Dawn Kelly 1958- *WhoWrEP 89*
Calloway, Doris Howes 1923- *WhoAm 90, WhoAmW 91*
Calloway, Jean Mitchener 1923- *WhoAm 90*
Calloway, Kirk 1960- *DrBlPA 90*
Calloway, Maureen 1964- *WhoAmW 91*
Calloway, Northern J. *BioIn 16, NewYTBS 90*
Calloway, Northern J 1948?- *DrBlPA 90*
Calloway, Stephen *BioIn 16*
Calloway, Vanessa Bell *BioIn 16*
Callsen, Christian E. 1938- *WhoAm 90*
Callsen, Christian Edward 1938- *St&PR 91*
Callum, Agnes Kane 1925- *WhoE 91*
Callum, Myles 1934- *WhoAm 90*
Calman, Donald R. 1928- *St&PR 91*
Calman, Robert Frederick 1932- *St&PR 91, WhoAm 90, WhoE 91*
Calman, W 1947- *WhoAmA 91*
Calmell del Solar, Fernando Javier 1949- *WhoWor 91*
Calmenson, Stephanie *BioIn 16*
Calmes, Richard Allen 1932- *St&PR 91*
Calmese, Linda 1947- *WhoAmW 91, WhoEmL 91, WhoWor 91*
Calmet, Antoine Augustin 1672-1757 *EncO&P 3*
Calnan, Arthur Francis 1926- *WhoE 91, WhoWor 91*
Calnan, Dennis John 1948- *St&PR 91*
Calnan, Thomas Ward 1945- *WhoSSW 91*
Calnon, Guin Corinne 1943- *WhoWrEP 89*
Calo, Joseph Manuel 1944- *WhoE 91*
Calobrisi, Dominick *BiDrAPA 89*
Calof, David Lorne 1949- *WhoEmL 91*
Calogero, Pascal Frank, Jr. 1931- *WhoAm 90*
Calonius, Ville Antti Guy 1950- *WhoWor 91*
Calore, James John 1948- *WhoWrEP 89*
Calpin, William Joseph, Jr. 1949- *St&PR 91*
Calrow, Robert F 1916- *WhoAmA 91*
Calsbeek, Franklin 1931- *WhoSSW 91*
Calsetta, Daryn Lee 1967- *WhoE 91*
Calson, Clayton Elwood, II 1939- *St&PR 91*
Calta, Louis 1913?-1990 *ConAu 132*
Caltabiano, Nerina Jane 1956- *WhoWor 91*
Caltagirone, Carmen Lillian 1950- *WhoAmW 91*
Caltagirone, Salvatore James 1942- *St&PR 91*
Calter, Paul 1934- *ConAu 31NR*
Calthorpe, Mena 1905- *FemiCLE*
Calton, Gary Jim 1943- *WhoE 91*
Calton, Martin Joel *BiDrAPA 89*
Caltrider, Arthur P. 1935- *St&PR 91*
Caluwaerts, Marc Joseph 1938- *WhoWor 91*
Calvaer, Andre Jules 1921- *WhoWor 91*
Calvani, Terry 1947- *WhoAm 90, WhoEmL 91*
Calvanico, Thomas Paul 1955- *WhoEmL 91*
Calvano, Conrad Anthony 1939- *St&PR 91*
Calvaruso, Joseph Anthony 1949- *WhoEmL 91*
Calve, Emma 1858-1942 *PenDiMP*
Calveley, Hugh *BioIn 16*
Calver, Richard Allen 1939- *WhoSSW 91*
Calverley, John Robert 1932- *WhoAm 90*
Calvert, Alan Hilary 1947- *WhoWor 91*
Calvert, Barbara Jean 1954- *WhoE 91, WhoEmL 91*
Calvert, Cecilius 1605-1675 *EncCRAm*
Calvert, Collin Michael 1952- *WhoEmL 91*
Calvert, Delbert William 1927- *WhoAm 90*
Calvert, Eddie 1922-1978 *OxCPMus*
Calvert, Elizabeth 1620?-1675 *BiDEWW*
Calvert, George 1580?-1632 *EncCRAm*
Calvert, George Henry 1803-1889 *BioIn 16*
Calvert, Gordon Lee 1921- *WhoAm 90*
Calvert, Horace Alton 1953- *St&PR 91*
Calvert, Jack George 1923- *WhoAm 90*
Calvert, James *AuBYP 90*
Calvert, James Francis 1920- *WhoAm 90*
Calvert, Jennie C 1878- *WhoAmA 91N*
Calvert, John David 1952- *WhoE 91*
Calvert, Jon Channing 1941- *WhoAm 90*
Calvert, Larrie S. 1935- *St&PR 91*
Calvert, Leonard 1606-1647 *EncCRAm*
Calvert, Lloyd P. 1936- *St&PR 91*
Calvert, Lois Wilson 1924- *WhoAmW 91*
Calvert, Melanie A. 1954- *WhoEmL 91*
Calvert, Patricia 1931- *BioIn 16, WhoWrEP 89*
Calvert, Paul 1917- *Ballpl 90*
Calvert, Richard Worcester 1931- *St&PR 91, WhoAm 90*
Calvert, Sam J., Jr. 1928- *St&PR 91*
Calvert, Shirley C. 1928- *St&PR 91*
Calvert, Stephen Edward 1935- *WhoAm 90*
Calvert, Terri Lynn *BiDrAPA 89*
Calvert, Terry L. 1949- *St&PR 91*
Calvert, Terry Lynn 1950- *WhoEmL 91*
Calvert, William Preston 1934- *WhoAm 90, WhoSSW 91, WhoWor 91*
Calverton, V. F. *EncAL*
Calvet Quartet *PenDiMP*
Calvet, Corinne 1925- *WhoAmW 91*
Calvet, Jacques Yves Jean 1931- *WhoWor 91*
Calvet, Joseph *PenDiMP*
Calvi, Leesa G. Wood 1957- *WhoEmL 91*
Calviello, Joseph Anthony 1933- *WhoAm 90*
Calvillo, Ricardo C. *BioIn 16, WhoAm 90*
Calvin, Allen David 1928- *WhoAm 90, WhoWor 91*
Calvin, Donald Lee 1931- *WhoAm 90*
Calvin, Dorothy Ver Strate 1929- *WhoAmW 91, WhoWor 91*
Calvin, Jean 1509-1564 *BioIn 16*
Calvin, Jerry Gene 1938- *St&PR 91*
Calvin, John 1509-1564 *BioIn 16, EncPaPR 91, WorAlBi, WrPh P*
Calvin, Lyle David 1923- *WhoAm 90*
Calvin, Melvin 1911- *WhoAm 90, WhoWor 91, WorAlBi*
Calvin, Monte D. 1944- *St&PR 91*
Calvin, Ronald L. 1941- *St&PR 91*
Calvin, Stafford Richard 1931- *WhoWor 91*
Calvino, Italo 1923-1985 *EuWr 13, MajTwCW, WorAlBi*
Calvino, Philippe Andre Marie 1939- *WhoWor 91*
Calvo, Alberto 1957- *WhoHisp 91*
Calvo, Francisco Omar 1948- *WhoHisp 91*
Calvo, Guillermo A. 1941- *WhoAm 90*
Calvo, Lino Novas *HispWr 90*
Calvo, Norman N. 1932- *ODwPR 91*
Calvo, Raymond B. 1953- *St&PR 91*
Calvo de Aguilar, Isabel 1916- *EncCoWW*
Calvo De Dios, Juan Jose 1942- *WhoWor 91*
Calvo Sotelo, Jose 1893-1936 *BioIn 16*
Calvo Sotelo, Leopoldo 1926- *WhoWor 91*
Calzadilla-Daguerre, Jesus Francisco 1954- *WhoWor 91*
Calzaretta, Frank G. 1936- *St&PR 91*
Calzetta, Frances Annette 1935- *WhoAmW 91*
Calzolari, Elaine 1950- *WhoAmA 91*
Cama, Rosalyn Anne 1954- *WhoE 91*
Camacci, Michael A. 1951- *WhoEmL 91*
Camacho, Alfredo 1951- *WhoSSW 91*
Camacho, Eliodoro 1831-1899 *BioIn 16*
Camacho, Ernest M. 1944- *WhoHisp 91*
Camacho, Ernie 1955- *Ballpl 90*
Camacho, Hector 1967- *WhoHisp 91*
Camacho, James Junior, Jr. 1956- *WhoE 91*
Camacho, Manuel Avila 1897-1955 *BioIn 16*
Camacho, Marcelino 1918- *BioIn 16*
Camacho, Marco Antonio 1960- *WhoHisp 91*
Camacho, Moises 1933- *Ballpl 90*
Camacho, Ralph Alberto 1954- *WhoHisp 91*
Camacho, Richard G. 1933- *St&PR 91*
Camacho, Ronaldo 1935- *Ballpl 90*
Camacho, Tomas Aguon 1933- *WhoAm 90*
Camadona, Juan *WhoHisp 91*
Camaglia, Ron 1950- *St&PR 91*
Camandari, Manuel Talamas 1917- *WhoAm 90*
Camani, Adrianna 1936- *IntWWM 90*
Camara, Amanda B *BiDrAPA 89*
Camara, Enrico G *BiDrAPA 89*
Camara, Iafai *WhoWor 91*
Camara-Peon, Nicolas *BiDrAPA 89*
Camarata, Martin L 1934- *WhoAmA 91*
Camarda, Rose Marie 1947- *WhoAmW 91*
Camardella, John 1944- *St&PR 91*
Camardo, Victor Joseph 1928- *St&PR 91*
Camaree, James P. 1959- *St&PR 91*
Camarena, Vicente 1941- *WhoWor 91*
Camarena Salazar, Enrique *BioIn 16*
Camargo, Alberto Lleras 1906-1990 *BioIn 16*
Camargo, Martin J. 1950- *WhoWrEP 89*
Camargo, Sergio 1930- *ArtLatA*
Camargo-Abib, Oswaldo *BiDrAPA 89*
Camarillo, Albert 1948- *BioIn 16, ConAu 132*
Camarillo, Albert Michael 1948- *WhoHisp 91*
Camarillo, Alberto *ConAu 132*
Camastro-Pritchett, Rose 1942- *WhoAmA 91*
Camayd-Freixas, Yohel 1948- *WhoE 91*
Camazine, S 1952- *ConAu 129*
Cambaceres, Eugenio 1843-1889 *BioIn 16*
Cambel, Ali Bulent 1923- *WhoAm 90*
Cambell, John F. 1917- *St&PR 91*
Camber, Diane Woolfe *WhoAmA 91*
Cambest, Lynn M. 1944- *St&PR 91*
Cambi, Jacopo *PenDiDA 89*
Cambier, Pierre L. J. J. 1949- *WhoWor 91*
Cambo, Francesc 1876-1947 *BioIn 16*
Cambon, Jules Martin 1845-1935 *BiDFrPL*
Cambor, C Glenn *BiDrAPA 89*
Cambosos, Bruce Michael *BiDrAPA 89*
Cambra, Juan *St&PR 91*
Cambrea, Ilie *EncCoWW*
Cambreling, Sylvain 1948- *PenDiMP*
Cambreling, Sylvian 1948- *IntWWM 90*
Cambria, Cathy A. 1955- *WhoEmL 91*
Cambria, Joseph *Ballpl 90*
Cambrice, Robert Louis 1947- *WhoEmL 91, WhoWor 91*
Cambridge, Ada 1844-1926 *FemiCLE*
Cambridge, Ed *DrBlPA 90*
Cambridge, Elizabeth 1893-1949 *FemiCLE*
Cambridge, Godfrey 1933-1976 *DrBlPA 90, WorAlBi*
Cambron, James Roy 1947- *St&PR 91*
Cambron, Richard Byron 1946- *WhoE 91*
Camden, Anthony 1938- *IntWWM 90*
Camden, Archie 1888-1979 *PenDiMP*
Camden, David George 1951- *WhoE 91*
Camden, William 1551-1623 *BioIn 16*
Camdessus, Michel 1933- *WhoWor 91*
Cameahwait *WhNaAH*
Camel, Edmond Joseph 1941- *St&PR 91*
Camelio, Cosmo Renato 1941- *St&PR 91*
Camell, Paul G. 1947- *St&PR 91, WhoAm 90*
Camera, Joan Ann 1955- *WhoEmL 91*
Camerano, Franklin 1936- *WhoE 91*
Camerlengo, Justin 1943- *ODwPR 91*
Camero, Elva Alejandro *BiDrAPA 89*
Cameron, Alan S 1918- *BiDrAPA 89*
Cameron, Alastair Duncan 1920- *St&PR 91, WhoAm 90*
Cameron, Alastair Graham Walter 1925- *WhoAm 90*
Cameron, Alexander 1827-1893 *DcCanB 12*
Cameron, Alison Stilwell 1921- *WhoWor 91*
Cameron, Andrew 1943- *WhoWor 91*
Cameron, Angus 1826-1897 *AmLegL*
Cameron, Angus Ewan 1906-1981 *DcScB S2*
Cameron, Ann 1943- *AuBYP 90*
Cameron, Anne 1938- *OxCCanT*
Cameron, Basil 1884-1975 *PenDiMP*
Cameron, Betsy *BioIn 16*
Cameron, Brooke Bulovsky *WhoAmA 91*
Cameron, Bruce 1937- *St&PR 91*
Cameron, Bruce Francis 1934- *WhoAm 90*
Cameron, Carey 1952- *ConLC 59 [port]*
Cameron, Caroline Emily Lovett 1844-1921 *FemiCLE*
Cameron, Charles Clifford 1920- *St&PR 91*
Cameron, Charles Metz, Jr. 1923- *WhoAm 90*
Cameron, Colin C. 1927- *St&PR 91*
Cameron, Colin Campbell 1927- *WhoAm 90*
Cameron, Colleen Irene 1952- *WhoAmW 91, WhoEmL 91*
Cameron, Constance Tegge *ODwPR 91*
Cameron, D. Pierre, Jr. 1934- *St&PR 91*
Cameron, Dale C 1912- *BiDrAPA 89*
Cameron, David Brian 1953- *WhoEmL 91*
Cameron, David Pierre Guyot, Jr. 1934- *WhoAm 90*
Cameron, Don R. 1937- *WhoE 91*
Cameron, Donald James 1947- *WhoSSW 91*
Cameron, Donald Nelson 1931- *St&PR 91*
Cameron, Donaldina M. 1869-1968 *BioAmW*
Cameron, Douglas *PenDiMP*

Cameron, Douglas Winston 1947- *WhoEmL 91*
Cameron, Duane Harold 1927- *St&PR 91*
Cameron, Duncan F 1930- *WhoAmA 91*
Cameron, Duncan Hume 1934- *WhoAm 90*
Cameron, Earl 1917- *DrBlPA 90*
Cameron, Eleanor 1912- *AuBYP 90, FemiCLE, MajTwCW*
Cameron, Eleanor Frances 1912- *WhoAm 90, WhoWrEP 89*
Cameron, Elizabeth Jane 1910-1976 *AuBYP 90*
Cameron, Elsa S 1939- *WhoAmA 91*
Cameron, Emmet G. 1911- *St&PR 91*
Cameron, Eric 1935- *WhoAmA 91*
Cameron, Eugene Foster 1945- *WhoAm 90*
Cameron, Eugene Nathan 1910- *WhoAm 90*
Cameron, Ewen *BioIn 16*
Cameron, Franklin Dane 1947- *WhoAm 90*
Cameron, George Frederick 1854-1885 *DcLB 99*
Cameron, Gerald Thomas, Sr. 1924- *St&PR 91*
Cameron, Gerry B. 1938- *St&PR 91*
Cameron, Glenn Nilsson 1956- *WhoEmL 91, WhoSSW 91*
Cameron, Gordon Murray 1932- *WhoWor 91*
Cameron, Harry 1881-1944 *BioIn 16*
Cameron, Heather Anne 1951- *St&PR 91*
Cameron, Herbert Daniel, Jr. 1950- *WhoEmL 91*
Cameron, Ian R *BiDrAPA 89*
Cameron, Irma Kyllikki 1948- *WhoAmW 91*
Cameron, J. Elliot 1923- *WhoAm 90*
Cameron, James 1911-1985 *DcNaB 1981*
Cameron, James Donald 1833-1918 *BiDrUSE 89*
Cameron, James Duke 1925- *WhoAm 90*
Cameron, James M. 1928- *WhoAm 90*
Cameron, James William, Jr. 1947- *St&PR 91*
Cameron, Jared S. *ODwPR 91*
Cameron, JoAnna *WhoAm 90, WhoWor 91*
Cameron, John Clifford 1946- *WhoEmL 91*
Cameron, John Ewen 1918- *IntWWM 90*
Cameron, John J. 1933- *ODwPR 91*
Cameron, John Lansing 1916- *WhoAm 90*
Cameron, John M. 1943- *St&PR 91*
Cameron, John Roderick 1922- *WhoAm 90*
Cameron, John Stuart 1951- *WhoWor 91*
Cameron, John Wilson 1936- *WhoE 91*
Cameron, JohnAlexander Duncan 1948- *WhoWor 91*
Cameron, Joseph Alexander 1942- *WhoSSW 91*
Cameron, Joseph J. 1936- *St&PR 91*
Cameron, Joy 1912- *ConAu 132*
Cameron, Judith Elaine Moellering 1943- *WhoAmW 91*
Cameron, Judith Lynne 1945- *WhoAmW 91, WhoEmL 91, WhoWor 91*
Cameron, Judy Lea 1948- *WhoEmL 91*
Cameron, Julia Margaret 1815-1879 *WorAlBi*
Cameron, Julia Margaret Pattle 1815-1879 *BioIn 16*
Cameron, Kenneth A. *St&PR 91*
Cameron, Kenneth M. 1931- *ConAu 129*
Cameron, Kirk *BioIn 16*
Cameron, Kirk 1970- *WorAlBi*
Cameron, Larry Melvin 1951- *St&PR 91*
Cameron, Laura Jean 1957- *WhoWor 91*
Cameron, Lou 1924- *WhoWrEP 89*
Cameron, Louis McDuffy 1935- *WhoAm 90*
Cameron, Malcolm Colin 1831-1898 *DcCanB 12*
Cameron, Malcolm Maben 1941- *WhoWor 91*
Cameron, Marion A. 1950- *St&PR 91*
Cameron, Mark Alan 1954- *WhoEmL 91*
Cameron, Mary King 1940- *St&PR 91*
Cameron, Mike Graham- 1931- *BioIn 16*
Cameron, Neil 1920-1985 *DcNaB 1981*
Cameron, Nicholas Allen 1939- *St&PR 91, WhoAm 90, WhoWor 91*
Cameron, Oliver Gene 1946- *BiDrAPA 89*
Cameron, Paul Archibald, Jr. 1931- *WhoSSW 91*
Cameron, Paul Francis 1950- *BiDrAPA 89*
Cameron, Peter Alfred Gordon 1930- *WhoAm 90, WhoE 91*
Cameron, Polly 1928- *AuBYP 90*
Cameron, Richard Douglas 1937- *BiDrAPA 89*
Cameron, Robert 1911- *BioIn 16*
Cameron, Robert Edwin *BiDrAPA 89*
Cameron, Robert M. 1925- *St&PR 91*
Cameron, Robert William 1911- *WhoAm 90*
Cameron, Roderick William 1823-1900 *DcCanB 12*
Cameron, Ronald W. 1934- *St&PR 91*
Cameron, Rondo 1925- *WhoAm 90*
Cameron, Rosaline Briskin *WhoE 91*
Cameron, Roy Eugene 1929- *WhoAm 90, WhoWor 91*
Cameron, Shirley 1944- *BiDWomA*
Cameron, Simon 1799-1889 *BiDrUSE 89, BioIn 16*
Cameron, Thomas S. 1935- *St&PR 91*
Cameron, Thomas William Lane 1927- *WhoAm 90*
Cameron, W.S. 1942- *St&PR 91*
Cameron, William Bleasdell 1862-1951 *DcLB 99 [port]*
Cameron, William Duncan 1925- *WhoSSW 91, WhoWor 91*
Cameron, William James 1926-1989 *BioIn 16*
Cameros, Alan L. 1935- *St&PR 91*
Cameros, Maurice 1907- *St&PR 91*
Camey, Pamela S. 1962- *WhoAmW 91*
Camfferman, Peter Marienus 1890-1957 *WhoAmA 91N*
Camfield, Elizabeth 1632-1716 *BiDEWW*
Camfield, William Arnett 1934- *WhoAm 90, WhoAmA 91*
Camhi, Morrie 1928- *WhoAmA 91*
Camicia, Nicholas T. 1916- *St&PR 91*
Camiel, Edwin Peter, Jr. *BiDrAPA 89*
Camiel, Edwin Peter, Jr. 1950- *WhoE 91*
Camilleri, Charles 1931- *IntWWM 90*
Camilleri, John Peter 1957- *WhoEmL 91*
Camilletti, Rob *BioIn 16*
Camilli, Carlo 1946- *WhoWor 91*
Camilli, Dolf 1907- *Ballpl 90*
Camilli, Doug 1936- *Ballpl 90*
Camillo, Michael Francis *BiDrAPA 89*
Camillone, Barbara 1937- *WhoE 91*
Camilo, Michel *BioIn 16*
Camilo, Michel 1954- *WhoHisp 91*
Caminiti, Ken 1963- *Ballpl 90*
Caminos, Horacio 1914- *WhoAm 90*
Caminos, Hugo 1921- *WhoE 91*
Camins, Jacques Joseph 1904- *WhoAmA 91*
Camisa, George Lincoln 1929- *WhoE 91*
Camisa, Kenneth Peter 1938- *St&PR 91*
Camisi, Domenick J. 1947- *WhoE 91*
Camlin, James A 1918-1982 *WhoAmA 91N*
Camm, Anne *BiDEWW*
Camm, Mabel *BiDEWW*
Camma, Philip 1923- *WhoWor 91*
Cammack, Caroline 1951- *WhoAmW 91*
Cammack, Dennis Robert 1948- *WhoEmL 91*
Cammack, Raymond Weldon 1942- *WhoSSW 91*
Cammack, Richard Lewis 1945- *WhoEmL 91*
Cammack, Trank Emerson 1919- *WhoAm 90*
Cammaker, Sheldon I. 1939- *St&PR 91*
Cammann, Schuyler Van Rensselaer 1912- *WhoAm 90*
Cammarata, Joseph 1958- *WhoEmL 91*
Cammarata, Joseph Toro 1953- *WhoE 91*
Cammarata, Sandra 1959- *BiDrAPA 89*
Cammarosano, Joseph Raphael 1923- *WhoAm 90*
Cammarota, Robert Michael 1949- *IntWWM 90*
Cammermeyer, Margarethe 1942- *WhoAmW 91*
Cammett, Stuart Hyland 1931- *St&PR 91*
Cammock, Earl E. 1926- *WhoAm 90*
Camnitz, Howie 1881-1960 *Ballpl 90*
Camoes, Luis Vaz De 1524?-1580 *WorAlBi*
Camosse, Henry J. 1930- *St&PR 91*
Camosy, Raymond J. 1950- *St&PR 91*
Camougis, George 1930- *WhoWor 91*
Camozzi, Victor E. 1916- *St&PR 91*
Camp, Alethea Taylor 1938- *WhoAmW 91*
Camp, Barbara Ann 1943- *WhoAmW 91*
Camp, Carson *BioIn 16*
Camp, Clifton Durrett, Jr. 1927- *WhoAm 90*
Camp, Corrine Marie 1936- *WhoWrEP 89*
Camp, Craig Charles 1958- *WhoE 91*
Camp, Ehney Addison, III 1942- *WhoSSW 91, WhoWor 91*
Camp, Ellis G. 1914- *St&PR 91*
Camp, Frances Spencer 1924- *WhoE 91*
Camp, Gretschen Dale 1958- *WhoEmL 91*
Camp, Harry *EarBlAP*
Camp, Hazel Lee Burt 1922- *WhoAmW 91, WhoE 91, WhoSSW 91, WhoWor 91*
Camp, Jack Tarpley, Jr. 1943- *WhoSSW 91*
Camp, Jeffrey 1944- *BioIn 16*
Camp, Joe *ConAu 129*
Camp, John *BioIn 16*
Camp, John Clayton 1923- *WhoE 91*
Camp, John Francis 1947- *WhoSSW 91*
Camp, Joseph Shelton, Jr. 1939- *ConAu 129, WhoAm 90*
Camp, Larry Michael 1948- *WhoEmL 91*
Camp, Laurie Smith 1953- *WhoAmW 91*
Camp, Lewis Forman, Jr. 1928- *St&PR 91*
Camp, Linda Joyce *WhoAmW 91*
Camp, Marva Jo 1961- *WhoE 91*
Camp, Max Wayne 1935- *IntWWM 90*
Camp, Mitch Owen 1964- *WhoSSW 91*
Camp, Norman M *BiDrAPA 89*
Camp, Orton P. 1922- *St&PR 91*
Camp, Richard D. *BioIn 16*
Camp, Richard W. *BioIn 16*
Camp, Rick 1953- *Ballpl 90*
Camp, Rose Elizabeth Thomas 1952- *WhoAmW 91*
Camp, Sokari Douglas 1958- *BiDWomA*
Camp, Toni Jean 1959- *BiDrAPA 89*
Camp, Walter 1859-1925 *WorAlBi*
Camp, Warren Victor 1946- *WhoSSW 91*
Camp, Wesley Douglass 1915- *WhoAm 90*
Camp, William P 1917- *BiDrAPA 89*
Camp, William Ragsdale 1945- *St&PR 91*
Camp-Brewer, Laura Marie 1962- *WhoAmW 91*
Campa, Arthur L 1905- *HispWr 90*
Campa, Arthur Leon 1905-1978 *BioIn 16*
Campagna, Richard Vincent 1952- *WhoEmL 91*
Campagnani, Cesar Augusto 1938- *WhoWor 91*
Campagnari, Francesco 1927- *WhoWor 91*
Campagne, Thomas Elmer 1950- *WhoEmL 91*
Campagni, Roberto *EncO&P 3*
Campagnuolo, Benjamin 1941- *St&PR 91*
Campaigne, Ernest Edwin 1914- *WhoAm 90*
Campan, Jeanne Louise Henriette 1752-1822 *EncCoWW*
Campana, Ana Isabel 1934- *WhoAmW 91, WhoE 91, WhoWor 91*
Campana, Joseph A. *St&PR 91*
Campana, Joseph A. 1937- *WhoAm 90*
Campana, Joseph E. 1952- *WhoEmL 91*
Campana, Richard John 1918- *WhoAm 90*
Campanalie, Richard Anthony 1946- *St&PR 91*
Campanaro, Lurana Tucker 1935- *WhoAmW 91*
Campanella, Alice 1955- *WhoAmW 91*
Campanella, Anton J. 1932- *WhoAm 90*
Campanella, Anton Joseph 1932- *St&PR 91*
Campanella, Carl 1947- *St&PR 91*
Campanella, Donna Madeline 1952- *WhoAmW 91*
Campanella, Joseph Alex 1942- *St&PR 91*
Campanella, Migdalia Cavazos 1961- *WhoHisp 91*
Campanella, Roy 1921- *Ballpl 90 [port], WorAlBi*
Campanella, Roy, Jr. 1949?- *DrBlPA 90*
Campanelli, Anthony Joseph 1935- *St&PR 91*
Campanelli, Dan 1949- *WhoAmA 91*
Campanelli, Pauline Eble *WhoAmA 91*
Campaneris, Bert 1942- *Ballpl 90 [port], WhoHisp 91*
Campani, Ferdinando Maria *PenDiDA 89*
Campanile, Samuel John 1952- *WhoEmL 91*
Campanini, Cleofonte 1860-1919 *PenDiMP*
Campanini, Italo 1845-1896 *PenDiMP*
Campanioni, Raul A. 1956-1990 *NewYTBS 90*
Campanis, Al *BioIn 16*
Campanis, Al 1916- *Ballpl 90*
Campbel, Ernest 1904- *St&PR 91*
Campbell, A.N. 1913- *St&PR 91*
Campbell, Alan Hugh *BioIn 16*
Campbell, Alan Keith 1923- *St&PR 91, WhoAm 90, WhoE 91*
Campbell, Alasdair Iain *ConAu 130*
Campbell, Albert A. *ConAu 129*
Campbell, Alexander 1822?-1892 *DcCanB 12*
Campbell, Alexander John 1904- *St&PR 91*
Campbell, Alistair Matheson 1905- *WhoAm 90*
Campbell, Allan Adams, Jr. 1945- *WhoEmL 91*
Campbell, Allan McCulloch 1929- *WhoAm 90*
Campbell, Alma Jacqueline Porter 1948- *WhoE 91*
Campbell, Almira Taylor 1920- *WhoAmW 91*
Campbell, Alvin Dean 1947- *St&PR 91*
Campbell, Andrea 1963- *BioIn 16*
Campbell, Andrew 1853- *DcCanB 12*
Campbell, Andrew Foil *BiDrAPA 89*
Campbell, Andrew Gordon 1948- *WhoWor 91*
Campbell, Andrew Hamilton 1932- *St&PR 91*
Campbell, Angus *ConAu 30NR*
Campbell, Angus 1910-1980 *ConAu 129*
Campbell, Angus K. 1904- *St&PR 91*
Campbell, Anthony 1955- *WhoSSW 91*
Campbell, Arlington Fichtner 1939- *WhoSSW 91*
Campbell, Arthur Andrews 1924- *WhoAm 90*
Campbell, Arthur Charles 1947- *St&PR 91*
Campbell, Arthur Samuel 1928- *BiDrAPA 89*
Campbell, Arthur V. 1954- *St&PR 91*
Campbell, Avril Kim 1947- *WhoAm 90, WhoAmW 91, WhoE 91*
Campbell, Barbara *BioIn 16*
Campbell, Barbara Ann 1935- *WhoAmW 91*
Campbell, Barbara T. *ODwPR 91*
Campbell, Barbara Vaughan 1947- *WhoEmL 91*
Campbell, Barry Innes 1960- *BiDrAPA 89*
Campbell, Bart 1924- *ODwPR 91*
Campbell, Bebe Moore *BioIn 16*
Campbell, Ben Nighthorse 1933- *WhoAm 90*
Campbell, Betty Becker Pinkston *BioIn 16*
Campbell, Betty Jean 1951- *WhoAmW 91*
Campbell, Beverly Ann 1938- *WhoSSW 91*
Campbell, Beverly-Claire 1954- *WhoAmW 91*
Campbell, Bill 1948- *Ballpl 90*
Campbell, Billy 1873-1957 *Ballpl 90*
Campbell, Bonnie Jean 1948- *WhoAmW 91*
Campbell, Bonnie Marie 1944- *WhoAmW 91*
Campbell, Bruce *AuBYP 90*
Campbell, Bruce 1909- *Ballpl 90*
Campbell, Bruce Crichton 1947- *WhoAm 90*
Campbell, Bruce Henry 1930- *St&PR 91*
Campbell, Bruce Irving 1947- *WhoEmL 91*
Campbell, Byron Chesser 1934- *WhoAm 90*
Campbell, C. John 1935- *St&PR 91*
Campbell, Calvin Arthur, Jr. 1934- *St&PR 91, WhoAm 90, WhoWor 91*
Campbell, Carl L. 1943- *St&PR 91*
Campbell, Carl Lester 1943- *WhoAm 90*
Campbell, Caroline Krause 1926- *WhoAmW 91*
Campbell, Carolyn Milburn 1961- *WhoEmL 91*
Campbell, Carroll Ashmore, Jr. 1940- *WhoAm 90, WhoSSW 91, WhoWor 91*
Campbell, Charles A. 1944- *St&PR 91*
Campbell, Charles Alton 1944- *WhoSSW 91*
Campbell, Charles Bryan 1922- *WhoAm 90*
Campbell, Charles D. 1905-1988 *BioIn 16*
Campbell, Charles Edwin 1942- *WhoAm 90*
Campbell, Charles J. 1915- *WhoAm 90*
Campbell, Charles Malcolm 1908-1985 *WhoAmA 91N*
Campbell, Charles Philip, Jr. 1948- *WhoEmL 91*
Campbell, Charles R. 1939- *St&PR 91*
Campbell, Charles Rodman *BioIn 16*
Campbell, Cheryl 1951- *ConTFT 8*
Campbell, Chris Lane 1937- *St&PR 91*
Campbell, Christian L. 1950- *St&PR 91*
Campbell, Christopher J. 1927- *St&PR 91*
Campbell, Christopher Jay 1950- *WhoEmL 91*
Campbell, Christopher John 1927- *WhoAm 90*
Campbell, Christopher Joseph 1955- *WhoE 91, WhoEmL 91*
Campbell, Clair Gilliland 1961- *WhoEmL 91*
Campbell, Claire Patricia 1933- *WhoAmW 91*
Campbell, Clara Shiver 1931- *St&PR 91*
Campbell, Clyde Del 1930- *WhoAm 90*
Campbell, Colin 1927- *WhoAm 90*
Campbell, Colin Dearborn 1917- *WhoAm 90*
Campbell, Colin Goetze 1935- *WhoAm 90*
Campbell, Colin Herald 1911- *WhoWor 91*
Campbell, Colin Kydd 1927- *WhoAm 90*
Campbell, Colin Percy 1877- *AmLegL*
Campbell, Coline *WhoAmW 91*
Campbell, Corbett *BiDrAPA 89*
Campbell, Courtney Lee 1957- *WhoEmL 91*
Campbell, Craig Christopher 1960- *BiDrAPA 89*
Campbell, Craig Sherman 1935- *St&PR 91, WhoSSW 91*
Campbell, Crom B. 1928- *St&PR 91*
Campbell, Dale W 1932- *BiDrAPA 89*
Campbell, Daniel Robert 1958- *WhoEmL 91*
Campbell, Dave 1942- *Ballpl 90*
Campbell, Dave 1951- *Ballpl 90*
Campbell, David *BioIn 16, NewYTBS 90*
Campbell, David 1953- *IntWWM 90*
Campbell, David Douglas 1929- *WhoAm 90*
Campbell, David George 1949- *WhoE 91*

Campbell, David Gwynne 1930- *WhoAm 90, WhoSSW 91*
Campbell, David N. 1941- *St&PR 91*
Campbell, David Ned 1929- *WhoAm 90*
Campbell, David P. 1939- *WhoSSW 91*
Campbell, David Paul 1936- *WhoAmA 91*
Campbell, David Ralph 1945- *WhoEmL 91*
Campbell, David White 1945- *WhoSSW 91*
Campbell, Debe L. 1957- *WhoWrEP 89*
Campbell, Deborah Kaye 1955- *WhoAmW 91*
Campbell, Debra Lynn 1954- *WhoAmW 91*
Campbell, Delois 1945- *WhoE 91*
Campbell, Dennis Marion 1945- *WhoAm 90*
Campbell, Dexter McPherson, Jr. 1949- *St&PR 91*
Campbell, Diana Butt 1943- *WhoE 91*
Campbell, Diane Hoye 1942- *BiDrAPA 89*
Campbell, Dick *EarBlAP*
Campbell, Dick 1903- *DrBlPA 90*
Campbell, Don *NewAgMG*
Campbell, Don E. 1924- *St&PR 91*
Campbell, Donald *BioIn 16*
Campbell, Donald 1940- *ConAu 30NR*
Campbell, Donald Alfred 1928- *WhoAm 90*
Campbell, Donald Broughton 1929- *St&PR 91*
Campbell, Donald Graham 1925- *St&PR 91, WhoAm 90*
Campbell, Donald Guy 1922- *WhoAm 90*
Campbell, Donald K. 1926- *WhoAm 90*
Campbell, Donald L. 1926- *St&PR 91*
Campbell, Donald L. 1944- *ODwPR 91*
Campbell, Donald Ross *BiDrAPA 89*
Campbell, Donald Thomas 1916- *WhoAm 90*
Campbell, Donald W. 1934- *St&PR 91*
Campbell, Donn Melvin 1931- *St&PR 91*
Campbell, Donna Waugh 1937- *WhoAmW 91*
Campbell, Doris Klein *WhoAmW 91*
Campbell, Dorothea Primrose 1793-1863 *FemiCLE*
Campbell, Dorothy Bostwick 1899- *WhoAmA 91*
Campbell, Douglas *NewYTBS 90*
Campbell, Douglas 1920- *St&PR 91*
Campbell, Douglas 1922- *OxCCanT [port]*
Campbell, Douglas Alexander 1948- *WhoWor 91*
Campbell, Douglass 1919- *WhoAm 90, WhoWor 91*
Campbell, Duncan G 1926- *BiDrAPA 89*
Campbell, E. P. *WhoAm 90*
Campbell, Earl *BioIn 16*
Campbell, Earl 1955- *WorAlBi*
Campbell, Early 1943- *WhoSSW 91*
Campbell, Edmund Douglas 1899- *WhoAm 90*
Campbell, Edmund S 1884-1950 *WhoAmA 91N*
Campbell, Edna Boyne *BioIn 16*
Campbell, Edward *BioIn 16*
Campbell, Edward C. *BioIn 16*
Campbell, Edward Clinton 1929- *WhoE 91, WhoWor 91*
Campbell, Edward Fay, Jr. 1932- *WhoAm 90*
Campbell, Edward George 1916- *St&PR 91*
Campbell, Edward J. 1928- *St&PR 91*
Campbell, Edward Joseph 1928- *WhoAm 90, WhoSSW 91*
Campbell, Edward Patrick 1949- *St&PR 91*
Campbell, Edwin Colin 1943- *WhoE 91*
Campbell, Edwin Denton 1927- *WhoAm 90*
Campbell, Elden *NewYTBS 90 [port]*
Campbell, Elizabeth A. *AuBYP 90*
Campbell, Elnora Frances 1948- *WhoAmW 91, WhoEmL 91*
Campbell, Eric Eldon 1929- *WhoAm 90*
Campbell, Eugene Paul 1907- *WhoE 91*
Campbell, Ewing 1940- *WhoSSW 91, WhoWrEP 89*
Campbell, Fenton Gregory 1939- *WhoAm 90*
Campbell, Finley Alexander 1927- *WhoAm 90*
Campbell, Frances Harvell *WhoAmW 91, WhoWor 91*
Campbell, Frances Stine 1935- *BiDrAPA 89*
Campbell, Francis James 1924- *WhoAm 90*
Campbell, Frank B., Jr. 1917- *St&PR 91*
Campbell, Frank Carter 1916- *WhoAm 90*
Campbell, Frank G *BioIn 16*
Campbell, Frank Paul 1931- *St&PR 91*
Campbell, Franklin F 1921- *BiDrAPA 89*
Campbell, Fremont Lee 1923- *WhoAm 90*
Campbell, Gary J. 1944- *St&PR 91*
Campbell, George Emerson 1932- *WhoAm 90*
Campbell, George Leroy 1940- *St&PR 91*
Campbell, George Washington 1768-1848 *BiDrUSE 89*
Campbell, George Wendal, Jr. 1947- *WhoEmL 91*
Campbell, Gilbert Sadler 1924- *WhoAm 90*
Campbell, Glen 1936- *OxCPMus, WorAlBi*
Campbell, Glenn F. 1929- *ODwPR 91*
Campbell, Gloria Mae 1925- *WhoAmW 91*
Campbell, Gordon Muir 1948- *WhoAm 90*
Campbell, Gordon Wallace 1932- *St&PR 91*
Campbell, Grace MacLennan 1895-1963 *FemiCLE*
Campbell, Gregory Scott 1948- *St&PR 91*
Campbell, Gretna 1922-1987 *BioIn 16*
Campbell, H. Stuart 1929- *WhoAm 90*
Campbell, Harold Andrew, III 1947- *WhoSSW 91*
Campbell, Harold Norman 1940- *WhoAm 90, WhoE 91*
Campbell, Harry C. 1912- *St&PR 91*
Campbell, Harry Woodson 1946- *WhoEmL 91*
Campbell, Harvey A. 1930- *St&PR 91*
Campbell, Harvey Devilloe, III 1954- *BiDrAPA 89*
Campbell, Harvey E. 1928- *St&PR 91*
Campbell, Hazel D. *FemiCLE*
Campbell, Hazel Vivian *HarlReB*
Campbell, Helen 1839-1918 *FemiCLE*
Campbell, Helen Louise 1939- *WhoAmW 91*
Campbell, Helen Stuart 1839-1918 *EncAL*
Campbell, Henry Cummings 1919- *WhoAm 90*
Campbell, Howard R *BiDrAPA 89*
Campbell, Hugh L. 1937- *St&PR 91*
Campbell, Hugh Lyle 1937- *WhoAm 90*
Campbell, Hugh P. 1934- *St&PR 91*
Campbell, Ian 1899-1978 *DcScB S2*
Campbell, Ian B. 1928- *St&PR 91*
Campbell, Ian David 1945- *IntWWM 90, WhoAm 90, WhoEmL 91*
Campbell, Ian David 1953- *ODwPR 91, WhoEmL 91*
Campbell, J.B. *St&PR 91*
Campbell, J.D., Jr. 1941- *St&PR 91*
Campbell, J. Louis, III 1946- *WhoE 91*
Campbell, Jack B. 1924- *St&PR 91*
Campbell, Jack James Ramsay 1918- *WhoAm 90*
Campbell, Jack M. 1916- *WhoAm 90*
Campbell, Jack Thomas 1937- *St&PR 91*
Campbell, Jackson Justice 1920- *WhoAm 90*
Campbell, James 1812-1893 *BiDrUSE 89*
Campbell, James Albert Barton 1940- *WhoSSW 91*
Campbell, James Arthur 1916-1989 *BioIn 16*
Campbell, James Arthur 1924- *WhoAm 90*
Campbell, James B. 1931- *St&PR 91*
Campbell, James Batchelder 1944- *WhoSSW 91*
Campbell, James Boyd 1931- *WhoAm 90*
Campbell, James D. 1946- *St&PR 91*
Campbell, James E. 1935- *St&PR 91*
Campbell, James Ernest *BiDrAPA 89*
Campbell, James Franklin 1938- *St&PR 91*
Campbell, James Fromhart 1912- *WhoWor 91*
Campbell, James Howard, Jr. 1958- *WhoEmL 91*
Campbell, James L. 1928- *St&PR 91*
Campbell, James Lawrence 1914- *WhoAmA 91*
Campbell, James M. *BioIn 16*
Campbell, James M 1938- *BiDrAPA 89*
Campbell, James Oliver 1932- *St&PR 91*
Campbell, James P. 1939- *St&PR 91*
Campbell, James Robert 1942- *WhoAm 90*
Campbell, James Sargent 1938- *WhoAm 90*
Campbell, Jan L *BiDrAPA 89*
Campbell, Jane *WhoWrEP 89*
Campbell, Jean *BioIn 16*
Campbell, Jean 1901- *FemiCLE*
Campbell, Jean 1925- *WhoAmW 91*
Campbell, Jeanna *WhoWrEP 89*
Campbell, Jeanne Begien 1913- *WhoAmA 91*
Campbell, Jeanne Marie 1940- *WhoAmW 91*
Campbell, Jefferey James 1952- *St&PR 91*
Campbell, Jeffrey Alan 1956- *St&PR 91*
Campbell, Jerry Dean 1945- *WhoAm 90*
Campbell, Jerry Lee 1934- *WhoSSW 91*
Campbell, Jewett 1912- *WhoAmA 91*
Campbell, Jill Frost 1948- *WhoAmW 91, WhoEmL 91*
Campbell, Jo 1950- *WhoAmW 91*
Campbell, Joan Brown 1931- *NewYTBS 90*
Campbell, Joan Salmon *WhoAm 90*
Campbell, John 1653-1728 *BioIn 16*
Campbell, John 1949- *BioIn 16*
Campbell, John B. 1922- *St&PR 91*
Campbell, John Coert 1911- *WhoAm 90*
Campbell, John Coleman 1935- *IntWWM 90*
Campbell, John David 1954- *St&PR 91*
Campbell, John Duncan 1940- *WhoWor 91*
Campbell, John H. 1942- *St&PR 91*
Campbell, John Joseph 1926- *WhoE 91*
Campbell, John Kelly 1929- *WhoAm 90*
Campbell, John L. 1950- *St&PR 91*
Campbell, John Morgan 1922- *WhoAm 90*
Campbell, John Nathan 1930- *St&PR 91*
Campbell, John Palmer 1923- *WhoAm 90*
Campbell, John Richard 1932- *WhoAm 90*
Campbell, John Robert 1915- *WhoSSW 91*
Campbell, John Roy 1933- *WhoAm 90, WhoSSW 91*
Campbell, John S. 1950- *St&PR 91*
Campbell, John Tucker 1912- *WhoAm 90, WhoSSW 91*
Campbell, John W 1910-1971 *MajTwCW, RGTwCSF*
Campbell, John William 1954- *WhoSSW 91*
Campbell, John Wood 1910-1971 *WorAlBi*
Campbell, Johnnie Jay 1946- *WhoSSW 91*
Campbell, Joseph 1904-1983 *EncO&P 3*
Campbell, Joseph 1904-1987 *BioIn 16, MajTwCW*
Campbell, Joseph Howard, Jr. 1952- *WhoEmL 91*
Campbell, Joseph Leonard, II 1938- *St&PR 91*
Campbell, Josiah Abigail Patterson 1830-1917 *AmLegL*
Campbell, Judith Lowe 1946- *BiDrAPA 89, WhoAm 90, WhoAmW 91, WhoEmL 91*
Campbell, Judith May 1938- *WhoAm 90*
Campbell, Julia *BioIn 16*
Campbell, Karlyn Kohrs 1937- *WhoAm 90, WhoAmW 91*
Campbell, Keith Allen 1948- *WhoEmL 91*
Campbell, Keith S. 1954- *St&PR 91*
Campbell, Keith Wilson 1921- *St&PR 91*
Campbell, Ken *BioIn 16*
Campbell, Kenneth 1899- *WhoAm 90*
Campbell, Kenneth 1922- *IntWWM 90*
Campbell, Kenneth, Mrs. 1919- *St&PR 91*
Campbell, Kenneth Eugene, Jr. 1943- *WhoAm 90*
Campbell, Kenneth Floyd 1925- *WhoAmA 91*
Campbell, Kenneth L. 1947- *St&PR 91*
Campbell, Kent Norman 1955- *WhoEmL 91*
Campbell, Kevin Peter 1952- *WhoAm 90*
Campbell, Kristine M *BiDrAPA 89*
Campbell, Larry E. 1941- *WhoAm 90*
Campbell, Laurence Bradford 1940- *St&PR 91*
Campbell, Lawrence 1914- *WhoE 91*
Campbell, Lawrence Claire 1929- *St&PR 91*
Campbell, Leah S *BiDrAPA 89*
Campbell, Leonard Gene 1933- *WhoSSW 91*
Campbell, Leonard Martin 1918- *WhoAm 90*
Campbell, Lesley Ann 1959- *WhoAmW 91*
Campbell, Levin Hicks 1927- *WhoAm 90, WhoE 91*
Campbell, Lewis Davis 1811-1882 *BioIn 16*
Campbell, Linda Ann 1961- *WhoAmW 91*
Campbell, Linda Katherine 1948- *WhoEmL 91*
Campbell, Linda Key 1943- *WhoSSW 91*
Campbell, Linn A 1924- *BiDrAPA 89*
Campbell, Linzy Leon 1927- *WhoAm 90*
Campbell, Lisa Ann 1961- *WhoE 91*
Campbell, Lou Ellen 1943- *WhoAmW 91*
Campbell, Louis Lorne 1928- *WhoAm 90*
Campbell, Louisa Dresser 1907-1989 *BioIn 16, ConAu 129*
Campbell, Louise 1937- *WhoWrEP 89*
Campbell, Lucy Barnes *WhoWor 91*
Campbell, Lyle Richard 1942- *WhoAm 90*
Campbell, Lynn Ann 1963- *WhoE 91*
Campbell, M. Rudolph *AuBYP 90*
Campbell, M. Steve 1949- *St&PR 91*
Campbell, Mack W. *St&PR 91*
Campbell, Magda 1928- *BiDrAPA 89*
Campbell, Malcolm Gregory 1943- *WhoWor 91*
Campbell, Margaret *BioIn 16, IntWWM 90, TwCCr&M 91*
Campbell, Margaret Amelia 1923- *WhoAm 90*
Campbell, Margaret M. 1928- *WhoAm 90, WhoAmW 91*
Campbell, Maria 1940- *FemiCLE*
Campbell, Maria Bouchelle 1944- *St&PR 91, WhoAm 90, WhoAmW 91*
Campbell, Maria Dolores Delgado 1943- *WhoHisp 91*
Campbell, Marion 1929- *WhoSSW 91*
Campbell, Mark Alan 1953- *WhoEmL 91*
Campbell, Mark Stephen 1949- *WhoSSW 91*
Campbell, Marsha Marie 1952- *WhoAmW 91*
Campbell, Marsha Mulford 1946- *WhoAmW 91*
Campbell, Martha Ann 1946- *BiDrAPA 89*
Campbell, Martha Jean 1926- *WhoAmW 91*
Campbell, Mary A. 1950- *WhoAmW 91*
Campbell, Mary Ann 1920- *WhoWor 91*
Campbell, Mary Beth 1952- *WhoEmL 91*
Campbell, Mary Grace 1928- *St&PR 91*
Campbell, Mary Kathleen 1944- *WhoAmW 91*
Campbell, Mary Kathryn 1939- *WhoAm 90, WhoAmW 91*
Campbell, Mary Rose 1934- *St&PR 91*
Campbell, Mary Schmidt *BioIn 16*
Campbell, Mary Virginia 1946- *WhoWrEP 89*
Campbell, Maurice Anthony 1961- *WhoSSW 91*
Campbell, McCoy Clempson, III 1918- *WhoAm 90*
Campbell, Michael *BioIn 16*
Campbell, Michael Duff 1943- *St&PR 91*
Campbell, Michael Edward 1947- *WhoE 91*
Campbell, Michael Jeffrey 1948- *WhoSSW 91*
Campbell, Michael Joseph 1964- *WhoE 91*
Campbell, Michael Leonard 1945- *WhoEmL 91*
Campbell, Mike 1964- *Ballpl 90*
Campbell, Milton Hugh 1928- *WhoAm 90*
Campbell, Mona Louise 1919- *WhoAm 90*
Campbell, Nancy A. 1961- *ODwPR 91*
Campbell, Nancy Edinger 1957- *WhoAmW 91, WhoE 91*
Campbell, Nancy Irene Barr 1955- *WhoAmW 91*
Campbell, Nancy L. 1939 *St&PR 91, WhoAm 90*
Campbell, Naomi *BioIn 16*
Campbell, Newton Allen 1928- *St&PR 91, WhoAm 90*
Campbell, Nina *BioIn 16*
Campbell, Norman Ambrose 1936- *WhoAm 90, WhoE 91*
Campbell, Orland 1890-1972 *WhoAmA 91N*
Campbell, P L 1944- *OxCCanT*
Campbell, Pamela Ann *BiDrAPA 89*
Campbell, Pat *WhoWrEP 89*
Campbell, Patricia Ann 1941- *WhoWrEP 89*
Campbell, Patricia Barbara 1947- *WhoAmW 91*
Campbell, Patricia Cawley 1949- *WhoAmW 91*
Campbell, Patricia J *BiDrAPA 89*
Campbell, Patrick, Mrs. 1865-1940 *BioIn 16, WorAlBi*
Campbell, Patrick G *BiDrAPA 89*
Campbell, Patton 1926- *WhoAm 90*
Campbell, Paul Barton 1930- *St&PR 91, WhoAm 90*
Campbell, Peter *AuBYP 90*
Campbell, Peter L 1941- *BiDrAPA 89*
Campbell, Peter W. *BioIn 16*
Campbell, Philip Allen 1936- *WhoAm 90*
Campbell, Phillip J., Jr. 1932- *St&PR 91*
Campbell, Pollyann S. 1949- *WhoEmL 91*
Campbell, R. Nelson 1964- *WhoE 91*
Campbell, R. Wright *TwCCr&M 91*
Campbell, R. Wright 1927- *SpyFic*
Campbell, R Wright 1927- *WhoWrEP 89*
Campbell, Randall Marvin 1927- *St&PR 91*
Campbell, Raymond, III 1948- *WhoEmL 91*
Campbell, Rea Burne 1954- *WhoEmL 91*
Campbell, Renoda Gisele 1963- *WhoAmW 91*
Campbell, Richard Alden 1926- *WhoAm 90*
Campbell, Richard Horton 1921- *WhoAmA 91*
Campbell, Richard J. 1929- *St&PR 91*
Campbell, Richard P. 1947- *WhoAm 90*
Campbell, Richard Rice 1923- *WhoAm 90*
Campbell, Roald Fay 1905-1988 *BioIn 16*
Campbell, Robert 1804-1879 *WhNaAH*
Campbell, Robert 1808-1894 *DcCanB 12, WhNaAH*
Campbell, Robert 1826-1898 *DcCanB 12*
Campbell, Robert 1927- *TwCCr&M 91*
Campbell, Robert 1937- *WhoAm 90*
Campbell, Robert, Jr. 1924- *St&PR 91*
Campbell, Robert Ayerst 1940- *WhoAm 90*
Campbell, Robert Charles 1924- *WhoAm 90*
Campbell, Robert Dale 1914- *WhoAm 90*
Campbell, Robert Edward 1928- *WhoSSW 91*
Campbell, Robert Emmett 1933- *St&PR 91*

Campbell, Robert George 1934- *St&PR 91*
Campbell, Robert H. 1948- *WhoAm 90, WhoE 91*
Campbell, Robert J, III *BiDrAPA 89*
Campbell, Robert Joseph 1935- *BiDrAPA 89*
Campbell, Robert Kenneth *St&PR 91N*
Campbell, Robert L. 1922- *St&PR 91*
Campbell, Robert L. 1951- *St&PR 91*
Campbell, Robert Merrill 1939- *WhoSSW 91*
Campbell, Robert Millett *BiDrAPA 89*
Campbell, Robert S. *St&PR 91*
Campbell, Robert W. *WhoAm 90*
Campbell, Robert W. 1922- *St&PR 91, WhoAm 90, WhoWor 91*
Campbell, Robert W. 1944- *WhoE 91*
Campbell, Robert Walter 1934- *WhoE 91*
Campbell, Rod *ODwPR 91*
Campbell, Rod 1945- *BioIn 16*
Campbell, Roger D. 1946- *St&PR 91, WhoAm 90*
Campbell, Roger Keith 1951- *WhoSSW 91*
Campbell, Rolla Bruce Dunbar 1950- *WhoEmL 91*
Campbell, Ronald 1948- *BiDrAPA 89*
Campbell, Ronald Bruce 1946- *WhoEmL 91, WhoWor 91*
Campbell, Ronald F. 1949- *St&PR 91*
Campbell, Ronald John 1930- *St&PR 91*
Campbell, Ronald Neil 1926- *WhoAm 90*
Campbell, Ronald Roy *BiDrAPA 89*
Campbell, Ronald William Fearnley 1946- *WhoWor 91*
Campbell, Rosemae Wells 1909- *AuBYP 90*
Campbell, Ross 1918- *WhoAm 90*
Campbell, Roy E. 1926- *St&PR 91, WhoAm 90*
Campbell, Russell G. 1940- *St&PR 91*
Campbell, Sam *BioIn 16*
Campbell, Samuel Gordon 1933- *WhoAm 90*
Campbell, Sandy 1956- *WhoEmL 91*
Campbell, Sara Wendell 1886-1960 *WhoAmA 91N*
Campbell, Scott Eugene 1957- *WhoSSW 91*
Campbell, Scott Robert 1946- *WhoAm 90*
Campbell, Selaura Joy 1944- *WhoAmW 91, WhoWor 91*
Campbell, Sharon Lynn 1955- *WhoWrEP 89*
Campbell, Sheila Hood 1952- *WhoAmW 91*
Campbell, Sherry Anita 1947- *WhoAmW 91*
Campbell, Sherry Dawn 1951- *WhoAmW 91*
Campbell, Stephen Donald Peter 1946- *WhoSSW 91*
Campbell, Stephen Mercer 1941- *St&PR 91*
Campbell, Stewart Fred 1931- *WhoAm 90*
Campbell, Susan Cunningham 1942- *WhoAmW 91*
Campbell, Susan Lee *BiDrAPA 89*
Campbell, Susan Pannill 1947- *WhoAmW 91*
Campbell, Suzann Kay 1943- *WhoAmW 91*
Campbell, Sylvia June 1957- *WhoAmW 91*
Campbell, T. Scott *St&PR 91*
Campbell, Tammy Ann 1966- *WhoEmL 91*
Campbell, Tammy DiAnne 1958- *WhoEmL 91*
Campbell, Teresa Ann 1957- *WhoAmW 91*
Campbell, Terry Allen 1957- *WhoEmL 91*
Campbell, Terry Leland 1941- *St&PR 91*
Campbell, Terry M. 1950- *St&PR 91*
Campbell, Thomas 1777-1844 *DcLB 93 [port]*
Campbell, Thomas 1943- *WhoAm 90*
Campbell, Thomas Bernard 1951- *WhoEmL 91*
Campbell, Thomas Colin 1934- *WhoAm 90*
Campbell, Thomas Corwith, Jr. 1920- *WhoAm 90*
Campbell, Thomas D *BiDrAPA 89*
Campbell, Thomas Douglas 1951- *WhoSSW 91*
Campbell, Thomas J. *BioIn 16*
Campbell, Thomas J. 1952- *WhoAm 90*
Campbell, Thomas Justin 1959- *WhoE 91*
Campbell, Thomas R. Brown 1938- *St&PR 91*
Campbell, Thomas Raymond *St&PR 91*
Campbell, Thomas W. 1930- *ODwPR 91*
Campbell, Thomas Way 1942- *BiDrAPA 89*
Campbell, Thomas Wood 1930- *St&PR 91*
Campbell, Tiko Frederick, V 1947- *WhoE 91*
Campbell, Tisha *BioIn 16*
Campbell, Tom George 1953- *BiDrAPA 89*
Campbell, Tom J. 1943- *St&PR 91*
Campbell, Travis Nebeker 1951- *WhoEmL 91*
Campbell, Van C. 1938- *St&PR 91*
Campbell, Vernon Deene 1944- *WhoWor 91*
Campbell, Vernon Leonard 1928- *St&PR 91*
Campbell, Vin 1888-1969 *Ballpl 90*
Campbell, Virginia Gwen Rush 1939- *WhoAmW 91*
Campbell, Virginia Owen 1956- *WhoSSW 91*
Campbell, Vivian 1919- *WhoAmA 91*
Campbell, W. Douglas *ODwPR 91*
Campbell, W. Glenn 1924- *BioIn 16*
Campbell, Wallace Arnold 1918- *St&PR 91*
Campbell, Wallace Justin 1910- *WhoAm 90*
Campbell, Wanda Jay *AuBYP 90*
Campbell, Wendell Jerome 1927- *WhoAm 90*
Campbell, Wendy L. 1953- *WhoWrEP 89*
Campbell, Wesley Glenn 1924- *WhoAm 90*
Campbell, Will D 1924- *WhoWrEP 89*
Campbell, Willard Donald 1901- *WhoAm 90*
Campbell, William Cecil 1930- *WhoAm 90*
Campbell, William Clarke 1918- *St&PR 91, WhoAm 90*
Campbell, William Coolidge 1954- *WhoEmL 91*
Campbell, William David 1929- *St&PR 91*
Campbell, William Edward 1927- *WhoAm 90*
Campbell, William Foley 1951- *WhoAm 90*
Campbell, William G 1952- *BiDrAPA 89*
Campbell, William Henry 1915- *WhoAmA 91, WhoE 91*
Campbell, William Henry, Jr. 1947- *WhoE 91*
Campbell, William Ian 1944- *St&PR 91*
Campbell, William J. 1905-1988 *BioIn 16*
Campbell, William J. 1958- *WhoSSW 91*
Campbell, William John 1931- *WhoAm 90*
Campbell, William L *BiDrAPA 89*
Campbell, William Leander, Jr. 1946- *WhoSSW 91*
Campbell, William Lester 1931- *St&PR 91*
Campbell, William McClure 1949- *St&PR 91*
Campbell, William Patrick 1914-1976 *WhoAmA 91N*
Campbell, William Russell 1931- *WhoE 91*
Campbell, William Steen 1919- *St&PR 91, WhoAm 90, WhoE 91, WhoWor 91*
Campbell, William Wilfred 1858-1918 *DcLB 92 [port]*
Campbell, Winnie B. 1925- *St&PR 91*
Campbell-Everett, Karan Yvette 1962- *WhoSSW 91*
Campbell-White, Annette Jane 1947- *WhoAm 90, WhoEmL 91*
Campden-Main, Brian C 1920- *BiDrAPA 89*
Campean, Basil 1920- *BiDrAPA 89*
Campeanu, Ioan Marius 1947- *BiDrAPA 89*
Campeas, Raphael 1953- *BiDrAPA 89*
Campeau, Jean 1931- *WhoAm 90*
Campeau, Keith Stewart *BiDrAPA 89*
Campeau, L. Gerald 1935- *St&PR 91*
Campeau, Robert 1923- *BioIn 16, News 90 [port], St&PR 91*
Campeau, Robert 1924- *WhoAm 90*
Campenni, Thomas Felix 1953- *WhoE 91, WhoWor 91*
Camper, John Jacob 1943- *WhoAm 90*
Camperlengo, Henry Antonio *BiDrAPA 89*
Campin, Robert 1378?-1444 *IntDcAA 90, WorAlBi*
Camping, Bantam Kirchberg 1918- *WhoWor 91*
Campins, Luis Herrera 1925- *BioIn 16*
Campion, Daniel Ray 1949- *WhoWrEP 89*
Campion, Donald Curry, III 1948- *WhoWor 91*
Campion, Donald R. 1921-1988 *BioIn 16*
Campion, Edmund 1540?-1581 *WorAlBi*
Campion, Edmund John 1949- *WhoSSW 91*
Campion, Frank D. 1921-1989 *BioIn 16*
Campion, Joan Berengaria *WhoWrEP 89*
Campion, John F. 1952- *WhoE 91*
Campion, John Francis 1952- *BiDrAPA 89*
Campion, Nardi Reeder 1917- *AuBYP 90*
Campion, Robert Emmet 1939- *BiDrAPA 89*
Campion, Robert Thomas 1921- *WhoAm 90, WhoWor 91*
Campion, Sarah 1906- *FemiCLE*
Campion, Thomas 1567-1620 *BioIn 16*
Campise, Tony *NewAgMG*
Camplin, Mark Eugene 1954- *WhoEmL 91*
Campling, Elizabeth 1948- *BioIn 16*
Campman, Christopher Kuller 1949- *WhoE 91, WhoEmL 91*
Campner, Lars Gustav 1947- *WhoWor 91*
Campo, Ana Elisa 1955- *BiDrAPA 89*
Campo, Anthony 1956- *BiDrAPA 89*
Campo, Arthur *BiDrAPA 89*
Campo, Benjamin Paul 1941- *WhoAm 90*
Campo, Carlos Ibanez del 1877-1960 *BioIn 16*
Campo, Estanislao de 1834-1880 *BioIn 16*
Campo, Frank Philip 1927- *IntWWM 90*
Campo, Fred S. 1949- *St&PR 91*
Campo, J. M. 1943- *WhoWor 91*
Campo, John Vincent 1956- *BiDrAPA 89*
Campo, John William 1920- *St&PR 91*
Campo Alange, Condesa de *EncCoWW*
Campobello, Nellie 1912- *ConAu 131, HispWr 90*
Campolettano, Thomas Alfred 1946- *WhoSSW 91*
Campoli, Alfredo 1906- *IntWWM 90, PenDiMP*
Campoli, Cosmo 1922- *WhoAmA 91*
Campoli, Ella Frances 1906- *WhoAmW 91*
Campoli, Lisa Maria 1957- *WhoE 91*
Campolongo, James Michael 1962- *WhoE 91*
Campolongo, Vincent Netal 1938- *St&PR 91*
Campomanes, Pedro Rodriguez de 1723-1802 *BioIn 16*
Campora, Giuseppe 1923- *IntWWM 90*
Campora, Hector Jose 1909-1980 *BioIn 16*
Camporese, Giovanni 1943- *St&PR 91*
Campos, Alvaro de 1888-1935 *BioIn 16*
Campos, Anisia *IntWWM 90*
Campos, Antonio C. 1930- *St&PR 91*
Campos, Eduardo Javier, Sr. 1949- *WhoHisp 91*
Campos, Elizabeth Marie 1955- *WhoHisp 91*
Campos, Gloria 1954- *WhoHisp 91*
Campos, Kenneth Lawrence 1957- *BiDrAPA 89*
Campos, Luis Manuel Braga da Costa 1950- *WhoWor 91*
Campos, Pedro Albizu 1891-1965 *BioIn 16*
Campos, Pete 1953- *WhoHisp 91*
Campos, Rafael 1935- *WhoHisp 91*
Campos, Robert *WhoHisp 91*
Campos, Robert J *BiDrAPA 89*
Campos, Rodolfo Estuardo 1967- *WhoHisp 91*
Campos, Rodolfo M 1928- *BiDrAPA 89*
Campos, Santiago E. 1926- *WhoAm 90*
Campos, Victor Manuel 1942- *WhoHisp 91*
Campos-Parsi, Hector 1922- *IntWWM 90*
Campra, Andre 1660-1744 *PenDiMPA*
Camps, Arnulf 1925- *ConAu 131*
Campus, Peter 1937- *WhoAm 90, WhoAmA 91*
Camras, Marvin 1916- *WhoAm 90*
Camron, Roxanne *WhoAmW 91, WhoWrEP 89*
Camurati, Mireya B. 1934- *WhoHisp 91*
Camus, Albert 1913-1960 *BiDFrPL, BioIn 16, ConLC 63 [port], EuWr 13, MajTwCW, WorAlBi, WrPh*
Camus, Philippe *EncO&P 3*
Camus, Raoul F. 1930- *IntWWM 90*
Can, Cu Huy 1919- *WhoWor 91*
Canaan, Antonio *BiDrAPA 89*
Canaan, Lee 1931- *ODwPR 91*
Canabas, Joseph Gegenbach 1712-1797 *PenDiDA 89*
Canabrava, Jose Stockler 1928- *WhoWor 91*
Canada, Catherine F *BiDrAPA 89*
Canada, Clarence Coleman 1935- *WhoSSW 91*
Canada, Karyn E. 1948- *WhoSSW 91*
Canada, Linda *BioIn 16*
Canada, Mary Whitfield 1919- *WhoAm 90*
Canaday, Harry Edsel 1925- *WhoSSW 91*
Canaday, John *TwCCr&M 91*
Canaday, John Edwin 1907-1985 *WhoAmA 91N*
Canadeo, Ernest Gerard 1955- *WhoEmL 91*
Canadian Brass, The *ConMus 4 [port]*
Canale, John Phillip *BiDrAPA 89*
Canale, Michael 1949-1989 *BioIn 16*
Canale-Parola, Ercole 1929- *WhoAm 90*
Canales, Antonio 1800-1852 *BioIn 16*
Canales, Oscar Mario 1939- *WhoHisp 91*
Canaletto 1697-1768 *WorAlBi*
Canaletto, Antonio 1697-1768 *IntDcAA 90*
Canalla *WhNaAH*
Canan, Elizabeth Levy 1963- *WhoAmW 91*
Canan, Janine Burford 1942- *BiDrAPA 89, WhoWrEP 89*
Canant, Louis Milton 1935- *St&PR 91*
Canapary, Herbert Carton 1932- *WhoAm 90*
Canapary, Leon J 1932- *BiDrAPA 89*
Canardo, Hernando Vicente 1957- *WhoEmL 91, WhoWor 91*
Canarina, John Baptiste 1934- *IntWWM 90*
Canarios, Michael Chris 1953- *St&PR 91*
Canaris, Wilhelm 1887-1945 *BioIn 16, WorAlBi*
Canary, John Joseph 1925- *WhoAm 90*
Canary, Martha B. 1852-1903 *BioAmW*
Canary, Nancy Halliday 1941- *WhoAm 90*
Canas, Jon 1940- *WhoAm 90*
Canas, Jose A. 1934- *St&PR 91*
Canas, Jose Marin 1904-1980 *BioIn 16*
Canasatego *WhNaAH*
Canassatego *WhNaAH*
Canatella, Carl E. 1941- *St&PR 91*
Canavan, Bernard 1936- *St&PR 91, WhoAm 90*
Canavan, Ellen McGee 1941- *WhoAmW 91*
Canavan, James McGregor, Jr. 1937- *St&PR 91*
Canavan, Thomas Gerard 1953- *WhoE 91*
Canavesio, Orlando 1915-1957 *EncPaPR 91*
Canavesio, Orlando 1916-1957 *EncO&P 3*
Canby, Edward Richard Sprigg 1817-1873 *WhNaAH*
Canby, Jeanny Vorys 1929- *WhoAmA 91*
Canby, Joan Alexander 1948- *WhoSSW 91*
Canby, John P. 1957- *WhoE 91*
Canby, William Cameron, Jr. 1931- *WhoAm 90*
Canby, William P. 1949- *St&PR 91*
Cancalosi, Mark Francis 1954- *WhoSSW 91*
Cancel, Adrian R. 1946- *WhoHisp 91*
Cancel, Luis R 1952- *WhoAmA 91*
Cancelarich, John 1930- *St&PR 91*
Cancellaro, Louis A 1933- *BiDrAPA 89*
Cancelliere, Joseph Albert 1923- *St&PR 91*
Cancellieri, Carmela *BiDrAPA 89*
Cancellieri, Frank R 1957- *BiDrAPA 89*
Cancellieri, Remo *BiDrAPA 89*
Cancemi, Richard John 1933- *BiDrAPA 89*
Canchiani, Celia 1949- *WhoHisp 91*
Canchola, Acencion 1934- *WhoHisp 91*
Canchola, Joe Paul 1935- *WhoHisp 91*
Canchola, Joseph Paul, Jr. 1954- *WhoHisp 91*
Canchola, Samuel Victor 1944- *WhoHisp 91*
Cancio, Norma Gloria 1961- *WhoHisp 91*
Cancro, Robert 1932- *BiDrAPA 89, WhoAm 90, WhoE 91*
Candace *WomWR*
Candace, Gratien 1873-1953 *BiDFrPL*
Candaele, Casey 1961- *Ballpl 90*
Candage, Howard Everett 1952- *WhoE 91*
Candales de Lopez, Maria D. 1930- *WhoHisp 91*
Candau, Eugenie 1938- *WhoAmA 91*
Candee, Marshall Greene 1915- *WhoWor 91*
Candee, Richard Alexander, Jr. 1947- *WhoWor 91*
Candee, Richard M. 1942- *WhoE 91*
Candeille, Amelie-Julie 1767-1834 *EncCoWW*
Candel, Miguel 1945- *WhoWor 91*
Candela, Frank Michael 1951- *WhoE 91*
Candela, John A. 1934- *St&PR 91*
Candelaria, Alberto 1941- *St&PR 91*
Candelaria, Cordelia 1943- *ConAu 131, HispWr 90*
Candelaria, Cordelia Chavez 1943- *WhoHisp 91*
Candelaria, John 1953- *Ballpl 90, BioIn 16*
Candelaria, Nash 1928- *BioIn 16, ConAu 32NR, HispWr 90, WhoHisp 91*
Candelario, John S. 1916- *WhoHisp 91*
Candell, Victor 1903-1977 *WhoAmA 91N*
Candella, Joseph Peter 1939- *St&PR 91*
Cander, Leon 1926- *WhoAm 90*
Candia, Alfredo Ovando 1918-1982 *BioIn 16*
Candia, Oscar A. 1935- *WhoAm 90*
Candib, Murray A. 1915- *WhoAm 90, WhoWor 91*
Candilis, Georges 1913- *WhoWor 91*
Candilis, Wray 1927- *WhoE 91*
Candini, Milo 1917- *Ballpl 90*
Candioti, Beatriz A *WhoAmA 91*
Candiotti, Alan 1947- *WhoE 91*
Candiotti, Tom 1957- *Ballpl 90*
Candland, Douglas Keith 1934- *WhoAm 90, WhoWor 91*
Candler, Ann 1740-1814 *FemiCLE*
Candler, Asa G. 1851-1929 *WorAlBi*
Candler, David Edward 1943- *WhoSSW 91*
Candler, John Slaughter, II 1908- *WhoAm 90, WhoSSW 91, WhoWor 91*
Candlish, Malcolm 1935- *St&PR 91, WhoAm 90*
Candolle, Augustine Pyrame De 1778-1841 *WorAlBi*
Candris, Laura A. 1955- *WhoEmL 91*
Candy, Ardis Jean 1924- *BiDrAPA 89*
Candy, John *BioIn 16*
Candy, John 1950- *CurBio 90 [port], WorAlBi*
Candy, John Franklin 1950- *WhoAm 90*

Candy, Robert 1920- *AuBYP 90*
Cane, David E. 1944- *WhoAm 90*
Cane, Melanie Beth 1961- *BiDrAPA 89*
Cane, Paula P. 1945- *WhoAmW 91*
Canedo, David Lawrence 1945- *St&PR 91*
Canedo, Joseph Anthony 1938- *WhoE 91*
Canedy, Charles Edwin 1931- *WhoAm 90*
Caneira, Ana Maria 1965- *WhoE 91*
Canel, Eli 1906-1980 *Ballpl 90*
Canelas, Dale Brunelle 1938- *WhoAm 90*
Canell, Beverly June 1949- *WhoE 91*
Canellakis, A. John 1958- *WhoE 91*
Canellakis, Martin 1942- *IntWWM 90*
Canellas, Dionisio J., IV 1935- *WhoHisp 91*
Canellos, George P. 1934- *WhoAm 90*
Canelo, Pureza 1946- *EncCoWW*
Canepa, Fernando 1947- *St&PR 91*
Canepa, John Charles 1930- *St&PR 91, WhoAm 90*
Canepa, Luis Enrique 1947- *BiDrAPA 89*
Canepa, Robert F. 1947- *St&PR 91*
Canepa, Sue *ODwPR 91*
Caner, George Colket, Jr. 1925- *WhoAm 90*
Canes, Michael Edwin 1941- *WhoE 91*
Canestri, Giovanni 1918- *WhoWor 91*
Canetti, Elias 1905- *EuWr 12, MajTwCW, WhoWor 91, WorAlBi*
Canetti, Nicolai *BioIn 16*
Caneva-Biggane, Terri Denise 1955- *WhoAmW 91, WhoEmL 91*
Canevari, Charles Daniel 1920- *WhoAm 90*
Canfield, Andrew Trotter 1953- *WhoE 91*
Canfield, Brian A. 1938- *WhoAm 90*
Canfield, Cass 1897-1986 *WorAlBi*
Canfield, Deborah Ann 1953- *WhoWrEP 89*
Canfield, Debra Beth McKay 1955- *WhoEmL 91*
Canfield, Earle Lloyd 1918- *WhoAm 90*
Canfield, Edward Francis 1922- *WhoAm 90*
Canfield, Ernest C. 1949- *St&PR 91*
Canfield, Francis Xavier 1920- *WhoAm 90*
Canfield, Frederick Weber 1930- *St&PR 91, WhoAm 90*
Canfield, Glenn, Jr. 1935- *WhoSSW 91*
Canfield, Grant Wellington, Jr. 1923- *WhoAm 90*
Canfield, James A. 1943- *ODwPR 91*
Canfield, Jane 1897-1984 *WhoAmA 91N*
Canfield, Joan Giltner 1921- *WhoWrEP 89*
Canfield, Louise Monette *WhoAmW 91*
Canfield, Lynda Rae 1947- *WhoAmW 91*
Canfield, Maurice C. 1920- *St&PR 91*
Canfield, Muriel Jean Nixon 1928- *WhoAmW 91, WhoE 91*
Canfield, Peter Crane 1954- *WhoEmL 91, WhoSSW 91*
Canfield, Richard Grant 1928- *St&PR 91*
Canfield, Thomas F. 1942- *St&PR 91*
Canfield, William Newton 1920- *WhoAm 90, WhoE 91*
Cangalovic, Miroslav 1921- *PenDiMP*
Canganelli, Michael Antonio 1951- *WhoEmL 91*
Canganelli, Vincent G 1927- *BiDrAPA 89*
Cangelosi, Carl J. 1942- *St&PR 91*
Cangelosi, John 1963- *Ballpl 90*
Cangemi, Joseph Peter 1936- *WhoAm 90*
Cangemi, Michael Paul 1948- *St&PR 91, WhoE 91, WhoEmL 91*
Cangemi, Phyllis *BioIn 16*
Cangurel, Susan Stone 1946- *WhoAmW 91*
Canham, Brian *BioIn 16*
Canham, Donald N. 1947- *St&PR 91*
Canham, Erwin Dain 1904-1982 *BioIn 16*
Canham, Hugh Oswald 1938- *WhoE 91*
Caniff, Milton 1907-1988 *EncACom, WorAlBi*
Caniff, Milton Arthur 1907-1988 *BioIn 16, WhoAmA 91N*
Caniggia, Gianfranco *BioIn 16*
Caniglia, Alan Scott 1956- *WhoE 91*
Caniglia, Maria 1905-1979 *PenDiMP*
Caniglia, Richard Gary 1948- *WhoE 91*
Canihac, Jean-Pierre 1947- *IntWWM 90*
Canin, Ethan *BioIn 16*
Canin, Ethan 1960- *ConAu 131*
Canin, Stuart V. 1926- *IntWWM 90*
Canin, Stuart Victor 1926- *WhoAm 90*
Canino, Bruno 1935- *IntWWM 90, PenDiMP*
Canino, Ian Alberto *BiDrAPA 89*
Canion, Joseph R. *BioIn 16*
Canion, Joseph R. 1945- *St&PR 91*
Canion, Joseph Rod 1945- *WhoAm 90, WhoSSW 91*
Canion, Kimberly Ann 1963- *WhoAmW 91*
Canion, Rod *BioIn 16*
Canipe, Stephen Lee 1946- *WhoSSW 91*
Canistraro, Salvatore Kenneth 1927- *St&PR 91*
Canive, Jose Miguel *BiDrAPA 89*
Canizalez, Thomas Manuel 1957- *WhoHisp 91*
Canizaro, Peter Corte 1935- *WhoAm 90*
Canizaro, Robert Host 1938- *WhoAm 90*
Cankosyan, Garbis 1923- *BiDrAPA 89*
Canlas, Edwin Acosta 1949- *WhoWor 91*
Canlon, Barbara 1955- *WhoWor 91*
Cann, Brian *St&PR 91*
Cann, Nancy Timanus *WhoAmW 91*
Cann, Rachel P. 1942- *WhoWrEP 89*
Cann, Ronald Edward 1947- *BiDrAPA 89*
Cann, Sharon Lee 1935- *WhoAmW 91*
Cann, Stephen R 1951- *BiDrAPA 89*
Cann, William Francis 1922- *WhoAm 90*
Cann, William Hopson 1916- *WhoAm 90*
Canna, Joseph John 1950- *St&PR 91*
Cannac, Yves Gabriel 1935- *WhoWor 91*
Cannady, Brett Phillips 1956- *St&PR 91*
Cannady, Bruce Riordan 1941- *St&PR 91*
Cannady, Edward Wyatt, Jr. 1906- *WhoWor 91*
Cannady, Frances P. 1920- *St&PR 91*
Cannady, Nathaniel Ellis, Jr. 1920- *St&PR 91*
Cannaliato, Vincent 1941- *St&PR 91*
Cannaliato, Vincent, Jr. 1941- *WhoAm 90, WhoE 91, WhoWor 91*
Cannam, Peggie 1925- *AuBYP 90*
Cannamela, David *St&PR 91*
Cannan, Joanna 1896-1961 *FemiCLE*
Cannan, Joanna 1898-1961 *TwCCr&M 91*
Cannan, May Wedderburn 1893-1973 *FemiCLE*
Cannan, Phyllis 1955- *IntWWM 90*
Cannarozzi, Michael 1948- *St&PR 91*
Cannava, Marie Elizabeth 1946- *WhoAmW 91*
Cannavo, Sal Michael 1928- *St&PR 91*
Canne Meyer, Cora 1929- *IntWWM 90*
Canned Heat *OxCPMus*
Cannedy, Curtis Dwight 1953- *St&PR 91*
Cannell, Charles Frederick 1913- *WhoAm 90*
Cannell, John Redferne 1937- *WhoAm 90*
Cannell, Lee Ora 1947- *St&PR 91*
Cannell, Peter B. 1926- *St&PR 91*
Cannell, Stephen J. *BioIn 16*
Cannell, Stephen Joseph 1941- *WhoAm 90*
Cannell, Thomas George 1946- *St&PR 91*
Cannella, John Matthew 1908- *WhoAm 90*
Cannella, Philip 1933- *WhoAm 90*
Cannella, Vincent David 1938- *St&PR 91*
Cannerelli, Carol Ann 1958- *WhoE 91*
Cannerelli, Kenneth A. 1948- *St&PR 91*
Canney, Donald James 1930- *WhoAm 90*
Canney, Walter A. 1934- *St&PR 91*
Canniff, Bryan Gregory 1948- *WhoAmA 91*
Canniff, Edward Timothy, Jr. 1942- *St&PR 91*
Canniff, Kiki 1948- *WhoWrEP 89*
Canning, Charlotte 1817-1861 *BioIn 16*
Canning, Curtis Ray *BiDrAPA 89*
Canning, Francis 1851-1899 *DcCanB 12*
Canning, Fred W. 1931- *St&PR 91*
Canning, George 1770-1827 *BioIn 16*
Canning, Gerald W. 1948- *St&PR 91*
Canning, Jessie M. *ODwPR 91*
Canning, Jessie Marie *WhoAm 90*
Canning, John *BioIn 16*
Canning, John A., Jr. *St&PR 91*
Canning, John Anthony, Jr. 1944- *WhoAm 90*
Canning, John J. 1941- *St&PR 91*
Canning, John Rafton 1927- *WhoAm 90*
Canning, Susan Carol 1955- *WhoSSW 91*
Canning, Suzanne B *BiDrAPA 89*
Canning, Victor 1911-1986 *SpyFic, TwCCr&M 91*
Cannistra, Linda M. 1955- *WhoAmW 91*
Cannistra, Philip 1954- *WhoEmL 91*
Cannistraci, Anthony 1951- *WhoE 91*
Cannistraro, Nicholas, Jr. 1939- *WhoAm 90*
Cannizzaro, Chris 1938- *Ballpl 90*
Cannizzaro, Paul Peter 1925- *WhoE 91*
Cannizzaro, Peter Louis 1944- *St&PR 91*
Canno, Leonard E. 1912- *St&PR 91*
Cannold, David L. *St&PR 91*
Cannon, Alexander 1896-1963? *EncO&P 3*
Cannon, Allen 1920- *IntWWM 90*
Cannon, Annie Jump 1863-1941 *BioIn 16, WorAlBi*
Cannon, Barbara Gayle 1941- *St&PR 91*
Cannon, Beekman Cox 1911- *IntWWM 90*
Cannon, Benjamin Winton 1944- *WhoWor 91*
Cannon, Bettie Waddell 1922- *BioIn 16*
Cannon, Bland Wilson 1920- *WhoSSW 91*
Cannon, Bradford 1907- *WhoAm 90*
Cannon, Cavendish Welles 1895-1962 *BioIn 16*
Cannon, Charles C. 1928- *WhoAm 90*
Cannon, Charles Dale 1928- *WhoAm 90*
Cannon, Christine Anne 1952- *WhoAmW 91*
Cannon, Christopher Perry 1953- *WhoEmL 91*
Cannon, Clarence 1879-1964 *WorAlBi*
Cannon, Cornelia James *BioIn 16*
Cannon, Craig Lee 1955- *WhoEmL 91*
Cannon, Curt *MajTwCW, TwCCr&M 91*
Cannon, Daniel Willard 1920- *WhoAm 90, WhoWor 91*
Cannon, Darrell Jay 1955- *WhoEmL 91, WhoSSW 91*
Cannon, David Price 1946- *WhoEmL 91*
Cannon, Deborah Lynn 1961- *WhoAmW 91*
Cannon, Debra Jean *BiDrAPA 89*
Cannon, Denise Thornsberry 1949- *WhoEmL 91*
Cannon, Dorothy Ann 1957- *WhoE 91*
Cannon, Douglas 1939- *WhoAm 90*
Cannon, Dyan *BioIn 16*
Cannon, Dyan 1937- *WhoAm 90, WorAlBi*
Cannon, Francis V., Jr. 1935- *WhoAm 90*
Cannon, Garland 1924- *ConAu 30NR, WhoAm 90*
Cannon, Gary Curtis 1951- *WhoEmL 91*
Cannon, Georgina *ODwPR 91*
Cannon, Gerald N. 1929- *St&PR 91*
Cannon, Glenn Scott 1949- *WhoEmL 91, WhoSSW 91*
Cannon, Grace Bert 1937- *WhoE 91*
Cannon, Hannah *BioIn 16*
Cannon, Harriet Starr 1823-1896 *BioAmW*
Cannon, Helen Leighton 1911- *WhoAm 90*
Cannon, Herbert Seth 1931- *WhoAm 90, WhoSSW 91*
Cannon, Howard Walter 1912- *WhoAm 90, WhoE 91*
Cannon, Hugh 1931- *WhoSSW 91, WhoWor 91*
Cannon, Ida Maud 1877-1960 *BioIn 16*
Cannon, Isabella Walton 1904- *WhoAm 90*
Cannon, J Alfred *BiDrAPA 89*
Cannon, J.W. 1943- *St&PR 91*
Cannon, James A. 1938- *St&PR 91*
Cannon, James Anthony 1938- *WhoAm 90*
Cannon, James Damon, Jr. 1933- *WhoSSW 91*
Cannon, James Patrick 1890-1974 *EncAL*
Cannon, Janet 1945- *WhoWrEP 89*
Cannon, Jimmy 1909-1973 *BioIn 16*
Cannon, Jimmy 1910-1973 *Ballpl 90*
Cannon, John, III 1954- *WhoEmL 91, WhoWor 91*
Cannon, John Haile 1942- *St&PR 91, WhoAm 90*
Cannon, John Joseph 1954- *WhoE 91*
Cannon, John Kemper 1932- *WhoAm 90*
Cannon, John M. 1932- *St&PR 91*
Cannon, Joseph 1836-1926 *WorAlBi*
Cannon, Katie G. *BioIn 16*
Cannon, Kenneth Dean 1943- *St&PR 91*
Cannon, Kevin 1948- *WhoAmA 91*
Cannon, Lynne Marple 1955- *WhoE 91, WhoWor 91*
Cannon, Mark 1950- *BiDrAPA 89*
Cannon, Mark Wilcox 1928- *WhoAm 90*
Cannon, Marlene Hutton 1934- *WhoAmW 91*
Cannon, Mary Ellen 1956- *WhoEmL 91*
Cannon, Mary Lou *BiDrAPA 89*
Cannon, Maurice L. 1949- *St&PR 91*
Cannon, Michael David 1947- *WhoEmL 91*
Cannon, Michael John 1940- *St&PR 91*
Cannon, Nancy Gladstein *WhoAmW 91*
Cannon, Norman Lawrence 1936- *WhoAm 90*
Cannon, Patrick Francis 1938- *WhoAm 90*
Cannon, Peter 1932- *WhoAm 90*
Cannon, Philip 1929- *IntWWM 90*
Cannon, R.A. 1927- *St&PR 91*
Cannon, Raymond G 1915- *BiDrAPA 89*
Cannon, Robert Edwin 1947- *St&PR 91*
Cannon, Robert Emmet 1929- *WhoAm 90*
Cannon, Robert Eugene 1945- *WhoAm 90, WhoSSW 91*
Cannon, Robert L. 1936- *St&PR 91*
Cannon, Robert Leo 1947- *WhoSSW 91*
Cannon, Robert William 1931- *WhoAm 90*
Cannon, Ronald Edgar 1926- *WhoSSW 91*
Cannon, Sarah Ophelia Colley 1912- *ConAu 129*
Cannon, Sebren Hatley 1922- *St&PR 91*
Cannon, Sheila S *BiDrAPA 89*
Cannon, Thomas Burt 1944- *St&PR 91*
Cannon, Walter Bradford 1871-1945 *BioIn 16*
Cannon, William Bernard 1920- *WhoAm 90*
Cannon, William Harold 1930- *St&PR 91*
Cannon, William Ragsdale 1916- *WhoAm 90*
Cannon, Woodrow Wilson 1911- *WhoSSW 91*
Cannon, Yolanda J. 1957- *WhoAmW 91*
Cannon-Ryan, Susan Kaye 1950- *WhoEmL 91*
Cannonchet 1630?-1676 *WhNaAH*
Cannone-McGill, Rosalie Antoinette 1943- *WhoAmW 91*
Cannuli, Richard Gerald 1947- *WhoAmA 91*
Canny, J. Francis *BioIn 16*
Canny, Jack *ODwPR 91*
Canny, Paula Kay 1955- *WhoAmW 91*
Cano, Alonso 1601-1667 *IntDcAA 90*
Cano, Carlos Eduardo 1955- *BiDrAPA 89*
Cano, Juan Sebastian Del 1460?-1526 *WorAlBi*
Cano, Kristin Maria 1951- *WhoEmL 91*
Cano, Linda Dulce 1949- *WhoSSW 91*
Cano, Margarita 1932- *WhoAmA 91*
Cano, Mario Stephen 1953- *WhoEmL 91*
Cano, Olivia Dean 1934- *WhoHisp 91*
Cano, Pablo D 1961- *WhoAmA 91*
Cano-Ballesta, Juan 1932- *WhoAm 90*
Canochet 1630?-1676 *WhNaAH*
Canoff, Karen Huston 1954- *WhoEmL 91*
Canon, L. Barton, Jr. 1953- *WhoEmL 91*
Canon, Nancy Anne 1939- *WhoAmW 91*
Canon, Robert Morris 1941- *WhoAm 90*
Canonchet 1630?-1676 *EncCRAm, WhNaAH*
Canoni, John David 1939- *WhoAm 90*
Canonicus 1565?-1647 *EncCRAm, WhNaAH*
Canopari, Gerald Eugene 1944- *St&PR 91*
Canosa, Albert Anthony 1946- *St&PR 91, WhoAm 90, WhoEmL 91*
Canosa, David J. 1952- *St&PR 91*
Canova, Antonio 1757-1822 *IntDcAA 90*
Canova, Carol Joy 1965- *WhoAmW 91*
Canova, Judy 1916- *OxCPMus*
Canovas, Isabel *BioIn 16*
Canovas, Isabel 1945- *WhoWor 91*
Canovas del Castillo, Antonio 1828-1897 *BioIn 16*
Canright, Marchelle Diane 1957- *WhoSSW 91*
Canright, Sarah Anne 1941- *WhoAmA 91*
Canseco, Jose *BioIn 16*
Canseco, Jose 1964- *Ballpl 90, News 90 [port], WhoAm 90, WhoHisp 91, WorAlBi*
Canseco, Jose Santiago 1958- *WhoHisp 91*
Cansler, Leslie Ervin 1920- *WhoAm 90*
Cantacuzene, Jean Michel 1933- *WhoWor 91*
Cantafio, Anthony W. 1942- *ODwPR 91*
Cantagalli, Giuseppe *PenDiDA 89*
Cantagalli, Ulisse 1839-1901 *PenDiDA 89*
Cantalupo, Barbara Anne 1947- *WhoAmW 91*
Cantalupo, Patrizia 1952- *BiDWomA*
Cantalupo, Paul 1937- *BiDrAPA 89*
Cantanese, Anthony 1942- *WhoAm 90*
Cantarella, Francesco Paguin 1932- *WhoAm 90*
Cantarella, Michael John 1940- *St&PR 91*
Cantarutti, Tracey Lerch 1955- *WhoAmW 91*
Cantees, Abe J. 1911- *St&PR 91*
Cantella, Vincent Michele 1917- *WhoAm 90*
Cantelli, Guido 1920-1956 *PenDiMP*
Cantelmi, Michael John 1945- *WhoE 91*
Cantelmo, John R. 1947- *St&PR 91*
Cantelmo, Marilee Ann 1948- *WhoE 91*
Cantelmo, Patricia Ann 1944- *WhoAmW 91, WhoE 91*
Cantelo, April 1928- *PenDiMP*
Cantelon, John Edward 1924- *WhoAm 90*
Canteloube, Joseph 1879-1957 *PenDiMP A*
Canter, Deborah Dean 1950- *WhoAmW 91*
Canter, Jerome Wolf 1930- *WhoE 91*
Canter, Pamela S. 1963- *WhoAmW 91*
Canter, Ralph Raymond 1921- *WhoAm 90*
Canter, Stanley D. 1923- *St&PR 91, WhoAm 90*
Canter, Stanley Stanton 1933- *WhoAm 90, WhoWor 91*
Canter, Stephen Edward 1945- *WhoAm 90*
Cantera, Jose Antonio Remon 1908-1955 *BioIn 16*
Canterbury, Randolph Jack, II 1951- *BiDrAPA 89*
Cantey, J. Willis 1917-1986 *EncABHB 7 [port]*
Cantey, Robert C. 1929- *St&PR 91*
Cantey, Sam Benton, III *WhoAmA 91N*
Canth, Minna 1844-1897 *DcScanL*
Canth, Wilhelmina Ulrika 1844-1897 *EncCoWW*
Cantilli, Edmund Joseph 1927- *WhoAm 90, WhoWor 91*
Cantillon, Richard 1680-1734 *BioIn 16*
Cantilo, Patrick Herrera 1954- *WhoEmL 91, WhoSSW 91, WhoWor 91*
Cantin, Augustin 1809-1893 *DcCanB 12*
Cantin, Marc 1933- *WhoAm 90*
Cantine, David 1939- *WhoAmA 91*
Cantini, Virgil D. 1920- *WhoAm 90, WhoAmA 91*
Cantlay, George Gordon 1920- *WhoAm 90*
Cantliffe, Jeri Miller 1927- *WhoAmW 91, WhoE 91*
Cantlin, Richard Anthony 1946- *WhoEmL 91*

Cantlon, Floyd 1932- *St&PR 91*
Cantlon, John Edward 1921- *WhoAm 90*
Canto, Benjamin Joseph 1932- *St&PR 91*
Canto, Diana Catherine 1939- *WhoAmW 91*
Canto, Jacqueline *BioIn 16*
Canton, Anthony Michael 1941- *WhoSSW 91*
Canton, Rafael 1921- *BiDrAPA 89*
Cantone, Vic 1933- *WhoAm 90, WhoAmA 91, WhoE 91*
Cantoni, Louis Joseph 1919- *WhoAm 90*
Cantor, Alan Everett 1950- *WhoEmL 91*
Cantor, B. Gerald 1916- *St&PR 91*
Cantor, B Gerald 1916- *WhoAmA 91*
Cantor, Bernard Gerald 1916- *WhoAm 90*
Cantor, Bernard Jack 1927- *WhoAm 90*
Cantor, Charles Robert 1942- *WhoAm 90*
Cantor, David Geoffrey 1935- *WhoAm 90*
Cantor, David Jules 1935- *WhoE 91*
Cantor, Eddie 1892-1964 *BioIn 16, OxCPMus, WorAlBi*
Cantor, Edward A. 1928- *St&PR 91*
Cantor, Eleanor Weschler 1913- *WhoAmW 91, WhoE 91*
Cantor, Eli 1913- *WhoWrEP 89*
Cantor, Fredrich 1944- *WhoAmA 91*
Cantor, Georg 1845-1918 *BioIn 16*
Cantor, George Nathan 1941- *WhoAm 90*
Cantor, Leonard *St&PR 91*
Cantor, Mira 1944- *WhoAmA 91*
Cantor, Morton B 1924- *BiDrAPA 89, WhoE 91*
Cantor, Muriel Goldsman 1923- *WhoAm 90, WhoAmW 91*
Cantor, Norman Frank 1929- *WhoAm 90*
Cantor, Pamela Corliss 1944- *WhoAmW 91, WhoE 91*
Cantor, Paul *BioIn 16*
Cantor, Richard Ira 1944- *WhoE 91*
Cantor, Robert Lloyd 1919-1986 *WhoAmA 91N*
Cantor, Samuel C. 1919- *WhoAm 90*
Cantor, Sherwood Roy 1943- *BiDrAPA 89*
Cantow, Lawrence A *BiDrAPA 89*
Cantrall, Edward Warren 1931- *WhoAm 90*
Cantrell, Andrea 1948- *WhoAmW 91*
Cantrell, Charles T. 1944- *St&PR 91*
Cantrell, Cheryl Kaye *BiDrAPA 89*
Cantrell, Coleen Sharon 1952- *WhoAmW 91*
Cantrell, Constance 1945- *WhoAmW 91*
Cantrell, Cyrus Duncan, III 1940- *WhoAm 90, WhoWor 91*
Cantrell, Derrick Edward 1926- *IntWWM 90*
Cantrell, Dorothy 1940- *St&PR 91*
Cantrell, James F. 1938- *St&PR 91*
Cantrell, Jim 1935- *WhoAmA 91*
Cantrell, Joe R 1924- *BiDrAPA 89*
Cantrell, John D. 1933- *St&PR 91*
Cantrell, John Frederick 1919- *WhoSSW 91*
Cantrell, John L. *St&PR 91*
Cantrell, Joseph D. 1944- *St&PR 91*
Cantrell, Lana 1943- *WhoAm 90*
Cantrell, Lavonne Opal 1933- *WhoAmW 91*
Cantrell, Mary 1915- *WhoAmW 91*
Cantrell, Richard Montgomery 1962- *WhoSSW 91*
Cantrell, Robert Wendell 1933- *WhoAm 90*
Cantrell, Ronald G. 1942- *St&PR 91*
Cantrell, Sharron Caulk 1947- *WhoAmW 91, WhoSSW 91*
Cantrell, Steve *ODwPR 91*
Cantrell, Tommy Glenn 1943- *WhoSSW 91*
Cantrell, Wesley Eugene, Sr. 1935- *WhoAm 90, WhoSSW 91*
Cantrell, William A 1920- *BiDrAPA 89*
Cantrell, William Allen 1920- *WhoAm 90*
Cantrell, William Arch, II 1953- *WhoSSW 91*
Cantrelle, Joseph, Sr. 1951- *WhoWor 91*
Cantrick, Robert Birdsall 1917- *IntWWM 90*
Cantril, Albert Hadley 1940- *WhoE 91*
Cantu, Antonio *PenDiDA 89*
Cantu, John Maurice 1928- *St&PR 91*
Cantu, Mauro *PenDiDA 89*
Cantu, Oralia E. 1933- *WhoHisp 91*
Cantu, Raquel S. 1960- *WhoEmL 91*
Cantu, Ricardo M. *WhoHisp 91*
Cantus, H. Hollister 1937- *WhoAm 90*
Cantwell, Alice Catherine 1927- *WhoAmW 91*
Cantwell, Ben 1902-1962 *Ballpl 90*
Cantwell, Betty L. 1923- *St&PR 91*
Cantwell, Dallas 1920- *St&PR 91*
Cantwell, Dan *BioIn 16*
Cantwell, Dennis Michael 1943- *St&PR 91*
Cantwell, Dennis P *BiDrAPA 89*
Cantwell, Don 1935- *WhoSSW 91*
Cantwell, John Dalzell, Jr. 1909- *WhoAm 90*
Cantwell, John Walsh 1922- *WhoAm 90*
Cantwell, Linda Walsh 1938- *WhoAmW 91*
Cantwell, Lois 1951- *WhoAmW 91, WhoE 91, WhoWor 91*
Cantwell, Mary *WhoAm 90*
Cantwell, Michael Louis *BiDrAPA 89*
Cantwell, Raymond J. 1916-1990 *BioIn 16*
Cantwell, Robert 1931- *WhoAm 90*
Cantwell, Sidney W. *AmLegL*
Cantwell, Thomas Joseph *BiDrAPA 89*
Cantwell, William Patterson 1921- *WhoAm 90*
Cantwell, William Richard 1947- *WhoAmA 91*
Canty, Eileen Maxwell 1933- *WhoAmW 91*
Canty, Marietta 1906?-1986 *DrBIPA 90*
Canty, Mary *AuBYP 90*
Canup, Ollow Edward 1943- *WhoSSW 91*
Canup, William 1945- *ODwPR 91*
Canut, A. Louis 1927- *St&PR 91*
Canvin, Jack H. 1921- *St&PR 91*
Canyon, Sky *NewAgMG*
Canzano, Edward D., Jr. 1907- *St&PR 91*
Canziani, Arnaldo M. 1951- *WhoWor 91*
Canziani, Estella 1887-1964 *BiDWomA*
Canziani, L. *BiDWomA*
Canzio, Michele *PenDiDA 89*
Canzoneri, Robert 1925- *WhoWrEP 89*
Canzoniero, Joseph A. 1923- *St&PR 91*
Cao Qiongde 1955- *BioIn 16*
Cao Tianqin *BioIn 16*
Cao Yu 1910- *WorAu 1980 [port]*
Cao, Thai-Hai 1954- *WhoWor 91*
Caos, Antonio 1952- *WhoSSW 91*
Caouette, David P. 1960- *ODwPR 91*
Caouette, John Bernard 1944- *WhoE 91*
Caouette, Thomas W. 1950- *St&PR 91*
Capa, Cornell 1918- *BioIn 16, WhoAm 90, WhoAmA 91, WhoE 91*
Capa, Robert 1913-1954 *BioIn 16, WorAlBi*
Capablanca, Fernando Aquiles 1944- *WhoSSW 91*
Capablanca, Jose Raul 1888-1942 *BioIn 16*
Capalbo, Carmen Charles 1925- *WhoAm 90*
Capalbo, Richard J. 1946- *St&PR 91*
Capalbo, Richard Joseph 1946- *WhoAm 90*
Capaldi, Anthony C. 1939- *WhoE 91*
Capaldi, Elizabeth Ann Deutsch 1945- *WhoAm 90*
Capaldo, Guy 1950- *WhoEmL 91*
Capano, David Vincent 1949- *St&PR 91*
Capants, J.M. 1936- *St&PR 91*
Capanzano, Charles Thomas 1949- *WhoEmL 91*
Caparn, Rhys 1909- *WhoAm 90*
Caparulo, Ralph Daniel 1939- *WhoE 91*
Capasso, Carl *BioIn 16*
Capasso, Federico 1949- *BioIn 16, WhoAm 90*
Capasso, Vincent 1934- *St&PR 91*
Capasso, Vincenzo 1945- *WhoWor 91*
Capati, Myrna V Galang *BiDrAPA 89*
Capaul, Raymond W. 1912- *St&PR 91*
Capcova *EncCoWW*
Capdeville, Anne Regina 1947- *BiDrAPA 89*
Cape, Judith *MajTwCW*
Cape, Ronald Elliot 1932- *St&PR 91, WhoAm 90*
Cape, Safford 1906-1973 *PenDiMP*
Cape, William Robert 1950- *St&PR 91*
Capecchi, Renato 1923- *IntWWM 90, PenDiMP*
Capece Minutolo, Francesco 1937- *WhoWor 91*
Capecelatro, Mark John 1948- *WhoE 91, WhoEmL 91*
Capehart, Anthony Ashbourne, Jr. 1922- *St&PR 91*
Capehart, Barney Lee 1940- *WhoAm 90*
Capehart, Homer Earl, Jr. 1922- *WhoAm 90*
Capehart, Martin Ellis, Jr. 1957- *WhoSSW 91, WhoWor 91*
Capek, Antoinette A. 1926- *WhoWrEP 89*
Capek, Karel 1890-1938 *BioIn 16, RGTwCSF, TwCLC 37 [port], WorAlBi*
Capek, Milic 1909- *WhoAm 90*
Capel, Guy B. 1938- *WhoAm 90*
Capelin, Joan 1938- *ODwPR 91*
Capell, Cydney Lynn 1956- *WhoAmW 91, WhoSSW 91*
Capellan, Angel 1942- *WhoE 91, WhoHisp 91*
Capellari, Elmer E *BiDrAPA 89*
Capellaro, John Joseph 1951- *St&PR 91*
Capelle, Barbara Frederica 1927- *WhoAmW 91*
Capelle, Christopher Brett *BiDrAPA 89*
Capelletti, Daniel 1958- *IntWWM 90*
Capelli, Elizabeth A. 1963- *WhoAmW 91*
Capelli, John Placido 1936- *WhoAm 90*
Capello, Dominick R. *BioIn 16*
Capello, Gabriele *PenDiDA 89*
Capello, Louis Anthony *BiDrAPA 89*
Capels, Valerie June 1962- *WhoE 91, WhoEmL 91*
Capen, Charles Chabert 1936- *WhoAm 90*
Capen, Richard Goodwin, Jr. 1934- *St&PR 91, WhoAm 90*
Capener, Regner Alvin 1942- *WhoWor 91*
Caper, Robert Alan 1942- *BiDrAPA 89*
Caper, Samuel Philip 1938- *WhoAm 90*
Capers, Charlotte 1913- *WhoAm 90*
Capers, Daniel G *BiDrAPA 89*
Capers, Gerald Mortimer, Jr. 1909- *WhoAm 90*
Capers, Mark Verdier 1955- *WhoSSW 91*
Capers, Olivia *BiDrAPA 89*
Capers, Theodore Russell, Jr. 1943- *WhoE 91*
Capers, Virginia 1925- *DrBIPA 90*
Caperton, Dee Kessel *WhoAmW 91*
Caperton, Gaston *BioIn 16*
Caperton, Gaston 1940- *WhoAm 90, WhoSSW 91*
Caperton, Richard Walton 1948- *WhoSSW 91*
Capes, Frederick Lloyd 1954- *WhoE 91*
Capes, Richard Edward 1942- *WhoAmA 91*
Capestany, Roberto A 1919- *BiDrAPA 89*
Capestrani, Timothy John 1956- *WhoAm 90*
Capet Quartet *PenDiMP*
Capet, Hugh 938?-996 *WorAlBi*
Capet, Lucien *PenDiMP*
Capezio, William Joseph 1950- *WhoE 91*
Capiaux, Raymond 1927- *WhoAm 90*
Capice, Philip Charles 1931- *WhoAm 90, WhoWor 91*
Capice, Phillip *WhoWrEP 89*
Capildeo, Rudranath 1920-1970 *BioIn 16*
Capilla, Doug 1952- *Ballpl 90*
Capin, Harlan 1930- *St&PR 91*
Capion, Iseut de *EncCoWW*
Capiro, Jose Regino 1957- *BiDrAPA 89*
Capistran, Eleno Pete, III 1958- *WhoHisp 91*
Capistrano, Francisco Victorino 1932- *WhoWor 91*
Capitaine, Jacques Albert 1950- *WhoWor 91*
Capitaine, Raul Ricardo *BiDrAPA 89*
Capitan, William Harry 1933- *WhoAm 90*
Capitant, Rene 1901-1970 *BiDFrPL*
Capitman, Barbara Baer *NewYTBS 90*
Capitman, Barbara Baer 1919-1990 *BioIn 16*
Capitman, Barbara Baer 1920-1990 *ConAu 131*
Capizzi, Anthony 1954- *WhoEmL 91*
Capizzi, Robert Lawrence 1938- *WhoAm 90*
Capizzi, Tracey Leigh Quante 1959- *WhoE 91, WhoWor 91*
Caplan, Albert Joseph 1908- *WhoAm 90*
Caplan, Amy Gail 1960- *WhoEmL 91*
Caplan, Arthur L 1950- *WhoWrEP 89*
Caplan, Benjamin 1916- *St&PR 91*
Caplan, Constance Rose 1935- *WhoE 91*
Caplan, David M. 1956- *ODwPR 91*
Caplan, Denise Boorstein 1958- *WhoAmW 91*
Caplan, Edwin Harvey 1926- *WhoAm 90*
Caplan, Elinor 1944- *WhoAmW 91*
Caplan, Frank *BioIn 16*
Caplan, Frank 1919- *St&PR 91*
Caplan, Gerald *BiDrAPA 89*
Caplan, Jerry L 1922- *WhoAmA 91*
Caplan, John David 1926- *WhoAm 90*
Caplan, Judith Shulamith Langer 1945- *WhoWrEP 89*
Caplan, Lazarus David 1940- *WhoAm 90*
Caplan, Lester 1924- *WhoSSW 91*
Caplan, Lloyd M *BiDrAPA 89*
Caplan, Louis Robert 1936- *WhoAm 90, WhoE 91*
Caplan, Marian Amy 1955- *BiDrAPA 89*
Caplan, Mischa 1920- *BiDrAPA 89*
Caplan, Murray S *BiDrAPA 89*
Caplan, Paula J 1947- *ConAu 129*
Caplan, Richard V. 1937- *WhoAm 90*
Caplan, Stanley H. 1944- *St&PR 91*
Caplan, Verla Louise 1914- *WhoAmW 91*
Caplan Ciarrochi, Sandra *WhoAmA 91*
Caplanides, Ignatios Michel 1948- *WhoSSW 91*
Caplat, Moran 1916- *IntWWM 90*
Caplen, Harry A. 1911- *St&PR 91*
Caplen, Larry 1963- *St&PR 91*
Caples, Barbara Barrett 1914- *WhoAmA 91*
Caples, John *NewYTBS 90 [port]*
Caples, John 1900-1990 *BioIn 16, ConAu 131*
Caples, Michael Edward 1951- *WhoEmL 91*
Caples, Richard James 1949- *WhoAm 90, WhoWor 91*
Caples, William Goff, IV 1946- *WhoEmL 91*
Caplin, Barbara Ellen 1954- *WhoAmW 91*
Caplin, Hymie 1901?-1949 *BioIn 16*
Caplin, Jerrold Leon 1930- *WhoE 91*
Caplin, Jo Ann *WhoAmW 91*
Caplin, Lee 1946- *WhoEmL 91*
Caplin, Loren-Paul 1948- *WhoEmL 91*
Caplin, Michael Andrew 1951- *WhoEmL 91*
Caplin, Mortimer Maxwell 1916- *WhoAm 90, WhoE 91*
Caplinger, Debra Ann 1954- *WhoSSW 91*
Caplinger, James T. *BioIn 16*
Caplinger, Kenneth Travers 1912- *WhoWor 91*
Caplinger, Paula Ruth 1948- *WhoAmW 91*
Caplovitz, Coleman David 1925- *WhoSSW 91*
Caplovitz, Iris Ann Smith 1944- *WhoAmW 91*
Caplow, Peter Joseph 1943- *St&PR 91*
Caplow, Theodore 1920- *WhoAm 90*
Capo, Bobby 1921-1989 *BioIn 16, WhoHisp 91N*
Capo, Helena Frances 1959- *WhoAmW 91*
Capobianco, Daniel Lauro 1962- *WhoEmL 91*
Capobianco, Domenick 1928- *WhoAmA 91*
Capobianco, Domenick J. *WhoE 91*
Capobianco, Eva Mary 1954- *WhoAmW 91*
Capobianco, Frank Joseph *BiDrAPA 89*
Capobianco, Lucia 1938- *St&PR 91*
Capobianco, Tito 1931- *IntWWM 90, WhoAm 90, WhoE 91*
Capocaccia, Lilia 1931- *WhoWor 91*
Capodiferro, Giovanni Francesco *PenDiDA 89*
Capodilupo, Elizabeth Jeanne Hatton 1940- *WhoAmW 91, WhoE 91, WhoWor 91*
Capoferri, Marco Alessandro 1943- *WhoWor 91*
Capois, Francois *BioIn 16*
Capolarello, Joe R. 1961- *WhoE 91, WhoEmL 91, WhoWor 91*
Capon, Dale E. 1929- *St&PR 91*
Capone, Al 1899-1947 *BioIn 16, WorAlBi*
Capone, Alphonse William 1919- *WhoAm 90*
Capone, Annette *WhoAm 90, WhoAmW 91*
Capone, Antonio 1926- *BiDrAPA 89, WhoE 91*
Capone, Charles August 1933- *St&PR 91*
Capone, Donald William 1943- *St&PR 91*
Capone, Lucien, Jr. *WhoAm 90, WhoWor 91*
Capone, Margaret Lynch 1907- *WhoAmW 91*
Capone, Patrick M *BiDrAPA 89*
Caponi, Anthony 1921- *WhoAmA 91*
Caponigro, Jeffrey R. 1957- *ODwPR 91*
Caponigro, Jeffrey Ralph 1957- *WhoAm 90*
Caponigro, Paul 1932- *WhoAmA 91*
Caponigro, Ralph Angelo 1932- *St&PR 91*
Caponio, Joseph F. 1926- *WhoAm 90*
Caporale, D. Nick 1928- *WhoAm 90*
Caporale, Patricia Jeane 1947- *WhoWrEP 89*
Caporaso, Pat Marie 1952- *WhoAmA 91*
Caporella, Nick A. 1937- *WhoAm 90*
Caporrino, Charlotte Katherine 1954- *WhoAmW 91*
Caposela, Ernest Michael 1953- *WhoE 91*
Capossela, James P. 1949- *WhoWrEP 89*
Capote, Truman 1924-1984 *BioIn 16, MajTwCW, WorAlBi*
Capouch, Jay B. 1945- *St&PR 91*
Capowich, Suzanne 1961- *WhoAmW 91*
Capozza, Richard Carl 1942- *St&PR 91*
Capozzi, Anthony 1958- *BiDrAPA 89*
Capozzi, Carolyn Ann 1947- *WhoAmW 91*
Capozzi, David Alvin 1956- *WhoE 91*
Capozzi, Della Marie 1963- *WhoAmW 91*
Capozzi, Louis 1947- *ODwPR 91*
Capozzi, Louis Joseph, Jr. 1961- *WhoEmL 91*
Capozzoli, Cathy 1959- *ODwPR 91*
Capp, Al 1909-1979 *EncACom, SmATA 61 [port], WhoAmA 91N, WorAlBi*
Capp, B. S. *ConAu 130*
Capp, Bernard 1943- *ConAu 130*
Capp, Keith Michael 1955- *St&PR 91*
Capp, Michael Paul 1930- *WhoAm 90*
Capp, Morris R. 1957- *St&PR 91*
Capp, Patrick O. 1951- *St&PR 91*
Capp, Robert R. 1946- *St&PR 91*
Capp, Ruth Harrell 1934- *BiDrAPA 89*
Capp, Sheldon N *BiDrAPA 89*
Cappa, B. *BiDWomA*
Cappa, Carl M. 1923- *St&PR 91*
Cappabianca, Patrick Silvio 1933- *WhoE 91*
Cappadona, Robert Santo 1926- *St&PR 91*
Cappaert, Michael Lynn 1943- *WhoSSW 91*
Cappaldi, Nicholas 1939- *WhoE 91*
Capparell, Homer V *BiDrAPA 89*

Capparucci, Edmund Michael 1957- WhoE 91
Cappe, Catharine 1744-1821 FemiCLE
Cappel, Constance 1936- WhoAmW 91, WhoWor 91
Cappeline, Gary Anthoney 1949- St&PR 91, WhoE 91
Cappell, Gerald A. 1925- St&PR 91
Cappelletti, Andrea 1961- IntWWM 90
Cappelletti, Chip 1951- St&PR 91
Cappelletti, Grace 1939- St&PR 91
Cappelletti, John Peter 1936- St&PR 91
Cappelletti, Joseph R. 1951- St&PR 91
Cappelletti, Marietta 1940- WhoAmW 91
Cappelletti, Salvatore 1945- WhoE 91
Cappelletti, Vincenzo 1930- WhoWor 91
Cappelli, Henry Charles 1934- St&PR 91
Cappelli, Louis Joseph 1931- St&PR 91
Cappellini, Louis A. St&PR 91
Cappello, A. Barry 1942- WhoWor 91
Cappello, Eve 1922- WhoAmW 91
Cappello, Gerard Karam 1961- WhoEmL 91
Cappello, Juan C. 1938- WhoAm 90
Cappello, Rosemary C. 1935- WhoWrEP 89
Cappello-Lorca, Juan Carlos 1938- St&PR 91
Capper, Aloysius Joseph, III 1955- WhoE 91
Capper, Robert 1930- BiDrAPA 89
Cappiello, Angela 1954- WhoAmW 91
Cappiello, Frank A., Jr. 1926- St&PR 91
Cappiello, Frank Anthony, Jr. 1926- WhoAm 90
Cappiello, Rosa 1942- FemiCLE
Cappitella, Mauro John 1934- WhoE 91
Cappo, Joseph C. BioIn 16
Cappo, Joseph C. 1936- WhoAm 90
Cappon, Alexander Patterson 1900- WhoAm 90
Cappon, Andre Alfred 1948- WhoE 91
Cappon, Daniel BiDrAPA 89
Capps, Benjamin 1922- BioIn 16
Capps, Brenda Gale Harden 1964- WhoSSW 91
Capps, Dianne Elizabeth 1956- WhoEmL 91
Capps, Katherine Herring 1957- WhoAmW 91
Capps, Kenneth P 1939- WhoAmA 91
Capps, Michael Edward 1956- WhoSSW 91
Capps, Milton F. 1948- ODwPR 91
Capps, Richard Huntley 1928- WhoAm 90
Capps, Sherrill Maynard 1941- St&PR 91
Capps, Thomas Edward 1935- St&PR 91, WhoAm 90, WhoSSW 91
Cappucci, Joseph D. 1931- St&PR 91
Cappuccilli, Piero 1929- IntWWM 90, PenDiMP
Capra, Buzz 1947- Ballpl 90
Capra, Frank 1897- BioIn 16, WhoAm 90, WorAlBi
Capra, Pierre Jens Frederic 1915- WhoWor 91
Capra, Richard D. 1932- WhoAm 90
Capraro, Franz 1941- WhoSSW 91
Capre, Alfred 1946- St&PR 91
Capretto, Neil Anthony 1955- BiDrAPA 89
Capria, Ernest Alvin 1941- WhoE 91
Capria, Frank Antonio 1951- WhoEmL 91
Capriati, Jennifer BioIn 16, NewYTBS 90 [port]
Capriati, Jennifer 1976- News 91-1 [port]
Capricci, Samuel Clement 1955- WhoE 91
Caprino, Luciano 1934- WhoWor 91
Caprio, Anthony S. 1945- WhoAm 90
Caprio, Betsy ConAu 30NR
Caprio, Elizabeth Blair 1933- ConAu 30NR
Caprio, Joseph Giuseppe 1914- WhoWor 91
Caprio, Virginia Stutsman 1916- WhoWor 91
Caprio-Stilwell, Julie Ann 1963- WhoEmL 91, WhoWor 91
Caprioli, Alberto 1956- IntWWM 90
Capriolo, John Anthony 1957- WhoEmL 91
Capriotti, Eugene Raymond WhoAm 90
Caprita, Barbara Jean 1949- WhoSSW 91
Capritto, Anthony Joseph 1931- WhoSSW 91
Capron, Adin Ballou 1841-1911 AmLegL
Capron, Alexander Morgan 1944- WhoAm 90
Capros, Pantelis 1954- WhoWor 91
Capsalis, Barbara D. 1943- St&PR 91
Capsalis, Barbara Damon 1943- WhoAm 90, WhoAmW 91
Capshaw, John Chandler 1932- St&PR 91
Capshaw, Kate BioIn 16
Captain & Tennille EncPR&S 89
Captain Beefheart 1941- OxCPMus
Captain Beefheart and the Magic Band EncPR&S 89
Captain Douglas DcCanB 12
Captain Jack 1840?-1873 WhNaAH
Captain Pipe WhNaAH
Captured The Gun Inside DcCanB 12
Capua, James Vincent 1949- WhoE 91
Capuana, Franco 1894-1969 PenDiMP
Capuano, Christine Marie 1953- WhoAmW 91
Capucilli, Terese BioIn 16
Capucine NewYTBS 90
Capucine 1933-1990 BioIn 16
Capuis, Matilde 1913- IntWWM 90
Caputa, Lewis Anthony 1924- WhoSSW 91
Capute, Joseph 1942- St&PR 91
Caputi, Anthony 1924- WhoAm 90, WhoE 91
Caputi, Jane 1953- ConAu 129
Caputi, William James, Jr. 1936- WhoAm 90
Caputo, Anne Spencer BioIn 16
Caputo, Anne Spencer 1947- WhoAmW 91
Caputo, Carmen Michael 1940- St&PR 91
Caputo, Dante WhoWor 91
Caputo, Dante Maria BioIn 16
Caputo, David Armand 1943- WhoAm 90
Caputo, Joseph Anthony 1940- WhoAm 90, WhoE 91
Caputo, Kevin Patrick BiDrAPA 89
Caputo, Lucio 1935- WhoWor 91
Caputo, Philip 1941- WorAu 1980 [port]
Caputo, Philip Joseph 1941- WhoAm 90, WhoWor 91, WhoWrEP 89
Capuzzo, Jill P. ODwPR 91
Capwell, Bobbi Lou Storseth 1956- WhoEmL 91
Capwell, Richard Leonard 1920- WhoAm 90
Capwell, Robin R 1947- BiDrAPA 89
Car, Michael Anthony 1946- WhoEmL 91
Cara, Irene 1959- DrBlPA 90, EncPR&S 89
Caraballo, Jose Noel 1955- WhoHisp 91
Caraballo, Luis Benito 1954- WhoHisp 91
Carabello, Vincent J. 1942- St&PR 91
Carabillo, Joseph Anthony 1946- WhoEmL 91
Carabillo, Virginia A. 1926- WhoAm 90
Carabin, Francois-Rupert 1862-1932 PenDiDA 89
Carabine, Michael D BiDrAPA 89
Caracci, Giovanni BiDrAPA 89
Caraccio, Babette B 1957- BiDrAPA 89, WhoE 91
Caracciolo, Andrew Bernard 1950- WhoSSW 91
Caracciolo, Enrichetta 1821-1901 EncCoWW
Caracciolo, Francis Samuel 1929- WhoSSW 91
Caracciolo, Frank Salvatore 1941- WhoE 91
Caracciolo, John R. 1942- St&PR 91
Caraci, Philip D. 1938- St&PR 91
Caradja, Catherine 1893- WhoAmW 91
Caradon, Lord 1907-1990 NewYTBS 90 [port]
Caradori-Allan, Maria 1800-1865 PenDiMP
Caradosso, Cristoforo Foppa 1452?-1526? PenDiDA 89
Carafello, William V. 1956- St&PR 91
Caragher, Jean Marie 1959- WhoSSW 91
Caraion, Ion 1923-1986 WorAu 1980 [port]
Caraley, Demetrios 1932- WhoAm 90
Caram, Dorothy Farrington 1933- WhoHisp 91
Caram, Eve 1934- WhoWrEP 89
Caram, Miguel Angel 1934- WhoSSW 91
Caramel, Jean-Pierre-Daniel-Edmond 1953- WhoWor 91
Caramello, Anne Olszewski 1951- WhoAmW 91
Carameros, George Demitrius, Jr. 1924- St&PR 91, WhoAm 90
Carancini, Francesco 1863- EncO&P 3
Carancini, Francesco 1863?-1940 EncPaPR 91
Caranfa, Patrick Louis 1943- St&PR 91
Carani, Dorothy Mariam 1927- WhoWrEP 89
Carapancea, Mihai Titus 1920- WhoWor 91
Carapella, Victor P. 1949- St&PR 91
Carapellucci, Daniel A. 1946- St&PR 91
Carapetyan, Armen 1908- IntWWM 90, WhoAm 90
Caras, Constantine George 1938- St&PR 91, WhoAm 90
Caras, George T BiDrAPA 89
Caras, J. Sheldon 1924- St&PR 91
Caras, Joseph Sheldon 1924- WhoAm 90
Caras, Roger A. BioIn 16
Caras, Roger Andrew 1928- WhoAm 90, WhoWrEP 89
Carasick, Gene Eric 1949- St&PR 91
Caratheodory, Constantin 1873-1950 BioIn 16
Carattini, Teodoro BiDrAPA 89
Carattini, Teodoro 1961- WhoE 91
Caravaggio 1571-1610 IntDcAA 90
Caravaggio, Michelangelo Merisi Da 1573-1610 WorAlBi
Caravajal y Saavedra, Mariana de 16--?-1664? EncCoWW
Caravatt, Paul Joseph, Jr. 1922- WhoAm 90
Caravedo, Baltazar 1915- BiDrAPA 89
Caraveo, Joseph Richard 1931- St&PR 91
Caravia, Manuel A. WhoHisp 91
Caraway, Betty Jones 1928- WhoAmW 91
Caraway, Caren 1939- BioIn 16
Caraway, Hattie W. 1878-1950 WorAlBi
Caraway, Pat 1906-1974 Ballpl 90
Caraway, Robert E 1932- BiDrAPA 89
Caray Family BioIn 16
Caray, Harry BioIn 16
Caray, Harry 1920- Ballpl 90
Caray, Skip 1939- Ballpl 90
Carazo Odio, Rodrigo 1926- BioIn 16
Carb, Evan Daniel 1960- WhoEmL 91
Carb, Stephen Ames 1930- WhoAm 90
Carbajal, Jose M. J. 1810?-1874 BioIn 16
Carbajal, Michael 1968- WhoHisp 91
Carbajal, Ulysses Mejia 1922- WhoWor 91
Carbajal G, Enrique WhoAmA 91
Carballada, R. Carlos 1935- St&PR 91
Carballido, Emilio BioIn 16
Carballido, Emilio 1925- HispWr 90
Carballo, Lourdes BiDrAPA 89
Carballo-Ricardo, Neyda 1941- WhoAmW 91
Carbaugh, John Edward, Jr. 1945- WhoE 91, WhoWor 91
Carberg, John ODwPR 91
Carberry, Deirdre WhoAmW 91
Carberry, James John 1925- WhoAm 90, WhoWor 91
Carberry, John A. WhoWrEP 89
Carberry, John J. 1904- WhoWor 91
Carberry, Michael Glen 1941- WhoAm 90
Carbine, Eugene J. 1936- St&PR 91
Carbo, Bernie 1947- Ballpl 90
Carbo, Kimberly Monique 1960- WhoAmW 91, WhoSSW 91
Carbo, Mariano Fortuny y 1838-1874 BioIn 16
Carbo, Robert Michael 1946- St&PR 91
Carbon, Max William 1922- WhoAm 90
Carbonari, Bruce A. 1955- St&PR 91
Carbonari, Claudia Mary 1952- BiDrAPA 89
Carbonari, James J. 1941- St&PR 91
Carbone, Alexander A. 1944- St&PR 91
Carbone, Alfonso R. 1921- St&PR 91
Carbone, Claudia 1941- WhoAmW 91
Carbone, David 1950- WhoAmA 91
Carbone, Dominick F. 1933- WhoE 91
Carbone, Edward A. 1940- St&PR 91
Carbone, Egidio 1940- St&PR 91
Carbone, Hubert A 1917- BiDrAPA 89
Carbone, John Vito 1922- WhoAm 90
Carbone, Joseph Robert BiDrAPA 89
Carbone, Lewis Peter 1949- WhoAm 90
Carbone, Lisa Ann M BiDrAPA 89
Carbone, Paul Peter 1931- WhoAm 90
Carbone, Vincent Peter 1951- St&PR 91
Carbonell, Dora 1946- WhoE 91
Carbonell, Frieda Wollmann WhoSSW 91
Carbonell, Nestor WhoHisp 91
Carbonell, Robert J. WhoAm 90
Carboni, Daniel S. WhoAm 90
Carboni, Pietro Angelo 1963- WhoE 91
Carboni, Robert O. 1929- ODwPR 91, St&PR 91
Carboni, Teresa Maria 1961- WhoE 91
Carcani, Adil 1922- WhoWor 91
Carcara, P. 1943- St&PR 91
Carcassi, Ugo Efisio Francesco 1921- WhoWor 91
Carcedo, Jo Zenaida 1956- WhoAmW 91
Carceller, Thierry Michel 1955- WhoWor 91
Carcich, James J. 1941- St&PR 91
Carcione, Joe BioIn 16
Card, Joseph Bartow 1941- St&PR 91
Card, June 1942- IntWWM 90
Card, Lewis WhoWrEP 89
Card, Orson Scott 1951- MajTwCW, RGTwCSF, WhoAm 90
Card, Royden 1952- WhoAmA 91
Card, Wesley Roy 1947- WhoEmL 91
Carda, R I EncCoWW
Cardalena, Peter Paul, Jr. 1943- WhoE 91
Cardamone, Jeanette M. 1940- WhoSSW 91
Cardamone, Louis J. 1926- St&PR 91
Cardamone, Richard J. 1925- WhoAm 90, WhoE 91
Cardamone, S Joseph BiDrAPA 89
Cardamone-Jackson, Donna 1937- IntWWM 90
Cardan, Jerome 1501-1576 EncO&P 3
Cardano, Girolamo 1501-1576 BioIn 16
Cardarelli, Michael 1958- WhoE 91
Cardell, Jose Emilio BiDrAPA 89
Cardell, Victor T. 1951- IntWWM 90
Cardella, Elaine 1963- BioIn 16
Cardella, Robert J. 1952- St&PR 91
Carden, Charles B. 1944- St&PR 91
Carden, Charles Buford 1944- WhoAm 90
Carden, George Patrick 1929- St&PR 91
Carden, James Matthew, Jr. 1956- WhoEmL 91
Carden, Joan Maralyn IntWWM 90
Carden, John M. 1938- St&PR 91
Carden, Norman Lester 1931- BiDrAPA 89
Carden, Priscilla AuBYP 90
Cardenal, Ernesto 1925- BioIn 16, ConAu 32NR, HispWr 90, MajTwCW
Cardenal, Jose 1943- Ballpl 90
Cardenal, Patricia 1949- WhoSSW 91
Cardenal Martinez, Ernesto 1925- ConAu 32NR
Cardenas, Cuauhtemoc BioIn 16
Cardenas, Henry WhoHisp 91
Cardenas, Jose A. 1930- WhoHisp 91
Cardenas, Juan Donoso 1963- WhoE 91
Cardenas, Lazaro 1895-1970 BioIn 16
Cardenas, Leo 1938- Ballpl 90
Cardenas, Leo Elias 1935- WhoHisp 91
Cardenas, Maria E. 1944- WhoSSW 91
Cardenas, Nick 1940- WhoHisp 91
Cardenas, Norma Alicia 1952- WhoAmW 91
Cardenas, Norma Yvette 1944- WhoHisp 91
Cardenas, Patricia Lorain Hicks 1939- WhoAmW 91, WhoWor 91
Cardenas, Raul 1937- WhoHisp 91
Cardenas, Renato E. WhoHisp 91
Cardenas, Rene F. 1933- St&PR 91, WhoHisp 91
Cardenas, Rene Fernando 1933- WhoSSW 91
Cardenas, Reyes 1948- HispWr 90
Cardenas, Robert Leon 1920- WhoHisp 91
Cardenas, Roberto L. 1920- BioIn 16
Cardenas, Santiago 1937- ArtLatA
Cardenas, Victor J 1926- BiDrAPA 89
Cardenas-Jaffe, Veronica 1947- WhoHisp 91
Cardenes, Andres Jorge 1957- WhoAm 90
Carder, David Allen 1961- WhoEmL 91
Carder, Frederick 1864-1963 PenDiDA 89
Carder, Scott Lamb BiDrAPA 89
Carder, Thomas Allen 1949- WhoSSW 91
Cardero, Jose 1766?-1810? WhNaAH
Cardew, Cornelius 1936-1981 ConAu 130
Cardew, Michael BioIn 16
Cardew, Michael 1901-1982 PenDiDA 89
Cardew, Michael 1901-1983 ConAu 30NR
Cardew, Michael Ambrose 1901-1983 DcNaB 1981
Cardew, William J. 1926- St&PR 91
Cardew, William Joseph WhoAm 90
Cardey, Keith R. 1924- St&PR 91
Cardi, Frank BioIn 16
Cardi, Mauro 1955- IntWWM 90
Cardi, Vincent 1948- WhoE 91
Cardia, Roy A. 1940- St&PR 91
Cardiff, Keith Curtis 1921- WhoAm 90
Cardigan, James Thomas Brudenell 1797-1868 BioIn 16
Cardile, Joseph S. 1953- St&PR 91
Cardilicchia, Tina Gail 1944- WhoAmW 91
Cardillo, Anthony Thomas 1953- WhoEmL 91
Cardillo, Jerry Edward 1920- St&PR 91
Cardillo, Joe 1951- WhoWrEP 89
Cardillo, Rimer Angel 1944- WhoAmA 91
Cardillo, Susan 1958- WhoE 91
Cardin, Benjamin Louis 1943- WhoAm 90, WhoE 91
Cardin, Frederick A. BioIn 16
Cardin, Herschel 1926- St&PR 91
Cardin, Jackie Darlene 1954- WhoEmL 91
Cardin, Lucien 1919-1988 AnObit 1988, BioIn 16
Cardin, Meyer M. 1907- WhoAm 90
Cardin, Pierre BioIn 16
Cardin, Pierre 1922- ConDes 90, WhoWor 91, WorAlBi
Cardin, Shoshana Shoubin 1926- WhoAmW 91
Cardin, Steven Harris 1950- St&PR 91
Cardin, Tommie Sullivan 1961- WhoEmL 91
Cardina, Claire Armstrong 1931- WhoSSW 91
Cardinal, Anthony J. 1934- St&PR 91
Cardinal, Anthony John 1934- WhoAm 90
Cardinal, Lawrence Michael, Jr. 1951- St&PR 91
Cardinal, Marcelin 1920- WhoAm 90, WhoAmA 91
Cardinal, Marie 1929- EncCoWW
Cardinal, Shirley Mae 1944- WhoAmW 91
Cardinale, Claudia 1939- BioIn 16, WhoWor 91
Cardinale, Kathleen Carmel 1933- WhoAmW 91
Cardinale, Rose Marie 1937- IntWWM 90
Cardinale, S. Gerald 1934- WhoE 91
Cardinali, Albert John 1934- WhoAm 90

Cardine, Godfrey Joseph 1924- *WhoAm 90*
Cardini 1895-1973 *BioIn 16*
Cardis, John W. 1939- *ODwPR 91*
Cardis, Michael N *BiDrAPA 89*
Cardish, Robert Jay 1948- *BiDrAPA 89*
Cardman, Lawrence S. 1944- *WhoAm 90*
Cardnell, Valerie Flora *IntWWM 90*
Cardon, Marriner Paul 1932- *WhoAm 90*
Cardona, Daniel Josue *BiDrAPA 89*
Cardona, Emilio Rene *BiDrAPA 89*
Cardona, Fernando 1935- *WhoHisp 91*
Cardona, Florencia Bisenta de Casillas M *WhoAmW 91*
Cardona, Jose A. Montes *St&PR 91*
Cardona, Manuel 1934- *WhoWor 91*
Cardona, Mari Lourdes 1963- *WhoAmW 91*
Cardona, Rodolfo 1924- *WhoAm 90*
Cardone, Angelo B., Jr. 1946- *St&PR 91*
Cardone, Bonnie Jean 1942- *WhoAm 90, WhoAmW 91*
Cardoni, Horace R. 1916- *St&PR 91*
Cardoni, Horace Robert 1916- *WhoAm 90*
Cardosa, John 1940- *St&PR 91*
Cardoso, Anthony 1930- *WhoAmA 91*
Cardoso, Anthony Antonio 1930- *WhoSSW 91, WhoWor 91*
Cardoso, Carlos A 1946- *BiDrAPA 89*
Cardoso, Fernando Henrique *BioIn 16*
Cardoso, Lynn *BioIn 16*
Cardoso, Onelio Jorge 1914-1986 *HispWr 90*
Cardot, Carlos Felice 1913-1986 *BioIn 16*
Cardoza, Anne de Sola 1941- *WhoAmW 91*
Cardoza, Edmund James 1944- *St&PR 91*
Cardoza, Jose Alfredo 1953- *WhoHisp 91*
Cardoza, Raul John 1944- *WhoHisp 91*
Cardoza, Robert J. 1943- *St&PR 91*
Cardoza y Aragon, Luis 1904- *HispWr 90*
Cardozier, Virgus R. 1923- *WhoAm 90*
Cardozo, Benjamin Mordecai 1915- *WhoAm 90*
Cardozo, Benjamin N. 1870-1938 *WorAlBi*
Cardozo, Lois *AuBYP 90*
Cardozo, Michael Hart 1910- *WhoAm 90, WhoE 91*
Cardozo, Patricia Velez 1941- *WhoAmA 91*
Cardozo, Richard Nunez 1936- *WhoAm 90*
Cardozo-Freeman, Inez 1928- *ConAu 131, HispWr 90*
Carducci, Giosue 1835-1907 *WorAlBi*
Carducci, Olivia Marie 1961- *WhoE 91*
Carducci, Vincent A 1953- *WhoAmA 91*
Carducci Artenisio, Giuseppe Giulio 1936- *WhoWor 91*
Carduff, Thomas Jerome 1940- *St&PR 91*
Cardullo, Alice Cecilia 1955- *WhoAmW 91*
Cardullo, Joseph *St&PR 91*
Cardus, David 1922- *WhoAm 90*
Cardus, Joseph-Oriol 1914- *WhoWor 91*
Cardwell, Don 1935- *Ballpl 90*
Cardwell, Henry A 1919- *BiDrAPA 89*
Cardwell, James William 1948- *WhoEmL 91*
Cardwell, John J. *NewYTBS 90*
Cardwell, Kenneth Donald 1936- *St&PR 91*
Cardwell, Kenneth Harvey 1920- *WhoAm 90*
Cardwell, Nancy Lee 1947- *WhoAm 90, WhoE 91*
Cardwell, Paul *AuBYP 90*
Cardwell, Richard Henry 1846-1931 *AmLegL*
Cardwell, Samuel Patterson 1931- *St&PR 91*
Cardwell, Sandra Gayle Bavido 1943- *WhoAmW 91*
Cardwell, Sue Poole 1952- *WhoAmW 91, WhoEmL 91, WhoSSW 91, WhoWor 91*
Cardwell, Thomas Augusta, III 1943- *WhoE 91, WhoSSW 91*
Cardwell, William Duvall 1868-1954 *AmLegL*
Cardy, Andrew Gordon *WhoAm 90*
Cardy, Patrick Robert Thomas 1953- *IntWWM 90*
Carek, Donald J 1931- *BiDrAPA 89*
Carek, Donald John 1931- *WhoAm 90*
Carelli, Gabor Paul 1915- *WhoAm 90*
Carelman *BioIn 16*
Caren, Robert Poston 1932- *WhoAm 90*
Carerra, Kathleen *ConAu 130*
Caret, Robert Laurent 1947- *WhoAm 90*
Caretti, Richard Louis 1953- *WhoWor 91*
Caretto, Albert Alexander 1928- *WhoAm 90*
Carew, Clementine 1615-1671 *BiDEWW*
Carew, Elizabeth 1585-1639 *BiDEWW*
Carew, George 1941- *WhoWor 91*
Carew, Jan 1925- *BioIn 16*
Carew, Jan Rynveld 1925- *WhoAm 90*
Carew, John C. 1947- *St&PR 91*
Carew, Lyndon Belmont, Jr. 1932- *WhoE 91*
Carew, Rod 1945- *Ballpl 90 [port], WorAlBi*
Carew, Thomas 1595?-1640 *LitC 13 [port]*
Carew, Topper 1943- *DrBlPA 90*
Carewe, John Maurice Foxall 1933- *IntWWM 90*
Carewe, Sylvia *WhoAmA 91N*
Carey, Alan Leslie 1944- *St&PR 91*
Carey, Andy 1931- *Ballpl 90*
Carey, Anthony Morris 1935- *WhoAm 90*
Carey, Arthur Bernard, Jr. 1950- *WhoAm 90*
Carey, Benjamin A *BiDrAPA 89*
Carey, Bernice *BioIn 16*
Carey, Beverly Jane 1927- *BiDrAPA 89*
Carey, Bruce Douglas 1923- *WhoAm 90*
Carey, Charles W. 1941- *St&PR 91*
Carey, Christopher Chad 1957- *WhoEmL 91*
Carey, Christopher Edwin 1958- *WhoEmL 91*
Carey, Clara Parker 1937- *WhoSSW 91*
Carey, Clementine 1615-1671 *BiDEWW*
Carey, Cynthia 1947- *WhoAmW 91, WhoEmL 91*
Carey, David Edward 1913- *WhoSSW 91*
Carey, David M. *ODwPR 91*
Carey, Dean L. 1925- *St&PR 91*
Carey, Dean Lavere 1925- *WhoAm 90, WhoWor 91*
Carey, Dennis Clarke 1949- *WhoAm 90*
Carey, Edward John 1944- *St&PR 91, WhoAm 90*
Carey, Edward Marshel, Jr. 1942- *WhoAm 90*
Carey, Elizabeth 1585-1639 *BiDEWW*
Carey, Ellen 1952- *WhoAmA 91*
Carey, Ernestine Gilbreth 1908- *WhoAm 90, WhoAmW 91, WhoWor 91*
Carey, Evangeline Ruth 1949- *WhoEmL 91*
Carey, Frances Elizabeth 1945- *WhoAmW 91, WhoWor 91*
Carey, Francis J., Jr. 1926- *St&PR 91*
Carey, Francis James 1926- *WhoAm 90, WhoWor 91*
Carey, G. Cheston, Jr. 1930- *St&PR 91*
Carey, George Leonard 1935- *NewYTBS 90*
Carey, Gerald John, Jr. 1930- *WhoAm 90*
Carey, Gerald R. 1930- *WhoSSW 91*
Carey, Gerard V. 1926- *St&PR 91, WhoAm 90*
Carey, Gregory Brian 1942- *WhoAm 90*
Carey, Gregory Dale 1950- *WhoWrEP 89*
Carey, Harry, Jr. 1921- *ConTFT 8*
Carey, Harry Hill 1922- *WhoAm 90*
Carey, Henry Charles 1793-1879 *BioIn 16, EncABHB 6 [port]*
Carey, Hugh L. *BioIn 16*
Carey, Hugh L. 1919- *WorAlBi*
Carey, J. Edwin 1923- *WhoAm 90*
Carey, Jack R. 1952- *St&PR 91*
Carey, Jacqueline *BioIn 16*
Carey, James Edward 1946- *WhoEmL 91*
Carey, James Henry 1932- *WhoAm 90*
Carey, James Joseph 1939- *WhoAm 90*
Carey, James William 1934- *WhoAm 90*
Carey, Jane Quellmalz 1952- *St&PR 91, WhoAmW 91, WhoEmL 91*
Carey, Jay A. *WhoSSW 91*
Carey, Jean Lebeis 1943- *WhoAmW 91, WhoE 91*
Carey, Jeanne Grace 1957- *WhoAmW 91*
Carey, John 1924- *WhoAm 90*
Carey, John A. 1949- *St&PR 91*
Carey, John Edward 1949- *WhoEmL 91*
Carey, John J. 1928- *WhoAm 90*
Carey, John Jesse 1931- *WhoAm 90*
Carey, John Joseph 1928- *St&PR 91*
Carey, John L. 1904-1987 *BioIn 16*
Carey, John Leo 1920- *WhoAm 90*
Carey, John M. 1933- *St&PR 91*
Carey, John P. *BioIn 16*
Carey, John Thomas 1917-1990 *WhoAmA 91N*
Carey, Kathryn Ann 1949- *WhoAmW 91, WhoEmL 91*
Carey, Ken *NewAgE 90*
Carey, Larry Campbell 1933- *WhoAm 90*
Carey, Laura *BioIn 16*
Carey, Lott 1780?-1828? *BioIn 16*
Carey, MacDonald 1913- *ConTFT 8, WorAlBi*
Carey, Marcia J. 1941- *WhoAmW 91*
Carey, Margaret Standish 1926- *WhoWrEP 89*
Carey, Margaret Theresa Logan 1931- *WhoAmW 91*
Carey, Martin Conrad 1939- *WhoWor 91*
Carey, Mary *BiDEWW*
Carey, Mary 1609?-1680 *FemiCLE*
Carey, Max *BioIn 16*
Carey, Max 1890-1976 *Ballpl 90 [port]*
Carey, Milburn Ernest 1912- *WhoAm 90*
Carey, Nancy Bunting 1949- *WhoAmW 91*
Carey, Norman B. 1936- *St&PR 91*
Carey, Olive 1896-1988 *BioIn 16*
Carey, Omer L. 1929- *WhoWrEP 89*
Carey, Patricia Elaine Stedman 1944- *WhoAmW 91*
Carey, Peggy Johnson 1933- *WhoSSW 91*
Carey, Peter 1943- *MajTwCW, WorAu 1980 [port]*
Carey, Peter Kevin 1940- *WhoAm 90*
Carey, Philip A. *BioIn 16*
Carey, R. John 1913- *St&PR 91*
Carey, Raymond B., Jr. 1926- *St&PR 91*
Carey, Raymond Bernard, Jr. 1926- *WhoAm 90*
Carey, Richard 1950- *St&PR 91*
Carey, Richard Adams 1951- *WhoWrEP 89*
Carey, Richard Fremont 1924- *WhoAm 90*
Carey, Richard Neal 1953- *St&PR 91*
Carey, Robert 1941- *St&PR 91*
Carey, Robert M. 1945- *St&PR 91*
Carey, Robert Munson 1940- *WhoAm 90*
Carey, Robert Williams 1918- *WhoAm 90*
Carey, Ron 1935- *ConTFT 8*
Carey, Rosa Nouchette 1840-1909 *BioIn 16, FemiCLE*
Carey, Sarah Collins 1938- *WhoAm 90, WhoAmW 91*
Carey, Steven Harry *BioIn 16*
Carey, Steven Harry 1946?-1989 *ConAu 129*
Carey, Thomas 1931- *IntWWM 90*
Carey, Thomas Devore 1931- *WhoAm 90*
Carey, Thomas Hilton 1944- *WhoAm 90*
Carey, Thomas Howell, II 1945- *WhoSSW 91*
Carey, Thomas Patrick 1954- *WhoEmL 91*
Carey, Tom 1908-1970 *Ballpl 90*
Carey, Valerie Scho 1949- *SmATA 60 [port]*
Carey, Willard Keith 1929- *WhoAm 90*
Carey, William 1761-1834 *BioIn 16*
Carey, William Bacon 1926- *WhoAm 90, WhoE 91*
Carey, William Joseph 1922- *WhoAm 90*
Carey, William P. 1941- *St&PR 91*
Carey, William Polk 1930- *St&PR 91, WhoAm 90, WhoWor 91*
Carey, William R., Jr. *BioIn 16*
Carez, Christian Charles-Marie 1938- *WhoWor 91*
Carfagni, Arthur B *BiDrAPA 89*
Carfagno, Anthony Michael *St&PR 91*
Carfagno, Robert F. 1951- *St&PR 91*
Carfagno, Theresa L. 1942- *WhoE 91*
Carfolite, David Warren 1954- *WhoEmL 91*
Carfora, John Michael 1950- *WhoE 91*
Cargas, Harry J 1932- *WhoWrEP 89*
Cargian, Donald 1935- *St&PR 91*
Cargile, David Lee 1946- *WhoSSW 91*
Cargile, James Thomas 1938- *WhoAm 90*
Cargile, Susan Walter 1942- *WhoAmW 91*
Cargill, Michael 1951- *ODwPR 91*
Cargill, Paula Marie 1943- *WhoAmW 91*
Cargo, David Francis 1929- *WhoAm 90*
Cargo, Gerald Thomas 1930- *WhoE 91*
Cargo, William Ira 1917- *WhoAm 90*
Cargoe, Richard *ConAu 31NR*
Carhart, E.M., III 1932- *St&PR 91*
Cariani, Paul Raymond 1940- *St&PR 91*
Carias, Antonio *BiDrAPA 89*
Carias, Julio A *BiDrAPA 89*
Carias Audino, Tiburcio 1876-1969 *BioIn 16*
Cariati, Donald Francis, Sr. 1941- *WhoSSW 91*
Caric, Helen Lora 1939- *WhoAmW 91, WhoE 91, WhoWor 91*
Caric, Louis Stephen 1945- *St&PR 91*
Caric, Steve Louis 1919- *St&PR 91*
Caricari, Carl 1938- *WhoE 91*
Caricato, Joan Leedy 1957- *WhoAmW 91*
Carico, Margie Helton 1938- *WhoSSW 91*
Carideo, James V. 1935- *St&PR 91*
Caridis, Andrew Anthony 1921- *St&PR 91*
Caridis, Miltiades 1923- *IntWWM 90*
Carifio, Michael Sweet 1957- *WhoSSW 91*
Carigiet, Alois 1902-1985 *BioIn 16*
Cariglia, Michael Anthony 1930- *St&PR 91*
Carignan, Luc 1945- *St&PR 91*
Carillo, Mary *BioIn 16*
Carillo, Michael A. 1951- *WhoHisp 91*
Carin, Anavel Osorio *BiDrAPA 89*
Carin, Michael 1951- *ConAu 132*
Carinci, Gabriele Giustino 1951- *WhoSSW 91*
Caringal, Cecilia G 1952- *BiDrAPA 89*
Caringi, Vincent Dominic 1940- *WhoE 91*
Carington, Peter Alexander Rupert 1919- *BioIn 16*
Carington, W Whateley 1884-1947 *EncO&P 3*
Carington, Walter Whately 1884-1947 *EncPaPR 91*
Carino, Aurora Lao *BiDrAPA 89*
Carino, Donald Lawrence 1948- *WhoEmL 91*
Carino, Fernando Jaico 1932- *BiDrAPA 89*
Carino, Janel Sparling 1943- *BiDrAPA 89*
Carino, Ronald Louis *BiDrAPA 89*
Cariola, Robert J 1927- *WhoAmA 91*
Cariola, Robert Joseph 1927- *WhoAm 90, WhoE 91*
Cariou, Len *BioIn 16*
Cariou, Len 1939- *OxCCanT, WorAlBi*
Cariou, Len Joseph 1939- *WhoAm 90*
Caris, Theodore 1934- *WhoAm 90*
Cariseo, David Joseph 1941- *WhoAm 90*
Carisetti, Domenic Andrew 1951- *St&PR 91*
Cariss, Richard J. 1943- *St&PR 91*
Carisse, Johanne Marguerite 1953- *WhoWrEP 89*
Carita, Lois Roxane 1949- *WhoAmW 91*
Caritat, Marie-Jean-Antoine-Nicholas de 1743-1794 *BioIn 16*
Carithers, Hugh Alfred 1913- *WhoAm 90*
Carithers, Jeanine Rutherford 1933- *WhoAm 90*
Carius, Robert Wilhelm 1929- *WhoAm 90, WhoSSW 91*
Carl XVI Gustaf 1946- *WhoWor 91, WorAlBi*
Carl, Charles W., Jr. *BiDrAPA 89*
Carl, Eugene Marion, Jr. 1953- *IntWWM 90*
Carl, Jean Geralyn 1959- *WhoAmW 91*
Carl, Joan 1926- *WhoAmA 91*
Carl, John 1932- *St&PR 91*
Carl, Judith Lee 1944- *WhoAmW 91*
Carl, Linda Christine 1949- *WhoE 91*
Carl, Robert D., III 1954- *St&PR 91*
Carl, Tommie Ewert 1921- *WhoAmW 91*
Carl, W.J. 1934- *St&PR 91*
Carlander, Kenneth Dixon 1915- *WhoAm 90*
Carlat, Paul B 1930- *BiDrAPA 89*
Carlaw, Bogart 1904-1979 *WorAlBi*
Carlberg, James Edwin 1950- *WhoEmL 91*
Carlberg, Jill Renee 1957- *WhoSSW 91*
Carlberg, Nancy Ellen 1947- *WhoAmW 91*
Carlberg, Norman Kenneth 1928- *WhoAmA 91*
Carlberg, Ralph 1943- *St&PR 91*
Carle, Eric *BioIn 16*
Carle, Frankie 1903- *OxCPMus*
Carle, Kevin George 1951- *WhoSSW 91*
Carle, Marlyn E. 1931- *St&PR 91*
Carlebach, Eli Chaim *BioIn 16, NewYTBS 90*
Carlebach, Shlomo 1926- *NewAgE 90*
Carlell, Lodowick 1602-1675 *BioIn 16*
Carlen, Alexander 1913- *BiDrAPA 89*
Carlen, Claudia 1906- *WhoAm 90*
Carlen, Raymond Nils 1919- *St&PR 91*
Carles, Arthur B. *BioIn 16*
Carles, Arthur B 1882-1952 *WhoAmA 91N*
Carlesimo, P. J. *BioIn 16*
Carleson, Robert Bazil 1931- *WhoAm 90, WhoWor 91*
Carleson, Rolf Alfred Douglas 1910- *EncO&P 3*
Carleston, Stephen Hamilton 1948- *IntWWM 90*
Carleton, Bukk Griffith 1909- *WhoWor 91*
Carleton, David 1955- *WhoEmL 91*
Carleton, Don Edward 1947- *WhoAm 90*
Carleton, Gaye 1952- *WhoAmW 91*
Carleton, Gordon Robert 1955- *WhoEmL 91*
Carleton, James Henry 1814-1873 *WhNaAH*
Carleton, John 1861-1936 *OxCCanT*
Carleton, John L 1925- *BiDrAPA 89*
Carleton, John T. 1944- *St&PR 91*
Carleton, Mary 1634?-1673 *BiDEWW, FemiCLE*
Carleton, Mary Ruth 1948- *WhoAmW 91*
Carleton, R. Milton 1899-1986 *AuBYP 90*
Carleton, Richard Allyn 1931- *WhoAm 90*
Carleton, Robert L. 1940- *St&PR 91, WhoAm 90*
Carleton, Tex 1906-1977 *Ballpl 90*
Carleton, Willard Tracy 1934- *WhoAm 90*
Carleton, William 1794-1869 *BioIn 16*
Carleton-Lausten, Esther 1912- *BioIn 16*
Carley, Charles Team, Jr. 1932- *WhoAm 90*
Carley, Floyd Lyndol 1921- *St&PR 91*
Carley, James French 1923- *WhoAm 90*
Carley, James Patrick, Jr. 1949- *St&PR 91*
Carley, John Halliday 1941- *WhoAm 90*
Carley, Joni Marie 1955- *WhoAmW 91*
Carley, Kurt 1962- *WhoEmL 91*
Carley, Laura Ann 1950- *WhoEmL 91*
Carley, Lionel 1936- *ConAu 132*
Carley, Robin Michele 1955- *WhoAmW 91*
Carli, Audrey Marilyn 1932- *WhoWrEP 89*
Carli, Giancarlo 1938- *WhoWor 91*
Carli, Thomas 1947- *BiDrAPA 89*
Carlier, Eugene Norman 1932- *St&PR 91*
Carlier, Jean Joachim 1926- *WhoWor 91*
Carlier, John Carmelo 1957- *WhoEmL 91*
Carlile, Henry David 1934- *WhoWrEP 89*

Carlile, Janet 1942- *WhoAmA 91*
Carlin, Anne Ilishabeth 1949- *WhoAmW 91*
Carlin, Clair Myron 1947- *WhoEmL 91*
Carlin, David R., Jr. *BioIn 16*
Carlin, David R., Jr. 1938- *WhoE 91*
Carlin, Diane *BioIn 16*
Carlin, Donald Walter 1934- *St&PR 91, WhoAm 90*
Carlin, Edward R. 1940- *St&PR 91*
Carlin, Edward Robert 1940- *WhoAm 90*
Carlin, Electra Marshall *WhoAmA 91*
Carlin, Eugene Austin, Jr. 1955- *WhoE 91*
Carlin, Gabriel S. 1921- *WhoAm 90*
Carlin, George Denis 1937- *WhoAm 90*
Carlin, Herbert J. 1917- *WhoAm 90*
Carlin, James 1910- *WhoAmA 91*
Carlin, Jean E *BiDrAPA 89*
Carlin, Jerry Fay 1946- *WhoEmL 91*
Carlin, John William 1940- *WhoAm 90*
Carlin, Joyce Kimberly 1959- *WhoE 91*
Carlin, Martin *PenDiDA 89*
Carlin, Melissa Joann 1949- *WhoHisp 91*
Carlin, Michael Kevin 1951- *WhoEmL 91*
Carlin, Vivian F. 1919- *ConAu 131*
Carlin, William J. C. *ODwPR 91*
Carliner, David 1918- *WhoAm 90*
Carliner, Kathryn *ODwPR 91*
Carliner, Michael Simon 1945- *WhoAm 90*
Carlini, Agostino *BioIn 16*
Carlini, James 1954- *WhoEmL 91*
Carlini, Lawrence J. 1949- *St&PR 91*
Carlino, Rose Therese 1928- *WhoE 91*
Carlinsky, Dan 1944- *WhoWrEP 89*
Carlisi, Dominick J 1912- *BiDrAPA 89*
Carlisle, Albert E. *St&PR 91*
Carlisle, Belinda *BioIn 16, EncPR&S 89*
Carlisle, Charles Roger 1929- *WhoWor 91*
Carlisle, Christopher E. 1948- *St&PR 91*
Carlisle, Clark *TwCCr&M 91*
Carlisle, Clark, Jr. *AuBYP 90*
Carlisle, Darlwin *BioIn 16*
Carlisle, Dean W. 1929- *St&PR 91*
Carlisle, Dwight L., Jr. 1935- *WhoSSW 91*
Carlisle, Dwight Lester 1935- *St&PR 91*
Carlisle, George D. 1913- *St&PR 91*
Carlisle, George Richard, Jr. 1949- *WhoEmL 91*
Carlisle, George W. 1919- *St&PR 91*
Carlisle, Isabella 1721-1795 *FemiCLE*
Carlisle, James Patton 1946- *WhoE 91, WhoEmL 91*
Carlisle, Jay Charles, II 1942- *WhoWor 91*
Carlisle, Jerry Dean 1946- *St&PR 91*
Carlisle, Jock Alan 1924- *WhoWrEP 89*
Carlisle, John Griffin 1835-1910 *BiDrUSE 89*
Carlisle, Joyce Ellen 1954- *WhoWrEP 89*
Carlisle, Kitty *BioIn 16*
Carlisle, Kitty 1914- *OxCPMus*
Carlisle, L Lee 1956- *BiDrAPA 89*
Carlisle, Leo 1935- *WhoSSW 91*
Carlisle, Lilian Matarose Baker 1912- *WhoAmW 91*
Carlisle, M. Eugene, Jr. 1933- *St&PR 91*
Carlisle, Margo Duer Black *WhoAm 90, WhoAmW 91*
Carlisle, Olga Andreyev 1930- *AuBYP 90*
Carlisle, Patricia Kinley 1949- *WhoAmW 91*
Carlisle, Robert Bruce 1928- *WhoAm 90*
Carlisle, Robert Marsden, Jr. 1931- *WhoSSW 91*
Carlisle, Robert Paul 1960- *WhoEmL 91*
Carlisle, Rosalind F Howard, Countess of 1845-1921 *BioIn 16*
Carlisle, Shirley Carolyn 1932- *St&PR 91*
Carlisle, Steven J 1932- *BiDrAPA 89*
Carlisle, Timothy Frank 1960- *WhoSSW 91*
Carlisle, Wallace *BioIn 16*
Carlisle, William Aiken 1918- *WhoAm 90*
Carlisle, William G. 1930- *St&PR 91*
Carlisle, Woodson Studebaker, Jr. 1934- *St&PR 91*
Carlitz, Leonard 1907- *WhoAm 90*
Carll, Elizabeth Kassay 1950- *WhoE 91*
Carlnas, Bengt Eric *WhoWor 91*
Carlo, Gerardo Adolfo 1942- *WhoAm 90*
Carlo, Ismael 1949- *BiDrAPA 89*
Carlo, Nelson 1938- *WhoHisp 91*
Carlock, Jon Thompson 1964- *WhoSSW 91*
Carlock, Mahlon Waldo 1926- *WhoWor 91*
Carlock, Richard Bruce 1951- *St&PR 91*
Carlock, Roger E. 1935- *St&PR 91*
Carlock, William Delos 1938- *BiDrAPA 89*
Carlon, Patrick John 1947- *WhoEmL 91*
Carlos III, King of Spain 1716-1788 *BioIn 16*
Carlos IV, King of Spain 1748-1819 *BioIn 16*
Carlos, Alfredo R 1929- *BiDrAPA 89*
Carlos, Cisco 1940- *Ballpl 90*
Carlos, Edward 1937- *WhoAmA 91*
Carlos, Iluminada T 1932- *BiDrAPA 89*
Carlos, Joao 1884-1950 *BioIn 16*
Carlos, Laurie *BioIn 16*
Carlos, Michael C. 1927- *St&PR 91*
Carlos, Wendy *NewAgMG*
Carlos, Wendy 1939- *IntWWM 90, PenDiMP*
Carlot *EncCoWW*
Carlotti, Francois 1907- *BioIn 16*
Carlozzi, Annette Dimeo 1953- *WhoAmA 91*
Carlozzi, Carlo, Jr. 1958- *WhoE 91*
Carlozzi, Nicholas 1952- *St&PR 91*
Carlquist, Sherwin 1930- *WhoAm 90*
Carls, David Henry 1938- *St&PR 91*
Carlsberg, Richard Presten 1937- *WhoAm 90*
Carlsen, Chris *ConAu 131*
Carlsen, Clifford N., Jr. 1927- *St&PR 91*
Carlsen, Clifford Norman, Jr. 1927- *WhoAm 90*
Carlsen, Deborah Eileen Bettray 1956- *WhoAmW 91*
Carlsen, Henning *BioIn 16*
Carlsen, Henrik Kurt 1915-1989 *BioIn 16*
Carlsen, James Caldwell 1927- *WhoAm 90*
Carlsen, Janet Haws 1927- *WhoAmW 91*
Carlsen, June Marie 1959- *WhoEmL 91*
Carlsen, Laurie Beth 1961- *WhoAmW 91*
Carlsen, Mary Baird 1928- *WhoAmW 91*
Carlsen, Nils 1945- *WhoWor 91*
Carlsen, Peter 1946-1989 *BioIn 16*
Carlsen, Ruth 1918- *AuBYP 90*
Carlsmith, James Merrill 1936- *WhoAm 90*
Carlsnaes, Walter Emanuel 1943- *WhoWor 91*
Carlson, Alan R. *St&PR 91*
Carlson, Anita Hoke 1942- *WhoAmW 91*
Carlson, Anita Lynne 1952- *WhoAmW 91*
Carlson, Ann *BioIn 16*
Carlson, Arnold R., Jr. 1928- *St&PR 91*
Carlson, Arnold W. 1928- *St&PR 91*
Carlson, Barbara Bigger 1939- *WhoAmW 91*
Carlson, Barbara Jean 1926- *WhoAmW 91*
Carlson, Ben 1936- *St&PR 91*
Carlson, Bernice Wells 1910- *AuBYP 90*
Carlson, Bille Chandler 1924- *WhoAm 90*
Carlson, Bradley Reed 1956- *WhoEmL 91*
Carlson, Brett Roberts 1951- *WhoWor 91*
Carlson, Brian Jay 1956- *WhoEmL 91*
Carlson, Bruce *St&PR 91*
Carlson, Byron Lee 1945- *WhoEmL 91*
Carlson, C. Herbert 1940- *St&PR 91*
Carlson, Carl A. 1917- *St&PR 91*
Carlson, Carl Linne 1935- *WhoSSW 91*
Carlson, Carmen Elizabeth 1963- *WhoAmW 91*
Carlson, Carol Sue 1946- *WhoAmW 91*
Carlson, Carol Weber 1960- *WhoAmW 91*
Carlson, Carolin McCormick Furst 1934- *WhoE 91*
Carlson, Charles K. 1937- *St&PR 91*
Carlson, Charlotte Booth 1920- *WhoAmW 91*
Carlson, Chester 1906-1968 *BioIn 16*
Carlson, Chester F. 1906-1968 *EncPaPR 91*
Carlson, Chris 1946- *ODwPR 91*
Carlson, Claudine *IntWWM 90*
Carlson, Curtis Keith 1946- *WhoEmL 91*
Carlson, Curtis L. 1914- *St&PR 91*
Carlson, Curtis LeRoy *BioIn 16*
Carlson, Curtis LeRoy 1914- *WhoAm 90*
Carlson, Curtis M. 1927- *St&PR 91*
Carlson, Cynthia J 1942- *WhoAmA 91*
Carlson, Cynthia Joanne 1942- *WhoAm 90*
Carlson, D.O. 1928- *St&PR 91*
Carlson, Dale 1935- *AuBYP 90*
Carlson, Dale A. 1956- *St&PR 91*
Carlson, Dale Alan 1959- *WhoEmL 91*
Carlson, Dale Arvid 1925- *WhoAm 90*
Carlson, Dale Bick 1935- *WhoAm 90, WhoAmW 91, WhoE 91, WhoWor 91*
Carlson, Dale Lynn 1946- *WhoE 91, WhoEmL 91, WhoWor 91*
Carlson, Daniel A. 1945- *St&PR 91*
Carlson, David A 1933- *BiDrAPA 89*
Carlson, David Arthur *BiDrAPA 89*
Carlson, David Blaine *BiDrAPA 89*
Carlson, David Bret 1918- *WhoAm 90*
Carlson, David Edwin 1946- *St&PR 91*
Carlson, David Emil 1942- *WhoAm 90*
Carlson, David George 1959- *WhoEmL 91*
Carlson, David M. 1940- *St&PR 91*
Carlson, David Martin 1940- *WhoAm 90*
Carlson, Dawn Marie 1956- *WhoAmW 91*
Carlson, Deborah Ann 1948- *WhoAmW 91*
Carlson, Dennis Lee 1946- *WhoEmL 91*
Carlson, DeVon McElvin 1917- *WhoAm 90*
Carlson, Don Marvin 1931- *WhoAm 90*
Carlson, Dorothy L 1928- *BiDrAPA 89*
Carlson, Douglas John 1955- *St&PR 91*
Carlson, Duane Stuart 1935- *WhoAm 90*
Carlson, Dwain C. 1942- *St&PR 91*
Carlson, Dwight Lloyd 1933- *BiDrAPA 89*
Carlson, Edward C. 1942- *WhoAm 90*
Carlson, Edward E. 1911-1990 *NewYTBS 90*
Carlson, Edward Elmer 1911-1990 *BioIn 16*
Carlson, Elizabeth Ann 1946- *WhoAm 90*
Carlson, Elof Axel 1931- *WhoAm 90*
Carlson, Elvin Palmer 1950- *WhoE 91*
Carlson, Eric T 1922- *BiDrAPA 89*
Carlson, Esther Elisabeth 1920- *AuBYP 90*
Carlson, Evans F. 1896-1947 *BioIn 16*
Carlson, Evans Fordyce 1896-1947 *WorAlBi*
Carlson, Frederick Paul 1938- *WhoAm 90*
Carlson, Gabrielle A 1942- *BiDrAPA 89*
Carlson, Gary 1950- *St&PR 91*
Carlson, Gary Albert 1946- *WhoEmL 91*
Carlson, Gary Lee 1954- *WhoEmL 91, WhoWor 91*
Carlson, George 1887-1962 *EncACom*
Carlson, George Arthur 1940- *WhoAm 90, WhoAmA 91*
Carlson, George Lewis 1946- *WhoEmL 91*
Carlson, Gerald K. 1943- *St&PR 91*
Carlson, Gerald Wesley 1947- *WhoEmL 91*
Carlson, Glen A., Jr. 1935- *St&PR 91*
Carlson, Graham B. 1927- *St&PR 91*
Carlson, Gretchen Elizabeth *BioIn 16*
Carlson, Guy Douglas 1956- *WhoSSW 91*
Carlson, Guy Raymond 1918- *WhoAm 90*
Carlson, Hal 1892-1930 *Ballpl 90*
Carlson, Harald D. 1952- *St&PR 91*
Carlson, Harold S. *NewYTBS 90*
Carlson, Harry *WhoAm 90*
Carlson, Harry 1919- *WhoAm 90*
Carlson, Jack Wilson 1933- *WhoAm 90*
Carlson, James R. 1942- *St&PR 91*
Carlson, James William 1951- *St&PR 91*
Carlson, Jane C 1928- *WhoAmA 91*
Carlson, Jane E. 1918- *IntWWM 90*
Carlson, Jane Rise 1949- *St&PR 91*
Carlson, Janet Frances 1957- *WhoAmW 91, WhoE 91*
Carlson, Janet Lynn 1952- *WhoAmW 91*
Carlson, Jay Cornel *BiDrAPA 89*
Carlson, Jeannie Ann 1955- *WhoAmW 91, WhoEmL 91, WhoSSW 91*
Carlson, Jerome Walter 1936- *St&PR 91*
Carlson, Jerry Alan 1936- *WhoAm 90, WhoWrEP 89*
Carlson, John E. 1930- *St&PR 91*
Carlson, John F. 1938- *St&PR 91, WhoAm 90*
Carlson, John Henry 1945- *WhoEmL 91*
Carlson, John P. *St&PR 91*
Carlson, John Tyler 1963- *WhoE 91*
Carlson, Jon Olaf 1942- *IntWWM 90*
Carlson, Jud L. 1942- *St&PR 91*
Carlson, Judith K *BiDrAPA 89*
Carlson, Karen *St&PR 91*
Carlson, Kenneth George 1949- *WhoEmL 91*
Carlson, Kenneth W. 1933- *St&PR 91*
Carlson, Kristi Mork 1955- *WhoAmW 91*
Carlson, Kurt I. 1932- *St&PR 91*
Carlson, Lance R 1950- *WhoAmA 91*
Carlson, Lanette Anne 1952- *WhoWrEP 89*
Carlson, Larry E. 1943- *St&PR 91*
Carlson, Larry Paul 1942- *St&PR 91*
Carlson, Lenus 1945- *IntWWM 90*
Carlson, Leroy T. 1916- *St&PR 91*
Carlson, Leroy T. 1946- *St&PR 91*
Carlson, LeRoy Theodore Sheridan, Sr. 1916- *WhoAm 90*
Carlson, Leslie Gail 1954- *WhoEmL 91*
Carlson, Loren Merle 1923- *WhoAm 90*
Carlson, Lynette L. 1960- *WhoSSW 91*
Carlson, Marian Bille 1952- *WhoAmW 91*
Carlson, Mark Alan *BiDrAPA 89*
Carlson, Martin Thomas 1950- *St&PR 91*
Carlson, Marvin Albert 1935- *WhoAm 90*
Carlson, Mary 1951- *WhoAmA 91*
Carlson, Mary Ann 1944- *WhoAmW 91*
Carlson, Mary Anne Jerow 1957- *WhoAmW 91*
Carlson, Mary Rebecca 1955- *WhoEmL 91*
Carlson, Mary Susan 1949- *WhoEmL 91*
Carlson, Matt *ODwPR 91*
Carlson, N. Taylor 1946- *WhoSSW 91*
Carlson, Nancy L. 1953- *BioIn 16*
Carlson, Nancy Lee 1950- *WhoAmW 91, WhoEmL 91*
Carlson, Natalie 1906- *AuBYP 90*
Carlson, Natalie Savage 1906- *WhoAm 90, WhoWrEP 89*
Carlson, Norman A. 1933- *WhoAm 90*
Carlson, Oscar Norman 1920- *WhoAm 90*
Carlson, Otto C. 1927- *St&PR 91*
Carlson, Patricia Warren 1947- *WhoEmL 91*
Carlson, Paul Edwin 1944- *WhoWor 91*
Carlson, Penny Jo 1964- *St&PR 91*
Carlson, Per J. 1938- *WhoWor 91*
Carlson, Ralph Lawrence 1944- *WhoAm 90*
Carlson, Ralph W. *St&PR 91*
Carlson, Randy Eugene 1948- *WhoEmL 91, WhoWor 91*
Carlson, Ria Marie 1961- *WhoAmW 91, WhoEmL 91, WhoWor 91*
Carlson, Richard A. *BioIn 16*
Carlson, Richard Allen 1944- *WhoSSW 91*
Carlson, Richard C. 1946- *St&PR 91*
Carlson, Richard Carl 1942- *WhoAm 90*
Carlson, Richard Ernest 1927- *St&PR 91*
Carlson, Richard Ernest 1953- *WhoEmL 91*
Carlson, Richard George 1930- *WhoAm 90*
Carlson, Richard Gregory 1949- *WhoAm 90, WhoEmL 91*
Carlson, Richard J *BiDrAPA 89*
Carlson, Richard Merrill 1925- *WhoAm 90*
Carlson, Richard Warner 1941- *BioIn 16, WhoAm 90, WhoE 91, WhoWor 91*
Carlson, Robert A. 1932- *St&PR 91*
Carlson, Robert Brian 1943- *St&PR 91*
Carlson, Robert Charles 1957- *WhoE 91*
Carlson, Robert Codner 1939- *WhoAm 90*
Carlson, Robert Edward 1936- *WhoAm 90*
Carlson, Robert Frederick, Jr. 1952- *WhoEmL 91*
Carlson, Robert G 1915- *BiDrAPA 89*
Carlson, Robert Gideon 1938- *WhoAm 90*
Carlson, Robert J. 1929- *St&PR 91*
Carlson, Robert James 1944- *WhoAm 90*
Carlson, Robert John 1929- *WhoAm 90*
Carlson, Robert Lee 1924- *WhoAm 90*
Carlson, Robert Marshall 1950- *WhoEmL 91*
Carlson, Robert Oskar 1921- *WhoAm 90, WhoWor 91*
Carlson, Robert W., Jr. 1947- *St&PR 91*
Carlson, Robert William, Jr. 1947- *WhoAm 90*
Carlson, Roderick 1928- *St&PR 91*
Carlson, Roger Allan 1932- *St&PR 91, WhoWor 91*
Carlson, Rolland Sigfrid 1932- *St&PR 91, WhoAm 90*
Carlson, Ronald Joseph 1950- *St&PR 91*
Carlson, Ronald Lee 1934- *WhoAm 90*
Carlson, Roy Perry Merritt 1923- *WhoAm 90*
Carlson, Ruggles B. 1933- *St&PR 91*
Carlson, Russell Charles 1926- *WhoAm 90*
Carlson, Russell L. 1923- *St&PR 91*
Carlson, Ruth Ellen 1952- *WhoAmW 91*
Carlson, Samuel La Verne 1936- *St&PR 91*
Carlson, Sarah Ann 1966- *WhoAmW 91*
Carlson, Sarah Raup 1955- *WhoEmL 91*
Carlson, Scott Alexander 1955- *St&PR 91*
Carlson, Stephen Curtis 1951- *WhoEmL 91*
Carlson, Stephen Oscar 1937- *St&PR 91*
Carlson, Suzanne Olive 1939- *WhoAm 90*
Carlson, Sven Hjalmar George 1916- *WhoE 91*
Carlson, Theodore Joshua 1919- *WhoAm 90, WhoE 91, WhoWor 91*
Carlson, Thomas Joseph 1953- *WhoAm 90*
Carlson, Timothy Don 1952- *BiDrAPA 89*
Carlson, Timothy P. 1938- *St&PR 91*
Carlson, Tina Marie 1958- *WhoAmW 91*
Carlson, Vada F. 1897- *AuBYP 90*
Carlson, Wallace *EncACom*
Carlson, Walter 1928- *ODwPR 91*
Carlson, Wayne Edward 1946- *WhoEmL 91*
Carlson, Wendell R. 1936- *WhoWrEP 89*
Carlson, William D. 1945- *WhoEmL 91*
Carlson, William D 1950- *WhoAmA 91*
Carlson, William Dwight 1928- *WhoAm 90*
Carlson-Pickering, Jane 1954- *WhoE 91*
Carlsson, Bernt 1938-1988 *BioIn 16*
Carlsson, Gunnar Erik 1952- *WhoAm 90*
Carlsson, Ingvar 1934- *BioIn 16*
Carlsson, Ingvar Gosta 1934- *WhoWor 91*
Carlsson, Jan Olof 1935- *WhoWor 91*
Carlsson, Percy Allan 1927- *WhoAm 90, WhoSSW 91*
Carlsson, Roine 1937- *WhoWor 91*
Carlstroem, Charles Mark 1955- *BiDrAPA 89*
Carlstrom, David E. *St&PR 91*
Carlstrom, Lucinda 1950- *WhoAmA 91*
Carlstrom, Nancy White *AuBYP 90*
Carlstrom, Nancy White 1948- *BioIn 16*
Carlstrom, Richard A. 1943- *St&PR 91*
Carlton 1881-1942 *BioIn 16*
Carlton, Alfred Pershing, Jr. 1947- *WhoEmL 91*
Carlton, Barry S *BiDrAPA 89*
Carlton, Bob 1950- *ConTFT 8*
Carlton, Bruce C. 1935- *St&PR 91*
Carlton, Carol Lee 1941- *WhoAmW 91*
Carlton, Charles Merritt 1928- *WhoAm 90*
Carlton, Claudia Dowdy 1955- *WhoAmW 91*
Carlton, Dean 1928- *WhoAm 90*
Carlton, Dennis William 1951- *WhoAm 90*

Carlton, Diane Michele 1950- *WhoEmL 91*
Carlton, Donald James 1947- *WhoEmL 91*
Carlton, Donald Morrill 1937- *WhoAm 90*
Carlton, Gerald Grant 1935- *St&PR 91*
Carlton, Irvin L 1924- *BiDrAPA 89*
Carlton, Joe R. 1923- *St&PR 91*
Carlton, Keith *AuBYP 90*
Carlton, Larry *BioIn 16*
Carlton, Lawrence Sumner 1924- *WhoE 91*
Carlton, Lonnie Calvin 1949- *WhoSSW 91*
Carlton, Marion Clade 1917- *WhoAmW 91*
Carlton, Mary Powell 1925- *St&PR 91*
Carlton, Michael Will 1936- *St&PR 91*
Carlton, Patrick William 1937- *WhoSSW 91*
Carlton, Paul Kendall 1921- *WhoAm 90*
Carlton, Richard Anthony 1951- *WhoWor 91*
Carlton, Richard H. 1943- *ODwPR 91*
Carlton, Richard M 1943- *BiDrAPA 89*
Carlton, Richard P. 1893-1953 *WorAlBi*
Carlton, Robert Bruce 1948- *WhoE 91*
Carlton, Steve *BioIn 16*
Carlton, Steve 1944- *Ballpl 90 [port], WorAlBi*
Carlton, Terry Scott 1939- *WhoAm 90*
Carlton, Thomas Grant 1943- *BiDrAPA 89*
Carlton, Will Yarborough *BiDrAPA 89*
Carlton, William L. 1945- *St&PR 91*
Carlton-Jones, Dennis 1930- *St&PR 91*
Carlu, Jean 1900- *ConDes 90*
Carlucci, Frank Charles *BioIn 16*
Carlucci, Frank Charles, III 1930- *BiDrUSE 89, WhoAm 90, WhoWor 91*
Carlyle, Jane 1801-1866 *FemiCLE*
Carlyle, Jane Welsh 1801-1866 *BioIn 16*
Carlyle, Joan Hildred 1931- *IntWWM 90*
Carlyle, Thomas 1795-1881 *BioIn 16, WorAlBi, WrPh*
Carlyon, Don J. 1924- *WhoAm 90*
Carlyon, Richard *BioIn 16*
Carlyss, Earl *PenDiMP*
Carlyss, Earl Winston 1939- *WhoAm 90*
Carlzon, Jan *BioIn 16*
Carlzon, Jan 1941- *WhoWor 91*
Carmack, Comer A., Jr. 1932- *St&PR 91*
Carmack, David English 1938- *WhoE 91*
Carmack, George 1907- *WhoAm 90*
Carmack, Paul R 1895-1977 *WhoAmA 91N*
Carmack, Paula Lenora 1951- *WhoAmW 91*
Carman, A.C., Mrs. *LiHiK*
Carman, Bliss 1861-1929 *DcLB 92 [port]*
Carman, Don 1959- *Ballpl 90*
Carman, Elaine Marion 1950- *WhoE 91*
Carman, George Henry 1928- *WhoAm 90*
Carman, Gregory Wright 1937- *WhoAm 90*
Carman, Holly Lynn 1953- *WhoAmW 91*
Carman, Hoy Fred 1938- *WhoAm 90*
Carman, James Russell 1920- *WhoE 91*
Carman, John Elwin 1946- *WhoAm 90*
Carman, John Scott *BiDrAPA 89*
Carman, Juanita Chenault 1923- *WhoWrEP 89*
Carman, Laura Junge 1952- *WhoSSW 91*
Carman, LauraLee 1964- *WhoAmW 91*
Carman, Michael Dennis 1938- *WhoAm 90*
Carman, Susan Lea 1952- *WhoWrEP 89*
Carman, Thomas W. 1951- *St&PR 91*
Carman, Toni Louise 1943- *BiDrAPA 89*
Carmazzi, R. Frank 1950- *WhoSSW 91*
Carmazzi, Robert Frank 1950- *St&PR 91*
Carmean, D.W. 1944- *St&PR 91*
Carmean, E A, Jr 1945- *WhoAmA 91*
Carmean, Jerry Richard 1938- *WhoWor 91*
Carmean, Michael L. 1945- *St&PR 91*
Carmel, Alan Stuart 1944- *WhoAm 90*
Carmel, Harold *BiDrAPA 89*
Carmel, Ida F *BiDrAPA 89*
Carmel, Simon Jacob 1938- *WhoAm 90*
Carmell, Pamela Lee 1950- *WhoWrEP 89*
Carmen, Dave 1948- *WhoE 91*
Carmen, Elaine *BiDrAPA 89*
Carmen, Elaine 1939- *WhoE 91*
Carmen, Eric *BioIn 16*
Carmen, Ira Harris 1934- *WhoAm 90, WhoWor 91*
Carmen, Julie *WhoHisp 91*
Carmen, Lawrence M 1926- *BiDrAPA 89*
Carmen Rubio y Lopez Guijarro, Maria del 1915- *EncCoWW*
Carmer, Carl Lamson 1893-1976 *AuBYP 90*
Carmer, Elizabeth 1904- *AuBYP 90*
Carmer, James Edward 1956- *St&PR 91*
Carmi, Eugenio 1920- *ConDes 90*
Carmi, Shlomo 1937- *WhoAm 90*
Carmichael, Alexander Douglas 1929- *WhoAm 90*
Carmichael, Amy *BioIn 16*
Carmichael, Ann Crocker 1955- *WhoAmW 91*
Carmichael, Anne Gaye 1961- *WhoEmL 91*
Carmichael, Archibald Hill 1864- *AmLegL*
Carmichael, Bruce Fenton 1946- *WhoE 91*
Carmichael, Carson, III 1954- *WhoEmL 91*
Carmichael, Carson, Jr. 1928- *St&PR 91*
Carmichael, Charles Wesley 1919- *WhoWor 91*
Carmichael, Charlotte Marie Breeden 1945- *WhoAmW 91*
Carmichael, David Burton 1923- *WhoAm 90*
Carmichael, David Edward 1947- *St&PR 91*
Carmichael, Deborah Murray 1956- *WhoEmL 91*
Carmichael, Dennis D 1927- *BiDrAPA 89*
Carmichael, Donald Ray 1922- *WhoAmA 91*
Carmichael, Donald Scott 1912- *WhoAm 90, WhoE 91*
Carmichael, Douglas 1923- *WhoAm 90*
Carmichael, Gilbert E. *WhoAm 90*
Carmichael, Harry 1908-1979 *TwCCr&M 91*
Carmichael, Harry W. 1922- *St&PR 91*
Carmichael, Hoagy 1899-1981 *OxCPMus, WorAlBi*
Carmichael, Hoagy 1899-1982 *BioIn 16*
Carmichael, Hugh 1906- *WhoAm 90*
Carmichael, Ian 1920- *ConAu 129, OxCPMus, WorAlBi*
Carmichael, Ian Stuart Edward 1930- *WhoAm 90*
Carmichael, Jae 1925- *WhoAmA 91*
Carmichael, James Dolph 1947- *WhoEmL 91*
Carmichael, Joel 1915- *AuBYP 90*
Carmichael, John P. 1902-1986 *Ballpl 90*
Carmichael, Joseph Patrick 1954- *St&PR 91*
Carmichael, Katherine Ann 1962- *WhoE 91*
Carmichael, Mary Mulloy 1916- *WhoAm 90*
Carmichael, Nelson *BioIn 16*
Carmichael, Richard Dudley 1942- *WhoSSW 91*
Carmichael, Robert William 1958- *WhoE 91*
Carmichael, Rowena Mary 1957- *IntWWM 90*
Carmichael, Sarah Elizabeth 1838-1901 *FemiCLE*
Carmichael, Stokely 1941- *BioIn 16, WorAlBi*
Carmichael, Sumter Miller *BiDrAPA 89*
Carmichael, Vicki 1950- *St&PR 91*
Carmichael, Virgil Wesly 1919- *WhoAm 90, WhoWor 91*
Carmichael, William Clyde 1942- *St&PR 91*
Carmichael, William Daniel 1929- *WhoAm 90*
Carmichael, William G 1925- *BiDrAPA 89*
Carmichael, William Jerome 1920- *WhoAm 90*
Carmien, J. Allen 1919- *St&PR 91*
Carmin, Robert Leighton 1918- *WhoAm 90*
Carmine, Leonard G. *ODwPR 91*
Carmine, Michael *BioIn 16*
Carmines, Pamela Kay 1955- *WhoAmW 91*
Carmirelli, Pina 1914- *PenDiMP*
Carmo 1881-1944 *BioIn 16*
Carmo, Antoninho Martinez 1940- *WhoWor 91*
Carmody, Ann K. *ODwPR 91*
Carmody, Arthur Roderick, Jr. 1928- *WhoAm 90, WhoWor 91*
Carmody, Charles Stuart 1960- *WhoSSW 91*
Carmody, Dennis Patrick 1948- *WhoEmL 91*
Carmody, George Edward 1931- *WhoE 91*
Carmody, James Albert 1945- *WhoEmL 91, WhoWor 91*
Carmody, Margaret Jean 1924- *WhoE 91*
Carmody, Robert Edward 1942- *WhoE 91, WhoWor 91*
Carmody, Susan Dolores 1953- *WhoAmW 91*
Carmody, Thomas Gaughan 1932- *St&PR 91*
Carmody, Thomas R. 1933- *St&PR 91*
Carmody, Thomas Roswell 1933- *WhoAm 90, WhoSSW 91*
Carmody, Victor Wallace, Jr. 1945- *WhoSSW 91*
Carmody, William Joseph 1945- *IntWWM 90*
Carmody-Arey, Christine 1938- *WhoAmW 91*
Carmon, James Foster 1941- *St&PR 91*
Carmona, Alicia Teresa 1942- *BiDrAPA 89*
Carmona, Benhur 1960- *WhoHisp 91*
Carmona, Walter *BiDrAPA 89*
Carmony, Donald Duane 1935- *WhoAm 90*
Carmony, Kevin Brackett 1959- *WhoEmL 91, WhoWor 91*
Carmony, Larry Glen 1960- *St&PR 91*
Carmony, Marvin Dale 1923- *WhoAm 90*
Carnac, Carol 1894-1958 *TwCCr&M 91*
Carnaggio, Charles Samuel 1948- *St&PR 91*
Carnahan, Brice 1933- *WhoAm 90*
Carnahan, C. Earl 1935- *St&PR 91*
Carnahan, Danny *NewAgMG*
Carnahan, David E. 1943- *St&PR 91*
Carnahan, Frances Morris 1937- *WhoAm 90, WhoAmW 91*
Carnahan, Frances Morris 1947- *WhoWrEP 89*
Carnahan, John Anderson 1930- *WhoAm 90*
Carnahan, John Mitchell 1934- *St&PR 91*
Carnahan, Lew Wallace 1946- *WhoEmL 91*
Carnahan, Marjorie R. *AuBYP 90*
Carnahan, Marvin R. 1941- *WhoWor 91*
Carnahan, Mel Eugene 1934- *WhoAm 90*
Carnahan, Orville Darrell 1929- *WhoAm 90*
Carnahan, Robert G 1913- *BiDrAPA 89*
Carnall, John Victor 1948- *WhoE 91*
Carnase, Thomas Paul 1939- *WhoAm 90*
Carnaval, Charles William 1952- *St&PR 91*
Carne, Marcel *BioIn 16*
Carne, Marcel Albert 1906- *WhoWor 91*
Carneal, Ann Holland Stambaugh 1947- *WhoSSW 91*
Carneal, George Upshur 1935- *WhoAm 90*
Carneal, James William 1918- *WhoAm 90*
Carnegie, Andrew 1835-1919 *BioIn 16, WorAlBi*
Carnegie, Dale 1888-1955 *BioIn 16, WorAlBi*
Carnegie, Deborah Mary 1952- *WhoEmL 91*
Carnegie, Lawrence Gales 1944- *WhoE 91*
Carneiro da Cunha Neto, Jose Maria 1942- *WhoSSW 91*
Carnell, Judith M. 1943- *WhoWrEP 89*
Carnell, Paul Herbert 1917- *WhoAm 90*
Carnella, Frank Thomas 1934- *St&PR 91*
Carner, Gary Raymond 1955- *IntWWM 90*
Carner, Joanne 1939- *WorAlBi*
Carner, William John 1948- *WhoEmL 91, WhoWor 91*
Carnera, Giovanna Maria 1947- *WhoAmW 91*
Carnes, Ben *BioIn 16*
Carnes, Betty 1905-1987 *BioIn 16*
Carnes, Clarence *BioIn 16*
Carnes, James Edward 1939- *WhoAm 90*
Carnes, James Robert 1909- *WhoAm 90*
Carnes, Kim 1947?- *EncPR&S 89*
Carnes, Kim 1948- *ConMus 4 [port]*
Carnes, Lamar 1923- *WhoSSW 91, WhoWor 91*
Carnes, Mark C 1950- *ConAu 30NR*
Carnes, Michael P. C. *WhoAm 90*
Carnes, Neil Patrick 1953- *WhoEmL 91*
Carnes, Patty *BioIn 16*
Carnes, R. Nelson 1932- *St&PR 91*
Carnes, Richard Albert 1940- *WhoSSW 91*
Carnes, Sam Abbott, Jr. 1946- *WhoSSW 91*
Carnes, Thomas Alton 1953- *WhoSSW 91*
Carnes, Wilson Woodrow 1924- *WhoAm 90*
Carnese, Paul Joseph, Jr. 1926- *WhoAm 90*
Carnesecca, Lou *BioIn 16*
Carnevale, Sally London 1954- *WhoAmW 91*
Carnevali, Emanuele 1897-1940? *BioIn 16*
Carnevall, Doris L. *WhoWrEP 89*
Carney, Art *BioIn 16*
Carney, Art 1918- *WorAlBi*
Carney, Arthur William Matthew 1918- *WhoAm 90*
Carney, Charles Seymour 1920- *WhoWrEP 89*
Carney, Claire T. *St&PR 91*
Carney, Claire Therese 1922- *WhoAmW 91*
Carney, Cynthia Claire 1961- *WhoSSW 91*
Carney, Deborah Leah Turner 1952- *WhoEmL 91*
Carney, Dennis Joseph 1921- *WhoAm 90*
Carney, Donald F., Jr. 1948- *WhoEmL 91*
Carney, Edward James 1930- *St&PR 91*
Carney, Frank Thomas 1956- *WhoEmL 91*
Carney, Gregory John 1946- *St&PR 91*
Carney, Harry 1910-1974 *OxCPMus*
Carney, Heath Joseph 1955- *WhoEmL 91*
Carney, Henry Allen 1939- *St&PR 91*
Carney, James Francis *BioIn 16*
Carney, Jean Kathryn 1948- *WhoAmW 91*
Carney, John D. 1944- *St&PR 91*
Carney, John Henry, Jr. 1964- *WhoEmL 91*
Carney, Joseph Patrick 1939- *WhoE 91*
Carney, Karen Lynne 1959- *WhoE 91*
Carney, Kate 1869-1950 *OxCPMus*
Carney, Kathleen L. 1947- *WhoAmW 91*
Carney, Kathy Klein *BiDrAPA 89*
Carney, Kay 1933- *WhoAmW 91*
Carney, Kim 1925- *WhoAm 90*
Carney, Nell Cardwell 1945- *WhoAm 90*
Carney, Pat 1876-1953 *Ballpl 90*
Carney, Patrick 1948- *St&PR 91*
Carney, Peter Roy 1931- *St&PR 91*
Carney, Phillita Toyia 1952- *WhoAmW 91*
Carney, Pomp Temple *BiDrAPA 89*
Carney, Raymond 1950- *WhoSSW 91*
Carney, Richard S. 1927- *St&PR 91*
Carney, Robert Alfred 1916- *WhoAm 90*
Carney, Robert Arthur 1937- *St&PR 91*
Carney, Robert B 1895-1990 *CurBio 90N, NewYTBS 90 [port]*
Carney, Robert Emmet *BiDrAPA 89*
Carney, Robert Thomas 1945- *WhoEmL 91*
Carney, Roger Francis Xavier 1933- *WhoE 91*
Carney, Thomas Daly 1947- *St&PR 91*
Carney, Thomas J.T. 1952- *WhoEmL 91*
Carney, Thomas Quentin 1949- *WhoEmL 91*
Carney, Vaden Jackson 1951- *St&PR 91*
Carney, W. Peter 1932- *ODwPR 91, St&PR 91*
Carney, William Paul 1941- *BiDrAPA 89*
Carney, William Ray 1940- *WhoAm 90*
Carney, William Vincent 1937- *St&PR 91*
Carniato, Donald Emmanual 1947- *WhoE 91*
Carnicero, Jorge E. 1921- *St&PR 91*
Carnicero, Jorge Emilio 1921- *WhoAm 90, WhoSSW 91*
Carnicke, Sharon Marie 1949- *WhoAmW 91*
Carnicom, Gene E. 1944- *WhoWor 91*
Carnie, Mary Catherine 1938- *WhoAmW 91*
Carniglia, Sherry *WhoAmW 91*
Carniglia, Stephen Davis 1950- *WhoAm 90*
Carnine, Roy Leland 1949- *WhoEmL 91*
Carniol, Paul J. 1951- *WhoE 91*
Carnival, John A. 1944- *St&PR 91*
Carnley, Samuel Fleetwood 1918- *WhoSSW 91*
Carnochan, Walter Bliss 1930- *WhoAm 90*
Carnogursky, Jan *WhoWor 91*
Carnohan, Christopher Patrick 1953- *WhoEmL 91*
Carnot, Gaetan 1938- *WhoWor 91*
Carnot, Lazare Nicholas Marguerite 1753-1823 *BioIn 16*
Carnot, Marie Francois Sadi 1837-1894 *BiDFrPL*
Carnot, Nicolas-Leonard Sadi 1796-1832 *WorAlBi*
Carnota-Cohen, Lidia Ruth *BiDrAPA 89*
Carnovale, Marco 1959- *WhoWor 91*
Carnow, Bertram W. *St&PR 91*
Carnoy, Martin 1938- *WhoAm 90*
Carnwath, Francis Anthony 1940- *WhoWor 91*
Carnwath, Squeak 1947- *WhoAmA 91*
Caro, Albert Joseph 1938- *St&PR 91*
Caro, Alfred 1931- *St&PR 91*
Caro, Anthony 1924- *BioIn 16, WhoWor 91*
Caro, Charles Crawford 1946- *WhoEmL 91, WhoSSW 91, WhoWor 91*
Caro, Francis 1938- *WhoAmA 91*
Caro, Ivor 1946- *WhoAm 90, WhoEmL 91*
Caro, Miguel Antonio 1843-1909 *BioIn 16*
Caro, Pauline 1835-1901 *EncCoWW*
Caro, Rafael 1952- *WhoHisp 91*
Caro, Robert A. *BioIn 16*
Caro, Warren 1907- *WhoAm 90*
Caro, William Allan 1934- *WhoAm 90*
Caro Mallen de Soto, Ana 1600?-1645? *EncCoWW*
Caroe, Olaf Kirkpatrick Krunse 1892-1981 *DcNaB 1981*
Caroff, Phyllis M. 1924- *WhoAm 90*
Caroff, Stanley N 1949- *BiDrAPA 89*
Caroff, Stanley Nathan 1949- *WhoE 91*
Carol, Jean J. 1937- *ODwPR 91*
Carolan, Douglas *WhoAm 90*
Carolan, Douglas M. 1942- *St&PR 91*
Carolan, James Anthony 1953- *WhoEmL 91*
Carolan, Vincent L. 1930- *St&PR 91*
Carolin, Carol A. 1948- *WhoE 91*
Carolin, Carol Anne *WhoAmW 91*
Carolin, Charles A. 1915- *St&PR 91*
Caroline, Princess of Monaco *BioIn 16*
Carollo, James Paul 1946- *St&PR 91*
Carolsfeld, Ludwig Schnorr von 1836-1865 *BioIn 16*
Carolus, James P. 1951- *St&PR 91*
Caron, Alan R. 1951- *St&PR 91*
Caron, Arthur Eugene 1937- *St&PR 91*
Caron, Chantal *BiDrAPA 89*

Caron, David Dennis 1952- *WhoEmL 91*
Caron, Edouard 1830-1900 *DcCanB 12*
Caron, Glenn *BioIn 16*
Caron, John B. 1924- *St&PR 91*
Caron, Leslie 1931- *WhoAm 90, WorAlBi*
Caron, Paul Lawrence 1957- *WhoEmL 91*
Caron, Phillip Anthony 1954- *WhoEmL 91*
Caron, Raymond 1906- *St&PR 91*
Caron-Parker, Laura Marie 1959- *WhoAmW 91, WhoEmL 91*
Carona, Philip 1925- *AuBYP 90*
Carondelet, Francois Louis Hector De 1748?-1807 *EncCRAm*
Carone, Frank 1927- *WhoAm 90*
Carone, Pasquale A 1914- *BiDrAPA 89*
Carone, Patrick F 1944- *BiDrAPA 89*
Carone, Richard C. *St&PR 91*
Carosella, Nicholas William *BiDrAPA 89*
Carosi, Alfred Charles, Jr. *BioIn 16, WhoAm 90*
Carosio, Margherita 1908- *IntWWM 90*
Carossa, Hans 1878-1956 *BioIn 16*
Carosso, Vincent Phillip 1922- *WhoAm 90*
Carota, Elvira M *BiDrAPA 89*
Carota, Richard J. 1937- *St&PR 91*
Carotenuto, Ralph Joseph 1945- *BiDrAPA 89*
Carothers, Barbara 1954- *WhoEmL 91*
Carothers, Charles Omsted 1923- *WhoAm 90*
Carothers, Durell 1909- *St&PR 91*
Carothers, Richard Alton 1935- *WhoAm 90*
Carothers, Robert Lee 1942- *WhoAm 90*
Carothers, Sean Brown *St&PR 91*
Carothers, Steven Michael 1954- *WhoAm 90, WhoEmL 91, WhoSSW 91*
Carothers, Wallace H. 1896-1937 *WorAlBi*
Carothers, Wallace Hume *BioIn 16*
Carousso, Dorothee Hughes 1909- *WhoE 91*
Caroutch, Yvonne 1937- *EncCoWW*
Carovano, John Martin 1935- *WhoAm 90*
Carow, Marsha S. 1942- *St&PR 91*
Carozza, Davy Angelo 1926- *WhoAm 90*
Carozza, Gerald Nicholas, Jr. 1960- *WhoEmL 91*
Carozza, William Victor 1961- *WhoE 91*
Carozzi, Albert Victor 1925- *WhoAm 90*
Carozzolo, Shirley Jean 1935- *WhoAmW 91*
Carp, Richard Irvin 1934- *WhoAm 90*
Carp, Richard Lawrence 1926- *WhoAm 90*
Carpaccio, Vittore 1465?-1526? *IntDcAA 90, WorAlBi*
Carpathios, Neil Emmanuel 1961- *WhoWrEP 89*
Carpel, Kenneth Richard 1941- *St&PR 91*
Carpelan, Bo Gustaf Berelsson 1926- *DcScanL*
Carpeneto, Gloria Ray 1947- *WhoAm 90*
Carpenter, Allan 1917- *WhoAm 90, WhoWrEP 89*
Carpenter, Amy B. 1956- *St&PR 91*
Carpenter, Anna-Mary Passier 1916- *WhoAm 90*
Carpenter, Arthur Espenet *WhoAmA 91*
Carpenter, Ben 1936- *WhoWrEP 89*
Carpenter, Ben H. 1924- *St&PR 91*
Carpenter, Benjamin Harrison, Jr. 1921- *WhoSSW 91*
Carpenter, Bill *Ballpl 90*
Carpenter, Bob 1917- *Ballpl 90*
Carpenter, Bobby R. 1947- *St&PR 91*
Carpenter, Bruce H. 1932- *WhoAm 90*
Carpenter, C. Neal 1932- *St&PR 91*
Carpenter, Carl Hatten 1932- *WhoAm 90*
Carpenter, Carlton Lanier 1930- *WhoSSW 91*
Carpenter, Carol Settle 1953- *WhoAmW 91*
Carpenter, Charles Bernard 1933- *WhoAm 90*
Carpenter, Charles Colcock Jones 1931- *WhoAm 90*
Carpenter, Charles Congden 1921- *WhoAm 90*
Carpenter, Charles D. 1946- *St&PR 91*
Carpenter, Charles Elford, Jr. 1944- *WhoSSW 91, WhoWor 91*
Carpenter, Christy 1949- *WhoAmW 91*
Carpenter, Clark Gilbert 1936- *St&PR 91*
Carpenter, Clayton D. 1940- *St&PR 91*
Carpenter, Cris 1965- *Ballpl 90*
Carpenter, Darrell Franklin 1955- *WhoEmL 91*
Carpenter, David Lloyd 1947- *WhoEmL 91*
Carpenter, David Roland 1939- *St&PR 91, WhoAm 90*
Carpenter, David William 1950- *WhoEmL 91*
Carpenter, Delma Rae, Jr. 1928- *WhoAm 90*
Carpenter, Dennis Wilkinson 1947- *WhoAmA 91*
Carpenter, Derr Alvin 1931- *WhoAm 90*
Carpenter, Donald Alfred 1907- *WhoWor 91*
Carpenter, Donald Blodgett 1916- *WhoWor 91*
Carpenter, Dorothy Fulton 1933- *WhoAmW 91*
Carpenter, Doug 1944- *WhoAm 90, WhoE 91*
Carpenter, Douglas Bruce 1936- *St&PR 91*
Carpenter, Earl L 1931- *WhoAmA 91*
Carpenter, Ed 1946?- *BioIn 16*
Carpenter, Edmund M. 1941- *St&PR 91*
Carpenter, Edmund Mogford 1941- *WhoAm 90, WhoE 91*
Carpenter, Edmund Nelson, II 1921- *WhoE 91, WhoWor 91*
Carpenter, Edmund Snow 1922- *AuBYP 90*
Carpenter, Edward 1844-1929 *BioIn 16*
Carpenter, Edward Monroe 1930- *St&PR 91*
Carpenter, Edward William 1955- *WhoSSW 91*
Carpenter, Elizabeth Jane 1949- *WhoAmW 91*
Carpenter, Elizabeth Sutherland 1920- *WhoAm 90, WhoAmW 91, WhoWrEP 89*
Carpenter, F. Scott *St&PR 91*
Carpenter, Frances 1890-1972 *AuBYP 90*
Carpenter, Frank A. 1925- *St&PR 91*
Carpenter, Frank Morton 1902- *WhoAm 90*
Carpenter, Frank Wilkinson 1931- *WhoAm 90*
Carpenter, Freddie 1908-1989 *ConTFT 8*
Carpenter, Gene Blakely 1922- *WhoAm 90*
Carpenter, Gene F. 1931- *St&PR 91*
Carpenter, George Thomas, III 1955- *BiDrAPA 89*
Carpenter, Gideon Judd 1823-1910 *AmLegL*
Carpenter, Gilbert Frederick 1920- *WhoAm 90, WhoAmA 91*
Carpenter, Gordon Russell 1920- *WhoSSW 91*
Carpenter, H. Paul 1927- *St&PR 91*
Carpenter, Healy Evans *AuBYP 90*
Carpenter, Henry Alan 1950- *St&PR 91*
Carpenter, Howard Grant, Jr. 1939- *St&PR 91, WhoAm 90*
Carpenter, Howard Ralph 1919- *IntWWM 90*
Carpenter, Hoyle Dameron 1909- *WhoE 91*
Carpenter, Humphrey 1946- *WorAu 1980 [port]*
Carpenter, Iris *BioIn 16*
Carpenter, J. Robert 1936- *WhoSSW 91*
Carpenter, Jake Burton *BioIn 16*
Carpenter, James Arthur 1939- *St&PR 91*
Carpenter, James Craig 1949- *WhoEmL 91*
Carpenter, James Morton 1914- *WhoAm 90, WhoAmA 91*
Carpenter, James W. 1932- *St&PR 91*
Carpenter, Jewel C. 1946- *WhoSSW 91*
Carpenter, John *BioIn 16*
Carpenter, John 1948- *ConTFT 8, WorAlBi*
Carpenter, John Henry 1854-1905 *AmLegL*
Carpenter, John Howard 1948- *WhoAm 90*
Carpenter, John Marland 1935- *WhoAm 90*
Carpenter, John Randell 1936- *WhoWrEP 89*
Carpenter, John William *BiDrAPA 89*
Carpenter, John Wilson, III 1916- *WhoAm 90*
Carpenter, Joseph E., Jr. 1953- *St&PR 91*
Carpenter, Joseph Robert 1934- *St&PR 91*
Carpenter, Jot David 1938- *WhoAm 90*
Carpenter, Karen 1950-1983 *BioIn 16, EncPR&S 89, OxCPMus, WorAlBi*
Carpenter, Karen H. 1943- *St&PR 91*
Carpenter, Kathryn Lyn 1961- *WhoAmW 91*
Carpenter, Kenneth B 1932- *BiDrAPA 89*
Carpenter, Kenneth E. 1936- *WhoAm 90*
Carpenter, Kenneth John 1923- *WhoAm 90*
Carpenter, Kevin Starr 1954- *WhoEmL 91*
Carpenter, Larry H. 1947- *St&PR 91*
Carpenter, Larry Horace 1947- *WhoAm 90*
Carpenter, Linda Buck 1952- *WhoAmA 91*
Carpenter, Linda Leigh 1960- *WhoAmW 91*
Carpenter, Lon P. 1936- *St&PR 91*
Carpenter, Lorne E *BiDrAPA 89*
Carpenter, Malcolm Breckenridge 1921- *WhoAm 90*
Carpenter, Malcolm Scott 1925- *WorAlBi*
Carpenter, Margaret Sarah 1793-1872 *BiDWomA*
Carpenter, Mark Joseph 1953- *WhoEmL 91*
Carpenter, Marshall L. 1937- *St&PR 91*
Carpenter, Marshall Le Roy 1937- *WhoAm 90*
Carpenter, Mary 1807-1877 *BioIn 16*
Carpenter, Mary Chapin *WhoNeCM*
Carpenter, Mary Laure 1953- *WhoAmW 91, WhoWor 91*
Carpenter, Mary Paige Abeel 1950- *WhoAmW 91*
Carpenter, Michael Alan 1947- *BioIn 16, St&PR 91*
Carpenter, Michele Annette 1964- *WhoWrEP 89*
Carpenter, Miles Burkholder 1889-1985 *MusmAFA*
Carpenter, Mimi Gregoire 1947- *ConAu 30NR*
Carpenter, Miriam Charlotte 1932- *WhoAmW 91, WhoSSW 91*
Carpenter, Myron Arthur 1938- *St&PR 91, WhoAm 90*
Carpenter, Nan Cooke 1912- *IntWWM 90*
Carpenter, Nancy A. 1944- *St&PR 91*
Carpenter, Nancy Carol 1956- *WhoAmW 91*
Carpenter, Nancy Sumrall 1955- *WhoSSW 91*
Carpenter, Noble O. 1929- *St&PR 91*
Carpenter, Noble Olds 1929- *WhoAm 90*
Carpenter, Norman Roblee 1932- *WhoAm 90, WhoWor 91*
Carpenter, Patricia 1920- *WhoAmW 91, WhoWrEP 89*
Carpenter, Patricia 1923- *WhoAm 90*
Carpenter, Paul Leonard 1920- *St&PR 91, WhoAm 90*
Carpenter, Peter F. 1940- *St&PR 91*
Carpenter, Philip David 1943- *WhoAm 90*
Carpenter, Raymond Leonard 1926- *WhoSSW 91*
Carpenter, Richard 1945- *EncPR&S 89*
Carpenter, Richard 1946- *OxCPMus*
Carpenter, Richard Amon 1926- *WhoAm 90*
Carpenter, Richard Michael 1943- *St&PR 91*
Carpenter, Robert Beach 1930- *WhoAm 90*
Carpenter, Robert Douglas 1925- *St&PR 91*
Carpenter, Robert Durward 1932- *WhoWor 91*
Carpenter, Robert Eddy 1924- *St&PR 91*
Carpenter, Robert Eugene 1929- *WhoSSW 91*
Carpenter, Robert Hunt 1948- *WhoSSW 91*
Carpenter, Robert James 1945- *WhoAm 90*
Carpenter, Robert Wayne 1949- *WhoEmL 91*
Carpenter, Roberta Lynn 1948- *WhoAmW 91*
Carpenter, Sandra Mitchell 1934- *St&PR 91*
Carpenter, Stanley Waterman 1921- *WhoE 91*
Carpenter, Stephen G. 1940- *St&PR 91*
Carpenter, Steve 1954- *WhoSSW 91*
Carpenter, Steven David 1953- *WhoSSW 91*
Carpenter, Susan Karen 1951- *WhoAm 90, WhoAmW 91*
Carpenter, Ted Galen 1947- *WhoAm 90*
Carpenter, Thelma 1922- *DrBIPA 90*
Carpenter, Thomas A. *St&PR 91*
Carpenter, Thomas Edgar, III 1936- *WhoAm 90*
Carpenter, Thomas Glenn 1926- *WhoAm 90, WhoSSW 91*
Carpenter, Thomas Oliver 1952- *WhoE 91*
Carpenter, Tim *BioIn 16*
Carpenter, Wallace Wright 1923- *St&PR 91*
Carpenter, Wayne Lewis 1945- *WhoEmL 91*
Carpenter, Wendy Joan 1955- *WhoAmW 91*
Carpenter, Will Dockery 1930- *St&PR 91, WhoAm 90*
Carpenter, William 1940- *WhoWrEP 89*
Carpenter, William Levy 1926- *WhoAm 90*
Carpenter, William T, Jr. 1936- *BiDrAPA 89*
Carpenter, Woodrow Wilson 1915- *St&PR 91*
Carpenter-Gorka, Barbara Jo 1951- *WhoAmW 91*
Carpenter-Mason, Beverly Nadine 1933- *WhoAmW 91, WhoE 91, WhoWor 91*
Carpenters, The *EncPR&S 89*
Carpentier, Alejo 1904-1980 *BioIn 16, HispWr 90*
Carpentier, Madeleine 1865-1939? *BiDWomA*
Carpentier y Valmont, Alejo 1904-1980 *HispWr 90*
Carpentieri, Theresa A. 1946- *WhoE 91*
Carper, Diane Clements 1945- *WhoAmW 91, WhoSSW 91, WhoWor 91*
Carper, Freda Smith 1953- *WhoAmW 91, WhoEmL 91*
Carper, Gertrude Esther 1921- *WhoAmW 91, WhoE 91, WhoWor 91*
Carper, Robert Allen 1947- *St&PR 91*
Carper, Thomas Richard 1947- *WhoAm 90, WhoE 91*
Carper, William Barclay 1946- *WhoEmL 91, WhoSSW 91*
Carpi, Aldo 1886-1973 *BioIn 16*
Carpien, Jannet Siegle 1943- *WhoAmW 91*
Carpinello, George Fortune 1950- *WhoE 91*
Carpino, Francesco 1905- *WhoWor 91*
Carpino, Louis A. 1927- *WhoAm 90*
Carpio, Julio Fernando 1947- *WhoHisp 91*
Carpio, Marco T 1936- *BiDrAPA 89*
Carpio Nicolle, Roberto 1930- *WhoWor 91*
Carples, Steven Arthur 1954- *WhoEmL 91*
Carpmael, Charles 1846-1894 *DcCanB 12*
Carpp, Edward Daniel 1952- *WhoE 91, WhoEmL 91*
Carr, Albert Bernard 1930- *WhoWrEP 89*
Carr, Alice Griffith 1887-1968 *BioIn 16*
Carr, Allan *WhoAm 90*
Carr, Alwyn Charles Ellison *PenDiDA 89*
Carr, Anne Elizabeth 1939- *WhoSSW 91*
Carr, Arthur Charles 1918- *WhoAm 90*
Carr, Arthur Henry 1947- *St&PR 91*
Carr, Arthur Japheth 1914- *WhoAm 90*
Carr, Audri Joan 1936- *WhoAmW 91*
Carr, Barbara J. 1950- *WhoAmW 91*
Carr, Barbara Kunkel 1945- *WhoAmW 91*
Carr, Barry Lynn 1953- *WhoEmL 91*
Carr, Bernadette Patricia *WhoAm 90, WhoAmW 91*
Carr, Bernard Francis 1919- *WhoAm 90*
Carr, Bernard John 1949- *EncPaPR 91*
Carr, Bessie 1920- *WhoSSW 91, WhoWor 91*
Carr, Beverly Anne 1942- *WhoAmW 91*
Carr, Bonnie Jean 1947- *WhoAmW 91, WhoWor 91*
Carr, Brenda Sue 1955- *WhoAmW 91*
Carr, Bruce 1938- *IntWWM 90*
Carr, C.A., Jr. 1944- *St&PR 91*
Carr, C. Wesley *St&PR 91*
Carr, Calvin Johnson 1960- *WhoSSW 91*
Carr, Carolyn K 1939- *WhoAmA 91*
Carr, Carolyn Kehlor 1948- *WhoEmL 91, WhoWor 91*
Carr, Carolyn Kinder 1939- *WhoE 91*
Carr, Carolyn Sue Dean 1943- *WhoSSW 91*
Carr, Cassandra C. 1944- *St&PR 91*
Carr, Charles Jelleff 1910- *WhoAm 90*
Carr, Charles William 1917- *WhoAm 90*
Carr, Charlie 1876-1932 *Ballpl 90*
Carr, Christopher C. 1950- *WhoEmL 91*
Carr, Colin Michael 1957- *IntWWM 90*
Carr, Daniel Barry 1948- *WhoWor 91*
Carr, Daniel Paul 1951- *WhoWrEP 89*
Carr, Darleen 1950- *ConTFT 8*
Carr, David 1905-1986 *BioIn 16*
Carr, David Brian 1946- *WhoSSW 91*
Carr, David F. *St&PR 91*
Carr, David Turner 1914- *WhoAm 90*
Carr, Diane Cole 1952- *WhoAmW 91*
Carr, Edward Albert, Jr. 1922- *WhoAm 90*
Carr, Edward Hallett 1892-1982 *BioIn 16, DcNaB 1981*
Carr, Edward S *BiDrAPA 89*
Carr, Emily 1871-1945 *BioIn 16, FemiCLE*
Carr, Eugene Asa 1830-1910 *WhNaAH*
Carr, F. James 1930- *ODwPR 91*
Carr, Frank Joseph 1929- *WhoAm 90*
Carr, Frank Osmond 1858-1916 *OxCPMus*
Carr, George 1895- *Ballpl 90*
Carr, George 1939- *St&PR 91*
Carr, George Carter 1929-1990 *BioIn 16*
Carr, George Francis, Jr. 1939- *WhoAm 90*
Carr, George Leroy 1927- *WhoAm 90*
Carr, George Watts, Jr. 1918- *St&PR 91*
Carr, Gerald Paul 1932- *WhoAm 90*
Carr, Geraldine Marie 1955- *WhoAmW 91, WhoEmL 91*
Carr, Gilbert R. 1928- *St&PR 91*
Carr, Gilbert Randle 1928- *WhoAm 90*
Carr, Glenna Dodson 1927- *WhoAmW 91*
Carr, Glyn 1908- *TwCCr&M 91*
Carr, Hal N. 1921- *St&PR 91*
Carr, Harold Noflet 1921- *WhoAm 90, WhoSSW 91*
Carr, Harriett Helen 1899- *AuBYP 90*
Carr, Hobart Cecil 1912-1990 *BioIn 16*
Carr, Howard Earl 1915- *WhoAm 90*
Carr, Howard Ernest 1908- *WhoSSW 91*
Carr, Hubert F. 1920-1989 *BioIn 16*
Carr, Hubert Franklin 1920- *WhoWor 91*
Carr, Hugh Emerson 1932- *St&PR 91*
Carr, Hugh Verne, Jr. 1952- *WhoSSW 91*
Carr, Jack David 1938- *St&PR 91*
Carr, Jack Neerken 1936- *BiDrAPA 89*
Carr, Jack Richard 1937- *St&PR 91, WhoAm 90*
Carr, James Duncan 1938- *St&PR 91*
Carr, James Francis 1946- *WhoEmL 91*

Carr, James Michael 1950- *WhoEmL 91*
Carr, James Patrick 1950- *WhoEmL 91*
Carr, James Saunders 1947- *WhoE 91*
Carr, Jay Phillip 1936- *WhoAm 90, WhoE 91*
Carr, Jeffrey *BioIn 16*
Carr, Jess 1930-1990 *ConAu 130*
Carr, Jesse Metteau, III 1952- *WhoEmL 91, WhoSSW 91*
Carr, John Dickson 1906-1976 *WorAlBi*
Carr, John Dickson 1906-1977 *ConAu 33NR, MajTwCW, TwCCr&M 91*
Carr, John Geoffrey 1927-1987 *BioIn 16*
Carr, John Hampton 1939- *WhoAm 90*
Carr, John Howard 1926- *WhoAm 90*
Carr, John Lyle, Jr. 1946- *WhoE 91*
Carr, John Mark 1953- *WhoEmL 91*
Carr, John Thomas 1927- *BiDrAPA 89*
Carr, John W *BiDrAPA 89*
Carr, Josephine Sussman 1952- *WhoAmW 91*
Carr, Kathryne Elizabeth 1955- *WhoAmW 91*
Carr, Kenneth C. 1937- *St&PR 91*
Carr, Kenneth L. 1932- *St&PR 91*
Carr, Kenneth Lloyd 1932- *WhoAm 90*
Carr, Kenneth Monroe 1925- *WhoAm 90*
Carr, Larry Dean 1947- *WhoEmL 91*
Carr, Lawrence Edward, Jr. 1923- *WhoAm 90*
Carr, Leonard Barrett *BiDrAPA 89*
Carr, Leonard T 1944- *BiDrAPA 89*
Carr, Leroy 1905-1935 *OxCPMus*
Carr, Les 1935- *WhoAm 90*
Carr, M. Emily 1871-1945 *BioIn 16*
Carr, M. L. *BioIn 16*
Carr, M. Robert 1943- *WhoAm 90*
Carr, Margaret *BioIn 16*
Carr, Margaret Nell 1933- *WhoSSW 91*
Carr, Marie Pinak 1954- *WhoAmW 91*
Carr, Mary Jane 1899- *AuBYP 90*
Carr, Mary Jane 1899-1988 *BioIn 16*
Carr, Mary Lois 1948- *WhoSSW 91*
Carr, Melanie Lee *BiDrAPA 89*
Carr, Michael 1904-1968 *OxCPMus*
Carr, Michael A. 1954- *St&PR 91*
Carr, Michael E. *St&PR 91*
Carr, Mortimer *AmLegL*
Carr, Neil David 1946- *BiDrAPA 89*
Carr, Nora Kathleen 1958- *WhoEmL 91*
Carr, Paddy 1808- *WhNaAH*
Carr, Pat 1932- *WhoWrEP 89*
Carr, Pat M 1932- *ConAu 31NR*
Carr, Patricia Warren 1947- *WhoAmW 91, WhoEmL 91*
Carr, Patrick F. 1951- *St&PR 91*
Carr, Paul d'Argaville 1961- *IntWWM 90*
Carr, Paul Henry 1935- *WhoAm 90*
Carr, Paul Martin 1928- *WhoAm 90*
Carr, Peter Emile 1950- *WhoWrEP 89*
Carr, Philippa *TwCCr&M 91*
Carr, Phyllis Mae 1943- *WhoAmW 91*
Carr, Rachel *AuBYP 90*
Carr, Rich *WhoWrEP 89*
Carr, Richard Joseph 1935- *WhoWrEP 89*
Carr, Richard L. 1929- *St&PR 91*
Carr, Robert Allen 1917- *WhoAm 90*
Carr, Robert Allen 1952- *WhoSSW 91*
Carr, Robert C. 1926- *St&PR 91*
Carr, Robert David 1948- *WhoAm 90*
Carr, Robert Locke 1930- *WhoWor 91*
Carr, Robert Wilson, Jr. 1934- *WhoAm 90*
Carr, Robin 1953- *WhoEmL 91*
Carr, Ronald Edward 1932- *WhoAm 90*
Carr, Ronald Gene 1946- *WhoAm 90*
Carr, Ruby Louise 1948- *WhoSSW 91*
Carr, Ruth Anne 1947- *WhoAmW 91*
Carr, Sally Swan *WhoAmA 91*
Carr, Sandra Gotham 1948- *WhoAmW 91*
Carr, Sherwyn T. *ODwPR 91*
Carr, Shirley G. E. *WhoAm 90*
Carr, Stephen Hamilton 1947- *St&PR 91*
Carr, Stephen Howard 1942- *WhoAm 90*
Carr, Steven D. 1952- *ODwPR 91*
Carr, Susan Jean *St&PR 91*
Carr, Susan Lynn *BiDrAPA 89*
Carr, Susan Price 1946- *WhoEmL 91*
Carr, Tara B *BiDrAPA 89*
Carr, Temple St. Clair *BioIn 16*
Carr, Thomas E. 1949- *St&PR 91*
Carr, Thomas Jefferson, Jr. 1942- *St&PR 91*
Carr, Thos C. 1932- *St&PR 91*
Carr, Twila Marie 1957- *WhoSSW 91*
Carr, Vikki *BioIn 16, WhoAm 90, WhoAmW 91*
Carr, Vikki 1940- *WhoHisp 91*
Carr, Vikki 1941- *WorAlBi*
Carr, Vikki 1942- *OxCPMus*
Carr, Walter James, Jr. 1918- *WhoAm 90*
Carr, Walter Stanley 1945- *WhoEmL 91*
Carr, Wayne 1948- *St&PR 91*
Carr, Wendell Hampton 1953- *WhoSSW 91*
Carr, Wilbur John 1870-1942 *BioIn 16, WorAlBi*
Carr, Wiley Nelson 1940- *WhoSSW 91*
Carr, Willard Zeller, Jr. 1927- *WhoAm 90*
Carr, William 1930- *St&PR 91*
Carr, William Anthony 1938- *St&PR 91, WhoAm 90*
Carr, William G. 1930- *St&PR 91*
Carr, William H. A. 1924- *ODwPR 91*
Carr, William Henry A. 1924- *WhoWor 91*
Carr-Harris, Ian Redford 1941- *WhoAmA 91*
Carr-Porrier, Sheryl A. 1961- *WhoE 91*
Carra, Andrew Joseph 1943- *WhoAm 90*
Carra, Angelo D *BiDrAPA 89*
Carra, Atilio F 1936- *BiDrAPA 89*
Carra, Carlo 1881-1966 *IntDcAA 90*
Carracci Family *WorAlBi*
Carracci, Agostino 1557?-1602 *WorAlBi*
Carracci, Annibale 1560?-1609 *IntDcAA 90 [port], WorAlBi*
Carracci, Ludovico 1555?-1619 *WorAlBi*
Carracino, Eugene 1951- *St&PR 91*
Carrad, David Clayton 1944- *WhoE 91*
Carradine, Calista *BioIn 16*
Carradine, David *BioIn 16*
Carradine, David 1936- *WhoAm 90, WorAlBi*
Carradine, Gail *BioIn 16*
Carradine, John 1906-1988 *AnObit 1988, BioIn 16*
Carradine, John 1906-1989 *WorAlBi*
Carradine, Keith 1949- *WorAlBi*
Carradine, Keith Ian 1949- *WhoAm 90*
Carragher, Audrey Ann 1924- *WhoAmW 91*
Carragher, Frank A. 1932- *St&PR 91*
Carragher, Frank Anthony 1932- *WhoAm 90*
Carraher, Charles Eugene, Jr. 1941- *WhoSSW 91*
Carrall, John D. 1930- *St&PR 91*
Carramani *WhNaAH*
Carranco, Lynwood 1921- *WhoWrEP 89*
Carranza, Jose 1937- *BiDrAPA 89, WhoSSW 91*
Carranza, Venustiano 1859-1920 *BioIn 16, WorAlBi*
Carrara, Arthur Alfonso 1914- *WhoAm 90*
Carraro, Mauro *BioIn 16*
Carrascal, Jose Maria 1930- *IntvSpW [port]*
Carrasco, Alejandro 1962- *WhoHisp 91*
Carrasco, Cecilia Carmina 1966- *WhoHisp 91*
Carrasco, Concepcion Arenal de Garcia 1820-1893 *BioIn 16*
Carrasco, Connie *WhoHisp 91*
Carrasco, David *BioIn 16*
Carrasco, David L. 1919- *WhoHisp 91*
Carrasco, Emma J. *ODwPR 91, WhoHisp 91*
Carrasco, Julian *WhoHisp 91*
Carrasco, Mario 1945- *WhoHisp 91*
Carrasquel, Alex 1921-1969 *Ballpl 90*
Carrasquel, Chico 1928- *Ballpl 90 [port]*
Carrasquilla, Tomas 1858-1940 *BioIn 16*
Carraway, Andrew 1947- *St&PR 91*
Carraway, Anthony Glenn *BiDrAPA 89*
Carre, Andre Daniel 1941- *WhoWor 91*
Carre, Ben 1883-1978 *ConDes 90*
Carre, Jean *PenDiDA 89*
Carre, Sara McDowell 1950- *WhoAmW 91, WhoEmL 91*
Carreker, James D. *WhoAm 90, WhoSSW 91*
Carrel, Alexis 1873-1944 *EncO&P 3, EncPaPR 91, WorAlBi*
Carrel, Clarence Wayne 1937- *St&PR 91*
Carrel, Mark *ConAu 31NR*
Carrell, Betty Lou 1941- *WhoAmW 91*
Carrell, Stewart 1934- *St&PR 91*
Carrell, Todd Alan *BiDrAPA 89*
Carrender, Michael Wendell 1953- *St&PR 91*
Carreno, Albert 1905-1964 *EncACom*
Carreno, Cenaida Carmen *BiDrAPA 89*
Carreno, Jose R. 1930- *WhoHisp 91*
Carreno, Richard Dennis 1946- *WhoE 91*
Carreno, Teresa 1853-1917 *BioIn 16, PenDiMP*
Carrens, Jane Neill 1939- *WhoSSW 91*
Carreon, Cam 1937-1987 *Ballpl 90*
Carrera, Carlos J 1948- *BiDrAPA 89, WhoE 91*
Carrera, Danilo Eduardo 1938- *WhoWor 91*
Carrera, Frank, III 1931- *BiDrAPA 89*
Carrera, Jose 1929- *BiDrAPA 89*
Carrera, Jose Luis 1932- *WhoHisp 91*
Carrera, Rafael 1814-1865 *BioIn 16*
Carrera, Victor Manuel 1954- *WhoEmL 91*
Carrera Andrade, Jorge 1903-1978 *HispWr 90*
Carrera Verdugo, Jose Miguel 1785-1821 *BioIn 16*
Carreras, Edmond Joseph 1936- *St&PR 91*
Carreras, Francisco Jose 1932- *WhoAm 90*
Carreras, James *NewYTBS 90*
Carreras, James 1910-1990 *BioIn 16*
Carreras, Jose 1946- *BioIn 16, IntWWM 90, PenDiMP*
Carreras, Jose 1947- *WhoWor 91*
Carreras, Leonardo Alfredo 1920- *WhoHisp 91*
Carrere, Charles Scott 1937- *WhoWor 91*
Carrere, Tia *BioIn 16*
Carrero, Jaime 1931- *BioIn 16, WhoAmA 91, WhoHisp 91*
Carret, Philip L. *BioIn 16*
Carret, Philip L. 1896- *St&PR 91*
Carretta, Albert Aloysius 1907- *WhoAm 90*
Carretta, Richard L. 1939- *St&PR 91*
Carretta, Vincent 1945- *ConAu 131*
Carretti, Guglielmo 1933- *WhoWor 91*
Carrey, Randi Lee 1958- *WhoAmW 91*
Carricato, G.V. 1933- *St&PR 91*
Carrick, Bill 1873-1932 *Ballpl 90*
Carrick, Bruce Robert 1937- *St&PR 91, WhoAm 90*
Carrick, Carol 1935- *SmATA 63 [port]*
Carrick, Donald *BioIn 16*
Carrick, Donald 1929-1989 *SmATA 63 [port]*
Carrick, Donald F 1929- *WhoAmA 91*
Carrick, Edward 1905- *ConDes 90*
Carrick, Janice R *BiDrAPA 89*
Carrick, John Lowell 1937- *BiDrAPA 89*
Carrick, Paula S. 1944- *WhoAmW 91*
Carrico, Christine Kathryn 1950- *WhoAmW 91*
Carrico, Harry Lee 1916- *WhoAm 90, WhoSSW 91*
Carrie, Doreen 1958- *WhoAmW 91*
Carrie, Grace *FemiCLE*
Carrie, Jacques Felix 1939- *WhoWrEP 89*
Carrie, Robert G *BiDrAPA 89*
Carrier, Allen E. 1954- *ODwPR 91*
Carrier, Constance 1908- *FemiCLE*
Carrier, Constance Virginia 1908- *WhoWrEP 89*
Carrier, Estelle Stacy 1913- *WhoAm 90*
Carrier, George Francis 1918- *WhoAm 90, WhoE 91*
Carrier, Glass Bowling, Jr. 1931- *WhoAm 90*
Carrier, Lark 1947- *BioIn 16*
Carrier, Louise *BiDrAPA 89*
Carrier, Mark *BioIn 16*
Carrier, Roch 1937- *ConAu 130, OxCCanT*
Carrier, Ronald Edwin 1932- *WhoAm 90, WhoSSW 91*
Carrier, Russell N *BiDrAPA 89*
Carrier, Samuel Crowe, III 1945- *WhoAm 90*
Carrier, W.P. 1923- *St&PR 91*
Carrier, Warren Pendleton 1918- *WhoAm 90*
Carrier, William David, III 1943- *WhoSSW 91*
Carrier, Willis Haviland 1876-1950 *BioIn 16*
Carrier-Belleuse, Albert-Ernest 1824-1887 *PenDiDA 89*
Carriera, Rafael Pedro 1936- *BiDrAPA 89*
Carriera, Rosalba 1675-1757 *IntDcAA 90*
Carriera, Rosalba Giovanna 1675-1757 *BioIn 16*
Carriere, Jacques *BiDrAPA 89*
Carriere, Jacques 1924- *St&PR 91*
Carriere, Jean-Claude *BioIn 16*
Carriere, Jean-Claude 1931- *ConTFT 8*
Carriero, Peter C. 1949- *St&PR 91*
Carries, Jean 1855-1894 *PenDiDA 89*
Carrig, Wayne Kenneth 1946- *St&PR 91*
Carrigan, Bill 1883-1969 *Ballpl 90 [port]*
Carrigan, David Owen 1933- *WhoAm 90, WhoWrEP 89*
Carrigan, Jim Richard 1929- *WhoAm 90*
Carrigan, John Richard 1948- *WhoEmL 91*
Carrigan, Joseph Michael 1916- *St&PR 91*
Carrigan, Martha Loretto 1961- *WhoAmW 91*
Carrigan, Patricia M. *BioIn 16*
Carrigan, Richard A., Jr. 1932- *ConAu 30NR*
Carriger, Albert Clayton, II 1945- *WhoSSW 91*
Carrigg, C. Eddie 1965- *St&PR 91*
Carrigg, James A. 1933- *WhoAm 90, WhoE 91*
Carrigg, James Andrew 1933- *St&PR 91*
Carrighar, Sally 1905?- *FemiCLE*
Carriker, Edward Henry 1925- *St&PR 91*
Carriker, Mary Ann Sloop 1957- *WhoEmL 91*
Carril, Pete *BioIn 16*
Carril, Peter J. 1931- *WhoHisp 91*
Carrill, John Howard 1949- *BiDrAPA 89*
Carrillo, Alejandro A *BiDrAPA 89*
Carrillo, Ana C. 1963- *WhoAmW 91*
Carrillo, Braulio 1800-1845 *BioIn 16*
Carrillo, Carlos *BioIn 16*
Carrillo, Carmen 1943- *WhoHisp 91*
Carrillo, Donna Gribben 1954- *WhoAmW 91*
Carrillo, Eduardo 1937- *BioIn 16*
Carrillo, Eduardo L. 1937- *WhoHisp 91*
Carrillo, Enrique Gomez 1873-1927 *BioIn 16*
Carrillo, Joe M., Jr. 1927- *WhoHisp 91*
Carrillo, Jose Arturo 1944- *WhoHisp 91*
Carrillo, Josefa 1810-1893 *BioIn 16*
Carrillo, Leo 1880?-1961 *BioIn 16, WorAlBi*
Carrillo, Lilia 1929-1974 *WhoAmA 91N*
Carrillo, Miguel Angel 1964- *WhoHisp 91*
Carrillo, Robert S. 1932- *WhoHisp 91*
Carrillo, Santiago 1915- *BioIn 16*
Carrillo-Abbott, Cheryl Lee 1953- *WhoAmW 91*
Carrillo-Beron, Carmen 1943- *WhoHisp 91*
Carringer, Paul Timothy 1958- *WhoEmL 91*
Carrington 1893-1932 *BiDWomA, FemiCLE*
Carrington, Charles Edmund 1897-1990 *ConAu 132*
Carrington, Dora de Houghton 1893-1932 *BioIn 16*
Carrington, Elaine 1892-1958 *FemiCLE*
Carrington, Elizabeth Ellen 1943- *WhoWrEP 89*
Carrington, Frank Gamble, Jr. 1936- *WhoWor 91*
Carrington, George C, Jr. 1928-1990 *ConAu 132*
Carrington, Grant Clark 1938- *WhoWrEP 89*
Carrington, Henry A. 1929- *St&PR 91*
Carrington, Henry Beebee 1824-1912 *WhNaAH*
Carrington, Hereward 1880-1958 *EncO&P 3, EncPaPR 91*
Carrington, Joy Harrell *WhoAmA 91*
Carrington, Judith *ODwPR 91*
Carrington, Judith 1939- *WhoAm 90*
Carrington, Leonora 1917- *ArtLatA, BiDWomA, BioIn 16*
Carrington, Mary Ann 1957- *WhoAmW 91*
Carrington, Noel 1894-1989 *AnObit 1989*
Carrington, Omar Raymond 1904- *WhoAmA 91*
Carrington, Patricia Mastrapa 1962- *BiDrAPA 89*
Carrington, Peter A R Carington, Baron 1919- *BioIn 16*
Carrington, Peter Alexander Rupert 1919- *WhoWor 91*
Carrington, Samuel Macon, Jr. 1939- *WhoAm 90*
Carrington, Simon Robert 1942- *IntWWM 90*
Carrington, Stephens D 1926- *BiDrAPA 89*
Carrington, Susan Schell 1951- *WhoAmW 91*
Carrington, Sylvia 1960- *WhoAmW 91*
Carrington, Terri Lyne *BioIn 16*
Carrino, A. Greg 1948- *St&PR 91*
Carrino, David 1959- *WhoAmA 91*
Carrio de la Vandera, Alonso *BioIn 16*
Carrion, Arturo Morales *BioIn 16, ConAu 131, HispWr 90*
Carrion, Audrey J. Sylvia 1958- *WhoEmL 91*
Carrion, Rafael, Jr. 1914- *WhoAm 90*
Carrion, Richard L. *WhoAm 90*
Carrion, Tanner Rae 1945- *WhoAmW 91*
Carrion, Teresita Milagros 1964- *WhoHisp 91*
Carris, Marcia Lynn 1956- *WhoAmW 91*
Carris, William H. 1944- *St&PR 91*
Carrithers, Don 1949- *Ballpl 90*
Carrithers, Robin Carole 1955- *WhoAmW 91*
Carrithers, Walter A, Jr. 1924- *EncO&P 3*
Carritt, David 1927-1982 *DcNaB 1981*
Carriveau, Michael Jon 1956- *WhoEmL 91*
Carro, John 1927- *WhoHisp 91*
Carro, John Placid 1920- *WhoHisp 91*
Carrodus, John Tiplady 1836-1895 *PenDiMP*
Carrol, Louis Leon 1923- *St&PR 91*
Carroli, Silvano 1938- *IntWWM 90*
Carroll, Adorna Occhialini 1952- *WhoAmW 91, WhoEmL 91*
Carroll, Albert 1914- *WhoAm 90*
Carroll, Alexander Spicer, Jr. *BiDrAPA 89*
Carroll, Ann Foley 1962- *WhoAmW 91*
Carroll, Anna E. 1815-1893 *BioAmW*
Carroll, Anna Ella 1815-1894 *BioIn 16*
Carroll, Anthony J. 1864- *AmLegL*
Carroll, Barbara Anne 1945- *WhoAmW 91*
Carroll, Barry Joseph 1944- *St&PR 91, WhoAm 90*
Carroll, Benajah Harvey 1843-1914 *BioIn 16*
Carroll, Bernard James 1940- *BiDrAPA 89, WhoAm 90*
Carroll, Billy Price 1920- *WhoAm 90*
Carroll, Bob 1936- *ConAu 129*
Carroll, Bobby *BioIn 16*
Carroll, Bonnie 1941- *WhoAmW 91*

Carroll, Bonnie Cooper 1947- WhoEmL 91
Carroll, Brenda Ann BiDrAPA 89
Carroll, Brendan T. 1960- BiDrAPA 89
Carroll, Brion Michael 1957- WhoE 91
Carroll, Carmal Edward 1923- WhoAm 90
Carroll, Catherine North 1948- WhoEmL 91
Carroll, Charles 1660-1720 BioIn 16
Carroll, Charles 1737-1832 BioIn 16, EncCRAm, WorAlBi
Carroll, Charles Coleman 1932- St&PR 91, WhoAm 90
Carroll, Charles F. 1927- ODwPR 91
Carroll, Charles Lemuel, Jr. 1916- WhoSSW 91, WhoWor 91
Carroll, Charles Michael 1921- IntWWM 90, WhoSSW 91, WhoWor 91
Carroll, Christopher ODwPR 91
Carroll, Chuck BioIn 16
Carroll, Clay 1941- Ballpl 90
Carroll, Cliff 1859-1923 Ballpl 90
Carroll, Crawford 1942- St&PR 91
Carroll, Curt AuBYP 90
Carroll, Cynthia Louise 1960- WhoE 91
Carroll, Daniel 1730-1796 BioIn 16
Carroll, Daniel T. 1926- St&PR 91
Carroll, David ConAu 129
Carroll, David L. 1942- ConAu 129
Carroll, David McKenzie 1954- WhoEmL 91
Carroll, David Shields 1917- WhoAm 90
Carroll, David Todd 1959- WhoEmL 91
Carroll, Deborah Jean BiDrAPA 89
Carroll, Diahann BioIn 16
Carroll, Diahann 1935- DrBlPA 90, WhoAmW 91, WorAlBi
Carroll, Earl 1893-1948 OxCPMus
Carroll, Earl Hamblin 1925- WhoAm 90
Carroll, Edward J BiDrAPA 89
Carroll, Edwin Winford 1912- WhoAm 90
Carroll, Elizabeth J. 1955- WhoEmL 91
Carroll, Elizabeth Joan 1944- St&PR 91, WhoAmW 91
Carroll, Frank Morris 1928- IntWWM 90
Carroll, Geneva Barr 1930- WhoAmW 91
Carroll, George Joseph 1917- WhoAm 90, WhoSSW 91
Carroll, Gerald J. 1934- St&PR 91
Carroll, Ginny 1948- ConAu 130
Carroll, Gladys Hasty 1904- WhoAm 90
Carroll, Gretchen Lou 1950- WhoAmW 91
Carroll, Harry 1892-1962 OxCPMus
Carroll, Harry M. 1932- ODwPR 91
Carroll, Holbert Nicholson 1921- WhoAm 90
Carroll, Inez Richardson 1929- WhoAmW 91
Carroll, Irwin Dixon 1934- WhoSSW 91
Carroll, J. Larry 1946- ConAu 129
Carroll, J. Roy, Jr. NewYTBS 90
Carroll, J. Speed 1936- WhoAm 90, WhoE 91
Carroll, J. Terry 1945- St&PR 91
Carroll, James 1943- WhoAm 90
Carroll, James Edward 1946- WhoWor 91
Carroll, James Joseph 1946- WhoEmL 91
Carroll, James K. ODwPR 91
Carroll, James L. 1931- WhoSSW 91
Carroll, James Langton 1931- St&PR 91
Carroll, James Larry 1946- WhoEmL 91
Carroll, James Michael 1943- WhoAm 90
Carroll, James S. 1925- St&PR 91
Carroll, James Vincent, III 1940- WhoAm 90
Carroll, Jane Hammond 1946- WhoWrEP 89
Carroll, Janice Ann Hicks 1957- WhoSSW 91
Carroll, Jeanne 1929- WhoAmW 91
Carroll, Jeanne Frances 1965- WhoE 91
Carroll, Jefferson Roy, Jr. 1904- WhoAm 90
Carroll, Joan 1932- IntWWM 90
Carroll, John BioIn 16
Carroll, John 1735-1815 EncCRAm, WorAlBi
Carroll, John 1809-1884 DcLB 99
Carroll, John 1892-1959 WhoAmA 91N
Carroll, John Bissell 1916- WhoAm 90
Carroll, John D. TwCCr&M 91
Carroll, John Douglas 1939- WhoAm 90, WhoE 91
Carroll, John M. 1939- St&PR 91
Carroll, John Michael, Jr. 1954- WhoSSW 91
Carroll, John P. 1939- WhoAm 90
Carroll, John Patrick 1928- St&PR 91
Carroll, John Phillip 1925- WhoSSW 91
Carroll, John Sawyer 1942- WhoAm 90
Carroll, Jonathan 1949- WhoWrEP 89
Carroll, Joseph BioIn 16
Carroll, Joseph Anthony BioIn 16
Carroll, Joseph J. 1931- St&PR 91
Carroll, Joseph John 1936- WhoAm 90, WhoE 91
Carroll, Judith Ann 1947- WhoWrEP 89
Carroll, Julian Morton 1931- WhoAm 90
Carroll, Kenneth Kitchener 1923- WhoAm 90
Carroll, Kent Jean 1926- WhoAm 90
Carroll, Kim Marie 1958- WhoAmW 91
Carroll, L. James 1940- St&PR 91
Carroll, Lee S. 1942- St&PR 91
Carroll, Leo G. 1892-1972 WorAlBi
Carroll, Leonard M. 1942- St&PR 91
Carroll, Lester Edward 1912- WhoAm 90
Carroll, Lewis AuBYP 90
Carroll, Lewis 1832-1898 BioIn 16, WorAlBi
Carroll, Llawanna Faye 1955- WhoAmW 91
Carroll, Loren Kenneth 1943- WhoAm 90
Carroll, Lucy E. 1946- IntWWM 90
Carroll, Lucy Ellen 1946- WhoWrEP 89
Carroll, Malcolm W. 1922- St&PR 91
Carroll, Margaret Ann 1929- WhoAmW 91
Carroll, Marilyn Jeanne 1950- WhoAmW 91
Carroll, Mark Sullivan 1924- WhoAm 90
Carroll, Mark Thomas 1956- WhoEmL 91
Carroll, Marshall Elliott 1923- WhoAm 90
Carroll, Mary ConAu 130, ODwPR 91
Carroll, Mary Colvert 1940- WhoAm 90
Carroll, MaryBeth Ann 1953- WhoEmL 91
Carroll, Michael Adrian 1946- WhoAm 90
Carroll, Michael Dennis 1955- WhoEmL 91
Carroll, Michael Peter 1946- WhoE 91
Carroll, Ownie 1902-1975 Ballpl 90
Carroll, Pat 1927- WhoAm 90
Carroll, Patricia L. 1958- WhoWrEP 89
Carroll, Patricia Mary 1939- WhoAmW 91
Carroll, Patricia Whitehead 1954- WhoWor 91
Carroll, Patrick J. 1939- St&PR 91
Carroll, Paul Ferguson 1928- St&PR 91
Carroll, Paula Marie 1933- WhoAmW 91
Carroll, Philip Joseph 1937- St&PR 91, WhoAm 90
Carroll, Phillip Patrick, III 1948- WhoEmL 91
Carroll, Raymond BioIn 16
Carroll, Raymond James 1949- WhoSSW 91
Carroll, Rebecca Ann 1946- WhoAmW 91
Carroll, Rebecca Lois 1952- WhoAmW 91
Carroll, Regina Martin BiDrAPA 89
Carroll, Richard BioIn 16
Carroll, Richard John 1940- St&PR 91
Carroll, Robert 1927- St&PR 91
Carroll, Robert Bruce 1949- WhoEmL 91
Carroll, Robert C. 1930- St&PR 91
Carroll, Robert Earl 1922- St&PR 91
Carroll, Robert Eugene 1957- WhoAm 90
Carroll, Robert G. H., III 1940- ODwPR 91
Carroll, Robert Henry 1932- WhoAm 90
Carroll, Robert Hoff BiDrAPA 89
Carroll, Robert Lynn 1938- WhoAm 90
Carroll, Robert W. 1923- WhoAm 90
Carroll, Robert Wayne 1930- WhoAm 90
Carroll, Robert William 1923- St&PR 91
Carroll, Ronnie Lee 1945- WhoSSW 91
Carroll, Rosemary Lalevee 1945- WhoAmW 91
Carroll, Stephen John, Jr. 1930- WhoAm 90
Carroll, Theodus Catherine 1928- WhoWrEP 89
Carroll, Theresa Jane 1962- WhoSSW 91
Carroll, Thomas Charles 1921- WhoAm 90
Carroll, Thomas Edward 1958- WhoSSW 91
Carroll, Thomas John 1929- WhoAm 90
Carroll, Thomas Joseph 1912- WhoAm 90
Carroll, Thomas Phillip 1955- WhoEmL 91
Carroll, Thomas S. 1919- St&PR 91
Carroll, Thomas Sylvester 1919- WhoAm 90
Carroll, Timothy Wayne 1951- WhoEmL 91
Carroll, Tom 1952- Ballpl 90
Carroll, Tony 1944- ODwPR 91
Carroll, Vinnette 1922- BioIn 16, DrBlPA 90, NotWoAT
Carroll, W. James BioIn 16
Carroll, Wallace E. 1907- St&PR 91
Carroll, Wallace Edward 1907- WhoAm 90
Carroll, William F.G. St&PR 91
Carroll, William H. 1930- St&PR 91
Carroll, William Jerome 1923- WhoAm 90
Carroll, William Joseph 1947- WhoE 91
Carroll, William Kenneth 1927- WhoAm 90
Carroll, William M. 1932- WhoSSW 91
Carroll Lange, Monica 1951- WhoAmW 91
Carroll-Smith, Elisabeth Nicole Eliane 1937- WhoAm 90
Carroll-Van Norman, Donna Lee 1958- WhoAmW 91
Carron, Arthur 1900-1967 PenDiMP
Carron, Maudee Lilyan WhoAmA 91
Carron de la Carriere, Guy Marie Aime 1929- WhoWor 91
Carrothers, Alfred William Rooke 1924- WhoAm 90
Carrothers, Gerald Arthur Patrick 1925- WhoAm 90
Carrow, Leon Albert 1924- WhoAm 90
Carrow, Milton Michael 1912- WhoAm 90
Carrow, Robert Duane 1934- WhoWor 91
Carrowan, Erwin Raeford 1937- St&PR 91
Carrozzi, Craig 1955- BioIn 16
Carrubba, Paul Anthony 1949- St&PR 91
Carrubba, Sandra J. McPherson 1943- WhoWrEP 89
Carruth, Charles Weldon 1921- WhoAm 90
Carruth, Clarence U., Jr. 1901- St&PR 91
Carruth, David Barrow 1926- WhoAm 90, WhoWor 91
Carruth, Ella AuBYP 90
Carruth, Gorton Veeder 1925- WhoAm 90, WhoWrEP 89
Carruth, Hayden 1921- BioIn 16, MajTwCW, WhoAm 90, WhoWrEP 89
Carruth, Paul H 1892-1961 WhoAmA 91N
Carruthers, Garrey Edward 1939- WhoAm 90, WhoWor 91
Carruthers, George Barry 1924- WhoWor 91
Carruthers, Glen Blaine 1954- IntWWM 90
Carruthers, John Robert 1935- WhoAm 90
Carruthers, Joyce Ann 1942- WhoSSW 91
Carruthers, Leo Martin 1949- WhoWor 91
Carruthers, Norman Harry 1935- WhoE 91
Carruthers, Peter Ambler 1935- WhoAm 90
Carruthers, S. George 1945- WhoAm 90
Carruthers, Sara Procter 1962- WhoAmW 91
Carruthers, Walter Edward Royden 1938- WhoAm 90
Carry, L. Ray 1932- WhoSSW 91, WhoWor 91
Carry, Myrtle Louise 1914- WhoSSW 91
Cars, The EncPR&S 89
Carsberg, Bryan BioIn 16
Carscallen, Howard B BiDrAPA 89
Carscallen, John D. 1832?- AmLegL
Carsch, Ruth Elizabeth 1945- WhoAmW 91
Carsell, Carolyn Kay 1938- WhoAmW 91
Carsen, Marjorie L BiDrAPA 89
Carsey, Julian Nance BioIn 16
Carsey, Kid 1870-1960 Ballpl 90
Carsey, Marcia Lee Peterson 1944- WhoAm 90, WhoAmW 91
Carsey, Marcy NewYTBS 90 [port]
Carsley, John F. 1931- St&PR 91
Carson, Anne 1950- ConAu 132
Carson, Benjamin BioIn 16
Carson, Benjamin Solomon 1951- WhoAm 90
Carson, Bud WhoAm 90
Carson, Carol S. 1939- WhoAmW 91
Carson, Charles R. 1945- WhoE 91
Carson, Cheryl Dawn 1961- WhoAmW 91
Carson, Christopher Houston 1809-1868 WhNaAH
Carson, Christopher Leonard 1940- WhoAm 90, WhoSSW 91
Carson, Clarence B. 1925- ConAu 130
Carson, Clarice 1936- IntWWM 90
Carson, Dale George 1922- WhoAm 90
Carson, David Costley 1921- WhoSSW 91
Carson, David E.A. 1934- St&PR 91
Carson, David Ellis Adams 1934- WhoAm 90
Carson, David Eugene 1959- WhoSSW 91
Carson, Dennis R. 1948- St&PR 91
Carson, Donald Prescott 1949- St&PR 91
Carson, Donita Faye 1956- WhoAmW 91
Carson, Doyle I 1936- BiDrAPA 89
Carson, Eben 1951- WhoEmL 91
Carson, Edward Mansfield 1929- St&PR 91, WhoAm 90
Carson, Florida Pearl 1906- WhoAmW 91
Carson, Gerald BioIn 16
Carson, Gerald 1899-1989 ConAu 130
Carson, Gerald Hewes 1899- WhoWrEP 89
Carson, Gordon Bloom 1911- WhoAm 90
Carson, Hamilton C. 1928- St&PR 91
Carson, Harry Albert 1913- WhoAm 90
Carson, Howard C. 1932- St&PR 91
Carson, Ira M BiDrAPA 89
Carson, Jack 1910-1963 WorAlBi
Carson, James Donald 1929- WhoAm 90
Carson, James E 1923- BiDrAPA 89
Carson, James Elijah 1923- WhoE 91
Carson, James Tyson 1925- St&PR 91
Carson, Joanna BioIn 16
Carson, John 1868-1949 OxCPMus
Carson, John David ConTFT 8
Carson, John F., Jr. 1932- St&PR 91
Carson, John Franklin 1920- AuBYP 90
Carson, John R. 1940- WhoSSW 91
Carson, John Robert 1935- St&PR 91
Carson, Johnny 1925- BioIn 16, WhoAm 90, WorAlBi
Carson, Joseph M., Jr. 1931- St&PR 91
Carson, Julia M. 1938- WhoAmW 91
Carson, Julia Margaret 1899- AuBYP 90
Carson, Kent 1930- WhoAm 90
Carson, Kent L. 1930- St&PR 91
Carson, Kit 1809-1868 BioIn 16, WorAlBi
Carson, Leonard Allen 1940- WhoAm 90, WhoSSW 91, WhoWor 91
Carson, Lettie Gay 1901- WhoAm 90
Carson, Margaret Marie 1944- WhoAmW 91
Carson, Marvin Wayne 1955- WhoEmL 91
Carson, Mary Silvano 1925- WhoAmW 91
Carson, Melinda BioIn 16
Carson, Michael 1946- ConAu 130
Carson, Nolan Wendell 1924- WhoAm 90
Carson, Norman Richard 1916- WhoWor 91
Carson, Philip L., Sr. 1941- St&PR 91
Carson, Rachel 1907-1964 BioIn 16, FemiCLE, WomFie [port]
Carson, Rachel Louise 1907-1964 BioAmW, DcScB S2, MajTwCW
Carson, Richard Nathaniel 1933- St&PR 91
Carson, Robert 1928- SmATA X [port]
Carson, Robert William 1948- WhoEmL 91
Carson, Ronald 1943- St&PR 91
Carson, Ronald Frank 1947- WhoWrEP 89
Carson, Ronald Thomas WhoE 91
Carson, Russell L. 1943- St&PR 91
Carson, Sam Leon 1955- BiDrAPA 89
Carson, Samuel Goodman 1913- WhoAm 90
Carson, Sara 1927- St&PR 91
Carson, Sharon BioIn 16
Carson, Sharon Lynn 1959- WhoSSW 91
Carson, Terry David 1943- WhoSSW 91
Carson, Tom C. 1941- St&PR 91
Carson, Vance Turner 1945- WhoE 91
Carson, Vincent A. BioIn 16, NewYTBS 90 [port]
Carson, William Harvey, Jr. BiDrAPA 89
Carson, William James 1952- WhoEmL 91
Carson, William L. 1918- St&PR 91
Carson, William M. 1947- St&PR 91
Carson, William Morris WhoE 91
Carstairs, George M BiDrAPA 89
Carstairs, John E. 1933- St&PR 91
Carstarphen, J. Martin BioIn 16
Carsten, Arlene Desmet 1937- WhoAmW 91
Carsten, Hugo Christiaan Georg 1926- WhoWor 91
Carsten, Mary E. 1922- WhoAm 90
Carsten, Mary Nash 1958- WhoAmW 91
Carstens, Conrad S. 1930- ODwPR 91
Carstens, Donald D. 1935- St&PR 91
Carstens, Harold Henry 1925- WhoAm 90, WhoWor 91
Carstens, Jane Ellen 1922- WhoSSW 91
Carstens, Laura Beth 1959- WhoEmL 91
Carstensen, Broder Helmut 1926- WhoWor 91
Carstensen, Edwin Lorenz 1919- WhoAm 90
Carstensen, Laurence William, Jr. 1954- WhoSSW 91
Carstensen, Roger Norwood 1920- WhoSSW 91
Carstensen, Vernon 1907- WhoAm 90
Carstenson, Cecil C 1906- WhoAmA 91
Carswell, Allan Ian 1933- WhoAm 90
Carswell, Bruce 1930- St&PR 91
Carswell, Carol Frances 1939- WhoAmW 91
Carswell, Catherine 1879-1946 BioIn 16, FemiCLE
Carswell, Dean 1940- St&PR 91
Carswell, Evelyn Medicus 1919- AuBYP 90
Carswell, Harmon 1926- St&PR 91
Carswell, Jane Triplett 1932- WhoAm 90
Carswell, John 1931- WhoAmA 91
Carswell, Lloyd Brooks 1910- WhoAm 90
Carswell, Mary 1933- WhoE 91
Carswell, Philip John, Jr. 1939- St&PR 91
Carswell, Robert 1928- WhoAm 90
Carswell, Robert Glenn 1926- St&PR 91
Carswell, Rodney 1946- WhoAmA 91
Carswell Cox, Diana Caryl 1945- WhoSSW 91
Cart, Dorothy Cariker 1923- WhoWrEP 89
Cart, Henri Philippe 1938- WhoWor 91
Cart, Pauline Harmon 1914- WhoAmW 91
Cart, Theodore S. BioIn 16
Carta, Phil 1948- WhoSSW 91
Cartagena, Luis A. 1946- WhoHisp 91
Cartagena, Roberto A. 1947- WhoHisp 91
Cartaino, Carol Ann 1944- WhoAmW 91
Cartales, John A. 1928- St&PR 91
Cartano, Tony 1944- ConAu 129
Carte, Bridget D'Oyly 1908-1985 DcNaB 1981
Carte, D'Oyly 1844-1901 WorAlBi

Carte, Richard D'Oyly 1844-1901 *BioIn 16, OxCPMus*
Carte, Suzanne Lewis 1943- *WhoAmW 91*
Carteciano, Teresita *BiDrAPA 89*
Cartee, Gary Lane 1954- *WhoEmL 91*
Cartee, L. T. *AmLegL*
Cartee, Leanne 1962- *WhoE 91*
Cartee, Roger Lee 1953- *WhoEmL 91*
Cartee, Thomas Edward, Jr. 1960- *WhoEmL 91*
Carter Family, The *OxCPMus, WhoNeCM C*
Carter, A.B. 1939- *St&PR 91*
Carter, A. Boyd 1950- *St&PR 91*
Carter, Alan Bruce 1936- *BiDrAPA 89*
Carter, Albert Marvin 1951- *WhoSSW 91*
Carter, Alden R 1947- *ChlLR 22 [port]*
Carter, Aldia Spiers 1936- *WhoAmW 91*
Carter, Alfred H 1939- *BiDrAPA 89*
Carter, Alvin Pleasant 1891-1960 *OxCPMus*
Carter, Amy *BioIn 16*
Carter, Angela 1940- *BioIn 16, FemiCLE, MajTwCW, WorAu 1980 [port]*
Carter, Anne Cohen 1919- *WhoAm 90, WhoAmW 91*
Carter, Anthony *BioIn 16*
Carter, Arnold N., Jr. 1929- *St&PR 91*
Carter, Arnold P *BiDrAPA 89*
Carter, Arthur *BioIn 16*
Carter, Arthur D., Jr. 1937- *WhoSSW 91*
Carter, Arthur Franklin 1935- *St&PR 91*
Carter, Augustus D 1895-1957 *WhoAmA 91N*
Carter, Avis Murton *ConAu 32NR*
Carter, Barbara E. 1925-1988 *BioIn 16*
Carter, Barry Edward 1942- *WhoAm 90, WhoWor 91*
Carter, Bear *WhoWrEP 89*
Carter, Ben 1912-1946 *DrBIPA 90*
Carter, Benjamin Carroll 1916- *WhoSSW 91*
Carter, Benny *BioIn 16*
Carter, Benny 1907- *DrBIPA 90, OxCPMus, WorAlBi*
Carter, Bernard A. 1926- *St&PR 91*
Carter, Betsy L. 1945- *WhoAm 90, WhoAmW 91, WhoE 91*
Carter, Betty *BioIn 16*
Carter, Betty 1930?- *DrBIPA 90*
Carter, Billy *BioIn 16*
Carter, Boake 1898-1944 *BioIn 16*
Carter, Bruce *AuBYP 90*
Carter, Bruce 1930- *WhoAmA 91*
Carter, Byron J 1863-1908 *EncABHB 4*
Carter, Byrum Earl 1922- *WhoAm 90*
Carter, Carla Cifelli 1949- *WhoAmW 91*
Carter, Carol A 1955- *WhoAmA 91*
Carter, Carolyn Houchin 1952- *WhoAm 90, WhoAmW 91*
Carter, Carolyn Howard 1950- *WhoAmW 91*
Carter, Charles Edward 1925- *WhoE 91*
Carter, Charles G. 1937- *ODwPR 91*
Carter, Charles McLean 1936- *WhoAm 90*
Carter, Churchhill 1930- *St&PR 91*
Carter, Cindy *BiDrAPA 89*
Carter, Clarence Holbrook 1904- *WhoAm 90, WhoAmA 91*
Carter, Colin *BioIn 16*
Carter, Connie Bernice 1943- *WhoAmW 91*
Carter, Connie Beverly 1926- *WhoAmW 91*
Carter, Constance Laverne 1945- *WhoEmL 91*
Carter, Craig Nash 1949- *WhoSSW 91*
Carter, Curtis Harold, Jr. 1939- *WhoWrEP 89*
Carter, Cynthia Susan *BiDrAPA 89*
Carter, D Linnea 1937- *BiDrAPA 89*
Carter, Dale P. 1944- *BiDrAPA 89*
Carter, Dan T. 1940- *WhoAm 90*
Carter, Dana Pierce 1931- *St&PR 91*
Carter, Daniel Paul 1948- *WhoE 91*
Carter, Darrell Lewis 1946- *WhoEmL 91*
Carter, Dauton Odell, Jr. 1943- *WhoSSW 91*
Carter, David Clifford 1929- *WhoE 91*
Carter, David Edward 1942- *WhoWor 91*
Carter, David George, Sr. 1942- *WhoE 91*
Carter, David Giles 1921- *WhoAmA 91, WhoE 91*
Carter, David L. *NewYTBS 90*
Carter, David Martin 1936- *WhoAm 90*
Carter, David R. *St&PR 91*
Carter, David Ray 1951- *WhoAm 90*
Carter, Dean 1922- *WhoAm 90, WhoAmA 91*
Carter, Debbie Rene *BiDrAPA 89*
Carter, Denis George 1947- *WhoSSW 91*
Carter, Dennis E. 1956- *St&PR 91*
Carter, Dennis L. 1930- *St&PR 91*
Carter, Dewey Gaston 1942- *WhoAm 90*
Carter, Diane Mason 1959- *WhoAmW 91*
Carter, Dixie 1939- *WorAlBi*
Carter, Don Earl 1917- *WhoAm 90*
Carter, Donald *WhoSSW 91*
Carter, Donald C 1922- *BiDrAPA 89*
Carter, Donald Lee 1937- *WhoSSW 91*
Carter, Donald Patton 1927- *WhoAm 90*
Carter, Dorothy *BiDEWW*
Carter, Doug C. 1952- *St&PR 91*
Carter, Douglas B *BiDrAPA 89*
Carter, Dudley Christopher 1891- *WhoAm 90, WhoAmA 91*
Carter, E. Leo *St&PR 91*
Carter, Edith Houston 1936- *WhoAmW 91*
Carter, Edward Carlos, II 1928- *WhoAm 90*
Carter, Edward W. 1911- *St&PR 91*
Carter, Edward William 1911- *WhoAm 90, WhoWor 91*
Carter, Edward William 1912?- *ConAmBL*
Carter, Eleanor Elizabeth 1954- *WhoAmW 91, WhoEmL 91*
Carter, Elizabeth 1717-1806 *BioIn 16, FemiCLE*
Carter, Elizabeth Marie 1963- *WhoAmW 91*
Carter, Elizabeth Naomi 1955- *WhoAmW 91*
Carter, Elliott 1908- *BioIn 16, IntWWM 90, PenDiMP A*
Carter, Elliott Cook, Jr. 1908- *WhoAm 90*
Carter, Emily Ann 1960- *WhoAmW 91*
Carter, Emily Suzanne 1942- *WhoSSW 91*
Carter, Ernest V. 1860-1933 *AmLegL*
Carter, Ernestine *ConAu 130*
Carter, Erskine 1948- *WhoWrEP 89*
Carter, Eugene Hudson 1912- *St&PR 91*
Carter, Eunice Roberta Hunton 1899-1970 *HarlReB [port]*
Carter, Felicity *TwCCr&M 91*
Carter, Frances Rosina 1952- *WhoSSW 91*
Carter, Franklin *BiDrAPA 89*
Carter, Frederic Bowker Terrington 1819-1900 *DcCanB 12*
Carter, Frederick Timmins 1925- *WhoAmA 91*
Carter, Gail Marie 1956- *WhoAmW 91*
Carter, Gary *BioIn 16*
Carter, Gary 1939- *BioIn 16, WhoAmA 91*
Carter, Gary 1954- *Ballpl 90 [port], WorAlBi*
Carter, Gary Kibler 1936- *St&PR 91*
Carter, Gary Lynn 1947- *St&PR 91*
Carter, Gene 1935- *WhoAm 90, WhoE 91*
Carter, George Carson 1957- *WhoEmL 91*
Carter, George H 1916- *BiDrAPA 89*
Carter, George Kent 1935- *WhoAm 90*
Carter, George W. *AmLegL*
Carter, Gerald Emmett 1912- *WhoAm 90, WhoE 91, WhoWor 91*
Carter, Gina Lee 1962- *WhoAmW 91*
Carter, Glen Harold 1946- *WhoAm 90*
Carter, Gordon Thomas 1956- *WhoEmL 91*
Carter, Granville W 1920- *WhoAmA 91*
Carter, Granville Wellington 1920- *WhoAm 90*
Carter, Harold Dee 1939- *St&PR 91*
Carter, Harold O. 1932- *WhoAm 90*
Carter, Harriet Manore 1929- *WhoAmA 91*
Carter, Harriet Vanessa *WhoSSW 91*
Carter, Harry Tyson 1924- *WhoAm 90*
Carter, Harvey 1945- *St&PR 91*
Carter, Helene 1887-1960 *WhoAmA 91N*
Carter, Henry Alpheus Peirce 1837-1891 *BioIn 16*
Carter, Henry Moore, Jr. 1932- *WhoAm 90*
Carter, Herbert Edmund 1910- *WhoAm 90*
Carter, Hodding, III 1935- *WhoAm 90*
Carter, Hugh Clendenin 1925- *WhoAm 90*
Carter, Hurricane *BioIn 16*
Carter, J. Wesley 1940- *St&PR 91*
Carter, Jack 1923- *BioIn 16, WorAlBi*
Carter, Jaine Marie 1946- *WhoAm 90, WhoWor 91*
Carter, James *AuBYP 90*
Carter, James Able 1926- *WhoSSW 91*
Carter, James Alfred 1941- *WhoSSW 91*
Carter, James Clarence 1927- *WhoAm 90, WhoSSW 91*
Carter, James E 1935- *WhoWrEP 89*
Carter, James Earl 1924- *BioIn 16*
Carter, James Earl, Jr. 1924- *ConAu 32NR, MajTwCW, WhoAm 90, WhoSSW 91, WhoWor 91*
Carter, James Edward 1941- *St&PR 91*
Carter, James Edward, Jr. 1906- *WhoSSW 91*
Carter, James H. 1935- *WhoAm 90*
Carter, James Hal, Jr. 1943- *WhoAm 90, WhoE 91*
Carter, James Harvey 1934- *BiDrAPA 89*
Carter, James J. 1949- *St&PR 91*
Carter, James McCord 1952- *WhoEmL 91, WhoSSW 91*
Carter, James Paul 1940- *WhoSSW 91*
Carter, James Raymond *BiDrAPA 89*
Carter, James Rose, Jr. 1933- *WhoAm 90*
Carter, James Stanley, Jr. 1955- *WhoEmL 91*
Carter, James Stephen 1940- *BiDrAPA 89*
Carter, Jane Foster 1927- *WhoAmW 91*
Carter, Janice Joene 1948- *WhoAmW 91, WhoEmL 91, WhoWor 91*
Carter, Jared 1939- *WhoWrEP 89*
Carter, Jean *EarBlAP*
Carter, Jeff *BioIn 16*
Carter, Jennifer 1963- *WhoAmW 91*
Carter, Jerry Lee 1955- *BiDrAPA 89*
Carter, Jerry Williams 1941- *WhoAmA 91*
Carter, Jessie *BioIn 16*
Carter, Jessie Anita 1948- *WhoAmW 91*
Carter, Jimmy *ConAu 32NR, MajTwCW*
Carter, Jimmy 1924- *BiDrUSE 89, BioIn 16, WorAlBi*
Carter, Joan P. 1943- *St&PR 91*
Carter, JoAnn Martin 1932- *WhoSSW 91*
Carter, Joe 1960- *Ballpl 90*
Carter, Joe Morris 1948- *WhoAm 90*
Carter, John *BioIn 16*
Carter, John Allen, Jr. 1934- *St&PR 91, WhoAm 90*
Carter, John Avery 1924- *WhoAm 90*
Carter, John B., Jr. 1924- *St&PR 91*
Carter, John Bernard 1934- *St&PR 91, WhoAm 90, WhoE 91, WhoWor 91*
Carter, John Boyd, Jr. 1924- *WhoAm 90*
Carter, John Coles 1920- *WhoAm 90*
Carter, John Dale 1944- *WhoAm 90, WhoWor 91*
Carter, John Douglas 1946- *WhoAm 90, WhoEmL 91*
Carter, John J. 1920- *St&PR 91*
Carter, John J, Jr. 1949- *BiDrAPA 89*
Carter, John Linus *BiDrAPA 89*
Carter, John M. 1918- *St&PR 91*
Carter, John Mack 1928- *WhoAm 90*
Carter, John Tilton, Jr. 1950- *WhoEmL 91*
Carter, John W. 1945- *WhoSSW 91*
Carter, Jon Michael 1945- *WhoEmL 91, WhoSSW 91*
Carter, Jonna Carol 1965- *WhoSSW 91*
Carter, Joseph A., III 1936- *St&PR 91*
Carter, Joseph C., Jr. 1927- *St&PR 91*
Carter, Joseph Carlyle, Jr. 1927- *WhoAm 90*
Carter, Joseph Chris 1960- *WhoAm 90*
Carter, Joseph Edwin 1915- *WhoAm 90*
Carter, Joseph Emerson 1920- *St&PR 91*
Carter, Joseph R. 1918- *St&PR 91*
Carter, Joseph Robert 1951- *WhoAm 90*
Carter, Josiah Mason 1813-1868 *AmLegL*
Carter, Joy Eaton 1923- *WhoAmW 91*
Carter, Joyce Lee 1929- *WhoWrEP 89*
Carter, Judith Henson *BiDrAPA 89*
Carter, Judith Rockwell 1939- *WhoAmW 91*
Carter, Julie 1956- *WhoEmL 91*
Carter, Katharine Tipton 1950- *WhoAmA 91*
Carter, Kathy Diane 1957- *WhoAmW 91*
Carter, Lark P. 1930- *WhoAm 90*
Carter, Larry J. *St&PR 91*
Carter, Larry Michael 1949- *WhoWor 91*
Carter, Larry Vince 1962- *WhoEmL 91*
Carter, Larry W. *BioIn 16*
Carter, Launor F. 1914-1986 *BioIn 16*
Carter, Lawrence Wayne 1942- *WhoSSW 91*
Carter, Leigh 1925- *St&PR 91, WhoAm 90*
Carter, Leslie 1853-1937 *LiHiK*
Carter, Leslie, Mrs. 1862-1937 *BioIn 16, NotWoAT*
Carter, Lewis A., Jr. 1941- *ODwPR 91*
Carter, Liane Kupferberg 1954- *WhoWrEP 89*
Carter, Lin 1930-1988 *ConAu 30NR*
Carter, Lisa Joyce 1959- *WhoAmW 91*
Carter, Lynda *BioIn 16*
Carter, Lynda 1951- *WorAlBi*
Carter, Lynda Cordoba *WhoHisp 91*
Carter, Mae Riedy 1921- *WhoAmW 91, WhoE 91, WhoWor 91*
Carter, Manson Hildreth 1923- *St&PR 91*
Carter, Margaret L. 1935- *WhoAmW 91*
Carter, Marie Kernan *BiDrAPA 89*
Carter, Marilyn *ConAu 32NR*
Carter, Marshall Nichols 1940- *WhoAm 90*
Carter, Marshall Sylvester 1909- *WhoAm 90*
Carter, Martha Elizabeth 1935- *WhoWor 91*
Carter, Mary *WhoAmA 91*
Carter, Mary 1931- *WhoE 91*
Carter, Mary Arkley *WhoWrEP 89*
Carter, Mary Eddie 1925- *WhoAm 90, WhoAmW 91*
Carter, Mary Helen 1926- *St&PR 91*
Carter, Mary Kennedy 1934- *BioIn 16*
Carter, Mary Thomas 1956- *WhoAmW 91*
Carter, Mason Carlton 1933- *WhoAm 90*
Carter, Mason N. *St&PR 91*
Carter, Matthew *BioIn 16*
Carter, Maybelle Addington 1909-1978 *OxCPMus*
Carter, Medora Abbott 1953- *WhoAmW 91*
Carter, Michael Allen 1947- *WhoAm 90*
Carter, Michael Ray 1953- *WhoEmL 91*
Carter, Michael Stephen *BioIn 16*
Carter, Mildred Brown 1927- *WhoAmW 91*
Carter, Nancy Young 1950- *WhoAmW 91*
Carter, Nanette Carolyn 1954- *WhoAmA 91*
Carter, Neal Andrew 1960- *WhoEmL 91*
Carter, Nell *BioIn 16*
Carter, Nell 1948- *DrBIPA 90*
Carter, Nevada *ConAu 31NR*
Carter, Neville Louis 1934- *WhoAm 90*
Carter, Nicholas S.F. 1935- *St&PR 91*
Carter, Nick *ConAu 30NR, SpyFic, TwCCr&M 91*
Carter, Noel 1942- *St&PR 91*
Carter, Nolan 1941- *WhoSSW 91*
Carter, O.K. 1943- *St&PR 91*
Carter, Olive Marie 1910- *WhoSSW 91*
Carter, Ollie *BioIn 16*
Carter, Orwin Lee 1942- *St&PR 91*
Carter, Page *AuBYP 90*
Carter, Pamela Lynn 1949- *WhoAmW 91*
Carter, Paul 1894-1984 *Ballpl 90*
Carter, Paul 1951- *ConAu 129*
Carter, Paul D. 1950- *WhoSSW 91*
Carter, Paul R. 1940- *St&PR 91*
Carter, Paul Richard 1922- *WhoAm 90*
Carter, Paul Stanley 1950- *WhoEmL 91*
Carter, Peggy Wolfe 1936- *WhoAmW 91*
Carter, Peter *PenDiMP*
Carter, Peter 1929- *BioIn 16*
Carter, Peter John Burnett 1935- *IntWWM 90*
Carter, Phil Norman 1934- *St&PR 91*
Carter, Phillip F. 1948- *ODwPR 91*
Carter, Phyllis Ann *AuBYP 90*
Carter, Polly Sue 1947- *WhoAmW 91*
Carter, Ralph 1961- *DrBIPA 90*
Carter, Rebecca Davilene 1932- *WhoAm 90*
Carter, Rebecca Marie Hunt 1955- *WhoAmW 91*
Carter, Richard *BiDrAPA 89*
Carter, Richard 1918- *WhoAm 90, WhoWrEP 89*
Carter, Richard Alton 1952- *WhoSSW 91*
Carter, Richard Duane *WhoAm 90, WhoE 91*
Carter, Richard Herrick 1920- *St&PR 91*
Carter, Robert 1728-1804 *BioIn 16*
Carter, Robert 1932- *ODwPR 91*
Carter, Robert Daniel 1927- *WhoSSW 91*
Carter, Robert Edward 1946- *St&PR 91*
Carter, Robert Estil 1939- *WhoSSW 91*
Carter, Robert Guild 1928- *St&PR 91*
Carter, Robert Philip, Sr. 1946- *WhoEmL 91*
Carter, Robert Powell 1957- *St&PR 91*
Carter, Robert Warren *St&PR 91N*
Carter, Robert Warren 1941- *WhoAm 90*
Carter, Roberta Eccleston *WhoAmW 91*
Carter, Rodney 1957- *WhoSSW 91*
Carter, Ron 1937- *BioIn 16*
Carter, Ronald 1937- *WhoAm 90*
Carter, Ronald Dale 1948- *WhoEmL 91*
Carter, Ronald Martin, Sr. 1925- *St&PR 91, WhoAm 90*
Carter, Rosalynn *BiDrAPA 89, BioIn 16*
Carter, Rosalynn 1927- *WorAlBi*
Carter, Rosalynn S. 1927- *BioAmW*
Carter, Rosalynn Smith 1927- *WhoAm 90, WhoAmW 91, WhoSSW 91*
Carter, Roy Ernest, Jr. 1922- *WhoAm 90*
Carter, Roy George *BiDrAPA 89*
Carter, Rubin *BioIn 16*
Carter, Russell Paul, Jr. 1927- *WhoSSW 91*
Carter, Ruth B. *WhoAmW 91, WhoE 91*
Carter, Sam John 1943- *WhoAmA 91*
Carter, Samuel 1904-1988 *BioIn 16*
Carter, Samuel, III 1904-1988 *SmATA 60*
Carter, Samuel Roberts, Jr. 1949- *WhoE 91, WhoWor 91*
Carter, Sara Dougherty 1889-1979 *OxCPMus*
Carter, Saralee Lessman 1951- *WhoAmW 91*
Carter, Sharon Maureen 1948- *BiDrAPA 89*
Carter, Sidney 1912- *BiDrAPA 89, WhoAm 90*
Carter, Stephen Louis 1954- *WhoSSW 91*
Carter, Stephen Michael 1946- *St&PR 91*
Carter, Steve 1930- *DrBIPA 90*
Carter, Stewart Arlen 1944- *WhoSSW 91*
Carter, Susie *BioIn 16*
Carter, T K *DrBIPA 90*
Carter, Ted *BioIn 16*
Carter, Terry *DrBIPA 90*
Carter, Theresa Howard 1929- *WhoAm 90*
Carter, Thomas *BioIn 16*
Carter, Thomas Allen 1935- *WhoSSW 91*
Carter, Thomas Barton 1949- *WhoEmL 91*
Carter, Thomas F 1932- *BiDrAPA 89*
Carter, Thomas Heyward, Jr. 1946- *WhoEmL 91*
Carter, Thomas Leslie 1926- *St&PR 91*

Carter, Thomas Smith, Jr. 1921- WhoAm 90, WhoWor 91
Carter, Victor M. 1909- St&PR 91
Carter, Virginia M. 1946- WhoAmW 91
Carter, Weld Saunders 1900-1989 BioIn 16
Carter, Wesley Byrd 1942- BiDrAPA 89
Carter, Wilbur Lee, Jr. 1922- WhoAm 90
Carter, Wilfred Wilson 1923- St&PR 91, WhoAm 90
Carter, William BioIn 16
Carter, William Caswell 1917- WhoAm 90
Carter, William D. BioIn 16
Carter, William E. 1926-1983 AuBYP 90
Carter, William Henry, II 1930- St&PR 91
Carter, William Hodding 1907-1972 AuBYP 90
Carter, William Julian, Jr. 1923- WhoE 91
Carter, William Lee 1925- WhoAm 90
Carter, William Minor 1940- St&PR 91
Carter, William S, Jr. 1922- BiDrAPA 89
Carter, William Walton 1921- WhoAm 90
Carter, Yvonne Pickering 1939- WhoAmA 91, WhoE 91
Carter Cash, June 1929- WorAlBi
Carter-Clayton, Connie Lynn 1956- WhoEmL 91
Carter-Scott, Cherie Untermeyer 1949- WhoEmL 91
Carter-Torres, Richard E BiDrAPA 89
Carteret, George 1610-1680 EncCRAm
Carteret, Philip 1639-1682 EncCRAm
Carterette, Edward Calvin Hayes 1921- WhoAm 90
Carteri, Rosanna 1930- IntWWM 90
Cartey, Wilfred 1931- BioIn 16
Cartey, Wilfred George Onslow 1931- WhoAm 90
Carthaus, James A. 1940- St&PR 91
Carthaus, James Arthur 1940- WhoAm 90
Carthel, Anne Fawver 1952- WhoAmW 91, WhoEmL 91
Carthen, Billy Burton 1950- WhoEmL 91, WhoSSW 91
Cartheuser, William EncO&P 3
Carthy, Mark Patrick 1960- WhoE 91
Cartier, Celine Paule 1930- WhoAm 90, WhoAmW 91
Cartier, Denise Marie 1952- WhoAmW 91
Cartier, Georges 1929- WhoWor 91
Cartier, Gerard Albert 1923- WhoE 91
Cartier, Jacques 1491-1557 BioIn 16, EncCRAm, WhNaAH, WorAlBi
Cartier, Janice BioIn 16
Cartier, Richard Wrye 1920- St&PR 91
Cartier-Bresson, Henri 1908- BioIn 16, WhoWor 91, WorAlBi
Cartimandua WomWR
Cartimandua, Queen of the Brigantes BioIn 16
Cartisano, Linda Ann 1953- WhoAmW 91
Cartland, Barbara 1901- FemiCLE, MajTwCW, WhoAm 90, WhoWor 91
Cartland, Barbara 1902- BioIn 16
Cartland, Barbara 1904- WorAlBi
Cartland, Bob WhoWrEP 89
Cartland, John Everett, III 1944- St&PR 91
Cartledge, Raymond Eugene 1929- St&PR 91, WhoAm 90, WhoE 91
Cartledge, William 1916- MusmAFA
Cartlidge, Michelle 1950- BioIn 16
Cartlidge, Richard L. 1954- St&PR 91
Cartmell, Harriet BioIn 16
Cartmell, Helen 1923- WhoAmA 91
Cartmell, James Robert 1931- St&PR 91
Cartmell, Jennifer B. 1953- St&PR 91
Cartmell, Vinton Aikins 1925- WhoAm 90
Cartmill, George Edwin, Jr. 1918- WhoAm 90
Cartmill, Matt 1943- WhoAm 90
Cartmill, Rick T. 1948- St&PR 91
Cartner, John A., III 1947- WhoSSW 91
Carto, Willis Allison 1926- WhoE 91
Carton, Cristina Silva-Bento 1928- WhoSSW 91
Carton, John E. BioIn 16
Carton, John Jay 1856-1934 AmLegL
Carton, Laurence Alfred 1918- WhoAm 90
Carton, Marvyn 1917- St&PR 91
Cartun, Steven Mark BiDrAPA 89
Cartwright, Alexander 1820-1892 Ballpl 90 [port]
Cartwright, Alton Stuart 1922- WhoAm 90
Cartwright, Angela BioIn 16
Cartwright, Carol F. ODwPR 91
Cartwright, Carroll L WhoAmA 91
Cartwright, Charles Nelson 1933- WhoSSW 91
Cartwright, Constance B WhoAmA 91
Cartwright, Donna J. 1960- WhoAmW 91
Cartwright, Edwin Orville 1901- St&PR 91
Cartwright, Frances Lynn 1948- WhoAmW 91
Cartwright, George BioIn 16
Cartwright, H., Mrs. FemiCLE
Cartwright, Howard Eugene 1924- WhoAm 90
Cartwright, Inez P. Gesell 1917- WhoWor 91
Cartwright, Joanna FemiCLE
Cartwright, Johanna BiDEWW
Cartwright, Joseph Michael 1954- WhoSSW 91
Cartwright, Julia Mary 1851-1924 BioIn 16
Cartwright, Lenora T. BioIn 16
Cartwright, Madeline NewYTBS 90 [port]
Cartwright, Mary Lou 1923- WhoAmW 91
Cartwright, Maxine BiDrAPA 89
Cartwright, Michael Wayne 1962- WhoEmL 91
Cartwright, Peter Swain 1937- St&PR 91
Cartwright, Reg 1938- SmATA 64 [port]
Cartwright, Rhonda Delrie 1952- St&PR 91, WhoAmW 91
Cartwright, Robert, Mrs. FemiCLE
Cartwright, Roberta A. 1938- St&PR 91
Cartwright, Rosalind Dymond BioIn 16
Cartwright, Sally 1923- AuBYP 90
Cartwright, Thomas Harold 1953- St&PR 91
Cartwright, Ursula 1647-1702 BiDEWW
Cartwright, Walter Joseph 1922- WhoAm 90
Cartwright, William Holman 1915- WhoAm 90, WhoWor 91
Carty, Arthur John 1940- WhoAm 90
Carty, Gerard James 1932- St&PR 91, WhoAm 90
Carty, John L. 1945- St&PR 91
Carty, John Lydon 1945- WhoE 91
Carty, John Wesley 1923- WhoWor 91
Carty, Leo 1931- BioIn 16
Carty, Raymond Thomas 1946- St&PR 91
Carty, Raymond Wesley 1956- WhoEmL 91
Carty, Rico 1941- Ballpl 90
Carty, Rita Mary 1937- WhoAmW 91
Caru, Bruno Eugene 1935- WhoWor 91
Caruana, Joseph Charles 1939- WhoWor 91
Caruba, Alan 1937- ODwPR 91
Carubelli, Raoul 1929- WhoSSW 91
Carucci, Joseph P. BioIn 16
Carucci, Samuel Anthony 1935- WhoAm 90
Carulla, Ramon 1938- WhoAmA 91
Carus, A. Ross WhoWrEP 89
Carus, Andre W. 1953- St&PR 91
Carus, Emma 1879-1927 BioIn 16
Carus, Frederick Leonard 1941- St&PR 91
Carus, Louis 1927- IntWWM 90
Carus, M. Blouke 1927- St&PR 91
Carus, Marianne 1928- WhoAm 90, WhoAmW 91
Carus, Marianne S. 1928- St&PR 91
Carus, Milton Blouke 1927- WhoAm 90
Carus, Paul 1923- St&PR 91
Carusillo, Joan Gloria 1931- WhoAmW 91
Caruso, Carol Ann 1945- WhoEmL 91
Caruso, Charles Michael 1950- WhoEmL 91
Caruso, Christine Ann 1954- WhoSSW 91
Caruso, Enrico 1873-1921 BioIn 16, PenDiMP, WorAlBi
Caruso, Joseph A. BioIn 16
Caruso, Marie Therese 1931- WhoAmW 91
Caruso, Michael G. ODwPR 91
Caruso, Nicholas Dominic 1957- WhoE 91, WhoEmL 91
Caruso, Robert Thomas 1945- WhoAm 90
Caruso, Salvatore Anthony 1941- WhoSSW 91
Caruso, Saverio BiDrAPA 89
Caruso, Thomas Paul 1952- WhoE 91
Caruso, Thomas Samuel 1950- St&PR 91
Caruso, Victor Guy 1948- WhoE 91
Caruso, Vincent John 1947- St&PR 91
Carusone, L. Michael 1936- St&PR 91
Caruthers, Barbara Sue Apgar 1943- WhoAmW 91
Caruthers, Bob 1864-1911 Ballpl 90
Caruthers, Candace DrBIPA 90
Caruthers, Frank Eugene 1963- WhoE 91
Caruthers, Henry D. BioIn 16
Caruthers, Marilynn Laird 1922- WhoAmW 91
Caruthers, William F. 1920- St&PR 91
Carvajal, Jose M. J. 1810-1874 BioIn 16
Carvajal Prado, Patricio 1916- WhoWor 91
Carvalho, Anna Marie 1955- WhoAmW 91, WhoEmL 91
Carvalho, Carlos Alberto Pereira 1937- WhoWor 91
Carvalho, Caroline 1827-1895 PenDiMP
Carvalho, Eugene Wade BiDrAPA 89
Carvalho, Flavio de Rezende 1899-1973 ArtLatA
Carvalho, Josely 1942- WhoAmA 91
Carvalho, Julie Ann 1940- WhoWor 91
Carvalho, Julio de WhoWor 91
Carvalho, Maria Judite de 1921- EncCoWW
Carvalho, Robert M. 1948- BiDrAPA 89
Carvalho, Roger P. 1951- ODwPR 91
Carvalho, Solomon Solis 1856-1942 BioIn 16
Carvallo, Jorge Nicolas 1945- WhoSSW 91
Carvallo, Marc Evangelista 1934- WhoWor 91
Carvel, Elbert N. 1910- St&PR 91
Carvel, Elbert Nostrand 1910- WhoWor 91
Carvel, Tom 1906-1990 NewYTBS 90 [port]
Carvell, Jedediah Slason 1832-1894 DcCanB 12
Carvell, Michael Charles 1950- BiDrAPA 89
Carven, Madame BioIn 16
Carven, Christopher J. BioIn 16
Carver, Mrs. FemiCLE
Carver, Ada Jack 1890-1972 BioAmW
Carver, Brent 1951- OxCCanT
Carver, Calvin R. 1925- St&PR 91
Carver, Calvin Reeve 1925- WhoAm 90
Carver, Charles Clifford, Jr. 1954- WhoE 91
Carver, Charles Mark 1960- WhoEmL 91
Carver, Charles Ray 1929- WhoSSW 91
Carver, Clevie Raymond BioIn 16
Carver, Darlene T. 1954- WhoAmW 91
Carver, David Harold 1930- WhoAm 90
Carver, Dorothy Lee Eskew 1926- WhoAmW 91
Carver, Eugene Pendleton, II 1928- St&PR 91
Carver, George Washington 1864?-1943 BioIn 16, WorAlBi
Carver, Hazel Irvin Oates 1918- IntWWM 90
Carver, James Lewis 1925- WhoSSW 91, WhoWor 91
Carver, Jeffrey Penn 1961- St&PR 91
Carver, John 1567?-1621 EncCRAm
Carver, John William, Jr. 1952- WhoSSW 91
Carver, Jonathan 1710-1780 EncCRAm, WhNaAH
Carver, Juanita 1929- WhoWor 91
Carver, Kendall Lynn 1936- WhoAm 90
Carver, Kevin Scott 1953- WhoEmL 91
Carver, Lawrence Morrow 1948- BiDrAPA 89
Carver, Loyce Cleo 1918- WhoAm 90
Carver, Martin G. 1948- BioIn 16
Carver, Martin Gregory 1948- St&PR 91, WhoAm 90, WhoEmL 91
Carver, Norman Francis, Jr. WhoAm 90
Carver, Randall 1948- BioIn 16
Carver, Raymond BioIn 16
Carver, Raymond 1938-1988 AnObit 1988, MajTwCW, WorAlBi
Carver, Robert Dale 1936- St&PR 91
Carver, Roy James, Jr. 1943- St&PR 91
Carver, Todd B. 1958- WhoEmL 91
Carvey, Dana BioIn 16
Carville, James G. 1932- St&PR 91
Carvor, Robert 1487-1566 BioIn 16
Carwell, Hattie Virginia 1948- WhoEmL 91
Carwell, L'Ann AuBYP 90
Cary, Alice 1820-1871 BioAmW, FemiCLE
Cary, Anne 1615?-1671 FemiCLE
Cary, Archibald 1721-1787 EncCRAm
Cary, Arthur Joyce Lunel 1888-1957 BioIn 16
Cary, Boyd Balford, Jr. 1923- WhoE 91
Cary, Charles Muse 1948- WhoEmL 91
Cary, Charles Oswald 1917- WhoAm 90
Cary, Chuck 1960- Ballpl 90
Cary, Cornelius Adams 1949- WhoAm 90
Cary, Elizabeth 1585-1639 BioIn 16
Cary, Elton Mikell 1929- St&PR 91
Cary, Emily Pritchard 1931- WhoWrEP 89
Cary, Falkland 1897-1989 ConTFT 8
Cary, Frank Taylor 1920- WhoAm 90
Cary, Freeman Hamilton 1926- WhoAm 90
Cary, Gene L 1928- BiDrAPA 89
Cary, Gene Leonard 1928- WhoE 91
Cary, Guy Clif, III BiDrAPA 89
Cary, Harry William, III 1945- WhoE 91
Cary, Hunsdon, III 1945- WhoSSW 91
Cary, James Donald 1919- WhoAm 90, WhoWrEP 89
Cary, John William 1945- WhoWor 91
Cary, Joyce 1888-1957 BioIn 16, DcLB 100 [port], WorAlBi, WrPh
Cary, Mary 1621?- BiDEWW
Cary, Mary 1621?-1653? FemiCLE
Cary, Mary 1622?-1693 FemiCLE
Cary, Mary Ann Camberton DcCanB 12
Cary, Mary Katherine 1953- WhoEmL 91
Cary, Phoebe 1824-1871 BioAmW, FemiCLE
Cary, Tristram Ogilvie 1925- IntWWM 90
Cary, Victor Lee 1917- St&PR 91
Cary, Walter L. 1935- St&PR 91
Cary, William Sterling 1927- WhoAm 90
Caryl, Jean 1926- AuBYP 90
Caryll, Ivan 1860-1921 OxCPMus
Carysfort, John Joshua Proby, Earl of 1751-1828 BioIn 16
Casa Loma Orchestra OxCPMus
Casa, Joann St&PR 91
Casa, Patricia BioIn 16
Casabal, Melecia Luna 1928- WhoWrEP 89
Casablancas, John BioIn 16
Casablancas i Domingo, Benet 1956- IntWWM 90
Casabon-Sanchez, Luis 1931- WhoHisp 91
Casabonne, Peter G. 1932- St&PR 91
Casabonne, Richard Joseph 1945- St&PR 91
Casaburi, Nicholas A BiDrAPA 89
Casaburro, John E. 1951- WhoE 91
Casaccia, Gabriel HispWr 90
Casaccia Bibolini, G 1907- HispWr 90
Casad, Robert Clair 1929- WhoAm 90
Casada, James Allen 1942- WhoSSW 91, WhoWrEP 89
Casademont, Angel Carlos 1936- BiDrAPA 89
Casadesus PenDiMP
Casadesus, Francis 1870-1954 PenDiMP
Casadesus, Gaby 1901- IntWWM 90, PenDiMP
Casadesus, Henri 1879-1947 PenDiMP
Casadesus, Jean 1927-1972 PenDiMP
Casadesus, Jean-Claude 1935- IntWWM 90, PenDiMP
Casadesus, Marcel 1882-1914 PenDiMP
Casadesus, Marius 1892-1981 PenDiMP
Casadesus, Robert 1899-1972 PenDiMP, WorAlBi
Casado, Andrew Richard 1950- WhoHisp 91
Casado, Antonio Francisco 1913- BioIn 16, WhoAm 90
Casado, Gustavo E. 1935- WhoHisp 91
Casadonte, Paul Peter 1944- BiDrAPA 89
Casady, Cort 1947- WhoWrEP 89
Casagrande, Louie B. AuBYP 90
Casal, Julian del 1863-1893 BioIn 16
Casal, Lourdes 1938-1981 BioIn 16
Casalaspro, Debra Ann 1956- WhoAmW 91
Casalaspro-Couls, Debra Ann 1956- WhoEmL 91
Casale, Carol Ann 1962- WhoE 91
Casale, Jerry 1933- Ballpl 90
Casale, John Francis, Jr. 1959- WhoSSW 91
Casale, Karen A. WhoAmW 91
Casale, Maria BioIn 16
Casale, Ralph P. 1928- St&PR 91
Casale, Ralph Patrick 1928- WhoE 91
Casale, Robert J. 1938- WhoAm 90
Casali, Antonio PenDiDA 89
Casali, John L 1913- BiDrAPA 89
Casali, Richard A. 1947- St&PR 91
Casalotti, Ronald Peter 1955- St&PR 91
Casals, Pablo 1876-1973 BioIn 16, PenDiMP, -A, WorAlBi
Casals, Rosemary 1948- WhoAm 90
Casals-Ariet, Christina Brock 1949- BiDrAPA 89
Casals-Ariet, Jordi 1911- WhoAm 90
Casalveri, Lauren Mary 1960- WhoAmW 91
Casani, John Richard 1932- WhoAm 90
Casano, Brenda Jo 1965- WhoAmW 91
Casanova, Aldo John 1929- WhoAm 90, WhoAmA 91
Casanova, Alicia L. 1937- WhoHisp 91
Casanova, Daniele 1909-1943 BiDFrPL
Casanova, Edda N BiDrAPA 89
Casanova, Giacomo 1725-1798 BioIn 16
Casanova, Giovanni Giacomo 1725-1798 WorAlBi
Casanova, Hector L. 1941- WhoHisp 91
Casanova, Jean-Claude 1934- WhoWor 91
Casanova, Jeffrey Steven 1971- WhoE 91
Casanova, Jose Manuel WhoHisp 91
Casanova, Laurent 1906-1972 BiDFrPL
Casanova, Paul WhoHisp 91
Casanova, Paul 1941- Ballpl 90
Casanova de Lutoslawski, Sofia Perez 1862-1958 EncCoWW
Casanova de Seingalt, Giovanni Jacopo 1725-1798 LitC 13 [port]
Casapietra, Celestina 1938- IntWWM 90
Casarella, Edmond 1920- WhoAmA 91
Casarella, William Joseph 1937- WhoAm 90
Casares, Adolfo Bioy HispWr 90, MajTwCW
Casares, Adolfo Bioy 1914- BioIn 16
Casarett, Alison Provoost 1930- WhoAm 90
Casarett, George William 1920- WhoAm 90
Casarez, Rosendo, Jr. 1943- WhoHisp 91
Casarez, Rosendo, Sr. 1910- WhoHisp 91
Casariego, Jorge Isaac BiDrAPA 89
Casariego, Jorge Isaac 1945- WhoAm 90
Casarino, John Philip 1940- BiDrAPA 89, WhoE 91
Casaroli, Agostino 1914- WhoWor 91
Casas, Bartolome de las 1474-1566 BioIn 16

Casas, Fernando 1946- WhoAmA 91
Casas, Melesio 1929- BioIn 16, WhoAmA 91
Casas, Melesio, III 1929- WhoHisp 91
Casas, Myrna 1934- WhoHisp 91
Casas, Roberto 1931- WhoHisp 91
Casas, Salvador G. 1950- WhoEmL 91
Casas Olascoaga, Raul Angel 1926- WhoWor 91
Casas-Pardo, Jose 1938- WhoWor 91
Casasent, David Paul 1942- WhoAm 90
Casavis, David Bingham 1952- WhoEmL 91
Casazza, Carol A. 1957- WhoAmW 91
Casazza, John Andrew 1924- WhoAm 90
Cascardi, Anthony J 1953- ConAu 132
Cascarella, Joe 1907- Ballpl 90
Casciano, Daniel Anthony 1941- WhoAm 90
Casciari, Raoul Joseph 1934- St&PR 91
Cascieri, Arcangelo 1902- WhoAmA 91
Cascino, Anthony Elmo, Jr. 1948- WhoEmL 91
Cascino, James Madison 1951- WhoEmL 91
Cascino, Mary Dory 1949- WhoAmW 91
Cascio, Anna Theresa 1955- WhoAmW 91
Cascio, Grace Catherine 1944- WhoSSW 91
Cascio, Michael Joseph 1950- WhoEmL 91
Casco Zelaya, Jorge Omar 1951- WhoWor 91
Cascorbi, Helmut Freimund 1933- WhoAm 90
Casdorph, Paul Douglas 1932- WhoSSW 91
Case, Anne Catherine 1958- WhoE 91
Case, Bonnie Nally 1949- WhoSSW 91
Case, Charles Carroll 1914- WhoAm 90
Case, Charles Dixon 1952- WhoEmL 91
Case, Charlie 1879-1964 Ballpl 90
Case, Colleen Mae 1952- WhoEmL 91
Case, David Knowlton 1938- WhoAm 90, WhoE 91
Case, David Leon 1948- WhoEmL 91
Case, Dean Wellington 1936- St&PR 91
Case, Douglas Manning 1947- WhoEmL 91, WhoWor 91
Case, Dwight Leland 1929- WhoAm 90
Case, Elinor 1914- AuBYP 90
Case, Elizabeth 1930- WhoAm 90, WhoAmA 91
Case, Eugene Lawrence 1937- WhoAm 90
Case, Everett Needham 1901- WhoAm 90
Case, Fred E 1918- ConAu 31NR
Case, George 1915- Ballpl 90
Case, George 1915-1989 BioIn 16
Case, George Phillip, Jr. 1929- WhoE 91
Case, Gerald Clarence 1937- WhoSSW 91
Case, Gordon Thomas Martin 1941- St&PR 91
Case, Hadley 1909- St&PR 91, WhoAm 90, WhoWor 91
Case, Harry L. 1929- St&PR 91
Case, I Clark BiDrAPA 89
Case, James Hebard 1920- WhoAm 90
Case, Jean 1930 St&PR 91
Case, John 1926- St&PR 91
Case, John Danford 1945- St&PR 91
Case, John Gouyd, Jr. 1954- BiDrAPA 89
Case, John Howard 1955- WhoEmL 91
Case, John J. 1930- St&PR 91
Case, John Philip 1952- WhoEmL 91
Case, Josephine Young NewYTBS 90
Case, Josephine Young 1907-1990 BioIn 16, ConAu 130
Case, Joyce BioIn 16
Case, Karen Ann 1944- WhoAm 90, WhoAmW 91
Case, Karen Beth 1958- WhoEmL 91
Case, Kenneth Eugene 1944- WhoAm 90
Case, L.L. WhoWrEP 89
Case, Larry D. 1943- WhoAm 90
Case, Laura Ferguson 1951- WhoSSW 91
Case, Manning Eugene, Jr. 1916- WhoAm 90
Case, Mary Elizabeth 1925- WhoAmW 91
Case, Matthew Alan 1957- WhoEmL 91
Case, Pamela Jane 1944- WhoE 91
Case, Paul Watson, Jr. 1949- WhoEmL 91
Case, Richard Thomas 1949- WhoEmL 91
Case, Rita Coleman WhoAmW 91
Case, Stephen W. St&PR 91
Case, Steve K. 1949- St&PR 91
Case, Terese Elizabeth 1946- WhoE 91
Case, Thomas Louis 1947- WhoSSW 91
Case, Thomas Louis 1952- WhoSSW 91
Case, Warren G. Jr. 1934- BiDrAPA 89
Case, Weldon W. 1921- St&PR 91
Case, Weldon Wood 1921- WhoAm 90
Case, William B. 1928- St&PR 91
Case, William Cullen 1836-1901 AmLegL
Casebeer, Edwin Frank, Jr. 1933- WhoAm 90
Casebeer, R. Scott 1955- St&PR 91
Casebere, James E 1953- WhoAmA 91
Casebere, James Edward 1953- WhoE 91
Casebolt, Victor Alan 1935- St&PR 91, WhoAm 90, WhoE 91
Casebolt, Wayne C. 1929- St&PR 91
Casei, Nedda WhoAm 90, WhoAmW 91
Casel, Mary Lynn 1943- WhoAmW 91
Caseley, Judith AuBYP 90
Caseley, Judith 1951- BioIn 16
Casell, Joachim WhoAmA 91
Casella, Charles W 1940- BiDrAPA 89
Casella, James V. 1929- St&PR 91
Casellas, Gilbert F. 1952- WhoHisp 91
Casellas, Joachim 1927- WhoAmA 91
Casellato, Renzo 1936- IntWWM 90
Caselli, Giuseppe PenDiDA 89
Caselli, Virgil P. 1940- WhoAm 90
Caselllato-Lamberti, Giorgio 1938- IntWWM 90
Casely-Hayford, Adelaide 1868-1960 FemiCLE
Casely-Hayford, Gladys 1904-1950 FemiCLE
Casenas, Emmanuel R BiDrAPA 89
Caserio, Patricia Bovich 1956- WhoEmL 91
Caserta, Maria Theresa BiDrAPA 89
Casewit, Curtis W. 1927- WhoWrEP 89
Casey, Albert Vincent 1920- WhoAm 90
Casey, Barbara A. Perea 1951- WhoAmW 91
Casey, Barbara Ann Perea 1951- WhoHisp 91
Casey, Barbara Sayre 1940- ODwPR 91
Casey, Bernie 1939- DrBIPA 90
Casey, Beverly Ann 1949- WhoAmW 91
Casey, Byron L. Jr. 1918- BiDrAPA 89
Casey, Caryl BiDrAPA 89
Casey, Catherine Elizabeth 1941- WhoAmW 91
Casey, Charles F. 1927- St&PR 91
Casey, Charles Francis 1927- WhoAm 90, WhoSSW 91
Casey, Charles Philip 1942- WhoAm 90
Casey, Coleman Hampton 1947- WhoE 91
Casey, Colleen Sue 1956- WhoEmL 91
Casey, Daniel Edward 1947- BiDrAPA 89
Casey, Daniel J 1937- WhoWrEP 89
Casey, David Allan BiDrAPA 89
Casey, Denise AuBYP 90
Casey, Denise Mapes 1955- WhoAmW 91
Casey, Dennis M. 1944- ODwPR 91
Casey, Doc 1870-1936 Ballpl 90
Casey, Don WhoAm 90
Casey, Donald Michael 1935- WhoAm 90
Casey, Donna Miller 1949- St&PR 91
Casey, Douglas R. St&PR 91
Casey, Douglas Robert 1946- WhoWrEP 89
Casey, E. Paul 1930- St&PR 91
Casey, Edward Dennis 1931- WhoAm 90
Casey, Edward Paul 1930- WhoAm 90
Casey, Edwin F. 1944- WhoE 91
Casey, Elizabeth Temple 1901-1990 WhoAmA 91N
Casey, Ethel Laughlin 1926- WhoAm 90, WhoWor 91
Casey, Genevieve Mary 1916- WhoAm 90
Casey, George Edward, Jr. 1946- WhoE 91
Casey, Gerald Wayne 1940- WhoWrEP 89
Casey, Gerard William 1942- WhoAm 90
Casey, Horace Craig, Jr. 1934- WhoAm 90
Casey, Hugh 1913-1951 Ballpl 90
Casey, Ira Lamont, Jr. BiDrAPA 89
Casey, J. Joseph 1921- WhoAm 90
Casey, J.W. St&PR 91
Casey, Jacqueline Shepard 1927- WhoAmA 91
Casey, James J. 1915- St&PR 91
Casey, James Joseph 1943- St&PR 91
Casey, James K. 1948- St&PR 91
Casey, James Martin BiDrAPA 89
Casey, James McLean 1930- St&PR 91
Casey, James P BiDrAPA 89
Casey, Janice Marie 1954- WhoAmW 91, WhoEmL 91
Casey, Jay C. 1931- WhoAm 90
Casey, Jerald Francis 1926- St&PR 91
Casey, Joan Kelleher ODwPR 91
Casey, John 1939- BioIn 16, ConLC 59 [port]
Casey, John A. 1927- St&PR 91
Casey, John Dennis 1949- St&PR 91
Casey, John Dudley 1939- WhoAm 90, WhoWrEP 89
Casey, John Joseph 1918- WhoAm 90
Casey, John Joseph 1926- BiDrAPA 89
Casey, John Joseph 1931- WhoAmA 91
Casey, John K. 1933- St&PR 91
Casey, John McLelland 1952- WhoSSW 91
Casey, John P. 1920- WhoAm 90
Casey, John P. 1928- ODwPR 91
Casey, John P. 1945- St&PR 91
Casey, John Patrick 1928- WhoAm 90
Casey, John Patrick, Jr. 1947- WhoE 91
Casey, John Richard 1944- St&PR 91
Casey, Joseph T. 1931- St&PR 91
Casey, June B. 1924- WhoAmW 91
Casey, Karen Anne 1955- WhoAmW 91, WhoEmL 91
Casey, Kathleen Heirich 1937- WhoAmW 91
Casey, Keith Allen 1961- WhoEmL 91
Casey, Kenneth Lyman 1935- WhoAm 90
Casey, Kerry BioIn 16
Casey, Kevin V.E. St&PR 91
Casey, Lawrence Joseph 1933- St&PR 91
Casey, Lynn M. 1955- ODwPR 91
Casey, Madelyn Bennett 1951- WhoAmW 91
Casey, Margaret Mary BiDrAPA 89
Casey, Marilyn 1943- ODwPR 91
Casey, Maureen Therese 1953- WhoEmL 91
Casey, Maurice Francis 1920- St&PR 91
Casey, Michael Gerard 1944- WhoWor 91
Casey, Michael Joseph 1949- WhoE 91
Casey, Michael Kirkland 1940- WhoSSW 91, WhoWor 91
Casey, Murray Joseph 1936- WhoWor 91
Casey, Patricia Marie 1955- WhoE 91
Casey, Patrick Alan 1957- BiDrAPA 89
Casey, Patrick Jon 1943- WhoSSW 91
Casey, Phillip E. 1942- St&PR 91
Casey, Phillip Earl 1942- WhoAm 90
Casey, Randall Charles 1954- WhoSSW 91
Casey, Raymond R. 1935- St&PR 91
Casey, Raymond Richard 1935- WhoAm 90
Casey, Richard Joseph 1918- St&PR 91
Casey, Robert E. 1938- St&PR 91
Casey, Robert P. 1932- WhoAm 90, WhoE 91, WhoWor 91
Casey, Robin Emmett 1953- St&PR 91
Casey, Samuel Alexander 1914- St&PR 91, WhoAm 90
Casey, Samuel B., Jr. 1927- St&PR 91
Casey, Solanus 1870-1957 BioIn 16
Casey, Terri M. 1954- WhoAmW 91
Casey, Thomas Joseph, III 1951- WhoEmL 91
Casey, Thomas Warren 1942- WhoE 91
Casey, Veronica Angela 1952- WhoAmW 91
Casey, Walter H. 1940- ODwPR 91
Casey, Walter Hamilton 1940- St&PR 91
Casey, Warren 1935-1988 BioIn 16
Casey, William J. BioIn 16, St&PR 91
Casey, William J. 1913-1987 WorAlBi
Casey, William Robert, Jr. 1944- WhoAm 90
Casey, William Van Etten 1914-1990 ConAu 131
Casgrain, Charlotte Ardoin 1940- WhoE 91
Cash, Alana 1950- WhoAmW 91
Cash, Alice Adelaide Hudnall 1948- IntWWM 90
Cash, Angela Burton 1963- WhoSSW 91
Cash, Audrey Sutton 1926- WhoAmW 91
Cash, Carl G. 1929- St&PR 91
Cash, Carol Vivian 1929- WhoAmW 91
Cash, Dave 1948- Ballpl 90
Cash, David Powell 1939- WhoSSW 91
Cash, Ellen Lewis Buell 1905-1989 BioIn 16, ConAu 130, SmATA 64
Cash, Francis W. 1942- St&PR 91
Cash, Francis Winford 1942- WhoAm 90, WhoE 91
Cash, Frank Errette, Jr. 1921- WhoAm 90
Cash, Gerald C. 1917- WhoWor 91
Cash, H. Ray 1929- St&PR 91
Cash, Hal Duncan BiDrAPA 89
Cash, James Barrett, Jr. 1921- WhoAm 90
Cash, Johnny 1932- EncPR&S 89, OxCPMus, WhoAm 90, WhoNeCM C [port], WorAlBi
Cash, Joseph Harper 1927- WhoAm 90
Cash, June Carter 1929- WhoAm 90
Cash, LaVerne 1956- WhoAmW 91
Cash, Mary Emma 1955- WhoSSW 91
Cash, Norm 1934-1986 Ballpl 90 [port]
Cash, Norman E. 1918-1990 BioIn 16
Cash, Pat BioIn 16
Cash, Paul E. 1932- St&PR 91
Cash, Paul T 1911- BiDrAPA 89
Cash, Paul Thalbert 1911- WhoAm 90, WhoWor 91
Cash, Renee M. 1941- St&PR 91
Cash, Robert Edward 1933- St&PR 91
Cash, Robert Joseph 1955- WhoEmL 91
Cash, Rosalind 1938- DrBIPA 90
Cash, Rosanne 1955- BioIn 16, WhoAmW 91, WhoNeCM [port], WorAlBi
Cash, Roy Don 1942- WhoAm 90
Cash, William Elbert, Jr. 1947- WhoSSW 91
Cash, William McKinley 1930- WhoSSW 91
Cashdan, Linda 1942- ConAu 132
Cashel, Thomas William 1930- WhoAm 90
Cashel, William S., Jr. 1920- St&PR 91
Cashell, Jane Gering 1948- WhoAmW 91
Cashell, Lois D. WhoAmW 91
Cashen, Eric WhoWrEP 89
Cashen, Henry Christopher, II 1939- WhoAm 90
Cashen, J. Frank WhoAm 90, WhoE 91
Cashen, Joseph Lawrence 1931- WhoWor 91
Cashen, Susan K. ODwPR 91
Casher, J P Blake BiDrAPA 89
Casher, Michael Ira 1951- BiDrAPA 89
Cashill, Jack BioIn 16
Cashin, Bonnie 1915- WhoAmW 91
Cashin, Edward A. 1905- St&PR 91
Cashin, Edward Joseph 1927- WhoSSW 91
Cashin, John Richard 1946- WhoE 91
Cashin, Richard Marshall 1924- WhoAm 90
Cashion, Barbara Tansey 1947- WhoSSW 91
Cashion, Bonnie Bingham 1926- WhoSSW 91
Cashion, Herschell A. St&PR 91
Cashion, James H. 1941- WhoSSW 91
Cashion, James Taylor 1940- St&PR 91
Cashion, Joe Mason 1938- WhoSSW 91
Cashion, Norma Louella 1953-1984 BioIn 16
Cashion, Robert Nesbit 1947- WhoSSW 91
Cashion, Shelley Jean 1955- WhoEmL 91
Cashion, William Neil 1946- St&PR 91
Cashman, Edmund Joseph, Jr. 1936- St&PR 91, WhoAm 90
Cashman, G.D. 1953- St&PR 91
Cashman, Georgia 1932- WhoAmW 91
Cashman, Joe Ballpl 90
Cashman, John G. 1931- St&PR 91
Cashman, John Richard 1935- WhoWrEP 89
Cashman, John W. 1923- WhoAm 90
Cashman, Margaret Anne 1951- BiDrAPA 89
Cashman, Michael Richard 1926- WhoWor 91
Cashman, Ray Dudley 1945- St&PR 91
Cashman, Thomas J., Jr. 1952- St&PR 91
Cashman, W. Timothy, II 1929- WhoAm 90
Cashman, William James, Jr. 1937- WhoE 91
Cashmore, Patsy Joy 1943- WhoAmW 91
Casian, Alexandra EncCoWW
Casiano, Americo, Jr. 1951- WhoHisp 91
Casiano, Luz Nereida 1950- WhoHisp 91
Casiano, Manuel A., Jr. BioIn 16
Casiano, Manuel A., Jr. 1931- WhoHisp 91
Casiano, Marlene Emelina 1956- BiDrAPA 89
Casida, John Edward 1929- WhoAm 90
Casida, Kati 1931- WhoAmA 91
Casier, Francis David 1918- St&PR 91
Casillas, Ernest A BiDrAPA 89
Casillas, Mark 1953- WhoEmL 91, WhoWor 91
Casillas, Miguel A BiDrAPA 89
Casimir, Georges Jean 1951- BiDrAPA 89
Casimir, H B G 1909- ConAu 129
Casimir, Hendrik ConAu 129
Casimir-Perier, Jean-Paul-Pierre 1847-1907 BiDFrPL
Casimiro, Jorge L. 1953- WhoHisp 91
Casimiro, Jorge Luis 1953- WhoSSW 91
Casino, Joanne 1951- WhoAmW 91
Casiraghi, Stefano NewYTBS 90 [port]
Casken, John 1949- IntWWM 90
Caskey, W J. 1949- St&PR 91
Caskey, William Joslin 1949- WhoE 91, WhoEmL 91
Caskie, Cabot Robison 1944- St&PR 91
Caslavska, Vera 1942- WhoWor 91
Caslavska, Vera Barbara 1934- WhoAmW 91
Caslow, Richard Walker 1933- St&PR 91
Casmir, Mina G. Halliday 1945- WhoEmL 91
Casner, A. James NewYTBS 90 [port]
Casner, A James 1907-1990 ConAu 132
Casner, Andrew James 1907- WhoAm 90
Caso, Adolph 1934- WhoWrEP 89
Caso, Gasper 1933- WhoAm 90, WhoE 91
Cason, Barbara 1933- ConTFT 8
Cason, Brenda Wright 1950- WhoSSW 91
Cason, Dick Kendall 1922- WhoSSW 91, WhoWor 91
Cason, Ellen Pearre 1948- WhoAmW 91
Cason, Frederick Leon 1928- St&PR 91
Cason, June Macnabb 1930- WhoE 91
Cason, Marilynn Jean 1943- St&PR 91
Cason, Mary Patricia BiDrAPA 89
Cason, Neal Martin 1938- WhoAm 90
Cason, Roger Lee 1930- WhoE 91
Casona, Alejandro ConAu 131, HispWr 90
Casoni, Bianca-Maria 1936- IntWWM 90
Casoria, Giuseppe 1908- WhoWor 91
Caspar, George J. 1933- St&PR 91
Caspar, George J., III 1933- WhoAm 90
Caspar, Walter PenDiMP
Caspary, Anita 1915- WhoAm 90
Caspary, Vera 1899- FemiCLE
Caspary, Vera 1904-1987 TwCCr&M 91
Casper, Barry Michael 1939- WhoAm 90
Casper, Billy 1931- WorAlBi
Casper, Cathy Moore 1956- WhoAmW 91
Casper, Cheri Luann 1949- WhoAmW 91
Casper, Dale E. 1947-1989 BioIn 16
Casper, Daniel David 1959- St&PR 91
Casper, David NewAgMG

Casper, David 1949- *WhoWor 91*
Casper, David Bernard 1936- *St&PR 91*
Casper, Edmund 1936- *BiDrAPA 89*
Casper, Ellen Frances 1951- *WhoEmL 91*
Casper, George L. 1908- *St&PR 91*
Casper, Gerhard 1937- *WhoAm 90*
Casper, Jeffrey Elliot 1956- *WhoEmL 91*
Casper, John Michael 1945- *WhoEmL 91*
Casper, Laura 1953- *WhoAmW 91*
Casper, Laurie Kae 1965- *WhoAmW 91*
Casper, Leonard Ralph 1923- *WhoAm 90, WhoWrEP 89*
Casper, Majorie Helen 1938- *St&PR 91*
Casper, Michael David 1959- *St&PR 91*
Casper, Paul Alexander 1947- *WhoAm 90*
Casper, Philip Wilson 1914- *St&PR 91*
Casper, Regine Klaere 1938- *BiDrAPA 89*
Casper, Richard 1927- *St&PR 91*
Casper, Robert J. 1943- *St&PR 91, WhoAm 90*
Casper, Steven Lee 1958- *St&PR 91*
Casper, Stewart Michael 1953- *WhoEmL 91*
Caspers, Mary Lou *WhoAmW 91*
Caspersen, Barbara Morris 1945- *St&PR 91, WhoAmW 91*
Caspersen, Finn M.W. 1941- *St&PR 91*
Caspersen, Finn Michael Westby 1941- *WhoAm 90, WhoE 91*
Caspersen, Freda R. 1908- *St&PR 91*
Caspi, Daniel 1939- *WhoE 91*
Caspi, David Joshua 1955- *WhoWrEP 89*
Casriel, Ronald Beryl 1932- *St&PR 91*
Cass, A. Carl *WhoAm 90*
Cass, April Lorraine 1957- *WhoE 91*
Cass, Bill 1954- *WhoAmA 91*
Cass, Cami *BioIn 16*
Cass, David 1937- *WhoAm 90, WhoE 91*
Cass, Edmund Francis, Jr. 1934- *St&PR 91*
Cass, George F. 1939- *St&PR 91*
Cass, George Frank 1939- *WhoAm 90*
Cass, George L. 1940- *WhoAm 90*
Cass, Hyla R 1946- *BiDrAPA 89*
Cass, Joan *AuBYP 90*
Cass, Leonard J. 1944- *St&PR 91*
Cass, Lewis 1782-1866 *BiDrUSE 89, BioIn 16, WhNaAH [port]*
Cass, Maxine Harriet 1952- *WhoEmL 91*
Cass, Millard 1916- *WhoAm 90*
Cass, Oliver Wilfred 1949- *WhoEmL 91*
Cass, Robert Michael 1945- *WhoWor 91*
Cass, Ronald 1923- *OxCPMus*
Cass, Ronald Andrew 1949- *WhoAm 90*
Cass, Thomas Richardson 1930- *WhoE 91*
Cass, William F., Jr. 1934- *St&PR 91*
Cass-Beggs, Barbara 1904- *SmATA 62 [port]*
Cassab, Judy 1920- *BioIn 16*
Cassado, Gaspar 1897-1966 *PenDiMP*
Cassady, B.W. 1921- *St&PR 91*
Cassady, Cheryl Gale 1949- *WhoEmL 91*
Cassady, Claude *ConAu 31NR*
Cassady, John Mac 1938- *WhoAm 90*
Cassady, Laura Taulbee 1958- *WhoAmW 91*
Cassady, Marsh Gary 1936- *WhoWrEP 89*
Cassady, Shawn Lawrence 1958- *WhoE 91*
Cassagne, Gilbert Michael 1956- *WhoEmL 91*
Cassagnol, Francois 1947- *WhoSSW 91*
Cassak, Albert Loeb 1917- *WhoWor 91*
Cassani, Kaspar V. *BioIn 16*
Cassani, Kaspar V. 1928- *WhoAm 90*
Cassani, Robert A. 1959- *WhoWor 91*
Cassano, Donald A. 1951- *WhoE 91*
Cassano, Peter V. 1932- *St&PR 91*
Cassano, Phyllis A.M. 1949- *WhoAmW 91*
Cassano, Vincent Frank 1943- *St&PR 91*
Cassanova, Lawrence Joseph, III 1948- *WhoE 91, WhoEmL 91*
Cassar, Arthur Ivo 1847- *WhoWor 91*
Cassar, Jon Francis 1958- *WhoEmL 91*
Cassara, Frank *WhoAmA 91*
Cassara, Frank 1913- *WhoAm 90*
Cassara, Michael D. 1947- *St&PR 91*
Cassat, Georganne 1950- *IntWWM 90*
Cassata, John J. 1908-1989 *BioIn 16*
Cassatt, Mary 1844-1926 *BioAmW, BioIn 16, IntDcAA 90, WorAlBi*
Cassatt, Mary Stevenson 1844-1926 *BiDWomA*
Cassavetes, John *BioIn 16*
Cassavetes, John 1929-1989 *AnObit 1989, WorAlBi*
Cassavetti, M. *BiDWomA*
Cassedy, Hiram 1820-1881 *AmLegL*
Cassedy, John H. 1930- *St&PR 91*
Cassedy, Sylvia 1930- *WhoWrEP 89*
Cassedy, Sylvia 1930-1989 *AuBYP 90, BioIn 16, SmATA 61*
Cassel, Carl Gustav 1866-1945 *BioIn 16*
Cassel, Christine Karen 1945- *WhoAmW 91*
Cassel, Cynthia Lou 1962- *WhoEmL 91*
Cassel, Daniel 1920- *St&PR 91*
Cassel, Dieter 1939- *WhoWor 91*
Cassel, Dona Julian 1946- *WhoAmW 91*
Cassel, Harrison H. 1917- *St&PR 91*
Cassel, John Elden 1934- *WhoSSW 91, WhoWor 91*
Cassel, John Harmon *WhoAmA 91N*
Cassel, John Walter 1910- *IntWWM 90*
Cassel, Neil Jonathon 1961- *WhoE 91, WhoEmL 91*
Cassel, Raymond L. 1957- *St&PR 91*
Cassel, Robert Harrison 1949- *St&PR 91*
Cassel, Robert Thomas 1931- *St&PR 91*
Cassel, Sylvia Ann 1938- *WhoAmW 91*
Cassel, Thomas A.V. 1946- *St&PR 91*
Cassel, Walter 1920- *WhoAm 90*
Casselberry, Robert Logan 1926- *St&PR 91*
Cassell, Beverly 1936- *WhoAmA 91*
Cassell, Dana Kay *WhoWrEP 89*
Cassell, Eric Jonathan 1928- *WhoAm 90*
Cassell, Frank Hyde 1916- *WhoAm 90*
Cassell, Kay Ann 1941- *WhoAm 90, WhoAmW 91*
Cassell, Martin Leroy 1910- *WhoAm 90*
Cassell, Ollan *BioIn 16*
Cassell, Richard Emmett 1949- *WhoEmL 91*
Cassell, Robert Bernard 1918- *WhoSSW 91*
Cassell, Wilfred A *BiDrAPA 89*
Cassell, William Comyn 1934- *WhoAm 90*
Cassell, William J. *BioIn 16*
Cassell, William Walter 1917- *WhoAm 90*
Cassella, Anthony *St&PR 91*
Cassella, William Nathan, Jr. 1920- *WhoAm 90*
Casselli, Henry C, Jr 1946- *WhoAmA 91*
Cassells, Cyrus Curtis 1957- *WhoWrEP 89*
Casselman, Juanita 1921- *BiDrAPA 89*
Casselman, Ruth Zagat *BioIn 16*
Casselman, William A. 1903-1989 *BioIn 16*
Casselman, William E., II 1941- *WhoAm 90, WhoE 91*
Cassels, Andrew *BioIn 16*
Cassels, Peter Andrew 1943- *WhoE 91*
Cassels-Brown, Alastair Kennedy 1927- *IntWWM 90, WhoAm 90*
Cassem, Edwin Hughes 1935- *BiDrAPA 89*
Casserly, Alvaro Alonso 1932- *St&PR 91, WhoWor 91*
Casserly, John Joseph 1927- *WhoAm 90*
Casserly, Joseph William 1929- *WhoAm 90*
Casserly, Mary Lou 1951- *WhoE 91*
Cassese, John 1934- *WhoE 91*
Cassese, John J. 1945- *St&PR 91*
Cassetty, Fred Joseph 1938- *St&PR 91*
Cassian, Nina 1924- *EncCoWW*
Cassibry, Fred James 1918- *WhoAm 90*
Cassiday, Benjamin Buckles, Jr. 1922- *WhoAm 90*
Cassidy, Butch 1866?- *BioIn 16*
Cassidy, Carl Eugene 1924- *WhoAm 90*
Cassidy, Claudia 1905?- *BioIn 16, NotWoAT*
Cassidy, David 1950- *ConTFT 8 [port], WorAlBi*
Cassidy, David Bede 1953- *WhoSSW 91*
Cassidy, Donald L. 1945- *WhoEmL 91*
Cassidy, Francis E. 1928- *WhoSSW 91*
Cassidy, Frederic Gomes 1907- *WhoAm 90*
Cassidy, Harold Gomes 1906- *WhoAm 90*
Cassidy, Jack 1927-1976 *WorAlBi*
Cassidy, Jack 1941- *WhoE 91, WhoWor 91*
Cassidy, James Joseph 1916- *WhoAm 90*
Cassidy, James Patrick 1925- *WhoAm 90*
Cassidy, Joan Kathryn 1927- *WhoAmW 91, WhoE 91*
Cassidy, Joe 1883-1906 *Ballpl 90*
Cassidy, John Harold 1925- *WhoAm 90*
Cassidy, John Rufus 1922- *SpyFic*
Cassidy, John Tobin *BioIn 16*
Cassidy, John Wayne *BiDrAPA 89*
Cassidy, Lawrence R. 1946- *WhoEmL 91*
Cassidy, Margaret Carol *WhoAmA 91*
Cassidy, Mariellen 1956- *WhoSSW 91*
Cassidy, Mary Catherine 1953- *WhoAmW 91*
Cassidy, Michael Stanley 1938- *WhoAm 90*
Cassidy, Patrick 1961- *ConTFT 8*
Cassidy, Paul *PenDiMP*
Cassidy, Raymond Jack 1933- *IntWWM 90*
Cassidy, Richard Thomas 1916- *WhoAm 90*
Cassidy, Robert *BioIn 16*
Cassidy, Robert Charles, Jr. 1946- *WhoAm 90*
Cassidy, Robert Edward 1931- *St&PR 91, WhoAm 90*
Cassidy, Robert Eustace 1935- *WhoE 91*
Cassidy, Robert J. 1930- *St&PR 91*
Cassidy, Robert Joseph 1930- *WhoAm 90*
Cassidy, Samuel M. 1932- *St&PR 91, WhoAm 90*
Cassidy, Suzanne Bletterman 1944- *WhoAmW 91*
Cassidy, Thomas Joseph 1925- *St&PR 91*
Cassidy, Thomas Louis 1928- *St&PR 91*
Cassidy, Thomas M 1932- *BiDrAPA 89*
Cassidy, Thomas Owen 1946- *St&PR 91*
Cassidy, W.D., III 1941- *St&PR 91*
Cassidy, Walter L *BiDrAPA 89*
Cassidy, William Arthur 1928- *WhoAm 90*
Cassidy, William Dunnigan, III 1941- *WhoE 91*
Cassidy, William Louis 1945- *St&PR 91*
Cassie *WhoWrEP 89*
Cassill, Herbert Carroll 1928- *WhoAm 90, WhoAmA 91*
Cassill, Karilyn *WhoWrEP 89*
Cassill, Ronald Verlin 1919- *WhoAm 90, WhoWrEP 89*
Cassilly, Richard 1927- *IntWWM 90, PenDiMP, WhoAm 90, WhoE 91*
Cassils, William 1832-1891 *DcCanB 12*
Cassimatis, Emmanuel G. 1944- *BiDrAPA 89*
Cassimatis, Peter John 1928- *WhoAm 90*
Cassin, James A. 1934- *St&PR 91*
Cassin, Rene 1887-1976 *WorAlBi*
Cassin, Rene Samuel 1887-1976 *BiDFrPL*
Cassin, Thomas Conway 1938- *St&PR 91*
Cassin, William Bourke 1931- *WhoAm 90, WhoSSW 91, WhoWor 91*
Cassin, William F. *BioIn 16*
Cassinelli, Anthony Pete 1940- *St&PR 91*
Cassinelli, Hector Juan *BiDrAPA 89*
Cassinelli, Joseph Patrick 1940- *WhoAm 90*
Cassingham, Randy C. 1959- *WhoWrEP 89*
Cassini, Giovanni Domenico 1625-1712 *WorAlBi*
Cassini, Igor 1915- *ConAu 129*
Cassini, Oleg *BioIn 16*
Cassinis, Elaine L. 1957- *WhoAmW 91*
Cassirer, Fritz 1871-1926 *PenDiMP*
Cassirer, Manfred 1920- *EncPaPR 91*
Cassirer, Nadine Gordimer 1923- *BioIn 16*
Cassisi, Elayne E 1936- *BiDrAPA 89*
Cassity, Turner 1929- *DcLB 105 [port]*
Cassner, Alvin B. 1913- *St&PR 91*
Cassner, John Daniel 1940- *St&PR 91*
Casso, Araceli Gonzalez *BiDrAPA 89*
Cassoday, John Bolivar 1830-1907 *AmLegL*
Cassoli, Piero 1918- *EncO&P 3, EncPaPR 91*
Casson, Hugh 1910- *ConDes 90*
Casson, Richard Frederick 1939- *St&PR 91*
Cassone, Dominick Joseph 1954- *WhoE 91*
Cassubhoy Oves, Hasani 1948- *WhoWor 91*
Cassuto, Alvaro 1938- *IntWWM 90*
Cassutt, Thomas Gerard 1960- *St&PR 91*
Cassyd, Syd 1908- *WhoAmA 91*
Cast, Anita Hursh 1939- *WhoAmW 91*
Casta, Aurora M *BiDrAPA 89*
Castagna, W. Norman 1923- *St&PR 91*
Castagnaro, Marie Renee 1944- *WhoAmW 91*
Castagne, Maurice 1920- *ODwPR 91*
Castagnetta, Grace Sharp 1912- *WhoAm 90*
Castagnini, Gene Joseph 1949- *WhoEmL 91*
Castagnino, Raul Hector 1914- *WhoWor 91*
Castagno, Andrea Del 1421?-1457 *WorAlBi*
Castaing, Francois J. *BioIn 16*
Castaing, Raimond Bernard 1921- *WhoWor 91*
Castaldi, Alexander Richard 1950- *St&PR 91*
Castaldi, David Lawrence 1940- *WhoAm 90*
Castaldo, John N. 1956- *WhoEmL 91*
Castaldo, Joseph 1927- *IntWWM 90*
Castaldo, Peter James 1948- *WhoE 91*
Castaldo, Vincenzo 1930- *BiDrAPA 89*
Castaneda, Antonio 1945- *WhoWor 91*
Castaneda, Carlos 1925?- *EncO&P 3, WhoHisp 91*
Castaneda, Carlos 1931?- *ConAu 32NR, HispWr 90, MajTwCW, WorAlBi*
Castaneda, Carlos Eduardo 1896-1958 *BioIn 16*
Castaneda, Hector-Neri 1924- *WhoAm 90*
Castaneda, Lina Luz M *BiDrAPA 89*
Castaneda, Roberto Rudolph 1956- *WhoEmL 91*
Castaneira Colon, Rafael 1936- *WhoHisp 91*
Castang, Veronica *BioIn 16*
Castania-Smith, Deborah Lynn 1963- *WhoEmL 91*
Castanis, Muriel 1926- *BioIn 16, WhoAmA 91*
Castanis, Muriel Julia Brunner 1926- *WhoE 91*
Castano, Elvira 1929- *WhoAmA 91*
Castano, Elvira Palmerio 1929- *WhoAmW 91, WhoE 91, WhoWor 91*
Castano, Giovanni 1896- *WhoAmA 91N*
Castano, Gregory Joseph 1929- *WhoE 91*
Castano, Sylvia Elizabeth 1953- *WhoEmL 91*
Castanuela, Mary-Helen 1950- *WhoHisp 91*
Caste, Jean F. 1929- *WhoAm 90, WhoWor 91*
Castedo, Elena 1937- *ConAu 132*
Castedo, Nicanor F 1928- *BiDrAPA 89*
Castedo-Ellerman, Elena *ConAu 132*
Casteel, Bette 1920- *WhoWrEP 89*
Casteel, Clyde Terrel 1953- *WhoEmL 91*
Casteel, DiAnn Brown 1953- *WhoSSW 91*
Casteel, J. Kenneth 1939- *St&PR 91*
Casteel, Lynn E. *ODwPR 91*
Casteel, Phillip Thomas 1951- *St&PR 91*
Casteel, Ronald Clay *WhoSSW 91*
Casteel, William J. 1929- *St&PR 91*
Casteen, John T., III 1943- *WhoAm 90, WhoSSW 91, WhoWor 91*
Castel, Gerard Joseph 1934- *WhoWor 91*
Castel, Jean Gabriel 1928- *WhoAm 90*
Castel, Nico 1931- *IntWWM 90*
Castel, Nico 1935- *WhoAm 90*
Castel, P. Kevin 1950- *WhoEmL 91*
Castel, Philippe 1956- *WhoWor 91*
Castel, Robert 1933- *ConAu 129*
Castelain, Pierre-Yves 1927- *WhoWor 91*
Castelbajac, Kate de *BioIn 16*
Castele, Theodore John 1928- *WhoWor 91*
Casteleyn, Mary 1941- *ConAu 131*
Castell, David Gerard 1945- *St&PR 91*
Castell, George Coventry 1936- *WhoE 91*
Castellan, Gilbert William 1924- *WhoAm 90*
Castellan, Norman John, Jr. 1939- *WhoAm 90*
Castellani, Alessandro 1823-1883 *PenDiDA 89*
Castellani, Armand J. 1917- *St&PR 91*
Castellani, Augusto 1829-1914 *PenDiDA 89*
Castellani, Pio Fortunato 1794-1865 *PenDiDA 89*
Castellani, Robert Joseph 1941- *WhoSSW 91*
Castellani, Sam U. *BiDrAPA 89*
Castellano, Giovanni *PenDiDA 89*
Castellano, Richard 1933-1988 *BioIn 16*
Castellanos, Carlos *BiDrAPA 89*
Castellanos, Daniel *BiDrAPA 89*
Castellanos, Diego Antonio 1933- *WhoHisp 91*
Castellanos, F. Xavier 1953- *BiDrAPA 89*
Castellanos, George N. 1944- *WhoE 91*
Castellanos, Jane 1913- *AuBYP 90*
Castellanos, Ricardo C. 1945- *WhoHisp 91*
Castellanos, Rosario *BioIn 16*
Castellanos, Rosario 1925-1974 *ConAu 131, HispWr 90*
Castellanos, Theodora 1940- *WhoHisp 91*
Castellarin, Sheila *ODwPR 91*
Castellarin, Sheila A. 1935- *St&PR 91*
Castellaw, Earlene Johnson 1928- *WhoAmW 91*
Castellett, Marisa *WhoAmA 91*
Castelli, Alexander Gerard 1929- *WhoAm 90*
Castelli, Dolores Bennett 1932- *WhoAmW 91*
Castelli, Francis Anthony 1951- *WhoE 91*
Castelli, Leo 1907- *WhoAm 90, WhoAmA 91*
Castelli-Ferrieri, Anna 1920- *ConDes 90*
Castellino, Francis Joseph 1943- *WhoAm 90*
Castellino, Ronald Augustus Dietrich 1938- *WhoAm 90*
Castellitto, George Paul 1949- *WhoE 91*
Castello, Cristiana 1961- *WhoWor 91*
Castello, Hugo Martinez 1914- *WhoHisp 91*
Castello, Joli Marion 1963- *WhoAmW 91*
Castellon, Augustin *BioIn 16*
Castellon, Federico 1914-1971 *BioIn 16*
Castellon, Michael Cary 1961- *WhoEmL 91*
Castelloza *EncCoWW*
Castells, Manuel F. 1942- *St&PR 91*
Castelluzzi, Donato Dan Michael 1949- *St&PR 91*
Castelmary, Armand 1834-1897 *PenDiMP*
Castelnau, Henriette Julie de 1670-1716 *EncCoWW*
Castelnau, Noel Marie Joseph Edouard de 1851-1944 *BiDFrPL*
Castelnuovo-Tedesco, Diana *ODwPR 91*
Castelnuovo-Tedesco, Mario 1895-1968 *PenDiMP A*
Castelnuovo-Tedesco, Pietro 1925- *BiDrAPA 89*
Castelo, Carlos Alberto Monteiro 1943- *WhoWor 91*
Castelo, Cecilia B *BiDrAPA 89*
Castelo Branco, Humberto de Alencar 1900-1967 *BioIn 16*

Casteloes, Susan Chambers 1939- *WhoAmW 91*
Castelvitch, Countess *EncO&P 3*
Casteneda, Carlos 1925?- *EncPaPR 91*
Castenschiold, Rene 1923- *WhoAm 90*
Caster, Bernard Harry 1921- *WhoAmA 91, WhoE 91, WhoWor 91*
Caster, David Udell *BiDrAPA 89*
Caster, George 1907-1955 *Ballpl 90*
Caster, Jeffery Edward 1965- *WhoE 91*
Casterborn, Lars Goran 1942- *St&PR 91*
Casterella, Anthony J. 1945- *St&PR 91*
Casterline, William Hale, Jr. 1951- *WhoEmL 91*
Castetter, Gregory Keelerr 1935- *BiDrAPA 89*
Casti, John Louis 1943- *WhoWor 91*
Castiello, Anastasio M. *BiDrAPA 89*
Castiglia, Athan F. *St&PR 91*
Castiglia, Joseph J. 1934- *St&PR 91*
Castiglia, Patricia Anne Thorson *WhoAmW 91, WhoSSW 91*
Castiglione, Giovanni Benedetto 1609-1663? *IntDcAA 90*
Castiglione, Pete 1921- *Ballpl 90*
Castiglione-Colonna, Duchess of *BiDWomA*
Castiglioni, Achille 1918- *ConDes 90, PenDiDA 89*
Castiglioni, Aldo Joseph, Jr. *BiDrAPA 89*
Castiglioni, Baldassare 1478-1549 *WorAlBi*
Castiglioni, Livio 1911-1979 *ConDes 90*
Castiglioni, Nicola 1932- *IntWWM 90*
Castiglioni, Pier Giacomo 1913-1968 *ConDes 90*
Castile, Rand 1938- *WhoAm 90, WhoAmA 91, WhoWor 91*
Castilla, Craig K. 1961- *St&PR 91*
Castilla, Ramon 1797-1867 *BioIn 16*
Castillo, Alba N. 1945- *WhoHisp 91*
Castillo, Ana 1953- *ConAu 131, HispWr 90, WhoHisp 91*
Castillo, Antonio Canovas del 1828-1897 *BioIn 16*
Castillo, Bernal Diaz del 1496-1584 *BioIn 16*
Castillo, Bob 1955- *Ballpl 90*
Castillo, Brenda Victoria 1962- *WhoHisp 91*
Castillo, Carlos *BiDrAPA 89*
Castillo, Carmen 1958- *Ballpl 90, WhoHisp 91*
Castillo, Craig Michael 1967- *WhoHisp 91*
Castillo, Diego Del *EncCRAm*
Castillo, Edgar *BiDrAPA 89*
Castillo, Edmund Luis 1924- *AuBYP 90*
Castillo, Edwin F *BiDrAPA 89*
Castillo, Gloria J. 1954- *WhoHisp 91*
Castillo, Gloria Jean 1954- *WhoEmL 91*
Castillo, Hal Stephen 1947- *WhoEmL 91*
Castillo, Helen M. 1936- *WhoHisp 91*
Castillo, Jaime Del 1951- *WhoWor 91*
Castillo, Javier M. 1967- *WhoHisp 91*
Castillo, John Roy 1948- *WhoHisp 91*
Castillo, Jorge 1933- *BioIn 16*
Castillo, Juan 1962- *Ballpl 90*
Castillo, Karen Sue 1948- *WhoAmW 91*
Castillo, Leonel J. 1939- *BioIn 16*
Castillo, Leonel Javier 1939- *WhoHisp 91*
Castillo, Luciano 1896-1980 *BioIn 16*
Castillo, Luis Enrique 1950- *WhoSSW 91*
Castillo, Manny 1957- *Ballpl 90*
Castillo, Manuel H. 1949- *WhoHisp 91*
Castillo, Mario Enrique 1945- *WhoWor 91*
Castillo, Marty 1957- *Ballpl 90*
Castillo, Mary 1947- *WhoHisp 91*
Castillo, Nilda 1956- *WhoHisp 91*
Castillo, Pedro Antonio 1926- *WhoAm 90, WhoHisp 91*
Castillo, Pura M *BiDrAPA 89*
Castillo, Rafael C. 1950- *WhoWrEP 89*
Castillo, Rafael Ernest 1952- *WhoEmL 91*
Castillo, Ramona 1928- *WhoHisp 91*
Castillo, Ricardo Orlando 1948- *WhoHisp 91*
Castillo, Richard Cesar 1949- *WhoHisp 91*
Castillo, Robert Charles 1952- *WhoHisp 91*
Castillo, Roberto Diaz 1931- *WhoWor 91*
Castillo, Rogelio Galam 1939- *BiDrAPA 89*
Castillo, Victor Rodriguez 1945- *WhoHisp 91*
Castillo, Walter M 1934- *BiDrAPA 89*
Castillo Armas, Carlos 1914-1957 *BioIn 16*
Castillo Lara, Rosalio Jose 1922- *WhoWor 91*
Castillo-Olimpo, Julita S. *BiDrAPA 89*
Castillo Puche, Jose Luis 1919- *IntvSpW [port]*
Castillo-Quinones, Isabel 1953- *WhoHisp 91*
Castillo-Tovar, Maria-Lourdes 1950- *WhoHisp 91*
Castilow, H. Carter 1943- *St&PR 91*
Castine, Michael Patrick 1954- *WhoE 91*
Castino, John 1954- *Ballpl 90*
Castle, Alfred L, Mrs 1886-1970 *WhoAmA 91N*
Castle, Anthony 1938- *ConAu 32NR*
Castle, Barbara 1910- *ConAu 130*
Castle, Bruce Edward 1958- *WhoEmL 91*
Castle, Connie Jo 1953- *WhoAmW 91*
Castle, David R. 1949- *St&PR 91*
Castle, Donald Robert 1936- *WhoSSW 91*
Castle, Douglas Bishop 1942- *St&PR 91*
Castle, Emery Neal 1923- *WhoAm 90*
Castle, Frank Allen 1934- *St&PR 91*
Castle, Frank E. 1932- *St&PR 91*
Castle, Gray 1931- *St&PR 91*
Castle, Irene 1893-1969 *BioIn 16, OxCPMus, WorAlBi*
Castle, James Cameron 1936- *St&PR 91, WhoAm 90, WhoE 91*
Castle, John K. 1940- *St&PR 91*
Castle, John Krob 1940- *WhoAm 90, WhoWor 91*
Castle, Kit *BioIn 16*
Castle, Lee *NewYTBS 90*
Castle, Leonard L. 1912?-1989 *ConAu 129*
Castle, Marian Johnson *WhoAm 90, WhoWrEP 89*
Castle, Michael N. 1939- *WhoAm 90, WhoE 91, WhoWor 91*
Castle, Paul *AuBYP 90*
Castle, Raymond Nielson 1916- *WhoAm 90, WhoWor 91*
Castle, Robert Woods 1925- *WhoAm 90*
Castle, Sharon Denise 1952- *WhoE 91*
Castle, Stephen Neil 1952- *WhoEmL 91*
Castle, Tony *ConAu 32NR*
Castle, Vernon 1887-1918 *BioIn 16, OxCPMus, WorAlBi*
Castle, Wendell 1932- *PenDiDA 89*
Castle, Wendell Keith 1932- *WhoAm 90, WhoAmA 91, WhoE 91*
Castle, William Eugene 1929- *WhoAm 90*
Castle, William Richards 1878-1963 *BioIn 16*
Castle Stewart, E M Guggenheim, Countess 1898- *BioIn 16*
Castleberry, Karen Wittler 1953- *WhoSSW 91*
Castleberry, May Lewis 1954- *WhoAm 90*
Castleberry, Robert Holmes 1955- *WhoEmL 91*
Castleberry, Vivian Lou Anderson 1922- *WhoAm 90*
Castleberry, William *BioIn 16*
Castleman, Albert Welford, Jr. 1936- *WhoAm 90*
Castleman, Charles 1941- *IntWWM 90*
Castleman, Foster 1931- *Ballpl 90*
Castleman, Harry W., Jr. 1950- *ODwPR 91*
Castleman, Louis Samuel 1918- *WhoAm 90*
Castleman, Paul Stanley 1941- *St&PR 91*
Castleman, Riva 1930- *WhoAm 90, WhoAmA 91*
Castleman, Slick 1913- *Ballpl 90*
Castlereagh, Robert Stewart 1769-1822 *BioIn 16*
Castles, James B. 1915 *St&PR 91*
Castles, John William 1947- *WhoEmL 91*
Castles, Leone Dexter Strickland 1923- *WhoAmW 91*
Castleton, Lane J. 1956- *St&PR 91*
Castling, Leon C. 1911- *St&PR 91*
Castloo, Shirley Annette 1943- *WhoSSW 91*
Castner, Edward John *BiDrAPA 89*
Casto, Dale G. 1936- *St&PR 91*
Casto, Dennis Lee 1954- *WhoEmL 91*
Casto, Leo V. 1933- *St&PR 91*
Casto, Sara Lynn 1952- *BiDrAPA 89*
Caston, Jesse Douglas 1932- *WhoAm 90*
Caston, John Chris 1946- *BiDrAPA 89*
Caston, Joseph 1936- *BiDrAPA 89*
Castonguay, Claude 1929- *St&PR 91, WhoAm 90, WhoWor 91*
Castor, C. William, Jr. 1925- *WhoAm 90*
Castor, Carol Jean 1944- *WhoSSW 91*
Castor, Elizabeth B. 1941- *WhoAmW 91*
Castor, Henry 1909- *AuBYP 90*
Castor, Susan Dee 1946- *WhoEmL 91*
Castor, Wilbur Wright 1932- *WhoWor 91*
Castor, William Stuart, Jr. 1926- *WhoAm 90*
Castoro, Rosemarie 1939- *WhoAmA 91*
Castranova, Vincent 1949- *WhoSSW 91*
Castrilla, Gregory John 1949- *St&PR 91*
Castriotta, Ralph John, Jr. *BiDrAPA 89*
Castro, Alfonso H. Peter, III 1955- *WhoHisp 91*
Castro, Alfred A. 1934- *WhoHisp 91*
Castro, Amado Alejandro 1924- *WhoWor 91*
Castro, Americo 1885-1972 *HispWr 90*
Castro, Antonio de *PenDiDA 89*
Castro, Beatriz M. 1961- *IntWWM 90*
Castro, Bill 1931- *WhoHisp 91*
Castro, Bill 1953- *Ballpl 90*
Castro, Brian Albert 1950- *WhoWor 91*
Castro, C. Elizabeth 1950- *WhoHisp 91*
Castro, Carlos Arturo, Sr. 1954- *WhoHisp 91*
Castro, Carmen de Lara *BioIn 16*
Castro, Celia 1949- *WhoHisp 91*
Castro, Cipriano 1858?-1924 *BioIn 16*
Castro, D.H. de *PenDiDA 89*
Castro, Eduardo *BiDrAPA 89*
Castro, Eduardo C *BiDrAPA 89*
Castro, Ernesto 1967- *WhoHisp 91*
Castro, Fidel 1926- *Ballpl 90, ConAu 129*
Castro, Fidel 1927- *BioIn 16, WhoWor 91, WorAlBi*
Castro, George 1939- *WhoHisp 91*
Castro, Giovanni 1946- *WhoAmA 91*
Castro, Hugo A. 1943- *St&PR 91*
Castro, Jaime 1943- *WhoHisp 91*
Castro, Jan Garden 1945- *WhoAm 90, WhoWrEP 89*
Castro, Jennie *BiDrAPA 89*
Castro, John M. 1951- *WhoHisp 91*
Castro, Jose Gil de 1785-1841 *ArtLatA*
Castro, Joseph Armand 1927- *WhoWor 91*
Castro, Joseph Ronald 1934- *WhoAm 90*
Castro, Lalo di *EncCoWW*
Castro, Leon Cortes 1882-1946 *BioIn 16*
Castro, Leonard Edward 1934- *WhoWor 91*
Castro, Lillian 1954- *WhoHisp 91*
Castro, Maria del Rosario 1947- *WhoHisp 91*
Castro, Maria del Rosario 1952- *WhoSSW 91*
Castro, Mario Humberto 1934- *WhoHisp 91*
Castro, Max Jose 1951- *WhoHisp 91*
Castro, Michael 1945- *ConAu 132, WhoHisp 91*
Castro, Miguel Antonio 1953- *BiDrAPA 89*
Castro, Mike *WhoHisp 91*
Castro, Providencia *BiDrAPA 89*
Castro, Rafael Yglesias 1861-1924 *BioIn 16*
Castro, Ramon Baldorioty de 1822-1889 *BioIn 16*
Castro, Raul *WhoWor 91*
Castro, Raul 1931- *BioIn 16*
Castro, Raul H. 1916- *BioIn 16, WhoHisp 91*
Castro, Raul Hector 1916- *WhoAm 90*
Castro, Rick R. 1938- *WhoHisp 91*
Castro, Rodolfo H. 1942- *WhoHisp 91*
Castro, Rosalia de 1837-1885 *BioIn 16, EncCoWW*
Castro, Salvador B. 1933- *BioIn 16*
Castro, Salvador Piccio, Jr. 1942- *WhoWor 91*
Castro, Sam Anthony 1923- *BiDrAPA 89*
Castro, Teresa Harper 1956- *WhoAmW 91*
Castro Alves, Antonio Frederico de 1847-1871 *BioIn 16*
Castro-Blanco, David *WhoHisp 91*
Castro-Caldas, Alexandre Lemos 1948- *WhoWor 91*
Castro-Gomez, Margaret 1959- *WhoHisp 91*
Castro-Neves, Oscar *NewAgMG*
Castro y Quesada, Americo 1885-1972 *HispWr 90*
Castroleal, Alicia 1945- *WhoHisp 91*
Castroll, Robert Stephen 1940- *BiDrAPA 89*
Castronovo, David 1945- *WhoE 91*
Castrop, Helmut 1936- *WhoWor 91*
Castroviejo, Santiago 1946- *WhoWor 91*
Castroviejo Blanco-Ciceron, Concha 1912- *EncCoWW*
Castruccio, Peter A 1925- *EncO&P 3*
Casty, Ronald G. 1945- *St&PR 91*
Casu, Nereide *BiDrAPA 89*
Casuso, Enrique Gustavo *BiDrAPA 89*
Casuso, W. Jill 1952- *WhoSSW 91*
Caswall, Emily Jane 1954- *WhoAmW 91*
Caswell, Dana Earl 1940- *St&PR 91*
Caswell, Donald Eugene 1948- *WhoEmL 91, WhoWrEP 89*
Caswell, Dorothy Ann Cottrell 1938- *WhoAmW 91*
Caswell, Helen 1923- *AuBYP 90*
Caswell, Helen Rayburn 1923- *WhoAmA 91*
Caswell, Herbert Hall, Jr. 1923- *WhoAm 90*
Caswell, Hollis L. 1901-1988 *BioIn 16*
Caswell, Hollis Leland 1931- *St&PR 91, WhoAm 90*
Caswell, James Donald 1935- *WhoSSW 91*
Caswell, Jeffrey Paul 1962- *WhoEmL 91, WhoSSW 91*
Caswell, Jeffry Claxton 1959- *WhoSSW 91*
Caswell, Jim 1948- *WhoAmA 91*
Caswell, John Beveridge 1938- *St&PR 91, WhoAm 90*
Caswell, Lyman Ray 1928- *WhoSSW 91*
Caswell, Michael Lynn 1948- *WhoSSW 91*
Caswell, Paul Hadley 1936- *WhoAm 90*
Caswell, W.B. 1934- *St&PR 91*
Caswell, W. Cameron 1916- *St&PR 91*
Caswick, Mary Ann *BiDrAPA 89*
Cat *BioIn 16*
Cata, Alfonso *NewYTBS 90*
Cata, Gabriel L 1928- *BiDrAPA 89*
Catabelle, Jean-Marie Henri 1941- *WhoWor 91*
Catabia, Ellen Coty 1948- *WhoAmW 91*
Catacalos, Rosemary 1944- *WhoHisp 91*
Catacosinos, William J. 1930- *St&PR 91*
Catacosinos, William James 1930- *WhoAm 90, WhoE 91*
Catahecassa 1740?-1831 *WhNaAH*
Catala, Mario E., II 1942- *WhoHisp 91*
Catala, Rafael 1942- *BioIn 16, ConAu 32NR, HispWr 90*
Catala, Rafael Enrique 1942- *WhoHisp 91, WhoWrEP 89*
Catala, Victor *EncCoWW*
Catalan, Edgardo Omar *WhoAmA 91*
Cataland, James Ronald 1944- *St&PR 91*
Catalani, Alfredo 1854-1893 *PenDiMP A*
Catalani, Angelica 1780-1849 *PenDiMP*
Catalano, Anthony Peter 1946- *St&PR 91*
Catalano, Carl Philip 1953- *WhoEmL 91*
Catalano, Charles Ross 1936- *St&PR 91*
Catalano, Joseph Michael 1945- *St&PR 91*
Catalano, Phillip Thomas 1929- *St&PR 91*
Cataldi, Anna *BioIn 16*
Cataldi, Oscar Blas *BiDrAPA 89*
Cataldo, Anthony Joseph, II 1957- *WhoEmL 91*
Cataldo, Bernard Francis 1907- *WhoWor 91*
Cataldo, Corinne Balog 1953- *WhoSSW 91*
Cataldo, John William 1924- *WhoAmA 91*
Cataldo, Joseph 1837-1928 *WhNaAH*
Cataldo, Patricia Ediin *WhoAmW 91*
Cataldo, Robert J. 1954- *St&PR 91*
Cataldo, Wallace A. 1950- *St&PR 91*
Catalfamo, Janice Stella 1936- *WhoAmW 91*
Catalfamo, Sal Frank 1951- *WhoE 91, WhoEmL 91*
Catalfo, Alfred, Jr. 1920- *WhoAm 90, WhoE 91, WhoWor 91*
Catalfo, Betty Marie 1942- *WhoAmW 91*
Catalfomo, Philip 1931- *WhoAm 90*
Catalinda de Albret *WomWR*
Catallo, Clarence Guerrino, Jr. 1940- *WhoAm 90*
Catanese, Anthony James 1942- *ConAu 32NR*
Catania, Anthony Charles 1936- *WhoAm 90*
Catania, Barbara Josephine 1939- *WhoAmW 91*
Catania, Joseph A. 1927- *St&PR 91*
Catania, Lorraine Laura 1942- *WhoAmW 91*
Catania, Ronald 1945- *St&PR 91, WhoEmL 91*
Catania, Thomas Francis 1932- *St&PR 91*
Catanzano, Attilio Bruce *BiDrAPA 89*
Catanzano, Frank Alexander 1947- *WhoEmL 91*
Catanzaro, Karen Barbara 1960- *WhoAmW 91*
Catanzaro, Ronald J 1934- *BiDrAPA 89*
Catanzaro, Tony *WhoAm 90*
Catapano, Joseph John 1935- *St&PR 91, WhoAm 90*
Catapano, Thomas F. 1949- *WhoHisp 91*
Catapano-Friedman, Lisa Karen 1952- *BiDrAPA 89, WhoE 91*
Catarino, Camilo Jose 1955- *WhoEmL 91*
Catasus, Jose Magin Perez 1942- *WhoSSW 91*
Catayee, Justin *BioIn 16*
Catchapaw, Dorothy Deane 1912- *WhoWrEP 89*
Catchi 1920- *WhoAmA 91*
Catchi, Catherine Oeland 1920- *WhoE 91*
Catchpole, Lawrence Welton 1952- *WhoSSW 91*
Catchpole, Margaret 1762-1819 *FemiCLE*
Cate, Benjamin Wilson Upton 1931- *WhoAm 90*
Cate, Charles H. 1938- *St&PR 91*
Cate, David Julian 1955- *WhoEmL 91*
Cate, John *ODwPR 91*
Cate, John S. 1948- *St&PR 91*
Cate, Phillip Dennis 1944- *WhoAm 90, WhoAmA 91*
Cate, Rex Neil 1958- *WhoEmL 91*
Cate, William Warner *AmLegL*
Cate, Wirt Armistead 1900- *WhoAm 90*
Catell, Robert Barry 1937- *St&PR 91, WhoAm 90, WhoE 91*
Cateora, Philip Rene 1932- *WhoAm 90*
Cater, Alice Ruth Wallace 1935- *WhoAmW 91*
Cater, Berkeley A. *BioIn 16*
Cater, Danny 1940- *Ballpl 90*
Cater, Douglass 1923- *WhoAm 90, WhoWrEP 89*
Cater, Ester Balatan *BiDrAPA 89*
Cater, Eugene F. 1940- *St&PR 91*
Cater, James Thomas 1948- *WhoSSW 91*
Cater, John T. 1935- *St&PR 91*

Cater, John Thomas 1935- WhoAm 90, WhoSSW 91
Cater, Steven Clyde 1953- WhoSSW 91
Cater, Wilhelmenia Mitchell 1933- WhoWor 91
Caterina da Bologna 1413-1463 EncCoWW
Caterina da Genova 1447-1510 EncCoWW
Caterina da Siena 1347?-1380 EncCoWW
Caterina Sforza 1462-1509 WomWR [port]
Caterine, Anthony James 1962- BiDrAPA 89
Caterino, Ronald F. 1944- St&PR 91
Cates, Charles Brad 1950- WhoEmL 91
Cates, Don Tate 1933- WhoAm 90, WhoSSW 91
Cates, Dudley Foulke 1917- St&PR 91
Cates, Edward William 1952- WhoWrEP 89
Cates, Gilbert 1934- WhoAm 90
Cates, Homer Willard 1930- WhoE 91
Cates, Jeanette Sue 1947- WhoAmW 91
Cates, Jennifer Ann 1956- WhoAmW 91, WhoEmL 91
Cates, John Robinson 1918- BiDrAPA 89
Cates, Kathleen Mary 1964- WhoAmW 91
Cates, Lydia Joe 1928- WhoWrEP 89
Cates, M. Stephen 1950- St&PR 91
Cates, Macfarlane L. 1898- St&PR 91
Cates, Macfarlane Lafferty, Jr. 1927- St&PR 91
Cates, Madelyn ConTFT 8 [port]
Cates, Marc Laurence 1952- WhoSSW 91
Cates, Marian Ward 1947- WhoAmW 91
Cates, Nelia Barletta de 1932- WhoWor 91
Cates, Phoebe BioIn 16
Cates, Phyllis Stork 1921- WhoAmW 91
Catesby, Mark 1679?-1749 EncCRAm
Cateura, Linda Brandi WhoE 91
Cath, Phyllis Jean BiDrAPA 89
Cath, Stanley H BiDrAPA 89
Catharine Parr, Queen 1512-1548 BioIn 16
Cathcart, Allen 1938- IntWWM 90
Cathcart, Christopher ODwPR 91
Cathcart, David Paul 1949- IntWWM 90
Cathcart, Harold Robert 1924- WhoAm 90
Cathcart, Jack Edward 1943- St&PR 91
Cathcart, Keith BioIn 16
Cathcart, Linda 1947- WhoAm 90, WhoAmW 91
Cathcart, Linda Louise WhoAmA 91
Cathcart, Margaret E. 1945- WhoEmL 91, WhoWrEP 89
Cathcart, Martha Kimball 1951- WhoAmW 91
Cathcart, Richard 1950- WhoEmL 91
Cathcart, Robert Stephen 1923- WhoAm 90
Cathcart, Silas Strawn 1926- St&PR 91
Cathell, David Wayne 1954- St&PR 91
Cather, Donald Warren 1926- WhoAm 90
Cather, James Newton 1931- WhoAm 90
Cather, Willa MajTwCW
Cather, Willa 1873-1947 BioIn 16, FemiCLE, WorAlBi, WrPh
Cather, Willa S. 1873-1947 BioAmW
Cather, Willa Sibert 1873-1947 MajTwCW
Catherall, Arthur 1906- AuBYP 90
Catherine WomWR
Catherine I 1683?-1727 WomWR
Catherine II 1729-1796 WorAlBi
Catherine Cornaro WomWR
Catherine de Foix WomWR
Catherine de Foix, Queen of Navarre 1470?-1517 BioIn 16
Catherine de Medicis 1519-1589 WomWR [port], WorAlBi
Catherine de Medicis, Queen 1519-1589 BioIn 16
Catherine I, Empress of Russia 1684?-1727 BioIn 16
Catherine II, Empress of Russia 1729-1796 EncCoWW
Catherine of Aragon 1485- WomWR [port]
Catherine of Aragon 1485-1536 WorAlBi
Catherine of Bologna, Saint 1413-1463 EncPaPR 91
Catherine of Braganza WomWR [port]
Catherine of Genoa, Saint 1447-1510 EncPaPR 91
Catherine, of Siena 1347-1380 BioIn 16
Catherine of Valois WomWR
Catherine the Great 1729-1796 WomWR [port]
Catherine II, the Great 1729-1796 BioIn 16
Catherman, Donna Elaine 1947- WhoAmW 91
Cathers, James O 1934-1982 WhoAmA 91N
Catherwood, C. Cummins WhoWrEP 89
Catherwood, Cummins BioIn 16
Catherwood, Cummins 1910-1990 WhoAm 90
Catherwood, Frederick 1799-1854 ArtLatA
Catherwood, Mary 1847-1902 FemiCLE
Cathey, John M. 1964- ODwPR 91
Cathey, M. Elizabeth 1946- WhoAmW 91, WhoEmL 91
Cathey, Marsha Pryor 1951- WhoEmL 91
Cathey, Marshall Lester 1941- St&PR 91
Cathey, William Fletcher 1953- WhoEmL 91
Cathey, Wm. Harve 1939- St&PR 91
Cathou, Renata Egone 1935- WhoAm 90, WhoAmW 91
Cathriner, Richard Lee 1930- WhoSSW 91
Cation, Kenneth L. 1940- St&PR 91
Catledge, Turner 1901-1983 BioIn 16
Catlett, David G. ODwPR 91
Catlett, David Gilman 1953- WhoE 91
Catlett, Elizabeth 1915- BiDWomA
Catlett, Elizabeth 1919- WhoAmA 91
Catlett, George Roudebush 1917- WhoAm 90
Catlett, James C., Jr. 1957- WhoSSW 91
Catlett, Richard H., Jr. 1921- WhoAm 90
Catlett, Richard Henry, Jr. 1921- St&PR 91
Catlett, Sid 1910-1951 BioIn 16
Catlett, Sidney 1910-1951 OxCPMus, WorAlBi
Catlett, W.H., Jr. 1948- St&PR 91
Catlett, Walter 1889-1960 OxCPMus
Catlin, Allen Burdett 1918- WhoAm 90
Catlin, Avery 1924- WhoAm 90
Catlin, B. Wesley 1917- WhoAmW 91
Catlin, David Eugene 1945- St&PR 91
Catlin, Donald Edward 1936- WhoE 91
Catlin, Francis Irving 1925- WhoAm 90
Catlin, George 1796-1872 WhNaAH, WorAlBi
Catlin, Harold Harvey 1949- WhoEmL 91
Catlin, Karl A BiDrAPA 89
Catlin, Randolph 1925- BiDrAPA 89
Catlin, Randolph, Jr. 1925- WhoE 91
Catlin, Robin John Oakley 1927- WhoSSW 91
Catlin, Stanton Loomis 1915- WhoAmA 91
Cato, David Edward 1948- WhoSSW 91
Cato, Dorothy A 1916- BiDrAPA 89
Cato, Jett C. 1953- St&PR 91
Cato, Jim Paul 1943- WhoSSW 91
Cato, Marcus Porcius 234BC-149BC WorAlBi
Cato, Minto 1900-1979 DrBlPA 90
Cato, Nancy 1917- FemiCLE
Cato, Robert Milton 1915- BioIn 16
Catoe, Bette Lorrina 1926- WhoAmW 91
Catoe, Sandra Clyburn 1937- WhoAmW 91
Catoe, William A. 1964- WhoSSW 91
Catok, Lottie Meyer WhoAmA 91
Catoline, Pauline Dessie 1937- WhoAmW 91
Caton, Betty Ann 1917- WhoAm 90
Caton, Buster 1896-1948 Ballpl 90
Caton, Charles Edwin 1928- WhoAm 90
Caton, David 1955- WhoAmA 91
Caton, John Collings 1937- St&PR 91
Caton, John E BiDrAPA 89
Caton, Jordi 1957- WhoWor 91
Caton, Nathan T. 1832- AmLegL
Caton-Thompson, Gertrude 1888-1985 DcNaB 1981
Catoni, Pedro Miguel 1957- WhoHisp 91
Catravas, George Nicholas 1919- WhoAm 90
Catron, David Lloyd 1939- WhoAm 90
Catron, Deborah Ann 1958- WhoAmW 91
Catron, Donald Gibson 1938- BiDrAPA 89
Catron, Louis E. WhoWrEP 89
Catron, Patricia D'Arcy WhoAmA 91
Catronio, Ronald Joseph 1951- WhoSSW 91
Catroux, Francois Philippe 1936- WhoWor 91
Catsimatidis, John A. 1948- St&PR 91
Catsimatidis, John Andreas 1948- WhoAm 90
Catt, Carrie Chapman 1859-1947 BioAmW, WorAlBi
Catt, Michael Cameron 1952- WhoSSW 91
Cattanach, Robert Edward, Jr. 1949- WhoEmL 91
Cattaneo, Jacquelyn Annette Kammerer 1944- WhoAmW 91
Cattaneo, Jo-Ann 1950- WhoAmW 91
Cattaneo, Kammerer 1944- WhoAmA 91
Cattani, David Arthur 1953- WhoEmL 91
Cattani, Debra 1953- WhoAmW 91
Cattani, Eduardo Hector 1946- WhoE 91
Cattani, Maryellen B. 1943- WhoAm 90, WhoAmW 91
Cattani, Richard J. 1936- WhoAm 90
Cattarulla, Elliot Reynold 1931- St&PR 91
Cattaui, Maria Livanos 1941- WhoWor 91
Cattaui, Stephane Aslan 1937- WhoWor 91
Cattell, James McKeen 1860-1944 BioIn 16
Cattell, James Paul 1916- BiDrAPA 89
Cattell, Lawrence A. 1947- St&PR 91
Cattell, Ray 1921- WhoAmA 91
Cattell, Raymond B. 1905- WhoAm 90
Cattell, Richard B 1927- BiDrAPA 89
Catterall, John Edward 1940- WhoAmA 91
Catterall, John W. 1941- St&PR 91
Catterall, Marlene 1939- WhoAmW 91
Catterall, William A. 1946- WhoAm 90
Cattermole Mancini, Eva 1849-1896 EncCoWW
Catterson, Francis Joseph 1931- St&PR 91
Catterson, Robert Kenneth 1930- St&PR 91
Cattey, James Paul 1935- WhoAm 90
Cattier, Jean NewYTBS 90
Cattier, Jean 1901-1990 BioIn 16
Cattier, John Francis 1954- WhoEmL 91
Cattle, Nancy E. 1959- WhoAmW 91
Catto, Graeme Robertson 1945- WhoWor 91
Catto, Henry Edward 1930- WhoAm 90, WhoWor 91
Catto, Isabel Gordon 1912- WhoAm 90
Catto, William James 1957- WhoEmL 91
Catto, William Martin 1938- St&PR 91
Catto of Cairncatto, Stephen Gordon 1923- WhoAm 90, WhoWor 91
Cattoi, Robert Louis 1926- St&PR 91, WhoAm 90
Catton, Bruce 1899-1978 WorAlBi
Catton, Ivan 1934- WhoAm 90
Catton, Jack Joseph 1920- WhoAm 90
Catton, William Bruce 1926- WhoAm 90
Cattrall, Kim 1956- ConTFT 8
Cattrell, William R. 1948- St&PR 91
Catts, Douglas Byard 1947- WhoEmL 91
Catudal, Michel 1940- OxCCanT
Catullus, Gaius Valerius 84?BC-54?BC WorAlBi
Caturano, Carlo 1939- WhoSSW 91
Catusco, Louis WhoAmA 91
Catuzzi, J. P., Jr. 1938- WhoAm 90
Caty, J.C. 1940- St&PR 91
Catz, Boris 1923- WhoWor 91
Cau, Jean 1925- WhoWor 91
Cauas, Jorge 1934- WhoWor 91
Cauble, Steven Loraine BiDrAPA 89
Cauce, Ana Mari 1956- WhoAmW 91
Cauchi, Gary Steven 1952- WhoEmL 91
Cauchois, Y. 1908- BioIn 16
Caudel, Gary Dewayne 1949- WhoEmL 91
Caudel, Stephen NewAgMG
Caudell, Joy Laraine 1948- WhoAmW 91, WhoSSW 91
Caudell, Marian BioIn 16
Caudill, Bill 1956- Ballpl 90
Caudill, David L. 1935- St&PR 91
Caudill, David Stanley 1951- WhoEmL 91
Caudill, Fred Welden, III 1961- BiDrAPA 89
Caudill, Harry M. NewYTBS 90
Caudill, Harry M. 1922- BioIn 16, LiHiK
Caudill, James 1950- ODwPR 91
Caudill, Maureen 1951- WhoAmW 91, WhoEmL 91, WhoWor 91
Caudill, Rebecca 1899-1985 AuBYP 90, LiHiK
Caudill, Rodney C BiDrAPA 89
Caudill, Samuel Jefferson 1922- WhoAm 90
Caudill, Terry L. 1947- St&PR 91
Caudill, Terry Lee 1947- WhoEmL 91
Caudill, Tom Holden 1945- WhoEmL 91
Caudill, Vaughn Edward 1952- WhoEmL 91
Caudle, Adrian Robert, Jr. 1930- WhoSSW 91
Caudle, James Gary 1937- St&PR 91
Caudle, John Allen 1938- BiDrAPA 89
Caudle, Jones Richard, Jr. 1911- WhoAm 90
Caudle, Michael Ray 1951- WhoEmL 91
Caudle, Neil 1952- ConAu 132
Caudrelier, Jean Robert Julien 1932- WhoWor 91
Caudwell, Sarah 1939- TwCCr&M 91
Cauffiel, Lowell 1951- ConAu 132
Caufield, G. Farlin 1927- St&PR 91
Caufield, James D. St&PR 91
Caufriez, Anne 1945- IntWWM 90
Caughey, David Alan 1944- WhoE 91
Caughey, James 1810-1891 DcCanB 12
Caughey, John Walton 1902- BioIn 16
Caughey, Patricia Ann 1926- BiDrAPA 89
Caughey, Robert Michael 1934- St&PR 91
Caughlan, Georgeanne Robertson 1916- WhoAm 90
Caughlin, Judith Ann 1941- St&PR 91
Caughlin, Stephenie Jane 1948- WhoEmL 91
Caughman, Belton D. 1929- BiDrAPA 89
Caughran, William Hermann, Jr. 1956- WhoEmL 91
Caulder, Mary Mezzanotte 1953- WhoAmW 91
Cauldwell, Frank ConAu 33NR, MajTwCW
Cauley, Betty K. 1951- St&PR 91
Cauley, James Robert 1952- WhoEmL 91
Cauley, John Francis 1932- St&PR 91
Cauley, John Henry, Jr. 1945- WhoEmL 91
Cauley, Linda Newbern 1952- WhoAmW 91
Cauley, Lorinda Bryan 1951- BioIn 16
Caulfield, Barbara Ann 1947- WhoAm 90
Caulfield, Carlota 1953- WhoWrEP 89
Caulfield, George F. 1924- ODwPR 91
Caulfield, H. J. 1936- BioIn 16
Caulfield, Henry John 1936- BioIn 16
Caulfield, Howard Donald, Jr. 1948- WhoAm 90
Caulfield, James Benjamin 1927- WhoAm 90, WhoSSW 91
Caulfield, Joan 1943- WhoAmW 91
Caulfield, Peggy F. 1926-1987 BioIn 16
Caulfield, Philip A. Jr. BiDrAPA 89
Caulkins, Curtis Henry 1932- St&PR 91
Caulkins, Tracy 1963- WorAlBi
Caulo, Ralph Daniel 1935- WhoAm 90, WhoSSW 91
Cauman, Samuel 1910-1971 BioIn 16
Caumont de la Force, Charlotte-Rose 1650-1724 EncCoWW
Cauna, Nikolajs 1914- WhoAm 90
Caunitz, William J. BioIn 16
Caunitz, William J. 1933- ConAu 130
Caunter, Harry Allen 1935- St&PR 91, WhoAm 90
Caupin, Jean Henri Georges 1910- WhoWor 91
Causby, Jerry Wilburn 1938- St&PR 91
Causey, Annette Denise 1960- WhoAmW 91
Causey, George Donald 1926- WhoE 91
Causey, J.P., Jr. 1943- St&PR 91
Causey, James Robert 1956- WhoEmL 91
Causey, John Paul, Jr. 1943- WhoAm 90
Causey, Marion Edward, II 1947- WhoSSW 91
Causey, Mike BioIn 16
Causey, Red 1893-1960 Ballpl 90
Causey, Robert Louis 1941- WhoAm 90
Causey, Wayne 1936- Ballpl 90
Caushaj, Philip Fillor 1954- WhoE 91
Caushois, Yvette 1908- BioIn 16
Causley, Charles 1917- AuBYP 90, MajTwCW
Caussade, Jose J BiDrAPA 89
Caussignac, Jacques 1945- St&PR 91
Caussy, Paul PenDiDA 89
Caussy, Pierre-Paul PenDiDA 89
Caust-Ellenbogen, Sanford Nathan 1954- WhoEmL 91
Caute, David 1936- ConAu 33NR
Cauthen, Charles Edward, Jr. 1931- WhoAm 90, WhoWor 91
Cauthen, Deloris Vaughan WhoWor 91
Cauthen, Irby Bruce, Jr. 1919- WhoAm 90
Cauthen, John Vaughan 1928- St&PR 91
Cauthen, Rea Kimbrell, Jr. 1953- WhoSSW 91
Cauthen, Steve 1960- WhoAm 90, WhoWor 91
Cauthen, Wiley M. 1935- St&PR 91
Cauthorn, Henry Sullivan 1828-1905 AmLegL
Cauthorn, Julia Loughborough 1918- WhoAm 90
Cautin, Murray 1941- St&PR 91
Caution-Davis, Ethel 1880-1981 HarlReB
Cauvet, Gilles-Paul 1731-1788 PenDiDA 89
Cauvin, Jean 1509-1564 BioIn 16
Cava, Carlo 1928- IntWWM 90
Cava, Edmund 1928- BiDrAPA 89
Cava, Esther L. 1916- WhoAmW 91
Cava, Michael Patrick 1926- WhoAm 90
Cava, Paul 1949- WhoAmA 91
Cava, Richard William 1942- St&PR 91
Cavacini, Lisa Ann 1961- WhoAmW 91
Cavaco Silva, Anibal 1939- WhoWor 91
Cavafy, Constantine P. 1863-1933 BioIn 16
Cavaglieri, Giorgio 1911- WhoAm 90
Cavaglieri, Mario 1887-1969 BioIn 16
Cavagna, Giancarlo Antonio 1938- WhoE 91
Cavagnaro, Maurizio 1938- WhoWor 91
Cavagnaro, Richard Ray 1939- St&PR 91
Cavaiana, Mabel S. 1919- WhoWrEP 89
Cavakis, Robert Allan 1947- WhoEmL 91
Cavalcanti, Emiliano di 1897-1976 ArtLatA
Cavalcanti, Newton 1930- ArtLatA
Cavalier, John C. 1939- St&PR 91
Cavaliere, Andrew L. 1938- St&PR 91
Cavaliere, Barbara ODwPR 91, WhoAmA 91
Cavaliere, Louis Daniel 1947- St&PR 91
Cavaliere, Paul Joseph 1947- St&PR 91
Cavalieri, Gianpaolo 1939- WhoWor 91
Cavalieri, Grace 1932- WhoWrEP 89
Cavalieri, Lina 1874-1944 PenDiMP
Cavallari, Alberto 1927- WhoWor 91
Cavallari, Robert Francis 1958- WhoE 91
Cavallaro, Ann 1918- SmATA 62
Cavallaro, Carmen BioIn 16
Cavallaro, Carmen 1913- OxCPMus

Cavallaro, Mary Caroline 1932- WhoAmW 91
Cavalletti, Sofia 1917- ConAu 130
Cavalli, Dick 1923- WhoAmA 91
Cavalli, Harriet Weymouth 1938- IntWWM 90
Cavalli, Pier-Francesco 1602-1676 PenDiMP A
Cavallini, Pietro 124-?-133-? IntDcAA 90
Cavallito, Albino 1905-1966 WhoAmA 91N
Cavallo, Diana 1931- WhoAm 90
Cavallo, Domingo WhoWor 91
Cavallo, Ernest J. 1933- St&PR 91
Cavallo, Evelyn MajTwCW
Cavallo, Giorgio 1923- WhoWor 91
Cavallo, Luis E BiDrAPA 89
Cavallo, Pamela Florence 1947- WhoE 91
Cavallo, Victor J. ODwPR 91
Cavallon, Betty Gabler 1918- WhoAmW 91, WhoE 91
Cavallon, Giorgio WhoAmA 91N
Cavallon, Giorgio 1904-1989 BioIn 16
Cavallon, Michel Francis, III 1936- WhoSSW 91
Cavan, Ann M. 1955- WhoWrEP 89
Cavan, Ruth Shonle 1896- BioIn 16
Cavan, Stephen Edward 1953- St&PR 91
Cavanagh, Brendan Edward 1940- WhoSSW 91
Cavanagh, Carroll John 1943- WhoE 91
Cavanagh, Denis WhoAm 90
Cavanagh, Edward Dean 1949- WhoEmL 91
Cavanagh, Francis X. 1933- St&PR 91
Cavanagh, Harrison Dwight 1940- WhoAm 90
Cavanagh, Helen 1939- BioIn 16
Cavanagh, James J BiDrAPA 89
Cavanagh, John Charles 1932- WhoAm 90
Cavanagh, John Edward 1918- WhoAm 90
Cavanagh, John Henry 1955- WhoAm 90
Cavanagh, Michael Francis 1940- WhoAm 90
Cavanagh, Richard Edward 1946- WhoAm 90, WhoE 91, WhoEmL 91, WhoWor 91
Cavanagh, Ronald J 1940- BiDrAPA 89
Cavanagh, Ronald Jerome 1940- WhoE 91
Cavanagh, Tom 1931- WhoWor 91
Cavanagh, Walter BioIn 16
Cavanagh, William Joseph 1954- St&PR 91
Cavanah, Frances 1899-1982 AuBYP 90
Cavanaugh, Dennis Miles 1937- St&PR 91, WhoAm 90
Cavanaugh, Gary Lynn BiDrAPA 89
Cavanaugh, Gordon 1928- WhoAm 90
Cavanaugh, James Henry 1937- WhoAm 90
Cavanaugh, James L, Jr. 1941- BiDrAPA 89
Cavanaugh, Jean 1924- WhoAmW 91
Cavanaugh, John 1920- ODwPR 91
Cavanaugh, John W 1921- WhoAmA 91N
Cavanaugh, Kenneth Clinton 1916- WhoAm 90
Cavanaugh, Marie 1953- St&PR 91
Cavanaugh, Niel Christian 1940- St&PR 91
Cavanaugh, Patric Lawrence BioIn 16
Cavanaugh, Patricia L. 1954- WhoEmL 91
Cavanaugh, Patrick Dennis 1947- WhoEmL 91
Cavanaugh, Raymond Robert BiDrAPA 89
Cavanaugh, Stephanie Von Ammon 1942- BiDrAPA 89
Cavanaugh, Stephen Ward 1946- St&PR 91
Cavanaugh, Tom Richard 1923- WhoAm 90
Cavanaugh, William, III 1939- St&PR 91, WhoSSW 91
Cavanaugh, William J. 1932- St&PR 91
Cavaney, Red 1943- WhoAm 90
Cavani, Liliana 1936- ConTFT 8
Cavanna, Betty 1909- AuBYP 90
Cavanna, Roberto 1927- EncO&P 3
Cavano, Francis J BiDrAPA 89
Cavano, Francis Joseph 1941- WhoE 91
Cavarretta, Phil 1916- Ballpl 90
Cavasina, Mary Magdalene 1927- WhoAmW 91, WhoE 91
Cavat, Irma WhoAmA 91
Cavathas, Constantine 1939- WhoWor 91
Cavato, Joseph A. 1945- WhoEmL 91
Cavazos, Ben 1950- WhoHisp 91
Cavazos, Joel WhoHisp 91
Cavazos, Lauro F. 1927- WhoHisp 91
Cavazos, Lauro Fred 1927- BiDrUSE 89, BioIn 16, WhoAm 90, WhoE 91, WhoWor 91
Cavazos, Miguel A., Jr. 1943- WhoHisp 91
Cavazos, Peggy Ann BioIn 16
Cavazos, Rosa I. 1954- WhoHisp 91
Cavazza, Fabio Luca 1927- WhoWor 91
Cave, Anita Margaret 1950- BiDrAPA 89
Cave, Catherine Anne N. 1956- WhoAmW 91
Cave, Daisy Wilson NewYTBS 90
Cave, George Harold, III 1957- WhoEmL 91
Cave, George Patton 1948- WhoWrEP 89
Cave, Hugh B. BioIn 16
Cave, Jane 1757?-1813 FemiCLE
Cave, John B. 1929- St&PR 91
Cave, Jon Robert 1954- WhoE 91
Cave, K.N. 1929- St&PR 91
Cave, Kirk Clark 1957- WhoEmL 91, WhoSSW 91
Cave, Leonard Edward 1944- WhoAmA 91
Cave, Mac Donald 1939- WhoAm 90
Cave, Penelope 1951- IntWWM 90
Cavell, Daniel A. 1954- WhoEmL 91
Cavell, John Anthony 1951- WhoEmL 91
Cavell, Stanley 1926- WhoAm 90
Cavelli, Dick 1923- EncACom
Cavelti, Elsa 1914- IntWWM 90
Caven, Howard S. 1919- St&PR 91
Cavenar, Jesse Oscar, Jr. 1939- BiDrAPA 89
Cavenaugh, Raymond W., Sr. 1920- St&PR 91
Cavender, William F 1933- BiDrAPA 89
Cavender, William Francis 1933- WhoE 91
Cavendish, Elizabeth BiDEWW
Cavendish, Elizabeth 1626-1663 FemiCLE
Cavendish, Henry 1731-1810 WorAlBi
Cavendish, Jane 1621-1669 BiDEWW, FemiCLE
Cavendish, Margaret 1623-1673 BiDEWW
Cavendish, Margaret 1624?-1674 BioIn 16
Cavendish, Thomas Edgar 1929- WhoAm 90
Caveney, Ike 1894-1949 Ballpl 90
Caveney, William Vincent 1926- St&PR 91
Caveny, Elmer L BiDrAPA 89
Caver, William Ralph 1932- WhoAmA 91
Caverly, Gardner A. 1910- WhoAm 90
Cavers, David Farquhar 1902-1988 BioIn 16
Cavers-Huff, Dasiea Yvonne 1961- WhoAmW 91
Cavert, Henry Mead 1922- WhoAm 90
Caves, Richard Earl 1931- WhoAm 90
Cavett, Dick 1936- ConTFT 8 [port], WhoAm 90, WorAlBi
Cavey, Carol Meredith 1947- BiDrAPA 89
Caviani, Ronald Joseph 1931- IntWWM 90
Cavicchioli, Gianfranco 1927- WhoWor 91
Caviedes, Juan del Valle y BioIn 16
Cavill, Ronald William 1944- WhoE 91
Cavin, Doyle K. 1936- St&PR 91
Cavin, F.G. 1930- St&PR 91
Cavin, Susan Elizabeth 1948- WhoE 91
Cavin, Wade Leonard 1915- WhoAm 90
Cavin, William Brooks 1914- WhoAm 90
Cavin, William Pinckney 1925- WhoAm 90
Caviness, Leon Harold 1920- BiDrAPA 89
Caviness, Madeline Harrison 1938- WhoAm 90
Cavior, Warren J. 1929- ODwPR 91
Cavior, Warren Joseph 1929- WhoAm 90
Cavitch, David 1933- WhoAm 90
Cavitt, Mark Allen BiDrAPA 89
Cavnar, Margaret Mary 1945- WhoAmW 91
Cavnar, Samuel Melmon 1925- WhoWor 91
Cavour, Camillo Benso, Conte De 1810-1861 WorAlBi
Cawein, Kathrin 1895- WhoAmA 91, WhoE 91
Cawein, Madison 1865-1914 LiHiK
Cawley, Barbara Ann 1942- WhoE 91
Cawley, Charles Nash 1937- WhoSSW 91
Cawley, Donald F. 1929-1990 NewYTBS 90
Cawley, Edward Philip 1912- WhoAm 90
Cawley, Joan Mae WhoAmA 91
Cawley, Lawrence J. 1934- St&PR 91
Cawley, Lawrence Joseph 1934- WhoAm 90
Cawley, Neil Patrick 1958- WhoSSW 91
Cawley, Richard A. BioIn 16
Cawley, William Arthur 1925- WhoSSW 91
Cawneen, Kevin Martin 1960- WhoEmL 91
Cawood, Elizabeth Jean 1947- WhoEmL 91
Cawood, Gary Kenneth 1947- WhoAmA 91
Cawood, Harry Edwin, III 1936- St&PR 91
Cawood, Hobart Guy 1935- WhoAm 90, WhoE 91
Cawrse, Celeste Powlus 1956- WhoAmW 91, WhoE 91
Caws, Mary Ann 1933- ConAu 31NR, WhoAm 90, WhoAmW 91
Caws, Peter James 1931- WhoAm 90, WhoWrEP 89
Cawse, Alfred J. 1909-1989 BioIn 16
Cawte, John E 1925- BiDrAPA 89
Cawthon, Frank H. 1930- WhoSSW 91
Cawthon, Frank Hill 1930- St&PR 91
Cawthon, William Connell 1922- WhoAm 90, WhoWor 91
Cawthon, Zelma Harrison 1911- WhoAmW 91
Cawthorn, Joseph 1867-1949 OxCPMus
Cawthorn, Robert E. 1935- St&PR 91
Cawthorn, Robert Elston 1935- WhoAm 90, WhoE 91
Cawthorn, T. Steven 1958- WhoEmL 91
Cawthorne, Kenneth Clifford 1936- St&PR 91, WhoAm 90
Caxias, Luis A de Lima e Silva, Duque de 1803-1880 BioIn 16
Caxton, William 1422-1491 WorAlBi
Cayaldo, Wallace A. 1950- St&PR 91
Cayatte, Andre 1903-1989 AnObit 1989
Cayatte, Andre 1909-1989 BioIn 16
Cayce, Charles Thomas Taylor 1942- NewAgE 90
Cayce, Edgar 1877-1945 BioIn 16, EncO&P 3, EncPaPR 91, NewAgE 90, WorAlBi
Cayce, Edgar Evans 1918- WhoWrEP 89
Cayce, Hugh Lynn 1907- EncO&P 3
Cayce, Hugh Lynn 1907-1982 NewAgE 90
Caycedo, Jorge H 1939- BiDrAPA 89
Cayetano, Benjamin Jerome 1939- WhoAm 90
Cayetano, David Mata 1909- WhoWor 91
Cayford, Philip BioIn 16
Cayias, Peter W.G. 1935- St&PR 91
Caylan, Lilian Jamito BiDrAPA 89
Cayleff, Susan Evelyn 1954- WhoAmW 91
Cayley, George 1773-1857 WorAlBi
Caylor, Anne Marie Sara 1954- WhoAmW 91
Caylor, Dee Jerlyn 1942- WhoAmW 91
Caylor, Marilyn Eleanor WhoSSW 91
Caylor, O P Ballpl 90
Caylus, Comtesse de 1673-1729 EncCoWW
Cayne, Bernard Stanley 1924- WhoAm 90, WhoWrEP 89
Cayne, James E. 1934- WhoAm 90, WhoE 91
Cayne, Merel Sue 1937- WhoE 91
Cayton, William D'Arcy 1918- St&PR 91
Caywood, Clarke Lawrence 1947- WhoEmL 91
Caywood, James Alexander 1923- St&PR 91
Caywood, John Millard 1941- St&PR 91
Caywood-Beauregard, Janice Eileen 1955- WhoE 91
Caza, Carlton C. 1937- St&PR 91, WhoAm 90
Cazalas, Mary Rebecca Williams 1927- WhoSSW 91, WhoWor 91
Cazalet-Keir, Thelma 1899-1989 AnObit 1989
Cazan, Matthew John 1912- WhoWor 91
Cazan, Sylvia Marie Buday 1915- WhoWor 91
Cazares, Roger 1941- WhoHisp 91
Cazden, Courtney Borden 1925- WhoAm 90, WhoAmW 91
Cazden, Elizabeth 1950- WhoEmL 91
Cazeau, Bernard Jean-Francois 1939- WhoWor 91
Cazeaux, Isabelle Anne-Marie 1926- IntWWM 90, WhoAm 90
Cazeneuve, Paul 1871-1925 OxCCanT
Cazenove, Christopher De Lerisson 1945- WhoEmL 91
Cazet, Denys 1938- BioIn 16
Cazimir, Otilia EncCoWW
Cazin, Marie 1844-1924 BiDWomA
Cazotte, Jacques 1720-1792 EncO&P 3
Cazzaniga, Riccardo Angelo 1932- St&PR 91
Cazzullo, Carlo Lorenzo BiDrAPA 89
Ce, Marco Cardinal 1925- WhoWor 91
Cea, Christine ODwPR 91
Cearlock, Dennis Bill 1941- WhoAm 90
Ceasar, Harold Paul 1945- BiDrAPA 89
Cease, Jane Hardy 1936- WhoAmW 91
Cease, Philip H. 1924- St&PR 91
Ceaser, Martin A 1943- BiDrAPA 89
Ceausescu, Elena BioIn 16
Ceausescu, Marin BioIn 16
Ceausescu, Nicolae BioIn 16
Ceausescu, Nicolae 1918-1989 AnObit 1989, CurBio 90N, News 90, WorAlBi
Ceazan, Gary Michael 1942- St&PR 91
Ceballos, Francisco J BiDrAPA 89
Ceballos, Nelson J 1935- BiDrAPA 89
Cebotari, Maria 1910-1949 PenDiMP
Cebrian, Teresa del Carmen 1960- WhoHisp 91
Cebrian Echarri, Juan Luis 1944- WhoWor 91
Cebrik, Melvin Lawrence 1947- WhoEmL 91
Cebrik, Michael M. 1943- St&PR 91
Cebuc, Alexandru Ion 1932- WhoWor 91
Cebula, James Michael 1952- WhoEmL 91
Cebulash, Mel 1937- ConAu 30NR
Cecala, Kathy Petersen BioIn 16
Ceccardi, Herman R. 1939- St&PR 91
Ceccarelli, Art 1930- Ballpl 90
Ceccarelli, John F. 1921- WhoE 91
Ceccato, Aldo 1934- IntWWM 90, PenDiMP
Cecchele, Gianfranco 1940- IntWWM 90
Cecchetti, Giovanni 1922- WhoAm 90
Cecchi, Franco 1950- WhoWor 91
Cecco, Richard Victor 1948- WhoE 91
Ceccon, Harry Leonard 1930- St&PR 91
Cece, Joseph W. WhoAm 90
Cecere, Gaetano 1894-1985 WhoAmA 91N
Cecere, Michael S. 1944-1989 BioIn 16
Cech, Thomas R. 1947- WorAlBi
Cech, Thomas Robert 1947- WhoAm 90, WhoWor 91
Ceci, Anthony Thomas 1917- WhoE 91
Ceci, Jesse Arthur 1924- WhoAm 90
Ceci, Louis J. 1927- WhoAm 90
Ceci, Lynn BioIn 16
Cecich, Donald Edward 1950- WhoE 91
Cecil, Alex Thomson 1930- WhoE 91
Cecil, Allan V. 1941- ODwPR 91
Cecil, Charles Harkless 1945- WhoAm 90, WhoAmA 91
Cecil, David 1902-1986 BioIn 16
Cecil, David George Brownlow 1905-1981 DcNaB 1981
Cecil, David Rolf 1935- WhoAm 90
Cecil, Dorcas Ann 1945- WhoAmW 91, WhoEmL 91
Cecil, Henry 1902-1976 TwCCr&M 91
Cecil, Jack Witten 1927- St&PR 91
Cecil, John Lamont 1909- St&PR 91, WhoAm 90
Cecil, Judith Sybil BiDrAPA 89
Cecil, Leonard Jay 1952- IntWWM 90
Cecil, Malcolm NewAgMG
Cecil, Paula B. 1927- WhoWrEP 89
Cecil, Paula Bernice 1927- WhoAmW 91
Cecil, Richard Thomas 1944- WhoWrEP 89
Cecil, Robert 1563-1612 BioIn 16
Cecil, Robert Arthur Talbot Gascoyne- 1830-1903 BioIn 16
Cecil, Robert Gascoyne 1864-1958 WorAlBi
Cecil, Robert Salisbury 1935- WhoAm 90
Cecil, Rosemary BiDrAPA 89
Cecil, Stephen Don 1958- WhoEmL 91
Cecil, Vander Bethea 1947- WhoEmL 91
Cecil-Stuart, Wendy M. 1948- ODwPR 91
Cecilia 1915- WhoAmA 91
Ceconi, Arthur Bruno, Jr. 1956- WhoE 91
Cecora, Raymond Eugene, Jr. 1947- WhoE 91
Cedar, Howard 1943- WhoWor 91
Cedar, Paul Arnold 1938- WhoWor 91
Cedarbaum, Miriam Goldman 1929- WhoAm 90, WhoAmW 91, WhoE 91
Cedars, Phyllis Irene 1951- BiDrAPA 89
Ceddia, Anthony Francis 1944- WhoAm 90, WhoE 91
Cedel, Melinda Irene 1957- WhoEmL 91, WhoSSW 91
Cedeno, Cesar 1951- Ballpl 90 [port], WhoHisp 91
Cedeno, George Luis 1936- WhoWor 91
Cederbaum, Lorenz Srulek WhoWor 91
Cederberg, C.W. 1897- St&PR 91
Cederberg, Dolores Katherine 1929- WhoE 91
Cederberg, John Edwin 1943- WhoAm 90
Cedercreutz, Axel Victor 1939- WhoWor 91
Cedering, Siv 1939- WhoWrEP 89
Cederlund, Candace Ray 1952- WhoWor 91
Cederquist, John 1946- WhoAmA 91
Cederquist, John Walfred BiDrAPA 89
Cederstrom, Carole A. WhoAmW 91
Cederstrom, Janice Joy 1953- BiDrAPA 89
Cederstrom, John Andrew 1929- WhoAm 90, WhoAmA 91
Cedoline, Anthony John 1942- WhoWor 91
Cedraschi, Tullio 1938- St&PR 91
Cedrone, Louis Robert, Jr. 1923- WhoAm 90
Ceely, Robert Paige 1930- IntWWM 90
Cefalo, Frank P. St&PR 91
Cefalo, Romeo Robert 1949- St&PR 91
Cefalu, Salvador J 1931- BiDrAPA 89
Cefaratti, James P. 1942- St&PR 91
Cefis, Adolfo M. 1937- WhoWor 91
Cegan, Patricia E. 1943- WhoAmW 91
Cegnar, Ronald William 1945- WhoAm 90
Ceha, Joseph A M 1931- BiDrAPA 89
Cehanovsky, George 1892- PenDiMP
Cehelsky, Priscilla 1959- WhoE 91
Cehelyk, Bohdan 1944- BiDrAPA 89
Ceja, Vicky BioIn 16
Cejas, Paul L. 1943- WhoHisp 91
Cejka, Jaroslav 1943- ConAu 132
Cekal, James Fredrick 1933- St&PR 91
Cekan, Paul Robert BiDrAPA 89

Cekela, Vincent Walter 1933- *St&PR 91*
Cela, Camilo Jose 1916- *BioIn 16, ConAu 32NR, ConLC 59 [port], CurBio 90 [port], EuWr 13, HispWr 90, IntvSpW [port], MajTwCW, WhoWor 91*
Cela, Jose Luis 1930- *WhoWor 91*
Celan, Paul *ConAu 33NR, MajTwCW*
Celan, Paul 1920-1970 *WorAlBi*
Celant, Germano 1940- *BioIn 16*
Celata, Steven Anthony 1957- *St&PR 91*
Celaya, Frank *WhoHisp 91*
Celaya, Haydee 1958- *St&PR 91*
Celaya, Mary Susan 1962- *WhoHisp 91*
Celebrezze, Anthony Joseph 1910- *BiDrUSE 89*
Celebrezze, Steven James 1959- *WhoEmL 91*
Celedon, Hernando 1936- *WhoWor 91*
Celender, Don 1931- *WhoAmA 91*
Celentano, Francis Michael 1928- *WhoAm 90, WhoAmA 91*
Celentano, Thomas Neil 1959- *WhoE 91*
Celentano, Ulad Dianna Vibert 1945- *WhoSSW 91*
Celenti, Dan Nicholas 1952- *WhoE 91*
Celentino, Theodore 1938- *St&PR 91*
Celenza, Michael Thomas 1946- *St&PR 91*
Celesia, Dorothea 1738?-1790 *FemiCLE*
Celesia, Gastone Guglielmo 1933- *WhoAm 90*
Celeste, Daniel Joseph 1942- *St&PR 91*
Celeste, Marie *ConAu 30NR*
Celeste, Richard F. 1937- *WhoAm 90, WhoWor 91*
Celestin, Papa 1884-1954 *OxCPMus*
Celestine V, Pope 1215-1296 *BioIn 16*
Celestino, Domenico 1935- *WhoWor 91*
Celibidache, Sergiu 1912- *IntWWM 90, PenDiMP, WhoWor 91*
Celik, Kubilay *BioIn 16*
Celine, Louis-Ferdinand *MajTwCW*
Celis, Frits 1929- *IntWWM 90*
Celis, Perez *BioIn 16*
Celis, Perez 1939- *WhoAmA 91*
Celkupa, Joseph Bruno 1940- *St&PR 91*
Cell, Gillian Townsend 1937- *WhoAm 90*
Cella, Francis Raymond 1909- *WhoAm 90*
Cella, Frank G. 1929- *St&PR 91*
Cella, Jane Murphy *ODwPR 91*
Cella, John J. 1940- *WhoAm 90*
Cella, Paolo 1925- *WhoWor 91*
Cellan-Jones, James Gwynne 1931- *WhoAm 90*
Cellar, Frank Andrew, Jr. *BiDrAPA 89*
Cellarova, Eva 1954- *WhoWor 91*
Celler, Emanuel 1888-1981 *WorAlBi*
Celli, Bartolome Romulo 1946- *WhoEmL 91*
Celli, Pasquale 1953- *St&PR 91*
Celli, Paul 1935- *WhoAmA 91*
Celli, Vincenzo 1900-1988 *BioIn 16*
Cellier, Alfred 1844-1891 *OxCPMus, PenDiMP, -A*
Cellier, Elizabeth *BiDEWW, FemiCLE*
Cellier, Francois 1849-1914 *OxCPMus, PenDiMP*
Cellier, Marcel 1925- *IntWWM 90*
Celliers, Peter J. *ODwPR 91*
Cellini, Benvenuto 1500-1571 *EncO&P 3, IntDcAA 90, PenDiDA 89, WorAlBi*
Cellini, Joseph 1924- *WhoAmA 91*
Cellini, William Quirino, Jr. 1951- *WhoE 91, WhoEmL 91*
Celor, Pierre Louis Joseph Jean 1902-1957 *BiDFrPL*
Celoron De Blainville, Pierre Joseph 1693-1759 *EncCRAm*
Celsius, Anders 1701-1744 *WorAlBi*
Ceman, T. 1931- *St&PR 91*
Cembalisty, Richard Henry 1951- *WhoE 91*
Cember, Herman 1924- *WhoAm 90*
Cemo, Michael John 1945- *St&PR 91*
Cempel, Czeslaw 1938- *WhoWor 91*
Cenac, Neville *WhoWor 91*
Cenac, Philip Louis, Jr. 1948- *BiDrAPA 89*
Cenarrusa, Pete T. 1917- *WhoAm 90, WhoHisp 91*
Cenci, Deborah Ann 1959- *WhoAmW 91*
Cenci, Silvana 1926- *WhoAmA 91*
Cendrars, Blaise *MajTwCW*
Cenkner, William 1930- *WhoAm 90*
Cennamo, Louis *NewAgMG*
Censabella, Laura Maria 1959- *WhoWrEP 89*
Censits, Richard John 1937- *St&PR 91, WhoAm 90*
Censor, Therese *WhoAmA 91*
Centa, William James 1952- *WhoEmL 91*
Centelles, Agusti 1909-1985 *BioIn 16*
Centelli, Maria Grazia 1518?-1602 *EncCoWW*
Centena, Edmundo Franco 1946- *BiDrAPA 89*
Centeno, Herbert Elliott 1948- *WhoHisp 91*
Center, Anthony 1949- *St&PR 91*
Center, Irvin Warren 1916- *St&PR 91*
Center, John William 1946- *WhoEmL 91*
Center, Leo Ehren 1918- *St&PR 91*
Center, Tony 1949- *WhoEmL 91*
Centgraf, Damian Louis 1957- *WhoEmL 91*
Centlivre, Susanna 1667?-1723 *BioIn 16*
Centlivre, Susanna 1669-1723 *FemiCLE*
Centlivre, Susanna 1670?-1723 *BiDEWW*
Centner, Charles William 1915- *WhoWor 91*
Centner, Marilyn Parker 1929- *WhoSSW 91*
Centracchio, Charlene Joan 1958- *WhoE 91*
Centrella, Charles J 1935- *BiDrAPA 89*
Centric, Ronald William *BiDrAPA 89*
Centrone, Sylvester T *BiDrAPA 89*
Centurione Scotto, Carlo *EncO&P 3*
Cepeda, Anne-Marie 1953- *BiDrAPA 89*
Cepeda, Claudio 1942- *BiDrAPA 89*
Cepeda, Manuel L 1944- *BiDrAPA 89*
Cepeda, Orlando 1937- *Ballpl 90 [port], BioIn 16*
Cepeda, Orlando Manuel Penne 1937- *WhoHisp 91*
Cepielik, Elizabeth Lindberg 1941- *WhoAmW 91*
Ceppos, Jerome Merle 1946- *WhoAm 90, WhoEmL 91*
Cera, Kenneth Blair 1960- *WhoEmL 91*
Cera, Lee Marie 1950- *WhoAm 90*
Cera, Pete *BioIn 16*
Cera, Robert Joseph 1962- *St&PR 91*
Cerago, Carl R. 1946- *St&PR 91*
Cerami, Anthony 1940- *WhoAm 90*
Ceramicoli, Carol Frances 1960- *WhoAmW 91*
Ceraolo, Salvatore Joseph 1962- *WhoE 91*
Cerasaro, Thomas Stephen 1953- *WhoSSW 91*
Cerasoli, Gregorio *PenDiDA 89*
Cerasuolo, Frank Michael *BiDrAPA 89*
Ceraul, David James 1955- *WhoEmL 91*
Ceravolo, Joseph 1934-1988 *BioIn 16*
Cercone, Timothy E. 1965- *WhoEmL 91*
Cerda, David 1927- *WhoHisp 91*
Cerda, Gabriela *WhoWrEP 89*
Cerda, Martin G. 1964- *WhoHisp 91*
Cerda, Pedro Aguirre 1878-1941 *BioIn 16*
Cere, Ronald Carl 1947- *WhoEmL 91, WhoWor 91*
Cereijo, Manuel Ramon 1938- *WhoHisp 91*
Cereta, Laura 1469-1499 *EncCoWW*
Cerezo, Adolfo 1952- *St&PR 91*
Cerezo, Carmen Consuelo 1940- *WhoAmW 91*
Cerezo, Hector S *BiDrAPA 89*
Cerezo, Vinicio 1942- *WhoWor 91*
Cerezo Arevalo, Vinicio *BioIn 16*
Cerf, Bennett 1898-1971 *AuBYP 90*
Cerf, Bennett A. 1898-1971 *WorAlBi*
Cerf, Genevieve Charbin 1943- *WhoWor 91*
Cerf, J. Georg 1941- *WhoE 91*
Cerf, Muriel 1951- *EncCoWW*
Cerf, Vinton G. *BioIn 16*
Cerf, Vinton Gray 1943- *WhoAm 90*
Cerfolio, Nina E *BiDrAPA 89*
Cergol, Gregory Gerard 1959- *WhoE 91*
Cergol, Jack *ODwPR 91*
Cerha, Friedrich 1926- *IntWWM 90*
Ceriani, Gary James 1947- *WhoEmL 91*
Ceriani, Peter John 1956- *WhoEmL 91*
Ceriello, Nancy Dee 1951- *WhoEmL 91*
Cerino, Angela Marie 1950- *WhoE 91, WhoEmL 91*
Cerino, Anne Catherine 1954- *WhoAmW 91*
Cerio, George A. *St&PR 91*
Cerio, Tom *BioIn 16*
Cerkas, Michael William 1956- *WhoEmL 91*
Cerlini, Celia L. *St&PR 91*
Cermak, Daniel O. 1932- *St&PR 91*
Cermak, Jack Edward 1922- *WhoAm 90*
Cermak, Josef Rudolf Cenek 1924- *WhoE 91*
Cerminara, Frank 1948- *St&PR 91*
Cerna, Christina Monica 1946- *WhoE 91*
Cerna, Enrique Santiago 1953- *WhoHisp 91*
Cernan, Eugene A. 1934- *WhoAm 90*
Cerne, Wence F. 1931- *WhoAm 90*
Cernek, Jeffrey T. 1958- *WhoEmL 91*
Cernera, Anthony Joseph 1950- *WhoAm 90*
Cerniglia, Joseph *BioIn 16*
Cernosek, Kitty 1938- *WhoSSW 91*
Cernovitch, Nicholas 1929- *WhoAm 90*
Cernuda, Luis 1902-1963 *ConAu 131, HispWr 90*
Cernuda y Bidon, Luis 1902-1963 *HispWr 90*
Cernugel, William John 1942- *St&PR 91, WhoAm 90*
Cernuschi, Alberto C *WhoAmA 91*
Cerny, Daniel J. 1945- *St&PR 91*
Cerny, Daniel John 1945- *WhoEmL 91*
Cerny, Douglas M. 1958- *St&PR 91*
Cerny, Janice Louise 1947- *WhoWrEP 89*
Cerny, Jeffrey Douglas 1951- *WhoSSW 91*
Cerny, Jiri 1940- *WhoWor 91*
Cerny, Joseph, III 1936- *WhoAm 90*
Cerny, Joseph Charles 1930- *WhoAm 90, WhoWor 91*
Cerny, Louis Thomas 1942- *WhoAm 90*
Cero, Joseph T. 1931- *St&PR 91*
Cerone, David P. 1941- *IntWWM 90*
Cerone, James Francis 1938- *WhoWor 91*
Cerone, Rick 1954- *Ballpl 90*
Cerottini, Jean-Charles 1938- *WhoWor 91*
Cerovsek, Corey *BioIn 16*
Cerquetti, Anita 1931- *IntWWM 90, PenDiMP*
Cerra, Luis R *BiDrAPA 89*
Cerra, Luis R. 1955- *WhoE 91*
Cerra, Roseanne 1950- *WhoAmW 91*
Cerra Fernandez, Domingo 1953- *BiDrAPA 89*
Cerrano, Robert Edward 1947- *WhoEmL 91*
Cerre, Jean Gabriel 1734-1805 *EncCRAm*
Cerrell, Joseph R. 1935- *ODwPR 91*
Cerreto, Mary Christine 1951- *WhoE 91*
Cerri, Lawrence J. 1923- *WhoWrEP 89*
Cerrito, Oratio Alfonso 1911- *WhoWor 91*
Cerro, Luis M. Sanchez 1889-1933 *BioIn 16*
Cerrone, Michael Anthony 1933- *St&PR 91*
Cerrone, Pamela Sue 1962- *WhoE 91*
Cerroni, Rose Elizabeth 1930- *WhoAmW 91*
Cerrotti, Eugene Don 1944- *St&PR 91*
Cerruti, James Lawrence 1953- *WhoE 91*
Cerruti, Piero John 1935- *BiDrAPA 89*
Cerruto, Gladys Y. 1929- *St&PR 91*
Cersosimo, Dominic *St&PR 91*
Cersosimo, Sally Ann 1963- *WhoEmL 91*
Certa, Kenneth Michael *BiDrAPA 89*
Certilman, Martha Anne 1945- *WhoAmW 91*
Certo, Dominic Nicholas 1950- *WhoWrEP 89*
Ceru, Andrea 1952- *WhoWor 91*
Cerul, Maurice S 1937- *BiDrAPA 89*
Cerulli, Enrico 1898-1988 *AnObit 1988*
Cerulli, Frank *BiDrAPA 89*
Cerullo, Edward Anthony 1950- *St&PR 91*
Cerullo, Lisa Ann 1959- *WhoE 91*
Ceruti, Giacomo 1698-1767 *IntDcAA 90*
Cerutti, James Frank 1952- *WhoAm 90*
Cerutti, John 1960- *Ballpl 90*
Cerv, Bob 1926- *Ballpl 90, BioIn 16*
Cervantes, Alfonso 1937- *WhoHisp 91*
Cervantes, Donald E. *WhoHisp 91*
Cervantes, Evelio 1937- *WhoHisp 91*
Cervantes, John Alexander 1954- *BiDrAPA 89*
Cervantes, Lorna Dee *BioIn 16*
Cervantes, Lorna Dee 1954- *ConAu 131, HispWr 90, WhoHisp 91*
Cervantes, Michael Anthony 1949- *WhoEmL 91*
Cervantes Saavedra, Miguel de 1547-1616 *BioIn 16, WorAlBi*
Cervantes Sahagun, Miguel 1959- *WhoHisp 91*
Cervantez, Pedro 1915- *BioIn 16, WhoHisp 91*
Cervarich, Peter Jerome, Jr. 1909- *St&PR 91*
Cervellero, Paul B. 1942- *St&PR 91*
Cerven, Ludevit 1918- *St&PR 91*
Cervena, Sona 1925- *IntWWM 90*
Cervene, Richard *WhoAmA 91*
Cervenka, Barbara 1939- *WhoAmA 91*
Cerveny, Kathryn M. 1939- *WhoAmW 91*
Cervetti, Sergio 1940- *IntWWM 90*
Cervi, Dennis Paul 1943- *WhoE 91*
Cervieri, John A., Jr. 1931- *St&PR 91*
Cervon, Lawrence John 1922- *St&PR 91*
Cesa, Marco 1958- *WhoWor 91*
Cesaire, Aime *BioIn 16*
Cesaire, Aime 1913- *MajTwCW, WorAlBi*
Cesar 1921- *BioIn 16*
Cesar, Isabelita T *BiDrAPA 89*
Cesar, Tort Oropeza 1928- *IntWWM 90*
Cesarani, Sal 1941- *WhoAm 90*
Cesare, Romiti 1923- *WhoWor 91*
Cesari, Joe *BioIn 16*
Cesario, James Alex 1942- *St&PR 91*
Cesario, Margaret Kannaly 1937- *WhoAmW 91, WhoE 91*
Cesario, Robert James 1951- *WhoSSW 91*
Cesario, Virginia Naill 1923- *WhoAm 90*
Cesarz, Joseph Andrew 1941- *St&PR 91*
Cesarz, Paul Michael 1956- *WhoEmL 91*
Ceschin, Marian *BioIn 16*
Cescon, Lawrence Anthony 1934- *WhoWor 91*
Ceserani, Remo 1933- *WhoWor 91*
Cesinger, Joan 1936- *WhoAmW 91*
Ceska, Miroslav 1932- *WhoWor 91*
Ceska, Zdenek 1929- *WhoWor 91*
Cesna, Joseph Vito 1932- *St&PR 91*
Cesnik, James Michael 1935- *WhoAm 90*
Cespedes, Carlos Manuel de 1819-1874 *BioIn 16*
Cess, Robert Donald 1933- *WhoAm 90*
Cessna, Clyde Vernon 1879-1954 *WorAlBi*
Cessna, John 1821-1893 *AmLegL*
Ceszkowski, Daniel David 1954- *WhoWor 91*
Cetani, Frank R. 1946- *St&PR 91*
Cetera, Peter 1944- *WorAlBi*
Ceterski, Dorothy 1950- *WhoAmW 91, WhoWor 91*
Ceterski, John Joseph 1948- *WhoEmL 91*
Cetin, Anton 1936- *WhoAmA 91*
Ceto, Nicholas, Jr. 1933- *WhoAm 90*
Cetola, Thomas Anthony 1933- *St&PR 91*
Cetron, Marvin Jerome 1930- *WhoAm 90, WhoSSW 91*
Cetrone, Gene Leonard 1958- *WhoEmL 91*
Cetta, Anthony Joseph 1949- *St&PR 91*
Ceulemans, Yvon Constant Jean 1905- *IntWWM 90*
Ceus, Faidherbe *BiDrAPA 89*
Ceva, Joseph C. 1926- *St&PR 91*
Cevallos, Rodrigo Borja 1935- *BioIn 16*
Cevc, Anica 1926- *WhoWor 91*
Cevenini, Roberto Mauro 1957- *WhoSSW 91*
Cey, Ron 1948- *Ballpl 90 [port], BioIn 16*
Cey, Ronald Charles 1948- *WhoAm 90*
Ceyer, Sylvia *WhoAmW 91*
Ceynar, Marvin Emil 1934- *WhoWrEP 89*
Cezanne, Paul 1839-1906 *BioIn 16, IntDcAA 90, WorAlBi*
Cezayirli, Cemil 1927- *BiDrAPA 89*
Cezayirli, Sevim *BiDrAPA 89*
Cezzar, Ruknet 1943- *WhoSSW 91*
Cha, Dong Se 1943- *WhoWor 91*
Cha, Jaeok *BiDrAPA 89*
Cha, Jaeok 1952- *WhoE 91*
Cha, Louis *BioIn 16*
Cha, Se Do 1942- *WhoWor 91*
Cha, Sigmund M 1939- *BiDrAPA 89*
Chaban-Delmas, Jacques Pierre Michel D. 1915- *BiDFrPL*
Chabanel, Claude Fernand 1946- *WhoWor 91*
Chabe, Mary Janice 1923- *WhoE 91*
Chaber, M. E. *TwCCr&M 91*
Chabert, Joseph 1831-1894 *DcCanB 12*
Chabon, Michael *BioIn 16*
Chabot, Albert David 1941- *WhoE 91*
Chabot, Aurore 1949- *WhoAmA 91*
Chabot, Elliot Charles 1955- *WhoEmL 91*
Chabot, Gerri Louise 1949- *WhoAmW 91*
Chabot, Herbert L. 1931- *WhoAm 90*
Chabot, Joseph Marcel 1932- *St&PR 91*
Chabot, Philip Louis, Jr. 1951- *WhoE 91, WhoEmL 91*
Chabot, Stephen L. *BiDrAPA 89*
Chabran, Richard 1950- *WhoHisp 91*
Chabre, Stephen William 1943- *WhoAm 90*
Chabrier, Emmanuel 1841-1894 *PenDiMP A*
Chabrol, Claude 1930- *BioIn 16, ConTFT 8, WorAlBi*
Chabus, Brent Ira *BiDrAPA 89*
Chaby, Diane 1935- *ODwPR 91*
Chaby, Diane Block 1935- *WhoAmW 91*
Chace, James 1931- *ConAu 30NR*
Chace, William Murdough 1938- *WhoAm 90, WhoE 91*
Chacel, Rosa 1898- *EncCoWW*
Chachkes, Jacob T 1933- *BiDrAPA 89*
Chachko, Faina *BiDrAPA 89*
Chacho, Raymond Andrew 1931- *St&PR 91*
Chacin Guzman, Juan 1929- *WhoWor 91*
Chackes, Kenneth Michael 1949- *WhoEmL 91*
Chacko, Chowallur D 1946- *BiDrAPA 89*
Chacko, David 1942- *ConAu 31NR*
Chacko, Elizabeth *BiDrAPA 89*
Chacko, George Kuttickal 1930- *WhoAm 90, WhoWor 91*
Chacko, Ranjit C 1948- *BiDrAPA 89*
Chacko, Rose *BiDrAPA 89*
Chacksfield, Frank 1914- *OxCPMus*
Chacon, Bobby *BioIn 16*
Chacon, Carlos R. 1959- *WhoHisp 91*
Chacon, Elio 1936- *Ballpl 90*
Chacon, Eusebio 1869-1948 *ConAu 131, HispWr 90*
Chacon, Felipe Maximiliano 1873- *BioIn 16*
Chacon, Jose Andres 1925- *BioIn 16*
Chacon, Peter R. 1925- *WhoHisp 91*
Chacon, Richard Frank 1945- *St&PR 91*
Chaconas, D. J. 1938- *AuBYP 90*
Chad and Jeremy *EncPR&S 89*
Chadabe, Joel A. 1938- *IntWWM 90*
Chadbourn, Alfred Cheney 1921- *WhoAmA 91*
Chadbourne, Chet 1884-1943 *Ballpl 90*
Chadbourne, Robert *St&PR 91*
Chadderdon, John Posey 1965- *WhoSSW 91*
Chaddha, Aroon Kumar 1939- *St&PR 91*

Chaddlesone, Sherman 1947- *WhoAmA 91*
Chaddock, Jack Bartley 1924- *WhoAm 90*
Chaddock, Paul Henry 1936- *St&PR 91*
Chadeayne, Robert Osborne 1897- *WhoAmA 91*
Chadha, Mohinder Kaur 1944- *BiDrAPA 89*
Chadha, Mohinder Partap 1948- *BiDrAPA 89*
Chadha, Parvinder S. 1955- *St&PR 91*
Chadik, Paul Arthur 1947- *WhoSSW 91*
Chadirji, Rifat Kamil 1926- *WhoWor 91*
Chadli, Bendjedid *BioIn 16*
Chadsey, Phillip Duke 1936- *WhoAm 90*
Chadsey, William Lloyd 1942- *St&PR 91*
Chadwell, Barbara Sue 1963- *WhoAmW 91*
Chadwell, Susie 1940- *WhoAmW 91*
Chadwell, Tracey Gillian 1959- *IntWWM 90*
Chadwick, Alan *BioIn 16*
Chadwick, Charles Eli 1818-1896 *DcCanB 12*
Chadwick, Charles Robb 1923- *St&PR 91*
Chadwick, Charles William 1912- *WhoSSW 91*
Chadwick, Edwin 1800-1890 *BioIn 16*
Chadwick, Elizabeth B. 1857-1907 *BioAmW*
Chadwick, Eric Bourne 1928- *IntWWM 90*
Chadwick, Florence 1918- *WorAlBi*
Chadwick, Helen 1953- *BiDWomA*
Chadwick, Henry 1824-1908 *Ballpl 90 [port]*
Chadwick, Henry 1920- *WhoWor 91*
Chadwick, Ian W. 1950- *WhoWrEP 89*
Chadwick, James 1891-1974 *DcScB S2*, *WorAlBi*
Chadwick, Jerome A 1937- *BiDrAPA 89*
Chadwick, Owen 1916- *WhoWor 91*
Chadwick, Paige Parrish 1960- *WhoAmW 91*
Chadwick, Peter 1931- *WhoWor 91*
Chadwick, Robert 1924- *WhoSSW 91*, *WhoWor 91*
Chadwick, Sara Jane Hawks 1942- *WhoAmW 91*
Chadwick, Sharon Stevens 1951- *WhoEmL 91*
Chadwick, Wallace Lacy 1897- *WhoAm 90*, *WhoWor 91*
Chadwick, Whitney 1943- *ConAu 132*, *WhoAmA 91*
Chadwick-Collins, Richard 1915- *WhoWor 91*
Chaet, Bernard 1924- *WhoAmA 91*
Chaet, Bernard Robert 1924- *WhoAm 90*
Chafe, Wallace L. 1927- *WhoAm 90*
Chafe, William Henry 1942- *WhoAm 90*
Chafee, Francis Hasseltine 1903- *WhoAm 90*
Chafee, John Hubbard 1922- *WhoAm 90*, *WhoE 91*, *WhoWor 91*
Chafee, Judith Davidson 1932- *WhoAm 90*
Chafel, Judith Ann 1945- *WhoAmW 91*
Chafer, Clive Derek 1954- *WhoEmL 91*
Chafetz, Barry Richard 1946- *WhoEmL 91*
Chafetz, Henry 1916-1978 *AuBYP 90*
Chafetz, Marc Edward 1953- *WhoEmL 91*
Chafetz, Marion Claire 1925- *WhoWrEP 89*
Chafetz, Morris Edward 1924- *WhoAm 90*
Chafetz, Sidney 1922- *WhoAmA 91*
Chaffart, Robby Ghislain 1958- *WhoEmL 91*
Chaffee, Adna Romanza 1842-1914 *WorAlBi*
Chaffee, Adna Romanza, Jr. 1884-1941 *WorAlBi*
Chaffee, C. David 1951- *WhoWrEP 89*
Chaffee, Charles David 1951- *WhoE 91*
Chaffee, Dennis A. *St&PR 91*
Chaffee, Frederic H., Jr. 1941- *WhoAm 90*
Chaffee, Jerome Bunty 1825-1886 *AmLegL*
Chaffee, John Densmore 1952- *WhoSSW 91*
Chaffee, Kevin St. Clair 1952- *WhoE 91*, *WhoEmL 91*, *WhoWor 91*
Chaffee, Nelson R. 1941- *St&PR 91*
Chaffee, Pamela Jane 1953- *WhoE 91*
Chaffee, Paul Stanley 1928- *WhoAm 90*
Chaffee, Sheila Marie 1966- *WhoAmW 91*
Chaffee, Steven Henry 1935- *WhoAm 90*
Chaffers, Richard *PenDiDA 89*
Chaffin *EncPaPR 91*
Chaffin, B.E. 1935- *St&PR 91*
Chaffin, Bill *St&PR 91*
Chaffin, Charlie Cole 1938- *WhoSSW 91*
Chaffin, Daniel S *BiDrAPA 89*
Chaffin, Douglas George 1943- *WhoE 91*
Chaffin, Gary 1937- *St&PR 91*
Chaffin, Gary Roger 1937- *WhoAm 90*
Chaffin, Glenn 1897-1978 *EncACom*
Chaffin, Goodloe Summers 1922- *St&PR 91*
Chaffin, Julie Eileen 1959- *WhoEmL 91*
Chaffin, Lillie 1925- *AuBYP 90*
Chaffin, Lillie D. *WhoWrEP 89*
Chaffin, Lillie D. 1925- *LiHiK*
Chaffin, Owen C. *St&PR 91N*
Chaffin, Randell C. 1948- *St&PR 91*
Chaffin, Richard J. 1932- *St&PR 91*
Chaffin, Thomas Lafayette 1938- *St&PR 91*
Chaffin, Tommy Lynn 1943- *WhoWor 91*
Chaffin, William Michael 1947- *WhoEmL 91*
Chaffinch, Richard A. 1939- *St&PR 91*
Chafflin *EncPaPR 91*
Chafin, Lydia Estepp 1956- *WhoAmW 91*
Chafin, Sara Susan 1952- *WhoAmW 91*, *WhoE 91*
Chafin, William Vernon, Jr. 1936- *WhoAm 90*
Chagall, Bella 1895-1944 *BioIn 16*
Chagall, David 1930- *WhoAm 90*
Chagall, Marc 1887-1985 *BioIn 16*, *IntDcAA 90 [port]*, *WorAlBi*
Chagami, Michael S. 1952- *St&PR 91*
Chagnon, Joseph V. 1929- *WhoE 91*, *WhoWor 91*
Chagnon, Leon 1902-1953 *Ballpl 90*
Chagnon, Lucille Tessier 1936- *WhoAmW 91*
Chagnon, Marcel 1916- *St&PR 91*
Chagnon, Napoleon A. 1938- *ConAu 130*
Chagnon, Richard Joseph 1942- *WhoE 91*
Chagnon, Roland 1910- *St&PR 91*
Chagnon, Sandra Trombley 1941- *WhoAmW 91*
Chahal, Balinder B S 1954- *BiDrAPA 89*
Chahal, Bhupinder Singh 1952- *BiDrAPA 89*
Chahid-Nourai, Behrouz J.P. 1938- *WhoWor 91*
Chahine, Moustafa Toufic 1935- *WhoAm 90*
Chahine, Youssef *BioIn 16*
Chahroudi, Martha L 1946- *WhoAmA 91*
Chai, Winberg 1932- *WhoAm 90*, *WhoWor 91*
Chaice, Herbert H. 1928- *WhoAm 90*
Chaides, Rudy L. *WhoHisp 91*
Chaidron, Andre 1935- *WhoWor 91*
Chaiet, Alan Howard 1943- *WhoAm 90*
Chaika, Stephen 1920- *St&PR 91*
Chaiken, Barry Paul 1956- *WhoE 91*
Chaiken, Eugene Barry 1940- *St&PR 91*
Chaiken, Sheldon A. 1934- *St&PR 91*
Chaikin, Alyce *WhoAmA 91*
Chaikin, Alyce 1923- *WhoE 91*
Chaikin, Bonnie Patricia 1953- *WhoAmW 91*, *WhoEmL 91*
Chaikin, Donald Joel 1933- *WhoE 91*
Chaikin, Miriam 1928- *BioIn 16*
Chaikin, Tommy *BioIn 16*
Chaiklin, Amy 1955- *WhoAmA 91*
Chaikovsky, Leo I *BiDrAPA 89*
Chaikovsky, P. I. 1840-1893 *BioIn 16*
Chailley, Jacques 1910- *IntWWM 90*
Chailly, Luciano 1920- *IntWWM 90*
Chailly, Riccardo 1953- *IntWWM 90*, *PenDiMP*
Chaim, Robert Alex 1947- *WhoWor 91*
Chaimowitz, Gary A 1956- *BiDrAPA 89*
Chain, Beverly Jean 1933- *WhoE 91*
Chain, Bobby Lee 1929- *WhoSSW 91*, *WhoWor 91*
Chain, Ernst B. 1906-1979 *WorAlBi*
Chain, Ernst Boris 1906-1979 *DcScB S2*
Chain, John T. *WhoAm 90*
Chairnoff, Hugh 1939- *St&PR 91*
Chaison, William *BioIn 16*
Chaisson, William T. 1931- *St&PR 91*
Chait, Arnold 1930- *WhoAm 90*
Chait, Lawrence G. 1917- *WhoAm 90*
Chait, Robert Harlan 1954- *WhoEmL 91*
Chait, Sallie Hope 1953- *WhoEmL 91*
Chait, William 1915- *WhoAm 90*
Chaitanya 1486-1534 *BioIn 16*
Chaitin, Anthony 1941- *St&PR 91*
Chaitin, Barry F 1943- *BiDrAPA 89*
Chaitin, Raymond M 1915- *BiDrAPA 89*
Chaitkin, David 1938- *IntWWM 90*
Chaitman, Edmund *BiDrAPA 89*
Chajet, Clive 1937- *WhoAm 90*
Chakales, Bob 1927- *Ballpl 90*
Chakava, Henry Miyinzi 1946- *WhoWor 91*
Chako, Nicholas 1910- *WhoAm 90*
Chakoian, George 1924- *WhoE 91*
Chakos, Miranda Helen 1954- *BiDrAPA 89*
Chakovsky, Aleksandr Borisovich 1913- *WhoWor 91*
Chakrabarti, Arun Kumar 1955- *WhoSSW 91*
Chakrabarti, Binay K *BiDrAPA 89*
Chakrabarti, Mukti *BiDrAPA 89*
Chakrabarti, Paritosh Mohan 1940- *St&PR 91*
Chakrabarti, Ramrenu 1951- *WhoWor 91*
Chakrabarti, Subrata Kumar 1941- *WhoAm 90*
Chakrabarty, Ananda Mohan 1938- *WhoAm 90*, *WhoWor 91*
Chakraborti, Champa *BiDrAPA 89*
Chakraborty, Ajita *BiDrAPA 89*
Chakraborty, Prasanta Kumar 1942- *BiDrAPA 89*
Chakravarty, Indranil 1954- *WhoSSW 91*
Chakravarty, Krishna *NewAgMG*
Chakravarty, Sudipto 1951- *WhoWor 91*
Chakravorty, Arun Kanta 1940- *WhoWor 91*
Chalabala, Zdenek 1899-1962 *PenDiMP*
Chalabi, A. Fattah 1924- *WhoAm 90*
C'halan, Reun ar 1923- *WhoAm 90*
Chalandon, Albin Paul Henri 1920- *BiDFrPL*
Chalas, John George 1926- *St&PR 91*
Chalasani, Subramanyeswara 1940- *BiDrAPA 89*
Chalbaud, Carlos Delgado 1909-1950 *BioIn 16*
Chalberg-Plunkett, Sherri Linell 1960- *WhoAmW 91*, *WhoEmL 91*
Chaleby, Kutaiba Salem 1947- *BiDrAPA 89*
Chalef, Rita M 1925- *BiDrAPA 89*
Chaleff, Carl Thomas 1945- *WhoEmL 91*
Chaleff, Norman *St&PR 91*
Chalem, Mark Lawrence 1951- *BiDrAPA 89*
Chalemian, Robert John *BiDrAPA 89*
Chalfant, C. Dana 1918- *St&PR 91*
Chalfant, Clyde 1905- *St&PR 91*
Chalfant, Edward Cole 1937- *WhoAm 90*, *WhoE 91*
Chalfant, T.W. 1931- *St&PR 91*
Chalfen, Judith Resnick 1925- *WhoAmW 91*
Chalfin, Ann *ODwPR 91*
Chalfin, Bernard 1934- *St&PR 91*
Chalfin, Lawrence S *BiDrAPA 89*
Chalfin, Norman Leonard 1913- *WhoWor 91*
Chalfin, Robert M 1936- *BiDrAPA 89*
Chalfin, Samuel 1910- *St&PR 91*
Chalfont, Alun Arthur G Jones, Baron 1919- *BioIn 16*
Chalgren, William S *BiDrAPA 89*
Chaliapin, Boris 1907-1979 *WhoAmA 91N*
Chaliapin, Feodor 1873-1938 *BioIn 16*
Chaliapin, Fyodor *PenDiMP*
Chaliapin, Fyodor 1873-1938 *WorAlBi*
Chalick, Morris Jay 1937- *BiDrAPA 89*
Chalif, Seymour Hunt 1927- *WhoAm 90*
Chalifoux, Alice *BioIn 16*
Chalifoux, Michael Thomas 1947- *St&PR 91*
Chalifoux, Thomas Eugene, Jr. 1948- *WhoEmL 91*, *WhoSSW 91*
Chalip, Alice Grace 1930- *WhoWrEP 89*
Chalk, Dave 1950- *Ballpl 90*
Chalk, Howard Wolfe 1922- *WhoAm 90*, *WhoE 91*
Chalk, John Allen 1937- *WhoAm 90*, *WhoSSW 91*
Chalk, Vincent *NewYTBS 90*
Chalk, Warren 1927-1987 *BioIn 16*
Chalke, John 1940- *WhoAmA 91*
Chalker, Brad Alan 1950- *WhoEmL 91*
Chalker, Bruce Orrin 1927- *St&PR 91*
Chalker, Durwood 1923- *St&PR 91*
Chalker, Robert Phelps 1914- *WhoWor 91*
Chalker, William Rogers 1920- *WhoAm 90*
Chalko, Alexander J, III *BiDrAPA 89*
Challakere, Kedarnath K *BiDrAPA 89*
Challand, Helen J. *AuBYP 90*
Challand, Helen J 1921- *SmATA 64*
Challans, Mary *AuBYP 90*
Challans, Mary 1905-1983 *BioIn 16*, *DcNaB 1981*
Challapalli, Roopa *BiDrAPA 89*
Challe, Maurice 1906- *BiDFrPL*
Challem, Jack Joseph 1950- *WhoWrEP 89*
Challender, Craig Alton 1946- *WhoSSW 91*
Challender, Stuart *PenDiMP*
Challender, Stuart 1948- *IntWWM 90*
Challenger, Rudy 1928- *DrBlPA 90*
Challinor, David 1920- *WhoAm 90*
Challis, Chris *ConAu 131*
Challis, Mary *TwCCr&M 91*
Challis, Norma Jean 1934- *WhoAmW 91*
Challis, Philip 1929- *IntWWM 90*
Challis, Richard Bracebridge 1920- *WhoAmA 91*
Challis, Simon *TwCCr&M 91*
Challis, Thomas Jack 1947- *WhoEmL 91*
Challis, Thomas William 1926- *WhoAm 90*
Challoner, David Reynolds 1935- *WhoAm 90*
Challoner, Rosemary Regina *WhoWrEP 89*
Chalmers, Audrey 1899- *AuBYP 90*
Chalmers, Bruce 1907-1990 *BioIn 16*
Chalmers, Bruce Abernethy 1915- *WhoSSW 91*
Chalmers, Catherine Faye 1959- *WhoWrEP 89*
Chalmers, David B. 1924- *St&PR 91*, *WhoAm 90*, *WhoSSW 91*
Chalmers, David Glenn 1860-1940 *AmLegL*
Chalmers, David Hamilton 1960- *IntWWM 90*
Chalmers, Douglas Raymond 1954- *WhoE 91*
Chalmers, E Laurence, Jr 1928- *WhoAmA 91*
Chalmers, Edwin Laurence, Jr. 1928- *WhoAm 90*
Chalmers, Floyd Sherman 1898- *OxCCanT*, *WhoAm 90*
Chalmers, George 1888-1960 *Ballpl 90*
Chalmers, Gordon James 1925- *St&PR 91*
Chalmers, Hugh 1873-1932 *EncABHB 4 [port]*
Chalmers, Irena *BioIn 16*
Chalmers, Jacqueline Louise 1952- *WhoEmL 91*
Chalmers, Margaret 1758- *FemiCLE*
Chalmers, Mary 1927- *AuBYP 90*
Chalmers, Neil Robert 1942- *WhoWor 91*
Chalmers, Penny *ConAu 130*
Chalmers, Rives 1918- *BiDrAPA 89*
Chalmers, Thomas Clark 1917- *WhoAm 90*
Chalmers, Thomas Scott 1925- *WhoAm 90*
Chalon, Jonathan William 1960- *WhoEmL 91*
Chaloupek, Guenther Karl 1947- *WhoWor 91*
Chalovich, Pamela Sue 1954- *WhoAmW 91*
Chalpinich *WhNaAH*
Chalsty, John S. 1933- *St&PR 91*
Chalsty, John Steele 1933- *WhoAm 90*, *WhoE 91*
Chaltiel, Victor M.G. 1941- *St&PR 91*
Chamasrour, Joseph Albert 1952- *WhoAm 90*
Chambelland, Bruno *BioIn 16*
Chamberlain, Adrian Raymond 1929- *WhoAm 90*
Chamberlain, Austen 1863-1937 *BioIn 16*
Chamberlain, Barbara Greene 1962- *WhoAmW 91*
Chamberlain, Barbara Jean 1949- *WhoAmW 91*
Chamberlain, Betty 1908-1983 *WhoAmA 91N*
Chamberlain, Brenda 1912-1971 *BiDWomA*
Chamberlain, Charles 1942- *WhoAmA 91*
Chamberlain, Charles Ernest 1917- *WhoAm 90*
Chamberlain, Charles James 1921- *WhoAm 90*
Chamberlain, Charlotte Appel 1946- *St&PR 91*
Chamberlain, Claudia Catherine 1940- *St&PR 91*
Chamberlain, Daniel Robert 1932 *WhoAm 90*, *WhoE 91*
Chamberlain, Darrell H *BiDrAPA 89*
Chamberlain, David 1949- *WhoAmA 91*
Chamberlain, Diane 1950- *WhoAmW 91*
Chamberlain, Donald William 1905- *WhoWrEP 89*
Chamberlain, Donna Jon 1937- *WhoWrEP 89*
Chamberlain, Douglas Anthony 1931- *WhoWor 91*
Chamberlain, E. Martin 1940- *St&PR 91*
Chamberlain, Elinor 1901- *AuBYP 90*
Chamberlain, Elwyn M. 1928- *ConAu 131*
Chamberlain, George Arthur, III 1935- *St&PR 91*, *WhoAm 90*
Chamberlain, Harriet Feigenbaum 1939- *BioIn 16*
Chamberlain, Henry 1796-1844 *ArtLatA*
Chamberlain, Houston Stewart 1855-1926 *EncO&P 3*
Chamberlain, Houston Stewart 1855-1927 *BioIn 16*
Chamberlain, Humphrey *PenDiDA 89*
Chamberlain, James M. 1947- *St&PR 91*
Chamberlain, James O. 1952- *St&PR 91*
Chamberlain, James Robert 1949- *WhoEmL 91*
Chamberlain, Jill Frances 1954- *WhoAmW 91*
Chamberlain, Jocelyn Olivia 1932- *WhoWor 91*
Chamberlain, John Angus 1927- *WhoAm 90*, *WhoAmA 91*
Chamberlain, John Harold, Jr. 1929- *WhoWor 91*
Chamberlain, John Rensselaer 1903- *WhoAm 90*
Chamberlain, Joseph 1836-1914 *BioIn 16*
Chamberlain, Joseph 1863-1937 *WorAlBi*
Chamberlain, Joseph Miles 1923- *WhoAm 90*

Chamberlain, Joseph Wyan 1928- *WhoAm 90*
Chamberlain, Karen 1942- *WhoWrEP 89*
Chamberlain, Kent Clair 1943- *WhoWrEP 89*
Chamberlain, Lawrence Henry 1906-1989 *BioIn 16*
Chamberlain, Linda Lee 1951- *WhoAmW 91*
Chamberlain, Lindy *BioIn 16*
Chamberlain, Marian Crowley 1943- *WhoSSW 91*
Chamberlain, Marisha Anne 1952- *WhoWrEP 89*
Chamberlain, Michael Barnard 1941- *St&PR 91*
Chamberlain, Neil Cornelius Wolverton 1915- *WhoAm 90*
Chamberlain, Neville 1869-1940 *BioIn 16, WorAlBi*
Chamberlain, Owen 1920- *WhoAm 90, WhoWor 91, WorAlBi*
Chamberlain, Richard *BioIn 16*
Chamberlain, Richard 1935- *WhoAm 90, WorAlBi*
Chamberlain, Richard Gray 1952- *WhoWrEP 89*
Chamberlain, Robert *PenDiDA 89*
Chamberlain, Robert Glenn 1926- *WhoAm 90*
Chamberlain, Robert N. 1856-1917 *AmLegL*
Chamberlain, Ross Edwin 1929- *St&PR 91*
Chamberlain, Samuel 1895-1975 *WhoAmA 91N*
Chamberlain, Steven Craig 1946- *WhoE 91*
Chamberlain, Theresa Nowak 1947- *WhoAmW 91*
Chamberlain, Thomas Taber, Jr. 1945- *WhoEmL 91*
Chamberlain, Velma *WhoWrEP 89*
Chamberlain, Walter *PenDiDA 89*
Chamberlain, Willard Thomas 1928- *St&PR 91, WhoAm 90*
Chamberlain, William Edwin, Jr. 1951- *WhoAm 90*
Chamberlain, William Woodrow 1914- *LiHiK*
Chamberlain, Wilt 1936- *BioIn 16, WorAlBi*
Chamberlain, Wilton Norman 1936- *WhoAm 90*
Chamberland, Bertrand Leo 1934- *WhoE 91*
Chamberland, Paul 1939- *BioIn 16*
Chamberlin, Powell and Bon *ConDes 90*
Chamberlin, Barbara Carol 1951- *BiDrAPA 89*
Chamberlin, C. Rick 1947- *WhoEmL 91*
Chamberlin, Cecil Rhodes, Jr. 1930- *BiDrAPA 89*
Chamberlin, Christine A. *WhoAmW 91*
Chamberlin, Dean *BioIn 16*
Chamberlin, Douglas Eric *BiDrAPA 89*
Chamberlin, Edward 1899-1967 *BioIn 16*
Chamberlin, Jo Hubbard *AuBYP 90*
Chamberlin, John Stephen 1928- *WhoAm 90*
Chamberlin, Lee *DrBIPA 90*
Chamberlin, Michael John 1937- *WhoAm 90*
Chamberlin, Peter 1919-1978 *ConDes 90*
Chamberlin, Peter Klotz- *BioIn 16*
Chamberlin, Ronald Eugene 1947- *St&PR 91*
Chamberlin, Rosetta E. 1945- *WhoAmW 91*
Chamberlin, Scott 1948- *WhoAmA 91*
Chamberlin, Terry McBride *WhoAmW 91*
Chamberlin, Ward Bryan *BioIn 16*
Chambers, Aidan 1934- *BioIn 16, ConAu 31NR, SmATA 12AS [port]*
Chambers, Alan Brent 1948- *WhoEmL 91*
Chambers, Albert M. 1941- *ODwPR 91*
Chambers, Allan 1937- *WhoWor 91*
Chambers, Anne Cox *WhoAm 90*
Chambers, Arther Eugene 1923- *St&PR 91*
Chambers, Arthur A. 1922- *St&PR 91*
Chambers, Aubrey Pat 1944- *BiDrAPA 89*
Chambers, Barbara Mae Fromm 1940- *WhoE 91*
Chambers, Bradford 1922-1984 *AuBYP 90*
Chambers, Bruce William 1941- *WhoAmA 91*
Chambers, C. Fred *BioIn 16*
Chambers, Carl D. 1934-1989 *BioIn 16*
Chambers, Carolyn S. 1931- *St&PR 91*
Chambers, Catherine E. *ConAu 32NR*
Chambers, Clarke Alexander 1921- *WhoAm 90*
Chambers, Cliff 1922- *Ballpl 90*
Chambers, Clytia M. *ODwPR 91*
Chambers, Curtis Allen 1924- *WhoAm 90*
Chambers, Dale 1953- *WhoSSW 91*
Chambers, Dave 1940- *WhoAm 90*
Chambers, David Edson 1938- *St&PR 91*
Chambers, Dennis *BioIn 16*
Chambers, Donald Seldon *BiDrAPA 89*
Chambers, Dorothy J. 1950- *WhoEmL 91*
Chambers, Earl Denton 1925- *St&PR 91, WhoAm 90*
Chambers, Edward Thomas 1930- *WhoAm 90*
Chambers, Elizabeth *BiDEWW*
Chambers, Emmett K. *St&PR 91*
Chambers, Erve Jefferson 1942- *WhoAm 90*
Chambers, Frank G. 1916- *St&PR 91*
Chambers, Fred 1912- *WhoAm 90*
Chambers, George Michael 1928- *BioIn 16*
Chambers, Glenn D. 1936- *WhoWor 91*
Chambers, Henry Carroll 1928- *WhoSSW 91*
Chambers, Ima Louise 1932- *WhoAmW 91*
Chambers, Imogene Klutts 1928- *WhoAmW 91*
Chambers, J.H.L., II 1927- *St&PR 91*
Chambers, J. Richard 1947- *St&PR 91*
Chambers, Jack A. 1932- *WhoAm 90*
Chambers, Jacqueline Alease 1962- *WhoE 91*
Chambers, James *BioIn 16*
Chambers, James Richard 1947- *WhoAm 90*
Chambers, Jane 1937-1983 *BioIn 16, FemiCLE, NotWoAT*
Chambers, Janet Haldeman 1962- *WhoAmW 91*
Chambers, Jean F *BiDrAPA 89*
Chambers, Jeffrey Roy *BiDrAPA 89*
Chambers, Jessie *MajTwCW*
Chambers, Jimmie Joe 1951- *WhoSSW 91*
Chambers, Joan Louise 1937- *WhoAm 90, WhoAmW 91*
Chambers, John 1931-1978 *WhoAmA 91N*
Chambers, John Darby 1939- *WhoWrEP 89*
Chambers, John Edward 1927- *St&PR 91*
Chambers, John W. 1933- *BioIn 16*
Chambers, Julius Burgess 1923- *WhoSSW 91*
Chambers, Julius LeVonne 1936- *WhoAm 90*
Chambers, Karen 1948- *WhoAmA 91*
Chambers, Karen Jean 1946- *WhoAmW 91*
Chambers, Kate *ConAu 32NR*
Chambers, Katherine Tyson 1922- *St&PR 91*
Chambers, Kenneth R. 1937- *St&PR 91*
Chambers, Leigh Ross 1932- *WhoAm 90*
Chambers, Leslie Ann 1963- *WhoAmW 91*
Chambers, Linda Dianne Thompson 1953- *WhoAmW 91, WhoSSW 91, WhoWor 91*
Chambers, Lois Irene 1935- *WhoAmW 91*
Chambers, Marian Tector 1926- *WhoSSW 91*
Chambers, Marianne *FemiCLE*
Chambers, Martin John 1944- *IntWWM 90*
Chambers, Merle Catherine 1946- *WhoAmW 91*
Chambers, Park A. Jr 1942- *WhoAmA 91*
Chambers, Patrick J. 1934- *St&PR 91*
Chambers, Paul 1904-1981 *DcNaB 1981*
Chambers, Paul 1935-1969 *BioIn 16*
Chambers, Peter 1924- *TwCCr&M 91*
Chambers, Phillip B. 1944- *WhoE 91*
Chambers, Ray Wayne 1931- *WhoSSW 91*
Chambers, Raymond G. *BioIn 16*
Chambers, Richard Everett 1931- *St&PR 91*
Chambers, Richard H. 1906- *WhoAm 90*
Chambers, Richard H. 1935- *St&PR 91*
Chambers, Richard Lee 1947- *WhoSSW 91*
Chambers, Robert *BioIn 16*
Chambers, Robert 1802-1871 *BioIn 16, EncO&P 3*
Chambers, Robert Ben 1949- *IntWWM 90*
Chambers, Robert Hunter, III 1939- *WhoAm 90*
Chambers, Robert Jeffferson 1930- *WhoAm 90*
Chambers, Robert Warner *AuBYP 90*
Chambers, Robert William 1943- *WhoSSW 91*
Chambers, Roy G *BiDrAPA 89*
Chambers, Royce Aldwin 1935- *St&PR 91*
Chambers, Russell Raymond 1948- *WhoEmL 91*
Chambers, Theodore D. 1931- *St&PR 91*
Chambers, Thomas Doane 1959- *WhoAm 90*
Chambers, Thomas Edward 1934- *WhoSSW 91*
Chambers, Thomas H. *St&PR 91*
Chambers, Thomas P. 1942- *St&PR 91*
Chambers, Tony Edward, Jr. 1951- *WhoSSW 91*
Chambers, Walter Ray, Jr. 1931- *St&PR 91*
Chambers, Whittaker *BioIn 16*
Chambers, Whittaker 1901-1961 *WorAlBi*
Chambers, Wicke Oliver 1937- *WhoSSW 91*
Chambers, William 1723-1796 *PenDiDA 89*
Chambers, William Douglas 1945- *WhoEmL 91*
Chambers, William E. *St&PR 91*
Chambers, William Eldridge 1931- *WhoSSW 91*
Chambers, William J 1945- *BiDrAPA 89*
Chambers, William John 1946- *St&PR 91*
Chambers, William N 1920- *BiDrAPA 89*
Chambers, William R *BiDrAPA 89*
Chambi, Martin 1891-1973 *WhoAmA 91N*
Chambial, D.C. 1950- *WhoWor 91*
Chamblee, John James, Jr. 1949- *WhoEmL 91*
Chamblee, Wendy Morie 1949- *St&PR 91*
Chambless, Jimmie Juanita 1935- *WhoSSW 91*
Chambliss, Chris 1948- *Ballpl 90 [port], BioIn 16*
Chambliss, H. Darden, Jr. 1929- *ODwPR 91*
Chambliss, Jac 1910- *St&PR 91*
Chambliss, John Davidson 1943- *WhoAm 90*
Chambliss, Karen Maria *BiDrAPA 89*
Chambliss, Leonard Perryman, Jr. 1949- *WhoSSW 91*
Chambliss, William Joseph 1933- *WhoAm 90*
Chambord, Henri, Comte de 1820-1883 *BiDFrPL*
Chambre, Paul L. 1918- *WhoAm 90*
Chambrette, Jacques *PenDiDA 89*
Chambrier, Janet Elene Herbert De 1953- *IntWWM 90*
Chamby, Gilbert Charles 1930- *WhoSSW 91*
Chameides, Walter A 1934- *BiDrAPA 89*
Chaminade, Cecile 1857-1944 *BioIn 16*
Chamine, Robert B. *BioIn 16*
Chamis, Alice Yanosko *WhoAmW 91*
Chamlee, Kenneth D. 1952- *WhoWrEP 89*
Chammas, Jacques 1950- *WhoWor 91*
Chammas, Sabah N *BiDrAPA 89*
Chamness, John Charles 1942- *St&PR 91*
Chamorro, Emiliano 1871-1966 *BioIn 16*
Chamorro, Frutos 1806-1855 *BioIn 16*
Chamorro, Pedro Joaquin *BioIn 16*
Chamorro, Violeta 1929- *CurBio 90 [port], WhoWor 91*
Chamorro, Violeta Barrios de *BioIn 16, NewYTBS 90 [port]*
Chamorro, Violeta Barrios de 1929- *WomWR, WorAlBi*
Chamorro Rappacioli, Fernando *BioIn 16*
Chamoun, Camille 1900-1987 *PolLCME*
Champ, Joseph C. 1929- *St&PR 91*
Champ, Norman B., Jr. 1928- *St&PR 91*
Champagne, Andree 1939- *WhoAmW 91*
Champagne, Betty June 1949- *WhoAmW 91, WhoEmL 91, WhoSSW 91*
Champagne, Carol Ziegler 1941- *WhoE 91*
Champagne, Charles F. 1941- *St&PR 91*
Champagne, Gayle Lynn 1950- *WhoAmW 91*
Champagne, Guy B. 1928- *St&PR 91*
Champagne, Joseph Ernest 1938- *WhoAm 90*
Champagne, Marie de 1145-1198 *EncCoWW*
Champagne, Ronald Oscar 1942- *WhoAm 90*
Champaigne, Philippe de 1602?-1674 *IntDcAA 90*
Champanhet, Bernard 1950- *WhoWor 91*
Champe, Flavia Waters 1902- *BioIn 16*
Champeil, Jean *PenDiMP*
Champena, Tito A 1933- *BiDrAPA 89*
Champeny, Susan Jean 1957- *WhoE 91*
Champion, Albert 1878-1927 *EncABHB 4 [port]*
Champion, Billy 1947- *Ballpl 90*
Champion, David 1937- *IntWWM 90*
Champion, David Warren 1939- *WhoSSW 91*
Champion, Debbie Slovak 1956- *WhoAmW 91*
Champion, Deborah 1753-1845 *EncCRAm*
Champion, Elizabeth Hollis 1945- *WhoWrEP 89*
Champion, Gower 1921-1980 *WorAlBi*
Champion, Hale 1922- *WhoAm 90*
Champion, Harry 1866-1942 *OxCPMus*
Champion, James Perry, Jr. 1918- *WhoSSW 91*
Champion, Lawrence A *BiDrAPA 89*
Champion, Marge 1923- *WhoAm 90, WorAlBi*
Champion, Maxine C. *St&PR 91*
Champion, Maxine Christina *WhoAm 90, WhoAmW 91*
Champion, Mike 1955- *Ballpl 90*
Champion, Patti Taylor 1961- *WhoSSW 91*
Champion, Pierre Dheilly 1936- *WhoWor 91*
Champion, Richard 1743-1791 *PenDiDA 89*
Champion, Robert Louis, Jr. 1944- *WhoAm 90*
Champion, Walter Thomas, Jr. 1950- *WhoEmL 91*
Champion, Wm. David, Jr. 1947- *St&PR 91*
Champion de Crespigny, Mary 1748?-1812 *FemiCLE*
Champion-Metardier, Isabelle 1947- *BiDWomA*
Champlain, Samuel de 1567-1635 *BioIn 16, EncCRAm, WhNaAH, WorAlBi*
Champlin, Charles Davenport 1926- *WhoAm 90, WhoWrEP 89*
Champlin, Edward James 1948- *WhoAm 90*
Champlin, Elizabeth Ellen 1962- *WhoAmW 91*
Champlin, Ezra Thomas 1839-1928 *AmLegL*
Champlin, George Charles 1938- *St&PR 91*
Champlin, Greta Virginia 1947- *WhoAmW 91*
Champlin, Herbert Alvin 1933- *St&PR 91*
Champlin, Malcolm McGregor 1911- *WhoAm 90*
Champlin, Marjorie Weeden 1921- *WhoAmW 91*
Champlin, Richard H. 1935- *St&PR 91, WhoAm 90*
Champlin, Rolland S. 1951- *St&PR 91*
Champlin, Sheila Ann 1946- *WhoWrEP 89*
Champney, Paul Arthur 1942- *St&PR 91*
Champney, Raymond Joseph 1940- *WhoSSW 91, WhoWor 91*
Champollion, Jean Francois 1790-1832 *BioIn 16, WorAlBi*
Champourcin, Ernestina de 1905- *EncCoWW*
Champseix, Gregoire de, Mme. *EncCoWW*
Chamson, Sandra Potkorony 1933- *WhoAmW 91*
Chan K'in *BioIn 16*
Chan, Benny 1948- *St&PR 91*
Chan, Carlyle Hung-Lun 1949- *BiDrAPA 89*
Chan, Chak-Fu 1918- *WhoWor 91*
Chan, Chin-Hong 1951- *BiDrAPA 89*
Chan, Chris 1948- *WhoWor 91*
Chan, Clara Suet-Phang 1949- *WhoE 91, WhoEmL 91*
Chan, Curtis Joseph 1953- *WhoEmL 91*
Chan, David *BioIn 16*
Chan, Don A. 1944- *St&PR 91*
Chan, Dwight Kung-Sang 1934- *WhoWor 91*
Chan, Eddy S.F. 1947- *St&PR 91*
Chan, Eliza Y. *WhoAmW 91*
Chan, George Moy 1948- *WhoE 91*
Chan, Jackie 1954- *BioIn 16*
Chan, James Wah-kong 1949- *WhoEmL 91*
Chan, Jerry Share Young 1932- *WhoWor 91*
Chan, Johnny *BioIn 16*
Chan, Johnny Kwongchai 1950- *WhoEmL 91*
Chan, Kai 1940- *BioIn 16*
Chan, Keng Loke 1961- *WhoE 91*
Chan, Kin-Chung 1947- *BiDrAPA 89*
Chan, Lai Kow *WhoAm 90*
Chan, Laris Chi-Man 1948- *WhoE 91*
Chan, Lau Chun 1928- *WhoE 91*
Chan, Lien 1936- *WhoWor 91*
Chan, Lo-Yi Cheung Yuen 1932- *WhoAm 90*
Chan, Marie Yee 1956- *WhoEmL 91*
Chan, Michael Alan 1956- *BiDrAPA 89*
Chan, Michael P. *BiDrAPA 89*
Chan, Ming Kong 1937- *WhoWor 91*
Chan, Patricia Ping 1953- *St&PR 91*
Chan, Phillip Paang 1946- *WhoAmA 91*
Chan, Raymond T. 1955- *St&PR 91*
Chan, Robert Hing Cheong *WhoWor 91*
Chan, Robin Yau-Hing 1932- *WhoWor 91*
Chan, Rodney H 1936- *BiDrAPA 89*
Chan, Roger T 1928- *BiDrAPA 89*
Chan, Sally Wingchong 1962- *WhoAmW 91*
Chan, Shih Hung 1943- *WhoAm 90*
Chan, Shu-Park 1929- *WhoAm 90*
Chan, Siu 1962- *WhoAmW 91*
Chan, Siu-Hung 1944- *WhoWor 91*
Chan, Stephen Yan-Tat 1951- *WhoWor 91*
Chan, Steven Roderick 1959- *WhoEmL 91*
Chan, Sunney Ignatius 1936- *WhoAm 90*
Chan, Tak Hang 1941- *WhoAm 90*
Chan, Tony Chi-Hung 1954- *WhoEmL 91*
Chan, Tze Yan 1961- *WhoEmL 91*
Chan, W. Y. 1932- *WhoAm 90*
Chan, Wai Ang 1953- *WhoSSW 91*
Chan, Wan Choon 1937- *WhoWor 91*
Chan, Wayne 1946- *St&PR 91*
Chan, Yim Hung 1959- *BiDrAPA 89*

Chan Keller, Lilian Man-Yim 1957- *WhoWor 91*
Chan Peck Tong, Evelyn 1940- *WhoWor 91*
Chanak, Adam George Steven 1954- *WhoEmL 91*
Chance, Bob 1940- *Ballpl 90*
Chance, Britton 1913- *WhoAm 90*
Chance, Dean 1941- *Ballpl 90*
Chance, Douglas Charles 1942- *WhoAm 90*
Chance, Frank 1877-1924 *Ballpl 90 [port], BioIn 16*
Chance, Henry Martyn, II 1912- *WhoAm 90*
Chance, Irma Rivera *BiDrAPA 89*
Chance, Jane 1945- *WhoSSW 91, WhoWrEP 89*
Chance, John Newton 1911-1983 *TwCCr&M 91*
Chance, Joseph Edgar 1940- *WhoSSW 91*
Chance, Kenneth Bernard 1953- *WhoEmL 91*
Chance, Lawrence Edwin, Jr. *BiDrAPA 89*
Chance, M Sue 1942- *WhoWrEP 89*
Chance, Mari Sue 1942- *BiDrAPA 89*
Chance, Michael 1960- *IntWWM 90*
Chance, Nancy Laird 1931- *IntWWM 90*
Chance, Terrianna Elaine 1959- *WhoSSW 91*
Chance, William *PenDiDA 89*
Chancellor, Christopher 1904-1989 *AnObit 1989*
Chancellor, Christopher John Howard 1904-1989 *BioIn 16*
Chancellor, Glenn A. 1937- *St&PR 91*
Chancellor, John 1927- *BestSel 90-4 [port], BioIn 16*
Chancellor, John William 1927- *WhoAm 90, WhoE 91*
Chancellor, Robert Tearle 1936- *WhoSSW 91*
Chancellor, William Joseph 1931- *WhoAm 90*
Chancey, Charles Clifton, III 1955- *WhoE 91*
Chancey, Malcolm Brant 1931- *St&PR 91*
Chand, Sheetal Karam 1942- *WhoE 91*
Chand, Suresh 1935- *BiDrAPA 89*
Chandarana, Paragini K *BiDrAPA 89*
Chandarana, Praful C 1944- *BiDrAPA 89*
Chandel, Vijaya K *BiDrAPA 89*
Chander, Ernest R 1940- *BiDrAPA 89*
Chandler, Adele Rico 1923- *WhoHisp 91*
Chandler, Albert B. 1898- *BioIn 16*
Chandler, Alfred Dupont *BioIn 16*
Chandler, Alfred Dupont, Jr. 1918- *WhoAm 90*
Chandler, Alice 1931- *WhoAmW 91*
Chandler, Arthur Bleakley 1926- *WhoAm 90*
Chandler, Arthur Louis 1912- *BiDrAPA 89*
Chandler, B. J. 1921- *WhoAm 90*
Chandler, Betty Hilyard 1927- *WhoAm 90*
Chandler, Carmen Ramos 1963- *WhoHisp 91*
Chandler, Caroline Augusta 1906-1979 *AuBYP 90*
Chandler, Chan 1960- *WhoEmL 91*
Chandler, Charles Quarles 1926- *St&PR 91, WhoAm 90*
Chandler, Clarke Ralph 1953- *St&PR 91*
Chandler, Colby H. *BioIn 16, WhoAm 90, WhoE 91, WhoWor 91*
Chandler, Collis Paul, Jr. 1926- *St&PR 91*
Chandler, Danny Ricardo 1962- *WhoSSW 91*
Chandler, David 1944- *WhoAm 90*
Chandler, David Lewis 1926- *St&PR 91*
Chandler, Dorothy Buffum *WhoAmW 91*
Chandler, E.G. 1905- *St&PR 91*
Chandler, Edgar H. S. 1904-1988 *BioIn 16*
Chandler, Edna Walker 1908-1982 *AuBYP 90*
Chandler, Edward William 1953- *WhoEmL 91*
Chandler, Edwin Russell 1932- *WhoAm 90*
Chandler, Elisabeth Gordon 1913- *WhoAm 90, WhoAmA 91, WhoAmW 91*
Chandler, Elizabeth 1807-1834 *FemiCLE*
Chandler, Frederick S *EncABHB 4*
Chandler, Gene 1937- *EncPR&S 89*
Chandler, Geoffrey *NewAgMG*
Chandler, George Alfred 1929- *St&PR 91, WhoAm 90*
Chandler, George N. 1938- *St&PR 91*
Chandler, Happy 1907- *Ballpl 90*
Chandler, Harold M *BiDrAPA 89*
Chandler, Harry 1864-1944 *BioIn 16, WorAlBi*
Chandler, Harry Edgar 1920- *WhoAm 90*
Chandler, Herbert Gray 1925- *St&PR 91*
Chandler, Hubert Thomas 1933- *WhoAm 90*
Chandler, Ira Ansel 1953- *WhoEmL 91, WhoSSW 91*
Chandler, J. Howard *ODwPR 91*
Chandler, J. Malloy 1946- *St&PR 91*
Chandler, James E. 1924- *St&PR 91, WhoAm 90*
Chandler, James Greenough 1917-1988 *BioIn 16*
Chandler, James John 1932- *WhoAm 90*
Chandler, James Lloyd *BiDrAPA 89*
Chandler, James W. 1932- *St&PR 91*
Chandler, James Williams 1904- *WhoAm 90*
Chandler, Jean Kover 1939- *WhoAmW 91*
Chandler, John, Jr. 1920- *WhoAm 90*
Chandler, John Brandon, Jr. 1939- *WhoSSW 91*
Chandler, John F. *ODwPR 91*
Chandler, John Herrick 1928- *WhoAm 90*
Chandler, John T. 1932- *St&PR 91*
Chandler, John Turbeville 1932- *WhoSSW 91*
Chandler, John Wesley 1923- *WhoAm 90*
Chandler, John William 1910- *WhoAmA 91*
Chandler, Joseph Ripley 1792-1880 *BioIn 16*
Chandler, Judith Anne 1948- *WhoEmL 91*
Chandler, Karyln Dorothy 1943- *WhoAmW 91*
Chandler, Katrina Pipkins 1955- *WhoAmW 91*
Chandler, Kay *WhoWrEP 89*
Chandler, Kenneth A. 1947- *WhoAm 90, WhoE 91*
Chandler, Kent, Jr. 1920- *WhoAm 90*
Chandler, Lana Jean 1954- *WhoEmL 91*
Chandler, Larry C. 1939- *St&PR 91*
Chandler, Larry Donald 1948- *WhoEmL 91*
Chandler, Lawrence Bradford, Jr. 1942- *WhoSSW 91, WhoWor 91*
Chandler, Leroy 1918- *St&PR 91*
Chandler, Lester Vernon 1905-1988 *BioIn 16*
Chandler, Lewis 1920- *WhoAm 90*
Chandler, Linda Cline 1946- *WhoAmW 91*
Chandler, Linda Hoffner 1947- *St&PR 91*
Chandler, Linda S 1929- *WhoWrEP 89*
Chandler, Louise Taylor 1944- *WhoAmW 91*
Chandler, Lynne Carol 1955- *WhoAmW 91*
Chandler, Marcia Shaw Barnard 1934- *WhoAmW 91*
Chandler, Margaret Kueffner 1922- *WhoAm 90, WhoAmW 91*
Chandler, Marguerite Nella 1943- *WhoAm 90, WhoWor 91*
Chandler, Mark Steven *BiDrAPA 89*
Chandler, Mary 1687-1745 *BioIn 16, FemiCLE*
Chandler, Mary Voelz 1948- *WhoEmL 91*
Chandler, Michael David 1959- *WhoSSW 91*
Chandler, Michael Robert 1950- *WhoAmA 91*
Chandler, Muriel Jane 1927- *WhoWor 91*
Chandler, Norman 1899-1973 *BioIn 16*
Chandler, Otis *BioIn 16*
Chandler, Otis 1927- *St&PR 91*
Chandler, Paul 1921- *St&PR 91*
Chandler, Raymond 1888-1959 *BioIn 16, ConAu 129, MajTwCW, TwCCr&M 91, WorAlBi*
Chandler, Richard H. 1943- *St&PR 91*
Chandler, Richard Hill 1943- *WhoAm 90*
Chandler, Richard William 1950- *WhoE 91*
Chandler, Robert Charles 1945- *WhoSSW 91*
Chandler, Robert Flint, Jr. 1907- *WhoAm 90, WhoWor 91*
Chandler, Robert Leslie 1948- *WhoE 91, WhoEmL 91*
Chandler, Robertsena Bateman 1945- *WhoSSW 91*
Chandler, Robin *BioIn 16*
Chandler, Rod Dennis 1942- *WhoAm 90*
Chandler, Ronald Jay 1949- *WhoEmL 91*
Chandler, Ronald Lee 1938- *WhoE 91*
Chandler, Ruth Forbes 1894-1978 *AuBYP 90*
Chandler, Sadie Arnette 1933- *WhoSSW 91*
Chandler, Seeley Dole 1940- *BiDrAPA 89*
Chandler, Spud *NewYTBS 90*
Chandler, Spud 1907- *Ballpl 90*
Chandler, Spud 1907-1990 *BioIn 16*
Chandler, Stephen Ray 1949- *WhoEmL 91*
Chandler, Stephen Saunders 1899-1989 *BioIn 16*
Chandler, Swithin 1830-1887 *AmLegL*
Chandler, Theodore Lindy, Jr. 1952- *WhoSSW 91*
Chandler, Thomas 1911- *AuBYP 90*
Chandler, Wallace L. 1926- *St&PR 91*
Chandler, Wallace Lee 1926- *WhoAm 90*
Chandler, William Eaton 1835-1917 *AmLegL, BiDrUSE 89*
Chandler, William Knox 1933- *WhoAm 90*
Chandler, Zachariah 1813-1879 *BiDrUSE 89*
Chandonnet, Ann Fox 1943- *WhoWrEP 89*
Chandonnet, Noel Andrew 1933- *St&PR 91*
Chandor, Douglas 1897-1953 *WhoAmA 91N*
Chandor, Karen Kayser 1950- *WhoAmW 91*
Chandor, Stebbins Bryant 1933- *WhoAm 90*
Chandora, Deen Bandhu *BiDrAPA 89*
Chandos, Cassandra, Duchess of 1670-1735 *FemiCLE*
Chandou, Francois Luc 1948- *WhoSSW 91*
Chandra, Agustinus 1946- *WhoWor 91*
Chandra, Aruna *BiDrAPA 89*
Chandra, Bhuvana *BiDrAPA 89*
Chandra, Hermanto 1959- *WhoWor 91*
Chandra, Pankaj Raj 1951- *WhoSSW 91*
Chandra, Pradeep Kumar 1949- *BiDrAPA 89*
Chandraiah, Shambhavi 1957- *BiDrAPA 89*
Chandrani, Prem Kumar Swamidas 1954- *WhoWor 91*
Chandrasekar, Krishnamurti 1935- *WhoE 91*
Chandrasekaran, Balakrishnan 1942- *WhoAm 90*
Chandrasekaran, Perinkolam Raman 1949- *WhoSSW 91*
Chandrasekhar, Bellur Sivaramiah 1928- *WhoAm 90*
Chandrasekhar, Subrahmanyan 1910- *WhoAm 90, WhoWor 91, WorAlBi*
Chandrasekhara, Muthaiah *BiDrAPA 89*
Chandrasekharan, Maya *BiDrAPA 89*
Chandrasekharan, Narayanan 1958- *WhoSSW 91*
Chandrasena, Ranjith 1949- *BiDrAPA 89*
Chandresh *NewAgMG*
Chandy, Kanianthra Mani 1944- *WhoAm 90*
Chane, George Warren 1910- *WhoAm 90*
Chanel, Coco 1883-1971 *BioIn 16*
Chanel, Gabrielle 1883-1971 *BioIn 16, ConDes 90, WorAlBi*
Chaneles, Sol 1926- *AuBYP 90*
Chanen, Franklin Allen 1933- *WhoAm 90*
Chanen, Steven Robert 1953- *WhoEmL 91, WhoWor 91*
Chaney, Dale Rex 1955- *WhoEmL 91*
Chaney, Darrel 1948- *Ballpl 90*
Chaney, Debora Anne 1965- *WhoWrEP 89*
Chaney, Don *WhoAm 90*
Chaney, Earlyne *NewAgE 90*
Chaney, Edward 1951- *ConAu 131*
Chaney, Francis Hall, II 1957- *WhoE 91, WhoEmL 91*
Chaney, James Earl 1943-1964 *BioIn 16*
Chaney, Jared P. 1952- *ODwPR 91*
Chaney, John *BioIn 16*
Chaney, Lon 1883-1930 *WorAlBi*
Chaney, Michael Eugene 1935- *St&PR 91*
Chaney, Michael Thomas 1948- *WhoEmL 91*
Chaney, Morris J. 1858- *AmLegL*
Chaney, Patrice Watson 1953- *WhoEmL 91*
Chaney, Peggy Velena 1955- *WhoWrEP 89*
Chaney, Ralph Works 1890-1971 *DcScB S2*
Chaney, Robert Eugene 1957- *WhoSSW 91*
Chaney, Robert Wayne 1947- *WhoEmL 91*
Chaney, Roy Gene 1947- *WhoEmL 91*
Chaney, Scott Clay 1941- *IntWWM 90*
Chaney, Verne Edward, Jr. 1923- *WhoAm 90*
Chaney, Vincent V. 1913- *St&PR 91*
Chaney, William Albert 1922- *WhoAm 90*
Chaney, William Calvin 1952- *WhoEmL 91*
Chaney, William R. 1932- *WhoAm 90*
Chang Chieh *WorAu 1980*
Chang Chun *NewYTBS 90*
Chang Hsien-Liang *WorAu 1980*
Chang, Allison Sheng Shiuan 1933- *WhoSSW 91*
Chang, Bertina Pang Loh 1957- *WhoEmL 91*
Chang, C. Morris 1931- *WhoAm 90*
Chang, C. Yul 1934- *WhoWor 91*
Chang, Chia-Lin 1959- *WhoE 91, WhoEmL 91*
Chang, Chiu Cheng 1940- *St&PR 91*
Chang, Christine Yuanchen *BiDrAPA 89*
Chang, Chun Sik *BiDrAPA 89*
Chang, Chun Yueh Jerry 1954- *WhoE 91*
Chang, Chung-Jan 1947- *WhoSSW 91*
Chang, Dai-chien 1899-1983 *BioIn 16*
Chang, Darwin Ray 1917- *WhoWor 91*
Chang, David Chung-Ching 1941- *WhoAm 90*
Chang, David Ping-Chung 1929- *St&PR 91, WhoAm 90*
Chang, David Wen-wei 1929- *ConAu 130*
Chang, Deborah Sook 1960- *WhoAmW 91*
Chang, Debra Wei Kuan 1952- *IntWWM 90*
Chang, Dennis *BioIn 16*
Chang, Ellison Toshiya *BiDrAPA 89*
Chang, Ernest Sun-Mei 1950- *WhoEmL 91*
Chang, Fen *BioIn 16*
Chang, Garma Chen-Chi 1920- *EncO&P 3*
Chang, Grace *BiDrAPA 89*
Chang, H. K. 1940- *WhoAm 90*
Chang, Harry 1916- *St&PR 91*
Chang, Hay Kyung 1956- *WhoEmL 91*
Chang, Henry Chung-Lien 1941- *WhoAm 90*
Chang, Hsi-Ya 1955- *WhoSSW 91*
Chang, Hubert Wen-Hu *BiDrAPA 89*
Chang, Iris J. 1935- *St&PR 91*
Chang, Jack Che-man 1941- *WhoAm 90*
Chang, Jae Chan 1941- *WhoWor 91*
Chang, Jo-Anne Marguerite 1960- *St&PR 91*
Chang, John C. H. 1936- *WhoWor 91*
Chang, John K. 1929- *St&PR 91*
Chang, Joyce Yung-Kuang 1956- *WhoSSW 91*
Chang, Judy Yukzun 1943- *WhoWor 91*
Chang, Kia-ngau 1889-1979 *BioIn 16*
Chang, Kwang-Chih 1931- *WhoAm 90*
Chang, Lawrence *BiDrAPA 89*
Chang, Lee *ConAu 31NR*
Chang, Leroy L. 1936- *WhoAm 90*
Chang, Li-Ly 1952- *IntWWM 90*
Chang, Lifu *BiDrAPA 89*
Chang, Ling Wei 1960- *WhoE 91*
Chang, Lulu H. 1935- *IntWWM 90*
Chang, Merry Low 1949- *WhoE 91*
Chang, Michael *BioIn 16*
Chang, Milton Mow-Tack 1943- *St&PR 91*
Chang, Min Chueh 1908- *WhoAm 90*
Chang, Pak Kean Willie 1954- *WhoSSW 91*
Chang, Pao-sheng Erich 1951- *WhoSSW 91*
Chang, Parris Hsu-cheng 1936- *WhoAm 90*
Chang, Patricia Davis 1945- *WhoAmW 91*
Chang, Peter Hon 1941- *St&PR 91*
Chang, Peter Tsu-Yuan 1935- *WhoSSW 91*
Chang, Robert Huei 1932- *WhoAm 90*
Chang, Robert Timothy 1958- *WhoAm 90*
Chang, Robin 1951- *St&PR 91*
Chang, Rodney Eie Joon 1945- *WhoWor 91*
Chang, Rodney Eiu Joon 1945- *WhoEmL 91*
Chang, Ronald Chiu Mun 1965- *WhoEmL 91*
Chang, Samuel Y *BiDrAPA 89*
Chang, Sheldon Shou Lien 1920- *WhoAm 90*
Chang, Sheng-Yen 1930- *WhoE 91*
Chang, Shi Ching 1947- *WhoEmL 91*
Chang, Shi-Kuo 1944- *WhoAm 90*
Chang, Shou-Shian 1929- *WhoWor 91*
Chang, Sidney Sinyih 1940- *BiDrAPA 89*
Chang, Stephen S. 1918- *BioIn 16, WhoAm 90, WhoWor 91*
Chang, Steve Chee-Shan 1933- *WhoE 91*
Chang, Steven Choon *BiDrAPA 89*
Chang, Suk Choo 1925- *BiDrAPA 89*
Chang, Sun-Yung Alice 1948- *WhoAmW 91*
Chang, Ta-ch'ien 1899-1983 *BioIn 16*
Chang, Ta-kuang 1955- *WhoEmL 91*
Chang, Terrill J. 1950- *St&PR 91*
Chang, Thomas Ming Swi 1933- *WhoAm 90*
Chang, Tisa 1941- *BioIn 16, NotWoAT*
Chang, Tong-Ying 1958- *WhoWor 91*
Chang, Vivian 1931-1989 *BioIn 16*
Chang, Weilin Parrish 1947- *WhoSSW 91*
Chang, William Shen Chie 1931- *WhoAm 90*
Chang, Y. Austin *WhoAm 90*
Chang, Yau-Fung Olivia 1963- *WhoAmW 91*
Chang, Young Soon *BiDrAPA 89*
Chang, Yu-Yi *BioIn 16*
Chang, Yuan 1934- *St&PR 91*
Chang, Yuan-Feng 1928- *WhoAm 90*
Chang-Diaz, Franklin Ramon 1950- *WhoHisp 91*
Chang-Mota, Roberto 1935- *WhoWor 91*
Chang-Rodriguez, Eugenio *WhoWrEP 89*
Chang-Rodriguez, Eugenio 1926- *WhoHisp 91*
Chang-Wailing, Kasion Joseph 1930- *WhoWor 91*
Chanin, Abraham L *WhoAmA 91N*
Chanin, Bernard 1932- *WhoAm 90*
Chanin, Luba A 1947- *BiDrAPA 89*
Chanin, Michael Henry 1943- *WhoAm 90*
Chanin, Mildred Maxine 1921- *WhoAmW 91*
Chanko, Mark S. 1928- *St&PR 91*
Chann, Jagmeet Kaur 1952- *BiDrAPA 89*
Channabasavanna, Sindhgi M *BiDrAPA 89*
Channel, Elinor *BiDEWW, FemiCLE*

Channell, Carl BioIn 16
Channell, Carl R NewYTBS 90 [port]
Channell, Mary Lincoln 1935- WhoAmW 91
Channer, Harold Hudson 1935- WhoWor 91
Channer, Stephen Dyer Stanton 1933- WhoWor 91
Channick, Herbert S. 1929- WhoAm 90
Channing, Carol BioIn 16
Channing, Carol 1921- NotWoAT, OxCPMus
Channing, Carol 1923- WhoAmW 91, WorAlBi
Channing, Edward Tyrrell 1790-1856 BioIn 16
Channing, Stacey Lisa 1957- WhoEmL 91
Channing, Stockard WhoAm 90, WhoAmW 91
Channing, Susan Rose 1943- WhoAmA 91
Channing, William Ellery 1780-1842 BioIn 16
Channing, William Ellery 1919- St&PR 91
Channing, William Henry 1810-1884 BioIn 16
Channon, E. M. 1875-1951 FemiCLE
Channon, Henry 1897-1958 BioIn 16
Channon, John 1711-1783? PenDiDA 89
Channon, Michael David Hudleston 1939- IntWWM 90
Channon, Paul 1935- WhoWor 91
Channon, Robert Arnold BiDrAPA 89
Chano, Fouad Georges 1947- WhoWor 91
Chanock, Martin Leon 1942- WhoWor 91
Chanoki, Fred WhoAm 90
Chanoski, Norman Walter 1934- St&PR 91
Chanover, Hyman 1920- BioIn 16
Chansky, Daniel BiDrAPA 89
Chansky, Norman Morton 1929- WhoWrEP 89
Chansky, Steven Harvey 1943- WhoE 91
Chant, Davis Ryan 1938- WhoE 91
Chant, Dixon S. 1913- St&PR 91
Chant, Donald Alfred 1928- WhoAm 90
Chantal, Jeanne-Francoise de 1572-1641 BioIn 16
Chanter, Charlotte 1828-1882 FemiCLE
Chanticleer, Raven 1933- DrBIPA 90
Chantres, Gerald Robert 1942- St&PR 91
Chantrey, Francis PenDiDA 89
Chantrey, Francis Legatt 1781-1841 BioIn 16
Chantry, Art BioIn 16
Chanut, Jean Yves 1951- WhoWor 91
Chao, Bei Tse 1918- WhoAm 90
Chao, C. Tien-Bao 1962- WhoEmL 91
Chao, Chih Hsu 1939- WhoAm 90
Chao, Chong-Yun 1930- WhoAm 90
Chao, Elaine BioIn 16
Chao, Elaine L. WhoAm 90, WhoAmW 91
Chao, Helen 1960- WhoAmW 91
Chao, James Min-Tzu 1940- WhoWor 91
Chao, Kwang-Chu 1925- WhoAm 90
Chao, Marshall S. 1924- WhoAm 90
Chao, Pie Chu BiDrAPA 89
Chaovalit Yongchaiyut BioIn 16
Chaowasilp, Pramote 1937- BiDrAPA 89
Chapa, Alfonso 1930- WhoHisp 91
Chapa, Amancio Jose, Jr. 1946- WhoHisp 91
Chapa, Elia Kay 1960- WhoHisp 91
Chapa, Joseph S. 1948- WhoHisp 91
Chapa, Judy J. 1957- WhoHisp 91
Chapa, Maria Estela 1956- WhoAmW 91
Chapa, Ramon, Jr. 1958- WhoHisp 91
Chapa, Raul Roberto 1948- WhoHisp 91
Chapa, Rodolfo Chino 1958- WhoHisp 91
Chapanis, Alphonse 1917- WhoAm 90, WhoWor 91
Chaparala, Dilip Kumar 1946- BiDrAPA 89
Chaparala, Sivaji 1947- BiDrAPA 89
Chaparro, Carmen 1947- WhoHisp 91
Chaparro, Luis F. 1947- WhoHisp 91
Chapdelaine, Henri Joseph 1934- WhoWrEP 89
Chapdelaine, Joan Murphy 1936- WhoAmW 91
Chapekis, Fred A. 1925- St&PR 91
Chapel, Alain 1937-1990 NewYTBS 90 [port]
Chapel, Burdette Alan 1941- St&PR 91
Chapel, Theron Theodore 1918- WhoSSW 91
Chapel, Thomas Joseph 1951- WhoSSW 91
Chapelle, Dickey BioIn 16
Chapelle, Jacques PenDiDA 89
Chapelle, Monique 1945- WhoAmW 91
Chapelle, Rene Adrien 1933- WhoSSW 91
Chapelli, Armando C., Jr. WhoHisp 91
Chapellier, George 1890-1978 WhoAmA 91N
Chapellier, Robert WhoAmA 91N
Chapellin, Helena WhoAmA 91
Chapello, Craig Alan 1956- WhoEmL 91
Chapi y Lorente, Ruperto 1851-1909 OxCPMus
Chapian, Grieg Hovsep 1913- WhoAm 90, WhoAmA 91
Chapin, Alene Olsen Dalton BioIn 16
Chapin, Alfred Clark 1848-1936 AmLegL
Chapin, Charles Fisher 1929- WhoAm 90
Chapin, Cornelia van Auken 1893-1972 BiDWomA
Chapin, Dwight Allan 1938- WhoAm 90
Chapin, Edward William 1908- WhoAm 90
Chapin, Eliphelet 1741-1807 PenDiDA 89
Chapin, Elliott Lowell 1917- WhoAm 90
Chapin, F. Stuart 1888-1974 BioIn 16
Chapin, Francis 1899-1965 WhoAmA 91N
Chapin, Francis Stuart 1888-1974 BioIn 16
Chapin, Frederic BioIn 16
Chapin, Frederick J BiDrAPA 89
Chapin, H.N. 1904- St&PR 91
Chapin, Harry 1942-1981 EncPR&S 89, OxCPMus
Chapin, Harvey N 1935- BiDrAPA 89
Chapin, Henry 1893-1983 AuBYP 90
Chapin, Horace Beecher 1917- WhoWor 91
Chapin, Hugh A. 1925- WhoAm 90
Chapin, Josephine M BiDrAPA 89
Chapin, Lauren BioIn 16
Chapin, Linda BioIn 16
Chapin, Linda Mari 1949- WhoE 91, WhoEmL 91
Chapin, Lloyd Walter 1937- WhoSSW 91
Chapin, Mary Real 1953- WhoEmL 91
Chapin, Melville 1918- St&PR 91, WhoAm 90
Chapin, Myron Butman 1887-1958 WhoAmA 91N
Chapin, Nancy Louise 1944- WhoAmW 91
Chapin, Ralph Baldwin 1915- St&PR 91
Chapin, Richard 1923- WhoAm 90
Chapin, Richard 1947- St&PR 91
Chapin, Richard Earl 1925- WhoAm 90
Chapin, Roy D., Jr. 1915- St&PR 91
Chapin, Roy Dikeman 1880-1936 BiDrUSE 89, EncABHB 4 [port]
Chapin, Roy Dikeman, Jr. 1915- EncABHB 5, WhoAm 90
Chapin, Schuyler Garrison 1923- IntWWM 90, WhoAm 90
Chapin, Selden 1899-1963 BioIn 16
Chapin, Suzanne Phillips 1930- WhoAmW 91, WhoE 91
Chapin, Walter Leeds 1902- WhoE 91
Chapin, William Franklin 1831-1885 AmLegL
Chapleau, Joseph-Adolphe 1840-1898 DcCanB 12
Chaplet, Ernest 1835-1909 PenDiDA 89
Chaplik, Arnold Sidney 1928- WhoAm 90
Chaplik, Michael BiDrAPA 89
Chaplik, Seymour BiDrAPA 89
Chaplin, Ansel Burt 1931- WhoAm 90, WhoWor 91
Chaplin, Charles 1825-1891 BioIn 16
Chaplin, Charles 1889-1977 WorAlBi
Chaplin, Charlie 1889-1977 BioIn 16, OxCPMus
Chaplin, D. Edward 1938- St&PR 91
Chaplin, Dora P. 1906?-1990 ConAu 132
Chaplin, George 1914- WhoAm 90
Chaplin, George Edwin 1931- WhoAmA 91, WhoE 91
Chaplin, Geraldine 1944- WhoAm 90, WorAlBi
Chaplin, Gervase Michael 1936- St&PR 91, WhoSSW 91
Chaplin, Herbert S. 1935- St&PR 91
Chaplin, Hugh, Jr. 1923- WhoAm 90
Chaplin, James Crossan, IV 1933- WhoAm 90
Chaplin, Jon Howick 1935- St&PR 91
Chaplin, Lorelei M. 1954- WhoEmL 91
Chaplin, Mark H. 1955- St&PR 91
Chaplin, Mark Harlan 1955- WhoEmL 91
Chaplin, Mary Ann 1946- WhoEmL 91
Chaplin, Patrice BioIn 16
Chaplin, Ralph H. 1887-1961 EncAL
Chaplin, Saul 1912- OxCPMus
Chaplin, Tiny 1905-1939 Ballpl 90
Chaplin, Wanda Louise 1950- WhoAmW 91
Chapline, Claudia Beechum 1930- WhoAmA 91
Chapman, Abigail Diamond 1937- WhoAmW 91
Chapman, Alan Jesse 1925- WhoAm 90
Chapman, Alfred George, Jr. 1962- WhoEmL 91
Chapman, Alger B. 1931- St&PR 91
Chapman, Alger Baldwin 1931- WhoAm 90
Chapman, Alvah H., Jr. BioIn 16
Chapman, Alvah H., Jr. 1921- St&PR 91
Chapman, Alvah Herman, Jr. 1921- WhoAm 90, WhoSSW 91
Chapman, Anne 1930-1986 WhoAmA 91N
Chapman, Anthony Colin Bruce 1928-1982 BioIn 16
Chapman, Arthur Harry BiDrAPA 89
Chapman, Barbara Della 1952- WhoEmL 91
Chapman, Ben 1908- Ballpl 90 [port]
Chapman, Bernard 1921- St&PR 91
Chapman, Bonita G BiDrAPA 89
Chapman, C. Joe 1923- St&PR 91
Chapman, Carleton Burke 1915- WhoAm 90
Chapman, Carolyn 1942- WhoAmW 91
Chapman, Charles 1880-1941 Ballpl 90
Chapman, Charles Alan 1949- WhoEmL 91
Chapman, Charles Jarvis 1938- St&PR 91
Chapman, Charles Shepard 1879-1962 WhoAmA 91N
Chapman, Charles Wayne IntWWM 90
Chapman, Charlotte Marie 1953- WhoSSW 91
Chapman, Christian Addison 1921- WhoE 91
Chapman, Cindy Lorraine Farr 1952- WhoWrEP 89
Chapman, Colin 1928-1982 BioIn 16, DcNaB 1981
Chapman, Conrad Daniel 1933- St&PR 91, WhoWor 91
Chapman, Constance Ann 1935- WhoWrEP 89
Chapman, David Lee, II 1943- St&PR 91
Chapman, Deborah Ann 1947- WhoAmW 91
Chapman, Donald D. 1917- WhoAm 90
Chapman, Donald Edward 1945- WhoSSW 91
Chapman, Douglas K. 1928- St&PR 91
Chapman, Douglas Kenneth 1928- WhoAm 90
Chapman, Earl Marshall 1925- St&PR 91
Chapman, Edward E. 1925- ODwPR 91
Chapman, Edward L. 1948- St&PR 91
Chapman, Edward William 1925- WhoAm 90
Chapman, Edwin Karl 1932- St&PR 91
Chapman, Esther 1904- FemiCLE
Chapman, Ethel A BiDrAPA 89
Chapman, Eugenia Sheldon 1923- WhoAmW 91
Chapman, F. H. Af 1721-1808 BioIn 16
Chapman, Frances Elizabeth Clausen 1920- WhoAmW 91
Chapman, Frank PenDiMP
Chapman, Frank Michler 1864-1945 DcScB S2
Chapman, Fred J. 1939- St&PR 91
Chapman, Frederick A. ODwPR 91
Chapman, Fredrik Henrik 1721-1808 BioIn 16
Chapman, G. Arnold 1917- WhoAm 90
Chapman, George 1559?-1634 BioIn 16
Chapman, George C. 1937- WhoAm 90
Chapman, Gerald Frederick 1948- WhoSSW 91
Chapman, Gerald T. 1942- St&PR 91
Chapman, Gilbert W., Jr. 1933- WhoAm 90
Chapman, Graham BioIn 16
Chapman, Graham 1941-1989 AnObit 1989, ConAu 129, ConTFT 8
Chapman, Harry Carrol 1930- St&PR 91
Chapman, Heidi Goldenberg 1953- WhoEmL 91
Chapman, Howard BioIn 16
Chapman, Howard Eugene 1913-1977 WhoAmA 91N
Chapman, Howard Kramer 1918- St&PR 91
Chapman, Howard Stuart 1941- WhoAm 90
Chapman, Hugh McMaster 1932- St&PR 91, WhoAm 90, WhoSSW 91
Chapman, Irwin WhoWrEP 89
Chapman, J. Thomas ODwPR 91
Chapman, Jack 1843-1916 Ballpl 90
Chapman, Jack Teague 1943- St&PR 91
Chapman, James 1919- ConAu 33NR
Chapman, James Claude 1931- St&PR 91, WhoAm 90
Chapman, James Edward 1927- WhoAm 90
Chapman, James Edward 1944- St&PR 91
Chapman, James L. 1945- WhoAm 90, WhoSSW 91
Chapman, James L. 1949- St&PR 91
Chapman, James Lee 1932- WhoAm 90
Chapman, Janet Carter Goodrich 1922- WhoAm 90, WhoE 91
Chapman, John 1774-1845 BioIn 16, WorAlBi
Chapman, John Andrew 1928- WhoSSW 91
Chapman, John Arthur 1933- WhoAm 90
Chapman, John Davis 1947- WhoSSW 91
Chapman, John Davol 1934- WhoAm 90
Chapman, John Edmon 1931- WhoAm 90
Chapman, John L. 1949- St&PR 91
Chapman, John S. 1897-1989 BioIn 16
Chapman, John Stanton Higham 1891-1972 AuBYP 90
Chapman, John Stewart 1908- WhoAm 90
Chapman, Josephine Lawton 1918- WhoE 91
Chapman, Kathleen Halloran 1937- WhoAmW 91
Chapman, Kenneth Stephen 1946- WhoE 91
Chapman, Laura Mae BiDrAPA 89
Chapman, Laurence Arthur 1949- WhoAm 90
Chapman, Lemmie Jerry 1934- WhoSSW 91
Chapman, Loren J. 1927- WhoAm 90
Chapman, Loring 1929- WhoAm 90, WhoWor 91
Chapman, Margaret Storm Jameson 1891-1986 BioIn 16
Chapman, Maristan AuBYP 90
Chapman, Mark David 1955- WorAlBi
Chapman, Mark Eugene 1959- WhoEmL 91
Chapman, Mary Ilsley AuBYP 90
Chapman, Michael 1935- ConTFT 8
Chapman, Michael Edward 1956- WhoSSW 91
Chapman, Michael James 1941- St&PR 91
Chapman, Michael Scott 1951- WhoE 91
Chapman, Nettles Ford, Jr. 1909- WhoSSW 91
Chapman, Norman Alan 1953- BiDrAPA 89
Chapman, Orville Lamar 1932- WhoAm 90
Chapman, Oscar Littleton 1896-1978 BiDrUSE 89
Chapman, Page 1909- St&PR 91
Chapman, Pat 1937- St&PR 91
Chapman, Paul A 1923- BiDrAPA 89
Chapman, Paul Ray 1937- St&PR 91
Chapman, Paula Anne 1960- WhoAmW 91
Chapman, Peter Herbert 1953- WhoAm 90, WhoE 91, WhoEmL 91
Chapman, Ray ODwPR 91
Chapman, Ray 1891-1920 Ballpl 90 [port]
Chapman, Reid Gillis 1920- WhoAm 90
Chapman, Richard F 1933- BiDrAPA 89
Chapman, Richard L. 1928- St&PR 91
Chapman, Richard Leroy 1932- WhoWor 91
Chapman, Richard P. 1905-1988 BioIn 16
Chapman, Robert Breckinridge, III 1917- WhoAm 90
Chapman, Robert Dale 1955- WhoEmL 91
Chapman, Robert E 1932- BiDrAPA 89
Chapman, Robert Eugene 1941- WhoSSW 91
Chapman, Robert Foster 1926- WhoAm 90
Chapman, Robert George 1919- St&PR 91
Chapman, Robert Glenn, III 1932- WhoSSW 91
Chapman, Robert Gordon 1941- WhoAmA 91
Chapman, Robert Gorham, Jr. 1940- WhoAm 90
Chapman, Robert H. 1945- St&PR 91
Chapman, Robert James 1936- BiDrAPA 89
Chapman, Robert Lee, III 1946- WhoSSW 91
Chapman, Roger Green 1952- WhoEmL 91
Chapman, Roger William 1949- WhoWor 91
Chapman, Roland H BiDrAPA 89
Chapman, Ronald Earl 1949- WhoEmL 91
Chapman, Ronald Thomas 1933- WhoE 91, WhoWor 91
Chapman, Roy Webster 1924- St&PR 91
Chapman, Russell Dale 1951- WhoEmL 91
Chapman, Sam 1916- Ballpl 90
Chapman, Samuel Greeley 1929- WhoAm 90
Chapman, Sara Simmons 1940- WhoAm 90, WhoAmW 91
Chapman, Stephen James 1954- WhoAm 90
Chapman, Susan Kardevan 1953- WhoAmW 91
Chapman, Sydney 1888-1970 DcScB S2
Chapman, Terry Glen 1952- St&PR 91
Chapman, Thomas William 1945- WhoE 91
Chapman, Tracy BioIn 16
Chapman, Tracy 1964- ConMus 4 [port], DrBIPA 90, WhoAmW 91
Chapman, Tracy 1965- WorAlBi
Chapman, Vera 1898- BioIn 16
Chapman, Verne M. 1938- WhoAm 90
Chapman, Walker MajTwCW
Chapman, Walter Howard 1912- WhoAmA 91, WhoWor 91
Chapman, Warren Howe 1925- WhoAm 90
Chapman, Wilbur E. 1937- St&PR 91
Chapman, William WhoAm 90
Chapman, William 1850-1917 DcLB 99 [port]

Chapman, William Francis 1925- WhoWor 91
Chapman, William Paul 1919- WhoAm 90
Chapman, William S., Jr. 1951- St&PR 91
Chapman, William Scott 1959- BiDrAPA 89
Chapman, Willie Dean 1958- WhoEmL 91
Chapnik-Gross, Elissa-Beth Lynda 1962- WhoE 91
Chapon, Claude Marie 1947- WhoWor 91
Chapone, Hester 1727-1801 FemiCLE
Chapone, Hester Mulso 1727-1801 BioIn 16
Chapone, Sarah 1699-1764 FemiCLE
Chappano, Perry Michael 1961- WhoEmL 91
Chappel, John Nelson 1931- BiDrAPA 89
Chappelear, Claude Keplar 1937- St&PR 91
Chappelear, Harold E. 1938- WhoAm 90
Chappelear, Patsy Stallings 1931- WhoAmW 91
Chappell & Co. OxCPMus
Chappell, Ann L 1943- BiDrAPA 89
Chappell, Annette M. 1939- WhoAm 90
Chappell, Anthony Gordon 1943- St&PR 91, WhoAm 90
Chappell, Barbara Kelly 1940- WhoAmW 91
Chappell, Berkley Warner 1934- WhoAmA 91
Chappell, Bill BioIn 16
Chappell, Charles A., Jr. 1924- St&PR 91
Chappell, Charles Franklin 1927- WhoAm 90
Chappell, Charles Richard 1943- WhoAm 90
Chappell, Clovis Gillham, Jr. 1911- WhoAm 90
Chappell, Danny Michael 1956- WhoEmL 91, WhoSSW 91, WhoWor 91
Chappell, Duncan 1939- WhoAm 90, WhoWor 91
Chappell, Fred 1936- ConAu 33NR, DcLB 105 [port], WhoWrEP 89, WorAu 1980 [port]
Chappell, Fred Davis 1936- WhoAm 90, WhoSSW 91
Chappell, George Lewis 1947- BiDrAPA 89
Chappell, Jim NewAgMG
Chappell, John Charles 1935- WhoAm 90
Chappell, John Francis 1936- St&PR 91, WhoAm 90
Chappell, Katherine Cheney 1945- St&PR 91
Chappell, Miles Linwood 1939- WhoAmA 91
Chappell, Miles Linwood, Jr. 1939- WhoAm 90
Chappell, Milton Leroy 1951- WhoEmL 91
Chappell, Phillip Branch BiDrAPA 89
Chappell, Richard Lee 1938- WhoE 91
Chappell, Robert E. 1944- WhoAm 90
Chappell, Robert Earl, Jr. 1936- St&PR 91, WhoAm 90
Chappell, Robert Harvey, Jr. 1926- St&PR 91, WhoAm 90
Chappell, Robert K. 1939- ODwPR 91
Chappell, Samuel OxCPMus
Chappell, Sandra 1950- WhoE 91
Chappell, Thomas M. BioIn 16
Chappell, Vere Claiborne 1930- WhoAm 90
Chappell, Walter 1925- WhoAm 90, WhoAmA 91, WhoWor 91
Chappell, Warren 1904- WhoAm 90
Chappell, Willard Ray 1938- WhoAm 90
Chappell, William 1809-1888 OxCPMus
Chappelle, Jerry Leon 1939- WhoAmA 91
Chappen, Edward Peter BiDrAPA 89
Chappen, Edward Peter 1925- WhoE 91
Chapple, Abby 1939- WhoAmW 91
Chapple, Brian 1945- IntWWM 90
Chapple, F. Colleen 1932- WhoAmW 91
Chapple, Paul William 1922- St&PR 91
Chapple, Stanley 1900- IntWWM 90
Chapple-Camacho, Marie Christine 1960- WhoHisp 91
Chappuis, Jack Emile BiDrAPA 89
Chapsal, Madeleine 1925- EncCoWW
Chapski, Peter F. 1928- ODwPR 91
Chapski, Peter Francis 1928- St&PR 91
Chaput-Rolland, Solange BioIn 16
Char, Carlene Mae 1954- WhoAmW 91, WhoEmL 91, WhoWrEP 89
Char, Jerome BiDrAPA 89
Char, Randall Yau Kunn 1952- WhoEmL 91
Char, Rene 1907-1988 AnObit 1988, BioIn 16, ConAu 32NR, MajTwCW
Char, Richard Jay 1959- WhoEmL 91
Char, Walter F 1920- BiDrAPA 89
Charabati, Victoria France 1954- WhoAmW 91, WhoE 91
Charache, Samuel 1930- WhoAm 90, WhoE 91
Characklis, William Gregory 1941- WhoAm 90
Charalampous, Kanellos D 1931- BiDrAPA 89
Charania, Barkat 1941- WhoSSW 91
Charap, Stanley Harvey 1932- WhoAm 90
Charatan, Debrah Lee 1957- WhoEmL 91
Charatan, Fred B 1921- BiDrAPA 89
Charbit, Andre 1936- WhoWor 91
Charbit, Michel 1953- WhoWor 91
Charbon, Gerard Anton 1924- WhoWor 91
Charboneau, Brian Paige 1949- WhoEmL 91
Charboneau, Joe 1955- Ballpl 90
Charbonneau, Guy 1922- WhoAm 90, WhoWor 91
Charbonneau, Jean 1875-1960 DcLB 92 [port]
Charbonneau, Jean Baptiste 1805-1866 WhNaAH
Charbonneau, Manon BiDrAPA 89
Charbonneau, Matthew A. 1941- St&PR 91
Charbonneau, Patricia ConTFT 8
Charbonneau, Rene 1932- BiDrAPA 89
Charbonneau, Rhona Mae 1928- WhoAmW 91, WhoE 91
Charbonneau, Roger 1914- WhoAm 90
Charbonneau, Sharon Mae 1953- WhoAmW 91
Charbonneau, Toussaint 1759?-1840? WhNaAH
Charbonnel, Armand-Francois-Marie de 1802-1891 DcCanB 12
Charbonnier, Pierre 1897-1978 ConDes 90
Charbonnier, Volker 1939- St&PR 91
Charby, Jay MajTwCW
Charcoal DcCanB 12
Charcot, Jean Martin 1825-1893 EncO&P 3, EncPaPR 91, WorAlBi
Chard, Chester Stevens 1915- WhoAm 90
Chard, Daniel BioIn 16
Chard, Geoffrey 1930- IntWWM 90
Chard, Judy 1916- ConAu 31NR
Chard, Rodney D. 1942- St&PR 91
Chard, Roland Turner 1907- WhoAm 90
Chardavoyne, David E. 1948- St&PR 91
Chardavoyne, David Edwin 1948- WhoE 91
Chardiet, Bernice Kroll 1930- WhoAm 90, WhoAmW 91, WhoWor 91
Chardin, Jean Baptiste 1699-1779 IntDcAA 90
Chardin, Jean-Baptiste-Simeon 1699-1779 BioIn 16
Chardin, Jean Simeon 1699-1779 WorAlBi
Chardin, Pierre Teilhard de BioIn 16
Chardonnet, Louis-Marie-Hilaire B. 1839-1924 WorAlBi
Chareau, Pierre 1883-1950 PenDiDA 89
Charek, Thomas Jack 1952- St&PR 91
Charen, Mona 1957- WhoAmW 91
Charen, Solomon WhoE 91
Charen, Walter David BiDrAPA 89
Ch'arents', Eghishe 1897-1937 BioIn 16
Charest, Jean J. 1958- WhoAm 90, WhoE 91
Charest, Joseph G. ODwPR 91
Charest, Roger David 1916- WhoE 91
Charette, Steve Vern 1952- WhoEmL 91
Charfoos, Lawrence Selig 1935- WhoAm 90
Chargaff, Erwin BioIn 16
Chargaff, Erwin 1905- WhoAm 90
Charger, Martin 1833-1900 WhNaAH
Chari, C.T.K. 1909- EncO&P 3
Chari, Cadambur Tiruvenkatachari K 1909- EncPaPR 91
Charig, Phil 1902-1960 OxCPMus
Charisse, Cyd 1923- WhoAm 90, WorAlBi
Charity, Neil Mitchell 1915- WhoWor 91
Charkatz, Harry M 1940- BiDrAPA 89
Charke, Charlotte 1713-1760 BioIn 16, FemiCLE
Charla, Joseph BioIn 16
Charla, Joseph, Jr. 1924- St&PR 91
Charlamb, Susan Dale BiDrAPA 89
Charlamow, Vsevolod BiDrAPA 89
Charlap, Anne E. 1956- WhoAmW 91
Charlemagne 742-814 EncO&P 3, WorAlBi
Charlemagne, Emperor 742-814 BioIn 16
Charleroy, Belinda Dorris 1942- WhoE 91
Charles I 1600-1649 LitC 13 [port]
Charles V 1500-1558 WorAlBi
Charles VII 1403-1461 WorAlBi
Charles, Archduke of Austria 1771-1847 BioIn 16
Charles, Duke of Burgundy 1433-1477 BioIn 16
Charles Edward, Prince 1720-1788 BioIn 16
Charles I, Emperor of Austria 1887-1922 BioIn 16
Charles XIV John 1763-1844 WorAlBi
Charles II, King of France 823-877 BioIn 16
Charles II, King of Great Britain 1630-1685 BioIn 16
Charles IV, King of Hungary 1887-1922 BioIn 16
Charles III, King of Spain 1716-1788 BioIn 16
Charles IV, King of Spain 1748-1819 BioIn 16
Charles Martel 688-741 WorAlBi
Charles, Prince 1948- WhoWor 91, WorAlBi
Charles, Prince of Wales 1948- BioIn 16
Charles, the Bald 823-877 BioIn 16
Charles, the Bold 1433-1477 BioIn 16
Charles the Great 742-814 BioIn 16, EncO&P 3
Charles, Allan David 1940- WhoSSW 91
Charles, Allan G. 1928- WhoAm 90
Charles, Andrew V 1939- BiDrAPA 89
Charles, Bertram 1918- WhoAm 90
Charles, Carol Morgan 1931- WhoAm 90
Charles, Caroline BioIn 16
Charles, Carolyn Stowell 1921- WhoSSW 91
Charles, Clayton 1913-1976 WhoAmA 91N
Charles, Durant WhoAmA 91
Charles, Ed 1935- Ballpl 90
Charles, Elizabeth 1828-1896 FemiCLE
Charles, Eugenia BioIn 16
Charles, Franklin TwCCr&M 91
Charles, George Frederic 1916- BioIn 16
Charles, Gerda 1914- FemiCLE
Charles, Glen BioIn 16
Charles, Henry ConAu 30NR
Charles, Henry Lee 1930- BiDrAPA 89
Charles, Isabel 1926- WhoAm 90
Charles, Jacques Alexandre Cesar 1746-1823 WorAlBi
Charles, Joel 1914- WhoSSW 91
Charles, John A. 1951- WhoHisp 91
Charles, John Franklyn 1937- WhoSSW 91
Charles, Jose Rodolfo 1953- WhoEmL 91
Charles, Joseph BioIn 16
Charles, Josh BioIn 16
Charles, Julie-Francoise Bouchaud 1784-1817 EncCoWW
Charles, Les BioIn 16
Charles, Lisa J. 1943- WhoAmW 91
Charles, Lyn Ellen 1951- WhoEmL 91
Charles, Lyria Michelle 1957- WhoAmW 91
Charles, Maggi ConAu 30NR
Charles, Marc Anthony BiDrAPA 89
Charles, Mary Eugenia 1919- WhoWor 91, WomWR
Charles, Norman BioIn 16
Charles, Philipp Lambert 1909- WhoWor 91
Charles, Ray BioIn 16
Charles, Ray 1930- DrBIPA 90, EncPR&S 89, OxCPMus, WhoAm 90, WorAlBi
Charles, Raymond Alanson 1919- WhoAm 90
Charles, Reid Shaver 1940- WhoE 91, WhoWor 91
Charles, Richard Alan BiDrAPA 89
Charles, Richard Lloyd 1939- St&PR 91
Charles, Robert Richard 1938- WhoE 91
Charles, Roderick E 1927- BiDrAPA 89
Charles, Sara C. 1934- ConAu 132
Charles, Sara Connor 1934- BiDrAPA 89
Charles, Will TwCCr&M 91
Charleson, Ian NewYTBS 90 [port]
Charleson, Ian 1949-1990 BioIn 16
Charlestein, Gary M. 1944- St&PR 91
Charleston, Oscar 1896-1954 Ballpl 90 [port]
Charlesworth, Brian 1945- WhoAm 90
Charlesworth, James H 1940- ConAu 130
Charlesworth, Maria Louisa 1819-1880 BioIn 16
Charlesworth, Marigold 1926- OxCCanT
Charlesworth, Sarah E 1947- WhoAmA 91
Charlesworth, Velma Lillian 1919- WhoAmW 91
Charleton, Margaret Ann 1947- WhoAmW 91
Charleux, Henri 1924- WhoWor 91
Charlevoix, Pierre Francois Xavier De 1682-1761 EncCRAm, WhNaAH
Charley, Philip J. 1921- St&PR 91
Charley, Philip James 1921- WhoAm 90
Charlie, Wayne Alexander 1945- WhoEmL 91
Charlier, Jean Pierre 1937- WhoWor 91
Charlier, Roger H 1921- ConAu 31NR
Charlier, Roger Henri 1921- WhoAm 90
Charlip, Remy 1929- AuBYP 90
Charlos 1831?-1900 WhNaAH
Charlot 1831?-1900 WhNaAH
Charlot, Andre 1882-1956 OxCPMus
Charlot, Jean 1898-1979 WhoAmA 91N
Charlot, Martin 1944- SmATA 64 [port]
Charlot, Martin Day 1944- WhoAmA 91
Charlotte WomWR
Charlotte WomWR
Charlotte, Grand Duchess of Luxembourg 1896-1985 BioIn 16
Charlson, Chauncey Rudolph, Jr. 1933- WhoAm 90
Charlson, David Harvey 1947- WhoAm 90, WhoEmL 91, WhoWor 91
Charlson, Michael Lloyd 1958- WhoEmL 91
Charlson, Murray T BiDrAPA 89
Charlson, Robert Jay 1936- WhoAm 90
Charlton, Betty Jo 1923- WhoAmW 91
Charlton, Gordon Taliaferro, Jr. 1923- WhoSSW 91
Charlton, Jesse Melvin, Jr. 1916- WhoAm 90
Charlton, John Fraser 1940- WhoWor 91
Charlton, John Kipp 1937- WhoAm 90
Charlton, Jon Wallace 1948- WhoE 91
Charlton, Mary FemiCLE
Charlton, Norm 1963- Ballpl 90
Charlton, Richard G. 1934- ODwPR 91
Charlu, Sreenivasapuram Sesha 1921- WhoWor 91
Charlupski, Allen 1918- WhoAm 90
Charlwood, Gary BioIn 16
Charm, Joel Barry WhoE 91
Charm, Leslie 1943- St&PR 91
Charmatz, Bill 1925- WhoAmA 91
Charmatz, Leslie Howard 1945- St&PR 91
Charmello, Catherine Mary 1942- WhoAmW 91
Charmet, Roch Pierre BioIn 16
Charnas, Michael 1947- WhoAm 90, WhoEmL 91
Charnas, Suzy M 1939- SmATA 61 [port]
Charnas, Suzy McKee 1939- FemiCLE, RGTwCSF
Charner, Ivan 1949- WhoE 91
Charness, Wayne Samuel 1954- WhoEmL 91
Charney, David H 1923- WhoWrEP 89
Charney, David L 1943- BiDrAPA 89
Charney, Dennis S BiDrAPA 89
Charney, Florence R. 1923- WhoSSW 91
Charney, James 1946- BiDrAPA 89
Charney, M. Jeffrey ODwPR 91
Charney, Melvin 1935- WhoAmA 91
Charney, Michele ODwPR 91
Charney, Seth Dragiff 1944- BiDrAPA 89
Charnick, Arnie BioIn 16
Charnin, Jade Hobson 1945- WhoAmW 91, WhoE 91, WhoWor 91
Charnin, Martin 1934- WhoAm 90
Charnley, John 1911-1982 DcNaB 1981
Charnock, Thomas 1526-1581 EncO&P 3
Charny, E Joseph 1927- BiDrAPA 89
Charochak, Dale Michael 1955- WhoE 91, WhoEmL 91
Charos, Evangelos Nikolaou 1953- WhoE 91
Charpentier, Alexandre 1856-1909 PenDiDA 89
Charpentier, Arthur A. 1919-1989 BioIn 16
Charpentier, Gabriel 1925- OxCCanT
Charpentier, Gail Wigutow 1946- WhoAmW 91, WhoEmL 91
Charpentier, Gustave 1860-1956 PenDiMP A
Charpentier, Helene Barbro 1945- WhoWor 91
Charpentier, Marcel PenDiMP
Charpentier De Castro, Eduardo 1927- IntWWM 90, WhoWor 91
Charpie, Robert A. 1925- St&PR 91
Charpie, Robert Alan 1925- WhoAm 90
Charrach, Josef 1946- WhoWor 91
Charren, Peggy 1928- ConAu 129, WhoAm 90, WhoAmW 91
Charretie, Anna Maria 1819-1875 BiDWomA
Charrier, Michael Edward 1945- WhoE 91, WhoEmL 91
Charriere, Belle de 1740-1805 EncCoWW
Charron, Andre 1936- WhoAm 90
Charron, Paul Richard 1942- WhoAm 90
Charron, Theodore J. BioIn 16
Charry, Dana BiDrAPA 89
Charry, Michael Ronald 1933- WhoAm 90
Chartak, Mike 1916-1967 Ballpl 90
Charteris, Leslie 1907- TwCCr&M 91, WhoAm 90
Charteris, Richard 1948- IntWWM 90
Charteris of Amisfield, Baron 1913- BioIn 16
Charters, Alexander Nathaniel 1916- WhoAm 90, WhoWor 91
Charters, Ann 1936- WhoAm 90
Charters, Ann D 1936- WhoWrEP 89
Charters, David H. 1942- St&PR 91
Chartier, Donna Marie 1955- WhoEmL 91
Chartier, Janellen Olsen 1951- WhoAmW 91
Chartier, Jeffrey David 1956- WhoEmL 91
Chartier, Vernon Lee 1939- WhoAm 90
Chartoff, Robert Irwin WhoAm 90
Charton, Donald Gene 1930- St&PR 91
Charton, Jean 1924- St&PR 91
Charton, Marvin 1931- WhoAm 90
Chartow, Harold 1920- St&PR 91

Chartrain-Hebbelinck, Marie-Jeanne 1909-1987 BioIn 16
Chartrand, Mark Ray, III 1943- WhoAm 90
Chartrand, Robert Lee 1928- WhoAm 90
Charue, Jean L. 1930- WhoWor 91
Charuvastra, V. Charles 1945- BiDrAPA 89
Charvat, Fedia Rudolf 1931- St&PR 91
Charvat, Jan Maria 1933- WhoWor 91
Charwat, Andrew Franciszek 1925- WhoAm 90
Charwat, Arthur Charles 1929- St&PR 91
Charwath, Walter 1928- St&PR 91
Charya, Vijayalakshmi Velagaleti 1956- WhoAmW 91
Charyk, Joseph V. 1920- St&PR 91
Charyk, Joseph Vincent 1920- WhoAm 90
Charyn, Jerome 1937- MajTwCW, TwCCr&M 91
Chasanow, Abraham BioIn 16
Chase, Agnes 1869-1963 WomFic [port]
Chase, Alan C. 1936- St&PR 91
Chase, Alice AuBYP 90
Chase, Alice Elizabeth 1906- AuBYP 90, WhoAmA 91
Chase, Allan WhoAmA 91
Chase, Allan Harrison 1945- WhoEmL 91
Chase, Allen 1911- WhoWor 91
Chase, Andy BioIn 16
Chase, Annazette DrBIPA 90
Chase, Arlen BioIn 16
Chase, Aurin Moody, Jr. 1904- WhoAm 90
Chase, Barrie BioIn 16
Chase, Brandon Lee 1932- WhoAm 90
Chase, Chevy 1943- News 90 [port], WhoAm 90, WorAlBi
Chase, Clarence W. 1913- IntWWM 90
Chase, Clinton Irvin 1927- WhoAm 90
Chase, Cochrane BioIn 16
Chase, Cochrane 1932- WhoAm 90
Chase, David Edward 1941- WhoWrEP 89
Chase, David Marion 1930- WhoE 91
Chase, David W. 1937- St&PR 91
Chase, Dawn Renee 1961- WhoEmL 91
Chase, Diane BioIn 16
Chase, Doris 1923- WhoAmA 91
Chase, Doris Totten 1923- WhoAm 90, WhoAmW 91, WhoE 91
Chase, Edward 1884-1965 WhoAmA 91N
Chase, Elaine Raco 1949- WhoWrEP 89
Chase, Elise BioIn 16
Chase, Eric Tobey WhoE 91
Chase, Ezra Bartholomew 1827-1864 AmLegL
Chase, Francis M. 1920- St&PR 91
Chase, Francis Russell 1818-1876 AmLegL
Chase, Frank Swift 1886-1958 WhoAmA 91N
Chase, Gary Alan BiDrAPA 89
Chase, George Anderson BioIn 16
Chase, George H 1874-1952 WhoAmA 91N
Chase, George J BiDrAPA 89
Chase, Gerard BiDrAPA 89
Chase, Gilbert 1906- IntWWM 90
Chase, Glen ConAu 31NR
Chase, Goodwin 1911- WhoAm 90
Chase, Hal 1883-1947 Ballpl 90 [port], BioIn 16
Chase, Helen Louise 1943- WhoAmW 91
Chase, Henry 1923-1988 BioIn 16
Chase, Henry Pahtahquahong 1818-1900 DcCanB 12
Chase, Ilka 1907-1978 FemiCLE
Chase, Irving E 1919- BiDrAPA 89
Chase, J Samuel BiDrAPA 89
Chase, Jack S 1941- WhoAmA 91
Chase, James Hadley 1906-1985 TwCCr&M 91
Chase, James Keller 1927- WhoAm 90
Chase, James Staton 1932- WhoAm 90
Chase, Jean Cox 1925- WhoAmW 91
Chase, Jeanne Norman 1929- WhoAmA 91
Chase, Jeff 1965- ODwPR 91
Chase, Jeffrey Stuart 1960- WhoE 91
Chase, Jerry David 1959- WhoSSW 91
Chase, Joan ConAu 129
Chase, John David 1920- WhoAm 90
Chase, John Saunders 1925- WhoAm 90
Chase, John William 1940- St&PR 91, WhoAm 90
Chase, Joseph Cummings 1878-1965 WhoAmA 91N
Chase, Joyce Elaine 1931- WhoAmW 91
Chase, Kate 1840-1899 BioAmW
Chase, Keith 1927- St&PR 91
Chase, Ken 1913- Ballpl 90
Chase, Laurie Regan ODwPR 91
Chase, Lida Gazlay 1938- WhoAmW 91
Chase, Linda Arville 1953- WhoAmW 91, WhoEmL 91
Chase, Loriene Eck 1934- WhoAmW 91, WhoWor 91
Chase, Louis S BiDrAPA 89
Chase, Louisa L 1951- WhoAmA 91
Chase, Lucius Peter 1902- WhoAm 90
Chase, Lyndon ConAu 31NR
Chase, Lynn Edward 1939- St&PR 91
Chase, Margaret Smith AuBYP 90
Chase, Marian Emma 1844-1905 BiDWomA
Chase, Marian Tyler BioIn 16
Chase, Mark Earle 1960- WhoEmL 91
Chase, Mary 1907-1981 AuBYP 90, BioIn 16, WorAlBi
Chase, Mary Coyle 1907-1981 NotWoAT
Chase, Mary Ellen 1887-1973 AuBYP 90, BioAmW, FemiCLE
Chase, Maurice BioIn 16
Chase, Merrill Wallace 1905- WhoAm 90
Chase, Michael Tilden 1950- WhoE 91
Chase, Michael William 1959- WhoSSW 91
Chase, Morris 1918- WhoAm 90, WhoWor 91
Chase, Naomi Feigelson 1932- WhoWrEP 89
Chase, Nicholas Joseph 1913- WhoAm 90, WhoE 91
Chase, Norman Eli 1926- WhoAm 90
Chase, Oscar Gottfried WhoAm 90
Chase, Otta Louise 1909-1987 ConAu 32NR
Chase, Peter R. 1947- St&PR 91
Chase, Richard 1904-1988 AuBYP 90, BioIn 16, SmATA 64
Chase, Richard J. 1922- St&PR 91
Chase, Richard Lionel St. Lucian 1933- WhoAm 90
Chase, Robert Arthur 1923- WhoAm 90
Chase, Robert M 1940- WhoAmA 91
Chase, Rochelle Ann 1961- WhoEmL 91
Chase, Salmon P. 1808-1873 EncABHB 6 [port], WorAlBi
Chase, Salmon Portland 1808-1873 BiDrUSE 89
Chase, Samuel 1741-1811 EncCRAm, WorAlBi
Chase, Seymour M. 1924- WhoAm 90
Chase, Sheldon 1944- BiDrAPA 89
Chase, Sidney M 1877-1957 WhoAmA 91N
Chase, Steve BioIn 16
Chase, Stuart Alan 1958- WhoE 91
Chase, Sylvia B. 1938- WhoAm 90
Chase, Thomas Newell 1932- WhoAm 90
Chase, Thomas Parker BiDrAPA 89
Chase, Vicki Verret 1950- St&PR 91
Chase, Victor E BiDrAPA 89
Chase, Victoria Byler 1954- WhoAmW 91, WhoEmL 91
Chase, W. Howard 1910- ODwPR 91
Chase, W. Rowell 1904- St&PR 91
Chase, W Thomas 1940- WhoAmA 91
Chase, Warren 1813-1891 EncO&P 3
Chase, William B. St&PR 91N
Chase, William Clifford 1960- WhoSSW 91
Chase, William Howard 1910- WhoAm 90
Chase, William Merritt 1849-1916 BioIn 16, WorAlBi
Chase, William Rowell 1904- WhoAm 90
Chase, William Thomas, III 1940- WhoAm 90
Chase-Riboud, Barbara 1936- BioIn 16
Chase-Riboud, Barbara 1939- WhoAmA 91
Chase-Riboud, Barbara Dewayne 1936?- BiDWomA
Chase-Riboud, Barbara Dewayne 1939- WhoAm 90, WhoAmW 91
Chasek, Judith AuBYP 90
Chaseman, Joel 1926- St&PR 91, WhoAm 90
Chasen, Jonathan Lee 1952- BiDrAPA 89
Chasen, Mignon C 1911- BiDrAPA 89
Chasen, Mignon Charney 1911- WhoE 91
Chasen, Nancy H. 1945- ConAu 130
Chasen, Robert E. 1916- St&PR 91, WhoAm 90
Chasen, Ronni ODwPR 91
Chasen, Sherwin A. 1938- St&PR 91
Chasen, Sylvan Herbert 1926- WhoAm 90
Chaset, Alan Jay 1946- WhoEmL 91
Chasey, Patrick Ross 1947- St&PR 91
Chasin, Martin 1938- WhoAmA 91
Chasin, Milton Jack 1919- St&PR 91
Chasin, Richard M 1936- BiDrAPA 89
Chasin, Werner David 1932- WhoAm 90, WhoE 91
Chasins, Abram 1903- AuBYP 90, IntWWM 90
Chasins, Edward A. 1920- WhoAm 90
Chasis, Herbert 1905- WhoAm 90
Chaskelson, Marsha Ina 1950- WhoAmW 91
Chaski, Hilda Cecelia 1951- WhoAmW 91
Chason, Jacob 1915- WhoAm 90
Chassaing, J. Patrick 1952- WhoEmL 91
Chassler, Seymour Murray 1919- WhoE 91
Chassman, Leonard Fredric 1935- WhoAm 90
Chasson, Ann Kathryn 1959- WhoE 91
Chast, Roz BioIn 16
Chastain, Deborah BioIn 16
Chastain, Dorothy Straughan 1950- WhoAmW 91
Chastain, Gary P. 1954- St&PR 91
Chastain, Larry Kent 1943- WhoAm 90
Chastain, Paul Raymond 1934- St&PR 91
Chastain, Randall Meads 1945- WhoSSW 91
Chastain, Sheila McClendon 1948- WhoSSW 91
Chastain, Thomas TwCCr&M 91
Chastain-Lorber, Katherine BiDrAPA 89
Chasteen, Michael Allen 1947- WhoEmL 91, WhoSSW 91
Chastek, C Terrence 1948- BiDrAPA 89
Chastek, James Walter BiDrAPA 89
Chastel, Andre 1912-1990 ConAu 132
Chastellaine, Nicolas 1795?-1892 DcCanB 12
Chastney, Michael Anthony 1944- WhoE 91
Chat, Emanuel 1909- BiDrAPA 89
Chateau, Jacques Marie 1935- St&PR 91
Chateau, John-Peter David 1942- St&PR 91, WhoAm 90
Chateaubriand, Francois Rene, Vicomte De 1768-1848 WorAlBi
Chatel, John Charles BiDrAPA 89
Chatelain, Carl J. 1932- St&PR 91
Chatelain, Nicolas 1795?-1892 DcCanB 12
Chatelaine, Nicolas 1795?-1892 DcCanB 12
Chatelan, Nicolas 1795?-1892 DcCanB 12
Chatelet-Lomont, Gabrielle-Emilie le 1706-1749 EncCoWW
Chatelus, Paul 1952- WhoE 91
Chater, James Michael 1951- IntWWM 90
Chater, Shirley Sears 1932- WhoAm 90, WhoAmW 91, WhoSSW 91
Chatfield, Cheryl Ann 1946- WhoAmW 91, WhoEmL 91
Chatfield, David Alan 1939- St&PR 91
Chatfield, H. Marshall 1935- St&PR 91
Chatfield, Henry Marshall 1935- WhoAm 90
Chatfield, Kenneth William 1930- St&PR 91
Chatfield, Mary Van Abshoven WhoAm 90, WhoE 91
Chatfield, Ruth Christina 1956- WhoAmW 91
Chatfield-Taylor, Adele BioIn 16
Chatfield-Taylor, Adele 1945- WhoAmW 91
Chatfield-Taylor, Robert BioIn 16
Chatham, Buster 1901-1975 Ballpl 90
Chatham, Edmund H. 1943- WhoSSW 91
Chatham, Gerry W. 1938- ODwPR 91
Chatham, James Ray 1931- WhoAm 90
Chatham, Ralph Ernest 1948- WhoE 91, WhoEmL 91
Chatham, Robert BioIn 16
Chatham, Russell 1939- News 90 [port]
Chatham-Showalter, Peggy E 1958- BiDrAPA 89
Chatillon, Dominique 1928- WhoWor 91
Chatlos, John Calvin, Jr. BiDrAPA 89
Chatlos, William E. 1927- ODwPR 91
Chatlos, William Edward 1927- WhoAm 90
Chatman, James Icelius 1926- St&PR 91
Chatman, Kay Lynn Wade 1963- WhoEmL 91
Chatman, Peter 1915-1988 BioIn 16
Chatmas, John T 1945- WhoAmA 91
Chato 1860?-1934 WhNaAH [port]
Chato, Donna Mae 1949- WhoEmL 91
Chato, John Clark 1929- WhoAm 90
Chato, Joseph Edward 1950- WhoEmL 91
Chatoff, Michael Alan 1946- WhoE 91, WhoEmL 91, WhoWor 91
Chatoor, Irene BiDrAPA 89
Chatoor, Irene Child 1937- WhoE 91
Chatot, Charles A. 1941- St&PR 91
Chatot-Travis, Judee J. 1948- St&PR 91
Chatowsky, Anthony Peter BiDrAPA 89
Chatrier, Philippe BioIn 16
Chatroo, Arthur Jay 1946- WhoEmL 91, WhoWor 91
Chatroop, Louis Carl 1951- WhoEmL 91
Chatsuthipan, Visit BiDrAPA 89
Chattah, Leon 1934- BiDrAPA 89
Chattalas, Michael John 1962- WhoE 91
Chattaway, Dwight Nelson 1936- St&PR 91
Chattaway, Thurland 1872-1947 OxCPMus
Chattelaine, Nicolas 1795?-1892 DcCanB 12
Chatterjee, Jay 1936- WhoAmA 91
Chatterjee, Lata Roy 1938- WhoE 91
Chatterjee, M. Jayanta 1936- WhoAm 90
Chatterjee, Manjusri 1950- BiDrAPA 89
Chatterjee, Pranab 1936- WhoAm 90
Chatterjee, Srabani WhoAmW 91
Chatterji, Debajyoti 1944- St&PR 91, WhoAm 90
Chatterley, James Philip 1923- WhoWor 91
Chatterton, Clarence Kerr 1880-1973 WhoAmA 91N
Chatterton, Georgiana 1806-1876 FemiCLE
Chatterton, N. Jerry 1939- WhoAm 90
Chatterton, Robert Treat, Jr. 1935- WhoAm 90
Chatterton, Roylance Wayne 1921- WhoWrEP 89
Chatterton, Sterling Gene 1928- St&PR 91
Chattha, Jaswinder K 1935- BiDrAPA 89
Chattin, Gilbert Marshall 1914- WhoSSW 91
Chatto, Alexa Johanna 1961- WhoE 91
Chatto, Alfred 1860?-1934 WhNaAH [port]
Chattopadhyay, Sukumar 1950- WhoWor 91
Chattopadhyaya, Kamaladevi 1903-1988 BioIn 16
Chattoraj, Sati Charan 1934- WhoE 91
Chatty, Habib 1916- WhoWor 91
Chatwin, Bruce BioIn 16
Chatwin, Bruce 1940-1989 AnObit 1989, ConLC 59 [port]
Chatzkel, Ben 1924- St&PR 91
Chau, Dang Viet BioIn 16
Chau, Timothy Yiu-Ki 1938- WhoWor 91
Chau, Wing Fan Thomas 1957- WhoWor 91
Chaucer, Daniel ConAu 132, MajTwCW
Chaucer, Geoffrey BioIn 16
Chaucer, Geoffrey 1340?-1400 WorAlBi
Chaucer, Geoffrey 1342?-1400 WrPh
Chaudhari, Praveen 1937- WhoAm 90
Chaudhary, Basudeo 1930- BiDrAPA 89
Chaudhary, Nazir Ahmad 1949- BiDrAPA 89
Chaudhri, Nonihal Singh 1945- BiDrAPA 89
Chaudhry, Dewat Ram 1942- BiDrAPA 89
Chaudhry, Jawade Osman 1957- WhoWor 91
Chaudhry, Naseem Mahmood 1957- BiDrAPA 89
Chaudhry, Rajnish Pratap 1949- BiDrAPA 89
Chaudhry, Rashid A. 1945- St&PR 91
Chaudhry, Vijay K. 1945- St&PR 91
Chaudhuri, Nirad C. 1897- BioIn 16
Chaudoin, John Randall 1940- WhoSSW 91
Chaudoir, Jacques 1929- WhoWor 91
Chaudry, Irshad Hussain 1945- WhoWor 91
Chauff, Eugene Henry 1950- St&PR 91
Chaugy, Francoise-Madeleine de 1611-1680 EncCoWW
Chauhan, Jagadish Narabherambhai 1951- WhoWor 91
Chauhan, Khurshid Ali 1947- WhoWor 91
Chauhan, Narendra 1952- BiDrAPA 89
Chauhan, Narinder Singh 1952- WhoE 91
Chauls, Robert Nathan 1942- IntWWM 90
Chaume, Jacqueline Thion de la BioIn 16
Chauncey, Susan Joan 1945- WhoAmW 91
Chauncy, Charles 1705-1787 EncCRAm
Chauncy, Nan 1900-1970 AuBYP 90
Chaunu, Pierre Rene 1923- WhoWor 91
Chaurette, Normand 1954- OxCCanT
Chausson, Ernest 1855-1899 PenDiMP A
Chaut, Robert ODwPR 91
Chautemps, Camille Gabriel 1885-1963 BiDFrPL
Chauveau, Pierre-Joseph-Olivier 1820-1890 DcLB 99 [port]
Chauvet, Guy 1933- IntWWM 90
Chauvette, Claude 1939- St&PR 91
Chauvin, Louis 1881-1908 OxCPMus
Chauvin, Mamie Jo 1929- WhoSSW 91
Chauvin, Nicolas WorAlBi
Chauvin, Remy 1913- EncO&P 3, EncPaPR 91
Chavali, Srinivas 1961- WhoE 91
Chavannes, Pierre Puvis de 1824-1898 BioIn 16
Chavarria, Adam, Jr. 1949- WhoHisp 91
Chavarria, Dawn Marie 1960- WhoAmW 91
Chavarria, Dolores Esparza 1952- WhoAmW 91
Chavarria, Doroteo WhoHisp 91
Chavarria, Ernest M., Jr. 1955- WhoHisp 91
Chavarria, Ernest Montes, Jr. 1955- WhoAm 90, WhoEmL 91, WhoSSW 91
Chavarria, Hector Manuel 1934- WhoHisp 91
Chavarria, Oscar 1947- WhoHisp 91
Chavarria, Phil 1929- WhoHisp 91
Chavarria, Rebecca 1956- WhoHisp 91
Chavarria, Rosemary Ann 1954- WhoAmW 91, WhoEmL 91
Chavee, Xavier Noel 1955- St&PR 91
Chaveriat, Andrew John 1963- WhoE 91
Chavern, Hugh Edward BiDrAPA 89
Chavers, P. W. BioIn 16
Chaves, Amado 1851-1930 AmLegL
Chaves, Federico 1882- BioIn 16

Chaves, Jose Andrade 1941- *St&PR 91*
Chaves, Jose Francisco 1833-1904 *BioIn 16*
Chaves, Jose Maria 1922- *WhoAm 90, WhoWor 91*
Chaves, Manuel Antonio 1818-1889 *BioIn 16*
Chaves, Richard 1951- *ConTFT 8*
Chaves-Carballo, Enrique 1936- *WhoHisp 91*
Chavez, Abel Max 1951- *WhoHisp 91*
Chavez, Abraham 1927- *WhoHisp 91*
Chavez, Abraham, Jr. 1927- *WhoAm 90*
Chavez, Alice Diaz 1956- *WhoHisp 91*
Chavez, Andrew 1939- *WhoHisp 91*
Chavez, Angelico *BioIn 16, ConAu 32NR, HispWr 90*
Chavez, Angelico, Fray *ConAu 32NR, HispWr 90*
Chavez, Cesar 1927- *BioIn 16, WorAlBi*
Chavez, Cesar Estrada 1927- *WhoAm 90, WhoHisp 91*
Chavez, Cesar Tizoc 1952- *WhoEmL 91*
Chavez, Cynthia 1967- *WhoHisp 91*
Chavez, Denise 1948- *ConAu 131, HispWr 90*
Chavez, Denise Elia 1948- *WhoHisp 91*
Chavez, Dennis 1888-1962 *BioIn 16*
Chavez, Dennis C. *WhoHisp 91*
Chavez, Dennis M. 1954- *WhoHisp 91*
Chavez, Don Antonio 1955- *WhoHisp 91*
Chavez, Eduardo Arcenio 1917- *WhoAm 90, WhoAmA 91, WhoHisp 91*
Chavez, Edward Arcenio 1917- *BioIn 16*
Chavez, Edward L. 1963- *WhoHisp 91*
Chavez, Eliverio 1940- *WhoHisp 91*
Chavez, Ernest L. 1949- *WhoHisp 91*
Chavez, Felipe 1835-1905 *BioIn 16*
Chavez, Felix P. 1933- *WhoHisp 91*
Chavez, Gabriel Anthony 1955- *WhoHisp 91*
Chavez, Gilbert Espinoza 1932- *WhoAm 90*
Chavez, Ida Lillian 1944- *WhoHisp 91*
Chavez, Janie Ignacia 1946- *WhoAmW 91*
Chavez, Joe Robert 1958- *WhoHisp 91*
Chavez, John J. 1935- *WhoHisp 91*
Chavez, John Montoya 1952- *WhoHisp 91*
Chavez, John Phillip 1950- *WhoWor 91*
Chavez, John R 1949- *HispWr 90*
Chavez, John Richard 1949- *WhoSSW 91*
Chavez, John Robert 1952- *WhoEmL 91*
Chavez, Joseph A. *BioIn 16*
Chavez, Joseph Arnold 1939- *WhoAmA 91, WhoHisp 91*
Chavez, Julio Cesar *BioIn 16, WhoHisp 91*
Chavez, Larry Sterling 1948- *WhoHisp 91*
Chavez, Linda *BioIn 16*
Chavez, Linda 1947- *WhoHisp 91*
Chavez, Luis 1953- *WhoHisp 91*
Chavez, Manuel 1910- *ConAu 32NR, HispWr 90*
Chavez, Manuel Camacho, Sr. 1930- *WhoHisp 91*
Chavez, Maria D. 1939- *WhoHisp 91*
Chavez, Mariano, Jr. *WhoHisp 91*
Chavez, Martin Joseph 1952- *WhoHisp 91*
Chavez, Mary 1952- *WhoHisp 91*
Chavez, Mauro 1947- *WhoHisp 91*
Chavez, Patricia L. 1954- *WhoHisp 91*
Chavez, Ray 1950- *WhoHisp 91*
Chavez, Raymond M. 1947- *WhoHisp 91*
Chavez, Robert B. 1946- *St&PR 91*
Chavez, Rodolfo Lucas 1950- *WhoHisp 91*
Chavez, Samuel 1958- *WhoEmL 91*
Chavez, Tito David 1947- *WhoHisp 91*
Chavez, Tony A. 1931- *WhoHisp 91*
Chavez, Victor B. 1945- *St&PR 91, WhoHisp 91*
Chavez, Victor Edwin 1930- *WhoAm 90*
Chavez, Victoria Marie 1933- *WhoHisp 91*
Chavez-Cornish, Patricia Marie 1951- *WhoHisp 91*
Chavez Morado, Jose 1909- *ArtLatA*
Chavez-Vasquez, Gloria *WhoHisp 91*
Chavin, Walter 1925- *WhoAm 90*
Chavinson, Melvin Jay 1938- *BiDrAPA 89*
Chavis, Douglas A 1946- *BiDrAPA 89*
Chavis, Melvin Lin 1944- *St&PR 91*
Chavis, Peggy Wilkins 1950- *WhoAmW 91*
Chavis-Mickey, Angela Yelverton 1950- *WhoAmW 91*
Chavkin, Wallace 1922- *St&PR 91*
Chavkin, Wendy 1952- *WhoAmW 91*
Chavonelle, Peter Bruce 1943- *WhoE 91*
Chavooshian, Marge *BioIn 16*
Chavooshian, Marge 1925- *WhoAmA 91, WhoAmW 91*
Chawla, Anwantbir Singh 1956- *BiDrAPA 89*
Chawla, Manmohan Singh 1940- *WhoE 91*
Chawla, Mantosh K. 1946- *St&PR 91*
Chayama, Yukihiko 1947- *WhoEmL 91*
Chayanne 1969- *WhoHisp 91*
Chayat, Sherry 1943- *WhoWrEP 89*
Chayefsky, Paddy 1923-1981 *WorAlBi*
Chayet, Martha 1956- *WhoE 91*
Chazan, Charlotte Saumaise de 1619-1693 *EncCoWW*
Chazanoff, Daniel 1923- *IntWWM 90*
Chazanoff, Jay D. 1945- *St&PR 91*
Chazen, Barbara G. *WhoSSW 91*
Chazen, David Franklin, II 1960- *WhoE 91*
Chazen, Gary David 1951- *St&PR 91*
Chazen, Hartley James 1932- *WhoAm 90*
Chazen, Jerome A. 1927- *St&PR 91, WhoAm 90*
Chazen, Robert Gordon 1943- *St&PR 91*
Chazin, Norman S *BiDrAPA 89*
Chazov, Yevgeny 1929- *WhoWor 91*
Chazz *NewAgMG*
Chbosky, Fred G. 1944- *St&PR 91*
Che, Chuang 1934- *WhoAmA 91*
Cheadle, William L. 1927- *St&PR 91*
Cheah, Jonathon Yoo Chong 1951- *WhoEmL 91*
Cheah, Keong Chye 1939- *BiDrAPA 89*
Cheal, Marylou *WhoAmW 91*
Cheaney, Lewis R. *WhoSSW 91*
Cheap Trick *EncPR&S 89*
Cheater, Angela Penelope 1947- *WhoWor 91*
Cheatham, Benjamin Franklin 1820-1886 *BioIn 16*
Cheatham, Clarence Donald 1923- *WhoSSW 91*
Cheatham, Daniel E. 1949- *WhoEmL 91*
Cheatham, David Todd 1956- *WhoEmL 91*
Cheatham, Doc *BioIn 16*
Cheatham, Edward W. 1937- *ODwPR 91*
Cheatham, Frank Reagan 1936- *WhoAmA 91*
Cheatham, Geoffrey D. 1941- *St&PR 91*
Cheatham, Glenn Wallace 1934- *WhoAm 90*
Cheatham, Henry Plummer 1857-1935 *BlkAmsC [port]*
Cheatham, James Spencer 1924- *BiDrAPA 89*
Cheatham, John Bane, Jr. 1924- *WhoAm 90*
Cheatham, John Henry, Jr. 1924- *St&PR 91*
Cheatham, John Lawrence, Jr. 1933- *St&PR 91*
Cheatham, K Follis *WhoWrEP 89*
Cheatham, Karyn Elizabeth 1943- *WhoWrEP 89*
Cheatham, Ollie V. 1945- *St&PR 91*
Cheatham, Robert Thomas 1952- *WhoSSW 91*
Cheatham, Robert William 1938- *WhoAm 90*
Cheatham, Thomas Edward, Jr. 1929- *WhoAm 90*
Cheatham, Thomas J. 1944- *WhoSSW 91*
Cheatheam, O. Newell 1946- *WhoSSW 91*
Cheatle, Leslie N., Jr. 1940- *St&PR 91*
Cheatwood, Roy Clifton 1946- *WhoEmL 91*
Cheban, Ion Konstantinovici 1927- *WhoWor 91*
Chebrikov, Viktor Mikhailovich 1923- *WhoWor 91*
Chebul, Charles Ray 1954- *WhoEmL 91*
Checa, Eduardo 1959- *WhoWor 91*
Checchi, Vincent V. 1918- *St&PR 91*
Checchi, Vincent Victor 1918- *WhoAm 90*
Chech, Charlie 1879-1938 *Ballpl 90*
Chechik, H.I. *St&PR 91*
Chechile, James S. 1942- *St&PR 91*
Check, Irene Jocius 1946- *WhoAmW 91*
Checka, Venkata Raju 1940- *WhoSSW 91*
Checkanow, Benjamin 1917- *St&PR 91*
Checker, Chubby 1941- *DrBIPA 90, EncPR&S 89, OxCPMus, WorAlBi*
Checkfield *NewAgMG*
Checkosky, Anne Catherine 1964- *WhoAmW 91*
Checkoway, Robert 1951- *WhoEmL 91*
Checota, Joseph Woodrow 1939- *St&PR 91*
Checton, John Burt 1952- *WhoE 91*
Chedgy, David George 1939- *WhoE 91*
Chediak, Elias 1939- *BiDrAPA 89*
Chediak, Natalio 1909- *WhoHisp 91*
Chedid, Andree 1920- *EncCoWW, FemiCLE, WorAu 1980*
Chedid, Antonio 1939- *WhoWor 91*
Chee, Anthony Ngik Choong 1942- *WhoSSW 91*
Chee, Cheng-Khee 1934- *WhoAmA 91*
Chee, Percival Hon Yin 1936- *WhoAm 90*
Cheech 1946- *WhoAm 90*
Cheech and Chong *EncPR&S 89*
Cheech & Chong *WorAlBi*
Cheeger, Thomas *BioIn 16*
Cheek, Barbara Lee 1935- *WhoAmW 91*
Cheek, Ben F., III 1936- *St&PR 91*
Cheek, Ben F., Jr. *St&PR 91N*
Cheek, Cheryl *BioIn 16*
Cheek, Dennis William 1955- *WhoE 91*
Cheek, Ed 1948- *WhoSSW 91*
Cheek, Hollis C. 1945- *St&PR 91*
Cheek, James Edward 1932- *BioIn 16, WhoAm 90*
Cheek, James Howe, III 1942- *WhoAm 90*
Cheek, James Richard 1936- *WhoAm 90, WhoWor 91*
Cheek, John 1948- *IntWWM 90*
Cheek, John Henry 1929- *WhoSSW 91*
Cheek, King Virgil, Jr. 1937- *WhoAm 90*
Cheek, Linda Parker 1942- *St&PR 91*
Cheek, Louis Eugene 1951- *WhoEmL 91*
Cheek, Malcolm 1950- *WhoWor 91*
Cheek, Ralph L. 1930- *St&PR 91*
Cheek, Ronald Edward 1942- *WhoAmA 91*
Cheek, Wayne *BioIn 16*
Cheek, Will Tompkins 1943- *WhoSSW 91*
Cheeks, Dorothy Ross 1922- *WhoAmW 91*
Cheeks, Maurice Edward 1956- *WhoAm 90*
Cheeks, Sherrill C *BiDrAPA 89*
Cheely, Daniel Joseph 1949- *WhoEmL 91*
Cheere, Henry 1703-1781 *BioIn 16*
Cheesbrough, Leon R. 1936- *St&PR 91*
Cheesbrough, Peter H. 1952- *St&PR 91*
Cheeseman, Douglas Taylor, Jr. 1937- *WhoWor 91*
Cheeseman, Elizabeth *BiDEWW*
Cheeseman, Raymond Joseph 1947- *WhoSSW 91*
Cheeseman, Valerie Christine 1949- *WhoAmW 91, WhoEmL 91, WhoSSW 91*
Cheeseman, William John 1943- *WhoAm 90*
Cheetham, Erika 1939- *ConAu 30NR*
Cheetham, Kenneth L. 1944- *ODwPR 91*
Cheetham, Richard W S 1915- *BiDrAPA 89*
Cheever, Benjamin 1948- *BioIn 16*
Cheever, Daniel Sargent 1916- *WhoAm 90*
Cheever, George Barrell 1807-1890 *BioIn 16*
Cheever, George Martin 1947- *WhoEmL 91*
Cheever, John 1912-1982 *BioIn 16, ConLC 64 [port], DcLB 102 [port], MajTwCW, WorAlBi*
Cheever, Susan Liley 1943- *WhoAmW 91*
Cheevers, Phil, Jr. *BioIn 16*
Cheevers, Sarah *BiDEWW*
Cheeves, Virgil 1901-1979 *Ballpl 90*
Cheffetz, Asa 1897-1965 *WhoAmA 91N*
Chefitz, Harold Neal 1935- *WhoAm 90*
Cheh, Huk Yuk 1939- *WhoAm 90, WhoE 91, WhoWor 91*
Chehab, Fuad 1903-1973 *PolLCME*
Chehabi, Houchang Esfandiar 1954- *WhoE 91*
Chehak, Susan Taylor 1951- *ConAu 130*
Chehrazi, Shahla Senehi *BiDrAPA 89*
Cheifetz, Cary Bennet 1954- *WhoEmL 91*
Cheifetz, Lorna Gale 1953- *WhoAmW 91*
Cheifetz, Philip Nathan *BiDrAPA 89*
Chein, Orin Nathaniel 1943- *WhoE 91*
Cheinstein, Julian Edward 1950- *WhoEmL 91*
Cheiro 1866-1936 *EncO&P 3*
Cheit, Earl Frank 1926- *WhoAm 90*
Chekhonin, Sergei *PenDiDA 89*
Chekhov, Anton 1860-1904 *WorAlBi*
Chekhov, Anton Pavlovich 1860-1904 *BioIn 16*
Chekki, Dan A 1935- *WhoWrEP 89*
Chelazzi, Giovanni 1936- *WhoWor 91*
Chelberg, Bruce S. 1934- *St&PR 91*
Chelberg, Bruce Stanley 1934- *WhoAm 90*
Cheldin, Erwin 1931- *St&PR 91*
Chelebian, Jack *BiDrAPA 89*
Chelf, John C *BiDrAPA 89*
Cheli, Henry Alan 1950- *St&PR 91*
Chelin, Steve Clyde 1942- *St&PR 91*
Chelios, Chris 1962- *WorAlBi*
Chelius, James Robert 1943- *WhoE 91*
Chell, Beverly C. 1942- *WhoAm 90, WhoAmW 91, WhoE 91*
Chellappa, Paul *BiDrAPA 89*
Chellappa, Ramalingam 1953- *WhoEmL 91*
Chellappan, Anand Babu 1944- *BiDrAPA 89*
Chellas, Brian Farrell 1941- *WhoAm 90*
Chellgren, Paul Wilbur 1943- *St&PR 91, WhoAm 90*
Chellis, Eugene Clifton 1954- *WhoEmL 91*
Chelnek, Irving *BiDrAPA 89*
Chelnov, Michael 1947- *WhoEmL 91*
Chelstrom, Marilyn Ann *WhoAmW 91, WhoWor 91*
Chelton, Alice Graybil 1923- *BiDrAPA 89*
Chely, Rudolph Anton *PenDiDA 89*
Chema, Peter *BioIn 16*
Chemeche, George 1934- *WhoAm 90, WhoAmA 91*
Chemerow, David I. 1951- *St&PR 91*
Chemerow, David Irving 1951- *WhoAm 90*
Chemiakin, Mihail 1940- *BioIn 16*
Chemparathy, George 1928- *WhoWor 91*
Chempin, Beryl Margaret *IntWWM 90*
Chen Boda 1904-1989 *AnObit 1989, BioIn 16*
Chen Chi 1912- *WhoAm 90, WhoE 91, WhoWor 91*
Chen Jiayan 1599-1683 *BioIn 16*
Chen Jingrun *BioIn 16*
Chen Junsheng 1927- *WhoWor 91*
Chen Muhua 1917- *WhoWor 91*
Chen Rong 1935- *WorAu 1980*
Chen Xieyang 1939- *IntWWM 90*
Chen Xitong *WhoWor 91*
Chen Xueqing 1967- *BioIn 16*
Chen, Albert K C 1936- *BiDrAPA 89*
Chen, Alexander Yu-Kuang 1954- *WhoE 91*
Chen, Alfonso *BiDrAPA 89*
Chen, Alice Tung-Hua 1949- *WhoAmW 91*
Chen, Anne Cooper 1944- *WhoAmW 91*
Chen, Bill Shun-Zer 1941- *St&PR 91, WhoAm 90*
Chen, Calvin H 1919- *BiDrAPA 89*
Chen, Cheng-Jen 1953- *BiDrAPA 89*
Chen, Chi-Tsong 1936- *WhoAm 90*
Chen, Chia Ting 1935- *WhoWor 91*
Ch'en, Chia-yen 1599-1683 *BioIn 16*
Chen, Chin-Tu 1951- *WhoEmL 91*
Chen, Ching-chih 1937- *WhoAmW 91, WhoWrEP 89*
Chen, Ching Jen 1936- *WhoAm 90*
Chen, Chuan Fang 1932- *WhoAm 90*
Chen, Chuanyu Ed 1933- *WhoE 91*
Chen, Chung-Kuang *BiDrAPA 89*
Chen, Clarence Lee 1949- *BiDrAPA 89, WhoE 91*
Chen, Concordia Chao *WhoWor 91*
Chen, Di 1929- *WhoAm 90*
Chen, Francis F. 1929- *WhoAm 90*
Chen, Ga-Lane 1953- *WhoEmL 91*
Chen, George A. 1943- *St&PR 91*
Chen, Grace Wei-Yin 1964- *WhoAmW 91*
Chen, Han-Seng 1897- *WhoWor 91*
Chen, Herbert H. 1942-1987 *BioIn 16*
Chen, Hilo 1942- *WhoAmA 91*
Chen, Hilo Chao-Hung 1942- *WhoE 91*
Chen, Ho-Hong H. H. 1933- *WhoE 91, WhoWor 91*
Chen, Huiyi 1926- *WhoWor 91*
Chen, James Tsung-tsun 1924- *WhoAm 90*
Chen, Jianer 1954- *WhoSSW 91*
Chen, Jim 1948- *WhoSSW 91*
Chen, Jin 1967- *WhoWor 91*
Chen, John-ren 1936- *WhoWor 91*
Chen, Joseph Tao 1925- *WhoAm 90*
Chen, Kao 1919- *WhoAm 90*
Chen, Keenan Jei 1920- *WhoWor 91*
Ch'en, Kenneth Kuan-Sheng 1907- *WhoAm 90*
Chen, Kok-Choo 1947- *WhoEmL 91*
Chen, Kun-Mu 1933- *WhoAm 90*
Chen, Kurt Chien Lun 1920- *WhoWor 91*
Ch'en, Li-li 1934- *WhoAm 90*
Chen, Lihtorng Robert 1952- *WhoE 91*
Chen, Lincoln Chin-ho 1942- *WhoAm 90*
Chen, Linda Li-Yueh Huang 1937- *WhoAmW 91*
Chen, Lung-chu 1935- *WhoWor 91*
Chen, Martha Alter 1944- *WhoAmW 91*
Chen, Michael Che 1926- *WhoSSW 91*
Chen, Michael Ming 1933- *WhoAm 90*
Chen, Michael Shih-ta 1945- *WhoWor 91*
Chen, Min-Chu 1949- *WhoSSW 91*
Chen, Ming 1934- *WhoWor 91*
Chen, Ming-Ming 1961- *WhoE 91*
Chen, Ming-Ming H. 1947- *WhoE 91*
Chen, Peter Pin-Shan 1947- *WhoAm 90*
Chen, Philip S., Jr. 1932- *WhoAm 90*
Chen, Ping-fan 1917- *WhoAm 90*
Chen, Raymond T. 1937- *St&PR 91*
Chen, Richard L. 1938- *St&PR 91*
Chen, Richard Li-chia 1938- *WhoAm 90*
Chen, Samuel Shih-Tsai 1911- *WhoE 91*
Chen, Shau-Tsyh 1936- *WhoAm 90*
Chen, Shoei-Sheng 1940- *WhoAm 90, WhoWor 91*
Chen, Sow-Hsin 1935- *WhoAm 90*
Chen, Stephen S *BiDrAPA 89*
Chen, Stuart Tsau Shiong 1933- *WhoAm 90*
Chen, Su-Chen *IntWWM 90*
Chen, T. C. *BioIn 16*
Chen, Tar Timothy 1945- *WhoE 91, WhoWor 91*
Chen, Tsai Yueh *BiDrAPA 89*
Chen, Wai-Kai 1936- *WhoAm 90*
Chen, Wan-Yu 1916- *WhoWor 91*
Chen, Wayne H. 1922- *WhoAm 90*
Chen, Wen-Tien 1945- *WhoE 91*
Chen, Wenxiong 1952- *WhoE 91*
Chen, Wesley 1954- *WhoWor 91*
Chen, William Hok-Nin 1950- *WhoEmL 91*
Chen, William Y *BiDrAPA 89*
Chen, Xiangkun 1946- *WhoSSW 91*
Chen, Yi 1953- *IntWWM 90*
Chen, Yi-Shung 1941- *St&PR 91*
Chen, Yuh-Ching 1930- *WhoWor 91*
Chen, Yuki Y. Kuo 1930- *WhoE 91*
Chen, Yung-Cheng J 1951- *BiDrAPA 89*

Chen, Zhibo 1947- WhoEmL 91
Chen, Zuohuang 1947- IntWWM 90, WhoWor 91
Chenard, Pierre Dominique 1961- St&PR 91
Chenault, Alice Adele 1944- BiDrAPA 89
Chenault, Henry Smith, Jr. 1933- WhoSSW 91
Chenault, James E., Jr. 1927- WhoAm 90
Chenault, Kenneth I. BioIn 16
Chenault, Kenneth Irvine 1951- WhoAm 90
Chenault, Lawrence E 1877- DrBIPA 90
Chenault, Lawrence R. 1897-1990 BioIn 16
Cheneau, Jacques Pierre Joseph 1927- WhoWor 91
Chenes, Barry A. 1936- St&PR 91
Chenetier, Marc 1946- WhoWor 91
Chenette, Jonathan Lee 1954- IntWWM 90
Chenevert, Edward Valmore, Jr. 1923- WhoAm 90
Cheney, Benjamin P. 1815-1895 WorAlBi
Cheney, Brainard 1900-1990 BioIn 16, ConAu 130, CurBio 90N
Cheney, C. R. 1906-1987 BioIn 16
Cheney, Christopher Robert 1906-1987 BioIn 16
Cheney, Cora 1916- AuBYP 90
Cheney, Daniel L. 1928- St&PR 91
Cheney, Daniel Lavern 1928- WhoAm 90
Cheney, Darwin Leroy 1940- WhoAm 90
Cheney, David Godwin, Jr. 1945- WhoEmL 91
Cheney, David Willi 1950- St&PR 91
Cheney, Dick 1941- WhoAm 90, WhoE 91, WhoWor 91
Cheney, Ednah Dow 1824-1904 FemiCLE
Cheney, Elisabeth Mary 1957- BiDrAPA 89
Cheney, Elliott Ward 1929- WhoAm 90
Cheney, Gerald V. 1942- St&PR 91
Cheney, Glenn Alan 1951- WhoE 91, WhoEmL 91
Cheney, Harriet FemiCLE
Cheney, Harriet Vaughan 1796-1889 DcLB 99
Cheney, Harry Morrison 1860- AmLegL
Cheney, James Addison 1927- WhoAm 90
Cheney, Janice Louanne 1954- WhoAmW 91
Cheney, John Max 1952- WhoSSW 91
Cheney, Larry 1886-1969 Ballpl 90
Cheney, Liana De Girolami 1942- WhoAmA 91
Cheney, Liana Degirolami 1942- WhoE 91
Cheney, Linda Gail 1949- WhoAmW 91
Cheney, Lynne Ann 1941- WhoAm 90, WhoAmW 91
Cheney, Lynne V 1941- News 90 [port]
Cheney, Max W. 1922- St&PR 91
Cheney, Meredith 1925- WhoAmW 91
Cheney, Paul E. 1927- St&PR 91
Cheney, Richard B. BioIn 16
Cheney, Richard B. 1941- WorAlBi
Cheney, Richard Bruce 1941- BiDrUSE 89
Cheney, Richard E. 1921- ODwPR 91
Cheney, Richard Eugene 1921- WhoAm 90
Cheney, Rita Mae 1951- WhoAmW 91
Cheney, Sheldon 1886-1980 WhoAmA 91N
Cheney, Theodore Albert 1928- WhoWrEP 89
Cheney, Thomas Charles 1868-1957 AmLegL
Cheney, Thomas Ward 1914- WhoAm 90
Cheney, Tom 1934- Ballpl 90
Cheney, Wendy Foster 1967- WhoEmL 91
Cheney, William A. 1923- St&PR 91
Cheney, William J. 1938- St&PR 91
Cheng, Boon Looi 1960- WhoSSW 91
Cheng, Ching Ho 1946-1989 BioIn 16
Cheng, Chu Yuan 1927- WhoWor 91
Cheng, David Hong 1920- WhoAm 90
Cheng, David Hung Sheng 1922- WhoAm 90
Cheng, David Keun 1918- WhoAm 90
Cheng, Dominic Toming 1949- WhoSSW 91
Cheng, Edward Teh-Chang 1946- WhoEmL 91
Cheng, Emily 1953- WhoAmA 91
Cheng, Franklin Yih 1936- WhoAm 90
Cheng, Fred Nai-Chung 1970- WhoWrEP 89
Cheng, Fu-Ding 1943- WhoAmA 91
Cheng, Herbert Su-Yuen 1929- WhoAm 90
Cheng, Hsien Kei 1923- WhoAm 90
Cheng, Irene Teresa 1954- WhoAmW 91, WhoE 91
Cheng, Jane Chi-ya 1954- WhoE 91
Cheng, Keith BiDrAPA 89
Cheng, Kenneth Tat-Chiu 1954- WhoEmL 91, WhoSSW 91
Cheng, Kuang Lu 1919- WhoAm 90, WhoWor 91
Cheng, Leslie Y BiDrAPA 89
Cheng, Lily W L BiDrAPA 89
Cheng, Linda Yi Hsien 1958- WhoEmL 91
Cheng, Myra BiDrAPA 89
Cheng, Nien 1915- BioIn 16
Cheng, Samson 1934- WhoWor 91
Cheng, Scarlet 1953- WhoWrEP 89
Cheng, Suan Soon 1953- WhoWor 91
Cheng, Thomas Clement 1930- WhoAm 90
Cheng, Tsen-Chung 1944- WhoAm 90
Cheng, Tsung O. 1925- WhoAm 90, WhoWor 91
Cheng, Tung Chao 1931- St&PR 91
Cheng, Wan-Lee 1945- WhoAm 90
Cheng, Wei-Yuan 1913- WhoWor 91
Cheng, Wilfred David 1948- WhoE 91
Cheng, William Wai Ling 1961- WhoEmL 91
Cheng, Yann-Chiou Wang 1949- WhoAmW 91
Cheng-Chun WomWR
Chenhall, Robert Gene 1923- WhoAm 90
Chenhall, Terry Stephen 1948- St&PR 91
Chenhalls, Anne Marie 1929- WhoAmW 91
Chenier, Clifton BioIn 16
Chenier, Yves Edouard BiDrAPA 89
Chennault, Anna Chan 1925- WhoAm 90, WhoAmW 91, WhoWor 91
Chennault, Claire 1890-1958 WorAlBi
Chennevieres-Pointel, marquis de 1820-1899 BioIn 16
Chenok, Philip Barry 1935- WhoAm 90
Chenoweth, Mrs. 1867-1936 EncPaPR 91
Chenoweth, Daniel Albert 1948- St&PR 91
Chenoweth, David M. 1949- ODwPR 91
Chenoweth, Dellzell WhoWrEP 89
Chenoweth, Francis A. 1819-1899 AmLegL
Chenoweth, J. Mark 1964- WhoSSW 91
Chenoweth, James M. 1931- St&PR 91
Chenoweth, Joe Elling 1936- WhoAm 90
Chenoweth, Rose Marie 1953- WhoEmL 91
Chenoweth, Vida S. 1938- IntWWM 90
Chentoff, Polia BioIn 16
Chenu, Marie-Dominique 1895-1990 BioIn 16
Chenven, Mark S 1948- BiDrAPA 89
Cheo, Peter Kiong-Liang 1930- WhoAm 90
Cheon, Sung Ai 1950- BiDrAPA 89
Cheops WorAlBi
Cheops, King of Egypt BioIn 16
Chepaitis, Elia BioIn 16
Chepiga, Pamela Rogers 1949- WhoEmL 91, WhoWor 91
Cheplen, Evelyn Cox 1923- WhoAmW 91
Chepow, Steven Barry 1943- St&PR 91
Chepponis, James Joseph 1956- IntWWM 90
Chepuru, Yadagiri BiDrAPA 89
Cher 1945- EncPR&S 89
Cher 1946- BioIn 16, WhoAm 90, WhoAmW 91, WorAlBi
Cher, Beatrice WhoAmA 91
Cheramie, Mildred 1928- WhoAmW 91
Cheran, Selvi 1949- BiDrAPA 89
Cherberg, John Andrew 1910- WhoAm 90
Cherbonnier, Alice Christie 1945- WhoE 91
Cherbuliez, Theodore BiDrAPA 89
Chercover, Murray 1929- WhoAm 90
Chercover, Murray H. 1929- St&PR 91
Chereau, Patrice BioIn 16
Chereau, Patrice 1944- CurBio 90 [port], IntWWM 90, WhoWor 91
Cherekos, George Steven 1928- St&PR 91
Cherem, Barbara Frances 1946- WhoAm 90
Cherenkov, Pavel 1904- WorAlBi
Cherenkov, Pavel Alexeyevich 1904- WhoAm 90, WhoWor 91
Cherenson, Lee 1929- ODwPR 91
Cherenzia, Peter Franklin 1937- St&PR 91
Cherepnin, Aleksandr Nikolaevich 1899-1977 BioIn 16
Chereskin, Alvin 1928- WhoAm 90
Cheret, Gustave Joseph 1838-1894 PenDiDA 89
Cherian, Annie BiDrAPA 89
Cherian, Dilip 1956- WhoWor 91
Cherian, Jacob 1935- St&PR 91
Cherian, Joy 1942- WhoAm 90
Cherian, Paul T BiDrAPA 89
Cherici, Coleen Ann 1950- WhoE 91
Cherici, Paolo 1952- IntWWM 90
Cherins, Robert H. 1940- St&PR 91
Cherins, Robert Howard 1940- WhoAm 90
Cheris, Elaine BioIn 16
Cheris, Samuel David 1945- WhoEmL 91
Cherkas, Constantine 1919- WhoAmA 91
Cherkas, Marshall S 1929- BiDrAPA 89
Cherkasky, Marny R 1946- BiDrAPA 89
Cherkasky, Martin 1911- WhoAm 90
Cherkasky, Rudy 1928- St&PR 91
Cherkassky, Shura 1911- CurBio 90 [port], IntWWM 90, PenDiMP
Cherken, Harry Sarkis, Jr. 1949- WhoEmL 91
Cherkis, Laura 1944- WhoAmW 91
Cherlin, Edward A BiDrAPA 89
Chermak, Gail Donna 1950- WhoEmL 91
Chermann, Jean Claude 1939- WhoWor 91
Chermayeff, Ivan 1932- BioIn 16, ConDes 90, WhoAmA 91
Chermayeff, Jane Clark BioIn 16
Chermayeff, Peter 1936- WhoAm 90
Chermayeff, Serge 1900- ConDes 90
Cherminova, M. BiDWomA
Chern, Shiing-Shen 1911- WhoAm 90
Chernaik, Stephen J 1948- BiDrAPA 89
Chernak, John A. 1929- St&PR 91
Chernenko, K. U. ConAu 132
Chernenko, Konstantin U 1911-1985 ConAu 132
Chernenko, Konstantin Ustinovich 1911-1985 BioIn 16
Cherner, Anne WhoWrEP 89
Cherner, Marvin 1924- WhoAm 90
Chernesky, Richard John 1939- WhoAm 90
Chernetzky, John BiDrAPA 89
Chernev, Melvin 1928- WhoAm 90
Cherney, Andrew Knox 1947- WhoEmL 91
Cherney, Brian 1942- IntWWM 90
Cherney, Carl D. 1952- St&PR 91
Cherney, James Alan 1948- WhoEmL 91
Cherney, Marvin WhoAmA 91N
Cherniack, Helen Wessel 1911- WhoAmW 91
Cherniack, Louis 1908- EncO&P 3
Cherniack, Neil Stanley 1931- WhoAm 90
Cherniack, Reuben Mitchell 1924- WhoAm 90
Cherniack, Saul Mark 1917- WhoAm 90
Chernichaw, Mark 1946- WhoAm 90
Chernick, Steven Roy 1949- St&PR 91
Chernikoff, Neil N. 1931- St&PR 91
Chernin, Fredric David 1939- St&PR 91, WhoAm 90
Chernin, Russell Scott 1957- WhoEmL 91
Chernish, Stanley Michael 1924- WhoAm 90, WhoWor 91
Cherno, Melvin 1929- WhoAm 90
Chernof, David 1935- WhoAm 90
Chernoff, Amoz Immanuel 1923- WhoAm 90, WhoE 91
Chernoff, Daniel Paregol 1935- WhoAm 90
Chernoff, Eugene M. 1926- St&PR 91
Chernoff, Herman 1923- WhoAm 90, WhoE 91
Chernoff, Hildegard 1926- St&PR 91
Chernoff, John Miller 1947- IntWWM 90
Chernoff, Martin 1943- St&PR 91
Chernoff, Mindy Lee 1957- WhoAmW 91
Chernoff, Nancy Robin WhoAmW 91
Chernoff, Sheryl Stern 1954- WhoEmL 91
Chernov, Viktor Mikhailovich 1873-1952 BioIn 16
Chernow, Allison 1958- WhoAmW 91
Chernow, Ann 1936- BiDWomA, WhoAmA 91
Chernow, Burt 1933- WhoAm 90, WhoAmA 91
Chernow, Claudia Groves BiDrAPA 89
Chernow, Claudia Groves 1957- WhoE 91
Chernow, David A. 1922- WhoAm 90
Chernow, Fred 1932- WhoAm 90
Chernus, Jack BiDrAPA 89
Chernus, Jack 1912-1989 BioIn 16
Cherny, Robert W 1943- ConAu 131
Cherny, Robert Wallace 1943- WhoAm 90
Chernyshevsky, Nikolay Gavrilovich 1828-1889 BioIn 16
Cheron, Phillip Scott 1952- WhoEmL 91
Cheroutes, Michael Louis 1940- WhoAm 90
Cherovsky, Erwin 1933- St&PR 91
Cherovsky, Erwin Louis 1933- WhoAm 90
Cherpes, James Lewis 1934- St&PR 91
Cherre, C. J. 1952?- BioIn 16
Cherrick, Bernard 1914-1988 BioIn 16
Cherrick, Henry Morton 1939- WhoAm 90
Cherry, Carol D. BioIn 16
Cherry, Charles Lewis 1926- WhoSSW 91, WhoWor 91
Cherry, Charles Walter 1939- St&PR 91
Cherry, Daniel Ronald 1948- WhoEmL 91
Cherry, Diane 1961- WhoE 91
Cherry, Don BioIn 16
Cherry, Don 1936- DrBIPA 90
Cherry, Dorothy BioIn 16
Cherry, Eagle-Eye BioIn 16
Cherry, Edward Earl 1926- WhoAm 90
Cherry, Francis Adams 1908-1965 BioIn 16
Cherry, Harold 1931- WhoAm 90
Cherry, Herbert S BiDrAPA 89
Cherry, Herman 1909- WhoAm 90, WhoAmA 91
Cherry, James Donald 1930- WhoAm 90
Cherry, James R., Jr. 1938- St&PR 91
Cherry, Joe Howard 1934- WhoSSW 91
Cherry, Joseph Andrew 1947- WhoSSW 91
Cherry, Karen J. 1938- St&PR 91
Cherry, Kathleen Ann 1946- ODwPR 91
Cherry, Kelly 1940- WhoWrEP 89
Cherry, Kenneth W. St&PR 91
Cherry, Kevin Patrick 1950- WhoSSW 91
Cherry, Mark Stuart 1957- WhoE 91
Cherry, Neneh BioIn 16
Cherry, Neneh 1964- ConMus 4 [port]
Cherry, Peter Ballard 1947- St&PR 91, WhoAm 90
Cherry, Richard L. 1936- St&PR 91
Cherry, Robert Douglas 1950- WhoEmL 91
Cherry, Robert Earl Patrick 1924- WhoAm 90
Cherry, Rona Beatrice 1948- WhoAm 90, WhoAmW 91
Cherry, Sabrina BiDrAPA 89
Cherry, Sandra Wilson 1941- WhoAmW 91
Cherry, Walter L. 1917- St&PR 91
Cherry, Walter Lorain 1917- WhoAm 90
Cherry, Wendell BioIn 16, WhoAm 90, WhoSSW 91
Cherry, Wendell 1935- St&PR 91
Cherry, William Ashley 1924- WhoAm 90
Cherry, William Bailey 1916- WhoSSW 91
Cherryh, C. J. 1942- RGTwCSF, WhoAm 90, WhoAmW 91
Cherryholmes, Anne AuBYP 90
Cherryholmes, James Gilbert 1917- WhoAm 90
Chertack, Melvin M. 1923- WhoAm 90
Chertkow, Louis 1945- St&PR 91
Chertoff, Harvey Ronald BiDrAPA 89
Chertoff, Judith M BiDrAPA 89
Chertoff, Lionel BiDrAPA 89
Chertoff, Michael BioIn 16
Chertok, David BioIn 16
Chertok, Haim BioIn 16
Chertok, Harvey BioIn 16
Chertok, Leon 1911- BiDrAPA 89
Chertok, Michael BioIn 16
Cherubini, Luigi 1760-1842 PenDiMP A
Cherubini, Victor Fred 1952- WhoEmL 91
Cherundolo, Robert Francis 1941- St&PR 91
Cheruvanky, Bharathi BiDrAPA 89
Cherven, Kenneth Patrick 1959- WhoSSW 91
Chervenak, Mary ODwPR 91
Chervin, Peter C. St&PR 91
Chervin, Ronda 1937- WhoWrEP 89
Chervitz, David Howard 1958- WhoEmL 91
Chervokas, John V 1936- ConAu 129
Chervokas, John Vincent 1936- WhoAm 90
Chervony, Daniel E BiDrAPA 89
Cherwin, Joel Ira 1942- WhoE 91
Chesak, Donna 1942- WhoAmW 91
Chesanow, Charles 1953- BiDrAPA 89
Chesarek, Ferdinand Joseph 1914- WhoAm 90
Chesbro, George C 1940- TwCCr&M 91
Chesbro, Jack 1874-1931 Ballpl 90 [port]
Chesebro, Caroline 1825-1873 FemiCLE
Chesebro, Kay B. 1930- St&PR 91
Chesebro, Robert E., Jr. 1937- St&PR 91
Cheseldine, Raymond M. BioIn 16
Chesen, Catherine Sue 1953- WhoAmW 91, WhoEmL 91
Chesen, Eli S 1944- BiDrAPA 89
Cheser, Ray NewAgMG
Cheshier, Stephen Robert 1940- WhoAm 90
Cheshire, Craig Gifford 1936- WhoAmA 91
Cheshire, David W 1927- BiDrAPA 89
Cheshire, Edney Brinn 1950- St&PR 91
Cheshire, McKinley, Jr. 1925- BiDrAPA 89
Cheshire, Molly Patterson 1961- WhoEmL 91
Cheshire, Sandra Kay 1958- WhoEmL 91
Cheshire, William Polk 1931- WhoAm 90
Chesimard, Joanne BioIn 16
Chesin, Sorrell Ely 1932- WhoE 91
Chesky, Frank Holmes 1933- BiDrAPA 89
Chesler, Bernice BioIn 16
Chesler, Don Bruce 1957- BiDrAPA 89
Chesler, Doris Adelle 1924- WhoSSW 91
Chesler, Victoria Aimee 1957- WhoAmW 91
Chesley, Paul Alexander 1946- WhoAmA 91
Chesley, Paul F. 1926- St&PR 91
Chesley, Robert NewYTBS 90
Chesner, Donald Walter 1944- WhoSSW 91
Chesnes, Bob 1921-1979 Ballpl 90
Chesney, Larry Wilfred 1952- WhoEmL 91
Chesney, Lee R, Jr 1920- WhoAmA 91
Chesney, Lee Roy, III 1945- WhoAmA 91
Chesney, Lee Roy, Jr. 1920- WhoAm 90, WhoWor 91
Chesney, Murphy Alvis, Jr. 1927- WhoAm 90

Chesney, Patricia Susan 1951- *WhoAmW 91, WhoSSW 91*
Chesney, Russell Wallace 1941- *WhoAm 90*
Chesney, Susan Talmadge 1943- *WhoAmW 91*
Chesney, W. Lamar 1949- *St&PR 91*
Chesni, Yves Gerard Alexandre 1920- *WhoWor 91*
Chesnick, Joyce Bailes 1925- *WhoAmW 91*
Chesnos, Ronald J. 1944- *St&PR 91*
Chesnut, Bruce Jones 1944- *WhoAm 90*
Chesnut, Carol Fitting 1937- *WhoAmW 91*
Chesnut, David Otis, III 1951- *WhoEmL 91*
Chesnut, Donald Blair 1932- *WhoAm 90*
Chesnut, Donald David 1932- *St&PR 91*
Chesnut, Franklin Gilmore 1919- *WhoAm 90*
Chesnut, Graham H 1926- *BiDrAPA 89*
Chesnut, John Edward 1925- *St&PR 91*
Chesnut, Mary B. 1823-1886 *BioAmW*
Chesnut, Mary Boykin 1823-1886 *FemiCLE*
Chesnutis, Gary F. 1957- *ODwPR 91*
Chesnutt, Charles W 1858-1932 *MajTwCW, WorAlBi*
Chesnutt, Charles Waddell *BioIn 16*
Chesnutt, Charles Waddell 1858-1932 *ShSCr 7 [port], TwCLC 39 [port]*
Chesrow, Cathleen Gwen 1947- *WhoWrEP 89*
Chess, Muriel Remes *WhoAmW 91, WhoE 91*
Chess, Richard B. 1953- *WhoSSW 91*
Chess, Stella 1914- *BiDrAPA 89*
Chess, Victoria 1939- *BioIn 16*
Chessa, Mario 1939- *St&PR 91*
Chessa, Paolo 1922- *ConDes 90*
Chessar, Isobel Jean *BiDrAPA 89*
Chessare, Joseph John 1924- *St&PR 91*
Chessen, Douglas H 1943- *BiDrAPA 89*
Chesser, Al H. 1914- *WhoAm 90*
Chesser, Barbara Russell 1941- *WhoWrEP 89*
Chesser, Douglas Stanley 1948- *WhoEmL 91*
Chesser, Kerry Royce 1956- *WhoEmL 91*
Chesser, Michael Joseph 1948- *St&PR 91*
Chessick, Richard D 1931- *BiDrAPA 89*
Chessler, Ronald J. 1957- *St&PR 91*
Chessley, Bara *WhoWrEP 89*
Chessman, Caryl 1921-1960 *WorAlBi*
Chesson, Eugene, Jr. 1928- *WhoAm 90*
Chesson, Gregory Lawrence *BioIn 16*
Chesson, Michael Bedout 1947- *WhoE 91*
Chesson, Reginald Eugene, Jr. 1953- *WhoEmL 91*
Chesson, Wesley Merritt 1927- *St&PR 91*
Chester, Alexander Campbell, III 1947- *WhoE 91*
Chester, Alice S *BiDrAPA 89*
Chester, Arthur Noble 1940- *WhoAm 90*
Chester, Barbara 1950- *WhoEmL 91*
Chester, Bob 1908- *BioIn 16*
Chester, Charles John 1953- *BiDrAPA 89*
Chester, Charlotte Wanetta *WhoAmA 91*
Chester, Clive Ronald 1930- *WhoE 91*
Chester, Douglas Barry 1952- *WhoE 91*
Chester, Douglas C. 1939- *St&PR 91*
Chester, Edward William 1935- *WhoAm 90, WhoWrEP 89*
Chester, Elizabeth 1637?-1719 *BiDEWW*
Chester, Francis 1936- *WhoSSW 91*
Chester, George M. 1922- *St&PR 91*
Chester, Giraud 1922- *WhoAm 90*
Chester, Hilda *Ballpl 90*
Chester, John Geoffrey 1951- *St&PR 91*
Chester, John Jonas 1920- *WhoAm 90*
Chester, Michael 1928- *AuBYP 90*
Chester, Nia Lane 1945- *WhoAmW 91*
Chester, Norman 1907-1986 *BioIn 16*
Chester, Norman Charles 1953- *WhoE 91*
Chester, P. Thomas 1947- *St&PR 91*
Chester, Peter *TwCCr&M 91*
Chester, Ralph Lawrence 1957- *BiDrAPA 89*
Chester, Russell Gilbert, Jr. 1947- *WhoEmL 91*
Chester, Slick 1900-1978 *DrBlPA 90*
Chester, Stephanie Ann 1951- *WhoEmL 91*
Chester, Tessa Rose 1950- *ConAu 130*
Chester, Thomas Jay 1951- *WhoEmL 91*
Chester, Thomas Lee 1949- *WhoEmL 91*
Chester, W. Lee *WhoAm 90*
Chester, W. Lee 1923- *St&PR 91*
Chester, Wayne Seagroves 1935- *WhoSSW 91*
Chester, Yvonne Elizabeth Wong 1958- *WhoAmW 91*
Chesterfield, Earl of 1694-1773 *DcLB 104 [port]*
Chesterfield, Elizabeth, Countess of *BiDEWW*
Chesterfield, John M. 1912- *St&PR 91*
Chesterfield, Norman *BioIn 16*
Chesterton, David 1930- *WhoAmA 91N*
Chesterton, G.K. 1874-1936 *BioIn 16, ConAu 132, DcLB 98 [port], MajTwCW, TwCCr&M 91*
Chesterton, G. K. 1874-1936 *WorAlBi*
Chesterton, G K 1874-1936 *WrPh*
Chesterton, Gilbert Keith 1874-1936 *BioIn 16, SpyFic*
Chestnov, Robert Eric 1948- *St&PR 91*
Chestnut, Harold 1917- *WhoAm 90*
Chestnut, Kathi Lynne 1959- *WhoEmL 91*
Chestnut, Lottie 1966- *WhoEmL 91*
Chestnut, Mark E. *St&PR 91*
Chestnut, Roberta 1940- *WhoAmW 91*
Chestnut, Wade Hampton, III 1944- *WhoWor 91*
Chestnutt, George Alexander, Jr. 1914- *WhoAm 90*
Chestnutwood, R.L. 1931- *St&PR 91*
Cheston, Charles Edward 1911- *WhoAm 90*
Cheston, George Morris 1917- *WhoAm 90*
Cheston, Sheila Carol 1958- *WhoEmL 91*
Cheston, Theodore C. 1922- *WhoAm 90*
Cheston, Warren Bruce 1926- *WhoAm 90*
Cheswick, Richard R. 1924- *St&PR 91*
Chet, Ilan 1939- *WhoWor 91*
Chetel, Gregory 1950- *WhoE 91*
Chetelat, Larree Daniel 1930- *WhoSSW 91*
Chetham, Charles *WhoAmA 91*
Chethlahe 1926-1984 *WhoAmA 91N*
Chetkovich, Michael N. 1916- *WhoAm 90*
Chetkowski, Ryszard Jerzy 1948- *WhoEmL 91*
Chetverikov, Sergei Sergeevich 1880-1959 *DcScB S2*
Chetwin, Grace *BioIn 16*
Chetwynd, Berry *ConAu 30NR*
Chetwynd, Lionel *WhoWor 91*
Chetwynd-Hayes, R 1919- *ConAu 30NR*
Cheung, Jeffrey 1950- *St&PR 91*
Cheung, John Yan-Poon 1950- *WhoSSW 91*
Cheung, Samson Si Sing 1952- *WhoWor 91*
Cheung, Siu-Fai 1948- *WhoWor 91*
Cheung, Tak Kee 1955- *WhoEmL 91*
Cheung, Yau Kay Tony 1952- *WhoWor 91*
Cheuse, Alan *BioIn 16*
Cheuvront, Thomas A. 1934- *St&PR 91*
Cheval, Ferdinand 1836-1924 *BioIn 16*
Cheval, Louis Joseph 1932- *WhoWor 91*
Chevalier, Albert 1862-1923 *OxCPMus*
Chevalier, Elizabeth Pickett 1896-1984 *LiHiK*
Chevalier, Gilles 1934- *St&PR 91*
Chevalier, Jacques E. 1926- *St&PR 91*
Chevalier, Jean-Pierre 1935- *WhoWor 91*
Chevalier, Marie George 1889- *EncO&P 3*
Chevalier, Maurice 1888-1972 *OxCPMus, WorAlBi*
Chevalier, Paul Edward 1939- *WhoAm 90*
Chevalier, Roger Alan 1949- *WhoAm 90*
Chevalier, Samuel Fletcher 1934- *St&PR 91, WhoAm 90, WhoE 91*
Chevalier De Saint Georges, Joseph B 1739-1799 *DrBlPA 90*
Chevallard, Philip Carl 1950- *IntWWM 90*
Chevallier, Andre-Marc 1930- *WhoWor 91*
Chevannes, Paul Hayden 1952- *WhoEmL 91*
Chevassus, Antoine Francois 1963- *WhoWor 91*
Chevenement, Jean-Pierre 1939- *BiDFrPL, WhoWor 91*
Chevers, Wilda Anita Yarde *WhoAmW 91*
Cheves, Harry Langdon, Jr. 1924- *WhoSSW 91, WhoWor 91*
Cheves, Langdon 1776-1857 *EncABHB 6 [port]*
Chevillard, Camille 1859-1923 *PenDiMP*
Chevins, Anthony *BioIn 16*
Chevins, Anthony Charles 1921- *WhoAm 90*
Chevins, Christopher M 1951- *WhoAmA 91*
Chevis, Cheryl Ann 1947- *WhoEmL 91*
Chevray, Rene 1937- *WhoAm 90*
Chevremont, Evaristo Ribera *HispWr 90*
Chevrette, Maurice 1942- *BiDrAPA 89*
Chevreuil, Leon Marie Martial 1852-1939 *EncO&P 3*
Chevreul, Michel Eugene 1786-1889 *BioIn 16, EncO&P 3*
Chevrier, Jean Marc 1916- *WhoAm 90*
Chevrillon, Olivier 1929- *WhoWor 91*
Chevrolet, Louis 1878-1941 *EncABHB 4 [port]*
Chevska, Maria 1948- *BiDWomA*
Chew, Anne *BiDEWW*
Chew, Elizabeth 1959- *WhoE 91*
Chew, Eng Chuan 1950- *WhoWor 91*
Chew, Frank Stephens 1937- *St&PR 91*
Chew, Geoffrey Alexander 1940- *IntWWM 90*
Chew, Geoffrey Foucar 1924- *WhoAm 90*
Chew, Harry 1925- *WhoAmA 91N*
Chew, James Albert 1946- *WhoSSW 91*
Chew, Leonard Guan 1941- *WhoWor 91*
Chew, Lim Kian 1949- *WhoWor 91*
Chew, Mary Catherine *WhoAmW 91*
Chew, Pamela Christine 1953- *WhoEmL 91*
Chew, Paul Albert 1925- *WhoAmA 91, WhoE 91*
Chew, Robert Z., III 1953- *ODwPR 91*
Chew, Ruth 1920- *BioIn 16, ConAu 31NR*
Chew, William H. *St&PR 91*
Chew-Freidenberg, Deanna Eileen 1952- *WhoEmL 91*
Chewett, Jocelyn 1906-1979 *BiDWomA*
Chewett, William Cameron 1828-1897 *DcCanB 12*
Chewning, Richard Carter 1933- *WhoAm 90*
Chewning, Robert Wills 1929- *WhoAm 90*
Chey, William Yoon 1930- *WhoAm 90*
Cheyer, Thomas Francis 1935- *St&PR 91*
Cheyette, Irving 1904- *IntWWM 90, WhoWrEP 89*
Cheyette, Ruth Marcus 1918- *WhoSSW 91*
Cheyne, Ian *St&PR 91*
Cheyne, Lisa Wilson 1959- *WhoE 91*
Cheyney, Arnold B 1926- *WhoWrEP 89*
Cheyney, Curtis Paul, III 1942- *WhoE 91, WhoWor 91*
Cheyney, Harry Stanton 1926- *St&PR 91*
Cheyney, Peter 1896-1951 *TwCCr&M 91*
Cheyney, Reginald Southouse 1896-1951 *SpyFic*
Cheysson, Claude 1920- *WhoWor 91*
Cheysson, Jean-Christian *BioIn 16*
Chezem, Curtis Gordon 1924- *WhoAm 90*
Chezy, Wilhelmine von 1783-1856 *EncCoWW*
Chhabria, Kiki Kanayalal 1934- *WhoWor 91*
Chi, Carl C 1940- *BiDrAPA 89*
Chi, Chen 1912- *WhoAmA 91*
Chi, Chia-Dann 1936- *St&PR 91*
Chi, Donald Nan-Hua 1939- *WhoE 91*
Chi, Youn Suck *BiDrAPA 89*
Chi-Lites *EncPR&S 89*
Chia, Edward H S *BiDrAPA 89*
Chia, Hsin Pao 1920- *St&PR 91*
Chia, Pei-Yuan 1939- *WhoAm 90*
Chia, Sandro 1946- *BioIn 16, CurBio 90 [port], WhoAmA 91*
Chia, Vivien Su 1945- *WhoEmL 91*
Chia, Yen On *BioIn 16*
Chiado, Paul S. 1930- *St&PR 91*
Chiaia, Ercole *EncO&P 3, EncPaPR 91*
Chiancone, Aldo 1936- *WhoWor 91*
Chianese, Carla Ann 1960- *WhoAmW 91*
Chiang Ching-Kuo 1910-1988 *AnObit 1988*
Chiang Kai-Shek 1887-1975 *WorAlBi*
Chiang, Benjamin Bi-Nin 1929- *WhoWor 91*
Chiang, Ch'ing 1910- *BioIn 16*
Chiang, Ching-kuo 1910-1988 *BioIn 16*
Chiang, Elizabeth 1953- *BiDrAPA 89*
Chiang, George Djia-Chee 1938- *WhoE 91*
Chiang, Hsiao-wen *BioIn 16*
Chiang, Huai Chang 1915- *WhoAm 90*
Chiang, Julie JoLee 1947- *WhoAmW 91*
Chiang, Kai-shek 1887-1975 *BioIn 16*
Chiang, Martin Kuang Ping 1933- *WhoWor 91*
Chiang, P.C. 1949- *WhoWor 91*
Chiang, Peter 1954- *WhoE 91*
Chiang, Samuel Edward 1959- *WhoSSW 91*
Chiang, Shiao-Hung 1929- *WhoE 91*
Chiang, Stephen C *BiDrAPA 89*
Chiang, Wen-Li 1946- *WhoEmL 91*
Chiang, Yawen Lee 1950- *WhoE 91*
Chiang Kai-Shek, Madame 1899- *WhoWor 91*
Ch'iao, Sung *ConAu 132*
Chiapella, Anne Page 1942- *WhoE 91*
Chiapella, Edward Emile 1889-1951 *WhoAmA 91N*
Chiappa, Francis William 1949- *WhoEmL 91*
Chiappardi, Stephanie Corp 1953- *WhoEmL 91*
Chiappe, Jean 1878-1940 *BiDFrPL*
Chiappelli, Fredi 1921-1990 *ConAu 131*
Chiapperini, Patricia Bignoli 1946- *WhoAmW 91*
Chiappetta, Carl Joseph 1948- *BiDrAPA 89*
Chiappetta, Thomas 1955- *ODwPR 91*
Chiara, Alan Robert 1936- *WhoAmA 91*
Chiara, Maria 1939- *IntWWM 90*
Chiara, Maria 1942- *PenDiMP*
Chiaramonte, Joseph Salvatore 1938- *WhoE 91*
Chiaramonte, Steven 1956- *WhoEmL 91*
Chiaramonte, Steven C. 1956- *St&PR 91*
Chiarandini, Irene L *BiDrAPA 89*
Chiarella, Peter Ralph 1932- *WhoAm 90*
Chiarella, Sam Vincent 1948- *WhoSSW 91*
Chiarelli, Brunetto Antonio 1934- *WhoWor 91*
Chiarelli, James Joseph 1908- *WhoAm 90*
Chiarelli, Joseph 1946- *WhoE 91, WhoWor 91*
Chiarello, Anthony James 1943- *St&PR 91*
Chiarello, Carmelo J *BiDrAPA 89*
Chiarello, Donald Frederick 1940- *WhoAm 90*
Chiarello, Robert J 1947- *BiDrAPA 89*
Chiarenza, Carl 1935- *WhoAm 90, WhoAmA 91*
Chiarenza, Frank John 1926- *WhoAm 90*
Chiari, Mario 1909-1989 *BioIn 16*
Chiari, Roberto F. 1905-1981 *BioIn 16*
Chiari, Rodolfo E. 1870-1937 *BioIn 16*
Chiariello, Luigi 1943- *WhoWor 91*
Chiarucci, Vincent A. 1929- *WhoAm 90*
Chiasson, Charles Edward 1947- *St&PR 91*
Chiasson, Donat 1930- *WhoAm 90*
Chiasson, John P 1913- *BiDrAPA 89*
Chiat, Jay *BioIn 16*
Chiat, Jay 1931- *WhoAm 90*
Chiavario, Nancy Anne 1947- *WhoAmW 91*
Chiaverini, John Edward 1924- *St&PR 91, WhoAm 90, WhoWor 91*
Chiazze, Leonard, Jr. 1934- *WhoAm 90, WhoE 91*
Chiba, Kaoru 1928- *IntWWM 90*
Chiba, Mototsugu 1935- *WhoWor 91*
Chiba, Shigeru *Ballpl 90*
Chiba, Tanetaka 1922- *WhoWor 91*
Chibas, Eduardo 1907-1951 *BioIn 16*
Chibbett, Harold 1900-1978 *EncO&P 3*
Chibeau, Edmond Victor 1947- *WhoEmL 91*
Chicago *EncPR&S 89*
Chicago, Judy 1939- *BiDWomA, BioIn 16, WhoAm 90, WhoAmA 91, WhoAmW 91, WhoWrEP 89*
Chicaneau, Pierre *PenDiDA 89*
Chicco, Giacomo Franco 1958- *WhoE 91*
Chicco, Gianfranco 1951- *ODwPR 91*
Chicherin, Georgii Vasil'evich 1872-1936 *BioIn 16*
Chichester, Connie Elizabeth 1954- *WhoEmL 91*
Chichester, David Nelson 1945- *St&PR 91*
Chichester, Frederick Donald 1937- *WhoE 91*
Chichester, Susan Mary 1936- *WhoAmW 91*
Chichester Clark, Emma 1955- *ConAu 132*
Chichetto, James William *WhoWrEP 89*
Chichon, Reginald Henry 1952- *WhoWor 91*
Chichura, Diane B *WhoAmA 91*
Chichura, Diane Bassi 1932- *WhoE 91*
Chick, Charles Eugene 1934- *St&PR 91*
Chick, Harriette 1875-1977 *DcScB S2*
Chickataubut *WhNaAH*
Chickering, Howard Allen 1942- *WhoE 91*
Chickering, Laura Lucille 1948- *WhoAmW 91*
Chickering, Marjorie *AuBYP 90*
Chickey, Rebecca Butler 1959- *WhoAmW 91*
Chicoine, Francis G. 1931- *St&PR 91*
Chicoine, Jerry L. 1942- *St&PR 91*
Chicorel, Marietta S. *WhoAm 90, WhoAmW 91*
Chidambaram, Rajagopala 1936- *WhoWor 91*
Chidananda, Swami 1916- *EncO&P 3*
Chiddix, James A. 1945- *St&PR 91*
Chiddix, James Alan 1945- *WhoE 91*
Chideckel, David Barry *BiDrAPA 89*
Chidester, Otis Holden 1903- *WhoAm 90*
Chidley, Katharine *FemiCLE*
Chidley, Katherine *BiDEWW*
Chidley, William G. 1951- *St&PR 91*
Chidnese, Patrick N. 1940- *WhoSSW 91*
Chieco, Michael Gerard 1953- *WhoEmL 91*
Chieco, Pasquale 1948- *WhoWor 91*
Chief Joseph *WhNaAH*
Chief Eagle, Charles Lince 1961- *WhoAmA 91*
Chiefari, Janet 1942- *BioIn 16*
Chieffalo, Mario Victor 1934- *WhoWor 91*
Chieffo, Clifford Toby 1937- *WhoAmA 91*
Chieger, Kathryn J. 1948- *ODwPR 91*
Chiego, William J 1943- *WhoAmA 91*
Chiel, Arthur A. 1920-1983 *BioIn 16*
Chielanski-Lallinger, Manuela von *BioIn 16*
Ch'ien Chung-shu 1910- *ConAu 130, MajTwCW*
Chien, Ching-Piao 1933- *BiDrAPA 89*
Chien, Kuei-Yuan 1941- *WhoE 91*
Ch'ien, Mu 1895- *BioIn 16*
Chien, Norbert Wei 1955- *WhoEmL 91*
Chien, Ring-Ling 1952- *WhoEmL 91*
Chieng, Ching-Chang 1946- *WhoWor 91*
Chiepe, Gaositwe Keagakwa Tibe 1922- *WhoWor 91*
Chierchia, Madeline Carmella 1943- *WhoAmW 91*
Chieri, Pericle Adriano C. 1905- *WhoAm 90, WhoSSW 91, WhoWor 91*
Chiericozzi, Pete R. 1943- *St&PR 91*
Chiesa, John Richard 1924- *WhoWrEP 89*

Chiesi, Alexander Robert 1937- *St&PR 91*
Chiffer, Floyd 1956- *Ballpl 90*
Chigas, Vessarios George *St&PR 91N*
Chiger, Jeffrey Stuart 1949- *WhoSSW 91*
Chigier, Norman 1933- *WhoAm 90*
Chigorin, Mikhail Ivanovich 1850-1908 *BioIn 16*
Chigos, David 1933- *WhoAm 90*
Chih, Chung-Ying 1916- *WhoWor 91*
Chihara, Carol Joyce 1941- *WhoAmW 91*
Chihara, Hideaki 1927- *WhoWor 91*
Chihorek, John Paul 1943- *WhoWor 91*
Chihuly, Dale Patrick 1941- *WhoAm 90, WhoAmA 91*
Chikamatsu Monzaemon 1653-1724 *EncJap*
Chikane, Frank *BioIn 16*
Chikofsky, Elliot Jay 1955- *WhoE 91*
Chila, Anthony George 1937- *WhoWor 91*
Chilaka, James Oguike 1942- *WhoE 91*
Chilakamarri, Ramesh 1954- *BiDrAPA 89*
Chilakamarri, Srinivas *BiDrAPA 89*
Chilcot, Harriet 1754-1784 *FemiCLE*
Chilcote, Lee A. 1908- *St&PR 91*
Chilcote, Lee A., Jr. 1942- *St&PR 91*
Chilcote, Lugean Lester 1929- *WhoAm 90*
Chilcote, Ronald H 1935- *WhoWrEP 89*
Chilcote, Samuel Day, Jr. 1937- *WhoAm 90, WhoE 91, WhoWor 91*
Chilcott, Barbara 1923- *OxCCanT*
Chilcott, Edward Hidinger 1948- *WhoE 91, WhoEmL 91*
Child, Anthony H. 1951- *St&PR 91*
Child, Arthur J.E. 1910- *St&PR 91*
Child, Arthur James Edward 1910- *WhoAm 90*
Child, Charles Judson, Jr. 1923- *WhoAm 90*
Child, Francis James 1825-1896 *BioIn 16*
Child, Frank Clayton 1921- *WhoAm 90*
Child, Harold L. 1920- *St&PR 91*
Child, Harry Ray 1928- *WhoSSW 91*
Child, Irvin L. 1915- *EncPaPR 91*
Child, Irvin Long 1915- *WhoAm 90*
Child, John Sowden, Jr. 1944- *WhoE 91, WhoWor 91*
Child, Joy Challender 1952- *WhoAmW 91, WhoEmL 91*
Child, Julia *BioIn 16*
Child, Julia 1912- *WorAlBi*
Child, Julia McWilliams 1912- *WhoAm 90, WhoAmW 91*
Child, Kent 1951- *St&PR 91*
Child, Lydia Maria 1802-1880 *BioAmW, FemiCLE, WhNaAH*
Child, Margaret Smillie 1929- *WhoAmW 91*
Child, Paul *BioIn 16*
Child, Philip 1898-1978 *BioIn 16*
Child, Richard Washburn 1881-1935 *BioIn 16*
Child, Ross *WhoWrEP 89*
Child, Thomas 1841?-1898 *BioIn 16*
Child, Vern D. 1944- *St&PR 91*
Childe, David Cyril 1963- *WhoE 91*
Childers, Betty Bivins 1913-1982 *WhoAmA 91N*
Childers, Bruce S. 1938- *St&PR 91*
Childers, Carol Lynn *BiDrAPA 89*
Childers, Cecil Adison, Jr. 1933- *BiDrAPA 89*
Childers, Charles Eugene 1932- *WhoAm 90*
Childers, Erskine 1870-1922 *BioIn 16, TwCCr&M 91*
Childers, Gary Steve 1960- *St&PR 91*
Childers, James Howard 1942- *St&PR 91*
Childers, James Monroe, IV 1953- *WhoEmL 91*
Childers, Joe F. 1928- *St&PR 91*
Childers, John Henry 1930- *WhoWor 91*
Childers, Judy Kaye 1946- *WhoAmW 91, WhoSSW 91*
Childers, Kathryn Clark 1947- *WhoSSW 91*
Childers, Malcolm Graeme 1945- *WhoAmA 91*
Childers, Michael Wayne 1945- *St&PR 91*
Childers, Norman Franklin 1910- *WhoAm 90*
Childers, Perry Robert 1932- *WhoAm 90, WhoSSW 91, WhoWor 91*
Childers, Richard Lee 1930- *WhoSSW 91*
Childers, Robert Erskine 1870-1922 *SpyFic*
Childers, Robert Lawson 1948- *WhoEmL 91*
Childers, Russell 1915- *MusmAFA*
Childers, Sheri Diane 1954- *WhoAmW 91*
Childers, Susan Lynn 1948- *WhoAmW 91*
Childress, Alice *EarBlAP*
Childress, Alice 1920- *AuBYP 90, BioIn 16, DrBlPA 90, FemiCLE, MajTwCW, NotWoAT, WhoAm 90*
Childress, Allen Bruce, Jr. 1942- *WhoSSW 91*
Childress, Alvin 1907?-1986 *DrBlPA 90*
Childress, Alvin 1908-1986 *EarBlAP*
Childress, Ann Catherine *BiDrAPA 89*
Childress, Barry Lee 1941- *WhoWor 91*
Childress, Dennis Robert 1945- *WhoEmL 91*
Childress, J. Donald 1948- *WhoSSW 91*
Childress, James Franklin 1940- *WhoAm 90*
Childress, James Gary 1947- *St&PR 91*
Childress, James J. 1942- *WhoAm 90*
Childress, Juanita Cherryl 1959- *WhoEmL 91*
Childress, Kristie Elaine Johnston 1956- *WhoEmL 91*
Childress, Margie Faye 1954- *WhoAmW 91*
Childress, Mark *BioIn 16*
Childress, Phyllis Ann 1937- *WhoAmW 91*
Childress, Rocky 1962- *Ballpl 90*
Childress, Scott Julius 1926- *WhoAm 90*
Childress, Steven Alan 1959- *WhoEmL 91*
Childress, Walter Dabney, III 1943- *WhoSSW 91*
Childress, William Dale 1933- *WhoWrEP 89*
Childs, Alan John 1962- *IntWWM 90*
Childs, Allen 1941- *BiDrAPA 89*
Childs, Barney Sanford 1926- *IntWWM 90*
Childs, Barton 1916- *WhoAm 90*
Childs, Bernard 1910-1985 *WhoAmA 91N*
Childs, Brevard Springs 1923- *WhoAm 90*
Childs, Carole Mai 1940- *WhoAmW 91*
Childs, Catherine Oeland 1920- *WhoE 91*
Childs, Cupid 1867-1912 *Ballpl 90*
Childs, David 1933- *ConAu 31NR*
Childs, David Thompson 1938- *IntWWM 90*
Childs, Diana Mary *St&PR 91*
Childs, Donnalea S 1932- *BiDrAPA 89*
Childs, Edward *EncO&P 3*
Childs, Elizabeth *BiDrAPA 89*
Childs, Frances Sergeant 1901-1988 *BioIn 16*
Childs, Frank Leighton 1944- *St&PR 91*
Childs, Gayle Bernard 1907- *WhoWor 91*
Childs, Hoyt Abner, Jr. 1945- *WhoSSW 91*
Childs, J. Mabon 1922- *St&PR 91*
Childs, James William 1935- *WhoAm 90*
Childs, John David 1939- *WhoWor 91*
Childs, John F. 1909- *St&PR 91*
Childs, John Farnsworth *AuBYP 90*
Childs, John Farnsworth 1909- *WhoAm 90*
Childs, Julian Bruce 1949- *WhoWor 91*
Childs, Julie 1950- *WhoEmL 91*
Childs, Lucinda *BioIn 16*
Childs, Lucinda 1940- *WhoAm 90*
Childs, Marjorie May Victoria 1918- *WhoAm 90, WhoAmW 91*
Childs, Marquis 1903-1990 *WorAlBi*
Childs, Marquis W 1903-1990 *ConAu 132, CurBio 90N, NewYTBS 90 [port]*
Childs, Marquis William 1903-1990 *BioIn 16, WhoWor 91*
Childs, Mary Jane 1936- *WhoAmW 91*
Childs, Maryanna 1910- *WhoWrEP 89*
Childs, Morris Elsmere 1923- *WhoAm 90*
Childs, Rand Hampton 1949- *WhoSSW 91*
Childs, Richard M 1929- *BiDrAPA 89*
Childs, Ronald Frank 1939- *WhoAm 90*
Childs, Rosemary Burke 1958- *WhoE 91*
Childs, Sally *BioIn 16*
Childs, Samuel S. 1863-1925 *WorAlBi*
Childs, Sheldon Mills 1922- *St&PR 91*
Childs, Shirle Moone 1936- *WhoAmW 91*
Childs, Steve Douglas 1956- *WhoSSW 91*
Childs, Terry A 1960- *WhoWrEP 89*
Childs, Thea Douglas Wise 1924- *WhoAmW 91*
Childs, Toni *BioIn 16*
Childs, Wylie Jones 1922- *WhoAm 90*
Chiles, Catherine *BiDrAPA 89*
Chiles, James 1798-1883 *AmLegL*
Chiles, John Adair 1940- *BiDrAPA 89*
Chiles, Lawton *BioIn 16*
Chiles, Lawton Mainor 1930- *WhoAm 90, WhoSSW 91*
Chiles, Lois *BioIn 16*
Chiles, Rich 1949- *Ballpl 90*
Chiles, Ross Pershing 1939- *WhoSSW 91*
Chiles, Stephen Michael 1942- *WhoAm 90*
Chilian, George William *St&PR 91*
Chilingarian, George Varos 1929- *WhoAm 90*
Chilingirian Quartet *PenDiMP*
Chilingirian, Levon *PenDiMP*
Chilingirian, Levon 1948- *IntWWM 90*
Chilivis, Nickolas Peter 1931- *WhoAm 90*
Chillida, Eduardo 1924- *BioIn 16*
Chillida Juantegui, Eduardo 1924- *WhoWor 91*
Chilly *WhoWrEP 89*
Chilman, Catherine Earles Street 1914- *WhoAm 90*
Chilman, John Howard 1932- *BiDrAPA 89*
Chilson, Nancy Lee 1944- *WhoAmW 91*
Chilstrom, Herbert Walfred 1931- *WhoAm 90*
Chilton, Alice Pleasance Hunter 1911- *WhoWor 91*
Chilton, Bradley Stuart, Jr. 1953- *WhoSSW 91*
Chilton, Constance *BioIn 16*
Chilton, Fred 1944- *WhoAmA 91*
Chilton, Horace Thomas 1923- *WhoAm 90*
Chilton, Jeanne L. *ODwPR 91*
Chilton, Kathryn Ward 1930- *WhoAmW 91*
Chilton, Lynn Louise Ambroz 1948- *WhoAmW 91*
Chilton, Mary-Dell Matchett 1939- *WhoAm 90, WhoAmW 91*
Chilton, Nick Ray 1946- *St&PR 91*
Chilton, Raymond Lee, Jr. 1936- *St&PR 91*
Chilton, St. John Poindexter 1909- *WhoAm 90*
Chiluly, Dale *PenDiDA 89*
Chilver, Henry *BioIn 16*
Chilver, Henry 1926- *WhoWor 91*
Chilvers, Derek 1940- *St&PR 91, WhoAm 90*
Chilvers, John James 1924- *St&PR 91*
Chimel, Robert George 1953- *WhoEmL 91*
Chimenti, James J. 1955- *St&PR 91*
Chimenti, Ronald Christopher 1944- *St&PR 91*
Chimento, John F. 1938- *St&PR 91*
Chimerine, Eileen 1942- *WhoE 91*
Chimerine, Lawrence 1940- *WhoAm 90*
Chimes, Philip Richard 1949- *WhoEmL 91*
Chimes, Thomas James 1921- *WhoAmA 91*
Chimiak, Susan Claire 1965- *WhoEmL 91*
Chimick, Claire Bessie Reifenheiser 1933- *WhoAmW 91*
Chimoff, Rapheal 1933- *St&PR 91*
Chimples, Constantine George 1948- *St&PR 91*
Chimples, George 1924- *WhoAm 90, WhoE 91*
Chimples, Thomas 1959- *St&PR 91*
Chimsky, Mark Evan 1955- *WhoAm 90*
Chimy, Jerome Isidore 1919- *WhoAm 90*
Ch'in Shih-huang, Emperor of China 259BC-210BC *BioIn 16*
Chin, Ai Kyung 1949- *BiDrAPA 89*
Chin, Albert *BioIn 16*
Chin, Alexander Foster 1937- *WhoSSW 91*
Chin, Ark Geow 1924- *WhoAm 90*
Chin, Carolyn Sue 1947- *WhoAm 90*
Chin, Cecilia Hui-Hsin *WhoAm 90, WhoAmW 91, WhoE 91*
Chin, Cindy Lai 1957- *WhoAmW 91, WhoEmL 91*
Chin, Cynthia D. *St&PR 91*
Chin, Danny 1960- *WhoE 91*
Chin, Daryl 1953- *WhoWrEP 89*
Chin, Der-Tau 1939- *WhoE 91*
Chin, Gilbert Yukyu 1934- *WhoAm 90*
Chin, Gordon 1948- *BioIn 16*
Chin, Hong Woo 1935- *WhoSSW 91, WhoWor 91*
Chin, Hsiao-Yi 1921- *WhoWor 91*
Chin, James Kee-Hong 1934- *WhoWor 91*
Chin, James Ying 1953- *WhoEmL 91*
Chin, Janet Jue 1930- *WhoAmW 91*
Chin, Janet Sau-Ying 1949- *WhoAmW 91*
Chin, Kenneth 1950- *St&PR 91*
Chin, Kim Hock 1957- *WhoWor 91*
Chin, Larry Wu-Tai *BioIn 16*
Chin, Lung *BioIn 16, NewYTBS 90*
Chin, Maria Theresa 1959- *WhoSSW 91*
Chin, Marilyn 1955- *ConAu 129*
Chin, Marilyn Mei Ling 1955- *WhoWrEP 89*
Ch'in, Michael Kuo-hsing 1921- *WhoWor 91*
Chin, Penny 1948- *WhoEmL 91*
Chin, Ric 1935- *WhoAmA 91*
Chin, Richard 1946- *BioIn 16*
Chin, Robert Allen 1950- *WhoSSW 91*
Chin, Sherry 1951- *WhoEmL 91*
Chin, Sue SooneMarian *WhoAmW 91, WhoWor 91*
Chin, Sylvia Fung 1949- *WhoAmW 91*
Chin, Tin S *BiDrAPA 89*
Chin, Wayne Tong Fe 1940- *WhoE 91*
Chinard, Francis Pierre 1918- *WhoAm 90*
Chinard, Jeanne *WhoAmW 91*
Chinburg, Kenneth G 1921- *BiDrAPA 89*
Chinea-Varela, Migdia 1952- *WhoAmW 91*
Chinen, Allan Bruce *BiDrAPA 89*
Ch'ing *PenDiDA 89*
Ch'ing Sheng-tsu 1654-1722 *BioIn 16*
Ching, Alfred Y T 1927- *BiDrAPA 89*
Ching, Chauncey T.K. 1940- *WhoWrEP 89*
Ching, Cyrus S. 1876-1967 *BioIn 16*
Ching, Dorothy K. 1926- *St&PR 91*
Ching, Eric San Hing 1951- *WhoEmL 91*
Ching, Frank 1940- *ConAu 129*
Ching, Hung Wo 1912- *St&PR 91*
Ching, Larry Fong Chow 1912- *WhoWor 91*
Ching, Laureen *WhoWrEP 89*
Ching, Louis Michael 1956- *WhoEmL 91*
Ching, Norman K.Y. 1932- *St&PR 91*
Ching, Philip H. 1931- *St&PR 91, WhoAm 90*
Ching, Wesley H. H. 1949- *WhoEmL 91*
Ching-hsia, Lin *WhoWor 91*
Chingren, Amanda M. *BioIn 16*
Chinh, Truong 1908-1988 *BioIn 16*
Chini, Galileo 1873-1956 *PenDiDA 89*
Chinigo, Salvatore A *BiDrAPA 89*
Chiniquy, Charles 1809-1899 *DcCanB 12*
Chinitz, Jody Anne Kolb 1953- *WhoAmW 91*
Chink, Alfred Carl 1936- *St&PR 91*
Chinmoy, Sri *NewAgMG*
Chinmoy, Sri 1931- *EncO&P 3, NewAgE 90*
Chinn and Chapman *OxCPMus*
Chinn, Herman Isaac 1913- *WhoAm 90*
Chinn, Nicky 1945- *OxCPMus*
Chinn, Peggy Lois 1941- *WhoAmW 91*
Chinn, Phyllis Zweig 1941- *WhoAmW 91*
Chinn, Robert Carson 1916- *WhoAm 90*
Chinn, Terrance A 1943- *BiDrAPA 89*
Chinn, Thomas Wayne 1909- *WhoWor 91*
Chinn, W. Franklyn *BioIn 16*
Chinn, Wesley Earl 1946- *St&PR 91*
Chinn-Hechter, Mamie May 1951- *WhoAmW 91, WhoEmL 91*
Chinnery, Carl Lloyd 1941- *St&PR 91*
Chinnery, Michael Alistair 1933- *WhoAm 90*
Chinni, Charles Ross 1944- *WhoAm 90*
Chinni, Peter Anthony 1928- *WhoAm 90, WhoAmA 91*
Chinoy, Helen Krich 1922- *BioIn 16, NotWoAT, WhoAm 90*
Chintapalli, Girija Sankar *BiDrAPA 89*
Chioco, Carmen Warren *BiDrAPA 89*
Chioco, Jose Sideo *BiDrAPA 89*
Chiodi, Charles Karoly 1932- *WhoE 91*
Chiodo, Gayle *BioIn 16*
Chiodo, Vincent Robert 1955- *WhoE 91, WhoEmL 91*
Chiogioji, Melvin Hiroaki 1939- *WhoAm 90*
Chiong, Desmond B 1949- *BiDrAPA 89*
Chiorazzi, Mary Lorraine 1944- *BiDrAPA 89*
Chiostri, Luigi *PenDiMP*
Chiou, George Chung-Yih 1934- *WhoAm 90*
Chiovetti, Robert, Jr. 1946- *WhoSSW 91*
Chiozza, Lou 1910-1971 *Ballpl 90*
Chip, William Waddington 1948- *WhoEmL 91*
Chipande, Alberto *WhoWor 91*
Chipchase, Robert *PenDiDA 89*
Chipka, Stephen Thomas 1953- *WhoSSW 91*
Chipkin, Irving 1912- *BiDrAPA 89*
Chipman, Bob 1918-1973 *Ballpl 90*
Chipman, Dennis C, Jr. 1934- *BiDrAPA 89*
Chipman, John *BioIn 16*
Chipman, John Somerset 1926- *WhoAm 90*
Chipman, Samuel 1790-1891 *DcCanB 12*
Chipman, Susan Elizabeth 1946- *WhoAmW 91*
Chipouras, Susan Cathleen Massina 1956- *St&PR 91*
Chipouras, Susan Massina 1956- *WhoEmL 91*
Chipp, Donald Leslie 1925- *BioIn 16*
Chippendale, Thomas 1718-1779 *PenDiDA 89, WorAlBi*
Chippendale, Thomas 1749-1822 *PenDiDA 89*
Chipperfield, Joseph Eugene 1912-1980? *AuBYP 90*
Chirac, Jacques 1932- *BioIn 16, WorAlBi*
Chirac, Jacques Rene 1932- *BiDFrPL, WhoWor 91*
Chircop, Michael Francis 1952- *WhoSSW 91*
Chirello, Stephen M. 1955- *ODwPR 91*
Chirgwin, G H 1854-1922 *OxCPMus*
Chirgwin, Thomas D. 1944- *St&PR 91*
Chiriboga, David Anthony 1941- *WhoSSW 91*
Chiriboga, Hernando Alfonso 1960- *WhoWor 91*
Chirico, Dominick F 1911- *BiDrAPA 89*
Chirico, Giorgio De 1888- *WorAlBi*
Chirigos, Michael Anthony 1924- *WhoE 91*
Chirikov, Alexei Ilyich 1703-1748 *EncCRAm*
Chirillo, Antonella Vanda 1962- *WhoE 91*
Chirlian, Paul Michael 1930- *WhoAm 90*
Chirlin, Elaine S. 1951- *BiDrAPA 89*
Chirot, Daniel 1942- *ConAu 132*
Chirovsky, Nicholas Ludomir 1919- *WhoAm 90*
Chirtea, George 1936- *St&PR 91*
Chirurg, James Thomas, Jr. 1944- *WhoAm 90*
Chisari, Andrew C. 1937- *St&PR 91*
Chisena, Ernest, III 1956- *WhoEmL 91*

Chisholm, Anthony Hewlings 1939- WhoWor 91
Chisholm, Carol Lee 1938- WhoAmW 91
Chisholm, Caroline 1808-1877 FemiCLE
Chisholm, Colin 1944- WhoWor 91
Chisholm, Donald Alexander 1927- WhoAm 90
Chisholm, Donald E. 1938- St&PR 91
Chisholm, Donald Herbert 1917- WhoAm 90
Chisholm, Donald William 1953- WhoEmL 91
Chisholm, Dugald Donald 1945- BiDrAPA 89
Chisholm, Frank A. 1910- St&PR 91
Chisholm, Geoffrey McKay 1965- WhoE 91
Chisholm, George 1915- OxCPMus
Chisholm, Jesse 1805?-1868 WhNaAH
Chisholm, Jesse 1806-1868? WorAlBi
Chisholm, Malcolm Harold 1945- WhoAm 90
Chisholm, Margaret Elizabeth 1921- WhoAm 90, WhoWor 91
Chisholm, Shirley 1924- BioIn 16, WorAlBi
Chisholm, Shirley Anita 1924- BlkAmsC [port]
Chisholm, Shirley Anita St. Hill 1924- WhoAm 90
Chisholm, Tague Clement 1915- WhoAm 90
Chisholm, Tommy 1941- St&PR 91, WhoAm 90, WhoSSW 91, WhoWor 91
Chisholm, William DeWayne 1924- WhoSSW 91
Chisholm, William H. 1917- St&PR 91
Chisholm, William Hardenbergh 1917- WhoAm 90
Chislett, Anne 1942- OxCCanT
Chislett, Gail 1948- BioIn 16
Chism, Geoffrey Paul 1952- WhoEmL 91
Chism, James Arthur 1933- WhoWor 91
Chism, Jeff P. 1960- St&PR 91
Chism, Robert W. 1942- St&PR 91
Chisner, Michael Brian 1959- WhoSSW 91
Chisolm, Margaret Smith BiDrAPA 89
Chisolm, O. Beirne, Jr. 1928- St&PR 91
Chisolm, Shirley 1924- BioIn 16
Chissano, Joachim 1939- CurBio 90 [port]
Chissano, Joaquim Alberto 1939- BioIn 16, WhoWor 91
Chissell, Herbert G., III BiDrAPA 89
Chissell, Joan Olive 1919- IntWWM 90
Chiste, Robert Matthew 1947- WhoAm 90
Chisum, Bessie Fisher 1945- WhoSSW 91
Chisum, David Edward 1955- WhoSSW 91
Chisum, T. Tolbert 1942- St&PR 91
Chiswick, Nancy Rose 1945- WhoAmW 91
Chitayat, Anwar 1927- St&PR 91
Chiti, Harry 1932- Ballpl 90, BioIn 16
Chittal, Nitin Mohan 1958- WhoSSW 91
Chittam, Dick 1952- WhoSSW 91
Chittemma, Nannapaneni BiDrAPA 89
Chittenden, Curtis D. 1935- St&PR 91
Chittenden, Hiram Martin 1858-1917 WhNaAH
Chittenden, Tanya Aletha 1958- WhoSSW 91
Chittenden, William A. 1927- St&PR 91
Chittick, David Rupert 1934- WhoE 91
Chittick, Elizabeth Lancaster 1918- WhoAm 90
Chittick, Rupert BiDrAPA 89
Chittick, Stanley Woodworth 1941- St&PR 91
Chittipeddi, Kumar 1955- WhoEmL 91
Chitto Harjo 1846-1912 WhNaAH
Chittum, Charles Lewis, Jr. 1938- WhoSSW 91
Chittum, Donald 1930- IntWWM 90
Chittum, Ida 1918- AuBYP 90
Chittur, Krishnan Shanker 1954- WhoEmL 91
Chitty, Arthur Benjamin, Jr. 1914- WhoAm 90, WhoWor 91
Chitty, Dennis Hubert 1912- WhoAm 90
Chitty, Elizabeth Nickinson 1920- WhoAmW 91, WhoSSW 91
Chituc, Mihai Adrian 1950- BiDrAPA 89
Chitwood, Frank Warren 1933- St&PR 91
Chitwood, Harold Otis 1930- St&PR 91, WhoAm 90
Chitwood, James L. 1943- WhoAm 90
Chitwood, Julius Richard 1921- WhoAm 90
Chitwood, Patricia May 1958- WhoAmW 91
Chitwood, Phyllis Ann 1959- WhoEmL 91
Chitwood Marshall, Lezlie Elaine 1955- WhoEmL 91
Chiu, David Tak Wai 1945- WhoAm 90
Chiu, Hungdah 1936- ConAu 31NR, WhoAm 90, WhoE 91
Chiu, Ing-Ming 1952- WhoEmL 91
Chiu, Ke-Chuan 1926- WhoWor 91
Chiu, Mary Lou 1964- WhoE 91
Chiu, Mary Man Ling 1946- WhoWor 91
Chiu, Peter Yee-Chew 1948- WhoWor 91
Chiu, Samantha Wai-Lim 1960- WhoE 91
Chiu, Thomas Lee 1935- BiDrAPA 89
Chiu, Yau-Sen 1943- WhoSSW 91
Chiulli, E. Antoinette 1950- WhoAmW 91
Chiulli, Joseph Giulio 1955- WhoE 91
Chiusano, Charles 1917- St&PR 91
Chivers, James Leeds 1939- WhoE 91
Chivers, Norman C 1914- BiDrAPA 89
Chivers, Thomas Holley 1807-1858 LiHiK
Chivington, John Milton 1821-1894 WhNaAH
Chivvis, A. 1954- St&PR 91
Chizauskas, Cathleen Jo 1954- WhoAmW 91
Chizeck, Susan Phyllis 1947- WhoEmL 91
Chizen, Harlan J. 1951- St&PR 91
Chizick, Jerry Lawrence 1948- St&PR 91
Chizinsky, Walter 1926- WhoE 91
Chizmadia, Stephen Mark 1950- WhoE 91, WhoEmL 91, WhoWor 91
Chizmadia, Thomas A. 1954- ODwPR 91
Chkheidze, Nikolai Semenovich 1864-1926 BioIn 16
Chladni, Ernst 1756-1827 WorAlBi
Chlan, Caryl Anne 1955- WhoSSW 91
Chlebowski, John Francis, Jr. 1945- St&PR 91, WhoAm 90
Chlopak, Donna Gayle 1950- WhoAm 90, WhoEmL 91
Chloupek, Frank James 1935- St&PR 91
Chludzinski-Mertz, Lisa Ann 1963- WhoEmL 91
Chlup, Joseph 1928- St&PR 91
Chluski, John J. 1923- WhoAm 90
Chmelir, Frank 1946- St&PR 91
Chmell, Samuel Jay 1952- WhoEmL 91
Chmely, Robert M. 1934- St&PR 91
Chmiel, Andrew Joseph 1940- BiDrAPA 89
Chmiel, Joseph Anthony, Jr. 1959- WhoEmL 91
Chmielewski, Margaret Ann 1946- WhoEmL 91
Chmielinski, Edward Alexander 1925- WhoAm 90, WhoE 91
Chmura, Edward 1940- St&PR 91
Chmura, Gabriel 1946- IntWWM 90, WhoE 91, WhoWor 91
Chmura, John A. 1943- St&PR 91
Chmurny, William Wayne 1941- WhoAm 90
Cho, Alfred Yi 1937- WhoAm 90
Cho, Anthony Chil BiDrAPA 89
Cho, Cheng Tsung 1937- WhoAm 90
Cho, Choong-Kun 1932- WhoWor 91
Cho, Choong Yul 1941- BiDrAPA 89
Cho, Choung Cha BiDrAPA 89
Cho, David 1950- WhoAmA 91
Cho, Dong-Il Dan 1958- WhoEmL 91
Cho, Doo Whan 1937- BiDrAPA 89
Cho, Hai-Hyung 1934- WhoWor 91
Cho, Hong BiDrAPA 89
Cho, Hyun Ju 1939- WhoAm 90
Cho, Jae Yone 1936- BiDrAPA 89
Cho, Jun Tae BiDrAPA 89
Cho, Kazunobu 1930- WhoWor 91
Cho, Lee-Jay 1936- WhoAm 90
Cho, Moon J 1945- BiDrAPA 89
Cho, Nam Yong 1943- BiDrAPA 89
Cho, Shinil 1951- WhoSSW 91
Cho, Soon 1928- WhoWor 91
Cho, Sung Hee 1957- WhoAmW 91, WhoSSW 91
Cho, Sung-Nai 1937- BiDrAPA 89
Cho, Sung-Ran 1940- BiDrAPA 89
Cho, Sung Yoon 1928- WhoE 91, WhoWor 91
Cho, Tai Yong 1943- WhoWor 91
Cho, Y J 1950- WhoAmA 91
Cho, Yoon Je 1952- WhoWor 91
Cho, Young Il 1949- WhoE 91
Cho, Young S. 1934- St&PR 91
Cho, Young Won 1931- WhoAm 90
Cho, Yuk-Kei Carlos 1940- WhoWor 91
Choain, Jean Georges 1917- WhoWor 91
Choate, Alan G. 1939- St&PR 91
Choate, Carl 1941- St&PR 91
Choate, Carolyn Hannah 1930- WhoAmW 91
Choate, Dimmitt N. 1943- St&PR 91
Choate, Eddie Allen 1954- WhoEmL 91
Choate, Edward Lee 1951- WhoEmL 91
Choate, Emily Teresa 1953- WhoEmL 91
Choate, Eugene 1936- St&PR 91
Choate, James Ralph 1950- WhoSSW 91
Choate, Jerry D. 1938- St&PR 91
Choate, Joseph 1900- WhoAm 90
Choate, Joseph Hodges 1832-1917 BioIn 16
Choate, Lewis Duane 1959- WhoEmL 91
Choate, Murray Rickliffe, II 1954- WhoSSW 91
Choate, Nathaniel 1899-1965 WhoAmA 91N
Choate, Robert Alden 1912- WhoAm 90
Choate, Roger Nye 1940- WhoWor 91
Chobanian, Aram Van 1929- WhoAm 90
Chobaut, Jean-Claude Charles 1946- WhoWor 91
Chobot, John Charles 1948- WhoEmL 91, WhoWor 91
Chobot-Sochet, Elzbieta J BiDrAPA 89
Choca, Santiago L BiDrAPA 89
Chocano, Jose Santos 1875-1934 BioIn 16, ConAu 131, HispWr 90
Chock, Alvin Keali'i 1931- WhoE 91, WhoWor 91
Chock, Eric Edward 1950- WhoWrEP 89
Chock, Jay Richard 1955- WhoEmL 91
Chockalingam, Periakaruppa 1943- WhoSSW 91
Chod, Jerry 1921- St&PR 91
Chodash, Charles Morton 1937- St&PR 91
Chodkowski, BettyAnn 1964- WhoAmW 91
Chodkowski, Henry, Jr 1937- WhoAmA 91
Chodl, Francis Thomas 1955- WhoEmL 91
Chodoff, Christopher BioIn 16
Chodoff, Paul 1914- BiDrAPA 89
Chodorkoff, Bernard 1925- BiDrAPA 89, WhoAm 90
Chodorov, Edward BioIn 16
Chodorow, Marvin 1913- WhoAm 90
Chodorow, Stanley Alan 1943- WhoAm 90
Chodos, Dale David Jerome 1928- WhoAm 90
Chodos, Gabriel 1939- IntWWM 90
Chodosh, Alan P. 1954- St&PR 91
Chodosh, H Louis 1925- BiDrAPA 89
Choe, Byung Rock BiDrAPA 89
Choe, Dong-Chull BiDrAPA 89
Choe, Hong Rak BiDrAPA 89
Choe, Kil Song 1940- WhoWor 91
Choe, Maria Il-Cha BiDrAPA 89
Choe, Won-Gil 1932- WhoAm 90
Choe, Yeon Chan 1940- BiDrAPA 89
Chogyam Trungpa 1940-1987 EncO&P 3
Chohn, Mijael WhoWrEP 89
Choi, Byung Ho 1928- WhoAm 90
Choi, Cyndia Sun BiDrAPA 89
Choi, Duk Shin 1914-1989 BioIn 16
Choi, Jae Hoon 1929- WhoWor 91
Choi, James Sangjin 1943- BiDrAPA 89
Choi, Jay Kenneth BiDrAPA 89
Choi, John Young 1944- BiDrAPA 89
Choi, Kyung Kook 1946- WhoEmL 91
Choi, Luke Sung Kyu 1947- WhoSSW 91
Choi, Man-Duen 1945- WhoAm 90
Choi, Myung D K BiDrAPA 89
Choi, Paul Soo-Woong 1943- WhoWor 91
Choi, Sang-il 1931- WhoAm 90
Choi, Sarah M BiDrAPA 89
Choi, Sei Young BiDrAPA 89
Choi, Seunghyun 1941- IntWWM 90
Choi, Sun Oak 1939- BiDrAPA 89
Choi, Won Il 1946- BiDrAPA 89
Choice, Harvey Leander 1950- WhoSSW 91
Chojiro PenDiDA 89
Chojiro 1516-1592 EncJap
Chojnacki, John Stephen 1940- St&PR 91
Chojnacki, Michael John 1944- BiDrAPA 89
Chojnacki, Paul Ervin 1950- WhoEmL 91
Chojnicki, Paul F 1947- St&PR 91
Chokhawala, Pankaj P 1948- BiDrAPA 89
Chokr, Ali Mohamad 1951- WhoSSW 91
Chokshi, Gaurang Navnitlal 1956- WhoEmL 91
Choksi, Aroon 1941- St&PR 91
Choksi, Jayendra C BiDrAPA 89
Choksi, Krutarth P BiDrAPA 89
Chol, Angelo BioIn 16
Cholak, Emmy Lou BiDrAPA 89
Cholakis, Constantine George 1930- WhoAm 90, WhoE 91
Cholawsky, Elizabeth Mary 1956- WhoE 91
Cholis, Thomas Joseph 1946- St&PR 91
Cholis, Thomas Joseph, Jr. 1946- WhoEmL 91
Chollar, Andrew S. ODwPR 91
Chollet, Jean Louis 1930- St&PR 91
Cholmley, Elisabeth BiDEWW
Cholmley, Margaret BiDEWW
Cholmondeley, Horace I BiDrAPA 89
Cholmondeley, Mary 1859-1925 BioIn 16, FemiCLE
Cholnoky, Imre BioIn 16
Cholodowski, Antonia Marie 1932- WhoE 91
Cholst, Sheldon 1924- BiDrAPA 89
Chome, Maryse IntWWM 90
Chomeau, Bernal T. 1931- St&PR 91
Chomeau, David Douglass 1937- St&PR 91, WhoAm 90
Chominski, Jozef Michal 1906- IntWWM 90
Chomitz, Morris A. 1925- St&PR 91
Choms, Wladyslawa 1891-1966 BioIn 16
Chomsky, Avram Noam 1928- WhoAm 90, WhoWor 91, WhoWrEP 89
Chomsky, Marvin J. 1929- WhoAm 90
Chomsky, Noam BioIn 16
Chomsky, Noam 1928- MajTwCW, WorAlBi
Chomsky, Noam 1929- EncAL
Chonez, Claudine 1917- EncCoWW
Chong, Chin Cheong 1960- WhoWor 91
Chong, Christopher Khiong 1948- WhoE 91
Chong, Clayton Elliott 1950- WhoEmL 91
Chong, Elaine Kui K BiDrAPA 89
Chong, Howard K.O., Jr. 1942- St&PR 91
Chong, Luis A. 1930- St&PR 91
Chong, Ping 1946- WhoAmA 91
Chong, Rae Dawn BioIn 16
Chong, Rae Dawn 1960?- DrBIPA 90
Chong, Shui-Fong 1954- WhoE 91, WhoEmL 91, WhoWor 91
Chong, Sooi P. St&PR 91
Chong, Sooi Peaw 1942- WhoAm 90
Chong, Thomas 1938- WhoAm 90
Chong, Vernon 1933- WhoAm 90, WhoSSW 91
Chongwitookit, Nakorn 1954- WhoWor 91
Chontos, Kathryn Lee 1951- WhoAmW 91
Choo, Caroline W H BiDrAPA 89
Choo, Chin S. BiDrAPA 89
Choo, Chunghi 1938- WhoAmA 91
Choo, Hun Oh BiDrAPA 89
Chook, Paul Howard 1929- WhoAm 90
Chookasian, Lili 1921- IntWWM 90
Chookaszian, Dennis H. 1943- St&PR 91
Chookaszian, Dennis Haig 1943- WhoAm 90
Choon, Tan Hock 1947- WhoWor 91
Choonhavan, Chatichai 1922- WhoWor 91
Chopdar, Amresh 1940- WhoWor 91
Choper, Jesse Herbert 1935- WhoAm 90
Chopin, Frederic 1810-1849 BioIn 16, WorAlBi
Chopin, Frederic Francois 1810-1849 PenDiMP A
Chopin, Kate 1850-1904 FemiCLE
Chopin, Kate 1851-1904 BioIn 16, WorAlBi
Chopin, Kate O. 1851-1904 BioAmW
Chopin, L. Frank 1942- WhoAm 90, WhoSSW 91
Chopin, Rene 1885-1953 DcLB 92
Chopin, Susan Gardiner 1947- WhoEmL 91
Choplin, John Max, II 1945- WhoAm 90, WhoEmL 91
Chopp, Gerald L. 1934- St&PR 91
Choppin, Gregory Robert 1927- WhoAm 90
Choppin, Purnell Whittington 1929- WhoAm 90, WhoE 91
Chopra, Anil Kumar 1941- WhoAm 90
Chopra, Hari Dass 1939- BiDrAPA 89
Chopra, Mohini 1947- St&PR 91
Chopra, Ravi 1947- WhoWor 91
Chopra, Roshan Mahendragir 1938- WhoWor 91
Chopra, Sudhir Kumar 1949- St&PR 91
Choptiany, Thor Ihor BiDrAPA 89
Choquet, Victorine EncCoWW
Choquette, Ernest 1852-1941 OxCCanT
Choquette, Paul J., Jr. 1938- St&PR 91
Choquette, Paul Joseph, Jr. 1938- WhoAm 90
Choquette, Philip Wheeler 1930- WhoAm 90
Choquette, William H. 1941- WhoAm 90
Choquette, William Henry 1941- St&PR 91
Chor, Philip Noble BiDrAPA 89
Chorbajian, John 1936- IntWWM 90
Chordia, Prakash L 1941- BiDrAPA 89
Chorell, Walentin 1912-1983 DcScanL
Chorin, Alexandre Joel 1938- WhoAm 90
Chorlton, David 1948- WhoWrEP 89
Chorlton, R.W. 1925- St&PR 91
Chormann, Richard F. 1937- St&PR 91, WhoAm 90
Chornesky, Adam Brett 1947- WhoE 91
Chornesky, George BiDrAPA 89
Chornesky, Samuel BiDrAPA 89
Chorney, Harold 1917- St&PR 91
Chorney, Shirley Ruth 1935- WhoE 91
Chorney, Theresa Rand 1955- WhoAmW 91, WhoEmL 91
Choromanski, Lynn Marie 1954- WhoAmW 91
Choromokos, James, Jr. 1929- WhoAm 90
Choron, Gaston BioIn 16
Choron, Jacques 1904-1972 AuBYP 90
Choronenko, Iwan 1937- WhoSSW 91
Chorot, Paloma 1958- WhoWor 91
Chorpenning, Charlotte 1872-1955 BioIn 16
Chorpenning, Charlotte Barrows 1873-1955 NotWoAT
Chorpenning, Nancy Ellen 1953- WhoAm 90
Choruby, Larry Nicholas 1938- St&PR 91
Chorzempa, Daniel 1944- PenDiMP
Chorzempa, Daniel Walter 1944- IntWWM 90
Chostner, Chrystal Lea 1963- WhoAmW 91

Chosy, John Eugene 1948- *WhoEmL 91*
Chotigeat, Tosporn 1945- *WhoSSW 91*
Chotiner, Kenneth Lee 1937- *WhoAm 90*
Chotjewitz, Peter O 1934- *ConAu 129*
Chou *PenDiDA 89*
Chou En-Lai 1898-1976 *WorAlBi*
Chou, Clarence Paul *BiDrAPA 89*
Chou, Clifford Chi Fong 1940- *WhoAm 90*
Chou, En-lai 1898-1976 *BioIn 16*
Chou, Eric 1915- *ConAu 132*
Chou, Erwin C. 1952- *WhoEmL 91*
Chou, Harry H. S. 1923- *WhoAm 90*
Chou, Henry Yuan *BiDrAPA 89*
Chou, Jack Chen 1936- *St&PR 91*
Chou, James C.-Y. 1959- *BiDrAPA 89*
Chou, James Ching-Yung 1959- *WhoE 91*
Chou, Kuo-Chen 1938- *WhoWor 91*
Chou, Ling-Tai Lynette 1955- *WhoAmW 91*
Chou, Maxine J. 1942- *WhoE 91*
Chou, Pei Chi 1924- *WhoAm 90*
Chou, Pei-Chuang 1913- *St&PR 91*
Chou, Raymond H. 1956- *WhoEmL 91*
Chou, Ri-Chee 1961- *WhoEmL 91*
Chou, Shelley Nien-chun 1924- *WhoAm 90*
Chou, Shingsan 1941- *BiDrAPA 89*
Chou, Timothy Chen Kuang 1954- *WhoEmL 91*
Chou, Ting-Chao 1938- *WhoE 91*
Chou, Wen-chung 1923- *IntWWM 90*, *WhoAm 90*
Chou, Wushow 1939- *WhoAm 90*
Chou, Youn-Min Amanda *WhoSSW 91*, *WhoWor 91*
Chou, Yu-Jui *ConAu 132*
Choudhury, A.P. Roy 1929- *St&PR 91*
Choudhury, Abdul Latif 1933- *WhoSSW 91*
Choudhury, Deo Chand 1926- *WhoWor 91*
Choudhury, Muazzam Sultan 1949- *WhoWor 91*
Choudry, Mayna Meah *BiDrAPA 89*
Chouinard, George Delphon 1936- *St&PR 91*
Chouinard, Guy 1944- *BiDrAPA 89*
Chouinard, Nelbert, Mrs *WhoAmA 91N*
Chouinard, Paul Lewellyn 1945- *WhoEmL 91*
Chouinard, Richard J. 1932- *St&PR 91*
Chouinard, Yvon *BioIn 16*
Choukas, Chris Nicholas 1955- *WhoEmL 91*
Choukas, Michael 1901-1989 *ConAu 129*
Choukas, Michael Eugene 1901-1989 *BioIn 16*
Chouteau, Auguste Pierre 1786-1838 *WhNaAH*
Chouteau, Jean Pierre 1758-1849 *WhNaAH*
Chouteau, Pierre, Jr. 1789-1865 *WhNaAH*
Chouteau, Rene Auguste 1749-1829 *EncCRAm*, *WhNaAH*
Chovan, Karen Ryan 1959- *WhoAmW 91*
Choveaux, Nicholas 1904- *IntWWM 90*
Chovnick, Harry *BiDrAPA 89*
Chow Chian-Chiu 1910- *WhoAmA 91*
Chow Leung Chen-Ying 1921- *WhoAmA 91*
Chow, Anthony Wei-Chik 1941- *WhoAm 90*
Chow, Charn Ki Kenneth 1953- *WhoWor 91*
Chow, Eileen Siu-Ha 1951- *WhoWor 91*
Chow, Franklin Szu-Chien 1956- *WhoEmL 91*, *WhoWor 91*
Chow, Gregory Chi-Chong 1929- *WhoAm 90*, *WhoE 91*
Chow, John Victor 1942- *St&PR 91*
Chow, Kao Liang 1918- *WhoAm 90*
Chow, Michael *BioIn 16*
Chow, Poo 1934- *WhoAm 90*
Chow, Rita Kathleen 1926- *WhoAm 90*, *WhoAmW 91*
Chow, Stephen Heung Wing 1954- *WhoWor 91*
Chow, Stephen Yee 1952- *WhoE 91*, *WhoEmL 91*
Chow, Tony 1953- *WhoWor 91*
Chow, Tse-Tsung 1916- *WhoAm 90*, *WhoWrEP 89*
Chow, Winston 1946- *WhoEmL 91*
Chow, Winston Win Sein 1944- *BiDrAPA 89*
Chow, Yuan Shih 1924- *WhoAm 90*
Chow, Yun Fat *BioIn 16*
Chow-Kai, Juan 1963- *WhoHisp 91*
Chowdhrey, M Salim *BiDrAPA 89*
Chowdhri, Kahkashan Jabeen *BiDrAPA 89*
Chowdhuri, Pritindra 1927- *WhoAm 90*, *WhoWor 91*
Chowdhury, Abdur Rahim 1953- *WhoEmL 91*
Chowdhury, Ashraful Aziz 1955- *WhoSSW 91*
Chowdhury, Eulie 1923- *WomArch*
Chowdhury, Eulie, & Elizabeth Ghuman *WomArch*
Chowdhury, Mizanur Rahman 1928- *WhoWor 91*
Chowhan, Shagufta Jabeen *BiDrAPA 89*
Chown, David Byron 1953- *St&PR 91*
Chown, Frank D. 1918- *St&PR 91*
Chown, Fred Roger 1950- *St&PR 91*
Chowning, John 1934- *IntWWM 90*
Chowpaknam, Griengsak 1947- *WhoSSW 91*
Choy, Herbert Young Cho 1916- *WhoAm 90*
Choy, Leona Frances 1925- *WhoWrEP 89*
Choy, Terence Tin-Ho 1941- *WhoAmA 91*
Choyce, David Peter 1919- *WhoWor 91*
Choyce, Lesley 1951- *ConAu 130*
Choyke, Phyllis May 1921- *WhoWrEP 89*
Choyke, Phyllis May Ford 1921- *WhoAmW 91*, *WhoWor 91*
Choynowski, Mieczyslaw 1909- *EncO&P 3*
Chozen, Harry 1915- *BioIn 16*
Chozick, Henry 1924- *St&PR 91*
Chozinski, Joseph Patric 1963- *BiDrAPA 89*
Chrabaszcz, Emil George 1928- *WhoE 91*
Chrein, Maxine 1950- *WhoEmL 91*
Chrencik, Frank 1914- *WhoAm 90*
Chretien De Troyes *WorAlBi*
Chretien, Heidi 1947- *WhoAmA 91*
Chretien, Jean *BioIn 16*
Chretien, Jean 1934- *CurBio 90 [port]*, *News 90 [port]*
Chretien, Joseph-Jacques Jean 1934- *WhoAm 90*
Chretien, Margaret Cecilia 1953- *WhoE 91*
Chretien, Michel 1936- *WhoAm 90*
Chretign, Paul Bernard 1931- *St&PR 91*
Chrey, Kristine Ann 1951- *WhoEmL 91*
Chrien, Robert Edward 1930- *WhoAm 90*
Chris the Wonder Dog *EncPaPR 91*
Chris, Emanuel Solon 1957- *BiDrAPA 89*
Chrisanthopoulos, Peter *WhoAm 90*
Chriscoe, Christine Faust 1950- *WhoAmW 91*
Chrisley, Neil 1931- *Ballpl 90*
Chrisman, Allan K 1945- *BiDrAPA 89*
Chrisman, Arthur Bowie 1889-1953 *AuBYP 90*
Chrisman, Bruce Lowell 1943- *WhoAm 90*
Chrisman, Cheryl Lynn 1945- *WhoAm 90*
Chrisman, Dale L. 1945- *ODwPR 91*
Chrisman, Diane J. 1937- *WhoAm 90*, *WhoE 91*
Chrisman, Harry E. *BioIn 16*
Chrisman, James Joseph 1954- *WhoEmL 91*, *WhoSSW 91*
Chrisman, Marlene Santia 1946- *WhoAmW 91*
Chrisman, Miriam Usher 1920- *ConAu 131*
Chrisman, Noel D. 1934- *St&PR 91*
Chrismer, Denny L. 1946- *St&PR 91*
Chrismer, Michael Peter 1940- *St&PR 91*
Chrismer, Ronald Michael 1954- *WhoE 91*
Chrisopulos, John 1946- *WhoEmL 91*
Chrisoscoleu, Sofia *EncCoWW*
Chriss, Irene Adrienne 1944- *WhoAmW 91*
Chriss, Nicholas C. 1928?-1990 *ConAu 131*
Chriss, William J 1956- *WhoEmL 91*
Christ *BioIn 16*, *EncPaPR 91*
Christ, Adolph E 1929- *BiDrAPA 89*
Christ, Albert Howard 1941- *WhoE 91*
Christ, Betsy Anne 1954- *WhoAmW 91*
Christ, Carl Finley 1923- *WhoAm 90*, *WhoE 91*
Christ, Carol Manlove *ODwPR 91*
Christ, Clifford Charles 1947- *WhoAm 90*
Christ, Donald Clough 1935- *WhoAm 90*
Christ, Duane Marland 1932- *WhoE 91*, *WhoWor 91*
Christ, Ellen Marie 1960- *WhoAmW 91*
Christ, Jacob 1926- *BiDrAPA 89*
Christ, Kathy Scott 1951- *WhoEmL 91*
Christ, Lena 1881-1920 *EncCoWW*
Christ, Marcus G. 1900-1988 *BioIn 16*
Christ, Nicholas M. 1951- *St&PR 91*
Christ, Sharon Jeanne 1958- *WhoAmW 91*
Christ, Thomas Warren 1944- *WhoAm 90*
Christ-Janer, Albert William 1910-1973 *WhoAmA 91N*
Christ-Janer, Arland F 1922- *WhoAmA 91*
Christ-Janer, Arland Frederick 1922- *WhoAm 90*
Christaal *NewAgMG*
Christainsen, Philip Lucian 1918- *BiDrAPA 89*
Christakos, Arthur Chris 1930- *WhoAm 90*
Christakos, Sylvia 1946- *WhoAmW 91*
Christel, Henry Eugene 1945- *St&PR 91*
Christelis, Constantine G. 1930- *WhoE 91*
Christen, Lynne Robbins 1946- *WhoAmW 91*
Christen, Paul R. 1929- *St&PR 91*
Christenberry, Boyd *St&PR 91*
Christenberry, William 1936- *BioIn 16*, *WhoAmA 91*
Christenbury, Edward S. *St&PR 91*
Christenbury, Edward Samuel 1941- *WhoAm 90*
Christenbury, Mary McMahan *BiDrAPA 89*
Christenen, Clayton M. 1952- *St&PR 91*
Christensen, Albert Kent 1927- *WhoAm 90*
Christensen, Albert Sherman 1905- *WhoAm 90*
Christensen, Allen Clare 1935- *WhoWor 91*
Christensen, Allen Thomas 1952- *WhoEmL 91*
Christensen, Arnold 1936- *WhoAm 90*
Christensen, Beth Elaine 1954- *IntWWM 90*
Christensen, Betty *WhoAmA 91*
Christensen, Bruce LeRoy 1943- *WhoAm 90*
Christensen, Burton Grant 1930- *St&PR 91*
Christensen, Caren *BioIn 16*
Christensen, Carl Roland 1919- *WhoAm 90*
Christensen, Carl Waldo 1916- *BiDrAPA 89*
Christensen, Carol Ann 1941- *WhoAmW 91*
Christensen, Carole Lynn 1937- *WhoSSW 91*
Christensen, Chris Dale 1949- *WhoEmL 91*
Christensen, Chris P. 1947- *St&PR 91*
Christensen, Clyde Martin 1905- *WhoAm 90*
Christensen, Coburn F. 1947- *St&PR 91*
Christensen, Corine *BioIn 16*
Christensen, Cyrus Robert 1926- *WhoSSW 91*
Christensen, Dan 1942- *WhoAmA 91*
Christensen, Daniel Dee 1949- *BiDrAPA 89*
Christensen, Daniel K. 1946- *St&PR 91*
Christensen, David Allen 1935- *St&PR 91*
Christensen, Dennis Wesley *BiDrAPA 89*
Christensen, Dieter 1932- *IntWWM 90*
Christensen, Don A. 1930- *St&PR 91*
Christensen, Don M. 1929- *WhoWor 91*
Christensen, Donna Radovich 1925- *WhoE 91*
Christensen, Douglas A. 1947- *St&PR 91*
Christensen, Earl William *BiDrAPA 89*
Christensen, Edwin Hans 1942- *St&PR 91*
Christensen, Eric Dean 1958- *WhoEmL 91*
Christensen, Ernest Martin 1933- *WhoE 91*
Christensen, Fern Eloise Breakenridge 1923- *WhoAmW 91*
Christensen, Gardell Dano 1907- *AuBYP 90*
Christensen, Gary Soren 1937- *St&PR 91*
Christensen, George Curtis 1924- *WhoAm 90*
Christensen, George M. 1921- *St&PR 91*
Christensen, George Theodore 1926- *St&PR 91*
Christensen, Gerald R. *St&PR 91*
Christensen, Glen E 1947- *BiDrAPA 89*
Christensen, Gordon Edward 1948- *WhoEmL 91*
Christensen, Gustav Amstrup 1947- *WhoEmL 91*
Christensen, Halvor Niels 1915- *WhoAm 90*
Christensen, Harold 1904-1989 *BioIn 16*
Christensen, Henry, III 1944- *WhoE 91*, *WhoWor 91*
Christensen, Howard A. 1933- *ODwPR 91*
Christensen, Howard Alan 1933- *WhoAm 90*
Christensen, Inger 1935- *DcScanL*, *EncCoWW*
Christensen, Jacob Sand 1953- *WhoWor 91*
Christensen, James Edward 1941- *WhoWor 91*
Christensen, Jan Friis 1948- *WhoE 91*
Christensen, Jens Knud 1933- *WhoWor 91*
Christensen, John William 1914- *WhoAm 90*
Christensen, Jon Hall 1939- *St&PR 91*
Christensen, Jorgen B. 1932- *St&PR 91*
Christensen, Julien Martin 1918- *WhoAm 90*
Christensen, Kai 1916- *WhoWor 91*
Christensen, Karen Dorothe 1947- *WhoEmL 91*
Christensen, Karen Kay 1947- *WhoEmL 91*
Christensen, Karen Messer *BiDrAPA 89*
Christensen, Karen Sue 1958- *WhoAmW 91*
Christensen, Kathleen Marie 1957- *WhoAmW 91*
Christensen, Kirk Le 1950- *WhoSSW 91*
Christensen, Larry R 1936- *WhoAmA 91*
Christensen, Lars 1945- *WhoWor 91*
Christensen, Lars Ivar 1965- *WhoWor 91*
Christensen, Lee Robert 1932- *St&PR 91*
Christensen, Lillian Langseth- *BioIn 16*
Christensen, Lydell Lee 1934- *WhoAm 90*
Christensen, Lynne Ellen 1955- *WhoEmL 91*
Christensen, M. Katherine *St&PR 91*
Christensen, Marc Douglas 1948- *St&PR 91*
Christensen, Margaret Jane 1938- *WhoAmW 91*, *WhoWor 91*
Christensen, Martha 1932- *WhoAm 90*
Christensen, Mary M. 1945- *WhoSSW 91*
Christensen, Mitchell Allen 1954- *WhoEmL 91*
Christensen, Nadia Margaret 1937- *WhoWor 91*
Christensen, Nikolas Ivan 1937- *WhoAm 90*
Christensen, Norma Sheppard 1924- *WhoAmW 91*
Christensen, Odin Dale 1947- *WhoEmL 91*
Christensen, Opal Marie 1930- *St&PR 91*
Christensen, Otto Bertel 1934- *WhoWor 91*
Christensen, P.S. 1930- *St&PR 91*
Christensen, Patricia Anne Watkins 1947- *WhoEmL 91*
Christensen, Paul 1943- *WhoWrEP 89*
Christensen, Paul Walter, Jr. 1925- *St&PR 91*, *WhoAm 90*
Christensen, Ralph 1897-1961 *WhoAmA 91N*
Christensen, Ray Richards 1922- *WhoAm 90*
Christensen, Robert A. 1933- *St&PR 91*
Christensen, Shara Dawn 1956- *WhoSSW 91*
Christensen, Sharlene 1939- *WhoAmA 91*
Christensen, Ted 1911- *WhoAmA 91*
Christensen, Terry N. *BioIn 16*
Christensen, Thomas Allen 1939- *St&PR 91*
Christensen, Thor G. 1936- *St&PR 91*
Christensen, Val Alan 1946- *WhoAmA 91*
Christensen, William Robert 1960- *WhoSSW 91*
Christensen, William Rozelle 1917- *WhoAm 90*
Christenson, Bob 1951- *St&PR 91*
Christenson, Brian C 1949- *BiDrAPA 89*
Christenson, Carolyn 1949- *ODwPR 91*
Christenson, Charles John 1930- *WhoAm 90*
Christenson, Clifford James 1949- *St&PR 91*
Christenson, Gary Alan-Hue *BiDrAPA 89*
Christenson, Gordon A. 1932- *WhoAm 90*, *WhoWor 91*
Christenson, Grant P. 1951- *St&PR 91*
Christenson, Hans-Jorgen Thorvald 1924-1983 *WhoAmA 91N*
Christenson, Joseph Charles 1958- *St&PR 91*
Christenson, Joseph L. *BiDrAPA 89*
Christenson, Larry 1953- *Ballpl 90*
Christenson, Le Roy Howard 1948- *WhoAm 90*
Christenson, Neil O. 1932- *St&PR 91*
Christenson, Philip Lawrence 1947- *WhoE 91*
Christenson, Randall Mark 1951- *BiDrAPA 89*
Christenson, Susan Elizabeth 1951- *WhoAmW 91*
Christenson, Wayne Allen, Jr. 1951- *BiDrAPA 89*
Christenson, William Newcome 1925- *WhoAm 90*, *WhoE 91*
Christesen, Russell J. 1923- *WhoAm 90*
Christesen, Russell James 1922- *St&PR 91*
Christgau, Peter Valdemar 1940- *WhoWor 91*
Christhilf, Bryson Gill 1918- *St&PR 91*
Christhilf, John Harwood 1946- *WhoEmL 91*, *WhoSSW 91*
Christi, Marilyn Patricia 1950- *WhoAmW 91*
Christiaanse, Jan Hendrikus 1932- *WhoWor 91*
Christian IV, King of Denmark 1577-1648 *BioIn 16*
Christian, Almeric Leander 1919- *WhoSSW 91*
Christian, Betty Jo 1936- *WhoAm 90*, *WhoAmW 91*
Christian, Charles F *BiDrAPA 89*
Christian, Charles Leigh 1926- *WhoAm 90*
Christian, Charlie 1916-1942 *BioIn 16*, *OxCPMus*
Christian, Chester Carsel 1926- *WhoSSW 91*
Christian, Dennis W. 1946- *St&PR 91*
Christian, Edward Kierin 1944- *BioIn 16*
Christian, Ernest Silsbee, Jr. 1937- *WhoAm 90*
Christian, Eugene Elmore *BiDrAPA 89*
Christian, Gary Dale 1937- *WhoAm 90*
Christian, Gary Irvin 1951- *WhoEmL 91*, *WhoSSW 91*, *WhoWor 91*

Christian, Gene H. 1932- St&PR 91
Christian, George ODwPR 91
Christian, George Eastland 1927- WhoAm 90
Christian, George Lloyd, Jr. 1937- WhoAm 90
Christian, James Wayne 1934- WhoAm 90
Christian, Joe Clark 1934- WhoAm 90
Christian, John Catlett, Jr. 1929- WhoAm 90, WhoSSW 91, WhoWor 91
Christian, John Edward 1917- WhoAm 90
Christian, John Kenton 1927- WhoAm 90
Christian, Joseph Ralph 1920- WhoAm 90
Christian, Karen Kay BiDrAPA 89
Christian, Lorraine A BiDrAPA 89
Christian, Louis Gordon 1923- St&PR 91
Christian, Marc BioIn 16
Christian, Mary Blount 1933- AuBYP 90
Christian, Mary Jo Dinan 1941- WhoE 91
Christian, Mary Nordean 1944- WhoAmW 91
Christian, Michael Spruce 1949- St&PR 91
Christian, Michael Tod 1943- WhoAm 90
Christian, Nelson Frederick 1949- WhoSSW 91
Christian, Paul 1811-1877 EncO&P 3
Christian, Paula 1953- WhoWrEP 89
Christian, Rebecca Anne 1952- WhoWrEP 89
Christian, Richard Carlton 1924- WhoAm 90, WhoWor 91
Christian, Richard S. BioIn 16
Christian, Robert 1939-1983 DrBIPA 90
Christian, Robert Henry 1922- WhoAm 90
Christian, Roland Carl 1938- WhoWrEP 89
Christian, Rudolph, Sr. 1951- WhoSSW 91
Christian, Samuel T. AuBYP 90
Christian, Sherril Duane 1931- WhoAm 90
Christian, Shirley 1938- BioIn 16
Christian, Spencer 1947- DrBIPA 90
Christian, Suzanne Hall 1935- WhoAmW 91
Christian, Thomas Embree 1953- WhoEmL 91
Christian, William David 1941- St&PR 91
Christian, Winslow 1926- WhoAm 90
Christian-Michaels, Stephen 1954- WhoEmL 91
Christiana, Edward 1912- WhoAmA 91
Christiana, Felix J. 1924- St&PR 91
Christiancy, Isaac Peckham 1812-1890 BioIn 16
Christiano, Nicholas, Jr. 1950- WhoE 91
Christiano, Paul P. 1942- WhoAm 90
Christians, Glenn Arthur 1923- St&PR 91
Christiansen, Alan Keith 1946- WhoEmL 91
Christiansen, Christian Carl, Jr. 1933- WhoAm 90, WhoE 91
Christiansen, Claire Beth 1947- WhoEmL 91
Christiansen, Clifford Glen 1924- St&PR 91
Christiansen, David K. 1952- WhoEmL 91
Christiansen, Deanne Marie 1945- BiDrAPA 89
Christiansen, Donald Barry 1939- St&PR 91
Christiansen, Donald David 1927- WhoAm 90, WhoWor 91
Christiansen, George W. 1915- St&PR 91
Christiansen, Hans 1866-1945 PenDiDA 89
Christiansen, James Edward 1930- WhoSSW 91
Christiansen, John Rees 1927- WhoAm 90
Christiansen, John Valdemar 1927- WhoAm 90
Christiansen, Kenneth Allen 1924- WhoAm 90
Christiansen, Lucille 1918- WhoAmW 91
Christiansen, Marjorie Miner 1922- WhoAmW 91
Christiansen, Norman Juhl 1923- WhoAm 90
Christiansen, Patricia Ann 1949- WhoEmL 91
Christiansen, Paul J. 1906- St&PR 91
Christiansen, Paula Sue 1956- WhoAmW 91
Christiansen, Philip C. 1922- St&PR 91
Christiansen, R. E. 1935- WhoAm 90
Christiansen, Richard Dean 1931- WhoAm 90
Christiansen, Richard Louis 1935- WhoAm 90
Christiansen, Robert L. 1927- St&PR 91
Christiansen, Russell 1935- WhoAm 90
Christiansen, Russell Eric 1935- St&PR 91
Christiansen, S. Edward V. 1941- St&PR 91
Christiansen, Sharon Lee 1956- WhoEmL 91
Christiansen, Sigurd 1891-1947 DcScanL
Christiansen, Ted Leo 1922- WhoAm 90
Christiansen, Vicky Lynn 1958- WhoEmL 91
Christiansen, Walter Henry 1934- WhoAm 90
Christiansen, William E.S. 1944- St&PR 91
Christianson, Bruce Wilton 1919- BiDrAPA 89
Christianson, Elin Ballantyne 1936- WhoAmW 91
Christianson, Frank L. 1946- St&PR 91
Christianson, James Duane 1952- WhoEmL 91
Christianson, Kevin Earl 1948- WhoWrEP 89
Christianson, Lloyd F. 1914- St&PR 91
Christianson, Lloyd Fenton 1914- WhoAm 90
Christianson, Marcia LaRaye 1947- WhoAmW 91
Christianson, Mary H F BiDrAPA 89
Christianson, Peter Robert 1957- WhoE 91
Christianson, Roger Gordon 1947- WhoEmL 91
Christianson, Warren George 1921- St&PR 91
Christie, Agatha 1890-1976 AuBYP 90, FemiCLE, MajTwCW, TwCCr&M 91, WorAlBi
Christie, Agatha 1891-1976 BioIn 16
Christie, Amalie 1913- IntWWM 90
Christie, Andrew Dobbie 1922- WhoAm 90, WhoE 91
Christie, Audrey BioIn 16
Christie, Carole Sullivan WhoAmW 91
Christie, Clarence J. 1930- St&PR 91, WhoAm 90
Christie, David G. 1930- St&PR 91
Christie, Donald Melvin, Jr. 1942- WhoE 91
Christie, Franklyn James 1933- St&PR 91
Christie, George 1934- IntWWM 90
Christie, George A. 1927- St&PR 91
Christie, George Custis 1934- WhoAm 90
Christie, George L BiDrAPA 89
Christie, George Nicholas 1924- WhoE 91, WhoWor 91
Christie, H. Frederick 1933- WhoAm 90
Christie, Hugh 1932- St&PR 91
Christie, James R 1952- ConAu 129
Christie, Jesse Roy 1889-1978 BioIn 16
Christie, John Donald 1937- WhoAm 90
Christie, Julie 1940- BioIn 16, WhoAm 90, WhoWor 91, WorAlBi
Christie, Laurence Glenn, Jr. 1930- WhoAm 90
Christie, Lindon Edwin, Jr. 1932- WhoE 91
Christie, Marie 1949- SmATA X [port]
Christie, Michael Jae 1956- WhoEmL 91
Christie, Michael Monte BiDrAPA 89
Christie, Nan 1960- IntWWM 90
Christie, Nigel B. 1948- WhoAm 90
Christie, Peter Alexander 1925- St&PR 91
Christie, Philippa AuBYP 90
Christie, R George 1920- BiDrAPA 89
Christie, Richard East 1918- St&PR 91
Christie, Robert 1913- OxCCanT
Christie, Robert Brent 1952- WhoAm 90
Christie, Robert Duncan 1946- WhoAmA 91
Christie, Robert J. 1954- ODwPR 91
Christie, Robert Michael BioIn 16
Christie, Robert S. 1953- St&PR 91
Christie, Scott Douglas BiDrAPA 89
Christie, Scott G. 1953- ODwPR 91
Christie, Scott Graham 1953- WhoEmL 91
Christie, Thomas Philip 1934- WhoAm 90
Christie, Tod Stephens 1958- WhoE 91
Christie, Tom E. 1934- St&PR 91
Christie, Walter Robert 1942- BiDrAPA 89, WhoE 91
Christie, Walter Scott 1922- WhoWor 91
Christie, William 1944- IntWWM 90, PenDiMP
Christie, William Joseph 1824-1899 DcCanB 12
Christie, William Mellis 1829-1900 DcCanB 12
Christin, Judith BioIn 16
Christina 1626-1689 WomWR [port]
Christina of Sweden 1626-1689 EncCoWW
Christina, Queen of Sweden 1626-1689 BioIn 16
Christine de Pizan 1363?-1429? FemiCLE
Christine of France WomWR
Christine, Dennis Brion, Jr. 1947- WhoEmL 91
Christine, Henri Marius 1867-1941 OxCPMus
Christine, Virginia Feld 1920- WhoAm 90
Christison, Caron S I BiDrAPA 89
Christison, George Wilburn BiDrAPA 89
Christison, Muriel B WhoAmA 91
Christison, William Henry, III 1936- WhoAm 90
Christlieb, Theophyle EncCoWW
Christman, Arthur Castner, Jr. 1922- WhoAm 90
Christman, Bert 1915-1942 EncACom
Christman, Bruce Lee 1955- WhoEmL 91
Christman, Elizabeth A 1914- WhoWrEP 89
Christman, Henry Max 1932- WhoAm 90, WhoWor 91, WhoWrEP 89
Christman, John Francis 1924- WhoAm 90
Christman, Kenneth Daniel 1949- WhoEmL 91
Christman, Lawrence Lee 1943- St&PR 91
Christman, Luther Parmalee 1915- WhoAm 90
Christman, Mark 1913-1976 Ballpl 90
Christman, Paul J. 1952- ConAu 132
Christman, Rebecca BioIn 16
Christman, Richard Marlo 1950- St&PR 91
Christman, Ronald A. 1939- St&PR 91
Christmann, Helmut 1924- WhoWor 91
Christmas, Eric 1916- OxCCanT
Christmas, Jeffrey L. 1953- ODwPR 91
Christmas, June Jackson 1924- BiDrAPA 89
Christner, David Lee 1949- WhoEmL 91
Christo 1935- BioIn 16, WhoAm 90, WhoAmA 91, WhoE 91, WorAlBi
Christo-Schlapp, Joi 1959- WhoAmW 91
Christodoulou, Aris Peter 1939- WhoAm 90, WhoWor 91
Christodoulou, Manolis A. 1955- WhoWor 91
Christodoulou, Renos John 1935- WhoWor 91
Christoff, Beth Graves 1936- WhoAmW 91
Christoff, Boris 1914- IntWWM 90, PenDiMP
Christoff, Boris 1919- WhoWor 91
Christoff, Carl 1936- St&PR 91
Christoff, Dimiter 1933- IntWWM 90
Christoff, George S. 1924- St&PR 91
Christoffersen, Arthur Lynn 1946- St&PR 91
Christoffersen, Jon Michael 1942- St&PR 91
Christoffersen, Leif Edvard 1935- WhoE 91
Christoffersen, Ralph Earl 1937- WhoAm 90
Christofferson, D. Todd 1945- St&PR 91
Christofferson, Kimberlee Killmer 1959- WhoE 91
Christoffersson, John Goran 1945- WhoAm 90
Christoffersson, Rea Raihala 1945- WhoAmW 91, WhoE 91
Christofi, Andreas Charalambos 1949- WhoE 91
Christofides, John Nicholas 1931- WhoWor 91
Christofidis, George 1943- St&PR 91
Christofilos, Nicholas C 1916-1972 DcScB S2
Christofle, Charles 1805-1863 PenDiDA 89
Christoforidis, A. John 1924- WhoAm 90, WhoWor 91
Christol, Carl Quimby 1913- WhoAm 90
Christomos, Timothy M. 1950- St&PR 91
Christopfel, Steven W. 1951- St&PR 91
Christoph, Frank Henry, Jr. WhoE 91
Christoph, James Bernard 1928- WhoAm 90
Christoph, Susan Catherine 1960- WhoAmW 91
Christophe, Henri 1767-1820 BioIn 16
Christopher, Alice Joanne BiDrAPA 89
Christopher, Barbara BioIn 16
Christopher, Beth ConAu 32NR
Christopher, Chris Constantine 1921- WhoWor 91
Christopher, Daniel Roy 1947- WhoEmL 91
Christopher, Elisabeth Neal 1910- WhoAmW 91
Christopher, F. Hudnall, Jr. 1933- St&PR 91
Christopher, F. Scott 1952- WhoEmL 91
Christopher, Garland R. 1946- WhoE 91
Christopher, George Edwin 1927- St&PR 91
Christopher, Harold 1936- St&PR 91
Christopher, James 1946- BiDrAPA 89
Christopher, James Walker 1930- WhoAm 90
Christopher, Joe 1935- Ballpl 90
Christopher, John 1922- BioIn 16
Christopher, John L. WhoE 91
Christopher, Lawrence C. 1923- ODwPR 91
Christopher, Matt 1917- BioIn 16
Christopher, Matthew F. 1917- AuBYP 90
Christopher, Matthew Frederick 1917- WhoWrEP 89
Christopher, Maurine Brooks WhoAm 90, WhoAmW 91, WhoWrEP 89
Christopher, Milbourne 1914-1984 EncO&P 3, EncPaPR 91
Christopher, Nancy 1957- ODwPR 91
Christopher, Paul J., Jr. 1948- WhoE 91
Christopher, Richard Scott 1953- WhoEmL 91
Christopher, Robert C. 1931- St&PR 91
Christopher, Robert Collins 1924- WhoAm 90
Christopher, Robert Paul 1932- WhoSSW 91
Christopher, Rochelle Alisa 1952- WhoE 91
Christopher, Russ 1917-1954 Ballpl 90
Christopher, Russell Lee 1946- BiDrAPA 89
Christopher, Russell Lewis 1930- WhoAm 90
Christopher, Sharon A. Brown 1944- WhoAm 90, WhoAmW 91
Christopher, Warren BioIn 16
Christopher, Warren 1925- WhoAm 90
Christopher, Wilford Scott 1916- WhoAm 90
Christopher, William BioIn 16, WhoAm 90
Christopher, William E 1929- BiDrAPA 89
Christopher, William R 1924-1973 WhoAmA 91N
Christopher-Colon, MarJorie Ann 1940- WhoAmW 91
Christophersen, Henning 1939- WhoWor 91
Christophersen, Robert L. 1936- St&PR 91
Christopherson, Karin Agnes 1948- WhoAmW 91
Christopherson, Leroy Omar 1935- WhoWrEP 89
Christopherson, Weston R. 1925- St&PR 91
Christopherson, Weston Robert 1925- WhoAm 90
Christopherson, William Martin 1916- WhoAm 90
Christopoulos, Angelos C BiDrAPA 89
Christopoulos, Arthur George 1930- St&PR 91
Christov, Solveig 1918- EncCoWW
Christoverson, Marcene H. St&PR 91
Christus, Petrus 1410?-1473? IntDcAA 90
Christy, Arthur Hill 1923- WhoAm 90, WhoWor 91
Christy, Audrey Meyer 1933- WhoAmW 91
Christy, Briceida 1950- WhoWor 91
Christy, Carolyn Thomas 1942- WhoAmW 91
Christy, David Hardacker 1955- WhoSSW 91
Christy, Doris 1942- St&PR 91
Christy, Edmund F. BioIn 16
Christy, Gary A. 1956- St&PR 91
Christy, Howard Chandler 1872-1952 WhoAmA 91N
Christy, James Walter 1938- WhoAm 90
Christy, John Gilray 1932- St&PR 91, WhoAm 90
Christy, Joseph Thomas, Jr. 1945- WhoE 91
Christy, June NewYTBS 90 [port]
Christy, June 1925-1990 OxCPMus
Christy, Kathleen Ann 1953- WhoAmW 91
Christy, Marian WhoAm 90
Christy, Myron M. 1917- St&PR 91
Christy, Nicholas Pierson 1923- WhoAm 90
Christy, Ralph L, Jr. BiDrAPA 89
Christy, Richard R 1952- BiDrAPA 89
Christy, Robert Allen 1956- WhoEmL 91, WhoSSW 91
Christy, Teresa E. 1927-1982 BioIn 16
Christy, William Paul 1953- WhoSSW 91
Chriswell, Barbara Ann 1943- St&PR 91
Chrobok, Jan M 1929- BiDrAPA 89
Chroman, Allan Stuart 1954- BiDrAPA 89
Chrominski, Andrew 1935-1989 BioIn 16
Chromulak, Michael Thomas 1929- St&PR 91
Chromy, James R. 1940- St&PR 91
Chrones, Lambros C BiDrAPA 89
Chronic, Byron John 1921- WhoAm 90
Chronister, Jay L. 1934- WhoSSW 91
Chronley, James Andrew 1930- WhoAm 90
Chrust, Steven G. 1949- St&PR 91
Chrysler, Walter P. 1875-1940 WorAlBi
Chrysler, Walter Percy 1875-1940 BioIn 16, EncABHB 5 [port]
Chrysler, Walter Percy 1909-1988 BioIn 16
Chrysostomos, Archbishop 1927- WhoWor 91
Chrysostomos of Oreoi 1945- WhoEmL 91
Chrysostomos of Oreoi, Bishop 1945- WhoAm 90
Chrysoulakis, Gennadios WhoWor 91
Chryssa 1933- BiDWomA, WhoAm 90, WhoAmA 91
Chryssafopoulos, Nicholas 1919- WhoAm 90
Chryssanthou, Alina Helen 1962- WhoEmL 91

Chryssicas, Valerie Foster 1955- WhoAmW 91
Chryssis, George Christopher 1947- St&PR 91, WhoE 91, WhoWor 91
Chryssoveryi, Crystallia 1862-1904 EncCoWW
Chryst, Gary 1949- WhoAm 90
Chrystal, John WhoAm 90
Chrystie, Frances N 1904-1986 SmATA 60
Chrystie, Frances Nicholson 1904- AuBYP 90
Chrystie, Thomas L. 1933- St&PR 91
Chrzan-Seelig, Patricia Ann 1954- WhoAmW 91
Chrzanowski, Diana Stella 1966- WhoE 91
Chrzanowski, Gerard 1913- BiDrAPA 89
Chrzanowski, Lionel Michel 1958- WhoWor 91
Chrzanowski, Ronald P. 1942- St&PR 91
Chrzavzez, Georges Ladislas 1939- WhoWor 91
Chu Teh 1886-1976 WorAlBi
Chu, Ann Maria WhoAmW 91
Chu, Benjamin Thomas Peng-Nien 1932- WhoAm 90
Chu, C. K. 1927- WhoAm 90
Chu, Chauncey C. 1924- St&PR 91
Chu, Chien-Hung 1919- WhoWor 91
Chu, Ching-Wu BioIn 16
Chu, Cho-Ho 1947- WhoWor 91
Chu, Chung-Bin 1923- WhoWor 91
Chu, Chung-Chou 1948- BiDrAPA 89
Chu, David S. C. 1944- WhoAm 90
Chu, David Yuk 1945- WhoE 91
Chu, Diane BiDrAPA 89
Chu, Donald Lee 1953- WhoSSW 91
Chu, Dong Sun BioIn 16
Chu, Ernest D. 1946- St&PR 91
Chu, Foo 1921- WhoE 91
Chu, Franklin Dean 1948- WhoWor 91
Chu, Gene 1936- WhoAmA 91
Chu, Hoi L. 1947- WhoE 91
Chu, Hung-Ming BiDrAPA 89
Chu, James Alexander 1950- BiDrAPA 89
Chu, Jeffrey Chuan 1919- WhoAm 90
Chu, Jen-Yih 1940- WhoAm 90
Chu, Johnson C H 1918- BiDrAPA 89
Chu, Johnson Chin Sheng 1918- WhoAm 90, WhoWor 91
Chu, Julia Nee 1940- WhoAmA 91
Chu, Kuang-Han 1919- WhoAm 90
Chu, Morgan 1950- WhoEmL 91
Chu, Paul BioIn 16
Chu, Paul Ching-Wu 1941- WhoAm 90, WhoSSW 91
Chu, Raphael KS BiDrAPA 89
Chu, Richard Chao-Fan 1933- WhoAm 90, WhoWor 91
Chu, Robin NewYTBS 90
Chu, Roderick Gong-Wah 1949- WhoAm 90, WhoE 91, WhoEmL 91, WhoWor 91
Chu, Shirley Shan-Chi 1929- WhoAmW 91
Chu, Steven 1948- WhoAm 90
Chu, Ta 1624?-1705? BioIn 16
Chu, Tsann Ming 1938- WhoAm 90
Chu, Valentin Yuan-ling 1919- WhoE 91, WhoWor 91
Chu, Victor Lap-Lik 1957- WhoWor 91
Chu, Wen-djang 1914- WhoAm 90
Chu, Wesley Wei-Chin 1936- WhoAm 90
Chu, Yee-Yeen 1949- WhoEmL 91
Chua, Boon-Chye BiDrAPA 89
Chua, Corazon N 1948- BiDrAPA 89
Chua, Evelyn Bautista 1950- WhoAmW 91
Chua, Leon O. 1936- WhoAm 90
Chua, Manuel Ortiga, Jr. 1948- BiDrAPA 89
Chua, Marietta M BiDrAPA 89
Chua, Primitivo D. 1935- WhoWor 91
Chua, Streamson Tan 1927- BiDrAPA 89
Chua, Tommy Dy 1955- WhoWor 91
Chua-Tasciotti, Nenita S BiDrAPA 89
Chuan, Leekpai 1938- WhoWor 91
Chuan, Victoria Keng-hua 1921- IntWWM 90
Chuang, Frank Shiunn-Jea 1942- WhoAm 90, WhoE 91
Chuang, Henry Tan 1952- BiDrAPA 89
Chuang, Shih S. 1940- St&PR 91
Chuaqui, Rolando Basim 1935- WhoWor 91
Chubar', Vlas IAkovlevich 1891-1939 BioIn 16
Chubb, Donald Burke 1924- St&PR 91
Chubb, Elmer MajTwCW
Chubb, Hilkka Aileen 1930- WhoWrEP 89
Chubb, Percy, III 1934- St&PR 91, WhoAm 90
Chubb, Stephen Darrow 1944- WhoAm 90
Chubb, Talbot Albert 1923- WhoAm 90
Chuber, August Bruce 1922- St&PR 91
Chubinsky, Peter Martin 1953- BiDrAPA 89
Chuck, Harry Cousins 1904- WhoE 91
Chuck, Terri M. 1944- St&PR 91
Chuck, Walter Goonsun 1920- WhoAm 90, WhoWor 91
Chud, Laurence S 1950- BiDrAPA 89
Chudek, Christopher William 1963- WhoEmL 91
Chudgar, Ashok Babulal 1951- WhoSSW 91
Chudkowski, Joseph Michael 1939- St&PR 91
Chudleigh, Mary 1656-1710 BiDEWW, BioIn 16, FemiCLE
Chudnoff, Jay 1945- St&PR 91
Chudnovsky, Christine Pardo 1958- WhoEmL 91
Chudoba, David Thomas 1953- WhoEmL 91
Chudobiak, Walter James 1942- WhoE 91, WhoWor 91
Chudzinski, Mark Adam 1956- WhoWor 91
Chueca, Federico 1846-1908 OxCPMus
Chuhan, Jagjit 1955- BiDWomA
Chuhran, Linda 1949- WhoAmW 91
Chuikov, Vasilii 1900-1982 WorAlBi
Chukhrai, Grigori 1921- BioIn 16
Chukovskaya, Lidia Korneevna 1907- EncCoWW
Chukovsky, Kornei 1882-1969 AuBYP 90
Chuks-Orji, Austin Ogonna 1943- WhoWor 91
Chulick, Alberta Bjorkman 1951- WhoEmL 91
Chumacero, Ali 1918- HispWr 90
Chuman, Dwight 1952- St&PR 91
Chumas, Constantine 1935- St&PR 91
Chumbris, Stephen Claude 1950- WhoEmL 91
Chumley, Donnie Ann 1942- WhoAmW 91
Chumley, John Wesley 1928- WhoAmA 91N
Chumley, Norris Jewett 1956- WhoEmL 91
Chumsky, Sandra Evelyn 1934- WhoAmW 91
Chun Doo Hwan 1931- WhoWor 91
Chun, Bonnie B C BiDrAPA 89
Chun, Dai Ho 1905- WhoWor 91
Chun, Doo Hwan BioIn 16
Chun, Edward Hong BiDrAPA 89
Chun, Kyung S 1937- BiDrAPA 89
Chun, Lowell Koon Wa 1944- WhoWor 91
Chun, Michael Sing Fong 1944- St&PR 91
Chun, Rupert Kaisun 1944- St&PR 91
Chun, Ryo Sook 1944- BiDrAPA 89
Chun, Se-Choong 1929- WhoWor 91
Chun, Theodore K J 1933- BiDrAPA 89
Chun, Thomas K. 1935- St&PR 91
Chun, Wallace K C 1928- BiDrAPA 89
Chun, Wendy Sau Wan 1951- WhoAmW 91, WhoWor 91
Chun, Yang Kog 1942- BiDrAPA 89
Chun-Hoon, Lowell Koon Ying 1949- WhoEmL 91
Chunawala, Shaista B BiDrAPA 89
Chundu, Sai Babu BiDrAPA 89
Chung Ling Soo 1861-1918 BioIn 16
Chung Se Yung 1923- WhoWor 91
Chung, Carol Yonge 1960- BiDrAPA 89
Chung, Chi Yung 1920- WhoWor 91
Chung, Chin-Suck 1935- BiDrAPA 89
Chung, Cho Man BiDrAPA 89
Chung, Cho Man 1918- WhoWor 91
Chung, Christopher K BiDrAPA 89
Chung, Connie BioIn 16, ConAu 132
Chung, Connie 1946- WorAlBi
Chung, Constance Yu-Hwa 1946- ConAu 132, WhoAm 90, WhoAmW 91, WhoE 91
Chung, Cynthia Norton 1955- WhoAmW 91, WhoEmL 91
Chung, Deborah Duen Ling 1952- WhoAmW 91
Chung, Dong-Ha 1942- BiDrAPA 89
Chung, Edward Kooyoung 1931- WhoAm 90
Chung, Fan R. K. 1949- WhoE 91
Chung, Gene Koo 1943- BiDrAPA 89
Chung, Gloria W BiDrAPA 89
Chung, Hack R 1937- BiDrAPA 89, WhoE 91
Chung, Hae Jin 1940- BiDrAPA 89
Chung, Henry 1962- BiDrAPA 89
Chung, Hwan Yung 1927- WhoWor 91
Chung, Hyungkun 1945- WhoWor 91
Chung, Jack Chun-Hsien 1953- WhoEmL 91
Chung, Jae Young BiDrAPA 89
Chung, Jane Yeoun BiDrAPA 89
Chung, Jay Hoon 1947- WhoWor 91
Chung, Joseph Sang-hoon 1929- WhoAm 90
Chung, Joyce Yong BiDrAPA 89
Chung, Jung Git 1922- WhoAm 90, WhoE 91
Chung, Kyung Cho 1921- WhoAm 90, WhoWor 91
Chung, Kyung-Wha 1948- IntWWM 90, PenDiMP, WhoWor 91
Chung, Myung-Wha 1944- PenDiMP
Chung, Myung-Whun 1953- CurBio 90 [port], IntWWM 90, PenDiMP
Chung, Paul Myungha 1929- WhoAm 90
Chung, Richard S. 1938- St&PR 91
Chung, Sae Youn 1942- BiDrAPA 89
Chung, Sandra L. 1938- WhoAmW 91
Chung, Soon-Hyung BiDrAPA 89
Chung, Stewart 1956- WhoEmL 91
Chung, Su Jin 1943- BiDrAPA 89
Chung, Sul 1934- BiDrAPA 89
Chung, Wai Mun 1932- St&PR 91
Chung, Young-Cho BiDrAPA 89
Chung, Young-iob 1928- WhoAm 90
Chung, Yung-Kul 1929- BiDrAPA 89
Chung, Yung Sik 1942- BiDrAPA 89
Chungviwatanant, Smith 1959- WhoWor 91
Chunn, Leona Hayes 1885- WhoWrEP 89
Chupa, Barbara Ann BiDrAPA 89
Chupack, Leah Sadovnick 1921- WhoAmW 91
Chupela, Dolores Carole 1952- WhoAmW 91
Chupik, Eugene Jerry 1931- WhoSSW 91
Chupka, William Andrew 1923- WhoAm 90
Chuprevich, Joseph W BiDrAPA 89
Chuprinko, John Andrew 1955- St&PR 91
Churan, J. Thomas 1940- St&PR 91
Churbanov, Yuri BioIn 16
Churberg, Fanny 1845-1892 BiDWomA
Church, Abiah A. 1922- WhoAm 90
Church, Alfred John 1829-1912 AuBYP 90
Church, Barton Kay 1926- WhoE 91
Church, Benjamin 1639-1718 EncCRAm, WhNaAH
Church, Benjamin 1734?-1778? BioIn 16
Church, Brooks Davis 1918- WhoAm 90
Church, Bubba 1924- Ballpl 90
Church, C. Howard 1904- WhoAm 90
Church, C Howard 1904- WhoAmA 91
Church, Carol Bauer AuBYP 90
Church, Charles H., Jr. 1926- St&PR 91
Church, Douglas M. 1950- St&PR 91
Church, Earlyn 1939- St&PR 91
Church, Earlyn Eva 1939- WhoE 91
Church, Edwin Arnold 1939- St&PR 91
Church, Edwin H 1925- BiDrAPA 89
Church, Edwin Harold 1925- WhoE 91
Church, Eugene Lent 1925- WhoAm 90
Church, F. Forrester BioIn 16
Church, Francis Pharcellus 1839-1906 BioIn 16
Church, Frank 1924-1984 WorAlBi
Church, Frank Forrester 1948- WhoAm 90
Church, Frederic Edwin 1826-1900 BioIn 16
Church, Frederick E 1826-1900 WhoAmA 91N
Church, Frederick Edwin 1826-1900 WorAlBi
Church, Gary Ray 1946- WhoSSW 91
Church, George Lyle 1903- WhoAm 90
Church, George Millord 1924- WhoSSW 91
Church, Henry 1836-1908 MusmAFA
Church, Henry C., Jr. 1905- St&PR 91
Church, Herbert Stephen, Jr. 1920- WhoAm 90
Church, Irene Zaboly 1947- WhoAmW 91
Church, James Arlan 1936- St&PR 91
Church, John A. 1920- St&PR 91
Church, John F., Jr. 1936- St&PR 91
Church, John Franklin, Jr. 1936- WhoAm 90
Church, John Irwin 1919- WhoWrEP 89
Church, John Stewart 1948- WhoEmL 91
Church, John Trammell 1917- St&PR 91, WhoAm 90
Church, Levi Ruggles 1836-1892 DcCanB 12
Church, Marguerite Stitt NewYTBS 90 [port]
Church, Marguerite Stitt 1892-1990 BioIn 16, CurBio 90N
Church, Martha Eleanor 1930- WhoAm 90, WhoAmW 91, WhoE 91
Church, Mary Ethel St&PR 91
Church, Maude 1949- WhoAmA 91
Church, Nancy Jeanne 1950- WhoEmL 91
Church, Philip Throop 1931- WhoAm 90, WhoE 91
Church, Randolph Warner, Jr. 1934- WhoAm 90
Church, Richard Dwight 1936- WhoE 91
Church, Russell Miller 1930- WhoAm 90
Church, Sonia Jane Shutter 1940- WhoAmW 91
Church, Stanley E. 1910- St&PR 91
Church, Theodore H. 1925- St&PR 91
Church, Thomas A. 1933- St&PR 91
Church, Thomas Gale 1940- St&PR 91
Church, Thomas Trowbridge 1919- WhoAm 90
Churchill, Brenda Carol BiDrAPA 89
Churchill, Buntzie Ellis WhoE 91
Churchill, Caryl BioIn 16
Churchill, Caryl 1938- FemiCLE, MajTwCW, WorAu 1980 [port]
Churchill, Cynthia Marie BiDrAPA 89
Churchill, Daniel Wayne 1947- WhoEmL 91
Churchill, Diane 1941- WhoAmA 91
Churchill, E Richard 1937- ConAu 30NR
Churchill, Frank 1901-1942 OxCPMus
Churchill, Glen D. 1934- St&PR 91
Churchill, Hugo M. 1939- St&PR 91
Churchill, J H 1920-1990 ConAu 131
Churchill, James Garton 1930- WhoAm 90
Churchill, James Paul 1924- WhoAm 90
Churchill, Jennie Jerome 1850-1921 BioAmW
Churchill, Jerry M. 1939- St&PR 91
Churchill, John 1650-1722 WorAlBi
Churchill, John William 1931- WhoE 91
Churchill, Lisa Taylor 1948- WhoAmW 91
Churchill, Mary C. ODwPR 91
Churchill, Neil Center 1927- WhoAm 90
Churchill, Randolph 1849-1895 WorAlBi
Churchill, Randolph Henry Spencer 1849-1895 BioIn 16
Churchill, Rogers Platt 1902-1989 ConAu 129
Churchill, Ruth Pierson 1896- WhoAmW 91
Churchill, Sarah 1914-1982 ConAu 129
Churchill, Savannah 1919- DrBlPA 90
Churchill, Scott Richard 1956- WhoSSW 91
Churchill, Stephen Wood 1941- BiDrAPA 89
Churchill, Stuart Winston 1920- WhoAm 90
Churchill, Thomas Bell Lindsay 1907-1990 ConAu 131
Churchill, Thomas James 1824-1905 BioIn 16
Churchill, Thomas John 1961- WhoEmL 91
Churchill, Verne Bartlett 1932- St&PR 91
Churchill, Winston 1874-1965 BioIn 16, DcLB 100 [port], MajTwCW, WorAlBi
Churchill, Winston John 1940- WhoAm 90
Churchill, Winston S 1940- ConAu 131
Churchland, Patricia Smith 1943- WhoAm 90
Churchman, Mary BiDEWW
Churchman, Norman P. 1910- St&PR 91
Churchville, Lida Holland 1933- WhoAmW 91
Churchward, James 1852-1936 EncO&P 3
Churg, Jacob 1910- WhoAm 90, WhoWor 91
Churg, P. Michel 1945- WhoWor 91
Churgin, Bathia Dina 1928- IntWWM 90, WhoWor 91
Churinske, Paul Joseph 1948- St&PR 91
Churm, Peter 1926- St&PR 91
Chused, Andrew Michael 1949- St&PR 91
Chused, Judith Fingert 1941- BiDrAPA 89
Chused, Paul Leon 1943- St&PR 91
Chusid, Judith Francine 1947- WhoAmW 91
Chusid, Martin 1925- IntWWM 90
Chusmir, Janet BioIn 16, WhoAmW 91
Chusmir, Janet NewYTBS 90
Chustek, Roy Stuart 1948- WhoE 91
Chustz, Harris J. 1915- St&PR 91
Chut, Frank Joseph 1934- St&PR 91
Chute, Arthur L. 1945- St&PR 91
Chute, B. J. 1913-1987 BioIn 16
Chute, Beatrice Joy 1913-1987 BioIn 16
Chute, Marchette 1909- DcLB 103 [port], WhoAm 90, WhoWrEP 89
Chute, Marchette Gaylord 1909- AuBYP 90
Chute, Peggy Jo 1951- WhoAmW 91
Chute, Robert A. 1938- St&PR 91
Chute, Robert M 1926- WhoWrEP 89
Chute, Robert Maurice 1926- WhoAm 90
Chutes, Brenda WhoWrEP 89
Chutich, Margaret Helen 1958- WhoAmW 91
Chutjian, Seta Leonie WhoAmA 91
Chutkow, Jerry Grant 1933- WhoAm 90
Chutkow, Lee Robinson 1927- BiDrAPA 89
Chvala, Robert J. 1944- St&PR 91
Chvany, Catherine Vakar 1927- WhoAmW 91
Chwalek, C.T. 1943- St&PR 91
Chwalk, Taras J. 1945- St&PR 91
Chwast, Seymour 1931- ConDes 90, WhoAm 90, WhoAmA 91
Chwat, Jacques BioIn 16
Chwatsky, Ann 1942- WhoAmW 91
Chylak, Nestor 1922-1982 Ballpl 90
Chynoweth, Alan Gerald 1927- WhoAm 90, WhoE 91
Chyriwski, John Richard 1957- St&PR 91
Chytil, Frank 1924- WhoAm 90
Chytilova, Vera 1929- BioIn 16
Chyu, Ho Chong BiDrAPA 89
Chyung, Chi Han 1933- WhoWor 91

Ciabattari, Jane Dotson 1946- WhoWrEP 89
Ciaburri, Joseph Victor 1929- St&PR 91
Ciacchi, Jacopo PenDiDA 89
Ciaccio-Crowley, Ritamarie 1966- WhoAmW 91
Ciafardini, Gino 1950- WhoWor 91
Ciak, Brenda Susan 1955- WhoAmW 91
Ciak, Jack 1947- WhoE 91
Ciak, Karl 1955- WhoE 91
Cialdea, James Giulio 1960- WhoE 91
Cialente, Fausta Terni- 1900- EncCoWW
Ciallella, Albert John 1951- WhoSSW 91
Cialli, Antonio PenDiDA 89
Cialli, Lorenzo PenDiDA 89
Cialone, Richard Michael 1948- St&PR 91
Ciampaglia, Carlo 1891-1975 WhoAmA 91N
Cianchette, Alton E. 1930- St&PR 91
Cianci, Vincent Albert, Jr. 1941- WhoAm 90
Ciancimino, David Eugene BiDrAPA 89
Ciancimino, Matthew Rudolph 1925- WhoAm 90
Ciancio, June 1920- WhoAmA 91
Ciancio, Sebastian Gene 1937- WhoAm 90
Cianciola, Charles Salvatore 1933- St&PR 91
Cianciulli, Robert Philip 1945- St&PR 91
Cianelli, Alfred A., Jr. 1930- St&PR 91
Cianfarani, Gina 1960- WhoWrEP 89
Cianflone, Francis Edward 1930- WhoSSW 91
Cianfoni, Emilio 1946- WhoAmA 91
Ciangio, Cynthia M. 1953- WhoWor 91
Ciangio, Donna Lenore 1949- WhoE 91
Ciani, Suzanne NewAgMG
Ciani, Suzanne Elizabeth 1946- IntWWM 90
Ciannella, Giuliano 1943- IntWWM 90
Ciao, Frederick J. WhoE 91
Ciappi, Mario Luigi 1909- WhoWor 91
Ciaramella, Donald A. ODwPR 91
Ciaramella, Raffaele Joseph 1949- St&PR 91
Ciaramelli, Letizia C BiDrAPA 89
Ciaranello, Roland David 1943- BiDrAPA 89
Ciarcia, James J 1948- BiDrAPA 89
Ciardi, John 1916-1986 AuBYP 90, BioIn 16, ConAu 33NR, MajTwCW, WorAlBi
Ciardiello, Joseph G 1953- WhoAmA 91
Ciark-Karstien, Diana Barbara 1946- WhoE 91
Ciarlette, David George 1952- St&PR 91
Ciarlillo, Marjorie Ann 1940- IntWWM 90
Ciarlo, John Louis 1945- St&PR 91
Ciarochi, Sandra Reichert 1943- WhoSSW 91
Ciarrocca, Norman St&PR 91
Ciarrochi, Ray WhoAmA 91
Ciarula, Thomas Alan 1948- WhoEmL 91
Ciasca, Richard Neil 1941- BiDrAPA 89
Ciatteo, Carmen Thomas 1921- BiDrAPA 89, WhoWor 91
Ciatto, Debi Lynn 1956- WhoAmW 91
Ciaverelli, Robert BiDrAPA 89
Ciavola, Louise Arlene 1933- WhoAmW 91
Ciavolino, Marco 1956- WhoE 91
Cibber, Caius Gabriel 1630-1700 BioIn 16
Cibber, Susanna 1714-1766 PenDiMP
Cibreiro Santalla, Pilar 1952- EncCoWW
Cibroski, Ronald Bryan 1945- St&PR 91
Cic, Milan 1932- WhoWor 91
Cicalese, Amy Luisa 1954- WhoEmL 91
Cicansky, Victor 1935- WhoAmA 91
Ciccarelli, John A. 1939- St&PR 91
Ciccarelli, Lawrence John 1949- St&PR 91
Ciccarelli, William E. 1920- St&PR 91
Ciccarone, Henry BioIn 16
Ciccarone, Richard Anthony 1952- WhoAm 90
Ciccaroni, Andrew John 1962- WhoE 91
Cicci, Henry Edward 1945- WhoSSW 91
Cicco, Martin John 1955- St&PR 91
Ciccolella, Anthony 1959- WhoE 91
Ciccolella, Catherine Anne 1944- WhoSSW 91
Ciccolini, Aldo 1925- IntWWM 90, PenDiMP
Ciccone, Amy Navratil 1950- WhoAmA 91
Ciccone, Anne Panepinto 1943- WhoAmW 91
Ciccone, J Richard 1943- BiDrAPA 89
Ciccone, J. Richard 1943- WhoAm 90
Ciccone, Joseph BiDrAPA 89
Ciccone, Marshall John 1947- St&PR 91, WhoEmL 91
Ciccone, Patrick Edwin 1944- BiDrAPA 89, WhoAm 90
Ciccotelli, Teresa T. 1951- St&PR 91
Cicen, John Randolph 1942- St&PR 91
Cicerelle, Carole Anne 1940- WhoAmW 91
Ciceri, Leo 1928-1970 OxCCanT
Cicero, Carmen L WhoAmA 91
Cicero, Carmen Louis 1926- WhoAm 90
Cicero, Frank, Jr. 1935- WhoAm 90
Cicero, Marcus Tullius 106BC-43BC BioIn 16, WorAlBi, WrPh P
Cicero, Mary Beth 1953- WhoEmL 91
Cicet, Donald James 1940- WhoSSW 91, WhoWor 91
Cichacki, Joseph C. 1949- St&PR 91
Cichoke, Anthony Joseph, Jr. 1931- WhoWor 91
Cichowski, Maryann Emily 1918- WhoAmW 91
Cicinelli, Richard Ray 1946- BiDrAPA 89
Ciciora, Walter Stanley 1942- St&PR 91, WhoAm 90
Cicippio, Joseph BioIn 16
Cicirelli, Victor George 1926- WhoAm 90
Cicolani, Angelo George 1933- WhoSSW 91, WhoWor 91
Cicotte, Al 1929-1982 Ballpl 90
Cicotte, Eddie 1884-1969 Ballpl 90 [port]
Cid 1043?-1099 BioIn 16
Cid Campeador 1043?-1099 BioIn 16
Cid, El 1043?-1099 WorAlBi
Cid, A. Louis 1923- WhoHisp 91
Cid Perez, Jose 1906- WhoHisp 91
Ciechandver, Joseph 1933- WhoE 91
Ciechanover, Joseph 1933- St&PR 91, WhoAm 90
Ciecieznski, Barbara Jean 1950- WhoSSW 91
Cielinski, Audrey Ann 1957- WhoAmW 91, WhoEmL 91, WhoSSW 91, WhoWor 91
Cielle, Cynthia Elizabeth 1949- WhoEmL 91
Ciereszko, Leon Stanley 1917- WhoAm 90
Cierva, Juan de la 1896-1936 BioIn 16
Ciervo, Frank J. ODwPR 91
Ciesinski, Kristine PenDiMP
Ciesinski, Kristine Frances 1952- IntWWM 90
Ciesla, Casimir Charles 1930- St&PR 91
Ciesla, Thomas K 1935- BiDrAPA 89
Cieslak, Arthur Kazimer 1915- WhoAm 90
Cieslewicz, Roman 1930- ConDes 90
Ciesniewski, Anthony Richard 1945- WhoEmL 91
Cifarelli, Frank 1918-1988 BioIn 16
Cifelli, Barbara Doris 1942- WhoAmW 91
Cifelli, John Louis 1923- WhoAm 90
Ciferri, Orio E. 1928- WhoWor 91
Cifolelli, Alberta 1931- WhoAmA 91
Cifolelli, Alberta Carmella 1931- WhoE 91
Cifu, Robert BiDrAPA 89
Cifuni, Joseph J. 1942- St&PR 91
Cigler, James Douglas 1953- WhoAm 90
Cigna, Gina 1900- IntWWM 90, PenDiMP
Cignetti, Franklin E. 1939- WhoE 91
Cihlar, Christine Carol 1948- WhoEmL 91, WhoWrEP 89
Cihlar, Frank Phillip 1943- WhoAm 90
Cihocki, Tobiann 1965- WhoAmW 91
Cikanek, Harry Arthur, III 1959- WhoEmL 91, WhoSSW 91
Cikker, Jan 1911- IntWWM 90
Cikovsky, Nicolai 1894-1984 WhoAmA 91N
Cikovsky, Nicolai, Jr. 1933- WhoAm 90, WhoAmA 91
Cilella, Salvatore G, Jr 1941- WhoAmA 91
Cilella, Salvatore George, Jr. 1941- WhoAm 90, WhoSSW 91
Ciletti, Christine Joy 1945- WhoAmW 91
Cilfone, Nicholas J. 1950- St&PR 91
Cilfone, Nicholas Joseph 1950- WhoAm 90
Cillan-Chung, Lauretta R 1933- BiDrAPA 89
Cillario, Carlo Felice 1915- IntWWM 90, PenDiMP
Cillie, Petrus Johannes 1917- WhoWor 91
Cillo, Larry Joseph 1955- WhoEmL 91
Cilluffo, John Mariano 1950- WhoEmL 91
Cilurzo, Stephen 1953- WhoEmL 91
Cima, Alex NewAgMG
Cima da Conegliano, Giovanni Battista 1459?-1517? IntDcAA 90
Cimabue 1240?-1302 IntDcAA 90
Cimabue, Giovanni 1240?-1302 WorAlBi
Cimadevilla, Francisco Javier 1961- WhoEmL 91
Cimarosa, Domenico 1749-1801 PenDiMP A
Cimbalo, Robert W WhoAmA 91
Cimbalo, Robert William 1935- WhoE 91
Cimeno, Thomas E., Jr. 1944- WhoAm 90
Ciment, Melvyn 1941- WhoE 91
Cimiluca, H. Thomas 1927- St&PR 91
Ciminello, Emanuel, Jr. WhoHisp 91
Ciminero, Gary L. 1943- St&PR 91
Ciminero, Gary Louis 1943- WhoAm 90
Cimini, Maria Dolores 1958- WhoAmW 91
Cimini, Theresa Ann 1947- WhoEmL 91
Cimino, Frank Joseph 1947- WhoEmL 91
Cimino, James Ernest 1928- WhoAm 90
Cimino, Joseph Anthony 1934- WhoAm 90
Cimino, Maria AuBYP 90
Cimino, Michael BioIn 16
Cimino, Michael 1948- WhoAm 90, WorAlBi
Cimino, Paul Luke 1963- WhoE 91
Cimino, Pete 1942- Ballpl 90
Cimino, Philip A. 1950- St&PR 91
Cimino, Richard Dennis 1947- WhoEmL 91
Cimino, Thomas 1935- St&PR 91
Cimmet, Gerald 1941- WhoE 91
Cimmino, Daniel Louis 1964- WhoE 91
Cimochowicz, Diane Marie 1955- WhoAmW 91
Cimoli, Gino 1929- Ballpl 90
Cimonetti, Thomas Curran 1928- BiDrAPA 89
Cimorell, Alberta May WhoAmW 91
Cimoszko, Bogy Boguslawa 1956- WhoEmL 91
Cimpl, David 1958- St&PR 91
Cina, Colin 1943- BioIn 16
Cinabro, Robert Henry 1948- WhoEmL 91
Cinader, Bernhard 1919- WhoAm 90
Cinader, Emily BioIn 16
Cinca, Eduardo E 1913- BiDrAPA 89
Cincinnatus, Lucius Quinctius 519?BC- WorAlBi
Cinciotta, Linda Ann 1943- WhoAmW 91
Cincotta, Anthony Welsh 1947- BiDrAPA 89
Cincotta, Gale BioIn 16
Cindrich, Stephen John BiDrAPA 89
Cineas, Fritz Nerval 1932- WhoWor 91
Cinense, Rosa Erce BiDrAPA 89
Cini, T.J. St&PR 91
Ciniglio, Ada Vivian 1935- WhoAmW 91
Cinlar, Erhan 1941- WhoE 91
Cinotti, Alfonse Anthony 1923- WhoAm 90
Cinquin, Emmanuelle 1908- ConAu 131
Cinquin, Emmanuelle, Sister ConAu 131
Cintorino, Richard P. 1936- St&PR 91
Cintron, Joseph M 1921- WhoAmA 91
Cintron, Martin 1948- WhoHisp 91
Ciobota, Constantin F BiDrAPA 89
Ciobotaru, Gillian 1936- BiDWomA
Cioccio, Ellen Lacey 1935- WhoAmW 91
Cioci, Gerald Robert 1942- St&PR 91
Cioffari, Richard J. 1943- IntWWM 90
Cioffi, Albert F BiDrAPA 89
Cioffi, Paul 1896-1989 BioIn 16
Ciolino, Charles Peter 1955- BiDrAPA 89, WhoE 91
Ciolli, Antoinette 1915- WhoAmW 91, WhoE 91, WhoWor 91
Cion, Judith Ann 1943- WhoAm 90
Cion, Maurice C BiDrAPA 89
Cion, Richard M. 1943- WhoAm 90
Cioni, Joseph Anthony 1939- St&PR 91
Cioni, Renato 1929- IntWWM 90
Cioran, E.M. 1911- ConLC 64 [port]
Cioroiu, Michael Gelu 1947- WhoE 91
Cioschi, Eugene Anthony 1950- WhoEmL 91
Ciotti, Eugene Barney 1928- WhoAm 90
Ciotti, Frank 1944- St&PR 91
Ciotti, George Anthony 1931- St&PR 91
Ciottone, Richard Thomas 1945- St&PR 91
Cipau, Gabriel R. 1941- St&PR 91
Cipich, Thomas Hilary 1939- St&PR 91
Ciplijauskaite, Birute 1929- ConAu 31NR, WhoAm 90
Cipoletti, Joy 1959- WhoAmW 91
Cipolla, Thomas Alphonse 1950- WhoEmL 91
Cipolla, Wilma Reid 1930- IntWWM 90
Cipollaro, Michael A. 1935- St&PR 91
Cipollina, Anthony 1928- St&PR 91
Cipollini, Mark Dennis 1951- St&PR 91
Cipollone, Antonio BioIn 16, NewYTBS 90
Cipollone, Nina A. 1953- WhoAmW 91
Cipriani, Arthur Andrew 1875-1945 BioIn 16
Cipriani, Frank Anthony 1933- WhoAm 90
Cipriani, Guido Emilio 1956- St&PR 91
Cipriani, John F., Sr. 1924- St&PR 91
Cipriani, Roberta 1967- WhoEmL 91
Cipriano, Fred Louis 1944- St&PR 91
Cipriano, Gaetano Peter 1956- St&PR 91
Cipriano, Grace Irene 1925- WhoAmW 91, WhoWor 91
Cipriano, Irene P. 1942- WhoHisp 91
Cipriano, Mary Lynn 1947- WhoAmW 91
Cipriano, Michael R 1942- WhoAmA 91
Cipriano, Michael Robert 1942- WhoE 91
Cipriano, Patricia Ann 1946- WhoWor 91
Cipriano, Peter A. 1921- St&PR 91
Cipriano, William Peter BiDrAPA 89
Ciprich, Sybilla Barry 1957- WhoEmL 91
Cipriotti, Vincent A BiDrAPA 89
Ciraulo, Domenic Anthony 1948- BiDrAPA 89
Ciraulo, Stephen Joseph 1960- WhoEmL 91, WhoSSW 91, WhoWor 91
Circeo, Louis Joseph, Jr. 1934- WhoSSW 91
Circle, Sybil Jean BiDrAPA 89
Circo, Dennis Paul 1947- WhoAm 90, WhoWor 91
Circus, Anthony TwCCr&M 91, WhoWrEP 89
Circus, Philip James 1951- WhoWor 91
Cirelli, Richard Anthony 1940- WhoE 91
Ciresi, Michael 1946- BioIn 16
Ciresi, Michael Vincent 1946- WhoEmL 91, WhoWor 91
Ciresi, Samuel Michael, Jr. 1965- WhoE 91, WhoEmL 91
Ciricillo, Rose Casale 1922- WhoAmW 91
Ciricillo, Samuel Francis 1920- St&PR 91
Ciriclio, Susan E. 1946- WhoAmW 91
Cirillo, John 1943- St&PR 91
Cirillo, Marie 1929- BioIn 16
Cirillo, Vivian Linda 1950- WhoAmW 91, WhoE 91
Cirilo, Amelia Medina 1925- WhoWor 91
Cirincion, John C. 1948- St&PR 91
Cirincione, John Robert 1931- WhoE 91
Cirino, Leonard John 1943- WhoWrEP 89
Cirker, Hayward 1917- WhoAm 90
Cirlot, Kay Cheshire 1940- WhoAmW 91
Cirmenho, Sebastian Rodriguez EncCRAm
Ciroli, J. Vincent, Jr. 1945- St&PR 91
Cirou, Ciquaire PenDiDA 89
Cirpili, Esat Ozcan BiDrAPA 89
Cirrincione, Joseph C. 1936- St&PR 91
Cirucci, Christina A. 1961- WhoEmL 91
Cirucci, Thomas G. 1945- St&PR 91
Cirulli, Albert Joseph 1929- St&PR 91
Cirulli, Vincent 1956- WhoE 91
Ciruti, Joan Estelle 1930- WhoAm 90, WhoAmW 91
Cisco, Galen 1937- Ballpl 90
Cisek, Carol Marie 1926- WhoAmW 91
Cisewski, Fred Louis 1935- St&PR 91
Cisin, Ira H. 1919-1987 BioIn 16
Cisler, Cynthia Marie 1962- WhoAmW 91
Cisler, Theresa Ann 1951- WhoAmW 91, WhoEmL 91
Cismaru, Pat K. 1933- WhoAmW 91
Cisneros, Antonio 1942- ConAu 131, HispWr 90
Cisneros, Carlos R. WhoHisp 91
Cisneros, Evelyn 1955- WhoHisp 91
Cisneros, Florencio Garcia WhoAmA 91
Cisneros, Francisco Jimenez de 1436?-1517 BioIn 16
Cisneros, Fred Andrew 1963- WhoEmL 91
Cisneros, George BioIn 16
Cisneros, Henry BioIn 16
Cisneros, Henry G. 1947- WhoAm 90, WhoSSW 91
Cisneros, Henry Gabriel 1947- WhoHisp 91
Cisneros, James M. 1951- WhoHisp 91
Cisneros, Joe Alvarado 1935- WhoHisp 91
Cisneros, Jose 1910- BioIn 16
Cisneros, Sandra ConAu 131, HispWr 90, WhoHisp 91
Cisney, Marcella WhoAmW 91
Cisney, Marcella BioIn 16
Cissell, Bill 1904-1949 Ballpl 90
Cissell, James Charles 1940- WhoAm 90
Cissey, Ernest Louis Octave Courtot de 1810-1882 BiDFrPL
Cissna, William David 1952- WhoEmL 91
Cissom, Mary Joan 1941- WhoWrEP 89
Cistone, Daniel Anthony, Jr. 1947- St&PR 91
Citarelli, Alessandro Andrea 1960- WhoWor 91
Citerley, Richard L. 1932- St&PR 91
Citino, David John 1947- WhoWrEP 89
Citrin, Andrew Ted 1961- WhoEmL 91
Citrin, Harold L. 1929- St&PR 91
Citrin, Phillip Marshall 1931- WhoAm 90
Citrin, Stephen Marc 1952- WhoEmL 91
Citrine, Walter McLennan 1887-1983 DcNaB 1981
Citrino, Robert Joseph 1933- St&PR 91
Citroen, Andre 1878-1935 BioIn 16
Citroen, Karel Adolf 1920- WhoWor 91
Citrola, Rosemary Nicolina 1958- WhoAmW 91
Citrome, Leslie Lucien BiDrAPA 89
Citron, Beatrice Sally 1929- WhoAmW 91
Citron, Burton 1930- St&PR 91
Citron, David B. 1947- St&PR 91
Citron, David Sanford 1920- WhoAm 90
Citron, Elizabeth Jean 1961- WhoAmW 91
Citron, Harvey Lewis 1942- WhoAmA 91
Citron, Marcia J. 1945- IntWWM 90
Citron, Minna 1896- BiDWomA
Citron, Minna Wright 1896- WhoAmA 91
Citron, Richard Ira 1944- WhoE 91
Citron, Thomas H. St&PR 91
Citry, Edgar BiDrAPA 89
Citton, Clare 1959- WhoEmL 91
Citty, Brenda Vinson 1959- WhoEmL 91
Ciuciura, Leoncjusz 1930- IntWWM 90
Ciuffo, Cynthia Louise 1946- WhoAmW 91, WhoEmL 91
Ciullo, Rosemary WhoAmW 91

Ciurea, Alexandru Ioan BiDrAPA 89
Ciurea, Lucia Elena BiDrAPA 89
Ciurlionis, Mikalojus Konstantinas 1875-1911 BioIn 16
Civale, Biagio A 1935- WhoAmA 91
Civale, Biagio Antonio 1935- WhoE 91
Civardi, Ernesto 1906- WhoWor 91
Civardi, Ernesto 1906-1989 BioIn 16
Civello, Anthony N. 1944- St&PR 91
Civello, Anthony Ned 1944- WhoAm 90
Civello, Ellis John, Jr. BiDrAPA 89
Civello, Teresa R. ODwPR 91
Cividino, Ugo Valentino 1947- IntWWM 90
Civil, Alan 1928-1989 AnObit 1989
Civil, Alan 1929-1989 BioIn 16, PenDiMP
Civiletti, Benjamin Richard 1935- BiDrUSE 89
Civit, Josep Maria 1954- WhoWor 91
Civitello, John Patrick 1939- WhoAmA 91
Civitico, Bruno 1942- WhoAmA 91
Cixi 1835-1908 WomWR [port]
Cixous, Helene 1937- EncCoWW, FemiCLE, MajTwCW
Cizek, Cathy Patrice 1949- WhoEmL 91
Cizek, David John 1959- WhoEmL 91
Cizik, Robert 1931- St&PR 91, WhoAm 90, WhoSSW 91
Cizmadia, Robert Arnold 1952- WhoSSW 91
Claar, John Bennett 1922- WhoAm 90
Claar, John E. 1923- St&PR 91
Claar, Nancy BioIn 16
Claas, Gerhard BioIn 16
Claassen, Manfred W. 1940- WhoWor 91
Claassen, Sharon Elaine 1953- WhoEmL 91
Clabaugh, Elmer Eugene, Jr. 1927- WhoWor 91
Clabaugh, Henry E. 1942- St&PR 91
Clabault, Robert A. 1928- St&PR 91
Clabby, William Robert 1931- St&PR 91, WhoAm 90
Clabes, Judith Grisham 1945- WhoAm 90
Clabin, Anne BiDEWW
Claborn, James R. 1942- St&PR 91
Clack, Douglas Mae 1943- WhoAmW 91
Clack, Jerry 1926- WhoAm 90, WhoE 91
Cladel, Charles E, Jr. BiDrAPA 89
Claes, Daniel John 1931- WhoAm 90, WhoWor 91
Claes, Michael 1951- ODwPR 91
Claes, Willy 1938- WhoWor 91
Claes-Vetter, Stephanie 1884-1974 EncCoWW
Claessens, Hendrik Ivon 1927- WhoWor 91
Claeys, Jerome Joseph, III 1942- WhoAm 90
Claeys, Richard G. ODwPR 91
Claeys Bouuaert, Ignace 1920- WhoWor 91
Claeyssens, Astere E 1924-1990 ConAu 132
Claflin Sisters EncO&P 3
Claflin, Edward 1949- AuBYP 90
Claflin, Robert Malden 1921- WhoAm 90
Claflin, Tennessee C. 1846-1923 BioAmW
Claflin, Tennessee Celeste 1845-1923 BioIn 16
Claflin, Tennessee Celeste 1846-1923 EncO&P 3
Claflin, Victoria 1838-1927 BioIn 16, EncO&P 3
Clagett, Arthur Frank, Jr. 1916- WhoAm 90, WhoWor 91
Clagett, Brice McAdoo 1933- WhoAm 90, WhoE 91
Clagett, Diana Wharton Sinkler 1943- WhoE 91
Clagett, John 1916- AuBYP 90, LiHiK
Clagett, Leslie Plummer 1956- WhoAmW 91
Clagett, Marshall 1916- WhoAm 90
Clagett, Oscar Theron 1908- WhoAm 90
Clagett, William H., IV 1938- WhoAm 90
Clagg, Thomas Lytle 1943- St&PR 91
Claghorn, James L 1935- BiDrAPA 89
Claghorn, James Lawrence 1817-1884 BioIn 16
Clagnaz, Peter John 1951- BiDrAPA 89
Clagstone, Paul 1871-1932 AmLegL
Clague, Frank 1865-1952 AmLegL
Clague, John Rogers 1928- WhoAmA 91
Claiborne, Craig 1920- WhoWrEP 89, WorAlBi
Claiborne, Elisabeth 1929- ConAmBL
Claiborne, Jerry BioIn 16
Claiborne, John H., III 1946- St&PR 91
Claiborne, Liz BioIn 16
Claiborne, Liz 1929- WhoAm 90, WhoAmW 91, WhoE 91, WhoWor 91
Claiborne, P. Michael 1949- St&PR 91
Claiborne, Robert BioIn 16
Claiborne, Robert NewYTBS 90
Claiborne, Robert 1919- ConAu 31NR
Claiborne, Robert 1919-1990 ConAu 130
Claiborne, William 1587-1677 EncCRAm
Claing, Karen Schaefer 1952- WhoAmW 91
Clair, Carolyn Green 1909- WhoAmW 91, WhoWor 91
Clair, David R. 1935- St&PR 91
Clair, Dick BioIn 16
Clair, Kenneth E. 1934- ODwPR 91
Claire, Allen Barry 1933- WhoE 91
Claire, Cyrielle BioIn 16
Claire, Elizabeth 1939- WhoWrEP 89
Claire, Ina 1892-1985 BioIn 16, NotWoAT
Claire, Thomas Andrew 1951- WhoE 91
Claire, William 1935- WhoWrEP 89
Clairmont, Mary Jane 1766-1841 BioIn 16
Clairmont, William Edward 1926- WhoWor 91
Claitor, Robert Gregory, Jr. 1959- St&PR 91
Claman, Lawrence 1925- BiDrAPA 89
Claman, Leoni Neumann 1900-1989 BioIn 16
Claman, Morris Theodore 1928- St&PR 91
Clamar, Aphrodite J. 1933- WhoAmW 91
Clambaneva, James 1942- WhoWor 91
Clamme, Marvin Leslie 1953- WhoEmL 91
Clammer, Samuel Robert 1936- St&PR 91
Clamon, Harleyne Dianne 1940- WhoAmW 91
Clampitt, Amy 1920- DcLB 105 [port], FemiCLE, WorAu 1980 [port]
Clampitt, Amy Kathleen 1920- WhoAm 90, WhoAmW 91, WhoWrEP 89
Clampitt, Martha Redding 1947- WhoSSW 91
Clampitt, Mary O'Briant 1931- WhoAmW 91, WhoE 91
Clancarty, Earl of 1911- EncO&P 3
Clancey, Jennifer 1958- WhoAmW 91
Clancy Brothers, The OxCPMus
Clancy, Anita Domigan 1931- WhoAmW 91
Clancy, Bud 1900-1968 Ballpl 90
Clancy, Colleen Marie 1963- WhoAmW 91
Clancy, Constance S. 1957- WhoSSW 91
Clancy, Deirdre BioIn 16
Clancy, Edward Bede 1923- WhoWor 91
Clancy, Frank Thomas 1937- St&PR 91
Clancy, George P. 1943- St&PR 91
Clancy, Gerald Joseph, Jr. 1918- St&PR 91
Clancy, Gerald P. St&PR 91
Clancy, James 1955- St&PR 91
Clancy, Jim 1955- Ballpl 90
Clancy, Joan Bennett 1935- WhoAmW 91
Clancy, John WhoAmA 91N
Clancy, John 1922- BiDrAPA 89
Clancy, John Joseph 1937- WhoAm 90
Clancy, Joseph E. 1930- St&PR 91
Clancy, Joseph P. 1928- AuBYP 90
Clancy, Joseph Patrick 1931- WhoAm 90
Clancy, Kevin J. 1942- St&PR 91
Clancy, King 1903-1986 BioIn 16
Clancy, Leo C. 1932- St&PR 91
Clancy, Louis John 1946- WhoAm 90
Clancy, Margaret Mary 1948- BiDrAPA 89
Clancy, Mary 1948- WhoAmW 91
Clancy, Patrick 1941- WhoAmA 91
Clancy, Richard G. 1954- ODwPR 91
Clancy, Robert A. 1934- St&PR 91
Clancy, Robert James 1949- St&PR 91
Clancy, Sean S. ODwPR 91
Clancy, Steven P 1956- WhoWrEP 89
Clancy, Thomas Hanley 1923- WhoSSW 91
Clancy, Thomas L., Jr. 1947- ConAu 131, MajTwCW, SpyFic
Clancy, Tom ConAu 131, MajTwCW
Clancy, Tom NewYTBS 90 [port]
Clancy, Tom 1947- BioIn 16, TwCCr&M 91, WorAlBi
Clannad NewAgMG
Clanon, T.L. 1929- BiDrAPA 89
Clanon, Thomas Lawrence 1929- WhoAm 90
Clanton, Donald B. 1942- St&PR 91
Clanton, Rony DrBlPA 90
Clapes, Louis NewYTBS 90
Clapham, C.F. 1920- St&PR 91
Clapham, J. H. 1873-1946 BioIn 16
Clapham, John Harold 1873-1946 BioIn 16
Clapman, Marcia 1940- St&PR 91
Clapman, Peter Carlyle 1936- St&PR 91, WhoAm 90
Clapp, Alfred C. 1903-1988 BioIn 16
Clapp, Allen Linville 1943- WhoSSW 91, WhoWor 91
Clapp, Arthur Warren 1915- St&PR 91
Clapp, Carol Shlifer 1947- WhoEmL 91
Clapp, Christopher Lee 1952- WhoEmL 91
Clapp, David D. 1939- St&PR 91
Clapp, Earl W. 1926- St&PR 91
Clapp, Edwin G. 1918- St&PR 91
Clapp, Eugene H., II 1913- St&PR 91
Clapp, Eugene Howard, II 1913- WhoAm 90
Clapp, James Ford, Jr. 1908- WhoAm 90
Clapp, John McMahon 1944- WhoE 91
Clapp, Joseph Mark 1936- St&PR 91, WhoAm 90
Clapp, Kenneth Wayne 1948- WhoEmL 91
Clapp, Lee Irving 1941- WhoE 91
Clapp, Malcolme A. 1929- St&PR 91
Clapp, Margaret 1910-1974 BioIn 16
Clapp, Mary Alice 1941- WhoAmW 91
Clapp, Mary Stuart 1941- WhoAmW 91
Clapp, Maude Caroline Ede 1876-1960 WhoAmA 91N
Clapp, Melvin Carl 1933- St&PR 91
Clapp, Norton BioIn 16
Clapp, Roger Alvin 1909- WhoAm 90
Clapp, Roger Howland 1928- WhoAm 90, WhoSSW 91
Clapp, Walter Lucas 1850-1901 AmLegL
Clapp, William L 1943- BiDrAPA 89
Clappe, Louise 1819-1906 FemiCLE
Clapper, Jack Woodrow BiDrAPA 89
Clapper, Jon C. 1949- St&PR 91
Clapper, Lyle Nielsen 1941- WhoAm 90
Clapper, Raymond 1892-1944 BioIn 16
Clapper-Coomer, Kathryn Accola 1942- WhoAmW 91
Claps, Gerard St&PR 91
Clapsaddle, Jerry 1941- WhoAmA 91
Clapton, Eric BioIn 16
Clapton, Eric 1945- EncPR&S 89, OxCPMus, WhoAm 90, WorAlBi
Clapton, Nicholas 1955- IntWWM 90
Clar Margarit, Maria Francisca EncCoWW
Clara d'Anduza 12--?- EncCoWW
Clarac EncCoWW
Claramunt, Morrall M. 1941- St&PR 91
Clardy, James Anthony 1958- BiDrAPA 89
Clardy, Jon Christel 1943- WhoAm 90
Clare of Assisi 1193-1253 EncCoWW
Clare, of Assisi 1194-1253 BioIn 16
Clare, David R. 1925- St&PR 91
Clare, David Ross 1925- WhoE 91
Clare, Fountain Stewart, III 1936- WhoSSW 91
Clare, George 1930- WhoSSW 91, WhoWor 91
Clare, Gloria BiDrAPA 89
Clare, Helen AuBYP 90
Clare, Henry E 1934- BiDrAPA 89
Clare, John 1793-1864 BioIn 16, DcLB 96 [port]
Clare, Richard Dexter 1949- WhoEmL 91
Clare, Robert Linn, Jr. 1914- WhoAm 90
Clare, Stewart 1913- WhoAm 90, WhoAmA 91
Clare, Thomas A. 1920- St&PR 91
Claremon, Glenda Ruth 1951- WhoEmL 91
Clarendon, Edward Hyde, Earl of 1609-1674 BioIn 16, DcLB 101 [port]
Clarendon, George W F Villiers, Earl of 1800-1870 BioIn 16
Clarendon, John Marsden 1946- WhoE 91
Clarens, John Gaston 1924- WhoAm 90
Clarey, Cynthia BioIn 16
Clarey, Donald Alexander 1950- WhoAm 90
Clarfield, Avram Mark 1949- WhoWor 91
Clarfield, Gerard Howard 1936- WhoAm 90
Claridge, Richard Allen 1932- WhoSSW 91
Clarie, Thomas C 1943- EncO&P 3
Clarin ConAu 131, HispWr 90
Clarin 1852-1901 BioIn 16
Clarity, Timothy Baldwin 1951- WhoEmL 91
Clarizia, Renato 1950- WhoWor 91
Clarizio, Josephine Delores 1922- WhoAm 90
Clark EncCoWW
Clark, Abraham 1726-1794 EncCRAm
Clark, Agi 1941- WhoAm 90, WhoAmW 91
Clark, Al C. TwCCr&M 91
Clark, Alan Barthwell 1936- WhoAm 90
Clark, Alan F. 1931- St&PR 91
Clark, Alan F. 1936- WhoAm 90
Clark, Alan Kelley 1948- WhoSSW 91
Clark, Albert Carl Vernon 1947- WhoWrEP 89
Clark, Albert Edwin 1946- WhoEmL 91
Clark, Alexander 1818-1898 DcCanB 12
Clark, Alfred, Jr. 1936- WhoAm 90
Clark, Alfred Samuel 1947- WhoEmL 91
Clark, Alice Thompson 1926- WhoAm 90
Clark, Alicia Garcia WhoAmW 91, WhoWor 91
Clark, Allan 1896-1950 WhoAmA 91N
Clark, Allan Richard 1953- St&PR 91
Clark, Allan William 1960- BiDrAPA 89
Clark, Allie 1923- Ballpl 90
Clark, Alson Skinner 1876-1949 WhoAmA 91N
Clark, Alvin John 1933- WhoAm 90
Clark, Andrea Taylor 1952- WhoAmW 91
Clark, Andrew BioIn 16
Clark, Andrew Lawrence 1926- St&PR 91
Clark, Andrew M. 1955- WhoSSW 91
Clark, Anita Louise 1950- WhoAm 90
Clark, Ann Blakeney 1958- WhoSSW 91
Clark, Ann Nolan 1896- AuBYP 90
Clark, Anne ConAu 31NR
Clark, Annie Troy BioIn 16
Clark, Anthony Morris 1923-1976 WhoAmA 91N
Clark, Arthur Dean 1932- BiDrAPA 89
Clark, Arthur Joseph, Jr. 1921- WhoWor 91
Clark, Arthur Watts 1922- St&PR 91, WhoAm 90
Clark, Badger ConAu 31NR
Clark, Badger 1883-1957 BioIn 16
Clark, Barry Wayne 1941- St&PR 91
Clark, Bernard F. 1921- WhoAm 90
Clark, Bernard Francis 1921- St&PR 91
Clark, Betty Jean 1920- WhoAmW 91
Clark, Beverly Jean 1939- WhoAmW 91
Clark, Bill BioIn 16
Clark, Billy Curtis 1928- LiHiK
Clark, Billy Pat 1939- WhoE 91, WhoWor 91
Clark, Blair 1917- WhoAm 90
Clark, Blake 1908- WhoAm 90
Clark, Bobby 1888-1960 OxCPMus
Clark, Bobby 1955- Ballpl 90
Clark, Bonnie Leigh 1961- WhoSSW 91
Clark, Booby 1950-1988 BioIn 16
Clark, Brackett David 1940- St&PR 91
Clark, Bradley Linthicum 1926- WhoWor 91
Clark, Brent David 1950- St&PR 91
Clark, Brian Thomas 1951- WhoEmL 91
Clark, Bruce Arlington, Jr. 1951- WhoEmL 91
Clark, Bruce Budge 1918- WhoAm 90
Clark, Bruce Robert 1941- WhoAm 90
Clark, Bryan 1956- Ballpl 90
Clark, Buddy 1912-1949 OxCPMus
Clark, Burton Robert 1921- WhoAm 90
Clark, Byron Standish, II 1959- WhoSSW 91
Clark, C. A. WhoAm 90
Clark, Candy WhoAm 90
Clark, Carl Arthur 1911- WhoWor 91
Clark, Carl Dwight 1946- WhoSSW 91
Clark, Carol 1947- WhoAmA 91
Clark, Carol Canda 1947- WhoAmW 91
Clark, Carol Lois 1948- WhoAmW 91, WhoEmL 91
Clark, Carol Morrow 1962- WhoEmL 91
Clark, Carolyn Archer 1944- WhoAmW 91, WhoWor 91
Clark, Carolyn Chambers 1941- WhoAmW 91, WhoWrEP 89
Clark, Carolyn Cochran 1941- WhoAm 90
Clark, Carroll 1880?-1933? DcAfAmP
Clark, Cathy Ann 1948- WhoE 91
Clark, Champ 1850-1921 WorAlBi
Clark, Champ 1923- BioIn 16, WhoAm 90, WhoWrEP 89
Clark, Chapin DeWitt 1930- WhoAm 90
Clark, Charles 1925- WhoAm 90, WhoSSW 91
Clark, Charles D 1917- WhoAmA 91
Clark, Charles Daniel St&PR 91N
Clark, Charles Daniel 1917- WhoSSW 91
Clark, Charles Edward 1949- WhoEmL 91
Clark, Charles F 1939- BiDrAPA 89
Clark, Charles Joseph 1939- WhoAm 90, WhoE 91
Clark, Charles Lester 1917- WhoAm 90
Clark, Charles Parsons, III 1944- WhoSSW 91
Clark, Charles Richard 1946- WhoSSW 91
Clark, Charles S. 1833-189-? AmLegL
Clark, Charles Taliferro 1917- WhoAm 90
Clark, Charles Winthrop 1952- WhoE 91
Clark, Cheryl Ann 1957- BiDrAPA 89
Clark, Cindy BioIn 16
Clark, Claude 1915- WhoAmA 91
Clark, Clayton 1912- WhoAm 90
Clark, Clifford Dale 1925- WhoAm 90
Clark, Clifford Edward, Jr. 1941- WhoAm 90
Clark, Clifton Bob 1927- WhoAm 90
Clark, Clinton Anthony 1941- St&PR 91
Clark, Colin 1905-1989 AnObit 1989, ConAu 129
Clark, Colleen Kelly 1944- WhoAm 90
Clark, Connie Mullins 1948- WhoAmW 91
Clark, Cornelius J BiDrAPA 89
Clark, Corydon G 1939- BiDrAPA 89
Clark, Craig Anthony BiDrAPA 89
Clark, Curt TwCCr&M 91
Clark, Cynthia Lynn 1963- WhoAmW 91
Clark, Daniel 1953- WhoEmL 91
Clark, Daniel C. 1933- St&PR 91
Clark, Daniel Cooper 1948- WhoSSW 91
Clark, Danny Miles 1937- WhoSSW 91
Clark, Dave BioIn 16
Clark, Dave 1942- EncPR&S 89, WorAlBi
Clark, Dave, Five EncPR&S 89
Clark, David 1939- ConAu 130
Clark, David Crawford 1925- St&PR 91
Clark, David Delano 1924- WhoAm 90
Clark, David Henry 1932- WhoE 91

Clark, David Howard 1950- *WhoEmL 91*
Clark, David Lee 1959- *WhoE 91*
Clark, David Leigh 1931- *WhoAm 90*
Clark, David Louis 1929- *WhoAm 90*
Clark, David M. 1940- *St&PR 91*
Clark, David Randolph 1943- *WhoAm 90, WhoSSW 91*
Clark, David Robert 1953- *WhoEmL 91*
Clark, David W., Jr. 1937- *St&PR 91*
Clark, David Willard 1930- *WhoAm 90*
Clark, Dayle Meritt 1933- *WhoSSW 91*
Clark, Debra Feiock 1958- *WhoAmW 91*
Clark, Denis *AuBYP 90*
Clark, Denise Lynn 1954- *WhoAmW 91, WhoEmL 91*
Clark, Dennis Byler 1952- *WhoSSW 91*
Clark, Dennis Michael 1963- *WhoE 91*
Clark, Dianna Lea 1956- *WhoAmW 91*
Clark, Dick *ConAu 130*
Clark, Dick 1928- *WhoAm 90*
Clark, Dick 1929- *BioIn 16, EncPR&S 89, WhoAm 90*
Clark, Diddo Ruth 1950- *WhoEmL 91*
Clark, Dixie Dugan 1940- *WhoWrEP 89*
Clark, Donald B. 1942- *St&PR 91*
Clark, Donald C. 1931- *St&PR 91*
Clark, Donald Cameron 1931- *WhoAm 90*
Clark, Donald Graham Campbell 1920- *WhoE 91*
Clark, Donald Judson 1932- *WhoE 91*
Clark, Donald M. 1915- *St&PR 91*
Clark, Donald Malin 1929- *WhoAm 90*
Clark, Donald McGillivray 1957- *St&PR 91*
Clark, Donald Otis 1934- *WhoAm 90, WhoE 91, WhoWor 91*
Clark, Donald Ralph 1935- *WhoAm 90*
Clark, Donald Robert 1924- *WhoAm 90*
Clark, Donna E. 1928- *St&PR 91*
Clark, Donna Marie 1954- *WhoEmL 91*
Clark, Donovan Deryl *BiDrAPA 89*
Clark, Dorothy Park 1899-1983 *LiHiK*
Clark, Dorothy Van Gelder 1915- *St&PR 91*
Clark, Douglas 1919- *TwCCr&M 91*
Clark, Douglas Bernard 1951- *WhoEmL 91*
Clark, Douglas Napier 1944- *WhoSSW 91*
Clark, Duncan Barnes 1952- *BiDrAPA 89, WhoE 91*
Clark, E. Roger 1947- *St&PR 91*
Clark, Earl 1907-1938 *Ballpl 90*
Clark, Earl D., Jr. 1923- *St&PR 91*
Clark, Earl Wesley 1901- *WhoAm 90*
Clark, Earnest Hubert, Jr. 1926- *St&PR 91, WhoAm 90*
Clark, Edgar Sanderford 1933- *WhoAm 90*
Clark, Edward 1888-1962 *PenDiMP*
Clark, Edward 1906- *WhoAm 90*
Clark, Edward 1926- *WhoAmA 91*
Clark, Edward Ferdnand 1921- *WhoAm 90*
Clark, Edwin Green, Jr. 1940- *WhoSSW 91*
Clark, Edwin Hill, II 1938- *WhoE 91*
Clark, Edwin John 1925- *St&PR 91*
Clark, Eleanor *WhoAm 90, WhoAmW 91, WhoWrEP 89*
Clark, Eleanor 1913- *FemiCLE*
Clark, Electa *AuBYP 90*
Clark, Eliot Candee 1883-1980 *WhoAmA 91N*
Clark, Elizabeth *WhoAm 90*
Clark, Elizabeth Ann 1950- *WhoAmW 91*
Clark, Elizabeth Annette 1934- *WhoAmW 91*
Clark, Elliott Earl 1948- *WhoE 91, WhoEmL 91*
Clark, Elmer J. 1919- *WhoAm 90*
Clark, Eloise Elizabeth 1931- *WhoAm 90, WhoAmW 91*
Clark, Emery *BioIn 16*
Clark, Emery Ann 1950- *WhoAmA 91*
Clark, Emily Frederick *FemiCLE*
Clark, Emma Chichester *ConAu 132*
Clark, Emory Eugene 1931- *WhoSSW 91*
Clark, Eric 1937- *SpyFic*
Clark, Eric Oden 1955- *WhoEmL 91*
Clark, Erika *BioIn 16*
Clark, Ernest Adams *St&PR 91N*
Clark, Ernest John 1905- *WhoAm 90*
Clark, Esther Frances 1929- *WhoAm 90, WhoAmW 91*
Clark, Eugene Corry 1941- *WhoSSW 91*
Clark, Eugenie 1922- *WhoAm 90*
Clark, Evert *BioIn 16*
Clark, Faye Louise 1936- *WhoAmW 91*
Clark, Felicia *BioIn 16, NewYTBS 90*
Clark, Forrester Andrew 1906- *St&PR 91*
Clark, Frances *BiDEWW*
Clark, Frank 1922- *AuBYP 90*
Clark, Frank Kingsley 1927- *WhoSSW 91*
Clark, Frank Rinker, Jr. 1912- *WhoAm 90*
Clark, Franklin Jacob, Jr. 1937- *WhoWor 91*
Clark, Fred 1930- *WhoE 91*
Clark, Fred Yarbrough 1931- *St&PR 91*
Clark, Frederick J. 1926- *St&PR 91*
Clark, Frederick R. 1916- *St&PR 91*
Clark, Frederick R. 1916-1990 *BioIn 16*
Clark, Freeman Thomas 1939- *WhoSSW 91*
Clark, G Fletcher 1899-1982 *WhoAmA 91N*
Clark, G. Peter 1948- *WhoEmL 91*
Clark, Garel *AuBYP 90, ConAu 130*
Clark, Garth Reginald 1947- *WhoAmA 91*
Clark, Geoffrey 1946- *WhoEmL 91, WhoSSW 91*
Clark, George A. 1929- *St&PR 91*
Clark, George Bryan 1925- *WhoAm 90*
Clark, George Lee 1950- *WhoE 91*
Clark, George M., Jr. 1932- *St&PR 91*
Clark, George R. 1752-1818 *WorAlBi*
Clark, George Robert 1940- *WhoSSW 91*
Clark, George Roberts 1910- *WhoAm 90*
Clark, George Rogers 1752-1818 *BioIn 16, EncCRAm [port], WhNaAH*
Clark, George Whipple 1928- *WhoAm 90*
Clark, Gerald Lamont 1932- *WhoAm 90*
Clark, Gerald R *BiDrAPA 89*
Clark, Gilbert *BioIn 16*
Clark, Gilbert Michael 1944- *WhoAm 90*
Clark, Glen Edward 1943- *WhoAm 90*
Clark, Glenwood 1926- *WhoAm 90*
Clark, Gordon Haddon 1902-1985 *BioIn 16*
Clark, Gordon Hostetter, Jr. 1947- *WhoE 91*
Clark, Gordon M. 1940- *St&PR 91*
Clark, Gordon Morrow 1934- *WhoSSW 91*
Clark, Gordon W. 1939- *ODwPR 91*
Clark, Graham 1941- *IntWWM 90*
Clark, Gregory Arnold 1947- *BiDrAPA 89*
Clark, Gregory C. 1947- *St&PR 91*
Clark, Gregory Cooper 1947- *WhoEmL 91*
Clark, Guy *WhoNeCM [port]*
Clark, H. Sol 1906- *WhoAm 90*
Clark, Halliday 1918- *WhoE 91*
Clark, Harold F. 1935- *St&PR 91*
Clark, Harold Steve 1947- *WhoAm 90*
Clark, Harry Westley *BiDrAPA 89*
Clark, Helen Elizabeth 1950- *WhoWor 91*
Clark, Henry G. 1945- *St&PR 91*
Clark, Henry Ray 1936- *MusmAFA*
Clark, Herbert Forrester 1943- *St&PR 91, WhoAm 90*
Clark, Howard Charles 1929- *WhoAm 90*
Clark, Howard Longstreth 1916- *WhoAm 90*
Clark, Howard Longstreth, Jr. 1944- *St&PR 91, WhoAm 90, WhoE 91*
Clark, Ian Douglas 1946- *WhoAm 90*
Clark, Isaac Edgar 1919- *WhoAm 90*
Clark, J. Bunker 1931- *IntWWM 90*
Clark, J. Desmond 1916- *BioIn 16*
Clark, J. Jill 1938- *WhoAmW 91*
Clark, J. Kenneth 1932- *ODwPR 91*
Clark, J. Peter 1942- *St&PR 91*
Clark, J R 1947- *WhoWrEP 89*
Clark, J. Reuben 1871-1961 *BioIn 16*
Clark, J. Thomas *WhoAm 90*
Clark, Jack *BioIn 16*
Clark, Jack 1932- *WhoAm 90, WhoSSW 91*
Clark, Jack 1955- *Ballpl 90, BioIn 16*
Clark, James *PenDiMP*
Clark, James A. *BioIn 16*
Clark, James A. 1930- *WhoAm 90*
Clark, James A. 1941- *St&PR 91*
Clark, James Averell, Jr. *NewYTBS 90*
Clark, James Benton 1914- *WhoAm 90*
Clark, James D. 1935- *St&PR 91*
Clark, James Edward 1926- *WhoE 91*
Clark, James Edward 1942- *WhoAm 90*
Clark, James H. 1944- *St&PR 91*
Clark, James Hamel 1960- *WhoEmL 91*
Clark, James Henry 1931- *WhoAm 90*
Clark, James Howard 1953- *WhoEmL 91*
Clark, James Milford 1930- *WhoAm 90, WhoE 91*
Clark, James Milo 1944- *St&PR 91*
Clark, James Norman 1932- *St&PR 91, WhoAm 90*
Clark, James Patrick 1947- *BiDrAPA 89*
Clark, James Robert 1943- *St&PR 91*
Clark, James Robert 1953- *WhoEmL 91*
Clark, James T. 1940- *St&PR 91*
Clark, James Walter 1948- *WhoSSW 91*
Clark, James Whitley 1930- *St&PR 91, WhoAm 90*
Clark, Jane Angela 1955- *WhoAmW 91*
Clark, Jane Currie 1906- *BioIn 16*
Clark, Jane Elizabeth 1946- *WhoAmW 91*
Clark, Janet Eileen 1940- *WhoAmW 91*
Clark, Janet Lee 1952- *WhoAmW 91*
Clark, Jay A. 1936- *ODwPR 91*
Clark, Jay D. 1936- *St&PR 91*
Clark, Jeffrey Charles 1960- *WhoEmL 91*
Clark, Jeffrey Wade 1950- *WhoE 91*
Clark, Jeffrey William 1961- *WhoSSW 91*
Clark, Jennifer *ODwPR 91*
Clark, Jim *BioIn 16*
Clark, Joan 1934- *BioIn 16*
Clark, Joan Faye Henry 1928- *WhoAmW 91*
Clark, Joanne 1951- *St&PR 91*
Clark, Joe *BioIn 16*
Clark, Joel Phillip 1944- *WhoE 91*
Clark, John 1821-1872 *AmLegL*
Clark, John Alden 1923- *WhoAm 90*
Clark, John Arthur 1920- *WhoAm 90*
Clark, John Bates 1847-1938 *BioIn 16*
Clark, John C *NewYTBS 90*
Clark, John Clinton, III 1943- *St&PR 91*
Clark, John Conrad 1913-1990 *BioIn 16*
Clark, John Desmond 1916- *BioIn 16, WhoAm 90*
Clark, John Drury 1907-1988 *BioIn 16*
Clark, John E. 1943- *St&PR 91*
Clark, John Elwood 1931- *WhoAm 90*
Clark, John F. 1920- *WhoAm 90*
Clark, John Foster 1950- *WhoEmL 91*
Clark, John Frederick 1953- *IntWWM 90*
Clark, John Grahame 1907- *WhoWor 91*
Clark, John H., Jr. 1928- *WhoAm 90*
Clark, John Hallett, III 1918- *WhoAm 90*
Clark, John Hamilton 1949- *WhoAm 90, WhoEmL 91*
Clark, John Holley, III 1918- *WhoE 91*
Clark, John J. 1924- *WhoAm 90, WhoWor 91*
Clark, John Joseph 1954- *WhoE 91*
Clark, John Leo 1945- *WhoEmL 91*
Clark, John Maurice 1884-1963 *BioIn 16*
Clark, John N., Jr. 1935- *St&PR 91*
Clark, John P. 1935- *St&PR 91*
Clark, John R. *St&PR 91*
Clark, John Robert, III 1954- *St&PR 91*
Clark, John Russell 1927- *WhoAm 90*
Clark, John S. 1928-1988 *BioIn 16*
Clark, John Stanley *BiDrAPA 89*
Clark, John Steven 1947- *WhoAm 90, WhoSSW 91*
Clark, John Walter, Jr. 1919- *WhoAm 90*
Clark, John Walter, Jr. 1946- *WhoE 91*
Clark, John Whitcomb 1918- *WhoAm 90*
Clark, Johnny Sullivan 1936- *WhoSSW 91*
Clark, Jon Frederic 1947- *WhoAmA 91*
Clark, Jonathan Redfield 1958- *WhoEmL 91*
Clark, Joseph *BioIn 16*
Clark, Joseph S. 1901-1990 *BioIn 16, ConAu 130, NewYTBS 90 [port]*
Clark, Joseph S., Jr. 1901-1990 *CurBio 90N*
Clark, Joshua Reuben 1871-1961 *BioIn 16*
Clark, Joyce Naomi Johnson 1936- *WhoAmW 91, WhoSSW 91, WhoWor 91*
Clark, Judith Wells 1943- *WhoSSW 91*
Clark, Julian Joseph 1935- *BiDrAPA 89*
Clark, Kanchan Puri *BiDrAPA 89*
Clark, Karen Elizabeth 1955- *WhoAmW 91, WhoEmL 91*
Clark, Karen Heath 1944- *WhoAmW 91*
Clark, Karen Marie 1953- *WhoAmW 91*
Clark, Karen Sue 1952- *WhoEmL 91*
Clark, Kate F. 1875-1957 *BioAmW*
Clark, Keith C. 1927- *IntWWM 90*
Clark, Kelly 1953- *WhoE 91, WhoEmL 91*
Clark, Kenneth 1903-1983 *BioIn 16, MajTwCW*
Clark, Kenneth 1942- *WhoSSW 91*
Clark, Kenneth Bancroft *BioIn 16*
Clark, Kenneth Bancroft 1914- *WhoAm 90*
Clark, Kenneth Courtright 1919- *WhoAm 90*
Clark, Kenneth Edwin 1914- *WhoAm 90*
Clark, Kenneth J. 1937- *St&PR 91*
Clark, Kenneth M 1924- *BiDrAPA 89*
Clark, Kenneth Mackenzie 1903-1983 *DcNaB 1981*
Clark, Kenneth Sears 1909- *WhoAm 90*
Clark, Kevin Anthony 1956- *WhoE 91*
Clark, Kim Bryce 1949- *WhoE 91*
Clark, Kirk A. 1946- *St&PR 91*
Clark, Kit *BioIn 16*
Clark, Krista Helen 1951- *WhoAmW 91*
Clark, Larry 1943- *WhoAm 90*
Clark, Larry Dale 1932- *WhoAm 90*
Clark, Larry Dalton 1942- *WhoWor 91*
Clark, Larry Duane 1945- *WhoSSW 91*
Clark, Laurie Jane 1951- *WhoAmW 91*
Clark, Laverne Harrell 1929- *WhoWrEP 89*
Clark, Lee Walter 1955- *BiDrAPA 89*
Clark, Lemuel B *BiDrAPA 89*
Clark, Leonard J., Jr. 1934- *St&PR 91*
Clark, Leonard P. 1919- *St&PR 91*
Clark, Leonard Vernon 1938- *WhoAm 90*
Clark, Leonor A. 1943- *WhoAmW 91*
Clark, Lester 1916- *St&PR 91*
Clark, Letitia Z. 1945- *WhoAmW 91*
Clark, Lewis F. *BioIn 16*
Clark, Lewis Gaylord 1808-1873 *BioIn 16*
Clark, Lewis H. 1925- *St&PR 91*
Clark, Lincoln H. *BioIn 16*
Clark, Linda Anne 1958- *WhoAmW 91*
Clark, Linda Wilson 1939- *WhoSSW 91*
Clark, Loren Joseph 1935- *St&PR 91*
Clark, Louis Morris, Jr. 1931- *WhoE 91*
Clark, Louise Stone *BiDrAPA 89*
Clark, Luther John 1941- *WhoAm 90*
Clark, Lygia 1920-1988 *ArtLatA*
Clark, Lyle Arthur *BiDrAPA 89*
Clark, Lynda Lea 1944- *WhoAmW 91*
Clark, M. Anne 1942- *WhoAmW 91*
Clark, M. Brooks 1948- *WhoSSW 91*
Clark, Mabel Beatrice Smith *WhoAmA 91N*
Clark, Malcolm Dowdles 1940- *WhoAm 90*
Clark, Margaret *BiDEWW*
Clark, Margaret 1949- *WhoAmW 91*
Clark, Margaret Ann 1949- *WhoEmL 91*
Clark, Margaret Goff 1913- *AuBYP 90, WhoWrEP 89*
Clark, Margaret Pruitt 1946- *WhoAmW 91*
Clark, Marguerite 1887-1940 *BioAmW*
Clark, Maria Caridad 1959- *WhoAmW 91, WhoSSW 91*
Clark, Marie *WhoAmA 91*
Clark, Marilyn Hall 1950- *St&PR 91*
Clark, Marjorie McCutchan 1938- *WhoAmW 91*
Clark, Mark 1896-1984 *WorAlBi*
Clark, Mark A 1931- *WhoAmA 91*
Clark, Mark Edwin 1933- *St&PR 91*
Clark, Mark Furman 1940- *WhoAm 90*
Clark, Mark Lee 1953- *WhoEmL 91*
Clark, Mark Sessel *BiDrAPA 89*
Clark, Marlene *DrBIPA 90*
Clark, Martha Ann 1949- *WhoEmL 91*
Clark, Martin Fillmore, Jr. 1959- *WhoEmL 91*
Clark, Martin Michael 1931- *St&PR 91*
Clark, Marveta Yvonne 1948- *WhoE 91*
Clark, Mary *BiDEWW*
Clark, Mary H Hoback 1950- *BiDrAPA 89*
Clark, Mary Higgins *BioIn 16*
Clark, Mary Higgins 1929- *MajTwCW, TwCCr&M 91, WhoWrEP 89*
Clark, Mary Higgins 1931- *WhoAm 90, WhoAmW 91*
Clark, Mary Margaret 1925- *WhoAm 90*
Clark, Mary Twibill *WhoAm 90*
Clark, Mason Alonzo 1921- *WhoWrEP 89*
Clark, Matt 1930- *WhoAm 90, WhoWrEP 89*
Clark, Matt 1936- *ConTFT 8 [port]*
Clark, Matthew Harvey 1937- *WhoAm 90, WhoE 91*
Clark, Mavis Thorpe *BioIn 16*
Clark, Maxine 1949- *WhoAm 90*
Clark, Mazie Earhart 1874-1958 *HarlReB*
Clark, Mel 1926- *Ballpl 90*
Clark, Melville, Jr. 1921- *WhoAm 90*
Clark, Melvin Eugene 1916- *WhoAm 90, WhoWor 91*
Clark, Meredith Kaye Plier 1927- *WhoAm 90*
Clark, Merrell Edward, Jr. 1922- *WhoAm 90*
Clark, Merrell Mays 1935- *WhoE 91*
Clark, Michael *BioIn 16*
Clark, Michael Erik 1943- *WhoE 91*
Clark, Michael Kirk 1965- *WhoE 91*
Clark, Michael Vinson 1946- *WhoAmA 91*
Clark, Michelle *BioIn 16*
Clark, Michelle O *BiDrAPA 89*
Clark, Mike 1938- *ODwPR 91*
Clark, Montague Graham, Jr. 1909- *WhoAm 90*
Clark, Muriel *BioIn 16*
Clark, Nancee Flesher 1948- *WhoSSW 91*
Clark, Nancy Claire 1954- *BiDrAPA 89*
Clark, Nancy Kissel 1919- *WhoAmA 91*
Clark, Nancy Lee 1948- *WhoAmW 91*
Clark, Nancy Randall 1938- *WhoAmW 91*
Clark, Nathan *BioIn 16*
Clark, Newcomb 1840- *AmLegL*
Clark, Nicholas 1959-1984 *ConAu 132*
Clark, Nolwen de Janze *BioIn 16*
Clark, Noreen Morrison 1943- *WhoAm 90*
Clark, Odette M 1925- *BiDrAPA 89*
Clark, Odis Morrison 1944- *WhoSSW 91*
Clark, Ouida Ouijella 1949- *WhoSSW 91*
Clark, Owen Edward 1938- *BiDrAPA 89*
Clark, Pamela Ann 1955- *WhoAmW 91*
Clark, Pat English 1940- *WhoAm 90*
Clark, Patricia Ann 1936- *WhoAmW 91*
Clark, Patricia Beans- *BioIn 16*
Clark, Paul C *BiDrAPA 89*
Clark, Paul Fenimore 1861- *AmLegL*
Clark, Paul N. 1947- *St&PR 91*
Clark, Paul Newton 1947- *WhoAm 90, WhoEmL 91, WhoWor 91*
Clark, Paul T. *ODwPR 91*
Clark, Paul Thomas 1954- *WhoE 91, WhoEmL 91*
Clark, Paul Wallace 1961- *St&PR 91*
Clark, Peggy 1915- *BioIn 16, NotWoAT, WhoAm 90*
Clark, Peggy Lynne 1937- *WhoAmW 91*
Clark, Peter Bruce 1928- *WhoAm 90*
Clark, Peter Joseph 1943- *WhoE 91*
Clark, Petula 1932- *OxCPMus, WorAlBi*
Clark, Petula 1933- *EncPR&S 89*
Clark, Philip *BioIn 16*
Clark, Philip Raymond 1930- *WhoE 91*
Clark, Phyllis 1955- *St&PR 91*
Clark, Phyllis Rhoda 1955- *WhoEmL 91*

Clark, R. Bradbury 1924- WhoAm 90, WhoWor 91
Clark, R. Thomas 1951- WhoE 91, WhoEmL 91, WhoWor 91
Clark, Ralph Barkley 1944- BiDrAPA 89
Clark, Ralph Barlow 1933- WhoAm 90
Clark, Ramsey 1927- WhoAm 90, WorAlBi
Clark, Ranville S BiDrAPA 89
Clark, Raymond B., Jr. 1927- WhoE 91
Clark, Raymond Robert 1938- WhoAm 90
Clark, Raymond Skinner 1913- St&PR 91, WhoAm 90
Clark, Reuben Grove, Jr. 1923- WhoAm 90
Clark, Rhea Kirby 1930- WhoSSW 91
Clark, Rich BioIn 16
Clark, Richard A. BioIn 16
Clark, Richard B. 1943- St&PR 91
Clark, Richard Dale 1933- St&PR 91
Clark, Richard Edward 1947- WhoEmL 91
Clark, Richard George 1943- WhoSSW 91
Clark, Richard J. 1943- IntWWM 90
Clark, Richard Lee 1940- WhoSSW 91
Clark, Richard McCourt 1937- WhoAm 90
Clark, Richard T. 1952- St&PR 91
Clark, Richard U. 1945- St&PR 91
Clark, Richard Wagstaff 1929- ConAu 130
Clark, Rickey 1946- Ballpl 90
Clark, Rita W 1936- BiDrAPA 89
Clark, Robert 1924- WhoWor 91
Clark, Robert A 1908- BiDrAPA 89
Clark, Robert Arthur 1923- WhoAm 90
Clark, Robert Carl 1956- BiDrAPA 89
Clark, Robert Charles 1920- WhoAmA 91
Clark, Robert Charles 1944- BioIn 16, WhoAm 90
Clark, Robert Foerst 1927- WhoE 91
Clark, Robert Henry, Jr. 1941- St&PR 91, WhoAm 90
Clark, Robert James 1932- St&PR 91
Clark, Robert King 1934- WhoAm 90
Clark, Robert Lloyd, Jr. 1945- WhoAm 90, WhoSSW 91
Clark, Robert Newhall 1925- WhoAm 90
Clark, Robert Phillips 1921- WhoAm 90
Clark, Robert Ronald 1937- BiDrAPA 89
Clark, Robert S 1922- BiDrAPA 89
Clark, Robert Samuel 1931- WhoSSW 91
Clark, Robert Sheffield 1934- WhoAm 90
Clark, Robert Stuart 1932- St&PR 91
Clark, Robert W. 1946- St&PR 91
Clark, Robert Wesley 1946- WhoEmL 91
Clark, Roberta Carter 1924- WhoAmA 91
Clark, Robin LaRae BiDrAPA 89
Clark, Roger Arthur 1932- WhoAm 90
Clark, Roger Gordon 1937- WhoAm 90
Clark, Roger Harrison 1939- WhoAm 90
Clark, Roger Lewis 1955- WhoEmL 91
Clark, Roland 1874-1957 WhoAmA 91N
Clark, Romane Lewis 1925- WhoAm 90
Clark, Ron 1943- Ballpl 90
Clark, Ron Dean 1947- WhoAm 90
Clark, Ronald Channing 1934- St&PR 91
Clark, Ronald Dean 1943- WhoAm 90
Clark, Ronald Hurley 1953- WhoEmL 91
Clark, Ronald Keith 1955- WhoEmL 91
Clark, Ronald Lewis 1952- WhoE 91
Clark, Ronald William AuBYP 90, BioIn 16
Clark, Ross Bert, II 1932- WhoSSW 91, WhoWor 91
Clark, Ross Godfrey 1949- WhoEmL 91
Clark, Ross Townsend 1956- WhoEmL 91
Clark, Roy 1933- WhoAm 90, WorAlBi
Clark, Roy D, Jr. 1943- BiDrAPA 89
Clark, Roy Thomas, Jr. 1922- WhoSSW 91
Clark, Rupert O 1929- BiDrAPA 89
Clark, Rush 1834-1879 AmLegL
Clark, Russell Gentry 1925- WhoAm 90
Clark, Samuel Delbert 1910- WhoAm 90
Clark, Samuel Smith 1932- WhoAm 90
Clark, Sandra Helen Becker 1938- WhoAmW 91
Clark, Sandra Lee 1949- WhoAmW 91
Clark, Sandra Marie 1942- WhoAmW 91
Clark, Sara Mott 1915- WhoAmW 91
Clark, Sarah P. 1959- St&PR 91
Clark, Scott Cameron 1956- BiDrAPA 89
Clark, Sedgwick 1946- IntWWM 90
Clark, Sheree L. 1956- WhoAmW 91
Clark, Sherry Parsons BioIn 16
Clark, Sheryl Marie 1944- WhoAmW 91
Clark, Shirley Reed, Jr. 1932- St&PR 91
Clark, Stanford E. 1917- St&PR 91, WhoAm 90
Clark, Stanley Lawrence 1943- WhoAm 90
Clark, Stephen C., Jr. 1882-1960 Ballpl 90
Clark, Stephen P. 1923- WhoSSW 91
Clark, Stephen R L 1945- ConAu 32NR
Clark, Steven English 1950- WhoEmL 91
Clark, Stuart John 1961- WhoEmL 91
Clark, Susan 1944- WhoAm 90, WhoAmW 91, WorAlBi
Clark, Susan Honeycutt BiDrAPA 89
Clark, Susan Jane 1953- WhoAmW 91
Clark, Susan Loraine 1952- BiDrAPA 89
Clark, Susan Matthews 1950- WhoAmW 91
Clark, Sylvia St&PR 91
Clark, Teresa Ellen 1959- WhoAmW 91
Clark, Terrence Andrew 1956- WhoEmL 91
Clark, Terrence Peter 1946- BiDrAPA 89
Clark, Terry 1960- Ballpl 90
Clark, Terry Wayne 1950- St&PR 91
Clark, Theodore F. 1838-1910 AmLegL
Clark, Theodore Rust 1926- BiDrAPA 89
Clark, Thomas Alonzo 1920- WhoAm 90
Clark, Thomas B. 1942- St&PR 91
Clark, Thomas C. 1899-1977 WorAlBi
Clark, Thomas Carlyle 1947- St&PR 91, WhoAm 90
Clark, Thomas Dionysius 1903- WhoAm 90
Clark, Thomas Garis 1925- WhoAm 90
Clark, Thomas Harold 1951- WhoAm 90
Clark, Thomas Harvey 1857- AmLegL
Clark, Thomas Henry 1893- WhoAm 90
Clark, Thomas Lloyd 1939- WhoAm 90
Clark, Thomas Rolfe 1941- WhoWor 91
Clark, Thomas Spencer 1954- WhoE 91
Clark, Thomas Willard 1941- WhoAm 90, WhoWrEP 89
Clark, Timothy John 1951- WhoAmA 91
Clark, Timothy Ross 1952- WhoAm 90
Clark, Timothy Warner 1953- St&PR 91
Clark, Tom 1941- Ballpl 90
Clark, Tom C. 1899-1977 BioIn 16
Clark, Tom Campbell 1899-1977 BiDrUSE 89
Clark, Valerie Susan 1959- WhoE 91
Clark, Verne Thomas 1932- WhoSSW 91
Clark, Vernon A. 1930- WhoAm 90
Clark, Vicky A WhoAmA 91, WhoE 91
Clark, Viola Anna 1930- WhoWrEP 89
Clark, Virginia AuBYP 90
Clark, Voris Chester 1930- St&PR 91
Clark, W. Lee 1937- St&PR 91
Clark, W. M. AmLegL
Clark, W. Michael 1950- St&PR 91
Clark, Wallis Hensman, Jr. 1937- WhoAm 90
Clark, Walter Burns 1913- St&PR 91
Clark, Walter H 1931- WhoWrEP 89
Clark, Walter Houston 1902- EncO&P 3, EncPaPR 91
Clark, Walter Van Tilburg 1909-1971 WorAlBi
Clark, Ward Christopher 1939- WhoAm 90
Clark, Warren, Jr. 1936- WhoAm 90, WhoWor 91
Clark, Warren F. BioIn 16
Clark, Watty 1902-1972 Ballpl 90
Clark, Wayne B. 1938- St&PR 91
Clark, Wesley Clarke 1907- WhoAm 90
Clark, Wesley James 1950- ConAu 31NR
Clark, Will BioIn 16
Clark, Will 1964- Ballpl 90, WhoAm 90, WorAlBi
Clark, William 1770-1838 BioIn 16, WhNaAH, WorAlBi
Clark, William, Jr. 1930- WhoAm 90, WhoE 91, WhoWor 91
Clark, William Arthur 1954- WhoSSW 91
Clark, William Donaldson 1916-1985 DcNaB 1981
Clark, William F. 1922- St&PR 91
Clark, William Francis, Jr. 1954- BiDrAPA 89
Clark, William G. 1932- St&PR 91
Clark, William George 1924- WhoAm 90
Clark, William Hartley 1930- WhoAm 90
Clark, William Howard, Jr. 1951- WhoE 91, WhoEmL 91, WhoWor 91
Clark, William J. 1923- St&PR 91
Clark, William James 1923- WhoAm 90, WhoWor 91
Clark, William James 1931- WhoE 91
Clark, William Kalar 1921- St&PR 91
Clark, William P. 1921- St&PR 91
Clark, William Patrick BioIn 16
Clark, William Patrick 1931- BiDrUSE 89
Clark, William Ramsey 1927- BiDrUSE 89
Clark, William Robert, Jr. 1951- WhoEmL 91
Clark, William Roger 1949- WhoAmA 91
Clark, William Stratton 1914- WhoAm 90
Clark, William W 1940- WhoAmA 91
Clark, Worley H., Jr. 1932- WhoAm 90
Clark-Brooks, Bronnie Denise 1954- WhoAmW 91
Clark-Cameron, Bonnie 1946- WhoAmW 91
Clark-Edge, Virginia Lee 1945- WhoAmW 91
Clark-Hurn, Paula Dawne 1952- WhoEmL 91
Clark-Pendarvis, China 1950- ConAu 129
Clark-Rubin, Lorna Jayne BiDrAPA 89
Clark-Schwarzenbach EncCoWW
Clarke, Alice BiDEWW
Clarke, Allen Bruce 1927- WhoAm 90
Clarke, Allen Richard 1957- WhoEmL 91
Clarke, Andrew William 1956- St&PR 91
Clarke, Ann 1944- WhoAmA 91
Clarke, Anna 1919- TwCCr&M 91
Clarke, Arthur C. 1917- BioIn 16, EncO&P 3, MajTwCW, RGTwCSF, WorAlBi
Clarke, Arthur Charles 1917- AuBYP 90, WhoWor 91
Clarke, Austin C 1934- ConAu 32NR
Clarke, B. Devane, Jr. 1929- St&PR 91
Clarke, Bobby 1949- WorAlBi
Clarke, Boileryard 1868-1959 Ballpl 90
Clarke, Bruce Cooper 1901-1988 BioIn 16
Clarke, Bryan 1949- St&PR 91
Clarke, Bryan Campbell 1932- WhoWor 91
Clarke, Bud 1941- WhoAmA 91
Clarke, Caitlin 1952- ConTFT 8
Clarke, Carter W., Jr. 1926- St&PR 91
Clarke, Charles C. 1928- ODwPR 91
Clarke, Charles Fenton 1916- WhoAm 90
Clarke, Christopher L.A. 1939- St&PR 91
Clarke, Clifford Montreville 1925- WhoAm 90, WhoSSW 91
Clarke, Clifton Boris BiDrAPA 89
Clarke, Conley BioIn 16
Clarke, Cordelia Kay Knight Mazuy 1938- WhoAm 90
Clarke, Cyril Astley 1907- WhoWor 91
Clarke, Danny O. 1949- St&PR 91
Clarke, David Barry 1930- WhoWor 91
Clarke, David Bruce 1945- WhoSSW 91
Clarke, David Bruce 1951- St&PR 91
Clarke, David H. 1941- WhoAm 90, WhoE 91
Clarke, David Marshall 1927- WhoAm 90
Clarke, David Robinson 1943- WhoAm 90
Clarke, Denise Elizabeth 1961- BiDrAPA 89
Clarke, Donald Dudley 1930- WhoAm 90
Clarke, Donald Lancaster 1941- St&PR 91
Clarke, Dora 1890?-1964? BiDWomA
Clarke, Doreen 1928- FemiCLE
Clarke, Edith 1883-1959 BioIn 16
Clarke, Edward Nielsen 1925- WhoAm 90
Clarke, Edward Owen, Jr. 1929- WhoAm 90
Clarke, Edward Rhea 1963- WhoSSW 91
Clarke, Edwin B. 1923- St&PR 91
Clarke, Edwin J. 1934- St&PR 91
Clarke, Edwin Kent 1932- WhoAm 90
Clarke, Edwin R. 1946- St&PR 91
Clarke, Edwin V., Jr. 1925- St&PR 91
Clarke, Ellis Emmanuel Innocent 1917- WhoWor 91
Clarke, Eric Thacher 1916- WhoAm 90
Clarke, Erwin Bennett 1922- St&PR 91, WhoAm 90
Clarke, Eugene C., Jr. 1921- St&PR 91
Clarke, Frank Eldridge 1913- WhoAm 90
Clarke, Frank Gay 1850-1901 AmLegL
Clarke, Franklyn R BiDrAPA 89
Clarke, Fred 1872-1960 Ballpl 90 [port]
Clarke, Fred G. AuBYP 90
Clarke, Frederic B., III 1942- WhoAm 90
Clarke, G. Modele BioIn 16
Clarke, Garry Evans 1943- WhoAm 90, WhoE 91
Clarke, Garry Kenneth Connal 1941- WhoAm 90
Clarke, Gary Kendrick 1939- WhoAm 90
Clarke, Gary O. 1936- St&PR 91
Clarke, George Leonard 1813-1890 AmLegL
Clarke, George Washington 1852-1936 AmLegL
Clarke, Gillian 1937- ConLC 61 [port], FemiCLE, WorAu 1980
Clarke, Grant 1891-1931 OxCPMus
Clarke, Gregory Vislav 1950- WhoE 91
Clarke, Greta Fields WhoAmW 91
Clarke, H. Weston, Jr. 1929- St&PR 91
Clarke, Harold Gravely 1927- WhoAm 90
Clarke, Henry De Brunner, Jr. 1933- St&PR 91
Clarke, Henry Leland 1907- IntWWM 90
Clarke, Hope DrBIPA 90
Clarke, Horace 1940- Ballpl 90, BioIn 16
Clarke, J. Calvitt, Jr. 1920- WhoAm 90, WhoSSW 91
Clarke, J. F. Gates NewYTBS 90
Clarke, J F Gates 1905-1990 ConAu 132
Clarke, Jack 1939- WhoSSW 91
Clarke, Jack Alden 1924- WhoAm 90
Clarke, Jack Graeme 1927- St&PR 91, WhoAm 90
Clarke, James Freeman 1810-1888 BioIn 16
Clarke, James McClure 1917- WhoAm 90, WhoSSW 91
Clarke, James Paul 1854-1916 BioIn 16
Clarke, James Weston 1937- WhoAm 90
Clarke, John 1609-1676 BioIn 16
Clarke, John 1942- WhoAm 90
Clarke, John Clem 1937- WhoAm 90, WhoAmA 91
Clarke, John Michael 1941- St&PR 91
Clarke, John P. 1930- St&PR 91
Clarke, John Patrick 1930- WhoAm 90
Clarke, John R 1913- WhoWrEP 89
Clarke, John R 1945- WhoAmA 91
Clarke, John U. 1952- St&PR 91
Clarke, Joseph Brian 1938- WhoAm 90, WhoE 91
Clarke, Joseph Henry 1930- WhoAm 90
Clarke, Karen Elisabeth 1946- WhoAmW 91
Clarke, Kay Knight ODwPR 91
Clarke, Kay Knight 1938- St&PR 91
Clarke, Ken Russell 1944- WhoAm 90
Clarke, Kenneth 1940- WhoWor 91
Clarke, Kenneth Kingsley 1924- WhoAm 90, WhoE 91
Clarke, Kenneth R. 1944- St&PR 91
Clarke, Kenneth Stevens 1931- WhoAm 90
Clarke, Kenny 1914-1985 BioIn 16, OxCPMus
Clarke, Kit Hansen 1944- WhoAmW 91
Clarke, Lambuth McGeehee 1923- WhoAm 90
Clarke, Larry D. 1925- St&PR 91
Clarke, Leslie Earle 1923- St&PR 91
Clarke, Lewis James 1927- WhoAm 90
Clarke, Linda Louise 1952- WhoAmW 91
Clarke, Lloyd Auton BiDrAPA 89
Clarke, Logan, Jr. 1927- St&PR 91, WhoAm 90
Clarke, Louis Semple 1866-1957 EncABHB 4 [port]
Clarke, Malcolm WhoAm 90
Clarke, Margaret 1941- ConAu 130
Clarke, Marion FemiCLE
Clarke, Martha 1944?- BioIn 16, WhoAmW 91
Clarke, Mary Caldwell 1943- WhoSSW 91
Clarke, Mary Cowden- 1809-1898 BioIn 16, FemiCLE
Clarke, Mary Elizabeth 1924- WhoAmW 91
Clarke, Maura BioIn 16
Clarke, Michael Bradshaw 1946- St&PR 91
Clarke, Milton Charles 1929- WhoAm 90
Clarke, Neil G. 1932- St&PR 91
Clarke, Nig 1882-1949 Ballpl 90
Clarke, Norma Veronica BiDrAPA 89
Clarke, Olivia 1785?-1845 FemiCLE
Clarke, Oscar Withers 1919- WhoAm 90
Clarke, Patrick E. 1936- St&PR 91
Clarke, Pauline 1921- AuBYP 90
Clarke, Peter 1936- WhoAm 90
Clarke, Philip R., Jr. 1914- St&PR 91
Clarke, Rebecca 1886-1979 BioIn 16
Clarke, Richard ConAu 31NR
Clarke, Richard A. WhoAm 90
Clarke, Richard Alan 1930- WhoAm 90
Clarke, Richard Gordon 1949- WhoSSW 91
Clarke, Richard Lewis 1948- WhoAm 90
Clarke, Robert ConAu 31NR
Clarke, Robert 1920- BioIn 16
Clarke, Robert B BiDrAPA 89
Clarke, Robert Bradstreet 1928- WhoAm 90, WhoE 91
Clarke, Robert E. BioIn 16
Clarke, Robert Earle 1949- WhoAm 90, WhoE 91
Clarke, Robert Emmett 1906- WhoWor 91
Clarke, Robert Fitzgerald 1942- St&PR 91
Clarke, Robert Francis 1915- WhoWor 91
Clarke, Robert J. 1947- WhoE 91
Clarke, Robert Logan 1942- WhoAm 90
Clarke, Robert Thorburn 1945- WhoAm 90
Clarke, Roger Glen 1948- WhoEmL 91
Clarke, Roger Henry 1940- WhoE 91
Clarke, Rosemary WhoAmW 91
Clarke, S. Bruce 1940- WhoSSW 91
Clarke, Sandra BioIn 16
Clarke, Shirley BioIn 16
Clarke, Shirley Alfretta 1934- St&PR 91
Clarke, Shirley Carl BiDrAPA 89
Clarke, Sidney 1831-1909 AmLegL
Clarke, Stanley BioIn 16
Clarke, Stephen David Justin 1964- IntWWM 90
Clarke, Steven Elliot 1949- BiDrAPA 89
Clarke, Steven Richard 1958- WhoSSW 91
Clarke, Symon Richard 1957- IntWWM 90
Clarke, T.C. 1932- St&PR 91
Clarke, T. E. B. 1907-1989 AnObit 1989
Clarke, T Paschal BiDrAPA 89
Clarke, Terence Michael 1937- WhoAm 90
Clarke, Terry WhoNeCM B
Clarke, Terry Bradley BiDrAPA 89
Clarke, Thomas A. 1941- St&PR 91
Clarke, Thomas Crawford 1932- WhoAm 90
Clarke, Thomas Earle 1940- WhoSSW 91
Clarke, Thomas Ernest Bennett 1907-1989 BioIn 16
Clarke, Thomas Hal 1914- WhoAm 90
Clarke, Thomas K. 1932- St&PR 91
Clarke, Thomas Paschal, III 1923- WhoSSW 91
Clarke, Tommy 1888-1945 Ballpl 90
Clarke, Urana 1902- WhoAmW 91

Clarke, Vaughn Anthony 1953- *WhoAm 90*
Clarke, W. Hall 1927- *WhoAm 90*
Clarke, Walter Sheldon 1934- *WhoAm 90*
Clarke, William *PenDiDA 89*
Clarke, William J. 1937- *St&PR 91*
Clarke, William Newton 1841-1912 *BioIn 16*
Clarke, Wm. A. Lee, III 1949- *WhoEmL 91*
Clarke-Hall, Edna 1879-1979 *BiDWomA*
Clarke-Halper, Carol Antoinette 1954- *WhoEmL 91*
Clarke-Stewart, K Alison 1943- *ConAu 32NR*
Clarkin, Donald J. 1929- *St&PR 91*
Clarkin, Michael Fitzgerald 1941- *St&PR 91*
Clarkin, Paul K. 1937- *St&PR 91*
Clarkson, Andrew MacBeth 1937- *WhoAm 90*
Clarkson, Bayard D, Jr. *BiDrAPA 89*
Clarkson, Bessie *BiDEWW*
Clarkson, Carole Lawrence 1942- *WhoAmW 91*
Clarkson, Charles 1947- *St&PR 91*
Clarkson, Charles Andrew 1945- *WhoSSW 91*
Clarkson, Cheryl Lee 1953- *WhoEmL 91*
Clarkson, Edith Margaret 1915- *BioIn 16*
Clarkson, Elisabeth Ann Hudnut 1925- *WhoAmW 91*
Clarkson, Gustav 1954- *IntWWM 90*
Clarkson, Harold 1949- *WhoWor 91*
Clarkson, Hugh M. *St&PR 91*
Clarkson, Jocelyn Adrene 1952- *WhoAmW 91*
Clarkson, John 1861-1909 *Ballpl 90 [port]*
Clarkson, Kenneth Wright 1942- *WhoAm 90, WhoWor 91*
Clarkson, Lawrence William 1938- *WhoAm 90*
Clarkson, Lindsay *BiDrAPA 89*
Clarkson, Max B.E. 1922- *St&PR 91*
Clarkson, Max Boydell Elliott 1922- *WhoAm 90*
Clarkson, Paul Richard 1935- *St&PR 91*
Clarkson, Robert Noel 1950- *WhoEmL 91, WhoWor 91*
Clarkson, Ross T. 1922- *St&PR 91*
Clarkson, Thomas William 1932- *WhoAm 90*
Clarkson, Walter 1878-1946 *Ballpl 90*
Clarkson, William D *BiDrAPA 89*
Clarkson, William Edwin 1925- *St&PR 91*
Clarkson, William Morris 1954- *WhoEmL 91*
Clarkson, William Wade 1949- *WhoSSW 91*
Clarkston, Ronne 1941- *WhoAmW 91*
Clarner, Walter J. 1947- *WhoE 91*
Claro, Jaime 1936- *St&PR 91, WhoAm 90*
Clarvit, Richard N. 1953- *WhoSSW 91*
Clarvit, Susan 1955- *BiDrAPA 89*
Clary, Alexia Barbara 1954- *WhoAmW 91*
Clary, Bradley Grayson 1950- *WhoEmL 91*
Clary, Bruce Maxfield 1939- *WhoE 91*
Clary, Cathryn M 1953- *BiDrAPA 89*
Clary, Elsie Ray 1948- *WhoAmW 91*
Clary, Everett Burton 1921- *WhoAm 90*
Clary, Jerome Edwin, Jr. 1956- *WhoSSW 91*
Clary, John G. 1926- *St&PR 91*
Clary, Linda Mixon 1946- *WhoEmL 91*
Clary, Richard Henry 1945- *BiDrAPA 89*
Clary, Richard Wayland 1953- *WhoEmL 91, WhoWor 91*
Clary, Robert 1926- *WhoAm 90*
Clary, Rosalie Brandon Stanton 1928- *WhoAmW 91*
Clary, William F 1927- *BiDrAPA 89*
Clasby, Mark Bower 1943- *St&PR 91*
Clasen, Robert Burke 1944- *WhoAm 90*
Clasgens, J.H., II 1924- *St&PR 91*
Clash, The *ConMus 4 [port], EncPR&S 89*
Clason, Clyde B. 1903- *TwCCr&M 91*
Clasper, Geoffrey S. 1949- *St&PR 91*
Claspill, James Louis 1946- *WhoEmL 91, WhoWor 91*
Class, Charles Andrew *BiDrAPA 89*
Class, Harold Martin 1932- *St&PR 91*
Class, Kelly *ODwPR 91*
Classon, Bruce D. 1932- *St&PR 91*
Classon, Bruce David 1932- *WhoAm 90*
Classon, Louise Laurette 1948- *WhoWrEP 89*
Classon, Rolf A. 1945- *St&PR 91*
Classon, Rolf Allan 1945- *WhoAm 90, WhoWor 91*
Claster, Jay B. 1931- *St&PR 91*
Claster, Jill Nadell *WhoAmW 91*
Claster, Mark L. 1952- *St&PR 91*
Clatsoff, William Adam 1940- *WhoSSW 91*
Clatworthy, Raymond Jack 1944- *WhoE 91*
Clauberg, Karl 1898-1957 *BioIn 16*
Claud, Joseph Gillette 1927- *St&PR 91, WhoAm 90*
Claude Lorrain 1600-1682 *IntDcAA 90, WorAlBi*
Claude, Abram, Jr. 1927- *St&PR 91*
Claude, Albert 1898-1983 *WorAlBi*
Claude, Anthony B. 1936- *St&PR 91*
Claude, Dietrich 1933- *WhoWor 91*
Claude, Inis Lothair, Jr. 1922- *WhoAm 90*
Claude, Pierre 1916- *WhoWor 91*
Claude, Richard Pierre 1934- *WhoE 91*
Claude, Robert Erwin 1929- *St&PR 91*
Claude, Thomas Eugene 1949- *St&PR 91*
Claudel, Camille 1864-1943 *BiDWomA, BioIn 16*
Claudel, Paul 1868-1955 *BioIn 16, WorAlBi*
Claudine 1451-1514 *WomWR*
Claudio, Pete 1956- *WhoHisp 91*
Claudius I 10BC-54AD *WorAlBi*
Claudius, Matthias 1740-1815 *DcLB 97 [port]*
Claudius-Petit, Eugene 1907-1989 *BioIn 16*
Claudon, Jean-Louis Rene 1950- *WhoWor 91*
Clauer, Calvin Robert 1910- *WhoWor 91*
Claughton, Hugh Dawson, Sr. 1928- *WhoSSW 91*
Claus, Carol Jean 1959- *WhoAmW 91*
Claus, Clyde Robert 1931- *St&PR 91, WhoAm 90*
Claus, Frederick Rochlitz 1934- *WhoSSW 91*
Claus, Joan Maxine 1954- *WhoEmL 91*
Claus, Kimberly Kay 1965- *WhoAmW 91*
Claus, Marcie Ruth 1951- *WhoEmL 91*
Claus, Roland D. 1934- *WhoE 91*
Clausell, Paul L *BiDrAPA 89*
Clausen, Alden Winship 1923- *WhoAm 90*
Clausen, Bent Andreas 1921- *WhoWor 91*
Clausen, Betty Jane Hansen 1925- *WhoAmW 91*
Clausen, Bret Mark 1958- *WhoEmL 91*
Clausen, Christopher 1942- *ConAu 130*
Clausen, Edgar Clemens 1951- *WhoSSW 91*
Clausen, Franciska 1899- *BiDWomA*
Clausen, George Edward 1929- *St&PR 91*
Clausen, Henry Christian 1905- *WhoAm 90*
Clausen, Hugh Joseph 1926- *WhoAm 90*
Clausen, Jan 1950- *FemiCLE*
Clausen, Jens Christen 1891-1969 *DcScB S2*
Clausen, Jerry Lee 1939- *BiDrAPA 89, WhoE 91*
Clausen, John Adam 1914- *WhoAm 90*
Clausen, Judith H. *WhoAmW 91*
Clausen, Niels Senius 1943- *WhoWor 91*
Clausen, Robert William 1947- *WhoEmL 91*
Clausen, Roger H. 1942- *St&PR 91*
Clausen, Sally Ilene 1945- *WhoAmW 91*
Clausen, Tom 1923- *EncABHB 7 [port]*
Clausen, Wendell Vernon 1923- *WhoAm 90, WhoWrEP 89*
Clauser, Barry Raymond 1953- *St&PR 91*
Clauser, Donald Roberdeau 1941- *WhoAm 90*
Clauser, Francis H. 1913- *WhoAm 90, WhoWor 91*
Clauser, Frederick Dale 1935- *St&PR 91*
Clausewitz, Karl Von 1780-1831 *WorAlBi*
Clausing, Arthur M. 1936- *WhoAm 90*
Clausius, Rudolf 1822-1888 *WorAlBi*
Clausman, Gilbert Joseph 1921- *WhoAm 90*
Clauson, James Wilson 1913- *WhoAm 90*
Clauson, Sharyn Ferne 1946- *WhoE 91, WhoEmL 91, WhoWor 91*
Clauson, Steven Lloyd 1955- *WhoEmL 91*
Clauson-Kaas, Niels Konrad Friedrich W. 1917- *WhoWor 91*
Clauss, Alfred 1906- *WhoAm 90*
Clauss, C. David 1948- *WhoEmL 91*
Clauss, Charles J. 1925- *St&PR 91*
Clauss, Peter Otto 1936- *WhoAm 90, WhoE 91, WhoWor 91*
Clauss, Philip John 1942- *St&PR 91*
Clauss, Valerie E. 1923- *St&PR 91*
Clauss, William A. 1952- *ODwPR 91*
Claussen, Darryll *BioIn 16*
Claussen, E.W. 1922- *St&PR 91*
Claussen, Howard Boyd 1946- *WhoEmL 91, WhoWor 91*
Claussen, Louise Keith 1947- *WhoSSW 91*
Claussen, Russell George 1934- *WhoE 91*
Claussen, Sophus Niels Christen 1865-1931 *DcScanL*
Clautice, William Gunther 1937- *WhoE 91, WhoSSW 91*
Clavadetscher, David Jerome 1935- *St&PR 91*
Clavano, Natividad Relucio 1932- *WhoWor 91*
Clave, Antoni 1913- *BioIn 16*
Clavel, Bernard Charles Henri 1923- *WhoWor 91*
Clavel, F.T.B. *EncO&P 3*
Clavel, Michel Dominique 1946- *WhoWor 91*
Clavell, James *EncJap*
Clavell, James 1924- *AuBYP 90, WhoAm 90, WorAlBi*
Clavell, James 1925- *MajTwCW*
Claver, Robert Earl 1928- *WhoAm 90*
Claverie, Melvin Juice 1960- *WhoEmL 91*
Clavet, Arthur Joseph 1957- *WhoE 91*
Clavier, David E. 1951- *ODwPR 91*
Claviere d'Hust, Anne-Marie de *BioIn 16*
Claviere d'Hust, Bernard de *BioIn 16*
Claw, Silas 1913- *MusmAFA*
Clawson, Carol A. 1946- *WhoAmW 91*
Clawson, Daniel Bruce 1946- *St&PR 91*
Clawson, David Kay 1927- *WhoAm 90*
Clawson, Harry Quintard Moore 1924- *WhoE 91*
Clawson, James Craig 1949- *St&PR 91*
Clawson, John Addison 1922- *WhoAm 90*
Clawson, John David 1934- *WhoSSW 91*
Clawson, John Gibbs 1928- *St&PR 91*
Clawson, Lance Douglas *BiDrAPA 89*
Clawson, Leanna Lynn 1949- *WhoEmL 91*
Clawson, Marion 1905- *BioIn 16*
Clawson, Michael Howard 1950- *St&PR 91*
Clawson, Michael J. 1950- *St&PR 91*
Clawson, Raymond Walden 1906- *WhoWor 91*
Clawson, Robert G. *St&PR 91*
Clawson, Robert Wayne 1939- *WhoAm 90, WhoWor 91*
Clawson, Roxann Eloise 1945- *WhoAmW 91, WhoE 91*
Clawson, Tony Charles 1955- *WhoEmL 91*
Clax, Freda Marie 1959- *WhoAmW 91*
Claxon, Michael William 1951- *WhoEmL 91*
Claxton, Adelaide 1835?-1900? *BiDWomA*
Claxton, Anthony L. *BiDrAPA 89*
Claxton, Florence 1835?- *BiDWomA*
Claxton, Harriett Maroy Jones 1930- *WhoAmW 91*
Claxton, Philander Priestley, Jr. 1914- *WhoE 91*
Claxton, Robert Howard 1942- *WhoSSW 91*
Clay, Albert Greene 1917- *WhoAm 90*
Clay, Alexander Stephens 1863-1910 *AmLegL*
Clay, Alexander Stephens 1942- *WhoAm 90*
Clay, Ambrose Whitlock Winston 1941- *WhoAm 90*
Clay, Andrew Dice *BioIn 16*
Clay, Andrew Dice 1958- *News 91-1 [port]*
Clay, Billy Jerrell 1940- *St&PR 91*
Clay, Carolyne 1952- *WhoAm 90, WhoAmW 91*
Clay, Cassius 1942- *BioIn 16*
Clay, Cassius Marcellus *BioIn 16*
Clay, Cassius Marcellus 1810-1903 *BioIn 16*
Clay, Catesby W. 1923- *St&PR 91*
Clay, Charles Horace 1925- *St&PR 91*
Clay, Clifton Ford 1939- *WhoWor 91*
Clay, Dain 1919- *Ballpl 90*
Clay, David S. 1923- *St&PR 91*
Clay, Diskin 1938- *WhoWrEP 89*
Clay, Donna Jean 1958- *WhoAmW 91*
Clay, Frederic 1838-1889 *OxCPMus*
Clay, George Harry 1911- *WhoAm 90*
Clay, Grady Edward 1916- *WhoAm 90, WhoSSW 91*
Clay, Harris Aubrey 1911- *WhoSSW 91, WhoWor 91*
Clay, Heidi Alexandra *BiDrAPA 89*
Clay, Henry *PenDiDA 89*
Clay, Henry 1777-1852 *BiDrUSE 89, BioIn 16, EncABHB 6 [port], WorAlBi*
Clay, Henry Allen 1930- *WhoAm 90*
Clay, James Franklin 1911- *WhoSSW 91*
Clay, James Harvey 1950- *WhoEmL 91*
Clay, James Jordan, Jr. 1962- *WhoEmL 91*
Clay, John A. 1939- *St&PR 91*
Clay, John Ernest 1921- *WhoAm 90*
Clay, John W., Jr. 1941- *WhoSSW 91*
Clay, John William 1913- *St&PR 91, WhoAm 90, WhoSSW 91*
Clay, Ken 1954- *Ballpl 90*
Clay, Landon Thomas 1926- *St&PR 91, WhoAm 90*
Clay, Larry David 1948- *St&PR 91*
Clay, Laura 1849-1941 *BioAmW*
Clay, Louis Davies 1930- *St&PR 91*
Clay, Lucius 1897-1978 *WorAlBi*
Clay, Lucius D. 1897-1978 *BioIn 16*
Clay, Lyell Buffington 1923- *St&PR 91, WhoAm 90*
Clay, Orson C. 1930- *St&PR 91, WhoAm 90, WhoSSW 91*
Clay, Patrice 1947- *BioIn 16*
Clay, Paul Eugene 1933- *St&PR 91*
Clay, Robert Bruce 1946- *St&PR 91*
Clay, Robert J. 1927- *ODwPR 91*
Clay, Ryburn Glover, Jr. 1928- *WhoSSW 91*
Clay, Thomas Howard *BiDrAPA 89*
Clay, Tommie Senior *WhoAmW 91*
Clay, W. Robert 1932- *St&PR 91*
Clay, William Lacy 1931- *BlkAmsC [port], WhoAm 90*
Clay, William Lacy, Jr. 1956- *WhoEmL 91*
Clay, William Robert 1932- *WhoAm 90*
Clayberger, Samuel Robert 1926- *WhoAmA 91*
Claybon, Patience H *BiDrAPA 89*
Clayburgh, Jill 1944- *BioIn 16, WhoAm 90, WorAlBi*
Claycomb, Cecil Keith 1920- *WhoAm 90*
Clayden, Raymond 1927- *St&PR 91*
Claydon, David A. 1935- *St&PR 91*
Claydon, J.H. 1934- *St&PR 91*
Claydon, Margaret 1923- *WhoAm 90*
Clayman, Gary A. 1954- *St&PR 91*
Clayman, Joel A. 1957- *St&PR 91*
Clayman, Lawrence Howard 1910- *WhoE 91*
Clayman, Martin J. 1925- *St&PR 91*
Claypoole, Robert Edwin 1936- *WhoAm 90*
Clayson, S Hollis *WhoAmA 91*
Clayton, Anita Louise Hammer 1956- *BiDrAPA 89*
Clayton, Anne *BiDEWW, FemiCLE*
Clayton, Barbara *AuBYP 90*
Clayton, Bernard Miles, Jr. 1953- *WhoEmL 91*
Clayton, Billy Wayne 1928- *WhoAm 90*
Clayton, Bruce Underhill 1947- *St&PR 91*
Clayton, Buck 1911- *BioIn 16, DrBlPA 90, OxCPMus*
Clayton, Byron Cordell 1957- *WhoEmL 91*
Clayton, Coy 1935- *St&PR 91*
Clayton, Cynthia Carlson 1943- *WhoAmW 91*
Clayton, David Lawrence 1952- *WhoSSW 91*
Clayton, David Russell 1943- *WhoE 91*
Clayton, Donald Delbert 1935- *WhoAm 90*
Clayton, Donald W. *WhoSSW 91*
Clayton, Donald W. 1942- *St&PR 91*
Clayton, Ellen Wright 1952- *WhoAmW 91*
Clayton, Evelyn Williams 1951- *WhoAmW 91*
Clayton, Frances Elizabeth 1922- *WhoAm 90, WhoAmW 91*
Clayton, Gregory Paul 1949- *WhoEmL 91*
Clayton, Herbert Kenneth 1920- *IntWWM 90*
Clayton, Hugh Newton 1907- *WhoAm 90, WhoWor 91*
Clayton, J. Don 1933- *St&PR 91*
Clayton, Jack *BioIn 16*
Clayton, Jack 1921- *WhoWor 91*
Clayton, James Edwin 1929- *WhoAm 90*
Clayton, Jay 1951- *WhoWrEP 89*
Clayton, Joan *WhoWrEP 89*
Clayton, JoAnn Cleveland 1935- *WhoE 91*
Clayton, Joe Todd 1924- *WhoAm 90*
Clayton, John Charles 1924- *WhoAm 90*
Clayton, John J. 1917- *WhoWor 91, WhoWrEP 89*
Clayton, John J 1935- *WhoWrEP 89*
Clayton, John Middleton 1796-1856 *BiDrUSE 89, BioIn 16*
Clayton, John Middleton, Jr. 1941- *WhoE 91*
Clayton, John S 1950- *BiDrAPA 89*
Clayton, Jonathan Alan 1937- *WhoAm 90*
Clayton, Joseph Coy 1935- *St&PR 91*
Clayton, Joy May 1947- *WhoAmW 91, WhoSSW 91*
Clayton, Keith Alan 1957- *WhoSSW 91*
Clayton, Kenneth P. 1931- *St&PR 91*
Clayton, Laura Ancelina 1960- *WhoEmL 91*
Clayton, Lawrence Ray 1938- *WhoSSW 91*
Clayton, Marvin Courtland 1938- *WhoSSW 91*
Clayton, Mary Jo *WhoAm 90*
Clayton, Michael 1947- *St&PR 91*
Clayton, Michael William 1946- *WhoSSW 91*
Clayton, Paula J 1934- *BiDrAPA 89*
Clayton, Peggy L. 1953- *WhoAmW 91*
Clayton, Peter A 1937- *ConAu 130*
Clayton, Powell 1833-1914 *BioIn 16*
Clayton, Preston Copeland 1903- *WhoAm 90*
Clayton, Ralph David 1946- *WhoSSW 91*
Clayton, Richard R. 1938- *St&PR 91*
Clayton, Richard Reese 1938- *WhoAm 90*
Clayton, Robert *WhoSSW 91*
Clayton, Robert Eugene 1929- *BiDrAPA 89*
Clayton, Robert Hugh 1957- *WhoEmL 91*
Clayton, Robert Norman 1930- *WhoAm 90*
Clayton, S. Lillian 1876-1930 *BioIn 16*
Clayton, Stephen John 1946- *WhoEmL 91*
Clayton, William E. 1938- *WhoAm 90*
Clayton, William Edward 1926- *St&PR 91*
Clayton, William Howard 1927- *WhoAm 90*

Clayton, William L. 1929- *St&PR 91, WhoAm 90*
Clayton, William Lewis 1930- *WhoAm 90*
Clayton, William Lockhart 1880-1966 *BioIn 16*
Claytor, James Emery 1954- *BiDrAPA 89*
Claytor, Murray *BiDrAPA 89*
Claytor, Robert B. 1922- *St&PR 91*
Claytor, Robert Buckner 1922- *WhoAm 90*
Claytor, W. Graham, Jr. *BioIn 16*
Claytor, William Graham, Jr. 1912- *WhoAm 90*
Cleall, Charles 1927- *IntWWM 90*
Clear, Albert F., Jr. 1920- *WhoAm 90*
Clear, Charles V *WhoAmA 91N*
Clear, Geoffrey P. 1950- *St&PR 91*
Clear, Geoffrey Posselt 1950- *WhoEmL 91*
Clear, John Michael 1948- *WhoEmL 91*
Clear, Mark 1956- *Ballpl 90*
Clear, Rosemary Elaine 1946- *WhoEmL 91*
Clearfield, Andrew Mark 1949- *WhoE 91*
Clearfield, Harris Reynold 1933- *WhoAm 90*
Cleary, Barbara B 1935- *WhoAmA 91*
Cleary, Beverly *BioIn 16*
Cleary, Beverly 1916- *Au&Arts 6 [port], AuBYP 90, MajTwCW, WorAlBi*
Cleary, Beverly Atlee *WhoAm 90, WhoAmW 91*
Cleary, Brian Gerald 1960- *WhoE 91*
Cleary, Edward H. *BioIn 16, NewYTBS 90*
Cleary, Edward William 1919- *WhoAm 90*
Cleary, Francis Charles 1932- *St&PR 91*
Cleary, Francis P. *St&PR 91*
Cleary, Frank Joseph 1930- *St&PR 91*
Cleary, Fritz 1913- *WhoE 91*
Cleary, Fritz 1914- *WhoAmA 91*
Cleary, James Charles, Jr. 1921- *WhoE 91*
Cleary, James Francis 1927- *WhoAm 90*
Cleary, James Roy 1926- *WhoAm 90*
Cleary, James Vincent 1828-1898 *DcCanB 12*
Cleary, James W. 1927- *WhoAm 90*
Cleary, Jean Marie 1964- *WhoEmL 91*
Cleary, John Anthony 1931- *St&PR 91*
Cleary, John V. *NewYTBS 90 [port]*
Cleary, John Vincent, Jr. 1928- *St&PR 91, WhoAm 90*
Cleary, John Washington 1911- *WhoAm 90*
Cleary, Jon 1917- *TwCCr&M 91*
Cleary, Joseph Aloysius, Jr. 1954- *St&PR 91*
Cleary, Joseph M. 1914- *St&PR 91*
Cleary, Lynda Woods 1950- *WhoAmW 91*
Cleary, Manon Catherine 1942- *WhoAmA 91, WhoAmW 91, WhoE 91, WhoWor 91*
Cleary, Michael Francis 1926- *BiDrAPA 89*
Cleary, Robert Edward 1932- *WhoAm 90*
Cleary, Russell George 1933- *St&PR 91, WhoAm 90*
Cleary, Shirley 1942- *WhoAmA 91*
Cleary, Thomas A. 1925- *St&PR 91*
Cleary, Thomas C. 1921- *St&PR 91*
Cleary, Thomas John 1939- *St&PR 91*
Cleary, Timothy Finbar 1925- *WhoAm 90*
Cleary, William B. 1921- *St&PR 91*
Cleary, William Richard 1933- *WhoWor 91*
Cleasby, John LeRoy 1928- *WhoAm 90*
Cleaton, Anne *FemiCLE*
Cleave, Mary *BioIn 16*
Cleave, Mary L. 1947- *WhoAmW 91*
Cleaveland, John B. 1948- *St&PR 91*
Cleaveland, Parker 1780-1858 *BioIn 16*
Cleavelin, Leonard Robert 1957- *WhoEmL 91*
Cleaver, C Perry *BiDrAPA 89*
Cleaver, Dale Gordon 1928- *WhoAmA 91*
Cleaver, Dorothy Marian *BiDrAPA 89*
Cleaver, Eldridge 1935- *BioIn 16*
Cleaver, Hylton 1891-1961 *BioIn 16*
Cleaver, Toni Evyonne *BiDrAPA 89*
Cleaver, Vera *AuBYP 90, BioIn 16*
Cleaver, Vera Allen 1919- *WhoAm 90, WhoWrEP 89*
Cleaver, William Joseph 1920-1981 *AuBYP 90*
Cleaver, William Lehn 1949- *WhoEmL 91*
Cleaver, William Pennington 1914- *WhoAm 90*
Cleaves, Margaret Ann 1946- *WhoWrEP 89*
Cleaves, Mark Andrew 1960- *WhoE 91*
Cleaves, Muriel Mattock *WhoAmA 91N*
Clecak, Peter Emmett 1938- *WhoAm 90*
Cleckley, Lula Shaw 1947- *WhoSSW 91*
Clede, Emile William, Jr. 1927- *WhoWrEP 89*
Clee, Jan Evert 1928- *WhoAm 90*
Cleek, Judy Ann 1948- *WhoEmL 91*
Cleese, John *BioIn 16*
Cleese, John 1939- *MajTwCW*
Cleese, John Marwood 1939- *WhoAm 90, WhoWor 91*
Cleeve, Brian 1921- *TwCCr&M 91*
Cleeve, Brian Brendan Talbot 1921- *SpyFic*
Cleeve, Lucas *FemiCLE*
Cleeves, Ann 1954- *TwCCr&M 91*
Cleff, William Carl 1942- *St&PR 91, WhoAm 90*
Cleffius, Lambert *PenDiDA 89*
Clegg, Charles T 1940- *BiDrAPA 89*
Clegg, Hugh Anthony 1900-1983 *DcNaB 1981*
Clegg, John 1928- *IntWWM 90*
Clegg, Johnny *BioIn 16*
Clegg, Karen Kohler 1949- *WhoEmL 91*
Clegg, Kathleen Anne *BiDrAPA 89*
Clegg, Marshall Terrell 1931- *St&PR 91*
Clegg, Milton Lee 1943- *St&PR 91*
Clegg, Roger Burton 1955- *WhoAm 90*
Cleghorn, Cheree Briggs 1945- *WhoE 91*
Cleghorn, John E. 1941- *St&PR 91*
Cleghorn, John Edward 1941- *WhoAm 90*
Cleghorn, John M *BiDrAPA 89*
Cleghorn, Leslie 1941- *St&PR 91*
Cleghorn, Reese 1930- *WhoAm 90, WhoWrEP 89*
Cleghorn, Robert A 1904- *BiDrAPA 89*
Cleghorn, Sarah 1876-1959 *FemiCLE*
Clehane, Diane *ODwPR 91*
Clein, Cheryl Lee 1948- *WhoAmW 91, WhoEmL 91*
Clein, Reubin *BioIn 16*
Cleland, Andrew Wallace 1946- *WhoE 91, WhoEmL 91*
Cleland, Charles A *BiDrAPA 89*
Cleland, Charles Carr 1924- *WhoAm 90*
Cleland, Douglas Stewart 1952- *WhoEmL 91*
Cleland, Edward Gordon 1949- *WhoEmL 91*
Cleland, Gladys Lee 1959- *WhoAmW 91*
Cleland, John 1709-1789 *WorAlBi*
Cleland, Joseph Maxwell 1942- *WhoAm 90, WhoSSW 91*
Cleland, Max 1942- *ConAu 129*
Cleland, Philip B. 1945- *St&PR 91*
Cleland, Ralph Erskine 1892-1971 *DcScB S2*
Cleland, Richard Henderson 1937- *St&PR 91*
Cleland, Robert Erksine 1932- *WhoAm 90*
Cleland, Robert Lindbergh 1927- *WhoAm 90*
Cleland, Sherrill 1924- *WhoAm 90*
Cleland, Thomas Maitland 1880-1964 *WhoAmA 91N*
Cleland, William Wallace 1930- *WhoAm 90*
Cleland, Winston Eugene 1943- *WhoE 91*
Clelland, Lamond 1921- *IntWWM 90*
Clelland, Richard Cook 1921- *WhoAm 90*
Clelland, Robert Theodore 1943- *WhoSSW 91*
Clem, Alan Leland 1929- *WhoAm 90*
Clem, Donald Y. 1926- *St&PR 91*
Clem, Elizabeth Ann Stumpf 1945- *WhoAmW 91*
Clem, Gary Lee 1948- *WhoSSW 91*
Clem, James Allen 1934- *St&PR 91*
Clem, John Richard 1938- *WhoAm 90*
Clem, Lester William 1934- *WhoAm 90*
Clem, Wendy Lee 1950- *WhoWrEP 89*
Clemans, Jerald Garrow 1930- *St&PR 91*
Clemans, William Vance 1920- *WhoAm 90, WhoWor 91*
Clemenceau, Georges 1841-1929 *BioIn 16, WorAlBi*
Clemenceau, Georges Eugene Benjamin 1841-1929 *BiDFrPL*
Clemencic, Rene 1928- *IntWWM 90, PenDiMP*
Clemens, Carl E. *BioIn 16*
Clemens, Clara *PenDiMP*
Clemens, Doug 1939- *Ballpl 90*
Clemens, Douglas H. 1939- *St&PR 91*
Clemens, Earl L. 1925- *IntWWM 90*
Clemens, Elizabeth Malm 1928- *WhoSSW 91*
Clemens, Frank Joseph, Jr. 1940- *St&PR 91*
Clemens, Jane L. 1803-1890 *BioAmW*
Clemens, Jon K. 1938- *St&PR 91*
Clemens, Mary Etcheverry 1953- *St&PR 91*
Clemens, Michael Terrence 1950- *WhoEmL 91, WhoWor 91*
Clemens, Norman A 1933- *BiDrAPA 89*
Clemens, P. Blaine 1937- *St&PR 91*
Clemens, Paul 1911- *WhoAmA 91*
Clemens, Peter John, III 1943- *St&PR 91*
Clemens, Philip A. 1949- *St&PR 91*
Clemens, Richard Glenn 1940- *WhoAm 90*
Clemens, Richard Phillip 1933- *St&PR 91*
Clemens, Roger *BioIn 16*
Clemens, Roger 1962- *Ballpl 90, WhoAm 90, WorAlBi*
Clemens, Ronald E. 1951- *St&PR 91*
Clemens, Samuel Langhorne *EncPaPR 91*
Clemens, Samuel Langhorne 1835-1910 *AuBYP 90, BioIn 16, EncO&P 3*
Clemens, T. Pat 1944- *WhoWor 91*
Clemens, Tammy L. 1958- *WhoAmW 91*
Clemens, Walter H. 1928- *St&PR 91*
Clemens, William Alvin 1932- *WhoAm 90*
Clement, Alain Gerard *WhoAmA 91*
Clement, Allan Montgomery, III 1955- *St&PR 91*
Clement, Alvis Macon 1912- *WhoAm 90*
Clement, Besse Alberta *WhoSSW 91*
Clement, Betsy Kay 1952- *WhoAmW 91*
Clement, Bob 1943- *WhoAm 90, WhoSSW 91*
Clement, Dale E. 1933- *St&PR 91*
Clement, Dallas Brent 1940- *WhoWrEP 89*
Clement, Franz 1780-1842 *PenDiMP*
Clement, Graham McMurray 1957- *WhoSSW 91*
Clement, Gregory Vance 1928- *WhoWrEP 89*
Clement, Hal 1922- *RGTwCSF*
Clement, Henry Joseph, Jr. 1942- *St&PR 91, WhoAm 90*
Clement, Hope Elizabeth Anna 1930- *WhoAm 90, WhoAmW 91*
Clement, Howard Wheeler 1917- *WhoAm 90*
Clement, Jacques 1566?-1589 *BioIn 16*
Clement, Janice Faye 1946- *WhoAmW 91*
Clement, Jean M. 1948- *WhoEmL 91*
Clement, John 1932- *St&PR 91*
Clement, Joseph Dale 1928- *WhoAm 90*
Clement, Josephine-Eleonore *DcCanB 12*
Clement, Kathi Dee 1951- *WhoEmL 91*
Clement, Kathleen 1928- *WhoAmA 91*
Clement, Meredith Owen 1926- *WhoAm 90*
Clement, Patricia Ellen 1951- *St&PR 91*
Clement, Philip A. 1944- *WhoAm 90*
Clement, Philip Alan 1944- *St&PR 91*
Clement, Richard F. 1906- *St&PR 91*
Clement, Richard Francis 1906- *WhoAm 90, WhoWor 91*
Clement, Robert William 1927- *WhoAm 90*
Clement, Roger 1950- *IntWWM 90*
Clement, Shirley 1922- *WhoAmA 91*
Clement, Shirley George 1926- *WhoAmW 91, WhoSSW 91*
Clement, Stephen M 1913- *BiDrAPA 89*
Clement, Thomas Earl 1932- *WhoAm 90*
Clement, Tim *NewAgMG*
Clement, Timothy Robert 1960- *St&PR 91*
Clemente, Alice Rodrigues 1934- *WhoAmW 91*
Clemente, Arthur Clarence 1947- *St&PR 91*
Clemente, Bartholomew 1921- *BiDrAPA 89*
Clemente, Carmine Domenic 1928- *WhoAm 90*
Clemente, Celestino 1922- *WhoAm 90*
Clemente, Charles C. 1935- *ODwPR 91*
Clemente, Dennis Taylor 1939- *St&PR 91*
Clemente, Fernando V M *BiDrAPA 89*
Clemente, Francesco 1952- *WhoAmA 91, WorAlBi*
Clemente, Frank 1945- *WhoAm 90*
Clemente, Holly A. 1951- *ODwPR 91*
Clemente, Jack Michael 1938- *BiDrAPA 89*
Clemente, Leopold M. 1938- *St&PR 91*
Clemente, Lilia C. *BioIn 16*
Clemente, Lilia C. 1941- *St&PR 91*
Clemente, Marc Gennaro *BiDrAPA 89*
Clemente, Mark Andrew 1951- *WhoEmL 91*
Clemente, Nicholas Jerome *BiDrAPA 89*
Clemente, Robert Stephen 1956- *WhoE 91*
Clemente, Roberto 1934-1972 *Ballpl 90 [port], BioIn 16, WorAlBi*
Clementel, Etienne 1864-1936 *BiDFrPL*
Clementi, Muzio 1752-1832 *BioIn 16*
Clementi, Stephan F. 1952- *ODwPR 91*
Clements, Allen, Jr. 1924- *WhoWor 91*
Clements, Arthur L 1932- *WhoWrEP 89*
Clements, Bernadette Stone 1943- *WhoAm 90*
Clements, Brian Matthew 1946- *WhoE 91*
Clements, Bruce 1931- *AuBYP 90*
Clements, C Glenn *BiDrAPA 89*
Clements, Calvin *BioIn 16*
Clements, Charles Adams 1953- *WhoSSW 91*
Clements, Dale Martin 1947- *St&PR 91*
Clements, Donald Ray 1949- *WhoEmL 91*
Clements, Emilia Gonzalez 1944- *WhoAmW 91*
Clements, Frank A. 1942- *AuBYP 90*
Clements, Fred Preston 1954- *WhoWrEP 89*
Clements, G. Paul 1916- *St&PR 91*
Clements, George *BioIn 16*
Clements, George Gerald 1939- *St&PR 91*
Clements, Harold *St&PR 91*
Clements, Irven H. 1937- *St&PR 91*
Clements, Jack 1864-1941 *Ballpl 90*
Clements, James David *BiDrAPA 89*
Clements, James David 1931- *WhoAm 90, WhoWor 91*
Clements, James Franklin 1927- *St&PR 91*
Clements, Jamie Hager 1957- *WhoEmL 91*
Clements, Janice C. *BioIn 16*
Clements, Jeffrey K. 1946- *St&PR 91*
Clements, John 1910-1988 *AnObit 1988, BioIn 16*
Clements, John Allen 1923- *WhoAm 90*
Clements, John B. 1928- *St&PR 91*
Clements, John Brian 1928- *WhoAm 90*
Clements, John David 1938- *St&PR 91*
Clements, John Robert 1950- *WhoEmL 91*
Clements, Joye Arline 1936- *WhoAmW 91*
Clements, Julia Anne 1953- *WhoAmW 91*
Clements, Kevin Anthony 1941- *WhoAm 90*
Clements, Kevin Paul 1946- *WhoWor 91*
Clements, Lynne Fleming 1945- *WhoAmW 91*
Clements, Michael Reid 1943- *St&PR 91*
Clements, Neal Woodson 1926- *WhoAm 90*
Clements, Newton Nash 1834-1900 *AmLegL*
Clements, Pat 1962- *Ballpl 90*
Clements, Richard Hamer 1926- *St&PR 91*
Clements, Richard L. 1956- *St&PR 91*
Clements, Robert 1932- *St&PR 91, WhoAm 90*
Clements, Robert Donald 1937- *WhoAmA 91*
Clements, Robert Earl 1928- *St&PR 91*
Clements, Robert John 1912- *WhoAm 90*
Clements, Stephen A. 1933- *St&PR 91*
Clements, Thomas 1898- *WhoAm 90*
Clements, Thomas Scott 1967- *WhoSSW 91*
Clements, Walter Alexander 1924- *WhoAm 90*
Clements, William Perry, Jr. 1917- *WhoAm 90, WhoSSW 91, WhoWor 91*
Clements, William Thomas 1947- *WhoE 91*
Clements, Woodrow Wilson 1914- *WhoAm 90*
Clemetson, Charles Alan Blake 1923- *WhoAm 90*
Cleminshaw, Frank Foster 1911- *WhoAm 90*
Cleminshaw, Helen K. Marie 1938- *WhoAmW 91*
Clemmens, Daryl *ODwPR 91*
Clemmens, Edward R 1914- *BiDrAPA 89*
Clemmens, Elisabeth B 1921- *BiDrAPA 89*
Clemmensen, Rick Lee 1953- *WhoSSW 91*
Clemments, Ralph W 1923- *BiDrAPA 89*
Clemmer, Leon 1926- *WhoE 91*
Clemmer, Mary 1839-1884 *BioIn 16*
Clemmer, Mary E. 1831-1884 *BioAmW*
Clemmey, John L., III 1945- *St&PR 91*
Clemmons, Barry Wayne 1949- *WhoEmL 91, WhoSSW 91*
Clemmons, David Robert 1947- *WhoEmL 91*
Clemmons, Frances Anne Mansell 1915- *WhoAmW 91, WhoSSW 91*
Clemmons, Gordon L. 1920- *St&PR 91*
Clemmons, James Glenn 1952- *WhoEmL 91*
Clemmons, Jane Goodrich 1934- *WhoAmW 91*
Clemmons, Slaton 1909- *WhoSSW 91*
Clemmow, Caroline Anne 1959- *IntWWM 90*
Clemo, Polly Gretchen Howe 1941- *WhoAmW 91*
Clemon, U. W. 1943- *WhoAm 90*
Clemons, D. Gradon 1947- *St&PR 91*
Clemons, Jimmie R 1935- *BiDrAPA 89*
Clemons, John Robert 1948- *WhoAm 90*
Clemons, Julie Payne 1948- *WhoAmW 91, WhoEmL 91*
Clemons, Ralph Hardy, Jr. 1926- *WhoAm 90*
Clemons, Verne 1892-1959 *Ballpl 90*
Clemons, Walter, Jr. 1929- *WhoAm 90*
Clendaniel, Fontaine Cowan 1951- *WhoEmL 91*
Clendenin, John L. *BioIn 16*
Clendenin, John L. 1934- *St&PR 91, WhoAm 90, WhoSSW 91*
Clendenin, Maria L. *St&PR 91*
Clendenin, William W *BiDrAPA 89*
Clendenning, William Edmund 1931- *WhoAm 90*
Clendenon, Donn 1935- *Ballpl 90*
Clennan, John Joseph 1951- *WhoEmL 91*
Clennon, David *ConTFT 8 [port]*
Clensy, Ronald E. 1946- *St&PR 91*
Cleobury, Nicholas Randall 1950- *IntWWM 90*
Cleobury, Stephen John 1948- *IntWWM 90*
Cleopatra I *WomWR*
Cleopatra II *WomWR*
Cleopatra III *WomWR*
Cleopatra VII 69BC- *WomWR [port]*
Cleopatra VII 69BC-30BC *WorAlBi*
Cleopatra of Cyrene *WomWR*
Cleopatra, Queen of Egypt *BioIn 16*
Cleopatra Thea *WomWR*

Cleopatra Tryphaena WomWR
Clephane, Thomas Painter 1942- WhoE 91
Clepper, Frank D. 1934- St&PR 91
Clerc, Doris BiDrAPA 89
Clerc, Jeanne Marie 1954- WhoAmW 91
Clerc, Oliver C., Jr. 1947- St&PR 91
Clergue, Lucien George 1934- WhoAm 90, WhoWor 91
Clerici, Felice PenDiDA 89
Clerico, John A. 1941- St&PR 91
Clerisme, Joseph Roosevelt 1950- BiDrAPA 89, WhoE 91
Clerissy, Antoine, I PenDiDA 89
Clerissy, Antoine, II 1673-1743 PenDiDA 89
Clerissy, Joseph 1649?-1684 PenDiDA 89
Clerissy, Pierre, I 1651?-1728 PenDiDA 89
Clerissy, Pierre, II 1704-1794 PenDiDA 89
Clerjeaud, Georges-Paul 1934- WhoWor 91
Clerk, N.W. ConAu 33NR
Clerk, N. W. MajTwCW
Clerk, Pierre 1928- WhoAmA 91
Clerke, Ellen Mary 1840-1906 FemiCLE
Clerkin, Eugene Patrick 1931- WhoAm 90
Clerkin, Thomas 1950- St&PR 91
Clerkin, Thomas A. 1950- WhoSSW 91
Clermont WhNaAH
Clermont, Jacques A BiDrAPA 89
Clermont, Yves Wilfrid 1926- WhoAm 90, WhoE 91
Clermore WhNaAH
Clermos WhNaAH
Clery-Melin, Bernard WhoSSW 91
Clesi, Bret Alden 1958- WhoSSW 91
Clesi, Frank Joseph 1928- St&PR 91
Cleva, Fausto 1902-1971 PenDiMP
Cleveland Quartet PenDiMP
Cleveland, Alan ODwPR 91
Cleveland, Barbara Palmer, Countess of BiDEWW
Cleveland, Barry NewAgMG
Cleveland, C.E. Thomas 1947- St&PR 91
Cleveland, Ceil Margaret Ellen 1938- WhoWrEP 89
Cleveland, Charles Robert 1954- WhoSSW 91
Cleveland, Chauncey Fitch 1799-1887 AmLegL
Cleveland, Cromwell Cook, Jr. 1948- WhoSSW 91
Cleveland, Cynthia Ann BiDrAPA 89
Cleveland, Dexter Alden 1947- WhoSSW 91
Cleveland, Donald Leslie 1938- WhoAm 90
Cleveland, Edward Allen 1950- WhoSSW 91
Cleveland, Frances Folsom BioIn 16
Cleveland, Grover 1837-1908 BiDrUSE 89, BioIn 16, WorAlBi
Cleveland, Harlan 1918- WhoAm 90, WhoWor 91
Cleveland, Helen Barth WhoAmA 91N
Cleveland, James 1931- DrBIPA 90
Cleveland, James Colgate 1920- WhoAm 90
Cleveland, Joan 1932- St&PR 91
Cleveland, John Edward 1940- St&PR 91
Cleveland, Kenneth Charles 1933- St&PR 91
Cleveland, Paul Matthews 1931- WhoAm 90, WhoWor 91
Cleveland, Peggy Rose Richey 1929- WhoAmW 91
Cleveland, Reggie 1948- Ballpl 90
Cleveland, Richard Joseph 1932- WhoAm 90
Cleveland, Robert Earl 1936- WhoAmA 91
Cleveland, Robert W. 1910- St&PR 91
Cleveland, Susan Elizabeth 1946- WhoAm 90, WhoAmW 91
Cleveland, William Charles 1926- WhoE 91
Cleveland, William West 1921- WhoAm 90
Cleven, Carol Chapman 1928- WhoAmW 91
Clevenger, Arthur Frank 1928- St&PR 91
Clevenger, Ernest A. 1953- St&PR 91
Clevenger, Ernest Allen, III 1953- WhoSSW 91
Clevenger, Frank A. 1928- St&PR 91
Clevenger, Jerry L. 1953- WhoEmL 91
Clevenger, Johanna BiDrAPA 89
Clevenger, Penelope 1940- WhoAmW 91
Clevenger, Raymond C., III 1937- WhoAm 90
Clevenger, Robert Vincent 1921- WhoAm 90, WhoWor 91
Clevenger, Roy Edward 1953- WhoE 91, WhoWor 91
Clevenger, Sarah 1926- WhoAm 90
Clevenger, Terri L. ODwPR 91
Clevenger, Tex 1932- Ballpl 90
Clevenger, Thomas Ramsey 1935- St&PR 91, WhoAm 90
Clevenger, William Thomas 1950- WhoSSW 91
Clever Hans EncPaPR 91
Clever, Geraldine 1930- St&PR 91
Clever, Linda Hawes WhoAm 90, WhoAmW 91
Clever, Marcia Sue 1956- BiDrAPA 89
Clever, Warren Glenn 1918- WhoAm 90
Cleverdon, Douglas 1903-1987 BioIn 16
Cleverdon, Walter Irving 1933- St&PR 91
Cleves, Marie de 1426-1487 EncCoWW
Clevett, Kenneth John 1934- WhoE 91
Clew, Harry T. St&PR 91
Clewes, Dorothy 1907- AuBYP 90
Clewett, Kenneth Vaughn 1923- WhoAm 90
Clewett, Richard Monroe 1911- WhoAm 90
Clewis, Charlotte Wright Staub 1935- WhoAmW 91
Clewlow, Carl William 1916- WhoAm 90
Cleworth, Charles W. BioIn 16
Clews, Henry 1834-1923 EncABHB 6 [port]
Clews, James PenDiDA 89
Clews, Ralph PenDiDA 89
Cleyn, Franz 1582-1648 PenDiDA 89
Cliburn, Stu 1956- Ballpl 90
Cliburn, Van 1934- BioIn 16, IntWWM 90, PenDiMP, WhoAm 90, WhoWor 91, WorAlBi
Click, David Forrest 1947- WhoEmL 91
Click, John William 1936- WhoSSW 91
Click, Paul R 1924- BiDrAPA 89
Clicquot-Ponsardin, Barbe-Nicole 1777-1866 BioIn 16
Cliett, Charles Buren 1924- WhoAm 90, WhoSSW 91
Cliett, Otis Jay, III 1944- WhoSSW 91
Cliff, Clarice 1899-1972 BioIn 16, PenDiDA 89
Cliff, Denis Antony 1942- WhoAmA 91
Cliff, Jimmy DrBIPA 90
Cliff, Jimmy 1949?- EncPR&S 89
Cliff, John William, Jr. 1949- WhoEmL 91
Cliff, Johnnie Marie 1935- WhoAmW 91
Cliff, Judith Anita 1941- WhoAmW 91
Cliff, Laddie 1891-1937 OxCPMus
Cliff, Linda A. 1951- WhoAmW 91
Cliff, Michael Peter Hedley 1942- WhoE 91
Cliff, Michelle 1946- FemiCLE
Cliff, Ronald Laird 1929- St&PR 91
Cliff, Steven Burris 1952- WhoEmL 91, WhoSSW 91
Cliff, Walter Conway 1932- WhoAm 90
Clifford, Ann T. WhoSSW 91
Clifford, Anne 1590-1676 BiDEWW, BioIn 16, FemiCLE
Clifford, Carmella Marie 1955- WhoE 91
Clifford, Carrie Williams 1862-1934 HarlReB [port]
Clifford, Cheryl Ann 1952- WhoE 91
Clifford, Clark M. 1906- BioIn 16
Clifford, Clark McAdams 1906- BiDrUSE 89, St&PR 91, WhoAm 90, WhoWor 91
Clifford, Donald Francis, Jr. 1935- WhoAm 90
Clifford, Earle Winchester, Jr. 1925- WhoAm 90
Clifford, Eth 1915- AuBYP 90, BioIn 16
Clifford, Francesca Bishop 1959- WhoAmW 91
Clifford, Francis 1917-1975 TwCCr&M 91
Clifford, Frederick Burr 1914- WhoAm 90
Clifford, Garry Carroll 1934- WhoAmW 91
Clifford, George Orr 1924- WhoAm 90
Clifford, Gerald BioIn 16
Clifford, Geraldine Marie Joncich 1931- WhoAm 90, WhoAmW 91
Clifford, Howard BioIn 16
Clifford, James L 1901-1978 DcLB 103 [port]
Clifford, John 1836-1912 BioIn 16
Clifford, John Leger 1950- WhoEmL 91
Clifford, Jutta WhoAmA 91
Clifford, Lawrence M. 1955- St&PR 91
Clifford, Leon Albert 1919- WhoE 91
Clifford, Lucy 1853?-1929 FemiCLE
Clifford, Lucy Lane 1855?-1929 BioIn 16
Clifford, Margaret Cort 1929- WhoAmW 91
Clifford, Margaret Louise 1920- WhoAmW 91
Clifford, Mary Ellen R BiDrAPA 89
Clifford, Mary Louise 1926- AuBYP 90
Clifford, Maurice Cecil 1920- WhoAm 90
Clifford, Michael Richard 1952- WhoSSW 91
Clifford, Morgan 1950- BioIn 16
Clifford, Nathan 1803-1881 BiDrUSE 89
Clifford, Nicholas Rowland 1930- WhoAm 90
Clifford, Paul Ingraham 1914- WhoSSW 91, WhoWor 91
Clifford, Peter Bulkeley 1931- WhoE 91
Clifford, Ralph D. 1954- WhoEmL 91
Clifford, Robert Anderson 1957- WhoEmL 91
Clifford, Robert L. 1924- WhoAm 90, WhoE 91
Clifford, Robert William 1937- WhoE 91
Clifford, Sidney, Jr. 1937- WhoE 91
Clifford, Steven A. 1942- St&PR 91
Clifford, Steven Francis 1943- WhoAm 90
Clifford, Stewart Burnett 1929- WhoAm 90, WhoE 91, WhoWor 91
Clifford, Sylvester 1929- WhoAm 90
Clifford, Terry W. 1937- St&PR 91
Clifford, Thomas John 1921- WhoAm 90
Clifford, Thomas Robert 1957- WhoEmL 91
Clifford, Timothy Earl 1954- WhoE 91
Clift, Charmian 1923-1969 FemiCLE
Clift, G.W. 1952- WhoWrEP 89
Clift, Harlond 1912- Ballpl 90
Clift, Montgomery 1920-1966 BioIn 16, WorAlBi
Clift, William 1944- BioIn 16
Clift, William Brooks 1944- WhoAmA 91
Clift, William Brooks, III 1944- WhoAm 90
Clift, William Orrin 1914- WhoAm 90
Clifton, Anne Rutenber 1938- WhoAmW 91, WhoE 91
Clifton, Charles 1853-1928 EncABHB 4 [port]
Clifton, Chester Victor, Jr. 1913- WhoAm 90
Clifton, Donald O. 1924- St&PR 91
Clifton, Elwyn Martin 1948- St&PR 91
Clifton, Fred J. BioIn 16
Clifton, Harold Ray 1946- WhoEmL 91
Clifton, Harry 1832-1872 OxCPMus
Clifton, James Albert 1923- WhoAm 90
Clifton, Jerry T 1928- BiDrAPA 89
Clifton, John Hill 1946- St&PR 91
Clifton, Josephine 1813-1847 BioIn 16, NotWoAT
Clifton, Judy Raelene 1946- WhoAmW 91
Clifton, Linda Jane 1940- WhoWrEP 89
Clifton, Lucille 1936- BioIn 16, FemiCLE, MajTwCW
Clifton, Lucille Thelma 1936- WhoAmW 91
Clifton, Merritt Robin 1953- WhoWrEP 89
Clifton, Michelle Gamm 1944- WhoAmA 91
Clifton, Nat NewYTBS 90
Clifton, Paul Hoot, Jr. 1947- WhoAm 90
Clifton, Phillip Max 1944- BiDrAPA 89
Clifton, Richard Randall 1950- WhoEmL 91
Clifton, Robert G. BioIn 16
Clifton, Robin Mary 1962- WhoAmW 91
Clifton, Rodney James 1937- WhoAm 90
Clifton, Russell B. 1930- WhoAm 90
Clifton, William Lacy 1920- St&PR 91
Clifton-Taylor, Alec 1907-1985 DcNaB 1981
Clignet, Marion BioIn 16
Cligrow, Edward Thomas, Jr. 1934- WhoAm 90
Climan, Richard Elliot 1953- WhoEmL 91
Clime, Winfield Scott 1881-1958 WhoAmA 91N
Climenko, Jesse 1904- St&PR 91
Climenson, Charles Maynard 1946- St&PR 91
Climent, Carlos E 1940- BiDrAPA 89
Climent, Silvia 1940- WhoHisp 91
Climer, James Alan 1954- WhoEmL 91
Climko, Robert P BiDrAPA 89
Climko, Robert Paul 1953- WhoE 91
Climo, Lawrence H 1938- BiDrAPA 89
Climo, Lawrence Hanon 1938- WhoE 91
Clinard, Marshall Barron 1911- WhoAm 90
Clinard, Robert Noel 1946- WhoEmL 91
Clinch, Duncan Lamont 1787-1849 WhNaAH
Clinch, J. Houstoun M., Jr. 1934- St&PR 91
Clinch, John Houstoun McIntosh 1902- WhoAm 90
Clinch, Peter Gladstone 1930- IntWWM 90
Clinchy, Richard Alexander, III 1943- WhoSSW 91
Clinchy, Walter G. 1911- St&PR 91
Clindinning, Robert Wilson 1815-1898 DcCanB 12
Cline, Alfred B., Jr. 1949- St&PR 91
Cline, Bobby James 1932- WhoAm 90
Cline, C. Bob 1946- St&PR 91
Cline, Carolyn Joan 1941- WhoAmW 91, WhoWor 91
Cline, Charles 1937- WhoWrEP 89
Cline, Charles Edward 1858- AmLegL
Cline, Charles William 1937- WhoAm 90, WhoWor 91
Cline, Clarence Lee 1905- WhoAm 90
Cline, Clinton C 1934- WhoAmA 91
Cline, Clyde D. 1907- St&PR 91
Cline, Craig 1959- St&PR 91
Cline, Darrell Eugene 1962- WhoEmL 91
Cline, David William 1935- BiDrAPA 89
Cline, Denna Lee 1943- St&PR 91
Cline, Dennis L. 1942- ODwPR 91
Cline, Dorothy May Stammerjohn 1915- WhoWor 91
Cline, Eileen Marie 1947- WhoAmW 91
Cline, Eileen Tate 1935- IntWWM 90
Cline, Foster W., Jr. 1940- BiDrAPA 89
Cline, Gibbons Dee 1941- St&PR 91
Cline, Glen Edwin 1920- WhoAm 90
Cline, Gregory Paul 1960- WhoEmL 91
Cline, Hayden Dwight 1944- WhoSSW 91
Cline, Herbert S BiDrAPA 89
Cline, J.A. 1936- St&PR 91
Cline, James Ralph, Jr. 1928- WhoSSW 91
Cline, Linda Blair 1950- WhoEmL 91
Cline, Linda Carol WhoAmW 91
Cline, Lucille Glasser 1927- WhoAmW 91
Cline, Maggie 1857-1934 BioIn 16
Cline, Martin Jay 1934- WhoAm 90
Cline, Michael Bruce 1957- WhoWor 91
Cline, Michael Robert 1949- WhoEmL 91
Cline, Nancy M. 1946- WhoAm 90
Cline, Ned A. 1938- WhoSSW 91
Cline, Patsy WhoNeCM C
Cline, Patsy 1932-1963 ConMus 5 [port], OxCPMus
Cline, Paul Charles 1933- WhoAm 90
Cline, Pauline M. 1947- WhoAmW 91
Cline, Peter Joseph 1946- St&PR 91
Cline, Philip Eugene 1933- St&PR 91
Cline, Ray Steiner 1918- WhoAm 90
Cline, Richard Allan 1961- WhoWrEP 89
Cline, Richard Allen 1955- WhoEmL 91
Cline, Richard Gordon 1935- St&PR 91, WhoAm 90
Cline, Richard Lee 1942- St&PR 91, WhoAm 90
Cline, Robert Alexander, Jr. 1935- St&PR 91
Cline, Robert Stanley 1937- St&PR 91, WhoAm 90
Cline, Robert Theodore 1941- St&PR 91
Cline, Robert Thomas 1925- WhoSSW 91
Cline, Roger M. 1935- St&PR 91
Cline, Ruth Eleanor Harwood 1946- WhoAmW 91
Cline, S L 1948- ConAu 129
Cline, Sally Irene 1938- WhoWor 91
Cline, Shelia Rhonda 1953- WhoAmW 91, WhoEmL 91, WhoSSW 91
Cline, Stewart Martin 1945- St&PR 91
Cline, Thomas Farrell 1953- WhoEmL 91
Cline, Thomas William 1932- WhoAm 90
Cline, Tim 1942- WhoWrEP 89
Cline, Ty 1939- Ballpl 90
Cline, William R BiDrAPA 89
Cline, William Richard 1941- WhoAm 90
Cline, Wilson Ettason 1914- WhoWor 91
Clinedinst, Katherine Parsons 1903- WhoAmA 91
Clinedinst, May Spear 1887- WhoAmA 91N
Clines, Gene 1946- Ballpl 90
Clineschmidt, Bradley Van 1941- WhoAm 90
Cling, Alice 1946- MusmAFA
Clingan, James William 1937- WhoE 91
Clingan, Robert Keith 1961- WhoWrEP 89
Clinger, Anthony R. 1939- ODwPR 91
Clinger, Arthur William, Jr. 1934- St&PR 91
Clinger, David M. 1933- ODwPR 91
Clinger, Orris W BiDrAPA 89
Clinger, William Alan BiDrAPA 89
Clinger, William Floyd, Jr. 1929- WhoAm 90, WhoE 91
Clingerman, Edgar Allen 1934- St&PR 91
Clingman, Billy 1869-1958 Ballpl 90
Clingman, William Herbert, Jr. 1929- WhoSSW 91, WhoWor 91
Clink, Stephen Henry 1911- WhoAm 90
Clink-Pubalowski, Lori Lee 1965- WhoAmW 91
Clinkenbeard, James Howard 1950- WhoSSW 91
Clinkscales, Anna Lee James 1931- WhoAmW 91
Clinkscales, William Abner, Jr. 1928- WhoAm 90
Clinton, Bill 1946- BioIn 16, WhoAm 90, WhoSSW 91, WhoWor 91
Clinton, Catherine 1952- ConAu 130
Clinton, Cathleen Ann 1950- WhoEmL 91
Clinton, D WhoWrEP 89
Clinton, De Witt 1769-1828 BioIn 16
Clinton, DeWitt 1769-1828 EncABHB 6 [port], WorAlBi
Clinton, Dirk MajTwCW
Clinton, Dorothy Louise 1925- WhoWrEP 89
Clinton, Elizabeth 1574?-1630? BiDEWW, BioIn 16
Clinton, F. G. TwCCr&M 91
Clinton, George 1686-1761 EncCRAm, WhNaAH
Clinton, George 1739-1812 BiDrUSE 89, EncCRAm [port], WhNaAH, WorAlBi
Clinton, George 1941- EncPR&S 89
Clinton, George Carl Wellesley 1931- IntWWM 90

Clinton, Gerry *WhoWrEP 89*
Clinton, Gordon Stanley 1920- *WhoAm 90*
Clinton, Henry 1738?-1795 *BioIn 16, EncCRAm, WorAlBi*
Clinton, Hillary Rodham 1947- *WhoEmL 91*
Clinton, J. Hart 1905- *St&PR 91*
Clinton, James 1733-1812 *WhNaAH*
Clinton, James Harmon 1946- *WhoAm 90*
Clinton, Jean Maria *BiDrAPA 89*
Clinton, Jeff *WhoWrEP 89*
Clinton, John Hart 1905- *WhoAm 90*
Clinton, Judith Mary Myers 1945- *WhoEmL 91*
Clinton, Larry 1909-1985 *BioIn 16*
Clinton, Larry 1909-1987 *OxCPMus*
Clinton, Lawrence P *BiDrAPA 89*
Clinton, Lawrence Paul 1945- *WhoEmL 91, WhoWor 91*
Clinton, Lloyd DeWitt 1946- *WhoWrEP 89*
Clinton, Lu 1937- *Ballpl 90*
Clinton, Mariann Hancock 1933- *WhoAm 90*
Clinton, Paul Arthur 1942- *WhoAmA 91*
Clinton, Richard Lee 1938- *WhoWrEP 89*
Clinton, Richard M. 1941- *WhoAm 90*
Clinton, Timothy Edward 1960- *WhoSSW 91*
Clinton, Tracy Peter, Sr. 1948- *WhoSSW 91*
Clinton-Baddeley, V C 1900-1970 *TwCCr&M 91*
Clippeleyr, Hans Edward 1957- *WhoWor 91*
Clippert, Charles Frederick 1931- *WhoAm 90, WhoWor 91*
Clipsham, Margery *FemiCLE*
Clipsham, Margery *BiDEWW*
Clipson, Margery *BiDEWW*
Clisby, Roger David 1939- *WhoAmA 91*
Clise, Alfred Hammer 1920- *St&PR 91*
Clitheroe, Baron 1901-1984 *DcNaB 1981*
Clive, Caroline 1801-1873 *BioIn 16, FemiCLE*
Clive, Catherine 1711-1785 *BioIn 16, FemiCLE*
Clive, John *ConAu 130*
Clive, John L. *NewYTBS 90 [port]*
Clive, John Leonard 1924-1990 *BioIn 16, ConAu 130*
Clive, Kitty 1711-1785 *PenDiMP*
Clive, Richard R 1912- *WhoAmA 91*
Clive, Robert 1725-1774 *BioIn 16, WorAlBi*
Clive-Ross, F 1921- *EncO&P 3*
Cliver, Dean Otis 1935- *WhoAm 90*
Cliver, Kendra-Jean *WhoAmA 91*
Clizbe, John Anthony 1942- *WhoAm 90, WhoE 91*
Clizer, Herald Kenneth 1932- *St&PR 91*
Cloak, Frank Theodore 1904- *WhoAm 90*
Cloar, Carroll 1913- *WhoAm 90, WhoAmA 91*
Cloar, James Allen 1939- *WhoAm 90*
Cloar, Patricia Ann Sandstead 1932- *WhoAmW 91*
Cloche, Maurice *NewYTBS 90*
Cloche, Maurice 1907-1990 *BioIn 16*
Clod, Bente 1946- *EncCoWW*
Clodagh *BioIn 16*
Clodfelter, Catherine Joy 1955- *WhoAmW 91*
Clodfelter, Daniel Gray 1950- *WhoEmL 91*
Clodfelter, Micheal 1946- *BioIn 16*
Clodfelter, Micheal D 1946- *ConAu 31NR*
Clodion 1738-1814 *IntDcAA 90*
Clodius, Julia Marie 1958- *WhoAmW 91*
Clodius, Robert LeRoy 1921- *WhoAm 90, WhoWor 91*
Clodman, Jo Mira 1954- *St&PR 91*
Cloer, Carl Thomas, Jr. 1945- *WhoSSW 91*
Clofine, Henry Lawrence 1940- *St&PR 91*
Clogan, Paul Maurice 1934- *WhoAm 90*
Clogg, Richard Bruce 1949- *WhoEmL 91*
Cloherty, John Joseph 1949- *WhoAm 90*
Cloherty, Michael J. 1947- *St&PR 91*
Clohesy, Stephanie J. 1948- *WhoEmL 91*
Clokey, Art *BioIn 16*
Clonan, Jeanette H. *ODwPR 91*
Clonch, Naaman George 1923- *St&PR 91*
Clond, Michael B. *St&PR 91*
Cloney, Richard M. 1941- *St&PR 91*
Cloney, Richard Morgan 1941- *WhoE 91*
Cloney, William Thomas, Jr. 1911- *WhoAm 90*
Cloninger, Claude Robert *BiDrAPA 89*
Cloninger, Claude Robert 1944- *WhoAm 90, WhoWor 91*
Cloninger, Eugene F. 1941- *St&PR 91*
Cloninger, Kriss, III 1947- *WhoAm 90*
Cloninger, Tony 1940- *Ballpl 90*
Clonts, Thomas Michael 1942- *St&PR 91*
Clontz, William Ralph 1947- *WhoE 91*
Cloonan, Clifford B. 1928- *WhoAm 90*
Cloonan, Edward Thomas 1951- *WhoE 91*
Cloonan, James Brian 1931- *WhoAm 90*
Clooney, George *BioIn 16*
Clooney, Rosemary 1928- *OxCPMus*
Clooney, Thomas J. 1948- *St&PR 91*
Clopine, Marjorie Showers 1914- *WhoAmW 91, WhoSSW 91, WhoWor 91*
Clopine, Sandra Lou 1936- *WhoAmW 91*
Clopton, Beverly Beck *WhoWrEP 89*
Clopton, Claudia Lou *BiDrAPA 89*
Clopton, David 1820-1892 *AmLegL*
Clopton, George Willis 1951- *WhoSSW 91*
Clore, Alan E. *BioIn 16*
Clore, Gideon Marius 1955- *WhoE 91*
Clorety, Joseph Anthony, III 1942- *St&PR 91, WhoAm 90*
Close, Charles Mollison 1927- *WhoAm 90*
Close, Charles Thomas 1940- *WhoAm 90*
Close, Chuck 1940- *BioIn 16, WhoAmA 91, WorAlBi*
Close, David Palmer 1915- *WhoAm 90*
Close, Dean Purdy 1905- *WhoAmA 91*
Close, Elizabeth Scheu 1912- *WhoAm 90, WhoAmW 91*
Close, Frank *WhoAmA 91*
Close, Frederick J. 1905-1989 *BioIn 16*
Close, Glenn *BioIn 16*
Close, Glenn 1947- *WhoAm 90, WhoAmW 91, WorAlBi*
Close, Harry Francis 1921- *St&PR 91*
Close, Jeffrey S. *ODwPR 91*
Close, Karen Elizabeth 1951- *WhoAmW 91*
Close, Katherine Anne *BiDrAPA 89*
Close, Marjorie 1899-1978 *WhoAmA 91N*
Close, Michael John 1943- *WhoE 91*
Close, Susanne Busey 1950- *St&PR 91*
Close, Upton 1894-1960 *BioIn 16*
Close, Winston Arthur 1906- *WhoAm 90*
Closen, Michael Lee 1949- *WhoEmL 91*
Closner, John James 1915- *St&PR 91*
Closon, Jacques Henri Lucien 1921- *WhoWor 91*
Closs, August 1898-1990 *ConAu 132*
Closs, Gerhard Ludwig 1928- *WhoAm 90*
Closse, William Denis 1940- *WhoWor 91*
Closser, Mary H 1953- *BiDrAPA 89*
Closser, Patrick Denton 1945- *WhoEmL 91, WhoSSW 91, WhoWor 91*
Closset, Gerard P. 1943- *St&PR 91*
Closset, Gerard Paul 1943- *WhoE 91*
Closson, John Eugene, Jr. 1947- *WhoWor 91*
Closson, Michael *BioIn 16*
Closson, Nanci Blair 1943- *WhoAmA 91*
Closson, William G, Jr. *BiDrAPA 89*
Clot, Archlyn Ann 1931- *WhoSSW 91*
Clotet, Lluis 1941- *BioIn 16*
Clotfelter, Beryl Edward 1926- *WhoAm 90*
Clotfelter, Charles T. 1947- *ConAu 131, WhoSSW 91*
Clotfelter, Lucile Dennison 1947- *BiDrAPA 89*
Clothier, Birchard Taylor 1936- *St&PR 91*
Clothier, Jeffrey Lane *BiDrAPA 89*
Clothier, Peter D. 1936- *WhoWrEP 89*
Clothier, Peter Dean 1936- *WhoAmA 91*
Clothier, Roy A. 1939- *St&PR 91*
Clotworthy, John Harris 1924- *WhoAm 90*
Clotworthy, William Baird, Jr. 1922- *BiDrAPA 89*
Cloud, Bruce Benjamin 1920- *St&PR 91*
Cloud, Bruce Benjamin, Sr. 1920- *WhoAm 90*
Cloud, Daniel Tuttle 1925- *WhoAm 90*
Cloud, David Eugene 1934- *WhoWrEP 89*
Cloud, Dolores Ona 1941- *WhoAmW 91*
Cloud, Harry E. 1947- *St&PR 91*
Cloud, Jack L 1925- *WhoAmA 91*
Cloud, Linda Beal 1937- *WhoAmW 91*
Cloud, Marina Taylor 1945- *WhoSSW 91*
Cloud, Peter J. 1942- *St&PR 91*
Cloud, Preston 1912- *WhoAm 90*
Cloud, Sanford, Jr. 1944- *St&PR 91*
Cloud, Sharon Lee 1948- *WhoEmL 91*
Cloud, Stanley Wills 1936- *WhoAm 90*
Cloud, Thomas Gordon 1950- *WhoSSW 91*
Cloud, William Frank 1947- *St&PR 91*
Cloud, William Larry 1943- *WhoSSW 91*
Cloudman 1790?-1862 *WhNaAH*
Cloudman, Francis Harold, III 1944- *WhoE 91*
Cloudman, Harry Howard, Jr. 1917- *WhoAm 90*
Cloudman, Ruth Howard 1948- *WhoAmA 91*
Cloudsley, Donald Hugh 1925- *WhoAm 90, WhoE 91*
Cloues, Edward Blanchard, II 1947- *St&PR 91*
Clouet, Francois 1515?-1572 *IntDcAA 90*
Clouet, Jean 1485?-1540? *IntDcAA 90*
Clough, Anne Jemima 1820-1892 *BioIn 16*
Clough, Arthur Hugh 1819-1861 *BioIn 16, NinCLC 27 [port]*
Clough, Charles E. 1930- *St&PR 91*
Clough, Charles Elmer 1930- *WhoAm 90, WhoE 91*
Clough, Charles M. 1928- *St&PR 91*
Clough, Charles Marvin 1928- *WhoAm 90*
Clough, Charles Sidney 1951- *WhoAmA 91*
Clough, David Alan 1955- *WhoEmL 91*
Clough, George James, Jr. 1932- *St&PR 91*
Clough, John Everett 1836-1910 *BioIn 16*
Clough, Nadine Doerr 1942- *WhoAmW 91*
Clough, Prunella 1919- *BiDWomA*
Clough, Ralph Nelson 1916- *WhoAm 90*
Clough, Ray William, Jr. 1920- *WhoAm 90*
Clough, Richard Hudson 1922- *WhoAm 90*
Clough, Richard John 1940- *St&PR 91*
Clough, Ronald H. 1935- *St&PR 91*
Clough, Shepard B. *NewYTBS 90 [port]*
Clough, Shepard B 1901-1990 *ConAu 131*
Clough, Shepard Bancroft 1901-1990 *BioIn 16*
Clougherty, Anne Marie *WhoE 91*
Cloughly, Cecilia Louise 1943- *WhoAmW 91*
Clous, James Melvin 1959- *WhoSSW 91*
Clouse, James Paul 1922- *WhoAm 90*
Clouse, Jan Louise 1945- *WhoEmL 91*
Clouse, Jerome Vincent 1943- *St&PR 91*
Clouse, John Daniel 1925- *WhoWor 91*
Clouse, Kenneth Earl 1954- *WhoSSW 91*
Clouse, Robert G. 1931- *BioIn 16*
Clouse, Robert Wilburn 1937- *WhoAm 90*
Clouse, Roger R. 1907- *St&PR 91*
Clouse, Ronald E. 1937- *St&PR 91*
Clouse, Roy *BiDrAPA 89*
Clouser, Christopher E. *ODwPR 91*
Clouser, Christopher E. 1952- *St&PR 91*
Clouser, Christopher E. 1953- *WhoAm 90*
Clouspy, William C. *St&PR 91*
Clouston, Judith Kay 1940- *WhoWrEP 89*
Clouston, Ross Neal 1922- *WhoAm 90*
Clout, Richard J.S. *St&PR 91*
Clouthier, Manuel 1934-1989 *BioIn 16*
Cloutier, Anne O'Rourke 1955- *WhoAmW 91*
Cloutier, Brian John 1957- *WhoE 91*
Cloutier, Cecile 1930- *BioIn 16*
Cloutier, Charlotte Berube 1942- *WhoE 91*
Cloutier, David Edward 1951- *WhoWrEP 89*
Cloutier, E George *BiDrAPA 89*
Cloutier, Gilles Georges 1928- *WhoAm 90*
Cloutier, Joan Elizabeth 1936- *BiDrAPA 89*
Cloutier, Joseph R. 1908-1989 *BioIn 16*
Cloutier, Leonce 1928- *WhoAm 90*
Cloutier, Patricia Ayotte 1938- *WhoAmW 91*
Cloutier, Richard Robert 1942- *St&PR 91*
Clouzot, Henri-Georges 1907-1977 *WorAlBi*
Clover, Don Kennedy, Jr. 1946- *WhoSSW 91*
Clover, Gerald T. 1929- *St&PR 91*
Clovers, The *EncPR&S 89*
Clovis, Albert L. 1935- *WhoAm 90*
Clovis, Donna Lucille 1957- *WhoE 91*
Clovis, James R. 1929- *St&PR 91*
Clovis, William L 1932- *BiDrAPA 89*
Clovis, William Leroy 1932- *WhoE 91*
Clow, Barbara Hand 1943- *WhoWrEP 89*
Clow, Gordon Henry 1942- *St&PR 91*
Clow, Lee *WhoAm 90*
Clow, Timothy James 1960- *WhoEmL 91*
Cloward, Esther Marie Fleming *BioIn 16*
Cloward, George R. 1935- *St&PR 91*
Cloward, Richard Andrew 1926- *WhoAm 90*
Cloward, Steven P. 1947- *St&PR 91*
Clowdis, Charles Wilburn, Jr. 1944- *WhoSSW 91*
Clowe, Kevin Nord 1950- *WhoE 91*
Clower, Clement Hogbin 1920- *WhoSSW 91*
Clower, Courtney *BiDrAPA 89*
Clower, Jerry *BioIn 16*
Clower, Robert Wayne 1926- *WhoAm 90*
Clower, Virginia L 1920- *BiDrAPA 89*
Clower, William Dewey 1935- *WhoAm 90*
Clowes, Allen Whitehill 1917- *WhoAmA 91*
Clowes, George H.A. 1915-1988 *BioIn 16*
Clowry, Suzanne Kathleen 1943- *WhoAmW 91*
Cloyd, Richard M. 1948- *ODwPR 91*
Cloyd, William P 1932- *BiDrAPA 89*
Clozier, Christian Robert Adrien 1945- *IntWWM 90*
Clubb, Bruce Edwin 1931- *WhoAm 90, WhoWor 91*
Clubb, Martin L. 1957- *St&PR 91*
Clubb, Oliver Edmund 1901-1989 *BioIn 16*
Clubbe, John Louis Edwin 1938- *WhoSSW 91*
Clube, Victor 1934- *ConAu 130*
Cluchey, David Paul 1946- *WhoE 91*
Cluchey, James P. 1947- *St&PR 91*
Cluff, E. Dale 1937- *WhoAm 90*
Cluff, Edward Fuller 1928- *WhoAm 90*
Cluff, Leighton Eggertsen 1923- *WhoAm 90*
Cluger, David *BioIn 16*
Clukey, Wayne P. 1939- *St&PR 91*
Clum, Dennis Patrick 1925- *WhoSSW 91*
Clum, John P. 1851-1932 *WhNaAH*
Clune, Henry W. 1890- *WhoWrEP 89*
Clune, Robert Bell 1920- *WhoAm 90*
Clurman, Ann *BioIn 16*
Clurman, Richard Michael 1924- *WhoAm 90, WhoWor 91*
Cluster *NewAgMG*
Clute, John E. 1934- *St&PR 91*
Clute, Karen Leslie 1956- *WhoAmW 91*
Clute, Robert Eugene 1924- *WhoAm 90*
Clutha, Janet Paterson Frame 1924- *MajTwCW*
Clutsam, George H. 1866-1951 *OxCPMus*
Clutter, Bertley Allen, III 1942- *WhoAm 90*
Clutter, Gayle Ann 1945- *WhoSSW 91*
Clutter, John Allen 1947- *WhoSSW 91*
Clutter, Mary E. *St&PR 91*
Clutter, Mary Elizabeth *WhoAm 90, WhoAmW 91*
Clutter, R. Marie *St&PR 91*
Clutton-Brock, Arthur 1868-1924 *DcLB 98 [port]*
Clutz, William 1933- *WhoAm 90, WhoAmA 91*
Cluver, Michael Albert 1942- *WhoWor 91*
Cluysenaar, Anne 1936- *BioIn 16, FemiCLE*
Cluytens, Andre 1905-1967 *PenDiMP*
Clybouw, Daniel Joseph 1934- *WhoWor 91*
Clyce, Thomas Ellis 1945- *St&PR 91*
Clyde, Calvin Geary 1924- *WhoAm 90*
Clyde, Constance 1872- *FemiCLE*
Clyde, David *BioIn 16*
Clyde, David 1955- *Ballpl 90*
Clyde, Debra Lynne 1953- *WhoE 91*
Clyde, Edward Wilbur 1917- *WhoAm 90*
Clyde, Glenda Estelle 1937- *WhoAmW 91*
Clyde, Jeremy 1941- *ConTFT 8*
Clyde, Norman 1885-1972 *BioIn 16*
Clyde, Wallace Alexander, Jr. 1929- *WhoSSW 91*
Clyman, James 1792-1881 *WhNaAH*
Clyman, Robert *BiDrAPA 89*
Clyman, Robert B. 1956- *BiDrAPA 89*
Clymer, Albert Anderson 1942- *WhoAmA 91*
Clymer, Brian William 1947- *WhoAm 90*
Clymer, David H. 1924- *St&PR 91*
Clymer, Eleanor 1906- *WhoAm 90, WhoWrEP 89*
Clymer, Eleanor Lowenton 1906- *AuBYP 90*
Clymer, Everett Stuart 1944- *St&PR 91*
Clymer, George 1739-1813 *BioIn 16, EncCRAm*
Clymer, John 1907-1989 *BioIn 16*
Clymer, John F 1907-1989 *WhoAmA 91N*
Clymer, John Marion 1960- *WhoEmL 91*
Clymer, John Tuttle 1925- *BiDrAPA 89*
Clymer, Otis 1880-1926 *Ballpl 90*
Clymer, R Swinburne 1878-1966 *EncO&P 3*
Clymer, Wayne Kenton 1917- *WhoAm 90*
Clymore, Sue Allison 1959- *WhoAmW 91*
Clynch, Edward John 1942- *WhoAm 90*
Clynch, Michael Richard 1951- *BiDrAPA 89*
Clyne, Irving M *BiDrAPA 89*
Clyne, John Clayton 1946- *WhoEmL 91*
Clyne, Julius S 1937- *BiDrAPA 89*
Clyne, Patricia Edwards *AuBYP 90*
Clyne, Patricia Edwards 1935- *WhoWrEP 89*
Clyne, Rosemarie Blackstone 1926- *WhoAmW 91*
Clynes, James J., Jr. 1924- *St&PR 91*
Clynes, Manfred 1925- *IntWWM 90*
Cmar, Janice Butko 1954- *WhoAmW 91*
Cmar, Karen A. 1955- *St&PR 91*
Cnattingius, Sven Harald Michael 1949- *WhoWor 91*
Cnong, Sooi Peaw 1942- *St&PR 91*
Co, Bun Tee, Jr. 1943- *BiDrAPA 89*
Co, George Go 1958- *WhoWor 91*
Co, Laurence T. *BiDrAPA 89*
Co, Rufino Tan 1951- *BiDrAPA 89*
Coaci, Vincenzo 1756-1794 *PenDiDA 89*
Coacoochee *WhNaAH*
Coad, Peter, Jr. 1953- *WhoSSW 91*
Coade, Eleanor 1733-1821 *BioIn 16*
Coady, Barbara Lee 1938- *WhoAm 90*
Coady, Edmond Patrick 1938- *WhoAm 90*
Coady, John Martin 1927- *WhoAm 90*
Coady, Michael Francis 1957- *WhoEmL 91*
Coady, Roger 1942- *ODwPR 91*
Coady, William Francis 1940- *WhoSSW 91*
Coady, William John 1939- *St&PR 91*
Coady-Weinand, Mary Ann 1959- *BiDrAPA 89*
Coahran, Norwin T. 1936- *St&PR 91*

Coake, Richard William 1952- St&PR 91
Coaker, James Whitfield 1946- WhoWor 91
Coakley, Andy 1882-1963 Ballpl 90
Coakley, Charles E., Mrs. WhoAmW 91
Coakley, John P. BioIn 16
Coakley, Robert S. 1931- St&PR 91
Coakley, Thomas Francis 1946- St&PR 91
Coakley, William 1951- St&PR 91
Coale, Ansley Johnson 1917- WhoAm 90
Coale, Edward H. 1920- St&PR 91
Coale, Elizabeth BiDEWW
Coale, John P. BioIn 16
Coan, Gil 1922- Ballpl 90
Coan, Pamela Elaine 1959- WhoAmW 91
Coapstick, Richard P. 1931- St&PR 91
Coar, Richard John 1921- WhoAm 90
Coasters, The ConMus 5 [port], EncPR&S 89, OxCPMus
Coate, D.F.S. 1931- St&PR 91
Coates, Albert 1882-1953 PenDiMP
Coates, Albert Andrew, Jr. 1954- WhoSSW 91
Coates, Ann S WhoAmA 91
Coates, Bradley Allen 1951- WhoEmL 91
Coates, Casey BioIn 16
Coates, Charles Lorimer 1940- St&PR 91
Coates, Clarence Leroy, Jr. 1923- WhoAm 90
Coates, David John 1953- WhoEmL 91
Coates, Dianne Kay 1945- WhoAmW 91
Coates, Donald Robert 1922- WhoAm 90
Coates, Edith 1908-1983 PenDiMP
Coates, Eric 1886-1957 OxCPMus
Coates, Eugene G BiDrAPA 89
Coates, G. Richard 1943- St&PR 91
Coates, Glenn Richard 1923- WhoAm 90, WhoWor 91
Coates, Gloria 1938- IntWWM 90
Coates, Helen Grace BioIn 16
Coates, James EncO&P 3
Coates, Jesse 1908- WhoAm 90
Coates, Jim 1932- Ballpl 90
Coates, John 1865-1941 PenDiMP
Coates, John Robert 1961- WhoSSW 91
Coates, Jon P. 1934- St&PR 91
Coates, Joseph Francis 1929- WhoAm 90
Coates, K. S. ConAu 130
Coates, Ken ConAu 130
Coates, Ken S. ConAu 130
Coates, Kenneth 1956- ConAu 130
Coates, Michael 1950- ODwPR 91
Coates, Nigel 1949- BioIn 16
Coates, Paul David 1947- St&PR 91
Coates, Robert Jay 1922- WhoAm 90
Coates, Robert M. 1897-1973 DcLB 102 [port], WhoAmA 91N
Coates, Robert Mercer 1938- WhoAm 90
Coates, Ross Alexander 1932- WhoAmA 91
Coates, Sam Joel BiDrAPA 89
Coates, Vincent J. St&PR 91
Coates, W Robert BiDrAPA 89
Coates, William Franklin 1935- St&PR 91
Coates, Willson H. 1899-1976 ConAu 33NR
Coates, Winslow Shelby 1891-1989 BioIn 16
Coates-Wilkes, Charlotte BiDrAPA 89
Coatman, Graham Robert 1952- IntWWM 90
Coatney, Sherry Kay 1960- WhoEmL 91
Coats, Andrew Montgomery 1935- WhoAm 90
Coats, Charles F. 1949- WhoSSW 91
Coats, Charles Warren 1956- BiDrAPA 89
Coats, Dan BioIn 16
Coats, Daniel R. 1943- WhoAm 90, WhoWor 91
Coats, Edwin Albert 1906- BiDrAPA 89
Coats, Gary Lee 1949- WhoSSW 91
Coats, Hugh B. 1925- St&PR 91
Coats, Keith Hal 1934- WhoAm 90
Coats, Laura Jane AuBYP 90
Coats, Linda Tuggles 1958- WhoAmW 91
Coats, Michael Edwin BiDrAPA 89
Coats, Michael Edwin 1954- WhoE 91
Coats, Peter 1910-1990 ConAu 132
Coats, Roy R. 1924- St&PR 91
Coats, Stephen E. 1948- WhoEmL 91
Coats, Wendell John, Jr. 1947- WhoEmL 91
Coats, William EncCRAm
Coats, William Sloan, III 1950- WhoEmL 91, WhoWor 91
Coatsworth, Elizabeth Jane 1893-1986 AuBYP 90, BioIn 16
Coba, Robert L. 1954- St&PR 91
Cobanoglu, Adnan 1951- WhoEmL 91
Cobb, A. Willard 1929- IntWWM 90
Cobb, Alice BiDEWW
Cobb, Alton B. 1928- WhoAm 90
Cobb, Alton H., Jr. 1954- St&PR 91
Cobb, Amasa 1823-1905 AmLegL
Cobb, Ann 1885-1960 LiHiK
Cobb, Arnett 1918-1989 AnObit 1989
Cobb, Arnett Cleophus 1918-1989 BioIn 16, DrBlPA 90
Cobb, Brenda Ann 1942- WhoSSW 91
Cobb, Bruce W. 1941- St&PR 91
Cobb, Byron Lee 1954- WhoSSW 91
Cobb, Calvin Hayes, Jr. 1924- WhoAm 90
Cobb, Carlee Conway, II 1949- WhoEmL 91
Cobb, Carolus Melville 1922- St&PR 91
Cobb, Carolyn Jane 1943- WhoAmW 91
Cobb, Charles E., Jr. 1936- WhoWor 91
Cobb, Charles Roger 1951- BiDrAPA 89
Cobb, Christine Marie 1952- WhoEmL 91
Cobb, Daniel W., Jr. 1921- WhoAm 90, WhoWor 91
Cobb, Donna Deanne Hill 1943- WhoAmW 91
Cobb, Douglas Romain 1942- St&PR 91
Cobb, Elizabeth Bliss Parkinson 1907- WhoAm 90
Cobb, Evelyn Laverne Burkhart 1945- WhoEmL 91
Cobb, Frank L. 1869-1923 BioIn 16
Cobb, G. Elliott, Jr. 1939- WhoAm 90
Cobb, George Hamilton 1911- St&PR 91, WhoAm 90
Cobb, George L. 1886-1942 OxCPMus
Cobb, George Leo 1886-1942 BioIn 16
Cobb, Henry Hammond, Jr. 1920- WhoAm 90
Cobb, Henry Nichols 1926- WhoAm 90
Cobb, Henry Van Zandt 1909- WhoAm 90
Cobb, Howell 1815-1868 BiDrUSE 89
Cobb, Howell 1922- WhoAm 90, WhoSSW 91
Cobb, Hubbard Hanford 1917- WhoAm 90
Cobb, Irvin S. 1876-1944 BioIn 16
Cobb, Irvin Shrewsbury 1876-1944 LiHiK
Cobb, James Charles 1947- ConAu 31NR
Cobb, James Richard 1942- St&PR 91
Cobb, Jewel Plummer 1924- WhoAmW 91
Cobb, John 1715?-1778 PenDiDA 89
Cobb, John 1942- IntWWM 90
Cobb, John Anthony 1927- WhoAm 90, WhoSSW 91
Cobb, John Boswell, Jr. 1925- WhoAm 90
Cobb, John Cecil, Jr. 1927- WhoAm 90
Cobb, John W. 1927- St&PR 91
Cobb, Lee J. 1911-1976 WorAlBi
Cobb, Leslie Davis 1935- St&PR 91, WhoAm 90
Cobb, Margaret Evelyn 1918- IntWWM 90
Cobb, Melinda Ann BiDrAPA 89
Cobb, Miles Alan 1930- WhoAm 90
Cobb, Morgan Thomas 1932- WhoSSW 91
Cobb, Patricia Ann 1939- WhoSSW 91
Cobb, Richard 1917- WorAu 1980 [port]
Cobb, Richard M. 1952- St&PR 91
Cobb, Roger K. ODwPR 91
Cobb, Ronald David 1945- WhoSSW 91
Cobb, Ruth 1914- WhoAm 90, WhoAmA 91, WhoAmW 91, WhoE 91
Cobb, Sharon A. 1953- WhoEmL 91
Cobb, Sharon Yvonne 1950- WhoSSW 91
Cobb, Shirley Ann 1936- WhoAmW 91, WhoWor 91
Cobb, Stephen Alonzo 1833-1878 AmLegL
Cobb, Sue BioIn 16
Cobb, Susan Clason 1953- WhoEmL 91
Cobb, Terri R. 1934- WhoSSW 91
Cobb, Thomas W. 1944- St&PR 91
Cobb, Timothy I. ODwPR 91
Cobb, Ty 1886-1961 Ballpl 90 [port], BioIn 16, WorAlBi
Cobb, Ty 1950- WhoEmL 91
Cobb, Vicki 1938- AuBYP 90
Cobb, Vincent 1943- WhoAm 90
Cobb, Virginia Horton 1933- WhoAm 90, WhoAmA 91
Cobb, W. Montague NewYTBS 90
Cobb, Will D. 1876-1930 OxCPMus
Cobb, William 1937- WhoWrEP 89
Cobb, William Allen 1947- St&PR 91
Cobb, William Ervin 1947- WhoSSW 91
Cobb, William Montague 1904- BioIn 16, WhoAm 90, WhoWor 91
Cobban, James Robert 1929- St&PR 91
Cobbe, Frances Power 1822-1904 BioIn 16, FemiCLE
Cobbe, Hugh Michael Thomas 1942- IntWWM 90
Cobbett, Stuart H. 1948- St&PR 91
Cobbett, William 1763-1835 BioIn 16
Cobble, Arthur Lee, Jr. 1947- St&PR 91
Cobble, James Wikle 1926- WhoAm 90
Cobbledick, Gordon 1899-1969 Ballpl 90
Cobbler, Edward Leroy 1947- WhoSSW 91
Cobbol-Hansum, Cathy Alane 1956- WhoE 91
Cobbold, Elizabeth 1764?-1824 FemiCLE
Cobbold, Richard Southwell Chevallier 1931- WhoAm 90
Cobbs, Cabell Flournoy 1927- WhoSSW 91
Cobbs, James Franklin, Jr. 1955- WhoE 91
Cobbs, James Harold 1928- WhoSSW 91
Cobbs, John Lewis 1917- WhoAm 90
Cobbs, Louise Bertram 1947- WhoEmL 91
Cobbs, Price M. BioIn 16
Cobbs, Price Mashaw BiDrAPA 89
Cobbs, Price Mashaw 1928- WhoAm 90
Cobden, Richard 1804-1865 BioIn 16
Cobden-Sanderson, Thomas James 1840-1922 PenDiDA 89
Cobe, Lori 1957- WhoEmL 91
Cobean, Warren Richardson, Jr. 1923- St&PR 91
Coben, William Allen 1932- WhoAm 90
Cober, Alan E. 1935- WhoAm 90, WhoAmA 91, WhoE 91
Cober, Richard G. 1928- St&PR 91
Coberly, C. Wheeler 1912- St&PR 91
Coberly, Camden Arthur 1922- WhoAm 90
Coberly, Daniel Leo 1954- WhoSSW 91
Coberly, William Bayley, Jr. 1908- WhoAm 90
Coberly, Wm. B., Jr. 1908- St&PR 91
Cobern, Martin E. 1946- St&PR 91
Cobery, Thomas John 1946- St&PR 91
Cobes, Madeline Joyce 1941- WhoAmW 91
Cobey, James Alexander 1913- WhoWor 91
Cobey, Ralph 1909- WhoAm 90
Cobham, Billy BioIn 16
Cobham, Billy 1947?- DrBlPA 90
Cobham, Michael John 1927- St&PR 91
Cobham, William Emanuel, Jr. 1944- WhoAm 90
Cobia, Paula Ivey 1957- WhoEmL 91
Cobiella, Grace Marie BiDrAPA 89
Cobiella, Robert Mario 1930- WhoWor 91
Cobiella, Robert S 1954- BiDrAPA 89
Coble, Bob WhoSSW 91
Coble, Daniel Bruce 1949- WhoSSW 91
Coble, Frederick Charles 1961- WhoSSW 91
Coble, Howard 1931- WhoAm 90, WhoSSW 91
Coble, Hugh Kenneth 1934- St&PR 91
Coble, Mary Susan 1949- WhoAmW 91, WhoEmL 91
Coble, Robert Louis 1928- WhoAm 90
Coble, William Carroll 1958- WhoEmL 91
Coblentz, Donald Richard 1948- WhoE 91
Coblentz, Gilbert S. 1949- St&PR 91
Coblentz, Jane Cudlip 1922- WhoAmW 91
Coblentz, William Kraemer 1922- WhoAm 90
Coblentz, William W. 1873-1962 WorAlBi
Coborn, Charles 1852-1945 OxCPMus
Cobos, Henry Diaz 1931- IntWWM 90
Coburn, Alvin Langdon 1882-1966 BioIn 16
Coburn, Andrew 1932- TwCCr&M 91
Coburn, Barry M. 1935- St&PR 91
Coburn, Bette Lee 1922- WhoAmA 91
Coburn, Charles 1877-1961 BioIn 16, WorAlBi
Coburn, Donald Lee 1938- WhoAm 90
Coburn, Frances Gullett 1919- WhoAmW 91
Coburn, Frank Emerson 1912- BiDrAPA 89
Coburn, Harry L. 1934- WhoAm 90
Coburn, James 1928- WhoAm 90, WorAlBi
Coburn, John Bowen 1914- AuBYP 90, WhoAm 90
Coburn, John P. 1953- St&PR 91
Coburn, Kathryn 1943- WhoAmW 91
Coburn, Lewis Alan 1940- WhoAm 90
Coburn, Marjorie Foster 1939- WhoAmW 91, WhoWor 91
Coburn, Michael B 1940- BiDrAPA 89
Coburn, Peggy Ann 1946- WhoAmW 91
Coburn, Ralph 1923- WhoAmA 91
Coburn, Richard Joseph 1931- St&PR 91, WhoE 91
Coburn, Robert Craig 1930- WhoAm 90
Coburn, Robert James 1949- IntWWM 90
Coburn, Ronald 1948- St&PR 91
Coburn, Theodore James 1926- WhoAm 90
Coburn, Thomas Bowen 1944- WhoE 91
Coburn, Warren B. 1926- St&PR 91
Coburn, Warren Baxter 1926- WhoAm 90
Cobuzzi, Barbara J. 1955- WhoAmW 91
Coca, Imogene BioIn 16
Coca, Joella Rosemary 1954- WhoHisp 91
Cocadiz, Norval Tardecilla 1943- WhoWor 91
Cocanougher, Arthur Benton 1938- WhoAm 90, WhoSSW 91, WhoWor 91
Cocanower, Jaime 1957- Ballpl 90
Cocanower, Liana Cheryl 1953- WhoAmW 91
Cocard, Luc 1946- WhoWor 91
Coccagna, Fred Joseph, Jr. 1945- WhoE 91
Coccaro, Emil Frank BiDrAPA 89
Coccaro, Shirley Lorraine 1943- WhoAmW 91
Cocchiarella, Alfonse Joseph 1948- WhoEmL 91
Coccioli, Carlo 1920- ConAu 31NR
Cocciolone, Vincent Scott 1964- WhoEmL 91
Coccoluto, Ralph Edward BiDrAPA 89
Cocea, Sofia 1839-1861 EncCoWW
Coche, Erich Henry Ernst 1941- WhoE 91
Cochin, Arnold Mitchell 1951- WhoE 91
Cochin, Denys Pierre Augustin 1851-1922 BiDFrPL
Cochin, Rita R. 1936- WhoAmW 91
Cochise 1812?-1874 WhNaAH, WorAlBi
Cochius, P.M. PenDiDA 89
Cochnar, Robert John 1939- WhoAm 90
Cochran, Alfred Williams 1950- IntWWM 90
Cochran, C. B. 1872-1951 OxCPMus
Cochran, Carole 1955- WhoEmL 91
Cochran, Carolyn 1934- WhoAmW 91
Cochran, Carolyn Collette 1951- WhoEmL 91
Cochran, Carolyn L. 1950- St&PR 91
Cochran, Chan 1942- ODwPR 91
Cochran, Chester G BiDrAPA 89
Cochran, Clark Jones, Jr. 1949- WhoEmL 91
Cochran, Connie E. 1947- WhoE 91
Cochran, David S. 1931- St&PR 91
Cochran, Dennis Grady 1947- St&PR 91
Cochran, Don Wayne 1952- WhoEmL 91
Cochran, Douglas E. 1932- St&PR 91
Cochran, Douglas Eugene 1932- WhoAm 90
Cochran, E Winston BiDrAPA 89
Cochran, Earl Vernon 1922- St&PR 91
Cochran, Eddie 1938-1960 EncPR&S 89, OxCPMus
Cochran, Eleanor Betts 1914- WhoAmW 91
Cochran, George Calloway, III 1932- St&PR 91, WhoAm 90, WhoSSW 91, WhoWor 91
Cochran, George McKee 1908- WhoAmA 91
Cochran, George Moffett 1912- WhoAm 90, WhoWor 91
Cochran, Helen Hege 1953- WhoAmW 91
Cochran, Howard E. 1938- St&PR 91
Cochran, Jacqueline 1910?-1980 WorAlBi
Cochran, Jacqueline Louise 1953- WhoAmW 91, WhoEmL 91
Cochran, Jaimie N 1927- BiDrAPA 89
Cochran, James Alan 1936- WhoAm 90
Cochran, Jim Ray 1945- WhoSSW 91
Cochran, John Arthur 1921- WhoAm 90
Cochran, John Charles 1935- WhoAm 90
Cochran, John Euell, Jr. 1944- WhoAm 90
Cochran, John Hughes 1838- AmLegL
Cochran, John Robert 1945- WhoEmL 91
Cochran, Joseph Wesley 1954- WhoEmL 91, WhoSSW 91
Cochran, Judith Ann WhoSSW 91
Cochran, Kathy Lynette Holcombe 1953- IntWWM 90
Cochran, Kendall Pinney 1924- WhoAm 90
Cochran, Larry WhoSSW 91
Cochran, Les 1935- WhoAm 90
Cochran, Leslie Hershel 1939- WhoAm 90
Cochran, Lewis W. 1915- WhoAm 90
Cochran, Lolly 1953- BioIn 16
Cochran, Michael David 1960- WhoSSW 91
Cochran, Olive Leigh Myatt 1907- WhoSSW 91
Cochran, Rebecca Sue 1959- WhoEmL 91
Cochran, Richard Michael 1951- WhoEmL 91
Cochran, Robert Glenn 1919- WhoAm 90
Cochran, Ronald Robert 1935- St&PR 91
Cochran, Ronald Waylon 1941- WhoAm 90, WhoWor 91
Cochran, Ruth Elaine Beardsley 1936- WhoAmW 91
Cochran, Sachiko Tomie 1945- WhoAmW 91
Cochran, Sandra Lynn 1953- WhoEmL 91
Cochran, Stephen Grey 1947- WhoEmL 91
Cochran, Steven K. 1934- St&PR 91
Cochran, Thad 1937- WhoAm 90, WhoSSW 91, WhoWor 91
Cochran, Thomas L 1936- BiDrAPA 89
Cochran, Wendell 1929- WhoAm 90
Cochran, William 1922- WhoWor 91
Cochran, William 1938- IntWWM 90
Cochran, William D. 1930- St&PR 91
Cochran, William Gemmell 1909-1980 DcScB S2
Cochran, William Granville 1844-1932 AmLegL
Cochran, William L BiDrAPA 89
Cochrane, Alfred S. BioIn 16
Cochrane, Andrew R. 1908- St&PR 91
Cochrane, Betsy Lane WhoAmW 91
Cochrane, Charles Alexander 1919- WhoWor 91
Cochrane, Edward G. 1954- St&PR 91
Cochrane, Elizabeth 1865-1922 FemiCLE
Cochrane, Elizabeth 1867-1922 BioIn 16
Cochrane, Francis Douglas 1920- St&PR 91, WhoAm 90
Cochrane, Frederick Pierce 1940- St&PR 91
Cochrane, Harwood 1911- WhoAm 90
Cochrane, Henry 1834?-1898 DcCanB 12

Cochrane, James Harwood, Jr. 1953- *WhoSSW 91*
Cochrane, James Louis 1942- *St&PR 91, WhoAm 90, WhoWor 91*
Cochrane, Jerry Wilson 1934- *St&PR 91*
Cochrane, Josephine Garis *BioIn 16*
Cochrane, Michael Harald 1958- *WhoE 91*
Cochrane, Mickey 1903-1962 *Ballpl 90 [port]*
Cochrane, Pauline Atherton 1929- *WhoAm 90*
Cochrane, Richard James Christopher 1945- *WhoE 91*
Cochrane, Robert H. 1924- *WhoAm 90*
Cochrane, Robert Lowe 1931- *WhoWor 91*
Cochrane, Ronald Dale 1946- *WhoSSW 91*
Cochrane, Sandra Victoria *BiDrAPA 89*
Cochrane, Shirley Graves 1925- *WhoWrEP 89*
Cochrane, Vincent W. 1916-1987 *BioIn 16*
Cochrane, William 1831-1898 *DcCanB 12*
Cochrane, William Henry 1912- *WhoAm 90, WhoWor 91*
Cocilovo, Vincenzo 1928- *BiDrAPA 89*
Cock, Richard Alan Charles 1949- *IntWWM 90*
Cockayne, Elizabeth 1895-1988 *AnObit 1988*
Cockayne, Robert Barton 1937- *WhoAm 90*
Cockburn, Alison 1713-1794 *BioIn 16, FemiCLE*
Cockburn, Bruce 1945- *BioIn 16*
Cockburn, Catherine 1679-1749 *BiDEWW*
Cockburn, Claud 1904-1981 *DcNaB 1981*
Cockburn, John F. 1928- *St&PR 91, WhoAm 90*
Cockburn, John Shearer 1942- *WhoWor 91*
Cockburn, Patricia 1914-1989 *AnObit 1989*
Cockcroft, Ann Jones 1934- *WhoE 91*
Cockcroft, John D. 1897-1967 *WorAlBi*
Cocke, Erle, Jr. 1921- *WhoAm 90*
Cocke, James William 1917- *St&PR 91*
Cocke, John *BioIn 16*
Cocke, Joseph Garber *BiDrAPA 89*
Cocke, Louisa Maxwell *BioIn 16*
Cocke, Norman A. 1945- *St&PR 91*
Cocke, Philip St. George, V 1950- *WhoEmL 91*
Cocke, Sally Shropshire *ODwPR 91*
Cocke, William Marvin, Jr. 1934- *WhoAm 90, WhoSSW 91*
Cockell, William Arthur, Jr. 1929- *WhoAm 90*
Cockenoe *WhNaAH*
Cocker, Barbara Joan *WhoAmW 91*
Cocker, Barbara Joan 1923- *WhoAmA 91*
Cocker, Joe 1944- *ConMus 4 [port], EncPR&S 89, OxCPMus, WorAlBi*
Cockerell, Charles Robert 1788-1863 *BioIn 16*
Cockerell, Christopher 1910- *WhoWor 91*
Cockerell, Sydney Morris 1906-1987 *BioIn 16*
Cockerham, Columbus Clark 1921- *WhoAm 90*
Cockerham, Donald Lewis 1934- *St&PR 91*
Cockerham, Haven Earl 1947- *St&PR 91*
Cockerham, James Edward 1948- *WhoEmL 91*
Cockerham, Lorris G. 1935- *WhoSSW 91*
Cockerham, Rodney Wayne 1948- *St&PR 91*
Cockerill, A W 1929- *ConAu 131*
Cockerill, James Wesley *BiDrAPA 89*
Cockerill, John Albert 1845-1896 *BioIn 16*
Cockerill, Kay *BioIn 16*
Cockerill, Thomas G., III 1933- *ODwPR 91*
Cockett, Abraham T. K. 1928- *WhoAm 90*
Cockfield, D.W. 1932- *St&PR 91*
Cockfield, Jamie Hartwell 1945- *WhoSSW 91*
Cockhill, Leslie Ann *BiDrAPA 89*
Cocking, John Brian 1936- *WhoWor 91*
Cocking, Matthew 1743-1799 *EncCRAm*
Cocklin, Kim Roland 1951- *St&PR 91*
Cocklin, Robert Frank 1919- *WhoAm 90*
Cockman, Richard Lee 1949- *WhoSSW 91*
Cockrel, Orvel H. 1920- *St&PR 91*
Cockrel, Sam Wesley 1945- *St&PR 91*
Cockrell, Debra Ann 1950- *WhoAmW 91*
Cockrell, Frank Boyd, II 1948- *WhoEmL 91*
Cockrell, Lila May Banks 1922- *WhoAm 90, WhoAmW 91*
Cockrell, Phil 1898-1946 *Ballpl 90*
Cockrell, Thomas A. 1939- *St&PR 91*
Cockrell, Wilburn A. *BioIn 16*
Cockrell, Wilburn Allen 1941- *WhoSSW 91*
Cockriel, Russell George, Sr. 1957- *WhoAm 90, WhoEmL 91*
Cockriel, Stephen Eugene 1948- *WhoEmL 91*
Cockrill, Robert Maurice 1923- *WhoAm 90*
Cockrill, Sherna *WhoAmA 91*
Cockrum, William Monroe, III 1937- *WhoAm 90, WhoWor 91*
Cocks, Franklin Hadley 1941- *WhoAm 90*
Cocks, George Gosson 1919- *WhoAm 90*
Cockshaw, Peter Albert 1934- *WhoE 91*
Cockshutt, Eric Philip 1929- *WhoAm 90*
Cockshutt, Malcolm William 1940- *WhoSSW 91*
Cockwell, Jack Lynn 1941- *WhoAm 90*
Coco, Charles Edward 1942- *WhoAm 90*
Coco, James *BioIn 16*
Coco, James 1930-1987 *WorAlBi*
Coco, Lewis Michael 1939- *WhoE 91*
Coco, Mark Steven 1952- *WhoEmL 91*
Coco, Peter M. 1959- *St&PR 91*
Coco, Samuel B., Jr. 1927- *St&PR 91*
Coco, Samuel Barbin 1927- *WhoAm 90, WhoE 91*
Coco, Thomas Michael 1949- *WhoSSW 91*
Cocordas, Eleni 1955- *WhoAmA 91*
Cocores, James A 1953- *BiDrAPA 89*
Cocores, James Alexander 1953- *WhoE 91*
Cocroft, Duncan Hunter 1943- *St&PR 91*
Cocron, Ronald Robert 1937- *WhoWor 91*
Cocteau, Jean 1889-1963 *BioIn 16, EncPaPR 91, MajTwCW, WorAlBi*
Cocuzzi, Kathleen Joan 1951- *WhoAmW 91*
Coda, Evis John 1920- *BiDrAPA 89*
Codacovi, Lawrence 1933- *St&PR 91*
Codd, Donald 1845?-1896 *DcCanB 12*
Codd, Edgar F. *BioIn 16*
Codd, Richard Trent, Jr. 1945- *WhoSSW 91*
Codding, Charles Harold, III 1947- *St&PR 91*
Codding, Frederick Hayden 1938- *WhoAm 90*
Codding, George Arthur, Jr. 1923- *WhoAm 90*
Codding, Hugh Bishop 1917- *St&PR 91*
Codding, Nellie Williams *St&PR 91N*
Coddington, Earl Alexander 1920- *WhoAm 90*
Coddington, Joseph, Jr. 1939- *WhoWrEP 89*
Coddington, R Dean 1924- *BiDrAPA 89*
Coddington, Robert H. *WhoWrEP 89*
Coddington, William 1601-1678 *EncCRAm*
Code, Arthur Dodd 1923- *WhoAm 90*
Code, Audrey 1937- *WhoAmA 91*
Code, James Manley Wayne 1930- *WhoSSW 91*
Code, Wayne 1930- *St&PR 91*
Codell, David Williams 1951- *St&PR 91*
Codell, J.C., Jr. 1919- *St&PR 91*
Codell, Julie Francia 1945- *WhoAmA 91*
Codella, John J. 1928- *ODwPR 91*
Coden, Michael Henri 1947- *St&PR 91, WhoE 91, WhoWor 91*
Coder, Samuel Maxwell 1902- *WhoAm 90*
Coderre, Paul Gerard 1958- *WhoE 91*
Codey, Lawrence R. 1944- *St&PR 91*
Codi, Joseph L. 1952- *St&PR 91*
Codina, Armando Mario 1946- *WhoHisp 91*
Codiroli, Chris 1958- *Ballpl 90*
Codispoti, Anthony 1946- *St&PR 91, WhoEmL 91*
Codispoti, Joseph D. 1944- *ODwPR 91*
Codispoti, Victoria Lisa 1952- *BiDrAPA 89*
Codman, William *PenDiDA 89*
Codo, Edward Anthony, Jr. 1954- *WhoEmL 91*
Codos, Richard Neil 1955- *St&PR 91*
Codraro, Lawrence Frederick 1926- *St&PR 91, WhoAm 90*
Codrescu, Andrei 1946- *WhoWrEP 89*
Codron, Michael Victor 1930- *WhoWor 91*
Codus, William R. *ODwPR 91*
Cody, Alan Morrow 1947- *WhoE 91, WhoEmL 91*
Cody, Andrea Rhodarmer 1958- *WhoEmL 91*
Cody, Edward Bryan 1946- *WhoEmL 91*
Cody, George Moore 1944- *WhoE 91*
Cody, Iron Eyes 1904- *BioIn 16*
Cody, J. Derrill 1938- *WhoSSW 91*
Cody, James Marion 1945- *WhoWrEP 89*
Cody, James P. 1932- *St&PR 91*
Cody, John M. 1942- *St&PR 91*
Cody, Kathleen Murphy *BiDrAPA 89*
Cody, Kevin Francis 1960- *WhoSSW 91*
Cody, Liza *ConAu 129*
Cody, Liza 1944- *TwCCr&M 91*
Cody, Mary Ellen *BiDrAPA 89*
Cody, Michael J. *BioIn 16*
Cody, Raymond G. 1946- *St&PR 91*
Cody, Thomas G. 1929- *St&PR 91*
Cody, Thomas Gerald 1929- *WhoAm 90*
Cody, Thomas Gerald 1941- *WhoAm 90*
Cody, Vivian 1943- *WhoAmW 91*
Cody, William F. 1846-1917 *WorAlBi*
Cody, William Frederic 1931- *St&PR 91, WhoAm 90*
Cody, William Frederick 1846-1917 *BioIn 16, WhNaAH [port]*
Cody, William J T 1926- *BiDrAPA 89*
Cody, William James Michael 1936- *WhoAm 90*
Cody, Wilmer St. Clair 1937- *WhoAm 90*
Coe, Alan Jason 1952- *BiDrAPA 89*
Coe, Anne Elizabeth *WhoAmA 91*
Coe, Benjamin Plaisted 1930- *WhoAm 90*
Coe, Bernice *WhoE 91*
Coe, Charles E. *BioIn 16*
Coe, Charles Norton 1915- *WhoAm 90*
Coe, Christopher Lane 1951- *WhoEmL 91*
Coe, Clark W. 1847-1919 *MusmAFA*
Coe, David Allan 1939- *BioIn 16, ConMus 4 [port]*
Coe, David Lewis 1948- *St&PR 91*
Coe, Donald Kirk 1934- *WhoAm 90*
Coe, Douglas *AuBYP 90*
Coe, Elizabeth Beaubien 1919- *WhoSSW 91*
Coe, Fred Atkins, Jr. 1916- *St&PR 91, WhoAm 90*
Coe, Fredric L. 1936- *WhoAm 90*
Coe, George Frank 1953- *WhoEmL 91*
Coe, Henry 1946- *WhoAmA 91*
Coe, Herring 1907- *WhoAm 90*
Coe, Ilse G. 1911- *WhoAmW 91*
Coe, J.W. 1920- *St&PR 91*
Coe, Jacques 1893- *St&PR 91*
Coe, Joe Ann 1934- *WhoWrEP 89*
Coe, John Emmons 1931- *WhoWor 91*
Coe, Jon *NewAgMG*
Coe, Judith Lynn 1945- *WhoAmW 91*
Coe, Linda Marlene Wolfe 1941- *WhoAmW 91*
Coe, Lloyd 1899-1977 *WhoAmA 91N*
Coe, Margaret Louise Shaw 1917- *WhoAmW 91*
Coe, Marian 1931- *WhoWrEP 89*
Coe, Marvin Parnick 1931- *WhoSSW 91*
Coe, Matchett Herring 1907- *WhoAmA 91*
Coe, Michael Douglas 1929- *WhoAm 90*
Coe, Miriam M. 1902- *WhoAm 90, WhoSSW 91, WhoWor 91*
Coe, Paul E., Jr. 1919- *St&PR 91*
Coe, Paul Francis 1909- *WhoAm 90*
Coe, Peter John Tudor 1959- *WhoWor 91*
Coe, Peter Trask 1936- *St&PR 91*
Coe, Ralph Tracy 1929- *WhoAmA 91*
Coe, Richard N. *BioIn 16*
Coe, Robert Campbell 1918- *WhoAm 90*
Coe, Robert Milton 1931- *IntWWM 90*
Coe, Robert Stanford 1919- *WhoAm 90*
Coe, Roland *WhoAmA 91N*
Coe, Sebastian 1956- *WorAlBi*
Coe, Sue *WhoAmA 91*
Coe, Sue 1951- *BiDWomA*
Coe, Tucker *TwCCr&M 91*
Coe, Ward Baldwin, Jr. 1913- *WhoAm 90*
Coe, William Charles 1930- *WhoAm 90*
Coechea, Ignacio Ellacuria Beas *BioIn 16*
Coeler, Joachim 1891- *BioIn 16*
Coelho, Anthony Mendes, Jr. 1947- *WhoSSW 91*
Coelho, Bernard *BiDrAPA 89*
Coelho, Duarte Pinto *BioIn 16*
Coelho, Helder Ferreira 1944- *WhoWor 91*
Coelho, Jose Dias 1949- *WhoWor 91*
Coelho, Joseph Richard 1946- *WhoE 91, WhoEmL 91*
Coelho, Marilena Cavalcanti 1942- *WhoWor 91*
Coelho, Tony 1942- *BioIn 16, WhoAm 90*
Coello, Claudio 1642-1696 *IntDcAA 90*
Coello, Dennis *ConAu 129*
Coello, Elena Coromoto 1952- *WhoAmW 91*
Coeme, Guy 1946- *WhoWor 91*
Coen, Lodewijk Karel Celina 1952- *WhoEmL 91*
Coen, Manus 1908- *St&PR 91*
Coen, Massimo 1933- *IntWWM 90*
Coen, Robert Joseph 1923- *WhoAm 90*
Coen, Stanley J 1937- *BiDrAPA 89*
Coen, Stanley Jerome 1937- *WhoE 91*
Coen, Victoria Lynn 1954- *WhoAmW 91*
Coene, Edgar T. 1930- *St&PR 91*
Coenen, Dale Stephen 1928- *St&PR 91*
Coenraets, Andre Jean 1930- *WhoWor 91*
Coenson, Barbara Ellen 1956- *WhoSSW 91*
Coerper, Milo George 1925- *WhoAm 90*
Coerr, Eleanor 1922- *AuBYP 90, BioIn 16*
Coertse, Mimi 1932- *IntWWM 90*
Coerver, Robert Albert, Jr. 1933- *St&PR 91*
Coes, Kent Day 1910- *WhoAm 90, WhoAmA 91*
Coetzee, J. M. 1940- *BioIn 16*
Coetzee, J M 1940- *MajTwCW*
Coetzee, Johannes Francois 1924- *WhoAm 90*
Coetzee, John M. 1940- *WhoWor 91*
Cofacci, Gino *BioIn 16*
Cofer, Charles Norval 1916- *WhoAm 90*
Cofer, Judith Ortiz 1952- *BioIn 16, ConAu 32NR, HispWr 90, WhoHisp 91, WhoWrEP 89*
Cofer-Shabica, Stephen Vale 1945- *WhoEmL 91*
Coffee, George 1938- *BiDrAPA 89*
Coffee, Gerald *BioIn 16*
Coffee, Harry Noell 1918- *St&PR 91*
Coffee, James Frederick 1918- *WhoAm 90*
Coffee, John Trousdale 1816-1890 *AmLegL*
Coffee, Joseph Denis, Jr. 1918- *WhoAm 90*
Coffee, Karen Lynn 1956- *WhoSSW 91*
Coffee, Richard Jerome, II 1954- *WhoEmL 91*
Coffee, Sue 1954- *WhoEmL 91*
Coffee, Virginia Claire 1920- *WhoAmW 91*
Coffee, William John *PenDiDA 89*
Coffen, Richard Wayne 1941- *WhoWrEP 89*
Coffeng, John Adrianus 1948- *WhoWor 91*
Coffer, Robert H, Jr. 1923- *BiDrAPA 89*
Coffey, Barbara Jane *BiDrAPA 89*
Coffey, Brian *MajTwCW, TwCCr&M 91*
Coffey, C Edward 1952- *BiDrAPA 89*
Coffey, C. Shelby *BioIn 16*
Coffey, C. Shelby, III *WhoAm 90*
Coffey, C. Shelby, III 1946- *St&PR 91*
Coffey, Dairine 1933- *AuBYP 90*
Coffey, Daniel 1950- *ConAu 131*
Coffey, Daniel Patrick 1954- *WhoEmL 91*
Coffey, David Mario 1949- *WhoSSW 91*
Coffey, Donald Straley 1932- *WhoAm 90*
Coffey, Douglas Robert 1937- *WhoAmA 91*
Coffey, Helen Ernestine 1934- *WhoAmW 91*
Coffey, James Franklin 1938- *St&PR 91*
Coffey, James Robert 1942- *St&PR 91*
Coffey, John Louis 1922- *WhoAm 90*
Coffey, John William 1954- *WhoSSW 91*
Coffey, John William, II 1954- *WhoAmA 91*
Coffey, Joseph Daniel 1938- *WhoAm 90*
Coffey, Joseph Irving 1916- *WhoAm 90*
Coffey, Kathryn Robinson *WhoAmW 91*
Coffey, Kelley Lynn 1961- *BiDrAPA 89*
Coffey, Kelly Ann 1954- *WhoEmL 91*
Coffey, Kendall Brindley 1952- *WhoEmL 91*
Coffey, Larry R. 1939- *St&PR 91*
Coffey, Mabel 1874-1949 *WhoAmA 91N*
Coffey, Margaret R *BiDrAPA 89*
Coffey, Matthew B. 1941- *WhoAm 90*
Coffey, Michael 1936- *St&PR 91*
Coffey, Nancy Ann *WhoAmW 91*
Coffey, Patrick Sean 1958- *WhoEmL 91*
Coffey, Paul 1951- *WorAlBi*
Coffey, Paul 1961- *WhoAm 90*
Coffey, Raymond Richard 1929- *WhoAm 90*
Coffey, Richard E. *BioIn 16*
Coffey, Robert Dennis 1950- *WhoEmL 91*
Coffey, Robert Thomas 1931- *BiDrAPA 89*
Coffey, Robert Tuttle *BiDrAPA 89*
Coffey, Rosemary Klineberg 1937- *WhoAmW 91*
Coffey, Sean Owen 1950- *WhoE 91*
Coffey, Shelby, III *BioIn 16*
Coffey, Smith Dwight 1946- *WhoSSW 91*
Coffey, Stephen Jacob 1948- *WhoSSW 91*
Coffey, Thomas Anthony 1953- *WhoSSW 91*
Coffey, Thomas Francis, Jr. 1923- *WhoAm 90*
Coffey, Thomas William 1959- *WhoEmL 91*
Coffey, Timothy 1941- *WhoAm 90*
Coffield, Conrad Eugene 1930- *WhoSSW 91*
Coffield, Deborah Jean 1961- *WhoE 91, WhoEmL 91*
Coffield, Lloyd Dexter 1937- *St&PR 91*
Coffield, Tom R. 1941- *St&PR 91*
Coffill, Marjorie Louise 1917- *WhoAmW 91, WhoWor 91*
Coffin, Bertha Louise 1919- *WhoAmW 91*
Coffin, C. Hayden 1862-1935 *OxCPMus*
Coffin, Charles A. 1844-1926 *WorAlBi*
Coffin, Charles Carleton 1823-1896 *BioIn 16*
Coffin, David L. 1925- *St&PR 91*
Coffin, David Linwood 1925- *WhoAm 90*
Coffin, David Robbins 1918- *WhoAm 90*
Coffin, Frank Morey 1919- *WhoAm 90*
Coffin, Geoffrey *AuBYP 90, TwCCr&M 91*
Coffin, Gordon Lee 1938- *WhoAm 90*
Coffin, Howard *BioIn 16*
Coffin, Howard E. 1873-1937 *EncABHB 4 [port]*
Coffin, John Devereux 1937- *WhoAm 90*
Coffin, John K. 1949- *WhoE 91*
Coffin, Joseph 1899- *AuBYP 90*
Coffin, Laurence Edmondston, Jr. 1928- *WhoAm 90*
Coffin, Louis Fussell, Jr. 1917- *WhoAm 90*
Coffin, Lyn 1943- *WhoWrEP 89*
Coffin, Peter *TwCCr&M 91*
Coffin, Ralston Hudson, Jr. 1933- *St&PR 91*

Coffin, Richard Keith 1940- WhoAm 90
Coffin, Robert Parker 1917- WhoWor 91
Coffin, Trenmor 1848- AmLegL
Coffin, Tristram 1912- WhoAm 90, WhoE 91, WhoWor 91
Coffin, Wayne Philip 1942- St&PR 91
Coffin, William Sloane BioIn 16
Coffin, William Sloane, Jr. 1924- News 90 [port], -90-3 [port], WorAlBi
Coffing, James Lee 1946- WhoEmL 91
Coffman, Cheryl Clance 1947- WhoEmL 91
Coffman, Christine Roberta 1914- WhoAmW 91
Coffman, Dallas Whitney 1957- WhoE 91, WhoEmL 91
Coffman, Deborah 1956- St&PR 91
Coffman, Delphos Otto 1909- BiDrAPA 89
Coffman, Diane Sharon 1952- WhoAmW 91
Coffman, Dick 1906-1972 Ballpl 90
Coffman, Edward McKenzie 1929- WhoAm 90
Coffman, Franklin Edward 1942- WhoAm 90
Coffman, Gregory M. 1947- St&PR 91
Coffman, Hal 1883-1958 WhoAmA 91N
Coffman, Jay Denton 1928- WhoAm 90
Coffman, Jeffrey Allyn BiDrAPA 89
Coffman, Kenneth Morrow 1921- St&PR 91
Coffman, Kevin 1965- Ballpl 90
Coffman, Orene Burton 1938- WhoAmW 91
Coffman, Phillip Hudson 1936- WhoAm 90
Coffman, Renae K. 1957- WhoAmW 91
Coffman, Roy Walter, III 1943- WhoAm 90
Coffman, Sandra Jeanne 1945- WhoAmW 91
Coffman, Sharon Kay WhoSSW 91
Coffman, Slick 1910- Ballpl 90
Coffman, Stanley Knight, Jr. 1916- WhoAm 90
Coffman, Virginia Sue 1954- WhoAmW 91
Coffman, Ward Denver, III 1953- WhoEmL 91
Coffman, William Brent 1945- WhoEmL 91
Coffman, William Eugene 1913- WhoAm 90
Coffrin, Albert Wheeler 1919- WhoAm 90, WhoE 91
Coffy, Michael Haskell 1936- St&PR 91
Cofield, Howard John 1926- WhoAm 90
Cofitachique, Lady of EncCRAm
Cofoid, Paul Brian 1945- WhoEmL 91
Cofresi-Aviles, Mariame 1942- BiDrAPA 89
Cofyn, Cornelius TwCCr&M 91
Cogan, Alma 1932-1966 OxCPMus
Cogan, Dana Lee 1947- BiDrAPA 89
Cogan, David Glendenning 1908- WhoAm 90
Cogan, Eddy BioIn 16
Cogan, Edward J. 1925- WhoAm 90
Cogan, James Richard 1928- WhoAm 90
Cogan, John BioIn 16
Cogan, John F., Jr. 1926- St&PR 91
Cogan, John Francis 1947- WhoAm 90
Cogan, John Francis, Jr. 1926- WhoAm 90
Cogan, Mark Charles 1956- WhoEmL 91
Cogan, Marshall S. 1937- WhoAm 90, WhoE 91
Cogan, Marshall Stuart 1937- St&PR 91
Cogan, Mike ConAu 30NR
Cogan, Mordechai 1939- WhoWor 91
Cogan, Robert David 1930- WhoAm 90
Cogan, Robert E. 1933- St&PR 91
Cogan, Sheila Walsh 1939- BiDrAPA 89
Cogbill, Tracy Lloyd 1942- BiDrAPA 89
Cogburn, Edmund Lewis 1932- WhoAm 90
Cogburn, Max Oliver 1927- WhoWor 91
Cogdell, John Blair 1928- St&PR 91
Cogen, Pierre 1931- IntWWM 90
Coggan, Bernard Frederick 1918- St&PR 91
Coggan, Chris BioIn 16
Coggan, Donald 1909- BioIn 16
Coggan, Frederick Donald 1909- WhoAm 90
Cogger, Barbara Sue 1965- WhoAmW 91
Cogger, Harold Willis 1935- St&PR 91
Coggeshall, Calvert NewYTBS 90
Coggeshall, Calvert 1907-1990 BioIn 16
Coggeshall, James Wells 1927- St&PR 91
Coggeshall, Janice R. 1935- WhoAmW 91
Coggeshall, Lowell T. 1901-1987 BioIn 16
Coggeshall, Norman David 1916- WhoSSW 91
Coggeshall, Peter Collin 1915- St&PR 91
Coggeshall, Randy Lynn 1955- WhoEmL 91
Coggin, Charlotte Joan 1928- WhoAm 90, WhoAmW 91
Coggin, Chris T. 1953- St&PR 91
Coggin, James Michael 1952- WhoEmL 91
Coggin, Maris Montgomery 1936- WhoSSW 91
Coggin, Walter Arthur 1916- WhoAm 90
Coggins, Cynthia Anne 1954- WhoAmW 91, WhoSSW 91
Coggins, Dana Chandler 1931- WhoAm 90
Coggins, Deborah R 1924- BiDrAPA 89
Coggins, Edward Vaughan 1931- St&PR 91
Coggins, Freeman Wescoat 1942- St&PR 91
Coggins, Herbert AuBYP 90
Coggins, Homer Dale 1922- WhoAm 90
Coggins, Jack Banham 1914- AuBYP 90, WhoAm 90, WhoAmA 91
Coggins, Nolan S. 1940- St&PR 91
Coggins, Oran Chalmers 1950- WhoSSW 91
Coggins, Paul Edward 1951- WhoEmL 91
Coggins, R. Stan 1947- St&PR 91
Coggins, Rich 1950- Ballpl 90
Coggins, Wilmer Jesse 1925- WhoAm 90
Coggiola, Donald Anthony 1939- WhoAm 90
Coggswell, Amos 1825-1892 AmLegL
Coghan, Bob St&PR 91
Coghe, David William 1942- BiDrAPA 89
Coghill, Harry MacLeod 1944- IntWWM 90
Coghill, Joy 1926- OxCCanT
Coghill, Marvin W. 1933- WhoAm 90, WhoSSW 91
Coghill, Timothy Lee 1942- St&PR 91
Coghlan, Alan 1947- WhoEmL 91
Coghlan, Alban J BiDrAPA 89
Coghlan, Kelly Jack 1952- WhoEmL 91, WhoSSW 91
Coghlan, Mary Ellen 1954- WhoAmW 91
Coghlan, Paul 1945- WhoAm 90, WhoEmL 91
Coghlan, Rosamond Marie 1852?-1932 NotWoAT
Coghlan, Rose 1853?-1932 BioIn 16
Coghlin, Fitzmaurice, Jr. 1920- St&PR 91
Cogliandro, Charles A. 1917- St&PR 91
Cogliandro, Charles E. 1953- St&PR 91
Cogliandro, Helene Lorraine 1954- St&PR 91
Coglianese, Fred Anthony 1930- St&PR 91
Cogman, George EarBlAP
Cognard, Philippe Pierre 1940- WhoWor 91
Cognet, Yves Andre 1950- WhoWor 91
Cogni, Giulio 1908- EncO&P 3
Cograve, John Edwin 1929- WhoAm 90
Cogswell, Arnold 1924- WhoAm 90
Cogswell, Dorothy McIntosh 1909- WhoAm 90, WhoAmA 91
Cogswell, Fred 1917- BioIn 16
Cogswell, Frederick William 1917- WhoAm 90, WhoWrEP 89
Cogswell, George Wallace 1923- WhoSSW 91
Cogswell, Glenn Dale 1922- WhoAm 90
Cogswell, John PenDiDA 89
Cogswell, John Heyland 1933- WhoAm 90
Cogswell, Margaret Price 1925- WhoAmA 91
Cogswell, Rick 1948- St&PR 91
Cogswell, Theodore R. 1918-1987 RGTwCSF
Cogswell, Thomas Edmund 1952- WhoSSW 91
Cohalan, John P. 1907-1988 BioIn 16
Cohall, Alwyn BioIn 16
Cohan, Andrew 1954- St&PR 91
Cohan, Anthony Robert 1939- WhoWrEP 89
Cohan, Carole WhoAmW 91
Cohan, George M. 1878-1942 BioIn 16, OxCPMus, WorAlBi
Cohan, George Sheldon 1924- WhoAm 90
Cohan, Georges S. 1924- ODwPR 91
Cohan, John Robert 1931- WhoAm 90
Cohan, Leon Sumner 1929- St&PR 91, WhoAm 90
Cohan, Leonard Lee BiDrAPA 89
Cohan, Norman H. 1922- St&PR 91
Cohan, Philip L. 1939- WhoAm 90
Cohan, Richard L. 1926- St&PR 91
Cohan, Stanford H. 1929- St&PR 91
Cohan, Zara R 1928- WhoAmA 91
Cohane, Heather Christina 1934- WhoAmW 91
Cohane, Jak T BiDrAPA 89
Cohane, John Francis 1951- WhoSSW 91
Cohane, Tim 1912-1989 BioIn 16
Cohane, Timothy F. 1952- St&PR 91
Cohea, Melinda Ruth 1961- WhoSSW 91
Coheen, Jack J 1921- BiDrAPA 89
Coheleach, Guy Joseph WhoAm 90, WhoAmA 91
Cohen, Aaron 1924- WhoSSW 91
Cohen, Aaron 1931- WhoAm 90
Cohen, Aaron 1956- WhoE 91
Cohen, Abraham B. BioIn 16
Cohen, Abraham Bernard 1922- WhoAm 90
Cohen, Abraham Ezekiel WhoE 91
Cohen, Abraham Ezekiel 1936- St&PR 91
Cohen, Abraham J. 1932- WhoAm 90, WhoWor 91
Cohen, Adele WhoAmA 91
Cohen, Adrian M BiDrAPA 89
Cohen, Adrian Nathaniel 1955- WhoEmL 91
Cohen, Ahren L. St&PR 91
Cohen, Alan Barry 1943- WhoAmA 91
Cohen, Alan Geoffrey 1958- WhoEmL 91
Cohen, Alan Irwin 1951- WhoSSW 91
Cohen, Alan Jay BiDrAPA 89
Cohen, Alan Jay 1956- BiDrAPA 89
Cohen, Alan Norman 1930- St&PR 91, WhoAm 90
Cohen, Alan Seymour 1926- WhoAm 90
Cohen, Albert 1914- St&PR 91
Cohen, Albert 1929- IntWWM 90, WhoAm 90
Cohen, Albert D. 1914- St&PR 91
Cohen, Albert J. 1940- St&PR 91
Cohen, Albert Jerome 1940- WhoAm 90
Cohen, Alex 1927- WhoAm 90
Cohen, Alexander Freeman 1960- WhoE 91
Cohen, Alexander H. 1920- WhoAm 90, WhoE 91, WorAlBi
Cohen, Alfred G. 1912- St&PR 91
Cohen, Alfred Martin 1941- WhoAm 90
Cohen, Alfred Simon 1958- IntWWM 90
Cohen, Allan Richard 1947- WhoAm 90
Cohen, Allan Yale 1939- WhoE 91
Cohen, Allen Joseph 1950- St&PR 91
Cohen, Alonzo Clifford, Jr. 1911- WhoSSW 91
Cohen, Alvin BiDrAPA 89
Cohen, Alysia BioIn 16
Cohen, Alysia 1952- WhoAmW 91
Cohen, Amy 1942- WhoE 91
Cohen, Andre 1948- St&PR 91
Cohen, Andrew H. 1957- WhoE 91
Cohen, Andrew Louis 1950- WhoE 91
Cohen, Andrew Stuart 1930- WhoAm 90
Cohen, Andy BioIn 16
Cohen, Andy 1904-1988 Ballpl 90
Cohen, Ann Ellen 1949- WhoE 91, WhoEmL 91
Cohen, Anne Hamlen BiDrAPA 89
Cohen, Anthea 1913- TwCCr&M 91
Cohen, Armond E. 1909- BioIn 16
Cohen, Arnaldo 1948- IntWWM 90
Cohen, Arnold 1949- St&PR 91
Cohen, Arnold A. 1914- WhoAm 90
Cohen, Arnold D 1927- BiDrAPA 89
Cohen, Arnold Robert 1938- BiDrAPA 89, WhoE 91
Cohen, Arthur 1919- St&PR 91
Cohen, Arthur 1927- WhoE 91
Cohen, Arthur G. 1930- WhoE 91
Cohen, Arthur Jay 1952- WhoAm 90
Cohen, Arthur Morris 1928- WhoAm 90, WhoAmA 91
Cohen, Audrey C. WhoAmW 91
Cohen, Avery S. 1936- St&PR 91
Cohen, B. Stanley 1923- WhoAm 90
Cohen, Barbara 1932- AuBYP 90
Cohen, Barbara Ann 1958- WhoWrEP 89
Cohen, Barbara Gloria 1952- WhoEmL 91
Cohen, Barbara Joanne 1951- St&PR 91
Cohen, Barbara Sugarman 1935- WhoE 91
Cohen, Barry Allan 1939- BiDrAPA 89
Cohen, Barry David 1952- WhoEmL 91
Cohen, Barry S. 1947- ODwPR 91
Cohen, Bella ConAu 131
Cohen, Benjamin Bernard 1922- WhoAm 90
Cohen, Bennett Jay 1925- WhoAm 90
Cohen, Bennett Joseph BiDrAPA 89
Cohen, Bernard BiDrAPA 89
Cohen, Bernard 1929- WhoAm 90
Cohen, Bernard B. 1927- WhoE 91
Cohen, Bernard Cecil 1926- WhoAm 90
Cohen, Bernard Leonard 1924- WhoAm 90
Cohen, Bertram David 1923- WhoAm 90
Cohen, Bertram M. 1931- St&PR 91
Cohen, Beverly Singer 1933- WhoAmW 91
Cohen, Boaz 1899-1968 BioIn 16
Cohen, Brian E. 1955- St&PR 91
Cohen, Brian Jeffrey 1953- WhoE 91
Cohen, Bruce M 1947- BiDrAPA 89
Cohen, Bruce Michael 1947- WhoAm 90
Cohen, Burton D. 1940- St&PR 91
Cohen, Burton Jerome 1933- WhoAm 90, WhoWor 91
Cohen, Burton Marcus 1925- WhoAm 90, WhoE 91, WhoWor 91
Cohen, Burton Ronald 1940- St&PR 91
Cohen, Carl Alexander 1952- WhoE 91
Cohen, Carl Ira 1947- BiDrAPA 89
Cohen, Carla Lynn 1937- WhoAmW 91
Cohen, Carol Jean 1948- BiDrAPA 89
Cohen, Caron Lee AuBYP 90
Cohen, Caryn Lee 1957- WhoAmW 91
Cohen, Cathi 1960- WhoAmW 91
Cohen, Charles NewAgMG
Cohen, Charles E 1942- WhoAmA 91
Cohen, Charles Emil 1942- WhoAm 90
Cohen, Charlotte J BiDrAPA 89
Cohen, Charlotte Smith 1933- WhoAm 90, WhoWor 91
Cohen, Cheryl Diane Durda 1947- WhoAmW 91, WhoEmL 91, WhoWor 91
Cohen, Claire Gorham 1934- St&PR 91
Cohen, Claire MaChere 1956- BiDrAPA 89
Cohen, Clarence Budd 1925- WhoAm 90
Cohen, Claudia BioIn 16
Cohen, Claudia 1950- WhoE 91
Cohen, Cora 1943- WhoAmA 91, WhoAmW 91
Cohen, Cynthia Goldstein BiDrAPA 89
Cohen, Cynthia Marylyn 1945- WhoAmW 91, WhoEmL 91, WhoWor 91
Cohen, D. David 1940- St&PR 91
Cohen, Daniel 1936- AuBYP 90, BioIn 16
Cohen, Daniel Elliot 1946- BiDrAPA 89
Cohen, Daniel Lawrence 1958- WhoE 91
Cohen, Daniel Morris 1930- WhoAm 90
Cohen, David 1882-1967 BioIn 16
Cohen, David 1946- ConAu 129
Cohen, David Charles 1942- WhoE 91
Cohen, David E. 1941- St&PR 91
Cohen, David Edward 1950- WhoEmL 91
Cohen, David Harris 1938- WhoAm 90
Cohen, David J. 1929- St&PR 91
Cohen, David Walter 1926- WhoAm 90
Cohen, David Walter 1947- WhoEmL 91
Cohen, Denise Jodi 1961- WhoAmW 91, WhoEmL 91
Cohen, Diane Berkowitz 1938- WhoAmW 91
Cohen, Diane Irene 1943- BiDrAPA 89
Cohen, Donald 1935- BiDrAPA 89
Cohen, Donald Jay 1940- BiDrAPA 89, WhoAm 90
Cohen, Donn Isaac 1930- WhoAm 90
Cohen, Donna Eden 1956- WhoAmW 91
Cohen, Douglas M. 1946- St&PR 91
Cohen, E. Judd 1944- ODwPR 91
Cohen, Earl BiDrAPA 89
Cohen, Edward 1921- WhoAm 90, WhoWor 91
Cohen, Edward 1954- WhoEmL 91
Cohen, Edward Barth 1949- WhoEmL 91
Cohen, Edward Herschel 1938- WhoAm 90
Cohen, Edward Philip 1932- WhoAm 90
Cohen, Edwin Samuel 1914- WhoAm 90, WhoWor 91
Cohen, Elaine Lustig 1927- WhoAmA 91
Cohen, Eli D. 1926- St&PR 91
Cohen, Eli Edward 1912- WhoAm 90
Cohen, Eliahu 1933- St&PR 91
Cohen, Elizabeth G. 1931- WhoAm 90
Cohen, Ellen Melissa BiDrAPA 89
Cohen, Elliot S 1942- BiDrAPA 89
Cohen, Eric Bruce 1951- BiDrAPA 89
Cohen, Eric David BiDrAPA 89
Cohen, Ernest BiDrAPA 89
Cohen, Esther Rhea 1937- WhoAmW 91
Cohen, Eta 1920- IntWWM 90
Cohen, Etahn Micah 1952- WhoEmL 91
Cohen, Ethan 1961- BioIn 16
Cohen, Eugene Erwin 1917- WhoAm 90
Cohen, Eugene Joseph 1918- WhoWor 91
Cohen, Evelyn L. 1914- WhoAm 90
Cohen, Ezechiel Godert David 1923- WhoAm 90
Cohen, Faith Hartman 1938- BiDrAPA 89
Cohen, Felix BiDrAPA 89
Cohen, Felix Asher 1943- St&PR 91, WhoAm 90
Cohen, Frances BiDrAPA 89
Cohen, Fred 1928- St&PR 91
Cohen, Gabriel Murrel 1908- WhoAm 90
Cohen, Gad Jacques 1964- WhoE 91
Cohen, Gary 1948- WhoE 91
Cohen, Gary N BiDrAPA 89
Cohen, Gary Ormond 1937- WhoE 91
Cohen, Gary Perris 1946- WhoEmL 91
Cohen, Gary S. 1948- WhoEmL 91
Cohen, Gene David 1944- BiDrAPA 89, WhoAm 90, WhoWor 91
Cohen, Geoffrey Frith 1931- WhoWor 91
Cohen, Geoffrey Merrill 1954- WhoE 91
Cohen, George Leon 1930- WhoAm 90
Cohen, George Michael WhoAmA 91
Cohen, Georges N. 1920- WhoWor 91
Cohen, Gerald A BiDrAPA 89
Cohen, Geraldine M. 1919- WhoAmW 91
Cohen, Gerry Farmer 1950- WhoEmL 91
Cohen, Gerson David 1924- BioIn 16, WhoAm 90
Cohen, Gloria Ernestine 1942- WhoAmW 91, WhoE 91, WhoWor 91
Cohen, Gordon R 1934- BiDrAPA 89
Cohen, Gordon Seth 1937- St&PR 91
Cohen, H George 1913-1980 WhoAmA 91N
Cohen, H. Reuben 1921- St&PR 91
Cohen, H. Rodgin BioIn 16
Cohen, Harley 1933- WhoAm 90
Cohen, Harold 1928- WhoAmA 91
Cohen, Harold Arthur BiDrAPA 89
Cohen, Harold Kenneth 1943- WhoE 91
Cohen, Harold Larry 1925- WhoAmA 91

Cohen, Harriet 1895-1967 *PenDiMP*
Cohen, Harriet Newman 1932- *WhoAmW 91*
Cohen, Harris B. 1921- *St&PR 91*
Cohen, Harry B. 1912- *St&PR 91*
Cohen, Harry X *BiDrAPA 89*
Cohen, Harvey Jay 1940- *WhoAm 90*
Cohen, Harvey Spencer 1947- *WhoE 91*
Cohen, Helmut *BiDrAPA 89*
Cohen, Hennig 1919- *WhoAm 90*
Cohen, Henry 1863-1952 *BioIn 16*
Cohen, Henry 1922- *WhoE 91*
Cohen, Herbert *BiDrAPA 89*
Cohen, Herbert Jay 1957- *WhoEmL 91*
Cohen, Herbert Jesse 1935- *WhoAm 90*
Cohen, Herman *NewYTBS 90*
Cohen, Herman 1894- *WhoAm 90*
Cohen, Herman 1894-1990 *BioIn 16*
Cohen, Herman H. *BioIn 16*
Cohen, Herman Jacob 1922- *WhoAm 90*
Cohen, Herman Jay 1932- *WhoAm 90*
Cohen, Herman Nathan 1949- *WhoE 91*
Cohen, Hermann 1842-1918 *BioIn 16, WrPh P*
Cohen, Hershel *BioIn 16*
Cohen, Hirsh Gerald 1925- *WhoE 91*
Cohen, Hirsh Joel 1942- *WhoAm 90*
Cohen, Howard 1927- *St&PR 91*
Cohen, Howard Jerome 1945- *WhoEmL 91*
Cohen, Howard L. 1941- *St&PR 91*
Cohen, Howard Mark *BiDrAPA 89*
Cohen, Howard Marvin 1926- *WhoE 91*
Cohen, Hy 1901- *WhoAmA 91*
Cohen, Hy 1931- *BioIn 16*
Cohen, I. Bernard 1914- *WorAu 1980 [port]*
Cohen, I. Roy 1922- *St&PR 91*
Cohen, Ida Bogin *WhoAmW 91*
Cohen, Ingram *BiDrAPA 89*
Cohen, Ira H. 1935- *WhoWrEP 89*
Cohen, Ira Myron 1937- *WhoAm 90*
Cohen, Ira Stanley 1922- *WhoAm 90*
Cohen, Irene A *BiDrAPA 89*
Cohen, Irvin H 1924- *BiDrAPA 89*
Cohen, Irvin Myron 1922- *BiDrAPA 89*
Cohen, Irving David 1945- *WhoE 91, WhoWor 91*
Cohen, Irving Elias 1946- *WhoE 91, WhoWor 91*
Cohen, Irwin 1936- *WhoE 91, WhoWor 91*
Cohen, Irwin J 1911- *BiDrAPA 89*
Cohen, Irwin Robert 1924- *WhoE 91*
Cohen, Isidore *PenDiMP*
Cohen, Isidore 1922- *IntWWM 90*
Cohen, Isidore Leonard 1922- *WhoAm 90*
Cohen, Israel 1912- *WhoAm 90, WhoE 91*
Cohen, Ivan Stuart *BiDrAPA 89*
Cohen, J. M. *ConAu 129*
Cohen, Jack Joseph 1919- *BioIn 16*
Cohen, Jack S 1938- *ConAu 130*
Cohen, Jack V. 1942- *St&PR 91*
Cohen, Jacob Joseph 1939- *WhoAm 90*
Cohen, James A. 1946- *St&PR 91*
Cohen, James Samuel 1946- *WhoEmL 91*
Cohen, Jane R 1938- *ConAu 130*
Cohen, Jay Adam 1962- *WhoEmL 91*
Cohen, Jay Allen 1951- *WhoE 91*
Cohen, Jay R. 1941- *St&PR 91*
Cohen, Jay Richard 1941- *WhoAm 90*
Cohen, Jean 1927- *WhoAmA 91*
Cohen, Jean R 1935- *WhoAmA 91*
Cohen, Jeanne Patterson *BiDrAPA 89*
Cohen, Jeffrey Alan 1953- *WhoE 91, WhoEmL 91*
Cohen, Jeffrey Lewis 1950- *WhoEmL 91*
Cohen, Jeffrey Lewis 1952- *BiDrAPA 89*
Cohen, Jeffrey M. 1940- *WhoAm 90*
Cohen, Jeffrey Steven 1952- *WhoE 91, WhoWor 91*
Cohen, Jene Barr *AuBYP 90*
Cohen, Jeremy 1953- *ConAu 130*
Cohen, Jeri 1962- *ODwPR 91*
Cohen, Jeri Fried 1956- *WhoAmW 91, WhoEmL 91*
Cohen, Jerome 1925- *WhoAm 90*
Cohen, Jerome Alan 1930- *ConAu 30NR, WhoAm 90*
Cohen, Jerome Bernard 1932- *WhoAm 90*
Cohen, Jerry D. 1948- *St&PR 91*
Cohen, Jill *ODwPR 91*
Cohen, Joan Lebold 1932- *ConAu 30NR, WhoAmA 91*
Cohen, Joan M. *BioIn 16*
Cohen, Joan Newman 1934- *WhoSSW 91*
Cohen, Joanne 1938- *IntWWM 90*
Cohen, Joe Naham 1933- *WhoSSW 91*
Cohen, Joel 1941- *BiDrAPA 89*
Cohen, Joel 1942- *IntWWM 90*
Cohen, Joel B. 1931- *St&PR 91*
Cohen, Joel David 1952- *WhoEmL 91*
Cohen, Joel Ephraim 1944- *WhoAm 90*
Cohen, Joel H. *AuBYP 90*
Cohen, Joel J. 1938- *WhoAm 90*
Cohen, Joel M. 1941- *WhoE 91*
Cohen, Joel Ralph 1926- *WhoE 91*
Cohen, John *PenDiMP*
Cohen, John Charles 1911- *St&PR 91*
Cohen, John Michael 1903-1989 *ConAu 129*
Cohen, Jon Stephan 1943- *WhoAm 90*
Cohen, Jonathan *BiDrAPA 89*
Cohen, Jonathan Allan *BiDrAPA 89*
Cohen, Jonathan Brewer 1944- *WhoAm 90*
Cohen, Jonathan David *BiDrAPA 89*
Cohen, Jonathan Jacob 1955- *WhoAmA 91*
Cohen, Jonathan L. 1939- *St&PR 91*
Cohen, Jonathan Little 1939- *WhoAm 90*
Cohen, Jonathan Stuart *BiDrAPA 89*
Cohen, Joseph 1926- *WhoSSW 91*
Cohen, Joseph A. 1917- *St&PR 91*
Cohen, Joseph H. 1921- *St&PR 91*
Cohen, Joseph M. 1937- *St&PR 91*
Cohen, Joyce E. 1937- *WhoAmW 91*
Cohen, Jozef 1921- *WhoAm 90*
Cohen, Judith Ann 1953- *BiDrAPA 89, WhoAmW 91*
Cohen, Judith Levitt 1948- *WhoEmL 91*
Cohen, Judith Lynne 1951- *WhoEmL 91*
Cohen, Judith R. 1949- *IntWWM 90*
Cohen, Judith Rachael 1954- *WhoAmW 91*
Cohen, Judith W. 1937- *WhoE 91*
Cohen, Judy W. 1954- *St&PR 91*
Cohen, Jules *BioIn 16*
Cohen, Jules 1931- *WhoAm 90, WhoE 91*
Cohen, Jules Simon 1937- *WhoAm 90*
Cohen, Julius G 1921- *BiDrAPA 89*
Cohen, Julius George 1921- *WhoE 91*
Cohen, Karl Paley 1913- *WhoAm 90*
Cohen, Keith 1945- *WhoWrEP 89*
Cohen, Kelli Ann *BiDrAPA 89*
Cohen, Kenneth Allan 1959- *BiDrAPA 89*
Cohen, Kenneth D 1928- *BiDrAPA 89*
Cohen, Kenneth David 1928- *WhoE 91*
Cohen, Kenneth H *BiDrAPA 89*
Cohen, Kenneth Robert 1951- *BiDrAPA 89*
Cohen, Lajla Jane 1928- *WhoAmW 91*
Cohen, Larry David 1953- *WhoSSW 91*
Cohen, Lauren Ann 1949- *WhoAmW 91*
Cohen, Lawrence 1926- *WhoAm 90*
Cohen, Lawrence Brent 1948- *WhoE 91*
Cohen, Lawrence N. 1932- *St&PR 91, WhoAm 90*
Cohen, Lawrence Sorel 1933- *WhoAm 90*
Cohen, Lawrence Steven *BiDrAPA 89*
Cohen, Lee Steven *BiDrAPA 89*
Cohen, Lee Steven 1959- *WhoE 91*
Cohen, Lee Stuart *BiDrAPA 89*
Cohen, Leonard *BioIn 16*
Cohen, Leonard 1925- *St&PR 91, WhoAm 90*
Cohen, Leonard 1934- *BioIn 16, MajTwCW, OxCPMus*
Cohen, Leonard Norman 1934- *IntWWM 90*
Cohen, Leslie B. 1923- *St&PR 91*
Cohen, Levi 1931- *BiDrAPA 89*
Cohen, Lewis Alan 1945- *St&PR 91*
Cohen, Lewis Carroll 1936- *WhoSSW 91*
Cohen, Lewis Cobrain 1947- *WhoE 91, WhoEmL 91*
Cohen, Lewis Isaac 1932- *WhoAm 90*
Cohen, Lewis M 1950- *BiDrAPA 89*
Cohen, Lila Beldock 1927- *WhoWrEP 89*
Cohen, Lloyd Robert 1947- *WhoEmL 91*
Cohen, Lois Ruth Kushner 1938- *WhoAm 90*
Cohen, Louis Hirsh 1949- *BiDrAPA 89*
Cohen, Louis N. 1911- *St&PR 91*
Cohen, Lynne G 1944- *WhoAmA 91*
Cohen, Madeline 1948- *ODwPR 91*
Cohen, Mae 1929- *IntWWM 90*
Cohen, Malcolm Martin 1937- *WhoAm 90*
Cohen, Marcy Sharon 1954- *WhoEmL 91*
Cohen, Margaret Ann 1953- *WhoAmW 91*
Cohen, Mariam C *BiDrAPA 89*
Cohen, Marion Deutsche 1943- *WhoWrEP 89*
Cohen, Marjorie Karen 1953- *WhoAmW 91*
Cohen, Mark H. 1932- *St&PR 91*
Cohen, Mark Herbert 1932- *WhoAm 90*
Cohen, Mark N. 1947- *WhoE 91, WhoEmL 91, WhoWor 91*
Cohen, Mark Steven 1948- *WhoE 91, WhoWor 91*
Cohen, Marlene L. 1945- *WhoAmW 91*
Cohen, Marlene Zichi 1951- *WhoEmL 91*
Cohen, Marshall *ODwPR 91, WhoAm 90*
Cohen, Marthe-Hermance *BioIn 16*
Cohen, Martin 1932- *St&PR 91, WhoAm 90*
Cohen, Martin 1934- *ODwPR 91*
Cohen, Martin Harvey 1932- *WhoAm 90*
Cohen, Martin Lee *BiDrAPA 89*
Cohen, Martin R. 1937- *St&PR 91*
Cohen, Marvin Lou 1935- *WhoAm 90*
Cohen, Marvin William 1936- *WhoE 91*
Cohen, Mary Ann 1943- *WhoAm 90, WhoAmW 91*
Cohen, Mary Ann Adler 1941- *BiDrAPA 89*
Cohen, Max 1918- *WhoWor 91*
Cohen, Max Harry 1940- *WhoAm 90*
Cohen, Max P 1924- *BiDrAPA 89*
Cohen, Maxine Bilsky 1961- *WhoSSW 91*
Cohen, Maynard Manuel 1920- *WhoAm 90*
Cohen, Melvin 1926- *St&PR 91*
Cohen, Melvin F 1925- *BiDrAPA 89*
Cohen, Melvin Irwin 1936- *WhoAm 90*
Cohen, Melvin Joseph 1928- *WhoAm 90*
Cohen, Melvin Lee 1950- *WhoSSW 91*
Cohen, Melvin R. 1911- *WhoAm 90*
Cohen, Melvin S. 1918- *St&PR 91*
Cohen, Melvin S. 1919- *St&PR 91*
Cohen, Melvin Samuel 1918- *WhoAm 90*
Cohen, Melvin Stephen 1919- *WhoAm 90*
Cohen, Melvin Warren *BiDrAPA 89*
Cohen, Michael 1930- *WhoAm 90*
Cohen, Michael 1939- *WhoAm 90*
Cohen, Michael Harris 1953- *WhoEmL 91*
Cohen, Michael I. 1935- *WhoAm 90*
Cohen, Michael J. 1940- *ConAu 129*
Cohen, Michael Paul 1947- *WhoE 91*
Cohen, Michael S 1936- *WhoAmA 91*
Cohen, Mickey L. 1923- *St&PR 91*
Cohen, Mildred Thaler 1921- *WhoAmA 91, WhoE 91*
Cohen, Miles Jon 1941- *WhoAm 90*
Cohen, Millard Stuart 1939- *St&PR 91, WhoWor 91*
Cohen, Milton *BiDrAPA 89*
Cohen, Milton Howard 1911- *WhoAm 90*
Cohen, Milton L. 1928- *St&PR 91*
Cohen, Miriam 1926- *SmATA 11AS [port]*
Cohen, Mitchell Harry 1904- *WhoAm 90*
Cohen, Mitchell Jay 1954- *St&PR 91*
Cohen, Mitchell Joseph *BiDrAPA 89*
Cohen, Morley M. 1917- *St&PR 91*
Cohen, Morrel Herman 1927- *WhoAm 90*
Cohen, Morris 1911- *WhoAm 90*
Cohen, Morris David *BiDrAPA 89*
Cohen, Morris Leo 1927- *WhoAm 90*
Cohen, Morris Raphael 1880-1947 *WorAlBi*
Cohen, Mortimer J. 1894-1972 *BioIn 16*
Cohen, Morton N. 1921- *AuBYP 90*
Cohen, Moses Elias 1937- *WhoAm 90*
Cohen, Murray 1926-1988 *BioIn 16*
Cohen, Murry Joseph 1941- *BiDrAPA 89, WhoE 91*
Cohen, Myer 1907- *WhoAm 90*
Cohen, Myron Leslie 1934- *St&PR 91, WhoE 91*
Cohen, N. Jerold 1935- *WhoAm 90*
Cohen, Nancy *ODwPR 91*
Cohen, Nancy Lin 1957- *WhoEmL 91*
Cohen, Nancy Rae *BiDrAPA 89*
Cohen, Nat 1906-1988 *AnObit 1988*
Cohen, Nathan 1923-1971 *OxCCanT*
Cohen, Nathan 1941- *BiDrAPA 89*
Cohen, Neal Lawrence 1946- *BiDrAPA 89*
Cohen, Nicholas 1938- *WhoAm 90*
Cohen, Nina *WhoAmW 91*
Cohen, Noel Lee 1930- *WhoAm 90*
Cohen, Noreen Marie 1955- *WhoAmW 91*
Cohen, Norm 1936- *WhoAm 90*
Cohen, Octavus Roy 1891-1959 *TwCCr&M 91*
Cohen, Orville Salvator 1922- *St&PR 91*
Cohen, Otto 1883-1979 *WorAlBi*
Cohen, Paul 1945- *BioIn 16*
Cohen, Paul M. *St&PR 91*
Cohen, Paula Beth 1963- *WhoAmW 91*
Cohen, Perry D. 1946- *WhoE 91, WhoEmL 91*
Cohen, Peter *BioIn 16, WhoAm 90*
Cohen, Peter 1947?- *BioIn 16*
Cohen, Peter M. 1947- *ODwPR 91*
Cohen, Peter Ronald 1948- *BiDrAPA 89*
Cohen, Peter William *BiDrAPA 89*
Cohen, Philip 1907- *WhoSSW 91*
Cohen, Philip 1931- *WhoAm 90*
Cohen, Philip 1948- *WhoEmL 91*
Cohen, Philip Francis 1911- *WhoAm 90*
Cohen, Philip Herman 1936- *WhoAm 90, WhoE 91, WhoWor 91*
Cohen, Philip Pacy 1908- *WhoAm 90*
Cohen, Phill I 1932- *BiDrAPA 89*
Cohen, Phillip 1919- *St&PR 91*
Cohen, Phillip A *BiDrAPA 89*
Cohen, Phillip T 1949- *BiDrAPA 89*
Cohen, Phyllis Claire 1960- *WhoAmW 91*
Cohen, R Robert *BiDrAPA 89*
Cohen, Rachelle Sharon 1946- *WhoAmW 91*
Cohen, Ralph 1917- *WhoAm 90*
Cohen, Ralph 1919- *WhoAm 90*
Cohen, Ralph H. 1935- *St&PR 91, WhoAm 90*
Cohen, Ralph L 1938- *BiDrAPA 89, WhoE 91*
Cohen, Randal Lee 1953- *WhoEmL 91*
Cohen, Raquel E *BiDrAPA 89*
Cohen, Raquel E. 1922- *WhoHisp 91*
Cohen, Raymond 1919- *IntWWM 90, PenDiMP*
Cohen, Raymond 1923- *WhoAm 90*
Cohen, Raymond L *BiDrAPA 89*
Cohen, Reina Joyce 1931- *WhoE 91*
Cohen, Richard 1952- *WhoAm 90*
Cohen, Richard 1955- *WhoEmL 91*
Cohen, Richard A *BiDrAPA 89*
Cohen, Richard Allen 1948- *St&PR 91*
Cohen, Richard Gerard 1931- *WhoAm 90*
Cohen, Richard Jack 1936- *WhoAm 90*
Cohen, Richard L *BiDrAPA 89*
Cohen, Richard M. *BioIn 16*
Cohen, Richard Neil 1953- *WhoEmL 91*
Cohen, Richard Norman 1923- *WhoAm 90*
Cohen, Richard Steven 1942- *St&PR 91, WhoAm 90*
Cohen, Richard Stockman 1937- *WhoAm 90*
Cohen, Robert 1929- *WhoE 91, WhoWor 91*
Cohen, Robert 1932- *WhoE 91*
Cohen, Robert 1957- *ConAu 131, WhoEmL 91*
Cohen, Robert 1959- *IntWWM 90, PenDiMP*
Cohen, Robert A 1909- *BiDrAPA 89*
Cohen, Robert Abraham 1909- *WhoAm 90*
Cohen, Robert Avram 1929- *WhoAm 90*
Cohen, Robert Carl 1930- *AuBYP 90*
Cohen, Robert Edward 1947- *WhoAm 90*
Cohen, Robert Harvey 1928- *St&PR 91*
Cohen, Robert L. 1929- *St&PR 91*
Cohen, Robert L. 1947- *WhoWrEP 89*
Cohen, Robert L. 1952- *WhoSSW 91*
Cohen, Robert Leonard 1937- *WhoAm 90*
Cohen, Robert P. 1927- *St&PR 91*
Cohen, Robert S. 1928- *St&PR 91*
Cohen, Robert Sonne 1923- *WhoAm 90, WhoWor 91*
Cohen, Robert Yale, II 1950- *WhoEmL 91*
Cohen, Roberta Sherri 1955- *WhoEmL 91*
Cohen, Roger L. 1935- *WhoAm 90*
Cohen, Ron *BioIn 16*
Cohen, Ron 1956- *WhoE 91*
Cohen, Rona Spector *BiDrAPA 89*
Cohen, Ronald 1930- *WhoAm 90*
Cohen, Ronald Eli 1937- *WhoAm 90*
Cohen, Ronald J. 1956- *WhoEmL 91*
Cohen, Ronald Jay 1948- *WhoEmL 91*
Cohen, Ronald K 1955- *BiDrAPA 89*
Cohen, Ronald Marc 1951- *WhoEmL 91*
Cohen, Ronald Paul 1944- *WhoE 91*
Cohen, Ronny H 1950- *WhoAmA 91*
Cohen, Ruben David 1956- *WhoSSW 91*
Cohen, Ruth Paula *BiDrAPA 89*
Cohen, Ruth Schiff 1957- *WhoAmW 91*
Cohen, Sally Ann 1942- *WhoAmW 91*
Cohen, Samuel 1909- *St&PR 91*
Cohen, Samuel Harris *BioIn 16*
Cohen, Samuel Israel 1933- *WhoE 91, WhoWor 91*
Cohen, Samuel Meir 1886-1945 *BioIn 16*
Cohen, Sander Harris 1937- *WhoE 91*
Cohen, Sandon Lee 1960- *WhoEmL 91*
Cohen, Sandra Irene *BiDrAPA 89*
Cohen, Sandra Kopit 1952- *BiDrAPA 89*
Cohen, Sanford I 1928- *BiDrAPA 89*
Cohen, Sanford Irwin 1928- *WhoAm 90, WhoSSW 91*
Cohen, Sanford Ned 1935- *WhoAm 90*
Cohen, Saul 1930- *St&PR 91*
Cohen, Saul Bernard 1925- *ConAu 130, WhoAm 90*
Cohen, Saul G. 1916- *WhoAm 90*
Cohen, Saul Zelman 1926- *WhoAm 90*
Cohen, Selma 1930- *WhoAmW 91*
Cohen, Selma Jeanne 1920- *WhoAm 90*
Cohen, Seth Alexander *BiDrAPA 89*
Cohen, Seymour 1917- *WhoAm 90*
Cohen, Seymour I 1936- *BiDrAPA 89*
Cohen, Seymour J. 1922- *BioIn 16*
Cohen, Seymour Jay 1922- *WhoAm 90*
Cohen, Seymour Stanley 1917- *WhoAm 90*
Cohen, Shari Sue 1950- *St&PR 91*
Cohen, Sharon Anne *WhoAmW 91*
Cohen, Sheldon B 1928- *BiDrAPA 89*
Cohen, Sheldon Gilbert 1918- *WhoAm 90*
Cohen, Sheldon Hersh 1934- *WhoAm 90*
Cohen, Sheldon Stanley 1927- *WhoAm 90*
Cohen, Shera *WhoAmW 91*
Cohen, Sidney 1910-1987 *BioIn 16*
Cohen, Sidney Louis 1926- *St&PR 91*
Cohen, Sidney M 1919- *BiDrAPA 89*
Cohen, Sidney Maximilian 1919- *WhoE 91*
Cohen, Sidney R. 1920- *St&PR 91*
Cohen, Sorel *WhoAmA 91*
Cohen, Spencer 1943- *St&PR 91*
Cohen, Stanley 1922- *WhoAm 90, WhoSSW 91, WhoWor 91, WorAlBi*
Cohen, Stanley 1937- *WhoAm 90, WhoWor 91*
Cohen, Stanley 1942- *WhoWor 91*
Cohen, Stanley Jack 1939- *St&PR 91*
Cohen, Stanley Norman 1935- *WhoAm 90*
Cohen, Stephanie D. *St&PR 91*
Cohen, Stephen A. 1937- *St&PR 91*
Cohen, Stephen F. *BioIn 16*
Cohen, Stephen Frand 1938- *WhoAm 90*
Cohen, Stephen Howard 1938- *WhoAm 90*
Cohen, Stephen M 1941- *BiDrAPA 89*
Cohen, Stephen Mark 1952- *WhoEmL 91*
Cohen, Stephen Marshall 1929- *WhoAm 90*
Cohen, Stephen Martin 1957- *WhoEmL 91*

Cohen, Stephen Michael 1957- *WhoEmL 91*
Cohen, Stephen Philip 1936- *WhoAm 90*
Cohen, Stephen Robert 1950- *WhoEmL 91*
Cohen, Steven 1947- *WhoEmL 91*
Cohen, Steven 1954- *WhoEmL 91*
Cohen, Steven Charles 1947- *WhoEmL 91*
Cohen, Steven Marc 1949- *WhoAm 90*
Cohen, Steven Roger *BiDrAPA 89*
Cohen, Susan Berk 1942- *WhoAmW 91*
Cohen, Susan Merle 1950- *WhoSSW 91*
Cohen, Sydney *BiDrAPA 89*
Cohen, Sylvan M. 1914- *St&PR 91, WhoAm 90*
Cohen, Ted 1939- *WhoAm 90*
Cohen, Theodore B 1923- *BiDrAPA 89*
Cohen, Thomas William *BioIn 16*
Cohen, Victor 1910- *BiDrAPA 89*
Cohen, Wallace M. 1908- *WhoAm 90, WhoE 91*
Cohen, Walter Stanley 1936- *WhoAm 90*
Cohen, Warren I. 1934- *WhoAm 90*
Cohen, Wendy C *BiDrAPA 89*
Cohen, Wilbur Joseph 1913-1987 *BiDrUSE 89, BioIn 16*
Cohen, William 1940- *WorAlBi*
Cohen, William Alan 1937- *WhoAm 90*
Cohen, William Benjamin 1941- *WhoAm 90*
Cohen, William L. *St&PR 91*
Cohen, William Mark 1949- *WhoAm 90*
Cohen, William Nathan 1935- *WhoAm 90*
Cohen, William R *BiDrAPA 89*
Cohen, William Sebastian 1940- *WhoAm 90, WhoE 91, WhoWor 91*
Cohen-Adad, Gerard Samuel 1955- *WhoWor 91*
Cohen-Berman, Naomi Eileen 1947- *WhoEmL 91*
Cohen-Cole, Steven Arnold 1948- *BiDrAPA 89*
Cohen-Mansfield, Jiska 1951- *WhoEmL 91*
Cohen-Solal, Michael Martin 1943- *WhoWor 91*
Cohen-Stratyner, Barbara Naomi 1951- *WhoE 91*
Cohenca, Jacques *St&PR 91*
Cohenca, Philip M. 1952- *St&PR 91*
Cohill, Maurice Blanchard, Jr. 1929- *WhoAm 90, WhoE 91*
Cohill, Robert Anthony 1939- *St&PR 91*
Cohl, Claudia Hope 1939- *WhoAmW 91*
Cohl, Michael *BioIn 16*
Cohl, Rita *WhoSSW 91*
Cohler, Anne M 1940?-1989 *ConAu 130*
Cohler, Bertram Joseph 1938- *WhoAm 90*
Cohler, Edmund U. 1928- *St&PR 91*
Cohler, Eric D. W. 1959- *ODwPR 91*
Cohlon, William 1941- *WhoAmA 91*
Cohn, Al 1925-1988 *AnObit 1988, BioIn 16*
Cohn, Alan Jay 1945- *BiDrAPA 89*
Cohn, Alan M. 1926-1989 *BioIn 16, ConAu 129*
Cohn, Anni G 1911- *BiDrAPA 89*
Cohn, Arnold N. 1934- *St&PR 91*
Cohn, Arthur 1910- *IntWWM 90*
Cohn, Avern Levin 1924- *WhoAm 90*
Cohn, Barry H. 1951- *WhoE 91*
Cohn, Benno 1897- *St&PR 91*
Cohn, Bernard Samuel 1928- *WhoAm 90*
Cohn, Bertram Josiah 1925- *WhoAm 90*
Cohn, Cal K 1942- *BiDrAPA 89*
Cohn, Clara Viebig 1860-1952 *BioIn 16*
Cohn, David Earl *BiDrAPA 89*
Cohn, David Herc 1923- *WhoAm 90*
Cohn, David Stephen 1945- *WhoEmL 91*
Cohn, David Valor 1926- *WhoWor 91*
Cohn, Derek 1947- *WhoEmL 91*
Cohn, Don Stephen 1950- *WhoEmL 91*
Cohn, Elchanan 1941- *WhoSSW 91*
Cohn, Frederick Donald 1931- *WhoAmA 91*
Cohn, George L 1926- *BiDrAPA 89*
Cohn, Gerald Martin 1948- *St&PR 91*
Cohn, Geraldine Lois 1934- *St&PR 91*
Cohn, Gregory Phil 1919- *WhoWor 91*
Cohn, Harvey 1923- *WhoAm 90, WhoE 91*
Cohn, Haskell 1901- *WhoAm 90, WhoWor 91*
Cohn, Herbert B. 1912- *WhoAm 90*
Cohn, Howard 1922- *WhoAm 90*
Cohn, Hugo *BioIn 16, NewYTBS 90*
Cohn, Ian J. 1950- *WhoEmL 91*
Cohn, Isadore H *BiDrAPA 89*
Cohn, Isidore, Jr. 1921- *WhoAm 90, WhoSSW 91*
Cohn, James 1928- *IntWWM 90*
Cohn, James R. 1949- *WhoE 91*
Cohn, Jan Kadetsky 1933- *WhoWrEP 89*
Cohn, Jane *ODwPR 91*
Cohn, Jane Shapiro 1935- *WhoAmW 91, WhoE 91*
Cohn, Janet Stone 1909- *WhoWrEP 89*
Cohn, Jay B 1922- *BiDrAPA 89*
Cohn, Jay Binswanger 1922- *WhoAm 90*
Cohn, Jeanne Terry 1957- *WhoEmL 91*
Cohn, Jerome 1923- *St&PR 91*
Cohn, Jerry S 1944- *BiDrAPA 89*
Cohn, Jess V 1908- *BiDrAPA 89*
Cohn, Jess Victor 1908- *WhoAm 90*
Cohn, Jim 1953- *WhoWrEP 89*
Cohn, Kenneth Doyle 1946- *St&PR 91*
Cohn, Lawrence H. 1937- *WhoAm 90*
Cohn, Lawrence S 1940- *BiDrAPA 89*
Cohn, Lawrence Steven 1945- *WhoEmL 91*
Cohn, Lee S 1931- *BiDrAPA 89*
Cohn, Leonard Allan 1929- *St&PR 91, WhoAm 90*
Cohn, Louis Franklin 1948- *WhoAm 90*
Cohn, Marcus 1913- *WhoAm 90*
Cohn, Marianne 1924-1944 *BioIn 16*
Cohn, Marianne Winter Miller 1928- *WhoAmW 91*
Cohn, Marjorie B 1939- *WhoAmA 91*
Cohn, Martin David 1925- *St&PR 91, WhoE 91*
Cohn, Marvin 1924-1990 *BioIn 16*
Cohn, Marvin 1928- *WhoAm 90*
Cohn, Marvin L 1924-1990 *ConAu 131*
Cohn, Max Arthur 1903- *WhoAmA 91, WhoE 91*
Cohn, Mildred 1913- *WhoAm 90, WhoAmW 91*
Cohn, Milton L. 1915- *St&PR 91*
Cohn, Nathan *St&PR 91N*
Cohn, Nathan 1918- *WhoWor 91*
Cohn, Nik 1946- *AuBYP 90*
Cohn, Norman Stanley 1930- *WhoAm 90*
Cohn, Richard A 1924- *WhoAmA 91*
Cohn, Richard Arnold 1940- *BiDrAPA 89*
Cohn, Richard Steven 1956- *WhoEmL 91*
Cohn, Robert 1922- *WhoE 91*
Cohn, Robert Allen 1949- *WhoE 91*
Cohn, Robert Charles *BiDrAPA 89*
Cohn, Robert E. 1945- *WhoAm 90*
Cohn, Robert Mark 1945- *WhoE 91, WhoEmL 91*
Cohn, Roberta Kimmel 1937- *WhoE 91*
Cohn, Robin Jean 1952- *WhoAmW 91*
Cohn, Ronald Ira 1936- *WhoAm 90*
Cohn, Roy 1927-1986 *BioIn 16*
Cohn, Ruby 1922- *BioIn 16, ConAu 32NR, NotWoAT*
Cohn, Ruth Sidonie *BiDrAPA 89*
Cohn, Sam 1929- *WhoAm 90*
Cohn, Samuel Maurice 1915- *WhoAm 90*
Cohn, Sherman Louis 1932- *WhoAm 90*
Cohn, Sidney Elliott 1908- *WhoAm 90*
Cohn, Sy *BioIn 16*
Cohn, Theodore 1923- *WhoAm 90*
Cohn, Timothy William 1962- *WhoEmL 91*
Cohn, Victor 1919- *BioIn 16*
Cohn, Victor Edward 1919- *WhoAm 90*
Cohn, Werner M 1913- *BiDrAPA 89*
Cohn, William Elliott 1951- *WhoEmL 91*
Cohn, Zanvil Alexander 1926- *WhoAm 90*
Cohn-Bendit, Daniel *BioIn 16*
Cohn-Bendit, Daniel 1945- *BiDFrPL*
Cohn-Haft, Hera Johnston 1947- *BiDrAPA 89*
Cohn-Haft, Hera Maria 1947- *WhoE 91*
Cohodes, Eli Aaron 1927- *WhoAm 90*
Cohoe 1854-1924 *WhNaAH*
Cohoe, Grey 1944- *WhoAmA 91*
Cohon, George *BioIn 16*
Cohoon, Christen Ann 1964- *WhoAmW 91*
Cohoon, David K. *WhoE 91*
Cohowicz, Lucy Ann 1950- *WhoAmW 91*
Cohrs, Jo-Anne *BioIn 16*
Cohrt, Poul Tor 1946- *WhoWor 91*
Cohune, James S. 1934- *ODwPR 91*
Coia, Jack Antonio 1898-1981 *DcNaB 1981*
Coier, Wimmer Lane 1939- *WhoAm 90*
Coignard, Gabrielle de *EncCoWW*
Coigney, Martha Wadsworth 1933- *BioIn 16, NotWoAT, WhoAm 90*
Coil, Charles Ray 1940- *WhoSSW 91*
Coin, Sheila Regan 1942- *WhoAmW 91*
Coincoin, Maria Theresa *BioIn 16*
Coiner, Charles T 1897-1989 *WhoAmA 91N*
Coiner, Charles T. 1898-1989 *BioIn 16*
Coins, Raymond 1904- *MusmAFA*
Coiscou, Jose Luis Gonzalez 1926- *BioIn 16*
Coish, Eric Calvin 1948- *WhoWrEP 89*
Coisne, Henri Paul 1923- *WhoWor 91*
Coit, Arthur Leon 1934- *WhoWrEP 89*
Coit, Dorothy 1889-1976 *BioIn 16, NotWoAT*
Coit, M B *WhoAmA 91*
Coit, Margaret Louise 1919- *AuBYP 90, WhoAm 90*
Coit, Michele Vivian 1954- *WhoAmW 91*
Cojuangco family *BioIn 16*
Cokburne, Alison 1713-1794 *FemiCLE*
Coke, Alfred Mack 1941- *WhoSSW 91*
Coke, Chauncey Eugene *WhoAm 90, WhoWor 91*
Coke, Dorothy Josephine 1897-1979 *BiDWomA*
Coke, Edward 1552-1634 *BioIn 16*
Coke, F Van Deren 1921- *WhoAmA 91*
Coke, Frank Van Deren 1921- *WhoAm 90*
Coke, Mary 1727-1811 *FemiCLE*
Coke, Van Deren 1921- *WhoWrEP 89*
Cokelet, Giles Roy 1932- *WhoAm 90*
Cokeley, John M *BiDrAPA 89*
Cokendolpher, Eunice Loraine 1931- *WhoAmA 91*
Coker, Bernard John 1952- *St&PR 91*
Coker, Carl David 1928- *WhoAmA 91*
Coker, Charles Westfield 1933- *St&PR 91, WhoAm 90, WhoSSW 91*
Coker, Claudia Germaine 1953- *WhoAmW 91*
Coker, Darby *BioIn 16*
Coker, Donald William 1945- *WhoEmL 91*
Coker, Elizabeth Boatwright 1909- *WhoAm 90, WhoAmW 91*
Coker, James Lide 1941- *St&PR 91*
Coker, Jimmie 1936- *Ballpl 90*
Coker, Linda Lou 1940- *WhoAmW 91*
Coker, Paul 1959- *IntWWM 90*
Coker, William A. 1930- *St&PR 91*
Coker, William R. 1936- *WhoWrEP 89*
Col, Jeanne-Marie 1946- *WhoEmL 91*
Col, Martin H. 1951- *St&PR 91*
Cola, Charles A. *BioIn 16*
Colabrese, Cary John 1948- *WhoWor 91*
Colacchio, Judith Maxine 1947- *St&PR 91*
Colacci, Irving Roger 1953- *WhoEmL 91*
Colaco, Joseph Phillip 1940- *St&PR 91*
Coladarci, Arthur Paul 1917- *WhoAm 90*
Coladarci, Paul H. 1944- *ODwPR 91*
Colaguori, June Carol 1955- *WhoAmW 91*
Colah, Jessy Jamshed *BiDrAPA 89*
Colahan, J. Randolph 1952- *St&PR 91*
Colahan, Peter D. 1956- *St&PR 91*
Colaiaco, Paul Arthur *BiDrAPA 89*
Colaiacovo, Philip E. *ODwPR 91*
Colaianni, Joseph Vincent 1935- *WhoAm 90*
Colaizzi, John Louis 1938- *WhoAm 90*
Colaizzi, Robert A., Jr. 1936- *ODwPR 91*
Colalucci, Francis Michael 1944- *St&PR 91*
Colamarino, Katrin Belenky 1951- *WhoAmW 91*
Colamarino, Leonard James 1951- *WhoEmL 91*
Colamasi, Cesare 1928- *WhoWor 91*
Colander, David Charles 1947- *WhoAm 90, WhoE 91*
Colander, Valerie Nieman 1955- *WhoWrEP 89*
Colaneri, Joseph 1955- *IntWWM 90*
Colangelo, Carmon 1957- *WhoSSW 91*
Colangelo, Jerry John 1939- *WhoAm 90*
Colani, Luigi 1928- *BioIn 16*
Colantoni, Alfred D. 1952- *St&PR 91*
Colantoni, Alfred Daniel 1952- *WhoE 91*
Colantuono, Anthony 1958- *WhoAmA 91*
Colao, Anthony F. 1927- *St&PR 91*
Colao, Ralph F. 1930- *St&PR 91*
Colao, Rudolph 1927- *WhoAmA 91*
Colapelle-Snodgrass, Natalie 1957- *BiDrAPA 89*
Colarco, Richard Frank 1949 *WhoEmL 91*
Colarik, Paul E. 1943- *St&PR 91*
Colarullo, Louis Anthony 1948- *WhoE 91*
Colarusso, Calvin A 1935- *BiDrAPA 89*
Colarusso, Corrine Camille 1952- *WhoAmA 91*
Colarusso, Joseph R. 1925- *St&PR 91*
Colas, Antonio Espada 1928- *WhoAm 90*
Colas, Emile Jules 1923- *WhoAm 90*
Colasanti, Brenda Karen 1945- *WhoAmW 91*
Colasanto, E.M. 1941- *St&PR 91*
Colasuonno, Louis Christopher 1948- *WhoAm 90*
Colasurd, Richard Michael 1928- *WhoAm 90*
Colatrella, Carol Ann 1957- *WhoE 91*
Colavita, Marianne Eugenia 1946- *WhoE 91*
Colavito, Rocky 1933- *Ballpl 90 [port], BioIn 16*
Colaw, Thomas Allan 1939- *WhoE 91*
Colbach, Edward M 1939- *BiDrAPA 89*
Colberg, Malcolm Gunnar 1924- *St&PR 91*
Colberg, Marshall Rudolph 1913- *WhoAm 90*
Colberg-Arroyo, Pedro *BiDrAPA 89*
Colbert, Annette Darcia 1959- *WhoEmL 91*
Colbert, Charles A. 1921- *St&PR 91*
Colbert, Charles Ralph 1921- *WhoAm 90*
Colbert, Claudette 1903- *WhoAm 90*
Colbert, Claudette 1905- *BioAmW, WorAlBi*
Colbert, Donald W. 1949- *St&PR 91*
Colbert, Edward G *BiDrAPA 89*
Colbert, Edwin Harris 1905- *BioIn 16, WhoAm 90*
Colbert, Elbert Lynn 1952- *WhoEmL 91*
Colbert, George 1764-1839 *WhNaAH*
Colbert, Heather 1950- *WhoAmW 91, WhoEmL 91*
Colbert, James E. 1951- *WhoSSW 91*
Colbert, James J. 1933- *St&PR 91*
Colbert, Jean-Baptiste 1619-1683 *EncCRAm, WorAlBi*
Colbert, John R. 1945- *St&PR 91*
Colbert, Lester L., Jr. 1934- *St&PR 91*
Colbert, Lester Lum 1905- *EncABHB 5 [port], WhoAm 90*
Colbert, Lester Lum, Jr. 1934- *WhoAm 90*
Colbert, Levi *WhNaAH*
Colbert, Nate 1946- *Ballpl 90*
Colbert, Olga 1959- *WhoEmL 91*
Colbert, Pittman *WhNaAH*
Colbert, Robert B., Jr. 1921- *WhoAm 90*
Colbert, Vince 1945- *Ballpl 90*
Colbert, William *WhNaAH*
Colbert-Kelly, Judith Ann 1956- *WhoAmW 91*
Colborn, Edward F. 1855- *BioIn 16*
Colborn, Gene Louis 1935- *WhoSSW 91*
Colborn, Harry Walter 1921- *WhoAm 90*
Colborn, Jane Taylor 1913-1983 *WhoAmA 91N*
Colborn, Jim 1946- *Ballpl 90*
Colborn, Patricia Harrison 1952- *WhoAmW 91*
Colborn, Theo E. 1927- *WhoAmW 91*
Colborne, Patricia Becker 1929- *St&PR 91*
Colbourn, Joseph Leason 1929- *WhoE 91*
Colbourn, Trevor 1927- *WhoSSW 91*
Colbow, Brian R. 1947- *St&PR 91*
Colbroth, Ronald John 1945- *WhoE 91*
Colburn, Carol *BioIn 16*
Colburn, Craig Paul 1943- *St&PR 91*
Colburn, Francis Peabody 1909-1984 *WhoAmA 91N*
Colburn, Gene Lewis 1932- *WhoWor 91*
Colburn, Gladys La Flamme 1910- *WhoWrEP 89*
Colburn, J. Brian 1943- *St&PR 91*
Colburn, James Edward 1924- *St&PR 91*
Colburn, Julia Katherine Lee 1927- *WhoAmW 91*
Colburn, Kenneth Albert 1953- *WhoE 91*
Colburn, Kenneth Hersey 1952- *St&PR 91, WhoAm 90*
Colburn, Philip William 1929- *St&PR 91, WhoAm 90*
Colburn, Richard Dunton 1911- *WhoAm 90*
Colburn, Robert Dickinson 1962- *WhoWrEP 89*
Colburn, Zerah 1804-1840 *BioIn 16*
Colby, Anne 1946- *WhoAmW 91*
Colby, Bainbridge 1869-1950 *BiDrUSE 89, BioIn 16*
Colby, Barbara Diane 1932- *WhoAm 90*
Colby, Barnard L. 1911- *St&PR 91*
Colby, Bill 1927- *WhoAmA 91*
Colby, Carroll Burleigh 1904-1977 *AuBYP 90*
Colby, Edith Lucille 1917- *WhoWrEP 89*
Colby, Ethel *WhoAm 90*
Colby, Homer Wayland 1874-1950 *WhoAmA 91N*
Colby, Jean Poindexter 1909- *AuBYP 90*
Colby, Jeff 1956- *WhoAmA 91*
Colby, John A. 1949- *WhoE 91*
Colby, Jonathan Elbridge 1946- *St&PR 91*
Colby, Joy Hakanson *WhoAm 90, WhoAmA 91*
Colby, Karen Lynn 1943- *WhoAmW 91*
Colby, Kenneth Mark *BiDrAPA 89*
Colby, Kenneth Poole 1908- *WhoAm 90*
Colby, Laura J. 1957- *WhoWor 91*
Colby, Lewis James, Jr. 1934- *St&PR 91*
Colby, Luther 1813-1894 *EncO&P 3*
Colby, Marvelle Seitman 1932- *WhoAmW 91*
Colby, Orrin Tether, Jr. 1940- *St&PR 91*
Colby, Patricia Farley 1958- *WhoAmW 91*
Colby, Robert Alan 1920- *WhoAm 90*
Colby, Victor E 1917- *WhoAmA 91*
Colby, Virginia Little 1917- *WhoAmW 91*
Colby, William Edward 1875- *BioIn 16*
Colby, William Egan 1920- *WhoAm 90, WhoE 91*
Colby, William George 1939- *St&PR 91*
Colby, William George, Jr. 1939- *WhoAm 90*
Colby-Hall, Alice Mary 1932- *WhoAm 90, WhoAmW 91*
Colclaser, H. Alberta 1911- *WhoAm 90*
Colclough, Jim 1900-1986 *MusmAFA*
Colclough, William F. 1905- *St&PR 91*
Colcord, Elmer Danforth 1895- *WhoE 91, WhoWor 91*
Colcord, Herbert N. 1951- *ODwPR 91*
Colcord, Herbert Nathaniel 1951- *St&PR 91*
Colcord, Linda Miller 1953- *WhoEmL 91*
Cold, Birgit 1936- *WomArch [port]*
Cold, Ulrik 1939- *IntWWM 90*
Colden, Cadwallader 1688-1776 *EncCRAm, WhNaAH*
Colden, Jane 1724-1766 *EncCRAm, WomFie*

Coldewey, T.S. 1912- *St&PR 91*
Colding-Jorgensen, Henrik 1944- *IntWWM 90*
Coldren, Diane 1945- *WhoAmW 91*
Coldren, Larry Allen 1946- *WhoAm 90*
Coldren, Scott 1964- *St&PR 91*
Coldrey, Jennifer *AuBYP 90*
Coldsmith, Don 1926- *BioIn 16, WhoWrEP 89*
Coldstream, John Nicolas 1927- *WhoWor 91*
Coldstream, William Menzies 1908-1987 *BioIn 16*
Coldwell, Philip Edward 1922- *WhoAm 90*
Coldwell, Raymond E. 1941- *St&PR 91*
Coldwell, Rodney Lloyd 1943- *St&PR 91*
Coldwell, Stephen O. 1939- *St&PR 91*
Cole, Alan Randolph *BiDrAPA 89*
Cole, Albert Leslie 1894-1989 *BioIn 16*
Cole, Alphaeus Philemon 1876-1988 *BioIn 16*
Cole, Anita Louise 1954- *WhoSSW 91*
Cole, Ann Marie 1937- *WhoWrEP 89*
Cole, Annette *AuBYP 90, ConAu 30NR*
Cole, Anthony F. 1955- *WhoE 91, WhoEmL 91*
Cole, Aubrey Louis 1923- *St&PR 91, WhoAm 90, WhoSSW 91*
Cole, Babette 1949- *SmATA 61 [port]*
Cole, Barbara Ruth 1941- *WhoAmW 91*
Cole, Barry Eliot *BiDrAPA 89*
Cole, Basil 1920- *St&PR 91*
Cole, Beatrice L. *BioIn 16*
Cole, Benjamin Richason 1916- *WhoAm 90*
Cole, Benjamin Theodore 1921- *WhoAm 90*
Cole, Bert 1896-1975 *Ballpl 90*
Cole, Betty Lou McDonel Shelton 1926- *WhoAmW 91, WhoWor 91*
Cole, Bob *EarBlAP*
Cole, Bob 1868-1911 *BioIn 16*
Cole, Brock 1938- *BioIn 16*
Cole, Bruce 1938- *WhoAmA 91*
Cole, Bruce Milan 1938- *WhoAm 90*
Cole, Byron Joseph 1941- *St&PR 91*
Cole, C. Richard 1949- *St&PR 91*
Cole, Carl W. 1947- *WhoSSW 91*
Cole, Carol 1944- *DrBlPA 90*
Cole, Carol Anne 1955- *WhoWrEP 89*
Cole, Carole Osborne 1936- *WhoWrEP 89*
Cole, Carolyn Jo 1943- *WhoAm 90, WhoE 91*
Cole, Cecil S. *WhoSSW 91*
Cole, Charles Chester, Jr. 1922- *WhoAm 90*
Cole, Charles David 1920- *St&PR 91*
Cole, Charles Dewey, Jr. 1952- *WhoEmL 91*
Cole, Charles E 1926- *BiDrAPA 89*
Cole, Charles T., Jr. 1946- *St&PR 91*
Cole, Charles Talmadge, Jr. 1946- *WhoAm 90*
Cole, Charles W., Jr. *WhoAm 90*
Cole, Charles William 1945- *St&PR 91*
Cole, Clarence Russell 1918- *WhoAm 90*
Cole, Clifford Adair 1915- *WhoAm 90*
Cole, Clyde Curtis, Jr. 1932- *WhoAm 90*
Cole, Cozy 1909-1981 *BioIn 16, DrBlPA 90, OxCPMus, WorAlBi*
Cole, Dave 1930- *Ballpl 90*
Cole, David Andrew 1942- *St&PR 91*
Cole, David C. 1936- *St&PR 91*
Cole, David Chamberlin 1928- *WhoE 91*
Cole, Davis *AuBYP 90*
Cole, Dawn Vroegop 1966- *WhoAmW 91*
Cole, Dayton Thomas 1954- *WhoEmL 91*
Cole, Diane *BioIn 16*
Cole, Diane Jackson 1952- *WhoAmW 91, WhoWor 91*
Cole, Donald 1930- *WhoAmA 91, WhoE 91*
Cole, Donald Foster 1957- *St&PR 91*
Cole, Donald Willard 1920- *WhoAm 90, WhoWor 91*
Cole, Doris M. 1905-1989 *BioIn 16*
Cole, Dorthy Gatlin 1933- *WhoAmW 91*
Cole, Douglas 1934- *WhoAm 90, WhoWrEP 89*
Cole, E R 1930- *ConAu 31NR, WhoWrEP 89*
Cole, Edward Nicholas 1909-1977 *EncABHB 5*
Cole, Edwin M 1904- *BiDrAPA 89*
Cole, Elaine Geneva 1932- *WhoWrEP 89*
Cole, Elizabeth *ConTFT 8*
Cole, Elma Phillipson 1909- *WhoAmW 91, WhoE 91, WhoWor 91*
Cole, Elsa Kircher 1949- *WhoAmW 91*
Cole, Ernest *BioIn 16, NewYTBS 90*
Cole, Eugene 1933- *St&PR 91*
Cole, Eugene Roger 1930- *WhoWor 91*
Cole, Evelyn Marie 1928- *WhoWor 91*
Cole, Floyd Clinton 1926- *St&PR 91*
Cole, Frances Kay 1941- *WhoSSW 91*
Cole, Franklin A. 1926- *St&PR 91*
Cole, Fremont 1856- *AmLegL*
Cole, G. Alexander 1943- *St&PR 91*
Cole, G D H 1889-1959 *TwCCr&M 91*
Cole, Galen L. 1925- *St&PR 91*
Cole, Gary *BioIn 16, ConTFT 8*
Cole, Gary Donald 1945- *St&PR 91*
Cole, George David 1925- *WhoAm 90*
Cole, George William 1948- *WhoEmL 91*
Cole, Gerald Albert 1913- *St&PR 91*
Cole, Ginger Sue 1946- *St&PR 91*
Cole, Gordon Bradley 1956- *St&PR 91*
Cole, Gordon H. 1912-1988 *BioIn 16*
Cole, Grace V *WhoAmA 91*
Cole, Gretchen Bornor 1927- *St&PR 91, WhoAmW 91*
Cole, H. S. D. *ConAu 130*
Cole, Harold 1906-1946 *BioIn 16*
Cole, Harold David 1940- *WhoAmA 91*
Cole, Harry A. *WhoAm 90, WhoE 91*
Cole, Heather E. 1942- *WhoAm 90*
Cole, Henry 1808-1882 *BioIn 16, PenDiDA 89*
Cole, Herbert Milton 1935- *WhoAmA 91*
Cole, Herbert Myrman 1937- *St&PR 91*
Cole, Howard John *BiDrAPA 89*
Cole, Hugo 1917- *IntWWM 90*
Cole, J. Bruce 1941- *St&PR 91*
Cole, J. Chase 1954- *WhoEmL 91*
Cole, J. Gregory 1922- *St&PR 91*
Cole, Jack 1914-1958 *EncACom*
Cole, Jack Eli 1915- *WhoE 91, WhoWor 91*
Cole, Jacqueline *BioIn 16*
Cole, James Anthony 1945- *WhoSSW 91*
Cole, James Mariner, Jr. 1915- *WhoSSW 91*
Cole, James Robert 1935- *St&PR 91*
Cole, James William 1944- *WhoSSW 91*
Cole, James Woodard, Jr. 1950- *WhoSSW 91*
Cole, Jane Bagby 1931- *WhoAmW 91*
Cole, Janet 1922- *WhoAm 90, WhoAmW 91*
Cole, Jeanette 1952- *WhoAmA 91*
Cole, Jeffrey A. 1941- *WhoAm 90*
Cole, Jeffrey Alan 1941- *St&PR 91*
Cole, Jerome Foster 1940- *WhoSSW 91*
Cole, Joan Hays 1929- *WhoAmW 91*
Cole, Joanna *BioIn 16*
Cole, Joanna 1944- *AuBYP 90*
Cole, John Brian 1937- *WhoAm 90*
Cole, John D. 1949- *St&PR 91*
Cole, John L. 1941- *ODwPR 91*
Cole, John L., II 1941- *St&PR 91*
Cole, John Nelson 1863-1922 *AmLegL*
Cole, John Pope, Jr. *BioIn 16*
Cole, John Pope, Jr. 1930- *WhoAm 90*
Cole, John Sterling 1954- *St&PR 91*
Cole, John Sterling, II 1954- *WhoEmL 91*
Cole, John Young 1940- *BioIn 16*
Cole, Johnnetta B. *BioIn 16*
Cole, Johnnetta Betsch 1936- *WhoAm 90, WhoAmW 91*
Cole, Jonathan O 1925- *BiDrAPA 89*
Cole, Jonathan Otis 1925- *WhoAm 90*
Cole, Jonathan Richard 1942- *WhoAm 90, WhoWor 91*
Cole, Joseph E. 1915- *St&PR 91*
Cole, Joseph Edmund 1915- *WhoAm 90*
Cole, Joseph J *EncABHB 4*
Cole, Joyce *WhoAmA 91*
Cole, Judith Lynne 1944- *WhoSSW 91*
Cole, Julia Patricia 1952- *WhoAmW 91*
Cole, Julie Kramer 1942- *WhoAmA 91*
Cole, June Robertson 1931- *WhoAmW 91, WhoWor 91*
Cole, Justine *WhoWrEP 89*
Cole, Karyl Gilbert 1947- *BiDrAPA 89*
Cole, Katherine Ione 1949- *WhoEmL 91*
Cole, Kathleen *BioIn 16*
Cole, Kellie Birdgett Arndt 1964- *WhoAmW 91*
Cole, Kenneth Duane 1932- *WhoAm 90*
Cole, Kenneth Dwight 1954- *WhoSSW 91*
Cole, King 1886-1916 *Ballpl 90*
Cole, Kris W. 1957- *WhoEmL 91*
Cole, Larry Lee 1941- *WhoSSW 91*
Cole, Laurence Anthony 1953- *WhoE 91*
Cole, Lawrence Allen, Jr. 1944- *St&PR 91*
Cole, Lawrence Frederick 1947- *WhoSSW 91*
Cole, Lee M. 1955- *WhoSSW 91*
Cole, Leon Jacob 1877-1948 *BioIn 16, DcScB S2*
Cole, Leon Monroe 1933- *WhoE 91*
Cole, Leonard Aaron 1933- *WhoE 91, WhoWor 91*
Cole, Leslie Allen 1945- *WhoSSW 91*
Cole, Lester 1904-1985 *BioIn 16*
Cole, Lewis George 1931- *WhoAm 90*
Cole, Linda Sue 1953- *BiDrAPA 89*
Cole, Lois Dwight 1903-1979 *AuBYP 90*
Cole, Luther Francis 1925- *WhoAm 90*
Cole, M. Dean 1946- *St&PR 91*
Cole, Malcolm Stanley 1936- *IntWWM 90*
Cole, Malvin 1933- *WhoWor 91*
Cole, Margaret 1893-1980 *FemiCLE, TwCCr&M 91*
Cole, Margaret Elizabeth 1960- *WhoAmW 91*
Cole, Mari L.J. *BiDrAPA 89*
Cole, Mary *BiDEWW*
Cole, Max 1937- *WhoAm 90, WhoAmA 91*
Cole, Michael 1947- *BioIn 16*
Cole, Michael E. 1913- *St&PR 91*
Cole, Michael Steven 1955- *WhoEmL 91*
Cole, Michelle 1940- *WhoAmW 91*
Cole, Monroe 1933- *WhoAm 90*
Cole, Murray L. 1922- *St&PR 91*
Cole, Nancy 1902- *WhoE 91*
Cole, Nancy Berkey 1936- *WhoSSW 91*
Cole, Nancy Stooksberry 1942- *WhoAm 90*
Cole, Nat 1917-1965 *OxCPMus*
Cole, Nat 1919-1965 *DrBlPA 90, WorAlBi*
Cole, Nat King 1919?-1965 *BioIn 16*
Cole, Natalie *BioIn 16*
Cole, Natalie 1950- *DrBlPA 90, EncPR&S 89, WorAlBi*
Cole, Natalie Maria 1950- *WhoAm 90*
Cole, Neil D., Jr. *St&PR 91*
Cole, Nelson Abner 1849-1930? *BioIn 16*
Cole, Nyla J *BiDrAPA 89*
Cole, Nyla Jessamine 1925- *WhoAmW 91*
Cole, Olivia *DrBlPA 90*
Cole, Olivia 1942- *ConTFT 8*
Cole, Patricia Ann Elizabeth 1958- *WhoAmW 91*
Cole, Paul Campbell 1954- *WhoSSW 91*
Cole, Randel F. 1950- *WhoE 91, WhoEmL 91*
Cole, Raymond Edward *BiDrAPA 89*
Cole, Richard 1949- *WhoWrEP 89*
Cole, Richard Allen 1939- *St&PR 91*
Cole, Richard Barry 1933- *WhoE 91*
Cole, Richard Cargill 1926- *WhoAm 90*
Cole, Richard Dennis 1933- *St&PR 91*
Cole, Richard Garfield 1926- *WhoWor 91*
Cole, Richard George 1948- *WhoEmL 91*
Cole, Richard John 1926- *WhoAm 90*
Cole, Richard K *BiDrAPA 89*
Cole, Richard Louis 1946- *WhoAm 90*
Cole, Richard P. 1948- *WhoEmL 91*
Cole, Richard Ray 1942- *WhoAm 90*
Cole, Richie *BioIn 16*
Cole, Robert 1869-1911 *DrBlPA 90*
Cole, Robert Alan *BiDrAPA 89*
Cole, Robert Allen 1952- *WhoEmL 91*
Cole, Robert Bates 1911- *St&PR 91, WhoAm 90*
Cole, Robert Benjamin 1956- *WhoEmL 91*
Cole, Robert Carlton 1937- *WhoE 91*
Cole, Robert Kenneth 1945- *WhoSSW 91*
Cole, Robert S. 1938- *ODwPR 91*
Cole, Robert Stanley, Jr. 1946- *WhoEmL 91*
Cole, Robert Theodore 1932- *WhoE 91*
Cole, Roger David 1924- *WhoAm 90*
Cole, Roger Edward 1955- *WhoE 91*
Cole, Roger Jerome 1951- *WhoSSW 91*
Cole, Ronald L. 1945- *St&PR 91*
Cole, Rosalie M. 1926- *WhoAmW 91*
Cole, Russell Warren 1915- *St&PR 91*
Cole, Ruth Elena 1918- *WhoWrEP 89*
Cole, Sam 1943- *ConAu 130*
Cole, Sarah *BiDEWW*
Cole, Sharon F. 1941- *WhoAmW 91*
Cole, Sharon Kay *BiDrAPA 89*
Cole, Sherman Ward *BiDrAPA 89*
Cole, Sherwood Orison 1930- *WhoAm 90*
Cole, Solon Robert 1937- *WhoE 91*
Cole, Sonya Kressler 1941- *WhoAmW 91*
Cole, Stanley M 1947- *BiDrAPA 89*
Cole, Stephan William 1947- *St&PR 91, WhoAm 90*
Cole, Stephen Adams 1940- *BiDrAPA 89, WhoE 91*
Cole, Sterne Kendall 1956- *WhoSSW 91*
Cole, Steven Patrick 1960- *WhoEmL 91*
Cole, Susan W. *ODwPR 91*
Cole, Susie Cleora *WhoAmW 91*
Cole, Sylvan 1918- *WhoAmA 91*
Cole, Sylvan, Jr. 1918- *WhoAm 90*
Cole, T.F.C. 1917- *St&PR 91*
Cole, Terri Lynn 1951- *WhoAm 90*
Cole, Terry Paul 1945- *WhoEmL 91*
Cole, Terry Ronald 1945- *WhoEmL 91*
Cole, Thomas 1801-1848 *BioIn 16, IntDcAA 90, WorAlBi*
Cole, Thomas Amor 1948- *WhoAm 90*
Cole, Thomas L. R., III 1958- *WhoSSW 91*
Cole, Thomas Winston, Jr. 1941- *WhoAm 90*
Cole, Toby 1916- *BioIn 16, NotWoAT*
Cole, Todd G. 1921- *St&PR 91, WhoAm 90, WhoSSW 91*
Cole, Ty Ray 1961- *WhoSSW 91*
Cole, Ulric 1905- *IntWWM 90*
Cole, Vinson *BioIn 16, WhoAm 90*
Cole, Virginia Starr 1953- *WhoAmW 91*
Cole, Ward Howard 1932- *WhoSSW 91*
Cole, Warner Booton 1938- *St&PR 91*
Cole, Wayne Herbert 1947- *WhoE 91*
Cole, Wayne Merritt 1941- *St&PR 91*
Cole, Wayne Stanley 1922- *WhoAm 90, WhoE 91*
Cole, Wendell Gordon 1914- *WhoAm 90*
Cole, William 1919- *AuBYP 90*
Cole, William Charles 1909- *IntWWM 90*
Cole, William Edward 1931- *WhoAm 90*
Cole, William Howard 1943- *WhoSSW 91*
Cole, William Kaufman 1914- *WhoAm 90*
Cole, William Lawren 1926- *St&PR 91*
Cole, William S. *WhoAm 90*
Cole-Appel, Barbara *BioIn 16*
Cole-Mc Guckin, Connie Jean 1947- *WhoEmL 91*
Cole-Schiraldi, Marilyn Bush 1945- *WhoAmW 91*
Cole-Talbert, Florence 1890-1961 *DcAfAmP*
Cole-Whittaker, Terry *NewAgE 90*
Colebank, Marshall N., Jr. 1942- *St&PR 91*
Colebrook, Elizabeth Poss 1923- *WhoAmW 91*
Colebrook, Joan *BioIn 16*
Coleburn, George Wallace 1930- *St&PR 91*
Colecchia, Francesca Maria *WhoAm 90*
Colegate, Isabel *BioIn 16*
Colegate, Isabel 1931- *MajTwCW, WorAu 1980 [port]*
Colegrove, Clare Lee 1930- *WhoWor 91*
Colehour, Jean Marie 1954- *WhoEmL 91*
ColeHuckeba, Paula Jill 1948- *WhoAmW 91*
Colella, Janice *BioIn 16*
Colella, Joseph John, Jr. 1940- *WhoE 91*
Colella, Raymond Francis *BiDrAPA 89*
Colella, Tom *BioIn 16*
Colella, Tommy *BioIn 16*
Colello, Alan R. 1949- *St&PR 91*
Coleman, A D 1943- *WhoAmA 91*
Coleman, Albert John 1918- *WhoAm 90*
Coleman, Alex 1949- *WhoE 91*
Coleman, Alfred N. 1930- *St&PR 91*
Coleman, Allan Douglass 1943- *WhoE 91*
Coleman, Allen Markley 1949- *WhoEmL 91*
Coleman, Almand Rouse 1905- *WhoAm 90*
Coleman, Amoss Lee 1913- *WhoAm 90*
Coleman, Angela Marie 1960- *WhoAmW 91*
Coleman, Angella Cobb 1962- *WhoAmW 91*
Coleman, Anita Scott 1890-1960 *HarlReB*
Coleman, Ann Raney 1810-1897 *BioIn 16*
Coleman, Annette Wilbois 1934- *WhoAmW 91*
Coleman, Arlene Hamlett 1946- *WhoE 91*
Coleman, Audrey *BioIn 16*
Coleman, Barbara *St&PR 91*
Coleman, Barbara Lee Weinstein 1948- *WhoAmW 91*
Coleman, Barry B.Z. 1931- *St&PR 91*
Coleman, Beatrice *NewYTBS 90*
Coleman, Beatrice 1916- *St&PR 91*
Coleman, Beatrice 1916-1990 *BioIn 16*
Coleman, Bernell 1929- *WhoAm 90*
Coleman, Bernice E 1925- *BiDrAPA 89*
Coleman, Bernice Greenbaum 1929- *St&PR 91*
Coleman, Bethany Baldwin 1950- *WhoAmW 91*
Coleman, Bob 1890-1959 *Ballpl 90*
Coleman, Brian Doyle *BiDrAPA 89*
Coleman, Bruce T. 1939- *St&PR 91*
Coleman, Bryan Douglas 1948- *WhoEmL 91, WhoSSW 91, WhoWor 91*
Coleman, C. Norman 1945- *WhoAm 90*
Coleman, Charles Calvin 1960- *BiDrAPA 89*
Coleman, Charles Clyde 1937- *WhoAm 90*
Coleman, Claire K. *ODwPR 91*
Coleman, Clarence William 1909- *WhoAm 90, WhoWor 91*
Coleman, Constance Depler 1926- *WhoAmA 91*
Coleman, Craig Steven 1957- *BiDrAPA 89*
Coleman, Cy 1929- *CurBio 90 [port], OxCPMus, WhoAm 90, WhoE 91*
Coleman, D. Jackson 1934- *WhoAm 90*
Coleman, Dabney 1932- *WorAlBi*
Coleman, Dabney W. 1932- *WhoAm 90*
Coleman, Daniel J. 1932- *St&PR 91*
Coleman, Daniel Joseph, II 1932- *WhoAm 90*
Coleman, Darrell Glenn 1953- *WhoEmL 91*
Coleman, David Cecil 1937- *WhoE 91*
Coleman, David Manley 1948- *WhoEmL 91*
Coleman, Deborah Ann 1951- *WhoEmL 91*
Coleman, Deborah Ann 1953- *WhoAmW 91*
Coleman, Desiree 1968?- *DrBlPA 90*
Coleman, Donald J 1927- *BiDrAPA 89*
Coleman, Donald John 1950- *St&PR 91*
Coleman, Donald K *BiDrAPA 89*
Coleman, Donna Ann 1949- *WhoAmW 91*
Coleman, Dorothy P. 1954- *WhoSSW 91*
Coleman, E. Thomas 1943- *WhoAm 90*
Coleman, Earl Maxwell 1916- *WhoAm 90, WhoWor 91*
Coleman, Ed 1901-1964 *Ballpl 90*
Coleman, Edmonia Sue *BioIn 16*

Coleman, Edmund Benedict 1926- *WhoAm 90*
Coleman, Edward C. 1931- *St&PR 91*
Coleman, Edward H 1928- *WhoAmA 91*
Coleman, Elisabeth *ODwPR 91*
Coleman, Elisabeth Charlotte 1945- *WhoE 91*
Coleman, Elizabeth *BiDEWW*
Coleman, Elizabeth 1937- *WhoAmW 91, WhoE 91*
Coleman, Elizabeth Anne *BiDrAPA 89*
Coleman, Elizabeth J. 1947- *WhoEmL 91*
Coleman, Ellen Schneid 1943- *WhoWrEP 89*
Coleman, Emily 1899-1974 *FemiCLE*
Coleman, Emmett *MajTwCW*
Coleman, Eric Norman 1925- *WhoWor 91*
Coleman, Erica *BioIn 16*
Coleman, Ernest Albert 1929- *WhoAm 90*
Coleman, Ernest Robert, Sr. 1936- *St&PR 91*
Coleman, F.D.R. 1939- *St&PR 91*
Coleman, Florence Squire *BiDrAPA 89*
Coleman, Floyd Willis 1939- *WhoAmA 91*
Coleman, Frances Aline 1955- *WhoAmW 91*
Coleman, Francis Xavier, Jr. 1930- *St&PR 91, WhoAm 90, WhoWor 91*
Coleman, Frederick S 1913- *BiDrAPA 89*
Coleman, Frederick W *BiDrAPA 89*
Coleman, G.A. John 1945- *St&PR 91*
Coleman, Gary *BioIn 16*
Coleman, Gary 1968- *DrBlPA 90, WorAlBi*
Coleman, Gayle 1954- *WhoAmA 91*
Coleman, Geoffrey Parker 1956- *WhoEmL 91*
Coleman, George Edward 1935- *WhoAm 90*
Coleman, George Michael 1953- *WhoEmL 91*
Coleman, George W. 1928- *St&PR 91*
Coleman, George Willard 1912- *WhoSSW 91*
Coleman, George William 1928- *WhoSSW 91*
Coleman, Gerald Christopher 1939- *WhoAm 90, WhoWor 91*
Coleman, Gleason Walter 1928- *St&PR 91*
Coleman, Gloria Jean 1952- *WhoEmL 91*
Coleman, Gordy 1934- *Ballpl 90*
Coleman, Henry Thomas 1931- *St&PR 91*
Coleman, Heyward Hamilton 1943- *WhoAm 90*
Coleman, Howard S. 1917- *WhoAm 90*
Coleman, Ivory Claudette 1947- *WhoAmW 91*
Coleman, J. D. 1930- *ODwPR 91*
Coleman, J.E. 1957- *St&PR 91*
Coleman, Jack 1958- *ConTFT 8*
Coleman, James Covington 1914- *WhoAm 90*
Coleman, James Edwin, Jr. 1923- *WhoAm 90*
Coleman, James Hallett 1936- *St&PR 91*
Coleman, James Julian 1915- *WhoAm 90, WhoWor 91*
Coleman, James Julian, Jr. 1941- *WhoSSW 91*
Coleman, James Malcolm 1935- *WhoAm 90*
Coleman, James N. 1931- *WhoWrEP 89*
Coleman, James Samuel 1926- *BioIn 16, WhoAm 90*
Coleman, Jane C. 1939- *WhoWrEP 89*
Coleman, Jane Rankin 1927- *St&PR 91*
Coleman, Jason Chandler 1958- *WhoEmL 91*
Coleman, Jason Gill 1961- *WhoEmL 91*
Coleman, Jean Black 1925- *WhoAmW 91*
Coleman, Jerry 1924- *Ballpl 90, BioIn 16*
Coleman, Joe 1922- *Ballpl 90*
Coleman, Joe 1947- *Ballpl 90*
Coleman, Joel Clifford 1930- *WhoAm 90*
Coleman, John 1863-1922 *Ballpl 90*
Coleman, John Alvin 1931- *St&PR 91*
Coleman, John Harrod 1926- *WhoSSW 91, WhoWor 91*
Coleman, John Hewson 1912- *St&PR 91, WhoAm 90*
Coleman, John Joseph 1937- *WhoE 91, WhoWor 91*
Coleman, John M. 1947- *St&PR 91*
Coleman, John Michael 1949- *WhoAm 90, WhoE 91*
Coleman, John Royston 1921- *St&PR 91, WhoAm 90*
Coleman, John Tinsley 1927- *St&PR 91*
Coleman, John Walter 1938- *St&PR 91*
Coleman, Jonathan *BioIn 16*
Coleman, Jonathan 1951?- *ConAu 129*
Coleman, Jonathan A. 1947- *St&PR 91*
Coleman, Jonathan Mark 1951- *WhoSSW 91*
Coleman, Joseph Michael 1945- *WhoE 91*
Coleman, Judy *BioIn 16*
Coleman, Judy 1944- *WhoAmA 91*
Coleman, Jules Victor 1907- *BiDrAPA 89*
Coleman, Katherine Ann *WhoAmW 91, WhoE 91*
Coleman, Kathleen 1856-1915 *FemiCLE*
Coleman, Ken *Ballpl 90*
Coleman, Kenneth 1916- *ConAu 33NR*
Coleman, Kenneth William 1930- *WhoWor 91*
Coleman, Larry Joseph 1949- *WhoEmL 91*
Coleman, Lee Alan *BiDrAPA 89*
Coleman, Lee Sorrels 1949- *WhoEmL 91*
Coleman, Lester E. 1930- *St&PR 91*
Coleman, Lester Earl 1930- *WhoAm 90*
Coleman, Lester L. 1942- *St&PR 91*
Coleman, Lester Laudy 1911- *WhoAm 90*
Coleman, Lewis Waldo 1942- *St&PR 91, WhoAm 90*
Coleman, Lillian Simons 1955- *WhoAmW 91*
Coleman, Linda R. *WhoAmW 91*
Coleman, Lisa Ane 1963- *WhoE 91*
Coleman, M L 1941- *WhoAmA 91*
Coleman, Malcolm James, Jr. 1947- *WhoEmL 91*
Coleman, Marcia Lepri *WhoAmW 91*
Coleman, Margaret Ann 1959- *WhoAmW 91*
Coleman, Mark Anthony 1958- *WhoSSW 91*
Coleman, Mark J. 1947- *St&PR 91*
Coleman, Marshall D 1925- *BiDrAPA 89*
Coleman, Martin M. 1926- *WhoSSW 91*
Coleman, Martin Stone 1913- *WhoAm 90*
Coleman, Mary Ann 1928- *WhoWrEP 89*
Coleman, Mary Catherine 1929- *WhoAmW 91*
Coleman, Mary Stallings *WhoAm 90*
Coleman, Melvin Douglas 1948- *WhoEmL 91*
Coleman, Michael 1946- *WhoAmA 91*
Coleman, Michael Dortch 1944- *WhoSSW 91*
Coleman, Michael Herder 1927- *EncPaPR 91*
Coleman, Michael Murray 1938- *WhoAm 90*
Coleman, Michael Patrick 1939- *St&PR 91*
Coleman, Miles 1931- *St&PR 91*
Coleman, Milton *BioIn 16*
Coleman, Monroe 1918- *WhoAm 90*
Coleman, Morton 1939- *WhoAm 90*
Coleman, Nancy C. *WhoWrEP 89*
Coleman, Nancy Pees 1955- *WhoAmW 91*
Coleman, Nathan W 1915- *BiDrAPA 89*
Coleman, Nelda Louise Spears 1943- *WhoSSW 91*
Coleman, Norman Arthur 1923- *WhoWor 91*
Coleman, Ornette *BioIn 16*
Coleman, Ornette 1930- *ConMus 5 [port], DrBlPA 90, OxCPMus, WhoAm 90, WorAlBi*
Coleman, Patricia Anne 1943- *WhoAmW 91*
Coleman, Paul Dare 1918- *WhoAm 90*
Coleman, Paul David 1927- *WhoAm 90*
Coleman, Paul Jerome, Jr. 1932- *WhoAm 90*
Coleman, Paul Timothy 1951- *WhoSSW 91*
Coleman, Pauline Hodgkinson *AuBYP 90*
Coleman, Peter James *BiDrAPA 89*
Coleman, Peter M. 1941- *St&PR 91*
Coleman, Peter Tali 1919- *WhoAm 90*
Coleman, Ralf 1898- *EarBlAP*
Coleman, Ralph Edward 1943- *WhoAm 90*
Coleman, Ralph P 1892-1968 *WhoAmA 91N*
Coleman, Randolph G. 1934- *St&PR 91*
Coleman, Randy Lee 1951- *St&PR 91*
Coleman, Ray 1922- *Ballpl 90*
Coleman, Rexford Lee 1930- *WhoAm 90, WhoWor 91*
Coleman, Richard Daly 1932- *St&PR 91*
Coleman, Rip 1931- *Ballpl 90*
Coleman, Robert E. 1925- *St&PR 91*
Coleman, Robert Griffin 1923- *WhoAm 90*
Coleman, Robert Lee 1929- *WhoAm 90, WhoWor 91*
Coleman, Robert Marshall 1925- *WhoAm 90*
Coleman, Robert S. 1953- *St&PR 91*
Coleman, Robert Winston 1942- *WhoAm 90*
Coleman, Rod 1957- *St&PR 91*
Coleman, Roger 1937- *ODwPR 91*
Coleman, Roger Dixon 1915- *WhoWor 91*
Coleman, Roger Lewis *BiDrAPA 89*
Coleman, Roger Lewis 1945- *WhoE 91, WhoEmL 91*
Coleman, Roger W. 1929- *St&PR 91, WhoAm 90*
Coleman, Ronald 1946- *ODwPR 91*
Coleman, Ronald D. 1941- *WhoAm 90, WhoSSW 91*
Coleman, Rosa Lee 1916- *WhoWrEP 89*
Coleman, Roy Melvin 1930- *BiDrAPA 89, WhoE 91*
Coleman, Ruth D. *BioIn 16*
Coleman, Sandra Sloan 1943- *WhoAm 90*
Coleman, Sheldon *BioIn 16*
Coleman, Sheldon, Jr. 1953- *News 90 [port]*
Coleman, Sheldon C. *St&PR 91*
Coleman, Sheldon Coffin, Jr. 1953- *WhoAm 90*
Coleman, Sheri Lynn 1960- *WhoAmW 91*
Coleman, Sherman Smoot 1922- *WhoAm 90*
Coleman, Sidney Richard 1937- *WhoAm 90*
Coleman, Stephen J *BiDrAPA 89*
Coleman, Stephen M. 1911- *WhoWrEP 89*
Coleman, Steve *BioIn 16*
Coleman, Steven Eugene 1955- *WhoSSW 91*
Coleman, Susan Wilson 1953- *WhoEmL 91*
Coleman, T.W. 1938- *St&PR 91*
Coleman, Thomas Britt 1952- *WhoSSW 91*
Coleman, Thomas Young 1949- *WhoEmL 91*
Coleman, Timothy John 1958- *WhoEmL 91*
Coleman, Timothy Louis 1946- *WhoSSW 91*
Coleman, Vince 1960- *Ballpl 90*
Coleman, Vince 1961- *WorAlBi*
Coleman, Vincent Robert 1925- *St&PR 91*
Coleman, Wade Hampton, III 1932- *WhoAm 90*
Coleman, Walter *BioIn 16*
Coleman, Walter Carpenter, Jr. 1928- *St&PR 91*
Coleman, Wanda 1946- *WhoWrEP 89*
Coleman, Warren *EarBlAP*
Coleman, William 1766-1829 *BioIn 16*
Coleman, William 1934-1988 *BioIn 16*
Coleman, William Dwight 1950- *IntWWM 90*
Coleman, William Edwin *BiDrAPA 89*
Coleman, William L. 1938- *BioIn 16*
Coleman, William Patrick, III 1948- *WhoEmL 91*
Coleman, William Stephen 1829-1904 *PenDiDA 89*
Coleman, William T. 1943- *ODwPR 91*
Coleman, William Thaddeus, Jr. 1920- *BiDrUSE 89, WhoAm 90*
Coleman, Willie *BioIn 16*
Coleman, Winifred Ellen 1932- *WhoAmW 91*
Coleman-Johnson, Debra Lynn 1966- *WhoAmW 91*
Coleman Wood, Krista Ann 1956- *WhoAmW 91*
Colen, B. D. 1946- *WhoAm 90*
Colen, Bradford Emil *BiDrAPA 89*
Colen, Donald Jerome 1917- *WhoAm 90*
Colenbrander, Theodorus 1841-1930 *PenDiDA 89*
Colenda, Christopher C, III 1952- *BiDrAPA 89*
Colenso, Frances 1849-1887 *FemiCLE*
Colenso, John William 1814-1883 *BioIn 16*
Coler, Myron Abraham 1913- *WhoAm 90, WhoWor 91*
Coleridge, Christabel 1843-1921 *FemiCLE*
Coleridge, Hartley 1796-1849 *DcLB 96 [port]*
Coleridge, Mary 1861-1907 *DcLB 98 [port], FemiCLE*
Coleridge, Mary Elizabeth 1861-1907 *BioIn 16*
Coleridge, Nicholas 1957- *BioIn 16*
Coleridge, Samuel Taylor 1772-1834 *BioIn 16, DcLB 93 [port], EncO&P 3, EncPaPR 91, WorAlBi, WrPh*
Coleridge, Sara 1802-1852 *BioIn 16, FemiCLE*
Coleridge-Taylor, Samuel 1875-1912 *DrBlPA 90*
Coles, Allen E. 1927- *St&PR 91*
Coles, Anna Louise Bailey 1925- *WhoAm 90, WhoAmW 91*
Coles, Charles, Jr. 1922- *St&PR 91*
Coles, Cynthia Ann *BiDrAPA 89*
Coles, Cyril Henry 1899-1965 *TwCCr&M 91*
Coles, Darnell 1962- *Ballpl 90*
Coles, Donald Earl 1924- *WhoAm 90*
Coles, Erostine *EarBlAP*
Coles, Honi 1911- *DrBlPA 90*
Coles, James Stacy 1913- *St&PR 91*
Coles, Jane Ellen 1952- *WhoAmW 91*
Coles, Jeffrey Link 1957- *WhoE 91*
Coles, Lorraine McClellan 1929- *WhoAmW 91*
Coles, Manning *SpyFic, TwCCr&M 91*
Coles, Manning 1899-1965 *WorAlBi*
Coles, Martin Robert 1929- *WhoAm 90*
Coles, Richard Warren 1939- *WhoAm 90*
Coles, Robert *BioIn 16*
Coles, Robert 1929- *ConAu 32NR, WhoAm 90, WhoWrEP 89, WorAlBi*
Coles, Robert Martin 1929- *AuBYP 90*
Coles, Robert S. 1920-1989 *BioIn 16*
Coles, Robert Traynham 1929- *WhoAm 90*
Coles, Thelma 1952- *WhoAmA 91*
Coles, Wesley Obert, III 1965- *WhoWrEP 89*
Coles, William Henry *WhoAm 90*
Coles, Zaida 1933- *DrBlPA 90*
Colescott, Robert 1925- *BioIn 16*
Colescott, Robert H 1925- *WhoAmA 91*
Colescott, Warrington W 1921- *WhoAmA 91*
Colescott, Warrington Wickham 1921- *WhoAm 90*
Colet, John 1467?-1519 *BioIn 16*
Colet, Louise Revoli 1810-1876 *EncCoWW*
Colett, Ilse Vivien *BiDrAPA 89*
Coletta, Carol C. *ODwPR 91*
Coletta, Paolo Enrico 1916- *ConAu 31NR*
Colette 1873-1954 *BioIn 16, ConAu 131, FemiCLE, MajTwCW, WorAlBi*
Colette 1952- *WhoAmA 91*
Colette, Deborah *BioIn 16*
Colette, Sidonie-Gabrielle 1873-1954 *EncCoWW*
Coletti, Chiara *WhoE 91*
Coletti, John Anthony 1952- *WhoE 91, WhoEmL 91, WhoWor 91*
Coletti, Joseph Arthur 1898-1973 *WhoAmA 91N*
Coletti, Paul Anthony 1958- *WhoEmL 91*
Coletti, Ralph Michael 1931- *WhoSSW 91*
Coley, Betty 1933- *WhoAm 90*
Coley, Betty Ann 1933- *WhoSSW 91*
Coley, Bill A. 1929- *St&PR 91*
Coley, Carol Ann 1947- *WhoAmW 91*
Coley, Caroline Rita 1962- *WhoAmW 91*
Coley, Dennis Howard 1945- *St&PR 91, WhoAm 90*
Coley, Eva Marie 1943- *WhoAmW 91*
Coley, Franklin Luke, Jr. 1958- *WhoEmL 91*
Coley, Mary P S 1926- *BiDrAPA 89*
Coley, Philip B. 1952- *WhoEmL 91*
Coley, Robert Bernard 1951- *WhoEmL 91, WhoWor 91*
Coley, Silas Bodie, Jr. 1934- *BiDrAPA 89*
Coley, Sussan Shahin 1957- *WhoE 91*
Coley, Thomas *BioIn 16*
Coley, Travis Carl 1947- *WhoEmL 91*
Colfax, Schuyler 1823-1885 *BiDrUSE 89, WorAlBi*
Colfer, Randy *BioIn 16*
Colfin, Bruce Elliott 1951- *WhoE 91, WhoEmL 91*
Colford, Francis Xavier 1952- *St&PR 91, WhoAm 90*
Colgan, Bill *BioIn 16*
Colgan, Charles Joseph 1926- *WhoSSW 91*
Colgan, Charles Thomas 1940- *WhoAm 90*
Colgan, Harry J *BiDrAPA 89*
Colgan, Michael Anthony 1950- *WhoWor 91*
Colgan, P. Barry 1930- *St&PR 91*
Colgan, Peter David 1933- *St&PR 91*
Colgan, Sumner 1934- *WhoE 91*
Colgan, William B. 1920- *WhoWrEP 89*
Colgate, Craig 1912-1989 *BioIn 16*
Colgate, Doris Eleanor 1941- *WhoAmW 91, WhoSSW 91*
Colgate, Kathleen Bishop 1953- *WhoEmL 91*
Colgate, Stephen 1935- *WhoE 91*
Colgate, William 1783-1857 *BioIn 16, WorAlBi*
Colglazier, John Perre 1936- *St&PR 91*
Colgrass, Michael 1932- *IntWWM 90, PenDiMP A*
Colgrass, Michael Charles 1932- *WhoAm 90, WhoE 91*
Colhoun, Howard Post 1935- *WhoAm 90*
Colhoun, J.L.A. 1920- *St&PR 91*
Coli, Guido John 1921- *WhoAm 90*
Colicos, John 1928- *ConTFT 8, OxCCanT*
Colin, Georges 1921- *IntWWM 90*
Colin, Georgia T *WhoAmA 91*
Colin, Georgia Talmey *WhoAmW 91*
Colin, Jean-Francois 1954- *WhoWor 91*
Colin, Jeanne 1924- *IntWWM 90*
Colin, John A. 1914- *St&PR 91*
Colin, Kim Renee 1957- *WhoEmL 91*
Colin, Lawrence 1931- *WhoAm 90*
Colin, Paul 1892-1985 *ConDes 90*
Colin, Philip G. 1902-1989 *BioIn 16*
Colin, Ralph Frederick 1900- *WhoAmA 91N*
Colina, Armando G 1935- *WhoAmA 91*
Coling, Michael L. 1947- *St&PR 91*
Colini, Ilona *IntWWM 90*
Colinon, Maurice 1922- *EncO&P 3*
Colis, George P. 1954- *St&PR 91*
Colish, Marcia Lillian 1937- *WhoAm 90*
Colizoli, Lucia De Leon 1947- *BiDrAPA 89*
Colker, Edward 1927- *WhoAm 90, WhoAmA 91*
Colker, Marvin Leonard 1927- *WhoAm 90*
Colker, Richard Frank 1945- *WhoWor 91*
Coll, Alberto Raoul 1955- *WhoEmL 91*

Coll, Daniel E. 1936- *St&PR 91*
Coll, Edward Girard, Jr. 1934- *WhoAm 90, WhoE 91*
Coll, Elizabeth Esteve- *BioIn 16*
Coll, Helen F. 1921- *WhoAm 90*
Coll, Ivonne *WhoHisp 91*
Coll, John Peter, Jr. 1943- *WhoAm 90*
Colladay, Martin Grimes 1925- *St&PR 91*
Colladay, Robert S. 1940- *WhoAm 90*
Collado, Emilio Gabriel 1910- *WhoAm 90, WhoWor 91*
Collado, Lisa 1944- *WhoAmA 91*
Collado, Raymond 1915- *BiDrAPA 89*
Collaert, Hans *PenDiDA 89*
Collamer, Jacob 1791-1865 *BiDrUSE 89*
Collamore, Thomas Jones 1959- *WhoAm 90*
Collan, Yrjo Urho 1941- *WhoWor 91*
Collar, Leo Linford 1930- *WhoAm 90*
Collard, Jean Philippe 1948- *IntWWM 90*
Collard, Joseph Arthur 1938- *WhoSSW 91*
Collard, Joseph Eugene, Jr. 1949- *WhoSSW 91*
Collard, Thomas Albert 1942- *WhoE 91*
Collard, Thomas Hardy, Jr. 1927- *WhoSSW 91*
Collarini Schlossberg, Antoinette Marie 1950- *WhoEmL 91*
Collas, Juan Garduno, Jr. 1932- *WhoAm 90*
Collazo, Carlos Erick 1956- *WhoAmA 91*
Collazo, Carlos Roberto *BiDrAPA 89*
Collazo, Francisco Jose 1928- *WhoHisp 91*
Collazo, Frank, Jr. 1931- *WhoHisp 91*
Collazo, Joe Manuel 1945- *WhoHisp 91*
Collazo, Jose Antonio 1943- *WhoAm 90, WhoHisp 91*
Collazo, Ramiro 1939- *St&PR 91*
Collazo, Salvador 1948- *WhoHisp 91*
Collazo-Camunas, Rafael E 1929- *BiDrAPA 89*
Collazo-Levy, Dora *BioIn 16*
Collbohm, Franklin R. *NewYTBS 90*
Collbohm, Franklin R. 1907-1990 *BioIn 16*
Collcutt, Martin Charles 1939- *WhoAm 90*
Collcutt, Thomas Edward 1840-1924 *PenDiDA 89*
Colledge, Charles Hopson 1911- *WhoAm 90*
Colleen, Robert Gene 1930- *St&PR 91*
Collen, Desire J. 1943- *WhoWor 91*
Collen, Jean McIntyre Campbell 1943- *IntWWM 90*
Collen, Morris Frank 1913- *WhoAm 90, WhoWor 91*
Collen, Robert Philip 1928- *St&PR 91*
Collen, Sheldon Orrin 1922- *WhoAm 90, WhoWor 91*
Collens, Lewis Morton 1938- *WhoAm 90*
Coller, Gary Hayes 1952- *WhoEmL 91*
Colleran, Kevin 1941- *WhoWor 91*
Colleran, L.C. 1922- *St&PR 91*
Collert, Fritz Anders Goran 1937- *WhoWor 91*
Collery, Arnold P. 1927-1989 *BioIn 16*
Collery, Paula 1954- *WhoAmA 91*
Collery, Peter Mitchell 1959- *St&PR 91, WhoE 91*
Colles, Gertrude 1869-1957 *WhoAmA 91N*
Collet, Ninon Germain 1959- *BiDrAPA 89*
Collett, Camilla 1813-1895 *DcScanL, EncCoWW*
Collett, David *NewAgMG*
Collett, Farrell Reuben 1907- *WhoAmA 91*
Collett, Joan *WhoAm 90, WhoAmW 91*
Collett, John Frederick 1951- *St&PR 91*
Collett, Ray E. 1903- *St&PR 91*
Collett, Robert Clement 1928- *St&PR 91*
Collett, Wayne Neville 1941- *WhoAm 90*
Collett-Sutton, Faye 1944- *WhoAmW 91*
Colletta, Patricia R. 1954- *WhoAmW 91*
Colletta, Richard A. 1952- *St&PR 91*
Colletta, Vincent Joseph 1923- *WhoE 91*
Collette, Alfred Thomas 1922- *WhoAm 90*
Collette, Buddy 1921- *OxCPMus*
Collette, Carolyn Penney 1945- *WhoAmW 91*
Collette, Christine 1947- *ConAu 132*
Collette, Craig D. 1942- *St&PR 91*
Collette, Frances Madelyn 1947- *WhoAmW 91*
Collette, Kevin J. 1952- *WhoEmL 91*
Collette, Renee Ann 1951- *WhoEmL 91*
Collette, Richard J. 1947- *St&PR 91*
Collette, Roderick Edward 1934- *St&PR 91*
Collette, Susan Harter 1948- *WhoAmW 91*
Collette, W.R. 1920- *St&PR 91*
Colletti, Anthony Bernard 1917- *WhoE 91*
Colley, Ann C 1940- *ConAu 30NR*
Colley, Carolyn Virginia 1926- *St&PR 91*
Colley, David 1940- *ConDes 90*
Colley, Don Pedro *DrBIPA 90*
Colley, John Leonard, Jr. 1930- *WhoAm 90*
Colley, Linda 1949- *ConAu 130*
Colley, Nathaniel Sextus 1918- *WhoAm 90*
Colley, Stephen Gallo 1953- *WhoEmL 91*
Colley, Thomas *EncO&P 3*
Colley, Thomas Neil 1949- *St&PR 91*
Colley, William, Jr 1910-1984 *WhoAmA 91N*
Colli, Bart Joseph 1948- *WhoEmL 91*
Colliander, Fritiof Tito 1904- *DcScanL*
Collias, Elsie Cole 1920- *WhoAmW 91*
Collias, Nicholas E 1914- *ConAu 131*
Collie, David Edwin 1956- *WhoSSW 91*
Collie, Norman 1859-1942 *BioIn 16*
Collier, Alan Caswell 1911- *WhoAm 90, WhoAmA 91*
Collier, Alberta 1911-1987 *WhoAmA 91N*
Collier, Barbara Lee 1959- *WhoAmW 91*
Collier, Barron G. 1873-1939 *WorAlBi*
Collier, Birtan Aka 1944- *WhoE 91*
Collier, Charles Arthur, Jr. 1930- *WhoAm 90*
Collier, Charlotte Mae Meier 1947- *WhoAmW 91*
Collier, Christopher 1930- *AuBYP 90, BioIn 16, ConAu 33NR*
Collier, Clarence Robert 1919- *WhoAm 90*
Collier, David Alan 1947- *WhoEmL 91*
Collier, David Franklin 1919- *WhoSSW 91*
Collier, Edmund *AuBYP 90*
Collier, Ellen Clodfelter 1927- *WhoAmW 91, WhoE 91*
Collier, Ethel 1903- *AuBYP 90*
Collier, Felton Moreland 1924- *WhoAm 90, WhoWor 91*
Collier, Fred 1923- *BioIn 16*
Collier, Gaylan Jane 1924- *WhoAm 90, WhoSSW 91*
Collier, Gilman Frederick 1929- *IntWWM 90*
Collier, Graham 1937- *OxCPMus*
Collier, Haywood Maurice 1955- *WhoSSW 91*
Collier, Herbert Isaac 1924- *WhoSSW 91*
Collier, Herman Edward, Jr. 1927- *WhoAm 90*
Collier, Holt *BioIn 16*
Collier, James Bruce, Jr. 1938- *WhoSSW 91*
Collier, James L. 1928- *ConAu 33NR*
Collier, James Lincoln 1928- *AuBYP 90, BioIn 16*
Collier, James Mitchell 1943- *WhoAmA 91*
Collier, James Warren 1940- *WhoAm 90*
Collier, Jane *WhoWrEP 89*
Collier, Jane 1710-1754? *FemiCLE*
Collier, Jeannine Henderson 1956- *WhoAmW 91*
Collier, John *BioIn 16*
Collier, John 1901-1980 *TwCCr&M 91*
Collier, John Robert 1939- *WhoSSW 91*
Collier, Julia E. *BioIn 16*
Collier, June *WhoAmW 91*
Collier, Ken 1944- *St&PR 91*
Collier, Leo Nathan 1884-1901 *WhoAmA 91N*
Collier, Marie 1926-1971 *PenDiMP*
Collier, Mary *BioIn 16*
Collier, Mary 1679-1762? *FemiCLE*
Collier, Mary 1690-1762? *DcLB 95*
Collier, Matthew Samuel 1957- *WhoAm 90*
Collier, Maxie Tyrone 1945- *BiDrAPA 89*
Collier, Michael Thomas 1950- *WhoE 91*
Collier, Miles Carnes *BioIn 16*
Collier, Nathan Morris 1924- *IntWWM 90*
Collier, Norma J. *ODwPR 91*
Collier, Norma Jean *WhoAmW 91*
Collier, Oscar 1924- *WhoAm 90*
Collier, Peter 1939- *BioIn 16*
Collier, Richard Earl 1927- *WhoSSW 91*
Collier, Robert Charles 1955- *WhoE 91*
Collier, Robert Oran 1945- *BiDrAPA 89*
Collier, Rodney M. 1935- *St&PR 91*
Collier, Shelley Hale, Jr. 1928- *WhoSSW 91*
Collier, Steven 1942- *SmATA 61 [port]*
Collier, Steven Edward 1952- *WhoSSW 91*
Collier, Susan 1938- *ConDes 90*
Collier, Susan/Campbell, Sarah *ConDes 90*
Collier, Thomas Casher, Jr. 1961- *WhoSSW 91*
Collier, Thomas J. 1938- *St&PR 91*
Collier, Tom W. 1948- *WhoWor 91*
Collier, William J., III 1953- *WhoEmL 91*
Collier, Zena 1926- *WhoWrEP 89*
Collier-Evans, Demetra Frances 1937- *WhoAmW 91*
Colliflower, Michael A. 1954- *St&PR 91*
Colligan, Francis X *BiDrAPA 89*
Colligan, Jack J. 1929- *St&PR 91*
Colligan, John 1951- *St&PR 91*
Colligan, Joseph F *BiDrAPA 89*
Colligan, Richard Vincent, Jr. 1951- *WhoAm 90*
Collin, Arthur Edwin 1929- *WhoAm 90*
Collin, Hedvig *AuBYP 90*
Collin, Richard Harvey 1932- *WhoSSW 91*
Collin, Robert Emanuel 1928- *WhoAm 90*
Collin, Thomas James 1949- *WhoEmL 91*
Colling, David John 1950- *WhoAm 90*
Colling, Mary 1805- *FemiCLE*
Collings, Albert Frederick 1941- *St&PR 91*
Collings, Betty 1934- *WhoAmA 91*
Collings, Charles L. 1925- *St&PR 91*
Collings, Charles LeRoy 1925- *WhoAm 90*
Collings, Ellsworth 1887- *AuBYP 90*
Collings, Lori Jo 1959- *WhoAmW 91*
Collings, Michael R 1947- *ConAu 30NR*
Collings, Michael Robert 1947- *WhoWrEP 89*
Collings, Ray Eugene 1949- *WhoSSW 91*
Collington, Peter *AuBYP 90, BioIn 16*
Collingwood, Charles 1917-1985 *BioIn 16*
Collingwood, Lawrance 1887-1982 *PenDiMP*
Collingwood, R. G. 1889-1943 *BioIn 16*
Collingwood, Richard J. 1939- *St&PR 91*
Collingwood, Robin George 1889-1943 *BioIn 16*
Collinot, Eugene-Victor *PenDiDA 89*
Collins & Milazzo *WhoAmA 91*
Collins, Alan 1928- *ConAu 132*
Collins, Albert 1932- *ConMus 4 [port]*
Collins, Albert 1944- *St&PR 91*
Collins, Allen *BioIn 16, NewYTBS 90*
Collins, Allen Howard 1942- *BiDrAPA 89*
Collins, An *BiDEWW, FemiCLE*
Collins, Andrew J. 1953- *WhoSSW 91*
Collins, Anita Marguerite 1947- *WhoAmW 91*
Collins, Ann Elizabeth Averitt 1934- *WhoAmW 91*
Collins, Anne 1943- *IntWWM 90*
Collins, Anthony 1893-1963 *PenDiMP*
Collins, Arlene Rycombel 1940- *WhoAmW 91, WhoE 91*
Collins, Arthur Cowan *BiDrAPA 89*
Collins, Arthur Worth, Jr. 1929- *ConAu 131*
Collins, Atwood, III 1947- *WhoEmL 91*
Collins, Barbara Geraghty 1948- *WhoAmW 91*
Collins, Barbara Jo 1958- *WhoAmW 91*
Collins, Barbara-Rose 1939- *WhoAmW 91*
Collins, Barret Hunt 1943- *St&PR 91*
Collins, Ben Arnold 1959- *BiDrAPA 89*
Collins, Bert 1934- *St&PR 91, WhoAm 90*
Collins, Bettye Fine 1936- *WhoAmW 91*
Collins, Bootsy *BioIn 16*
Collins, Brian Alan 1947- *WhoSSW 91*
Collins, Bruce Dennis 1951- *WhoE 91*
Collins, Bud *ConAu 131*
Collins, Byron Griggs 1939- *WhoSSW 91*
Collins, Candace Brown 1950- *WhoAmW 91*
Collins, Cardiss 1931- *BlkAmsC [port], WhoAm 90, WhoAmW 91*
Collins, Carl Russell, Jr 1926- *WhoAm 90*
Collins, Carter Compton 1925- *WhoAm 90*
Collins, Carvel *NewYTBS 90*
Collins, Carvel 1912-1990 *BioIn 16, ConAu 131*
Collins, Catherine French 1955- *WhoAmW 91*
Collins, Cecil 1908-1989 *AnObit 1989, BioIn 16*
Collins, Charles, Jr. 1954- *WhoSSW 91*
Collins, Charles Floyd 1928- *St&PR 91*
Collins, Charles Frederick 1916- *IntWWM 90*
Collins, Charles R. 1934- *St&PR 91*
Collins, Charles Williams 1954- *BiDrAPA 89*
Collins, Christie Woolcock 1906- *WhoAmW 91*
Collins, Christiane C *WhoAmA 91*
Collins, Christopher Carl 1950- *WhoE 91, WhoEmL 91*
Collins, Copp 1914- *WhoAm 90*
Collins, Craig Allan 1959- *WhoWor 91*
Collins, Curtis Allan 1940- *WhoAm 90*
Collins, Cyrus S. 1917- *St&PR 91*
Collins, Cyrus Stickney 1917- *WhoAm 90*
Collins, Dan 1951- *ODwPR 91*
Collins, Dan 1954- *WhoAmA 91*
Collins, Dana J. 1956- *St&PR 91*
Collins, Dana Jon 1956- *WhoEmL 91*
Collins, Daniel Allen *BiDrAPA 89*
Collins, Daniel F. 1942- *St&PR 91*
Collins, Daniel W. 1946- *WhoAm 90*
Collins, Dave 1952- *Ballpl 90*
Collins, David Browning 1922- *WhoAm 90*
Collins, David Edward 1949- *IntWWM 90*
Collins, David Monroe *BioIn 16*
Collins, David Raymond 1940- *AuBYP 90, WhoWrEP 89*
Collins, Dean T 1928- *BiDrAPA 89*
Collins, Deborah Russell 1958- *WhoAmW 91*
Collins, Delano M 1934- *BiDrAPA 89*
Collins, Dennis Arthur 1940- *WhoAm 90*
Collins, Diana Josephine 1944- *WhoAmW 91*
Collins, Diana Marie 1958- *WhoAmW 91*
Collins, Diane Elizabeth 1948- *WhoAmW 91*
Collins, Don Cary 1951- *WhoEmL 91*
Collins, Donald Francis 1928- *WhoE 91*
Collins, Donald Henry 1953- *WhoSSW 91*
Collins, Donald L. 1918- *St&PR 91*
Collins, Donald Lynn 1952- *St&PR 91*
Collins, Donald Ogden 1934- *WhoAm 90*
Collins, Doris 1918?- *EncO&P 3*
Collins, Dorothy Walker 1911- *St&PR 91*
Collins, Douglas Charles 1953- *St&PR 91*
Collins, Earlean *WhoAmW 91*
Collins, Eddie 1887-1951 *Ballpl 90 [port]*
Collins, Eddie Lee 1936- *WhoE 91*
Collins, Edgar Ernest 1941- *BiDrAPA 89*
Collins, Edward James, Jr. 1933- *WhoAm 90*
Collins, Eileen Louise 1942- *WhoAmW 91, WhoE 91*
Collins, Elisabeth B *BiDrAPA 89*
Collins, Eliza G. C. 1938- *ConAu 129*
Collins, Fleda Mae 1935- *WhoSSW 91*
Collins, Francis Winfield 1927- *WhoE 91*
Collins, Frank Charles, Jr. 1927- *WhoAm 90, WhoSSW 91*
Collins, Gary *BioIn 16*
Collins, Gary 1934- *WhoWrEP 89*
Collins, Gary Dean 1951- *WhoEmL 91*
Collins, George J. 1940- *St&PR 91*
Collins, George Joseph *WhoAm 90*
Collins, George R 1917- *WhoAmA 91*
Collins, George W. 1837- *AmLegL*
Collins, George Washington 1925-1972 *BlkAmsC [port]*
Collins, Gerald Chester 1946- *WhoEmL 91*
Collins, Gerald E. 1924- *St&PR 91*
Collins, Geraldine Teresa 1935- *WhoSSW 91*
Collins, Gerard 1938- *WhoWor 91*
Collins, Gladys *BioIn 16*
Collins, Gordon Scott, Jr. 1942- *St&PR 91*
Collins, Gregory Bruce 1945- *BiDrAPA 89*
Collins, Gretchen M *BiDrAPA 89*
Collins, Gwendolyn Beth 1943- *WhoAmW 91, WhoSSW 91*
Collins, Harker 1924- *St&PR 91, WhoAm 90, WhoWor 91*
Collins, Harry David 1931- *WhoSSW 91, WhoWor 91*
Collins, Harvey Arnold 1927- *WhoAmA 91*
Collins, Helen Johnson 1911- *WhoAmW 91*
Collins, Henry Hill, Jr. 1907-1961 *AuBYP 90*
Collins, Henry James, III 1927- *WhoAm 90*
Collins, Herschel Douglas 1928- *WhoAm 90*
Collins, Howard Burton 1946- *St&PR 91*
Collins, Howard F 1922- *WhoAmA 91*
Collins, Hub 1864-1892 *Ballpl 90*
Collins, Hunt *AuBYP 90, MajTwCW, TwCCr&M 91*
Collins, J. Michael 1935- *WhoAm 90, WhoE 91*
Collins, J.P. 1942- *St&PR 91*
Collins, Jackie *BioIn 16, WorAlBi*
Collins, Jackie 1941- *BestSel 90-4 [port]*
Collins, Jacqueline *BiDrAPA 89*
Collins, Jacqueline Wight 1930- *WhoAmW 91*
Collins, James A. 1926- *St&PR 91*
Collins, James Alexander, II 1944- *WhoAm 90*
Collins, James Andrew 1964- *WhoSSW 91*
Collins, James Arthur 1926- *WhoAm 90*
Collins, James Carstairs 1930- *St&PR 91*
Collins, James Evans 1936- *BiDrAPA 89*
Collins, James F. 1905-1989 *BioIn 16*
Collins, James Foster 1922- *WhoAm 90*
Collins, James Francis 1953- *WhoSSW 91*
Collins, James Harold Lee 1946- *WhoEmL 91*
Collins, James Ignatius 1949- *WhoEmL 91*
Collins, James Lawton, Jr. 1917- *WhoAm 90, WhoSSW 91*
Collins, James Lincoln, Sr. *BiDrAPA 89*
Collins, James M. 1916-1989 *BioIn 16*
Collins, James P. 1947- *ODwPR 91*
Collins, James Pittenger 1929- *WhoAm 90*
Collins, James Thomas 1946- *WhoSSW 91*
Collins, James William 1942- *WhoAm 90*
Collins, Janet 1917- *DrBIPA 90*
Collins, Java L. 1960- *WhoAmW 91*
Collins, Jeffrey Hamilton 1930- *WhoAm 90*
Collins, Jeffrey Townes *BiDrAPA 89*
Collins, Jeremiah James 1931- *St&PR 91*
Collins, Jerome A *BiDrAPA 89*
Collins, Jerry Allan 1936- *WhoAm 90*
Collins, Jess 1934- *WhoAmA 91*
Collins, Jill *ODwPR 91*
Collins, Jill Harrison 1957- *WhoAmW 91, WhoEmL 91*
Collins, Jim 1934- *WhoAmA 91*
Collins, Jimmy *Ballpl 90*
Collins, Jimmy 1870-1943 *Ballpl 90 [port]*
Collins, Joan *BioIn 16*
Collins, Joan 1933- *ConTFT 8 [port]*
Collins, Joan Henrietta 1933- *WhoAm 90, WhoAmW 91, WhoWor 91*

Collins, Jocko 1905-1986 Ballpl 90
Collins, Joe 1909- St&PR 91
Collins, Joe 1922- Ballpl 90
Collins, Joe 1922-1989 BioIn 16
Collins, John BioIn 16
Collins, John 1905-1982 DcNaB 1981
Collins, John 1945- WhoWor 91
Collins, John G. 1936- St&PR 91
Collins, John Ireland 1926-1982 WhoAmA 91N
Collins, John Joseph 1921- WhoWor 91
Collins, John Joseph, Jr. 1934- WhoAm 90
Collins, John M 1921- ConAu 31NR
Collins, John Patrick 1942- WhoWor 91
Collins, John Roger 1941- St&PR 91, WhoAm 90, WhoSSW 91
Collins, John Timothy BioIn 16
Collins, Jose 1887-1958 OxCPMus
Collins, Joseph Bernard 1953- WhoE 91
Collins, Joseph Edmund 1855-1892 DcCanB 12
Collins, Joseph J. 1944- WhoAm 90
Collins, Joseph Thomas 1939- WhoWrEP 89
Collins, Joseph V. 1936- St&PR 91, WhoAm 90
Collins, Joy Hanft 1931- WhoE 91
Collins, Judy 1939- ConMus 4 [port], OxCPMus, WorAlBi
Collins, Judy Marjorie 1939- WhoAm 90
Collins, Julie 1959- ConAu 131
Collins, Karen Linda 1959- WhoE 91
Collins, Kathleen BioIn 16
Collins, Kathleen 1953- WhoE 91, WhoWor 91
Collins, Kathleen Dawn 1954- BiDrAPA 89
Collins, Kathleen Elizabeth 1951- WhoAmW 91
Collins, Kenneth 1935- IntWWM 90
Collins, Kenneth Bruce 1939- WhoAm 90
Collins, Kenneth E. 1926- WhoWor 91
Collins, Kent Howes 1940- St&PR 91
Collins, Kevin Joseph 1939- St&PR 91
Collins, Kreigh EncACom
Collins, Kreigh 1908-1974 WhoAmA 91N
Collins, Larry 1929- WhoAm 90
Collins, Larry Richard 1945- WhoAmA 91, WhoEmL 91
Collins, Larry Wayne 1937- St&PR 91
Collins, Lee 1901-1960 BioIn 16
Collins, Lena Vestal 1933- WhoAmW 91
Collins, Leroy, Jr. 1934- WhoAm 90
Collins, Lester Albertson 1914- WhoAm 90
Collins, Linda Carol 1952- WhoSSW 91
Collins, Lisa 1920- WhoAmW 91
Collins, Lorin Cone, Jr. 1848-1940 AmLegL
Collins, Lottie 1866-1910 OxCPMus
Collins, Louis BioIn 16
Collins, Lowell Daunt 1924- WhoAmA 91
Collins, Lucy Emerson 1942- BiDrAPA 89, WhoE 91
Collins, Mabel 1851-1922? EncO&P 3
Collins, Mabelle S BiDrAPA 89
Collins, Marcus E., Sr. 1927- WhoSSW 91
Collins, Margaret Anne BiDrAPA 89
Collins, Margaret Helen 1950- WhoEmL 91
Collins, Maribeth Wilson 1918- WhoAm 90
Collins, Marilee Fassero 1945- WhoSSW 91
Collins, Mark Jerome BiDrAPA 89
Collins, Marshall J., Jr. 1941- St&PR 91
Collins, Martha 1940- WhoWrEP 89
Collins, Martha Layne 1936- WhoAm 90, WhoAmW 91
Collins, Marva BioIn 16
Collins, Marva Deloise Nettles 1936- WhoAm 90, WhoAmW 91
Collins, Mary 1940- WhoAm 90, WhoAmW 91, WhoE 91
Collins, Mary Alice 1937- WhoAmW 91
Collins, Mary Beth 1925- WhoAmW 91
Collins, Mary Elizabeth 1953- WhoAmW 91
Collins, Mary Ellen Kennedy 1939- WhoWor 91
Collins, Max Allan 1948- TwCCr&M 91
Collins, Maya Janice 1956- WhoSSW 91
Collins, Merle FemiCLE
Collins, Michael ODwPR 91, WhoWrEP 89
Collins, Michael 1890-1922 WorAlBi
Collins, Michael 1924- BioIn 16, TwCCr&M 91
Collins, Michael 1930- BioIn 16, WhoAm 90, WhoWor 91, WorAlBi
Collins, Michael 1962- IntWWM 90
Collins, Michael Augustus 1948- IntWWM 90
Collins, Michael B. 1930- IntWWM 90
Collins, Michael Edward, Jr. 1957- WhoEmL 91
Collins, Michael James 1944- WhoAm 90
Collins, Michael Ray 1958- WhoSSW 91
Collins, Michael Sean 1951- WhoEmL 91
Collins, Miki 1959- ConAu 131
Collins, Monica Ann 1951- WhoAm 90
Collins, Nancy Elizabeth 1954- WhoAmW 91
Collins, Nancy M BiDrAPA 89
Collins, Natalie A. WhoAmW 91
Collins, Norman Richard 1907-1982 DcNaB 1981
Collins, Pat 1896-1960 Ballpl 90
Collins, Pat Lowery 1932- WhoWrEP 89
Collins, Paul ODwPR 91
Collins, Paul 1936- WhoAmA 91
Collins, Paul John 1936- WhoAm 90, WhoWor 91
Collins, Pauline BioIn 16
Collins, Pauline 1940- ConTFT 8, WhoAm 90, WhoAmW 91, WhoWor 91
Collins, Phil BiDrAPA 89, EncPR&S 89, WhoAm 90
Collins, Phil 1901-1948 Ballpl 90
Collins, Phil 1951- OxCPMus
Collins, Philip Reilly 1921- WhoAm 90
Collins, Ralph Earl, III 1939- WhoE 91, WhoWor 91
Collins, Ralph T BiDrAPA 89
Collins, Ray 1887-1970 Ballpl 90
Collins, Raymond C. 1931- WhoSSW 91
Collins, Richard B. 1942- St&PR 91
Collins, Richard Berry 1948- WhoEmL 91
Collins, Richard L. 1927- IntWWM 90
Collins, Richard Lawrence 1933- WhoAm 90
Collins, Richard Raoul 1936- WhoE 91
Collins, Richard S. 1929- ODwPR 91
Collins, Richard William 1930- WhoWor 91
Collins, Rip 1896-1968 Ballpl 90
Collins, Ripper 1904-1970 Ballpl 90
Collins, Robert Clarkson, II 1949- WhoEmL 91
Collins, Robert Edward 1934- St&PR 91
Collins, Robert Edward 1949- WhoE 91
Collins, Robert Ellwood 1932- WhoE 91, WhoWor 91
Collins, Robert Emmet 1913- WhoAm 90
Collins, Robert Frederick 1931- WhoAm 90, WhoSSW 91
Collins, Robert Herschel, Jr. 1935- St&PR 91
Collins, Robert J. 1930- St&PR 91
Collins, Robert Joseph 1923- WhoAm 90
Collins, Robert Joseph 1927- WhoAm 90
Collins, Robert Keith 1947- WhoEmL 91
Collins, Robert L. 1929- St&PR 91
Collins, Robert L. 1931- St&PR 91
Collins, Robert McVickar 1930- St&PR 91, WhoAm 90
Collins, Robert Oakley 1933- WhoAm 90, WhoWrEP 89
Collins, Roger Buckner 1953- St&PR 91
Collins, Ronald W. WhoAm 90
Collins, Ross Edmond, Jr. 1957- BiDrAPA 89
Collins, Roy H WhoAmA 91N
Collins, Royal Eugene 1925- WhoAm 90
Collins, Rupert Mark 1955- IntWWM 90
Collins, Russell M., Jr. 1933- WhoAm 90
Collins, Sally Mae 1956- WhoAmW 91
Collins, Sam 1826-1865 OxCPMus
Collins, Samuel W., Jr. 1923- WhoE 91
Collins, Saxon Lynn 1963- WhoAmW 91
Collins, Shano 1885-1955 Ballpl 90 [port]
Collins, Shirley Jean 1952- WhoAmW 91
Collins, Stanley E. 1931- ODwPR 91
Collins, Stephen Barksdale 1932- WhoAm 90
Collins, Stephen Bruce 1962- WhoSSW 91
Collins, Susan ODwPR 91
Collins, Susan Ballantyne 1938- WhoAmW 91
Collins, Suzanne Mallory 1956- WhoAmW 91
Collins, Terrence T. 1942- St&PR 91
Collins, Terry Gene 1948- WhoSSW 91
Collins, Theodore Joseph 1932- WhoAm 90
Collins, Thomas Asa 1921- WhoAm 90
Collins, Thomas C. 1948- St&PR 91
Collins, Thomas E., III WhoAm 90
Collins, Thomas Joseph 1936- WhoAm 90
Collins, Thomas M., III BiDrAPA 89
Collins, Thomas William 1926- WhoWor 91
Collins, Timothy John 1954- WhoE 91
Collins, Tom BioIn 16, TwCCr&M 91
Collins, Tricia BioIn 16, WhoAmA 91
Collins, Truman Edward 1919- WhoAm 90
Collins, Vincent Patrick 1912- WhoAm 90
Collins, Vincent Peter 1947- WhoWor 91
Collins, Virginia Riddick 1963- WhoSSW 91
Collins, W Stuart BiDrAPA 89
Collins, Walker Harbour 1940- WhoAm 90
Collins, Walter Regis, Jr. 1935- St&PR 91
Collins, Walter Stowe 1926- IntWWM 90
Collins, Wayne Dale 1951- WhoEmL 91
Collins, Wayne Forrest 1941- WhoAm 90
Collins, Wilkie 1824-1889 BioIn 16, TwCCr&M 91A, WorAlBi
Collins, William EncPR&S 89
Collins, William Arthur, III 1943- WhoSSW 91
Collins, William Edgar 1935- WhoAm 90
Collins, William Edward 1932- WhoAm 90
Collins, William F. 1929- St&PR 91
Collins, William F., Jr. 1924- WhoAm 90
Collins, William Leroy 1942- WhoWor 91
Collins, William Lewis 1954- WhoEmL 91
Collins, William Thomas 1922- WhoAm 90
Collins, Winifred Quick WhoAmW 91, WhoE 91
Collins, Zip 1892-1983 Ballpl 90
Collins-Eiland, Karen Wisler 1949- WhoAmW 91, WhoSSW 91, WhoWor 91
Collins-Wright, Robert John 1927- St&PR 91
Collinson, Brent Patrick 1952- WhoEmL 91
Collinson, Dale Stanley 1938- WhoAm 90
Collinson, John Theodore 1926- St&PR 91, WhoAm 90
Collinson, William R. WhoAm 90
Collinson-Ghesquiere, Lynn Christine 1946- WhoEmL 91
Collis, Charles 1920- WhoAm 90
Collis, Christopher Henry 1948- WhoWor 91
Collis, Eric Rand 1947- WhoEmL 91
Collis, George Richard PenDiDA 89
Collis, Kay Lynn 1958- WhoEmL 91
Collis, Robert J M 1934- BiDrAPA 89
Collis, Sidney Robert 1924- WhoAm 90
Collishaw, Raymond BioIn 16
Collishaw, Robert J. 1934-1990 BioIn 16
Collishaw, Robert James St&PR 91N
Collison, Curtis Lee, Jr. 1940- St&PR 91, WhoAm 90
Collison, Diane Wittrock 1939- WhoAmW 91
Collison, Robert Lewis 1914-1989 BioIn 16
Collister, Donna Marie 1959- WhoAmW 91
Collmer, Robert George 1926- WhoAm 90
Collo, Luis Cariaso, Jr. 1944- BiDrAPA 89
Collodi, C. AuBYP 90
Colloff, Margery A. 1945- WhoEmL 91
Colloff, Roger David 1946- St&PR 91, WhoAm 90, WhoE 91
Collomb, Bertrand C. 1942- St&PR 91
Collomb, Bertrand Pierre 1942- WhoAm 90, WhoSSW 91
Collons, Rodger Duane 1935- WhoAm 90
Collopy, Christopher Stephen 1952- WhoEmL 91
Collopy, Edward Michael 1959- BiDrAPA 89
Collor, Fernando 1949- CurBio 90 [port]
Collor de Mello, Fernando BioIn 16, NewYTBS 90 [port]
Collor de Mello, Fernando 1949- CurBio 90 [port], WhoWor 91
Colloredo-Mansfeld, Ferdinand 1939- St&PR 91
Collot, Pierre PenDiDA 89
Collot, Serge PenDiMP
Collot, Victor 1751?-1805 WhNaAH
Colloton, J. Edmund ODwPR 91
Colloton, John William 1931- WhoAm 90
Collson, Mary 1870-1953 BioAmW
Collum, Jackie 1927- Ballpl 90
Collum, Robert Edward 1928- St&PR 91
Collumb, Peter John 1942- WhoSSW 91
Collura, J.A. 1949- St&PR 91
Collura, Michael J. 1948- St&PR 91
Collura, Natalie 1962- WhoAmW 91
Collyer, Charles Ralph 1930- St&PR 91
Collyer, Mary BioIn 16
Collyer, Mary 1716?-1762? FemiCLE
Collyer, Robin 1949- WhoAmA 91
Collyns, C. Napier 1927- ODwPR 91
Colman, Arthur EncO&P 3
Colman, Arthur D BiDrAPA 89
Colman, Ben 1907-1988 BioIn 16
Colman, Claire S 1946- BiDrAPA 89
Colman, Edward 1905- BioIn 16
Colman, Henry ConTFT 8
Colman, Hila AuBYP 90, BioIn 16
Colman, James Alan 1949- St&PR 91
Colman, John Charles 1927- St&PR 91, WhoAm 90
Colman, Martin 1928- BiDrAPA 89
Colman, Michael D 1942- BiDrAPA 89
Colman, Norman Jay 1827-1911 BiDrUSE 89
Colman, Richard Thomas 1935- WhoE 91
Colman, Robert Wolf 1935- WhoAm 90
Colman, Ronald 1891-1958 WorAlBi
Colman, Stephanie G. 1952- WhoEmL 91
Colman, Timothy Henry 1959- WhoWor 91
Colman, Virginia O'Connell WhoAmA 91, WhoE 91
Colman, Wendy 1950- WhoAmW 91
Colman, William Gerald 1914- WhoE 91
Colmano, Germille 1921- WhoSSW 91
Colmano, Marino Giovanni Augusto 1948- WhoEmL 91
Colmans, David J. ODwPR 91
Colmenares, Margarita Hortensia 1957- WhoHisp 91
Colmenares, Narses Jose 1945- WhoE 91
Colmer, Roy David WhoAmA 91
Colmery, Harry W., Jr. 1924- St&PR 91
Colmus, Mary Anne 1946- WhoAmW 91
Colner, Gregory Henry 1957- WhoE 91
Colnes, Martin B. 1927- St&PR 91
Colnon, William Lydon 1928- WhoAm 90
Colodne, Angela 1956- WhoAmW 91
Colodny, Dorothy BiDrAPA 89
Colodny, Edwin I. 1926- St&PR 91
Colodny, Edwin Irving 1926- WhoAm 90, WhoSSW 91
Colodny, John David 1965- WhoSSW 91
Colodny, Robert Garland 1915- WhoAm 90
Colodzin, Martin 1929- BiDrAPA 89
Colodzin, Robert S. ODwPR 91
Colokathis, Jane 1951- WhoEmL 91
Colom, George A BiDrAPA 89
Colom, Vilma M. WhoHisp 91
Colomb, Herman D 1933- BiDrAPA 89
Colombel, George I 1936- BiDrAPA 89
Colombik, Richard Michael 1953- WhoEmL 91
Colombine EncCoWW
Colombini, Gino 1915- PenDiDA 89
Colombini, Susan Murphy WhoAmA 91
Colombo, Charles 1927- WhoAmA 91
Colombo, Cristoforo BioIn 16
Colombo, Frank V. 1956- St&PR 91
Colombo, Frederick J. 1916- WhoWor 91
Colombo, Furio 1931- ConAu 30NR
Colombo, Furio Marco 1931- WhoAm 90, WhoWor 91
Colombo, Giovanni 1902- WhoWor 91
Colombo, Joe 1930-1971 BioIn 16, ConDes 90
Colombo, Joe Cesare 1930-1971 PenDiDA 89
Colombo, John Robert 1936- BioIn 16, EncO&P 3, WhoAm 90, WhoWrEP 89
Colombo, Louis John 1947- WhoEmL 91
Colombo, Umberto Paolo 1927- WhoWor 91
Colomer, Jaime Arturo 1945- WhoWor 91
Colon, Alicia V. 1944- WhoHisp 91
Colon, Anthony Ezequiel 1955- WhoHisp 91
Colon, Arthur Alan 1947- WhoSSW 91
Colon, Diego L. 1943- WhoHisp 91
Colon, Eduardo A 1953- BiDrAPA 89
Colon, Gilberto 1963- WhoHisp 91
Colon, Janette BioIn 16
Colon, Jesus 1901- ConAu 131, HispWr 90
Colon, Jesus 1901-1974 BioIn 16
Colon, Juan B. Rivera 1940- St&PR 91
Colon, Leonardo, Jr. 1958- WhoHisp 91
Colon, Lydia M. 1947- WhoAmW 91, WhoWor 91
Colon, Miriam 1945- BioIn 16, NotWoAT, WhoHisp 91
Colon, Nelson 1960- WhoHisp 91
Colon, Nicholas, Jr. 1909- WhoHisp 91
Colon, Oscar A. 1937- WhoHisp 91
Colon, Pastor BiDrAPA 89
Colon, Phyllis Janet 1938- WhoAmW 91
Colon, Rafael Hernandez- BioIn 16
Colon, Vanessa BioIn 16
Colon, William Ralph 1930- WhoHisp 91
Colon, Willie 1950- WhoHisp 91
Colon-Pacheco, Rico 1927- WhoHisp 91
Colon-Quetglas, Edward W 1934- BiDrAPA 89
Colon-Rivera, Luis Raul BiDrAPA 89
Colon-Vargas, Manuel J BiDrAPA 89
Colonel, Sheri L. 1955- St&PR 91
Colonel, Sheri Lynn 1955- WhoAmW 91
Coloney, Wayne H. 1925- St&PR 91
Coloney, Wayne Herndon 1925- WhoAm 90, WhoSSW 91, WhoWor 91
Colonius, Ray Edward 1935- St&PR 91
Colonna, Edward 1862-1948 PenDiDA 89
Colonna, Enzo M. 1943- St&PR 91
Colonna, Vittoria 1492-1547 EncCoWW
Colonna, William Mark 1956- WhoEmL 91
Colonne, Edouard 1838-1910 PenDiMP
Colonnier, Marc Leopold 1930- WhoAm 90
Colony, Henry S BiDrAPA 89
Colony-Cokely, Pamela Cameron 1947- WhoAmW 91, WhoE 91
Colorado WhNaAH
Colorado, Antonio J 1903- ConAu 32NR, HispWr 90
Colorado, Charu 1920- WhoAmA 91
Colorado Capella, Antonio J 1903- ConAu 32NR
Colorow 1810?-1888 WhNaAH

Colosi, Nick 1927- *Ballpl 90*
Colosi, Thomas Richard 1934- *St&PR 91*
Colosimo, Antonio 1949- *WhoEmL 91*
Colosimo, Robert 1929- *WhoAm 90*
Colot, Roseann Marie 1957- *WhoAmW 91*
Colotka, Peter 1925- *WhoWor 91*
Colovas, Stephen William 1957- *WhoAm 90*
Colp, Ralph, Jr. 1924- *BiDrAPA 89, WhoE 91*
Colpacci, Viorica *WhoAmA 91*
Colpitt, Frances 1952- *WhoAmA 91*
Colquhoun, Archibald 1912-1964 *ConAu 129*
Colquhoun, Ithell 1906-1988 *BiDWomA*
Colquitt, Charles G., II 1938- *St&PR 91*
Colquitt, Geoffrey Lynd 1954- *WhoEmL 91*
Colquitt, James Earl 1942- *WhoSSW 91*
Colquitt, John C. 1848-1913 *AmLegL*
Colquitt, Landon Augustus 1919- *WhoAm 90*
Colsky, Liane Caryl 1958- *BiDrAPA 89*
Colson, Andree 1924- *IntWWM 90*
Colson, Ardanna Oran 1953- *WhoAmW 91*
Colson, Charles W. *BioIn 16*
Colson, Charles W. 1931- *WorAlBi*
Colson, Charles Wendell 1931- *WhoAm 90, WhoWrEP 89*
Colson, Cherrill Wilcox 1941- *WhoAmW 91*
Colson, Chester E 1917-1985 *WhoAmA 91N*
Colson, Earl M. 1930- *WhoAm 90*
Colson, Elizabeth Florence 1917- *WhoAm 90, WhoAmW 91*
Colson, Janet *BioIn 16*
Colson, Joseph S., Jr. *BioIn 16*
Colson, Steve 1949- *IntWWM 90*
Colson, Steven Douglas 1941- *WhoAm 90*
Colson, Wendell H. *WhoSSW 91*
Colt, Alexander T. *BioIn 16, NewYTBS 90*
Colt, John Nicholson 1925- *WhoAmA 91*
Colt, Martin *AuBYP 90*
Colt, Maximilian *BioIn 16*
Colt, Samuel 1814-1862 *WorAlBi*
Coltelli, Laura 1941- *WhoWor 91*
Coltelli, Laura Rauch 1958- *WhoEmL 91, WhoSSW 91*
Colten, Harvey Radin 1939- *WhoAm 90*
Colter, Cleveland *BioIn 16*
Colter, Cyrus 1910- *WhoAm 90, WhoWrEP 89*
Colter, John 1775?-1813 *WhNaAH*
Colter, Mel Archie 1947- *WhoWor 91*
Colthart, James M. 1944- *St&PR 91*
Colthart, Shirley M *BiDrAPA 89*
Coltman, Edward Jeremiah 1948- *WhoEmL 91*
Coltman, Felicity Ann 1933- *IntWWM 90*
Coltman, John Wesley 1915- *WhoAm 90*
Coltoff, Beth Jamie 1955- *WhoAmW 91*
Colton, Clark Kenneth 1941- *WhoAm 90, WhoWor 91*
Colton, David 1936- *St&PR 91*
Colton, David Lem 1943- *WhoAm 90*
Colton, Don Jared 1946- *St&PR 91*
Colton, E.G., Jr. 1929- *St&PR 91*
Colton, Ed Lynn, Jr. 1951- *WhoEmL 91*
Colton, Frank Benjamin 1923- *WhoAm 90*
Colton, Frank W. 1928- *St&PR 91*
Colton, Grant A., Jr. 1940- *St&PR 91*
Colton, Gregg Byron 1953- *St&PR 91*
Colton, Gustavus A. 1828-1894 *AmLegL*
Colton, Hugh Wilkens *BioIn 16*
Colton, Joel 1918- *WhoAm 90*
Colton, John O. *WhoSSW 91*
Colton, John P. 1935- *St&PR 91*
Colton, Judith 1943- *WhoAmA 91*
Colton, Kendrew H. 1955- *WhoEmL 91*
Colton, Kent W. 1943- *WhoAm 90*
Colton, Nathan H 1905- *BiDrAPA 89*
Colton, Nelson Burton 1930- *WhoAm 90*
Colton, Richard 1951- *WhoAm 90*
Colton, Roberta Ann 1957- *WhoEmL 91*
Colton, Roy Charles 1941- *WhoWor 91*
Colton, Sterling D. 1929- *St&PR 91*
Colton, Sterling Don 1929- *WhoAm 90*
Colton, Theodore 1933- *WhoE 91*
Colton, Theodore J. 1932- *St&PR 91*
Colton, V. Robert 1930- *WhoWor 91*
Coltrain, Juanita Holliday 1917- *WhoSSW 91*
Coltrane, Alice *BioIn 16*
Coltrane, James 1937- *SpyFic*
Coltrane, John 1926-1967 *BioIn 16, ConMus 4 [port], DrBlPA 90, OxCPMus, WorAlBi*
Coltrane, Loretta Elaine 1949- *WhoE 91*
Coltrera, Joseph T 1923- *BiDrAPA 89*
Coltrin, Mark Steven 1948- *WhoSSW 91*
Coltrin, Stephen Hugh 1945- *WhoWor 91*
Colucci, Anthony Joseph, III 1958- *WhoEmL 91*
Colucci, Giuseppe 1955- *WhoWor 91*
Colucci, Tommaso 1931- *WhoE 91*
Coluccio, Bob 1951- *Ballpl 90*
Colum, Padraic 1881-1972 *AuBYP 90, MajTwCW*
Columbare, Stephen James 1951- *St&PR 91*
Columbo, Charlie *BioIn 16*
Columbo, Russ 1908-1934 *BioIn 16, OxCPMus*
Columbro, Madeline Mary 1934- *IntWWM 90*
Columbus, Christopher *BioIn 16*
Columbus, Christopher 1451?-1506 *EncCRAm [port], WhNaAH, WorAlBi*
Columbus, Robert Howard 1952- *WhoEmL 91*
Colussy, Dan Alfred 1931- *St&PR 91, WhoAm 90, WhoE 91*
Colvard, David F 1952- *BiDrAPA 89*
Colvard, Dean Wallace 1913- *WhoAm 90*
Colvard, Michael David 1954- *WhoEmL 91, WhoWor 91*
Colver, Alice Mary 1892- *AuBYP 90*
Colver, Anne 1908- *AuBYP 90*
Colver, Richard C. 1927- *St&PR 91*
Colvert, Cheryl Lynn 1956- *WhoSSW 91*
Colvett, Caron Elaine 1962- *WhoAmW 91*
Colvile, Eden 1819-1893 *DcCanB 12*
Colvill, Robin 1945- *IntWWM 90*
Colville, Alexander 1920- *WhoAmA 91*
Colville, David Alexander 1920- *WhoAm 90*
Colville, Elizabeth *BiDEWW, BioIn 16*
Colville, John 1930- *WhoWor 91*
Colville, Kenneth H., Jr. 1923- *St&PR 91*
Colville, W. J. 1859-1917 *EncO&P 3*
Colvin, Amelia E. 1957- *WhoAmW 91*
Colvin, Bill D. 1940- *WhoAm 90*
Colvin, Burton Houston 1916- *WhoAm 90, WhoE 91*
Colvin, Clark Sherman 1958- *WhoEmL 91*
Colvin, David Paul 1945- *BiDrAPA 89*
Colvin, Harry Walter, Jr. 1921- *WhoAm 90*
Colvin, Henry McCollough 1940- *WhoAm 90*
Colvin, Herbert, Jr. 1923- *WhoAm 90*
Colvin, Iris 1914- *St&PR 91*
Colvin, James *MajTwCW*
Colvin, John *AmLegL*
Colvin, John Kim 1954- *WhoEmL 91*
Colvin, Karen *BioIn 16*
Colvin, Lloyd Dayton 1915- *St&PR 91*
Colvin, Milton 1923- *WhoAm 90*
Colvin, Neil J. *BioIn 16*
Colvin, Robert Allan 1952- *WhoEmL 91*
Colvin, Sharon Kay 1947- *WhoAmW 91*
Colvin, Shawn *BioIn 16*
Colvin, Thomas Stuart 1947- *WhoWrEP 89*
Colvin, Walter Bishop 1946- *St&PR 91*
Colvin, William E. 1929- *St&PR 91*
Colvin, William Given 1951- *WhoEmL 91*
Colvin-Harrison, Laura *BioIn 16*
Colway, James R 1920- *WhoAmA 91*
Colwell, Bryan York 1961- *WhoEmL 91*
Colwell, David Bruce 1959- *IntWWM 90*
Colwell, Edwin Clinton 1933- *St&PR 91*
Colwell, Howard Otis 1929- *WhoAm 90*
Colwell, John Amory 1928- *WhoAm 90*
Colwell, Louise Grieff 1933- *St&PR 91*
Colwell, Richard 1930- *IntWWM 90*
Colwell, Richard James 1930- *WhoAm 90*
Colwell, Rita Rossi 1934- *WhoAm 90, WhoAmW 91, WhoE 91*
Colwell, Scott David 1957- *WhoEmL 91*
Colwell, Thomas G. 1930- *St&PR 91*
Colwell, William B. *ODwPR 91*
Colwill, Jack Marshall 1932- *WhoAm 90*
Colwin, Arthur Lentz 1911- *WhoAm 90*
Colwin, Laurie 1944- *MajTwCW*
Colwyn, Stewart 1910-1988 *SmATA X*
Coly, Eileen 1916- *EncPaPR 91*
Coly, Lisette 1950- *EncPaPR 91, WhoAmW 91*
Colyar, Ardell Benton 1914- *WhoAm 90*
Colyer, Dale Keith 1931- *WhoSSW 91*
Colyer, Ken 1928-1988 *AnObit 1988, OxCPMus*
Colyer, Ralph Joseph 1935- *WhoE 91*
Colyer, Sheryl Lynn 1959- *WhoAmW 91*
Colyer, Vincent 1825-1888 *WhNaAH*
Colzani, Anselmo 1918- *IntWWM 90*
Coman, Charlotte 1833-1924 *BiDWomA*
Coman, Nicolae 1936- *IntWWM 90*
Coman, William LeRoy 1948- *WhoE 91*
Comanduras, Peter Diacoumis *NewYTBS 90*
Comanduras, Peter Diacoumis 1908-1990 *BioIn 16*
Comaneci, Nadia 1961- *WhoWor 91, WorAlBi*
Comaneci, Nadia 1962- *BioIn 16*
Comanescu, Denisa 1954- *EncCoWW*
Comanor, William S. 1937- *WhoAm 90*
Comans, Marc de *PenDiDA 89*
Comas Bacardi, Adolfo T. 1944- *WhoAm 90, WhoHisp 91*
Comay, Eli Bernard 1927- *BiDrAPA 89*
Comay, Sholom David 1937- *St&PR 91, WhoAm 90, WhoE 91*
Comba, Davida H 1928- *BiDrAPA 89*
Comba, Davida Hotz 1928- *WhoE 91*
Combe, Bernard Marie-Joel 1947- *WhoWor 91*
Combe, Christopher Bryan 1947- *St&PR 91*
Combe, David Alfred 1942- *WhoAm 90*
Combe, Ivan DeBlois 1911- *WhoAm 90*
Combe, John Clifford, Jr. 1939- *WhoAm 90*
Combe, Joseph *PenDiDA 89*
Combemale, Patrick Abel 1953- *WhoWor 91*
Comber, Bernard E 1933- *BiDrAPA 89*
Comber, Neil M. 1951- *WhoHisp 91*
Comber, Ronald Edward 1951- *IntWWM 90*
Comberford, Mary *BiDEWW*
Comberg, Dietrich Wilhelm 1928- *WhoWor 91*
Comberiate, Josephine Bertolini 1917- *WhoWrEP 89*
Combes, Emile Justin Louis 1835-1921 *BiDFrPL*
Combes, Richard Snyder 1948- *WhoEmL 91*
Combes, Simon 1940- *BioIn 16*
Combest, Craig 1944- *St&PR 91*
Combest, Larry Ed 1945- *WhoAm 90, WhoSSW 91*
Combier, Elizabeth Irene 1949- *WhoE 91*
Combopiano, Charles Angelo 1935- *IntWWM 90*
Combrinck-Graham, Lee 1941- *BiDrAPA 89*
Combs, Austin Olin 1917- *WhoWor 91*
Combs, Charles Donald 1952- *WhoEmL 91*
Combs, Charles S. 1940- *St&PR 91*
Combs, Clarence Murphy 1925- *WhoAm 90*
Combs, Dan Jack 1924- *WhoAm 90*
Combs, Earle 1899-1976 *Ballpl 90*
Combs, Gene Norman, Jr. *BiDrAPA 89*
Combs, George M. 1956- *St&PR 91*
Combs, Harry 1913- *ConAu 129*
Combs, Jack Lewis, Jr. 1960- *WhoEmL 91*
Combs, Jack M., Jr. 1949- *St&PR 91*
Combs, James Boyd 1942- *St&PR 91*
Combs, Jo Karen Kobeck 1944- *WhoAmW 91*
Combs, John F. 1950- *St&PR 91*
Combs, John Hayden 1929- *St&PR 91*
Combs, Leslie, II *BioIn 16*
Combs, Leslie, II *NewYTBS 90*
Combs, Linda Jones 1948- *WhoAmW 91, WhoSSW 91*
Combs, Linda Morrison 1946- *WhoAm 90*
Combs, Maxine Ruth Solow 1937- *WhoWrEP 89*
Combs, Paul Joseph 1960- *WhoEmL 91, WhoSSW 91*
Combs, Randall Jay 1956- *WhoEmL 91*
Combs, Ray *BioIn 16*
Combs, Richard Alexander *WhoWrEP 89*
Combs, Richard J. *WhoAm 90*
Combs, Robert J. *ODwPR 91*
Combs, Thomas Neal 1942- *St&PR 91, WhoAm 90*
Combs, Wallace Earl *BiDrAPA 89*
Combs, William David 1938- *WhoSSW 91*
Combs, William G. 1930- *WhoAm 90*
Combs, William George 1930- *St&PR 91*
Combs, William Henry, III 1949- *WhoEmL 91, WhoWor 91*
Combs-Jordan, Valda Jean 1956- *WhoAmW 91*
Comchoc, Rudolph A. *WhoSSW 91*
Comchoc, Rudolph A. 1935- *St&PR 91*
Comcomly 1765?-1830 *WhNaAH*
Comden, Betty 1917- *OxCPMus*
Comden, Betty 1918- *NotWoAT*
Comden, Betty 1919- *BioIn 16, FemiCLE, WhoAm 90, WhoAmW 91, WorAlBi*
Comeau, Andre Victor 1932- *St&PR 91*
Comeau, Barbara Jeanne 1928- *St&PR 91*
Comeau, James Raymond *BiDrAPA 89*
Comeau, Lorene Anita Emerson 1952- *WhoAmW 91*
Comeau, Louis Roland 1941- *WhoAm 90*
Comeau, Robert Lee 1947- *St&PR 91*
Comeau Yager, Kimberly Kay 1954- *WhoWrEP 89*
Comeaux, Douglas James 1958- *WhoEmL 91*
Comedian Harmonists *OxCPMus*
Comedy Harmonists *OxCPMus*
Comeforo, Jean Elizabeth 1947- *WhoAmW 91*
Comegys, George 1839-1901 *AmLegL*
Comegys, Walker Brockton 1929- *WhoAm 90*
Comegys, William A. 1847?- *AmLegL*
Comella, Patricia Ann Egan 1941- *WhoAmW 91*
Comenitz, Elliot 1925- *St&PR 91*
Comenitz, Louis 1916- *St&PR 91*
Comenius, John Amos 1592-1670 *WorAlBi*
Comer, Anjanette 1942- *BioIn 16*
Comer, Braxton Bragg, II 1951- *WhoEmL 91, WhoSSW 91, WhoWor 91*
Comer, Carla A. 1949- *WhoAmW 91*
Comer, Clara Prada *BiDrAPA 89*
Comer, Clarence C. 1948- *St&PR 91, WhoSSW 91*
Comer, Debra Ruth 1960- *WhoAmW 91*
Comer, Donald, III 1938- *St&PR 91, WhoAm 90*
Comer, Elma M *BiDrAPA 89*
Comer, Elma M. 1918-1989 *BioIn 16*
Comer, Evan Philip 1927- *WhoAm 90*
Comer, Gregg Thomas 1953- *WhoEmL 91*
Comer, James P. *BioIn 16*
Comer, James P 1934- *BiDrAPA 89*
Comer, James Pierpont 1934- *St&PR 91, WhoAm 90, WhoE 91*
Comer, John Edward 1938- *St&PR 91*
Comer, John Fletcher, Jr. 1946- *WhoSSW 91*
Comer, Kelvie Cureton 1946- *WhoAmW 91*
Comer, Maggie 1904- *BioIn 16*
Comer, Nathan L *BiDrAPA 89*
Comer, Nathan Lawrence 1923- *WhoE 91*
Comer, Owen A. 1933- *St&PR 91*
Comer, Patricia Ann 1949- *WhoSSW 91*
Comer, Russell Wayne 1959- *WhoEmL 91*
Comer, Steve 1954- *Ballpl 90*
Comer, Wayne 1944- *Ballpl 90*
Comer, Wilson Sidney, Jr. 1950- *BiDrAPA 89*
Comerer, Harold A. 1949- *WhoAm 90*
Comerford, James J. 1901-1988 *BioIn 16*
Comerford, Philip M. 1931- *St&PR 91*
Comers, Russell D. 1939- *St&PR 91*
Comery, Robert Whitfield 1918- *WhoE 91*
Comes, Jennifer Lynn 1955- *WhoAmW 91*
Comes, Liviu 1918- *IntWWM 90*
Comes, Marcella *WhoAmA 91*
Comes, Robert George 1931- *WhoWor 91*
Comess, Leonard J 1924- *BiDrAPA 89*
Comet, Catherine *WhoAmW 91*
Comet-Epstein, Sharon 1950- *WhoAmW 91*
Cometti, Giacomo 1863-1938 *PenDiDA 89*
Comey, Dale R. 1941- *St&PR 91*
Comey, J. Martin 1934- *St&PR 91, WhoAm 90*
Comey, James Hugh 1947- *WhoWrEP 89*
Comfort, Alex 1920- *WorAlBi*
Comfort, Alexander 1920- *BiDrAPA 89, WhoAm 90*
Comfort, Hartley B. 1909- *St&PR 91*
Comfort, J. L. *AuBYP 90*
Comfort, Jane Levington 1903- *AuBYP 90*
Comfort, Joe *BioIn 16*
Comfort, Priscilla Maria 1947- *WhoAmW 91*
Comfort, Ted Paul 1950- *St&PR 91*
Comfort, Thomas Edwin 1921- *WhoAm 90*
Comfort, William Twyman, Jr. 1937- *WhoAm 90*
Comfort, William Wistar 1933- *WhoAm 90, WhoE 91*
Comiez, Maynard Sheldon 1931- *WhoE 91*
Comine, Lawrence, Jr. 1939- *St&PR 91*
Comines, Philippe de 1445?-1511 *BioIn 16*
Comings, David Edward 1935- *WhoAm 90*
Comings, John Paul 1945- *WhoEmL 91*
Comings, William Daniel, Jr. 1938- *WhoAm 90*
Comini, Alessandra 1934- *WhoAm 90, WhoAmA 91*
Cominos, Achilles Zachariah 1911- *WhoWor 91*
Cominsky, Lynn Ruth 1953- *WhoAmW 91*
Cominsky, Ronald John 1940- *WhoSSW 91*
Comiskey, Charlie 1859-1931 *Ballpl 90 [port]*
Comiskey, Eugene Edward 1936- *WhoAm 90*
Comiskey, J. Louis 1885-1939 *Ballpl 90*
Comiskey, James August 1926- *WhoAm 90*
Comiskey, Michael Peter 1948- *WhoEmL 91*
Comisky, Marvin 1918- *WhoAm 90*
Comissiona, Robinne 1928- *IntWWM 90*
Comissiona, Sergiu 1928- *IntWWM 90, PenDiMP, WhoAm 90, WhoWor 91*
Comitas, Lambros 1927- *WhoAm 90*
Comito, Carmelo Ciro 1949- *St&PR 91*
Comizio-Assante, Delva Maria 1964- *WhoE 91*
Comley, Nancy Rich 1935- *WhoAmW 91*
Comly, Harry R. 1845- *AmLegL*
Comly, Hunter H 1919- *BiDrAPA 89*
Comly, Kathleen Mckeag *BiDrAPA 89*
Commack, William E. 1929- *St&PR 91*
Commack, William Earl 1929- *WhoAm 90*
Commager, Henry Steele 1902- *AuBYP 90, BioIn 16, MajTwCW, WhoAm 90, WorAlBi*
Command, Michele 1946- *IntWWM 90*
Commanday, Robert 1922- *IntWWM 90*
Commander, Shari L. 1950- *WhoAmW 91*

Commella, William Oliver 1913- WhoSSW 91
Commerford, Kathleen Anne 1951- WhoAmW 91
Commes, Thomas A. 1942- WhoAm 90
Commes, Thomas Allen 1942- St&PR 91
Commins, Dorothy Berliner AuBYP 90
Commins, James Alton 1927- St&PR 91
Commins, Michael William 1948- WhoWrEP 89
Commire, Anne WhoAm 90, WhoWrEP 89
Commisa, Vincent J. 1921-1990 BioIn 16
Commito, Richard William 1951- WhoWor 91
Commito, Thomas F. 1948- St&PR 91
Common, Frank Breadon, Jr. 1920- St&PR 91, WhoAm 90, WhoWor 91
Commoner, Barry 1917- BioIn 16, ConAu 33NR, MajTwCW, WhoAm 90, WorAlBi
Commons, Donald William 1951- WhoEmL 91
Commons, Dorman L 1918- ConAu 129
Commons, John R. 1862-1945 BioIn 16
Commons, Kathleen Marie 1954- WhoE 91
Commynes, Philippe de 1445?-1511 BioIn 16
Comninou, Maria 1947- WhoAmW 91
Como, Francis W. 1931- St&PR 91
Como, Odoardo 1961- WhoWor 91
Como, Perry 1912- OxCPMus, WorAlBi
Como, Perry 1913- BioIn 16, WhoAm 90
Como, Ronald A. 1935- St&PR 91
Como, William 1925-1989 BioIn 16
Como, William Michael WhoWrEP 89
Comola, James Paul 1931- WhoAm 90, WhoSSW 91
Comollo, Thomas C. 1947- St&PR 91
Comor, Henry BioIn 16
Comorosky, Adam 1904-1951 Ballpl 90
Comotto, Robert Paul 1948- WhoEmL 91
Compagnet, Alex WhoHisp 91
Compagnon, Jean George Andre 1916- WhoWor 91
Compain, Rita 1926- WhoAmW 91
Compaine, Andrew Guy 1959- BiDrAPA 89
Compaore, Blaise WhoWor 91
Comparin, Robert Anton 1928- WhoAm 90
Compel, Deborah Catherine 1955- WhoAmW 91
Comper, F.A. 1945- St&PR 91
Compere, Clinton Lee 1911- WhoAm 90
Compernolle, Theo Hector 1946- WhoWor 91
Compes, Peter Constantin 1930- WhoWor 91
Compiseno, Deborah Loraine 1956- WhoEmL 91
Compo, Sandra Irene 1950- WhoEmL 91
Composers Quartet PenDiMP
Compton, Alan Bertrand BiDrAPA 89
Compton, Allan R 1934- BiDrAPA 89
Compton, Allen T. 1938- WhoAm 90
Compton, Ann Woodruff 1947- WhoAm 90, WhoAmW 91
Compton, Ariel S BiDrAPA 89
Compton, Arthur H. 1892-1962 WorAlBi
Compton, Asbury Christian 1929- WhoAm 90
Compton, Charles B. 1926- St&PR 91
Compton, Charles Daniel 1915- WhoAm 90
Compton, David Bruce 1952- WhoEmL 91, WhoWor 91
Compton, David Orville, Jr. 1959- WhoSSW 91
Compton, Elizabeth BiDEWW
Compton, Elizabeth J. 1829- EncO&P 3
Compton, Erlinda Rae 1947- WhoHisp 91
Compton, George Lough 1928- St&PR 91
Compton, James Carl 1926- WhoAm 90
Compton, James F. 1940- St&PR 91
Compton, Jennifer 1949- FemiCLE
Compton, John Carroll 1941- WhoSSW 91, WhoWor 91
Compton, John George 1926- WhoWor 91
Compton, John George Melvin 1926- BioIn 16
Compton, John Robinson 1923- WhoAm 90
Compton, Joseph E. 1925- St&PR 91
Compton, Laurence B. 1925- St&PR 91
Compton, Mary Beatrice Brown 1923- WhoAmW 91, WhoE 91
Compton, Norma Haynes 1924- WhoAm 90, WhoAmW 91
Compton, Olin Randall 1925- WhoAm 90
Compton, Paul Martin BiDrAPA 89
Compton, Ralph Theodore, Jr. 1935- WhoAm 90
Compton, Raymond Hayden 1927- St&PR 91
Compton, Robert C. 1947- St&PR 91
Compton, Ronald E. 1933- WhoAm 90, WhoE 91
Compton, Shannon Leigh 1953- WhoAmW 91
Compton, Susan LaNell 1917- WhoAmW 91, WhoSSW 91, WhoWor 91
Compton, W. Dale 1929- WhoAm 90
Compton, William Thomas 1945- WhoWor 91
Compton, Wilson M, III BiDrAPA 89
Compton-Burnett, I. 1884-1969 BioIn 16, MajTwCW
Compton-Burnett, Ivy 1884-1969 BioIn 16, FemiCLE
Comras, Jay 1934- St&PR 91
Comras, Rema 1936- WhoAm 90, WhoSSW 91
Comras, Rosemary 1940- St&PR 91
Comrey, Cynthia 1949- BiDrAPA 89
Comrie, Allan 1919- St&PR 91
Comrie, Keith Brian 1939- WhoAm 90
Comrie, Sandra Melton 1940- St&PR 91, WhoAmW 91
Comstock, Anna Botsford 1854-1930 BioIn 16
Comstock, Anna Botsford 1864-1930 WomFie
Comstock, Betsy Smith BiDrAPA 89
Comstock, C.B. 1930- St&PR 91
Comstock, Cyrus Ballou 1831-1910 BioIn 16
Comstock, Dale Robert 1934- WhoAm 90
Comstock, Donald W. 1928- St&PR 91
Comstock, Donna Lee 1929- WhoAm 90, WhoAmW 91
Comstock, Glen David 1945- WhoAm 90, WhoEmL 91
Comstock, James William 1946- WhoEmL 91
Comstock, John A. 1883- BioIn 16
Comstock, Keith 1955- Ballpl 90
Comstock, R. W. 1930- ODwPR 91
Comstock, Ralph J., Jr. 1917- St&PR 91
Comstock, Robert BioIn 16
Comstock, Robert Donald, Jr. 1921- WhoSSW 91
Comstock, Robert Francis 1936- WhoE 91, WhoWor 91
Comstock, Robert Ray 1927- WhoAm 90
Comte, Auguste 1798-1857 WorAlBi, WrPh P
Comte, William H. 1953- WhoSSW 91
Comvalius, Lawrence Austin 1940- WhoE 91
Comyns, Barbara BioIn 16
Comyns, Barbara 1909- WorAu 1980 [port]
Comyns, Barbara 1912- FemiCLE
Comyns-Carr, Barbara 1909- WorAu 1980 [port]
Conabee, Earl Edward 1937- St&PR 91
Conable, Barber B., Jr. 1922- WhoAm 90, WorAlBi
Conaboy, Richard Paul 1925- WhoAm 90
Conacher, Desmond John 1918- WhoAm 90
Conafay, Stephen Rogers 1943- WhoAm 90
Conaghan, Dorothy Dell 1930- WhoAmW 91
Conal, Robbie BioIn 16
Conal, Robbie 1941- WhoAmA 91
Conan, Abraham P. BioIn 16
Conan, Laure 1845-1924 DcLB 99 [port], FemiCLE
Conan, Robert James, Jr. 1924- WhoAm 90
Conant, Allah B., Jr. 1939- WhoAm 90
Conant, Barton C. 1928- St&PR 91
Conant, Colleen Christner 1947- WhoAm 90, WhoAmW 91
Conant, Deborah Henson- BioIn 16
Conant, Doris S. 1925- St&PR 91
Conant, Herbert D. 1924- St&PR 91, WhoE 91
Conant, Howard R. 1924- St&PR 91
Conant, Howard Rosset 1924- WhoAm 90
Conant, Howard Somers 1921- WhoAm 90, WhoAmA 91
Conant, J H, Mrs. 1831-1875 EncO&P 3
Conant, James Bryant BioIn 16
Conant, James Bryant 1893-1978 DcScB S2, WorAlBi
Conant, Jan Royce 1930- WhoAmA 91, WhoE 91
Conant, Jon Frederick 1957- WhoEmL 91
Conant, L. Victor 1946- St&PR 91
Conant, Miriam Bernheim 1931- WhoAm 90
Conant, Ralph Gordon, Jr. 1929- St&PR 91
Conant, Ralph W 1926- ConAu 31NR
Conant, Richard Paul 1941- IntWWM 90
Conant, Robert Scott 1928- IntWWM 90, WhoAm 90
Conant, Roger 1592?-1679 EncCRAm
Conant, Roger Royce 1938- WhoAm 90
Conant, Roger Vincent 1936- St&PR 91
Conant, Roy Kenyon 1945- WhoSSW 91
Conant, Shari 1947- WhoAmW 91
Conant, Steven George 1949- BiDrAPA 89, WhoWor 91
Conant-Lawer, Marcie Lee 1960- WhoAmW 91
Conant-Norville, David Oliver BiDrAPA 89
Conard, Diane Joy 1959- WhoAmW 91
Conard, Elsie G. 1929- St&PR 91
Conard, Frederick Underwood, Jr. 1918- WhoAm 90
Conard, John Joseph 1921- WhoAm 90
Conard, Virgil Warren 1921- WhoSSW 91
Conarroe, Joel Osborne 1934- WhoAm 90
Conarty, Murray Rogers 1963- WhoEmL 91
Conary, David Arlan 1937- WhoE 91, WhoWor 91
Conaton, Michael Joseph 1933- St&PR 91, WhoAm 90
Conaway, Christine Y. 1901-1989 BioIn 16
Conaway, Gerald 1933- WhoAmA 91
Conaway, Harry BioIn 16
Conaway, J. Michal 1948- St&PR 91, WhoAm 90
Conaway, James D 1932- WhoAmA 91
Conaway, Jane Ellen 1941- WhoAmW 91
Conaway, Jeff 1950- BioIn 16
Conaway, Orrin Bryte 1918- WhoAm 90
Conboy, Thomas F., III 1955- St&PR 91
Concaison, John Silva 1963- WhoWrEP 89
Concannon, Ann Worth 1946- WhoAmA 91
Concannon, Richard James 1933- WhoAm 90
Concar, John R. 1937- St&PR 91
Concepcion Espina EncCoWW
Concepcion, Dave 1948- Ballpl 90 [port], WhoHisp 91
Concepcion, Onix 1957- Ballpl 90
Concha Espina 1869-1955 EncCoWW
Concha Ortiz, Luis Malaquias 1859-1921 BioIn 16
Concheri, Kathleen Elsie 1963- WhoAmW 91
Concholar, Dan Robert 1939- WhoAm 90
Conchon, Georges NewYTBS 90
Conchon, Georges 1925-1990 ConAu 132
Conconi, Diana Alexis 1962- WhoE 91
Concordia, Charles 1908- WhoAm 90
Condax, Kate Delano 1945- WhoE 91
Condayan, John 1933- WhoAm 90
Conde, Alice 1946- WhoAmW 91
Conde, Anselmo 1944- WhoHisp 91
Conde, Carlos D. 1936- WhoHisp 91
Conde, Carmen 1907- IntvSpW [port]
Conde, Mario BioIn 16
Conde, Maryse ConAu 30NR
Conde, Maryse 1937- WorAu 1980
Conde, Michael Hugo 1939- WhoAm 90
Conde, Paul Henri Louis 1930- WhoWor 91
Conde, Richard L 1922- BiDrAPA 89
Condello, Russell Anthony 1958- WhoEmL 91, WhoSSW 91
Condello, Virginia BiDrAPA 89
Conder, Robert Lake, Jr. 1950- WhoSSW 91
Conder, Robert M. 1930- St&PR 91
Condeso, Orlando 1947- WhoAmA 91
Condict, Edgar Rhodes 1940- WhoE 91, WhoWor 91
Condie, Carol Joy 1931- WhoAmW 91
Condie, Donald Bryant 1951- BiDrAPA 89
Condie, Robert Stevens 1950- WhoEmL 91
Condie, Thomas M.J. 1929- St&PR 91
Condino, Joan ODwPR 91
Condit, Albert P. 1829-1901 AmLegL
Condit, Bradley Wade 1958- WhoE 91
Condit, Carl W. BioIn 16
Condit, Carl Wilbur 1914- WhoAm 90
Condit, Doris Elizabeth WhoAm 90
Condit, Frances Cathleen 1943- WhoSSW 91
Condit, Gary A. WhoAm 90
Condit, Gary Adrian 1948- BioIn 16
Condit, Hilary E. 1954- ODwPR 91
Condit, Louise 1914- WhoAm 90
Condit, Madeleine Kay Bryant 1941- WhoAmW 91
Condit, Philip Murray 1941- WhoAm 90
Condo, James Robert 1952- WhoEmL 91
Condo, Nucci 1946- IntWWM 90
Condom, Pierre Philippe 1941- WhoWor 91
Condon, Breen O'Malley 1944- WhoAm 90
Condon, Daniel Deal 1956- St&PR 91
Condon, David Bruce 1949- WhoEmL 91
Condon, Donald L. 1931- St&PR 91
Condon, Eddie 1904-1973 BioIn 16
Condon, Eddie 1905-1973 OxCPMus
Condon, Edward John, Jr. 1940- WhoAm 90
Condon, Edward U 1902-1974 EncO&P 3
Condon, Francis Edward 1919- WhoAm 90
Condon, Frederick Hughes 1934- St&PR 91
Condon, G.J. 1947- St&PR 91
Condon, George Edward 1916- WhoAm 90
Condon, James Edward 1950- St&PR 91
Condon, James Michael 1914- WhoSSW 91
Condon, Jane Frances 1951- WhoE 91
Condon, John F. X. BioIn 16
Condon, Joseph F. 1925- St&PR 91, WhoAm 90
Condon, Lester Patrick 1922- WhoAm 90
Condon, Patrick Ian 1936- WhoWor 91
Condon, Richard BioIn 16
Condon, Richard 1915- BestSel 90-3 [port], MajTwCW, TwCCr&M 91, WorAlBi
Condon, Richard Bernard, Jr. 1955- WhoSSW 91
Condon, Richard Thomas 1915- SpyFic, WhoAm 90
Condon, Robert Edward 1929- WhoAm 90
Condon, Robert Howard 1944- WhoE 91
Condon, Robert Lewis 1937- St&PR 91
Condon, Thomas 1822-1907 BioIn 16
Condon, Thomas J. 1930- WhoAm 90
Condon, Thomas J. 1945- St&PR 91
Condon, Verner Holmes, Jr. 1926- WhoAm 90
Condon, William P. 1937- St&PR 91
Condorcet, Marie de Caritat, Marquis de 1743-1794 BioIn 16
Condorcet, Marie Jean, Marquis De 1743-1794 WorAlBi
Condos, Barbara BioIn 16
Condos, Barbara Seale 1925- WhoAmW 91
Condos, George 1953- St&PR 91
Condos, George Augustus 1931- St&PR 91
Condos, James Alexander 1959- WhoEmL 91
Condos, Marios John 1924- WhoWor 91
Condos, Steve NewYTBS 90
Condra, Allen Lee 1950- WhoEmL 91, WhoWor 91
Condra, Frances Rife 1929- WhoAmW 91
Condra, Norma Lee 1925- WhoAmW 91
Condran, Cynthia Marie 1953- WhoAmW 91
Condravy, Joan Carol 1952- WhoAmW 91
Condray, Ansel Lynn 1942- St&PR 91
Condrill, Jo Ellaresa 1935- WhoAmW 91, WhoE 91, WhoWor 91
Condron, Brian P 1944- BiDrAPA 89
Condry, Dorothea June 1935- WhoWrEP 89
Condry, Robert Stewart 1941- WhoAm 90
Cone, Bonnie Ethel 1907- WhoAmW 91
Cone, Carl Bruce 1916- WhoAm 90
Cone, Carol L. 1950- ODwPR 91
Cone, Carol Lynn 1950- WhoAm 90
Cone, Claribel 1864-1929 BioAmW
Cone, Daniel York 1962- WhoSSW 91
Cone, Danny M. ODwPR 91
Cone, David BioIn 16
Cone, David 1963- Ballpl 90
Cone, Dorothy BioIn 16
Cone, Edward Christopher 1937- WhoE 91
Cone, Edward T. 1917- IntWWM 90
Cone, Edward Toner 1917- WhoAm 90
Cone, Etta 1870-1949 BioAmW
Cone, Ferne Geller 1921- WhoAmW 91
Cone, Frances McFadden 1938- WhoAmW 91
Cone, George Wallis 1945- WhoSSW 91
Cone, Gerrit Craig 1947- WhoAmA 91
Cone, James Hal 1938- WhoAm 90
Cone, Joseph Jay 1955- WhoAm 90
Cone, Karen Elizabeth 1961- WhoAmW 91
Cone, Marvin 1891-1964 WhoAmA 91N
Cone, Mary 1923- WhoAmW 91
Cone, Max R. 1939- St&PR 91
Cone, Molly 1918- SmATA 11AS [port]
Cone, Molly Lamken 1918- AuBYP 90
Cone, Ruby WhoWrEP 89
Cone, Spencer Burtis 1910- WhoAm 90
Cone, Spencer Houghton 1785-1855 BioIn 16
Cone, Sydney M., III 1930- WhoAm 90
Cone, Thomas Conrad 1948- WhoEmL 91, WhoSSW 91
Cone, Tom 1947- OxCCanT
Cone, Virgie Horne Hyman 1912- WhoAmW 91
Cone, Virginia Williams WhoAmW 91
Cone, William BioIn 16
Cone, William Alan BiDrAPA 89
Cone, William Drury 1924- BiDrAPA 89
Cone, William H BiDrAPA 89
Cone-Skelton, Annette 1942- WhoAmA 91
Coneglio, Vince 1950- St&PR 91
Conejero, Manuel Angel 1943- WhoWor 91
Conejo, Mary Lynn 1951- WhoHisp 91
Conell, Lawrence Joseph BiDrAPA 89
Conerly, Erlene Brinson 1938- WhoAmW 91
Conerly, R.P. 1924- St&PR 91
Conerly, Richard Pugh 1924- WhoAm 90
Conery, Candida BioIn 16
Conesa, Eduardo Raul 1937- WhoWor 91
Conesa, Miguel A 1952- WhoAmA 91
Conese, Eugene Paul 1929- WhoAm 90
Coneway, Steve 1946- St&PR 91
Coney, Aims C., Jr. 1929- WhoAm 90

Coney, Carole Anne 1944- *WhoAmW 91*
Coney, John 1655-1722 *PenDiDA 89*
Coney, Mattie Rice *BioIn 16*
Coney, Michael G 1932- *SmATA 61 [port]*
Confalonieri, Giulio 1936- *ConDes 90*
Confer, Barbara Ann 1961- *WhoEmL 91*
Confer, Bernard A. *BioIn 16*
Confer, Ogden William 1945- *St&PR 91*
Confer, Thomas A. 1951- *St&PR 91*
Confer, William Clarence 1925- *St&PR 91*
Conford, Ellen *BioIn 16*
Conford, Ellen 1942- *AuBYP 90*
Conford, Milton Bernard *BioIn 16*
Conforte, Renee *WhoAmA 91*
Conforti, Emile Ralph 1928- *St&PR 91*
Conforti, Joanne 1944- *WhoAmW 91*
Conforti, John J. 1934- *St&PR 91*
Conforti, Michael Peter 1945- *WhoAm 90, WhoAmA 91*
Conforti, Salvatore J. *St&PR 91*
Conforto, Tracie Ruiz- *BioIn 16*
Confrey, Zez *BioIn 16*
Confrey, Zez 1895-1971 *OxCPMus*
Confucius *BioIn 16*
Confucius 551?BC-479BC *WorAlBi, WrPh P*
Congalton, Bunk 1875-1937 *Ballpl 90*
Congalton, Christopher William 1946- *WhoEmL 91*
Congalton, Susan Tichenor 1946- *WhoAm 90*
Congar, Marie Joseph *ConAu 130*
Congar, Y. M. *ConAu 130*
Congar, Yves *ConAu 130*
Congar, Yves M. J. *ConAu 130, -130*
Congar, Yves Marie-Joseph 1904- *ConAu 130*
Congdon, Constance *BioIn 16*
Congdon, James *BiDrAPA 89*
Congdon, John Rhodes 1933- *WhoAm 90*
Congdon, Lee 1939- *ConAu 130*
Congdon, Marsha B. 1947- *St&PR 91*
Congdon, Paul U. 1922- *WhoE 91*
Congdon, Raymond J. 1927- *St&PR 91*
Congdon, Rita Isabel 1948- *WhoHisp 91*
Congdon, Sarah-Braeme 1952- *WhoAmW 91*
Congdon, Thomas B., Jr. 1931- *WhoAm 90*
Congdon, William 1912- *WhoAmA 91*
Congel, Frank Joseph 1943- *WhoE 91*
Conger, Beach 1941- *BioIn 16*
Conger, Bob Vernon 1938- *WhoAm 90*
Conger, Clement E 1912- *WhoAmA 91*
Conger, Clement Ellis 1912- *WhoAm 90*
Conger, Edwin Hurd 1843-1907 *BioIn 16*
Conger, Elizabeth Tompkins 1942- *WhoE 91*
Conger, Franklin Barker 1929- *WhoAm 90*
Conger, Harry M. 1930- *St&PR 91*
Conger, Harry Milton 1930- *WhoAm 90*
Conger, James Gordon *BiDrAPA 89*
Conger, Jay A. 1952- *ConAu 132*
Conger, John Janeway 1921- *WhoAm 90*
Conger, Kenneth William 1936- *St&PR 91*
Conger, Kyril B. 1913- *WhoAm 90*
Conger, Lesley *WhoWrEP 89*
Conger, Marion *AuBYP 90*
Conger, Marion 1915-1990 *ConAu 130*
Conger, Marion C. 1915-1990 *BioIn 16*
Conger, Stephen Halsey 1927- *St&PR 91, WhoAm 90*
Conger, Sue Ann 1947- *WhoSSW 91*
Conger, Virginia Lee 1961- *WhoAmW 91*
Conger, Virginia Louise 1945- *WhoAmW 91, WhoSSW 91*
Conger, Willard F 1948- *BiDrAPA 89*
Conger, William 1937- *WhoAmA 91*
Conger, William Frame 1937- *WhoAm 90*
Congleton, Conley Cole, III 1945- *WhoEmL 91*
Congleton, Joseph Patrick 1947- *WhoEmL 91*
Congleton, Laura Helen 1962- *WhoAmW 91*
Congleton, William Harold 1922- *St&PR 91*
Congreve, William 1670-1729 *WorAlBi*
Congtang, Phungmai T 1932- *BiDrAPA 89*
Conhagen, Alfred *St&PR 91*
Conhagen, Alfred 1897- *WhoSSW 91*
Coniaris, John Charles 1925- *BiDrAPA 89*
Conibear, Shirley A. 1946- *St&PR 91*
Conibear, Shirley Ann 1946- *WhoAmW 91*
Conidi, Daniel Joseph 1957- *WhoEmL 91, WhoWor 91*
Conidi, Jennifer 1950- *WhoSSW 91*
Conigilaro, Phyllis Ann 1932- *WhoE 91*
Conigliaro, Billy 1947- *Ballpl 90*
Conigliaro, Tony *BioIn 16*
Conigliaro, Tony *NewYTBS 90*
Conigliaro, Tony 1945- *Ballpl 90*
Conigliaro, Tony 1945-1990 *CurBio 90N, News 90, -90-3*
Conigliaro, Vincent S *BiDrAPA 89*
Coniglio, Cynthia Ann *BiDrAPA 89*
Coniglione, Roy 1938- *St&PR 91*
Conijn, Gerard L. 1941- *St&PR 91*
Conine, Ernest 1925- *WhoAm 90*
Conine, Kevin Alan 1957- *WhoEmL 91*
Conine, Thomas Edmund, Jr. 1951- *WhoEmL 91, WhoWor 91*
Coningsby, Thomas *BioIn 16*
Conix, Andre Jan 1925- *WhoWor 91*
Conk, Richard Vincent 1947- *St&PR 91*
Conkey, Ruth C. *BioIn 16*
Conkey, Sharyn Yanoshak 1945- *WhoWrEP 89*
Conkin, Paul Keith 1929- *WhoAm 90*
Conkle, Daniel Oliver 1953- *WhoEmL 91*
Conkle, Donald Steven 1948- *WhoWrEP 89*
Conklin, Andrew Sterrett 1961- *WhoAmA 91*
Conklin, Anna Immaculata G. 1951- *WhoAmW 91*
Conklin, Charles Russell 1922- *St&PR 91*
Conklin, David Arnold 1930- *St&PR 91, WhoAm 90, WhoWor 91*
Conklin, Dean 1936- *ODwPR 91*
Conklin, Diane L. 1953- *St&PR 91*
Conklin, Donald Ransford 1936- *WhoAm 90, WhoE 91*
Conklin, Frances Phillips 1924- *WhoAmW 91*
Conklin, Gary Eldon 1935- *St&PR 91*
Conklin, George Melville 1921- *WhoAm 90*
Conklin, George T., Jr. 1914- *St&PR 91*
Conklin, Gladys 1903- *AuBYP 90*
Conklin, Gloria Zamko 1925- *WhoAmA 91*
Conklin, Gordon Leroy 1927- *WhoAm 90*
Conklin, Harold Colyer 1926- *WhoAm 90*
Conklin, Hugh Randolph 1911- *WhoAm 90*
Conklin, J. B. *EncO&P 3*
Conklin, Jack Lariviere 1942- *WhoE 91*
Conklin, James LaRue 1922- *St&PR 91*
Conklin, Janice G. *ODwPR 91*
Conklin, John Evan 1943- *WhoAm 90*
Conklin, John Roger 1933- *St&PR 91*
Conklin, Kenneth Edward 1939- *WhoAm 90*
Conklin, Mara L. *ODwPR 91*
Conklin, Mary Washburn 1907- *BioIn 16*
Conklin, Paul *AuBYP 90*
Conklin, Richard J. 1945- *St&PR 91*
Conklin, Robert Elliot 1936- *WhoAm 90*
Conklin, Robert Murray 1916- *St&PR 91*
Conklin, Susan Jean 1950- *WhoEmL 91*
Conklin, Susan Joan 1950- *WhoAmW 91*
Conklin, Thomas J. 1946- *St&PR 91*
Conklin, Thomas Joseph *BiDrAPA 89*
Conklin, Thomas William 1938- *WhoAm 90*
Conklin, William Spencer 1940- *St&PR 91*
Conklin, William T. *BioIn 16, NewYTBS 90 [port]*
Conklin-Andreski, Barbara Jeanne-Anne 1959- *WhoSSW 91*
Conkling, Fleur *AuBYP 90*
Conkling, Hilda 1910-1986 *BioIn 16*
Conkling, Roger Linton 1917- *WhoAm 90*
Conkling, Roscoe 1829-1888 *WorAlBi*
Conkwright, John M. 1944- *St&PR 91*
Conlan, Gary D. 1936- *St&PR 91*
Conlan, Jocko 1899- *Ballpl 90 [port]*
Conlan, Jocko 1899-1989 *AnObit 1989, BioIn 16*
Conlan, Richard John 1924- *St&PR 91*
Conlan, Terrence J. 1940- *St&PR 91*
Conlan, William H. 1928- *ODwPR 91*
Conland, Stephen 1916- *WhoAm 90*
Conlee, Cecil D. 1936- *St&PR 91*
Conley *EncPaPR 91*
Conley, Barbara 1949- *BioIn 16*
Conley, Barbara Bernadette *WhoAmW 91*
Conley, Carroll Lockard 1915- *WhoAm 90*
Conley, Christopher John 1946- *WhoEmL 91*
Conley, Clare Dean 1929- *WhoAm 90*
Conley, Colleen Alice 1952- *BiDrAPA 89*
Conley, David R. 1944- *St&PR 91*
Conley, Donal Thayer *BiDrAPA 89*
Conley, Earl Thomas *WhoNeCM [port]*
Conley, Eugene Allen 1925- *St&PR 91, WhoAm 90*
Conley, Eugene J 1933- *BiDrAPA 89*
Conley, Gene 1930- *Ballpl 90*
Conley, Gene Raymond 1952- *WhoEmL 91*
Conley, Howard Harry, Jr. 1915- *WhoAm 90*
Conley, James Daniel 1928- *WhoAm 90*
Conley, James Edward 1913- *WhoAm 90*
Conley, James Michael 1944- *St&PR 91*
Conley, James Patrick 1938- *WhoAm 90*
Conley, Jeffrey B. *ODwPR 91*
Conley, Jerry Lynn 1946- *WhoSSW 91*
Conley, John Ellis, II *BiDrAPA 89*
Conley, Joseph H. *St&PR 91*
Conley, Joseph Howard 1941- *WhoE 91*
Conley, Lakita 1955- *WhoE 91*
Conley, M Catherine 1954- *BiDrAPA 89*
Conley, Margaret Elizabeth 1960- *WhoEmL 91*
Conley, Mariita Arosemena 1951- *WhoAmW 91*
Conley, Michael Clark 1938- *St&PR 91*
Conley, Nancy MacConnell 1959- *WhoEmL 91*
Conley, Ned Leroy 1925- *WhoAm 90, WhoSSW 91, WhoWor 91*
Conley, Patricia 1961- *ODwPR 91*
Conley, Philip I. 1919- *St&PR 91*
Conley, Philip James, Jr. 1927- *WhoAm 90*
Conley, Richard Michael 1910- *St&PR 91*
Conley, Richard Michael 1943- *St&PR 91*
Conley, Robert 1928- *WhoE 91*
Conley, Robert Francis 1923- *WhoAm 90*
Conley, Robert Russell 1956- *BiDrAPA 89*
Conley, Steven W. 1952- *St&PR 91*
Conley, Tim James 1958- *WhoSSW 91*
Conley, Tom Clark 1943- *WhoAm 90*
Conley, Walter Leslie 1941- *St&PR 91*
Conley, William Donald 1927- *St&PR 91*
Conley, Zeb Bristol, Jr 1936- *WhoAmA 91*
Conlin, Alfred Thomas 1921- *WhoAm 90*
Conlin, Joanne 1955- *WhoAmW 91*
Conlin, Kellie Ann 1964- *WhoEmL 91*
Conlin, Nancy Marie 1949- *WhoAmW 91*
Conlin, Olive Westberry 1943- *WhoAmW 91*
Conlin, Roxanne Barton 1944- *WhoAm 90, WhoAmW 91*
Conlin, Thomas R. 1943- *ODwPR 91*
Conlin, Thomas William 1949- *St&PR 91*
Conlin, William P. 1933- *St&PR 91*
Conlin, William Patrick 1933- *WhoAm 90*
Conlisk, Elizabeth *ODwPR 91*
Conlogue, William Paul 1963- *WhoWrEP 89*
Conlon, April Harrington 1958- *WhoAmW 91*
Conlon, Ellen Catherine 1940- *St&PR 91*
Conlon, Eugene 1925- *WhoAm 90*
Conlon, Jack Martin 1931- *WhoAm 90*
Conlon, James 1950- *IntWWM 90, PenDiMP*
Conlon, James Edward 1935- *WhoAmA 91*
Conlon, James Joseph 1950- *WhoAm 90*
Conlon, Joseph 1937- *St&PR 91*
Conlon, Kathleen 1943- *ConAu 130*
Conlon, Kathryn Ann 1958- *WhoAmW 91*
Conlon, Kevin John 1961- *WhoE 91*
Conlon, Michael William 1946- *WhoAm 90*
Conlon, Patrick St. John *BiDrAPA 89*
Conlon, Peter John, Jr. 1951- *WhoEmL 91, WhoSSW 91*
Conlon, Richard 1930-1988 *BioIn 16*
Conlon, Robert Kenneth 1937- *WhoAm 90*
Conlon, Suzanne B. 1939- *WhoAmW 91*
Conlon, Thomas James 1935- *WhoWor 91*
Conlon, Timothy J. *ODwPR 91*
Conlon, Vicki Lynn 1952- *WhoEmL 91*
Conlon, William Martin 1953- *WhoEmL 91*
Conly, Jane Leslie *AuBYP 90*
Conly, John Franklin 1933- *WhoAm 90*
Conly, Robert Leslie *AuBYP 90*
Conmy, Peter Thomas 1901- *WhoAm 90*
Conn, A.C. 1947- *St&PR 91*
Conn, Adina 1962- *WhoAmW 91*
Conn, Arthur Leonard 1913- *WhoAm 90*
Conn, Carol 1952- *WhoEmL 91, WhoWrEP 89*
Conn, Christopher 1948- *WhoWrEP 89*
Conn, Claude Bowen, Jr. 1932- *WhoSSW 91*
Conn, David Edward 1941- *WhoAmA 91*
Conn, Eric Edward 1923- *WhoAm 90*
Conn, Eunice Marie Janicki 1938- *WhoAmW 91*
Conn, Frances 1925- *AuBYP 90*
Conn, Hadley Lewis, Jr. 1921- *WhoAm 90, WhoWor 91*
Conn, Harold O. 1925- *WhoAm 90*
Conn, Jacob H *BiDrAPA 89*
Conn, James Warren 1943- *BiDrAPA 89*
Conn, Jan E 1952- *ConAu 31NR*
Conn, Jerome W. 1907- *WhoAm 90*
Conn, Joseph Bert 1950- *WhoEmL 91*
Conn, Laurence 1945- *WhoAmA 91*
Conn, Lewis *BioIn 16*
Conn, Lois Marie 1953- *BiDrAPA 89*
Conn, Malcolm 1831-1898 *BioIn 16*
Conn, Paul Harding, Jr. 1955- *WhoEmL 91*
Conn, Raymond Allen 1933- *BiDrAPA 89*
Conn, Rex Boland, Jr. 1927- *WhoAm 90*
Conn, Richard 1960- *St&PR 91*
Conn, Richard George 1928- *WhoAmA 91*
Conn, Robert Henry 1925- *WhoAm 90*
Conn, Robert William 1942- *WhoAm 90*
Conn, Stephen R. 1938- *ODwPR 91*
Conn, Virginia Louise Starbuck 1916- *WhoAmW 91*
Connable, Alfred Barnes 1904- *WhoAm 90*
Connally, Ernest Allen 1921- *WhoAm 90*
Connally, John B. 1917- *St&PR 91, WorAlBi*
Connally, John B., Jr. *BioIn 16*
Connally, John Bowden 1917- *BiDrUSE 89*
Connally, Michael W. 1957- *WhoEmL 91*
Connally, Sarge 1898-1978 *Ballpl 90*
Connar, Richard Grigsby 1920- *WhoAm 90*
Connaughton, James Patrick 1931- *BiDrAPA 89*
Connavino, Nicholas Anthony 1946- *WhoAm 90*
Connaway, Jay Hall 1893-1970 *WhoAmA 91N*
Connaway, Robert Wallace 1956- *WhoSSW 91*
Conneally, P. Michael *WhoAm 90*
Connealy, Laurence Allen 1929- *St&PR 91*
Conneely, John 1944- *St&PR 91*
Conneen, Jane W 1921- *WhoAmA 91*
Conneen, Mari M 1946- *WhoAmA 91*
Connell, Alastair McCrae 1929- *WhoAm 90*
Connell, Byron Patrick 1941- *WhoE 91*
Connell, Charles John 1951- *WhoEmL 91*
Connell, Charles Richard, III 1932- *WhoWor 91*
Connell, Clyde 1900- *BioIn 16*
Connell, Coleman Joseph 1929- *St&PR 91*
Connell, Daniel W. 1948- *St&PR 91*
Connell, Elizabeth 1946- *IntWWM 90, PenDiMP*
Connell, Elizabeth Bishop 1925- *WhoAmW 91*
Connell, Elizabeth Day 1952- *BiDrAPA 89*
Connell, Evan S., Jr. 1924- *MajTwCW*
Connell, Evan Shelby, Jr. 1924- *WhoAm 90, WhoWrEP 89*
Connell, Gene McCain, Jr. 1958- *WhoEmL 91*
Connell, George Edward 1930- *WhoAm 90*
Connell, George Herman, Jr. 1944- *WhoSSW 91*
Connell, Grover 1918- *WhoAm 90*
Connell, Harold Lee 1943- *St&PR 91*
Connell, Hugh P. 1931- *St&PR 91*
Connell, James Patrick *BioIn 16*
Connell, Jim *BioIn 16*
Connell, Jim O. 1942- *St&PR 91*
Connell, John Alexander *BiDrAPA 89*
Connell, John G. 1944- *St&PR 91*
Connell, John Gibbs, Jr. 1914- *WhoAm 90*
Connell, Joseph Edward 1930- *St&PR 91, WhoAm 90*
Connell, Karl 1924- *St&PR 91*
Connell, Kathleen Sullivan 1937- *WhoAm 90, WhoAmW 91, WhoE 91*
Connell, Lawrence *BioIn 16*
Connell, Lawrence 1936- *WhoAm 90*
Connell, Linda Marie 1957- *WhoAmW 91*
Connell, Michael L 1935- *BiDrAPA 89*
Connell, Peter *ODwPR 91*
Connell, Philip F. 1924- *St&PR 91*
Connell, Philip Francis 1924- *WhoAm 90*
Connell, Philip Henry *BiDrAPA 89*
Connell, Roy, II 1933- *WhoSSW 91*
Connell, Sandra Kay *BiDrAPA 89*
Connell, Shirley Hudgins 1946- *WhoAmW 91, WhoE 91, WhoEmL 91*
Connell, Terry 1950- *WhoAm 90*
Connell, Thomas A. 1947- *St&PR 91*
Connell, Thomas Alfred 1960- *BiDrAPA 89*
Connell, Wilfred 1937- *St&PR 91*
Connell, William Francis 1938- *WhoAm 90, WhoE 91*
Connell-Tatum, Elizabeth Bishop 1925- *WhoAm 90*
Connelly, Albert R. 1908- *WhoAm 90*
Connelly, Anne 1950- *St&PR 91*
Connelly, Becky Lou 1940- *WhoAmW 91*
Connelly, Carolyn Thomas 1941- *WhoAmW 91*
Connelly, Chuck 1955- *WhoAmA 91*
Connelly, Cornelia 1809-1879 *BioAmW*
Connelly, Daniel F. 1939- *St&PR 91*
Connelly, David Warren 1945- *WhoEmL 91*
Connelly, Donald Albert 1945- *WhoE 91*
Connelly, Donald P. 1939- *St&PR 91*
Connelly, Donald Preston 1939- *WhoAm 90*
Connelly, Donald Webb 1930- *WhoAm 90*
Connelly, Eileen Bernadette 1965- *WhoAmW 91*
Connelly, Eric 1910- *St&PR 91*
Connelly, John Coleman 1939- *BiDrAPA 89*
Connelly, John Dooley 1946- *WhoEmL 91*
Connelly, John E., Jr. 1904- *St&PR 91*
Connelly, John Edward, III 1935- *WhoE 91*
Connelly, John Edward, Jr. 1904- *WhoAm 90*
Connelly, John F. *St&PR 91N*
Connelly, John Francis 1905- *WhoAm 90, WhoE 91*
Connelly, John J. 1946- *St&PR 91*
Connelly, John Matthew 1942- *St&PR 91, WhoAm 90*
Connelly, Kathleen Fitzgerald 1949- *ODwPR 91*
Connelly, Linda McLean 1950- *WhoE 91*
Connelly, Marc 1890-1980 *ConAu 30NR, WorAlBi*

Connelly, Marilyn L. 1949- St&PR 91
Connelly, Martin J. 1931- St&PR 91
Connelly, P. Kevin 1950- WhoEmL 91
Connelly, Patricia Lorraine 1948- WhoAmW 91
Connelly, Patrick O'Neil 1946- WhoE 91
Connelly, Reg 1895-1963 OxCPMus
Connelly, Richard J. ODwPR 91
Connelly, Robert Bourke 1935- WhoWrEP 89
Connelly, Robert J. 1939- WhoSSW 91
Connelly, Sally S. 1953- St&PR 91
Connelly, Sharon Rudolph 1940- WhoAm 90
Connelly, Stephen A. 1944- St&PR 91
Connelly, Terrence Ralph 1943- WhoAm 90
Connelly, Timothy John, Jr. 1909- St&PR 91
Connelly, William Arthur 1935- St&PR 91
Connelly, William Howard 1920- WhoAm 90
Connelly, William Joseph 1931- WhoWor 91
Connelly-Sistovaris, Anne-Francoise 1959- WhoWor 91
Conner, Ann 1948- WhoAmA 91
Conner, Archie Hampton 1941- WhoSSW 91
Conner, Bruce 1933- WhoAm 90, WhoAmA 91
Conner, Carl Watson 1950- WhoE 91
Conner, Charlotte Barnes 1818-1863 BioIn 16, NotWoAT
Conner, Cindy Dixon 1951- WhoWrEP 89
Conner, Colleen Colgan 1949- WhoAmW 91
Conner, David Allen 1939- WhoSSW 91
Conner, David McDonald 1957- BiDrAPA 89
Conner, Dennis BioIn 16
Conner, Don R. 1949- WhoWrEP 89
Conner, Donald Gene 1936- St&PR 91
Conner, Donald Matthew 1951- WhoSSW 91
Conner, Gary Lee BioIn 16
Conner, Gay Arterburn 1962- WhoAmW 91
Conner, Harry W. 1929- ODwPR 91
Conner, Hugh Mcdonald, Jr. BiDrAPA 89
Conner, James Arnel 1940- St&PR 91
Conner, James Edward 1927- WhoE 91
Conner, Janet Austin 1946- WhoAmW 91
Conner, Janet Chestelynn 1953- WhoAmW 91
Conner, Jeanette Jones 1934- WhoAmW 91
Conner, Joan Fish 1947- WhoSSW 91
Conner, John Davis 1911- WhoAm 90
Conner, John Ramsey 1869-1952 WhoAmA 91N
Conner, John Wayne 1919- WhoAm 90
Conner, Judy Sue 1947- WhoAmW 91
Conner, Karen Jean 1941- WhoAmW 91
Conner, Kathryn Gamble 1959- WhoEmL 91
Conner, Kenyon BioIn 16
Conner, Larry Edward 1945- WhoSSW 91
Conner, Linda Adcock 1959- WhoEmL 91
Conner, Lindsay Andrew 1956- WhoEmL 91
Conner, Lynda Marie 1962- WhoEmL 91
Conner, Nadine 1914- IntWWM 90
Conner, Phillip Lee 1953- WhoEmL 91
Conner, Roger W. 1948- ODwPR 91
Conner, Sherry Johnson 1952- WhoSSW 91
Conner, Stewart Edmund 1941- WhoSSW 91
Conner, Timothy James 1954- WhoEmL 91
Conner, Timothy V. ODwPR 91
Conner, Troy Blaine, Jr. 1926- WhoAm 90
Conner, Virginia Lea 1935- WhoAmW 91
Conner, Virginia S. 1950- WhoHisp 91
Conner, W.B. 1923- St&PR 91
Conner, Wallace J. 1933- St&PR 91
Conner, Walter 1947- ODwPR 91
Conner, William Boudinot 1913- WhoWor 91
Conner, William C 1934- BiDrAPA 89
Conner, William Joseph, Jr. 1923- St&PR 91
Conner, William Lawrence, III 1952- WhoEmL 91
Conner, William P. 1941- St&PR 91
Connerly, Dianna Jean 1947- WhoAmW 91
Conners, John Brendan 1945- St&PR 91, WhoAm 90
Conners, John Reed 1954- WhoEmL 91
Conners, Keith 1962- WhoEmL 91
Conners, Keith J. 1948- WhoEmL 91
Conners, Kerry B. 1957- WhoEmL 91
Conners, William Patrick 1938- St&PR 91
Connerty, Mary Constance 1956- WhoE 91
Connery, Bob 1879-1967 Ballpl 90
Connery, Carol Jean 1948- WhoAmW 91
Connery, Jason BioIn 16
Connery, Robert Howe 1907- WhoAm 90
Connery, Sean BioIn 16
Connery, Sean 1930- News 90 [port], WhoAm 90, WorAlBi
Connett, Dee M 1935- WhoAmA 91
Connett, Richard James 1943- WhoE 91
Conney, Allan Howard 1930- WhoAm 90
Conney, David 1953- BiDrAPA 89
Connick, Charles Milo 1917- WhoAm 90
Connick, George P. WhoAm 90
Connick, Girard Briant 1944- WhoSSW 91
Connick, Harry, Jr. BioIn 16
Connick, Harry, Jr. 1967- ConMus 4 [port], CurBio 90 [port], News 91-1 [port]
Connick, Harry, Sr. BioIn 16
Connick, Robert Elwell 1917- WhoAm 90
Connie WhoWrEP 89
Conniff, Gregory 1944- WhoAmA 91
Conniff, Ray 1916- IntWWM 90, OxCPMus, WhoAm 90
Connington, J. J. 1880-1947 TwCCr&M 91
Connochie, Robert Gordon 1941- St&PR 91
Connock, Stuart Wallace 1925- WhoSSW 91
Connola, Donald Pascal, Jr. 1948- WhoE 91
Connolly, Arthur G. 1905- St&PR 91
Connolly, Arthur Guild 1905- WhoAm 90
Connolly, Billy BioIn 16
Connolly, Brian ODwPR 91
Connolly, Brian Andrew 1946- BiDrAPA 89
Connolly, Brian E. 1945- St&PR 91
Connolly, Brian Michael 1941- WhoSSW 91
Connolly, Brigid BiDrAPA 89
Connolly, Charles H. 1934- ODwPR 91, St&PR 91
Connolly, Cyril 1903-1974 BioIn 16, DcLB 98 [port], MajTwCW
Connolly, David I. 1934- St&PR 91, WhoAm 90
Connolly, Donna Marie 1953- WhoEmL 91
Connolly, Ed 1939- Ballpl 90
Connolly, Edward J. 1915-1989 BioIn 16
Connolly, Elizabeth Anne 1957- WhoAmW 91
Connolly, Elma Troutman 1931- WhoAmW 91
Connolly, Eugene B., Jr. 1932- WhoAm 90
Connolly, Eugene Bernard, Jr. 1932- St&PR 91
Connolly, Eugene T., Jr. 1931- St&PR 91
Connolly, George P. 1917- St&PR 91
Connolly, Gerald Edward 1943- WhoAm 90
Connolly, Gerald Joseph 1948- WhoE 91
Connolly, H. Andrew 1945- WhoEmL 91
Connolly, J. Wray 1934- St&PR 91
Connolly, James 1868-1916 BioIn 16, EncAL
Connolly, James M. 1942- St&PR 91
Connolly, Jane Terrell 1942- WhoAmW 91
Connolly, Janet F. 1929- WhoAmW 91
Connolly, Janna L. 1956- St&PR 91
Connolly, Jerome Patrick 1931- WhoAmA 91
Connolly, Joanne Marie 1958- WhoE 91
Connolly, Joe 1888-1943 Ballpl 90
Connolly, John Earle 1923- WhoAm 90, WhoWor 91
Connolly, John J. 1939- St&PR 91
Connolly, John Joseph 1940- WhoAm 90, WhoE 91
Connolly, John Michael 1947- WhoWor 91
Connolly, John Stephen 1936- WhoAm 90
Connolly, John Thomas 1925- WhoSSW 91
Connolly, John William Domville 1938- WhoSSW 91
Connolly, Joseph 1950- ConAu 130
Connolly, Joseph Edward 1932- St&PR 91
Connolly, Joseph Francis, II 1944- WhoSSW 91, WhoWor 91
Connolly, Justin Riveagh 1933- IntWWM 90
Connolly, Kathy Ann Schultz 1952- WhoEmL 91
Connolly, L. William 1923- WhoAm 90
Connolly, Leo Augustine 1941- WhoSSW 91
Connolly, Margaret Theresa 1942- WhoAmW 91
Connolly, Marie Loyola 1960- WhoEmL 91
Connolly, Mark Edward 1952- WhoEmL 91
Connolly, Martin F. 1949- WhoEmL 91
Connolly, Matthew Bernard, Jr. 1941- WhoAm 90
Connolly, Maureen 1934-1969 WorAlBi
Connolly, Maureen Ann 1958- WhoAmW 91
Connolly, Michael BioIn 16
Connolly, Michael Brian 1939- WhoSSW 91
Connolly, Michael I. 1956- St&PR 91
Connolly, Michael Joseph 1947- WhoAm 90, WhoE 91
Connolly, Peggy 1951- WhoAmW 91
Connolly, Peter 1935- BioIn 16
Connolly, Peter K. ODwPR 91
Connolly, Roberta Sue 1947- WhoAmW 91
Connolly, Ronald C. 1932- St&PR 91
Connolly, Selden Wolcott 1925- St&PR 91
Connolly, Stephen J., III 1920- St&PR 91
Connolly, Stephen John, IV 1949- St&PR 91
Connolly, Sybil BioIn 16
Connolly, Thomas Arthur 1899- WhoAm 90
Connolly, Thomas Edward 1942- WhoE 91, WhoWor 91
Connolly, Thomas Joseph 1957- WhoEmL 91, WhoWor 91
Connolly, Tom 1870-1963 Ballpl 90
Connolly, Trudye ODwPR 91
Connolly, Vera Leona 1888-1964 BioIn 16
Connolly, Walter Justin, Jr. 1928- St&PR 91, WhoAm 90, WhoE 91
Connolly, William Gerard 1937- WhoE 91
Connolly, William Joseph 1929- St&PR 91
Connolly-O'Neill, Barrie Jane 1943- WhoAmW 91, WhoWor 91
Connon, Thomas 1832-1899 DcCanB 12
Connor, Brian Nichols 1946- WhoE 91
Connor, Charles Peter BiDrAPA 89
Connor, Charles Robert 1939- WhoSSW 91
Connor, Constance Gibson Wehrman 1935- WhoAmW 91, WhoSSW 91
Connor, Daniel Fredrick 1953- BiDrAPA 89
Connor, David J. 1942- St&PR 91
Connor, David John 1953- WhoEmL 91, WhoWor 91
Connor, David Michael 1935- WhoE 91
Connor, Edward BioIn 16
Connor, Geoffrey Michael 1946- St&PR 91, WhoAm 90
Connor, George Carley, Jr. 1936- WhoSSW 91
Connor, Henry Groves 1852-1924 AmLegL
Connor, Huell E, Jr. BiDrAPA 89
Connor, Hugh F. ODwPR 91
Connor, J. Robert 1927- WhoAm 90, WhoWrEP 89
Connor, Jack A. 1923- St&PR 91
Connor, James AuBYP 90
Connor, James Edward, Jr. 1924- WhoAm 90
Connor, James Richard 1928- WhoAm 90
Connor, James Russell 1940- WhoWor 91
Connor, James W. 1926- St&PR 91
Connor, Jeffrey C. 1948- ODwPR 91
Connor, John Anthony 1930- WhoAm 90
Connor, John Edwin 1959- WhoWrEP 89
Connor, John Francis 1944- St&PR 91
Connor, John M. 1952- St&PR 91
Connor, John Thomas 1914- BiDrUSE 89, WhoAm 90
Connor, John Thomas, Jr. 1941- WhoAm 90
Connor, John Thorp, II 1944- WhoE 91
Connor, Joseph Andrew 1952- WhoEmL 91
Connor, Joseph E. 1931- WhoAm 90
Connor, Joseph Patrick, III 1953- WhoE 91, WhoWor 91
Connor, Katherine Elizabeth 1958- WhoEmL 91
Connor, Kenneth Luke 1947- WhoSSW 91
Connor, Laura Louise 1962- WhoAmW 91
Connor, Lawrence Stanton 1925- WhoAm 90
Connor, Linda Stevens 1944- WhoAmA 91
Connor, Margo 1943- WhoAmW 91
Connor, Marie Stella 1918- WhoAmW 91
Connor, Martin Edward 1945- WhoE 91
Connor, Martin J., Jr. 1933- St&PR 91
Connor, Patrick Edward 1820-1891 WhNaAH
Connor, Patrick F. 1939- ODwPR 91
Connor, Paul Eugene 1921- WhoE 91, WhoWor 91
Connor, Ralph 1860-1937 DcLB 92 [port]
Connor, Richard Hallowell 1946- St&PR 91
Connor, Richard L. 1947- WhoAm 90
Connor, Robert Brian BiDrAPA 89
Connor, Robert T. 1919- WhoE 91
Connor, Roger 1857-1931 Ballpl 90 [port], BioIn 16
Connor, Seymour Vaughan 1923- WhoAm 90, WhoWrEP 89
Connor, Sidney Gregg 1947- WhoEmL 91
Connor, Stephen Brian BiDrAPA 89
Connor, Susan 1958- WhoAmW 91
Connor, Thomas Byrne 1921- WhoAm 90
Connor, Thomas G. 1938- St&PR 91
Connor, Tony 1930- WhoWrEP 89
Connor, Walter Fischer 1938- St&PR 91
Connor, Walter Robert 1934- WhoAm 90
Connor, Whitfield 1916-1988 BioIn 16
Connor, Wilda 1947- WhoAmW 91, WhoEmL 91
Connor, William Elliott 1921- WhoAm 90
Connors, Basil J. 1927- St&PR 91
Connors, Carol 1940- BioIn 16
Connors, Catherine Louise 1960- WhoAmW 91
Connors, Chuck 1921- Ballpl 90, WorAlBi
Connors, Chuck Kevin Joseph 1921- WhoAm 90
Connors, Cornelia Kathleen 1958- WhoEmL 91
Connors, Dorsey WhoAm 90, WhoAmW 91
Connors, Edward M. 1940- St&PR 91
Connors, Eugene Kenneth 1946- WhoAm 90
Connors, James Joseph 1930- St&PR 91
Connors, James Patrick 1952- WhoEmL 91
Connors, James T. 1935- St&PR 91, WhoAm 90
Connors, Jimmy 1952- BioIn 16, WhoAm 90, WhoWor 91, WorAlBi
Connors, John A. 1928- St&PR 91
Connors, John J. 1931- St&PR 91
Connors, John James BiDrAPA 89
Connors, John Michael, Jr. 1942- WhoAm 90
Connors, John Patrick BioIn 16
Connors, Joseph Aloysius, III 1946- WhoEmL 91, WhoSSW 91, WhoWor 91
Connors, Joseph Conlin 1948- WhoEmL 91
Connors, Kathryn Dughi 1947- WhoAmW 91
Connors, Kenneth Antonio 1932- WhoAm 90
Connors, Leo G. 1927- St&PR 91
Connors, Leo Gerard 1927- WhoAm 90
Connors, Mary Eileen 1953- WhoAmW 91
Connors, Michele Perrott 1952- WhoSSW 91
Connors, Mike 1925- WhoAm 90
Connors, Richard James 1931- St&PR 91
Connors, Robert Leo 1940- WhoE 91
Connors, Thomas E. 1929- WhoWrEP 89
Connors, Thomas H. 1959- WhoEmL 91
Connors, Thomas Joseph 1924- WhoAm 90
Connors, Timothy John 1947- St&PR 91
Connors, Tracy Daniel 1939- WhoE 91
Connors, W.F. 1940- St&PR 91
Connors, William P. BioIn 16
Connuck, Paul Dennis 1951- WhoEmL 91
Conoby, Joseph Francis 1930- WhoE 91, WhoWor 91
Conole, Clement Vincent 1908- WhoAm 90, WhoWor 91
Conole, Richard Clement 1936- WhoWor 91
Conoley, Gillian 1955- WhoWrEP 89
Conoley, Joann Shipman 1931- WhoAmW 91, WhoWor 91
Conolly, Henry Neal 1952- WhoE 91
Conolly, R.N. 1913- St&PR 91
Conomy, John Paul 1938- WhoAm 90
Conor, Henry M. 1925- St&PR 91
Conoscenti, Thomas C. 1945- St&PR 91
Conour, William Frederick 1947- WhoEmL 91
Conover, Arthur Verner, III 1942- St&PR 91
Conover, Brooks William, III 1959- WhoEmL 91
Conover, Carole Ann 1941- WhoAmW 91
Conover, Catherine 1949- WhoAmW 91
Conover, Charles Todd 1939- WhoAm 90
Conover, Chris 1950- AuBYP 90, BioIn 16
Conover, Claude 1907- WhoAmA 91
Conover, Harvey 1925- WhoAm 90
Conover, Heather C. 1952- ODwPR 91
Conover, Mark BioIn 16
Conover, Nellie Coburn 1921- WhoAmW 91
Conover, Robert Fremont 1920- WhoAmA 91
Conover, Roger L 1950- ConAu 130
Conover, Sarah Miller 1965- WhoAmW 91
Conover, Simon Barclay 1840-1908 AmLegL
Conover, Ted 1958- ConAu 129
Conover, Val Vagts 1930- WhoAmW 91, WhoE 91
Conover, Warren BioIn 16
Conover, William Jay 1936- WhoAm 90, WhoWor 91
Conquering Bear WhNaAH
Conquest, Edwin Parker, Jr. 1931- WhoE 91
Conquest, Richard Lee 1949- St&PR 91
Conquest, Robert 1917- WhoAm 90
Conrace, Joseph Ettor, Jr. BiDrAPA 89
Conrad, Barbara 1945- IntWWM 90
Conrad, Barbara Kay 1946- WhoAmW 91
Conrad, Beverly Ann 1953- WhoE 91
Conrad, Brenda TwCCr&M 91

Conrad, Bruce Phillips 1943- WhoE 91
Conrad, Carlton J. 1922- St&PR 91
Conrad, Charles, Jr. 1930- WhoAm 90, WorAlBi
Conrad, Charles Mynn 1804-1878 BiDrUSE 89
Conrad, Clyde Lee BioIn 16
Conrad, Con 1891-1938 BioIn 16, OxCPMus
Conrad, Constance Hoevel 1948- St&PR 91
Conrad, Cynthia Dale 1948- BiDrAPA 89
Conrad, David Edward 1941- St&PR 91
Conrad, David Paul 1946- WhoSSW 91
Conrad, Diethelm 1933- WhoWor 91
Conrad, Doda 1905- PenDiMP
Conrad, Donald Glover 1930- WhoAm 90, WhoE 91
Conrad, Douglas Michael BiDrAPA 89
Conrad, Edward Craig 1958- WhoEmL 91
Conrad, George 1916- WhoAmA 91
Conrad, George John 1943- WhoE 91
Conrad, Gladys K BiDrAPA 89
Conrad, Glenn Carl 1950- WhoE 91
Conrad, Hans 1922- WhoAm 90
Conrad, Harold T 1934- BiDrAPA 89
Conrad, Harold Theodore 1934- WhoSSW 91, WhoWor 91
Conrad, Harry Lester, Jr. 1917- St&PR 91
Conrad, Helen Bott 1918- WhoAmW 91
Conrad, Jerome Charles 1947- WhoEmL 91
Conrad, John R. 1915- St&PR 91, WhoAm 90
Conrad, John Regis 1955- WhoEmL 91
Conrad, John W 1935- WhoAmA 91
Conrad, Joseph 1857-1924 BioIn 16, ConAu 131, DcLB 98 [port], MajTwCW, SpyFic, WorAlBi, WrPh
Conrad, Kathryn Jo 1956- WhoAmW 91
Conrad, Kay Ann 1945- WhoAmW 91
Conrad, Kenneth Allen 1946- WhoEmL 91
Conrad, Kent 1948- WhoAm 90, WhoWor 91
Conrad, Kimberley BioIn 16
Conrad, Larry Wayne 1961- WhoEmL 91
Conrad, Laurie Margaret 1946- WhoEmL 91
Conrad, Marcel Edward 1928- WhoAm 90, WhoSSW 91
Conrad, Michael Patrick 1958- BiDrAPA 89
Conrad, Michael Van 1952- WhoSSW 91
Conrad, Nancy R 1940- WhoAmA 91
Conrad, Natalie Teresa 1953- WhoAmW 91
Conrad, Osmond 1936- St&PR 91, WhoAm 90
Conrad, Pam 1947- BioIn 16
Conrad, Paul 1921- WhoAm 90
Conrad, Paul Edward 1956- WhoEmL 91
Conrad, Paul Ernest 1927- WhoAm 90
Conrad, Paul Francis 1924- WhoAm 90, WhoAmA 91
Conrad, Paul Leslie 1918- BiDrAPA 89
Conrad, Peter 1948- WorAu 1980
Conrad, Peter A. 1949- St&PR 91
Conrad, Phillip Gordon 1957- WhoEmL 91
Conrad, Ralph Willis 1924- St&PR 91
Conrad, Robert BioIn 16
Conrad, Robert 1935- WhoAm 90, WorAlBi
Conrad, Sally Y. WhoAmW 91
Conrad, Simon J BiDrAPA 89
Conrad, Stanley W 1920- BiDrAPA 89
Conrad, Susan Lynne 1948- WhoAmW 91
Conrad, Sybil 1921- AuBYP 90
Conrad, William 1920- WhoAm 90, WorAlBi
Conrad, William Charles 1936- St&PR 91
Conrad Regan, Terri Jo 1961- WhoEmL 91
Conrade, Augustin PenDiDA 89
Conrade, Baptiste PenDiDA 89
Conrade, Dominique PenDiDA 89
Conradi, Eugene Paul 1929- St&PR 91
Conrads, Robert John 1947- WhoAm 90
Conradsen, Cliff D. 1941- St&PR 91
Conradson, Edgar BioIn 16
Conradson, Leonard 1945- BiDrAPA 89
Conradt, Jody BioIn 16
Conran, Harold W 1912- BiDrAPA 89
Conran, Helen Josephine BiDrAPA 89
Conran, Mary 1957- St&PR 91
Conran, Shirley 1932- MajTwCW
Conran, Terence 1931- ConDes 90
Conrat, Richard Fraenkel WhoAm 90
Conreid, Hans 1915-1982 WorAlBi
Conrey, Charles Keith 1948- St&PR 91
Conrey, Theron Albert 1948- WhoEmL 91
Conroe, Bruce Alan 1931- WhoE 91
Conroe, Henry Gerald 1946- BiDrAPA 89, WhoEmL 91
Conron, John Phelan 1921- WhoAm 90, WhoWor 91
Conrow, James Willard 1952- WhoAm 90
Conrow, Wilford Seymour 1880- WhoAmA 91N
Conroy, Al ConAu 30NR, TwCCr&M 91
Conroy, Albert ConAu 30NR, TwCCr&M 91
Conroy, Augustine Edward, II 1934- WhoAm 90
Conroy, Catherine M. BioIn 16
Conroy, Catherine M. 1948- ODwPR 91
Conroy, Cathryn Devan 1954- WhoWrEP 89
Conroy, Charles William 1947- WhoSSW 91
Conroy, Daniel J. BioIn 16
Conroy, David J. 1929- St&PR 91
Conroy, Donald Patrick 1945- WhoAm 90, WhoWrEP 89
Conroy, Frank 1936- BioIn 16, WorAu 1980 [port]
Conroy, Frank John 1942- WhoWor 91
Conroy, Georgetta Ann 1946- WhoAmW 91
Conroy, Harold William 1906-1989 BioIn 16
Conroy, Jack ConAu 131
Conroy, Jack 1899- EncAL, WhoWrEP 89
Conroy, Jack 1899-1990 BioIn 16
Conroy, Jennifer 1944- WhoWor 91
Conroy, John Wesley 1899-1990 ConAu 131
Conroy, Leslie McCoy 1959- BiDrAPA 89
Conroy, Maryellen ODwPR 91
Conroy, Normabelle 1918- BiDrAPA 89
Conroy, Pat 1945- MajTwCW
Conroy, Pat 1955- WorAlBi
Conroy, Richard C 1933- BiDrAPA 89
Conroy, Robert AuBYP 90
Conroy, Robert John 1953- WhoEmL 91
Conroy, Robert Stephen 1932- WhoAm 90
Conroy, Robert W 1938- BiDrAPA 89
Conroy, Robert Warren 1938- WhoAm 90
Conroy, Rose Maureen 1953- WhoAmW 91
Conroy, Sarah Booth 1927- WhoAm 90
Conroy, Stephen 1947- ODwPR 91
Conroy, Stephen Martin 1959- WhoEmL 91
Conroy, Thomas Francis 1938- St&PR 91
Conroy, Tim 1960- Ballpl 90
Conroy, Wid 1877-1959 Ballpl 90
Conroy, William Eugene 1933- St&PR 91
Conroyd, Danielle St&PR 91
Conroyd, W. Daniel 1920- WhoAm 90
Conry, Thomas Francis 1942- WhoAm 90
Cons, Jean Marie Abele 1934- WhoAmW 91
Consagra, Pier Luigi 1954- WhoAmA 91
Consagra, Pietro 1920- WhoWor 91
Consagra, Sophie Chandler 1927- WhoAm 90
Consalvi, Ercole 1757-1824 BioIn 16
Consdorf, Frank 1936- St&PR 91
Conselheiro, Antonio 1835-1897 EncO&P 3
Conselman, Frank Buckley 1910- WhoAm 90
Conser, Geraldine M. WhoAmW 91
Consese, Eugene Paul 1929- St&PR 91
Consey, Kevin E 1952- WhoAmA 91
Considerant, Victor-Prosper 1808-1893 BioIn 16
Considine, Ann-Marie Gwiazdowski 1962- WhoAmW 91
Considine, Bob 1906-1975 BioIn 16
Considine, Bob 1907-1975 Ballpl 90
Considine, Frank W. 1921- St&PR 91
Considine, Frank William 1921- WhoAm 90
Considine, James F BiDrAPA 89
Considine, John ConTFT 8
Considine, John Joseph 1941- WhoAm 90
Considine, John R. 1950- St&PR 91
Considine, Michael Anthony 1953- St&PR 91
Considine, Richard 1933- St&PR 91
Considine, Robert 1906-1975 WorAlBi
Considine, Susan M. 1958- St&PR 91
Considine, Susan Mary 1958- WhoAmW 91, WhoEmL 91
Considine, Timothy James 1953- WhoE 91
Consiglio, John 1948- WhoE 91
Consiglio, Louis V. 1934- St&PR 91
Consiglio, Luigi 1955- WhoWor 91
Consiglio, Ronald Joseph 1943- St&PR 91
Consilio, Barbara Ann 1938- WhoAmW 91
Console, David A BiDrAPA 89
Console, F.M. 1924- St&PR 91
Consoli, Marc-Antonio 1941- IntWWM 90, WhoAm 90
Consoli, Robert J. 1948- St&PR 91
Consoli, Rotraut Bohlmann 1946- WhoWor 91
Consoli, Scott P. 1961- WhoEmL 91
Consolino, Thomas Patrick 1939- St&PR 91
Consolmagno, Donald L. 1935- ODwPR 91
Consolo, Billy 1934- Ballpl 90
Consolver, Jay Paul BiDrAPA 89
Constable, Elinor Greer 1934- WhoAm 90, WhoAmW 91, WhoWor 91
Constable, John 1776-1837 BioIn 16, IntDcAA 90, WorAlBi
Constable, John Robert 1934- IntWWM 90
Constable, Robert Lee 1942- WhoE 91
Constable, Rosalind WhoAmA 91
Constable, William BioIn 16
Constable, William G. 1950- St&PR 91
Constable, William George 1887-1976 WhoAmA 91N
Constan, Evan 1927- BiDrAPA 89
Constan, Louis Leonard 1947- WhoEmL 91
Constance WomWR
Constance 1127-1163? WomWR
Constance 1154-1198 WomWR
Constance, Diana Marie BiDrAPA 89
Constance, George BioIn 16
Constance, Helen BioIn 16
Constance, Thomas Ernest 1936- WhoAm 90
Constandy, John Peter 1924- WhoAm 90
Constans, Henry Philip, Jr. 1928- WhoSSW 91
Constans, Jean Antoine Ernest 1833-1913 BiDFrPL
Constant, Alberta 1908-1981 AuBYP 90
Constant, Clinton 1912- WhoAm 90, WhoWor 91
Constant, F. Woodbridge 1904-1988 BioIn 16
Constant, Franz 1910- IntWWM 90
Constant, George 1892-1978 WhoAmA 91N
Constant, George A BiDrAPA 89
Constant, Joseph 1956- WhoEmL 91
Constant, Marius 1925- IntWWM 90
Constant, Samuel Victor BioIn 16
Constant, William David 1954- WhoSSW 91
Constant Botelho de Magalhaes, Benjamin 1836-1891 BioIn 16
Constanten, Thomas Charles Sture Hills 1944- IntWWM 90
Constantia Munda BiDEWW
Constantin, James Alford 1922- WhoAm 90
Constantin, Maurice Charles 1928- WhoWor 91
Constantin-Weyer, Maurice 1881-1964 DcLB 92 [port]
Constantinau, Walea Lokelani 1962- WhoEmL 91
Constantine I 280?-337 WorAlBi
Constantine Bereng Seeiso 1938- WhoWor 91
Constantine I, Emperor of Rome BioIn 16
Constantine Pavlovich 1779-1831 BioIn 16
Constantine, Jan Friedman 1948- WhoAm 90, WhoAmW 91, WhoE 91, WhoWor 91
Constantine, Jean M. WhoWrEP 89
Constantine, K. C. TwCCr&M 91
Constantine, Louise BioIn 16
Constantine, Michael 1927- WorAlBi
Constantine, Mildred 1914- WhoAmA 91
Constantinescu, Dan 1931- IntWWM 90
Constantinescu, Mihai 1926- IntWWM 90
Constantini, JoAnn M. 1948- WhoAmW 91
Constantini, Louis Orlando 1948- WhoEmL 91
Constantinides, Dinos Demetrios 1929- WhoAm 90
Constantinides, Ellen 1946- St&PR 91
Constantinidi, Emil R 1928- BiDrAPA 89
Constantino, Carol L. 1948- St&PR 91
Constantino, Mark A. NewYTBS 90
Constantino-Bana, Rose Eva 1940- WhoAmW 91
Constas, Robert L 1936- BiDrAPA 89
Constine, Louis Sanders, Jr. 1914- BiDrAPA 89
Conston, Henry S. 1928- St&PR 91
Conston, Henry Siegismund 1928- WhoAm 90
Conston, Stanley Ross 1958- WhoEmL 91
Consuegra, Sandy 1920- Ballpl 90
Conta, Bart Joseph 1914- WhoAm 90
Conta, Lewis Dalcin 1912- WhoAm 90
Conta, Richard Vincent 1946- WhoE 91
Contaldi, Robert Gaetano BiDrAPA 89
Contamine, Philippe 1932- WhoWor 91
Contantine, Greg John 1938- WhoAmA 91
Contardi, Evaldo 1915- St&PR 91
Conte, Albert 1932- St&PR 91, WhoAm 90
Conte, Andrea 1941- WhoAmW 91
Conte, Anthony C. 1945- St&PR 91
Conte, Charles V. ODwPR 91
Conte, David 1955- IntWWM 90
Conte, Frederick Henry 1951- St&PR 91
Conte, Jean Jacques 1938- WhoWor 91
Conte, Jean-Paul 1956- WhoWor 91
Conte, Jeanne Larner 1928- WhoAmA 91
Conte, John Louis 1947- St&PR 91
Conte, Joseph John, II 1932- WhoAm 90
Conte, Lansana 1944- WhoWor 91
Conte, Louis Robert 1935- BiDrAPA 89
Conte, Maryanne Micchelli 1959- WhoAmW 91
Conte, Patrick John 1934- St&PR 91
Conte, Richard Nicholas 1918- WhoAm 90
Conte, Richard R. 1947- WhoAm 90
Conte, Robert Francis 1942- St&PR 91
Conte, Samuel Daniel 1917- WhoAm 90
Conte, Silvio Otto 1921- WhoAm 90, WhoE 91
Conte, William R 1921- BiDrAPA 89
Contenti, John Anthony 1948- St&PR 91
Conterato, Bruno Paul 1920- WhoAm 90
Conti, Carl Joseph 1937- St&PR 91, WhoAm 90
Conti, Corrado 1933- WhoWor 91
Conti, Daniel Joseph 1949- WhoEmL 91
Conti, Fred A. 1941- St&PR 91
Conti, Isabella 1942- WhoAmW 91
Conti, James Joseph 1930- WhoAm 90
Conti, John V. 1944- ODwPR 91
Conti, Laurie Ann 1961- WhoAmW 91
Conti, Nicoletta 1957- IntWWM 90
Conti, Paul Anthony 1947- BiDrAPA 89
Conti, Peter Selby 1934- WhoAm 90
Conti, Primo 1900-1988 AnObit 1988
Conti, Samuel 1922- WhoAm 90
Conti, Samuel Francis 1931- WhoAm 90
Conti, Tom 1941- WhoAm 90, WhoWor 91
Conti, Vincent Roy 1943- WhoSSW 91
Conticchio, Linda Anne 1953- WhoAmW 91
Contie, Leroy John, Jr. 1920- WhoAm 90
Contiguglia, John 1937- IntWWM 90
Contiguglia, Joseph Justin 1948- WhoSSW 91
Contiguglia, Richard 1937- IntWWM 90
Contini, Anita 1944- WhoAmA 91
Contini, Edgardo BioIn 16, NewYTBS 90
Contini, Gianfranco 1910-1990 BioIn 16
Contini, Gianfranco 1912-1990 ConAu 130
Contino, Carla 1961- WhoE 91
Contino, Vincent Nicholas 1952- WhoEmL 91
Contney, John Joseph 1932- WhoAm 90, WhoWor 91
Contos, Larry D. 1940- St&PR 91, WhoAm 90
Contrada, Joseph Guy 1950- St&PR 91
Contreni, John Joseph, Jr. 1944- WhoAm 90
Contreras, Abraham 1965- WhoHisp 91
Contreras, Adela Marie 1960- WhoHisp 91
Contreras, Alonso de 1582- BioIn 16
Contreras, Carl Toby 1957- WhoHisp 91
Contreras, Don L. 1962- WhoHisp 91
Contreras, Eleazar Lopez 1883-1973 BioIn 16
Contreras, Emilio BiDrAPA 89
Contreras, Esther Cajahuaringa 1962- WhoHisp 91
Contreras, James WhoHisp 91
Contreras, Joseph J. 1941- St&PR 91
Contreras, Luis A. 1952- WhoHisp 91
Contreras, Matias Ricardo 1946- WhoHisp 91
Contreras, Nancy 1955- ODwPR 91
Contreras, Philip A. 1934- St&PR 91
Contreras, Salvador A BiDrAPA 89
Contreras, Vincent John 1943- WhoHisp 91
Contreras-Sweet, Maria WhoHisp 91
Contreras-Velasquez, Simon Rafael 1956- WhoHisp 91
Contursi, Paul 1953- WhoWrEP 89
Contway, Jay 1934- BioIn 16
Conver, Stephen K. 1944- WhoAm 90
Conversano, Henry M. 1931- St&PR 91
Converse, Andrea Lee 1940- WhoSSW 91
Converse, Elizabeth Richter 1946- WhoAmA 91
Converse, Frederick F BiDrAPA 89
Converse, Frederick Shepherd 1871-1940 PenDiMP A
Converse, George Leroy 1827-1897 AmLegL
Converse, George Marquis 1940- WhoSSW 91
Converse, James Clarence 1942- WhoAm 90
Converse, Mary Parker 1872-1961 BioIn 16
Converse, Philip Ernest 1928- WhoAm 90
Converse, Thomas Allen BiDrAPA 89
Converse, William Rawson Mackenzie 1937- WhoAm 90
Conversi, Marcello 1917-1988 BioIn 16
Converti, Vincenzo 1925- WhoAm 90
Convertino, Victor Anthony 1949- WhoAm 90
Convey, Raymond Arthur 1949- St&PR 91
Conviser, Richard James 1938- WhoAm 90
Convisser, Theodora S. 1947- St&PR 91
Convy, Bert 1934- WhoAm 90
Convy, Richard John 1954- St&PR 91
Conway, Alice Frances 1907- WhoWrEP 89
Conway, Alvin James 1925- WhoAm 90

Conway, Anne *BiDEWW*
Conway, Anne 1631-1679 *FemiCLE*
Conway, Betty Ann 1930- *WhoAmW 91*
Conway, Brian Peter 1942- *WhoAm 90*
Conway, Casey Anthony 1953- *WhoWor 91*
Conway, Charles Francis 1931- *St&PR 91*
Conway, Clayton R. 1942- *St&PR 91*
Conway, David Antony 1941- *WhoAm 90*
Conway, Dwight Colbur 1930- *WhoAm 90*
Conway, E. Virgil 1929- *St&PR 91, WhoAm 90*
Conway, Elias Nelson 1812-1892 *BioIn 16*
Conway, French Hoge 1918- *WhoSSW 91, WhoWor 91*
Conway, Gerald G. *BioIn 16*
Conway, Gerald W. 1937- *St&PR 91*
Conway, Gordon Richard 1938- *WhoE 91*
Conway, Gregory Charles 1941- *St&PR 91*
Conway, Harold Eugene 1936- *WhoSSW 91*
Conway, Harry Donald 1917- *WhoAm 90*
Conway, Helene *AuBYP 90*
Conway, Hobart McKinley, Jr. 1920- *WhoAm 90*
Conway, Honoria 1815?-1892 *DcCanB 12*
Conway, Jack Steven 1956- *BiDrAPA 89*
Conway, Jack T. 1917- *St&PR 91*
Conway, James Donald 1946- *WhoSSW 91*
Conway, James F., Jr. *WhoAm 90*
Conway, James F., Jr. 1924- *St&PR 91*
Conway, James Sevier 1798-1855 *BioIn 16*
Conway, James Valentine Patrick 1917- *WhoAm 90*
Conway, Jill K. 1934- *BioIn 16, ConAu 130*
Conway, Jill Kathryn Ker 1934- *WhoAm 90, WhoAmW 91, WhoE 91*
Conway, Joan I. 1949- *St&PR 91*
Conway, John L. 1932- *St&PR 91*
Conway, John R. 1952- *WhoWrEP 89*
Conway, John S. 1929- *WhoAm 90*
Conway, John Thomas 1924- *WhoAm 90*
Conway, Joseph *ODwPR 91*
Conway, Joseph P. 1930- *WhoAm 90*
Conway, Karen 1959- *WhoEmL 91*
Conway, Katharine St John 1867-1950 *FemiCLE*
Conway, Kenneth Edward 1943- *WhoSSW 91*
Conway, Kenneth Francis *BiDrAPA 89*
Conway, Kevin 1942- *WhoAm 90*
Conway, Kevin G. 1948- *St&PR 91*
Conway, Laura W. 1958- *ODwPR 91*
Conway, Lawrence Charles 1943- *St&PR 91*
Conway, Lynn Ann 1938- *WhoAm 90, WhoAmW 91*
Conway, Mark *BiDrAPA 89*
Conway, Mary Elizabeth 1923- *WhoAm 90, WhoAmW 91*
Conway, Maureen Ann 1945- *WhoAmW 91*
Conway, Michael Anthony 1947- *WhoAm 90*
Conway, Michael J. 1945- *St&PR 91, WhoAm 90*
Conway, Morna Helen 1945- *WhoEmL 91*
Conway, Neil James, III 1950- *WhoEmL 91*
Conway, Richard Ashley 1931- *WhoAm 90*
Conway, Richard James, Jr. 1952- *WhoEmL 91*
Conway, Richard Walter 1931- *WhoAm 90*
Conway, Rita M. 1953- *WhoEmL 91*
Conway, Robert A. 1927- *St&PR 91*
Conway, Robert Alfred 1927- *WhoAm 90*
Conway, Robert George, Jr. 1951- *WhoEmL 91*
Conway, Robert Hunter 1947- *St&PR 91*
Conway, Robert P. 1946- *WhoAm 90*
Conway, Ronald J. 1944- *St&PR 91*
Conway, Russ 1927- *OxCPMus*
Conway, Stephen J. 1938- *St&PR 91*
Conway, Stephen T. 1947- *ODwPR 91*
Conway, Terence James 1944- *WhoSSW 91*
Conway, Thomas 1735-1800? *EncCRAm, WorAlBi*
Conway, Thomas A. 1910- *St&PR 91*
Conway, Thomas James 1913- *WhoAm 90*
Conway, Tim 1933- *BioIn 16, WhoAm 90, WorAlBi*
Conway, Verona Margaret 1910-1986 *BioIn 16*
Conway, William Augustine 1948- *WhoEmL 91*
Conway, William Edward 1927- *St&PR 91*
Conway, William Gaylord 1929- *WhoAm 90*
Conway, William Judson 1947- *WhoEmL 91*
Conway Carey, Allison Brandes 1957- *WhoAmW 91*
Conwell, Anne Fletcher 1958- *St&PR 91*
Conwell, Brian 1958- *St&PR 91*
Conwell, Esther Marly 1922- *WhoAm 90, WhoAmW 91*
Conwell, Halford Roger 1924- *WhoWor 91*
Conwell, Michael James 1946- *WhoSSW 91*
Conwell, Russell Herman 1843-1925 *BioIn 16*
Conwell, Theresa Gallo 1947- *WhoAmW 91*
Conwell, Yeates *BiDrAPA 89*
Conwill, Alan F. 1921-1989 *BioIn 16*
Conwill, Houston E 1947- *WhoAmA 91*
Cony, Steven Richard 1947- *St&PR 91*
Conybeare, Charles Augustus *MajTwCW*
Conyers, John, Jr. 1929- *BlkAmsC [port], WhoAm 90*
Conyngham, Barry Ernest 1944- *IntWWM 90*
Conza, A.P. *St&PR 91*
Conzen, W.H. 1913- *St&PR 91*
Coo, Robert Gaston 1941- *St&PR 91*
Cooder, Ry 1947- *ConTFT 8, EncPR&S 89, WhoAm 90*
Coodin, Shalom Zalman *BiDrAPA 89*
Coodley, Alfred E 1922- *BiDrAPA 89*
Coodley, Alfred Edgar 1922- *WhoAm 90*
Coody, Dale *BioIn 16*
Cooey, William Randolph 1942- *WhoSSW 91*
Coogan, Alice 1944- *WhoAmW 91*
Coogan, Jackie 1914-1984 *WorAlBi*
Coogan, Philip Shields 1938- *WhoAm 90*
Coogan, Robyn Kay Ankney 1951- *WhoAmW 91*
Coogan, Susan C. 1954- *St&PR 91*
Coogle, Joseph Moore, Jr. 1933- *St&PR 91, WhoAm 90*
Cook, A. Philip, Jr. 1944- *St&PR 91*
Cook, A. Samuel 1921- *WhoAm 90*
Cook, Addison Gilbert 1933- *WhoAm 90*
Cook, Albert Spaulding 1925- *WhoAm 90, WhoWrEP 89*
Cook, Albert Thomas Thornton, Jr. 1940- *WhoWor 91*
Cook, Alexander Burns 1924- *WhoWor 91*
Cook, Anda Suna 1935- *WhoAmW 91*
Cook, Andrew Devereux 1946- *BiDrAPA 89*
Cook, Ann *FemiCLE*
Cook, Ann Jennalie 1934- *WhoAm 90, WhoAmW 91*
Cook, Anthony M. 1939- *St&PR 91*
Cook, Arthur L. 1926- *St&PR 91*
Cook, Audella 1948- *WhoEmL 91*
Cook, August Charles 1897- *WhoAmA 91*
Cook, Barbara 1927- *OxCPMus*
Cook, Barry L. 1949- *St&PR 91*
Cook, Bart R. 1950- *WhoAm 90*
Cook, Ben H. 1926- *St&PR 91*
Cook, Benjamin Hopson 1926- *WhoAm 90*
Cook, Bernadine Hladik 1949- *WhoAmW 91*
Cook, Beryl 1937- *BiDWomA*
Cook, Beth Marie 1933- *WhoAmW 91*
Cook, Bette Walker Philpott 1941- *WhoAmW 91*
Cook, Betty Jean Shelly 1941- *WhoSSW 91*
Cook, Blanche McLane 1901- *WhoAmW 91*
Cook, Blanche Wiesen 1941- *WhoAm 90, WhoAmW 91*
Cook, Bob 1961- *SpyFic*
Cook, Boyd McCoy 1930- *St&PR 91*
Cook, Brian Lynne 1954- *BiDrAPA 89*
Cook, Brian Rayner 1945- *IntWWM 90*
Cook, Bryan Douglas 1951- *WhoEmL 91*
Cook, Bryson Leitch 1948- *WhoEmL 91*
Cook, Burleigh Don 1932- *St&PR 91*
Cook, Byron Curtis 1954- *WhoSSW 91*
Cook, Camille Wright *WhoAm 90*
Cook, Carl J. 1927- *St&PR 91*
Cook, Charles Addison 1952- *St&PR 91*
Cook, Charles Beckwith, Jr. 1929- *WhoAm 90*
Cook, Charles Caruthers 1932- *St&PR 91*
Cook, Charles Davenport 1919- *WhoAm 90*
Cook, Charles David 1924- *WhoAm 90, WhoWor 91*
Cook, Charles Edward, Jr. 1953- *WhoEmL 91*
Cook, Charles Emerson 1926- *WhoAm 90*
Cook, Charles Francis 1941- *St&PR 91, WhoAm 90*
Cook, Charles Wilkerson, Jr. 1934- *St&PR 91, WhoAm 90, WhoSSW 91*
Cook, Charles William 1927- *WhoAm 90*
Cook, Charlotte Dasher 1948- *WhoEmL 91*
Cook, Chauncey William Wallace 1909- *WhoAm 90*
Cook, Christopher Capen 1932- *WhoAm 90, WhoAmA 91, WhoE 91*
Cook, Cindy Kaye 1952- *WhoAmW 91*
Cook, Clarence Edgar 1936- *WhoAm 90*
Cook, Clarence Sharp 1918- *WhoAm 90*
Cook, Claude P., Sr. 1916- *St&PR 91*
Cook, Clayton Henry 1912- *WhoSSW 91, WhoWor 91*
Cook, Clyde *WhoAm 90*
Cook, Clyde 1891-1984 *BioIn 16*
Cook, Colin *BioIn 16*
Cook, Colin Burford 1927- *WhoE 91, WhoWor 91*
Cook, Connie Sue 1951- *WhoEmL 91*
Cook, David Alastair 1942- *WhoAm 90*
Cook, David C. 1912-1990 *BioIn 16*
Cook, David Charles, III 1912- *WhoWrEP 89*
Cook, David G. 1938- *St&PR 91*
Cook, David Lee 1952- *WhoEmL 91*
Cook, David Phillips 1949- *St&PR 91*
Cook, David S. 1921- *WhoAm 90*
Cook, David Sheldon 1921- *St&PR 91*
Cook, David Sherman 1952- *WhoEmL 91*
Cook, Deborah *IntWWM 90*
Cook, Dennis 1962- *Ballpl 90*
Cook, Dennis David *BiDrAPA 89*
Cook, Desmond C. 1949- *WhoSSW 91*
Cook, Diane Grefe 1943- *WhoAmW 91*
Cook, Doc 1886-1973 *Ballpl 90*
Cook, Don 1920- *WhoAm 90*
Cook, Donald E. 1928- *WhoAm 90*
Cook, Donald Eugene 1935- *WhoSSW 91, WhoWor 91*
Cook, Donald Frederick 1937- *IntWWM 90*
Cook, Donald H. 1930- *St&PR 91*
Cook, Donald Jack 1915- *WhoAm 90*
Cook, Donald Jean 1920- *WhoAm 90*
Cook, Donald Wilfred 1938- *WhoSSW 91*
Cook, Doris Marie 1924- *WhoAm 90, WhoAmW 91, WhoSSW 91, WhoWor 91*
Cook, Douglas Neilson 1929- *WhoAm 90*
Cook, Dwight Ray 1951- *WhoEmL 91*
Cook, Edgar L 1923- *BiDrAPA 89*
Cook, Edward Joseph 1925- *WhoAm 90*
Cook, Edward Willingham 1922- *WhoAm 90, WhoSSW 91*
Cook, Edwin Haynes, Jr. 1955- *BiDrAPA 89*
Cook, Eileen Marie 1950- *WhoWrEP 89*
Cook, Elisha, Jr. 1906- *ConTFT 8*
Cook, Eliza 1817-1889 *FemiCLE*
Cook, Eliza 1818-1889 *BioIn 16*
Cook, Elizabeth Taylor 1945- *WhoSSW 91*
Cook, Ellen Ann De Corte 1943- *WhoAmW 91*
Cook, Elsa Estelle 1932- *WhoAmW 91*
Cook, Elton Straus 1909- *WhoAm 90*
Cook, Emily Ann 1941- *WhoSSW 91*
Cook, Emory Giddings 1913- *BioIn 16*
Cook, Ernest Ewart 1926- *St&PR 91*
Cook, Eugene Augustus 1938- *WhoAm 90, WhoSSW 91, WhoWor 91*
Cook, Eugene E. 1922- *St&PR 91*
Cook, Eung-Do 1935- *WhoAm 90*
Cook, Fannie 1893-1949 *FemiCLE*
Cook, Fielder *WhoAm 90*
Cook, Florence 1856-1904 *EncO&P 3*
Cook, Florence Eliza 1856-1904 *EncPaPR 91*
Cook, Frances *BiDEWW, FemiCLE*
Cook, Frances D. 1945- *WhoAm 90, WhoAmW 91, WhoWor 91*
Cook, Francis Edward 1916- *St&PR 91*
Cook, Frank Eugene 1950- *WhoSSW 91*
Cook, Fred James 1911- *AuBYP 90, WhoAm 90*
Cook, Fred S. 1915- *WhoWrEP 89*
Cook, Frederick A. 1865-1940 *WorAlBi*
Cook, Frederick Albert 1865-1940 *BioIn 16*
Cook, Gail Fairman 1937- *WhoE 91*
Cook, Galen B. 1930- *WhoSSW 91*
Cook, Gary M. 1942- *St&PR 91*
Cook, Gary Raymond 1950- *WhoAm 90, WhoSSW 91*
Cook, Gayle Freeman 1949- *WhoEmL 91*
Cook, Gene Paul 1945- *St&PR 91*
Cook, Geoffrey Arthur 1946- *WhoWrEP 89*
Cook, George Edward 1938- *WhoAm 90*
Cook, George Henry, Jr. 1951- *WhoEmL 91*
Cook, George Valentine 1927- *WhoAm 90*
Cook, George Wallace Foster 1919- *WhoAm 90*
Cook, Gerald 1937- *WhoAm 90*
Cook, Gillian Elizabeth 1934- *WhoSSW 91*
Cook, Gladys Emerson 1899- *AuBYP 90, WhoAmA 91N*
Cook, Gloria Houston 1933- *WhoAmW 91*
Cook, H. Gordon *St&PR 91*
Cook, Harold Dale 1924- *WhoAm 90, WhoSSW 91*
Cook, Harold Rodney 1944- *WhoWor 91*
Cook, Harry Clayton, Jr. 1935- *WhoAm 90, WhoWor 91*
Cook, Harvey Carlisle 1936- *WhoE 91*
Cook, Herbert S. 1915- *St&PR 91*
Cook, Howard Norton 1901-1980 *WhoAmA 91N*
Cook, Hugh 1956- *ConAu 132*
Cook, J Alan 1939- *BiDrAPA 89*
Cook, J M 1910- *ConAu 130*
Cook, Jack Augustine 1940- *WhoE 91*
Cook, Jack H. 1939- *St&PR 91*
Cook, James 1728-1779 *BioIn 16, EncCRAm, WhNaAH, WorAlBi*
Cook, James 1926- *WhoAm 90, WhoWrEP 89*
Cook, James Francis 1960- *WhoSSW 91*
Cook, James H, II *BiDrAPA 89*
Cook, James Harry 1959- *WhoEmL 91*
Cook, James Ivan 1925- *WhoAm 90*
Cook, James Stuart 1943- *St&PR 91*
Cook, James Talmadge, III 1943- *WhoSSW 91*
Cook, James Wallace 1940- *St&PR 91*
Cook, James Winfield Clinton 1908- *WhoWor 91*
Cook, Jay Michael 1942- *WhoAm 90*
Cook, Jeannine Salvo 1929- *WhoE 91*
Cook, Jeff *BioIn 16*
Cook, Jeff Holland 1940- *IntWWM 90*
Cook, Jeffrey Alan 1949- *WhoAm 90*
Cook, Jeffrey Ross 1934- *WhoAm 90*
Cook, Jess 1934- *ODwPR 91*
Cook, John *WhoSSW 91*
Cook, John 1805-1892 *DcCanB 12*
Cook, John 1930- *WhoAmA 91*
Cook, John A *BiDrAPA 89*
Cook, John Alfred 1930- *WhoAm 90*
Cook, John Alvin 1952- *WhoEmL 91*
Cook, John E. *ODwPR 91*
Cook, John Laird 1941- *St&PR 91*
Cook, John R. *ODwPR 91*
Cook, John Rowland 1941- *St&PR 91, WhoAm 90*
Cook, John William 1929- *WhoSSW 91*
Cook, Jon Leslie 1943- *WhoE 91*
Cook, Joseph C., Jr. 1942- *St&PR 91*
Cook, Joseph Jay 1924- *AuBYP 90*
Cook, Joseph Leslie 1952- *WhoSSW 91*
Cook, Joseph S 1936- *WhoAmA 91*
Cook, Juanita 1948- *WhoAmW 91*
Cook, Judith 1933- *ConAu 132*
Cook, Judith A H 1941- *BiDrAPA 89*
Cook, Judith Ellen 1959- *WhoEmL 91*
Cook, Julian Abele, Jr. 1930- *WhoAm 90*
Cook, Karen Sue 1960- *WhoAmW 91*
Cook, Kate Selina 1859-1923 *EncPaPR 91*
Cook, Kathleen *BioIn 16*
Cook, Kathryn Ann 1965- *WhoAmW 91*
Cook, Kathryn Ella 1945- *WhoAmW 91*
Cook, Kathryn Malloy 1958- *WhoEmL 91*
Cook, Katie 1859-1923 *EncO&P 3*
Cook, Kenneth 1929- *ConAu 130*
Cook, Kenneth Ray 1953- *WhoSSW 91*
Cook, Kenneth Totman 1950- *WhoEmL 91*
Cook, Kevin Douglas 1945- *WhoSSW 91*
Cook, Kimra Kay *BiDrAPA 89*
Cook, Lawrence *DrBlPA 90*
Cook, LeAnn Cecilia 1950- *WhoAmW 91, WhoEmL 91*
Cook, Leonard Clarence 1936- *WhoAm 90*
Cook, Leonard Paul 1924- *WhoAm 90*
Cook, LeRoy Franklin, Jr. 1931- *WhoAm 90*
Cook, Lewis H. 1943- *St&PR 91*
Cook, Lia 1942- *WhoAmA 91*
Cook, Linda Sue 1945- *St&PR 91*
Cook, Lodwrick M. *BioIn 16*
Cook, Lodwrick Monroe 1928 *WhoAm 90, WhoWor 91*
Cook, Lucretia 1606-1694 *BiDEWW*
Cook, Lyle Edwards 1918- *WhoAm 90, WhoSSW 91*
Cook, Marian Alice 1928- *WhoAmW 91*
Cook, Marion Belden *AuBYP 90*
Cook, Marjorie Ellen 1942- *WhoAmW 91*
Cook, Marjorie Ruth Cochrane 1920- *WhoWrEP 89*
Cook, Marv *BioIn 16*
Cook, Mary Ann 1929- *St&PR 91*
Cook, Mary Frances 1962- *WhoAmW 91*
Cook, Mary Joene 1943- *WhoAmW 91, WhoSSW 91*
Cook, Mary Lynn B. 1934- *WhoAmW 91*
Cook, Mary Margaret 1944- *WhoAmW 91*
Cook, Mary Rozella 1936- *WhoAmW 91*
Cook, Melinda 1954- *WhoSSW 91*
Cook, Melville 1912- *IntWWM 90*
Cook, Melvin 1929- *St&PR 91*
Cook, Melvin Garfield 1940- *WhoAm 90*
Cook, Mercer 1903- *EarBlAP*
Cook, Michael 1933- *OxCCanT*
Cook, Michael Allan 1940- *WhoAm 90*
Cook, Michael Anthony 1956- *WhoE 91, WhoEmL 91*
Cook, Michael Blanchard 1942- *WhoAm 90*
Cook, Michael C. 1939- *St&PR 91*
Cook, Michael David 1953- *WhoAmA 91*
Cook, Michael Ian 1951- *BiDrAPA 89*
Cook, Michael Jackson 1947- *WhoWor 91*
Cook, Michael L. 1933- *ODwPR 91*
Cook, Michael Lewis 1944- *WhoAm 90*
Cook, Michael Lyles 1946- *WhoEmL 91*
Cook, Michael Stephen, Sr. 1951- *WhoEmL 91*
Cook, Milton Olin 1933- *WhoAm 90*
Cook, Nancy Anne 1953- *WhoEmL 91*
Cook, Nancy W. 1936- *WhoAmW 91*
Cook, Nathan 1950-1988 *DrBlPA 90*

Cook, Neville George Wood 1938- *WhoAm 90*
Cook, Nicholas John 1950- *IntWWM 90*
Cook, Olive Rambo 1892- *AuBYP 90*
Cook, Pat Moffitt 1956- *WhoAmW 91*
Cook, Paul Christopher 1953- *WhoEmL 91*
Cook, Paul K. *BioIn 16*
Cook, Paul M. *WhoAm 90*
Cook, Paul Martin, II 1942- *WhoSSW 91*
Cook, Paul Maxwell 1924- *St&PR 91*
Cook, Peggy Jo 1931- *WhoSSW 91*
Cook, Peggy Lou 1935- *WhoAmW 91*
Cook, Peter 1915- *WhoAmA 91*
Cook, Peter Emile 1948- *BiDrAPA 89*
Cook, Peter Geoffrey 1915- *WhoE 91*
Cook, Petronelle Marguerite Mary 1925- *WhoWrEP 89*
Cook, Philip Jackson 1946- *WhoSSW 91*
Cook, R Scott *WhoAmA 91*
Cook, Ralph Franklin 1922- *St&PR 91*
Cook, Reagan *BioIn 16*
Cook, Rebecca Johnson *WhoAmW 91*
Cook, Richard A. 1921- *St&PR 91*
Cook, Richard A. 1937- *St&PR 91*
Cook, Richard Borreson 1937- *WhoAm 90*
Cook, Richard Burton 1944- *WhoE 91*
Cook, Richard F., Jr. 1951- *St&PR 91*
Cook, Richard K. 1910- *BioIn 16*
Cook, Richard Kelsey 1931- *WhoAm 90*
Cook, Richard L. 1935- *St&PR 91*
Cook, Richard Wallace 1907- *WhoAm 90*
Cook, Robert C. 1947- *St&PR 91*
Cook, Robert Crossland 1947- *WhoEmL 91*
Cook, Robert Donald 1929- *St&PR 91, WhoAm 90*
Cook, Robert Edgar 1941- *St&PR 91*
Cook, Robert Edward 1943- *St&PR 91, WhoAm 90, WhoSSW 91*
Cook, Robert Edward 1946- *WhoAm 90*
Cook, Robert Fred, Jr. 1933- *WhoAm 90*
Cook, Robert Howard 1921- *WhoAmA 91*
Cook, Robert John 1951- *WhoEmL 91*
Cook, Robert John 1954- *WhoEmL 91*
Cook, Robert Lee, Jr. 1928- *St&PR 91*
Cook, Robert Nevin 1912- *WhoWor 91*
Cook, Robert P *BiDrAPA 89*
Cook, Robert S. 1935- *St&PR 91*
Cook, Robin *TwCCr&M 91*
Cook, Robin 1940- *BioIn 16, WhoAm 90, WorAlBi, WorAu 1980 [port]*
Cook, Rodney Mims 1924- *WhoSSW 91*
Cook, Roy *MajTwCW*
Cook, Roy E. 1952- *St&PR 91*
Cook, Ruby Davis 1921- *BioIn 16*
Cook, Ruth Ellen 1929- *WhoAmW 91*
Cook, S. N. *EarBlAP*
Cook, Sam *BioIn 16*
Cook, Sam B. 1922- *WhoAm 90*
Cook, Sam Bryan 1951- *WhoEmL 91*
Cook, Samuel DuBois 1928- *WhoAm 90, WhoWor 91*
Cook, Samuel Ronald 1924- *St&PR 91*
Cook, Sharon Evonne 1941- *WhoWor 91*
Cook, Sherman R. *AuBYP 90*
Cook, Sid Frank 1953- *WhoEmL 91*
Cook, Stanton R. 1925- *WhoAm 90, WhoWor 91*
Cook, Stephani 1944- *WhoWrEP 89*
Cook, Stephen Arthur 1939- *WhoAm 90*
Cook, Stephen Bernard 1947- *WhoAm 90, WhoEmL 91*
Cook, Stephen C 1944- *BiDrAPA 89*
Cook, Stephen D 1951- *WhoAmA 91*
Cook, Stephen Hubbard 1960- *WhoEmL 91*
Cook, Stephen K. 1949- *ODwPR 91*
Cook, Steven 1957- *WhoEmL 91*
Cook, Steven Robert 1955- *St&PR 91*
Cook, Stuart Donald 1936- *WhoAm 90*
Cook, Susan Farwell 1953- *WhoAmW 91*
Cook, Susan Linda 1949- *WhoE 91*
Cook, Tennessee Celeste Claflin, Lady 1845-1923 *BioIn 16*
Cook, Terry Lee 1955- *WhoEmL 91*
Cook, Thomas H. 1947- *ConAu 32NR*
Cook, Thomas Henry 1915- *St&PR 91*
Cook, Thomas Herbert 1936- *WhoE 91*
Cook, Thomas Nelson, Jr. 1956- *WhoE 91*
Cook, Thurlow Adrean 1939- *WhoE 91*
Cook, Todd McClure 1962- *WhoSSW 91*
Cook, Tom L. 1950- *St&PR 91*
Cook, Truman Frederick 1915- *WhoSSW 91*
Cook, Victor Joseph, Jr. 1938- *WhoSSW 91, WhoWor 91*
Cook, Vincent N. *WhoAm 90*
Cook, Waldo S 1927- *BiDrAPA 89*
Cook, Walter Blackwell 1930- *St&PR 91, WhoAm 90*
Cook, Walter Gresham 1927- *St&PR 91*
Cook, Walter Roudley 1954- *WhoWor 91*
Cook, Walter William Spencer 1888-1962 *WhoAmA 91N*
Cook, Warren Ayer 1900- *WhoWor 91*
Cook, Wayne Michael 1943- *WhoAm 90*
Cook, Wendel Winston 1931- *St&PR 91*
Cook, Will A. *EarBlAP*
Cook, Will Marion *EarBlAP*
Cook, Will Marion 1869-1944 *DcAfAmP, DrBlPA 90, OxCPMus*
Cook, Will Mercer *BioIn 16*
Cook, William Campbell 1923- *St&PR 91*
Cook, William Holmes 1920- *WhoAm 90*
Cook, William Howard 1924- *WhoAm 90*
Cook, William John 1929- *WhoAm 90*
Cook, William S. 1922- *St&PR 91*
Cook, William Wilber 1921- *WhoAm 90, WhoWor 91*
Cook-Jacobson, Ellen *BiDrAPA 89*
Cook-Kollars, Kaye V. 1950- *WhoAmW 91*
Cook-Lynn, Elizabeth 1930- *WhoWrEP 89*
Cooke, A. Curts 1936- *WhoAm 90*
Cooke, Albert Curts 1960- *WhoE 91*
Cooke, Alfred Alistair 1908- *BioIn 16, WhoAm 90*
Cooke, Alistair 1908- *BioIn 16, ConTFT 8, WorAlBi*
Cooke, Anne 1528?-1610 *BioIn 16*
Cooke, Arnold Atkinson 1906- *IntWWM 90*
Cooke, Arthur H. 1912-1987 *BioIn 16*
Cooke, Audrey *WhoWrEP 89*
Cooke, Barbara *AuBYP 90*
Cooke, Barbara Ayres 1936- *WhoAmW 91*
Cooke, Bette Louise 1929- *WhoAmW 91*
Cooke, Bob *BioIn 16*
Cooke, Carlton Lee, Jr. 1944- *WhoAm 90, WhoSSW 91*
Cooke, Cassandra 1744-1826 *FemiCLE*
Cooke, Charles 1904?-1977 *AuBYP 90*
Cooke, Charles Mather 1844-1909 *AmLegL*
Cooke, Chester W. 1943- *St&PR 91*
Cooke, Claude Everett, Jr. 1929- *WhoSSW 91*
Cooke, Colleen *BioIn 16*
Cooke, Constance Blandy 1935- *WhoAm 90, WhoAmW 91*
Cooke, Danny Frank 1948- *St&PR 91*
Cooke, David C. 1927- *St&PR 91*
Cooke, David Coxe 1917- *AuBYP 90*
Cooke, David Ohlmer 1920- *WhoAm 90*
Cooke, Donald Ewin 1916-1985 *AuBYP 90*
Cooke, Dorothy Helena Cosby 1941- *WhoAmW 91*
Cooke, Dusty 1907- *Ballpl 90*
Cooke, Edward 1552-1634 *BioIn 16*
Cooke, Edward William 1921- *WhoAm 90*
Cooke, Edward William, III 1946- *WhoSSW 91*
Cooke, Eileen Delores 1928- *WhoAm 90*
Cooke, Elisha 1637-1715 *EncCRAm*
Cooke, Elizabeth 1948- *ConAu 129*
Cooke, Fred Charles 1915- *WhoSSW 91*
Cooke, Genevieve 1869-1928 *BioIn 16*
Cooke, George A. 1941- *St&PR 91*
Cooke, Gerald Edward 1925- *WhoWor 91*
Cooke, Gillian Lewis 1935- *WhoAmW 91*
Cooke, Grace *EncO&P 3*
Cooke, Herbert Basil Sutton 1915- *WhoAm 90*
Cooke, Hereward Lester 1916-1973 *WhoAmA 91N*
Cooke, Holland 1950- *WhoEmL 91*
Cooke, Jack Kent 1912- *BioIn 16, WhoAm 90, WhoE 91*
Cooke, Jacob Ernest 1924- *WhoAm 90*
Cooke, Janet *BioIn 16*
Cooke, Jay 1821-1905 *EncABHB 6 [port], WorAlBi*
Cooke, Jean 1927- *BiDWomA*
Cooke, Jeffrey Allen 1945- *WhoEmL 91*
Cooke, Jody Helen 1922- *WhoAmA 91*
Cooke, John Cary, III 1939- *BiDrAPA 89*
Cooke, John Estes *MajTwCW*
Cooke, John William 1930- *IntWWM 90*
Cooke, Joseph Peter 1947- *WhoAm 90*
Cooke, Judy 1940- *WhoAmA 91*
Cooke, Karen *BioIn 16*
Cooke, Kathleen McKeith 1908-1978 *WhoAmA 91N*
Cooke, Kenneth 1932- *WhoAm 90*
Cooke, Kenneth Lloyd 1925- *WhoAm 90*
Cooke, Kim *BioIn 16*
Cooke, Lawrence Henry 1914- *WhoAm 90, WhoE 91, WhoWor 91*
Cooke, Lee *WhoSSW 91*
Cooke, Lloyd Miller 1916- *WhoAm 90*
Cooke, M. E. *MajTwCW, TwCCr&M 91*
Cooke, M. Todd 1920- *St&PR 91*
Cooke, Margaret *MajTwCW*
Cooke, Marjorie Benton 1876-1920 *FemiCLE*
Cooke, Mary A. 1944- *WhoAmW 91*
Cooke, Maxwell Joseph Lorimer 1924- *IntWWM 90*
Cooke, Merrita Marie 1934- *WhoE 91*
Cooke, Merritt Todd 1920- *WhoAm 90*
Cooke, Mervyn John 1963- *IntWWM 90*
Cooke, Michael G. *NewYTBS 90*
Cooke, Michael G. 1934-1990 *ConAu 132*
Cooke, Mordecai Cubitt 1825-1914 *BioIn 16*
Cooke, Morris Dawes, Jr. 1954- *WhoEmL 91*
Cooke, Noreen Ann 1943- *WhoAmW 91*
Cooke, Pamela Suzanne 1961- *WhoEmL 91*
Cooke, Philip Pendleton 1816-1850 *BioIn 16*
Cooke, R.W. 1925- *St&PR 91*
Cooke, Richard C 1904- *BiDrAPA 89*
Cooke, Richard Caswell, Jr. 1935- *WhoE 91*
Cooke, Richard Earle 1934- *St&PR 91*
Cooke, Robert Edmond 1920- *BiDrAPA 89, WhoAm 90*
Cooke, Robert John 1923- *WhoAm 90, WhoWor 91*
Cooke, Robert William 1935- *WhoAm 90*
Cooke, Robin Brunskill 1926- *WhoWor 91*
Cooke, Roger Anthony 1948- *St&PR 91*
Cooke, Rose 1827-1892 *FemiCLE*
Cooke, Russell *BioIn 16*
Cooke, Sam *BioIn 16*
Cooke, Sam 1935-1964 *DrBlPA 90, EncPR&S 89, OxCPMus, WorAlBi*
Cooke, Samuel Tucker 1941- *WhoAmA 91*
Cooke, Sandra Dee 1960- *WhoE 91*
Cooke, Sara Graff 1935- *WhoAmW 91*
Cooke, Sarah Belle 1910- *WhoAmW 91*
Cooke, Suzanne *BioIn 16*
Cooke, Suzanne Gamsby 1945- *WhoSSW 91*
Cooke, Terence James 1921-1983 *WorAlBi*
Cooke, Terence Stuart 1946- *St&PR 91*
Cooke, Theodore Frederic, Jr. 1913- *WhoAm 90*
Cooke, Thomas Fowke, II 1959- *WhoEmL 91*
Cooke, William Bridge 1908- *WhoAm 90*
Cooke, William Donald 1918- *WhoAm 90*
Cooke, William Peter 1932- *WhoWor 91*
Cooker, Philip George 1942- *WhoSSW 91*
Cookesley, Margaret Murray 1860?-1927 *BiDWomA*
Cooks, Kelvin *BioIn 16*
Cooksey, Crit Reon 1957- *BiDrAPA 89*
Cooksey, David Carl 1944- *St&PR 91*
Cooksey, Joe B. 1946- *St&PR 91*
Cooksey, Thomas Lynch 1950- *WhoSSW 91*
Cooksey, Virginia Epting 1949- *WhoSSW 91*
Cookson, Alan Howard 1939- *WhoAm 90*
Cookson, Albert Ernest 1921- *WhoAm 90*
Cookson, Andrea N *BiDrAPA 89*
Cookson, Catherine *BioIn 16*
Cookson, Catherine 1906- *FemiCLE, MajTwCW*
Cookson, Catherine Ann 1906- *WhoAm 90*
Cookson, Elizabeth 1954- *BiDrAPA 89*
Cookson, Grace Elizabeth 1948- *WhoAmW 91*
Cookson, Jane 1939- *WhoAmW 91*
Cookson, John Simmons 1944- *St&PR 91*
Cookson, Peter 1913-1990 *BioIn 16, ConAu 130, NewYTBS 90*
Cookson, Peter Willis, Jr. 1942- *WhoE 91, WhoWor 91*
Cookson, Sybil *WhoWor 91*
Cookson, William 1939- *ConAu 30NR*
Cookson, William Buckley 1952- *WhoE 91*
Cookworthy, William 1705-1780 *PenDiDA 89*
Cool, David Harry 1933- *St&PR 91, WhoAm 90*
Cool, Delphine de 1830-1911? *BiDWomA*
Cool, Gary Paul 1963- *St&PR 91*
Cool, Judd R. 1935- *St&PR 91*
Cool, Kim Patmore 1940- *WhoAmW 91*
Cool, Rodney L. 1920-1988 *BioIn 16*
Cool, Thomas Edward 1950- *WhoSSW 91*
Cool-Foley, Alicia Ann 1956- *WhoAmW 91*
Coolbaugh, Frank 1908- *St&PR 91*
Coolbaugh, Ronald Charles 1944- *WhoAm 90*
Coolbrith, Ina 1841-1928 *BioAmW*
Coolbrith, Ina 1842-1928 *FemiCLE*
Coolbroth, Frederick James 1951- *WhoEmL 91*
Cooler, Amanda Jeffers 1955- *WhoWrEP 89*
Cooley, Adelaide N 1914- *WhoAmA 91*
Cooley, Andrew Lyman 1934- *WhoAm 90, WhoWor 91*
Cooley, Arthur Maxwell 1951- *St&PR 91*
Cooley, Ben Furman 1954- *WhoSSW 91*
Cooley, Charles Lindy, Sr. 1931- *WhoSSW 91*
Cooley, Claudia 1944- *WhoAm 90*
Cooley, Deanna Kay 1945- *WhoSSW 91*
Cooley, Denton A. 1920- *BioIn 16*
Cooley, Denton Arthur 1920- *WhoAm 90*
Cooley, Dixie 1896- *WhoAmA 91N*
Cooley, Duff 1873-1937 *Ballpl 90*
Cooley, Edward H. 1922- *WhoAm 90*
Cooley, Elsie Marie Endress 1932- *WhoAmW 91*
Cooley, Floyd 1949- *WhoAm 90*
Cooley, George Farmer 1931- *St&PR 91*
Cooley, Gladys Cecilia 1954- *WhoAmW 91*
Cooley, Harold Eugene 1929- *St&PR 91*
Cooley, Hilary Elizabeth 1953- *WhoAmW 91*
Cooley, Howard Dager 1934- *WhoAm 90*
Cooley, Isabelle *DrBlPA 90*
Cooley, Ivory Lee 1951- *WhoE 91, WhoEmL 91*
Cooley, James Franklin 1926- *WhoSSW 91*
Cooley, James William 1926- *WhoAm 90*
Cooley, John R. 1937- *WhoWrEP 89*
Cooley, Kathleen Shannon 1939- *WhoAmW 91*
Cooley, Lawrence Sachse 1948- *WhoE 91*
Cooley, Leland Frederick 1909- *WhoWor 91*
Cooley, Louise Ellen 1948- *WhoEmL 91*
Cooley, M Cecilia *BiDrAPA 89*
Cooley, Marie Szpiruk 1935- *WhoAmW 91*
Cooley, Nancy Colver *WhoAm 90, WhoWor 91*
Cooley, Peter 1940- *DcLB 105 [port]*
Cooley, Peter John 1940- *WhoWrEP 89*
Cooley, R.H. 1924- *St&PR 91*
Cooley, Richard Pierce 1923- *St&PR 91, WhoAm 90*
Cooley, Robert Earl 1930- *WhoAm 90*
Cooley, Robert Holmes 1944- *St&PR 91*
Cooley, Robert James 1929- *St&PR 91*
Cooley, Roger B. 1940- *St&PR 91*
Cooley, Ron *NewAgMG*
Cooley, Samuel P. 1931- *St&PR 91*
Cooley, Spade 1910-1969 *OxCPMus*
Cooley, Thomas McIntyre, II 1910- *WhoAm 90*
Cooley, Warren W. 1922- *St&PR 91*
Cooley, Wils LaHugh 1942- *WhoSSW 91*
Coolidge, Calvin 1872-1933 *BiDrUSE 89, BioIn 16, WorAlBi*
Coolidge, David A., Jr. 1956- *WhoE 91*
Coolidge, Edwin Channing 1925- *WhoAm 90*
Coolidge, Grace Anna Goodhue 1879-1957 *BioIn 16*
Coolidge, Grace G. 1879-1957 *BioAmW*
Coolidge, Harold Lane 1933- *St&PR 91*
Coolidge, John 1913- *WhoAmA 91*
Coolidge, Lawrence 1936- *St&PR 91*
Coolidge, Martha *BioIn 16*
Coolidge, Martha 1946- *ConTFT 8, WhoAmW 91*
Coolidge, Martha Henderson 1925- *WhoAmW 91*
Coolidge, Nathaniel Silsbee 1939- *St&PR 91*
Coolidge, Olivia Ensor 1908- *AuBYP 90*
Coolidge, Richard Ard 1929- *IntWWM 90*
Coolidge, Rita 1944- *EncPR&S 89*
Coolidge, Rita 1945- *WhoAm 90*
Coolidge, Thomas Jefferson 1831-1920 *BioIn 16*
Coolidge, Thomas Richards 1934- *St&PR 91*
Coolidge, William D. 1873-1975 *WorAlBi*
Coolidge, William David 1873-1975 *DcScB S2*
Cools, Alta Marie 1941- *WhoWrEP 89*
Cools, Jan Neal 1953- *BiDrAPA 89*
Cools, Joseph M *BiDrAPA 89*
Coomaraswamy, Ananda K 1877-1947 *WhoAmA 91N*
Coombe, Edmund Jay 1940- *WhoSSW 91*
Coombe, George W. 1925- *St&PR 91*
Coombe, George William, Jr. 1925- *WhoAm 90*
Coombe, Jack D. 1922- *WhoWrEP 89*
Coombe, V. Anderson 1926- *St&PR 91, WhoAm 90*
Coombe-Tenant, Winifred *EncPaPR 91*
Coombe-Tennant, Winifred Margaret S 1874-1956 *EncO&P 3*
Coombes, Rame Spignul 1940- *St&PR 91*
Coombes, Robert Law 1929- *St&PR 91*
Coombs, Ann *ConAu 130*
Coombs, Bertha I. 1961- *WhoHisp 91*
Coombs, Bradley Maxwell 1953- *St&PR 91*
Coombs, C'Ceal Phelps *WhoAmW 91, WhoWor 91*
Coombs, Charles Ira 1914- *AuBYP 90*
Coombs, Chick *AuBYP 90*
Coombs, Clyde Hamilton 1912-1988 *BioIn 16*
Coombs, Danny 1942- *Ballpl 90*
Coombs, Francis Place 1915-1990 *BioIn 16*
Coombs, Frank L. 1853-1934 *BioIn 16*
Coombs, Frank Leslie 1853-1934 *AmLegL*
Coombs, H. C. 1906- *BioIn 16*
Coombs, Herbert Cole 1906- *BioIn 16*
Coombs, J. Curtis 1939- *St&PR 91*
Coombs, Jack 1882-1957 *Ballpl 90*
Coombs, John Wendell 1905- *WhoAm 90*
Coombs, Lee C. *BioIn 16*
Coombs, Murdo *TwCCr&M 91*
Coombs, Nina *ConAu 130*
Coombs, Patricia 1926- *AuBYP 90, BioIn 16*
Coombs, Philip H 1915- *WhoWrEP 89*

Coombs, Robert Holman 1934- *WhoAm 90*
Coombs, Vicki J. 1956- *WhoAmW 91*
Coombs, Walter Paul 1920- *WhoAm 90*
Coombs, William Fremont, Jr. 1934- *WhoSSW 91*
Coomer, Anne *AuBYP 90*
Coomer, Joe 1958- *LiHiK, WhoWrEP 89*
Coon, Carlton 1894-1932 *OxCPMus*
Coon, Charles Edward 1933- *St&PR 91*
Coon, Charles P. 1943- *St&PR 91*
Coon, Julian Barham 1939- *St&PR 91, WhoAm 90*
Coon, Kenneth Charles 1950- *St&PR 91*
Coon, Max Alan 1934- *St&PR 91*
Coon, Miles Anthony 1938- *St&PR 91*
Coon, Minor Jesser 1921- *WhoAm 90*
Coon, Richard A. 1945- *St&PR 91*
Coon, William Richard 1927- *St&PR 91*
Coon-Sanders Orchestra *OxCPMus*
Coonan, Sheila M. *BioIn 16*
Coonen, Richard D. 1925- *St&PR 91*
Cooney, Barbara 1917- *AuBYP 90, BioIn 16, ChlLR 23 [port], WhoAm 90, WhoAmW 91*
Cooney, Caroline B. 1947- *Au&Arts 5 [port], BioIn 16*
Cooney, Charles Leland 1944- *WhoAm 90*
Cooney, Christine Joyce 1954- *WhoAmW 91*
Cooney, David Francis 1954- *WhoEmL 91, WhoSSW 91, WhoWor 91*
Cooney, David M. 1930- *St&PR 91*
Cooney, David Martin 1930- *WhoAm 90*
Cooney, Diane *WhoAmW 91*
Cooney, Ellen 1948- *WhoWrEP 89*
Cooney, Eugene Joseph 1948- *WhoEmL 91, WhoSSW 91*
Cooney, Gary M. 1951- *St&PR 91*
Cooney, Harold Anthony 1937- *St&PR 91*
Cooney, James Allen 1947- *WhoE 91*
Cooney, James Patrick, Jr. 1933- *WhoAm 90*
Cooney, Jane Margaret 1943- *WhoAm 90*
Cooney, Jimmy 1894- *Ballpl 90*
Cooney, Joan Ganz 1920- *WorAlBi*
Cooney, Joan Ganz 1929- *St&PR 91, WhoAm 90, WhoAmW 91*
Cooney, John Gerard 1952- *WhoEmL 91*
Cooney, John Gordon 1930- *WhoAm 90, WhoE 91, WhoWor 91*
Cooney, John Thomas 1927- *WhoAm 90*
Cooney, Johnny 1901- *Ballpl 90*
Cooney, Kevin Packard 1952- *St&PR 91*
Cooney, Lenore *WhoAmW 91*
Cooney, Lenore C. *ODwPR 91*
Cooney, Lynn Futch 1961- *WhoEmL 91*
Cooney, Mike 1954- *WhoAm 90*
Cooney, Miriam P. 1925- *WhoAmW 91*
Cooney, Nancy Evans 1932- *AuBYP 90*
Cooney, Patricia Ruth *WhoAmW 91, WhoE 91, WhoWor 91*
Cooney, Patrick Ronald 1934- *WhoAm 90*
Cooney, Ray 19--?- *ConLC 62 [port]*
Cooney, Robert Lincoln 1934- *St&PR 91*
Cooney, Terry 1933- *Ballpl 90*
Cooney, Thomas D. 1926- *St&PR 91*
Cooney, Thomas Michael 1926- *St&PR 91, WhoAm 90*
Coonfield, Ed 1941- *WhoWrEP 89*
Coonrad, Douglas V. 1945- *WhoEmL 91*
Coonrod, Anne Taylor 1944- *WhoAmW 91*
Coonrod, Gregory Loran 1956- *St&PR 91*
Coonrod, Richard Allen 1931- *St&PR 91, WhoAm 90*
Coonrod, William C. 1934- *St&PR 91*
Coons, Barbara 1948- *ODwPR 91*
Coons, Clifford V. 1911-1990 *BioIn 16*
Coons, David Joel 1947- *BiDrAPA 89, WhoEmL 91*
Coons, E. N. *BioIn 16*
Coons, Edwin Joseph, Jr. 1932- *WhoSSW 91*
Coons, Eldo Jess, Jr. 1924- *WhoSSW 91*
Coons, James William 1957- *St&PR 91*
Coons, Lisa Karol 1955- *WhoSSW 91*
Coons, Marion M. 1915- *St&PR 91*
Coons, Marion McDowell 1915- *WhoAm 90*
Coons, Patricia Ann 1940- *WhoE 91*
Coons, Peter 1875-1955 *EncO&P 3*
Coons, Philip M 1945- *BiDrAPA 89*
Coons, Richard E *BiDrAPA 89*
Coons, Ronald Edward 1936- *WhoAm 90*
Coons, Theodore W. 1950- *St&PR 91*
Coons, William Ellsworth 1949- *WhoEmL 91*
Coontz, Eric John 1949- *WhoEmL 91, WhoWor 91*
Coontz, Morris Stephen 1946- *WhoEmL 91*
Coontz, Stephanie *ConAu 132*
Coop, Donald Charles 1955- *WhoSSW 91*
Coop, Frederick Robert 1914- *WhoAm 90*
Coop, Jane Austin 1950- *IntWWM 90*
Coop, William Steven 1953- *WhoSSW 91*
Coopee, Thomas L. 1946- *St&PR 91*
Cooper, Lord 1908-1988 *AnObit 1988*
Cooper, Alan Bruce 1928- *BiDrAPA 89*
Cooper, Alan Michael *BiDrAPA 89*
Cooper, Alan Robert 1942- *WhoE 91*
Cooper, Alan Samuel 1942- *WhoAm 90*
Cooper, Alice *BioIn 16*
Cooper, Alice 1948- *EncPR&S 89, OxCPMus, WorAlBi*
Cooper, Allen David 1942- *WhoAm 90*
Cooper, Andrew *BioIn 16*
Cooper, Andrew 1948- *ODwPR 91*
Cooper, Andrew Charles 1952- *WhoSSW 91*
Cooper, Ann Eisenberg 1936- *WhoAmW 91*
Cooper, Anna J. 1859-1964 *BioAmW*
Cooper, Anna Julia *EarBlAP*
Cooper, Anna Julia 1856-1964 *HarlReB [port]*
Cooper, Anna Julia 1859?-1964 *FemiCLE*
Cooper, Anthony Ashley 1801-1885 *BioIn 16*
Cooper, Anthony J 1907- *WhoAmA 91*
Cooper, April Helen 1951- *WhoEmL 91*
Cooper, Arlin B 1909- *BiDrAPA 89*
Cooper, Arlin R 1942- *BiDrAPA 89*
Cooper, Armah Jamale *BiDrAPA 89*
Cooper, Arnold M 1923- *BiDrAPA 89*
Cooper, Arnold Michael 1923- *WhoAm 90*
Cooper, Arthur Irving 1922- *WhoAm 90*
Cooper, Arthur Martin 1937- *WhoAm 90, WhoWrEP 89*
Cooper, Arthur Wells 1931- *WhoAm 90*
Cooper, B. Jay 1950- *WhoAm 90*
Cooper, Barbara Mary 1949- *WhoWrEP 89*
Cooper, Barry Anthony Raymond 1949- *IntWWM 90*
Cooper, Ben 1920- *St&PR 91*
Cooper, Bennett J. *BioIn 16*
Cooper, Bernard Richard 1936- *WhoAm 90*
Cooper, Betsy Jane *BiDrAPA 89*
Cooper, Betty Jane 1945- *WhoSSW 91*
Cooper, Betty Ruth 1941- *WhoSSW 91*
Cooper, Billy Norman 1937- *WhoWrEP 89*
Cooper, Blanche *EncO&P 3, EncPaPR 91*
Cooper, Brian 1919- *TwCCr&M 91*
Cooper, Calvin Gordon 1925- *St&PR 91*
Cooper, Camille Sutro 1946- *St&PR 91, WhoAmW 91*
Cooper, Carl B. 1939- *St&PR 91*
Cooper, Carol Ann 1940- *WhoAmW 91*
Cooper, Carol Diane 1953- *WhoEmL 91*
Cooper, Carol Joan 1938- *WhoE 91*
Cooper, Caroline Ann 1943- *WhoAmW 91*
Cooper, Carolyn Helen *WhoAmW 91*
Cooper, Carter Vanderbilt *BioIn 16*
Cooper, Cary Wayne 1939- *WhoAm 90*
Cooper, Cecil *BioIn 16*
Cooper, Cecil 1949- *Ballpl 90 [port]*
Cooper, Charles Alan 1929- *St&PR 91*
Cooper, Charles B. 1938- *St&PR 91*
Cooper, Charles Byron 1938- *WhoAm 90*
Cooper, Charles Edward 1933- *WhoAm 90, WhoWor 91*
Cooper, Charles G. 1928- *St&PR 91, WhoAm 90*
Cooper, Charles Gerson 1932- *WhoE 91*
Cooper, Charles Gordon 1927- *WhoAm 90*
Cooper, Charles Grafton 1927- *WhoAm 90*
Cooper, Charles Howard 1920- *WhoAm 90*
Cooper, Charles Jasper 1929- *WhoAm 90, WhoE 91, WhoSSW 91*
Cooper, Charles Justin 1952- *WhoAm 90*
Cooper, Charles M. *BioIn 16*
Cooper, Charles William, Jr. 1931- *WhoE 91*
Cooper, Charlotte B. 1941- *St&PR 91*
Cooper, Charlotte Wynn 1941- *WhoAmW 91*
Cooper, Chester Lawrence 1917- *WhoE 91*
Cooper, Claire Virginia *BiDrAPA 89*
Cooper, Clare Dunlap 1938- *WhoAmW 91*
Cooper, Claude 1892-1974 *Ballpl 90*
Cooper, Constance 1945- *IntWWM 90*
Cooper, Constance Carter 1935- *WhoAm 90*
Cooper, Corinne 1952- *WhoEmL 91*
Cooper, Cynthia Lee 1964- *WhoAmW 91*
Cooper, Dalton *St&PR 91*
Cooper, Daniel 1931- *WhoAm 90*
Cooper, Darlene Rae 1943- *WhoSSW 91*
Cooper, David Anthony 1949- *IntWWM 90*
Cooper, David B., Jr. 1956- *St&PR 91*
Cooper, David Booth, Jr. 1956- *WhoAm 90*
Cooper, David E 1942- *ConAu 31NR*
Cooper, David Lee 1949- *WhoSSW 91*
Cooper, David R. 1942- *St&PR 91*
Cooper, David Samuel 1955- *WhoEmL 91*
Cooper, Dayton Charles, Jr. 1947- *WhoEmL 91*
Cooper, Deborah Robinson 1958- *WhoEmL 91*
Cooper, Debra Lynn 1957- *WhoEmL 91*
Cooper, Dennis Lamar 1941- *WhoE 91*
Cooper, Diana 1892-1986 *BioIn 16*
Cooper, Dick *ODwPR 91*
Cooper, Dolores Ann 1935- *WhoAmW 91*
Cooper, Dolores G. 1922- *WhoAmW 91*
Cooper, Dona Hanks 1950- *WhoAmW 91*
Cooper, Donald 1927- *St&PR 91*
Cooper, Donald Lee 1928- *WhoAm 90*
Cooper, Donald M. 1939- *St&PR 91*
Cooper, Doris Jean 1934- *WhoAmW 91*
Cooper, Dorothy W. 1955- *WhoAmW 91*
Cooper, Douglas 1911-1984 *BioIn 16, ConAu 130, DcNaB 1981*
Cooper, Douglass William 1956- *WhoEmL 91*
Cooper, E. Camron 1939- *WhoAm 90*
Cooper, Edgar S. *WhoWrEP 89*
Cooper, Edith Emma 1862-1913 *BioIn 16*
Cooper, Edmund 1926-1982 *ConAu 31NR*
Cooper, Edward Hayes 1941- *WhoAm 90*
Cooper, Edward Holmes 1927- *WhoWor 91*
Cooper, Edward Russell 1951- *WhoE 91*
Cooper, Edward S. *BioIn 16*
Cooper, Edwin Lowell 1936- *WhoAm 90*
Cooper, Eileen 1953- *BiDWomA*
Cooper, Elizabeth *FemiCLE*
Cooper, Elizabeth Keyser *BioIn 16*
Cooper, Elizabeth M. 1954- *WhoAmW 91*
Cooper, Emil 1877-1960 *PenDiMP*
Cooper, Emma 1837-1912? *BiDWomA*
Cooper, Eugene Bruce 1933- *WhoAm 90*
Cooper, Evan 1949- *ODwPR 91*
Cooper, Floyd C, III 1930- *BiDrAPA 89*
Cooper, Francis Loren 1919- *WhoAm 90*
Cooper, Frank 1922- *BioIn 16*
Cooper, Frank Evans 1928- *WhoAm 90*
Cooper, Franklin Seaney 1908- *WhoAm 90*
Cooper, Fred 1936- *St&PR 91*
Cooper, Fred G 1883-1962 *WhoAmA 91N*
Cooper, Frederick Eansor 1942- *St&PR 91, WhoAm 90*
Cooper, Fredric Milton 1923- *WhoSSW 91*
Cooper, Frieda Louise 1944- *WhoAmW 91*
Cooper, Garrett Wayne 1952- *WhoEmL 91*
Cooper, Gary 1901-1961 *BioIn 16, WorAlBi*
Cooper, Gary Allan 1947- *WhoEmL 91*
Cooper, Gary Keith 1954- *WhoEmL 91*
Cooper, Gary Martin 1928- *St&PR 91*
Cooper, George Brinton 1916- *WhoAm 90*
Cooper, George Robert 1921- *WhoAm 90*
Cooper, George William 1928-1990 *BioIn 16*
Cooper, George Wilson 1927- *St&PR 91*
Cooper, Gerald Lewis 1945- *WhoE 91*
Cooper, Gershon N. 1949- *St&PR 91*
Cooper, Gladys L. 1951- *St&PR 91*
Cooper, Gloria 1931- *WhoAm 90*
Cooper, Gloria 1937- *WhoAmW 91*
Cooper, Gordon 1932- *AuBYP 90*
Cooper, Gordon Mayo 1925- *St&PR 91, WhoAm 90*
Cooper, Grant B. *NewYTBS 90*
Cooper, Grant B. 1903-1990 *BioIn 16*
Cooper, Guy *BioIn 16*
Cooper, H. Jackie 1939- *St&PR 91*
Cooper, H. Lee 1938- *St&PR 91*
Cooper, Hal 1923- *WhoAm 90*
Cooper, Hal Dean 1934- *WhoAm 90*
Cooper, Harris 1937- *St&PR 91*
Cooper, Harry P., Jr. 1911- *St&PR 91*
Cooper, Helen 1947- *ConAu 129*
Cooper, Helen Allen 1947- *WhoSSW 91*
Cooper, Helmar Augustus *DrBlPA 90*
Cooper, Henry F. *BioIn 16*
Cooper, Henry St. John *MajTwCW*
Cooper, Herbert K, III 1946- *BiDrAPA 89*
Cooper, Horace Jackie 1939- *WhoSSW 91*
Cooper, Howard N 1922- *BiDrAPA 89*
Cooper, Howard Norvin 1922- *WhoE 91*
Cooper, Imogen 1949- *IntWWM 90*
Cooper, Irmgard Marie 1946- *WhoEmL 91*
Cooper, Irving Ben 1902- *WhoAm 90*
Cooper, Ivan Leveson 1925- *WhoWor 91*
Cooper, J. Daniel Cooper 1948- *WhoSSW 91*
Cooper, J. Danny 1948- *WhoSSW 91*
Cooper, Jack M. 1939- *St&PR 91*
Cooper, Jack Ross 1924- *WhoAm 90*
Cooper, Jackie 1921- *WorAlBi*
Cooper, Jackie 1922- *ConTFT 8 [port], WhoAm 90*
Cooper, Jacqueline Marie 1947- *WhoEmL 91*
Cooper, James C. 1935- *St&PR 91, WhoAm 90*
Cooper, James Carter, II 1945- *BiDrAPA 89*
Cooper, James Fenimore 1789-1851 *AuBYP 90, BioIn 16, NinCLC 27 [port], SpyFic, WhNaAH [port], WorAlBi*
Cooper, James Ford 1935- *WhoAm 90, WhoWor 91*
Cooper, James Hayes Shofner 1954- *WhoAm 90, WhoSSW 91*
Cooper, James M., Jr. 1941- *St&PR 91*
Cooper, James Michael 1939- *WhoAm 90*
Cooper, James Richard *BiDrAPA 89*
Cooper, James Richard 1943- *WhoAm 90*
Cooper, James Wayne 1904-1989 *BioIn 16*
Cooper, Jane Elizabeth 1937- *WhoAmW 91*
Cooper, Jane Todd 1943- *WhoAmW 91*
Cooper, Janis C. 1947- *ODwPR 91, St&PR 91*
Cooper, Jay Leslie 1929- *WhoAm 90*
Cooper, Jean H 1903- *BiDrAPA 89*
Cooper, Jean Saralee 1946- *WhoAm 90*
Cooper, Jeanine Grace 1964- *WhoE 91*
Cooper, Jeffrey 1950- *WhoEmL 91*
Cooper, Jeffrey B. 1950- *WhoWrEP 89*
Cooper, Jeffrey Stuart 1947- *WhoE 91*
Cooper, Jerome A. 1913- *WhoAm 90*
Cooper, Jerome Maurice 1930- *WhoAm 90, WhoSSW 91*
Cooper, Jerrold Stephen 1942- *WhoAm 90*
Cooper, Jerry Lee, Jr. 1963- *WhoEmL 91*
Cooper, Jerry William 1937- *ODwPR 91*
Cooper, Jessie Allen *NewAgMG*
Cooper, Jessie F. 1932- *MusmAFA*
Cooper, Jilly 1937- *ConAu 30NR*
Cooper, Jimmy Lee 1942- *WhoSSW 91*
Cooper, Joann G. 1938- *St&PR 91*
Cooper, Joel 1943- *WhoAm 90*
Cooper, Joel J. 1958- *WhoEmL 91*
Cooper, John *BioIn 16*
Cooper, John A., Jr. 1938- *St&PR 91*
Cooper, John Alfred 1906- *WhoAm 90, WhoSSW 91*
Cooper, John Alfred, Jr. 1938- *WhoAm 90, WhoSSW 91*
Cooper, John Allen Dicks 1918- *WhoAm 90, WhoWor 91*
Cooper, John Anthony 1959- *WhoEmL 91*
Cooper, John Arnold 1917- *WhoWor 91*
Cooper, John Arthur 1943- *BiDrAPA 89*
Cooper, John Byrne, Jr. 1942- *WhoSSW 91*
Cooper, John C 1933- *ConAu 30NR*
Cooper, John Charles 1933- *WhoWrEP 89*
Cooper, John Frederick 1956- *WhoEmL 91*
Cooper, John Ireland 1955- *WhoEmL 91*
Cooper, John J. 1924- *St&PR 91*
Cooper, John Joseph 1924- *WhoAm 90*
Cooper, John L. 1937- *St&PR 91*
Cooper, John Madison 1939- *WhoAm 90*
Cooper, John Milton, Jr. 1940- *WhoAm 90*
Cooper, John Sherman *BioIn 16*
Cooper, John Sherman 1901- *WorAlBi*
Cooper, John Thomas 1945- *WhoSSW 91*
Cooper, Joseph 1933- *WhoAm 90, WhoWor 91*
Cooper, Joseph Elliott Needham 1912- *IntWWM 90*
Cooper, Joseph V. 1920- *St&PR 91*
Cooper, Josephine S. *ODwPR 91*
Cooper, Josephine Smith 1945- *WhoAmW 91, WhoE 91*
Cooper, Joshua Edward Synge 1901-1981 *DcNaB 1981*
Cooper, Judith *WhoWrEP 89*
Cooper, Julian M. 1945- *ConAu 130*
Cooper, Karen Elizabeth Mauser 1955- *WhoEmL 91*
Cooper, Katherine 1841-1894 *FemiCLE*
Cooper, Kathleen Bell 1945- *WhoAm 90*
Cooper, Kathy Nelle 1956- *WhoWrEP 89*
Cooper, Keith Harvey 1936- *WhoAm 90*
Cooper, Ken Errol 1939- *WhoAm 90*
Cooper, Kenneth 1941- *IntWWM 90, PenDiMP*
Cooper, Kenneth Banks 1923- *WhoAm 90*
Cooper, Kenneth Carlton 1948- *WhoEmL 91, WhoWrEP 89*
Cooper, Kenneth H. *BioIn 16*
Cooper, Kenneth Stanley 1948- *WhoEmL 91, WhoSSW 91*
Cooper, Kent 1880-1965 *BioIn 16*
Cooper, Kent D. 1952- *St&PR 91*
Cooper, Kristina Marie 1955- *WhoAmW 91*
Cooper, L. Gordon, Jr. 1927- *WorAlBi*
Cooper, Lance Eugene 1943- *St&PR 91*
Cooper, Larry B. 1943- *St&PR 91*
Cooper, Larry Paige *BiDrAPA 89*
Cooper, Larry Preston 1936- *St&PR 91*
Cooper, Laurie A. 1952- *WhoEmL 91*
Cooper, Lee E. *BioIn 16*
Cooper, Lee Pelham 1926- *AuBYP 90*
Cooper, Leon 1925- *WhoSSW 91*
Cooper, Leon 1929- *St&PR 91*
Cooper, Leon Melvin 1924- *WhoAm 90*
Cooper, Leon N. 1930- *St&PR 91, WhoAm 90, WhoE 91, WhoWor 91, WorAlBi*
Cooper, Leonard Jay 1938- *WhoAm 90*
Cooper, Leroy Gordon, Jr. 1927- *WhoAm 90*
Cooper, Lettice 1897- *BioIn 16, FemiCLE*
Cooper, Linda Frances 1961- *WhoAmW 91*
Cooper, Linda Groomes 1954- *WhoEmL 91*
Cooper, Lisa Ivy 1961- *WhoAmW 91*
Cooper, Louise Field 1905- *WhoAm 90*
Cooper, Lyman B. 1854-1913 *AmLegL*
Cooper, Malcolm E. *St&PR 91*
Cooper, Margaretta S. *EncO&P 3*
Cooper, Margery Wilkens 1947- *WhoAmW 91*

Cooper, Maria Susanna 1738-1807 *FemiCLE*
Cooper, Marilyn Mace 1950- *WhoEmL 91*
Cooper, Mario 1905- *WhoAmA 91*
Cooper, Marsh Alexander 1912- *St&PR 91, WhoAm 90*
Cooper, Martha Rose 1956- *WhoE 91, WhoEmL 91*
Cooper, Martin 1928- *WhoAm 90*
Cooper, Martin M. *ODwPR 91*
Cooper, Martin Mayer 1954- *BiDrAPA 89*
Cooper, Martin Michael 1941- *St&PR 91*
Cooper, Marve H 1939- *WhoAmA 91*
Cooper, Marvin Arthur 1933- *St&PR 91*
Cooper, Marvin Meyer 1931- *WhoE 91*
Cooper, Mary A. 1927- *St&PR 91*
Cooper, Mary Adrienne 1927- *WhoAm 90, WhoAmW 91*
Cooper, Mary Ann 1935- *WhoSSW 91*
Cooper, Maury M. 1944- *St&PR 91*
Cooper, Melbourne J 1901- *BiDrAPA 89*
Cooper, Merri-Ann 1946- *WhoAmW 91*
Cooper, Michael *BioIn 16*
Cooper, Michael Allen 1936- *St&PR 91*
Cooper, Michael Anthony 1936- *WhoAm 90*
Cooper, Michael Charles 1956- *BiDrAPA 89*
Cooper, Michael J. 1953- *WhoSSW 91*
Cooper, Michael R. 1946- *St&PR 91*
Cooper, Milton 1929- *St&PR 91, WhoAm 90*
Cooper, Mort 1913- *Ballpl 90*
Cooper, Morton 1917- *St&PR 91*
Cooper, Muriel *ConDes 90*
Cooper, Murray W. 1932- *St&PR 91*
Cooper, Nathan 1946- *St&PR 91*
Cooper, Neil 1950- *St&PR 91*
Cooper, Norman 1931- *WhoAm 90*
Cooper, Norman John 1950- *WhoEmL 91*
Cooper, Norman Streich 1920- *WhoAm 90*
Cooper, Norton *BioIn 16*
Cooper, Norton J. 1931- *St&PR 91, WhoAm 90*
Cooper, Olin Cecil, Jr. 1925- *WhoSSW 91*
Cooper, Pamela Mary 1950- *St&PR 91*
Cooper, Patricia Ann 1949- *WhoEmL 91*
Cooper, Patricia Dawkins 1944- *WhoAmW 91*
Cooper, Patricia Gorman 1946- *WhoEmL 91*
Cooper, Patricia Jacqueline 1958- *WhoEmL 91*
Cooper, Paul 1926- *IntWWM 90, WhoAm 90*
Cooper, Paul Douglas 1941- *WhoAm 90*
Cooper, Paul Fenimore *BioIn 16*
Cooper, Paul W. *BioIn 16*
Cooper, Paula *BioIn 16*
Cooper, Paula 1938- *WhoAmA 91*
Cooper, Paulette Marcia 1942- *WhoAmW 91, WhoE 91, WhoWrEP 89*
Cooper, Peter 1791-1883 *WhNaAH, WorAlBi*
Cooper, Peter Brian 1927- *IntWWM 90*
Cooper, Peter Dirr 1940- *St&PR 91*
Cooper, Phyllis Anne Greene 1927- *WhoSSW 91*
Cooper, R. John, III 1942- *WhoAm 90*
Cooper, Rachel Elizabeth 1963- *IntWWM 90*
Cooper, Ralph *DrBIPA 90*
Cooper, Randall K. 1948- *St&PR 91*
Cooper, Randall L. 1951- *St&PR 91*
Cooper, Rebecca 1957- *WhoAmW 91*
Cooper, Reginald Rudyard 1932- *WhoAm 90*
Cooper, Rene Victor 1924- *WhoSSW 91*
Cooper, Rhonda H 1950- *WhoAmA 91*
Cooper, Rhonda Helene 1950- *WhoE 91*
Cooper, Richard 1945-1979 *WhoAmA 91N*
Cooper, Richard A. 1927- *St&PR 91*
Cooper, Richard A 1936- *BiDrAPA 89*
Cooper, Richard Alan 1936- *WhoAm 90*
Cooper, Richard Alan 1953- *WhoEmL 91*
Cooper, Richard F. 1951- *St&PR 91*
Cooper, Richard Lee 1946- *WhoAm 90*
Cooper, Richard Melvin 1942- *WhoAm 90*
Cooper, Richard Newell 1934- *WhoAm 90*
Cooper, Robert A. 1926- *St&PR 91*
Cooper, Robert Arthur, Jr. 1932- *WhoAm 90*
Cooper, Robert Elbert 1920- *WhoAm 90*
Cooper, Robert Gerald 1931- *WhoSSW 91*
Cooper, Robert Gordon 1953- *WhoEmL 91*
Cooper, Robert Harold 1925- *St&PR 91*
Cooper, Robert Joe *BiDrAPA 89*
Cooper, Robert Louis 1919- *WhoE 91*
Cooper, Robert Rodney 1938- *WhoE 91*
Cooper, Robert Vernon, Jr. 1954- *WhoSSW 91*
Cooper, Robin Julia *BiDrAPA 89*
Cooper, Rochella 1933- *WhoAmW 91*
Cooper, Roger Frank 1944- *WhoAm 90*
Cooper, Roger Merlin 1943- *WhoAm 90*
Cooper, Ron 1943- *WhoAmA 91*
Cooper, Ronald E. 1931- *MusmAFA*
Cooper, Rosaleen 1894-1989 *ConAu 129*
Cooper, Rubin Seymour 1946- *WhoE 91*
Cooper, Ruffin 1942- *WhoAmA 91*
Cooper, Russell 1918- *St&PR 91*
Cooper, Rustomjee Cavasjee 1922- *WhoWor 91*
Cooper, Ruthie Mae 1948- *WhoEmL 91*
Cooper, Samuel 1608?-1672 *IntDcAA 90 [port]*
Cooper, Sandra Lenore 1934- *WhoWrEP 89*
Cooper, Scott Francis 1953- *WhoEmL 91*
Cooper, Sharon Elizabeth 1951- *WhoE 91*
Cooper, Sharon Marsha 1944- *WhoAmW 91*
Cooper, Sidney 1920- *St&PR 91*
Cooper, Sol 1916- *St&PR 91*
Cooper, Stanley Bernard 1944- *WhoE 91*
Cooper, Stephen 1948- *BiDrAPA 89*
Cooper, Stephen C. 1951- *ODwPR 91*
Cooper, Stephen Herbert 1939- *WhoAm 90*
Cooper, Steve Neil 1944- *WhoE 91*
Cooper, Steven *NewAgMG*
Cooper, Steven J. 1957- *BiDrAPA 89*
Cooper, Stuart Leonard 1941- *WhoAm 90*
Cooper, Susan 1935- *AuBYP 90, BioIn 16, SmATA 64 [port]*
Cooper, Susan 1947- *WhoAmA 91*
Cooper, Susan Fenimore 1813-1894 *FemiCLE*
Cooper, Susan Vera 1902- *PenDiDA 89*
Cooper, Sylvia Jane 1936- *WhoAmW 91*
Cooper, Terrance G. 1942- *WhoAm 90*
Cooper, Terry Lane 1946- *WhoEmL 91*
Cooper, Theodore 1928- *St&PR 91, WhoAm 90*
Cooper, Theodore A 1943- *WhoAmA 91*
Cooper, Thomas 1759-1840 *BioIn 16*
Cooper, Thomas 1805-1892 *BioIn 16*
Cooper, Thomas Butler 1817-1885 *AmLegL*
Cooper, Thomas Frederick 1921-1984 *DcNaB 1981*
Cooper, Thomas Luther 1917- *WhoAm 90*
Cooper, Thomas O. *AmLegL*
Cooper, Tony *ODwPR 91*
Cooper, Walker 1915- *Ballpl 90 [port]*
Cooper, Wallace J. 1926- *WhoAm 90*
Cooper, Warren S. 1922- *St&PR 91*
Cooper, Warren Stanley 1922- *WhoAm 90*
Cooper, Wayne 1942- *WhoAmA 91*
Cooper, Wendy Fein 1946- *WhoAmW 91, WhoEmL 91*
Cooper, Wendy Leigh 1960- *WhoSSW 91*
Cooper, Wilbur 1892-1973 *Ballpl 90 [port]*
Cooper, William Allen 1943- *WhoAm 90*
Cooper, William Clark 1912- *WhoWor 91*
Cooper, William Edward 1921- *WhoWor 91*
Cooper, William Edward 1930- *St&PR 91*
Cooper, William Eugene 1924- *WhoAm 90*
Cooper, William Ewing, Jr. 1929- *WhoAm 90*
Cooper, William Frazier 1932- *WhoAm 90*
Cooper, William James 1945- *WhoSSW 91*
Cooper, William James, Jr. 1940- *WhoAm 90*
Cooper, William Marion 1919- *WhoAm 90*
Cooper, William Secord 1935- *WhoAm 90*
Cooper, William Thomas 1938- *WhoE 91, WhoWor 91*
Cooper, William Wager 1914- *WhoAm 90*
Cooper, Wray Thomas, Jr. 1943- *WhoSSW 91*
Cooper-Fedler, Pamela Ann 1959- *WhoEmL 91*
Cooper-Lewter, Marcia Jean 1959- *WhoAmW 91*
Cooper-Scott, Nedra Denise 1953- *WhoAmW 91, WhoEmL 91, WhoWor 91*
Cooperman, Barry S. 1941- *WhoAm 90*
Cooperman, Bruce 1937- *St&PR 91*
Cooperman, Elliot Mark 1945- *BiDrAPA 89*
Cooperman, Hasye 1909- *WhoWrEP 89*
Cooperman, Leon *BioIn 16*
Cooperman, Leon G. 1943- *St&PR 91, WhoAm 90*
Cooperman, Lewis J. 1936- *St&PR 91*
Cooperman, Martin 1914- *BiDrAPA 89*
Cooperman, Oliver Burton 1946- *BiDrAPA 89*
Cooperman, Saul 1934- *WhoAm 90, WhoE 91*
Cooperman, Selma Shaffer 1926- *BiDrAPA 89*
Cooperman, Sheila Ann *BiDrAPA 89*
Cooperman, Suzanne Kay 1948- *BiDrAPA 89*
Cooperrider, Tom Smith 1927- *WhoAm 90*
Coopersmith, Barry 1946- *St&PR 91*
Coopersmith, Bernard Ira 1914- *WhoWor 91*
Coopersmith, Brant *BioIn 16*
Coopersmith, Georgia A 1950- *WhoAmA 91*
Coopersmith, Georgia Ann 1950- *WhoE 91*
Coopersmith, Harvey J. 1937- *WhoE 91*
Coopersmith, Jeffrey Alan 1946- *St&PR 91, WhoEmL 91*
Coopersmith, Jerome 1925- *AuBYP 90*
Coopersmith, Martin Joseph 1940- *St&PR 91*
Coopersmith, Richard C *BiDrAPA 89*
Coopersmith, Shirley Ann 1944- *WhoAmW 91*
Cooperstein, Martin 1924- *St&PR 91*
Cooperstein, Paul Andrew 1953- *WhoEmL 91*
Cooperstein, Sherwin Jerome 1923- *WhoAm 90*
Cooperstock, Andrew Bryan 1960- *IntWWM 90*
Coopman, Bill *BioIn 16*
Coopwood, William E *BiDrAPA 89*
Coor, Lattie Finch 1936- *WhoAm 90*
Cooray, Thomas 1901-1988 *BioIn 16*
Coords, Robert H. *WhoSSW 91*
Coore, David 1925- *WhoWor 91*
Coors Family *ConAmBL*
Coors, George J. 1922- *St&PR 91*
Coors, Jeffrey H. *BioIn 16*
Coors, Jeffrey H. 1945- *WhoAm 90*
Coors, Joseph 1917- *ConAmBL, WhoAm 90*
Coors, Peter Hanson 1946- *ConAmBL*
Coors, William K. 1916- *ConAmBL, St&PR 91, WhoAm 90*
Coorts, Gerald Duane 1932- *WhoAm 90*
Coote, Richard 1636-1701 *EncCRAm*
Cooter, Dale A. 1948- *WhoWor 91*
Cootes, Frank Graham 1879-1960 *WhoAmA 91N*
Coots, Daniel Jay 1951- *St&PR 91*
Coots, J. Fred 1897- *OxCPMus*
Coots, John Frederick 1897-1985 *BioIn 16*
Coover, David B. 1932- *St&PR 91*
Coover, Edward John 1945- *St&PR 91*
Coover, Elizabeth Barbara 1959- *WhoSSW 91*
Coover, Harry Wesley 1919- *WhoAm 90*
Coover, Harry Wesley, Jr. *BioIn 16*
Coover, Harry Wesley, Jr. 1919- *St&PR 91*
Coover, James B. 1925- *IntWWM 90, WhoWrEP 89*
Coover, John Edgar 1872-1938 *EncO&P 3, EncPaPR 91*
Coover, Paula Louise 1947- *WhoAmW 91*
Coover, Robert 1922- *Ballpl 90 [port]*
Coover, Robert 1932- *MajTwCW*
Coover-Clark, Carol 1955- *WhoAmW 91, WhoEmL 91*
Coox, Alvin David 1924- *WhoAm 90*
Copa, Kathleen Therese 1955- *WhoAmW 91*
Copacino, William Charles 1950- *St&PR 91*
Copage, Marc 1962- *DrBIPA 90*
Copans, Kenneth Gary 1946- *WhoEmL 91*
Copans, Stuart Alan 1943- *BiDrAPA 89, WhoE 91*
Cope, Alfred Haines 1912- *WhoE 91, WhoWor 91*
Cope, Alice Nelson 1941- *WhoWor 91*
Cope, Betty 1927- *St&PR 91*
Cope, Brenda Louise 1956- *WhoAmW 91*
Cope, David Edge 1948- *WhoWrEP 89*
Cope, Esther Sidney 1942- *WhoAmW 91*
Cope, Everton B., Jr. 1932- *St&PR 91*
Cope, Harold Cary 1918- *WhoAm 90*
Cope, Hester Lee 1940- *WhoAmW 91*
Cope, Jackson Irving 1925- *WhoAm 90*
Cope, James Dudley 1932- *WhoAm 90*
Cope, John Robert 1942- *WhoAm 90, WhoWor 91*
Cope, Joseph Adams 1945- *WhoEmL 91*
Cope, Kenneth Wayne 1924- *WhoAm 90*
Cope, Kevin Lee 1957- *WhoSSW 91*
Cope, Larry Morgan 1946- *WhoSSW 91*
Cope, Lewis 1934- *WhoAm 90*
Cope, Louise Todd 1930- *WhoAmA 91*
Cope, Nancy Elizabeth 1952- *WhoAmW 91*
Cope, Randolph Howard, Jr. 1927- *WhoAm 90*
Cope, Roger W. 1945- *St&PR 91*
Cope, Wendy 1945- *FemiCLE*
Cope, William Scott 1948- *St&PR 91*
Copeau, Jacques 1879-1949 *BioIn 16*
Copel, Ken 1962- *WhoEmL 91*
Copelan, Aubrey I *BiDrAPA 89*
Copelan, John Jefferson, Jr. 1951- *WhoEmL 91*
Copeland, A. Clayton 1933- *St&PR 91*
Copeland, Adrian D *BiDrAPA 89*
Copeland, Adrian Dennis 1928- *WhoE 91*
Copeland, Alvin *BioIn 16*
Copeland, Alvin Charles 1944- *WhoAm 90*
Copeland, Anne Pitcairn 1951- *WhoAmW 91*
Copeland, Arthur Richard 1949- *WhoSSW 91*
Copeland, Carolyn Abigail 1931- *WhoAmW 91*
Copeland, Conrad Grant 1924- *St&PR 91*
Copeland, D. Robert 1923- *WhoSSW 91*
Copeland, Darryl W. 1936- *St&PR 91*
Copeland, Donald Eugene 1912- *WhoAm 90*
Copeland, Douglas Wallace, Jr. 1952- *WhoEmL 91*
Copeland, Edward Jerome 1933- *WhoAm 90*
Copeland, Elaine Wilson 1944- *WhoAmW 91*
Copeland, Eric A., Jr. 1936- *St&PR 91*
Copeland, Erma Riddick 1948- *WhoWrEP 89*
Copeland, Eugene Leroy 1939- *WhoAm 90, WhoWor 91*
Copeland, Floyd Dean 1939- *WhoAm 90*
Copeland, Frances Virginia *AuBYP 90*
Copeland, Hal 1931- *ODwPR 91*
Copeland, Henry Jefferson, Jr. 1936- *WhoAm 90*
Copeland, Hunter Armstrong 1918- *WhoAm 90*
Copeland, Jacqueline Lanz 1944- *WhoE 91*
Copeland, Jane Conyers 1941- *WhoAmW 91*
Copeland, Joan Miller *WhoAm 90*
Copeland, John Alexander, III 1941- *WhoAm 90*
Copeland, John Wesley 1935- *St&PR 91, WhoAm 90*
Copeland, John Wilson 1922- *WhoAm 90*
Copeland, Joseph J. 1907-1990 *BioIn 16*
Copeland, Joseph John 1907-1990 *NewYTBS 90 [port]*
Copeland, Josephine *HarlReB*
Copeland, Keith Lamont 1946- *WhoEmL 91*
Copeland, Lee Gordon 1937- *WhoAm 90*
Copeland, Leticia Salvatierra 1962- *WhoHisp 91*
Copeland, Lila 1922- *WhoAm 90, WhoAmA 91*
Copeland, Linda Jane 1947- *WhoEmL 91*
Copeland, Marcia *BioIn 16*
Copeland, Mark Robert 1962- *St&PR 91*
Copeland, Maxine 1956- *WhoAmW 91*
Copeland, Morris Albert 1895-1989 *BioIn 16*
Copeland, Patrick *St&PR 91*
Copeland, Patrick Joseph 1944- *WhoAm 90*
Copeland, Paul Clifford *BiDrAPA 89*
Copeland, Paul W. *AuBYP 90*
Copeland, R. Bruce 1930- *ODwPR 91*
Copeland, Robert Bodine 1938- *WhoAm 90*
Copeland, Robert Glenn 1941- *WhoAm 90*
Copeland, Robert Marshall 1945- *IntWWM 90, WhoE 91*
Copeland, Robert Tayloe 1947- *WhoEmL 91*
Copeland, Ronald Max *WhoAm 90*
Copeland, Stewart *BioIn 16*
Copeland, Suzanne Johnson 1943- *WhoAmW 91*
Copeland, Tatiana Brandt *WhoAmW 91*
Copeland, Terrilyn Denise 1954- *WhoAmW 91, WhoEmL 91*
Copeland, Thomas C., III 1940- *St&PR 91*
Copeland, Vicki Renae 1959- *WhoEmL 91*
Copeland, William Edgar 1920- *WhoAm 90*
Copeland, William George 1926- *St&PR 91*
Copeland, William John 1918- *WhoAm 90*
Copeland, Wilma T. 1940- *WhoAmW 91*
Copenhaver, Brian Paul 1942- *WhoAm 90*
Copenhaver, Ida Louise 1945- *WhoEmL 91*
Copenhaver, John Thomas, Jr. 1925- *WhoAm 90*
Copenhaver, William Pierce 1924- *St&PR 91*
Coper, Hans 1920-1981 *PenDiDA 89*
Copernicus, Nicolas 1473-1543 *WorAlBi*
Copernicus, Nicolaus 1473-1543 *BioIn 16*
Copes, Marvin Lee 1938- *WhoSSW 91, WhoWor 91*
Copess, Joyce Travis 1947- *WhoAmW 91*
Copestakes, Vesta 1949- *WhoEmL 91*
Copi, Irving Marmer 1917- *WhoAm 90*
Copi, Margaret Ruth 1955- *BiDrAPA 89*
Copier, Andries Dirk 1901- *PenDiDA 89*
Copin, Charis Wagner 1949- *St&PR 91*
Copithorne, Alton Russell 1920- *WhoE 91*
Copitorne, David *ODwPR 91*
Coplan, Alfred I. 1925- *St&PR 91*
Coplan, Alfred Irving 1925- *WhoAm 90*
Coplan, Daniel Jonathan 1955- *WhoEmL 91*
Coplan, Jeremy David *BiDrAPA 89*
Coplan, Julius N. 1946- *St&PR 91*
Coplan, Neil Lawrence 1954- *WhoE 91*
Coplan, Norman Allan 1919- *WhoAm 90*
Copland, Aaron 1900- *BioIn 16, EncAL, IntWWM 90, PenDiMP A, WhoAm 90, WhoWor 91, WorAlBi*
Copland, Aaron 1900-1990 *News 91-2*
Copland, Elizabeth Ann 1951- *WhoAmW 91*

Copland, Henry 1720-1753 *PenDiDA 89*
Coplans, John 1920- *WhoAmA 91*
Coplans, John Rivers 1920- *WhoAm 90*
Coplar, Nancy Lockhart 1958- *WhoAmW 91*
Cople, William James, III 1955- *WhoE 91*
Copley, Helen K. 1922- *St&PR 91, WorAlBi*
Copley, Helen Kinney 1922- *WhoAm 90, WhoAmW 91*
Copley, Ira Clifton 1864-1947 *BioIn 16*
Copley, John 1933- *IntWWM 90, WhoWor 91*
Copley, John Singleton 1738-1815 *EncCRAm, IntDcAA 90, WorAlBi*
Copley, Lionel *EncCRAm*
Copley, Patrick O'Neil 1933- *WhoAm 90*
Copley, Stephen Michael 1936- *WhoAm 90*
Copley, William McKinley, III 1943- *WhoSSW 91*
Copley, William Nelson 1919- *WhoAmA 91*
Coplin, Mark David 1928- *WhoAm 90*
Coplin, Paul Robert *BiDrAPA 89*
Coplin, William D 1939- *ConAu 32NR*
Coplin, William David *WhoAm 90*
Coplon, Dee Anne 1963- *WhoAmW 91*
Coplon, Fredric Jay 1942- *BiDrAPA 89*
Coplon, Michael Carl 1942- *BiDrAPA 89*
Coplon, Ronald H. 1935- *St&PR 91*
Copman, Louis 1934- *WhoWor 91*
Copp, Douglas Harold 1915- *WhoAm 90*
Copp, Earle Morse, III 1955- *WhoEmL 91*
Copp, Emmanuel Anthony 1945- *WhoAm 90*
Copp, James Harris 1925- *WhoAm 90*
Copp, Laurel Archer 1931- *WhoAmW 91*
Copp, Susan *BiDrAPA 89*
Copp, William Walter 1826-1894 *DcCanB 12*
Coppa, George *BiDrAPA 89*
Coppedge, Arthur L 1938- *WhoAmA 91*
Coppedge, Christy 1955- *WhoAmW 91*
Coppedge, Robert Locke 1958- *WhoEmL 91*
Coppel, Alfred 1921- *WhoAm 90*
Coppel, Harry Charles 1918- *WhoAm 90*
Coppel Kelly, Ernesto Jesus 1947- *WhoWor 91*
Coppen, Alec 1923- *BiDrAPA 89*
Coppenrath, Robert A.M. 1928- *St&PR 91*
Coppens, Patrick John 1952- *St&PR 91*
Coppens, Philip 1930- *WhoAm 90*
Coppens, Thomas Adriaan 1923- *WhoE 91*
Copper Family *OxCPMus*
Copper, Basil 1924- *TwCCr&M 91*
Copper, Bob 1915- *OxCPMus*
Copper, J. Robert 1939- *St&PR 91*
Copper, James Robert 1939- *WhoAm 90*
Copper, Jill Susan 1945- *OxCPMus*
Copper, John Franklin 1940- *WhoAm 90, WhoSSW 91, WhoWor 91*
Copper, John James 1949- *OxCPMus*
Copper, Robert Arnold de Vignier 1938- *WhoE 91*
Copperfield, David *BioIn 16*
Copperfield, David 1956- *WhoAm 90*
Copperman, Stuart Morton 1935- *WhoAm 90, WhoWor 91*
Coppersmith, Randall S. *ODwPR 91*
Coppi, Charles N. *St&PR 91*
Coppie, Comer Swift 1932- *St&PR 91, WhoAm 90*
Copping, Allen Anthony 1927- *WhoAm 90, WhoSSW 91*
Copping, Craig P. 1943- *St&PR 91*
Copping, Robert Edward 1932- *St&PR 91*
Coppinger, John Joseph 1937- *St&PR 91*
Coppinger, Raymond Parke 1937- *WhoAm 90*
Coppini, Pompeo Luigi 1870-1957 *WhoAmA 91N*
Copple, Christine D. 1950- *St&PR 91*
Copple, Michael Andrew 1951- *WhoEmL 91*
Copple, Robert C. 1953- *St&PR 91*
Copple, Robert Francis 1955- *WhoEmL 91*
Coppoc, Harriet Kagay 1940- *IntWWM 90*
Coppock, Charles 1906- *AuBYP 90*
Coppock, David M. 1942- *St&PR 91*
Coppock, John Terence 1921- *WhoWor 91*
Coppock, Thomas William 1923- *WhoE 91*
Coppola, Albert Anthony 1933- *St&PR 91*
Coppola, Allison Marie 1965- *WhoAmW 91*
Coppola, Andrew 1941- *WhoAmA 91*
Coppola, Anthony 1935- *WhoAm 90*
Coppola, August 1934- *WhoAm 90*
Coppola, Carl *St&PR 91*
Coppola, Carlo 1938- *WhoWrEP 89*
Coppola, Carmine 1910- *WhoAm 90*
Coppola, Francis 1939- *BioIn 16*
Coppola, Francis Ford 1939- *WhoAm 90, WorAlBi*
Coppola, Jean Frances 1964- *WhoE 91*
Coppola, Joseph 1928- *BiDrAPA 89*
Coppola, Lenora Elaine Davis 1948- *WhoAmW 91*
Coppola, Nancy Walters 1945- *WhoAmW 91*
Coppola, Piero 1888-1971 *PenDiMP*
Coppola, Richard Alexander 1929- *St&PR 91*
Coppolechia, Yillian Castro 1948- *WhoAmW 91, WhoHisp 91*
Coppoletti, John H. 1942- *St&PR 91*
Coppolillo, Henry P 1926- *BiDrAPA 89*
Coppolino, Dominic Louis 1919- *BiDrAPA 89*
Coppotelli, H. Catherina 1944- *WhoAmW 91*
Copps, Donald W. 1914- *St&PR 91*
Copps, Frederic Chandler 1946- *WhoAm 90*
Copps, Michael William 1939- *WhoAm 90*
Copps, Sheila Maureen 1952- *WhoAmW 91*
Copps, Thomas Richard 1939- *St&PR 91*
Copsetta, Norman George 1932- *WhoWor 91*
Copulsky, Lewis 1958- *WhoE 91*
Copway, George 1818?-1863? *BioIn 16, WhNaAH*
Coquilla, Beatriz Hordista 1948- *WhoAmW 91, WhoEmL 91*
Coquillette, Lorene 1933- *St&PR 91*
Coquillette, William Hollis 1949- *WhoEmL 91*
Coquillette-Dean, Daniel Robert 1944- *WhoAm 90, WhoWor 91*
Cora, Lee Frank 1931- *St&PR 91*
Corace, Joseph Russell 1953- *WhoAm 90*
Corace, William Ross Carle 1940- *St&PR 91*
Corah, Deborah Jean 1960- *WhoAmW 91*
Corales, Enedino R *BiDrAPA 89*
Coram, Edward Clinton 1947- *WhoE 91, WhoEmL 91*
Coran, Arnold Gerald 1938- *WhoAm 90, WhoWor 91*
Coraor, John E 1955- *WhoAmA 91*
Corasanti, Eugene R. 1930- *St&PR 91*
Corato, Wendi Cheryl 1958- *WhoAmW 91*
Coray, Hans *PenDiDA 89*
Coray, Stephanie Mary 1938- *WhoAmW 91*
Corazzini, Arthur John 1939- *WhoE 91*
Corballis, Paul Thomas 1934- *WhoE 91*
Corbally, John Edward 1924- *WhoAm 90*
Corbato, Charles Edward 1932- *WhoAm 90*
Corbato, Fernando Jose 1926- *WhoAm 90*
Corbaux, Fanny 1812-1883 *BiDWomA*
Corbaux, Louisa 1808-1881? *BiDWomA*
Corbeil, Jean *WhoAm 90, WhoE 91*
Corben, Herbert Charles 1914- *WhoAm 90*
Corber, Robert Jack, I 1926- *WhoAm 90, WhoWor 91*
Corbero, Ana *BioIn 16*
Corbet, David Lewis 1953- *St&PR 91, WhoE 91*
Corbet, Donald Lee 1959- *WhoEmL 91*
Corbet, Leo F., Jr. 1936- *WhoAm 90*
Corbet, Timothy Boyd 1948- *St&PR 91*
Corbett, Bruce Loring 1955- *St&PR 91*
Corbett, Carolyn Susanne 1951- *WhoAmW 91, WhoE 91*
Corbett, Doris Ree *BioIn 16*
Corbett, Doug 1952- *Ballpl 90*
Corbett, Edward M 1919-1971 *WhoAmA 91N*
Corbett, Elizabeth Burgoyne 1846-1922? *FemiCLE*
Corbett, Elizabeth Frances 1887-1961 *FemiCLE*
Corbett, Elizabeth Sullivan 1946- *WhoSSW 91*
Corbett, Frank E. *AmLegL*
Corbett, Frank Joseph 1917- *WhoAm 90*
Corbett, Gail Sherman 1871-1952 *WhoAmA 91N*
Corbett, Gerard Francis 1950- *ODwPR 91, WhoEmL 91*
Corbett, Gloria Ann *WhoSSW 91*
Corbett, Harold John 1927- *St&PR 91*
Corbett, Harry 1918-1989 *AnObit 1989*
Corbett, Henry Winslow 1827-1903 *EncABHB 6 [port]*
Corbett, Hilary 1929- *OxCCanT*
Corbett, Howard Lewis 1924- *St&PR 91*
Corbett, Idna Maritza 1960- *WhoAmW 91*
Corbett, J. Elliott 1920- *St&PR 91*
Corbett, J. Ralph 1898-1988 *BioIn 16*
Corbett, Jack Elliott 1920- *WhoE 91, WhoWor 91*
Corbett, James Edward 1875- *AuBYP 90*
Corbett, James J. 1866-1933 *WorAlBi*
Corbett, James Otho 1945- *WhoSSW 91*
Corbett, James Robert 1945- *WhoEmL 91*
Corbett, James T 1923- *BiDrAPA 89*
Corbett, James William 1928- *WhoAm 90, WhoE 91*
Corbett, Joan Dufner 1928- *WhoAmW 91*
Corbett, Joe 1875-1945 *Ballpl 90*
Corbett, John Dudley 1926- *WhoAm 90*
Corbett, John Frank 1935- *St&PR 91*
Corbett, John Richard 1928- *St&PR 91*
Corbett, Joseph Edward 1921- *St&PR 91*
Corbett, Keith Bernard 1956- *St&PR 91*
Corbett, Larry R. 1945- *St&PR 91*
Corbett, Leon H., Jr. 1937- *WhoAm 90*
Corbett, Lionel *BiDrAPA 89*
Corbett, Lorraine T. 1954- *WhoAmW 91*
Corbett, Mary Ellen 1941- *WhoE 91*
Corbett, Michael Alan 1951- *St&PR 91, WhoAm 90, WhoE 91*
Corbett, Michael B. *WhoE 91*
Corbett, Michael Derrik 1929- *WhoWor 91*
Corbett, Mike *BioIn 16*
Corbett, Peter Frank 1959- *WhoE 91*
Corbett, Roger L. 1931- *St&PR 91*
Corbett, Scott 1913- *AuBYP 90, WhoAm 90, WhoWrEP 89*
Corbett, Sidney 1960- *IntWWM 90*
Corbett, Suzanne Elaine 1953- *WhoAmW 91*
Corbett, Thomas John 1951- *WhoEmL 91*
Corbett, W. J. *BioIn 16*
Corbett, William 1675?-1748 *BioIn 16*
Corbett, William J. 1937- *ODwPR 91*
Corbett, William John 1937- *WhoAm 90, WhoE 91*
Corbett, William Thomas, Jr. 1960- *WhoEmL 91*
Corbett Ashby, Margery Irene 1882-1981 *DcNaB 1981*
Corbie, Leo A. 1930- *WhoAm 90, WhoE 91*
Corbin, Albert H. *BioIn 16*
Corbin, Arnold 1911- *WhoAm 90*
Corbin, Charles, Jr. 1924- *BiDrAPA 89*
Corbin, Charles B 1940- *ConAu 31NR*
Corbin, Christine Marie 1947- *WhoAmW 91*
Corbin, Claire 1913- *WhoAm 90*
Corbin, Clayton 1928- *DrBlPA 90*
Corbin, David C. 1901- *St&PR 91*
Corbin, David Randolph 1956- *WhoE 91, WhoEmL 91*
Corbin, Earl Leo 1932- *WhoWor 91*
Corbin, Edwin I 1909- *BiDrAPA 89*
Corbin, Everett Jimmy 1932- *WhoSSW 91*
Corbin, Frank G. M. 1925- *ODwPR 91*
Corbin, George Allen 1941- *WhoAmA 91*
Corbin, Hazel 1893-1988 *BioIn 16*
Corbin, Herbert L. 1940- *ODwPR 91*
Corbin, Herbert Leonard 1940- *St&PR 91, WhoAm 90*
Corbin, John Albert 1931- *WhoWor 91*
Corbin, John B 1935- *WhoWrEP 89*
Corbin, John Stephen 1946- *WhoEmL 91*
Corbin, Kendall Brooks 1907- *WhoAm 90*
Corbin, Krestine Margaret 1937- *WhoAmW 91, WhoWor 91*
Corbin, Lauren L. 1959- *WhoEmL 91*
Corbin, Margaret C. 1751-1800 *BioAmW*
Corbin, Margaret Cochran 1751-1800 *EncCRAm*
Corbin, Paul *BioIn 16*
Corbin, Paul *NewYTBS 90*
Corbin, Ralph A. 1934-1989 *BioIn 16*
Corbin, Ralph Arthur *St&PR 91N*
Corbin, Ray 1949- *Ballpl 90*
Corbin, Richard 1911-1988 *BioIn 16*
Corbin, Richard Henry 1936- *WhoWor 91*
Corbin, Richard J. 1939- *St&PR 91*
Corbin, Robert Edward 1935- *St&PR 91*
Corbin, Robert Keith 1928- *WhoAm 90*
Corbin, Rori Cooper 1951- *WhoAmW 91*
Corbin, Rosemary Mac Gowan 1940- *WhoAmW 91*
Corbin, Sabra Lee *AuBYP 90*
Corbin, Scott Douglas 1950- *WhoSSW 91*
Corbin, Sol Neil 1927- *WhoAm 90*
Corbin, Steven 1953- *ConAu 131*
Corbin, William *AuBYP 90*
Corbin, William J. 1945- *WhoSSW 91*
Corbin, William Lewis 1935- *St&PR 91*
Corbin, William S. 1945- *St&PR 91*
Corbino, John 1905-1964 *WhoAmA 91N*
Corbino, Marcia Norcross *WhoAmA 91*
Corbino, Orso Mario 1876-1937 *DcScB S2*
Corbishley, David Edward 1946- *St&PR 91*
Corbitant *WhNaAH*
Corbitt, Cary Carder 1953- *WhoAm 90, WhoSSW 91*
Corbley, John James 1926- *WhoE 91*
Corbman, Eric Stuart 1952- *WhoE 91*
Corbman, Gene R 1947- *BiDrAPA 89*
Corbo, Alan Gerald 1927- *St&PR 91*
Corbo, Joseph *BiDrAPA 89*
Corboy, James John 1929- *St&PR 91*
Corboy, James McNally 1940- *WhoWor 91*
Corboy, Michael Robert 1930- *St&PR 91*
Corboy, Michele LaRue 1952- *WhoAmW 91*
Corboy, Philip Harnett 1924- *WhoAm 90*
Corboz, Michel 1934- *PenDiMP*
Corbridge, James Noel, Jr. 1934- *WhoAm 90*
Corbusier, Le 1887-1965 *WorAlBi*
Corby, Ellen 1913- *WorAlBi*
Corby, Francis M., Jr. 1944- *St&PR 91*
Corby, Francis Michael, Jr. 1944- *WhoAm 90*
Corby, James Clewell 1945- *BiDrAPA 89*
Corby, Michael Charles 1960- *WhoEmL 91*
Corcella, John 1926- *BiDrAPA 89*
Corces, Loretta Cueto 1943- *WhoSSW 91*
Corchado, Alfredo 1960- *WhoHisp 91*
Corcia, John T. 1945- *St&PR 91*
Corcoran, Andrew Patrick, Jr. 1948- *WhoEmL 91*
Corcoran, Barbara Asenath 1911- *WhoAm 90*
Corcoran, Clare Mary 1929- *WhoAmW 91*
Corcoran, David 1947- *WhoAm 90*
Corcoran, David M. 1903- *St&PR 91*
Corcoran, Dennis Michael 1945- *WhoEmL 91*
Corcoran, Eileen Lynch 1917- *WhoAm 90*
Corcoran, Eugene Francis 1916- *WhoSSW 91*
Corcoran, George R. 1928- *ODwPR 91*
Corcoran, Howard F. 1906-1989 *BioIn 16*
Corcoran, J. Walter 1938- *St&PR 91*
Corcoran, James C. 1926- *St&PR 91*
Corcoran, James F T 1937- *BiDrAPA 89*
Corcoran, James Martin, Jr. 1932- *WhoAm 90*
Corcoran, James Thomas 1929- *St&PR 91*
Corcoran, John *BioIn 16*
Corcoran, John 1937- *WhoAm 90*
Corcoran, John Joseph 1920- *WhoAm 90*
Corcoran, Larry 1859-1891 *Ballpl 90*
Corcoran, Leigh *ODwPR 91*
Corcoran, Mary Barbara 1924- *WhoAm 90, WhoAmW 91, WhoE 91*
Corcoran, Maureen Elizabeth 1944- *WhoAm 90, WhoAmW 91*
Corcoran, Michael Patrick 1957- *WhoEmL 91*
Corcoran, Paul John 1934- *WhoAm 90*
Corcoran, Robert Lee, Jr. 1944- *WhoAm 90, WhoWor 91*
Corcoran, Thomas Joseph 1920- *WhoAm 90, WhoWor 91*
Corcoran, Thomas M. 1955- *St&PR 91*
Corcoran, Tim 1953- *Ballpl 90*
Corcoran, Tommy 1869-1960 *Ballpl 90 [port]*
Corcoran, W. W. 1798-1888 *EncABHB 6 [port]*
Corcoran, William Richard *BiDrAPA 89*
Corcoran-Gadsby, Barbara Ann 1945- *WhoAmW 91*
Corcos, Lucille 1908-1973 *AuBYP 90, WhoAmA 91N*
Corcos, Vittorio 1859-1933 *BioIn 16*
Cord, Alex 1933- *WhoAm 90*
Cord, Barry Kieselstein- *BioIn 16*
Cord, Cece Kieselstein- *BioIn 16*
Cord, Errett Lobban 1894-1974 *EncABHB 5*
Cord, Joseph Anthony 1956- *WhoSSW 91*
Cordano, Vira Elda 1918- *WhoAmW 91*
Cordaro, Matthew C. 1943- *St&PR 91*
Cordaro, Matthew Charles 1943- *WhoAm 90*
Cordaro, Michael J. 1958- *St&PR 91*
Cordasco, Anna 1961- *ODwPR 91*
Cordasco, Francesco 1920- *WhoAm 90, WhoWrEP 89*
Corday, Barbara *BioIn 16*
Corday, Barbara 1944- *WhoAmW 91*
Corday, Charlotte 1768-1793 *WorAlBi*
Corday, Robert Jay 1922- *BiDrAPA 89*
Corddry, Paul Imlay 1936- *St&PR 91, WhoAm 90, WhoE 91*
Cordeiro, Joseph 1918- *WhoWor 91*
Cordeiro, Margaret C. 1945- *WhoAmW 91*
Cordek, Lawrence Donald 1946- *St&PR 91*
Cordell, Alfred H. 1928- *St&PR 91*
Cordell, Edwin B. 1958- *St&PR 91*
Cordell, Joe B. 1927- *St&PR 91, WhoAm 90, WhoSSW 91*
Cordell, Martin Lewis 1950- *WhoEmL 91*
Cordell, Philip Marvin, Jr. 1922- *St&PR 91*
Cordell, Robert James 1917- *WhoSSW 91, WhoWor 91*
Cordell, Steven Mark 1955- *WhoEmL 91*
Corden, Warner Max 1927- *WhoE 91*
Corder, Billie Farmer 1934- *WhoAmW 91*
Corder, Duane Ralph 1925- *WhoAm 90*
Corder, Eddie Charles 1949- *St&PR 91*
Corder, Henry R. *St&PR 91*
Corder, Linda Jane 1949- *WhoE 91*
Corder, Steven Lynn *BiDrAPA 89*
Cordero, Angel *BioIn 16*
Cordero, Angel, Jr. 1942- *WorAlBi*
Cordero, Angel T., Jr. 1942- *WhoAm 90*
Cordero, Angel Tomas, Jr. 1942- *WhoHisp 91*
Cordero, Brenda Sue 1967- *WhoHisp 91*
Cordero, Edward C. *WhoHisp 91*
Cordero, Fausto 1954- *WhoHisp 91*
Cordero, Helen 1915- *MusmAFA*
Cordero, Joseph A. 1953- *WhoHisp 91*
Cordero, Juan 1824-1884 *ArtLatA*

Cordero, Roque 1917- DrBIPA 90, IntWWM 90
Cordero, Sylvia D. 1959- WhoHisp 91
Cordero de Noriega, Diane C. 1943- WhoHisp 91
Cordero-Santiago, Rafael 1942- WhoAm 90, WhoHisp 91
Cordero-Spampinato, Sylvia D. 1959- WhoHisp 91
Cordery, Sara Brown 1920- WhoAmW 91
Cordes, Alexander Charles 1925- WhoAm 90
Cordes, Charles K 1934- BiDrAPA 89
Cordes, Clifford Frederick, III 1946- WhoEmL 91
Cordes, Donald Wesley 1917- WhoAm 90
Cordes, Doris Kaiser 1934- WhoAmW 91
Cordes, Eugene Harold 1936- WhoAm 90
Cordes, James F. St&PR 91
Cordes, James F. 1940- WhoAm 90, WhoSSW 91
Cordes, Kathryn ODwPR 91
Cordes, Loverne Christian 1927- WhoAm 90
Cordes, Marcel 1920- IntWWM 90
Cordes, Mary Kenrick 1933- WhoAmW 91
Cordier, Herbert 1925- WhoAm 90
Cordier, Hubert Victor 1917- WhoAm 90
Cordier, William K. 1927- St&PR 91
Cording, Edward James 1937- WhoAm 90
Cordingley, John Stuart 1953- WhoEmL 91
Cordingley, Mary Bowles 1918- WhoAmA 91
Cordingley, Mary Jeanette Bowles 1918- WhoAmW 91, WhoWor 91
Cordis, Francis 1939- WhoE 91
Cordis, Maria 1929- WhoAm 90
Cordner, Denise Francoise 1961- WhoWrEP 89
Cordner, Jacqueline Willingham 1922- WhoWrEP 89
Cordner, John 1816-1894 DcCanB 12
Cordoba, Basilio Carlos BiDrAPA 89
Cordoba, Basilio Carlos 1947- WhoE 91
Cordoba, Becky Abbate 1956- WhoHisp 91
Cordoba, J Bernard 1949- BiDrAPA 89
Cordoba, Oscar A 1949- BiDrAPA 89
Cordomi, Manuel Luis 1928- WhoWor 91
Cordon, David Jay BiDrAPA 89
Cordon, Frank Joseph 1925- St&PR 91
Cordon, Jenean C. 1943- St&PR 91
Cordonnier, Gerard Anatole F. 1907- EncO&P 3
Cordova, Francisco Ray 1963- WhoHisp 91
Cordova, J. Gustavo 1949- WhoHisp 91
Cordova, Johnny Amezquita 1946- WhoHisp 91
Cordova, Karen Sue 1951- WhoAmW 91
Cordova, Linda L. 1957- WhoHisp 91
Cordova, Manuel 1949- WhoHisp 91
Cordova, Maria de Lourdes 1961- BiDrAPA 89
Cordova, Moses E. WhoHisp 91
Cordova, Ralph Aguirre 1933- WhoHisp 91
Cordova-Salinas, Maria Asuncion 1941- WhoAmW 91
Cordover, Ronald H. 1943- St&PR 91
Cordover, Ronald Harvey 1943- WhoAm 90
Cordovero, Moses EncO&P 3
Cordoves, Margarita 1947- WhoHisp 91
Cordovez, Diego BioIn 16
Cordovez, Diego 1935- WhoWor 91
Cordray, Richard Lynn 1952- WhoEmL 91
Cordrey, Richard Stephen 1933- WhoAm 90
Cordry, V. Ray 1947- BiDrAPA 89
Cords, Fred W. 1930- St&PR 91
Cordy-Collins, Alana 1944- WhoAmA 91
Core, Carol Byrd 1938- WhoSSW 91
Core, Mary Carolyn W. Parsons 1949- WhoAmW 91, WhoEmL 91, WhoWor 91
Core, Philip 1951-1989 AnObit 1989
Corea, Chick BioIn 16
Corea, Chick 1941- WhoAm 90
Corea, Luigi 1939- WhoWor 91
Corea, Luis Felipe 1910- WhoAm 90
Corea, Roger C. 1943- St&PR 91
Corell, Belle Oliver 1902- WhoAmW 91
Corell, Robert Walden 1934- WhoAm 90
Corella, John C. WhoHisp 91
Corelli, Franco 1921- IntWWM 90, PenDiMP, WorAlBi
Corelli, Marie 1855-1924 BioIn 16, FemiCLE
Coren, Arthur 1933- St&PR 91
Coren, Harry Z 1937- BiDrAPA 89
Coren, Lance Scott 1949- WhoEmL 91, WhoWor 91
Coren, Stu ODwPR 91
Coren, Victoria 1972- ConAu 131
Corena, Fernando 1916-1984 PenDiMP
Coreth, Joseph Herman 1937- WhoE 91
Corette, John E. 1908- WhoAm 90
Corey, Bob L. 1951- St&PR 91
Corey, Dean WhoE 91
Corey, Donald Lee 1932- St&PR 91
Corey, Elias James 1928- WhoAm 90, WhoWor 91
Corey, Gordon Richard 1914- WhoAm 90
Corey, Irene 1925- BioIn 16, NotWoAT
Corey, Jeff 1914- BioIn 16, ConTFT 8 [port], WhoAm 90
Corey, John C. 1947- St&PR 91
Corey, Kenneth Edward 1938- WhoAm 90
Corey, Leslie Norman, Jr. 1949- WhoEmL 91
Corey, Melinda Ann 1957- WhoAmW 91
Corey, Michael R. 1942- St&PR 91
Corey, Orlin Russell 1926- WhoAm 90
Corey, Paul Frederick 1903- WhoAm 90
Corey, Rebecca Ann 1959- WhoSSW 91
Corey, Ronald 1938- WhoAm 90, WhoE 91
Corey, Stephen Dale 1948- WhoWrEP 89
Corey, William E. 1866-1934 WorAlBi
Corey Archer, Pamela 1940- WhoAmW 91
Corfman, Stanley Luccock 1953- WhoEmL 91
Cori, Carl F. 1896-1984 WorAlBi
Cori, Domenico di Niccolo de' PenDiDA 89
Cori, Gerty T. 1896-1957 WorAlBi
Cori, Gregory Salvatore 1925- WhoAm 90, WhoWor 91
Coriaty, George Michael 1933- WhoE 91
Coriden, Michael Warner 1948- WhoEmL 91
Coriell, Lewis Lemon 1911- WhoAm 90
Corigliano, John 1938- BioIn 16, IntWWM 90, PenDiMP A
Corigliano, John Paul 1938- WhoAm 90
Corina EncCoWW
Corinaldi, Austin 1921- WhoAm 90
Corinna EncCoWW
Corinth, Lovis 1858-1925 BioIn 16, IntDcAA 90 [port]
Coriolis, Gustave-Gaspard De 1792-1843 WorAlBi
Corish, Brendan NewYTBS 90
Corish, Brendan 1919-1990 BioIn 16
Corish, Joseph Ryan 1909-1988 WhoAmA 91N
Corita BioIn 16
Cork, D. Bradley 1950- St&PR 91
Cork, Dennis Bradley 1950- WhoEmL 91
Cork, Donald Burl 1949- WhoEmL 91
Cork, Edwin Kendall WhoAm 90
Cork, Herbert V. 1933- St&PR 91
Cork, John Robert 1947- St&PR 91
Cork, Linda Katherine 1936- WhoAm 90, WhoAmW 91
Cork, Susan Phifer 1953- St&PR 91
Corke, Helen 1882-1978 FemiCLE
Corke, Patricia P BiDrAPA 89
Corker, Charles Edward 1917- WhoAm 90
Corker, Frank Thomas 1935- WhoSSW 91
Corker, R. Stephen 1941- St&PR 91
Corker, William Russell 1949- WhoEmL 91
Corkern, Carl Bruce 1961- St&PR 91
Corkery, Christopher Jane 1946- WhoWrEP 89
Corkery, James Caldwell 1925- WhoAm 90
Corkery, Tim 1931- WhoAmA 91
Corkhill, Arlene Finatti 1946- St&PR 91
Corkin, Cary J. 1951- St&PR 91
Corkin, Suzanne Hammond 1937- WhoE 91
Corkindale, William M., Jr. 1918- St&PR 91
Corkins, Gary Charles 1935- St&PR 91
Corkins, Mike 1946- Ballpl 90
Corle, Frederic William, II 1945- WhoE 91, WhoEmL 91
Corless, Harry 1928- St&PR 91, WhoAm 90, WhoE 91
Corlett-Thielmann, Emma Jean 1926- WhoWor 91
Corley, Bruce E. 1926- St&PR 91
Corley, Carol A. 1948- St&PR 91
Corley, Georgia Buckner 1923- WhoAmW 91
Corley, Joyce WhoAmW 91
Corley, Leslie M. 1946- WhoE 91, WhoEmL 91
Corley, Linda Gail 1947- WhoSSW 91
Corley, Marshall Bennett 1932- St&PR 91
Corley, Neil Bradford 1940- WhoE 91
Corley, Reynard Alton 1937- WhoSSW 91
Corley, William Edward 1942- WhoAm 90
Corley, William Gene 1935- WhoAm 90
Corley, William J. 1953- St&PR 91
Corlieto, Martin, III 1954- WhoSSW 91
Corliss, Beth BioIn 16
Corliss, John Ozro 1922- WhoAm 90
Corliss, Richard Nelson 1944- WhoAm 90
Corll, Vivian Morgan 1940- WhoWrEP 89
Cormac, C.D. WhoWrEP 89
Cormack, Allan MacLeod 1924- WhoAm 90, WhoE 91, WhoWor 91, WorAlBi
Cormack, George 1870-1953 WorAlBi
Cormack, Malcolm 1935- WhoAmA 91
Cormack, Maribelle 1902-1984 AuBYP 90
Cormack, Robert George Hall 1904- WhoAm 90
Corman, Alan Gary 1939- BiDrAPA 89
Corman, Avery 1935- WhoAm 90, WhoWrEP 89
Corman, Cid 1924- WhoAm 90, WhoWrEP 89
Corman, Clifford Lennard 1946- BiDrAPA 89
Corman, Eugene Harold 1927- WhoAm 90
Corman, Gene BioIn 16
Corman, Harvey H 1922- BiDrAPA 89
Corman, James Allen 1952- WhoEmL 91
Corman, Karen Marie 1962- WhoAmW 91
Corman, Patrick 1943- ODwPR 91
Corman, Roger BioIn 16
Corman, Roger William 1926- WhoAm 90
Corman, William Franklin 1916- St&PR 91
Cormey, John R. 1947- St&PR 91
Cormie, Donald Mercer BioIn 16
Cormie, Donald Mercer 1922- WhoAm 90, WhoWor 91
Cormier, Andrew M. St&PR 91
Cormier, Bruno M 1919- BiDrAPA 89
Cormier, David Emile 1939- WhoE 91
Cormier, Elizabeth Ferguson 1925- WhoSSW 91
Cormier, Hugues Jean 1953- BiDrAPA 89
Cormier, Jean G. 1941- WhoAm 90
Cormier, Jessie Ann LeBlanc 1955- WhoEmL 91
Cormier, Lawrence E 1953- BiDrAPA 89
Cormier, Ramona Theresa 1923- WhoAm 90
Cormier, Robert BioIn 16
Cormier, Robert 1925- MajTwCW
Cormier, Robert Edmund 1925- WhoAm 90, WhoWrEP 89
Cormier, Robert John 1932- WhoAmA 91
Corn Plant 1735?-1836 WhNaAH [port]
Corn, Alfred DeWitt 1943- WhoAm 90, WhoWrEP 89
Corn, Jack W. 1929- WhoAm 90
Corn, James Louis 1928- St&PR 91
Corn, John W. 1955- St&PR 91
Corn, Joseph Edward, Jr. 1932- WhoAm 90
Corn, Julius Alfred 1931- St&PR 91
Corn, Larry R. 1941- St&PR 91
Corn, Leslie Joan 1949- WhoAmW 91
Corn, Lovick Pierce 1922- St&PR 91
Corn, Mary Louise Johnston 1948- WhoSSW 91
Corn, Merton 1934- WhoAm 90
Corn, Milton 1928- WhoAm 90
Corn, Morton 1933- WhoAm 90
Corn, Pauline Gordon 1931- St&PR 91
Corn, Wanda M 1940- WhoAmA 91, WhoAmW 91
Cornacchio, Joseph Vincent 1934- WhoAm 90
Cornacchio, Peter Anthony 1941- St&PR 91
Cornatzer, William Eugene 1918- WhoAm 90
Cornblath, Marvin 1925- WhoAm 90
Cornblatt, Max 1906- WhoAm 90
Cornehlsen, James Harsh 1942- St&PR 91
Corneille 1922- BioIn 16
Corneille, Pierre 1606-1684 WorAlBi
Cornejo, Jeffrey Martin 1959- WhoHisp 91
Cornejo-Polar, Antonio 1936- WhoHisp 91
Cornelia, Edward J. 1939- WhoE 91
Cornelia, Marion Johnson 1924- WhoE 91
Corneliano, Mario Nasalli Rocca di 1903-1988 BioIn 16
Cornelio, Albert C. 1930- St&PR 91
Cornelio, Albert Carmen 1930- WhoAm 90
Cornelis, Frans Charles 1957- WhoWor 91
Cornelis, Pieter Arsene 1927- WhoWor 91
Cornelisen, Ann 1926- WorAu 1980 [port]
Cornelison, David Richard 1957- St&PR 91
Cornelison, Floyd S, Jr. 1918- BiDrAPA 89
Cornelison, Floyd Shovington, Jr. 1918- WhoAm 90, WhoE 91
Cornelissen, Michael Adriaan 1943- WhoAm 90
Cornelius Luke BioIn 16
Cornelius, Catherine Petrey 1941- WhoAmW 91
Cornelius, Charles Edward 1927- WhoAm 90
Cornelius, Dennis Alfred 1942- St&PR 91
Cornelius, Don 1937?- DrBIPA 90
Cornelius, Gordon A. 1928- St&PR 91
Cornelius, H. Thomas 1933- St&PR 91
Cornelius, Jack Randall 1954- BiDrAPA 89
Cornelius, James Alfred 1936- WhoAm 90
Cornelius, James M. 1943- St&PR 91
Cornelius, James Milton WhoAm 90
Cornelius, James Russell 1953- WhoSSW 91
Cornelius, Jeffrey Michael 1943- IntWWM 90
Cornelius, Kay LaVerne 1935- WhoSSW 91
Cornelius, Kay Oldham 1933- WhoWrEP 89
Cornelius, Kenneth C., Jr. 1944- St&PR 91
Cornelius, Kenneth Cremer, Jr. 1944- WhoAm 90
Cornelius, Lester Ernest 1953- WhoE 91
Cornelius, Linda Louise 1953- WhoAmW 91
Cornelius, Mark Richard 1953- WhoEmL 91
Cornelius, Marty 1913-1979 WhoAmA 91N
Cornelius, Peter 1824-1874 PenDiMP A
Cornelius, Peter Klaus 1960- WhoWor 91
Cornelius, Sara M. 1941- St&PR 91
Cornelius, Virginia H. 1922- St&PR 91
Cornelius, Walter Felix 1922- WhoSSW 91
Cornelius, William Edward 1931- St&PR 91, WhoAm 90
Cornell, A D 1923- EncO&P 3
Cornell, A. Jefferson 1941- WhoWrEP 89
Cornell, Alonzo B. 1832-1904 AmLegL
Cornell, Anthony Donald 1923- EncPaPR 91
Cornell, Carl Allin 1938- WhoAm 90
Cornell, Christy E. BiDrAPA 89
Cornell, Corwin David 1924- WhoAm 90, WhoWor 91
Cornell, David BioIn 16
Cornell, David E 1939- WhoAmA 91
Cornell, Douglas B., Mrs. 1920- WhoAmW 91
Cornell, Edgar 1918- St&PR 91
Cornell, Eugenia Ann 1943- BiDrAPA 89
Cornell, Ezra 1807-1874 WorAlBi
Cornell, George W. 1896-1988 BioIn 16
Cornell, George Ware, Jr. 1950- WhoEmL 91
Cornell, George Washington, II 1920- WhoAm 90
Cornell, Harry M., Jr. 1928- WhoAm 90
Cornell, Henry Watson, III 1932- St&PR 91
Cornell, Howard Vernon 1947- WhoE 91
Cornell, Ian Beaumont 1960- WhoEmL 91
Cornell, James 1955- ODwPR 91
Cornell, James Mark 1953- WhoEmL 91
Cornell, John William 1929- WhoE 91
Cornell, Jonas 1938- WhoWor 91
Cornell, Joseph 1903- WorAlBi
Cornell, Joseph 1903-1972 BioIn 16, WhoAmA 91N
Cornell, Katharine 1893-1974 BioIn 16, NotWoAT
Cornell, Katharine 1898-1974 BioAmW
Cornell, Katherine 1893-1974 WorAlBi
Cornell, M.K. 1936- St&PR 91
Cornell, Michael V. 1955- St&PR 91
Cornell, Minnie Jo 1926- St&PR 91
Cornell, Nancy Trinka 1954- WhoSSW 91
Cornell, Paul Grant 1918- WhoAm 90
Cornell, Paul Harold 1952- WhoSSW 91
Cornell, Peter Joseph 1952- WhoE 91
Cornell, Peter McCaul 1926- WhoAm 90
Cornell, Ralph Lawrence, Jr. 1951- WhoE 91
Cornell, Rhonda Holmes 1951- WhoSSW 91
Cornell, Richard Garth 1930- WhoAm 90
Cornell, Robert Arthur 1936- WhoAm 90
Cornell, Robert Witherspoon 1925- WhoWor 91
Cornell, Tanis Jill 1953- WhoAmW 91
Cornell, Thomas Browne 1937- WhoAm 90, WhoAmA 91
Cornell, William Daniel 1919- WhoAm 90
Cornelsen, Paul F. 1923- St&PR 91
Cornelsen, Paul Frederick 1923- WhoWor 91
Cornelsen, Rufus 1914- WhoAm 90
Cornelson, George Henry 1931- WhoAm 90
Cornely, Paul Bertau 1906- WhoAm 90
Corner, Bruce E. 1949- St&PR 91
Corner, Christopher J BiDrAPA 89
Corner, Elena Lucrezia 1648-1684 EncCoWW
Cornes, Cleon L BiDrAPA 89
Corness, Colin Ross 1931- WhoWor 91
Cornet, Antonio Gaudi Y 1852-1926 BioIn 16
Cornet, Ken 1941- WhoE 91
Cornett, Chester 1913-1981 MusmAFA
Cornett, John David 1958- St&PR 91
Cornett, Laureen Elizabeth 1946- WhoAmW 91, WhoEmL 91
Cornett, Lloyd Harvey, Jr. 1930- WhoAm 90
Cornett, Richard Orin 1913- WhoAm 90
Cornett, Robert Mack 1939- St&PR 91
Cornett, Roger 1937- St&PR 91
Cornett, William Forrest, Jr. 1919- WhoAm 90
Cornette, James Lawson 1935- WhoAm 90
Cornette, Marvin Clifford BiDrAPA 89
Cornette, Mary Elizabeth 1909- WhoAmA 91

Cornette, William Magnus 1945- *WhoAm 90, WhoEmL 91*
Cornette de Saint-Cyr, Bernard 1944- *WhoWor 91*
Corney, Robert T 1932- *BiDrAPA 89*
Cornez, Gerald H. 1946- *WhoAm 90, WhoEmL 91*
Cornez, Marie C. 1959- *ODwPR 91*
Cornfeld, Bernie *BioIn 16*
Cornfeld, Betty S. *BioIn 16*
Cornfeld, Dave Louis 1921- *WhoAm 90*
Cornfeld, David 1926- *WhoE 91*
Cornfeld, Richard Steven 1950- *WhoEmL 91*
Cornfield, Melvin 1927- *WhoAm 90*
Cornfield, Richard Borek *BiDrAPA 89*
Cornford, Frances 1886-1960 *BioIn 16, FemiCLE*
Cornforth, John Warcup 1917- *WhoAm 90, WhoWor 91*
Corngold, Stanley Alan 1934- *ConAu 32NR, WhoAm 90*
Cornic, Jean-Claude Louis-Jacques 1946- *WhoWor 91*
Cornicelli, Joseph Anthony 1951- *WhoAm 90*
Cornick, Walter Francis 1926- *St&PR 91*
Cornin, Jon 1905- *WhoAmA 91*
Corning, Joy Cole 1932- *WhoAmW 91*
Corning, Merv 1926- *BioIn 16*
Corning, Nathan E. 1931- *St&PR 91*
Cornish, Donovan Eugene 1930- *St&PR 91*
Cornish, Edward Seymour 1927- *WhoAm 90, WhoWor 91, WhoWrEP 89*
Cornish, Elizabeth Turverey 1919- *WhoAmW 91*
Cornish, Frank Louis, III *BiDrAPA 89*
Cornish, G. P. *BioIn 16*
Cornish, Geoffrey St. John 1914- *WhoAm 90*
Cornish, George 1828?-1895 *DcCanB 12*
Cornish, George A. *BioIn 16*
Cornish, Graham Peter *BioIn 16*
Cornish, James W 1946- *BiDrAPA 89*
Cornish, Jeannette Carter 1946- *WhoEmL 91*
Cornish, Larry Brian 1946- *St&PR 91*
Cornish, Marie Angela 1960- *WhoAmW 91*
Cornish, Mary Held 1957- *BiDrAPA 89*
Cornish, Richard Joseph 1925- *WhoWor 91*
Cornish, Sam 1935- *BioIn 16*
Cornish, Scott Charles 1960- *WhoEmL 91*
Cornman, Guy Leslie, Jr. 1923- *WhoSSW 91*
Corno, Fabio Martino 1958- *WhoWor 91*
Cornog, Robert Andrew 1940- *St&PR 91*
Cornplanter 1735?-1836 *WhNaAH [port]*
Cornstalk 1720?-1777 *EncCRAm, WhNaAH*
Cornsweet, Carol 1958- *WhoAmW 91*
Cornuelle, Herbert Cumming 1920- *WhoAm 90*
Cornwall, Deborah J. 1946- *St&PR 91*
Cornwall, Deborah Joyce 1946- *WhoAmW 91, WhoE 91, WhoEmL 91*
Cornwall, J. Michael 1935- *St&PR 91*
Cornwall, James Handyside Marshall- 1887-1985 *DcNaB 1981*
Cornwall, John Michael 1934- *WhoAm 90*
Cornwall, John Michael 1935- *WhoAm 90*
Cornwall, Richard S. 1932- *WhoAm 90*
Cornwall, Robert Maynard 1921- *St&PR 91*
Cornwall, Thomas Paul 1944- *BiDrAPA 89*
Cornwallis, Caroline Frances 1786-1858 *FemiCLE*
Cornwallis, Charles 1738-1805 *EncCRAm [port]*
Cornwallis, Jane 1581-1659 *BiDEWW*
Cornwalls, Charles 1738-1805 *WorAlBi*
Cornwell, Betty Ann 1954- *St&PR 91*
Cornwell, Charles Daniel 1924- *WhoAm 90*
Cornwell, David 1931- *ConAu 33NR, MajTwCW*
Cornwell, David George 1927- *WhoAm 90*
Cornwell, David John Moore *WhoWor 91*
Cornwell, David John Moore 1931- *BioIn 16, SpyFic, WhoAm 90, WhoWor 91*
Cornwell, Dean 1892-1960 *WhoAmA 91N*
Cornwell, Gibbons Gray, III 1933- *WhoAm 90*
Cornwell, Gilbert Darwyn 1943- *St&PR 91*
Cornwell, Harold *BioIn 16*
Cornwell, Ilene Jones *WhoAmW 91*
Cornwell, Ilene Jones 1942- *WhoWrEP 89*
Cornwell, Jerald Moyer 1928- *WhoAm 90*
Cornwell, Karl Burdell 1931- *St&PR 91*
Cornwell, Smith *WorAu 1980*
Cornyn-Selby, Alyce P. 1946- *WhoWrEP 89*
Cornyn-Selby, Alyce Patricia 1946- *WhoEmL 91*
Coro, Alicia Comacho 1937- *WhoHisp 91*
Corogin, John Solon 1925- *St&PR 91*
Corogin, Peter J. 1956- *St&PR 91*
Corona, Bert N. 1918- *BioIn 16, WhoHisp 91*
Corona, Juan *BioIn 16*
Corona, Richard Patrick 1962- *WhoHisp 91*
Corona, Salvador 1895- *BioIn 16*
Coronado, Beatriz 1960- *WhoHisp 91*
Coronado, Edward H, III *BiDrAPA 89*
Coronado, Elaine Marie 1959- *WhoHisp 91*
Coronado, Francisco Vasquez De 1510-1554 *EncCRAm, WhNaAH, WorAlBi*
Coronado, Gil 1936- *WhoHisp 91*
Coronado, Jose 1950- *WhoHisp 91*
Coronado, Jose Cesareo 1939- *WhoSSW 91*
Coronado, Jose R. 1932- *WhoHisp 91*
Coronado, Jose Ricardo 1932- *WhoAm 90, WhoSSW 91*
Coronado, Primitiva C 1928- *BiDrAPA 89*
Coronado, Rafael Alberto 1948- *WhoWor 91*
Coronado, Rizalino H *BiDrAPA 89*
Coronado, Salvacion H *BiDrAPA 89*
Coronado, Shirley Jeanne 1948- *WhoEmL 91*
Coronado-Greeley, Adela 1934- *WhoHisp 91*
Coronas, Jose J. 1942- *WhoHisp 91*
Coronel, Antonio 1817-1894 *BioIn 16*
Coronel, Francisco Faustino 1948- *WhoHisp 91*
Coronel, Helen Christine 1962- *WhoSSW 91*
Coroniti, Ferdinand Vincent 1943- *WhoAm 90*
Corot, Jean-Baptiste-Camille 1796-1875 *BioIn 16, IntDcAA 90, WorAlBi*
Corotis, Ross Barry 1945- *WhoAm 90*
Corp, Charles Lewworthy *IntWWM 90*
Corp, Dawn Holder 1938- *IntWWM 90*
Corp, Harriet *FemiCLE*
Corp, Patrick John *BiDrAPA 89*
Corpi, Lucha 1945- *ConAu 131, HispWr 90, WhoHisp 91*
Corpis, Richard Peter 1927- *St&PR 91*
Corporon, John Robert 1929- *WhoAm 90*
Corporon, Nancy Ann 1949- *WhoAmW 91*
Corprew-Beverly, Theresa Louise 1958- *WhoAmW 91*
Corpron, Carlotta M 1901-1988 *WhoAmA 91N*
Corpuz, Teresa Agrifina 1951- *WhoAmW 91, WhoEmL 91*
Corr, D. Joseph 1941- *WhoAm 90*
Corr, Edgar Boatwright 1959- *WhoEmL 91*
Corr, Edwin Gharst 1934- *WhoAm 90*
Corr, Fitzhugh Lee 1934- *WhoAm 90*
Corr, James D 1931- *WhoAmA 91*
Corr, James Vanis 1922- *WhoAm 90*
Corr, Joan Marie *BiDrAPA 89*
Corr, Joseph E. *BioIn 16*
Corrada del Rio, Baltasar 1935- *WhoAm 90*
Corradi, Ariello Rolando 1947- *WhoSSW 91*
Corradi, Richard B 1934- *BiDrAPA 89*
Corradino, Le Roy Michael 1932- *St&PR 91*
Corrado, Albert V, Jr. 1924- *BiDrAPA 89*
Corrado, Doris Golda 1950- *WhoWrEP 89*
Corrado, Fred 1940- *St&PR 91, WhoAm 90, WhoE 91*
Corral, Edward Anthony 1931- *WhoHisp 91, WhoSSW 91*
Corral, Maria D R *BiDrAPA 89*
Corralejo, Robert A. 1935- *WhoHisp 91*
Corrales, Jose 1937- *BioIn 16, WhoHisp 91*
Corrales, Ophelia *EncO&P 3*
Corrales, Oralia Lillie 1940- *WhoHisp 91*
Corrales, Pat 1941- *Ballpl 90, WhoHisp 91*
Corrales, Patrick 1941- *WhoAm 90*
Corrales, Scott Fidel 1963- *WhoHisp 91*
Corrao, Joseph Frank 1953- *WhoE 91*
Corre, Giselle Aviva *BiDrAPA 89*
Corre, Nita Levy 1938- *WhoAmW 91*
Correa, Charles M. 1930- *WhoWor 91*
Correa, Douce Fleming *BioIn 16*
Correa, Ed 1966- *Ballpl 90*
Correa, Eileen Israel 1950- *WhoSSW 91*
Correa, Elsa I *BiDrAPA 89*
Correa, Flora Horst 1908- *WhoAmA 91*
Correa, Gerald A 1949- *BiDrAPA 89*
Correa, Gustavo 1914- *WhoAm 90*
Correa, Henry A. 1917- *WhoAm 90, WhoWor 91*
Correa, Joao Jorge Guerra 1936- *WhoWor 91*
Correa, Julio Roberto *BiDrAPA 89*
Correa, Marie E. 1963- *ODwPR 91*
Correa, Raul *BiDrAPA 89*
Correa-Coronas, Rafael 1935- *WhoSSW 91*
Correa da Costa, Zazi Aranha 1944- *WhoWor 91*
Correa-Villasenor, Adolfo 1946- *WhoE 91*
Corredor, Livia Margarita 1960- *WhoEmL 91*
Correggio 1489?-1534 *IntDcAA 90, WorAlBi*
Correia, Alberto Abrantes 1956- *WhoE 91, WhoEmL 91*
Correia, Antone 1945- *St&PR 91*
Correia, Armand S. 1946- *St&PR 91*
Correia, Clarisse Ann 1943- *WhoAmW 91*
Correia, John F. 1939- *WhoE 91*
Correia, Natalia de Oliveira 1923- *EncCoWW*
Correia de Lima, Jose 1814-1857 *ArtLatA*
Correjolles, Gerald Lee *St&PR 91*
Correll, A.D. 1941- *St&PR 91*
Correll, Alston Dayton, Jr. 1941- *WhoSSW 91*
Correll, Charles 1890-1972 *WorAlBi*
Correll, Helen Butts 1907- *WhoAmW 91*
Correll, Joanna Rae 1948- *WhoEmL 91*
Correll, John Thomas 1939- *WhoAm 90*
Correll, Vic 1946- *Ballpl 90*
Correns, Carl Wilhelm 1893-1980 *DcScB S2*
Correnti, Elizabeth Elaine 1954- *BiDrAPA 89, WhoWor 91*
Correnti, James *BioIn 16*
Correnti, Lawrence M *BiDrAPA 89*
Correoso, Anthony B *BiDrAPA 89*
Correra, Francis X. 1938- *St&PR 91*
Correro, Anthony James, III 1941- *WhoAm 90, WhoSSW 91*
Corretjer, Juan Antonio *BioIn 16*
Correvon, Henry 1854-1939 *BioIn 16*
Correy, Lee *ConAu 30NR*
Corrick, Ann Marjorie *WhoAm 90*
Corridan, Thomas J. 1935- *WhoSSW 91*
Corridon, Frank 1880-1941 *Ballpl 90*
Corrie, John Roy 1945- *St&PR 91*
Corrier, Lucille V. *ODwPR 91*
Corriere, Joseph N., Jr. 1937- *WhoSSW 91*
Corrigall, Don Joseph 1929- *St&PR 91*
Corrigan, Charles Lawrence 1936- *WhoSSW 91*
Corrigan, Daniel Joseph 1947- *St&PR 91*
Corrigan, Douglas *BioIn 16*
Corrigan, E. Gerald 1941- *St&PR 91, WhoAm 90*
Corrigan, Edward C. *BioIn 16*
Corrigan, Edward William 1925- *St&PR 91*
Corrigan, Frederick W. 1946- *ODwPR 91*
Corrigan, Fredric H. 1914- *WhoAm 90*
Corrigan, Harold 1927- *St&PR 91*
Corrigan, Harold Cauldwell 1927- *WhoAm 90*
Corrigan, James F. *BioIn 16*
Corrigan, James Henry, Jr. 1926- *St&PR 91, WhoAm 90*
Corrigan, James John, Jr. 1935- *WhoAm 90*
Corrigan, Jeanne *ODwPR 91*
Corrigan, John Edward 1931- *WhoAm 90*
Corrigan, John Edward, Jr. 1922- *WhoAm 90*
Corrigan, John T. *BioIn 16*
Corrigan, John Thomas 1936- *WhoWrEP 89*
Corrigan, Joseph Thomas 1942- *St&PR 91*
Corrigan, Leo F., Jr. 1925- *St&PR 91*
Corrigan, Lynda Dyann 1949- *WhoAmW 91, WhoEmL 91, WhoSSW 91, WhoWor 91*
Corrigan, Mairead 1944- *BioIn 16*
Corrigan, Mark H N *BiDrAPA 89*
Corrigan, Maura Denise 1948- *WhoAmW 91*
Corrigan, Michael Edward 1955- *WhoEmL 91, WhoSSW 91*
Corrigan, Michael Joseph 1951- *St&PR 91*
Corrigan, Paul James, Jr. 1933- *WhoAm 90, WhoSSW 91*
Corrigan, Richard Lawrence 1940- *St&PR 91*
Corrigan, Robert Anthony 1935- *WhoAm 90*
Corrigan, Robert Emmett 1920- *WhoSSW 91*
Corrigan, Robert Foster 1914- *WhoAm 90*
Corrigan, Robert Willoughby 1927- *WhoAm 90*
Corrigan, Timothy 1951- *ConAu 129*
Corrigan, Timothy Patrick Penningon B. 1957- *WhoWor 91*
Corrigan, William Thomas 1921- *WhoAm 90*
Corrigan-Maguire, Mairead 1944- *WhoWor 91*
Corrin, Adaline E 1947- *BiDrAPA 89*
Corrin, Sara 1918- *BioIn 16*
Corrin, Stephen *BioIn 16*
Corrington, John William 1932- *WhoWrEP 89*
Corrington, Richard Fitch 1931- *St&PR 91, WhoSSW 91*
Corripio Ahumada, Ernesto 1919- *WhoAm 90, WhoWor 91*
Corris, Peter 1942- *TwCCr&M 91*
Corriveau, Joseph-Eugene 1885-1947 *OxCCanT*
Corrody, Carol Ann 1957- *WhoWrEP 89*
Corroon, Robert F. 1922- *St&PR 91*
Corrothers, Helen Gladys 1937- *WhoAmW 91, WhoWor 91*
Corry, Andrew Francis 1922- *WhoAm 90*
Corry, Charles A. *BioIn 16*
Corry, Charles Albert 1932- *St&PR 91, WhoAm 90, WhoE 91*
Corry, James Michael 1947- *WhoE 91*
Corry, Kathryn Mary 1948- *WhoEmL 91*
Corry, Lawrence Lee 1939- *St&PR 91, WhoAm 90*
Corry, Martha Lucille 1919- *WhoAm 90*
Corry, Robert John 1934- *WhoAm 90*
Cors, Allan D. 1936- *St&PR 91*
Corsa, Helen Storm 1915- *WhoAm 90*
Corsale, Mark James *BiDrAPA 89*
Corsaro, Frank Andrew 1924- *WhoAm 90*
Corse, John Doggett 1924- *WhoAm 90*
Corse, Richard Michael 1946- *WhoWor 91*
Corsello, Catherine Jane *BiDrAPA 89*
Corsello, Florence *St&PR 91*
Corsello, Lily Joann 1953- *WhoWor 91*
Corsello, Samuel I. 1928- *St&PR 91*
Corser, David Hewson 1930- *WhoAm 90*
Corseri, Gary Steven 1946- *WhoWrEP 89*
Corsi, Armando 1939- *WhoWor 91*
Corsi, Deborah Eranda 1953- *WhoWrEP 89*
Corsi, Jim 1961- *Ballpl 90*
Corsi, Patrick 1951- *WhoWor 91*
Corsi, Philip Donald 1928- *WhoAm 90*
Corsi, Pietro 1937- *WhoWrEP 89*
Corsiglia, Louis A. 1932- *St&PR 91*
Corsini, Andrew Cammeron 1935- *St&PR 91*
Corsini, Raymond Joseph 1914- *WhoAm 90, WhoWrEP 89*
Corso, Gregory 1930- *MajTwCW*
Corso, Gregory Nunzio 1930- *WhoAm 90, WhoWrEP 89*
Corso, John Fiermonte 1919- *WhoWor 91*
Corso, Joseph R. *NewYTBS 90*
Corso, Samuel 1953- *WhoAmA 91*
Corson, Constance 1947- *BiDrAPA 89*
Corson, Dale Raymond 1914- *WhoAm 90*
Corson, Don Edward 1956- *WhoEmL 91*
Corson, Dorthy Scheide 1927- *St&PR 91*
Corson, John J 1905-1990 *ConAu 132*
Corson, Keith D. 1935- *St&PR 91*
Corson, Keith Daniel 1935- *WhoAm 90*
Corson, Lynn H. 1931- *St&PR 91*
Corson, Richard Howell 1931- *WhoSSW 91*
Corson, Robert W. *St&PR 91*
Corson, Thomas H. 1927- *St&PR 91*
Corson, Thomas Harold 1927- *WhoAm 90, WhoWor 91*
Corsover, Meryl L. 1954- *WhoE 91*
Cort, Bud *BioIn 16*
Cort, Bud 1951- *WhoAm 90*
Cort, Diana 1934- *WhoAmW 91*
Cort, Winifred Mitchell 1917- *WhoAmW 91*
Corta, Nancy Ruth 1957- *WhoAmW 91*
Cortada, James N. 1914- *WhoAm 90*
Cortada, Rafael Leon 1934- *WhoAm 90, WhoE 91, WhoHisp 91*
Cortazar, Julio 1914-1984 *BioIn 16, ConAu 32NR, HispWr 90, MajTwCW, ShSCr 7 [port], WorAlBi*
Corte, Lawrence Julius 1954- *WhoEmL 91*
Corte Real, Gaspar 1450?-1501? *WhNaAH*
Corteguera, Homero Joseph 1930- *BiDrAPA 89*
Cortelazzo, Antonio 1819-1903 *PenDiDA 89*
Cortell, Jason Merrill 1936- *WhoE 91*
Cortelyou, Ethaline Hartge 1909- *WhoE 91*
Cortelyou, George Bruce 1862-1940 *BiDrUSE 89*
Cortelyou, John R. 1914- *WhoAm 90*
Cortes, Carlos E. 1934- *BioIn 16*
Cortes, Carlos Eliseo 1934- *WhoHisp 91*
Cortes, Cesar Augusto *BiDrAPA 89*
Cortes, Ernesto *BioIn 16*
Cortes, Hernan 1485-1547 *WorAlBi*
Cortes, Hernando 1485-1547 *EncCRAm*
Cortes, Juan Donoso 1809-1853 *BioIn 16*
Cortes, Marcos Henrique Camillo 1935- *WhoWor 91*
Cortes, Pedro Juan 1950- *WhoHisp 91*
Cortes, Robert 1955- *WhoEmL 91*
Cortes, William Antony 1947- *WhoHisp 91*
Cortes, William Patrick 1955- *WhoEmL 91, WhoWor 91*
Cortes Castro, Leon 1882-1946 *BioIn 16*
Cortes-Hwang, Adriana 1928- *WhoE 91*
Cortese, Alfred William, Jr. 1937- *WhoAm 90*
Cortese, Don F 1934- *WhoAmA 91*
Cortese, Edward Fortunato 1922- *WhoAmA 91*
Cortese, Jorge Daniel 1957- *WhoSSW 91*
Cortese, Joseph Samuel, II 1955- *WhoEmL 91*

Cortese, Leonardo *BiDrAPA 89*
Cortese, Richard Anthony 1942- *WhoAm 90*
Cortesi, Lawrence *WhoWrEP 89*
Cortesi, Roger *BioIn 16*
Corteway, Robert C. 1944- *St&PR 91, WhoAm 90*
Cortez, Angela Denise 1964- *WhoHisp 91*
Cortez, Angelina Guadalupe 1949- *WhoHisp 91*
Cortez, Carlos Alfredo 1923- *WhoHisp 91*
Cortez, Edwin Michael 1951- *WhoAm 90*
Cortez, Gilbert Diaz, Sr. 1942- *WhoHisp 91*
Cortez, Gregorio 1875-1916 *BioIn 16*
Cortez, Hernan Torres *BioIn 16*
Cortez, Jayne 1936- *ConAu 31NR, FemiCLE*
Cortez, Johnny J. 1950- *WhoHisp 91*
Cortez, Manuel J 1934- *BiDrAPA 89*
Cortez, Manuel J. 1939- *WhoHisp 91*
Cortez, Mauro *BioIn 16*
Cortez, Stanley 1908- *BioIn 16*
Cortez, Viorica 1935- *IntWWM 90, PenDiMP*
Cortez-Gentner, Celia M. 1964- *WhoHisp 91*
Corthell, Lisa Lia 1959- *BiDrAPA 89*
Corti, Maria 1915- *EncCoWW*
Cortiglia, Niccolo 1893- *WhoAmA 91N*
Cortina, Alberto *BioIn 16*
Cortina, Jorge Alberto 1959- *BiDrAPA 89*
Cortina, Juan Nepomuceno 1824-1892 *BioIn 16*
Cortina, Mauricio G *BiDrAPA 89*
Cortina, Rodolfo Jose 1946- *WhoHisp 91*
Cortinez, Veronica 1958- *WhoE 91*
Cortinovis, Dan 1947- *WhoWrEP 89*
Cortissoz, Paul 1924- *WhoAm 90*
Cortland, Nicholas *BioIn 16*
Cortner, Jean Alexander 1930- *WhoAm 90*
Cortney, David E. 1958- *St&PR 91*
Cortor, Eldzier 1916- *WhoAm 90, WhoAmA 91*
Cortot, Alfred 1877-1962 *BioIn 16, PenDiMP*
Cortrera, Richard A. 1945- *St&PR 91*
Cortright, Steven M 1942- *WhoAmA 91*
Corts, Thomas Edward 1941- *WhoAm 90, WhoSSW 91*
Cortsen, Henry A. 1941- *St&PR 91*
Corum, B. H. 1933- *WhoAm 90*
Corum, Bill 1894-1958 *Ballpl 90*
Corum, Bill 1918- *St&PR 91*
Corum, Caroline Ferguson *WhoE 91*
Corum, Grover Allen 1926- *WhoSSW 91*
Corum, Wm. M. 1942- *St&PR 91*
Corva, Angelo Francis 1948- *WhoE 91*
Corvalan, Juan C *BiDrAPA 89*
Corvino, Frank Anthony 1949- *WhoE 91*
Corvino, Joseph M 1945- *BiDrAPA 89*
Corvino, Ron L. 1960- *WhoEmL 91*
Corvo, Nicolangelo 1950- *WhoEmL 91*
Corwell, Ann E. *ODwPR 91*
Corwell, Marion *ODwPR 91*
Corwen, Leonard 1921- *WhoE 91*
Corwin, Adele Beatrice Lewis 1922-1990 *ConAu 131*
Corwin, Al 1926- *Ballpl 90*
Corwin, Arthur B. 1956- *St&PR 91*
Corwin, Bert Clark 1930- *WhoAm 90*
Corwin, Bruce Charles 1963- *WhoE 91*
Corwin, David Lewis *BiDrAPA 89*
Corwin, David Murray *BiDrAPA 89*
Corwin, Douglas Henry 1958- *St&PR 91*
Corwin, Franklin 1818-1879 *AmLegL*
Corwin, Frederic W. 1947- *St&PR 91*
Corwin, Garrison R. *BioIn 16*
Corwin, H. Hobart 1944- *St&PR 91*
Corwin, Hal Michael 1953- *WhoSSW 91*
Corwin, Howard A 1932- *BiDrAPA 89*
Corwin, Isidore *BioIn 16*
Corwin, Jeannette H 1933- *BiDrAPA 89*
Corwin, John Paul 1947- *BiDrAPA 89*
Corwin, Joyce Elizabeth Stedman *WhoAmW 91, WhoWor 91*
Corwin, Judith H 1946- *ConAu 32NR*
Corwin, Kim Henson 1957- *WhoAmW 91*
Corwin, Margaret Ann 1949- *WhoEmL 91*
Corwin, Marvin S. *BioIn 16*
Corwin, Norman 1910- *WhoAm 90*
Corwin, Philip Seth 1950- *WhoEmL 91*
Corwin, Richard L. 1952- *St&PR 91*
Corwin, Ronald G 1932- *WhoWrEP 89*
Corwin, Scott L. 1958- *St&PR 91*
Corwin, Scott Laurence 1958- *WhoEmL 91*
Corwin, Sherman Phillip 1917- *WhoAm 90*
Corwin, Sophia M *WhoAmA 91*
Corwin, Stanley Joel 1938- *WhoAm 90*
Corwin, Swift Churchill 1916- *WhoAm 90*
Corwin, Thomas 1794-1865 *BiDrUSE 89, BioIn 16*
Corwin, Thomas Michael 1952- *WhoE 91*
Corwin, Vera-Anne Versfelt *WhoAmW 91*
Corwin, Walter Horton 1924- *St&PR 91*
Corwin, William *BiDrAPA 89*
Corwin, William 1908- *WhoSSW 91, WhoWor 91*
Corwine, David Brooks 1937- *St&PR 91*
Cory, Charles R. *BioIn 16*
Cory, Christopher T. 1940- *ODwPR 91*
Cory, Desmond 1928- *TwCCr&M 91*
Cory, Eleanor Thayer 1943- *WhoAm 90*
Cory, Fanny 1877-1972 *EncACom*
Cory, Gordon Lee 1939- *St&PR 91*
Cory, Jim 1953- *WhoWrEP 89*
Cory, John Mackenzie 1914-1988 *BioIn 16*
Cory, Margaret F. 1911- *WhoAmW 91*
Cory, Pamela Mitchell 1962- *WhoEmL 91*
Cory, Paul R. 1926- *St&PR 91*
Cory, Paul Russell 1926- *WhoAm 90, WhoWor 91*
Cory, Peter deC. 1925- *WhoAm 90*
Cory, Ralph Noel 1943- *WhoSSW 91*
Cory, Ronald Joseph 1932- *St&PR 91*
Cory, Susan Elizabeth 1953- *WhoEmL 91*
Cory, Timothy Robert 1961- *WhoEmL 91*
Cory, William Eugene 1927- *WhoAm 90*
Cory, William Johnson 1823-1892 *BioIn 16*
Corydon, George Patrick 1948- *St&PR 91*
Coryell, Daniel Carl 1951- *WhoWor 91*
Coryell, Glynn Heath 1929- *WhoAm 90*
Coryell, Larry *BioIn 16*
Coryell, Roger Charles 1916- *WhoAm 90*
Coryell, Roger H. 1921- *ODwPR 91*
Coryell, William Henry 1948- *BiDrAPA 89*
Corzilius, Max W. 1924- *St&PR 91*
Corzine, Jon Stevens 1947- *WhoAm 90*
Corzo, Hector R 1947- *BiDrAPA 89*
Corzo Moody, Alfonso 1922- *BiDrAPA 89*
Cos, Louis Robert 1942- *WhoE 91*
Cosand, Joseph Parker, Jr. 1914- *WhoAm 90*
Cosbey, Robert C. 1952- *St&PR 91*
Cosby, Bill 1937- *BioIn 16, DrBlPA 90, WhoAm 90, WhoWrEP 89, WorAlBi*
Cosby, Camille *BioIn 16*
Cosby, Clair Golihew 1944- *WhoWrEP 89*
Cosby, Erinn *BioIn 16*
Cosby, Jae Traina 1960- *WhoAmW 91*
Cosby, Robert Edward, Jr. 1950- *WhoSSW 91*
Cosby, Stephen Lee 1951- *BiDrAPA 89*
Cosby, William F. 1939- *St&PR 91*
Coscarart, Pete 1931- *Ballpl 90*
Cosell, Howard 1918- *WhoAm 90, WorAlBi*
Cosell, Howard 1920- *Ballpl 90, BioIn 16*
Cosens, Barry L *BiDrAPA 89*
Cosentino, Frank 1937- *ConAu 132*
Cosentino, Louis C. 1943- *St&PR 91*
Cosenza, Arthur George 1924- *WhoAm 90, WhoSSW 91*
Cosenza, Vincent John 1962- *WhoEmL 91*
Coser, Lewis A. 1913- *BioIn 16*
Coser, Lewis Alfred 1913- *WhoAm 90*
Cosford, P.R. *St&PR 91*
Cosgrave, J O'Hara, II 1908-1968 *WhoAmA 91N*
Cosgrave, Liam 1920- *BioIn 16*
Cosgrave, Peggy *ConTFT 8 [port]*
Cosgriff, Stuart Worcester 1917- *WhoAm 90, WhoWor 91*
Cosgrove, Allen Herbert 1944- *WhoE 91*
Cosgrove, Beatrice Mary 1917- *WhoAmW 91*
Cosgrove, Emmet Lawrence 1948- *WhoEmL 91*
Cosgrove, John Darrell 1934- *WhoAm 90*
Cosgrove, John Patrick 1918- *WhoAm 90*
Cosgrove, Joseph William 1947- *WhoEmL 91*
Cosgrove, Kathleen Ann 1958- *St&PR 91*
Cosgrove, Margaret 1926- *AuBYP 90, BioIn 16*
Cosgrove, Maryellen Smith 1948- *WhoSSW 91*
Cosgrove, Michael Joseph *BiDrAPA 89*
Cosgrove, Mike 1951- *Ballpl 90*
Cosgrove, R. Dennis 1926- *St&PR 91*
Cosgrove, Stanley 1911- *WhoAmA 91*
Cosgrove, Stephen 1945- *BioIn 16*
Cosgrove, Terence Joseph 1957- *WhoEmL 91*
Coshal, Balbir Singh 1935- *BiDrAPA 89*
Cosier, Richard A. 1947- *WhoAm 90*
Cosindas, Marie 1925- *WhoWor 91*
Cosio Villegas, Daniel 1898-1976 *BioIn 16*
Cositore, Joseph Kealy 1948- *St&PR 91*
Coskey, Evelyn 1932- *AuBYP 90*
Cosla, O K *WhoAmA 91N*
Coslet, Bruce N. 1946- *WhoAm 90, WhoE 91*
Coslet, Dorothy Gawne 1924- *WhoWrEP 89*
Coslett, Charles Reynolds 1952- *WhoEmL 91*
Cosley, Jerry W. 1935- *St&PR 91*
Coslow, Richard David 1942- *WhoE 91*
Coslow, Sam 1902- *OxCPMus*
Cosma, Guillermo W 1937- *BiDrAPA 89*
Cosma, Octavian Lazar 1933- *IntWWM 90*
Cosma, Viorel 1923- *IntWWM 90*
Cosman, Ian *NewYTBS 90*
Cosman, Jeffrey M. 1951- *St&PR 91*
Cosnard, Marthe 1614-1659 *EncCoWW*
Cosner, Charles Kinian, Jr. 1950- *WhoEmL 91*
Cosner, Jerry Lee 1936- *St&PR 91*
Cosner, Melvin 1929- *St&PR 91*
Cosner, Shaaron Louise 1940- *WhoWrEP 89*
Cosper, William Huston 1948- *St&PR 91*
Cospolich, James Donald 1944- *St&PR 91*
Coss, Edward W, Jr. *BiDrAPA 89*
Coss, Herbert David 1934- *St&PR 91*
Coss, John Edward 1947- *WhoEmL 91*
Cossa, Alfonso 1833-1902 *DcScB S2*
Cossa, Dominic 1935- *IntWWM 90*
Cossa, Dominic Frank 1935- *WhoAm 90*
Cossa, Francesco del 1435?-1477? *IntDcAA 90*
Cosse, Jacques C. 1934- *ODwPR 91*
Cosse, R. Paul 1956- *WhoSSW 91*
Cossee de Maulde, Guy Jean 1935- *WhoWor 91*
Cossette, Jacquelin 1933- *BiDrAPA 89*
Cossiga, Francesco *BioIn 16*
Cossiga, Francesco 1928- *WhoWor 91*
Cossins, Edwin Albert 1937- *WhoAm 90*
Cossman, Joanne Patricia Tully 1949- *WhoAmW 91*
Cossons, Neil 1939- *WhoWor 91*
Cossotto, Fiorenza 1935- *IntWWM 90, PenDiMP, WhoAm 90, WhoWor 91*
Cossu, Scott *NewAgMG*
Cossutta, Araldo Alfred 1925- *WhoAm 90*
Cossutta, Carlo 1932- *IntWWM 90, PenDiMP*
Cost, James Peter 1923- *WhoAm 90, WhoAmA 91*
Cost, John Joseph 1934- *WhoAm 90*
Cost, Richard Scott 1966- *WhoE 91*
Costa, Catherine Aurora 1926- *WhoAmW 91, WhoE 91*
Costa, Charles Kenneth 1948- *St&PR 91*
Costa, Claudio Manuel da 1729-1789 *BioIn 16*
Costa, Daniel Joseph 1948- *WhoEmL 91*
Costa, Donna Marie 1955- *WhoAmW 91*
Costa, Eduardo *WhoAmA 91*
Costa, Ernest Fiorenzo 1926- *WhoAm 90*
Costa, Felix Augusto *BiDrAPA 89*
Costa, Fernando 1953- *WhoSSW 91*
Costa, Frank J. *WhoHisp 91*
Costa, Giovanni 1826-1903 *BioIn 16*
Costa, Gustavo 1930- *WhoAm 90*
Costa, H. Marie 1951- *WhoEmL 91*
Costa, Helen Marie 1951- *WhoWrEP 89*
Costa, James 1952- *WhoWor 91*
Costa, Jaunita 1948- *St&PR 91*
Costa, Joaquim Jose Soares 1938- *WhoWor 91*
Costa, John Joseph 1922- *St&PR 91*
Costa, Joseph 1904-1988 *BioIn 16*
Costa, Kimberly Anne 1963- *WhoEmL 91*
Costa, Linda Alice 1949- *WhoSSW 91*
Costa, Lucio Guido 1954- *WhoEmL 91*
Costa, Maria de Fatima Bivar Velho da 1938- *EncCoWW*
Costa, Marithelma 1955- *WhoHisp 91*
Costa, Mary *WhoAmW 91*
Costa, Mary D. *BioIn 16*
Costa, Maryanne Sugarman 1959- *WhoAmW 91*
Costa, Michael 1808-1884 *PenDiMP*
Costa, Olga 1913- *BioIn 16*
Costa, Pat Vincent 1943- *St&PR 91, WhoAm 90, WhoE 91*
Costa, Peter *BioIn 16*
Costa, Petronilo R *BiDrAPA 89*
Costa, Ralph Charles 1956- *WhoHisp 91*
Costa, Robert Nicholas 1938- *WhoAm 90, WhoSSW 91*
Costa, Robert Richard 1928- *WhoAm 90*
Costa, Rui Carlos Martins 1945- *WhoWor 91*
Costa, Victor *BioIn 16*
Costa, Victor Charles 1935- *WhoAm 90*
Costa, Walter Henry 1924- *WhoAm 90*
Costa E Silva, Jorge A *BiDrAPA 89*
Costa-Gaudiosi, Roberta Frances 1952- *WhoEmL 91*
Costa-Gavras *BioIn 16*
Costa-Gavras 1933- *WorAlBi*
Costa y Martinez, Joaquin 1846-1911 *BioIn 16*
Costagliola, Francesco 1917- *WhoE 91, WhoWor 91*
Costagliola, John 1962- *St&PR 91*
Costain, Anne-Marie 1950- *WhoWor 91*
Costain, Robert George 1939- *St&PR 91*
Costain, Thomas Bertram 1885-1965 *AuBYP 90*
Costakis, George 1912-1990 *BioIn 16, NewYTBS 90 [port]*
Costales, Federico *WhoHisp 91*
Costan, Chris 1950- *WhoAmA 91*
Costantini, Humberto 1924?-1987 *ConAu 131, HispWr 90, WorAu 1980 [port]*
Costantini, Lana Ellen 1955- *WhoEmL 91*
Costantini, Louis C *BiDrAPA 89*
Costantini, William Paul 1947- *St&PR 91*
Costantino, Lorine Protzman 1921- *WhoAmW 91*
Costanza da Varano 1426-1447 *EncCoWW*
Costanza, Angelo Anthony 1926- *St&PR 91*
Costanza, John Joseph 1924- *WhoAmA 91*
Costanza, Margaret Midge 1932- *WhoAm 90*
Costanzo, Frank T. 1948- *St&PR 91*
Costanzo, Henry John 1925- *WhoAm 90*
Costanzo, Hilda Alba *WhoAm 90, WhoAmW 91*
Costanzo, John Anthony 1946- *WhoE 91*
Costanzo, Michael Francis 1957- *BiDrAPA 89*
Costanzo, Santino 1958- *WhoSSW 91*
Costanzo, W. Kenneth 1952- *St&PR 91*
Costas, Bob *BioIn 16*
Costas, Bob 1952- *WhoAm 90*
Costas, Robert Quinlan 1952- *WhoAm 90*
Costas-Lozada, Haydee 1943- *BiDrAPA 89*
Coste, Ramona *BiDrAPA 89*
Coste-Floret, Paul 1911-1979 *BiDFrPL*
Costea, Nicolas Vincent 1927- *WhoAm 90*
Costede, Jurgen Reinhard 1939- *WhoWor 91*
Costell, Ronald M 1940- *BiDrAPA 89*
Costellese, Linda E. Grace 1950- *WhoE 91*
Costello, A.M. *St&PR 91*
Costello, Albert J. 1935- *St&PR 91*
Costello, Albert Joseph 1935- *WhoAm 90*
Costello, Allan John 1956- *St&PR 91*
Costello, Amelia Fusco 1946- *WhoE 91*
Costello, Bonnie 1950- *ConAu 129*
Costello, Charles H. 1907- *St&PR 91*
Costello, Christine Ann 1958- *WhoAmW 91*
Costello, Christine Claire 1968- *WhoAmW 91*
Costello, Claudia J. 1954- *WhoAmW 91*
Costello, Cynthia Ann 1952- *WhoAmA 91, WhoE 91*
Costello, Daniel Brian 1950- *WhoEmL 91*
Costello, Daniel Walter 1930- *WhoAm 90*
Costello, David L. 1951- *St&PR 91*
Costello, Dawn Elizabeth Barnes 1940- *WhoAmW 91*
Costello, Dorothy Stassun 1954- *St&PR 91*
Costello, Eileen Marie 1949- *WhoEmL 91*
Costello, Elvis *BioIn 16, WhoNeCM B [port]*
Costello, Elvis 1954- *WhoAm 90*
Costello, Elvis 1955- *EncPR&S 89, OxCPMus*
Costello, Frank 1891-1973 *BioIn 16*
Costello, Gerald Michael 1931- *WhoAm 90*
Costello, Harry *ODwPR 91*
Costello, J. Robert 1918- *St&PR 91*
Costello, James Joseph 1930- *St&PR 91*
Costello, Jerry F. *WhoAm 90*
Costello, Jerry F. 1949- *BioIn 16*
Costello, John 1960- *Ballpl 90*
Costello, John B. 1936- *St&PR 91*
Costello, John Francis, Jr. 1935- *WhoAm 90*
Costello, John H., III 1947- *WhoAm 90, WhoEmL 91*
Costello, John Michael, Jr. 1961- *WhoEmL 91*
Costello, John Richard 1954- *WhoEmL 91*
Costello, John Robert 1942- *WhoAm 90, WhoWor 91*
Costello, John Robert 1947- *WhoSSW 91*
Costello, Joseph B. *BioIn 16*
Costello, Joseph Mark, III 1940- *WhoAm 90*
Costello, Lawrence B. 1948- *St&PR 91*
Costello, Lawrence P. 1941- *BiDrAPA 89*
Costello, Lou *BioIn 16*
Costello, Lou 1906-1959 *WorAlBi*
Costello, Louisa Stuart 1799-1870 *FemiCLE*
Costello, Mark Gregory 1960- *WhoE 91*
Costello, Mary 1940- *WhoAmW 91*
Costello, Melissa *BioIn 16*
Costello, Michael Joseph 1952- *WhoEmL 91*
Costello, Michael Mark 1948- *WhoE 91*
Costello, Patrick Raymond 1948- *St&PR 91*
Costello, Richard James 1945- *WhoAm 90*
Costello, Richard King 1927- *WhoAm 90*
Costello, Richard Neumann 1943- *WhoAm 90*
Costello, Robert L. 1951- *St&PR 91*
Costello, Russell Hill 1904- *WhoAm 90*
Costello, Shawn Randolph 1960- *WhoAmW 91*
Costello, Thomas Joseph 1929- *WhoAm 90*
Costello, Thomas Patrick 1931- *St&PR 91*
Costello, Tom 1863-1943 *OxCPMus*
Costello, William F. 1946- *St&PR 91*
Costenbader, Charles Michael 1935- *WhoE 91*
Costenbader, Cynthia Lou 1956- *WhoAmW 91*

Costenuck, Gloria Anne 1944- St&PR 91
Coster, Anne Vallayer- 1744-1818 BioIn 16
Coster, Nancy L. 1941- WhoAmW 91
Costes, Nicholas Constantine 1926- WhoAm 90
Costi, Jack 1946- St&PR 91
Costigan, Alexander James 1944- St&PR 91
Costigan, Constance Frances 1935- WhoAm 90, WhoAmA 91
Costigan, Daniel M 1929- ConAu 31NR
Costigan, Edward John 1914- WhoAm 90, WhoWor 91
Costigan, Giovanni NewYTBS 90
Costigan, Giovanni 1905-1990 BioIn 16
Costigan, John Edward 1888-1972 WhoAmA 91N
Costigan, John Mark 1942- St&PR 91, WhoAm 90
Costigan, John Robert 1953- BiDrAPA 89
Costiglio, Peter ODwPR 91
Costikyan, Edward Nazar 1924- WhoAm 90
Costikyan, Granger 1907- St&PR 91
Costilla, Miguel Hidalgo y 1753-1811 BioIn 16
Costin, Darryl J. 1946- WhoAm 90
Costin, Eugene 1935- St&PR 91
Costin, Frank WhoAmA 91
Costin, J. Laurence 1941- St&PR 91
Costin, Michael Craig 1947- St&PR 91
Costle, Douglas Michael 1939- WhoE 91
Costley, Bill 1942- WhoWrEP 89
Costley, Gary Edward 1943- St&PR 91, WhoAm 90
Costley, Jennifer L. 1956- WhoAmW 91
Costley-Jacobs, Averille Esther 1947- WhoAmA 91
Costlow, Curt C. 1942- St&PR 91
Costner, Kevin BioIn 16
Costner, Kevin 1955- CurBio 90 [port], WhoAm 90, WorAlBi
Costo, Jose A BiDrAPA 89
Costoff, Theodore 1925- WhoAm 90
Coston, Gale Norman 1937- WhoSSW 91
Coston, James E. 1955- WhoEmL 91
Coston, Neeoma Lee 1935- WhoAmW 91
Costrell, Louis 1915- WhoAm 90
Costrell, Robert Michael 1950- WhoEmL 91
Cosulich, Paolo Ulisse 1916- WhoWor 91
Cosway, Richard 1917- WhoAm 90
Cot, Pierre 1895-1977 BiDFrPL
Cota, A. James 1947- St&PR 91
Cota, Glenn Lowell 1929- St&PR 91
Cota, John Francis 1924- St&PR 91, WhoAm 90
Cota, Karen L. 1957- WhoAmW 91
Cota, Manuelito WhNaAH
Cota-Robles, Eugene Henry 1926- WhoHisp 91
Cotant, Marilyn Jean 1950- WhoAmW 91
Cotchett, Joseph Winters 1939- WhoAm 90
Cote, Alan 1937- WhoAmA 91
Cote, Gilles A 1902- BiDrAPA 89
Cote, Henri G. 1914- St&PR 91
Cote, Isabelle 1961- BiDrAPA 89
Cote, Joseph A.C. 1939- St&PR 91
Cote, Louise Roseann 1959- WhoAmW 91, WhoEmL 91
Cote, Pierre 1926- St&PR 91, WhoAm 90
Cote, Raynald BiDrAPA 89
Cote, Richard Norman 1945- WhoSSW 91
Cote, Robert Andrew 1958- WhoEmL 91
Cote, Roger Burton 1949- WhoEmL 91
Cote, Sally Spilker 1946- WhoAmW 91
Cote, Scott M. 1950- WhoE 91
Cote, William Alfred 1942- St&PR 91
Cote-Beaupre, Camille Yvette 1926- WhoAmW 91
Cote-O'Hara, Jocelyne BioIn 16
Cote-O'Hara, Jocelyne M. 1945- St&PR 91
Cotellessa, Robert Francis 1923- WhoAm 90
Cotera, Martha P. 1938- WhoHisp 91
Cotes, Roger 1682-1716 BioIn 16
Cothorn, John Arthur 1939- WhoAm 90
Cothorne, Robin J. 1961- WhoAmW 91
Cothran, Andrew Neilson 1929- WhoAm 90
Cothran, Bettina Kluth 1952- WhoSSW 91
Cothran, Cynthia Lynn 1957- WhoSSW 91
Cothran, Tilman Christopher 1918- WhoAm 90
Cothran, William T. St&PR 91
Cothren, Michael Watt 1951- WhoAmA 91, WhoE 91
Cotlar, Mischa 1913- EncO&P 3
Cotlar, Morton 1928- WhoAm 90
Cotler, Leslie B. 1938- St&PR 91
Cotler, Marvin Aaron 1932- WhoE 91
Cotliar, George BioIn 16
Cotlov, Jerry L. 1951- St&PR 91
Cotlov, Jerry Louis 1951- WhoEmL 91
Cotlove, Candace 1952- BiDrAPA 89
Cotlove, Elaine Wolf 1921- BiDrAPA 89
Cotman, John Sell 1782-1842 IntDcAA 90
Cotman, Shirley Ann WhoAmW 91
Cotner, C. Beth 1952- St&PR 91
Cotner, Carol Beth 1952- WhoAmW 91
Cotner, Kathleen Yvonne 1963- WhoEmL 91
Cotner, Mary Y. 1952- St&PR 91
Cotner, Roger Garner 1952- WhoEmL 91
Coto, Juan Carlos 1966- WhoHisp 91
Coto, Pedro BiDrAPA 89
Cotoia, Margaret Ann 1960- WhoEmL 91
Coton, Carlos David 1950- WhoEmL 91, WhoSSW 91
Coton, Luis Donovan 1947- WhoEmL 91
Cotran, Ramzi S. 1932- WhoAm 90, WhoE 91
Cotronea, Francesco J BiDrAPA 89
Cotros, Charles H. 1937- WhoSSW 91
Cotrubas, Ileana WhoAm 90, WhoWor 91
Cotrubas, Ileana 1939- IntWWM 90, PenDiMP
Cotsen, Lloyd E. 1929- St&PR 91
Cotsen, Tobey BioIn 16
Cotsonas, Nicholas John, Jr. 1919- WhoAm 90
Cotsworth, J.B. 1925- St&PR 91
Cotsworth, Staats 1908-1979 WhoAmA 91N
Cott, Allan 1910- BiDrAPA 89
Cott, Craig John BiDrAPA 89
Cott, Jean Cahan WhoAmA 91
Cott, Jonathan 1942- AuBYP 90
Cott, Peter 1924- ODwPR 91
Cott, Ted 1932- ODwPR 91
Cotta, Johann Friedrich 1764-1832 BioIn 16
Cottam, Grant 1918- WhoAm 90
Cottam, Keith M. 1941- WhoAm 90
Cotten, Catheryn Deon 1952- WhoAmW 91, WhoEmL 91
Cotten, Daniel G. 1951- St&PR 91
Cotten, Joseph WhoAm 90
Cotten, Joseph 1905- WorAlBi
Cotter, Berchmans Paul, Jr. 1937- WhoAm 90
Cotter, Clifton Joseph 1926- St&PR 91
Cotter, Daniel A. 1934- St&PR 91, WhoAm 90
Cotter, Ernest Robert, III 1951- WhoAm 90
Cotter, George Edward 1918- WhoAm 90
Cotter, Holland 1947- WhoAmA 91
Cotter, James Edward 1944- WhoAmA 91
Cotter, James J. BioIn 16
Cotter, James Michael 1942- WhoE 91
Cotter, John BioIn 16
Cotter, Joseph Francis 1927- St&PR 91, WhoAm 90
Cotter, Joseph Seamon 1861-1949 LiHiK
Cotter, Joseph Seamon, Jr. 1895-1919 EarBlAP, LiHiK
Cotter, Joseph Seamon, Sr. 1861-1949 EarBlAP
Cotter, Lloyd Harry 1922- BiDrAPA 89
Cotter, Lucy Ann 1957- WhoAmW 91
Cotter, Richard J. 1928- St&PR 91
Cotter, Shirley Ann WhoAmW 91
Cotter, Veronica Irene 1949- WhoAmW 91
Cotter, Vincent P. 1927- St&PR 91
Cotter, Vincent Paul 1927- WhoAm 90
Cotter, Wayne Billings 1949- WhoEmL 91
Cotter, William Donald 1921- WhoAm 90
Cotter, William Joseph 1921- WhoAm 90
Cotter, William Reckling 1936- WhoAm 90
Cotterill, Carl Hayden 1918- WhoAm 90
Cotterill, David Lee 1937- St&PR 91, WhoAm 90, WhoWor 91
Cotterill, Edmund PenDiDA 89
Cotterill, Nancy Ann 1950- WhoAmW 91
Cotterill, Ronald Wayne 1948- WhoE 91
Cotterill, Sarah L. 1948- WhoWrEP 89
Cotterman, D. Brant 1938- St&PR 91
Cottet, Jack L. 1944- WhoE 91
Cotti, Flavio 1939- WhoWor 91
Cotti, Gianfranco 1929- WhoWor 91
Cottier, Chuck 1936- Ballpl 90
Cottin, Angelique EncO&P 3
Cottin, Marie-Sophie Risteau 1770-1807 EncCoWW
Cotting, James Charles 1933- St&PR 91, WhoAm 90, WhoWor 91
Cottingham, Bob BioIn 16
Cottingham, Laura Josephine 1959- WhoAmA 91
Cottingham, Robert 1935- WhoAmA 91, WhoE 91
Cottingham, Stephen Kent 1951- WhoSSW 91
Cottingham, Tracy Thomas, III 1947- WhoEmL 91
Cottingham, William B. 1933- St&PR 91
Cottingham, William Brooks 1933- WhoAm 90
Cottington, Angela BiDEWW
Cottington, Eliza BiDEWW
Cottington, Linda Renee 1948- WhoAmW 91
Cottle, Carey Gordon, Jr. 1960- BiDrAPA 89
Cottle, Charles ConAu 130
Cottle, David William 1942- WhoSSW 91
Cottle, Gail 1951- St&PR 91
Cottle, John V. 1936- St&PR 91
Cottle, Robert Duquemin 1935- WhoAm 90, WhoE 91, WhoWor 91
Cottler, Ilene S. 1946- BiDrAPA 89
Cotto, Antonio, II 1939- WhoHisp 91
Cotto, Carmen M BiDrAPA 89
Cotto, Henry 1961- Ballpl 90
Cotto, Mario 1938- WhoWor 91
Cottom, Frederick Arthur Sefton 1928- IntWWM 90
Cotton, Aime-Auguste 1869-1951 DcScB S2
Cotton, Albert E. 1939- St&PR 91
Cotton, Alfred J., Jr. 1942- ODwPR 91
Cotton, Anne 1933- WhoAmW 91
Cotton, Aylett Borel 1913- WhoAm 90
Cotton, Aylett Rains 1826-1912 AmLegL
Cotton, Billy 1899-1969 OxCPMus
Cotton, Bruce C. 1931- St&PR 91
Cotton, Dana Meserve 1905- WhoAm 90
Cotton, Donald Lloyd 1914- St&PR 91
Cotton, Dorothy Foreman WhoAm 90
Cotton, Eugene 1914- WhoAm 90
Cotton, Frank Albert 1930- WhoAm 90
Cotton, Gary Douglas 1940- St&PR 91
Cotton, James 1938- WhoSSW 91
Cotton, James Perry, Jr. 1939- WhoAm 90
Cotton, Joe Walter 1926- WhoSSW 91
Cotton, John 1584-1652 EncCRAm, WorAlBi
Cotton, John 1938- WhoAm 90
Cotton, Lillian 1901-1962 WhoAmA 91N
Cotton, Lori Lee 1956- WhoAmW 91
Cotton, Norris 1900-1989 BioIn 16
Cotton, Patricia Alice 1940- WhoAmW 91
Cotton, Paul Gerald 1945- BiDrAPA 89
Cotton, Priscilla BiDEWW, FemiCLE
Cotton, Ryan D. BioIn 16
Cotton, Vincent John, Jr. 1957- WhoEmL 91
Cotton, William Davis 1904- WhoAm 90
Cotton, William Henry 1880-1958 WhoAmA 91N
Cotton, William Robert 1931- WhoE 91
Cottone, Benedict Peter 1909- WhoAm 90
Cottone, James Anthony 1947- WhoEmL 91
Cottone, Linda Marie 1945- WhoAmW 91
Cottongame, Charlotte Brock 1947- WhoEmL 91
Cottor, Robert E 1932- BiDrAPA 89
Cottrau, Teodoro 1827-1879 OxCPMus
Cottrell, Comer J. 1931- St&PR 91
Cottrell, David George 1952- WhoWor 91
Cottrell, Dorothy 1902-1957 FemiCLE
Cottrell, Frank S. 1942- St&PR 91
Cottrell, Frank Stewart 1942- WhoAm 90
Cottrell, G. Walton 1939- WhoAm 90
Cottrell, J. Thomas, Jr. 1925- St&PR 91
Cottrell, James Edward 1933- St&PR 91
Cottrell, Janet Ann 1943- WhoAmW 91
Cottrell, Jenay Southwick ODwPR 91
Cottrell, Kathleen ODwPR 91
Cottrell, Leonard 1913-1974 AuBYP 90
Cottrell, Mary-Patricia Tross 1934- WhoAmW 91, WhoE 91
Cottrell, Paul 1951- WhoE 91
Cottrell, Richard 1936- ConAu 130
Cottrell, Stanley Lee 1949- WhoSSW 91
Cottrell, Stuart Rogers 1946- WhoWor 91
Cottrell, Wilbert Curtis, Jr. 1933- St&PR 91
Cottrol, Cheryl Henrietta BiDrAPA 89
Cotts, Cynthia L. 1958- WhoWrEP 89
Cotts, Gertrude V 1909- BiDrAPA 89
Coty, Francois Spaturno 1874-1934 BiDFrPL
Coty, Rene 1882-1962 BiDFrPL
Cotzen, Donna Joyce 1947- BiDrAPA 89
Couani, Anna 1948- FemiCLE
Coubertin, Pierre, Baron De 1863-1937 WorAlBi
Couch, B. Joyce 1954- WhoAmW 91
Couch, Deborah Lynn BiDrAPA 89
Couch, Harvey Crowley, III 1936- WhoAm 90
Couch, J. Foy, Jr. 1926- St&PR 91
Couch, J. O. Terrell 1920- WhoAm 90
Couch, James Houston 1919- WhoAm 90
Couch, Jesse Wadsworth 1921- WhoAm 90
Couch, John Charles 1939- St&PR 91, WhoAm 90
Couch, John Nathaniel 1896-1986 BioIn 16
Couch, Johnny 1891-1975 Ballpl 90
Couch, Johnson 1943- St&PR 91
Couch, Margaret Wheland 1941- WhoAmW 91
Couch, Michael Jaye 1952- St&PR 91
Couch, Robert Barnard 1930- WhoAm 90
Couch, Robert Franklin 1947- WhoE 91
Couch, Urban 1927- WhoAmA 91
Couchenour, Donna Lee 1950- WhoSSW 91
Couchet, Richard Lee 1939- St&PR 91
Couchman, Donald Louis 1931- St&PR 91
Couchman, Mary Catherine 1945- WhoAmW 91, WhoWor 91
Couchman, Robert George James 1937- WhoAm 90
Coudenhove, Ida 1901- EncCoWW
Couderc, Louis A. BioIn 16
Coudert, Ferdinand Wilmerding 1909- WhoAm 90
Coudert, Victor Raphael, Jr. 1926- WhoE 91
Coudriet, Charles Edward 1946- St&PR 91, WhoAm 90
Coue, Emile 1857-1926 EncO&P 3
Coues, W. Pearce St&PR 91
Couey, Duane Emerson 1924- WhoAm 90
Coufal, Franz Anton 1927- WhoWor 91
Coufal, Ronald Louis 1952- St&PR 91
Cougar, John BioIn 16
Couger, James Daniel 1929- WhoAm 90
Coughenour, John Clare 1941- WhoAm 90
Coughlan, Basil Joseph, II 1940- WhoAm 90
Coughlan, Gary Patrick 1944- St&PR 91, WhoAm 90
Coughlan, John Appleby 1929- WhoAm 90
Coughlan, Joseph Daly 1934- St&PR 91
Coughlan, Kenneth Lewis 1940- WhoAm 90
Coughlan, Margaret N. 1925- AuBYP 90
Coughlan, Patrick Campbell 1940- WhoAm 90
Coughlan, Robert 1914- WhoAm 90, WhoWrEP 89
Coughlan, William David 1946- WhoAm 90, WhoSSW 91
Coughlin, Barring 1913- WhoAm 90
Coughlin, Bernard John 1922- WhoAm 90
Coughlin, Bill 1877-1943 Ballpl 90
Coughlin, Charles E. 1891-1979 WorAlBi
Coughlin, Charles Edward 1891-1979 BioIn 16
Coughlin, Colleen 1962- WhoEmL 91
Coughlin, Cornelius Edward 1927- WhoWor 91
Coughlin, Daniel J. 1940- St&PR 91
Coughlin, Elizabeth Ann 1945- WhoAmW 91
Coughlin, Francis Raymond, Jr. 1927- WhoAm 90, WhoE 91
Coughlin, Jack 1932- WhoAm 90, WhoAmA 91
Coughlin, James P. St&PR 91
Coughlin, James Porter 1938- St&PR 91
Coughlin, Joseph P. 1934- St&PR 91
Coughlin, Kathleen 1941- WhoAmW 91
Coughlin, Kenneth Morgan 1952- WhoE 91
Coughlin, Lawrence WhoAm 90, WhoE 91
Coughlin, Magdalen 1930- WhoAm 90
Coughlin, Margaret Ann 1955- WhoAmW 91
Coughlin, Peter Joseph 1952- WhoE 91, WhoEmL 91
Coughlin, Peter Lutz 1945- WhoEmL 91
Coughlin, Richard Francis 1932- St&PR 91
Coughlin, Richard John 1931- WhoAm 90
Coughlin, Richard Joseph 1923- St&PR 91
Coughlin, Stephen NewAgMG
Coughlin, Terrance J. 1948- WhoEmL 91
Coughlin, Thomas Martin 1949- St&PR 91, WhoAm 90
Coughlin, Thomas Patrick 1954- WhoEmL 91
Coughlin, Thomas Stanley 1942- St&PR 91
Coughlin, Timothy Crathorne 1942- WhoE 91
Coughran, Bruce Edward 1955- WhoEmL 91
Coughran, Tom Bristol 1906- WhoAm 90, WhoWor 91
Couillard, Fernand BiDrAPA 89
Coulange, Edouard Andre 1950- WhoWor 91
Coulbourn, John ODwPR 91
Coulbourn, Thomas Edgar 1940- St&PR 91
Couleur, John T. 1945- St&PR 91
Coulier, David BioIn 16
Coulling, Sidney Baxter 1924- WhoAm 90
Coulman, George Albert 1930- WhoAm 90
Coulmas, Florian 1949- ConAu 132
Coulomb, Charles Augustin De 1736-1806 WorAlBi
Coulombe, Andre Normand 1953- WhoEmL 91
Coulombe, Cecile 1925- St&PR 91
Coulombe, Raymond R. 1924- St&PR 91
Coulouris, George 1903-1989 AnObit 1989, BioIn 16, ConTFT 8
Coulshed, Norman 1922- WhoWor 91
Coulson, Arlene Ann 1935- WhoAmW 91
Coulson, Carolyn Lu 1937- WhoAmW 91
Coulson, Jesse Edward 1940- WhoSSW 91
Coulson, Jimmie T.G. 1933- St&PR 91
Coulson, John S. 1915- St&PR 91
Coulson, John Selden 1915- WhoAm 90

Coulson, Kinsell Leroy 1916- WhoAm 90
Coulson, Norman M. WhoAm 90
Coulson, Patricia Bunker 1942- WhoAmW 91
Coulson, Robert 1924- St&PR 91, WhoAm 90
Coulson, Roland Armstrong 1915- BioIn 16
Coulson, Tracy Noreen 1957- WhoEmL 91
Coulson, William Roy 1949- WhoEmL 91
Coulson, Zoe Elizabeth 1932- St&PR 91, WhoAm 90, WhoAmW 91
Coultas, James C. 1921- St&PR 91
Coulter, Andrea McCandless 1938- WhoE 91
Coulter, Barbara Clare 1950- WhoEmL 91
Coulter, Borden McKee 1917- WhoWor 91
Coulter, Cathrine Ann 1957- St&PR 91
Coulter, Clare 1942- OxCCanT
Coulter, Cynthia A. ODwPR 91
Coulter, Earl Grant 1923- St&PR 91
Coulter, Elizabeth Jackson 1919- WhoAm 90, WhoAmW 91, WhoWor 91
Coulter, Hope Norman 1961- ConAu 129
Coulter, Jack Benson, Jr. 1947- WhoEmL 91, WhoSSW 91
Coulter, James Bennett 1920- WhoAm 90
Coulter, John 1888-1980 OxCCanT
Coulter, John Breitling, III 1941- WhoSSW 91, WhoWor 91
Coulter, Kyle Jane 1937- WhoAmW 91
Coulter, L William BiDrAPA 89
Coulter, Mary Elise 1946- WhoSSW 91
Coulter, Michael David 1953- St&PR 91
Coulter, Myron Lee 1929- WhoAm 90, WhoSSW 91
Coulter, N Arthur, Jr. 1920- WhoWrEP 89
Coulter, Norman Arthur, Jr. 1920- WhoAm 90
Coulter, Olivia W. 1915?-1989 ConAu 129
Coulter, Paul David Todd 1938- WhoAm 90
Coulter, Philip Wylie 1938- WhoAm 90
Coulter, Sara ODwPR 91
Coulter, Stephen 1914- SpyFic, TwCCr&M 91
Coulter, Theodore Anthony 1945- St&PR 91
Coulter, Thomas Henry 1911- St&PR 91
Coulter, William John 1934- St&PR 91
Coulter, Wilson Huxley 1936- WhoSSW 91
Coulton, Martha Jean Glasscoe 1927- WhoAmW 91
Coultrap, Connie Ann 1946- WhoEmL 91
Coultry, Barbara A. 1945- WhoWrEP 89
Coumbe, Fritz 1889-1978 Ballpl 90
Coumides, Andreas Demosthenous 1928- WhoWor 91
Counce-Nicklas, Sheila Jean 1927- WhoAm 90
Counceller, John 1946- St&PR 91
Council, Brenda Joyce 1953- WhoEmL 91
Council, Pauline Carter 1950- WhoEmL 91, WhoSSW 91
Councilor, James Allan, III 1947- WhoE 91
Counen, Michael N. 1929- St&PR 91
Counihan, Darlyn Joyce 1948- WhoAmW 91
Counihan, Noel 1913-1986 BioIn 16
Counihan, Timothy Brendan 1923- WhoWor 91
Counio, Gilbert Albert 1942- WhoWor 91
Counsell, Paul Stone 1936- St&PR 91
Counsell, Raymond Ernest 1930- WhoAm 90
Counselman, Charles Claude, III 1943- WhoAm 90
Counselman, Eleanor Frey 1946- WhoEmL 91
Counselman, Elizabeth Burke 1954- WhoAmW 91
Counsil, William Glenn 1937- BioIn 16, WhoAm 90
Counsilman, Doc BioIn 16
Counsilman, James Edward 1920- WhoAm 90
Countee, Sandra Flowers 1943- WhoAmW 91
Counterman, Sharon Ann WhoAmW 91
Countess of Septimania EncCoWW
Countiss, Richard Neil 1936- WhoSSW 91
Countryman, Dayton Wendell 1918- WhoAm 90
Countryman, Edward Francis 1944- WhoAm 90
Countryman, Frank W 1920- BiDrAPA 89
Countryman, Gary Lee 1939- St&PR 91, WhoAm 90, WhoE 91
Countryman, John Russell 1933- WhoAm 90
Countryman, Keith R. 1951- St&PR 91
Countryman, Richard Alva 1926- WhoWor 91
Countryman, Vern 1917- WhoAm 90
Counts, Catherine Ann 1962- WhoAmW 91
Counts, George S. 1889-1974 BioIn 16
Counts, James Curtis 1915- WhoAm 90
Counts, Justice Fuller 1941- St&PR 91
Counts, Mary Lou 1933- WhoSSW 91
Counts, Robert M 1924- BiDrAPA 89
Counts, Stanley Thomas 1926- WhoAm 90
Counts, Wayne Boyd 1936- WhoSSW 91
Coupe, Irene Fay 1928- WhoAm 90
Coupe, James Warnick 1949- WhoEmL 91
Coupe, John Donald 1931- WhoAm 90
Coupe, Suzanne Jean 1965- WhoE 91
Couper, Charles Alexander 1924- WhoAmA 91
Couper, James M 1937- WhoAmA 91
Couper, Richard W. 1922- St&PR 91
Couper, Richard Watrous 1922- WhoAm 90
Couper, William 1853-1942 BioIn 16
Couperin, Francois 1668-1733 PenDiMP A
Cour, Paul la DcScanL
Courage, Piers BioIn 16
Courant, Ernest David 1920- WhoAm 90
Couraud, Katherine Seaman 1955- WhoAmW 91
Couraud, Marcel 1912- IntWWM 90, PenDiMP
Courbet, Gustave 1819-1877 BioIn 16, IntDcAA 90, WorAlBi
Courchene, Ernest E., Jr. 1932- St&PR 91
Courey, Michael Herbert 1947- WhoSSW 91
Couri, George J. BioIn 16
Couriard, Pelagia Petrovna 1848-1898 BiDWomA
Courier, Jim BioIn 16
Courlander, Harold 1908- AuBYP 90, BioIn 16
Cournand, Andre F. 1895-1988 BioIn 16
Cournos, Francine 1945- BiDrAPA 89
Cournot, Antoine Augustin 1801-1877 BioIn 16
Cournoyer, Barry Roger 1947- WhoEmL 91
Cournoyer, Jocelyne BiDrAPA 89
Cournoyer, Michele Louise 1960- WhoEmL 91
Cournoyer, R.O. 1933- St&PR 91
Courreges, Andre 1923- ConDes 90
Courrier-Carpenter, Elaine F. 1919- WhoAmW 91
Cours, John Dave 1934- WhoE 91
Coursen, Christopher Dennison 1948- WhoE 91
Coursen, H. R. 1932- WhoWrEP 89
Courshon, Arthur Howard 1921- St&PR 91, WhoAm 90
Courshon, Carol Biel 1923- WhoAmW 91
Coursin, David Reyburn 1947- BiDrAPA 89
Courson, John Edward 1944- WhoSSW 91
Courson, Leland C. 1956- WhoAm 90
Courson, Marna B. P. 1951- WhoAmW 91
Courson, Steve BioIn 16
Court, Arnold 1914- WhoWor 91
Court, Hazel 1926- BioIn 16
Court, Jean de PenDiDA 89
Court, Kathryn Diana 1948- WhoAm 90, WhoAmW 91
Court, Lee Winslow 1903- WhoAmA 91
Court, Leonard 1947- WhoAm 90, WhoEmL 91, WhoSSW 91
Court, Margaret Smith 1942- WorAlBi
Court, Wesli WhoWrEP 89
Courtade, Judy Louise 1951- St&PR 91
Courtaud, Bernard Jean-Jacques 1945- WhoWor 91
Courtauld, Augustus 1686?-1751 PenDiDA 89
Courtauld, George 1938- ConAu 129
Courtauld, Samuel 1720-1765 PenDiDA 89
Courtemanche, Albert Douglas 1929- WhoAm 90
Courtemanche, Leo Maurice 1959- WhoE 91
Courtenai de la Fosse-Ronde, Sophie de EncCoWW
Courtenay, Adrian Henry, III 1942- WhoE 91
Courtenay, Bryce 1933- ConLC 59 [port]
Courtenay, Irene Doris 1920- WhoAmW 91
Courtenay, Tom 1937- WorAlBi
Courtenay, William James 1935- WhoAm 90
Courtenaye, Richard Hubert 1923- WhoAm 90
Courter, Amy S. 1961- WhoAmW 91
Courter, Jack E. 1933- St&PR 91
Courter, James A. 1936- St&PR 91
Courter, James A. 1941- WhoAm 90, WhoE 91
Courter, James Andrew 1936- WhoAm 90
Courter, Jeanne Lynn 1953- WhoE 91, WhoEmL 91
Courter, John Edward 1941- IntWWM 90
Courter, Joseph A. 1904- St&PR 91
Courter, William R. 1930- St&PR 91
Courteys, Jean PenDiDA 89
Courteys, Martial PenDiDA 89
Courteys, Pierre 1520?-1586? PenDiDA 89
Courths-Mahler, Hedwig 1867-1950 EncCoWW
Courtice, Rody Kenny WhoAmA 91N
Courtice, Thomas Barr 1943- WhoAm 90
Courtier, S H 1904-1974 TwCCr&M 91
Courtieu, Andre-Louis 1925- WhoWor 91
Courtiss, Eugene Howard 1930- WhoAm 90, WhoE 91
Courtmans-Berchmans, Johanna Desideria 1811-1890 EncCoWW
Courtneidge, Cicely 1893-1980 OxCPMus
Courtney, Barbara Wood 1929- WhoAmA 91
Courtney, Charles Edward 1936- WhoAm 90
Courtney, Clint 1927-1975 Ballpl 90
Courtney, David Richard 1953- WhoEmL 91
Courtney, Dayle WhoWrEP 89
Courtney, Diane Trossello 1951- WhoE 91
Courtney, Donald E. 1930- St&PR 91
Courtney, E 1932- ConAu 129
Courtney, Edward 1932- WhoAm 90
Courtney, Ernie 1875-1920 Ballpl 90
Courtney, Eugene Whitmal 1936- WhoAm 90
Courtney, Gladys 1930- WhoAm 90
Courtney, Henry 1898-1954 Ballpl 90
Courtney, Henry Thomas 1941- WhoSSW 91
Courtney, Howard Perry 1911- WhoAm 90
Courtney, J. E. 1865-1954 FemiCLE
Courtney, James Edmond 1931- St&PR 91, WhoAm 90
Courtney, Jon Earl BiDrAPA 89
Courtney, Keith 1956- BiDrAPA 89
Courtney, Keith Townsend 1949- WhoAmA 91
Courtney, Nicholas 1944- ConAu 32NR
Courtney, Patti Lynn 1957- WhoAmW 91
Courtney, Richard Augustus 1953- WhoEmL 91
Courtney, Robert MajTwCW
Courtney, Rohan Richard 1948- WhoWor 91
Courtney, Rosemary 1961- WhoEmL 91
Courtney, Suzan 1947- WhoAmA 91
Courtney, Suzan Lee 1947- WhoE 91
Courtney, Ward EarBlAP
Courtney, William Francis 1914- WhoAm 90
Courtois, Edmond Jacques 1920- St&PR 91, WhoAm 90
Courtois, Jean PenDiDA 89
Courtois, Martial PenDiDA 89
Courtois, Pierre 1520?-1586? PenDiDA 89
Courtright, Anne Comfort 1926- BiDrAPA 89
Courtright, Robert 1926- WhoAmA 91
Courts, Andrew J BiDrAPA 89
Courts, Barbara Jane 1931- WhoAmW 91, WhoWor 91
Courts, Richard Winn 1896- St&PR 91
Courtsal, Donald Preston 1929- WhoAm 90
Courvoisie, Helen E BiDrAPA 89
Courvoisier, Georges Rene 1946- WhoWor 91
Coury, Ameel Sam 1936- WhoSSW 91
Coury, Beverly Sue 1945- WhoAmW 91
Coury, Bruce E. 1946- St&PR 91
Coury, John, Jr. 1921- WhoAm 90
Couse, Blake Thomas 1928- St&PR 91
Couse, Philip Edward BioIn 16
Cousens, Gabriel K BiDrAPA 89
Couser, William Griffith 1939- WhoAm 90
Cousin, Jean 1490?-1560? IntDcAA 90
Cousin, Jean-Paul 1948- St&PR 91
Cousin, Maribeth Anne 1949- WhoAmW 91
Cousin, Philip R. 1933- WhoAm 90
Cousin, Rebecca Elizabeth 1932- WhoAmW 91
Cousineau, Bonnie Jean 1939- WhoE 91
Cousineau, Pierre 1948- WhoEmL 91
Cousinet, Ambroise-Nicolas PenDiDA 89
Cousinet, Henri-Nicolas PenDiDA 89
Cousinet, Roger 1881-1973 BioIn 16
Cousino, Bernard A. 1902- St&PR 91
Cousino, Gerald A. 1928- St&PR 91
Cousino, Ralph Emmett 1932- St&PR 91
Cousins, Bernice Brigando 1937- WhoAmW 91
Cousins, Deborah Jane BiDrAPA 89
Cousins, George H. 1952- St&PR 91
Cousins, Kenneth Eddleman 1939- WhoAm 90
Cousins, Linda 1946- WhoWrEP 89
Cousins, Margaret 1905- AuBYP 90, WhoAm 90
Cousins, Norman BioIn 16
Cousins, Norman 1915- MajTwCW, WhoAm 90, WhoWrEP 89, WorAlBi
Cousins, Norman 1915-1990 ConAu 33NR, NewYTBS 90
Cousins, Robert John 1941- WhoAm 90
Cousins, Thomas G. 1931- St&PR 91
Cousins, William Edward 1902-1988 BioIn 16
Cousins, William M., Jr. 1924- St&PR 91
Cousland, Charles Patrick 1930- St&PR 91
Couso, Linda Marie 1959- WhoEmL 91
Coussa, F. St&PR 91
Cousteau, Jacques 1910- WorAlBi
Cousteau, Jacques Yves BioIn 16
Cousteau, Jacques-Yves 1910- MajTwCW, WhoAm 90, WhoWor 91
Cousy, Bob 1928- WorAlBi
Cousy, Bob Joseph 1928- WhoAm 90
Coutagne, Denis 1947- WhoWor 91
Coutant, Helen AuBYP 90
Coutant, William R BiDrAPA 89
Coutard, Christian Edmond 1945- WhoWor 91
Coutaud, Lucien 1904-1977 ConDes 90
Coutin, Florence 1922- St&PR 91
Coutin, Ronald Steven 1949- St&PR 91
Couto, C. Douglass 1950- WhoEmL 91
Couto, Robert 1946- St&PR 91
Couts, Cave Johnson 1821-1874 BioIn 16
Couts, Shirley Ashley 1943- WhoWrEP 89
Coutts, Angela Georgina Burdett- 1814-1906 BioIn 16
Coutts, John R. 1936- St&PR 91
Coutts, John Wallace 1923- WhoAm 90
Coutts, Lawrence Robert 1948- WhoEmL 91
Coutu, Joseph Henry 1932- St&PR 91
Couture, Andrea Marie 1943- WhoAmW 91
Couture, Charles E. 1940- St&PR 91
Couture, Jean G. 1924- WhoAm 90
Couture, Jean Guy 1929- WhoAm 90
Couture, Maurice 1926- WhoAm 90
Couture, Robert E. 1921- St&PR 91
Couture, Ronald David 1944- WhoAm 90
Couturier, Marion B WhoAmA 91
Couturier, Marion Beatris WhoE 91
Couturier, Ronald Lee 1949- WhoE 91, WhoEmL 91, WhoSSW 91, WhoWor 91
Couve de Murville, Jacques Maurice 1907- BiDFrPL
Couvreux Family BioIn 16
Couwenberg, Servatius Willem 1926- WhoWor 91
Couzens, James 1872-1936 EncABHB 4 [port]
Couzyn, Jeni 1942- FemiCLE
Couzzo, Michael Ralph, Jr. 1954- WhoSSW 91
Coval-Apel, Naomi Miller WhoAm 90
Covalt, Robert B. St&PR 91
Covalt, Robert Byron 1931- WhoAm 90
CoVan, James Parker 1940- WhoSSW 91
Covarrubias, Leopoldo H 1942- BiDrAPA 89
Covarrubias, Patricia Olivia 1951- WhoAmW 91
Covault, Lloyd R 1928- BiDrAPA 89
Covault, Lloyd R., Jr. 1928- WhoAm 90, WhoWor 91
Cove, Jeffrey A. 1946- St&PR 91
Cove, Laurence A BiDrAPA 89
Cove, Lindsay Suzanne 1940- WhoAmW 91
Cove, Rosemary 1936- WhoAmA 91
Coveleski, Harry 1886-1950 Ballpl 90
Coveleski, Stan 1889-1984 Ballpl 90 [port]
Coveleskie, Stan 1889-1984 Ballpl 90 [port]
Covell, Alan Carter 1952- WhoAmA 91
Covell, Christopher Greene 1947- WhoE 91
Covell, Lyman David 1922- St&PR 91
Covell, Richard B. 1929- St&PR 91
Covell, Roger David 1931- IntWWM 90
Covelli, Joy Allene 1941- WhoAmW 91
Covello, Alfred Vincent 1933- WhoAm 90, WhoE 91
Covello, Philip J. 1954- St&PR 91
Covello, Vincent Thomas 1946- WhoE 91
Coven, Berdeen 1941- WhoAmW 91
Coveney, Richard Marean 1933- St&PR 91
Covenko, Howard Louis 1942- St&PR 91
Coventry, Anne, Countess of 1673-1763 BiDEWW, FemiCLE
Cover, Albert David 1947- WhoEmL 91
Cover, E. McIntosh 1933- WhoAm 90
Cover, Eva Nast Timrud 1946- WhoAmW 91
Cover, Franklin 1928- ConTFT 8 [port]
Cover, Franklin Edward 1928- WhoAm 90
Cover, Fred W. 1952- St&PR 91
Cover, Norman Bernard 1935- WhoSSW 91
Coverdale, Glen E. 1930- St&PR 91
Coverdale, Glen Eugene 1930- WhoAm 90
Coverdale, Shirley Evelyn 1945- WhoEmL 91
Coverdell, Paul D. WhoAm 90
Coveri, Enrico 1952- ConDes 90
Coverman, Franye Jill 1949- WhoAmW 91
Coverston, David Yost 1920- WhoWrEP 89
Coverston, Harry Scott 1953- WhoSSW 91

Covert, Calvin C. 1924- *St&PR 91*
Covert, Charles Betts *BiDrAPA 89*
Covert, Eugene Edzards 1926- *WhoAm 90*
Covert, John 1882-1960 *WhoAmA 91N*
Covert, Kersti V *BiDrAPA 89*
Covert, Michael Henri 1949- *WhoAm 90*
Covert, Robert John 1938- *St&PR 91*
Covert, Roberta Marsha 1950- *WhoAmW 91*
Covert, Thomas C. 1934- *St&PR 91*
Covey, Arthur 1878-1960 *WhoAmA 91N*
Covey, Charles William 1918- *WhoAm 90*
Covey, Cyclone 1922- *WhoAm 90, WhoSSW 91*
Covey, Edward *BioIn 16*
Covey, Elizabeth 1873- *FemiCLE*
Covey, F. Don 1934- *St&PR 91, WhoAm 90, WhoSSW 91*
Covey, Frank Michael, Jr. 1932- *WhoAm 90*
Covey, Harold D. 1930- *St&PR 91*
Covey, Harold Dean 1930- *WhoAm 90*
Covey, Norma Scott 1924- *WhoAmW 91*
Covey, Preston King, Jr. 1942- *WhoE 91*
Covey, Richard O. 1946- *BioIn 16*
Covey, Ronald H. 1932- *St&PR 91*
Covey, Ronald H., Jr. 1956- *St&PR 91*
Covey, Susan Singer 1943- *WhoE 91*
Covey, Victor Charles B 1916- *WhoAmA 91*
Covey, William Roderic 1929- *St&PR 91*
Covey, Wilton Warner *BiDrAPA 89*
Covey-Crump, Rogers *IntWWM 90*
Covi, Dario A 1920- *WhoAmA 91*
Covi, Dario Alessandro 1920- *WhoAm 90*
Covi, Lino 1926- *BiDrAPA 89, WhoE 91*
Covici, Edward Norman 1942- *St&PR 91*
Coviello, Jenny *ODwPR 91*
Coviello, Robert Frank 1941- *WhoE 91*
Covil, James P. 1952- *St&PR 91*
Coville, Andrea *ODwPR 91*
Coville, Bruce 1950- *WhoWrEP 89*
Covin, Theron Michael 1947- *WhoSSW 91*
Covina, Gina 1952- *WhoWrEP 89*
Covington, Alice Lucille 1955- *WhoEmL 91*
Covington, Ann K. 1942- *WhoAmW 91*
Covington, Bathild June 1950- *WhoAmW 91*
Covington, Calvin Blackwell 1955- *WhoEmL 91*
Covington, Charles J. 1914- *WhoWor 91*
Covington, Clarence Allen 1917- *St&PR 91*
Covington, Don Kingsley, Jr. 1920- *St&PR 91*
Covington, Donald Ray 1945- *WhoSSW 91*
Covington, Duncan Seay 1949- *St&PR 91*
Covington, Edward Conner, Jr. 1946- *BiDrAPA 89*
Covington, Frank Lee, Jr. *BiDrAPA 89*
Covington, Gail Lynn 1950- *WhoAmW 91*
Covington, George M. 1935- *St&PR 91*
Covington, George Morse 1942- *WhoAm 90*
Covington, Glen E. *BioIn 16*
Covington, Harold Douglas 1935- *WhoAm 90*
Covington, Harrison Wall 1924- *WhoAmA 91*
Covington, J. Harriss 1920- *St&PR 91*
Covington, James Walter, Jr. 1954- *WhoAm 90*
Covington, John *AuBYP 90*
Covington, John R. 1913- *St&PR 91*
Covington, Loran D. 1929- *St&PR 91*
Covington, Marie E. *ODwPR 91*
Covington, Mary W. 1940- *ODwPR 91*
Covington, Oscar Brandford, Jr. 1932- *St&PR 91*
Covington, Pamela Jean 1956- *WhoAmW 91*
Covington, Patricia Ann 1946- *WhoAmW 91, WhoEmL 91, WhoWor 91*
Covington, Robert Newman 1936- *WhoAm 90*
Covington, Ruth *BiDrAPA 89*
Covington, Saundra Ella *BiDrAPA 89*
Covington, Susan 1949- *WhoE 91*
Covington, Virginia Seay 1915- *St&PR 91*
Covington, Waymon Thomas 1943- *WhoSSW 91*
Covington, Wes 1932- *Ballpl 90*
Covington, William Clyde, Jr. 1932- *WhoAm 90*
Covino, Benjamin Gene 1930- *WhoAm 90*
Covino, Charles P. 1923- *St&PR 91*
Covino, Michael *WhoWrEP 89*
Covino, Michael 1950- *ConAu 132*
Covinsky, Jeffrey Neal 1947- *St&PR 91*
Covitch, Michael Judah 1949- *WhoEmL 91*
Covitz, Carl D. 1939- *WhoAm 90*
Covone, James Michael 1948- *WhoE 91, WhoEmL 91*
Cowan, Abe M 1900- *BiDrAPA 89*
Cowan, Agnes 1839-1893 *DcCanB 12*
Cowan, Aileen Hooper 1926- *WhoAmA 91*
Cowan, Andrew Glenn 1951- *WhoEmL 91*
Cowan, Barton Zalman 1934- *WhoAm 90*
Cowan, Billy 1938- *Ballpl 90*
Cowan, Charles Douglas 1950- *St&PR 91*
Cowan, Charles Gibbs 1928- *St&PR 91, WhoAm 90*
Cowan, David A. 1931- *St&PR 91*
Cowan, Deborah Ann 1955- *WhoEmL 91*
Cowan, Douglas Wayne 1943- *St&PR 91*
Cowan, Dwaine Oliver 1935- *WhoAm 90*
Cowan, Edward 1933- *WhoAm 90*
Cowan, Fairman Chaffee 1915- *WhoAm 90*
Cowan, Frederic Joseph 1945- *WhoAm 90, WhoSSW 91, WhoWor 91*
Cowan, Gary Allan 1937- *BiDrAPA 89*
Cowan, Gary Lawrence 1934- *WhoAm 90*
Cowan, Geni 1955- *WhoAmW 91*
Cowan, George M 1909- *BiDrAPA 89*
Cowan, Gertrude *BioIn 16*
Cowan, Henry Jacob 1919- *WhoWor 91*
Cowan, Homer H., Jr. 1923- *St&PR 91*
Cowan, Irving 1932- *WhoAm 90*
Cowan, J Milton 1907- *WhoAm 90*
Cowan, James Douglas 1920- *WhoAm 90*
Cowan, James Rankin, Jr. *BiDrAPA 89*
Cowan, Jerry Louis 1927- *WhoAm 90*
Cowan, Jerry S 1931- *BiDrAPA 89*
Cowan, Judith 1954- *BiDWomA*
Cowan, Katherine Ann *BiDrAPA 89*
Cowan, Lester *NewYTBS 90*
Cowan, Mark Douglas 1949- *WhoAm 90*
Cowan, Michael Heath 1937- *WhoAm 90*
Cowan, Ned Nathaniel 1939- *BiDrAPA 89*
Cowan, Paul *BioIn 16*
Cowan, R. Guy 1884-1957 *BioIn 16*
Cowan, Ralph Wolfe 1931- *WhoAm 90, WhoAmA 91*
Cowan, Richard B T 1940- *BiDrAPA 89*
Cowan, Richard Wayne 1942- *St&PR 91*
Cowan, Robert Bruce, Jr. 1945- *BiDrAPA 89*
Cowan, Robert Jenkins 1937- *WhoAm 90*
Cowan, Robert Vern 1939- *St&PR 91*
Cowan, Ruth Baldwin 1902- *BioIn 16*
Cowan, Stanley Merle 1916- *St&PR 91*
Cowan, Stuart DuBois 1917- *WhoAm 90*
Cowan, Stuart Marshall 1932- *WhoWor 91*
Cowan, Susan Kaufman 1959- *WhoEmL 91*
Cowan, Ted 1947- *WhoSSW 91*
Cowan, Thomas David 1957- *WhoEmL 91, WhoSSW 91, WhoWor 91*
Cowan, Timothy Scott 1950- *St&PR 91*
Cowan, Wallace Edgar 1924- *St&PR 91, WhoAm 90*
Cowan, Warren *ODwPR 91*
Cowan, Warren J. *WhoAm 90*
Cowan, William Maxwell 1931- *WhoAm 90*
Cowan, Woodson Messick 1886-1977 *WhoAmA 91N*
Coward, Barry 1941- *ConAu 131*
Coward, Carroll L. 1957- *St&PR 91*
Coward, Floyd Allen 1928- *St&PR 91*
Coward, Fred Leon 1938- *St&PR 91*
Coward, Henry 1849-1944 *PenDiMP*
Coward, Noel *BioIn 16*
Coward, Noel 1899-1973 *MajTwCW, OxCPMus, PenDiMP A, WorAlBi*
Coward, Richard Anthony 1949- *IntWWM 90*
Coward, Rosalind *FemiCLE*
Cowardin, Camilla Ann 1931- *BiDrAPA 89*
Cowart, Barry Gene 1963- *WhoSSW 91*
Cowart, Bill Frank 1932- *WhoAm 90*
Cowart, David 1947- *ConAu 30NR*
Cowart, Elgin Courtland, Jr. 1923- *WhoAm 90*
Cowart, Elizabeth *BiDEWW*
Cowart, Jack 1945- *WhoAm 90, WhoE 91*
Cowart, Jess R. 1923- *St&PR 91*
Cowart, Richard Merrill 1951- *WhoEmL 91*
Cowart, Thomas David 1953- *WhoEmL 91, WhoSSW 91, WhoWor 91*
Cowboy Junkies *ConMus 4 [port]*
Cowden, Chester Lyle 1917- *WhoWor 91*
Cowden, David W. 1926- *St&PR 91*
Cowden, John William 1945- *WhoEmL 91*
Cowden, Julianan *WhoAmW 91*
Cowden, Robert Laughlin 1933- *WhoAm 90*
Cowden, William Bruce 1917- *WhoAm 90*
Cowden-Clarke, Mary 1809-1898 *BioIn 16*
Cowderoy, James Anthony 1960- *WhoE 91*
Cowderoy, Peter Sutherland 1918- *IntWWM 90*
Cowdery, Charles Kendrick 1951- *WhoEmL 91*
Cowdery, Jebez Franklin 1835?-1914 *AmLegL*
Cowdery, Joy Rise 1954- *WhoAmW 91*
Cowdery, Mae Virginia 1909-1953 *HarlReB*
Cowdery, Oliver *BioIn 16*
Cowdery, R. Joe 1952- *St&PR 91*
Cowdrey, H E J 1926- *ConAu 129*
Cowdrey, Mary Bartlett 1910-1974 *WhoAmA 91N*
Cowdry, Rex William 1947- *BiDrAPA 89, WhoE 91*
Cowee, John Widmer 1918- *WhoAm 90*
Cowell, Allan Tyler 1950- *WhoEmL 91*
Cowell, Daniel D 1934- *BiDrAPA 89*
Cowell, David Arthur 1938- *WhoE 91*
Cowell, Ensign Jay 1941- *St&PR 91*
Cowell, Frank Richard 1897- *AuBYP 90*
Cowell, Gary R. 1940- *St&PR 91*
Cowell, Henry 1897-1965 *BioIn 16*
Cowell, John Franklin, III 1944- *St&PR 91, WhoAm 90*
Cowell, Marion A., Jr. 1934- *St&PR 91*
Cowell, Marion Aubrey, Jr. 1934- *WhoAm 90*
Cowell, Richard Dudly 1930- *WhoE 91*
Cowell, Sam 1820-1864 *OxCPMus*
Cowen, Bruce D. 1953- *St&PR 91*
Cowen, Daniel C. 1927- *St&PR 91*
Cowen, David Elias 1957- *WhoEmL 91*
Cowen, Donald Eugene 1918- *WhoWor 91*
Cowen, Eugene Sherman 1925- *WhoAm 90*
Cowen, George N. *St&PR 91*
Cowen, Ida 1898- *SmATA 64*
Cowen, Jill Bernice 1943- *WhoE 91*
Cowen, John *BiDrAPA 89*
Cowen, Joseph Robert 1923- *BiDrAPA 89, WhoE 91*
Cowen, Joshua Lionel 1880-1965 *WorAlBi*
Cowen, Michael Bruce 1939- *WhoSSW 91*
Cowen, Philip R. 1942- *St&PR 91*
Cowen, Robert E. 1930- *WhoAm 90*
Cowen, Robert Henry 1915- *WhoAm 90*
Cowen, Robert Nathan 1948- *St&PR 91, WhoAm 90*
Cowen, Roy Chadwell, Jr. 1930- *WhoAm 90*
Cowen, Wilson 1905- *WhoAm 90*
Cowen, Zelman 1919- *WhoWor 91*
Cowens, Al 1951- *Ballpl 90*
Cowens, Dave 1948- *WorAlBi*
Cowens, David William 1948- *WhoAm 90*
Cowgill, F. Brooks 1932- *St&PR 91*
Cowgill, Frank Brooks 1932- *WhoAm 90*
Cowgill, George L. *BioIn 16*
Cowgill, Thomas A. 1840-1906 *AmLegL*
Cowgill, Ursula Moser 1927- *WhoAm 90*
Cowherd, Edwin R. 1921- *St&PR 91*
Cowhig, Michael Thomas 1947- *St&PR 91*
Cowhill, William Joseph 1928- *WhoAm 90*
Cowie, Bruce Edgar 1938- *WhoAm 90*
Cowie, Catherine Christine 1953- *WhoAmW 91, WhoE 91*
Cowie, David M A *BiDrAPA 89*
Cowie, Edward 1943- *IntWWM 90, PenDiMP A*
Cowie, Ivan Alexander 1955- *WhoSSW 91*
Cowie, Lennox Lauchlan 1950- *WhoAm 90*
Cowie, Peter *BioIn 16*
Cowie, Terrence James 1934- *WhoSSW 91*
Cowie, William Henry, Jr. 1931- *St&PR 91*
Cowin, Daniel 1922- *St&PR 91*
Cowin, Eileen 1947- *WhoAmA 91*
Cowin, John Albert 1947- *WhoSSW 91*
Cowin, Lawrence R., Jr. *St&PR 91N*
Cowin, Stephen Corteen 1934- *WhoAm 90, WhoE 91*
Cowing, Walter Lishman 1926- *WhoAm 90*
Cowitz, Bernard *BiDrAPA 89*
Cowl, Gorham A. 1935- *St&PR 91*
Cowl, Jane 1884-1950 *BioIn 16, NotWoAT*
Cowl, John Geoffrey 1942- *BiDrAPA 89*
Cowles, Anne Roosevelt 1855-1931 *BioAmW*
Cowles, Betsey Mix 1810-1876 *BioIn 16*
Cowles, Bruce Kipling 1936- *WhoAm 90*
Cowles, Charles 1941- *WhoAm 90, WhoAmA 91*
Cowles, Chauncey Deming, IV 1946- *WhoEmL 91*
Cowles, Donald Harry 1917-1989 *BioIn 16*
Cowles, Fleur *WhoAm 90, WhoAmA 91*
Cowles, Frederick Oliver 1937- *WhoE 91*
Cowles, Gardner 1861-1946 *BioIn 16*
Cowles, Gardner 1903-1985 *BioIn 16*
Cowles, Harold Andrews, Jr. 1924- *WhoAm 90*
Cowles, Joe Richard 1941- *WhoAm 90*
Cowles, John N. 1914- *St&PR 91*
Cowles, John N. 1950- *St&PR 91*
Cowles, Mary Beth 1942- *BiDrAPA 89*
Cowles, Mary Ellen 1925- *IntWWM 90, WhoSSW 91*
Cowles, Mike 1903-1985 *BioIn 16*
Cowles, Milly 1932- *WhoAm 90, WhoAmW 91*
Cowles, Neill Jacobi, III 1961- *WhoEmL 91*
Cowles, Patrick Michael 1952- *St&PR 91*
Cowles, Robert S. 1937- *St&PR 91*
Cowles, Roger William 1945- *WhoAm 90, WhoE 91, WhoWor 91*
Cowles, Russell 1887-1979 *WhoAmA 91N*
Cowles, Symon *BioIn 16*
Cowles, William H., III *BioIn 16*
Cowles, William Hutchinson, III 1932- *WhoAm 90*
Cowley, Abraham 1618-1667 *BioIn 16*
Cowley, Clifford C. 1928- *St&PR 91*
Cowley, Deborah Suzanne *BiDrAPA 89*
Cowley, Edward P 1925- *WhoAmA 91*
Cowley, Elmer 1939- *St&PR 91*
Cowley, Hannah 1743-1809 *FemiCLE*
Cowley, Hannah Parkhouse 1743-1809 *BioIn 16*
Cowley, Joe 1958- *Ballpl 90*
Cowley, John Maxwell 1923- *WhoAm 90*
Cowley, John Wade 1946- *St&PR 91*
Cowley, Joseph Gilbert 1923- *WhoWrEP 89*
Cowley, Joy 1913- *FemiCLE*
Cowley, Joy 1936- *AuBYP 90*
Cowley, Luis M 1921- *BiDrAPA 89, WhoAm 90*
Cowley, Malcolm 1898-1989 *AnObit 1989, BioIn 16, MajTwCW*
Cowley, Roderick Spencer 1937- *WhoE 91*
Cowley, Samuel P. 1934- *St&PR 91*
Cowley, Samuel Parkinsan 1934- *WhoAm 90*
Cowley, William E. 1909- *St&PR 91*
Cowley, William Eugene 1909- *WhoAm 90*
Cowling, Denny Patrick 1954- *WhoSSW 91*
Cowling, Necie Brown 1961- *WhoSSW 91*
Cowling, William 1925- *WhoAm 90*
Cowlishaw, Mary Lou 1932- *WhoAmW 91*
Cowman, Edward Floyd 1942- *WhoAm 90*
Cowman, Harold Arthur 1931- *St&PR 91*
Cownie, Douglas H *BiDrAPA 89*
Cownie, Douglas H. 1917- *WhoE 91*
Cownie, James Sloan *BioIn 16*
Cownie, John Bowler 1940- *WhoAm 90*
Cowper, Mary 1685-1724 *BiDEWW, FemiCLE*
Cowper, Sarah 1644-1720 *BiDEWW, FemiCLE*
Cowper, Stephen Cambreleng 1938- *WhoAm 90, WhoWor 91*
Cowper, William 1731-1800 *BioIn 16, DcLB 104 [port], WorAlBi*
Cowperthwaite, John James, Sr. 1944- *WhoWor 91*
Cowperthwaite, John Milton, Jr. 1912- *WhoE 91*
Cowser, Danny Lee 1948- *WhoEmL 91*
Cox, Ainslee 1936-1988 *BioIn 16*
Cox, Albert Harrington, Jr. 1932- *WhoAm 90*
Cox, Albert R., Jr. 1946- *St&PR 91*
Cox, Albert Reginald 1928- *WhoAm 90*
Cox, Allan J. *BioIn 16*
Cox, Allan J. 1937- *WhoAm 90*
Cox, Allan Keefer 1948- *WhoSSW 91*
Cox, Allyn 1896-1982 *WhoAmA 91N*
Cox, Alvin Earl 1918- *WhoAm 90*
Cox, Alvin Joseph, Jr. 1907- *WhoAm 90*
Cox, Andrew Brian 1950- *WhoEmL 91*
Cox, Andrew Hood 1917- *WhoAm 90*
Cox, Andrew J. 1941- *St&PR 91*
Cox, Andrew Paul, Jr. 1937- *WhoSSW 91*
Cox, Ann 1644-1716 *BiDEWW*
Cox, Ann Bruger *WhoAmW 91*
Cox, Anna Lee 1931- *WhoAmW 91*
Cox, Anne Louise 1954- *BiDrAPA 89*
Cox, Archibald 1912- *BioIn 16, WhoAm 90, WorAlBi*
Cox, Archibald, Jr. 1940- *WhoAm 90*
Cox, Aris W *BiDrAPA 89*
Cox, Barbara Roose 1951- *WhoAmW 91*
Cox, Barry 1931- *SmATA 62*
Cox, Bert G. 1920- *St&PR 91*
Cox, Betsy 1951- *WhoSSW 91*
Cox, Betty 1938- *ODwPR 91*
Cox, Beverley Lenore 1929- *WhoAmW 91*
Cox, Beverly Elaine 1945- *WhoAmW 91*
Cox, Bill *BioIn 16*
Cox, Billy 1919-1978 *Ballpl 90*
Cox, Bobby 1941- *Ballpl 90, WhoAm 90, WhoSSW 91*
Cox, Brenda Gale 1948- *WhoEmL 91*
Cox, Brent Taylor 1950- *BiDrAPA 89*
Cox, Britton Parks 1957- *WhoEmL 91*
Cox, Bruce Baldwin 1931- *St&PR 91*
Cox, Bruce Keven 1957- *WhoSSW 91*
Cox, C. Christopher 1952- *BioIn 16, WhoAm 90, WhoEmL 91*
Cox, C.R. 1937- *St&PR 91*
Cox, Carol Ann 1950- *WhoAmW 91*
Cox, Carol Grace 1942- *WhoAm 90*
Cox, Carol M. 1942- *St&PR 91*
Cox, Carol Moore 1946- *WhoWrEP 89*
Cox, Carole Ann 1958- *WhoSSW 91*
Cox, Carrie Lee 1956- *WhoEmL 91*
Cox, Casey 1941- *Ballpl 90*
Cox, Cathleen Ruth 1948- *WhoAmW 91*
Cox, Chapman Beecher 1940- *WhoAm 90*
Cox, Charles C. 1945- *WhoAm 90*
Cox, Charles Daniel, III 1946- *St&PR 91*
Cox, Charles Ernest, Jr. 1929- *St&PR 91*
Cox, Charles Robert 1942- *St&PR 91*
Cox, Charles Shipley 1922- *WhoAm 90*

Cox, Christopher William Machell 1899-1982 *DcNaB 1981*
Cox, Clair Edward, II 1933- *WhoAm 90*
Cox, Clarence Ronald 1927- *WhoSSW 91*
Cox, Clark 1943- *WhoSSW 91*
Cox, Clark Burgess 1929- *WhoWor 91*
Cox, Clifton B. 1916- *St&PR 91*
Cox, Courteney *BioIn 16*
Cox, Cynthia Lee 1960- *WhoEmL 91*
Cox, Danny 1959- *Ballpl 90*
Cox, David 1916- *IntWWM 90*
Cox, David 1933- *BioIn 16*
Cox, David Austin 1955- *WhoEmL 91*
Cox, David Brummal 1940- *WhoE 91*
Cox, David Buchtel 1927- *St&PR 91*
Cox, David C. 1937- *St&PR 91*
Cox, David Carson 1937- *WhoAm 90*
Cox, David Eugene 1949- *WhoEmL 91*
Cox, David Jackson 1934- *WhoAm 90*
Cox, David Walter 1951- *WhoEmL 91*
Cox, Dennis Edwin 1948- *WhoSSW 91*
Cox, Desmond 1903-1966 *OxCPMus*
Cox, Donald Clyde 1937- *WhoAm 90, WhoWor 91*
Cox, Donald William 1931- *WhoAm 90*
Cox, Dorothy Deasy 1937- *WhoAmW 91*
Cox, Douglas Lynn 1945- *WhoAm 90*
Cox, E. Morris 1903- *St&PR 91*
Cox, E Morris 1903- *WhoAmA 91*
Cox, Ebbie L. 1927- *St&PR 91*
Cox, Ebbie Lee 1927- *WhoAm 90*
Cox, Eddie R. 1944- *WhoSSW 91*
Cox, Edward Charles 1937- *WhoAm 90*
Cox, Edward William 1809-1879 *EncO&P 3, EncPaPR 91*
Cox, Eileen Frances Hinshaw 1935- *WhoAmW 91*
Cox, Elizabeth *BioIn 16*
Cox, Elizabeth 1942- *ConAu 130*
Cox, Elizabeth B 1952- *BiDrAPA 89*
Cox, Emily *BioIn 16*
Cox, Emmett Ripley 1935- *WhoAm 90, WhoSSW 91*
Cox, Eric Frederick 1932- *WhoE 91*
Cox, Ernest Lee 1937- *WhoAmA 91*
Cox, Ernest S. 1929- *St&PR 91*
Cox, Exum Morris 1903- *WhoAm 90*
Cox, F. Kim 1952- *St&PR 91*
Cox, Fred B. 1934- *St&PR 91*
Cox, Frederick Moreland 1928- *WhoAm 90*
Cox, Gary Forrest 1949- *WhoEmL 91*
Cox, Gary Lee 1950- *WhoSSW 91*
Cox, Gary Robert 1953- *WhoEmL 91*
Cox, Gene Spracher 1921- *WhoAm 90*
Cox, Geoffrey Arnold 1951- *IntWWM 90*
Cox, George *NewYTBS 90*
Cox, George A. 1923- *St&PR 91*
Cox, George Walter 1912- *St&PR 91*
Cox, Gerald Everett 1932- *St&PR 91*
Cox, Geraldine Vang 1944- *WhoAm 90, WhoAmW 91*
Cox, Gerry McMillian 1949- *WhoAmW 91*
Cox, Gilbert Edwin 1917- *WhoAm 90*
Cox, Glenn Andrew 1929- *St&PR 91*
Cox, Glenn Andrew, Jr. 1929- *WhoAm 90, WhoSSW 91*
Cox, Gregg Clayton 1954- *WhoSSW 91*
Cox, Grover Arnold 1933- *WhoE 91*
Cox, Harry Seymour 1923- *WhoAm 90*
Cox, Harvey Gallagher *BioIn 16*
Cox, Harvey Gallagher 1929- *WhoAm 90*
Cox, Headley Morris, Jr. 1916- *WhoAm 90*
Cox, Heinrich Leonard 1935- *WhoWor 91*
Cox, Helen Parks 1949- *WhoEmL 91*
Cox, Helen Ruth 1939- *WhoAmW 91*
Cox, Henry 1935- *WhoAm 90*
Cox, Herbert Bartle 1944- *St&PR 91*
Cox, Hollis Utah 1944- *WhoAm 90*
Cox, Howard Andrew 1958- *WhoSSW 91*
Cox, Howard Ellis 1912-1989 *BioIn 16*
Cox, Howard Ellis, Jr. 1944- *WhoAm 90*
Cox, Howard Wayne 1938- *WhoSSW 91*
Cox, Ida 1896-1967 *BioIn 16, OxCPMus*
Cox, Ivan William Robert 1950- *WhoEmL 91*
Cox, J Halley 1910- *WhoAmA 91N*
Cox, J. Tom 1929- *St&PR 91*
Cox, J. William 1928- *WhoAm 90*
Cox, Jacob Dolson, Jr. 1828-1900 *BiDrUSE 89*
Cox, James *PenDiDA 89*
Cox, James A, Jr. 1920- *BiDrAPA 89*
Cox, James Andrew 1942- *WhoWrEP 89*
Cox, James Carl, Jr. 1919- *WhoWor 91*
Cox, James D. 1943- *WhoAm 90*
Cox, James Darrell 1950- *WhoSSW 91*
Cox, James David 1945- *WhoAm 90*
Cox, James L D 1927- *BiDrAPA 89*
Cox, James M. 1870-1957 *BioIn 16*
Cox, James Melville 1925- *WhoAm 90*
Cox, James O., III 1946- *ODwPR 91*
Cox, James Oliver, III 1946- *WhoAm 90*
Cox, James S. 1946- *St&PR 91*
Cox, James Sidney 1950- *WhoEmL 91*
Cox, James Talley 1921- *WhoAm 90*
Cox, James William 1937- *WhoAm 90*
Cox, Janet *BioIn 16*
Cox, Jean 1922- *IntWWM 90, PenDiMP*
Cox, Jeffery G. 1947- *St&PR 91*
Cox, Jerome Rockhold, Jr. 1925- *WhoAm 90*
Cox, Jerry 1943- *St&PR 91*
Cox, Jerry W. 1954- *ODwPR 91*
Cox, Jessie Lynn 1929- *St&PR 91*
Cox, Joanne Furtek 1947- *WhoEmL 91*
Cox, Joe Bruce 1939- *WhoAm 90*
Cox, Joe Neal 1953- *WhoEmL 91*
Cox, John 1946- *WhoWor 91*
Cox, John Carroll 1933- *St&PR 91*
Cox, John F. 1929- *ODwPR 91*
Cox, John Foreman, III 1963- *WhoEmL 91*
Cox, John Francis 1929- *St&PR 91, WhoAm 90*
Cox, John Fremont 1852-1911 *AmLegL*
Cox, John Henry *PenDiDA 89*
Cox, John Henry 1928- *St&PR 91*
Cox, John M. *BioIn 16*
Cox, John Phillip 1927- *BiDrAPA 89*
Cox, John R. 1944- *St&PR 91*
Cox, John Robertson 1939- *WhoE 91*
Cox, John Thomas, Jr. 1943- *WhoSSW 91*
Cox, John W. 1948- *St&PR 91*
Cox, John William 1950- *WhoAm 90*
Cox, Joseph King 1950- *WhoEmL 91*
Cox, Joseph Lamoin 1932- *WhoAm 90*
Cox, Joseph Mason Andrew 1930- *WhoWrEP 89*
Cox, Joseph Merrells, II 1949- *WhoEmL 91*
Cox, Joseph William 1937- *WhoAm 90*
Cox, Joy Dean 1940- *WhoAmW 91, WhoWor 91*
Cox, Joyce Stegall 1957- *WhoSSW 91*
Cox, Justin Brantlin 1934- *WhoWrEP 89*
Cox, Karen Sue 1953- *WhoAmW 91*
Cox, Kenneth Allen 1916- *WhoAm 90*
Cox, Kenneth K. 1952- *St&PR 91*
Cox, Kermitt L. 1943- *St&PR 91*
Cox, Kevin Keith 1958- *BiDrAPA 89*
Cox, Larry 1947- *Ballpl 90*
Cox, Larry Duane 1955- *WhoEmL 91*
Cox, Laura Joan 1959- *WhoSSW 91*
Cox, Laurence A., Jr. 1939- *St&PR 91*
Cox, Lawrence 1950- *St&PR 91*
Cox, Lawrence Henry 1947- *WhoE 91*
Cox, Lawrence M. *BioIn 16*
Cox, Lee Ann 1956- *WhoAmW 91*
Cox, Lester Lee 1922- *St&PR 91, WhoAm 90*
Cox, Lewis Franklin 1949- *WhoEmL 91, WhoWor 91*
Cox, Linda Blankenship 1952- *WhoAmW 91*
Cox, Lisa Czirjak 1958- *WhoAmW 91*
Cox, Louis Howland Andres 1959- *WhoSSW 91*
Cox, Louise Howland King 1865-1945 *BioIn 16*
Cox, Madison *BioIn 16*
Cox, Marilyn Arlene 1960- *WhoAmW 91*
Cox, Marion Averal *WhoAmA 91*
Cox, Mark Baker 1958- *WhoSSW 91*
Cox, Mark Stanley 1953- *WhoEmL 91*
Cox, Marsden Haigh, III 1950- *WhoEmL 91*
Cox, Marshall 1932- *WhoAm 90*
Cox, Martha Jean 1956- *WhoAmW 91*
Cox, Marvin Dean 1953- *WhoE 91*
Cox, Marvin M., Jr. 1953- *St&PR 91*
Cox, Marvin Melvin, Jr. 1953- *WhoEmL 91*
Cox, Mary E *BiDrAPA 89*
Cox, Mary E. 1937- *WhoAmW 91*
Cox, Mary Lathrop 1930- *WhoE 91*
Cox, Mary Linda 1946- *WhoAmW 91*
Cox, Melvin Monroe 1947- *WhoEmL 91*
Cox, Michael Walter 1942- *St&PR 91*
Cox, Myron Keith 1926- *WhoWor 91*
Cox, Norman Lee 1947- *WhoSSW 91*
Cox, Orrin Blaine, Jr. 1940- *St&PR 91*
Cox, Orville Woodrow 1934- *WhoWor 91*
Cox, Owen Stephenson 1944- *St&PR 91*
Cox, P. Thomas 1930- *WhoWor 91*
Cox, Palmer 1840-1924 *AuBYP 90*
Cox, Pamela L. 1957- *WhoAmW 91*
Cox, Patricia Jan 1943- *WhoSSW 91*
Cox, Philip D. 1923- *St&PR 91*
Cox, Raymond 1954- *St&PR 91*
Cox, Raymond H. 1926- *St&PR 91*
Cox, Raymond Whitten, III 1949- *WhoEmL 91*
Cox, Renee *BioIn 16*
Cox, Richard 1931- *ConAu 30NR*
Cox, Richard Garner 1928- *IntWWM 90*
Cox, Richard Horton 1920- *WhoAm 90*
Cox, Richard Joseph 1929- *WhoAm 90*
Cox, Richard William 1942- *WhoAmA 91*
Cox, Rita Agler 1951- *WhoEmL 91*
Cox, Robert Andrew 1963- *WhoE 91*
Cox, Robert Delayette 1934- *WhoHisp 91*
Cox, Robert Gene 1929- *WhoAm 90, WhoWor 91*
Cox, Robert George 1941- *St&PR 91*
Cox, Robert H. 1940- *St&PR 91*
Cox, Robert Osborne 1917- *WhoSSW 91*
Cox, Robert Sayre, Jr. 1925- *WhoAm 90*
Cox, Rody Powell 1926- *WhoAm 90*
Cox, Roger Frazier 1939- *WhoE 91*
Cox, Roger Stephen 1957- *WhoEmL 91*
Cox, Ron *BioIn 16*
Cox, Ronald Baker 1943- *WhoAm 90*
Cox, Ronald O. 1938- *St&PR 91*
Cox, Sammie Tyree 1943- *WhoAmW 91*
Cox, Samuel Sullivan 1824-1889 *BioIn 16*
Cox, Scott Lee 1951- *WhoSSW 91*
Cox, Stephen 1966- *ConAu 130*
Cox, Stephen M *BiDrAPA 89*
Cox, Steven Allen 1944- *St&PR 91*
Cox, Steven McKay 1952- *WhoEmL 91*
Cox, Taylor Howard 1926- *WhoWor 91*
Cox, Ted 1955- *Ballpl 90*
Cox, Terrence Guy 1956- *WhoE 91, WhoEmL 91, WhoWor 91*
Cox, Terry Allen 1939- *WhoAm 90*
Cox, Thad S. 1936- *WhoSSW 91*
Cox, Thad Scott 1936- *St&PR 91*
Cox, Thelma Banks 1928- *WhoAmW 91*
Cox, Thomas L. 1930- *St&PR 91*
Cox, Thomas P. 1954- *St&PR 91*
Cox, Thomas R. 1951- *St&PR 91*
Cox, Timothy Martin 1948- *WhoWor 91*
Cox, Verne E. 1930- *St&PR 91*
Cox, Vincent Daniel 1932- *St&PR 91*
Cox, Virgil M, Jr. 1931- *BiDrAPA 89*
Cox, Wally 1924-1973 *WorAlBi*
Cox, Walter Maddox 1932- *St&PR 91*
Cox, Walter Thompson, III 1942- *WhoAm 90*
Cox, Warren Jacob 1935- *WhoAm 90*
Cox, Warren M *BiDrAPA 89*
Cox, Warren Murdock, IV 1951- *BiDrAPA 89*
Cox, Whitson William 1921- *WhoAm 90*
Cox, Wilford Donald 1925- *WhoAm 90*
Cox, William Albert, Jr. 1927- *WhoSSW 91*
Cox, William Andrew 1925- *WhoAm 90, WhoSSW 91, WhoWor 91*
Cox, William Arthur 1937- *WhoE 91*
Cox, William Bruce 1951- *WhoSSW 91*
Cox, William Drought *BioIn 16*
Cox, William Edward 1915- *EncO&P 3, EncPaPR 91*
Cox, William Frederick *BiDrAPA 89*
Cox, William H *BiDrAPA 89*
Cox, William Huff 1939- *WhoSSW 91*
Cox, William Jackson 1921- *WhoAm 90*
Cox, William Jay 1947- *WhoEmL 91*
Cox, William K. 1950- *St&PR 91*
Cox, William Martin 1922- *WhoE 91, WhoWor 91*
Cox, William Plummer 1915- *WhoAm 90*
Cox, William R. 1901-1988 *BioIn 16*
Cox, William R 1901-1989 *TwCCr&M 91*
Cox, William R. 1933- *ODwPR 91*
Cox, William Robert 1901- *AuBYP 90*
Cox, William Sebron 1939- *EncO&P 3*
Cox, William Trevor 1928- *MajTwCW, WhoWor 91*
Cox, Willis Franklin 1927- *WhoWrEP 89*
Cox, Winston H. 1941- *St&PR 91, WhoE 91*
Cox-Jones, Carla Lynn *BiDrAPA 89*
Cox-Pursley, Carol Sue 1951- *WhoSSW 91*
Coxe, Daniel 1673-1739 *EncCRAm*
Coxe, Eckley Brinton, IV 1922- *St&PR 91*
Coxe, George Harmon 1901-1984 *TwCCr&M 91*
Coxe, Thomas C., III 1930- *WhoAm 90*
Coxe, Thomas Chatterton, III 1930- *St&PR 91*
Coxen-Glover, Michelle Denise 1957- *WhoE 91*
Coxeter, Harold Scott Macdonald 1907- *WhoAm 90*
Coxeter, John *ODwPR 91*
Coxey, Jacob S. 1854-1951 *WorAlBi*
Coxon, Jonathan *PenDiDA 89*
Coxwell, Melvin Rogers 1929- *St&PR 91*
Coy, Arvel Jean 1951- *WhoEmL 91*
Coy, David Lavar 1951- *WhoWrEP 89*
Coy, Elba Boone 1924- *WhoSSW 91*
Coy, Harold 1902- *AuBYP 90*
Coy, John F. 1944- *ODwPR 91*
Coy, Patricia Ann 1952- *WhoAmW 91*
Coy, Thomas Richard 1948- *WhoE 91*
Coy, Timothy Kirk 1958- *WhoEmL 91*
Coyer, Anthony Joseph, Jr. 1955- *St&PR 91*
Coyer, Max R 1954- *WhoAmA 91*
Coyle, Bernard Hugh, Jr. 1951- *St&PR 91*
Coyle, Brent Richard 1960- *BiDrAPA 89*
Coyle, Carlos Cortez 1871-1962 *MusmAFA*
Coyle, Deborah Anne 1953- *BiDrAPA 89*
Coyle, Deborah Knott 1932- *WhoAmW 91*
Coyle, Dennis P. 1938- *St&PR 91*
Coyle, Donald Walton 1922- *WhoSSW 91*
Coyle, Edward John 1956- *WhoEmL 91*
Coyle, Elizabeth Alling 1959- *WhoE 91*
Coyle, Elliott Rodgers 1909- *St&PR 91*
Coyle, Grady Ellis 1946- *IntWWM 90*
Coyle, Harry *BioIn 16*
Coyle, J J 1928- *ConAu 129*
Coyle, Joseph Thomas, Jr. *BiDrAPA 89*
Coyle, Katherine Gallagher 1947- *WhoAmW 91*
Coyle, Mara Genevieve 1961- *WhoE 91*
Coyle, Marie 1935- *WhoAmW 91*
Coyle, Marie Bridget 1935- *WhoAmW 91*
Coyle, Martin Adolphus 1941- *St&PR 91*
Coyle, Martin Adolphus, Jr. 1941- *WhoAm 90*
Coyle, Mary Lynn *ODwPR 91*
Coyle, Michael Anthony 1946- *St&PR 91*
Coyle, Peter Francis 1951- *St&PR 91*
Coyle, Rhonda May 1957- *WhoEmL 91*
Coyle, Richard Jay 1948- *ODwPR 91*
Coyle, Robert Everett 1930- *WhoAm 90*
Coyle, Terence 1925- *WhoAmA 91*
Coyle, Timothy L. 1953- *WhoAm 90*
Coyle, William 1917- *WhoAm 90*
Coyne, Bob 1898-1976 *Ballpl 90*
Coyne, Carol Ann 1939- *WhoSSW 91*
Coyne, Catherine *BioIn 16*
Coyne, Charles Cole 1948- *WhoE 91*
Coyne, Elizabeth Ann 1962- *WhoAmW 91*
Coyne, Frank H. 1925- *St&PR 91*
Coyne, James K. 1946- *St&PR 91*
Coyne, John Michael 1950- *WhoAmA 91*
Coyne, John Thomas 1927- *St&PR 91*
Coyne, Joseph 1867-1941 *OxCPMus*
Coyne, Joseph Gillick 1934- *WhoAm 90*
Coyne, Karen Ann 1948- *St&PR 91*
Coyne, Lisa Ann 1952- *WhoEmL 91*
Coyne, M. Colleen 1958- *WhoAmW 91*
Coyne, M. Jeanne 1926- *WhoAm 90, WhoAmW 91*
Coyne, Nancy Carol 1949- *WhoAm 90*
Coyne, Nancy M 1940- *BiDrAPA 89*
Coyne, Ruth P Kane *BiDrAPA 89*
Coyne, Thomas Anthony 1957- *WhoWor 91*
Coyne, Thomas Joseph 1933- *WhoAm 90*
Coyne, Thomas R. 1926- *St&PR 91*
Coyne, William Joseph 1936- *WhoAm 90, WhoE 91*
Coyner, C.P. 1942- *St&PR 91*
Coyner, Martin Boyd, Jr. 1928- *WhoAm 90*
Coyner, Randolph Stratton 1944- *WhoSSW 91*
Coyner, Russell R. 1932- *St&PR 91*
Coysevox, Antoine 1640-1720 *IntDcAA 90*
Cozad, James W. 1927- *St&PR 91, WhoAm 90*
Cozad, John Condon 1944- *WhoAm 90*
Cozan, Lee *WhoAm 90*
Cozart, John Roger 1955- *WhoSSW 91*
Cozart, William Hoyt, III 1960- *WhoSSW 91*
Coze-Dabija, Paul 1903-1975 *WhoAmA 91N*
Cozen, Sidney 1924- *St&PR 91*
Cozens, John Robert 1752-1799 *IntDcAA 90*
Cozens, Roger A. 1950- *St&PR 91*
Cozette, Cynthia 1953- *IntWWM 90*
Cozette, Pierre-Francois *PenDiDA 89*
Cozier, Robert V. 1867- *AmLegL*
Cozort, Amber Lynne 1963- *WhoEmL 91*
Cozy, Carl A. 1930- *St&PR 91*
Cozza, Patrick A. 1955- *St&PR 91*
Cozza, Stephen John *BiDrAPA 89*
Cozzarelli, Guidoccio di Giovanni *BioIn 16*
Cozzarelli, Isabelle Mary 1961- *WhoAmW 91*
Cozzarelli, Nicholas R. 1938- *WhoAm 90*
Cozzens, Betty *BioIn 16*
Cozzens, James Gould 1903-1978 *MajTwCW, WorAlBi*
Cozzi, Geminiano 1728-1797 *PenDiDA 89*
Cozzi, Hugo Louis 1934- *BiDrAPA 89, WhoAm 90*
Cozzolino, Dorothy Aramini 1938- *WhoAmW 91, WhoE 91*
Cozzolino, Salvatore James 1924- *St&PR 91, WhoAm 90*
Cprek, Kent Gordon 1953- *WhoE 91, WhoEmL 91*
Craane, Janine *BioIn 16*
Craane, Janine Lee 1961- *WhoHisp 91*
Craane, Valery *BioIn 16*
Crabb, Alfred Leland 1883-1980 *LiHiK*
Crabb, Barbara Brandriff 1939- *WhoAm 90, WhoAmW 91*
Crabb, Kenneth Wayne 1950- *WhoEmL 91*
Crabb, Lawrence J., Jr. 1944- *ConAu 31NR*
Crabbe, Armand 1883-1947 *PenDiMP*
Crabbe, Buster 1908- *WorAlBi*
Crabbe, Edward Luis *BioIn 16*
Crabbe, George 1754-1832 *BioIn 16, DcLB 93 [port]*
Crabbe, Henry Francis 1949- *BiDrAPA 89*
Crabbe, Jean 1927- *WhoWor 91*
Crabbe, John Crozier 1914- *WhoAm 90*
Crabbe, Katharyn W. 1945- *ConAu 130*
Crabbs, Roger Alan 1928- *WhoAm 90*
Crabe, James 1931-1989 *BioIn 16*
Crabill, Robert Louis 1937- *WhoSSW 91*

Crable, James Harbour 1939- WhoAmA 91
Crable, Richard Ellsworth 1947- WhoAm 90
Crabtree, Beverly June 1937- WhoAm 90
Crabtree, Bill Preston 1952- WhoEmL 91
Crabtree, Bruce Ibester, Jr. 1923- St&PR 91
Crabtree, Bruce Isbester, III 1951- WhoEmL 91, WhoSSW 91
Crabtree, Bruce Isbester, Jr. 1923- WhoAm 90
Crabtree, Clovis A 1929- BiDrAPA 89
Crabtree, David H. 1944- St&PR 91
Crabtree, Estel 1903-1967 Ballpl 90
Crabtree, Harold L. 1935- St&PR 91
Crabtree, Jack Turner 1936- WhoAm 90
Crabtree, James Alan 1931- WhoAm 90
Crabtree, James Bruce 1918- WhoE 91
Crabtree, Jean Louise 1958- WhoAmW 91
Crabtree, Joel J. 1938- St&PR 91
Crabtree, John Henry, Jr. 1925- WhoAm 90
Crabtree, John Michael 1949- WhoSSW 91
Crabtree, Joseph Blair 1956- BiDrAPA 89
Crabtree, Judith 1928- SmATA 63 [port]
Crabtree, Larry Alston 1943- St&PR 91
Crabtree, Loren H, Jr. BiDrAPA 89
Crabtree, Lotta 1847-1924 BioAmW, BioIn 16, NotWoAT
Crabtree, Mark Anderson 1959- WhoSSW 91
Crabtree, Richard Alan 1946- St&PR 91
Cracco, Roger Quinlan 1934- WhoAm 90
Crace, Frederick 1779-1859 PenDiDA 89
Crace, John C. 1754-1819 PenDiDA 89
Crace, John Diblee 1838-1917 PenDiDA 89
Crace, John Gregory 1809-1889 PenDiDA 89
Crace, Joseph Brent 1954- WhoWor 91
Crace, Robert Kelly 1960- WhoSSW 91
Craciunescu, Ioana 1950- EncCoWW
Crackel, Theodore Joseph 1938- WhoAm 90
Cracovaner, John Lee 1953- St&PR 91
Cracraft, Bruce Noel 1921- WhoAm 90
Cracraft, Elbridge C. AmLegL
Cracraft, Ivan Wayne 1933- St&PR 91
Craddock, Campbell 1930- WhoAm 90
Craddock, Frank Wootters 1928- St&PR 91
Craddock, Fred B 1928- ConAu 132
Craddock, Frederick G. Foster EncO&P 3
Craddock, J.T. 1963- St&PR 91
Craddock, Mark C. 1949- St&PR 91
Craddock, Melville V. St&PR 91N
Craddock, Peter Trevor 1936- IntWWM 90
Craddock, Stephen James 1951- WhoEmL 91
Craddock, Thomas Wofford 1946- WhoAm 90
Crader, Rebecca Jane 1951- WhoWrEP 89
Cradle, William A. ODwPR 91
Craft, Alice May 1947- WhoEmL 91
Craft, Brigetta Ditomaso 1954- WhoAmW 91
Craft, C. Douglas 1953- WhoEmL 91
Craft, Charles E. ODwPR 91
Craft, David Ralph 1945- WhoAmA 91
Craft, Donald Bruce 1935- WhoE 91
Craft, Douglas D 1924- WhoAmA 91
Craft, Douglas Durwood 1924- WhoAm 90, WhoE 91
Craft, Edmund Coleman 1939- St&PR 91, WhoAm 90
Craft, Ellen BioIn 16
Craft, George Sullivan 1947- WhoEmL 91
Craft, Harold Dumont, Jr. 1938- WhoAm 90
Craft, Harry 1915- Ballpl 90, BioIn 16
Craft, Helle BioIn 16
Craft, Jack Johnson 1930- St&PR 91
Craft, James Pressley, Jr. 1913- WhoSSW 91
Craft, Jerome Walter 1932- WhoSSW 91
Craft, John Richard 1909- WhoAmA 91
Craft, Joyce Pressley 1942- WhoAmW 91
Craft, Marjorie 1945- WhoEmL 91
Craft, Mark E. 1954- ODwPR 91
Craft, Polly Harding 1943- BiDrAPA 89
Craft, Randal Robert, Jr. 1941- WhoAm 90, WhoE 91
Craft, Richard Earl 1947- WhoEmL 91
Craft, Robert BioIn 16
Craft, Robert 1923- IntWWM 90, PenDiMP
Craft, Robert H. 1906- St&PR 91
Craft, Robert Homan 1906- WhoAm 90
Craft, Robert J. 1900-1989 BioIn 16
Craft, Robert Merrill 1958- WhoEmL 91
Craft, Roy B. 1931- St&PR 91
Craft, Ruth AuBYP 90
Craft, Stuart Morrow 1949- WhoSSW 91
Craft, William BioIn 16
Crafton, Andrew Allen 1957- WhoEmL 91
Crafton, Clifford Gene 1943- BiDrAPA 89
Crafton-Masterson, Adrienne 1926- WhoSSW 91, WhoWor 91
Crafts, Clayton Edward 1848-1920 AmLegL
Crafts, John Smith 1927- St&PR 91
Crafts, Mary Elizabeth 1941- WhoAmW 91
Crafts, Richard BioIn 16
Crafts, Robert Glen, Sr. 1943- St&PR 91
Crafts-Lighty, Anita Louise 1954- WhoWor 91
Cragen, John P. 1950- St&PR 91
Crager, Bruce Lee 1952- WhoSSW 91
Crager, Jay Cecil, Jr. 1928- St&PR 91
Crager, Ted J. 1925- IntWWM 90
Cragg, Ernest E. BioIn 16
Cragg, Ernest Elliott 1927- WhoAm 90
Cragg, Laurence Harold 1912- WhoAm 90
Cragg, Richard Thompson 1912- St&PR 91
Craghead, James Douglas 1950- WhoWor 91
Cragoe, Arthur C. 1927- St&PR 91
Crahan, Jack Bertsch 1923- St&PR 91, WhoAm 90
Craib, Kenneth Bryden 1938- WhoAm 90
Craib, Ralph Grant 1925- WhoAm 90
Craig, A. A. AuBYP 90, MajTwCW
Craig, Alan Daniel 1935- WhoE 91
Craig, Alan Gordon BiDrAPA 89
Craig, Albert Morton 1927- WhoAm 90
Craig, Alexander Robert 1941- St&PR 91
Craig, Alisa TwCCr&M 91
Craig, Allen Robbins 1956- BiDrAPA 89
Craig, Andrew Billings, III 1931- St&PR 91, WhoAm 90
Craig, Angela Heitert 1956- WhoSSW 91
Craig, Ben H. 1921- St&PR 91
Craig, Bernard Duffy 1909- WhoAm 90
Craig, Bruce Christopher 1956- WhoE 91
Craig, Bryn 1932- BioIn 16
Craig, Burlon 1914- MusmAFA
Craig, Cairns 1949- ConAu 131
Craig, Carol Lynn BiDrAPA 89
Craig, Charles 1919- IntWWM 90
Craig, Charles 1920- PenDiMP
Craig, Charles Grant 1957- WhoEmL 91
Craig, Charles Raymond 1940- St&PR 91
Craig, Charles Samuel 1943- WhoE 91
Craig, Christine 1943- FemiCLE
Craig, Christopher John 1956- WhoEmL 91
Craig, Curtis Lee 1955- WhoSSW 91
Craig, Daniel H. 1811-1895 BioIn 16
Craig, Darlene Stetson 1939- WhoSSW 91
Craig, David Clarke 1955- WhoEmL 91, WhoSSW 91
Craig, David Jeoffrey 1925- WhoAm 90
Craig, David W. 1925- WhoAm 90
Craig, Donald Leland 1948- WhoSSW 91
Craig, Douglas Broward 1929- WhoE 91
Craig, Douglas Warren 1942- WhoE 91
Craig, E. Wilson 1930- St&PR 91
Craig, Edith 1869-1947 FemiCLE
Craig, Edward Armstrong, III 1934- WhoAm 90
Craig, Edward Gordon 1872-1966 BioIn 16
Craig, Elaine 1958- WhoEmL 91
Craig, Floyd William 1933- St&PR 91
Craig, Gail Heidbreder 1941- WhoAmW 91, WhoWor 91
Craig, George WhoAm 90
Craig, George Brownlee, Jr. 1930- WhoAm 90
Craig, George Dennis 1936- WhoSSW 91
Craig, George R. 1901- St&PR 91
Craig, Glendon Brooks 1933- WhoAm 90
Craig, Gordon Alexander 1913- WhoAm 90
Craig, Gregory Lewis 1961- WhoEmL 91
Craig, Harald Franklin 1930- WhoAm 90
Craig, Harmon 1926- WhoAm 90
Craig, Helen AuBYP 90, BioIn 16
Craig, Holly Lynn 1959- WhoE 91
Craig, Hurshel Eugene 1932- WhoWor 91
Craig, Isa 1831-1903 FemiCLE
Craig, James B BiDrAPA 89
Craig, James Duhadway 1943- WhoWrEP 89
Craig, James Lynn 1933- St&PR 91, WhoAm 90, WhoWor 91
Craig, James Robert 1913- WhoWor 91
Craig, James S. 1925- St&PR 91
Craig, James William 1921- WhoAm 90
Craig, Janice L BiDrAPA 89
Craig, Jean 1937- WhoAm 90, WhoAmW 91
Craig, Jim BioIn 16
Craig, John Eland AuBYP 90
Craig, John G. 1942- St&PR 91
Craig, John Gilbert, Jr. 1933- WhoAm 90, WhoE 91
Craig, John Grant 1942- WhoAm 90
Craig, John Merrill 1913- BiDrAPA 89, WhoE 91
Craig, Johnny 1926- EncACom
Craig, Jonathan 1919-1984 TwCCr&M 91
Craig, Juanita Moose 1941- WhoAmW 91
Craig, Judith 1937- WhoAm 90, WhoAmW 91
Craig, Karen Lynn 1959- WhoAmW 91
Craig, Kenneth Denton 1937- WhoAm 90
Craig, Kyle T. 1947- WhoAm 90
Craig, Larry Edwin 1945- WhoAm 90
Craig, Laura J. 1958- WhoAmW 91
Craig, Lexie Ferrell 1921- WhoAmW 91
Craig, M. Jean AuBYP 90
Craig, Malcolm Everett 1930- WhoAm 90
Craig, Margaret Wilcox 1934- WhoAmW 91
Craig, Martha Ann 1952- WhoAmW 91
Craig, Mary Francis AuBYP 90
Craig, Mary Francis Shura 1923- WhoAm 90, WhoWrEP 89
Craig, Matthew Mark 1932- St&PR 91
Craig, Maureen Wetmore 1962- WhoEmL 91
Craig, Michael Edward 1951- WhoE 91
Craig, Nancy Ellen WhoAm 90
Craig, Peter Stebbins 1928- WhoE 91
Craig, Richard James 1959- WhoE 91
Craig, Robert Charles 1921- WhoAm 90
Craig, Robert George 1923- WhoAm 90
Craig, Robert James 1958- WhoEmL 91
Craig, Robert Mark, III 1948- WhoEmL 91
Craig, Robert Michael 1944- WhoSSW 91
Craig, Robert Sanderson 1932- St&PR 91
Craig, Roger 1931- Ballpl 90
Craig, Roger 1960- BioIn 16, WorAlBi
Craig, Roger Alan 1944- WhoE 91
Craig, Roger Timothy 1960- WhoAm 90
Craig, Stanley Russel, Jr. 1947- St&PR 91
Craig, Stephen John 1954- WhoEmL 91
Craig, Stephen Wright 1932- WhoAm 90
Craig, Stuart N. 1942- WhoAm 90, WhoWor 91
Craig, Susan V 1948- WhoAmA 91
Craig, Thomas Franklin 1943- WhoSSW 91
Craig, Thomas J.H. 1931- BiDrAPA 89
Craig, Thomas John BiDrAPA 89
Craig, Thomas Lee 1937- WhoAm 90
Craig, Wallace BioIn 16
Craig, Wallace Mason, Jr. 1953- WhoSSW 91
Craig, William C. 1939- St&PR 91
Craig, William Francis 1931- St&PR 91
Craig, William Ooley 1931- WhoE 91
Craig, Yvonne 1941- BioIn 16
Craige, Ernest 1918- WhoAm 90
Craighead, David 1924- IntWWM 90
Craighead, Frank Cooper, Jr. 1916- WhoAm 90
Craighead, George P. BioIn 16
Craighead, George Palmer 1929- WhoAm 90
Craighead, John J. 1916- WhoAm 90
Craighead, Rodkey 1916- WhoAm 90
Craighead, Wendel Lee 1936- WhoWor 91
Craighill, Francis Hopkinson, III 1939- WhoAm 90
Craigie, Hugh B BiDrAPA 89
Craigie, Pearl Mary Teresa Richards 1867-1906 BioIn 16
Craigie, Walter Williams St&PR 91N
Craigmile, D. H. 1933- St&PR 91
Craigmile, David F. 1928- St&PR 91
Craigmile, David Francis 1928- WhoAm 90
Craigmile, Thomas Kay 1924- WhoAm 90
Craigo, Gordon Earl 1951- WhoEmL 91
Craik, Charles Scott 1954- WhoEmL 91
Craik, Dinah 1826-1887 FemiCLE
Craik, Dinah Maria Mulock 1826-1887 BioIn 16
Craik, Elizabeth M 1939- ConAu 131
Craik, Eva Lee 1919- WhoAmW 91
Craik, Helen 1750?-1825 FemiCLE
Craik, Peggy Sue 1943- WhoSSW 91
Craik, Philip Lee 1952- WhoSSW 91
Crain, Alan Rau, Jr. 1951- WhoEmL 91
Crain, Bluford Walter, Jr. 1914- WhoAm 90
Crain, C. William 1941- St&PR 91, WhoAm 90
Crain, Charles Anthony 1931- St&PR 91, WhoAm 90
Crain, Chester Ray 1944- WhoE 91
Crain, Cullen Malone 1920- WhoAm 90
Crain, Darrell Clayton, Jr. 1910- WhoE 91
Crain, Gertrude Ramsay WhoAm 90, WhoAmW 91
Crain, Irving J. 1914- WhoE 91
Crain, Irving Jay 1914- BiDrAPA 89
Crain, J. Wendell 1918- St&PR 91
Crain, James Francis 1931- St&PR 91, WhoAm 90
Crain, James T., Jr. 1937- St&PR 91
Crain, James Walter 1949- WhoEmL 91
Crain, Jeanne 1925- WorAlBi
Crain, John Walter 1944- WhoAm 90, WhoSSW 91
Crain, Lacy E. 1910- St&PR 91, WhoSSW 91
Crain, Margie Lynn 1912- St&PR 91
Crain, Nancy L. 1953- WhoAmW 91
Crain, Peter Michael 1944- BiDrAPA 89
Crain, Stanley Wilson 1925- St&PR 91
Crain, Stephen Lee 1948- WhoEmL 91
Crain, William DrBlPA 90
Crain, William Edwin 1929- WhoAm 90
Crain, William Forrest 1953- WhoEmL 91
Crain, William Henry 1917- WhoAm 90, WhoSSW 91
Craine, Thomas Knowlton 1942- WhoAm 90
Crainer, Herchel Americus, III 1955- WhoEmL 91
Crainz, Vittorio 1918- WhoWor 91
Crais, Thomas Floyd, Jr. 1943- WhoWor 91
Crakes, Gary Michael 1953- WhoE 91
Crall, Frank T. 1951- WhoSSW 91
Crall, James Monroe 1914- WhoAm 90
Cram, Donald J. 1919- BioIn 16, WorAlBi
Cram, Donald James 1919- WhoAm 90, WhoWor 91, WhoWrEP 89
Cram, Ira Higgins, Jr. 1929- St&PR 91
Cram, Phillip J. 1943- St&PR 91
Cram, Reginald Maurice 1914- WhoAm 90
Cramb, Milina F. 1918- St&PR 91
Cramblett, Henry Gaylord 1929- WhoAm 90
Cramer, Betty F. 1920- WhoAm 90
Cramer, Conrad Charles 1927- St&PR 91
Cramer, Dale Lewis 1924- WhoAm 90
Cramer, Doc 1905- Ballpl 90 [port]
Cramer, Douglas S. BioIn 16, WhoAmA 91
Cramer, Douglas Schoolfield WhoAm 90
Cramer, Edward Morton 1925- WhoAm 90
Cramer, Eugene Casjen 1935- IntWWM 90
Cramer, Fred 1912-1989 BioIn 16
Cramer, Friedrich Detmar 1923- WhoWor 91
Cramer, George Bennett 1903- WhoSSW 91
Cramer, George H. 1947- WhoSSW 91
Cramer, H. Eugene 1932- St&PR 91
Cramer, Hans Max 1920- WhoWor 91
Cramer, Harold 1927- WhoAm 90
Cramer, Howard Ross 1925- WhoAm 90
Cramer, James P. BioIn 16
Cramer, James Perry 1947- WhoAm 90, WhoE 91
Cramer, Johann Baptist 1771-1858 BioIn 16
Cramer, John Gleason, Jr. 1934- WhoAm 90
Cramer, John Scott 1930- WhoAm 90
Cramer, Jonathan Paul 1955- WhoE 91
Cramer, Joseph B 1914- BiDrAPA 89
Cramer, Kirby L. 1936- St&PR 91
Cramer, Lee H. 1945- St&PR 91, WhoAm 90, WhoE 91
Cramer, Marian H. 1934- WhoWrEP 89
Cramer, Marjorie 1941- WhoAmW 91
Cramer, Mark Clifton 1954- WhoEmL 91
Cramer, Mercade Adonis, Jr. 1932- WhoAm 90
Cramer, Michael William 1924- WhoWor 91
Cramer, Morgan Joseph, Jr. 1906- WhoAm 90
Cramer, Nancy Higgins 1934- WhoSSW 91
Cramer, Owen Carver 1941- WhoAm 90
Cramer, Patrick Roe 1950- WhoEmL 91
Cramer, Peter WhoAmA 91
Cramer, Richard A. WhoAm 90
Cramer, Richard Charles 1932- WhoAm 90, WhoAmA 91
Cramer, Richard F., Jr. 1947- St&PR 91
Cramer, Richard Raymond 1937- St&PR 91, WhoAm 90
Cramer, Robert Eli 1919- WhoAm 90
Cramer, Robert Louis 1931- WhoAm 90
Cramer, Robert Vern 1933- WhoAm 90
Cramer, Roxanne Herrick 1934- WhoAmW 91
Cramer, Stanley Howard 1933- WhoAm 90
Cramer, Teresa Lynn 1964- WhoWrEP 89
Cramer, Walter H. 1928- St&PR 91
Cramer, William Anthony 1938- WhoAm 90
Cramer, William F. 1923- WhoAm 90
Cramer, William Mitchell 1948- WhoEmL 91
Cramer, William Smith 1914- WhoAm 90
Crames, Mark David 1955- WhoE 91
Cramm, D. C. 1925- St&PR 91
Cramond, Elizabeth BiDEWW
Cramond, Elizabeth, Baroness of FemiCLE
Cramond, Richard, Jr. 1945- WhoEmL 91
Cramp, David S. 1935- WhoE 91
Cramp, Donald Arthur 1936- WhoAm 90
Cramp, Donald Arthur, Sr. 1936- WhoWor 91
Cramp, H. St. G. 1912- ConAu 130
Cramp, John Franklin 1923- WhoE 91
Crampton, Alton B. BioIn 16
Crampton, Charles Gregory 1911- WhoAm 90

Crampton, Freda Henrietta Carline 1906- *IntWWM 90*
Crampton, Henry Edward 1875-1956 *DcScB S2*
Crampton, John Philip 1941- *WhoAm 90*
Crampton, Juanita *BioIn 16*
Crampton, Norman J. 1933- *ODwPR 91*
Crampton, Patricia *BioIn 16*
Crampton, Rollin 1886-1970 *WhoAmA 91N*
Crampton, Scott Paul 1913- *WhoAm 90*
Crampton, Stuart Jessup Bigelow 1936- *WhoAm 90*
Crampton, William DeVer 1920- *WhoAm 90*
Cramton, Peter Conant 1957- *WhoE 91*
Cramton, Roger Conant 1929- *WhoAm 90*
Cranach, Lucas 1472-1553 *IntDcAA 90, WorAlBi*
Cranage, Kathleen Lynn 1952- *WhoAmW 91*
Crancer, Lester Allen, Jr. 1932- *St&PR 91*
Crandal, Jack *WhoWrEP 89*
Crandall, Albert Earl 1943- *WhoE 91*
Crandall, Alissa Joy 1954- *WhoEmL 91*
Crandall, Arlene Bernadette 1956- *WhoAmW 91, WhoE 91*
Crandall, Charles Jordan 1958- *WhoWrEP 89*
Crandall, Dale Eugene 1944- *St&PR 91*
Crandall, Del 1930- *Ballpl 90*
Crandall, Derrick Allan 1951- *WhoE 91*
Crandall, Doc 1887-1951 *Ballpl 90*
Crandall, Drew Martin 1955- *WhoEmL 91*
Crandall, Edward David 1938- *WhoAm 90*
Crandall, Ella Phillips 1871-1938 *BioIn 16*
Crandall, Gilbert Albert 1915- *WhoWrEP 89*
Crandall, Grant Fotheringham 1947- *WhoEmL 91*
Crandall, Honie B *BiDrAPA 89*
Crandall, Ira Carlton 1931- *WhoAm 90*
Crandall, James A. 1947- *ODwPR 91*
Crandall, Jerry C 1935- *WhoAmA 91*
Crandall, John K. *St&PR 91*
Crandall, John Karl 1931- *WhoWrEP 89*
Crandall, John Lynn 1927- *St&PR 91, WhoWor 91*
Crandall, Judith Ann 1948- *WhoAmA 91*
Crandall, Lee Walter 1913- *WhoAm 90*
Crandall, Louis van Buren 1958- *WhoE 91*
Crandall, Mark Winthrop *BiDrAPA 89*
Crandall, Mark Winthrop 1948- *WhoE 91*
Crandall, Michael Grain 1940- *WhoAm 90*
Crandall, Nancy Lee 1940- *WhoAmW 91*
Crandall, Nelson David, III 1954- *WhoEmL 91, WhoWor 91*
Crandall, Norma Rand *WhoWrEP 89*
Crandall, Prudence 1803-1889 *BioAmW*
Crandall, Reed 1917-1982 *EncACom*
Crandall, Richard G. 1946- *St&PR 91*
Crandall, Richard L. 1943- *St&PR 91*
Crandall, Riel Stanton 1914- *WhoE 91*
Crandall, Robert G 1928- *BiDrAPA 89*
Crandall, Robert L. *BioIn 16*
Crandall, Robert L. 1935- *NewYTBS 90 [port]*
Crandall, Robert Lloyd 1935- *St&PR 91, WhoAm 90, WhoSSW 91, WhoWor 91*
Crandall, Robert Mason 1928- *St&PR 91*
Crandall, Roderick Pendleton 1948- *WhoEmL 91*
Crandall, Sonia Jane 1952- *WhoAmW 91*
Crandall, Stephen Harry 1920- *WhoAm 90*
Crandall, Suzanne 1934- *WhoAmW 91*
Crandall, Vern Jay 1939- *WhoWor 91*
Crandall, Victoria *BioIn 16, NewYTBS 90*
Crandall, Vine, III 1943- *St&PR 91*
Crandall, Walter Ellis 1916- *WhoAm 90*
Crandell, Allan Edward *BiDrAPA 89*
Crandell, Archie 1900- *BiDrAPA 89*
Crandell, Bradshaw *WhoAmA 91N*
Crandell, Dewitt L *BiDrAPA 89*
Crandell, Dwight Samuel 1943- *WhoAm 90*
Crandell, J. Wayne 1933- *St&PR 91*
Crandell, Kenneth James 1957- *WhoEmL 91, WhoSSW 91, WhoWor 91*
Crandles, George Marshal 1917- *WhoAm 90*
Crandon, John Howland 1912- *WhoAm 90, WhoWor 91*
Crandon, Le Roi Goddard 1873-1939 *EncPaPR 91*
Crandon, Mina S. 1890?-1941 *BioAmW*
Crandon, Mina Stinson 1888-1941 *EncO&P 3*
Crandon, Mina Stinson 1889-1941 *EncPaPR 91*
Crane *WhNaAH*
Crane, Alan 1901- *AuBYP 90*
Crane, Andrew B. 1946- *WhoAm 90*
Crane, Andrew Marion 1946- *St&PR 91*
Crane, Angus Edgar 1955- *WhoEmL 91*
Crane, Barbara Bachmann 1928- *WhoAm 90, WhoAmA 91*
Crane, Barbara Jean 1945- *WhoSSW 91*
Crane, Barbara Joyce 1934- *WhoAm 90, WhoWrEP 89*
Crane, Benjamin Field 1929- *WhoAm 90*
Crane, Bonnie L 1930- *WhoAmA 91*
Crane, Bonnie Loyd 1930- *WhoE 91*
Crane, Burton *WhoWrEP 89*
Crane, C. J. 1946- *St&PR 91*
Crane, C. Lincoln *BioIn 16*
Crane, Cannonball 1862-1896 *Ballpl 90*
Crane, Caroline 1930- *AuBYP 90*
Crane, Charles F. 1949- *St&PR 91*
Crane, Charles R. 1858-1939 *BioIn 16*
Crane, Charlotte 1951- *WhoEmL 91*
Crane, Cheryl *BioIn 16*
Crane, Cora H. 1868-1910 *BioAmW*
Crane, Cora Howarth Stewart Taylor 1868-1910 *BioIn 16*
Crane, Daniel Lionel *BiDrAPA 89*
Crane, David Franklin 1953- *WhoAmA 91*
Crane, David G *BiDrAPA 89*
Crane, David Mark 1948- *WhoE 91*
Crane, Debra Ohnmacht 1956- *WhoAmW 91*
Crane, Diane 1939- *BioIn 16*
Crane, Douglas Allen 1949- *WhoEmL 91*
Crane, Douglas F *BiDrAPA 89*
Crane, Dwight Burdick 1937- *WhoAm 90*
Crane, Edward Harrison, III 1944- *WhoAm 90*
Crane, Edward J. 1928- *St&PR 91*
Crane, Eileen Cunningham 1935- *WhoAmW 91*
Crane, Elana Suezanne 1960- *WhoSSW 91*
Crane, Faye 1947- *WhoEmL 91*
Crane, Fenwick James 1923- *WhoAm 90*
Crane, Florence *AuBYP 90*
Crane, Frances 1896- *TwCCr&M 91*
Crane, Frances Hawkins 1928- *WhoSSW 91*
Crane, Francis George 1916- *St&PR 91*
Crane, Gary Wade 1957- *WhoSSW 91*
Crane, Gerald William 1938- *St&PR 91*
Crane, Glenda Paulette 1946- *WhoAmW 91*
Crane, Gregory *BioIn 16*
Crane, H. Richard *BioIn 16*
Crane, Hart 1899-1932 *BioIn 16, MajTwCW, WorAlBi*
Crane, Hewitt David 1927- *WhoAm 90*
Crane, Horace Richard 1907- *WhoAm 90*
Crane, Howard C. 1937- *ODwPR 91, St&PR 91*
Crane, Irving *AuBYP 90*
Crane, Irving Donald 1913- *WhoAm 90*
Crane, James 1877-1974 *MusmAFA*
Crane, James Gordon 1927- *WhoWor 91*
Crane, Jameson 1926- *St&PR 91, WhoAm 90*
Crane, Jean 1933- *WhoAmA 91*
Crane, Jim 1927- *WhoAmA 91*
Crane, John Bruce 1939- *BiDrAPA 89*
Crane, John William 1940- *WhoE 91*
Crane, Julia Gorham 1925- *WhoAm 90*
Crane, Kent Bruce 1935- *WhoAm 90, WhoWor 91*
Crane, L. Stanley *BioIn 16*
Crane, Laura Jane 1941- *WhoAm 90*
Crane, Lawrence L., Jr. 1938- *WhoAm 90*
Crane, Leo Stanley 1915- *WhoAm 90*
Crane, Lila Goolsby 1951- *WhoEmL 91*
Crane, Louis Arthur 1922- *WhoAm 90*
Crane, Margaret Ann 1940- *WhoAmW 91*
Crane, Marilyn N. 1930- *WhoSSW 91*
Crane, Mark 1930- *WhoAm 90*
Crane, Mary L. 1919- *St&PR 91*
Crane, Michael Patrick 1948- *WhoAm 90, WhoAmA 91*
Crane, Neal D. 1916- *St&PR 91*
Crane, Neal Dahlberg 1916- *WhoAm 90*
Crane, Norman T. 1901 1990 *BioIn 16*
Crane, Patrick F. 1946- *St&PR 91*
Crane, Philip Miller 1930- *WhoAm 90*
Crane, Ray 1923- *St&PR 91*
Crane, Regina Ann 1961- *WhoAmW 91*
Crane, Robert *ConAu 131*
Crane, Robert Carl 1938- *St&PR 91*
Crane, Robert Kendall 1935- *WhoAm 90*
Crane, Robert Q. 1926- *WhoAm 90, WhoE 91*
Crane, Robert Sellers, Jr. 1922- *St&PR 91, WhoAm 90*
Crane, Ronald S 1886-1967 *WorAu 1980*
Crane, Ronald Salmon 1886-1967 *BioIn 16*
Crane, Roy 1901-1977 *EncACom, WhoAmA 91N*
Crane, Sam 1894-1955 *Ballpl 90*
Crane, Stephen 1871-1900 *BioIn 16, ShSCr 7 [port], WorAlBi*
Crane, Stephen Andrew 1945- *St&PR 91, WhoAm 90*
Crane, Stephen Joel 1946- *WhoEmL 91*
Crane, Stuart 1930- *WhoAm 90*
Crane, Terese Ann 1947- *WhoEmL 91*
Crane, Walter 1845-1915 *BioIn 16, PenDiDA 89*
Crane, William C. 1918- *St&PR 91*
Crane, William M. *ODwPR 91*
Crane, Winthrop Murray 1910- *St&PR 91*
Cranefield, Paul Frederic 1925- *WhoAm 90*
Cranendonk, John 1919- *BiDrAPA 89*
Craney, Myrna 1936- *WhoAmW 91*
Cranfield, Kenneth M. 1939- *St&PR 91*
Cranfill, Linda Williamson 1949- *WhoAmW 91*
Cranford, Brett Joel 1964- *WhoSSW 91*
Cranford, Henry Lee 1928- *St&PR 91*
Cranford, J. Wayne 1933- *St&PR 91*
Cranford, James Blease 1950- *WhoSSW 91*
Cranford, James E *BiDrAPA 89*
Cranford, Luke 1939- *St&PR 91*
Cranford, Page DeRonde 1935- *St&PR 91, WhoAm 90*
Cranford, Steven Leon 1951- *WhoEmL 91*
Crang, Richard Francis Earl 1936- *WhoAm 90*
Crangle, Edward C. 1923- *St&PR 91*
Crangle, Robert Dale 1943- *St&PR 91*
Cranin, Marilyn Sunners 1932- *WhoAmW 91, WhoE 91*
Crank, Charles Edward, Jr. 1923- *WhoSSW 91*
Crank, H Harlan 1908- *BiDrAPA 89*
Crank, J. David 1954- *St&PR 91*
Crank, Ruth Elizabeth 1938- *WhoAmW 91*
Crankshaw, Edward 1909-1984 *DcNaB 1981*
Cranmer, Damian 1943- *IntWWM 90*
Cranmer, David Charles 1954- *WhoE 91, WhoEmL 91*
Cranmer, Frank Wilson 1948- *WhoE 91*
Cranmer, James Paul 1938- *St&PR 91*
Cranmer, Philip 1918- *IntWWM 90*
Cranmer, Thomas 1489-1556 *WorAlBi*
Crann, Gordon Parker 1952- *WhoWor 91*
Cranna, Rick Lee 1956- *WhoSSW 91*
Crannell, David J. 1947- *St&PR 91*
Crannell, Richard 1953- *St&PR 91*
Cranois, Nicole Simone 1949- *WhoWor 91*
Cranor, John Marion, III 1946- *WhoAm 90*
Cranshaw, Whitney *BioIn 16*
Cranston, Alan *BioIn 16*
Cranston, Alan 1914- *NewYTBS 90 [port], WhoAm 90, WhoWor 91*
Cranston, Alan M. 1914- *WorAlBi*
Cranston, Caroline Wood 1925- *WhoAmW 91*
Cranston, Henry Young 1789-1864 *AmLegL*
Cranston, Howard Stephen 1937- *WhoWor 91*
Cranston, John 1625-1680 *EncCRAm*
Cranston, John Montgomery 1909- *WhoAm 90*
Cranston, John Welch 1931- *WhoSSW 91*
Cranston, Mary B. 1947- *WhoAmW 91*
Cranston, Maurice 1920- *WhoWor 91*
Cranston, Robert W *BiDrAPA 89*
Cranston, Wilber Charles 1933- *WhoWor 91*
Cranstone, B A L 1918-1989 *ConAu 129*
Cranstone, Bryan 1918-1989 *AnObit 1989*
Cranton, John R *BiDrAPA 89*
Cranton, Nina Renee 1949- *WhoEmL 91*
Crants, D. Robert, Jr. 1944- *St&PR 91*
Crants, Doctor Robert, Jr. 1944- *WhoWor 91*
Crantz, Frank Richard 1948- *WhoSSW 91*
Crapanzano, Kathleen A *BiDrAPA 89*
Crapo, Sheila Anne 1951- *WhoAmW 91*
Crapper, Thomas 1837-1910 *WorAlBi*
Crapsey, Adelaide 1878-1914 *BioAmW, FemiCLE*
Crary, Edward Dallas 1927- *St&PR 91*
Crary, Jonathan Knight *WhoAmA 91*
Crary, Margaret Coleman 1906- *AuBYP 90*
Crary, Mildred Rodgers 1925- *WhoWrEP 89*
Crary, Miner Dunham, Jr. 1920- *WhoAm 90*
Crase, Douglas 1944- *WhoWrEP 89*
Crasemann, Bernd 1922- *WhoAm 90*
Crash 1961- *WhoAmA 91*
Crashawe, Elizabeth *BiDEWW*
Crasilneck, Harold Bernard 1921- *WhoWor 91*
Craske, Leonard *WhoAmA 91N*
Craske, Margaret *BioIn 16, NewYTBS 90*
Crasnaru, Daniela 1950- *EncCoWW*
Crass, David P *BiDrAPA 89*
Crass, David Paul 1948- *WhoSSW 91*
Crass, Franz 1928- *IntWWM 90, PenDiMP*
Crass, James E., IV 1940- *St&PR 91*
Crassaris, Leonidas George 1935- *WhoWor 91*
Crasta, Jovita M *BiDrAPA 89*
Crasto, Justin M. 1947- *St&PR 91*
Craswell, Ellen 1932- *WhoAmW 91*
Cratcha, Daniel Stanley 1956- *WhoEmL 91*
Crate, Stephen Church 1952- *WhoE 91, WhoEmL 91, WhoWor 91*
Craton, Joseph Michael 1946- *WhoEmL 91*
Craton, Roger P. 1932- *St&PR 91*
Cratty, Alfred R. *Ballpl 90*
Cratty, Mabel 1868-1928 *BioAmW*
Cratz, Benjimin Arthur 1888- *WhoAmA 91N*
Craugh, Carolyn 1929- *WhoSSW 91*
Craugh, Joseph P., Jr. 1934- *St&PR 91*
Craugh, Joseph Patrick, Jr. 1934- *WhoE 91*
Craumer, Robert Charles 1926- *St&PR 91*
Craun Brown, Tammy Lee 1963- *WhoAmW 91*
Crausman, Israel L. *BioIn 16*
Cravalho, Ernest George 1939- *WhoAm 90*
Cravath, Gavvy 1881-1963 *Ballpl 90 [port]*
Cravath, Glenn *WhoAmA 91N*
Cravatts, Richard Louis 1949- *WhoEmL 91*
Craven, Carolyn *AuBYP 90*
Craven, Charles *WhNaAH*
Craven, David James 1946- *WhoAmA 91*
Craven, Donald Neil 1924- *WhoAm 90*
Craven, Douglas Gary 1957- *WhoSSW 91*
Craven, Elizabeth Berkeley Craven 1750-1828 *BioIn 16*
Craven, Frank J. 1939- *St&PR 91*
Craven, Gemma 1950- *OxCPMus*
Craven, Homer Henry, Jr. 1925- *WhoWor 91*
Craven, John Pinna 1924- *WhoAm 90*
Craven, John W. 1927- *St&PR 91*
Craven, Keith J. 1935- *St&PR 91*
Craven, Robert H. 1922- *St&PR 91*
Craven, Robin Gray 1948- *WhoSSW 91*
Craven, Roy Curtis, Jr. 1924- *WhoAm 90, WhoAmA 91*
Craven, Thomas 1889-1969 *AuBYP 90*
Craven, Wanda Parrett 1932- *WhoSSW 91*
Craven, Wayne 1930- *WhoAmA 91*
Craven, Wes *BioIn 16*
Craven, Wes 1939- *Au&Arts 6 [port]*
Craven, William Wallace 1935- *St&PR 91*
Cravens, James Hewitt 1919- *WhoAm 90*
Cravens, Margaret *BioIn 16*
Cravens, Nancy Lee 1936- *WhoWor 91*
Cravens, Raymond Lewis 1930- *WhoAm 90*
Cravens, William Lewis 1947- *WhoSSW 91*
Craver, Adelaide Austell 1942- *St&PR 91*
Craver, Carrol Mickey 1924- *St&PR 91*
Craver, Catherine Carlile 1945- *WhoSSW 91*
Craver, James Bernard 1943- *St&PR 91, WhoAm 90*
Cravero, Roberto *BioIn 16*
Cravey, Robin T. 1951- *WhoWrEP 89*
Cravez, Glenn Edward 1957- *WhoEmL 91*
Craviotto, Darlene Susan 1950- *WhoEmL 91*
Craw, Freeman *WhoAm 90*
Crawford, Ann MacCollom 1927- *WhoAmW 91*
Crawford, Anne *BioIn 16*
Crawford, Anne F. *ODwPR 91*
Crawford, Arlene Angela *BiDrAPA 89*
Crawford, Bettye E. 1929- *St&PR 91*
Crawford, Bill 1941- *WhoAmA 91*
Crawford, Broderick 1911-1986 *WorAlBi*
Crawford, Bruce D. 1952- *St&PR 91*
Crawford, Bruce Edgar 1929- *WhoAm 90, WhoE 91*
Crawford, Bruce Mabry 1945- *St&PR 91*
Crawford, Bryce Low, Jr. 1914- *WhoAm 90*
Crawford, Burnett Hayden 1922- *WhoSSW 91, WhoWor 91*
Crawford, Byron *BiDrAPA 89*
Crawford, Caren 1954- *WhoAmW 91*
Crawford, Carl Benson 1923- *WhoAm 90*
Crawford, Carl Wayne 1949- *WhoEmL 91*
Crawford, Carmela Racanelli 1954- *WhoAmW 91*
Crawford, Carol A. 1945- *ODwPR 91*
Crawford, Carole Ann 1942- *WhoSSW 91*
Crawford, Catherine Betty 1910- *WhoAmA 91*
Crawford, Charles 1946- *ODwPR 91*
Crawford, Charles McNeil 1918- *WhoAm 90*
Crawford, Charles Merle 1924- *WhoAm 90*
Crawford, Charlotte Ray 1943- *WhoSSW 91*
Crawford, Cheryl 1902-1986 *BioIn 16, NotWoAT*
Crawford, Christina 1939- *BioIn 16*
Crawford, Christopher Miller 1942- *St&PR 91*
Crawford, Cindy *BioIn 16*
Crawford, Craig *St&PR 91*
Crawford, Curtis J. *BioIn 16*
Crawford, D. Gwyn *BiDrAPA 89*
Crawford, Daniel Eldon 1939- *St&PR 91*
Crawford, Daniel L. 1944- *St&PR 91*
Crawford, David Benn *BiDrAPA 89*
Crawford, David Coleman 1930- *WhoAm 90*

Crawford, David Eugene 1939- *IntWWM 90*
Crawford, David Scott 1956- *BiDrAPA 89*
Crawford, Dawn Constance 1919- *IntWWM 90*
Crawford, Debra Fossett 1959- *WhoAmW 91*
Crawford, Dewey Byers 1941- *WhoAm 90*
Crawford, Diana Jean 1945- *WhoAmW 91*
Crawford, Don D. 1936- *St&PR 91*
Crawford, Dorothy Lamb 1933- *IntWWM 90*
Crawford, Duke Bernard 1950- *WhoSSW 91*
Crawford, E. David 1947- *WhoAm 90*
Crawford, E.H. 1925- *St&PR 91*
Crawford, Earl 1890-1960 *WhoAmA 91N*
Crawford, Earl Boyd 1906- *WhoAm 90, WhoWor 91*
Crawford, Edward Hamon 1925- *WhoAm 90*
Crawford, Elouise S. 1949- *WhoAmW 91*
Crawford, Frances F. 1933- *IntWWM 90*
Crawford, Gary William 1953- *WhoWrEP 89*
Crawford, George Washington 1798-1872 *BiDrUSE 89*
Crawford, Gordon *BioIn 16*
Crawford, Hal Wayne 1940- *BiDrAPA 89*
Crawford, Hank *ConAu 132*
Crawford, Harold Bernard 1934- *WhoAm 90*
Crawford, Hazle Reid 1939- *WhoAm 90*
Crawford, Holly 1961- *WhoE 91*
Crawford, Homer 1916- *WhoE 91, WhoWor 91*
Crawford, Howard A. 1917- *St&PR 91*
Crawford, Howard Allen 1917- *WhoAm 90*
Crawford, Hugh W. 1923- *St&PR 91*
Crawford, Ira S. *St&PR 91*
Crawford, Isabel Alice Hartley 1865-1961 *BioIn 16*
Crawford, Isabella Valancy 1850-1887 *DcLB 92 [port], FemiCLE*
Crawford, James D. 1950- *St&PR 91*
Crawford, James Douglas 1932- *WhoAm 90*
Crawford, James Ellis, III 1945- *WhoEmL 91*
Crawford, James W 1927- *BiDrAPA 89*
Crawford, James Weldon 1927- *WhoAm 90*
Crawford, Jane *WhoE 91*
Crawford, Jean Andre 1941- *WhoAmW 91*
Crawford, Jean Gray 1924- *St&PR 91*
Crawford, Jennifer Lynn 1956- *WhoEmL 91*
Crawford, Jeriann *ODwPR 91*
Crawford, Jerry 1947- *Ballpl 90*
Crawford, Jerry N. 1937- *St&PR 91*
Crawford, Jesse 1895-1962 *OxCPMus*
Crawford, Jim 1950- *Ballpl 90*
Crawford, Joan 1908-1977 *BioAmW, BioIn 16, WorAlBi*
Crawford, Joe Allen 1961- *WhoWrEP 89*
Crawford, John C. 1924- *St&PR 91*
Crawford, John Charlton 1931- *IntWWM 90*
Crawford, John D. 1945- *St&PR 91*
Crawford, John Edward 1924- *WhoAm 90*
Crawford, John F. 1940- *WhoWrEP 89*
Crawford, John Fort 1937- *WhoWor 91*
Crawford, John Franklin, Jr. 1943- *WhoSSW 91*
Crawford, John M., Jr. *BioIn 16*
Crawford, John Milton, Jr. 1939- *WhoSSW 91*
Crawford, John Patrick 1952- *WhoEmL 91*
Crawford, John W 1914- *ConAu 30NR*
Crawford, John William 1930- *WhoAm 90*
Crawford, Jon Gregory 1943- *WhoSSW 91*
Crawford, Jonathan Michael 1965- *WhoE 91*
Crawford, Judith Ann 1952- *WhoAmW 91*
Crawford, Judith L. 1945- *St&PR 91*
Crawford, Karen Taylor *BiDrAPA 89*
Crawford, Keith Edward 1953- *St&PR 91*
Crawford, Kelly Griffith 1951- *WhoEmL 91*
Crawford, Kenneth Charles 1918- *WhoAm 90*
Crawford, Kenneth G. 1902-1983 *BioIn 16*
Crawford, Kevin Scott 1957- *WhoEmL 91*
Crawford, Lewis Cleaver 1925- *WhoAm 90*
Crawford, Lewis O. 1943- *St&PR 91*
Crawford, Linda *St&PR 91*
Crawford, Linda Carole 1944- *WhoAmW 91*
Crawford, Linda Louise 1949- *WhoAmW 91*
Crawford, Linda Sibery 1947- *WhoAmW 91, WhoE 91, WhoEmL 91, WhoWor 91*
Crawford, Linnea Ruth 1952- *WhoAmW 91*
Crawford, Lisa *BioIn 16*
Crawford, Lynn S. 1940- *St&PR 91*
Crawford, Mabel Sharman *FemiCLE*
Crawford, Margaret Anne 1952- *WhoSSW 91*
Crawford, Maria Luisa 1939- *WhoAm 90*
Crawford, Maria Lusia *BioIn 16*
Crawford, Marian Schumacher 1929- *WhoAmW 91*
Crawford, Mark Alan 1956- *WhoEmL 91*
Crawford, Mark Maxwell 1955- *WhoEmL 91*
Crawford, Martelia Theresa 1956- *WhoEmL 91, WhoSSW 91*
Crawford, Mary Anne 1952- *WhoAmW 91*
Crawford, Mary B. 1949- *WhoAmW 91*
Crawford, Mary Louise Perri *WhoAmW 91*
Crawford, Meredith Pullen 1910- *WhoAm 90*
Crawford, Michael *BioIn 16, ConMus 4 [port]*
Crawford, Michael 1942- *OxCPMus*
Crawford, Michael Solomon 1950- *WhoE 91*
Crawford, Michael Thomas 1946- *St&PR 91*
Crawford, Morris DeCamp, Jr. 1915- *WhoAm 90*
Crawford, Muriel Laura *WhoAm 90, WhoAmW 91*
Crawford, Norma Vivian 1936- *WhoAmW 91*
Crawford, Norman Crane, Jr. 1930- *WhoAm 90*
Crawford, Oliver Ray 1925- *WhoSSW 91*
Crawford, Pamela E. 1950- *WhoAmW 91*
Crawford, Peter Baker 1939- *St&PR 91*
Crawford, Purdy *WhoAm 90*
Crawford, Ralston 1906-1977 *WhoAmA 91N*
Crawford, Randy Charles 1952- *St&PR 91*
Crawford, Raymond Maxwell, Jr. 1933- *WhoAm 90*
Crawford, Richard 1935- *WhoAm 90*
Crawford, Richard A. 1930- *St&PR 91*
Crawford, Richard Bradway 1933- *WhoAm 90*
Crawford, Richard Eben, Jr. 1930- *WhoWor 91*
Crawford, Richard G. 1926- *St&PR 91*
Crawford, Richard Jay 1947- *WhoE 91*
Crawford, Robert *TwCCr&M 91*
Crawford, Robert B. 1926-1987 *BioIn 16*
Crawford, Robert Clement 1929- *WhoE 91*
Crawford, Robert George 1943- *WhoAm 90*
Crawford, Robert S. 1914- *St&PR 91*
Crawford, Roger Brentley 1951- *WhoWor 91*
Crawford, Ronald Lyle 1947- *WhoWor 91*
Crawford, Roy Edgington, III 1938- *WhoAm 90*
Crawford, Ruth 1901-1953 *BioIn 16*
Crawford, Sally Sue 1944- *WhoAmW 91*
Crawford, Sam 1880-1968 *Ballpl 90 [port]*
Crawford, Sarah Carter 1938- *WhoAmW 91*
Crawford, Shag 1921- *Ballpl 90*
Crawford, Sheila Simmons 1948- *WhoAmW 91*
Crawford, Stanley Edward 1932- *St&PR 91, WhoSSW 91*
Crawford, Stanley Luke *BiDrAPA 89*
Crawford, Steve 1958- *Ballpl 90*
Crawford, Susan Jean 1947- *WhoAm 90, WhoAmW 91*
Crawford, Susan N. Young *WhoAm 90*
Crawford, T.E. 1940- *St&PR 91*
Crawford, Terrence Michael 1945- *ConAu 129*
Crawford, Terry *ConAu 129*
Crawford, Thelmar Wyche 1905- *AuBYP 90*
Crawford, Thom Cooney 1944- *WhoAmA 91*
Crawford, Thomas Henry 1931- *WhoSSW 91*
Crawford, Thomas Joey 1955- *St&PR 91*
Crawford, Thomas Raymond 1954- *WhoEmL 91*
Crawford, Timothy Terry 1948- *IntWWM 90*
Crawford, W. J. 188-?-1920 *EncO&P 3*
Crawford, William Avery 1915- *WhoE 91*
Crawford, William Basil, Jr. 1941- *WhoAm 90*
Crawford, William C. 1930- *St&PR 91*
Crawford, William David 1947- *WhoE 91*
Crawford, William F. 1911- *WhoAm 90*
Crawford, William H 1913- *WhoAmA 91N*
Crawford, William Harris 1772-1834 *BiDrUSE 89, BioIn 16*
Crawford, William Howard, Jr. 1937- *WhoAm 90*
Crawford, William Jackson 1881-1920 *EncPaPR 91*
Crawford, William Randall 1899-1989 *BioIn 16*
Crawford, William Rex, Jr. 1928- *WhoAm 90*
Crawford, William Richard 1936- *WhoAm 90*
Crawford, William W. 1928- *St&PR 91*
Crawford, Willie 1946- *Ballpl 90*
Crawford-Compton, William 1915-1988 *AnObit 1988*
Crawford-Kummer, Sondra 1950- *WhoAmW 91*
Crawford-Mason, Clare Wootten 1936- *WhoAm 90*
Crawley, A. Bruce 1946- *ODwPR 91*
Crawley, Clifford 1929- *IntWWM 90*
Crawley, Edward Francis 1954- *WhoE 91*
Crawley, Jacqueline Nina 1950- *WhoAmW 91*
Crawley, James B. 1926- *St&PR 91*
Crawley, Jane Carolyn 1950- *WhoEmL 91*
Crawley, John Boevey 1946- *WhoAm 90, WhoE 91*
Crawley, Judith Rosemary 1914- *WhoWrEP 89*
Crawley, Leonard George 1903-1981 *DcNaB 1981*
Crawley, Philip 1944- *WhoWor 91*
Crawley, Robert Allen 1950- *WhoSSW 91*
Crawley, Robert Evans 1937- *St&PR 91*
Crawley, Thomas Michael 1963- *WhoEmL 91*
Crawley, Tony 1938- *ConAu 129*
Crawshaw, Alwyn 1934- *WhoWor 91*
Crawshaw, Ralph 1921- *WhoAm 90*
Crawshaw, Ralph S 1921- *BiDrAPA 89*
Craxi, Bettino *BioIn 16*
Craxi, Bettino 1934- *WhoWor 91, WorAlBi*
Cray, Cloud Lanor, Jr. 1922- *St&PR 91, WhoAm 90, WhoWor 91*
Cray, Richard B. 1927- *St&PR 91*
Cray, Robert *BioIn 16*
Cray, Robert 1953- *WhoAm 90*
Cray, Seymour R. 1925- *WhoAm 90*
Craycraft, Carl LeRoy 1935- *WhoE 91, WhoWor 91*
Craycroft, John E. 1950- *St&PR 91*
Craycroft, Joseph L., Jr. 1937- *St&PR 91*
Crayder, Dorothy 1906- *AuBYP 90*
Crayder, Teresa *AuBYP 90*
Crayencour, Marguerite de *BioIn 16, EncCoWW*
Crayford, Helen Elizabeth 1953- *IntWWM 90*
Crayne, Richard S *BiDrAPA 89*
Craypo, Charles 1936- *WhoAm 90*
Crayton, John Wendell 1939- *BiDrAPA 89*
Crayton, Render 1933- *St&PR 91*
Craz, Albert G. 1926- *AuBYP 90*
Craze, Steven Lee 1950- *WhoEmL 91, WhoSSW 91*
Crazy Gang, The *OxCPMus*
Crazy Horse *EncPR&S 89*
Crazy Horse 1842?-1877 *WhNaAH*
Crazy Horse 1845?-1877 *WorAlBi*
Crazy Snake *WhNaAH*
Crbanek, Karel *WhoWor 91*
Crea, Enzo Francesco Saverio 1927- *WhoWor 91*
Crea, Samatha *WhoWrEP 89*
Creadick, Wayne Samuel, Jr. 1962- *WhoE 91*
Creagan, Clarence Wayne 1929- *St&PR 91*
Creagan, David John 1954- *WhoAm 90*
Creagan, Robert Joseph 1919- *WhoAm 90*
Creager, Clifford Raymond 1937- *WhoWor 91*
Creager, Cynthia Ruth 1947- *WhoAm 90*
Creager, Joan Guynn 1932- *WhoAmW 91*
Creager, Joe Scott 1929- *WhoAm 90*
Creager, Maureen 1931- *WhoWrEP 89*
Creagh, Richard P. 1946- *St&PR 91*
Cream *OxCPMus*
Cream, The *EncPR&S 89*
Creamer, Andrew G. 1929- *St&PR 91*
Creamer, Claude Wendell 1936- *St&PR 91*
Creamer, David E. 1947- *St&PR 91*
Creamer, Dustin Walter *St&PR 91*
Creamer, Henry *EarBlAP*
Creamer, Henry 1879-1930 *OxCPMus*
Creamer, Jack Major 1954- *WhoEmL 91*
Creamer, James J. 1928- *St&PR 91*
Creamer, John Edward 1953- *WhoWor 91*
Creamer, Joseph M. *BioIn 16*
Creamer, Linda Edith 1954- *WhoAmW 91*
Creamer, Robert 1922- *Ballpl 90*
Creamer, Robert 1958- *St&PR 91*
Creamer, Robert Watts 1922- *WhoE 91*
Creamer, Thomas F. 1917- *St&PR 91*
Creamer, William Henry, III 1927- *St&PR 91, WhoAm 90*
Crean, John C. 1925- *St&PR 91, WhoAm 90*
Crean, John Gale 1910- *St&PR 91, WhoAm 90*
Creany, Cathleen Annette 1950- *WhoAm 90*
Creasey, David E. 1944- *WhoE 91*
Creasey, David Edward *BiDrAPA 89*
Creasey, John 1908-1973 *MajTwCW, SpyFic, TwCCr&M 91, WorAlBi*
Creasman, William Paul 1952- *St&PR 91, WhoEmL 91*
Creasman, William Thomas 1934- *WhoAm 90*
Creason, Gary Wayne 1948- *WhoEmL 91*
Creason, John Paul 1942- *WhoAm 90*
Creason, Kenneth Claude 1940- *St&PR 91*
Creath, Charlie 1890-1951 *BioIn 16*
Creath, Donald Blades 1931- *WhoE 91*
Creaturo, Barbara 1943- *ConAu 129*
Creaturo, Barbara 1943-1990 *ConAu 132*
Creaven, Patrick Joseph 1933- *WhoAm 90*
Crecine, John Patrick 1939- *WhoAm 90, WhoSSW 91, WhoWor 91*
Crede, Brian H. 1952- *WhoE 91*
Crede, Robert Henry 1915- *WhoAm 90*
Credidio, Louis A. *BioIn 16*
Credit, Samuel L. 1940- *St&PR 91*
Credle, Constance Clover 1934- *WhoAmW 91*
Credle, Ellis 1902- *AuBYP 90*
Credo *MajTwCW*
Credo, Alvaro J. de *ConAu 131, HispWr 90*
Cree, Birdie 1882-1942 *Ballpl 90*
Creech, Franklin Underwood 1941- *WhoAmA 91*
Creech, Fulton Hunter 1929- *WhoAm 90*
Creech, Hugh John 1910- *WhoAm 90*
Creech, Jay Heyward 1956- *WhoEmL 91*
Creech, John Lewis 1920- *WhoAm 90*
Creech, Wilbur Lyman 1927- *WhoAm 90*
Creecy, Herbert Lee 1939- *WhoAmA 91*
Creed, Edmond M. 1921- *St&PR 91*
Creed, James Bennett, Jr. 1946- *BiDrAPA 89*
Creed, Kay 1940- *IntWWM 90*
Creed, Nellie Anne 1955- *WhoWrEP 89*
Creed, Robert Payson, Sr. 1925- *WhoAm 90*
Creed, Thomas G. 1933- *WhoSSW 91*
Creed, Thomas Gary 1933- *St&PR 91*
Creed, Thomas Wayne 1943- *WhoSSW 91*
Creedence Clearwater Revival *EncPR&S 89, OxCPMus*
Creedon, John J. 1924- *St&PR 91, WhoAm 90, WhoE 91, WhoWor 91*
Creedon, Seamus 1952- *WhoWor 91*
Creedon, Timothy *WhoAm 90*
Creedon, Timothy 1928- *St&PR 91*
Creedon, William Henry 1938- *St&PR 91*
Creegan, Robert Francis 1915- *WhoAm 90*
Creeger, Allan D. 1921- *St&PR 91*
Creeger, Lawrence Allan 1947- *St&PR 91*
Creekmore, Marion Virgil, Jr. 1939- *WhoAm 90, WhoWor 91*
Creekmore, William Brown 1959- *WhoSSW 91*
Creel, Austin Bowman 1929- *WhoAm 90*
Creel, David Russel 1949- *WhoEmL 91*
Creel, Diane C. 1948- *St&PR 91*
Creel, Frank L *BiDrAPA 89*
Creel, Frank Warner 1941- *WhoE 91*
Creel, George 1876-1956 *BioIn 16*
Creel, Joe 1912- *WhoWor 91*
Creel, Keith 1959- *Ballpl 90*
Creel, Luther Edward, III 1937- *WhoAm 90*
Creel, Michael Allen 1953- *WhoEmL 91*
Creel, Roger Ellis 1933- *St&PR 91*
Creeley, Robert 1926- *BioIn 16, MajTwCW*
Creeley, Robert White 1926- *WhoAm 90, WhoWrEP 89*
Creelman, James 1859-1915 *BioIn 16*
Creelman, Samuel 1808-1891 *DcCanB 12*
Creelman, Wayne Lewis 1951- *BiDrAPA 89, WhoE 91*
Creer, Carl R. 1942- *St&PR 91*
Creer, Philip Douglas 1903- *WhoAm 90*
Creery Sisters *EncPaPR 91*
Creery, Alice *EncPaPR 91*
Creery, Emily *EncPaPR 91*
Creery, Kathleen *EncPaPR 91*
Creery, Mary *EncPaPR 91*
Creery, Maud *EncPaPR 91*
Creese, Elwin H. 1931- *St&PR 91*
Creese, Walter Littlefield 1919- *WhoAm 90, WhoAmA 91*
Creevey, Lucy Ellsworth 1940- *WhoE 91*
Creevy, Bill 1942- *WhoAmA 91, WhoE 91*
Creevy, Donald Charles 1936- *WhoAm 90*
Creffeld, Rosanna 1945- *IntWWM 90*
Cregan, Jerry *BioIn 16*
Cregan, John Barry 1930- *St&PR 91*
Cregan, John P. 1937- *St&PR 91*
Creger, Carolyn Sue 1939- *WhoAmW 91*
Cregger, Morris M. 1939- *St&PR 91*
Cregier, Don M 1930- *WhoWrEP 89*
Cregier, Don Mesick 1930- *WhoE 91*
Crehan, Joseph Edward 1938- *WhoAm 90, WhoWor 91*
Crehan, Michael Joseph 1954- *St&PR 91*
Crehore, John Davenport 1891- *EncO&P 3*
Creigh, Thomas, Jr. 1912- *St&PR 91, WhoAm 90*
Creighton, Alex E. *St&PR 91N*
Creighton, Basil *BioIn 16*

Creighton, Dale Edward 1934- St&PR 91, WhoAm 90
Creighton, David O' Neil 1938- St&PR 91
Creighton, Edward 1932- St&PR 91
Creighton, Harriet Baldwin 1909- WhoAmW 91
Creighton, Helen 1899-1989 ConAu 130, SmATA 64
Creighton, James 1841-1862 Ballpl 90
Creighton, John Douglas 1928- WhoAm 90
Creighton, John W., Jr. 1932- St&PR 91, WhoAm 90
Creighton, Joseph R. 1920- St&PR 91
Creighton, Letitia 1827-1896 DcCanB 12
Creley, Jack 1926- OxCCanT
Crelin, Edmund Slocum 1923- WhoAm 90
Crelly, William Richard 1924- WhoAmA 91
Cremazie, Octave 1827-1879 DcLB 99 [port]
Creme, Benjamin 1922- EncO&P 3, NewAgE 90
Cremer, Jack Edward 1956- WhoSSW 91
Cremer, Lawrence Edward 1941- WhoAm 90
Cremer, Leon Earl 1945- WhoE 91, WhoWor 91
Cremer, Lothar 1905- BioIn 16
Cremer, Mabelle A. 1927- WhoAmW 91
Cremer, W. PenDiDA 89
Cremers, Clifford John 1933- WhoAm 90
Cremin, Lawrence A. NewYTBS 90 [port]
Cremin, Lawrence A 1925-1990 ConAu 132
Cremin, Lawrence Arthur 1925- WhoAm 90, WhoE 91
Cremin, Susan E. 1947- WhoAmW 91
Cremins, Bobby BioIn 16
Cremins, James Joseph 1946- WhoE 91
Cremins, William Carroll 1957- WhoSSW 91
Cremisi, Julius S. 1931- St&PR 91
Cremona, Girolamo da BioIn 16
Cremona, Luigi 1945- WhoWor 91
Cremona, Vincent Anthony 1925- WhoAm 90
Cremony, John C. 1815-1879 WhNaAH
Crenna, Charles David 1944- WhoWrEP 89
Crenna, James Alan 1950- St&PR 91, WhoEmL 91
Crenna, Karen Kathleen 1959- WhoAmW 91
Crenna, Richard 1926- WorAlBi
Crenna, Richard 1927- WhoAm 90
Crenne, Helisenne de EncCoWW
Crenner, James Joseph 1922- WhoAm 90
Crenshaw, Albert Burford 1942- WhoAm 90
Crenshaw, Ben BioIn 16
Crenshaw, Ben 1952- WhoAm 90
Crenshaw, Carlton Boyd 1945- St&PR 91
Crenshaw, Claudia Regan 1951- WhoAmW 91
Crenshaw, Dorothy W. 1955- ODwPR 91
Crenshaw, Elizabeth Wells 1948- WhoSSW 91
Crenshaw, Francis Nelson 1922- WhoAm 90
Crenshaw, Gordon L. 1922- St&PR 91
Crenshaw, Gordon Lee 1922- WhoAm 90, WhoSSW 91
Crenshaw, Jan Carol 1945- WhoSSW 91
Crenshaw, Karen Bruce 1952- WhoAmA 91
Crenshaw, Kevin Mills 1960- WhoEmL 91
Crenshaw, Kristina 1943- WhoSSW 91
Crenshaw, Marion Carlyle, Jr. 1931- WhoAm 90
Crenshaw, Marshall 1954?- ConMus 5 [port]
Crenshaw, Marva Louise 1951- WhoAmW 91
Crenshaw, Patricia Shryack 1941- WhoAmW 91
Crenshaw, Roger Timothy 1943- BiDrAPA 89
Crenshaw, Theresa L 1942- BiDrAPA 89
Crenshaw, Thomas Bedford, Jr. 1926- St&PR 91
Crenshaw, Walter Henry 1817-1878 AmLegL
Crenson, Matthew Allen 1943- WhoAm 90
Crenwelge, Dayton R. 1937- St&PR 91
Creo, Matthew J., Jr. 1929- St&PR 91
Creo, Robert Angelo 1952- WhoEmL 91
Crepeau, Michel Edouard Jean 1930- BiDFrPL
Crepeau, Richard Charles 1941- WhoSSW 91
Crepet, William Louis 1946- WhoAm 90
Creppel, Claire Binet 1936- WhoAmW 91
Creps, Gerald A 1939- WhoAmA 91
Creps, James R 1929- BiDrAPA 89
Creps, Philp Lloyd 1951- WhoWor 91
Creque, Halimena Montelaire BiDrAPA 89
Crerand, Mary J. 1933- St&PR 91
Crernejewski, Larry Craig 1949- St&PR 91
Cresap, Theda Beatty 1943- WhoAmW 91
Crescas, Robert Michael 1952- WhoE 91
Crescentii WomWR
Crescenzo, Peter Joseph 1923- St&PR 91
Cresci, Joseph V, Jr. BiDrAPA 89
Creslein, William Edward, III 1930- WhoSSW 91
Creson, Daniel L BiDrAPA 89
Creson, Lenore Sapinsley 1940- St&PR 91
Crespel, Etienne 1935- WhoWor 91
Crespi, Creepy 1918- Ballpl 90
Crespi, Giuseppe Maria 1665-1747 IntDcAA 90
Crespi, Irving 1926- WhoAm 90
Crespi, Michael Albert 1946- WhoEmL 91
Crespi, Pachita 1900- AuBYP 90
Crespi, Pachita 1900-1971 WhoAmA 91N
Crespin, George Ernest 1936- WhoHisp 91
Crespin, Leslie A 1947- WhoAmA 91
Crespin, Paul 1694-1770 PenDiDA 89
Crespin, Regine WhoAm 90, WhoAmW 91
Crespin, Regine 1927- IntWWM 90, PenDiMP
Crespo, Alice BioIn 16
Crespo, Cynthia Ann 1952- St&PR 91
Crespo, Hilda Linda 1949- WhoE 91
Crespo, Joaquin 1845-1898 BioIn 16
Crespo, Luis 1952- WhoWor 91
Crespo, Michael Lowe 1947- WhoAmA 91, WhoSSW 91
Crespo Casares, Alfredo Eduardo 1927- WhoWor 91
Cress, Charles H 1920- BiDrAPA 89
Cress, Floyd Cyril 1920- WhoWrEP 89
Cress, George Ayers 1921- WhoAm 90, WhoAmA 91
Cress, George H. 1936- St&PR 91
Cress, Sally 1954- St&PR 91
Cresse, Richard Staunton 1928- St&PR 91
Cressent, Charles 1685-1768 PenDiDA 89
Cressey, Donald Ray 1919-1987 BioIn 16
Cressey, Verne E 1921- BiDrAPA 89
Cressler, David Morgan 1953- St&PR 91
Cressler, John Charles 1915- WhoE 91
Cressman, Edward Howard 1945- St&PR 91
Cressman, Luther Sheeleigh 1897- BioIn 16
Cressman, Ralph Dwight 1909- WhoAm 90
Cresson, Edith 1934- BiDFrPL
Cresson, Jacques-Louis 1743-1795 PenDiDA 89
Cresson, Jean-Baptiste PenDiDA 89
Cresson, Louis 1706-1761 PenDiDA 89
Cresson, Louis, II PenDiDA 89
Cresson, Margaret 1889-1973 WhoAmA 91N
Cresson, Michel 1709-1773? PenDiDA 89
Cresswell, Lady BiDEWW
Cresswell, George F 1948- BiDrAPA 89
Cresswell, Helen 1934- AuBYP 90, BioIn 16
Cresswell, Lyell Richard 1944- IntWWM 90
Cresswell, Ronald M. 1934- St&PR 91
Cresswell, Ronald Morton 1934- WhoAm 90
Cressy, David 1946- ConAu 130
Cresti, Mauro 1945- WhoWor 91
Creston, Paul 1906-1985 PenDiMP A
Creswell, Dorothy Anne 1943- WhoAmW 91, WhoWor 91
Creswell, John Angel James 1828-1891 BiDrUSE 89
Cretan, Gladys 1921- AuBYP 90
Cretara, Domenic Anthony 1946- WhoAmA 91
Creteau, Raymond Joseph 1927- St&PR 91
Cretekos, Constantine J 1933- BiDrAPA 89
Cretella, Henry Emile BiDrAPA 89
Cretin, Shan 1946- WhoAmW 91
Cretser, Gary Allen 1942- WhoAm 90
Crette, Louis PenDiDA 89
Cretzianu, Miza 1905-1978 EncCoWW
Cretzmeyer, Stacy Megan 1959- WhoWrEP 89
Creutz, Edward Chester 1913- WhoAm 90
Creutz, Gustaf Philip 1731-1785 DcScanL
Creuzot, Percy 1924- St&PR 91
Crevecoeur, J. Hector St. John de 1735-1813 BioIn 16
Crevecoeur, Michel-Guillaume Jean De 1735-1813 EncCRAm, WorAlBi
Crevel, Rene 1900-1935 WorAu 1980 [port]
Crevelt, Dwight Eugene 1957- WhoEmL 91, WhoWor 91
Crever, Robert 1936- St&PR 91
Crevier, Roger L. 1939- St&PR 91
Creviston, Robert Louis 1940- St&PR 91
Crevoiserat, Patricia Jill 1955- WhoAmW 91, WhoE 91
Crew, Carl Leon, Jr. 1946- BiDrAPA 89
Crew, Fleming H. AuBYP 90
Crew, Henry 1859-1953 DcScB S2
Crew, John Neal 1954- St&PR 91
Crew, Linda 1951- ConAu 130
Crew, Louie 1936- WhoAm 90
Crew, Richard Marion 1949- St&PR 91
Crew, Wynn D. St&PR 91
Crewdson, John 1945- ConAu 132
Crewdson, John Mark 1945- WhoAm 90
Crewe, Albert Victor 1927- WhoAm 90
Crewe, Trenton Guy, Jr. 1950- WhoEmL 91
Crews, C.H., Jr. 1925- St&PR 91
Crews, Charles F. 1932- St&PR 91
Crews, Donald BioIn 16
Crews, Donald 1938- WhoE 91
Crews, Donald R. 1943- St&PR 91
Crews, Donald Roy 1943- WhoAm 90
Crews, Esca Holmes, Jr. 1922- WhoAm 90
Crews, Eugene Lyndon, III 1944- BiDrAPA 89
Crews, Frederick Campbell 1933- WhoAm 90, WhoWrEP 89
Crews, Harry 1935- MajTwCW, WorAlBi
Crews, Harry Eugene 1935- WhoAm 90, WhoWrEP 89
Crews, John Eric 1946- WhoEmL 91, WhoWor 91
Crews, John Russell 1956- St&PR 91
Crews, Judith Carol 1948- WhoEmL 91
Crews, Kenneth Donald 1955- WhoEmL 91
Crews, Kimberly Anne 1962- WhoE 91
Crews, Laura Hope 1879?-1942 BioIn 16, NotWoAT
Crews, Richard Douglas 1951- WhoEmL 91
Crews, Richard L BiDrAPA 89
Crews, Robert Thornton 1933- WhoSSW 91
Crews, Ruthellen 1927- WhoAm 90, WhoAmW 91
Crews, Stephen G. ODwPR 91
Crews, Tim 1961- Ballpl 90
Crews, William Odell, Jr. 1936- WhoAm 90
Crewse, Leonard Lee 1934- St&PR 91
Crewson, Walter F.J. 1938- St&PR 91
Criaerd, Antoine-Mathieu 1724- PenDiDA 89
Criaerd, Mathieu 1689-1776 PenDiDA 89
Criaerd, Sebastien-Mathieu PenDiDA 89
Cribari, Stephen Jon 1947- WhoE 91, WhoSSW 91
Cribb, Jeffery E. 1925- St&PR 91
Cribb, Peter Harold 1931- WhoAm 90
Cribb, Roy Steven 1959- WhoSSW 91
Cribbet, John Edward 1918- WhoAm 90, WhoWor 91
Cribbs, Jeffrey Scott, Sr. 1945- WhoEmL 91
Cricco-Lizza, Roberta 1952- WhoAmW 91
Crice, Douglas B. 1941- St&PR 91
Crichigno, Gerardo A BiDrAPA 89
Crichlow, Ernest 1914- BioIn 16
Crichton, Charles 1910- ConTFT 8
Crichton, David Rodney 1938- St&PR 91
Crichton, John H. 1920- St&PR 91
Crichton, John Michael 1942- WhoAm 90, WhoWrEP 89
Crichton, Michael 1942- BioIn 16, MajTwCW, TwCCr&M 91, WorAlBi
Crichton, Ronald Henry 1913- IntWWM 90
Crichton, Theodore P. 1927- St&PR 91
Crichton-Brown, Robert 1919- WhoWor 91
Crichton-Harris, Margaret Ann 1936- WhoE 91
Crick, Francis 1916- BioIn 16
Crick, Francis H. C. 1916- WorAlBi
Crick, Francis Harry Compton 1916- WhoAm 90, WhoWor 91
Crickboom, Mathieu 1871-1947 PenDiMP
Crickmore, Leon 1932- IntWWM 90
Criddle, Mary Ann 1805-1880 BiDWomA
Criden, Frank M BiDrAPA 89
Crider, Andrew Blake 1936- WhoAm 90
Crider, Bill 1941- ConAu 30NR, TwCCr&M 91
Crider, Cora Elizabeth 1927- WhoAmW 91
Crider, David S. 1948- St&PR 91
Crider, Donald B 1925- BiDrAPA 89
Crider, Irene Perritt 1921- WhoAmW 91, WhoSSW 91
Crider, Jerry 1941- Ballpl 90
Crider, Karen Koch 1945- WhoEmL 91
Crider, Kenneth Gordon 1927- WhoSSW 91
Crider, Robert Agustine 1935- WhoWor 91
Crider, Stephen W. 1939- St&PR 91
Crider, Stephen Wayne 1939- WhoAm 90
Crider, William Ahtee, Jr. 1939- WhoSSW 91
Cridim, Claudia EncCoWW
Cridlin, W.G., Jr. 1946- St&PR 91
Criel, Jan Andre 1943- WhoWor 91
Crier, Catherine BioIn 16
Criger, Lou 1872-1934 Ballpl 90
Criger, Nancy S. 1951- WhoAmW 91, WhoEmL 91
Crigler, B. Waugh 1948- WhoEmL 91
Crigler, T. P. 1933- WhoAm 90
Crigler, Trusten Frank 1935- WhoAm 90, WhoWor 91
Crile, George, Jr. 1907- WhoAm 90
Crile, Susan 1942- BiDWomA, WhoAm 90, WhoAmA 91, WhoAmW 91
Crilly, Karen Ann 1963- WhoAmW 91
Crilly, Stephen Richard 1952- WhoEmL 91
Crim, Alonzo A. 1928- WhoAm 90
Crim, Cheryl Leigh 1956- WhoWor 91
Crim, Chuck 1961- Ballpl 90
Crim, Howard Emmett 1942- WhoSSW 91
Crim, Jack C. 1930- St&PR 91, WhoAm 90
Crim, Keith Renn 1924- WhoE 91
Crim, R. Sidney 1942- St&PR 91
Crim, Reuben Sidney 1942- WhoSSW 91
Crimi, Alfred D 1900- WhoAmA 91
Crimi, Alfred DiGiorgio 1900- WhoAm 90
Crimi, Felipe BiDrAPA 89
Crimian, Jack 1926- Ballpl 90
Criminale, William Oliver, Jr. 1933- WhoAm 90
Crimlisk, Anthony Trevor 1935- IntWWM 90
Crimmins, Alfred Stephen, Jr. 1934- WhoAm 90, WhoE 91
Crimmins, Jerry WhoAmA 91
Crimmins, Jerry 1940- WhoAmA 91, WhoE 91
Crimmins, John Blaine, Jr. 1928- St&PR 91
Crimmins, John Frank 1933- St&PR 91
Crimmins, Philip Patrick 1930- WhoAm 90
Crimmins, Robert BioIn 16
Crimp, Douglas 1944- WhoAmA 91
Crinella, Francis Michael 1936- WhoAm 90
Criner, Beatrice AuBYP 90
Criner, Calvin AuBYP 90
Criner, Clyde 1952- IntWWM 90
Criner, Douglas E. 1942- St&PR 91
Criner, George NewAgMG
Criner, John Lawrence 1960- WhoWrEP 89
Criner, Katy Lynn 1960- WhoAmW 91
Crinion, Gregory Paul 1959- WhoEmL 91, WhoSSW 91
Criniti, Mary Pauline 1931- WhoWrEP 89
Crinkley, Richmond 1940-1989 BioIn 16, ConTFT 8
Crino, Marjanne Helen 1933- WhoAmW 91
Cripe, Jerome H 1929- BiDrAPA 89
Cripe, Michael J. 1941- St&PR 91
Cripe, Nicholas McKinney 1913- WhoAm 90
Cripe, Richard L. 1958- St&PR 91
Cripe, Wyland S. 1921- WhoAm 90
Crippen, Hawley Harvey 1862-1910 BioIn 16
Crippen, Robert Laurel 1937- WhoAm 90
Crippin, Byron Miles, Jr. 1928- WhoAm 90
Cripps, Howard D. 1932- St&PR 91
Cripps, Peter Kendall 1947- St&PR 91
Cripps, William PenDiDA 89
Criquette WhoAmA 91
Criqui, William Edmund 1922- WhoAm 90
Crisa, John Baptist 1927- St&PR 91
Crisafulli, Barbara Ann 1960- WhoE 91
Crisafulli, Frank, Jr. 1940- St&PR 91
Crisafulli, Stephen W. 1940- St&PR 91
Crisalli, Anthony P. 1929- St&PR 91
Crisan, Susana WhoHisp 91
Crisanti, John A. 1940- St&PR 91
Crisci, Mathew G. 1941- WhoAm 90
Criscillis, Paul A., Jr. 1949- St&PR 91
Crisco, Kelly Reid 1963- WhoAmW 91
Criscoe, Arthur Hugh 1939- WhoSSW 91
Criscuolo, Jack J. St&PR 91
Criscuolo, Wendy Laura 1949- WhoAmW 91, WhoEmL 91, WhoWor 91
Crise, Richard 1925- St&PR 91
Crise, Robert 1929- St&PR 91
Criser, Marshall M. 1928- St&PR 91, WhoAm 90, WhoSSW 91
Crisler, Charles Robert 1948- WhoEmL 91
Crisley, Francis Daniel 1926- WhoAm 90
Crisman, Mary Frances Borden 1919- WhoAm 90, WhoWor 91
Crisman, Stephen BioIn 16
Crisman, Thomas Lynn 1941- WhoAm 90
Crismond, Linda F. 1943- BioIn 16
Crisona, James Joseph 1907- WhoAm 90
Crisostomo, Juanchito Delval 1953- BiDrAPA 89
Crisostomo, Lolita BiDrAPA 89
Crisostomo, Manny WhoAm 90
Crisp, David James 1946- St&PR 91
Crisp, Donald 1880-1974 WorAlBi

Crisp, Elizabeth Amanda 1922- *WhoAmW 91*
Crisp, Norman James 1923- *SpyFic*
Crisp, Polly Lenore 1952- *WhoAmW 91*
Crisp, Shelley Jean 1951- *WhoAmW 91*
Crisp, Terry Arthur 1943- *WhoAm 90*
Crispell, Kenneth Raymond 1916- *WhoAm 90*
Crispen, Elaine D. *ODwPR 91*
Crispin, A C 1950- *ConAu 32NR*
Crispin, Andre Arthur 1923- *St&PR 91, WhoAm 90*
Crispin, Edmund 1921-1978 *TwCCr&M 91, WorAlBi*
Crispin, James Hewes 1915- *WhoWor 91*
Crispin, Mildred Swift *WhoAmW 91*
Crispin, Robert William 1946- *WhoAm 90*
Crispini, Patrick 1955- *IntWWM 90*
Crispo, Dick 1945- *WhoAmA 91*
Crispo, Lawrence Walter 1934- *WhoAm 90*
Criss, Abraham Lincoln 1914- *MusmAFA*
Criss, Cecil M. 1934- *WhoSSW 91*
Criss, Darlene June 1931- *WhoAmW 91, WhoWor 91*
Criss, Diane Ramsey 1941- *WhoSSW 91*
Criss, Francis H 1901-1973 *WhoAmA 91N*
Criss, Lynne Elizabeth 1936- *WhoE 91*
Criss, Mildred 1890- *AuBYP 90*
Criss, William Sotelo 1949- *WhoEmL 91*
Crissey, William Stoddart 1811-1888 *BioIn 16*
Crissinger, Karen Denise 1956- *WhoAmW 91*
Crissman, James Hudson 1937- *WhoAm 90*
Crist, Cynthia Louise 1950- *WhoEmL 91*
Crist, Darlene Trew *ODwPR 91*
Crist, Earl 1925- *St&PR 91*
Crist, Eda 1909- *AuBYP 90*
Crist, George Brainard 1931- *WhoAm 90*
Crist, James Fontaine, Jr. 1935- *WhoSSW 91*
Crist, Judith Klein 1922- *WhoAm 90, WhoAmW 91*
Crist, Mary Jane 1946- *WhoAmW 91*
Crist, Richard 1947- *IntWWM 90*
Crist, Richard Harrison 1909- *AuBYP 90*
Crist, Robert H 1930- *BiDrAPA 89*
Crist, Stephen Alan 1957- *IntWWM 90*
Crist, Steven *BioIn 16*
Crist, William Gary 1937- *WhoAmA 91*
Crist, William Miles 1943- *WhoAm 90*
Cristaldi, Anthony Joseph 1957- *WhoSSW 91*
Cristall, Ann Batten 1769-1816? *FemiCLE*
Criste, Rita 1898- *BioIn 16, NotWoAT*
Cristi, John *BioIn 16*
Cristiani, Alfredo *BioIn 16*
Cristiani, Alfredo 1947- *CurBio 90 [port], WhoWor 91*
Cristiani, Francesco *BioIn 16*
Cristiani, Luca Giovanni 1957- *WhoWor 91*
Cristiano, Joseph P. 1940- *St&PR 91*
Cristiano, Marilyn Jean 1954- *WhoEmL 91*
Cristiano, Paul Anthony, Jr. 1955- *St&PR 91*
Cristillo, Louis Francis *BioIn 16*
Cristin, Lilli Fong 1947- *WhoAmA 91*
Cristina, Princess 1965- *BioIn 16*
Cristina, Donna Marie 1948- *WhoAmW 91*
Cristini, Angela Louise 1948- *WhoAmW 91*
Cristobal de Augusta *PenDiDA 89*
Cristobal, Adrian Empremiado 1932- *WhoWor 91*
Cristofalo, Vincent Joseph 1933- *WhoAm 90*
Cristofer, Michael 1945- *WhoAm 90*
Cristol, Allan H *BiDrAPA 89*
Cristol, Stanley Jerome 1916- *WhoAm 90*
Cristy, George 1924- *WhoSSW 91*
Criswell, Arthurine 1953- *WhoAmW 91*
Criswell, Charles Harrison 1943- *WhoWor 91*
Criswell, Francis Marion 1935- *BiDrAPA 89*
Criswell, Kathleen Jean 1949- *WhoAmW 91*
Criswell, Kimberly Ann 1957- *WhoAmW 91, WhoEmL 91*
Criswell, Paul Lindsay 1954- *WhoEmL 91*
Critchell, Brian John 1953- *St&PR 91*
Critchell, Ferd Brian 1926- *St&PR 91*
Critchett, David Loren 1935- *St&PR 91*
Critchfield, Jack B. 1933- *WhoSSW 91*
Critchfield, Jack Barron 1933- *St&PR 91*
Critchfield, Richard Patrick 1931- *WhoAm 90*
Critchley, D. Ellen 1948- *WhoEmL 91*
Critchley, Lynne *WhoWrEP 89*
Critchlow, B. Vaughn 1927- *WhoAm 90*
Critchlow, Charles Howard 1950- *WhoEmL 91*
Critchlow, Dale Leverne 1932- *WhoAm 90*
Critchlow, Hubert Nathaniel 1884-1958 *BioIn 16*
Critchlow, Paul W. *BioIn 16*
Critchlow, Paul W. 1946- *ODwPR 91*
Critchlow, Robert Howard 1950- *WhoWor 91*
Critchlow, Susan Melissa 1950- *WhoAmW 91, WhoWor 91*
Crite, Allan Rohan 1910- *WhoAmA 91*
Critelli, Frank 1929- *St&PR 91*
Critelli, Paul Joseph 1949- *WhoEmL 91*
Critelli, Tecla Linda *BiDrAPA 89*
Crites, Dorothy Adele 1919- *WhoWrEP 89*
Crites, E.F. 1926- *St&PR 91*
Crites, Omar Don, Jr. 1928- *WhoAm 90*
Crites, Richard Ray 1952- *WhoEmL 91, WhoWor 91*
Criticos, Aristotelis S. 1924- *BiDrAPA 89*
Critoph, Eugene 1929- *WhoAm 90*
Critser, Gary Lee 1949- *WhoEmL 91*
Crittenden, Eugene Dwight, Jr. 1927- *WhoAm 90, WhoE 91*
Crittenden, Gazaway Lamar 1918- *WhoAm 90*
Crittenden, Jack 1928- *St&PR 91*
Crittenden, John J. 1787-1863 *WorAlBi*
Crittenden, John Jordan 1787-1863 *BiDrUSE 89*
Crittenden, Lee J. 1945- *ODwPR 91*
Crittenden, Linda Adkins 1947- *WhoSSW 91*
Crittenden, Otis Smith 1933- *St&PR 91*
Crittenden, Sophie Marie 1926- *WhoAmW 91*
Crittenden, Toya Cynthia 1958- *WhoWrEP 89*
Crittenden, Victoria Lynn 1956- *WhoAmW 91*
Crittendon, Robert Russell 1930- *St&PR 91*
Crittin, Joel T. 1939- *WhoWor 91*
Critz, Hughie 1900-1980 *Ballpl 90*
Critz, Richard Laurens 1922- *WhoAm 90*
Critzer, Rex L. 1947- *St&PR 91*
Critzer, William Ernest 1934- *WhoAm 90*
Crivelli, Carlo 1430?-1495? *IntDcAA 90*
Crivelli, Elaine 1950- *WhoAmA 91*
Crivelli, Joseph D. 1936- *WhoE 91*
Crivelli, Joseph Louis 1947- *WhoAm 90*
Crivellone, Angelo Anthony 1919- *St&PR 91*
Crivellone, Ernest L. 1956- *St&PR 91*
Crncich, Tony Joseph 1930- *St&PR 91, WhoAm 90*
Crnic, Linda Smith 1948- *WhoAmW 91, WhoEmL 91*
Crnkovic, Leslie Allen 1961- *WhoSSW 91*
Crnkovich, Nick George 1926- *St&PR 91*
Croak, Henry *St&PR 91*
Croall, Jonathan 1941- *ConAu 130*
Croasmun, Robert McHenry 1946- *WhoEmL 91*
Croatti, Aldo A. 1917- *St&PR 91*
Crobaugh, Emma Adelia 1903- *WhoWrEP 89*
Crocco, John Anthony 1934- *WhoE 91*
Crocco, Richard A 1937- *BiDrAPA 89*
Croce, Arlene Louise 1934- *WhoAm 90, WhoAmW 91*
Croce, Benedetto 1866-1952 *TwCLC 37 [port], WorAlBi*
Croce, Charles *ODwPR 91*
Croce, Jim 1942-1973 *WorAlBi*
Croce, Jim 1943-1973 *OxCPMus*
Crochet, Gregory Randolph 1957- *WhoEmL 91*
Crochet, Laura Browning 1953- *WhoEmL 91*
Crochiere, Ronald Eldon *WhoAm 90*
Crocitto, Peter 1957- *St&PR 91*
Crocker, Albert Rudolph 1914- *WhoWor 91*
Crocker, Benjamin 1946- *BiDrAPA 89*
Crocker, Bristol B. 1926- *St&PR 91*
Crocker, Bruce E. 1942- *St&PR 91*
Crocker, Charles 1822-1888 *WorAlBi*
Crocker, Chester A 1941- *CurBio 90 [port]*
Crocker, Chester Arthur 1941- *WhoAm 90*
Crocker, David *BiDrAPA 89*
Crocker, David Arthur Edward 1943- *IntWWM 90*
Crocker, Dennis John 1953- *IntWWM 90*
Crocker, Dorothy Brin 1913- *IntWWM 90*
Crocker, Edgar 1930- *St&PR 91*
Crocker, Frankie *BioIn 16*
Crocker, Frankie 1944?- *DrBIPA 90*
Crocker, Frederick Greeley, Jr. 1937- *St&PR 91, WhoAm 90*
Crocker, Gary Lamar 1951- *St&PR 91*
Crocker, George Allen *BioIn 16*
Crocker, George F. *AmLegL*
Crocker, Hannah 1752-1829 *FemiCLE*
Crocker, Jack J. 1924- *St&PR 91*
Crocker, Kenneth Franklin 1950- *WhoEmL 91*
Crocker, Lester Gilbert 1912- *WhoAm 90*
Crocker, Lillian Carol 1946- *WhoSSW 91*
Crocker, Malcolm John 1938- *WhoAm 90, WhoWor 91*
Crocker, Richard L. 1927- *IntWWM 90*
Crocker, Richard R. 1938- *WhoAm 90*
Crocker, Ryan *NewYTBS 90 [port]*
Crocker, Saone Baron 1943- *WhoAmW 91*
Crocker, Thomas P. 1960- *St&PR 91*
Crockett, Arthur H. 1917- *St&PR 91*
Crockett, Barbara A 1943- *BiDrAPA 89*
Crockett, Barbara Anastasia 1943- *WhoE 91*
Crockett, Betty 1936- *St&PR 91*
Crockett, Christopher Yates 1946- *WhoE 91*
Crockett, Clyll Webb 1934- *WhoAm 90*
Crockett, Davey 1786-1836 *WorAlBi*
Crockett, David 1786-1836 *WhNaAH*
Crockett, Davy 1786-1836 *BioIn 16*
Crockett, Don Warren 1938- *WhoE 91*
Crockett, Donald 1951- *IntWWM 90*
Crockett, Ethel Stacy 1915- *WhoAm 90*
Crockett, George William, Jr. 1909- *BlkAmsC [port], WhoAm 90*
Crockett, Gib 1912- *WhoAmA 91*
Crockett, Gibson M. 1912- *WhoAm 90*
Crockett, James Edwin 1924- *WhoWor 91*
Crockett, James Grover, III 1937- *WhoAm 90*
Crockett, Jerry Bruce 1930- *WhoAm 90*
Crockett, Joseph Turner *BiDrAPA 89*
Crockett, Lori Lee 1963- *WhoWrEP 89*
Crockett, Mavis *WhoAmW 91*
Crockett, Mortimer Crane 1919- *St&PR 91*
Crockett, Phyllis Darlene 1950- *WhoAmW 91, WhoE 91*
Crockett, Raymond Foster 1951- *WhoWor 91*
Crockett, Rex Jerold 1940- *St&PR 91*
Crockett, Richard Hayden 1947- *WhoE 91*
Crockett, Ronald D. 1951- *WhoAm 90*
Crockett, Shan 1944- *BiDrAPA 89*
Crockett-Smith, D. L. *WhoWrEP 89*
Crockford, Robert David 1948- *St&PR 91*
Crockwell, Douglas 1904-1968 *WhoAmA 91N*
Crocq, Marc-Antoine 1955- *BiDrAPA 89*
Croel, Philip M. 1938- *St&PR 91*
Croes, Gilbert Francois 1938- *BioIn 16*
Croes, Keith John 1952- *WhoWrEP 89*
Croesus *EncPaPR 91*
Croff, Davide *BioIn 16*
Crofford, Emily 1927- *SmATA 61 [port]*
Crofford, Harry R. 1921- *St&PR 91*
Crofford, Helen Lois 1932- *WhoAmW 91*
Crofford, Oscar Bledsoe, Jr. 1930- *WhoAm 90*
Crofford, Tom R. 1951- *St&PR 91*
Croft, Alvin C. 1926- *ODwPR 91*
Croft, Barbara Yoder 1940- *WhoAmW 91*
Croft, Caroline Jane 1947- *WhoE 91*
Croft, Giles Lawrence 1957- *WhoWor 91*
Croft, Harry A *BiDrAPA 89*
Croft, Harry Allen 1943- *WhoAm 90*
Croft, Hugo William 1945- *WhoEmL 91*
Croft, James 1517?-1590 *BioIn 16*
Croft, James Edwin 1929- *IntWWM 90, WhoSSW 91*
Croft, John-Ed *BioIn 16*
Croft, Katherine May-ing 1939- *WhoAmW 91*
Croft, Leonard Mathias 1930- *St&PR 91, WhoAm 90*
Croft, Michael Flynt 1941- *WhoAmA 91*
Croft, P. Howard, Jr. 1927- *St&PR 91*
Croft, Susan *ODwPR 91*
Croft, Susan Elizabeth 1958- *WhoWor 91*
Croft, William Crosswell 1918- *St&PR 91*
Croft-Cooke, Rupert *TwCCr&M 91*
Crofton, John Edward 1937- *WhoSSW 91*
Crofts, Antony Richard 1940- *WhoAm 90*
Crofts, Freeman Willis 1879-1957 *WorAlBi*
Crofts, Freeman Wills 1879-1957 *TwCCr&M 91*
Crofts, Inez Altman *IntWWM 90*
Crofts, Lisa Christine 1955- *WhoAmW 91*
Crofut, Robert Joel 1951- *WhoE 91*
Crogan, Neva Lynne 1957- *WhoEmL 91*
Croghan, Dennis Michael 1956- *WhoSSW 91, WhoWor 91*
Croghan, Gary Alan 1954- *WhoE 91, WhoEmL 91, WhoWor 91*
Croghan, George *EncCRAm*
Croghan, George 1720?-1782 *WhNaAH*
Croghan, George 1791-1849 *WhNaAH*
Crohn, Max Henry, Jr. 1934- *WhoAm 90*
Crois, John Henry 1946- *WhoEmL 91, WhoWor 91*
Croise, Jacques *EncCoWW*
Croiset, Gerard 1909-1980 *EncO&P 3, EncPaPR 91*
Croissant, Raymond B 1911- *BiDrAPA 89*
Croitoru, Nathan 1927- *WhoWor 91*
Croiza, Claire 1882-1946 *PenDiMP*
Croke, Jerome Patrick 1933- *St&PR 91*
Croke, Thomas Michael, IV 1952- *WhoE 91*
Croker, B. M. 1849?-1920 *FemiCLE*
Croker, Margaret 1773- *FemiCLE*
Croker, Robert Arthur 1932- *WhoE 91*
Croley, Jack Glenn 1916- *WhoSSW 91*
Croley, Steven Wayne *BiDrAPA 89*
Croll, Carolyn 1945- *BioIn 16*
Croll, Robert Frederick 1934- *WhoWor 91*
Croll, S.W. 1949- *St&PR 91*
Crollius, Oswaldus 1580-1609 *EncO&P 3*
Crols, Henri Marcel 1931- *WhoWor 91*
Croly, Herbert David 1869-1930 *BioIn 16*
Croly, Jane Cunningham 1829?-1901 *BioIn 16*
Crom, Debora L. *St&PR 91*
Crom, James Oliver 1933- *WhoAm 90*
Crom, Thomas Le Roy, III 1955- *WhoEmL 91*
Cromack, Margot Schlegel 1952- *WhoAmW 91*
Cromar, Michael Earl 1947- *WhoWor 91*
Cromartie, Eric Ross 1955- *WhoEmL 91*
Cromartie, Warren *BioIn 16*
Cromartie, Warren 1953- *Ballpl 90*
Cromartie, William James 1913- *WhoAm 90*
Cromarty, Deas *FemiCLE*
Cromarty, George *NewAgMG*
Crombie, David Edward 1936- *WhoAm 90*
Crombie, Douglass Darnill 1924- *WhoAm 90*
Crome, John 1768-1821 *IntDcAA 90*
Cromer, Benjamin Dean 1954- *WhoEmL 91*
Cromer, Gretchen L. 1954- *BiDrAPA 89*
Cromer, Jenny Lu 1954- *WhoAmW 91*
Cromer, Ortell Diane *WhoE 91*
Cromie, Alice 1914- *AuBYP 90*
Cromie, Judith E. 1943- *St&PR 91*
Cromie, Peter E. 1920- *St&PR 91*
Cromie, Robert George 1929- *WhoE 91*
Cromie, William Joseph 1930- *AuBYP 90, WhoE 91*
Cromiller, Harold Lee 1920- *WhoAm 90*
Cromley, Allan Wray 1922- *WhoAm 90*
Cromley, Carter B. *ODwPR 91*
Cromley, Jon Lowell 1934- *WhoWor 91*
Cromley, Raymond Avolon 1910- *WhoAm 90, WhoWor 91*
Crommelin, May 1850?-1930 *FemiCLE*
Crommelin, Quentin *BioIn 16*
Crompton, Anne Eliot 1930- *AuBYP 90*
Crompton, Arnold 1914- *WhoWor 91*
Crompton, Louis William 1925- *WhoAm 90*
Crompton, Richmal 1890-1969 *BioIn 16, FemiCLE*
Crompton, Thomas Charles 1953- *WhoEmL 91*
Cromwell, Adelaide M. 1919- *WhoAm 90*
Cromwell, Anna 1623?- *BiDEWW*
Cromwell, David Marshall 1944- *WhoAm 90*
Cromwell, Douglas Henry 1950- *St&PR 91*
Cromwell, Edwin Boykin 1909- *WhoAm 90*
Cromwell, Elizabeth *BiDEWW*
Cromwell, Florence Stevens 1922- *WhoAm 90, WhoAmW 91*
Cromwell, James David 1943- *WhoE 91*
Cromwell, James H. R. *NewYTBS 90 [port]*
Cromwell, James H R 1897?-1990 *ConAu 131, CurBio 90N*
Cromwell, James H. R. 1898-1990 *BioIn 16*
Cromwell, James Robert 1948- *WhoEmL 91*
Cromwell, Jarvis, II 1958- *ODwPR 91*
Cromwell, John L. *St&PR 91*
Cromwell, Leslie 1924- *WhoAm 90*
Cromwell, Margrit Else 1946- *WhoEmL 91*
Cromwell, Norman Henry 1913- *WhoAm 90*
Cromwell, Oliver 1599-1658 *BioIn 16, EncCRAm, WorAlBi*
Cromwell, Oliver Dean 1950- *WhoAm 90, WhoEmL 91*
Cromwell, Rue LeVelle 1928- *WhoAm 90*
Cromwell, Sharon Lee 1947- *WhoWrEP 89*
Cromwell, Thomas 1485?-1540 *WorAlBi*
Cromwell, William Nelson 1854-1948 *BioIn 16*
Cron, Edward Leroy 1937- *St&PR 91*
Cron, Jennifer Lynne 1956- *WhoEmL 91*
Cronan, Daniel 1807-1892 *DcCanB 12*
Cronan, Donald George 1924- *WhoE 91*
Cronan, Douglas P. 1956- *St&PR 91*
Cronan, Kathleen Michele 1953- *WhoEmL 91*
Cronan, Michael Patrick *BioIn 16*
Cronau, Rebecca Lynn 1962- *WhoAmW 91, WhoEmL 91*
Cronauer, Adrian *BioIn 16*
Cronbach, Lee Joseph 1916- *WhoAm 90*
Cronbach, Robert M. 1908- *WhoAm 90, WhoAmA 91*
Crone, Bill L. 1927- *St&PR 91*
Crone, Christine Hess 1917- *WhoAmW 91*
Crone, Dana *BioIn 16*
Crone, John Porter *WhoAm 90*
Crone, John William, Jr. 1923- *WhoSSW 91*
Crone, Rainer F 1942- *WhoAmA 91*

Crone, Ray 1931- *Ballpl 90*
Crone, Richard Allan 1947- *WhoEmL 91*
Crone, Richard Irving 1909- *WhoAm 90*
Crone, Richard Kenneth 1957- *WhoEmL 91*
Crone, Ruth 1919- *AuBYP 90*
Crone, Tan *IntWWM 90*
Crone-Rawe, Bernard Gerhard 1924- *WhoWor 91*
Croneberger, Robert Bruce, Jr. 1937- *WhoAm 90, WhoE 91*
Cronemiller, Philip Douglas 1918- *WhoAm 90*
Cronen, Arthur Clark 1946- *BiDrAPA 89, WhoE 91*
Cronenberg, David *BioIn 16*
Cronenwett, Wilson R. 1913- *ODwPR 91*
Cronenworth, Charles Douglas 1921- *St&PR 91, WhoAm 90*
Croney, J. Kenneth 1942- *St&PR 91*
Cronhjort, Bjorn Torvald 1934- *WhoWor 91*
Cronholm, Lois S. 1930- *WhoAm 90, WhoAmW 91*
Cronick, Anne B *BiDrAPA 89*
Cronin, A. J. 1896-1981 *BioIn 16*
Cronin, Ambrose M., III 1930- *St&PR 91*
Cronin, Archibald Joseph 1896-1981 *BioIn 16, DcNaB 1981*
Cronin, Bonnie Kathryn Lamb 1941- *WhoAm 90*
Cronin, Daniel Anthony 1927- *WhoAm 90, WhoE 91*
Cronin, David Alan 1949- *WhoEmL 91*
Cronin, Francis J. *St&PR 91*
Cronin, James W. 1931- *WorAlBi*
Cronin, James Watson 1931- *WhoAm 90, WhoWor 91*
Cronin, Jeremiah P. *St&PR 91*
Cronin, Joe 1906-1984 *Ballpl 90 [port]*
Cronin, John 1874-1929 *Ballpl 90*
Cronin, John Daniel *BioIn 16*
Cronin, John Garrett 1936- *St&PR 91*
Cronin, John T. 1949- *WhoEmL 91*
Cronin, John W. *BioIn 16*
Cronin, John Welsch 1944- *St&PR 91*
Cronin, Joseph M 1935- *ConAu 31NR*
Cronin, Lawrence R *BiDrAPA 89*
Cronin, Patrick Reilly 1946- *St&PR 91*
Cronin, Patti Adrienne Wright 1943- *WhoAmW 91*
Cronin, Paul William 1938- *St&PR 91, WhoAm 90*
Cronin, Philip Mark 1932- *WhoAm 90*
Cronin, Raymond Valentine 1924- *WhoAm 90*
Cronin, Robert 1936- *WhoAmA 91*
Cronin, Robert Francis Patrick 1926- *WhoAm 90*
Cronin, Robert Lawrence 1936- *WhoAm 90*
Cronin, Robert Neil 1947- *WhoE 91*
Cronin, Stephen G 1937- *BiDrAPA 89*
Cronin, Timothy Cornelius 1927- *St&PR 91*
Cronin, Timothy Cornelius, III 1927- *WhoE 91*
Cronin, Timothy Xavier 1924- *St&PR 91*
Cronin, Tony *WhoAmA 91N*
Croninger, George Julian 1905- *St&PR 91*
Cronk, Randall D. 1950- *ODwPR 91*
Cronkhite, Leland James 1933- *WhoAm 90*
Cronkhite, Leonard Wolsey, Jr. 1919- *WhoAm 90*
Cronkhite, Vern Eugene 1922- *St&PR 91, WhoAm 90*
Cronkite, Eugene Pitcher 1914- *WhoAm 90*
Cronkite, Walter *BioIn 16*
Cronkite, Walter 1916- *WhoAm 90, WhoE 91, WorAlBi*
Cronn, Dagmar Rais 1946- *WhoAmW 91, WhoEmL 91*
Cronon, Edmund David, Jr. 1924- *WhoAm 90*
Cronon, William 1954- *WhoAm 90, WhoEmL 91*
Cronquist, Arthur John 1919- *WhoAm 90, WhoWor 91*
Cronson, Alvin Joseph *BiDrAPA 89*
Cronson, Caroline Mary 1962- *WhoE 91*
Cronson, Harold Andrew 1952- *BiDrAPA 89*
Cronson, Harry Marvin 1937- *WhoAm 90*
Cronson, Robert Granville 1924- *WhoAm 90*
Cronstein, Ralph 1918- *St&PR 91*
Cronvall, Aarno Erik 1945- *IntWWM 90*
Cronyn, Hume *BioIn 16*
Cronyn, Hume 1911- *OxCCanT [port], WhoAm 90, WorAlBi*
Cronyn, J.B. 1920- *St&PR 91*
Cronyn, James B. 1921- *St&PR 91*
Cronyn, Marshall William 1919- *WhoAm 90*
Crook, Alan Peter 1954- *IntWWM 90*
Crook, Colin 1942- *St&PR 91*
Crook, David S. 1954- *St&PR 91*
Crook, Donald Martin 1947- *St&PR 91, WhoAm 90*
Crook, George 1828-1890 *WhNaAH [port]*
Crook, George 1829-1890 *WorAlBi*
Crook, Herman *BioIn 16*
Crook, J.A.F. 1936- *St&PR 91*
Crook, John 1852-1922 *OxCPMus*
Crook, John Robert 1947- *WhoE 91*
Crook, Reginald Douglas 1901-1989 *BioIn 16*
Crook, Robert Lacey 1929- *WhoSSW 91*
Crook, Robert Wayne 1936- *WhoAm 90*
Crook, Roy M. 1945- *St&PR 91*
Crook, Sean Paul 1953- *WhoEmL 91*
Crook, Sharon Marie 1965- *WhoEmL 91*
Crook, Stephen Richard 1963- *WhoEmL 91, WhoWor 91*
Crook, Tressa Helen 1956- *WhoAmW 91*
Crook, Walter Joseph 1952- *BiDrAPA 89*
Crook, William G. 1917- *ConAu 129*
Crook of Carshalton, Baron 1901-1989 *BioIn 16*
Crookall, Robert 1890-1981 *ConAu 30NR, EncO&P 3, EncPaPR 91*
Crooke, Edward A. 1938- *St&PR 91, WhoAm 90*
Crooke, James Stratton *WhoE 91*
Crooke, Rosanne Muzyka 1955- *WhoAmW 91*
Crooke, Stanley Thomas 1945- *St&PR 91, WhoAm 90*
Crooke, Theresa Whitt *WhoSSW 91*
Crooker, Barbara 1945- *WhoWrEP 89*
Crooker, John H., Jr. 1914- *WhoAm 90*
Crookes, Joyce Fuda 1941- *WhoWrEP 89*
Crookes, William 1832-1919 *EncO&P 3, EncPaPR 91, WorAlBi*
Crooks, Bruce Philip 1944- *WhoE 91*
Crooks, Edwin William 1919- *WhoAm 90*
Crooks, G. Walter 1955- *WhoEmL 91*
Crooks, Hulda *BioIn 16*
Crooks, John A. 1936- *St&PR 91*
Crooks, Richard Marius 1943- *WhoSSW 91*
Crooks, W Spencer 1917- *WhoAmA 91*
Crooks, W. Spencer 1917- *WhoE 91*
Crooks, William Clayton 1948- *St&PR 91*
Crookshank, Anne 1927- *BioIn 16*
Crookshanks, Barbara Malone 1928- *WhoAmW 91*
Crookshanks, Betty Dorsey 1944- *WhoAmW 91*
Crookshanks, Michael Donald 1938- *St&PR 91*
Croom, Adam *BioIn 16*
Croom, Frederick Hailey 1941- *WhoSSW 91*
Croom, Henrietta Brown 1940- *WhoAmW 91*
Croom, John Henry 1932- *St&PR 91*
Croom, John Henry, III 1932- *WhoAm 90, WhoE 91*
Croom, Lucille *WhoE 91*
Croom, Robert Edward, Jr. 1942- *WhoSSW 91*
Crooms, Charles Gary 1943- *WhoSSW 91*
Cropley, Arthur John 1935- *WhoWor 91*
Cropper, M Elizabeth 1944- *WhoAmA 91*
Cropper, Peter *PenDiMP*
Cropper, Rebecca Lynn 1957- *WhoEmL 91*
Cropper, Stephen L. 1950- *St&PR 91*
Cropper, Susan Peggy 1941- *WhoAmW 91, WhoE 91*
Cropper, William A. 1939- *St&PR 91, WhoAm 90*
Cropsey, Jeanne Elizabeth 1947- *WhoEmL 91*
Cropsey, Joseph 1919- *WhoAm 90*
Cros, Edmond Georges 1931- *WhoWor 91*
Cros, Georges Noel 1930- *WhoWor 91*
Cros, Henri 1840-1907 *PenDiDA 89*
Crosa, Michael L. 1942- *WhoHisp 91*
Crosbie, Alfred Linden 1942- *WhoAm 90*
Crosbie, Allan H.T. 1941- *St&PR 91*
Crosbie, Helen Blair *WhoAmA 91*
Crosbie, Henry R. *AmLegL*
Crosbie, John 1931- *CurBio 90 [port]*
Crosbie, John Carnell *BioIn 16*
Crosbie, John Carnell 1931- *WhoAm 90, WhoE 91, WhoWor 91*
Crosbie, John S 1920- *WhoWrEP 89*
Crosbie, Lester Lyle 1945- *St&PR 91*
Crosbie, Robert 1849-1919 *NewAgE 90*
Crosbie, Vincent B. 1955- *St&PR 91*
Crosbie, William Perry 1947- *IntWWM 90*
Crosby, Stills, Nash *OxCPMus*
Crosby, Stills, Nash & Young *EncPR&S 89*
Crosby, Stills, Nash and Young *OxCPMus*
Crosby, Alexander L. 1906-1980 *AuBYP 90*
Crosby, Alfred Worcester 1931- *WhoAm 90*
Crosby, B.P. 1938- *St&PR 91*
Crosby, Bing 1903-1977 *OxCPMus, WorAlBi*
Crosby, Bing 1904-1977 *BioIn 16*
Crosby, Bob 1913- *BioIn 16, OxCPMus, WorAlBi*
Crosby, Brian 1933- *IntWWM 90*
Crosby, Caresse 1892-1970 *BioIn 16, FemiCLE*
Crosby, Clanrick 1804?-1871 *AmLegL*
Crosby, David *BioIn 16*
Crosby, David 1941- *EncPR&S 89, OxCPMus, WorAlBi*
Crosby, David P. 1940- *St&PR 91*
Crosby, Denise *BioIn 16, ConTFT 8*
Crosby, Ed 1949- *Ballpl 90*
Crosby, Fanny 1820-1915 *BioAmW*
Crosby, Faye Jacqueline 1947- *WhoEmL 91*
Crosby, Fred McClellan 1928- *WhoAm 90*
Crosby, Gary M. 1953- *St&PR 91*
Crosby, Glenn Arthur 1928- *WhoAm 90*
Crosby, Gordon E., Jr. 1920- *St&PR 91*
Crosby, Gordon Eugene, Jr. 1920- *WhoAm 90*
Crosby, Harry 1898-1929 *BioIn 16*
Crosby, Israel 1919-1962 *BioIn 16*
Crosby, J. Lamont 1940- *St&PR 91*
Crosby, J. Richard 1924- *St&PR 91*
Crosby, Jeffrey Wayne 1958- *WhoEmL 91*
Crosby, Joan Carew 1934- *WhoAm 90*
Crosby, John 1926- *IntWWM 90*
Crosby, John Bartlett 1947- *WhoEmL 91*
Crosby, John Campbell 1912- *WhoAm 90*
Crosby, John Griffith 1943- *WhoE 91*
Crosby, John O'Hea 1926- *WhoAm 90*
Crosby, Kenneth Gerald 1928- *WhoAm 90*
Crosby, Lindsay 1938-1989 *BioIn 16*
Crosby, Lindsey L. 1948- *St&PR 91*
Crosby, Nickey Aaron, Sr. 1936- *WhoE 91*
Crosby, Norman Lawrence 1927- *WhoAm 90*
Crosby, Percy L. 1891-1964 *EncACom*
Crosby, Peter Alan 1945- *WhoEmL 91*
Crosby, Philip 1922- *WhoSSW 91*
Crosby, Philip B. 1926- *St&PR 91*
Crosby, Philip Bayard 1926- *WhoWor 91*
Crosby, Phoebe *AuBYP 90*
Crosby, R.W. 1902- *St&PR 91*
Crosby, Ralph D. *St&PR 91*
Crosby, Ralph Wolf 1933- *WhoE 91*
Crosby, Ranice W 1915- *WhoAmA 91*
Crosby, Richard A. 1930- *St&PR 91*
Crosby, Richard John 1934- *St&PR 91*
Crosby, Robert Eugene 1939- *WhoE 91*
Crosby, Sumner McKnight 1909-1982 *WhoAmA 91N*
Crosby, Susan 1945- *WhoAmW 91*
Crosby, Theo 1925- *ConDes 90*
Crosby, Thomas 1683-1751? *BioIn 16*
Crosby, Thomas Anthony 1947- *WhoE 91*
Crosby, Thomas M., Jr. 1938- *St&PR 91*
Crosby Metzger, Lisa M. 1960- *WhoWrEP 89*
Crosdill, John 1775-1825 *PenDiMP*
Crose, George C. *AmLegL*
Crosetti, Frank 1910- *BioIn 16*
Crosetti, Frankie 1910- *Ballpl 90 [port]*
Crosfield, John F. *BioIn 16*
Croshal, Kathleen Klotz 1947- *WhoAmW 91*
Crosier, John David 1937- *WhoE 91*
Crosland, Camilla 1812-1895 *FemiCLE*
Crosland, Edward Burton 1912- *WhoAm 90*
Crosland, John, Jr. 1928- *St&PR 91, WhoAm 90, WhoSSW 91*
Crosland, Newton, Mrs. 1812-1895 *EncO&P 3*
Crosland, Page Dahl *ODwPR 91*
Crosland, Philip Crawford 1943- *St&PR 91*
Crosley, Powel, Jr. 1886-1961 *EncABHB 5 [port], WorAlBi*
Crosley, Powell, Jr. 1887-1961 *Ballpl 90*
Crosley, William Allen 1926- *St&PR 91*
Crosman, Christopher Byron 1946- *WhoAm 90, WhoAmA 91*
Croson, Donald C. 1936- *St&PR 91*
Cross, Alan Elliott 1951- *WhoSSW 91*
Cross, Alexander Dennis 1932- *St&PR 91, WhoAm 90*
Cross, Alvin F. 1927- *WhoAm 90*
Cross, Amanda 1926- *BioIn 16, TwCCr&M 91, WorAlBi*
Cross, Aureal Theophilus 1916- *WhoAm 90*
Cross, Betty Felt 1920- *WhoAmW 91, WhoSSW 91*
Cross, Bob R. 1948- *WhoSSW 91*
Cross, Burton B. 1940- *St&PR 91*
Cross, C. Deborah 1940- *BiDrAPA 89*
Cross, Carroll N. 1903- *St&PR 91*
Cross, Chester Joseph 1931- *WhoWor 91*
Cross, Christopher 1951- *EncPR&S 89, WhoAm 90*
Cross, Clyde Cleveland 1918- *WhoAm 90*
Cross, Dale L. 1947- *St&PR 91*
Cross, Darryl Geoffrey 1949- *WhoWor 91*
Cross, Dennis Gerald 1945- *WhoEmL 91*
Cross, Dewain Kingsley 1937- *St&PR 91*
Cross, Dolores E. 1937- *WhoAmW 91*
Cross, Dorothy Abigail 1924- *WhoAmW 91, WhoWor 91*
Cross, Earle Albright 1925- *WhoSSW 91*
Cross, Eason, Jr. 1925- *WhoAm 90*
Cross, Elmo Garnett, Jr. 1942- *WhoSSW 91*
Cross, Eric L. 1943- *St&PR 91*
Cross, Frank Moore, Jr. 1921- *WhoAm 90, WhoE 91, WhoWrEP 89*
Cross, Gary D. 1933- *St&PR 91*
Cross, George Alan Martin 1942- *WhoAm 90*
Cross, George Lynn 1905- *WhoAm 90*
Cross, George R. 1923- *WhoAm 90*
Cross, George S. 1949- *St&PR 91*
Cross, Gilbert B. 1939- *BioIn 16, SmATA 60 [port]*
Cross, Gillian 1945- *BioIn 16*
Cross, Glenn Griffin 1923- *St&PR 91*
Cross, Harry Maybury 1913- *WhoAm 90*
Cross, Henry 1837-1918 *WhNaAH*
Cross, Irv *WhoAm 90*
Cross, Irvie Keil 1917- *WhoAm 90*
Cross, Jacob Thomas *BiDrAPA 89*
Cross, James 1916- *WhoAm 90*
Cross, James E. 1921- *St&PR 91*
Cross, James Edwin 1921- *WhoAm 90*
Cross, James Estes, Jr. 1947- *WhoEmL 91*
Cross, James Millard 1945- *WhoEmL 91, WhoSSW 91*
Cross, James Paul 1954- *WhoEmL 91*
Cross, Jane Ellen 1961- *WhoEmL 91*
Cross, Janice Eileen 1944- *WhoAmW 91*
Cross, Jayne Roberta 1953- *WhoAmW 91*
Cross, Jennifer Mary 1932- *WhoAm 90*
Cross, Jeremy Ladd 1939- *WhoWor 91*
Cross, Joan 1900- *IntWWM 90, PenDiMP*
Cross, Joan Elaine 1945- *WhoEmL 91*
Cross, John Keir 1914-1967 *AuBYP 90*
Cross, John M. *St&PR 91*
Cross, John R. 1936- *St&PR 91*
Cross, Joseph 1843-1913 *AmLegL*
Cross, June Victoria 1954- *WhoE 91*
Cross, L. Wallace 1929- *St&PR 91*
Cross, Laura Elizabeth *WhoAmW 91, WhoE 91, WhoWor 91*
Cross, Lave 1866-1927 *Ballpl 90 [port]*
Cross, Leland Briggs, Jr. 1930- *WhoAm 90*
Cross, Lenora Routon 1920- *WhoAm 90*
Cross, Leslie Eric 1923- *WhoAm 90*
Cross, Linda Grace 1938- *BiDrAPA 89*
Cross, Linda Kames 1949- *BiDrAPA 89*
Cross, Lowell 1938- *IntWWM 90*
Cross, M. Lucille 1923- *St&PR 91*
Cross, Mary Ann Evans 1819-1880 *BioIn 16*
Cross, Mary Frances 1956- *WhoWrEP 89*
Cross, Maxwell S. 1912- *WhoSSW 91*
Cross, Milton 1897-1975 *WorAlBi*
Cross, Monte 1869-1934 *Ballpl 90*
Cross, O. Dee 1948- *St&PR 91*
Cross, Paul Thomas 1962- *St&PR 91*
Cross, Philip Sidney 1922- *St&PR 91*
Cross, Ralph Emerson 1910- *WhoAm 90*
Cross, Ray G. 1941- *St&PR 91*
Cross, Raymond Edward 1922- *St&PR 91*
Cross, Rex D. 1922- *St&PR 91*
Cross, Rex Devers 1922- *WhoWor 91*
Cross, Richard Assheton 1823-1914 *BioIn 16*
Cross, Richard E. 1910- *St&PR 91*
Cross, Richard Eugene 1910- *WhoAm 90*
Cross, Richard John 1929- *WhoAm 90*
Cross, Richard Vernon 1935- *St&PR 91, WhoAm 90*
Cross, Robert Brandt 1914- *WhoAm 90*
Cross, Robert Clark 1939- *WhoAm 90*
Cross, Robert William 1937- *St&PR 91*
Cross, Ronald 1929- *IntWWM 90, WhoE 91, WhoWor 91*
Cross, Ronald Anthony 1937- *WhoWrEP 89*
Cross, Russell S., Jr. 1930- *St&PR 91*
Cross, Samuel S. 1919- *WhoAm 90, WhoWor 91*
Cross, Sandra Lee 1946- *WhoEmL 91*
Cross, Shelley Ann 1948- *WhoEmL 91*
Cross, Steven Jasper 1954- *WhoEmL 91*
Cross, Susan Lee 1960- *WhoAmW 91*
Cross, Theodore Lamont 1924- *WhoAm 90, WhoE 91*
Cross, Thomas G. 1947- *St&PR 91*
Cross, Thomas Gary 1947- *WhoE 91, WhoWor 91*
Cross, Thomas N 1920- *BiDrAPA 89*
Cross, Timothy D. 1947- *WhoSSW 91*
Cross, Veronica 1937- *IntWWM 90*
Cross, Victoria *FemiCLE*
Cross, Virginia Rose 1950- *WhoAmW 91, WhoEmL 91*
Cross, Watson, Jr 1918- *WhoAmA 91*
Cross, Wilbur J. 1942- *St&PR 91*
Cross, William Herbert 1945- *WhoAm 90*
Cross, William Redmond, Jr. 1917- *WhoAm 90*
Cross, Zora 1890-1964 *FemiCLE*
Crossan, Donald Franklin 1926- *WhoE 91*
Crossan, Geordie John 1959- *WhoEmL 91*
Crosscup, Richard 1905- *AuBYP 90*
Crosse, Andrew 1784-1855 *EncO&P 3*
Crosse, Gordon 1937- *IntWWM 90, PenDiMP A*

Crosse, Rupert 1927?-1973 *DrBlPA 90*
Crosse, Victoria *FemiCLE*
Crossen, Frank Marvin 1923- *St&PR 91, WhoAm 90*
Crossen, Henry M. 1921- *St&PR 91*
Crossen, John Jacob 1932- *WhoSSW 91*
Crossen, Ken 1910-1981 *TwCCr&M 91*
Crossen, Margaret Lee 1958- *WhoEmL 91*
Crosser, Michael Richard *BiDrAPA 89*
Crossett, Daniel Joseph 1952- *WhoSSW 91*
Crossett, Judith H. W. 1947- *BiDrAPA 89*
Crossett, Kevin Stephen 1960- *WhoE 91*
Crossfield, Albert Scott 1921- *WhoAm 90*
Crossfield, Valerie L. 1965- *WhoEmL 91*
Crossgrove, Roger Lynn 1921- *WhoAmA 91*
Crosskill, W. E. 1904- *ConAu 129*
Crossland, Anthony 1931- *IntWWM 90*
Crossland, Harriet Kent 1902- *WhoAmW 91, WhoWor 91*
Crossland, Martin Dale 1953- *WhoAm 90*
Crossland, Richard Irving, Jr. 1948- *WhoEmL 91*
Crossley, Frank Alphonso 1925- *WhoAm 90*
Crossley, Gary Exley 1951- *WhoE 91*
Crossley, H. Buffinton 1925- *ODwPR 91*
Crossley, Kay Frances 1946- *WhoAmW 91, WhoEmL 91*
Crossley, Linda Susan 1950- *WhoAmW 91*
Crossley, Lytton F. 1935- *St&PR 91*
Crossley, Mark Larry *WhoSSW 91*
Crossley, Paul 1944- *IntWWM 90, PenDiMP*
Crossley, Randolph Allin 1904- *WhoAm 90*
Crossley, Reno E. 1957- *St&PR 91*
Crossley-Holland, Kevin 1941- *AuBYP 90*
Crossley-Holland, Peter Charles 1916- *IntWWM 90*
Crossman, Anne E. 1957- *WhoAmW 91*
Crossman, Edgar O., II 1930- *St&PR 91*
Crossman, Patrick F. 1931- *St&PR 91*
Crossman, R. H. S. 1907-1974 *BioIn 16*
Crossman, Richard Howard Stafford 1907-1974 *BioIn 16*
Crossman, William Whittard 1927- *WhoAm 90*
Crossman-Hecht, Eva *BioIn 16*
Crossno, Charles Lee 1956- *WhoEmL 91*
Crosson, Albert J. 1934- *WhoAm 90*
Crosson, David Earl 1948- *WhoAm 90*
Crosson, Frank 1943- *St&PR 91*
Crosson, Frederick James 1926- *WhoAm 90*
Crosson, James David 1961- *WhoE 91*
Crosson, James Edward 1933- *WhoE 91*
Crosson, W. David *ODwPR 91*
Crosswell, Charles Miller 1825-1886 *AmLegL*
Crosswell, Laurie Ellen 1956- *WhoAmW 91*
Crosswhite, Beverly Ann 1953- *WhoAmW 91*
Crosswhite, Jeanette Elvira 1941- *IntWWM 90*
Crosswhite, Jessie Sowers 1934- *WhoAmW 91*
Crosswhite, Randal Neal 1953- *St&PR 91*
Crosswhite, Victor William 1936- *St&PR 91*
Crost, Lyn *BioIn 16*
Crosten, William Loran 1909- *IntWWM 90*
Crosthwait, D. Lloyd, Jr. 1942- *St&PR 91*
Croswell, Edgar D. *NewYTBS 90 [port]*
Croswell, Robert S *BiDrAPA 89*
Croteau, Julie *BioIn 16*
Croteau, Robert Francis 1950- *St&PR 91*
Crothers, Donald Morris 1937- *WhoAm 90*
Crothers, Joan Helsel 1946- *WhoAmW 91*
Crothers, Larry Alan 1947- *WhoEmL 91*
Crothers, Rachel 1870?-1958 *BioIn 16, NotWoAT*
Crothers, Rachel 1878-1958 *BioAmW, FemiCLE*
Crothers, Scatman *BioIn 16*
Crothers, Scatman 1910-1986 *DrBlPA 90*
Crotto, Paul 1922- *WhoAmA 91*
Crotts, Glenn David 1953- *WhoSSW 91*
Crotty, John Joseph, Jr. 1934- *St&PR 91*
Crotty, Leo William 1927- *St&PR 91*
Crotty, Michael F. 1947- *WhoEmL 91*
Crotty, Peter *BioIn 16*
Crotty, Philip Thomas 1929- *WhoE 91*
Crotty, Wayne E. 1913- *St&PR 91*
Crotty, Willard Edwin *St&PR 91N*
Crotty, William 1936- *WhoAm 90*
Crotty, William M. 1937- *St&PR 91*
Crouch, Andrae *DrBlPA 90*
Crouch, Barbara Lee 1936- *WhoAmW 91*
Crouch, Bill W. 1947- *St&PR 91*
Crouch, Carol Denise *BiDrAPA 89*
Crouch, Clarence David 1957- *WhoSSW 91*
Crouch, Constance W. 1941- *WhoAmW 91*
Crouch, Daniel Everett 1956- *WhoEmL 91*
Crouch, David 1948- *ConAu 129*
Crouch, Eldon L. 1948- *St&PR 91*
Crouch, Florella G. 1953- *WhoAmW 91*
Crouch, Fordyce William 1914- *WhoAm 90*
Crouch, Gary Clinton 1956- *WhoEmL 91*
Crouch, Gary L. 1941- *St&PR 91*
Crouch, Helen Olive 1925- *WhoAmW 91*
Crouch, Howard Earle 1918- *WhoE 91, WhoWor 91*
Crouch, James Ensign 1908- *WhoAm 90*
Crouch, James Michael 1949- *WhoEmL 91*
Crouch, Jennifer Elaine 1952- *WhoAmW 91*
Crouch, Jordan Jones 1909- *WhoAm 90*
Crouch, Joyce Greer 1925- *WhoAmW 91*
Crouch, Leon 1928- *WhoSSW 91*
Crouch, Leona G. *BioIn 16*
Crouch, Les 1946- *St&PR 91*
Crouch, Margaret Ann 1956- *WhoAmW 91*
Crouch, Marilee S. 1951- *WhoAmW 91*
Crouch, Michelle Elaine 1964- *WhoAmW 91*
Crouch, Mickey Morgan 1935- *BiDrAPA 89*
Crouch, Ned Philbrick 1948- *WhoAmA 91*
Crouch, Richard W. 1950- *WhoSSW 91*
Crouch, Ruth 1637-1710 *BiDEWW*
Croucher, Frank 1914-1980 *Ballpl 90*
Crough, Daniel Francis 1936- *WhoE 91*
Croughan, Jack Lester *BiDrAPA 89*
Croughton, Amy H 1880-1951 *WhoAmA 91N*
Crounse, Frederick 1940- *WhoSSW 91*
Crounse, George P. 1912- *St&PR 91*
Crouse, Anna *AuBYP 90*
Crouse, Buck 1897-1983 *Ballpl 90*
Crouse, Clifford F. 1918- *St&PR 91*
Crouse, Edwin R. 1920- *St&PR 91*
Crouse, Farrell R 1932- *BiDrAPA 89*
Crouse, Farrell Rondall 1932- *WhoAm 90*
Crouse, James Robert 1949- *WhoEmL 91*
Crouse, Joseph Robert 1946- *WhoAm 90*
Crouse, Karen Jean 1962- *WhoWrEP 89*
Crouse, Lindsay 1948- *WhoAm 90, WhoAmW 91*
Crouse, Lloyd Roseville 1918- *WhoAm 90, WhoE 91*
Crouse, Michael Glenn 1949- *WhoAmA 91*
Crouse, R.J. 1920- *St&PR 91*
Crouse, Richard Paul 1939- *St&PR 91*
Crouse, Roger Leslie 1944- *WhoE 91*
Crouse, Russel 1893-1966 *OxCPMus, WorAlBi*
Crouse, Russel M. 1893-1966 *AuBYP 90*
Crouse, Ted *WhoSSW 91*
Crouse, William Harry 1907- *AuBYP 90*
Croushore, Dean Darrell 1956- *WhoE 91*
Crout, Elizabeth Roop 1925- *WhoAmW 91*
Crout, John Richard 1929- *WhoAm 90*
Crout, Teresa Elizabeth Kochmar 1945- *WhoWrEP 89*
Crouter, Richard Earl 1937- *WhoAm 90*
Crouton, Francois 1921- *WhoAmA 91*
Crouwel, Wim 1928- *ConDes 90*
Crouzat, Jacques *PenDiDA 89*
Crovello, James N 1937- *BiDrAPA 89*
Croves, Hal *MajTwCW*
Crovitz, Louis Gordon 1958- *WhoE 91*
Crovo, Frank Anthony, Jr. 1930- *St&PR 91*
Crow Dog 1835?-1910 *WhNaAH [port]*
Crow King *WhNaAH*
Crow, Barry L. 1943- *St&PR 91*
Crow, Bettina Lum *AuBYP 90*
Crow, Betty Lee 1929- *St&PR 91*
Crow, C. Gary 1936- *St&PR 91*
Crow, Carl Arnold, Jr. 1951- *WhoEmL 91*
Crow, Carol 1915- *WhoAmA 91*
Crow, Cecile Marie 1938- *WhoAmW 91*
Crow, Edwin Louis 1916- *WhoAm 90*
Crow, Elizabeth 1946- *BioIn 16, St&PR 91*
Crow, Elizabeth Smith *WhoAm 90, WhoAmW 91*
Crow, Harold Eugene 1933- *WhoAm 90, WhoWor 91*
Crow, Howard G *BiDrAPA 89*
Crow, James Franklin 1916- *WhoAm 90*
Crow, James Sylvester 1915- *WhoAm 90*
Crow, James T. *BioIn 16*
Crow, John Armstrong 1906- *WhoAm 90*
Crow, John French 1943- *BiDrAPA 89*
Crow, John William *BioIn 16*
Crow, John William 1937- *WhoAm 90, WhoWor 91*
Crow, Leo J. 1926- *St&PR 91*
Crow, Leslie Ellen 1954- *WhoAmW 91*
Crow, Lynne Campbell Smith 1942- *WhoAmW 91*
Crow, Marvin Boyd 1932- *St&PR 91*
Crow, Mary Lynn 1934- *WhoAmW 91*
Crow, Maureen B. *ODwPR 91*
Crow, Nancy Rebecca 1948- *WhoEmL 91*
Crow, Neil Edward 1926- *WhoAm 90*
Crow, Paul Abernathy, Jr. 1931- *WhoAm 90, WhoWor 91*
Crow, Richard Ronald 1915- *St&PR 91*
Crow, Richard Thomas 1939- *WhoSSW 91*
Crow, Richard ValJean 1924- *WhoSSW 91*
Crow, Robin *NewAgMG*
Crow, Sam Alfred 1926- *WhoAm 90*
Crow, Terry Tom 1931- *WhoAm 90*
Crow, Todd 1945- *IntWWM 90*
Crow, Todd William 1945- *WhoEmL 91*
Crow, Trammell *BioIn 16*
Crow, Trammell 1914- *ConAmBL, St&PR 91*
Crow, Walter 1936- *St&PR 91*
Crow, Walter, Jr. 1936- *WhoAm 90*
Crow, William Cecil 1904- *WhoAm 90*
Crow, William Langstaff 1910- *WhoAm 90*
Crowden, George Michael 1956- *WhoEmL 91*
Crowder, Anita Pauline 1933- *WhoAmW 91*
Crowder, Barbara Lynn 1956- *WhoAmW 91, WhoEmL 91, WhoWor 91*
Crowder, Beth Marie 1957- *WhoEmL 91*
Crowder, Bruce Houck 1942- *St&PR 91*
Crowder, Charles H. *St&PR 91N*
Crowder, David Herman 1950- *WhoEmL 91*
Crowder, David Lester 1941- *WhoAm 90*
Crowder, Elizabeth *WhoAmW 91*
Crowder, Enoch H. 1859-1932 *BioIn 16*
Crowder, General 1899-1972 *Ballpl 90*
Crowder, Helen L. 1928- *St&PR 91*
Crowder, Jack *ConTFT 8*
Crowder, James Caswell 1941- *St&PR 91*
Crowder, Jaye Douglas *BiDrAPA 89*
Crowder, John E 1946- *BiDrAPA 89*
Crowder, Judy Alicia 1960- *WhoEmL 91*
Crowder, Linda Fay 1952- *WhoWrEP 89*
Crowder, Michael 1934-1988 *AnObit 1988, BioIn 16*
Crowder, Miles Keeney 1943- *BiDrAPA 89*
Crowder, Moncure Gravatt 1940- *St&PR 91*
Crowder, Rebecca *ODwPR 91*
Crowder, Richard Thomas 1939- *WhoAm 90, WhoE 91*
Crowder, Wade Allen *BiDrAPA 89*
Crowder, William Stinson 1940- *IntWWM 90*
Crowdus, Clark 1949- *WhoEmL 91*
Crowdus, Gary Alan 1945- *WhoAm 90, WhoWrEP 89*
Crowe, Brenda Stone 1946- *WhoSSW 91*
Crowe, Byron A. *St&PR 91*
Crowe, Cameron 1957- *BioIn 16*
Crowe, Cameron Macmillan 1931- *WhoAm 90*
Crowe, Catherine 1790?-1872 *FemiCLE*
Crowe, Catherine 1800?-1876 *BioIn 16*
Crowe, Charles Lawson 1928- *WhoAm 90*
Crowe, Colin 1913-1989 *AnObit 1989*
Crowe, Daniel L. 1947- *St&PR 91*
Crowe, David Barr 1956- *BiDrAPA 89*
Crowe, Devon George 1948- *WhoSSW 91*
Crowe, Eugene Bertrand 1916- *WhoAm 90, WhoWor 91*
Crowe, George 1923- *Ballpl 90*
Crowe, J.D. 1937- *ConMus 5 [port]*
Crowe, James Joseph 1935- *St&PR 91, WhoAm 90*
Crowe, John *TwCCr&M 91, WhoWrEP 89*
Crowe, John 1924- *BioIn 16*
Crowe, John Carl 1937- *St&PR 91, WhoAm 90*
Crowe, John Joseph 1930- *WhoSSW 91*
Crowe, John T. 1938- *WhoWor 91*
Crowe, Joseph Francis 1938- *St&PR 91*
Crowe, Martin A. *St&PR 91*
Crowe, Martin Joseph, III 1930- *St&PR 91*
Crowe, Patrick James 1944- *St&PR 91*
Crowe, Raymond R 1942- *BiDrAPA 89*
Crowe, Robert Alan 1950- *WhoEmL 91*
Crowe, Robert William 1924- *WhoAm 90*
Crowe, Ronald Girardeau 1932- *WhoWrEP 89*
Crowe, Thomas Kealey 1957- *WhoEmL 91*
Crowe, Tonya *BioIn 16*
Crowe, W.R. 1925- *St&PR 91*
Crowe, William J. 1925- *BioIn 16*
Crowe, William James, Jr. 1925- *WhoAm 90, WhoSSW 91*
Crowell, Ann *AuBYP 90*
Crowell, Bradford Allan, Jr. 1960- *BiDrAPA 89*
Crowell, Caleb 1932- *St&PR 91*
Crowell, Carol Ann 1958- *WhoAmW 91, WhoEmL 91*
Crowell, Charles Byron 1943- *St&PR 91*
Crowell, Douglas John 1954- *St&PR 91*
Crowell, Edward Prince 1926- *WhoAm 90*
Crowell, Eldon Hubbard 1924- *WhoAm 90*
Crowell, Frances Elisabeth 1875-1950 *BioIn 16*
Crowell, Gentry 1932-1989 *BioIn 16*
Crowell, J.B. 1933- *St&PR 91*
Crowell, J.L. 1916- *St&PR 91*
Crowell, James T. *AmLegL*
Crowell, John B., Jr. 1930- *WhoAm 90*
Crowell, John Chambers 1917- *WhoAm 90*
Crowell, Joseph T. *AmLegL*
Crowell, Judith Ann *BiDrAPA 89*
Crowell, Kay Upton 1947- *WhoSSW 91*
Crowell, Kenneth Leland 1933- *WhoE 91*
Crowell, Lucius 1911-1988 *WhoAmA 91N*
Crowell, Nancy Melzer 1948- *WhoEmL 91*
Crowell, Ohmer O. 1924- *St&PR 91*
Crowell, Ohmer Oreal 1924- *WhoAm 90*
Crowell, Raymond E. 1926- *St&PR 91*
Crowell, Richard Henry 1928- *WhoAm 90, WhoE 91*
Crowell, Richard Lane 1930- *WhoAm 90*
Crowell, Robert L 1909- *SmATA 63 [port]*
Crowell, Robert Leland 1909- *WhoAm 90, WhoE 91*
Crowell, Rodney *BioIn 16, WhoNeCM [port]*
Crowell, Ronald Keith 1948- *St&PR 91*
Crowell, Rosemary Elaine 1942- *WhoAmW 91*
Crowell, Warren H. 1905- *St&PR 91*
Crowell, Wayne Franklin 1937- *St&PR 91*
Crowell, William M *BiDrAPA 89*
Crowers, Richard T. 1923- *St&PR 91*
Crowfoot 1821-1890 *WhNaAH [port]*
Crowfoot, Barbara Lynne 1945- *WhoAmW 91*
Crowl, Gary Michael 1955- *WhoEmL 91*
Crowl, John Allen 1935- *WhoAm 90*
Crowl, Martha Jean 1941- *WhoAmW 91*
Crowl, R. Bern 1931- *St&PR 91*
Crowl, Richard Bern 1931- *WhoAm 90*
Crowl, Samuel Renninger 1940- *WhoAm 90*
Crowle, Alfred John 1930- *WhoAm 90*
Crowley, Aleister 1875-1947 *BioIn 16, EncO&P 3, EncPaPR 91, WorAlBi*
Crowley, Brian 1933- *BiDrAPA 89*
Crowley, Brian Scott 1950- *WhoEmL 91*
Crowley, Carol Dee 1931- *WhoWrEP 89*
Crowley, Daniel John 1921- *WhoAm 90*
Crowley, David Benjamin 1954- *WhoE 91*
Crowley, Denis Mark 1922- *St&PR 91*
Crowley, Diane 1939- *WhoAm 90*
Crowley, E.J. 1938- *St&PR 91*
Crowley, Edward Denis 1926- *St&PR 91*
Crowley, Elizabeth Marlene 1940- *WhoAmW 91*
Crowley, Ellen Teresa 1943- *St&PR 91*
Crowley, Francis E. 1934- *St&PR 91*
Crowley, Francis L *BiDrAPA 89*
Crowley, Geoffrey Thomas 1952- *St&PR 91*
Crowley, George J. 1939- *St&PR 91*
Crowley, James Farrell 1946- *WhoAm 90*
Crowley, James T. 1943- *WhoAm 90*
Crowley, James Worthington 1930- *St&PR 91, WhoAm 90*
Crowley, Jane F *BiDrAPA 89*
Crowley, Jerome J., Jr. 1939- *St&PR 91*
Crowley, Jerome Joseph, Jr. 1939- *WhoAm 90*
Crowley, Jill 1950- *BioIn 16*
Crowley, John Crane 1919- *WhoWor 91*
Crowley, John Dale 1961- *BiDrAPA 89*
Crowley, John Joseph, Jr. 1928- *WhoAm 90*
Crowley, John P. 1924- *St&PR 91*
Crowley, John Robert 1929- *WhoWor 91*
Crowley, John Schaft 1923- *St&PR 91*
Crowley, John William 1945- *WhoAm 90*
Crowley, Joseph B. 1905- *WhoAm 90*
Crowley, Joseph C., Jr. 1936- *St&PR 91*
Crowley, Joseph Michael 1940- *WhoAm 90*
Crowley, Joseph Neil 1933- *WhoAm 90*
Crowley, Joseph Paul 1944- *St&PR 91, WhoSSW 91*
Crowley, Joseph R. 1915- *WhoAm 90*
Crowley, Kate *BioIn 16*
Crowley, Keith L. 1934- *St&PR 91*
Crowley, Kevin D. 1958- *WhoEmL 91*
Crowley, Leonard James 1921- *WhoAm 90*
Crowley, Lisa A. *St&PR 91*
Crowley, Maria Elena 1943- *WhoSSW 91*
Crowley, Mark 1933- *St&PR 91*
Crowley, Nicholas Pearse 1949- *WhoEmL 91*
Crowley, Pat *ConTFT 8*
Crowley, Pat 1938- *WhoAm 90*
Crowley, Patricia *ConTFT 8*
Crowley, Patrick J. 1941- *St&PR 91*
Crowley, Patty *BioIn 16*
Crowley, Ray E. 1932- *WhoAm 90, WhoSSW 91*
Crowley, Raymond *WhoAm 90*
Crowley, Richard Allerton 1949- *WhoEmL 91*
Crowley, Richard M. 1935- *St&PR 91*
Crowley, Richard Martyn 1931- *St&PR 91*
Crowley, Robert Dale 1949- *St&PR 91*
Crowley, Terry 1947- *Ballpl 90*
Crowley, Thomas B. 1914- *WhoAm 90*
Crowley, Thomas J. 1931- *St&PR 91*
Crowley, Thomas Joseph 1930- *St&PR 91*
Crowley, Thomas Robert 1947- *St&PR 91*
Crowley, William Francis, Jr. 1943- *WhoAm 90*
Crowley, William Gary 1948- *WhoAm 90*
Crowley, William J 1927- *BiDrAPA 89*
Crowley, William James *BiDrAPA 89*

Crowley, William Morris 1940- *WhoE 91*
Crowley-Long, Kathleen 1958- *WhoAmW 91*
Crowling, Patrick McGuire, Jr. 1942- *WhoSSW 91*
Crowll, John Lee 1954- *WhoSSW 91*
Crown, Aric Steven 1952- *St&PR 91*
Crown, Charles W *BiDrAPA 89*
Crown, David Allan 1928- *WhoAm 90*
Crown, Frederick Smith, Jr. 1949- *WhoEmL 91*
Crown, Henry *NewYTBS 90 [port]*
Crown, Henry 1896- *St&PR 91, WhoAm 90*
Crown, Henry 1896-1990 *CurBio 90N*
Crown, John P. 1922- *St&PR 91*
Crown, Judith Ann 1952- *WhoE 91*
Crown, Keith Allen 1918- *WhoAmA 91*
Crown, Lester 1925- *St&PR 91, WhoAm 90*
Crown, Nancy Elizabeth 1955- *WhoAmW 91, WhoEmL 91*
Crowner, Sara Louise 1957- *BiDrAPA 89*
Crownfield, Gertrude 1867-1945 *AuBYP 90*
Crowninshield, Benjamin Williams 1772-1851 *BiDrUSE 89*
Crownover, James Darragh 1929- *St&PR 91*
Crows, Harry 1921- *St&PR 91*
Crowson, James L. 1938- *St&PR 91*
Crowson, Robert E., Jr. 1947- *St&PR 91*
Crowston, Wallace Bruce Stewart 1934- *WhoAm 90*
Crowther, Bosley 1905-1981 *WorAlBi*
Crowther, Brian *TwCCr&M 91*
Crowther, Christy Lynn 1958- *WhoAmW 91*
Crowther, G. Rodney, III 1927- *WhoE 91, WhoWor 91*
Crowther, H. David 1930- *St&PR 91, WhoAm 90*
Crowther, James E. 1930- *St&PR 91*
Crowther, James Earl 1930- *WhoAm 90*
Crowther, James Gerald 1899- *AuBYP 90*
Crowther, Patricia Anne 1925- *BiDrAPA 89*
Crowther, Richard Layton 1910- *WhoAm 90*
Crowther-Alwyn, Peter 1944- *WhoWor 91*
Croxford, Eileen 1924- *IntWWM 90*
Croxford, Lynne Louise 1947- *WhoAmW 91*
Croxson, Jeremy P. G. *WhoAm 90*
Croxson, Morva Olwyn 1934- *IntWWM 90*
Croxton, Frederick Emory, Jr. 1923- *WhoAm 90*
Croy, Dan Jack 1933- *BiDrAPA 89*
Croy, Daniel Albert 1951- *WhoSSW 91*
Croy, Elisabeth de *BioIn 16*
Croydon, Michael Benet 1931- *WhoAmA 91*
Croyle, John *BioIn 16*
Croyle, Thomas J. 1949- *St&PR 91*
Croyle, William R. 1920- *St&PR 91*
Crozat-Williams, Madeleine *BioIn 16*
Crozaz, Ghislaine 1939- *WhoAmW 91*
Crozer, John Price 1793-1866 *BioIn 16*
Crozet, Claudius 1790-1864 *BioIn 16*
Crozier, Catharine 1914- *IntWWM 90*
Crozier, Eric John 1914- *IntWWM 90*
Crozier, John Huntington 1935- *St&PR 91*
Crozier, Lorna 1948- *ConAu 32NR*
Crozier, Lucille Breeding 1907- *WhoAmW 91*
Crozier, Michel 1922- *WhoWor 91*
Crozier, Michel J. 1922- *ConAu 130*
Crozier, Ouida G. 1947- *WhoWrEP 89*
Crozier, Prudence Slitor 1940- *WhoAmW 91, WhoE 91*
Crozier, Richard Lewis 1944- *WhoAmA 91*
Crozier, St George 1814-1892 *DcCanB 12*
Crozier, William K, Jr 1926- *WhoAmA 91*
Crozier, William Marshall, Jr. 1932- *St&PR 91, WhoAm 90*
Cruce, Teresia Benedicta a *EncCoWW*
Cruchet, Jean-Denis 1939- *WhoE 91, WhoWor 91*
Cruciger, Alfred 1937- *St&PR 91*
Crucke, Koen 1952- *IntWWM 90*
Crudden, Charles Henry 1908- *BiDrAPA 89*
Crudden, Joseph Courtney 1930- *St&PR 91*
Cruden, Joan Patricia 1951- *WhoAmW 91*
Cruden, John Charles 1946- *WhoEmL 91*
Crudge, Vernon 1912-1989 *BioIn 16*
Crudup, Arthur 1905- *EncPR&S 89*
Crudup, Carl W *DrBlPA 90*
Cruess, Leigh Saunders 1958- *WhoEmL 91*
Cruess, Richard Leigh 1929- *WhoAm 90*
Cruet, Jorge Luis 1952- *WhoE 91*
Cruft, Edgar Frank 1933- *St&PR 91*
Cruger, F. Christopher 1935- *St&PR 91*
Cruger, Mary 1834-1908 *FemiCLE*
Cruger, Michael H. 1945- *St&PR 91*
Cruice, Francis Joseph 1957- *WhoE 91*
Cruickshank, Alexander Middleton 1919- *WhoAm 90*
Cruickshank, Andrew 1907-1988 *AnObit 1988*
Cruickshank, Helen 1907- *AuBYP 90*
Cruickshank, James Stanley 1946- *St&PR 91*
Cruickshank, John Malcolm 1938- *WhoWor 91*
Cruickshank, Michael James 1929- *WhoAm 90, WhoWor 91*
Cruickshank, Sheila Ethel 1937- *WhoAmW 91*
Cruickshank, William Mellon 1915- *WhoAm 90*
Cruikshank, George 1792-1878 *BioIn 16*
Cruikshank, John W., III 1933- *WhoAm 90*
Cruikshank, Nelson Hale 1902-1986 *BioIn 16*
Cruikshank, Robert James 1930- *WhoAm 90*
Cruikshank, Robert Lane 1936- *WhoAm 90*
Cruikshank, Thomas Henry 1931- *St&PR 91, WhoAm 90, WhoSSW 91*
Cruikshank, Warren Lott 1916- *WhoAm 90*
Cruise, Francis Augustine 1932- *St&PR 91*
Cruise, John R. 1941- *St&PR 91*
Cruise, Tom *BioIn 16*
Cruise, Tom 1962- *WhoAm 90, WorAlBi*
Cruise, Walt 1890-1975 *Ballpl 90*
Crull, Linda Befeld 1947- *WhoAmW 91*
Crull, Timm F. 1931- *WhoAm 90*
Crum, Albert B 1931- *BiDrAPA 89*
Crum, Albert Byrd 1931- *WhoE 91*
Crum, David 1938- *WhoAmA 91*
Crum, Denny 1937- *WorAlBi*
Crum, Denny Edwin 1937- *WhoAm 90*
Crum, Fred C., Jr. 1944- *St&PR 91*
Crum, George Francis, Jr. 1926- *WhoAm 90*
Crum, James Francis 1934- *WhoAm 90*
Crum, John Kistler 1936- *WhoAm 90*
Crum, Katherine B 1941- *WhoAmA 91*
Crum, Lawrence Lee 1933- *WhoAm 90*
Crum, Rosa Maria *BiDrAPA 89*
Crum, Steven Dale 1954- *WhoEmL 91*
Crumb, George *BioIn 16*
Crumb, George 1929- *IntWWM 90, PenDiMP A*
Crumb, George Henry 1929- *WhoAm 90*
Crumb, Owen J. 1925- *ODwPR 91*
Crumb, Owen Joseph 1925- *WhoAm 90*
Crumb, Robert 1932- *EncACom*
Crumb-Wolfe, Brenda Jean 1962- *WhoAmW 91*
Crumbaker-Lomax, Mary Kathryn *WhoWor 91*
Crumbaugh, James C 1912- *EncO&P 3*
Crumbaugh, Lee Forrest 1947- *WhoAm 90*
Crumbley, D. Larry *BioIn 16*
Crumbley, Donald Larry 1941- *WhoAm 90*
Crumbley, Esther Helen 1928- *WhoSSW 91*
Crumbley, R. Alex 1942- *WhoSSW 91*
Crumbo, Minisa 1942- *WhoAmW 91*
Crume, Lou Ann *BiDrAPA 89*
Crumes, William Edward 1914- *WhoAm 90*
Crumit, Frank 1889-1943 *OxCPMus*
Crumley, Beth Bailey 1962- *WhoSSW 91*
Crumley, Bruce L. 1948- *St&PR 91*
Crumley, David Oliver 1949- *WhoSSW 91*
Crumley, Frank Edward 1936- *BiDrAPA 89*
Crumley, James 1939- *TwCCr&M 91, WhoWrEP 89*
Crumley, James Harold 1953- *WhoAm 90*
Crumley, James Robert, Jr. 1925- *WhoAm 90, WhoSSW 91*
Crumley, John Walter 1944- *WhoSSW 91*
Crumley, Laura Lee 1949- *WhoWor 91*
Crumley, Martha Ann 1910- *WhoSSW 91*
Crumley, Roger Lee 1941- *WhoAm 90*
Crumlin, Rosemary Anne 1932- *WhoWor 91*
Crumlish, James Patrick 1944- *St&PR 91*
Crumlish, Joseph Dougherty 1922- *WhoE 91*
Crummer, Murray Thomas, Jr. 1922- *WhoAm 90*
Crummette, Hugh David 1937- *St&PR 91*
Crummie, Robert G 1938- *BiDrAPA 89*
Crump, Caryn McQuilkin 1953- *WhoEmL 91*
Crump, Charles H. 1926- *WhoWrEP 89*
Crump, Charles Metcalf 1913- *WhoSSW 91*
Crump, Constance A. 1948- *WhoAmW 91*
Crump, Elizabeth Burford 1932- *St&PR 91*
Crump, G. Lindsay 1922- *St&PR 91*
Crump, Galbraith Miller 1929- *WhoAm 90*
Crump, Harold Craft 1931- *St&PR 91*
Crump, J. Irving 1901-1979 *BioIn 16*
Crump, James Gleason 1930- *St&PR 91*
Crump, James Irving 1887-1979 *AuBYP 90*
Crump, James Noble 1908- *St&PR 91*
Crump, Judy Gail 1955- *WhoWrEP 89*
Crump, Kathleen 1884-1977 *WhoAmA 91N*
Crump, Larry 1953- *WhoWor 91*
Crump, Larry Cameron 1948- *WhoEmL 91*
Crump, Mary Nola 1919- *St&PR 91*
Crump, Neville *BioIn 16*
Crump, Peter Norman 1928- *IntWWM 90*
Crump, Ronald Cordell 1951- *WhoEmL 91*
Crump, Spencer *WhoAm 90*
Crump, Stuart Faulkner, Jr. 1945- *WhoSSW 91*
Crump, Thomas Fletcher 1956- *St&PR 91, WhoAm 90*
Crump, W Leslie 1894-1962 *WhoAmA 91N*
Crump, Walter Moore, Jr 1941- *WhoAmA 91*
Crumpacker, Carol A. 1958- *WhoAmW 91*
Crumpler, Donna Burt 1950- *WhoSSW 91*
Crumpley, Wayne E. 1943- *St&PR 91*
Crumpton, Charles Whitmarsh 1946- *WhoEmL 91*
Crumpton, Lisa M *BiDrAPA 89*
Crunden, John 1740-1828? *PenDiDA 89*
Crupi, Thomas James 1946- *WhoE 91*
Crupie, Joseph E 1924- *BiDrAPA 89*
Crusat, Paulina 1900- *EncCoWW*
Cruse, C. Lansford 1956- *St&PR 91*
Cruse, Donald, Jr. 1932- *St&PR 91*
Cruse, Elise Wandel *BioIn 16*
Cruse, Emily E. 1952- *WhoAmW 91*
Cruse, Fredrich James 1947- *WhoEmL 91*
Cruse, Irma Belle Russell 1911- *WhoAmW 91, WhoSSW 91, WhoWor 91*
Cruse, Irma R. *BioIn 16*
Cruse, Irma Russell 1911- *WhoWrEP 89*
Cruse, Julius Major, Jr. 1937- *WhoAm 90, WhoSSW 91, WhoWor 91*
Cruse, R.L. 1932- *St&PR 91*
Cruser, George E. 1930- *St&PR 91*
Crusham, Michael S. 1950- *St&PR 91*
Crusinberry, James 1879-1960 *Ballpl 90*
Crutcher, Anita Maria 1951- *WhoSSW 91*
Crutcher, Chris 1946- *BioIn 16*
Crutcher, Christopher C. 1946- *WhoWrEP 89*
Crutcher, Frances Hill 1905- *IntWWM 90*
Crutcher, Gerald Henry 1942- *WhoSSW 91*
Crutcher, Harold Trabue, Jr. 1938- *WhoAm 90*
Crutcher, Howard K., Jr. *BiDrAPA 89*
Crutcher, John William 1916- *WhoAm 90*
Crutcher, Lawrence McVickar 1942- *St&PR 91*
Crutcher, Nancy Lee Price 1944- *WhoSSW 91*
Crutchfield, Barbara Ann Johnson *WhoSSW 91*
Crutchfield, Charles Calvin, Jr. 1948- *WhoEmL 91*
Crutchfield, Charles H. 1912- *St&PR 91*
Crutchfield, Edward Elliott, Jr. 1941- *St&PR 91, WhoAm 90, WhoSSW 91*
Crutchfield, James Andrew 1938- *WhoWrEP 89*
Crutchfield, Jimmie 1910- *Ballpl 90*
Crutchfield, Oscar Minor 1800-1861 *AmLegL*
Crutchfield, Robert J. *ODwPR 91*
Crutchfield, Sam Shaw, Jr. 1934- *WhoAm 90*
Crutchfield, William Richard 1932- *WhoAm 90, WhoAmA 91*
Crutchley, Carolynn Adele *BiDrAPA 89*
Crutchley, Carolynn Adele 1951- *WhoE 91*
Crutchley, Rosalie 1921- *ConTFT 8*
Crute, O. Jacqueline 1947- *WhoSSW 91*
Cruthers, David Crowell 1955- *WhoE 91*
Cruthers, James Winter 1924- *St&PR 91*
Cruthird, Robert Lee 1944- *WhoWor 91*
Cruthirds, Elizabeth Harper 1952- *WhoSSW 91*
Crutsinger, Robert Keane 1930- *St&PR 91, WhoAm 90*
Cruttenden, Walter W., Jr. 1923- *St&PR 91*
Cruver, Philip Charles 1945- *WhoSSW 91*
Cruver, Suzanne Lee 1942- *WhoAmW 91*
Cruys, George *ODwPR 91*
Cruz, Abraham 1949- *WhoHisp 91*
Cruz, Albert Raymond 1933- *WhoHisp 91*
Cruz, Andres Santa 1792-1865 *BioIn 16*
Cruz, Antonio L. *WhoHisp 91*
Cruz, Arturo, Jr. 1954?- *ConAu 131, HispWr 90*
Cruz, Aurelio R. 1934- *WhoHisp 91*
Cruz, B. Roberto 1941- *WhoHisp 91*
Cruz, Ben Ruben 1918- *WhoHisp 91*
Cruz, Carlos 1940- *WhoHisp 91*
Cruz, Catherine Stannie 1960- *WhoAmW 91*
Cruz, Celia *WhoHisp 91*
Cruz, Cristina *BiDrAPA 89*
Cruz, Daniel Louis 1951- *WhoHisp 91*
Cruz, Emilio *WhoAmA 91*
Cruz, Erasmo, Sr. 1940- *WhoHisp 91*
Cruz, Erasmo R, Jr. 1948- *BiDrAPA 89*
Cruz, Georgina 1945- *ODwPR 91*
Cruz, Gilbert R 1929- *ConAu 131, HispWr 90, WhoHisp 91*
Cruz, Gilberto Rafael *ConAu 131, HispWr 90*
Cruz, Gregory A. *WhoHisp 91*
Cruz, Hector 1953- *Ballpl 90*
Cruz, Herbert Angel *BiDrAPA 89*
Cruz, Jose 1947- *Ballpl 90 [port]*
Cruz, Jose A *BiDrAPA 89*
Cruz, Jose Bejar 1932- *WhoAm 90*
Cruz, Juana Ines de la 1651-1695 *BioIn 16*
Cruz, Julia Margarita 1948- *WhoHisp 91*
Cruz, Julio 1954- *Ballpl 90*
Cruz, Luis F. Gonzalez- 1943- *BioIn 16*
Cruz, Manuel Franklin 1937- *WhoE 91*
Cruz, Migdalia 1958- *WhoHisp 91*
Cruz, Miguel A. 1957- *WhoSSW 91*
Cruz, Miriam Cosca 1946- *BiDrAPA 89*
Cruz, Nicomedes Santa *HispWr 90*
Cruz, Norma Oropesa 1943- *WhoAmW 91*
Cruz, Norma Picio 1941- *BiDrAPA 89*
Cruz, Phillip 1955- *WhoHisp 91*
Cruz, Pura *WhoAmA 91*
Cruz, Ralph 1935- *St&PR 91*
Cruz, Raul Apolinario 1946- *WhoAm 90*
Cruz, Raymond 1953- *WhoHisp 91*
Cruz, Renier 1952- *WhoSSW 91*
Cruz, Ricardo A. 1950- *St&PR 91*
Cruz, Richard L 1953- *BiDrAPA 89*
Cruz, Roque Gonzalez de Santa 1576-1628 *BioIn 16*
Cruz, Secundino 1938- *WhoHisp 91*
Cruz, Sherry Laraine 1945- *WhoAmW 91*
Cruz, Silvia 1959- *WhoHisp 91*
Cruz, Tim R. 1959- *WhoHisp 91*
Cruz, Todd 1955- *Ballpl 90*
Cruz, Victor 1957- *Ballpl 90*
Cruz, Victor Hernandez 1949- *BioIn 16, ConAu 32NR, HispWr 90, WhoHisp 91*
Cruz, Victor M *BiDrAPA 89*
Cruz, Willie *WhoHisp 91*
Cruz Aponte, Ramon Aristides 1927- *WhoAm 90, WhoHisp 91, WhoWor 91*
Cruz-Cuebas, Blanca 1939- *WhoSSW 91*
Cruz-Diez, Carlos 1923- *ArtLatA, WhoWor 91*
Cruz e Souza, Joao da 1861-1898 *BioIn 16*
Cruz-Emeric, Jorge A. 1951- *WhoHisp 91*
Cruz-Igartua, Arnaldo *BiDrAPA 89*
Cruz-Lim, Maria Ami *BiDrAPA 89*
Cruz Monclova, Lidio 1899- *HispWr 90*
Cruz-Rodriguez, Escolastico 1931- *WhoHisp 91*
Cruz-Romo, Gilda *WhoAm 90, WhoHisp 91*
Cruz-Romo, Gilda 1940- *IntWWM 90*
Cruz-Velez, David Francisco 1951- *WhoHisp 91*
Cruzan, Clarah Catherine 1913- *WhoSSW 91*
Cruzan, Joe *BioIn 16*
Cruzan, Nancy *BioIn 16*
Cruzat, Roscoe Modesta *BioIn 16*
Cruze, Alvin M. 1939- *St&PR 91, WhoAm 90*
Cruze, Kenneth 1927- *WhoE 91*
Cruzen, James John 1942- *BiDrAPA 89*
Cryan, Allison Foil 1961- *WhoAmW 91*
Cryan, Jeffrey L. 1951- *WhoE 91*
Cryan, Pete Scott 1953- *WhoSSW 91, WhoWor 91*
Cryer, Edward John 1935- *WhoE 91*
Cryer, Eugene Edward 1935- *WhoAm 90, WhoSSW 91*
Cryer, Gretchen 1935- *WhoAm 90*
Cryer, Jon *BioIn 16*
Cryer, Theodore Hudson 1946- *WhoE 91*
Crymes, Ronald Jack 1935- *WhoSSW 91*
Crynes, Billy Lee 1938- *WhoAm 90*
Crystal *NewAgMG*
Crystal, Allan A. 1929- *St&PR 91*
Crystal, Andrew Joseph 1950- *WhoE 91*
Crystal, Billy *BioIn 16*
Crystal, Billy 1947- *WhoAm 90, WorAlBi*
Crystal, Boris 1931- *WhoAmA 91*
Crystal, David, II 1938- *WhoE 91*
Crystal, Graef Slater 1934- *WhoAm 90*
Crystal, James William 1937- *WhoE 91, WhoWor 91*
Crystal, Joel Frome 1945- *WhoEmL 91*
Crystal, John C. 1920-1988 *BioIn 16*
Crystal, Lester Martin 1934- *WhoAm 90*
Crystal, Robert Abraham 1956- *WhoE 91*
Crystals, The *EncPR&S 89*
Csabina, Sandor Fanos 1951- *WhoWor 91*
Csajbok, Terezia 1930- *IntWWM 90*
Csanady, Gabriel Tibor 1925- *WhoAm 90*
Csanalosi, Irma B 1921- *BiDrAPA 89*
Csanyi-Salcedo, Zoltan F. 1964- *WhoHisp 91*
Csapo, Gyula 1955- *IntWWM 90*
Csaposs, Jean Fox 1931- *WhoAmW 91*
Csavinszky, Peter John 1931- *WhoAm 90*
Cseh, William M *BiDrAPA 89*
Csehak, Judit 1940- *WhoWor 91*

Csencsits, Christopher Joseph WhoE 91
Csendes, Ernest 1926- WhoWor 91
Csengery, Adrienne 1950- IntWWM 90
Csenki, Imre 1912- IntWWM 90
Cseres, Tibor 1915- WhoWor 91
Csermely, Thomas John 1931- WhoE 91, WhoWor 91
Csernansky, John Gary BiDrAPA 89
Csernus, Tibor 1927- WhoAmA 91
Cserny, Edith 1907- BiDrAPA 89
Cserr, Robert 1936- BiDrAPA 89, WhoAm 90
Csetri, C Frank 1931- BiDrAPA 89
Csia, Susan Rebecca 1945- WhoAm 90
Csik, Miklos 1930- IntWWM 90
Csikos, Rezso 1930- WhoWor 91
Csikszentmihalyi, Mihaly 1934- WhoAm 90
Csiszar, Antal 1946- WhoWor 91
Csiszar, Paul Leslie 1957- WhoEmL 91
Csoka, Stephen WhoAmA 91N
Csoka, Stephen 1897-1989 BioIn 16
Csonka, Larry BioIn 16
Csonka, Larry 1946- WorAlBi
Csoori, Sandor 1930- WorAu 1980 [port]
Csorgo, Miklos 1932- WhoAm 90
Cua, Antonio S. 1932- WhoAm 90
Cua, Rosita Lee BiDrAPA 89
Cuadra, Carlos Albert 1925- WhoAm 90
Cuadra, Julio Cesar 1946- WhoEmL 91
Cuadra, Pablo Antonio 1912- BioIn 16, ConAu 131, HispWr 90
Cuadrado, Carlos Mellizo ConAu 130
Cuadrado, John J. WhoHisp 91
Cuadros, Alvaro Julio 1926- WhoHisp 91
Cuadros, Carlos BiDrAPA 89
Cuarenta, Jayne Stephanie 1959- WhoHisp 91
Cuaresma, Luz Bunuan 1946- BiDrAPA 89
Cuaron, Alicia Valladolid 1939- WhoHisp 91
Cuaron, Marco A. 1944- WhoHisp 91
Cuatrecasas, Pedro Martin 1936- WhoWor 91
Cuba, Ernesto N BiDrAPA 89
Cubalchini, Linda Sharon 1956- WhoEmL 91
Cubas, Jose M. WhoHisp 91
Cubas, Jose Manuel 1930- WhoAm 90, WhoE 91
Cubbage, Mike 1950- Ballpl 90
Cubberley, Ellwood Patterson 1868-1941 BioIn 16
Cubberley, Robert R. 1948- St&PR 91
Cubberley, William Charles 1945- WhoE 91
Cubbins, Robert Fulton 1929- WhoE 91
Cubbins, William R. 1924- BioIn 16
Cubena 1941- WhoHisp 91
Cuberli, Lella BioIn 16
Cuberli, Lella 1950- IntWWM 90
Cubeta, Paul Marsden 1925- WhoAm 90
Cubine, Margaret Virginia 1919- WhoAmW 91
Cubita, Peter Naylor 1957- WhoE 91, WhoEmL 91
Cubr, Antonin 1904- IntWWM 90
Cuccaro, Ronald Anthony 1944- WhoE 91
Cucchi, Giancarlo 1936- WhoWor 91
Cucci, Anthony WhoE 91
Cucci, Cesare Eleuterio 1925- WhoAm 90
Cucci, Domenico Filippo 1630?-1705 PenDiDA 89
Cucci, Francis X. BioIn 16
Cuccinelli, Kenneth T. 1945- St&PR 91
Cuccinelli, Kenneth Thomas 1945- WhoWor 91
Cuccinello, Tony 1907- Ballpl 90
Cucco, Salvatore Nicholas 1948- St&PR 91
Cucco, Ulisse P. 1929- WhoAm 90
Cuccumos, Filippo PenDiDA 89
Cucinotta, Philip L. St&PR 91
Cucksey, John Davenport 1934- St&PR 91
Cuckston, Alan George 1940- IntWWM 90
Cuculic, Zarko BiDrAPA 89
Cuculo, Paula Marie 1955- WhoE 91
Cudahy, Dorothy BioIn 16
Cudahy, Edward A. 1860-1941 WorAlBi
Cudahy, Michael 1841-1910 WorAlBi
Cudahy, Richard D. 1926- WhoAm 90
Cudd, Ben Keaton, III 1945- WhoSSW 91
Cuddahy, John P. 1930- WhoAm 90
Cuddahy, John Patrick 1930- St&PR 91
Cuddeback, James Edward 1934- St&PR 91
Cuddehe, Judith Link 1961- WhoAmW 91
Cuddihy, John C. ODwPR 91
Cuddihy, Robert V., Jr. 1959- St&PR 91
Cuddihy, Robert Vincent, Jr. 1959- WhoE 91
Cuddon, Eric 1905- EncO&P 3
Cude, Bobby Lee 1925- WhoSSW 91
Cude, Reginald Hodgin 1936- WhoE 91
Cudemo, Regina BiDrAPA 89
Cudlin, Robert L. 1949- St&PR 91
Cudlip, Charles Thomas 1940- WhoE 91
Cudlip, Jack Merlin 1924- St&PR 91
Cudlipp, Alice Verner 1941- WhoAmW 91
Cudmore, Peter Lucian 1957- IntWWM 90
Cudney, Marsha BioIn 16
Cudworth, Allen 1929- St&PR 91
Cudworth, Allen L. 1929- WhoAm 90
Cudworth, Damaris 1658-1708 BiDEWW
Cudworth, Marsha Elizabeth 1947- WhoWrEP 89
Cudworth, Raymond P. 1938- St&PR 91
Cudzilo, Cheryle Ann 1957- WhoEmL 91
Cuellar, Alfredo M. 1946- WhoHisp 91
Cuellar, Enrique Roberto 1955- WhoEmL 91, WhoHisp 91
Cuellar, Gilbert, Jr. WhoHisp 91
Cuellar, John A. 1945- St&PR 91
Cuellar, Michael J. 1956- WhoHisp 91
Cuellar, Mike 1937- Ballpl 90, WhoHisp 91
Cuellar, Robert Aleman 1939- WhoSSW 91
Cuellar, Salvador M., Jr. 1949- WhoHisp 91
Cuellar, Virginia Adrien 1967- WhoSSW 91
Cuellar Medina, Celso 1826?- AmLegL
Cuello, Adoree Q BiDrAPA 89
Cuello, Augusto Claudio Guillermo 1939- WhoAm 90
Cuello, Luz Fule BiDrAPA 89
Cuenca, Peter Nicolas 1943- WhoHisp 91
Cuenca Garcia, Eduardo 1951- WhoWor 91
Cuenod, Hugues 1902- IntWWM 90, PenDiMP
Cueny, Burke William 1959- WhoEmL 91
Cuerdon, Don BioIn 16
Cuerno Verde WhNaAH
Cuesta, Roberto BiDrAPA 89
Cueto, Maximo Librada, Jr. 1946- BiDrAPA 89
Cueva, Jeanette Eulalia BiDrAPA 89
Cuevas, Alex F. 1943- St&PR 91
Cuevas, Betty 1953- WhoHisp 91
Cuevas, Carlos M. 1951- WhoHisp 91
Cuevas, David BioIn 16
Cuevas, Helen 1952- WhoHisp 91
Cuevas, Hipolito 1966- WhoHisp 91
Cuevas, Jose Luis 1934- WhoAm 90, WhoAmA 91, WhoWor 91
Cuevas, Joseph B. 1942- WhoHisp 91
Cuevas, Milton Joseph 1934- WhoAm 90
Cuevas, Plotino 1880-1962 BioIn 16
Cuevas, Rosemary 1958- WhoEmL 91
Cuevas, Vivian del Carmen BiDrAPA 89
Cuff, Charlotte D. 1941- ODwPR 91
Cuff, Dennis James 1942- St&PR 91
Cuff, Douglas George 1961- WhoWrEP 89
Cuff, Kevin Michael 1964- WhoE 91
Cuff, William 1942- St&PR 91
Cuffe, Paul 1759-1817 BioIn 16
Cuffe, Stafford Sigesmund 1949- WhoEmL 91
Cuffee-Browne, Patsy Anne 1949- WhoSSW 91
Cugat, Xavier 1900- BioIn 16, WorAlBi
Cugat, Xavier 1900-1990 ConAu 132, NewYTBS 90 [port], News 91-2, OxCPMus
Cugler-Poni, Matilda 1851-1931 EncCoWW
Cuiffo, Steven Robert 1944- WhoSSW 91
Cuil De Stratclut, Alecsandr Alastair 1931- WhoE 91, WhoWor 91
Cuillo, Robert Sal 1935- WhoSSW 91
Cuisenier, Jean Henri Eugene 1927- WhoWor 91
Cuisinier, Jeanne A L 1890- EncO&P 3
Cuison, Laura Miranda BiDrAPA 89
Cukaro, Kate 1955- EncCoWW
Cukier, Rona 1951- St&PR 91
Cukor, George 1899-1983 WorAlBi
Cukor, Peter 1936- WhoAm 90
Culberg, Paul S. 1942- St&PR 91
Culberson, Anne B. Gwynn 1952- WhoSSW 91
Culberson, Chicita Frances 1931- WhoAmW 91
Culberson, James M., Jr. 1928- St&PR 91
Culberson, James O. 1932- WhoSSW 91
Culberson, John Andrew 1947- WhoEmL 91
Culberson, Leon 1919- Ballpl 90
Culberson, Leon 1919-1989 BioIn 16
Culberson, Robert Allan 1935- St&PR 91
Culberson, William Louis 1929- WhoAm 90
Culbert, David H 1943- ConAu 31NR
Culbert, Joyce Laura 1945- WhoAmW 91
Culbert, Kenneth Edward 1948- WhoE 91
Culbertson, Dooley Ewell 1936- St&PR 91, WhoAm 90
Culbertson, Ely 1891-1955 WorAlBi
Culbertson, James Francis, Jr. 1949- St&PR 91
Culbertson, James Thomas 1904-1989 BioIn 16
Culbertson, Janet Lynn 1932- WhoAm 90, WhoAmA 91
Culbertson, Joe Campbell 1945- BiDrAPA 89
Culbertson, John Mathew 1921- WhoAm 90
Culbertson, Judi 1941- ConAu 31NR
Culbertson, Katheryn Campbell 1920- WhoAm 90
Culbertson, Philip Edgar 1925- WhoAm 90
Culbreath, Hugh Lee, Jr. 1921- St&PR 91, WhoAm 90, WhoSSW 91
Culbreth, Arnold Arthur, Jr. 1934- St&PR 91
Culbreth, Carl R 1952- WhoAmA 91
Culbreth, Eric Douglas 1959- WhoE 91
Culbreth, Luann Janine 1961- WhoAmW 91
Culhaci, Hayri 1956- WhoWor 91
Culham, Clifford BioIn 16
Culhane, Floyd C. 1945- St&PR 91
Culhane, James Edward 1941- WhoAm 90
Culhane, James F. 1930- St&PR 91
Culhane, John William 1934- WhoE 91
Culhane, Patrick J. St&PR 91N
Culhane, Shamus 1908- WhoAm 90
Culhane, Shamus H 1908- WhoAmA 91
Culick, Fred Ellsworth Clow 1933- WhoAm 90
Culik, Karel 1934- WhoSSW 91
Culin, Walter Georg 1930- St&PR 91
Culkin, Elizabeth Anne 1950- WhoE 91
Culkin, John Michael 1928- WhoAmA 91
Culkin, John Michael 1962- WhoE 91
Cull, Chris Alan 1947- WhoEmL 91
Cull, Robert Robinette 1912- WhoAm 90
Cullander, Cecil C H 1921- BiDrAPA 89
Cullell, Agustin 1928- IntWWM 90
Cullem-Kristian, Florence Mary 1922- WhoWrEP 89
Cullen, Bernard Anthony 1950- WhoWor 91
Cullen, Bill NewYTBS 90 [port]
Cullen, Bill 1920-1990 CurBio 90N, WorAlBi
Cullen, Brian Dennis 1940- St&PR 91
Cullen, Charles David 1951- WhoEmL 91
Cullen, Charles Thomas 1940- WhoAm 90
Cullen, Christopher T. 1958- ODwPR 91
Cullen, Countee 1903-1946 BioIn 16, EarBlAP, MajTwCW, TwCLC 37 [port]
Cullen, Countee 1903-1949 DrBlPA 90
Cullen, Curtis Anthony 1937- WhoE 91
Cullen, Daniel Scott 1949- WhoE 91
Cullen, Donna Marie 1953- WhoEmL 91
Cullen, Elizabeth Rita 1965- WhoSSW 91
Cullen, Frederick Landis 1947- St&PR 91, WhoAm 90
Cullen, Gail Frederick 1940- St&PR 91
Cullen, Harry Patrick, II 1949- WhoSSW 91
Cullen, Helen Frances 1919- WhoAmW 91
Cullen, Hugh R. 1881-1957 WorAlBi
Cullen, J. Russell, Jr. 1939- St&PR 91
Cullen, Jack Sydney George Bud 1927- WhoAm 90
Cullen, James Donald 1947- WhoEmL 91
Cullen, James Douglas 1945- WhoAm 90
Cullen, James Patrick 1944- WhoE 91
Cullen, James Thaddeus, Jr. 1935- WhoAm 90
Cullen, John 1947- ODwPR 91
Cullen, John B. 1911- WhoAm 90
Cullen, John Gavin 1936- IntWWM 90
Cullen, John Terry 1937- BiDrAPA 89
Cullen, Joseph Gregory 1960- IntWWM 90
Cullen, Kathleen Christina WhoAmW 91
Cullen, Leah Oseas 1952- BiDrAPA 89
Cullen, Linda Jo Krozser 1955- WhoAmW 91, WhoEmL 91
Cullen, Lynn 1948- WhoEmL 91
Cullen, Margaret 1924- WhoWrEP 89
Cullen, Marygael 1951- WhoAmW 91
Cullen, Michael A. 1961- St&PR 91
Cullen, Randall Keith BiDrAPA 89
Cullen, Robert Edward 1929- St&PR 91
Cullen, Stephen Leonard, Jr. 1940- WhoE 91
Cullen, Terrance Michael 1953- WhoEmL 91
Cullen, Thomas Francis, Jr. 1949- WhoEmL 91
Cullen, Tim 1942- Ballpl 90
Cullen, Vicky 1941- WhoE 91
Cullenbine, Clair Stephens 1905- WhoAm 90
Cullenbine, Roy 1915- Ballpl 90
Cullens, William Scott 1930- WhoAm 90
Cullens, Williams Scott 1930- St&PR 91
Culler, Arthur Dwight 1917- WhoAm 90
Culler, Cheryle Faye Leach 1955- WhoAmW 91
Culler, Dick 1915-1964 Ballpl 90
Culler, Floyd LeRoy, Jr. 1923- WhoAm 90
Culler, Joe Henry 1928- St&PR 91
Culler, Jonathan D. BioIn 16
Culler, Jonathan Dwight 1944- WhoAm 90, WhoWrEP 89
Culler, Robert Ransom 1950- WhoSSW 91
Culler, Robert W. 1933- St&PR 91
Culler-Penney, Annette Lorena 1916- WhoAmW 91
Cullerne Brown, Matthew 1956- ConAu 132
Cullers, James J. 1930- St&PR 91
Cullers, Jeffery Bryan 1957- WhoEmL 91
Cullers, Mark Eugene 1958- WhoEmL 91
Culleton, James F 1918- BiDrAPA 89
Culley, Grant Burdette, Jr. 1921- St&PR 91
Culley, James Spencer 1950- WhoSSW 91
Culley, John Henry 1947- WhoEmL 91
Culley-Foster, Anthony Robert 1947- WhoE 91, WhoEmL 91
Culliford, Ingrid PenDiMP
Culliford, Sydney B. 1932- St&PR 91
Culligan, John W. 1916- St&PR 91
Culligan, John William 1916- WhoAm 90
Culligan, Thomas J. 1944- St&PR 91
Cullimore, Kelvyn Henry, Jr. 1956- St&PR 91
Cullina, William Michael 1921- WhoAm 90
Cullinan, Brendan Peter 1927- WhoWor 91
Cullinan, Catherine BiDrAPA 89
Cullinan, Elizabeth 1933- WhoWrEP 89
Cullinan, Richard 1923- St&PR 91
Cullinan, Thomas William 1951- WhoEmL 91, WhoSSW 91
Cullinane, Daniel C., Jr. St&PR 91
Cullinane, Joe St&PR 91
Cullinane, John J. 1934- WhoAm 90
Cullinane, Joseph 1930- ODwPR 91
Cullinane, Maureen 1949- BioIn 16
Cullinane, Timothy M 1954- BiDrAPA 89
Culling, Laurie 1950- WhoEmL 91
Culling, Richard Edward 1951- WhoAmA 91
Cullingford, Cecil H D 1904-1990 ConAu 132
Cullingford, Guy 1907- TwCCr&M 91
Cullingford, Hatice S. 1945- WhoAmW 91, WhoWor 91
Cullington, John Donald 1937- IntWWM 90
Cullingworth, L. Ross 1939- St&PR 91
Cullingworth, Larry Ross 1939- WhoAm 90
Cullis, Christopher Paul 1956- St&PR 91
Cullis, Ford Miller 1919- St&PR 91
Cullis, Rita IntWWM 90
Cullison, William Lester 1931- WhoAm 90, WhoWor 91
Culliton, Barbara J. 1943- WhoAm 90
Culliton, Edward F. 1941- St&PR 91
Culliton, Edward Milton 1906- WhoAm 90
Cullman, Edgar M. 1918- St&PR 91
Cullman, Edgar Meyer 1918- WhoAm 90
Cullman, Elissa BioIn 16
Cullman, Hugh 1923- St&PR 91, WhoAm 90
Cullman, Joseph F., III 1912- St&PR 91
Cullman, Lewis B. 1919- St&PR 91
Cullom, Hale Ellicott 1935- St&PR 91, WhoAm 90
Cullom, Shelby Moore 1829-1914 AmLegL
Cullom, William Otis 1932- WhoAm 90, WhoSSW 91, WhoWor 91
Cullop, Nick 1900-1978 Ballpl 90
Cullum, Albert AuBYP 90
Cullum, Andrew R., III 1939- St&PR 91
Cullum, Charles Gillespie 1916- St&PR 91, WhoAm 90
Cullum, Debbie Lynn 1954- WhoSSW 91
Cullum, Gay Nelle 1952- WhoAmW 91
Cullum, John Michael 1959- WhoEmL 91
Cullum, Robert David 1946- WhoAm 90
Cullwick, Hannah 1833-1909 BioIn 16, FemiCLE
Cully, Zara 1892-1978 DrBlPA 90
Culman, John Kelley 1927- St&PR 91
Culmer, Cara Lee 1949- WhoAmW 91
Culmer, Marjorie Mehne 1912- WhoAm 90
Culos, Peter R. 1926- St&PR 91
Culotta, Denise Fern 1958- WhoAmW 91
Culotta, Shawna NewAgMG
Culp, Charles Allen 1930- WhoAm 90
Culp, Cliff Thomas 1952- WhoEmL 91
Culp, Clifford L, Jr. 1934- BiDrAPA 89
Culp, Clyde E., III 1942- WhoAm 90
Culp, E. Ronald 1947- ODwPR 91
Culp, Edward Ronald 1947- WhoEmL 91
Culp, Even Asher 1952- WhoSSW 91
Culp, George Hart 1938- WhoSSW 91
Culp, Gordon Louis 1939- WhoAm 90
Culp, Iris Land 1960- WhoSSW 91
Culp, James David 1951- WhoWor 91
Culp, James Stanley 1935- St&PR 91
Culp, Joe Carl 1933- WhoAm 90, WhoSSW 91
Culp, John Stephen 1947- WhoSSW 91
Culp, Judy Lee 1943- WhoSSW 91
Culp, Marvin Edward 1948- WhoSSW 91
Culp, Michael 1952- WhoE 91, WhoWor 91
Culp, Mildred Louise 1949- WhoAmW 91, WhoEmL 91
Culp, Ralph Borden 1929- WhoAm 90
Culp, Ray 1941- Ballpl 90

Culp, Raymond Mayo BiDrAPA 89
Culp, Robert BioIn 16
Culp, Robert 1930- WhoAm 90, WorAlBi
Culp, Robert George, III 1946- St&PR 91
Culp, Sandra C. ODwPR 91
Culp, Terry P. 1946- St&PR 91
Culp, W.N., Jr. 1923- St&PR 91
Culp, W.S. 1949- St&PR 91
Culp, William H. WhoAm 90
Culp, William Newton 1923- WhoAm 90
Culpeper, Thomas 1635-1689 EncCRAm
Culpepper, Anne BiDEWW
Culpepper, Dennis Wayne 1940- St&PR 91
Culpepper, Jerri Lea 1958- WhoAmW 91
Culpepper, John Blair 1937- St&PR 91
Culpepper, Leon 1937- St&PR 91
Culpepper, Nicolas 1616-1654 NewAgE 90
Culpepper, Robert Byron BiDrAPA 89
Culpepper, Wm. Warren 1928- St&PR 91
Culpitt, David Alan 1933- WhoWor 91
Culture Club EncPR&S 89
Culvahouse, Arthur Boggess, Jr. 1948- WhoEmL 91
Culver, Barbara Green 1926- WhoAm 90
Culver, Cathryn Ann 1940- BiDrAPA 89
Culver, Charles George 1937- WhoE 91
Culver, Charles M 1934- BiDrAPA 89
Culver, Dan Louis 1957- WhoEmL 91, WhoSSW 91
Culver, David M. 1924- St&PR 91
Culver, David S. ODwPR 91
Culver, Dennis BioIn 16
Culver, Edward H. 1918- St&PR 91
Culver, Edward Holland 1918- WhoAm 90
Culver, Ernest Wayne 1938- WhoE 91, WhoWor 91
Culver, Florence Morrow 1915- WhoAmW 91
Culver, George 1943- Ballpl 90
Culver, James 1939- WhoAm 90
Culver, Janet BioIn 16
Culver, John Eskridge 1932- St&PR 91, WhoAm 90
Culver, Linda S. 1953- St&PR 91
Culver, Martin S. BioIn 16
Culver, Michael L 1947- WhoAmA 91
Culver, Rennie Wynn BiDrAPA 89
Culver, Robert Elroy 1926- WhoAm 90
Culver, Robert J. 1937- St&PR 91
Culver, Timothy J. TwCCr&M 91
Culver, Walter Julius 1937- WhoAm 90
Culverhouse, Hugh Franklin 1919- WhoAm 90, WhoSSW 91
Culverhouse, Joy McCann 1920- WhoAm 90
Culverhouse, Renee Daniel 1950- WhoAmW 91
Culverwell, Albert Henry 1913- WhoAm 90
Culverwell, Ronald LeRoy 1936- St&PR 91
Culverwell, Rosemary Jean 1934- WhoAmW 91
Culwell, Charles Louis 1927- WhoAm 90
Cumber, Carol Jane 1956- WhoEmL 91
Cumber, Joseph BioIn 16
Cumberland, Joanna 1944- ODwPR 91
Cumberland, John 1947- Ballpl 90
Cumberland, John Hammett 1924- WhoE 91
Cumberland, Margaret C., Countess of 1560-1616 BiDEWW
Cumberland, Richard 1732-1811 BioIn 16
Cumbest, Elvis Mark 1953- WhoEmL 91
Cumbey, Constance Elizabeth 1944- WhoWor 91
Cumbie, Billy Joe 1954- WhoSSW 91
Cumbie-Drake, David E 1952- BiDrAPA 89
Cumbo, Lawrence James, Jr. 1947- WhoSSW 91
Cumbow, Robert Charles 1946- WhoEmL 91
Cumbuka, Ji-Tu 1942- DrBlPA 90
Cumella, Antoni 1913- PenDiDA 89
Cumerford, William Richard 1916- WhoAm 90
Cumfer, Donald Alonzo 1924- WhoSSW 91
Cuming, Beatrice 1903-1975 WhoAmA 91N
Cuming, Bernice BioIn 16
Cuming, David Brompton 1932- St&PR 91
Cuming, George Scott 1915- WhoAm 90
Cumings, Edwin Harlan 1933- WhoE 91
Cumings, Thayer 1904-1989 BioIn 16
Cumiskey, Colin Edward 1942- St&PR 91
Cummens, Linda Talaba WhoAmA 91
Cummer, William Jackson 1922- St&PR 91, WhoAm 90
Cummin, Alfred Samuel 1924- St&PR 91, WhoAm 90, WhoE 91, WhoWor 91
Cumming, David Robert, Jr. 1927- WhoAm 90
Cumming, David T. 1943- St&PR 91
Cumming, Donald A. 1937- St&PR 91
Cumming, Glen Edward 1936- WhoAm 90, WhoAmA 91, WhoE 91
Cumming, Ian M. 1940- WhoAm 90
Cumming, Ian Macneill 1940- St&PR 91
Cumming, John Battin 1936- St&PR 91, WhoAm 90
Cumming, Joseph Bryan 1836-1922 AmLegL
Cumming, Kate 1838-1909 BioIn 16
Cumming, L.W. 1930- St&PR 91
Cumming, Patricia Arens 1932- WhoWrEP 89
Cumming, Peter 1951- ConAu 129
Cumming, Peter Hood Ballantine BioIn 16
Cumming, Richard 1928- IntWWM 90
Cumming, Richard Jackson 1928- WhoE 91
Cumming, Robert 1935- WhoWrEP 89
Cumming, Robert Emil 1933- WhoAm 90
Cumming, Robert Gordon BiDrAPA 89
Cumming, Robert H 1943- WhoAmA 91
Cumming, Robert Hugh 1943- WhoAm 90
Cumming, Thomas Alexander 1937- WhoAm 90
Cummings, Abbott L. WhoAm 90
Cummings, Ann WhoWrEP 89
Cummings, Barton A. 1914- St&PR 91
Cummings, Bernard J. ODwPR 91
Cummings, Betty Ellen 1940- WhoAmW 91
Cummings, Betty Sue 1918- WhoWrEP 89
Cummings, Beverly A. 1953- St&PR 91
Cummings, Brian T. 1945- ODwPR 91
Cummings, Brian Thomas 1945- WhoAm 90
Cummings, Bruce Frederick 1889-1919 BioIn 16
Cummings, Candy 1848-1924 Ballpl 90 [port]
Cummings, Carol Ann 1957- WhoE 91
Cummings, Catherine J. ODwPR 91
Cummings, Charles Edgeworth, Jr. 1946- St&PR 91
Cummings, Charles Rogers 1930- WhoAm 90
Cummings, Charles William 1935- WhoAm 90
Cummings, Claudia 1941- IntWWM 90
Cummings, Conrad Milton 1933- WhoSSW 91
Cummings, Constance WhoAm 90, WhoAmW 91
Cummings, Daniel 1820-1861 AmLegL
Cummings, David Michael 1942- IntWWM 90
Cummings, David William 1937- WhoAm 90, WhoAmA 91, WhoE 91
Cummings, Diana 1941- IntWWM 90
Cummings, Diana K. 1943- WhoAmW 91, WhoWor 91
Cummings, E E AuBYP 90
Cummings, E. E. 1894-1962 BioIn 16
Cummings, E E 1894-1962 ConAu 31NR, MajTwCW
cummings, e. e. 1894-1962 WorAlBi
Cummings, Edmund George 1928- WhoE 91
Cummings, Edward Estlin 1894-1962 AuBYP 90, BioIn 16
Cummings, Edward L. 1948- St&PR 91
Cummings, Elizabeth BioIn 16
Cummings, Elizabeth Veronica 1962- WhoAmW 91
Cummings, Erika Helga WhoAmW 91
Cummings, Erwin Karl 1954- WhoEmL 91, WhoWor 91
Cummings, Frank 1929- WhoAm 90, WhoE 91, WhoWor 91
Cummings, Frank C. WhoHisp 91
Cummings, Frank C. 1929- WhoAm 90, WhoE 91
Cummings, Frederick J. NewYTBS 90
Cummings, Frederick James 1933-1990 WhoAmA 91N
Cummings, George F., Jr. 1921- St&PR 91
Cummings, George Richard 1912- St&PR 91
Cummings, George Wilson 1809-1891 AmLegL
Cummings, Geraldine Dorothy 1890-1968 EncPaPR 91
Cummings, Glenn D. 1934- St&PR 91
Cummings, Gordon Eric Myles 1940- WhoAm 90
Cummings, Harold Joseph St&PR 91N
Cummings, Homer Stille 1870-1956 BiDrUSE 89
Cummings, Howard D. 1948- WhoEmL 91
Cummings, Janis Marie Stahl 1936- WhoAmW 91, WhoSSW 91
Cummings, Jean 1930- WhoWrEP 89
Cummings, Jeanette Glenn 1949- WhoAm 90
Cummings, Jeffrey Lee BiDrAPA 89
Cummings, John F. 1950- St&PR 91
Cummings, John Hugh 1923- WhoWor 91
Cummings, John Rodgers 1933- St&PR 91
Cummings, Joseph Ballpl 90
Cummings, Josephine Anna 1949- WhoAm 90, WhoAmW 91
Cummings, Keith PenDiMP
Cummings, Keith 1906- IntWWM 90
Cummings, Kraig Ward 1943- WhoSSW 91
Cummings, Larry E. 1952- St&PR 91
Cummings, Larry Lee 1937- WhoAm 90
Cummings, Lee Philip 1945- St&PR 91
Cummings, Linda Marie BiDrAPA 89
Cummings, Maizie Jean 1961- WhoE 91
Cummings, Marie Ellen WhoAmW 91
Cummings, Martin Marc 1920- WhoAm 90, WhoE 91
Cummings, Mary B. ODwPR 91
Cummings, Mary Dappert 1922- WhoAmW 91
Cummings, Mary T 1951- WhoAmA 91
Cummings, Merilyn Lloy 1939- WhoAmW 91
Cummings, Michael Allen BiDrAPA 89
Cummings, Nancy Boucot 1927- WhoAm 90, WhoAmW 91
Cummings, Nathan 1896-1985 ConAmBL
Cummings, Nicholas Allen BiDrAPA 89
Cummings, Nicholas Andrew 1924- WhoAm 90, WhoWor 91
Cummings, Parke 1902-1987 BioIn 16
Cummings, Pat 1950- BioIn 16
Cummings, Patrick Henry 1941- WhoSSW 91
Cummings, Paul WhoAmA 91
Cummings, Paul 1933- BioIn 16
Cummings, Ray 1887-1957 ConAu 31NR
Cummings, Richard AuBYP 90
Cummings, Richard Howe 1921- St&PR 91
Cummings, Richard M. 1938- WhoE 91
Cummings, Rita 1950- WhoEmL 91
Cummings, Robert 1908-1990 NewYTBS 90 [port]
Cummings, Robert 1910- WorAlBi
Cummings, Robert E. 1926- St&PR 91
Cummings, Robert R 1946- BiDrAPA 89
Cummings, Rose Beheler 1959- WhoAmW 91
Cummings, Ross W. 1930- ODwPR 91
Cummings, Sam R. 1944- WhoAm 90
Cummings, Sandra Bielawa 1961- WhoAmW 91
Cummings, Spangler 1936- WhoWor 91
Cummings, Sue Carol 1941- WhoAmW 91
Cummings, Terry BioIn 16
Cummings, Thomas Gerald 1944- WhoAm 90
Cummings, Thomas L., III 1954- St&PR 91
Cummings, Victor 1925- WhoAm 90
Cummings, Victoria E. St&PR 91
Cummings, Virginia J. WhoAmW 91
Cummings, Walter J. 1916- WhoAm 90
Cummings, Willard E BiDrAPA 89
Cummings, Yvonne Eutrelda BiDrAPA 89
Cummins, Alfred Byron 1905- WhoAm 90
Cummins, Ben Milton 1934- BiDrAPA 89
Cummins, Brian John 1960- WhoSSW 91
Cummins, Charles Albert, II 1930- St&PR 91
Cummins, Clessie L EncABHB 5
Cummins, Daniel 1820-1861 AmLegL
Cummins, Delmer Duane 1935- WhoAm 90
Cummins, Evelyn Freeman 1904- WhoWor 91
Cummins, George Wilson 1809-1891 AmLegL
Cummins, Georgette Jaber 1931- WhoE 91
Cummins, Geraldine Dorothy 1890-1968 EncO&P 3
Cummins, Herman Zachary 1933- WhoAm 90
Cummins, James 1909- St&PR 91
Cummins, James Dale 1929- WhoE 91
Cummins, John David 1946- WhoAm 90
Cummins, John Stephen 1928- WhoAm 90
Cummins, Joseph Hervey 1916- WhoAm 90
Cummins, Karen Gasco 1945- WhoAmA 91
Cummins, Karen Muir 1959- WhoAmW 91
Cummins, Kathryn Lewis 1908- WhoAmW 91
Cummins, Kenneth Burdette 1911- WhoAm 90
Cummins, Kenneth Copeland 1943- St&PR 91, WhoAm 90
Cummins, Larry E 1937- BiDrAPA 89
Cummins, Lin M. ODwPR 91
Cummins, Maria 1827-1866 FemiCLE
Cummins, Nancyellen Heckeroth 1948- WhoAmW 91
Cummins, Pauline 1949- BiDWomA
Cummins, Robert L. 1926- St&PR 91
Cummins, Robert Patrick 1933- WhoAm 90, WhoWor 91
Cummins, Shirley Jean 1948- WhoAmW 91
Cummins, Susan Amy 1957- WhoEmL 91
Cummins, Walter 1936- WhoWrEP 89
Cummins-Hoxsey, Patricia Ann 1945- WhoAmW 91, WhoEmL 91
Cummiskey, J. Kenneth 1928- WhoAm 90
Cummock, Vicky BioIn 16
Cumpston, Gary Robert 1947- St&PR 91
Cunard, Nancy 1896-1965 BioIn 16, FemiCLE
Cunard, Samuel 1787-1865 WorAlBi
Cunarro, Julia A. BiDrAPA 89
Cundari, Dominick L. St&PR 91
Cundey, Paul Edward, Jr. 1936- WhoSSW 91
Cundiff, Carl Copeland 1941- WhoAm 90, WhoWor 91
Cundiff, Edward William 1919- WhoAm 90
Cundiff, James Nelson 1954- WhoEmL 91
Cundiff, Leslie Wolfe- BioIn 16
Cundiff, Margaret Joan 1932- ConAu 30NR
Cundiff, Paul Arthur 1909- WhoAm 90
Cundy, Rhonda Gail 1941- IntWWM 90
Cundy, Richard M. 1949- St&PR 91
Cundy, Vic Arnold 1950- WhoSSW 91
Cuneo, Dennis Clifford 1950- WhoWor 91
Cuneo, Ernest L. 1905-1988 BioIn 16
Cuneo, Jack A. 1947- St&PR 91
Cuneo, John BioIn 16
Cuneo, John F. 1931- St&PR 91
Cunetto, Dominic Joseph 1932- WhoSSW 91
Cuney-Hare, Maud 1874-1936 EarBlAP, FemiCLE
Cunha, Christine Denise 1957- BiDrAPA 89
Cunha, Euclydes da 1866-1909 BioIn 16
Cunha, George Martin 1911- WhoSSW 91, WhoWor 91
Cunha, Joao Carlos Brito e 1884-1950 BioIn 16
Cunha, Jose Anastacio da 1744-1787 BioIn 16
Cunha, Mark Geoffrey 1955- WhoEmL 91, WhoWor 91
Cunha, Richard E. BioIn 16
Cunha, Sergio Pereira 1842- WhoWor 91
Cunha, Timothy Martin 1951- St&PR 91
Cunha, Tony Joseph 1916- WhoAm 90
Cunin, John Raymond 1924- St&PR 91
Cuninggim, Whitty Daniel 1918- WhoAmW 91
Cuningham, Elizabeth Bayard WhoAmA 91
Cunion, Earl Eugene 1927- St&PR 91
Cunliffe, Charles H. 1930- St&PR 91
Cunliffe, Marcus NewYTBS 90
Cunliffe, Marcus 1922-1990 ConAu 132
Cunliffe, Sydney Joseph 1919- WhoAm 90
Cunnane, James Joseph 1938- St&PR 91, WhoAm 90
Cunnane, Patricia S. 1946- WhoAmW 91
Cunneen, Charles T. 1928- St&PR 91
Cunneen, Joseph 1923- WhoWrEP 89
Cunneen, Michael James 1944- St&PR 91
Cunnien, Alan James 1953- BiDrAPA 89
Cunniff, Gregory Nixon 1947- WhoEmL 91
Cunniff, John WhoAm 90, WhoE 91
Cunniff, Leo C. 1926- St&PR 91
Cunniff, Nelda Norene 1935- WhoAmW 91
Cunniff, Patrick Francis 1933- WhoAm 90
Cunniffe, Charles Lawrence 1951- WhoWor 91
Cunning, Jan Elizabeth 1944- WhoAmW 91
Cunningham, Agnes 1923- WhoAmW 91
Cunningham, Alan Gordon 1887-1983 DcNaB 1981
Cunningham, Alant T. 1942- St&PR 91
Cunningham, Albert James 1833-1912 AmLegL
Cunningham, Allan 1784-1842 BioIn 16
Cunningham, Alma BioIn 16
Cunningham, Arthur 1928- IntWWM 90
Cunningham, Arthur Francis 1922- WhoAm 90
Cunningham, Arthur H 1928- DrBlPA 90
Cunningham, Atlee Marion, Jr. 1938- WhoSSW 91, WhoWor 91
Cunningham, Ben 1904-1975 BioIn 16
Cunningham, Benjamin Frazier 1904-1975 WhoAmA 91N
Cunningham, Bert 1865-1952 Ballpl 90
Cunningham, Bill 1895-1953 Ballpl 90
Cunningham, Bill 1896-1960 Ballpl 90
Cunningham, Billy 1943- WhoAm 90
Cunningham, Bob Dale 1935- St&PR 91
Cunningham, Bradley 1925-1988 BioIn 16
Cunningham, Brian Timothy 1936- St&PR 91
Cunningham, Bridget Eugenia 1952- WhoEmL 91
Cunningham, Bruce 1905-1984 Ballpl 90
Cunningham, Bruce 1943- WhoAmA 91
Cunningham, Bruce Arthur 1940- WhoAm 90
Cunningham, C. Donald 1947- St&PR 91
Cunningham, Carl Robert 1931- WhoAm 90

Cunningham, Caroline M. 1925- *IntWWM 90*
Cunningham, Charles *BioIn 16*
Cunningham, Charles Baker 1941- *St&PR 91*
Cunningham, Charles Baker, III 1941- *WhoAm 90, WhoSSW 91*
Cunningham, Charles Crehore 1910-1979 *WhoAmA 91N*
Cunningham, Charles J., Jr. *St&PR 91*
Cunningham, Clarence J. 1931- *WhoAm 90*
Cunningham, Clark Edward 1934- *WhoAm 90*
Cunningham, Colette Lauri *BiDrAPA 89*
Cunningham, Colin McAllister, Jr. 1945- *WhoAm 90*
Cunningham, Curt James *BiDrAPA 89*
Cunningham, Dale Everett 1927- *St&PR 91*
Cunningham, Darrel Eugene 1938- *WhoSSW 91*
Cunningham, David *WhoWor 91*
Cunningham, David Jowett 1925- *St&PR 91*
Cunningham, Deborah Lynn 1954- *WhoWrEP 89*
Cunningham, Dennis Dean 1939- *WhoAm 90*
Cunningham, Dorothy Jane 1927- *WhoAm 90*
Cunningham, Dorothy Ruth 1951- *WhoAmW 91*
Cunningham, E C 1956- *WhoAmA 91*
Cunningham, E. V. *AuBYP 90*
Cunningham, E.V. *ConAu 33NR*
Cunningham, E. V. *WhoWrEP 89*
Cunningham, E. V. 1914- *TwCCr&M 91*
Cunningham, Earl 1893-1977 *MusmAFA*
Cunningham, Earlene Brown 1930- *WhoE 91, WhoWor 91*
Cunningham, Edward Joseph 1938- *St&PR 91*
Cunningham, Ellen 1940- *WhoAmW 91*
Cunningham, Emory O. *St&PR 91*
Cunningham, Ernest 1936- *WhoSSW 91*
Cunningham, Evangeline C 1944- *BiDrAPA 89*
Cunningham, Francis 1931- *WhoAmA 91, WhoE 91*
Cunningham, Gail Blair 1950- *WhoAmW 91*
Cunningham, Gary Bruce 1947- *WhoSSW 91*
Cunningham, Gary Lee 1948- *WhoEmL 91*
Cunningham, George 1894-1972 *Ballpl 90*
Cunningham, George Gray 1951- *WhoEmL 91*
Cunningham, George Woody 1930- *WhoAm 90*
Cunningham, Germaine Nadine 1964- *WhoEmL 91*
Cunningham, Glenn 1909-1988 *BioIn 16*
Cunningham, Glenn Clarence 1912- *WhoAm 90*
Cunningham, Gordon *BioIn 16*
Cunningham, Harry Blair 1907- *ConAmBL*
Cunningham, Imogen 1883-1976 *BioAmW, BioIn 16, WhoAmA 91N, WorAlBi*
Cunningham, Isabella Clara Mantovani 1942- *WhoAm 90, WhoSSW 91*
Cunningham, J 1940- *WhoAmA 91*
Cunningham, J. Thalia 1953- *WhoEmL 91*
Cunningham, Jack Lynn, Jr. 1944- *St&PR 91*
Cunningham, Jack Wayne 1962- *WhoSSW 91*
Cunningham, Jacqueline Lemme 1941- *WhoAmW 91*
Cunningham, James Calvin 1947- *WhoEmL 91*
Cunningham, James Everett 1923- *St&PR 91, WhoAm 90*
Cunningham, James F 1918- *BiDrAPA 89*
Cunningham, James Floyd 1949- *IntWWM 90*
Cunningham, James Gerald 1930- *St&PR 91*
Cunningham, James Gerald, Jr. 1930- *WhoAm 90*
Cunningham, James Lee 1936- *WhoAm 90*
Cunningham, James Michael 1945- *St&PR 91*
Cunningham, James Robert *BiDrAPA 89*
Cunningham, Jean DiGiorgio 1961- *WhoAmW 91*
Cunningham, Jeffrey Milton 1952- *WhoAm 90*
Cunningham, Jennifer Lewis 1958- *WhoE 91*
Cunningham, Jerry Joe 1946- *St&PR 91*
Cunningham, Joe 1931- *Ballpl 90*
Cunningham, Joel Luther 1944- *WhoAm 90, WhoE 91*
Cunningham, John David 1953- *WhoE 91*
Cunningham, John Fabian 1928- *WhoAm 90, WhoE 91*
Cunningham, John Francis 1943- *WhoAm 90*
Cunningham, John R. 1925- *St&PR 91*
Cunningham, John Talley, Jr. 1877-1945 *AmLegL*
Cunningham, Joseph John, Jr. 1949- *WhoEmL 91*
Cunningham, Joseph Oliver 1918- *St&PR 91*
Cunningham, Joseph Thomas 1859-1935 *DcScB S2*
Cunningham, Judy R. 1942- *ODwPR 91*
Cunningham, Julia 1916- *AuBYP 90*
Cunningham, Julia Woolfolk 1916- *WhoAm 90, WhoWrEP 89*
Cunningham, Karin Olsen 1959- *WhoAmW 91*
Cunningham, Karon Lynette 1950- *WhoEmL 91*
Cunningham, Keith Allen 1922- *WhoWor 91*
Cunningham, Keith Allen, II 1948- *St&PR 91*
Cunningham, Kenneth R. 1945- *St&PR 91*
Cunningham, Larry Hugh 1944- *St&PR 91*
Cunningham, Larry J. 1944- *WhoAm 90*
Cunningham, Laura 1947- *WhoEmL 91*
Cunningham, Lawrence David 1936- *WhoSSW 91*
Cunningham, Leon William 1927- *WhoAm 90*
Cunningham, Leslie *BiDrAPA 89*
Cunningham, Lorinne Mitchell 1909- *WhoAmW 91*
Cunningham, Lowell King 1922- *BiDrAPA 89*
Cunningham, Madonna Marie 1933- *WhoAm 90*
Cunningham, Marcia Lynn 1955- *WhoWrEP 89*
Cunningham, Margaret *FemiCLE*
Cunningham, Marion 1911- *WhoAmA 91N*
Cunningham, Mary *AuBYP 90*
Cunningham, Mary Elizabeth *BioIn 16*
Cunningham, Mary Elizabeth 1931- *WhoAmW 91*
Cunningham, Mary Elizabeth 1951- *WhoAmW 91*
Cunningham, Mary Louise 1954- *WhoAmW 91*
Cunningham, Matthew Zachary 1961- *WhoEmL 91*
Cunningham, Maureen Mala *WhoSSW 91*
Cunningham, Merce *BioIn 16, WhoAm 90, WhoE 91*
Cunningham, Merce 1922- *WorAlBi*
Cunningham, Michael 1952- *BioIn 16*
Cunningham, Michael E. 1933- *St&PR 91*
Cunningham, Michael W. 1948- *St&PR 91*
Cunningham, Milton Alexander 1922- *WhoSSW 91*
Cunningham, Morris 1917- *WhoAm 90*
Cunningham, Murray Hunt, Jr. 1942- *WhoE 91*
Cunningham, Neil Lewis 1924- *St&PR 91, WhoAm 90*
Cunningham, Nina Strickler 1947- *WhoAmW 91*
Cunningham, Patricia Marr 1943- *WhoSSW 91*
Cunningham, Patrick 1943- *St&PR 91*
Cunningham, Patrick Joseph, III 1950- *WhoEmL 91, WhoWor 91*
Cunningham, Paul Johnston 1928- *WhoSSW 91*
Cunningham, Paul Raymond Goldwyn 1949- *WhoEmL 91, WhoSSW 91*
Cunningham, Pierce Edward 1934- *WhoAm 90*
Cunningham, R. John 1926- *WhoAm 90*
Cunningham, R. Walter 1932- *WhoAm 90*
Cunningham, Ralph Sanford 1940- *WhoAm 90*
Cunningham, Randall *BioIn 16*
Cunningham, Randall 1963- *News 90 [port], WhoAm 90, WorAlBi*
Cunningham, Randy 1941- *BioIn 16*
Cunningham, Raymond Clement 1931- *WhoAm 90, WhoSSW 91*
Cunningham, Reba Pierce 1897- *BioIn 16*
Cunningham, Rebecca Commans 1956- *St&PR 91*
Cunningham, Richard Greenlaw 1921- *WhoAm 90*
Cunningham, Robert C. 1936- *WhoAm 90*
Cunningham, Robert Cyril 1914- *WhoAm 90*
Cunningham, Robert Henry 1945- *St&PR 91*
Cunningham, Robert Maris, Jr. 1909- *WhoAm 90*
Cunningham, Robert Morton 1907- *WhoAm 90*
Cunningham, Robert Shannon, Jr. 1958- *WhoEmL 91*
Cunningham, Roger L. 1914- *St&PR 91*
Cunningham, Ronald 1942- *St&PR 91*
Cunningham, Russell Harold 1934- *WhoAm 90*
Cunningham, Russell McWhorter, III 1941- *St&PR 91*
Cunningham, Scott Alan 1957- *WhoSSW 91*
Cunningham, Scott Lance 1956- *BiDrAPA 89*
Cunningham, Sue 1932- *WhoAmA 91*
Cunningham, Sue Carol 1940- *WhoAmW 91*
Cunningham, Susan Delavan 1948- *BiDrAPA 89*
Cunningham, T. Jefferson, III *St&PR 91*
Cunningham, Thom W. 1943- *WhoE 91*
Cunningham, Thomas David, Jr. 1950- *WhoSSW 91*
Cunningham, Thomas Earle, Jr. 1950- *WhoEmL 91*
Cunningham, Thomas H. 1947- *St&PR 91*
Cunningham, Thomas William 1911- *WhoAm 90*
Cunningham, Timothy White 1952- *WhoEmL 91*
Cunningham, Tom 1838-1900 *BioIn 16*
Cunningham, Tom Alan 1946- *WhoWor 91*
Cunningham, Van Hugh 1928- *WhoSSW 91*
Cunningham, Vicki Frances 1963- *WhoAmW 91*
Cunningham, Virginia 1909- *AuBYP 90*
Cunningham, Walter Jack 1917- *WhoAm 90*
Cunningham, William 1849-1919 *BioIn 16*
Cunningham, William Francis, Jr. 1931- *WhoAm 90*
Cunningham, William Gerard 1933- *St&PR 91*
Cunningham, William Henry 1930- *WhoAm 90, WhoWor 91*
Cunningham, William Hughes 1944- *WhoAm 90, WhoSSW 91, WhoWor 91*
Cunningham, William Palmer 1968- *WhoSSW 91*
Cunningham-Dunlop, G. Richard 1932- *St&PR 91*
Cunninghame Graham, R. B. 1852-1936 *BioIn 16*
Cunninghame Graham, Robert Bontine 1852-1936 *BioIn 16*
Cunnion, Doris Sorg 1919- *St&PR 91*
Cunnold, Derek Martin 1940- *WhoSSW 91*
Cunnyngham, Jon 1935- *WhoAm 90*
Cunnyngham, Maxine Brown 1949- *WhoSSW 91*
Cunyus, George Marvin 1930- *St&PR 91, WhoAm 90*
Cuoco, Daniel A. 1937- *St&PR 91*
Cuoco, Daniel Anthony 1937- *WhoAm 90*
Cuomo, Ana-Marie Patricia 1960- *WhoAmW 91*
Cuomo, Andrew *BioIn 16*
Cuomo, George 1929- *WhoWrEP 89*
Cuomo, Maria *BioIn 16*
Cuomo, Mario *BioIn 16*
Cuomo, Mario 1932- *Ballpl 90, WorAlBi*
Cuomo, Mario Matthew 1932- *WhoAm 90, WhoE 91, WhoWor 91*
Cuomo, Matilda *BioIn 16*
Cuomo, Ralph Albert 1925- *St&PR 91*
Cuoq, Jean-Andre 1821-1898 *DcCanB 12*
Cuozzi, William Francis, III 1952- *WhoEmL 91*
Cuozzo, Steven David 1950- *WhoAm 90*
Cupala, Homai J *BiDrAPA 89*
Cupala, Jitendra B *BiDrAPA 89*
Cupers, Jean-Louis 1946- *IntWWM 90*
Cupery, Robert Rink 1944- *WhoWor 91*
Cupiccia, Louis A. 1928- *St&PR 91*
Cupid, Elsa Joan Elizabeth 1953- *WhoWor 91*
Cupido, Alberto 1952- *IntWWM 90*
Cupino, Elmer *BiDrAPA 89*
Cupler, Edward James *BiDrAPA 89*
Cupler, J.A. 1945- *St&PR 91*
Cupler, John A., III 1945- *WhoE 91*
Cupp, David Foster 1938- *WhoAm 90*
Cupp, John S., Jr. 1950- *WhoEmL 91*
Cupp, Lucy Paschall 1949- *WhoAmW 91*
Cupp, Paul J. *BioIn 16*
Cupp, Robert Erhard 1939- *WhoAm 90*
Cupp, Stephen G. *St&PR 91*
Cupp, William Franklyn 1939- *St&PR 91*
Cuppaidge, Virginia 1943- *WhoAmA 91*
Cupper, Ralph John 1954- *IntWWM 90*
Cuppett, Sharon D. *ODwPR 91*
Cupples, Andrew M. 1951- *St&PR 91*
Cupples, Janet Cummings 1942- *WhoAmW 91*
Cupples, William S. 1955- *WhoSSW 91*
Cuppy, Nig 1869-1922 *Ballpl 90*
Cuprien, Frank W 1871-1948 *WhoAmA 91N*
Cura, Alice Miller 1959- *WhoAmW 91*
Curan, Michael E. 1931- *St&PR 91*
Curato, Randy Joseph 1958- *WhoEmL 91*
Curatola, Dorothy Margaret 1938- *St&PR 91*
Curatolo, Alphonse Frank 1936- *WhoAm 90*
Curb, Michael Charles 1944- *WhoAm 90*
Curbelo, Jose-Luis 1955- *WhoWor 91*
Curboy, Robert Edward 1928- *WhoSSW 91*
Curchoe, Carl A. 1944- *WhoE 91*
Curcie, Bonnie E. 1952- *WhoAmW 91*
Curcio, Barbara Ann 1951- *WhoAmW 91*
Curcio, Christopher Frank 1950- *WhoEmL 91, WhoWor 91*
Curcio, Cynthia Davies 1947- *WhoEmL 91*
Curcio, Edward Paul 1942- *BiDrAPA 89*
Curcio, Frances Rena 1951- *WhoAmW 91*
Curcio, Jack *BioIn 16*
Curcio, John Baptist *BioIn 16*
Curcio, John Baptist 1934- *St&PR 91, WhoAm 90, WhoE 91*
Curcuru, Felix C. 1947- *St&PR 91*
Curd, Howard R. 1939- *St&PR 91*
Curdue, Kathryn Jeanette 1951- *BiDrAPA 89*
Curdy, Harold M. 1947- *St&PR 91*
Cure D'Ars 1786-1859 *EncO&P 3*
Cure of Ars 1786-1859 *EncPaPR 91*
Cure, Carol Campbell 1944- *WhoAmW 91*
Cure, Michel Yves Marie 1937- *WhoWor 91*
Cure, Susan Carol Flint 1940- *WhoWor 91*
Cureau, Frank Raymond 1955- *WhoEmL 91, WhoWor 91*
Cureton, Bryant Lewis 1938- *WhoAm 90*
Curfew, James V. 1946- *WhoSSW 91*
Curfman, David Ralph 1942- *IntWWM 90, WhoE 91, WhoWor 91*
Curfman, Lawrence Everett 1909- *WhoAm 90*
Curfman, Wayne Corbet 1949- *BiDrAPA 89*
Curiae, Amicus *AuBYP 90*
Curie, Eve 1904- *WhoAmW 91, WhoWor 91*
Curie, Irene Joliot- 1897-1956 *BioIn 16*
Curie, Leonardo Rodolfo 1950- *WhoHisp 91*
Curie, Marie 1867-1934 *BioIn 16, WorAlBi*
Curie, Pierre 1859-1906 *BioIn 16, WorAlBi*
Curiel, Herman F., II 1934- *WhoHisp 91*
Curien, Hubert *BioIn 16*
Curkendall, Brenda Irene 1954- *WhoAmW 91, WhoEmL 91*
Curko, Kathleen Ann 1950- *WhoE 91*
Curl, A. Delmour 1925- *St&PR 91*
Curl, Blake, Jr. 1940- *St&PR 91*
Curl, Frank Gordon 1925- *WhoSSW 91*
Curl, Gregory Lynn 1948- *St&PR 91, WhoAm 90*
Curl, Richard L. 1932- *St&PR 91*
Curl, Robert Floyd, Jr. 1933- *WhoAm 90*
Curl, Samuel Everett 1937- *WhoAm 90*
Curl, Steven M. 1954- *St&PR 91*
Curle, Robin Lea 1950- *WhoAmW 91*
Curlee, Dorothy Sumner 1921- *WhoSSW 91*
Curlee, Steven A. 1951- *St&PR 91*
Curler, Howard J. 1925- *WhoAm 90*
Curler, Jeffrey H. 1950- *St&PR 91*
Curless, Carroll D. 1938- *St&PR 91*
Curless, Larry 1931- *St&PR 91*
Curlett, Howard D. 1945- *St&PR 91*
Curley, Arthur 1938- *WhoAm 90, WhoE 91*
Curley, Carlo 1952- *IntWWM 90*
Curley, Clare Mary 1961- *WhoAmW 91*
Curley, Daniel *BioIn 16*
Curley, Daniel 1918-1988 *SmATA 61*
Curley, Denis Michael 1947- *St&PR 91*
Curley, Donald Houston 1940- *WhoAmA 91*
Curley, Edwin Munson 1937- *WhoAm 90*
Curley, Eileen Sara 1936- *WhoAmW 91*
Curley, Frank Donald 1929- *St&PR 91*
Curley, James O. 1941- *St&PR 91*
Curley, John Francis, Jr. 1939- *St&PR 91, WhoAm 90, WhoWor 91*
Curley, John J. *BioIn 16*
Curley, John J. 1938- *St&PR 91, WhoAm 90, WhoSSW 91*
Curley, John Peter 1952- *WhoAm 90*
Curley, Mary Kay O'Brien 1959- *WhoAmW 91*
Curley, Michael Edward 1947- *WhoAm 90*
Curley, Robert M. 1947- *St&PR 91*
Curley, Sarah Sharer *WhoAmW 91*
Curley, Thomas 1948- *WhoAm 90*
Curley, Thomas F. 1925- *WhoWrEP 89*
Curley, Thomas J., Jr. 1957- *WhoEmL 91*
Curley, Tom *BioIn 16*
Curley, Walter J.P. 1922- *St&PR 91*
Curley, Walter Joseph Patrick, Jr. 1922- *WhoAm 90, WhoWor 91*
Curlik, Sharon Marie *BiDrAPA 89*
Curlin, Frederick J *BiDrAPA 89*
Curlin, Jack V. 1917- *St&PR 91*
Curlin, John Paschal 1939- *WhoSSW 91*
Curling Hair 1750?-1825 *WhNaAH*
Curll, Daniel B., III 1942- *St&PR 91*

Curlook, Walter 1929- *St&PR 91, WhoAm 90*
Curly 1859?-1923 *WhNaAH*
Curly Headed Doctor *WhNaAH*
Curmano, Billy 1949- *WhoAmA 91*
Curnen, Tim 1945- *WhoEmL 91*
Curnin, Thomas Francis 1933- *WhoAm 90*
Curnock, Audrey Geraldine 1961- *WhoWor 91*
Curnow, Barry *BioIn 16*
Curnow, James Edward 1943- *WhoSSW 91*
Curnow, W. Leslie *EncO&P 3*
Curnow, William J. 1946- *ODwPR 91*
Curns, Eileen Bohan 1927- *WhoAmW 91*
Curns, John R *BiDrAPA 89*
Curnutt, Esther *ODwPR 91*
Curnutte, Mark William 1954- *WhoEmL 91, WhoSSW 91*
Curphey, Margaret 1938- *IntWWM 90*
Curran, Alvin *NewAgMG*
Curran, Alvin 1938- *IntWWM 90*
Curran, Barbara E 1941- *BiDrAPA 89*
Curran, Caitlin Tavenner 1963- *WhoAmW 91*
Curran, Cecily *BioIn 16*
Curran, Charles 1921-1980 *ConAu 130*
Curran, Charles 1934- *WhoWrEP 89*
Curran, Charles Eschman, III 1946- *St&PR 91*
Curran, Clifford L. *BioIn 16*
Curran, Connie 1947- *WhoAmW 91, WhoEmL 91, WhoWor 91*
Curran, Cyril James *BiDrAPA 89*
Curran, D. Patrick 1944- *St&PR 91*
Curran, Darryl Joseph 1935- *WhoAm 90, WhoAmA 91*
Curran, David Bernard, Jr. 1959- *WhoSSW 91*
Curran, Desmond *BiDrAPA 89*
Curran, Donald Charles 1933- *WhoAm 90*
Curran, Donna Rae 1955- *WhoAmW 91*
Curran, Dorothy Elizabeth 1952- *WhoE 91, WhoEmL 91*
Curran, Douglas Edward 1952- *WhoAmA 91*
Curran, Edward Milford 1922- *WhoWor 91*
Curran, Edward Owen *BioIn 16, NewYTBS 90*
Curran, Edwin H. 1928- *St&PR 91*
Curran, Eleanor Gavigan 1924- *WhoAmW 91*
Curran, Frank Earl 1912- *WhoAm 90*
Curran, Frank J. *St&PR 91*
Curran, Frank J 1904- *BiDrAPA 89*
Curran, Frank Joseph 1904-1989 *BioIn 16*
Curran, George William, III 1953- *WhoE 91, WhoEmL 91*
Curran, Guernsey, III 1931- *St&PR 91*
Curran, Harold Thomas 1935- *St&PR 91*
Curran, Hilda Patricia 1938- *WhoAmW 91*
Curran, J. Joseph, Jr. 1931- *WhoAm 90, WhoE 91*
Curran, James F. 1932- *St&PR 91*
Curran, James Patrick 1930- *St&PR 91*
Curran, Jane Mary 1948- *IntWWM 90*
Curran, Janet S. 1953- *WhoEmL 91*
Curran, Jerry Lynne *WhoAmW 91*
Curran, John Howard, Mrs. 1881-1937 *EncO&P 3*
Curran, John J *BiDrAPA 89*
Curran, John P. 1930- *St&PR 91*
Curran, Johnny Walter 1952- *WhoEmL 91*
Curran, Joseph *EncAL*
Curran, Joseph E. 1906-1981 *WorAlBi*
Curran, Kevin J. 1945- *St&PR 91*
Curran, Kimberly A. 1966- *WhoEmL 91*
Curran, Kristine Charnowski 1954- *WhoAmW 91, WhoEmL 91*
Curran, M. Christina 1962- *WhoEmL 91*
Curran, Madeline Mc Grath 1947- *WhoWrEP 89*
Curran, Marilyn R 1928- *BiDrAPA 89*
Curran, Mark A. *St&PR 91*
Curran, Michael Walter 1935- *WhoAm 90, WhoWor 91*
Curran, Paul Saether 1960- *WhoEmL 91*
Curran, Pearl Lenore 1883-1937 *EncPaPR 91*
Curran, Peter Vincent 1947- *WhoWor 91*
Curran, Richard C. 1920- *St&PR 91*
Curran, Richard F 1931- *BiDrAPA 89*
Curran, Robert Allen 1938- *St&PR 91*
Curran, Robert Bruce 1948- *WhoEmL 91*
Curran, Robert W. 1927- *St&PR 91*
Curran, Ross William 1952- *IntWWM 90*
Curran, S. M. *AmLegL*
Curran, Samuel Crowe 1912- *WhoWor 91*
Curran, Stuart Alan 1940- *WhoAm 90*
Curran, Susan 1952- *WhoWor 91*
Curran, T. Aidan, III 1959- *WhoWor 91*
Curran, Thomas A. 1957- *St&PR 91*
Curran, Thomas J. 1924- *WhoAm 90*
Curran, Vincent 1945- *ODwPR 91*
Curran, William Edward 1938- *St&PR 91*
Curran, William F. 1948- *St&PR 91*
Curran, William Patrick, III 1953- *WhoEmL 91*
Curran, William Stephen 1935- *WhoSSW 91*
Currat, Claude Auguste 1951- *St&PR 91*
Curray, Robert W., Jr. 1948- *St&PR 91*
Currelley, Lorraine 1951- *WhoWrEP 89*
Curren, Francis H. 1923- *St&PR 91*
Curren, Tommy *BioIn 16*
Currence, Richard Morrison 1938- *St&PR 91*
Currence, William Mack 1938- *St&PR 91*
Current, Joretta Louise 1960- *WhoAmW 91*
Current, Richard Nelson 1912- *WhoAm 90*
Current-Garcia, Eugene 1908- *WhoAm 90*
Curreri, Anthony J. 1937- *St&PR 91*
Curreri-Alibrandi, Gaetano 1927- *WhoE 91*
Currey, Agneta *BioIn 16*
Currey, Brownlee *BioIn 16*
Currey, Frederick *BioIn 16*
Currey, Richard 1949- *WhoWrEP 89*
Currey, Richard F. 1928- *St&PR 91*
Currey, William R. 1944- *ODwPR 91*
Curria, Carol Jean 1963- *WhoEmL 91*
Currid, Cheryl Clarke 1950- *WhoAmW 91, WhoSSW 91*
Currie, Arthur 1875-1933 *BioIn 16*
Currie, Barbara Flynn 1940- *WhoAmW 91*
Currie, Bruce 1911- *WhoAm 90, WhoAmA 91*
Currie, Charles Peter 1924- *St&PR 91*
Currie, Clarence 1878-1941 *Ballpl 90*
Currie, Clifford William Herbert 1918- *WhoAm 90, WhoWor 91*
Currie, David Park 1936- *WhoAm 90*
Currie, Dean Winn 1947- *WhoEmL 91*
Currie, Earl James 1939- *St&PR 91, WhoAm 90*
Currie, Edward Jones, Jr. 1951- *WhoEmL 91*
Currie, Eileen *WhoAmW 91*
Currie, Gilbert A. *St&PR 91*
Currie, Glenn Kenneth 1943- *WhoAm 90*
Currie, Ian Hamilton 1948- *WhoWor 91*
Currie, James Angus 1919- *St&PR 91*
Currie, Jane Moore 1953- *WhoSSW 91*
Currie, Kenneth Max 1947- *WhoE 91, WhoSSW 91*
Currie, Leonard James 1913- *WhoAm 90*
Currie, Madeline Ashburn 1922- *WhoAmW 91*
Currie, Malcolm Roderick 1927- *St&PR 91, WhoAm 90*
Currie, Mary Montgomerie Lamb 1843-1905 *BioIn 16*
Currie, Michael Robert 1952- *WhoEmL 91*
Currie, Neal J. 1929- *St&PR 91*
Currie, Norman T. 1928- *St&PR 91*
Currie, Richard James 1937- *WhoAm 90*
Currie, Robert *BioIn 16*
Currie, Stanley R. 1921- *St&PR 91*
Currie, Steve 1954- *WhoAmA 91*
Currier, Barry Arthur 1946- *WhoEmL 91, WhoSSW 91*
Currier, Benjamin Atkinson 1933- *St&PR 91*
Currier, Chester S. 1945- *ConAu 129*
Currier, Cyrus Bates 1868- *WhoAmA 91N*
Currier, Frank Dunklee 1853-1921 *AmLegL*
Currier, Frederick Plumer 1923- *WhoAm 90*
Currier, George E *BiDrAPA 89*
Currier, Jeffrey Lee 1940- *St&PR 91*
Currier, Laurence M 1916- *BiDrAPA 89*
Currier, Maria Beatriz *BiDrAPA 89*
Currier, Meriel 1954- *St&PR 91*
Currier, Nathaniel 1813-1888 *BioIn 16, WorAlBi*
Currier, Richard Agnew 1940- *St&PR 91*
Currier, Robert David 1925- *WhoAm 90, WhoWor 91*
Currier, Ruth 1926- *WhoAm 90*
Currier, Susan Anne 1949- *WhoAmW 91*
Currier, Thomas Sholars 1932- *WhoAm 90*
Currimbhoy, Nayana *AuBYP 90*
Currin, George Spencer 1936- *St&PR 91*
Currin, Julie Amarie 1960- *WhoEmL 91*
Currin, Margaret Person 1950- *WhoAmW 91*
Currin, Michael Franklin 1951- *WhoSSW 91*
Currin, Russell Ashmore, Jr. 1935- *WhoSSW 91*
Curris, Constantine William 1940- *WhoAm 90*
Currivan, John Daniel 1947- *WhoWor 91*
Curror, Ian Munro 1949- *IntWWM 90*
Curry, Alan C. 1933- *St&PR 91*
Curry, Alan Chester 1933- *WhoAm 90*
Curry, Alton Frank 1933- *WhoAm 90*
Curry, Beatrice Chesrown 1932- *WhoAmW 91*
Curry, Bernard Francis 1918- *WhoAm 90*
Curry, Catharine Terrill 1950- *WhoSSW 91*
Curry, D Troy *BiDrAPA 89*
Curry, Daniel A. 1937- *St&PR 91*
Curry, Daniel Arthur 1937- *WhoAm 90*
Curry, David Jerome 1944- *WhoAm 90*
Curry, David Lee 1942- *WhoWrEP 89*
Curry, David Park 1946- *WhoAmA 91*
Curry, Denise 1952- *WhoAmW 91*
Curry, Donald Robert 1943- *WhoWor 91*
Curry, Duncan Steele 1940- *St&PR 91*
Curry, Edwin Mathew 1962- *WhoSSW 91*
Curry, Elizabeth R. 1934- *WhoWrEP 89*
Curry, Francis John 1911- *WhoAm 90*
Curry, Francis R. 1910- *St&PR 91*
Curry, Horace Edward 1939- *WhoSSW 91*
Curry, Hugh Robert 1948- *WhoSSW 91*
Curry, James Edwin 1950- *WhoEmL 91*
Curry, James T. 1936- *St&PR 91*
Curry, James Trueman, Jr. 1936- *WhoAm 90*
Curry, Jane Louise 1932- *AuBYP 90, BioIn 16, WhoAm 90, WhoWrEP 89*
Curry, Jerry Ralph 1932- *WhoAm 90*
Curry, John A. *WhoAm 90*
Curry, John Anthony 1949- *WhoAm 90*
Curry, John Joseph 1936- *WhoAm 90*
Curry, John Michael 1942- *WhoE 91*
Curry, John Patrick 1934- *WhoWor 91*
Curry, Kathi Joy *BiDrAPA 89*
Curry, Kathleen Bridget 1931- *WhoAmW 91*
Curry, Kelly E. 1955- *St&PR 91*
Curry, Kelly Edwin 1955- *WhoAm 90*
Curry, Kevin Lee 1957- *WhoAmA 91*
Curry, Leyla Cambel 1953- *WhoAmW 91*
Curry, Mary Earle Lowry 1917- *WhoWrEP 89*
Curry, Mary Grace 1947- *WhoAmW 91*
Curry, Michael Paul 1952- *WhoEmL 91*
Curry, Nancy Ann 1950- *BiDrAPA 89*
Curry, Nancy Ellen 1931- *WhoAm 90, WhoAmW 91*
Curry, Norval Herbert 1914- *WhoAm 90*
Curry, Parran Helena 1947- *WhoSSW 91*
Curry, Peggy Simson 1911-1987 *BioIn 16*
Curry, Richard A. 1926- *St&PR 91*
Curry, Richard Orr 1931- *WhoAm 90*
Curry, Robert A. 1931- *St&PR 91*
Curry, Robert L. 1923- *St&PR 91*
Curry, Robert Lee 1923- *WhoAm 90*
Curry, Roy Lee, Jr. 1939- *BiDrAPA 89*
Curry, Ruby Cotton 1907- *WhoAmW 91*
Curry, Stephen Allen 1954- *WhoEmL 91*
Curry, Stephen Leroy 1940- *WhoAm 90*
Curry, Thomas Edward, Jr. 1953- *WhoSSW 91*
Curry, Thomas Fortson 1926- *WhoAm 90*
Curry, Tray *BioIn 16*
Curry, William Charles 1942- *St&PR 91*
Curry, William Thomas, Jr. 1947- *WhoSSW 91*
Curschmann, Michael Johann Hendrik 1936- *WhoAm 90*
Cursmith, David *WhoAmA 91*
Curson, Theodore 1935- *WhoAm 90*
Curtain, Antonette McIntosh 1948- *WhoEmL 91*
Curtas, William Warren 1947- *St&PR 91*
Curteis, Ian Bayley 1935- *WhoWor 91*
Curthoys, Norman P. 1944- *WhoAm 90*
Curti, Merle Eugene 1897- *WhoAm 90*
Curti, Silvio 1953- *IntWWM 90*
Curtice, Harlow Herbert 1893-1962 *EncABHB 5 [port]*
Curtin, Brian Joseph 1921- *WhoAm 90, WhoE 91, WhoWor 91*
Curtin, Catherine Marie 1951- *WhoAmW 91*
Curtin, Christopher James 1951- *WhoEmL 91*
Curtin, Daniel John 1951- *WhoSSW 91*
Curtin, Dave 1955- *ConAu 132*
Curtin, David Stephen 1955- *WhoAm 90*
Curtin, Forrest J. 1926- *St&PR 91*
Curtin, J. Lawrence 1939- *St&PR 91*
Curtin, James B. 1929- *St&PR 91*
Curtin, Jane 1947- *WorAlBi*
Curtin, Jane Therese 1947- *WhoAm 90, WhoAmW 91*
Curtin, Joe Lawrence 1950- *WhoEmL 91*
Curtin, John D., Jr. 1932- *St&PR 91*
Curtin, John Joseph, Jr. 1933- *WhoAm 90*
Curtin, John T. 1921- *WhoAm 90*
Curtin, Joseph Stanley, Jr. 1943- *WhoE 91*
Curtin, Lawrence *BioIn 16*
Curtin, Michael Edward 1939- *WhoAm 90*
Curtin, Patricia Romero *ConAu 31NR*
Curtin, Philip De Armond 1922- *WhoAm 90*
Curtin, Phyllis *WhoAm 90*
Curtin, Phyllis 1921- *IntWWM 90*
Curtin, Phyllis 1922- *PenDiMP*
Curtin, Richard Daniel 1915- *WhoAm 90*
Curtin, S. Scott 1951- *WhoSSW 91*
Curtin, Valerie *ConAu 130*
Curtin, Virginia Marie 1958- *WhoAmW 91*
Curtin Caldeira, Tracy A. 1958- *ODwPR 91*
Curtis, Alan 1934- *IntWWM 90*
Curtis, Alan 1937- *St&PR 91, WhoAm 90*
Curtis, Albert Bradley, II 1957- *WhoEmL 91, WhoSSW 91*
Curtis, Albert Eugene, III 1951- *WhoE 91*
Curtis, Alice Bertha *AuBYP 90*
Curtis, Alice Turner 1860-1958 *AuBYP 90*
Curtis, Alton Kenneth 1939- *WhoE 91*
Curtis, Alva Marsh 1911- *WhoAmW 91*
Curtis, Arnold Bennett 1940- *WhoAm 90*
Curtis, Asahel 1874- *BioIn 16*
Curtis, Benjamin R. 1809-1874 *WorAlBi*
Curtis, Brigitte *BiDrAPA 89*
Curtis, Bruce *BioIn 16*
Curtis, Carl Thomas 1905- *WhoAm 90*
Curtis, Carol *ODwPR 91*
Curtis, Carol Joan 1941- *WhoE 91*
Curtis, Charles 1860-1936 *BiDrUSE 89, WhNaAH, WorAlBi*
Curtis, Charles Brent 1860-1936 *BioIn 16*
Curtis, Charles Edward 1931- *WhoAm 90*
Curtis, Charles G. 1933- *St&PR 91*
Curtis, Charles Melvin 1926- *St&PR 91*
Curtis, Charles Ravan 1938- *WhoAm 90*
Curtis, Charlotte 1928-1978 *WorAlBi*
Curtis, Chester Harris 1913- *WhoAm 90*
Curtis, Chet *BioIn 16*
Curtis, Christopher Dean 1961- *WhoSSW 91*
Curtis, Christopher Michael 1934- *WhoAm 90*
Curtis, Clark Britten 1951- *WhoEmL 91, WhoWor 91*
Curtis, Cliff 1883-1943 *Ballpl 90*
Curtis, Constance *WhoAmA 91N*
Curtis, Cyrus 1850-1933 *WorAlBi*
Curtis, Cyrus Hermann Kotzschmar 1850-1933 *BioIn 16*
Curtis, David Arnold 1939- *WhoE 91*
Curtis, David William, Jr. 1945- *WhoEmL 91*
Curtis, Dolly Powers 1942- *WhoAmA 91*
Curtis, Don K. 1949- *St&PR 91*
Curtis, Donald James 1941- *WhoAm 90*
Curtis, Douglas B. 1933- *St&PR 91*
Curtis, Douglas Homer 1934- *WhoAm 90*
Curtis, Dunstan Michael Carr 1910-1983 *DcNaB 1981*
Curtis, Edward Clinton 1865-1920 *AmLegL*
Curtis, Edward P. 1897-1987 *BioIn 16*
Curtis, Edward Sheriff 1868-1952 *WhNaAH [port]*
Curtis, Ever Louise 1915- *BiDrAPA 89*
Curtis, Frances *BiDEWW*
Curtis, Frank R. 1946- *WhoAm 90*
Curtis, Franklin R. 1925- *St&PR 91*
Curtis, Frederick Augustus, Jr. 1922- *WhoAm 90*
Curtis, George C 1926- *BiDrAPA 89*
Curtis, George Edward 1942- *St&PR 91*
Curtis, George W. N. *AmLegL*
Curtis, George William 1824-1892 *BioIn 16*
Curtis, Glenda Morris 1939- *WhoAmW 91*
Curtis, Gregory Dyer 1947- *WhoAm 90, WhoE 91, WhoEmL 91*
Curtis, Hallie Vea 1930- *WhoWrEP 89*
Curtis, Homer C 1917- *BiDrAPA 89*
Curtis, Horace Brogdon 1927- *WhoSSW 91*
Curtis, Ivan L. 1928- *St&PR 91*
Curtis, Jack 1937- *Ballpl 90*
Curtis, Jack 1943- *WhoE 91*
Curtis, James Breckenridge 1859-1922 *AmLegL*
Curtis, James L 1922- *BiDrAPA 89, WhoE 91*
Curtis, James P. 1953- *St&PR 91*
Curtis, James Richard 1930- *WhoWor 91*
Curtis, James Richard 1953- *WhoEmL 91*
Curtis, James Robert 1905- *St&PR 91*
Curtis, James Theodore 1923- *WhoE 91, WhoWor 91*
Curtis, Jamie Lee *BioIn 16*
Curtis, Jamie Lee 1958- *WorAlBi*
Curtis, Jean Trawick *WhoAm 90*
Curtis, Jeff Bain 1953- *WhoEmL 91*
Curtis, Jesse William, Jr. 1905- *WhoAm 90*
Curtis, Jo Dee 1964- *WhoEmL 91*
Curtis, John 1948- *Ballpl 90*
Curtis, John R 1934- *BiDrAPA 89*
Curtis, Karen Janann 1947- *WhoEmL 91*
Curtis, Kenneth Stewart 1925- *WhoAm 90*
Curtis, Kevin A. 1951- *St&PR 91*
Curtis, Kipp Allen 1953- *WhoEmL 91*
Curtis, Lamont William 1937- *St&PR 91*
Curtis, Laurence 1893-1989 *BioIn 16*
Curtis, Lawrence Henry 1958- *WhoE 91, WhoWor 91*
Curtis, Lewis G. 1934- *WhoAm 90*
Curtis, Linda Lee 1950- *WhoWrEP 89*
Curtis, Luther Cullens 1946- *WhoSSW 91*
Curtis, Marcia 1931- *WhoAm 90*
Curtis, Marianne Rose 1952- *WhoEmL 91*
Curtis, Mark 1921- *ODwPR 91*
Curtis, Mark Hubert 1920- *WhoAm 90, WhoWor 91*
Curtis, Mary Cranfill 1925- *WhoAmA 91*
Curtis, Mary Ellen 1946- *WhoAm 90*

Curtis, Mary Pacifico 1953- *WhoAmW 91*
Curtis, Michael *BiDrAPA 89*
Curtis, Michael Raymond 1923- *WhoWrEP 89*
Curtis, Nanci-Ames E *BiDrAPA 89*
Curtis, Nancy Ruth 1937- *WhoAmW 91*
Curtis, Natalie Jacobson *BioIn 16*
Curtis, Nevius Minot 1929- *St&PR 91, WhoAm 90*
Curtis, Orlie Lindsey, Jr. 1934- *WhoAm 90*
Curtis, Patricia Ellen 1930- *WhoAmW 91*
Curtis, Penny Johnson 1957- *WhoEmL 91*
Curtis, Peter *AuBYP 90*
Curtis, Philip 1920- *SmATA 62 [port]*
Curtis, Philip C. 1907- *WhoAm 90, WhoWor 91*
Curtis, Philip Campbell 1907- *WhoAmA 91*
Curtis, Philip Chadsey, Jr. 1928- *WhoAm 90*
Curtis, Philip James 1918- *WhoAm 90*
Curtis, Price *MajTwCW*
Curtis, Raymond Frank 1927- *IntWWM 90*
Curtis, Regina M *BiDrAPA 89*
Curtis, Richard 1937- *AuBYP 90*
Curtis, Richard Anson 1926- *St&PR 91*
Curtis, Richard Earl 1930- *WhoAm 90*
Curtis, Richard Earl 1957- *BiDrAPA 89*
Curtis, Richard Hale *ConAu 31NR*
Curtis, Richard Kenneth 1924- *WhoAm 90*
Curtis, Robert D 1948- *WhoAmA 91*
Curtis, Robert Emmett, Jr. 1965- *WhoE 91*
Curtis, Robert H. *AuBYP 90*
Curtis, Robert Joseph 1945- *WhoE 91, WhoEmL 91*
Curtis, Robert Kern 1940- *WhoE 91*
Curtis, Robert W. 1867-1939 *Ballpl 90*
Curtis, Roger William 1910- *WhoAm 90, WhoAmA 91*
Curtis, Rosemary Ann 1935- *AuBYP 90*
Curtis, Samuel Ralston, Jr. 1919- *WhoAm 90*
Curtis, Sheldon 1932- *St&PR 91, WhoAm 90*
Curtis, Sherry Lynn 1954- *WhoSSW 91*
Curtis, Solomon M. 1818-1904 *AmLegL*
Curtis, Staton Russell 1921- *WhoAm 90*
Curtis, Ted 1937- *St&PR 91*
Curtis, Terry Wayne 1951- *WhoAmA 91*
Curtis, Thomas Allan *BiDrAPA 89*
Curtis, Thomas E 1927- *BiDrAPA 89*
Curtis, Thomas Jennifer 1838-1898 *AmLegL*
Curtis, Thompson 1941- *St&PR 91*
Curtis, Tony 1925- *WhoAm 90, WorAlBi*
Curtis, Verna P *WhoAmA 91*
Curtis, Verna P. 1940- *WhoAmW 91*
Curtis, Wade *ConAu 30NR*
Curtis, Walter W. 1913- *WhoAm 90*
Curtis, Willbur N., Jr. 1933- *St&PR 91*
Curtis, William 1746-1799 *BioIn 16*
Curtis, William 1953- *St&PR 91*
Curtis, William David 1948- *IntWWM 90*
Curtis, William Edgar 1914- *IntWWM 90, WhoAm 90*
Curtis, William Hall 1915- *WhoAm 90*
Curtis, William Nicholas *WhoSSW 91*
Curtis-Hall, Vondie *DrBlPA 90*
Curtis-Smith, Curtis Otto Bismarck 1941- *IntWWM 90*
Curtis-Verna, Mary 1927- *IntWWM 90*
Curtiss, Charles Francis 1921- *WhoAm 90*
Curtiss, David Pierce, Jr. 1938- *BiDrAPA 89*
Curtiss, Elden F. 1932- *WhoAm 90*
Curtiss, Gayle Laura 1953- *WhoSSW 91*
Curtiss, Glenn H. 1878-1930 *WorAlBi*
Curtiss, Glenn Hammond 1878-1930 *BioIn 16*
Curtiss, Howard Crosby, Jr. 1930- *WhoAm 90*
Curtiss, Jeffrey Eugene 1948- *St&PR 91*
Curtiss, Roy, III 1934- *WhoAm 90*
Curtiss, Sidney Quinn 1917- *WhoE 91*
Curtiss, Thomas, Jr. 1941- *WhoAm 90, WhoWor 91*
Curtiss, Trumbull Cary 1940- *WhoAm 90*
Curtiss, Ursula 1923- *TwCCr&M 91*
Curtright, Guy 1912- *Ballpl 90*
Curts, Constance Elaine 1957- *WhoAmW 91*
Curts, Harold Layne 1957- *WhoEmL 91, WhoSSW 91*
Curty, Judith A. 1957- *WhoWor 91*
Curva, Leoncio Gaite 1929- *BiDrAPA 89*
Curwen, Alice *FemiCLE*
Curwen, Alice 1620?-1679 *BiDEWW*
Curwen, Randall William 1946- *WhoAm 90*
Curwin, Ronald 1930- *St&PR 91, WhoAm 90*
Curzan, Myron Paul 1940- *WhoWor 91*
Curzi, Cesare 1926- *IntWWM 90*
Curzio, Elaine Mary 1947- *WhoE 91*
Curzio, Francis X. *BioIn 16*
Curzio, Francis Xavier 1944- *WhoE 91*
Curzon, Clare 1922- *TwCCr&M 91*
Curzon, Clifford 1907-1982 *PenDiMP*
Curzon, Clifford Michael 1907-1982 *DcNaB 1981*
Curzon, Daniel *WhoWrEP 89*
Curzon, Frederic 1899-1973 *OxCPMus*
Curzon, George Nathaniel 1859-1925 *WorAlBi*
Curzon, Mary 1870-1906 *BioIn 16*
Curzon, Mary Leiter 1870-1906 *BioAmW*
Curzon, Sarah 1833-1898 *FemiCLE*
Curzon, Sarah Anne *DcCanB 12*
Curzon, Sarah Anne 1833-1898 *DcLB 99 [port], OxCCanT [port]*
Curzon, Susan Carol 1947- *WhoEmL 91*
Cusa, Thomas Leonard 1943- *St&PR 91*
Cusack, Cyril James 1910- *WhoWor 91*
Cusack, Donald James 1926- *St&PR 91*
Cusack, Dymphna 1902-1981 *FemiCLE*
Cusack, Gerald William 1939- *St&PR 91*
Cusack, James Campbell 1936- *St&PR 91*
Cusack, Joan *BioIn 16*
Cusack, John *BioIn 16*
Cusack, John 1966- *ConTFT 8*
Cusack, John Thomas 1935- *WhoAm 90*
Cusack, Margaret 1945- *BioIn 16*
Cusack, Margaret Weaver 1945- *WhoAmA 91*
Cusack, Mary Josephine 1935- *WhoAmW 91*
Cusack, Michael Joseph 1928- *WhoAm 90*
Cusack, Thomas Joseph 1938- *WhoE 91*
Cusano, Anthony John 1950- *WhoE 91*
Cusano, Cristino 1941- *WhoAm 90*
Cusano, Paul Philip, Jr. *BiDrAPA 89*
Cuscela, Frank P. 1933- *St&PR 91*
Cusco *NewAgMG*
Cuse, Carlton 1959- *WhoEmL 91*
Cusenza, Vito P. 1930- *St&PR 91*
Cush, Joseph Wilbur 1929- *WhoSSW 91*
Cushing, Caleb 1800-1879 *BiDrUSE 89*
Cushing, Eliza 1794-1854? *FemiCLE*
Cushing, Eliza Lanesford 1794-1886 *DcLB 99*
Cushing, Ellen Howard Winsor 1840-1915 *BioIn 16*
Cushing, Enid Louise *FemiCLE*
Cushing, Frank Hamilton 1857-1900 *WhNaAH*
Cushing, Frederic Sanford 1920- *WhoAm 90*
Cushing, John D. 1922-1987 *BioIn 16*
Cushing, Kay Smith 1944- *WhoAmW 91, WhoE 91*
Cushing, Margaret Channing 1941- *WhoAmW 91*
Cushing, Pamela Higley 1943- *WhoAmW 91*
Cushing, Peter Wilton 1913- *WhoWor 91*
Cushing, Richard J. 1895-1970 *WorAlBi*
Cushing, Robert Hunter 1953- *WhoAm 90*
Cushing, Steven 1948- *WhoAm 90, WhoE 91, WhoEmL 91, WhoWor 91*
Cushing, Thomas Francis, Sister *BioIn 16*
Cushing, Winifred 1907-1990 *ConAu 132*
Cushman, Aaron D. 1924- *ODwPR 91, WhoAm 90*
Cushman, Allerton, Jr. 1936- *St&PR 91*
Cushman, Ann Louise 1961- *WhoAmW 91*
Cushman, Charles Whitacre 1917- *St&PR 91*
Cushman, Charlotte 1816-1876 *BioIn 16*
Cushman, Charlotte S. 1816-1876 *BioAmW*
Cushman, Charlotte Saunders 1816-1876 *NotWoAT*
Cushman, David Wayne 1939- *WhoAm 90*
Cushman, Edward L. 1914- *WhoAm 90*
Cushman, George, Jr. 1922- *St&PR 91*
Cushman, Helen Merle Baker *WhoAm 90*
Cushman, Jerome *AuBYP 90*
Cushman, John Holloway 1921- *WhoAm 90*
Cushman, Judith *ODwPR 91*
Cushman, Laura Ann 1958- *WhoAmW 91*
Cushman, Margaret Jane 1948- *WhoAmW 91*
Cushman, Mary Susan Livingstone 1932- *WhoSSW 91*
Cushman, Michael Larry 1947- *WhoEmL 91*
Cushman, Paul 1930- *WhoE 91*
Cushman, Paulette Bessire 1931- *WhoAmW 91*
Cushman, Pauline 1833-1893 *BioAmW*
Cushman, Phillip Wayne 1941- *BiDrAPA 89*
Cushman, Robert 1916- *St&PR 91*
Cushman, Robert Earl 1913- *WhoAm 90*
Cushman, Robert Fairchild 1918- *WhoAm 90*
Cushman, Robert W. *St&PR 91*
Cushman, Stewart *BioIn 16*
Cushman, Timothy James 1958- *WhoEmL 91*
Cushman, Walter Herbert 1929- *St&PR 91*
Cushmore, Carole Lee *WhoAm 90*
Cushwa, Charles Benton, III 1934- *St&PR 91*
Cushwa, William Wallace 1937- *St&PR 91, WhoAm 90*
Cusi, Antonio 1951- *BiDrAPA 89*
Cusic, Donald F. 1948- *WhoSSW 91*
Cusick, Albert 1846- *WhNaAH*
Cusick, Mary Lynn 1955- *ODwPR 91*
Cusick, Nancy Taylor *WhoAmA 91*
Cusick, Ralph A., Jr. 1934- *St&PR 91, WhoAm 90*
Cusick, Ralph J, Jr. *BiDrAPA 89*
Cusick, Robert Erik 1964- *WhoEmL 91*
Cusick, Thomas A. 1944- *St&PR 91*
Cusimano, Adeline Mary 1939- *WhoE 91*
Cusimano, James Michael 1949- *WhoEmL 91*
Cusseaux, Selma Ulease Small 1925- *WhoSSW 91*
Cussen, Jack Donald 1937- *WhoAm 90*
Cussen, June 1944- *WhoWrEP 89*
Cussimanio, Brian Scott 1964- *WhoE 91*
Cussler, Clive 1931- *BestSel 90-4 [port], TwCCr&M 91*
Cussler, Clive Eric 1931- *SpyFic, WhoAm 90*
Cusson-Cobb, Jody Marie 1957- *WhoAmW 91*
Custance, D.A. 1942- *St&PR 91*
Custance, Olive 1874-1944 *BioIn 16*
Custer, Benjamin Scott, Jr. 1937- *WhoAm 90, WhoE 91*
Custer, Betty Lou *BioIn 16*
Custer, Charles Francis 1928- *WhoAm 90*
Custer, Clarence P., Jr. *BioIn 16*
Custer, Clint *ConAu 31NR*
Custer, Diane Edith 1962- *BiDrAPA 89*
Custer, Elizabeth 1842-1933 *FemiCLE*
Custer, George Armstrong 1839-1876 *BioIn 16, WhNaAH [port], WorAlBi*
Custer, Gilbert Joseph, Jr. *BiDrAPA 89*
Custer, John Charles 1934- *WhoE 91*
Custer, Laurenz 1930- *IntWWM 90*
Custer, Quessnal Stewart, Jr. 1931- *WhoSSW 91*
Custer, R. Philip 1903-1989 *BioIn 16*
Custer, Richard Lewis Payzant 1940- *WhoE 91*
Custer, Robert 1927-1990 *ConAu 132*
Custer, Robert L 1927- *BiDrAPA 89*
Custin, Mildred 1906- *WhoAm 90*
Custine, Adam-Philibert, Comte de *PenDiDA 89*
Custodio, Deogracias Banaban 1935- *WhoWor 91*
Custureri, Mary Catherine Foca 1929- *WhoAmW 91*
Custureri, Richard Domenick 1957- *WhoSSW 91*
Cusumano, Charles Louis 1936- *WhoSSW 91*
Cusumano, Gary M. 1943- *St&PR 91*
Cusumano, James Anthony 1942- *WhoAm 90*
Cusumano, Stefano 1912-1975 *WhoAmA 91N*
Cutbush, James D. 1947- *St&PR 91*
Cutbush, Murray S. *WhoAm 90*
Cutcheon, Sullivan M. 1843-1900 *AmLegL*
Cutchins, C.A., III 1923- *St&PR 91*
Cutchins, Clifford Armstrong, III 1923- *WhoAm 90*
Cutchins, Clifford Armstrong, IV 1948- *St&PR 91, WhoEmL 91*
Cutchins, Judy *AuBYP 90, BioIn 16*
Cutchins, Malcolm Armstrong 1935- *WhoSSW 91*
Cutforth, David Ecroyd 1923- *IntWWM 90*
Cutforth, Roger 1944- *WhoAmA 91*
Cuthbert, Saint 653?-687 *BioIn 16*
Cuthbert, Alan William 1932- *WhoWor 91*
Cuthbert, Betty 1938- *BioIn 16*
Cuthbert, Geraldine Ruth 1931- *WhoSSW 91*
Cuthbert, Marion Vera 1896- *HarlReB [port]*
Cuthbert, Richard I. *ODwPR 91*
Cuthbert, Robert Allen *WhoAm 90*
Cuthbert, Virginia 1908- *WhoAmA 91*
Cuthbert, William R. 1919- *WhoAm 90*
Cuthbertson, Allan 1920-1988 *AnObit 1988*
Cuthbertson, Betsy Alice 1952- *WhoEmL 91*
Cuthbertson, Catherine *FemiCLE*
Cuthbertson, David 1900-1989 *AnObit 1989*
Cuthbertson, David Granville 1932- *WhoAm 90*
Cuthbertson, John Brown 1929- *St&PR 91*
Cuthbertson, Richard W. 1935- *St&PR 91*
Cuthbertson, Richard Wiley 1935- *WhoAm 90*
Cuthbertson, Robert Anthony *BiDrAPA 89*
Cuthbertson, William D., Jr. 1920- *St&PR 91*
Cuthill, J. Ivan 1930- *St&PR 91*
Cuthrell, Carl Edward 1934- *WhoAm 90*
Cutietta, Robert Alan 1953- *IntWWM 90*
Cutilletta, Thomas Paul 1943- *St&PR 91, WhoAm 90*
Cutkosky, Richard Edwin 1928- *WhoAm 90*
Cutler, Alexander Macdonald 1951- *St&PR 91, WhoAm 90*
Cutler, Andrew Hall 1956- *WhoEmL 91*
Cutler, Andrew Jon *BiDrAPA 89*
Cutler, Ann *AuBYP 90*
Cutler, Arnold Robert 1908- *WhoAm 90, WhoE 91, WhoWor 91*
Cutler, Bernard Joseph 1924- *WhoAm 90*
Cutler, Bess 1949- *WhoAmA 91*
Cutler, Beverly Winslow 1949- *WhoAmW 91*
Cutler, Bruce 1930- *WhoWrEP 89*
Cutler, Cassius Chapin 1914- *WhoAm 90*
Cutler, Charles Russell 1924- *WhoAm 90*
Cutler, Christopher Ashton 1950- *St&PR 91*
Cutler, Cynthia Ann 1953- *WhoAmW 91*
Cutler, David Lloyd *BiDrAPA 89*
Cutler, Devorah Ann 1952- *WhoEmL 91*
Cutler, Ebbitt 1923- *AuBYP 90*
Cutler, Edward I. 1913- *WhoAm 90*
Cutler, Ellen *ODwPR 91*
Cutler, Ethel Rose *WhoAmA 91, WhoE 91*
Cutler, Everette Wayne 1938- *WhoSSW 91*
Cutler, Frank Charles 1949- *WhoEmL 91*
Cutler, Glenn *BioIn 16*
Cutler, Grayce E *WhoAmA 91*
Cutler, Howard Armstrong 1918- *WhoAm 90*
Cutler, Jane 1936- *WhoWrEP 89*
Cutler, Janis Lynne 1957- *BiDrAPA 89*
Cutler, Jay B. 1930- *WhoE 91*
Cutler, John Charles 1915- *WhoAm 90*
Cutler, John Frederick 1937- *WhoAm 90*
Cutler, Kay Robinson 1921- *BiDrAPA 89*
Cutler, Kenneth B. 1932- *St&PR 91*
Cutler, Kenneth Burnett 1932- *WhoAm 90*
Cutler, Laurel *BioIn 16*
Cutler, Laurel 1926- *WhoAm 90, WhoAmW 91*
Cutler, Lauren Elizabeth Savage 1961- *WhoAmW 91*
Cutler, Laurence Stephan 1940- *WhoAm 90*
Cutler, Leonard Samuel 1928- *WhoAm 90*
Cutler, Leroy Respess 1934- *WhoSSW 91, WhoWor 91*
Cutler, Lloyd Norton 1917- *WhoAm 90*
Cutler, Lynn Germain 1938- *WhoAmW 91*
Cutler, Manasseh 1742-1823 *WhNaAH*
Cutler, Mark Owen 1947- *BiDrAPA 89, WhoE 91*
Cutler, Mary Levin 1933- *WhoWor 91*
Cutler, Max 1912- *St&PR 91*
Cutler, Morene Parten 1911- *WhoAmW 91*
Cutler, Neal Richard 1949- *BiDrAPA 89*
Cutler, Ralph W. *BioIn 16*
Cutler, Rhoda *WhoAmW 91*
Cutler, Richard J. 1931- *St&PR 91*
Cutler, Richard M. 1920- *St&PR 91*
Cutler, Richard Woolsey 1917- *WhoAm 90*
Cutler, Robert P 1917- *BiDrAPA 89*
Cutler, Robert Porter 1917- *WhoAm 90*
Cutler, Robert Ward 1905- *WhoAm 90*
Cutler, Ronnie 1924- *WhoAmA 91*
Cutler, Ruth Ellen Lemon 1928- *WhoAmW 91*
Cutler, Scott Bruce 1951- *BiDrAPA 89*
Cutler, Stephen D. 1936- *St&PR 91*
Cutler, Stephen Joel 1943- *WhoAm 90*
Cutler, Suzanne 1939- *St&PR 91*
Cutler, Tarrant 1926- *St&PR 91*
Cutler, Theodore John 1941- *WhoAm 90*
Cutler, Thomas Joshua 1947- *WhoE 91*
Cutler, Timothy Rookwood 1931- *St&PR 91*
Cutler, Walter Leon 1931- *WhoAm 90, WhoWor 91*
Cutler, William Parker 1812-1889 *BioIn 16*
Cutler, Winnifred Berg 1944- *WhoAmW 91*
Cutler-Shaw, Joyce *WhoAmA 91*
Cutlip, Gary C. 1942- *St&PR 91*
Cutlip, Randall Brower 1916- *WhoAm 90, WhoWor 91*
Cutlip, Scott Munson 1915- *WhoAm 90*
Cutlip, Thomas A. 1941- *St&PR 91*
Cutmore, Ross H. 1929- *St&PR 91*
Cutmore, Ross Herbert James 1929- *WhoAm 90*
Cutner, Solomon *BioIn 16*
Cutrell, Benjamin Elwood 1923- *WhoAm 90*
Cutrer, Hebron D. 1938- *St&PR 91*
Cutri, William J. 1949- *St&PR 91*
Cutrie, Sherri Ann 1948- *WhoAmW 91*
Cutright, Phillips 1930- *WhoAm 90*
Cutright, William Marcus 1952- *WhoEmL 91*
Cutro, Dyan 1949- *ODwPR 91*
Cutrona, Anthony Joseph 1938- *St&PR 91*
Cutrone, Candace Ann 1956- *BiDrAPA 89*

Cutrone, Lee David 1947- *St&PR 91*
Cutrone, Lee David, Jr. 1947- *WhoAm 90*
Cutrone, Lee J. 1948- *St&PR 91*
Cutrone, Luigi Cutrone 1950- *WhoWor 91*
Cutrone, Ronnie Blaise 1948- *WhoAmA 91*
Cutrubus, Christina N. 1934- *WhoAmW 91*
Cutsforth, Marshall Marvin 1936- *WhoE 91*
Cutshall, Roger Ackard *BiDrAPA 89*
Cutshaw, George 1887-1973 *Ballpl 90*
Cutshaw, Kenneth Andrew 1953- *WhoAm 90, WhoEmL 91*
Cutten, John H *EncO&P 3*
Cutter, Alan B. 1934- *St&PR 91*
Cutter, Albert V 1914- *BiDrAPA 89*
Cutter, Charles Richard, III 1924- *WhoAm 90*
Cutter, David L. 1929- *St&PR 91*
Cutter, David L., Jr. 1952- *St&PR 91*
Cutter, David Lee 1929- *WhoAm 90*
Cutter, Dennis A. 1941- *St&PR 91*
Cutter, Dennis M. 1945- *St&PR 91*
Cutter, Edward A. 1939- *St&PR 91*
Cutter, Edward Ahern 1939- *WhoAm 90*
Cutter, John A. 1954- *St&PR 91*
Cutter, John Michael 1952- *WhoEmL 91*
Cutter, Margaret Mead 1953- *WhoWrEP 89*
Cutter, Philip D 1936- *BiDrAPA 89*
Cutter, Portia Lynette 1938- *WhoAmW 91*
Cutter, Ralph Frederick 1955- *WhoWrEP 89*
Cutter, Richard Ammi 1902- *WhoAm 90*
Cutter Modlin, Beverly Wright 1947- *WhoEmL 91*
Cutting, Charles L. 1926- *St&PR 91*
Cutting, Heyward 1921- *WhoAm 90*
Cutting, Robert Thomas 1929- *WhoAm 90*
Cutting, Thomas *PenDiMP*
Cuttle, Tracy Donald 1908- *WhoAm 90*
Cuttler, Charles David 1913- *WhoAmA 91*
Cutts, Mrs. *FemiCLE*
Cutts, Charles Eugene 1914- *WhoAm 90*
Cutts, Norma E. 1892-1988 *BioIn 16*
Cutts, Peter Warwick 1937- *IntWWM 90*
Cutts, Robert I *BiDrAPA 89*
Cutugno, Leonard F. 1952- *WhoE 91*
Cuvier, Georges 1769-1832 *WorAlBi*
Cuvillier, Charles 1877-1955 *OxCPMus*
Cuvillier, Philippe 1930- *WhoWor 91*
Cuvillies, Francois 1695-1768 *PenDiDA 89*
Cuyler, Kiki 1899-1950 *Ballpl 90 [port]*
Cuyler, Lewis B. *BioIn 16*
Cuyp, Aelbert 1620-1691? *IntDcAA 90*
Cuyp, Albert 1620?-1691 *WorAlBi*
Cuypers, Jan Hendrik 1936- *WhoWor 91*
Cuyvers, Luc 1954- *WhoE 91*
Cuza, Alexandru 1857-1946 *BioIn 16*
Cuza Male, Belkis 1942- *ConAu 131, HispWr 90, WhoHisp 91*
Cuzzetto, Charles Edward 1954- *WhoEmL 91*
Cuzzocrea, Dominic David 1945- *St&PR 91, WhoAm 90*
Cuzzone, Mary Jo 1953- *WhoAmW 91*
Cuzzoni, Francesca 1698?-1770 *PenDiMP*
Cuzzort, R. P. 1926- *WhoWrEP 89*
Cuzzort, Ray Paul 1926- *WhoAm 90*
Cvejic, Biserka 1923- *PenDiMP*
Cvejin, Snezana Z *BiDrAPA 89*
Cvelbar, Anthony W. 1943- *St&PR 91*
Cveljo, Katherine *WhoAmW 91*
Cvengros, Mike 1901-1970 *Ballpl 90*
Cvetan-Gardner, Marcia Ellen 1951- *IntWWM 90*
Cvetko, Dragotin 1911- *IntWWM 90*
Cvetkovic, Nikola Berndt 1945- *WhoEmL 91*
Cvijanovic, Alex 1923- *St&PR 91, WhoE 91*
Cwik, John Peter 1947- *WhoSSW 91*
Cwirko, Tracey Alice 1963- *WhoAmW 91*
Cwynar, Michael John 1944- *BiDrAPA 89*
Cybul, Richard Mark 1963- *WhoE 91*
Cybulski, Joanne Karen 1950- *WhoAm 90*
Cyccone, Louis A. 1956- *WhoEmL 91*
Cyert, Richard Michael 1921- *BioIn 16, WhoAm 90, WhoE 91, WhoWor 91*
Cyffle, Paul-Louis 1724-1806 *PenDiDA 89*
Cyker, Marvin M. *St&PR 91*
Cyker, Marvin Myer 1929- *WhoAm 90*
Cyker, Michael *St&PR 91*
Cyker, Michael 1930- *WhoAm 90*
Cykler, Edmund A. 1903- *IntWWM 90*
Cylke, Frank Kurt 1932- *WhoAm 90*
Cymbala, Robert J. *BioIn 16*
Cymbala, Robert J. 1937- *St&PR 91*
Cymbala, Robert Joseph 1937- *WhoAm 90*
Cymerman, Sandra Rae 1942- *WhoAmW 91, WhoE 91*
Cymet, Tyler Childs 1963- *WhoWrEP 89*
Cyn, T. G. 1948- *WhoAmW 91, WhoWor 91*
Cynader, Max Sigmund 1947- *WhoAm 90*
Cynar, Sandra Jean 1941- *WhoAmW 91*
Cynkar, Maribeth 1951- *WhoEmL 91*
Cynkin, Thomas Michael 1958- *WhoEmL 91, WhoWor 91*
Cynman, Selig Abraham *BiDrAPA 89*
Cypert, Jimmy Dean 1934- *WhoAm 90*
Cypher, Michael Jerome 1941-1975 *BioIn 16*
Cypher, Robert Leonard 1938- *St&PR 91*
Cypher, Victor Joseph 1938- *St&PR 91*
Cyphers, Edward J. 1946- *St&PR 91*
Cyphers, James Michael 1949- *WhoSSW 91*
Cyphers, Peggy K 1954- *WhoAmA 91*
Cyphers, Ronald Alan 1940- *WhoSSW 91*
Cyphers, Stanley P. 1944- *St&PR 91*
Cyphert, Frederick Ralph 1928- *WhoAm 90*
Cyphus, Anthony Lattimore 1926- *IntWWM 90*
Cypress, Conrad Sigmond 1927- *St&PR 91*
Cypress, F.G. 1928- *St&PR 91*
Cyr, Arthur 1945- *WhoAm 90*
Cyr, Conrad Keefe 1931- *WhoAm 90, WhoE 91*
Cyr, Ellie R. 1942- *WhoAmW 91*
Cyr, Gordon Conrad 1925- *IntWWM 90*
Cyr, J.V. Raymond 1934- *St&PR 91*
Cyr, J. V. Raymond 1934- *WhoAm 90, WhoE 91, WhoWor 91*
Cyr, Jennifer Hubbard *BiDrAPA 89*
Cyr, Joanne *BiDrAPA 89*
Cyr, Maurice J. 1932- *St&PR 91*
Cyran, Francis Michael 1952- *BiDrAPA 89*
Cyran, William John 1954- *WhoSSW 91*
Cyrankiewicz, Jozef 1911-1989 *AnObit 1989*
Cyrano De Bergerac, Savinien 1619-1655 *WorAlBi*
Cyren, Gunnar 1931- *ConDes 90*
Cyrille, Andrew *BioIn 16*
Cyrlin, Marshall Nelson 1950- *WhoEmL 91*
Cyrus The Great 600?BC-529BC *WorAlBi*
Cyrus, Pamela Ann 1962- *BiDrAPA 89*
Cyrus, Teriece Dyer 1912- *WhoAmW 91*
Cysarz, Jan M. 1931- *St&PR 91*
Cysarz, Janusz Marian 1931- *WhoE 91*
Cysewski, Gerald R. 1949- *St&PR 91*
Cytowic, Richard Edmund 1952- *WhoAm 90*
Cytraus, Aldona Ona 1947- *WhoEmL 91*
Cytryn, Jack 1916- *St&PR 91*
Cytryn, Leon *BiDrAPA 89*
Cyvas, Edmund V. *BiDrAPA 89*
Czach, Marie *WhoAmA 91*
Czachowski, Robert Joseph 1933- *WhoSSW 91*
Czaja, Mary Forest McLean 1928- *WhoAmW 91*
Czaja, Mike *BioIn 16*
Czajka, James Vincent 1950- *WhoE 91, WhoEmL 91*
Czajka, Stanislaw Antoni 1941- *WhoWor 91*
Czajka, Stephen 1953- *WhoE 91, WhoWor 91*
Czajkouski, Francis D. 1937- *St&PR 91*
Czajkowski, Eva Anna 1961- *WhoAmW 91, WhoEmL 91*
Czajkowski, Nancy Gallardo 1961- *WhoE 91*
Czander, Walter W. 1931- *St&PR 91*
Czapanskiy, Karen 1947- *WhoEmL 91*
Czapiewski, Susan Elizabeth *BiDrAPA 89*
Czapnik, Sheldon Jacob 1947- *WhoE 91*
Czarlinsky, Randall Gregg 1954- *WhoE 91*
Czarnecki, Alan Joseph 1951- *WhoEmL 91*
Czarnecki, Caroline MaryAnne 1929- *WhoAm 90*
Czarnecki, Edward 1937- *St&PR 91*
Czarnecki, Eugene Bielen 1947- *WhoWor 91*
Czarnecki, Gerald Milton 1940- *St&PR 91, WhoAm 90*
Czarnecki, Michael Frank *BiDrAPA 89*
Czarnecki, Richard Edward 1931- *WhoAm 90*
Czarnecki, Rita Marie Reymann 1939- *IntWWM 90*
Czarnecky, David Joseph 1943- *St&PR 91*
Czarnezki, Joseph John 1954- *WhoEmL 91*
Czarniecki, M J, III 1948- *WhoAmA 91*
Czarniecki, Myron James, III 1948- *WhoAm 90, WhoEmL 91*
Czarnik, Marvin Ray 1932- *WhoAm 90*
Czarra, Edgar F., Jr. 1928- *WhoAm 90*
Czech Quartet *PenDiMP*
Czech, Michael Paul 1945- *WhoAm 90*
Czechowicz, Dorynne Joan *BiDrAPA 89*
Czechowicz, Harry *BiDrAPA 89*
Czekalski, Loni Raven 1948- *WhoAmW 91*
Czemerda, Linda Ann 1964- *WhoE 91*
Czempiel, Ernst-Otto 1927- *WhoWor 91*
Czepowicz, Violetta D *BiDrAPA 89*
Czerniakow, Adam 1880-1942 *BioIn 16*
Czerny, Carl 1791-1857 *BioIn 16, PenDiMP*
Czerny, Charles 1791-1857 *BioIn 16*
Czerny-Stefanska, Halina 1922- *PenDiMP*
Czeropski, Walter P., Jr. 1925- *St&PR 91*
Czerwenka, Oscar 1924- *IntWWM 90*
Czerwenka, Oskar 1924- *PenDiMP*
Czerwinski, Edward Joseph 1929- *WhoAm 90, WhoE 91, WhoWor 91*
Czerwinski, Henry Richard 1933- *St&PR 91, WhoAm 90*
Czestochowski, Joseph Stephen 1950- *WhoAmA 91*
Czetli, Nancy *BioIn 16*
Czibulka, Alphons 1842-1894 *OxCPMus*
Cziffra, Gyorgy 1921- *IntWWM 90, PenDiMP*
Czigany, Lorant 1935- *ConAu 130*
Czimbalmos, Magdolna Paal *WhoAmA 91*
Czimbalmos, Szabo Kalman 1914- *WhoAmA 91*
Czin, Felicia Tedeschi 1950- *WhoAmW 91*
Czirr, Ruth Patrice 1954- *WhoAmW 91*
Czolgosz, Leon 1873-1901 *EncAL*
Czolgosz, Leon F. 1873-1901 *WorAlBi*
Czubaroff, Valentine B 1944- *BiDrAPA 89*
Czufin, Rudolf 1901-1979 *WhoAmA 91N*
Czuj, Chester Francis, Jr. 1955- *WhoE 91, WhoEmL 91*
Czuma, Stanislaw J 1935- *WhoAmA 91*
Czurda, Elfriede 1946- *EncCoWW*
Czuszak, Janis Marie 1956- *WhoAmW 91*
Czygan, Franz-Christian 1934- *WhoWor 91*
Czyz, Henryk 1923- *IntWWM 90*
Czyzewska, Elzbieta *BioIn 16*

D

D, E *BiDEWW*
D.O.C. *BioIn 16*
D. P. *MajTwCW*
Daamen, Maximiliaan *BiDrAPA 89*
Daane, Adrian Hill 1919- *WhoAm 90*
Daane, J. Dewey 1918- *St&PR 91*
Daane, James Dewey 1918- *WhoAm 90*
Daane, Mary Ann 1932- *WhoAmW 91*
Daaood, Kamau *BioIn 16*
D'Abadie, Jeannette *EncO&P 3*
Dabagia, Lee Warren *St&PR 91*
D'Abate, Janina Monica 1921- *WhoAmW 91, WhoE 91*
D'Abate, JoAnn Therese 1946- *WhoEmL 91, WhoWor 91*
Dabbagh, Mamoun *BiDrAPA 89*
D'Abbieri, Philip 1938- *St&PR 91*
Dabbs, Edwin Gerald 1937- *BiDrAPA 89*
Dabbs, Helen Bernice 1936- *WhoE 91*
Dabbs, Henry Erven 1932- *WhoAm 90*
Dabbs, Robert Lowell 1937- *St&PR 91*
Dabbs, Theron Randolph, Jr. 1940- *WhoSSW 91*
Dabby, Sabah Salman 1946- *St&PR 91, WhoAm 90*
Dabcovich, Lydia *AuBYP 90*
Dabcovich, Lydia 1935- *BioIn 16*
Daberko, David A. 1945- *St&PR 91, WhoAm 90*
Dabich, Danica 1930- *WhoAmW 91*
Dabich, Eli, Jr. 1939- *WhoAm 90*
Dabill, Phillip Alvin 1942- *WhoAm 90*
Dabipi, Ibibia Karisemie 1955- *WhoSSW 91*
Dabit, Eugene 1898-1936 *BioIn 16*
Dabkowski, John 1933- *WhoWor 91*
Dablow, Dean Clint 1946- *WhoAmA 91*
Dabner, Jack Duane 1930- *WhoWor 91*
Dabney, Anita Elizabeth 1951- *WhoAmW 91*
Dabney, Betty Lou Lovett 1933- *WhoSSW 91*
Dabney, Ford T. 1883-1958 *OxCPMus*
Dabney, Hovey S. 1923- *St&PR 91*
Dabney, Hovey Slayton 1923- *WhoAm 90, WhoSSW 91*
Dabney, June Bosley 1935- *IntWWM 90*
Dabney, Michelle Sheila 1959- *WhoAmW 91*
Dabney, Seth Mason, III 1918- *WhoAm 90*
Dabney, Virginius 1901- *WhoAm 90*
Dabney, Watson Barr 1923- *WhoAm 90*
Dabney, William Kroehle 1933- *St&PR 91, WhoAm 90*
Dabney-Smith, Lois *BioIn 16*
Dabo, Leon 1868-1960 *WhoAmA 91N*
Daborne, Robert *BioIn 16*
d'Aboville, Benoit 1942- *WhoWor 91*
Dabrowska, Maria 1889-1965 *EncCoWW*
Dabrowski, Edward Michael 1944- *St&PR 91*
Dabrowski, Joseph Michael 1933- *St&PR 91*
Dabrowski, Richard C. 1947- *St&PR 91*
Dabrowski, Robert Albert 1938- *St&PR 91*
Dabrowski, Stanislaw 1922- *BiDrAPA 89*
Dabundo, Charles 1961- *WhoE 91*
Dacanay-Raj, Veronica 1933- *BiDrAPA 89*
D'Accone, Frank A. 1931- *IntWWM 90*
D'Accone, Frank Anthony 1931- *WhoAm 90*
Dacek, Raymond Francis 1930- *WhoAm 90*
Dacey, Eileen M. 1948- *WhoAmW 91*
Dacey, George Clement 1921- *WhoAm 90*
Dacey, Judith Elaine 1946- *WhoEmL 91*
Dacey, Kathleen Ryan *WhoAm 90, WhoAmW 91*
Dacey, Philip 1939- *ConAu 32NR, DcLB 105 [port], WhoWrEP 89*
Dach, Eugene W 1921- *BiDrAPA 89*
Dach, John Richard 1945- *WhoEmL 91*
Dache, Lilly *BioIn 16, NewYTBS 90 [port]*
Dache, Lilly 1892?-1989 *CurBio 90N*
Dachenhausen, Theodore 1925-1988 *BioIn 16*
Dachowski, Marjorie McCormick 1932- *WhoAmW 91*
Dachowski, Peter Richard 1948- *St&PR 91, WhoAm 90*
Dachtera-Bobowski, Celina *BiDrAPA 89*
Dachtler, Jilene Rae 1961- *WhoAmW 91*
Dacier, Anne 1654-1720? *FemiCLE*
Dacier, Anne Lefebvre 1647?-1720 *EncCoWW*
Daciuk, Myron Michael 1919- *WhoAm 90*
Dack, Charles J 1950- *BiDrAPA 89*
Dack, Jerilyn *WhoAmW 91*
Dack, Simon 1908- *WhoAm 90*
Dackawich, S. John 1926- *WhoAm 90*
Dackis, Charles Andrew 1951- *BiDrAPA 89*
Dackis, William C. 1924- *St&PR 91*
Dackow, Orest Taras 1936- *St&PR 91, WhoAm 90*
Dackow, Sandra Katherine 1951- *IntWWM 90, WhoEmL 91*
Da Costa, Ana M. 1957- *WhoAmW 91*
Da Costa, Claudio Manuel 1729-1789 *BioIn 16*
Dacosta, David H. 1950- *St&PR 91*
Da Costa, Dennis 1959- *ODwPR 91*
Dacosta, Edward H. 1918- *St&PR 91*
DaCosta, Edward Hoban 1918- *WhoAm 90*
Da Costa, Gaspard Louis 1943- *WhoWor 91*
Da Costa, Granville *BiDrAPA 89*
DaCosta, Jacqueline 1927- *WhoAmW 91*
Da Costa, Maria Manuela *BiDrAPA 89*
Da Costa, Morton 1914-1989 *AnObit 1989, BioIn 16*
Da Costa, Noel 1930- *DrBIPA 90*
D'Acquisto, John 1951- *Ballpl 90*
Dacre, Barbarina Brand 1768-1854 *FemiCLE*
Dacre, Charlotte 1782?- *FemiCLE*
Dacre, Harry 1860-1922 *OxCPMus*
Dacres, Dorothy 1605-1698 *BiDEWW*
Dacri, Stephen R. 1952- *WhoEmL 91*
Da Cunha, Euclydes 1866-1909 *BioIn 16*
Da Cunha, Jose Anastacio 1744-1787 *BioIn 16*
Da Cunha, Julio 1929- *WhoAmA 91*
Dacy, John F. 1949- *St&PR 91*
Dadaglio, Luigi *NewYTBS 90 [port]*
D'Adamo, Dominic Frank 1947- *St&PR 91*
D'Adamo, Eugene J *BiDrAPA 89*
Dadamo, Vincent Michael 1948- *St&PR 91*
Dadd, Ronald Frederick 1943- *St&PR 91*
D'Addabbo, Michael Patrick 1921- *St&PR 91*
Daddario, Emilio Quincy 1918- *WhoAm 90*
Daddi, Bernardo 1290?-1348 *IntDcAA 90*
Daddi, William G. *ODwPR 91*
Daddino, Anthony Francis 1940- *St&PR 91*
Daddona, Joseph S. *WhoAm 90*
Dadds, Harry Leon, II 1950- *WhoEmL 91*
Dade, Francis Langhorne 1790?-1835 *WhNaAH*
Dade, Lonnie Paul 1951- *Ballpl 90*
Dade, Malcolm G. 1931- *St&PR 91*
Dadea, Gianmaria 1941- *WhoWor 91*
Dadekian, Gary Arsen 1955- *St&PR 91*
Dadgar, Mohammed Reza *BioIn 16*
Dadic, Boris 1929- *BiDrAPA 89*
Dadie-Roberg, Dagmar 1897- *BiDWomA*
Dadisman, Joseph Carrol 1934- *WhoAm 90, WhoSSW 91*
Dadley, Arlene Jeanne 1941- *WhoAmW 91*
d'Adolf, Stuart Victor 1925- *WhoAm 90*
Dadourian, Dadour *NewYTBS 90*
Dadrian, Vahakn Norair 1926- *WhoAm 90*
Dadson, Ebenezer William 1845-1900 *DcCanB 12*
Dadvand, Mahmood *BiDrAPA 89*
Daech, Etteen Marie 1952- *WhoSSW 91*
Daecke, Sigurd Martin 1932- *WhoWor 91*
Daehler, Robert T 1937- *BiDrAPA 89*
Daele, Jacques Joseph 1947- *WhoWor 91*
Daemmrich, Horst Sigmund 1930- *WhoAm 90*
Daen, Phyllis Helene 1931- *WhoE 91*
Daenzer, Bernard John 1916- *St&PR 91, WhoAm 90*
Daering, Duane Howard 1929- *St&PR 91*
Daerr, Richard L., Jr. 1944- *St&PR 91*
Daerr, Richard Leo, Jr. 1944- *WhoAm 90*
Daeschner, Charles William, Jr. 1920- *WhoAm 90*
Daeschner, Richard Wilbur 1917- *WhoAm 90*
Daessler, Mathias 1951- *WhoWor 91*
Daeuble, Louis 1912- *WhoAm 90*
DaFano, Marc 1926- *St&PR 91*
Dafermos, Constantine Michael 1941- *WhoAm 90*
Daffer, Stephanie Lee 1952- *WhoAmW 91*
Daffern, Shari Lynn 1949- *WhoAmW 91, WhoSSW 91*
Daffin, Carol Farwell 1953- *WhoWor 91*
Daffin, Irl Alonzo 1902- *WhoAm 90*
D'Afflitti, Joseph Paul 1946- *BiDrAPA 89*
Daffner, Gregg 1954- *WhoEmL 91*
Daffos, Fernand Alain 1947- *WhoWor 91*
Daffron, Mary Elizabeth Foley 1965- *WhoAmW 91*
Daffron, MaryEllen 1946- *WhoAm 90, WhoAmW 91*
Dafoe, Willem *BioIn 16*
Dafoe, Willem 1955- *CurBio 90 [port], WhoAm 90, WorAlBi*
Da Fonseca, Manuel Deodoro 1827-1892 *BioIn 16*
Dafora, Asadata 1890-1965 *DrBIPA 90*
Dafov, Yordan 1940- *WhoWor 91*
Daft, Jack Robert 1929- *WhoAm 90*
Daga, Andrew William 1957- *St&PR 91, WhoE 91*
Daga, Meryl Ann 1963- *St&PR 91*
Dagadakis, Christos S 1948- *BiDrAPA 89*
Da Gama, Vasco 1469-1524 *BioIn 16*
Dagan, Avigdor 1912- *ConAu 30NR*
Dagar, Faiyazuddin *BioIn 16*
Dagastine, Gary P. 1955- *ODwPR 91*
D'Agati, Donald Craig 1950- *BiDrAPA 89*
Dagdag, Faustino 1949- *St&PR 91*
Dagdeviren, Emre 1946- *WhoWor 91*
Dagenais, Marcel Gilles 1935- *WhoAm 90*
Dagenais, Pierre 1924- *OxCCanT*
Dagenais, Sandra Lee 1958- *WhoAmW 91*
Dagenhart, Larry Jones 1932- *WhoAm 90*
Dager, Fernando E. 1961- *WhoHisp 91*
Dager, Stephen Roger 1953- *BiDrAPA 89*
Dagerman, Stig 1923-1954 *DcScanL*
Dagg, John Leadley 1794-1884 *BioIn 16*
Dagg, Steven Gregory 1959- *WhoSSW 91*
Dagg, Tom 1930- *St&PR 91*
Daggatt, Walter Russell 1919- *WhoAm 90*
Dagger, William Carson 1949- *WhoEmL 91*
Daggett, Andrea Stuhlman 1952- *WhoEmL 91*
Daggett, Beverly Clark 1945- *WhoAmW 91*
Daggett, Donald R 1922- *BiDrAPA 89*
Daggett, Lorin Reid 1945- *BiDrAPA 89*
Daggett, Robert *St&PR 91*
Daggett, Robert Sherman 1930- *WhoAm 90, WhoWor 91*
Daggett, Tim *BioIn 16*
Daggett, William Athern 1937- *St&PR 91, WhoAm 90*
Daggs, Charles W., III 1947- *St&PR 91*
Daghestani, Amin N 1944- *BiDrAPA 89*
Daghlian, John Edward 1946- *WhoE 91*
Dagincourt, Paul G 1955- *BiDrAPA 89*
Dagirmanjian, Rose 1930- *WhoAmW 91*
Dagit, Charles Edward, Jr. 1943- *WhoAm 90*
Dagley, Larry Jack 1948- *St&PR 91*
Daglian, John Peter 1946- *WhoE 91*
Dagly, Gerhard *PenDiDA 89*
Dagna, Lawrence R. 1950- *St&PR 91*
Dagnan, Owen Gregory 1939- *St&PR 91*
D'Agnese, Helen Jean 1922- *WhoAmW 91*
Dagnese, Joseph M. 1927-1989 *BioIn 16*
Dagnon, James Bernard 1940- *St&PR 91*
Dago, Pedro Luis 1962- *BiDrAPA 89*
Dagon, Eugene M *BiDrAPA 89*
D'Agosta, Dominick *WhoE 91*
D'Agosta, Joseph *BioIn 16*
D'Agostino, Anthony Carmen 1939- *WhoE 91*
D'Agostino, Anthony M 1941- *BiDrAPA 89*
D'Agostino, Anthony M. 1957- *St&PR 91*
D'Agostino, Arthur D. 1948- *St&PR 91*
D'Agostino, Diane G. 1948- *St&PR 91*
D'Agostino, Douglas 1952- *St&PR 91*
D'Agostino, James Samuel, Jr 1946- *WhoAm 90*
D'Agostino, Joseph Salvatore 1928- *WhoE 91*
Dagostino, Ken A. 1929- *St&PR 91*
D'Agostino, Mae A. 1954- *WhoEmL 91*
D'Agostino, Matthew Paul 1948- *WhoE 91*
D'Agostino, Peppino *NewAgMG*
D'Agostino, Peter Pasquale 1945- *WhoAmA 91*
D'Agostino, Ralph Benedict 1940- *WhoAm 90, WhoE 91, WhoWor 91*
D'Agostino, Richard Daniel 1957- *WhoE 91*
D'Agostino, Robert Michael 1952- *WhoE 91*
D'Agostino, Stephen I. 1933- *St&PR 91, WhoAm 90*

D'Agostino, Vincent Ralph 1954- *WhoEmL 91*
D'Agostino, Vito Julius 1933- *St&PR 91*
Dagoty, Pierre-Louis *PenDiDA 89*
DaGraca, George *BioIn 16*
D'Agrosa, Peter D. 1925- *St&PR 91*
D'Aguanno, Silvio Vincent 1944- *WhoE 91*
Dague, Mark 1961- *St&PR 91*
Dague, Paul David 1931- *St&PR 91*
Dague, William Francis 1917- *St&PR 91*
Daguerre, Louis 1789-1851 *WorAlBi*
Dagum, Camilo 1925- *WhoWor 91*
Dagys, Jacob 1905-1989 *WhoAmA 91N*
Dagys, Marc Christopher 1955- *St&PR 91*
Dahan, Andre *AuBYP 90*
Daheim, Hansjurgen 1929- *WhoWor 91*
Daher, James D. 1945- *WhoAm 90*
Dahill, E. Kevin 1947- *St&PR 91*
Dahill, Thomas Henry, Jr 1925- *WhoAmA 91*
DaHinden, Dean Richard 1939- *St&PR 91*
Dahinden, Justus 1925- *WhoWor 91*
Dahir, Carol Ann 1950- *WhoE 91*
Dahl, Andrew Wilbur 1943- *WhoWor 91*
Dahl, Arlene 1928- *WhoAm 90, WhoAmW 91, WhoE 91, WhoWor 91, WorAlBi*
Dahl, Arthur Ernest 1916- *WhoAm 90*
Dahl, Bard 1926- *WhoWrEP 89*
Dahl, Bernt Olle 1950- *WhoWor 91*
Dahl, Borghild 1890-1984 *AuBYP 90*
Dahl, Bren Bennington 1954- *WhoAmW 91*
Dahl, Charles R. 1921- *St&PR 91*
Dahl, Chester George 1946- *St&PR 91*
Dahl, Curtis 1920- *WhoAm 90*
Dahl, Daniel Carl 1960- *BiDrAPA 89*
Dahl, Diane Margaret 1951- *BiDrAPA 89*
Dahl, Eugene 1924- *WhoAm 90*
Dahl, Eugene R. 1924- *St&PR 91*
Dahl, Francis W 1907-1973 *WhoAmA 91N*
Dahl, Gardar Godfrey, Jr. 1946- *WhoEmL 91*
Dahl, Gerald LuVern 1938- *WhoWor 91*
Dahl, Gregory C. 1948- *WhoE 91*
Dahl, H. Wayne *WhoAm 90*
Dahl, Harry Waldemar 1927- *WhoAm 90, WhoWor 91*
Dahl, Hartvig *BiDrAPA 89*
Dahl, Ingeborg *EncO&P 3*
Dahl, Jeffrey Alan 1953- *WhoEmL 91*
Dahl, Johan Christian 1788-1857 *IntDcAA 90*
Dahl, John Anton 1922- *WhoAm 90*
Dahl, John Carlton 1934- *St&PR 91*
Dahl, Joyle Cochran 1935- *WhoAm 90*
Dahl, Lawrence Frederick 1929- *WhoAm 90*
Dahl, Marilyn Gail 1946- *WhoEmL 91, WhoSSW 91*
Dahl, Mary B. *AuBYP 90*
Dahl, Michael Stephen 1955- *WhoEmL 91*
Dahl, Nancy Marie 1960- *WhoAmW 91*
Dahl, Reynold Paul 1924- *WhoAm 90*
Dahl, Roald *BioIn 16*
Dahl, Roald 1916- *AuBYP 90, ConAu 32NR, MajTwCW, WhoAm 90, WorAlBi*
Dahl, Roald 1916-1990 *NewYTBS 90 [port], News 91-2*
Dahl, Robert A 1915- *ConAu 30NR*
Dahl, Robert Alan 1915- *WhoAm 90*
Dahl, Robert R. 1923- *St&PR 91*
Dahl, Tyrus Vance, Jr. 1949- *WhoEmL 91*
Dahl Eriksen, Richard 1918- *IntWWM 90*
Dahl-Wolfe, Louise *BioIn 16*
Dahl-Wolfe, Louise 1895-1989 *ConAu 130*
Dahlben, Salin A 1945- *BiDrAPA 89*
Dahlberg, Albert 1908- *WhoAm 90, WhoWor 91*
Dahlberg, Albert Edward 1938- *WhoAm 90*
Dahlberg, Alfred William 1940- *WhoAm 90, WhoSSW 91*
Dahlberg, Alfred William, III 1940- *St&PR 91*
Dahlberg, Arnold R. 1923- *St&PR 91*
Dahlberg, Arthur O. *BioIn 16*
Dahlberg, Arthur O. 1898?-1989 *ConAu 129*
Dahlberg, Carl Fredrick, Jr. 1936- *WhoSSW 91*
Dahlberg, Charles C *BiDrAPA 89*
Dahlberg, Edward 1900-1977 *ConAu 31NR, MajTwCW, WrPh*
Dahlberg, Edwin Lennart 1901-1984 *WhoAmA 91N*
Dahlberg, Gunnar 1893-1956 *DcScB S2*
Dahlberg, John E. 1947- *St&PR 91*
Dahlberg, Joyce Karen 1943- *WhoWrEP 89*
Dahlberg, LeRoy Waldo 1904- *WhoAm 90*
Dahlberg, Marvin H. 1942- *St&PR 91*
Dahlberg, Peter Black 1952- *St&PR 91*
Dahlberg, Richard E. 1939- *St&PR 91*
Dahlberg, Rlene H 1925- *WhoWrEP 89*
Dahlberg, Stefan 1955- *IntWWM 90*
Dahlberg, William Stewart 1956- *St&PR 91*
Dahlberg, William W 1939- *BiDrAPA 89*
Dahle, Daniel John 1958- *WhoEmL 91*
Dahle, Karen 1945- *WhoAmW 91*
Dahle, Ralph Edwin 1947- *BiDrAPA 89*
Dahle, Raymond Keith 1941- *St&PR 91*
Dahlem, Maurice Jacob 1912- *WhoAm 90*
Dahlen, Bill 1870-1950 *Ballpl 90 [port]*
Dahlen, Edward 1926- *St&PR 91*
Dahlenburg, Lyle Marion 1935- *WhoAm 90*
Dahler, John Spillers 1930- *WhoAm 90*
Dahler, Warren 1897-1961 *WhoAmA 91N*
Dahlerup, Ulla 1942- *EncCoWW*
Dahlgren, Babe 1912- *Ballpl 90*
Dahlgren, Bo Arne Bertil 1924- *WhoWor 91*
Dahlgren, Carl H. P. 1929- *IntWWM 90*
Dahlgren, Carl Herman Per 1929- *WhoAm 90*
Dahlgren, Charles Marshall, Jr. 1950- *St&PR 91*
Dahlgren, Christine Kenyon 1949- *WhoAmW 91*
Dahlgren, Dan Lee 1949- *WhoEmL 91*
Dahlgren, Leslie Patrice 1955- *WhoE 91*
Dahlgren, Madeleine 1825-1898 *FemiCLE*
Dahlie, Paul Norman 1940- *St&PR 91*
Dahlig, Piotr Wincenty 1953- *IntWWM 90*
Dahlin, Donald Clifford 1941- *WhoAm 90*
Dahlin, Nils *PenDiDA 89*
Dahling, Daniel Fred 1957- *WhoEmL 91*
Dahling, Gerald Vernon 1947- *WhoWor 91*
Dahlinger, Kathleen Gayle 1942- *WhoAmW 91*
Dahlinger, Randolph 1953- *WhoEmL 91*
Dahlke, Daniel Frank 1954- *WhoEmL 91*
Dahlke, Donald W. 1930- *St&PR 91*
Dahlke, Jane Brush *BiDrAPA 89*
Dahlke, Walter Emil 1910- *WhoAm 90*
Dahlke, Wayne T. 1941- *St&PR 91*
Dahlman, Barbro Elsa 1946- *WhoEmL 91*
Dahlman, Richard Alan 1951- *WhoEmL 91*
Dahlman, Steven Ray 1961- *St&PR 91, WhoEmL 91*
Dahlmann, David Scott 1949- *St&PR 91*
Dahlquist, Eric 1937- *ODwPR 91*
Dahlquist, Eric Eugene 1937- *WhoAm 90*
Dahlquist, Robert A. *St&PR 91*
Dahlsen, John Christian 1935- *WhoWor 91*
Dahlskog, Ewald Albin Filip 1894-1950 *PenDiDA 89*
Dahlstedt, Marden 1921- *AuBYP 90*
Dahlsten, Donald L. 1933- *ConAu 132*
Dahlstroem, H. Norbert 1936- *WhoAm 90*
Dahlstrom, Carl Peter 1700-1794 *PenDiDA 89*
Dahlstrom, Donald Albert 1920- *WhoAm 90*
Dahlstrom, Joe F. 1943- *WhoSSW 91*
Dahlstrom, Nancy Gail 1948- *WhoAmA 91*
Dahlstrom, William Grant 1922- *WhoAm 90*
Dahltorp, Bruce L. 1937- *St&PR 91*
Dahly, John H. 1940- *St&PR 91*
Dahm, Alfons George 1942- *WhoE 91*
Dahm, Bernhard Otto Julius 1932- *WhoWor 91*
Dahmen, Erik Verner Harald 1916- *WhoWor 91*
Dahmer, Ann 1956- *WhoAmW 91*
Dahmer, Claude Lafayette, Jr. 1922- *WhoE 91*
Dahmer, E. Joe 1943- *St&PR 91*
Dahmer, Edward C. 1941- *St&PR 91*
Dahmes, Robert Allan 1949- *BiDrAPA 89*
Dahms, Douglas George 1949- *WhoWor 91*
Dahms, Janet H. 1919- *WhoWrEP 89*
Dahms, William J. 1943- *St&PR 91*
Dahn, Daniela 1949- *EncCoWW*
Dahne, Micki *EncO&P 3*
Dahnke, Keith Francis 1947- *WhoSSW 91*
Dahod, Aarif Mansur 1952- *WhoEmL 91*
Dahood, Michael K. 1947- *St&PR 91*
Dahrendorf, Ralf Gustav 1929- *WhoWor 91*
Dai Qing *BioIn 16*
Dai, Jing Ling 1927- *WhoAmW 91*
Daichendt, Gary James 1951- *St&PR 91*
Daiches, David 1912- *BioIn 16, WhoWor 91*
Daichman, Ricardo 1935- *BiDrAPA 89*
Daicoff, Cathy L. 1955- *St&PR 91*
Daidola, John Chris 1947- *WhoE 91*
Daidone, Lewis Eugene 1957- *WhoE 91, WhoEmL 91, WhoWor 91*
Daie, Jaleh 1948- *WhoAmW 91*
Daifuku, Hiroshi 1920- *WhoE 91*
Daiger, William H., Jr. 1935- *WhoAm 90, WhoE 91*
Daigle, Bradley Allan 1942- *BiDrAPA 89*
Daigle, David James 1935- *St&PR 91*
Daigle, Gilles A. *BioIn 16*
Daigle, Janice B. 1955- *WhoAmW 91*
Daigle, John M. 1932- *WhoAm 90*
Daigle, Lennet Joseph, Jr. 1948- *WhoSSW 91*
Daigle, Mark Denis 1958- *BiDrAPA 89*
Daigle, Paul Nelson 1938- *WhoAm 90*
Daigle, Pierre Varmon 1923- *WhoWrEP 89*
Daigle, Wilfred C. 1926- *St&PR 91*
Daignault, Francis M 1928- *BiDrAPA 89*
Daigneault, Diane Sue 1955- *WhoAmW 91*
Daigneault, Marilyn Yvonne 1935- *WhoAmW 91*
Daigon, Ruth 1933- *WhoWrEP 89*
Daigre, Jean Francois *BioIn 16*
Dail, Hilda Lee 1920- *WhoAmW 91*
Dail, Joseph Garner, Jr. 1932- *WhoAm 90*
Daileda, David Allen 1949- *WhoE 91*
Dailey, Angela Zizzi 1948- *ODwPR 91*
Dailey, Benjamin Peter 1919- *WhoAm 90*
Dailey, Bill 1935- *Ballpl 90*
Dailey, Charles Martel 1953- *WhoSSW 91*
Dailey, Chuck 1935- *WhoAmA 91*
Dailey, Coleen Hall 1955- *WhoAmW 91*
Dailey, Cornelius Edwin, Jr. 1959- *WhoEmL 91*
Dailey, Dan 1917-1978 *WorAlBi*
Dailey, Dan 1947- *WhoAmA 91*
Dailey, Daniel Owen 1947- *WhoAm 90*
Dailey, David Kevin 1947- *BiDrAPA 89*
Dailey, Donald Earl 1914- *WhoAm 90*
Dailey, Fred William 1908- *WhoWor 91*
Dailey, Irene 1920- *WhoAm 90*
Dailey, Irene Eleanor 1952- *WhoAmW 91*
Dailey, Janet *BioIn 16*
Dailey, Janet 1944- *MajTwCW, WhoAm 90, WhoAmW 91, WhoWrEP 89*
Dailey, John Howard 1920- *WhoSSW 91*
Dailey, Joseph Charles *WhoAmA 91*
Dailey, Kathleen Humphreys 1956- *WhoAmW 91*
Dailey, Lee Kenneth 1940- *WhoE 91*
Dailey, Michael Dennis 1938- *WhoAmA 91*
Dailey, Patricia H *BiDrAPA 89*
Dailey, Peter Heath 1930- *WhoAm 90*
Dailey, Priscilla Fieder 1947- *WhoE 91*
Dailey, Ralph Edwin 1906- *St&PR 91*
Dailey, Richard R. 1928- *WhoAm 90*
Dailey, Richard T. 1926- *St&PR 91*
Dailey, Robert Duane 1956- *BiDrAPA 89*
Dailey, Robert M. 1929- *St&PR 91*
Dailey, Roger F. 1940- *St&PR 91*
Dailey, Terry Jo 1953- *WhoE 91*
Dailey, Thomas E. 1932- *St&PR 91*
Dailey, Victoria Keilus 1948- *WhoAmA 91*
Dailey, Virginia Flood 1927- *WhoSSW 91*
Daily, Ellen Wilmoth Matthews 1949- *WhoAmW 91*
Daily, Evelynne Mess 1903- *WhoAmA 91*
Daily, Fay Kenoyer 1911- *WhoAmW 91*
Daily, Francis Willson 1920- *WhoSSW 91*
Daily, Frank Jerome 1942- *WhoAm 90*
Daily, James L., Jr. 1929- *WhoAm 90*
Daily, James Wallace 1913- *WhoAm 90*
Daily, Jay Elwood 1923- *WhoAm 90*
Daily, Jeanette Marie 1965- *WhoAmW 91*
Daily, Joseph Ignatius, Jr. 1923- *WhoE 91*
Daily, Louis 1919- *WhoSSW 91, WhoWor 91*
Daily, Lowell Robert 1927- *WhoAm 90*
Daily, Lynn Y. 1955- *WhoHisp 91*
Daily, One Arm 1857- *Ballpl 90*
Daily, Rebecca Susan 1958- *BiDrAPA 89*
Daily, Richard W. 1945- *WhoEmL 91*
Daily, Thomas V 1927- *News 90 [port], WhoAm 90, WhoE 91*
Daim, Aminudin 1953- *WhoWor 91*
Daim, Wilfried 1923- *EncO&P 3*
Daimler, Gottlieb *BioIn 16*
Daimler, Gottlieb Wilhelm 1834-1900 *WorAlBi*
Dain, Harvey Joshua *BiDrAPA 89*
Dain, Sandia Elizabeth 1955- *WhoEmL 91*
Daingerfield, Foxhall 1887-1933 *LiHiK*
Daingerfield, Marjorie Jay *WhoAmA 91N*
Dains, Mary Kathleen 1936- *WhoAmW 91*
Dainwood, James Darwin 1955- *WhoSSW 91*
Daisak, Barbara Nina 1961- *WhoAmW 91*
Daisak, Stephen Theodore 1957- *WhoE 91*
Daisey, Edward Lora 1936- *St&PR 91*
Daisley, William Prescott 1935- *WhoAm 90*
Daitch, Jacqueline Shirley 1935- *WhoAmW 91*
Daitch, Peggy 1946- *WhoAmW 91*
Daitch, Sheldon 1948- *WhoEmL 91, WhoWor 91*
Daiter, Donald 1922- *BiDrAPA 89*
D'Aiutolo, Diane Virginia 1959- *WhoEmL 91*
Dajani, M S 1951- *ConAu 132*
Dajani, Mahmoud T. 1932- *St&PR 91*
Dakan, Norman E. 1926- *WhoAm 90*
Dakan, Wayne *BioIn 16*
Dake, Marcia Allene 1923- *WhoAm 90*
Dake, Theodore, Jr. 1930- *BiDrAPA 89*
Dake, Toney Suzanne 1952- *WhoSSW 91*
Dakers, Elaine Kidner 1905-1978 *ConAu 30NR*
Dakers, Lionel 1924- *IntWWM 90*
Dakin, Alice R 1917- *BiDrAPA 89*
Dakin, Arthur Hazard 1905- *WhoE 91*
Dakin, Christine Whitney 1949- *WhoAm 90*
Dakin, Florence 1868-1958 *BioIn 16*
Dakin, Henry Drysdale 1880-1952 *DcScB S2*
Dakin, Mary Meier 1956- *WhoAmW 91*
Dakoske, Catherine Anne *BiDrAPA 89*
Dal, Gunnar 1923- *WhoWor 91*
Dalack, Gregory W. 1959- *BiDrAPA 89*
Daladier, Edouard 1884-1970 *BiDFrPL, WorAlBi*
Dalager, Jon Karl 1956- *WhoEmL 91*
Dalai Lama 1935- *WhoWor 91, WorAlBi*
Dalai Lama VIII 1876-1933 *BioIn 16*
Dalai Lama XIV 1935- *BioIn 16*
Dalal, Saeeda 1934- *BiDrAPA 89*
Dalayrac, Nicolas 1753-1809 *PenDiMP A*
d'Alb, Camille *EncCoWW*
Dalbak, Verlyn M. 1942- *St&PR 91*
Dalbeck, Elizabeth Ann 1959- *WhoEmL 91*
Dalbeck, Richard Bruce 1929- *St&PR 91, WhoAm 90*
Dalbeck, Richard Warren 1948- *St&PR 91, WhoAm 90*
D'Albergaria, Nancy Keck 1956- *WhoAmW 91*
D'Albert, Charles Louis Napoleon 1809-1886 *OxCPMus*
D'Albert, Eugen 1864-1932 *BioIn 16*
D'Albert, Eugene *PenDiMP*
Dalberto, Michel 1955- *PenDiMP*
Dalberto, Michel Jean Jacques 1955- *IntWWM 90*
D'Albora, John Matthew 1941- *WhoE 91*
Dalby, Alan J. 1937- *St&PR 91*
Dalby, Alan James 1937- *WhoAm 90, WhoE 91*
Dalby, Clive Desmond 1935- *BiDrAPA 89*
Dalby, Liza Crihfield 1948- *EncJap*
Dalby, Martin 1942- *IntWWM 90*
Dal Canton, Bruce 1942- *Ballpl 90*
Dale, Benjamin Moran 1889-1951 *WhoAmA 91N*
Dale, Brenda Stephens 1942- *WhoAmW 91*
Dale, Charlene Boothe 1942- *WhoE 91*
Dale, Chris 1949- *St&PR 91*
Dale, Christopher J. 1952- *WhoSSW 91*
Dale, Clamma 1948- *DrBlPA 90, IntWWM 90*
Dale, D Duane *BiDrAPA 89*
Dale, Dave Fowler 1916- *St&PR 91*
Dale, David C. 1940- *WhoAm 90*
Dale, Douglas Don 1950- *WhoEmL 91*
Dale, Elizabeth *BiDEWW*
Dale, Erwin Randolph 1915- *WhoAm 90*
Dale, Francis Lykins 1921- *WhoAm 90*
Dale, Gene 1889-1958 *Ballpl 90*
Dale, George E. *MajTwCW*
Dale, George William 1912- *WhoSSW 91*
Dale, H.L. 1923- *St&PR 91*
Dale, Harald K *BiDrAPA 89*
Dale, Harvey Philip 1937- *WhoAm 90*
Dale, Jerry 1933- *Ballpl 90*
Dale, Jim 1935- *WhoAm 90*
Dale, John D. 1916- *St&PR 91*
Dale, John Denny 1916- *WhoAm 90, WhoE 91*
Dale, John Wesley 1937- *BiDrAPA 89*
Dale, Judy Ries 1944- *WhoAmW 91, WhoSSW 91*
Dale, Larry H. 1946- *St&PR 91*
Dale, Laura A 1919-1983 *EncO&P 3*
Dale, Laura Abbott 1919-1983 *EncPaPR 91*
Dale, Leon Andrew 1921- *WhoAm 90, WhoWor 91*
Dale, Lorraine Henderson 1942- *WhoAmW 91*
Dale, Madeline Houston McWhinney 1922- *WhoAm 90*
Dale, Mae *WhoWrEP 89*
Dale, Martin Albert 1932- *WhoAm 90, WhoE 91, WhoWor 91*
Dale, Nan A. 1942- *WhoAmW 91*
Dale, Norman *AuBYP 90*
Dale, Paul Ross 1915- *WhoWor 91*
Dale, Paul W *BiDrAPA 89*
Dale, Richard L. 1950- *St&PR 91*
Dale, Robert D. 1940- *ConAu 33NR*
Dale, Robert Gordon 1920- *WhoAm 90*
Dale, Ron G 1949- *WhoAmA 91*
Dale, Ronald L. 1950- *St&PR 91*
Dale, Ruth Bluestone *AuBYP 90*
Dale, Sharer Susan 1966- *WhoEmL 91*
Dale, Stephen Glenn 1955- *WhoSSW 91*
Dale, Theresa Marie 1957- *WhoEmL 91*
Dale, Thomas *EncCRAm*
Dale, Thomas R 1930- *BiDrAPA 89*
Dale, Timothy *WhoWrEP 89*
Dale, Veronica *WhoWrEP 89*

Dale, Virginia House 1951- WhoAmW 91
Dale, Wesley John 1921- WhoAm 90
Dale, William TwCCr&M 91
Dale, William Allen 1957- WhoEmL 91
Dale, William Andrew 1920- WhoAm 90
Dale, William Brown 1924- WhoAm 90
Dale, William Scott Abell 1921- WhoAmA 91
Dalecio, Leslie Anthony 1940- St&PR 91
D'Alembert, Jean Le Rond 1717-1783 BioIn 16
Dalen, James Eugene 1932- WhoAm 90
Dalenberg, Robert Van Raalte 1929- WhoAm 90
D'Alene, Alixandria Frances 1951- WhoAmW 91, WhoEmL 91
Dales, Richard Clark 1926- WhoAm 90
Dales, Samuel 1927- WhoAm 90
Dalessandro, Angela 1956- WhoAmW 91
D'Alessandro, Angelo Michael 1930- WhoAm 90
D'Alessandro, Anna BioIn 16
D'Alessandro, Daniel Anthony 1949- WhoEmL 91
D'Alessandro, David F. ODwPR 91
D'Alessandro, David Francis 1951- WhoAm 90
D'Alessandro, Edward A. BioIn 16
D'Alessandro, Frank S. BioIn 16
D'Alessandro, Mary Patricia 1924- WhoE 91
D'Alessandro, Paul BioIn 16
D'Alessandro, Richard William 1948- WhoEmL 91
Dalessandrri, Kathie Marie 1947- WhoAmW 91
Dalessio, A.J. 1933- St&PR 91
Dalessio, Donald John 1931- WhoAm 90
D'Alessio, Gregory 1904- WhoAmA 91
D'Alessio, Hilda Terry WhoAmA 91
D'Alessio, Jacqueline Ann 1943- WhoAmW 91
D'Alessio, Kitty BioIn 16
D'Alessio, Kitty 1929- WhoAmW 91
D'Alessio, Natalie Marino WhoAmA 91
D'Alessio, Natalie Marino 1947- WhoE 91
Daleuski, Edward Joseph 1931- WhoSSW 91
Dalewitz, Alan 1948- St&PR 91
D'Alexander, William Joseph 1927- WhoAm 90
Daley, A. Gordon 1920- St&PR 91
Daley, Arthur Ballpl 90
Daley, Arthur James 1916- WhoAm 90
Daley, Arthur Stuart 1908- WhoAm 90
Daley, Buddy 1932- Ballpl 90
Daley, C. Michael 1936- St&PR 91
Daley, Charles Leon 1932- WhoAm 90
Daley, Donald O. 1934- St&PR 91
Daley, James A. 1927- St&PR 91
Daley, Jodi 1957- WhoE 91
Daley, John 1948- WhoWrEP 89
Daley, John F. 1939- St&PR 91
Daley, Joseph A. 1927- ODwPR 91
Daley, Kevin Francis 1961- WhoE 91
Daley, Laverne Doyle WhoAmA 91
Daley, Leslie G. 1947- St&PR 91
Daley, Matthew James 1955- WhoEmL 91
Daley, Michael Dennis 1950- WhoSSW 91
Daley, Michael John William 1953- WhoWor 91
Daley, Michael Joseph, Jr. 1949- WhoSSW 91
Daley, Owen 1932- ODwPR 91
Daley, Paul Hubert 1919- WhoAm 90
Daley, Paul Patrick 1941- WhoE 91
Daley, Pete 1930- Ballpl 90
Daley, Richard J. 1902-1976 BioIn 16, WorAlBi
Daley, Richard M. BioIn 16
Daley, Richard M. 1942- WhoAm 90, WorAlBi
Daley, Robert BioIn 16
Daley, Robert Edward 1939- St&PR 91, WhoAm 90
Daley, Robert Emmett 1933- WhoAm 90
Daley, Robert James, Jr. 1953- St&PR 91
Daley, Royston Tuttle 1929- St&PR 91, WhoAm 90
Daley, Sherri BioIn 16
Daley, Susan J. 1959- WhoEmL 91
Daley, Victor N. 1943- St&PR 91
Daley, William PenDiDA 89
Daley, William P 1925- WhoAmA 91
Daley, William Patrick 1925- WhoAm 90
D'Alfonsi, Saturno J. 1932- St&PR 91
D'Alfonso, Antonio 1953- ConAu 129
Dalgarno, Alexander 1928- WhoAm 90
Dalgliesh, Alice 1893-1979 AuBYP 90
Dalglish, Jamie 1947- WhoAmA 91
Dalglish, Malcolm NewAgMG
Dalglish, Meredith Rennels 1941- WhoAmA 91
Dalhouse, Warner Norris 1934- St&PR 91, WhoAm 90, WhoSSW 91
Dali, 'Abd al'Aziz al- WhoWor 91
Dali, Paul ODwPR 91
Dali, Salvador 1904- IntDcAA 90
Dali, Salvador 1904-1989 AnObit 1989, BioIn 16, ModArCr 1 [port], WhoAmA 91N, WorAlBi
Dalichau, Harald Gustav Joachim 1934- WhoWor 91
Dalies, Carl A. AmLegL
Daligand, Daniel 1942- WhoWor 91
Dalin, Olof von 1708-1763 DcScanL
Dalinka, Murray Kenneth 1938- WhoAm 90
Dalis, Irene 1925- WhoAm 90
Dalis-Loinaz, Irene 1925- IntWWM 90
D'Alisa, Rose 1948- WhoAmW 91
Dalitz, Moe BioIn 16
Dalitz, Morris Barney BioIn 16
Dalke, Barbara Helen 1946- WhoSSW 91
Dalke, Constance Olivia Logan 1950- WhoAmW 91
Dalke, Robert Lynn 1945- WhoE 91
Dalkoff, Morris Sidney 1948- WhoEmL 91
Dall, Caroline Healey 1822-1912 FemiCLE
Dall, Jes J. 1921- St&PR 91
Dall, Peter Andrew 1951- WhoSSW 91
Dalla-Vicenza, Mario J. 1938- St&PR 91
Dalla-Vicenza, Mario Joseph 1938- WhoAm 90
Dalladay, Arthur 1894-1989 BioIn 16
Dal Lago, Frank E. 1927- St&PR 91
Dallal, Salim S. 1940- St&PR 91
Dallal Khalili, Marylouise 1937- WhoAmW 91
Dallam, Timothy Michael 1948- WhoEmL 91
Dallapiccola, Luigi 1904-1975 PenDiMP A
Dallapozza, Adolf 1940- IntWWM 90
Dallas, Alexander James 1759-1817 BiDrUSE 89
Dallas, Claude, Jr. BioIn 16
Dallas, Donald Edward, Jr. 1931- WhoE 91
Dallas, Dorothy B WhoAmA 91
Dallas, George Mifflin 1792-1864 BiDrUSE 89, BioIn 16
Dallas, George Sherman 1956- St&PR 91
Dallas, Helen Alexandria 1856-1944 EncO&P 3
Dallas, L. B. BioIn 16
Dallas, Neil Lessels 1926- WhoWor 91
Dallas, Noelle Marie 1959- WhoAmW 91
Dallas, Peter August 1935- St&PR 91
Dallas, Ruth 1919- FemiCLE
Dallas, Thomas A. 1923- St&PR 91
Dallas, Thomas Abraham 1923- WhoAm 90
Dalle, Beatrice BioIn 16
Dalle Molle, Daniel 1950- St&PR 91
Dalle Palle, Gianbattista PenDiDA 89
D'Allegro, Diane Phyllis 1952- BiDrAPA 89
Dallenbach, Karl M. 1887-1971 BioIn 16
DallePezze, John Raymond 1943- WhoAm 90
Daller, W.E. St&PR 91
Dallery, Jacques Andre 1951- WhoE 91
Dallessandro, Dom 1913-1988 Ballpl 90
Dallett, Janet O. BioIn 16
Dalley, George Albert 1941- WhoAm 90
Dalley, John PenDiMP
Dalley, Joseph Winthrop A. 1918- WhoAm 90
Dallin, Alexander 1924- WhoAm 90
Dallin, Leon 1918- IntWWM 90
Dallion, Susan BioIn 16
Dallis, David Bear 1956- St&PR 91
Dallis, Herbert 1930- St&PR 91
Dallis, Nicholas P 1911- BiDrAPA 89
Dallis, Nicholas Peter 1911- WhoAm 90
Dallman, Elaine Gay WhoWrEP 89
Dallman, Paul Jerald 1939- WhoAm 90
Dallman, Peter Richard 1929- WhoAm 90
Dallman, Raymond P. 1943- WhoAm 90
Dallman, Steven Robert 1954- WhoEmL 91
Dallmann, Daniel F. 1942- WhoAm 90
Dallmann, Daniel Forbes 1942- WhoAmA 91
Dallmann-Schaper, Mary Louise 1951- WhoAmW 91, WhoEmL 91
Dallmayr, Winfried Reinhard 1928- WhoAm 90
Dallmeier, Francisco 1953- WhoHisp 91
Dallmeyer, Dorothy Marie 1923- WhoAmW 91
Dallmeyer, Mary Dorinda Gilmore 1952- WhoAmW 91, WhoSSW 91
Dallons, Berna Lou Wright 1928- WhoAmW 91
Dallos, Peter John 1934- WhoAm 90
Dallosto, Raymond Michael 1952- WhoEmL 91
Dalloway, Marie 1945- WhoWrEP 89
Dally, James William 1929- WhoAm 90
Dally, Peter 1928- BioIn 16
Dalman, Gisli Conrad 1917- WhoAm 90
D'Almeida, George 1934- WhoAmA 91
Dal Monte, Toti 1893-1975 PenDiMP
D'Alo, Louise Katherine 1966- WhoE 91
D'Aloia, G. Peter 1945- St&PR 91
D'Aloia, Giambattista Peter 1945- WhoAm 90
Daloisio, Alfonso, Jr. 1953- St&PR 91
D'Aloisio, Virginia Marie 1951- WhoAmW 91
Dalpasso, Tommaso PenDiDA 89
Dalpayrat, Adrien-Pierre 1844-1910 PenDiDA 89
Dalpe, Jean Normand 1960- BiDrAPA 89
Dalpes, Linda Frances 1938- WhoAmW 91
Dal Piaz, Giorgio 1872-1962 DcScB S2
Dal Pont, Jean-Pierre 1937- St&PR 91
Dal Pozzo, E Earlene BiDrAPA 89
d'Alpuget, Blanche 1944- FemiCLE
Dalquist, Dorothy Margerite 1925- St&PR 91
Dalquist, H. David 1918- St&PR 91
Dalrymple, Abner 1857-1939 Ballpl 90
Dalrymple, Clay 1936- Ballpl 90
Dalrymple, Donald Wylie 1947- WhoEmL 91
Dalrymple, Eric Gordon 1940- St&PR 91, WhoAm 90, WhoE 91
Dalrymple, Gary Brent 1937- WhoAm 90
Dalrymple, Gordon Bennett 1924- WhoAm 90
Dalrymple, Ian 1903-1989 AnObit 1989
Dalrymple, Jean 1910- BioIn 16, NotWoAT
Dalrymple, Jean Van Kirk 1902- WhoAm 90, WhoAmW 91
Dalrymple, John Kern 1954- WhoAm 90
Dalrymple, Keith L. 1938- St&PR 91
Dalrymple, Ronald Gerald 1949- WhoWrEP 89
Dalrymple, Thomas Lawrence 1921- WhoAm 90
Dalrymple, Willard 1921- BiDrAPA 89
Dalrymple, Windsor Howard 1923- WhoE 91
Dal Santo, Diane 1949- WhoAmW 91
Dal Santo, John 1928- WhoWor 91
Dal Santo, Paula WhoAmW 91
DalSanto, Robert J. 1955- St&PR 91
Dalsass, Diana 1947- ODwPR 91
Dalshaug, Allan Emory 1931- WhoAm 90
Dalsimer, Andrew S 1941- BiDrAPA 89
Dalsimer, James S 1937- BiDrAPA 89
Dalsimer, Walter 1928- BiDrAPA 89
Dalsin, Judith BiDrAPA 89
Dalsin, T.J. 1940- St&PR 91
Dalston, Jeptha William 1931- WhoAm 90, WhoSSW 91
Daltas, Arthur John 1945- WhoAm 90, WhoE 91
Dalton Gang Ballpl 90
Dalton, Alene BioIn 16
Dalton, Ben S. 1943- St&PR 91
Dalton, Caryl 1949- WhoAmW 91
Dalton, Claudette Ellis Harloe 1947- WhoAmW 91
Dalton, Daniel J. 1949- WhoE 91
Dalton, David L. 1948- St&PR 91
Dalton, Debbie Jo 1966- WhoAmW 91
Dalton, Dennis 1938- BiDrAPA 89
Dalton, Dennis Gilmore 1938- WhoAm 90
Dalton, Dick N. 1937- St&PR 91
Dalton, Dorothy 1915- WhoWrEP 89
Dalton, Douglas 1929- WhoAm 90
Dalton, Edgardo O BiDrAPA 89
Dalton, Edward Aloysius, Jr. 1938- WhoE 91
Dalton, Edwina P. 1936- WhoAmW 91
Dalton, Fred C 1922- BiDrAPA 89
Dalton, H. J., Jr. 1927- ODwPR 91
Dalton, Harry 1928- BioIn 16, WhoAm 90
Dalton, Howard E. 1937- St&PR 91
Dalton, Jack 1885- Ballpl 90
Dalton, James Edward 1930- WhoAm 90
Dalton, James F. 1950- St&PR 91
Dalton, James Scott 1960- WhoSSW 91
Dalton, James Warren 1932- St&PR 91
Dalton, Jennifer Faye 1959- WhoEmL 91, WhoSSW 91
Dalton, John 1766-1844 WorAlBi
Dalton, John Charles 1931- WhoAm 90
Dalton, Kevin Michael 1955- WhoEmL 91
Dalton, Lacy J. 1948- BioIn 16
Dalton, Larry Raymond 1945- WhoAm 90
Dalton, Louisiana 1936- WhoWrEP 89
Dalton, Margaret Anne 1951- WhoEmL 91
Dalton, Phyllis Irene 1909- WhoAmW 91
Dalton, Pleasant Hunter, III 1948- St&PR 91
Dalton, Priscilla TwCCr&M 91
Dalton, Richard F., Jr. 1949- BiDrAPA 89
Dalton, Roger M. 1936- St&PR 91
Dalton, Ted 1901-1989 BioIn 16
Dalton, Thomas EncO&P 3
Dalton, Thomas 1948- BioIn 16
Dalton, Timothy BioIn 16
Dalton, Tristram 1738-1817 BioIn 16
Dalton, William Lee 1949- WhoSSW 91
Dalton, William Matthews 1922- St&PR 91
Dalton, William Stephen 1930- WhoE 91
Daltrey, Roger 1944- OxCPMus, WhoAm 90
Daluege, Kurt 1897-1946 BioIn 16
da Luz, Amaro Alexandre 1934- WhoWor 91
Daluz, Cornelia Rosque 1953- BiDrAPA 89
D'Alvarenga, Joao Pedro 1961- IntWWM 90
Dalven, Joseph NewYTBS 90
Dalven, Joseph 1899-1990 BioIn 16
Dalvi, Abdul Ghani Ishaque 1947- WhoWor 91
Daly, Anthony V. 1945- ODwPR 91
Daly, Augustin 1838-1899 BioIn 16, OxCPMus
Daly, Barrett Bond 1954- WhoEmL 91
Daly, Benedict Dudley Thomas, Jr. 1939- WhoAm 90
Daly, Carroll John 1889-1958 TwCCr&M 91
Daly, Charles Joseph 1933- WhoAm 90
Daly, Charles Patrick 1930- St&PR 91, WhoE 91
Daly, Charles Ulick 1927- WhoAm 90
Daly, Christopher Joseph 1951- WhoEmL 91
Daly, Chuck BioIn 16
Daly, David G. 1936- St&PR 91
Daly, Denis J. 1940- St&PR 91
Daly, Denis Jon 1940- WhoAm 90
Daly, Edward Francis 1947- BiDrAPA 89
Daly, Edwin A. 1917- St&PR 91
Daly, Eleanor Theresa 1929- St&PR 91
Daly, Elizabeth 1878-1967 FemiCLE, TwCCr&M 91
Daly, Francis Leslie, III BiDrAPA 89
Daly, Gay 1951- ConAu 131
Daly, Gene Benedict 1919- WhoAm 90
Daly, Jack ODwPR 91
Daly, James Joseph BiDrAPA 89
Daly, James Joseph 1921- WhoAm 90
Daly, James M. 1935- St&PR 91
Daly, James Michael, III 1958- WhoEmL 91
Daly, James William 1931- WhoAm 90
Daly, Janet Morgan 1937- WhoAmW 91, WhoWrEP 89
Daly, Joe Ann Godown 1924- WhoAm 90
Daly, John Charles 1914- BioIn 16
Daly, John Charles, Jr. 1914- WhoAm 90, WorAlBi
Daly, John Dennis 1936- St&PR 91, WhoAm 90, WhoSSW 91
Daly, John E. 1919-1989 BioIn 16
Daly, John J., Jr. ODwPR 91
Daly, John M. 1947- WhoAm 90
Daly, John Neal 1937- WhoAm 90
Daly, John Patrick 1932- St&PR 91
Daly, Joseph Leo 1942- WhoWor 91
Daly, Joseph Michael 1922- WhoAm 90
Daly, Joseph R. 1910- St&PR 91
Daly, Joseph R. 1918- St&PR 91
Daly, Joseph Raymond 1918- WhoAm 90
Daly, Judith Marie 1950- WhoAmW 91
Daly, Julian 1929- St&PR 91
Daly, Kathleen 1898- WhoAmA 91
Daly, Kathleen Ann 1955- BiDrAPA 89
Daly, Kathleen N. AuBYP 90
Daly, Kenneth H. St&PR 91
Daly, Liam Noel BiDrAPA 89
Daly, Lloyd W. 1910-1989 BioIn 16
Daly, M. Virginia BioIn 16
Daly, Marcus 1841-1900 WorAlBi
Daly, Maria Vega 1950- WhoHisp 91
Daly, Mary BioIn 16
Daly, Mary 1928- ConAu 30NR, FemiCLE, MajTwCW
Daly, Mary F. WhoAmW 91
Daly, Maureen BioIn 16
Daly, Maureen 1921- Au&Arts 5 [port], AuBYP 90
Daly, Michael C. 1948- St&PR 91
Daly, Nancy Jane 1932- WhoAmW 91, WhoWor 91
Daly, Niki 1946- BioIn 16
Daly, Norman 1911- WhoAmA 91
Daly, Patricia Marie 1963- WhoAmW 91
Daly, Peter Francis, Jr. 1956- WhoE 91
Daly, R.A., Jr. 1914- St&PR 91
Daly, Radley Hutchinson 1925- WhoE 91
Daly, Richard Farrell 1926- St&PR 91
Daly, Richard James 1942- BiDrAPA 89
Daly, Richard T. BioIn 16
Daly, Robert Anthony 1936- WhoAm 90
Daly, Robert J 1936- BiDrAPA 89
Daly, Robert M 1935- BiDrAPA 89
Daly, Robert Michael 1935- WhoE 91
Daly, Robert Ward 1932- BiDrAPA 89, WhoE 91
Daly, Roberta Abele BioIn 16
Daly, Saralyn R. 1924- WhoWrEP 89
Daly, Seaton Maurice, Jr. 1945- WhoEmL 91
Daly, Sheila John 1929- AuBYP 90
Daly, Simeon Philip John 1922- WhoAm 90
Daly, Stephen Jeffrey 1942- WhoAmA 91
Daly, Stephen L 1917- BiDrAPA 89
Daly, Susan Campbell BiDrAPA 89

Daly, Susan Carol Campbell 1948- WhoAmW 91
Daly, Susan Loftus 1951- WhoEmL 91
Daly, Susan S. 1939- WhoAmW 91
Daly, Thomas F. 1903-1990 BioIn 16
Daly, Thomas Francis Gilroy 1931- WhoAm 90, WhoE 91
Daly, Thomas Milton 1946- St&PR 91
Daly, Timothy 1956- ConTFT 8
Daly, Tom 1866-1939 Ballpl 90
Daly, Tyne BioIn 16
Daly, Tyne 1947- WhoAm 90, WhoAmW 91, WorAlBi
Daly, Walter Joseph 1930- WhoAm 90
Daly, William F. 1942- St&PR 91
Daly, William Gerald 1924- WhoAm 90
Daly, William James 1917- WhoAm 90
Daly, William Joseph 1928- WhoAm 90
Daly, William P. 1931- St&PR 91
Dalyai, Stephen Attila 1938- St&PR 91
Dalyell, Tam BioIn 16
Dalzell, Fred Briggs 1922- WhoAm 90
Dalzell, Grace Rosalie 1936- WhoAmW 91, WhoSSW 91
Dalzell, Jan 1938- WhoAmW 91
Dalzell, Robert Fenton, Jr. 1937- WhoAm 90
Dalzell, Robert James, Jr. 1928- St&PR 91
Dalzell, Steven William 1958- St&PR 91
Dalziel, Charles Meredith, Jr. 1956- WhoEmL 91
Dalziel, Robert David 1934- WhoE 91
Dam Quang Trung WhoWor 91
Dam, Hans 1945- WhoWor 91
Dam, Henrik 1895-1976 DcScB S2
Dam, Hien Quang 1942- BiDrAPA 89
Dam, Jose van PenDiMP
Dam, Kenneth W. 1932- WhoAm 90, WhoE 91
Damadian, Raymond 1936- St&PR 91
Damadian, Raymond Vahan 1936- WhoAm 90
Daman, Ernest Ludwig 1923- WhoAm 90
Daman, Harlan Richard 1941- WhoE 91, WhoWor 91
Damarati, Luciano 1942- IntWWM 90
Damas, David 1926- ConAu 132
Damaska, Mirjan Radovan 1931- WhoAm 90
Damaskenides, Anthony N. 1910- WhoWor 91
Damaskos, James Constantine 1924- WhoAm 90
Damast, Elba Cecilia 1944- WhoAmA 91
D'Amato, Alex 1919- AuBYP 90
D'Amato, Alfonse BioIn 16
D'Amato, Alfonse M. 1937- WhoAm 90, WhoE 91, WhoWor 91
D'Amato, Anthony 1937- WhoAm 90
D'Amato, Anthony Roger 1931- WhoAm 90, WhoWor 91
D'Amato, Anthony S. 1930- St&PR 91, WhoAm 90
Damato, Bertil Eric 1953- WhoWor 91
Damato, David Joseph 1953- WhoSSW 91
D'Amato, Domenico Donald 1911- WhoAm 90
D'Amato, Ellen A. 1948- St&PR 91
D'Amato, Frederick M. 1954- St&PR 91
D'Amato, Gabriel BiDrAPA 89
D'Amato, Janet 1925- AuBYP 90
D'Amato, Janet Potter WhoAmA 91
D'Amato, Jean Marie 1945- WhoAmW 91, WhoSSW 91
D'Amato, Michael Angelo 1953- WhoE 91
D'Amato, Patrick Antonio 1918- WhoE 91
D'Amato, Salvatore F. 1928- St&PR 91
D'Amato, Salvatore Francis 1928- WhoAm 90
Damaz, Paul F. 1917- WhoAm 90, WhoAmA 91
Dambis, Lee Victor 1935- St&PR 91
D'Amboise, Charlotte BioIn 16
D'Amboise, Christopher BioIn 16
d'Amboise, Jacques Joseph 1934- WhoAm 90
D'Ambrosio, Blanche Fada Grawe 1926- WhoAmW 91
D'Ambrosio, Charles A. 1932- WhoWrEP 89
D'Ambrosio, Charles Anthony 1932- WhoAm 90
D'Ambrosio, Eugene Joseph 1921- St&PR 91, WhoAm 90
D'Ambrosio, Richard Michael 1946- St&PR 91
D'Ambrosio, Vinnie-Marie WhoWrEP 89
Dame, Edna Genevieve Otto 1906- WhoWrEP 89
Dame, Enid 1943- WhoWrEP 89
Dame, Paul Hartley 1953- WhoSSW 91
Dame, William E. 1858- AmLegL
Dame, William Page, III 1940- WhoE 91
Damen, Piet Christiaan 1943- WhoWor 91
Damer, Anne 1748-1828 FemiCLE
Damer, Annie 1858-1915 BioIn 16
Damera, Bhaskar Rao BiDrAPA 89
Dameron, Larry Wright 1949- WhoEmL 91
Dameron, Tadd 1917-1965 OxCPMus
Dameron, Thomas Barker, Jr. 1924- WhoAm 90
Damerow, Mae Wright 1956- WhoAmW 91, WhoEmL 91
Damerst, Lisa Yvonne 1958- WhoAmW 91, WhoE 91
Dames, Joan Foster 1934- WhoAm 90
Dameshek, Harold Lee 1937- WhoAm 90, WhoE 91
Dameson, Louis G., Jr. 1923- St&PR 91
Damgard, John Michael 1939- WhoAm 90
Damholt, Ronald James 1951- WhoEmL 91
Damian, Guillermo Rustia 1925- WhoWor 91
Damian, John EncO&P 3
Damian, Michael BioIn 16
Damian, Walter Edward 1940- St&PR 91
Damiani, Elizabeth Jane 1928- WhoE 91
Damiani, Enrico EncPaPR 91
Damiano, Chris W. 1930- St&PR 91
Damiano, Robert 1936- St&PR 91
Damianos, Sylvester 1933- WhoAm 90
D'Amico, Andrew John 1942- WhoAm 90
Damico, Debra Lynn 1956- WhoAmW 91, WhoEmL 91
D'Amico, Esteban L. 1935- St&PR 91
D'Amico, Fedele BioIn 16
Damico, Frank J. 1947- St&PR 91
D'Amico, Giuseppe 1929- WhoWor 91
Damico, James Anthony 1932- WhoSSW 91
D'Amico, James P. 1945- St&PR 91
D'Amico, John Anthony, Sr. 1931- St&PR 91
D'Amico, John F. BioIn 16
D'Amico, Joseph Allen 1962- WhoSSW 91
D'Amico, Joseph Thomas 1930- St&PR 91
D'Amico, Louis Edward 1922- St&PR 91
D'Amico, Maria Vittoria 1941- WhoWor 91
Damico, Nicholas Peter 1937- WhoE 91
D'Amico, Paul M. 1947- St&PR 91
D'Amico, Richard Joseph 1938- WhoE 91
D'Amico, Theodore 1954- St&PR 91
D'Amico, Tommaso 1939- WhoWor 91
Damien, Father 1840-1889 BioIn 16, WorAlBi
Damisch, Harriet Darley 1927- WhoAmW 91
Damjan, Mischa 1914- AuBYP 90
Damjanov, Andrea 1940- WhoAmW 91
Damluji, Namir Faisal BiDrAPA 89
Damm, Guy France 1945- WhoWor 91
Damm, James E. 1946- St&PR 91
Dammann, Gordon Edward 1945- WhoEmL 91
Dammann, Richard W. St&PR 91N
Dammann, Richard Weil 1911-1988 BioIn 16
D'Ammassa, Donald Eugene 1946- St&PR 91
Dammerman, Dennis Dean 1945- St&PR 91, WhoAm 90
Dammeyer, Robert P. 1948- St&PR 91
Dammeyer, Rod F. 1940- St&PR 91
Dammin, Gustave John 1911- WhoAm 90
Dammon, James R. 1943- St&PR 91
Dammouse, Albert-Louis 1848-1926 PenDiDA 89
Damned, The OxCPMus
Damocles HispWr 90
Damon, Betsy 1940- BiDWomA
Damon, Constance Tiffany WhoWrEP 89
Damon, E. Kent 1918- St&PR 91
Damon, Edmund Holcombe 1929- St&PR 91, WhoAm 90, WhoE 91
Damon, Franklin Lee 1944- WhoAm 90
Damon, Gene 1933- WhoAmW 91
Damon, Jacqueline Ruth 1951- WhoE 91
Damon, John D 1926- WhoWrEP 89
Damon, Laura Provost 1938- WhoAmW 91
Damon, Ralph S. 1897-1956 WorAlBi
Damon, Richard Winslow 1923- WhoAm 90
Damon, Stewart Wilbur 1925- WhoAm 90
Damon, Valerie Hubbard 1945- WhoWrEP 89
Damon, William Van Buren 1944- WhoAm 90
Damone, Vic 1928- OxCPMus, WorAlBi
Damonte, James Charles 1949- St&PR 91
Damoose, George Lynn 1938- WhoAm 90
Damora, Robert Matthew WhoAm 90
D'Amore, Victor 1943- WhoE 91
Damos, Diane Lynn 1949- WhoAmW 91
Damoth, Gene Richard 1953- WhoEmL 91
DaMotta, Lorraine 1957- WhoE 91, WhoEmL 91
DaMoude, Denise Ann 1953- WhoEmL 91
D'Amour, Claire Marie 1956- WhoAmW 91
D'Amour, Donald H. 1943- St&PR 91
D'Amours, Norman Edward 1937- WhoAm 90
Damov, Daniel 1927- St&PR 91
Dampeer, John Lyell 1916- WhoAm 90
Dampier, William 1652-1715 BioIn 16, WorAlBi
Dampierre, Alfonso de Borbon y 1936-1989 BioIn 16
Damptz, Robert Edward BiDrAPA 89
Damri, Kersi Phiroze 1951- WhoSSW 91
Damro, DiAnne M. BioIn 16
Damron, Kay 1954- WhoSSW 91
Damron, Thomas Anthony 1934- WhoSSW 91
Damron, Virginia Lee 1937- WhoAmW 91
Damrosch, Barbara 1942- WhoAmW 91
Damrosch, Leopold BioIn 16
Damrosch, Leopold 1832-1885 PenDiMP
Damrosch, Lori Fisler 1953- WhoEmL 91
Damrosch, Shirley Petchel WhoE 91
Damrosch, Walter 1862-1950 PenDiMP, WorAlBi
Damrow, Dick ODwPR 91
Damrow, Donald E. 1934- St&PR 91
Damsbo, Ann Marie 1931- WhoAm 90, WhoAmW 91
Damschroder, Michael E. 1952- St&PR 91
Damsel, Richard A. 1942- WhoAm 90
Damsey, Joan 1931- WhoAmW 91
Damsky, Kenneth L. 1946- St&PR 91
Damson, Barrie M. 1936- St&PR 91
Damson, Barrie Morton 1936- WhoAm 90
Damste, Pieter Helbert 1925- WhoWor 91
Damsteegt, Don Calvin 1946- WhoEmL 91
Damstra, Donald D. 1946- St&PR 91
Damtoft, Walter Atkinson 1922- WhoAm 90
Damukaitis, Thomas S. 1950- St&PR 91
Dan, A. EncCoWW
Dan, F. I. 1871-1947 BioIn 16
Dan, Lidiia 1878-1963 BioIn 16
Dana, Amber ConAu 31NR
Dana, Charles A., Jr. 1945- ODwPR 91
Dana, Charles Anderson 1819-1897 BioIn 16
Dana, Edward Runkle 1919- WhoAm 90
Dana, Frank Mitchell 1942- WhoAm 90
Dana, Freeman TwCCr&M 91
Dana, Grosvenor BioIn 16
Dana, Jayne WhoWrEP 89
Dana, Jerilyn Denise 1949- WhoAm 90
Dana, Lauren Elizabeth 1950- WhoEmL 91
Dana, Michael Ray 1947- WhoEmL 91
Dana, Richard ConAu 31NR
Dana, Richard Henry 1815-1882 BioIn 16
Dana, Richard Henry, Jr. 1815-1882 WorAlBi
Dana, Rose ConAu 32NR
Danadjieva, Angela BioIn 16
Danaher, James William 1929- WhoAm 90
Danaher, John A. NewYTBS 90 [port]
Danaher, John Anthony 1899- WhoAm 90
Danaher, Mallory Millett 1939- WhoWor 91
Danaher, Michael John BioIn 16
Danaher, Susan Marie 1957- WhoEmL 91
Danaher, Thomas Anthony 1957- WhoSSW 91
Danahey, Thomas Joseph, III 1935- BiDrAPA 89
D'Anania, Giovanni Lorenzo EncO&P 3
Danatos, Steven Clark 1951- WhoE 91
Danburg, Debra 1951- WhoAmW 91
Danby, Frank 1861-1916 FemiCLE
Danby, Ken 1940- WhoAmA 91
Danby, Kenneth Edison 1940- WhoAm 90
Dance, Charles BioIn 16
Dance, Daryl Cumber 1938- ConAu 131
Dance, Francis Esburn Xavier 1929- WhoAm 90
Dance, Gloria Fenderson 1932- WhoAm 90, WhoSSW 91
Dance, Maurice Eugene 1923- WhoAm 90
Dance, Robert Bartlett 1934- WhoAmA 91
Dance, Tom Fred 1934- WhoSSW 91
Dance, Walter David 1917- St&PR 91
Danceanu, Liviu 1954- IntWWM 90
Dancel, Mary Lou BiDrAPA 89
Dancer, John Benjamin 1812-1887 BioIn 16
Dancer, John T. 1928- St&PR 91
Dancer, Winston C. 1917- St&PR 91
Dancewicz, John Edward 1949- WhoAm 90, WhoEmL 91
Dancey, Charles Lohman 1916- WhoAm 90
Dancey, Travis E 1905- BiDrAPA 89
Danchak, Anne Marie Rose 1964- WhoAmW 91
Dancik, Daniel BiDrAPA 89
Dancis, Joseph 1916- WhoAm 90
Danckwerts, Peter Victor 1916-1984 DcNaB 1981
Danco, Gerard J. BioIn 16
Danco, Leon A. 1923- BioIn 16, St&PR 91
Danco, Leon Antoine 1923- WhoAm 90
Danco, Linda Marie 1961- WhoAmW 91
Danco, Suzanne BioIn 16
Danco, Suzanne 1911- IntWWM 90, PenDiMP
D'Ancona, Vito 1825-1884 BioIn 16
Dancy, John Albert 1936- WhoAm 90
Dancy, Linda Smith 1947- WhoEmL 91
Dancy, Mel 1937- DrBIPA 90
Dancy, Patricia Laura 1938- WhoE 91
Dancz, Roger L. 1930- IntWWM 90
Dandalides, John P. 1923- WhoAm 90
Dandavate, Madhu 1924- WhoWor 91
Dandavino, Rita Rachele 1953- WhoWor 91
Dandliker, Rene 1939- WhoWor 91
Dando, A. Jeffrey 1938- WhoAm 90
Dandora, Nathu R. 1942- St&PR 91
Dandoy, Maxima Antonio WhoAm 90
Dandoy, Suzanne Eggleston 1935- WhoAm 90, WhoAmW 91
D'Andrade, Hugh Alfred 1938- St&PR 91, WhoAm 90, WhoE 91
D'Andrea, Albert Philip 1897-1983 WhoAmA 91N
D'Andrea, Alphonse F. BioIn 16
Dandrea, Carmine 1929- WhoWrEP 89
D'Andrea, Denise Marie 1961- WhoAmW 91
D'Andrea, Francis Joseph 1933- St&PR 91
D'Andrea, Jeanne 1925- WhoAmA 91
D'Andrea, Kate ConAu 30NR
D'Andrea, Mark 1960- WhoSSW 91
D'Andrea, Mark A BiDrAPA 89
D'Andrea, Vincent J 1930- BiDrAPA 89
D'Andrea Mohr, Guillermo Jorge 1950- WhoWor 91
Dandridge, Dorothy 1920-1965 OxCPMus
Dandridge, Dorothy 1923?-1965 DrBIPA 90, WorAlBi
Dandridge, Ray BioIn 16
Dandridge, Ray 1913- Ballpl 90
Dandridge, Rita Bernice WhoSSW 91
Dandridge, Ruby 1904-1987 DrBIPA 90
Dandridge, William Shelton 1914- WhoSSW 91, WhoWor 91
Dandrieux, Edouard Pierre Olivier 1941- WhoWor 91
D'Andrilli, Stephen BioIn 16
Dandro, David Warren 1937- St&PR 91
Dandrow, C. George 1899-1988 BioIn 16
Dandy Dan BioIn 16
Dandy, Robert Herbert 1931- St&PR 91
Dandy, W.E. 1932- St&PR 91
Dane, Bill 1938- WhoAmA 91
Dane, Clemence 1887-1965 BioIn 16
Dane, Clemence 1888-1965 FemiCLE
Dane, Jane PenDiMP
Dane, John Hunter 1933- WhoE 91
Dane, Kate Nelson 1952- WhoEmL 91
Dane, Leila Finlay 1936- WhoAmW 91
Dane, Mark TwCCr&M 91
Dane, Mary TwCCr&M 91
Dane, Maxwell 1906- St&PR 91, WhoAm 90
Dane, Peter D. 1947- St&PR 91
Dane, William Jerald 1925- WhoAmA 91
Daneels, Axel Jean Herman Adrien Edward 1941- WhoWor 91
Daneels, Francois 1921- IntWWM 90
Danehy, Diane Dobrowski 1960- WhoEmL 91
Danehy, John J 1924- BiDrAPA 89
Danek, Larry J. 1949- St&PR 91
Danelski, David Joseph 1930- WhoAm 90, WhoWor 91
Danelz, Debbie Hilliard 1953- WhoSSW 91
Danenberg, Harold 1930- St&PR 91, WhoAm 90
Danenhauer, Sid David 1942- St&PR 91
Danesh, Ali B BiDrAPA 89
Daney, Tamara Kay 1957- WhoAmW 91
Danford, Ardath Anne 1930- WhoAm 90
Danford, Darla Erhard 1945- WhoE 91
Danford, Robert Edward 1947- WhoE 91
Danford, Thaddus S. 1956- WhoEmL 91
Danforth, Arthur Edwards 1925- WhoAm 90, WhoWor 91
Danforth, Dave 1890-1970 Ballpl 90
Danforth, David Newton, Jr. 1942- WhoE 91, WhoWor 91
Danforth, Douglas Dewitt 1922- WhoAm 90, WhoE 91
Danforth, Elliot, Jr. 1933- WhoAm 90
Danforth, Frances Louise Adams 1903- IntWWM 90
Danforth, Frances Mueller 1914- WhoAmW 91
Danforth, John Claggett 1936- WhoAm 90, WhoWor 91
Danforth, Linda Mangold 1944- WhoAmW 91
Danforth, Louis F. 1913- St&PR 91
Danforth, Louis Fremont 1913- WhoAm 90
Danforth, Nicholas BiDrAPA 89
Danforth, Nicholas Williamson BioIn 16
Danforth, Robert Wallace 1931- St&PR 91
Danforth, Wendy 1936- WhoAm 90
Danforth, William Henry 1926- WhoAm 90, WhoWor 91
Dang, Hien D. BiDrAPA 89
Dang, Jagdish C 1940- BiDrAPA 89

Dang, Jagdish Chander 1940- WhoE 91
Dang, Marvin S.C. 1954- WhoEmL 91, WhoWor 91
Dang, Minh Ngoc 1958- WhoEmL 91
Dang-Vu, Chan BiDrAPA 89
Dangaard, Kay ODwPR 91
Dangeard, Frank Emmanuel 1958- WhoWor 91
D'Angeli, Miriam Toigo- BioIn 16
D'Angelico, Michael John 1943- WhoAm 90, WhoE 91
D'Angelo, Andrea BioIn 16
D'Angelo, Anthony William 1960- WhoE 91
D'Angelo, Antonio 1924- BiDrAPA 89
D'Angelo, Arthur BioIn 16
D'Angelo, Beverly BioIn 16
D'Angelo, Christopher Scott 1953- WhoEmL 91, WhoWor 91
D'Angelo, Dolores Amidon 1947- WhoE 91
D'Angelo, Elmer Mauro 1922- St&PR 91
D'Angelo, Ernest Eustachio 1944- WhoE 91
D'Angelo, Frances Bonacorsa 1914- WhoAmW 91
D'Angelo, Gianna 1929- IntWWM 90
D'Angelo, Joseph Francis 1930- WhoAm 90
D'Angelo, Laura J BiDrAPA 89
D'Angelo, Marc Scott 1952- WhoSSW 91
D'Angelo, Nicholas 1937- St&PR 91
D'Angelo, Pascal 1894-1932 BioIn 16
D'Angelo, Robert William 1932- WhoAm 90
Dangerfield, Balfour AuBYP 90
Dangerfield, Enoch BiDrAPA 89
Dangerfield, Harlan ConAu 30NR
Dangerfield, Rodney 1921- WorAlBi
Dangerfield, Rodney 1922- WhoAm 90
D'Angio, Giulio John 1922- WhoAm 90
Danglade, Joyce Ann 1933- WhoSSW 91
Danglade, Ruth Ellen 1940- WhoAmW 91
Dangler, LeRoy Stout 1916- WhoSSW 91, WhoWor 91
Dangler, Richard Reiss 1940- WhoAm 90, WhoE 91
Dangoia, Robert J. 1940- St&PR 91
Dangol, Balram Das 1935- WhoWor 91
D'Angola, Patrick M. 1952- St&PR 91
Dangoor, David Ezra Ramsi 1949- WhoAm 90
Dangremond, Dale Joan 1957- WhoAmW 91
Dangremond, David W. 1952- WhoAm 90, WhoE 91, WhoWor 91
Danhausen, Eldon WhoAmA 91
Danhauser, Josef Ulrich 1780-1829 PenDiDA 89
Danica, Elly BioIn 16
Daniec, Danuta Anna BiDrAPA 89
Daniel, Alan 1939- BioIn 16
Daniel, Albro Dickinson 1943- St&PR 91
Daniel, Andrea ODwPR 91
Daniel, Anita 1893?-1978 AuBYP 90
Daniel, Anne AuBYP 90, ConAu 30NR
Daniel, Ansseril E 1944- BiDrAPA 89
Daniel, Aubrey Monroe 1925- St&PR 91
Daniel, Becky 1947- BioIn 16
Daniel, Beth 1956- WhoAm 90, WhoAmW 91
Daniel, Brenda Jean 1957- WhoSSW 91
Daniel, Carlton Ralph, III 1952- WhoSSW 91
Daniel, Carol Gene 1945- WhoE 91
Daniel, Cathy Brooks 1946- WhoEmL 91, WhoSSW 91
Daniel, Cecile Margaret 1956- WhoAmW 91
Daniel, Charles Dwelle, Jr. 1925- WhoAm 90
Daniel, Christopher Hobart 1958- WhoSSW 91
Daniel, Clifton, Jr. 1912- WorAlBi
Daniel, Dan BioIn 16
Daniel, Dan 1890-1981 Ballpl 90
Daniel, David Gordon 1956- BiDrAPA 89
Daniel, David Grant BiDrAPA 89
Daniel, David Logan 1906- WhoAm 90
Daniel, David Ronald 1930- WhoAm 90
Daniel, Donald Knight 1946- St&PR 91
Daniel, E. Clifton 1912- WhoE 91
Daniel, E. Leon WhoSSW 91
Daniel, E. Ralph 1928- St&PR 91
Daniel, Eleanor A. 1940- WhoAmW 91
Daniel, Eleanor Sauer 1917- WhoAmW 91, WhoE 91, WhoWor 91
Daniel, Elmer Leon 1936- St&PR 91
Daniel, Evelyn Hope 1933- WhoAm 90, WhoAmW 91
Daniel, Frederick K. 1910-1990 BioIn 16
Daniel, Gary Wayne 1948- WhoEmL 91
Daniel, Gerard Lucian 1927- WhoE 91, WhoWor 91
Daniel, Glyn 1914-1986 ConAu 30NR
Daniel, Glyn Edmund 1914-1986 BioIn 16
Daniel, Hardie William 1933- WhoWrEP 89
Daniel, Harry B., II 1951- St&PR 91
Daniel, Herbert Gustav Karl 1926- WhoWor 91
Daniel', IUlii 1925-1988 BioIn 16
Daniel, James 1916- WhoAm 90
Daniel, James Edward 1955- WhoEmL 91
Daniel, James Richard 1940- WhoSSW 91
Daniel, James Richard 1947- St&PR 91, WhoAm 90
Daniel, Jaquelin James 1916- WhoAm 90
Daniel, John J. 1925- St&PR 91
Daniel, John Sagar 1942- WhoAm 90
Daniel, Kenneth Rule 1913- WhoAm 90, WhoWor 91
Daniel, Leon 1931- WhoAm 90
Daniel, Lewis C 1901-1952 WhoAmA 91N
Daniel, Mark D. 1950- St&PR 91
Daniel, Marva Jeane 1943- WhoAmW 91
Daniel, Marvin Valerius 1946- WhoEmL 91
Daniel, Michael Roland 1940- WhoAm 90
Daniel, Milly Hawk AuBYP 90
Daniel, Oliver 1911- IntWWM 90
Daniel, Paul 1945- IntWWM 90
Daniel, Price 1910-1988 BioIn 16
Daniel, Raymond John 1942- St&PR 91, WhoE 91
Daniel, Raymond Martin 1957- WhoSSW 91
Daniel, Rebecca Susan 1959- WhoAmW 91, WhoEmL 91
Daniel, Richard C. 1966- WhoHisp 91
Daniel, Richard H. 1946- St&PR 91
Daniel, Richard I. 1926- St&PR 91
Daniel, Richard Nicholas 1935- St&PR 91, WhoAm 90, WhoE 91
Daniel, Robert E. 1939- St&PR 91
Daniel, Robert Edwin 1906- WhoAm 90
Daniel, Robert L. 1926- St&PR 91
Daniel, Robert Williams, Jr. 1936- WhoAm 90
Daniel, Royal, III 1945- WhoAm 90, WhoEmL 91
Daniel, Royal Thomas, III 1956- WhoE 91, WhoEmL 91
Daniel, Samuel 1562-1619 BioIn 16
Daniel, Simeon 1934- WhoWor 91
Daniel, Thomas J. 1956- St&PR 91
Daniel, Thomas Wilder 1818-1892 DcCanB 12
Daniel, Victor James, Jr. 1916- WhoAm 90
Daniel, Vivi Susan BiDrAPA 89
Daniel, William Gerald, Jr. 1942- WhoSSW 91
Daniel, William Marvin 1949- St&PR 91
Daniel, William Verner 1928- St&PR 91
Daniel, Yuli 1925-1988 AnObit 1988
Daniel, Yvette Felice 1959- WhoAmW 91
Daniel-Dreyfus, Susan B. Russe 1940- WhoAmW 91, WhoE 91, WhoWor 91
Daniel-Lesur, Jean Yves 1908- IntWWM 90, WhoWor 91
Danielak, Christopher 1959- St&PR 91
Daniele, Joseph A. 1938- St&PR 91
Daniele, Maria Theresa 1942- BiDrAPA 89
Danielian, Leon 1920- WhoAm 90
Daniell, Ellen 1947- WhoEmL 91
Daniell, Eugene S. 1904-1988 BioIn 16
Daniell, Herman Burch 1929- WhoAm 90
Daniell, Jere Rogers 1932- WhoAm 90
Daniell, Mark Haynes 1955- WhoWor 91
Daniell, Robert F. BioIn 16
Daniell, Robert F. 1933- WhoAm 90, WhoE 91, WhoWor 91
Daniell, Robert Fisher 1933- St&PR 91
Daniell, Warren Fisher, Jr. 1926- St&PR 91
Danielli, James Frederic 1911-1984 DcNaB 1981
Daniello, Jean Lois 1954- WhoE 91
Daniells, Helen E 1916- BiDrAPA 89
Danielou, Alain 1907- ConAu 31NR
Daniels, Aaron Martin BioIn 16
Daniels, Albert Peet 1914- St&PR 91
Daniels, Alex BioIn 16
Daniels, Alfred Harvey 1912- WhoAm 90
Daniels, Alrie McNiff 1962- WhoAmW 91
Daniels, Arthur N. AmLegL
Daniels, Astar 1920- WhoAmA 91
Daniels, Barbara 1946- IntWWM 90
Daniels, Barbara Wiedner 1946- WhoAm 90
Daniels, Bebe 1901-1971 OxCPMus
Daniels, Bennie 1932- Ballpl 90
Daniels, Bert 1882-1958 Ballpl 90
Daniels, Bill BioIn 16
Daniels, Bill 1920- St&PR 91
Daniels, Billy BioIn 16
Daniels, Billy 1915?-1988 AnObit 1988, DrBlPA 90, OxCPMus
Daniels, Brett MajTwCW
Daniels, C. Eugene 1943- St&PR 91
Daniels, Calvin L. 1936- St&PR 91
Daniels, Carlos Ruben 1928- WhoHisp 91
Daniels, Carolyn Elizabeth 1946- WhoAmW 91
Daniels, Cecil Edwin, III 1961- WhoE 91
Daniels, Celia Annette 1958- WhoWrEP 89
Daniels, Charles Neil 1878-1943 BioIn 16, OxCPMus
Daniels, Charlie 1936- WhoAm 90, WorAlBi
Daniels, Charlie 1937- OxCPMus
Daniels, Cindy Lou 1959- WhoAmW 91
Daniels, David 1933- IntWWM 90
Daniels, David M 1927- WhoAmA 91
Daniels, David Mark 1959- St&PR 91
Daniels, Deanna L BiDrAPA 89
Daniels, Deborah J. WhoAmW 91
Daniels, Dee Arlane 1955- WhoAmW 91
Daniels, Diana M. WhoAm 90
Daniels, Diana M. 1949- St&PR 91
Daniels, Doria Lynn 1951- WhoAmW 91, WhoEmL 91
Daniels, Doris Groshen 1931- ConAu 131
Daniels, Edward M 1921- BiDrAPA 89
Daniels, Edwin A., Jr. 1925- St&PR 91
Daniels, Elizabeth Adams 1920- WhoAm 90
Daniels, Elton G. St&PR 91
Daniels, Emma Alexandra St&PR 91
Daniels, Erik William 1954- WhoEmL 91
Daniels, Faith BioIn 16
Daniels, Farrington 1889-1972 DcScB S2
Daniels, Frank Arthur, Jr. 1931- WhoAm 90, WhoSSW 91
Daniels, Frank Emmett 1963- WhoEmL 91
Daniels, Frank W. 1934- St&PR 91
Daniels, George Benjamin 1953- WhoEmL 91
Daniels, George Goetz 1925- WhoWrEP 89
Daniels, Ginnette F. ODwPR 91
Daniels, Gladys Roberta Steinman 1912- WhoWrEP 89
Daniels, Glenn Earl BiDrAPA 89
Daniels, Gregory L. BioIn 16
Daniels, Guy BioIn 16
Daniels, Guy 1919- AuBYP 90
Daniels, Guy 1919-1989 SmATA 62
Daniels, Hadassah S BiDrAPA 89
Daniels, Hilda Jean 1942- WhoE 91
Daniels, Hope Mary 1947- WhoWrEP 89
Daniels, James D. 1946- ODwPR 91
Daniels, James Maurice 1924- WhoAm 90
Daniels, Jeff BioIn 16
Daniels, Jeffrey Irwin 1951- WhoEmL 91
Daniels, Jeremy Lynn 1941- St&PR 91
Daniels, Jerry 1945- St&PR 91
Daniels, Jesse L. 1936- WhoSSW 91
Daniels, Jim 1956- WhoWrEP 89
Daniels, John Clifford 1936- WhoE 91
Daniels, John Dean 1949- WhoEmL 91
Daniels, John H. 1921- St&PR 91
Daniels, John Hancock 1921- WhoAm 90
Daniels, John Mark 1958- WhoSSW 91
Daniels, John Peter 1937- WhoAm 90
Daniels, Jonathan 1902-1981 AuBYP 90
Daniels, Jonathan B. NewYTBS 90
Daniels, Joseph Anton 1940- St&PR 91
Daniels, Joseph Jerard 1953- WhoE 91
Daniels, Josephus 1862-1948 BiDrUSE 89, BioIn 16
Daniels, Kal 1963- Ballpl 90
Daniels, Karlheinz 1928- WhoWor 91
Daniels, Kettlie Joseph BiDrAPA 89
Daniels, Lashanda BioIn 16
Daniels, Laura Kidd 1957- WhoAmW 91
Daniels, Laurie Jean 1954- WhoEmL 91
Daniels, Lee S. 1925- St&PR 91
Daniels, Linda Brint BiDrAPA 89
Daniels, Lloyd BioIn 16
Daniels, Lydia M. 1932- WhoWor 91
Daniels, M.A. 1946- St&PR 91
Daniels, Madeline Marie 1948- WhoWrEP 89
Daniels, Malcolm L. 1926- St&PR 91
Daniels, Marc BioIn 16
Daniels, Marc 1912?-1989 ConTFT 8
Daniels, Marcel Ludolphe C.M. 1952- WhoWor 91
Daniels, Marcia L 1950- BiDrAPA 89
Daniels, Marilyn Snell 1925- WhoAmW 91
Daniels, Melvin L. 1931- IntWWM 90
Daniels, Michael Alan 1946- WhoWor 91
Daniels, Michael Anthony 1945- WhoE 91
Daniels, Michael D 1943- BiDrAPA 89
Daniels, Michael Paul 1930- WhoAm 90
Daniels, Molly WhoWrEP 89
Daniels, Myra Janco WhoAm 90
Daniels, Norma WhoAmW 91
Daniels, Norman 1942- WhoAm 90, WhoWrEP 89
Daniels, Norman A. TwCCr&M 91
Daniels, Owen Laurence BiDrAPA 89
Daniels, Paul 1938- BioIn 16
Daniels, Philip TwCCr&M 91
Daniels, Phyllis Hyder 1951- WhoAmW 91
Daniels, Ralph 1921- WhoAm 90
Daniels, Rebecca Joye 1961- WhoSSW 91
Daniels, Richard L. 1937- St&PR 91
Daniels, Richard M. 1942- ODwPR 91
Daniels, Robert ODwPR 91
Daniels, Robert Alan 1944- WhoE 91
Daniels, Robert Anthony 1945- WhoE 91
Daniels, Robert S 1927- BiDrAPA 89
Daniels, Robert Sanford 1927- WhoAm 90
Daniels, Robert Vincent 1926- WhoAm 90
Daniels, Ronald Earl 1948- WhoE 91
Daniels, Rosemary Murnighan 1918- St&PR 91
Daniels, Roy Gwynne 1928- St&PR 91, WhoE 91
Daniels, Sandy Lee 1958- WhoE 91
Daniels, Sarah 1957- FemiCLE
Daniels, Shouri WhoWrEP 89
Daniels, Stephen M. 1947- WhoAm 90
Daniels, Steven 1948- St&PR 91
Daniels, Terrence D. 1943- St&PR 91
Daniels, Thaddeus Lee 1951- WhoSSW 91
Daniels, Tricia 1961- WhoEmL 91
Daniels, Virginia Annamae 1907- WhoWrEP 89
Daniels, Wilbur 1923- WhoAm 90
Daniels, William 1927- WorAlBi
Daniels, William Albert 1937- WhoE 91
Daniels, William Burton 1930- WhoAm 90
Daniels, William Carlton, Jr. 1920- WhoAm 90
Daniels, William David 1927- WhoAm 90
Daniels, William Dohn 1949- St&PR 91
Daniels, William Lewis 1944- WhoAm 90
Daniels, William Ward, Jr. 1951- BiDrAPA 89
Daniels Weinert, Patti Marie 1932- WhoWrEP 89
Danielsen, Clifford R. 1949- St&PR 91
Danielsen, Harland Allen 1964- WhoEmL 91
Danielski, Linda Sharon 1955- WhoAmW 91
Danielson, Anders Jerker 1957- WhoWor 91
Danielson, Clifford 1899- St&PR 91
Danielson, Dale Lee 1955- WhoSSW 91
Danielson, Donald C. 1919- St&PR 91
Danielson, Doris K. 1940- ODwPR 91
Danielson, Elizabeth Kay 1949- WhoEmL 91
Danielson, Gary R. 1953- WhoEmL 91, WhoWor 91
Danielson, Gordon Kenneth, Jr. 1931- WhoAm 90
Danielson, Jerry Craig 1953- WhoEmL 91
Danielson, Kenneth Leroy 1950- St&PR 91
Danielson, Leon Charles 1945- St&PR 91
Danielson, Patricia Rochelle Frank 1941- WhoAmW 91
Danielson, Phyllis I WhoAmA 91, WhoAmW 91
Danielson, Stacy Ann 1963- WhoAmW 91
Danielson, Ursel 1935- BiDrAPA 89
Danielson, Ursel Rehding 1935- WhoE 91
Danielson, Wayne Allen 1929- WhoAm 90
Danikian, Caron Le Brun 1942- WhoAmA 91
Danilek, Donald J. 1937- WhoAm 90
Daniloff, Nicholas BioIn 16
Danilov, Victor Joseph 1924- WhoAm 90
Danilova, Alexandra BioIn 16, WhoAm 90, WorAlBi
Danilowicz, Delores Ann 1935- WhoAm 90
Danilowicz, L. Paul 1936- St&PR 91
Daniluk, Agnes BioIn 16
Daniluk, Paul BioIn 16
Danin, Mary Ann 1928- WhoAm 90
Danis, Julie Marie 1955- WhoEmL 91
Danis, Marcel 1943- WhoAm 90
Danis, Peter G., Jr. 1932- St&PR 91
Danis, Richard Ralph 1943- St&PR 91, WhoAm 90
Danise, Giuseppe PenDiMP
Danish, Roy Bertram 1919- WhoAm 90
Danisman, Mustafa Cihat 1947- WhoWor 91
Danitz, Marilynn Patricia WhoAmW 91, WhoE 91, WhoWor 91
Danjczek, David William 1951- WhoWor 91
Danjczek, William Emil 1913- WhoWor 91
Dank, Gerald M 1930- BiDrAPA 89
Dank, Gloria 1955- BioIn 16
Dank, Leonard D 1929- WhoAmA 91
Dank, Leonard Dewey 1929- WhoAm 90
Dankanyin, R.J. 1934- St&PR 91
Dankanyin, Robert John 1934- WhoAm 90
Danker, Frederick J. 1923- St&PR 91
Dankin, Alexander Harry 1916- St&PR 91
Dankin, Peter Alfred 1942- St&PR 91
Dankmeyer, Theodore Rognald 1938- St&PR 91, WhoAm 90
Dankner, Jay Warren 1949- WhoEmL 91
Dankner-Rosen, Dawn ODwPR 91
Danko, Barbara Daly 1953- WhoAmW 91
Danko, Joseph O., Jr. 1926- St&PR 91
Danko, Kevin Stephen 1959- WhoEmL 91
Danko, Natalia Yakovnievna 1892-1942 BiDWomA

Danko, Patricia St. John 1944- *WhoAmW 91, WhoSSW 91*
Danko, William David 1952- *WhoEmL 91*
Danko-Alexseyenko, Natalia Yakovnievna 1892-1942 *BiDWomA*
Danks, Elizabeth *BiDEWW*
Dankworth, Charles Henry 1950- *WhoEmL 91*
Dankworth, Clementina Dinah 1927- *WhoAm 90, WhoAmW 91, WhoE 91*
Dankworth, John 1927- *OxCPMus, PenDiMP*
Dankworth, John Philip William 1927- *IntWWM 90*
Danky, James Philip 1947- *WhoWrEP 89*
Danly, Donald Robert 1923- *WhoAm 90*
Danly, Susan 1948- *WhoAmA 91*
Dann, Elliot W. *BioIn 16*
Dann, Emily 1932- *WhoAmW 91, WhoE 91*
Dann, Jack 1945- *ConAu 30NR, RGTwCSF*
Dann, Jack M. 1945- *WhoWrEP 89*
Dann, Laurie Wasserman *BioIn 16*
Dann, Max 1955- *SmATA 62*
Dann, Norman 1927- *St&PR 91*
Dann, O Townsend 1935- *BiDrAPA 89*
Dann, Rosemary Weinstein 1948- *WhoEmL 91*
Dann, Steven Arthur 1953- *IntWWM 90*
Dann, Theodore E. 1917- *St&PR 91*
Dann, Thomas Semmes 1952- *WhoEmL 91*
D'Anna, Angelo Nino 1924- *St&PR 91*
D'Anna, Anthony S. 1926- *St&PR 91*
Danna, Carl 1930- *WhoWrEP 89*
D'Anna, Carmen Vito 1920- *WhoE 91*
Danna, Diane 1952- *WhoE 91*
Danna, Dorothy R 1920- *BiDrAPA 89*
Danna, Jo J. *WhoAmW 91*
Danna, Margaret Ann 1942- *WhoAmW 91*
Danna, Mychael *NewAgMG*
Danna, Robert 1951- *WhoEmL 91*
Dannatt, George 1915- *IntWWM 90*
Dannay, Frederic *TwCCr&M 91*
Dannay, Frederic 1905-1982 *AuBYP 90, MajTwCW*
Danneberg, Kenneth I. 1927- *St&PR 91*
Dannecker, Johann Heinrich *PenDiDA 89*
Dannecker, Theodor 1913-1945 *BioIn 16*
Danneels, Godfried 1933- *WhoWor 91*
Dannehl, Mary Zeitler 1959- *WhoAmW 91*
Danneker, James Anthon 1951- *WhoEmL 91*
Danneker, Joseph Martin 1953- *WhoEmL 91*
Dannemeyer, William Edwin 1929- *WhoAm 90*
Dannemiller, John C. 1938- *WhoAm 90*
Dannenbaum, Paul O. 1916- *St&PR 91*
Dannenberg, Arthur Milton, Jr. 1923- *WhoAm 90*
Dannenberg, Martin E. 1915- *St&PR 91*
Dannenberg, Martin Ernest 1915- *WhoAm 90*
Dannenfeldt, Paula *ODwPR 91*
Dannenmann, Otto Karl 1915- *WhoWrEP 89*
Danner, Blythe 1943- *WorAlBi*
Danner, Blythe Katharine 1944- *WhoAm 90*
Danner, Bobby Charles 1930- *St&PR 91*
Danner, Dean W. 1950- *St&PR 91*
Danner, Dean Wilson 1950- *WhoEmL 91*
Danner, Donald G. 1944- *St&PR 91*
Danner, George W. *St&PR 91*
Danner, Jeanne Elisa 1959- *WhoSSW 91*
Danner, Lawrence Melville 1949- *WhoSSW 91*
Danner, Patsy Ann 1934- *WhoAm 90, WhoAmW 91*
Danner, Raymond L. 1925- *WhoAm 90, WhoSSW 91*
Danner, Richard Allen 1947- *WhoAm 90*
Danner, Robert P. 1924- *St&PR 91*
Danner, Stephen George 1952- *WhoSSW 91*
Danner, William Theodore 1931- *St&PR 91*
Dannhofer, Joseph Philipp *PenDiDA 89*
D'Anniballe, Priscilla Lucille 1950- *WhoAmW 91*
Dannible, Carmin D. 1929- *St&PR 91*
Danning, Harry 1911- *Ballpl 90, BioIn 16*
Dannis-Applegate, Fern Sue 1953- *WhoAmW 91*
Dannreuther, Edward 1844-1905 *PenDiMP*
Dannreuther, John West 1948- *St&PR 91*
D'Annunzio, Gabriele 1863-1938 *BioIn 16, TwCLC 40 [port], WorAlBi*
D'Annunzio, Joseph C. 1925- *St&PR 91*
Danny and the Juniors *EncPR&S 89*
Dano, Paul Kenneth 1935- *St&PR 91*
Dano, Royal 1922- *ConTFT 8*
Da Nobrega, Mailson *BioIn 16*
Danoff, I. Michael 1940- *WhoAm 90*
Danoff, I Michael 1940- *WhoAmA 91*
Danoff, Jascha Wolsey *BiDrAPA 89*
Danoff, Susan Beth 1953- *WhoE 91*
Danoff-Kraus, Pamela Sue 1946- *WhoAmW 91, WhoEmL 91*
Danois-Maricq, Etienne M. 1955- *WhoWor 91*
Danon, Giuliana Maria 1957- *WhoEmL 91*
Danon, Oscar 1913- *PenDiMP*
Danos, Robert McClure 1929- *St&PR 91, WhoAm 90*
Danovitch, Gerry *BioIn 16*
Danquah, Mabel 1910?- *FemiCLE*
Danrell, John Rayment 1942- *IntWWM 90*
Dansak, Daniel Albert 1943- *BiDrAPA 89, WhoSSW 91*
Dansby, Eunice Lillith 1927- *IntWWM 90, WhoWor 91*
Dansby, John Walter 1944- *St&PR 91, WhoAm 90*
Danser, Bonita Kay 1949- *WhoAmW 91, WhoEmL 91*
Danser, Harold Wesley, III 1945- *WhoEmL 91, WhoWor 91*
Danser, Mary Helen 1940- *WhoAmW 91, WhoWor 91*
Dansereau, Jean-Joseph *BiDrAPA 89*
Dansereau, Muriel Tannehill *BioIn 16*
Dansereau, Pierre 1911- *WhoAm 90*
Dansie, Kim Duncan *BiDrAPA 89*
Danskin, Wesley Robert 1952- *WhoEmL 91*
Dansky, Brad Lee 1957- *BiDrAPA 89*
Danson, Stephen Michael 1943- *WhoAm 90*
Danson, Ted *BioIn 16*
Danson, Ted 1947- *CurBio 90 [port], WhoAm 90, WorAlBi*
Dante 1883-1955 *BioIn 16*
Dante Alighieri 1265-1321 *WrPh WorAlBi*
Dante, Harris Loy 1912- *WhoAm 90*
Dante, Lee Gerard 1947- *BiDrAPA 89*
Dante, Robert David 1953- *WhoWrEP 89*
Dantes, Edmund *WhoWrEP 89*
d'Antibes, Germain *ConAu 129, MajTwCW*
Dantin, Louis 1865-1945 *DcLB 92*
Dantini, Julie Ann 1947- *WhoE 91*
Dantley, Adrian 1956- *WhoAm 90, WorAlBi*
Danto, Arthur Coleman 1924- *BioIn 16, WhoAm 90, WhoWrEP 89*
Danto, Bruce L 1927- *BiDrAPA 89*
Danton, Georges 1759-1794 *WorAlBi*
Danton, Georges Jacques 1759-1794 *BioIn 16*
Danton, Joseph Periam 1908- *WhoAm 90*
Danton, Rebecca *WhoWrEP 89*
Dantone, Jerry B. 1942- *St&PR 91*
D'Antoni, David J. *BioIn 16*
D'Antonio, Anthony A. 1933- *ODwPR 91*
D'Antonio, Gregory Douglas 1951- *WhoWor 91*
D'Antonio, James Joseph 1959- *WhoEmL 91*
D'Antonio, Joseph C 1950- *BiDrAPA 89*
D'Antonio, Thomas Samuel 1957- *WhoEmL 91*
D'Antuono, D.J. 1943- *St&PR 91*
Dantzic, Cynthia Maris 1933- *WhoAmA 91, WhoE 91*
Dantzig, David Van 1900-1959 *DcScB S2*
Dantzig, George Bernard 1914- *WhoAm 90*
Dantzig, Rudi Van 1933- *WhoWor 91*
Dantzler, John William, Jr. 1953- *WhoEmL 91*
Danubrata, Mohammad Noor 1932- *WhoWor 91*
Danusugondho, Sumarto 1936- *WhoWor 91*
D'Anvers, Alicia 1667?-1725 *FemiCLE*
D'Anvers, Alicia 1668-1725 *BiDEWW*
Danyluk, Paul R. 1937- *St&PR 91*
Danyluk, Steven Simeon 1933- *WhoAm 90*
Danza, John *BioIn 16*
Danza, Tony *BioIn 16*
Danza, Tony 1951- *WorAlBi*
Danzberger, Alexander Harris 1932- *WhoAm 90*
D'Anzi, Francis A *BiDrAPA 89*
Danzig, Aaron Leon 1913- *WhoAm 90*
Danzig, Amy 1950- *ODwPR 91*
Danzig, Ethel 1931-1989 *BioIn 16*
Danzig, Frederick Paul 1925- *WhoAm 90*
Danzig, Jerome Alan 1913- *WhoAm 90*
Danzig, Lisa 1958- *St&PR 91, WhoAmW 91*
Danzig, Richard Jeffrey 1944- *WhoAm 90*
Danzig, Robert James 1932- *WhoAm 90*
Danzig, Sarah H. Palfrey 1912- *WhoAm 90*
Danzig, Sheila Ring 1948- *WhoAmW 91, WhoEmL 91, WhoSSW 91*
Danzig, William Harold 1947- *WhoEmL 91, WhoSSW 91, WhoWor 91*
Danziger, Avery C 1953- *WhoAmA 91*
Danziger, Debra Rosenblum 1954- *WhoAmW 91*
Danziger, Frederick B 1934- *BiDrAPA 89*
Danziger, Frederick Michael 1940- *St&PR 91*
Danziger, Gertrude *St&PR 91*
Danziger, Gertrude Seelig 1919- *WhoAmW 91*
Danziger, Glenn Norman 1930- *WhoE 91*
Danziger, Howard 1941- *St&PR 91*
Danziger, Ivan John 1936- *WhoWor 91*
Danziger, Jeffrey Arlen 1956- *BiDrAPA 89*
Danziger, Jerry 1924- *WhoAm 90*
Danziger, Joan 1934- *WhoAmA 91, WhoAmW 91*
Danziger, Lewis *BiDrAPA 89*
Danziger, Louis 1923- *ConDes 90, WhoAm 90*
Danziger, Martin Breitel 1931- *WhoAm 90*
Danziger, Michael Roy 1954- *WhoEmL 91*
Danziger, Nick 1958- *ConAu 129*
Danziger, Paula 1944- *BioIn 16, SmATA 63 [port]*
Danziger, Richard Ira 1956- *St&PR 91*
Danziger, Richard Martin 1938- *WhoE 91*
Danziger, Seymour I. *St&PR 91N*
Danziger, Sidney 1903- *St&PR 91*
Danzis, Colin Michael 1938- *WhoWor 91*
Danzis, Jo-Ann Fine 1941- *WhoAmW 91*
Danzis, Rose Marie *WhoAm 90*
Dao, Thi-Hong-Trang 1957- *BiDrAPA 89*
Daoud, Abraham Joseph, IV 1957- *WhoSSW 91*
Daoud, Daoud Selim 1953- *WhoWor 91*
Daoud, Mohamed 1947- *WhoEmL 91*
Daoudi, M S 1946- *ConAu 132*
Daouk, Nadim Fawzi 1948- *WhoWor 91*
Daoust, Donald Roger 1935- *St&PR 91, WhoAm 90*
Daoust, Hubert 1928- *WhoAm 90*
D'Aoust, Jean-Jacques 1924- *WhoSSW 91*
Daoust, Julien 1866-1943 *OxCCanT [port]*
Dapaz Strout, Lilia 1930- *WhoSSW 91*
Daphne *EncCoWW*
Daphne, Emily *EncCoWW*
Daphnis, Nassos 1914- *WhoAm 90, WhoAmA 91*
D'Apice, Joseph P *BiDrAPA 89*
Dapice, Ronald R. 1937- *WhoAm 90*
Dapogny, James Elliot 1940- *IntWWM 90*
D'Apolito, David Joseph 1955- *WhoE 91*
Da Ponte, Lorenzo 1749-1838 *BioIn 16*
DaPonte, Ronald Gennaro 1948- *WhoEmL 91*
Dapper, G. Steven 1946- *WhoAm 90*
Dapples, Edward Charles 1906- *WhoAm 90*
D'Appolonia, David J. 1944- *St&PR 91*
Dapprich, John William 1937- *WhoWor 91*
Dapron, Elmer Joseph, Jr. 1925- *WhoWor 91*
Dapuzzo, Peter James 1941- *St&PR 91, WhoAm 90*
D'Aquili, Eugene Guy *BiDrAPA 89*
D'Aquin, Mordecai *EncO&P 3*
d'Aquino, Thomas 1940- *WhoAm 90, WhoWor 91*
D'Aquisto, Jim *BioIn 16*
D'Aquisto, Thomas William 1945- *St&PR 91*
Dara, Enzo 1938- *IntWWM 90*
Darabi, Homa *BiDrAPA 89*
Darack, Arthur J. 1918- *WhoAm 90, WhoWrEP 89*
D'Aranyi, Jelly *PenDiMP*
Darazidi, James Joseph 1949- *St&PR 91*
Darazsdi, James Joseph 1949- *WhoAm 90*
D'Arbanville, Patti *BioIn 16*
Darbe, Shantharam *BiDrAPA 89*
Darbelnet, Jean Louis 1904- *WhoWrEP 89*
D'Arbeloff, George Vladimir 1945- *St&PR 91, WhoEmL 91*
D'Arblay, Frances Burney 1752-1840 *BioIn 16*
Darbo, Bakary Bunja 1946- *WhoWor 91*
Darboven, Hanne 1941- *WhoAmA 91*
Darby, Ada Claire 1883- *AuBYP 90*
Darby, Daniel Lee 1947- *BiDrAPA 89*
Darby, Douglas Alan 1946- *St&PR 91*
Darby, Edwin Wheeler 1922- *WhoAm 90*
Darby, Elton H. 1918- *St&PR 91*
Darby, Elton H., Jr. 1961- *St&PR 91*
Darby, Henry Clifford 1909- *BioIn 16*
Darby, J. N. *AuBYP 90*
Darby, Janice Ann 1961- *WhoE 91*
Darby, Jay Rodney 1953- *WhoEmL 91, WhoWor 91*
Darby, Jerome S. 1950- *St&PR 91*
Darby, John Kenneth 1941- *BiDrAPA 89*
Darby, Joseph Branch, Jr. 1925- *WhoAm 90*
Darby, Kenneth M. 1946- *St&PR 91*
Darby, Michael Rucker 1945- *WhoAm 90*
Darby, Michele Leonardi 1949- *WhoSSW 91*
Darby, Raymond 1912- *AuBYP 90*
Darby, Stephen John, Jr. 1933- *St&PR 91*
D'Arby, Terence Trent *BioIn 16*
D'Arby, Terence Trent 1962- *EncPR&S 89*
Darby, Walter Lee, III *BiDrAPA 89*
Darby, William E 1920- *BiDrAPA 89*
Darby, William Jefferson, Jr. 1913- *WhoAm 90*
Darby, William Leonard 1919- *WhoAm 90*
D'Arc, Victor 1924- *BiDrAPA 89*
D'Arcangelo, Allan M 1930- *WhoAmA 91*
D'Arcangelo, Allan Matthew 1930- *WhoAm 90*
Darcera, Carlito Duron 1952- *BiDrAPA 89*
D'Archambeau, Felicien *PenDiMP*
D'Archambeau, Iwan *PenDiMP*
Darcie, Grace *BiDEWW*
Darclee, Hariclea 1860-1939 *PenDiMP*
D'Arcy, Adelyse Marie 1934- *WhoAmW 91*
D'Arcy, Ella 1851-1939 *FemiCLE*
D'Arcy, Ella 1887-1965 *BioIn 16*
Darcy, George R. 1920- *ODwPR 91*
Darcy, George Robert 1920- *WhoAm 90, WhoE 91, WhoWor 91*
D'Arcy, Gerald Paul 1933- *WhoAm 90*
Darcy, Harold P. 1929- *WhoE 91*
Darcy, James J. 1947- *WhoE 91*
D'Arcy, John Michael 1932- *WhoAm 90*
Darcy, Keith T. 1948- *St&PR 91*
Darcy, Keith Thomas 1948- *WhoE 91, WhoEmL 91*
D'Arcy, Margaretta 1934- *ConAu 31NR*
Darcy, Pat 1950- *Ballpl 90*
D'Arcy, Rosemary V. 1944- *WhoAmW 91*
D'Arcy, Willard *TwCCr&M 91*
Dard, Jacques 1937- *WhoE 91*
Dardano, Guillermo J 1925- *BiDrAPA 89*
Dardas, Charles L. 1953- *St&PR 91*
Darden, Charles Franklin 1958- *WhoSSW 91*
Darden, Dawn L. 1963- *WhoAmW 91*
Darden, Edwin Speight, Sr. 1920- *WhoAm 90*
Darden, George Washington, III 1943- *WhoAm 90, WhoSSW 91*
Darden, Joseph S., Jr. *BioIn 16*
Darden, Joseph Samuel, Jr. 1925- *WhoE 91*
Darden, R. Scott 1955- *St&PR 91*
Darden, Richard Truman 1944- *WhoSSW 91*
Darden, Sam H., Jr. 1921- *BiDrAPA 89*
Darden, Severn 1929- *ConTFT 8 [port]*
Darden, Severn Teackle *WhoAm 90*
Darden, William E. 1916- *St&PR 91*
Darden, William Howard, Jr. 1937- *WhoAm 90*
Dardes, Jack Andrew 1946- *WhoE 91*
Dardick, Kenneth Regen 1946- *WhoAm 90*
Dardick, Leon M. 1926- *St&PR 91*
Dardon, Carlos Alfred *BiDrAPA 89*
DaRe, Aldo *ConTFT 8*
Dare, Arthur Newman 1850-1923 *AmLegL*
Dare, Michael 1951- *WhoEmL 91*
Dare, Phyllis 1890-1975 *OxCPMus*
Dare, Virginia 1587- *EncCRAm*
Dare, Virginia 1587-1587? *WorAlBi*
Dare, Zena 1887-1975 *OxCPMus*
Dareff, Hal 1920- *AuBYP 90, WhoAm 90, WhoWrEP 89*
Darehshori, Anne C. *BioIn 16*
Darehshori, Nader F. 1936- *St&PR 91*
Darell, Edward Wilke *BiDrAPA 89*
Daresta, James Edward 1946- *WhoSSW 91*
Darewski, Herman 1883-1947 *OxCPMus*
Darewski, Max 1894-1929 *OxCPMus*
D'Arezzo, James David 1951- *St&PR 91*
Darga, Jerome Paul 1944- *St&PR 91*
Dargan, James Vernon 1923- *St&PR 91*
Dargan, Mary Palmer Kelley 1954- *WhoWor 91*
Dargan, Olive 1869-1968 *FemiCLE*
Dargan, Olive Tilford 1869-1968 *LiHiK*
Dargan, Surinder K 1947- *BiDrAPA 89*
Dargaud, Georges *NewYTBS 90*
Darge, Moniek 1952- *IntWWM 90*
Dargene, Carl 1930- *St&PR 91*
D'Argenio, Raymond 1930- *St&PR 91, WhoAm 90*
D'Argenson, Marc-Antoine-Rene 1722-1787 *BioIn 16*
Darger, Henry J. 1892-1973 *MusmAFA*
Darger, Stanford Parley 1920- *St&PR 91*
Dargie, Bryan Alfred 1941- *IntWWM 90*
D'Argnac, Jesse *WhoWrEP 89*
Dargomizhsky, Alexander 1813-1869 *PenDiMP A*
Darian, Ralph 1925- *St&PR 91*
Darie, Sandu 1908- *ArtLatA*
Darien, Steven Martin 1942- *St&PR 91, WhoE 91*
Darin, Bobby 1936-1973 *ConMus 4 [port], EncPR&S 89, OxCPMus, WorAlBi*
Dario, Ruben 1867-1916 *BioIn 16, ConAu 131, HispWr 90, MajTwCW*
Darion, Joe 1917- *WhoAm 90*
Darius I 550BC-486BC *WorAlBi*
Darius, Denyll 1942-1976 *WhoAmA 91N*
Darjany, John C. 1948- *St&PR 91*

Darjany, John Charles 1948- *WhoEmL 91*
Dark, Alvin 1922- *Ballpl 90 [port]*
Dark, Alvin Ralph 1922- *WhoAm 90*
Dark, Eleanor 1901-1985 *FemiCLE*
Dark, Philip John Crosskey 1918- *WhoAm 90*
Darke, Harold 1888-1976 *PenDiMP*
Darke, Richard Francis 1943- *St&PR 91*
Darke, Roy A 1914- *BiDrAPA 89*
Darken, Marjorie Alice 1915- *WhoSSW 91*
Darken, Teresa Joan Joyce 1961- *WhoAmW 91*
Darkey, Kermit Louis 1930- *WhoWor 91*
Darko, Denis F. 1947- *BiDrAPA 89*
Darkovich, Sharon Marie 1949- *WhoAmW 91*
Darlan, Francois 1881-1942 *BiDFrPL, BioIn 16*
Darland, Nancy Ann Wilson 1958- *WhoSSW 91*
Darley, Felix Octavius Carr 1822-1888 *WhNaAH*
Darley, George 1795-1846 *DcLB 96 [port]*
Darley, Jeffrey S. 1958- *St&PR 91*
Darley, John McConnon 1938- *WhoAm 90*
Darley, William Joseph 1928- *St&PR 91*
Darling, Alberta Statkus 1944- *WhoAmW 91, WhoWor 91*
Darling, Byron Thorwell 1912- *WhoAm 90*
Darling, Darlene Duffy *BioIn 16*
Darling, David *NewAgMG*
Darling, David J 1953- *SmATA 60 [port]*
Darling, Debra Beth 1953- *WhoAmW 91*
Darling, Edward *BioIn 16*
Darling, Frank Clayton 1925- *WhoAm 90*
Darling, George Bapst, Jr. 1905- *WhoAm 90*
Darling, Grace *BioIn 16*
Darling, Jay Norwood 1876-1962 *BioIn 16, WhoAmA 91N*
Darling, Joan 1935?- *BioIn 16*
Darling, John Albert 1937- *St&PR 91*
Darling, John Dallas 1944- *St&PR 91*
Darling, John Rothburn, Jr. 1937- *WhoAm 90, WhoSSW 91, WhoWor 91*
Darling, Ken 1940- *ODwPR 91*
Darling, Lois 1917- *AuBYP 90*
Darling, Lois MacIntyre 1917-1989 *BioIn 16, ConAu 130, SmATA 64*
Darling, Louis, Jr. 1916-1970 *AuBYP 90*
Darling, Marie C 1963- *WhoAmW 91*
Darling, Mark Paul 1949- *St&PR 91*
Darling, Michael James Auchinleck 1960- *WhoE 91*
Darling, Michael Roy Norman 1946- *WhoWor 91*
Darling, Paul C. *NewYTBS 90*
Darling, Ralph Clement 1927- *WhoAm 90*
Darling, Richard Harrison 1925- *St&PR 91*
Darling, Richard Lewis 1925- *AuBYP 90*
Darling, Robert Edward 1937- *WhoAm 90*
Darling, Ron *BioIn 16*
Darling, Ron 1960- *Ballpl 90*
Darling, Scott Edward 1949- *WhoEmL 91, WhoWor 91*
Darling, Scott Martin 1953- *St&PR 91*
Darling, Sharon Kathleen 1959- *WhoAmW 91*
Darling, Sharon Sandling 1943- *WhoAmA 91*
Darling, Stephen Edward 1949- *WhoEmL 91*
Darling, Sturgis W. 1932- *St&PR 91*
Darling, Tom 1917- *St&PR 91*
Darling, Toni O'Reilly *BioIn 16*
Darling, William 1951- *WhoSSW 91*
Darling, William Ritchie 1933- *WhoWrEP 89*
Darlinger, Copper 1954- *WhoEmL 91*
Darlington, Cyril Dean 1903-1981 *DcNaB 1981, DcScB S2*
Darlington, David William 1945- *WhoEmL 91*
Darlington, Henry, Jr. 1925- *WhoE 91, WhoWor 91*
Darlington, Jared Lloyd 1933- *WhoWor 91*
Darlington, Judith Mabel 1942- *WhoAmW 91*
Darlington, Lloyd F. 1945- *St&PR 91*
Darlington, Oscar Gilpin 1909- *WhoAm 90*
Darlington, Richard Benjamin 1937- *WhoAm 90*
Darlington, Sidney 1906- *WhoAm 90*
Darlington, Stephen Mark 1952- *IntWWM 90*
Darlington, W.D. 1932- *St&PR 91*
Darlow, Denys 1921- *IntWWM 90*
Darlow, Julia Donovan 1941- *WhoAm 90, WhoAmW 91*
Darlow, Mark Howard 1941- *St&PR 91*
Darlow, Sheldon Jay 1935- *St&PR 91*
Darly, Matthias *PenDiDA 89*
Darman, Richard *BioIn 16*
Darman, Richard Gordon 1943- *NewYTBS 90 [port], WhoAm 90*
Darmanian, Denise G. 1957- *St&PR 91*
Darmojuwono, Justin 1914- *WhoWor 91*
Darmon, Robert L. 1925- *St&PR 91*
Darmory, Franklin P. *BioIn 16*
D'Arms, John Haughton 1934- *WhoAm 90*
Darmstandler, Harry Max 1922- *WhoAm 90*
Darnall, Dennis Wayne 1941- *WhoAm 90*
Darnall, Michael Steven 1947- *St&PR 91*
Darnall, Robert J. *WhoAm 90*
Darnall, Roberta Morrow 1949- *WhoEmL 91*
Darnall, Thomas S., Jr. 1936- *St&PR 91*
Darnand, Aime Joseph Auguste 1897-1945 *BiDFrPL*
Darneille, Wallace Lambert 1951- *WhoSSW 91*
Darnell, August *BioIn 16*
Darnell, Betty Jean 1942- *WhoAmW 91*
Darnell, Coleman Howard, Jr. 1923- *St&PR 91*
Darnell, Gary Peter *BiDrAPA 89*
Darnell, James Edwin, Jr. 1930- *WhoAm 90*
Darnell, James Oral 1955- *WhoEmL 91*
Darnell, Leonard Robert 1957- *WhoEmL 91, WhoWor 91*
Darnell, Linda 1921-1965 *WorAlBi*
Darnell, Nicholas Henry 1807-1885 *AmLegL*
Darnell, Patricia Ann 1954- *WhoWor 91*
Darnell, Quinton L. 1928- *St&PR 91*
Darnell, Riley Carlisle 1940- *WhoSSW 91*
Darney, Philip Dempsey 1943- *WhoAm 90*
Darney, William Joseph, Jr. 1940- *St&PR 91*
Darnton, Robert 1939- *WorAu 1980 [port]*
Darnyi, Tamas *BioIn 16*
Daroff, Karen *BioIn 16*
Daroff, Robert Barry 1936- *WhoAm 90, WhoWor 91*
Daronco, Richard J. 1931-1988 *BioIn 16*
da Roza, Victoria Cecilia 1945- *WhoAmW 91*
Darphin, Sarah Winifred 1949- *WhoAmW 91*
D'Arpino, Tony 1951- *WhoWrEP 89*
Darquier de Pellepoix, Louis 1897-1980 *BioIn 16*
Darr, Alice Louise 1951- *WhoEmL 91*
Darr, Ann Russell 1920- *WhoWrEP 89*
Darr, Barbara Harman 1927- *WhoAmW 91*
Darr, George *BiDrAPA 89*
Darr, James Earl, Jr. 1943- *WhoAm 90*
Darr, James Franklin *BioIn 16*
Darr, John 1951- *St&PR 91, WhoEmL 91*
Darr, John K. 1944- *St&PR 91*
Darr, Milton Freeman, Jr. 1921- *WhoAm 90*
Darr, Robert Charles 1937- *St&PR 91*
Darrach, Orlin Ward 1928- *St&PR 91*
Darragh, Cavan J. 1916- *St&PR 91*
Darragh, Daniel Meyer 1946- *WhoEmL 91*
Darragh, James Hilton 1924- *WhoAm 90*
Darragh, John K. 1929- *St&PR 91, WhoAm 90*
Darragh, Lydia Barrington 1729-1789 *EncCRAm*
Darrah, Katherine Simpson 1937- *WhoAmW 91*
Darrah, Lucy Morgan 1946- *WhoSSW 91*
Darre, Bernard John 1939- *St&PR 91*
Darre, Jeanne-Marie 1905- *PenDiMP*
Darre, Walther *BioIn 16*
Darrell, Evelyn Boyden *WhoAmW 91*
Darrell, George Albert 1931- *WhoAm 90*
Darrell, Norris 1899-1989 *BioIn 16*
Darrell, Norris, Jr. 1929- *WhoAm 90*
Darrell, R. D. 1903-1988 *BioIn 16*
Darrell, Robert Donaldson 1903-1988 *BioIn 16*
Darriau, Jean-Paul 1929- *WhoAmA 91*
Darrigan, Robert Joseph, Jr. 1958- *WhoE 91*
Darroca, William Celis *BiDrAPA 89*
Darrone, Donald William 1916- *St&PR 91, WhoAm 90*
Darrone, Richard William 1941- *St&PR 91*
Darrow, Clarence 1857-1938 *BioIn 16, WorAlBi*
Darrow, Henry *WhoHisp 91*
Darrow, Katharine 1943- *BioIn 16*
Darrow, Katherine Prager 1943- *WhoAmW 91*
Darrow, Paul Gardner *WhoAmA 91*
Darrow, Robert Arthur 1911- *WhoAm 90*
Darrow, Ruth 1895-1956 *BioIn 16*
Darrow, Terri Lynn 1955- *WhoWrEP 89*
Darrow, Whitney 1909- *AuBYP 90*
Darrow, Whitney, Jr 1909- *WhoAmA 91*
Darrow, William Richard 1939- *WhoE 91, WhoWor 91*
Dars, Rene 1921- *WhoWor 91*
Darsey, Betty Jean 1931- *WhoAmW 91*
Darsey, Susan Bowen 1940- *BiDrAPA 89*
Darshan-Stanton, Abigail M *BiDrAPA 89*
Darsky, Julius 1907- *WhoSSW 91*
Darsky, Richard H. 1941- *St&PR 91*
Darsonval, Vincent Andre 1948- *WhoWor 91*
Darsot, Ismail *BioIn 16*
Darst, David Martin 1947- *WhoE 91, WhoEmL 91*
Dart, Charles Edward 1915- *WhoAm 90*
Dart, Jack Calhoon 1912- *St&PR 91*
Dart, John Robert 1925- *WhoE 91*
Dart, John Seward 1936- *WhoAm 90*
Dart, Raymond 1893-1988 *AnObit 1988*
Dart, Raymond A. 1893-1988 *BioIn 16*
Dart, Rollin B. 1925- *St&PR 91*
Dart, Thurston 1921-1971 *PenDiMP*
Darter, Jeffrey Allen 1958- *WhoEmL 91*
Darter, Steven Mark 1949- *WhoEmL 91*
Dartez, Franklin 1934- *WhoAm 90*
Dartez, Louis Avery 1925- *WhoSSW 91*
Darting, Edith Anne 1945- *WhoAmW 91*
Dartnall, Gary 1937- *St&PR 91*
Darton, Christopher 1945- *WhoAmA 91*
Dartt, Roger Wallace 1941- *St&PR 91*
Daruma *EncJap*
Daruna, Paul Alfred 1943- *BiDrAPA 89*
Daruni, Sam K. *St&PR 91*
Darvarova, Elmira *WhoAm 90*
Darvas, Endre Peter 1946- *WhoEmL 91*
Darvasula, Viswa B *BiDrAPA 89*
Darver, Gerald B. 1944- *St&PR 91*
Darvi, Andrea *ConAu 130*
Darwall, Mary 1738-1825 *FemiCLE*
Darwall, Mary Whately *BioIn 16*
Darwich, Samir A. 1937- *WhoWor 91*
Darwin, Allen Charles 1948- *St&PR 91*
Darwin, Beverly Levenson 1935- *WhoE 91*
Darwin, Bobby 1943- *Ballpl 90*
Darwin, Charles 1809-1882 *BioIn 16, WrPh P*
Darwin, Charles R. 1809-1882 *WorAlBi*
Darwin, Charles Robert 1809-1882 *BioIn 16*
Darwin, Christopher *BioIn 16*
Darwin, Danny 1955- *Ballpl 90*
Darwin, Erasmus 1731-1802 *DcLB 93 [port]*
Darwin, Gary Robert 1952- *St&PR 91*
Darwin, George H. 1845-1912 *WorAlBi*
Darwin, John Walter 1953- *WhoEmL 91*
Darwin, Natalie W. 1923- *St&PR 91*
Darwin, Rebecca *BioIn 16*
Darwin, Rebecca Wesson 1953- *WhoAm 90, WhoAmW 91*
Darwin, Sidney 1915- *St&PR 91*
Darwisch, Tiffany *BioIn 16*
Dary, David Archie 1934- *WhoAm 90*
Daryanani, Raj 1961- *WhoE 91*
Daryush, Elizabeth 1887-1977 *BioIn 16, FemiCLE*
Das, Arabinda *BiDrAPA 89*
Das, Chitta Ranjan 1870-1925 *BioIn 16*
Das, Kalyan 1956- *WhoEmL 91, WhoWor 91*
Das, Kamala 1934- *FemiCLE*
Das, Kshitish C *BiDrAPA 89*
Das, Manjusri 1946- *WhoAmW 91*
Das, Mohan P *BiDrAPA 89*
Das, Natendra Nath 1936- *BiDrAPA 89*
Das, Pradip Kumar 1951- *WhoE 91*
Das, Purnananda 1939- *BiDrAPA 89*
Das, Rathin C. 1948- *WhoAm 90*
Das, Renu P *BiDrAPA 89*
Das, Santhi Kumara *BiDrAPA 89*
Das, T. K. 1938- *WhoE 91*
Das Gupta, Krishna 1957- *BiDrAPA 89*
Das Gupta, Narenda Kumar 1910- *EncO&P 3*
Dasarathy, Belur Venkatachalan *WhoSSW 91*
Dasari, Balasundaram *BiDrAPA 89*
Dasberg, Haim *BiDrAPA 89*
Dasburg, Andrew 1887-1979 *BioIn 16*
Dasburg, Andrew Michael 1887-1979 *WhoAmA 91N*
Dasburg, John H. 1943- *St&PR 91*
Dasburg, John Harold 1944- *WhoAm 90, WhoE 91*
Dascalescu, Constantin *WhoWor 91*
Daschbach, James M. 1932- *WhoAm 90*
Dascher, Paul Edward 1942- *WhoAm 90*
Daschle, Thomas Andrew 1947- *WhoAm 90, WhoWor 91*
D'Ascoli, Bernard 1958- *IntWWM 90, PenDiMP*
Dascoli, Frank 1915- *Ballpl 90*
Dasenbrock, Doris Voss 1939- *WhoAmA 91*
Dasent, George Webbe 1817-1896 *SmATA 62*
Dasgupta, Apurba Kumar 1935- *WhoWor 91*
Dash, La Comtesse *EncCoWW*
Dash, Barry Harold 1931- *St&PR 91*
Dash, Harvey Dwight 1924- *WhoAmA 91*
Dash, Jack *BioIn 16*
Dash, Jack 1907-1989 *AnObit 1989*
Dash, Joan 1925- *ConAu 31NR*
Dash, Julie *DrBlPA 90*
Dash, Leon 1944- *BioIn 16*
Dash, Leon DeCosta, Jr. 1944- *WhoAm 90*
Dash, Robert 1934- *WhoAmA 91*
Dash, Samuel 1925- *WhoAm 90*
Dash, Tracy 1958- *WhoAmW 91*
Dashef, Stephen S 1941- *BiDrAPA 89*
Dashef, Stephen Sewell 1941- *WhoE 91*
Dashen, Roger Frederick 1938- *WhoAm 90*
Dasher, Michael Joseph 1949- *St&PR 91*
Dasher, Samuel P 1908- *BiDrAPA 89*
Dashiell, George Easley 1924- *St&PR 91*
Dashiell, L. Travis 1869-1924 *AmLegL*
Dashkova, Ekaterina Romanovna 1743-1810 *EncCoWW*
Dashnaw, Richard L. 1937- *St&PR 91*
Dashow, James 1944- *WhoWor 91*
Da Silva, Howard 1909-1986 *WorAlBi*
Da Silva, Jose Carlos *BiDrAPA 89*
Da Silva, Jose P *BiDrAPA 89*
DaSilva, Mark Edward 1955- *WhoEmL 91*
DaSilva, Pat *WhoHisp 91*
Dasilva, Paul R. 1964- *St&PR 91*
Da Silva Martins, Antonio Augusto De F. 1931- *WhoWor 91*
Da Silva Nunes, Armando Jorge 1938- *WhoWor 91*
da Silveira, Oscar Marques 1930- *WhoWor 91*
Daskal, Robert H. 1941- *St&PR 91*
Daskaloff, Gyorgy 1923- *WhoAmA 91*
Daskam, Josephine Dodge 1876-1961 *BioIn 16*
Dasmann, Raymond Fredric 1919- *WhoAm 90*
D'Aspilette, Marie *EncO&P 3*
Daspit, Laurence F. 1945- *ODwPR 91*
Dass, Dean A. 1955- *WhoEmL 91*
Dass, Dean Allen 1955- *WhoAmA 91*
Dass, Manoj K *BiDrAPA 89*
Dass, Petter 1647-1707 *DcScanL*
Dassanowsky-Harris, Robert 1956- *WhoWrEP 89*
Dassanowsky-Harris, Robert von 1956- *WhoEmL 91*
DasSarma, Basudeb 1923- *WhoSSW 91*
Dassault, Marcel Ferdinand 1892-1986 *BiDFrPL*
Dassdorf, Karl Wilhelm 1750-1812 *BioIn 16*
Dassenko, Paul Edward 1951- *WhoEmL 91*
Dassin, Jules 1911- *ConAu 132*
Dassler, A. Fred 1936- *WhoWor 91*
Dasso, Jerome Joseph 1929- *WhoAm 90, WhoWor 91*
Dasson, Henri 1825-1896 *PenDiDA 89*
Dassori, Frederic Davis, Jr. 1942- *WhoAm 90*
D'Asta, Nicholas A. 1953- *St&PR 91*
D'Astolfo, Frank Joseph 1943- *WhoE 91*
Dastur, Kersy B. 1946- *St&PR 91*
Data, Joann Lucille 1944- *WhoAm 90, WhoAmW 91*
Datan, Nancy *BioIn 16*
Datars, William Ross 1932- *WhoAm 90*
Date, Elaine S. 1957- *WhoAmW 91*
Date, Hikaru 1927- *WhoWor 91*
Date, Toshihiro 1931- *WhoWor 91*
Dater, Judy 1941- *WhoAmA 91*
Dater, Judy Lichtenfeld 1941- *WhoAm 90*
Dates, Herbert W. *BioIn 16*
Dates, Lois Ann 1952- *WhoE 91*
Dathan, John Rodney Ellis 1940- *WhoWor 91*
Dathe, Robert F. 1951- *St&PR 91*
Dati, James Donald 1958- *WhoEmL 91*
Datiles, Manuel Bernaldes, III 1951- *WhoE 91*
Datlof, Steven *BiDrAPA 89*
Dato Iradier, Eduardo 1856-1921 *BioIn 16*
Datoo, Bashir Ahmed 1941- *St&PR 91*
Datre, Donna M. 1956- *ODwPR 91*
D'Atri, Joseph Eugene 1938- *WhoAm 90*
Datri, Tamara Jo 1960- *WhoAmW 91*
Datshkovsky, Jacob 1931- *BiDrAPA 89*
Datskovsky, Boris Abramovich 1960- *WhoE 91*
Datsolai 1835?-1925 *WhNaAH [port]*
Datsolalee 1835?-1925 *WhNaAH [port]*
Datta, Ambika Charan 1928- *BiDrAPA 89*
Datta, Biswa Nath 1941- *WhoWor 91*
Datta, Gouri *BiDrAPA 89*
Datta, Pabitra Kumar *BiDrAPA 89*
Datta, Satya Pall 1926- *BiDrAPA 89*
Datta, Subhendu Kumar 1936- *WhoAm 90*
Dattan, Christopher L *BiDrAPA 89*
D'Attellis, Carlos Enrique 1946- *WhoWor 91*
Dattilo, Anton Michael 1953- *WhoEmL 91*
Dattilo, Dominick A. 1926- *St&PR 91*
Dattilo, Vincent Joseph 1967- *WhoE 91*
Dattner, Richard 1937- *WhoAm 90*
Datuin, Alejandro M *BiDrAPA 89*
Datus, Jay 1914-1974 *WhoAmA 91N*
Datyner, Harry 1923- *IntWWM 90*
Datz, A Mark 1889- *WhoAmA 91N*
Datz, Israel Mortimer 1928- *WhoAm 90*
Datz, Sheldon 1927- *WhoSSW 91*
Dau, John J. 1926- *St&PR 91*
Daub, Gerald Jacob 1953- *WhoEmL 91*

Daub, Hal 1941- *WhoAm 90*
Daub, Matthew Forrest 1951- *WhoAmA 91*
Daub, Peggy E. 1949- *IntWWM 90*
Daub, Richard Paul 1946- *WhoSSW 91*
Daube, David 1909- *WhoAm 90*
Daubel, James Francis 1941- *St&PR 91*
Dauben, Joseph Warren 1944- *WhoE 91*
Dauben, William Garfield 1919- *WhoAm 90*
Daubenas, Jean Dorothy Tenbrinck *WhoAmW 91*
Daubenspeck, Albert Warren 1951- *St&PR 91*
Daubenspeck, Nora Jane 1950- *WhoAmW 91*
Daubenspeck, Robert Donley 1926- *WhoAm 90*
Dauber, Arthur George 1943- *St&PR 91*
Dauber, William P. 1960- *St&PR 91*
Daubert, David Bruce 1945- *WhoEmL 91*
Daubert, Jake 1884-1924 *Ballpl 90 [port]*
Daubert, Thomas Frederick 1930- *WhoE 91*
D'Aubigne, Agrippa 1552-1630 *BioIn 16*
D'Aubigny, Julie *PenDiMP*
Daubler, Wolfgang 1939- *WhoWor 91*
Daubon, Ramon E. 1945- *WhoHisp 91*
Daubs, James Franklin, Jr. 1952- *WhoSSW 91*
Daubs, Michael Steven 1943- *St&PR 91*
D'Aubuisson, Roberto *BioIn 16*
Dauch, Richard E. 1942- *WhoAm 90*
Dauch, Richard Eugene 1942- *St&PR 91*
Daucsavage, Bruce L. 1952- *St&PR 91*
Daud, Ben H. 1939- *St&PR 91*
Daud, Munawar 1954- *WhoWor 91*
Daudelin, Charles 1920- *WhoAmA 91*
Daudet, Alphonse 1840-1897 *AuBYP 90, WorAlBi*
Daudet, Leon 1867-1942 *BiDFrPL, BioIn 16*
Daudt, Valter M 1942- *BiDrAPA 89*
Dauenhauer, Erich Paul 1935- *WhoWor 91*
Dauer, Edward Arnold 1944- *WhoAm 90*
Dauer, Francis Watanabe 1939- *WhoAm 90*
Dauer, Rich 1952- *Ballpl 90*
Daufin, Evie-Kaiulani 1960- *WhoAmW 91*
Daughaday, William Hamilton 1918- *WhoAm 90*
Daughdrill, James Harold, Jr. 1934- *WhoAm 90*
Daughdrill, Roy Wilson 1942- *WhoSSW 91*
Daughenbaugh, Randall J. 1948- *St&PR 91*
Daughenbaugh, Randall Jay 1948- *WhoEmL 91*
Daughenbaugh, Terry L. 1939- *WhoE 91*
Daugherty, Alfred Clark 1923- *St&PR 91, WhoAm 90*
Daugherty, Betty Jane 1920- *WhoAmW 91*
Daugherty, Bettye Dillingham 1936- *WhoAmW 91*
Daugherty, Billy Joe 1923- *WhoAm 90*
Daugherty, Carroll Roop 1900-1988 *BioIn 16*
Daugherty, Charles A. 1917- *St&PR 91*
Daugherty, Charles Michael 1914- *AuBYP 90*
Daugherty, David Martin, Jr. 1951- *WhoEmL 91*
Daugherty, David Reams 1947- *BiDrAPA 89*
Daugherty, Edward Payson 1956- *WhoEmL 91*
Daugherty, Franklin W. 1927- *WhoAm 90*
Daugherty, Frederick Alvin 1914- *WhoAm 90*
Daugherty, Gail Trask 1957- *WhoSSW 91*
Daugherty, Gerald E. 1936- *St&PR 91*
Daugherty, Harris Micajah 1860-1941 *BiDrUSE 89*
Daugherty, Jack Edward 1947- *WhoSSW 91*
Daugherty, James Henry 1889-1974 *AuBYP 90*
Daugherty, James Henry 1898-1974 *WhoAmA 91N*
Daugherty, Jean M. 1931- *WhoAmW 91*
Daugherty, John Thomas 1938- *WhoSSW 91*
Daugherty, Louis E. 1946- *St&PR 91*
Daugherty, Marshall Harrison 1915- *WhoAmA 91*
Daugherty, Martha Jane 1928- *WhoSSW 91*
Daugherty, Michael Dennis 1948- *WhoEmL 91*
Daugherty, Michael F 1942- *WhoAmA 91*
Daugherty, Michele Marie 1963- *WhoSSW 91*
Daugherty, Milton *BiDrAPA 89*
Daugherty, R.C. 1950- *St&PR 91*
Daugherty, Raymond Edward 1946- *St&PR 91*
Daugherty, Richard Bernard 1915- *WhoAm 90*
Daugherty, Robert Melvin, Jr. 1934- *WhoAm 90*
Daugherty, Robert Michael 1949- *IntWWM 90, WhoAm 90, WhoEmL 91*
Daugherty, William L. 1927- *St&PR 91*
Daughters, Robert A 1929- *WhoAmA 91*
Daughton, Christian Gaaei 1948- *WhoEmL 91*
Daughton, Donald 1932- *WhoAm 90, WhoWor 91*
Daughtrey, Max E. 1947- *St&PR 91*
Daughtry, DeWitt Cornell 1914- *WhoAm 90*
Daughtry, Leah Denyatta 1963- *WhoAmW 91*
Daughtry, Pamela 1961- *WhoAmW 91*
Daugs, Edward Herold 1931- *St&PR 91*
Dauguet, Marie 1860-1942 *EncCoWW*
D'Augusta, Alfred M. 1941- *St&PR 91*
Dauk, Regis A. 1941- *St&PR 91*
Daul, George Cecil, Jr. 1942- *BiDrAPA 89*
D'Aulaire, Edgar Parin 1898-1986 *AuBYP 90, BioIn 16, ChlLR 21 [port], WhoAmA 91N*
D'Aulaire, Ingri 1904-1980 *AuBYP 90, ChlLR 21 [port]*
Dauler, L. Van V., Jr. 1943- *St&PR 91*
Dauler, Lee Van Voorhis, Jr. 1943- *WhoE 91*
Dauler, Thomas Pearce *BiDrAPA 89*
D'Aulnoy, Marie *AuBYP 90*
Dault, Raymond Arthur 1923- *WhoAm 90, WhoWor 91*
Daulte, Francois 1928- *BioIn 16*
Daulton, Darren 1962- *Ballpl 90*
Daulton, David Coleman 1937- *St&PR 91, WhoAm 90*
Daum, Annette *BioIn 16*
Daum, Bryan Edwin 1949- *WhoEmL 91*
Daum, Conrad Henry 1943- *BiDrAPA 89, WhoSSW 91*
Daum, David Ernest 1939- *St&PR 91, WhoAm 90*
Daum, Gregory Lee 1947- *WhoE 91*
Daum, John H. 1907- *St&PR 91*
Daum, Kenneth Arno 1931- *St&PR 91*
Daum, Nancy Lee 1957- *WhoEmL 91*
Daum, Robert Charles 1952- *WhoEmL 91*
Dauman, Anatole *BioIn 16*
Dauman, Jan Victor 1942- *WhoWor 91*
Daume, Daphne Marie 1924- *WhoAmW 91*
Daumier, Honore 1808-1879 *BioIn 16, IntDcAA 90, WorAlBi*
Daumus, George Theodore, Jr. 1931- *St&PR 91*
Daun, Mary Agnes 1945- *WhoAmW 91*
Daunis, Alexander B. 1940- *St&PR 91*
Daunt, Jon 1951- *WhoWrEP 89*
Daunter, Maria Teresa 1946- *WhoEmL 91*
Dauphinais, George Arthur 1918- *WhoAm 90*
Dauphinais, I Deborah *BiDrAPA 89*
Dauphinee, James *BioIn 16*
D'Auri, Gino *NewAgMG*
D'Auria, Mark 1955- *WhoE 91*
D'Aurora, James Joseph 1949- *WhoEmL 91*
Daus, Anita Dacpano 1935- *WhoAmW 91*
Daus, Arthur T, Jr. 1934- *BiDrAPA 89*
Daus, George August 1889-1963 *Ballpl 90*
Dauscher, Raymond George 1929- *St&PR 91*
Dauser, Kimberly Ann 1947- *WhoAmW 91, WhoEmL 91*
Dauser, Steven Kent 1952- *WhoSSW 91*
Dauses, Joseph E. 1950- *St&PR 91*
Dauss, Hooks 1889-1963 *Ballpl 90*
Dausset, Jean 1916- *WhoAm 90, WhoWor 91, WorAlBi*
Daussman, Grover Frederick 1919- *WhoAm 90, WhoSSW 91, WhoWor 91*
Daust, Mary Frances 1964- *WhoAmW 91*
Dauster, William Gary 1957- *WhoE 91*
Daut, Steven William 1951- *WhoEmL 91*
Dautel, Charles Shreve 1923- *WhoAm 90*
Dauten, Kent P. *BioIn 16*
Dauterman, Carl Christian *WhoAmA 91*
Dauterman, Carl Christian 1908-1989 *BioIn 16*
Dauterman, James Russell 1941- *St&PR 91*
Dauterman, Steven Lynn 1954- *WhoEmL 91*
Dauth, Frances Kutcher 1941- *WhoAm 90*
D'Autremont, Chester C 1920- *BiDrAPA 89*
Dautresme, Beatrice *BioIn 16*
Dauzat, Samuel Varner 1942- *WhoSSW 91*
Davalillo, Vic 1939- *Ballpl 90*
Davalos, Carlos J. 1951- *WhoHisp 91*
Davancaze, Rosalie Katherine 1964- *WhoAmW 91*
Davani, Bahman Faghaie 1953- *WhoSSW 91*
Davanloo, Habib *BiDrAPA 89*
Davant, James Waring 1917- *WhoAm 90*
Davantzis, Constantine James *BiDrAPA 89*
Davantzis, Maria 1963- *WhoE 91*
D'Avanzo, Victor Nunzio 1935- *WhoSSW 91*
Davar, Adi J. 1935- *WhoE 91*
Davarova, Elmira *WhoAm 90*
Davda, Paresh Jayantilal 1949- *St&PR 91*
Dave, Bhasker J 1943- *BiDrAPA 89*
Dave, Mahendra J 1949- *BiDrAPA 89*
Dave, Mahesh Ratilal 1950- *BiDrAPA 89*
Dave, Peter 1954- *ODwPR 91*
Dave, Raju S. 1958- *WhoEmL 91*
Dave, Uday Vinodray 1937- *WhoSSW 91*
D'Avella, John C. 1948- *St&PR 91*
Daveluy, Raymond 1926- *IntWWM 90*
Davenant, Charles 1656-1714 *BioIn 16*
Davenant, William 1606-1668 *BioIn 16, LitC 13 [port]*
Davenport Brothers *EncO&P 3, EncPaPR 91*
Davenport, Alan Garnett 1932- *WhoAm 90*
Davenport, Ann Adele Mayfield 1941- *WhoAmW 91*
Davenport, Betty Joan 1954- *WhoAmW 91*
Davenport, Carolyn Wesley 1952- *WhoEmL 91*
Davenport, Charles W 1935- *BiDrAPA 89*
Davenport, Chester 1940- *WhoAm 90*
Davenport, Christopher V *BiDrAPA 89*
Davenport, Cow-Cow 1894-1955 *OxCPMus*
Davenport, Dave 1890-1954 *Ballpl 90*
Davenport, David 1950- *WhoAm 90*
Davenport, Debra Ann 1955- *WhoSSW 91*
Davenport, Dona Lee 1931- *WhoAm 90*
Davenport, Edith Fairfax 1880-1957 *WhoAmA 91N*
Davenport, Edwin C. 1940- *St&PR 91*
Davenport, Effie Leighton 1951- *BiDrAPA 89*
Davenport, Elvin L. *BioIn 16*
Davenport, Ernest Harold 1917- *WhoAm 90*
Davenport, Eugene F. *St&PR 91*
Davenport, Fanny Lily Gypsy 1850-1898 *BioIn 16, NotWoAT*
Davenport, Forrest N. 1925- *St&PR 91*
Davenport, Fountain St. Clair 1914- *WhoSSW 91*
Davenport, Glyn 1948- *IntWWM 90*
Davenport, Guy 1927- *LiHiK [port]*
Davenport, Guy Mattison 1927- *WhoWrEP 89*
Davenport, Guy Mattison, Jr. 1927- *WhoAm 90*
Davenport, Gwen 1910- *WhoAm 90, WhoWrEP 89*
Davenport, Gwen Leys 1910-1960 *LiHiK*
Davenport, Harold 1907-1969 *DcScB S2*
Davenport, Homer Calvin 1867-1912 *BioIn 16*
Davenport, Horace Willard 1912- *WhoAm 90*
Davenport, Ira Erastus 1839-1877 *EncPaPR 91*
Davenport, Ira Erastus 1839-1911 *EncO&P 3*
Davenport, James Robert 1943- *WhoSSW 91*
Davenport, Jim 1933- *Ballpl 90*
Davenport, John 1597-1669 *EncCRAm*
Davenport, John 1597?-1670 *WorAlBi*
Davenport, John Alun 1946- *IntWWM 90*
Davenport, John L. 1906-1988 *BioIn 16*
Davenport, John T. 1930- *St&PR 91*
Davenport, Joseph Dale 1931- *WhoSSW 91*
Davenport, Karen Odom 1953- *WhoWrEP 89*
Davenport, Kay 1950- *St&PR 91*
Davenport, LaNoue 1922- *IntWWM 90*
Davenport, Lawrence Franklin 1944- *WhoAm 90*
Davenport, Lee L. 1915- *St&PR 91*
Davenport, Linda G. 1949- *St&PR 91*
Davenport, Manuel Manson 1929- *WhoAm 90*
Davenport, Marcia 1903- *AuBYP 90*
Davenport, Millia 1895- *BioIn 16*
Davenport, Millia Crotty 1895- *NotWoAT*
Davenport, Pamela Beaver 1948- *WhoAmW 91*
Davenport, Patricia Jennings 1959- *WhoAmW 91*
Davenport, Patricia Marie 1948- *WhoE 91*
Davenport, Paul *WhoAm 90*
Davenport, Paul 1946- *ConAu 132*
Davenport, Paul S., Jr. 1941- *St&PR 91*
Davenport, Ray 1926- *WhoAmA 91*
Davenport, Rebecca Read 1943- *WhoAmA 91*
Davenport, Robert *BioIn 16*
Davenport, Roger 1946- *ConAu 131*
Davenport, Selina 1779-1856? *FemiCLE*
Davenport, Thomas Ira 1923- *WhoAm 90*
Davenport, Wilbur Bayley, Jr. 1920- *WhoAm 90*
Davenport, William David 1954- *WhoSSW 91*
Davenport, William Harold 1935- *WhoSSW 91*
Davenport, William Henry 1841-1877 *EncO&P 3*
Davenport, William Henry 1841-1911 *EncPaPR 91*
Davenport, William Kirk 1928- *St&PR 91*
Davenport, William Wyatt 1916- *WhoWor 91*
Davenport, Wortham David 1935- *WhoE 91*
Daver, Edul Minoo 1944- *St&PR 91*
Daverat, Jean Vincent 1927- *WhoWor 91*
Daverne, Gary Michiel 1939- *IntWWM 90*
Da Verrazano, Giovanni 1485?-1527 *BioIn 16*
Daversa, Joseph James, Jr. 1940- *BiDrAPA 89*
Daves, Mark Duane 1960- *WhoSSW 91*
Daves, Michael 1938- *AuBYP 90*
Davey, Anthony John 1925- *WhoAm 90*
Davey, Bruce James 1927- *St&PR 91, WhoAm 90*
Davey, Charles Bingham 1928- *WhoAm 90*
Davey, Clark William 1928- *St&PR 91, WhoAm 90*
Davey, Don *BioIn 16*
Davey, Frank 1850-1937 *AmLegL*
Davey, Frank 1940- *ConAu 32NR*
Davey, Gerard Paul 1949- *WhoEmL 91*
Davey, Janet Calonge 1956- *WhoWrEP 89*
Davey, Janet Christopherson 1928- *WhoAmW 91*
Davey, Jocelyn 1908- *TwCCr&M 91*
Davey, Keith *BioIn 16*
Davey, Kenneth George 1932- *WhoAm 90*
Davey, Kent Ritter 1952- *WhoSSW 91*
Davey, Lycurgus Michael 1918- *WhoAm 90, WhoWor 91*
Davey, Randall 1887-1964 *WhoAmA 91N*
Davey, Robert Charles 1938- *WhoE 91*
Davey, Ronald A *WhoAmA 91*
Davey, S. John 1864-1891 *EncPaPR 91*
Davey, S. T. *EncO&P 3*
Davi, Antonio E. 1924- *St&PR 91*
Davi, Robert *BioIn 16*
Davia, Federico 1933- *IntWWM 90*
Daviau, Donald G 1927- *ConAu 32NR*
David 11--?BC-973?BC *WorAlBi*
David, King of Israel *BioIn 16*
David, Ariel *BiDrAPA 89*
David, Avram 1930- *IntWWM 90*
David, Bruce Edward 1952- *WhoWrEP 89*
David, Bruce Kent 1947- *WhoEmL 91*
David, Catherine Anne 1963- *WhoAmW 91*
David, Charles B 1912- *BiDrAPA 89*
David, Clive 1934- *WhoAm 90, WhoWor 91*
David, Cyril Frank 1920- *WhoAmA 91*
David, Don Raymond 1906- *WhoAmA 91, WhoE 91*
David, Edward Emil, Jr. 1925- *WhoAm 90*
David, Edward Joseph 1942- *WhoE 91*
David, Eric Henri 1943- *WhoWor 91*
David, Eugene *AuBYP 90*
David, Ferdinand 1810-1873 *PenDiMP*
David, Gabriel Samuel 1951- *WhoE 91, WhoEmL 91*
David, Gabrielle 1947- *WhoEmL 91*
David, Gary Lynn 1964- *WhoE 91*
David, George *BiDrAPA 89*
David, George 1948- *St&PR 91*
David, George Alfred Lawrence 1942- *WhoAm 90*
David, George Franklin, III 1923- *St&PR 91*
David, Gerard 1450?-1523 *IntDcAA 90*
David, Hal *WhoAm 90*
David, Heinz 1931- *WhoWor 91*
David, Henry Philip 1923- *WhoE 91*
David, Herbert Aron 1925- *WhoAm 90*
David, Hugh 1954- *ConAu 129*
David, Iosif Leib *BiDrAPA 89*
David, Jack 1946- *ConAu 30NR*
David, Jack E. 1937- *St&PR 91*
David, Jacqueline 1951- *WhoE 91*
David, Jacques-Henri *BioIn 16*
David, Jacques Louis 1748-1825 *IntDcAA 90, PenDiDA 89, WorAlBi*
David, James Milton 1942- *St&PR 91*
David, Jean Robert 1931- *WhoWor 91*
David, Joe 1947- *ODwPR 91*
David, Joseph Jordan 1953- *BiDrAPA 89*
David, Judy Breiner 1938- *WhoAm 90, WhoAmW 91*
David, Keith *ConTFT 8 [port]*
David, Larry *NewAgMG*
David, Laurent-Olivier 1824-1926 *OxCCanT*
David, Leon Thomas 1901- *WhoWor 91*
David, Lloyd 1941- *WhoE 91*
David, Lynn Allen 1948- *WhoEmL 91*
David, Mark Steven 1951- *WhoEmL 91*
David, Martha Lena Huffaker 1925- *WhoAmW 91*
David, Martin A. 1939- *WhoWrEP 89*
David, Martin Heidenhain 1935- *WhoAm 90*

David, Melvin J. 1915- *St&PR 91*
David, Michael William 1949- *WhoWor 91*
David, Michel Louis 1945- *WhoAm 90*
David, Mildred 1935- *WhoAmW 91*
David, Miles 1926- *WhoAm 90*
David, Miriam Lang 1945- *WhoAmW 91*
David, Murphy Samuel 1931- *WhoWor 91*
David, Neal O. 1950- *St&PR 91*
David, Panakkal U S *BiDrAPA 89*
David, Paul *BiDrAPA 89*
David, Paul P *BiDrAPA 89*
David, Paul Theodore 1906- *WhoAm 90*
David, Philip 1931- *St&PR 91, WhoE 91, WhoWor 91*
David, Pierre *BiDrAPA 89*
David, R. W. *ConAu 129*
David, Richard 1912- *ConAu 129*
David, Richard Francis 1938- *WhoAm 90*
David, Richard H. 1931- *St&PR 91*
David, Robert Jefferson 1943- *WhoWor 91*
David, Robyn Sue 1958- *WhoE 91*
David, Romeo Soliman 1934- *WhoWor 91*
David, Ronald Albert 1951- *WhoEmL 91*
David, Ronald C. *ODwPR 91*
David, Ronald S 1940- *BiDrAPA 89*
David, Shirley Hart 1949- *WhoEmL 91*
David, Stefansson *DcScanL*
David, Stephen Paul 1957- *WhoEmL 91*
David, Theresa 1959- *WhoAmW 91*
David, Therese de Sonneville- 1938-1988 *BioIn 16*
David, Thomas Christian 1925- *IntWWM 90*
David, Thomas Meredith 1941- *WhoAm 90*
David, Traci Lynn *BiDrAPA 89*
David, Wilfred Lascelles 1938- *WhoE 91*
David-Neel, Alexandra 1868-1969 *EncO&P 3*
David-Weill, Michel Alexandre 1932- *WhoAm 90*
David-West, Haig 1946- *ConDes 90*
Davidek, Stefan 1924- *WhoAmA 91*
Davidge, Robert Cunninghame, Jr. 1942- *WhoAm 90*
Davidian, Tim N. 1946- *St&PR 91*
Davidman, Howard *BiDrAPA 89*
Davidoff, E. Martin 1952- *WhoE 91*
Davidoff, Howard 1956- *WhoEmL 91*
Davidoff, Leonore 1932- *WhoWor 91*
Davidoff, Robert George 1926- *St&PR 91*
Davidoff, Roger 1949- *WhoE 91*
Davidoff, Ronald Jay *BiDrAPA 89*
Davidoff, Stephen Harry 1938- *WhoE 91*
Davidoff, Zino *BioIn 16*
Davidoff-Hirsch, Helen 1929- *BiDrAPA 89*
Davidon, William Cooper 1927- *WhoAm 90*
Davidova-Medene, Lea 1921- *BiDWomA*
Davidovich, Bella *BioIn 16*
Davidovich, Bella 1928- *IntWWM 90, PenDiMP, WhoAm 90, WhoAmW 91*
Davidovich, Jaime 1936- *WhoAmA 91, WhoE 91*
Davidovici, Robert 1946- *IntWWM 90*
Davidoviciu, Adrian Victor Gheorghe A. 1938- *WhoWor 91*
Davidovsky, Mario 1934- *IntWWM 90, WhoAm 90, WorAlBi*
Davidow, Glenn Robert 1958- *WhoEmL 91*
Davidow, Jeffrey 1944- *WhoAm 90, WhoWor 91*
Davidow, Leonard S. 1900-1989 *BioIn 16*
Davidow, Robert 1947- *WhoAm 90, WhoEmL 91*
Davidow, Stanley *St&PR 91*
Davidow, William Henry 1935- *St&PR 91*
Davidowitz, Sherman 1927- *St&PR 91*
Davids, Daniel Joseph 1955- *WhoEmL 91*
Davids, Glenn Corey 1951- *WhoEmL 91*
Davids, Hollace Goodman 1947- *WhoEmL 91*
Davids, L. Roberts 1926- *Ballpl 90*
Davids, Meryl Anne 1961- *WhoEmL 91*
Davids, Norman 1918- *WhoAm 90*
Davids, Robert Norman 1938- *WhoWor 91*
Davidse, Gerard John, II 1953- *WhoE 91*
Davidsen, Arthur F. 1944- *WhoAm 90*
Davidson, Abraham A. 1935- *WhoAm 90, WhoAmA 91*
Davidson, Alan John 1938- *St&PR 91*
Davidson, Alexander Turnbull 1947- *St&PR 91*
Davidson, Alfred E. 1911- *WhoAm 90*
Davidson, Alice Joyce 1932- *BioIn 16*
Davidson, Allain G., Jr. 1943- *St&PR 91*
Davidson, Allan Albert 1913-1988 *WhoAmA 91N*
Davidson, Allen E *BiDrAPA 89*
Davidson, Anne Stowell 1949- *WhoAmW 91*
Davidson, Anne Stripling *BiDrAPA 89*
Davidson, Anthony Lewis *BioIn 16*
Davidson, Arnold 1912- *BiDrAPA 89*
Davidson, Audrey Jean Ekdahl 1930- *IntWWM 90*
Davidson, Avram 1923- *RGTwCSF*
Davidson, Barbara Taylor 1920- *WhoAmW 91*
Davidson, Barry Rodney 1943- *WhoSSW 91*
Davidson, Bill *AuBYP 90, BioIn 16*
Davidson, Bill 1918- *WhoWor 91*
Davidson, Brian Y. 1933- *St&PR 91, WhoAm 90*
Davidson, Bruce Merrill 1924- *WhoAm 90*
Davidson, Carl B. 1933- *WhoAm 90*
Davidson, Carl Barry 1933- *St&PR 91*
Davidson, Carl Thomas, Jr. 1961- *WhoSSW 91*
Davidson, Cathy Notari 1949- *WhoAm 90*
Davidson, Chalmers Gaston 1907- *WhoAm 90, WhoWrEP 89*
Davidson, Charles Henry 1920- *WhoAm 90*
Davidson, Charles Sprecher 1910- *WhoAm 90, WhoE 91*
Davidson, Charles T. 1940- *St&PR 91*
Davidson, Charles Tompkins 1940- *WhoAm 90, WhoSSW 91*
Davidson, Charlotte Dale *St&PR 91*
Davidson, Cheryl Adair 1949- *St&PR 91*
Davidson, Chester D. *AmLegL*
Davidson, Colin Henry 1928- *WhoAm 90*
Davidson, Crow Girard 1910- *WhoAm 90*
Davidson, Dalwyn Robert 1918- *WhoAm 90*
Davidson, Daniel Everett 1949- *WhoEmL 91*
Davidson, David L *BiDrAPA 89*
Davidson, David Scott 1925- *WhoAm 90*
Davidson, Deborah 1951- *WhoAmW 91*
Davidson, Dennis Keith 1941- *St&PR 91*
Davidson, Don *BioIn 16*
Davidson, Don-Lee M. 1930- *St&PR 91*
Davidson, Donald *BioIn 16*
Davidson, Donald 1917- *WorAu 1980 [port]*
Davidson, Donald 1921- *St&PR 91*
Davidson, Donald Herbert 1917- *WhoAm 90*
Davidson, Donald Matthew 1958- *WhoEmL 91*
Davidson, Donald William 1938- *WhoAm 90, WhoE 91*
Davidson, Douglas Alvin 1936- *St&PR 91*
Davidson, Duane Clarc 1937- *WhoE 91*
Davidson, Duncan Mowbray 1953- *WhoEmL 91*
Davidson, Edith Young 1940- *WhoE 91*
Davidson, Edmund B. 1936- *St&PR 91*
Davidson, Edward W., Jr. 1937- *St&PR 91*
Davidson, Edwin M 1925- *BiDrAPA 89*
Davidson, Eldon Ray 1958- *WhoSSW 91*
Davidson, Elizabeth H Donnally 1948- *WhoAmA 91*
Davidson, Eric Harris 1937- *WhoAm 90*
Davidson, Ernest Roy 1936- *WhoAm 90*
Davidson, Eugene Abraham 1930- *WhoAm 90*
Davidson, Eugene Arthur 1902- *WhoAm 90*
Davidson, Ezra C., Jr. *BioIn 16*
Davidson, Ezra C., Jr. 1933- *WhoAm 90*
Davidson, Faye Rowe 1929- *WhoSSW 91*
Davidson, Fred, III 1941- *WhoAm 90*
Davidson, Frederic McShan 1941- *WhoAm 90*
Davidson, G. Don, Jr. 1919- *St&PR 91*
Davidson, Gary 1946- *St&PR 91*
Davidson, Gary Edward 1959- *WhoEmL 91*
Davidson, George A., Jr. 1938- *WhoAm 90, WhoE 91*
Davidson, George H. 1944- *St&PR 91*
Davidson, Glen Everette 1925- *St&PR 91*
Davidson, Glen Harris 1941- *WhoAm 90, WhoSSW 91*
Davidson, Gloria Lockett 1928- *WhoSSW 91*
Davidson, Gordon 1933- *WhoAm 90*
Davidson, Gordon Byron 1926- *WhoAm 90*
Davidson, Gordon Chambers 1927- *St&PR 91*
Davidson, Grace Evelyn 1920- *WhoAmW 91*
Davidson, Greg 1961- *ConAu 129*
Davidson, H. Justin 1930- *St&PR 91*
Davidson, Harold H 1923- *BiDrAPA 89*
Davidson, Harry Lee 1956- *WhoEmL 91*
Davidson, Herbert Alan 1932- *WhoAm 90*
Davidson, Herbert Laurence 1930- *WhoAmA 91*
Davidson, Herbert M., Jr. 1925- *WhoAm 90*
Davidson, Herbert S. 1922- *St&PR 91*
Davidson, Honey Iris 1959- *WhoAmW 91*
Davidson, Howard Steven 1955- *St&PR 91*
Davidson, Ian Bruce 1931- *St&PR 91*
Davidson, Ian J 1925- *WhoAmA 91*
Davidson, Israel 1870-1939 *BioIn 16*
Davidson, Jack Leroy 1927- *WhoAm 90*
Davidson, James A. *BioIn 16*
Davidson, James Arthur 1946- *WhoEmL 91*
Davidson, James Dale 1947- *WhoE 91*
Davidson, James E. 1957- *St&PR 91*
Davidson, James Joseph, Jr. 1904- *WhoAm 90*
Davidson, Jean *WhoAmA 91*
Davidson, Jeannie *BioIn 16*
Davidson, Jeffery H. 1946- *St&PR 91*
Davidson, Jeffrey H. 1952- *WhoEmL 91*
Davidson, Jessica Ursula 1914- *IntWWM 90*
Davidson, Jill Elaine 1962- *WhoAmW 91*
Davidson, Jo 1883-1952 *WhoAmA 91N*
Davidson, Joan *BiDrAPA 89*
Davidson, Joan 1894-1985 *DcNaB 1981*
Davidson, Joan K. 1927- *St&PR 91*
Davidson, John *BiDrAPA 89*
Davidson, John 1916- *WhoAm 90*
Davidson, John 1941- *BioIn 16, WhoAm 90, WorAlBi*
Davidson, John F. *BioIn 16*
Davidson, John Frederick 1908-1989 *BioIn 16*
Davidson, John Herbert 1938- *St&PR 91*
Davidson, John Keay, III 1922- *WhoAm 90*
Davidson, John Kenneth, Sr. 1939- *WhoAm 90, WhoWor 91*
Davidson, John Lefler, Jr. 1915- *WhoAm 90*
Davidson, John Melvin 1929- *BiDrAPA 89*
Davidson, John Pirnie 1924- *WhoAm 90*
Davidson, Jonathan R T 1943- *BiDrAPA 89*
Davidson, Joy 1940- *IntWWM 90*
Davidson, Joy Elaine 1940- *WhoAm 90*
Davidson, Juli 1960- *WhoAmW 91*
Davidson, Karen Sue 1950- *WhoAmW 91, WhoWor 91*
Davidson, Kenneth Harvey 1941- *WhoE 91*
Davidson, Lacinda Susan 1958- *WhoAmW 91*
Davidson, Laura *ODwPR 91*
Davidson, Leah 1926- *BiDrAPA 89, WhoE 91*
Davidson, Lionel 1922- *TwCCr&M 91*
Davidson, Lorimer A. 1902- *St&PR 91*
Davidson, Louis Douglas 1956- *WhoE 91*
Davidson, Lucretia Maria 1808-1825 *FemiCLE*
Davidson, Lucy Ellen 1950- *BiDrAPA 89*
Davidson, Lynda S. 1934- *St&PR 91*
Davidson, M. Bernice 1935- *WhoAmW 91*
Davidson, Marcella Schools 1952- *WhoAmW 91*
Davidson, Margaret 1787-1844 *FemiCLE*
Davidson, Margaret 1936- *AuBYP 90*
Davidson, Margaret M. 1823-1838 *BioAmW*
Davidson, Margaret Miller 1823-1838 *FemiCLE*
Davidson, Marie Diane 1924- *WhoAmW 91*
Davidson, Marina Elaina Papailiou 1945- *WhoE 91*
Davidson, Mark 1961- *Ballpl 90*
Davidson, Mark Steven 1959- *WhoSSW 91*
Davidson, Marshall B. *BioIn 16*
Davidson, Marshall B 1907-1989 *ConAu 129*
Davidson, Martha Ellen *BiDrAPA 89*
Davidson, Marty *BioIn 16*
Davidson, Mary Frances Logue 1958- *WhoAmW 91*
Davidson, Mary S 1940- *SmATA 61 [port]*
Davidson, Mary Wallace 1935- *IntWWM 90*
Davidson, Max D. 1899-1977 *BioIn 16*
Davidson, Maxwell, III 1939- *WhoAmA 91*
Davidson, Mayer B. 1935- *WhoAm 90*
Davidson, Melanie *ConAu 129*
Davidson, Melvin L. 1936- *St&PR 91*
Davidson, Michael 1940- *WhoAm 90*
Davidson, Michael Howard 1947- *WhoSSW 91*
Davidson, Michael Walker 1947- *WhoAm 90*
Davidson, Mike T. 1936- *WhoSSW 91*
Davidson, Morris 1898-1979 *WhoAmA 91N*
Davidson, Nancy *WhoAmA 91*
Davidson, Nancy Brachman 1943- *WhoE 91*
Davidson, Norman Ralph 1916- *WhoAm 90*
Davidson, Odie Ray 1930- *St&PR 91*
Davidson, P. Marques 1939- *St&PR 91*
Davidson, P Waverly, III 1934- *BiDrAPA 89*
Davidson, Park R. 1934- *St&PR 91*
Davidson, Paul 1930- *WhoSSW 91*
Davidson, Paul L. 1911- *St&PR 91*
Davidson, Paul Patrick 1956- *WhoEmL 91*
Davidson, Peter J 1956- *BiDrAPA 89*
Davidson, Peter Warner 1959- *WhoE 91*
Davidson, Philip D. 1931- *St&PR 91*
Davidson, Philip Harold 1944- *WhoAm 90*
Davidson, Phillip B. 1915- *ConAu 130*
Davidson, Phillip T. 1925- *St&PR 91*
Davidson, Ralph *BioIn 16*
Davidson, Ralph Kirby 1921- *WhoAm 90*
Davidson, Ralph Parsons 1927- *St&PR 91, WhoAm 90, WhoE 91*
Davidson, Richard Dodge 1945- *WhoSSW 91*
Davidson, Richard John 1954- *St&PR 91*
Davidson, Richard K. 1942- *St&PR 91, WhoAm 90*
Davidson, Richard Laurence 1941- *WhoAm 90*
Davidson, Robert A. 1947- *St&PR 91*
Davidson, Robert Bruce 1945- *WhoAm 90, WhoEmL 91*
Davidson, Robert E 1936- *BiDrAPA 89*
Davidson, Robert Gage 1940- *WhoSSW 91*
Davidson, Robert Laurenson Dashiell 1909- *WhoAm 90*
Davidson, Robert Lee, III 1923- *WhoWrEP 89*
Davidson, Robert Meyer 1943- *St&PR 91*
Davidson, Robert Michael 1941- *WhoE 91*
Davidson, Roger Harry 1936- *WhoAm 90*
Davidson, Ronald Crosby 1941- *WhoAm 90*
Davidson, Ronald Jay 1946- *BiDrAPA 89*
Davidson, Sandra 1935- *AuBYP 90*
Davidson, Sandra Lee Dresman 1947- *WhoEmL 91*
Davidson, Satch 1936- *Ballpl 90*
Davidson, Sigmund Edward 1922- *St&PR 91*
Davidson, Simon David 1927- *St&PR 91*
Davidson, Stanley 1894-1981 *DcNaB 1981*
Davidson, Steven C. 1953- *St&PR 91*
Davidson, Steven Durbin 1961- *WhoEmL 91*
Davidson, Suzette Morton 1911- *WhoAmA 91*
Davidson, Ted 1939- *Ballpl 90*
Davidson, Thomas Maxwell 1937- *St&PR 91, WhoAm 90*
Davidson, Thomas N. 1939- *St&PR 91*
Davidson, Thomas Noel 1939- *WhoAm 90*
Davidson, Thyra 1926- *BioIn 16, WhoAmA 91*
Davidson, Tina 1952- *IntWWM 90*
Davidson, Van Michael, Jr. 1945- *WhoWor 91*
Davidson, Virginia M T 1940- *BiDrAPA 89*
Davidson, Walter A. *BioIn 16*
Davidson, Wendell Arthur 1927- *St&PR 91*
Davidson, William *AuBYP 90, WhoSSW 91*
Davidson, William D *BiDrAPA 89*
Davidson, William Ellis *BiDrAPA 89*
Davidson, William George, III 1938- *WhoWor 91*
Davidson, William M. 1921- *WhoAm 90*
Davidson, William Ward, III 1940- *WhoWor 91*
Davidson, Young Ock 1936- *BiDrAPA 89*
Davie, Alastair *ODwPR 91*
Davie, Audrey Nelsene 1961- *WhoAmW 91*
Davie, Donald 1922- *MajTwCW*
Davie, Donald Alfred 1922- *WhoAm 90*
Davie, Elspeth *BioIn 16, FemiCLE*
Davie, Emily 1915-1989 *BioIn 16*
Davie, John L. 1850-1934 *BioIn 16*
Davie, Joseph Myrten 1939- *WhoAm 90*
Davie, Malcolm Henderson 1918- *WhoE 91, WhoWor 91*
Davie, Maxie 1935- *ODwPR 91*
Davie, Ronald B. 1934- *WhoAm 90*
Davie, Theodore 1852-1898 *DcCanB 12*
Davie, William Richardson 1756-1820 *BioIn 16*
Daviee, Jerry Michael 1947- *WhoAmA 91*
Davies, Alan V. *BioIn 16*
Davies, Alfred Robert 1933- *WhoAm 90*
Davies, Alma *WhoE 91*
Davies, Arabella 1753-1787 *FemiCLE*
Davies, Arthur 1950- *IntWWM 90*
Davies, Arthur B. 1862-1928 *BioIn 16*
Davies, Arthur Bowen 1862-1928 *WorAlBi*
Davies, Barbara Jane 1948- *WhoE 91*
Davies, Ben 1858-1943 *PenDiMP*
Davies, Bob *NewYTBS 90*
Davies, Bob 1920-1990 *BioIn 16*
Davies, Brian Ewart 1937- *WhoWor 91*
Davies, C.J. David 1936- *St&PR 91*
Davies, Catherine Therese 1955- *WhoAmW 91*
Davies, Cecilia 1750?-1836 *PenDiMP*
Davies, Christopher J. 1959- *WhoEmL 91*
Davies, Cyril 1932-1964 *EncPR&S 89*
Davies, Daniel R. 1911- *WhoAm 90*
Davies, David *BioIn 16*
Davies, David George 1928- *WhoAm 90*
Davies, David Keith 1940- *WhoAm 90, WhoWor 91*
Davies, David Llewellyn 1941- *WhoE 91*
Davies, David Reginald 1927- *WhoAm 90*

Davies, David Somerville 1954- IntWWM 90
Davies, Dennis Russell 1944- IntWWM 90, PenDiMP
Davies, Donald Lewis BiDrAPA 89
Davies, Donald Thomas 1948- WhoWor 91
Davies, Donald Watts 1924- WhoWor 91
Davies, Duane Alan 1953- St&PR 91
Davies, Dwight Randell 1946- WhoE 91
Davies, E. Jerry 1941- ODwPR 91
Davies, Edward James 1933- St&PR 91
Davies, Eiluned IntWWM 90
Davies, Eleanor 1590-1652 BiDEWW
Davies, Eleanor 1598?-1652 BioIn 16
Davies, Eleanor 1603-1652 EncO&P 3
Davies, Elizabeth Ursula 1958- WhoWor 91
Davies, Elmer David 1926- WhoSSW 91
Davies, Emily 1830-1921 BioIn 16, FemiCLE
Davies, Evan Thomas 1919- St&PR 91
Davies, Fanny 1861-1934 PenDiMP
Davies, Frank Edward 1923- WhoAm 90
Davies, Gail 1948- BioIn 16
Davies, Gareth John 1944- WhoAm 90
Davies, George M 1926- BiDrAPA 89
Davies, Gerald Andrew 1957- WhoWrEP 89
Davies, Gerald Keith 1944- WhoSSW 91
Davies, Glyn 1919- WhoWor 91
Davies, Graham John 1953- St&PR 91
Davies, Gregory Lane 1951- WhoEmL 91
Davies, Harry Clayton 1940- WhoAmA 91
Davies, Haydn Llewellyn 1921- WhoAmA 91
Davies, Hazel Anne 1937- IntWWM 90
Davies, Helen 1940- IntWWM 90
Davies, Horton Marlais 1916- WhoAm 90
Davies, Hugh Llewelyn 1924- WhoWor 91
Davies, Hugh Marlais 1948- WhoAm 90, WhoAmA 91
Davies, Hugh Seymour 1943- IntWWM 90
Davies, Hunter 1936- BioIn 16
Davies, Ioan PenDiMP
Davies, Jack L. 1923- St&PR 91
Davies, James A. 1939- ConAu 129
Davies, James Arthur 1930- WhoAm 90
Davies, James Chowning 1918- WhoAm 90
Davies, James Garfield BioIn 16
Davies, James Scott 1958- WhoEmL 91
Davies, Jane Badger 1913- WhoAmW 91, WhoE 91
Davies, Joan 1934- BioIn 16
Davies, John Arthur 1927- WhoAm 90
Davies, John B. 1937- St&PR 91
Davies, John Benjamin 1931- BiDrAPA 89
Davies, John Dale 1927- St&PR 91
Davies, John E. 1936- St&PR 91
Davies, John Edward 1936- WhoE 91
Davies, John H. 1936- St&PR 91
Davies, John Huw 1935- IntWWM 90
Davies, John Nigel 1950- IntWWM 90
Davies, John Paton 1908- BioIn 16
Davies, John Picton 1920- WhoWor 91
Davies, John Sherrard 1917- WhoAm 90
Davies, Joseph Edward 1876-1958 BioIn 16
Davies, Kenneth 1928- WhoAm 90
Davies, Kenneth Southworth 1925- WhoAmA 91
Davies, Kent Richard 1947- WhoWrEP 89
Davies, L P 1914- TwCCr&M 91
Davies, Lee A. ODwPR 91
Davies, Lee A. 1950- St&PR 91
Davies, Lyndon 1944- IntWWM 90
Davies, Marcus Owen 1928- St&PR 91
Davies, Marianne 1744-1818? PenDiMP
Davies, Marilyn Anne 1949- WhoEmL 91
Davies, Marion 1900-1961 WorAlBi
Davies, Marion C. 1897-1961 BioAmW
Davies, Marvin H. 1907- St&PR 91
Davies, Meredith 1922- IntWWM 90, PenDiMP
Davies, Merlyn Kingsley 1940- St&PR 91
Davies, Michael John 1944- WhoAm 90, WhoE 91
Davies, Michael L. St&PR 91
Davies, Ogden R. 1913- St&PR 91
Davies, Olive Morris BiDrAPA 89
Davies, P C W ConAu 31NR
Davies, Paul 1946- ConAu 31NR
Davies, Paul Lewis, Jr. 1930- WhoAm 90
Davies, Peter 1937- BioIn 16
Davies, Peter John 1940- WhoAm 90
Davies, Peter Maxwell 1934- IntWWM 90, PenDiMP A, WhoWor 91
Davies, Ray 1944- ConMus 5 [port], WorAlBi
Davies, Ray George Andrew 1939- WhoWor 91
Davies, Raymond Douglas 1944- WhoAm 90
Davies, Richard Llewelyn 1912-1981 DcNaB 1981
Davies, Richard Townsend 1920- WhoAm 90
Davies, Richard Warren 1946- St&PR 91
Davies, Robert 1940- St&PR 91
Davies, Robert Abel, III 1935- WhoAm 90
Davies, Robert Allan 1928- WhoWrEP 89
Davies, Robert Ernest 1919- WhoAm 90
Davies, Robert Evan 1931- St&PR 91
Davies, Robert K 1936- BiDrAPA 89
Davies, Robert Terry 1943- St&PR 91
Davies, Robertson 1913- BioIn 16, MajTwCW, OxCCanT, WhoAm 90, WhoWrEP 89, WorAlBi
Davies, Ronald Edward George 1921- WhoE 91
Davies, Ronald F. 1932- St&PR 91
Davies, Ryland 1943- IntWWM 90, PenDiMP
Davies, S. Connally 1961- WhoAmW 91
Davies, Samuel 1723-1761 EncCRAm
Davies, Stanley Smyth 1923- St&PR 91
Davies, Suzanne Kaye 1940- St&PR 91
Davies, Terence BioIn 16
Davies, Theodore Peter 1928- WhoAm 90, WhoAmA 91
Davies, Thomas Mockett, Jr. 1940- WhoAm 90
Davies, Tudor 1892-1958 PenDiMP
Davies, Victor 1939- IntWWM 90
Davies, Vonda Sines 1947- WhoAmW 91
Davies, William D., Jr. 1928- WhoAm 90
Davies, William Robertson 1913- BioIn 16
Davies, Wyn 1952- IntWWM 90
Davies-McNair, Jane 1922- WhoWor 91
Davies-Owens, Shirley 1937- WhoWrEP 89
Daviess, Maria Thompson 1872-1924 LiHiK
Davignon, Etienne 1932- BioIn 16
Davila, Bill NewAgMG
Davila, Elisa 1944- WhoAmW 91
Davila, Maritza 1952- WhoAmA 91
Davila, Robert Refugio 1932- WhoHisp 91
Davila, Sonia J. 1942- WhoHisp 91
Davila, Virgilio 1869-1943 ConAu 131, HispWr 90
Davila, William 1931- WhoHisp 91
Davila, William S. 1931- WhoAm 90
Davila-Colon, Luis R. 1952- WhoHisp 91
Davila-Johnston, Ruth Marie 1960- WhoAmW 91
Davila-Katz, Nicolas BiDrAPA 89
Davin, D M 1913- ConAu 30NR
Davin, Dan ConAu 30NR
Davin, James Manson 1945- St&PR 91, WhoWor 91
Davin, James Martin 1958- WhoSSW 91
Davin, Nicholas Flood 1840?-1901 DcLB 99 [port]
Davin, Nicholas Flood 1843-1901 OxCCanT
Da Vinci, Leonardo 1452-1519 BioIn 16
Davio, Joseph A. 1951- St&PR 91
Davion, Anthony EncCRAm
Davion, Ethel Johnson 1948- WhoAmW 91
Daviot, Gordon TwCCr&M 91
Daviot, Gordon 1896-1952 BioIn 16
Davis, A. Arthur 1928- WhoAm 90
Davis, A. Dano 1945- St&PR 91, WhoAm 90, WhoSSW 91
Davis, A. Jann 1941- WhoWrEP 89
Davis, Adelle 1904-1974 ConAu 30NR, WorAlBi
Davis, Al BioIn 16
Davis, Al 1929- WorAlBi
Davis, Alan Jay 1937- WhoAm 90
Davis, Alan V. 1953- St&PR 91
Davis, Albert 1923- St&PR 91
Davis, Alexander Jackson 1803-1892 BioIn 16, PenDiDA 89
Davis, Alfred Carl 1941- WhoSSW 91
Davis, Alfred Lewis 1941- WhoSSW 91
Davis, Alice J. 1929- WhoAmW 91
Davis, Alice Taylor 1903- BioIn 16
Davis, Alice Taylor 1903-1989 ConAu 129
Davis, Alice V. Gunn 1918- IntWWM 90
Davis, Alison ODwPR 91
Davis, Allan S. 1926- St&PR 91
Davis, Allen 1929- WhoAm 90
Davis, Allen, III 1929- WhoWrEP 89
Davis, Allen Freeman 1931- WhoAm 90
Davis, Alonzo Joseph 1942- WhoAmA 91
Davis, Alvin 1960- Ballpl 90
Davis, Alvin E 1914- BiDrAPA 89
Davis, Amos BiDrAPA 89
Davis, Andrea Denise 1964- WhoAmW 91
Davis, Andrew 1944- PenDiMP
Davis, Andrew Frank 1944- IntWWM 90, WhoAm 90, WhoE 91
Davis, Andrew George 1956- WhoEmL 91
Davis, Andrew Hambley, Jr. 1937- WhoE 91, WhoWor 91
Davis, Andrew Jackson 1826-1910 EncO&P 3, EncPaPR 91
Davis, Angela 1944- EncAL, WorAlBi
Davis, Angela Y. 1944- BioAmW, FemiCLE
Davis, Angela Yvonne 1944- BioIn 16
Davis, Ann Janette 1942- WhoAmW 91
Davis, Ann-Marie 1951- WhoWrEP 89
Davis, Anna Marie 1946- WhoAmW 91
Davis, Annette Brock 1909- WhoSSW 91
Davis, Anthony BioIn 16
Davis, Anthony 1938- WhoWor 91
Davis, Anthony 1951- CurBio 90 [port], WhoAm 90
Davis, Anthony Michael John 1939- WhoSSW 91
Davis, Archie Darryl 1945- WhoSSW 91
Davis, Arnold 1947- WhoEmL 91
Davis, Arthur D. 1947- St&PR 91
Davis, Arthur David WhoAm 90
Davis, Arthur Edward 1943- WhoSSW 91
Davis, Arthur Horace 1917- WhoAm 90, WhoWor 91
Davis, Arthur Quentin 1920- WhoAm 90
Davis, Arthur Vining 1867-1962 BioIn 16
Davis, Asa Eugene Johnny 1941- WhoSSW 91
Davis, Audrey ConAu 31NR
Davis, Audrey Elizabeth 1957- WhoSSW 91
Davis, B. Lynch HispWr 90, MajTwCW
Davis, Barbara Jean 1942- WhoAmW 91
Davis, Barbara Jean Siemens 1931- WhoAmW 91
Davis, Barbara Mae 1926- WhoAmW 91
Davis, Barry K. BioIn 16
Davis, Barry Randolph 1956- WhoEmL 91
Davis, Ben 1947- WhoAmA 91
Davis, Ben Hill, Jr. 1944- WhoSSW 91
Davis, Benjamin, Jr. 1903-1964 EncAL
Davis, Benjamin George 1941- WhoE 91
Davis, Benjamin O. 1877-1970 WorAlBi
Davis, Benjamin O. 1880-1970 BioIn 16
Davis, Benjamin O., Jr. 1912- WorAlBi
Davis, Bennie Luke 1928- WhoAm 90
Davis, Bernard David 1916- WhoAm 90
Davis, Bertha 1918- WhoAmA 91
Davis, Bertha G. 1911- WhoAmW 91
Davis, Bertram George 1919- WhoAm 90
Davis, Bertram Hylton 1918- WhoAm 90
Davis, Bette ConAu 129
Davis, Bette 1908-1989 AnObit 1989, BioAmW, BioIn 16, ConTFT 8 [port], News 90, WorAlBi
Davis, Betty Gale 1937- WhoSSW 91
Davis, Betty Harrington 1936- WhoAmW 91
Davis, Betty Jean Bourbonia 1931- WhoAmW 91
Davis, Billie Johnston 1933- WhoAmW 91, WhoWor 91
Davis, Billy BioIn 16
Davis, Billy Humes 1922- WhoAm 90
Davis, Billy Michael 1955- WhoSSW 91
Davis, Bob 1952- Ballpl 90
Davis, Bobbye Hudson 1950- WhoSSW 91
Davis, Bonni G. 1957- St&PR 91
Davis, Bonnie B. 1926- St&PR 91
Davis, Bonnie Christell 1949- WhoEmL 91
Davis, Brad 1942- WhoAmA 91
Davis, Brenda Washington 1950- WhoSSW 91
Davis, Brian BioIn 16
Davis, Brian Francis BiDrAPA 89
Davis, Brian Warren 1947- WhoAm 90
Davis, Britt Duane 1933- St&PR 91
Davis, Britton BioIn 16
Davis, Britton 1860-1930 WhNaAH
Davis, Britton Anthony 1936- WhoAm 90
Davis, Brock 1943- Ballpl 90
Davis, Bruce Allen 1948- WhoEmL 91
Davis, Bruce Henry 1948- WhoEmL 91
Davis, Bruce Livingston, Jr. 1929- WhoAm 90
Davis, Bruce Owen 1935- St&PR 91
Davis, Bunki Bankaitis- BioIn 16
Davis, Burke 1913- AuBYP 90
Davis, Burl Edward 1930- WhoAm 90
Davis, C Nelson BiDrAPA 89
Davis, Cabell Seal, Jr. 1926- WhoAm 90
Davis, Calla Lea 1944- WhoSSW 91
Davis, Calvin De Armond 1927- WhoAm 90
Davis, Campbell M 1941- BiDrAPA 89
Davis, Carl George 1937- WhoAm 90
Davis, Carl L 1930- BiDrAPA 89
Davis, Carle E. 1920- WhoAm 90
Davis, Carol Ann 1957- St&PR 91
Davis, Carol Lyn 1953- WhoAmW 91
Davis, Carol Lynn 1963- WhoAmW 91
Davis, Carole Joan 1942- WhoAmW 91
Davis, Carolyn 1958- WhoEmL 91
Davis, Carolyn Kahle 1932- WhoAmW 91
Davis, Carolyn Sue 1954- WhoEmL 91
Davis, Carrol R. 1924- St&PR 91
Davis, Cedreck Gene 1950- WhoSSW 91
Davis, Chandler 1926- WhoAm 90
Davis, Charles A BiDrAPA 89
Davis, Charles Burdis, III 1945- WhoAmA 91
Davis, Charles Carroll 1911- WhoAm 90
Davis, Charles Dwain, Jr. 1958- WhoSSW 91
Davis, Charles E. 1936- St&PR 91
Davis, Charles E., Sr. 1933- St&PR 91
Davis, Charles Edward 1928- St&PR 91
Davis, Charles Edwin 1940- WhoSSW 91
Davis, Charles F. 1949- St&PR 91
Davis, Charles Francis, Jr. 1908- WhoAm 90
Davis, Charles Hargis 1938- WhoAm 90
Davis, Charles M 1941- BiDrAPA 89
Davis, Charles Mitchell, Jr. 1925- WhoSSW 91
Davis, Charles Patrick 1945- WhoSSW 91
Davis, Charles T. 1945- St&PR 91
Davis, Charles Talcott 1951- BiDrAPA 89
Davis, Charles Till 1929- WhoAm 90
Davis, Charles William 1948- WhoSSW 91
Davis, Cheryl Ann 1962- WhoAmW 91
Davis, Cheryl Driver 1959- WhoSSW 91
Davis, Chester P., Jr. 1922- St&PR 91
Davis, Chester R., Jr. 1930- WhoAm 90, WhoWor 91
Davis, Chili 1960- Ballpl 90
Davis, Chip BioIn 16, ConMus 4
Davis, Christine Salkin 1957- WhoEmL 91
Davis, Christopher 1928- AuBYP 90, WhoWrEP 89
Davis, Christopher Lee 1950- WhoEmL 91
Davis, Christopher Patrick 1954- WhoEmL 91
Davis, Claude-Leonard 1944- WhoSSW 91
Davis, Clayton Arthur Larsh 1955- WhoEmL 91, WhoSSW 91
Davis, Clifton BioIn 16
Davis, Clifton 1945- WorAlBi
Davis, Clifton B BiDrAPA 89
Davis, Clifton D 1945- DrBlPA 90
Davis, Clive Edward 1914- AuBYP 90
Davis, Clive Jay 1935- WhoAm 90
Davis, Coleen Cockerill 1930- WhoAmW 91
Davis, Colin 1927- PenDiMP
Davis, Colin Rex 1927- IntWWM 90, WhoWor 91
Davis, Courtland Harwell, Jr. 1921- WhoAm 90
Davis, Craig Alphin 1940- St&PR 91, WhoAm 90
Davis, Curt 1903-1965 Ballpl 90
Davis, Curtis Carroll 1916- WhoE 91
Davis, Cynthia Jeanne 1948- WhoAmW 91
Davis, D. Dwight 1908-1965 DcScB S2
Davis, D. Frank 1946- WhoEmL 91
Davis, D Jack 1938- WhoAmA 91
Davis, Daisy Sidney 1944- WhoAmW 91
Davis, Dale Allen 1955- WhoSSW 91
Davis, Daniel BiDrAPA 89
Davis, Daniel Edward 1922- WhoAm 90
Davis, Daniel J. 1946- St&PR 91
Davis, Daniel Walter 1930- WhoAm 90
Davis, Danny 1925- WhoAm 90
Davis, Darrel BioIn 16
Davis, Darrell 1939- WhoWor 91
Davis, Darwin N. BioIn 16
Davis, Dave M 1937- BiDrAPA 89
Davis, Dave McAlister 1937- WhoSSW 91
Davis, David 1927- BiDrAPA 89, WhoAm 90
Davis, David 1932- WhoAm 90
Davis, David Brion 1927- WhoAm 90
Davis, David E. 1909- St&PR 91
Davis, David Ensos 1920- WhoAmA 91
Davis, David F. 1934- St&PR 91
Davis, David George 1945- WhoAm 90
Davis, David James 1938- WhoSSW 91, WhoWor 91
Davis, David MacFarland 1926- WhoE 91, WhoWor 91
Davis, David Mark 1948- BiDrAPA 89
Davis, David McCall 1946- WhoSSW 91
Davis, David Oliver 1933- WhoAm 90
Davis, Deane Chandler NewYTBS 90 [port]
Davis, Deane Chandler 1900- WhoAm 90
Davis, Deborah 1949- ConAu 129
Davis, Deborah Griffith 1954- IntWWM 90
Davis, Deborah Hanson 1945- WhoAmW 91
Davis, Deborah Lynn 1948- WhoEmL 91
Davis, Deforest P., Jr. 1943- St&PR 91
Davis, Delmont Alvin, Jr. 1935- WhoAm 90
Davis, Dennis John 1940- St&PR 91
Davis, Diane G. 1939- ODwPR 91
Davis, Dick 1953- Ballpl 90
Davis, Dix F. 1937- St&PR 91
Davis, Dixie 1890-1944 Ballpl 90
Davis, Don Clarence 1943- WhoSSW 91
Davis, Don K. 1945- St&PR 91
Davis, Don Ray 1924- WhoAm 90, WhoWor 91
Davis, Donald 1928- OxCCanT [port]
Davis, Donald Alan 1939- WhoAm 90
Davis, Donald Gordon, Jr. 1939- WhoAm 90
Davis, Donald Irvin 1942- BiDrAPA 89
Davis, Donald James 1929- WhoAm 90
Davis, Donald Marc 1952- WhoEmL 91
Davis, Donald Marshall 1924- St&PR 91
Davis, Donald McEnry 1953- WhoSSW 91
Davis, Donald Miller 1945- WhoE 91
Davis, Donald Ray 1934- WhoAm 90
Davis, Donald Robert 1909- WhoAmA 91

Davis, Donald Romain 1957- WhoEmL 91
Davis, Donald W. 1921- St&PR 91
Davis, Donald Walter 1921- WhoAm 90, WhoE 91
Davis, Donna 1960- WhoEmL 91
Davis, Donna Rae 1942- WhoAmW 91
Davis, Dorinne Sue Taylor Lovas 1949- WhoAmW 91
Davis, Dorothy BioIn 16, NewAgE 90
Davis, Dorothy Salisbury 1916- ConAu 32NR, TwCCr&M 91, WhoAm 90, WhoAmW 91
Davis, Doryne Shari 1960- WhoE 91
Davis, Douglas Charles 1949- St&PR 91
Davis, Douglas Matthew 1933- WhoAm 90, WhoAmA 91
Davis, Douglas Richard 1944- St&PR 91
Davis, Duane Lee 1950- WhoSSW 91
Davis, Dwight 1948- WhoAm 90
Davis, Dwight Filley 1879-1945 BiDrUSE 89
Davis, Dwight John 1953- WhoSSW 91
Davis, E. Harold St&PR 91
Davis, E. Marcus 1951- WhoEmL 91
Davis, E. W. AmLegL
Davis, Earl James 1934- WhoAm 90
Davis, Earon Scott 1950- WhoEmL 91
Davis, Eddie 1921-1986 OxCPMus
Davis, Eddie Joe 1945- WhoSSW 91
Davis, Edgar Glenn 1931- St&PR 91, WhoAm 90
Davis, Edward B. 1927- St&PR 91
Davis, Edward Bertrand 1933- WhoAm 90
Davis, Edward Braxton, III 1938- WhoSSW 91
Davis, Edward H. BioIn 16
Davis, Edward H. 1927-1989 BioIn 16
Davis, Edward Joseph, Jr. 1930- WhoWrEP 89
Davis, Edward Mott 1918- WhoSSW 91
Davis, Edward N. 1927- St&PR 91
Davis, Edward Wilson 1935- WhoAm 90
Davis, Edwin Clark BioIn 16
Davis, Edwin Dyer 1925- WhoSSW 91
Davis, Eleanor Kay 1935- WhoSSW 91
Davis, Eleanor Lauria 1923- WhoAmW 91
Davis, Elise Miller 1915- WhoAmW 91
Davis, Elisha W. 1828-1887 AmLegL
Davis, Elizabeth AuBYP 90
Davis, Elizabeth Ann 1941- WhoAmW 91
Davis, Elizabeth Ann 1955- WhoSSW 91
Davis, Elizabeth B 1920- BiDrAPA 89
Davis, Elizabeth Mary 1948- WhoAm 90
Davis, Ellabelle 1907-1960 BioIn 16, DcAfAmP, DrBIPA 90
Davis, Ellen N 1937- WhoAmA 91
Davis, Ellsworth J. 1862-1949 AmLegL
Davis, Elmer 1890-1958 BioIn 16
Davis, Elmo Wright, Jr. 1946- WhoSSW 91
Davis, Emery Stephen 1940- WhoAm 90, WhoSSW 91
Davis, Emma R. 1944- WhoAmW 91
Davis, Eric BioIn 16
Davis, Eric 1962- Ballpl 90, WorAlBi
Davis, Eric Clark 1952- WhoEmL 91
Davis, Eric Keith 1962- WhoAm 90
Davis, Erick Malone 1951- BiDrAPA 89
Davis, Ernest 1917- St&PR 91
Davis, Ernie 1939-1963 BioIn 16
Davis, Erroll Brown, Jr. 1944- St&PR 91, WhoAm 90
Davis, Eschol Eugene 1920- BiDrAPA 89
Davis, Esther M 1893-1974 WhoAmA 91N
Davis, Eunice Beatrice 1936- WhoSSW 91
Davis, Evan Anderson 1944- WhoE 91
Davis, Evelyn Cadenhead 1948- WhoAmW 91
Davis, Evelyn Marguerite Bailey IntWWM 90
Davis, Evelyn Y. WhoAm 90, WhoWor 91
Davis, Everett M. 1934- WhoE 91
Davis, Ferd Leary, Jr. 1941- WhoSSW 91
Davis, Finis E. 1911- WhoAm 90
Davis, Fitzroy 1912-1980 ConAu 31NR
Davis, Florea Jean 1953- WhoEmL 91
Davis, Florence Elizabeth BiDrAPA 89
Davis, Floyd Russell 1951- WhoEmL 91
Davis, Foster B., Jr. 1917- St&PR 91
Davis, Frances Elliot 1882-1965 BioIn 16
Davis, Frances Kay 1952- WhoAmW 91, WhoEmL 91
Davis, Frances M. 1925- WhoAm 90, WhoAmW 91
Davis, Francis E 1922- BiDrAPA 89
Davis, Francis Gordon 1908- WhoWor 91
Davis, Francis Kaye 1918- WhoWor 91
Davis, Francis Keith 1928- WhoAm 90
Davis, Francis Raymond 1920- WhoE 91, WhoWor 91
Davis, Francis W. 1905- St&PR 91
Davis, Frank 1892-1990 ConAu 131
Davis, Frank B. 1928- WhoAm 90
Davis, Frank Edward 1956- WhoEmL 91
Davis, Frank French 1920- St&PR 91
Davis, Frank Isaac 1919- WhoAm 90
Davis, Frank N. 1925- St&PR 91
Davis, Frank Tradewell, Jr. 1938- WhoAm 90, WhoWor 91
Davis, Fred C. 1928- St&PR 91
Davis, Fred Swanton, Jr. 1922- St&PR 91
Davis, Frederick B 1931- BiDrAPA 89
Davis, Frederick C 1902-1977 TwCCr&M 91
Davis, Frederick H BiDrAPA 89
Davis, Frederick Townsend 1945- WhoAm 90
Davis, G. Lynn St&PR 91
Davis, Gail Yvette 1953- WhoEmL 91
Davis, Gale Elwood 1909- WhoAm 90
Davis, Gary Charles 1945- WhoSSW 91
Davis, Gary Lynn 1949- WhoEmL 91, WhoSSW 91
Davis, Gary Mark 1959- WhoSSW 91
Davis, Gary Myron BiDrAPA 89
Davis, Gary R 1926- BiDrAPA 89
Davis, Geena BioIn 16, WhoAm 90, WhoAmW 91
Davis, Geena 1957- WorAlBi
Davis, Gene B 1920-1985 WhoAmA 91N
Davis, Gene Carlton 1917- WhoAm 90
Davis, George St&PR 91, -91N
Davis, George 1870-1940 Ballpl 90 [port]
Davis, George A. 1928- St&PR 91
Davis, George Alfred 1928- WhoAm 90
Davis, George Donald 1942- WhoAm 90
Davis, George Edward 1928- WhoAm 90, WhoSSW 91, WhoWor 91
Davis, George Edwin 1952- BiDrAPA 89
Davis, George Gordon 1941- WhoE 91
Davis, George Holmes 1936- St&PR 91
Davis, George Kelso 1910- WhoAm 90
Davis, George Linn 1934- WhoAm 90
Davis, George Lynn 1940- WhoAm 90
Davis, George Osmond 1957- WhoEmL 91
Davis, George Vestal 1936- BiDrAPA 89
Davis, George Wilmot 1933- WhoAm 90
Davis, Georgeann L. 1954- WhoAmW 91
Davis, Georgia Ann BiDrAPA 89
Davis, Gerald Hinkle 1930- WhoSSW 91
Davis, Gerald Titus 1932- WhoAm 90
Davis, Gil 1941- ODwPR 91
Davis, Gilbert S. 1924- St&PR 91
Davis, Gilla Prizant 1951- BiDrAPA 89
Davis, Ginger Fields 1934- WhoSSW 91
Davis, Glenn BioIn 16
Davis, Glenn 1961- Ballpl 90
Davis, Glenn Craig 1946- BiDrAPA 89
Davis, Glenn R. 1914-1988 BioIn 16
Davis, Glenn W. 1924- BioIn 16
Davis, Gloria 1940- WhoAmW 91, WhoSSW 91
Davis, Gordon ConAu 31NR, EncPaPR 91, TwCCr&M 91
Davis, Gordon Richard Fuerst 1925- WhoAm 90
Davis, Grace Montanez 1926- WhoHisp 91
Davis, Grania 1943- BioIn 16
Davis, Gregory Lewis 1951- St&PR 91
Davis, Gregory Todd 1959- WhoWrEP 89
Davis, Guillett Gervaise, III 1932- St&PR 91
Davis, Gussie Lord 1863-1899 BioIn 16, DcAfAmP
Davis, Hal BioIn 16
Davis, Hal F. NewYTBS 90
Davis, Hal Scott 1957- WhoEmL 91
Davis, Harlow M. 1927- St&PR 91
Davis, Harold WhoAm 90
Davis, Harold 1950- WhoAm 90, WhoEmL 91
Davis, Harold 1953- WhoEmL 91
Davis, Harold Dean 1951- WhoEmL 91
Davis, Harold Eugene 1902-1988 BioIn 16
Davis, Harold Fenimore 1916- WhoAm 90
Davis, Harold L. 1924- St&PR 91
Davis, Harold L. 1925- WhoAm 90
Davis, Harold Truscott 1895- WhoAm 90
Davis, Harold William 1929- St&PR 91
Davis, Harrison BioIn 16
Davis, Harry 1873-1947 Ballpl 90 [port]
Davis, Harry 1909- WhoAm 90
Davis, Harry Allen 1914- WhoAmA 91
Davis, Harry Floyd 1925- WhoAm 90
Davis, Harry Francis BiDrAPA 89
Davis, Harry K 1926- BiDrAPA 89
Davis, Harry L. 1927- St&PR 91
Davis, Harry Lee, Jr. 1952- WhoEmL 91
Davis, Harry Rex 1921- WhoAm 90
Davis, Harry Scott, Jr. 1943- St&PR 91, WhoAm 90
Davis, Hartwell 1906- WhoAm 90
Davis, Harvey Leonard 1926- St&PR 91
Davis, Hayden E. 1933- St&PR 91
Davis, Helen Gordon 1924- WhoAmW 91
Davis, Helen Nancy Matson 1905- WhoAmW 91, WhoWor 91
Davis, Helena Lang 1942- WhoE 91
Davis, Henry Andrew BiDrAPA 89
Davis, Henry Barnard, Jr. 1923- WhoWor 91
Davis, Henry Jefferson, Jr. 1929- WhoAm 90
Davis, Herbert Lowell 1933- St&PR 91, WhoAm 90
Davis, Herbert W. 1927- St&PR 91
Davis, Hiram Logan 1943- WhoAm 90
Davis, Holly 1951- WhoAmW 91
Davis, Hope Hale 1903- WhoWrEP 89
Davis, Horance Gibbs, Jr. 1924- WhoAm 90
Davis, Howard PenDiMP
Davis, Howard 1940- IntWWM 90
Davis, Howard C., Jr. 1932- St&PR 91
Davis, Howard Eckert 1933- WhoAm 90
Davis, Howard Ted 1937- WhoAm 90
Davis, Howard W 1945- BiDrAPA 89
Davis, Howard Walter 1945- WhoAm 90, WhoSSW 91
Davis, Howard Wells 1945- WhoEmL 91
Davis, Hubert 1904- AuBYP 90
Davis, Inger Pedersen 1927- WhoAmW 91
Davis, Irvin 1926- ODwPR 91, St&PR 91, WhoWrEP 89
Davis, Ivan 1932- IntWWM 90, PenDiMP
Davis, Ivan W., Jr. 1932- St&PR 91
Davis, J. Alan 1961- WhoEmL 91
Davis, J. B. 1935- IntWWM 90
Davis, J. Clarke 1951- WhoSSW 91
Davis, J. Douglas 1954- ODwPR 91
Davis, J. Luther 1924- St&PR 91
Davis, J Madison 1951- WhoWrEP 89
Davis, J. Michael 1947- WhoAm 90
Davis, J. Morton 1929- St&PR 91, WhoAm 90
Davis, J. Spencer 1946- ODwPR 91
Davis, J. Steve 1945- WhoAm 90
Davis, Jack 1926- EncACom
Davis, Jack Beason 1924- BiDrAPA 89
Davis, Jack C. 1938- St&PR 91, WhoAm 90
Davis, Jack D. 1927- St&PR 91
Davis, Jack R WhoAmA 91
Davis, Jacqueline Marie Vincent WhoAm 90
Davis, Jacquelyn Kay 1950- WhoE 91, WhoEmL 91
Davis, James 1901-1974 WhoAmA 91N
Davis, James Allan 1953- WhoAm 90
Davis, James Anthony 1941- BiDrAPA 89, WhoE 91
Davis, James B. 1950- St&PR 91
Davis, James Carl 1945- WhoSSW 91
Davis, James E. 1907- St&PR 91
Davis, James Edward 1921- St&PR 91
Davis, James Eugene 1934- WhoE 91
Davis, James Evans 1918- WhoAm 90, WhoSSW 91, WhoWor 91
Davis, James Granberry 1931- WhoAmA 91
Davis, James Harold 1937- WhoSSW 91
Davis, James Harold 1943- WhoAm 90
Davis, James Henry 1932- WhoAm 90
Davis, James Holland 1920- St&PR 91
Davis, James Hornor, III 1928- WhoAm 90
Davis, James Hornor, IV 1953- WhoAm 90
Davis, James Howard 1955- WhoEmL 91
Davis, James John 1873-1947 BiDrUSE 89
Davis, James John 1946- St&PR 91, WhoAm 90
Davis, James Kirby 1956- WhoEmL 91
Davis, James Luther 1924- WhoAm 90
Davis, James M. 1936- St&PR 91
Davis, James Minor, Jr. 1936- WhoAm 90
Davis, James Norman 1939- WhoAm 90
Davis, James Othello 1916- WhoAm 90
Davis, James P. St&PR 91
Davis, James Paxton 1925- WhoWrEP 89
Davis, James Robbins BiDrAPA 89
Davis, James Robert 1945- WhoAm 90, WhoAmA 91
Davis, James Verlin 1935- WhoAm 90
Davis, James Wesley 1940- WhoAmA 91
Davis, Jan 1943- WhoAmW 91
Davis, Jane Strauss 1944- WhoAmW 91
Davis, Janice Ann 1953- WhoAmW 91
Davis, Jarita Delores 1958- WhoAmW 91
Davis, Jasper Claud 1920- St&PR 91
Davis, Jay Alan 1956- BiDrAPA 89
Davis, Jay Michael 1946- WhoAm 90
Davis, Jean McArthur 1924- St&PR 91
Davis, Jeanine Marie 1955- WhoAmW 91
Davis, Jeannine M. 1948- St&PR 91
Davis, Jeff 1862-1913 BioIn 16
Davis, Jefferson 1808-1889 BiDrUSE 89, BioIn 16, WorAlBi
Davis, Jefferson Clark, Jr. 1931- WhoAm 90, WhoSSW 91
Davis, Jefferson J. 1913- St&PR 91
Davis, Jeffrey J. 1947- WhoEmL 91
Davis, Jennifer ODwPR 91
Davis, Jeremy Matthew 1953- WhoEmL 91
Davis, Jerrold 1926- WhoAmA 91
Davis, Jerrold Calvin 1926- WhoAm 90
Davis, Jerry Donald 1938- St&PR 91
Davis, Jerry Ray 1938- WhoAm 90
Davis, Jill Renea 1966- WhoAmW 91
Davis, Jim BioIn 16
Davis, Jim 1924- Ballpl 90
Davis, Jim 1945- WorAlBi
Davis, Jimmie 1902- OxCPMus
Davis, Jimmie Dan 1940- WhoAm 90
Davis, Jimmy Frank 1945- WhoEmL 91
Davis, JoAn 1947- WhoAmW 91
Davis, Joanne King Herring WhoAmW 91, WhoSSW 91, WhoWor 91
Davis, Jodi A. 1964- WhoAmW 91
Davis, Jody 1956- Ballpl 90
Davis, Joe Louis 1943- St&PR 91
Davis, Joe R. 1952- WhoSSW 91
Davis, Joe William 1918- WhoSSW 91
Davis, Joel 1934- St&PR 91, WhoAm 90
Davis, Joel 1965- Ballpl 90
Davis, Joel Anthony 1948- WhoEmL 91
Davis, Joel Foster 1953- WhoEmL 91
Davis, John 1550?-1605 EncCRAm, WorAlBi
Davis, John 1916-1986 BioIn 16
Davis, John 1963- Ballpl 90
Davis, John A. BioIn 16
Davis, John Adams, Jr. 1944- WhoE 91
Davis, John Anderson 1924- WhoAm 90
Davis, John Byron 1922- WhoAm 90, WhoWrEP 89
Davis, John Chandler Bancroft 1822-1907 BioIn 16
Davis, John Charles 1943- WhoAm 90
Davis, John Clements 1938- WhoAm 90
Davis, John Donald 1927- WhoAm 90
Davis, John Dwelle 1928- WhoAm 90
Davis, John Edward WhoWor 91
Davis, John Edward NewYTBS 90
Davis, John Edward 1913-1990 BioIn 16
Davis, John Edward 1942- WhoAm 90
Davis, John F. NewYTBS 90
Davis, John F.X. 1932- WhoSSW 91
Davis, John H. 1927- WhoAm 90, WhoE 91
Davis, John Herschel 1924- WhoAm 90, WhoE 91
Davis, John I. 1917- St&PR 91
Davis, John James 1936- WhoAm 90
Davis, John Joseph 1942- St&PR 91
Davis, John Joseph, Jr. 1948- WhoSSW 91
Davis, John K. 1940- St&PR 91
Davis, John Kennerly, Jr. 1945- WhoAm 90
Davis, John Leonard 1926- WhoAm 90
Davis, John Louis, II 1934- WhoSSW 91
Davis, John M 1933- BiDrAPA 89
Davis, John MacDougall 1914- WhoAm 90
Davis, John Marcell 1933- WhoAm 90
Davis, John Mason 1935- WhoAm 90
Davis, John Michael 1948- WhoEmL 91
Davis, John Norman 1954- WhoEmL 91
Davis, John Phillips, Jr. 1925- WhoAm 90
Davis, John Reed 1927- WhoE 91
Davis, John Roger, Jr. 1927- WhoAm 90, WhoWor 91
Davis, John Rowland 1927- WhoAm 90
Davis, John Sherwood 1942- WhoAmA 91N
Davis, John Staige, IV 1931- WhoAm 90
Davis, John Vincent 1954- BiDrAPA 89
Davis, John Weldon 1931- St&PR 91
Davis, John Wesley 1799-1859 AmLegL
Davis, John William 1873-1955 BioIn 16
Davis, John William 1926- WhoAm 90
Davis, Jolene Bryant 1942- WhoAmW 91
Davis, Jon Edward 1952- WhoWrEP 89
Davis, Joseph C BiDrAPA 89
Davis, Joseph Edward 1926- St&PR 91, WhoAm 90
Davis, Joseph Frank 1939- St&PR 91
Davis, Joseph H. BioIn 16
Davis, Joseph Lloyd 1927- WhoAm 90
Davis, Joseph S. St&PR 91
Davis, Joseph Samuel 1930- WhoAm 90
Davis, Josh D BiDrAPA 89
Davis, Joy Lee 1931- WhoAmW 91
Davis, Joy Lynn Edwards 1945- WhoAmW 91, WhoWrEP 89
Davis, Joyce Nannette 1958- WhoAmW 91
Davis, Juana St&PR 91
Davis, Judith M 1936- BiDrAPA 89
Davis, Judy Ann 1942- WhoAmW 91
Davis, Julia McBroom 1930- WhoAm 90, WhoAmW 91
Davis, Julie Lynn 1956- WhoEmL 91
Davis, Julie Mann 1960- WhoAmW 91
Davis, K. V. 1936- WhoAm 90
Davis, Karen Padgett 1942- WhoAm 90, WhoAmW 91, WhoE 91
Davis, Katharine Bement 1860-1935 BioIn 16
Davis, Katharine Cleland 1907- WhoAmW 91, WhoSSW 91, WhoWor 91
Davis, Kathleen Ann 1955- WhoAmW 91
Davis, Kathleen O BiDrAPA 89
Davis, Kathlyne Mary Elizabeth 1954- WhoEmL 91
Davis, Kathlyne Skillas 1954- St&PR 91
Davis, Kathryn Ann 1952- WhoEmL 91
Davis, Kathryn Leola 1954- WhoAmW 91
Davis, Kathryn Wasserman 1907- WhoAm 90, WhoAmW 91
Davis, Kathy BioIn 16
Davis, Katie BioIn 16
Davis, Keith E. 1920- St&PR 91
Davis, Keith Eugene 1936- WhoAm 90
Davis, Keith Frederic 1952- WhoAmA 91

Davis, Keith Irwin 1952- *WhoEmL 91*
Davis, Kenn 1932- *TwCCr&M 91*
Davis, Kenneth *BioIn 16*
Davis, Kenneth A. 1949- *WhoAm 90*
Davis, Kenneth Boone, Jr. 1947- *WhoEmL 91*
Davis, Kenneth Culp 1908- *WhoAm 90*
Davis, Kenneth Ira 1941- *WhoE 91*
Davis, Kenneth J. *BioIn 16*
Davis, Kenneth Leon *BiDrAPA 89*
Davis, Kenneth Ray 1951- *WhoSSW 91*
Davis, Kenneth S 1912- *ConAu 30NR*
Davis, Kenneth Sidney 1912- *WhoAm 90*
Davis, Kenneth Wayne 1945- *WhoEmL 91*
Davis, Kevin Adam 1962- *WhoWrEP 89*
Davis, Kevin R. 1945- *WhoWrEP 89*
Davis, Kevin Robert 1945- *WhoEmL 91*
Davis, Kevin T. 1958- *St&PR 91*
Davis, Kim McAlister 1958- *WhoAmW 91*
Davis, Kimberly Brooke 1953- *WhoAmA 91*
Davis, Kimberly Vance 1956- *WhoEmL 91*
Davis, Kingsley 1908- *WhoAm 90*
Davis, Kristin Woodford 1944- *WhoAmW 91*
Davis, L Clarice 1929- *WhoAmA 91*
Davis, L. Clay 1939- *St&PR 91*
Davis, L. D. 1942- *ODwPR 91*
Davis, Lance Alan 1939- *WhoAm 90*
Davis, Lance Edwin 1928- *WhoAm 90*
Davis, Larry Marvin *BiDrAPA 89*
Davis, Larry Michael 1947- *WhoWor 91*
Davis, Latham Windsor 1942- *WhoAm 90*
Davis, Laura Ann 1959- *WhoAmW 91, WhoSSW 91*
Davis, Laura Arlene 1935- *WhoAm 90, WhoAmW 91*
Davis, Laurence Laird 1915- *WhoAm 90*
Davis, Lavinia 1909- *AuBYP 90*
Davis, Lawrence Edward 1947- *WhoE 91*
Davis, Lawrence Stanley 1925- *St&PR 91*
Davis, Lee Edward 1966- *WhoE 91*
Davis, Lefty 1875-1919 *Ballpl 90*
Davis, Lennard J. 1949- *WhoE 91*
Davis, Leodis 1933- *WhoAm 90*
Davis, Leon Glenn 1931- *WhoSSW 91*
Davis, Leonard McCutchan 1919- *WhoAm 90*
Davis, Lester T. 1930- *WhoAm 90*
Davis, Leverett, Jr. 1914- *WhoAm 90*
Davis, Levi R. *AmLegL*
Davis, Lew E 1910-1979 *WhoAmA 91N*
Davis, Lewis 1925- *WhoAm 90*
Davis, Lewis Berkley 1944- *WhoE 91*
Davis, Lila Ross 1941- *WhoAmW 91*
Davis, Linda J. 1946- *St&PR 91*
Davis, Linda Jacobs 1955- *WhoAmW 91*
Davis, Linda Prewett 1946- *WhoSSW 91*
Davis, Linda Rooney 1953- *WhoAmW 91*
Davis, Linden Allen 1946- *St&PR 91*
Davis, Lindsay *BioIn 16*
Davis, Lloyd Edward 1929- *WhoAm 90*
Davis, Lois Ann 1945- *WhoAmW 91*
Davis, Lori Ann 1963- *WhoSSW 91*
Davis, Lori Lynne *BiDrAPA 89*
Davis, Lorraine Jensen 1924- *WhoAm 90, WhoAmW 91*
Davis, Lou Bryant 1955- *WhoEmL 91*
Davis, Lou Ellen 1936- *AuBYP 90*
Davis, Louise Spiers 1911- *WhoAmW 91*
Davis, Lourie Irene Bell 1930- *WhoAmW 91*
Davis, Loyd Evan 1939- *WhoSSW 91*
Davis, Luther 1921- *WhoAm 90*
Davis, Luther, Jr. 1922- *WhoAm 90*
Davis, Lydia Joanna 1958- *WhoAmW 91, WhoWor 91*
Davis, Lyle E. 1927- *St&PR 91*
Davis, Lyn E. 1911- *St&PR 91*
Davis, Lynn Harry 1949- *WhoE 91, WhoEmL 91, WhoWor 91*
Davis, M. G. 1930- *WhoSSW 91*
Davis, Mac 1941- *EncPR&S 89*
Davis, Mac 1942- *OxCPMus, WhoAm 90, WorAlBi*
Davis, Maceo Nathaniel 1948- *WhoAm 90, WhoE 91, WhoEmL 91*
Davis, Maggie S. 1942- *BioIn 16*
Davis, Mallory Donald, Jr. 1957- *WhoEmL 91*
Davis, Maralee G. *WhoWrEP 89*
Davis, Marc I. 1934- *WhoWrEP 89*
Davis, Marcia Welch 1949- *WhoAmW 91*
Davis, Margaret A. 1952- *WhoWrEP 89*
Davis, Margaret Bryan 1931- *WhoAmW 91*
Davis, Margy-Ruth 1949- *WhoEmL 91*
Davis, Marian B 1911- *WhoAmA 91*
Davis, Marie Henrietta 1929- *WhoAmW 91*
Davis, Marilynn A. 1952- *WhoE 91*
Davis, Marion Pease 1918- *WhoAmW 91, WhoE 91, WhoWor 91*
Davis, Mark 1960- *Ballpl 90, WorAlBi*
Davis, Mark Hezekiah, Jr. 1948- *WhoWor 91*
Davis, Mark Jefferson 1954- *WhoEmL 91*
Davis, Mark Randall 1955- *WhoAm 90*
Davis, Marsha Ross 1952- *WhoAmW 91*
Davis, Marsha Sue 1948- *WhoAmW 91*
Davis, Martha *BioIn 16*
Davis, Martha Algenita Scott 1950- *WhoEmL 91*
Davis, Martha Demeter 1949- *WhoAmW 91*
Davis, Martin David 1928- *WhoAm 90*
Davis, Martin S. *BioIn 16*
Davis, Martin S. 1927- *St&PR 91, WhoAm 90, WhoE 91, WhoWor 91*
Davis, Marvin *BioIn 16*
Davis, Marvin Arnold 1937- *WhoWor 91*
Davis, Marvin Harold 1925- *ConAmBL*
Davis, Mary 1852-1909 *FemiCLE*
Davis, Mary A *BiDrAPA 89*
Davis, Mary Bronaugh 1937- *IntWWM 90*
Davis, Mary Gould 1882- *AuBYP 90*
Davis, Mary Helen *BiDrAPA 89*
Davis, Mary Helen 1949- *BiDrAPA 89, WhoAmW 91, WhoEmL 91*
Davis, Mary Ione 1942- *WhoAmW 91*
Davis, Mary Jane 1951- *WhoAmW 91*
Davis, Mary Josephine 1947- *WhoAmW 91*
Davis, Mary Kathleen Oros 1947- *WhoEmL 91*
Davis, Mary Lee 1935- *AuBYP 90*
Davis, Mary Louise 1942- *WhoSSW 91*
Davis, Mary Paul *BiDrAPA 89*
Davis, Maryellen S *BiDrAPA 89*
Davis, Mattie Belle Edwards 1910- *WhoAm 90, WhoWor 91*
Davis, Mel *ConAu 129*
Davis, Melodie M. 1951- *ConAu 33NR*
Davis, Melvin Clayton 1929- *St&PR 91*
Davis, Meredith J 1948- *WhoAmA 91*
Davis, Michael David 1937- *WhoAm 90*
Davis, Michael James 1942- *WhoAm 90*
Davis, Michael Leonard 1954- *WhoE 91*
Davis, Michael Todd 1963- *WhoSSW 91*
Davis, Michael W. R. 1931- *ODwPR 91*
Davis, Michael William 1949- *WhoEmL 91*
Davis, Michelle Y. *BioIn 16*
Davis, Mike 1959- *Ballpl 90*
Davis, Miles *BioIn 16*
Davis, Miles 1926- *DrBIPA 90, OxCPMus, WorAlBi*
Davis, Miles Dewey 1926- *WhoAm 90*
Davis, Milton 1922- *St&PR 91*
Davis, Milton Simon *BiDrAPA 89*
Davis, Milton Wickers, Jr. 1923- *WhoAm 90, WhoWor 91*
Davis, Minette *BiDrAPA 89*
Davis, Minnie Delores 1945- *WhoAm 90*
Davis, Monique 1936- *WhoAmW 91*
Davis, Monnett Bain 1893-1953 *BioIn 16*
Davis, Monte Hill 1932- *IntWWM 90*
Davis, Monte Vincent 1923- *WhoAm 90*
Davis, Morris Schuyler 1919- *WhoAm 90*
Davis, Moshe 1916- *BioIn 16, WhoAm 90*
Davis, Mouse *BioIn 16*
Davis, Muller 1935- *WhoAm 90, WhoWor 91*
Davis, Murray 1924- *OxCCanT*
Davis, Nan Doak- *BioIn 16*
Davis, Nancy Dumond 1928- *BiDrAPA 89*
Davis, Nancy Jane 1947- *WhoEmL 91*
Davis, Nancy Redemann *WhoSSW 91*
Davis, Natalie 1928- *FemiCLE*
Davis, Natalie Zemon 1928- *WhoAm 90, WhoAmW 91, WorAu 1980 [port]*
Davis, Nathan Joseph 1955- *IntWWM 90*
Davis, Nathan M *BiDrAPA 89*
Davis, Nathan Tate 1937- *WhoAm 90*
Davis, Nathaniel *BioIn 16*
Davis, Nathaniel 1925- *WhoAm 90*
Davis, Nelson Kent 1950- *St&PR 91*
Davis, Nicholas Homans Clark 1938- *WhoAm 90*
Davis, Nissen 1933- *ODwPR 91*
Davis, Noel *News 90, -90-3*
Davis, Norman Hezekiah 1878-1944 *BioIn 16*
Davis, Norman R. 1921- *St&PR 91*
Davis, O. L., Jr. 1928- *WhoSSW 91*
Davis, Olivia Abrego *BiDrAPA 89*
Davis, Orlando Ross 1961- *BiDrAPA 89*
Davis, Orlin Ray 1937- *WhoAm 90*
Davis, Orval C. 1920- *St&PR 91*
Davis, Orval Clifton 1920- *WhoAm 90*
Davis, Oscar F 1928- *BiDrAPA 89*
Davis, Oscar H. 1914-1988 *BioIn 16*
Davis, Ossie *EarBlAP*
Davis, Ossie 1917- *BioIn 16, DrBIPA 90, WhoAm 90, WorAlBi*
Davis, Otto Anderson 1934- *WhoAm 90*
Davis, Ovide Joseph 1930- *WhoSSW 91*
Davis, Pamela Bowes 1949- *WhoAmW 91*
Davis, Pamela Cralle 1945- *WhoWor 91*
Davis, Pamela Eileen 1956- *WhoAmW 91*
Davis, Pamela Sue 1959- *WhoSSW 91*
Davis, Patricia A. 1939- *St&PR 91*
Davis, Patricia Alison 1963- *IntWWM 90*
Davis, Patricia LuAnn 1959- *WhoEmL 91*
Davis, Patrick 1943- *MusmAFA*
Davis, Patrick Reese 1935- *St&PR 91*
Davis, Patti *BioIn 16*
Davis, Paul 1938- *BioIn 16*
Davis, Paul 1951- *WhoSSW 91*
Davis, Paul Brooks 1938- *WhoAm 90*
Davis, Paul Francis 1947- *WhoSSW 91*
Davis, Paul Harvey 1938- *BiDrAPA 89*
Davis, Paul Joseph 1937- *WhoAm 90*
Davis, Paul Michael 1940- *WhoSSW 91*
Davis, Paulette Jean Turner 1946- *WhoAmW 91*
Davis, Paxton 1925- *WhoAm 90*
Davis, Peaches 1905- *Ballpl 90*
Davis, Peggy Cooper 1943- *WhoAmW 91*
Davis, Perry John 1932- *WhoE 91*
Davis, Peter 1937- *BioIn 16*
Davis, Peter Bennett 1942- *St&PR 91*
Davis, Peter Frank 1937- *WhoAm 90*
Davis, Peter Kerpich Byng 1933- *WhoWor 91*
Davis, Phil *WhoAmA 91N*
Davis, Phil 1906-1964 *EncACom*
Davis, Philip 1952- *WhoEmL 91*
Davis, Philip Charles 1921- *WhoAmA 91*
Davis, Philip J. 1923- *WhoAm 90*
Davis, Philip P. 1938- *St&PR 91*
Davis, Phillip Howard 1946- *WhoSSW 91*
Davis, Phyllis 1891- *OxCCanT*
Davis, Phyllis Burke 1931- *St&PR 91, WhoAm 90*
Davis, Piper *BioIn 16*
Davis, Piper 1917- *Ballpl 90*
Davis, Preston Homer 1913- *St&PR 91*
Davis, R. Joseph 1934- *WhoAm 90*
Davis, R. Kent 1956- *WhoEmL 91*
Davis, R. Lee 1901- *St&PR 91*
Davis, Rachel Lee Mostert 1952- *WhoSSW 91*
Davis, Ralph 1866-1952 *AmLegL*
Davis, Ralph E. 1919- *WhoAm 90*
Davis, Ralph E. 1934- *St&PR 91*
Davis, Ralph Manning 1926- *St&PR 91*
Davis, Ramona Elaine 1928- *BiDrAPA 89*
Davis, Randall Paul 1956- *WhoWrEP 89*
Davis, Randy 1952- *St&PR 91*
Davis, Ray Burt 1926- *WhoE 91*
Davis, Ray C. 1941- *St&PR 91*
Davis, Ray Charles 1943- *BiDrAPA 89*
Davis, Ray Prince 1941- *WhoSSW 91*
Davis, Raymond, Jr. 1914- *WhoAm 90*
Davis, Raythea Gale 1943- *WhoAmW 91*
Davis, Rebecca 1831-1910 *FemiCLE*
Davis, Rebecca Ann Henry 1948- *WhoSSW 91*
Davis, Rebecca B. 1831-1910 *BioAmW*
Davis, Reda *AuBYP 90*
Davis, Reese Ballew 1909- *St&PR 91*
Davis, Rex Darwin 1924- *WhoE 91*
Davis, Rex Lloyd 1929- *WhoAm 90*
Davis, Rex Randall 1959- *WhoSSW 91*
Davis, Richard 1930- *WhoAm 90*
Davis, Richard Bradley 1926- *WhoAm 90*
Davis, Richard Bruce 1940- *WhoAm 90*
Davis, Richard E *BiDrAPA 89*
Davis, Richard Francis 1936- *WhoAm 90*
Davis, Richard Harding 1864-1916 *BioIn 16, WorAlBi*
Davis, Richard Joel 1946- *WhoAm 90*
Davis, Richard L. 1949- *WhoEmL 91*
Davis, Richard Macomber 1929- *WhoAm 90*
Davis, Richard Malone 1918 *WhoAm 90*
Davis, Richard Owen 1949- *WhoEmL 91*
Davis, Richard R. 1936- *St&PR 91*
Davis, Richard Ralph 1936- *WhoAm 90*
Davis, Richard Rodney 1944- *WhoAm 90*
Davis, Richard Whitlock 1935- *WhoAm 90*
Davis, Rick Anthony 1961- *WhoE 91*
Davis, Robbie *BioIn 16*
Davis, Robert 1915- *ODwPR 91*
Davis, Robert 1933- *WhoAmA 91*
Davis, Robert Aldine 1928- *WhoAm 90, WhoWor 91*
Davis, Robert Arthur *BiDrAPA 89*
Davis, Robert Carlton 1944- *WhoE 91*
Davis, Robert Charles 1946- *WhoEmL 91*
Davis, Robert Dennis 1945- *WhoEmL 91*
Davis, Robert E. 1942- *St&PR 91*
Davis, Robert Edward 1931- *WhoAm 90*
Davis, Robert Edwin 1931- *St&PR 91, WhoAm 90, WhoE 91*
Davis, Robert Eugene *St&PR 91N*
Davis, Robert Frederick 1943- *WhoE 91*
Davis, Robert Gorham 1908- *WhoAm 90*
Davis, Robert H *BiDrAPA 89*
Davis, Robert Harry 1927- *WhoAm 90*
Davis, Robert Hart *TwCCr&M 91*
Davis, Robert Hugh, Jr. 1949- *BiDrAPA 89*
Davis, Robert Jeffrey 1952- *BiDrAPA 89*
Davis, Robert Jocelyn 1951- *WhoE 91, WhoEmL 91*
Davis, Robert Leach 1924- *WhoAm 90*
Davis, Robert Lee 1937- *St&PR 91*
Davis, Robert Lee, Jr. 1901- *WhoSSW 91*
Davis, Robert Louis 1927- *WhoAm 90*
Davis, Robert M. 1923- *St&PR 91*
Davis, Robert M. 1947- *St&PR 91*
Davis, Robert Mitchell 1949- *WhoSSW 91*
Davis, Robert Nason 1938- *WhoE 91*
Davis, Robert Paul 1926- *WhoAm 90*
Davis, Robert Phillip 1941- *St&PR 91*
Davis, Robert S. 1914- *St&PR 91*
Davis, Robert Spink 1919- *St&PR 91*
Davis, Robert T. *WhoAm 90*
Davis, Robert Thomas 1927- *St&PR 91*
Davis, Robert Tyler 1904- *WhoAmA 91N*
Davis, Robert W *BiDrAPA 89*
Davis, Robert William 1932- *WhoAm 90*
Davis, Robert Wyche 1849-1929 *AmLegL*
Davis, Robin Ray 1948- *WhoSSW 91*
Davis, Rod 1946- *WhoWrEP 89*
Davis, Roderick William 1936- *St&PR 91*
Davis, Roger Dale 1954- *WhoEmL 91*
Davis, Roger Edwin 1928- *St&PR 91, WhoAm 90*
Davis, Roger Huntley 1923- *WhoAm 90*
Davis, Roger Kenneth 1937- *St&PR 91*
Davis, Roman T.H. 1961- *St&PR 91*
Davis, Ron 1955- *Ballpl 90*
Davis, Ronald 1937- *WhoAm 90, WhoAmA 91*
Davis, Ronald Clark 1943- *St&PR 91*
Davis, Ronald Farlandi, Jr. 1946- *WhoEmL 91*
Davis, Ronald L. 1937- *St&PR 91*
Davis, Ronald Stephen 1946- *WhoSSW 91*
Davis, Ronald W. 1941- *WhoAm 90*
Davis, Ronald Wayne 1954- *WhoWrEP 89*
Davis, Ross Dane 1919- *WhoAm 90*
Davis, Roy Tasco 1889-1975 *BioIn 16*
Davis, Roy Walton, Jr. 1930- *WhoSSW 91*
Davis, Russ Erik 1941- *WhoAm 90*
Davis, Russell Ray 1954- *WhoEmL 91*
Davis, Russell S. 1923- *St&PR 91*
Davis, Russell Stewart, Jr. 1923- *WhoAm 90, WhoSSW 91*
Davis, Ruth C. 1943- *WhoAmW 91*
Davis, Ruth Elizabeth 1908-1989 *ConAu 129*
Davis, Ruth Frances 1952- *IntWWM 90*
Davis, Ruth Lenore 1910- *WhoAmW 91*
Davis, Ruth Margaret 1928- *WhoAm 90, WhoAmW 91, WhoSSW 91, WhoWor 91*
Davis, Ruth V. *BioIn 16*
Davis, Sam A., II 1948- *St&PR 91*
Davis, Sam H. 1921- *St&PR 91*
Davis, Sammi *BioIn 16*
Davis, Sammy, Jr. *BioIn 16*
Davis, Sammy, Jr. 1923-1990 *CurBio 90N*
Davis, Sammy, Jr. 1925- *DrBIPA 90, IntWWM 90*
Davis, Sammy, Jr. 1925-1990 *ConAu 131, ConMus 4 [port], NewYTBS 90 [port], News 90, OxCPMus, WhoAm 90, WorAlBi*
Davis, Sammy, Sr. *BioIn 16*
Davis, Samuel 1834-1895 *DcCanB 12*
Davis, Samuel 1931- *WhoAm 90*
Davis, Samuel Bernhard 1942- *St&PR 91*
Davis, Sandra H. 1942- *St&PR 91*
Davis, Sandra Irene 1949- *WhoEmL 91*
Davis, Sandra Lynne 1960- *WhoSSW 91*
Davis, Sara A. 1956- *WhoAmW 91*
Davis, Sara Lea 1951- *WhoAmW 91, WhoSSW 91, WhoWor 91*
Davis, Sarah Irwin 1923- *WhoWrEP 89*
Davis, Scott Jonathan 1952- *WhoEmL 91*
Davis, Scott Livingston 1941- *WhoAm 90*
Davis, Scott Murray 1954- *BiDrAPA 89*
Davis, Seth Richard 1954- *WhoEmL 91*
Davis, Sharla Jane 1963- *WhoAmW 91*
Davis, Sharon Marie 1939- *St&PR 91*
Davis, Sharron Kay 1953- *WhoAmW 91, WhoEmL 91*
Davis, Shelby Cullom 1909- *WhoAm 90*
Davis, Shelby M.C. 1937- *St&PR 91*
Davis, Shelby M. C. 1937- *WhoAm 90*
Davis, Shelley Lorraine 1956- *WhoE 91*
Davis, Sheree Renee 1965- *WhoAmW 91*
Davis, Sid 1927- *WhoAm 90*
Davis, Sidney M. 1918-1988 *BioIn 16*
Davis, Skeeter 1931- *OxCPMus*
Davis, Sonia *WhoWrEP 89*
Davis, Spud 1904-1984 *Ballpl 90*
Davis, Stanley Nelson 1924- *WhoAm 90*
Davis, Stanton, Jr. 1945- *WhoEmL 91*
Davis, Stephen 1945- *WhoAmA 91*
Davis, Stephen Allen 1947- *WhoEmL 91*
Davis, Stephen Edward 1925- *St&PR 91, WhoAm 90*
Davis, Stephen F. *BioIn 16*
Davis, Stephen Howard 1939- *WhoAm 90*
Davis, Stephen Jeffrey 1943- *WhoAm 90*
Davis, Stephen John 1945- *WhoAm 90*
Davis, Stephen Marshall 1955- *WhoE 91*
Davis, Stephen Oliver 1942- *WhoE 91*
Davis, Stephen R. 1923- *WhoAm 90*
Davis, Stephen W. 1953- *WhoWrEP 89*
Davis, Steve *ODwPR 91*
Davis, Steven Bruce 1963- *WhoSSW 91*
Davis, Steven Jay 1940- *BiDrAPA 89*
Davis, Stewart 1918- *St&PR 91*
Davis, Stewart Thorpe 1951- *WhoEmL 91, WhoSSW 91, WhoWor 91*
Davis, Storm 1961- *Ballpl 90*
Davis, Stuart *EncAL, WhoAm 90*
Davis, Stuart 1894-1964 *BioIn 16, IntDcAA 90, WhoAmA 91N, WorAlBi*

Davis, Stuart 1916- *St&PR 91*
Davis, Susan Ann *BioIn 16*
Davis, Susan Elizabeth 1955- *WhoAmW 91*
Davis, Susan Emily 1951- *WhoAm 90*
Davis, Susan Frances 1939- *WhoAmW 91, WhoSSW 91*
Davis, Susan Gloria 1957- *WhoAmW 91*
Davis, Susan Jean *WhoWrEP 89*
Davis, Suzanne Gould 1947- *WhoAmW 91, WhoEmL 91*
Davis, Swep T. 1945- *St&PR 91*
Davis, Sybil Alicia 1954- *WhoAmW 91*
Davis, Sydney C. *BioIn 16*
Davis, T. Eleanor 1960- *WhoAmW 91*
Davis, Tamara Petrosian 1945- *St&PR 91*
Davis, Tamra Kathleen 1958- *WhoAmW 91*
Davis, Ted E. 1923- *St&PR 91*
Davis, Terrence Donavon 1945- *St&PR 91*
Davis, Terri M. 1947- *WhoAmW 91*
Davis, Terry Alan 1950- *BiDrAPA 89*
Davis, Terry Michael 1957- *WhoWrEP 89*
Davis, Theodore R. 1840-1894 *BioIn 16*
Davis, Thetton William Grenville 1929- *WhoAm 90*
Davis, Thomas Albert 1940- *BiDrAPA 89*
Davis, Thomas Crawley, III 1945- *WhoSSW 91*
Davis, Thomas Edward 1932- *St&PR 91, WhoAm 90*
Davis, Thomas H. 1918- *St&PR 91*
Davis, Thomas Henry 1918- *WhoAm 90*
Davis, Thomas Jerome 1946- *WhoEmL 91*
Davis, Thomas N, III 1919- *BiDrAPA 89*
Davis, Thomas Robin MacLeod 1947- *WhoE 91*
Davis, Thomas Swift 1941- *WhoE 91*
Davis, Thomas William 1927- *St&PR 91*
Davis, Thomas William 1946- *WhoAm 90*
Davis, Tim Douglas 1956- *WhoEmL 91*
Davis, Tine Wayne, Jr. 1946- *St&PR 91*
Davis, Tom Ivey, II 1946- *WhoSSW 91*
Davis, Tommy 1939- *Ballpl 90 [port]*
Davis, True 1919- *WhoAm 90*
Davis, Tyrone 1938- *BioIn 16*
Davis, Ulysses 1913- *MusmAFA*
Davis, V Terrell 1911- *BiDrAPA 89*
Davis, Varina Howell 1826-1906 *BioAmW*
Davis, Verda Merlyn 1936- *WhoSSW 91*
Davis, Veronica A. 1959- *WhoAmW 91*
Davis, Vestie 1903-1978 *MusmAFA*
Davis, Vickie Beene 1951- *WhoAmW 91*
Davis, Victor *BioIn 16*
Davis, Victor 1964-1989 *AnObit 1989*
Davis, Vikki Ann 1952- *WhoAmW 91*
Davis, Vincent 1930- *WhoAm 90, WhoWor 91*
Davis, Virginia Marie 1947- *WhoAmW 91*
Davis, W.J. 1953- *St&PR 91*
Davis, Wade 1953- *ConAu 131*
Davis, Walter *WhoAmA 91*
Davis, Walter 1912- *WhoWrEP 89*
Davis, Walter 1932-1990 *BioIn 16*
Davis, Walter, Jr. *NewYTBS 90 [port]*
Davis, Walter, Mrs *WhoAmA 91*
Davis, Walter Bond 1930- *WhoE 91*
Davis, Walter J., Jr. 1936- *WhoAm 90, WhoE 91*
Davis, Walter Lewis 1937- *WhoAmA 91*
Davis, Walter Richard 1935- *WhoAm 90*
Davis, Walter Stanley 1928- *WhoE 91*
Davis, Walter Stewart 1924- *St&PR 91, WhoAm 90, WhoSSW 91*
Davis, Wanda Rose 1937- *WhoAmW 91*
Davis, Warren Earl 1926- *WhoWor 91*
Davis, Warwick *BioIn 16*
Davis, Wayne Alton 1931- *WhoAm 90*
Davis, Wayne Lambert 1904-1988 *WhoAmA 91N*
Davis, Wendell, Jr. 1933- *WhoAm 90*
Davis, William *PenDiDA 89*
Davis, William 1923- *St&PR 91*
Davis, William Albert 1946- *WhoAm 90*
Davis, William Arthur 1932- *WhoAm 90*
Davis, William Columbus 1910- *WhoAm 90, WhoWor 91*
Davis, William Currier *BiDrAPA 89*
Davis, William D 1936- *WhoAmA 91*
Davis, William Eugene 1921- *WhoAm 90*
Davis, William Eugene 1929- *WhoAm 90*
Davis, William Eugene 1936- *WhoAm 90*
Davis, William F. 1946- *St&PR 91*
Davis, William H *BiDrAPA 89*
Davis, William Harry 1925- *WhoAm 90*
Davis, William Heath 1822-1909 *BioIn 16*
Davis, William Howard 1922- *WhoAm 90*
Davis, William Howard 1951- *WhoEmL 91*
Davis, William Hugh 1933- *WhoAm 90*
Davis, William K. 1926- *St&PR 91*
Davis, William Kruger 1926- *WhoE 91*
Davis, William L., Jr. 1931- *St&PR 91*
Davis, William M. 1940- *St&PR 91*
Davis, William Maxie, Jr. 1932- *WhoSSW 91, WhoWor 91*
Davis, William Potter, Jr. 1924- *WhoAm 90*
Davis, William Randall 1952- *WhoSSW 91*
Davis, William Richard, Jr. 1947- *WhoSSW 91*
Davis, William Robert 1929- *WhoAm 90*
Davis, William Roger *BiDrAPA 89*
Davis, William S *BiDrAPA 89*
Davis, William S, Jr. *BiDrAPA 89*
Davis, William Stanley 1922- *St&PR 91*
Davis, William Steeple 1884-1961 *WhoAmA 91N*
Davis, William Virgil 1940- *WhoWrEP 89*
Davis, William Wootton, Jr. 1933- *WhoSSW 91*
Davis, Willie 1940- *Ballpl 90 [port]*
Davis, Wyatt 1931- *St&PR 91*
Davis, Wylie Herman 1919- *WhoAm 90*
Davis, Yvonne Dolores 1947- *WhoAmW 91*
Davis, Yvonne Singleton 1952- *WhoAmW 91*
Davis Aspinwall, Gail Ann 1959- *WhoWrEP 89*
Davis-Banks, Phyllis Eileen *WhoAmA 91*
Davis-Culbertson, Evelyn H. Johnson 1915- *IntWWM 90*
Davis-Grossman, Carol Gail 1952- *WhoAm 90*
Davis-Millis, Nina Jo 1953- *IntWWM 90*
Davison, Arthur Clifford Percival *IntWWM 90*
Davison, Barbara 1936- *WhoAmW 91*
Davison, Beaumont 1929- *WhoAm 90*
Davison, Beverly *WhoAm 90*
Davison, Bill 1906-1989 *BioIn 16*
Davison, Bill 1941- *WhoAmA 91*
Davison, Calvin 1932- *WhoAm 90, WhoE 91*
Davison, Carole Sawyer 1934- *WhoE 91*
Davison, Charles Hamilton 1926- *WhoAm 90, WhoE 91*
Davison, Charles Hamilton, Jr. 1959- *St&PR 91*
Davison, Daniel P. 1925- *St&PR 91*
Davison, Daniel Pomeroy 1925- *WhoAm 90, WhoE 91*
Davison, Dean 1960- *ODwPR 91*
Davison, Derek Harold 1923- *WhoWor 91*
Davison, Edward Doran 1819-1894 *DcCanB 12*
Davison, Edward Joseph 1938- *WhoAm 90*
Davison, Emily Wilding *BioIn 16*
Davison, Endicott Peabody 1923- *WhoAm 90*
Davison, Frederick Corbet 1929- *WhoAm 90*
Davison, George Frederick, Jr. 1950- *WhoEmL 91*
Davison, Harry Pomeroy 1867-1922 *BioIn 16*
Davison, Helen Irene 1926- *WhoAmW 91, WhoWor 91*
Davison, Imogene 1924- *WhoAmW 91*
Davison, Jeffrey Blair 1956- *WhoEmL 91*
Davison, John Herbert 1930- *IntWWM 90, WhoAm 90*
Davison, Kenneth Edwin 1924- *WhoAm 90*
Davison, Lawrence H. *MajTwCW*
Davison, Lisette G *BiDrAPA 89*
Davison, Martha Frances *BiDrAPA 89*
Davison, Maxine Baker 1912- *St&PR 91*
Davison, Michael Edward 1955- *WhoAm 90*
Davison, Nancy Reynolds 1944- *WhoAmW 91*
Davison, Paul Sioussa 1955- *WhoEmL 91, WhoSSW 91*
Davison, Peter *ConTFT 8, NewAgMG*
Davison, Peter 1948- *IntWWM 90*
Davison, Peter Hubert 1928- *WhoAm 90, WhoWrEP 89*
Davison, Richard 1936- *WhoAm 90*
Davison, Robert Manning 1937- *St&PR 91*
Davison, Roderic Hollett 1916- *WhoAm 90*
Davison, Stanley Martin 1928- *St&PR 91*
Davison, Thomas Cornell Barringer 1948- *WhoEmL 91*
Davison, Walter Todd *BiDrAPA 89*
Davison, Wild Bill 1906-1989 *AnObit 1989, BioIn 16, OxCPMus*
Davison-McLane, Denise Rosetta 1963- *WhoAmW 91*
Daviss, David Burleson 1936- *St&PR 91*
Daviss, Steven Roy *BiDrAPA 89*
Davisson, Clinton J. 1881-1958 *WorAlBi*
Davisson, Homer G 1866- *WhoAmA 91N*
Davisson, Lee David 1936- *WhoAm 90*
Davisson, Sharon Ryan 1940- *WhoAmW 91*
Davisson, Vanessa Teresa 1958- *WhoEmL 91*
Davitt, Margaret Mary Herlihy 1929- *WhoE 91*
Davol, Benjamin Dean 1960- *WhoSSW 91*
Davol, Peter B 1942- *BiDrAPA 89*
d'Avray, David L. *ConAu 129*
Davuluri, Narayana Laksmi 1943- *WhoWor 91*
Davy, Gloria 1931- *BioIn 16, DrBlPA 90, IntWWM 90*
Davy, Humphrey 1778-1829 *WorAlBi*
Davy, Nadine Irene 1958- *WhoEmL 91*
Davy, Philip Sheridan 1915- *WhoAm 90*
Davy, Richard Gordon, Jr. 1948- *St&PR 91*
Davy, Samuel Jackson 1922- *St&PR 91*
Davy, Sarah 1635?-1667 *BiDEWW*
Davy, Sarah 1639?-1670 *FemiCLE*
Davy, Woods 1949- *WhoAmA 91*
Davye, John Joseph 1929- *IntWWM 90*
Davys, Mary 1674-1732 *BiDEWW, BioIn 16, FemiCLE*
Davys, Michael G D *BiDrAPA 89*
Daw Khin Kyi *BioIn 16*
Daw Khin Kyi 1911-1988 *AnObit 1988*
Daw, Harold John 1926- *WhoAm 90*
Daw, Jane L 1952- *BiDrAPA 89*
Daw, Leila 1940- *BiDWomA*
Daw, Lenore E. *WhoAmW 91*
Dawalt, Kenneth Francis 1911- *WhoAm 90*
Dawbarn, Elizabeth *FemiCLE*
Dawbarn, H.D., Jr. 1942- *St&PR 91*
Dawbarn, Henry Dunlop 1914- *St&PR 91*
Dawber, Pam *WhoAm 90*
Dawber, Pam 1951- *WorAlBi*
Dawdy, Doris Ostrander *WhoAmA 91*
Dawdy, Faye Marie Catania 1954- *WhoAmW 91*
Dawe, David H. 1945- *St&PR 91*
Dawe, Mathew *BiDrAPA 89*
Dawe, Roger *BioIn 16*
Dawes, Carol J. 1931- *WhoAm 90*
Dawes, Charles G. 1865-1951 *EncABHB 7 [port], WorAlBi*
Dawes, Charles Gates 1865-1951 *BiDrUSE 89, BioIn 16*
Dawes, David Ford 1909- *WhoWor 91*
Dawes, Douglas Charles 1952- *WhoEmL 91*
Dawes, Geoffrey Sharman 1918- *WhoAm 90*
Dawes, Henry Laurens 1816-1903 *WhNaAH*
Dawes, Henry M. 1877-1952 *WorAlBi*
Dawes, Jerome Martin 1947- *St&PR 91*
Dawes, Lydia G *BiDrAPA 89*
Dawes, Lyell Clark 1931- *WhoE 91*
Dawes, Michael Anthony *BiDrAPA 89*
Dawes, Michael V. 1944- *St&PR 91*
Dawes, Richard Irving 1919- *WhoAm 90*
Dawes, Richard M 1929- *BiDrAPA 89*
Dawes, Robert Taylor 1904- *St&PR 91*
Dawes, Robyn Mason 1936- *WhoAm 90*
Dawid, Igor Bert 1935- *WhoAm 90*
Dawida, Michael M. 1949- *WhoE 91*
Dawidoff, Nicholas *BioIn 16*
Dawidowicz, Lucy S. *BioIn 16*
Dawidowicz, Lucy S. 1915-1990 *NewYTBS 90 [port]*
Dawidowicz, Lucy Schildkret 1915- *WhoAm 90*
Dawidowicz, Samuel 1951- *St&PR 91*
Dawis, Rene V. 1928- *WhoAm 90*
Dawison, Bogumil 1818-1872 *BioIn 16*
Dawkins, Cecil 1927- *WhoWrEP 89*
Dawkins, Charles N. 1932- *WhoAm 90*
Dawkins, Darryl *BioIn 16*
Dawkins, David Michael 1948- *WhoSSW 91*
Dawkins, Diantha Dee 1942- *WhoSSW 91*
Dawkins, Jacquelinn Hawkins 1938- *WhoAmW 91*
Dawkins, John Sydney 1947- *WhoWor 91*
Dawkins, Marva Phyllis 1948- *WhoAmW 91*
Dawkins, Maurice A. *BioIn 16*
Dawkins, Pete *BioIn 16*
Dawkins, Vickie Lynn 1960- *WhoWrEP 89*
Dawkins, William James 1948- *St&PR 91*
Dawkins, William Lee 1960- *WhoEmL 91*
Dawley, Bill 1958- *Ballpl 90*
Dawley, Donald Lee 1936- *WhoWor 91*
Dawley, Harry F. 1934- *St&PR 91*
Dawley, John P. 1929- *St&PR 91*
Dawley, Joseph William 1936- *WhoAmA 91*
Dawley, Melvin Emerson 1905-1989 *BioIn 16*
Dawley, Robert Michael 1948- *IntWWM 90*
Dawn, Clarence Ernest 1918- *WhoAm 90*
Dawn, David *BioIn 16*
Dawn, Hazel *BioIn 16*
Dawn, Helga *BioIn 16*
Dawn, Marpessa 1935- *DrBlPA 90*
Dawney, Michael William 1942- *IntWWM 90*
Dawood, Muhammad 1945- *BiDrAPA 89*
Dawood, Qazi Mohammad 1961- *WhoEmL 91*
Daws, Jerry Wayne 1944- *St&PR 91*
Dawson, Allen Daniel 1955- *St&PR 91*
Dawson, Allen W. 1926- *St&PR 91*
Dawson, Andre *BioIn 16*
Dawson, Andre 1954- *Ballpl 90 [port], WorAlBi*
Dawson, Andre Fernando 1954- *WhoAm 90*
Dawson, Anna Mae Harne 1931- *WhoAmW 91*
Dawson, Anne 1955- *IntWWM 90*
Dawson, Annie L. 1953- *WhoEmL 91*
Dawson, Barbara Jean 1957- *WhoE 91*
Dawson, Bess Phipps *WhoAmA 91*
Dawson, Bonnie Jean 1955- *WhoWrEP 89*
Dawson, Carol Gene 1937- *WhoAmW 91*
Dawson, Charles Edward 1921- *WhoSSW 91*
Dawson, Charles Robert 1925- *WhoE 91*
Dawson, Clay *ConAu 31NR*
Dawson, Clayton Leroy 1921- *WhoAm 90*
Dawson, Cleo 1909- *LiHiK*
Dawson, Craig Gayden 1954- *WhoEmL 91*
Dawson, David George 1947- *St&PR 91*
Dawson, Dawn Paige 1956- *WhoAmW 91*
Dawson, Dennis R. 1948- *St&PR 91*
Dawson, Dennis Ray 1948- *WhoAm 90, WhoEmL 91*
Dawson, Diane 1954- *WhoAmW 91*
Dawson, Donald C. 1937- *St&PR 91*
Dawson, Doug 1944- *WhoAmA 91*
Dawson, Earl Bliss 1930- *WhoSSW 91*
Dawson, Edith Robinson 1862-1928? *BioIn 16*
Dawson, Edward Joseph 1944- *WhoWor 91*
Dawson, Eve *WhoAmA 91N*
Dawson, George 1951- *BiDrAPA 89*
Dawson, George Amos 1924- *WhoWrEP 89*
Dawson, George Glenn 1925- *WhoAm 90*
Dawson, Gerald L. 1935- *ODwPR 91*
Dawson, Horace Greeley, Jr. 1926- *WhoAm 90*
Dawson, Howard 1953- *WhoEmL 91*
Dawson, Howard Athalone, Jr. 1922- *WhoAm 90*
Dawson, James A. 1937- *St&PR 91*
Dawson, James P. 1896-1953 *Ballpl 90*
Dawson, Jennifer 1929- *FemiCLE*
Dawson, Jim William 1934- *WhoSSW 91*
Dawson, Joan Helen 1941- *WhoAmW 91*
Dawson, JoAnn Overton 1934- *WhoAmW 91*
Dawson, Joe 1897-1978 *Ballpl 90*
Dawson, John Alan 1949- *WhoE 91*
Dawson, John Allan 1946- *WhoAmA 91*
Dawson, John Frederick 1930- *WhoAm 90*
Dawson, John Huger, Jr. 1943- *St&PR 91*
Dawson, John Myrick 1930- *WhoAm 90*
Dawson, John Scott 1953- *WhoEmL 91, WhoSSW 91*
Dawson, John Virgil 1956- *WhoSSW 91*
Dawson, John William 1820-1899 *DcCanB 12*
Dawson, Kenneth Robert *BiDrAPA 89*
Dawson, Leighton Brooks 1910- *WhoSSW 91*
Dawson, Len 1935- *WorAlBi*
Dawson, Leslie D. 1903- *St&PR 91*
Dawson, Lynne 1953- *IntWWM 90*
Dawson, M. Taylor, Jr. 1929- *St&PR 91*
Dawson, Mark H. *WhoAm 90*
Dawson, Mary Ann Weyforth *BioIn 16*
Dawson, Mary Elizabeth 1961- *WhoAmW 91*
Dawson, Mary Martha 1908- *WhoWrEP 89*
Dawson, Mary Ruth 1931- *WhoAm 90*
Dawson, Michelle Henderson- *BioIn 16*
Dawson, Mimi 1944- *WhoAm 90, WhoAmW 91*
Dawson, Mimi Weyforth *BioIn 16*
Dawson, Mitchell 1890- *AuBYP 90*
Dawson, Nathaniel Henry Rhodes 1829-1895 *AmLegL*
Dawson, Nelson 1859-1941 *BioIn 16*
Dawson, Nelson Lloyd 1939- *WhoSSW 91*
Dawson, O. Douglas 1944- *St&PR 91*
Dawson, Pamela *ODwPR 91*
Dawson, Peter 1882-1961 *OxCPMus, PenDiMP*
Dawson, Peter 1933- *BioIn 16*
Dawson, Peter John 1928- *WhoSSW 91*
Dawson, Ralph B 1910- *BiDrAPA 89*
Dawson, Ray Fields 1911- *WhoAm 90*
Dawson, Raymond Howard 1927- *WhoAm 90*
Dawson, Rhett Brewer 1943- *St&PR 91*
Dawson, Richard 1932- *ConTFT 8, WorAlBi*
Dawson, Richard T. 1945- *St&PR 91*
Dawson, Richard Thomas 1945- *WhoAm 90*
Dawson, Robert C. 1923- *St&PR 91*
Dawson, Robert Earle 1923- *WhoAm 90*
Dawson, Robert Edward, Sr. 1918- *WhoAm 90, WhoSSW 91, WhoWor 91*
Dawson, Robert Kent 1946- *WhoAm 90*
Dawson, Robert Kevin 1953- *WhoEmL 91*
Dawson, Robert Oscar 1939- *WhoAm 90*
Dawson, Robert Victor 1939- *St&PR 91*

Dawson, Samuel Cooper, Jr. 1909- WhoAm 90
Dawson, Seth Ray 1951- WhoEmL 91
Dawson, Stephen Edwin 1949- WhoEmL 91
Dawson, Stephen Everette 1946- WhoEmL 91
Dawson, Stuart Owen 1935- WhoAm 90
Dawson, Sue Ellen 1955- WhoAmW 91, WhoSSW 91
Dawson, Thomas Cleland 1865-1912 BioIn 16
Dawson, Thomas Cleland, II 1948- WhoAm 90
Dawson, Thomas Wayne 1947- WhoSSW 91
Dawson, Wallace Douglas, Jr. 1931- WhoAm 90
Dawson, Wilfred Thomas 1928- WhoAm 90
Dawson, William 1885-1972 BioIn 16
Dawson, William 1901- MusmAFA
Dawson, William James, Jr. 1930- WhoAm 90
Dawson, William Johnson, Jr. 1925- WhoSSW 91
Dawson, William L. 1899-1990 NewYTBS 90
Dawson, William Levi 1886-1970 BlkAmsC [port]
Dawson, William Levi 1898- DrBlPA 90
Dawson, William Levi 1899- DcAfAmP, IntWWM 90
Dawson, William Levi 1899-1990 BioIn 16
Dawson, William P. 1943- St&PR 91
Dawson, William Ryan 1927- WhoAm 90
Dawson, William Thomas 1938- St&PR 91
Dawson-Scott, Catharine Amy EncO&P 3
Dax, E Cunningham 1908- BiDrAPA 89
Daxhelet, Jean Paul 1958- WhoWor 91
Day, A. Grove 1904- BioIn 16
Day, Aidan 1952- ConAu 132
Day, Alexandra 19--?- ChlLR 22 [port]
Day, Ali Mae 1959- WhoAmW 91
Day, Anne Glendenning White Parker 1926- WhoAmW 91
Day, Anne Leitch ODwPR 91
Day, Anthony 1933- WhoAm 90
Day, Arthur Grove 1904- BioIn 16, WhoAm 90
Day, Audrey WhoWrEP 89
Day, Barry Leonard 1934- WhoAm 90
Day, Benjamin Henry 1810-1889 BioIn 16
Day, Beth 1924- AuBYP 90
Day, Bill BioIn 16
Day, Boots 1947- Ballpl 90
Day, Brigitte Kapitaen 1951- WhoAmW 91
Day, Bruce W. 1945- St&PR 91
Day, Burnis Calvin 1940- WhoAmA 91
Day, Caroline Bond Stewart 1889-1948 HarlReB
Day, Castle Nason 1933- St&PR 91, WhoAm 90
Day, Cecil LeRoy 1922- WhoAm 90
Day, Charles E. ODwPR 91
Day, Chester L BiDrAPA 89
Day, Chon 1907- WhoAm 90, WhoAmA 91
Day, Clarence NewYTBS 90
Day, Clarence 1874-1935 WorAlBi
Day, Clarence 1901-1990 BioIn 16
Day, Clifford Grant 1948- WhoE 91
Day, Colin Leslie 1944- WhoAm 90
Day, Daniel Edgar 1913- WhoAm 90
Day, David 1825-1893 AmLegL
Day, David Allen 1924- WhoAm 90
Day, David Owen 1958- WhoSSW 91
Day, Dennis 1917-1988 AnObit 1988, BioIn 16, OxCPMus
Day, Donald Clifford 1928- St&PR 91
Day, Donald Lee 1947- WhoE 91
Day, Donald Morfoot 1954- WhoEmL 91
Day, Donald Sheldon 1924- WhoAm 90
Day, Doris 1922- OxCPMus
Day, Doris 1924- WhoAm 90, WorAlBi
Day, Dorothy 1897- WorAlBi
Day, Dorothy 1897-1980 BioAmW, BioIn 16, FemiCLE
Day, Dorothy G. 1930- St&PR 91
Day, Edith 1896-1971 OxCPMus
Day, Edward Francis, Jr. 1946- WhoE 91, WhoEmL 91, WhoWor 91
Day, Elise 1955- St&PR 91
Day, Emerson 1913- WhoAm 90
Day, Eugene Davis, Sr. 1925- WhoAm 90, WhoSSW 91
Day, Frances 1908- OxCPMus
Day, Frank Parker 1881-1950 DcLB 92 [port]
Day, Frank R. 1931- WhoAm 90
Day, Gary Eugene 1954- WhoEmL 91
Day, Gary Lewis 1950- WhoAmA 91
Day, George C. 1948- St&PR 91
Day, George H 1851-1907 EncABHB 4 [port]
Day, George R. 1950- WhoWrEP 89
Day, Gerald J. WhoAm 90
Day, Gerald W. WhoAm 90
Day, Graham BioIn 16
Day, Gregg Alan 1952- WhoEmL 91
Day, Guy Brian BioIn 16
Day, H. Willis, Jr. 1925- St&PR 91
Day, Holliday T 1936- WhoAmA 91
Day, Horace Talmage 1909- WhoAmA 91N
Day, Ingeborg 1940- EncCoWW
Day, J. Alan 1945- WhoE 91
Day, Jack Theodore 1934- WhoSSW 91
Day, James E. 1940- ODwPR 91
Day, James Edward 1914- BiDrUSE 89, WhoAm 90, WhoE 91
Day, James Edward 1940- St&PR 91
Day, James L 1946- BiDrAPA 89
Day, James Milton 1931- WhoAm 90
Day, Jennie D. WhoAmW 91
Day, Joe Campbell 1955- WhoSSW 91
Day, Joel M. 1941- St&PR 91
Day, John 1574-1640? BioIn 16
Day, John 1932-1984 WhoAmA 91N
Day, John 1944- ODwPR 91
Day, John A. 1957- WhoSSW 91
Day, John Arthur 1956- WhoEmL 91, WhoSSW 91
Day, John B. Ballpl 90, BioIn 16
Day, John Denton 1942- WhoWor 91
Day, John Francis 1920- WhoAm 90
Day, John Franklin 1928- WhoAm 90
Day, John M. 1935- St&PR 91
Day, John Sidney 1917- WhoAm 90
Day, John W. 1933- WhoAm 90
Day, Jonny Mac 1946- St&PR 91
Day, Joseph Dennis 1942- WhoAm 90
Day, Larry 1921- WhoAmA 91
Day, Larry D. 1944- St&PR 91
Day, Lawrence Elwood 1947- WhoEmL 91
Day, Leon 1916- Ballpl 90
Day, LeRoy Edward 1925- WhoAm 90
Day, Lewis Foreman 1845-1910 PenDiDA 89
Day, Lila WhoWrEP 89
Day, Lucienne 1917- ConDes 90, PenDiDA 89
Day, Lucille Elizabeth 1947- WhoAmW 91, WhoEmL 91
Day, Lynda ConTFT 8
Day, Lynne Karen BiDrAPA 89
Day, Mabel K 1884- WhoAmA 91N
Day, Marie 1933- OxCCanT
Day, Mary Jane Thomas 1927- WhoAmW 91
Day, Marylouise Muldoon WhoAmW 91
Day, Maurice Jerome 1913- St&PR 91, WhoAm 90
Day, Max 1923- BiDrAPA 89, WhoE 91
Day, Melvin Sherman 1923- WhoAm 90, WhoE 91
Day, Michael H. 1949- St&PR 91
Day, Morris 1958?- DrBlPA 90
Day, Nancy I. 1944- St&PR 91
Day, Pat 1954?- BioIn 16
Day, Paul Richard 1922- WhoAm 90
Day, Peggy Jean 1946- WhoAmW 91, WhoSSW 91
Day, Peter William 1944- WhoSSW 91
Day, Pomeroy 1906- WhoAm 90
Day, Richard 1896-1972 ConDes 90
Day, Richard Cortez 1927- LiHiK, WhoWrEP 89
Day, Richard Curtis 1934- St&PR 91
Day, Richard Earl 1929- WhoWor 91
Day, Richard Elledge 1939- WhoWor 91
Day, Richard L. 1905-1989 BioIn 16
Day, Richard Putnam 1930- St&PR 91
Day, Rob BioIn 16
Day, Robert Androus 1924- WhoAm 90
Day, Robert Edgar 1919- WhoAm 90
Day, Robert Jennings 1925- St&PR 91, WhoAm 90
Day, Robert Malcolm 1954- WhoSSW 91
Day, Robert Winsor 1930- WhoAm 90
Day, Robin 1915- ConDes 90, PenDiDA 89
Day, Roland Bernard 1919- WhoAm 90
Day, Ronald Elwin 1933- WhoE 91, WhoWor 91
Day, Ruth S BiDrAPA 89
Day, Sharon Hoelscher BioIn 16
Day, Sharon Hoelscher 1952- WhoEmL 91
Day, Stacey Biswas 1927- WhoAm 90, WhoE 91, WhoWor 91
Day, Stanley R. 1925- WhoAm 90
Day, Stephen 1594?-1668 EncCRAm
Day, Stephen Leo 1945- WhoEmL 91
Day, Stephen Martin 1931- WhoAm 90
Day, Stephen Peter 1938- WhoWor 91
Day, Steven Guy 1954- WhoE 91
Day, Suzanne Marie 1953- WhoAmW 91
Day, Terry Lee 1955- WhoAmW 91
Day, Thomas Brennock 1932- WhoAm 90
Day, Timothy T. 1937- St&PR 91
Day, Tod Eugene 1964- WhoSSW 91
Day, Valerie BioIn 16
Day, Wayne Allan 1955- WhoSSW 91
Day, Wilbur 1864-1924 BioIn 16
Day, William Hudson 1937- WhoAm 90
Day, William Rufus 1849-1923 BiDrUSE 89, BioIn 16
Day, Willie S. 1947- St&PR 91
Day, Worden 1916-1986 WhoAmA 91N
Day Lewis, C. TwCCr&M 91
Day Lewis, C 1904-1972 MajTwCW
Day-Lewis, Daniel BioIn 16, WhoWor 91
Day-Lewis, Daniel 1958?- CurBio 90 [port]
Day-Lewis, Sean 1931- ConAu 132
Dayal, Parmeshwar 1931- EncPaPR 91
Dayal, Rajeshwar 1909- ConAu 130
Dayan, Ezra 1913- St&PR 91
Dayan, Jacob 1944- St&PR 91
Dayan, Moshe 1915-1981 BioIn 16, PolLCME, WorAlBi
Dayan, Rodney S. 1933- WhoAm 90, WhoE 91, WhoWor 91
Dayan, Sara Beth BiDrAPA 89
Dayananda, Mysore Ananthamurthy 1934- WhoAm 90
Dayani, John Hassan, Sr. 1947- WhoEmL 91
Dayboch, Barry Irnest 1954- WhoE 91, WhoEmL 91
Daye, Eliza FemiCLE
Dayharsh, Virginia Fiengo 1942- WhoAmW 91
Dayhoff, Charles Sidney, III 1948- WhoEmL 91
Dayhoff, Jocelyn Rausch 1956- WhoEmL 91
Dayley, Ken 1959- Ballpl 90
Dayman, Craig Ryan 1961- WhoEmL 91
Dayne, Taylor BioIn 16
Dayne, Taylor 1963- ConMus 4 [port]
Daysh, George Henry John 1901-1987 BioIn 16
Dayson, Diane Harris 1953- WhoE 91
Dayton, Anne Harker 1938- WhoE 91
Dayton, Donald C. 1914-1989 BioIn 16
Dayton, Douglas J. 1924- St&PR 91
Dayton, Irene Catherine 1922- WhoWrEP 89
Dayton, John Webster 1945- WhoSSW 91
Dayton, Jonathan 1760-1824 BioIn 16, WorAlBi
Dayton, Nancy Elizabeth 1945- WhoAmW 91
Dayton, Richard Lee 1934- WhoAm 90
Dayton, Robert Jackson 1942- WhoAm 90
Dayton, S. Grey, Jr. 1921- St&PR 91
Dayton, Samuel Grey, Jr. 1921- WhoAm 90
Dayton, William Lewis 1807-1864 BioIn 16
Daywalt, Theodore Lewis 1949- WhoSSW 91
Daza, Pedro 1925- WhoWor 91
Dazai, Osamu 1909-1948 BioIn 16
Daze, Colleen Janice 1950- WhoE 91
Daze, David Timothy 1949- WhoEmL 91
Dazey, Agnes AuBYP 90
Dazey, Charles T. 1855-1938 LiHiK
Dazey, Frank M. AuBYP 90
Dazey, William Boyd 1915- WhoAm 90
D'Azzara, Lewis 1935- BiDrAPA 89
D'Azzo, John Joachim 1919- WhoAm 90
D'Costa, Jean 1937- FemiCLE
De, Bibhas Ranjan 1946- WhoWor 91
Doo, Donald Don 1954- WhoE 91
Dea, Margaret Mary 1946- WhoAmW 91
Dea, Phoebe Kin-Kin 1946- WhoAmW 91, WhoEmL 91
Deacon, Donald M. 1920- St&PR 91
Deacon, George Edward Raven 1906-1984 DcNaB 1981
Deacon, Paul Septimus 1922- WhoAm 90
Deacon, Richard ConAu 32NR
Deacon, Robert H. 1926- St&PR 91
Deacons, Prudentia 1581-1645 BiDEWW
De Acosta, Joseph 1540-1600 BioIn 16
Deacy, Thomas Edward, Jr. 1918- WhoAm 90
Deaderick, Jimmy R. 1947- WhoE 91
Deaderick, Joseph 1930- WhoAmA 91
Deadman, John C BiDrAPA 89
Deadman, Leonard John 1932- WhoAm 90
Deadman, Ronald 1919-1988? BioIn 16
Deagon, Ann 1930- WhoWrEP 89
De Ahna, Heinrich PenDiMP
De Ahna, Pauline PenDiMP
Deak, Csaba 1932- IntWWM 90
Deak, Edit 1948- WhoAmA 91
Deak, Franklin Harry 1948- WhoEmL 91
Deak, Istvan 1926- WhoAm 90
Deakin, Edward B. 1943- WhoAm 90
Deakin, James 1929- WhoAm 90, WhoWor 91
Deakins, Anthony Duke 1946- WhoSSW 91
Deakins, John David 1942- St&PR 91
Deakins, Susan Margaret BiDrAPA 89
Deakins, Warren Whitney 1938- St&PR 91, WhoAm 90
Deakyne, S. Graham 1928- St&PR 91, WhoAm 90
Deal, Alphonso B. BioIn 16
Deal, Bruce Elmer 1927- WhoAm 90
Deal, Charlie 1891-1979 Ballpl 90
Deal, Coite Oscar 1929- WhoSSW 91
Deal, Ernest L 1918-1984 ConAu 132
Deal, Ernest L., Jr. 1929- St&PR 91
Deal, Ernest Linwood, Jr. 1929- WhoAm 90, WhoSSW 91
Deal, G. Ralph 1940- St&PR 91
Deal, George A. 1914- St&PR 91
Deal, George Edgar 1920- WhoAm 90, WhoWor 91
Deal, Grady Abee 1944- St&PR 91
Deal, James William 1932- WhoE 91
Deal, Janet Jean 1936- WhoAmW 91
Deal, Joe 1947- WhoAmA 91
Deal, Michael J BiDrAPA 89
Deal, Richard Allen 1929- St&PR 91
Deal, Roger Wiley 1943- BiDrAPA 89
Deal, Shirley Mae Herd 1935- WhoWrEP 89
Deal, Susan Strayer 1948- WhoWrEP 89
Deal, Terrance E. 1939- ConAu 130
Deal, William Brown 1936- WhoAm 90
De Alarcon, Pedro Antonio 1833-1891 BioIn 16
de Albuquerque Fortes, Jose R 1924- BiDrAPA 89
Deale, Henry Vail, Jr. 1915- WhoAm 90
Deale, Shirley 1925- BiDrAPA 89
De Alencar, Jose Martiniano 1829-1877 BioIn 16
Dealessandro, Joseph P. 1930- St&PR 91
DeAlessandro, Joseph Paul 1930- WhoAm 90, WhoWor 91
Dealexandris, Robert A. 1941- St&PR 91
Dealey, Amanda Mayhew 1950- WhoSSW 91
Dealey, George Bannerman 1859-1946 BioIn 16
Dealey, Joseph MacDonald, Jr. 1947- WhoSSW 91
De Almeida, Anibal Traga 1950- WhoWor 91
De Almeida, Antonio PenDiMP
DeAlmeida, Marcella J. 1922- WhoAmW 91
De Almeida, Robert Anthony 1954- WhoEmL 91
De Alwis, Susanta 1932- WhoWor 91
Dealy, James J. 1935- St&PR 91
Dealy, John Francis 1939- WhoAm 90
Dealy, John Michael 1937- WhoAm 90
Deamer, Dulcie 1890-1972 FemiCLE
Deamer, Richard M 1941- BiDrAPA 89
De Amicis, Anna Lucia 1733?-1816 PenDiMP
Dean, Alan Loren 1918- WhoAm 90
Dean, Andrea Oppenheimer 1935- WhoE 91
Dean, Anna Rose 1940- WhoAmW 91
Dean, Anne Frey 1942- WhoAmW 91
Dean, Anthony Taylor 1945- St&PR 91
Dean, Arthur Hobson 1898-1987 BioIn 16
Dean, Beale 1922- WhoAm 90, WhoSSW 91
Dean, Bennett Wayne, Sr. 1942- WhoSSW 91, WhoWor 91
Dean, Betty Marlene 1941- WhoAmW 91
Dean, Bruce Campbell 1958- WhoEmL 91
Dean, Burton Victor 1924- WhoAm 90
Dean, Carl L. 1927- St&PR 91
Dean, Carold A., Jr. 1944- St&PR 91
Dean, Catherine Jean 1950- WhoAmW 91
Dean, Charles Henry, Jr. 1925- WhoAm 90
Dean, Charles Thomas 1918- WhoAm 90
Dean, Chubby 1916-1970 Ballpl 90
Dean, Cynthia Bailey 1956- WhoWrEP 89
Dean, David 1942- St&PR 91
Dean, David Jerome 1948- WhoEmL 91
Dean, Dearest 1911- WhoAmW 91
Dean, Deborah Gore BioIn 16
Dean, Deborah Gore 1954- WhoAm 90, WhoAmW 91
Dean, Denis Allen 1942- WhoSSW 91
Dean, Dewey Hobson, Jr. 1920- St&PR 91
Dean, Dizzy 1911-1974 Ballpl 90 [port], WorAlBi
Dean, Don R. 1941- St&PR 91
Dean, Donald B 1927- BiDrAPA 89
Dean, Donna Joyce 1947- WhoAmW 91
Dean, E Douglas 1916- EncPaPR 91
Dean, E. H. Rick 1946- WhoSSW 91
Dean, E. Joseph 1949- WhoEmL 91
Dean, Earl F 1915- BiDrAPA 89
Dean, Edward S 1914- BiDrAPA 89
Dean, Edwin Becton 1940- WhoSSW 91, WhoWor 91
Dean, Elizabeth M. 1948- WhoEmL 91
Dean, Eric BioIn 16
Dean, Eric Douglas 1916- EncO&P 3
Dean, Ernest Wilfrid WhoAmA 91N
Dean, Frances Childers 1930- WhoAm 90, WhoAmW 91
Dean, Frederick B. 1927- St&PR 91
Dean, G Adrian 1939- BiDrAPA 89
Dean, Geoffrey 1940- WhoAm 90
Dean, George Alden 1929- WhoAm 90
Dean, Graham M. 1904- AuBYP 90
Dean, Harold Leon 1950- WhoSSW 91
Dean, Harry Todrick 1947- St&PR 91
Dean, Helen Barbara 1945- WhoAmW 91
Dean, Helen Henrietta 1905- WhoAmW 91

Dean, Henry L BiDrAPA 89
Dean, Hope Sweetser BioIn 16, NewYTBS 90
Dean, Howard 1948- WhoAm 90, WhoE 91
Dean, Howard Brush 1921- WhoAm 90
Dean, Howard M., Jr. 1937- WhoAm 90
Dean, Jack Pearce 1931- WhoAm 90
Dean, Jaclynn Lee 1947- WhoAmW 91
Dean, Jacquelyn Marie 1954- WhoAmW 91
Dean, James 1931- WhoAmA 91
Dean, James 1931-1955 BioIn 16, WorAlBi
Dean, James B. 1941- WhoAm 90
Dean, James Edward 1944- WhoSSW 91
Dean, James Wendell 1948- WhoSSW 91
Dean, Jane Susan 1953- WhoE 91
Dean, Jerry Robert 1935- St&PR 91
Dean, Jimmy 1928- St&PR 91, WhoAm 90, WorAlBi
Dean, Joe Alan 1950- WhoEmL 91
Dean, John Aurie 1921- WhoAm 90, WhoWor 91
Dean, John Clemet, Jr. 1947- WhoSSW 91
Dean, John Gunther 1926- WhoAm 90
Dean, John Stanley 1939- St&PR 91
Dean, John Theodore 1934- IntWWM 90
Dean, John W., III 1938- WorAlBi
Dean, John Wilson, Jr. 1918- WhoAm 90
Dean, Julia 1830-1868 BioIn 16, NotWoAT
Dean, Julie 1951- WhoE 91
Dean, Karen Strickler 1923- BioIn 16
Dean, Kathy Jean Davis 1962- WhoSSW 91
Dean, Larry A. 1942- St&PR 91
Dean, Laura BioIn 16
Dean, Laura 1945- WhoAmW 91
Dean, Leigh AuBYP 90
Dean, Lydia Margaret Carter 1919- WhoAm 90, WhoAmW 91, WhoWor 91
Dean, Lynda G. 1945- St&PR 91
Dean, Lynn 1923- St&PR 91
Dean, Malcolm 1948- ConAu 31NR
Dean, Margaret Mahler 1944- WhoAmW 91
Dean, Margo 1927- WhoAmW 91, WhoSSW 91
Dean, Mary Ann 1941- WhoAmW 91
Dean, Mary Elisabeth 1933- WhoE 91
Dean, Mary Elizabeth 1947- WhoEmL 91
Dean, Michael M. 1933- WhoAm 90, WhoWor 91
Dean, Michael Patrick 1946- WhoEmL 91
Dean, Morris Jonathan 1931- WhoAm 90
Dean, Nancy Ann 1959- WhoAmW 91
Dean, Nat 1956- WhoAmA 91
Dean, Nathaniel 1956- WhoE 91
Dean, Nell 1910- AuBYP 90
Dean, Nicholas Brice 1933- WhoAmA 91
Dean, Norman E. 1943- St&PR 91
Dean, Norman Emerson 1943- WhoAm 90
Dean, Norman Kent 1943- WhoSSW 91
Dean, Norman L. 1939- WhoE 91
Dean, Paul 1913-1981 Ballpl 90
Dean, Paul John 1941- WhoAm 90, WhoWrEP 89
Dean, Paul Regis 1918- WhoAm 90
Dean, Penny BioIn 16
Dean, Peter 1939- WhoAmA 91
Dean, Peter 1941- WhoAm 90
Dean, Peter Laurence 1956- WhoE 91
Dean, Phillip Hayes DrBlPA 90
Dean, Ralph James, Sr. 1944- WhoSSW 91, WhoWor 91
Dean, Richard Anthony 1935- St&PR 91
Dean, Richard Whaley 1942- St&PR 91
Dean, Robert A. 1926- St&PR 91
Dean, Robert Bruce 1949- WhoE 91
Dean, Robert Charles 1903- WhoAm 90
Dean, Robert Charles, Jr. 1928- WhoAm 90
Dean, Robert Couslor 1947- BiDrAPA 89
Dean, Robert George 1904?-1989 ConAu 130
Dean, Robert Scott 1955- WhoE 91, WhoEmL 91
Dean, Robert T., Jr. 1927- BiDrAPA 89
Dean, Robert Walter, Jr. 1950- WhoEmL 91
Dean, Roger Thornton 1948- IntWWM 90
Dean, Ronald L. 1945- St&PR 91
Dean, Rosemary WhoWrEP 89
Dean, Roxane 1956- WhoAmW 91
Dean, Roy Marvin, Jr. 1953- WhoSSW 91
Dean, S. F. X. TwCCr&M 91
Dean, Sidney Walter, Jr. 1905- WhoAm 90
Dean, Spencer TwCCr&M 91
Dean, Stafford PenDiMP
Dean, Stafford 1937- IntWWM 90
Dean, Stanley R BiDrAPA 89
Dean, Stanley Rochelle 1908- WhoAm 90, WhoWor 91
Dean, Stephen Odell 1936- WhoAm 90
Dean, Talmage Whitman 1915- IntWWM 90
Dean, Thelma J. 1944- WhoAmW 91
Dean, Thomas H. 1928- St&PR 91
Dean, Thomas Scott 1924- WhoAm 90
Dean, Tommy 1945- Ballpl 90
Dean, Vincent W. 1948- St&PR 91
Dean, Walter L. 1927- St&PR 91
Dean, Walter Nelson 1919- WhoAm 90
Dean, Warren Michael 1944- St&PR 91
Dean, Warwick R BiDrAPA 89
Dean, Wayland 1902-1930 Ballpl 90
Dean, Wayne Dickerson 1925- WhoWor 91
Dean, William Evans 1930- St&PR 91, WhoAm 90
Dean, William George 1921- WhoAm 90
Dean, William L. 1926- St&PR 91
Dean, William Mark 1943- BiDrAPA 89
Dean, William Shirley 1947- WhoEmL 91
Dean, Winton Basil 1916- IntWWM 90
Dean-Zubritsky, Cynthia Marian 1950- WhoAmW 91, WhoE 91, WhoEmL 91
De Anda, Arnold 1946- WhoHisp 91
DeAnda, James 1925- WhoAm 90, WhoSSW 91
De Anda, Peter 1940- DrBlPA 90
De Anda, Raul WhoHisp 91
De Andino, Jean-Pierre M 1946- WhoAmA 91
de Andino, Jean-Pierre Martinez 1946- WhoE 91
de Andrade, Carlos Drummond ConAu 132
De Andrade, Mario 1893-1945 BioIn 16
De Andrade, Mario 1928-1990 BioIn 16
de Andrade, Mario Pinto 1928-1990 NewYTBS 90
DeAndrea, William L 1952- TwCCr&M 91
Deane, Ada Emma EncO&P 3
Deane, Anne BiDEWW
Deane, Edwin G. 1928- St&PR 91
Deane, Elaine 1958- WhoEmL 91
Deane, Frederick, Jr. BioIn 16
Deane, Frederick, Jr. 1926- St&PR 91, WhoAm 90, WhoSSW 91
Deane, Frederick R M 1936- BiDrAPA 89
Deane, Herbert Andrew 1921- WhoAm 90
Deane, James Garner 1923- WhoAm 90, WhoWor 91, WhoWrEP 89
Deane, James R. 1935- St&PR 91
Deane, John Cutting 1947- WhoAm 90
Deane, John Herbert 1952- WhoE 91
Deane, Joseph R. 1926- St&PR 91
Deane, Lyttleton Nicholas 1954- WhoEmL 91
Deane, Norman MajTwCW, TwCCr&M 91
Deane, Philip Redpath 1947- IntWWM 90
Deane, Sally Jan 1948- WhoAmW 91, WhoEmL 91
Deane, Silas 1737-1789 BioIn 16, EncCRAm [port], WorAlBi
Deane, Thomas Andersen 1921- St&PR 91, WhoAm 90
Deane, William John 1938- St&PR 91
Deaner, R. Milton 1924- WhoAm 90
DeAngeli, Carlo Frua 1944- St&PR 91
De Angeli, Marguerite 1889- AuBYP 90
De Angeli, Marguerite Lofft 1889-1987 BioIn 16
De Angelis, Anthony A. 1938- ODwPR 91
De Angelis, Barbara BestSel 90-3 [port]
De Angelis, Deborah Ann Ayars 1948- WhoAmW 91
Deangelis, Elsa J. St&PR 91
DeAngelis, John A. 1913- St&PR 91
DeAngelis, John E. St&PR 91
DeAngelis, John Louis, Jr. 1951- WhoSSW 91
Deangelis, Joseph Anthony 1955- St&PR 91
Deangelis, Joseph Rocco 1938- WhoAmA 91
Deangelis, Kay ODwPR 91
DeAngelis, Lorraine Theresa 1960- WhoEmL 91
DeAngelis, Margaret Scalza 1936- WhoAmW 91, WhoWor 91
DeAngelis, Peter 1929- St&PR 91
DeAngelis, Robert Neal 1942- WhoSSW 91
DeAngelis, Susan Penny 1950- WhoAmW 91
Deangelo, John 1928- St&PR 91
Deano, Paula Mayard 1957- WhoSSW 91
Deans, Angela Vick 1957- WhoAmW 91
Deans, Janice P. 1958- WhoEmL 91
Deans, Thomas Seymour 1946- WhoEmL 91
Deans, William Ronald 1935- WhoSSW 91
De Antoni, Edward Paul 1941- WhoAm 90
De Antonio, Carlo Peter 1920- BiDrAPA 89
De Antonio, Emile BioIn 16
de Antonio, Emile 1922-1989 ConAu 130
De Antonio, Mark 1954- BiDrAPA 89
De Antonio, Miriam F BiDrAPA 89
DeAntonis, G.W., Jr. 1940- St&PR 91
Dear, David Ollie 1941- St&PR 91
De Aragon, RaGena Cheri 1952- WhoEmL 91
Dearborn, Donald Edward 1939- WhoE 91
Dearborn, Henry 1751-1829 BiDrUSE 89, EncCRAm, WhNaAH
Dearborn, Laura WhoAmW 91
Dearborn, Maureen Markt 1948- WhoAmW 91, WhoE 91
De Arce, Jaime Borrios Perez BioIn 16
Dearden, Douglas E. 1921- St&PR 91
Dearden, James BioIn 16
Dearden, John BioIn 16
Dearden, William Edgar Chambers 1922- St&PR 91, WhoAm 90
Deardorf, David Allen 1937- St&PR 91
Deardourff, John D. 1933- WhoAm 90
Deare, Jennifer Laurie 1952- WhoEmL 91
Dearie, Blossom BioIn 16
Dearing, Audrey Traugott 1929- St&PR 91
Dearing, David A. 1948- St&PR 91
Dearing, Deborah Carter 1957- WhoEmL 91
Dearing, Michael Eugene 1955- WhoE 91
Dearing, Reinhard Josef 1947- WhoEmL 91, WhoSSW 91
Dearing, Vinton Adams 1920- WhoAm 90, WhoWrEP 89
Dearman, Henry B BiDrAPA 89
Dearman, Henry Hursell 1934- WhoAm 90
DeArman, Richard L. 1947- St&PR 91
De Armand, Frances Ullmann 1904?-1984 AuBYP 90
de Armas, Frederick A. 1945- WhoHisp 91
De Armas, Frederick Alfred 1945- WhoAm 90
De Armas, Jorge Benito 1931- St&PR 91
DeArment, George S. 1913- St&PR 91
DeArment, William Almon 1915- St&PR 91
De Arment, William S. 1947- St&PR 91
De Armond, Anna Janney 1910- WhoAmW 91
De Armond, Dale B WhoAmA 91
De Armond, Murray M 1935- BiDrAPA 89
Dearmont, Nelson Strother 1930- WhoE 91
Dearmore, Thomas Lee 1927- WhoAm 90
Dearnley, Christopher 1930- PenDiMP
Dearnley, Christopher Hugh 1930- IntWWM 90
Dearnley, Dorothy Alice 1914- IntWWM 90
De Arriaga, Julian BioIn 16
Dears, Robert Alan 1948- IntWWM 90
Dearsley, Gwenda Margaret 1944- IntWWM 90
Dearth, Jeffrey L. 1950- WhoAm 90
Dearth, Robert Alfred, Jr. 1944- WhoAm 90
Dearth, William Benton, III 1950- St&PR 91
Deary, Roy Grant, Jr. 1930- St&PR 91
Deary, Terry 1946- BioIn 16
Deas, Charles 1818-1867 WhNaAH
Deas, David John 1929- BiDrAPA 89
Deas, Richard Ryder, III 1927- WhoSSW 91
Dease, Ann Wilks 1938- WhoSSW 91
Deasey, Michael Keith 1947- IntWWM 90
Deason, Edward Joseph 1955- WhoWor 91
Deason, Glen Albert 1941- WhoSSW 91
Deason-Lee, Patricia Ann 1950- WhoEmL 91
Deasy, Cornelius Michael 1918- WhoAm 90
Deasy, John Michael 1945- WhoEmL 91
Deasy, Kevin 1953- WhoEmL 91
Deasy, Mark ODwPR 91
Deasy, Patrick G. 1938- St&PR 91
Deasy, Theresa 1958- WhoAmW 91
Deasy, William John 1937- St&PR 91, WhoAm 90
Deat, Marcel 1894-1955 BiDFrPL
Deatherage, Joann BiDrAPA 89
Deatherage, Martha Martin WhoSSW 91
Deatly, Richard Henry 1928- St&PR 91
Deaton, Angus Stewart 1945- WhoAm 90
Deaton, Bobby Charles 1936- WhoSSW 91
Deaton, Brian Jason 1948- WhoE 91
Deaton, Charles 1921- WhoAmA 91, WhoWor 91
Deaton, Daniel Harry 1927- St&PR 91
Deaton, Donald C. ODwPR 91
Deaton, Fae Adams 1932- WhoWor 91
Deaton, Frank A. 1925- St&PR 91
Deaton, Michael Paul 1951- WhoEmL 91
Deaton, Rodney J S 1957- BiDrAPA 89
Deaton, Tammie Lynn 1964- WhoEmL 91
Deaton, Teresa Pressley 1951- WhoAmW 91
Deats, John R. 1943- ODwPR 91
Deats, Margaret 1942- WhoAmA 91
Deats, Paul Edwin 1946- WhoEmL 91
Deats, Paul Kindred, Jr. 1918- WhoAm 90
Deats, Richard Warren 1945- WhoEmL 91
D'Eau, Jean ConAu 132
D'Eaubonne, Jean 1903-1970 ConDes 90
Deaver, Bobby Gray 1932- WhoSSW 91
Deaver, Darwin Holloway 1914- St&PR 91, WhoAm 90
Deaver, E. Allen 1935- WhoAm 90
Deaver, Julie Reece 1953- ConAu 129
Deaver, Michael K. BioIn 16
Deaver, Pete Eugene 1936- WhoWor 91
Deaver, Phillip Lester 1952- WhoEmL 91, WhoWor 91
Deavers, Karl A. 1934- St&PR 91
Deavers, Karl Alan 1934- WhoAm 90
De Aycinena, Juan Jose 1792?-1865 BioIn 16
De Azevedo, Belmiro BioIn 16
De Azevedo, Lorenco 1958- WhoHisp 91
Deb, Arun Kumar 1936- St&PR 91
Deb Sikdar, Brajendra M 1929- BiDrAPA 89
de Back, John, Jr. BiDrAPA 89
DeBakey, George Toufee 1949- WhoAm 90, WhoWor 91
DeBakey, Lois WhoAm 90, WhoSSW 91
Debakey, Michael 1908- WorAlBi
DeBakey, Michael Ellis 1908- WhoAm 90, WhoWor 91
DeBakey, Selma WhoAm 90, WhoWor 91
De Balboa, Vasco Nunez 1475-1519 BioIn 16
De Balbuena, Bernardo 1561?-1627 BioIn 16
DeBane, Pierre 1938- WhoAm 90
deBarbadillo, John Joseph 1942- WhoAm 90
de Barbaro, Bogden BiDrAPA 89
De Barbieri, Mary Ann 1945- WhoAmW 91
De Barbieri, Roy Louis 1947- WhoEmL 91
Debard, Daniel Lee 1954- St&PR 91
De Bardeleben, Arthur 1918- WhoAm 90
DeBardeleben, John Thomas, Jr. 1926- WhoAm 90, WhoE 91
DeBardeleben, Marian Zalis 1946- WhoAmW 91
DeBardeleben, Prince, Jr. 1924- St&PR 91
De Barriault, Lee 1952- WhoEmL 91, WhoSSW 91
DeBartolo, Edward J., Sr. BioIn 16
DeBartolo, Edward J., Sr. 1919- WhoAm 90, WhoE 91
DeBartolo, Edward John 1919?- ConAmBL
DeBartolo, Edward John, Jr. 1946- WhoAm 90
de Bary, William Theodore 1919- WhoAm 90
DeBaryshe, B. Delano 1929- WhoE 91
Debas, Haile T. 1937- WhoAm 90
DeBat, Donald Joseph 1944- WhoAm 90
Debayle, Luis Somoza 1922-1967 BioIn 16
Debb, Larry 1955- St&PR 91
Debbaut, Jan 1949- WhoWor 91
Debbold, Lester Irving BiDrAPA 89
Debe, A. Joseph 1927- St&PR 91
deBear, Richard Stephen 1933- WhoWor 91
De Beaumarchais, Pierre Augustin Caron 1732-1799 BioIn 16
de Beausse, Jacques 1932- WhoWor 91
de Beauvoir, Simone MajTwCW
De Beauvoir, Simone 1908-1986 BioIn 16, EuWr 12
DeBeck, Billy 1890-1942 EncACom [port]
De Beenhouwer, Jozef 1948- IntWWM 90
De Beer, E S 1895-1990 ConAu 132
DeBeer, Frederick S., Jr. 1921- St&PR 91
De Beer, Gavin Rylands 1899-1972 DcScB S2
De Beer, Patrice 1942- WhoWor 91
De Begnis, Giuseppe 1793-1849 PenDiMP
De Begnis, Giuseppina Ronzi PenDiMP
de Behar, Lisa Block 1937- WhoWor 91
DeBekker, Jay TwCCr&M 91
Debelius-Enemark, Peter C BiDrAPA 89
Debeljak, Ales 1961- WhoWor 91
De Bell, Daryl Everett BiDrAPA 89
De Bell, Peter John, Jr. BiDrAPA 89
DeBella, Tore Thomas 1945- St&PR 91
de Belleval, Denis 1939- WhoAm 90
DeBellis, Michael Damingo BiDrAPA 89
De Benedetti, Carlo BioIn 16
De Benedetti, Carlo 1934- CurBio 90 [port]
DeBenedetti, Carlo 1934- WhoWor 91
De Benedetti, Carlo 1934- WorAlBi
De Benedetti, Enzo Enrico 1935- St&PR 91
De Benedictis, Dario 1918- WhoAm 90
DeBenedittis, Charles A. 1931- St&PR 91
De Benko, Eugene 1917- WhoAm 90
de Benoist, Alain de 1943- BiDFrPL
Debenport, Don 1934- St&PR 91
DeBerardinis, Robert Andrew, Jr. 1949- WhoEmL 91
DeBerge, Gary A. 1947- St&PR 91
De Beriot, Charles-Auguste PenDiMP
de Bernard, Lionel Oswald BiDrAPA 89
DeBerry, Hank 1893-1951 Ballpl 90
DeBerry, James Ralph 1960- WhoEmL 91
DeBerry, Robert B. St&PR 91
de Bethune, Andre 1943- WhoWor 91
De Betz, Barbara H BiDrAPA 89

Debevoise, Dickinson Richards 1924- *WhoAm 90*
Debevoise, Eli Whitney *St&PR 91N*
Debevoise, Eli Whitney 1899-1990 *NewYTBS 90*
Debevoise, Thomas McElrath 1929- *WhoAm 90*
DeBiagi, Anna Lillian 1930- *WhoAmW 91*
DeBiasi, Ralph Michael 1920- *St&PR 91*
Debicki, Andrew Peter 1934- *WhoAm 90*
de Bie, Alexis Irenee du Pont 1943- *WhoSSW 91, WhoWor 91*
Debien, Barbara JoAnn 1946- *WhoSSW 91*
Debillemont, Gabrielle 1860-1947 *BiDWomA*
Debillemont-Chardon, Gabrielle 1860-1947 *BiDWomA*
Debin, George J. 1945- *St&PR 91*
De Binder, Todd C. 1931- *St&PR 91*
De Biragues, Flaminio *EncO&P 3*
De Blank, Joost 1908-1968 *BioIn 16*
De Blaquier, Nelly Arrieta *BioIn 16*
De Blasi, Anthony 1933- *WhoAm 90, WhoAmA 91*
De Blasi, Armando 1933- *WhoAm 90*
De Blasi, Pasquale, Jr. 1941- *WhoE 91*
Deblasio, Ernest F. 1926- *St&PR 91*
DeBlasio, Michael P. 1937- *St&PR 91*
De Blasio, Michael Peter 1937- *WhoAm 90*
DeBlasis, Donna Maria 1946- *WhoAmW 91*
De Blasis, James Michael 1931- *IntWWM 90, WhoAm 90*
De Blauwe, Jozef Leo 1940- *WhoWor 91*
Deble, Lluis 1923- *WhoWor 91*
de Blij, Harm Jan 1935- *WhoAm 90*
Deblinger, Michelle Suzanne Portell 1955- *WhoAmW 91*
De Board, Janeen Sloan 1953- *WhoWrEP 89*
DeBobes, Leo Joseph, III 1955- *WhoE 91*
DeBock, Florent Alphonse 1924- *WhoAm 90*
DeBock, Lance Eric 1956- *WhoEmL 91*
Deboer, Dave M. 1951- *St&PR 91*
de Boer, Engbert 1930- *WhoWor 91*
De Boer, John F. 1942- *St&PR 91*
DeBoer, Kathryn Anne 1960- *WhoEmL 91*
De Boer, Martinus Stephanus Johannes 1930- *WhoWor 91*
De Boer, Pieter Cornelis Tobias 1930- *WhoAm 90*
DeBofsky, Greta 1928- *ODwPR 91*
DeBofsky, Greta M. 1928- *WhoAmW 91*
DeBois, James Adolphus 1929- *St&PR 91, WhoAm 90*
de Boissieu, Philippe Henry 1936- *WhoWor 91*
de Bold, Adolfo J. 1942- *WhoAm 90*
DeBolt, Joanna Lawrence 1937- *WhoAmW 91*
De Bolt, Merlan Edward 1922- *BiDrAPA 89*
DeBolt, Richard Howard 1926- *St&PR 91*
DeBon, George A. *WhoAm 90*
De Boni, Gastone 1908-1986 *EncO&P 3, EncPaPR 91*
De Bonnevault, Maturin *EncO&P 3*
de Bono, Edward 1933- *MajTwCW*
de Boor, Carl 1937- *WhoAm 90*
Deborah *WomWR [port]*
Debord, Donald Edward 1933- *St&PR 91*
Debord, Guy 1931- *BioIn 16*
DeBord, Marilyn Anne 1936- *WhoAmW 91*
De Borhegyi, Stephen 1921-1969 *WhoAmA 91N*
De Borhegyi, Suzanne Catherine Sims *AuBYP 90*
De Boschnek, Chris 1947- *WhoAmA 91*
De Boskey, Ross A *BiDrAPA 89*
De Bosset, Farideh *BiDrAPA 89*
De Botton, Jean Philippe *WhoAmA 91N*
de Bouchard d'Aubeterre, Hubert Guy 1912- *WhoWor 91*
De Bouter, Eduard Cornelis 1949- *WhoWor 91*
De Boville, Charles 1470?-1550 *EncO&P 3*
DeBow, Jay 1932- *ODwPR 91, St&PR 91*
DeBow, Lee Richard *BiDrAPA 89*
Debow, Stanley Lawrence 1940- *BiDrAPA 89*
DeBow, Thomas C. 1940- *ODwPR 91*
DeBow, Thomas Joseph, Jr. 1936- *WhoE 91, WhoWor 91*
DeBra, Daniel B. 1930- *WhoAm 90*
De Brahm, William Gerhard 1717-1799 *EncCRAm*
De Brath, Stanley 1854-1937 *EncO&P 3*
Debre, Michel Jean-Pierre 1912- *BiDFrPL*
Debrecht, Donald Robert 1946- *St&PR 91*
Debreczeny, Paul 1932- *WhoAm 90*
De Bremaecker, Jean-Claude 1923- *WhoAm 90*
Debret, Jean-Baptiste 1768-1848 *ArtLatA*
Debrett, Hal *TwCCr&M 91*
De Bretteville, Sheila Levrant 1940- *WhoAmA 91*
Debreu, Gerard 1921- *WhoAm 90, WhoWor 91, WorAlBi*
Debrey, Adele F. 1924- *St&PR 91*
Debrey, Andrew Dale 1922- *St&PR 91*
Debrey, Drew Stephen 1953- *St&PR 91, WhoEmL 91*
De Brier, Donald Paul 1940- *WhoAm 90*
de Brissac, Malcolm *ConAu 31NR*
Debro, Julius 1931- *WhoAm 90*
De Broca, Philippe 1933- *BioIn 16, WorAlBi*
DeBrosse, James Gerard 1962- *WhoE 91*
Debrot, Peter 1960- *WhoE 91*
DeBrow, Mical E. 1954- *WhoEmL 91*
De Bruhl, Arthur Marshall 1935- *WhoAm 90*
De Bruijn, Chris Henry 1946- *WhoWor 91*
De Bruin, David Lee 1955- *WhoEmL 91*
De Bruin, Jerome Edward 1941- *WhoWrEP 89*
DeBruler, Roger O. 1934- *WhoAm 90*
de Brun, Shauna Doyle 1956- *WhoAmW 91*
De Brunhoff, Laurent 1925- *BioIn 16*
DeBrunner, Gerald Joseph 1937- *WhoAm 90*
Debrunner, Peter George 1931- *WhoAm 90*
Debruycker, Dirk H A 1955- *WhoAmA 91*
De Bruyn, H. Donald 1912- *St&PR 91*
De Bruyn, Harold Ferdinand 1924- *WhoE 91*
De Bruyn, Peter Paul Henry 1910- *WhoAm 90*
De Bruyn, Robert Lee 1934- *WhoWrEP 89*
de Bruyn Kops, Julian 1908- *WhoAm 90*
De Bruyne, Paul 1953- *WhoWor 91*
Debs, Barbara Knowles 1931- *WhoAm 90, WhoWor 91*
Debs, Eugene V. 1855-1926 *EncAL [port], WorAlBi*
Debs, Richard A. 1930- *St&PR 91, WhoAm 90, WhoWor 91*
Debs, Victor Selim 1909- *WhoE 91*
Debschitz, Wilhelm von 1871-1948 *PenDiDA 89*
Debski, Jo Ann 1959- *WhoAmW 91*
Debuhr, Ted 1947- *St&PR 91*
De Burciaga, Cecilia Preciado 1945- *BioIn 16*
De Burgos, Julia 1916-1953 *BioIn 16*
De Burgos, Rafael Fruhbeck *PenDiMP*
de Burlo, Comegys Russell, Jr. *WhoAm 90, WhoWor 91*
Debus, Allen G 1926- *ConAu 31NR*
Debus, Allen George 1926- *WhoAm 90*
Debus, Alvin Philip 1933- *St&PR 91*
Debus, Eleanor Viola 1920- *WhoAmW 91, WhoWor 91*
Debus, John R. 1957- *BiDrAPA 89*
Debus, Mary *ODwPR 91*
DeBusk, Edith M. 1912- *WhoAm 90, WhoWor 91*
DeBusk, Manuel Conrad 1914- *WhoAm 90*
DeBusschere, Dave 1940- *Ballpl 90, WorAlBi*
DeBussey, Judy Brown 1958- *WhoEmL 91*
Debussy, Claude 1862-1918 *BioIn 16, PenDiMP A, WorAlBi*
De Bustamante, Heitor T 1950- *BiDrAPA 89*
De Bustros, Serge Nicolas 1953- *WhoE 91*
DeButts, Robert Edward Lee 1927- *St&PR 91*
De Buys, Coenraad 1761- *BioIn 16*
Debye, Peter J. W. 1884-1966 *WorAlBi*
Decadt, Jan 1914- *IntWWM 90*
Decaminada, Joseph P. 1935- *St&PR 91*
Decaminada, Joseph Pio 1935- *WhoAm 90*
De Camp, Catherine Crook *AuBYP 90*
DeCamp, Graydon 1934- *WhoAm 90*
DeCamp, L. Sprague 1907- *RGTwCSF*
De Camp, L Sprague 1907- *WhoWrEP 89*
De Camp, L. Sprague 1907- *WorAlBi*
De Camp, Lyon 1907- *AuBYP 90*
de Camp, Lyon Sprague 1907- *WhoAm 90*
DeCamp, Rosemary Shirley 1910- *WhoAm 90*
de Camp, William Schuyler 1934- *WhoAm 90*
DeCampi, John Webb 1939- *WhoE 91*
De Campo, Estanislao 1834-1880 *BioIn 16*
De Campomanes, Pedro Rodriguez 1723-1802 *BioIn 16*
DeCamps, Charles Michael 1950- *WhoEmL 91*
Decancq, H. George *BioIn 16*
de Cani, John Stapley 1924- *WhoAm 90*
Decanini, Jesus Mario *BiDrAPA 89*
DeCanio, Salvatore Michael, Jr. 1953- *WhoSSW 91*
Decaprio, Alice 1919- *WhoAmA 91*
DeCarava, Roy R. *WhoAm 90*
Decarava, Roy Rudolph 1919- *WhoAmA 91*
De Carbonnel, Francois Eric 1946- *St&PR 91, WhoAm 90, WhoWor 91*
De Cardenas, Cristina 1938- *WhoSSW 91*
De Cardenas, Gilbert Lorenzo 1941- *WhoHisp 91*
Decareau, Eugene Francis 1929- *St&PR 91*
De Caritat, Marie-Jean-Antoine-Nicolas 1743-1794 *BioIn 16*
DeCarli, Ralph Peter 1958- *WhoEmL 91*
De Carlo, Andrea 1952- *ConAu 132*
De Carlo, Leonard Dominick 1939- *WhoWrEP 89*
DeCarlo, Michael 1960- *WhoEmL 91*
Decarlo, Yvonne 1922- *WorAlBi*
DeCaro, Angelo *WhoAm 90*
De Caro, Angelo 1943- *St&PR 91*
de Caro, Frank Anthony 1943- *WhoSSW 91*
DeCaro, John Cecil 1923- *WhoSSW 91*
de Caro, Marc Clement 1920- *WhoE 91*
De Carolis, Phillip Fiore 1949- *WhoE 91*
de Cartagena, Teresa 14--?- *EncCoWW*
De Carvajal Perez, Jose Federico 1930- *WhoWor 91*
De Carvalho, Manoel Joaquim, Jr. 1925- *WhoWor 91*
DeCasale, Secchi *BioIn 16*
de Castelbajac, Jean-Charles 1949- *ConDes 90*
De Castelbajac, Kate *BioIn 16*
DeCastro, Donald John 1930- *St&PR 91*
De Castro, Edson D. 1938- *St&PR 91, WhoAm 90, WhoE 91*
de Castro, Hugo Daniel 1935- *WhoAm 90*
De Castro, Jose Manuel Borges 1939- *WhoWor 91*
De Castro, Lorraine 1946- *WhoAmA 91*
De Castro, Ramon Baldorioty 1822-1889 *BioIn 16*
De Castro, Raymond Millan 1952- *BiDrAPA 89*
De Castro, Rosalia 1837-1885 *BioIn 16*
Decastro, Stephen Alan 1956- *St&PR 91*
Decater, Steven *BioIn 16*
Decatur, Art 1894-1966 *Ballpl 90*
Decatur, Stephen 1779-1820 *BioIn 16, WorAlBi*
Decaux, Alain 1925- *WhoWor 91*
Decavele, Casimir Alois 1937- *WhoWor 91*
Decazes, Louis Charles Elie Armanieu 1819-1886 *BiDFrPL*
Deccio, David M. 1946- *St&PR 91*
Decea, Steven 1955- *St&PR 91*
de Cecco, Marcello 1939- *WhoWor 91*
De Cecco, Raymond Joseph 1924- *St&PR 91*
Decesare, James C. 1931- *St&PR 91*
DeCesare, Jeanne Anne 1949- *WhoAmW 91*
DeCesare, Mike *ODwPR 91*
DeCesare, Paula Doreen 1936- *WhoAmW 91, WhoE 91*
De Cesare, Ruth 1923- *IntWWM 90*
de Cespedes, Alba 1911- *EncCoWW*
de Cespedes, Carlos M. *WhoHisp 91*
De Cespedes, Carlos Manuel 1819-1874 *BioIn 16*
Dechabert-Ostland, Jean G 1909- *BiDrAPA 89*
De Chamorro, Violeta Barrios *BioIn 16*
de Champeaux de la Boulaye, Denis Marie 1929- *WhoWor 91*
De Champlain, Samuel 1567-1635 *BioIn 16*
De Champlain, Vera Chopak *WhoAmA 91*
de Champlain, Vera Chopak 1928- *WhoAmW 91*
Dechamps, Bruno Josef Gerhard 1925- *WhoWor 91*
Dechant, John J. 1934- *St&PR 91*
Dechant, Virgil C. 1930- *WhoAm 90*
De Chantal, Jeanne-Francoise 1572-1641 *BioIn 16*
Dechar, Peter 1942- *WhoAmA 91*
Dechar, Peter Henry 1942- *WhoAm 90*
Dechario, Tony Houston 1940- *IntWWM 90*
Dechary, Jenet Lynn 1946- *WhoAmW 91*
de Chastelain, Alfred John Gardyne D. 1937- *WhoAm 90*
Dechene, James Charles 1953- *WhoEmL 91*
Dechene, Joseph Fernand 1959- *WhoEmL 91*
Dechenne, James Allen 1943- *WhoSSW 91*
Decher, Rudolf 1927- *WhoAm 90*
Decherd, Robert *BioIn 16*
Decherd, Robert William 1951- *St&PR 91, WhoAm 90, WhoSSW 91*
De Cherney, Alan Hersh 1942- *WhoAm 90*
DeCherney, Deanna Saver 1943- *WhoE 91, WhoWor 91*
De Cherney, H George *BiDrAPA 89*
Dechert, Joseph P. 1916- *St&PR 91*
Dechert, Michael Salvatore Alfred 1958- *WhoSSW 91*
Dechery, Bertrand F. 1950- *St&PR 91*
De Chirico, Giorgio 1888-1978 *IntDcAA 90*
Dechnik, James Edward 1946- *St&PR 91, WhoEmL 91*
Dechristopher, Joseph L. 1936- *St&PR 91*
Dechter, Warren *WhoAm 90*
Deci, Edward Lewis 1942- *WhoAm 90*
Deci, Mary D. 1947- *St&PR 91*
Deci, Paul Andrew 1960- *BiDrAPA 89*
Deciccio, Donald R. 1934- *St&PR 91*
Decicco, Anne Lommel 1950- *WhoAmW 91, WhoE 91*
De Cillis, Steven Edward 1951- *WhoE 91*
Decina, Paolo 1944- *BiDrAPA 89*
DeCinces, Doug 1950- *Ballpl 90*
Decio, Arthur J. 1931- *St&PR 91*
Decio, Arthur Julius 1930- *WhoAm 90*
deCiutiis, Alfred Charles Maria 1945- *WhoAm 90, WhoEmL 91, WhoWor 91*
de Ciutiis, Vincent Louis 1924- *WhoWor 91*
Deck, Allan Figueroa 1945- *WhoHisp 91*
Deck, Joseph Francis 1907- *WhoAm 90*
Deck, Joseph-Theodore 1823-1891 *PenDiDA 89*
Deck, Larry L. 1945- *St&PR 91*
Deckelbaum, Nelson 1928- *WhoAm 90, WhoWor 91*
Decker, Albert 1895-1988 *BioIn 16*
Decker, Alonzo Galloway, Jr. 1908- *St&PR 91*
Decker, Barbara Bodine 1929- *WhoAmW 91*
Decker, Bernard Martin 1904- *WhoAm 90*
Decker, Bruce 1946- *BiDrAPA 89*
Decker, C. Lawrence 1940- *St&PR 91*
Decker, Charles David 1945- *WhoAm 90*
Decker, Charles L. *WhoAm 90*
Decker, Charles Richard 1937- *WhoAm 90*
Decker, David Garrison 1917- *WhoAm 90*
Decker, David Howard 1956- *BiDrAPA 89*
Decker, David John 1952- *WhoWor 91*
Decker, Debra Elnora 1946- *WhoAmW 91*
Decker, Don M. 1935- *ODwPR 91*
Decker, Dorothy Sexton 1922- *WhoSSW 91*
Decker, Duane Walter 1910-1964 *AuBYP 90*
Decker, Edward W. 1952- *St&PR 91*
Decker, Edwin Albert 1929- *St&PR 91*
Decker, Elizabeth Anne 1952- *WhoAmW 91*
Decker, Erwin Louis 1925- *St&PR 91, WhoAm 90*
Decker, Franz-Paul 1923- *IntWWM 90, PenDiMP*
Decker, Gilbert Felton 1937- *WhoAm 90, WhoSSW 91*
Decker, Gregory Allen 1951- *WhoSSW 91*
Decker, Hannah Shulman 1937- *WhoSSW 91*
Decker, Hans Wilhelm 1929- *WhoE 91*
Decker, Howard Elwood 1922- *St&PR 91*
Decker, James H. 1827- *AmLegL*
Decker, James Harrison, Jr. 1948- *WhoEmL 91*
Decker, James Thomas 1944- *WhoWor 91*
Decker, Jerome L. 1948- *St&PR 91*
Decker, Joe 1947- *Ballpl 90*
Decker, Joey 1955- *WhoEmL 91*
Decker, John 1895- *WhoAmA 91N*
Decker, John Barry 1929- *BiDrAPA 89*
Decker, John Charles 1941- *St&PR 91*
Decker, John Laws 1921- *WhoAm 90*
Decker, John Louis 1946- *WhoEmL 91*
Decker, John Robert 1952- *WhoEmL 91*
Decker, John William 1948- *WhoEmL 91*
Decker, Josephine I. 1933- *WhoAmW 91*
Decker, Judith Elaine 1940- *WhoAmW 91*
Decker, Karrie Lynn 1956- *WhoAmW 91*
Decker, Kurt Hans 1946- *WhoEmL 91*
Decker, Martha Ilene 1954- *WhoAmW 91, WhoWrEP 89*
Decker, Mary *BioIn 16*
Decker, Mary Locher 1936- *WhoWrEP 89*
Decker, Michael Bryan 1949- *St&PR 91*
Decker, Michael Lynn 1953- *WhoEmL 91*
Decker, Norman 1936- *BiDrAPA 89*
Decker, Paul 1677-1713 *PenDiDA 89*
Decker, Peter 1893-1988 *BioIn 16*
Decker, Peter William 1919- *WhoWor 91*
Decker, Raymond Frank 1930- *WhoAm 90*
Decker, Rebecca Linda 1961- *WhoEmL 91*
Decker, Richard K. 1913- *St&PR 91*
Decker, Richard Knore 1913- *WhoAm 90*
Decker, Richard W. 1945- *WhoE 91*
Decker, Robert Owen 1927- *WhoE 91, WhoWor 91*
Decker, Robert Wayne 1927- *WhoAm 90*
Decker, Ruth Marie 1928- *WhoE 91*
Decker, Sam 1912- *BiDrAPA 89*
Decker, Thomas Andrew 1946- *St&PR 91, WhoAm 90*
Decker, Vicki Lynn 1951- *WhoEmL 91*
Decker, Virginia Ann 1942- *WhoWrEP 89*
Decker, W. Patrick *St&PR 91*
Decker, Wayne Leroy 1922- *WhoAm 90*
Decker, Willard Lee 1929- *St&PR 91*
Decker, William A 1921- *BiDrAPA 89*
Decker Slaney, Mary Teresa 1958- *WhoAmW 91*
Decker-Ward, James Gordon 1943- *St&PR 91*

Deckert, David William BiDrAPA 89
Deckert, Donna Kay 1963- WhoAmW 91
Deckert, Gordon H 1930- BiDrAPA 89
Deckert, Gordon Harmon 1930- WhoAm 90
Deckert, Myrna Jean 1936- WhoAmW 91
Deckert, Ralph E. 1952- St&PR 91
Deckert, Robert Allen 1935- WhoWrEP 89
Deckinger, Elliott Lawrence 1917- WhoAm 90
Deckys, Elena BiDrAPA 89
De Clara, Roberto 1955- IntWWM 90
DeClaris, Nicholas 1931- WhoAm 90
De Claviere d'Hust, Anne-Marie BioIn 16
De Claviere d'Hust, Bernard BioIn 16
Declemente, Donna Marie 1958- WhoEmL 91
DeClements, Barthe 1920- BioIn 16, ChlLR 23 [port], WhoWrEP 89
de Clercq, Willy 1927- WhoWor 91
de Cleyre, Voltairine 1866-1912 EncAL, FemiCLE
Declue, Stephen S. 1944- St&PR 91
DeCock, Frederick Mitchell 1958- WhoEmL 91
Decolta, Ramon TwCCr&M 91
De Comines, Phillipe 1445?-1511 BioIn 16
DeConcini, Dennis BioIn 16
De Concini, Dennis 1937- WhoAm 90, WhoWor 91
DeConcini, John Cyrus 1918- WhoAm 90
DeCongelio, Frank Joseph 1948- St&PR 91
De Coninck, Herman 1944- WhoWor 91
De Coningh, Edward Hurlbut 1902- St&PR 91, WhoAm 90, WhoWor 91
De Contreras, Alonso 1582- BioIn 16
DeCook, Richard Cyril 1942- WhoAm 90
Decora, Little 1797-1887 WhNaAH
Decora, Spoon 1730?-1816 WhNaAH
Decora, Waukon WhNaAH
Decorchemont, Francois-Emile 1880-1971 PenDiDA 89
De Cordova, Fred BioIn 16
de Cordova, Frederick Timmins 1910- WhoAm 90
De Cormier-Shekerjian, Regina WhoWrEP 89
de Corse, Marie BiDrAPA 89
De Corte, Marie-Therese 1942- WhoWor 91
De Cosmos, Amor 1825-1897 DcCanB 12
DeCosse, Sheila Flynn 1935- WhoE 91
De Costa, Edwin J. 1906- WhoAm 90
DeCosta, Peter F. WhoE 91
Decoste, Paul St&PR 91
De Coster, Cyrus Cole 1914- WhoAm 90
Decoster, Leonard L. 1921- St&PR 91
De Coster, William 1920- WhoWor 91
DeCoteau, Ann M. 1946- St&PR 91
DeCoteau, Dennis 1937- BioIn 16
Decotis, Deborah Anne 1952- WhoAmW 91
De Cotret, Robert Rene 1944- WhoAm 90, WhoE 91, WhoWor 91
DeCou, John E. 1934- ODwPR 91
Decourcelle, Gerard WhoAm 90
Decourcelle, Gerard Raymond 1942- St&PR 91
DeCourcy, Kim Gary 1948- St&PR 91
DeCoursey, Michael 1946- St&PR 91
Decourtray, Albert 1923- WhoWor 91
Decoust, Michel 1936- IntWWM 90
De Coux, Janet WhoAmA 91
de Coux, Janet 1904- WhoAm 90
Decrane, Alfred Charles, Jr. 1931- St&PR 91, WhoAm 90, WhoE 91, WhoWor 91
DeCrane, Karen Stuart- BioIn 16
De Crane, Victor C. 1932- St&PR 91
De Crayencour, Marguerite BioIn 16
de Crayencour, Michel-Francois 1936- WhoWor 91
De Creeft, Jose 1884-1982 WhoAmA 91N
De Creeft, Lorrie J 1927- WhoAmA 91
De Crescentis, James 1948- WhoWrEP 89
DeCrescenzo, Jame Melisse 1955- WhoEmL 91, WhoSSW 91
De Crescenzo-Rivard, Sarah Carole 1941- WhoAmW 91
De Crespigny, Rose Champion 1860-1935 EncO&P 3
De Cressac Bachelerie, Bertrande 1899- EncO&P 3
De Crevecoeur, J. Hector St. John 1735-1813 BioIn 16
Decristoforo, Thomas P. 1957- St&PR 91
Decroix, Jean-Louis Maurice 1934- WhoWor 91
DeCrosta, Susan Elyse 1956- WhoAmW 91, WhoE 91
De Crow, Karen 1937- WhoAm 90, WhoAmW 91
Decrow, Karen 1937- WhoWrEP 89
De Croy, Elisabeth BioIn 16
De Cruccio, John F. 1933- St&PR 91
Decsenyi, Janos 1927- IntWWM 90
De Csillery, Bela 1915- IntWWM 90
Decter, Betty Eva 1927- WhoAmA 91
Decter, Midge 1927- WhoAm 90, WhoWrEP 89
de Cuevas, M. Francisco EncCoWW
DeCuir, Clint Thomas 1948- St&PR 91
De Curtis, David Samuel 1930- WhoAm 90
Decyk, Roxanne Jean 1952- St&PR 91, WhoAm 90, WhoAmW 91
Dedania, Kishorkumar G 1956- BiDrAPA 89
Deddens, James Carroll 1928- St&PR 91, WhoAm 90
Dedek, Clent 1935- WhoSSW 91
Dedekind, Richard 1831-1916 BioIn 16
Deden, Otto 1925- IntWWM 90
De Deo, Joseph E. 1937- St&PR 91
Dederer, Carl Christian 1957- IntWWM 90
Dederer, Michael E. 1932- ODwPR 91
Dederer, Michael Eugene 1932- WhoAm 90
Dederer, William Bowne 1945- IntWWM 90
Dederich-Pejovich, Susan Russell 1951- WhoAm 90
Dederick, Donald Henry 1935- WhoE 91
Dederick, Margarida M BiDrAPA 89
Dederick, Robert Gogan 1929- WhoAm 90
Dederick, Ronald Osburn 1935- WhoAm 90
Dedering, August WhoWor 91
Dedert, Nancy Ann 1941- St&PR 91
Dedert, Steven Ray 1953- WhoEmL 91
Dedeurwaerder, Jose J. BioIn 16
Dedeurwaerder, Jose Joseph 1932- WhoAm 90
De Diego, Julio 1900-1979 WhoAmA 91N
De Diego Nafria, Mariano 1943- WhoWor 91
Dedijer, Vladimir 1914- WhoWor 91
Dedijer, Vladimir 1914-1990 NewYTBS 90
Dedik, Patricia Jacqueline 1949- WhoE 91
Dedini, Eldon Lawrence 1921- WhoAm 90, WhoAmA 91
Dedinsky, Mary Lee 1948- WhoAmW 91
Dediu, Constantin 1932- IntWWM 90
Dediu, Michael Mihai 1943- WhoE 91
de Divitiis, Enrico 1935- WhoWor 91
Dedman, Bertram Cottingham 1914- WhoAm 90
Dedman, Bill WhoAm 90, WhoSSW 91
Dedman, Malcolm John 1948- IntWWM 90
Dedman, Robert Henry 1926- WhoAm 90
Dedmon, Donald Newton 1931- WhoAm 90, WhoSSW 91
Dedmon, Jeff 1960- Ballpl 90
Dedo, Dorothy Junell Turner 1920- WhoAmW 91
De Dogorza, Patricia 1936- WhoAmA 91
Dedomenico, Paskey BioIn 16
Dedomenico, Vincent Michael 1915- St&PR 91
DeDominicis, Aldo BioIn 16
Dedona, Francis A. 1924- St&PR 91
DeDonato, David Michael 1947- WhoSSW 91
DeDonato, Donald Michael 1952- WhoEmL 91
De Donato, Louis 1934- WhoAmA 91
DeDonato, Richard E. 1955- WhoEmL 91
DeDonder, Leon Gerard 1951- WhoEmL 91
Dedrick, John Rockwell 1939- St&PR 91
Dedrick, Kenneth C. 1947- St&PR 91
De Dube, Brett St&PR 91
de Duve, Christian Rene 1917- WhoAm 90, WhoWor 91
Dee, Alan G. 1948- ODwPR 91
Dee, Elaine Evans 1924- WhoAmA 91
Dee, James Francis 1947- BiDrAPA 89
Dee, Joey BioIn 16
Dee, Joey 1940- EncPR&S 89
Dee, Joey, and the Starlighters EncPR&S 89
Dee, John 1527-1608 BioIn 16, EncO&P 3
Dee, Leo Joseph 1931- WhoAmA 91
Dee, Pacita Chan 1939- BiDrAPA 89
Dee, Peter Sycip 1941- WhoWor 91
Dee, Philip Ivor 1904-1983 DcNaB 1981
Dee, Raymond C. 1942- St&PR 91
Dee, Robert F. 1924- St&PR 91
Dee, Robert Forrest 1924- WhoAm 90
Dee, Ruby BioIn 16, WhoAm 90
Dee, Ruby 1923- DrBlPA 90, WorAlBi
Dee, Ruby 1924- NotWoAT
Dee, Sandra 1942- BioIn 16, WorAlBi
Dee, Thomas D., II 1920- St&PR 91
Dee, Vivien 1944- WhoAmW 91
Deean, Ibeyaima D BiDrAPA 89
Deeb, Edward Emile 1923- St&PR 91
Deeb, Robert M BiDrAPA 89
Deecken, George Christian 1922- WhoAm 90
Deed, Martha Louise 1941- WhoE 91
Deedy, John Gerard, Jr. 1923- WhoAm 90, WhoWrEP 89
Deedy, Joyce 1928- WhoWrEP 89
Deegan, Arthur X., II 1929- WhoSSW 91
Deegan, Bill 1935- Ballpl 90
Deegan, Denis James 1954- St&PR 91
Deegan, Derek James 1940- St&PR 91, WhoAm 90
Deegan, Gail 1946- St&PR 91
Deegan, John, Jr. 1944- WhoAm 90
Deegan, John Edward 1935- WhoE 91
Deegan, John Edward, Jr. 1936- St&PR 91
Deegan, Nan Marie 1952- WhoEmL 91
Deegan, Paul Joseph 1937- BioIn 16
Deegan, Robert 1948- IntWWM 90
Deegan, Russell B. 1944- St&PR 91
Deegear, James Otis, III 1948- WhoEmL 91
Deeik, Khalil George 1937- WhoWor 91
Deeken, Michael George 1952- BiDrAPA 89
Deel, Frances Quinn 1939- WhoAm 90, WhoAmW 91
de Elejalde, Fernando 1921- BiDrAPA 89
Deeley, Walter G. BioIn 16
De Elorza, John 1919- St&PR 91
Deely, Catharine B. 1950- ODwPR 91
Deem, George 1932- WhoAm 90, WhoAmA 91
Deem, Howard H. 1926- St&PR 91
Deemer, Bill 1945- WhoWrEP 89
Deemer, Candy Kaelin 1954- WhoAmW 91
Deems, Nyal David 1948- WhoEmL 91
Deems, Richard E. 1913- St&PR 91
Deems, Richard Emmet 1913- WhoAm 90
Deen, Edith Alderman 1905- WhoAmW 91
Deen, Lewis Stanley BiDrAPA 89
Deen, Robert R 1915- BiDrAPA 89
Deen, Talat BiDrAPA 89
Deen, Thomas Blackburn 1928- WhoAm 90
Deener, Larry Colby 1950- WhoEmL 91
Deeney, Virginia I. 1933- WhoE 91
Deenik, Ronald Wayne 195?- WhoEmL 91
Deep Chin ConAu 132
Deep Purple EncPR&S 89, OxCPMus
Deep, Ira Washington 1927- WhoAm 90
Deepe, Beverly BioIn 16
Deephouse, Christopher Vaughn 1954- WhoE 91
Deer, Donald M. 1932- St&PR 91
Deer, James W. 1917- St&PR 91
Deer, James Willis 1917- WhoAm 90, WhoE 91, WhoWor 91
Deer, Richard Elliott 1932- WhoAm 90
Deer, Rob 1960- Ballpl 90
Deer-In-Water, Jessie BioIn 16
De Ercilla y Zuniga, Alonso 1533-1584 BioIn 16
De Erdely, Francis 1904-1959 WhoAmA 91N
Deere, Cyril Thomas 1924- WhoAm 90
Deere, John 1804-1886 BioIn 16
Deere, Joy Lucretia BiDrAPA 89
Deere, Louis Edward BiDrAPA 89
Deerfoot DcCanB 12
Deering, Allan Brooks 1934- WhoAm 90
Deering, Anthony Wayne Marion 1945- WhoAm 90
Deering, Fred A. 1928- St&PR 91
Deering, Fred Arthur 1928- WhoAm 90
Deering, George E 1917- BiDrAPA 89
Deering, George Edwin 1917- WhoE 91
Deering, John R. 1936- St&PR 91
Deering, Joseph William 1940- St&PR 91, WhoAm 90
Deering, Richard Jon 1947- IntWWM 90
Deering, Ronald Franklin 1929- WhoSSW 91, WhoWor 91
Deerwester, Eric Stanley 1944- WhoAm 90
Dees, C. Stanley 1938- WhoAm 90
Dees, James Parker 1915- WhoAm 90
Dees, Lynne 1954- WhoAmW 91
Dees, Morris Seligman, Jr. 1936- WhoAm 90, WhoWor 91
Dees, Richard Lee 1955- WhoEmL 91
Dees, Sandra Kay Martin 1944- WhoAmW 91, WhoSSW 91
Deese, James Earle 1921- WhoAm 90
Deese, James LaMotte 1944- WhoE 91
Deese, Sebelle Kyle Gates 1944- WhoAmW 91
De Espronceda, Jose 1808-1842 BioIn 16
Deeter, Bernard S. 1924- St&PR 91
Deeter, Elizabeth Jean 1918- WhoAmW 91
Deets, Charles D. 1936- St&PR 91
Deets, Dwain Aaron 1939- WhoAm 90
Deets, Floyd H. 1929- St&PR 91
Deets, Horace 1938- WhoAm 90
Deevey, Edward S. 1914-1988 BioIn 16
Deevy, Teresa 1903-1963 FemiCLE
DeFabis, Mike 1932- WhoAm 90
De Fabritiis, Oliviero 1902-1982 PenDiMP
De Fabritus, John T. 1924- St&PR 91
DeFalaise, Louis 1945- WhoAm 90
DeFalco, Anthony Joseph 1936- St&PR 91
DeFalco, Frank Damian 1934- WhoAm 90
Defauw, Desire 1885-1960 PenDiMP
DeFazio, Frank 1925- St&PR 91
De Fazio, John 1959- WhoAmA 91
DeFazio, Lynette Stevens 1930- WhoAmW 91, WhoWor 91
DeFazio, Peter A. 1947- WhoAm 90
DeFazio, Thomas C. 1941- WhoAm 90
De Feis, Frederic Orpheus 1926- WhoE 91
DeFelice, Dennis Joseph 1949- WhoEmL 91
DeFelice, Eugene Anthony 1927- WhoAm 90, WhoWor 91
DeFelice, Eugene Vincent 1958- WhoE 91, WhoWor 91
DeFelice, Kimberle Levin 1963- WhoAmW 91
DeFelice, Lois Anne 1950- WhoEmL 91
De Felitta, Frank Paul WhoAm 90
De Fels, Laure BioIn 16
Defenbaugh, Richard Eugene 1946- WhoSSW 91
Defendorf, Charles E. 1912- St&PR 91
DeFeo, Jay 1929-1989 BioIn 16
De Fermat, Pierre 1601-1665 BioIn 16
De Ferranti, Basil 1930-1988 BioIn 16
De Ferranti, Sebastian Ziani 1864-1930 BioIn 16
De Ferrari, Gabriella 1941- WhoAm 90
De Ferrari, Gian Antonio 1928- St&PR 91
De Ferreire, Mary Elizabeth 1949- WhoSSW 91
Defesche, Charles Leon 1948- St&PR 91
De Feure, Georges 1868-1943 BioIn 16
Defeyter, David W. 1954- St&PR 91
Deffaugt, Jean BioIn 16
Deffenbaugh, David R. 1941- St&PR 91
Defferre, Gaston Paul Charles 1910-1986 BiDFrPL
Deffeyes, Robert J. 1935- St&PR 91
Deffeyes, Robert Joseph 1935- WhoAm 90, WhoSSW 91
Defibaugh, Patricia J. 1946- St&PR 91
De Figueiredo, Desmond Peter 1938- St&PR 91
de Figueiredo, John M BiDrAPA 89
De Filippi, Amedeo 1900- IntWWM 90
DeFilippo, Allan John 1946- St&PR 91
de Filippo, Eduardo 1900-1984 ConAu 132, MajTwCW
De Filippo, Gaetano A 1940- BiDrAPA 89
Defilippo, Robert C. 1952- St&PR 91
Defilla, Steivan 1959- WhoWor 91
Define, William Thomas 1941- WhoAm 90
DeFiore, Celeste Antoinette 1963- WhoSSW 91
DeFiore, Elizabeth Ann 1940- WhoE 91
DeFiore, Joseph C., Jr. 1938- WhoSSW 91
Defleur, Lois B. 1936- WhoAm 90
DeFleur, Melvin Lawrence 1923- WhoAm 90
De Fleury, Maria FemiCLE
Defliese, Philip Leroy 1915- WhoAm 90
De Flon, Cassius Adair 1941- BiDrAPA 89
Deflorez, Suzanne Humphreys 1915- St&PR 91
DeFlorio, Mary Lucy WhoE 91
Defoe, Daniel 1660?-1731 DcLB 101 [port], -95 [port], WorAlBi
Defoe, Daniel 1661?-1731 BioIn 16
De Folter, Leo C. 1941- St&PR 91
Defonte, Robert G. 1950- St&PR 91
De Fontenay, Guillaume 1861-1914 EncO&P 3
DeFoor, James Allison, II 1953- WhoSSW 91, WhoWor 91
Defoor, Jerry W. 1952- St&PR 91
DeFoor, Keith Alex 1960- WhoSSW 91
Defoor, Nathan Dwight 1952- WhoEmL 91, WhoSSW 91, WhoWor 91
DeFord, David Wayne 1952- WhoSSW 91
Deford, Frank BioIn 16
Deford, Frank 1938- WhoAm 90
DeFord, Horace A 1927- BiDrAPA 89
DeFord, Paul Steven 1956- WhoEmL 91
deFord, Sara Whitcraft 1916- WhoAm 90
De Ford, Sara Whitcraft 1916- WhoWrEP 89
Deford, Thomas McAdams 1942- WhoWor 91
De Forest, Charlotte B. 1879-1971 AuBYP 90
De Forest, James Vincent 1926- St&PR 91
De Forest, Lee 1873-1961 WorAlBi
De Forest, Roy Dean 1930- WhoAmA 91
De Forest, Sherwood Searle 1921- WhoAm 90
De Forest, Taber 1940-1987 BioIn 16
DeForest, Walter Pattison, III 1944- WhoE 91, WhoWor 91
De Forster, Estrella BiDrAPA 89
De Fortabat, Amalia BioIn 16
Defossez, Rene IntWWM 90
De Fouw, Eugene Allen 1941- St&PR 91
De Foy, Walter Josin 1941- BiDrAPA 89
De Fraites, Emanuel G, Jr. BiDrAPA 89
Defrance, Harry Anthony 1929- St&PR 91
Defrance, Newilda 1944- St&PR 91
DeFranceaux, George W. 1913- St&PR 91
Defrances, Lisa Krul 1957- WhoAmW 91

Defrancesch, Thomas John 1955- *St&PR 91*
Defrancesco, Italo I 1901-1967 *WhoAmA 91N*
DeFrancesco, John B., Jr. 1936- *ODwPR 91*
De Francesco, John Blaze, Jr. 1936- *WhoAm 90*
De Francesco, Josephine Catherine 1923- *WhoAmW 91*
DeFrancesco, Mark L. 1962- *St&PR 91*
DeFrancesco, Raymond P. 1960- *St&PR 91*
De Francia, Jose Gaspar Rodriguez 1766-1840 *BioIn 16*
DeFrancis, Frank J. 1924-1989 *BioIn 16*
De Francis, James Upton 1943- *WhoAm 90*
DeFrancis, Suellen Maria 1946- *WhoAmW 91*
De Francisci, Anthony 1887-1964 *WhoAmA 91N*
De Francisco, Cesar Perez 1940- *BiDrAPA 89*
De Francisco, Don Fredric *BiDrAPA 89*
DeFrancisco, Ignatuis 1927- *St&PR 91*
DeFrancisco, Joseph E. 1942- *BioIn 16*
DeFranco, Buddy 1923- *BioIn 16*
DeFranco, Buddy 1933- *WorAlBi*
Defrank, Anthony Alfred 1924- *St&PR 91*
De Frank, Vincent 1915- *IntWWM 90, WhoAm 90*
DeFrantz, Anita *BioIn 16*
DeFrees, Douglas John 1952- *WhoEmL 91*
DeFrees, John Stallard 1938- *WhoSSW 91*
DeFrees, Madeline 1919- *DcLB 105 [port], WhoWrEP 89*
Defreitas, Robert Frederick 1924- *St&PR 91*
DeFreitas, Rui M. Aragon F. 1929- *WhoSSW 91*
De Freitas Branco, Pedro *PenDiMP*
Defren, Ken *ODwPR 91*
De Fries, John Clarence 1934- *WhoAm 90*
De Fries, Zira 1917- *BiDrAPA 89*
De Froment, Louis *PenDiMP*
De Froment, Louis Georges Francois 1921- *IntWWM 90*
De Frondeville, Bertrand Lambert 1934- *WhoE 91*
De Fry, Cyril Trevor 1947- *WhoWor 91*
DeFurio, Susan Snelling 1948- *WhoAmW 91*
De Furstenberg, Maximilien 1904-1988 *BioIn 16*
De Gaay Fortman, Bastiaan 1937- *WhoWor 91*
De Gaeta, Albert M. *St&PR 91*
De Gaeta, Edythe C. *St&PR 91*
De Gaetani, Barbara Ann 1934- *St&PR 91*
DeGaetani, Jan 1933-1989 *AnObit 1989, BioIn 16, PenDiMP*
DeGagne, A. J. *WhoE 91*
Degala, Ajita *BiDrAPA 89*
Degala, Ramamohana P 1945- *BiDrAPA 89*
Degala, Satyanarayana V *BiDrAPA 89*
DeGalleford, Fred *St&PR 91*
De Galvez, Jose 1720-1787 *BioIn 16*
Degan, Robert Anderson 1939- *St&PR 91*
Deganawida *WhNaAH*
Deganawidah *WhNaAH*
De Ganay, Birgitte *BioIn 16*
Degand, Lynne Marie 1955- *WhoEmL 91*
Deganello, Paolo *PenDiDA 89*
DeGange, Robert James 1945- *WhoEmL 91*
de Garcia, Lucia 1941- *WhoHisp 91*
De Garcia, Orlando Frank 1947- *WhoHisp 91*
De Garcia Carrasco, Concepcion Arenal 1820-1893 *BioIn 16*
Degarmo, George 1938- *St&PR 91*
DeGarmo, Lindley Grant 1953- *WhoEmL 91*
DeGarmo, Mark Borden *WhoE 91*
DeGarmo, Robert M. 1945- *St&PR 91*
De Garmo, Sheryl Frances 1952- *WhoWrEP 89*
De Garza, Patricia *AuBYP 90*
Degas, Edgar 1834-1917 *BioIn 16, IntDcAA 90, WorAlBi*
Degas, Hilaire Germain Edgar 1834-1917 *BioIn 16*
De Gasparin, Agenor 1810-1871 *EncO&P 3*
De Gasperi, Alcide 1881-1954 *WorAlBi*
Degast, Hilaire G. 1928- *St&PR 91*
De Gaster, Zachary 1926- *WhoAm 90*
deGategno, Paul James 1949- *WhoSSW 91*
DeGaugh, Jackie L. 1951- *WhoSSW 91*
De Gaulle, Charles 1890-1970 *BioIn 16, ConAu 130, WorAlBi*
DeGavre, Robert T. 1940- *St&PR 91*
deGavre, Robert Thompson 1940- *WhoAm 90*
Degbor, Anku Francis 1940- *WhoWor 91*
De Geer, Ingrid 1927- *IntWWM 90*
Degen, Bernard John, II 1937- *WhoAm 90*
Degen, Bruce *AuBYP 90*
Degen, Bruce 1945- *BioIn 16*
Degen, G. Richard 1948- *St&PR 91*
Degen, Helmut 1911- *IntWWM 90*
Degen, Kathleen 1945- *BiDrAPA 89*
De Genaro, Jennie Jennings 1932- *WhoWrEP 89*
Degener, Curtis Don 1930- *St&PR 91*
Degener, Richard Bowman 1937- *St&PR 91*
De Generes, Lanford H 1922- *BiDrAPA 89*
DeGeneste, Henry I. 1941- *WhoE 91*
Degenevieve, Barbara 1947- *WhoAmA 91*
Degenford, James Edward 1938- *WhoAm 90*
Degenhardt, Dawn Carole 1935- *WhoE 91*
Degenhart, Pearl C. *WhoAmW 91*
DeGennaro, Paul T. 1951- *WhoE 91*
De Gennaro, Richard 1926- *WhoAm 90*
de Gennes, Pierre G. 1932- *WhoWor 91*
Degenstein, Lester Ernest *WhoE 91*
DeGeorge, Francis Donald 1929- *WhoAm 90*
DeGeorge, Lawrence J. 1916- *St&PR 91*
De George, Lawrence Joseph 1916- *WhoAm 90*
De George, Richard Thomas 1933- *WhoAm 90*
De Gerenday, Laci, Mrs. *WhoAmW 91*
de Gerenday, Laci Anthony 1911- *WhoAm 90*
De Gering, Etta Fowler 1898- *AuBYP 90*
Degerness, Kenneth W. 1932- *ODwPR 91*
De Gerson, Jean Charlier 1363-1429 *EncO&P 3*
Degerstedt, Ross Maurice 1958- *WhoEmL 91*
De Gert, Berthomine *EncO&P 3*
De Geus, Ary 1925- *WhoWor 91*
DeGeus, Wendell Ray 1948- *WhoEmL 91*
DeGhetto, Kenneth Anselm 1924- *WhoAm 90*
Degi, Keith Joseph *BiDrAPA 89*
Degioanni, Henri *St&PR 91*
De Giorgi, Ennio 1928- *WhoWor 91*
DeGiovanni-Donnelly, Rosalie Frances 1926- *WhoAm 90*
DeGiusti, Dominic Lawrence 1911- *WhoAm 90*
de Givenchy, Hubert 1927- *ConDes 90*
De Givenchy, Hubert James Marcel Taffin 1927- *WhoAm 90, WhoWor 91*
Degkwitz, Eva Gertrud 1926- *WhoWor 91*
Degler, Carl Neumann 1921- *WhoAm 90*
Degler, Stanley E. 1929- *St&PR 91*
Degnan, Elizabeth J. 1927- *WhoAmW 91*
Degnan, Herbert Raymond 1921- *WhoAm 90*
Degnan, James J. 1932- *St&PR 91*
Degnan, John James, III 1945- *WhoEmL 91*
Degnan, Joseph 1955- *WhoAm 90*
Degnan, Kim E. 1956- *WhoAmW 91*
Degnan, Thomas Leonard 1909- *WhoAm 90*
Degner, Robert Lindell 1924- *St&PR 91*
Degner, Robert Louis 1942- *WhoSSW 91*
De Godoy, Manuel 1767-1851 *BioIn 16*
De Goede, Hendrik 1948- *WhoWor 91*
De Goeij, Ad D.M. 1939- *WhoWor 91*
De Gogorza, Emilio *PenDiMP*
de Gogorza, Patricia 1936- *WhoE 91*
De Golia, Van Dyke 1951- *BiDrAPA 89*
DeGonia, Mary Elise 1954- *WhoAmW 91*
Degos, Claude-Francois 1939- *WhoWor 91*
de Gosson de Varennes, Maurice Alexis 1948- *WhoWor 91*
Degoullons, Jules 1671?-1738 *PenDiDA 89*
De Goulon, Jules 1671?-1738 *PenDiDA 89*
De Graaff, Jan 1903-1989 *BioIn 16*
DeGrace, Charles A.H. 1926- *St&PR 91*
Degrada, Francesco 1940- *IntWWM 90*
Degraff, David Charles 1954- *WhoE 91*
Degraff, Robin L. *St&PR 91*
DeGraffenreid, Brenda Jean 1947- *WhoAmW 91*
de Graffenried, Velda Mae Camp *WhoAmW 91*
DeGrandi, Joseph Anthony 1927- *WhoAm 90*
De Grandpre, A. Jean *BioIn 16*
De Grandpre, Albert Jean 1921- *St&PR 91, WhoAm 90*
De Grandpre, Pierre 1946- *St&PR 91*
de Grassi, Alex *NewAgMG*
DeGrassi, Leonard Rene 1928- *WhoWor 91*
DeGrave, Philip *TwCCr&M 91*
de Gravelles, William Decatur, Jr. 1928- *WhoAm 90*
DeGraw, Bette Feather 1946- *WhoEmL 91*
De Graw, Darrel Garvin 1934- *WhoSSW 91*
De Gray, Julian 1905- *IntWWM 90, WhoE 91*
de Grazia, Edward 1927- *ConAu 129*
De Grazia, Ettore Ted 1909-1982 *WhoAmA 91N*
De Grazia, Loretta Theresa 1955- *WhoAmW 91*
de Grazia, Sebastian 1917- *WhoAm 90*
De Greef, Arthur 1862-1940 *PenDiMP*
Degreef, Gustav 1953- *BiDrAPA 89*
Degregorio, Michael A. 1954- *St&PR 91*
De Gregory, Alfred D. 1941- *St&PR 91*
De Greiff, Monica *BioIn 16*
De Greve, Marcel 1922- *WhoWor 91*
de Grey, Roger 1918- *WhoWor 91*
DeGrilla, Robert J. 1942- *WhoSSW 91*
De Grimaldi, Jean-Marie 1796-1874 *BioIn 16*
De Grip, Andries 1954- *WhoWor 91*
Degroat, Diane 1947- *WhoAmA 91*
DeGroat, Gail Barbara 1937- *WhoAmW 91*
De Groat, George Hugh 1917- *WhoAmA 91*
DeGroat, Joanne E. 1951- *WhoAmW 91*
deGroat, William Chesney 1938- *WhoAm 90*
De Groen, Alma 1941- *FemiCLE*
DeGroff, Ralph Lynn, Jr. 1936- *WhoE 91*
de Groot, Christopher Mark *BiDrAPA 89*
De Groot, Huub Johannes Maria 1958- *WhoWor 91*
De Groot, Johannes 1914-1972 *DcScB S2*
Degroot, Leslie Jacob 1928- *WhoAm 90*
DeGroot, Morris H. 1931-1989 *BioIn 16*
de Groot, Stephen F. 1961- *WhoEmL 91*
De Groote, David Glenn 1958- *WhoE 91*
DeGroote, Michael G. 1930- *WhoAm 90*
De Groote, Philip *PenDiMP*
De Groote, Steven *BioIn 16*
de Gruchy, John W 1939- *ConAu 131*
De Gruchy, Nigel *BioIn 16*
De Grummond, Lena *AuBYP 90*
De Grummond, Lena Young *BioIn 16, SmATA 62 [port]*
De Grunwald, Dimitri *BioIn 16*
DeGruson, Eugene Henry 1932- *WhoAm 90*
De Gruson, Gene 1932- *WhoWrEP 89*
De Guatemala, Joyce 1938- *WhoAmA 91, WhoE 91*
Deguchi, Yoshiaki 1929- *WhoWor 91*
Deguillaume, Jean-Charles 1949- *WhoWor 91*
DeGulis, Albert Joseph 1934- *St&PR 91*
Degutyte, Janina 1928- *EncCoWW*
DeGuzman, Betty Freehill *WhoAmW 91*
De Guzman, Evelyn Lopez 1947- *WhoAmA 91*
De Guzman, Julita Mapalad *BiDrAPA 89*
Deguzman, Melvin Berdon 1955- *WhoE 91*
De Guzman, Rafael M *BiDrAPA 89*
De Haan, Byron 1926- *ODwPR 91*
De Haan, Marvin R 1926- *BiDrAPA 89*
DeHaan, Norman Richard *NewYTBS 90*
DeHaan, Norman Richard 1927- *WhoAm 90*
De Haan-Puls, Joyce Elaine 1941- *WhoAmW 91*
DeHaas, H. Tony 1940- *ODwPR 91*
DeHaas, John Neff, Jr. 1926- *WhoAm 90*
De Habsburgo-Lorena, Inmaculada *BioIn 16*
Dehaene, Jean-Luc 1940- *WhoWor 91*
De Hamel, Christopher 1950- *BioIn 16*
De Harak, Rudolph 1924- *ConDes 90*
DeHart, Barbara Boudreau 1946- *WhoEmL 91*
De Hart, Cor *BiDrAPA 89*
De Hart, David 1949- *St&PR 91*
DeHart, David Glenn 1958- *WhoEmL 91*
De Hart, Flora Ballowe 1931- *WhoSSW 91*
De Hart, Harold C. 1938- *St&PR 91*
DeHart, James French, Jr. 1961- *WhoEmL 91*
DeHart, James Louis 1946- *WhoEmL 91*
DeHart, Robert Charles 1917- *WhoAm 90*
DeHart, Robert L. 1933- *St&PR 91*
De Hartog, Jan 1914- *BioIn 16, WhoWor 91*
DeHaven, Gloria 1925- *BioIn 16*
DeHaven, Kenneth Le Moyne 1913- *WhoWor 91*
DeHaven, Robert Claude 1945- *WhoEmL 91*
De Haven, Tom 1949- *WhoWrEP 89*
de Havilland, Olivia 1916- *BioAmW, WorAlBi*
de Havilland, Olivia Mary 1916- *WhoAm 90, WhoWor 91*
de Havilland, Peter *NewAgMG*
DeHay, John Carlisle, Jr. 1922- *WhoAm 90*
DeHayes, Daniel Wesley 1941- *WhoAm 90*
De Hegedus, Coloman 1942- *St&PR 91*
Dehejia, Makarand V. 1934- *St&PR 91*
Dehennin, Herman 1929- *WhoAm 90*
De Herrera, Luis Alberto 1873-1959 *BioIn 16*
De Herrera, Rick *WhoHisp 91*
De Heusch, Lucio 1946- *WhoAmA 91*
De Hidalgo, Elvira *PenDiMP*
Dehkharghani, Farangis A *BiDrAPA 89*
Dehlendorf, Robert O., II 1931- *St&PR 91*
Dehler, Martin D. 1941- *St&PR 91*
Dehlinger, Peter 1917- *WhoAm 90*
Dehmelt, Hans G. 1922- *WorAlBi*
Dehmelt, Hans Georg 1922- *WhoAm 90, WhoWor 91*
Dehmer, Carlos 1949- *WhoEmL 91*
Dehmler, Mari Lynch 1953- *WhoWrEP 89*
Dehmlow, Louis H.T. 1927- *St&PR 91*
Dehmlow, Louis Henry Theodore, III 1927- *WhoAm 90*
Dehmlow, Nancy 1952- *St&PR 91*
Dehn, Adolf 1895-1968 *WhoAmA 91N*
Dehn, Joseph William, Jr. 1928- *WhoAm 90*
Dehn, Letha Arlene 1916- *WhoAmW 91*
Dehn, Paula Faye 1951- *WhoAmW 91*
Dehne, Carl A. 1957- *St&PR 91*
Dehnel, Luther L *BiDrAPA 89*
Dehner, Amie M. *ODwPR 91*
Dehner, Dorothy *WhoAm 90*
Dehner, Dorothy 1901- *WhoAmA 91*
Dehner, Dorothy Florence 1901- *BiDWomA*
Dehnert, Edmund John 1931- *IntWWM 90*
De Hoffmann, Frederic 1924-1989 *BioIn 16*
De Hont, Raymond Joseph 1954- *St&PR 91*
DeHoog, Rosemary Luther 1939- *WhoE 91*
de Hoop, Adrianus Teunis 1927- *WhoWor 91*
DeHope, Edward Kim 1952- *WhoE 91*
DeHority, Edward Havens, Jr. 1930- *WhoAm 90*
De Hostos, Eugenio Maria 1839-1903 *BioIn 16*
De Hoyos, Angela *BioIn 16, ConAu 131*
De Hoyos, Angela 1940- *WhoHisp 91*
de Hoyos, Linda 1944- *BiDrAPA 89*
De Ibarbourou, Juana 1895-1979 *BioIn 16*
Deibel, Charles Louis 1934- *WhoSSW 91*
Deibel, David C. 1950- *St&PR 91*
Deibel, Jerome P. 1924- *St&PR 91*
Deibel, Robert F., Jr. 1917- *St&PR 91*
Deibler, Barbara Ellen 1943- *WhoAmW 91, WhoE 91, WhoWor 91*
Deibler, Marie Phillips *WhoAmW 91, WhoWor 91*
Deibler, William Edwin 1932- *WhoAm 90*
Deichert, Anne Van Nuys 1924- *WhoAmW 91*
Deiches, Isadore William 1933- *WhoWor 91*
Deichler, Deborah 1948- *BioIn 16*
Deichmann, Dick H. 1928- *St&PR 91*
Deichmann, Hans *BioIn 16*
Deichmann, Paul 1898- *BioIn 16*
Deicken, Raymond Friedrich *BiDrAPA 89*
Deieso, Donald Allan 1949- *WhoAm 90*
Deighton, Len *ConAu 33NR, MajTwCW*
Deighton, Len 1929- *Au&Arts 6 [port], TwCCr&M 91, WhoAm 90, WhoWor 91, WorAlBi*
Deighton, Leonard Cyril 1929- *ConAu 33NR, MajTwCW, SpyFic*
Deignan, Daniel James 1947- *WhoSSW 91*
Deihl, Richard Harry 1928- *St&PR 91, WhoAm 90, WhoWor 91*
Deikel, Theodore *WhoAm 90*
Deikman, Arthur J 1929- *BiDrAPA 89*
Deiler, Deana Davis 1959- *WhoAmW 91*
Deily, James H. 1946- *St&PR 91*
Deily, James Richard 1921- *St&PR 91, WhoE 91*
Deily, Linnet Frazier 1945- *WhoAm 90, WhoAmW 91*
Deimer, Lorena Ruth Murrill 1926- *WhoWrEP 89*
Deimler, Kathryn George *IntWWM 90*
Deimling, George F. 1945- *St&PR 91*
Deinert, Herbert 1930- *WhoAm 90*
Deines, E Hubert 1894-1967 *WhoAmA 91N*
Deininger, James Paul 1950- *WhoEmL 91*
Deininger, John 1932- *WhoAm 90*
Deininger, William Dwight 1956- *WhoWor 91*
Deinzer, George William 1934- *WhoWor 91*
Deiotte, Margaret Tukey 1952- *WhoAmW 91*
Deisenhofer, Johann 1943- *BioIn 16, WhoAm 90, WhoSSW 91, WhoWor 91*
Deisenroth, Clinton Wilbur 1941- *WhoAm 90*
Deisler, Paul Frederick, Jr. 1926- *WhoAm 90*
Deiss, William Paul, Jr. 1923- *WhoAm 90*
Deissler, Robert George 1921- *WhoAm 90, WhoWor 91*
Deister, Irwin Frederick, Jr. 1929- *St&PR 91*
Deitch, Arline Douglis 1922- *WhoAmW 91*
Deitch, Donna Marie *WhoAmW 91*
Deitch, Irene M. 1930- *WhoAmW 91*

Deitch, James Michael 1954- WhoE 91
Deitch, Jeffrey 1952- WhoAmA 91
Deitch, Marc W. 1942- St&PR 91
Deitch, Stewart 1941- St&PR 91
Deitch, William 1933- St&PR 91
Deitcher, Herbert 1933- St&PR 91, WhoAm 90
Deitchle, Gerald W. 1951- St&PR 91
Deitchman, Robert B 1920- BiDrAPA 89
Deitchman, Seymour Jacob 1923- WhoE 91
Deiters, Joan Adele 1934- WhoAm 90, WhoAmW 91
Deitrich, Merrill Arthur 1920- St&PR 91
Deitrick, William Edgar 1944- WhoAm 90
Deitsch, Marian Mimi 1933- WhoAmW 91
De Iturbide, Agustin 1783-1824 BioIn 16
Deitz, Ira Jeffrey 1949- BiDrAPA 89
Deitz, Owen David 1952- WhoE 91
Deitz, Paula 1938- WhoAm 90
Deitz, Robert David 1926- St&PR 91
Deitz, Susan Rose 1934- WhoAmW 91
Deitzler, George Washington 1826-1884 AmLegL
De Jaager, Gerald 1946- WhoEmL 91
DeJacimo, Alexandria Welzien 1951- WhoEmL 91
de Jager, Cornelis 1921- WhoWor 91
DeJarnette, Edward 1938- WhoAm 90
De Jary, J.J. St&PR 91
De Jesus, Carlos I 1958- BiDrAPA 89
De Jesus, Edwin 1961- WhoE 91
De Jesus, Enrique Angeles BiDrAPA 89
De Jesus, Esteban 1951-1989 BioIn 16
DeJesus, Hiram Raymon 1957- WhoHisp 91
DeJesus, Ivan 1953- Ballpl 90
De Jesus, Jaime Manuel 1945- WhoSSW 91
De Jesus, Magdeleine 1898-1989 BioIn 16
De Jesus, Maria Leonora Vasquez 1950- WhoWor 91
De Jesus, Nydia Rosa 1930- WhoAm 90
De Jesus-Burgos, Sylvia Teresa 1941- WhoHisp 91
De Jesus-Torres, Migdalia 1944- WhoHisp 91
Dejmek, Kazimierz 1924- WhoWor 91
Dejmek, Linda Marie 1953- WhoAmW 91
De John, Charles S 1940- BiDrAPA 89
DeJohnette, Jack BioIn 16
De Johnette, Jack 1942- WhoAm 90
De Jong, Arthur Jay 1934- WhoAm 90
DeJong, Bruce Allen 1946- WhoEmL 91
De Jong, Caspar B.M. 1925- St&PR 91
De Jong, Conrad J. 1934- IntWWM 90
De Jong, David Cornel 1905-1967 AuBYP 90
De Jong, David John 1951- WhoEmL 91
De Jong, David Samuel 1951- WhoE 91, WhoEmL 91, WhoWor 91
De Jong, Dola 1911- AuBYP 90
de Jong, Eveline D 1948- ConAu 130
DeJong, Gerben 1946- WhoE 91
De Jong, Gerrit, Jr 1892-1979 WhoAmA 91N
De Jong, Henk Wouter 1925- WhoWor 91
De Jong, Jacob 1926- BiDrAPA 89
De Jong, Jan Willem 1942- WhoWor 91
De Jong, Meindert 1906- AuBYP 90
De Jong, Norman Klay 1930- St&PR 91
De Jong, Robert Duris 1945- WhoWrEP 89
De Jong, Russell N 1907-1990 ConAu 132
DeJong, Russell Nelson NewYTBS 90
De Jong, Russell Nelson, Jr. 1945- WhoE 91
de Jong, Stef J. M. Chr. 1955- WhoWor 91
De Jonge, Curt Edward 1922- St&PR 91
DeJonge, David Earl 1959- WhoEmL 91
Dejonge, Joanne E. 1943- BioIn 16
De Jonge, Nicolaas Marinus 1920- BioIn 16
De Jongh, James Laurence 1942- WhoWrEP 89
De Jonghe, Marcel 1943- IntWWM 90
DeJoseph, Jeff 1955- WhoEmL 91
De Josselin de Jong, Patrick Edward 1922- BioIn 16
De Journett, Rosalie Sue Cottrill 1937- IntWWM 90
De Jouvenel, Bertrand 1903-1987 BioIn 16
de Jouvenel, Hugues Alain 1946- ConAu 130
De Jovellanos, Gaspar 1744-1811 BioIn 16
De Juan, Ronaldo 1931-1989 BioIn 16
DeJur, Ralph A. BioIn 16
Dekanahwidah WhNaAH
Dekanawida WhNaAH
Dekanawidah WhNaAH
Dekanawidah 1550?-1600? EncCRAm
Dekanisora 1650?-1730 WhNaAH
Dekanisoura 1650?-1730 WhNaAH
Dekany, Bela 1928- IntWWM 90
DeKay, Dennis Alan 1952- WhoEmL 91
deKay, James Tertius 1930- WhoE 91
de Kazinczy, Ferenc Andor 1929- WhoWor 91
De Keersmaeker, Anne Teresa BioIn 16
Deken, Agatha 1741-1804 EncCoWW
De Kerchove, Gerald 1946- St&PR 91
De Kergommeaux, Duncan 1927- WhoAmA 91
De Kerpel, Jo Lucien Felix 1959- WhoWor 91
DeKeysek, Michael August 1943- St&PR 91
DeKeyser, James C. 1937- St&PR 91
DeKeyser, William Richard, Jr. 1948- WhoE 91
DeKeyserlingk, Doris Muser BioIn 16
Dekker, Carl AuBYP 90, TwCCr&M 91, WhoWrEP 89
Dekker, Eugene Earl 1927- WhoAm 90
Dekker, Evelyn E. St&PR 91
Dekker, George Gilbert 1934- WhoAm 90
Dekker, Gerard 1931- WhoWor 91
Dekker, Harriett Gromb 1942- WhoAmW 91
Dekker, Howard R. 1920- St&PR 91
Dekker, Jacob Christoph Edmond 1921- WhoE 91
Dekker, Jerry Allen 1954- St&PR 91
Dekker, Marcel 1931- WhoAm 90
Dekker, Maurits 1899- WhoAm 90
Dekker, Randall M. 1922- St&PR 91
Dekker, Rudolf M 1951- ConAu 132
Dekker, Thomas 1572?-1632 BioIn 16
Dekker, Wisse BioIn 16
Dekker, Wisse 1924- WhoAm 90
Dekko, Thomas L. 1927- St&PR 91
Dekle, Larry Carlton 1942- BiDrAPA 89
de Klerk, F W 1936- CurBio 90 [port], News 90 [port]
De Klerk, F. W. 1936- WorAlBi
De Klerk, Frederik Willem BioIn 16
de Klerk, Frederik Willem 1936- NewYTBS 90 [port], WhoWor 91
De Klerk, Willem 1928- BioIn 16
Dekmejian, Richard Hrair 1933- WhoAm 90
Deknatel, Frederick Brockway 1905-1973 WhoAmA 91N
De Knight, Avel 1933- WhoAmA 91
De Kock, Gerhard 1926-1989 BioIn 16
De Kock, Josse 1933- WhoWor 91
De Koenigswarter, Pannonica 1913-1988 BioIn 16
de Koff, John Peter 1954- WhoE 91
Dekoker, Richard Carroll 1929- WhoSSW 91
De Kooning, Elaine Marie Catherine 1920-1989 BioIn 16, WhoAmA 91N
De Kooning, Lisa BioIn 16
De Kooning, Willem 1904- BioIn 16, IntDcAA 90, WhoAm 90, WorAlBi
De Kooning, William 1904-1988 WhoAmA 91N
De Korne, Betsy 1923- St&PR 91
De Korne, David J. 1956- St&PR 91
De Korne, Jack E. 1947- St&PR 91
De Korne, Jack M. 1923- St&PR 91
De Korte, Rudolf Willem 1936- WhoWor 91
de Koster, Henri Johan 1914- WhoWor 91
De Koven, Reginald 1859-1920 OxCPMus
De Kovner-Mayer, Barbara 1938- WhoWrEP 89
DeKozan, Raymond L. 1936- St&PR 91
Dekret, Jeffrey J 1950- BiDrAPA 89
Dekret, Jeffrey Joseph 1950- WhoE 91
De Kroon, Ciro BioIn 16
DeKruif, Jack H. 1921- St&PR 91
De Kruif, Paul 1890-1971 BioIn 16
DeKruif, Robert M. 1919- WhoAm 90
Dekster, Boris Veniamin 1938- WhoWor 91
Dektor, Leslie BioIn 16
de Kurz, Carmen de Rafael Mares 1911- EncCoWW
Del Vikings EncPR&S 89
Dela Cruz, Jose Santos 1948- WhoEmL 91, WhoWor 91
de la Bandera, Elna Marie 1936- WhoE 91
Delabarre, Ginger Ann 1954- WhoAmW 91
DeLabarre, S. P. AmLegL
DelaBarre Powers, Nancy May 1941- WhoAmW 91
de la Bedoyere, Charlotte 1931- WhoWor 91
de Laboulaye, Francois Rene 1917- WhoWor 91
Delabre, Kevin Michael 1952- WhoEmL 91
De La Cancela, Victor 1952- WhoHisp 91
Delacato, Carl Henry 1923- WhoAm 90
Delacey, Deborah Hartwell 1952- WhoAmW 91
De La Chapelle, Alain A 1940- BiDrAPA 89
De la Chaume, Jacqueline Thion BioIn 16
De la Cierva, Juan 1896-1936 BioIn 16
de la Colina, Rafael 1898- WhoAm 90
Delacote, Jacques IntWWM 90
Delacote, Jacques 1942- PenDiMP
Delacour, Yves Jean Claude Marie 1943- WhoWor 91
De Lacretelle, Jacques 1888-1985 BioIn 16
Delacroix, Eugene 1798-1863 BioIn 16, IntDcAA 90, WorAlBi
Delacroix, Pauline 1863-1912 BiDWomA
De La Croix, Robert AuBYP 90
de la Croix-Vaubois, Bruno 1958- WhoEmL 91
De La Cruz, Antonio Vergel de Dios 1943- WhoWor 91
de la Cruz, Carlos Manuel, Sr. 1941- WhoHisp 91
De La Cruz, Eduardo R 1948- BiDrAPA 89
De La Cruz, Emmanuel A BiDrAPA 89
De La Cruz, Francisco 1938- WhoWor 91
De La Cruz, Jerry John 1948- WhoHisp 91
De la Cruz, Juana Ines 1651-1695 BioIn 16
De La Cruz, Silvestre S 1947- BiDrAPA 89
de la Cuadra, Bruce WhoHisp 91
De la Cueva, Julio Jose Iglesias WhoWor 91
DeLacy, Sarah Rosalee 1941- WhoAmW 91
De La Falaise, Lucie BioIn 16
De La Falaise, Maxime BioIn 16
Delafield, E. M. 1890-1943 BioIn 16, FemiCLE
De La Flor, Eduardo Pablo 1926- BiDrAPA 89
Delafon, Remigio Andres EncCoWW
Delafosse, Jean-Charles 1734-1789 PenDiDA 89
De La Fresnaye, Roger 1885-1925 BioIn 16
De La Fressange, Ines BioIn 16
DeLaFuente, Charles 1945- WhoE 91
de la Fuente, Fernando 1930- WhoE 91
De La Fuente, Gita 1921- IntWWM 90
De La Fuente, Jose Ramon 1951- WhoEmL 91
De La Fuente, Juan Ramon 1951- BiDrAPA 89
De La Fuente, Maria Elena G BiDrAPA 89
de la Fuente, Roque WhoHisp 91
De La Gandara, Jose E. 1942- BiDrAPA 89
Delagardelle, Norma Jean 1934- St&PR 91
De la Garza, E. 1927- BioIn 16
de la Garza, Ekika 1927- WhoAm 90, WhoSSW 91
de la Garza, Eligio 1927- WhoHisp 91
de la Garza, Kika 1927- WhoHisp 91
de la Garza, Leonardo 1937- WhoHisp 91
de la Garza, Luis Adolfo 1943- WhoHisp 91
De La Garza, Pete 1945- WhoHisp 91
de la Garza, Rodolfo O. 1942- WhoHisp 91
Delage, Carol Anne 1958- WhoAmW 91, WhoEmL 91
Delagi, Edward Francis 1911- WhoAm 90
De Lago, Joseph Thomas 1923- St&PR 91
De la Guardia, Ernesto 1904-1983 BioIn 16
de la Guardia, Mario Francisco 1936- WhoAm 90
De la Guardia, Ricardo Adolfo 1899-1970 BioIn 16
De la Guerre, Elisabeth Claude Jacquet 1659-1729 BioIn 16
Del Aguila, Ralph W. 1939- St&PR 91
de Laguna, Frederica 1906- WhoAm 90, WhoAmW 91
Delahanty, Ed 1867-1903 Ballpl 90 [port]
Delahanty, Jim 1879-1953 Ballpl 90
Delahanty, Linda Michele 1957- WhoAmW 91
Delahay, Paul 1921- WhoAm 90
Delahaye, Guy 1888-1969 DcLB 92
Delahaye, Michael John 1946- SpyFic
Delaherche, Auguste 1857-1940 PenDiDA 89
de la Hoz, Mike 1939- Ballpl 90
De la Hunty, Shirley 1925- BioIn 16
De La Iglesia, Felix Alberto 1939- WhoAm 90
D'Elaine 1932- WhoAmA 91
De Laine, Franklin Pierce 1929- WhoAm 90
De Laittre, Eleanor 1911- WhoAmA 91
Delakas, Daniel Liudviko 1921- WhoAm 90, WhoWor 91
De La Lastra, Albert 1936- St&PR 91
del Alcazar-Silvela, Diego 1950- WhoWor 91
Delalic, Zdenka Joan WhoAmW 91
DeLalio, George M. 1929- St&PR 91
Delalio, Louis D. 1926- St&PR 91
Delalio, Marilyn 1928- St&PR 91
De Lalla, Marta BiDrAPA 89
de la Llave, Rafael 1957- WhoSSW 91
Delaloye, Bernard 1928- WhoWor 91
De La Luz, Nilsa 1946- WhoHisp 91
de Lama, George 1957- WhoHisp 91
De la Madrid Hurtado, Miguel BioIn 16
de la Madrid Hurtado, Miguel 1934- WhoAm 90, WhoSSW 91, WhoWor 91
Delamain, Henry PenDiDA 89
De Lamarck, Jean Baptiste Pierre Antoine 1744-1829 BioIn 16
Delamare, Daniel BioIn 16
de la Mare, Walter 1873-1956 ChlLR 23 [port], WorAlBi
De La Mare, Walter John 1873-1956 AuBYP 90
De la Martinez, Odaline PenDiMP
DeLamater, James Newton 1912- WhoAm 90
DeLaMater, Robert Griffin 1959- WhoEmL 91, WhoWor 91
DeLamatter, Donna Anne 1942- WhoAmW 91
De La Maza, Antonio 1936- BiDrAPA 89
De La Maza, Sebastian 1937- BiDrAPA 89
DeLambily, Robert Walter, Jr. 1950- WhoE 91
De Lamennais, Felicite Robert 1782-1854 BioIn 16
Delamonica, Roberto 1933- WhoAmA 91
Delamuraz, Jean-Pascal 1936- WhoWor 91
De Lancey Family EncCRAm
DeLancey, Bill 1901-1946 Ballpl 90
De Lancey, Etienne EncCRAm
De Lancey, James 1703-1760 EncCRAm
De Lancey, James 1732-1800 EncCRAm
De Lancey, John Oliver Lang 1951- WhoEmL 91
De Lancey, Oliver 1718-1785 EncCRAm
DeLancey, Robert Houston, Jr. 1936- WhoSSW 91
DeLancey, Teresa Hammack 1954- WhoSSW 91
De Lancie, John 1921- IntWWM 90, PenDiMP
De Lancre, Pierre 1553-1631 EncO&P 3
Delancy, Michael Robinson 1948- WhoEmL 91
De Land, Edward Charles 1922- WhoAm 90
Deland, Margaret 1857-1945 BioAmW, FemiCLE
De Land, Michelle Karen 1954- WhoWrEP 89
Deland, Raymond John 1927- WhoAm 90
De Landsheere, Gilbert Leopold Baron 1921- WhoWor 91
Delaney, Andrew 1920- WhoSSW 91, WhoWor 91
Delaney, Art 1895-1970 Ballpl 90
Delaney, Arthur Andrews 1931- WhoE 91
Delaney, Beauford 1902-1979 WhoAmA 91N
Delaney, Beverly Renay BiDrAPA 89
Delaney, C. Timothy 1957- WhoEmL 91
DeLaney, Charles Oliver 1925- WhoSSW 91
Delaney, Edward Norman 1927- WhoAm 90, WhoE 91, WhoWor 91
Delaney, Franey ConAu 31NR, MajTwCW
Delaney, Gary Martin 1939- St&PR 91
Delaney, George F., Jr. 1924- St&PR 91
Delaney, George Joseph 1936- St&PR 91
Delaney, Gerard Michael 1953- WhoSSW 91
Delaney, Gina WhoWrEP 89
Delaney, Harold 1919- WhoE 91
DeLaney, Herbert Wade, Jr. 1925- WhoWor 91
Delaney, Jack Lee 1956- IntWWM 90
Delaney, James V. BioIn 16
Delaney, Janet Clare 1952- WhoAmA 91
Delaney, John Adrian 1956- WhoEmL 91
Delaney, John Francis 1938- BiDrAPA 89, WhoAm 90
Delaney, John R 1934- BiDrAPA 89
Delaney, John W. St&PR 91
Delaney, Joseph P. 1934- WhoAm 90, WhoSSW 91
Delaney, Katherine Carroll 1941- WhoAmW 91
Delaney, Kathleen Hanley 1938- WhoAmW 91
Delaney, Kevin Francis 1958- WhoEmL 91
Delaney, Lawrence John 1935- WhoAm 90
Delaney, Logan D., Jr. 1949- St&PR 91
Delaney, Marion Patricia 1952- WhoAmW 91, WhoEmL 91
Delaney, Mark Steven 1952- WhoSSW 91
Delaney, Martin Donohue, III BiDrAPA 89
Delaney, Mary Anne 1948- BiDrAPA 89
Delaney, Mary Margaret 1950- WhoAmW 91
Delaney, Michael Brian 1957- WhoEmL 91
Delaney, Nancy Jo 1941- WhoAmW 91
Delaney, Pamela DeLeo 1947- WhoEmL 91
Delaney, Patrick Arthur 1932- St&PR 91
Delaney, Patrick E. 1953- St&PR 91
Delaney, Patrick James 1940- WhoAm 90
Delaney, Paul 1933- BioIn 16
Delaney, Philip Alfred 1928- St&PR 91, WhoAm 90, WhoWor 91
Delaney, Richard James 1946- WhoAm 90

Delaney, Robert Finley 1925- *WhoWor 91*
DeLaney, Robert J., Jr. 1931- *St&PR 91*
Delaney, Robert Patrick 1961- *WhoE 91*
Delaney, Robert Richard, Jr. 1954- *WhoEmL 91*
Delaney, Robert V. 1934- *St&PR 91*
Delaney, Robert Vernon 1936- *WhoAm 90*
Delaney, Robert William 1929- *St&PR 91*
Delaney, Shelagh 1939- *BioIn 16, ConAu 30NR, FemiCLE, MajTwCW*
Delaney, Terry W. 1949- *WhoEmL 91*
Delaney, Thomas Caldwell, Jr. 1918- *WhoAm 90*
Delaney, Thomas P. 1934- *St&PR 91*
Delaney, William Francis, Jr. *WhoAm 90*
Delaney, William Timothy 1937- *St&PR 91*
DeLaney Adams, Donna Marie 1952- *WhoEmL 91*
Delaney-Mech, Susan Delphine 1948- *BiDrAPA 89*
DeLange, Dirk 1948- *St&PR 91*
de Lange, Hans *WhoAm 90*
De Lange, Jeff *BioIn 16*
De Langlade, Charles Michel 1729-1801? *EncCRAm*
Delanne, Gabriel 1857-1926 *EncO&P 3, EncPaPR 91*
Delano, Columbus 1809-1893 *BiDrUSE 89*
Delano, Gerard Curtis 1890-1972 *BioIn 16*
Delano, Hugh Stafford 1933- *WhoE 91*
Delano, Jack 1914- *IntWWM 90*
De Lano, James Edwards, Jr. 1943- *BiDrAPA 89*
Delano, James G *BiDrAPA 89*
Delano, Jane Arminda 1862-1919 *BioIn 16*
Delano, Jonathan William 1949- *WhoE 91*
Delano, Lester Almy, Jr. 1928- *WhoAm 90*
Delano, Marcia Patricia 1939- *WhoAmW 91*
Delano, Robert Barnes, Jr. 1956- *WhoEmL 91*
Delanois, Louis 1731-1792 *PenDiDA 89*
De Lanoy, Charles James 1956- *WhoEmL 91*
Delany, Clarissa M. Scott 1901-1927 *HarlReB [port]*
Delany, Dana *WhoAmW 91*
Delany, Edward L. *WhoAm 90*
Delany, Hubert T. *NewYTBS 90 [port]*
Delany, Irene Beissner 1945- *WhoAmW 91*
Delany, Logan D. 1949- *St&PR 91*
Delany, Logan Drummond, Jr. 1949- *WhoE 91*
Delany, Martin Robinson 1812-1885 *BioIn 16*
Delany, Mary 1700-1788 *FemiCLE*
Delany, Mary Granville Pendarves 1700-1788 *BioIn 16*
Delany, Samuel 1942- *WorAlBi*
Delany, Samuel R 1942- *MajTwCW, RGTwCSF*
Delap, J. Q., Jr. 1948- *WhoEmL 91, WhoSSW 91*
Delap, Tony 1927- *WhoAm 90, WhoAmA 91*
De la Parra, Teresa 1890-1936 *BioIn 16*
de la Parte, Louis Anthony, Jr. 1929- *WhoAm 90*
De la Pasture, Elizabeth 1866-1945 *FemiCLE*
De la Pau, Maria *PenDiMP*
de La Pena, George 1956- *WhoAm 90*
de la Pena, Nonny 1963- *WhoHisp 91*
De La Pena Fuentes, Rosendo 1947- *WhoWor 91*
de la Piedra, Jorge 1923- *WhoSSW 91*
Delaplain, Theresa Rachel 1959- *IntWWM 90*
Delaplane, James Michael *BiDrAPA 89*
Delaplane, Stanton Hill 1907-1988 *BioIn 16*
De la Pole, William *BioIn 16*
De La Porte, Gayle Larson 1961- *St&PR 91*
Delaporte, Theophile *ConAu 33NR, MajTwCW*
DeLapp, Albert Ashley, II 1931- *St&PR 91, WhoAm 90*
Delappe, Irving Pierce 1915- *WhoAm 90*
De La Quintinie, Jean 1626-1688 *BioIn 16*
Delaquis, Noel 1934- *WhoAm 90*
de Lara, Hector G., Jr. *WhoHisp 91*
De Lara, Jose Garcia 1940- *WhoHisp 91*
De Lara Castro, Carmen *BioIn 16*
De la Ramee, Louise 1839-1908 *BioIn 16*
De la Renta, Oscar *BioIn 16*
De La Renta, Oscar 1932- *ConDes 90, WhoAm 90, WhoE 91, WhoHisp 91, WorAlBi*
De Large, Robert Carlos 1842-1874 *BlkAmsC [port]*
De Larios, Dora 1933- *WhoAmA 91*
De La Rocha, Manuel A 1930- *BiDrAPA 89*
de la Roche, Mazo 1879-1961 *ConAu 30NR, FemiCLE, SmATA 64 [port]*
DeLaRosa, Denise Maria 1954- *WhoAmW 91, WhoWor 91*
De La Rosa, Edna Elnore 1918- *WhoWrEP 89*
De la Rosa, Francisco Martinez 1787-1862 *BioIn 16*
De la Rosa, Javier *BioIn 16*
De Larra, Mariano Jose 1809-1837 *BioIn 16*
De Larrocha, Alicia *BioIn 16*
de Larrocha, Alicia 1923- *WhoAm 90, WhoAmW 91, WhoWor 91, WorAlBi*
De Larrocha, Alicia De La Calle 1923- *IntWWM 90*
Delaryd, Bengt 1929- *WhoWor 91*
Delasalle, Angele 1867-1938? *BiDWomA*
De Las Casas, Bartolome 1474-1566 *BioIn 16*
de las Casas, Walter Mario 1947- *WhoHisp 91*
de las Heras, Gonzalo 1940- *WhoAm 90*
DeLashmet, Gordon Bartlett 1928- *WhoWor 91*
de la Sierra, Jordan *NewAgMG*
De Lastic, Georges 1927-1988 *BioIn 16*
de la Teja, Elpidio Leoncio 1943- *WhoE 91*
de la Torre, Adrian Louis 1924- *WhoHisp 91*
De La Torre, Alberto A 1923- *BiDrAPA 89*
De La Torre, David Joseph 1948- *WhoAmA 91, WhoHisp 91*
de la Torre, Homero R. 1943- *WhoHisp 91*
de la Torre, JoLynn Kae Hinger 1960- *WhoSSW 91*
De La Torre, Jorge G *BiDrAPA 89*
De La Torre, Jose I 1931- *BiDrAPA 89*
De La Torre, Jose Manuel *BiDrAPA 89*
De La Torre, Lillian 1902- *AuBYP 90, TwCCr&M 91*
De La Torre, Lily Shu *BiDrAPA 89*
De La Torre, Luis G 1917- *BiDrAPA 89*
De La Torre, Manuel 1948- *WhoHisp 91*
DeLaTorre, Phillip Eugene 1953- *WhoEmL 91*
De La Torre, Rolando E *BiDrAPA 89*
De la Torre, Victor Raul Haya 1895-1979 *BioIn 16*
De La Torre-Leano, Jose Adolfo 1942- *WhoE 91*
de la Torriente, Alicia A. 1955- *WhoHisp 91*
Delauder, William B. *WhoAm 90*
DeLauer, Richard 1918-1990 *BioIn 16*
DeLauer, Richard D. *NewYTBS 90*
DeLaughter, Thomas Glenn 1948- *WhoEmL 91*
Delaunay, Charles 1911-1988 *AnObit 1988*
DeLaunay, Marcus 1956- *ODwPR 91*
Delaunay, Nicolas 1655?-1727 *PenDiDA 89*
Delaunay, Robert 1885-1941 *BioIn 16, IntDcAA 90*
Delaunay, Sonia 1885-1979 *BiDWomA, BioIn 16, ConDes 90*
Delaunay-Terk, Sonia 1885-1979 *BiDWomA*
Delaune, Etienne 1518?-1583 *PenDiDA 89*
Delaune, Lynn *AuBYP 90, WhoWrEP 89*
De Launoy, Jean 1603-1678 *EncO&P 3*
DeLaura, David Joseph 1930- *WhoAm 90, WhoWrEP 89*
DeLaura, Michael Anthony 1960- *WhoSSW 91*
De Laurentiis, Dino *BioIn 16*
De Laurentiis, Dino 1919- *WhoAm 90, WhoWor 91, WorAlBi*
DeLaurentis, Louise Budde 1920- *WhoWrEP 89*
DeLauro, Albert A. 1946- *St&PR 91*
Delauro, Joseph Nicola 1916- *WhoAmA 91*
DeLauro, Rosa *WhoAmW 91*
DeLauro, Thomas Michael 1951- *WhoE 91*
Delaval, Elizabeth 1649-1717 *BiDEWW, FemiCLE*
De Lavallade, Carmen 1931- *DrBlPA 90*
De La Vega, Antonio 1927- *WhoAmA 91, WhoE 91*
De La Vega, Diana Patricia *BiDrAPA 89*
de La Vega, Dianne Winifred DeMarinis *WhoAmW 91*
De La Vega, Enrique Miguel 1935- *WhoAmA 91*
de la Vega, Francis Joseph 1919- *WhoHisp 91*
De la Vega, Garcilaso 1539-1616 *BioIn 16*
De la Vega, Oscar Unzaga 1916-1959 *BioIn 16*
De La Verriera, Jean-Jacques *WhoAmA 91*
Delawar, Mohamed Sherif 1940- *WhoWor 91*
Delaware Prophet *WhNaAH*
De La Warr, George 1904-1969 *EncPaPR 91*
De la Warr, George 1905-1969 *EncO&P 3*
De La Warr, Thomas West 1577-1618 *EncCRAm*
Delawie, Homer Torrence 1927- *WhoAm 90*
De Lawter, Hilbert H 1920- *BiDrAPA 89*
Delay, Claude 1944- *ConAu 33NR*
Delay, Dorothy 1917- *IntWWM 90, WhoAm 90, WhoAmW 91*
Delay, Eugene Raymond 1948- *WhoEmL 91*
Delay, Jean *BiDrAPA 89*
De Lay, Robert Francis 1919- *WhoAm 90*
DeLay, Thomas D. 1947- *WhoAm 90, WhoSSW 91*
De Layo, Leonard Joseph 1921- *WhoAm 90*
Delbaen, Freddy 1946- *WhoWor 91*
Delbanco, Nicholas F. 1942- *WhoWrEP 89*
Delbanco, Thomas Lewis 1939- *WhoAm 90*
del Barco, Lucy Salamanca 1900?-1989 *ConAu 130, SmATA 64*
Del Bello, Bernard Nicholas 1935- *St&PR 91*
Del Bene, Adriana Ferrarese *PenDiMP*
Del Bergiolo, Fabio 1959- *WhoWor 91*
Delblanc, Sven Axel Herman 1931- *DcScanL*
Delbono, Elizabeth Anne 1951- *WhoAmW 91*
Delbono, Flavio 1959- *WhoWor 91*
Delborgo, Elliot Anthony 1938- *IntWWM 90*
Del Bosque, Hugo *BiDrAPA 89*
Delbruck, Hermann 1943- *WhoWor 91*
Delbruck, Max 1906-1981 *BioIn 16, WorAlBi*
Delbrueck, Peter Gerd 1947- *WhoWor 91*
Del Bufalo, Dario 1958- *WhoWor 91*
Del Buono, Antonio 1900-1975 *BioIn 16*
Del Busto, Nora *BiDrAPA 89*
Delcamp, Natalie Lowey 1923- *WhoSSW 91*
Del Campillo, Miguell J. 1960- *WhoHisp 91*
del Campo, Ann Laura 1955- *WhoE 91*
Del Campo, Carlos Ibanez 1877-1960 *BioIn 16*
Del Campo, Jose A *BiDrAPA 89*
Del Carmen, Rebecca 1957- *WhoAmW 91*
Del Caro, Adrian 1952- *WhoSSW 91*
Del Casal, Julian 1863-1893 *BioIn 16*
Delcasse, Theophile Pierre 1852-1923 *BiDFrPL*
Del Castillo, Guillermo, Jr. 1932- *BiDrAPA 89*
Del Castillo, Ines 1927- *WhoHisp 91*
del Castillo, Jeanne Louise Taillac 1933- *WhoAmW 91*
Del Castillo, Mary Virginia 1865- *WhoAmA 91N*
Del Castillo, Melinda T *BiDrAPA 89*
Del Castillo, Ramon R. 1949- *WhoHisp 91*
del Castillo, Ricardo A. 1946- *WhoHisp 91*
Del Castillo, Violeta *BiDrAPA 89*
Del Castillo, Virginia Lyn Moreno 1956- *WhoHisp 91*
Delchamps, Alfred Frederick, Jr. *St&PR 91N*
Delchamps, Harold John, Jr. 1920- *BiDrAPA 89*
Delchamps, O.H., Jr. 1933- *St&PR 91*
Delchamps, Oliver H., Jr. 1933- *WhoAm 90*
Delchamps, Randolph *WhoAm 90*
Delchamps, Randolph 1943- *St&PR 91*
Del Chiaro, Mario A 1925- *WhoAmA 91*
Del Chiaro, Mario Aldo 1925- *WhoAm 90*
Delco, Wilhelmina *BioIn 16*
Del Colliano, Gerard Anthony 1946- *WhoE 91, WhoWor 91*
Del Corio, Rosemarie Anne 1942- *WhoE 91*
Delcotto, Pamela Marie 1956- *WhoAmW 91*
Delcourt, Benoit Rene 1947- *WhoEmL 91*
Delden, Lex Van 1947- *IntWWM 90*
Delderfield, George Edward 1919- *IntWWM 90*
Del Duce, Gregory J. 1942- *St&PR 91*
Dele, Dorothy A. *WhoWrEP 89*
Delear, Frank J. 1914- *AuBYP 90*
Delecki, Kenneth Lee 1958- *WhoE 91*
De Lecuona, Juan Manuel *BiDrAPA 89*
Deledda, Grazia 1871-1936 *EncCoWW*
de Ledebur, Juan Carlos 1954- *WhoSSW 91*
Deledicque, Alain-Georges 1944- *WhoWor 91*
De Lee, Joseph B. 1869-1942 *BioIn 16*
DeLee, Joseph B. 1869-1942 *BioIn 16*
de Leenheer, Andre Prudent 1941- *WhoWor 91*
De Leeuw, Adele 1899-1988 *BioIn 16*
DeLeeuw, Adele 1899-1988 *BioIn 16*
De Leeuw, Adele Louise 1899- *AuBYP 90*
DeLeeuw, Bert Jay *BioIn 16*
De Leeuw, Cateau 1903-1975 *AuBYP 90*
de Leeuw, Frank 1930- *WhoE 91*
De Leeuw, Leon 1931- *WhoAmA 91*
De Leeuw, Ton 1926- *IntWWM 90*
DeLeeuw, Willem Hermanus 1929- *WhoWor 91*
Delehant, Joseph Henry 1950- *WhoEmL 91*
Delehant, Raymond Leonard 1937- *WhoE 91, WhoWor 91*
Delehanty, Edward John 1929- *WhoAm 90*
Delehanty, Hugh *BioIn 16*
Delehanty, Mary Joan 1936- *WhoAmW 91*
Delehanty, Peter Michael 1954- *WhoEmL 91*
Delehanty, Suzanne E 1944- *WhoAmA 91*
De Leizaola, Jesus Maria 1896-1989 *BioIn 16*
Delella, Diane M. 1951- *St&PR 91*
De Lemos, Gaston P 1928- *BiDrAPA 89*
DeLemos, Richard Alan 1946- *WhoEmL 91, WhoSSW 91, WhoWor 91*
de Lemos, Sheila Victoria 1949- *WhoAmW 91, WhoSSW 91*
De Leo, Dennis Michael 1939- *St&PR 91*
DeLeo, Dennis Michael 1939- *WhoAm 90*
DeLeo, Maryann 1952- *WhoAmW 91*
de Leon, Armando 1934- *WhoHisp 91*
Deleon, Armando Juan 1956- *WhoSSW 91*
DeLeon, Arthur Eugene 1942- *WhoWor 91*
de Leon, Carmen Maria 1956- *WhoSSW 91*
De Leon, Cesar 1934- *WhoHisp 91*
De Leon, Charles A *BiDrAPA 89*
De Leon, Cira Jane 1949- *BiDrAPA 89*
De Leon, Daniel 1852-1914 *BioIn 16*
DeLeon, Daniel 1852-1914 *EncAL*
De Leon, Edwin 1818-1891 *BioIn 16*
De Leon, Fernando Don *St&PR 91*
de Leon, Gloria I. 1952- *WhoHisp 91*
De Leon, Jose 1959- *BiDrAPA 89*
DeLeon, Jose 1960- *Ballpl 90*
De Leon, Jose 1960- *WhoHisp 91*
DeLeon, Jose R., Jr. 1928- *WhoHisp 91*
de Leon, Lidia Maria 1957- *WhoAm 90, WhoAmW 91*
DeLeon, Luis 1957- *Ballpl 90*
DeLeon, Morris Jack 1941- *WhoSSW 91*
De Leon, Naphtali 1945- *BioIn 16*
De Leon, Nephtali 1945- *HispWr 90*
de Leon, Oscar Eduardo 1937- *WhoHisp 91*
De Leon, Ovidio Albert 1939- *BiDrAPA 89*
DeLeon, Patricia Anastasia 1944- *WhoAmW 91*
Deleon, Patrick Henry 1943- *WhoAm 90*
de Leon, Perla Maria 1952- *WhoHisp 91*
De Leon, Val *WhoHisp 91*
De Leon-Jones, Frank A *BiDrAPA 89*
DeLeone, Carmon 1942- *WhoAm 90*
Delerme, Felix A 1928- *BiDrAPA 89*
DeLerno, Joseph 1924- *St&PR 91*
Delescluze, Louis-Charles 1809-1871 *BiDFrPL*
De Lesseps, Tauni 1920- *WhoAmA 91*
Delessert, Etienne 1941- *BioIn 16*
DeLessio, Frank Anthony, Jr. 1943- *WhoE 91*
Delessio-Neubauer, Elizabeth Mary 1950- *WhoAmW 91*
Deletang-Tardif, Yanette 1902-1976 *EncCoWW*
Deleuran, Aage 1925- *WhoWor 91*
Deleuze, Jean Philippe Francois 1753-1835 *EncO&P 3*
Delevie, Harold Jacob 1931- *WhoAm 90*
Delevoryas, Lillian Grace 1932- *WhoAmA 91*
De Ley, Jozef 1924- *WhoWor 91*
Delfano, M. M. *WhoWrEP 89*
Delfausse, Peter B 1943- *BiDrAPA 89*
DelFavero-Campbell, Patricia Graciela 1957- *WhoSSW 91*
Delfin, Stephen M. 1952- *ODwPR 91*
Delfiner, Henry *St&PR 91*
Delfino, Joseph John 1941- *WhoSSW 91*
Delfino, Mario 1948- *WhoWor 91*
Delfino, Michelangelo 1950- *WhoEmL 91*
Delfino, Paula Marie 1956- *WhoE 91*
Delfonics *EncPR&S 89*
Delfont, Bernard 1909- *WhoWor 91*
Del Forno, Anton 1950- *IntWWM 90*
Del Forno, Anton Joseph 1950- *WhoEmL 91*
Delgadillo, Larry 1950- *WhoHisp 91*
Delgadito 1830?-1870? *WhNaAH*
Delgado, Abelardo 1931- *BioIn 16*
Delgado, Abelardo B 1931- *ConAu 131, HispWr 90*
Delgado, Abelardo Barrientos 1931- *WhoHisp 91*
Delgado, Alma I. 1954- *WhoHisp 91*
Delgado, Carmelo Joseph 1945- *WhoE 91*
Delgado, Daniel *BioIn 16*
Delgado, Doris M 1927- *BiDrAPA 89*
Delgado, Dwighd Dubied 1950- *WhoSSW 91*
Delgado, Edmundo R. 1932- *WhoHisp 91*
Delgado, Gloria 1953- *WhoHisp 91*
Delgado, Hope Lena 1927- *WhoHisp 91*

Delgado, Jane L. 1953- *WhoHisp 91*
Delgado, Jose 1923- *BiDrAPA 89, WhoE 91*
Delgado, Jose 1950- *WhoHisp 91*
Delgado, Jose Arturo *BiDrAPA 89*
Delgado, Lenore R. 1948- *WhoAmW 91*
Delgado, Lucia De La Caridad 1964- *WhoAmW 91*
Delgado, M. Conchita 1942- *WhoHisp 91*
Delgado, Miguel Aquiles, Jr. 1943- *WhoHisp 91*
Delgado, Natalia 1953- *WhoEmL 91*
Delgado, Olga I. 1943- *WhoHisp 91*
Delgado, Pedro Lazaro *BiDrAPA 89*
Delgado, Rafael A 1921- *BiDrAPA 89*
Delgado, Ramon Louis 1937- *WhoHisp 91*
Delgado, Rene Torres 1947- *WhoHisp 91*
Delgado, Robert C *BiDrAPA 89*
Delgado, Robert Charles 1949- *WhoE 91*
Delgado, Tomas Edwin, Sr. 1948- *WhoSSW 91*
Delgado, Zoraida 1965- *WhoHisp 91*
Delgado-Baguer, Raul 1916- *WhoHisp 91*
Delgado Chalbaud, Carlos 1909-1950 *BioIn 16*
Delgado-Fourzan, Enrique 1918- *BiDrAPA 89*
Delgado-Hurtado, Cesar A *BiDrAPA 89*
Delgado-P., Guillermo 1950- *WhoHisp 91*
Delgado-Rivera, Lourdes J 1960- *BiDrAPA 89*
Delgado-Rivera, Lourdes Janette 1960- *WhoE 91*
Delgado-Simonet, Rafael Antonio 1933- *WhoSSW 91*
Del Galdo, Bice *WhoAmW 91*
Del Ghingaro, Virgil B. 1931- *St&PR 91*
Del Giorno, Mystical *BioIn 16*
Del Giudice, Amore *BiDrAPA 89*
Del Giudice, Amore 1913- *WhoAm 90*
Del Giudice, Michael J. 1943- *WhoAm 90*
Del Giudice, Vincent A. 1958- *WhoAm 90*
Delgorio, Frances Ann 1954- *WhoAmW 91*
Del Greco, Bobby 1933- *Ballpl 90*
del Greco, Francesco 1923- *WhoAm 90*
Delgrego, Andrew A. 1942- *St&PR 91*
DelGrego, Andrew August 1942- *WhoAm 90*
Del Guercio, Louis Richard Maurice 1929- *WhoAm 90, WhoWor 91*
Delguidice, Michael J. 1943- *St&PR 91*
Delhaye, Alain Jacques 1936- *St&PR 91*
Delhey, John Donald 1923- *WhoAm 90*
DelHomme, Beverly A. 1954- *WhoEmL 91*
Delia, Albert Arrigo 1960- *WhoSSW 91*
D'Elia, Frank G 1920- *BiDrAPA 89*
D'Elia, Gerardo Antonio, Jr. 1942- *WhoE 91*
Delia, Jesse Graves 1944- *WhoAm 90*
Delia, Michael A. 1930- *ODwPR 91*
D'Elia, Nicholas 1959- *WhoEmL 91*
Delia, Sylvia 1954- *WhoAmW 91*
Delianides, George 1931- *St&PR 91*
DeLibero, Mary Smellie 1950- *WhoAmW 91*
Delibes, C. P. Leo 1836-1891 *WorAlBi*
Delibes, Claude *ODwPR 91*
Delibes, Claude Blanche 1932- *WhoAmW 91*
Delibes, Leo 1836-1891 *PenDiMP A*
Delibes, Miguel *ConAu 32NR, HispWr 90, MajTwCW*
Delibes, Miguel 1920- *IntvSpW [port]*
Delibes Setien, Miguel 1920- *ConAu 32NR, HispWr 90, MajTwCW*
Delich, John M. 1930- *WhoAm 90*
Delifer, Jean-Pierre *BioIn 16*
Deligiorgis, Stavros G. 1933- *WhoAm 90*
Deligne, Pierre *WhoWor 91*
DeLilla, Celina 1934- *WhoWrEP 89*
DeLillo, Don *BioIn 16*
DeLillo, Don 1936- *MajTwCW, WhoAm 90*
De Lima, Clarence A 1932- *BiDrAPA 89*
De Lima, Jorge 1893-1953 *BioIn 16*
DeLima, Richard Ford 1930- *St&PR 91*
De Lima, Sigrid 1921- *WhoWrEP 89*
deLinde, Mark Terry 1956- *WhoEmL 91*
Delinsky, Barbara 1945- *ConAu 30NR*
De Lio, Anthony Peter 1928- *WhoWor 91*
Delio, Richard Peter 1943- *St&PR 91*
De Lisa, Gene 1957- *IntWWM 90*
DeLisi, Charles 1941- *WhoAm 90, WhoWor 91*
De Lisi, Joanne 1951- *WhoEmL 91*
Delisi, Lynn E *BiDrAPA 89*
Delisi, Samuel Dante 1941- *BiDrAPA 89*
Delisi, Vincent J. 1931- *St&PR 91*
De Lisio, Michael *WhoAmA 91*
De Lisio, Stephen Scott 1937- *WhoAm 90*
De Lisle *EncO&P 3*
Delisle, James Robert 1953- *WhoEmL 91*
Delisle, Jeffrey Dewey 1956- *BiDrAPA 89*
DeLisle, Lawrence *BioIn 16*
DeLisle, Marc *BiDrAPA 89*
DeLisle, Peter Andrew 1949- *WhoSSW 91*
de Lisle, Suzanne Turner 1948- *WhoEmL 91*
Delisle, Victor A. 1927- *St&PR 91*
Deliso, Joseph J., Sr. 1909- *St&PR 91*
Delissa Joseph, L. *BiDWomA*
Delissio, John F. 1930- *St&PR 91*
Delius, Frederick 1862-1934 *BioIn 16, PenDiMP A, WorAlBi*
Deliyannides, Deborah A *BiDrAPA 89*
Deliyannis, Constantine Christos 1938- *WhoE 91*
DeLizasoain, Patricia Maria 1962- *WhoAmW 91*
del Junco, Tirso 1925- *WhoHisp 91*
Delk, Ira Edwin 1930- *St&PR 91, WhoAm 90*
Delker, David Glen 1952- *WhoEmL 91*
Dell, Christine Marie 1963- *WhoEmL 91*
Dell, David Donald 1953- *WhoEmL 91*
Dell, Diana Lynn 1948- *WhoAmW 91*
Dell, Ernest Robert 1928- *WhoAm 90, WhoE 91, WhoWor 91*
Dell, Ethel M. 1881-1939 *FemiCLE*
Dell, Ethel May 1881-1939 *BioIn 16*
Dell, Floyd *EncAL*
Dell, Gabriel *BioIn 16*
Dell, Gary S. *BioIn 16*
Dell, Mary Lynn 1959- *BiDrAPA 89*
Dell, Michael *BioIn 16*
Dell, Michael John 1954- *WhoEmL 91*
Dell, Michael S. 1965- *St&PR 91*
Dell, Paul Carl 1945- *WhoEmL 91*
Dell, Paul Everett 1937- *WhoSSW 91*
Dell, Philip *AmLegL*
Dell, Ralph Bishop 1935- *WhoAm 90*
Dell, Robert Christopher 1950- *WhoAmA 91*
Dell, Robert E. 1935- *St&PR 91*
Dell, Ruth Hartman 1918- *WhoAmW 91*
Dell, Sidney S. *NewYTBS 90*
Dell, W. Frank 1945- *St&PR 91*
Dell, Warren Frank, II 1945- *WhoE 91, WhoEmL 91*
Dell, Wheezer 1887-1966 *Ballpl 90*
Dell, Willie Jones 1930- *WhoSSW 91*
Della, Phyllis *BioIn 16*
Della Badia, Eugene Louis, Jr. 1943- *BiDrAPA 89, WhoE 91*
Della Casa, Lisa 1919- *IntWWM 90, PenDiMP*
Dellacato, Christine Lisa 1965- *WhoAmW 91*
Della Clara, Aranco Abis 1940- *WhoWor 91*
Dellacroce, Nick *BioIn 16*
Della Femina, Jerry 1936- *BioIn 16, ConAmBL, WhoAm 90*
DellaFera, Mary Ann 1954- *WhoAmW 91*
Della Franco, Thomas J. 1952- *St&PR 91*
Dell'Aglio, Frank James 1954- *St&PR 91*
Dellagnena, Gail Lynn 1956- *WhoAmW 91*
Dellamaddalena, Carlos *ODwPR 91*
Della Maddalena, Otto Carlos 1930- *BiDrAPA 89*
Della Monica, Joseph G. 1927- *St&PR 91*
Dellamore, John J. 1946- *St&PR 91*
de Llanos, Myrka Barbara 1965- *WhoHisp 91*
Dell'Antonia, Jon Charles 1941- *St&PR 91*
Dellapa, John Anthony 1961- *WhoEmL 91*
Della Paolera, Elisabeth 1950- *WhoAmW 91*
Della Pergola, Edith 1918- *IntWWM 90*
Della Pia, Max Harold 1953- *WhoEmL 91*
Dellaquila, Stephen J. 1938- *St&PR 91*
Dell'Ario, Alfred Valare *BiDrAPA 89*
Della Robbia, Luca *PenDiDA 89*
Della Robbia, Luca 1399?-1482 *WorAlBi*
Della Rocca, Gerald Francis 1949- *St&PR 91*
Dellarocco, Kenneth Anthony 1952- *WhoEmL 91*
Dellas, Robert Dennis 1944- *WhoAm 90*
Della Sala, Robert 1964- *WhoE 91*
Della Santa, Raffaello 1938- *WhoWor 91*
Della-Terza, Dante Michele 1924- *WhoAm 90*
Della Torre, Edward 1934- *WhoAm 90*
Dellatorre, Thomas L. 1947- *St&PR 91*
Della Valle, Francesco 1937- *WhoWor 91*
Della-Volpe, Ralph Eugene 1923- *WhoAmA 91, WhoE 91*
Dellecave, Frank Anthony 1933- *St&PR 91*
Dellemann, Kenneth H. 1935- *St&PR 91*
Dellenback, John Richard 1918- *WhoAm 90*
Deller, Alfred 1912-1979 *PenDiMP*
Deller, Harris 1947- *WhoAmA 91, WhoEmL 91*
Deller, Mark 1938- *PenDiMP*
Deller, Mark Damian 1938- *IntWWM 90*
Dell'Ergo, Robert James 1918- *WhoWor 91*
Delleur, Jacques William 1924- *WhoAm 90*
Delli Colli, Humbert Thomas 1944- *WhoAm 90*
Delli-Pizzi, Antonia Elena 1920- *BiDrAPA 89*
Delligatti, Michael F. 1952- *St&PR 91*
Delligatti, Patrick 1924- *St&PR 91*
Dellinger, Charles Wade 1949- *WhoSSW 91*
Dellinger, David *BioIn 16*
Dellinger, David 1915- *EncAL, WhoWrEP 89*
DelliQuadri, Pardo Frederick 1915-1989 *BioIn 16*
Dellis, Arlene B 1927- *WhoAmA 91*
Dellis, Fredy M. 1945- *St&PR 91*
Dellis, Fredy Michel 1945- *WhoAm 90*
Dell'Isola, Anthony, Jr. 1955- *WhoE 91*
Dell'Isola, Salvatore *BioIn 16*
Dello Iacono, Paul Michael 1957- *WhoEmL 91*
Dello Joio, Justin Norman 1955- *IntWWM 90*
Dello Joio, Norman 1913- *BioIn 16, PenDiMP A, WhoAm 90*
Delloiacono, Alfred 1941- *St&PR 91*
Dell'Olio, Louis *BioIn 16*
Dell'Olio, Louis 1948- *WhoAm 90*
Dellomo, Frank A. 1933- *WhoAm 90*
Dellomo, James Robert 1940- *St&PR 91, WhoE 91*
Dellomo, Patricia Turvey 1938- *WhoAmW 91*
Dellora, Ralph Stephen 1940- *WhoWor 91*
Dell'Osso, Louis Frank 1941- *WhoAm 90*
Dell'Osso, Luino, Jr. 1939- *St&PR 91, WhoAm 90*
Dellow, Reginald Leonard 1924- *WhoAm 90*
Dellow, Ronald Graeme 1924- *IntWWM 90*
Dellsy, Harlan M. 1948- *St&PR 91*
Delluc, Gilles 1934- *WhoWor 91*
Dellums, C. L. 1900-1989 *BioIn 16*
Dellums, Cottrell Laurence 1900-1989 *BioIn 16*
Dellums, Erik *BioIn 16*
Dellums, Ronald V. 1935- *BioIn 16, BlkAmsC [port], WhoAm 90*
Dellums, Roscoe *BioIn 16*
del Maestro, Richard *NewAgMG*
Delman, Eric Martin 1955- *St&PR 91*
Delman, Ralph 1933- *St&PR 91*
Delman, Stephen Bennett 1942- *WhoAm 90*
Del Mar, Alice Ann Robinson 1951- *WhoSSW 91*
Del Mar, Bruce *St&PR 91*
Delmar, Eugene Anthony 1928- *WhoAm 90*
Del Mar, Jonathan Rene 1951- *IntWWM 90*
Del Mar, Norman 1919- *PenDiMP*
Del Mar, Norman Rene 1919- *IntWWM 90*
Delmar, Vina 1905-1990 *ConAu 130*
Delmarsh, Anna Lane 1940- *St&PR 91*
Delmas, Pierre Dominique 1950- *WhoWor 91*
Del Mastro, Rick Anthony 1945- *WhoAm 90*
del Mazo Gonzalez, Alfredo 1943- *WhoWor 91*
Delmege, Dale J. *St&PR 91*
Del Monaco, Mario 1915-1982 *PenDiMP*
Delmonico, Crist *BioIn 16*
Del Monte, Eugenio Senon 1928- *St&PR 91*
Delmonte, John 1913- *St&PR 91*
Delmonte, Linnie Aragon *BiDrAPA 89*
Del Monte, William R *BiDrAPA 89*
Delmore, Diana *WhoWrEP 89*
Delmore, Harry 1880?- *DcAfAmP*
Delmotte, Olivier 1951- *WhoWor 91*
Del Muro, Angela *BiDrAPA 89*
Del Negro, Vin *BioIn 16*
Del Negro, Vinny *BioIn 16*
Delo, David M. 1905- *BioIn 16*
De Loach, Allen Wayne 1939- *WhoE 91*
de Loach, Anthony Cortelyou 1934- *WhoAm 90*
De Loach, Bernard Collins, Jr. 1930- *WhoAm 90*
DeLoach, Harris Eugene, Jr. 1944- *WhoAm 90*
DeLoach, Robert Earl, II 1937- *WhoSSW 91*
DeLoach, Saran L. 1966- *WhoSSW 91*
Deloatch, Willie Thomas 1939- *WhoE 91*
DeLoatche, C. Darrell 1949- *St&PR 91*
Delobelle, Camille *PenDiMP*
De Lobkowicz, Robert *BioIn 16*
DeLoca, Cornelius Edward, Jr. 1930- *WhoE 91*
Delock, Ike 1929- *Ballpl 90*
Delogu, Gaetano 1934- *IntWWM 90*
Delohery, Holly 1952- *WhoAmW 91*
De Lollis, Michael Victor 1951- *BiDrAPA 89*
del Olmo, Frank P. 1948- *WhoHisp 91*
Delon, Alain 1935- *WhoWor 91, WorAlBi*
Delon, Dennis J. 1948- *St&PR 91*
Delon, Floyd G. 1929- *WhoWrEP 89*
Deloncle, Eugene 1890-1942 *BiDFrPL*
De Lone, H. Francis 1915- *WhoAm 90*
DeLone, William Hook 1946- *WhoE 91*
Deloney, Jack Clouse 1940- *WhoAmA 91*
Deloney, Mack Hatch 1937- *St&PR 91*
DeLong, Betty Jo 1923- *St&PR 91*
De Long, Charles C 1936- *BiDrAPA 89*
Delong, Charles E. 1831?-1876 *BioIn 16*
De Long, Dale Ray 1959- *WhoEmL 91*
De Long, Edward Ewing 1909- *BiDrAPA 89*
DeLong, Embert Harry 1940- *St&PR 91*
De Long, Erika Venta 1925- *WhoAmW 91*
Delong, F. Joe 1920- *St&PR 91*
DeLong, Frederick Joseph, III 1950- *St&PR 91*
DeLong, Gregory Grover 1955- *St&PR 91*
Delong, Jack E. 1933- *St&PR 91*
De Long, Jacob Edward 1939- *WhoE 91*
DeLong, James Clifford 1940- *WhoAm 90*
De Long, Katharine 1927- *WhoAmW 91*
DeLong, Lois Anne 1955- *WhoAmW 91*
DeLong, Robert E. 1923- *St&PR 91*
DeLong, Roberta Kay 1946- *WhoAmW 91*
DeLong, Scott Hauxhurst 1919- *St&PR 91*
DeLonga, Leonard Anthony 1925- *WhoAm 90, WhoAmA 91*
Delonis, Robert Joseph 1952- *St&PR 91*
Delony, Patty Litton 1948- *WhoAm 90*
DeLoof, Rita Denise Michele 1954- *WhoWor 91*
De Looper, Willem 1932- *WhoAmA 91*
De Looper, Willem Johan 1932- *WhoAm 90*
Delord, Terry Joseph *BiDrAPA 89*
De Lorean, Cristina *BioIn 16*
DeLorean, John Zachary 1925- *EncABHB 5 [port]*
De Lorenzo, A J Darin *BiDrAPA 89*
DeLorenzo, Annette 1941- *ODwPR 91*
De Lorenzo, Annette Marie 1941- *WhoAm 90*
DeLorenzo, Anthony G. 1914- *ODwPR 91*
De Lorenzo, Anthony G. 1914- *St&PR 91*
DeLorenzo, David Joseph 1932- *WhoAm 90*
DeLorey, John Alfred 1924- *WhoAm 90*
Deloria, Escolastico A, Jr. 1933- *BiDrAPA 89*
Deloria, Vine *BioIn 16*
Deloria, Vine *BioIn 16*
Deloria, Vine, Jr. 1933- *MajTwCW*
Deloria, Vine Victor, Jr. 1933- *WhoAm 90, WhoWrEP 89*
Delorme, Adrien *PenDiDA 89*
Delorme, Alexis *PenDiDA 89*
Delorme, Francois Faizelot 1691-1768 *PenDiDA 89*
Delorme, Jacques 1950- *WhoWor 91*
Delorme, Jean 1902- *WhoAm 90*
Delorme, Jean-Louis-Faizelot *PenDiDA 89*
DeLorme, Thomas Albert 1928- *WhoSSW 91*
Delors, Jacques *BioIn 16*
Delors, Jacques 1925- *News 90 [port], WhoWor 91*
Delors, Jacques Lucien Jean 1925- *BiDFrPL*
De Lory, Peter 1948- *WhoAmA 91*
De Los Angeles, Reynaldo A *BiDrAPA 89*
De Los Angeles, Reynaldo Adrillana 1945- *WhoSSW 91*
De los Angeles, Victoria *PenDiMP*
De Los Angeles, Victoria 1923- *IntWWM 90*
De Los Heros, Reinaldo O 1951- *BiDrAPA 89*
Deloso, Uldarico Drazba 1931- *WhoWor 91*
De Los Reyes, Harding Robert, Jr. 1946- *WhoHisp 91*
de los Reyes, Ramon *WhoHisp 91*
de los Reyes, Raul Alberto 1953- *WhoHisp 91*
de los Reyes, Telesforo Javellana, Jr. 1932- *WhoWor 91*
De Los Rios, Francisco Giner 1839-1915 *BioIn 16*
de los Santos, Alfredo G., Jr. 1936- *WhoHisp 91*
De Los Santos, Andreina 1953- *BiDrAPA 89*
De Los Santos, Renato Chiong *BiDrAPA 89*
Delott, Jerome Jack 1921- *St&PR 91*
Deloughery, Grace Leona 1933- *WhoAmW 91*
Deloyht-Arendt, Isobel 1927- *WhoAmA 91*
Delozier, Donald Edward 1942- *St&PR 91*
Delp, Charles William, Jr. 1926- *WhoAm 90*
Delp, Edwin Jay 1953- *WhoSSW 91*
Delp, George C. 1908- *St&PR 91*
Delp, George William 1929- *WhoAm 90*
Delp, John Verne 1943- *WhoWor 91*
Delp, Michael W. 1948- *WhoWrEP 89*
Delp, Wilbur Charles, Jr. 1934- *WhoAm 90*
Del Papa, Frankie Sue 1949- *WhoAm 90, WhoAmW 91*

Delpech, Marc Jean-Laurens 1953- *WhoWor 91*
Del Pero, Joseph Edward 1947- *St&PR 91*
Del Pesco, Susan Marie Carr 1946- *WhoEmL 91*
Delph, Donna Jean 1931- *WhoAm 90*
Delph, Eric *ODwPR 91*
Delphin, Jacques M 1929- *BiDrAPA 89*
Delphin, Jacques Mercier 1929- *WhoE 91, WhoWor 91*
DelPiero-Ross, Jean M 1959- *BiDrAPA 89*
Del Pinal, Jorge Huascar 1945- *WhoHisp 91*
Del Pizzo, Nancy Ann 1962- *WhoAmW 91*
Delporte, Antoon Gustaaf 1923- *WhoWor 91*
del Poza, Ivania 1947- *WhoHisp 91*
Del Pozo Veintimilla, Luis Guillermo 1954- *WhoWor 91*
Del Prado, Jorge 1910- *BioIn 16*
del Prado, Yvette 1932- *WhoHisp 91*
Del Prete, Arthur Eugene 1935- *WhoE 91*
Del Puerto, Daniel Bernardo 1965- *WhoE 91*
Del Re, Marisa *WhoAmA 91*
del Regato, Juan Angel 1909- *WhoAm 90*
Del Rey, Alfred John 1918- *BiDrAPA 89*
Del Rey, Lester 1915- *AuBYP 90, MajTwCW, RGTwCSF, WhoAm 90, WhoWrEP 89, WorAlBi*
Del Riego, Teresa 1876-1968 *OxCPMus*
Del Riego de Del Castillo, Lilia 1948- *WhoWor 91*
Del Rio, Carlos Alberto Arroyo 1893-1969 *BioIn 16*
Del Rio, Carlos H. 1949- *WhoHisp 91*
Del Rio, Dolores 1908-1983 *WorAlBi*
Del Rio, Fernando Rene 1932- *WhoHisp 91*
Del Rio, Joaquin 1941- *WhoHisp 91*
Del Rio, Luis 1942- *WhoWor 91*
Del Rio, Luis Raul 1939- *WhoHisp 91*
Del Rio, Martin Antoine 1551-1608 *EncO&P 3*
Del Rio Diaz, Estyne 1945- *WhoAmW 91, WhoEmL 91*
Del Rosario, Vivencio G 1925- *BiDrAPA 89*
Del Rossi, Paul R. 1942- *St&PR 91*
DelRosso, Diane 1949- *WhoEmL 91*
Delrosso, M.R. 1951- *St&PR 91*
Del Rosso, Paul J. 1944- *St&PR 91*
Del Ruth, Thomas 1942- *BioIn 16*
Delsack, Katherine Landey 1959- *WhoEmL 91*
Delsanter, Charles Douglas 1940- *St&PR 91*
Del Santo, Lawrence A. 1934- *WhoAm 90*
Del Sardo, Helen Ann 1954- *WhoAmW 91, WhoEmL 91*
Delsarte, Jean Frederic Auguste 1903-1968 *DcScB S2*
Delse, Frederick C 1941- *BiDrAPA 89*
Delshay 1835?-1874 *WhNaAH*
Del Signore, Thomas P. *ODwPR 91*
Del Sindaco, Joseph Michael 1950- *St&PR 91*
Delsing, Jim 1925- *Ballpl 90*
Delson, Edward Paul 1939- *St&PR 91*
Delson, Elizabeth 1932- *WhoAm 90, WhoAmA 91*
Delson, Max 1903-1988 *BioIn 16*
Delson, Robert 1905- *WhoAm 90*
Delson, Sidney Leon 1932- *WhoAm 90*
del Tasso, Battista di Marco 1500-1555 *PenDiDA 89*
Del Tasso, Domenico di Francesco 1440-1508 *PenDiDA 89*
Delton, Judy 1931- *Au&Arts 6 [port]*
Del Toro, Angelo 1947- *WhoHisp 91*
del Toro, Raul *WhoHisp 91*
Del Toro, Russell A. 1924- *WhoAm 90*
Del Tredici, David 1937- *IntWWM 90, PenDiMP A, WhoAm 90*
Del Tufo, Robert J. 1933- *WhoAm 90, WhoE 91*
delTufo, Theresa Lallana Izon 1943- *WhoAm 90*
de Lubac, Henri Sonier 1896- *WhoWor 91*
De Luca, Andrea 1950- *WhoE 91, WhoEmL 91*
DeLuca, Angelina Frances 1950- *WhoE 91*
DeLuca, Anthony Bart 1942- *WhoE 91*
De Luca, Anthony Michael 1943- *St&PR 91*
Deluca, August F. 1943- *St&PR 91*
DeLuca, Barbara H. *WhoAmW 91*
De Luca, C Mary Louise 1954- *BiDrAPA 89*
De Luca, Carlo John 1943- *WhoAm 90, WhoE 91*
DeLuca, Diane Lynelle 1955- *WhoAmW 91*
De Luca, Donald Paul 1940- *St&PR 91*
DeLuca, Donald Paul 1940- *WhoAm 90*
DeLuca, Frederick A. *BioIn 16*
De Luca, Giuseppe 1876-1950 *PenDiMP, WorAlBi*
DeLuca, Grace Mary 1947- *St&PR 91*
De Luca, Grace Mary 1947- *WhoAmW 91*
De Luca, Jean-Claude 1948- *ConDes 90*
De Luca, Joseph Victor 1935- *WhoAmA 91*
De Luca, Marina 1962- *BiDrAPA 89*
DeLuca, Mary 1960- *WhoSSW 91*
Deluca, Michael J *BiDrAPA 89*
DeLuca, Patrick Phillip 1935- *WhoAm 90*
De Luca, Peter J. 1927- *St&PR 91, WhoAm 90*
De Luca, Robert A. 1948- *St&PR 91*
DeLuca, Ronald 1924- *WhoAm 90*
De Luca, Thomas George 1950- *WhoEmL 91*
DeLuca, Tom *BioIn 16*
De Luca, Vincent Arthur 1940- *WhoWrEP 89*
DeLucca, Daniel Neil 1931- *WhoAm 90*
Delucca, John J. 1943- *St&PR 91*
DeLucca, Leopoldo Eloy 1952- *WhoEmL 91*
Delucchi, George Paul 1938- *WhoWor 91*
De Lucchi, Michele 1951- *ConDes 90*
deLuccia, Emil Robert 1904- *WhoAm 90, WhoWor 91*
DeLuccie, Karen Marie 1958- *WhoEmL 91*
DeLuccio, Jerome Joseph 1953- *WhoEmL 91*
DeLuce, Christine Garvey 1959- *WhoEmL 91*
de Luce, Virginia 1921- *WhoAmW 91, WhoE 91, WhoWor 91*
Deluce, William *BioIn 16*
DeLuchi, Stephen Frank 1952- *WhoEmL 91*
De Lucia, Diane Marie 1964- *WhoAmW 91*
De Lucia, Fernando 1860-1925 *BioIn 16, PenDiMP*
De Lucia, Frank Charles 1943- *WhoAm 90*
DeLucia, Gene Anthony 1952- *WhoWor 91*
De Lue, Donald 1897-1988 *BioIn 16*
Delugach, Albert Lawrence 1925- *WhoAm 90*
De Lugo, Ron 1930- *BioIn 16, WhoAm 90, WhoHisp 91, WhoSSW 91*
Deluigi, Janice Cecilia *WhoAmA 91*
DeLuigi, Janice Cecilia Weil Lefton 1915- *WhoAm 90*
De Luise, Dom 1933- *WhoAm 90, WorAlBi*
DeLuise, Peter *BioIn 16*
Delulio, Jim *ODwPR 91*
DeLuna, Carlos *BioIn 16*
DeLuna, Diane Goncalves 1954- *WhoEmL 91*
De Luna, Vickie Guzman *BioIn 16*
DeLustro, Frank Anthony 1948- *WhoAm 90*
De Lutis, Donald Conse 1934- *WhoAm 90*
Del Vacchio, Anthony Joseph 1944- *St&PR 91*
Delval, Robert Richard 1947- *WhoWor 91*
del Valle, Antonio M. 1954- *WhoHisp 91*
Del Valle, Carlos Sergio 1951- *WhoHisp 91*
Del Valle, Cezar Jose 1945- *WhoE 91*
Del Valle, Fernando *BiDrAPA 89*
Del Valle, Hector L. 1963- *WhoHisp 91*
Del Valle, Ignacio G. 1944- *St&PR 91*
Del Valle, Jose Cecilio 1777-1834 *BioIn 16*
Del Valle, Jose Luis 1954- *WhoWor 91*
Del Valle, Joseph Bourke 1919- *WhoAmA 91*
Del Valle, M. 1931- *WhoHisp 91*
del Valle, Manuel Luis 1924- *WhoAm 90*
Del Valle, Michael Francis 1921- *St&PR 91*
del Valle, Miguel 1951- *WhoHisp 91*
Delvalle, Philip Brandon 1914- *St&PR 91*
Del Valle, Raul *BioIn 16*
Delvalle Henriquez, Eric Arturo 1933- *WhoWor 91*
Del Valle-Inclan, Ramon 1870-1936 *BioIn 16*
Del Valle-Jacquemain, Jean Marie 1961- *WhoHisp 91*
Delvaux, Albert 1913- *IntWWM 90*
Delvaux, Andre 1926?- *BioIn 16*
Delvaux, Laurent 1696-1778 *BioIn 16*
Delvaux, Paul 1897- *IntDcAA 90*
Delvaux, Paul E. 1897- *WhoWor 91*
Del Vecchio, Dan Reeves 1950- *WhoEmL 91*
Del Vecchio, Francis *BioIn 16*
Delvecchio, Jules A. 1943- *St&PR 91*
Del Vecchio, Laura *WhoWrEP 89*
Del Vecchio, Michael A 1941- *BiDrAPA 89*
del Vendrell, Countess 1956- *WhoSSW 91*
Delventhal, Bruce Warren 1949- *WhoE 91*
Delventhal, Jerald Alan 1953- *WhoEmL 91*
Del Villar, Hugo Enrique *BiDrAPA 89*
Delwiche, Eugene Albert 1917- *WhoAm 90*
Dely, Steven 1943- *St&PR 91, WhoAm 90*
DeLynn, Jane *BioIn 16*
DeLyon, Jo *ODwPR 91*
De Lyrot, Alain Herve 1926- *WhoAm 90*
Delys, Chantal 1953- *WhoAmW 91*
Delysia, Alice 1889-1979 *OxCPMus*
Delz, Christoph 1950- *IntWWM 90*
Delz, William Ronald 1932- *WhoAm 90*
Delza-Munson, Elizabeth *WhoAm 90*
Delzell, Charles Floyd 1920- *WhoSSW 91*
deMaar, Natalie 1950- *WhoAmW 91*
De Macedo, Gilberto *BiDrAPA 89*
De Madrazo y Kuntz, Federico 1815-1894 *BioIn 16*
DeMaestri, Joe 1928- *Ballpl 90*
DeMaet, K.L. 1926- *St&PR 91*
DeMaeyer, Bruce Raymond 1938- *WhoAm 90*
De Maeyer, Jan Irma Maria 1949- *IntWWM 90*
Demaeyer, Thomas R. 1942- *St&PR 91*
De Maeztu, Ramiro 1875-1936 *BioIn 16*
De Magalhaes, Benjamin Constant Botelho 1836-1891 *BioIn 16*
De Maille, Leon Scott 1963- *WhoE 91*
Demain, Dominique Jacques 1935- *WhoWor 91*
De Main, John 1944- *IntWWM 90, WhoAm 90*
DeMaio, Dorothy J. 1927- *WhoAmW 91*
DeMaio, Ernest 1908-1990 *BioIn 16*
De Maio, Marie Rose 1940- *WhoE 91*
Demaire, Larry 1942- *St&PR 91*
de Maiziere, Lothar 1940- *CurBio 90 [port], WhoWor 91*
De Majo, W M 1917- *ConDes 90*
Demakes, John N. 1945- *St&PR 91*
Demakes, Nicholas Euthymios 1910- *St&PR 91*
Demala, David M. 1949- *ODwPR 91*
De Man, Paul *BioIn 16*
de Man, Paul 1919-1983 *MajTwCW, WorAu 1980 [port]*
De Mance, Henri 1871-1948 *WhoAmA 91N*
Demanche, Edna Louise 1915- *WhoAmW 91*
Demanche, Michel S 1953- *WhoAmA 91*
Demant, Vigo Auguste 1893-1983 *DcNaB 1981*
D'Emanuele, May Ann 1934- *WhoAmW 91*
Demar, Claire 1799?-1833 *EncCoWW*
de Mar, Leoda Miller 1929- *WhoAmW 91, WhoE 91*
Demarais, Yves Didier 1943- *WhoWor 91*
DeMaranville, Daisy Nicanor *BiDrAPA 89*
Demaray, Ronald Benjamin 1959- *WhoEmL 91*
De Marchi, Agostino *PenDiDA 89*
Demarchi, Ernest Nicholas 1939- *WhoAm 90*
De Marchi, Wilhelmina Jannetje Griep *BiDrAPA 89*
DeMarco, Anita Joyce 1933- *WhoAmW 91*
DeMarco, Diane Lynn 1958- *WhoAmW 91*
DeMarco, Gino Paul 1961- *WhoEmL 91*
de Marco, Guido 1931- *WhoWor 91*
De Marco, Jean Antoine 1898-1990 *WhoAmA 91N*
DeMarco, John J., Jr. *St&PR 91*
DeMarco, Louis Francis 1925- *WhoAm 90*
DeMarco, Michael J. 1910- *St&PR 91*
De Marco, Natalie Anne 1961- *WhoAmW 91*
DeMarco, Pam *BioIn 16*
DeMarco, Ralph John 1924- *WhoWor 91*
DeMarco, Robert Thomas 1950- *WhoAm 90*
DeMarco, Roland R. 1910- *WhoAm 90, WhoE 91*
De Marco, Thomas Joseph 1942- *WhoAm 90*
DeMarco, Tom *BioIn 16*
De Mare, Anthony *BioIn 16*
Demare, Nick 1954- *St&PR 91*
Demaree, Al 1886-1962 *Ballpl 90*
Demaree, Betty 1918- *WhoAmA 91*
Demaree, Frank 1910-1958 *Ballpl 90*
Demaree, Gary D. 1951- *ODwPR 91*
Demaree, Robert Glenn 1920- *WhoSSW 91*
Demarest, Clifford J. 1932- *St&PR 91*
Demarest, Daniel Anthony 1924- *WhoAm 90*
Demarest, David Franklin, Jr. 1951- *WhoAm 90*
Demarest, Frank C., Jr. 1927- *ODwPR 91*
Demarest, Philip S. 1936- *St&PR 91*
Demarest, Sylvia M. 1944- *WhoAm 90*
Demarest, Thomas William 1817-1894 *AmLegL*
Demarest, William 1892-1983 *WorAlBi*
de Margerie, Jean-M. 1927- *WhoAm 90*
de Margerie, Roland *NewYTBS 90*
de Margitay, Gedeon 1924- *WhoE 91, WhoWor 91*
DeMaria, Alfred Anthony, Jr. 1952- *WhoEmL 91*
De Maria, Anthony John 1931- *WhoAm 90*
DeMaria, Anthony Nicholas 1943- *WhoAm 90*
DeMaria, Dennis Michael 1946- *WhoEmL 91*
DeMaria, Joseph Angelo 1957- *WhoEmL 91*
DeMaria, Peter A, Jr. *BiDrAPA 89*
DeMaria, Peter James 1934- *St&PR 91*
Demaria, Walter 1935- *WhoAm 90*
De Maria, Walter 1935- *WhoAmA 91*
De Marigny, Enguerrand *EncO&P 3*
Demarines, Jane Mied 1949- *ODwPR 91*
DeMarinis, Bernard Daniel 1946- *WhoE 91*
De Marino, Donald Nicholson 1945- *WhoE 91*
De Maris, Harry Dean *BiDrAPA 89*
Demaris, Ovid 1919- *WhoAm 90, WhoWrEP 89*
DeMark, Richard Reid 1925- *WhoAm 90*
de Marneffe, Barbara Rowe 1929- *WhoAmW 91*
de Marneffe, Francis 1924- *WhoAm 90, WhoSSW 91*
de Marneffe, Francis L A 1924- *BiDrAPA 89*
De Marr, Mary Jean 1932- *WhoAm 90, WhoAmW 91*
De Marrais, Herbert J. 1928- *St&PR 91*
De Mars, Caron Emerson 1955- *WhoAmW 91, WhoEmL 91*
De Mars, Dan Richard 1943- *St&PR 91*
DeMars, Dan Richard 1943- *WhoAm 90*
Demars, Jean-Pierre *BiDrAPA 89*
DeMars, Richard B. 1918- *St&PR 91*
De Martelly, John Stockton 1903-1980 *WhoAmA 91N*
DeMartin, Charles Peter 1952- *WhoEmL 91*
DeMartin, Richard Lee 1926- *St&PR 91*
De Martini, Alfred Eugene 1916- *St&PR 91*
DeMartini, Frank Thomas 1962- *WhoEmL 91*
De Martini, Joseph 1896- *WhoAmA 91N*
DeMartini, Marilyn 1955- *WhoSSW 91*
DeMartini, Richard Michael 1952- *WhoE 91*
Demartini, Robert John 1919- *St&PR 91, WhoAm 90*
DeMartino, Alison Pulver 1958- *ODwPR 91*
DeMartino, Anthony Gabriel 1931- *WhoAm 90*
De Martino, Carl 1925- *St&PR 91*
De Martino, Ernesto 1908- *EncO&P 3*
De Martino, John A. 1939- *St&PR 91*
DeMartino, Joseph William 1964- *WhoE 91*
Demartino, Tony 1958- *ODwPR 91*
Demartis, James J 1926- *WhoAmA 91*
Demas, Thomas Theodore 1942- *St&PR 91*
Demas, William Gilbert 1929- *WhoWor 91*
Demas, William N. 1937- *St&PR 91*
DeMascio, Robert Edward 1923- *WhoAm 90*
DeMasi, Jack Bernard 1946- *WhoEmL 91*
De Masi, Jack Bernard 1946- *WhoWrEP 89*
De Maso, David Ray *BiDrAPA 89*
DeMaso, David Ray 1949- *WhoE 91*
Demaso, L. William 1941- *St&PR 91*
De Massa, Jessie G. *WhoAmW 91, WhoWor 91*
DeMasse, Robert John 1953- *WhoSSW 91*
Demasson, Hubert P. 1880-1917 *BioIn 16*
De Mastry, John A. 1930- *WhoSSW 91*
Demastus, Melodye Rose 1958- *St&PR 91, WhoAmW 91*
Demattei, Angelo F. 1926- *St&PR 91*
Dematteo, Albert 1932- *St&PR 91*
DeMatteo, Gene Joseph 1933- *WhoWor 91*
DeMatteo, Gloria Jean 1943- *WhoAmW 91*
DeMatteo, Madelyn M. 1948- *St&PR 91*
deMatties, Nicholas Frank 1939- *WhoAm 90*
Dematties, Nick 1939- *WhoAmA 91*
De Mattos, Gregorio 1636-1695 *BioIn 16*
de Mauriac, Caroline Marie 1959- *WhoEmL 91*
deMause, Lloyd 1931- *WhoAm 90*
Demay, Jean-Baptiste-Bernard 1759-1848 *PenDiDA 89*
DeMay, John Andrew 1925- *WhoWor 91*
DeMay, Karl F. 1922- *St&PR 91*
De May, Mary Genevieve 1955- *BiDrAPA 89*
Demay, Sami Zakaria *BiDrAPA 89*
de Mayo, Paul 1924- *WhoAm 90*
Demb, Howard B 1931- *BiDrAPA 89*
Dembeck, Mary Grace 1931- *WhoAmW 91, WhoE 91, WhoWor 91*

Dember, William Norton 1928- *WhoAm 90*
Dembert, Mark Lawrence 1949- *BiDrAPA 89*
Dembiak, Dorothy Ann 1946- *WhoEmL 91*
Dembitz, Nanette 1912-1989 *BioIn 16*
Dembling, Paul Gerald 1920- *WhoAm 90*
Dembner, Red *ConAu 131*
Dembner, S. Arthur 1920-1990 *BioIn 16, ConAu 131, NewYTBS 90*
Dembo, Joseph T. *WhoE 91*
Dembo, Lawrence Sanford 1929- *WhoAm 90*
Dembofsky, Thomas Joseph 1927- *WhoAm 90*
Dembow, David E. 1925- *St&PR 91*
Dembowski, Frederick Lester 1948- *WhoEmL 91*
Dembowski, Hermann 1928- *WhoWor 91*
Dembowski, Peter Florian 1925- *WhoAm 90*
Dembro, Melissa Lee 1960- *WhoE 91*
Dembroski, George Steven 1934- *WhoAm 90*
Dembry, George E. 1929- *St&PR 91*
Dembski, Stephen Michael 1949- *IntWWM 90, WhoEmL 91*
Demby, Betty J. *WhoWrEP 89*
Demby, Bill *BioIn 16*
Demby, Constance *NewAgMG*
Demby, Karen Bowks 1958- *WhoEmL 91*
Demchak, David Allen 1955- *WhoEmL 91*
De Medicis, Catherine 1519-1589 *BioIn 16*
De Medina, Louisa Honor 1813?-1838 *BioIn 16*
De Meester, Louis August Edmond Hendrik 1904- *IntWWM 90*
De Meester, Paul Jozef August 1935- *WhoWor 91*
Demel, Gerald F. 1941- *St&PR 91*
Demel, Sol 1933- *St&PR 91*
DeMelio, Joseph John 1930- *St&PR 91, WhoSSW 91*
Demelle, Arthur William 1940- *St&PR 91*
De Mello, Adragon Eastwood *BioIn 16*
De Mello, Anthony 1931-1987 *BioIn 16*
Demello, Louise Ann 1948- *WhoE 91*
de Mello-Franco, Affonso Arinos 1930- *WhoWor 91*
De Melo, Eurico 1925- *WhoWor 91*
De Melo Neto, Joao Cabral 1920- *BioIn 16*
De Mendelssohn, George H. *BioIn 16*
de Meneses, Mary Roades 1939- *WhoAmW 91*
DeMenil, Dominique 1908- *WhoAm 90*
De Menil, John 1904-1973 *WhoAmA 91N*
Dement, Gridley 1919- *St&PR 91*
De Ment, Ira 1931- *WhoWor 91*
Dement, Jay M. 1951- *St&PR 91*
Dement, William Charles 1928- *EncO&P 3*
Dementei, Nikolai Ivanovich 1931- *WhoWor 91*
Dementey, Nikolay Ivanovich 1931- *WhoWor 91*
Demento, Sandra Jo 1956- *WhoEmL 91*
Demeo, Martha Elizabeth 1964- *WhoE 91*
De Meo, Michael David *BiDrAPA 89*
Demer, Ronald 1937- *WhoSSW 91*
Demeranville, Mark Irving 1952- *WhoEmL 91*
Demerath, Nicholas Jay, III 1936- *WhoAm 90*
Demere, Robert H. 1924- *St&PR 91*
Demere, Robert Houstoun 1924- *WhoSSW 91*
De Mere-Dwyer, Leona 1928- *WhoAmW 91, WhoSSW 91, WhoWor 91*
Demerec, Milislav 1895-1966 *DcScB S2*
Demeree, Gloria 1931- *WhoAmW 91*
De Meritt, Bromley, Jr. 1935- *St&PR 91*
De Meritt, Carol Hutchinson 1928- *WhoE 91*
DeMerle, Les *BioIn 16*
DeMerritt, Ted C. 1932- *St&PR 91, WhoAm 90*
Demers, Jacques 1944- *WhoAm 90*
DeMers, Judy Lee 1944- *WhoAmW 91*
Demers, Michel 1949- *OxCCanT*
Demers, Raymond 1937- *St&PR 91*
Demers, Robert G *BiDrAPA 89*
Demers, Walter V., Jr. 1928- *St&PR 91*
Demery, Barbara Bell 1947- *WhoAmW 91*
Demery, Larry 1953- *Ballpl 90*
Demessieux, Jeanne 1921-1968 *PenDiMP*
De Mestral, Georges *BioIn 16, NewYTBS 90*
Demet, Margadette Moffatt 1927- *WhoAmW 91*
Demeter, Don 1935- *Ballpl 90*
Demetra, Tula Alexandra 1958- *WhoEmL 91*
Demetrakas, Gregory George 1933- *WhoE 91*
Demetre, S. Gordon 1943- *St&PR 91*
Demetree, Frances Mary 1943- *WhoSSW 91*
Demetrescu, Mihai Constantin 1929- *WhoWor 91*
Demetrion, James Thomas 1930- *WhoAm 90, WhoAmA 91, WhoE 91*
Demetrion, Jim J. 1926- *St&PR 91*
Demetrios, George 1896-1974 *WhoAmA 91N*
Demetriou, Michael 1927- *WhoE 91*
Demetrius, Beverley Allison 1945- *WhoSSW 91*
Demetrius, James Kleon 1924- *WhoAm 90*
Demetry, James Steve 1936- *WhoAm 90*
Demetry-Jeynes, Mary Kay 1941- *WhoAmW 91*
DeMetsenaere, Patricia *ODwPR 91*
Demetter, Richard A. 1940- *St&PR 91*
DeMetz, Kathleen Susan 1952- *WhoEmL 91*
Demetz, Peter 1922- *WhoAm 90*
Demeuldre, Michel 1944- *WhoWor 91*
De Meuse, Donald H. 1936- *St&PR 91*
De Meuse, Donald Howard 1936- *WhoAm 90*
De Mey, Hubert Roland 1946- *WhoWor 91*
De Meyer, Leopold 1816-1883 *BioIn 16*
Demharter, Cheryl Ann Marie 1955- *WhoWor 91*
Demi 1942- *BioIn 16*
Demian, Barbu Adrian 1940- *WhoSSW 91*
Demianoff, Renee Lockhart 1910-1962 *WhoAmA 91N*
de Michaelis, Jeremiah James 1945- *WhoE 91*
DeMichele, Michael Francis 1949- *St&PR 91*
De Michele, O. Mark *ODwPR 91*
De Michele, O. Mark 1934- *St&PR 91, WhoAm 90*
DeMichele, Robert Michael 1944- *St&PR 91*
De Michelis, Gianni 1940- *WhoWor 91*
Demichev, Petr Nilovich 1918- *WhoWor 91*
Demick, Paul Andrew 1956- *WhoSSW 91*
De Micoli, Salvatore 1939- *St&PR 91, WhoAm 90, WhoWor 91*
Demidovich, Stephen F. 1939- *St&PR 91*
Demiene, William L. 1932- *St&PR 91*
DeMieri, Joseph L. 1940- *WhoAm 90*
Demigot, Vittorio *PenDiDA 89*
De Miguel, Jesus Manuel 1947- *WhoWor 91*
Demijohn, Thom *MajTwCW*
DeMik, Anita Lorraine 1945- *WhoAmW 91*
De Milio, Lawrence 1951- *BiDrAPA 89*
DeMilio, Lawrence Thomas 1951- *WhoE 91*
De Mille, Agnes *BioIn 16, ConAu 30NR, WhoAm 90, WhoAmW 91*
De Mille, Agnes 1905?- *NotWoAT*
De Mille, Agnes 1909- *WorAlBi*
De Mille, Agnes George *IntWWM 90*
DeMille, Cecil B. 1881-1959 *WorAlBi*
DeMille, Darcy *WhoAmW 91*
De Mille, James 1833-1880 *DcLB 99 [port]*
De Mille, Leslie Benjamin 1927- *WhoAmA 91*
De Mille, Nelson *ConAu 31NR*
DeMille, Nelson 1943- *BestSel 90-3 [port], TwCCr&M 91*
De Mille, Nelson Richard 1943- *WhoE 91, WhoWrEP 89*
Demille, Wallace John 1929- *St&PR 91*
Demilliere, Bernard Henri Joseph 1931- *WhoWor 91*
DeMillion, Julianne 1955- *WhoAmW 91*
Demilt, Kenneth E. 1924- *St&PR 91*
De Milt, William A. 1941- *St&PR 91*
DeMilto, Lori 1960- *WhoE 91*
Deming, Alison Hawthorne 1946- *WhoWrEP 89*
Deming, Anne Louise 1939- *WhoAmW 91*
Deming, David Lawson 1943- *WhoAmA 91*
Deming, Donald Livingston 1924- *WhoAm 90, WhoWor 91*
Deming, Dorothy 1893- *AuBYP 90*
Deming, Dorothy 1893-1972 *BioIn 16*
Deming, Edward *EncJap*
Deming, Frederick Lewis 1912- *WhoAm 90*
Deming, Frederick Wilson 1935- *WhoAm 90*
Deming, Henry Champion 1815-1872 *AmLegL*
Deming, James Edwin, Jr. 1957- *BiDrAPA 89*
Deming, Michael G *BiDrAPA 89*
Deming, Richard 1915- *AuBYP 90*
Deming, Richard 1915-1983 *TwCCr&M 91*
Deming, Robert Herschel 1934- *WhoAm 90*
Deming, W. Edwards *BioIn 16*
Deming, William Edwards *WhoAm 90*
Deming, Willis Riley 1914- *St&PR 91, WhoAm 90*
De Minico, Charles P 1923- *BiDrAPA 89*
De Mino, Leonard Joseph 1930- *St&PR 91*
de Miollis Dussart, Anne *WhoWor 91*
Demir, Ramsey *St&PR 91*
De Miranda, Francisco 1750-1816 *BioIn 16*
Demirel, Suleyman 1924- *BioIn 16, PolLCME*
Demirjian, Gerald Jerier 1932- *St&PR 91*
De Miskey, Julian *WhoAmA 91N*
De Mita, Ciriaco *BioIn 16*
De Mita, Francis Anthony 1927- *WhoE 91*
De Mita, Luigi Ciriaco *BioIn 16*
De Mita, Luigi Ciriaco 1928- *WhoWor 91*
DeMitchell, Terri Ann 1953- *WhoAmW 91*
Demitrack, Mark A 1957- *BiDrAPA 89*
Demitz, Heinz-Jurgen 1946- *IntWWM 90*
Demjanjuk, John *BioIn 16*
Demke, Thomas Alan 1956- *WhoEmL 91*
Demko, George J. 1933- *BioIn 16*
Demko, Paul, Jr. 1944- *St&PR 91*
Demkovich, Paul Bryan 1956- *WhoEmL 91*
Demler, Frederick Russel 1953- *WhoE 91*
Demler, Linda Kass 1954- *WhoAmW 91, WhoEmL 91*
Demler, Marvin Christian 1909- *WhoE 91*
Demling, Robert Hugh 1943- *WhoAm 90*
Demma, Frank Joseph 1948- *BiDrAPA 89*
Demme, Jonathan *BioIn 16*
Demme, Jonathan 1944- *WhoAm 90*
Demmer, Paul G. 1927- *St&PR 91*
Demmer, Richard A. 1931- *St&PR 91*
Demmer, William R. 1933- *St&PR 91*
Demmer, William Roy 1933- *WhoAm 90*
Demmitt, Ray 1884-1956 *Ballpl 90*
Demmler, Albert William, Jr. 1929- *WhoE 91*
Demmler, Eugene F. 1936- *St&PR 91*
Demmler, John Henry 1932- *WhoAm 90*
Demmler, Ralph Henry 1904- *WhoAm 90*
Demmy, Merlyn Ray 1927- *BiDrAPA 89*
Demo 1--?- *EncCoWW*
Democritus 460?BC-370BC *WorAlBi, WrPh P*
Demoff, Samuel Louis 1909- *WhoAm 90*
De Mola, Don 1952- *Ballpl 90*
De Molina, Raul 1959- *WhoHisp 91*
De Monchaux, John *WhoAm 90*
Demond, Joan *WhoAmW 91*
Demond, Walter Eugene 1947- *WhoEmL 91*
Demone, Henry *WhoAm 90*
DeMone, Robert Stephen 1932- *WhoAm 90*
De Money, Fred William 1919- *WhoAm 90*
Demont, Edwin G. 1942- *St&PR 91*
De Mont, Willem *PenDiMP*
Demont-Breton, Virginie Elodie 1859-1935 *BiDWomA*
De Montbrial, Thierry 1943- *WhoWor 91*
De Monte, Claudia 1947- *WhoAmA 91*
DeMonte, Claudia Ann 1947- *WhoAm 90*
De Montebello, Philippe *BioIn 16*
de Montebello, Philippe Lannes 1936- *WhoAm 90, WhoAmA 91, WhoE 91, WhoWor 91*
de Montherlant, Henry *MajTwCW*
DeMontier, Paulette LaPointe 1948- *WhoAmW 91*
de Montigny, Claude A *BiDrAPA 89*
deMontmollin, Philip 1940- *WhoAm 90*
DeMontreville, Gene 1874-1962 *Ballpl 90*
De Monville, Francois-Nicolas-Henri R 1737-1794 *BioIn 16*
DeMoor, Barbara Jean 1956- *WhoAmW 91*
De Moor, Chris 1949- *IntWWM 90*
DeMoor, Thomas Murray 1960- *BiDrAPA 89*
Demopulos, Chris 1924- *WhoAm 90*
DeMore, Jane Elyse 1950- *WhoAmW 91*
Demorest, Ellen C. 1825-1898 *BioAmW*
Demorest, Jean-Jacques 1920- *WhoAm 90*
Demorest, Joan Florence 1947- *WhoEmL 91*
Demorest, Robert L. 1945- *St&PR 91*
De Morgan, Augustus 1806-1871 *EncO&P 3, EncPaPR 91*
De Morgan, William *BioIn 16*
De Morgan, William Frend 1839-1917 *PenDiDA 89*
De Mori, Renato 1941- *WhoAm 90*
De Mornay, Rebecca *BioIn 16*
Demornay, Rebecca 1962- *WorAlBi*
de Morsella, Guy Christopher 1926- *WhoWor 91*
Demorsky, Susan Anne *WhoSSW 91*
Demos, George James 1928- *St&PR 91*
Demos, Jean McMorran 1902- *WhoWor 91*
Demos, Jeffrey Charles 1954- *WhoEmL 91*
Demos, John 1931- *St&PR 91*
Demos, John Putnam 1937- *WhoAm 90*
Demos, Victoria Camille 1959- *WhoAmW 91*
De Mosquera, T. C. 1798-1878 *BioIn 16*
DeMoss, Bingo 1889-1965 *Ballpl 90*
De Moss, Deborah Lynne 1960- *WhoE 91*
DeMoss, Emmett Roland, Jr. 1936- *St&PR 91*
DeMoss, Harold R., Jr. 1930- *WhoAm 90, WhoSSW 91*
DeMoss, Jon W. 1947- *WhoAm 90*
DeMoss, Kathryn E. 1932- *St&PR 91*
DeMoss, Nancy *BioIn 16*
De Moss, Robert George 1928- *WhoAm 90*
Demosthene, Antoine Yvan *BiDrAPA 89*
Demosthenes 384BC-322BC *WorAlBi*
Demott, Benjamin Hailer 1924- *WhoWrEP 89*
De Mott, John Edward 1923- *WhoSSW 91*
DeMott, Peter *BioIn 16*
DeMott, Richard Melvin 1940- *WhoE 91*
DeMotte, Mary Burton *WhoSSW 91*
DeMotto, Benjamin Albert 1933- *St&PR 91*
Demoula, Kike 1931- *EncCoWW*
Demoulas, Telemachus A. 1923- *WhoAm 90*
DeMoulin, Raymond Henry 1930- *WhoAm 90*
Demoulin, Robert-Leon 1911- *WhoWor 91*
De Moura, Patricia Brown 1948- *WhoE 91*
De Moura, Venancio *BioIn 16*
De Moura Sobral, Luis 1943- *WhoAmA 91*
De Mourgues, Odette *BioIn 16*
Demouth, Robin Madison 1939- *WhoAm 90*
de Moville, David Brent 1952- *WhoSSW 91*
de Moya, Victor Felipe *BiDrAPA 89*
Dempewolff, Rita *BioIn 16*
Dempsey, Bernard Shanley 1929- *St&PR 91*
Dempsey, Brian P. 1937- *St&PR 91*
Dempsey, Bruce Harvey 1941- *WhoAm 90, WhoAmA 91, WhoSSW 91*
Dempsey, Charles Nathan 1938- *WhoSSW 91*
Dempsey, Francis Burke 1962- *WhoE 91*
Dempsey, Frank Joseph 1925-1988 *BioIn 16*
Dempsey, Gail Rolader 1949- *WhoAmW 91*
Dempsey, Glenn Michael 1941- *BiDrAPA 89*
Dempsey, Gregory 1931- *IntWWM 90*
Dempsey, Howard Stanley 1939- *WhoAm 90*
Dempsey, Hugh Michael 1948- *WhoE 91*
Dempsey, Jack 1895-1983 *BioIn 16, WorAlBi*
Dempsey, Jackson Tyler 1955- *BiDrAPA 89*
Dempsey, James Howard, Jr. 1916- *WhoAm 90*
Dempsey, James Raymon 1921- *St&PR 91, WhoAm 90*
Dempsey, Jerry Edward 1932- *St&PR 91, WhoAm 90, WhoWor 91*
Dempsey, John 1915-1989 *AnObit 1989*
Dempsey, John Cornelius 1914- *WhoAm 90*
Dempsey, John M., Jr. 1928- *St&PR 91*
Dempsey, John Nicholas 1923- *WhoAm 90*
Dempsey, John Noel 1915-1989 *BioIn 16*
Dempsey, John Richard 1945- *WhoAm 90*
Dempsey, Kathleen E *BiDrAPA 89*
Dempsey, Levon Franklin 1934- *St&PR 91*
Dempsey, Louis Francis, III 1926- *WhoAm 90*
Dempsey, Mary Joseph 1856-1939 *BioIn 16*
Dempsey, Michael Francis *BiDrAPA 89*
Dempsey, Michael James 1957- *WhoEmL 91*
Dempsey, Patrick *BioIn 16*
Dempsey, Raymond J. 1935- *WhoAm 90*
Dempsey, Raymond Leo, Jr. 1949- *WhoE 91*
Dempsey, Richard W 1909- *WhoAmA 91N*
Dempsey, Rick 1949- *Ballpl 90*
Dempsey, Stanley 1939- *St&PR 91*
Dempsey, Stephen Brian 1921- *St&PR 91*
Dempsey, Thomas L. 1926- *St&PR 91*
Dempsey, Wallace Guy 1925- *St&PR 91*
Dempsey, William H. 1925- *St&PR 91*
Dempsey, William Henry 1930- *WhoAm 90*
Dempsey, William Stanton 1932- *WhoE 91*
Dempster, Barry 1952- *ConAu 32NR*
Dempster, Charlotte 1835-1913 *FemiCLE*
Dempster, Lauramay Tinsley 1905- *WhoAmW 91*
Dempster, Stuart 1936- *IntWWM 90*
Demsetz, Harold 1930- *WhoAm 90*
Demsey, Barbara Blackstone 1921- *WhoAmW 91*

Demsey, David B. 1955- IntWWM 90
Demske, James Michael 1922- WhoAm 90, WhoE 91
Demski, Robert S 1937- BiDrAPA 89
De Munecas, J Anthony 1924- BiDrAPA 89
Demuro, Paul Robert 1954- WhoEmL 91
De Murska, Ilma PenDiMP
Demus, Jorg 1928- PenDiMP
Demus, Jorg Wolfgang 1928- IntWWM 90
Demus, Lee Anne 1959- WhoAmW 91
Demusz, Waldemar Henryk 1959- St&PR 91
Demusz, Walter 1933- St&PR 91
Demuth, Charles 1883-1935 BioIn 16, IntDcAA 90, WorAlBi
DeMuth, Christopher Clay 1946- WhoAm 90
DeMuth, David Peter 1945- St&PR 91
De Muth, David Wallis 1936- BiDrAPA 89
Demuth, Edwin Leopold BiDrAPA 89
DeMuth, George W BiDrAPA 89
Demuth, Laurence Wheeler, Jr. 1928- St&PR 91
Demuth, Marvin L. 1930- St&PR 91
Demuth, Patricia 1948- BioIn 16
Demuth, Richard Holzman 1910- WhoE 91
Demuyt, Don J. 1943- St&PR 91
De Muzquiz y Goyeneche, Miguel 1719-1785 BioIn 16
Demy, Jacques 1931- BioIn 16
Demy, Jacques 1931-1990 NewYTBS 90
Demyan, Jeanne Rauch 1951- WhoAmW 91
De Myer, Marian K H BiDrAPA 89
Denaburg, Charles Robert 1935- WhoSSW 91
De Nagy, Eva WhoAmA 91
De Nagy, Tibor 1910- WhoAmA 91
de Nagy, Tibor Julius 1910- WhoAm 90
Denahan, Joseph Anthony 1936- St&PR 91, WhoAm 90, WhoSSW 91
De Napoli, George Anthony 1932- WhoWor 91
De Napoli, Jorge H 1930- BiDrAPA 89
Denard, Roslyn 1924- St&PR 91
De Nardo, Mary Alice BiDrAPA 89
Denaro, Anthony T BiDrAPA 89
Denaro, Anthony Thomas 1929- WhoE 91
Denaro, Charles T. 1953- St&PR 91
Denaro, Charles Thomas 1953- WhoEmL 91
Denaro, Gregory 1954- WhoEmL 91, WhoSSW 91
De Natale, Andrew Peter 1950- WhoEmL 91
DeNatale, Carole Egan 1954- WhoAmW 91, WhoE 91
DeNatale, Regina Ann 1958- WhoAmW 91
DeNault, John B. 1919- St&PR 91
De Naut, James Eric 1940- St&PR 91
Denbeaux, Fred 1914- WhoAm 90
Denber, Herman C B BiDrAPA 89
Den Besten, Allan Lee 1945- St&PR 91
Den Besten, Ronald Wayne 1948- St&PR 91
Denbigh, Susan, Countess of BiDEWW
Denbo, Elic A BiDrAPA 89
Denbo, Nancy J 1948- BiDrAPA 89
den Boer, Cornelis Wilhelmus 1939- WhoWor 91
Den Braber, Joyce Elaine 1947- St&PR 91
Den Breeijen, Arie BiDrAPA 89
Denburg, Dorian Sue 1954- WhoEmL 91
Denburg, Sheldon 1925- St&PR 91
Denby, Charles BioIn 16
Denby, Charles 1830-1904 BioIn 16
Denby, Charles 1861-1938 BioIn 16
Denby, Charles, II 1953- BiDrAPA 89
Denby, Edwin 1870-1929 BiDrUSE 89
Denby, Edwin 1903-1983 WorAu 1980
Denby, Peter 1929- WhoAm 90
Denby, Walter A. 1951- St&PR 91
Dence, Edward William, Jr. 1938- WhoAm 90
Dence, Michael Robert 1931- WhoAm 90
Dencer, Derrick 1921- WhoWor 91
Dench, Judith Olivia 1934- WhoWor 91
Dencker-Jensen, Aksel Ingvard 1914- IntWWM 90
Denckhoff, Robert H., Jr. 1940- St&PR 91
Dende-Gallio, Lusia Marie 1953- WhoAmW 91
Dendinger, Martha Jo 1957- WhoSSW 91
Dendo, Albert Ulysses 1923- WhoAm 90
Dendy, Errol Barr 1946- BiDrAPA 89
Denea, Russell William 1947- BiDrAPA 89
De Neal, Gary Robert 1944- WhoWrEP 89
De Neal, Judy Kay 1947- WhoWrEP 89
de Necochea, Fernando WhoHisp 91
Deneen, Daniel Guy 1957- WhoEmL 91
De Neergaard, Pierre Paul Ferdinand M 1907-1987 BioIn 16
Denefe, Janet 1953- ODwPR 91
Denefield, Beatrice A BiDrAPA 89
Denegall, John Palmer, Jr. 1959- WhoE 91, WhoEmL 91
Denegre, George 1923- St&PR 91, WhoAm 90
Denegre, Stanhope Bayne-Jones 1952- WhoEmL 91
Denegre-Tosun, Louise 1958- WhoEmL 91
Denehy, Bill 1946- Ballpl 90
Denehy, Harry A. BioIn 16
Denehy, Robert Corneilius 1931- St&PR 91
Denenberg, Ed 1937- St&PR 91
Denenberg, Herbert Sidney 1929- WhoAm 90, WhoE 91
Denenberg, Victor Hugo 1925- WhoAm 90
Denenmark, Frieda BiDrAPA 89
DeNero, Nancy Sturdy 1946- WhoAmW 91
Deneroff, Shelley BioIn 16
Denerstein, Ezra J. 1918- St&PR 91
Denes, Agnes WhoAmA 91
Denes, Agnes C. 1938- WhoAm 90
Denes, Magda WhoAmW 91, WhoE 91, WhoWor 91
Denes, Vera PenDiMP
Denes, Zsofia 1885-1988 EncCoWW
DeNesnera, Alexander Peter 1957- BiDrAPA 89
de Nesnera, Alexander Peter 1957- WhoE 91
DeNeuf, Donald K. BioIn 16
de Neufville, Richard Lawrence 1939- WhoAm 90, WhoWor 91
Deneuve, Catherine BioIn 16
Deneuve, Catherine 1943- WhoAm 90, WhoWor 91, WorAlBi
Denevan, William Maxfield 1931- WhoAm 90
de Nevers, Roy Olaf 1922- WhoWor 91
Denevi, Marco 1922- BioIn 16, HispWr 90
Deney, Richard L. 1949- St&PR 91
Deng Xiaoping 1904- BioIn 16, WhoWor 91
Dengler, Jana Elizabeth 1956- WhoAmW 91
Dengler, Robert Anthony 1947- WhoWor 91
Dengler, Sandy 1939- BioIn 16, ConAu 30NR
Dengler, W.C. 1931- St&PR 91
Dengrove, Edward 1913- BiDrAPA 89
Dengrove, Ida Libby 1918- WhoAmW 91
Dengrove, Robert Stephen BiDrAPA 89
Dengrove, Robert Stephen 1948- WhoE 91
Dengyo Daishi EncJap
Denhaan, George Gerard 1947- St&PR 91
Denham, Caroline Virginia 1937- WhoSSW 91
Denham, Frederick Ronald 1929- WhoAm 90
Denham, Helen M 1921- BiDrAPA 89
Denham, John 1615-1669 BioIn 16
Denham, Mary Washko 1957- WhoAmW 91
Denham, Patricia Eileen Keller 1952- WhoAmW 91
Denham, Vernon Robert, Jr. 1948- WhoEmL 91, WhoSSW 91
Denhardt, David Tilton 1939- WhoAm 90
Denhart, Gun 1945- WhoAmW 91
Den Hartog, J. P. 1901-1989 BioIn 16
Den Hartog, Jacob Pieter 1901-1989 BioIn 16
Den Hartog, Lodewijk Christiaan 1951- WhoWor 91
Denhof, Miki WhoAm 90
Denholm, Diana B. 1944- WhoSSW 91
Denholtz, Myron S 1925- BiDrAPA 89
Denicke, George 1887- BioIn 16
Denicoff, Kirk David 1955- BiDrAPA 89
De Nicola, Peter Francis 1954- WhoE 91, WhoEmL 91
Denig, Edwin T. 1812-1858 WhNaAH
Denig, Stephen Joseph 1948- WhoE 91
DeNigris, Ernest G. 1944- WhoE 91
DeNigro, Anthony J. 1935- ODwPR 91
DeNike, James H. 1932- St&PR 91
DeNike, Lynette ODwPR 91
De Nike, Michael Nicholas 1923- WhoAmA 91
Deniker, Pierre G 1917- BiDrAPA 89
Denikin, Anton 1872-1947 WorAlBi
Denikin, Anton Ivanovich 1872-1947 BioIn 16
DeNinnis, Michele 1962- WhoAmW 91
Denio, Dale William 1947- St&PR 91
Denio, Lena Sue 1955- WhoEmL 91
Denious, Robert Wilbur 1936- WhoAm 90
De Niro, Robert 1943- WorAlBi
De Niro, Robert 1945?- BioIn 16
DeNiro, Robert 1945- WhoAm 90
Denis, Julio ConAu 32NR, HispWr 90, MajTwCW
Denis, Leon 1846-1927 EncO&P 3
Denis, Lorimer 1904-1957 EncO&P 3
Denis, Louis J. 1933- WhoWor 91
Denis, Paul-Yves 1932- WhoAm 90
Denis, Sylvain 1958- BiDrAPA 89
DeNisco, Jeanette Marie 1958- WhoSSW 91
Denisco, John Anthony 1948- WhoE 91
DeNisco, S.G. 1918- St&PR 91
Denise, Robert Phillips 1936- WhoAm 90
Denise, Theodore Cullom 1919- WhoAm 90
Denish, Darrell L. 1957- St&PR 91
Denisoff, R. Serge 1939- WhoAm 90
Denison, Anthony BioIn 16
Denison, Carol AuBYP 90
Denison, Dan Leyland 1939- St&PR 91
Denison, Edward Fulton 1915- WhoAm 90, WhoE 91
Denison, Floyd G. 1943- St&PR 91
Denison, Floyd Gene 1943- WhoAm 90
Denison, Frederick Charles 1846-1896 DcCanB 12
Denison, Glen H. 1924- St&PR 91
Denison, John B. 1940- St&PR 91
Denison, John Law 1911- IntWWM 90
Denison, Mary 1826-1911 FemiCLE
Denison, Mary Boney 1956- WhoEmL 91
Denison, Merrill 1893-1975 DcLB 92 [port], OxCCanT
Denison, Muriel AuBYP 90
Denison, Thomas Renau 1960- WhoEmL 91
Denison, William Rae 1937- IntWWM 90, WhoSSW 91
Denisov, Edison 1929- IntWWM 90
Denitz, Peter Jonathan 1954- WhoEmL 91
Denius, Franklin Wofford 1925- St&PR 91, WhoAm 90, WhoSSW 91, WhoWor 91
Denius, Homer Rainey 1914- WhoWor 91
Deniz, Clare Frances 1945- IntWWM 90
Deniz Espinos, Jose Antonio 1942- WhoWor 91
Denize, Nadine 1943- IntWWM 90
Denjoy, Arnaud 1884-1974 DcScB S2
Denke, Paul Herman 1916- WhoWor 91
Denkensohn, Barry David 1945- WhoEmL 91
Denker, Hans-Werner 1941- WhoWor 91
Denker, Henry 1912- ConAu 31NR, WhoAm 90, WhoWor 91
Denker, Martin Wm 1943- BiDrAPA 89
Denker, Randall Elizabeth 1950- WhoEmL 91
Denker, Susan A 1948- WhoAmA 91, WhoE 91
Denkinger, Don 1936- Ballpl 90
Denktas, Rauf Raif 1924- WhoWor 91
Denlea, Leo E., Jr. 1932- St&PR 91
Denlea, Leo Edward, Jr. 1932- WhoAm 90
Denley, Catherine IntWWM 90
Denlinger, Charles Good 1940- WhoE 91
Denlinger, Edgar Jacob 1939- WhoAm 90
Denlinger, John Kenneth 1942- WhoAm 90
Denman, Catherine Cheryl 1958- WhoAmW 91
Denman, Charles Frank 1934- WhoAm 90
Denman, Eugene Dale 1928- WhoAm 90
Denman, Frank AuBYP 90
Denman, Jill A. ODwPR 91
Denman, Joe C., Jr. 1923- St&PR 91
Denman, Joe Carter, Jr. 1923- WhoAm 90, WhoSSW 91
Denman, John Anthony 1933- IntWWM 90
Denman, Mary Elizabeth 1922- WhoAmW 91
Denman, Patricia Price 1932- WhoAmA 91
Denman, Rose Mary BioIn 16
Denman, William Foster 1929- WhoAm 90
Denmark, Bernhardt 1917- WhoAm 90
Denmark, Florence L. BioIn 16
Denmark, Harrison MajTwCW
Denmark, John Clifford 1924- WhoWor 91
Denmark, Lawrence Jay 1953- WhoWor 91
Denmark, Stanley Jay 1927- WhoE 91
Denmead, Doris Louise 1933- WhoAmW 91
Denmon, Melanie Patricia 1954- WhoAmW 91, WhoEmL 91
Denn, Cyril Joseph 1948- WhoEmL 91, WhoWor 91
Denn, Morton Mace 1939- WhoAm 90
Dennard family BioIn 16
Dennard, Cleveland Leon 1929- WhoAm 90
Dennard, David Brooks 1950- WhoEmL 91
Dennard, James Richard 1949- WhoSSW 91
Dennard, Peggy Etheridge 1937- WhoAmW 91
Dennard, Robert Heath 1932- WhoAm 90
Denne, Dorothy 1618?- BiDEWW
Denneen, John Paul 1940- WhoAm 90
Dennegar, Lee 1929- ODwPR 91
Dennehy, Brian BioIn 16
Dennehy, Brian 1939- WhoAm 90
Dennehy, Brian 1940- WorAlBi
Dennehy, Daniel Paul 1938- St&PR 91
Dennehy, John Joseph 1930- WhoE 91
Dennehy, W.E. 1923- St&PR 91
Dennen, David Warren 1932- WhoAm 90
Denneny, James Clinton, Jr. 1924- WhoAm 90
Denner, Melvin Walter 1933- WhoAm 90
Dennery, Moise Waldhorn 1915- WhoAm 90
Dennett, Daniel Clement 1942- WhoAm 90
Dennett, Douglas E BiDrAPA 89
Dennett, Ellen Loughrin 1960- WhoAmW 91
Dennett, Ian Gordon 1944- St&PR 91
Dennett, Tyler 1883-1949 BioIn 16
Denney, Arthur Hugh 1916- WhoAm 90
Denney, Charles Eugene 1951- WhoEmL 91
Denney, Donald Berend 1927- WhoAm 90
Denney, Donald Duane 1930- BiDrAPA 89
Denney, George Covert, Jr. 1921- WhoAm 90
Denney, James Buell 1946- BiDrAPA 89
Denney, Jim 1953- WhoAmA 91
Denney, Laura Falin 1948- WhoEmL 91, WhoSSW 91
Denney, Robert Gordon 1936- BiDrAPA 89
Denney, William Duhamel 1873-1953 AmLegL
Dennie, Deborah Thomas 1939- WhoAmW 91
Dennie, Joseph 1768-1812 BioIn 16
Dennies, Sandra Lee 1951- WhoAmW 91, WhoE 91
Denning, Brenda Fay 1949- WhoAmW 91
Denning, Darryl 1939- IntWWM 90
Denning, Dorothy Elizabeth Robling 1945- WhoAmW 91
Denning, Eileen Bonar 1944- WhoAmW 91
Denning, Gregory John 1946- WhoEmL 91
Denning, Hazel May 1907- WhoAmW 91
Denning, Joseph P. 1907-1990 BioIn 16
Denning, Julio V BiDrAPA 89
Denning, Leslie Barbara 1952- WhoAmW 91
Denning, Michael Marion 1943- WhoWor 91
Denning, Paul F. 1942- St&PR 91
Denning, Peter James 1942- WhoAm 90
Denning, Richard Lynn 1947- St&PR 91
Denninger, Al BioIn 16
Denninger, John William 1943- WhoE 91
Dennis, Aaron Seth 1938- St&PR 91
Dennis, Alfred Lewis Pinneo 1874-1930 BioIn 16
Dennis, Amel J. 1954- St&PR 91
Dennis, Arthur 1933- WhoAm 90
Dennis, Arthur W. 1846-1920 AmLegL
Dennis, Beatrice Markley 1956- WhoEmL 91
Dennis, Betty Jo 1935- WhoAmW 91
Dennis, Brian Christopher 1952- WhoEmL 91
Dennis, Brian Jonathan Charles 1941- IntWWM 90
Dennis, Bryan Dale 1927- WhoSSW 91
Dennis, Burt Morgan 1892-1960 WhoAmA 91N
Dennis, C. W. Lesley 1922- WhoSSW 91
Dennis, Candy S. 1952- WhoAmW 91
Dennis, Charles H. 1860-1943 BioIn 16
Dennis, Charles Houston 1921- WhoAmA 91
Dennis, Charles L., III 1947- St&PR 91
Dennis, Clarence 1909- WhoAm 90
Dennis, Darienne L. ODwPR 91
Dennis, Darienne Leigh 1956- WhoAmW 91
Dennis, David William 1959- WhoEmL 91
Dennis, Diane Lipton 1950- WhoAmW 91, WhoE 91
Dennis, Don 1942- Ballpl 90
Dennis, Don Clark 1951- WhoSSW 91
Dennis, Don W 1923- WhoAmA 91
Dennis, Donald Daly 1928- WhoAm 90
Dennis, Donald Patrick 1947- WhoSSW 91
Dennis, Doneldon Michael 1948- WhoEmL 91
Dennis, Donna BioIn 16, WhoAmW 91
Dennis, Donna Frances 1942- WhoAmA 91
Dennis, Dorothy WhoWor 91
Dennis, Elwyn 1941- IntWWM 90
Dennis, Eugene EncAL
Dennis, Frank BiDrAPA 89
Dennis, Frank George, Jr. 1932- WhoAm 90
Dennis, Gail 1943- WhoAmW 91, WhoE 91
Dennis, Gary Jay 1950- WhoE 91
Dennis, Gary Owen 1946- WhoSSW 91
Dennis, George Harold BioIn 16
Dennis, Gertrude Weyhe WhoAmA 91
Dennis, Ivanette Jones 1940- WhoWrEP 89
Dennis, J. C. 1948- ODwPR 91

Dennis, Jack Bonnell 1931- *WhoAm 90*
Dennis, James Hilary *BiDrAPA 89*
Dennis, James Leon 1936- *WhoAm 90, WhoSSW 91*
Dennis, James Michael 1940- *St&PR 91*
Dennis, Jerry L 1952- *BiDrAPA 89*
Dennis, Joe 1911- *WhoAm 90*
Dennis, John 1658-1734 *DcLB 101 [port]*
Dennis, John Emory, Jr. 1939- *WhoAm 90*
Dennis, John S. 1935- *St&PR 91*
Dennis, Kenneth Ralph 1925- *WhoAm 90*
Dennis, L.W. 1920- *St&PR 91*
Dennis, Lawrence William 1947- *WhoSSW 91*
Dennis, Leland Wayne *BiDrAPA 89*
Dennis, Lloyd B. 1936- *ODwPR 91*
Dennis, Lynette Colleen 1946- *WhoAmW 91*
Dennis, Matt 1914- *OxCPMus*
Dennis, Michael David 1949- *WhoSSW 91*
Dennis, Michael Fordham 1947- *WhoE 91*
Dennis, Morgan 1891?-1960 *AuBYP 90*
Dennis, Nicholas John 1950- *St&PR 91*
Dennis, Nigel 1912- *MajTwCW*
Dennis, Nigel 1912-1989 *AnObit 1989, BioIn 16, ConAu 129*
Dennis, Patricia Diaz 1946- *BioIn 16, WhoAm 90, WhoAmW 91, WhoHisp 91*
Dennis, Patrick Harley 1932- *WhoAm 90, WhoSSW 91*
Dennis, Ralph E. 1925- *St&PR 91*
Dennis, Rhonda Marie R. 1954- *WhoEmL 91*
Dennis, Richard Alan 1946- *WhoSSW 91*
Dennis, Richard Irwin 1934- *St&PR 91, WhoAm 90*
Dennis, Robert 1933- *WhoAm 90*
Dennis, Robert A. 1948- *St&PR 91*
Dennis, Robert Davis 1949- *WhoEmL 91*
Dennis, Robert Franklin 1939- *WhoSSW 91*
Dennis, Robert G. 1927- *St&PR 91*
Dennis, Robert K. *ODwPR 91*
Dennis, Roger 1902- *BioIn 16*
Dennis, Roger Wilson 1902- *WhoAmA 91*
Dennis, Ruth 1907- *WhoAmW 91, WhoWrEP 89*
Dennis, Rutledge Melvin 1939- *WhoSSW 91*
Dennis, Samuel Sibley, III 1910- *WhoAm 90*
Dennis, Sandy *BioIn 16*
Dennis, Sandy 1937- *WhoAm 90, WorAlBi*
Dennis, Sharina Marie 1963- *WhoAmW 91*
Dennis, Steven Pellowe 1960- *WhoAm 90*
Dennis, Thomas *PenDiDA 89*
Dennis, Thomas H. 1846- *AmLegL*
Dennis, Ward Brainerd 1922- *WhoAm 90*
Dennis, Ward Haldan 1938- *WhoAm 90*
Dennis, Wesley 1903-1966 *AuBYP 90*
Dennis-Hollis, Robbie Smagula 1957- *WhoAmW 91*
Dennis-Sykes, Carolyn Alice 1949- *WhoE 91*
Dennish, George William, III 1945- *WhoAm 90*
Dennison, Allen Mansfield 1952- *WhoE 91*
Dennison, Brian Kenneth 1949- *WhoSSW 91*
Dennison, Byron Lee 1930- *WhoAm 90*
Dennison, Charles Stuart 1918- *WhoAm 90*
Dennison, David Mathias 1900-1976 *DcScB S2*
Dennison, David Severin 1932- *WhoAm 90*
Dennison, David Short, Jr. 1918- *WhoAm 90*
Dennison, George 1925-1987 *BioIn 16*
Dennison, Helen *ODwPR 91*
Dennison, John Manley 1934- *WhoAm 90*
Dennison, Keith Elkins 1939- *WhoAmA 91*
Dennison, Peter John 1942- *IntWWM 90*
Dennison, Richard W. 1945- *St&PR 91*
Dennison, Sally Elizabeth 1946- *WhoWrEP 89*
Dennison, Stanley Scott 1920- *WhoAm 90, WhoWor 91*
Dennison, Sylvia Jean *BiDrAPA 89*
Dennison, Theresa Marie 1965- *WhoAmW 91*
Dennison, Thomas Anand 1953- *BiDrAPA 89*
Dennison, William 1815-1882 *BiDrUSE 89*
Denniston, Baron T *BiDrAPA 89*
Denniston, Douglas 1921- *WhoAmA 91*
Denniston, George 1917- *St&PR 91*
Denniston, Marjorie McGeorge 1913- *WhoAmW 91, WhoE 91*
Denniston, Pamela Boggs 1948- *WhoAmW 91*
Denniston, Richard Stokes 1959- *WhoSSW 91*
Denno, Zetta Lee 1943- *WhoAmW 91*
Dennstedt, Frederick DeVere 1918- *WhoAm 90*
Denny, Anthony 1501-1549 *BioIn 16*
Denny, Arthur Armstrong 1822-1899 *AmLegL*
Denny, Bill, Jr. *NewAgMG*
Denny, Brewster Castberg 1924- *WhoAm 90*
Denny, Charles Morton, Jr. 1931- *St&PR 91*
Denny, David Ray 1949- *WhoEmL 91, WhoSSW 91*
Denny, Floyd Wolfe, Jr. 1923- *WhoAm 90*
Denny, Frank W. 1935- *WhoSSW 91*
Denny, J. William 1935- *St&PR 91*
Denny, James M. *WhoSSW 91*
Denny, James McCahill 1932- *St&PR 91, WhoAm 90*
Denny, James William 1935- *WhoAm 90*
Denny, Jerry 1859-1927 *Ballpl 90*
Denny, John 1952- *Ballpl 90*
Denny, John Todd *BiDrAPA 89*
Denny, Judith Ann 1946- *WhoAmW 91, WhoE 91*
Denny, Kevin Mark *BiDrAPA 89*
Denny, Laurence A 1943- *BiDrAPA 89*
Denny, Leon A., Jr. 1930- *St&PR 91*
Denny, Mary Lu Magasano 1949- *WhoAmW 91*
Denny, Norman George 1901-1982 *AuBYP 90*
Denny, Peter *BioIn 16*
Denny, Presley 1845?-1900 *AmLegL*
Denny, Richard Alden, Jr. 1931- *WhoAm 90*
Denny, Robert Myron 1944- *WhoSSW 91*
Denny, William E. 1937- *St&PR 91*
Denny, William Murdoch, Jr. 1934- *WhoE 91, WhoWor 91*
De No, Rafael Lorente 1902-1990 *BioIn 16*
Denoga, Eufrosina C *BiDrAPA 89*
DeNoma, Bernard Louis 1925- *St&PR 91*
Denomme, Robert Thomas 1930- *WhoAm 90*
Denomme, Sharon Lynn 1958- *WhoAmW 91*
Denomme, Thomas Gerald 1939- *St&PR 91*
de Nonancourt, Bernard Marie 1920- *WhoWor 91*
Denonville, Jacques deBrisay, Marquis de 1637-1710 *EncCRAm*
Denoon, Clarence England, Jr. 1915- *WhoAm 90*
Denoon, David Baugh Holden 1945- *WhoAm 90*
DeNoto, Joanne 1953- *WhoEmL 91*
Den Otter, Willem 1938- *WhoWor 91*
De-Nour, Atara Kaplan 1932- *BiDrAPA 89*
Denov, Sam 1923- *WhoAm 90*
De Novellis, Anna *BiDrAPA 89*
DeNovio, Susan Williams 1948- *WhoWor 91*
DeNovo, John August 1916- *WhoAm 90*
DeNoyer, Georgia Ann 1948- *WhoAmW 91*
Densberger, Stephen James 1950- *St&PR 91*
Densen, Paul Maximillian 1913- *WhoAm 90*
Densen, Peter M. 1942- *St&PR 91*
Densen-Gerber, Judianne *BiDrAPA 89*
Densen-Gerber, Judianne 1934- *AuBYP 90, WhoAm 90*
Denslow, Deborah Pierson 1947- *WhoAmW 91, WhoE 91, WhoEmL 91, WhoWor 91*
Denslow, Dorothea Henrietta 1900-1971 *WhoAmA 91N*
Denslow, Suzette Poupore 1956- *WhoEmL 91*
Densmore, Ann 1941- *WhoAmW 91*
Densmore, John A. 1928- *St&PR 91*
Densmore, Morris Aubrey 1923- *WhoAm 90*
Densmore, William Phillips 1924- *WhoAm 90*
Densmore, William Phillips, Jr. 1953- *WhoE 91*
Denson, Alexander Bunn 1936- *WhoSSW 91*
Denson, Bruce P. 1938- *St&PR 91*
Denson, John Eley 1937- *St&PR 91*
Denson, Michael 1956- *WhoEmL 91*
Denson, Michael White *BiDrAPA 89*
Denson, William Frank, III 1943- *St&PR 91, WhoAm 90*
Dent, Aubrey O Neal 1934- *BiDrAPA 89*
Dent, Bucky 1951- *Ballpl 90, BioIn 16, WhoAm 90*
Dent, Edward Eugene 1948- *WhoSSW 91*
Dent, Ernest DuBose, Jr. 1927- *WhoWor 91*
Dent, Frederick Baily 1922- *BiDrUSE 89, St&PR 91, WhoAm 90*
Dent, Frederick Baily, Jr. 1947- *WhoSSW 91*
Dent, Geoffrey Nicholas 1948- *WhoE 91*
Dent, Georgette Amantha 1956- *WhoSSW 91*
Dent, John Francis 1814?-1898 *AmLegL*
Dent, John H. 1908-1988 *BioIn 16*
Dent, John Natale 1948- *WhoSSW 91*
Dent, Katherine Ann *BiDrAPA 89*
Dent, Lawrence M. 1939- *St&PR 91*
Dent, Lester 1904-1959 *TwCCr&M 91*
Dent, Paul R. 1922- *St&PR 91*
Dent, Richard 1960- *WorAlBi*
Dent, Richard Lamar 1960- *WhoAm 90*
Dent, V. Edward 1918- *WhoAm 90*
Dentan, Rene P. *BioIn 16*
Dente, Sam 1922- *Ballpl 90*
Dentice, Thomas Santo 1939- *WhoAm 90*
Dentiere, Marie 1500?-1561 *EncCoWW*
Dentinger, Stephen *TwCCr&M 91, WhoWrEP 89*
Dentino, Andrew Neal 1959- *WhoEmL 91*
Dentino, Karl *BioIn 16*
Dentiste, Paul George 1930- *WhoAm 90, WhoSSW 91*
Dentler, Robert Arnold 1928- *WhoAm 90*
Denton, Arnold Eugene 1925- *WhoAm 90, WhoE 91*
Denton, Betty Lou 1925- *WhoAmW 91*
Denton, Charles M. 1924- *ODwPR 91*
Denton, Charles Mandaville 1924- *WhoAm 90*
Denton, Charles Mandaville 1957- *WhoEmL 91*
Denton, D. Keith 1948- *WhoAm 90*
Denton, David Edward 1935- *WhoAm 90*
Denton, David W. 1926- *St&PR 91*
Denton, Emma Maney 1905- *WhoAmW 91, WhoWor 91*
Denton, Eric 1923- *WhoWor 91*
Denton, Eugene K. 1888-1988 *BioIn 16*
Denton, Frank Marion 1935- *St&PR 91*
Denton, George H. 1929- *St&PR 91*
Denton, George Hurst 1929- *WhoE 91*
Denton, George W. *BioIn 16*
Denton, Gisele Ann 1937- *WhoAmW 91*
Denton, Graham Williams, Jr. 1945- *WhoAm 90*
Denton, Herbert H. 1943-1989 *BioIn 16*
Denton, Jere Michael 1947- *St&PR 91, WhoEmL 91*
Denton, Jeremiah A., Jr. 1924- *ConAu 31NR*
Denton, Jerome F. 1951- *St&PR 91*
Denton, Joe D. 1924- *St&PR 91*
Denton, John Joseph 1915- *WhoAm 90*
Denton, Karl Robert 1959- *WhoEmL 91, WhoWor 91*
Denton, Laurie R. 1951- *WhoE 91*
Denton, Louise W. *WhoAmW 91*
Denton, Mary F. 1857-1947 *BioAmW*
Denton, Michael John 1956- *WhoEmL 91*
Denton, Patry 1943- *WhoAmA 91*
Denton, Ray Douglas 1937- *WhoWor 91*
Denton, Rebecca Liegh 1958- *WhoAmW 91*
Denton, Richard A. 1914- *St&PR 91*
Denton, Richard Todd 1932- *WhoAm 90*
Denton, Robert Albert, Jr. 1939- *WhoAm 90*
Denton, Robert Randall 1950- *St&PR 91*
Denton, Robert William 1944- *WhoSSW 91*
Denton, Roger Marius 1946- *WhoEmL 91, WhoSSW 91, WhoWor 91*
Denton, Sidney Benny 1928- *St&PR 91*
Denton, Thomas Wade 1952- *WhoSSW 91*
Denton, Wayne Holt 1956- *BiDrAPA 89*
Denton, Wayne K. 1939- *St&PR 91*
Denton, William 1823-1883 *EncO&P 3*
Denton, William J. 1944- *St&PR 91*
Denton, William R. 1930- *St&PR 91, WhoAm 90*
D'Entremont, Edward Joseph 1954- *WhoE 91*
d'Entremont, Marc Paul 1950- *WhoE 91*
Dentry, Robert *ConAu 130*
Dentsch, Arnold Philip 1935- *BiDrAPA 89*
Dentz, Jeffrey W. 1948- *St&PR 91*
Dentzel, Carl Schaefer 1913-1980 *WhoAmA 91N*
Dentzer, William Thompson, Jr. 1929- *St&PR 91*
DeNuccio, Raymond Adolph 1933- *St&PR 91*
De Nuccio, Raymond Adolph 1933- *WhoAm 90*
Denune, David Perry *BiDrAPA 89*
DeNunzio, Ralph D. 1931- *St&PR 91*
DeNunzio, Ralph Dwight 1931- *WhoAm 90*
DeNunzio, Sharon Kistler 1959- *WhoAmW 91*
De-Nur, Amnon 1926- *St&PR 91*
DeNuzzio, Albert S. 1921- *St&PR 91*
DeNuzzo, Rinaldo Vincent 1922- *WhoAm 90, WhoWor 91*
Denver, Bob *BioIn 16*
Denver, Bob 1935- *WorAlBi*
Denver, Daniel Joseph 1944- *WhoSSW 91, WhoWor 91*
Denver, Eileen Ann 1942- *WhoAm 90, WhoAmW 91*
Denver, John *NewAgE 90*
Denver, John 1943- *ConTFT 8 [port], EncPR&S 89, OxCPMus, WhoAm 90, WorAlBi*
Denver, Rod *ConAu 30NR*
Denvers, Robert Eugene 1942- *WhoAm 90, WhoWor 91*
Denvir, James Peter, III 1950- *WhoEmL 91*
Denyes, James Richard 1948- *WhoSSW 91*
Denysyk, Bohdan 1947- *WhoAm 90, WhoEmL 91, WhoWor 91*
Denza, Luigi 1846-1922 *OxCPMus*
Denzel, Herman Alfred 1927- *BiDrAPA 89*
Denzin, Norman K 1941- *ConAu 30NR*
Denzler, Robert 1892-1972 *PenDiMP*
Deo, Marjoree Nee 1907- *WhoAmA 91*
Deo, Narsingh 1936- *WhoAm 90*
Deohring, Richard Clayton 1936- *St&PR 91*
Deol, Prabhjot Singh 1954- *BiDrAPA 89*
Deol, Sharon Rose 1962- *WhoAmW 91*
Deola, Linda Lee *WhoAmW 91*
De Oliveira, Manuel Mendes 1951- *WhoWor 91*
D'Eon, Leonard Joseph 1929- *WhoWrEP 89*
Deon, Richard Phillip 1956- *WhoE 91*
De Ona, Pedro 1570-1643? *BioIn 16*
Deones, Jack E. 1931- *St&PR 91, WhoAm 90*
Deora, Man Singh 1947- *WhoWor 91*
De Orellana, Francisco 1500-1550 *BioIn 16*
Deorio, Anthony Joseph 1945- *WhoWor 91*
DeOrio, David James 1959- *WhoE 91*
DeOrio, George Louis 1945- *WhoE 91*
De Oriol e Ybarra, Miguel *BioIn 16*
De Orlov, Lino Sigismondo Lipinsky 1908-1988 *BioIn 16*
De Osma, Lupe *AuBYP 90*
Deoul, Neal 1931- *WhoE 91, WhoWor 91*
DePace, John Gordon 1962- *WhoWor 91*
DePace, Nicholas Louis 1953- *WhoE 91*
De Pachmann, Vladimir *PenDiMP*
De Pachmann, Vladimir 1848-1933 *BioIn 16*
DePalma, Anthony *BioIn 16*
De Palma, Anthony Robert 1952- *WhoWrEP 89*
De Palma, Brett 1949- *WhoAmA 91*
De Palma, Brian *BioIn 16*
DePalma, Brian Russell 1940- *WhoAm 90*
De Palma, Eugene A. 1935- *WhoAm 90*
DePalma, Kimberly Anne 1955- *WhoEmL 91*
DePalma, Philip Nicholas, Jr. 1947- *WhoEmL 91*
De Palma, Ralph 1883-1956 *BioIn 16*
DePalma, Ralph George 1931- *WhoAm 90*
DePalma, Robert A. 1935- *St&PR 91*
De Palma, Sandro 1957- *IntWWM 90*
Depalo, Armand M. 1949- *St&PR 91*
de Palo, Armand Michael 1949- *WhoEmL 91*
De Paola, Thomas Anthony 1934- *BioIn 16*
De Paola, Tomie 1934- *BioIn 16*
DePaola, Tomie 1934- *BioIn 16, WhoAmA 91*
De Paoli, Alexander 1936- *WhoAm 90*
DePaoli, Geri Mary 1941- *WhoAmW 91*
De Paoli, Mario 1940- *BiDrAPA 89*
dePaolis, Potito Umberto 1925- *WhoWor 91*
De Paolis, Rosemary 1962- *WhoWrEP 89*
De Paolo, Joseph John 1930- *St&PR 91*
dePaolo, Ronald Francis 1938- *WhoAm 90*
de Papp, Elise Wachenfeld 1933- *WhoAmW 91*
Depara, Manuel Moises *BiDrAPA 89*
Depardieu, Gerard 1948- *ConTFT 8 [port], News 91-2 [port], WhoWor 91*
DeParle, Jason *BioIn 16*
De Pas, Penney 1951- *WhoEmL 91*
Depasqua, Louis Paul 1938- *St&PR 91*
De Pasquale, John Anthony 1942- *WhoAm 90*
de Pasquale, Joseph 1919- *WhoAm 90*
Depasquale, N.H. 1941- *St&PR 91*
De Pasquale, R.H. 1905- *St&PR 91*
De Pasqually, Martines 1710-1774 *EncO&P 3*
De Passe, Derrel *ODwPR 91*
De Passe, Suzanne *BioIn 16, WhoAm 90, WhoAmW 91*
de Passe, Suzanne 1946?- *News 90 [port]*
De Pater, Anton Dammes 1920- *WhoWor 91*
De Paul, Gene Vincent 1919-1988 *OxCPMus*
Depaul, John D. 1931- *St&PR 91*
De Paula, Geraldine F 1941- *BiDrAPA 89*
De Paula, Roberto M V *BiDrAPA 89*
De Paulo, J Raymond 1946- *BiDrAPA 89*

De Paulo, Joseph Raymond, Jr. 1946- *WhoE 91*
De Paur, Leonard 1919- *DrBlPA 90*
De Paur, Leonard Etienne 1914- *DcAfAmP*
De Pauw, Gommar Albert 1918- *WhoAm 90, WhoWor 91*
De Pauw, Linda 1940- *AuBYP 90*
De Pauw, Linda Grant 1940- *WhoAm 90, WhoAmW 91*
De'Pazzi, Ellen E. 1915- *WhoWrEP 89*
Depeche Mode *ConMus 5 [port]*
De Pedery-Hunt, Dora 1913- *WhoAmA 91*
De Pellegrin, M.L. 1938- *St&PR 91*
De Pelsmaker, Helena H.L. 1957- *WhoWor 91*
DePersio, Richard John 1949- *WhoSSW 91*
De Petris, Carla Nicole Capirone *WhoWor 91*
Depetris, R.A. 1942- *St&PR 91*
DePetris, Susan Abrahams 1946- *WhoE 91*
DePew, Carol Ann 1962- *WhoEmL 91*
Depew, Charles G. 1930- *St&PR 91*
Depew, Charles Gardner 1930- *WhoAm 90*
Depew, Chauncey Mitchell 1834-1928 *BioIn 16*
Depew, Jeffrey Scott 1955- *WhoEmL 91, WhoWor 91*
Depew, Joseph D. *BioIn 16*
DePew, Marie Kathryn 1928- *WhoAmW 91*
DePew, William Earl 1948- *WhoWor 91*
De Peyer, Gervase 1926- *PenDiMP*
De Peyer, Gervase Alan 1926- *IntWWM 90*
dePeyster, Frederic Augustus 1914- *WhoAm 90*
De Pfyffer, Andre 1928- *WhoWor 91*
De Pierola, Nicolas 1839-1913 *BioIn 16*
De Pietri, Stephen *BioIn 16*
D'Epifanio, Lugi 1954- *WhoWor 91*
Depillars, Murry N 1938- *WhoAmA 91*
DePinna, Vivian 1883-1978 *WhoAmA 91N*
Depkovich, Francis John 1924- *WhoAm 90*
DePlonty, Duane Earl 1923- *WhoSSW 91*
Deplws, Guy Gaston Simon 1924- *IntWWM 90*
De Pol, John 1913- *WhoAm 90, WhoAmA 91*
DePolo, Anthony R. 1942- *WhoE 91*
Depoltova, Eva 1945- *IntWWM 90*
Depommier, Pierre Henri 1925- *WhoAm 90*
De Pont, Jan Joep Hubert Henri Maria 1942- *WhoWor 91*
de Pontbriand, Gael Jean 1947- *WhoWor 91*
De Ponte, Velma Alana 1949- *WhoAmW 91*
De Poorter, Pierre-Emmanuel 1919- *WhoWor 91*
De Portago, Alfonso 1928-1957 *BioIn 16*
De Portola, Gaspar 1723?-1784 *BioIn 16*
de Posada, Robert G. 1966 *WhoHisp 91*
de Pouzilhac, Alain Duplessis 1945- *WhoWor 91*
Depovic-Palmer, Jasminka *BiDrAPA 89*
Depoy, Jerry C. 1938- *St&PR 91*
Depp, Johnny *BioIn 16*
Depp, Johnny 1963- *WorAlBi*
Depp, Richard, III 1938- *WhoAm 90*
Deppe, Henry A. 1920- *WhoAm 90, WhoWor 91*
Deppe, Steven L. 1948- *St&PR 91*
Deppe, Victoria Lynn 1963- *WhoAmW 91*
Deppeler, James Gregory 1946- *WhoE 91*
Depperschmidt, Thomas Orlando 1935- *WhoAm 90*
De Pratz, Claire *FemiCLE*
de Pre, Jean-Anne *TwCCr&M 91*
DePree, D. J. 1891-1990 *NewYTBS 90 [port]*
De Pree, Max O. 1924- *WhoAm 90*
De Pree, Willard Ames 1928- *WhoAm 90, WhoWor 91*
DePreist, James 1936- *CurBio 90 [port], IntWWM 90*
De Preist, James Anderson 1936- *WhoAm 90*
De Premonville, Myrene *BioIn 16*
de Presno, Odd 1944- *WhoWor 91*
Depreux, Edouard Gustave 1898-1981 *BiDFrPL*
De Prey, Juan *WhoAmA 91N*
Deprez, Claudia 1948- *WhoAmW 91*
DePrez, Gene 1940- *St&PR 91*
DePrez, Gene Edward 1940- *WhoE 91*
De Prez, James Anthony 1935- *St&PR 91*
DePriest, Darryl *BioIn 16*
DePriest, Desiree Lynne 1956- *WhoAmW 91*
DePriest, James 1936- *BioIn 16*
De Priest, James 1936- *DrBlPA 90*
De Priest, Mary 1945- *WhoAmW 91*
De Priest, Oscar Stanton 1871-1951 *BlkAmsC [port]*
DePriest, Reah *WhoAmW 91*
De Prima, Charles Raymond 1918- *WhoAm 90*
Deprit, Andre Albert 1926- *WhoAm 90*
Depry, Dennis Lee 1938- *BiDrAPA 89*
DePue, Josephine Helen 1948- *WhoAmW 91*
DePui, Vine *BioIn 16*
Depuit, Thomas Harry 1950- *St&PR 91*
Depukat, Thaddeus Stanley 1936- *WhoWor 91*
De Puma, Richard Daniel 1942- *WhoAmA 91*
Deputy, William Jerry 1944- *St&PR 91*
DePuy, Charles Herbert 1927- *WhoAm 90*
DePuy, Henry W. *AmLegL*
Dequaine, Lester Joseph 1930- *St&PR 91*
De Quardo, John Robert *BiDrAPA 89*
DeQuattro, Vincent Louis 1933- *WhoAm 90*
De Queiroz, Dinah Silviera *BioIn 16*
De Queiroz, Rachel *BioIn 16*
De Quincy, Thomas 1785-1859 *WorAlBi*
De Raaff, Gert Henricus 1954- *WhoWor 91*
Derago, Anthony Francis 1928- *St&PR 91*
Derain, Andre 1880-1954 *BioIn 16, IntDcAA 90*
Deraismes, Maria 1828-1894 *EncCoWW*
DeRaleau, Roger L. 1924- *St&PR 91*
D'Eramo, Mark Anthony *BiDrAPA 89*
DeRamus, Betty Jean 1941- *WhoAm 90*
Deramus, William N. 1915-1989 *BioIn 16*
Deramus, William N., III *St&PR 91N*
De Ran, Susan Louise 1952- *WhoAmW 91*
DeRan, Timothy Michael 1951- *WhoEmL 91*
De Ranieri, Albert F *BiDrAPA 89*
Derasari, Sohan Sanat *BiDrAPA 89*
Derasmo, Jack Michael 1950- *St&PR 91*
de Ravel d'Esclapon, Pierre F. 1946- *WhoE 91*
Derber, Dana M. 1955- *WhoAmW 91*
Derber, Milton 1915- *WhoAm 90*
Derbes, Albert Joseph, III 1940- *WhoSSW 91*
Derbes, Daniel William 1930- *St&PR 91, WhoAm 90*
Derbin, James Philip *BiDrAPA 89*
Derboven, Paul Henri 1936- *BiDrAPA 89*
Derby, Cheryl Ann 1946- *WhoAmW 91*
Derby, Ernest Stephen 1938- *WhoAm 90*
Derby, George Horatio 1823-1861 *BioIn 16*
Derby, Norman Clyde 1952- *WhoSSW 91*
Derby, Richard William 1951- *IntWWM 90*
Derbyshire, Harry S. 1925- *St&PR 91*
D'Erchia, Peter John 1951- *St&PR 91*
Derchin, Michael Wayne 1942- *St&PR 91, WhoAm 90, WhoE 91*
Derck, Gary Stephen 1958- *WhoSSW 91*
Derden, John Kenneth 1947- *WhoSSW 91*
Derdenger, Patrick 1946- *WhoAm 90, WhoEmL 91, WhoWor 91*
Derderian, Yeghishe *BioIn 16*
Derderian, Yeghishe 1910?-1990 *ConAu 130*
Derdeyn, Andre P 1937- *BiDrAPA 89*
Derdzinski, Daniel M. 1957- *ODwPR 91*
Derdzinski, Kenneth Joseph 1929- *St&PR 91*
Derecktor, Nathan Edward *BioIn 16*
De Regniers, Beatrice Schenk 1914- *AuBYP 90, WhoAm 90*
Derek and the Dominos *EncPR&S 89*
Derek, Bo *BioIn 16*
Derek, John 1926- *WorAlBi*
DeRemee, Richard Arthur 1933- *WhoAm 90*
Deren, Edward Alison 1951- *WhoE 91*
Deren, Maya 1917-1961 *BioIn 16*
Derendinger, Pierre Fritz 1943- *WhoWor 91*
De Renne, Wymberley Jones 1853-1916 *BioIn 16*
Deresiewicz, Herbert 1925- *WhoAm 90*
De Reszke, Edouard 1853-1917 *PenDiMP*
De Reszke, Jean 1850-1925 *BioIn 16, PenDiMP*
De Reszke, Josephine 1855-1891 *PenDiMP*
Dereszynski, Jeffrey 1959- *St&PR 91*
de Reviers de Mauny, Bertrand Marie J. 1942- *WhoWor 91*
Derevyanny, Yelizaveta 1948- *BiDrAPA 89*
DeReynier, James E. 1942- *St&PR 91*
Derfelt, Grant William 1932- *St&PR 91*
Derfler, Melissa *BiDrAPA 89*
Dergalis, George 1928- *WhoAmA 91, WhoWor 91*
Dergarabedian, Paul 1922- *WhoAm 90*
Derge, David Richard 1928- *WhoAm 90*
Derge, Klaus Fritz 1937- *St&PR 91*
Derham, Anthony R. *BioIn 16, NewYTBS 90*
de Rham, Casimir, Jr. 1924- *WhoAm 90*
De Rham, David P. 1931- *St&PR 91*
Derham, Matthew Joseph 1928- *WhoWrEP 89*
Derham, Richard Andrew 1940- *WhoAm 90*
Der Harootian, Khoren 1909- *WhoAm 90*
Der-Houssikian, Haig 1938- *WhoAm 90*
Der Hovanessian, Diana *WhoWrEP 89*
Deri, John 1950- *BiDrAPA 89*
de Ribaupierre, Anik 1946- *WhoWor 91*
De Ribes, Jacqueline *BioIn 16*
De Ricco, Hank 1946- *WhoAmA 91*
DeRicco, Lawrence Albert 1923- *WhoAm 90*
DeRidder, Lawrence Melsen 1919- *WhoSSW 91*
De Riemer, Daniel Louis 1950- *WhoEmL 91, WhoSSW 91*
De Rienzo, William Thomson 1955- *WhoSSW 91*
Derieteanu, George 1918- *IntWWM 90*
DeRiggi, Raymond Joseph 1948- *St&PR 91*
Derijcke, Valeer 1939- *WhoWor 91*
Derin, Greg David 1954- *WhoEmL 91*
Derise, Nellie Louise 1937- *WhoSSW 91*
DeRita, Frank Edward 1952- *WhoE 91*
De Ritter, Lois May *BiDrAPA 89*
Derivan, Albert Thomas 1939- *BiDrAPA 89, WhoE 91*
De Rivas, Carmela F 1920- *BiDrAPA 89*
de Rivas, Carmela Foderaro 1920- *WhoAm 90*
De Rivera, Jose 1904-1985 *WhoAmA 91N*
De Rivera, Jose Antonio Primo 1903-1936 *BioIn 16*
De Rivera, Jose Luis Gonzalez 1944- *BiDrAPA 89*
Derksen, Bob *St&PR 91*
Derlacki, Eugene Lubin 1913- *WhoAm 90*
Derleth, August 1909-1971 *TwCCr&M 91*
Derleth, August William 1909-1971 *AuBYP 90, RGTwCSF*
Derloshon, Jack H. 1929- *St&PR 91*
Derman, Cyrus 1925- *WhoAm 90*
Derman, Robert M 1935- *BiDrAPA 89*
Der Manuelian, Lucy *WhoAmW 91*
DerMarderosian, Diran Robert 1940- *WhoE 91*
Dermer, Stanley Winston 1942- *BiDrAPA 89*
Dermid, Robert Aaron 1951- *WhoSSW 91*
D'Ermilio, Louis 1960- *ODwPR 91*
Derminio, David Erman 1953- *WhoEmL 91*
Dermody, Joseph *BioIn 16, NewYTBS 90*
Dermota, Anton 1910-1989 *AnObit 1989, BioIn 16, PenDiMP*
Dermout, Maria *EncCoWW*
Dermout-Ingerman, Helena Anthonia Maria 1888-1962 *EncCoWW*
Dern, Bruce 1936- *WorAlBi*
Dern, Bruce MacLeish 1936- *WhoAm 90*
Dern, Edouard *PenDiMP*
Dern, F Carl 1936- *WhoAmA 91*
Dern, George Henry 1872-1936 *BiDrUSE 89*
Dern, Laura *BioIn 16*
Dernburg, Ernest Aaron *BiDrAPA 89*
Dernesch, Helga 1939- *IntWWM 90, PenDiMP*
Dernier, Bob 1957- *Ballpl 90*
Dernorsek, Joseph J. 1924- *St&PR 91*
Dernovich, Donald Frederick 1942- *WhoAmA 91*
Dernulc, Leslie Ann 1965- *WhoAmW 91*
Deroanne, Claude Leon 1944- *WhoWor 91*
De Roburt, Hammer 1923- *WhoWor 91*
De Rocco, Andrew Gabriel 1929- *WhoAm 90*
Deroche, E.H. 1947- *St&PR 91*
Deroche, John Walter 1932- *St&PR 91*
DeRoche, Julie Paula 1958- *WhoE 91*
DeRoche, Peter Lavinis *BiDrAPA 89*
De Rochemont, John Frederick 1930- *St&PR 91*
De Rochemont, Louis 1899-1978 *BioIn 16*
de Roe Devon, Marchioness 1934- *WhoAmW 91*
Deroeck, Walter A. 1942- *St&PR 91*
De Roes, Nanda Yvonne 1945- *WhoAm 90*
Deroin, Jeanne 1805-1894 *EncCoWW*
DeRojas, Juan Jose 1954- *WhoE 91*
Derom, Fritz 1927- *WhoWor 91*
Derome, Jacques-Antoine 1696-1760 *PenDiDA 89*
Derome, Jacques Florian 1941- *WhoAm 90*
Derome, Nicholas-Denis 1731-1788 *PenDiDA 89*
de Romilly, Jacqueline 1913- *WhoWor 91*
De Roo, Remi Joseph 1924- *WhoAm 90*
de Rooij, Nicolaas Frans 1951- *WhoWor 91*
de Roquemaurel, Jacques Marie 1937- *WhoWor 91*
de Roquetaillade, Jean *EncO&P 3*
DeRosa, D. William 1945- *WhoE 91*
DeRosa, Dean Arthur 1948- *WhoE 91*
Derosa, Donald John 1943- *St&PR 91*
DeRosa, Joseph Charles 1954- *WhoEmL 91*
DeRosa, Mary Catherine 1952- *WhoAmW 91*
DeRosa, Patti Jean 1946- *WhoAmW 91*
De Rosa, Peter Gerald 1939- *BiDrAPA 89*
de Rosales, Ramona Arrequin *WhoHisp 91*
De Rosas, Juan Manuel Jose Domingo Ortiz 1793-1877 *BioIn 16*
DeRosbil, Andrea Marie 1965- *WhoAmW 91*
DeRose, Katherine Anne 1957- *WhoAmW 91*
De Rose, Louis John 1952- *WhoE 91*
De Rose, Mary Frances 1957- *WhoAmW 91*
De Rose, Peter 1900-1953 *OxCPMus*
De Rose, Peter Louis 1947- *WhoEmL 91*
De Rose, Rose *BioIn 16*
De Rose, Sandra Michele *WhoAmW 91*
DeRose, Umberto Joseph *WhoE 91*
DeRosear, David William 1947- *St&PR 91*
DeRosear, Lori *BiDrAPA 89*
DeRosier, Arthur Henry, Jr. 1931- *WhoAm 90*
Derosier, David John 1939- *WhoAm 90*
Derosier, H. Peter 1934- *St&PR 91*
De Rosis, Edward L 1954- *BiDrAPA 89*
De Rosis, Helen A *BiDrAPA 89*
De Rosis, Heloise E *BiDrAPA 89*
De Rosis, Louis E 1917- *BiDrAPA 89*
De Rothschild, Beatrice *BioIn 16*
De Rothschild, Donna Maria Beatrice *BioIn 16*
De Rothschild, Dorothy *BioIn 16*
De Rothschild, Eric *BioIn 16*
De Rothschild, Evelyn 1931- *WhoWor 91*
de Rothschild, Guy 1909- *ConAu 129*
De Rothschild, Marie-Helene *BioIn 16*
De Rothschild, Olimpia *BioIn 16*
Deroubaix, Jeanne 1927- *IntWWM 90*
Derouin, Raymond E. 1937- *St&PR 91*
Deroulede, Paul 1846-1914 *BiDFrPL*
Derounian, Steven Boghos 1918- *WhoAm 90*
De Rousse, Louis Theodore 1844-1921 *AmLegL*
de Routisie, Albert *MajTwCW*
De Rouvray, Bernard 1922- *WhoWor 91*
Deroux, Daniel Edward 1951- *WhoAmA 91*
Derow, Peter Alfred 1940- *WhoAm 90*
Derpinghaus, Patrick James 1955- *WhoEmL 91*
Derr, Amandus John 1949- *WhoE 91*
Derr, Harold James, Jr. 1927- *St&PR 91*
Derr, Jack 1927- *St&PR 91*
Derr, James Thomas 1958- *WhoE 91*
Derr, John Frederick 1936- *St&PR 91*
Derr, Joy Reese 1941- *WhoAmW 91*
Derr, Kenneth T. *WhoAm 90, WhoWor 91*
Derr, Kenneth Tindall 1936- *St&PR 91*
Derr, Lee E. 1948- *WhoEmL 91*
Derr, Mark David 1951- *WhoEmL 91*
Derr, Mark Edward 1960- *WhoE 91*
Derr, Richard Edward 1933- *WhoAm 90*
Derr, Robert A., II 1946- *St&PR 91*
Derr, Russell F. 1942- *WhoSSW 91*
Derr, Teresa Marie 1953- *WhoAmW 91*
Derr, Thomas Burchard 1929- *WhoWor 91*
Derr, Thomas Sieger 1931- *WhoWor 91*
Derr, Vernon Ellsworth 1921- *WhoAm 90*
Derrenberger, John Paul 1945- *WhoSSW 91*
Derrenger, William Harry 1941- *WhoE 91*
Derrey, Robert Fairbairn 1931- *St&PR 91*
Derrick, Butler 1936- *BioIn 16*
Derrick, Butler Carson, Jr. 1936- *WhoAm 90, WhoSSW 91*
Derrick, Charles Warren, Jr. 1935- *WhoAm 90*
Derrick, Gary Wayne 1953- *WhoEmL 91*
Derrick, Homer 1906- *WhoSSW 91*
Derrick, Jack Holley 1947- *WhoEmL 91*
Derrick, John Edward 1930- *St&PR 91*
Derrick, John M., Jr. 1940- *St&PR 91*
Derrick, Malcolm 1933- *WhoAm 90*
Derrick, Michael Lionel 1957- *WhoEmL 91*
Derrick, Robert Parker 1931- *WhoAm 90*
Derrick-White, Elizabeth 1940- *WhoAmW 91*
Derricks, Cleavant *DrBlPA 90*
Derrickson, Steve Bruce 1952- *WhoAmA 91*
Derrickson, William Borden 1940- *St&PR 91, WhoAm 90, WhoWor 91*
D'Errico, Edward Peter 1951- *WhoE 91*
Derricotte, Toi 1941- *ConAu 32NR*
Derricotte, Toi M. 1941- *WhoWrEP 89*
Derrida, Jacques *BioIn 16*
Derrig, Andrea Marie 1953- *WhoEmL 91*
Derrig, Leslie Anne 1951- *WhoAmW 91*
Derringer, Carol Ventresca 1945- *WhoEmL 91*
Derringer, Paul 1906-1988 *Ballpl 90 [port]*

Derringer, Rick 1949- EncPR&S 89
Derringer, Steele WhoWrEP 89
Derrough, Lee A. 1944- St&PR 91
Derrough, Neil E. 1936- WhoAm 90
Derrow, David D. 1923- St&PR 91
Derry, R. Michael 1937- St&PR 91
Derry, Ronald L. St&PR 91
Derryberry, Andy Lynn 1952- WhoEmL 91
Derryberry, Phillip Eugene 1952- St&PR 91
Dersch, John 1923- St&PR 91
Dersch, Thomas Mark 1957- St&PR 91
Dersh, Rhoda E. 1934- WhoAmW 91, WhoE 91, WhoWor 91
Dershowitz, Alan Morton 1938- WhoAm 90
Dersonnes, Jacques ConAu 129, MajTwCW
Dertel, John N. 1943- St&PR 91
Derthick, Martha Ann 1933- WhoAm 90
Dertien, Donald Charles 1936- WhoWor 91
Dertien, James LeRoy 1942- WhoAm 90
DeRubertis, Patricia Sandra 1950- WhoAmW 91, WhoEmL 91
Derucher, Kenneth Noel 1949- WhoE 91, WhoWor 91
de Ruiter, Johan Lourens 1957- WhoWor 91
DeRuiter, Peter Louis BiDrAPA 89
Derujinsky, Gleb W 1888-1975 WhoAmA 91N
Derunov, Konstantin Nikolaevich 1866-1929 BioIn 16
De Rupecissa, Johannes EncO&P 3
Derus, Patricia Irene 1947- WhoAmW 91
Derus, Stephen J. 1943- St&PR 91
Derusha, Gerald F. 1937- St&PR 91
Derusha, William Charles 1950- St&PR 91
De Ruth, Jan 1922- WhoAmA 91
DeRuth, Jan 1922- WhoE 91
De Ruyter, Adrianus Julius 1954- BiDrAPA 89
deRuyter, Carol 1948- WhoAmW 91
Dervaes, Claudine Lucienne 1954- WhoEmL 91
Dervan, Edward Cunningham 1947- St&PR 91
Dervan, Peter Anthony 1945- WhoWor 91
Dervan, Peter Brendan 1945- WhoAm 90
Dervaux, Pierre 1917- IntWWM 90, PenDiMP
Dervin, Brenda Louise 1938- WhoAm 90
Derwin, Jordan 1931- WhoE 91, WhoWor 91
Derwinski, Edward J. BioIn 16
Derwinski, Edward Joseph 1926- BiDrUSE 89, WhoAm 90, WhoE 91, WhoWor 91
Dery, Peter Poreku 1918?- BioIn 16
de Rycke, Laurence Joseph 1907-1989 ConAu 129
De Rycke, Paul H. 1938- WhoWor 91
Der Yeghiayan, Garbis H. 1949- WhoWor 91
Der-Yeghiayan, Samuel 1952- WhoEmL 91
Derzai, Matthew 1928- WhoWor 91
Derzon, Gordon M. 1934- WhoAm 90
Derzon, Robert Alan 1930- WhoAm 90
Desa-Matos, Marta Teresa 1950- WhoEmL 91
De Sa Pereira, Elisabeth A V BiDrAPA 89
de Saavedra, Ruben NewYTBS 90
De Sabata, Victor 1892-1967 PenDiMP
De Sabran, Eleonore 1750- BioIn 16
Desafey, Thomas 1930- St&PR 91
De Sagun, Manuel Biscocho 1945- BiDrAPA 89
De Sahagun, Bernardino BioIn 16
Desai, Amit B 1953- BiDrAPA 89
Desai, Amita S BiDrAPA 89
Desai, Amrit 1932- NewAgE 90
Desai, Angeline C N BiDrAPA 89
Desai, Anita 1937- BioIn 16, ConAu 33NR, FemiCLE, MajTwCW, SmATA 63 [port]
Desai, Barin G BiDrAPA 89
Desai, Barin G. 1933- WhoE 91
Desai, Bipin Manmarlal BiDrAPA 89
Desai, Cawas Jal 1938- St&PR 91, WhoE 91
Desai, Chandrakant S. 1936- WhoAm 90
Desai, Devanshu Dolatrai BiDrAPA 89
Desai, Dinkar H BiDrAPA 89
Desai, Geeta BiDrAPA 89
Desai, Jagdish I 1940- BiDrAPA 89
Desai, Jitendra S BiDrAPA 89
Desai, Kiran A. 1948- WhoEmL 91
Desai, Mahesh R 1957- BiDrAPA 89
Desai, Manikant V BiDrAPA 89
Desai, Maya Gautam 1946- BiDrAPA 89
Desai, Meghnad C. 1952- BiDrAPA 89
Desai, Meghnad Jagdischandra 1940- WhoWor 91
Desai, Morarji 1896- WorAlBi
Desai, Mukesh Indubhai 1954- BiDrAPA 89
Desai, Naresh Nanubhai 1953- WhoWor 91
Desai, Pradipkumar BiDrAPA 89
Desai, Praful C 1948- BiDrAPA 89
Desai, Prakash N BiDrAPA 89
Desai, Rajesh B BiDrAPA 89
Desai, Rohit Mojilal 1938- WhoE 91
Desai, Sangita Chetan BiDrAPA 89
Desai, Shrivatsa Pandurangrao 1946- WhoWor 91
Desai, Sreenivasa R 1939- BiDrAPA 89
Desai, Sudha Manubhai 1936- BiDrAPA 89
Desai, Suresh P 1945- BiDrAPA 89
Desai, Sureshchandra BiDrAPA 89
Desai, Vajendra J BiDrAPA 89
Desai-Vaidya, Devyani Nainan 1957- BiDrAPA 89
De Saint Phalle, Francois 1946- St&PR 91
De Saint-Phalle, Niki BioIn 16
De Saint Phalle, Therese 1930- WhoWrEP 89
de Saint Phalle, Thibaut 1918- WhoAm 90
de Saint Roman, Arnaud MajTwCW
de Sainte Marie d'Agneaux, Christian F. 1957- WhoWor 91
Desaloms, Armando 1938- BiDrAPA 89
De Salva, Salvatore Joseph 1924- WhoAm 90, WhoWor 91
DeSalvo, Deborah Lynn 1954- WhoAmW 91
De Sam Lazaro, Alda Margarida BiDrAPA 89
De Sampaio Godoy, Solange 1940- WhoWor 91
Desan, Wilfrid WhoAm 90
De San Martin, Jose 1778?-1850 BioIn 16
DeSana, Jimmy 1949-1990 NewYTBS 90
DeSanctis, Roman William 1930- WhoAm 90
De Sanctis, Vincent Joseph 1926- St&PR 91
de Santa Ana, Julio 1934- ConAu 132
De Santa Anna, Antonio Lopez 1794?-1876 BioIn 16
Desante, William F. 1955- St&PR 91
Desanti, Carole J. 1958- St&PR 91
DeSanti, Frederick D. 1950- St&PR 91
DeSantis, Camille Ann 1961- WhoAmW 91
DeSantis, Daniel Louis 1931- WhoAm 90
De Santis, F. A. 1946- WhoAm 90
DeSantis, Francesco 1901-1984 BioIn 16
DeSantis, Gerald F. St&PR 91
DeSantis, James R. ODwPR 91
DeSantis, James Robert 1944- WhoE 91
De Santis, Joe 1909-1989 BioIn 16
DeSantis, Judith Marian 1956- WhoEmL 91
De Santis, Larry 1929- WhoAm 90
DeSantis, Louis Alexander 1948- WhoE 91
De Santis, Mary Ann Theresa 1938- WhoAmW 91
DeSantis, Nunzio P. 1951- St&PR 91
De Santis, Vincent Paul 1916- WhoAm 90
De Santis, Vincent Paul 1947- BiDrAPA 89
De Santo, Donald James 1942- WhoE 91
DeSanto, Gerarda Marie 1955- WhoAmW 91
De Santo, Stephen C 1951- WhoAmA 91
de Santos, Robin King 1958- WhoEmL 91
Desanty, James R. 1934- St&PR 91
DeSapio, Gerard Joseph 1954- WhoEmL 91
De Saram, Rohan 1939- IntWWM 90, PenDiMP
De Sarasate, Pablo PenDiMP
DeSassure, Charles 1961- WhoEmL 91
Desaulniers DcCanB 12
Desaulniers, Andre 1941- St&PR 91
Desaulniers, Gonzalve 1863-1934 DcLB 92
Desaulniers, Lorraine 1941- St&PR 91
Desaulniers, Marc Joseph 1951- WhoEmL 91
Desaulniers, Yvon J. 1936- St&PR 91
Desautelle, William Peter 1939- St&PR 91, WhoAm 90
Desautels, Anne Catherine 1956- WhoEmL 91
Desautels, Claude 1941- St&PR 91
Desautels, Gene 1907- Ballpl 90
Desautels, Rene BiDrAPA 89
De Sautuola, Maria 1870-1946 BioIn 16
De Sayn-Wittgenstein, Carolyne 1819-1887 BioIn 16
Desbarats, George-Edouard 1838-1893 DcCanB 12
Desbarats, Peter Hullett 1933- WhoAm 90
Desberg, Daniel 1925- WhoSSW 91
Des Bois, Louis Cameron 1931- St&PR 91
Desbordes-Valmore, Marceline Felicite J 1786-1859 EncCoWW
Desbrandes, Robert 1924- WhoAm 90, WhoWor 91
DesBrisay, Mather Byles 1828-1900 DcCanB 12
Desbruyeres, Daniel Marie 1945- WhoWor 91
Descalzi, Guillermo 1947- WhoHisp 91
Descamps, Eugene Paul 1922- BiDFrPL
Descamps, Johan Jozef Arthur 1951- WhoWor 91
Descarpentries, Jean-Marie BioIn 16
Descartes, Rene 1596-1650 BioIn 16, WorAlBi, WrPh P
Desch, Carl William 1915- WhoAm 90
Desch, Mary Margaret BiDrAPA 89
Desch, Robert T. 1945- St&PR 91
Desch, Theodore Edward 1931- WhoAm 90
Deschaine, Barbara Ralph 1930- WhoAmW 91
De Schamphelaere, Lucien 1931- WhoWor 91
Deschamps, Francois WhoAmA 91
Deschamps, Gary W. 1951- WhoEmL 91
Des Champs, Nicholas Howard 1937- St&PR 91
Deschamps, Yvon 1935- OxCCanT
Deschanel, Caleb 1944- ConTFT 8, WhoAm 90
Deschanel, Paul Eugene Louis 1855-1922 BiDFrPL
Desche, Pierre Maurice 1936- WhoWor 91
Deschenes, Bruno 1955- IntWWM 90
Deschenes, Denise BiDrAPA 89
Deschenes, Georges-Honore 1841-1892 DcCanB 12
Deschenes, Marcelle IntWWM 90
Deschevaux-Dumesnil, Suzanne BioIn 16
Deschillie, Mamie 1920- MusmAFA
Deschner, Eleanor Elizabeth 1928- WhoE 91
De Schryver, Frans Carl 1939- WhoWor 91
DeSchutter, Richard U. 1940- WhoAm 90
De Schweinitz, Karl 1887-1956 AuBYP 90
Descoteaux, Carol J. 1948- WhoAmW 91
D'Escoto, Miguel 1933- WhoWor 91
Desderi, Claudio 1945- IntWWM 90
Desdier, Steven Ross 1952- WhoEmL 91
de Seguin des Hons, Luc Donald 1919- WhoWor 91
de Selding, Edward Bertrand 1926- WhoAm 90
DeSena, Alphonse Thomas 1947- WhoAm 90, WhoE 91
Desens, Richard Emil 1941- St&PR 91
De Senti, C. Mildred 1917- St&PR 91
De Senti, William L. 1916- St&PR 91
De Serigny, Eugenia BioIn 16
de Serres, Frederick Joseph 1929- WhoAm 90
Deserres, Roger 1914- St&PR 91
Desert Rose Band ConMus 4 [port]
Desert Rose Band, The WhoNeCM [port]
Desert, Alexis-Jaime W. 1961- WhoE 91
Deserti, Luigi 1915- WhoWor 91
Desertis, V.C. EncO&P 3
DeSesa, Michael Anthony 1927- WhoAm 90
DeSeta, Donna BioIn 16
Desforges, Bruno 1925- St&PR 91
Desforges, Jane Fay 1921- WhoAm 90
Desgranges, Louis 1944- BiDrAPA 89
des Granges, Maino 1918- WhoWor 91
Deshaies, Jim 1960- Ballpl 90
Deshaies, Kenneth Joseph 1946- WhoEmL 91
De Shalit-Agmon, Nechama BiDrAPA 89
De Shane, William Wesley 1938- St&PR 91
DeShaney, Melody BioIn 16
De Shazor, Ashley Dunn 1919- WhoAm 90
Desherow, James Dartmouth 1940- St&PR 91
DeShetler, Kenneth Edward 1928- St&PR 91, WhoAm 90
Deshields, Teresa Leigh 1959- WhoAmW 91
DeShong, Jimmie 1909- Ballpl 90
Deshotels, James Michael 1956- WhoE 91
Deshoulieres, Antoinette du Ligier 1634?-1694 EncCoWW
Deshpande, Rohit 1951- WhoE 91, WhoEmL 91
Deshpande, Shashi FemiCLE
DeSiano, Francis P 1945- ConAu 31NR
De Sica, Vittorio 1901-1974 WorAlBi
Desiderio Da Settignano 1428?-1464? IntDcAA 90
Desiderio, Anthony Joseph 1936- St&PR 91
Desiderio, Dominic Morse, Jr. 1941- WhoAm 90
Desiderio, Robert BioIn 16
Desiderio, Vincent 1955- WhoAmA 91
De Sieghardt, Frederick Otto 1925- St&PR 91
Desieno, John Anthony 1949- WhoEmL 91
Desikan, Gita BiDrAPA 89
Desilets, Pierre Andre 1961- WhoE 91
De Silva, Bernard 1939- BiDrAPA 89
de Silva, Colin WhoAm 90
De Silva, Colvin R. BioIn 16
De Silva, Constance P BiDrAPA 89
De Silva, Herbert Poshitha Janaka 1944- WhoWor 91
De Silva, Himasiri BiDrAPA 89
De Silva, Nihal 1944- BiDrAPA 89
De Silva, Oliver Ivan Peter 1946- WhoWor 91
De Silva, Priyani M BiDrAPA 89
De Silva, S Paul BiDrAPA 89
De Silva, Sriyawathie May BiDrAPA 89
De Silverio, Robert V BiDrAPA 89
Desimone, Angie DiFerdinando BioIn 16
Desimone, Anthony Vincent 1937- St&PR 91
De Simone, Daniel V. 1932- WhoAm 90
De Simone, Donna Marie BiDrAPA 89
deSimone, Jack 1920- ODwPR 91
DeSimone, Jack A. 1920- St&PR 91
De Simone, James William 1932- St&PR 91
DeSimone, Livio Diego 1936- St&PR 91
De Simone, Livio Diego 1936- WhoAm 90
Desimone, Robert A. IntWWM 90
DeSimone, Rory Jean 1941- WhoAmW 91
De Simone, V Theresa 1927- BiDrAPA 89
DeSimone, Vincent BioIn 16
Desind, Philip 1910- WhoAmA 91, WhoE 91, WhoWor 91
Desing, Donald Edward 1926- St&PR 91
De Sio, Anthony W. 1930- St&PR 91
De Sio, Robert J. 1934- St&PR 91
De Sipio, George 1925- WhoAm 90
Desir, Bertholet BiDrAPA 89
Desir, Harlem 1959- BioIn 16
Desir, Nicolina M 1912- BiDrAPA 89
De Sismondi, Jean Charles Leonard S 1773-1842 BioIn 16
DeSisto, Elizabeth Agnes 1954- WhoAmW 91
Desjardins, Andre Luc 1955- IntWWM 90
DesJardins, Charles Francis 1931- WhoE 91
DesJardins, Charles Raymond 1936- WhoE 91
Desjardins, Christopher John 1948- St&PR 91
Des Jardins, John Rolph 1932- St&PR 91
Desjardins, Marie-Catherine EncCoWW
Desjardins, Marie Catherine Hortense 1632-1683 FemiCLE
Desjardins, Raoul 1933- WhoAm 90, WhoWor 91
Desjardins, Robert James 1937- St&PR 91
Des Jarlais, David Conway 1948- BiDrAPA 89
Desjarlais, Erika Else 1934- WhoAmW 91
Desjarlais, John Joseph 1953- WhoEmL 91
Desjarlait, Robert D 1946- WhoAmA 91
Deskey, Donald BioIn 16
Deskey, Donald 1894- ConDes 90, PenDiDA 89
Deskey, Donald 1894-1989 AnObit 1989
Deskins, Wilbur Eugene 1927- WhoAm 90
Deskur, Andrzej Maria 1924- WhoWor 91
Desloge, Edward Augustine 1926- WhoAm 90
Desloge, George Burdeau 1924- St&PR 91
Desloge, Louis, Jr. 1922- St&PR 91
Desloge, Taylor S. 1921- St&PR 91
Desloge, Theodore P., Jr. 1939- St&PR 91
Deslongchamps, Pierre 1938- WhoAm 90
Deslys, Gaby 1883-1920 OxCPMus
Desmarais, Charles Joseph 1949- WhoAm 90, WhoAmA 91
Desmarais, Gilles M BiDrAPA 89
Des Marais, Louise Mercier 1923- WhoE 91, WhoWrEP 89
Desmarais, Maurice Andrew 1946- WhoE 91
Des Marais, Paul 1920- IntWWM 90
Desmarais, Paul 1927- WhoAm 90
Desmarais, Paul Guy 1927- St&PR 91
Des Marais, Pierre, II 1934- St&PR 91, WhoAm 90
Desmarecaux, Philippe WhoE 91
Desmarescaux, Philippe 1938- WhoAm 90, WhoWor 91
DesMarteau, Darryl Dwayne 1940- WhoAm 90
De Smet, Gilbert A.R. 1921- WhoWor 91
De Smet, Lorraine 1928- WhoAmA 91
De Smet, Pierre Jean 1801-1873 WhNaAH
De Smet, Raoul C. R. 1936- IntWWM 90
De Smet, Robin John 1935- IntWWM 90
de Smidt, Marc 1941- WhoWor 91
DeSmidt, Robert J. 1947- St&PR 91
Desmidt, Thomas H 1944- WhoAmA 91
De Smit, Bart N W 1930- BiDrAPA 89
De Smith, Rod 1925- St&PR 91
Desmond, Adrian J. 1947- BioIn 16
Desmond, Alice 1897- AuBYP 90
Desmond, Alice Curtis 1897- WhoAm 90
Desmond, Astra 1893-1973 PenDiMP
Desmond, Daniel Joseph 1942- St&PR 91
Desmond, Florence 1907- OxCPMus

Desmond, Gary Christopher 1948- *IntWWM 90*
Desmond, Gerald *EncO&P 3*
Desmond, John Jacob 1922- *WhoAm 90*
Desmond, John S. 1944- *St&PR 91*
Desmond, Johnny 1920-1985 *OxCPMus*
Desmond, Kathleen Mae 1940- *WhoAmW 91*, *WhoSSW 91*
Desmond, Mae 1887-1982 *BioIn 16*, *NotWoAT*
Desmond, Mark L. 1958- *St&PR 91*
Desmond, Patricia Ann 1956- *WhoE 91*
Desmond, Paul 1924-1977 *BioIn 16*, *OxCPMus*, *WorAlBi*
Desmond, Richard L. 1937- *St&PR 91*
Desmond, Richard Michael 1934- *St&PR 91*
Desmond, Robert Edward 1954- *BiDrAPA 89*
Desmond, Shaw 1877-1960 *EncO&P 3*
Desmond, Thomas Edward 1931- *St&PR 91*
Desmond, Walter Thomas, Jr. 1953- *WhoWrEP 89*
Desmono, John R. *St&PR 91*
De Smul, Pierre Hector 1959- *WhoEmL 91*
Desnick, Robert John 1943- *WhoAm 90*, *WhoE 91*
Desnoes, Peter Blaise *BioIn 16*
Desoer, Charles Auguste 1926- *WhoAm 90*
de Soet, J. F. A. *WhoAm 90*, *WhoE 91*
De Sofi, Oliver Julius 1929- *WhoSSW 91*, *WhoWor 91*
De Sola, Isabella Miriam 1955- *WhoAmW 91*
De Sola, Ralph 1908- *WhoAm 90*, *WhoWor 91*
De Sole, Daniel E *BiDrAPA 89*
De Solis, Frank W. 1950- *St&PR 91*
de Solminihac, Marc Carleton 1955- *BiDrAPA 89*
DeSomogyi, Aileen Ada 1911- *WhoAmW 91*, *WhoE 91*, *WhoWor 91*
De Sonneville-David, Therese 1938-1988 *BioIn 16*
DeSoo, F. Kenneth 1931- *St&PR 91*
D'Esopo, Donato Anthony 1897-1989 *BioIn 16*
Desor, Jeannette Ann 1942- *WhoAmW 91*
Desormeaux, Kent 1970- *News 90 [port]*
Desormier-Cartwright, Anne Maria 1959- *WhoSSW 91*
Desormiere, Roger 1898-1963 *PenDiMP*
de Soto, Alvaro 1943- *WhoWor 91*
Desoto, Clinton Burgel 1931- *WhoAm 90*, *WhoE 91*
De Soto, Danilo Arquimedes 1963- *BiDrAPA 89*
DeSoto, Ernest 1954- *WhoHisp 91*
De Soto, Hector 1951- *WhoHisp 91*
De Soto, Hernando *BioIn 16*
De Soto, Hernando 1496?-1542 *WhNaAH*
De Soto, Hernando 1498?-1542 *EncCRAm*
De Soto, Hernando 1499?-1542 *WorAlBi*
De Soto, Hernando 1500?-1542 *BioIn 16*
Desoto, Lewis D 1954- *WhoAmA 91*
Desoto, Mateo F *BiDrAPA 89*
DeSoto, Pete 1939- *St&PR 91*
Desoto, Rafael M *WhoAmA 91*
De Soto, Rosana *WhoHisp 91*
de Soto, Simon 1925- *WhoAm 90*
Desouky, Abdellatif M 1943- *BiDrAPA 89*
De Sousa, Alan *BiDrAPA 89*
Desousa, Dhanalakshmi A *BiDrAPA 89*
De Sousa, Dudley Joseph 1926- *St&PR 91*
DeSousa, Karen Evans *WhoAmW 91*
De Sousa, Maria Joao Leal *BioIn 16*
De Sousa, Paulo Teixeira 1947- *WhoEmL 91*
De Sousa Mendes, Aristides 1885-1954 *BioIn 16*
De Souter, Paul Dominique Desire 1944- *WhoWor 91*
De Souza, Alwyn Arthur 1933- *St&PR 91*
De Souza, Anthony Robert 1943- *WhoE 91*
Desouza, Cherilyn Martha *BiDrAPA 89*
De Souza, Ralph *PenDiMP*
De Soysa, K.V. Srimathie Florence 1946- *WhoWor 91*
D'Espagnet, Jean *EncO&P 3*
DeSpain, Sara Ellen 1949- *WhoEmL 91*
Despard, Charlotte 1844-1939 *FemiCLE*
Despard, Rosina Clara 1863- *EncPaPR 91*
Despenser, Rachel Fanny Antonina 1773-1829 *FemiCLE*
D'Esperance, Elizabeth 1855-1919 *EncO&P 3*, *EncPaPR 91*
Desphy, Jupiter Aranza, Jr. 1951- *WhoEmL 91*
Despommier, Dickson Donald 1940- *WhoAm 90*
Desportes, Ulysse Gandvier 1920- *WhoAmA 91*
Despres, Gina Helen 1941- *WhoAmW 91*
Despres, Jean 1903-1988 *BioIn 16*
Despres, Leo Arthur 1932- *WhoAm 90*
Despres, Leon Mathis 1908- *WhoAm 90*
Despres, Robert 1924- *WhoAm 90*
Despres, Robert Leon 1940- *WhoE 91*
Despres, Stephen *BioIn 16*
Des Pres, Terrence 1939-1987 *BioIn 16*
Desrenmaulx, Wuillaume *PenDiDA 89*
des Rioux, Deena Victoria Coty 1941- *WhoAm 90*
Desroche, Jerold J. 1937- *St&PR 91*
DesRochers, Gerard Camille 1922- *WhoE 91*, *WhoWor 91*
Desrochers, L. 1941- *St&PR 91*
Desrochers, L. S. *WhoAm 90*
Desrochers, Paul Emile 1929- *BiDrAPA 89*
Des Roches, Antoine 1924- *WhoAm 90*
Des Roches, Benoit Phillippe *BiDrAPA 89*
DesRoches, Diane Blanche 1947- *WhoAmW 91*, *WhoEmL 91*
DesRosiers, Roger I. 1935- *WhoAm 90*
Dessalines, Jean Jacques 1758-1806 *BioIn 16*
Dessar, Louis Paul 1867-1952 *WhoAmA 91N*
Dessart, Donald Joseph 1928- *WhoAm 90*
Dessaso, Deborah Ann 1952- *WhoAmW 91*
Dessau, Ingrid 1923- *ConDes 90*
Dessau, Randy Scot 1959- *WhoEmL 91*
Dessauer, Carin 1963- *WhoAmW 91*
Dessauer, Herbert Clay 1921- *WhoAm 90*
Dessauer, John Hans 1905- *WhoAm 90*, *WhoWor 91*
Dessauer, John Phillip 1936- *WhoE 91*
Dessauer, Rolf 1926- *WhoE 91*
Dessaulles, Louis-Antoine 1818-1895 *DcCanB 12*
Dessaulles, Louis-Antoine 1819-1895 *DcLB 99 [port]*
Dessaur, Catharina Irma 1931- *EncCoWW*
Dessel, Arnold M. 1921- *St&PR 91*
Dessel, Arnold Martin 1921- *WhoE 91*
Desselberger, Ulrich 1937- *WhoWor 91*
Dessem, R. Lawrence 1951- *WhoEmL 91*
Dessemontet, Francois Olivier Arnaud 1948- *WhoWor 91*
Dessen, Edgar Lee 1917- *St&PR 91*
Dessen, Stanley B. 1938- *St&PR 91*
Dessen, Stanley Benjamin 1938- *WhoAm 90*, *WhoWor 91*
Desser, Maxwell Milton *WhoAm 90*, *WhoAmA 91*, *WhoE 91*
Dessert, Lynn Marie 1960- *WhoAmW 91*
Dessibourg, Paul *BioIn 16*
Dessin, Carolyn Louise 1957- *WhoEmL 91*
Dessing, Paulus Jacobus 1945- *WhoWor 91*
Dessler, Alexander Jack 1928- *WhoAm 90*
Dessner, Murray 1934- *WhoAmA 91*
Dessoir, Max 1867-1947 *EncO&P 3*, *EncPaPR 91*
Dessonville, Loren Edward 1953- *WhoEmL 91*
Dessy, Blane Kent 1951- *WhoAm 90*
De St. Vrain, Ceran de Hault de Lassus 1802-1870 *BioIn 16*
De Staebler, Stephen 1933- *BioIn 16*
DeStaebler, Stephen 1933- *BioIn 16*
De Stael, Nicolas 1914-1955 *BioIn 16*, *IntDcAA 90*
de Stains, Ian 1948- *WhoWor 91*
D'Este, Mary Ernestine 1941- *WhoAmW 91*
De Stefani, Livia 1913- *EncCoWW*
Destefano, Daniel Michael 1941- *BiDrAPA 89*
DeStefano, John J. 1932- *St&PR 91*
DeStefano, Michael Thomas 1946- *St&PR 91*
DeStefano, Steven 1960- *WhoEmL 91*
Destefano, Thomas 1945- *WhoE 91*
De Stena, A.V. 1932- *St&PR 91*
deStevens, George 1924- *WhoAm 90*
Destine, Jean-Leon 1928- *DrBIPA 90*
Destinn, Emmy 1878-1930 *PenDiMP*
Destino, Ralph, Jr. 1936- *WhoAm 90*
Destler, I. Mac 1939- *WhoAm 90*
Destouches, Louis-Ferdinand 1894-1961 *MajTwCW*
Destounis, Nicholas 1927- *BiDrAPA 89*
D'Estrube, Pierre F 1923- *BiDrAPA 89*
de Stwolinski, Gail Rounce Boyd 1921- *WhoAm 90*
De Sucre, Antonio Jose 1795-1830 *BioIn 16*
de Suze, Jacques Christophe 1944- *WhoSSW 91*
Desy, Luc O. *St&PR 91*
Desylva, B. G. 1895-1950 *WorAlBi*
DeSylva, Buddy 1895-1950 *OxCPMus*
de Takacsy, Nicholas Benedict 1939- *WhoAm 90*
DeTar, DeLos F. 1920- *WhoSSW 91*
deTarnowsky, Nixon 1913- *WhoE 91*
De Tata, Juan C 1932- *BiDrAPA 89*
DeTata, Richard Anthony 1931- *St&PR 91*
Detben, John Peter 1939- *St&PR 91*
De Tejada, Sebastian Lerdo 1823-1889 *BioIn 16*
Detels, Roger 1936- *WhoAm 90*
Deter, Francis Harvey, Jr. 1936- *WhoE 91*
Deter, Robert Edward 1944- *St&PR 91*
Deterding, James Martin 1928- *St&PR 91*
Deterding, Mark Walter 1959- *St&PR 91*, *WhoEmL 91*
Deterling, Ralph Alden, Jr. 1917- *WhoAm 90*
Determan, James R. 1934- *St&PR 91*
Determan, John David 1933- *WhoAm 90*
Deters, James Raymond 1937- *WhoAm 90*, *St&PR 91*
de Terson, Suzon 1657-1685 *EncCoWW*
Detert, Yvonne Lembi- *BioIn 16*
Detert-Moriarty, Judith Anne 1952- *WhoAmW 91*, *WhoEmL 91*
Dethero, J. Hambright 1932- *WhoAm 90*
Dethier, Vincent Gaston 1915- *WhoAm 90*
Dethlefsen, George Russell, Jr. 1948- *St&PR 91*
Dethloff, Henry Clay 1934- *WhoAm 90*
De Thomas, Antonio, Jr. *BiDrAPA 89*
DeThomasis, Louis 1940- *WhoAm 90*
DeThorne, Jacquelyn Marie 1957- *WhoAmW 91*
de Thurah, Thomas 1963- *WhoWor 91*
Dethy, Ray Charles 1928- *WhoAm 90*
de Tirtoff, Romain 1892-1990 *ConAu 131*
De Tivoli, Serafino 1826-1892 *BioIn 16*
Detjen, James Thomas 1948- *WhoE 91*
Detkos, George J. 1934- *St&PR 91*
Detlefs, Richard Lyle 1950- *WhoSSW 91*
Detlefsen, Guy-Robert 1919- *WhoAm 90*
Detman, Art, Jr. 1938- *ODwPR 91*
Detmar-Pines, Gina Louise 1949- *WhoAmW 91*, *WhoE 91*, *WhoEmL 91*
Detmer, Don Eugene 1939- *WhoAm 90*
Detmers, Maruschka *BioIn 16*
Detmers, William Raymond 1942- *WhoAmA 91*
De Tocqueville, Alexis *BioIn 16*
de Toledano, Ralph *ConAu 31NR*
de Toledo, Catherine Holt 1954- *WhoAmW 91*
Detolve, Ethel June *St&PR 91*
De Tommasi, Anthony John 1937- *BiDrAPA 89*
de Tonnancour, Paul Roger Godefroy 1926- *WhoAm 90*
De Tonquedec, Joseph 1868-1962 *EncO&P 3*
De Tore, John E 1902-1975 *WhoAmA 91N*
de Tornyay, Rheba 1926- *WhoAm 90*, *WhoAmW 91*
de Torres, Manuel *WhoHisp 91*
DeTorres, Manuel Ramon 1924- *St&PR 91*
De Toth, Andre *BioIn 16*
Detra, Ralph William 1925- *St&PR 91*, *WhoAm 90*, *WhoE 91*
Detrano, John Michael 1927- *WhoE 91*
Detre, Katherine Maria 1926- *WhoAm 90*
Detre, Thomas 1924- *WhoAm 90*
Detre, Thomas P 1924- *BiDrAPA 89*
De Treaux, Tamara *NewYTBS 90*
deTreville, Robert Treat Paine 1925- *WhoSSW 91*
De Trevino, Elizabeth Borton 1904- *BioIn 16*
Detrez, Conrad 1937-1985 *ConAu 132*
Detrich, Tamas *BioIn 16*
Detrick, Richard William 1933- *St&PR 91*
Detrick, Thomas H. 1934- *St&PR 91*
Detrinis, Robert Benedict 1952- *BiDrAPA 89*
DeTroye, Jeff Eliot 1955- *WhoSSW 91*
Detsch, Donald D. 1947- *WhoEmL 91*
de T'serclaes, Jacques-Etienne de 1947- *WhoWor 91*
Dett, R Nathaniel 1882-1943 *DcAfAmP*
Dett, Robert Nathaniel 1882-1943 *DrBIPA 90*
Dettbarn, Wolf-Dietrich 1928- *WhoAm 90*
Dette, Walter *BioIn 16*
Dettelbach, Iona Schaffer 1935- *WhoAmW 91*
Detter, Brian R. *ODwPR 91*
Detter, Marshall Lee 1932- *St&PR 91*
Dettinger, Garth Bryant 1921- *WhoAm 90*
Dettinger, Warren W. 1954- *St&PR 91*
Dettinger, Warren Walter 1954- *WhoEmL 91*
Dettlaff, Theodore H. 1930- *St&PR 91*
Dettmann, Terry Robert 1947- *WhoEmL 91*
Dettmer, Robert G. 1919- *St&PR 91*
Dettmer, Robert G. 1931- *St&PR 91*
Dettmer, Robert Gerhart 1931- *WhoAm 90*
Dettmer, Scott Charles 1957- *WhoEmL 91*
Dettmering, William O'Neal, Jr. 1948- *WhoEmL 91*
Dettore, Raymond James 1943- *St&PR 91*
Dettore, Tom 1947- *Ballpl 90*
Dettore, Ugo 1905- *EncPaPR 91*
Detuno, Joseph Edward 1931- *WhoAm 90*
De Turczynowicz, Wanda 1908- *WhoAmA 91*
DeTurk, Deborah Suzanne 1953- *WhoAmW 91*
DeTurk, Frederick Walter 1928- *St&PR 91*
De Turk, Frederick Walter 1928- *WhoAm 90*
DeTurk, Pamela Elizabeth 1946- *WhoEmL 91*
De Turner, Clorinda Matto 1852-1909 *BioIn 16*
Detweiler, David Kenneth 1919- *WhoAm 90*
Detweiler, Marie Louise 1934- *WhoAmW 91*
Detweiler, Meade David 1920- *St&PR 91*
Detweiler, Robert Chester 1938- *WhoAm 90*
Detweiler, Roy Robert 1930- *WhoE 91*
Detweiler, Willard Stover, Jr. 1933- *WhoE 91*
Detwiler, Donald Scaife 1933- *WhoWor 91*
Detwiler, George 1825- *AmLegL*
Detwiler, Howard Fred, Jr. *BiDrAPA 89*
Detwiler, John Travers 1938- *St&PR 91*, *WhoAm 90*
Detwiler, Kathleen *ODwPR 91*
Detwiler, Paul I., Jr. 1933- *St&PR 91*
Detwiler, Paul Norman 1952- *WhoEmL 91*
Detwiler, Peter M. 1928- *St&PR 91*
Detwiler, Peter Mead 1928- *WhoAm 90*
Detwiler, Ralph Paul 1955- *WhoEmL 91*
Detwiler, Susan 1956- *BioIn 16*
Detwiler, Susan Margaret 1953- *WhoEmL 91*
Detz, Joan Marie 1951- *WhoWrEP 89*
Deuber-Pauli, Erica *BioIn 16*
Deuble, Stephen G. 1947- *St&PR 91*
Deubler, Donald L. 1946- *St&PR 91*
Deubner, Franz Ludwig 1934- *WhoWor 91*
Deucher, Richard S *BiDrAPA 89*
Deuchler, Philip George 1927- *St&PR 91*, *WhoAm 90*
Deuchler, Suzanne Louise 1929- *WhoAmW 91*
Deuel, Frank Paul 1959- *WhoEmL 91*
D'Eugenio, David P. 1957- *WhoSSW 91*
Deukmejian, George 1928- *WhoAm 90*, *WhoWor 91*
Deumens, Erik 1955- *WhoSSW 91*
Deumie, Louis C *BiDrAPA 89*
Deupi, Carlos 1936- *WhoHisp 91*
Deupree, Marvin Mattox 1917- *St&PR 91*, *WhoAm 90*
Deupree, Michael Harold 1946- *WhoEmL 91*
DeuPree, Robert Marshall 1912- *WhoWor 91*
Deur, Jan Lee 1944- *WhoSSW 91*
Deur, Lynne A. 1941- *WhoWrEP 89*
Deurmyer, James Joseph 1946- *WhoEmL 91*, *WhoWor 91*
De Urquiza, Justo Jose 1800?-1870 *BioIn 16*
Deuschl, Dennis Erwin 1940- *WhoE 91*
Deuschle, James Konrad 1956- *WhoEmL 91*
Deuschle, Kurt Walter 1923- *WhoAm 90*
Deuschle, Thomas Arthur 1957- *WhoEmL 91*
Deuss, Jean *WhoAm 90*, *WhoAmW 91*, *WhoE 91*
Deussen, Nancy Bloomer 1931- *IntWWM 90*
Deutch, John Mark 1938- *WhoAm 90*
Deutekom, Cristina 1932- *IntWWM 90*, *PenDiMP*
Deuter, Chaitanya Hari *NewAgMG*
Deuter, Karla Jean 1960- *WhoAmW 91*
Deutsch, Alexander 1933- *BiDrAPA 89*
Deutsch, Babette 1895-1982 *FemiCLE*
Deutsch, Barbara G 1937- *BiDrAPA 89*
Deutsch, Barbara Lynn 1962- *WhoE 91*
Deutsch, Cynthia Jane 1946- *WhoEmL 91*
Deutsch, David 1943- *BioIn 16*, *WhoAmA 91*
Deutsch, David 1952- *WhoEmL 91*
Deutsch, Edward J. 1922- *St&PR 91*
Deutsch, Ellen Beth 1960- *WhoEmL 91*
Deutsch, Ellen Sue 1942- *WhoAmW 91*
Deutsch, Florence Elayne Goodill 1923- *WhoAmW 91*
Deutsch, Helene 1884-1982 *WorAlBi*
Deutsch, Hunting Folger 1952- *St&PR 91*
Deutsch, James Bernard 1948- *WhoAm 90*, *WhoEmL 91*
Deutsch, James William *BiDrAPA 89*
Deutsch, Jaqueline Eileen *BiDrAPA 89*
Deutsch, Jo Ann 1946- *WhoWor 91*
Deutsch, Judith Sharon 1953- *WhoEmL 91*
Deutsch, Judith Sloan 1947- *WhoAm 90*
Deutsch, Karl Wolfgang 1912- *BioIn 16*, *WhoAm 90*, *WhoWor 91*
Deutsch, L Peter *BiDrAPA 89*
Deutsch, Lawrence *BiDrAPA 89*
Deutsch, Leonard J 1931- *BiDrAPA 89*
Deutsch, Lionel Gilbert *BiDrAPA 89*
Deutsch, Lynn Herkowitz *BiDrAPA 89*
Deutsch, Lynnore Susan 1962- *WhoAmW 91*
Deutsch, Marshall Emanuel 1921- *WhoAm 90*, *WhoE 91*
Deutsch, Martin Bernard Joseph 1931- *WhoAm 90*, *WhoWor 91*
Deutsch, Michael Joseph 1948- *St&PR 91*

Deutsch, Morton 1920- *BioIn 16, WhoAm 90*
Deutsch, Nina *IntWWM 90*
Deutsch, Pamela 1947- *ODwPR 91*
Deutsch, Robert William 1924- *WhoAm 90*
Deutsch, Ronald I. 1935- *ODwPR 91*
Deutsch, Ruth F 1927- *BiDrAPA 89*
Deutsch, Sheldon F *BiDrAPA 89*
Deutsch, Sid 1918- *WhoAm 90*
Deutsch, Stanley 1930- *WhoAm 90*
Deutsch, Stuart Jay 1943- *WhoAm 90*
Deutsch, Stuart Lewis 1945- *WhoEmL 91*
Deutsch, Sylvia 1924- *BioIn 16, WhoAmW 91*
Deutsch, Thomas Alan 1954- *WhoEmL 91*
Deutsch, William E. 1926- *WhoAm 90*
Deutscher, Allan 1940- *St&PR 91*
Deutscher, Isaac 1907-1967 *BioIn 16*
Deutscher, Lisa *BiDrAPA 89*
Deutscher, Tamara 1913?-1990 *ConAu 132*
Deutschlaender, Leo *BioIn 16*
Deutschman, Daniel Allen 1938- *BiDrAPA 89*
Deutschman, Louise Tolliver 1921- *WhoAmA 91*
Deutz, Natalie Rubinstein *WhoAmW 91*
Dev, Vasu 1933- *WhoAm 90*
Deva, M Parameshvara 1941- *BiDrAPA 89*
Devabhaktuni, Raghu Venkata *BiDrAPA 89*
Devadutt, Vinjamuri E. 1908-1990 *BioIn 16*
De Valera, Eamon 1882-1975 *WorAlBi*
De Valera, Eamonn 1882-1975 *BioIn 16*
De Vallbona, Rima 1931- *BioIn 16*
De Valois, Ninette 1898- *IntWWM 90, WorAlBi*
De Valpine, Jean England 1921- *St&PR 91*
Devan, Fred 1929- *St&PR 91*
Devanand, Davangere P *BiDrAPA 89*
Devanand, Davangere Prahalad 1955- *WhoE 91*
Devane, Denis James 1938- *WhoAm 90, WhoSSW 91*
Devane, Milton Phillips 1929- *St&PR 91*
Devane, William 1937- *WhoAm 90, WorAlBi*
DeVaney, Cynthia Ann 1947- *WhoAmW 91*
Devaney, Dennis Martin 1946- *WhoAm 90*
Devaney, Dominic Joseph 1939- *St&PR 91*
Devaney, Everett M. 1948- *WhoAm 90, WhoSSW 91*
Devaney, James Michael 1943- *WhoE 91*
Devaney, John 1926- *AuBYP 90*
Devaney, John Francis 1926- *WhoE 91*
Devaney, John Martin 1929- *St&PR 91*
Devaney, Michelle Cobb 1963- *WhoSSW 91*
Devanney, William T., Jr. 1955- *St&PR 91*
Devanny, Jean 1894-1962 *FemiCLE*
Devant, David 1868-1941 *BioIn 16*
Devantier, Paul W. 1946- *WhoAm 90*
Devarajan, Odhikadu *BiDrAPA 89*
Devarajan, Raj 1961- *BiDrAPA 89, WhoE 91*
Devarajan, Yogeswari *BiDrAPA 89*
De Vargas, Diego 1643-1704 *EncCRAm*
Devaris, Dionisios P *BiDrAPA 89*
DeVaris, Jeannette Mary 1947- *WhoAmW 91*
De Varis, Panayotis Eric 1932- *WhoE 91*
Devaron, Lorna Cooke 1921- *IntWWM 90*
de Varon, Lorna Cooke 1921- *WhoAm 90*
De Varona, Donna *BioIn 16*
de Varona, Esperanza Bravo *WhoHisp 91*
De Varona, Francisco Jose 1943- *WhoHisp 91*
DeVarso, James F. 1948- *St&PR 91*
Devas, Nicolette 1911- *FemiCLE*
De Vaucouleurs, Antoinette *BioIn 16*
de Vaucouleurs, Gerard Henri 1918- *WhoAm 90*
De Vaughn, Deborah A. 1955- *WhoAmW 91*
De Vaughn, Thomas Patrick 1952- *BiDrAPA 89*
DeVaughn-Stokes, Diane 1951- *WhoEmL 91*
De Vaul, Richard Allan *BiDrAPA 89*
De Vaul, Richard Allan 1940- *WhoAm 90*
Devault, David V. 1954- *St&PR 91*
De Vault, George H. 1907- *St&PR 91*
Devault, Maria Pineda *BiDrAPA 89*
De Vault, Virgil Thomas 1901- *WhoAm 90*
De Vaux, George R. 1941- *St&PR 91*
DeVaux, George Russell 1941- *WhoSSW 91*
Deveau, Francis Joseph 1953- *WhoEmL 91*
Deveau, Jack Thomas 1927- *St&PR 91*
De Veaugh-Geiss, Joseph 1946- *BiDrAPA 89*
De Veaux, Alexis 1948- *BioIn 16*
De Veaux, Richard Donald 1951- *WhoE 91*
Deveer, Robert K. 1946- *St&PR 91*
deVeer, Robert K., Jr. 1946- *WhoAm 90, WhoE 91*
De Vega, Jose *BioIn 16*
De Vega, Jose, Jr. *WhoHisp 91N*
Devegatales, Jugo 1946- *WhoAmA 91*
Deveines, Diane Jean *BiDrAPA 89*
De Veirman, Georges H. G. E. 1946- *WhoWor 91*
Devejian, Albert G. 1929- *St&PR 91*
de Velasco, Luisa Sigea 1530?-1560? *EncCoWW*
de Velez, Eileen McLellan 1955- *WhoAmW 91*
Develin, Rita *BioIn 16*
Devellano, James Charles 1943- *WhoAm 90*
Devendorf, David S. 1935- *St&PR 91*
Devendorf, David Stuart 1935- *WhoAm 90*
Devendorf, Don *BioIn 16*
Deveney, John L. 1921- *St&PR 91*
Devening, R. Randolph 1942- *St&PR 91*
Devening, Robert Randolph 1942- *WhoAm 90*
Devenney, David Paul 1958- *IntWWM 90*
DeVenny, Lillian Nickell *WhoSSW 91*
Devenport, Douglas Dean 1935- *WhoAm 90*
Devens, Charles 1820-1891 *BiDrUSE 89*
Devens, Paul 1931- *WhoAm 90*
Devenyi, Agnes *BiDrAPA 89*
De Venzio, Huck 1947- *WhoEmL 91*
Dever, James A. 1911- *St&PR 91*
Dever, James L. 1927- *St&PR 91*
Dever, Jeffrey Lloyd 1953- *WhoEmL 91*
Devera, Jesse Raymundo 1949- *BiDrAPA 89*
DeVera Fernandez, Manuel Ignacio 1949- *WhoSSW 91*
Devereaux, J. Peter 1956- *WhoEmL 91*
Devereaux, James Oliver 1927- *St&PR 91*
Devereaux, Marilyn 1941- *St&PR 91*
Devereaux, Mike 1963- *Ballpl 90*
Devereaux, Wanda Davis 1946- *WhoEmL 91*
Deverell, Mary 1731?- *FemiCLE*
Deverell, Rex 1941- *ConAu 132, OxCCanT*
Devereux, Frances *WhoAmW 91*
Devereux, George 1908- *EncO&P 3*
Devereux, James P. S. 1903-1988 *BioIn 16*
Devereux, Lane Gustafson 1950- *WhoAmW 91*
Devereux, Lawrence H. 1929- *St&PR 91*
Devereux, Lawrence Hackett 1929- *WhoAm 90*
Devereux, Owen Francis 1937- *WhoAm 90*
Devereux, Timothy Edward 1932- *St&PR 91, WhoAm 90*
Deverka, Louis T. 1932- *St&PR 91*
Deverka, Patricia Ann *BiDrAPA 89*
Deverka, Patricia Ann 1958- *WhoE 91*
Devers, Darryl Trimble 1955- *WhoEmL 91*
Devers Roberts, Gail *BioIn 16*
De Verter, John Scott 1936- *BiDrAPA 89*
Devery, Kieran M. 1937- *St&PR 91*
Devesi, Baddeley 1941- *WhoWor 91*
De Vesme, Cesar Baudi 1862-1938 *EncO&P 3*
Devi, Mahasveta 1926- *FemiCLE*
Devia, Mariella 1948- *IntWWM 90*
de Viana, Robert Fernandez 1938- *WhoWor 91*
De Vicq, Rene Francois 1932- *WhoWor 91*
de Vicq de Cumptich, Emmanuel 1933- *WhoWor 91*
De Vido, Alfredo Eduardo 1932- *WhoAm 90*
Devienne, Francois 1759-1803 *PenDiMP*
De Vigne, Jean-Paul Emile 1946- *BiDrAPA 89*
Devigne, Karen Cooke 1943- *WhoAmW 91*
DeVilbiss, Daniel Wesley 1955- *WhoSSW 91*
Devilla, Jose Francisco 1959- *WhoWor 91*
De Villanova, Arnold *EncO&P 3*
De Villars, l'Abbe de Montfaucon 1635-1673 *EncO&P 3*
Deville, Michel *BioIn 16*
DeVille, Paul Vincent 1908- *St&PR 91*
deVille, Vicki Lynne 1950- *WhoEmL 91*
DeVille, Willy 1950?- *EncPR&S 89*
de Villemejane, Bernard 1930- *WhoWor 91*
de Villenfagne de Vogelsanck, Jean I. 1949- *WhoWor 91*
Devillers, Marina 1947- *WomArch*
Devillers, Marina, & Lena Perot *WomArch*
De Villier, Albert B 1936- *BiDrAPA 89*
Devillier, Linda *ODwPR 91*
De Villiers, Florence *BioIn 16*
de Villiers, Nelson Adalberto 1949- *WhoAm 90*
Devin, David Allan 1966- *WhoE 91*
Devin, Edward J. 1937- *St&PR 91*
Devin, John J. *St&PR 91*
Devin, Judi *BioIn 16*
Devin, Lee 1938- *WhoAm 90*
Devin, Richard *BioIn 16*
Devinatz, Allen 1922- *WhoAm 90*
De Vincenzo, Richard Anthony 1947- *St&PR 91*
De Vinck, Jose M. 1912- *WhoWrEP 89*
Devine, Adrian 1951- *Ballpl 90*
Devine, Ann Marie 1936- *WhoE 91*
DeVine, B. Mack 1945- *WhoAm 90*
Devine, Betty 1937- *IntWWM 90*
Devine, Brian Kiernan 1942- *St&PR 91, WhoAm 90*
Devine, C. Robert *NewYTBS 90*
Devine, C. Robert 1917- *WhoAm 90*
Devine, C. Robert 1917-1990 *BioIn 16*
DeVine, Charles Donald 1943- *St&PR 91*
Devine, Charles Joseph, Jr. 1923- *WhoAm 90*
Devine, Charles V., Jr. 1948- *WhoEmL 91*
Devine, David F. 1929- *St&PR 91*
Devine, Dominic *TwCCr&M 91*
Devine, Donald J. 1937- *WhoAm 90*
Devine, Donald R. 1941- *St&PR 91*
Devine, Donald T 1919- *BiDrAPA 89*
Devine, Donn 1929- *WhoE 91*
DeVine, Edmond Francis 1916- *WhoAm 90*
Devine, Elaine T. 1924- *St&PR 91*
Devine, Frank A. 1946- *St&PR 91*
Devine, Grant 1944- *WhoAm 90*
Devine, Hugh James, Jr. 1938- *St&PR 91*
Devine, James Brendan 1936- *WhoAm 90*
Devine, James Joseph 1926- *WhoE 91*
Devine, James Richard 1948- *WhoEmL 91*
Devine, Jay *ODwPR 91*
Devine, Joe 1895-1951 *Ballpl 90*
De Vine, John Bernard 1920- *WhoAm 90*
Devine, John Gerard *BiDrAPA 89*
Devine, John M. 1944- *WhoAm 90*
Devine, John P. *BioIn 16*
Devine, Joseph Anthony 1927- *WhoAm 90*
Devine, Katherine 1951- *WhoAmW 91*
DeVine, Lawrence 1935- *WhoAm 90*
Devine, Loretta 1953?- *DrBlPA 90*
Devine, Michael Buxton 1953- *WhoE 91, WhoEmL 91, WhoWor 91*
Devine, Michael J. 1945- *WhoEmL 91*
Devine, Michael Joseph 1952- *WhoSSW 91*
Devine, Richard Kevin 1959- *WhoSSW 91*
Devine, Richard William 1938- *St&PR 91*
Devine, Sean Fearon 1950- *St&PR 91*
Devine, Shane 1926- *WhoAm 90*
Devine, Thomas Francis *NewYTBS 90*
Devine, Thomas John 1927- *St&PR 91*
Devine, William Charles 1932- *WhoAmA 91*
Devine, William Douglas 1962- *WhoSSW 91*
Devine, William H. 1937- *St&PR 91*
De Vine-Kirk, Valaria Ann 1951- *WhoAmW 91*
DeViney, Elizabeth Catherine 1943- *WhoAmW 91*
Deviney, Marvin Lee, Jr. 1929- *WhoAm 90, WhoWor 91*
Devinney, Timothy Michael 1956- *WhoEmL 91*
Devino, William Stanley 1926- *WhoAm 90*
De Viri, Anne *WhoWrEP 89*
DeVise, Pierre Romain 1924- *WhoAm 90*
De Visee, Robert *PenDiMP*
Devisme, Leopold 1816-1900 *DcCanB 12*
de Visscher, Francois Marie 1953- *WhoE 91, WhoWor 91*
De Vita, Joseph Stephen 1941- *St&PR 91*
DeVita, Raymond A. 1936- *St&PR 91*
De Vita, Sharon Louise 1950- *WhoWrEP 89*
DeVita, Vincent T. *BioIn 16*
DeVita, Vincent Theodore, Jr. 1935- *WhoAm 90*
De Vito, Albert 1919- *IntWWM 90*
De Vito, Danny *BioIn 16*
Devito, Danny 1944- *WorAlBi*
Devito, Danny Michael 1944- *WhoAm 90*
De Vito, Gioconda 1907- *IntWWM 90, PenDiMP*
De Vito, Joseph Anthony 1938- *WhoWrEP 89*
DeVito, Karen Smith 1953- *WhoE 91*
DeVito, Mathias J. 1930- *St&PR 91*
DeVito, Mathias Joseph 1930- *WhoAm 90*
DeVito, Richard Anthony 1940- *WhoAm 90*
de Vito, Robert 1935- *WhoAm 90*
de Vito, Robert A 1935- *BiDrAPA 89*
Devito, Robert A. 1937- *St&PR 91*
De Vitry D'Avaucourt, Arnaud 1926- *WhoWor 91*
Devitt, Charles Kent *BiDrAPA 89*
Devitt, Craig Vincent 1943- *St&PR 91*
Devitt, Edward James 1911- *WhoAm 90*
Devitt, James Edward 1920- *St&PR 91*
Devitt, Michael James 1938- *WhoE 91*
De Vivero, Fernando Leon 1906- *BioIn 16*
DeVivo, Ange 1925- *WhoAmW 91, WhoSSW 91, WhoWor 91*
De Vivo, Darryl Claude 1937- *WhoAm 90*
DeVivo, Sal J. 1937- *WhoAm 90, WhoE 91*
DeVizia, Joseph Francis 1942- *WhoE 91*
De Vlaminck, Rene Jan 1927- *WhoWor 91*
Devlesaver, Philippe Louis 1938- *WhoWor 91*
Devlin, Anne 1951- *FemiCLE*
Devlin, Art 1879-1948 *Ballpl 90 [port]*
Devlin, Barbara Jo 1947- *WhoAmW 91*
Devlin, Bernadette 1947- *BioIn 16, WorAlBi*
Devlin, Francis James 1943- *WhoSSW 91*
Devlin, Harry 1918- *WhoAmA 91*
Devlin, J. Richard 1950- *St&PR 91*
Devlin, James K. 1938- *St&PR 91*
Devlin, James Richard 1950- *WhoAm 90*
Devlin, Jean Theresa 1947- *WhoAmW 91*
Devlin, Jim 1849-1883 *Ballpl 90*
Devlin, John Byrne 1951- *St&PR 91*
Devlin, Johnny *EncACom*
Devlin, Joseph Aloysius 1932- *St&PR 91*
Devlin, Mary Margaret 1945- *WhoEmL 91*
Devlin, Michael 1942- *IntWWM 90*
Devlin, Michael Coles 1942- *WhoAm 90*
Devlin, Michael Gerard 1947- *WhoE 91*
Devlin, Michael James 1956- *BiDrAPA 89*
Devlin, Michael Patrick 1950- *WhoEmL 91*
Devlin, Paul 1903-1989 *BioIn 16*
Devlin, Philip Martin 1957- *BiDrAPA 89*
Devlin, Robert Manning 1941- *St&PR 91, WhoAm 90*
Devlin, Thomas *AuBYP 90*
Devlin, Thomas McKeown 1929- *WhoAm 90*
Devlin, Timothy Paul 1940- *St&PR 91*
Devlin, Wende 1918- *WhoAmA 91*
Devlin, Willard R. 1949- *St&PR 91*
Devney, Robert Bernard 1952- *BiDrAPA 89*
Devo *EncPR&S 89*
DeVoe, Christopher Howard 1957- *WhoE 91*
Devoe, Chuck 1943- *WhoSSW 91*
Devoe, James K. 1937- *St&PR 91*
Devoe, James Kent 1937- *St&PR 91, WhoAm 90*
DeVoe, Richard Franklin, Jr. 1948- *WhoEmL 91, WhoSSW 91*
DeVogt, John Frederick 1930- *WhoAm 90*
de Vogue, Ghislain 1933- *WhoWor 91*
Devokaitis, Judith Ohlson 1944- *WhoAmW 91*
Devol, George Charles, Jr. 1912- *WhoWor 91*
Devol, Kenneth Stowe 1929- *WhoAm 90*
De Volt, Artiss *IntWWM 90*
Devon, John Anthony *ConAu 31NR*
Devon, Wesley Scott 1939- *St&PR 91*
Devona, Thomas C. 1905- *St&PR 91*
Devons, Samuel 1914- *WhoAm 90*
Devonshire, Duchess of 1920- *BioIn 16*
Devonshire, Elizabeth, Duchess of 1757-1824 *FemiCLE*
Devonshire, Georgiana, Duchess of 1757-1806 *FemiCLE*
Devonshuk, Joseph Edward 1955- *WhoEmL 91*
DeVore, Carl Brent 1940- *WhoAm 90*
DeVore, Daun Aline 1955- *WhoEmL 91*
DeVore, Gilbert 1918- *St&PR 91*
Devore, John Edwin 1940- *St&PR 91*
Devore, Josh 1887-1954 *Ballpl 90*
DeVore, Judith T. 1959- *WhoAmW 91*
DeVore, Margaret Bowen 1930- *WhoAm 90*
De Vore, Mary Alice 1940- *WhoWrEP 89*
DeVore, Paul Cameron 1932- *WhoAm 90*
De Vore, Paul Warren 1926- *WhoAm 90*
De Vore, Richard E 1933- *WhoAmA 91*
Devore, Richard Owen 1956- *IntWWM 90*
De Vore, Sheryl Lynn 1956- *WhoWrEP 89*
DeVore, William D. 1936- *St&PR 91*
Devos, Louis 1926- *IntWWM 90, PenDiMP*
de Vos, Peter Jon 1938- *WhoE 91*
DeVos, Richard M. 1926- *St&PR 91*
Devos, Richard Marvin 1926- *ConAmBL, WhoAm 90*
DeVos, Richard Marvin, Jr. 1955- *WhoAm 90*
DeVoss, James Thomas 1916- *WhoAm 90*
De Voto, Bernard A. 1897-1955 *WorAlBi*
De Voto, Bernard Augustine 1897-1955 *BioIn 16*
Devoto, Juan E. Pivel 1910- *BioIn 16*
Devoto, Mark Bernard 1940- *IntWWM 90*
Devoto, W. Wesley 1940- *St&PR 91*
Devoyon, Pascal 1953- *IntWWM 90*
Devree, Howard 1890-1966 *WhoAmA 91N*
De Vree, Johan Karel 1938- *WhoWor 91*
Devreese, Frederic 1929- *IntWWM 90*
Devrient, Eduard 1801-1877 *PenDiMP*
De Vries, Barend Arie 1925- *WhoE 91*
DeVries, Bernard Jerin 1909- *WhoAm 90*
De Vries, Charles H. 1932- *ODwPR 91*
De Vries, Cornelis Geert 1935- *WhoWor 91*
De Vries, David Pietersen 1592?-1655? *EncCRAm*

DeVries, Donald Lawson 1917- *WhoAm 90*
de Vries, Ernst Bart 1939- *WhoWor 91*
DeVries, Glenn Fredrick 1952- *WhoEmL 91*
DeVries, Hans Wybren 1944- *WhoWor 91*
De Vries, Hugo Marie 1848-1935 *BioIn 16, WorAlBi*
DeVries, J.D. 1936- *St&PR 91*
DeVries, Jack *WhoAm 90*
DeVries, Jack Brownell 1944- *WhoWor 91*
de Vries, Jacobus E. 1934- *WhoE 91*
De Vries, Jacques Alexandre 1952- *St&PR 91*
Devries, James Howard 1932- *St&PR 91*
Devries, John A. 1923- *St&PR 91*
De Vries, Kenneth Lawrence 1933- *WhoAm 90*
de Vries, Lois Jean 1946- *WhoEmL 91*
de Vries, Margaret Garritsen 1922- *WhoAm 90, WhoE 91*
De Vries, Marten W 1948- *BiDrAPA 89*
DeVries, Nancy Lynne 1956- *WhoAmW 91*
deVries, Nicholas 1953- *WhoEmL 91*
De Vries, Peter 1910- *MajTwCW, WhoAm 90, WhoWrEP 89, WorAlBi*
De Vries, Peter J.M. 1941- *St&PR 91*
de Vries, Rimmer 1929- *WhoAm 90*
DeVries, Robert K. 1932- *WhoAm 90*
DeVries, Scott Philip 1954- *WhoEmL 91*
DeVries, William C. *BioIn 16*
Devries, William C. 1943- *WorAlBi*
DeVries, William Castle 1943- *WhoAm 90*
Devroy, Neil J. 1947- *ODwPR 91*
de Vryer, Miepje A 1931- *BiDrAPA 89*
De Vryer, Pieter *BiDrAPA 89*
DeVuono, Andrea Jane 1962- *WhoAmW 91*
de Vuyst, Bruno Michel 1950- *WhoWor 91*
Dew, Cecil Coleman 1930- *St&PR 91*
Dew, Charles Burgess 1937- *WhoAm 90*
Dew, Donald F. 1924- *St&PR 91*
Dew, Jess Edward 1920- *WhoSSW 91, WhoWor 91*
Dew, Joan King 1932- *WhoWor 91*
Dew, Kathi Rattin 1950- *WhoEmL 91*
Dew, Linda Sue 1956- *WhoAmW 91*
Dew, Mary Amanda 1955- *WhoAmW 91*
Dew, Susanna 1637-1707 *BiDEWW*
Dew, William Waldo, Jr. 1935- *WhoAm 90*
De Waal, Ronald Burt 1932- *WhoAmA 91*
De Waart, Edo 1941- *BioIn 16, CurBio 90 [port], IntWWM 90, PenDiMP, WhoAm 90, WhoWor 91*
de Waart, Paul Jacobus Ignatius Maria 1932- *WhoWor 91*
Dewaele, Jean-Claude *PenDiMP*
de Wagenaar, Dirk 1932- *WhoWor 91*
De Wahl, David Allen 1924- *St&PR 91*
DeWalch, Donald P. 1933- *St&PR 91*
Dewald, Ernest Leroy 1907- *WhoAm 90*
Dewald, Gretta Moll 1929- *WhoAmW 91*
Dewald, Howard Dean 1958- *WhoEmL 91*
Dewald, John 1947- *St&PR 91*
DeWald, John Edward 1946- *WhoEmL 91*
Dewald, Paul A 1920- *BiDrAPA 89*
Dewald, Paul Adolph 1920- *WhoAm 90*
DeWall, Beth Barclay 1954- *WhoAmW 91*
DeWall, Richard Allison 1926- *WhoAm 90*
Dewan, Mantosh 1951- *BiDrAPA 89*
Dewan, Mantosh Jaimani 1951- *WhoE 91*
Dewan, Naakesh Amrit 1962- *BiDrAPA 89*
De Wan-Carlson, Anna *WhoAmA 91*
De Wandeleer, Patrick Jules 1949- *WhoWor 91*
Dewane, John Richard 1934- *WhoWor 91*
Dewar, Daniel Bevis 1932- *WhoAm 90*
Dewar, David R 1913-1990 *ConAu 131*
Dewar, James 1842-1923 *WorAlBi*
Dewar, James McEwen 1943- *WhoWor 91*
Dewar, Mary Reed 1922- *WhoAmW 91*
Dewar, Michael James Steuart 1918- *WhoAm 90*
Dewar, Norman E. 1930- *St&PR 91*
Dewart, Edward Hartley 1828-1903 *DcLB 99*
De Waziers, Fernand 1954- *St&PR 91*
Dewberry, Betty Bauman 1930- *WhoAmW 91, WhoSSW 91*
Dewberry, Claire DeArment 1937- *WhoAmW 91*
Dewberry, J. Terry 1943- *St&PR 91*
Dewberry, James Terry 1943- *WhoAm 90*
Dewdney, Christopher 1951- *BioIn 16*
Dewdney, Selwyn 1909-1979 *SmATA 64*
Deweerd, Terrence Bruce 1942- *St&PR 91*
DeWeerdt, Jackie Lynn 1951- *St&PR 91*
Dewees, Barbara 1945- *WhoSSW 91*
DeWees, Dal *WhoAm 90*
DeWees, Darwin Dallas 1940- *St&PR 91*
Dewees, Donald Charles 1931- *WhoE 91*
DeWees, James H. 1933- *WhoAm 90*
Dewees, John Garrett 1951- *St&PR 91*
Dewees, Laura DeCou 1959- *WhoEmL 91*
Dewees, Peter Malcolm 1935- *WhoAm 90*
De Weese, Gene 1934- *AuBYP 90*
DeWeese, James Arville 1925- *WhoAm 90*
De Weese, Jean *AuBYP 90*
DeWeese, Marion Spencer 1915- *WhoAm 90*
De Weese, Thomas Eugene *AuBYP 90*
Dewein, Edward G 1933- *BiDrAPA 89*
Dewel, Gary E. *St&PR 91*
Dewell, Michael 1931- *WhoAm 90*
Dewenter, Donald Richard 1926- *St&PR 91*
DeWerth, Gordon Henry 1939- *WhoAm 90*
De Westbrook, Cicero *WhoWrEP 89*
de Wetter, Herman Peter 1920- *WhoAm 90*
DeWetter, Peter 1920- *St&PR 91*
Dewey, Anne Elizabeth Marie 1951- *WhoAmW 91, WhoEmL 91*
Dewey, Annie Godfrey *BioIn 16*
Dewey, Arthur Eugene 1933- *WhoAm 90*
Dewey, Barbara 1923- *WhoWrEP 89*
Dewey, Bradley, III 1943- *WhoAm 90*
Dewey, Daniel *BioIn 16*
Dewey, David Lawrence 1952- *WhoEmL 91*
Dewey, Davis Rich 1858-1942 *EncABHB 6 [port]*
Dewey, Dolores Gay 1932- *WhoAmW 91*
Dewey, Donald Odell 1930- *WhoAm 90*
Dewey, Donald William 1933- *WhoAm 90, WhoWor 91, WhoWrEP 89*
Dewey, Edward Allen 1932- *WhoAm 90*
Dewey, Gene Lawrence 1938- *WhoAm 90*
Dewey, George 1837-1917 *BioIn 16, WorAlBi*
Dewey, George W. 1923- *St&PR 91*
Dewey, Jennifer *BioIn 16*
Dewey, Joe *BioIn 16*
Dewey, John 1859-1952 *EncAL, WorAlBi, WrPh P*
Dewey, John Russell 1953- *WhoEmL 91*
Dewey, Kirk *BioIn 16*
Dewey, Larry Voss 1950- *BiDrAPA 89*
Dewey, Linda Sue 1955- *WhoEmL 91*
Dewey, Mary Elizabeth Brown 1853-1936 *BioIn 16*
Dewey, Melvil 1851-1931 *BioIn 16, WorAlBi*
Dewey, Pat Parker 1923- *WhoAmW 91, WhoSSW 91*
Dewey, Phelps 1928- *WhoAm 90*
Dewey, Richard L. 1929- *St&PR 91*
Dewey, Robert J. 1935- *St&PR 91*
Dewey, Ronald L. 1939- *St&PR 91*
Dewey, S. Dayton 1944- *WhoWor 91*
Dewey, Thomas B 1915- *TwCCr&M 91*
Dewey, Thomas E. 1902-1971 *BioIn 16, WorAlBi*
Dewey, Thomas E., Jr. 1932- *St&PR 91*
Dewez, Patrick Jean 1950- *WhoWor 91*
Dewhirst, Jeffrey Alan 1949- *St&PR 91*
Dewhurst, Charles Kurt 1948- *WhoAm 90*
Dewhurst, Colleen *BioIn 16*
Dewhurst, Colleen 1926- *NotWoAT, WhoAm 90, WhoAmW 91, WorAlBi*
Dewhurst, Eileen 1929- *TwCCr&M 91*
Dewhurst, William G 1926- *BiDrAPA 89*
Dewhurst, William George 1926- *WhoAm 90, WhoWor 91*
Dewhurst, William H 1929- *BiDrAPA 89*
DeWilde, David Allen 1934- *St&PR 91*
deWilde, David Michael 1940- *WhoAm 90, WhoWor 91*
De Windt, Herma Ilean 1933- *WhoAmW 91*
DeWine, Richard Michael 1947- *WhoAm 90*
Dewing, Maria Richards 1845-1927 *BiDWomA*
Dewing, Merlin Eugene 1934- *WhoAm 90*
de Winne, Terence Leslie 1940- *WhoWor 91*
DeWinter, Charles Mark 1941- *St&PR 91*
deWir, Harriet 1948- *WhoAmW 91*
DeWire, Fred C. 1934- *St&PR 91*
DeWire, John W. *NewYTBS 90*
DeWitt, Barbara Ann 1929- *WhoE 91*
De Witt, Bryce Seligman 1923- *WhoAm 90*
DeWitt, Calvin 1894-1989 *BioIn 16*
DeWitt, Charles Barbour 1950- *WhoE 91*
DeWitt, Dennis Carroll 1945- *St&PR 91*
DeWitt, Diana Leigh 1941- *WhoSSW 91*
DeWitt, Douglas Bryan 1956- *WhoSSW 91*
DeWitt, Elizabeth Kathleen 1947- *WhoEmL 91*
De Witt, Eugene A. 1943- *WhoAm 90*
Dewitt, Frank J. 1929- *St&PR 91*
DeWitt, Frank John 1929- *WhoAm 90*
DeWitt, Franklin Roosevelt 1936- *WhoSSW 91*
De Witt, James *AuBYP 90*
De Witt, James Edward 1931- *BiDrAPA 89*
Dewitt, Jamie *AuBYP 90*
De Witt, Johan 1625-1672 *BioIn 16*
DeWitt, John Hibbett, Jr. 1906- *WhoAm 90*
DeWitt, John Howard *BiDrAPA 89*
DeWitt, Karen Kelly 1963- *WhoAmW 91*
De Witt, Katherine 1867-1963 *BioIn 16*
Dewitt, Katherine Louise 1948- *WhoEmL 91*
DeWitt, Kimber 1956- *WhoEmL 91*
DeWitt, Lew *NewYTBS 90*
Dewitt, Linda Ross 1951- *WhoEmL 91*
DeWitt, Mary Schiller 1948- *WhoAmW 91*
De Witt, Michael Edward *BiDrAPA 89*
De Witt, Susan 1778-1824 *FemiCLE*
DeWitt, Thomas Jay 1947- *St&PR 91*
DeWitt, Walter N. 1937- *WhoAm 90*
Dewitt, Walter Newton 1937- *St&PR 91*
De Witt, William Gerald 1937- *WhoAm 90*
De Witt-Morette, Cecile 1922- *WhoAm 90*
Dewitte, Luc Willem 1949- *WhoWor 91*
Dewitz, Jean Laura 1946- *WhoAmW 91*
Dewitz, Robert Donald 1934- *St&PR 91*
De Wohl, Louis 1903-1961 *EncO&P 3*
de Wolf, David Alter 1934- *WhoAm 90*
DeWolf, Karyn Sue 1962- *WhoE 91*
De Wolfe, Anne *ODwPR 91*
DeWolfe, Elsie 1865-1950 *BioAmW*
DeWolfe, John Chauncey, Jr. 1913- *WhoAm 90*
DeWolfe, L. Donald 1934- *St&PR 91*
DeWolfe, Martha Rose 1959- *WhoAmW 91, WhoEmL 91*
De Wolff, Louis *WhoSSW 91*
Dewolff, Maurice Konrad 1941- *St&PR 91, WhoAm 90*
DeWoody, Barbara McKenna 1966- *WhoE 91*
DeWoody, James *BioIn 16*
DeWorsop, Richard *BiDrAPA 89*
DeWoskin, Alan Ellis 1940- *WhoWor 91*
Dewoskin, Irvin S. 1909- *St&PR 91*
De Wright, Yvonne *WhoHisp 91*
Dews, Laronald Warren 1944- *WhoSSW 91*
Dews, Pamela Jean 1959- *WhoSSW 91*
Dews, Peter Booth 1922- *WhoAm 90*
Dewsbury, Donald Allen 1939- *WhoAm 90*
Dewsnap, Barbara Everitt 1933- *WhoAmW 91*
Dewson, Molly 1874-1962 *BioIn 16*
De Wulf, Kathryn Colleen 1959- *WhoWrEP 89*
DeWyer, Gary Alton 1940- *St&PR 91*
De Wyngaert, Laura Patricia *WhoAmW 91, WhoE 91*
Dex, Laura Louise 1962- *WhoEmL 91*
Dexheimer, Henry Phillip, II 1925- *WhoWor 91*
Dexheimer, Marion Louise 1920- *WhoAmW 91*
Dextar, Baron of 1934- *WhoWor 91*
Dexter, Annette Ruby 1953- *WhoSSW 91*
Dexter, Charlie 1876-1934 *Ballpl 90*
Dexter, Colin 1930- *TwCCr&M 91*
Dexter, Dallas-Lee 1950- *WhoAmW 91, WhoWor 91*
Dexter, Dean Joseph 1948- *WhoE 91*
Dexter, Deirdre O'Neil Elizabeth 1956- *WhoAmW 91*
Dexter, Donald Harvey 1928- *WhoAm 90*
Dexter, Frederick Jay 1947- *WhoE 91*
Dexter, Harold 1920- *IntWWM 90*
Dexter, Jerry D. 1947- *WhoWrEP 89*
Dexter, John 1925- *IntWWM 90*
Dexter, John 1925-1990 *BioIn 16, CurBio 90N, NewYTBS 90 [port]*
Dexter, Keith 1928-1989 *BioIn 16*
Dexter, Lewis 1910- *WhoAm 90*
Dexter, Mary Jane *BiDrAPA 89*
Dexter, Myron *BiDrAPA 89*
Dexter, Pete 1943- *ConAu 131, MajTwCW*
Dexter, Peter Whittemore 1943- *WhoAm 90*
Dexter, Ron *NewAgMG*
Dexter, Samuel 1761-1816 *BiDrUSE 89*
Dexter, Stephen *BioIn 16*
Dexter, Stephen Cartwright 1942- *WhoE 91*
Dexter, Theodore Henry 1923- *WhoAm 90*
Dexter-Rosell, Mildred 1932- *WhoAmW 91*
Dey, Carol Ruth 1943- *WhoAmW 91*
Dey, John William 1912-1978 *MusmAFA*
Dey, K. V. R., Jr. *WhoAm 90*
Dey, Richard Dennis 1948- *WhoSSW 91*
Dey, Samuel E 1958- *BiDrAPA 89*
Dey, Susan *BioIn 16*
Dey, Susan 1952- *WorAlBi*
De Yanez, Nidia *BiDrAPA 89*
de Yanez, Nidia 1936- *WhoE 91*
Deyer, Kirk Donald 1947- *St&PR 91*
Deyerle, James Arthur, Jr. 1931- *WhoSSW 91*
Deyermond, Kelli Pogue 1961- *WhoEmL 91*
Deyglun, Henry 1903-1971 *OxCCanT*
Deyo, Steve Harold 1949- *WhoSSW 91*
Deyo, Steven Mark 1957- *WhoWrEP 89*
Deyoe, Alan Maurice, Jr. 1927- *WhoAm 90*
Deyoe-Chiullan, Rita Maxine 1947- *WhoSSW 91*
DeYoung, Billie Schaefer 1936- *WhoSSW 91*
DeYoung, David Ralph 1945- *St&PR 91*
DeYoung, Karen Jean 1949- *WhoAmW 91*
De Young, Lynden E. 1923- *IntWWM 90*
De Young, M. H. 1849-1925 *BioIn 16*
De Young, Michel Harry 1849-1925 *BioIn 16*
DeYoung, Russell 1909-1988 *BioIn 16*
DeYoung, Stephen Paul 1953- *St&PR 91*
De Young, Stephen Paul 1953- *WhoEmL 91*
DeYoung, Yvonne Marie 1951- *WhoAmW 91, WhoEmL 91*
Deyrup, Astrith 1923- *AuBYP 90*
Deysher, Paul Evans 1923- *WhoE 91, WhoWor 91*
De Yturbe, Jean *BioIn 16*
De Yturbe, Sandy *BioIn 16*
De Yurre, Victor Henry 1953- *WhoHisp 91*
Deza, Ernesto C *BiDrAPA 89*
Deza, Plaridel C 1931- *BiDrAPA 89*
Deza, Roberto Jose 1946- *WhoHisp 91*
Dezaki, Sumio 1935- *WhoWor 91*
De Zavala, Adina 1861-1955 *BioIn 16*
De Zavala, Lorenzo 1788-1836 *BioIn 16*
de Zayas, Jose A 1927- *BiDrAPA 89*
DeZee, Matthew Raymond 1946- *WhoSSW 91*
de Zeeuw, Gerard 1936- *WhoWor 91*
Dezell, James E. 1933- *St&PR 91*
Dezell, James E., Jr. *BioIn 16*
Dezer, Michael *BioIn 16*
Dezern, Kay Langley 1945- *WhoSSW 91*
de Zevallos, Edward Phillipe, Jr. 1943- *WhoSSW 91*
Dezort, Jacquelyn Louise Link 1950- *WhoEmL 91*
Dezura, Daniel John *BiDrAPA 89*
De Zwirek, M George *BiDrAPA 89*
DeZwirek, Phillip J. 1937- *St&PR 91*
D'Gabriel, Carlos Leonardo 1930- *WhoSSW 91*
Dhadphale, Manohar 1930- *BiDrAPA 89*
Dhaemers, Robert August 1926- *WhoAmA 91*
D'Haeze, Thomas M. *St&PR 91*
Dhaliwal, Vimal Singh 1960- *IntWWM 90*
D'Halluin, Michel 1928- *St&PR 91*
Dhammarungruang, Jajjai 1949- *WhoWor 91*
Dhanabalan, Suppiah 1937- *WhoWor 91*
Dhanak, Amritlal Maganlal 1925- *WhoAm 90*
Dhanani, Alnoor H.K.J. 1955- *St&PR 91*
Dhanjal, Surjeet Singh 1923- *WhoSSW 91*
Dhanjani, Vanita Suresh *BiDrAPA 89*
Dhar, Vinod K. *BiDrAPA 89*
Dharam, Vir 1946- *WhoWor 91*
D'Harambure, Ludovic 1949- *WhoWor 91*
Dharamsi, Kishore Devji 1951- *WhoWor 91*
Dharanipragada, Ramalinga Murty 1956- *WhoEmL 91*
Dharmawara Mahathera *BioIn 16*
Dharmay, Roland S *BiDrAPA 89*
d'Harnoncourt, Anne *WhoAm 90, WhoAmW 91, WhoE 91*
D'Harnoncourt, Anne 1943- *WhoAmA 91*
Dharwadkar, Kumar Vishwas 1945- *St&PR 91*
Dhawan, Jagdish Chandra 1946- *WhoSSW 91*
Dhayer, Gerald Douglas 1951- *St&PR 91*
Dhesi, Autar Singh 1936- *WhoWor 91*
Dhillon, Avtar Singh 1952- *BiDrAPA 89*
Dhillon, Inderpal 1958- *BiDrAPA 89*
Dhingra, Davinder H *BiDrAPA 89*
Dhingra, Upma *BiDrAPA 89*
Dhinsa, Surjit Singh *BiDrAPA 89*
Dhir, Krishna Swaroop 1944- *WhoSSW 91, WhoWor 91*
D'Hollander, Jos Werner Renilde 1934- *IntWWM 90*
Dhondt, Steven Thomas 1944- *WhoE 91*
Dhondy, Farrukh 1944- *ConAu 132*
Dhouda *EncCoWW*
D'Huart, Annabelle *BioIn 16*
Dhungel, Dambar Prasad 1941- *WhoWor 91*
Dhuoda *BioIn 16*
Dhutiyabhodhi, Uthai 1925- *WhoWor 91*
Dia, The Countess of *EncCoWW*
Dia, Ali Rida *BiDrAPA 89*
Diab, Elfateh Eltahir 1936- *IntWWM 90*
Diab, Mohammad Ide 1944- *WhoWor 91*
Diaco, Michael Anthony 1953- *WhoE 91*
Diaconis, Persi W. 1945- *WhoAm 90*
Diaconoff, Ted 1928- *IntWWM 90*
Diaconu, Adrian 1959- *WhoWor 91*
Diacumakos, Elaine G. 1930- *WhoAm 90*
Diaghilev, Serge 1872-1929 *BioIn 16*
Diaghilev, Sergei 1872-1929 *WorAlBi*
Diago, Carlos Augusto Jesus 1941- *WhoSSW 91*
Diagonale, Josephine Carmela 1941- *WhoAmW 91*
DiAiso, Robert Joseph 1940- *WhoE 91*

Dial, Frederick Clark 1950- St&PR 91
Dial, Garry BioIn 16
Dial, James Hampton 1955- WhoE 91
Dial, Joe BioIn 16
Dial, Michael Curtis 1941- St&PR 91
Dial, Nathaniel Victor 1938- WhoWor 91
Dial, Oliver Eugene 1922- WhoAm 90
Dial, Richard 1955- MusmAFA
Dial, Ronald Owen 1950- WhoEmL 91
Dial, Teresa A. St&PR 91
Dial, Thornton, Jr. 1953- MusmAFA
Dial, Thornton, Sr. 1928- MusmAFA
Dial, William Henry 1907- WhoAm 90
Dialdriver, E. WhoSSW 91
Diallo, Abdoulaye WhoWor 91
Dials, Lou 1904- Ballpl 90
Diaman, N. A. 1936- WhoWrEP 89
Diamand, Peter 1913- IntWWM 90
Diamandis, Peter G. BioIn 16
Diamandopoulos, Peter 1928- WhoAm 90, WhoE 91, WhoWor 91
Diamano, Silmang MajTwCW
Diamant, Alfred 1917- WhoAm 90
Diamant, Anita WhoAm 90
Diamant, Barbara Greenstein 1932- WhoAmW 91
Diamant, Gregory Eric 1949- WhoE 91
Diamant, Lincoln 1923- WhoE 91
Diamant-Cohen, Betsy Maria 1957- WhoWor 91
Diamantstein, Tibor 1925- WhoWor 91
Diament, Paul 1938- WhoAm 90
Diamond, Aaron M. 1918-1989 BioIn 16
Diamond, Abel Joseph 1932- WhoAm 90
Diamond, Adelina 1927- WhoAmW 91
Diamond, Alisa Robin 1962- WhoAmW 91
Diamond, Ann Berkman 1951- WhoAmW 91
Diamond, Arthur Mansfield, Jr. 1953- WhoEmL 91
Diamond, Bernard L 1912- BiDrAPA 89
Diamond, Bernard Lee 1912- WhoAm 90
Diamond, Beverly Esther Jean 1956- WhoSSW 91
Diamond, Bobby BioIn 16
Diamond, Cheryl Beth BiDrAPA 89
Diamond, Christopher Shaun 1946- St&PR 91
Diamond, Darryl M BiDrAPA 89
Diamond, David 1915- BioIn 16, PenDiMP A
Diamond, David Bruce 1944- BiDrAPA 89
Diamond, David Leo 1915- IntWWM 90, WhoAm 90, WhoWor 91
Diamond, Diana Louise 1937- WhoWor 91
Diamond, Dickson BiDrAPA 89
Diamond, Dorothy B. 1918- WhoAmW 91
Diamond, Elayne Fern 1945- WhoE 91, WhoEmL 91
Diamond, Elyse WhoWrEP 89
Diamond, Eugene Christopher 1952- WhoEmL 91, WhoWor 91
Diamond, Fred I. 1925- WhoAm 90
Diamond, Freda WhoAm 90
Diamond, G. William 1945- WhoAm 90, WhoE 91
Diamond, Gustave 1928- WhoAm 90, WhoE 91
Diamond, Harley David 1959- WhoEmL 91
Diamond, Harold J. 1934- IntWWM 90
Diamond, Harvey Jerome 1928- WhoSSW 91, WhoWor 91
Diamond, Heidi Janice 1958- WhoE 91
Diamond, Herbert BiDrAPA 89
Diamond, Howard 1941- St&PR 91
Diamond, I. A. L. 1920-1988 AnObit 1988, BioIn 16
Diamond, Irving T. 1922- BioIn 16
Diamond, Irwin 1923- St&PR 91
Diamond, Isadore 1918- St&PR 91
Diamond, Israel 1914- WhoAm 90
Diamond, James Edward, Jr. 1946- WhoAm 90
Diamond, James Thomas 1926- St&PR 91
Diamond, James William 1939- St&PR 91, WhoAm 90
Diamond, Jane Sydney 1952- WhoAmW 91
Diamond, Jay 1934- ConAu 33NR
Diamond, Jay Harrison 1951- WhoEmL 91
Diamond, Jeffrey Brian 1950- WhoEmL 91
Diamond, Jessica WhoAmA 91
Diamond, John 1898?-1931 WorAlBi
Diamond, John M 1953- BiDrAPA 89
Diamond, John P. 1936- St&PR 91
Diamond, Joni Lynn 1956- WhoWor 91
Diamond, Josef 1907- St&PR 91
Diamond, Lee Gregory 1946- WhoSSW 91
Diamond, Leon 1924- BiDrAPA 89
Diamond, Leon S BiDrAPA 89
Diamond, Leonard BiDrAPA 89
Diamond, Leonard 1927- St&PR 91
Diamond, Linda Ann 1951- WhoE 91
Diamond, Lisa Carol 1959- BiDrAPA 89
Diamond, M. Jerome 1942- WhoAm 90
Diamond, Malcolm Luria 1924- WhoAm 90
Diamond, Maria Sophia 1958- WhoEmL 91
Diamond, Marian Cleeves BioIn 16
Diamond, Marian Cleeves 1926- WhoAm 90
Diamond, Mark Wayne BiDrAPA 89
Diamond, Matthew Philip 1951- WhoAm 90
Diamond, Michael Nathan 1945- WhoSSW 91
Diamond, Michael Steven BiDrAPA 89
Diamond, Murray A 1910- BiDrAPA 89
Diamond, Neil BioIn 16
Diamond, Neil 1941- EncPR&S 89, OxCPMus, WorAlBi
Diamond, Neil Leslie 1941- WhoAm 90
Diamond, Olivia Harriet 1947- WhoWrEP 89
Diamond, Pamela Ann 1963- WhoAmW 91
Diamond, Paul 1942- WhoAmA 91
Diamond, Paul Steven 1953- WhoEmL 91
Diamond, Peter Arthur 1940- WhoAm 90
Diamond, Philip Ernest 1925- WhoAm 90, WhoWor 91
Diamond, Richard Edward 1932- WhoAm 90
Diamond, Richard John 1941- St&PR 91
Diamond, Robert Francis 1951- WhoEmL 91
Diamond, Robert Paul 1948- BiDrAPA 89
Diamond, Robert S. 1939- St&PR 91
Diamond, Robert Stephen 1939- WhoAm 90
Diamond, Ronald J 1946- BiDrAPA 89
Diamond, Russell W. 1956- St&PR 91
Diamond, Seymour 1925- WhoAm 90
Diamond, Shari Seidman 1947- WhoAmW 91
Diamond, Sidney 1929- WhoAm 90
Diamond, Sigmund 1920- WhoAm 90
Diamond, Stanley Jay 1927- WhoAm 90
Diamond, Steven Elliot 1949- WhoSSW 91
Diamond, Stuart 1942- WhoAmA 91
Diamond, Stuart 1948- WhoAm 90
Diamond, Stuart Samuel 1950- WhoEmL 91
Diamond, Susan Zee 1949- WhoAmW 91
Diamond, William 1917- WhoE 91
Diamondstein, Nelson Lee 1950- WhoE 91
Diamondstone, Lawrence 1928- St&PR 91, WhoE 91, WhoWor 91
Diamonstein, Arthur A. 1930- St&PR 91
Diamonstein, Barbaralee WhoAmA 91
Diamonstein, Richard Gartner 1957- St&PR 91
Diamonstein-Spielvogel, Barbaralee WhoAm 90
Dian, August J 1906- BiDrAPA 89
Diana, Princess 1961- WhoWor 91
Diana, Princess of Wales 1961- BioIn 16
Diana, John Nicholas 1930- WhoAm 90
Diana, Joseph A. 1924- WhoAm 90
Diana, Michael A. 1909-1989 BioIn 16
Diane of Poitiers 1499-1566 WomWR [port]
Diangi, Carmella 1920- St&PR 91
Dianich, Michael B., Sr. 1942- St&PR 91
Dianis, Walter Joseph 1918- WhoAm 90
Diano, Joseph 1904-1987 BioIn 16
Diao, David 1943- WhoAmA 91
Diao, Kenneth BioIn 16
Diar, Prakash BioIn 16
Dias, Aleksander I 1937- BiDrAPA 89
Dias, Antonio Goncalves 1823-1864 BioIn 16
Dias, Frederic 1962- WhoE 91
Dias, P Kithsen K BiDrAPA 89
Dias-Agudo, Fernando Roldao 1925- WhoWor 91
Dias Blue, Anthony BioIn 16
Dias Da Graca, Carlos Alberto WhoWor 91
Dias-Mandoly, Phillip C F 1951- BiDrAPA 89
Diassi, Patrick A. 1926- St&PR 91
Diaz, A. Michel 1945- WhoWor 91
Diaz, Abby Morton 1821-1904 FemiCLE
Diaz, Agustin 1936- St&PR 91
Diaz, Albert 1930- WhoHisp 91
Diaz, Albert 1958- WhoHisp 91
Diaz, Alek 1944- WhoAm 90
Diaz, Alicia 1956- WhoHisp 91
Diaz, Alirio 1923- PenDiMP
Diaz, Ana Rosa 1963- WhoAmW 91
Diaz, Angela C BiDrAPA 89
Diaz, Anthony Joseph 1944- WhoSSW 91
Diaz, Antonio R. 1935- WhoHisp 91
Diaz, Antonio Rimando, Jr. BiDrAPA 89
Diaz, Antonio Rufino 1935- St&PR 91
Diaz, Arthur Fred 1938- WhoHisp 91
Diaz, Barbara Andrea BiDrAPA 89
Diaz, Bartholomew 1450?-1500 EncCRAm
Diaz, Bo 1953- Ballpl 90, WhoHisp 91
Diaz, Carlos 1951- WhoHisp 91
Diaz, Carlos 1958- Ballpl 90
Diaz, Carlos Francisco 1950- WhoHisp 91
Diaz, Carlos Miguel 1919- WhoHisp 91
Diaz, Clemente 1949- WhoHisp 91
Diaz, Dalia 1946- WhoHisp 91
Diaz, David 1933- WhoHisp 91
Diaz, David 1952- WhoSSW 91
Diaz, David R BiDrAPA 89
Diaz, Donna P. 1958- WhoSSW 91
Diaz, Eduardo Acevedo 1851-1921 BioIn 16
Diaz, Eduardo Ibarzabal 1961- WhoHisp 91
Diaz, Elizabeth 1958- WhoHisp 91
Diaz, Emilio Orozco 1909-1987 BioIn 16
Diaz, Esperanza BiDrAPA 89
Diaz, Evelio F 1916- BiDrAPA 89
Diaz, Fernando G. 1946- WhoHisp 91
Diaz, Fernando Gustavo 1946- WhoSSW 91
Diaz, Francisco Antonio Pinto 1785-1858 BioIn 16
Diaz, Frank E. 1942- WhoHisp 91
Diaz, Frank Edward 1942- St&PR 91
Diaz, George 1931- BiDrAPA 89
Diaz, Gerald Joseph, Jr. 1952- WhoEmL 91
Diaz, Gerardo 1939- WhoHisp 91
Diaz, Guarione M. 1941- WhoHisp 91
Diaz, Gwendolyn 1950- WhoHisp 91
Diaz, H. Joseph WhoHisp 91
Diaz, H. Joseph 1930- St&PR 91
Diaz, Hector 1956- BiDrAPA 89
Diaz, Hector L. WhoHisp 91
Diaz, Henry F. 1948- WhoHisp 91
Diaz, Herminio 1941- WhoHisp 91
Diaz, Higinio Guido 1936- BiDrAPA 89
Diaz, Humberto 1937- BiDrAPA 89
Diaz, Ismael 1951- WhoHisp 91
Diaz, Israel 1961- WhoHisp 91
Diaz, James 1927- WhoHisp 91
Diaz, James Conrad, Sr. 1943- WhoHisp 91
Diaz, Jesus Adolfo 1954- WhoHisp 91
Diaz, Jesus Ernesto 1965- WhoHisp 91
Diaz, Joaquin 1947- IntWWM 90
Diaz, Jorge BioIn 16
Diaz, Jorge 1930- HispWr 90
Diaz, Jose Angel 1955- IntWWM 90, WhoHisp 91
Diaz, Jose W. WhoHisp 91
Diaz, Julio Cesar 1948- WhoHisp 91
Diaz, Justino 1939- IntWWM 90
Diaz, Justino 1940- PenDiMP, WhoAm 90
Diaz, Kris A. 1955- WhoHisp 91
Diaz, Lope Max WhoAmA 91
Diaz, Luis Florentino 1946- WhoEmL 91, WhoHisp 91
Diaz, Luis Wilfredo 1961- WhoEmL 91
Diaz, Manuel G. 1921- WhoHisp 91
Diaz, Margarita B 1956- BiDrAPA 89
Diaz, Maria Cristina 1955- WhoHisp 91
Diaz, Mario WhoHisp 91
Diaz, Maximo, Jr. 1944- WhoHisp 91
Diaz, Melchior EncCRAm
Diaz, Mercedes 1938- WhoHisp 91
Diaz, Michael A. 1944- WhoHisp 91
Diaz, Michael A 1950- BiDrAPA 89
Diaz, Mike 1960- Ballpl 90
Diaz, Nelson A. 1947- WhoHisp 91
Diaz, Nelson Angel 1947- WhoE 91
Diaz, Nils J. 1938- WhoHisp 91
Diaz, Octavio 1951- WhoHisp 91
Diaz, Porfirio 1830-1915 BioIn 16, WorAlBi
Diaz, Rafael, Jr. 1939- WhoHisp 91
Diaz, Rafael del Pino BioIn 16
Diaz, Raul de Jesus 1947- WhoSSW 91
Diaz, Raul J. 1947- WhoHisp 91
Diaz, Rene M. WhoHisp 91
Diaz, Rene Michel 1961- WhoSSW 91
Diaz, Ricardo 1951- WhoHisp 91
Diaz, Ricardo A. 1942- St&PR 91
Diaz, Robert James 1946- WhoHisp 91
Diaz, Rudolph A. 1942- WhoHisp 91
Diaz, Samuel T BiDrAPA 89
Diaz, Sharon 1946- WhoEmL 91
Diaz, Steven A. WhoE 91
Diaz, Steven A. 1948- WhoHisp 91
Diaz, Theodore Peter 1947- WhoSSW 91
Diaz, William Adams 1945- WhoAm 90, WhoHisp 91
Diaz-Alejandro, Carlos F 1937-1985 ConAu 131, HispWr 90
Diaz-Alejandro, Carlos Frederico 1937-1985 BioIn 16
Diaz-Arrastia, George Ravelo 1959- WhoEmL 91
Diaz-Azcuy, Orlando BioIn 16
Diaz-Balart, Jose A. 1960- WhoHisp 91
Diaz-Blanco, Eduardo J. 1944- WhoHisp 91
Diaz Bosch, Mario 1944- WhoHisp 91
Diaz-Cabal, Ramiro 1955- BiDrAPA 89
Diaz-Coller, Carlos 1916- WhoAm 90
Diaz-Cruz, Jorge Hatuey 1914- WhoHisp 91
Diaz Cruz, Luis Ramon 1951- WhoHisp 91
Diaz de Chumaceiro, Cora Luisa 1941- WhoWor 91
Diaz del Castillo, Bernal 1496-1584 BioIn 16
Diaz de Torres, Myrtha I. 1944- WhoAmW 91
Diaz de Vivar, Rodrigo 1043?-1099 BioIn 16
Diaz-Duque, Ozzie Francis 1955- WhoHisp 91
Diaz-Hernandez, Jaime Miguel 1950- WhoHisp 91
Diaz-Herrera, Jorge Luis 1950- WhoHisp 91
Diaz Miron, Salvador 1858-1928 HispWr 90
Diaz-Oliver, Remedios 1938- WhoHisp 91
Diaz Ordaz, Gustavo 1911-1979 BioIn 16
Diaz Pena, Mateo 1925- WhoWor 91
Diaz-Perez, Angel R 1948- BiDrAPA 89
Diaz-Peterson, Rosendo 1935- WhoHisp 91
Diaz-Pino, Margarita Beatriz 1956- WhoE 91
Diaz-Pinto, Migdonia Maria 1964- WhoHisp 91
Diaz-Plaja, Guillermo 1909-1984 ConAu 131, HispWr 90
Diaz Rodriguez, Manuel 1868-1927 BioIn 16
Diaz-Silveira, Carlos F 1931- BiDrAPA 89
Diaz Valcarcel, Emilio 1929- HispWr 90
Diaz-Velez, Felix 1942- WhoHisp 91
Diaz-Verson, Salvador 1951- St&PR 91
Diaz-Verson, Salvador, Jr. 1951- WhoAm 90, WhoHisp 91, WhoSSW 91, WhoWor 91
Diaz y Perez, Elias 1933- WhoHisp 91
DiBagno, Ricardo John 1955- WhoE 91
DiBartola, Wayne 1933- St&PR 91
DiBartolomeo, Diane Lynn 1956- WhoEmL 91
di Bassetto, Corno MajTwCW
DiBattiste, Carol 1951- WhoE 91, WhoEmL 91
Dibb, David Walter 1943- WhoSSW 91
Dibb, June Anne BiDrAPA 89
Dibble, Charles Elliott 1909- WhoAm 90
Dibble, Francis Daniel, Jr. 1947- WhoEmL 91
Dibble, George 1904- WhoAmA 91
Dibble, Gordon Lynch 1928- WhoAm 90
Dibble, James Birney 1925- WhoWrEP 89
Dibble, Rob 1964- Ballpl 90
Dibble, Russell Kurt 1945- WhoSSW 91
Dibble, Suzanne Gerdy 1939- St&PR 91
Dibdin, Charles 1745-1814 BioIn 16, OxCPMus, PenDiMP A
Dibdin, Michael 1947- TwCCr&M 91
Dibela, Kingsford 1932- WhoWor 91
Di Belardino, Aldo BioIn 16
Dibeler, John Borden 1957- WhoE 91
Dibelius, Friedrich Karl Otto 1880-1967 BioIn 16
Dibell, Helen Marie 1941- WhoAmW 91
Di Bella, Geoffrey Angelo 1941- BiDrAPA 89
DiBella, Joseph Carmen 1950- WhoSSW 91
DiBella, Joseph Patrick 1940- St&PR 91
DiBella, Lucy Leola 1951- WhoEmL 91
DiBenedetti, Paul E. R. 1937- WhoE 91
DiBenedetto, Al, III 1943- St&PR 91
DiBenedetto, Anthony Thomas 1933- WhoAm 90
di Benedetto, Antonio 1922- HispWr 90
DiBenedetto, Gussie BioIn 16
DiBenedetto, Paul J. 1949- St&PR 91
DiBeneditto, Barbara Jean 1959- WhoAmW 91
DiBerardino, Marie Antoinette 1926- WhoAm 90
Di Bernardo, Giuliano 1939- WhoWor 91
Dibert, Rita Jean 1946- WhoAmA 91
Dibert, William R. 1938- St&PR 91
Dibia, Peter Okonkwo 1932- WhoWor 91
DiBiaggio, John 1932- WhoAm 90, WhoWor 91
Dibianca, Joseph P. 1954- WhoAm 90
Di Bianca, Loretta Mary 1964- WhoEmL 91
Di Bianco, Joseph T 1933- BiDrAPA 89
DiBiase, Joseph Ralph 1940- WhoE 91
DiBiase, Michael 1957- WhoEmL 91
DiBiasio, Linda April 1944- WhoAmW 91
DiBitonto, Daryl Dean 1952- WhoSSW 91
DiBlasi, John Peter 1955- WhoEmL 91
DiBlasi, Philip James 1954- WhoSSW 91
Dible, William Trotter 1925- St&PR 91
Dibley, Nancy Priscilla 1931- IntWWM 90
Dibner, Bern St&PR 91N
Dibner, Bern 1897-1988 BioIn 16
Dibner, David R. 1926- St&PR 91
Dibner, David Robert 1926- WhoAm 90
Dibner, Martin 1911- WhoE 91, WhoWrEP 89
Dibona, Anthony 1896- WhoAmA 91N
DiBona, Charles Joseph 1932- WhoAm 90
Dibrell, Louis Nelson, III 1945- St&PR 91, WhoAm 90, WhoEmL 91
Dibui, W.J. 1943- St&PR 91
DiBuono, Anthony Joseph 1930- St&PR 91, WhoAm 90

DiBuono, Mark V. 1954- BiDrAPA 89
DiCamillo, Debra Allen 1957- WhoAmW 91
DiCamillo, Gary T. BioIn 16
DiCamillo, Gary Thomas 1950- WhoAm 90, WhoEmL 91
DiCamillo, Loretta Smimmo 1935- WhoAmW 91
Dicanio, Frank 1916- St&PR 91
Dicapua, Edmund Charles 1956- IntWWM 90
Di Capua, Edoardo 1864-1917 OxCPMus
DiCara, Lawrence Salvatore 1949- WhoE 91
DiCarlo, Armand Joseph 1945- WhoE 91
DiCarlo, Dominick L. 1928- WhoAm 90
DiCarlo, Edward Francis William 1953- WhoE 91
DiCarlo, Guy, Jr. 1933- WhoE 91
DiCarlo, Louis Michael 1903- WhoAm 90, WhoWor 91
DiCarlo, Mario 1922- WhoE 91
DiCarlo, Susanne Helen 1956- WhoAmW 91
Dicasali, Raymond Lee 1948- St&PR 91
Dicciani, Nance Katherine 1947- WhoEmL 91
Dice, Elizabeth Jane 1919- WhoAmA 91
Dice, Rhondalee Rohleder 1958- WhoAmW 91
Dicello, John Francis, Jr. 1938- WhoAm 90, WhoWor 91
Di Censo, Remo 1927- BiDrAPA 89
di Cenzo, Colin Domenic 1923- WhoAm 90
DiCenzo, George ConTFT 8
Di Cerbo, Michael 1947- WhoAmA 91
Dicerto, Anthony R. 1941- St&PR 91
Di Certo, Joseph J 1933- SmATA 60 [port]
Di Cesare, Ezio 1939- IntWWM 90
Dich, Lois Boyd 1944- WhoAmW 91
Dicharry, Douglas Clark 1951- BiDrAPA 89
Dichiara, Armand 1943- St&PR 91
DiChiera, David BioIn 16
Dichiera, David 1937- IntWWM 90
Di Chiera, David 1937- WhoAm 90
Dichter, Barry Joel 1950- WhoE 91, WhoEmL 91
Dichter, Cipa 1944- PenDiMP
Dichter, Ernest 1907- WhoAm 90
Dichter, Howard N 1950- BiDrAPA 89
Dichter, Lionel BiDrAPA 89
Dichter, Mischa 1945- PenDiMP
Dichter, Misha 1945- IntWWM 90, WhoAm 90
Dichter, Scott 1953- WhoSSW 91
Dichter, Tobey G. 1944- ODwPR 91
Di Cicco, Pier Giorgio 1949- BioIn 16
DiCicco, Susan Ailene 1959- WhoE 91
Dick, Albert Blake 1856-1934 WorAlBi
Dick, Albert Blake 1918-1989 BioIn 16
Dick, Anne FemiCLE
Dick, Bertram Gale, Jr. 1926- WhoAm 90
Dick, Catherine Lillian BiDrAPA 89
Dick, Charles BiDrAPA 89
Dick, Charles H. WhoAm 90
Dick, Charles Mathews, Jr. 1924- WhoE 91
Dick, Dennis Eugene 1939- St&PR 91
Dick, Donald Albert 1933- St&PR 91
Dick, Douglas Patrick 1953- St&PR 91
Dick, Earl Philip BiDrAPA 89
Dick, Eleanor 1918- IntWWM 90
Dick, Emanuel 1915- St&PR 91
Dick, Harold L. 1943- WhoAm 90
Dick, Henry Henry 1922- WhoAm 90
Dick, Henry Noble 1932- St&PR 91
Dick, Jerry Wayne 1947- St&PR 91
Dick, John 1917- BioIn 16
Dick, John Alexander 1949- WhoWor 91
Dick, John Antony 1934- WhoWor 91
Dick, John R. 1936- St&PR 91
Dick, Justin 1957- WhoEmL 91
Dick, Kay 1915- BioIn 16
Dick, Kenneth John 1950- WhoEmL 91
Dick, Louise Lattomus 1937- WhoSSW 91
Dick, Nancy E. 1930- WhoAm 90, WhoAmW 91
Dick, Norman Charles 1956- WhoEmL 91
Dick, Patricia Macke 1956- WhoEmL 91
Dick, Paul Wyatt 1940- WhoAm 90, WhoE 91
Dick, Philip K 1928-1982 MajTwCW, RGTwCSF, WorAlBi, WorAu 1980
Dick, Raymond Dale 1930- WhoAm 90
Dick, Richard Irwin 1935- WhoAm 90
Dick, Rollin Merle 1931- WhoAm 90
Dick, Stacy S. 1956- St&PR 91
Dick, Thomas Michael 1955- WhoSSW 91
Dick, Trella Lamson 1889-1974 AuBYP 90
Dickason, James Frank 1922- WhoAm 90
Dickason, John Hamilton 1931- WhoAm 90
Dickason, L. King, Jr. 1942- St&PR 91
Dickason, Olive Patricia 1920- ConAu 132
Dickason, Richard R. 1946- St&PR 91
Dicke, Arnold Arthur 1942- St&PR 91
Dicke, Candice Edwards 1949- WhoAm 90
Dicke, James Frederick, II 1945- WhoAm 90
Dicke, Robert Henry 1916- WhoAm 90, WhoWor 91
Dickelman, James Howard 1947- St&PR 91
Dicken, Craig Lee 1950- WhoEmL 91
Dicken, Cynthia S. ODwPR 91
Dickens, Bernard Morris 1937- WhoAm 90
Dickens, Brian Scott 1942- St&PR 91
Dickens, Charles 1812-1870 AuBYP 90, BioIn 16, EncO&P 3, EncPaPR 91, TwCCr&M 91A, WorAlBi
Dickens, Charles Allen 1932- WhoSSW 91
Dickens, Doris Lee BiDrAPA 89, WhoAmW 91, WhoE 91, WhoWor 91
Dickens, Esther Anne 1931- WhoAmW 91
Dickens, Gordon Lee, III 1952- WhoSSW 91
Dickens, Homer BioIn 16
Dickens, Inez Elizabeth 1949- WhoAmW 91
Dickens, Lloyd E. BioIn 16
Dickens, Mary 1862-1948 FemiCLE
Dickens, Monica 1915- BioIn 16, FemiCLE
Dickens, Monica Enid 1915- AuBYP 90
Dickens, Robert Allen BiDrAPA 89
Dickens, Roy S. 1938-1986 BioIn 16
Dickens, Timothy 1947- BiDrAPA 89
Dickens, Vera Josie 1933- WhoAmW 91
Dickens, William Arthur 1957- WhoSSW 91
Dickenson, Henry Boyd 1924- WhoAm 90
Dickenson, J.T. 1930- St&PR 91
Dickenson, James William 1940- IntWWM 90
Dickenson, Mollie 1935- ConAu 129
Dickenson, Vic 1906-1984 BioIn 16, OxCPMus
Dickenson, Victor St&PR 91
Dicker, Richard 1914- St&PR 91
Dicker, Robert Howard BiDrAPA 89
Dickerman, Allen Briggs 1914- WhoWor 91
Dickerman, Herbert William 1928- WhoAm 90
Dickerman, John M. 1914- ODwPR 91
Dickerman, John Melvin 1914- WhoE 91
Dickerman, Leo 1896-1982 Ballpl 90
Dickerman, Robert S. 1919- St&PR 91
Dickerson, Albert Myron 1947- WhoSSW 91
Dickerson, Amy Elizabeth 1965- WhoAmW 91
Dickerson, Arthur J. 1929- St&PR 91
Dickerson, Brian S 1951- WhoAmA 91
Dickerson, Charles W. 1944- St&PR 91
Dickerson, Claire Moore 1950- WhoAmW 91, WhoEmL 91
Dickerson, Daniel Jay 1922- WhoAmA 91
Dickerson, David W. 1929- St&PR 91
Dickerson, Edward Ted 1932- WhoAmA 91
Dickerson, Eric BioIn 16
Dickerson, Eric 1960- WorAlBi
Dickerson, Eric Demetric 1960- WhoAm 90
Dickerson, Frank Secor, III 1939- St&PR 91, WhoAm 90
Dickerson, Frederick Reed 1909- WhoAm 90, WhoWor 91
Dickerson, Frieda Esther Worrell 1922- WhoE 91
Dickerson, Gary Don 1950- St&PR 91
Dickerson, Graham David 1951- IntWWM 90
Dickerson, Ilse Agnes 1924- WhoAm 90
Dickerson, Jack David 1949- WhoSSW 91
Dickerson, James Wiley BiDrAPA 89
Dickerson, John Gillette 1943- WhoE 91
Dickerson, John Ray 1952- WhoEmL 91
Dickerson, Linda Ann 1961- St&PR 91
Dickerson, Mahlon 1770-1853 BiDrUSE 89
Dickerson, Mildred Thornhill 1951- WhoEmL 91
Dickerson, Monar Stephen 1947- WhoSSW 91
Dickerson, Nancy BioIn 16
Dickerson, Nancy Hanschman WhoAm 90, WhoAmW 91
Dickerson, Pamela May 1961- WhoAmW 91
Dickerson, Robert Charles 1960- St&PR 91
Dickerson, Robert D. 1949- St&PR 91
Dickerson, Robert Donald 1949- WhoAm 90
Dickerson, Robert K. 1946- St&PR 91
Dickerson, Thomas Pasquali 1950- WhoE 91
Dickerson, Vera Mason 1946- WhoAmA 91
Dickerson, Warner Lee 1937- WhoSSW 91
Dickerson, William J 1928- BiDrAPA 89
Dickerson, William J 1943- WhoAmA 91
Dickerson, William Judson 1904- WhoAmA 91N
Dickerson, William Roy 1928- WhoWor 91
Dickes, Richard A 1942- BiDrAPA 89
Dickes, Richard Alexander 1942- WhoE 91
Dickes, Robert 1912- BiDrAPA 89, WhoAm 90
Dickeson, Jana B. 1961- St&PR 91
Dickeson, Ludmila Weir 1941- WhoAmW 91
Dickeson, Robert Celmer 1940- WhoAm 90
Dickey, Bette Ellyn 1936- WhoAmW 91
Dickey, Bill 1907- Ballpl 90 [port]
Dickey, Boh A. 1944- St&PR 91
Dickey, Charles Richard 1935- St&PR 91
Dickey, David Herschel 1951- WhoSSW 91, WhoWor 91
Dickey, Duval Frederick 1916- WhoAm 90
Dickey, George Edward 1940- WhoE 91
Dickey, Glenn Ernest, Jr. 1936- WhoAm 90
Dickey, Jack E. 1928- St&PR 91
Dickey, James BioIn 16
Dickey, James 1923- MajTwCW, WhoAm 90, WhoWor 91, WorAlBi
Dickey, Jill 1955- WhoE 91
Dickey, John Horace 1914- WhoAm 90
Dickey, John Miller NewYTBS 90
Dickey, John Miller 1911-1990 WhoAm 90
Dickey, John Patrick 1935- WhoAm 90
Dickey, John Sloan, Jr. 1941- WhoSSW 91
Dickey, Julia Edwards 1940- WhoAmW 91
Dickey, Kenneth C. 1926- St&PR 91
Dickey, Louise Parke 1942- IntWWM 90, WhoAmW 91
Dickey, Robert Marvin 1950- WhoEmL 91
Dickey, Robert Preston 1936- WhoAm 90
Dickey, Sarah Ann 1838-1904 BioAmW
Dickey, Sharon Ruthane 1959- WhoAmW 91
Dickey, Steven Ryan 1947- WhoEmL 91
Dickey, Thomas Atherton 1917- WhoE 91
Dickey, Thomas Oscar, III 1952- BiDrAPA 89
Dickey, William 1928- WhoAm 90
Dickhoff, Robert Ernest EncO&P 3
Dickhoner, William H. 1921- St&PR 91
Dickhut, Heinrich Balduin 1937- WhoSSW 91
Dickhut, J.K. PenDiDA 89
Dickie, Brian James 1941- IntWWM 90
Dickie, John 1953- IntWWM 90
Dickie, Lloyd Merlin 1926- WhoAm 90
Dickie, M. Heather 1955- WhoEmL 91
Dickie, Margaret McKenzie 1935- WhoAm 90
Dickie, Murray 1924- IntWWM 90, PenDiMP
Dickie, Shirley Dalme 1946- WhoSSW 91
Dickinson, Alfred James 1916- WhoAm 90
Dickinson, Angie BioIn 16
Dickinson, Angie 1931- WhoAm 90, WorAlBi
Dickinson, Blanche Taylor 1896- HarlReB
Dickinson, Bob ODwPR 91
Dickinson, Bradley William 1948- WhoAm 90
Dickinson, Brian Ward 1937- WhoE 91
Dickinson, Calhoun 1931- WhoAm 90
Dickinson, Catherine Schatz 1927- WhoAmW 91
Dickinson, Charles Cameron, III 1936- WhoAm 90, WhoSSW 91, WhoWor 91
Dickinson, Dana Lynne 1951- WhoAmW 91
Dickinson, Daniel Stevens 1800-1866 BioIn 16
Dickinson, David Budd, Jr. 1936- WhoAm 90
Dickinson, David Charles 1940- WhoAmA 91
Dickinson, David Franklin 1953- WhoEmL 91
Dickinson, David Kelly 1948- WhoE 91
Dickinson, David W. WhoAm 90
Dickinson, Donald Charles 1927- WhoAm 90
Dickinson, Donald McDonald 1846-1917 BiDrUSE 89
Dickinson, Donald R. 1923- St&PR 91
Dickinson, Dorothy Helen 1941- IntWWM 90
Dickinson, Edmund 1624-1707 EncO&P 3
Dickinson, Edward 1803-1874 BioIn 16
Dickinson, Edward 1861-1898 BioIn 16
Dickinson, Edwin W 1891-1979 WhoAmA 91N
Dickinson, Eleanor Creekmore 1931- WhoAm 90, WhoAmA 91
Dickinson, Ellen S BiDrAPA 89
Dickinson, Emily 1830-1866 WorAlBi
Dickinson, Emily 1830-1886 BioAmW, BioIn 16, FemiCLE, PoeCrit 1 [port], WrPh
Dickinson, Emily Drake 1959- WhoEmL 91
Dickinson, Emily Norcross 1804-1882 BioIn 16
Dickinson, Ernest Milton 1905- WhoAm 90
Dickinson, Fairleigh S., Jr. 1919- St&PR 91
Dickinson, Fairleigh Stanton, Jr. 1919- WhoAm 90, WhoWor 91
Dickinson, George H. Ballpl 90
Dickinson, Jacob John Louis 1957- WhoEmL 91
Dickinson, Jacob McGavock 1851-1928 BiDrUSE 89
Dickinson, James Gordon 1940- WhoAm 90
Dickinson, Jane W. 1919- WhoAmW 91
Dickinson, Janet WhoWrEP 89
Dickinson, Jimmy Leon 1942- St&PR 91
Dickinson, JoAnne Walton 1936- WhoAmW 91, WhoSSW 91, WhoWor 91
Dickinson, John 1732-1808 BioIn 16, EncCRAm [port], WorAlBi
Dickinson, John Francis 1927- St&PR 91
Dickinson, John Taylor 1961- WhoE 91
Dickinson, Jonathan 1688-1747 EncCRAm
Dickinson, Joshua Clifton, Jr. 1916- WhoAm 90
Dickinson, Lawrence William 1946- St&PR 91
Dickinson, Linda Knowles 1951- WhoE 91
Dickinson, Luren Errol 1951- WhoEmL 91
Dickinson, Mary BioIn 16
Dickinson, Mary 1949- BioIn 16
Dickinson, Mary Alison Joseph 1959- WhoE 91
Dickinson, Meriel 1940- IntWWM 90, PenDiMP
Dickinson, Moss Kent 1822-1897 DcCanB 12
Dickinson, Ned 1861-1898 BioIn 16
Dickinson, Norman 1921- WhoAmA 91
Dickinson, Paul R. WhoHisp 91
Dickinson, Peter 1927- AuBYP 90, ConAu 31NR, SmATA 62 [port], TwCCr&M 91
Dickinson, Peter 1934- IntWWM 90, WhoWor 91
Dickinson, Richard Donald Nye 1929- WhoAm 90
Dickinson, Richard Henry 1944- WhoE 91
Dickinson, Richard R. 1931- St&PR 91
Dickinson, Richard Raymond 1931- WhoAm 90
Dickinson, Robert Duke 1916- IntWWM 90
Dickinson, Robert Earl 1940- WhoAm 90
Dickinson, Robert Hugh 1918- BiDrAPA 89
Dickinson, Robert Vance 1941- WhoAm 90
Dickinson, Roger Allyn 1929- WhoAm 90
Dickinson, Samuel D. 1850- AmLegL
Dickinson, Selden Jerome 1927-1990 BioIn 16
Dickinson, Steve R. 1942- St&PR 91
Dickinson, Thomas George 1955- IntWWM 90
Dickinson, Velvalee BioIn 16
Dickinson, Wade 1926- WhoAm 90
Dickinson, Wendy Armour 1957- WhoAmW 91
Dickinson, William Boyd, Jr. 1931- WhoAm 90
Dickinson, William Louis WhoAm 90, WhoSSW 91
Dickinson, William Trevor 1939- WhoAm 90
Dickinson-McDonald, Victoria Ann 1951- WhoAmW 91
Dickison, Carolyn Hope Carpenter 1933- WhoAmW 91
Dickler, Robert M. 1945- WhoAm 90
Dickman, Earl 1925- St&PR 91
Dickman, Emerson 1914-1981 Ballpl 90
Dickman, Francois Moussiegt 1924- WhoAm 90
Dickman, Gary 1951- St&PR 91
Dickman, Howard Stanley 1935- St&PR 91
Dickman, James Bruce 1949- WhoAm 90
Dickman, Marcus 1960- IntWWM 90
Dickman, Marshall ODwPR 91
Dickman, William A BiDrAPA 89
Dickmann, Dale Sidney 1931- St&PR 91
Dickmeyer, Lowell A. 1939- BioIn 16
Dickol, Edward H. 1926- St&PR 91
Dicks, Jack William 1949- WhoEmL 91, WhoSSW 91
Dicks, John Barber 1926- WhoAm 90
Dicks, Joyce Carolee 1936- WhoAmW 91
Dicks, Norman De Valois 1940- WhoAm 90
Dicks, Robert F. 1948- St&PR 91
Dicks, Robert Wilson, Jr. 1945- St&PR 91

Dicksee, Margaret Isabel 1858-1903 BiDWomA
Dickshot, Johnny 1910- Ballpl 90
Dickson, A.T. 1931- St&PR 91
Dickson, Alan T. 1931- WhoAm 90, WhoSSW 91
Dickson, Alex Dockery 1926- WhoAm 90
Dickson, Arthur L. 1902- St&PR 91
Dickson, Barbara 1947- OxCPMus
Dickson, Brian 1916- WhoAm 90, WhoE 91, WhoWor 91
Dickson, Carol Jean 1955- WhoAmW 91
Dickson, Carol Ward 1951- WhoAmW 91, WhoEmL 91
Dickson, Carr ConAu 33NR, MajTwCW, TwCCr&M 91
Dickson, Carroll J. 1905- WhoAm 90
Dickson, Carter ConAu 33NR, MajTwCW, TwCCr&M 91
Dickson, Catherine A. 1931- St&PR 91
Dickson, Daniel H. 1951- St&PR 91
Dickson, David Catchings 1815-1880 AmLegL
Dickson, David Watson Daly 1919- WhoAm 90
Dickson, Dianne Marie 1954- WhoEmL 91
Dickson, Dorothy 1896- OxCPMus
Dickson, Eleanor Shaler BioIn 16
Dickson, Eva Mae 1922- WhoAmW 91
Dickson, Frederic Howard 1946- WhoEmL 91
Dickson, Frederick Seller 1924- St&PR 91
Dickson, Gail Watkins 1943- WhoSSW 91
Dickson, Gean Harvill 1940- WhoSSW 91
Dickson, Gordon 1923- WorAlBi
Dickson, Gordon R. 1923- RGTwCSF
Dickson, Herbert J. 1925- St&PR 91
Dickson, James Edwin, II 1943- WhoE 91
Dickson, James Francis, III 1924- WhoAm 90
Dickson, James Lothar 1949- WhoAm 90
Dickson, Jane Leone 1952- WhoAmA 91, WhoE 91
Dickson, Jennifer Joan 1936- WhoAmA 91
Dickson, Jim 1938- Ballpl 90
Dickson, Joan 1921- IntWWM 90
Dickson, John 1916- WhoWrEP 89
Dickson, John H. 1943- St&PR 91, WhoAm 90
Dickson, John R. 1930- WhoAm 90
Dickson, Joseph M. 1935- WhoAm 90
Dickson, Karen Kenney 1955- BiDrAPA 89
Dickson, Katharine Hayland 1904- WhoSSW 91
Dickson, Lesley Ruth 1947- BiDrAPA 89
Dickson, Louis L BiDrAPA 89
Dickson, M. Chris 1935- St&PR 91
Dickson, Marguerite 1873-1953 AuBYP 90
Dickson, Mark Amos 1946- WhoAmA 91
Dickson, Markham Allen 1922- WhoSSW 91
Dickson, Murry 1916- Ballpl 90
Dickson, Murry 1916-1989 BioIn 16
Dickson, Paul BioIn 16
Dickson, Paul 1905- WhoAm 90
Dickson, Paul Andrew 1939- WhoE 91
Dickson, Paul Wesley, Jr. 1931- WhoAm 90, WhoWor 91
Dickson, Phyllis Webster 1926- WhoAmW 91
Dickson, R. Stuart 1929- St&PR 91
Dickson, Robert George 1930- St&PR 91
Dickson, Robert J. 1933- St&PR 91
Dickson, Robert Jay 1947- WhoEmL 91
Dickson, Robert John, Jr. 1949- WhoEmL 91
Dickson, Robert Lee 1932- WhoAm 90
Dickson, Roger E. 1947- WhoSSW 91
Dickson, Rush Stuart 1929- WhoAm 90, WhoSSW 91
Dickson, Ruth Ann 1953- BiDrAPA 89
Dickson, Sally ODwPR 91
Dickson, Sally Isabelle WhoAm 90
Dickson, Thomas David BioIn 16
Dickson, W.D. 1948- St&PR 91
Dickson, Walt 1878-1918 Ballpl 90
Dickson, William H. AmLegL
Dickson-Porter, Claudia Blair 1925- WhoAmW 91, WhoWor 91
Dickstein, Cynthia Diane 1946- WhoE 91, WhoEmL 91
Dickstein, Frank BioIn 16
Dickstein, George ODwPR 91
Dickstein, Leah Joan 1934- BiDrAPA 89
Dickstein, Michael Ethan 1959- WhoEmL 91
Dickstein, Sidney 1925- WhoAm 90
Dickstein, Simone Andrea 1957- WhoEmL 91
Dickstein, Stephen S BiDrAPA 89
DiCocco, Lou 1951- St&PR 91
DiComo, Michael Paul 1948- St&PR 91
Dicorcia, Edward T. 1930- St&PR 91
Di Cori, Ferruccio A BiDrAPA 89
DiCosimo, Charles John, II 1948- WhoE 91
Di Cosimo, Joanne Violet 1953- WhoAm 90
Di Cosola, Lois 1935- WhoAmA 91
DiCostanzo, Geraldine 1938- St&PR 91
DiCroce, Deborah Marie 1952- WhoSSW 91
Dicterow, Glenn 1948- IntWWM 90
Dicterow, Glenn Eugene 1948- WhoAm 90
Dicus, Clarence Howard, Jr. 1921- WhoAm 90
Dicus, John Carmack 1933- WhoAm 90
Dicus, Stephen Howard 1948- WhoEmL 91
Diczok, Paul D. 1943- St&PR 91
Didda WomWR
Diddel, Katha BioIn 16
Didden, George A., Jr. 1909- St&PR 91
Diddle, Deborah Kay 1949- WhoWrEP 89
Diddley, Bo BioIn 16, EncPR&S 89
Diddley, Bo 1928- DrBIPA 90, OxCPMus, WorAlBi
Diderot, Denis 1713-1784 BioIn 16, WorAlBi
Dides, Jurji Wadi BiDrAPA 89
Didi, Mestre 1917- ArtLatA
Didieo, James 1949- St&PR 91, WhoAm 90
Didier Brothers EncO&P 3
Didier, Adolph EncO&P 3
Didier, Alexis EncO&P 3
Didier, Alexis 1847?-1888? EncPaPR 91
Didier, Bob 1949- Ballpl 90
Didier, Michelle Ann WhoAmW 91
Didimamoff, Stephen Patrick 1945- St&PR 91
DiDio, Liberato John Alphonse 1920- WhoAm 90
Didion, Doug 1949- St&PR 91
Didion, Gilbert 1921- St&PR 91
Didion, James J. BioIn 16, WhoAm 90
Didion, Joan BioIn 16
Didion, Joan 1934- BioAmW, FemiCLE, MajTwCW, WhoAm 90, WhoAmW 91, WhoWrEP 89, WorAlBi
Didisheim, Ricarda J BiDrAPA 89
Di Domenica, Robert 1927- IntWWM 90
Di Domenica, Robert Anthony 1927- WhoAm 90
DiDomenico, Donald M. 1944- St&PR 91
DiDomenico, Mauro, Jr. 1937- WhoAm 90
Didomenico, Nikki 1948- WhoAmA 91
DiDomizio, Robert Anthony, Jr. 1955- WhoE 91, WhoEmL 91
DiDonato, Edward Joseph 1954- WhoE 91
Di Donato, Louis Michael 1946- WhoSSW 91
Di Donato, Pietro 1911- BioIn 16
Didone, Joseph 1926- St&PR 91
DiDonna, Richard A. St&PR 91, WhoAm 90
Didrickson, Loleta Anderson 1941- WhoAmW 91
Didriksen, Caleb H., III 1955- WhoEmL 91
Didrikson, Babe 1911-1956 BioIn 16
Didrikson, Mildred BioAmW
Di Drusco, Giovanni 1930- WhoWor 91
Didur, Adam 1874-1946 PenDiMP
Didzerekis, Paul Patrick 1939- WhoWor 91
Die Neuberin EncCoWW
Die, Ann Marie Hayes 1944- WhoAmW 91
Dieb, Dennis Rodney 1942- St&PR 91
Dieball, Dana Vincent 1953- WhoSSW 91
Diebel, Donald Ray 1947- WhoSSW 91, WhoWrEP 89
Diebel, Ronald C BiDrAPA 89
Diebel, William 1905- St&PR 91
Diebenkorn, Richard 1911- WorAlBi
Diebenkorn, Richard 1922- BioIn 16, WhoAmA 91
Diebenkorn, Richard Clifford, Jr. 1922- WhoAm 90
Diebold, Foster Frank 1932- WhoAm 90, WhoE 91
Diebold, Jim BioIn 16
Diebold, John 1926- BioIn 16, WhoAm 90
Diebold, John Mark 1957- WhoSSW 91
Diebold, Paul Horst 1944- WhoWor 91
Diebold, Raymond Joseph 1940- St&PR 91
Dieck, Daniel William 1951- WhoEmL 91
Dieck, E. Leopold 1940- WhoWor 91
Diecke, Friedrich Paul Julius 1927- WhoAm 90
Dieckert, Jurgen 1935- WhoWor 91
Dieckmann, Ed, Jr. 1920- WhoWrEP 89
Dieckmann, Karl W. 1928- St&PR 91
Dieckmann, O. Karl 1913- St&PR 91
Dieckmann, Wallace C. 1943- St&PR 91
Diederich, Anne Marie 1943- WhoAmW 91
Diederich, Daniel Kevin 1957- WhoEmL 91
Diederich, Helmut Anton 1928- WhoWor 91
Diederich, John William 1929- St&PR 91, WhoAm 90, WhoSSW 91, WhoWor 91
Diederich, R. David 1942- St&PR 91
Diederichs, Janet 1929- ODwPR 91
Diederichs, Janet Wood WhoAmW 91
Diederichs, John Kuensting 1921- WhoAm 90, WhoWor 91
Diedrich, Richard John 1936- St&PR 91, WhoWor 91
Diedrich, Richard Joseph 1936- WhoSSW 91
Diedrich, Susanne L BiDrAPA 89
Diedrich, William Lawler 1923- WhoAm 90
Diedrick, Arthur Hill, Jr. 1937- St&PR 91
Diedrick, George Vernon 1936- St&PR 91
Diefenbach, Pamela BiDrAPA 89
Diefenbach, Viron Leroy 1922- WhoAm 90
Diefenbaker, John 1895-1979 WorAlBi
Diefenderfer, William Martin, III 1945- WhoAm 90
Diefendorf, Arthur Ashley 1935- St&PR 91
Diegnan, Norman 1941- ODwPR 91
Diegnan, Norman Francis 1941- WhoE 91
Diego, Gerardo 1896-1987 HispWr 90
Diego, Rafaela BiDrAPA 89
Dieguez, Richard P. 1960- WhoHisp 91
Dieguez, Richard Peter 1960- WhoEmL 91
Diehl, Alden Edgar 1931- St&PR 91
Diehl, Alice 1844-1912 FemiCLE
Diehl, Charles Edward 1922- WhoE 91
Diehl, Chuck BioIn 16
Diehl, Deborah Hilda 1951- WhoEmL 91
Diehl, Digby Robert 1940- WhoAm 90
Diehl, Gerald George 1916- WhoAm 90
Diehl, Guy Louis 1949- WhoAmA 91
Diehl, Hans-Jurgen 1940- WhoAmA 91
Diehl, Harrison Lueders, Jr. 1935- St&PR 91
Diehl, Kenneth Laverne 1961- WhoEmL 91
Diehl, Lauren Traynor 1955- WhoEmL 91
Diehl, Lesley Ann 1943- WhoAmW 91
Diehl, Mark Emory 1951- WhoEmL 91
Diehl, Richard Kurth 1935- WhoAm 90
Diehl, Richard Lee 1928- St&PR 91
Diehl, Russell R. 1946- St&PR 91
Diehl, Sevilla S WhoAmA 91
Diehl, Stephen Anthony 1942- WhoAm 90, WhoE 91
Diehl, Thomas Franklin 1951- St&PR 91
Diehl, Timothy Jerel 1949- WhoE 91
Diehl, Walter Francis, Jr. 1935- St&PR 91, WhoAm 90
Diehl, Werner Karl St&PR 91
Diehl-Callaway, Linda Jo 1955- WhoAmW 91
Diehm, James Warren 1944- WhoAm 90
Diehm, Russell Charles 1946- WhoEmL 91
Diehn, Kate 1900- BiDWomA
Diehr, Beverly Hunt 1954- WhoEmL 91
Diekema, Anthony J. 1933- WhoAm 90
Diekema, Gerrit John 1859-1930 AmLegL
Dieker, Charles W. 1935- St&PR 91
Diel, Delores Kay 1953- WhoEmL 91
Dielman, Terry Edward 1952- WhoSSW 91
Diels, Gero BiDrAPA 89
Diels, Jean-Pierre Frederic 1949- St&PR 91
Diels, Otto P. H. 1876-1954 WorAlBi
Diem, Ngo Dinh 1901-1963 WorAlBi
Diem, Robert James 1944- St&PR 91
Diemar, Robert Emery, Jr. 1942- WhoAm 90
Diemecke, Paulo Roberto 1950- IntWWM 90
Diemente, Edward Philip 1923- IntWWM 90
Diemer, Arthur William 1925- WhoSSW 91
Diemer, Emma Lou BioIn 16
Diemer, Emma Lou 1927- IntWWM 90, WhoAm 90
Diemer, Jean Claude 1929- WhoWor 91
Diemer, Louis 1843-1919 PenDiMP
Dien, Philippe Nguyen Kim 1921-1988 BioIn 16
Dienemann, Paul Francis 1939- WhoE 91
Diener, Bert 1915- WhoAm 90, WhoE 91
Diener, Betty Jane 1940- WhoAm 90, WhoAmW 91
Diener, Eugenia 1925- EncCoWW
Diener, Ira Howard 1942- St&PR 91
Diener, Jerry L. St&PR 91
Diener, Robert Benjamin BiDrAPA 89
Diener, Robert Benjamin 1963- WhoEmL 91
Diener, Robert L.B. 1948- St&PR 91
Diener, Royce 1918- WhoAm 90
Diener, Theodor Otto 1921- WhoAm 90, WhoWor 91
Dienes, Sari 1898- BiDWomA, WhoAmA 91
Dienesch, Marie-Madeleine 1914- BiDFrPL
Dienst, Evelyn 1943- WhoAmW 91
Dienst, Henry W. 1935- St&PR 91
Dienstag, Eleanor Foa WhoE 91
Dienstbier, Jiri 1937- WhoWor 91
Dienstfrey, Harris David 1934- WhoAm 90
Diep, Do Ngoc 1950- WhoWor 91
Diepenbrock, Melchior von EncO&P 3
Dieperink, Willem 1933- BiDrAPA 89
Diepgen, Eberhard 1941- WhoWor 91
Diepholz, David Lester 1962- WhoEmL 91
Dieppe, Peter J. 1949- WhoSSW 91
Dier, Kelly E. 1949- St&PR 91
Dier, Raymond BioIn 16
Dierauf, Leslie Ann 1948- WhoAm 90, WhoAmW 91
Dierberg, James BioIn 16
Dierckman, Nicholas Bernard 1951- WhoSSW 91
Diercks, Chester William, Jr. 1926- WhoAm 90
Diercks, Frederick Otto 1912- WhoAm 90, WhoSSW 91, WhoWor 91
Diercks, John Henry 1927- IntWWM 90
Diercks, Mark Jeffrey 1955- BiDrAPA 89
Diercks, Walter Elmer 1945- WhoAm 90
Dierdorf, Dan BioIn 16
Dierdorf, Daniel Lee 1949- WhoAm 90
Dierdorff, John Ainsworth 1928- WhoAm 90
Dieren, Bernard Van 1887-1936 BioIn 16
Diering, Chuck 1923- Ballpl 90
Dieringer, Cindy Sue 1949- WhoEmL 91
Dierkens, Jean Charles 1926- WhoWor 91
Dierker, Larry 1946- Ballpl 90
Dierkes, John H. 1963- St&PR 91
Dierkes, Meinolf 1941- WhoWor 91
Dierkesmann, Rainer E. 1942- WhoWor 91
Dierks, Henry T. 1931- St&PR 91
Dierks, Richard Ernest 1934- WhoAm 90
Dierks, Terry A. 1946- St&PR 91
Dierman, Gerald F. 1942- St&PR 91
Dierna, Joseph Biaggio 1959- WhoE 91, WhoEmL 91
Diernisse, Villy 1928- WhoWrEP 89
Diers, Cynthia Dell 1952- WhoEmL 91
Diers, Hank H. 1931- WhoAm 90
Diers, Michael Everett 1961- WhoEmL 91
Diersen, David John 1948- WhoEmL 91
Diersen, Karen Annette 1950- WhoAmW 91
Diersen, Michael Larry 1954- WhoEmL 91
Dierstein, Rudiger 1930- WhoWor 91
Dies, Bruce F. 1939- St&PR 91
Dies, Douglas Hilton 1913- WhoAm 90
Dies, Martin 1901-1972 WorAlBi
Dies, Rose Ann 1958- St&PR 91
Diesch, Stanley La Verne 1925- WhoAm 90
Dieschbourg, Edward J. 1955- St&PR 91
Diesel, John P. 1926- St&PR 91
Diesel, John Phillip 1926- WhoAm 90
Diesel, Paul M. 1944- St&PR 91
Diesel, Rudolf 1858-1913 WorAlBi
Diesem, Charles David 1921- WhoAm 90
Diesem, John Lawrence 1941- WhoAm 90
Diesendruck, Leo 1920- WhoWor 91
Diesenhofer, Johann 1943- WorAlBi
Dieskau, Dietrich Fischer- 1925- BioIn 16
Diessner, Ardell W 1923- BiDrAPA 89
Diestelkamp, Dawn Lea 1954- WhoAmW 91
Dietch, Henry Xerxes 1913- WhoAm 90
Dietch, Robert 1938- St&PR 91
Dietel, Gregory Louis 1948- St&PR 91
Dietel, James Edwin 1941- WhoE 91
Dietel, William Moore 1927- WhoAm 90
Dieter, Alice Hunt 1928- WhoAmW 91
Dieter, Allen Charles 1942- St&PR 91
Dieter, Charles 1922-1986 MusmAFA
Dieter, F. Robert 1930- St&PR 91
Dieter, George E., Jr. 1928- WhoAm 90
Dieter, Joseph Marshall, Jr. 1951- WhoE 91
Dieter, Mary 1949- WhoE 91
Dieter, Raymond Andrew, Jr. 1934- WhoAm 90
Dieter, Richard Charles 1952- WhoE 91
Dieter, William Fred 1947- St&PR 91
Dieter, William G., Jr. 1942- St&PR 91
Dieter, William J. 1939- St&PR 91
Dieterich, Douglas Thomas 1951- WhoEmL 91
Dieterich, Ernest Johnston 1923- WhoE 91
Dieterich, Hans Jost 1933- WhoWor 91
Dieterich, Heinz K. 1930- St&PR 91
Dieterle, Donald Lyle 1908- WhoAm 90
Diethelm, Arnold Gillespie 1932- WhoAm 90
Diethelm, Caspar J. 1926- IntWWM 90
Diethelm, Oskar BiDrAPA 89
Diethorn, Gregory Andrew 1946- WhoE 91, WhoEmL 91
Diethrich, Edward Bronson 1935- WhoAm 90
Dietl, Bo BioIn 16
Dietl, Charles Albert 1948- WhoWor 91
Dietmeyer, Donald Leo 1932- WhoAm 90
Dietrich, A. Louise 1878-1962 BioIn 16
Dietrich, Alan D. 1950- St&PR 91
Dietrich, Anne Marie BiDrAPA 89
Dietrich, Anthony Paul 1942- BiDrAPA 89
Dietrich, Bill 1910-1978 Ballpl 90
Dietrich, Bruce Leinbach 1937- WhoAm 90, WhoAmA 91, WhoE 91, WhoWor 91

Dietrich, Christian Peter 1944- *St&PR 91*
Dietrich, Christian Wilhelm Ernst *PenDiDA 89*
Dietrich, Dean Joseph 1942- *St&PR 91*
Dietrich, E. Jerry 1926- *St&PR 91*
Dietrich, George Charles 1927- *WhoAm 90, WhoWor 91*
Dietrich, Glenn *St&PR 91*
Dietrich, Harley Harrison, Jr. 1951- *WhoE 91*
Dietrich, Joachim *PenDiDA 89*
Dietrich, John Hassler, II 1951- *WhoEmL 91*
Dietrich, Joseph Jacob 1932- *WhoAm 90*
Dietrich, Karl 1927- *IntWWM 90*
Dietrich, Kurt E. 1951- *St&PR 91*
Dietrich, Laura Jordan 1952- *WhoAm 90*
Dietrich, Manfred 1937- *WhoWor 91*
Dietrich, Manfried Leonhard Georg 1935- *WhoWor 91*
Dietrich, Marion C. 1922- *St&PR 91*
Dietrich, Marlene 1901- *WorAlBi*
Dietrich, Marlene 1904- *BioIn 16, OxCPMus, WhoAm 90, WhoWor 91*
Dietrich, Martha Jane 1916- *WhoAmW 91*
Dietrich, Nancy Bishop 1946- *St&PR 91*
Dietrich, Paul Emil 1926- *WhoAm 90*
Dietrich, Paul George 1949- *WhoAm 90*
Dietrich, Rainer 1944- *WhoWor 91*
Dietrich, Renee Long 1937- *WhoAmW 91, WhoE 91*
Dietrich, Richard Farr 1936- *WhoSSW 91*
Dietrich, Richard Vincent 1924- *WhoAm 90*
Dietrich, Robert *TwCCr&M 91*
Dietrich, Robert Anthony 1933- *WhoAm 90*
Dietrich, Suzanne Claire 1937- *WhoAmW 91*
Dietrich, Wendell E. 1940- *St&PR 91*
Dietrich, Wilhelm Otto 1881-1964 *DcScB S2*
Dietrich, William Alan 1951- *WhoAm 90*
Dietrich, William Allen 1923- *WhoAm 90*
Dietrich, William Colman 1949- *St&PR 91*
Dietrich, William Gale 1925- *WhoAm 90*
Dietrich, William Peter 1944- *St&PR 91*
Dietrichs, Marilyn Dixon Altrock 1927- *IntWWM 90*
Dietrichson, Mathilde 1837-1921 *BiDWomA*
Dietsch, Alfred John 1931- *St&PR 91, WhoAm 90*
Dietsch, C Percival 1881-1961 *WhoAmA 91N*
Dietsch, James William 1950- *IntWWM 90*
Dietterlin, Wendel *PenDiDA 89*
Dietterlin, Wendel 1551-1599 *PenDiDA 89*
Diettrich, Robert John 1954- *WhoE 91*
Dietz, Albert George Henry 1908- *WhoAm 90*
Dietz, Allen 1951- *WhoEmL 91*
Dietz, Arthur T. 1923- *WhoSSW 91*
Dietz, Betty Warner *AuBYP 90*
Dietz, Charles Lemoyne 1910- *WhoAmA 91*
Dietz, Charlton Henry 1931- *St&PR 91, WhoAm 90*
Dietz, Chester R *BiDrAPA 89*
Dietz, Dick 1941- *Ballpl 90*
Dietz, Donald Elmore, III 1946- *St&PR 91, WhoAm 90*
Dietz, Donald William 1935- *St&PR 91*
Dietz, Dutch 1912-1972 *Ballpl 90*
Dietz, E. Camilla 1942- *St&PR 91*
Dietz, Earl Daniel 1928- *WhoAm 90*
Dietz, Edmund *St&PR 91*
Dietz, Elisabeth Hoffmann *BioIn 16*
Dietz, Elizabeth Camilla 1942- *WhoAm 90*
Dietz, Elizabeth H. 1908- *AuBYP 90*
Dietz, F.S. 1926- *St&PR 91*
Dietz, Frank Herbert 1940- *WhoSSW 91*
Dietz, George Robert 1931- *St&PR 91*
Dietz, Gerald Paul 1933- *WhoSSW 91*
Dietz, Gertrud *EncCoWW*
Dietz, Gunter 1928- *WhoWor 91*
Dietz, Howard 1896-1983 *OxCPMus, WorAlBi*
Dietz, J. Randolph 1951- *WhoEmL 91*
Dietz, Janet 1938- *ODwPR 91*
Dietz, Janis Camille 1950- *WhoAmW 91*
Dietz, John Raphael 1912- *St&PR 91, WhoAm 90*
Dietz, Lew 1907- *AuBYP 90*
Dietz, Linda C. 1952- *St&PR 91*
Dietz, Lori Smith 1962- *WhoSSW 91*
Dietz, Margaret Jane 1924- *WhoAmW 91*
Dietz, Milton S. 1931- *St&PR 91, WhoAm 90*
Dietz, Park Elliott 1948- *BiDrAPA 89*
Dietz, Robert Barron 1942- *WhoE 91*
Dietz, Robert Sinclair 1914- *WhoAm 90*
Dietz, Sharon Lynn 1958- *WhoAmW 91*
Dietz, Susan Ellen 1954- *WhoSSW 91*
Dietz, Timothy Jon 1955- *St&PR 91*
Dietz, William Ronald 1942- *WhoAm 90*
Dietze, Claus J *BiDrAPA 89*
Dietze, Dayrel Elizabeth 1961- *WhoAmW 91*
Dietze, Gottfried 1922- *WhoAm 90*
Dietzgen, Walter Carl 1922- *St&PR 91*
Dietzman, Leslie *WhoAm 90*
Dietzman, Leslie Edward 1942- *St&PR 91*
Dieu, Ron *BioIn 16*
Dieuzaide, Jean 1921- *WhoWor 91*
Dievler, David Harold 1929- *St&PR 91*
Diez, Blanca *BiDrAPA 89*
Diez, Charles F. *WhoHisp 91*
Diez, Gerald F. *WhoHisp 91*
Diez, Maria Consuelo 1958- *IntWWM 90*
Diez, Sherry Mae 1968- *WhoHisp 91*
Diezmo, Rafael Fermo *BiDrAPA 89*
Di Fabio, Dominick F *BiDrAPA 89*
Di Falco, Laura 1910- *EncCoWW*
Di Falco, Leonard D. *BioIn 16*
Di Fate, Vincent 1945- *WhoAmA 91*
DiFederico, Elaine M *BiDrAPA 89*
DiFeliciantonio, Tina Marie 1961- *WhoEmL 91*
Di Ferdinand, Rosalie Chillemi 1955- *WhoE 91*
Diffee, James Edward 1934- *WhoSSW 91*
Diffenbaugh, John Nicholas 1954- *WhoSSW 91*
Diffendaffer, Gary Lee 1946- *WhoEmL 91*
Diffenderfer, Hope Anker 1917- *WhoAm 90*
Diffenderfer, Robert Charles 1936- *St&PR 91*
Difford, Winthrop Cecil 1921- *WhoAm 90*
Diffrient, Niels 1928- *ConDes 90, WhoAm 90, WhoE 91*
DiFilippo, Fernando, Jr. 1948- *WhoEmL 91, WhoWor 91*
DiFilippo, Francine Carmella 1950- *WhoAmW 91, WhoSSW 91*
DiFilippo, Nando 1948- *St&PR 91*
DiFillippo, Anthony Francis 1927- *St&PR 91, WhoAm 90*
DiFlorio, Anthony, III 1959- *WhoEmL 91*
Diforio, Robert G. 1940- *WhoAm 90*
Diforio, Robert George 1940- *St&PR 91*
DiFranco, Anthony M. 1945- *WhoWrEP 89*
Di Franco, Loretta 1942- *IntWWM 90*
Di Franco, Loretta Elizabeth 1942- *WhoAm 90*
DiFranza, Americo 1919- *BioIn 16*
Difranza, Americo M 1919- *WhoAmA 91*
Di Fulvio, Marguerite Miller 1949- *WhoE 91*
DiFuria, Arthur Joseph 1933- *St&PR 91*
Di Furia, Giulio 1925- *BiDrAPA 89, WhoAm 90*
DiGaetano, Dolores Maria 1952- *BiDrAPA 89*
DiGangi, Frank Edward 1917- *WhoAm 90*
Di Gangi, Mary Vincenza 1939- *BiDrAPA 89*
Di Gaudio, Paul Thomas *BiDrAPA 89*
Digby, Beatrice *BiDEWW*
Digby, Lyle Martin 1943- *St&PR 91*
DiGennaro, Michael Dominic 1941- *WhoE 91*
DiGennaro, Robert C. 1947- *St&PR 91*
DiGeronimo, Claire R. 1965- *WhoAmW 91*
DiGeronimo, Joseph 1944- *St&PR 91*
Digesare, Joseph D. 1947- *St&PR 91*
Digges, Deborah Lea 1950- *WhoWrEP 89*
Digges, Dudley Perkins 1918- *WhoAm 90*
Digges, Edward Simms, Jr. 1946- *WhoE 91, WhoWor 91*
Digges, John Joseph 1932- *St&PR 91*
Digges, Sam Cook *NewYTBS 90 [port]*
Digges, Sam Cook 1916- *WhoAm 90*
Diggins, James Patrick 1947- *St&PR 91*
Diggins, Julia E. *AuBYP 90*
Diggins, Peter Sheehan 1938- *WhoAm 90*
Diggs, Charles Clayton 1947- *WhoE 91*
Diggs, Charles Coles, Jr. 1922- *BlkAmsC [port]*
Diggs, Elizabeth Francis 1939- *WhoWrEP 89*
Diggs, Jesse Frank 1917- *WhoAm 90*
Diggs, Lynne Dorothy 1960- *WhoAmW 91*
Diggs, Matthew O., Jr. 1933- *St&PR 91*
Diggs, Matthew O'Brien, Jr. 1933- *WhoAm 90*
Diggs, Phyllis Allen 1926- *WhoAmW 91*
Diggs, Walter Edward 1936- *St&PR 91*
Diggs, Walter Edward, Jr. 1936- *WhoAm 90*
Diggs, Walter Whitley 1932- *WhoSSW 91*
Dighans-Wittkopp, Marita Yvonne 1958- *WhoSSW 91*
Dighe, Judith Ginaine 1938- *WhoAmW 91*
Dighiero, Guillermo Juan 1941- *WhoWor 91*
Dighton, John Basil 1931- *St&PR 91*
Digia, Robert M. 1924- *St&PR 91*
Di Giacinto, Sharon 1960- *WhoAmA 91*
DiGiacomo, Anna Catherine 1967- *WhoEmL 91*
DiGiacomo, David Robert 1952- *WhoEmL 91*
DiGiacomo, James J 1924- *ConAu 30NR*
Di Giacomo, Joseph 1931- *BiDrAPA 89*
Digiacomo, Joseph A. 1935- *St&PR 91*
Di Giacomo, Thomas Anthony 1941- *WhoAm 90, WhoWor 91*
Di Giacomo, Wayne Peter *WhoSSW 91*
DiGiamarino, Marian Eleanor 1947- *WhoAmW 91*
Di Gioia, Anthony Michael, Jr. 1934- *WhoAm 90*
Di Giorgio, Anthony J. *WhoAm 90*
Di Giorgio, Joseph 1874?-1951 *BioIn 16*
DiGiorgio, Joseph 1931- *BioIn 16*
Digiorgio, Joseph J 1931- *WhoAmA 91*
Di Giovachino, John 1955- *WhoE 91*
DiGiovanna, Joseph Thomas 1927- *St&PR 91*
Di Giovanni, Anthony 1919- *WhoAm 90*
Di Giovanni, Cleto, Jr. *BiDrAPA 89*
DiGiovanni, Eleanor Elma 1944- *WhoAmW 91, WhoE 91, WhoWor 91*
Di Giovanni, Eric Paul 1965- *WhoEmL 91*
DiGiovanni, Hugo J. 1912- *St&PR 91*
DiGiovanni, Jack L. *BioIn 16*
Di Giovanni, Jack Leonard 1935- *WhoAm 90*
DiGiovanni, Larry Joseph 1948- *WhoE 91, WhoEmL 91*
DiGiovanni, Leonard Jerome 1928- *WhoE 91, WhoWor 91*
Di Giovanni, Pamela 1946- *WhoAmW 91*
DiGirolamo, Joseph 1923- *St&PR 91*
Di Giuseppe, Enrico 1932- *IntWWM 90*
Digiusto, Gerald N 1929-1987 *WhoAmA 91N*
DiGiusto, Walter 1949- *St&PR 91*
Digman, Lester Aloysius 1938- *WhoWor 91*
Dignac, Geny 1932- *WhoAm 90, WhoAmA 91*
Dignam, Mark 1909-1989 *AnObit 1989*
Dignam, Robert Joseph 1925- *WhoAm 90*
Dignam, William Joseph 1920- *WhoAm 90*
Dignan, James Haley 1920- *St&PR 91*
Dignan, Thomas Gregory, Jr. 1940- *WhoAm 90, WhoE 91, WhoWor 91*
Digney, Beryl R. *St&PR 91*
Digney, Girard 1950- *ODwPR 91*
Digney, James Brian 1946- *St&PR 91*
Digoutte, Jean-Pierre 1927- *WhoWor 91*
DiGregorio, Albert J. 1921- *St&PR 91*
Di Gregorio, Mario A 1950- *ConAu 131*
DiGuglielmo, Antoinette Teresa 1964- *WhoAmW 91*
Diguisto, Carlo A. 1947- *St&PR 91*
Dihe, Yvon C. *BioIn 16*
Dihigo, Martin 1905-1971 *Ballpl 90*
Dihle, Albrecht G. F. 1923- *WhoWor 91*
Di Ienno, Joseph A *BiDrAPA 89*
Di James, Pascal 1926- *WhoAm 90*
Diji, Augustine *BiDrAPA 89*
Dijkstra, Edsger Wybe 1930- *WhoAm 90*
DiJulio, Joseph Michael 1923- *St&PR 91*
Dik, Susan Lee 1956- *WhoEmL 91*
Dike, Azuka Anthony *WhoWor 91*
Dike, Fatima 1948- *FemiCLE*
Dike, Kenneth O. 1917-1983 *BioIn 16*
Dike, Margaret Hopcraft 1921- *WhoAmW 91*
Dike, Phil 1906- *WhoAm 90*
Dikel, William 1951- *BiDrAPA 89*
Dikeman, Michael Lee 1949- *St&PR 91*
Diker, Charles Michael 1934- *St&PR 91*
Diker, M. Rifat 1948- *WhoWor 91*
Dikmen, John William 1951- *WhoSSW 91*
Dikmen, Ned F. *WhoWrEP 89*
Dikstein, Shabtay 1931- *WhoWor 91*
Diktas, Christos James 1955- *WhoE 91, WhoEmL 91*
Diktonius, Elmer 1896-1961 *DcScanL*
Di Lampedusa, Giuseppe Tomasi 1896-1957 *BioIn 16*
Dilatush, Robert E., Jr. 1929- *St&PR 91*
DiLaura, Kenneth Anthony 1945- *St&PR 91*
Dilaurenti, Marco Italo 1933- *WhoAmA 91*
Dilcher, David Leonard 1936- *WhoAm 90*
Dilda, Kenneth Wayne 1945- *WhoSSW 91*
Dilday, Russell Hooper 1930- *WhoAm 90*
Dileepan, Kanakam *BiDrAPA 89*
Di Lella, Alexander Anthony 1929- *WhoAm 90*
Dilella, James Theodore 1951- *St&PR 91*
Di Lello, Denise-Marie *WhoAmW 91*
DiLello, Marjorie Denise Guthrie 1951- *WhoAm 90*
Dilenschneider, Robert L. 1943- *ODwPR 91*
Dilenschneider, Robert Louis 1943- *St&PR 91, WhoAm 90*
Di Leo, Francesco B 1940- *BiDrAPA 89*
Di Leo, Francesco Biagio 1940- *WhoE 91*
Dileo, Leonard Michael *BiDrAPA 89*
DiLeonardi, Joan Wall 1935- *WhoAmW 91*
Di Leone, Helaine 1945- *WhoSSW 91*
Dileski, Patricia Parra *WhoHisp 91*
Dilg, Robert Fred, Jr. 1958- *St&PR 91*
Dilgard, Robert Carl 1932- *St&PR 91*
Dilger, Lorraine Ann 1959- *WhoAmW 91*
Dilger, Mark Sherman *BiDrAPA 89*
DiLiberto, John Gerard 1950- *St&PR 91*
Di Liello, Salvatore 1958- *WhoEmL 91*
Di Liscia, Julio C 1912- *EncO&P 3*
Dilke, Emilia Francis 1840-1904 *FemiCLE*
Dilks, Kenneth Rowland 1937- *WhoSSW 91*
Dilks, Park Bankert, Jr. 1928- *WhoAm 90*
Dill, Anne Holden 1920- *WhoAmW 91*
Dill, Charles A. 1939- *St&PR 91*
Dill, Charles Anthony 1939- *WhoAm 90*
Dill, Charles William 1955- *IntWWM 90*
Dill, Edith Palliser 1925- *WhoWrEP 89*
Dill, Ellen Renee 1949- *WhoAmW 91, WhoEmL 91, WhoWor 91*
Dill, Ellis Harold 1932- *WhoAm 90*
Dill, Evelena 1958- *WhoAmW 91*
Dill, Guy Girard 1946- *WhoAmA 91*
Dill, John Francis 1934- *St&PR 91, WhoAm 90*
Dill, John J. 1939- *St&PR 91*
Dill, John Junior 1939- *WhoAm 90*
Dill, Karole Edwyna 1961- *WhoAmW 91*
Dill, Laddie John 1943- *WhoAm 90, WhoAmA 91*
Dill, M. Reese, Jr. 1937- *WhoE 91*
Dill, Mary Alyson 1951- *WhoAmW 91, WhoEmL 91, WhoSSW 91*
Dill, Michele Andrus *WhoWrEP 89*
Dill, Richard Everett 1952- *WhoEmL 91*
Dill, Robert Clifton 1943- *St&PR 91*
Dill, Virginia S. 1938- *WhoAm 90*
Dill, William Allen 1918- *WhoE 91*
Dill, William Joseph 1935- *WhoAm 90*
Dill, William Rankin 1930- *WhoAm 90, WhoE 91*
Dillaber, Philip Arthur 1922- *WhoAm 90, WhoE 91, WhoWor 91*
Dillah, Kenrick L. 1944- *WhoE 91*
Dillahunty, Leslie Edmon 1947- *St&PR 91*
Dillard, Alex 1950- *WhoAm 90, WhoSSW 91*
Dillard, Annie *BioIn 16*
Dillard, Annie 1945- *Au&Arts 6 [port], ConLC 60 [port], FemiCLE, MajTwCW, WhoAm 90, WhoAmW 91, WhoWrEP 89*
Dillard, David Brownrigg 1935- *WhoAm 90*
Dillard, David Hugh 1923- *WhoAm 90*
Dillard, Dennis Alexander 1950- *St&PR 91*
Dillard, Dudley 1913- *WhoAm 90, WhoWor 91*
Dillard, Emil Lee 1921- *WhoWrEP 89*
Dillard, Godfrey Joseph 1948- *WhoEmL 91*
Dillard, Harrison *BioIn 16*
Dillard, J L 1924- *ConAu 31NR*
Dillard, J. Michael 1951- *WhoAm 90, WhoSSW 91*
Dillard, Jerry Wayne 1944- *WhoSSW 91*
Dillard, Joan Helen 1951- *WhoAmW 91*
Dillard, John Martin 1945- *WhoWor 91*
Dillard, John Robert 1955- *WhoEmL 91*
Dillard, Kirk Whitfield 1955- *WhoEmL 91*
Dillard, Lula *BioIn 16*
Dillard, Marilyn Dianne 1940- *WhoAmW 91, WhoWor 91*
Dillard, Max Murray 1935- *St&PR 91*
Dillard, Nancy Rose 1950- *WhoAmW 91*
Dillard, Richard Henry Wilde 1937- *WhoAm 90*
Dillard, Robert Carl 1931- *St&PR 91*
Dillard, Robert G. 1931- *St&PR 91*
Dillard, Robert Lionel, Jr. 1913- *WhoAm 90*
Dillard, Rodney Jefferson 1939- *WhoAm 90, WhoSSW 91*
Dillard, Steve 1951- *Ballpl 90*
Dillard, W. Thomas 1941- *WhoAm 90*
Dillard, W.W. 1920- *St&PR 91*
Dillard, William 1910?- *DrBIPA 90*
Dillard, William 1914- *BioIn 16, St&PR 91*
Dillard, William, II 1945- *WhoAm 90, WhoSSW 91*
Dillard, William Carroll 1958- *WhoEmL 91*
Dillard, William Reese 1937- *WhoSSW 91*
Dillard, William T. 1914- *WhoAm 90, WhoSSW 91*
Dillard-McGeoch, M. Anne 1950- *WhoEmL 91*
Dillards, The *WhoNeCM A*
Dillaway, Robert Beacham 1924- *WhoSSW 91*
Dille, Earl Kaye 1927- *St&PR 91, WhoAm 90*
Dille, Guy 1929- *St&PR 91*
Dille, John Flint, Jr. 1913- *WhoAm 90, WhoWor 91*
Dille, John Robert 1931- *WhoAm 90, WhoWor 91*

Dille, Roland Paul 1924- WhoAm 90
Dillehay, Pamela Ann 1957- WhoAmW 91
Dillen, John Thomas 1930- St&PR 91
Dillenberg, Stanley M BiDrAPA 89
Dillenberger, John 1918- WhoAm 90
Dillenburg, Carolyn Eva Lauer 1934- WhoAmW 91
Diller, Allen E. 1921- St&PR 91
Diller, Angela AuBYP 90
Diller, Barry 1942- News 91-1 [port], WhoAm 90, WorAlBi
Diller, Burgoyne 1906-1965 WhoAmA 91N
Diller, Charles Herbert, Jr. 1945- St&PR 91, WhoE 91, WhoEmL 91
Diller, Emmeline Ann 1955- BiDrAPA 89, WhoE 91
Diller, Hans Jurgen 1934- WhoWor 91
Diller, John C. WhoAm 90, WhoE 91
Diller, Phyllis 1917- BioIn 16, WhoAm 90, WhoWrEP 89, WorAlBi
Dillett, Gregory C. 1943- St&PR 91
Dillett, Gregory Craft 1943- WhoAm 90
Dilley, Barbara Jean 1938- WhoAmW 91
Dilley, David Wayne 1963- WhoWrEP 89
Dilley, James Willis BiDrAPA 89
Dilley, Margarita K. 1957- St&PR 91
Dilley, Richard A. 1936- WhoAm 90
Dilley, Thomas Robert 1953- WhoEmL 91
Dilley, Timothy Eugene 1958- WhoEmL 91
Dilley, Wanda Reiss 1918- WhoAmW 91
Dillier, Helen Jean 1939- WhoAmW 91
Dillin, John Woodward, Jr. 1936- WhoAm 90
Dillin, Samuel Hugh 1914- WhoAm 90
Dilling, Kirkpatrick Wallwick 1920- WhoAm 90, WhoWor 91
Dillinger, Bob 1918- Ballpl 90
Dillinger, John 1902-1934 WorAlBi
Dillinger, John 1903-1934 BioIn 16
Dillingham, Charles, III 1942- WhoAm 90
Dillingham, Daniel Jay 1958- WhoWrEP 89
Dillingham, Dorothy Hoyt 1909- WhoE 91
Dillingham, John Albert 1927- St&PR 91
Dillingham, John Allen 1939- WhoAm 90
Dillingham, Jon Milton 1951- St&PR 91
Dillingham, Marjorie Carter 1915- WhoAmW 91, WhoWor 91
Dillingham, Rick, II 1952- WhoAmA 91
Dillingham, Robert Bulger 1932- WhoAm 90, WhoE 91
Dillingham, William Addison Pitt 1824-1871 AmLegL
Dillingham, William Byron 1930- WhoAm 90, WhoSSW 91
Dillingham, William S 1939- BiDrAPA 89
Dillion, Theresa Lee 1948- WhoAmW 91
Dilliplaine, Wayne F. 1942- St&PR 91
Dillman, Bill 1945- Ballpl 90
Dillman, Bradford 1930- WhoAm 90, WorAlBi
Dillman, Darryl Grant BiDrAPA 89
Dillman, Grant 1918- WhoAm 90
Dillman, L. Thomas 1931- WhoAm 90
Dillman, Lewis 1918- St&PR 91
Dillman, Linda W. 1940- ODwPR 91
Dillman, Matthew Alan 1952- WhoSSW 91
Dillman, Robert John 1941- WhoAm 90, WhoSSW 91
Dillmann, Edward B. 1935- St&PR 91
Dillmann, Nancy Cameron 1947- WhoWrEP 89
Dillon, Andrew Dee 1956- WhoE 91
Dillon, Andrew Joseph 1947- WhoEmL 91
Dillon, Brandy WhoWrEP 89
Dillon, C. Douglas 1909- EncABHB 7 [port]
Dillon, C Douglas 1909- WhoAmA 91
Dillon, Clarence Douglas 1909- BiDrUSE 89, WhoAm 90
Dillon, Clifford Brien 1921- WhoAm 90
Dillon, David B. 1951- St&PR 91
Dillon, David Brian 1951- WhoAm 90
Dillon, David Charles 1947- BiDrAPA 89
Dillon, Dean WhoNeCM [port]
Dillon, Debra Jean 1952- WhoWrEP 89
Dillon, Diane BioIn 16
Dillon, Diane 1933- AuBYP 90
Dillon, Diane Claire Sorber 1933- WhoAm 90
Dillon, Donald Francis 1940- St&PR 91
Dillon, Donald Ward 1936- WhoAm 90
Dillon, Douglas 1909- BioIn 16
Dillon, Eilis 1920- AuBYP 90
Dillon, Eleanor Hyle Farley 1912- WhoSSW 91
Dillon, Enoch LaRoy 1925- WhoE 91
Dillon, Francis Patrick 1937- WhoWor 91
Dillon, Frank 1873-1931 Ballpl 90
Dillon, G. Michael 1938- St&PR 91
Dillon, Gary G. 1934- St&PR 91
Dillon, George C. 1922- St&PR 91
Dillon, George Chaffee 1922- WhoAm 90
Dillon, Gregory Russell 1922- St&PR 91
Dillon, Howard Burton 1935- WhoWor 91
Dillon, Jackson C BiDrAPA 89
Dillon, James 1950- IntWWM 90
Dillon, James Edward BiDrAPA 89
Dillon, James Lee 1928- St&PR 91, WhoAm 90
Dillon, James M. 1933- WhoAm 90
Dillon, James McNulty 1933- St&PR 91
Dillon, Jeff ODwPR 91
Dillon, John Andrew 1954- WhoE 91
Dillon, John B. 1911- WhoAm 90
Dillon, John C. 1919- St&PR 91
Dillon, John C., III 1920- St&PR 91
Dillon, John H. 1938- St&PR 91
Dillon, John Robert 1941- St&PR 91
Dillon, John Robert, III 1941- WhoAm 90
Dillon, John T. 1938- St&PR 91
Dillon, John Zimmerman, II 1956- WhoE 91
Dillon, Joy 1942- WhoSSW 91
Dillon, Judy Reep 1944- WhoAmW 91
Dillon, Julie Rosenfeld 1960- WhoEmL 91
Dillon, Karl Douglas St&PR 91
Dillon, Keith Gregory 1946- WhoE 91
Dillon, Kevin 1965- ConTFT 8
Dillon, Leo 1933- AuBYP 90, BioIn 16
Dillon, Marcia K BiDrAPA 89
Dillon, Mary Christine 1960- WhoE 91
Dillon, Maryann 1951- WhoAmW 91
Dillon, Matt BioIn 16
Dillon, Matt 1964- WhoAm 90, WorAlBi
Dillon, Merton Lynn 1924- WhoAm 90
Dillon, Michael Roy 1938- WhoWor 91
Dillon, Mildred 1907- WhoAmA 91
Dillon, Millicent 1925- WhoWrEP 89
Dillon, Neal Winfield 1925- WhoAm 90
Dillon, Oneil Singh 1940- BiDrAPA 89
Dillon, Oscar Wendell, Jr. 1928- WhoAm 90
Dillon, Paul Sanford 1943- WhoAm 90, WhoAmA 91
Dillon, Paul Wilson 1926- WhoAm 90
Dillon, Ralph D. 1940- St&PR 91, WhoAm 90, WhoSSW 91
Dillon, Ralph I. St&PR 91
Dillon, Ray William 1954- WhoSSW 91
Dillon, Richard Hugh 1924- WhoAm 90, WhoWrEP 89
Dillon, Robert Morton 1923- WhoAm 90
Dillon, Sharon Saseen 1949- BioIn 16
Dillon, Thomas L BiDrAPA 89
Dillon, Thomas Ray 1948- WhoEmL 91
Dillon, Vincence F, Sr. BiDrAPA 89
Dillon, W. Martin 1910- WhoAm 90
Dillon, William BioIn 16
Dillon, Wilton Sterling 1923- WhoAm 90
Dillon-McHugh, Cathleen Theresa 1951- WhoE 91
Dillont, M Nathalie 1910- BiDrAPA 89
Dillow, John David 1946- WhoEmL 91
Dillow, L. Gwen 1955- St&PR 91
Dillow, Nancy E 1928- WhoAmA 91
Dillport, Janet Files 1951- WhoEmL 91
Dills, Carol Ingle 1953- WhoSSW 91
Dills, James Arlof 1930- WhoAm 90
Dills, James Carl 1954- WhoSSW 91
Dillwyn, E. A. 1845-1935 FemiCLE
Dillwyn, Lewis Llewellyn PenDiDA 89
Dilone, Miguel 1954- Ballpl 90
DiLorenzo, Gary P. 1956- St&PR 91
DiLorenzo, John F., Jr. 1940- St&PR 91
Di Lorenzo, John Florio, Jr. 1940- WhoAm 90
DiLorenzo, Joseph L. WhoSSW 91
DiLorenzo, Louis Patrick 1952- WhoEmL 91
DiLoreto, Ann Marie 1953- WhoEmL 91
DiLouis, Anthony 1945- St&PR 91
Dils, Allen Cook 1948- St&PR 91
Dils, Henry H., Jr. 1914- St&PR 91
Dilsaver, Steven Charles 1953- BiDrAPA 89
Dilsizian, Rick BioIn 16
Dilsizian, Rick Charles 1946- WhoE 91
Dilts, David Michael 1950- WhoAm 90
Dilts, Joseph Lee 1956- WhoEmL 91
Dilts, Mervin Robert 1938- WhoAm 90
Dilts, Michael C. 1956- St&PR 91
Dilts, Stephen Leist 1940- BiDrAPA 89
Dilucente, Desiree A. 1964- WhoAmW 91
DiLuco, Dora 1922- St&PR 91
DiLuca, Eugene 1919- St&PR 91
Diluzio, C.B. 1955- St&PR 91
DiLuzio, Frank 1913-1990 BioIn 16
Dilweg, Anthony BioIn 16
Dilworth, Ann E. 1947- St&PR 91
Dilworth, Ann Evans 1947- WhoAm 90, WhoEmL 91
Dilworth, Billy D. 1934- WhoSSW 91
Dilworth, Edwin Earle 1914- WhoAm 90
Dilworth, Grace Dorothy 1930- WhoAm 90
Dilworth, James Weldon 1928- WhoAm 90
Dilworth, Stephen James 1959- WhoSSW 91
Dilworth-Leslie, Samuel 1937- IntWWM 90
Dim WhoWrEP 89
Dim, Bomen Hifzi BiDrAPA 89
DiMaggio, Dom 1917- Ballpl 90 [port], BioIn 16
DiMaggio, Frank Louis 1929- WhoAm 90
DiMaggio, Joe BioIn 16
DiMaggio, Joe 1914- Ballpl 90 [port], WorAlBi
Di Maggio, Joseph Paul 1914- WhoAm 90
DiMaggio, Vince 1912- Ballpl 90
DiMaio, Virginia Sue 1921- WhoAmW 91
Dimakis, John 1929- WhoAm 90
Diman, Homer 1914-1974 WhoAmA 91N
Dimant, Jacob 1947- WhoE 91, WhoWor 91
Di Mantova, Walter Dario 1958- WhoEmL 91
Di Marco, Gabriel Robert 1927- WhoAm 90
DiMarco, Joseph M. 1950- St&PR 91
DiMaria, Charles C. 1923- St&PR 91
Dimaria, Valerie T. 1957- ODwPR 91
Di Maria, Valerie Theresa 1957- WhoAmW 91
DiMario, Joseph F. 1931- St&PR 91
DiMartino, Joseph S. 1943- St&PR 91
Di Martino, Rita 1937- WhoHisp 91
DiMartino, Thomas Calvin BiDrAPA 89
Di Mascio, John Philip 1944- WhoE 91
Di Mascio, William 1943- ODwPR 91
Di Massa, Ernani Vincenzo, Jr. 1947- WhoEmL 91
DiMassa, Erni BioIn 16
DiMatteo, John R. 1931- St&PR 91, WhoAm 90, WhoE 91
DiMatteo, Maryanne Robin 1952- WhoAmW 91
DiMatteo, Philip Stephen 1947- WhoEmL 91
DiMattia, Ernest Anthony, Jr. 1940- WhoE 91
Di Mattia, Judy 1944- WhoE 91
Dimayuga, Victoria P BiDrAPA 89
Dimbath, Merle F. 1939- WhoWor 91
Dimbleby, David 1938- WhoWor 91
Dimedio, Annette Maria 1958- IntWWM 90
DiMeglio, Ralph 1926- St&PR 91
Dimen, Muriel Vera 1942- WhoAmW 91, WhoE 91
Diment, Adam SpyFic
Di Meo, Dominick 1927- WhoAm 90, WhoAmA 91
Dimeo, R. Steven 1945- WhoWrEP 89
Dimeo, Thomas P. 1930- WhoAm 90
DiMicco, Wendy Ann 1948- WhoAmW 91
Di Miceli, Caroline Regina 1959- WhoWor 91
Dimiceli, Vincent J. 1918- WhoWor 91
Dimich, William Michael 1931- St&PR 91
DiMichael, Salvatore George 1914- WhoAm 90
di Michele, Mary 1949- FemiCLE
Dimick, Walter S. 1950- WhoEmL 91
Dimijian, Gregory G BiDrAPA 89
Diminno, Frank S. St&PR 91
Dimino, Alfonso 1920- St&PR 91
DiMino, Andre Anthony 1955- St&PR 91
Di Mino, Andre Anthony 1955- WhoE 91, WhoEmL 91
Dimino, Charles BiDrAPA 89
Dimino, Franklin Joseph 1933- St&PR 91
Dimino, Sylvia Theresa 1955- WhoAmW 91, WhoEmL 91
Dimitman, Merlin 1928- BiDrAPA 89
Dimitras, Panayote Elias 1953- WhoWor 91
Dimitri, Konstantin BiDrAPA 89
Dimitrios I, Ecumenical Patriarch 1914- WhoWor 91
Dimitriou, Stavros George 1952- WhoWor 91
Dimitriou, Theodore 1926- St&PR 91
Dimitris, James C 1931- BiDrAPA 89
Dimitroff, Pashanko 1924- ConAu 129
Dimitrouleas, William Peter 1951- WhoEmL 91
Dimitrov, Boyko Georgiev 1941- WhoWor 91
Dimitrov, Georgi 1882-1949 BioIn 16
Dimitrova, Blaga 1922- EncCoWW
Dimitrova, Ghena BioIn 16
Dimitrova, Ghena 1941- IntWWM 90, WhoWor 91
Dimitruk, Paul Arthur 1949- WhoWor 91
Dimitry, Alexander 1805-1883 BioIn 16
Dimitry, John Randolph 1929- WhoAm 90
Dimitry, Theodore George 1937- WhoAm 90
Dimler, George Richard 1931- WhoWrEP 89
Dimling, David Stanton 1932- WhoAm 90
Dimling, James Sledge 1938- St&PR 91
Dimling, John BioIn 16
Dimling, John Arthur 1938- WhoAm 90, WhoE 91
Dimma, William Andrew 1927- St&PR 91
Dimma, William Andrew 1928- WhoAm 90
Dimmerman, Harry T. 1929- St&PR 91
Dimmick, Carolyn Reaber 1929- WhoAm 90, WhoAmW 91
Dimmick, Charles William 1940- WhoAm 90
Dimock, Marshall Edward 1903- WhoAm 90
Dimock, Rodney Claude 1946- St&PR 91
Dimon, Garth Fremont 1926- WhoAm 90
Dimon, James 1956- St&PR 91
Dimon, John E. 1916- St&PR 91
Dimond, Albert Kenneth 1923- St&PR 91
Dimond, Bridgit Carolyn 1941- WhoWor 91
Dimond, Marie Therese 1916- WhoAmW 91, WhoE 91
Dimond, Robert Edward 1936- WhoAm 90
Dimond, Stanley E. 1905-1989 BioIn 16
Dimond, Thomas 1916- WhoE 91
Dimondstein, Morton 1920- WhoAmA 91
Dimos, Jimmy 1938- WhoSSW 91
Dimoula, Kiki EncCoWW
Dimpel, Hal Curtis 1928- St&PR 91
Dimsdale, Joel Edward 1947- BiDrAPA 89, WhoEmL 91
Dimsey, Peter BioIn 16
Dimson, Theo Aeneas 1930- WhoAmA 91
Di Muccio, Mary Jo 1930- WhoAm 90
DiMuro, Lou 1931-1982 Ballpl 90
Di Murska, Ilma 1836-1889 PenDiMP
Dinaburg, Daniel Carl 1943- BiDrAPA 89
Dinaburg, Mary Ellen 1954- WhoAmW 91
Dinakarrao, Hassan S BiDrAPA 89
Dinale, Margherita Silvi 1928- WhoAmW 91
Dinallo, Gregory S. 1941- ConTFT 8 [port], SpyFic
Dinan, Carolyn BioIn 16
Dinan, Donald Robert 1949- WhoE 91
Dinan, Patrick Ann 1950- WhoEmL 91
Dinand, Pierre BioIn 16
DiNapoli, Frank A. 1933- St&PR 91
DiNapoli, Patrick Anthony 1942- St&PR 91
Dinapoli, Thomas John 1943- St&PR 91
DiNardo, George P. 1937- St&PR 91
Dinardo, Marilynn 1937- WhoWrEP 89
DiNardo, Mary Lou ODwPR 91
DiNardo, Thomas P. 1964- WhoE 91
DiNatale, Paul Peter 1951- WhoEmL 91
Dinc, Alev Necile WhoAmA 91
Dincauze, Dena Ferran 1934- WhoE 91
Dince, Paul R 1926- BiDrAPA 89
Dinces, Franklin Gary 1958- WhoEmL 91
Dinculeanu, Nicolae 1925- WhoAm 90
Dindorf, Joseph Lee 1940- St&PR 91
D'Indy, Vincent PenDiMPA
Dine, James 1935- WhoAmA 91
Dineen, Bill 1876-1955 Ballpl 90
Dineen, Daniel Thomas 1948- St&PR 91
Dineen, Donal Adrian 1947- WhoWor 91
Dineen, John K. 1928- WhoAm 90
Dineen, Peter 1925-1989 BioIn 16
Dineen, Robert E. 1903-1989 BioIn 16
Dineen, Robert J. 1923- St&PR 91
Dineen, Robert Joseph 1929- WhoAm 90
Dinehart, Scott Michael 1957- WhoSSW 91
Dinel, Richard Henry 1942- WhoWor 91
Diner, Bradley Canada BiDrAPA 89
Diner, Judithanne 1949- WhoAmW 91
Diner, Ralph Gordon 1951- WhoWor 91
Diner, Wilma Canada 1926- WhoAmW 91
Dinerman, Lisa 1953- WhoEmL 91
Dinerstein, Laura Ellen BiDrAPA 89
Dinerstein, Robert David 1953- WhoEmL 91
Dinerstein, Russell H 1923- BiDrAPA 89
Dines, Franklin H 1947- BiDrAPA 89
Dines, Glen 1925- AuBYP 90
Dines, James M. 1927- St&PR 91
Dines, Philipp BiDrAPA 89
Dinescu, Violeta 1953- IntWWM 90
Dinesen, Isak MajTwCW
Dinesen, Isak 1885-1962 BioIn 16, DcScanL, EncCoWW, FemiCLE, ShSCr 7 [port], WorAlBi, WrPh
Dinet, Rene Georges 1923- WhoWor 91
DiNetta, Dianne Connell 1951- WhoEmL 91
Ding, Chen 1919- WhoE 91
Dingell, John D. BioIn 16
Dingell, John David, Jr. 1926- WhoAm 90
Dinges, Richard Allen 1945- WhoEmL 91, WhoWor 91
Dingle, Donna Victoria 1952- WhoWrEP 89
Dingle, Edwin John 1881-1972 EncO&P 3
Dingle, Kevin S. St&PR 91
Dingle, Margaret Concetta Spargo 1918- WhoAmW 91
Dingle, Richard Douglas Hugh 1936- WhoAm 90
Dingle, Steven Franklin BiDrAPA 89
Dingle, Susan 1950- WhoAmW 91, WhoEmL 91
Dingley, Nelson, Jr. 1832-1899 AmLegL
Dinglinger, Johann Melchior 1664-1731 PenDiDA 89

Dingman, Avon Marie 1962- *WhoAmW 91*
Dingman, C. Wesley, II 1932- *BiDrAPA 89*
Dingman, Dennis Keith 1945- *St&PR 91*
Dingman, James Daniel 1954- *WhoEmL 91*
Dingman, Linda Susan 1942- *WhoAmW 91*
Dingman, M. Howard 1925- *St&PR 91*
Dingman, Mark R. 1949- *St&PR 91*
Dingman, Michael D. *BioIn 16*
Dingman, Michael D. 1931- *St&PR 91*
Dingman, Michael David 1931- *WhoAm 90*
Dingman, Robert John 1941- *St&PR 91*
Dingman, Robert Lewis 1931- *WhoSSW 91*
Dingman, Robert Walter 1926- *WhoAm 90*
Dingman, Sheila Elaine 1965- *WhoAmW 91*
Dings, John Linton 1937- *St&PR 91*
Dingus, David Hamilton 1948- *St&PR 91*
Dingus, Michael H.R. 1948- *St&PR 91*
Dingus, Phillip Rick 1951- *WhoAmA 91*
Dingwall, E J 1890-1986 *EncO&P 3*
Dingwall, Eric John 1890-1986 *EncPaPR 91*
Dingwell, David W. 1936- *St&PR 91*
Dingwell, Everett W. 1931- *WhoAm 90*
Dinh, Khanh *BioIn 16*
Dinhofer, Shelly Mehlman 1927- *WhoAmA 91*
Dini, John F. 1951- *St&PR 91*
Di Nicola, Albert 1917- *WhoWrEP 89*
Dinicola, David Dante *BiDrAPA 89*
DiNicola, John W. 1938- *St&PR 91*
Dinielli, Nicholas 1930- *St&PR 91*
Dinielli, Nicholas Anthony 1930- *WhoAm 90*
Dinin, David 1946- *WhoE 91*
Dininno, Steve *BioIn 16*
Dininny, Ferral C. 1818-1901? *AmLegL*
Dininny, Jacelyn Brown 1933- *WhoAmW 91*
Dinitz, Simon 1926- *WhoAm 90*
Dinius, E. Lowell 1940- *St&PR 91*
Dinkel, John George 1944- *WhoAm 90*
Dinkel, Philippe 1956- *IntWWM 90*
Dinkelspiel, Paul Gaines 1935- *WhoAm 90, WhoWor 91*
Dinkelspiel, Richard Coleman 1913- *WhoAm 90*
Dinkin, Alvin *PenDiMP*
Dinkins, Carol Eggert 1945- *WhoAm 90, WhoAmW 91*
Dinkins, David 1927- *BioIn 16, CurBio 90 [port], News 90 [port]*
Dinkins, David N. 1927- *WhoAm 90, WhoE 91*
Dinkins, Larry M. *St&PR 91*
Dinkins, Paul Newton 1919- *St&PR 91*
Dinkins, Thomas Allen, III 1946- *WhoEmL 91*
Dinkov, Vasiliy Alexandrovich 1924- *WhoWor 91*
Dinman, Bertram David 1925- *WhoAm 90*
Dinn, Winifreda Louise 1910- *IntWWM 90*
Dinndorf, Thomas E. 1934- *St&PR 91*
Dinneen, Betty 1929- *SmATA 61*
Dinneen, Edward Gorman 1925- *St&PR 91*
Dinneen, Gerald Paul 1924- *WhoAm 90*
Dinneen, James Francis 1915- *St&PR 91, WhoAm 90*
Dinneen, Michael Paul *BiDrAPA 89*
Dinner, Janice Marie 1957- *WhoEmL 91*
Dinner, Miles 1954- *WhoE 91*
Dinnerstein, Harvey *BioIn 16*
Dinnerstein, Harvey 1928- *WhoAm 90, WhoAmA 91*
Dinnerstein, Leonard 1934- *WhoAm 90*
Dinnerstein, Lois 1932- *WhoAmA 91*
Dinnerstein, Myra 1934- *WhoAmW 91*
Dinnerstein, Simon A 1943- *WhoAmA 91*
Dinniman, Andrew Eric 1944- *WhoE 91*
Dinning, James Smith 1922- *WhoAm 90*
Dinning, Mark 1933-1985? *EncPR&S 89*
Dinnocenzo, Deborah Anne 1964- *WhoAmW 91*
D'Innocenzo, Nick 1934- *WhoAmA 91*
D'Innocenzo, Phillis 1942- *St&PR 91*
Dinon, Richard A. 1944- *St&PR 91*
Dinorscia, Joseph 1929- *St&PR 91*
Dinos, Nicholas 1934- *WhoAm 90*
Dinoso, Vicente Pescador, Jr. 1936- *WhoAm 90*
DiNovo, Theresa Christine 1958- *WhoAmW 91*
Dinsch, F. Lawrence 1938- *St&PR 91*
Dinse, Curt W. 1958- *St&PR 91*
Dinse, John Merrell 1925- *WhoAm 90*
Dinsmoor, James Arthur 1921- *WhoAm 90*
Dinsmoor, Mara Jean 1956- *WhoAmW 91*
Dinsmoor, Samuel Perry 1843-1932 *MusmAFA*
Dinsmoor, William Bell 1923-1988 *BioIn 16*
Dinsmoore, Lee 1947- *ODwPR 91*
Dinsmore, David Allen 1951- *WhoEmL 91*
Dinsmore, Gordon Griffith 1917- *WhoAm 90*
Dinsmore, Paul Rich 1932- *BiDrAPA 89*
Dinsmore, Philip Wade 1942- *WhoAm 90*
Dinsmore, Roberta Joan Maier 1934- *WhoAmW 91, WhoE 91*
Dinsmore, Ronald E. 1926- *St&PR 91*
Dinsmore, Stephen Pul 1952- *WhoAmA 91*
Dinsmore, Thomas Hall 1953- *St&PR 91*
Dintaman, James L. 1943- *St&PR 91*
Dintenfass, Julius 1910- *WhoE 91*
Dintenfass, Mark 1941- *WhoWrEP 89*
Dintenfass, Terry *WhoE 91*
Dintenfass, Terry 1920- *WhoAmA 91*
Dintino, Justin J. *WhoE 91*
Dintzis, Renee Zlochover 1927- *WhoAmW 91*
Dinuscheonnia *WhoWrEP 89*
DiNuzzo, Nuccio 1962- *WhoEmL 91*
Dinwiddie, George L., Jr. 1924- *St&PR 91*
Dinwiddie, John Alexander 1931- *St&PR 91*
Dinwiddie, Robert 1693-1770 *EncCRAm, WhNaAH*
Dinwiddie, Stephen H 1955- *BiDrAPA 89*
Dinwiddy, J R 1939-1990 *ConAu 131*
Dinwiddy, John *ConAu 131*
Dinwoodie, Nancy D *BiDrAPA 89*
Dio, Ronnie James *EncPR&S 89*
Diocletian 245-316 *WorAlBi*
Dioda, Adolph T 1915- *WhoAmA 91*
Dioda, Adolph Tito 1915- *WhoE 91*
Diodene, Alonzo Nelson 1941- *WhoSSW 91*
Diogenes 412?BC-323BC *WorAlBi*
Dioguardi, Michael Joseph 1943- *St&PR 91*
Diohep, John Lewis 1933- *St&PR 91*
Diomede, Matthew 1940- *WhoWrEP 89*
Dion 1939- *BioIn 16, ConMus 4 [port], EncPR&S 89, WorAlBi*
Dion, Alain 1959- *BiDrAPA 89*
Dion, Gerard 1912- *WhoAm 90*
Dion, James Edmond 1948- *St&PR 91*
Dion, Philip J. 1944- *St&PR 91*
Dion, Philip Joseph 1944- *WhoAm 90*
Dion, Robert L. 1932- *St&PR 91*
Dion, Ronald P. 1936- *St&PR 91*
Dion, Thomas Raymond 1946- *WhoSSW 91*
Dionis *EncCoWW*
Dionisio, Lorenzita A *BiDrAPA 89*
Dionne Quintuplets *WorAlBi*
Dionne, Albert 1905- *St&PR 91*
Dionne, Dorothy Kay 1960- *WhoAmW 91*
Dionne, Douglas Paul 1945- *BiDrAPA 89*
Dionne, Gerald Francis 1935- *WhoE 91, WhoWor 91*
Dionne, Joseph L. *BioIn 16*
Dionne, Joseph L. 1933- *St&PR 91*
Dionne, Joseph Lewis 1933- *WhoAm 90, WhoE 91*
Dionysius I, of Syracuse 430?BC-367BC *BioIn 16*
Diop, Birago 1906-1989 *AnObit 1989, BioIn 16, ConAu 130, MajTwCW, SmATA 64*
Dior, Christian 1905-1957 *BioIn 16, WorAlBi*
Diori, Hamani 1916-1989 *BioIn 16*
D'Iorio, Antoine 1925- *WhoAm 90*
Diorio, Margaret Toarello *WhoWrEP 89*
DiOrio, Robert Michael 1947- *WhoEmL 91*
Diosdado, Ana 1938- *EncCoWW*
Diotalevi, Robert Nicholas 1959- *WhoEmL 91*
Diotte, Alfred P. 1925- *St&PR 91*
Diotte, Alfred Peter 1925- *WhoAm 90*
Diouf, Abdou 1935- *WhoWor 91*
DiPaglia, Raymond 1929- *St&PR 91*
DiPalma, Joseph Rupert 1916- *WhoAm 90*
DiPalma, Susan *St&PR 91*
Di Paola, Camille Patricia 1949- *WhoE 91*
Di Paola, Robert Arnold 1933- *WhoE 91*
Di Paolo, Bruno 1953- *WhoWor 91*
Di Paolo, Joseph Amadeo 1924- *WhoAm 90, WhoE 91*
DiPaolo, Peter Thomas 1937- *WhoSSW 91*
Dipasqua, Lucy Ann 1927- *WhoAmW 91*
Dipasquale, Dominic Theodore 1932- *WhoAmA 91*
Di Pasquale, Emanuel 1943- *WhoWrEP 89*
DiPentima, Renato Anthony 1941- *WhoAm 90*
Diperna, Frank Paul 1947- *WhoAmA 91*
DiPerna, Paula 1949- *WhoEmL 91*
DiPiazza, Michael Charles 1953- *WhoE 91*
DiPiero, Andrew Edward, Jr. 1952- *WhoEmL 91*
DiPierro, Karen P. 1964- *WhoAmW 91*
DiPierro, Patrick M. 1940- *St&PR 91*
Di Pietrantonj, Francesco 1932- *WhoWor 91*
DiPietro, Janice Diane 1957- *WhoAmW 91*
DiPietro, Mark Joseph 1947- *WhoEmL 91*
DiPietro, Melanie 1944- *WhoE 91*
DiPietro, Ralph Anthony 1942- *WhoAm 90*
Di Pietro, Robert Joseph 1932- *WhoAm 90*
Di Pietro, Rocco 1949- *IntWWM 90*
DiPillo, Frank William 1929- *WhoE 91*
DiPino, Frank 1956- *Ballpl 90*
Di Pinto, Teresita L *BiDrAPA 89*
DiPlacido, Donald Frank 1924- *WhoE 91*
DiPlacido, Lisa Ann 1967- *WhoAmW 91*
Diplock, Kenneth 1907-1985 *DcNaB 1981*
Di Ponio, Concetta Celia *WhoWor 91*
Dipple, William M. 1923- *St&PR 91*
Dippo, Cathryn Suzette 1947- *WhoE 91*
D'Ippolito, Anthony 1962- *WhoEmL 91*
Dippy, George B. 1900-1988 *BioIn 16*
Dippy, George Bradner, III 1934- *WhoE 91*
Dippy, Walter E 1933- *BiDrAPA 89*
DiPrete, Edward D. 1934- *WhoAm 90, WhoE 91, WhoWor 91*
Di Prima, Diane 1934- *FemiCLE, WhoWrEP 89*
Di Prima, Stephanie Marie 1952- *WhoEmL 91, WhoWor 91*
Di Primo, Marie Ann 1952- *WhoAmW 91*
DiProva, Robert Alan 1947- *St&PR 91*
Dirac, Paul A. M. 1902-1984 *WorAlBi*
Dirac, Paul Adrien Maurice 1902-1984 *BioIn 16, DcNaB 1981, DcScB S2*
Diracles, James Constantine 1948- *WhoEmL 91*
Diracles, John Michael, Jr. 1944- *St&PR 91, WhoAm 90*
Diranian, Nancy Lucille 1954- *WhoAmW 91*
Dircks, Robert J. 1927- *St&PR 91*
Dircks, William Joseph 1929- *WhoAm 90*
Dire Straits *EncPR&S 89*
Director, Kenneth Louis 1948- *BiDrAPA 89*
Director, Stephen William 1943- *WhoAm 90, WhoWor 91*
Direen, Harry George, Jr. 1955- *WhoEmL 91*
Direnfeld, Lorne Kenneth 1949- *WhoEmL 91*
DiRenzo, Gordon James 1934- *WhoAm 90*
Direnzo, Ted 1949- *St&PR 91*
Dirichlet, Gustav Peter Lejeune 1805-1859 *BioIn 16*
Dirico, Alfred *St&PR 91*
DiRico, Ernest J. 1948- *ODwPR 91*
Dirico, Henry 1927- *St&PR 91*
Dirico, Joseph F. 1912- *St&PR 91*
Dirig, Richelle Marie 1965- *WhoAmW 91*
Dirk *AuBYP 90*
Dirk, Lisa 1956- *WhoAmW 91*
Dirk, Nathaniel 1896-1961 *WhoAmA 91N*
Dirken, Johan Maurits 1935- *WhoWor 91*
Dirkin, Shirley 1959- *ODwPR 91*
Dirks, Bruce Lane 1950- *WhoSSW 91*
Dirks, Dennis J. 1948- *St&PR 91*
Dirks, John *EncACom*
Dirks, Kenneth Ray 1925- *WhoAm 90, WhoWor 91*
Dirks, Lee Edward 1935- *WhoAm 90*
Dirks, Leslie Chant 1936- *WhoAm 90*
Dirks, Rudolph *WhoAmA 91N*
Dirks, Rudolph 1877-1968 *EncACom*
Dirks, Vickie Ellen 1953- *WhoAmW 91, WhoEmL 91*
Dirks, Willy 1916- *BioIn 16*
Dirkse, Ronald John 1945- *BiDrAPA 89*
Dirksen, Everett McKinley 1896-1969 *AuBYP 90, BioIn 16, WorAlBi*
Dirksen, Gordon F. 1943- *St&PR 91*
Dirksen, John Stuart 1959- *BiDrAPA 89*
Dirksen, Richard Wayne 1921- *WhoAm 90*
Dirksing, John Walter 1941- *St&PR 91*
Dirlewanger, Oskar 1895-1945 *BioIn 16*
Dirmeier, Michael Dennis 1950- *WhoE 91*
Diroff, Joe *BioIn 16*
Dirrane, Brian Michael 1945- *St&PR 91*
Dirring, William Andrew 1946- *WhoEmL 91*
Dirube, Rolando Lopez 1928- *WhoAmA 91*
Dirvin, Gerald Vincent 1937- *St&PR 91, WhoAm 90*
Di Sabato, Joseph Patrick, Jr. 1947- *WhoEmL 91*
Di Sabato, Louis Roman 1931- *WhoAm 90*
DiSaia, Philip John 1937- *WhoAm 90, WhoWor 91*
Di Salvo, Arthur Francis 1932- *WhoSSW 91*
DiSalvo, Frank Paul 1946- *WhoE 91, WhoEmL 91*
Di Salvo, Nicholas Armand 1920- *WhoAm 90*
DiSalvo-Ryan, DyAnne 1954- *BioIn 16*
DiSanti, Alexander Donald 1958- *WhoEmL 91*
Di Santo, Grace Johanne DeMarco 1924- *WhoAm 90, WhoAmW 91*
Disbrow, Janet Alice 1946- *WhoEmL 91*
Disbrow, Michael Ray 1959- *WhoWor 91*
Disbrow, Richard E. 1930- *St&PR 91*
Disbrow, Richard Edwin 1930- *WhoAm 90, WhoWor 91*
Disbrowe, Nicholas *PenDiDA 89*
Disch, Thomas M. *BioIn 16*
Disch, Thomas M 1940- *MajTwCW, RGTwCSF*
Disch, Thomas Michael 1940- *AuBYP 90, WhoAm 90*
Disch, Tom *MajTwCW*
Disch, Wolfgang K. A. 1937- *WhoWor 91*
Dischner, Donald D. 1932- *St&PR 91*
Di Sciascio, Eve Francesca 1954- *WhoWrEP 89*
DiSciullo, Alan Michael 1950- *WhoEmL 91*
DiSciullo, William James 1946- *St&PR 91*
Dise, J.C. 1920- *St&PR 91*
DiSenso, Daniel Richard 1944- *St&PR 91*
DiSerio, Frank Joseph 1931- *WhoE 91*
D'Isernia, Richard 1906- *BiDrAPA 89*
Disharoon, Barbara Schaeffer 1946- *WhoAmW 91*
Disharoon, Leslie Benjamin 1932- *WhoAm 90*
Disher, J. William 1933- *St&PR 91*
Disheroon, Fred Russell 1931- *WhoE 91*
Dishman, Leonard I. 1920- *WhoAm 90*
Dishon, Carol A. 1953- *WhoSSW 91*
Dishotsky, Norman I 1940- *BiDrAPA 89*
Dishy, Bob *WhoAm 90*
Disick, Renee 1941- *WhoAmW 91*
Di Simone, Giorgio 1925- *EncPaPR 91*
Di Simoni, Frank Gerald 1941- *WhoE 91*
Disinger, John Franklin 1930- *WhoAm 90*
Disinger, Roland Thomas 1953- *WhoE 91, WhoEmL 91*
Diska *WhoAmA 91*
Diska 1924- *BiDWomA*
Diska, Pat *AuBYP 90*
Diskant, Gregory L. 1948- *WhoEmL 91*
Diskin, Marshal Andrew, II 1958- *WhoSSW 91*
Diskin, Robert Joseph 1957- *WhoEmL 91*
Disle, Michel 1934- *WhoWor 91*
d'Isly, Georges *ConAu 129, MajTwCW*
Dismorr, Jessica Stewart 1885-1939 *BiDWomA*
Dismuke, Fred Wynne, Jr. 1937- *St&PR 91*
DiSmukes, Carol Jaehne 1938- *WhoAmW 91*
Dismukes, Dizzy 1890-1961 *Ballpl 90*
Dismukes, Mary Ethel *WhoAmA 91N*
Disney, Doris Miles 1907-1976 *TwCCr&M 91*
Disney, Dorothy Cameron 1903- *TwCCr&M 91*
Disney, Frances Lou 1929- *WhoAmW 91*
Disney, Michael George 1955- *WhoEmL 91*
Disney, Richard Randolph 1830-1891 *DcCanB 12*
Disney, Walt 1901-1966 *BioIn 16, WorAlBi*
Dispeker, Thea *WhoAm 90*
Dispenza, Robet Gerard 1946- *St&PR 91*
Di Spigna, Tony 1943- *WhoAm 90*
Disque, Carol Sue 1951- *WhoAmW 91, WhoEmL 91*
Disraeli, Benjamin 1804-1881 *BioIn 16, WorAlBi*
Diss, David Mark 1953- *WhoSSW 91*
Dissait, Francois Louis 1950- *WhoWor 91*
Dissen, Paul Theodor 1920- *BiDrAPA 89*
Dissette, Alyce Marie 1952- *WhoAmW 91*
Dissette, G. Keith 1944- *St&PR 91*
Disston, Harry 1899- *WhoWor 91*
Disston, Harry 1899-1989 *BioIn 16*
DiStasio, James Shannon 1947- *WhoAm 90*
DiStasio, Richard P. 1954- *St&PR 91*
DiStefano, Alan A. 1945- *St&PR 91*
DiStefano, Ana Maria 1961- *WhoHisp 91*
Di Stefano, Anna Maria 1947- *WhoEmL 91*
Di Stefano, Anthony Ferdinand 1945- *WhoAm 90*
Distefano, Benny *BioIn 16*
DiStefano, Francis Glenn 1945- *WhoSSW 91*
Di Stefano, Giuseppe 1921- *IntWWM 90, PenDiMP*
DiStefano, Joseph John, III 1938- *WhoAm 90*
Distefano, Joseph Patrick 1936- *IntWWM 90*
DiStefano, Joseph Robert 1938- *St&PR 91*
Di Stefano, Julia Mary *WhoE 91*
Distefano, Peter Andrew 1939- *WhoWor 91*
Distel, Sacha 1933- *OxCPMus*
Distelhorst, Craig Tipton 1941- *WhoSSW 91, WhoWor 91*
Distelhorst, Garis Fred 1942- *WhoAm 90*
Distelhorst, Michael 1949- *WhoEmL 91*
Distelman, William L *BiDrAPA 89*
Distenfeld, Yvonne Schlafstein 1956- *WhoAm 90*
Dister, Arthur Charles 1933- *WhoSSW 91*

Distin *OxCPMus*
Distin, John Henry 1793-1863 *OxCPMus*
Distin, Theodore 1823-1893 *OxCPMus*
Distler, Martha Mary 1963- *WhoE 91*
Distler, William Francis 1917- *WhoAm 90*
Distler, William Joseph 1942- *St&PR 91*
Diston, David George 1932- *St&PR 91*
Di Suvero, Mark 1933- *WhoAm 90, WhoAmA 91*
Di Sylvester, Victor 1941- *WhoE 91*
Ditch, Steve 1956- *WhoE 91*
Ditchfield, Allan W. 1937- *St&PR 91*
Ditchoff, Pamela Jane 1950- *WhoWrEP 89*
Di Tella, Torcuato Salvador 1929- *WhoWor 91*
Di Tella, Vincenzo 1942- *WhoWor 91*
Dith, Pran *BioIn 16*
Dithridge, Betty 1920- *WhoAmW 91, WhoWor 91*
Ditka, Michael Keller 1939- *WhoAm 90*
Ditka, Mike 1939- *BioIn 16, WorAlBi*
Ditko, Steve 1927- *EncACom*
Ditkowsky, Keith Scott *BiDrAPA 89*
Ditlev Simonsen, Per *WhoWor 91*
Ditlevsen, Tove 1918-1976 *DcScanL*
Ditman, Keith S *BiDrAPA 89*
Ditmar, Art 1929- *Ballpl 90*
Ditmars, Raymond Lee 1876-1942 *AuBYP 90*
Ditmore, Dana C. 1940- *St&PR 91*
Ditmore, Michael Conrad 1943- *WhoAm 90*
Ditmore, Robert Keith 1934- *WhoAm 90*
Dito, John Allen 1935- *WhoAm 90*
DiTomaso, Gino 1940- *St&PR 91*
Ditomassi, George Robert 1934- *St&PR 91*
Diton, Carl 1886-1962 *DrBlPA 90*
DiTonno, Daniel Christian 1951- *WhoE 91*
DiTorrice, Guy Louis 1952- *WhoEmL 91*
Ditrapani, G. 1950- *St&PR 91*
D'Itri, Frank Michael 1933- *WhoAm 90*
Ditte, Andre Jacques 1916- *St&PR 91*
Dittemore, Ernest *BioIn 16*
Dittenber, Hal *ODwPR 91*
Dittenhafer, Brian Douglas 1942- *St&PR 91, WhoAm 90*
Ditter, John William, Jr. 1921- *WhoAm 90*
Ditterline, John R. 1950- *St&PR 91*
Dittert, J. Lee, Jr. 1931- *WhoAm 90*
Dittert, Lewis William 1934- *WhoAm 90*
Dittes, James Edward 1926- *WhoAm 90*
Dittman, Duane Arthur 1924- *WhoAm 90*
Dittman, Mark Allen 1950- *WhoEmL 91*
Dittmann, Lorenz 1928- *WhoWor 91*
Dittmann, Reidar 1922- *WhoAm 90*
Dittmer, Clark Martin 1936- *WhoAm 90*
Dittmer, Donald Charles 1927- *WhoAm 90*
Dittmer, Fred A *BiDrAPA 89*
Dittmer, Jack 1928- *Ballpl 90*
Dittmer, Petronella Elizabeth Kendrick 1948- *IntWWM 90*
Dittmer, Stevan W. 1952- *WhoWrEP 89*
Ditto, Arthur Harry 1941- *St&PR 91*
Ditto, Daniel Thomas 1954- *WhoEmL 91*
Ditto, Jane Ellen McPhail 1940- *IntWWM 90*
Ditto, Kane 1944- *WhoSSW 91*
Ditto, Michael E. 1943- *St&PR 91*
Ditton, James *TwCCr&M 91*
Dittrich, Gregory Duane 1960- *WhoEmL 91*
Dittrich, Joseph H. 1924- *St&PR 91*
Dittrich, Raymond Joseph 1932- *WhoAm 90*
Dittrich, Raymond Robert 1949- *St&PR 91*
Dittrich, Robert J. 1931- *St&PR 91*
Dittrich, Thomas Stayton 1954- *WhoEmL 91*
Ditty, Harry L. 1935- *WhoAm 90*
Ditucci, Luciano 1938- *St&PR 91*
DiTullo, Michael Joseph 1952- *WhoE 91*
DiTurno, Barbara Rose 1963- *WhoAmW 91*
Ditz, John Adams 1921- *WhoAm 90*
Ditzel, Paul Calvin 1926- *AuBYP 90, WhoWrEP 89*
Ditzen, Rudolf 1893-1947 *BioIn 16*
Ditzion, Grace *WhoAmA 91*
Ditzion, Grace 1914- *WhoAmW 91*
Ditzler, Daniel Edwin 1955- *WhoWrEP 89*
Ditzler, John William 1939- *St&PR 91*
Ditzler, Robert Lisle 1931- *St&PR 91*
DiUlio, Albert Joseph 1943- *WhoAm 90*
Divac, Ivan 1932- *WhoWor 91*
Divac, Vlado *BioIn 16*
DiValerio, Richard Michael 1930- *St&PR 91*
Divall, Richard S. 1945- *IntWWM 90*
Divall, Robert Keith 1923- *St&PR 91*
Divcic, Borivoj S *BiDrAPA 89*
Divelbiss, Terry L. 1947- *St&PR 91*
Dively, George Samuel 1902-1988 *BioIn 16*
Dively, John A., Jr. 1958- *WhoEmL 91*
Divendal, Joost 1955- *ConAu 132*
DiVento, Anthony John 1945- *St&PR 91*
DiVenuto, John Paul 1940- *WhoE 91*
Diver, Colin S. 1944- *BioIn 16*
Diver, Maud 1867-1945 *FemiCLE*
Diver, William 1921- *WhoAm 90*
Divic, Josif M 1930- *BiDrAPA 89*
di Vimercate, Alberto de Capitani 1942- *WhoE 91*
Divine *BioIn 16*
Divine 1945-1988 *AnObit 1988*
Divine, Arthur Durham 1904-1987 *BioIn 16*
Divine, B. Lees 1937- *St&PR 91*
Divine, Dick *BioIn 16*
Divine, Harold S. *WhoAm 90*
Divine, Harold S. 1921- *St&PR 91*
Divine, John David 1953- *WhoSSW 91*
Divine, Mona *BioIn 16*
Divine, Robert Alexander 1929- *WhoAm 90*
Divine, William Robinson 1915- *WhoAm 90*
Divinsky, N. J. *ConAu 132*
Divinsky, Nathan 1925- *ConAu 132*
Divird, D. Thomas 1942- *St&PR 91*
Divita, Eugene C 1933- *BiDrAPA 89*
Divita, James 1941- *St&PR 91*
Divita, Phillip S. *St&PR 91*
Divok, Mario J. *WhoWrEP 89*
Divola, John Manford, Jr 1949- *WhoAmA 91*
Diwan, Joyce Johnson 1940- *WhoAmW 91*
Diwan, Romesh Kumar 1933- *WhoAm 90*
Diwan, Satyendra K *BiDrAPA 89*
Diwoky, Roy John 1910- *WhoAm 90*
Dix, Barbara 1944- *IntWWM 90*
Dix, Beulah 1876-1970 *FemiCLE*
Dix, Beulah M. 1876-1970 *BioAmW*
Dix, David Wayne 1954- *WhoSSW 91*
Dix, Dorothea L. 1802-1887 *WorAlBi*
Dix, Dorothea Lynde 1802-1887 *BioAmW, BioIn 16*
Dix, Dorothy 1870-1951 *BioAmW, BioIn 16*
Dix, Fred Andrew, Jr. 1931- *WhoAm 90*
Dix, John Adams 1798-1879 *BiDrUSE 89, BioIn 16*
Dix, Linda Skidmore 1948- *WhoAmW 91, WhoEmL 91*
Dix, Otto 1891-1969 *BioIn 16, IntDcAA 90*
Dix, Paula McNicholas 1942- *WhoAmW 91*
Dix, Robert H. *WhoAm 90*
Dix, Rollin Cumming 1936- *WhoAm 90*
Dix, Ronald Lee 1951- *St&PR 91*
Dix, William Bradley 1911- *St&PR 91*
Dixey, Frank 1892-1982 *DcNaB 1981*
Dixey, Henry E. 1859-1943 *OxCPMus*
Dixie, Florence 1855-1905 *FemiCLE*
Dixie, Florence Douglas 1857-1905 *BioIn 16*
Dixit, Anita S. 1946- *St&PR 91*
Dixit, Balwant Narayan 1933- *WhoAm 90*
Dixit, Bhushit S. 1956- *BiDrAPA 89*
Dixit, Ganesh Datta 1935- *WhoWor 91*
Dixit, Kaivalya Mahendra 1942- *St&PR 91*
Dixon, Alan John 1927- *WhoAm 90, WhoWor 91*
Dixon, Albert Vernon, Jr. 1946- *BiDrAPA 89*
Dixon, Alexandreena Delaida 1945- *WhoEmL 91*
Dixon, Amy Lynne 1960- *WhoAmW 91*
Dixon, Andrew Derart 1925- *WhoAm 90*
Dixon, Andrew Douglas 1958- *WhoE 91, WhoEmL 91, WhoWor 91*
Dixon, Andrew Lee, Jr. 1942- *WhoE 91*
Dixon, Annemarie Anderson 1962- *WhoAmW 91*
Dixon, Armendia Pierce 1937- *WhoE 91*
Dixon, Billy Gene 1935- *WhoAm 90*
Dixon, Bonnie Lynn 1955- *WhoEmL 91*
Dixon, Carla Suzette *BiDrAPA 89*
Dixon, Carol Lois 1948- *WhoSSW 91*
Dixon, Carole 1943- *WhoAmW 91*
Dixon, Carolyn Sue 1940- *BiDrAPA 89*
Dixon, Carrie Mae *BioIn 16*
Dixon, Connie Lorraine 1965- *WhoAmW 91*
Dixon, Dabney White 1949- *WhoAmW 91*
Dixon, Daniel Iverson 1948- *WhoSSW 91*
Dixon, Dean 1915-1976 *DrBlPA 90, PenDiMP*
Dixon, Diane B. 1951- *St&PR 91*
Dixon, Don *BioIn 16*
Dixon, Donald D. 1935- *St&PR 91*
Dixon, Dorothy Beatrice 1921- *WhoAmW 91*
Dixon, Douglas Stephen 1945- *WhoEmL 91*
Dixon, Earl H. 1925- *St&PR 91*
Dixon, Ella Hepworth 1857-1932 *FemiCLE*
Dixon, Ernest Thomas, Jr. 1922- *WhoAm 90*
Dixon, Eva Crawford Johnson 1909- *WhoWor 91*
Dixon, Fitz Eugene, Jr. 1923- *WhoAm 90*
Dixon, Francis S 1879-1967 *WhoAmA 91N*
Dixon, Frank James 1920- *WhoAm 90*
Dixon, Frank James 1951- *WhoEmL 91*
Dixon, Frederick Augustus 1843-1919 *OxCCanT*
Dixon, Gale Harllee 1944- *WhoSSW 91*
Dixon, George F., Jr. 1918- *St&PR 91*
Dixon, George Francis, Jr. 1918- *WhoAm 90*
Dixon, George Hall 1920- *St&PR 91*
Dixon, George Lane, Jr. 1928- *WhoAm 90*
Dixon, George Sumter, Jr. 1938- *WhoSSW 91*
Dixon, Glenn T. 1943- *St&PR 91*
Dixon, Gordon Henry 1930- *WhoAm 90*
Dixon, Guy E. 1920- *St&PR 91*
Dixon, Guy Edwin, III 1946- *St&PR 91*
Dixon, Harvey Lewis 1927- *WhoAm 90*
Dixon, Henry H, Jr. 1928- *BiDrAPA 89*
Dixon, Herbert *BioIn 16*
Dixon, Huw David 1958- *WhoWor 91*
Dixon, Irma Muse 1952- *WhoAmW 91*
Dixon, Ivan 1931- *ConTFT 8*
Dixon, Ivan N., III 1931- *DrBlPA 90*
Dixon, Jacqueline 1949- *WhoAmW 91*
Dixon, James Andrew, Jr. 1951- *WhoAm 90, WhoEmL 91*
Dixon, James Payson, Jr. 1917- *WhoAm 90*
Dixon, Jeane *WhoAm 90, WhoWor 91, WhoWrEP 89*
Dixon, Jeane 1918- *EncO&P 3*
Dixon, Jeane P. 1918- *BioAmW*
Dixon, Jeane Pinckert 1918- *EncPaPR 91*
Dixon, Jeanette T. 1949- *WhoAmW 91*
Dixon, Jenny 1950- *WhoAmA 91*
Dixon, John Aldous 1923- *WhoAm 90*
Dixon, John Allen, Jr. 1920- *WhoSSW 91*
Dixon, John Edward 1933- *St&PR 91, WhoAm 90*
Dixon, John Fulton 1946- *WhoEmL 91*
Dixon, John Morris 1933- *WhoAm 90*
Dixon, John R. 1927- *WhoAm 90*
Dixon, John Ronald 1927- *St&PR 91*
Dixon, John Spencer 1957- *WhoSSW 91*
Dixon, John Wainwright 1920-1989 *BioIn 16*
Dixon, John Wesley, Jr. 1919- *WhoAm 90*
Dixon, Julian C. 1934- *BlkAmsC [port]*
Dixon, Julian Carey 1934- *WhoAm 90*
Dixon, Karen Sue 1946- *WhoAmW 91*
Dixon, Katharine N 1943- *BiDrAPA 89*
Dixon, Kelvin Norman 1959- *WhoE 91*
Dixon, Ken 1943- *WhoAmA 91*
Dixon, Ken 1960- *Ballpl 90*
Dixon, Kent 1937- *WhoAm 90*
Dixon, Larry Dean 1942- *WhoSSW 91*
Dixon, Lawrence Paul 1938- *WhoE 91*
Dixon, Linda Diane 1960- *WhoAmW 91*
Dixon, Lisa *BiDrAPA 89*
Dixon, Louis Frederick 1928- *WhoAm 90*
Dixon, Louis M. *WhoAm 90*
Dixon, Louise *ODwPR 91*
Dixon, MacIntyre 1931- *ConTFT 8*
Dixon, Marjorie 1887- *AuBYP 90*
Dixon, Markus K. 1945- *St&PR 91*
Dixon, Melvin 1950- *ConAu 132*
Dixon, Michael Albert 1948- *WhoEmL 91*
Dixon, Michael Wayne 1942- *WhoWor 91*
Dixon, Michel LaVon 1945- *WhoEmL 91, WhoSSW 91, WhoWor 91*
Dixon, Moses Devon 1928- *WhoSSW 91*
Dixon, Norman F 1922- *ConAu 130*
Dixon, Norman Rex 1932- *WhoAm 90*
Dixon, Norval W. 1931- *St&PR 91*
Dixon, Paige *AuBYP 90*
Dixon, Phelon *EarBlAP*
Dixon, Phillip Ray, Sr. 1949- *WhoEmL 91*
Dixon, Rap 1902-1945 *Ballpl 90*
Dixon, Reginald 1905-1985 *OxCPMus*
Dixon, Richard C. 1929- *St&PR 91*
Dixon, Richard Cressie 1929- *WhoAm 90*
Dixon, Richard Dean 1944- *WhoWor 91*
Dixon, Richard T. 1925- *St&PR 91*
Dixon, Richard Wayne 1936- *WhoAm 90, WhoE 91*
Dixon, Robert James 1920- *WhoAm 90*
Dixon, Robert Joseph 1951- *WhoE 91*
Dixon, Robert Michel 1951- *WhoE 91, WhoEmL 91*
Dixon, Ronney Theodore 1954- *WhoEmL 91*
Dixon, Sandra D *BiDrAPA 89*
Dixon, Sarah 1671- *FemiCLE*
Dixon, Sharon Pratt 1944- *St&PR 91, WhoAmW 91*
Dixon, Sheila D. 1948- *St&PR 91*
Dixon, Sheree Jones *BiDrAPA 89*
Dixon, Shirley Juanita 1935- *WhoAmW 91, WhoWor 91*
Dixon, Sonny 1924- *Ballpl 90*
Dixon, Stephen 1936- *WhoWrEP 89*
Dixon, Stephen Wiles 1950- *WhoSSW 91*
Dixon, Steven Bedford 1945- *WhoEmL 91*
Dixon, Stewart Strawn 1930- *WhoAm 90*
Dixon, Strother P 1940- *BiDrAPA 89*
Dixon, Terry Phillip 1946- *WhoEmL 91*
Dixon, Thomas Francis 1916- *WhoAm 90, WhoE 91*
Dixon, Thomas Lloyd 1957- *WhoEmL 91*
Dixon, Tod O. 1939- *St&PR 91*
Dixon, Tom 1955- *Ballpl 90*
Dixon, Vincent W. 1942- *St&PR 91*
Dixon, Vincent William 1942- *WhoAm 90*
Dixon, Warren Arthur 1934- *WhoSSW 91*
Dixon, Wendell L. 1923- *St&PR 91*
Dixon, Wesley Moon, Jr. 1927- *St&PR 91, WhoAm 90*
Dixon, Wilfrid Joseph *WhoAm 90*
Dixon, Willard 1942- *WhoAmA 91*
Dixon, William Cornelius 1904- *WhoAm 90, WhoWor 91*
Dixon, William L. 1931- *St&PR 91*
Dixon, William Robert 1917- *WhoAm 90*
Dixon, William Robert 1925- *WhoAm 90*
Dixon, William T 1918- *BiDrAPA 89*
Dixon, Willie *BioIn 16*
Dixon, Willie James 1915- *WhoAm 90*
Dixson, Cynthia Fisher 1949- *WhoE 91*
Dixson, J. B. *ODwPR 91*
Dixson, Robert J. 1907-1989 *BioIn 16*
Dixson, Robert John 1907- *WhoAm 90*
Dixson, Robert Morgan 1948- *St&PR 91*
Diz, Adolfo Cesar 1931- *WhoWor 91*
Diz, Harry Richard 1947- *St&PR 91*
Diz Pi, Olga 1939- *BiDrAPA 89*
Dizard, Wilson Paul, Jr. 1922- *WhoAm 90*
Dizdar, Marijan A. 1943- *St&PR 91*
Dizdarevic, Raif 1926- *WhoWor 91*
Dizenhuz, Israel M 1931- *BiDrAPA 89*
di Zerega, Thomas William 1927- *WhoAm 90*
Di Zio, Stephen David *BiDrAPA 89*
Dizmang, Larry H 1937- *BiDrAPA 89*
Dizon, Darian *WhoE 91*
Dizon, Dianella V. 1949- *BiDrAPA 89*
Dizon-Farrales, Elouisa V *BiDrAPA 89*
DJ Jazzy Jeff 1965?- *ConMus 5 [port]*
DJ Jazzy Jeff and the Fresh Prince *ConMus 5 [port]*
Djahanbakhch, Ovrang 1944- *WhoWor 91*
Djaparidze, Ludwig Alexander 1957- *IntWWM 90*
Djebar, Assia 1936- *WorAu 1980*
Djedje, Jacqueline Cogdell 1948- *IntWWM 90*
Djenderedjian, Armen Harout 1945- *BiDrAPA 89*
Djerassi, Carl 1923- *ConAu 131, WhoAm 90*
Djerassi, Isaac 1925- *WhoAm 90*
Djerejian, Edward Peter 1939- *WhoAm 90, WhoWor 91*
Djerejian, Robert A. 1931- *St&PR 91*
Djermakoye, Moumouni Adamou 1939- *WhoWor 91*
Djilas, Milovan 1911- *BioIn 16*
Djindjihashvili, Nodar *BioIn 16*
Djirlic, Aida E. 1949- *WhoWor 91*
Djohar, Said Mohamed *WhoWor 91*
Djordjevic, Cirila 1926- *WhoAm 90*
Djordjevic, Dimitrije 1922- *WhoAm 90*
Djordjevich, Michael 1936- *St&PR 91, WhoAm 90*
Djuranovic, Veselin 1925- *WhoWor 91*
Djurovic, Robert 1958- *WhoEmL 91*
Djwa, Sandra 1939- *ConAu 131*
Dlab, Vlastimil 1932- *WhoAm 90, WhoWor 91*
Dlamini, Obed Mfanyana *WhoWor 91*
Dlamini, Sotsha Ernest 1940- *WhoWor 91*
D'Lauro, Frank Andrew, Jr. 1940- *St&PR 91, WhoE 91, WhoWor 91*
Dlesk, George 1914- *WhoAm 90*
Dlin, Barney M 1924- *BiDrAPA 89*
Dlouhy, Annette Stephanie 1952- *WhoAmW 91*
Dlouhy, Phillip Edward 1941- *WhoAm 90*
Dlouhy, Vladimir *WhoWor 91*
D'Lower, Del 1912- *WhoE 91*
Dlugoff, Marc Alan 1955- *WhoE 91*
Dlugolenski, Ella M. 1951- *St&PR 91*
Dluhy, John M 1937- *BiDrAPA 89*
D'Mato, Patrick M. 1938- *St&PR 91*
D'Mello, Dale Alfred 1952- *BiDrAPA 89*
Dmitriev, Aleksander *IntWWM 90*
Dmitzak, Amy H. 1948- *ODwPR 91*
Dmitzak, Lee J. 1945- *ODwPR 91*
Dmochowski, John Francis 1944- *BiDrAPA 89*
Dmyterko, Michael Philip 1948- *WhoEmL 91*
Dmytruk, Ihor R 1938- *WhoAmA 91*
Dmytryk, Edward *BioIn 16*
Dmytryshyn, Basil 1925- *WhoAm 90, WhoWor 91*
Dneprov, Anatoly 1919-1975 *RGTwCSF*
Dnes, Antony William 1956- *WhoWor 91*
Do Muoi 1911- *WhoWor 91*
Do, Kim V 1954- *WhoAmA 91*
Do'a *NewAgMG*
Doa, Vincent, Sr. *WhoHisp 91*
Doak, Bill 1891-1954 *Ballpl 90*
Doak, Janice Askew 1925- *WhoAmW 91*
Doak, Robert A., Jr. 1928- *St&PR 91*
Doak, Sheila Jean *St&PR 91*

Doak, William Nuckles 1882-1933 *BiDrUSE 89*
Doak-Davis, Nan *BioIn 16*
Doamaral, Diogo Freitas 1941- *WhoWor 91*
Doan, Charles Austin *NewYTBS 90*
Doan, Charles Austin 1896-1990 *BioIn 16*
Doan, Cortland Charles 1926- *WhoAm 90*
Doan, James Kenton 1941- *St&PR 91*
Doan, John *NewAgMG*
Doan, Kirk Hugh 1953- *WhoEmL 91*
Doan, Patricia Nan 1930- *WhoSSW 91*
Doan, Peter Leisenring 1955- *WhoEmL 91, WhoSSW 91*
Doan, Richard Joseph *BiDrAPA 89*
Doan, Richard K. *BioIn 16*
Doan, Tuan Anh 1961- *WhoEmL 91*
Doan, Xuyen Van 1949- *WhoWor 91*
Doane, David Green 1921- *WhoAm 90, WhoWor 91*
Doane, Kathleen Frances 1945- *WhoE 91*
Doane, Pelagie 1906-1966 *AuBYP 90*
Doane, Roseanne Marie 1950- *WhoEmL 91*
Doane, William Howard 1832-1915 *BioIn 16*
Doar, William Walter, Jr. 1935- *WhoSSW 91*
Doat, Taxile 1851-1938 *PenDiDA 89*
Doban, Robert Charles 1924- *St&PR 91*
Dobard, Raymond Gerard 1947- *WhoAmA 91*
Dobashi, Masayuki 1938- *Ballpl 90*
Dobbel, Rodger Francis 1934- *WhoWor 91*
Dobbert, Daniel Joseph 1946- *WhoEmL 91*
Dobbert, Dean Roger 1954- *WhoE 91*
Dobbertien, Mark Alan *BiDrAPA 89*
Dobbie, Dorothy 1945- *WhoAmW 91*
Dobbie, George Herbert 1918- *St&PR 91, WhoAm 90*
Dobbin, James Cochran 1814-1857 *AmLegL, BiDrUSE 89*
Dobbins, David Foster 1928- *WhoAm 90*
Dobbins, Edmund J. *WhoAm 90*
Dobbins, Frank 1943- *IntWWM 90*
Dobbins, James Hamilton 1939- *WhoE 91*
Dobbins, James Joseph 1924- *WhoAm 90*
Dobbins, John Joseph 1940- *St&PR 91*
Dobbins, John Joseph 1946- *WhoSSW 91*
Dobbins, Marcus D. 1828-1871 *AmLegL*
Dobbins, Robert Newton 1904- *WhoE 91*
Dobbins, William D. *ODwPR 91*
Dobbins, William Octavius, III 1932- *WhoAm 90*
Dobbs, Andrew James 1960- *WhoEmL 91*
Dobbs, Dan Byron 1932- *WhoAm 90*
Dobbs, Donald Edwin 1931- *St&PR 91*
Dobbs, Ella Victoria 1866-1952 *WhoAmA 91N*
Dobbs, Farrell 1907-1983 *EncAL*
Dobbs, Frank Wilbur 1932- *WhoAm 90*
Dobbs, George Albert 1943- *WhoSSW 91, WhoWor 91*
Dobbs, Gregory Allan 1946- *WhoAm 90*
Dobbs, Jack Percival Baker 1922- *IntWWM 90*
Dobbs, James C. 1944- *St&PR 91*
Dobbs, John 1876-1934 *Ballpl 90*
Dobbs, John Barnes 1931- *WhoAm 90, WhoAmA 91*
Dobbs, Karen Keith 1957- *WhoAmW 91*
Dobbs, Kathryn Barry 1933- *WhoE 91*
Dobbs, Mattiwilda *IntWWM 90*
Dobbs, Mattiwilda 1925- *BioIn 16, DcAfAmP, DrBIPA 90, PenDiMP*
Dobbs, Rosalyne Brown 1933- *WhoWrEP 89*
Dobbs, Rose *AuBYP 90*
Dobbs, Tim Allen 1960- *WhoSSW 91*
Dobbs, Tracy Lloyd 1954- *WhoSSW 91*
Dobbs, William H 1924- *BiDrAPA 89*
Dobbs-Wiggins, Paula C *BiDrAPA 89*
Dobbyn, Edward T., Jr. 1916- *St&PR 91*
Dobbyn, Jerome W. 1942- *St&PR 91*
Dobeck, Peggy Sue *BiDrAPA 89*
Dobeck, Robert Bradley 1954- *WhoEmL 91*
Dobeck, Timothy G. 1961- *WhoEmL 91*
Dobelis, Inge Nachman 1933- *WhoAmW 91*
Dobell, Byron Maxwell 1927- *WhoAm 90, WhoWrEP 89*
Dobell, Mercy *WhoWrEP 89*
Doberczak, Bohdan W *BiDrAPA 89*
Doberenz, Alexander R. 1936- *WhoAm 90*
Doberneck, Raymond C. 1932- *WhoAm 90*
Doberstein, Audrey K. 1932- *WhoAmW 91, WhoE 91*
Doberstein, Carole Jean 1957- *St&PR 91*
Dobes, William Lamar, Jr. 1943- *WhoWor 91*
Dobey, James Kenneth 1919- *WhoAm 90*
Dobie, Dorcas Jean *BiDrAPA 89*
Dobie, James Frank 1888-1964 *WorAlBi*
Dobie, Jeanne *WhoAmA 91*
Dobie, Shirley Ann Bartlett 1951- *WhoSSW 91*
Dobilas, John J. 1946- *St&PR 91*
Dobilas, Ronald John 1942- *St&PR 91*
Dobin, Michael H. 1949- *WhoAm 90, WhoEmL 91*
Dobis, Joan Pauline 1944- *WhoAmW 91*
Dobish, Sidney *BioIn 16*
Dobkin, Alexander 1908-1975 *WhoAmA 91N*
Dobkin, David Paul 1948- *WhoAm 90*
Dobkin, Donald 1922- *St&PR 91*
Dobkin, Irving Bern 1918- *WhoAm 90, WhoWor 91*
Dobkin, James Allen 1940- *WhoAm 90*
Dobkin, John *BioIn 16*
Dobkin, John Howard 1942- *WhoAm 90, WhoAmA 91*
Dobkin, Lawrence *BioIn 16*
Doble family *BioIn 16*
Dobler, Conrad *BioIn 16*
Dobler, Donald William 1927- *WhoAm 90*
Dobler, Merri Louise Bailey 1956- *WhoWrEP 89*
Dobler, Norma 1917- *WhoAmW 91*
Dobles, Fabian 1918- *HispWr 90*
Doblin, Alfred 1878-1957 *BioIn 16*
Doblin, Jay 1920-1989 *BioIn 16, ConDes 90*
Dobmeier, Clarence Joseph, Jr. 1952- *WhoEmL 91*
Dobo, Steven *BiDrAPA 89*
Dobo, William 1935- *St&PR 91*
Dobois, Alan Beekman 1935- *WhoAmA 91*
Dobos, Albert Michael 1942- *St&PR 91*
Dobos, David M. *BiDrAPA 89*
Dobos, Donald Jack 1948- *St&PR 91*
Dobraczynski, Jan 1910- *WhoWor 91*
Dobranski, Bernard 1939- *WhoAm 90*
Dobratz, Betty Ann 1947- *WhoEmL 91*
Dobratz, Carl George 1933- *St&PR 91*
Dobree, Georgina 1930- *IntWWM 90*
Dobrenic, Denice Jo 1958- *WhoEmL 91*
Dobriansky, Lev Eugene 1918- *WhoAm 90, WhoWor 91*
Dobriansky, Paula Jon 1955- *WhoAm 90, WhoAmW 91*
Dobrich, Fulvio V. 1947- *St&PR 91*
Dobrin, Arnold 1928- *AuBYP 90*
Dobrin, Arthur Barry 1943- *WhoWrEP 89*
Dobrin, Bernard Robert 1937- *WhoAm 90*
Dobrin, Sheldon L. 1945- *WhoEmL 91*
Dobrinsky, Herbert Colman 1933- *WhoE 91, WhoWor 91*
Dobrinsky, Jaroslav *BiDrAPA 89*
Dobrish, Robert Zachary 1940- *WhoE 91*
Dobrjanskyj, Danylo Borys 1956- *WhoE 91*
Dobrofsky, Shirley *BiDrAPA 89*
Dobrovolny, Jerry Stanley 1922- *WhoAm 90*
Dobrow, Alan *BiDrAPA 89*
Dobrowen, Issay 1891-1953 *PenDiMP*
Dobrowolski, Andrzej 1921- *IntWWM 90*
Dobry, Stanley Thomas 1948- *WhoEmL 91*
Dobry, Sylvia Hearn 1938- *WhoAmW 91, WhoWor 91*
Dobrynin, Anatoly F. 1919 *WhoAm 90, WhoWor 91*
Dobscha, Steven Keith *BiDrAPA 89*
Dobschensky, Carolyn Sue 1943- *WhoAmW 91*
Dobsevage, Alvin Philip 1922- *WhoE 91, WhoWor 91*
Dobson, Alan 1928- *WhoAm 90*
Dobson, Alastair Graham 1948- *WhoWor 91*
Dobson, Allen 1943- *WhoAm 90*
Dobson, Andrew 1957- *ConAu 132*
Dobson, Brian 1934- *St&PR 91*
Dobson, Brian G. 1945- *ODwPR 91*
Dobson, Bridget McColl Hursley 1938- *WhoAm 90, WhoAmW 91, WhoWor 91*
Dobson, Christopher 1927- *ConAu 31NR*
Dobson, Chuck 1944- *Ballpl 90*
Dobson, Clarence A. 1921- *St&PR 91*
Dobson, David 1940- *WhoWor 91*
Dobson, David Irving 1883-1957 *WhoAmA 91N*
Dobson, Donald Alfred 1928- *WhoAm 90*
Dobson, Gavin Richard 1951- *WhoEmL 91*
Dobson, Geoffrey Martin 1937- *WhoAm 90*
Dobson, Harold 1922- *WhoWor 91*
Dobson, James *NewYTBS 90 [port]*
Dobson, James C. 1936- *BioIn 16*
Dobson, Jean Gabrielle Austin 1923- *IntWWM 90*
Dobson, Joe 1917- *Ballpl 90*
Dobson, John *BioIn 16*
Dobson, John 1930- *IntWWM 90*
Dobson, John McCullough 1940- *WhoAm 90*
Dobson, John P *BiDrAPA 89*
Dobson, John Robert 1930- *St&PR 91*
Dobson, Judith Elise 1934- *WhoSSW 91*
Dobson, Julia 1941- *BioIn 16*
Dobson, Karen 1932- *WhoE 91*
Dobson, Kathi A. 1958- *WhoEmL 91*
Dobson, Kevin 1943- *WhoAm 90*
Dobson, Margaret June 1931- *WhoAmW 91*
Dobson, Mark Michael 1948- *WhoEmL 91*
Dobson, Pat 1942- *Ballpl 90*
Dobson, Richard *WhoNeCM [port]*
Dobson, Richard Lawrence 1928- *WhoAm 90*
Dobson, Robert Albertus, IV 1957- *WhoSSW 91*
Dobson, Rosemary 1920- *FemiCLE*
Dobson, Sharon Kay 1936- *WhoAmW 91*
Dobson, Stuart Halstead 1935- *St&PR 91*
Dobson, Susann Douglas 1949- *WhoAmW 91*
Dobson, Susannah *FemiCLE*
Dobson, Tamara 1947- *DrBIPA 90*
Dobson, Terrance James 1940- *St&PR 91, WhoAm 90*
Dobson, Warren Theodore, II 1958- *WhoEmL 91*
Dobson, William 1611-1646? *IntDcAA 90*
Dobson, William F. 1946- *ODwPR 91*
Doby, Larry *BioIn 16*
Doby, Larry 1923- *Ballpl 90 [port]*
Dobyns, Audrey Harridge 1905- *WhoSSW 91*
Dobyns, Henry F 1925- *ConAu 32NR*
Dobyns, Jerome Middleton 1926- *St&PR 91*
Dobyns, M Meredith 1943- *BiDrAPA 89*
Dobyns, Nancy Annette 1956- *WhoEmL 91*
Dobyns, Norman L. 1933- *St&PR 91*
Dobyns, Robert Floyd *BiDrAPA 89*
Dobyns, Stephen 1941- *TwCCr&M 91*
Dobzhansky, Theodosius 1900-1975 *DcScB S2*
Dobzhansky, Theodosius Grigorievich 1900-1975 *BioIn 16*
DoCarmo, Winston G. 1942- *St&PR 91*
Docherty, James L. *TwCCr&M 91*
Docherty, John Patrick 1944- *BiDrAPA 89, WhoE 91*
Dock, Deborah L. 1955- *St&PR 91*
Dock, Lavinia L. 1858-1956 *BioIn 16*
Dock, William *NewYTBS 90*
Docken, Edsel Ardean, Sr. 1928- *WhoE 91*
Dockendorff, Charles H. 1933- *St&PR 91*
Dockendorff, Emma 1953- *ODwPR 91*
Docker, Ralph J. 1929- *St&PR 91*
Dockery, Cindi Jo 1965- *WhoAmW 91*
Dockery, Herbert Donald 1954- *WhoSSW 91*
Dockery, J. Lee 1932- *WhoAm 90*
Dockery, Joseph R. 1936- *St&PR 91*
Dockery, Robert W., Jr. *BioIn 16*
Dockery, Ronald Carl 1948- *WhoEmL 91*
Dockhorn, Robert John 1934- *WhoAm 90, WhoWor 91*
Docking, Robert Blackwell 1925- *WhoAm 90*
Docking, Thomas Robert 1954- *WhoAm 90*
Dockrell, William Bryan 1929- *ConAu 32NR*
Dockser, William Barnet 1937- *WhoAm 90*
Dockson, Robert Ray 1917- *St&PR 91, WhoAm 90*
Dockstader, Frederick J. 1919- *WhoAm 90, WhoAmA 91*
Dockstader, Lew 1856-1924 *OxCPMus*
Dockter, Selmer R. 1936- *WhoSSW 91*
Docobo, Richard Douglas 1956- *WhoHisp 91*
Docter, Charles Alfred 1931- *WhoAm 90*
Docter, Glenn Joseph 1949- *St&PR 91*
Docter, Lloyd W. 1954- *St&PR 91*
Docter, Sarah *BioIn 16*
Docterman, Gert 1933- *St&PR 91*
Docteur, Gerald John 1942- *WhoE 91*
Doctor Baseball *ConAu 130*
Doctor John, The Night Tripper 1940- *EncPR&S 89*
Doctor, Prerak Manibhai 1959- *BiDrAPA 89*
Doctor-Canham, Rhonda Lynn 1964- *WhoAmW 91*
Doctoroff, Martin Myles 1933- *WhoAm 90*
Doctorow, Donald 1922- *WhoE 91*
Doctorow, E. L. 1931- *BioIn 16*
Doctorow, E.L. 1931- *ConAu 33NR, MajTwCW*
Doctorow, E. L. 1931- *WorAlBi*
Doctorow, Edgar Lawrence 1931- *WhoAm 90, WhoWrEP 89*
Docwra, Ann 1640?-1710 *BiDEWW*
Docwra, Anne 1624?-1710 *FemiCLE*
Dodd, Alan D. 1953- *ODwPR 91*
Dodd, Anita Adreon 1946- *WhoSSW 91*
Dodd, Anne Wescott 1940- *WhoWrEP 89*
Dodd, Bobby 1908-1988 *BioIn 16*
Dodd, Carol Kelley 1947- *WhoAmW 91*
Dodd, Catherine Elizabeth 1939- *St&PR 91*
Dodd, Catherine Isabel 1860-1932 *FemiCLE*
Dodd, Charles Gardner 1915- *WhoAm 90*
Dodd, Charles M. *St&PR 91*
Dodd, Christine *BioIn 16*
Dodd, Christopher J. *BioIn 16*
Dodd, Christopher J. 1944- *WhoAm 90, WhoE 91, WhoWor 91*
Dodd, Darlene Mae 1935- *WhoAmW 91*
Dodd, David L. *BioIn 16*
Dodd, Deborah Jane 1947- *WhoEmL 91*
Dodd, Donald Bradford 1940- *WhoWrEP 89*
Dodd, Ed 1902- *EncACom*
Dodd, Edward *ConAu 31NR*
Dodd, Edward Benton 1902- *WhoAm 90*
Dodd, Edward H. 1905-1988 *BioIn 16*
Dodd, Edward Howard, Jr. 1905-1988 *ConAu 31NR*
Dodd, Edwin Dillon 1919- *St&PR 91, WhoAm 90*
Dodd, Emmeline Irwin 1939- *WhoSSW 91*
Dodd, Eric M *WhoAmA 91*
Dodd, Gary Wayne 1958- *WhoEmL 91*
Dodd, Gerald Dewey, Jr. 1922- *WhoAm 90*
Dodd, Glenn W. 1938- *St&PR 91*
Dodd, Howell Eugene, Jr. 1910- *St&PR 91*
Dodd, Jack Edward, Jr. *BiDrAPA 89*
Dodd, Jack Gordon, Jr. 1926- *WhoAm 90*
Dodd, Jack L 1938- *BiDrAPA 89*
Dodd, James Robert 1934- *WhoAm 90*
Dodd, James W *BiDrAPA 89*
Dodd, Joe David 1920- *WhoWor 91*
Dodd, John Francis 1931- *St&PR 91*
Dodd, Keith L. 1925- *St&PR 91*
Dodd, L.G. 1940- *St&PR 91*
Dodd, Lamar 1909- *WhoAmA 91*
Dodd, Lawrence Roe 1944- *WhoSSW 91*
Dodd, Lionel G. 1940- *WhoAm 90*
Dodd, Lois 1927- *WhoAmA 91, WhoE 91*
Dodd, Lowell A. 1938- *St&PR 91*
Dodd, M Irene 1941- *WhoAmA 91*
Dodd, Margaret E *BiDrAPA 89*
Dodd, Marie Walters 1936- *St&PR 91*
Dodd, Martha *ConAu 132*
Dodd, Michael Joseph 1952- *WhoEmL 91*
Dodd, Peter Frederic 1946- *WhoE 91*
Dodd, Raymond Henry 1929- *IntWWM 90*
Dodd, Robert Bruce 1921- *WhoAm 90*
Dodd, Roger James 1951- *WhoEmL 91, WhoSSW 91*
Dodd, Sara Mae Palmer *WhoE 91*
Dodd, Terry Gene 1938- *WhoSSW 91*
Dodd, Virginia Marilyn 1950- *WhoAmW 91*
Dodd, William Edward 1869-1940 *BioIn 16*
Dodde, Nantko Lieven 1932- *WhoWor 91*
Dodderidge, Richard William 1926- *WhoAm 90*
Doddi, Seshagiri Rao 1949- *BiDrAPA 89*
Doddridge, John E. *WhoAm 90*
Dodds, Baby 1898-1959 *BioIn 16*
Dodds, Brenda Kay 1961- *WhoEmL 91*
Dodds, C. William 1926- *St&PR 91*
Dodds, Claudette La Vonn 1947- *WhoAmW 91, WhoEmL 91*
Dodds, Dale Irvin 1915- *WhoWor 91*
Dodds, Eric Robertson 1893-1979 *EncO&P 3, EncPaPR 91*
Dodds, Frances Alison 1950- *WhoEmL 91*
Dodds, Gerald Cribbs 1932- *St&PR 91*
Dodds, James A. 1929- *St&PR 91*
Dodds, Joan *St&PR 91*
Dodds, John Wendell 1902- *AuBYP 90*
Dodds, Johnny 1892-1940 *BioIn 16, OxCPMus*
Dodds, Michael Bruce 1952- *WhoEmL 91*
Dodds, Rebecca 1950- *WhoSSW 91*
Dodds, Robert C. *BioIn 16*
Dodds, Robert J, III 1943- *WhoAmA 91*
Dodds, Robert James, Jr. 1916- *WhoAm 90*
Dodds, Russell E. *St&PR 91*
Dodds, Wayne S. 1918- *St&PR 91*
Dodds, William Farrell 1952- *WhoEmL 91*
Dodds, William Robert, Jr. 1952- *St&PR 91*
Doddy, Reginald Nathaniel 1952- *WhoEmL 91*
Dodek, Samuel Mayer 1902- *WhoE 91*
Doderer, Gerhard 1944- *IntWWM 90*
Doderer, Minnette Frerichs 1923- *WhoAmW 91*
Dodes, Lance M 1946- *BiDrAPA 89*
Dodge family *BioIn 16*
Dodge, Arnold J. 1920- *St&PR 91*
Dodge, Arthur Bryon, Jr. 1923- *St&PR 91*
Dodge, Arthur Byron, Jr. 1923- *WhoWor 91*
Dodge, Augustus Caesar 1812-1883 *BioIn 16*
Dodge, Bertha Sanford 1902- *AuBYP 90*
Dodge, Charles 1942- *IntWWM 90*
Dodge, Charles Malcolm 1942- *WhoAm 90*
Dodge, Cleveland Earl, Jr. 1922- *WhoAm 90*
Dodge, David 1910- *TwCCr&M 91*
Dodge, Donald T *BiDrAPA 89*

Dodge, Douglas Daniel 1933- WhoE 91
Dodge, Douglas Walker 1932- St&PR 91
Dodge, Earl F. 1932- WhoAm 90
Dodge, George Alan 1957- WhoEmL 91
Dodge, Gil AuBYP 90
Dodge, Grace H. 1856-1914 BioAmW
Dodge, H. Percival 1870-1936 BioIn 16
Dodge, Harlan B. 1919- St&PR 91
Dodge, Hazel 1903-1957 WhoAmA 91N
Dodge, Henry 1782-1867 WhNaAH
Dodge, Henry Chee 1857?-1947 WhNaAH
Dodge, Henry Lafayette 1810-1856 WhNaAH
Dodge, Horace Elgin 1868-1920 EncABHB 4 [port], WorAlBi
Dodge, Janet FemiCLE
Dodge, John 1889-1916 Ballpl 90
Dodge, John F. 1864-1920 BioIn 16, WorAlBi
Dodge, John Francis 1864-1920 EncABHB 4 [port]
Dodge, John Vilas 1909- WhoAm 90
Dodge, Joseph Jeffers 1917- WhoAmA 91, WhoSSW 91
Dodge, Joseph M. 1890-1964 WorAlBi
Dodge, Joseph Morrell 1890-1964 BioIn 16
Dodge, Langdon ConAu 131
Dodge, Mark S. 1946- St&PR 91
Dodge, Mary 1831-1905 AuBYP 90
Dodge, Mary Abigail 1833-1896 BioIn 16, FemiCLE
Dodge, Mary Mapes 1831-1905 WorAlBi
Dodge, N.S., Jr. St&PR 91
Dodge, Nancy Noble 1957- WhoAmW 91
Dodge, Peter Hampton 1929- WhoAm 90
Dodge, Philip Rogers 1923- WhoAm 90
Dodge, Ralph Edward 1936- WhoSSW 91
Dodge, Richard Irving 1827-1895 WhNaAH
Dodge, Robert G 1939- WhoAmA 91
Dodge, Stuart David 1940- St&PR 91
Dodge, Terry Craig 1955- WhoSSW 91
Dodge, Theodore Ayrault 1911- WhoWor 91
Dodge, Waldo E. 1922- St&PR 91
Dodge, William Douglas 1937- WhoAm 90
Dodge, William Earl 1805-1883 WhNaAH
Dodgen, Harold Warren 1921- WhoAm 90
Dodger Sym-Phony Ballpl 90
Dodgion, Dottie 1929- BioIn 16
Dodgion, Lee A. 1935- St&PR 91
Dodgson, Charles Lutwidge 1832-1898 AuBYP 90, BioIn 16
Dodgson, Stephen 1924- IntWWM 90
Dodin, Charles-Nicolas PenDiDA 89
Dodington, Sven H. M. 1912- WhoAm 90
Dodohara, Jean Noton 1934- WhoAmW 91
Dodrill, Dale W. 1944- St&PR 91
Dodrill, Donald Lawrence 1922- WhoAmA 91
Dodro, Robert Stephen 1949- St&PR 91
Dods, Walter Arthur, Jr. 1941- St&PR 91
Dodshon, Frances 1714-1793 FemiCLE
Dodsley, Robert 1703-1764 BioIn 16, DcLB 95 [port]
Dodson, Billy 1944- St&PR 91
Dodson, Carl Edward 1956- WhoSSW 91, WhoWor 91
Dodson, Cecilia Faith 1940- WhoSSW 91
Dodson, D. Keith 1943- WhoAm 90, WhoWor 91
Dodson, Daniel Boone 1918- WhoWor 91
Dodson, Daryl Theodore 1934- WhoAm 90
Dodson, David Charles 1959- WhoE 91
Dodson, Donald Mills 1937- St&PR 91, WhoAm 90
Dodson, Elaine 1944- WhoAmW 91
Dodson, Jack 1931- ConTFT 8
Dodson, James Graham 1949- St&PR 91
Dodson, James Robert 1951- WhoE 91, WhoEmL 91
Dodson, Jerry Wayne BiDrAPA 89
Dodson, John Edward 1952- St&PR 91
Dodson, John W. 1929- St&PR 91
Dodson, Linda S. 1952- WhoAmW 91, WhoEmL 91
Dodson, Marvin Hunter 1943- BiDrAPA 89
Dodson, Norman Elmer 1909- WhoSSW 91
Dodson, Oscar Henry 1905- WhoAm 90, WhoWor 91
Dodson, Owen 1914-1983 BioIn 16, DrBIPA 90, EarBIAP, WorAu 1980 [port]
Dodson, R. J. 1929- WhoAmW 91
Dodson, Samuel Robinette, III 1943- WhoAm 90
Dodson, Susan 1941- BioIn 16
Dodson, Thomas Andrew 1949- St&PR 91
Dodson, Timothy Daniel 1951- WhoWor 91
Dodson, Vanessa Mealaine 1958- WhoAmW 91
Dodson, William W 1950- BiDrAPA 89
Dodson, Wilmer Byrd 1925- St&PR 91
Dodson-Edgars, Jeannie Elizabeth 1950- WhoEmL 91
Dodt, Bruce Ilard BiDrAPA 89
Dodwell, C R 1922- ConAu 129
Dodworth, Allen Stevens 1938- WhoAmA 91
Dodworth, Dorothy L. AuBYP 90
Dody, Sandford 1918- ConAu 129
Doe, Bruce Roger 1931- WhoE 91
Doe, Patricia Louise 1948- WhoE 91
Doe, Richard Philip 1926- WhoAm 90
Doe, Samuel 1952-1990 News 91-1
Doe, Samuel K 1951-1990 CurBio 90N
Doe, Samuel K. 1952- WhoWor 91
Doe, Samuel Kanyon BioIn 16
Doe, Weldon W., Jr. 1918- St&PR 91
Doe, William Harvey AmLegL
Doebbeling, Minda Kay 1942- WhoAmW 91
Doebele, Justin William 1960- WhoE 91
Doebler, Leland Kent 1947- WhoSSW 91
Doebler, Paul Dickerson 1930- WhoAm 90
Doeblin, Richard Stephen 1940- WhoWor 91
Doede, John Henry 1937- St&PR 91, WhoAm 90
Doeff, Jan Willem 1933- BiDrAPA 89, WhoE 91
Doehne, Edward F 1933- BiDrAPA 89
Doek, Jakob Egbert 1942- WhoWor 91
Doel, Kenneth John 1948- St&PR 91, WhoAm 90
Doell, Aubrey Clarence 1918- St&PR 91
Doell, Mary Rae 1940- St&PR 91
Doelling-Baker-Erbisch, Carol Suzanne WhoAmW 91
Doellinger, Steve 1949- St&PR 91
Doelp, Florinda Donato 1936- St&PR 91
Doelp, Paul Robert 1934- St&PR 91
Doelz, Melvin Louis 1918- WhoAm 90
D'Oench, Ellen Gates 1930- WhoAmA 91, WhoE 91
D'Oench, Russell St&PR 91
D'Oench, Russell Grace, Jr. 1927- WhoE 91
D'Oench, Woodbridge Adams 1931- St&PR 91
Doenecke, Carol Anne 1942- WhoAmW 91
Doenecke, Justus Drew WhoSSW 91
Doenges, Byron Frederick 1922- WhoAm 90, WhoE 91
Doenges, Debra Lynne 1956- WhoEmL 91
Doenges, Norman Arthur 1926- WhoAm 90
Doenges, Rudolph Conrad 1930- WhoAm 90
Doenitz, Karl 1891-1980 WorAlBi
Doenlen, Henry Alexander, III 1957- BiDrAPA 89
Doepp, Adrienne Reed 1956- WhoE 91
Doeppner, Thomas Walter 1920- WhoAm 90, WhoWor 91
Doerfler, Leo G. 1919- WhoAm 90
Doerfler, Ronald John 1941- St&PR 91
Doerfler, Walter Hans 1933- WhoWor 91
Doerfling, Hank 1936- WhoWor 91
Doerflinger, Marlys Irene 1943- WhoAmW 91
Doerger, Gerald Lawrence 1944- St&PR 91
Doerhoff, Dale Charles 1946- WhoEmL 91
Doering, Amy Lewis 1960- WhoAmW 91
Doering, Barbara Jeanne 1947- WhoAmW 91
Doering, Charles Rogers 1956- WhoE 91
Doering, George Irey 1926- St&PR 91
Doering, James Dean 1936- St&PR 91
Doering, Werner Siegfried 1911- WhoWor 91
Doering, William von Eggers 1917- WhoAm 90
Doerksen, Nan 1934- BioIn 16
Doermann, Humphrey 1930- WhoAm 90
Doermann, Paul Edmund 1926- WhoAm 90
Doermann, Perry Edward 1947- WhoAm 90
Doermer, Richard T. 1922- St&PR 91
Doernbach, Robert Chris 1929- St&PR 91
Doernberger, William Le Claire 1951- St&PR 91
Doerper, John Erwin 1943- WhoWor 91
Doerr, Arthur Harry 1924- WhoAm 90
Doerr, Bobby 1918- Ballpl 90 [port], BioIn 16
Doerr, Christopher Lee 1949- St&PR 91
Doerr, Edwin Charles, Jr. 1950- St&PR 91
Doerr, Harriet BioIn 16
Doerr, Howard P. 1929- WhoAm 90
Doerr, Howard Paul 1929- St&PR 91
Doerr, Lexia Ethel 1931- WhoAmW 91
Doerr, R. Chris 1946- St&PR 91
Doerr, Ronald H. 1940- St&PR 91, WhoAm 90
Doerr Zegers, Otto 1936- BiDrAPA 89
Doerrie, Doris 1955- ConAu 130
Doerries, Reinhard Rene 1934- WhoWor 91
Doersam, Charles Henry, III 1957- WhoE 91
Doersam, Charles Henry, Jr. 1921- WhoE 91
Doerschuk, Jeanclaire Oakes 1925- WhoAmW 91
Doesberg, Alexandrina Munro 1931- WhoAmW 91
Doescher, William F. 1937- ODwPR 91
Doescher, William Frederick 1937- St&PR 91
Doese, Helena 1946- IntWWM 90
Doetsch, Douglas Allen 1957- WhoEmL 91
Doetsch, Karl Maximilian 1941- WhoSSW 91
Doettling, Robert L. 1937- St&PR 91
Doeung, Sok T. 1936- WhoSSW 91
Doezema, Edward R 1918- BiDrAPA 89
Doff, Neel EncCoWW
Doft, Alan 1933- St&PR 91
Doft, Avrom I. 1938- St&PR 91
Doft, Martin D 1936- BiDrAPA 89
Dogali, Jo Marie 1949- WhoEmL 91
Dogan, Mattei 1920- ConAu 30NR
Dogancay, Burhan C. 1929- WhoAm 90, WhoE 91
Dogancay, Burhan Cahit 1929- WhoAmA 91
Dogbe, Korsi 1940- WhoSSW 91
Dogen 1200-1253 EncJap
Dogger, Allen J. 1947- WhoEmL 91, WhoSSW 91
Doggett, Aubrey Clayton, Jr. 1928- WhoAm 90
Doggett, Burton Lee, Jr. 1928- WhoE 91
Doggett, James Rogal 1933- WhoSSW 91
Doggett, Lloyd 1946- WhoAm 90
Doggett, Lori Ann 1961- WhoAmW 91
Doggett, Mary BiDEWW
Doggett, Ron E. 1934- St&PR 91
Doggrell, Henry Patton 1948- WhoEmL 91, WhoSSW 91
Doghramji, Karl 1954- BiDrAPA 89
Dogin, Judith W Y BiDrAPA 89
Dogoloff, Lee Israel 1939- WhoE 91
Dogra, Bal Raj 1937- WhoAm 90
Dogyear, Drew ConAu 30NR
Dohaney, Jean ConAu 129
Dohaney, M.T. ConAu 129
Dohanian, Diran Kavork 1931- WhoAm 90
Dohanos, S. Peter BioIn 16
Dohanos, Stevan 1907- WhoAmA 91
Dohasan WhNaAH
Dohen, Dorothy BioIn 16
Doheny, David Armour 1931- WhoAm 90
Doheny, Donald Aloysius 1924- WhoAm 90, WhoWor 91
Doheny, Ed 1874-1916 Ballpl 90
Doheny, Edward L. 1856-1935 WorAlBi
Doheny, Steven Peter 1949- BiDrAPA 89
Doherty, Ann 1786- FemiCLE
Doherty, Barbara 1931- WhoAm 90, WhoAmW 91
Doherty, Berlie 19--?- ChILR 21 [port]
Doherty, Berlie 1943- ConAu 131
Doherty, Briggs A., Jr. BioIn 16
Doherty, Dan ODwPR 91
Doherty, David M. 1932- St&PR 91
Doherty, Edward Denvir 1935- St&PR 91
Doherty, Edward J. 1917- ODwPR 91
Doherty, Edward James 1950- WhoE 91
Doherty, Eileen Claire 1946- St&PR 91
Doherty, Eileen Patricia 1952- WhoAmW 91, WhoEmL 91
Doherty, Elizabeth Rose 1958- WhoAmW 91
Doherty, Evelyn Marie 1941- WhoAmW 91, WhoE 91
Doherty, Francis J., Jr. 1931- ODwPR 91
Doherty, George William 1941- WhoWor 91
Doherty, Gerald Dean 1937- St&PR 91
Doherty, Harry Patrick 1942- WhoE 91
Doherty, Henry Joseph 1933- WhoAm 90
Doherty, Henry L. 1870-1939 WorAlBi
Doherty, Herbert Joseph, Jr. 1926- WhoAm 90
Doherty, James Edward, III 1923- WhoAm 90
Doherty, Joe BioIn 16
Doherty, John Joseph 1940- WhoE 91
Doherty, John L. 1934- WhoE 91
Doherty, John Patrick 1947- WhoWrEP 89
Doherty, John Stephen AuBYP 90
Doherty, Joseph J. 1933- St&PR 91
Doherty, Joseph Leo, Jr. 1953- WhoEmL 91
Doherty, Karen Ann 1952- WhoAmW 91
Doherty, Kathleen Ann 1963- WhoE 91
Doherty, Kathy ODwPR 91
Doherty, Kevin 1949- SpyFic
Doherty, Leonard E. 1940- St&PR 91
Doherty, Leonard Edward 1940- WhoAm 90
Doherty, Lowell Ralph 1930- WhoAm 90
Doherty, Mary Margaret 1960- WhoAmW 91
Doherty, Mary Patricia BiDrAPA 89
Doherty, Michael Stephen 1948- WhoAmA 91
Doherty, Michel George 1930- WhoAm 90, WhoAmW 91, WhoSSW 91
Doherty, Norman S. 1937- St&PR 91
Doherty, Patricia Ann 1959- WhoE 91
Doherty, Patricia M. 1951- St&PR 91
Doherty, Paul Edward 1937- St&PR 91
Doherty, Raymond R. 1945- St&PR 91
Doherty, Rebecca Feeney 1952- WhoAmW 91
Doherty, Robert Cunningham 1930- WhoAm 90
Doherty, Shannen BioIn 16
Doherty, Thomas 1935- WhoAm 90
Doherty, Thomas A. 1938- St&PR 91
Doherty, Thomas Anthony 1938- WhoAm 90, WhoE 91
Doherty, Thomas Joseph 1933- WhoAm 90, WhoWor 91
Doherty, William Gary 1956- WhoEmL 91
Doherty, William Thomas, Jr. 1923- WhoAm 90
Doherty-Chapman, Margaret Ann 1952- WhoAmW 91
Dohl, Torrence William 1924- St&PR 91
Dohmen, Erwin John 1927- St&PR 91
Dohmen, John F. 1955- St&PR 91
Dohmen, Robert Charles 1951- St&PR 91
Dohn, Betty Kirksey 1939- St&PR 91
Dohn, Henry Harris 1951- BiDrAPA 89
Dohnal, David Edward 1937- St&PR 91
Dohnanyi, Christoph von BioIn 16
Dohnanyi, Christoph Von 1929- IntWWM 90, PenDiMP
Dohnanyi, Erno 1877-1960 BioIn 16
Dohnanyi, Ernst von PenDiMP
Dohnanyi, Oliver 1955- IntWWM 90
Dohner, John P. 1936- St&PR 91
Dohollau, Heather 1925- EncCoWW
Dohrenwend, Bruce Philip 1927- WhoAm 90
Dohrmann, Richard Martin 1947- WhoEmL 91
Dohrmann, Russell William 1942- WhoAm 90
Dohrmann, Stephan A. BioIn 16
Dohrmann, Walter Paul 1927- St&PR 91
Dohrn, Bernadine 1942- WorAlBi
Dohrn, Madelyn WhoWrEP 89
Doi Takako 1928- EncJap
Doi Takeo EncJap
Doi, Akoka WhoWor 91
Doi, Dorothy Mitsue 1934- WhoAmW 91
Doi, Isami 1903-1965 WhoAmA 91N
Doi, James Isao 1923- WhoAm 90
Doi, Lois 1951- WhoEmL 91
Doi, Mary Ellen 1933- WhoAmW 91
Doi, Masayuki 1933- WhoWor 91
Doi, Stanley Toshio 1935- St&PR 91
Doi, Takako 1928- BioIn 16, WhoWor 91
Doi, Takeo 1920- BiDrAPA 89
Doig, Ivan 1939- WhoAm 90
Doig, James Conroy 1929- WhoSSW 91
Doig, Jameson W. 1933- ConAu 32NR
Doig, Jameson Wallace 1933- WhoAm 90
Doig, John 1958- IntWWM 90
Doig, Raymond Allen 1936- St&PR 91
D'Oisly, Maurice PenDiMP
Doisneau, Robert Sylvain 1912- WhoWor 91
Dojc, Yuri BioIn 16
Dojka, Edwin Sigmund 1924- WhoAm 90, WhoE 91
Dojny, Richard Francis 1940- WhoAm 90, WhoE 91
Dok Hye, Princess of Korea BioIn 16
Doke, Marshall J., Jr. 1934- WhoAm 90, WhoSSW 91
Doke, Timothy J. 1952- ODwPR 91
Dokic, Petar 1941- WhoWor 91
Doko, Toshiwo 1896-1988 BioIn 16
Dokoudovsky, Nina Ludmila 1947- WhoAmW 91, WhoEmL 91
Dokshitser, Timofey 1921- PenDiMP
Doktor, Karl 1885-1949 PenDiMP
Doktor, Paul 1919-1989 BioIn 16, PenDiMP
Doktor, Paul Karl 1919- IntWWM 90
Doku, Hristo Chris 1928- WhoAm 90
Dokupil, Inez Lott 1937- WhoAmW 91
Dokurno, Anthony David 1957- WhoE 91, WhoEmL 91, WhoWor 91
Dolack, Denise Ann 1962- WhoAmW 91
Dolak, David John 1945- St&PR 91
Dolak, Terence Martin 1951- WhoE 91
Dolan, Anna T BiDrAPA 89
Dolan, Beverly Franklin 1927- St&PR 91, WhoAm 90, WhoE 91
Dolan, Brian P. 1955- ODwPR 91
Dolan, Brian Patrick 1955- St&PR 91
Dolan, Charles H., Jr. ODwPR 91
Dolan, Clifford Wilson 1930- St&PR 91
Dolan, Cozy 1872-1907 Ballpl 90
Dolan, Cozy 1889-1958 Ballpl 90
Dolan, Dennis Joseph 1946- WhoEmL 91, WhoSSW 91
Dolan, Edward Corcoran 1952- WhoE 91

Dolan, Edward Francis 1924- *AuBYP 90*
Dolan, G. Keith 1927- *WhoWrEP 89*
Dolan, Hubert G. 1927- *St&PR 91*
Dolan, J. Terrance, III 1938- *WhoAm 90*
Dolan, James Aloysius 1949- *WhoE 91*
Dolan, James Francis 1930- *WhoAm 90*
Dolan, James Michael, Jr. 1937- *WhoAm 90*
Dolan, James Patrick 1949- *WhoEmL 91*
Dolan, James T., Jr. 1926- *St&PR 91, WhoAm 90*
Dolan, James Vincent 1938- *WhoAm 90*
Dolan, Joe 1873-1938 *Ballpl 90*
Dolan, John E. 1923- *WhoAm 90*
Dolan, John J. 1956- *St&PR 91*
Dolan, John Patrick 1935- *BiDrAPA 89, WhoE 91*
Dolan, John Ralph 1926- *St&PR 91, WhoAm 90*
Dolan, Joseph J. *St&PR 91*
Dolan, Kevin L. 1937- *St&PR 91*
Dolan, Kevin Leo 1937- *WhoAm 90*
Dolan, Louis Robert 1937- *St&PR 91*
Dolan, Louise Ann 1950- *WhoAmW 91*
Dolan, Margaret Baggett 1914-1974 *BioIn 16*
Dolan, Margo 1946- *WhoAmA 91, WhoE 91*
Dolan, Mary Anne 1947- *WhoAmW 91*
Dolan, Maryanne McLorn 1924- *WhoAmW 91, WhoWor 91*
Dolan, Michael G. 1949- *St&PR 91*
Dolan, Michael J. *WhoAm 90*
Dolan, Michael William 1942- *WhoAm 90*
Dolan, Paul 1929- *St&PR 91*
Dolan, Paul Gregory 1928- *St&PR 91*
Dolan, Peter Brown 1939- *WhoAm 90*
Dolan, Peter Robert 1956- *WhoEmL 91*
Dolan, Raymond Bernard 1923- *St&PR 91, WhoAm 90*
Dolan, Richard Edwin 1933- *St&PR 91*
Dolan, Robert Dale 1930- *WhoE 91*
Dolan, Robert Emmett 1906-1972 *OxCPMus*
Dolan, Robert Glennon 1939- *St&PR 91*
Dolan, Robert Lee 1943- *St&PR 91*
Dolan, Ronald J. 1947- *St&PR 91*
Dolan, Ronald Vincent 1942- *St&PR 91, WhoAm 90*
Dolan, Terrence Raymond 1940- *WhoAm 90*
Dolan, Terry *BioIn 16*
Dolan, Thomas C. 1921- *St&PR 91*
Dolan, Thomas Ironside 1927- *St&PR 91, WhoAm 90*
Dolan, Tom 1956- *WhoEmL 91*
Dolan, William David, Jr. 1913- *WhoAm 90*
Dolan, William F. 1933- *St&PR 91*
Dolan, William G. 1927- *St&PR 91*
Dolan, William P. 1953- *St&PR 91*
Dolan, William Thomas 1937- *St&PR 91*
Dolanc, Stane 1925- *WhoWor 91*
Doland, Judy Ann 1940- *WhoAmW 91*
Doland, Michael Terry 1942- *St&PR 91*
Dolata, Albert 1939- *St&PR 91*
Dolbear, F. Trenery, Jr. 1935- *WhoAm 90*
Dolben, David Howland 1935- *St&PR 91*
Dolber, Wendy 1949- *St&PR 91*
Dolberg, Steve *St&PR 91*
Dolbier, Maurice 1912- *AuBYP 90*
Dolby, Charlotte 1821-1885 *PenDiMP*
Dolby, Ray Milton 1933- *BioIn 16, WhoAm 90*
Dolby, Thomas *BioIn 16*
Dolce, Carl John 1928- *WhoAm 90*
Dolce, John 1911-1989 *BioIn 16*
Dolce, Thomas A. 1948- *St&PR 91*
Dolch, Edward W. 1889-1961 *BioIn 16*
Dolch, Marguerite P. 1891-1978 *BioIn 16*
Dolch, Norman Allen 1947- *WhoSSW 91*
Dolch, William Lee 1925- *WhoAm 90*
Dolderer, Alan 1958- *WhoEmL 91*
Dole, Arthur Alexander 1917- *WhoAm 90*
Dole, Bob 1923- *NewYTBS 90 [port]*
Dole, Burton Andrew, Jr. 1937- *St&PR 91*
Dole, Dorcas *FemiCLE*
Dole, Dorcas *BiDEWW*
Dole, Elizabeth 1936- *News 90 [port]*
Dole, Elizabeth Hanford 1936- *BiDrUSE 89, BioIn 16, WhoAm 90, WhoAmW 91, WhoE 91, WhoWor 91*
Dole, Richard Fairfax, Jr. 1936- *WhoAm 90*
Dole, Robert J. 1923- *BioIn 16, WhoAm 90, WhoWor 91, WorAlBi*
Dole, Robert Malcolm, Jr. 1937- *WhoE 91*
Dole, Robert Paul 1923- *St&PR 91, WhoAm 90*
Dole, S. R., Jr. 1937- *WhoAm 90, WhoSSW 91*
Dole, Sanford Ballard 1844-1926 *BioIn 16*
Dole, Vincent Paul, III 1944- *WhoE 91*
Dole, Wanda Victoria 1942- *WhoAmW 91*
Dole, William 1917-1983 *WhoAmA 91N*
Dole, William Page 1928- *St&PR 91*
Doleac, Charles Bartholomew 1947- *WhoE 91, WhoEmL 91, WhoWor 91*
Dolensek, Emil P. *BioIn 16, NewYTBS 90 [port]*
Dolenz, Ami *BioIn 16*
Dolenz, Micky *BioIn 16*
Doler, Daniel C. 1926- *St&PR 91*
Dolese, Constance Cuccia 1923- *WhoSSW 91*
Doley, Harold Emanuel, Jr. 1947- *WhoAm 90*
Dolezal, Dale Francis 1936- *WhoE 91, WhoWor 91*
Dolezal, Karel 1948- *IntWWM 90*
Dolezal, Leo Thomas 1944- *WhoSSW 91*
Dolezal, Peter 1943- *WhoAm 90*
Dolezelova-Velingerova, Milena 1932- *WhoWrEP 89*
Dolganos, Ellen M *BiDrAPA 89*
Dolge, Alfred Karl 1926- *St&PR 91*
Dolgen, Jonathan *BioIn 16*
Dolger, Jonathan 1938- *WhoAm 90, WhoWrEP 89*
Dolgin, Bernard 1924- *St&PR 91*
Dolgin, Daniel Roy 1957- *WhoEmL 91*
Dolgin, Martin 1919- *WhoAm 90*
Dolgin, Steve Alan 1949- *St&PR 91*
Dolgins, Stuart 1936- *St&PR 91*
Dolgoff, Robert K *BiDrAPA 89*
Dolgoff, Sam *NewYTBS 90*
Dolgoff, Sam 1902-1990 *ConAu 132*
Dolgon, Howard 1957- *ODwPR 91*
Dolibois, John 1918- *BioIn 16*
Dolich, Andrew Bruce 1947- *WhoAm 90, WhoEmL 91*
Dolich, Ira Richard 1935- *St&PR 91*
D'Olier, Henry Mitchell 1946- *WhoAm 90, WhoEmL 91, WhoWor 91*
Dolim, Mary Nuzum 1925- *AuBYP 90*
Dolin, Albert Harry 1913- *WhoAm 90*
Dolin, Anton 1904-1983 *DcNaB 1981*
Dolin, Lonny H. 1954- *WhoAmW 91, WhoWor 91*
Dolin, Michelle Cynthia 1952- *WhoAmW 91*
Dolin, Mitchell F. 1956- *WhoEmL 91*
Dolin, Samuel 1917- *IntWWM 90*
Dolin, Samuel Joseph 1917- *WhoAm 90*
Dolinac, Peter Anthony 1949- *St&PR 91*
Dolinar, Louis John 1950- *BiDrAPA 89*
DoLiner, Roy George 1932- *WhoE 91*
Dolinger, M. B. 1921- *ODwPR 91*
Dolinich, Christine 1950- *WhoAmW 91*
Dolins, Ilene L. 1938- *WhoE 91*
Dolins, Richard S *BiDrAPA 89*
Dolinsky, Aaron 1926- *BiDrAPA 89*
Dolinsky, Howard 1950- *BiDrAPA 89*
Dolitsky, Linda Roselle *BiDrAPA 89*
Dolive, Earl 1917- *WhoAm 90*
D'Oliviera, Evadne 1942- *FemiCLE*
Doll, Bernard L 1930- *BiDrAPA 89*
Doll, Catherine Ann *WhoAmA 91*
Doll, Donald Arthur 1937- *WhoAmA 91*
Doll, Edgar Arnold *BioIn 16*
Doll, Elizabeth Jane 1952- *WhoAmW 91*
Doll, Eugenia Delarova *NewYTBS 90*
Doll, Linda A 1942- *WhoAmA 91*
Doll, Lynne *ODwPR 91*
Doll, Lynne Marie 1961- *WhoAmW 91*
Doll, Mary A 1940- *ConAu 130*
Doll, Mary Aswell 1940- *WhoSSW 91*
Doll, Paddy Ann 1928- *WhoWor 91*
Doll, Patricia Marie 1960- *WhoE 91, WhoEmL 91*
Doll, Robert B. 1939- *WhoAm 90*
Doll, William Elder, Jr. 1931- *WhoSSW 91*
Dollahite, David Curtis 1958- *WhoSSW 91*
Dollar Brand *BioIn 16*
Dollar, Diane 1933- *BioIn 16*
Dollar, Helen E *BiDrAPA 89*
Dollar, Jim *ConAu 129, EncCoWW*
Dollar, Thomas Roby, Jr. 1938- *WhoSSW 91*
Dollard, Virginia Marie 1952- *WhoSSW 91*
Dollen, Charles Joseph 1926- *WhoWrEP 89*
Dollerup, Erik Cay Krebs 1939- *WhoWor 91*
Dollerup, Robert Fin Krebs 1942- *WhoWor 91*
Dolley, Joseph Norman 1860-1936 *AmLegL*
Dollfuss, Engelbert 1892-1934 *WorAlBi*
Dollier de Casson, Francois 1636-1701 *EncCRAm*
Dollieslager, David P. 1945- *WhoSSW 91*
Dollimore, Jonathan 1948- *ConAu 132*
Dollin, Martin 1911- *BiDrAPA 89*
Dollinger, Joel I. 1942- *St&PR 91*
Dollinger, Toni Rae *BiDrAPA 89*
Dollison, Dwight G. 1943- *St&PR 91*
Dolliver, Brian Kemp 1961- *WhoE 91*
Dolliver, James Morgan 1924- *WhoAm 90*
Dolliver, Robert Henry 1934- *WhoAm 90*
Dolly Sisters *OxCPMus*
Dolly, Jennie 1902-1941 *OxCPMus*
Dolly, John Patrick 1942- *WhoAm 90*
Dolly, Rosie 1892-1970 *OxCPMus*
Dolman, John P. 1915- *St&PR 91*
Dolman, John Phillips, Jr. 1944- *WhoAm 90, WhoE 91*
Dolmatch, Theodore Bieley 1924- *WhoAm 90*
Dolmetsch, Arnold 1858-1940 *PenDiMP*
Dolmetsch, Carl 1911- *PenDiMP*
Dolmetsch, Carl Frederick 1911- *IntWWM 90*
Dolmetsch, Jean-Marie 1942- *IntWWM 90*
Dolmetsch, Mabel 1874-1963 *PenDiMP*
Dolmetsch, Marguerite Mabel 1942- *IntWWM 90*
Dolnick, David Benjamin 1950- *WhoEmL 91*
Dolores, Michael A *BiDrAPA 89*
Dolowitz, David Augustus 1913- *WhoWor 91*
Dolph, Charles Laurie 1918- *WhoAm 90*
Dolph, Robert Norman 1925- *WhoAm 90*
Dolph, Terence *NewAgMG*
Dolph, Wilbert Emery 1923- *WhoAm 90*
Dolphin, James 1949- *St&PR 91*
Dolphin, John Leo 1924- *St&PR 91*
Dolphy, Eric *BioIn 16*
Dolphy, Eric 1928-1964 *OxCPMus*
Dols, Jerome H. *BioIn 16*
Dolson, Donald 1937- *St&PR 91*
Dolson, Franklin Robert 1933- *WhoAm 90, WhoE 91*
Dolson, Vivian Antoinette 1925- *WhoAmW 91*
Doltolo, Joseph J *BiDrAPA 89*
Doluisio, James Thomas 1935- *WhoAm 90*
Dom, John A. 1941- *St&PR 91*
Domac, Dragutin Charles *WhoWrEP 89*
Domagala, Richard Edward 1947- *WhoE 91*
Domalakes, Lawrence David 1957- *WhoE 91*
Doman, Elvira *WhoAmW 91*
Doman, Janet Joy 1948- *WhoAm 90, WhoAmW 91, WhoEmL 91*
Doman, Nicholas R. 1913- *WhoAm 90*
Domanico, Noreen Kelly 1954- *St&PR 91*
Domaninska, Libuse 1924- *IntWWM 90*
Domanska, Janina *AuBYP 90*
Domansky, Hanus 1944- *IntWWM 90*
Domar, Evsey David 1914- *WhoAm 90, WhoE 91*
Domaradzki, Theodore Felix 1910- *WhoAm 90, WhoWrEP 89*
Domash, Michael Dennis *BiDrAPA 89*
Domash, Samuel G. *BioIn 16*
Domb, Jane Alice *BiDrAPA 89*
Dombeck, John Conrad 1939- *St&PR 91*
Dombeck, Sol *BiDrAPA 89*
Dombeck, Thomas Walter 1945- *WhoEmL 91*
Dombek, Blanche M *WhoAmA 91N*
Dombek, Charles E. 1956- *WhoEmL 91*
Dombek, Curtis Michael 1958- *WhoEmL 91*
Dombroff, Mark Andrew 1947- *WhoEmL 91*
Dombroski, Paul G. 1950- *WhoSSW 91*
Dombrowski, Anne Wesseling 1948- *WhoEmL 91*
Dombrowski, Bill 1934- *ODwPR 91*
Dombrowski, Charles F. 1954- *St&PR 91*
Dombrowski, Eugene Joseph 1931- *St&PR 91*
Dombrowski, Frank Paul, Jr. 1943- *WhoE 91, WhoWor 91*
Dombrowski, James Anderson 1897-1983 *EncAL*
Dombrowski, Joseph John 1945- *BiDrAPA 89*
Dombrowski, Leon Charles 1927- *St&PR 91*
Dombrowski, Mary Hain 1960- *WhoE 91*
Dombrowski, Maureen Marie 1950- *WhoAmW 91*
Dombrowski, Mitchell Paul 1953- *WhoEmL 91*
Dombrowski, Thomas Ralph 1945- *St&PR 91*
Dome, Douglas 1961- *ODwPR 91*
Domecq, H Bustos *HispWr 90, MajTwCW*
Domeier, David J. 1953- *St&PR 91*
Domeier, David John 1953- *WhoAm 90*
Domen, Haruo 1930- *WhoWor 91*
Domenech, Manuel 1943- *WhoSSW 91*
Domenichino 1581-1641 *IntDcAA 90, WorAlBi*
Domenici, Pete 1932- *WhoAm 90, WhoWor 91*
Domenico, di Bartolo 1400-1445 *BioIn 16*
Domenico di Niccolo de' Cori *PenDiDA 89*
Domenico Veneziano 1405?-1461 *IntDcAA 90*
Domenico, Pietro Di 1457-1501? *BioIn 16*
Domer, Floyd Ray 1931- *WhoAm 90*
Domer, Judith Elaine 1939- *WhoAmW 91*
Domeracki, Walter Arthur 1939- *St&PR 91*
Domes, Juergen 1932- *ConAu 129*
Domes, Jurgen Otto 1932- *WhoWor 91*
Domeshek, David G. 1957- *ODwPR 91*
Domeyer, Nancy 1941- *WhoAmW 91*
d'Omezon, Yves Paul Christian 1939- *WhoWor 91*
Domgraf-Fassbaender, Willi 1897-1978 *PenDiMP*
Domin, Hilde 1912- *BioIn 16*
Domingo, Danilo V *BiDrAPA 89*
Domingo, Jose Julian 1925- *BiDrAPA 89*
Domingo, Manuel I *BiDrAPA 89*
Domingo, Placido *BioIn 16*
Domingo, Placido 1934- *PenDiMP*
Domingo, Placido 1941- *IntWWM 90, WhoAm 90, WhoWor 91, WorAlBi*
Domingo, Wilfred A. 1889-1968 *EncAL*
Domingue, Emery 1926- *WhoAm 90*
Domingue, Gerald James 1937- *WhoAm 90, WhoWor 91*
Domingue, John Boring 1936- *WhoSSW 91*
Domingue, Nicole Zuber 1932- *WhoAm 90*
Domingue, Susan Gay 1947- *WhoAmW 91*
Dominguez, A. M., Jr. 1943- *WhoHisp 91*
Dominguez, Abraham A. 1927- *WhoHisp 91*
Dominguez, Angel De Jesus 1950- *WhoHisp 91*
Dominguez, Cari M. 1949- *WhoHisp 91*
Dominguez, Eddie 1957- *WhoAmA 91*
Dominguez, Eduardo Ramiro 1953- *WhoHisp 91*
Dominguez, Emilio J 1936- *BiDrAPA 89*
Dominguez, Florentino *BiDrAPA 89*
Dominguez, Francisco Atanasio *EncCRAm*
Dominguez, Jorge Ignacio 1945- *WhoAm 90*
Dominguez, Kathryn Mary 1960- *WhoE 91*
Dominguez, Luis *BiDrAPA 89*
Dominguez, Oralia 1927- *IntWWM 90, PenDiMP*
Dominguez, Rene O. 1943- *St&PR 91*
Dominguez, Robert A 1948- *BiDrAPA 89*
Dominguez, Roberto 1955- *WhoHisp 91*
Dominguez, Russell Guadalupe 1960- *WhoHisp 91*
Dominguez, Sergio D Elizondo *ConAu 131*
Dominguez, Steven 1942- *St&PR 91*
Dominguez, Virginia Rosa 1952- *WhoEmL 91*
Dominguez Alba, Bernardo 1902- *BioIn 16*
Dominguez-Mayoral, Rodrigo 1947- *WhoSSW 91*
Domini, Rey *MajTwCW*
Dominiak, George Marion *BiDrAPA 89*
Dominiak, George Marion 1955- *WhoE 91*
Dominiak, Geraldine Florence 1934- *WhoAm 90, WhoSSW 91*
Dominianni, Emilio Anthony 1931- *St&PR 91*
Dominic, de Guzman 1170-1221 *BioIn 16*
Dominic, R. B. *TwCCr&M 91*
Dominick, David DeWitt 1937- *WhoAm 90*
Dominick, Fred Adam 1925- *St&PR 91*
Dominie, Albert Duane 1943- *St&PR 91*
Dominik, Jack Edward 1924- *WhoAm 90*
Dominique *MajTwCW*
Dominique, Joe C. 1947- *St&PR 91*
Dominique, John August 1893- *WhoAmA 91*
Dominique, Lise Marie 1956- *WhoAmW 91, WhoEmL 91*
Dominique, Meg *ConAu 130*
Domino, Antoine 1928- *EncPR&S 89*
Domino, Edward F 1924- *BiDrAPA 89*
Domino, Edward Felix 1924- *WhoAm 90*
Domino, Fats 1928- *DrBlPA 90, OxCPMus, WorAlBi*
Domino, Gilbert George 1926- *St&PR 91*
Domino, Laurence Edward 1953- *BiDrAPA 89*
Domino, Valorie Jean *BiDrAPA 89*
Dominoes, The *EncPR&S 89*
Dominowski, Roger Lynn 1939- *WhoWrEP 89*
Domis, Raymond C. 1944- *St&PR 91*
Domit, Moussa M 1932- *WhoAmA 91*
Domitilla, Mary 1889-1955 *BioIn 16*
Domitrovich, Stephanie 1954- *WhoEmL 91*
Domjan, Joseph 1907- *AuBYP 90, WhoAm 90, WhoAmA 91*
Domjan, Laszlo Karoly 1947- *WhoEmL 91, WhoWor 91*
Domke, Herbert Reuben 1919- *WhoAm 90*
Domke, Kerry Lynn 1950- *St&PR 91, WhoEmL 91*
Domm, Alice 1954- *WhoAmW 91, WhoWor 91*
Domm, Sally A. 1945- *ODwPR 91*
Dommel, Darlene Hurst 1940- *WhoAmW 91*
Dommen, Arthur John 1934- *WhoAm 90*
Dommer, Ian Jerald 1951- *WhoEmL 91*
Dommermuth, William Peter *WhoAm 90, WhoWor 91*
Dommeyer, Frederick C 1909- *EncO&P 3*
Domo, Aki *NewAgMG*
Domokos, Gabor 1933- *WhoAm 90*
Domondon, Oscar 1924- *WhoWor 91*

Domonkos, Patricia Mahoney 1949- WhoAmW 91
Domont, Gilberto Barbosa 1934- WhoWor 91
Domosi, Pal Bela 1943- WhoWor 91
Domotor, Tekla 1914- ConAu 132
Dompierre, Judith Evlyn 1957- WhoE 91
Dompierre, Lyse Monique 1952- BiDrAPA 89
Domres, Harold C, Jr. 1937- BiDrAPA 89
Domres, Terry A. 1943- St&PR 91
Domroe, Barbara 1939- WhoAmA 91
Doms, Keith 1920- WhoAm 90
Doms, Vernon Albert 1920- BiDrAPA 89
Domsic, Dennis Michael 1949- WhoEmL 91
Domzalski, Kenneth Stanley 1949- WhoEmL 91
Don Francisco BioIn 16
Don Pino PenDiDA 89
Don, Agustin E 1928- BiDrAPA 89
Don, Alexander M 1935- BiDrAPA 89
Don, Arthur 1953- WhoEmL 91
Don, James K. 1936- St&PR 91, WhoSSW 91
Don, Michael H. 1956- St&PR 91
Don, Richard 1929- St&PR 91
Dona Isabel BioIn 16
Donabedian, Avedis 1919- WhoAm 90
Donachie, Nancy Davis BiDrAPA 89
Donadeo, John 1915- BiDrAPA 89
Donadio, Leonard E. 1928- St&PR 91
Donagan, Alan Harry 1925- WhoAm 90
Donagh, Rita 1939- BiDWomA
Donaghey, George Washington 1856-1937 BioIn 16
Donaghue, Ethel F. BioIn 16, NewYTBS 90
Donaghue, John Ames 1937- St&PR 91
Donaghy, Debra Ann 1957- WhoAmW 91, WhoEmL 91
Donaghy, Henry James 1930- WhoAm 90
Donaghy, James Edison 1934- St&PR 91
Donaghy, Patrick Christopher 1933- St&PR 91, WhoAm 90, WhoE 91
Donagi, Ron 1956- WhoE 91
Donahey, James Harrison 1875-1949 WhoAmA 91N
Donahey, William 1884-1970 AuBYP 90
Donahoe, David Lawrence 1949- WhoAm 90
Donahoe, Patricia BioIn 16
Donahoe, Thomas P. 1950- St&PR 91
Donahoo, Melvin Lawrence 1930- WhoE 91
Donahue, Barbara Lynn Sean 1956- WhoAmW 91
Donahue, Benedict, Sr WhoAmA 91N
Donahue, Charlotte Mary 1954- WhoAmW 91, WhoE 91, WhoEmL 91, WhoWor 91
Donahue, Claire Gertrude 1929- WhoAmW 91
Donahue, Daniel J. 1933- St&PR 91
Donahue, Donald Jordan 1924- WhoAm 90
Donahue, Donald P. 1917- St&PR 91
Donahue, Elinor BioIn 16
Donahue, Elinor 1937- WhoAm 90
Donahue, Hayden H 1912- BiDrAPA 89
Donahue, Hayden Hackney 1912- WhoAm 90, WhoWor 91
Donahue, Irving James, Jr. 1922- St&PR 91
Donahue, Jack 1892-1930 OxCPMus
Donahue, Jacolynne 1939- WhoAmW 91
Donahue, James 1927- St&PR 91
Donahue, James, Jr. ODwPR 91
Donahue, James E., III 1947- ODwPR 91
Donahue, James M 1934- BiDrAPA 89
Donahue, Janine Elizabeth 1962- BiDrAPA 89
Donahue, Jayne Keirn 1953- WhoEmL 91
Donahue, Jerry 1934- St&PR 91
Donahue, Jiggs 1879-1913 Ballpl 90
Donahue, Jill B. 1953- WhoAmW 91
Donahue, John Donald 1937- St&PR 91
Donahue, John F. 1924- St&PR 91
Donahue, Judith L. 1950- St&PR 91
Donahue, Judith Linnea 1950- WhoAmW 91
Donahue, Laura Kent 1949- WhoAmW 91
Donahue, Lauri Michele 1961- WhoEmL 91
Donahue, Mary Elizabeth 1965- WhoE 91
Donahue, Mary Rosenberg 1932- WhoE 91
Donahue, Michael James 1953- WhoE 91
Donahue, Michael Joseph 1947- WhoEmL 91
Donahue, Michael Richard 1949- WhoEmL 91
Donahue, Nancy Keirans 1932- WhoE 91
Donahue, Patrice Noreen BiDrAPA 89
Donahue, Phil 1935- WhoAm 90
Donahue, Philip Michael 1919- St&PR 91
Donahue, Philip Richard 1943- WhoAmA 91
Donahue, Red 1873-1913 Ballpl 90
Donahue, Sam 1918-1974 OxCPMus
Donahue, Suzanne Mary 1956- WhoAmW 91
Donahue, Terry 1944- BioIn 16
Donahue, Thomas Michael 1921- WhoAm 90, WhoWor 91
Donahue, Thomas R. BioIn 16
Donahue, Thomas Reilly 1928- WhoAm 90
Donahue, Tim 1870-1902 Ballpl 90
Donahue, Timothy Patrick 1955- WhoSSW 91
Donahue, Troy 1936- ConTFT 8, WorAlBi
Donahue, William J. 1950- St&PR 91
Donahugh, Robert Hayden 1930- WhoAm 90
Donakowski, Conrad Louis 1936- IntWWM 90
Donald, Alexander G BiDrAPA 89
Donald, Alexander Grant 1928- WhoAm 90, WhoSSW 91, WhoWor 91
Donald, Atley 1910- Ballpl 90
Donald, Beulah Mae BioIn 16
Donald, Bruce R. 1958- WhoE 91
Donald, David Herbert 1920- WhoAm 90
Donald, Earl P. 1944- WhoSSW 91
Donald, Eric Paul 1930- WhoAm 90
Donald, Hugh 1908-1989 AnObit 1989
Donald, Ian WhoAm 90
Donald, James L. 1931- WhoSSW 91
Donald, Joe Kennan 1942- St&PR 91
Donald, John Robert Brodie 1961- WhoWor 91
Donald, John W. 1955- St&PR 91
Donald, Larry Watson 1945- WhoAm 90
Donald, Michael BioIn 16
Donald, Milton Louis 1946- WhoEmL 91
Donald, Norman Henderson, III 1937- WhoAm 90
Donald, Paul Aubrey 1929- WhoWor 91
Donald, Peter James 1946- WhoWor 91
Donald, Robert Graham 1943- WhoAm 90
Donald, William Clyde, II 1918- WhoWor 91
Donalds, Gordon AuBYP 90
Donaldson, Alexander MacFarland 1953- WhoEmL 91
Donaldson, Asa L. 1941- St&PR 91
Donaldson, Billy Joe, Jr. 1954- WhoSSW 91
Donaldson, Coleman duPont 1922- WhoAm 90
Donaldson, Daniel Reed 1940- St&PR 91
Donaldson, Darcy Miller 1953- WhoAmW 91
Donaldson, David Howard, Jr. 1951- WhoEmL 91
Donaldson, David Marbury 1938- WhoAm 90
Donaldson, Deanna Lyn 1961- WhoAmW 91
Donaldson, Donald Ray 1940- St&PR 91
Donaldson, Edward Mossop 1939- WhoAm 90
Donaldson, Eric Leonhart 1960- WhoEmL 91
Donaldson, Ethelbert Talbot 1910-1987 BioIn 16
Donaldson, Frank Arthur 1919- St&PR 91
Donaldson, Frank Arthur, Jr. 1919- WhoAm 90
Donaldson, Gordon 1913- SmATA 64
Donaldson, James Adrian 1930- WhoAm 90
Donaldson, Jane Ellen 1947- WhoAmW 91
Donaldson, Jean Ann 1925- WhoAmW 91
Donaldson, Jeff R 1932- WhoAmA 91
Donaldson, Jeff Richardson 1932- WhoAm 90
Donaldson, Jesse Monroe 1885-1970 BiDrUSE 89
Donaldson, Jesse Philip 1940- WhoSSW 91
Donaldson, Joan BioIn 16
Donaldson, John 1737-1801 PenDiDA 89
Donaldson, John 1892-1970 Ballpl 90
Donaldson, John 1943- Ballpl 90
Donaldson, John Anthony 1938- St&PR 91, WhoAm 90
Donaldson, John Cecil, Jr. 1933- WhoE 91, WhoWor 91
Donaldson, John Edward 1945- St&PR 91
Donaldson, John Ira 1948- WhoEmL 91
Donaldson, John Y 1940- BiDrAPA 89
Donaldson, Lauren R. 1903- WhoAm 90
Donaldson, Leonard Ross 1945- WhoE 91
Donaldson, Marjory 1926- WhoAmA 91
Donaldson, Marlowe Helen BiDrAPA 89
Donaldson, Mary Kendrick 1937- WhoAmW 91
Donaldson, Merle Richard 1920- WhoAm 90
Donaldson, Myrtle Norma 1923- IntWWM 90
Donaldson, Norma DrBlPA 90
Donaldson, Raymond Canute 1958- WhoAm 90
Donaldson, Richard Miesse 1929- WhoAm 90
Donaldson, Robert Charles 1924- WhoAm 90
Donaldson, Robert Herschel 1943- WhoAm 90, WhoSSW 91
Donaldson, Robert Macartney, Jr. 1927- WhoAm 90
Donaldson, Sam BioIn 16
Donaldson, Sam 1934- WorAlBi
Donaldson, Samuel Andrew 1934- WhoAm 90, WhoE 91
Donaldson, Scott 1928- WhoAm 90
Donaldson, Stephen Reeder 1947- WhoAm 90, WhoWrEP 89
Donaldson, Thomas Pollock 1941- WhoAm 90
Donaldson, Walter 1893-1947 BioIn 16, OxCPMus, WorAlBi
Donaldson, William H. 1931- St&PR 91
Donaldson, William James 1927- St&PR 91
Donaldson, William R. ODwPR 91
Donaldson, Willis Lyle 1915- WhoAm 90
Donalson, Linda Kinnard 1941- WhoSSW 91
Donars, Paul W. 1932- St&PR 91
Donarski, David P 1934- BiDrAPA 89
Donas, Marthe 1885-1967 BiDWomA
do Nascimento, Alexander 1925- WhoWor 91
Donat, George 1920- WhoAm 90
Donat, Robert 1905-1958 WorAlBi
Donat, Thomas C. 1952- St&PR 91
Donat, Walter Kennedy 1954- WhoEmL 91
Donat, Zdislava 1939- IntWWM 90
Donatelli, Anthony BiDrAPA 89
Donatelli, Augie 1914- Ballpl 90
Donatelli, Augie 1914-1990 BioIn 16
Donatelli, Delia Elsa 1941- WhoE 91
Donatelli, Luciano Pietro 1947- WhoWor 91
Donatello 1383?-1466 IntDcAA 90
Donatello 1386?-1466 WorAlBi
Donath, David Alan 1951- WhoE 91
Donath, Fred Arthur 1931- WhoAm 90
Donath, Helen 1940- IntWWM 90, PenDiMP
Donath, Ludwig 1900-1967 BioIn 16
Donath, Robert E. 1945- WhoWrEP 89
Donath, Therese 1928- WhoAmW 91, WhoWor 91
Donati, Dale A. 1953- St&PR 91
Donati, Danilo 1926- ConDes 90
Donati, Enrico 1909- BioIn 16, WhoAm 90, WhoAmA 91
Donati, Gian Carlo 1929- WhoWor 91
Donati, Robert Mario 1934- WhoAm 90, WhoWor 91
Donato, Alfred Virgil 1917- WhoE 91
Donato, Alma Delia 1956- WhoHisp 91
Donato, Anthony 1909- IntWWM 90
Donato, Arthur Thomas, Jr. 1955- WhoEmL 91
Donato, Belen Q BiDrAPA 89
Donato, Debora E 1951- WhoAmA 91
Donato, Frank J. 1945- St&PR 91
Donato, Gerald BioIn 16
Donato, Giuseppe 1881-1965 WhoAmA 91N
Donato, Guido A. 1926- St&PR 91
Donato, Myrna Merle 1939- WhoAmW 91
Donato, Nola 1955- WhoAmW 91
Donato, Samuel Joseph 1941- St&PR 91
Donatoni, Franco 1927- IntWWM 90, WhoWor 91
Donavan, Douglas A. 1949- St&PR 91
Donavan, John TwCCr&M 91
Donavanik, Chanin BioIn 16
Donavel, David Frank 1946- WhoWrEP 89
Donbavand, James Joseph, Jr. 1947- WhoEmL 91
Doncaster, Hilary Louise 1960- WhoE 91
Donch, Karl 1915- IntWWM 90
Donchak, Andrew F. 1951- St&PR 91, WhoAm 90, WhoE 91
Donches, Stephen G. 1945- St&PR 91
Donchess, Barbara M. 1922- WhoWrEP 89
Donchian, Richard D. 1905- St&PR 91
Donchian, Richard Davoud 1905- WhoAm 90
Donchin, Emanuel 1935- WhoAm 90
Donckers, Richard H. 1950- St&PR 91
Donda, Russell Scott 1955- WhoSSW 91
Dondanville, John Wallace 1937- WhoAm 90
Dondanville, Leo John, Jr. 1930- St&PR 91
Donders, Jozef G 1929- ConAu 129
Dondershine, Harvey Edward 1942- BiDrAPA 89
Dondes, Robert Jonathan 1960- WhoE 91
Donegan, Charles Edward 1933- WhoAm 90
Donegan, Dorothy 1924- DrBlPA 90
Donegan, Frank BioIn 16
Donegan, James Edward 1945- St&PR 91
Donegan, James Edward 1959- WhoE 91
Donegan, Lonnie 1931- OxCPMus
Donegan, Patricia Lucille 1931- WhoAmW 91
Donegan, Robert E. 1953- St&PR 91
Donegan, Thomas James 1907- WhoAm 90
Donehogawa WhNaAH
Donehue, John Douglas 1928- WhoAm 90, WhoSSW 91
Doneker, I. Irene St&PR 91
Donelan, Francis P. 1939- St&PR 91
Donelan, Peter Andrew 1953- WhoSSW 91
Donelian, Armen BioIn 16
Donelian, Armen Hrant 1950- WhoEmL 91
Donell, Donald Ray 1929- St&PR 91
Donelli, Gianfranco 1943- WhoWor 91
Donelson, Andrew Jackson 1799-1871 BioIn 16
Donelson, Angie Fields Cantrell Merritt 1914- WhoAmW 91, WhoWor 91
Donelson, Daniel S. 1801-1863 AmLegL
Donelson, Emily 1808-1836 BioIn 16
Donelson, John Everett 1943- WhoAm 90
Donelson, Kenneth L. 1927- WhoWrEP 89
Donely, George Anthony Thomas, III 1934- WhoE 91, WhoWor 91
Donen, Stanley BioIn 16
Donenfeld, Kenneth J. 1946- ODwPR 91
Donenfeld, Kenneth Jay 1946- WhoAm 90
Donenfeld, Michael Simon 1933- St&PR 91
Donepudi, Suresh Kumar BiDrAPA 89
Doner, Colonel V. 1948- BioIn 16
Doner, Dean Benton 1923- WhoAm 90
Doner, Frederick Nathan 1943- WhoAm 90
Doner, Gary William 1951- WhoEmL 91
Doner, John Robert 1942- WhoSSW 91
Doner, Wilfred B. 1914-1990 BioIn 16
Doneson, Ira Nathaniel 1938- BiDrAPA 89
Donetta ConAu 130
Donetti, Arturo Guido 1941- WhoWor 91
Donewirth, Donald Jack 1927- St&PR 91
Doney, Brian H. 1941- St&PR 91
Doney, Judith Karen 1942- WhoAmW 91
Doney, Willis Frederick 1925- WhoAm 90
Donfried, Karl Paul 1940- WhoAm 90
Dong, Alvin Lim 1955- WhoE 91, WhoEmL 91, WhoWor 91
Dong, Kathleen Julia BiDrAPA 89
Donge, Bernard 1935- WhoWor 91
Donges, Juergen B. 1940- WhoWor 91
Dongier, Maurice H-J 1925- BiDrAPA 89
Donham, Philip NewYTBS 90
Donham, Russell G. 1944- St&PR 91
Donhauser, Paul Stefan 1936- WhoAmA 91
Donheiser, Walter Joseph 1927- WhoWor 91
Donhoff, Marion 1909- EncCoWW
Donhoffer, Dieter Karl 1939- WhoWor 91
Donhowe, Peter Arthur 1938- WhoAm 90
Donica, Thomas M BiDrAPA 89
Donicht, James Douglas 1938- St&PR 91
Donicht, Joyce Mae 1949- WhoAmW 91
Doniger, Nancy BioIn 16
Doniger, Wendy 1940- WhoAm 90
Doninger, Joseph Eugene 1939- St&PR 91
Donington, Robert 1907- IntWWM 90
Donington, Robert 1907-1990? ConAu 130
Donini, Gerald P. 1941- St&PR 91
Donini, Gerri BioIn 16
Donini, Rickey David 1949- WhoSSW 91
Doniphan, Alexander William 1808-1887 WhNaAH
Donisthorpe, Christine Ann 1932- WhoAmW 91
Donitz, Karl 1891-1980 BioIn 16
Donizetti, Gaetano 1797-1848 PenDiMP A, WorAlBi
Donizetti, Mario 1932- WhoWor 91
Donker, Ab J. 1935- WhoWor 91
Donker, Richard Bruce 1950- WhoWor 91
Donkervoet, Richard Cornelius 1930- WhoAm 90
Donkin, Eric 1929- OxCCanT
Donkor, Alex Ambrose 1950- WhoE 91
Donlan, Robert F. 1929- St&PR 91
Donleavy, Gabriel Douglas 1946- WhoWor 91
Donleavy, J P 1926- MajTwCW
Donleavy, J. P. 1926- WorAlBi
Donleavy, James Patrick 1926- WhoAm 90
Donlevy, Brian 1903-1972 WorAlBi
Donlevy, John Dearden 1933- WhoAm 90
Donley, Clifford Tappen 1941- WhoSSW 91
Donley, Edward 1921- St&PR 91, WhoAm 90
Donley, G.L. 1937- St&PR 91
Donley, Glenda Jane 1954- WhoEmL 91
Donley, James L 1946- BiDrAPA 89
Donley, James W. 1934- ODwPR 91
Donley, Joseph Francis 1952- WhoEmL 91
Donley, Michael Bruce 1952- WhoAm 90
Donley, Patrick J BiDrAPA 89
Donley, Richard D. 1930- St&PR 91
Donley, Robert Morris 1934- WhoAmA 91
Donley, Roger Thomas 1937- St&PR 91
Donley, Rosemary WhoAm 90
Donley, Russell Lee, III 1939- WhoAm 90
Donley, Terrance Kanear 1929- St&PR 91

Donlin, Mike 1878-1923 BioIn 16
Donlin, Mike 1878-1933 Ballpl 90
Donlin, Terence James 1931- St&PR 91
Donlon, Edward Joseph 1941- WhoE 91
Donlon, J.P. 1948- WhoE 91
Donlon, Joseph Thomas 1929- St&PR 91
Donlon, Patrick T 1937- BiDrAPA 89
Donlou, John BioIn 16
Donlou, John Nicholas 1945- BiDrAPA 89
Donn, Edward J. 1924- St&PR 91
Donn, Steven Mark 1949- WhoEmL 91
Donna, Natalie 1934-1979 AuBYP 90
Donna, Roberto 1961- WhoE 91
Donnaconna WhNaAH
Donnahoe, Alan S. 1916- St&PR 91
Donnahoe, Alan Stanley 1916- WhoAm 90
Donnally, Patricia Broderick 1955- WhoAm 90, WhoAmW 91
Donnars, Jacques 1919- EncO&P 3
Donnay, Albert BioIn 16
Donne, Eddy Marie Joseph 1934- WhoWor 91
Donne, Gaven 1914- WhoWor 91
Donne, John 1572-1631 BioIn 16, PoeCrit 1 [port], WorAlBi, WrPh
Donnell, Barry B. 1939- St&PR 91
Donnell, Brian James 1955- WhoEmL 91
Donnell, Bruce Bolton 1946- WhoE 91, WhoEmL 91
Donnell, Edward S. 1919- St&PR 91
Donnell, Harold Eugene, Jr. 1935- WhoAm 90
Donnell, Jeff 1921-1988 BioIn 16
Donnell, John Randolph 1912- WhoAm 90, WhoWor 91
Donnell, Mildred Webster 1951- WhoE 91
Donnell, Richard Spaight 1820-1867 AmLegL
Donnella, Michael Andre 1954- WhoEmL 91
Donnellan, Andrew B., Jr. 1952- St&PR 91
Donnellan, Edmond Joseph BiDrAPA 89
Donnellan, Joseph Anthony 1959- BiDrAPA 89, WhoE 91
Donnellan, Lynda A. 1957- WhoWrEP 89
Donnellan, Shaun Kevin 1944- WhoAm 90
Donnelley, James Russell 1935- St&PR 91
Donnelley, Laura BioIn 16
Donnelley, Thomas E. 1867-1955 WorAlBi
Donnelly, Barbara Schettler 1933- WhoAmW 91, WhoSSW 91, WhoWor 91
Donnelly, Blix 1914-1976 Ballpl 90
Donnelly, Brian 1946- WhoAm 90, WhoE 91
Donnelly, Candice 1954- ConTFT 8
Donnelly, Charles Lawthers, Jr. 1929- WhoAm 90
Donnelly, Charles Robert 1921- WhoAm 90
Donnelly, Craig Lanier BiDrAPA 89
Donnelly, David H. 1932- St&PR 91
Donnelly, Dennis W 1942- BiDrAPA 89
Donnelly, Edward James, Jr. 1946- WhoSSW 91
Donnelly, Edwin Harold 1947 WhoSSW 91
Donnelly, Gerard Kevin 1933- WhoAm 90, WhoWor 91
Donnelly, Harry J. BioIn 16
Donnelly, Ignatius 1831-1901 EncO&P 3, NewAgE 90
Donnelly, James WhoAm 90
Donnelly, James C. 1945- St&PR 91
Donnelly, James S. 1913-1989 BioIn 16
Donnelly, John 1914- BiDrAPA 89, WhoAm 90
Donnelly, John Casgrain 1953- St&PR 91
Donnelly, John F. 1947- St&PR 91
Donnelly, John Francis 1929- WhoAm 90
Donnelly, John J. AmLegL
Donnelly, John M, II BiDrAPA 89
Donnelly, John P. 1932- ODwPR 91
Donnelly, Joseph Dennis 1947- WhoAm 90
Donnelly, Joseph Lennon 1929- St&PR 91
Donnelly, Joseph Michael 1942- St&PR 91
Donnelly, Kathleen Ann 1951- WhoEmL 91
Donnelly, Lloyd W. 1927- WhoAm 90
Donnelly, Lori Ann 1963- WhoAmW 91
Donnelly, Lynne Carol 1955- WhoAmW 91
Donnelly, Malcolm Douglas 1943- IntWWM 90
Donnelly, Margarita Patricia 1942- WhoWrEP 89
Donnelly, Marian Card 1923- WhoAm 90, WhoAmA 91
Donnelly, Mary ODwPR 91
Donnelly, Mary E 1898-1963 WhoAmA 91N
Donnelly, Maureen 1950- BiDrAPA 89
Donnelly, Mavis Joan 1954- BiDrAPA 89
Donnelly, Michael Joseph 1951- WhoSSW 91
Donnelly, Peter Lane 1947- St&PR 91
Donnelly, Ralph Langdon 1936- St&PR 91
Donnelly, Raymond F., Jr. 1950- ODwPR 91
Donnelly, Richard Edwin 1939- WhoE 91
Donnelly, Robert Edward 1940- St&PR 91
Donnelly, Robert Oliver 1929- St&PR 91
Donnelly, Robert True 1924- WhoAm 90
Donnelly, Russell James 1930- WhoAm 90, WhoWor 91
Donnelly, Sheila ODwPR 91
Donnelly, Thomas J. BioIn 16
Donnelly, Thomas J. 1925- St&PR 91
Donnelly, Thomas J. 1930- St&PR 91
Donnelly, Thomas Joseph 1925- WhoAm 90
Donnelly, Timothy J. 1952- St&PR 91
Donnelly, Walter Joseph 1896-1970 BioIn 16
Donnem, Roland William 1929- WhoWor 91
Donnem, Ronald William 1929- WhoAm 90
Donnem, Sarah Lund 1936- WhoAmW 91, WhoWor 91
Donner, Christie Jean 1961- WhoSSW 91
Donner, Clive 1926- BioIn 16
Donner, Fred McGraw 1945- WhoEmL 91
Donner, Frederic Garrett 1902-1987 EncABHB 5 [port]
Donner, Jan-Hein BioIn 16
Donner, Jorn 1933- BioIn 16, DcScanL
Donner, Jorn Johan 1933- WhoWor 91
Donner, Kenneth 1915- St&PR 91
Donner, Martin Walter 1920- WhoAm 90
Donner, Paul Christopher 1959- WhoEmL 91
Donner, Paul G 1922- BiDrAPA 89
Donner, Richard WhoAm 90
Donner, William Irving 1936- WhoSSW 91
Donner, William T 1921- BiDrAPA 89
Donner, William Troutman 1921- WhoE 91
Donnerstein, Edward Irving 1945- WhoAm 90
Donneson, Seena WhoAmA 91
Donneson, Seena Sand WhoAm 90, WhoE 91
Donnet, Jean Baptiste 1923- WhoWor 91
Donnett, William Edward 1922- WhoE 91
Donnici, Peter Joseph 1939- WhoWor 91
D'Onofrio, Albert Marshall 1931- St&PR 91
D'Onofrio, Anthony Joseph 1929- WhoAm 90
Donofrio, Edward Patrick 1943- WhoE 91
Donofrio, Frederick Allen 1942- St&PR 91
Donofrio, Joseph R. 1946- St&PR 91
Donofrio, Karen Alena 1955- WhoAmW 91
D'Onofrio, Michael F. 1952- St&PR 91
Donofrio, Peter Daniel 1950- WhoSSW 91
Donofrio, Richard Michael 1938- St&PR 91, WhoAm 90
Donoghue, Dennis EarBlAP
Donoghue, Doris Mary BiDrAPA 89
Donoghue, John F. 1928- WhoAm 90, WhoSSW 91
Donoghue, John Timothy 1935- WhoE 91
Donoghue, Kenneth L. ODwPR 91
Donoghue, Mildred Ransdorf WhoAm 90, WhoAmW 91
Donoghue, William Thomas 1932- WhoSSW 91
Donohie, H. Gerard 1929- WhoE 91
Donoho, Burnett W. 1939- St&PR 91
Donoho, James D. 1948- St&PR 91
Donohoe, Edward F. 1907- St&PR 91
Donohoe, Francis X. 1925- St&PR 91
Donohoe, James Albert 1936- WhoAm 90, WhoSSW 91
Donohoe, James Aloysius, Jr. 1915- St&PR 91
Donohoe, Jerome F. 1939- St&PR 91
Donohoe, Jerome Francis 1939- WhoAm 90
Donohoe, Kevin Gerard 1948- St&PR 91
Donohoe, Leonard Charles 1928- St&PR 91
Donohoe, Mark Thomas 1942- WhoE 91
Donohoe, Peter 1953- PenDiMP
Donohoe, Peter Howard 1953- IntWWM 90
Donohoe, Thomas Ward 1936- WhoE 91
Donohoe, Victoria WhoAmA 91
Donohoo, Donovan L. 1936- WhoWor 91
Donohue, Andrew John 1950- St&PR 91
Donohue, Brenda 1950-1979 OxCCanT
Donohue, Carroll John 1917- WhoAm 90, WhoWor 91
Donohue, David Lee 1950- WhoSSW 91
Donohue, David Patrick 1931- WhoSSW 91
Donohue, Delaine R. 1931- St&PR 91
Donohue, Edith M. 1938- WhoAmW 91
Donohue, Elizabeth Anne 1961- WhoAmW 91
Donohue, George L. 1944- St&PR 91
Donohue, Gerald Joseph, Jr. 1959- WhoEmL 91
Donohue, Irene Mary WhoWrEP 89
Donohue, Janet ODwPR 91
Donohue, Jerry P. 1937- St&PR 91
Donohue, Jim 1938- Ballpl 90
Donohue, Joe 1953- ODwPR 91
Donohue, John F. 1956- St&PR 91
Donohue, John Joseph 1953- WhoEmL 91
Donohue, John Patrick 1930- WhoAm 90
Donohue, Joyce Morrissey 1940- WhoAmW 91
Donohue, Marc David 1951- WhoAm 90
Donohue, Margaret Anne 1953- WhoEmL 91
Donohue, Patricia Carol 1946- WhoAmW 91
Donohue, Patrick A. 1950- St&PR 91
Donohue, Pete 1900-1988 Ballpl 90
Donohue, Peter Joseph 1949- WhoAm 90
Donohue, Richard Harney 1950- WhoEmL 91
Donohue, Robert Peter 1942- WhoAm 90, WhoSSW 91
Donohue, Terence 1946- WhoEmL 91
Donohue, Thomas Joseph 1938- WhoAm 90
Donohue, Thomas Michael 1930- St&PR 91
Donohue, William V 1930- BiDrAPA 89
Donohue-Babiak, Amy Lorraine 1961- WhoAmW 91
Donohugh, Donald Lee 1924- WhoWor 91
Donor, Mary Elizabeth 1938- WhoAmW 91
Donosky, Theodore 1943- BiDrAPA 89
Donoso, Jose BioIn 16
Donoso, Jose 1924- ConAu 32NR, HispWr 90, MajTwCW, WhoWor 91
Donoso Cortes, Juan 1809-1853 BioIn 16
Donoso Yanez, Jose 1924- ConAu 32NR
Donough, Robert J. 1924- St&PR 91
Donoughe, Lisa ODwPR 91
Donovan 1943- WorAlBi
Donovan 1946- OxCPMus
Donovan, Alan Barton 1937- WhoAm 90
Donovan, Allen Francis 1914- WhoAm 90
Donovan, Althea Ann 1957- BiDrAPA 89
Donovan, Bruce Elliot 1937- WhoAm 90
Donovan, Charles Francis 1912- WhoAm 90
Donovan, Cornelia M 1938- BiDrAPA 89
Donovan, Dalvin E. 1923- St&PR 91
Donovan, Dan 1901-1986 OxCPMus
Donovan, Daniel Hatheway BiDrAPA 89
Donovan, David Gerard 1921- WhoAm 90
Donovan, David T. ODwPR 91
Donovan, Deborah Carolyn 1951- WhoEmL 91
Donovan, Denis M. 1946- WhoSSW 91
Donovan, Diane C. 1956- WhoWrEP 89
Donovan, Dianne Francys 1948- WhoAm 90
Donovan, Dick 1842-1934 TwCCr&M 91
Donovan, Dick 1927- Ballpl 90
Donovan, Donna Mae 1952- WhoAm 90, WhoE 91
Donovan, Donna Marie 1945- WhoE 91, WhoEmL 91
Donovan, Doran Warren 1941- St&PR 91
Donovan, Edward Michael 1921- WhoE 91
Donovan, Egbert Herbert 1913- WhoAm 90
Donovan, Eugene J. 1935- St&PR 91
Donovan, Eugene T BiDrAPA 89
Donovan, Francis C BiDrAPA 89
Donovan, Frank Robert 1906-1975 AuBYP 90
Donovan, Gary Richard 1947- BiDrAPA 89
Donovan, George Joseph 1935- WhoAm 90
Donovan, Gerald Alton 1925- WhoAm 90
Donovan, Geralyn Marie 1960- WhoAmW 91
Donovan, Gregory Edward 1950- WhoWrEP 89
Donovan, Hedley BioIn 16
Donovan, Hedley 1914-1990 ConAu 132, CurBio 90N, NewYTBS 90 [port]
Donovan, Hedley Williams 1914- WhoAm 90
Donovan, Herbert Alcorn, Jr. 1931- WhoAm 90, WhoSSW 91
Donovan, James St&PR 91N
Donovan, James F BiDrAPA 89
Donovan, James H. NewYTBS 90 [port]
Donovan, James J. 1915-1988 BioIn 16
Donovan, James Joseph, III 1954- WhoEmL 91
Donovan, James Patrick 1945- WhoE 91
Donovan, Jane Ellen 1957- WhoAmW 91
Donovan, Jean BioIn 16
Donovan, Jerome Francis 1936- WhoAm 90
Donovan, John Britt 1945- WhoE 91
Donovan, John Carl 1930- WhoSSW 91
Donovan, John Joseph, Jr. 1916- WhoWor 91
Donovan, John Peter 1926- St&PR 91
Donovan, Katherine Lee BiDrAPA 89
Donovan, Lowava Denise 1958- WhoAmW 91
Donovan, Lynley Kay 1962- WhoAmW 91
Donovan, Madeline Frances 1926- WhoAmW 91
Donovan, Margaret 1950- WhoAmW 91
Donovan, Marie Phillips WhoAmW 91, WhoWor 91
Donovan, Mark 1960- WhoWrEP 89
Donovan, Mary Patricia 1943- WhoE 91
Donovan, Michael Dennis 1959- WhoEmL 91
Donovan, Nancy BioIn 16
Donovan, Nancy S. 1951- WhoAm 90
Donovan, Patricia BiDrAPA 89
Donovan, Patsy 1865-1953 Ballpl 90 [port]
Donovan, Paul M. 1915- St&PR 91
Donovan, Raymond James 1930- BiDrUSE 89, BioIn 16
Donovan, Richard Edward BiDrAPA 89
Donovan, Richard Edward 1952- WhoEmL 91
Donovan, Richard Paul 1941- St&PR 91
Donovan, Robert Alan 1921- WhoAm 90
Donovan, Robert Edward 1941- WhoAm 90
Donovan, Robert Emmet 1952- WhoEmL 91
Donovan, Robert J 1923- BiDrAPA 89
Donovan, Robert John 1912- WhoAm 90
Donovan, Robert Orovan 1914- WhoWrEP 89
Donovan, Sandra Steranka 1942- WhoAmW 91
Donovan, Stephen BiDrAPA 89
Donovan, Stephen Patrick, Jr. 1941- St&PR 91, WhoAm 90
Donovan, Thomas F. 1933- St&PR 91
Donovan, Thomas Roy 1937- WhoAm 90
Donovan, Timothy Paul 1927- WhoAm 90
Donovan, Walter Edgar 1926- WhoAm 90
Donovan, Warren J. BioIn 16
Donovan, Wild Bill 1876-1923 Ballpl 90 [port]
Donovan, William 1883-1959 WorAlBi
Donovan, William B 1935- BiDrAPA 89
Donovan, William Daniel BiDrAPA 89
Donovan, Woodrow M BiDrAPA 89
Donovan-Kachavos, Kathryn Agnes 1937- BiDrAPA 89, WhoE 91
Donshik, Jacob BiDrAPA 89
Donson, Nathaniel 1937- BiDrAPA 89
Donth, Joseph Leonard 1946- St&PR 91
Donwen, William John 1936- St&PR 91
Donyu PenDiDA 89
Donze, Sara Lee 1925- AuBYP 90
Donzel-Gargand, Bernard 1955- IntWWM 90
Donzella, La Compiuta 12--?- EncCoWW
Donzelli, Rinaldo 1921- ConDes 90
Donziger, Michael 1932- St&PR 91
Doo Da Post 1949- WhoAmA 91
Doob, Joseph Leo 1910- WhoAm 90
Doob, Leonard William 1909- AuBYP 90, WhoAm 90
Doobie Brothers, The EncPR&S 89
Doochin, Jerald H. 1931- St&PR 91
Doochin, Michael David 1953- St&PR 91, WhoSSW 91
Doochin, Robert S. 1940- St&PR 91
Doodoh, Alfons Francis 1939- WhoWor 91
Doody, Agnes G. WhoE 91
Doody, Alison BioIn 16
Doody, Alton Frederick 1934- WhoWor 91
Doody, Barbara Pettett 1938- WhoAmW 91, WhoSSW 91, WhoWor 91
Doody, Daniel John 1952- St&PR 91
Doody, J. Robert 1930- St&PR 91
Doody, Louis Clarence, Jr. 1940- WhoSSW 91
Doody, Margaret Anne 1939- WhoAm 90, WhoAmW 91
Doody, William Joseph 1931- WhoWor 91
Dooge, James Clement Ignatius 1922- WhoWor 91
Doogs, Carol Wallace Kaki 1941- WhoAmW 91
Doohan, James BioIn 16
Doohan, James 1920- ConTFT 8 [port]
Dooher, Muredach Joseph 1913- WhoAm 90
Dooher, Thomas Jerome 1935- St&PR 91
Dooin, Red 1879-1952 Ballpl 90
Doolan, Mickey 1880-1951 Ballpl 90
Dooley, Ann Elizabeth 1952- WhoAm 90
Dooley, Arch Richard 1925- WhoAm 90
Dooley, Charles Richard 1913- St&PR 91
Dooley, Daniel Anthony 1959- WhoEmL 91
Dooley, Delmer John 1920- WhoAm 90
Dooley, Donald John 1921- WhoAm 90
Dooley, Douglas John 1955- WhoWor 91
Dooley, Edmund Robert 1940- St&PR 91
Dooley, George Elijah 1918- WhoAm 90
Dooley, Helen Bertha 1907- WhoAmA 91
Dooley, J. Gordon 1935- WhoWor 91
Dooley, Jo Ann Catherine 1930- WhoAmW 91, WhoWor 91
Dooley, John A., III 1944- WhoE 91
Dooley, Lawrence W. 1944- St&PR 91

Dooley, Mary Agnes 1923- WhoAmW 91, WhoE 91
Dooley, Maura Denise 1957- WhoWor 91
Dooley, Patrick Kiaran 1942- WhoAm 90
Dooley, Richard Gordon 1929- St&PR 91, WhoAm 90
Dooley, Robert Daniel 1923- WhoAm 90
Dooley, Roger B 1920- WhoWrEP 89
Dooley, Ronald Drinnan 1939- St&PR 91
Dooley, Sue Ann WhoAmW 91
Dooley, Thomas Howard 1934- WhoAm 90, WhoE 91
Dooley, Vince 1932- BioIn 16
Dooley, William 1932- IntWWM 90
Doolin, James Lawrence 1932- WhoAmA 91
Doolin, John B. 1918- WhoSSW 91
Doolittle, Bev BioIn 16
Doolittle, Diane Lewis 1959- WhoEmL 91
Doolittle, Hilda 1886-1961 BioAmW, BioIn 16, MajTwCW, WorAlBi
Doolittle, James H. WhoAm 90
Doolittle, James H. 1896- WorAlBi
Doolittle, James Harold 1896- BioIn 16
Doolittle, James Rood 1815-1897 WhNaAH
Doolittle, Jesse William, Jr. 1929- WhoAm 90
Doolittle, Mary 1810-1886 FemiCLE
Doolittle, Robert Frederick 1902- WhoAm 90
Doolittle, Russell Francis 1931- WhoAm 90
Doolittle, Sheila Rose 1956- WhoAmW 91
Doolittle, Sidney Newing 1934- St&PR 91, WhoAm 90
Doolittle, Tilton Edwin 1825-1896 AmLegL
Doolittle, William Hotchkiss 1929- WhoAm 90
Doolos, James W 1920- BiDrAPA 89
Dooly, Weyman I., Jr. 1932- St&PR 91
Dooly-Manning, Cathryn Rozanne 1953- WhoE 91
Dooman, Calvert 1927- St&PR 91
Doone, Michele Marie 1942- WhoAmW 91
Dooner, Peter Samuel, Jr. 1929- St&PR 91
Doongaji, Dinshaw R 1932- BiDrAPA 89
Doonican, Val 1928- OxCPMus
Doop, Raymond BioIn 16
Doores, Brad L. 1950- St&PR 91
Doorley, Michael G. 1955- St&PR 91
Doornbos, Johannes Fokko 1923- WhoWor 91
Doors, The ConMus 4 [port], EncPR&S 89, OxCPMus
Dooskin, Herbert P. 1941- St&PR 91, WhoAm 90
Dopf, Glenn William 1953- WhoEmL 91
Dopfer, Kurt 1939- WhoWor 91
Do Pico, Alfredo J 1934- BiDrAPA 89
Dopkins, Leonard A. 1929- St&PR 91
Dopkins, Leonard Arnold 1929- WhoSSW 91
Doppler, Christian Johann 1803-1853 WorAlBi
Doppstadt, William K. 1932- St&PR 91
Dopson, Cecil Clifton, Jr. 1948- BiDrAPA 89
Dopson, John 1963- Ballpl 90
Doqui, Robert DrBlPA 90
Dor, Yoram 1945- St&PR 91, WhoAm 90
Dor-Ner, Zvi Richard 1941- WhoE 91
Dora d'Istria EncCoWW
Dora, Joan Teresa 1935- WhoAmW 91
Dorado, Marianne Gaertner 1956- WhoEmL 91
Doran, Allen Robert 1948- BiDrAPA 89
Doran, Barbara Lee 1953- WhoAmW 91, WhoE 91
Doran, Bill 1958- Ballpl 90
Doran, Charles E. 1928- St&PR 91
Doran, Charles Edward 1928- WhoAm 90
Doran, Christopher M 1946- BiDrAPA 89
Doran, David A. 1941- St&PR 91
Doran, David Stephen 1942- IntWWM 90
Doran, Diane BioIn 16
Doran, Doris Jeanne 1932- WhoSSW 91
Doran, Dorothy Mary 1934- WhoE 91
Doran, Felix, III 1924- St&PR 91
Doran, Gerald Charles 1935- St&PR 91
Doran, James Martin 1933- WhoAm 90
Doran, John M. 1910- St&PR 91
Doran, Judith Ann 1953- WhoEmL 91
Doran, Kenneth John 1950- WhoEmL 91
Doran, Leo A. ODwPR 91
Doran, Mark Joseph 1962- WhoE 91
Doran, Matt 1921- IntWWM 90
Doran, Robert Stuart 1937- WhoSSW 91, WhoWor 91
Doran, Russell Del 1957- St&PR 91
Doran, Stephen Mark 1925- BiDrAPA 89
Doran, William M. 1940- St&PR 91
Dorantes, Ruth E. 1955- WhoHisp 91
Dorati, Antal BioIn 16
Dorati, Antal 1906-1988 AnObit 1988, PenDiMP, WorAlBi
Dorato, Peter 1932- WhoAm 90
Doray, Andrea Wesley 1956- WhoAmW 91, WhoEmL 91, WhoWrEP 89
Doray, Audrey Capel 1931- WhoAmA 91
D'Orazio, Harold E. 1939- WhoAm 90
D'Orazio, Nicholas Joseph 1949- BiDrAPA 89
Dorchester, John D. 1935- St&PR 91
Dordal, Erl 1927- WhoAm 90
Dordelman, William Forsyth 1940- WhoAm 90
Dordick, Johanna 1935- WhoAm 90
Dore, Anita Wilkes 1914- WhoAmW 91
Dore, Bonny Ellen 1947- WhoAm 90, WhoAmW 91, WhoWor 91
Dore, Fred Hudson 1925- WhoAm 90
Dore, Gordon Elwin, Jr. 1948- WhoE 91
Dore, Gustave 1832-1883 IntDcAA 90
Dore, J. Elliot 1954- St&PR 91
Dore, James Francis 1946- WhoSSW 91
Dore, Janet 1950- WhoEmL 91
Dore, Jean WhoE 91
Dore, Richard H. ODwPR 91
Dore, Stephen Edward, Jr. 1918- WhoAm 90
Doreen, Judy Strain 1938- WhoSSW 91
Do Rego, Jose Lins 1901-1957 BioIn 16
Doreman, Robert 1927- St&PR 91
Doremus, John 1933- WhoAm 90
Doremus, John C., Jr. 1931- WhoAm 90
Doremus, John Clinton, Jr. 1931- St&PR 91
Doremus, Ogden 1921- WhoAm 90
Doremus, Robert Heward 1928- WhoAm 90
Doren, A 1935- WhoAmA 91
Doren, Henry J T 1929- WhoAmA 91
Doren, Konstantin 1956- WhoWrEP 89
Doren, Marion Walker 1928- BioIn 16
Dorenfeld, Alan S. 1945- St&PR 91
Dorenfest, Sheldon I. 1935- St&PR 91
Dorer, Fred Harold 1936- WhoAm 90
Dorer, Michael A. 1952- St&PR 91
Doret, Gustave 1866-1943 PenDiMP
Dorez, Barthelemy PenDiDA 89
Dorf, Bob 1949- ODwPR 91
Dorf, Ilene A. 1948- ODwPR 91
Dorf, James J. 1946- St&PR 91
Dorf, Jerome 1936- St&PR 91, WhoAm 90
Dorf, Joan R. 1932- WhoE 91
Dorf, Philip ODwPR 91, WhoAm 90, WhoE 91
Dorf, Richard Carl 1933- WhoAm 90
Dorf, Robert L. 1949- WhoAm 90
Dorfan, Herbert I 1933- BiDrAPA 89
Dorfer, Ingemar 1939- ConAu 130
Dorff, Daniel 1956- IntWWM 90
Dorff, Ervin K. 1932- St&PR 91
Dorff, Joseph Ruppert 1936- St&PR 91
Dorfi, Klaus G. 1942- St&PR 91
Dorfler, Willibald 1944- WhoWor 91
Dorflinger, Christian 1828-1915 PenDiDA 89
Dorflinger, Max F. 1938- St&PR 91
Dorflinger, Peter Glen 1951- St&PR 91
Dorfman, Allen Bernard 1930- WhoAm 90, WhoWor 91
Dorfman, Andrea Randall 1959- WhoAmW 91
Dorfman, Ariel BioIn 16
Dorfman, Ariel 1942- ConAu 130, HispWr 90, WhoWor 91
Dorfman, Bruce 1936- WhoAmA 91
Dorfman, Colleen Kinney ODwPR 91
Dorfman, Dan BioIn 16
Dorfman, David BioIn 16
Dorfman, Elsa 1959- WhoAmA 91
Dorfman, Elsa S. 1937- WhoE 91
Dorfman, Fred 1946- WhoAmA 91
Dorfman, Isaiah S. 1907- WhoAm 90
Dorfman, J. Robert 1937- WhoAm 90
Dorfman, Joel Marvin 1951- WhoAm 90
Dorfman, John Charles 1925- WhoAm 90
Dorfman, John Ivor 1950- BiDrAPA 89
Dorfman, Leon Monte 1922- WhoAm 90
Dorfman, Margaret Jeanne 1950- BiDrAPA 89
Dorfman, Mark Stanley 1945- WhoSSW 91
Dorfman, Matthew Scott 1947- WhoEmL 91
Dorfman, Myron Herbert 1927- WhoAm 90
Dorfman, Paul Michael 1939- St&PR 91
Dorfman, Robert 1916- WhoAm 90, WhoE 91
Dorfman, Simon 1928- BiDrAPA 89
Dorfman, Steven David 1935- WhoAm 90
Dorfman, Vernon Gary BiDrAPA 89
Dorfman, Wilfred 1909- BiDrAPA 89, WhoE 91
Dorfmont, Linda Bernice 1947- WhoEmL 91
Dorfmuller, Kurt 1922- IntWWM 90
Dorfsman, Lou BioIn 16
Dorfsman, Louis 1918- ConDes 90
Dorfsman, Michael Jay 1947- WhoE 91
Dorgan, Byron Leslie 1942- WhoAm 90
Dorgan, John Joseph 1923- St&PR 91
Dorgan, John Joseph, Jr. 1923- WhoAm 90
Dorgan, Richard Joseph 1939- St&PR 91
Dorgan, Tad 1877-1929 EncACom
Dorgeles, Roland 1886-1973 BioIn 16
Dorgelo, Hendrik Berend 1894-1961 DcScB S2
Dorgeres, Henri Auguste d'Halluin 1897-1985 BiDFrPL
Dorham, Kenny 1924-1972 BioIn 16
Doria, Anthony Notarnicola 1927- WhoAm 90, WhoWor 91
Doria, Charles WhoWrEP 89
Doria, Leonida Tamondong 1946- WhoAmW 91
Doria, Marie E 1943- BiDrAPA 89
Doria, Sante Joseph 1927- St&PR 91
Doria, Vincent Mark 1947- WhoE 91
Dorian, Edward S., Jr. 1954- St&PR 91
Dorian, Edward S., Sr. St&PR 91
Dorian, Frederick 1902- IntWWM 90
Dorian, Harry A. 1928- St&PR 91
Dorian, Harry Aram 1928- WhoAm 90
Dorian, Linda Colvard WhoAmW 91
Dorian, Nancy Currier 1936- WhoAm 90, WhoAmW 91
Doriani, William 1891- MusmAFA
Dorigo, Werner Fritz, Jr. 1947- WhoSSW 91, WhoWor 91
Dorin, Bernard J. 1929- WhoWor 91
Dorin, Patrick C. 1939- BioIn 16
Dorin, William Joseph 1950- WhoEmL 91
Doring, De ODwPR 91
D'Orio, Barbara Marie BiDrAPA 89
Dorion, Antoine-Aime 1818-1891 DcCanB 12
Dorion, Marie 1786-1853? WhNaAH
Dorion, Pierre 1940- BiDrAPA 89
Dorion, Pierre, Jr. WhNaAH
Dorion, Pierre, Sr. 1750?-1820? WhNaAH
Doriot, Georges F. 1899-1987 WorAlBi
Doriot, Jacques Maurice 1898-1945 BiDFrPL
Doris Ann 1917- WhoAm 90
Dorish, Harry 1921- Ballpl 90
Dority, John Jerome 1953- St&PR 91
Dorius, Kermit Parrish 1926- WhoAm 90
Dorius, Richard Gordon, Jr. 1942- St&PR 91
Dorjahn, Renee Victoria 1960- WhoAmW 91
Dorji, Tobgye Sonam 1947- WhoWor 91
Dorkey, Charles Edward, III 1948- WhoE 91
Dorkin, Frederic Eugene 1932- WhoAm 90
Dorl-Adams, Donna Marie 1948- WhoEmL 91
Dorland, Byrl Brown 1915- WhoAmW 91, WhoWor 91
Dorland, Dodge Oatwell 1948- WhoE 91, WhoEmL 91, WhoWor 91
Dorland, Gilbert Meding 1912- St&PR 91
Dorlas, Johan Christiaan 1925- WhoWor 91
Dorleac, Catherine WhoWor 91
Dorman, Albert A. 1926- St&PR 91, WhoAm 90
Dorman, Craig Emery BioIn 16
Dorman, Daniel 1936- BiDrAPA 89
Dorman, Gerald Charles 1937- WhoE 91
Dorman, Gerald Huntington 1931- St&PR 91
Dorman, Hattie Lawrence 1932- WhoAmW 91
Dorman, Jack BiDrAPA 89
Dorman, James 1928- WhoSSW 91
Dorman, John Frederick 1928- WhoAm 90
Dorman, Karen Gail 1952- WhoAmW 91
Dorman, Kathryn Lynn 1957- WhoE 91
Dorman, Kenneth Randall BiDrAPA 89
Dorman, Linneaus Cuthbert 1935- WhoAm 90
Dorman, Michael 1932- AuBYP 90
Dorman, Rex Lee 1934- St&PR 91, WhoAm 90
Dorman, Richard Frederick, Jr. 1944- WhoE 91
Dorman, Richard Lee 1922- WhoAm 90
Dorman, Robert Joseph 1929- St&PR 91
Dorman, Sanford Alan 1950- WhoAm 90
Dorman, Sonya 1924- RGTwCSF
Dormann, Genevieve 1933- EncCoWW
Dormann, Henry O. 1932- WhoAm 90, WhoE 91
Dorme, Patrick John 1935- WhoAm 90
D'Ormesson, Jean 1925- WhoWor 91
Dormesy, Karl Dieudonne 1953- BiDrAPA 89
Dorminey, David Harley 1941- St&PR 91
Dorminey, Elizabeth Kline 1956- WhoAmW 91
Dorminey, Henry Clayton, Jr. 1949- WhoEmL 91
Dormire, Corwin Brooke 1942- WhoE 91
Dormire, John Carl 1931- St&PR 91
Dormitzer, Henry, II 1935- WhoAm 90
Dormon, Carrie 1888-1971 WomFie [port]
Dormont, Paul BiDrAPA 89
Dorn, Annita Lynne WhoAmW 91
Dorn, Charles Meeker 1927- WhoAm 90, WhoSSW 91
Dorn, David Norman 1944- WhoE 91
Dorn, Dolores WhoAm 90
Dorn, Edward Harvey 1952- WhoEmL 91
Dorn, Edward Merton 1929- WhoAm 90
Dorn, Ernest F., Jr. 1932- St&PR 91
Dorn, Gertrud EncCoWW
Dorn, Jacob 1944- WhoSSW 91
Dorn, James Andrew 1945- WhoAm 90, WhoE 91
Dorn, Janice Bebe 1938- BiDrAPA 89
Dorn, Jennifer Lynn 1950- WhoAm 90, WhoAmW 91, WhoE 91
Dorn, John Matthew BiDrAPA 89
Dorn, Joseph L. 1915- St&PR 91
Dorn, Lisa Jane BiDrAPA 89
Dorn, Peter Klaus 1932- WhoAmA 91
Dorn, Philip Brian 1947- WhoSSW 91
Dorn, Robert M 1921- BiDrAPA 89
Dorn, Robert Murray 1921- WhoAm 90
Dorn, Roosevelt F. 1935- WhoWor 91
Dorn, Ruth 1925- WhoAmA 91
Dorn, Samuel O. 1946- WhoSSW 91
Dorn, Wanda Faye 1945- WhoAmW 91
Dorn, William Schroeder 1928- WhoAm 90
Dornan, Candace Butler 1952- WhoAmW 91, WhoEmL 91
Dornan, John Neill 1944- WhoSSW 91
Dornan, Robert Kenneth 1933- WhoAm 90
D'Ornano, Hubert BioIn 16
D'Ornano, Isabelle BioIn 16
Dornberg, John Robert 1931- AuBYP 90
Dornblazer, George Henry, V 1950- BiDrAPA 89
Dornburgh, Fred David 1942- St&PR 91
Dornburgh, William Walter 1931- St&PR 91, WhoAm 90
Dornbusch, Arthur A., II 1943- St&PR 91, WhoAm 90
Dornbusch, Joan Louise Falquet 1932- WhoWrEP 89
Dornbusch, Rudiger 1942- WhoAm 90
Dornbusch, Sanford Maurice 1926- WhoAm 90
Dornbush, Charles F. 1947- St&PR 91
Dornbush, Darwin Cecil 1930- St&PR 91
Dornbush, Kirk T. 1933- St&PR 91
Dornbush, Rhea L. WhoAmW 91
Dorner, Alexander 1893- WhoAmA 91N
Dorner, Barbara Emilia 1945- WhoE 91
Dorner, Clifford O. 1933- St&PR 91
Dorner, Gus 1876-1956 Ballpl 90
Dorner, Marie-Christine 1960- BioIn 16
Dorner, Peter Paul 1925- WhoAm 90
Dorner-Andelora, Sharon Agnes Haddon 1943- WhoAmW 91, WhoE 91, WhoWor 91
Dornfeld, James L. 1954- St&PR 91
Dornfest, Burton Saul 1930- WhoE 91
Dornin, Catharine Quillen 1946- IntWWM 90, WhoE 91
Dorning, John Joseph 1938- WhoAm 90
Dornon, Robert F BiDrAPA 89
Dornsife, H.W. 1915- St&PR 91
Dornsife, Samuel Jonathan 1916- WhoE 91
Dornstauder, Jeanne Helen 1961- WhoSSW 91
Doro, Marie 1882-1956 BioIn 16, NotWoAT
Doro, Marion Elizabeth 1928- WhoAm 90, WhoAmW 91
Dorobek, J.S., II 1940- St&PR 91
Dorobiala, John Vincent 1931- St&PR 91
Dorocke, Lawrence Francis 1946- WhoEmL 91
Doromal, Noel M. 1944- WhoE 91
Doronina, Tatyana Vasiliyevna 1933- WhoWor 91
Doros, Maria Heczey 1937- WhoAmW 91
Doroschak, John Z. 1928- WhoWor 91
Dorosh, Daria 1943- WhoAmA 91
Doroski, Victor S 1946- BiDrAPA 89
Dorothe Engelbretsdatter DcScanL
Dorough, Bob BioIn 16
Dorough, H. Wyman 1936- WhoAm 90
Dorough, Prince Leon 1939- WhoSSW 91
Dorough, Tracey Leigh 1963- WhoAmW 91
Dorow, Dorothy 1930- IntWWM 90
Dorpat, Theodore L 1925- BiDrAPA 89
Dorpat, Theodore Lorenz 1925- WhoAm 90
Dorr, Aimee 1942- WhoAm 90
Dorr, Jackson G. WhoWrEP 89
Dorr, James Suhrer 1941- WhoWrEP 89
Dorr, Julia 1825-1913 FemiCLE
Dorr, Kathleen May 1955- WhoE 91
Dorr, Nell 1893- WhoAmA 91N
Dorr, Rheta Childe 1866-1948 BioIn 16
Dorr, Thomas O 1918- BiDrAPA 89
Dorra, Henri 1924- WhoAm 90, WhoAmA 91
Dorrance, Anson BioIn 16
Dorrance, G. Morris, Jr. 1922- St&PR 91
Dorrance, George Morris, Jr. 1922- WhoAm 90
Dorrance, John T., Jr. BioIn 16

Dorrel-Craven, Marla W. 1951- St&PR 91
Dorrie, Charles Theodore 1925- WhoE 91
Dorrie, Doris ConAu 130
Dorrien, Carlos Guillermo 1948- WhoAmA 91
Dorrier, Lindsay Gordon, Jr. 1943- WhoSSW 91
Dorrill, William Franklin 1931- WhoAm 90, WhoWor 91
Dorris, Catherine Ann 1963- WhoAmW 91
Dorris, Michael BioIn 16
Dorris, Michael Anthony 1945- WhoAm 90
Dorris, Peggy Rae 1933- WhoAmW 91
Dorritie, John Francis 1934- WhoAm 90, WhoWor 91
Dorros, Irwin 1929- WhoAm 90
Dors, Diana BioIn 16
Dors, Diana 1931-1984 DcNaB 1981
Dors, Joanne Lee 1946- WhoE 91
Dorsa, Madonna Deegan 1936- WhoE 91
Dorsan, Luc ConAu 129, MajTwCW
Dorsange, Jean ConAu 129, MajTwCW
Dorsch, Charles R. 1931- St&PR 91
Dorsen, David Milton 1935- WhoWor 91
Dorsen, Norman 1930- WhoAm 90
Dorset, Countess of BiDEWW
Dorset, John F Sackville, Duke of 1745-1799 BioIn 16
Dorset, Ruth ConAu 32NR
Dorset, Thomas Sackville, Earl of 1536-1608 BioIn 16
Dorsett, Charles Irvin 1945- WhoEmL 91, WhoSSW 91, WhoWor 91
Dorsett, Dovalee 1933- WhoSSW 91
Dorsett, Herbert Franklin 1933- WhoSSW 91
Dorsett, John Russel 1950- St&PR 91
Dorsett, John Russel, III 1950- WhoAm 90
Dorsett, Joseph J. 1929- St&PR 91
Dorsett, Judith Adele 1944- WhoWrEP 89
Dorsett, Lewis Howard, Jr. 1949- WhoSSW 91
Dorsett, Loyd George 1917- St&PR 91
Dorsett, Martha Janette 1943- WhoWrEP 89
Dorsett, Mary Janeen 1943- WhoWrEP 89
Dorsett, Patricia Jean Poole 1935- WhoAmW 91
Dorsett, Peter Elwood BiDrAPA 89
Dorsett, Tony BioIn 16
Dorsett, Tony 1954- WorAlBi
Dorsey, Albert Rich, Jr. 1921- St&PR 91
Dorsey, Ann Bahrani 1936- BiDrAPA 89
Dorsey, Anna 1815-1896 FemiCLE
Dorsey, Benjamin 1924- St&PR 91
Dorsey, David I. 1941- St&PR 91
Dorsey, Denise L 1951- BiDrAPA 89
Dorsey, Dennis Basil 1912- WhoSSW 91
Dorsey, Dolores Florence 1928- WhoAm 90
Dorsey, Donald Merrill 1953- WhoEmL 91
Dorsey, E Richard 1943- BiDrAPA 89
Dorsey, Edward C 1930- BiDrAPA 89
Dorsey, Eugene Carroll 1927- WhoAm 90
Dorsey, Frank James 1930- St&PR 91, WhoAm 90
Dorsey, Gail Ann BioIn 16
Dorsey, George C, Jr. 1927- BiDrAPA 89
Dorsey, Gray Lankford 1918- WhoAm 90
Dorsey, Helen Danner 1928- WhoAm 90
Dorsey, James Owen 1848-1895 WhNaAH
Dorsey, James Wilkinson, Jr. 1953- WhoWrEP 89
Dorsey, Jimmy 1904-1957 BioIn 16, OxCPMus, WorAlBi
Dorsey, John Frederick 1956- WhoEmL 91
Dorsey, John Henry St&PR 91N
Dorsey, John Russell 1938- WhoAm 90
Dorsey, John Wesley, Jr. 1936- WhoAm 90
Dorsey, Joseph R BiDrAPA 89
Dorsey, Laurens 1925- WhoE 91
Dorsey, Lee 1924-1986 OxCPMus
Dorsey, Lucia Iannone 1959- WhoAmA 91
Dorsey, Michael A 1949- WhoAmA 91
Dorsey, Norbert M. 1929- WhoAm 90, WhoSSW 91
Dorsey, Peter 1922- WhoAm 90
Dorsey, Rhoda Mary 1927- WhoAm 90, WhoAmW 91, WhoE 91
Dorsey, Richard P., III 1959- WhoEmL 91
Dorsey, Robert EarBlAP
Dorsey, Robert Francis 1947- St&PR 91
Dorsey, Sarah 1829-1879 FemiCLE
Dorsey, Thomas A. 1899- OxCPMus
Dorsey, Thomas Andrew 1899- DrBlPA 90
Dorsey, Thomas B. 1928-1988 BioIn 16
Dorsey, Tommy 1905-1956 BioIn 16, OxCPMus, WorAlBi
Dorsey, William E 1931- BiDrAPA 89
Dorsey, William Oscar Parks, III 1948- WhoEmL 91
Dorskind, Albert A. 1922- St&PR 91
Dorsky, Joshua Isaac BiDrAPA 89
Dorsky, Lydia 1955- ODwPR 91
Dorsky, Morris 1918- WhoAmA 91
Dorsky, Samuel 1914- WhoAmA 91
Dorst, Claire V 1922- WhoAmA 91
Dorst, John Phillips 1926- WhoAm 90
Dorst, Mary Crowe WhoAmA 91
Dorst, Tankred 1925- ConAu 30NR
Dort, Charles Webb BiDrAPA 89
Dort, Josiah Dallas 1861-1924 EncABHB 4 [port]
Dorta-Duque, Jorge Jesus BiDrAPA 89
Dortch, Carl Raymond 1914- WhoAm 90
Dortch, Richard BioIn 16
Dortch, William Theophilas 1824-1889 AmLegL
Dorton, David Lynn 1955- WhoEmL 91
Dorton, Patricia Ellen 1959- WhoSSW 91
Dorton, Phyllis Jean 1937- WhoSSW 91
Dortu, Frederic-Louis 1786-1860? PenDiDA 89
Dortu, Jacob 1749-1819 PenDiDA 89
Dorus, Walter 1942- BiDrAPA 89
Dorus-Gras, Julie 1805-1896 PenDiMP
Dorval, Gold Smith 1948- BiDrAPA 89
Dorval, Marie 1798-1849 EncCoWW
Dorval, Romeo E. 1924- St&PR 91
Dorvillier, William Joseph 1908- WhoAm 90
Dorward, Judith A. 1941- WhoAmW 91
Dorward, William 1929- WhoWor 91
Dorwart, Bonnie Brice 1942- WhoAmW 91
Dorwart, Mary Lucille 1948- WhoEmL 91
Dorwart, Paul Gregg 1944- St&PR 91
Dorwart, Robert Alan 1947- BiDrAPA 89, WhoE 91
Dorweiler, John P. 1926- WhoAm 90
Dorzab, Joe Henry 1940- BiDrAPA 89
Dos, Serge Jacques 1934- WhoWor 91
Dosanjh, Darshan Singh 1921- WhoAm 90
Doscher, Dennis Allen 1940- St&PR 91
Dosdall, Thomas Edward 1930- St&PR 91
Dose, Klaus 1928- WhoWor 91
Dosedel, James Anthony 1951- WhoWrEP 89
Dosemagen, Carol BioIn 16
Dosen, Susan Gail 1951- WhoEmL 91
Dosh, Steven Allan 1950- WhoEmL 91
Dosher, John Rodney 1936- WhoAm 90
Doshi, Bipin 1939- St&PR 91
Doshi, Jitendra Bhagwandas 1946- WhoEmL 91
Doshi, Priyakant S 1942- BiDrAPA 89
Doshi, Ramesh H BiDrAPA 89
Dosier, John Franklin 1951- WhoSSW 91
Dosio, Ernest J. 1950- St&PR 91
Dosio, John F. 1930- St&PR 91
Doskey, John Stanley 1927- WhoWrEP 89
Doskocil, Karl V BiDrAPA 89
Doskocil, Larry 1932- WhoSSW 91
Dosland, William Buehler 1927- St&PR 91, WhoAm 90
Dosovitz, Ira 1948- BiDrAPA 89
Dos Passos, John BioIn 16
Dos Passos, John 1896-1970 EncAL, MajTwCW, WorAlBi, WrPh
Dospil-Julian, Margaret Louise 1958- WhoEmL 91
Doss, Albert Hugh T 1909- BiDrAPA 89
Doss, Bob BioIn 16
Doss, Bruce Randy 1960- WhoSSW 91
Doss, Diana Lynn 1957- WhoAmW 91
Doss, Donald James 1952- WhoEmL 91
Doss, George W 1927- BiDrAPA 89
Doss, Helen 1918- AuBYP 90
Doss, Lawrence Paul 1927- WhoAm 90
Doss, Margot AuBYP 90
Doss, Marion Kenneth 1939- WhoAm 90
Doss, Richard H 1923- BiDrAPA 89
Doss, Richard William 1942- St&PR 91
Doss, Rita Gaynell 1942- WhoSSW 91
Doss, Robert Paul 1945- WhoEmL 91
Dossage, Jean ConAu 129, MajTwCW
Dos Santos, Alexandre Jose Maria 1924- WhoWor 91
Dos Santos, Deoscoredes ArtLatA
dos Santos, Domitilia M. WhoAmW 91
Dos Santos, Enrique BiDrAPA 89
Dos Santos, Jose Eduardo 1942- BioIn 16, WhoWor 91
Dos Santos, M Julia 1942- BiDrAPA 89
Dos Santos, Marcelino 1929- BioIn 16
Dos Santos, Nelson Pereira 1928- BioIn 16
Dossary, M, & Ghada Abdul Aziz Al-Mogren WomArch
Dossary, Mona Khalid Al 1965- WomArch
Dossena, Alceo 1878-1937 BioIn 16
Dossenbach, William R. 1943- St&PR 91
Dossetor, J. B. 1925- WhoAm 90
Dossett, Walter B., Jr. 1927- St&PR 91
Dossett, Walter Brown, Jr. 1927- WhoSSW 91
Dossey, Richard L. 1937- WhoAm 90
Dossi, Dosso 1490?-1542 IntDcAA 90
Dossick, Stephen Edward 1947- BiDrAPA 89
Dossin, Ernest Joseph, III 1941- WhoE 91
Dossor, Harry Lancelot 1916- IntWWM 90
Dostal, Nico 1895-1981 OxCPMus
Dostal, Raymond F. 1943- St&PR 91
Dostal, Robert Joseph 1947- WhoE 91
Dostart, Paul Joseph 1951- WhoEmL 91
Doster, Gayl William 1938- St&PR 91
Doster, Joseph C. 1928- WhoAm 90, WhoSSW 91
Dostoevskii, Fedor Mikhailovich 1821-1881 BioIn 16
Dostoevsky, Feodor 1821-1881 WrPh
Dostoevsky, Fyodor 1821-1881 AuBYP 90
Dostou, Steven St&PR 91
Dostoyevsky, Fyodor 1821-1881 BioIn 16, WorAlBi
Doswald, Herman Kenneth 1932- WhoAm 90
Doswell, Mary Cummings 1958- WhoAmW 91
Dote, Ralph BioIn 16
Doten, Elizabeth 1829-1913 EncO&P 3
Doten, George William 1923- WhoAm 90
Dothard, E. C. BioIn 16
Doto, Joseph Francis 1943- St&PR 91
Doto, Paul Jerome 1917- WhoE 91, WhoWor 91
Dotson, David Casto 1934- St&PR 91
Dotson, Donald L. 1938- WhoAm 90
Dotson, Gary BioIn 16
Dotson, George Stephen 1940- St&PR 91, WhoAm 90, WhoSSW 91
Dotson, James William 1959- BiDrAPA 89
Dotson, Jarine Ann 1953- St&PR 91
Dotson, John Louis, Jr. 1937- WhoAm 90
Dotson, Linda Sue 1951- WhoAmW 91
Dotson, Raymond Paul 1933- WhoWrEP 89
Dotson, Rich 1959- Ballpl 90
Dotson, Robert Charles 1946- WhoAm 90
Dotson, Robert E. 1936- St&PR 91
Dotson, Rodger A. 1948- St&PR 91
Dotson, Terry Lee 1950- St&PR 91
Dott, Jackson York 1958- St&PR 91
Dott, Robert Henry, Jr. 1929- WhoAm 90
Dott, Sharon Gail BiDrAPA 89
Dotts, M. Franklin 1929- WhoSSW 91
Dotts, Maryann J 1933- ConAu 30NR
Doty, Anne Elizabeth 1959- WhoAmW 91
Doty, Carl K. 1931- St&PR 91
Doty, Carolyn House 1941- WhoWrEP 89
Doty, Charles Stewart 1928- WhoAm 90
Doty, David Singleton 1929- WhoAm 90
Doty, Della Corrine 1945- WhoAmW 91
Doty, Donald D. 1928- St&PR 91
Doty, Donna Sue 1944- IntWWM 90
Doty, George E. 1918- St&PR 91
Doty, Gordon Leroy 1931- WhoAm 90
Doty, Gresdna Ann 1931- WhoSSW 91
Doty, Huberta M. 1904- St&PR 91
Doty, James Edward 1922- WhoAm 90
Doty, James Robert 1940- WhoAm 90
Doty, Jean Slaughter 1919- AuBYP 90
Doty, Jimmy Anderson 1950- WhoSSW 91
Doty, Matthew Emerson 1959- WhoEmL 91
Doty, Philip Edward 1943- WhoAm 90
Doty, Robert McIntyre 1933- WhoAmA 91
Doty, Robert Walter 1942- WhoAm 90
Doty, Robert William 1920- WhoAm 90
Doty, Rodney Oren 1948- St&PR 91
Doty, Roger F. 1934- St&PR 91
Doty, Ruth 1947- WhoWrEP 89
Doty, Sandra Ann 1965- WhoE 91
Doty, Wendell E. 1902- St&PR 91
Dotzauer, Earl G. 1931- St&PR 91
Douaihy, Saliba 1915- WhoAm 90, WhoAmA 91
Douaire, Daniel Lawlor 1934- St&PR 91
Douarinou, Alain BioIn 16
Doub, William Offutt 1931- WhoAm 90, WhoE 91, WhoWor 91
Doubek, Fayola Marie 1952- WhoEmL 91
Double Fantasy NewAgMG
Double Image NewAgMG
Doubleday, Abner 1819-1893 Ballpl 90, WorAlBi
Doubleday, Frank Nelson 1862-1934 WorAlBi
Doubleday, Nelson BioIn 16, WhoE 91
Doubleday, Veronica 1948- ConAu 129
Doubleday, William Alan 1951- WhoEmL 91
Doubledee, Sara Lynn 1946- WhoEmL 91
Doubler, Kenneth Francis 1946- WhoEmL 91
Doubles, Malcolm Carroll 1932- WhoSSW 91
Doubles, Michael J. 1945- St&PR 91
Douce, Patrice 1942- WhoWor 91
Douce, Wayne Richard 1928- WhoAm 90
Doucet, Michael BioIn 16
Doucet, Suzanne NewAgMG
Doucette, David Robert 1946- WhoE 91, WhoWor 91
Doucette, Edward I. 1929- St&PR 91
Doucette, Hubert Joseph 1930- St&PR 91
Doucette, James W. 1951- St&PR 91
Doucette, Joseph J. 1929- St&PR 91
Doucette, Mary-Alyce 1924- WhoAmW 91
Doucette, Michael David BiDrAPA 89
Doud, Donald Joseph 1940- St&PR 91
Doud, Jacqueline WhoAm 90
Doud, James John, Jr. 1938- St&PR 91
Doud, Robert Skinner 1931- St&PR 91
Doud, Wallace C. 1925- WhoAm 90
Doud, William F. 1935- St&PR 91
Doudera, Gerard 1932- WhoAmA 91
Doudna, Donald J. 1949- St&PR 91
Doudney, Sarah 1843-1926 FemiCLE
Doudoumopoulos, Alexander N 1924- BiDrAPA 89
Douenias, Natalie 1940- WhoAmA 91
Dougal, Arwin Adelbert 1926- WhoAm 90, WhoWor 91
Dougall, Lily 1858-1923 DcLB 92 [port], FemiCLE
Dougan, Diana Lady 1943- WhoAmW 91
Dougan, Paul Marriott 1938- St&PR 91
Dougan, Pauline Virginia 1928- St&PR 91
Dougan, Robert Ormes 1904- WhoAm 90
Doughan, James 1933- St&PR 91
Dougher, Colleen Marie 1962- WhoWrEP 89
Dougherty, Barbara Carolyne 1937- WhoAmW 91
Dougherty, Betsey Olenick 1950- WhoAmW 91
Dougherty, Brian James 1955- WhoEmL 91
Dougherty, Carolann Jackson 1957- WhoAmW 91
Dougherty, Cathy West 1956- WhoE 91
Dougherty, Charles 1850-1915 AmLegL
Dougherty, Charles John 1949- WhoAm 90
Dougherty, Charles Joseph 1919- WhoAm 90
Dougherty, Dana Dean Lesley WhoAmW 91
Dougherty, David J. 1936- St&PR 91
Dougherty, Dennis A. 1952- WhoEmL 91
Dougherty, Donald 1935- ODwPR 91
Dougherty, Donald Earl BiDrAPA 89
Dougherty, Donna 1958- WhoEmL 91
Dougherty, Douglas Wayne 1943- WhoAm 90
Dougherty, Elmer Lloyd, Jr. 1930- WhoAm 90
Dougherty, F. Jay 1950- WhoEmL 91
Dougherty, Flavian NewYTBS 90
Dougherty, Flavian 1913?-1990 ConAu 130
Dougherty, Flavian 1923-1990 BioIn 16
Dougherty, George Gehr, Jr. 1949- BiDrAPA 89
Dougherty, George Wighton 1921- WhoAm 90
Dougherty, H.W. 1916- St&PR 91
Dougherty, James 1926- WhoAm 90, WhoE 91, WhoWor 91
Dougherty, James Douglas 1936- St&PR 91, WhoAm 90, WhoE 91
Dougherty, James Henry 1936- St&PR 91
Dougherty, James Joseph 1951- WhoEmL 91
Dougherty, James Thomas 1935- St&PR 91
Dougherty, Jay Edwin 1959- WhoWrEP 89
Dougherty, John Archer 1958- WhoSSW 91
Dougherty, John Chrysostom, III 1915- WhoAm 90, WhoSSW 91, WhoWor 91
Dougherty, John F. 1912- St&PR 91
Dougherty, John J. 1925- St&PR 91
Dougherty, John Vincent 1950- WhoE 91
Dougherty, Jude Patrick 1930- WhoAm 90
Dougherty, June Eileen 1929- WhoAmW 91
Dougherty, Kathleen Clare 1956- BiDrAPA 89
Dougherty, Michael J. ODwPR 91
Dougherty, Molly Crocker 1944- WhoAmW 91
Dougherty, Molly Ireland 1949- WhoAmW 91, WhoEmL 91
Dougherty, Patsy 1876-1940 Ballpl 90
Dougherty, Paul BioIn 16
Dougherty, Paul John 1953- WhoEmL 91
Dougherty, Peter Hansen 1953- WhoE 91
Dougherty, Philip H. 1923-1988 BioIn 16
Dougherty, Ray 1942- WhoAmA 91
Dougherty, Richard Dean 1938- St&PR 91
Dougherty, Richard Hamlen 1952- WhoEmL 91
Dougherty, Richard M. BioIn 16
Dougherty, Richard Martin 1935- WhoAm 90
Dougherty, Robert Anthony 1928- WhoAm 90
Dougherty, Robert P. 1921- St&PR 91
Dougherty, Robert Ward 1945- St&PR 91
Dougherty, Rodolfo L. 1936- WhoWor 91
Dougherty, Ronald Jary 1936- St&PR 91
Dougherty, Russell Elliott 1920- St&PR 91, WhoAm 90, WhoWor 91
Dougherty, Samuel Allen 1917- WhoWrEP 89
Dougherty, Sherilyne Earnest 1950- WhoAmW 91
Dougherty, Thomas John 1933- WhoAm 90
Dougherty, Thomas Paul, Jr. 1948- WhoEmL 91

Dougherty, Ursel T. *ODwPR 91*
Dougherty, Ursel Thielbeule 1942- *WhoAmW 91, WhoWor 91*
Dougherty, William John 1933- *WhoAm 90*
Doughman, Donald J. 1933- *WhoAm 90*
Doughten, Gertrude S 1930- *BiDrAPA 89*
Doughten, Paul D 1955- *BiDrAPA 89*
Doughtie, Charles *AuBYP 90*
Doughton, Rufus Alexander 1857- *AmLegL*
Doughty, Charles Montagu 1843-1926 *BioIn 16*
Doughty, Dorothy *PenDiDA 89*
Doughty, George Franklin 1946- *WhoAm 90*
Doughty, Julian Orus 1933- *WhoSSW 91*
Doughty, Larry 1940- *WhoAm 90, WhoE 91*
Doughty, Michael Dean 1947- *WhoSSW 91*
Doughty, Richard E. 1938- *St&PR 91*
Doughty, Richard G. 1945- *WhoEmL 91*
Doughty, Robert Alan 1952- *ODwPR 91*
Doughty, Robert Allen 1945- *WhoAm 90, WhoWor 91*
Doughty, Susan Elaine 1960- *WhoEmL 91*
Douglas *WhNaAH*
Douglas, Captain *DcCanB 12*
Douglas, A. Vibert *BioIn 16*
Douglas, Aaron 1898-1979 *BioIn 16*
Douglas, Aaron 1900-1979 *WhoAmA 91N*
Douglas, Alan *BioIn 16*
Douglas, Amanda 1831-1916 *FemiCLE*
Douglas, Archibald 1929- *St&PR 91*
Douglas, Arthur *TwCCr&M 91*
Douglas, Arthur Eugene, Jr. 1934- *BiDrAPA 89*
Douglas, Barbara *ConAu 130*
Douglas, Barry *BioIn 16*
Douglas, Barry 1960- *IntWWM 90, PenDiMP*
Douglas, Bruce Lee 1925- *WhoAm 90*
Douglas, Bryce 1924- *WhoAm 90*
Douglas, Buster 1960?- *News 90 [port]*
Douglas, Carolyn Jory 1953- *BiDrAPA 89, WhoE 91*
Douglas, Cathie M. *WhoWrEP 89*
Douglas, Charles Albert 1946- *WhoSSW 91*
Douglas, Charles Francis 1930- *WhoAm 90*
Douglas, Charles G. 1942- *BioIn 16*
Douglas, Charles Gwynne, III 1942- *WhoAm 90, WhoE 91*
Douglas, Claire Lynette 1954- *WhoAmW 91*
Douglas, Clarence James, Jr. 1924- *WhoSSW 91*
Douglas, Clifford Eric 1958- *WhoEmL 91*
Douglas, Daniel Roger 1954- *St&PR 91*
Douglas, Diandra *BioIn 16*
Douglas, Donald B *BiDrAPA 89*
Douglas, Donald W. 1892-1981 *WorAlBi*
Douglas, Dorothy C. 1944- *St&PR 91*
Douglas, Douglas 1948- *St&PR 91*
Douglas, Dwight Oliver 1941- *WhoAm 90*
Douglas, Edna 1918- *WhoAm 90*
Douglas, Edwin Perry 1935- *WhoAmA 91*
Douglas, Eileen 1946- *WhoAmW 91*
Douglas, Eleanor *BiDEWW*
Douglas, Eleanor 1590-1652 *FemiCLE*
Douglas, Eleanor 1598-1652 *BioIn 16*
Douglas, Elizabeth Asche 1930- *WhoE 91*
Douglas, Ellen 1921- *WorAu 1980 [port]*
Douglas, Frank Fair 1945- *WhoAm 90*
Douglas, Frederic Huntington 1897-1956 *WhoAmA 91N*
Douglas, Frederick John 1928- *WhoAm 90*
Douglas, Gary Michael 1954- *WhoEmL 91*
Douglas, George 1825-1894 *DcCanB 12*
Douglas, George 1842-1893 *FemiCLE*
Douglas, George Norman 1868-1952 *BioIn 16*
Douglas, Gordon Watkins 1921- *WhoAm 90*
Douglas, Gregory A. *WhoWrEP 89*
Douglas, Harriet 1790-1872 *BioAmW*
Douglas, Helen Gahagan 1900-1980 *BioIn 16, NotWoAT, WorAlBi*
Douglas, Herbert Paul, Jr. 1922- *WhoAm 90, WhoWor 91*
Douglas, Herschel Lewis 1935- *WhoAm 90*
Douglas, Jack 1908-1989 *BioIn 16*
Douglas, James *NewYTBS 90 [port], WhoAm 90*
Douglas, James 1914- *WhoAm 90*
Douglas, James 1932- *IntWWM 90*
Douglas, James Henderson 1899-1988 *BioIn 16*
Douglas, James Holley 1951- *WhoE 91*
Douglas, James Stuart 1868-1949 *EncABHB 7 [port]*
Douglas, James W. 1951- *St&PR 91*
Douglas, Jocelyn Fielding 1927- *WhoAm 90*
Douglas, John *TwCCr&M 91*
Douglas, John Breed, III 1953- *WhoAm 90*
Douglas, John H. 1941- *St&PR 91*
Douglas, John Hoffmann 1920- *WhoE 91, WhoWor 91*
Douglas, John Robert Tomkys 1939- *WhoWor 91*
Douglas, John Scott *AuBYP 90*
Douglas, Johnny 1920- *IntWWM 90*
Douglas, Joseph Mahlon 1939- *BiDrAPA 89*
Douglas, Joseph Pickens, III 1946- *WhoEmL 91*
Douglas, Josephine *St&PR 91*
Douglas, Josephine 1928-1988 *AnObit 1988*
Douglas, Juliet 1962- *ConTFT 8 [port]*
Douglas, Kathleen Mary Harrigan 1950- *WhoSSW 91*
Douglas, Kathryn *AuBYP 90*
Douglas, Keith 1920-1944 *TwCLC 40 [port]*
Douglas, Kenneth 1922- *St&PR 91*
Douglas, Kenneth Dale 1943- *WhoSSW 91*
Douglas, Kenneth Jay 1922- *WhoAm 90*
Douglas, Kirk 1916- *BestSel 90-4 [port], BioIn 16*
Douglas, Kirk 1918- *WhoAm 90, WorAlBi*
Douglas, L J 1948- *WhoAmA 91*
Douglas, Lalette 1931- *WhoWrEP 89*
Douglas, Lauren Wright 1947- *ConAu 129*
Douglas, Lee *WhoWrEP 89*
Douglas, Leonard 1920- *SmATA X [port]*
Douglas, Leslie 1914- *St&PR 91, WhoAm 90*
Douglas, Leslie Gay 1949- *St&PR 91*
Douglas, Lester 1894-1961 *WhoAmA 91N*
Douglas, Lewis W. 1894-1974 *BioIn 16*
Douglas, Lewis Williams 1894-1974 *EncABHB 7 [port]*
Douglas, Lindsey Russell 1950- *WhoSSW 91*
Douglas, Lloyd Evans 1951- *WhoE 91*
Douglas, Louise Theresa 1955- *WhoAmW 91*
Douglas, Lucy Stovall 1959- *WhoAmW 91*
Douglas, Malcolm Angus 1931- *St&PR 91*
Douglas, Marion Joan 1940- *WhoAmW 91, WhoWor 91*
Douglas, Marjorie Jamison 1926- *WhoAmW 91*
Douglas, Marjory Stoneman *BioIn 16*
Douglas, Mary Tew 1921- *WhoAm 90*
Douglas, Melvyn 1901-1981 *WorAlBi*
Douglas, Michael *BioIn 16, MajTwCW, TwCCr&M 91*
Douglas, Michael 1902-1988 *SmATA X [port], -X*
Douglas, Michael 1944- *WorAlBi*
Douglas, Michael Kirk 1944- *WhoAm 90*
Douglas, Michael William 1945- *WhoEmL 91*
Douglas, Nancy L. 1940- *ODwPR 91*
Douglas, Nancy W. 1958- *St&PR 91*
Douglas, Nigel 1929- *IntWWM 90*
Douglas, Norman 1868-1952 *BioIn 16*
Douglas, O. 1877-1948 *FemiCLE*
Douglas, O. 1878-1948 *BioIn 16*
Douglas, Otis *BioIn 16*
Douglas, Paul 1907-1959 *WorAlBi*
Douglas, Paul H. 1892-1976 *WorAlBi*
Douglas, Paul W. 1926- *St&PR 91*
Douglas, Paul Wolff 1926- *WhoAm 90, WhoE 91*
Douglas, Peggy *ODwPR 91*
Douglas, Phil 1890-1952 *Ballpl 90, BioIn 16*
Douglas, R. Gordon 1898-1989 *BioIn 16*
Douglas, Richard Carl 1944- *WhoSSW 91*
Douglas, Robert Gordon, Jr. 1934- *WhoAm 90*
Douglas, Robert Langton *WhoAmA 91N*
Douglas, Rod D. 1925- *St&PR 91*
Douglas, Ronald George 1938- *WhoE 91*
Douglas, Ronald L. 1954- *St&PR 91*
Douglas, Roxanne Grace 1951- *WhoAmW 91*
Douglas, Roy 1924- *ConAu 30NR*
Douglas, Sarah *BioIn 16*
Douglas, Stephen A. 1813-1861 *WorAlBi*
Douglas, Stephen A. 1907-1967 *EncACom*
Douglas, Stephen Lane 1952- *WhoEmL 91, WhoSSW 91*
Douglas, Steve *NewAgMG*
Douglas, Sue McKnight 1939- *WhoSSW 91*
Douglas, Susan 1946- *WhoAmW 91, WhoEmL 91, WhoWor 91*
Douglas, Suzzanne *BioIn 16*
Douglas, T. C. 1904-1986 *BioIn 16*
Douglas, Teresa Lynn 1956- *WhoAmW 91*
Douglas, Terri 1957- *ODwPR 91*
Douglas, Thomas Clement 1904-1986 *BioIn 16*
Douglas, Thomas Edward 1937- *St&PR 91*
Douglas, Thomas Harrelson, III 1936- *St&PR 91*
Douglas, Thomas O'Neal 1935- *St&PR 91*
Douglas, Tom Howard 1957- *WhoAmA 91*
Douglas, Vincent Frederic 1949- *St&PR 91*
Douglas, Wade *WhoWrEP 89*
Douglas, Warren M 1924- *BiDrAPA 89*
Douglas, William C., Jr. 1955- *St&PR 91*
Douglas, William Ernest 1930- *WhoAm 90*
Douglas, William John 1938- *St&PR 91*
Douglas, William O. 1898-1980 *WorAlBi*
Douglas, William Orville 1898-1980 *AuBYP 90*
Douglas, William Randolph 1921- *WhoAm 90*
Douglas, William W *BiDrAPA 89*
Douglas, Zachariah Hicklin 1959- *BiDrAPA 89*
Douglas-Hamilton, Margaret M. *St&PR 91*
Douglas-Hill, Otto Douglas 1897-1972 *PenDiDA 89*
Douglas-Home, Alec 1903- *BioIn 16*
Douglas-Home, Charles Cospatrick 1937-1985 *DcNaB 1981*
Douglas-Home, David Alexander 1943- *WhoWor 91*
Douglass, Andrew Ian 1943- *St&PR 91*
Douglass, Beverly Jane 1951- *WhoAmW 91*
Douglass, Billie *ConAu 30NR*
Douglass, Bruce E. 1917- *WhoAm 90*
Douglass, Carl Dean 1925- *WhoAm 90*
Douglass, Carroll *BioIn 16*
Douglass, Edward Trent, Jr. 1906- *WhoSSW 91*
Douglass, Enid Hart 1926- *WhoAmW 91*
Douglass, Fenner 1921- *WhoAm 90*
Douglass, Frederick 1817?-1895 *BioIn 16, WorAlBi*
Douglass, George L. *AmLegL*
Douglass, Harry Robert 1937- *WhoAm 90, WhoSSW 91, WhoWor 91*
Douglass, James Frederick 1934- *WhoSSW 91*
Douglass, Jane Dempsey 1933- *WhoAm 90, WhoAmW 91*
Douglass, Jim *BioIn 16*
Douglass, John Michael 1939- *WhoAm 90*
Douglass, Kimberly Plaster 1960- *WhoSSW 91*
Douglass, Kingman 1923- *St&PR 91*
Douglass, Klondike 1872-1953 *Ballpl 90*
Douglass, Marion A, III *BiDrAPA 89*
Douglass, Melvin Isadore 1948- *WhoAm 90, WhoE 91*
Douglass, Paul 1904-1988 *BioIn 16*
Douglass, Ramona Elizabeth 1949- *WhoEmL 91, WhoWor 91*
Douglass, Robert Duncan 1941- *WhoE 91*
Douglass, Robert Raymond 1901-1988 *BioIn 16*
Douglass, Robert Royal 1931- *St&PR 91, WhoAm 90, WhoE 91*
Douglass, Robert Steven 1945- *WhoEmL 91*
Douglass, Roy William 1939- *WhoSSW 91*
Douglass, Sam Preston 1932- *St&PR 91*
Douglass, Shelley *BioIn 16*
Douglass, Truman B. 1901-1969 *WorAlBi*
Douglass, Wilford David 1927- *WhoSSW 91*
Douglass, William D. 1937- *St&PR 91*
Douglis, Avron 1918- *WhoAm 90*
Douhairet, Armande *BioIn 16*
Douke, Daniel W 1943- *WhoAmA 91*
Doukides, Panagiotis T *BiDrAPA 89*
Doulis, Thomas John 1931- *WhoWrEP 89*
Doull, James A, Jr. *BiDrAPA 89*
Doulos, Charles James 1935- *St&PR 91*
Doulton, Charles William 1923- *St&PR 91*
Doulton, Meridith *BioIn 16*
Doulton, Valerie Frances 1949- *WhoWor 91*
Douma, Harry Hein 1933- *WhoWor 91*
Douma, Jacob Hendrick 1912- *WhoAm 90*
Doumani, Shelley J *BiDrAPA 89*
Doumar, Robert George 1930- *WhoAm 90*
Doumas, Gena Kathleen 1963- *WhoAmW 91*
Doumas, Michael P. 1944- *St&PR 91*
Doumato, Lamia 1947- *WhoAmA 91, WhoE 91*
Doumer, Paul 1857-1932 *BiDFrPL*
Doumergue, Gaston 1863-1937 *BiDFrPL*
Doumlele, John A., Jr. 1946- *St&PR 91*
Doumlele, Ruth Hailey 1925- *WhoAmW 91, WhoSSW 91*
Doupe, Allison Jane *BiDrAPA 89*
Doupe, Joseph 1910- *EncO&P 3*
Douque, Willem Rudolf Carl 1942- *WhoWor 91*
Dourado, Autran 1926- *ConLC 60 [port], WorAu 1980 [port]*
Dourado, Esmeralda 1953- *WhoWor 91*
D'Ourches, Comte *EncO&P 3*
Douriez, Didier 1938- *WhoWor 91*
Dourif, Brad *BioIn 16*
Douris, George 1928- *ODwPR 91*
Dourlet, Ernest Francis 1924- *St&PR 91*
Dournovo, Pierre Alexandre 1945- *WhoWor 91*
Douskey, Franz 1941- *ConAu 129*
Douskey, Franz Thomas 1941- *WhoWrEP 89*
Doussan, Thomas H. 1931- *St&PR 91*
Doust, Arthur F. 1923- *St&PR 91*
Dout, Anne Jacqueline 1955- *WhoEmL 91*
Douthat, James Evans 1946- *WhoAm 90*
Douthit, Heather Maria 1959- *WhoAmW 91*
Douthit, Taylor 1901- *Ballpl 90*
Douthitt, Claude Alton 1928- *St&PR 91*
Douthitt, Shirley Ann 1947- *WhoAmW 91*
Douthwaite, Graham 1913- *WhoWrEP 89*
Doutt, Geraldine Moffatt 1927- *WhoWor 91*
Doutt, Richard Leroy 1916- *WhoAm 90*
Douty, Esther 1911- *AuBYP 90*
Douty, Horace Dale 1932- *WhoSSW 91*
Douty, Lucy Evelyn 1951- *WhoAmW 91*
Douty, Norman F 1899- *ConAu 31NR*
Douvan, Elizabeth 1926- *WhoAm 90*
Douville, Arthur John 1945- *St&PR 91*
Douville, Jean 1943- *St&PR 91*
Douville, Philip 1932- *St&PR 91*
Douwens, Carlos 1950- *WhoWor 91*
Douwes, Arnold 1906- *BioIn 16*
Douyon, Richard 1956- *BiDrAPA 89*
DoVale, Antonio Joseph, Jr. 1954- *WhoE 91, WhoWor 91*
Dovalina, Fernando, Jr. 1942- *WhoHisp 91*
Dovalina, Mario A., Jr. 1954- *St&PR 91*
Dovalina, Mario Alonzo 1924- *St&PR 91*
Do Valle, Cyro Eyer 1937- *WhoWor 91*
Dovberg, Norman Joseph 1946- *BiDrAPA 89*
Dove, Arthur Garfield 1880-1946 *BioIn 16, WhoAmA 91N*
Dove, Christopher Collier 1948- *St&PR 91*
Dove, Grant Alonza 1928- *St&PR 91, WhoAm 90*
Dove, Henry W *BiDrAPA 89*
Dove, Jeffrey Austin 1959- *WhoEmL 91*
Dove, Kathleen Meg Lindemann 1953- *WhoAmW 91*
Dove, Kenneth John 1935- *St&PR 91*
Dove, Richard Allan 1958- *WhoEmL 91*
Dove, Ricky Joe 1955- *WhoSSW 91*
Dove, Rita 1952- *WorAu 1980 [port]*
Dove, Rita Frances 1952- *WhoAm 90, WhoAmW 91, WhoWrEP 89*
Dove, Thomas Gene 1926- *St&PR 91*
Dove, Toni 1946- *WhoAmA 91*
Dove, White *WhoWrEP 89*
Dove, William E. 1937- *St&PR 91*
Dove, William Olson 1947- *WhoE 91*
Dove-Lowther, Sandra Elizabeth 1955- *WhoAmW 91*
Dovell, Diane *BioIn 16*
Dovenmuehle, Robert H 1924- *BiDrAPA 89*
Dover, James Burrell 1927- *WhoAm 90*
Dover, Joseph Yorke, Baron 1724-1792 *BioIn 16*
Dover, Kenneth James 1920- *WhoWor 91*
Dovey, Brian Hugh 1941- *WhoAm 90*
Dovey, W. C. *AmLegL*
Doviak, Robert F., II 1960- *WhoEmL 91, WhoSSW 91*
Dovima *BioIn 16, NewYTBS 90 [port]*
Dovlatov, Sergei *BioIn 16*
Dovlatov, Sergei 1941-1990 *ConAu 132, NewYTBS 90 [port]*
Dovlatov, Sergey 1941-1990 *WorAu 1980 [port]*
Dovorany, Richard J. 1946- *St&PR 91, WhoEmL 91*
Dovre, Paul John 1935- *WhoAm 90*
Dovring, Karin Elsa Ingeborg 1919- *WhoAmW 91, WhoWor 91*
Dovydenas, Elizabeth Dayton *BioIn 16*
Dow, Andrew Robert 1950- *BiDrAPA 89*
Dow, Arthur 1948- *WhoEmL 91*
Dow, Avard Morton, Sr. 1916- *St&PR 91*
Dow, Charles Henry 1851-1902 *BioIn 16*
Dow, Charles W. 1906-1989 *BioIn 16*
Dow, Daniel Gould 1930- *WhoAm 90*
Dow, Dorothy 1920- *IntWWM 90*
Dow, Edward *St&PR 91*
Dow, Frederick Neal 1840-1934 *AmLegL*
Dow, Frederick Warren 1917- *WhoAm 90*
Dow, Helen Jeannette 1926- *WhoAmA 91*
Dow, Herbert H. 1866-1930 *WorAlBi*
Dow, Herbert Henry 1866-1930 *BioIn 16*
Dow, Irving Apgar, Jr. 1920- *WhoE 91*
Dow, Janet A. *ODwPR 91*
Dow, Jean Louise 1955- *WhoAmW 91, WhoEmL 91, WhoWor 91*
Dow, Jerald R. 1939- *St&PR 91*
Dow, Kevin *St&PR 91*
Dow, Leslie Wright 1938- *WhoAmW 91*
Dow, Lois Weyman 1942- *WhoAmW 91, WhoE 91*
Dow, Mary Alexis 1949- *WhoAmW 91, WhoEmL 91*
Dow, Michael Craig 1947- *WhoAm 90*
Dow, Nelson Paxton 1901- *WhoSSW 91*
Dow, Patricia Ann Susan 1958- *IntWWM 90*
Dow, Peter Anthony 1933- *St&PR 91, WhoAm 90*
Dow, Peter Burton 1932- *St&PR 91*
Dow, Teresa Elmerick 1957- *WhoSSW 91*
Dow, Thomas W 1939- *BiDrAPA 89*

Dow, Tony Fares 1947- *WhoWor 91*
Dow, Tood Joseph *BioIn 16*
Dow, Wilbur Egerton, Jr. 1906- *WhoAm 90*
Dow, William Gould 1895- *WhoAm 90, WhoWor 91*
Dowaliby, Margaret Susanne 1924- *WhoAmW 91*
Doward, Bruce *BioIn 16*
Dowben, Carla Lurie 1932- *WhoAmW 91*
Dowben, Robert Morris 1927- *WhoAm 90*
Dowbenko, Uri 1951- *WhoWrEP 89*
Dowcett, James Michael 1949- *WhoEmL 91*
Dowd, A. Joseph 1929- *St&PR 91*
Dowd, Andrew Joseph 1929- *WhoAm 90*
Dowd, David Joseph 1924- *WhoAm 90*
Dowd, Donald G. 1933- *ODwPR 91*
Dowd, Edward J. 1934- *St&PR 91*
Dowd, Frances Smardo 1947- *WhoSSW 91*
Dowd, Harriet R. 1950- *St&PR 91*
Dowd, J. Richard 1956- *St&PR 91*
Dowd, James Edward 1922- *St&PR 91*
Dowd, Janice Lee 1948- *WhoAmW 91*
Dowd, Jeffrey Marc 1948- *St&PR 91*
Dowd, John Michael, Jr. 1935- *St&PR 91*
Dowd, Kenneth Lowell, Jr. 1940- *WhoAm 90*
Dowd, Kevin Michael 1961- *WhoEmL 91*
Dowd, Kevin P. 1948- *St&PR 91*
Dowd, Michael Burke 1958- *WhoWor 91*
Dowd, Michael Edward 1934- *St&PR 91*
Dowd, Morgan Daniel 1933- *WhoAm 90*
Dowd, Patrick 1813?-1891 *DcCanB 12*
Dowd, Peter J. 1942- *ODwPR 91*
Dowd, Peter Jerome 1942- *WhoAm 90, WhoWor 91*
Dowd, Robert 1937- *WhoAmA 91*
Dowd, Ronald 1914- *IntWWM 90*
Dowd, Tommy 1869-1933 *Ballpl 90*
Dowdall, Katherine *BiDEWW*
Dowdall, Mary Frances Harriet 1876-1939 *FemiCLE*
Dowdell, Dorothy Florence 1910- *WhoAmW 91*
Dowdell, Kevin Crawford 1961- *WhoE 91*
Dowdell, Lisa 1959- *ODwPR 91*
Dowden, Albert Ricker 1941- *St&PR 91, WhoAm 90, WhoWor 91*
Dowden, Anne Ophelia 1907- *WhoE 91*
Dowden, Anne Ophelia Todd 1907- *AuBYP 90, WhoAmA 91*
Dowden, Carroll Vincent 1933- *WhoAm 90*
Dowden, Charles Wingate 1955- *St&PR 91*
Dowden, George 1932- *WhoWrEP 89*
Dowden, Hester 1868-1949 *EncO&P 3*
Dowden, Richard Michael 1954- *WhoEmL 91*
Dowden, Thomas Clark 1935- *WhoSSW 91, WhoWor 91*
Dowden, Wilfred Sellers 1917- *WhoSSW 91*
Dowding, Clara M. 1928- *St&PR 91*
Dowding, Hugh Caswall 1882-1970 *WorAlBi*
Dowding, Hugh Caswall Tremenheere 1882-1970 *EncO&P 3*
Dowding, Nicholas *PenDiMP*
Dowding Duncan, Maria Lavonne 1954- *WhoAmW 91, WhoEmL 91*
Dowdle, James C. *BioIn 16*
Dowdle, John Nutie 1943- *WhoSSW 91*
Dowdle, John Robert 1938- *St&PR 91*
Dowdle, Nash James 1923- *St&PR 91*
Dowdle, Patrick Dennis 1948- *WhoEmL 91, WhoWor 91*
Dowds, Gertrude *AuBYP 90*
Dowds, John Joseph 1938- *WhoAm 90*
Dowdy, Helen *DcAfAmP, DrBlPA 90*
Dowdy, James T. 1960- *St&PR 91*
Dowdy, Joan Lee 1951- *IntWWM 90*
Dowdy, John Vernard 1912- *WhoSSW 91*
Dowdy, John Wesley 1912- *WhoAm 90*
Dowdy, John Wesley, Jr. 1935- *WhoWor 91*
Dowdy, Regera, Mrs. *ConAu 30NR*
Dowdy, Robert Eugene 1936- *St&PR 91*
Dowdy, Ronald Raymond 1944- *WhoAm 90*
Dowell, Anthony 1943- *WorAlBi*
Dowell, Anthony James 1943- *WhoAm 90, WhoWor 91*
Dowell, Boyd Max 1934- *WhoSSW 91*
Dowell, Coleman 1925-1985 *ConLC 60 [port], LiHiK*
Dowell, David Ray 1942- *WhoAm 90*
Dowell, David Scott 1960- *BiDrAPA 89*
Dowell, Earl Hugh 1937- *WhoAm 90*
Dowell, Flonnie 1947- *WhoEmL 91*
Dowell, George Howard *BiDrAPA 89*
Dowell, James 1942- *St&PR 91*
Dowell, James Calvin 1950- *WhoEmL 91*
Dowell, John E, Jr 1941- *WhoAmA 91*
Dowell, Michael Brendan 1942- *WhoAm 90*
Dowell, Patti Jo *WhoAmW 91*
Dowell, Richard Patrick 1934- *WhoSSW 91, WhoWor 91*
Dowell, Robert James 1942- *WhoSSW 91*
Dowell, Robert Vernon 1947- *WhoEmL 91*
Dowell, Travis Gordon, Sr. 1950- *WhoEmL 91*
Dowen, Thomas, Jr. 1931- *St&PR 91, WhoAm 90*
Dower, Catherine A. 1924- *IntWWM 90*
Dowey, James L. 1949- *St&PR 91*
Dowgiallo, William Walter 1955- *WhoEmL 91*
Dowgiewicz, Michael John 1952- *WhoEmL 91*
Dowgray, John Gray Laird, Jr. 1922- *WhoAm 90*
Dowie, Menie Muriel 1866-1945 *FemiCLE*
Dowis, Dee *BioIn 16*
Dowis, Lenore 1934- *WhoAmW 91*
Dowis, Richard *ODwPR 91*
Dowiyogo, Bernard 1946- *WhoWor 91*
Dowler, David P 1944- *WhoAmA 91*
Dowler, H. Logan 1939- *St&PR 91*
Dowless, Ernest Clark 1946- *WhoSSW 91*
Dowlin, Kenneth Everett 1941- *WhoAm 90*
Dowling, A Scott 1929- *BiDrAPA 89*
Dowling, Anthony J *BiDrAPA 89*
Dowling, Brendan Robert 1947- *WhoWor 91*
Dowling, Brian *BioIn 16*
Dowling, Eddie 1895- *OxCPMus*
Dowling, Edward Thomas 1938- *WhoAm 90*
Dowling, Hubert Aloysius 1921- *St&PR 91*
Dowling, Jacques MacCuiston 1906- *WhoAmW 91, WhoWor 91*
Dowling, James H. 1931- *ODwPR 91*
Dowling, James Stephen 1951- *WhoWrEP 89*
Dowling, Jean M *BiDrAPA 89*
Dowling, Jerome John 1935- *BiDrAPA 89*
Dowling, John Edward 1947- *WhoAm 90*
Dowling, John Elliott 1935- *WhoAm 90*
Dowling, Joseph Albert 1926- *WhoAm 90*
Dowling, Kevin Vincent 1951- *WhoSSW 91*
Dowling, Mary Ann 1939- *WhoSSW 91*
Dowling, Michael Anthony 1953- *WhoEmL 91*
Dowling, Michael John 1866-1921 *AmLegL*
Dowling, Patrick John 1935- *BiDrAPA 89*
Dowling, Ralph Wayne 1952- *St&PR 91, WhoSSW 91*
Dowling, Raymond J. 1928- *St&PR 91*
Dowling, Regina Nell 1930- *WhoE 91*
Dowling, Robert Murray 1932- *WhoE 91*
Dowling, Robert W 1895-1973 *WhoAmA 91N*
Dowling, Roderick A. 1940- *St&PR 91*
Dowling, Roderick Anthony 1940- *WhoAm 90*
Dowling, Thomas Allan 1941- *WhoAm 90*
Dowling, Thomas F. 1951- *St&PR 91*
Dowling, Walter 1905-1977 *BioIn 16*
Dowling, William P. 1933- *WhoAm 90*
Dowling-Bachand, Patricia Ann 1934- *WhoAmW 91*
Down, John Frederick 1946- *WhoEmL 91*
Down, William Blake 1921- *St&PR 91*
Downen, Byron H. 1924- *St&PR 91*
Downen, David Earl 1940- *St&PR 91, WhoAm 90*
Downen, Richard V. 1951- *St&PR 91*
Downen, Robert L. *ODwPR 91*
Downer, Anne *BiDEWW*
Downer, Eugene Debs, Jr. 1939- *WhoAm 90*
Downer, Jerol C. 1941- *St&PR 91*
Downer, Lesley 1949- *ConAu 131*
Downer, Marion 1892?-1971 *AuBYP 90*
Downer, Richard Fenton 1940- *WhoSSW 91*
Downer, William Clark 1936- *St&PR 91*
Downes, Andrew 1950- *IntWWM 90*
Downes, Edward 1924- *PenDiMP*
Downes, Edward O. D. 1911- *IntWWM 90*
Downes, Edward Olin Davenport 1911- *WhoAm 90*
Downes, Edward Thomas 1924- *IntWWM 90*
Downes, Gregory 1939- *St&PR 91*
Downes, John Michael 1954- *BiDrAPA 89*
Downes, Mollie Panter- 1906- *BioIn 16*
Downes, Quentin *TwCCr&M 91*
Downes, Rackstraw 1939- *WhoAm 90, WhoAmA 91*
Downes, Ralph 1904- *PenDiMP*
Downes, Ralph William 1904- *IntWWM 90*
Downes, Robert Eugene 1942- *St&PR 91*
Downes, Sue *BioIn 16*
Downey, Arthur Harold, Jr. 1938- *WhoAm 90*
Downey, Bernard L. 1923- *St&PR 91*
Downey, Brian William 1960- *WhoEmL 91*
Downey, Charles Hart 1930- *WhoSSW 91*
Downey, Daniel Granville, Jr. 1947- *St&PR 91*
Downey, D'Ann Barbara 1940- *WhoAmW 91*
Downey, Deoborah Ann 1958- *WhoAmW 91, WhoEmL 91, WhoWor 91*
Downey, Douglas Worth 1929- *St&PR 91*
Downey, Fairfax *NewYTBS 90*
Downey, Fairfax 1893-1990 *BioIn 16, CurBio 90N*
Downey, Fairfax D 1893-1990 *ConAu 131*
Downey, Fairfax Davis 1893- *AuBYP 90*
Downey, Frederick Fish 1948- *St&PR 91*
Downey, J. Patrick 1944- *St&PR 91*
Downey, James 1939- *WhoAm 90*
Downey, James J. *BioIn 16*
Downey, James Russell, Jr. 1948- *St&PR 91*
Downey, Janice Lee *BiDrAPA 89*
Downey, Jean Ann 1928- *St&PR 91*
Downey, Jennifer Ianthe *BiDrAPA 89*
Downey, Joan Carol 1931- *WhoAmW 91*
Downey, John 1927- *IntWWM 90*
Downey, John Charles 1926- *WhoAm 90*
Downey, John Francis 1914- *WhoAm 90*
Downey, John Harold 1956- *WhoEmL 91*
Downey, John Wilham 1927- *WhoAm 90*
Downey, Joseph Arthur 1923- *St&PR 91*
Downey, Joseph W. 1945- *WhoEmL 91*
Downey, Juan 1940- *WhoAmA 91*
Downey, Juan Antonio 1940- *WhoAm 90*
Downey, Judith Ann 1940- *WhoAmW 91*
Downey, Laurence J. 1950- *St&PR 91*
Downey, Loretta M. 1945- *WhoAm 90*
Downey, Michael J. *WhoAm 90*
Downey, Michael Peter 1942- *WhoAm 90*
Downey, Michael S *BiDrAPA 89*
Downey, Mortimer Leo, III 1936- *WhoAm 90*
Downey, Morton, Jr. *BioIn 16*
Downey, Patricia Ann 1953- *WhoAmW 91*
Downey, Patrick D. 1943- *St&PR 91*
Downey, Paul Anthony 1939- *WhoAm 90*
Downey, Peter 1956- *IntWWM 90*
Downey, Richard Ralph 1934- *WhoE 91, WhoWor 91*
Downey, Robert *ConTFT 8*
Downey, Robert, Jr. *BioIn 16*
Downey, Robert, Jr. 1965- *WorAlBi*
Downey, Stephen M. 1937- *ODwPR 91*
Downey, Stephen Wheeler 1839-1902 *AmLegL*
Downey, Thomas Joseph 1949- *WhoAm 90, WhoE 91*
Downey, Thomas R *BiDrAPA 89*
Downey, Tom 1884-1961 *Ballpl 90*
Downey, Tony *BioIn 16*
Downey, William Hugh 1945- *St&PR 91*
Downey, William John 1927- *St&PR 91*
Downham, John F. 1929- *St&PR 91*
Downham, Michael Thomas 1948- *St&PR 91*
Downie, Allan 1901-1988 *AnObit 1988*
Downie, David, IV 1953- *BiDrAPA 89*
Downie, John Francis 1934- *St&PR 91, WhoAm 90*
Downie, Leonard 1942- *BioIn 16*
Downie, Leonard, Jr. 1942- *WhoAm 90, WhoE 91, WhoWrEP 89*
Downie, Robert Charles 1947- *St&PR 91*
Downie, Romana Anzi 1925- *WhoAmA 91*
Downie, Sandra Carroll 1939- *WhoAmW 91*
Downie, Thomas Moore 1936- *St&PR 91*
Downing, Al 1941- *Ballpl 90*
Downing, Brian 1950- *Ballpl 90*
Downing, Brian T. 1947- *St&PR 91*
Downing, Brian Thomas 1947- *WhoAm 90*
Downing, Christine Rosenblatt 1931- *WhoAmW 91*
Downing, David 1943- *DrBlPA 90*
Downing, Donald Stuart 1946- *St&PR 91*
Downing, Edith E. 1857-1910? *BiDWomA*
Downing, Elizabeth Ann 1946- *WhoSSW 91*
Downing, Ellen M. 1961- *ODwPR 91*
Downing, Forrest William 1949- *WhoE 91*
Downing, George Walter 1924- *St&PR 91*
Downing, Grace Louise *BiDrAPA 89*
Downing, Gwendolyn 1960- *WhoAmW 91, WhoSSW 91*
Downing, Harriet *FemiCLE*
Downing, Henry F. 1846?-1928 *EarBlAP*
Downing, Jeffrey Melvin 1948- *St&PR 91*
Downing, Joan Forman 1934- *WhoAm 90*
Downing, John A. 1916- *St&PR 91*
Downing, John Edward 1937- *WhoSSW 91*
Downing, John Lawrence 1934- *WhoE 91*
Downing, Joseph H. 1955- *IntWWM 90*
Downing, Joseph J 1924- *BiDrAPA 89*
Downing, Linda Lou 1954- *WhoAmW 91*
Downing, Liz *BioIn 16*
Downing, Lowell M. 1916- *St&PR 91*
Downing, Lynda 1949- *WhoAmW 91*
Downing, Margaret Mary 1952- *WhoAmW 91*
Downing, Mary Brigetta 1938- *WhoAmW 91, WhoWrEP 89*
Downing, Paul A. 1925- *St&PR 91*
Downing, Robin Wilson 1962- *WhoAmW 91, WhoE 91*
Downing, William Edward 1940- *St&PR 91*
Downs, Andrew 1811-1892 *DcCanB 12*
Downs, Anthony 1930- *St&PR 91, WhoAm 90, WhoE 91*
Downs, Bernard Boozer, Jr. 1950- *WhoSSW 91*
Downs, Charity Ann 1943- *WhoAmW 91*
Downs, David Adam, Jr. 1955- *BiDrAPA 89*
Downs, David Lee 1929- *St&PR 91*
Downs, David R. 1937- *St&PR 91*
Downs, Diarmuid 1922- *WhoWor 91*
Downs, Douglas Walker 1945- *WhoAmA 91*
Downs, Florella McIntyre 1921- *WhoAmW 91*
Downs, Harry 1932- *St&PR 91, WhoAm 90*
Downs, Hartley H., III 1949- *WhoEmL 91, WhoWor 91*
Downs, Hugh 1921- *WorAlBi*
Downs, Hugh Malcolm 1921- *WhoAm 90, WhoE 91*
Downs, James H. 1927- *St&PR 91*
Downs, James L. 1940- *St&PR 91*
Downs, James William 1927- *WhoE 91*
Downs, Jerral Wayne 1943- *St&PR 91*
Downs, Joetta 1944- *WhoAmW 91*
Downs, John Henry 1919- *WhoE 91*
Downs, Jon Franklin 1938- *WhoSSW 91, WhoWor 91*
Downs, Joseph Edward 1932- *WhoSSW 91*
Downs, Kathleen Anne 1951- *WhoAmW 91, WhoEmL 91*
Downs, Kelly 1960- *Ballpl 90*
Downs, Larry R. 1949- *St&PR 91*
Downs, Linda Anne 1945- *WhoAmA 91*
Downs, Linn Hedwig 1954- *WhoEmL 91*
Downs, Mel 1933- *St&PR 91*
Downs, Michael Charles 1941- *WhoSSW 91*
Downs, Ramona Jo 1848- *WhoAmW 91*
Downs, Richard Scott 1947- *St&PR 91*
Downs, Richard Tinsley 1947- *WhoSSW 91*
Downs, Robert Bingham 1903- *WhoAm 90*
Downs, Robert C.S. 1937- *WhoWrEP 89*
Downs, Robert John 1936- *St&PR 91*
Downs, Shirley Gwinn 1936- *WhoAmW 91*
Downs, Steven Edward 1960- *WhoE 91, WhoEmL 91, WhoWor 91*
Downs, Stuart Clifton 1950- *WhoAmA 91*
Downs, Susan Pauline 1950- *WhoAmW 91*
Downs, Thomas M. 1960- *WhoSSW 91*
Downs, Thomas Michael 1943- *WhoAm 90, WhoE 91*
Downs, Wilbur George 1913- *WhoE 91*
Downum, Lawrence Morgan, Jr. 1939- *St&PR 91*
Dowriche, Anne *BiDEWW, FemiCLE*
Dows, David Alan 1928- *WhoAm 90*
Dowse, Granton Hall, Jr. 1911- *St&PR 91*
Dowsett, Connie M. 1955- *St&PR 91*
Dowsett, Patrick W. 1946- *St&PR 91*
Dowsett, Robert Chipman 1929- *St&PR 91, WhoAm 90*
Dowsett, William J. 1918- *St&PR 91*
Dowson, Ernest 1867-1900 *WorAlBi*
Dox, Ida 1927- *WhoE 91*
Doxsee, Lawrence Edward 1934- *WhoAm 90*
Doyama, Masao 1927- *WhoWor 91*
Doyle, Alfred Alan 1964- *WhoEmL 91*
Doyle, Arthur Conan 1859-1930 *AuBYP 90, BioIn 16, EncO&P 3, EncPaPR 91, MajTwCW, SpyFic, TwCCr&M 91, WorAlBi*
Doyle, Arthur J. 1923- *St&PR 91*
Doyle, Arthur James 1923- *WhoAm 90*
Doyle, Arthur Louis 1933- *WhoE 91*
Doyle, Beverly Ann 1945- *WhoAmW 91*
Doyle, Billy 1881-1939 *Ballpl 90*
Doyle, Brian 1935- *ChlLR 22 [port]*
Doyle, Brian Bowles 1941- *BiDrAPA 89*
Doyle, Brian King 1957- *St&PR 91*
Doyle, Carl 1912-1951 *Ballpl 90*
Doyle, Charles Thomas 1934- *WhoSSW 91*
Doyle, Charlotte Lackner 1937- *WhoAm 90*
Doyle, Conan 1859-1930 *BioIn 16*
Doyle, Constance Talcott Johnston 1945- *WhoAmW 91, WhoWor 91*
Doyle, Daniel Patrick 1944- *WhoE 91*
Doyle, Danny 1917- *Ballpl 90*
Doyle, David Allen 1959- *WhoSSW 91*
Doyle, Donald Earl 1930- *St&PR 91*
Doyle, Donovan *AuBYP 90*
Doyle, Eugenie Fleri 1921- *WhoAm 90*
Doyle, Frank Lawrence 1926- *WhoSSW 91*
Doyle, Frank P. 1931- *St&PR 91*
Doyle, Frank Stephen 1935- *St&PR 91*
Doyle, Frederick Joseph 1920- *WhoAm 90*
Doyle, George Edward 1948- *St&PR 91*
Doyle, George F *BiDrAPA 89*
Doyle, Gerard Francis 1942- *WhoAm 90*

Doyle, Harry A 1945- *BiDrAPA 89*
Doyle, Hugh 1876-1925 *Ballpl 90*
Doyle, Irene Elizabeth 1920- *WhoAmW 91*
Doyle, Jack 1869-1958 *Ballpl 90*
Doyle, Jack 1953- *WhoEmL 91*
Doyle, James Alexander 1904- *WhoAm 90*
Doyle, James Aloysius 1921- *WhoAm 90*
Doyle, James Edward 1931- *St&PR 91*
Doyle, James Edwin 1902-1989 *BioIn 16*
Doyle, James F. 1952- *St&PR 91*
Doyle, James M., Jr. 1932- *St&PR 91*
Doyle, James Paul 1952- *WhoE 91*
Doyle, James Stephen 1935- *WhoSSW 91*
Doyle, James Thomas 1933- *St&PR 91, WhoAm 90*
Doyle, Jeanne Marian *BiDrAPA 89*
Doyle, Jennifer Lydia 1953- *WhoAmW 91*
Doyle, Jerome 1909-1989 *BioIn 16*
Doyle, Joe 1941- *WhoAmA 91*
Doyle, John *MajTwCW*
Doyle, John 1955- *St&PR 91*
Doyle, John A. 1944- *St&PR 91*
Doyle, John Edward, III *BiDrAPA 89*
Doyle, John Laurence 1931- *WhoAm 90*
Doyle, John Lawrence 1939- *WhoAm 90, WhoAmA 91*
Doyle, John Robert, Jr. 1910- *WhoAm 90, WhoSSW 91, WhoWor 91*
Doyle, Joseph Anthony 1920- *WhoAm 90*
Doyle, Joseph Theobald 1918- *WhoAm 90*
Doyle, Joyce Ann 1937- *WhoAm 90, WhoAmW 91, WhoE 91*
Doyle, Judith Stovall 1940- *WhoAmW 91*
Doyle, Judith Warner 1943- *WhoAmW 91*
Doyle, Justin Emmett 1935- *WhoAm 90*
Doyle, Katherine Lee Lee 1932- *WhoAm 90, WhoAmW 91*
Doyle, Kathleen Marie 1937- *WhoE 91*
Doyle, Kevin F. 1934- *St&PR 91*
Doyle, Kevin John 1943- *WhoAm 90, WhoE 91*
Doyle, King 1922- *St&PR 91*
Doyle, L.F. Boker 1931- *St&PR 91*
Doyle, Larry 1886-1974 *Ballpl 90 [port], BioIn 16*
Doyle, Laura *BiDrAPA 89*
Doyle, Lawrence Sawyer 1943- *St&PR 91*
Doyle, Lori *ODwPR 91*
Doyle, Marcia Ann 1943- *WhoAmW 91*
Doyle, Margaret McCaffrey 1961- *WhoEmL 91*
Doyle, Mary Ellen 1938- *WhoAmA 91*
Doyle, Mary Glading 1925- *WhoAmW 91*
Doyle, Mathias Francis 1933- *WhoAm 90, WhoE 91*
Doyle, Matthew Wallace 1958- *WhoWor 91*
Doyle, Michael *BioIn 16*
Doyle, Michael Anthony 1937- *WhoAm 90*
Doyle, Michael Francis 1951- *WhoE 91*
Doyle, Michael James 1941- *St&PR 91*
Doyle, Michael O'Brien 1948- *WhoSSW 91*
Doyle, Mills Henry, III 1958- *WhoSSW 91*
Doyle, Morris McKnight 1909- *WhoAm 90*
Doyle, Ned 1902-1989 *BioIn 16*
Doyle, Owen Paul 1925- *St&PR 91*
Doyle, P. Jill 1955- *WhoAmW 91*
Doyle, Patricia Anne 1953- *WhoAmW 91*
Doyle, Patrick John 1926- *WhoAm 90*
Doyle, Patrick L. 1929- *St&PR 91*
Doyle, Patrick Lee 1929- *WhoAm 90*
Doyle, Patrick Thomas 1941- *WhoWor 91*
Doyle, Patrick William 1924- *St&PR 91*
Doyle, Paul A. 1925- *WhoWrEP 89*
Doyle, Peter Thomas 1928- *St&PR 91*
Doyle, Richard J. *WhoAm 90*
Doyle, Richard James 1923- *WhoAm 90*
Doyle, Richard L. 1926-1988 *BioIn 16*
Doyle, Robert Alan *BiDrAPA 89*
Doyle, Roland M. 1930- *St&PR 91*
Doyle, Sam 1906-1985 *MusmAFA*
Doyle, Sheila Marie 1958- *WhoAmW 91*
Doyle, Slow Joe 1881-1947 *Ballpl 90*
Doyle, Theresa Lipari 1957- *WhoAmW 91*
Doyle, Thomas James, III 1935- *St&PR 91*
Doyle, Thomas L 1925- *BiDrAPA 89*
Doyle, Tom *BioIn 16*
Doyle, Tom 1928- *WhoAmA 91, WhoE 91*
Doyle, Wilfred Emmett 1913- *WhoAm 90*
Doyle, William 1942- *ConAu 130*
Doyle, William Burroughs, Jr. 1959- *WhoEmL 91*
Doyle, William Edward 1923- *St&PR 91*
Doyle, William Jay, II 1928- *WhoWor 91*
Doyle, William Patrick 1932- *WhoSSW 91*
Doyle, William Stowell 1944- *WhoAm 90, WhoWor 91*
Doyle, William Thomas 1925- *WhoAm 90*
Doyle, Zita Maria 1961- *WhoAmW 91*
Doyle-Farrell, Anne J. 1948- *WhoAmW 91*
D'Oyly Carte, Bridget 1908-1985 *DcNaB 1981*
Doyon, Gerard Maurice 1923- *WhoAmA 91*
Doyon, Michael *St&PR 91*
Doza, Lawrence O. 1938- *St&PR 91, WhoAm 90*
Dozier, Ann Marie 1954- *WhoEmL 91*
Dozier, Brent A. *WhoWrEP 89*
Dozier, Bruce Emmitt 1948- *WhoEmL 91*
Dozier, David Charles, Jr. 1938- *WhoAm 90*
Dozier, Donna *ODwPR 91*
Dozier, Glenn Joseph 1950- *WhoAm 90*
Dozier, Graham Pinson, III 1932- *St&PR 91*
Dozier, Herbert Lee, Jr. 1936- *WhoSSW 91*
Dozier, James Lee 1931- *WhoAm 90*
Dozier, Jesse Emmett, Jr. *BiDrAPA 89*
Dozier, Julian D. 1943- *St&PR 91*
Dozier, Ollin Kemp 1929- *St&PR 91*
Dozier, Peter Marquis *BiDrAPA 89*
Dozier, Thomas Jefferson 1954- *WhoEmL 91*
Dozier, Velma Davis 1901-1988 *BioIn 16*
Dozier, William 1908- *WhoAm 90*
Dozier, William Everett, Jr. 1922- *WhoAm 90*
Dozoretz, Jerry 1947- *WhoEmL 91*
Dozoretz, Linda *ODwPR 91*
Dozoretz, Louis *BiDrAPA 89*
Dozoretz, Ronald I *BiDrAPA 89*
Dr. A *MajTwCW*
Dr Brute 1940- *WhoAmA 91*
Dr. J *BioIn 16*
Dr. Judy *ConAu 132*
Dr. Science *ConAu 131*
Draayer, Jerry P. 1942- *WhoAm 90*
Draba, Roman A. 1953- *St&PR 91*
Drabanski, Emily Ann 1952- *WhoAmW 91*
Drabb, Michael J. 1933- *St&PR 91*
Drabble, Bernard James 1925- *WhoAm 90*
Drabble, Margaret 1939- *BioIn 16, FemiCLE, MajTwCW, WhoAm 90, WhoWor 91, WorAlBi*
Drabeck, Bernard A. 1932- *ConAu 129*
Drabek, Doug 1962- *Ballpl 90*
Drabek, Paula Jane 1942- *WhoSSW 91*
Drabinsky, Garth 1948- *BioIn 16*
Drabinsky, Garth H. 1948- *St&PR 91*
Drabkin, Irving L. 1920- *St&PR 91*
Drabkin, Lester Y. 1918- *St&PR 91*
Drabkin, Murray 1928- *WhoAm 90*
Drabkin, Naomi Weiss 1932- *BiDrAPA 89*
Drabkin, Stella 1900-1976 *WhoAmA 91N*
Drabowicz, Barbara Linnea 1953- *WhoEmL 91*
Drabowsky, Moe 1935- *Ballpl 90*
Drach, George Wisse 1935- *WhoAm 90*
Drach, John Charles 1939- *WhoAm 90*
Drach, Michel *NewYTBS 90*
D'Rachael *NewAgMG*
Drachkovitch, Milorad M. 1921- *WhoAm 90*
Drachler, Norman 1912- *WhoAm 90*
Drachman, Daniel Bruce 1932- *WhoAm 90*
Drachman, David Alexander 1932- *WhoAm 90*
Drachman, Harold 1926- *St&PR 91*
Drachman, Theodore S. 1904-1988 *BioIn 16*
Drachmann, Holger 1846-1908 *DcScanL*
Drachnik, Catherine Meldyn 1924- *WhoWor 91*
Drack, Paul Edward 1928- *St&PR 91*
Drackett, Phil 1922- *BioIn 16*
Dracopoulos, Constantine Andreas 1929- *WhoWor 91*
Dracula *EncO&P 3*
Dracula 1431-1476 *BioIn 16*
Draddy, Vincent de Paul *NewYTBS 90 [port]*
Draeger, John Carl *BiDrAPA 89*
Draeger, Wayne Harold 1946- *St&PR 91, WhoAm 90*
Draenger, Shimshon 1917-1943? *BioIn 16*
Draenger, Tova 1917-1943? *BioIn 16*
Draffin, Cyril William, Jr. 1950- *St&PR 91*
Drag, Michelle Mary 1963- *WhoAmW 91*
Drage, Michelle S. 1965- *WhoAmW 91*
Drage, Starla Rae 1932- *WhoAmW 91*
Drager, Bertha Ours 1905- *WhoSSW 91*
Drager, Nick 1949- *WhoWor 91*
Dragesco, Jean *BioIn 16*
Dragging Canoe 1730?-1792 *EncCRAm, WhNaAH*
Dragich, Theodore 1925- *St&PR 91*
Dragics, David Lee 1945- *WhoEmL 91*
Dragisic, John 1940- *St&PR 91*
Drago, Dick 1945- *Ballpl 90*
Drago, Dorothy Ann 1946- *WhoE 91*
Drago, Joseph 1950- *St&PR 91*
Drago, Russell Stephen 1928- *WhoAm 90*
Dragoiu, John A. 1947- *St&PR 91*
Dragomir *WomWR*
Dragon, Carmen 1914-1984 *OxCPMus*
Dragon, Daryl 1942- *WorAlBi*
Dragon, Elizabeth Alice 1948- *WhoEmL 91*
Dragon, Normand *BiDrAPA 89*
Dragon, William, Jr. 1942- *St&PR 91, WhoAm 90*
Dragone, A. George 1939- *WhoAm 90*
Dragone, Allan R. 1926- *WhoE 91*
Dragone, Allan Rudolph 1926- *St&PR 91*
Dragonette, Joseph J. 1937- *ODwPR 91*
Dragonetti, Domenico 1763-1846 *PenDiMP*
Dragoni, John Ralph 1925- *St&PR 91*
Dragonwagon, Crescent *BioIn 16*
Dragonwagon, Crescent 1952- *WhoAm 90, WhoEmL 91*
Dragoo, Don W. 1925-1988 *BioIn 16*
Dragoo, John William 1949- *WhoEmL 91*
Dragotta, Richard *WhoAm 90*
Dragotta, Robert Gene 1950- *WhoE 91*
Dragoumis, James 1940- *WhoAm 90*
Dragoumis, Paul 1934- *St&PR 91, WhoAm 90*
Dragt, Alexander James 1936- *WhoAm 90*
Dragun, Osvaldo *BioIn 16*
Dragun, Osvaldo 1929- *HispWr 90*
Draheim, Edward Ray 1927- *St&PR 91*
Drahmann, Theodore 1926- *WhoAm 90*
Drahomira *WomWR*
Drahos, Leslie Ann 1942- *WhoWrEP 89*
Drain, Albert Sterling 1925- *WhoAm 90*
Drain, John Charles 1844?-1891 *AmLegL*
Drain, John F. 1932- *St&PR 91*
Drain, Lee 1925- *WhoAm 90*
Drain, Trisha McMahon *WhoAmW 91*
Drainie, Bronwyn 1945- *ConAu 129*
Drake, Albert Estern 1927- *WhoAm 90*
Drake, Alfred 1914- *OxCPMus*
Drake, Anne M. 1931- *ODwPR 91*
Drake, Barbara Leigh 1950- *WhoEmL 91*
Drake, Bonnie *ConAu 30NR*
Drake, Bryan Ernest Hare 1925- *IntWWM 90*
Drake, Charles Lum 1924- *WhoAm 90*
Drake, Charles Richard 1924- *St&PR 91*
Drake, Charles Whitney 1926- *WhoAm 90*
Drake, Cheryl Susan 1950- *WhoEmL 91*
Drake, Christine Spata 1946- *WhoWrEP 89*
Drake, Christopher *ODwPR 91*
Drake, David Allen 1945- *WhoWrEP 89*
Drake, David Allyn 1937- *WhoSSW 91*
Drake, David Rice 1946- *WhoEmL 91*
Drake, Delos 1886-1965 *Ballpl 90*
Drake, Donald Charles 1935- *WhoAm 90*
Drake, Edwin L. 1819-1880 *WorAlBi*
Drake, Eileen *ODwPR 91*
Drake, Elisabeth Mertz 1936- *WhoAm 90*
Drake, Ellen Tan 1927- *WhoAmW 91*
Drake, Emerson Hadley 1916- *WhoE 91*
Drake, Eric S. 1948- *WhoE 91*
Drake, Ervin Maurice 1919- *IntWWM 90*
Drake, Fabia *NewYTBS 90 [port]*
Drake, Fabia 1904-1990 *BioIn 16, ConTFT 8*
Drake, Fenton George *BiDrAPA 89*
Drake, Francis 1540?-1596 *BioIn 16, WorAlBi*
Drake, Francis 1543?-1596 *EncCRAm*
Drake, Francis E., Jr. 1915- *St&PR 91*
Drake, Frank Donald 1930- *WhoAm 90*
Drake, Frank R, Sr. *BiDrAPA 89*
Drake, Frank Rodney, Jr. 1940- *BiDrAPA 89*
Drake, Franklin G. 1928- *St&PR 91*
Drake, Galen *BioIn 16*
Drake, George Albert 1934- *WhoAm 90*
Drake, George Warren James 1939- *IntWWM 90*
Drake, Grace L. 1926- *WhoAmW 91*
Drake, Harrington 1919- *St&PR 91, WhoAm 90*
Drake, Hudson Billings 1935- *WhoAm 90*
Drake, Jack *BioIn 16*
Drake, James 1946- *WhoAmA 91*
Drake, James A. 1944- *ConAu 130*
Drake, Jessica *BioIn 16*
Drake, Jimmy D. 1943- *St&PR 91*
Drake, John 1927- *St&PR 91*
Drake, John Walter 1932- *WhoAm 90, WhoSSW 91*
Drake, John Warren 1930- *WhoAm 90*
Drake, Judith *BiDEWW, FemiCLE*
Drake, Kingsley D. 1937- *St&PR 91*
Drake, Larry *BioIn 16*
Drake, Leah Bodine 1904-1964 *LiHiK*
Drake, Linda Kay 1957- *WhoAmW 91, WhoEmL 91, WhoWor 91*
Drake, Lucius C., Jr. 1946- *WhoEmL 91*
Drake, Lynn Annette 1949- *WhoAmW 91*
Drake, Marsha Lorraine 1939- *WhoWrEP 89*
Drake, Melvin A *BiDrAPA 89*
Drake, Meredith *BioIn 16*
Drake, Michael L. 1936- *St&PR 91*
Drake, Michael W. 1953- *St&PR 91*
Drake, Michael Wayne 1953- *WhoEmL 91*
Drake, Nicholas *WhoWrEP 89*
Drake, Pamela Dawn *BiDrAPA 89*
Drake, Pamela O'Bryant 1957- *WhoEmL 91*
Drake, Patricia Ann Glasscock 1955- *WhoAmW 91*
Drake, Peter 1957- *WhoAmA 91*
Drake, Philip Meurer 1925- *WhoAm 90*
Drake, Rex Eugene 1926- *St&PR 91*
Drake, Richard Matthews 1906- *WhoAm 90*
Drake, Robert B. 1913- *St&PR 91*
Drake, Robert Eldon, Jr. 1949- *BiDrAPA 89*
Drake, Robert Grant 1945- *BiDrAPA 89*
Drake, Robert Mortimer, Jr. 1920- *WhoAm 90*
Drake, Rodman Leland 1943- *St&PR 91, WhoAm 90*
Drake, Sarah Frances Ashford 1943- *WhoAmW 91, WhoWor 91*
Drake, St. Clair 1911-1990 *BioIn 16, ConAu 131, CurBio 90N, NewYTBS 90 [port]*
Drake, Stan 1921- *EncACom*
Drake, Stillman 1910- *WhoAm 90*
Drake, Sylvia *WhoWrEP 89*
Drake, Sylvie 1930- *BioIn 16, NotWoAT, WhoAm 90*
Drake, Vaughn Paris, Jr. 1918- *WhoSSW 91*
Drake, William Edwin, Jr. 1954- *WhoEmL 91*
Drake, William Everett 1939- *WhoAm 90*
Drake, William Frank, Jr. 1932- *St&PR 91, WhoAm 90*
Drake, William McClellan 1932- *WhoAm 90*
Drake, William W. 1922- *St&PR 91*
Drake, William Whiting, Jr. 1922- *WhoAm 90*
Drake-Brockman, Henrietta 1901-1968 *FemiCLE*
Drakeman, Donald Lee 1953- *WhoAm 90, WhoEmL 91*
Drakopoulou, Theone 1883-1968 *EncCoWW*
Drakos, Charles Peter 1945- *WhoAm 90*
Drakos, Irene Sasso 1932- *WhoAmW 91*
Drakos, Nicholas Anthony *BiDrAPA 89*
Dralle, Carl William 1926- *St&PR 91*
Dramatics, The *EncPR&S 89*
Drammis, Hilary Patricia 1954- *WhoAmW 91*
Dran, Robert Joseph 1947- *WhoAm 90, WhoEmL 91*
Drance, Elisabeth Joan 1959- *BiDrAPA 89*
Drane, Edwin Byrd 1949- *WhoSSW 91*
Drane, Walter Harding 1915- *WhoAm 90*
Draney, Cyril L. 1939- *St&PR 91*
Dranginis, Peter J. 1944- *St&PR 91*
Dranias, Dean A. 1936- *ODwPR 91*
Dranias, Dean Anthony 1936- *WhoAm 90*
Dranoff, Linda Silver 1939- *ConAu 129*
Dranow, John Theodore 1948- *WhoEmL 91, WhoWrEP 89*
Dransfield, Michael 1948-1973 *ConAu 30NR*
Drantz, Veronica Ellen 1943- *WhoAmW 91*
Drapeau, Donald Francis 1932- *St&PR 91*
Drapeau, Pamela Kathryn *BiDrAPA 89*
Drapeau, Phillip David 1938- *St&PR 91, WhoAm 90*
Drapeau, Stanislas 1821-1893 *DcCanB 12*
Drapell, Joseph 1940- *WhoAmA 91*
Draper, Barbara Ann 1943- *WhoAmW 91*
Draper, Brice M. 1937- *St&PR 91*
Draper, Cecil R. 1914- *St&PR 91*
Draper, Cecil Vanoy 1940- *St&PR 91*
Draper, Charles 1869-1952 *PenDiMP*
Draper, Colin J. 1924- *St&PR 91*
Draper, Daniel Clay 1920- *WhoAm 90*
Draper, David Elliott 1943- *IntWWM 90*
Draper, Dorothy 1889-1969 *BioAmW, BioIn 16*
Draper, E. Linn *BioIn 16*
Draper, E. Linn, Jr. 1942- *St&PR 91, WhoSSW 91*
Draper, Earle Sumner 1893- *WhoAm 90*
Draper, Edgar 1926- *BiDrAPA 89*
Draper, Edith Augusta *BioIn 16*
Draper, Eileen Marie Adams 1954- *WhoWrEP 89*
Draper, Everett T., Jr. 1939- *WhoE 91*
Draper, Frances E. 1956- *St&PR 91*
Draper, Frances M. 1947- *St&PR 91*
Draper, Frances Murphy 1947- *WhoEmL 91*
Draper, Francis Collier 1837-1894 *DcCanB 12*
Draper, Gary James 1957- *WhoEmL 91*
Draper, Hal *BioIn 16*
Draper, Hal *NewYTBS 90*
Draper, Hal 1914-1990 *ConAu 130*
Draper, Haydn 1889-1934 *PenDiMP*
Draper, James David 1943- *WhoAm 90*
Draper, James Ross 1938- *St&PR 91*
Draper, James Wilson 1926- *WhoAm 90*
Draper, John Clayton 1945- *WhoE 91*
Draper, John H., III 1939- *St&PR 91*
Draper, John William Christopher 1922- *WhoE 91*
Draper, Josiah Everett 1915- *WhoAmA 91*
Draper, Kenneth Harry *BiDrAPA 89*
Draper, Line Bloom *WhoAm 90, WhoSSW 91, WhoWor 91*

Draper, Margaret Green 1730?-1807? BioIn 16
Draper, Mary Lytton WhoAmW 91
Draper, Muriel 1886-1952 FemiCLE
Draper, Nancy AuBYP 90
Draper, Norman Richard 1931- WhoAm 90
Draper, Polly BioIn 16, ConTFT 8
Draper, Randall Edwin BiDrAPA 89
Draper, Ronald John 1928- BiDrAPA 89
Draper, Ruth 1884-1956 BioAmW, BioIn 16, NotWoAT
Draper, Theodore 1912- WhoAm 90
Draper, Verden Rolland 1916- WhoAm 90
Draper, William David 1949- WhoSSW 91
Draper, William Franklin 1912- WhoAm 90, WhoAmA 91, WhoE 91
Draper, William Henry 1894-1974 BioIn 16
Draper, William Henry, III 1928- WhoAm 90
Drapkin, Arnold Howard 1931- WhoAm 90
Drapkin, D. G. WhoAm 90
Drasar, Pavel 1948- WhoWor 91
Drasco, Dennis J. 1948- WhoEmL 91
Drasen, Richard F. 1930- ODwPR 91
Drasher, Glenn D. ODwPR 91
Drasin, Dena Kippen 1940- BiDrAPA 89
Draskoczy, Paul R BiDrAPA 89
Draskovich, Zlatana Jennie 1948- WhoAmW 91
Drasner, Robert Joseph 1949- WhoEmL 91
Drassinower, Samuel Boris BiDrAPA 89
Drattell, Deborah WhoAmW 91
Drattell, Eric Marc 1958- WhoEmL 91
Draucker, Claire Burke 1955- WhoAmW 91
Drauden, Gail 1948- WhoEmL 91
Draudt, Donald A. 1925- St&PR 91
Draudt, Richard J. 1948- St&PR 91
Draughon, Edwin Smith, Jr. BiDrAPA 89
Draughon, Scott Wilson 1952- WhoEmL 91
Draughon, Terry Wayne 1947- St&PR 91
Draus, Frank John 1929- WhoAm 90
Draut, John Edward Paul 1950- WhoEmL 91
Dravecky, Dave BioIn 16
Dravecky, Dave 1956- Ballpl 90
Draves, Diane Christine 1947- WhoSSW 91
Draves, William August 1917- WhoWrEP 89
Drawbaugh, Roy Eugene 1930- St&PR 91
Drawert, James George 1941- St&PR 91
Dray, Mark S. 1943- WhoSSW 91
Dray, Monte Jan BiDrAPA 89
Dray, William Herbert 1921- WhoAm 90, WhoWrEP 89
Drayer, Calvin S BiDrAPA 89
Drayer, Calvin Searle, Jr. 1939- WhoE 91
Drayer, Frank 1926- St&PR 91
Drayham, James MajTwCW
Drayna, Roger D. 1930- ODwPR 91
Drayton, Eugenie Barbour 1950 WhoE 91
Drayton, Frank James, III 1958- WhoEmL 91
Drayton, William 1943- WhoAm 90
Drayton, William Henry 1742-1779 EncCRAm
Drazen, Erica L. 1946- St&PR 91
Drazen, Sydney BioIn 16
Drazin, Lisa 1953- WhoAmW 91
Drazin, Louis A. St&PR 91
Drazinic, Ivan Ivo 1942- IntWWM 90
D'Realo, Duke WhoWrEP 89
Dreaper, Richard Edward 1935- WhoAmA 91
Dreben, Burton Spencer 1927- WhoAm 90
Dreben, Raya Spiegel 1927- WhoAm 90
Drebing, Barbara Gail 1955- WhoE 91
Drebinger, John Ballpl 90
Dreblow, Darlene DeMarie 1952- WhoEmL 91
Drebsky, Dennis Jay 1946- WhoAm 90
Drebus, Richard William 1924- WhoAm 90, WhoE 91, WhoWor 91
Drechsel, Edwin Jared 1914- WhoAm 90
Drechsler, Dorothy Roberta 1949- WhoAmW 91
Drechsler, Heike 1964- BioIn 16
Drechsler, Randall Richard 1945- WhoWor 91
Drechsler, Richard Ernest 1934- St&PR 91
Drechsler-Parks, Deborah Marie 1952- WhoEmL 91
Drecoll, J. Cameron 1954- St&PR 91
Dredge, Thomas E 1902- BiDrAPA 89
Dredge, Thomas Everett, Jr. BiDrAPA 89
Dreer, Herman 1889- EarBlAP
Drees, Willem 1886-1988 BioIn 16
Drees, Willem, Sr 1886-1988 AnObit 1988
Drefs, Jerolene Amelia 1935- St&PR 91
Dreger, Dwight Elliot 1957- St&PR 91
Dreger, Jonathan M. 1947- St&PR 91
Dregne, Harold Ernest 1916- WhoAm 90
Dreher, Adolph BioIn 16
Dreher, Donald Dean 1949- St&PR 91
Dreher, Nancy C. 1942- WhoAmW 91
Dreher, Otmar 1940- St&PR 91
Dreher, P. Michael 1934- St&PR 91
Drehmer, Vernon J. St&PR 91
Dreiband, Laurence 1944- WhoAmA 91
Dreibelbis, Eric Paul 1952- WhoE 91
Dreicer, Maurice Charles 1911-1989 BioIn 16
Dreicer, Nancy 1949- St&PR 91
Dreier, David Timothy 1952- WhoAm 90
Dreier, Douglas H. WhoAm 90
Dreier, Katherine S 1877-1952 WhoAmA 91N
Dreier, Katherine Sophie 1877-1952 BiDWomA
Dreier, Mark Edward 1952- WhoEmL 91
Dreier, R. Chad 1947- St&PR 91
Dreier, Theodore BiDrAPA 89
Dreifke, Gerald Edmond 1918- WhoAm 90
Dreifus, Charles Robert 1944- WhoAm 90
Dreifus, David 1952- WhoEmL 91
Dreifuss, Fritz Emanuel 1926- WhoAm 90
Dreijer, Niels 1954- WhoWor 91
Dreikausen, Margret 1937- WhoAmA 91, WhoE 91
Dreiling, Harry R. 1921- St&PR 91
Dreiling, Mark Jerome 1940- WhoSSW 91
Dreilinger, Charles Lewis 1945- WhoAm 90
Dreimanis, Aleksis 1914- WhoAm 90
Dreisbach, Albert Russel, Jr. 1934- WhoSSW 91
Dreisbach, Albert William 1935- St&PR 91
Dreisbach, Clarence Ira 1903- WhoAmA 91
Dreisbach, John Gustave 1939- WhoWor 91
Dreisbach, Timothy Arthur 1949- WhoEmL 91
Dreiser, Theodore 1871-1945 BioIn 16, ConAu 132, DcLB 102 [port], MajTwCW, WorAlBi, WrPh
Dreisinger, Albert BiDrAPA 89
Dreiss, L. Jack 1948- WhoAm 90
Dreitler, Joseph Richard 1950- WhoEmL 91
Dreitzer, Albert J 1902- WhoAmA 91
Drekonja, Gerhard 1939- WhoWor 91
Drelich, Iris M. 1951- WhoSSW 91
Drell, Hyman Joseph BiDrAPA 89
Drell, Leonard B. 1919- St&PR 91
Drell, Sidney D. 1926- BioIn 16
Drell, Sidney David 1926- WhoAm 90
Drell, William 1922- WhoAm 90
Drell, William Kadison 1958- BiDrAPA 89
Drellich, Karen Kinney 1942- WhoWrEP 89
Drendel, Frank Matthew 1945- WhoAm 90
Drenik, Douglas Jay 1943- St&PR 91
Drenik, Gary William 1950- WhoEmL 91
Drennan, Carl Edward, Jr. 1952- WhoSSW 91
Drennan, Donna Jane 1944- WhoAmW 91
Drennan, George Eldon 1921- WhoAm 90
Drennan, Janice S. 1950- WhoWrEP 89
Drennan, Jeffrey Lloyd 1950- BiDrAPA 89
Drennan, Joseph Peter 1956- WhoE 91, WhoEmL 91, WhoWor 91
Drennan, Merrill William 1915- WhoAm 90
Drennan, Michael David BiDrAPA 89
Drennan, Michael Eldon 1946- WhoEmL 91
Drennen, Felix M., III 1951- St&PR 91
Drennen, Gordon 1947- WhoSSW 91
Drennen, John C. 1947- St&PR 91
Drennen, Marcia Simonton 1915- WhoWrEP 89
Drennen, William Miller 1914- WhoAm 90
Drennig, Manfred 1940- WhoWor 91
Drennon, Cindy-Jo Simmons 1956- WhoEmL 91
Drennon, Kay Byrom 1949- WhoAmW 91
Drenth, Pieter Johan Diederk 1935- WhoWor 91
Drentwett Family PenDiDA 89
Drentwett, Abraham PenDiDA 89
Drentwett, Abraham 1647?-1727 PenDiDA 89
Drentwett, Philip Jacob 1694-1754 PenDiDA 89
Drenz, Charles Francis 1930- WhoAm 90
Dreruf, John W. 1922- St&PR 91
Dresbach, David Philip 1947- WhoEmL 91
Dresch, Stephen Paul 1943- WhoAm 90
Drescher, David Robert 1937- WhoAm 90
Drescher, Fran BioIn 16
Drescher, Henrik 1955- BioIn 16
Drescher, Jack BiDrAPA 89
Drescher, Joan Elizabeth 1939- AuBYP 90
Drescher, Joseph Gerard 1940- St&PR 91
Drescher, Judith Altman 1946- WhoAm 90, WhoAmW 91, WhoSSW 91
Drescher, Scott Fredric 1961- WhoSSW 91
Drescher, Seymour 1934- WhoAm 90
Drescher, William P 1944- BiDrAPA 89
Dreschhoff, Gisela Auguste Marie 1938- WhoAm 90
Dresden, Mark Kenyon, Jr. WhoE 91
Dresdnere, Simon 1920- WhoAmA 91
Dresdow, Mary A. 1943- St&PR 91
Drese, Claus Helmut 1922- WhoWor 91
Dresel, Ellis Loring 1865-1925 BioIn 16
Dresher, James T. 1919- St&PR 91
Dresher, Paul NewAgMG
Dresher, Paul Joseph 1951- IntWWM 90
Dresher, William Henry 1930- WhoAm 90
Dreskin, Erving Arthur 1919- WhoWor 91
Dreskin, Jane Ellen 1943- BiDrAPA 89
Dreskin, Jeanet Steckler 1921- WhoAmA 91
Dresler, Paul 1879-1950 PenDiDA 89
Dresmal, James Eugene 1939- St&PR 91
Dresner, Albert BiDrAPA 89
Dresner, Bruce Lee 1946- BiDrAPA 89
Dresner, Mara Susan 1961- WhoEmL 91
Dresner, Nehama 1960- BiDrAPA 89
Dresner, Samuel H. 1923- BioIn 16
Dresner, Thomas Leland 1948- WhoEmL 91
Dresnin, Sandor George 1941- BiDrAPA 89
Dresnok, Joseph 1945- WhoEmL 91
Dress, Joe Anthony 1923- St&PR 91
Dress, Katherine Chang 1941- WhoAmW 91
Dress, Susan Hildebrant 1948- WhoE 91
Dressel, Barry 1947- WhoAm 90
Dressel, Birgit BioIn 16
Dressel, Deane Lisette 1955- WhoAmW 91
Dressel, Henry Francis 1914- WhoE 91
Dressel, Roy Robert 1923- WhoAm 90
Dresselhaus, Mildred 1930- BioIn 16
Dresselhaus, Mildred Spiewak 1930- WhoAm 90, WhoAmW 91
Dressen, Chuck 1898-1966 Ballpl 90
Dressen, Freddy Simeon 1946- WhoWor 91
Dressendofer, Jo-Anne 1960- WhoAmW 91
Dresser, Christopher 1834-1904 BioIn 16, PenDiDA 89
Dresser, David Owen 1948- WhoWor 91
Dresser, David W. St&PR 91
Dresser, Davis TwCCr&M 91
Dresser, Elizabeth AuBYP 90
Dresser, Jesse Dale 1906- WhoAm 90
Dresser, Louisa 1907-1988 WhoAmA 91N
Dresser, Louisa 1907-1989 BioIn 16
Dresser, Norine 1931- ConAu 132
Dresser, Paul 1857-1906 BioIn 16, OxCPMus
Dresser, Paul A., Jr. 1942- St&PR 91
Dresser, Paul Alton, Jr. 1942- WhoAm 90
Dresser, Robert C. 1955- St&PR 91
Dresser, Robert L. 1925- St&PR 91
Dresser, Roblyn Lafferty 1957- WhoEmL 91
Dresser, William Donald 1947- St&PR 91
Dressler, Brenda Joyce 1943- WhoAmW 91
Dressler, Brian Robert 1957- WhoEmL 91
Dressler, David Charles 1928- St&PR 91, WhoAm 90, WhoE 91
Dressler, David Michael 1939- BiDrAPA 89
Dressler, Frederic Michael 1941- St&PR 91
Dressler, Marie 1869-1934 BioIn 16, NotWoAT, OxCPMus, WorAlBi
Dressler, Marion S 1915- BiDrAPA 89
Dressler, Michael Barry 1950- WhoEmL 91
Dressler, Rob 1954- Ballpl 90
Dressler, Robert 1925- WhoAm 90
Dressler, Robert A. 1945- WhoAm 90
Dressler, Robert Eugene 1922- WhoAm 90
Dressner, Howard Roy 1919- WhoAm 90
Dressner, Paul Robert 1955- WhoEmL 91, WhoSSW 91
Dreste, Caspar PenDiDA 89
Dreszer, Andrew E. 1951- ODwPR 91
Drets, Maximo Eduardo 1930- WhoWor 91
Dreumont, Antonio Alcides 1939- WhoHisp 91
Dreux, Joan Albert 1951- WhoAmW 91
Dreves, Katharine Jane Densford 1890-1978 BioIn 16
Dreves, Veronica R. 1927-1986 BioIn 16
Drew, Betty Berg 1929- WhoAmW 91
Drew, Charles Richard 1904-1950 BioIn 16, WorAlBi
Drew, Clifford James 1943- WhoAm 90
Drew, Daniel 1797-1879 EncABHB 6 [port]
Drew, David 1930- IntWWM 90
Drew, Derek C. 1956- WhoWrEP 89
Drew, Donald Allen 1945- WhoAm 90
Drew, Elizabeth 1935- WhoAm 90, WhoAmW 91, WorAu 1980 [port]
Drew, Elizabeth Heineman 1940- WhoAm 90, WhoAmW 91
Drew, Ernest Harold 1937- St&PR 91, WhoAm 90, WhoE 91
Drew, Fraser Bragg Robert 1913- WhoAm 90
Drew, George 1943- WhoWrEP 89
Drew, Horace Rainsford, Jr. 1918- WhoSSW 91
Drew, James 1929- IntWWM 90
Drew, James Mulcro 1929- WhoAm 90
Drew, Jane 1911- WomArch [port]
Drew, Jane Beverly 1911- WhoWor 91
Drew, John E. WhoE 91
Drew, Judith Lowery 1950- WhoAmW 91
Drew, Judy Morine 1951- WhoAmW 91, WhoEmL 91
Drew, K. 1939- WhoAmW 91
Drew, Katherine Fischer 1923- WhoAm 90, WhoAmW 91
Drew, Louisa Lane 1820-1897 BioIn 16, NotWoAT
Drew, Lucas 1935- IntWWM 90
Drew, Lucille Haluska 1934- St&PR 91
Drew, Mary Shirley 1942- WhoSSW 91
Drew, Mindy Gunther 1950- St&PR 91
Drew, Morrill Newman 1862-1917 AmLegL
Drew, Paul 1935- WhoAm 90, WhoWor 91
Drew, Russell Cooper 1931- WhoAm 90
Drew, Stephen Richard 1949- WhoEmL 91
Drew, Thomas Arthur 1945- WhoEmL 91
Drew, Thomas Stevenson 1802-1867 BioIn 16
Drew, Walter H. 1935- St&PR 91
Drew, Walter Harlow 1935- WhoAm 90
Drewal, Henry John 1943- WhoAmA 91
Drewer, Milton L., Jr. BioIn 16
Drewery, Corinne BioIn 16
Drewery, Ida Mae Moore 1927- WhoAmW 91
Drewes, Charles E. 1941- St&PR 91
Drewes, Lester Richard 1943- WhoAm 90
Drewes, Werner 1899-1985 WhoAmA 91N
Drewet, Mary BiDEWW
Drewett, John Ernest 1952- WhoSSW 91
Drewitz, Ingeborg 1923-1986 EncCoWW
Drewlowe, Eve 1924-1988 WhoAmA 91N
Drewnowski, Jan 1908- ConAu 129, WhoWor 91
Drewry, Edwin Charles 1911- St&PR 91
Drewry, Guy Carleton 1901- WhoWrEP 89
Drews, Bernard H. 1924- St&PR 91
Drews, Karl 1920-1963 Ballpl 90
Drews, Mark William 1960- WhoEmL 91
Drews, Richard 1953- WhoAm 90
Drews, Robert S BiDrAPA 89
Drewsen, Edmond Titus, Jr. 1932- WhoAm 90
Drewsen, Jette 1943- EncCoWW
Drewyer WhNaAH
Drexel, Anthony Joseph 1826-1893 EncABHB 6 [port]
Drexel, Charles Francis 1923- St&PR 91
Drexel, Katharine Mary 1858-1955 BioIn 16
Drexel, R. Patrick 1943- St&PR 91
Drexler, Arthur 1925-1987 BioIn 16
Drexler, Arthur Justin 1925-1987 WhoAmA 91N
Drexler, Bradley Mark 1960- WhoE 91
Drexler, Caryl Ring 1951- WhoAmW 91
Drexler, Deborah Lynn 1957- WhoEmL 91
Drexler, Fred 1915- WhoAm 90
Drexler, Hans Bernd BiDrAPA 89
Drexler, J F ConAu 31NR
Drexler, Jerome 1927- St&PR 91
Drexler, K. Eric BioIn 16
Drexler, Karen Glaze BiDrAPA 89
Drexler, Kim Eric 1955- WhoEmL 91
Drexler, Lawrence Samuel 1957- WhoEmL 91
Drexler, Lloyd A. 1918- St&PR 91
Drexler, Lynne BioIn 16, WhoAmA 91
Drexler, Marci BioIn 16
Drexler, Mark Andrew 1953- WhoEmL 91
Drexler, Mary Sanford 1954- WhoAmW 91
Drexler, Michael David 1938- WhoAm 90
Drexler, Millard S 1944- News 90 [port], -90-3 [port], WhoAm 90
Drexler, Richard Allan 1947- St&PR 91, WhoAm 90
Drexler, Rosalyn BioIn 16
Drexler, Rosalyn 1926- BiDWomA, FemiCLE, NotWoAT
Drey, Leo BioIn 16
Dreyer, Barbara Jean 1938- St&PR 91
Dreyer, Carl Theodor 1889-1968 BioIn 16
Dreyer, Dave 1894- OxCPMus
Dreyer, Eugene Rubin 1921- WhoE 91
Dreyer, Floyd BioIn 16
Dreyer, Franklin Delano 1936- St&PR 91
Dreyer, Gay 1915- WhoAmA 91
Dreyer, James A. 1946- St&PR 91

Dreyer, Jerome Lee 1930- *WhoAm 90*
Dreyer, Joel S 1937- *BiDrAPA 89*
Dreyer, John Louis Emil 1852-1926 *BioIn 16*
Dreyer, Leslie I. 1930- *IntWWM 90*
Dreyer, Marla Lynn 1955- *WhoEmL 91*
Dreyer, Randolph Eugene 1957- *WhoE 91*
Dreyer, Robert H. 1937- *St&PR 91*
Dreyfus, Albert Etienne *BiDrAPA 89*
Dreyfus, Albert Etienne 1915- *WhoE 91*
Dreyfus, Alfred 1859-1935 *BiDFrPL, BioIn 16, WorAlBi*
Dreyfus, Alfred Stanley 1921- *WhoAm 90*
Dreyfus, Enrique *WhoWor 91*
Dreyfus, George 1928- *IntWWM 90*
Dreyfus, George Joseph 1920- *WhoAm 90*
Dreyfus, Huguette 1928- *PenDiMP*
Dreyfus, Huguette Pauline 1928- *IntWWM 90*
Dreyfus, Joseph E 1919- *BiDrAPA 89*
Dreyfus, Julia Louis- *BioIn 16*
Dreyfus, Pierre 1907- *WorAlBi*
Dreyfus, Richard Baeck 1958- *WhoEmL 91*
Dreyfus, Robert Louis- *BioIn 16*
Dreyfus, Robert M 1937- *BiDrAPA 89*
Dreyfuss, Daniel Abraham *BiDrAPA 89*
Dreyfuss, Henry 1903-1972 *PenDiDA 89*
Dreyfuss, Henry 1904-1972 *ConDes 90*
Dreyfuss, Jeramie *BioIn 16*
Dreyfuss, John Alan 1933- *WhoAm 90*
Dreyfuss, Nancy Matis 1954- *WhoAmW 91, WhoEmL 91*
Dreyfuss, Norman *St&PR 91*
Dreyfuss, Patricia 1932- *WhoAmW 91*
Dreyfuss, Richard 1947- *BioIn 16, WorAlBi*
Dreyfuss, Richard Stephan 1947- *WhoAm 90*
Dreyfuss-Diederich, Ginette 1938- *BiDrAPA 89*
Dreyschock, Alexander 1818-1869 *BioIn 16*
Dreyspool, Anthony Alan 1945- *WhoEmL 91*
Drezdzon, William Lawrence 1934- *WhoWor 91*
Drezga, Lyerka B *BiDrAPA 89*
Drezner, Jeffrey Lewis *BiDrAPA 89*
Dreznes, John Joseph *St&PR 91*
Drgac, Peter Paul 1883-1976 *MusmAFA*
Dribben, Irving S *BiDrAPA 89*
Dribin, Dennis 1946- *St&PR 91*
Dribinsky, Loren Rae *BiDrAPA 89*
Drickamer, Harry George 1918- *WhoAm 90*
Driebe, Edward K. 1916- *St&PR 91*
Drieberg, Denver Chris 1955- *WhoEmL 91*
Drieberg, Keith Lambert 1952- *WhoEmL 91*
Driehaus, Robert J. 1928- *St&PR 91*
Driehaus, Robert Joseph 1928- *WhoAm 90*
Drielsma, Willem Frans Carel 1919- *WhoE 91, WhoSSW 91*
Driemen, Pearl M *BiDrAPA 89*
Dries, David C *BiDrAPA 89*
Driesbach, David Fraiser 1922- *WhoAmA 91*
Driesbach, Walter Clark, Jr 1929- *WhoAmA 91*
Driesch, Hans 1867-1941 *EncO&P 3*
Driesch, Hans Adolf Eduard 1867-1941 *EncPaPR 91*
Drieschner, Michael 1939- *WhoWor 91*
Driese, Edward Clark 1933- *St&PR 91*
Driesel, Timothy Michaels 1951- *WhoWor 91*
Driesen, Jerome E *BiDrAPA 89*
Driessel, A. Berkley 1937- *WhoWrEP 89*
Driessen, Angela Kosta *WhoAmA 91*
Driessen, Dan 1951- *Ballpl 90*
Driessens, Ferdinand Clemens M. 1937- *WhoWor 91*
Drieu la Rochelle, Pierre Eugene 1893-1945 *BiDFrPL*
Drifters, The *EncPR&S 89, OxCPMus*
Driftmier, Richard Prentice 1948- *WhoEmL 91*
Driggers, Wallace Gerald 1927- *WhoE 91*
Driggs, Allan F. 1951- *St&PR 91*
Driggs, Charles Mulford 1924- *WhoAm 90*
Driggs, David M. 1953- *WhoE 91*
Driggs, Don C. 1934- *WhoAm 90*
Driggs, Don Wallace 1924- *WhoAm 90*
Driggs, Douglas Harmon 1901- *WhoAm 90, WhoWor 91*
Driggs, Elsie 1898- *BiDWomA, WhoAmA 91*
Driggs, Frank *BioIn 16*
Driggs, Gary H. 1934- *St&PR 91*
Driggs, Gary Harmon 1934- *WhoAm 90*
Driggs, Guy Kenneth 1921- *WhoSSW 91*
Driggs, Junius E. 1907- *St&PR 91*
Driggs, Margaret 1909- *WhoWor 91*
Drigo, Paola 1876-1938 *EncCoWW*
Driker, Eugene 1937- *WhoAm 90*
Drillette, Elysa Jean 1960- *WhoAmW 91*
Drillman, Paula *WhoAmW 91*
Drimmer, Eric Jonathan *BiDrAPA 89*
Drimmer, Frederick *SmATA 60 [port]*
Drimmer, Melvin 1934- *WhoAm 90*
Drinan, Robert Frederick 1920- *WhoAm 90, WhoE 91*
Drinka, George F *BiDrAPA 89*
Drinka, Joseph Mark 1953- *BiDrAPA 89*
Drinkard, Barbara Felio 1936- *WhoSSW 91*
Drinkard, James D 1931- *BiDrAPA 89*
Drinkard, Lawrence W. 1939- *St&PR 91, WhoAm 90*
Drinker, Catharine Ann 1841-1922 *BiDWomA*
Drinker, Elizabeth 1734-1807 *FemiCLE*
Drinker, Elizabeth Sandwith 1735-1807 *EncCRAm*
Drinko, John Deaver 1921- *WhoAm 90, WhoWor 91*
Drinkward, Cecil William 1927- *St&PR 91*
Drinkwater, Robert Edward 1935- *WhoAm 90*
Drinkwater, Terry *BioIn 16*
Drinkwine, Edward Allen 1946- *WhoEmL 91*
Drinnan, Alan John 1932- *WhoAm 90*
Drinnon, Doris Jean 1930- *WhoWrEP 89*
Drinnon, Elizabeth McCants 1925- *WhoWrEP 89*
Drinnon, Richard 1925- *WhoAm 90*
Driscoll, A. Storer 1942- *St&PR 91*
Driscoll, Abigail Julia Hannah 1958- *WhoAmA 91*
Driscoll, Alan Horace 1941- *WhoAm 90*
Driscoll, Brigid *WhoAmW 91*
Driscoll, Dawn-Marie 1946- *WhoAmW 91*
Driscoll, Donald Thomas 1931- *WhoE 91*
Driscoll, Edgar Joseph, Jr 1920- *WhoAmA 91, WhoE 91*
Driscoll, Edward Carroll 1929- *WhoAm 90*
Driscoll, Edward Carroll, Jr. 1952- *St&PR 91*
Driscoll, Ellen *WhoAmA 91*
Driscoll, Genevra Z 1916- *BiDrAPA 89*
Driscoll, Glen Robert 1920- *WhoAm 90*
Driscoll, Holly *BioIn 16*
Driscoll, Jack 1946- *WhoWrEP 89*
Driscoll, James G. 1932- *St&PR 91*
Driscoll, James Michael 1939- *WhoAm 90*
Driscoll, Jeanne Marie 1956- *WhoEmL 91*
Driscoll, Jeanne Watson 1949- *WhoEmL 91*
Driscoll, John Brian 1946- *WhoAm 90*
Driscoll, John Gerard 1933- *WhoAm 90, WhoE 91*
Driscoll, John H. *NewYTBS 90*
Driscoll, John M. *BioIn 16*
Driscoll, John Patrick 1935- *St&PR 91*
Driscoll, John Paul 1949- *WhoAmA 91*
Driscoll, John S. 1934- *WhoE 91*
Driscoll, Kevin Irving 1957- *WhoEmL 91*
Driscoll, Lee F., Jr. 1926- *St&PR 91*
Driscoll, Lee Francis, Jr. 1926- *WhoAm 90*
Driscoll, Loren 1928- *IntWWM 90*
Driscoll, Mary Harris 1928- *WhoWrEP 89*
Driscoll, Patricia Anne 1955- *WhoEmL 91*
Driscoll, Peter 1942- *TwCCr&M 91*
Driscoll, Peter John 1942- *SpyFic*
Driscoll, Richard Dennis 1931- *WhoAm 90, WhoE 91*
Driscoll, Richard K. 1922- *St&PR 91*
Driscoll, Robert E. 1949- *WhoE 91*
Driscoll, Robert George 1949- *WhoEmL 91*
Driscoll, Robert L. 1939- *WhoAm 90*
Driscoll, Robert S. 1947- *St&PR 91*
Driscoll, Thomas F. 1925- *St&PR 91*
Driscoll, Thomas Frank 1925- *WhoAm 90*
Driscoll, William B. 1926- *St&PR 91*
Driscoll, William Mark 1953- *WhoE 91*
Driscoll, William Michael 1929- *WhoAm 90*
Driscoll, William Patrick 1955- *WhoEmL 91*
Driskell, David Clyde 1931- *WhoAmA 91*
Driskell, Leon V. 1932- *LiHiK*
Driskill, Charles Dwayne 1954- *WhoSSW 91*
Driskill, Clarence 1945- *WhoAm 90, WhoE 91*
Driskill, Frank A. 1912- *ConAu 130*
Driskill, John Ray 1934- *WhoAm 90*
Drisko, Elliot Hillman 1917- *WhoAm 90*
Drissel, John *PenDiDA 89*
Drissell, Norman E. 1928- *St&PR 91*
Drissell, Norman Earl 1928- *WhoAm 90*
Driver, C J 1939- *ConAu 30NR*
Driver, C. Stephen 1936- *WhoE 91*
Driver, Cheryl Anne 1954- *WhoAmW 91*
Driver, Donald *BioIn 16*
Driver, Elwood Thomas 1921- *WhoE 91*
Driver, Frances C *BiDrAPA 89*
Driver, Frank L., III 1930- *St&PR 91*
Driver, Lottie Elizabeth 1918- *WhoAm 90*
Driver, Rodney David 1932- *WhoE 91*
Driver, Sharon Humphreys 1949- *WhoAmW 91*
Driver, Tom Faw 1925- *WhoAm 90*
Driver, William Raymond, Jr. 1907- *St&PR 91, WhoAm 90*
D'Rivera, Paquito *BioIn 16*
Drizul, Aleksandr Arvidovich 1920- *WhoWor 91*
Drlica, Karen Janette 1948- *BiDrAPA 89*
Drlik, John Martin *BiDrAPA 89*
Drnovsek, Janez 1950- *WhoWor 91*
Drob, Max 1887-1959 *BioIn 16*
Droba, Krzysztof 1946- *IntWWM 90*
Droba, Marian Patricia 1955- *BiDrAPA 89*
Drobashevsky, Vladimir 1929- *WhoE 91*
Drobatschewski, Ellen *BioIn 16*
Drobis, David R. 1941- *ODwPR 91*
Drobnes, Sidney *BiDrAPA 89*
Drobnick, Jack Anthony 1940- *St&PR 91*
Drobot, Eve 1951- *ConAu 131*
Droege, Anthony Joseph, II 1943- *WhoAmA 91*
Droege, Arthur J. 1948- *St&PR 91*
Droege, Franz 1937- *WhoWor 91*
Droege, Marie Therese 1961- *WhoEmL 91*
Droegemueller, William 1934- *WhoAm 90*
Droegkamp, Janis Mildred 1946- *WhoAmW 91*
Drogalis, Robert Michael 1960- *St&PR 91*
Drogendijk, Arie Corstiaan 1932- *WhoWor 91*
Drogheda, Earl of 1910- *WhoAm 90*
Drogheda, Lord 1910-1989 *AnObit 1989*
Drogin, Mark *BiDrAPA 89*
Drogkamp, Charles *WhoAmA 91N*
Drohan, John 1890-1969 *Ballpl 90*
Drohan, Thomas A. 1933- *ODwPR 91, St&PR 91*
Drohan, Thomas H. 1936- *WhoAm 90*
Drohan, William Michael 1954- *WhoEmL 91*
Drohlich, Robert A. *ODwPR 91*
Drohojowska, Hunter 1952- *WhoAmA 91*
Droit, Michel 1923- *ConAu 32NR*
Droke, Rose Mary 1935- *WhoSSW 91*
Drole, Luann 1955- *WhoAmW 91*
Drolet, Cynthia June 1945- *WhoEmL 91*
Drolet, Gene 1931- *St&PR 91*
Drolet, Michele Therese 1953- *WhoE 91*
Droll, Marian Clarke 1931- *WhoAm 90*
Drollet, Dag *BioIn 16*
Drollinger, John, Jr. 1924- *St&PR 91*
Drollinger, John M. 1946- *WhoEmL 91*
Drom, Robert Edwin 1929- *BiDrAPA 89*
Drombetta, Larry *St&PR 91*
Dromgoole, Catherine *BiDrAPA 89*
Droms, William George 1944- *WhoE 91, WhoWor 91*
Dronamraju, Rama B 1959- *BiDrAPA 89*
Drongoski, Cynthia 1957- *WhoEmL 91*
Drooby, Ala'Ud-Din S 1925- *BiDrAPA 89*
Drood, Eugene E. 1929- *St&PR 91*
Droog, Tom *BioIn 16*
Drook, Gary G. 1945- *St&PR 91*
Drooz, Daniel Bernard 1945- *WhoEmL 91*
Drooz, Richard B *BiDrAPA 89*
Dropo, Walt 1923- *Ballpl 90*
Droppers, Garrett 1860-1927 *BioIn 16*
Droppers, Neil Anthony 1928- *St&PR 91*
Drosd, Jacqueline Jean 1947- *WhoSSW 91*
Drosdick, John G. 1943- *St&PR 91*
Drosdick, John Girard 1943- *WhoAm 90*
Drosdoff, Daniel Aaron 1941- *WhoAm 90*
Drosdowsky, Michel Anatole 1930- *WhoWor 91*
Droske, Lloyd Z 1925- *BiDrAPA 89*
Dross, Raymond L. 1921- *St&PR 91*
Drossel, Norlen Eltoft 1944- *WhoAmW 91*
Drossman, Evan Harvey 1949- *WhoE 91*
Drosson, Roger Louis 1938- *WhoWor 91*
Drost, Marianne 1950- *St&PR 91, WhoAm 90, WhoEmL 91*
Drost-Hansen, Walter 1925- *WhoSSW 91*
Droste, Keith Joseph 1933- *St&PR 91*
Droste-Hulshoff, Annette von 1797-1848 *EncCoWW*
Drotar, Paul Peter 1946- *St&PR 91*
Drotman, Doug *ODwPR 91*
Drotning, John Evan 1932- *WhoAm 90*
Drott, Dick 1936-1985 *Ballpl 90*
Drouet, Juliette 1806-1883 *EncCoWW*
Drought, Brian Dennis 1943- *St&PR 91*
Drought, Rose Alice *WhoWor 91*
Drouilhet, Paul Raymond, Jr. 1933- *WhoAm 90, WhoE 91*
Drouillard, George *WhNaAH*
Drouin, Jacques 1931- *BiDrAPA 89*
Drouin, Pamela McIntyre 1956- *WhoE 91, WhoEmL 91*
Drouin, Richard *WhoAm 90*
Droukas, Ann Hantis 1923- *WhoAmW 91*
Droullard, Steven Maurice 1951- *WhoEmL 91, WhoWor 91*
Drower, G M F 1954- *ConAu 131*
Drower, Sara Ruth 1938- *WhoAmA 91*
Drown, Lucy Lincoln 1848-1934 *BioIn 16*
Drown, Merle 1943- *WhoWrEP 89*
Drown, Ruth B. 1891-1943? *EncO&P 3*
Drowota, Frank F., III 1938- *WhoAm 90, WhoSSW 91*
D'Royce, Jeric *WhoWrEP 89*
Droz, Henry 1926- *WhoAm 90*
Droz, Kenneth Mark 1957- *WhoEmL 91*
Drozak, Frank *BioIn 16*
Drozd, Andrew Peter 1947- *WhoEmL 91*
Drozda, Helen Dorothy 1924- *WhoAmW 91*
Drozda, Joseph Peter 1945- *WhoEmL 91*
Drozdov, Mark 1963- *WhoEmL 91*
Drozdowicz, Carol Elaine 1933- *WhoSSW 91*
Drozdowski, Stanley Michael 1938- *St&PR 91*
Drozdziel, Marion John 1924- *WhoE 91, WhoWor 91*
Drozeski, Leo Cornelius, Jr. 1940- *St&PR 91*
Drubach, Daniel A *BiDrAPA 89*
Drubel, James Michel 1931- *St&PR 91*
Druce, Howard Martin 1953- *WhoEmL 91*
Druck, Kalman B. 1914- *ODwPR 91*
Druck, Kalman Breschel 1914- *WhoAm 90*
Druck, Mark *WhoAm 90*
Drucke, Louis 1888-1955 *Ballpl 90*
Drucker, Aaron 1922- *St&PR 91*
Drucker, Alan Jay *BiDrAPA 89*
Drucker, Bertram Morris 1919- *WhoAm 90*
Drucker, Cynthia R. 1959- *ODwPR 91*
Drucker, Daniel Charles 1918- *WhoAm 90, WhoSSW 91*
Drucker, Debra M *BiDrAPA 89*
Drucker, Franklin 1934- *BiDrAPA 89*
Drucker, George David *ODwPR 91*
Drucker, Jakob Richard 1946- *WhoE 91*
Drucker, John Joseph, Jr. 1948- *BiDrAPA 89*
Drucker, Kenneth A. 1945- *St&PR 91*
Drucker, Kenneth Alan 1945- *WhoAm 90*
Drucker, Malka 1945- *BioIn 16, ConAu 31NR*
Drucker, Marvin 1929- *BiDrAPA 89*
Drucker, Melvin Bruce 1927- *WhoSSW 91*
Drucker, Mindy M. 1957- *WhoAmW 91*
Drucker, Miriam Koontz 1925- *WhoAm 90*
Drucker, Mort 1929- *BioIn 16, WhoAm 90*
Drucker, Nathan J. 1949- *St&PR 91*
Drucker, Peter F. 1909- *WorAlBi*
Drucker, Peter Ferdinand 1909- *BioIn 16, WhoAm 90, WhoWor 91*
Drucker, Stanley 1929- *IntWWM 90*
Drucker, William Richard 1922- *WhoAm 90*
Druckman, Jacob 1928- *IntWWM 90, PenDiMP A*
Druckman, Jacob Raphael 1928- *WhoAm 90*
Drude, Kenneth Paul 1945- *WhoEmL 91*
Drudge, Junior Harold 1922- *WhoAm 90*
Drudi, John Louis 1935- *WhoWor 91*
Drudy, Patrick 1943- *WhoE 91*
Drudy, Patrick Joseph 1942- *WhoWor 91*
Druecke, Jacqueline Paula 1957- *WhoAmW 91*
Druen, W. Sidney 1942- *St&PR 91*
Druesedow, John Edward, Jr. 1939- *IntWWM 90*
Drufenbrock, Diane Joyce 1929- *WhoAmW 91*
Drugan, Cornelius Bernard 1946- *WhoEmL 91*
Druggan, Terrance Lee 1960- *WhoSSW 91*
Druick, Douglas Wesley 1945- *WhoAm 90*
Druinin, Fyodor *PenDiMP*
Druke, Helene 1918- *IntWWM 90*
Druker, Henry Leo 1953- *WhoE 91*
Druker, Scott Douglas 1955- *WhoSSW 91*
Drukker, Austin C. 1934- *St&PR 91*
Drukteinis, Albert M *BiDrAPA 89*
Drulard, Frederick Fisher 1940- *St&PR 91*
Drum, Joan Marie McFarland 1932- *WhoAmW 91*
Drum, Joan McFarland 1932- *WhoWrEP 89*
Drum, Sydney Maria 1952- *WhoAmA 91*
Drumbor, George A. *ODwPR 91*
Drumetz, Michel Jean Camille 1928- *WhoWor 91*
Drumheller, Dan Parkes 1948- *St&PR 91*
Drumheller, George Jesse 1933- *WhoWor 91*
Drumheller, Linda Beth 1947- *WhoEmL 91*
Drumheller, Oscar 1920- *St&PR 91*
Drumheller, Philip Malloy 1953- *WhoE 91*
Drumm, Chris 1949- *WhoWrEP 89*
Drumm, Don 1935- *WhoAmA 91*
Drumm, John Edward 1942- *WhoWor 91*
Drumm, John G. 1936- *St&PR 91*
Drumm, Raymond F. 1933- *St&PR 91*
Drummer, Donald Raymond 1941- *St&PR 91, WhoAm 90*
Drummer, Dorothy Jean 1949- *WhoEmL 91*
Drummer, William Richard 1925- *WhoAmA 91*
Drummond, A. H. *AuBYP 90*
Drummond, Aleta *BiDrAPA 89*
Drummond, Arthur A 1891- *WhoAmA 91N*

Drummond, Cal 1917-1970 *Ballpl 90*
Drummond, Carmen R 1925- *BiDrAPA 89*
Drummond, Carol Cramer 1933- *WhoAmW 91*
Drummond, Charles *TwCCr&M 91*
Drummond, David Joseph 1957- *WhoEmL 91*
Drummond, Donald Francis 1917- *WhoAm 90*
Drummond, Donald M. 1929- *St&PR 91*
Drummond, Doris Wiggins 1938- *WhoAmW 91*
Drummond, Edward H 1953- *BiDrAPA 89*
Drummond, Gerard Kasper 1937- *WhoAm 90*
Drummond, Gillian M. 1943- *WhoAmW 91*
Drummond, Ivor *TwCCr&M 91*
Drummond, J. *TwCCr&M 91*
Drummond, James Everman 1932- *WhoAm 90*
Drummond, James Henry 1946- *WhoSSW 91*
Drummond, John A. 1929- *WhoAm 90*
Drummond, John Dodds 1944- *IntWWM 90, WhoWor 91*
Drummond, John Richard Gray 1934- *IntWWM 90*
Drummond, Josiah Hayden 1827-1902 *AmLegL*
Drummond, June 1923- *TwCCr&M 91*
Drummond, Kay *BioIn 16*
Drummond, LaVena May 1931- *WhoWrEP 89*
Drummond, Lee *AuBYP 90*
Drummond, Luther *BioIn 16*
Drummond, May 1710?-1772 *FemiCLE*
Drummond, Michael *NewYTBS 90 [port]*
Drummond, Pamela Johnson 1946- *WhoSSW 91*
Drummond, Robert Kendig 1939- *WhoAm 90*
Drummond, Robert W. *BioIn 16*
Drummond, Roscoe 1902-1983 *BioIn 16*
Drummond, Sally Hazelet 1924- *WhoAm 90, WhoAmA 91*
Drummond, Walter *AuBYP 90, MajTwCW*
Drummond, William B *BiDrAPA 89*
Drummond, William Henry 1854-1907 *DcLB 92 [port]*
Drummond, Winslow 1933- *WhoAm 90*
Drummond de Andrade, Carlos *BioIn 16*
Drummond de Andrade, Carlos 1902-1987 *ConAu 132*
Drumont, Edouard Adolphe 1844-1917 *BiDFrPL*
Drungole, Paula Elaine 1963- *WhoEmL 91*
Drury, Allen Stuart 1918- *WhoAm 90, WhoWrEP 89*
Drury, Anna 182-?- *FemiCLE*
Drury, Catherine Anne 1939- *WhoAmW 91*
Drury, Charles Louis, Jr. 1955- *WhoAm 90*
Drury, Chris *BioIn 16*
Drury, Daniel Patrick 1936- *St&PR 91*
Drury, Drummond 1912-1989 *BioIn 16*
Drury, Francis T. 1947- *St&PR 91*
Drury, John E. 1944- *WhoSSW 91*
Drury, John Robin 1944- *WhoWor 91*
Drury, L. Wayne 1951- *St&PR 91*
Drury, Leonard Leroy 1928- *WhoAm 90*
Drury, Morley 1903-1989 *BioIn 16*
Drury, Noel Drake 1944- *BiDrAPA 89*
Drury, Patricia Ann 1947- *WhoEmL 91*
Drury, Regina Rose 1951- *WhoEmL 91*
Drury, Richard B. 1949- *St&PR 91*
Drury, Robert B 1916- *BiDrAPA 89*
Drury, Robert Edward 1916- *WhoAm 90*
Drury, Roger W. 1914- *AuBYP 90*
Drury, Walter Lee 1934- *St&PR 91*
Drury, William H 1888-1960 *WhoAmA 91N*
Drury, William Martin 1953- *WhoSSW 91*
Druse, Margaret Dobson 1921- *WhoAmW 91*
Druss, Richard G 1933- *BiDrAPA 89*
Drutt, Helen Williams 1930- *BioIn 16, WhoAmA 91*
Drutz, June 1920- *WhoAmA 91*
Druvenga, Gordon Dale 1956- *WhoEmL 91*
Druyan, Mary Ellen 1938- *WhoAmW 91*
Druzbacka, Elzbieta 1695?-1765? *EncCoWW*
Drvota, Mojmir 1923- *WhoAm 90*
Dry, Morris E. *NewYTBS 90*
Dryburgh, Bruce Sinclair 1943- *St&PR 91, WhoAm 90*
Dryden, Charles 1869-1931 *Ballpl 90*
Dryden, Hugh Latimer 1898-1965 *DcScB S2*
Dryden, James Dale 1937- *WhoSSW 91*
Dryden, John 1613-1700 *WorAlBi*
Dryden, John 1631-1700 *DcLB 101 [port], WrPh*
Dryden, John Fairfield 1839-1911 *BioIn 16*
Dryden, Leo 1863-1939 *OxCPMus*
Dryden, Martin Francis, Jr. 1915- *WhoAm 90*
Dryden, Mary Elizabeth 1949- *WhoAmW 91*
Dryden, Pamela *ConAu 32NR*
Dryden, Phyllis Kay 1947- *WhoAm 90*
Dryden, Robert Charles 1936- *St&PR 91, WhoAm 90*
Dryden, Robert Eugene 1927- *WhoAm 90, WhoWor 91*
Dryden, Robert L. 1933- *St&PR 91*
Drye, Richard Arthur, Jr. 1950- *WhoEmL 91, WhoSSW 91*
Drye, Robert C *BiDrAPA 89*
Drye, Robert Caldwell 1927- *WhoE 91*
Drye, William James 1939- *WhoE 91*
Dryer, Donna A *BiDrAPA 89*
Dryer, Dorothea Merrill *WhoAmW 91, WhoE 91, WhoWor 91*
Dryer, Douglas Poole 1915- *WhoAm 90, WhoWrEP 89*
Dryer, Fred 1946- *BioIn 16, WorAlBi*
Dryer, Moira Jane 1957- *WhoAmA 91*
Dryer, Murray 1925- *WhoAm 90*
Dryfoos, Nancy *WhoAmA 91*
Dryfoos, Nancy Proskauer *WhoAmW 91*
Dryfoos, Orvil Eugene 1912-1963 *BioIn 16*
Drygulski, John Stanley 1949- *WhoE 91*
Dryhurst, Edward *ConAu 129*
Dryhurst, Glenn 1939- *WhoAm 90*
Drykerman, Dan 1948- *St&PR 91*
Drykos, William Ronald 1939- *St&PR 91*
Drylie, Lori L. *WhoAmW 91*
Drymalski, Raymond Hibner 1936- *WhoAm 90*
Drymiotis, Andrew D *BiDrAPA 89*
Drynan, Margaret Isobel 1915- *WhoAmW 91*
Dryovage, Mary Margaret 1954- *WhoEmL 91*
Drysdale, Don 1936- *Ballpl 90 [port], BioIn 16, WorAlBi*
Drysdale, Donald Scott 1936- *WhoAm 90*
Drysdale, Elaine Ruth *BiDrAPA 89*
Drysdale, Kenneth Gordon Thomas 1929- *St&PR 91*
Drysdale, M. Dickey *BioIn 16*
Drysdale, Nancy McIntosh 1931- *WhoAmA 91*
Dryzer, Scott Randall *BiDrAPA 89*
Dryzga, John Adam 1963- *WhoE 91*
Drzewiecki, Tadeusz Maria 1943- *WhoE 91*
D'Sa, Derek 1942- *St&PR 91*
Dsika, E.L., Jr. 1946- *St&PR 91*
D'Souza, Anthony Frank 1929- *WhoAm 90*
D'Souza, Bernadette B *BiDrAPA 89*
D'Souza, Eunice 1951- *BiDrAPA 89*
D'Souza, Michael Joseph 1959- *WhoEmL 91*
Du, Julie Yi-Fang Tsai 1937- *WhoAmW 91*
Du, Mingxin 1928- *IntWWM 90*
Du, Nang *BiDrAPA 89*
Du, Romeo Regner 1939- *WhoWor 91*
Du, Ying Tzyong 1947- *St&PR 91*
Dua, Hari Krishan 1937- *WhoWor 91*
Duall, John William 1928- *St&PR 91, WhoAm 90*
Duane, Daniel Joseph 1946- *St&PR 91*
Duane, Diane 1952- *BioIn 16*
Duane, Herbert Tobias, Jr. 1935- *WhoE 91*
Duane, Morris 1901- *WhoAm 90*
Duane, Robert Edward 1928- *St&PR 91*
Duane, Tanya *WhoAmA 91N*
Duane, Thomas David 1917- *WhoAm 90*
Duane, William 1760-1835 *BioIn 16*
Duane, William John 1780-1865 *BiDrUSE 89*
Duangploy, Orapin 1946- *WhoEmL 91, WhoSSW 91*
Duany, Luis Alberto 1965- *WhoHisp 91*
Duarte, Amalia Maria 1962- *WhoHisp 91*
Duarte, Augusto Rodrigues 1848-1888 *ArtLatA*
Duarte, Bienvenido 1927- *BiDrAPA 89*
Duarte, Cristobal G. 1929- *WhoWor 91*
Duarte, Jose Napoleon *BioIn 16*
Duarte, Jose Napoleon 1925-1990 *ConAu 131, CurBio 90N, NewYTBS 90 [port], News 90, -90-3, WorAlBi*
Duarte, Juan Pablo 1813-1876 *BioIn 16*
Duarte, Ramon Gonzalez 1948- *WhoWor 91*
Duarte, Roberto Jose 1938- *WhoSSW 91*
Duarte, Y. E. 1948- *WhoHisp 91*
Duarte Fuentes, Jose Napoleon 1925-1990 *CurBio 90N*
Duarte-Marshall, Patricia 1938- *WhoAmW 91, WhoE 91*
Duax, William Leo 1939- *WhoAm 90*
Dub, Anthony V. 1949- *St&PR 91, WhoAm 90*
Duba, Arlo Dean 1929- *WhoAm 90*
Duba, Roger Ernest 1938- *St&PR 91*
Duback, Charles S 1926- *WhoAmA 91*
Duback, Steven Rahr 1944- *St&PR 91, WhoAm 90*
Du Bain, Myron 1923- *WhoAm 90*
Dubal, David *IntWWM 90*
Duban, Beverly Ann 1944- *WhoAmW 91*
Dubanevich, Arlene 1950- *BioIn 16*
Dubanevich, Keith Scott 1957- *WhoEmL 91*
Dubaniewicz, Peter Paul 1913- *WhoAmA 91*
Du Bar, Jules Ramon 1923- *WhoAm 90*
Du Barry, Comtesse 1743-1793 *WorAlBi*
Dubarry, John 1938- *IntWWM 90*
Dubasky, Valentina 1951- *WhoAmA 91, WhoE 91*
DuBay, Daniel Joseph Alexander 1949- *WhoEmL 91*
Dubay, Eugene N. 1948- *St&PR 91*
Dubay, Gwen Ann 1951- *WhoAmW 91, WhoEmL 91*
Dubay, Stephen Newton 1941- *WhoSSW 91*
Dubberke, Jane Carol 1947- *WhoAmW 91*
Dubberly, Ronald Alvah 1942- *WhoSSW 91*
Dubbert, Patricia Marie 1947- *WhoAmW 91*
Dubbs, Robert Morton 1943- *St&PR 91*
Dubcek, Alexander *BioIn 16*
Dubcek, Alexander 1921- *WhoWor 91*
Dube, Armand Lucien 1931- *WhoE 91*
Dube, Daniel 1908- *St&PR 91*
Dube, James L. 1949- *St&PR 91*
Dube, Jean-Eudes 1926- *WhoAm 90, WhoE 91*
Dube, John 1899- *WhoAm 90, WhoE 91, WhoWor 91*
Dube, Kalika Charan 1913- *BiDrAPA 89*
Dube, Lawrence Edward, Jr. 1948- *WhoEmL 91*
Dube, Marcel 1930- *ConAu 129, OxCCanT*
Dube, Miriam *St&PR 91*
Dube, Noreen Mary 1941- *WhoE 91, WhoWor 91*
Dube, Oscar 1940- *St&PR 91*
Dube, Peter 1958- *St&PR 91*
Dube, Richard Lawrence 1950- *WhoE 91*
Dube, Robert Donald 1941- *St&PR 91*
Dube, Sanjay 1954- *BiDrAPA 89*
Dubeau, Donald Norman 1935- *St&PR 91*
Dubeau, Robert C. 1934- *St&PR 91*
Dubedout, Hubert 1922-1986 *BiDFrPL*
Dubelaar, Thea 1947- *SmATA 60 [port]*
Du Bellay, Joachim 1522?-1560 *WorAlBi*
Duberg, John Edward 1917- *WhoAm 90, WhoSSW 91, WhoWor 91*
Duberman, Lewis Donald 1940- *St&PR 91*
Duberman, Martin B. *BioIn 16*
Duberman, Martin Bauml 1930- *WhoAm 90*
Duberstein, Barbara Fern 1958- *St&PR 91*
Duberstein, Helen Laura 1926- *WhoWrEP 89*
Duberstein, Kenneth *BioIn 16*
Dubes, George Richard 1926- *WhoAm 90*
Dubes, Michael J. 1942- *WhoAm 90*
Dubes, Richard Charles 1931- *WhoAm 90*
Dubester, Michael Steven 1947- *St&PR 91*
Dubester, Sherry Nadine 1960- *BiDrAPA 89*
Dubey, Joseph M 1935- *BiDrAPA 89*
Dubey, Stephen Arthur 1947- *WhoEmL 91*
Dubie, Norman 1945- *WorAu 1980 [port]*
Dubief, Jean 1903- *WhoWor 91*
Dubiel, Donald E. *St&PR 91*
Dubiel, Mark Baldwin *BiDrAPA 89*
Dubiel, Monk 1919-1969 *Ballpl 90*
Dubiel, Thomas Wieslaw 1929- *WhoWor 91*
Dubin, Al 1891-1945 *OxCPMus*
Dubin, Alvin 1914- *WhoAm 90*
Dubin, Arthur Detmers 1923- *WhoAm 90*
Dubin, Charles Leonard 1921- *WhoAm 90*
Dubin, E. Beverly 1945- *WhoWor 91*
Dubin, Ellen Fenton 1953- *WhoAmW 91*
Dubin, Fred *BioIn 16*
Dubin, Gerald H *BiDrAPA 89*
Dubin, Howard Victor 1938- *WhoAm 90*
Dubin, James Michael 1946- *WhoAm 90*
Dubin, Joseph William 1948- *WhoE 91*
Dubin, Leonard 1934- *WhoAm 90*
Dubin, Mark William 1942- *WhoAm 90*
Dubin, Martin David 1927- *WhoAm 90*
Dubin, Mel 1923- *St&PR 91*
Dubin, Michael 1943- *WhoE 91, WhoWor 91*
Dubin, Morton Donald 1931- *WhoAm 90*
Dubin, Neil Stanford 1951- *BiDrAPA 89*
Dubin, Samuel *BiDrAPA 89*
Dubin, Seth Harris 1933- *WhoAm 90*
Dubin, Sheri 1953- *WhoAmW 91*
Dubin, Stephen Elliot 1946- *BiDrAPA 89*
Dubin, Stephen V. 1938- *St&PR 91*
Dubin, Steven Hugh 1948- *WhoE 91, WhoWor 91*
Dubin, Wesley P. *BioIn 16*
Dubin, William R 1947- *BiDrAPA 89*
Dubinin, Nikolai Petrovich 1907- *WhoWor 91*
Dubinin, Yuri V. *BioIn 16*
Dubinski, Gerald Z., Sr. 1928- *St&PR 91*
Dubinskis, Anda 1952- *WhoAmA 91*
Dubinsky, David 1892-1982 *WorAlBi*
Dubinsky, Inna 1938- *BiDrAPA 89*
Dubinsky, John P. 1943- *St&PR 91*
Dubinsky, Rostislav *BioIn 16, PenDiMP*
Dubis, Charles Stanley 1948- *WhoSSW 91*
Dubkin, Lois 1911- *AuBYP 90*
Dublac, Robert Revak 1938- *WhoAmA 91, WhoE 91*
Dublanc, Jean Marc 1954- *St&PR 91*
Duble, Ethel Mokhiber 1956- *WhoEmL 91*
Duble, Harold Grover 1938- *St&PR 91*
Duble, Lu 1896-1970 *WhoAmA 91N*
Dublin, Elvie Wilson 1937- *WhoAmW 91*
Dublin, Frederick Raymond 1945- *WhoE 91*
Dublin, James R. 1948- *ODwPR 91*
Dublin, Sascha *BioIn 16*
Dublin, Thomas David 1912- *WhoAm 90*
Dublis, Astrid Maria 1938- *BiDrAPA 89*
Dublis, Robert Adam 1939- *BiDrAPA 89*
Dubner, Harold H *BiDrAPA 89*
Dubner, Neil P 1936- *BiDrAPA 89*
Dubner, Ronald 1934- *WhoAm 90*
Dubnick, Bernard 1928- *WhoAm 90*
Dubnick, Mel 1946- *ConAu 30NR*
Dubnow, Simon 1860-1941 *BioIn 16*
Dubo, Sara *BiDrAPA 89*
Duboc, Charles A. 1923- *St&PR 91*
DuBoc, Roland George 1932- *WhoWor 91*
Duboczy, John Bela 1942- *BiDrAPA 89*
Du Boff, Eugene Alan 1937- *BiDrAPA 89*
Duboff, Robert Samuel 1948- *WhoE 91, WhoEmL 91*
Dubofsky, Jean Eberhart 1942- *WhoAm 90*
Dubofsky, Melvyn 1934- *WhoE 91*
Dubois, Abraham 1777?-1807 *PenDiDA 89*
Dubois, Alain 1955- *WhoE 91*
DuBois, Alan Beekman 1935- *WhoAm 90*
Dubois, Andre 1939- *WhoE 91*
DuBois, Arthur 1932- *St&PR 91*
Du Bois, Arthur Brooks 1923- *WhoAm 90*
DuBois, Barbara Rattray 1926- *WhoWrEP 89*
Dubois, Carol Stamp *BiDrAPA 89*
Dubois, Christine 1956- *WhoWrEP 89*
Dubois, Danuta Rosalia 1946- *IntWWM 90*
Du Bois, Dorothea 1728-1774 *FemiCLE*
DuBois, Gazell Macy 1929- *WhoWor 91*
Dubois, George E. 1951- *St&PR 91*
Dubois, Gerard Claude Eugene Albert 1936- *WhoWor 91*
Du Bois, Guy Pene 1884-1958 *BioIn 16, WhoAmA 91N*
DuBois, Howard J. 1936- *St&PR 91*
Dubois, Jacques 1693?-1763 *PenDiDA 89*
Dubois, Jacques E. 1921- *St&PR 91*
Dubois, Ja'net 1938- *DrBlPA 90*
DuBois, Jean Gabriel 1926- *WhoWor 91*
Dubois, Louis 1732-1790? *PenDiDA 89*
DuBois, Louis H. 1930- *St&PR 91*
Dubois, Macy 1929- *WhoAmA 91*
Dubois, Marie 1858-1940 *WorAlBi*
DuBois, Mark Benjamin 1955- *WhoWor 91*
DuBois, Melodee Ann 1948- *WhoAmW 91*
Du Bois, Paul Zinkhan 1936- *WhoAm 90*
Dubois, Peter Alan 1958- *IntWWM 90*
Du Bois, Philip Hunter 1903- *WhoAm 90, WhoWor 91*
Du Bois, Raoul Pene 1914-1985 *ConDes 90*
Dubois, Raphael-Horace 1849-1929 *DcScB S2*
Dubois, Rene 1737-1799 *PenDiDA 89*
Dubois, Rene-Daniel 1955- *OxCCanT*
Dubois, Rhoda Nicole Alexandra 1953- *WhoE 91*
Dubois, Robert *PenDiDA 89*
Dubois, Robert Wilfred 1947- *WhoEmL 91*
DuBois, Samuel S.M. 1931- *St&PR 91*
Du Bois, Shirley 1906-1977 *FemiCLE*
Du Bois, Shirley Graham *AuBYP 90*
Du Bois, Shirley Graham 1906-1977 *BioIn 16*
DuBois, Shirley Graham 1906-1977 *EarBlAP*
Du Bois, Theodora 1890- *AuBYP 90*
Du Bois, W. E. B. 1868-1963 *BioIn 16*
Du Bois, W.E.B. 1868-1963 *ConLC 64 [port]*
DuBois, W. E. B. 1868-1963 *EarBlAP*
Du Bois, W. E. B. 1868-1963 *EncAL*
Du Bois, W E B 1868-1963 *MajTwCW*
Dubois, W. E. B. 1868-1963 *WorAlBi*
DuBois, W. E. B., Mrs. 1906-1977 *EarBlAP*
Du Bois, William Edward Burghardt 1868-1963 *BioIn 16*
Du Bois, William Pene 1916- *BioIn 16*
Du Bois, William Sherman Pene 1916- *AuBYP 90*
Dubois-Jallais, Denise 1931- *EncCoWW*
Du Boise, Kim Rees 1953- *WhoSSW 91*

Dubon, Luis E. 1901- *St&PR 91*
Dubos, Jean 1918-1988 *BioIn 16*
DuBose, Barbara Jane 1922- *WhoAmW 91*
DuBose, Carol Ann 1954- *WhoAmW 91*
DuBose, Carroll Jones 1937- *St&PR 91*
DuBose, Charles Wilson 1949- *WhoEmL 91*
DuBose, Darryl Thomas 1940- *WhoAm 90*
DuBose, Maria Deborah 1952- *WhoHisp 91*
DuBose, Pamela *ODwPR 91*
Dubose, Reagan Layne, Jr. 1932- *St&PR 91*
Du Boulay, F R H 1920- *ConAu 131*
du Boulay, Shirley 1933- *ConAu 129*
Dubourg, Victoria 1840-1926 *BiDWomA*
DuBoux, Patricia Jane 1956- *WhoAmW 91*
Dubov, Larry Herbert 1936- *St&PR 91*
Dubovsky, Steven Lew 1944- *BiDrAPA 89*
Dubovy, Herbert 1934- *WhoE 91*
Dubow, Arthur Myron 1933- *WhoAm 90*
Dubow, Susan Diane 1948- *WhoEmL 91*
Dubowsky, Steven 1942- *WhoAm 90*
Dubowy, Burton Stephen 1939- *St&PR 91*
Duboy, Antonio 1963- *WhoHisp 91*
Dubreuil, Andre *BioIn 16*
Dubreuil, Pierre 1872-1944 *BioIn 16*
DuBridge, Lee Alvin 1901- *WhoAm 90*
DuBrin, Andrew J. 1935- *ConAu 33NR*
DuBrin, Andrew John 1935- *WhoAm 90, WhoE 91*
Dubrish, Douglas Martin 1953- *WhoEmL 91*
Dubriwny, Michael D 1939- *BiDrAPA 89*
Dubro, James 1946- *ConAu 129*
Dubrovay, Laszlo 1943- *IntWWM 90*
Dubrow, Marsha Ann 1948- *WhoAmW 91, WhoEmL 91*
DuBrul, Stephen M., Jr. 1929- *St&PR 91*
Dubs, Adolph 1920-1979 *BioIn 16*
Dubs, Patrick Christian 1947- *WhoAm 90*
Dubsky, Robert F. 1945- *St&PR 91*
Dubuc, Andre 1945- *WhoAm 90*
Dubuc, Carroll Edward 1933- *WhoAm 90, WhoE 91*
Dubuc, Jean 1888-1958 *Ballpl 90*
Dubuc, Mary Ellen 1950- *WhoAmW 91*
Dubuc, Serge 1939- *WhoAm 90*
Dubuffet, Jean 1901-1985 *IntDcAA 90*
Dubuque, Cheryl Anne 1952- *WhoWrEP 89*
Dubuque, Frank Thomas 1918- *St&PR 91*
Dubus, Andre 1936- *BioIn 16*
Dubus, Andre, III 1959- *ConAu 132*
Dubuss, Robert Francis 1935- *St&PR 91*
Duby, Paul Francois 1933- *WhoAm 90*
Duby, William Ralph *NewAgE 90*
Duca, Alfred Milton 1920- *WhoAm 90, WhoAmA 91*
Duca, Carmine A. *St&PR 91*
Ducan, Todd 1900- *OxCPMus*
Ducanis, Alex Julius 1931- *WhoAm 90*
duCann, Edward 1924- *WhoWor 91*
Ducas, Diane Athena *BiDrAPA 89*
Ducas, Dorothy 1905- *AuBYP 90*
Ducasse, C J 1881-1969 *EncO&P 3*
Ducasse, Curt John 1881-1969 *EncPaPR 91*
Ducate, Suzanne Elaine 1963- *BiDrAPA 89*
Ducatt, Jody Lynn 1962- *WhoAmW 91*
Ducceschi, James Martin Michael 1936- *WhoSSW 91*
Duccio Di Buoninsegna 1255?-1318? *IntDcAA 90, WorAlBi*
Duceppe, Jean 1924- *OxCCanT*
Du Cerceau, Jacques Androuet 1520?-1584? *PenDiDA 89*
Duch, Edward K. 1949- *St&PR 91*
Duch Martorell, Cesar 1950- *WhoWor 91*
Duchac, Kenneth Farnham 1923-1989 *BioIn 16*
Duchacek, Ivo D. 1913-1988 *BioIn 16*
Duchamp, Marcel 1887-1968 *BioIn 16, IntDcAA 90, WorAlBi*
Duchamp, Suzanne 1889-1963 *BiDWomA*
Duchamp-Villon, Raymond 1876-1918 *IntDcAA 90*
DuChanois, Lee Scott 1961- *St&PR 91*
Ducharme, Rejean *BioIn 16*
Ducharme, Rejean 1942- *OxCCanT*
Ducharme, Rene 1952- *BiDrAPA 89*
Ducharme, Roger Charles 1942- *St&PR 91*
Duche, Andrew 1709-1778 *PenDiDA 89*
Duchen, Charles 1918- *WhoAm 90*
Duchesne, Antoinette *ConAu 31NR*
Duchesne, Kay Ellen 1942- *WhoAmW 91*
Duchesne, Rose Philippine *BioIn 16*
Duchesne, Shadi 1960- *BiDrAPA 89*
Duchesne-Guillemin, Jacques 1910- *WhoWor 91*
Duchess of Marlborough *ConAu 131*
Duchet, Roger Benoit 1906-1981 *BiDFrPL*
Duchin, Eddy 1909-1951 *WorAlBi*
Duchin, Eddy 1910-1951 *OxCPMus*
Duchin, Louis Karl 1957- *BiDrAPA 89*
Duchin, Peter *BioIn 16*
Duchin, Peter 1937- *WorAlBi*
Duchin, Peter Oelrichs 1937- *WhoAm 90*
Duchossois, Richard L. 1921- *St&PR 91*
Duchossois, Richard Louis 1921- *WhoAm 90*
Duchowny, Irv Allan 1949- *St&PR 91*
Duchowny, Jack 1920- *St&PR 91*
Ducich, Dan 1951- *St&PR 91*
Ducie, Charles John, Jr. 1935- *WhoAm 90*
Ducie, Charles Jon, Jr. 1935- *St&PR 91*
Duck, June Moody 1947- *WhoEmL 91*
Duck, Stephen 1705?-1756 *DcLB 95 [port]*
Ducke, Kenneth F. 1943- *St&PR 91*
Ducken, Lynn K. *St&PR 91*
Duckenfield, Brida Sylvia 1933- *IntWWM 90*
Duckenfield, Thomas A. 1935- *St&PR 91*
Ducker, Bruce 1938- *WhoAm 90*
Ducker, James H. 1950- *ConAu 130*
Ducker, Paul Stephen 1942- *BiDrAPA 89*
Duckers, Ronald Lee 1935- *WhoSSW 91*
Duckert, Audrey Rosalind 1927- *WhoAm 90*
Duckett, Ann Lorraine 1951- *WhoEmL 91*
Duckett, Joan 1934- *WhoAmW 91*
Duckett, Karen Irene 1947- *WhoAmW 91, WhoSSW 91*
Duckett, Kermit Earl 1936- *WhoSSW 91*
Duckles, Sue Piper 1946- *WhoAmW 91*
Duckman, Jerome *BiDrAPA 89*
Duckman, Robert H. 1944- *WhoE 91*
Duckwitz, Georg Ferdinand 1904-1973 *BioIn 16*
Duckworth, Amanda 1958- *ODwPR 91*
Duckworth, Carol Kay 1941- *WhoAmW 91*
Duckworth, Geoffrey S 1942- *BiDrAPA 89*
Duckworth, Guy 1923- *WhoAm 90*
Duckworth, Henry Edmison 1915- *WhoAm 90*
Duckworth, Herbert Spencer 1900-1990 *BioIn 16*
Duckworth, Jim 1939- *Ballpl 90*
Duckworth, Kim Pelto 1956- *WhoAmW 91*
Duckworth, Lynn Allison 1948- *WhoAmW 91*
Duckworth, Marilyn 1935- *FemiCLE*
Duckworth, Nancy C H 1941- *BiDrAPA 89*
Duckworth, Paula Oliver 1940- *WhoSSW 91*
Duckworth, Robert Hunt 1932- *St&PR 91*
Duckworth, Ruth *PenDiDA 89*
Duckworth, Ruth 1919- *WhoAmA 91*
Duckworth, Walter Donald 1935- *WhoAm 90*
Duckworth, William Ervin 1943- *IntWWM 90*
Duckworth, Winston Howard 1918- *WhoAm 90*
Duclerc, Charles Theodore Eugene 1812-1892 *BiDFrPL*
Duclon, Warren Eugene 1924- *St&PR 91*
Duclos, Jacques 1896-1975 *BiDFrPL*
Duclos, Jeff *ODwPR 91*
Duclos, Keith Francis 1959- *WhoEmL 91*
Duclos, Warren Eugene, Jr. 1945- *WhoSSW 91*
Ducloux, Walter Ernest 1913- *IntWWM 90*
Duco, Josephine Diane 1947- *WhoAmW 91*
Ducoffe, Keith Rich 1950- *WhoWor 91*
Ducoin, Pierre *PenDiDA 89*
Ducommun, Charles E. 1913- *St&PR 91*
Ducommun, Charles Emil 1913- *WhoAm 90*
Ducommun, Edmond G. 1918- *St&PR 91*
Ducommun, Rick *BioIn 16*
Ducommun-Nagy, Catherine *BiDrAPA 89*
Ducornet, Erica 1943- *AuBYP 90*
Ducornet, Guy *AuBYP 90*
Ducornet, Rikki *AuBYP 90*
Ducote, Marjorie Ellen 1938- *WhoAmW 91*
Ducote-Cooper, Margaret Ann 1961- *WhoAmW 91*
Ducrest, Stephanie 1746- *EncCoWW*
Ducret, Lucette 1948- *WhoAmW 91, WhoWor 91*
Ducros, Pierre *BioIn 16*
Ducy, Patricia Cornelia 1945- *WhoSSW 91*
Duczek, Richard L. 1942- *St&PR 91*
Duda, Betty Ann 1932- *WhoSSW 91*
Duda, Cathy 1959- *WhoEmL 91*
Duda, John *BioIn 16*
Duda, John Larry 1936- *WhoAm 90*
Duda, Michael J. 1946- *St&PR 91*
Duda, Ronald P. 1942- *St&PR 91*
Duda, Zenon Michael 1955- *WhoEmL 91*
Dudack, Gail M. 1948- *St&PR 91*
Dudack, Gail Marie 1948- *WhoAm 90*
Dudak, John Joseph 1954- *WhoSSW 91*
Dudar, Abdur-Rahim Dib 1940- *WhoSSW 91*
Dudarova, Veronika 1916- *IntWWM 90*
Dudas, Louis Anthony 1935- *St&PR 91*
Dudash, Linda Christine *WhoAmW 91*
Duddeck, Heinz Werner 1928- *WhoWor 91*
Dudden, Arthur Power 1921- *WhoAm 90*
Duddles, Charles W. 1940- *St&PR 91*
Duddles, Charles Weller 1940- *WhoAm 90*
Duddy, Philip G. 1947- *St&PR 91*
du Deffand, Madame 1697-1780 *EncCoWW*
Dudek, Anthony Edward 1953- *WhoEmL 91*
Dudek, Beverly A *BiDrAPA 89*
Dudek, Henry Thomas 1929- *WhoE 91, WhoWor 91*
Dudek, Richard Albert 1926- *WhoAm 90*
Dudek, Stephanie Zuperko 1921- *WhoAm 90*
Dudek, William Michael 1956- *St&PR 91*
DuDell, Laura 1948- *ODwPR 91*
Duden, Anne 1942- *EncCoWW*
Duden, Joseph Francis 1933- *St&PR 91*
Dudeney, Alice 1866-1945 *FemiCLE*
Dudenhoeffer, Frank Edward 1926- *WhoAm 90*
Duderstadt, James Johnson 1942- *WhoAm 90, WhoWor 91*
Dudevant, Amantine Lucile Aurore Dupin 1804-1876 *BioIn 16*
Dudewicz, Edward John 1942- *WhoAm 90*
Dudey, Norman D. 1937- *St&PR 91*
Dudgeon, Dan Ed 1947- *WhoAm 90*
Dudgeon, Ralph Thomas 1948- *IntWWM 90*
Dudgeon, Stephen Murray 1949- *St&PR 91*
Dudick, Michael Joseph 1917- *WhoAm 90, WhoE 91*
Dudics-Dean, Susan Elaine 1950- *WhoAmW 91*
Dudley, Alden Woodbury, Jr. 1937- *WhoSSW 91*
Dudley, Alfred E. *St&PR 91*
Dudley, Alfred Edward 1928- *WhoAm 90*
Dudley, Bobby G. 1928- *WhoWrEP 89*
Dudley, Calmeze Henike, Jr. 1947- *BiDrAPA 89*
Dudley, Charles B., III *WhoSSW 91*
Dudley, Clise 1903- *Ballpl 90*
Dudley, David Watson 1954- *BiDrAPA 89*
Dudley, Dennis Wayne 1951- *WhoEmL 91*
Dudley, Elizabeth Hymer 1937- *WhoAmW 91*
Dudley, Gail 1951- *ODwPR 91*
Dudley, George Austin 1914- *WhoAm 90*
Dudley, Glenna Gail 1944- *WhoAmW 91*
Dudley, Guilford, Jr. *BioIn 16*
Dudley, H. Philip 1908- *WhoE 91*
Dudley, Hardy Drewrey 1912- *St&PR 91*
Dudley, Horace Chester 1909- *WhoWor 91*
Dudley, James F. 1942- *ConAu 130*
Dudley, James Michael 1941- *St&PR 91*
Dudley, Jane *BioIn 16*
Dudley, John 1951- *BiDrAPA 89*
Dudley, John A. 1931- *St&PR 91*
Dudley, Joseph 1647-1720 *EncCRAm*
Dudley, Kenneth Eugene 1937- *St&PR 91*
Dudley, LaQuita Joy 1932- *WhoAmW 91*
Dudley, Linda Jean 1946- *WhoEmL 91*
Dudley, Mark R. 1958- *St&PR 91*
Dudley, Mary 1750-1823 *FemiCLE*
Dudley, Merle Bland 1929- *WhoWor 91*
Dudley, Michael James 1960- *WhoEmL 91*
Dudley, Nancy *AuBYP 90*
Dudley, Patricia Lynn 1956- *BiDrAPA 89*
Dudley, Peggy Loucelle 1943- *WhoWrEP 89*
Dudley, Richard G, Jr. 1946- *BiDrAPA 89*
Dudley, Richard Mansfield 1938- *WhoAm 90, WhoE 91*
Dudley, Rick 1949- *WhoAm 90, WhoE 91*
Dudley, Robert *AuBYP 90*
Dudley, Robert 1532?-1588 *BioIn 16*
Dudley, Robert Edward 1942- *BiDrAPA 89*
Dudley, Robert Hamilton 1933- *WhoAm 90*
Dudley, Robert Stanley 1925- *WhoWor 91*
Dudley, Robert Thane 1916- *St&PR 91*
Dudley, Ronald G. 1939- *St&PR 91*
Dudley, S. H. *EarBlAP*
Dudley, Sherri Denise 1965- *WhoWrEP 89*
Dudley, Terri Crawford 1929- *WhoE 91*
Dudley, Thomas 1576-1653 *EncCRAm*
Dudley, Tilford E. *NewYTBS 90*
Dudley, Tilford E. 1907-1990 *BioIn 16*
Dudley, Wayne Carroll 1931- *St&PR 91*
Dudley, Wilbur George 1946- *WhoSSW 91*
Dudley, William Craig 1948- *WhoEmL 91*
Dudley, William G. *BioIn 16*
Dudley, William H C 1928- *BiDrAPA 89*
Dudley, William Henry 1932- *St&PR 91*
Dudley, William J. 1920- *St&PR 91*
Dudley-Smith, T. *TwCCr&M 91*
Dudman, Bryan L. 1956- *St&PR 91*
Dudman, Richard Beebe 1918- *WhoAm 90*
Dudney, William Cross, III 1948- *BiDrAPA 89*
Dudnick, Solis 1922- *St&PR 91*
Dudrick, Stanley John 1935- *WhoAm 90, WhoWor 91*
Duduit, James Michael 1954- *WhoEmL 91*
Dudziak, Edward Daniel 1941- *St&PR 91*
Dudzic, Joseph James 1963- *WhoE 91*
Dudzinski, Andrzej 1945- *BioIn 16*
Due, Jean Margaret 1921- *WhoAm 90*
Due, John Fitzgerald 1915- *WhoAm 90*
Due, Linnea A. 1948- *SmATA 64*
Dueber, Charles LeRoy 1945- *St&PR 91*
Duechting, Werner 1933- *WhoWor 91*
Duecker, Heyman Clarke 1929- *WhoAm 90*
Duecker, Robert Sheldon 1926- *WhoAm 90*
Duecker, Stephen Allen 1948- *WhoEmL 91*
Duecy, Charles Michael 1912- *WhoAm 90*
Duell, Daniel 1952- *BioIn 16*
Duell, Daniel Paul 1952- *WhoAm 90*
Duello, George Vincent 1954- *WhoEmL 91*
Duemer, Joseph 1951- *WhoWrEP 89*
Duemling, Robert Werner 1929- *WhoAm 90*
Duenas, Francisco *BioIn 16*
Duenewald, Doris *BioIn 16*
Duensing, James Arlin 1959- *WhoEmL 91*
Duer, David Edward 1954- *WhoWrEP 89*
Duer, Ellen Ann Dagon 1936- *WhoE 91, WhoWor 91*
Duer, Erika Waltraud 1937- *WhoWor 91*
Duer, Thomas C. *WhoAm 90*
Duer, Thomas Charles 1936- *St&PR 91*
Duer, William 1747-1799 *EncCRAm*
Duerbeck, Heidi Barbara 1947- *WhoEmL 91*
Duerig, Alfred W. 1926- *ConAu 129*
Duerinck, Louis T. 1929- *WhoAm 90*
Duerksen, Christopher James 1948- *WhoEmL 91*
Duerksen, George Louis 1934- *IntWWM 90, WhoAm 90*
Duerksen, Gregory J. 1957- *St&PR 91*
Duerksen-Hughes, Penelope Jayne 1960- *WhoSSW 91*
Duerr, Alfred *WhoAm 90*
Duerr, Dianne Marie 1945- *WhoAmW 91, WhoE 91, WhoEmL 91*
Duerr, Herman George 1931- *WhoAm 90*
Duerr, J. Stephen 1943- *St&PR 91*
Duerr, Jeannette Ferguson 1950- *ODwPR 91*
Duerr, Mary Jane 1955- *WhoAmW 91*
Duerr, Paula Cumming 1929- *WhoWrEP 89*
Duerre, John Arden 1930- *WhoAm 90*
Duerrenmatt, Friedrich 1921- *MajTwCW*
Duerrenmatt, Friedrich 1921-1990 *ConAu 33NR*
Duers, John Allen 1938- *BiDrAPA 89*
Duerson, David Russell 1960- *WhoWor 91*
Dues, Hal 1954- *Ballpl 90*
Dues, Theodore Roosevelt, Jr. 1953- *WhoSSW 91, WhoWor 91*
Duesberg, Peter Heinz Hermann 1936- *WhoAm 90*
Duesberry, Joellyn 1944- *WhoAmA 91*
Duesberry, Joellyn Toler 1944- *WhoE 91*
Duesbury, William 1725-1786 *PenDiDA 89*
Duesenberg, August *EncABHB 5*
Duesenberg, Frederick *EncABHB 5 [port]*
Duesenberg, Richard William 1930- *St&PR 91, WhoAm 90*
Duesenberg, Robert H. 1930- *St&PR 91, WhoAm 90, WhoWor 91*
Duesenberry, John 1950- *IntWWM 90*
Duesing, Dale 1950- *IntWWM 90*
Duesing, Dale L. 1945- *WhoAm 90*
Duet, Kendrick Joseph 1953- *WhoSSW 91*
Duetsch, John Edwin 1915- *WhoE 91*
Dueweke, Donald Gordon 1944- *St&PR 91*
Duewel, James L. *St&PR 91*
Duez-Donato, Debora *WhoAmA 91*
Dufallo, Richard 1933- *PenDiMP*
Dufallo, Richard John 1933- *IntWWM 90*
Dufau, Helene 1869-1937 *BiDWomA*
Dufault, Wilfrid Joseph 1907- *WhoAm 90*
Dufaure, Jules Armand Stanislas 1798-1881 *BiDFrPL*
Dufendach, Carl William 1953- *WhoEmL 91*
Duff, Allen Jerome, Jr. 1947- *WhoSSW 91*
Duff, Ann Macintosh *WhoAmA 91*
Duff, Annis J. *BioIn 16*
Duff, Brian Barnett 1930- *WhoAm 90*
Duff, Cloyd Edgar 1915- *WhoAm 90*
Duff, Daniel Vincent 1916- *WhoAm 90*
Duff, David Carroll 1933- *St&PR 91*
Duff, David Potter 1947- *WhoEmL 91*
Duff, Donald D. 1928- *St&PR 91*
Duff, Donald F 1930- *BiDrAPA 89*
Duff, Duane R. 1940- *St&PR 91*
Duff, Ernest Arthur 1929- *WhoSSW 91*
Duff, Francis Arthur 1916- *WhoWor 91*
Duff, George Alexander 1931- *WhoAm 90*
Duff, George Edwin 1912- *St&PR 91*
Duff, Howard 1913-1990 *NewYTBS 90 [port]*
Duff, Jack L. 1946- *St&PR 91*
Duff, James George 1938- *St&PR 91, WhoAm 90*
Duff, James H 1943- *WhoAmA 91*

Duff, James Henry 1943- *WhoAm 90, WhoE 91*
Duff, James Michael 1954- *WhoSSW 91*
Duff, Jane B. *ODwPR 91*
Duff, John Bernard 1931- *WhoAm 90*
Duff, John Ewing 1943- *WhoAm 90, WhoAmA 91*
Duff, Margaret K. 1916- *BioIn 16*
Duff, Mary Ann 1794-1857 *BioIn 16, NotWoAT*
Duff, Philip Nicholas 1957- *St&PR 91*
Duff, Raymond Stanley 1923- *WhoAm 90*
Duff, Ronald G. 1936- *WhoAm 90*
Duff, Virginia Anne 1957- *BiDrAPA 89*
Duff, William Grierson 1936- *WhoAm 90, WhoSSW 91, WhoWor 91*
Duff, William Leroy, Jr. 1938- *WhoAm 90*
Duff, William R 1941- *BiDrAPA 89*
Duff Gordon, Lucie 1821-1869 *BioIn 16*
Duffalo, Jim 1935- *Ballpl 90*
Duffee, Daniel J., Jr. 1918- *St&PR 91*
Duffee, Richard Anthony 1930- *St&PR 91*
Duffens, Robert Eugene 1924- *St&PR 91*
Duffett, John C. 1927- *St&PR 91*
Duffey, Donald Berrey 1933- *WhoSSW 91*
Duffey, H. Lyle 1922- *St&PR 91*
Duffey, Jeanne Christakos 1945- *WhoAmW 91*
Duffey, Joseph Daniel 1932- *WhoAm 90, WhoE 91*
Duffey, Lee 1959- *ODwPR 91*
Duffey, Merlee H. 1939- *WhoAmW 91*
Duffey, Michael S. 1954- *St&PR 91*
Duffey, Robert Joseph, II 1945- *St&PR 91*
Duffey, William Simon, Jr. 1952- *WhoEmL 91*
Dufficy, Rafael G, Jr. *BiDrAPA 89*
Duffie, Bruce 1951- *IntWWM 90*
Duffie, Edward R. 1929- *St&PR 91*
Duffie, Gerald Stover 1932- *WhoSSW 91*
Duffie, John Atwater 1925- *WhoAm 90*
Duffie, John Cochran 1957- *WhoSSW 91*
Duffie, Tommie C. 1929- *St&PR 91*
Duffie, Virgil W., Jr. 1935- *St&PR 91*
Duffie, Virgil Whatley, Jr. 1935- *WhoAm 90*
Duffield, David *BioIn 16*
Duffield, Don Forrest 1935- *St&PR 91*
Duffield, Mary Elizabeth 1819-1914 *BiDWomA*
Duffield, Thomas Andrew 1925- *St&PR 91*
Duffield, Timothy 1941- *WhoE 91*
Duffin, Michael B. 1948- *St&PR 91*
Duffin, Richard James 1909- *WhoAm 90*
Duffin, Simon 1844?-1900 *DcCanB 12*
Duffourc, Rene Charles, III 1945- *BiDrAPA 89*
Duffus, John Logie Lyall 1946- *IntWWM 90*
Duffus, Roy 1923- *ODwPR 91*
Duffus, Roy A. 1923- *St&PR 91*
Duffy, Adrian D 1932- *BiDrAPA 89*
Duffy, Betty Minor 1922- *WhoAmA 91*
Duffy, Brian J. 1941- *St&PR 91*
Duffy, Brian William 1951- *St&PR 91*
Duffy, Bruce Cary 1938- *St&PR 91*
Duffy, Carol Ann 1955- *FemiCLE*
Duffy, Dave 1948- *St&PR 91*
Duffy, David A. 1939- *ODwPR 91*
Duffy, Earl Gavin 1926- *WhoAm 90*
Duffy, Edmund 1899-1962 *WhoAmA 91N*
Duffy, Edward W. 1919-1988 *BioIn 16*
Duffy, Elaine Marie 1954- *WhoAmW 91*
Duffy, Esther Rodgers 1911- *WhoAmW 91*
Duffy, Francis Martin, Jr. 1949- *WhoE 91*
Duffy, Francis R 1915- *ConAu 30NR*
Duffy, Francis Ramon 1915- *WhoAm 90*
Duffy, Frank 1946- *Ballpl 90*
Duffy, Gary Wayne 1950- *WhoEmL 91*
Duffy, Gloria B 1944- *BiDrAPA 89*
Duffy, Helen Paton 1934- *BiDrAPA 89*
Duffy, Hugh 1866-1954 *Ballpl 90 [port]*
Duffy, J. O'Neill 1926- *St&PR 91*
Duffy, Jacques Wayne 1922- *WhoAm 90*
Duffy, James 1923- *ConAu 129*
Duffy, James Desmond 1956- *BiDrAPA 89*
Duffy, James H 1929- *BiDrAPA 89*
Duffy, James H 1934- *ConAu 131*
Duffy, James Henry 1934- *WhoAm 90*
Duffy, John 1915- *WhoAm 90*
Duffy, John 1928- *IntWWM 90*
Duffy, John C 1934- *BiDrAPA 89*
Duffy, John Charles 1934- *WhoAm 90*
Duffy, John Joseph 1931- *WhoAm 90, WhoSSW 91*
Duffy, John Louis 1933- *BiDrAPA 89*
Duffy, John Peter *BiDrAPA 89*
Duffy, Joseph Daniel 1946- *St&PR 91*
Duffy, Joseph Patrick, III 1949- *WhoAm 90*
Duffy, Julia *BioIn 16*
Duffy, Julia 1951- *WorAlBi*
Duffy, Katherine Plough *BiDrAPA 89*
Duffy, Kent Haviland 1951- *WhoEmL 91*
Duffy, Kevin 1943- *St&PR 91*
Duffy, Kevin Thomas 1933- *WhoAm 90*
Duffy, Lawrence Kevin 1948- *WhoWor 91*
Duffy, Malachy James, II 1951- *WhoE 91*
Duffy, Margaret Ann 1942- *SpyFic*
Duffy, Martin H. 1951- *St&PR 91*
Duffy, Maureen 1933- *BioIn 16, ConAu 33NR, FemiCLE, MajTwCW*
Duffy, Nancy Keogh 1947- *WhoAmW 91, WhoE 91*
Duffy, Patricia Mary 1955- *WhoEmL 91*
Duffy, Patrick *BioIn 16*
Duffy, Patrick 1949- *WhoAm 90, WorAlBi*
Duffy, Patrick C. 1937- *St&PR 91*
Duffy, Paul Gerald 1930- *St&PR 91*
Duffy, Philip Edmund 1943- *IntWWM 90*
Duffy, Richard A. 1928- *St&PR 91*
Duffy, Richard E. A. 1928- *ODwPR 91*
Duffy, Robert Aloysius 1921- *WhoAm 90*
Duffy, Robert Edward 1945- *WhoAm 90*
Duffy, Robert Thomas 1949- *WhoEmL 91*
Duffy, Robert Townsend 1926- *WhoSSW 91*
Duffy, Russell E. *St&PR 91*
Duffy, Stephen *BioIn 16*
Duffy, Terence 1922-1985 *DcNaB 1981*
Duffy, Thomas Brogan 1953- *St&PR 91*
Duffy, Thomas Edward 1947- *WhoAm 90*
Duffy, Thomas M 1943- *BiDrAPA 89*
Duffy, Thomas Patrick 1937- *St&PR 91*
Duffy, Vincent R. 1933- *ODwPR 91*
Duffy, W. Leslie 1939- *WhoAm 90*
Duffy, William Joseph, Jr. 1946- *WhoE 91*
Duffy, William Ray 1945- *WhoSSW 91*
Duffy, William Smith 1946- *St&PR 91*
Duffy, Yvonne Helen Patricia *WhoWrEP 89*
Duffy-Edwards, Sarah *ODwPR 91*
Duflos de Saint-Amand, Hubert 1936- *WhoWor 91*
Dufner, Edward 1871-1957 *WhoAmA 91N*
Dufner, Mary E *BiDrAPA 89*
Dufner, Max 1920- *WhoAm 90*
Dufoix, Georgina 1943- *BiDFrPL*
Dufour, Darlene 1944- *WhoWrEP 89*
Dufour, E. James 1934- *St&PR 91*
Dufour, Gregory Andre 1960- *WhoEmL 91*
Dufour, Joseph *PenDiDA 89*
Dufour, Lael Grey 1946- *WhoWor 91*
Dufour, Paul *BioIn 16*
Dufour, Paul Arthur 1922- *WhoAmA 91*
Dufour, Paul V. 1939- *St&PR 91*
DuFour, Richard William, Jr. 1940- *WhoAm 90*
Dufour, Val 1927- *WhoAm 90*
Dufourcq, Norbert 1904- *IntWWM 90*
Dufrene, Maurice 1876-1955 *PenDiDA 89*
Dufrenoy, Adelaide-Gillette 1765-1825 *EncCoWW*
Dufresne, Armand Alphee, Jr. 1909- *WhoAm 90*
Dufresne, Dewayne J. 1930- *St&PR 91*
Dufresne, Guy 1915- *OxCCanT*
Dufresne, Guy Georges 1941- *WhoAm 90*
Dufresne, Isabelle Collin *BioIn 16*
Dufresne, Jacques 1844-1896 *DcCanB 12*
Dufresne, Jerilyn Clare 1947- *WhoAmW 91, WhoEmL 91*
du Fresne, Yvonne 1929- *FemiCLE*
Duft, Cheryl G. *ODwPR 91*
Dufy, Raoul 1877-1953 *BioIn 16, IntDcAA 90, WorAlBi*
Dugal, Dianne Marie 1961- *WhoE 91*
Dugal, Louis Paul 1911- *WhoAm 90*
Dugan, Alan 1923- *CurBio 90 [port]*
Dugan, Charles Francis, II 1939- *WhoAm 90*
Dugan, Daniel J. 1953- *WhoAm 90*
Dugan, David Lawrence 1929- *WhoSSW 91*
Dugan, Denis K. 1939- *St&PR 91*
Dugan, Dennis *BioIn 16*
Dugan, Dennis 1946- *ConTFT 8*
Dugan, Dixie *WhoWrEP 89*
Dugan, Edward F. 1934- *St&PR 91*
Dugan, Edward Francis 1934- *WhoAm 90*
Dugan, Francis R. *St&PR 91*
Dugan, Francis Robert 1927- *St&PR 91*
Dugan, Frank P. *AmLegL*
Dugan, Hugh Patrick 1914- *WhoAm 90*
Dugan, Ida Annelle 1938- *WhoSSW 91*
Dugan, James Francis, III 1943- *WhoSSW 91*
Dugan, Joe 1897-1982 *Ballpl 90*
Dugan, John James, Jr. 1940- *St&PR 91*
Dugan, John Leslie, Jr. 1921- *WhoAm 90*
Dugan, John Michael 1909- *WhoAm 90*
Dugan, John Raymond, Jr. 1948- *WhoEmL 91*
Dugan, Joseph Harry 1926- *WhoAm 90*
Dugan, Karen Vernon *WhoAmA 91*
Dugan, Kimiko Hatta 1924- *WhoAmW 91*
Dugan, Linda Herrington *WhoAmW 91*
Dugan, Luan Martin 1952- *WhoSSW 91*
Dugan, Mary Deborah 1939- *WhoE 91*
Dugan, Mary E. *St&PR 91*
Dugan, Michael 1947- *ConAu 32NR*
Dugan, Patrick Raymond 1931- *WhoAm 90*
Dugan, Raymond C. 1930- *St&PR 91*
Dugan, Richard D. 1948- *WhoAm 90*
Dugan, Robert Michael 1953- *WhoEmL 91*
Dugan, Robert Perry, Jr. 1932- *WhoAm 90*
Dugan, Sean Francis Xavier 1951- *WhoEmL 91*
Dugan, Stanley Paul 1932- *BiDrAPA 89*
Dugan, Thomas Allen 1925- *St&PR 91*
Dugan, Timothy Francis *BiDrAPA 89*
Dugan, William Theodore, Jr. 1966- *WhoE 91*
Dugas, Lester J., Jr. 1924- *St&PR 91*
Dugas, Louis, Jr. 1928- *WhoAm 90*
Dugas, Marcel 1883-1947 *DcLB 92 [port]*
Dugazon, Louise-Rosalie 1755-1821 *PenDiMP*
Dugdale, Raymond J. 1949- *St&PR 91*
Dugdale, Sandra *IntWWM 90*
Duggan, Alfred Leo 1903-1964 *AuBYP 90*
Duggan, Andrew 1923-1988 *BioIn 16*
Duggan, Carol Cook 1946- *WhoAmW 91, WhoSSW 91*
Duggan, Charles Perkins 1922- *St&PR 91*
Duggan, Dennis Michael 1927- *WhoAm 90*
Duggan, Edward James 1931- *St&PR 91*
Duggan, Eileen 1894-1972 *FemiCLE*
Duggan, Elizabeth *BioIn 16*
Duggan, Ervin S. *BioIn 16*
Duggan, Herbert Garrison 1919- *WhoAm 90*
Duggan, J. Roy 1916- *WhoAm 90*
Duggan, James Edgar 1961- *WhoEmL 91*
Duggan, James H. 1935- *St&PR 91, WhoSSW 91*
Duggan, James Michael 1938- *BiDrAPA 89*
Duggan, James Roy 1916- *St&PR 91*
Duggan, Jerome Timothy 1914- *WhoAm 90*
Duggan, Joan 1935- *WhoAmW 91*
Duggan, John M. 1928-1988 *BioIn 16*
Duggan, John Patrick 1952- *WhoEmL 91*
Duggan, Kelly Marie 1963- *WhoAmW 91*
Duggan, Kevin 1944- *WhoSSW 91*
Duggan, M. Jane 1949- *WhoAmW 91*
Duggan, Mary Kay 1938- *IntWWM 90*
Duggan, Patrick O'Neill 1953- *WhoEmL 91*
Duggan, Peter James 1946- *St&PR 91*
Duggan, Robert E. 1939- *St&PR 91*
Duggan, Thomas Michael 1950- *WhoEmL 91*
Duggan, Thomas Patrick 1946- *WhoEmL 91*
Duggan, Timothy John 1928- *WhoAm 90*
Dugger, Charles B., Jr. 1944- *St&PR 91*
Dugger, Dorothy E G *BiDrAPA 89*
Dugger, Edwin Ellsworth 1940- *WhoAm 90*
Dugger, Jerold Orville 1927- *WhoAm 90*
Dugger, Julia Burns 1942- *WhoWrEP 89*
Dugger, Layne Ray 1964- *WhoSSW 91*
Dugger, Richard L. 1945- *St&PR 91*
Dugger, Ronnie E. 1930- *WhoAm 90, WhoWrEP 89*
Dugger, Willie Mack, Jr. 1919- *WhoAm 90*
Duggin, Lorraine Jean 1941- *WhoWrEP 89*
Duggins, Marian Barber 1925- *WhoAmW 91*
Duggleby, Bill 1874-1944 *Ballpl 90*
Duggleby, Brian David 1952- *WhoEmL 91*
Dugle, William M. 1942- *St&PR 91*
Dugmore, Clifford W 1909-1990 *ConAu 132*
Dugmore, Edward 1915- *WhoAm 90, WhoAmA 91*
Dugoff, Howard Jay 1936- *WhoAm 90*
Dugoni, Arthur A. 1925- *WhoAm 90*
Dugonjic, Zvonimir Furst 1923- *WhoWor 91*
Dugourc, Jean-Demosthene 1749-1825 *PenDiDA 89*
Duguay, Bernadette Ann 1963- *WhoAmW 91*
Duguay, Robert M *BiDrAPA 89*
Du Guesclin, Bertrand 1320?-1380 *BioIn 16*
Duguid, David 1832-1907 *EncO&P 3*
Dugundji, John 1925- *WhoAm 90*
Duhaime, Ricky Edward 1953- *WhoSSW 91*
Duhalde, Eduardo *WhoWor 91*
Duhamel, Georges 1855-1892 *DcCanB 12*
Duhamel, Georges 1884-1966 *BioIn 16, MajTwCW*
Duhamel, Joseph 1834-1894 *DcCanB 12*
Duhamel, Monique Julianne 1966- *WhoWrEP 89*
Duhamel, Pierre Albert 1920- *WhoAm 90*
Duhaylungsod, Toribio M 1939- *BiDrAPA 89*
Duhe, John Malcolm, Jr. 1933- *WhoAm 90, WhoSSW 91*
Duhl, Leonard J 1926- *BiDrAPA 89, WhoAm 90*
Duhl, Michael Foster 1944- *WhoAm 90*
Duhm, Kenneth David 1952- *WhoEmL 91*
Duhme, Carol McCarthy 1917- *WhoAmW 91, WhoWor 91*
Duhme, H Richard, Jr 1914- *WhoAmA 91*
Duhme, Herman Richard, Jr. 1914- *WhoAm 90*
Duhms, Martin 1947- *St&PR 91*
Duhnke, Robert Emmet, Jr. 1935- *WhoWor 91*
Duhon, Randy Reese 1948- *WhoSSW 91*
Duhr, Allen W. 1938- *St&PR 91*
Duignan, Peter James 1926- *WhoAm 90*
Duillo, Elaine *BioIn 16*
Duinker, Magreet 1953- *WomArch*
Duintjer, Otto Dirk 1932- *WhoWor 91*
Duis, Rita *WhoAmA 91*
Duisberg, Richard E H *BiDrAPA 89*
Duitch, Deborah Rachel *BiDrAPA 89*
Du Jardin, Gussie 1918- *WhoAmA 91*
Du Jardin, Rosamond 1902-1963 *AuBYP 90*
Dujardin de Calonne, Andre Bernard 1942- *WhoWor 91*
Duka, Ivo 1913-1988 *BioIn 16*
Duka, John 1949-1989 *BioIn 16*
Dukakis, Kara *BioIn 16*
Dukakis, Katharine *WhoAm 90, WhoAmW 91, WhoE 91*
Dukakis, Kitty *BioIn 16*
Dukakis, Michael *BioIn 16*
Dukakis, Michael 1933- *WorAlBi*
Dukakis, Michael Stanley 1933- *WhoAm 90, WhoE 91, WhoWor 91*
Dukakis, Olympia *BioIn 16*
Dukakis, Olympia 1931- *WhoAm 90, WhoAmW 91*
Dukakis, Olympia 1932- *WorAlBi*
Dukas, Christopher James 1955- *WhoE 91*
Dukas, Nick George 1947- *WhoSSW 91*
Dukas, Paul 1865-1935 *WorAlBi*
Dukas, Peter 1919- *WhoAm 90*
Dukas, Philip Alexander 1954- *WhoEmL 91*
Duke, A. W., Jr. 1931- *WhoSSW 91*
Duke, Angier Biddle 1915- *BioIn 16, WhoAm 90, WhoWor 91*
Duke, Anna Marie 1946- *ConAu 130*
Duke, Anthony D., Jr. 1942- *St&PR 91*
Duke, Benjamin N. 1855-1929 *WorAlBi*
Duke, Bernie 1927- *St&PR 91*
Duke, Bill 1943?- *DrBlPA 90*
Duke, C. H. *WhoSSW 91*
Duke, Charles Bryan 1938- *WhoAm 90*
Duke, Chris Charles 1961- *WhoSSW 91*
Duke, Clifford Frank 1953- *WhoSSW 91*
Duke, David *BioIn 16*
Duke, David 1951?- *News 90 [port]*
Duke, David Allen 1935- *St&PR 91, WhoAm 90*
Duke, David Carroll 1932- *St&PR 91*
Duke, Donald Norman 1929- *WhoAm 90*
Duke, Doris 1912- *BioIn 16*
Duke, Ellen Kay 1952- *WhoAmW 91, WhoEmL 91*
Duke, Emanuel 1916- *WhoAm 90*
Duke, Gary James 1947- *WhoSSW 91*
Duke, Gary Philip 1957- *WhoEmL 91*
Duke, Harold Benjamin, Jr. 1922- *St&PR 91, WhoAm 90*
Duke, Henry 1920- *IntWWM 90*
Duke, James *BioIn 16*
Duke, James Alan 1929- *WhoAm 90*
Duke, James Buchanan 1856-1925 *WorAlBi*
Duke, James Herring, Jr. 1950- *St&PR 91*
Duke, Jesse W. 1927- *St&PR 91*
Duke, John Wayne 1943- *St&PR 91*
Duke, Kate *AuBYP 90*
Duke, Katie Sue 1942- *WhoE 91*
Duke, Kenneth Jason 1957- *WhoEmL 91*
Duke, Lance Brittain 1958- *WhoSSW 91*
Duke, Lawrence Kenneth 1956- *WhoWor 91*
Duke, Leilani Lattin 1943- *WhoAmA 91*
Duke, Lois Lovelace 1935- *WhoAmW 91, WhoSSW 91*
Duke, Marshall Perry 1942- *WhoSSW 91*
Duke, Mary Bohland 1919- *WhoSSW 91*
Duke, Mathilde Weaver 1911- *WhoWrEP 89*
Duke, Patty *BioIn 16, ConAu 130*
Duke, Patty 1946- *WhoAm 90, WhoAmW 91, WorAlBi*
Duke, Paul Robert 1929- *WhoAm 90*
Duke, Red *BioIn 16*
Duke, Robert Dominick 1928- *St&PR 91, WhoAm 90, WhoE 91*
Duke, Robin *BioIn 16*
Duke, Robin Chandler Tippett 1923- *WhoAmW 91*
Duke, Steven Barry 1934- *WhoAm 90*
Duke, Vernon 1903-1969 *BioIn 16, OxCPMus*
Duke, Veronica Murray 1931- *WhoAmW 91*
Duke, W. Thomas 1933- *ODwPR 91*
Duke, Will *TwCCr&M 91*
Dukek, Nancy Bowman 1916- *WhoAmW 91, WhoE 91*
Dukeminier, Jesse 1925- *WhoAm 90*
Dukert, Betty Cole 1927- *WhoAm 90, WhoAmW 91, WhoE 91*
Dukert, Joseph Michael 1929- *AuBYP 90*
Dukes, Caroline *WhoAmA 91*
Dukes, Charles A. *St&PR 91*

Dukes, David 1945- *WhoAm 90, WhoEmL 91*
Dukes, Joan *WhoAmW 91*
Dukes, Joseph 1811-1861 *WhNaAH*
Dukes, Joyce Leak 1954- *WhoAmW 91*
Dukes, Paul 1889-1967 *EncO&P 3*
Dukes, Rebecca Weathers 1934- *WhoAmW 91, WhoE 91*
Dukes, Shirley *BioIn 16*
Dukes, Tamara Downham 1962- *WhoAmW 91*
Dukes, Tom 1942- *Ballpl 90*
Dukes, William W., Jr. 1917- *St&PR 91*
Dukes, Yvonne B. *St&PR 91*
Dukkony, Ruth Adams 1932- *WhoE 91*
Dukler, Abraham Emanuel 1925- *WhoAm 90*
Dukore, Bernard Frank 1931- *WhoSSW 91*
Dula, Gloria Elisabeth 1958- *WhoEmL 91*
Dula, Lucile Noell 1914- *WhoAmW 91*
Dula, Norman Lee 1924- *St&PR 91*
Dula, William A. 1932- *St&PR 91*
Dulai, Surjit Singh *WhoAm 90*
Dulan, Harold Andrew 1911- *WhoAm 90*
Dulaney, Frank Alan 1929- *St&PR 91*
Dulaney, Luther Carroll 1925- *WhoSSW 91*
Dulaney, Richard Alvin 1948- *WhoEmL 91*
Dulaney, Robert *BioIn 16*
Dulany, Charles Reihl 1934- *St&PR 91*
Dulany, Daniel 1685-1753 *EncCRAm*
Dulany, Elizabeth Gjelsness 1931- *WhoAm 90, WhoAmW 91*
Dulany, Franklin Reed, Jr. 1931- *St&PR 91*
Dulany, William Bevard 1927- *St&PR 91, WhoE 91*
DuLaux, Russell Frederick 1918- *WhoE 91, WhoWor 91*
Dulay, Dion Joseph 1948- *WhoWor 91*
Dulay, Elisa Tabique 1946- *BiDrAPA 89, WhoE 91*
Dulbecco, Patrick 1947- *WhoWor 91*
Dulbecco, Renato 1914- *WhoAm 90, WhoWor 91, WorAlBi*
Dulcan, Mina Karen 1948- *BiDrAPA 89*
Dulchinos, Peter 1935- *WhoE 91, WhoWor 91*
Duley, Margaret 1894-1968 *FemiCLE*
Duley, Susan Inge 1947- *WhoAmW 91*
Duliba, Bob 1935- *Ballpl 90*
Dulieu, Jean *ConAu 31NR*
Dulik, Arthur, Jr. 1946- *St&PR 91*
Dulin, Bill Joe 1935- *WhoSSW 91*
Dulin, Carol Jo *WhoE 91*
Dulin, Eric Saunders 1944- *St&PR 91*
Dulin, Jacques M. 1934- *St&PR 91*
Dulin, John P. 1938- *WhoSSW 91*
Dulin, Patricia Ann 1952- *WhoAmW 91, WhoEmL 91*
Dulin, Thomas N. 1949- *WhoEmL 91*
Dulin, William A. 1949- *WhoE 91*
Duling, Frank Samuel, Jr. 1923- *WhoSSW 91*
Duling, Richard E. 1933- *St&PR 91*
Dulit, Everett Paul 1929- *BiDrAPA 89*
Dulit, Rebecca Ann *BiDrAPA 89*
Dulka, Joseph Steven *BiDrAPA 89*
Dull Knife 1810?-1883 *WhNaAH*
Dull, Charles W. 1940- *St&PR 91*
Dull, Dallas Kevin 1961- *WhoSSW 91*
Dull, William Martin 1924- *WhoAm 90*
Dulla, Steven Glenn *BiDrAPA 89*
Dulla, Steven Glenn 1947- *WhoEmL 91*
Dullea, Charles W. *WhoAm 90*
Dullemen, Inez Van 1925- *EncCoWW*
Dulles, Allen 1893-1969 *WorAlBi*
Dulles, Allen Welsh 1893-1969 *SpyFic*
Dulles, Avery 1918- *WhoAm 90, WhoE 91*
Dulles, Avery Robert 1918- *BioIn 16*
Dulles, Eleanor L. 1895- *BioAmW*
Dulles, Eleanor Lansing 1895- *WhoAm 90*
Dulles, John Foster 1888-1959 *BiDrUSE 89, BioIn 16, WorAlBi*
Dullinger, Gloria 1962- *WhoAmW 91*
Dullnig, Michael M *BiDrAPA 89*
Dullum, Mervin E. 1922- *St&PR 91*
Dully, Frank Edward, Jr. 1932- *WhoWor 91*
Dulski, Thaddeus 1915-1988 *BioIn 16*
Dultz, Ron William 1943- *WhoWrEP 89*
Dulude, Donald O. 1928- *St&PR 91*
Dulude, Donald Owen 1928- *WhoAm 90*
Dulude, Richard 1933- *St&PR 91, WhoAm 90*
Duluth, Daniel Greysolon 1636-1710 *EncCRAm*
Duluth, Daniel Greysolon, Sieur 1636-1710 *WhNaAH*
Dulzin, Leon 1913-1989 *BioIn 16*
Duma, Richard Joseph 1933- *WhoAm 90*
Dumaine, F.C. 1902- *St&PR 91*
Dumaine, Marian Lee 1945- *WhoEmL 91*
Duman, Daniel 1948- *ConAu 129*
Dumaresq, John Edward 1913- *WhoAm 90*
Dumars, Joe *BioIn 16*
Dumars, Joe 1963- *WorAlBi*
Dumas, Alexandre 1802-1870 *BioIn 16, WorAlBi*
Dumas, Alexandre 1824-1895 *DrBIPA 90, WorAlBi*
Dumas, Andre A 1908- *EncO&P 3*
Dumas, Antoine 1932- *WhoAmA 91*
Dumas, Catherine Mary 1945- *WhoSSW 91*
Dumas, Claudia Jean 1959- *WhoAmW 91*
Dumas, Dick *BioIn 16*
Dumas, Henry 1934-1968 *BioIn 16, ConLC 62 [port]*
Dumas, Jacqueline 1946- *BioIn 16*
Dumas, Jerry 1930- *EncACom*
Dumas, Linda Jean 1959- *WhoAmW 91*
Dumas, Loretta Ponton *BioIn 16*
Dumas, Peter A *BiDrAPA 89*
Dumas, Philippe 1940- *BioIn 16*
Dumas, Rhetaugh Etheldra Graves 1928- *WhoAm 90, WhoAmW 91*
Dumas, Roland 1922- *CurBio 90 [port], WhoWor 91*
Dumaual, Cherry *ODwPR 91*
du Maurier, Daphne 1907-1989 *AnObit 1989, BioIn 16, ConLC 59 [port], FemiCLE, MajTwCW, SmATA 60, TwCCr&M 91, WorAlBi*
Du Maurier, George 1834-1896 *BioIn 16*
Dumay, Augustin 1949- *PenDiMP*
Dumbacher, Robert *St&PR 91*
Dumbaugh, George David 1930- *St&PR 91*
Dumbauld, Edward 1905- *ConAu 129, WhoAm 90*
Dumbleton, Duane Dean 1939- *WhoSSW 91*
Dumbrille, Dorothy 1897-1983? *FemiCLE*
Dumbutshena, Enoch 1920- *WhoWor 91*
Dumdi, Eleanor Stiles 1932- *WhoAmW 91*
Dumec, Roger 1930- *WhoWor 91*
Dumelin, Bruce Clayton 1948- *St&PR 91*
Dumeny, Marcel Jacque 1950- *St&PR 91, WhoAm 90, WhoEmL 91*
Dumerauf, James Robert *BiDrAPA 89*
Dumesnil, Carla Davis 1946- *WhoE 91, WhoEmL 91*
Dumesnil, Eugene Frederick, Jr. 1924- *St&PR 91*
Dumesnil, Suzanne Deschevaux- *BioIn 16*
Dumett, Clement Wallace, Jr. 1927- *St&PR 91, WhoAm 90*
Dumezil, Georges 1898-1986 *BioIn 16*
Dumin, Robert Neil 1950- *BiDrAPA 89*
Dumit, Thomas A. 1942- *WhoAm 90*
Dumit, Thomas Anthony 1942- *St&PR 91*
Dumitrescu, Claudia *ODwPR 91*
Dumitrescu, Domnita *WhoAmW 91*
Dumitrescu, Iancu Ioan 1944- *IntWWM 90*
Dumitriu, Petru 1924- *WhoWor 91*
Dumitru, Vincentiu I. 1934- *WhoWor 91*
Dumke, Glenn S. 1917-1989 *BioIn 16, ConAu 129, -31NR*
Dumke, William Edner 1930- *St&PR 91*
Dumm, Demetrius Robert 1923- *WhoAm 90*
Dumm, Edwina *NewYTBS 90*
Dumm, Edwina 1893-1990 *EncACom*
Dumm, Frances Edwina 1893-1990 *BioIn 16*
Dummer, Jeremiah 1645-1718 *EncCRAm, PenDiDA 89*
Dummer, Jeremiah 1679-1739 *EncCRAm*
Dummett, Clifton Orrin 1919- *WhoAm 90*
Dummett, Michael Anthony Eardley 1925- *WhoWor 91*
Dummit, Eldon Steven, III 1958- *WhoEmL 91*
Dumnire, Ronald Warren 1937- *St&PR 91*
Dumonceaux, Leonard *BiDrAPA 89*
Du Mond, Frank V 1865-1951 *WhoAmA 91N*
Dumond, Jesse William Monroe 1892-1976 *DcScB S2*
Dumonet, Andre A. 1930- *St&PR 91*
Dumont, Allan Eliot 1924- *WhoAm 90*
Dumont, Arthur, III *BiDrAPA 89*
Dumont, Arthur Edgar 1945- *WhoEmL 91*
Dumont, Daniel *BiDrAPA 89*
Dumont, Ebenezer 1814-1871 *AmLegL*
Dumont, Gabriel 1837-1906 *WhNaAH [port]*
Dumont, George 1895-1956 *Ballpl 90*
DuMont, Nicolas 1954- *BiDrAPA 89*
Du Mont, Nicolas 1954- *WhoHisp 91*
Dumont, Rene Fernand 1904- *BiDFrPL*
Dumont, Robert Craig 1934- *WhoAm 90*
Du Mont, Robert James, Sr. 1942- *WhoE 91*
Du Mont, Rosemary Ruhig 1947- *WhoAm 90*
Dumont, Sandra Jean 1955- *WhoAmW 91*
Dumont, Serge 1934- *WhoWor 91*
Dumont, William Kirby 1949- *WhoSSW 91*
Dumont-dit-Voitel, Charles Frederic C. 1916- *WhoWor 91*
Dumont du Voitel, Roland Jean 1947- *WhoWor 91*
Dumouchel, J. Robert 1936- *WhoWrEP 89*
Dumouchel, Paul 1911- *WhoAm 90*
Dumoulin, Jacques 1942- *St&PR 91*
Dumovich, Loretta 1930- *WhoAm 90*
Dumpas, M. Stevens 1937- *St&PR 91*
Dumstone, H Carter *BiDrAPA 89*
Dun, Dennis *BioIn 16*
Dun, Edwin 1848-1931 *BioIn 16*
Dunagan, Doris Deane 1933- *WhoAmW 91*
Dunagan, J. Conrad 1914- *WhoSSW 91*
Dunagin, Jack A 1920- *BiDrAPA 89*
Dunand, Jean 1877-1942 *PenDiDA 89*
Dunant, Henri 1828-1910 *BioIn 16*
Dunant, Jean Henri 1828-1910 *WorAlBi*
Dunant, Jean Henri Frederic 1934- *WhoWor 91*
Dunant, Sarah 1950- *ConAu 131*
Dunathan, Harmon Craig 1932- *WhoAm 90*
Dunavan, Ilena Abrams 1938- *WhoAmW 91*
Dunaway, Charles Ray 1934- *WhoSSW 91*
Dunaway, Donald L. 1937- *St&PR 91*
Dunaway, Donald Lucius 1937- *WhoAm 90*
Dunaway, Faye *BioIn 16*
Dunaway, Faye 1941- *WhoAm 90, WhoAmW 91, WorAlBi*
Dunaway, Trudy Vincent 1951- *WhoEmL 91*
Dunaway, Wayland Fuller 1912- *St&PR 91*
Dunaway, William Burns 1939- *St&PR 91*
Dunaway, William Preston 1936- *WhoSSW 91*
Dunayevskaya, Alla 1920- *WhoAmW 91*
Dunayevskaya, Raya 1910-1987 *ConAu 130, EncAL*
Dunayevsky, Isaak Osipovitch 1900-1955 *OxCPMus*
Dunbar, Alice *MajTwCW*
Dunbar, Alice Moore *MajTwCW*
Dunbar, Andrea 1961- *FemiCLE*
Dunbar, Bonnie 1949- *BioIn 16*
Dunbar, Bonnie J. 1949- *WhoAmW 91*
Dunbar, Bruce C. 1949- *St&PR 91*
Dunbar, Carl Owen 1891-1979 *DcScB S2*
Dunbar, Charles Edward, III 1926- *WhoAm 90*
Dunbar, Charles Franklin 1937- *WhoAm 90, WhoWor 91*
Dunbar, David Wesley 1952- *WhoSSW 91*
Dunbar, Dirk R. 1954- *St&PR 91*
Dunbar, Edward Caswell 1925- *St&PR 91*
Dunbar, Evelyn Mary 1906-1960 *BiDWomA*
Dunbar, Frank Rollin 1953- *WhoAm 90*
Dunbar, Holly Jean 1960- *WhoAmW 91*
Dunbar, Isobel Moira 1918- *WhoAm 90, WhoAmW 91*
Dunbar, Jack 1923?- *BioIn 16*
Dunbar, Jacob Ross, III 1952- *WhoSSW 91*
Dunbar, James V., Jr. 1937- *WhoAm 90*
Dunbar, Janet 1901-1989? *ConAu 129*
Dunbar, Jill H 1949- *WhoAmA 91, WhoE 91*
Dunbar, John Burton 1929- *WhoAm 90*
Dunbar, John Raine 1911- *WhoAm 90*
Dunbar, Joyce *AuBYP 90*
Dunbar, Leslie Wallace 1921- *WhoAm 90*
Dunbar, Louise Anderson *BiDrAPA 89*
Dunbar, Maxwell John 1914- *WhoAm 90*
Dunbar, Michael Austin 1947- *WhoAmA 91*
Dunbar, Paul Edward 1952- *IntWWM 90*
Dunbar, Paul Laurence 1872-1906 *BioIn 16, EarBlAP*
Dunbar, Paul Laurence, Mrs. 1875-1935 *EarBlAP*
Dunbar, Paul Lawrence 1872-1906 *WorAlBi*
Dunbar, Prescott Nelson 1942- *WhoSSW 91*
Dunbar, Ralph Oregon 1845-1912 *AmLegL*
Dunbar, Richard Paul 1951- *WhoEmL 91, WhoWor 91*
Dunbar, Robert J. 1948- *St&PR 91*
Dunbar, Robert Standish, Jr. 1921- *WhoAm 90*
Dunbar, Russell Raymond 1927- *WhoAmA 91*
Dunbar, Wallace 1931- *St&PR 91*
Dunbar, Wallace Huntington 1931- *WhoAm 90*
Dunbar, Walter Scott, Jr. 1941- *WhoE 91*
Dunbar, Wylene Wisby 1949- *WhoEmL 91*
Dunbar-Nelson, Alice *MajTwCW*
Dunbar-Nelson, Alice 1875-1935 *BioAmW, FemiCLE*
Dunbar-Nelson, Alice Moore *MajTwCW*
Dunbar-Nelson, Alice Moore 1875-1935 *EarBlAP*
Dunbar-Nelson, Alice Ruth Moore 1875-1935 *HarlReB*
Dunbar-Webb, Evelyn Louise 1954- *WhoAmW 91*
Dunbebin, Clarence Uhlar 1929- *WhoSSW 91*
Dunbeck, Joseph Ridenour 1936- *WhoAm 90*
Dunbier, Augustus W. 1888-1977 *BioIn 16*
Dunca, C. *EncCoWW*
Dunca, C. de *EncCoWW*
Dunca-Schiau, Constanta 1843- *EncCoWW*
Duncalf, Deryck 1926- *WhoAm 90*
Duncan, A. Baker 1927- *St&PR 91, WhoAm 90*
Duncan, Alan Eugene 1951- *WhoEmL 91*
Duncan, Alastair Robert Campbell 1915- *WhoAm 90*
Duncan, Alfred E *BiDrAPA 89*
Duncan, Ann Huberty 1933- *WhoAmW 91*
Duncan, Bruce Alan 1939- *St&PR 91*
Duncan, Buell Gard, Jr. 1928- *St&PR 91, WhoAm 90, WhoSSW 91*
Duncan, Carl Neil 1945- *WhoEmL 91*
Duncan, Carl Porter 1921- *WhoAm 90*
Duncan, Charles Clifford 1907- *WhoAm 90, WhoWor 91*
Duncan, Charles Howard 1924- *WhoAm 90*
Duncan, Charles Lee 1939- *WhoAm 90*
Duncan, Charles Tignor 1924- *WhoAm 90*
Duncan, Charles William, Jr. 1926- *BiDrUSE 89, WhoAm 90*
Duncan, Claudia Louise 1955- *WhoSSW 91*
Duncan, Cloyce L *BiDrAPA 89*
Duncan, Daniel Ward 1956- *WhoEmL 91*
Duncan, Dave 1945- *Ballpl 90*
Duncan, David 1913- *BioIn 16*
Duncan, David Douglas *BioIn 16*
Duncan, David Douglas 1916- *WorAlBi*
Duncan, David S. 1958- *St&PR 91*
Duncan, Dixie *BioIn 16*
Duncan, Donal Baker 1925- *WhoAm 90*
Duncan, Donald Pendleton 1916- *WhoAm 90*
Duncan, Donald William 1932- *WhoAm 90*
Duncan, Dorothy Wilber 1908- *WhoAmW 91*
Duncan, Elaine Hermoine 1922- *WhoSSW 91*
Duncan, Elizabeth Belle 1957- *WhoE 91*
Duncan, Elizabeth Charlotte 1919- *WhoAmW 91, WhoWor 91*
Duncan, Ellen C. 1959- *ODwPR 91*
Duncan, Elmore Edward 1932- *BiDrAPA 89*
Duncan, Eric Newton 1954- *WhoEmL 91*
Duncan, Erica Joan 1953- *BiDrAPA 89, WhoE 91*
Duncan, Frances Mary 1942- *BioIn 16*
Duncan, Frances Murphy 1920- *WhoAmW 91*
Duncan, Francis 1922- *WhoAm 90*
Duncan, Frank 1901-1973 *Ballpl 90*
Duncan, George H. 1931- *WhoAm 90*
Duncan, Glen M 1926- *BiDrAPA 89*
Duncan, Gordon Stuart 1933- *St&PR 91*
Duncan, Gregory *AuBYP 90*
Duncan, Harry Alvin 1916- *WhoAmA 91*
Duncan, Hearst Randolph 1905- *WhoAm 90*
Duncan, Helen Victoria 1898-1956 *EncO&P 3, EncPaPR 91*
Duncan, Isadora 1877-1927 *BioAmW, EncAL*
Duncan, Isadora 1878-1927 *BioIn 16, WorAlBi*
Duncan, J. Russell *St&PR 91*
Duncan, James Alan 1945- *WhoEmL 91*
Duncan, James Daniel 1941- *St&PR 91*
Duncan, James Herbert C. 1925- *St&PR 91*
Duncan, James Herbert Cavanaugh, Sr. 1925- *WhoAm 90*
Duncan, James Ward 1963- *WhoEmL 91*
Duncan, Jane *AuBYP 90*
Duncan, Jane 1910-1976 *FemiCLE*
Duncan, Jeff 1930-1989 *BioIn 16*
Duncan, Jeffrey Burt 1941- *WhoE 91*
Duncan, John Bonner 1910- *WhoAm 90*
Duncan, John C. 1920- *St&PR 91, WhoAm 90*
Duncan, John Dean, Jr. 1950- *WhoAm 90*
Duncan, John J. *BioIn 16*
Duncan, John J., Jr. 1947- *WhoAm 90, WhoSSW 91*
Duncan, John Lapsley 1933- *WhoAm 90, WhoSSW 91*
Duncan, Jon Allan 1954- *WhoEmL 91*
Duncan, Joseph Wayman 1936- *St&PR 91, WhoAm 90*
Duncan, Joyce Louise 1946- *WhoAmW 91*
Duncan, Julia Erin Nunnally 1956- *WhoSSW 91*
Duncan, Kelly Kay 1960- *WhoEmL 91*
Duncan, Kenneth V. 1938- *St&PR 91*
Duncan, Kent Whitney 1915- *WhoAm 90*
Duncan, Klari De Szecsanyi *WhoAmA 91*
Duncan, Lane Scot 1943- *WhoAm 90*
Duncan, Lois 1934- *AuBYP 90, BioIn 16*
Duncan, Lonnie Ernest 1929- *St&PR 91*

Duncan, Loretta Laverne BiDrAPA 89
Duncan, Lowell C., Jr. 1944- St&PR 91
Duncan, Malcolm P BiDrAPA 89
Duncan, Margaret Caroline 1930- WhoAm 90
Duncan, Mariano 1963- Ballpl 90, WhoHisp 91
Duncan, Marie C BiDrAPA 89
Duncan, Mark 1952- ConAu 130
Duncan, Nanna Sue 1936- WhoAmW 91
Duncan, Nora Kathryn 1946- WhoEmL 91
Duncan, Norman 1871-1916 DcLB 92 [port]
Duncan, Pat 1893-1960 Ballpl 90
Duncan, Penny R. 1953- WhoAmW 91
Duncan, Peter A. 1942- St&PR 91
Duncan, Phillip Marshall 1954- WhoSSW 91
Duncan, Pope Alexander 1920- WhoAm 90, WhoSSW 91
Duncan, Quince 1940- HispWr 90
Duncan, Raymond Glenn 1952- WhoEmL 91
Duncan, Richard 1944- WhoAmA 91
Duncan, Richard Fred 1951- WhoEmL 91
Duncan, Richard Fredrick, Jr. 1947- WhoEmL 91
Duncan, Richard James 1941- St&PR 91
Duncan, Robert 1919-1988 AnObit 1988, MajTwCW, PoeCrit 2 [port]
Duncan, Robert Bannerman 1942- WhoAm 90
Duncan, Robert Case 1958- WhoEmL 91
Duncan, Robert Clifton 1923- WhoAm 90
Duncan, Robert D. 1939- St&PR 91
Duncan, Robert H BiDrAPA 89
Duncan, Robert L. TwCCr&M 91
Duncan, Robert L. 1942- St&PR 91
Duncan, Robert Lipscomb 1927- SpyFic
Duncan, Robert Michael 1951- WhoWor 91
Duncan, Robert Walmsley BiDrAPA 89
Duncan, Rodger Dean 1944- ODwPR 91
Duncan, Rosetta 1900-1959 OxCPMus
Duncan, Russell Cushman, III 1947- WhoEmL 91
Duncan, Ruth 1908- WhoAmA 91
Duncan, Sandy BioIn 16
Duncan, Sandy 1946- WhoAm 90, WorAlBi
Duncan, Sara Jeanette 1861-1922 FemiCLE
Duncan, Sara Jeannette 1861-1922 DcLB 92 [port]
Duncan, Sheena 1932- BioIn 16
Duncan, Starkey Davis, Jr. 1935- WhoAm 90
Duncan, Stephen Mack 1941- WhoAm 90
Duncan, Steven Andrew 1947- St&PR 91
Duncan, Thelma Myrtle 1902- EarBlAP, HarlReB
Duncan, Thomas Lowe 1948- WhoEmL 91
Duncan, Thomas Michael Cavanaugh 1962- WhoEmL 91
Duncan, Timothy Brian 1950- WhoE 91
Duncan, Timothy Harold 1959- WhoEmL 91
Duncan, Todd 1903- DcAfAmP, DrBlPA 90
Duncan, Trevor 1924- OxCPMus
Duncan, Vern 1890-1954 Ballpl 90
Duncan, Virgil D. 1920- St&PR 91
Duncan, Vivian 1902- OxCPMus
Duncan, Wallace Lee 1956- WhoEmL 91
Duncan, William 1832-1918 WhNaAH
Duncan, William C. 1944- St&PR 91
Duncan, William Louis 1945- WhoEmL 91, WhoWor 91
Duncan, William M. 1939- St&PR 91
Duncan, William Millen 1939- WhoAm 90, WhoE 91
Duncan-Poitier, Johanna Monica 1955- WhoAmW 91
Duncan-Shorrock, Sarah Esther Janina 1953- IntWWM 90
Duncanson, Harry Richard 1947- WhoSSW 91
Duncanson, Robert 1817-1872 WhoAmA 91N
Duncomb, Virginia C. 1914-1988 BioIn 16
Duncombe, Raynor Bailey 1942- WhoE 91
Duncombe, Raynor Lockwood 1917- WhoAm 90, WhoWor 91
Duncombe, Susanna 1725-1812 FemiCLE
Dundas, Anthony J. 1946- St&PR 91
Dundas, John A L BiDrAPA 89
Dundas, Philip Blair, Jr. 1948- WhoWor 91
Dundas, R. Hugh, Jr. 1926- ODwPR 91
Dundee, John Graham of C, Viscount 1648-1689 BioIn 16
Dunderdale, David PenDiDA 89
Dundes, Alan 1934- WhoAm 90
Dundes, Jules 1913- WhoAm 90
Dundes, Lester BioIn 16
Dundish, Harold Ian 1946- St&PR 91
Dundon, Arthur F 1921- BiDrAPA 89
Dundon, Brian R. 1946- WhoAm 90
Dundon, Susan BioIn 16
Dundon, Suzanne E 1948- BiDrAPA 89
Dundon, Thomas Edward 1960- WhoEmL 91
Dundore, Dwight Arthur 1922- WhoE 91
Dune, Steve Charles 1931- St&PR 91, WhoAm 90, WhoWor 91
Dunea, George 1933- WhoAm 90
Duneier, Debra Hope 1954- WhoAmW 91
Dunetz, Lora E. WhoWrEP 89
Dunfee, David Edward 1952- St&PR 91
Dunfee, Earl William 1934- St&PR 91
Dunfee, Thomas Wylie 1941- WhoAm 90
Dunfey, Patrick 1958- BioIn 16
Dunfey, Robert John, Jr. 1951- WhoEmL 91
Dunfey, Walter James BioIn 16
Dunford, Karen Lynn 1957- WhoAmW 91
Dunford, Max Patterson 1930- WhoAm 90
Dunford, Penelope Ann 1947- WhoWor 91
Dunford, Robert A. 1931- St&PR 91, WhoAm 90
Dungan, Malcolm Thon 1922- WhoAm 90
Dungan, Ronald S. 1939- St&PR 91
Dungan, Ronald Samuel 1939- WhoE 91
Dungan, Sam 1866-1939 Ballpl 90
Dungan, Travis Patrick 1952- WhoAm 90
Dungan, Vicki Lou 1951- WhoEmL 91
Dungan, William Joseph, Jr. 1956- WhoEmL 91, WhoWor 91
Dungey, Gordon S. 1926- St&PR 91
Dungey, Joan Marie 1944- WhoWrEP 89
Dunham, Alice Clarke 1905- WhoAmW 91
Dunham, Aneva Jo 1938- WhoAmW 91
Dunham, Archie W. WhoAm 90
Dunham, Benjamin Starr 1944- IntWWM 90, WhoAm 90
Dunham, Bertha Mabel 1881-1957 FemiCLE
Dunham, Carroll 1949- BioIn 16
Dunham, Christine BioIn 16
Dunham, Christopher Brian 1958- BiDrAPA 89
Dunham, Corydon Bushnell 1927- WhoAm 90
Dunham, D. Ross 1928- WhoAm 90
Dunham, David Barr 1953- WhoSSW 91
Dunham, David Wheeler 1932- WhoE 91
Dunham, Donald Carl 1908- WhoAm 90
Dunham, Donald Harrison 1913- WhoWor 91
Dunham, Frank L. 1940- WhoAm 90
Dunham, Gilbert H. 1930- St&PR 91
Dunham, Halstead F. 1928- ODwPR 91
Dunham, James PenDiMP
Dunham, James Ira 1942- St&PR 91
Dunham, Jay Spencer 1948- St&PR 91
Dunham, Jeffrey Alan 1961- WhoEmL 91
Dunham, Joanne Krok 1957- WhoAmW 91
Dunham, Katherine BioIn 16
Dunham, Katherine 1910- BioAmW, DrBlPA 90, HarlReB [port], WorAlBi
Dunham, Katherine 1912- NotWoAT
Dunham, Kingsley Charles 1910- WhoWor 91
Dunham, Meggin Marie 1956- WhoAmW 91
Dunham, Philip Bigelow 1937- WhoAm 90
Dunham, Robert A. St&PR 91
Dunham, Selena L. 1952- WhoAmW 91
Dunham, Sherrie Ann 1949- WhoWrEP 89
Dunham, Wolcott Balestier, Jr. 1943- WhoAm 90
Dunham-Cragg, Melissa Kay 1956- WhoEmL 91
Dunham-Griggs, Margaret 1922- WhoAmA 91
Dunhill, Michael 1942- WhoWor 91
Dunhill, Robert H. 1929- WhoAm 90
Dunhill, Robert Hugo 1929- St&PR 91
Dunican, John James 1932- St&PR 91
Dunietz, Jack 1950- BiDrAPA 89
Dunigan, Carmon BiDrAPA 89
Dunigan, Dennis Wayne 1952- WhoEmL 91
Dunigan, Kevin BioIn 16
Dunigan, Robert Francis 1959- WhoE 91
Dunin-Wasowicz, Edward 1951- WhoEmL 91
Duning, George 1908- BioIn 16
Dunion, James William 1959- WhoE 91
Dunipace, Ian Douglas 1939- WhoAm 90
Dunitz, Jack David 1923- WhoWor 91
Dunitz, Jay 1956- WhoAmA 91
Duniway, Abigail 1834-1915 FemiCLE
Duniway, Abigail Scott 1834-1915 BioAmW, BioIn 16
Dunk, George Montagu 1716-1771 EncCRAm
Dunk, William 1938- ODwPR 91
Dunkas, Nicholas BiDrAPA 89
Dunkel, Arthur 1932- WhoWor 91
Dunkel, Florence Vaccarello 1942- WhoAmW 91
Dunkel, James Michael 1949- St&PR 91
Dunkel, Tom Richard 1950- WhoWrEP 89
Dunkelberg, Walter R 1928- BiDrAPA 89
Dunkell, Samuel BiDrAPA 89
Dunkelman, Loretta 1937- WhoAmA 91
Dunkelman, Martha Levine 1947- WhoAmA 91
Dunkelman, Robert BiDrAPA 89
Dunker, Robert F. 1931- St&PR 91
Dunkerley, James 1953- ConAu 131
Dunkerley, William 1942- WhoE 91
Dunkerson, Dennis L. 1947- St&PR 91
Dunkin, Catherine S. ODwPR 91
Dunkin, Pamela Ann 1956- BiDrAPA 89
Dunkins, Ronnie BioIn 16
Dunkirk, Alan B. 1947- St&PR 91
Dunklau, Rupert Louis 1927- WhoAm 90
Dunkle, Cathleen Brooke 1963- WhoAmW 91
Dunkle, Davey 1872-1941 Ballpl 90
Dunkle, Eleanor C. 1941- St&PR 91
Dunkle, Frank H. 1924- WhoAm 90
Dunkle, Joseph Lee 1943- WhoWor 91
Dunkle, W. E. 1917- BioIn 16
Dunkle, William E. 1917- BioIn 16
Dunkle, William F. 1942- St&PR 91
Dunklebarger, Eddie L. 1954- St&PR 91
Dunkley, Christopher 1944- WhoWor 91
Dunlap, Bradley Russell 1951- WhoSSW 91
Dunlap, Bruce St&PR 91
Dunlap, Carla BioIn 16
Dunlap, Charles Lee 1943- WhoAm 90
Dunlap, Connie 1924- WhoAm 90
Dunlap, Connie Sue Zimmerman 1952- WhoEmL 91
Dunlap, David Houston 1947- WhoEmL 91
Dunlap, Douglas R. 1948- St&PR 91
Dunlap, E. T. 1914- WhoAm 90
Dunlap, Ellen S. 1951- WhoAm 90, WhoAmA 91, WhoAmW 91
Dunlap, Estelle Cecilia Diggs 1912- WhoWor 91
Dunlap, F. Thomas 1951- St&PR 91
Dunlap, Fred 1859-1902 Ballpl 90
Dunlap, G.A. 1925- St&PR 91
Dunlap, Gary 1953- ODwPR 91
Dunlap, George Carter 1936- WhoAm 90
Dunlap, Gerard Willard 1956- WhoE 91
Dunlap, Henry Francis 1916- WhoSSW 91
Dunlap, James Cecil 1908- St&PR 91
Dunlap, James Lapham 1937- St&PR 91, WhoAm 90
Dunlap, James R BiDrAPA 89
Dunlap, James Riley 1925- St&PR 91
Dunlap, Jane ConAu 30NR, FemiCLE
Dunlap, Jane Elizabeth 1932- St&PR 91
Dunlap, Joe Everett 1930- WhoWrEP 89
Dunlap, John 1746-1792 PenDiDA 89
Dunlap, John Franklin 1943- St&PR 91
Dunlap, Kathleen Powers 1958- WhoAmW 91
Dunlap, Len D. 1923- St&PR 91
Dunlap, Linda Louise 1954- WhoAmW 91
Dunlap, Lon AuBYP 90
Dunlap, Loren Edward 1932- WhoAmA 91
Dunlap, Malinda BioIn 16
Dunlap, Paul D. 1930- St&PR 91, WhoAm 90
Dunlap, Philip Stanley 1918- WhoE 91
Dunlap, Rufus Thornwell, Jr. 1931- WhoSSW 91
Dunlap, Samuel 1752-1830 PenDiDA 89
Dunlap, Sandra Kathleen 1958- WhoE 91
Dunlap, Stanton Parks 1934- WhoSSW 91
Dunlap, Susan 1943- TwCCr&M 91
Dunlap, Tavner Branham 1953- WhoEmL 91
Dunlap, Thomas Winsper, Jr. 1929- WhoE 91
Dunlap, William 1766-1839 BioIn 16, EncCRAm
Dunlap, William Crawford 1918- WhoAm 90
Dunlap, William D. 1938- St&PR 91
Dunlap, William DeWayne, Jr. 1938- WhoAm 90
Dunlap, William Gray 1937- WhoSSW 91
Dunlap-Baker, Joyce Ann 1950- WhoAmW 91
Dunlavey, Dean Carl 1925- WhoAm 90
Dunlavey, Mary Ann 1929- WhoAmW 91
Dunleavy, Gareth Winthrop 1923- WhoAm 90
Dunleavy, Janet Egleson 1928- WhoWrEP 89
Dunleavy, Janet Frank Egleson 1928- WhoAm 90
Dunleavy, Kristie Lyn 1957- WhoAmW 91
Dunleavy, Mike WhoAm 90
Dunleavy, Richard Michael 1933- WhoAm 90
Dunleavy, Rosemary BioIn 16, WhoE 91
Dunleavy, Thomas J. 1938- St&PR 91
Dunlevy, James Frederick 1925- St&PR 91
Dunlevy, Jerome Michael 1926- St&PR 91
Dunlevy, Marion B. 1930- WhoWrEP 89
Dunlevy, Ralph Donald 1925- St&PR 91, WhoAm 90
Dunlevy, Richard J. 1934- St&PR 91
Dunlevy, Susan Danielsen BiDrAPA 89
Dunlop, Agnes Mary Robertson AuBYP 90
Dunlop, Becky Norton 1951- WhoAmW 91
Dunlop, David Wallace 1942- WhoE 91
Dunlop, Eileen 1938- BioIn 16, ConAu 32NR, SmATA 12AS [port]
Dunlop, Eliza 1796-1880 FemiCLE
Dunlop, Frank 1927- WhoWor 91
Dunlop, George Rodgers 1906- WhoAm 90
Dunlop, John Barrett 1942- WhoAm 90
Dunlop, John Boyd 1840-1921 WorAlBi
Dunlop, John T. 1944- St&PR 91
Dunlop, John Thomas 1914- BiDrUSE 89, WhoAm 90
Dunlop, Lois T BiDrAPA 89
Dunlop, Robert G. 1909- St&PR 91
Dunlop, Robert Galbraith 1909- WhoAm 90
Dunlop, Robert Hugh 1929- WhoAm 90
Dunlop, Stephen R 1944- BiDrAPA 89
Dunlop, Steve 1955- WhoE 91
Dunlop, William 1792-1848 DcLB 99 [port]
Dunman, Leonard Joe, III 1952- WhoSSW 91
Dunmeyer, Sarah Louise Fisher 1935- WhoAmW 91
Dunmire, Carole Ruth BiDrAPA 89
Dunmire, Fred A. 1933- St&PR 91
Dunmire, Jeffrey Scott 1957- WhoSSW 91
Dunmire, Philip L. 1946- St&PR 91
Dunmire, Ronald W. 1937- St&PR 91
Dunmire, Ronald Warren 1937- WhoAm 90
Dunmire, Ruth March 1930- WhoAmW 91
Dunmire, William Werden 1930- WhoAm 90
Dunmore, Albert J. BioIn 16
Dunmore, David Bruce 1954- WhoE 91
Dunmore, Helen 1952- FemiCLE
Dunmore, John Murray, Earl of 1732-1809 BioIn 16, EncCRAm, WhNaAH
Dunmore, Timothy 1948- ConAu 129
Dunn, A. Dale 1923- St&PR 91, WhoAm 90
Dunn, Adolphus William 1922- WhoSSW 91
Dunn, Alan 1900-1974 WhoAmA 91N
Dunn, Andrew Fletcher 1922- WhoAm 90
Dunn, Anne-Marie ODwPR 91
Dunn, Arnold Samuel 1929- WhoAm 90
Dunn, Arthur F BiDrAPA 89
Dunn, Arthur J. 1933- St&PR 91
Dunn, Arvin Gail 1930- WhoAm 90
Dunn, Ben 1933- ODwPR 91
Dunn, Bob 1908-1989 BioIn 16, EncACom
Dunn, Bonnie Brill 1953- WhoAmW 91
Dunn, Bruce A. 1931- St&PR 91
Dunn, Bruce Edward 1951- WhoWrEP 89
Dunn, Bruce Sidney 1948- WhoAm 90
Dunn, C Gibson, II 1946- BiDrAPA 89
Dunn, Cal 1915- WhoAmA 91
Dunn, Catherine WhoAm 90
Dunn, Catherine Lynn 1950- BiDrAPA 89
Dunn, Charles DeWitt 1945- WhoAm 90
Dunn, Charles T. 1930- St&PR 91
Dunn, Charles William 1915- WhoAm 90
Dunn, Cheryl T 1945- BiDrAPA 89
Dunn, Clark Allan 1901- WhoAm 90
Dunn, Darlene Sheree 1956- WhoEmL 91
Dunn, David 1943- St&PR 91
Dunn, David 1953- IntWWM 90
Dunn, David E. 1935- WhoAm 90
Dunn, David J. 1930- St&PR 91, WhoAm 90
Dunn, David Joseph 1930- WhoAm 90
Dunn, David Lynn 1960- WhoSSW 91
Dunn, David Nelson 1940- St&PR 91
Dunn, David S. 1943- St&PR 91
Dunn, David Walter 1953- WhoE 91
Dunn, Dean Alan 1954- WhoSSW 91, WhoWor 91
Dunn, Deborah Dechellis 1960- WhoAmW 91
Dunn, Deborah Jane 1954- WhoAmW 91
Dunn, Delmer Delano 1941- WhoAm 90
Dunn, Dennis 1947- St&PR 91
Dunn, Dennis J 1942- ConAu 129
Dunn, Donald Jack 1945- WhoE 91
Dunn, Donald M. 1903- St&PR 91
Dunn, Donna Hudson 1958- WhoSSW 91
Dunn, Dorothy Jean 1933- WhoAmW 91
Dunn, Douglas 1942- ConAu 33NR, MajTwCW
Dunn, E. Paul 1953- St&PR 91
Dunn, Edward ODwPR 91
Dunn, Edward Clare 1913- WhoAm 90
Dunn, Edward K., Jr. 1935- WhoAm 90
Dunn, Edward S., Jr. 1943- WhoAm 90
Dunn, Edward Sennett, Jr. 1943- St&PR 91
Dunn, Elsie 1893-1963 BioIn 16
Dunn, Elwood 1906- WhoAm 90
Dunn, Evans, Jr. 1932- St&PR 91
Dunn, Floyd 1924- BioIn 16, WhoAm 90
Dunn, Fontaine WhoAmA 91
Dunn, Francis Vivian 1908- OxCPMus
Dunn, Geoffrey Richard 1949- WhoWor 91
Dunn, George C, Jr. 1938- BiDrAPA 89
Dunn, George J. 1935- St&PR 91

Dunn, Gerald A. 1934- *St&PR 91*
Dunn, Grace Veronica *WhoAmW 91*
Dunn, H. Stewart, Jr. 1929- *WhoAm 90*
Dunn, Hampton 1916- *WhoWrEP 89*
Dunn, Harvey T 1884-1952 *WhoAmA 91N*
Dunn, Henry Hampton 1916- *WhoAm 90, WhoSSW 91, WhoWor 91*
Dunn, Holly *WhoNeCM [port]*
Dunn, Horton, Jr. 1929- *WhoAm 90*
Dunn, Howard James 1931- *St&PR 91*
Dunn, J.S. 1942- *St&PR 91*
Dunn, J. Willcox *BioIn 16*
Dunn, Jack 1872-1928 *Ballpl 90*
Dunn, James Melvin 1948- *WhoEmL 91*
Dunn, James Michael, Jr. 1931- *St&PR 91*
Dunn, James Milton 1932- *WhoE 91*
Dunn, James Patrick, Jr. 1936- *St&PR 91*
Dunn, James Robert 1921- *WhoAm 90*
Dunn, Jeffrey Allyn 1955- *WhoEmL 91, WhoSSW 91, WhoWor 91*
Dunn, Jeffrey Marc 1946- *WhoEmL 91*
Dunn, Jeffrey William 1947- *WhoEmL 91*
Dunn, Jerry Camarillo, Jr. 1947- *WhoEmL 91*
Dunn, Jerry R. 1935- *St&PR 91*
Dunn, Jessie Joyce 1930- *WhoSSW 91*
Dunn, Jim Edward 1948- *WhoEmL 91, WhoSSW 91*
Dunn, Joe Pender 1945- *WhoSSW 91*
Dunn, John Benjamin 1948- *WhoEmL 91*
Dunn, John David 1945- *St&PR 91*
Dunn, John F *BiDrAPA 89*
Dunn, John M 1927- *BiDrAPA 89*
Dunn, John Maximillian 1945- *WhoEmL 91*
Dunn, John Michael 1927- *WhoAm 90, WhoWor 91*
Dunn, John R. 1934- *St&PR 91*
Dunn, John Raymond, Jr. 1937- *WhoWor 91*
Dunn, John Thomas 1838-1907 *AmLegL*
Dunn, John W. 1944- *St&PR 91*
Dunn, Jon Michael 1941- *WhoAm 90*
Dunn, Jonah Marshall 1913- *WhoWrEP 89*
Dunn, Jonathan 1944- *BiDrAPA 89*
Dunn, Joseph Charles 1938- *WhoSSW 91*
Dunn, Joseph Franklin 1936- *WhoSSW 91*
Dunn, Joseph M. 1926- *St&PR 91*
Dunn, Joseph McElroy 1926- *WhoAm 90*
Dunn, Julia 1953- *WhoWrEP 89*
Dunn, Katherine *BioIn 16*
Dunn, Kathleen Ann 1961- *WhoE 91*
Dunn, Keith *BioIn 16*
Dunn, Keith Mervin 1959- *WhoEmL 91*
Dunn, Lawrence Anthony *BiDrAPA 89*
Dunn, Leo James 1931- *WhoAm 90*
Dunn, Leon A., Jr. 1938- *St&PR 91*
Dunn, Leslie Clarence 1893-1974 *DcScB S2*
Dunn, Linda Kay 1947- *WhoAmW 91*
Dunn, Loretta Lynn 1955- *WhoAmW 91*
Dunn, Lydia *BioIn 16*
Dunn, M. Catherine 1934- *WhoAm 90*
Dunn, Margaret Mary Coyne 1909- *WhoAmW 91*
Dunn, Marian Eisenberg 1937- *WhoE 91*
Dunn, Martin Joseph 1935- *WhoE 91*
Dunn, Marvin Irvin 1927- *WhoAm 90*
Dunn, Mary Beth 1949- *WhoAmW 91*
Dunn, Mary Elizabeth 1954- *WhoSSW 91*
Dunn, Mary Lois 1930- *AuBYP 90*
Dunn, Mary Maples 1931- *WhoAm 90, WhoAmW 91, WhoE 91*
Dunn, Matthew Joseph 1958- *WhoEmL 91*
Dunn, Maurice 1910- *BiDrAPA 89*
Dunn, Melvin Bernard 1936- *St&PR 91, WhoAm 90*
Dunn, Michael Brown 1954- *WhoEmL 91*
Dunn, Michael David 1944- *WhoWor 91*
Dunn, Michael G. 1952- *ODwPR 91*
Dunn, Michael Robert 1953- *WhoSSW 91*
Dunn, Mignon *WhoAm 90*
Dunn, Mignon 1931- *IntWWM 90*
Dunn, Morris Douglas 1944- *WhoAm 90*
Dunn, Murray Aaron 1955- *WhoE 91*
Dunn, Nell 1936- *BioIn 16, FemiCLE*
Dunn, Norman S. 1921- *St&PR 91*
Dunn, Norman Samuel 1921- *WhoAm 90*
Dunn, Parker Southerland 1910- *St&PR 91, WhoAm 90*
Dunn, Patrice Mary *BiDrAPA 89*
Dunn, Patricia *BioIn 16, NewYTBS 90*
Dunn, Patricia Ann 1942- *WhoAmW 91*
Dunn, Patricia Ellen 1958- *WhoAmW 91*
Dunn, Patrick Walter 1965- *WhoSSW 91*
Dunn, Paul M. 1898-1988 *BioIn 16*
Dunn, Pauline *IntWWM 90*
Dunn, Paxton Tays *BioIn 16*
Dunn, Peter Bruce 1946- *BiDrAPA 89*
Dunn, Peter L. 1945- *St&PR 91*
Dunn, Phillip Charles 1947- *WhoAmA 91*
Dunn, Phoebe *BioIn 16*
Dunn, Randy Edwin 1954- *WhoEmL 91*
Dunn, Raymond Elmer, Jr. 1956- *WhoE 91*
Dunn, Rebecca Diane 1948- *WhoAmW 91*
Dunn, Richard Brandner 1927- *WhoAm 90*
Dunn, Richard F. 1963- *ODwPR 91*
Dunn, Richard John 1938- *WhoAm 90*
Dunn, Richard Rogge 1957- *WhoEmL 91*
Dunn, Robert Alex 1946- *St&PR 91*
Dunn, Robert C. *St&PR 91*
Dunn, Robert Francis 1928- *WhoAm 90*
Dunn, Robert H *BiDrAPA 89*
Dunn, Robert Hayes, Jr. 1927- *St&PR 91*
Dunn, Robert Joseph 1908-1989 *BioIn 16*
Dunn, Robert Vincent 1929- *St&PR 91, WhoAm 90*
Dunn, Roger Terry 1946- *WhoAmA 91, WhoE 91*
Dunn, Ronald Holland 1937- *WhoSSW 91, WhoWor 91*
Dunn, Sandra Puncsak 1946- *WhoAmW 91*
Dunn, Stephen 1939- *DcLB 105 [port]*
Dunn, Stephen Elliott 1939- *WhoWrEP 89*
Dunn, Stephen Michael 1950- *WhoEmL 91*
Dunn, Susan 1954- *WhoAm 90, WhoAmW 91*
Dunn, Susan Marie 1956- *WhoEmL 91*
Dunn, Susan Rhea 1946- *WhoE 91*
Dunn, Suzan McVay 1953- *WhoAmW 91*
Dunn, Terence Sean *BiDrAPA 89*
Dunn, Thelma B. 1900- *BioIn 16*
Dunn, Theresa Rose 1962- *WhoAmW 91*
Dunn, Thomas 1925- *IntWWM 90*
Dunn, Thomas G. 1921- *WhoE 91*
Dunn, Thomas Parker 1944- *St&PR 91*
Dunn, Timothy Charles 1948- *St&PR 91*
Dunn, Timothy Hibbard 1816-1898 *DcCanB 12*
Dunn, Vicki Lynn 1949- *WhoAmW 91*
Dunn, Walter Scott, Jr. 1928- *WhoAm 90*
Dunn, Warren H. 1934- *St&PR 91*
Dunn, Warren Howard 1934- *WhoAm 90*
Dunn, Wendell Earl, III 1945- *WhoAm 90, WhoEmL 91*
Dunn, Wesley Brankley 1951- *WhoEmL 91*
Dunn, Wesley John 1924- *WhoAm 90*
Dunn, William Bruna, III 1947- *WhoAm 90, WhoSSW 91*
Dunn, William M.S. 1931- *St&PR 91*
Dunn, William Randolph 1935- *St&PR 91, WhoAm 90*
Dunn, William Warren 1936- *St&PR 91*
Dunn-Kinney, Brenda 1955- *WhoEmL 91*
Dunnagan, Robert Jones 1918- *WhoSSW 91*
Dunnahoo, Terry 1927- *ConAu 31NR, WhoAm 90*
Dunnam, Edwin Earl 1923- *St&PR 91*
Dunnam, Francis Eugene, Jr. 1931- *WhoAm 90*
Dunnam, Freda A *BiDrAPA 89*
Dunnan, Weaver White 1923- *WhoAm 90*
Dunnavan, Carol Chamblin 1954- *WhoAmW 91*
Dunne, Dana Philip C. 1963- *WhoE 91*
Dunne, Diane C. *WhoE 91, WhoWor 91*
Dunne, Dominick *BestSel 90-4 [port], BioIn 16*
Dunne, Finley Peter 1867-1936 *BioIn 16*
Dunne, Harry Powers, Jr. 1942- *WhoE 91*
Dunne, Irene 1898?-1990 *NewYTBS 90 [port], OxCPMus*
Dunne, Irene 1901- *WorAlBi*
Dunne, Irene 1904?-1990 *CurBio 90N*
Dunne, J W 1875-1949 *EncO&P 3*
Dunne, James Arthur 1934- *WhoAm 90, WhoWor 91*
Dunne, James L. 1940- *St&PR 91*
Dunne, James Robert 1929- *WhoSSW 91*
Dunne, John Edward 1944- *BiDrAPA 89*
Dunne, John Gregory 1932- *BioIn 16, WhoWrEP 89, WorAlBi*
Dunne, John Richard 1930- *WhoAm 90*
Dunne, John W. 1866-1949 *EncPaPR 91*
Dunne, Mary 1914- *AuBYP 90*
Dunne, Mike 1962- *Ballpl 90*
Dunne, Philip 1908- *WhoAm 90*
Dunne, Philip Roemer 1932- *ODwPR 91*
Dunne, Phillip George 1934- *St&PR 91*
Dunne, Richard *NewYTBS 90 [port]*
Dunne, Richard C. 1937- *ODwPR 91*
Dunne, Thomas 1943- *WhoAm 90*
Dunne, Thomas Gregory 1930- *WhoAm 90*
Dunne, Thomas L. *BioIn 16*
Dunne, Thomas Leo 1946- *WhoAm 90*
Dunne, Thomas P. 1943- *St&PR 91*
Dunnell, Rebecca Anne Noel 1952- *IntWWM 90*
Dunnell, Robert Chester 1942- *WhoAm 90*
Dunner, David Louis 1940- *BiDrAPA 89*
Dunner, Frederick J 1945- *BiDrAPA 89*
Dunner, Frederick Jules 1945- *WhoEmL 91*
Dunner, Leslie B. *BioIn 16*
Dunnery, John Anthony 1957- *WhoEmL 91*
Dunnett, Dorothy 1923- *TwCCr&M 91*
Dunnette, Marvin Dale 1926- *WhoAm 90*
Dunnewald, David Alan 1960- *WhoEmL 91*
Dunnick, John M. *St&PR 91N*
Dunnigan, Brian Leigh 1949- *WhoE 91*
Dunnigan, Frank Joseph *NewYTBS 90 [port]*
Dunnigan, Frank Joseph 1914- *WhoAm 90*
Dunnigan, Mary Catherine 1922- *WhoAmA 91*
Dunnigan, T. Kevin 1938- *WhoAm 90, WhoE 91*
Dunnigan, Thomas John 1921- *WhoAm 90*
Dunnigan, Thomas Kevin 1938- *St&PR 91*
Dunnihoo, Dale Russell 1928- *WhoSSW 91, WhoWrEP 89*
Dunning, Ann Marie 1942- *WhoAmW 91*
Dunning, Arthur Stephen 1924- *AuBYP 90*
Dunning, Ethel Flo 1935- *WhoWrEP 89*
Dunning, Herbert Neal 1923- *WhoAm 90*
Dunning, James L. 1938- *St&PR 91*
Dunning, James Morse 1904- *WhoAm 90*
Dunning, John R. 1907-1975 *WorAlBi*
Dunning, John S. 1905- *BioIn 16*
Dunning, Karen Ellen 1956- *WhoAmW 91*
Dunning, Lawrence 1931- *WhoWrEP 89*
Dunning, Steve 1949- *Ballpl 90*
Dunning, Thomas Earl 1944- *WhoAm 90*
Dunninger, Joseph 1892-1975 *BioIn 16*
Dunnington, Walter G., Jr. 1927- *St&PR 91*
Dunnington, Walter Grey, Jr. 1927- *WhoAm 90, WhoWor 91*
Dunnock, Mildred 1900- *BioIn 16, ConTFT 8*
Dunnock, Mildred Margaret 1900- *NotWoAT*
Dunoff, Richard 1952- *WhoEmL 91*
Dunow, Esti 1948- *WhoAmA 91*
Dunoyer, Philippe 1930- *St&PR 91, WhoAm 90*
Dunphy, Don 1909?- *BioIn 16*
Dunphy, Edward Joseph 1930- *St&PR 91*
Dunphy, Herbert George, Jr. 1929- *St&PR 91*
Dunphy, John Patrick 1932- *St&PR 91*
Dunphy, Maureen Ann 1949- *WhoAmW 91, WhoEmL 91*
Dunphy, T.J. Dermot 1932- *St&PR 91*
Dunquat *WhNaAH*
Dunrea, Olivier 1953- *BioIn 16*
Dunrossil, John William Morrison 1926- *WhoWor 91*
Duns Scotus, John 1266?-1308 *WrPh P*
Dunsby, Jonathan Mark 1953- *IntWWM 90*
Dunscomb, John Richard 1938- *IntWWM 90*
Dunsire, P. Kenneth 1932- *St&PR 91*
Dunsire, Peter Kenneth 1932- *WhoAm 90*
Dunsky, Anne 1949- *WhoE 91*
Dunsky, Menahem 1930- *WhoAm 90*
Dunsmoor, Barbara Janet 1944- *WhoAmW 91*
Dunsmore, Joseph Matthew, III 1948- *WhoE 91*
Dunson, William Albert 1941- *WhoAm 90, WhoE 91*
Dunst, Laurence David 1941- *WhoAm 90*
Dunstan, Saint 910?-988 *BioIn 16*
Dunstan, Daniel G. 1944- *St&PR 91*
Dunstan, Donald Lee 1945- *WhoEmL 91*
Dunstan, G R 1917- *ConAu 130*
Dunstan, Garland Herrington, Jr. 1957- *WhoSSW 91*
Dunstan, Larry Kenneth 1948- *WhoEmL 91*
Dunster, Henry 1609?-1659 *BioIn 16, WorAlBi*
Dunster, Ron Allan 1940- *St&PR 91*
Dunston, Mary Cottrell 1951- *WhoE 91*
Dunston, Shawon 1963- *Ballpl 90*
Dunstone, David Carter 1941- *BiDrAPA 89*
Dunstone, William Henry 1930- *St&PR 91*
Dunsworth, Francis A 1920- *BiDrAPA 89*
Dunteman, George Henry 1935- *WhoAm 90*
Dunton, Harlow D *BiDrAPA 89*
Dunton, James Gerald 1899- *WhoSSW 91*
Dunton, James Kegebein 1938- *St&PR 91*
Duntov, Zora Arkus- *BioIn 16*
Dunville, T. E. 1868-1924 *OxCPMus*
Dunwell, J.L. 1939- *St&PR 91*
Dunwich, Gerina 1959- *WhoE 91, WhoEmL 91*
Dunwiddie, Charlotte *WhoAmA 91*
Dunwiddie, Charlotte 1907- *WhoAm 90, WhoAmW 91*
Dunwiddie, Foster Wilfred 1925- *WhoAm 90*
Dunwody, Kenneth Webster, Jr. 1926- *St&PR 91*
Dunwoody, Kenneth Reed 1953- *WhoAm 90, WhoWrEP 89*
Dunwoody, Robert Cecil 1933- *St&PR 91*
Dunworth, John 1924- *WhoAm 90*
Duome, Joseph J. 1921- *ODwPR 91*
Duong, Hao Quang *BiDrAPA 89*
Duong, Nghiep Bao 1935- *WhoWor 91*
Duong, Su Duy 1942- *BiDrAPA 89*
Duong, Thieu 1936- *WhoE 91*
Dupanloup, Felix-Antoine-Philibert 1802-1878 *BiDFrPL*
Du Paquier, Claudius Innocentius *PenDiDA 89*
Duparc, Elisabeth *PenDiMP*
Dupasquier, Philippe 1955- *ConAu 130*
Du Pasquier, Shelby Robert 1960- *WhoWor 91*
Dupea, Bobby *ConAu 129*
Dupell, Raymond Robert, Jr. 1951- *WhoE 91*
Du Pen, Everett George 1912- *WhoAm 90, WhoAmA 91*
Duperreault, Brian 1947- *St&PR 91*
du Perry, Jean *ConAu 129, MajTwCW*
Dupey, Michele Mary 1953- *WhoAmW 91, WhoEmL 91*
Dupies, Donald Albert 1934- *WhoAm 90*
Dupin, Amandine-Aurore-Lucie 1804-1876 *EncCoWW*
Dupiton, Sandra *BioIn 16*
Duplant, Max Stephanie 1956- *WhoEmL 91*
Duplantier, Adrian Guy 1929- *WhoAm 90*
Dupler, Gerald E *BiDrAPA 89*
Dupler, Sharron Elizabeth *BiDrAPA 89*
Du Plessis, Barend Jacobus 1940- *WhoWor 91*
Du Plessis, Frederick J. *BioIn 16*
Duplessis, Gregory, Jr. 1950- *WhoEmL 91*
Duplessis, Guy 1947- *St&PR 91*
Du Plessis, Hubert 1922- *IntWWM 90*
Duplessis, Jean-Claude *PenDiDA 89*
Duplessis, Jean-Claude-Thomas *PenDiDA 89*
Duplessis, Neil M. *St&PR 91*
Duplessis, Suzanne 1940- *WhoAmW 91*
Duplessis, Yvonne 1912- *EncPaPR 91*
Du Poilloue de Saint-Mars, Gabrielle-A 1804-1872 *EncCoWW*
Dupond, Patrick *WhoWor 91*
Dupong, William Gregg 1911- *WhoE 91, WhoWor 91*
Dupont, Andrew Joseph, Jr. 1941- *St&PR 91*
Dupont, Colyer Lee 1957- *WhoWor 91*
Dupont, Daniel Georges-Valere 1931- *WhoWor 91*
DuPont, David Michael 1941- *St&PR 91*
Du Pont, E Paul *EncABHB 5*
DuPont, Edward Bradford 1934- *St&PR 91*
DuPont, Eleuthere I. 1921- *St&PR 91*
Du Pont, Eleuthere Irenee 1771-1834 *WorAlBi*
Du Pont, Francis Irenee 1873-1942 *WorAlBi*
Dupont, Henry F 1880-1969 *WhoAmA 91N*
DuPont, Herbert Lancashire 1938- *WhoAm 90*
Dupont, Jacqueline 1934- *WhoAm 90*
Dupont, Jacques 1908-1988 *BioIn 16*
Dupont, Jacques 1915- *ConAu 130*
Dupont, Jacques Pierre 1929- *WhoWor 91*
DuPont, James Richard 1937- *St&PR 91*
DuPont, John Joseph 1930- *WhoAm 90*
Dupont, Pierre *PenDiDA 89*
Dupont, Pierre 1944- *WhoWor 91*
Du Pont, Pierre S. 1870-1954 *BioIn 16*
Du Pont, Pierre S. 1911-1988 *BioIn 16*
du Pont, Pierre Samuel 1870-1954 *EncABHB 5 [port], WorAlBi*
Dupont, Ralph Paul 1929- *WhoAm 90, WhoE 91*
Dupont, Renee Marie *BiDrAPA 89*
Du Pont, Robert L, Jr. 1936- *BiDrAPA 89*
Du Pont, Robert Louis, Jr. 1936- *WhoAm 90*
Dupont, Stephen J. 1962- *ODwPR 91*
Du Pont, Thomas C. 1863-1930 *WorAlBi*
Dupont, Todd F. 1942- *WhoAm 90*
Du Pont De Nemours, Pierre Samuel 1739-1817 *WorAlBi*
DuPont-Morales, Maria A. Toni 1948- *WhoHisp 91*
Duport, Jean-Pierre 1741-1818 *PenDiMP*
Du Potet de Sennevoy, Baron 1796-1881 *EncO&P 3*
Dupouy, Jean *PenDiMP*
Duppstadt, Marlyn Henry 1947- *WhoAm 90, WhoEmL 91*
Dupre, Amalia 1845-1928 *BiDWomA*
Dupre, Anne-Marie 1962- *WhoAmW 91*
Dupre, Desmond 1916-1974 *PenDiMP*
Dupre, Heather 1949- *IntWWM 90*
Dupre, Henry Garland 1873-1924 *AmLegL*
Du Pre, Jacqueline 1945-1987 *BioIn 16, PenDiMP*
Dupre, John L *BiDrAPA 89*
Dupre, Judith Ann Neil 1945- *WhoAmW 91*
Dupre, Louis *WhoAm 90*
Dupre, Marcel 1886-1971 *PenDiMP*
Dupre, Patricia Dianne 1957- *WhoE 91*
Dupre, Thomas L. 1933- *WhoAm 90*
Dupre, Wilhelm 1936- *WhoWor 91*
Dupree, Anderson Hunter 1921- *WhoAm 90*

Dupree, Andrew Lane, Sr. 1956- *WhoEmL 91, WhoWor 91*
Dupree, Charles 1934- *St&PR 91*
DuPree, Clifford H.R. 1950- *St&PR 91*
DuPree, Clifford H. R. 1950- *WhoAm 90, WhoEmL 91*
Dupree, David H. 1959- *WhoEmL 91*
Dupree, F. Gene 1935- *St&PR 91*
Dupree, Franklin Taylor, Jr. 1913- *WhoAm 90*
Dupree, Jack 1910- *OxCPMus*
Dupree, James Edmund 1950- *WhoE 91*
Dupree, Louis 1925-1989 *BioIn 16*
Dupree, Mary Herron 1944- *IntWWM 90*
Dupree, Richard Wayne 1946- *St&PR 91*
Dupree, Sandra Kay 1956- *WhoSSW 91*
Dupree, Thomas Andrew 1950- *WhoE 91*
DuPree-Martin, Jean 1950- *WhoSSW 91*
Du Prel, Carl 1839-1899 *EncO&P 3*
Duprey, Janet Marie 1945- *WhoAmW 91*
Duprey, Jean 1947- *WhoWor 91*
Duprey, Thomas Donald 1951- *WhoEmL 91*
Duprey, Wilson Gilliland 1924- *WhoAm 90*
Duprey-Gutierrez, Irene Cathy 1941- *WhoAmW 91*
Duprez, Gilbert 1806-1896 *PenDiMP*
Dupuch, Etienne, Jr. 1931- *WhoWor 91*
Dupuis, Andre 1937- *BiDrAPA 89*
Dupuis, Bonnie Jeanne 1949- *WhoAmW 91*
Dupuis, Charles Francois 1742-1809 *EncO&P 3*
Dupuis, Gerard Adrien 1937- *St&PR 91, WhoE 91*
Dupuis, Phyllis Ann 1957- *WhoSSW 91*
Dupuis, Russell Dean 1947- *WhoAm 90, WhoWor 91*
Dupuis, Sylvio Louis 1934- *WhoAm 90, WhoE 91*
Dupuis, Victor Lionel 1934- *WhoAm 90*
Dupuit, Jules 1804-1866 *BioIn 16*
Dupuy, Charles Alexandre 1851-1923 *BiDFrPL*
DuPuy, Elbert Newton 1904- *WhoWor 91*
Dupuy, Eliza 1814-1880? *FemiCLE*
Dupuy, Ernest *BiDrAPA 89*
Dupuy, Frank Russell, Jr. 1907- *WhoAm 90*
Dupuy, Howard Moore, Jr. 1929- *WhoAm 90, WhoWor 91*
Dupuy, Jean 1925- *WhoAmA 91*
Dupuy, John B. 1919- *St&PR 91*
Dupuy, Ralph Anthony 1925- *St&PR 91*
Dupuy, Sidney J, III *BiDrAPA 89*
Dupuy, Trevor Nevitt 1916- *AuBYP 90, WhoAm 90*
Dupuy, William L., Jr. *ODwPR 91*
Duquaine, William Raymond 1937- *St&PR 91*
Duque, Sarah 1929- *WhoAmW 91*
Duquenoy, Linda Irene 1960- *WhoAmW 91*
Duquesne, Albert 1890-1956 *OxCCanT*
Duquette, Donald Richard 1954- *St&PR 91*
Duquette, Jean-Pierre 1939- *WhoAm 90*
Duquette, Joseph E., III 1944- *WhoSSW 91*
Duquette, Roderick Daniel 1956- *WhoEmL 91*
Duquette, Tony *BioIn 16*
Dur, Philip Francis 1914- *WhoAm 90*
Durachko, Michael Joseph 1955- *WhoWrEP 89*
Durack, Mary 1913- *FemiCLE*
Durai, Deivan 1955- *WhoEmL 91*
Durai, U N B 1955- *BiDrAPA 89*
Durairajan, Veerama Reddiar 1930- *WhoWor 91*
Durall, Keith Leighton 1928- *St&PR 91*
Duran Duran *ConMus 4 [port], EncPR&S 89, OxCPMus*
Duran, Alfredo G. 1936- *WhoHisp 91*
Duran, Andrew J. 1932- *St&PR 91*
Duran, Arthur Eligio 1937- *WhoHisp 91*
Duran, Beverly 1948- *WhoHisp 91*
Duran, Dianna J. 1955- *WhoHisp 91*
Duran, Herman Cesar 1939- *WhoAm 90*
Duran, Juan Antonio *BiDrAPA 89*
Duran, Karin Jeanine 1948- *WhoAmW 91, WhoHisp 91*
Duran, Lois Janine 1952- *WhoEmL 91*
Duran, Michael Carl 1953- *WhoEmL 91, WhoWor 91*
Duran, Miguel *BioIn 16*
Duran, Monina Acuna *BiDrAPA 89*
Duran, Natalie 1955- *WhoHisp 91*
Duran, Natividad Perez 1946- *WhoWrEP 89*
Duran, Roberto *BioIn 16*
Duran, Roberto 1951- *WhoHisp 91, WorAlBi*
Duran, Roberto 1953- *ConAu 131, HispWr 90*
Duran, Servet Ahmet 1920- *WhoAm 90*
Duran, Victor Manuel 1947- *WhoHisp 91*
Duran Salguero, Carlos 1956- *WhoHisp 91*
Durand, Asher Brown 1796-1886 *BioIn 16, WorAlBi*
Durand, Catherine Louise 1948- *WhoAmW 91*
Durand, Charles *BiDrAPA 89*
Durand, Charles 1820-1900 *AmLegL*
Durand, Claudette *BiDrAPA 89*
Du Rand, Curtiss Joel 1943- *BiDrAPA 89*
Durand, Harrison F. 1903- *St&PR 91*
Durand, Harvey S. 1941- *St&PR 91*
Durand, Louis *PenDiDA 89*
Durand, Loyal, III 1931- *WhoAm 90*
Durand, Lucile 1930- *BioIn 16*
Durand, Michael *ODwPR 91*
Durand, Pierre O *BiDrAPA 89*
Durand, Prosper-Guillaume *PenDiDA 89*
Durand, Ralph Scott 1933- *St&PR 91*
Durand, Ruth Sawyer *AuBYP 90*
Durand-Hollis, Gabriel 1932- *BiDrAPA 89*
Durang, Christopher 1949- *WorAu 1980 [port]*
Durano, Ramon 1905-1988 *BioIn 16*
Durant, Frederick Clark, III 1916- *WhoAm 90*
Durant, John 1902- *AuBYP 90*
Durant, John H. 1923- *St&PR 91*
Durant, John Ridgeway 1930- *WhoAm 90*
DuRant, John Wesley, III 1963- *WhoSSW 91*
Durant, Marc 1947- *WhoEmL 91*
Durant, Nancy A 1928- *BiDrAPA 89*
Durant, Paul D., II 1931- *St&PR 91*
Durant, Peter Montgomery 1950- *WhoEmL 91*
Durant, Susan 1820?-1873 *BiDWomA*
Durant, Thomas C. 1820-1885 *WorAlBi*
Durant, Will 1885-1981 *MajTwCW*
Durant, William C *EncABHB 5 [port]*
Durant, William C. 1861-1947 *WorAlBi*
Durant, William Crapo 1861-1947 *BioIn 16, EncABHB 4 [port]*
Durant, William James 1885-1981 *WorAlBi*
Durante, Jimmy 1893-1980 *BioIn 16, OxCPMus, WorAlBi*
Durante, Louis Michael 1919- *St&PR 91*
Durante, Sheila M. 1952- *ODwPR 91*
Duranti, Francesca 1935- *EncCoWW*
Duranti, Pietro *PenDiDA 89*
Durantine, Peter J. 1958- *WhoE 91*
Durantino *PenDiDA 89*
Duranty, Walter 1884-1957 *BioIn 16*
Duras, duchesse de 1778?-1828 *EncCoWW*
Duras, Marguerite 1914- *BioIn 16, EncCoWW, FemiCLE, MajTwCW, WhoWor 91, WorAlBi*
Durasov, Vladimir Aleksandrovich 1935- *WhoWor 91*
Duray-Bito, Siegfried Peter 1957- *WhoEmL 91*
Durazo, Maria Elena *WhoHisp 91*
Durazo, Ray 1942- *ODwPR 91*
Durazo, Raymond 1942- *WhoHisp 91*
D'Urban, Benjamin 1777-1849 *BioIn 16*
Durbec, Martin R. 1943- *St&PR 91*
Durbetaki, Pandeli 1928- *WhoAm 90*
Durbin, Daniel B. 1946- *WhoEmL 91, WhoSSW 91*
Durbin, Deanna 1921- *OxCPMus*
Durbin, Deanna 1922- *WorAlBi*
Durbin, Donald Dean 1928- *St&PR 91*
Durbin, Enoch Job 1922- *WhoAm 90*
Durbin, M. Rosamond 1952- *St&PR 91*
Durbin, Martin Robert 1960- *WhoSSW 91*
Durbin, Richard Joseph 1944- *WhoAm 90*
Durbin, Richard Louis, Jr. 1955- *WhoAm 90*
Durbin, Richard Louis, Sr. 1928- *WhoAm 90, WhoSSW 91*
Durbin, Robert Cain 1931- *WhoAm 90*
Durbin, Robert Francis 1936- *St&PR 91*
Durbin, Ronald E. 1937- *St&PR 91*
Durbin, Rosamond 1952- *WhoAmW 91*
Durbin, Russell L. 1936- *ODwPR 91*
Durboraw, Wayne A. 1944- *St&PR 91*
Durbridge, Francis 1912- *TwCCr&M 91*
Durbrow, Elbridge 1903- *BioIn 16*
Durburg, John Robert 1938- *BiDrAPA 89*
Durchholz, Dale Leroy 1948- *WhoEmL 91*
Durchholz, Patricia 1933- *WhoWor 91*
Durck, Craig Harold 1953- *WhoEmL 91*
Durda, Daniel Joseph 1948- *WhoEmL 91, WhoWor 91*
Durdahl, Carol Lavaun 1933- *WhoAmW 91*
Durden, Charles Dennis 1930- *St&PR 91, WhoAm 90*
Durden, Christopher John 1940- *WhoAm 90*
Durden, Jimmy David 1945- *WhoEmL 91, WhoSSW 91*
Durden, Lois Mills *St&PR 91*
Durden, Mark Watkins 1966- *WhoSSW 91*
Durden, Robert Franklin 1925- *WhoAm 90*
Durden-Simmons, Gwendolyn Marie *WhoAmW 91*
Durdy, James Dirk 1957- *WhoWor 91*
Dureau, Milton Maurice, Jr. 1952- *WhoSSW 91*
Duregger, Karen Marie 1952- *WhoAmW 91*
Dureich, Patricia S. 1942- *WhoAmW 91*
Durein, Joseph F. 1912- *St&PR 91*
Durell, Ann *AuBYP 90*
Durell, Ann 1930- *WhoAm 90*
Durell, Jack 1928- *BiDrAPA 89, WhoE 91*
Durell, Jay Glenn 1956- *WhoEmL 91*
Duren, Barry Ross 1957- *WhoSSW 91*
Duren, Carl Thomas, Jr. 1935- *WhoSSW 91*
Duren, David Loren 1951- *WhoEmL 91*
Duren, Francis S. 1945- *ODwPR 91*
Duren, Peter Larkin 1935- *WhoAm 90*
Duren, Ryne 1929- *Ballpl 90*
Duren, Stephen D 1948- *WhoAmA 91*
Durenberger, David *BioIn 16*
Durenberger, David Ferdinand 1934- *WhoAm 90, WhoWor 91*
Durer, Albrecht 1427-1502 *PenDiDA 89*
Durer, Albrecht 1471-1528 *BioIn 16, IntDcAA 90, PenDiDA 89, WorAlBi*
Durer, Michael *BioIn 16*
Duret, Theodore 1838-1927 *BioIn 16*
Durette, Andrew F. 1942- *St&PR 91*
Durette, Philippe Lionel 1944- *WhoE 91*
Durfee, Amy Lee McElheny 1954- *WhoEmL 91*
Durfee, Dick W. *St&PR 91*
Durfee, Harold Allen 1920- *WhoAm 90*
Durfee, John R. 1946- *St&PR 91*
Durfee, Louis, Jr. 1923- *St&PR 91*
Durfee, Robert L. 1936- *St&PR 91*
Durfee, Thomas 1826-1901 *AmLegL*
Durfee, Waite D., Jr. 1920- *St&PR 91*
Durfey, Robert Walker 1925- *WhoAm 90*
D'Urfey, Thomas 1653-1723 *OxCPMus*
Durffe, Francis L. 1935- *St&PR 91*
Durflinger, Duane Lee 1945- *St&PR 91*
Durgavati *WomWR*
Durgawati *WomWR*
Durgin, Diane 1946- *St&PR 91, WhoAm 90, WhoAmW 91*
Durgin, Don 1924- *St&PR 91*
Durgin, Francis J 1930- *BiDrAPA 89*
Durgin, Frank Albert, Jr. 1923- *WhoAm 90*
Durgin, Katherine Baldwin 1944- *St&PR 91*
Durgin, William R. 1950- *WhoE 91*
Durgin, William Walker 1942- *WhoE 91*
Durgnat, Raymond Eric 1932- *WhoWor 91*
Durham, Ashley Grey 1959- *WhoE 91*
Durham, Barbara 1942- *WhoAm 90, WhoAmW 91*
Durham, Carolyn Richardson 1947- *WhoSSW 91*
Durham, Charles William 1917- *St&PR 91*
Durham, Christine Meaders 1945- *WhoAmW 91*
Durham, Clarence R. 1930- *St&PR 91*
Durham, Daniel Cassell 1959- *WhoSSW 91*
Durham, David *TwCCr&M 91*
Durham, David Joe 1952- *WhoE 91*
Durham, Davis Godfrey 1914- *WhoAm 90*
Durham, Ed 1907-1976 *Ballpl 90*
Durham, Eddie 1906-1987 *OxCPMus*
Durham, Ernestine 1951- *WhoAmW 91*
Durham, G. Robert *BioIn 16*
Durham, G. Robert 1929- *St&PR 91*
Durham, Henry Francis 1923- *St&PR 91*
Durham, James Geoffrey 1951- *WhoEmL 91*
Durham, James Michael 1950- *WhoAm 90, WhoE 91*
Durham, Jeanette R 1945- *WhoAmA 91*
Durham, John *ConAu 31NR*
Durham, John George Lambton, Earl of 1792-1840 *BioIn 16*
Durham, Kenneth M. 1953- *WhoWrEP 89*
Durham, Lee B., Jr. 1930- *St&PR 91*
Durham, Leon 1957- *Ballpl 90*
Durham, Marilyn Jean 1930- *WhoWrEP 89*
Durham, Michael J. 1951- *St&PR 91*
Durham, Michael Jonathan 1951- *WhoEmL 91*
Durham, Norman Nevill 1927- *WhoAm 90*
Durham, Peggy J. 1941- *WhoAmW 91*
Durham, Richard Monroe 1954- *WhoEmL 91*
Durham, Roland Pierce, Jr. 1945- *BiDrAPA 89*
Durham, Sandra Kay 1953- *WhoSSW 91*
Durham, Sharon Feeney 1951- *WhoAmW 91*
Durham, Thomas Grady 1952- *WhoEmL 91, WhoWor 91*
Durham, William 1937- *WhoAmA 91, WhoE 91*
Durham, William Andrew 1956- *WhoEmL 91*
Durham, William D. 1936- *WhoAm 90*
Durham, William Emory, Jr. 1931- *St&PR 91*
Durham, William L. 1928- *St&PR 91*
Durham-McLoud, Dianna 1947- *WhoAmW 91*
Durica, A. James 1947- *St&PR 91*
Duricko, Michael W. 1944- *St&PR 91*
Duricko, Michael William 1944- *WhoE 91*
Durieu, Paul 1830-1899 *DcCanB 12*
Durin, George Warren 1957- *St&PR 91*
Durina, Michael F. 1954- *St&PR 91*
During, Marcel H. 1925- *St&PR 91*
During, Theobald 1912- *WhoE 91*
Duritz, Linda Feldman 1941- *BiDrAPA 89*
DuRivage, Donald Jay 1927- *St&PR 91*
Durk, Marion G. *ODwPR 91*
Durk, Marion G. 1947- *St&PR 91*
Durkan, Jenny Anne 1958- *WhoEmL 91*
Durkan, Michael Joseph 1925- *WhoAm 90*
Durkee, Jackson Leland 1922- *WhoAm 90*
Durkee, Michael C. 1938- *St&PR 91*
Durkee, Sarah Bruce 1955- *WhoAmW 91*
Durkee, William Robert 1923- *WhoAm 90*
Durkes, Richard Warren 1950- *St&PR 91*
Durkheim, Emile 1858-1917 *WorAlBi*
Durkin, Charles Joseph, Jr. 1943- *St&PR 91*
Durkin, Diane Barbara 1960- *WhoEmL 91*
Durkin, Dorothy Angela 1945- *WhoAmW 91, WhoE 91*
Durkin, Harry A, Jr. *BiDrAPA 89*
Durkin, James Patrick, II *BiDrAPA 89*
Durkin, Lisa Marie 1957- *WhoEmL 91*
Durkin, Martin Anthony, Jr. 1957- *WhoEmL 91*
Durkin, Martin Joseph 1943- *BiDrAPA 89*
Durkin, Martin Patrick 1894-1955 *BiDrUSE 89*
Durko, Zsolt 1934- *IntWWM 90*
Durlach, Christopher Lee 1951- *WhoEmL 91*
Durlach, Marcus Russell 1911- *WhoAmA 91, WhoSSW 91*
Durlacher, Ed *AuBYP 90*
Durlacher, Gerhard Leopold 1928- *WhoWor 91*
Durland, Jack Raymond 1916- *WhoAm 90*
Durland, Leslie L. 1947- *St&PR 91*
Durling, C. Correll 1952- *St&PR 91*
Durlofsky, Larry 1956- *BiDrAPA 89*
Durmer, William Howard 1940- *St&PR 91*
Durn, Raymond Joseph 1925- *WhoAm 90*
Durnbaugh, Donald Floyd 1927- *WhoAm 90*
Durney, Harry A. 1924- *St&PR 91*
Durney, Lawrence John, III 1948- *WhoE 91*
Durney, Michael Cavalier 1943- *WhoAm 90*
Durnford, James Henry 1915- *St&PR 91*
Durnin, Richard Gerry 1920- *WhoE 91*
Durning, Charles 1923- *WhoAm 90*
Durno, John D. 1936- *St&PR 91*
Durnovo, P. N. 1845-1915 *BioIn 16*
Durnovo, Peter Nikolaevich 1845-1915 *BioIn 16*
Durocher, Cort Louis 1946- *WhoAm 90, WhoE 91*
DuRocher, Frances Antoinette 1943- *WhoAmW 91*
Durocher, Jeanne Marie 1951- *WhoEmL 91*
DuRocher, Kevin Howard *BiDrAPA 89*
Durocher, Leo 1905- *Ballpl 90 [port], BioIn 16*
Durocher, Leo 1906- *WorAlBi*
Duron, Armando 1954- *WhoHisp 91*
Duron, Ysabel 1947- *WhoHisp 91*
Duroni, Charles E. 1933- *St&PR 91*
Duroni, Charles Eugene 1933- *WhoAm 90*
DuRose, Richard Arthur 1937- *WhoAm 90*
DuRose, Stanley Charles, Jr. 1923- *St&PR 91, WhoAm 90*
Durosko, Jeffrey S. *ODwPR 91*
Durosko, Jeffrey Scott 1959- *WhoE 91*
Durosko, Philip J. 1927- *St&PR 91*
Durost, Henry B 1925- *BiDrAPA 89*
Durost-Fish, Rebecca Bernice 1958- *WhoEmL 91*
Durova, Nadezhda *BioIn 16*
Durova, Nadezhda 1783-1866 *EncCoWW*
Durovic, Lubomir Jan 1925- *WhoWor 91*
Durr, Alfred 1918- *IntWWM 90*
Durr, Ernst 1927- *WhoWor 91*
Durr, Heinz 1933- *WhoWor 91*
Durr, Michael J 1934- *BiDrAPA 89*
Durr, Pat *WhoAmA 91*
Durr, Robert Joseph 1932- *WhoAm 90*
Durr, Rolf 1933- *WhoWor 91*
Durr, Virginia Foster *BioIn 16*
Durr, Walther 1932- *IntWWM 90*
Durrani, Sajjad Haidar 1928- *WhoAm 90*
Durrant, Colin John 1950- *IntWWM 90*
Durrant, Devin *BioIn 16*
Durrant, Geoffrey Hugh 1913- *WhoAm 90*
Durrant, Jennifer 1942- *BiDWomA*
Durrant, Theo *TwCCr&M 91*
Durrell, Amy Stewart 1962- *WhoSSW 91*
Durrell, Gerald 1925- *MajTwCW*

Durrell, Gerald Malcolm 1925- AuBYP 90, BioIn 16, WhoAm 90, WhoWor 91
Durrell, Jim WhoE 91
Durrell, Lawrence BioIn 16
Durrell, Lawrence 1912- MajTwCW, WorAlBi
Durrell, Lawrence 1912-1990 ConAu 132, DcLB Y90N [port], NewYTBS 90 [port]
Durrell, Lawrence George 1912- WhoWor 91
Durrell, Martin 1943- WhoWor 91
Durrell, Oliver H. BioIn 16
Durrenberger, William John 1917- WhoAm 90
Durrence, James Larry 1939- WhoSSW 91
Durrenmatt, Friedrich ConAu 33NR, MajTwCW
Durrenmatt, Friedrich 1921- EuWr 13, WhoWor 91, WorAlBi
Durrenmatt, Friedrich 1921-1990 NewYTBS 90 [port], TwCCr&M 91B
Durrer, Christopher Thomas 1949- WhoSSW 91
Durrett, Dewey Bert 1929- WhoWor 91
Durrett, George Mann 1917- St&PR 91
Durrett, Jackie Paul 1948- WhoSSW 91
Durrett, James Frazer, Jr. 1931- WhoAm 90
Durrett, Joseph Park 1945- WhoAm 90
Durrett, Mary Ellen 1921-1988 BioIn 16
Durrett, Richard Lamar 1939- St&PR 91
Durrie, J. Michael 1937- WhoAm 90
Durrigan, Ann Marie 1937- St&PR 91
Durruthy, Stephanie S. BiDrAPA 89
Dursin, Henry L. 1921- St&PR 91
Dursin, Henry Louis 1921- WhoE 91, WhoWor 91
Durslag, Melvin Ballpl 90
Durslag, Melvin 1921- WhoAm 90
D'Urso, Andrew Francis 1943- WhoSSW 91
Durso, Emily Frances 1950- WhoE 91
D'Urso, Joe 1943- BioIn 16
D'Urso, Joseph 1943- ConDes 90
Durso, Joseph A. 1928- St&PR 91
D'Urso, Joseph Paul 1943- WhoAm 90
D'Urso, William Joseph 1934- WhoE 91
Durst, Cedric 1896-1971 Ballpl 90
Durst, Gary Michael 1945- WhoEmL 91
Durst, James NewAgMG
Durst, Linda Shuman BiDrAPA 89
Durst, Milo G 1951- BiDrAPA 89
Durst, Robert Theodore, Jr. 1953- WhoE 91
Durst, Steven F. 1941- St&PR 91
Dursteler, J. Glade 1938- St&PR 91
Durston, Roger Andrew Cadle 1948- IntWWM 90
Dursunkaya, Defne BiDrAPA 89
Durtsche, Sheldon V. 1935- WhoAm 90
Durufle, Maurice IntWWM 90
Durufle, Maurice 1902-1986 PenDiMP, -A
Duruh, Anthony Nwanekwu 1938- WhoSSW 91
Durum, Daryl Eugene 1940- St&PR 91
Durutti Column NewAgMG
Durvasula, Srirama Sastri 1938- WhoWor 91
Durve, Mohan Jagannath 1948- WhoEmL 91
Durville, Gaston EncO&P 3
Durville, Hector 1849-1923 EncO&P 3
Durville, Henri 1888- EncO&P 3
Dury, Ian 1942- OxCPMus
Dury, Ian 1943- EncPR&S 89
Dury, Ronald E. 1950- St&PR 91
Duryea, Charles Edgar 1861-1938 EncABHB 4
Duryea, Dan 1907-1968 WorAlBi
Duryea, Elias J. BioIn 16
Duryea, James Frank EncABHB 4
Duryea, Ladd 1930- St&PR 91
Duryea, Lovejoy Reeves 1944- WhoWor 91
Duryea, Perry Belmont, Jr. 1921- WhoAm 90
Duryea, Philip Elias J. BioIn 16
Duryee, A. Wilbur 1899- WhoAm 90
Duryee, Harold Taylor 1930- WhoAm 90
Durzak, Manfred H. 1938- WhoWor 91
Du Sable, Jean Baptiste Point 1745?-1818 WorAlBi
Dusak, Erv 1920- Ballpl 90
Dusard, Jay 1937- WhoAmA 91
Dusay, John Murray BiDrAPA 89
Duscha, Julius Carl 1924- WhoAm 90
Duscha, Lloyd Arthur 1925- WhoAm 90
Duschek, Karl 1947- ConDes 90
Duse, Eleanora 1858-1924 WorAlBi
Duse, Eleonora 1858-1924 BioIn 16
Dusek, Frank Arthur 1946- WhoEmL 91
Dusenberry, Ann ConTFT 8
Dusenberry, Phil BioIn 16
Dusenberry, Philip Bernard 1936- WhoAm 90
Dusenberry, Vernon Edward 1935- St&PR 91
Dusenbery, Walter 1939- WhoAmA 91
Dusenbery, Walter Condit 1939- WhoAm 90
Dusenbury, Linda 1959- WhoAmW 91
Duseph, Florence 1949- WhoAmW 91
Duseuil, Augustin 1673-1746 PenDiDA 89
Du Shane, James William 1912- WhoAm 90
DuShane, Phyllis Miller 1924- WhoAmW 91
Dushkin, Harvey Brent 1948- St&PR 91
Dushkin, Samuel 1891-1976 PenDiMP
Du Shon, Jean DrBlPA 90
Du Simitiere, Pierre Eugene 1736?-1784 BioIn 16
Dusing, Reginald William 1946- WhoEmL 91
Dusio, Penelope A. 1943- St&PR 91
Duska, Ronald Felix 1937- WhoE 91
Dusold, Laurence Richard 1944- WhoE 91, WhoWor 91
Duson, Curley Pharr, Jr. 1921- WhoSSW 91
Dussault, Marie F. 1954- St&PR 91
Dussault, Marilyn Black 1943- WhoAmW 91
Dussault, Richard E. 1927- St&PR 91
Dussault, William Leonard Ernest 1947- WhoEmL 91
d'Usseau, Arnaud NewYTBS 90
D'Usseau, Arnaud 1916-1990 BioIn 16, ConAu 130, CurBio 90N
Dusseau, John LaFontaine 1912- WhoAm 90
Dusseault, C. Dean 1938- WhoAm 90
Dusseault, Norman Paul 1930- St&PR 91
Dussek, Jan Ladislav 1760-1812 BioIn 16
Dussert, Claudine V. 1942- WhoE 91
Dussman, Judith Ann 1947- WhoEmL 91
Dustan, Hannah 1657-1736? WhNaAH
Dusthimer, Thomas Lee 1934- St&PR 91
Dustin, Cedric Herbert, Jr. 1925- St&PR 91
Dustin, Hannah 1657-1736? WhNaAH
Dustin, M. BioIn 16
Dustman, Jack 1922- St&PR 91
Dusto, Frederick R. 1928- St&PR 91
Duston, Hannah 1657-1736? EncCRAm
Duston, Hannah Emerson 1657-1736? WhNaAH
Duszek, Roman 1935- ConDes 90
Duszenko, Michael 1951- WhoWor 91
Duszlak, Carla Gresian 1952- BiDrAPA 89
Duszynski, Donald Walter 1943- WhoAm 90
Duszynski, Richard James 1957- St&PR 91
Dutch, Stephen J., Jr. BiDrAPA 89
Dutchak, Denise Ann BiDrAPA 89
Dutcher, Andrew 1822- AmLegL
Dutcher, Charles, III BioIn 16
Dutcher, Flora Mae 1908- WhoAmW 91
Dutcher Thornton, Alice Marilyn 1934- WhoAmW 91
Du Temple, Octave Joseph 1920- WhoAm 90
Duthie, Angus Macdonald 1940- St&PR 91
Duthler, Julius 1921- St&PR 91
Dutil, Marcel St&PR 91
Dutile, Richard R. 1937- St&PR 91
Dutile, Trudy G. 1939- St&PR 91
Dutilleux, Henri 1916- IntWWM 90, PenDiMP A
Dutka, Andrew Joseph 1951- WhoE 91
Dutka, Robert Joseph 1951- WhoEmL 91
Dutkay, Katalin Kende BiDrAPA 89
Dutmers, Barbara Kay BiDrAPA 89
Dutmers, James E. 1943- St&PR 91
Dutoit, Charles BioIn 16
Dutoit, Charles 1936- IntWWM 90, PenDiMP, WhoAm 90, WhoE 91
Dutoit, Julius Ronald 1934- IntWWM 90
Dutourd, Jean 1920- ConAu 31NR
Dutournier, Alain BioIn 16
Dutov, Alexsandr Il'ich 1864-1921 BioIn 16
Dutra, Miguelzinho 1810-1875 ArtLatA
Dutram, Kay Lynn 1958- WhoAmW 91
Dutrisac, Maurice G. 1948- St&PR 91
Dutro, John Thomas, Jr. 1923- WhoAm 90
Dutro, Walter J. 1904- St&PR 91
Dutson, Brent Rogers 1950- St&PR 91
Dutt, Hank PenDiMP
Dutt, James Lee 1925- St&PR 91
Dutt, Lakshman S 1951- BiDrAPA 89
Dutt, Toru 1856-1877 FemiCLE, NinCLC 29 [port]
Dutta, Ajit Singh 1944- WhoE 91
Dutta, Prabhat Kumar, II 1940- WhoWrEP 89
Dutter, William Michael 1946- WhoSSW 91
Dutton, Allen A 1922- WhoAmA 91
Dutton, Anne 1621-1678? FemiCLE
Dutton, Anne 1692-1765 FemiCLE
Dutton, Brenton Price 1950- IntWWM 90
Dutton, Charles S DrBlPA 90
Dutton, Clarence Benjamin 1917- WhoAm 90
Dutton, Dan M. 1947- St&PR 91
Dutton, Denise Kitashima 1965- WhoAmW 91
Dutton, Diana B. 1943- ConAu 129
Dutton, Diana Cheryl 1944- WhoAm 90
Dutton, Edward N BiDrAPA 89
Dutton, Frank Elroy 1946- WhoEmL 91, WhoSSW 91, WhoWor 91
Dutton, Frederic Booth 1906- WhoAm 90
Dutton, Frederick Gary 1923- WhoAm 90
Dutton, Geoffrey 1936- St&PR 91
Dutton, George Doug, Jr. 1934- WhoSSW 91
Dutton, George E. 1913- St&PR 91
Dutton, George Roy 1925- St&PR 91
Dutton, Guy G. S. WhoAm 90
Dutton, John Altnow 1936- WhoAm 90
Dutton, John B. 1945- St&PR 91
Dutton, John Bartow 1945- WhoSSW 91
Dutton, John Coatsworth 1918- WhoAm 90
Dutton, Lawrence 1954- IntWWM 90
Dutton, Lois Ann 1939- WhoAmW 91
Dutton, Mary Ann Enloe 1931- IntWWM 90
Dutton, Michael Robert 1949- WhoE 91, WhoSSW 91
Dutton, Paul 1943- ConAu 31NR
Dutton, Pauline Mae WhoAmW 91
Dutton, Richard Edward 1929- WhoSSW 91
Dutton, Robert Edward, Jr. 1924- WhoAm 90, WhoWor 91
Dutton, Robert Wilbur 1944- WhoAm 90
Dutton, Ruth A. 1944- WhoAmW 91
Dutton, Steven 1946- BiDrAPA 89
Dutton, Susan Scott 1957- WhoSSW 91
Dutton, Wilmer Coffman, Jr. 1920- WhoAm 90, WhoE 91
Duttweiler, Donald Lars 1944- WhoAm 90
Duty, J. Bruce 1951- St&PR 91
Duty, Michael Shannon 1948- St&PR 91
Duty, Robert R. 1945- WhoEmL 91
Duty, Tony Edgar 1928-1990 WhoAm 90, WhoSSW 91, WhoWor 91
Duun, Olav 1876-1939 DcScanL
Duus, Peter 1933- WhoAm 90
Duva, Donna Marie 1956- WhoAmW 91, WhoWor 91
Duva, Lou BioIn 16
Duva, Philip 1945- St&PR 91, WhoAm 90
D'Uva, Robert Carmen 1920- WhoWor 91
Duval, Abdelwahad 1948- WhoWor 91
Duval, Addison M BiDrAPA 89
Duval, Albert Frank 1920- WhoAm 90
Duval, Barry Eugene 1959- WhoSSW 91
Duval, Betty Ann 1921- WhoAm 90
DuVal, Clive Livingston, II 1912- WhoSSW 91
Duval, Cynthia 1932- WhoAm 90
Duval, Daniel Webster 1936- WhoAm 90
Duval, David Paul 1945- St&PR 91
Du Val, David Rollin BioIn 16
Duval, Denise 1921- IntWWM 90, PenDiMP
Duval, Fabrice 1955- BiDrAPA 89
Duval, Gaetan 1930- WhoWor 91
Duval, John Tabb 1940- WhoWrEP 89
Duval, Laure BiDrAPA 89
Duval, Leon-Etienne 1903- WhoWor 91
Duval, Mary Ellen 1945- WhoAmW 91
Duval, Michael 1938- WhoAm 90
DuVal, Miles P., Jr. 1896-1989 ConAu 130
Duval, Raymond A. 1933- St&PR 91
Duval, Robert 1937- WhoAm 90
Duvalier, Francois 1907-1971 BioIn 16, WorAlBi
Duvalier, Jean-Claude BioIn 16
Duvalier, Jean-Claude 1951- WorAlBi
Duvalier, Jean-Claude 1952- WhoWor 91
Duvall, Arndt John, III 1931- WhoAm 90
Duvall, Barbra Marie 1956- IntWWM 90
Duvall, C. Dale 1933- WhoAm 90
Duvall, Charles Farmer 1935- WhoAm 90
Duvall, Charles Patton 1936- WhoE 91
DuVall, Jack 1946- WhoSSW 91, WhoWor 91
Duvall, John Edward 1947- WhoEmL 91
DuVall, Lorraine 1925- WhoAmW 91
DuVall, Patricia Arlene 1950- WhoAmW 91
Duvall, Robert 1931- WhoAm 90, WorAlBi
Duvall, Robert C BiDrAPA 89
Duvall, Shelley BioIn 16
Duvall, Shelley 1949- WhoAm 90, WhoAmW 91, WorAlBi
Duvall-Itjen, Phyllis 1951- WhoAmW 91
Duvall-Kellar, Donna Susann 1951- WhoAmW 91
Duvar DcCanB 12
Duvar, Ivan E.H. 1939- St&PR 91
Duvar, Ivan Ernest Hunter 1939- WhoAm 90
Duveen, Anneta 1924- WhoAmA 91
Duveen, Joseph 1869-1939 BioIn 16
Duvegerre, Suzanne BiDEWW
Duver-Miclot, Stephanie Anne 1956- WhoAmW 91, WhoEmL 91
Du Verger, Susan FemiCLE
Duveyrier, Henri 1840-1892 BioIn 16
Duvick, Donald Nelson 1924- WhoAm 90
Du Vigneaud, Vincent 1901-1978 WorAlBi
Duvin, Robert Phillip 1937- WhoAm 90
Duvivier, Claude PenDiDA 89
Duvivier, George BioIn 16
Duvivier, Henri-Joseph PenDiDA 89
DuVivier, Katharine Keyes 1953- WhoEmL 91
Duvo, Mechelle Louise 1962- WhoAmW 91
Duvoisin, Roger 1904-1980 BioIn 16, ChlLR 23 [port], WhoAmA 91N
Duvoisin, Roger Antone 1904-1980 AuBYP 90
Duvoisin, Roger C 1927- ConAu 132
Duvvi, Appalaraju 1926- BiDrAPA 89
Duvvi, Kamalamma A BiDrAPA 89
Duwe, Brian Miles 1941- WhoSSW 91
Duwe, James Arthur 1955- WhoAm 90
Duwe, John 1941- St&PR 91
Dux, Pierre 1908-1990 NewYTBS 90
Duxbury, Nancy Anne 1941- WhoSSW 91
Duyckinck, Evert Augustus 1816-1878 BioIn 16
Duyguluer, Feridun 1951- WhoWor 91
Duytschaver, Linda Lyvonne 1949- WhoEmL 91
Duzan, S.A. 1941- St&PR 91
Duzan, Stephen Andrew 1941- WhoAm 90
Duzer, Roger 1926- WhoWor 91
Duzy, Albert Frank 1921- WhoAm 90
Duzy, Merrilyn Jeanne 1946- WhoAmA 91
Dvarackas, Peter BioIn 16
Dveirin, Jack L. 1958- WhoEmL 91
Dvoor, Deborah Ann 1959- WhoAmW 91
Dvoracek, Jiri 1928- IntWWM 90
Dvorak, Allen Dale 1943- WhoAm 90
Dvorak, Ann Marie Tompkins 1938- WhoE 91
Dvorak, Antonin 1841-1904 BioIn 16, PenDiMP A, WorAlBi
Dvorak, David Alexander 1955- WhoSSW 91
Dvorak, Donald Allen 1933- St&PR 91
Dvorak, Donald Frank 1933- WhoAm 90
Dvorak, Harold F. 1937- WhoAm 90
Dvorak, Josef Cermin 1945- WhoE 91
Dvorak, Ray P. 1931- WhoWor 91
Dvorak, Stanley Joseph 1935- St&PR 91
Dvorak, Thomas L. 1941- IntWWM 90
Dvorak, Wilfred Paul 1940- WhoE 91
Dvorakova, Ludmila 1923- IntWWM 90, PenDiMP
Dvorchak, Dennis 1940- St&PR 91
Dvorchak, Thomas Edward 1933- St&PR 91, WhoAm 90
Dvores, Neil 1949- St&PR 91
Dvoretski, Alter 1906-1942 BioIn 16
Dvoretsky, Edward 1930- ConAu 31NR
Dvorin, Stephen 1941- BiDrAPA 89
Dvorine, Israel BioIn 16
Dvorkin, Donald 1942- WhoAm 90
Dvorsky, Peter 1951- IntWWM 90
Dvorsky, Petr 1951- PenDiMP
Dvoskin, Marcos Ramon 1950- WhoWor 91
Dvoskin, Philip Bryan 1941- BiDrAPA 89
Dwan, William Edward 1941- St&PR 91
Dwass, Meyer 1923- WhoAm 90
Dweck, Susan 1943- WhoAmW 91
Dwek, Cyril S. 1936- WhoAm 90, WhoWor 91
Dwenger, Randall Ralph BiDrAPA 89
Dwiggins, Clare 1874-1958 WhoAmA 91N
Dwiggins, Clare Victor 1874-1958 EncACom
Dwiggins, Claudius William, Jr. 1933- WhoSSW 91, WhoWor 91
Dwiggins, Don 1913- AuBYP 90
Dwiggins, Don 1913-1988 SmATA 60
Dwiggins, William Addison 1880-1956 BioIn 16, WhoAmA 91N
Dwight, Donald Rathbun 1931- St&PR 91, WhoAm 90, WhoE 91
Dwight, Edward Harold 1919-1981 WhoAmA 91N
Dwight, James Scutt, Jr. 1934- WhoAm 90
Dwight, John 1635?-1703 PenDiDA 89
Dwight, Olivia WhoWrEP 89
Dwight, Reginald Kenneth 1947- WhoAm 90, WhoWor 91
Dwight, Timothy 1752-1817 EncCRAm [port]
Dwight, William, Jr. 1929- WhoAm 90, WhoE 91
Dwinell, James Fisher 1939- St&PR 91
Dwinger, Philip 1914- WhoAm 90
Dwivedi, Suresh C BiDrAPA 89
Dwon, Larry 1913- WhoAm 90
Dworetsky, Steven David 1954- BiDrAPA 89
Dworetz, Arthur BiDrAPA 89
Dworetz, Marcia ODwPR 91
Dworetzky, Murray 1917- WhoAm 90
Dworin, Jeffrey Zolla 1950- St&PR 91
Dworken, Dudley Carter 1949- St&PR 91

Dworkin, Andrea 1946- *FemiCLE, MajTwCW*
Dworkin, David Lee 1943- *WhoAm 90*
Dworkin, Howard Jerry 1932- *WhoAm 90*
Dworkin, Martin 1927- *WhoAm 90*
Dworkin, Michael Leonard 1947- *WhoEmL 91*
Dworkin, Ronald Myles 1931- *WhoE 91*
Dworkin, Samuel Franklin 1933- *WhoAm 90*
Dworkin, Sidney 1921- *St&PR 91*
Dworschack, James Francis 1953- *WhoEmL 91*
Dworsky, Clara Weiner 1918- *WhoAmW 91*
Dworsky, Daniel Leonard 1927- *WhoAm 90*
Dworsky, Leonard B. 1915- *WhoAm 90*
Dworsky, Lynn Staton *BiDrAPA 89*
Dworzan, George R 1924- *WhoAmA 91*
Dwyer, Andrew T. 1948- *WhoAm 90*
Dwyer, Andrew Thompson 1948- *St&PR 91*
Dwyer, Ann *BioIn 16*
Dwyer, Ann Elizabeth 1953- *WhoAmW 91, WhoE 91*
Dwyer, Bernard James 1921- *WhoAm 90, WhoE 91*
Dwyer, Brian Michael 1940- *St&PR 91*
Dwyer, Daniel P. 1959- *St&PR 91*
Dwyer, Daniel Thomas 1942- *St&PR 91*
Dwyer, Deanna *MajTwCW, TwCCr&M 91*
Dwyer, Dennis D. 1943- *WhoWor 91*
Dwyer, Dennis Grant 1947- *WhoSSW 91*
Dwyer, Dennis Richard 1943- *St&PR 91*
Dwyer, Diane Marie 1958- *WhoAmW 91*
Dwyer, Doriot Anthony *WhoAm 90*
Dwyer, Doriot Anthony 1922- *IntWWM 90*
Dwyer, Eugene Joseph 1943- *WhoAmA 91*
Dwyer, Frank 1868-1943 *Ballpl 90*
Dwyer, Gary Joseph 1958- *WhoEmL 91*
Dwyer, Gerald Paul, Jr. 1947- *WhoEmL 91*
Dwyer, Gregg Allan 1943- *St&PR 91*
Dwyer, James 1921- *WhoAmA 91*
Dwyer, James Gormley 1913- *St&PR 91*
Dwyer, James L. 1932- *St&PR 91*
Dwyer, James Richard 1949- *WhoEmL 91*
Dwyer, James Robert 1947- *WhoEmL 91*
Dwyer, James Thomas, III 1957- *WhoE 91*
Dwyer, Jim *BioIn 16*
Dwyer, Jim 1950- *Ballpl 90*
Dwyer, Johanna Todd 1938- *WhoAmW 91*
Dwyer, John C. 1930- *ConAu 32NR*
Dwyer, John Denis 1927- *St&PR 91*
Dwyer, John H *BiDrAPA 89*
Dwyer, John Joseph 1917- *St&PR 91*
Dwyer, John R., Jr. 1937- *St&PR 91*
Dwyer, K. R. *MajTwCW, TwCCr&M 91*
Dwyer, Lawrence E. 1925- *St&PR 91*
Dwyer, Margaret Ann *WhoAmW 91*
Dwyer, Mary Ellen 1946- *WhoAmW 91*
Dwyer, Michael Thomas 1945- *St&PR 91*
Dwyer, Nancy Jean 1945- *WhoWrEP 89*
Dwyer, P. Clarke 1932- *St&PR 91*
Dwyer, Patrick C. 1939- *St&PR 91*
Dwyer, Philip Clarke 1932- *WhoAm 90*
Dwyer, Robert Francis 1911- *St&PR 91*
Dwyer, Robert Francis, Jr. 1936- *St&PR 91*
Dwyer, Sandra Sunderman 1946- *WhoAmW 91*
Dwyer, Terrence Edward 1945- *WhoE 91, WhoWor 91*
Dwyer, Thomas S. *BioIn 16*
Dwyer, Virginia Alice 1921- *WhoAm 90*
Dwyer, Walter W 1894- *EncO&P 3*
Dwyer-Dobbin, Mary Alice 1942- *WhoAmW 91*
Dwyre, Douglas Golding, Jr. 1932- *St&PR 91*
Dwyre, William Patrick 1944- *WhoAm 90*
Dy, Boniface *BiDrAPA 89*
Dy, Cynthia Hernandez 1953- *WhoWor 91*
Dy, Faustino *BioIn 16*
Dy, Sylvia Naval *BiDrAPA 89*
Dy Liacco, Tomas Enciso 1920- *WhoAm 90*
Dyakowski, Anthony 1948- *St&PR 91*
Dyakowski, Shannon *St&PR 91*
Dyal, William M., Jr. *BioIn 16*
Dyal, William M., Jr. 1928- *WhoAm 90, WhoE 91*
Dyar, Kathryn Wilkin 1945- *WhoAmW 91*
Dyas, Robert Edward 1923- *St&PR 91*
Dyas, Thomas Winning 1845-1899 *DcCanB 12*
Dybas, Susan Louise 1961- *WhoAmW 91*
Dybeck, Alfred Charles 1928- *WhoAm 90*
Dybeck, Dennis Joseph 1940- *WhoWrEP 89*
Dybek, Stuart John 1942- *WhoWrEP 89*
Dybell, Elizabeth Anne Sledden 1958- *WhoAmW 91*
Dybenko, Pavel Efimovich 1889-1938 *BioIn 16*
Dybiec, Linda J. 1944- *St&PR 91*
Dybing, Robert A. 1948- *St&PR 91*
Dybzinski, Jerry 1955- *Ballpl 90*
Dych, Joseph A. 1942- *St&PR 91*
Dyche, David B. 1902-1990 *BioIn 16*
Dyche, David Bennett, Jr. 1932- *WhoAm 90*
Dychkowski, Linda Ann 1947- *WhoE 91*
Dychtwald, Ken 1950- *BioIn 16*
Dychtwald, Maddy Kent 1952- *WhoAmW 91*
Dyck, princesse de Salm-Reifferscheid- 1767-1845 *EncCoWW*
Dyck, Andrew Roy 1947- *WhoAm 90*
Dyck, Anthonie Van 1599-1641 *BioIn 16*
Dyck, Arthur James 1932- *WhoAm 90*
Dyck, Ernest van *PenDiMP*
Dyck, George 1937- *BiDrAPA 89, WhoAm 90*
Dyck, Jim 1922- *Ballpl 90*
Dyck, Manfred F. 1935- *St&PR 91*
Dyck, Paul 1917- *WhoAmA 91*
Dyck, Peter Bern 1952- *BiDrAPA 89*
Dyck, Walter Peter 1935- *WhoAm 90*
Dyckman, Alice Ann *WhoE 91*
Dyckman, Richard Harris 1960- *WhoE 91*
Dyckman, Thomas Richard 1932- *WhoAm 90*
Dyckman, William T. 1917- *St&PR 91*
Dyckoff, Heidi Mae 1961- *WhoAmW 91*
Dyde, James F 1920- *BiDrAPA 89*
Dye, Alan Page 1946- *WhoE 91, WhoEmL 91*
Dye, Bradford Johnson, Jr. 1933- *WhoSSW 91*
Dye, Cecil Marion 1940- *WhoE 91*
Dye, Clifford W. 1930- *St&PR 91*
Dye, Daniel Mark 1956- *BiDrAPA 89*
Dye, David Ray 1951- *WhoEmL 91*
Dye, Geneva Cureton 1927- *St&PR 91*
Dye, Glenn W. 1921- *WhoE 91*
Dye, Henry 1941- *ODwPR 91*
Dye, James Louis 1927- *WhoAm 90*
Dye, Judy Ann 1950- *WhoAmW 91*
Dye, Kenneth Malcolm 1936- *WhoAm 90*
Dye, Kimberly Anderson 1961- *WhoAmW 91*
Dye, Molly Ball 1951- *WhoAmW 91*
Dye, Paul 1925- *WhoAm 90*
Dye, Robert C. 1943- *St&PR 91*
Dye, Sherman 1915- *WhoAm 90*
Dye, Thomas Alfred 1954- *WhoEmL 91*
Dye, Thomas Roy 1935- *WhoAm 90*
Dyekman, Gregory Chris 1955- *WhoEmL 91*
Dyen, Isidore 1913- *WhoAm 90*
Dyens, Georges Maurice 1932- *WhoAmA 91*
Dyer, Alexander P. 1932- *St&PR 91*
Dyer, Alexander Patrick 1932- *WhoAm 90*
Dyer, Alfred George 1918- *WhoE 91*
Dyer, Alice Mildred 1929- *WhoAmW 91*
Dyer, Allen Ralph 1944- *BiDrAPA 89, WhoE 91*
Dyer, Brien William *BiDrAPA 89*
Dyer, Calvin M. 1943- *St&PR 91*
Dyer, Carol Ann *BiDrAPA 89*
Dyer, Carolyn Price 1931- *WhoAmA 91*
Dyer, Charles Arnold 1940- *WhoWor 91*
Dyer, Charles Herbert 1949- *WhoEmL 91*
Dyer, Cromwell Adair, Jr. 1932- *WhoWor 91*
Dyer, Daniel L. *BioIn 16*
Dyer, Darrell Dean 1933- *St&PR 91*
Dyer, David William 1910- *WhoAm 90*
Dyer, Derrick Fenton 1932- *WhoWor 91*
Dyer, Doris Anne 1944- *WhoAmW 91, WhoE 91*
Dyer, Duffy 1945- *Ballpl 90*
Dyer, Eddie 1900-1964 *Ballpl 90*
Dyer, Edward S *AmLegL*
Dyer, Elaine Dedrickson 1923- *WhoAmW 91*
Dyer, Elizabeth 1928- *WhoAmW 91*
Dyer, Frederick Charles 1918- *WhoAm 90, WhoE 91*
Dyer, Frederick Robert 1944- *WhoAm 90*
Dyer, George 1755-1841 *DcLB 93 [port]*
Dyer, George Lewis, Jr. 1931- *WhoAm 90*
Dyer, Geraldine Ann 1921- *WhoAmW 91, WhoWor 91*
Dyer, Graham Francis 1955- *IntWWM 90*
Dyer, Gregory Clark 1947- *WhoEmL 91*
Dyer, Hugh David 1937- *WhoE 91*
Dyer, J. David, Jr. 1947- *WhoSSW 91*
Dyer, J. Lawson 1908- *St&PR 91*
Dyer, James Harrison 1952- *WhoWor 91*
Dyer, James M. 1950- *St&PR 91*
Dyer, James Mark *WhoAm 90*
Dyer, James Mason, Jr. 1928- *St&PR 91*
Dyer, James Simpson 1943- *WhoAm 90*
Dyer, Jasper Lee 1928- *BiDrAPA 89*
Dyer, Jaye F. 1927- *St&PR 91*
Dyer, Jaye Floyd 1927- *WhoAm 90*
Dyer, John 1699-1757 *DcLB 95 [port]*
Dyer, John Martin 1920- *WhoAm 90, WhoSSW 91*
Dyer, John T 1930- *BiDrAPA 89*
Dyer, Joseph Edward 1924- *St&PR 91*
Dyer, Kenneth Edwin 1949- *WhoWor 91*
Dyer, Kevin L. 1946- *St&PR 91*
Dyer, Lyndall Ellen 1936- *St&PR 91*
Dyer, M Wayne 1950- *WhoAmA 91*
Dyer, Mary *BiDEWW, FemiCLE*
Dyer, Mary 1610?-1660 *EncCRAm*
Dyer, Michael George 1930- *IntWWM 90*
Dyer, Norris William 1936- *WhoSSW 91*
Dyer, Peter Swinnerton- *BioIn 16*
Dyer, Richard 1941- *IntWWM 90*
Dyer, Richard Kerry 1952- *BiDrAPA 89*
Dyer, Richard Sanders, Sr. 1929- *St&PR 91*
Dyer, Robert 1943- *St&PR 91*
Dyer, Robert C. 1913- *St&PR 91*
Dyer, Robert Francis, Jr. 1926- *WhoE 91, WhoWor 91*
Dyer, Robert Stuart *BiDrAPA 89*
Dyer, Rod 1935- *BioIn 16*
Dyer, Samuel Edwin 1925- *St&PR 91, WhoAm 90*
Dyer, Stephen Edward 1946- *St&PR 91*
Dyer, Susan Kristine *WhoAmW 91*
Dyer, Walter Sullivan, III 1957- *WhoEmL 91, WhoWor 91*
Dyer, Wayne Walter 1940- *WhoAm 90*
Dyer, William A., Jr. 1902- *St&PR 91*
Dyer, William Allan, Jr. 1902- *WhoAm 90*
Dyess, Bobby Dale 1935- *WhoAm 90, WhoSSW 91*
Dyess, Cynthia Lee *BiDrAPA 89*
Dygard, Thomas J. 1931- *AuBYP 90, BioIn 16*
Dygert, Dave L. 1943- *St&PR 91*
Dygert, Jimmy 1884-1936 *Ballpl 90*
Dyhouse, Henry Norval 1945- *WhoAm 90*
Dyk, George Van 1943- *St&PR 91*
Dyk, Timothy Belcher *BioIn 16*
Dyk, Timothy Belcher 1937- *WhoAm 90*
Dyke, Charles William 1935- *WhoAm 90*
Dyke, Douglas M. 1942- *St&PR 91*
Dyke, James T. 1937- *St&PR 91*
Dyke, James Trester 1937- *WhoAm 90*
Dyke, Kermit Robert 1947- *St&PR 91*
Dykema, Dorothy Ethel 1923- *WhoAmW 91*
Dykema, Henry L. 1939- *WhoAm 90*
Dykema, Jeffrey Lynn 1950- *St&PR 91*
Dykema, John Russel 1918- *WhoAm 90*
Dykema, Rosemary 1922- *BiDrAPA 89*
Dykeman, Alice M. *ODwPR 91*
Dykeman, Therese Marie Boos 1936- *WhoAmW 91*
Dykeman, Wilma *FemiCLE*
Dykens, James Warren 1921- *BiDrAPA 89*
Dykes, Archie Reece 1931- *St&PR 91, WhoAm 90*
Dykes, Aubrey H. *WhoSSW 91*
Dykes, Bill G. 1947- *WhoSSW 91*
Dykes, C. Allen 1949- *St&PR 91*
Dykes, C.H. 1928- *St&PR 91*
Dykes, Clifford Earl, Jr. 1941- *WhoSSW 91*
Dykes, Eva Beatrice 1893-1986 *HarlReB*
Dykes, Hart Lee *BioIn 16*
Dykes, Iva Ree 1942- *WhoWrEP 89*
Dykes, James Edgar 1919- *WhoAm 90*
Dykes, Jimmy 1896-1976 *Ballpl 90 [port]*
Dykes, John Henry 1934- *St&PR 91*
Dykes, John Henry, Jr. 1934- *WhoAm 90*
Dykes, John S *BioIn 16*
Dykes, Julius A. 1943- *St&PR 91*
Dykes, Michael H. M. 1931- *WhoAm 90*
Dykes, Reno Jackson, Jr. *BiDrAPA 89*
Dykes, Virginia Chandler 1930- *WhoAmW 91*
Dykes Bower, John 1905-1981 *DcNaB 1981*
Dykhouse, David B. 1948- *St&PR 91*
Dykhouse, David Jay 1936- *WhoAm 90*
Dykhuizen, Daniel Edward 1942- *WhoE 91*
Dykshoorn, Marinus Bernardus 1920- *EncO&P 3, WhoE 91*
Dyksterhuis, Edsko Jerry 1908- *WhoSSW 91*
Dykstra, Charles Alan 1942- *St&PR 91*
Dykstra, Daniel D. 1955- *WhoEmL 91*
Dykstra, Daniel James 1916- *WhoAm 90*
Dykstra, David Allen 1938- *WhoWor 91*
Dykstra, David Charles 1941- *WhoAm 90*
Dykstra, Doward William 1933- *St&PR 91*
Dykstra, John *ConTFT 8*
Dykstra, Lenny 1963- *Ballpl 90*
Dykstra, Mary Elizabeth 1939- *WhoAm 90*
Dykstra, Paul Hopkins 1943- *WhoAm 90*
Dykstra, Robert Rozeboom 1930- *WhoAm 90*
Dykstra, Robert T. 1918- *St&PR 91*
Dykstra, Vergil Homer 1925- *WhoAm 90*
Dykstra, William Dwight 1927- *WhoWor 91*
Dykstra, William Henry 1928- *St&PR 91, WhoAm 90*
Dylan, Bob 1941- *BioIn 16, EncPR&S 89, OxCPMus, WhoAm 90, WorAlBi*
Dyles, C Lyn 1956- *BiDrAPA 89*
Dym, Andrew R. 1959- *St&PR 91*
Dym, Clive Lionel 1942- *WhoAm 90*
Dym, Diane S. *ODwPR 91*
Dymally, Mervyn Malcolm 1926- *BlkAmsC [port], WhoAm 90*
Dymek, James S. *St&PR 91*
Dymetryszyn, Rose *BiDrAPA 89*
Dymiotis, Petros 1940- *WhoWor 91*
Dymond, Barbara Louise 1956- *WhoAmW 91*
Dymond, Lewis Wandell 1920- *WhoAm 90, WhoWor 91*
Dyne, Michael 1918-1989 *BioIn 16*
Dynely, James *AuBYP 90*
Dynkin, Eugene B. 1924- *WhoAm 90*
Dynna, Harold Olaf 1935- *St&PR 91*
Dyon, Charles Raymond 1929- *St&PR 91*
Dyott, Richard Burnaby 1924- *WhoAm 90*
D'Youville, Marguerite 1701-1771 *BioIn 16*
Dyregaard, Jens Helge 1944- *WhoWor 91*
Dyregrov, Michael 1931- *WhoWor 91*
Dyreks, Raymond R. 1914- *St&PR 91*
Dyrud, Jarl E 1921- *BiDrAPA 89*
Dyrud, Jarl Edvard 1921- *WhoAm 90*
Dyrud, Jarl Edvard, Jr. *BiDrAPA 89*
Dysart, Benjamin Clay, III 1940- *WhoAm 90*
Dysart, Dorsey William, Jr. *BiDrAPA 89*
Dysart, Joel Alyn 1940- *WhoAm 90*
Dysart, Richard 19--?- *WorAlBi*
Dysart, Robert Lewis 1956- *WhoEmL 91*
Dysinger, Paul William 1927- *WhoAm 90*
Dysinger, Robert H *BiDrAPA 89*
Dysken, Maurice W 1942- *BiDrAPA 89*
Dysken, Signe Midelfort 1943- *BiDrAPA 89*
Dyson, Allan Judge 1942- *WhoAm 90*
Dyson, Anthony James 1953- *WhoE 91*
Dyson, Arthur Thomas 1940- *St&PR 91, WhoWor 91*
Dyson, Brian 1944- *WhoAmA 91*
Dyson, Brian G. 1935- *WhoSSW 91*
Dyson, Charles H. 1909- *St&PR 91*
Dyson, Esther *BioIn 16*
Dyson, Freeman J. 1923- *BioIn 16, WorAu 1980 [port]*
Dyson, Freeman John 1923- *WhoAm 90*
Dyson, John *NewAgMG*
Dyson, Ketaki 1940- *FemiCLE*
Dyson, Raymond Clegg 1902- *WhoAm 90, WhoWor 91*
Dyson, Robert Harris 1927- *WhoAm 90, WhoE 91*
Dyson, Ronnie 1950- *DrBlPA 90*
Dyson, Roy 1948- *WhoAm 90, WhoE 91*
Dyson, Ruth 1917- *IntWWM 90*
Dyson, Thomas Russell 1947- *WhoE 91*
Dyson, William L 1915- *BiDrAPA 89*
Dyson Perrins, Charles William *PenDiDA 89*
Dystel, Jane Dee 1945- *WhoAm 90, WhoAmW 91*
Dystel, Oscar 1912- *WhoAm 90, WorAlBi*
Dyvig, Peter P. 1934- *WhoAm 90, WhoWor 91*
Dywan, Jeffery Joseph 1949- *WhoEmL 91*
Dywasuk, Colette Marie 1941- *WhoAmW 91*
Dyyon, Frazier 1946- *WhoAm 90, WhoAmA 91*
Dyzes, Jean *PenDiDA 89, -89*
Dzerzhinskii, Feliks Edmundovich 1877-1926 *BioIn 16*
Dzhigarkhanian, Armen Borisovich 1935- *WhoWor 91*
Dzhirkvelov, Ilya *BioIn 16*
Dzhumagulov, Apas Dzhumagulovich 1934- *WhoWor 91*
Dzhurov, Dobri Marinov 1916- *WhoWor 91*
Dziadek, Fred 1934- *WhoE 91*
Dziak, Rosemary 1946- *WhoAmW 91*
Dziarski, Agnes 1949- *WhoAmW 91*
Dziedziak, Bryan John 1958- *WhoEmL 91*
Dziedzic, John Edward 1932- *WhoAm 90*
Dzielak, Richard Anthony 1943- *St&PR 91*
Dzielski, Miroslaw *BioIn 16*
Dzienius, Lorraine 1967- *WhoSSW 91*
Dzierski, Vincent Paul 1930- *WhoAmA 91*
Dziewanowski, Marian Kamil 1913- *WhoAm 90*
Dziewonski, Adam Marian 1936- *WhoAm 90*
Dziewulska, Maria Amelia 1909- *IntWWM 90*
Dzigurski, Alex 1911- *WhoAmA 91*
Dziuba, Henry Frank 1918- *WhoAm 90*
Dziuba, Joanne Carol 1951- *WhoAmW 91*
Dziuban, Steven Edwin 1951- *WhoEmL 91*
D'Zmura, Thomas Leo 1929- *BiDrAPA 89*
Dzodin, Harvey Cary 1947- *WhoE 91*
Dzombak, Agnes Marie 1931- *WhoE 91*
Dzubas, Friedel 1915- *WhoAmA 91*
Dzubera, Patricia 1951- *WhoAmW 91*
Dzubinski, David Lee *BiDrAPA 89*
Dzurinko, Joseph J. 1947- *WhoAm 90*

E

E, Sheila *WhoHisp 91*
E., Sheila 1958- *DrBlPA 90*
E., Sheila 1959- *EncPR&S 89*
Eaborn, Colin 1923- *WhoWor 91*
Eacho, William Carlton, Jr. 1923- *St&PR 91*
Eachus, Joseph Jackson 1911- *WhoAm 90*
Eackles, Ledell *BioIn 16*
Eacott, James H., Jr. 1923- *St&PR 91*
Eacott, James Henry, III 1948- *St&PR 91*
Eaddy, Wildon Brooks 1933- *St&PR 91*
Eade, Alfred Thompson 1891-1988 *BioIn 16*
Eade, George James 1921- *St&PR 91, WhoAm 90*
Eade, Lucy Gaye 1948- *WhoEmL 91*
Eadens, Barry Lynn 1952- *WhoEmL 91*
Eades, Barnett R 1939- *BiDrAPA 89*
Eades, James Beverly, Jr. 1923- *WhoAm 90, WhoE 91*
Eades, James F 1932- *BiDrAPA 89*
Eades, Kenneth Murray 1949- *WhoSSW 91*
Eades, Luis Eric 1923- *WhoAmA 91*
Eades, R Charles 1923- *BiDrAPA 89*
Eades, Ronald Wayne 1948- *WhoEmL 91*
Eadie, Arlan *BioIn 16*
Eadie, John William 1935- *WhoAm 90*
Eads, George Curtis 1942- *WhoAm 90*
Eads, James Buchanan 1820-1887 *BioIn 16*
Eads, Lyle Willis 1916- *WhoSSW 91, WhoWor 91*
Eads, M. Adela 1920- *WhoAmW 91*
Eads, Ora Wilbert 1914- *WhoAm 90*
Eads, Ronald Preston 1948- *WhoSSW 91*
Eady, Carol Murphy 1918- *WhoAm 90*
Eady, Cornelius Robert 1954- *WhoWrEP 89*
Eagan, Claire V. 1950- *WhoEmL 91*
Eagan, James Richard 1930- *WhoE 91*
Eagan, Kevin Gerard 1955- *WhoE 91*
Eagan, M. Patricia 1952- *WhoAmW 91*
Eagan, Marie T. 1952- *WhoAmW 91, WhoE 91*
Eagan, Michael 1942- *OxCCanT*
Eagan, Sherman G. 1942- *WhoAm 90, WhoE 91*
Eagan, Shirley C. 1942- *WhoAmW 91*
Eagar, Frances 1940-1978 *BioIn 16*
Eagar, Stephen J. *St&PR 91*
Eagel, Seymour 1927- *St&PR 91*
Eagels, Jeanne 1890?-1929 *NotWoAT*
Eagels, Jeanne 1894-1929 *BioAmW, BioIn 16*
Eagen, Christopher T 1956- *WhoAmA 91*
Eagen, James Michael, III 1957- *WhoE 91*
Eager, Edward McMaken 1911-1964 *AuBYP 90*
Eager, George B. 1921- *BioIn 16*
Eager, George Sidney, Jr. 1915- *WhoAm 90*
Eager, John Howard, III 1928- *St&PR 91*
Eager, Richard Alvin 1945- *WhoEmL 91*
Eager, Stephen J. 1927- *St&PR 91*
Eager, William E. 1946- *St&PR 91*
Eagerton, Robert Pierce 1940- *WhoAmA 91*
Eagle, Brook Medicine *NewAgMG*
Eagle, Candy Kerr 1949- *WhoAmW 91*
Eagle, Charles A. 1936- *St&PR 91*
Eagle, David Malcolm 1955- *IntWWM 90*
Eagle, Deanne *ODwPR 91*
Eagle, Ellen 1953- *SmATA 61 [port]*
Eagle, Harry 1905- *WhoAm 90*
Eagle, Jack 1926- *WhoE 91*
Eagle, James Philip 1837-1904 *AmLegL, BioIn 16*
Eagle, JoAnn Marie 1955- *WhoAmW 91*
Eagle, John M. *St&PR 91*
Eagle, John R *BiDrAPA 89*
Eagle, Kathleen 1947- *WhoWrEP 89*
Eagle, Kevin Dale 1954- *St&PR 91*
Eagle, Leonard R. 1954- *St&PR 91*
Eagle, Paula Frances 1951- *BiDrAPA 89*
Eagleburger, Lawrence Sidney 1930- *WhoAm 90*
Eaglen, Jane 1960- *IntWWM 90*
Eaglen, Roger William 1945- *WhoSSW 91*
Eagler, Jean-Marie 1951- *WhoAmW 91, WhoSSW 91*
Eagles, The *EncPR&S 89, OxCPMus, WhoNeCM A [port]*
Eagles, Lee N. 1947- *St&PR 91*
Eagles, Sidney Smith, Jr. 1939- *WhoAm 90*
Eagles, Stuart Ernest 1929- *WhoAm 90*
Eaglesfield, Francis *EncO&P 3*
Eagleson, Alan *BioIn 16*
Eagleson, David 1943- *St&PR 91*
Eagleson, David Newton *WhoAm 90*
Eagleson, Freeman T. 1876- *AmLegL*
Eagleson, George A. 1932- *St&PR 91*
Eagleson, Peter Sturges 1928- *WhoAm 90*
Eagleson, William Boal, Jr. 1925- *WhoAm 90*
Eagleson, William J. 1937- *WhoAm 90*
Eagleson, William James 1937- *St&PR 91*
Eagleston, Paul David 1924- *St&PR 91*
Eaglet, Robert Danton 1934- *WhoAm 90*
Eagleton, Beth B. 1950- *WhoEmL 91*
Eagleton, G. T. 1894-1988 *AnObit 1988*
Eagleton, Lee Chandler 1923- *WhoAm 90*
Eagleton, Richard Ernest 1930- *WhoAm 90*
Eagleton, Robert Don 1937- *WhoAm 90*
Eagleton, Terence 1943- *MajTwCW*
Eagleton, Terry *MajTwCW*
Eagleton, Terry 1943- *ConLC 63 [port], WorAu 1980 [port]*
Eagleton, Thomas F. 1929- *WorAlBi*
Eagleton, William Lester, Jr. 1926- *WhoAm 90*
Eaglin, Ronald G. 1940- *WhoAm 90*
Eaglstein, William Howard 1940- *WhoAm 90*
Eagly, Alice Hendrickson 1938- *WhoAmW 91*
Eagon, Donald E., Jr. 1942- *ODwPR 91*
Eaione, Joseph Henry 1949- *WhoE 91*
Eakeley, Douglas Scott 1946- *WhoEmL 91*
Eaken, Roderick Ford 1932- *St&PR 91*
Eaker, Charles William 1949- *WhoSSW 91*
Eaker, Ira 1922- *WhoAm 90, WhoE 91*
Eaker, Kenneth August 1952- *St&PR 91*
Eaker, Sherry Ellen 1949- *WhoEmL 91*
Eakin, David McClellan 1950- *WhoEmL 91*
Eakin, Margaretta Morgan 1941- *WhoWor 91*
Eakin, Randall L. 1962- *WhoEmL 91*
Eakin, Thomas Capper 1933- *WhoAm 90, WhoWor 91*
Eakin, Thomas Robert 1954- *St&PR 91*
Eakin, Tom S., Jr. 1927- *St&PR 91*
Eakin, Tom Scott, Jr. 1927- *WhoAm 90*
Eakin, William Wayne 1949- *WhoEmL 91*
Eakins, George H. 1928- *St&PR 91*
Eakins, Kenneth E. 1935- *St&PR 91*
Eakins, Patricia 1942- *WhoWrEP 89*
Eakins, Susan 1851-1938 *BiDWomA*
Eakins, Thomas 1844-1916 *BioIn 16, IntDcAA 90, WorAlBi*
Eakins, William Shannon 1951- *WhoE 91*
Eakle, Arlene H. 1936- *WhoAmW 91*
Ealy, Lawrence Orr 1915- *WhoAm 90, WhoWor 91*
Ealy, Robert Phillip 1914- *WhoAm 90*
Eamer, Richard K. 1928- *St&PR 91*
Eamer, Richard Keith 1928- *WhoAm 90*
Eames, Benjamin Tucker 1818-1901 *AmLegL*
Eames, Charles 1907-1978 *ConDes 90, PenDiDA 89, WorAlBi*
Eames, Emma 1865-1952 *PenDiMP*
Eames, G. Clifton 1927- *St&PR 91*
Eames, Genevieve Torrey *AuBYP 90*
Eames, Herbert Howell, Jr. 1934- *St&PR 91, WhoAm 90*
Eames, John Heagan 1900- *WhoAm 90, WhoAmA 91*
Eames, Larry Ray 1936- *St&PR 91*
Eames, Ray *BioIn 16*
Eames, Ray 1916-1988 *AnObit 1988, ConDes 90*
Eames, Wilmer Ballou 1914- *WhoAm 90*
Eanes, Joseph Cabel, Jr. 1935- *St&PR 91, WhoAm 90*
Eanes, Michael Bailey 1941- *St&PR 91*
Eanes, Wanda Marie 1958- *WhoSSW 91*
Eapen, Eldho 1949- *WhoWor 91*
Eardley, Cynthia 1946- *WhoAmA 91*
Eardley, Joan 1921-1963 *BiDWomA*
Earhart, Amelia 1898-1937 *BioIn 16, WorAlBi*
Earhart, Amelia M. 1898-1937 *BioAmW*
Earhart, Donald Marion 1944- *WhoAm 90*
Earhart, Eileen Magie 1928- *WhoAm 90*
Earl, Anthony Scully 1936- *WhoAm 90*
Earl, Don Charles 1925- *WhoSSW 91*
Earl, Harley Jefferson 1893-1969 *EncABHB 5 [port]*
Earl, Jack Eugene 1934- *WhoAmA 91*
Earl, James 1761-1796 *BioIn 16*
Earl, Jeanne *BiDrAPA 89*
Earl, John William 1939- *WhoE 91*
Earl, Lewis Harold 1918- *WhoAm 90*
Earl, Peter M. 1949- *St&PR 91*
Earl, Richard William 1943- *WhoE 91*
Earl, Ronnie *ConMus 5 [port]*
Earl, William John 1950- *WhoEmL 91*
Earl, William Lee 1945- *WhoEmL 91*
Earle M. *BioIn 16*
Earle, Alice Morse 1853?-1911 *AuBYP 90*
Earle, Arthur Percival 1922- *St&PR 91, WhoAm 90*
Earle, Brent Nicholson *BioIn 16*
Earle, Brian Vigors 1922- *BiDrAPA 89*
Earle, Clifford John, Jr. 1935- *WhoAm 90, WhoE 91*
Earle, David Prince, Jr. 1910- *WhoAm 90*
Earle, Douglas Vandyke 1955- *St&PR 91*
Earle, Edward W 1951- *WhoAmA 91*
Earle, Harry Woodward 1924- *St&PR 91, WhoAm 90*
Earle, Hubert Potter 1918- *St&PR 91*
Earle, Jean 1909- *FemiCLE*
Earle, Jean Buist 1951- *WhoAmW 91*
Earle, Julius Richard, Jr. 1954- *BiDrAPA 89*
Earle, Kenneth Martin 1919- *WhoAm 90*
Earle, Larry C. 1952- *WhoSSW 91*
Earle, Melvyn Stuart 1956- *IntWWM 90*
Earle, Peter T. 1933- *ODwPR 91*
Earle, Ralph 1751-1801 *EncCRAm*
Earle, Ralph, II 1928- *WhoAm 90, WhoE 91*
Earle, Richard Laurence 1930- *WhoWor 91*
Earle, Richard Millar 1932- *St&PR 91, WhoAm 90*
Earle, Roderick *IntWWM 90*
Earle, Steve *BioIn 16, WhoNeCM [port]*
Earle, Sylvia A. 1935- *BioIn 16*
Earle, Sylvia Alice 1935- *WhoAm 90, WhoAmW 91*
Earle, Victor M. *BioIn 16*
Earle, Victor Montagne, III 1933- *WhoAm 90*
Earle, Wendell G. *BioIn 16*
Earle, William *ConAu 30NR*
Earle, William George 1940- *WhoAm 90*
Earles, Dorothy Robertson 1946- *WhoAmW 91*
Earles, Richard Lee 1952- *St&PR 91*
Earley, Anthony *BioIn 16*
Earley, Anthony F. 1949- *St&PR 91*
Earley, Anthony Francis, Jr. 1949- *WhoAm 90*
Earley, Arnie 1933- *Ballpl 90*
Earley, Charity Adams 1918- *ConAu 132*
Earley, Daniel L. 1942- *St&PR 91*
Earley, Diane Marie 1963- *WhoE 91*
Earley, Ernest Benton 1906- *WhoAm 90*
Earley, Joseph Francis 1924- *St&PR 91*
Earley, Robert Horn 1948- *St&PR 91*
Earley, Teresita E *BiDrAPA 89*
Earley, Tom 1917-1988 *Ballpl 90*
Earley, William Guthrie 1941- *St&PR 91*
Earley, William Hugh *BiDrAPA 89*
Earll, Jerry Miller 1928- *WhoAm 90*
Earlougher, Robert Charles, Sr. 1914- *WhoAm 90, WhoSSW 91*
Earls, Clifford Dewight 1935- *St&PR 91*
Earls, Felton James 1942- *BiDrAPA 89*
Earls, Irene Anne *WhoAmW 91*
Earls, Jim Howard *BiDrAPA 89*
Earls, Paul 1934- *IntWWM 90, WhoAmA 91, WhoE 91*
Earls, Priscilla Sue 1945- *St&PR 91*
Earls-Solari, Bonnie 1951- *WhoAmA 91*
Earlston, Robert Paul 1928- *WhoE 91*
Early, Bert Hylton 1922- *WhoAm 90, WhoWor 91*
Early, Glen Alan 1948- *WhoSSW 91*
Early, Jack Dent 1929- *WhoAm 90*
Early, Jack Gavin, Jr. 1953- *WhoEmL 91, WhoSSW 91*
Early, Jack Jones 1925- *St&PR 91, WhoAm 90*
Early, Jake 1915- *Ballpl 90*
Early, Jim Lee 1933- *WhoSSW 91*
Early, John Collins 1919- *WhoWor 91*
Early, John Firman 1944- *WhoE 91*
Early, Jon *ConAu 30NR*
Early, Joseph Daniel 1933- *WhoAm 90, WhoE 91*
Early, Jubal 1816-1894 *WorAlBi*
Early, Jubal Anderson 1816-1894 *BioIn 16*
Early, Karen Helene 1954- *WhoAmW 91*

Early, Margaret Henderson 1952- *WhoEmL 91*
Early, Martin W. 1929- *St&PR 91*
Early, Patrick Joseph 1933- *WhoAm 90*
Early, Rodney Clyde 1950- *WhoE 91*
Early, Ronald Gayle 1944- *BiDrAPA 89*
Early, Stephen 1889-1951 *BioIn 16*
Early, Stephen Barry 1945- *St&PR 91*
Early, Terrence Stephen 1955- *BiDrAPA 89*
Early, William Bernard 1936- *St&PR 91*
Early, William James 1921- *WhoAm 90*
Earner, George Edward 1930- *WhoE 91, WhoWor 91*
Earnest, George H. 1908- *St&PR 91*
Earnest, Jack E. 1928- *St&PR 91*
Earnest, Jack Edward 1928- *WhoAm 90*
Earnest, William *St&PR 91*
Earnhardt, Dale *BioIn 16*
Earnhardt, Dale 1952- *WorAlBi*
Earnhardt, Edward 1938- *St&PR 91*
Earnhardt, R. Dale *WhoAm 90*
Earnhart, Don Brady 1925- *WhoAm 90*
Earnhart, Mark Warren 1955- *WhoEmL 91*
Earnshaw, Donald Van Arsdale 1925- *WhoE 91*
Earnshaw, George 1900-1976 *Ballpl 90*
Earp, Curtis Duncan, Jr. 1938- *WhoSSW 91*
Earp, James Francy 1935- *WhoSSW 91*
Earp, Josephine Marcus *BioIn 16*
Earp, Wyatt 1848-1929 *BioIn 16, WorAlBi*
Earth, Wind & Fire *EncPR&S 89*
Easbey, Marion Moriarty 1930- *WhoAmW 91, WhoE 91*
Easby, Dudley T, Jr 1905-1973 *WhoAmA 91N*
Easdale, Joan Adeney 1913- *FemiCLE*
Easdon, Don 1947- *WhoAm 90*
Easler, Lucian Russell, Jr. *WhoSSW 91*
Easler, Mike 1950- *Ballpl 90*
Easley, Betty 1929- *WhoAmW 91*
Easley, David Preston *BiDrAPA 89*
Easley, Dick L. 1935- *St&PR 91*
Easley, John Allen, Jr. 1922- *WhoAm 90*
Easley, Loyce Anna 1918- *WhoAmW 91*
Easley, Mack 1916- *WhoAm 90*
Easley, Matthew S. 1956- *St&PR 91*
Easley, Patsy Fletcher 1931- *WhoAmW 91, WhoSSW 91*
Easley, Robert Sheldon 1950- *WhoWor 91*
Easley, Waverly 1925- *St&PR 91*
Easlick, David Kenneth 1921- *WhoAm 90*
Eason, Carl Edward, Jr. 1954- *WhoEmL 91*
Eason, Clifton W. 1943- *St&PR 91*
Eason, David Mac 1956- *BiDrAPA 89*
Eason, Forrest K. 1940- *St&PR 91*
Eason, James Oscar 1947- *St&PR 91*
Eason, James Oscar, Jr. 1947- *WhoAm 90*
Eason, James S. 1926- *St&PR 91*
Eason, Jimmie Jerome 1940- *St&PR 91*
Eason, Mal 1879-1970 *Ballpl 90*
Eason, Randolph Arthur 1946- *St&PR 91*
Eason, Robert Gaston 1924- *WhoAm 90*
Eason, Thomas Frederick 1940- *St&PR 91*
Eason, Thomas K. 1911- *St&PR 91*
Eason, William Everette, Jr. 1943- *WhoAm 90*
Easson, William M *BiDrAPA 89*
Easson, William McAlpine 1931- *WhoAm 90*
East, Caprice Dorean 1951- *WhoAmW 91*
East, Charles 1924- *WhoWrEP 89*
East, Charles David 1934- *WhoAm 90*
East, Charles E. 1924- *WhoAm 90*
East, Charles E., Jr. 1949- *WhoEmL 91, WhoSSW 91*
East, Darrell 1956- *St&PR 91*
East, David J. 1927- *St&PR 91*
East, Ernest Earl 1942- *St&PR 91, WhoAm 90*
East, F. Howard 1937- *St&PR 91*
East, Frank Howard 1937- *WhoAm 90*
East, Isaac C *BiDrAPA 89*
East, John Delos 1945- *St&PR 91*
East, John Michael 1929- *IntWWM 90*
East, Maurice Alden 1941- *WhoAm 90*
East, Michael *MajTwCW*
Eastburn, David P. 1921- *St&PR 91*
Eastby, Allen Gerhard 1946- *WhoWrEP 89*
Eastcott, Robert Wayne 1943- *WhoAmA 91*
Eastep, Larry Gene 1938- *WhoSSW 91, WhoWor 91*
Easter, Eric James 1957- *WhoSSW 91*
Easter, Joyce Adele 1948- *BiDrAPA 89*
Easter, Luke 1915-1979 *Ballpl 90 [port]*
Easter, Olen Cordell 1917- *St&PR 91*
Easter, Stephen Sherman, Jr. 1938- *WhoAm 90*
Easter, Steven Wycliffe 1941- *St&PR 91*
Easterbrook, Ernest Fred 1908-1989 *BioIn 16*
Easterbrook, Frank *BioIn 16*
Easterbrook, James Arthur 1923- *WhoAm 90*
Easterbrook, Kenneth Brian 1935- *WhoAm 90*
Easterday, Bernard Carlyle 1929- *WhoAm 90*
Easterday, Jack Kahl 1932- *St&PR 91*
Easterday, Jerry L *BiDrAPA 89*
Easterday, Richard Lee 1938- *St&PR 91, WhoAm 90*
Easterfield, Trevor John 1939- *IntWWM 90*
Easterlin, Donald J. 1942- *St&PR 91*
Easterlin, Donald Jacob, III 1942- *WhoAm 90*
Easterlin, John Howard 1962- *WhoEmL 91*
Easterlin, Richard Ainley 1926- *WhoAm 90*
Easterling, Charles Armo 1920- *WhoSSW 91*
Easterling, Cynthia SoRelle 1953- *WhoEmL 91*
Easterling, Howard *Ballpl 90*
Easterling, Walter Sidney 1924- *BiDrAPA 89*
Easterling, William Ewart, Jr. 1930- *WhoAm 90*
Easterly, Clark 1926- *St&PR 91*
Easterly, David Eugene 1942- *WhoAm 90*
Easterly, Jamie 1953- *Ballpl 90*
Easterly, Ted 1885-1951 *Ballpl 90*
Easterly, Thomas B. 1947- *St&PR 91*
Easterly, Thomas M. 1809-1882 *WhNaAH*
Easterly, Thomas Martin 1809-1882 *BioIn 16*
Easterly, Valerie Frances 1951- *WhoAmW 91*
Easterman, Daniel 1949- *SpyFic*
Easterwood, Henry Lewis 1934- *WhoAm 90, WhoAmA 91*
Eastham, Alan Walter, Jr. 1951- *WhoAm 90*
Eastham, Dennis M. 1946- *St&PR 91*
Eastham, Dennis Michael 1946- *WhoAm 90*
Eastham, John F. 1952- *St&PR 91*
Eastham, Thomas 1923- *WhoAm 90*
Easthope, Antony 1939- *ConAu 130*
Eastin, Keith E. 1940- *WhoAm 90*
Eastin, W.J. 1904- *St&PR 91*
Eastlake, Charles Lock 1836-1906 *PenDiDA 89*
Eastlake, Elizabeth Rigby 1809-1893 *BioIn 16*
Eastlake, William Derry 1917- *WhoAm 90, WhoWrEP 89*
Eastland, James O. 1904-1986 *WorAlBi*
Eastland, Terry *BioIn 16*
Eastland, Woods Eugene 1945- *St&PR 91, WhoAm 90*
Eastlick, John Taylor 1912-1990 *BioIn 16*
Eastline, Dorothy 1929- *WhoAmW 91*
Eastline, Richard Leonard 1926- *St&PR 91*
Eastman, Albert Theodore 1928- *WhoAm 90, WhoE 91*
Eastman, Alvin Clark 1894-1959 *WhoAmA 91N*
Eastman, Caroline Merriam 1946- *WhoAmW 91*
Eastman, Carolyn Ann 1946- *WhoAmW 91*
Eastman, Carolyn Bertha 1933- *WhoAmW 91*
Eastman, Charles Alexander 1858-1939 *WhNaAH*
Eastman, Creswell John 1940- *WhoWor 91*
Eastman, Dean Eric 1940- *WhoAm 90*
Eastman, Elaine 1863-1953 *FemiCLE*
Eastman, Forest David 1950- *WhoEmL 91*
Eastman, Gene M 1926- *WhoAmA 91*
Eastman, George 1854-1932 *BioIn 16, WorAlBi*
Eastman, Harland Horace 1929- *WhoAm 90*
Eastman, Harold S. 1939- *WhoAm 90*
Eastman, Harry Claude MacColl 1923- *WhoAm 90*
Eastman, James Earl 1946- *WhoSSW 91*
Eastman, James Michael 1936- *St&PR 91*
Eastman, James Warren 1940- *BiDrAPA 89*
Eastman, Janet Louise 1957- *WhoEmL 91*
Eastman, John *BioIn 16*
Eastman, John 1916-1989 *BioIn 16*
Eastman, John Richard 1917- *WhoAm 90*
Eastman, Joseph M. 1941- *St&PR 91*
Eastman, Lester C. 1918- *St&PR 91*
Eastman, Lester Fuess 1928- *WhoAm 90*
Eastman, Linda Suzanne 1946- *WhoAmW 91*
Eastman, Mary 1818-1887 *FemiCLE*
Eastman, Max *EncAL*
Eastman, Max 1883-1969 *BioIn 16*
Eastman, P. Dwight 1917- *St&PR 91*
Eastman, Philip Dey 1909-1986 *AuBYP 90*
Eastman, Richard Morse 1916- *WhoAm 90*
Eastman, Samuel Coffin 1837-1917 *AmLegL*
Eastman, Seth 1809-1875 *WhNaAH*
Eastman, Wilbur F. *BioIn 16*
Eastman, William Don 1931- *WhoAm 90*
Eastman, William Joseph 1881-1950 *WhoAmA 91N*
Eastment, George T., III 1945- *St&PR 91*
Eastment, Thomas James 1950- *WhoE 91*
Easton, Carol Lee 1939- *WhoAmW 91*
Easton, Charles C., Jr. 1930- *St&PR 91*
Easton, Donald R *BiDrAPA 89*
Easton, Florence 1882-1955 *PenDiMP*
Easton, Frank Lorence 1884- *WhoAmA 91N*
Easton, Glenn Hanson, Jr. *WhoAm 90, WhoWor 91*
Easton, Jill Johanna 1949- *WhoAmW 91*
Easton, Joan Marie 1935- *WhoAmW 91*
Easton, John Edward 1935- *St&PR 91, WhoAm 90*
Easton, John Jay, Jr. 1943- *WhoAm 90*
Easton, Jonathan 1956- *BiDrAPA 89*
Easton, Joseph Wayne 1950- *WhoAm 90*
Easton, Karl 1926- *BiDrAPA 89*
Easton, Kelly Mark 1963- *WhoSSW 91*
Easton, Loyd David 1915- *WhoAm 90*
Easton, Michael Scott *BiDrAPA 89*
Easton, Michelle 1950- *WhoAm 90, WhoAmW 91*
Easton, Norman L *BiDrAPA 89*
Easton, Richard 1933- *OxCCanT*
Easton, Robert 1915- *WhoAm 90, WhoWor 91*
Easton, Roger David 1923- *WhoAmA 91*
Easton, Sheena 1959- *EncPR&S 89, WhoAmW 91*
Easton, Sidney 1891- *EarBlAP*
Easton, Stanley 1919- *St&PR 91*
Easton, Thomas W. *WhoE 91*
Easton, William Edgar 1861- *EarBlAP*
Easton, William Heyden 1916- *WhoAm 90*
Easton-Hafkenschiel, Cynthia Ruth 1949- *WhoEmL 91*
Eastwick, Ivy Ethel Olive *AuBYP 90*
Eastwick, Rawley 1950- *Ballpl 90*
Eastwood, Alice 1859- *WomFie [port]*
Eastwood, Clint *BioIn 16, NewYTBS 90 [port]*
Eastwood, Clint 1930- *WhoAm 90, WhoWor 91, WorAlBi*
Eastwood, Dana Alan 1947- *WhoE 91, WhoEmL 91, WhoWor 91*
Eastwood, DeLyle 1932- *WhoAmW 91*
Eastwood, Diane Roselyn 1940- *IntWWM 90*
Eastwood, Douglas William 1918- *WhoAm 90*
Eastwood, Eric 1910-1981 *DcNaB 1981*
Eastwood, Gregory Lindsay 1940- *WhoAm 90*
Eastwood, Hartley William 1933- *St&PR 91*
Eastwood, Martin Anthony 1935- *WhoWor 91*
Eastwood, Thomas Hugh 1922 *IntWWM 90*
Eastwood, William Scott 1942- *St&PR 91*
Easum, Donald B. 1923- *WhoAm 90, WhoE 91*
Easwaran, Eknath *BioIn 16*
Eatherly, Claude 1920?-1978 *BioIn 16*
Eathorne, Wendy 1939- *IntWWM 90*
Eatinger, Robert Joseph, Jr. 1957- *WhoEmL 91*
Eatmon, Randolph Ray 1950- *St&PR 91*
Eaton, Allen Hendershott 1878-1962 *WhoAmA 91N*
Eaton, Allen Ober 1910- *WhoAm 90*
Eaton, Alvin Ralph 1920- *WhoAm 90, WhoWor 91*
Eaton, Ann Berrien 1960- *WhoAmW 91*
Eaton, Ariana van der Heyden 1955- *WhoAmW 91*
Eaton, Audrey Barbara 1959- *WhoEmL 91*
Eaton, Ben 1963- *St&PR 91*
Eaton, Ben A. 1940- *WhoSSW 91*
Eaton, Berrien Clark 1919- *WhoAm 90, WhoWor 91*
Eaton, Charles Edward 1916- *WhoAm 90, WhoWrEP 89*
Eaton, Charlotte Anne 1788-1859 *FemiCLE*
Eaton, Clara Barbour 1930- *WhoAm 90*
Eaton, Conrad Paul 1941- *WhoAm 90*
Eaton, Curtis Howarth 1945- *WhoWor 91*
Eaton, Cyrus 1918- *BioIn 16*
Eaton, Cyrus S. 1883-1979 *WorAlBi*
Eaton, David Caldwell 1964- *WhoE 91*
Eaton, Dorla Dean 1929- *WhoAmW 91*
Eaton, E. Neal 1921- *St&PR 91*
Eaton, E.P., Jr. 1923- *St&PR 91*
Eaton, Edgar Philip, Jr. 1923- *WhoE 91, WhoWor 91*
Eaton, Edna Dorothy 1938- *WhoAmW 91*
Eaton, Edwin H., Jr. 1938- *St&PR 91*
Eaton, Evelyn Sybil Mary 1902- *BioIn 16, FemiCLE*
Eaton, Frederick Howard 1933- *St&PR 91, WhoAm 90*
Eaton, Gareth Richard 1940- *WhoAm 90*
Eaton, Gary Mayer 1944- *BiDrAPA 89*
Eaton, George 1929- *St&PR 91*
Eaton, George Benjamin 1958- *WhoE 91, WhoEmL 91, WhoWor 91*
Eaton, George L. *AuBYP 90, ConAu 131*
Eaton, Gordon Pryor 1929- *WhoAm 90, WhoWor 91*
Eaton, Haven McCrillis 1926- *St&PR 91*
Eaton, Henry F. 1925- *ODwPR 91*
Eaton, Henry Felix 1925- *WhoAm 90*
Eaton, Iris Kathleen 1954- *WhoSSW 91*
Eaton, James S. 1912- *St&PR 91*
Eaton, James S, Jr. 1936- *BiDrAPA 89*
Eaton, Janet 1932- *SmATA X [port]*
Eaton, Jean Bonnie 1951- *WhoAmW 91*
Eaton, Jeanette 1886-1968 *AuBYP 90*
Eaton, John 1935- *PenDiMP A*
Eaton, John A. 1925- *St&PR 91*
Eaton, John C. 1935- *IntWWM 90, WhoAm 90*
Eaton, John H. 1945- *St&PR 91*
Eaton, John Henry 1790-1856 *BiDrUSE 89*
Eaton, John LeRoy 1939- *WhoSSW 91*
Eaton, John Stanley 1932- *St&PR 91*
Eaton, Joseph Oriel *EncABHB 4*
Eaton, Joseph W. 1919- *WhoAm 90*
Eaton, Judith 1938- *BiDrAPA 89*
Eaton, Karl F. 1925- *St&PR 91*
Eaton, Katherine Cecelia 1934- *WhoE 91*
Eaton, Katherine Girton 1924- *WhoAmW 91*
Eaton, Kim Diane 1956- *WhoEmL 91*
Eaton, Larry Ralph 1944- *WhoAm 90*
Eaton, Leonard James, Jr. 1934- *St&PR 91, WhoAm 90, WhoSSW 91*
Eaton, Leonard Kimball 1922- *WhoAm 90*
Eaton, Leslie Kay 1945- *BiDrAPA 89*
Eaton, Lewis Swift 1919- *St&PR 91, WhoAm 90*
Eaton, Louise F *BiDrAPA 89*
Eaton, Lynda Lou 1946- *WhoAmW 91*
Eaton, Margaret 1799-1879 *BioAmW*
Eaton, Margaret Ann 1953- *WhoAmW 91*
Eaton, Mark *BioIn 16*
Eaton, Mark F. 1954- *WhoSSW 91*
Eaton, Mark R. 1952- *St&PR 91*
Eaton, Merrill T 1920- *BiDrAPA 89*
Eaton, Merrill Thomas 1920- *WhoAm 90*
Eaton, Nancy Jean 1932- *WhoE 91*
Eaton, Nancy L. 1943- *WhoAm 90, WhoAmW 91*
Eaton, Pauline 1935- *WhoAmA 91, WhoAmW 91*
Eaton, Reginald C 1917- *BiDrAPA 89*
Eaton, Richard Gillette 1929- *WhoE 91, WhoWor 91*
Eaton, Robert Charles 1946- *WhoWrEP 89*
Eaton, Robert Edward Lee 1909- *WhoWor 91*
Eaton, Robert J. *BioIn 16*
Eaton, Robert James 1940- *St&PR 91, WhoWor 91*
Eaton, Roy 1930- *DrBlPA 90*
Eaton, Roy F. 1930- *WhoE 91*
Eaton, Sandra Shaw 1946- *WhoAmW 91, WhoEmL 91*
Eaton, Theodore A. 1950- *St&PR 91*
Eaton, Theophilus 1590-1658 *EncCRAm*
Eaton, Thomas B. 1930- *St&PR 91*
Eaton, Thomas Clark 1952- *WhoWor 91*
Eaton, Thomas Newton *WhoAmA 91*
Eaton, Tom 1940- *WhoAmA 91*
Eaton, W. Thompson 1938- *St&PR 91*
Eaton, Willard Lee 1848- *AmLegL*
Eaton, William Charles 1927- *St&PR 91, WhoAm 90*
Eaton, William Lawrence 1946- *WhoEmL 91*
Eaton, William Lee 1947- *WhoEmL 91*
Eaton, William Mellon 1924- *WhoAm 90*
Eaton, William Wallace 1816-1898 *AmLegL*
Eaton, Wyatt 1849-1896 *DcCanB 12*
Eatwell, John Leonard 1945- *WhoAm 90*
Eaves, Allen Charles Edward 1941- *WhoAm 90*
Eaves, Anthony Corston 1928- *St&PR 91*
Eaves, Debra Johanna 1958- *WhoE 91*
Eaves, Elsie 1898-1983 *BioIn 16*
Eaves, George Newton 1935- *WhoAm 90*
Eaves, Jackson 1925- *St&PR 91*
Eaves, Morris Emery 1944- *WhoAm 90*
Eaves, Patricia Ann 1959- *St&PR 91*
Eaves, Reuben Elco 1944- *WhoE 91*
Eaves, Ronald Weldon 1937- *WhoAm 90*
Ebacher, Roger 1936- *WhoAm 90*
Ebalo, Carmen M *BiDrAPA 89*
Eban, Abba 1915- *BioIn 16, WhoWor 91*
Ebarb, William Lawrence 1950- *WhoEmL 91*
Ebata, Keisuke 1940- *BiDrAPA 89*
Ebaugh, Albert L 1937- *BiDrAPA 89*

Ebaugh, Frank Wright 1901- *WhoSSW 91, WhoWor 91*
Ebaugh, Franklin Gessford, Jr. 1921- *WhoAm 90*
Ebaugh, Helen Rose 1942- *WhoAm 90*
Ebaugh, Irvin Atwood, Jr. 1935- *BiDrAPA 89*
Ebb, Fred 1932- *OxCPMus*
Ebb, Lawrence Forrest 1918- *WhoE 91*
Ebb, Nina Zdenka 1923- *WhoE 91, WhoWor 91*
Ebben, James A. *WhoAm 90*
Ebben, Joyce Marie 1952- *WhoAmW 91*
Ebbers, Larry Harold 1941- *WhoAm 90*
Ebbers, Laura Kay 1954- *WhoEmL 91*
Ebbert, Arthur, Jr. 1922- *WhoAm 90*
Ebbert, Donald C. 1921- *St&PR 91*
Ebbert, Martin B., Jr. 1939- *St&PR 91*
Ebbert, Nancy E 1950- *BiDrAPA 89*
Ebbert, Robert 1910- *St&PR 91*
Ebbesen, Peter 1936- *WhoWor 91*
Ebbets, Charlie 1859-1925 *Ballpl 90*
Ebbing, Darrell Delmar 1933- *WhoAm 90*
Ebbitt, Kenneth Cooper 1908- *WhoAm 90*
Ebbitt, Kenneth Cooper, Jr. 1941- *WhoE 91*
Ebbott, Ralph Denison 1927- *WhoAm 90*
Ebbs, George Heberling, Jr. 1942- *WhoE 91*
Ebbs, Joyce *BiDEWW*
Ebeid, Russell Joseph 1940- *St&PR 91, WhoAm 90, WhoWor 91*
Ebel, Charles William 1951- *WhoWrEP 89*
Ebel, David M. 1940- *WhoAm 90*
Ebel, Gudrun 1948- *IntWWM 90*
Ebel, Marvin Emerson 1930- *WhoAm 90*
Ebel, Richard G. 1932- *ODwPR 91*
Ebel, Suzanne *ConAu 31NR*
Ebel, Wilfred Louis 1930- *WhoAm 90*
Ebeling, Charles 1943- *ODwPR 91*
Ebeling, John Altman 1937- *WhoAm 90*
Ebeling, Klaus 1930- *WhoE 91*
Ebell, Cecil Walter 1947- *WhoEmL 91*
Ebeltoft, Gary L. 1949- *St&PR 91*
Eben, Lois Ellen 1922- *WhoWrEP 89*
Eben, Petr 1929- *IntWWM 90*
Ebendorf, Robert *BioIn 16*
Ebener, Brian Scott 1961- *WhoEmL 91*
Ebener, Charlotte *BioIn 16*
Ebenhoeh, Patrick E 1936- *BiDrAPA 89*
Ebenstein, Judith 1948- *BiDrAPA 89*
Eber, Bruce Frank 1959- *WhoE 91*
Eber, Dorothy *BioIn 16*
Eber, Herbert Wolfgang 1928- *WhoSSW 91*
Eberdt, Mary Gertrude 1932- *WhoWrEP 89*
Eberhard, Franz Valentin 1947- *WhoWor 91*
Eberhard, John Paul 1927- *WhoAm 90*
Eberhardt, Charles Christopher 1871-1965 *BioIn 16*
Eberhardt, Cornelius 1932- *IntWWM 90*
Eberhardt, H. Alfred 1924- *St&PR 91*
Eberhardt, Isabelle 1877-1904 *BioIn 16, EncCoWW*
Eberhardt, James Joseph 1942- *WhoE 91*
Eberhardt, Jerrold Lee 1941- *St&PR 91*
Eberhardt, Mark 1954- *BioIn 16*
Eberhart, Guy F. *ODwPR 91*
Eberhart, Mary Ann Petesie 1940- *WhoAm 90, WhoSSW 91*
Eberhart, Mignon 1899- *FemiCLE, WorAlBi*
Eberhart, Mignon G 1899- *TwCCr&M 91*
Eberhart, Richard 1904- *MajTwCW, WhoAm 90, WhoWor 91, WhoWrEP 89, WorAlBi*
Eberhart, Robert Clyde 1937- *WhoAm 90*
Eberhart, Steve A. 1931- *WhoAm 90*
Eberhart, Steven Wesley 1952- *WhoEmL 91, WhoWor 91*
Eberius, Klaus Otto 1940- *WhoAm 90*
Eberl, Edward G. 1951- *St&PR 91*
Eberl, Julianne 1950- *IntWWM 90*
Eberle, Abastenia 1878-1942 *BiDWomA*
Eberle, Anne Rinehart 1932- *WhoAmW 91*
Eberle, August William 1916- *WhoAm 90, WhoWor 91*
Eberle, Charles Edward 1928- *WhoAm 90*
Eberle, Edward Samuel 1944- *WhoAmA 91*
Eberle, Irmengarde 1898-1979 *AuBYP 90*
Eberle, Kathy Mae 1966- *WhoAmW 91*
Eberle, Merab *WhoAmA 91N*
Eberle, Peter H. 1942- *St&PR 91*
Eberle, Richard Michael 1942- *WhoWor 91*
Eberle, Robert Frank 1946- *St&PR 91*
Eberle, Robert William 1931- *WhoAm 90*
Eberle, Todd Bailey 1946- *WhoSSW 91*
Eberle, William Denman 1923- *WhoAm 90, WhoE 91*
Eberlein, Gerald L. 1930- *WhoWor 91*
Eberlein, Johann Friedrich 1693?-1749 *PenDiDA 89*
Eberlein, Patricia James 1925- *WhoAm 90*
Eberlein, Shirley Ann 1932- *WhoAmW 91*
Eberley, Helen-Kay 1947- *WhoAm 90, WhoAmW 91, WhoEmL 91*
Eberling, Edward Robert, Jr. 1967- *WhoEmL 91*
Eberly, Harry Landis 1924- *WhoAm 90*
Eberly, Joseph Henry 1935- *WhoAm 90*
Eberly, Robert Edward 1918- *St&PR 91, WhoAm 90*
Eberly, Vickie 1956- *WhoAmA 91*
Eberman, Edwin 1905-1988 *WhoAmA 91N*
Ebers, Clara 1902- *IntWWM 90*
Ebersberger, Arthur Darryl 1946- *WhoE 91*
Ebersol, Dick *BioIn 16*
Ebersole, A V, Jr. 1919- *ConAu 31NR*
Ebersole, Christine *BioIn 16*
Ebersole, George D. 1936- *St&PR 91*
Ebersole, J. Glenn, Jr. 1947- *WhoE 91, WhoWor 91*
Ebersole, Mark Chester 1921- *WhoAm 90*
Ebersole, Mary Ellen Frances 1940- *WhoAmW 91*
Ebersole, Patricia Sue 1952- *WhoAmW 91, WhoEmL 91*
Eberson, Drew *BioIn 16*
Eberspacher, E. C. 1949- *WhoEmL 91*
Eberspacher, Nelson Ernest 1925- *WhoWrEP 89*
Eberstadt, Ferdinand 1890-1969 *BioIn 16*
Eberstadt, Frederick *AuBYP 90*
Eberstadt, Frederick 1926- *WhoE 91*
Eberstadt, Isabel 1934?- *AuBYP 90*
Eberstadt, Nicholas Nash 1955- *WhoE 91*
Eberstadt, Rudolph, Jr. 1923- *St&PR 91*
Eberstein, Arthur 1928- *WhoAm 90*
Ebert, Alfred H., Jr. 1929- *WhoAm 90*
Ebert, Barry Austin 1945- *St&PR 91*
Ebert, Bruce J. 1934- *St&PR 91*
Ebert, Carol Anne 1945- *St&PR 91*
Ebert, Carroll Erich 1924- *St&PR 91*
Ebert, Charles H. V. 1924- *WhoAm 90*
Ebert, Darlene Marie 1951- *WhoEmL 91*
Ebert, Douglas Edmund 1945- *St&PR 91*
Ebert, G. Donald 1932- *St&PR 91*
Ebert, Henry 1929- *St&PR 91*
Ebert, James David 1921- *WhoAm 90, WhoE 91, WhoWor 91*
Ebert, James Ian 1948- *WhoEmL 91*
Ebert, James Joel 1940- *St&PR 91*
Ebert, Jennifer Ann 1966- *WhoAmW 91*
Ebert, Larry P. *BioIn 16*
Ebert, Larry Paul 1952- *WhoEmL 91*
Ebert, Michael Hobart *BiDrAPA 89*
Ebert, Norma J. 1931- *WhoAmW 91*
Ebert, Paul Allen 1932- *WhoAm 90*
Ebert, Peter 1918- *IntWWM 90*
Ebert, Peter DeC. 1942- *St&PR 91*
Ebert, Richard Vincent 1912- *WhoAm 90*
Ebert, Robert Alvin 1915- *WhoAm 90*
Ebert, Robert Higgins 1914- *WhoAm 90*
Ebert, Roger Joseph 1942- *WhoAm 90, WhoWrEP 89*
Ebert, Velina Gail Hammond 1954- *WhoSSW 91*
Ebert, Ward Lyman 1944- *WhoE 91*
Eberth, Friedrich 1928- *WhoWor 91*
Eberts, Brian Wesley 1960- *BiDrAPA 89*
Eberts, Michael Albert 1955- *WhoWrEP 89*
Ebetino, Frank Hallock 1956- *WhoEmL 91*
Ebie, William D. 1942- *WhoAm 90*
Ebie, William Dennis 1942- *WhoAmA 91*
Ebigbo, Peter Onyekwere 1947- *WhoWor 91*
Ebin, Eva Veronica 1926- *BiDrAPA 89*
Ebin, Robert Felix 1940- *WhoAm 90*
Ebina, Yousuke 1947- *WhoWor 91*
Ebitz, Elizabeth Kelly 1950- *WhoAmW 91*
Eblan, Corinne Joy 1959- *WhoE 91*
Eble, Martin J. *St&PR 91*
Eble, Susan Louise 1961- *WhoAmW 91*
Eble, Timothy Eugene 1952- *WhoEmL 91*
Eblen, George Thomas 1936- *WhoAm 90*
Ebling, Timothy Andrew 1958- *WhoAm 90*
Ebner, Alan M. 1939- *St&PR 91*
Ebner, Heinrich Florian 1947- *WhoWor 91*
Ebner, Jeannie 1918- *EncCoWW*
Ebner, Kurt Ewald 1931- *WhoAm 90*
Ebner, Margarethe 1291-1351 *EncCoWW*
Ebner, Paul Jeffrey 1957- *St&PR 91*
Ebneshahrashoob, Morteza 1950- *WhoSSW 91*
Ebnet, Paul John 1955- *WhoEmL 91*
Ebon, Martin 1917- *EncO&P 3, EncPaPR 91*
Eboue, Felix Adolphe Sylvestre 1884-1944 *BiDFrPL*
Ebrahim, Giul M *BiDrAPA 89*
Ebrahim, Omar 1956- *IntWWM 90*
Ebrahimi, Fereshteh 1951- *WhoAmW 91*
Ebrahimzadeh, Shideh Delrahim 1962- *WhoEmL 91*
Ebright, George W. 1939- *St&PR 91*
Ebright, George Watson 1938- *WhoAm 90, WhoE 91*
Ebright, Mitchell A. 1943- *St&PR 91*
Ebrom, Ralph P. 1943- *St&PR 91*
Ebsen, Alf K 1908- *WhoAmA 91*
Ebsen, Buddy 1908- *WorAlBi*
Ebstein, Gemma Fontanella 1961- *WhoE 91*
Ebuskun *WomWR*
Eby, B Russell 1951- *BiDrAPA 89*
Eby, Cecil DeGrotte 1927- *WhoAm 90, WhoWrEP 89*
Eby, Charles Sidney 1936- *WhoSSW 91*
Eby, Frank Shilling 1924- *WhoAm 90*
Eby, John Robert 1935- *St&PR 91*
Eby, Lois Christine 1908- *AuBYP 90*
Eby, Martin K., Jr. 1934- *St&PR 91*
Eby, Martin Keller, Jr. 1934- *WhoAm 90*
Eccard, Walter Thomas 1946- *WhoAm 90*
Eccles, Viscountess 1912- *WhoAm 90*
Eccles, Charlotte O'Conor *FemiCLE*
Eccles, George S. 1900-1982 *EncABHB 7 [port]*
Eccles, John Carew 1903- *WhoAm 90, WhoWor 91, WorAlBi*
Eccles, John Edward 1932- *St&PR 91*
Eccles, Margot Lacy 1935- *St&PR 91*
Eccles, Marriner S. 1890-1977 *EncABHB 7 [port], WorAlBi*
Eccles, Spencer Fox *BioIn 16*
Eccles, Spencer Fox 1934- *St&PR 91, WhoAm 90*
Eccles, Thomas Allen *BiDrAPA 89*
Eccleston, Joan 1945- *BiDrAPA 89*
Eccleston, John J. *ODwPR 91*
Eccleston, John James 1926- *WhoE 91*
Eccleston, Thomas Robert 1948- *St&PR 91*
Ecclestone, Giles 1936-1990 *ConAu 132*
Ecclestone, Priscilla 1627-1694 *BiDEWW*
Ecevit, Bulent 1925- *BioIn 16, PolLCME, WhoWor 91*
Ecford, Brenda Swan 1952- *WhoSSW 91*
Echandi Jimenez, Mario 1915- *BioIn 16*
Echandia Olaya, Dario 1897-1989 *BioIn 16*
Echauren, Federico Errazuriz 1850-1901 *BioIn 16*
Echaurren, Roberto Matta 1911- *ArtLatA*
Echegaray, Jose 1832-1916 *ConAu 32NR, HispWr 90, MajTwCW*
Echegaray y Eizaguirre, Jose 1832-1916 *ConAu 32NR, HispWr 90, MajTwCW, WorAlBi*
Echegoyen, Luis Dernelio 1938- *WhoHisp 91*
Echement, John R. 1935- *St&PR 91, WhoAm 90*
Echenique, Miguel 1923- *WhoHisp 91*
Echevarria, Alvarado Ana H. *WhoSSW 91*
Echevarria, Angel M. *WhoHisp 91*
Echevarria, Efrain Franco, Jr. 1949- *WhoHisp 91*
Echevarria, Felicita de Rodriguez 1931- *WhoSSW 91*
Echevarria, Juan-Carlos *BiDrAPA 89*
Echevarria, Marta G *BiDrAPA 89*
Echevarria, Rocky *ConTFT 8*
Echevarria, Victor 1943- *WhoAm 90*
Echeverri, Eeva Irmeli 1958- *BiDrAPA 89*
Echeverri, Juan Bautista 1945- *WhoSSW 91*
Echeverri-Carroll, Elsie Lucia 1959- *WhoHisp 91*
Echeverria, Esteban 1805-1851 *BioIn 16*
Echeverria Alvarez, Luis 1922- *BioIn 16, WorAlBi*
Echikson, Richard 1929- *WhoE 91*
Echlin, Bernard Joseph 1918- *WhoAm 90*
Echlin, Elizabeth 1704?-1783? *FemiCLE*
Echo *MajTwCW*
Echo and the Bunnymen *EncPR&S 89*
Echo-Hawk, Walter *BioIn 16*
Echohawk, Brummett 1922- *WhoAmA 91*
Echohawk, John Ernest 1945- *WhoEmL 91*
Echols, Ann Thomas *BiDrAPA 89*
Echols, Dorothy Jung 1916- *WhoAmW 91*
Echols, Harrison 1933- *WhoAm 90*
Echols, Ivor Tatum 1919- *WhoAmW 91, WhoWor 91*
Echols, James Franklin 1932- *WhoSSW 91*
Echols, James Richard, Sr. 1935- *WhoSSW 91*
Echols, M. Eileen 1951- *WhoAmW 91*
Echols, Margaret J. 1938- *St&PR 91*
Echols, Mary Evelyn 1915- *WhoAm 90*
Echols, Paul Clinton 1944- *IntWWM 90*
Echols, Robert Wootten, Jr. 1928- *St&PR 91*
Echols, Thomas Matthew 1925- *St&PR 91*
Echsner, Stephen Herre 1954- *WhoEmL 91*
Echtenkamp, Mike G. 1934- *St&PR 91*
Ecin, Maria *EncCoWW*
Eck, Andrea Louise 1962- *WhoAmW 91*
Eck, Charles Paul 1956- *WhoEmL 91*
Eck, David John 1953- *WhoE 91*
Eck, Dorothy Fritz 1924- *WhoAmW 91*
Eck, Franklin Edward 1923- *St&PR 91*
Eck, James John 1946- *St&PR 91*
Eck, Joseph E. 1939- *St&PR 91*
Eck, Kenneth Christopher 1960- *WhoE 91*
Eck, Mary Kay *ODwPR 91*
Eck, Richard Allan 1945- *St&PR 91*
Eck, Ronald Warren 1949- *WhoSSW 91*
Eckam, Robert C. 1926- *St&PR 91*
Eckard, Ralph Edgar 1927- *WhoSSW 91*
Eckard, Ronald David 1944- *WhoSSW 91*
Eckard, Winfred W. 1924- *St&PR 91*
Eckard-Gaudino, Lorraine Michelle 1961- *WhoEmL 91*
Eckardt, A Roy 1918- *ConAu 31NR*
Eckardt, Arthur Roy 1918- *WhoAm 90*
Eckardt, Carl R. 1931- *WhoAm 90*
Eckardt, Charles Lincoln 1930- *WhoE 91*
Eckardt, Gladys Evangeline 1912- *WhoAmW 91*
Eckardt, Marianne H 1913- *BiDrAPA 89*
Eckardt, Richard William 1938- *WhoAm 90*
Eckart, Carl Henry 1902-1973 *DcScB S2*
Eckart, Christian 1959- *WhoAmA 91*
Eckart, Dennis Edward 1950- *WhoAm 90*
Eckart, Emile P, Jr. 1920- *BiDrAPA 89*
Eckart, Gabriele 1954- *EncCoWW*
Eckartshausen, Karl von 1752-1803 *EncO&P 3*
Eckaus, Richard Samuel 1926- *WhoAm 90, WhoE 91*
Eckaus, Theodore M. 1922- *St&PR 91*
Eckbert, William Fox, Jr. 1940- *BiDrAPA 89*
Eckbo, Garrett 1910- *WhoAm 90*
Eckdahl, Donald Edward 1924- *WhoAm 90*
Ecke, Betty Tseng Yu-Ho *WhoAmA 91*
Ecke, Gustav *WhoAmA 91N*
Ecke, Wolfgang 1927-1983 *AuBYP 90*
Eckebrecht, Betty Marie 1958- *WhoEmL 91*
Eckehart, Meister 1260-1327 *WrPh P*
Eckel, Edwin Butt 1906- *WhoAm 90*
Eckel, Eugene Joseph 1924- *St&PR 91*
Eckel, James A. 1943- *St&PR 91*
Eckel, Michael John 1961- *WhoEmL 91*
Eckelberry, Don Richard 1921- *WhoAmA 91*
Eckelberry, John Evans 1933- *St&PR 91*
Eckelberry, Richard Keith *BiDrAPA 89*
Eckelman, Paul John 1950- *WhoEmL 91*
Eckelman, Richard Joel, Sr. 1951- *WhoEmL 91*
Eckelmann, Frank Donald 1929- *WhoAm 90*
Eckels, Paul Glenn 1931- *WhoSSW 91*
Eckels, Thomas Paul 1962- *WhoSSW 91*
Eckelson, Robert Alan 1947- *WhoSSW 91*
Eckenfelder, William Wesley, Jr. 1926- *WhoAm 90, WhoSSW 91*
Eckenhoff, Edward Alvin 1943- *WhoWor 91*
Eckenhoff, James Benjamin 1943- *WhoAm 90*
Eckenhoff, James Edward 1915- *WhoAm 90*
Eckenrode, J. Thaddeus 1958- *WhoEmL 91*
Eckenrode, Robert J. 1931- *WhoAm 90*
Ecker, Allan B. 1921- *St&PR 91*
Ecker, Allan Benjamin 1921- *WhoAm 90*
Ecker, Arthur David *BiDrAPA 89*
Ecker, Arthur David 1913- *WhoE 91*
Ecker, Carol Adele 1940- *WhoAm 90*
Ecker, Charles R. 1948- *ODwPR 91*
Ecker, Charlesanna Daily 1955- *WhoE 91*
Ecker, G. T. Dunlop 1940- *WhoAm 90*
Ecker, H. Allen 1935- *WhoAm 90*
Ecker, Howard J. 1953- *St&PR 91*
Ecker, John Frederick *BioIn 16*
Ecker, Jonathan 1946- *BiDrAPA 89, WhoE 91*
Ecker, Michael Wade 1950- *WhoWrEP 89*
Ecker, Paul G 1919- *BiDrAPA 89*
Ecker, Paul Gerard 1919- *WhoE 91*
Ecker, Susan Marie 1945- *St&PR 91*
Ecker, Vivian Lea *BiDrAPA 89*
Eckerd, Frank Raymond 1945- *St&PR 91*
Eckerd, William M 1947- *BiDrAPA 89*
Eckerle, David Edward 1943- *St&PR 91*
Eckerling, Stanley *St&PR 91*
Eckerman, Dale H., Jr. 1940- *St&PR 91*
Eckerman, Jerome 1925- *WhoAm 90*
Eckermann, Gerald Carlton 1934- *WhoWor 91*
Eckersley, Dennis 1954- *Ballpl 90, BioIn 16*
Eckersley, Norman C. 1924- *St&PR 91*
Eckersley, Richard Laurence 1948- *WhoE 91*
Eckersley, Thomas Cyril 1941- *WhoAmA 91, WhoE 91*
Eckersley, Tom 1914- *ConDes 90*
Eckerson, Nancy Fiedler 1940- *WhoAmW 91*
Eckert, Alfred Carl, III 1948- *WhoAm 90*
Eckert, Allan W. 1931- *AuBYP 90, WhoAm 90*
Eckert, Arlene Gail 1956- *WhoAmW 91, WhoEmL 91, WhoSSW 91*
Eckert, Brenda Lynne 1961- *WhoAmW 91*

Eckert, Carter H. 1942- *St&PR 91*
Eckert, Charles Alan 1938- *WhoAm 90*
Eckert, Elke D *BiDrAPA 89*
Eckert, Ernst R. G. 1904- *WhoAm 90*
Eckert, Geraldine Gonzales 1948- *WhoAmW 91*
Eckert, Helen Ann 1940- *WhoAmW 91*
Eckert, Jacquelyn Maria 1952- *WhoAmW 91*
Eckert, Jean Patricia 1935- *WhoAmW 91*
Eckert, Lisa Loretta 1961- *WhoAmW 91*
Eckert, Lou 1928- *WhoAmA 91*
Eckert, Marlene MacNeal 1952- *WhoEmL 91*
Eckert, Michael 1949- *WhoWor 91*
Eckert, Michael 1950- *IntWWM 90*
Eckert, Michael Joseph 1947- *WhoSSW 91*
Eckert, Opal Effie 1905- *WhoAmW 91*
Eckert, R Christa 1935- *BiDrAPA 89*
Eckert, Ralph John 1929- *WhoAm 90*
Eckert, Reagan Al 1950- *St&PR 91*
Eckert, Roger Earl 1926- *WhoAm 90*
Eckert, Stephen Paul 1955- *WhoEmL 91*
Eckert William 1909-1971 *Ballpl 90*
Eckert, William Dean 1927- *WhoAmA 91*
Eckert, William Terry 1948- *WhoEmL 91*
Eckert, Yates P. 1929- *St&PR 91*
Eckert-Burton, Suzanne Mary 1960- *WhoAmW 91*
Eckerty, R. David 1946- *St&PR 91*
Eckes, Alfred Edward, Jr. 1942- *WhoAm 90*
Eckhard, Johannes 1260?-1327? *WorAlBi*
Eckhardt, Andreas 1943- *IntWWM 90*
Eckhardt, August Gottlieb 1917- *WhoAm 90*
Eckhardt, Bruce N. 1949- *WhoEmL 91*
Eckhardt, Caroline Davis 1942- *WhoAm 90*
Eckhardt, Craig Jon 1940- *WhoAm 90*
Eckhardt, Donald D. 1929- *St&PR 91*
Eckhardt, Ferdinand *WhoAmA 91*
Eckhardt, Juliane 1946- *WhoWor 91*
Eckhardt, Lloyd Ostrum *BiDrAPA 89*
Eckhardt, Maria 1943- *IntWWM 90*
Eckhardt, Ox 1901-1951 *Ballpl 90*
Eckhardt, Richard Dale 1918- *WhoAm 90*
Eckhardt, Sandor, Jr. 1927- *WhoWor 91*
Eckhardt, William E. 1933- *St&PR 91, WhoAm 90*
Eckhart, James Mc Kinley 1931- *St&PR 91, WhoAm 90*
Eckhart, Janis Gail 1952- *IntWWM 90*
Eckhart, Myron, Jr. 1923- *WhoAm 90*
Eckhart, Walter 1938- *WhoAm 90*
Eckhaus, Eleanor Annette 1956- *WhoAmW 91*
Eckhaus, Jay Elliot 1944- *WhoE 91, WhoWor 91*
Eckhert, Kenneth Harry, Jr. 1940- *WhoE 91*
Eckhoff, Carl D. 1933- *WhoE 91*
Eckhoff, Rosalee 1930- *WhoAmW 91*
Eckhoff, Tias *PenDiDA 89*
Eckhoff, Tias 1926- *ConDes 90*
Eckhold, Scott Reed 1953- *WhoEmL 91*
Eckholm, William Arthur 1951- *St&PR 91*
Eckl, William Wray 1936- *WhoWor 91*
Eckland, Diane Marie 1958- *WhoAmW 91*
Eckland, Jeff Howard 1957- *WhoEmL 91*
Ecklar, George Patrick 1951- *WhoEmL 91*
Eckle, Julie Kay 1962- *WhoEmL 91*
Eckler, John Alfred 1913- *WhoAm 90*
Eckler, Norman S. *St&PR 91*
Eckles, William F. 1933- *St&PR 91*
Eckley, Alicia Kathryn 1959- *WhoAmW 91, WhoEmL 91*
Eckley, Gerald Boice 1926- *St&PR 91*
Eckley, Robert Earl 1932- *WhoAm 90*
Eckley, Robert Spence 1921- *WhoAm 90*
Eckley, Wilton Earl, Jr. 1929- *WhoAm 90*
Ecklin, M Irenita 1908- *WhoAmA 91*
Ecklin, Robert L. 1938- *St&PR 91*
Ecklin, Robert Luther 1938- *WhoE 91, WhoWor 91*
Ecklund, Harry Vincent 1908- *WhoWrEP 89*
Ecklund, LeRoy Alfred 1930- *BiDrAPA 89*
Ecklund, N. Russell *St&PR 91*
Eckman, Carl Earl, Jr. 1928- *St&PR 91*
Eckman, David Walter 1942- *WhoAm 90*
Eckman, Fern Marja *WhoAm 90*
Eckman, John W. 1919- *St&PR 91*
Eckman, John Whiley 1919- *WhoAm 90, WhoWor 91*
Eckmann, Harold A. 1922- *St&PR 91*
Eckmann, Jeffrey A. 1952- *St&PR 91*
Eckmann, Otto 1865-1902 *PenDiDA 89*
Eckrich, Kurt B. 1939- *St&PR 91*
Ecks, John A 1935- *BiDrAPA 89*
Eckstein, Arthur 1923- *WhoE 91*
Eckstein, Jerome 1925- *WhoAm 90*
Eckstein, John William 1923- *WhoAm 90*
Eckstein, Marlene R. 1948- *WhoAmW 91*
Eckstein, Michael Lehman 1954- *WhoEmL 91*
Eckstein, Pavel 1911- *IntWWM 90*
Eckstein, Richard W 1911- *BiDrAPA 89*
Eckstein, Ruth 1916- *WhoAmA 91*
Eckstein, Steven Douglas 1946- *WhoEmL 91*
Eckstine, Billy *BioIn 16*
Eckstine, Billy 1914- *DrBlPA 90, OxCPMus, WhoAm 90*
Eckstrom, Daniel W. 1947- *WhoHisp 91*
Eckstrom, Marian Gerlich 1955- *ODwPR 91*
Eckstut, Michael Kauder 1952- *St&PR 91, WhoEmL 91*
Eco, Umberto *BioIn 16*
Eco, Umberto 1932- *ConAu 33NR, ConLC 60 [port], MajTwCW, WhoWor 91*
Economaki, Chris Constantine 1920- *WhoAm 90*
Economakis, Olga *AuBYP 90*
Econome, Kathryn Christine *BiDrAPA 89*
Economides, Nicholas George 1949- *WhoSSW 91*
Economides, Peter Achilles 1953- *WhoWor 91*
Economos, George Louis 1932- *St&PR 91*
Economos, Michael E 1936- *WhoAmA 91*
Economou, George 1934- *WhoWrEP 89*
Economou, George Aristotle 1923- *St&PR 91*
Economou, Richard E. 1947- *WhoE 91*
Economou, Steve George 1922- *WhoAm 90*
Economou-Pease, Bessie Carasoulas 1933- *WhoE 91*
Economy, James 1929- *WhoAm 90*
Ecroyd, Lawrence Gerald 1918- *WhoAm 90*
Ecton, Donna R. 1947- *WhoAm 90, WhoAmW 91*
Ed *EncCoWW*
Ed, Carl 1890-1959 *WhoAmA 91N*
Eda-Pierre, Christiane 1932- *IntWWM 90, PenDiMP*
Edamura, Sumio 1932- *WhoWor 91*
Edan, Mark 1950- *WhoEmL 91*
Eda'nsa 1810?-1894 *DcCanB 12*
Edberg, Rolf Filip 1912- *WhoWor 91*
Edberg, Stefan *BioIn 16*
Edde, Howard Jasper 1937- *WhoAm 90*
Eddinger, Gerald W. 1930- *St&PR 91*
Eddings, Claire Neff *AuBYP 90*
Eddings, Michael Charles 1945- *WhoEmL 91*
Eddington, Edward C. 1944- *St&PR 91*
Eddington, Susan J. *BioIn 16*
Eddington, Thomas L. 1960- *WhoE 91*
Eddins, James William, Jr. 1944- *WhoSSW 91*
Eddins-Folensbee, Florence Favre 1957- *BiDrAPA 89*
Eddis, Jerry 1941- *St&PR 91*
Eddison, Elizabeth Bole 1928- *WhoAmW 91, WhoE 91*
Eddison, John Corbin 1919- *WhoAm 90*
Eddleman, Douglas Dwayne 1956- *WhoSSW 91*
Eddleman, Floyd Eugene 1930- *WhoSSW 91*
Eddleman, G. David 1936- *IntWWM 90*
Eddleman, Henry Clay, III 1947- *BiDrAPA 89*
Eddleman, J. Dalton *WhoWrEP 89*
Eddleman, William Roseman 1913- *WhoAm 90, WhoWor 91*
Eddleston, Frank Warren 1923- *St&PR 91*
Eddowes, Elizabeth Anne 1931- *WhoAmW 91, WhoSSW 91*
Eddy Brothers *EncO&P 3*
Eddy, Charles Alan 1948- *WhoEmL 91, WhoWor 91*
Eddy, Charles Phillips 1941- *WhoAm 90*
Eddy, Charles Russell, Jr. 1940- *St&PR 91*
Eddy, Colette Ann 1950- *WhoAmW 91, WhoWor 91*
Eddy, Daniel Clarke 1823-1896 *AmLegL*
Eddy, Darlene Mathis 1937- *WhoAm 90, WhoAmW 91*
Eddy, David Latimer 1936- *St&PR 91, WhoAm 90*
Eddy, Don 1944- *WhoAm 90, WhoAmA 91, WhoE 91*
Eddy, Donald Davis 1929- *WhoAm 90*
Eddy, Donna Elizabeth 1955- *WhoEmL 91*
Eddy, Duane 1938- *EncPR&S 89, OxCPMus, WorAlBi*
Eddy, Edward Blaine 1928- *WhoSSW 91*
Eddy, Edward Danforth 1921- *WhoAm 90, WhoE 91*
Eddy, Elsbeth Marie 1934- *WhoE 91*
Eddy, Esther Dewitz 1926- *WhoAmW 91*
Eddy, Harrison P 1921- *BiDrAPA 89*
Eddy, Helen Jerome *BioIn 16, NewYTBS 90*
Eddy, Horatio *EncO&P 3*
Eddy, Horatio Henderson 1855?- *AmLegL*
Eddy, John Joseph 1933- *WhoAm 90*
Eddy, John S. 1933- *St&PR 91*
Eddy, Joseph Clifford 1961- *WhoEmL 91*
Eddy, Latimar B. 1937- *St&PR 91*
Eddy, Linda Joan 1949- *WhoAmW 91*
Eddy, Margaret *BioIn 16*
Eddy, Margaret Ruth *NewYTBS 90*
Eddy, Mary Baker 1821-1910 *BioAmW, BioIn 16, EncPaPR 91, FemiCLE, WorAlBi*
Eddy, Mary Morse 1821-1910 *EncO&P 3*
Eddy, Nelson 1901-1967 *OxCPMus, PenDiMP, WorAlBi*
Eddy, Roger C 1934- *BiDrAPA 89*
Eddy, Roger Graham 1940- *WhoWor 91*
Eddy, Thomas Alexander 1930- *St&PR 91*
Eddy, William *EncO&P 3*
Eddy, William Crawford 1902-1989 *BioIn 16*
Eddy, William David *BioIn 16*
Eddy, William Lindsay 1933- *St&PR 91*
Ede, H S 1895-1990 *ConAu 131*
Ede, Jim *ConAu 131*
Ede, Joyce Kinlaw 1936- *WhoAmW 91*
Ede, Terence W. 1938- *St&PR 91*
Edebo, Ralph Bertil 1932- *WhoWor 91*
Edel, Abraham 1908- *WhoAm 90*
Edel, Doris Rita 1936- *WhoWor 91*
Edel, Edwin E. 1932- *ODwPR 91, WhoAm 90*
Edel, Joseph Leon 1907- *BioIn 16*
Edel, Leon 1907- *BioIn 16, DcLB 103 [port], WhoAm 90, WhoWrEP 89*
Edel, Marjorie *ConAu 132*
Edelcup, Norman S. 1935- *St&PR 91*
Edelcup, Norman Scott 1935- *WhoAm 90*
Edelen, Mary Beaty 1944- *WhoAmW 91*
Edelhart, Michael 1951- *ConAu 129*
Edelhart, Mike *ConAu 129*
Edelhauser, Hans 1947- *WhoWor 91*
Edelheit, Martha *WhoAmA 91*
Edelin, Ramona Hoage *WhoAmW 91*
Edell, Dunnan D. 1955- *St&PR 91*
Edell, Joseph E. 1927- *St&PR 91*
Edell, Nancy 1942- *WhoAmA 91*
Edell, William Steven 1953- *WhoE 91*
Edelman, Alan Irwin 1958- *WhoE 91, WhoEmL 91, WhoWor 91*
Edelman, Allan 1933- *St&PR 91*
Edelman, Alvin 1916- *WhoAm 90*
Edelman, Andrew 1947- *St&PR 91*
Edelman, Ann *WhoAmA 91*
Edelman, Arthur Jay 1925- *WhoAm 90*
Edelman, Asher B. *BioIn 16*
Edelman, Asher Barry 1939- *WhoAm 90, WhoSSW 91*
Edelman, Cornelis Hendrik 1903-1964 *DcScB S2*
Edelman, Daniel Amos 1954- *WhoEmL 91*
Edelman, Daniel J. *BioIn 16*
Edelman, Daniel J. 1920- *ODwPR 91, St&PR 91*
Edelman, Daniel Joseph 1920- *WhoAm 90*
Edelman, Elaine *BioIn 16, WhoWrEP 89*
Edelman, Gerald M. 1929- *WorAlBi*
Edelman, Gerald Maurice 1929- *WhoAm 90, WhoE 91, WhoWor 91*
Edelman, Harold 1923- *WhoAm 90*
Edelman, Harry R., III 1928- *St&PR 91*
Edelman, Harry Rollings, III 1928- *WhoAm 90*
Edelman, Hendrik 1937- *WhoAm 90*
Edelman, Henry D. 1948- *BioIn 16*
Edelman, Irving *St&PR 91*
Edelman, Isidore Samuel 1920- *WhoAm 90*
Edelman, Joel 1931- *WhoAm 90*
Edelman, John *ODwPR 91*
Edelman, John Andrew 1928- *St&PR 91*
Edelman, Judith Hochberg 1923- *WhoAm 90, WhoAmW 91*
Edelman, Jules *St&PR 91*
Edelman, Kenneth Alan *BiDrAPA 89*
Edelman, Lily 1915-1981 *AuBYP 90*
Edelman, Lony Maria 1930- *WhoAmW 91*
Edelman, Marek 1921- *BioIn 16*
Edelman, Marian Wright *BioIn 16*
Edelman, Marian Wright 1939- *News 90 [port], WhoAm 90, WhoAmW 91*
Edelman, Mark Leslie 1943- *WhoAm 90, WhoWor 91*
Edelman, Martin Philip 1940- *WhoE 91*
Edelman, Maurice 1911-1975 *SpyFic*
Edelman, Max 1906-1989 *BioIn 16*
Edelman, Michelle Robyn 1964- *WhoAmW 91*
Edelman, Milton M *BiDrAPA 89*
Edelman, Murray Jacob 1919- *WhoAm 90*
Edelman, Murray R. 1939- *WhoAm 90*
Edelman, Murray Richard 1939- *St&PR 91*
Edelman, Norman H. 1937- *WhoAm 90*
Edelman, Paul Sterling 1926- *WhoAm 90, WhoWor 91*
Edelman, Peter Benjamin 1938- *WhoAm 90*
Edelman, Peter Raymond 1933- *BiDrAPA 89*
Edelman, Raymond E 1931- *BiDrAPA 89*
Edelman, Reed Stephen 1957- *WhoEmL 91*
Edelman, Richard J 1924- *BiDrAPA 89*
Edelman, Richard Winston 1954- *WhoAm 90*
Edelman, Rita 1930- *WhoAmA 91*
Edelman, Samuel Irving 1929- *WhoAm 90*
Edelman, Stuart Edward 1947- *BiDrAPA 89, WhoE 91*
Edelman, Susan Laurie *BiDrAPA 89*
Edelman, Terri Diane 1956- *WhoE 91*
Edelman, Thomas Jeffery 1951- *St&PR 91*
Edelmann, Chester Monroe, Jr. 1930- *WhoAm 90*
Edelmann, Heinz 1934- *BioIn 16, ConDes 90*
Edelmann, Otto Karl 1917- *IntWWM 90*
Edelmann, Sergei 1960- *IntWWM 90*
Edelmuth, Evelyn R. 1958- *BiDrAPA 89*
Edelsberg, Herman *BioIn 16*
Edelschick, Daniel Frederick 1944- *St&PR 91*
Edelsohn, Gail Ann *BiDrAPA 89*
Edelson, Alan Martin 1937- *WhoAm 90*
Edelson, Allan J. 1942- *St&PR 91*
Edelson, Burton Irving 1926- *WhoAm 90*
Edelson, Debra Erin 1963- *BiDrAPA 89*
Edelson, Edward 1932- *AuBYP 90, BioIn 16, WhoAm 90*
Edelson, Gilbert S 1928- *WhoAmA 91*
Edelson, Gilbert Seymour 1928- *WhoAm 90*
Edelson, Hana *BiDrAPA 89*
Edelson, Ira J. 1946- *WhoAm 90*
Edelson, Marshall 1928- *BiDrAPA 89, WhoAm 90*
Edelson, Mary Beth *WhoAmA 91, WhoAmW 91, WhoE 91*
Edelson, Mary Beth 1945?- *BiDWomA*
Edelson, Morris 1937- *WhoWrEP 89*
Edelson, Stanley 1931- *St&PR 91*
Edelson, Stuart R 1933- *BiDrAPA 89*
Edelson, Zelda Sarah Toll 1929- *WhoAmW 91*
Edelstein, Alvin 1936- *WhoE 91*
Edelstein, Barbara F *BiDrAPA 89*
Edelstein, Bernard Michael *BiDrAPA 89*
Edelstein, Bernard W. 1945- *St&PR 91*
Edelstein, Carole Kwass *BiDrAPA 89*
Edelstein, Chaim Y. 1942- *WhoAm 90*
Edelstein, David Northon 1910- *WhoAm 90*
Edelstein, David R 1947- *BiDrAPA 89*
Edelstein, Haskell 1933- *WhoAm 90*
Edelstein, J M 1924- *WhoAmA 91*
Edelstein, Jack P 1931- *BiDrAPA 89*
Edelstein, Jacob 1903-1944 *BioIn 16*
Edelstein, Jerome Melvin 1924- *WhoAm 90*
Edelstein, Joel K *BiDrAPA 89*
Edelstein, Joel Kenneth 1945- *WhoE 91*
Edelstein, Larry Bruce *BiDrAPA 89*
Edelstein, Lewis M. 1934- *St&PR 91*
Edelstein, Mark David *BiDrAPA 89*
Edelstein, Michael V *BiDrAPA 89*
Edelstein, Mortimer 1904-1990 *BioIn 16*
Edelstein, Phillip *BiDrAPA 89*
Edelstein, Phyllis *BiDrAPA 89*
Edelstein, Raymond Lewis 1954- *WhoEmL 91*
Edelstein, Richard David 1952- *BiDrAPA 89*
Edelstein, Rose Marie 1935- *WhoAmW 91*
Edelstein, Ruben 1918- *St&PR 91*
Edelstein, Scott Samuel 1954- *WhoWrEP 89*
Edelstein, Teri J 1951- *WhoAmA 91*
Edelstein, Tilden G. 1931- *WhoAm 90*
Edelstein, Victor *BioIn 16*
Edelstien, Maurice G 1928- *BiDrAPA 89*
Edelstone, Gordon 1927- *St&PR 91*
Eden and Tamir *PenDiMP*
Eden, Alvin N. *BioIn 16*
Eden, Anthony 1897-1977 *BioIn 16, WorAlBi*
Eden, Barbara *BioIn 16*
Eden, Barbara 1934- *WorAlBi*
Eden, Barbara Janiece 1951- *WhoEmL 91*
Eden, Bracha 1928- *PenDiMP*
Eden, Bronson B 1949- *WhoAmA 91*
Eden, David *BiDrAPA 89*
Eden, Diane Burn *BioIn 16*
Eden, Diane Holly 1958- *BiDrAPA 89*
Eden, Emily 1797-1869 *BioIn 16, FemiCLE*
Eden, F Brown 1916- *WhoAmA 91*
Eden, Florence Brown 1916- *WhoSSW 91*
Eden, Glenda Lee 1959- *WhoWrEP 89*
Eden, Glenn 1951- *WhoAmA 91*
Eden, James Gary 1950- *WhoAm 90*
Eden, James Joseph 1951- *WhoE 91*
Eden, Jerome 1925- *EncO&P 3*
Eden, Kate *WhoWrEP 89*
Eden, Lee Smythe 1937- *WhoAm 90*
Eden, Murray 1920- *WhoAm 90*
Eden, Nathan E. 1944- *WhoSSW 91, WhoWor 91*
Eden, Raymond Ler 1925- *WhoAm 90*
Eden, Richard Carl 1939- *WhoAm 90*
Eden, Robert 1741-1784 *EncCRAm*
Eden, Ronald William 1931- *St&PR 91*

Eden-Fetzer, Dianne Toni 1946- *WhoAmW 91*
Edenfield, Berry Avant 1934- *WhoAm 90, WhoSSW 91*
Edenfield, James C. *St&PR 91*
Edenfield, MaryAnn 1945- *WhoSSW 91*
Edens, Clarence J 1935- *BiDrAPA 89*
Edens, Cooper 1945- *BioIn 16*
Edens, Donald Keith 1928- *WhoAm 90*
Edens, Gary Denton 1942- *St&PR 91, WhoAm 90*
Edens, P. Clifton 1930- *St&PR 91*
Edens, Samuel Vinson 1930- *St&PR 91*
Edensa 1810?-1894 *DcCanB 12*
Edensaw 1810?-1894 *DcCanB 12*
Edensaw 1839-1924 *WhNaAH*
Edenshaw 1810?-1894 *DcCanB 12*
Edenshaw, Charles 1839-1924 *WhNaAH*
Eder, George Jackson 1900- *WhoAm 90*
Eder, Helmut 1916- *IntWWM 90*
Eder, Howard Abram 1917- *WhoAm 90*
Eder, James A. 1945- *St&PR 91*
Eder, James Alvin 1942- *WhoAmA 91*
Eder, Klaus 1946- *WhoWor 91*
Eder, Richard 1932- *ConAu 130*
Eder, Richard Gray 1932- *WhoAm 90*
Eder, Stephen K. 1952- *St&PR 91*
Eder, Susan Louise *BiDrAPA 89*
Ederer, Fred 1926- *WhoE 91*
Ederer-Schwartz, Jane 1939- *WhoAmW 91*
Ederle, Douglas Richard 1962- *WhoE 91*
Ederle, Gertrude 1906- *WorAlBi*
Ederma, Arvo Bruno 1928- *WhoSSW 91*
Edersheim, Maurits E. 1918- *St&PR 91*
Edersheim, Maurits Ernst 1918- *WhoAm 90*
Edes, Benjamin 1732-1803 *BioIn 16*
Edes, Nik Bruce 1943- *WhoAm 90, WhoSSW 91*
Edey, Dianne N. 1943- *St&PR 91*
Edey, Johanne Lynne 1956- *WhoEmL 91*
Edey, Maitland Armstrong 1910- *WhoAm 90*
Edfelt, Bo Johannes 1904- *DcScanL*
Edfors, Hugh Terrance 1946- *WhoEmL 91*
Edgar, Allan G. 1934- *St&PR 91*
Edgar, Allan George, Jr. 1934- *WhoSSW 91*
Edgar, David 1948- *MajTwCW*
Edgar, Gordon Russell 1948- *St&PR 91*
Edgar, Irving I *BiDrAPA 89*
Edgar, James David 1841-1899 *DcCanB 12*
Edgar, James Macmillan, Jr. 1936- *WhoAm 90*
Edgar, James Roy 1945- *BiDrAPA 89*
Edgar, Janelle Diane Ward 1955- *WhoEmL 91*
Edgar, Jim 1946- *WhoAm 90*
Edgar, John Douglas, Jr. 1962- *BiDrAPA 89*
Edgar, John E. 1940- *ODwPR 91*
Edgar, Kimberly Sue 1964- *WhoAmW 91*
Edgar, Robert Allan 1940- *WhoAm 90*
Edgar, Robert Benson 1951- *WhoAmA 91*
Edgar, Ruth R. 1930- *WhoAmW 91*
Edgar, Thomas Flynn 1945- *WhoAm 90*
Edgar, Walter Bellingrath 1943- *WhoAm 90*
Edgar, William 1944- *IntWWM 90*
Edgar, William John 1933- *WhoAm 90*
Edgcumbe, Ursula 1900-1984 *BiDWomA*
Edge 1961- *BioIn 16*
Edge, Alice *BiDEWW*
Edge, Charles Geoffrey 1920- *WhoAm 90*
Edge, David Owen 1932- *WhoWor 91*
Edge, Donald Joseph 1955- *WhoEmL 91*
Edge, Douglas Benjamin 1942- *WhoAmA 91*
Edge, Findley Bartow 1916- *WhoAm 90*
Edge, Harold Lee 1933- *WhoAm 90*
Edge, Hoyt L. 1944- *EncPaPR 91*
Edge, Irene Elizabeth 1961- *WhoAmW 91*
Edge, James Lafayette, III 1934- *WhoE 91*
Edge, Jodie Lee 1926- *BiDrAPA 89*
Edge, Lawrence Lott 1945- *St&PR 91*
Edge, Murray Claybourn 1936- *WhoSSW 91*
Edge, Norris Lagrand 1931- *St&PR 91*
Edge, Robert Laneer 1925- *WhoAm 90*
Edge, Ronald Dovaston 1929- *WhoAm 90*
Edge, Walter Evans 1873-1956 *BioIn 16*
Edge-Maldonado, Lillian 1952- *WhoE 91*
Edgecomb, William S 1924- *BiDrAPA 89*
Edgecombe, Nydia R. 1951- *WhoHisp 91*
Edgell, Annias Waitman, III 1950- *WhoSSW 91*
Edgell, Peter G 1918- *BiDrAPA 89*
Edgell, Robert Louis 1922- *WhoAm 90*
Edgell, Zoe *FemiCLE*
Edger, R.J. 1946- *St&PR 91*
Edger, Robert Reynolds 1950- *BiDrAPA 89*
Edgerly, Len 1950- *St&PR 91*
Edgerly, William S. 1927- *St&PR 91*
Edgerly, William Skelton 1927- *WhoAm 90*
Edgerton, A. Freeman 1919- *WhoSSW 91*
Edgerton, Brenda Evans 1949- *WhoAmW 91*
Edgerton, Charles N. 1944- *St&PR 91*
Edgerton, Clyde 1944- *BioIn 16*
Edgerton, David Allison 1940- *St&PR 91*
Edgerton, David George 1950- *WhoEmL 91*
Edgerton, Harold E 1903-1990 *ConAu 130, CurBio 90N, NewYTBS 90 [port]*
Edgerton, Harold Eugene 1903-1990 *BioIn 16*
Edgerton, J. Howard 1908- *St&PR 91*
Edgerton, James Robert 1925- *St&PR 91*
Edgerton, Lynne Todd 1947- *WhoAmW 91*
Edgerton, Mills Fox, Jr. 1931- *WhoAm 90*
Edgerton, Milton Thomas, Jr. 1921- *WhoAm 90*
Edgerton, Richard 1911- *WhoSSW 91, WhoWor 91*
Edgerton, Robert B. 1953- *WhoEmL 91*
Edgerton, Stephenie Grover 1931- *WhoAmW 91*
Edgerton, William B. 1914- *WhoAm 90*
Edgerton, Winfield Dow 1924- *WhoAm 90*
Edgett, Steven Dennis 1948- *WhoEmL 91*
Edgett, William Maloy 1926- *WhoAm 90*
Edgeworth, Alan C. 1945- *St&PR 91*
Edgeworth, Francis Ysidro 1845-1926 *BioIn 16*
Edgeworth, Maria 1767-1849 *BioIn 16*
Edgeworth, Maria 1768-1849 *FemiCLE*
Edgeworth, Robert Joseph 1947- *WhoSSW 91*
Edgin, Edward Clark 1939- *WhoSSW 91*
Edginton, John Arthur 1935- *WhoAm 90*
Edginton, May 1883-1957 *FemiCLE*
Edgreen, Robert J. 1946- *WhoE 91*
Edgren, Anne Charlotte *DcScanL, EncCoWW*
Edgren, E.G. 1934- *St&PR 91*
Edgren, Gary Robert 1947- *WhoAmA 91*
Edgren, Gretchen Grondahl 1931- *WhoAmW 91*
Edgren, Jorn Christer 1946- *WhoWor 91*
Edgy, Wardore *ConAu 30NR*
Edhie, Sarwo *BioIn 16*
Edholm, Rand Alan 1955- *WhoEmL 91*
Edick, Glenn Ellis 1918- *WhoAm 90*
Edidin, Michael Aaron 1939- *WhoAm 90*
Edidin, Ruth Glicenstein 1936- *WhoE 91*
Ediger, Lewis W. 1931- *St&PR 91*
Ediger, Nicholas Martin 1928- *St&PR 91, WhoAm 90*
Ediger, Robert Ike 1937- *WhoAm 90*
Edinberg, Joyce Felsen 1928- *WhoAmW 91*
Edinburgh, Philip, Duke of 1921- *BioIn 16*
Edinga, Kent Johnson 1950- *St&PR 91*
Edinger, Charles B. 1934- *WhoE 91*
Edinger, Edward F *BiDrAPA 89*
Edinger, Fred 1936- *St&PR 91, WhoE 91*
Edinger, J. Raymond 1914- *St&PR 91*
Edinger, Johanna Gabrielle Ottilie 1897-1967 *DcScB S2*
Edinger, Lewis Joachim 1922- *WhoAm 90*
Edinger, Lois Virginia 1925- *WhoAm 90*
Edington, Ernest McElroy, Jr. 1938- *WhoSSW 91*
Edington, Robert Lyle 1957- *WhoEmL 91*
Edington, Robert Van 1935- *WhoAm 90*
Edisen, Clayton B 1927- *BiDrAPA 89*
Edison, Allen Ray 1926- *WhoAm 90*
Edison, Bernard Alan 1928- *St&PR 91, WhoAm 90*
Edison, Charles 1890-1969 *BiDrUSE 89*
Edison, Donna Lucile 1945- *BiDrAPA 89*
Edison, George S. *St&PR 91*
Edison, Hali Jean 1953- *WhoAmW 91, WhoEmL 91*
Edison, Harry 1915- *BioIn 16, OxCPMus*
Edison, Irving *St&PR 91N*
Edison, Irving 1899-1989 *BioIn 16*
Edison, Julian I. 1929- *WhoAm 90*
Edison, Neil Harvey 1943- *BiDrAPA 89*
Edison, Peter Cornelius 1944- *WhoSSW 91*
Edison, Robert G. 1928- *St&PR 91*
Edison, Sweets 1915- *BioIn 16*
Edison, Thomas A. 1847-1931 *BioIn 16*
Edison, Thomas Alva 1847-1931 *EncPaPR 91, WorAlBi*
Edkins, Michael 1734-1811 *PenDiDA 89*
Edler, Anne 1918-1976 *FemiCLE*
Edler, Brett Arthur 1952- *IntWWM 90*
Edler, Robert Weber 1936- *WhoAm 90*
Edler, Tim 1948- *BioIn 16*
Edley, Christopher F., Jr. *BioIn 16*
Edlich, Richard French 1939- *WhoAm 90*
Edlich, Stephen 1944-1989 *BioIn 16*
Edlin, Rita Melamed 1929- *WhoAmW 91*
Edllin, Mari L. 1952- *ODwPR 91*
Edloe, Leonard Levi 1947- *WhoEmL 91, WhoSSW 91*
Edlosi, Mario *WhoWrEP 89*
Edlow, Esther 1925- *WhoAmW 91*
Edlow, Robert Blair 1946- *St&PR 91*
Edlund, Matthew J 1954- *BiDrAPA 89*
Edlund, Matthew Jonathan 1954- *WhoE 91*
Edlund, Mikael 1950- *IntWWM 90*
Edlund, Milton Carl 1924- *WhoAm 90*
Edly, Alan John 1935- *St&PR 91, WhoAm 90*
Edman, Janet Lee 1956- *WhoEmL 91*
Edman, John Richard 1927- *St&PR 91, WhoAm 90*
Edmands, Susan Banks 1944- *WhoAmW 91*
Edmark, David Stanley 1951- *WhoSSW 91*
Edminister, Edward Joseph, Jr. 1935- *WhoAm 90*
Edmisten, Jack *BiDrAPA 89*
Edmisten, Jane Moretz 1938- *WhoAmW 91*
Edmisten, Patricia Taylor 1939- *ConAu 132*
Edmisten, Rufus Ligh 1941- *WhoAm 90*
Edmister, Ivan F *BiDrAPA 89*
Edmister, Richard Riley 1939- *St&PR 91, WhoAm 90*
Edmiston, David Crockett, Jr. 1930- *St&PR 91*
Edmiston, Henry Duncan 1937- *St&PR 91*
Edmiston, James R. 1912- *St&PR 91*
Edmiston, Marilyn 1934- *WhoAmW 91*
Edmiston, Mark *BioIn 16*
Edmiston, Mark Morton 1943- *WhoAm 90, WhoE 91*
Edmiston, Norma 1956- *WhoAmW 91, WhoEmL 91*
Edmiston, Robert Gray 1954- *WhoEmL 91*
Edmiston, Ronald Lee 1946- *WhoSSW 91*
Edmiston, Sara Joanne 1935- *WhoAmA 91*
Edmiston, Theresa F. 1950- *WhoAmW 91*
Edmond, Lauris 1924- *WorAu 1980 [port]*
Edmond, Rayful, III *BioIn 16*
Edmonds, Anne Carey 1924- *WhoAm 90, WhoAmW 91*
Edmonds, Charles *ConAu 132*
Edmonds, David A. 1938- *St&PR 91*
Edmonds, David Carson 1937- *WhoWrEP 89*
Edmonds, David G. 1934- *St&PR 91*
Edmonds, Elizabeth Mayhew *FemiCLE*
Edmonds, Henry Valentine 1837-1897 *DcCanB 12*
Edmonds, I. G. 1917- *AuBYP 90*
Edmonds, I G 1917- *ConAu 30NR*
Edmonds, John 1816-1874 *EncPaPR 91*
Edmonds, John Worth 1799-1874 *EncO&P 3*
Edmonds, Kenny *BioIn 16*
Edmonds, Lawrence Vernon 1949- *WhoE 91*
Edmonds, Michael Darnell 1960- *WhoSSW 91*
Edmonds, Randolph 1900-1983 *EarBlAP*
Edmonds, Richard W. *AuBYP 90*
Edmonds, Robert 1913-1990 *ConAu 132*
Edmonds, S. Emma E. 1841-1898 *BioIn 16*
Edmonds, S Randolph 1900- *DrBlPA 90*
Edmonds, Sarah 1841-1898 *WorAlBi*
Edmonds, Sarah Emma Evelyn 1841-1898 *BioIn 16*
Edmonds, Thomas Andrew 1938- *WhoAm 90*
Edmonds, Walter Dumaux 1903- *AuBYP 90, WhoAm 90*
Edmonds, William Fleming 1923- *St&PR 91, WhoAm 90*
Edmonds, William Joseph 1932- *WhoSSW 91*
Edmondson, Abigail 1697?- *BiDEWW*
Edmondson, Charles Milton 1942- *WhoSSW 91*
Edmondson, David V. 1927- *St&PR 91*
Edmondson, Frank K. 1912- *WhoAm 90*
Edmondson, Harold Elbert 1930- *St&PR 91*
Edmondson, J. Richard 1927- *St&PR 91*
Edmondson, Jack Bernhard 1927- *St&PR 91*
Edmondson, James Larry 1947- *WhoAm 90*
Edmondson, James William 1930- *St&PR 91, WhoAm 90*
Edmondson, Jane P. 1946- *WhoAmW 91*
Edmondson, John Baldwin 1933- *IntWWM 90*
Edmondson, John Richard 1927- *WhoAm 90*
Edmondson, Keith Henry 1924- *WhoAm 90*
Edmondson, Leonard 1916- *WhoAmA 91*
Edmondson, Madeleine *AuBYP 90*
Edmondson, Mary 1647?-1732 *BiDEWW*
Edmondson, W. Thomas 1916- *BioIn 16*
Edmondson, Wallace *MajTwCW*
Edmondson, Wallace Thomas 1916- *WhoAm 90*
Edmondson, William 1870?-1951 *MusmAFA*
Edmondson, William Brockway 1927- *WhoAm 90*
Edmonson, Alan Lee 1935- *BiDrAPA 89*
Edmonson, Dan Hutcheson 1916- *WhoAm 90*
Edmonson, Lowell Russell, Jr. 1936- *St&PR 91*
Edmonson, Munro Sterling 1924- *WhoAm 90*
Edmonson, Randall W 1947- *WhoAmA 91*
Edmonson, Susan Marie 1958- *WhoEmL 91*
Edmonson, Thomas L., Jr. 1934- *WhoSSW 91*
Edmonston, Paul 1922- *WhoAmA 91*
Edmonston, William Edward, Jr. 1931- *WhoAm 90*
Edmund, Robert M. 1948- *St&PR 91*
Edmunds, Allan Logan 1949- *WhoAmA 91*
Edmunds, Dave 1944?- *EncPR&S 89*
Edmunds, George Franklin 1828-1919 *AmLegL*
Edmunds, Jack B., Jr. 1934- *St&PR 91*
Edmunds, Jane Clara 1922- *WhoAm 90*
Edmunds, Jeffrey Garth 1953- *WhoEmL 91*
Edmunds, John C. *St&PR 91*
Edmunds, Joseph Edsel 1935- *WhoAm 90*
Edmunds, Juana I *BiDrAPA 89*
Edmunds, Lowell 1938- *WhoAm 90*
Edmunds, Simeon 1917- *EncO&P 3*
Edmundson, Ann 1646?-1726 *BiDEWW*
Edmundson, Lida Lacy *BiDrAPA 89*
Edney, Palma Carter 1906- *WhoSSW 91*
Edney, Ruth Ann 1944- *WhoAmW 91*
Edney, William Milton 1925- *St&PR 91*
Ednie, Eileen Rose 1951- *WhoAmW 91*
Ednie, Kathryn Jean *BiDrAPA 89*
Ednie, Thomas Frew 1931- *BiDrAPA 89*
Edouard, Julio *BiDrAPA 89*
Edouard, Pierre 1959- *WhoAmA 91*
Edpuganti, Surya T *BiDrAPA 89*
Edris, C. Lawrence 1942- *St&PR 91*
Edris, Charles Lawrence 1942- *WhoAm 90*
Edris, Dwight Pierce 1946- *St&PR 91*
Edris, Paul Milburn 1909- *WhoAm 90*
Edrozo, Rosalyn Sue 1959- *WhoAmW 91*
Edsall, Howard Linn 1904- *WhoE 91, WhoWor 91*
Edsall, John Tileston 1902- *WhoAm 90*
Edsall, Marian 1920- *AuBYP 90*
Edsall, Thomas Byrne 1941- *WhoAm 90, WhoE 91*
Edschmid, Kasimir 1890-1966 *BioIn 16*
Edson, Andrew S. 1946- *ODwPR 91*
Edson, Bruce James 1958- *BiDrAPA 89*
Edson, David M. 1949- *St&PR 91*
Edson, Edward Marshall 1947- *WhoSSW 91*
Edson, Eugene Hirsh 1924- *St&PR 91*
Edson, Gary F 1937- *WhoAmA 91*
Edson, Herbert Robbins 1931- *WhoWor 91*
Edson, J T 1928- *ConAu 30NR*
Edson, John Thomas 1928- *BioIn 16*
Edson, Kay L. 1946- *St&PR 91*
Edson, Kent E. 1942- *St&PR 91*
Edson, Marian Louise 1940- *WhoAmW 91*
Edson, Martha Janet 1933- *St&PR 91*
Edson, Mary Christine 1959- *WhoEmL 91*
Edson, Nat 1909- *EncACom*
Edson, Ralph A. 1929- *St&PR 91*
Edson, Virginia Elizabeth 1936- *WhoAmW 91*
Edson, William Alden 1912- *WhoAm 90*
Edson, William Arthur 1951- *WhoEmL 91*
Edstrom, Eric Wayne 1950- *St&PR 91*
Edstrom, John Olof 1926- *WhoWor 91*
Edstrom, Lars Axel Simon 1935- *WhoWor 91*
Edvi Illes, Emma *WhoAmA 91*
Edvinsson, Johan Henrik Leif 1946- *WhoWor 91*
Edwalds, Robert M 1925- *BiDrAPA 89*
Edward VIII 1894-1972 *WorAlBi*
Edward Albert, Prince of Wales 1894-1972 *BioIn 16*
Edward, Duke of Windsor 1894-1972 *BioIn 16*
Edward I, King of England 1239-1307 *BioIn 16*
Edward III, King of England 1312-1377 *BioIn 16*
Edward VI, King of England 1537-1553 *BioIn 16*
Edward VII, King of Great Britain 1841-1910 *BioIn 16*
Edward VIII, King of Great Britain 1894-1972 *BioIn 16*
Edward, Prince of Great Britain 1964- *BioIn 16*
Edward, David Alexander Ogilvy 1934- *WhoWor 91*
Edward, David Andrew 1962- *WhoSSW 91*
Edward, H. F. V. 1898-1973 *EarBlAP*
Edward, John Thomas 1919- *WhoAm 90*
Edward, Nickolas W. 1928- *St&PR 91*
Edwardes, Annie 1830?-1896 *FemiCLE*
Edwardes, George 1855-1915 *OxCPMus*
Edwards, Alberta Roon 1926- *WhoAmW 91*

Edwards, Alfred Cecil *BiDrAPA 89*
Edwards, Alva Eugene 1928- *WhoWor 91*
Edwards, Amelia 1831-1892 *FemiCLE*
Edwards, Amelia Ann Blanford 1831-1892 *BioIn 16*
Edwards, Amy Williams 1930- *WhoAmW 91*
Edwards, Anne 1927- *ConAu 33NR*
Edwards, Annie 1830?-1896 *FemiCLE*
Edwards, Armstead *BioIn 16*
Edwards, Arthur Anderson 1926- *WhoAm 90*
Edwards, Arthur C. 1909- *IntWWM 90*
Edwards, Audrey 1947- *BioIn 16*
Edwards, Austin Burton 1909-1960 *DcScB S2*
Edwards, Ben *BioIn 16*
Edwards, Benjamin Franklin, III 1931- *St&PR 91, WhoAm 90*
Edwards, Benjamin Joseph 1838-1914 *BioIn 16*
Edwards, Bert Tvedt 1937- *WhoAm 90*
Edwards, Beryl Margaret 1932- *WhoAmW 91*
Edwards, Betty *BioIn 16, WhoAmW 91*
Edwards, Blake 1922- *BioIn 16, ConAu 32NR, WorAlBi*
Edwards, Bob 1947- *WhoAm 90*
Edwards, Bruce 1923-1975 *Ballpl 90*
Edwards, Bruce Kenneth 1960- *WhoE 91*
Edwards, Bruce Lynn 1948- *WhoEmL 91*
Edwards, Bryon Taggart 1937- *WhoAm 90*
Edwards, C. Webb 1947- *St&PR 91*
Edwards, Calvin Wayne 1954- *WhoSSW 91*
Edwards, Carl Bernard 1936- *WhoSSW 91*
Edwards, Carl E. 1941- *St&PR 91*
Edwards, Carl Normand 1943- *WhoE 91*
Edwards, Carole A. 1954- *WhoAmW 91*
Edwards, Cecile Pepin 1916- *AuBYP 90*
Edwards, Charlene Whitney 1948- *WhoEmL 91*
Edwards, Charles 1925- *WhoAm 90, WhoSSW 91*
Edwards, Charles Berkley 1942- *WhoSSW 91*
Edwards, Charles C. 1947- *St&PR 91*
Edwards, Charles C., Jr. 1947- *WhoAm 90*
Edwards, Charles Cornell 1923- *WhoAm 90*
Edwards, Charles Elvin, Jr. 1953- *WhoEmL 91*
Edwards, Charles Harris Wesley 1951- *WhoSSW 91*
Edwards, Charles L 1939- *BiDrAPA 89*
Edwards, Charles Lloyd 1940- *WhoAm 90*
Edwards, Charlotte Pack 1949- *WhoE 91*
Edwards, Christine Utley 1951- *WhoAmW 91*
Edwards, Claudia Jane 1943- *WhoWrEP 89*
Edwards, Cliff 1895-1972 *OxCPMus*
Edwards, Cliff 1897-1971 *WorAlBi*
Edwards, Clifford Murray 1952- *WhoEmL 91*
Edwards, Connie Lynn 1946- *WhoAmW 91*
Edwards, Consuelo M 1926- *BiDrAPA 89*
Edwards, Cynthia Ann 1954- *WhoAmW 91*
Edwards, Daniel James 1928- *WhoE 91*
Edwards, Daniel Walden 1950- *WhoEmL 91, WhoWor 91*
Edwards, Darrell *WhoE 91*
Edwards, Dave 1954- *Ballpl 90*
Edwards, David Allen 1953- *WhoE 91*
Edwards, David Arbenz, Sr. 1926- *St&PR 91*
Edwards, David Charles 1937- *WhoAm 90*
Edwards, David Kimberley 1942- *WhoE 91*
Edwards, David Northrop 1923- *WhoSSW 91*
Edwards, David Olaf 1932- *WhoAm 90*
Edwards, David Sheridan 1941- *St&PR 91*
Edwards, Dawn Ann 1956- *WhoE 91, WhoEmL 91*
Edwards, Deanne Bahr 1960- *WhoAmW 91*
Edwards, Deborah Joy 1951- *WhoEmL 91*
Edwards, Del Mount 1953- *WhoSSW 91, WhoWor 91*
Edwards, Denise Althea Michelle 1965- *WhoAmW 91*
Edwards, Dianne Carol 1945- *WhoEmL 91*
Edwards, Doc 1937- *Ballpl 90*
Edwards, Don 1915- *WhoAm 90*
Edwards, Donald James 1952- *WhoE 91*
Edwards, Donald Kenneth 1932- *WhoAm 90*
Edwards, Donald Mervin 1938- *WhoAm 90*
Edwards, Donna Reed 1955- *WhoAmW 91*
Edwards, Doris Anne 1937- *BiDrAPA 89*
Edwards, Doris Porter 1962- *WhoEmL 91*
Edwards, Douglas *BioIn 16*
Edwards, Douglas 1917-1990 *ConAu 132, NewYTBS 90 [port]*
Edwards, Douglas Alan 1959- *WhoWor 91*
Edwards, Dwayne Dee 1948- *WhoEmL 91*
Edwards, E. Everett 1937- *St&PR 91*
Edwards, Earnest Jonathan 1938- *St&PR 91*
Edwards, Eddie *BioIn 16*
Edwards, Edgar O. 1919- *WhoE 91*
Edwards, Edward W. 1943- *St&PR 91*
Edwards, Edwin Washington 1927- *WhoAm 90*
Edwards, Eleanor Cecile 1940- *WhoAmW 91*
Edwards, Eleanor Mattiasich 1938- *WhoAmW 91*
Edwards, Eli *MajTwCW*
Edwards, Elizabeth A. 1951- *St&PR 91*
Edwards, Ella Chandler 1934- *WhoSSW 91*
Edwards, Ellender Morgan *WhoAmA 91*
Edwards, Ellis Duncan 1947- *WhoAm 90, WhoSSW 91*
Edwards, Emma Jean 1961- *WhoAmW 91*
Edwards, Emmet 1907- *WhoAmA 91N*
Edwards, Ernest Preston 1919- *WhoAm 90*
Edwards, Esther *WhoAm 90*
Edwards, Ethel *WhoAmA 91*
Edwards, Eva K. 1942- *WhoAmW 91*
Edwards, Frances Sue 1933- *WhoAmW 91*
Edwards, Francis Charles 1947- *WhoE 91*
Edwards, Francis Gordon 1924- *St&PR 91*
Edwards, Frank 1908-1967 *EncO&P 3*
Edwards, Frank J. *BioIn 16*
Edwards, Franklin R. 1937- *WhoAm 90*
Edwards, Geoffrey Hartley 1936- *WhoAm 90, WhoSSW 91*
Edwards, George 1855-1915 *OxCPMus*
Edwards, George 1943- *IntWWM 90*
Edwards, George Alva 1916- *WhoAm 90*
Edwards, George Clifton, Jr. 1914- *WhoAm 90*
Edwards, George Danny 1951- *St&PR 91*
Edwards, George Herbert, III 1935- *WhoE 91*
Edwards, George Kent 1939- *WhoAm 90*
Edwards, George Lee 1937- *St&PR 91*
Edwards, George W. 1939- *St&PR 91*
Edwards, George W., Jr. 1939- *WhoAm 90, WhoE 91*
Edwards, George Wharton 1869-1950 *WhoAmA 91N*
Edwards, Gilbert Franklin 1915- *WhoAm 90*
Edwards, Glen 1935- *BioIn 16*
Edwards, Glenn Allen 1934- *St&PR 91*
Edwards, Glenn Thomas 1931- *WhoAm 90*
Edwards, Gloria *BioIn 16, DrBIPA 90*
Edwards, Gregory J. 1944- *St&PR 91*
Edwards, Gus 1879-1945 *BioIn 16, OxCPMus, WorAlBi*
Edwards, Gus 1939?- *DrBIPA 90*
Edwards, Guy H. 1939- *St&PR 91*
Edwards, H Berryman 1948- *BiDrAPA 89*
Edwards, Haden William 1952- *St&PR 91*
Edwards, Hammond Eugene, Jr. 1932- *WhoSSW 91*
Edwards, Hank 1919-1988 *Ballpl 90*
Edwards, Harold Mills 1930- *WhoAm 90*
Edwards, Harold Mortimer 1936- *WhoAm 90*
Edwards, Harry *BioIn 16*
Edwards, Harry 1893-1976 *EncO&P 3, EncPaPR 91*
Edwards, Harry LaFoy 1936- *WhoSSW 91, WhoWor 91*
Edwards, Harry Leon 1921- *St&PR 91, WhoAm 90*
Edwards, Harry T. 1940- *WhoAm 90*
Edwards, Harvey 1929- *AuBYP 90*
Edwards, Helen Jean 1937- *WhoWrEP 89*
Edwards, Helen Thom 1936- *WhoAm 90, WhoAmW 91*
Edwards, Henry E 1936- *BiDrAPA 89*
Edwards, Henry P. 1873-1948 *Ballpl 90*
Edwards, Henry Percival 1939- *WhoAm 90, WhoWor 91*
Edwards, Hero Joseph 1933- *St&PR 91*
Edwards, Hollis A *BiDrAPA 89*
Edwards, Horace Burton 1925- *St&PR 91, WhoAm 90*
Edwards, Howard Dawson 1923- *WhoAm 90*
Edwards, Howard L. 1931- *St&PR 91*
Edwards, Howard Lee 1931- *WhoAm 90*
Edwards, Howard M., III 1955- *IntWWM 90*
Edwards, Ian Keith 1926- *WhoAm 90, WhoWor 91*
Edwards, Ian Kenneth 1953- *WhoEmL 91*
Edwards, Ida Wierschem 1938- *WhoAmW 91*
Edwards, India *BioIn 16, NewYTBS 90*
Edwards, India 1895?-1990 *CurBio 90N*
Edwards, India 1896?-1990 *ConAu 130*
Edwards, J.M.B. 1935- *WhoWrEP 89*
Edwards, J. Michele 1945- *WhoEmL 91*
Edwards, Jack 1928- *WhoAm 90*
Edwards, Jack A. 1948- *WhoEmL 91*
Edwards, Jack Donald 1933- *WhoSSW 91*
Edwards, James 1916-1970 *DrBIPA 90*
Edwards, James 1927- *BiDrUSE 89*
Edwards, James Burrows 1927- *WhoAm 90, WhoSSW 91*
Edwards, James Christopher 1916- *WhoWrEP 89*
Edwards, James Clifford 1930- *WhoAm 90*
Edwards, James Cook 1923- *WhoAm 90*
Edwards, James Dallas, III 1937- *WhoWor 91*
Edwards, James Earl *BiDrAPA 89*
Edwards, James Edwin 1914- *WhoSSW 91, WhoWor 91*
Edwards, James Eugene *BiDrAPA 89*
Edwards, James F 1948- *WhoAmA 91*
Edwards, James Kennedy 1943- *WhoAm 90*
Edwards, James Lynn 1952- *WhoEmL 91*
Edwards, James Malone 1931- *WhoAm 90*
Edwards, James Owen 1943- *WhoE 91*
Edwards, James Preston 1952- *WhoSSW 91, WhoWor 91*
Edwards, James Richard 1951- *WhoEmL 91*
Edwards, James Scott 1945- *St&PR 91*
Edwards, Jane Elizabeth 1932- *WhoWrEP 89*
Edwards, Jane Katherine 1936- *WhoAmW 91*
Edwards, Jay T. 1931- *St&PR 91*
Edwards, Jay Thomas 1931- *WhoAm 90, WhoSSW 91*
Edwards, Jean Marie Grunklee 1952- *WhoAm 90*
Edwards, Jerome 1912- *WhoAm 90*
Edwards, Jesse Efrem 1911- *WhoAm 90*
Edwards, Jesse G. 1926- *St&PR 91*
Edwards, Jim Joe 1894-1965 *Ballpl 90*
Edwards, Jimmy 1920-1988 *AnObit 1988*
Edwards, Joell Louise *WhoAmW 91*
Edwards, John 1671-1746 *PenDiDA 89*
Edwards, John 1815-1894 *AmLegL*
Edwards, John Charles *WhoWrEP 89*
Edwards, John Charles 1941- *St&PR 91*
Edwards, John Duncan 1953- *WhoEmL 91*
Edwards, John G. *BioIn 16*
Edwards, John H 1944- *BiDrAPA 89*
Edwards, John Hamilton 1922- *WhoAm 90*
Edwards, John Kenneth 1944- *St&PR 91, WhoAm 90*
Edwards, John P. 1942- *St&PR 91*
Edwards, John Ralph 1937- *WhoAm 90*
Edwards, John Ray 1945- *BiDrAPA 89*
Edwards, John T. 1944- *ODwPR 91*
Edwards, John T., Jr. 1925- *St&PR 91*
Edwards, John White *WhoAm 90*
Edwards, John William 1930- *WhoWor 91*
Edwards, John Womer 1958- *WhoEmL 91*
Edwards, Johnny 1938- *Ballpl 90*
Edwards, Jonathan 1703-1758 *EncCRAm [port], WhNaAH, WorAlBi*
Edwards, Jorge *BioIn 16*
Edwards, Joseph *PenDiDA 89*
Edwards, Joseph Castro 1909- *WhoAm 90*
Edwards, Joseph Daniel, Jr. 1924- *WhoAm 90*
Edwards, Joseph Rowland Goodman 1915- *WhoWor 91*
Edwards, Joseph Vincent 1956- *BiDrAPA 89*
Edwards, Josh *ConAu 31NR*
Edwards, Joshua Leroy 1918- *WhoAm 90*
Edwards, Judith Ann 1939- *BiDrAPA 89*
Edwards, Judy 1949- *WhoSSW 91*
Edwards, Julia Brandt 1916- *BiDrAPA 89*
Edwards, Julia Spalding 1920- *WhoAm 90*
Edwards, Julian 1855-1910 *OxCPMus*
Edwards, Julie *BioIn 16*
Edwards, Julie 1935- *AuBYP 90*
Edwards, Julius Howard 1914- *WhoAm 90*
Edwards, Karen Kosiba 1956- *WhoE 91*
Edwards, Kathryn Inez 1947- *WhoAmW 91, WhoEmL 91*
Edwards, Kathryn Louise 1947- *WhoAmW 91*
Edwards, Kelvin *BioIn 16*
Edwards, Kenneth 1917- *WhoAm 90*
Edwards, Kenneth Joseph 1914- *St&PR 91*
Edwards, Kevin Dale 1957- *WhoWrEP 89*
Edwards, L. Ward 1936- *St&PR 91*
Edwards, Larry A. 1935- *WhoAm 90*
Edwards, Larry David 1937- *WhoAm 90*
Edwards, Laura L. *EarBIAP*
Edwards, Laurie Ellen 1951- *WhoAmW 91*
Edwards, Leverett 1902-1989 *BioIn 16*
Edwards, Lillian Brown 1921- *St&PR 91*
Edwards, Lillie Johnson 1952- *WhoEmL 91*
Edwards, Linda *BioIn 16*
Edwards, Linda 1951- *WhoAmA 91*
Edwards, Linda Ann 1944- *WhoWrEP 89*
Edwards, Lonzy Fitzgerald, Sr. 1949- *WhoSSW 91*
Edwards, Louis L. 1936- *BioIn 16*
Edwards, Louis Ward, Jr. 1936- *WhoAm 90*
Edwards, Lydia Justice 1937- *WhoAmW 91*
Edwards, Lynn *WhoWrEP 89*
Edwards, M.E. 1947- *St&PR 91*
Edwards, Macon *ODwPR 91*
Edwards, Mae 1878-1937 *OxCCanT [port]*
Edwards, Marc Scott 1961- *BiDrAPA 89*
Edwards, Margaret A. 1902-1988 *BioIn 16*
Edwards, Marie Babare *WhoAmW 91*
Edwards, Marisette L. *BioIn 16*
Edwards, Marjorie H. 1930- *St&PR 91*
Edwards, Mark 1959- *WhoEmL 91*
Edwards, Mark Allan 1954- *WhoAm 90*
Edwards, Mark Brownlow 1939- *WhoSSW 91*
Edwards, Martin H. 1931- *St&PR 91*
Edwards, Marvin Raymond 1921- *WhoSSW 91*
Edwards, Mary 1635?-1715 *BiDEWW*
Edwards, Mary 1949- *WhoAmW 91*
Edwards, Mary Ellen 1839-1908 *BiDWomA*
Edwards, Mary Janice 1939- *WhoSSW 91*
Edwards, Mary L. 1943- *WhoAmW 91*
Edwards, Matilda Betham- 1836-1919 *BioIn 16*
Edwards, Mauri *ODwPR 91*
Edwards, Michael David 1955- *WhoWor 91*
Edwards, Michael Donn 1949- *WhoSSW 91*
Edwards, Michael Paul 1950- *WhoWor 91*
Edwards, Mickey 1937- *WhoAm 90, WhoSSW 91*
Edwards, Mike 1952- *Ballpl 90*
Edwards, Morgan 1722-1795 *BioIn 16*
Edwards, Nancee Paula 1960- *St&PR 91*
Edwards, Neil Bonham *BiDrAPA 89*
Edwards, Oswald Carnac 1907-1988 *BioIn 16*
Edwards, Otis Carl, Jr. 1928- *WhoAm 90*
Edwards, Owain Tudor 1940- *IntWWM 90*
Edwards, Owen *BioIn 16*
Edwards, P. E. *WhoWrEP 89*
Edwards, Page 1941- *BioIn 16*
Edwards, Page Lawrence, Jr. 1941- *WhoAm 90*
Edwards, Palmer 1952- *BiDrAPA 89*
Edwards, Palmer Lowell 1923- *WhoSSW 91*
Edwards, Pat *AuBYP 90*
Edwards, Patrick Ross 1940- *WhoAm 90*
Edwards, Paul *NewAgMG*
Edwards, Paul Beverly 1915- *WhoSSW 91*
Edwards, Paul Burgess *WhoAmA 91*
Edwards, Paul Burgess 1934- *WhoAmA 91, WhoE 91*
Edwards, Paul Michael 1952- *IntWWM 90*
Edwards, Peter S., Jr. 1921- *St&PR 91*
Edwards, Peter Stuart Allenby 1948- *WhoWor 91*
Edwards, Philip Knox 1943- *WhoE 91*
Edwards, Philip Yonge 1957- *St&PR 91*
Edwards, Phillip Milton 1933- *WhoE 91*
Edwards, Phyllis Ann 1947- *WhoEmL 91*
Edwards, Phyllis Mae 1921- *WhoAmW 91*
Edwards, Presley W. 1904- *St&PR 91, WhoAm 90*
Edwards, R. LaVell 1930- *WhoAm 90*
Edwards, Ralph M. 1933- *WhoAm 90*
Edwards, Randall Hamilton 1961- *WhoSSW 91*
Edwards, Raoul D. 1928-1987 *BioIn 16*
Edwards, Ray Conway 1913- *St&PR 91, WhoE 91, WhoWor 91*
Edwards, Ray Dean 1932- *St&PR 91*
Edwards, Rayburn F. 1940- *St&PR 91*
Edwards, Raymond D. 1918- *WhoAm 90*
Edwards, Redick 1947- *St&PR 91*
Edwards, Renee Camille 1961- *WhoAmW 91*
Edwards, Rheba L *BiDrAPA 89*
Edwards, Richard 1523?-1566 *BioIn 16*
Edwards, Richard Alan 1957- *WhoEmL 91*
Edwards, Richard Ambrose 1922- *WhoAm 90*
Edwards, Richard Charles 1948- *WhoEmL 91*
Edwards, Richard Clark 1944- *WhoAm 90*
Edwards, Richard Lester 1928- *St&PR 91*
Edwards, Richard Thomas 1941- *WhoSSW 91*
Edwards, Rob 1963- *WhoEmL 91*
Edwards, Robert 1879-1948 *WhoAmA 91N*
Edwards, Robert 1925- *ConAu 129*
Edwards, Robert G. 1947- *St&PR 91*
Edwards, Robert H. 1902- *St&PR 91*
Edwards, Robert Hazard 1935- *WhoAm 90*
Edwards, Robert John 1951- *St&PR 91*
Edwards, Robert Nelson 1946- *St&PR 91*
Edwards, Robert Roy 1947- *WhoAm 90*
Edwards, Robert S. 1927- *St&PR 91*
Edwards, Robert Valentino 1940- *WhoAm 90*
Edwards, Roger P. 1933- *St&PR 91*
Edwards, Roger Yorke 1924- *WhoAm 90*
Edwards, Ronald Lee 1952- *WhoEmL 91*
Edwards, Ross 1943- *IntWWM 90*

Edwards, Roy A. Jr. *BiDrAPA 89*
Edwards, Roy Anderson, III 1945- *WhoAm 90*
Edwards, Ruth Ann Wheeler 1945- *WhoEmL 91*
Edwards, Ryan Hayes *WhoAm 90*
Edwards, Samuel 1705-1762 *PenDiDA 89*
Edwards, Samuel 1914-1988 *SmATA X*
Edwards, Samuel Frederick 1928- *WhoWor 91*
Edwards, Sarah 1710-1758 *FemiCLE*
Edwards, Sarah P. 1710-1758 *BioAmW*
Edwards, Sarah Pierpont 1710-1758 *EncCRAm*
Edwards, Scott Samuel, Jr. 1915- *WhoSSW 91*
Edwards, Sebastian 1953- *WhoAm 90*
Edwards, Sharon R. *ODwPR 91*
Edwards, Sian *WhoWor 91*
Edwards, Sian 1950- *IntWWM 90*
Edwards, Sian 1959- *PenDiMP*
Edwards, Stanley Dean 1941- *WhoAmA 91*
Edwards, Stanley Ewart 1921- *St&PR 91*
Edwards, Stephen E. 1944- *St&PR 91*
Edwards, Steve 1930- *WhoAm 90*
Edwards, Steve 1946- *WhoEmL 91*
Edwards, Steven Charles 1957- *IntWWM 90*
Edwards, Susan Arville Reynolds 1944- *WhoAmW 91*
Edwards, Susan Harris 1948- *WhoAmA 91*
Edwards, Susan Roddy Shaw 1954- *WhoSSW 91*
Edwards, Susie Laverne Matthews 1920- *WhoAmW 91*
Edwards, Sylvia Lorene 1946- *WhoEmL 91*
Edwards, Teresa *BioIn 16*
Edwards, Theodore R. 1925- *St&PR 91*
Edwards, Thomas 1701-1755 *PenDiDA 89*
Edwards, Thomas Ashton 1960- *WhoE 91*
Edwards, Thomas Blaine 1947- *WhoEmL 91*
Edwards, Thomas Marvin, III 1953- *WhoEmL 91*
Edwards, Thomas Robert, Jr. 1928- *WhoAm 90*
Edwards, Tommy 1922-1969 *DrBIPA 90*
Edwards, Tracy *BioIn 16*
Edwards, Victor Henry 1940- *WhoSSW 91*
Edwards, Vincent 1928- *WorAlBi*
Edwards, Virginia Davis 1927- *WhoAmW 91*
Edwards, Virginia S 1919- *BiDrAPA 89*
Edwards, W. Cary, Jr. 1944- *WhoAm 90*
Edwards, Wallace Winfield 1922- *WhoAm 90*
Edwards, Walter Meayers 1908- *WhoAm 90*
Edwards, Ward Dennis 1927- *WhoAm 90*
Edwards, Warwick Anthony 1944- *IntWWM 90*
Edwards, Wayne Forrest 1934- *WhoAm 90*
Edwards, Wayne Pennelton 1950- *WhoSSW 91*
Edwards, Wendell Edward 1937- *WhoSSW 91*
Edwards, Wilbur Shields 1916- *WhoAm 90*
Edwards, William *PenDiDA 89*
Edwards, William Brundige, III 1942- *WhoSSW 91*
Edwards, William C., Jr. 1930- *St&PR 91*
Edwards, William Cleveland 1928- *WhoAm 90*
Edwards, William F. *St&PR 91*
Edwards, William Henry 1917- *WhoAm 90*
Edwards, William I., III 1931- *St&PR 91*
Edwards, William J. 1939- *St&PR 91*
Edwards, William James 1915- *WhoAm 90, WhoWor 91*
Edwards, William Kirkpatrick 1812-1878 *AmLegL*
Edwards, William L. 1931- *St&PR 91*
Edwards, William Newton 1929- *St&PR 91*
Edwards, William Rowland, Jr. 1942- *WhoSSW 91*
Edwards, William Seymour 1856-1915 *AmLegL*
Edwards, William Sterling, III 1920- *WhoAm 90*
Edwards, William Thomas, Jr. 1956- *WhoEmL 91*
Edwards-Clarke, Sarah Louise 1961- *WhoE 91*
Edwards Helsel, Diane Marie 1961- *BiDrAPA 89*
Edwards-Thompson, Pauline *BiDrAPA 89*
Edwards-Tucker, Yvonne 1941- *WhoAmA 91*
Edwardson, Donald Walker *BiDrAPA 89*
Edwardson, John Albert, Jr. 1949- *St&PR 91, WhoAm 90*
Edwardson, Phillip Louis 1937- *BiDrAPA 89*
Edwin, John Reed 1930- *WhoAm 90, WhoSSW 91*
Edwynel, Rev. *WhoWrEP 89*
Eedes, Judith *BiDEWW*
Eek, Nathaniel Sisson 1927- *WhoAm 90*
Eekman, Thomas Adam 1923- *WhoAm 90*
Eells, Chris Allen 1955- *WhoSSW 91*
Eells, Richard 1917- *WhoAm 90, WhoWor 91*
Eells, Richard S F 1917- *ConAu 132*
Eells, William Hastings 1924- *WhoAm 90*
Eenhorn, Lambertus van *PenDiDA 89*
Eenhorn, Lambertus van 1651-1721 *PenDiDA 89*
Eenhorn, Samuel van *PenDiDA 89*
Eenhorn, Wouter van *PenDiDA 89*
Eerdmans, Ingrid *BiDrAPA 89*
Eerdmans, Johannes *NewYTBS 90*
Eernisse, Errol Peter 1940- *WhoAm 90*
Eerola, Lasse Olavi 1945- *IntWWM 90*
Eesteren, Cornelis van 1897-1988 *BioIn 16*
Efaw, Cary R. 1949- *WhoE 91*
Eff, Elaine *BioIn 16*
Effenberger, Eugene 1931- *IntWWM 90*
Effenberger, John A. 1934- *St&PR 91*
Efferson, John Norman 1912- *WhoAm 90*
Effimoff, Igor 1946- *St&PR 91*
Effinger, Cecil 1914- *IntWWM 90, WhoAm 90*
Effinger, Cecil 1914-1990 *NewYTBS 90*
Effinger, Harold J. 1952- *WhoEmL 91*
Effinger, Wm. L. 1943- *St&PR 91*
Effingham, Francis Howard 1643-1695 *BioIn 16*
Effrat, Edward Adrian 1925- *St&PR 91*
Effrat, Louis 1910-1988 *BioIn 16*
Effren, Gary Ross 1956- *WhoEmL 91*
Effron, Abraham S 1917- *BiDrAPA 89*
Efird, Hugh M. 1924- *St&PR 91*
Efird, James M 1932- *ConAu 31NR*
Efland, Simpson Lindsay 1913- *WhoSSW 91*
Efner, Howard Franklyn 1944- *WhoSSW 91*
Eforo, John Francis 1930- *WhoAm 90*
Efrat, Isaac 1957- *WhoE 91*
Efremoglou, Minas Demitriou 1925- *WhoWor 91*
Efremov, Georgi Dimitar 1932- *WhoWor 91*
Efron, Arthur 1931- *WhoWrEP 89*
Efron, Jeanette Oshman 1912- *WhoSSW 91*
Efron, Meryl Joy 1957- *WhoAmW 91*
Efron, Samuel 1915- *WhoAm 90, WhoE 91, WhoWor 91*
Efros, Ellen Ann 1950- *WhoEmL 91*
Efros, Norbert 1930- *St&PR 91*
Efroymson, Daniel R. 1941- *St&PR 91*
Efstathianos, Kimon *BiDrAPA 89*
Efthimiades, Michael Constantine 1958- *WhoE 91*
Efting, Gail K. 1948- *WhoWor 91*
Egami, Hisayoshi 1944- *WhoE 91*
Egan *WhNaAH*
Egan, Bruce Anthony 1939- *St&PR 91*
Egan, Catherine Denise 1952- *WhoAmW 91*
Egan, Charles Joseph, Jr. 1932- *WhoAm 90*
Egan, Charles Michael 1936- *WhoAm 90*
Egan, Daniel Francis 1915- *WhoAm 90*
Egan, Dave *BioIn 16*
Egan, Dick 1884-1947 *Ballpl 90*
Egan, Dick 1937- *Ballpl 90*
Egan, Donald John *BiDrAPA 89*
Egan, Dorothy Ann 1934- *WhoAmW 91*
Egan, Edward F. 1919- *St&PR 91*
Egan, Edward M. 1932- *WhoAm 90*
Egan, Eileen Mary *WhoAm 90, WhoAmW 91*
Egan, Ferol 1923- *WhoWrEP 89*
Egan, Frank T. 1933- *WhoAm 90*
Egan, Harold A., Jr. 1926- *St&PR 91*
Egan, James Clayton 1956- *WhoEmL 91*
Egan, James Harold 1938- *BiDrAPA 89*
Egan, James J., Jr. 1939- *St&PR 91*
Egan, James T. 1933- *St&PR 91*
Egan, Jocelyn Ann 1962- *WhoE 91*
Egan, John *BioIn 16*
Egan, John 1846?- *AmLegL*
Egan, John Frederick 1935- *St&PR 91, WhoAm 90, WhoE 91, WhoWor 91*
Egan, John Patrick, II 1944- *WhoE 91*
Egan, John T. 1927- *St&PR 91*
Egan, John Tinnerman 1948- *WhoEmL 91*
Egan, John V. 1934- *St&PR 91*
Egan, John W. 1939- *St&PR 91*
Egan, Joseph Edward 1936- *St&PR 91*
Egan, Joseph Richard 1954- *WhoE 91*
Egan, Kevin James 1950- *WhoEmL 91*
Egan, Laury Agnes 1950- *WhoE 91*
Egan, Leonard Joseph 1945- *St&PR 91*
Egan, Leslie *TwCCr&M 91*
Egan, Merritt H 1918- *BiDrAPA 89*
Egan, Michael Frederick 1958- *BiDrAPA 89*
Egan, Michael Joseph 1926- *WhoAm 90*
Egan, Patricia Geithman 1947- *WhoEmL 91*
Egan, Patrick 1841-1919 *BioIn 16*
Egan, Pierce 1772-1849 *BioIn 16*
Egan, Raymond Davis 1931- *WhoSSW 91*
Egan, Richard Burke 1931- *St&PR 91*
Egan, Richard John 1936- *WhoAm 90*
Egan, Richard Leo 1917- *WhoAm 90*
Egan, Robert Thomas 1952- *WhoEmL 91*
Egan, Roger Edward 1921- *WhoAm 90, WhoWor 91*
Egan, Rory Bernard 1942- *WhoAm 90*
Egan, Shirley Anne *WhoAm 90, WhoAmW 91*
Egan, Sylvia 1930- *WhoAm 90*
Egan, Thomas J. 1944- *St&PR 91*
Egan, Timothy John 1953- *BiDrAPA 89*
Egan, Tom 1946- *Ballpl 90*
Egan, Vincent Joseph 1921- *WhoAm 90*
Egan, William Edward 1944- *WhoE 91*
Egan, William H 1940- *BiDrAPA 89*
Egan, William M. 1929- *St&PR 91*
Egan, William P 1934- *BiDrAPA 89*
Egan, Wish 1881-1951 *Ballpl 90*
Egart, William V. 1939- *St&PR 91*
Egas, Camilo 1897-1962 *WhoAmA 91N*
Egas, Camilo 1899-1962 *ArtLatA*
Egashira, Matasuke 1932- *WhoWor 91*
Egatz, Laura Ann Brugos 1942- *WhoAmW 91*
Egbert, Elizabeth Frances 1945- *WhoAmA 91*
Egbert, Emerson Charles 1924- *WhoAm 90*
Egbert, John Clarence 1938- *St&PR 91*
Egbert, John S. 1955- *WhoSSW 91*
Egbert, Richard Cook 1927- *WhoAm 90*
Egdahl, Richard Harrison 1926- *WhoAm 90, WhoE 91*
Ege, Arvia MacKaye *BioIn 16*
Ege, H. Ray 1937- *St&PR 91*
Ege, Otto F 1888-1951 *WhoAmA 91N*
Egea, Fernando M 1937- *BiDrAPA 89*
Egekvist, W. Soren 1918- *WhoAm 90*
Egel, Martin 1949- *IntWWM 90*
Egeland, Elizabeth Vowell 1936- *WhoAmW 91*
Egeli, Peter Even 1934- *WhoAmA 91*
Egell, Paul 1691-1752 *PenDiDA 89*
Egelman, Edward Herschel 1952- *WhoE 91*
Egelston, Diane Carroll 1955- *WhoEmL 91*
Egelston, Robert Burnley 1930- *St&PR 91*
Egelston, Roberta Riethmiller 1946- *WhoAmW 91*
Egen, Richard Bell 1938- *St&PR 91*
Egendorf, Norma Lucy 1928- *WhoAmW 91*
Egensteiner, Donald Thomas 1932- *WhoAm 90*
Eger, Akiba 1761-1837 *BioIn 16*
Eger, Edmond I., II 1930- *WhoAm 90*
Eger, John B. 1940- *St&PR 91*
Eger, Joseph 1925- *WhoAm 90*
Eger, William H *BiDrAPA 89*
Egeri, Karl von *PenDiDA 89*
Egeria *EncCoWW*
Egermann, Friedrich 1777-1864 *PenDiDA 89*
Egert, Bruce 1955- *WhoEmL 91*
Egerter, Elise Ann *BiDrAPA 89*
Egerton, Arthur 1923- *St&PR 91*
Egerton, Bridget *BiDEWW*
Egerton, Daniel Thomas 1800?-1842 *ArtLatA*
Egerton, Elizabeth *BiDEWW*
Egerton, George 1859-1945 *BioIn 16, FemiCLE*
Egerton, John Walden 1935- *WhoAm 90, WhoWrEP 89*
Egerton, Raymond Frank 1944- *WhoAm 90*
Egerton, Sarah 1670?-1723 *BioIn 16*
Egerton, Sarah Fyge 1669?-1722 *BiDEWW*
Egertson, Darrell Jerlow 1933- *WhoAm 90*
Egg, Augustus Leopold 1816-1863 *BioIn 16*
Eggan, Andrew Michael 1949- *WhoEmL 91*
Eggan, Fred F. 1906- *BioIn 16*
Eggan, Fred Russell 1906- *WhoAm 90*
Eggar, Samantha 1939- *BioIn 16, ConTFT 8, WhoAm 90, WorAlBi*
Eggard, Julius *PenDiMP*
Egged, Molly M. 1950- *St&PR 91*
Eggen, Gilbert Richard *BiDrAPA 89*
Eggen, John Albert, Jr. 1934- *WhoAm 90*
Eggen, Olin Jeuck 1919- *WhoAm 90*
Eggener, Brian Joseph *BiDrAPA 89*
Egger, Albert E. 1911- *St&PR 91*
Egger, Carl Thomas 1937- *St&PR 91*
Egger, George E. 1905- *St&PR 91*
Egger, George Edward 1905- *WhoAm 90*
Egger, Laurence G. 1928- *St&PR 91*
Egger, Michael Lee 1949- *BiDrAPA 89*
Egger, Roscoe L., Jr. 1920- *WhoAm 90*
Egger, Stephen Edwin 1942- *St&PR 91*
Eggerbrecht, Peter *PenDiDA 89*
Eggerding, Herbert F., Jr. 1937- *St&PR 91*
Eggermont, Lodewuk 1938- *WhoWor 91*
Eggers, Alfred J., Jr. 1922- *WhoAm 90, WhoWor 91*
Eggers, Allan E. 1925- *ODwPR 91, St&PR 91*
Eggers, Cecilia Demovich 1942- *WhoAmW 91*
Eggers, David Frank, Jr. 1922- *WhoAm 90*
Eggers, Ernest Russell 1931- *WhoAm 90*
Eggers, George William 1883-1958 *WhoAmA 91N*
Eggers, George William Nordholtz, Jr. 1929- *WhoAm 90*
Eggers, Idamarie Rasmussen 1925- *WhoAmW 91*
Eggers, Mark Lee 1956- *WhoEmL 91*
Eggers, Melvin Arnold 1916- *WhoAm 90, WhoE 91*
Eggers, Paul Walter 1919- *WhoAm 90, WhoSSW 91, WhoWor 91*
Eggers, Renee Marlene 1956- *WhoAmW 91*
Eggers, Richard F 1918-1979 *WhoAmA 91N*
Eggers, Valdemar Kay Henrik 1929- *WhoWor 91*
Eggers, William Alfred, Jr. 1940- *St&PR 91*
Eggers, William J., III 1939- *WhoWor 91*
Eggert, Alan R. 1949- *St&PR 91*
Eggert, Delmer C 1934- *BiDrAPA 89*
Eggert, Gerald Gordon 1926- *WhoAm 90*
Eggert, H. Fletcher *BioIn 16*
Eggert, Paul Richard 1954- *WhoEmL 91*
Eggert, Richard 1933- *St&PR 91*
Eggert, Robert J. 1913- *St&PR 91*
Eggert, Robert John, Sr. 1913- *WhoAm 90, WhoWor 91*
Eggert, Russell Raymond 1948- *WhoWor 91*
Eggert, Theodore Philip 1929- *WhoE 91*
Eggerth, Marta *PenDiMP*
Eggerts, Arthur H *BiDrAPA 89*
Eggertsen, Ben Thomas 1953- *WhoEmL 91*
Eggertsen, Claude Andrew 1909- *WhoAm 90*
Eggertsen, Paul F 1925- *BiDrAPA 89*
Eggertsson, Gudmundur 1933- *WhoWor 91*
Eggimann, Harry Luis 1953- *WhoWor 91*
Egginton, Geoffrey Twining 1940- *WhoE 91*
Egginton, Wynn Meagher 1944- *WhoAmW 91*
Eggland, Haakon G. 1921- *St&PR 91*
Eggleston, Alan Earl 1949- *WhoWrEP 89*
Eggleston, Alan P. 1953- *St&PR 91*
Eggleston, Claud Hunt, III 1954- *WhoEmL 91*
Eggleston, David Robert 1951- *St&PR 91*
Eggleston, George Dudley 1936- *WhoSSW 91*
Eggleston, George T 1906-1990 *ConAu 132, NewYTBS 90*
Eggleston, Joseph C. 1936-1989 *BioIn 16*
Eggleston, Kent Lee 1936- *St&PR 91*
Eggleston, Robert Dale 1949- *WhoEmL 91*
Eggleston, Robert L 1934- *BiDrAPA 89*
Eggleston, Wilfrid 1901-1986 *DcLB 92 [port]*
Eggleston, William 1939- *BioIn 16*
Eggleton, Arthur C. *WhoAm 90, WhoE 91*
Eggleton, Charles Edward 1937- *WhoE 91*
Eggli, Donald F. 1932- *St&PR 91*
Eggum, John 1913- *St&PR 91*
Eghbal, Morad 1952- *WhoE 91*
Egholm, Per Hillebrandt 1958- *IntWWM 90*
Egi, Yasushi 1929- *WhoWor 91*
Egide, James Allen 1934- *St&PR 91*
Egielski, Richard *BioIn 16*
Egill Skallagrimsson *DcScanL*
Egilsson, Vilhjalmur 1952- *WhoWor 91*
Eginton, Charles Theodore 1914- *WhoAm 90*
Eginton, Warren William 1924- *WhoAm 90, WhoE 91*
Egk, Werner 1901-1983 *PenDiMP A*
Eglee, Charles Hamilton 1951- *WhoEmL 91*
Egler, Frederick Norton 1922- *WhoAm 90*
Egleson, Jim 1907- *WhoAmA 91N*
Egleston, Roger Lee 1935- *WhoE 91*
Egleston, Truman G 1931- *WhoAmA 91*
Egleton, Clive 1927- *TwCCr&M 91*
Egleton, Clive Frederick William 1927- *SpyFic*
Eglevsky, Andre 1917-1977 *WorAlBi*
Eglevsky, Leda Anchutina *BioIn 16*
Egley, Loren Edward 1931- *St&PR 91*
Egley, Thomas Arthur 1945- *WhoEmL 91*
Egley, Thomas M. 1946- *St&PR 91*
Egli, David Lambert *BiDrAPA 89*
Egli, Herbert H. 1930- *St&PR 91*
Egli, Urs Martin 1961- *IntWWM 90*
Eglinton, Douglas 1930- *ODwPR 91*
Eglinton, William 1857-1933 *EncPaPR 91*

Eglinton, William 1858-1933 EncO&P 3
Eglitis, Irma L. 1907- WhoAmW 91
Eglitis, Laimons 1929- WhoAmA 91
Egloff, Frank R L 1925- BiDrAPA 89
Egloff, Julius, III 1946- WhoWor 91
Eglseder, Ludwig Joseph 1928- BiDrAPA 89
Egly, Dewayne 1950- St&PR 91
Egmond, Max van PenDiMP
Egmond, Max Van 1936- IntWWM 90
Egner, Betty Jane 1951- WhoAmW 91
Egner, John David 1957- WhoEmL 91
Egnor-Brown, Rose Marie WhoWrEP 89
Egoff, Sheila A. 1918- ConAu 132
Egorov, Youri BioIn 16
Egorov, Yuri PenDiMP
Egoyan, Atom BioIn 16
Egozi, David 1932- St&PR 91
Egri, Gladys BiDrAPA 89
Egri, Gladys 1930- WhoHisp 91
Egri, Ted 1913- WhoAmA 91
Eguchi, Hideto 1927- WhoWor 91
Eguchi, Michael Steven 1947- WhoEmL 91
Eguchi, Yasu 1938- WhoAm 90
Eguren, Jose Maria 1874-1942 BioIn 16
Eguzkitza, Andolin 1953- WhoWor 91
Egypt, Ophelia Settle 1903-1984 BioIn 16
Ehara, Shozo 1928- WhoWor 91
Ehbrecht, Martha E BiDrAPA 89
Ehgartner, George Joseph, Jr. 1962- WhoE 91
Ehik, Julius BiDrAPA 89
Ehinger, Albert Louis, Jr. 1927- WhoE 91
Ehinger, Charles E. 1928- St&PR 91
Ehinger, Charles Edward 1928- WhoAm 90
Ehinger, Kenneth Ray 1953- St&PR 91
Ehinger, Thomas G. 1947- St&PR 91, WhoSSW 91
Ehle, Jay Sutton 1950- St&PR 91
Ehle, John 1925- WhoWrEP 89, WorAu 1980 [port]
Ehle, John Marsden, Jr. 1925- WhoAm 90, WhoWor 91
Ehlen, Judy 1944- WhoAmW 91
Ehler, Joan G 1933- BiDrAPA 89
Ehlerman, Paul Michael 1938- St&PR 91, WhoAm 90
Ehlers, Carol A 1952- WhoAmA 91
Ehlers, Charles H. 1930- St&PR 91
Ehlers, E Michael 1943- BiDrAPA 89
Ehlers, Eleanor May Collier 1920- WhoAmW 91, WhoWor 91
Ehlers, Gregory Allen, Sr. 1947- WhoEmL 91
Ehlers, John Andrew 1932- St&PR 91
Ehlers, Jurgen 1948- WhoWor 91
Ehlers, Kathryn Hawes 1931- WhoAm 90
Ehlers, Larry Lee 1953- WhoEmL 91, WhoWor 91
Ehlers, Lee St&PR 91
Ehlers, Lyle M. 1947- St&PR 91
Ehlers, Michael Gene 1951- WhoEmL 91
Ehlers, Ralph G. 1915- St&PR 91
Ehlers, Walter George 1933- WhoAm 90
Ehlers, William A. 1921- St&PR 91
Ehlers, William A 1942- BiDrAPA 89
Ehlert, Lois 1934- AuBYP 90
Ehley, Scott William 1955- WhoEmL 91
Ehlinger, Richard Joseph St&PR 91N
Ehm, Phillip Dean 1932- St&PR 91
Ehman, Michael Frederick 1945- WhoEmL 91
Ehmann, Anthony Valentine 1935- WhoWor 91
Ehmann, Carl William 1942- St&PR 91
Ehmann, David Benedict 1937- St&PR 91
Ehmann, Frank A. 1933- St&PR 91, WhoAm 90
Ehmann, Johanna Lombardo 1952- WhoAmW 91
Ehmann, Nancy Gallagher 1932- WhoSSW 91
Ehmann, William Donald 1931- WhoAm 90, WhoSSW 91
Ehmer, Marjy Arduina Niccoll 1927- WhoAmW 91, WhoE 91
Ehmke, Howard 1894-1959 Ballpl 90 [port]
Ehnamani 1825-1902 WhNaAH
Ehni, Bruce Loyal 1948- WhoAm 90, WhoSSW 91
Ehntholt, Daniel James 1945- WhoE 91, WhoEmL 91
Ehramani, Artemus 1825-1902 WhNaAH
Ehre, Edward NewYTBS 90
Ehre, Edward 1905-1990 BioIn 16
Ehre, Ida 1900-1989 BioIn 16
Ehre, Victor Tyndall 1913- St&PR 91, WhoAm 90
Ehren, Charles Alexander, Jr. 1932- WhoAm 90
Ehren, Dennis Randolph 1950- WhoEmL 91
Ehren, Fritz Henry 1928- WhoAm 90
Ehren, James Bernard 1946- St&PR 91
Ehrenberg, Edward 1930- St&PR 91, WhoAm 90
Ehrenberg, Eileen Dona BiDrAPA 89
Ehrenberg, Hannes Christian 1949- WhoWor 91
Ehrenberg, Ilya 1891-1967 WorAlBi
Ehrenberg, John Michael, Jr. 1937- WhoAm 90
Ehrenberg, Miriam Colbert 1930- WhoAmW 91
Ehrenberg, Robert John 1953- WhoEmL 91
Ehrenberg, Ruth BiDrAPA 89
Ehrenberg, Wolfgang 1909- EncO&P 3
Ehrenburg, Ilya 1891-1967 BioIn 16, ConLC 62 [port]
Ehrencron-Kidde, Astrid EncCoWW
Ehrencron-Kidde, Astrid Margrethe 1874-1960 EncCoWW
Ehrencron-Muller, Astrid EncCoWW
Ehreneweisen, H. Von BiDWomA
Ehrenfeld, Elizabeth Enloe 1959- WhoWor 91
Ehrenfeld, John Henry 1917- WhoAm 90
Ehrenfeld, Phyllis Rhoda 1932- WhoE 91
Ehrenfried, Albert D. 1922- St&PR 91
Ehrenhaft, Felix 1879-1952 DcScB S2
Ehrenhaft, Johann Leo 1915- WhoAm 90
Ehrenhaft, Peter David 1933- WhoAm 90
Ehrenhalt, Samuel M. BioIn 16
Ehrenkrantz, Ezra David 1932- WhoAm 90
Ehrenkrantz, Louis 1934- WhoE 91
Ehrenkranz, Shirley Malakoff 1920- WhoAm 90, WhoAmW 91
Ehrenman, Vicki 1949- WhoEmL 91
Ehrenpreis, Seymour 1927- WhoAm 90
Ehrenreich, Barbara 1941- BestSel 90-4 [port], MajTwCW, WhoAm 90
Ehrenreich, Donald L 1928- BiDrAPA 89
Ehrenreich, Henry 1928- WhoAm 90
Ehrenreich, Johann Eberhard Ludwig PenDiDA 89
Ehrenreich, Mark Jay 1958- BiDrAPA 89
Ehrensberger, Charles J. 1923- St&PR 91
Ehrensberger, Ray 1904- WhoAm 90
Ehrensing, Rudolph H BiDrAPA 89
Ehrenstrom, James William 1936- St&PR 91
Ehrensvard, Thomasine G. DcScanL
Ehrenwald, Jan 1900-1988 BioIn 16, EncO&P 3, EncPaPR 91
Ehrenwerth, David Harry 1947- WhoEmL 91
Ehresmann, Charles 1905-1979 DcScB S2
Ehresmann, Donald Louis 1937- WhoAmA 91
Ehret, Arnold 1866-1922 NewAgE 90
Ehret, Georg Dionys 1710-1770 BioIn 16
Ehrhardt, Helmut E BiDrAPA 89
Ehrhardt, Laurence White 1940- St&PR 91
Ehrhardt, Manfred Guenther 1933- WhoWor 91
Ehrhardt, Robert W. 1942- St&PR 91
Ehrhardt, Rube 1894-1980 Ballpl 90
Ehrhardt, Thomas Andrew 1961- WhoEmL 91
Ehrhart, Carl Yarkers 1918- WhoAm 90
Ehrhart, Daniel Diehl 1929- St&PR 91
Ehrhart, W. D. 1948- BioIn 16
Ehrhart, William Daniel 1948- BioIn 16, WhoWrEP 89
Ehrhorn, Richard William 1934- WhoAm 90
Ehrich, Fredric F. 1928- WhoE 91
Ehrich, Hans 1942- ConDes 90
Ehrich, Marion 1945- WhoSSW 91
Ehrich, Robert William 1908- WhoAm 90
Ehringer, Albert T. BioIn 16
Ehringer, Susann 1960- WhoAmW 91
Ehrke, David E. 1947- IntWWM 90
Ehrle, Roy W. 1928- WhoAm 90
Ehrle, William Lawrence 1932- WhoWor 91
Ehrlein, Hans-Jorg 1933- WhoWor 91
Ehrler, Bremer WhoAm 90, WhoSSW 91
Ehrler, H. Whit 1941- St&PR 91
Ehrlich, Abel 1915- IntWWM 90
Ehrlich, Alvin McIntyre 1950- WhoEmL 91
Ehrlich, Alvin Q. St&PR 91N
Ehrlich, Amy 1942- ConAu 32NR, WhoAm 90
Ehrlich, Arnold 1923-1989 BioIn 16, ConAu 129
Ehrlich, Ava 1950- WhoAmW 91
Ehrlich, Bernard Herbert 1927- WhoAm 90
Ehrlich, Bettina Bauer 1903- AuBYP 90
Ehrlich, Burtt R. 1939- St&PR 91
Ehrlich, Clarence Eugene 1938- WhoAm 90
Ehrlich, Clifford John 1938- St&PR 91, WhoAm 90
Ehrlich, Cyril 1925- IntWWM 90
Ehrlich, Elizabeth 1954- WhoAmW 91
Ehrlich, Evelyn Joan 1950- WhoAmW 91
Ehrlich, Frances E BiDrAPA 89
Ehrlich, Frederick 1932- WhoWor 91
Ehrlich, Frederick M 1930- BiDrAPA 89
Ehrlich, George 1925- WhoAmA 91
Ehrlich, George Edward 1928- WhoAm 90
Ehrlich, Geraldine Elizabeth 1939- WhoAmW 91, WhoWor 91
Ehrlich, Gert 1926- WhoAm 90
Ehrlich, Gertrude 1923- WhoAm 90
Ehrlich, Grant Conklin 1916- WhoAm 90
Ehrlich, Henry B BiDrAPA 89
Ehrlich, Henry Lutz 1925- WhoE 91
Ehrlich, Ira Robert 1926- WhoAm 90
Ehrlich, Joel Julius 1949- WhoE 91
Ehrlich, Kingston W. 1914- St&PR 91
Ehrlich, Leslie Sharon 1952- WhoAmW 91
Ehrlich, Margaret Elizabeth Gorley 1950- WhoAmW 91
Ehrlich, Mel 1938- ODwPR 91, WhoAm 90
Ehrlich, Morton 1934- St&PR 91, WhoAm 90
Ehrlich, Paul 1854-1915 WorAlBi
Ehrlich, Paul 1923- WhoAm 90
Ehrlich, Paul Ewing 1948- WhoSSW 91
Ehrlich, Paul Henry 1957- IntWWM 90
Ehrlich, Paul Ralph 1932- WhoAm 90
Ehrlich, Raymond 1918- WhoAm 90, WhoSSW 91
Ehrlich, Richard 1924- WhoAm 90
Ehrlich, Robert R. 1908- St&PR 91
Ehrlich, Roy E 1932- BiDrAPA 89
Ehrlich, Saul Paul, Jr. 1932- WhoAm 90
Ehrlich, Susan Marie BiDrAPA 89
Ehrlich, Thomas 1934- WhoAm 90, WhoWor 91
Ehrlich, Vivian Fenster 1942- WhoE 91
Ehrlicher, Werner Ludwig 1920- WhoWor 91
Ehrlichman, John 1925- SpyFic
Ehrlichman, John D. 1925- WorAlBi
Ehrlichman, John Daniel 1925- WhoAm 90, WhoWrEP 89
Ehrling, Robert Francis 1939- St&PR 91
Ehrling, Sixten 1918- IntWWM 90, PenDiMP, WhoAm 90, WhoWor 91
Ehrman, Frederick L 1906-1973 WhoAmA 91N
Ehrman, Joachim Benedict 1929- WhoAm 90
Ehrman, Joseph S. 1931- WhoAm 90
Ehrman, Lee 1935- WhoAm 90, WhoAmW 91
Ehrman, Madeline Elizabeth 1942- WhoAmW 91
Ehrman, Samuel K. 1943- St&PR 91
Ehrmann, Alexander 1926- St&PR 91
Ehrmann, Mariane 1755-1795 EncCoWW
Ehrmann, Thomas William 1935- WhoAm 90
Ehrnschwender, Arthur R. 1922- St&PR 91
Ehrnschwender, Arthur Robert 1922- WhoAm 90
Ehrnst, Craig Francis 1964- WhoEmL 91
Ei, Susan Michelle 1952- WhoAmW 91
Eiben, Robert Michael 1922- WhoAm 90
Eibenschutz, Ilona 1872-1967 BioIn 16
Eiber, Rick 1944- BioIn 16
Eiberger, Carl Frederick 1931- WhoAm 90
Eiberson, Harold 1913- WhoAm 90
Eibert, John M. 1925- St&PR 91
Eibl-Eibesfeldt, Irenaeus 1928- WhoWor 91
Eich, Margaret Holder 1948- WhoSSW 91
Eichacker, George 1930- St&PR 91
Eichbaum, Heinrich Alexander 1914- IntWWM 90
Eichberg, Joseph 1906- St&PR 91
Eichedinger, F.R. 1929- St&PR 91
Eichel, Edward W 1932- WhoAmA 91
Eichel, Gloria Lillian 1914- WhoWor 91
Eichel, Julius BioIn 16
Eichel, Paul Martin 1932- St&PR 91
Eichel, Roger Madison 1948- St&PR 91
Eichelbaum, Marvin WhoAm 90
Eichelbaum, Samuel 1894-1967 BioIn 16
Eichelbaum, Stanley 1926- WhoAm 90
Eichelberger, Ethyl BioIn 16
Eichelberger, Ethyl 1945-1990 ConAu 132, NewYTBS 90
Eichelberger, Juan 1953- Ballpl 90
Eichelberger, Robert L. 1886-1961 BioIn 16
Eichelman, Burr S 1943- BiDrAPA 89
Eichelman, Sarah Moreman 1952- WhoSSW 91
Eichenbaum, Andrew Charles 1962- St&PR 91
Eichenbaum, Bernard 1924- St&PR 91
Eichenberg, Fritz NewYTBS 90
Eichenberg, Fritz 1901- BioIn 16, WhoAm 90, WhoAmA 91
Eichendorff, Joseph Von 1788-1857 WorAlBi
Eichenfield, Samuel St&PR 91
Eichenholtz, Lewis Edward 1947- St&PR 91
Eichenwald, Heinz Felix 1926- WhoAm 90
Eicher, George John 1916- WhoAm 90
Eicher, Joanne Bubolz 1930- WhoAm 90, WhoAmW 91
Eicher, Leslie ODwPR 91
Eicher, Robin BiDrAPA 89
Eicher, Wolf 1940- WhoWor 91
Eichert, Arnold H 1913- BiDrAPA 89
Eichert, Jerome H. 1928- St&PR 91, WhoAm 90
Eichfeld, Timothy Joseph 1946- WhoEmL 91
Eichhold, Louis B. 1943- St&PR 91
Eichholz, Geoffrey Gunther 1920- WhoAm 90
Eichhorn, Arthur David 1953- WhoEmL 91
Eichhorn, Bradford Reese 1954- WhoEmL 91
Eichhorn, Frederick Foltz, Jr. 1930- WhoAm 90
Eichhorn, Gunther Louis 1927- WhoAm 90
Eichhorn, Heinrich Karl 1927- WhoAm 90
Eichhorn, Mark 1960- Ballpl 90
Eichhorn, Roger 1931- WhoAm 90
Eichhorn, Wolfgang Friedrich 1933- WhoWor 91
Eichinger, Marilynne H. WhoAm 90, WhoAmW 91
Eichleay, George Frederick 1948- St&PR 91
Eichleay, John William, Jr. 1946- St&PR 91
Eichler, Carla Elise 1960- WhoAmW 91
Eichler, Franklin Roosevelt 1933- St&PR 91, WhoAm 90
Eichler, Fred Sheldon 1948- St&PR 91
Eichler, Hans Joachim 1940- WhoWor 91
Eichler, Menahem Max 1870-1927 BioIn 16
Eichler, Ned 1930- ConAu 132
Eichler, Peter James 1928- St&PR 91
Eichler, Richard Samuel 1931- St&PR 91
Eichler, Seth BiDrAPA 89
Eichler, Thomas P. 1944- WhoAm 90
Eichler, Tyrrell Burton 1903- St&PR 91
Eichler, Tyrrell Burton, Jr. 1934- St&PR 91
Eichling, Mary Tourond 1947- WhoAmW 91
Eichman, Barbara V BiDrAPA 89
Eichman, Dale Bruce 1953- WhoEmL 91
Eichman, Margaret M. ODwPR 91
Eichman, Mary Redner 1919- BiDrAPA 89
Eichman, Peter Liebert 1925- WhoAm 90
Eichman, Russell John 1936- St&PR 91
Eichmann, Adolf 1906-1962 BioIn 16, WorAlBi
Eichner, Alfred S. 1937-1988 BioIn 16
Eichner, Claus-Rainer 1949- WhoWor 91
Eichner, Donald William St&PR 91N
Eichner, Hans 1921- WhoAm 90
Eichner, Ira A. 1931- St&PR 91
Eichner, L. John 1921- St&PR 91
Eichner, William Eduard 1937- WhoE 91
Eichold, Samuel 1916- WhoAm 90
Eichorn, John F.G., Jr. 1924- St&PR 91
Eichorn, John Frederick Gerard, Jr. 1924- WhoAm 90
Eichorst, Terry Alan 1948- WhoSSW 91
Eichstadt, Frank Thomas 1956- WhoSSW 91
Eichstadt, Hermann Werner 1948- WhoWor 91
Eichten, John Gregory 1943- BiDrAPA 89
Eichten, Patricia Jean 1960- WhoAmW 91
Eicke, Theodor 1892-1943 BioIn 16
Eickelberg, W. Warren Barbour 1925- WhoE 91
Eicken, Tonya Jo 1961- WhoSSW 91
Eickhof, Norbert 1943- WhoWor 91
Eickhoff, Barbara B. 1939- WhoAmW 91
Eickhoff, Dennis R. 1944- St&PR 91
Eickhoff, Dennis Raymond 1944- WhoAm 90
Eickhoff, Harold Walter 1928- WhoAm 90, WhoE 91
Eickhoff, Janie BioIn 16
Eickhoff, Theodore Carl 1931- WhoAm 90
Eickhorst, William Sigurd 1941- WhoAmA 91
Eickleberg, John Edwin 1944- WhoAm 90
Eickman, Jennifer Lynn 1946- WhoAmW 91
Eid, George Mtanos 1958- WhoE 91
Eid, Judy Salem 1940- WhoSSW 91
Eid, Steven Allen 1950- WhoSSW 91
Eide, Erling 1940- WhoWor 91
Eide, John 1943- WhoAmA 91, WhoE 91
Eide, Marlene 1932- WhoAmW 91
Eide, Melvin O. 1930- St&PR 91
Eide, Palmer 1906- WhoAmA 91
Eidelberg, Martin 1941- WhoAmA 91
Eidell, Ronald G. 1944- St&PR 91
Eidell, Ronald George 1944- WhoAm 90
Eidelman, David Robert 1944- St&PR 91
Eidelman, Gene 1958- WhoSSW 91
Eidelman, Jack R 1913- BiDrAPA 89
Eiden, Vera M 1906- BiDrAPA 89
Eidenbenz, Hermann 1902- ConDes 90

Eidenberg, Eugene 1939- *St&PR 91*
Eidenberg, Gene *ODwPR 91*
Eidenshink, Carla Kay 1959- *WhoAmW 91*
Eidlin, Fred Howard 1942- *WhoWor 91*
Eidsness, Paul Tobias 1944- *St&PR 91*
Eidson, Barbara Elaine 1938- *WhoSSW 91*
Eidson, Thomas E. 1944- *ODwPR 91, WhoAm 90*
Eidson, William Whelan 1935- *WhoAm 90*
Eidt, C.M., Jr. 1935- *St&PR 91*
Eidt, Clarence Martin, Jr. 1935- *WhoAm 90*
Eidt, John Charles *BioIn 16*
Eidus, Robert 1948- *WhoE 91, WhoEmL 91*
Eie, Olaf 1943- *WhoWor 91*
Eierman, Warren Harding 1922- *St&PR 91*
Eiermann, Harry J. 1915- *WhoE 91*
Eiesland, Mark Leon 1952- *WhoEmL 91*
Eiferman, Sharon Rees 1948- *WhoWrEP 89*
Eifert, Kevin Carl 1954- *WhoSSW 91*
Eifert, Virginia Louise 1911-1966 *AuBYP 90*
Eiff, Hansjoerg Hugo 1933- *WhoWor 91*
Eiffel, Alexandre-Gustave 1832-1923 *WorAlBi*
Eiffert, Jack Warden 1921- *St&PR 91*
Eiffler-Orton, Carol Ann 1948- *WhoAmW 91*
Eifler, Carl Frederick 1906- *WhoWor 91*
Eifler, Carl Morgan 1948- *St&PR 91*
Eifrig, David Eric 1935- *WhoAm 90*
Eig, Norman 1941- *WhoAm 90*
Eigel, Edwin George, Jr. 1932- *WhoAm 90*
Eigen, Barbara Helen 1945- *WhoAmW 91*
Eigen, Howard 1942- *WhoAm 90*
Eigen, Manfred 1927- *WhoAm 90, WhoWor 91, WorAlBi*
Eigenbrodt, Harold John 1928- *WhoAm 90*
Eiger, Richard William 1933- *WhoAm 90, WhoE 91, WhoWor 91*
Eiger, Rodney Ira *BiDrAPA 89*
Eighmey, Douglas Joseph, Jr. 1946- *WhoEmL 91*
Eighner, Renna Burkes 1958- *WhoAmW 91*
Eigner, William Whitling 1959- *WhoEmL 91*
Eigsti, Karl *BioIn 16*
Eigsti, Roger Harry 1942- *St&PR 91*
Eiguren, Roy *WhoHisp 91*
Eihusen, Virgil R. 1930- *St&PR 91, WhoAm 90*
Eikasia *EncCoWW*
Eike, Bonnie Maye 1928- *WhoAmW 91*
Eikelberger, Rand Jeffrey 1947- *St&PR 91*
Eikenberry, Arthur Raymond 1920- *WhoWor 91, WhoWrEP 89*
Eikenberry, Ching Yuan 1947- *WhoAmW 91, WhoWor 91*
Eikenberry, Jill *BioIn 16*
Eikenberry, Jill 1947- *WhoAm 90, WorAlBi*
Eikenberry, Kenneth Otto 1932- *WhoAm 90*
Eikerman, Alma *WhoAmA 91*
Eikermann, William Conrad *BiDrAPA 89*
Eikhenbaum, Vsevolod Mikhailovich 1882-1945 *BioIn 16*
Eikum, Rex L. 1932- *IntWWM 90*
Eiland, David C, Jr. *BiDrAPA 89*
Eiland, Dianna Kay 1957- *IntWWM 90*
Eiland, Gary Wayne 1951- *WhoEmL 91*
Eilber, Warren S. 1927- *St&PR 91*
Eilbracht, Lee Paul 1924- *WhoAm 90*
Eileen, Phyllis 1918- *WhoAmA 91*
Eilen, Howard Scott 1954- *WhoEmL 91*
Eilenberg, Julia *BiDrAPA 89*
Eilenberg, Matthew L. 1958- *WhoEmL 91*
Eilenberg, Samuel 1913- *WhoAm 90*
Eilenberger, Bruce F. 1947- *St&PR 91*
Eilenfeldt, Robert K. 1944- *St&PR 91*
Eiler, James Willard 1951- *St&PR 91*
Eiler, Kathryn Anne *BiDrAPA 89*
Eiler, Larry T. 1939- *ODwPR 91*
Eilers, Dave 1936- *Ballpl 90*
Eilers, Fred *WhoAmA 91*
Eilers, Robert Paul 1949- *BiDrAPA 89, WhoE 91*
Eilers, Steven Gerard *BiDrAPA 89*
Eilers, Warner William 1936- *St&PR 91*
Eilert, Richard E. 1947- *ConAu 129*
Eilert, Rick *ConAu 129*
Eils, Richard George 1937- *St&PR 91, WhoAm 90*
Eilts, Hermann Frederick 1922- *BioIn 16*
Eilts, Karin Lynn 1956- *WhoWrEP 89*
Eimer, Theodor Gustav Heinrich 1843-1898 *DcScB S2*
Eimermann, Daniel Allen 1952- *BiDrAPA 89*
Eimers, Robert Conrad 1948- *St&PR 91*
Eimicke, Victor William 1925- *WhoAm 90*
Ein, Melvin Bennett 1932- *WhoAm 90*
Einan, Menachem 1939- *WhoWor 91*
Einar Benediktsson *DcScanL*
Einarsson, Tomas Ragnar 1953- *IntWWM 90*
Einaudi, Marco Tullio 1939- *WhoAm 90*
Einbender, Alvin H. 1929- *WhoAm 90*
Einbender, Alvin Herbert 1929- *St&PR 91*
Einbinder, Eli 1943- *BiDrAPA 89*
Einbond, Bernard Lionel 1937- *WhoWrEP 89*
Einck, Dean Robert 1957- *WhoEmL 91*
Einem, Gottfried Von 1918- *IntWWM 90, PenDiMP A*
Einertson, Norris Leonard 1930- *WhoAm 90*
Einhorn, Bruce Jeffrey 1954- *WhoEmL 91*
Einhorn, David 1809-1879 *BioIn 16*
Einhorn, David Allen 1961- *WhoE 91, WhoEmL 91, WhoWor 91*
Einhorn, Eddie 1936- *Ballpl 90*
Einhorn, Edward H 1919- *BiDrAPA 89*
Einhorn, Edward Martin 1936- *WhoAm 90*
Einhorn, Eric John 1948- *WhoAm 90*
Einhorn, Hillel J. *BioIn 16*
Einhorn, Ira *BioIn 16*
Einhorn, Keith Lee *BiDrAPA 89*
Einhorn, Lawrence Henry 1942- *WhoAm 90*
Einhorn, Marcel *St&PR 91*
Einhorn, Michael Allan 1952- *WhoE 91*
Einhorn, Steven G. *BioIn 16*
Einhorn, Steven Gary 1948- *WhoAm 90*
Einiger, Carol B. *BioIn 16*
Einiger, Carol Blum 1949- *St&PR 91, WhoAmW 91*
Einiger, Roger William 1947- *St&PR 91*
Einisman, Vladimir 1941- *BiDrAPA 89*
Eino 1940- *WhoAmA 91*
Einoder, Camille Elizabeth 1937- *WhoAmW 91, WhoWor 91*
Einreinhofer, Nancy Anne 1943- *WhoAmA 91*
Einreinhofer, Roy John 1939- *WhoE 91*
Eins, Stefan 1941- *WhoAmA 91*
Einspahr, Larry William *BiDrAPA 89*
Einspruch, Burton C 1935- *BiDrAPA 89*
Einspruch, Burton Cyril 1935- *WhoWor 91*
Einspruch, Norman Gerald 1932- *WhoAm 90, WhoSSW 91*
Einstein, Albert *EncAL*
Einstein, Albert 1879-1955 *BioIn 16, MajTwCW, WorAlBi*
Einstein, Carl 1885-1940 *BioIn 16*
Einstein, Charles 1926- *Ballpl 90*
Einstein, Cliff *BioIn 16*
Einstein, Clifford Jay 1939- *WhoAm 90*
Einstein, Gilbert W 1942- *WhoAmA 91*
Einstein, Jeffrey Paul 1952- *WhoEmL 91*
Einstein, Kurt W. *BioIn 16*
Einstein, Lewis David 1877-1967 *BioIn 16*
Einstein, Mandy *BioIn 16*
Einstein, Margery A. 1943- *WhoAmW 91*
Einstein, Stephen Jan 1945- *WhoWor 91*
Einsweiler, Robert Charles 1929- *WhoAm 90, WhoWor 91*
Einzig, Barbara Ellen 1951- *WhoWrEP 89*
Eipper, Michael G. 1950- *St&PR 91*
Eipperle, Trude 1910- *IntWWM 90*
Eirich, Frederick Roland 1905- *WhoAm 90, WhoWor 91*
Eiriksdottir, Karolina 1951- *IntWWM 90*
Eis, Loryann Malvina 1938- *WhoAmW 91*
Eisai 1141-1215 *EncJap*
Eisaman, Josiah Reamer, III 1924- *WhoAm 90*
Eisaman, Ralph Herbert 1932- *BiDrAPA 89*
Eisberg, James Stephen 1938- *St&PR 91*
Eisberg, Robert Martin 1928- *WhoAm 90*
Eisch, Erwin 1927- *PenDiDA 89*
Eisch, John Joseph 1930- *WhoAm 90*
Eischeid, Theodore Joseph 1950- *St&PR 91*
Eischen, Michael Hugh 1931- *WhoAm 90*
Eisdorfer, Carl 1930- *BiDrAPA 89, WhoAm 90*
Eisele, Donn *BioIn 16*
Eisele, Edward Harrison, III 1941- *WhoAm 90*
Eisele, Garnett Thomas 1923- *WhoAm 90, WhoSSW 91*
Eisele, John Allan 1929- *WhoWor 91*
Eisele, John Evans 1940- *WhoSSW 91*
Eisele, John William 1952- *WhoSSW 91*
Eisele, Robert Henry 1948- *WhoEmL 91*
Eisele, William David 1927- *WhoSSW 91*
Eiseley, Loren 1907-1977 *Au&Arts 5 [port]*
Eiseley, Loren C. 1907-1977 *BioIn 16*
Eiseley, Loren Corey 1907-1977 *WorAlBi*
Eiseman, Alberta 1925- *AuBYP 90*
Eiseman, Barbara Ann 1955- *St&PR 91*
Eiseman, Fredrick A *BiDrAPA 89*
Eiseman, Neal Martin 1955- *WhoEmL 91*
Eisemann, Alexander, Jr. 1924- *St&PR 91*
Eisemann, Kate Helen 1956- *WhoEmL 91*
Eisen, Arthur 1933- *BiDrAPA 89*
Eisen, Charles J. 1914- *St&PR 91*
Eisen, Edward N. 1936- *ODwPR 91*
Eisen, Edwin Otto 1940- *WhoSSW 91*
Eisen, Frederic Stanton 1941- *WhoSSW 91*
Eisen, Harold M. 1932- *St&PR 91*
Eisen, Harvey Phillip 1942- *WhoAm 90*
Eisen, Henry 1921- *WhoAm 90*
Eisen, Herman Nathaniel 1918- *WhoAm 90*
Eisen, Irving M. 1927- *St&PR 91*
Eisen, Jane Louise *BiDrAPA 89*
Eisen, Jay Loeb 1957- *St&PR 91*
Eisen, Lawrence Edward 1944- *St&PR 91*
Eisen, Leonard 1934- *WhoAm 90*
Eisen, Leslie Ann 1964- *WhoE 91*
Eisen, Mark *BioIn 16*
Eisen, Morton *NewYTBS 90*
Eisen, Peter Ronald 1933- *BiDrAPA 89*
Eisen, Ronald J. 1932- *ODwPR 91*
Eisen, Simon Thomas 1945- *BiDrAPA 89*
Eisen, Steven *BiDrAPA 89*
Eisen, Steven Jeffrey 1958- *WhoEmL 91*
Eisen, Sydney B 1929- *BiDrAPA 89*
Eisenacher, Craig E. 1947- *St&PR 91*
Eisenbach, Michael 1945- *WhoWor 91*
Eisenbarth, Gary Lee 1947- *St&PR 91*
Eisenbeis, Robert A. 1941- *WhoAm 90*
Eisenberg, Adi 1935- *WhoAm 90*
Eisenberg, Alan 1935- *WhoAm 90, WhoE 91*
Eisenberg, Alan I. 1950- *St&PR 91*
Eisenberg, Albert Joel 1925- *St&PR 91*
Eisenberg, Amy Marcie 1956- *WhoAmW 91*
Eisenberg, Anne Frances 1960- *WhoEmL 91*
Eisenberg, Azriel Louis 1903- *AuBYP 90*
Eisenberg, Barbara Anne K. 1945- *WhoAm 90*
Eisenberg, Bart 1950- *ODwPR 91*
Eisenberg, Bertram William 1930- *WhoE 91*
Eisenberg, Carola *BiDrAPA 89*
Eisenberg, David Henry 1936- *St&PR 91*
Eisenberg, David Samuel 1939- *WhoAm 90*
Eisenberg, Edward Franklin 1947- *BiDrAPA 89*
Eisenberg, Eleanor 1941- *WhoAmW 91*
Eisenberg, Frank *BiDrAPA 89*
Eisenberg, Frank David 1945- *WhoE 91*
Eisenberg, Gail Charlene 1951- *BiDrAPA 89*
Eisenberg, George Henry Gilbert, Jr. 1940- *WhoE 91*
Eisenberg, George T. 1926- *St&PR 91*
Eisenberg, Harold J 1910- *BiDrAPA 89*
Eisenberg, Harry Victor 1945- *WhoSSW 91*
Eisenberg, Harve 1935- *St&PR 91*
Eisenberg, Harvey Ellis 1949- *WhoEmL 91*
Eisenberg, James 1930- *St&PR 91, WhoAm 90*
Eisenberg, Jerome Martin 1930- *WhoAmA 91*
Eisenberg, Joe Davidson 1920- *St&PR 91*
Eisenberg, John Meyer 1946- *WhoAm 90*
Eisenberg, Joseph Martin 1944- *WhoE 91, WhoWor 91*
Eisenberg, Karen Sue Byer 1954- *WhoAmW 91, WhoEmL 91, WhoWor 91*
Eisenberg, Larry H. 1952- *WhoEmL 91*
Eisenberg, Lee B. 1946- *WhoAm 90, WhoE 91, WhoEmL 91*
Eisenberg, Leon 1922- *BiDrAPA 89, WhoAm 90, WhoE 91*
Eisenberg, Lisa 1949- *BioIn 16*
Eisenberg, Marc S 1948- *WhoAmA 91*
Eisenberg, Marilyn 1941- *WhoAmW 91*
Eisenberg, Marvin *WhoAmA 91*
Eisenberg, Marvin 1922- *WhoAm 90*
Eisenberg, Maurice 1900-1972 *PenDiMP*
Eisenberg, Melvin 1929- *St&PR 91*
Eisenberg, Melvin A. 1934- *WhoAm 90*
Eisenberg, Meyer 1931- *WhoAm 90, WhoE 91*
Eisenberg, Milton 1928- *WhoAm 90*
Eisenberg, Morton S *BiDrAPA 89*
Eisenberg, Murray 1939- *WhoE 91*
Eisenberg, Pablo Samuel 1932- *WhoE 91*
Eisenberg, Peter A. 1932- *St&PR 91*
Eisenberg, Peter L. 1940-1988 *BioIn 16*
Eisenberg, R. Neal 1936- *WhoE 91*
Eisenberg, Richard K. 1944- *St&PR 91*
Eisenberg, Richard M. 1942- *WhoAm 90*
Eisenberg, Richard S. 1943- *WhoAm 90*
Eisenberg, Robin Ledgin 1951- *WhoAmW 91*
Eisenberg, Ron Aaron *ODwPR 91*
Eisenberg, Ronald Lee 1941- *St&PR 91*
Eisenberg, Ruth *BioIn 16*
Eisenberg, Seth Gregg *BiDrAPA 89*
Eisenberg, Sidney Edwin 1913- *WhoE 91*
Eisenberg, Sonja Miriam 1926- *WhoAmA 91, WhoAmW 91*
Eisenberg, Stephen *BioIn 16*
Eisenberg, Steven Allen 1947- *St&PR 91*
Eisenberg, Steven Dale 1958- *WhoEmL 91*
Eisenberg, Steven E. 1958- *St&PR 91*
Eisenberg, Stuart Richard *BiDrAPA 89*
Eisenberg, Wendy Fay 1931- *WhoAmA 91*
Eisenberger, Gary D. 1934- *St&PR 91, WhoAm 90*
Eisenberger, Herbert *WhoWor 91*
Eisenberger, J. Leon 1939- *St&PR 91*
Eisenberger, Mario Alfredo 1949- *WhoE 91*
Eisenberger, Robert Alan 1958- *WhoEmL 91*
Eisenbise, Janet K. 1941- *WhoAmW 91*
Eisenbraun, Doreen Karen 1942- *WhoAmW 91*
Eisenbraun, Eric Charles 1955- *WhoEmL 91*
Eisenbraun, Robert Alfred 1928- *St&PR 91*
Eisenbruch, I Maurice *BiDrAPA 89*
Eisenbud, Jule 1908- *BiDrAPA 89, EncO&P 3, EncPaPR 91*
Eisenbud, Merril 1915- *WhoAm 90*
Eisenbud, Monika M 1943- *BiDrAPA 89*
Eisenbud, Monika Margaret 1943- *WhoE 91*
Eisendorfer, Arnold *BiDrAPA 89*
Eisendrath, David B. 1914-1988 *BioIn 16*
Eisendrath, Edwin *BioIn 16*
Eisendrath, Robert M *BiDrAPA 89*
Eisendrath, Stuart James 1948- *BiDrAPA 89*
Eisener, Laura Dawn 1955- *WhoAmW 91*
Eisenhardt, Otto F *BiDrAPA 89*
Eisenhardt, Roy 1939- *WhoAm 90*
Eisenhart, Blake H. 1952- *St&PR 91*
Eisenhart, S. Forry, Jr. 1950- *St&PR 91*
Eisenhauer, Gail Lynn 1953- *BiDrAPA 89*
Eisenhauer, Thomas Walter 1936- *St&PR 91*
Eisenhauer, Wayne Harold 1949- *WhoEmL 91*
Eisenhauer, William Joseph 1934- *St&PR 91*
Eisenhaure, David Baker 1945- *WhoE 91*
Eisenhower, Dwight D. 1890-1969 *BioIn 16*
Eisenhower, Dwight David 1890-1969 *BiDrUSE 89, WorAlBi*
Eisenhower, Jean Ann 1952- *WhoAmW 91*
Eisenhower, John S D 1922- *ConAu 32NR*
Eisenhower, John Sheldon Doud 1922- *WhoAm 90, WhoE 91*
Eisenhower, Mamie Doud 1896-1979 *BioAmW, BioIn 16*
Eisenhower, Milton Stover 1899-1985 *BioIn 16, WorAlBi*
Eisenhower-Turner, E Susanna *BiDrAPA 89*
Eisenhuth, Elizabeth *BioIn 16*
Eisenkraft, Arthur *BioIn 16*
Eisenkraft, Arthur 1950- *WhoE 91*
Eisenkramer, Charles C. 1937- *St&PR 91*
Eisenlohr, David L. 1954- *St&PR 91*
Eisenlohr, Edward G 1873-1961 *WhoAmA 91N*
Eisenlohr, Mike J. 1955- *St&PR 91*
Eisenman, Alvin 1921- *WhoAm 90*
Eisenman, Peter 1932- *BioIn 16*
Eisenman, Peter David 1932- *WhoAm 90*
Eisenman, Sheldon *BiDrAPA 89*
Eisenman, Trudy Fox 1940- *WhoAmW 91*
Eisenmann, James R. 1941- *St&PR 91*
Eisenmann, Josef 1928- *WhoWor 91*
Eisenmann, Olivier Daphnis 1940- *WhoWor 91*
Eisenmann, Roberto *BioIn 16*
Eisenmenger, Robert Waltz 1926- *St&PR 91, WhoAm 90*
Eisenoff, Robert 1926- *WhoE 91*
Eisenpreis, Alfred 1924- *WhoAm 90*
Eisenrauch, Alvin Joseph 1943- *WhoE 91*
Eisenreich, David L. 1943- *St&PR 91*
Eisenreich, Jim 1959- *Ballpl 90*
Eisenschmid, Kurt Robert 1959- *WhoE 91*
Eisenshtat, Sidney Herbert 1914- *WhoAm 90*
Eisenstadt, Abraham S. 1920- *WhoAm 90*
Eisenstadt, Arlene Ellen 1954- *WhoAmW 91*
Eisenstadt, David 1944- *ODwPR 91*
Eisenstadt, Debbie Miriam 1951- *WhoAmW 91*
Eisenstadt, G. Michael 1928- *WhoAm 90*
Eisenstadt, Jill *BioIn 16*
Eisenstadt, Pauline Doreen Bauman 1938- *WhoAmW 91*
Eisenstadt, Samuel 1922- *St&PR 91*
Eisenstaedt, Alfred *BioIn 16*
Eisenstaedt, Alfred 1898- *WhoAm 90*
Eisenstat, Albert A. 1930- *St&PR 91*
Eisenstat, Benjamin 1915- *WhoAmA 91*
Eisenstat, Harry 1915- *Ballpl 90*
Eisenstat, Maxine Edith 1945- *WhoAmW 91*
Eisenstein, Alfred 1899- *IntWWM 90*
Eisenstein, Bruce Allan 1941- *WhoAm 90*
Eisenstein, Elizabeth Lewisohn 1923- *WhoAm 90*
Eisenstein, Ira 1906- *BioIn 16*
Eisenstein, Julian 1921- *WhoAmA 91*
Eisenstein, Julian, Mrs *WhoAmA 91*

Eisenstein, Julian Calvert 1921- *WhoE 91*
Eisenstein, Laurence Jay 1960- *WhoEmL 91*
Eisenstein, Lawrence M 1938- *BiDrAPA 89*
Eisenstein, Michael 1950- *WhoE 91, WhoEmL 91, WhoWor 91*
Eisenstein, Paul Allan 1953- *WhoWrEP 89*
Eisenstein, Richard Barry 1934- *BiDrAPA 89*
Eisenstein, Sam 1936- *WhoSSW 91*
Eisenstein, Samuel 1913- *BiDrAPA 89*
Eisenstein, Sergei 1898-1948 *BioIn 16, WorAlBi*
Eisenstein, Sheryl Fay 1961- *WhoAmW 91*
Eisenstein, Theodore Donald 1930- *WhoE 91, WhoWor 91*
Eisenstein, Toby K. 1942- *WhoAm 90*
Eisenstock, James A. 1928- *St&PR 91*
Eisenthal, Kenneth B. 1933- *WhoAm 90*
Eisentrager, James A 1929- *WhoAmA 91*
Eisenzimmer, Betty Wenner 1939- *WhoAmW 91*
Eiserer, Leonard Albert Carl 1916- *WhoE 91, WhoWor 91*
Eiserling, Frederick Allen 1938- *WhoAm 90*
Eisermann, Walter Friedrich 1922- *WhoWor 91*
Eisert, Debra Claire 1952- *WhoAmW 91*
Eisert, Edward Gaver 1948- *WhoEmL 91*
Eisfeld, Rainer 1941- *WhoWor 91*
Eisinger, Harry 1932- *WhoAmA 91*
Eisinger, Irene 1903- *IntWWM 90*
Eisinger, Miki Lynne 1948- *WhoAmW 91*
Eisinger, Peter Kendall 1942- *WhoAm 90*
Eisler, Colin Tobias 1931- *WhoAm 90*
Eisler, Edith 1925- *IntWWM 90*
Eisler, Georg 1928- *WhoWor 91*
Eisler, Nathan Mark 1958- *WhoEmL 91*
Eisler, Riane Tennenhaus 1931- *WhoAmW 91*
Eisler, Robert L 1926- *BiDrAPA 89*
Eisler, Susan Krawetz 1946- *St&PR 91, WhoAmW 91*
Eisley, Anthony *BioIn 16*
Eisma, Will Leendert 1929- *IntWWM 90*
Eisman, Esther 1950- *WhoAmW 91*
Eisman, Hyam 1927- *WhoE 91*
Eismont, Diane S. 1944- *St&PR 91*
Eisner, Alan M. 1939- *St&PR 91*
Eisner, Carole Swid 1937- *WhoAmA 91, WhoE 91*
Eisner, Christine Leuthold 1959- *WhoAmW 91*
Eisner, Dorothy 1906- *WhoAmA 91N*
Eisner, Elliot Wayne 1933- *WhoAmA 91*
Eisner, Eugene A *BiDrAPA 89*
Eisner, Harvey Brian 1958- *WhoEmL 91*
Eisner, Henry 1929- *BiDrAPA 89*
Eisner, Henry W. 1920- *St&PR 91*
Eisner, Howard 1935- *WhoAm 90*
Eisner, Janet Margaret 1940- *WhoAm 90, WhoAmW 91, WhoE 91*
Eisner, Joseph 1929- *WhoE 91*
Eisner, Kurt 1867-1919 *BioIn 16*
Eisner, Lawrence Brand 1951- *WhoE 91*
Eisner, Marvin M. 1938- *St&PR 91*
Eisner, Marvin Michael 1938- *WhoAm 90*
Eisner, Michael *BioIn 16*
Eisner, Michael 1942- *WorAlBi*
Eisner, Michael D. 1942- *St&PR 91*
Eisner, Michael Dammann 1942- *WhoAm 90*
Eisner, Peter Norman 1950- *WhoAm 90*
Eisner, Robert 1922- *WhoAm 90*
Eisner, Sandra *BioIn 16*
Eisner, Susanne Glock 1950- *WhoEmL 91*
Eisner, Thomas 1929- *WhoAm 90*
Eisner, Will 1917- *BioIn 16, EncACom, WhoAm 90*
Eisner, William 1927- *St&PR 91*
Eisnitz, Alan J *BiDrAPA 89*
Eison, Irving I. 1927- *St&PR 91*
Eiss, David H. 1942- *St&PR 91*
Eissenstat, Eric Spencer 1958- *WhoEmL 91*
Eissler, Holly *BioIn 16*
Eissler, Kurt Robert *BiDrAPA 89*
Eissler, Ruth S *BiDrAPA 89*
Eissler, Veda Alicia 1960- *WhoAmW 91*
Eissman, Mark Paul 1958- *WhoAm 90*
Eissmann, Robert Fred 1924- *WhoE 91*
Eissner, Bruce Allyn *BiDrAPA 89*
Eissner, Bruce Allyn 1944- *WhoE 91*
Eist, Harold I *BiDrAPA 89*
Eiswerth, Barry Neil 1942- *WhoAm 90*
Eiszner, James R. 1927- *St&PR 91*
Eiszner, James Richard 1927- *WhoAm 90, WhoE 91*
Eitan, Raphael 1926- *WhoWor 91*
Eitel, Cliffe Dean 1909- *WhoAmA 91N*
Eitel, Karl Emil 1928- *St&PR 91, WhoAm 90*
Eiteljorg, Harrison 1904- *WhoAmA 91*
Eiten, Geoffrey Joel 1950- *WhoEmL 91*
Eitinger, Leo *BiDrAPA 89*
Eitingon, Max *BioIn 16*
Eitner, Lorenz E A 1919- *WhoAmA 91*
Eitner, Lorenz Edwin Alfred 1919- *WhoAm 90*
Eitnier, Cynthia Kay 1953- *WhoAmW 91*
Eitzen, David Stanley 1934- *WhoAm 90*
Eizenstat, Stuart E. 1943- *WhoAm 90*
Eizou, Yokoyama 1929- *WhoWor 91*
Ejaz, Tahseen Ejaz 1934- *WhoWor 91*
Eji *WomWR*
Ejzak, Paul J. 1945- *St&PR 91*
Ek, Alan Ryan 1942- *WhoAm 90*
Ek, Harald 1936- *IntWWM 90*
Ekaireb, Hannah 1914- *BiDrAPA 89*
Ekandem, Dominic Ignatius 1917- *WhoWor 91*
Ekberg, Carl Edwin, Jr. 1920- *WhoAm 90*
Ekberg, David Jerome 1929- *St&PR 91*
Ekberg, Delores June 1939- *WhoWrEP 89*
Ekberg, Josef *PenDiDA 89*
Ekberg, Kent Francis 1947- *WhoEmL 91*
Ekblad, Stig Henrik Johan 1952- *WhoWor 91*
Ekblom, Harry Edward 1928- *WhoAm 90*
Ekdahl, Janis Kay 1946- *WhoAmA 91*
Ekdale, Allan Anton 1946- *WhoEmL 91*
Ekeblad, Frederick Alfred 1917- *WhoAm 90*
Ekedahl, James George 1946- *St&PR 91*
Ekelof, Gunnar 1907-1968 *DcScanL, EuWr 12, WorAlBi*
Ekelund, John Joseph 1928- *WhoAm 90*
Ekelund, Vilhelm 1880-1949 *DcScanL*
Eken, Elizabeth B 1917- *BiDrAPA 89*
Ekengard, Inger Aurora Maria 1949- *WhoWor 91*
Ekenstierna, Harvey Scott 1935- *WhoWor 91*
Eker, Dorothy 1925- *WhoWrEP 89*
Ekern, George Patrick 1931- *St&PR 91, WhoAm 90*
Ekern, Herman Lewis 1872-1954 *AmLegL*
Ekernas, Sven Anders 1945- *WhoE 91*
Ekert-Rotholz, Alice 1900- *EncCoWW*
Ekert-Rotholz, Alice Maria 1900- *ConAu 129*
Ekgren, Jacqueline Pattison 1937- *IntWWM 90*
Ekholm, Collyer Marden 1957- *BiDrAPA 89*
Ekholm, Ragnar Erik Gustaf 1921- *WhoWor 91*
Ekinci, Mehmet *BiDrAPA 89*
Ekins, Roger Robin 1945- *WhoEmL 91*
Ekins, William George 1956- *St&PR 91*
Ekizian, Michelle Lynne 1956- *IntWWM 90*
Ekland, Britt 1942- *BioIn 16, WorAlBi*
Ekle, Thomas Charles 1951- *St&PR 91, WhoEmL 91*
Eklof, Svea Christine 1951- *WhoAm 90*
Eklund, Donald Arthur 1929- *WhoAm 90*
Eklund, Donald Bruce 1944- *St&PR 91*
Eklund, George J. 1943- *St&PR 91*
Eklund, Gordon 1945- *RGTwCSF*
Eklund, Gordon Stewart 1945- *WhoWrEP 89*
Eklund, Hans 1927- *IntWWM 90*
Eklund, Louis E., Jr. 1931- *St&PR 91*
Eklund, Paul Joseph 1963- *WhoEmL 91*
Eklund, Reginald Ronald 1940- *St&PR 91*
Eklund, Robert L. 1931- *St&PR 91*
Eklund, Wayne O. 1929- *St&PR 91*
Ekman, Jan *BioIn 16*
Ekman, Kerstin 1933- *DcScanL*
Ekman, Lea Ann 1946- *WhoEmL 91*
Ekman, Paul 1934- *WhoAm 90*
Ekman, Richard *WhoAm 90*
Ekman, Thomas Arthur 1957- *WhoSSW 91*
Eknath Easwaran *BioIn 16*
Ekong, Etim Samuel 1953- *WhoE 91*
Ekonomou, Yvonne Patrice *BiDrAPA 89*
Ekovich, Steven Rudy 1948- *WhoWor 91*
Ekpu, Ray *BioIn 16*
Ekrom, Roy Herbert 1929- *WhoAm 90*
Ekselius, Eva 1942- *WhoWor 91*
Ekstract, Richard Evan 1931- *WhoAm 90*
Ekstrand, Bruce Rowland 1940- *WhoAm 90*
Ekstrand, John P *BiDrAPA 89*
Ekstrand, Margaret Elizabeth 1952- *WhoAmW 91*
Ekstrom, Bjorn Fredrik 1950- *WhoWor 91*
Ekstrom, Katina Bartsokas 1929- *WhoAmW 91*
Ekstrom, Michael Paul 1939- *WhoAm 90*
Ekstrom, Molly Anne 1929- *WhoWrEP 89*
Ekstrom, Norris K. 1927- *St&PR 91*
Ekstrom, Parmenia Migel 1908-1989 *BioIn 16, ConAu 130*
Ekstrom, Robert Carl 1917- *IntWWM 90, WhoWor 91*
Ekstrom, Ruth Burt 1931- *WhoAmW 91, WhoE 91*
Ekstrom, Walter F. 1927- *WhoAm 90*
Ekstrom, Walter F. 1937- *St&PR 91*
Ekstrom, William Ferdinand 1912- *WhoAm 90*
Ektare, Arun 1945- *WhoEmL 91*
Ekuan, Kenji 1929- *ConDes 90*
Ekvall, Bernt 1915- *WhoWor 91*
Ekwall, Merton L 1922- *BiDrAPA 89*
Ekwensi, C.O.D. *MajTwCW*
Ekwensi, Cyprian 1921- *MajTwCW*
El Greco 1541-1614 *BioIn 16*
El Huitlacoche *ConAu 131, HispWr 90*
El Mocho *WhNaAH*
El, Yusuf Ali 1948- *WhoWrEP 89*
El-Achkar, Issam 1962- *WhoE 91*
El-Akkad, Mohamed Ahmed 1954- *WhoWor 91*
El-Ansary, Adel Ibrahim 1941- *WhoAm 90*
El-Ayashy, Mamdouh Mahmoud 1954- *WhoWor 91*
El-Beshir, Abdel Monem M *BiDrAPA 89*
El-Borno, Bassam M.A. 1956- *BiDrAPA 89*
El-Dabh, Halim 1921- *IntWWM 90*
El Daly, Manzour Ahmed 1934- *WhoWor 91*
El-Duweini, Aadel Khalaf 1945- *WhoWor 91*
El-Fayoumy, Joanne Quinn 1930- *WhoAmW 91*
El-Gabalawy, Mohamed Hamed 1954- *BiDrAPA 89*
El Gabaly, Sherif-Mostafa 1949- *WhoWor 91*
El-Guebaly, Nady *BiDrAPA 89*
El-Hamalaway, Mohamed-Younis 1947- *WhoWor 91*
El Hanani, Jacob 1947- *WhoAmA 91*
El Khadem, Hassan S. 1923- *WhoAm 90, WhoWor 91*
El-Khalil, Khazem *BioIn 16*
El-Khalili, Nizar *BiDrAPA 89*
El Khatib, Isa Mahmoud 1934- *WhoWor 91*
El-Khazindar, Mohamed Ahmed 1931- *WhoWor 91*
El-Kholy, Samha 1925- *IntWWM 90*
El Kodsi, Baroukh 1923- *WhoE 91*
El-Mahdi, Anas Morsi 1935- *WhoAm 90*
El-Mahgoub, Rifaat 1926- *WhoWor 91*
El Mallakh, Kamal *BioIn 16*
El-Mallawany, J Jin *BiDrAPA 89*
El Mashhady, Afaf Abdel S *BiDrAPA 89*
El-Masry, Sayed Kassem 1936- *WhoWor 91*
El-Mufti, Said 1898-1989 *BioIn 16*
El-Nadi, Fathi Ali 1940- *WhoWor 91*
El-Najdawi, Eva 1950- *WhoEmL 91*
El-Qaddafi, Muammar 1942- *WorAlBi*
El-Rafei, Nabil Hassan 1913- *BiDrAPA 89*
El Saadawi, Nawal 1931- *FemiCLE*
El-Sabaawi, Mohamed A *BiDrAPA 89*
El-Sabaawi, Mohamed Abdel-Aziz 1948- *WhoE 91*
El Sabeh, Hani A. 1944- *St&PR 91*
El-Sadat, Anwar 1918-1981 *WorAlBi*
El Saffar, Ruth Snodgrass 1941- *WhoAm 90, WhoAmW 91*
El Sarraj, Eyad Rajab *BiDrAPA 89*
El-Sayed, Hosney Hussein 1925- *WhoWor 91*
El-Sayed, Mostafa Amr 1933- *WhoAm 90*
El-Shabazz, El Hajj Malik *MajTwCW*
El Shammaa, Norma N *BiDrAPA 89*
El-Shawan Castelo-Branco, Salwa 1950- *IntWWM 90*
El-Sherbini, Abdel-Aziz 1926- *WhoWor 91*
El-Turk, Said Nejam 1946- *WhoWor 91*
El-Yousef, M Khaled *BiDrAPA 89*
Ela, Erik 1957- *WhoE 91*
Elad, Emanuel 1935- *WhoAm 90*
Elafros, Bernard 1927- *St&PR 91*
Elam, Albert Garland, II 1955- *WhoEmL 91*
Elam, Andres Gregory, II 1932- *ODwPR 91*
Elam, Andrew Gregory, II 1932- *WhoSSW 91*
Elam, Gene G. 1939- *St&PR 91*
Elam, Harper Johnston, III 1926- *St&PR 91, WhoAm 90*
Elam, Harry B. 1929- *St&PR 91*
Elam, Joe 1931- *St&PR 91*
Elam, John Carlton 1924- *WhoAm 90*
Elam, Joseph Barton 1821-1885 *AmLegL*
Elam, Leslie Albert 1938- *WhoAm 90*
Elam, Lloyd C 1928- *BiDrAPA 89*
Elam, Lloyd Charles 1928- *WhoAm 90*
Elam, Merrill 1943- *WomArch [port]*
Elam, Sam Ray 1932- *St&PR 91*
Elam, Sandra Michael *BiDrAPA 89*
Elam, W. Dale 1948- *St&PR 91*
Elander, Eugene Francis 1937- *WhoE 91*
Elander, Richard Paul 1932- *WhoE 91*
Elarth, Vernon Allison 1944- *St&PR 91*
Elashkar, Mursi Mahmoud 1927- *WhoWor 91*
Elath, Eliahu 1903-1990 *ConAu 132, NewYTBS 90 [port]*
Elaw, Zilpha *FemiCLE*
Elbaum, Charles 1926- *WhoAm 90*
Elbaum, Jerome David 1939- *WhoE 91*
Elbaum, Melvin 1934- *St&PR 91*
Elbaum-David, Jean 1960- *WhoAmW 91*
Elberfeld, Kid 1875- *Ballpl 90*
Elberg, Dale Allen 1950- *St&PR 91*
Elberg, Darryl Gerald 1944- *WhoAm 90*
Elberg, Sanford Samuel 1913- *WhoAm 90*
Elberger, Ronald Edward 1945- *WhoEmL 91*
Elberry, Zainab Abdelhaliem 1948- *WhoEmL 91*
Elberson, Elwood L. 1918- *St&PR 91*
Elberson, Robert E. 1928- *St&PR 91*
Elberson, Robert Evans 1928- *WhoAm 90*
Elbert, Edwin A. *BioIn 16*
Elbert, Lisa Marie 1958- *WhoEmL 91*
Elbert, Virginie Fowler 1912- *AuBYP 90*
Elbery, Kathleen Marie 1959- *WhoAmW 91*
Elbilia, Bruce David 1958- *St&PR 91*
Elbirlik, Kemal H 1922- *BiDrAPA 89*
Elble, Rodger Jacob 1948- *WhoEmL 91*
Elchamo, Jason *HispWr 90*
Elchamo, Sebastian *ConAu 132*
Elchynski, Theodore Frank 1936- *St&PR 91*
Elcock, W.B., Jr. 1920- *St&PR 91*
Elconin, Michael Henry 1953- *WhoEmL 91*
Eldeiry, Bahig Riad 1944- *WhoE 91*
Eldem, Sedad Hakki 1908-1988 *BioIn 16*
Elden, Douglas Lloyd 1947- *WhoEmL 91*
Elden, Gary Michael 1944- *WhoAm 90*
Elder, Alexander *BiDrAPA 89*
Elder, Alfred Stratton 1936- *WhoSSW 91*
Elder, Andrew William 1951- *St&PR 91*
Elder, Arthur John 1874- *WhoAmA 91N*
Elder, Carol 1935- *WhoAmW 91*
Elder, David Morton 1936- *WhoAmA 91*
Elder, Dean *BioIn 16*
Elder, Douglas P. 1951- *St&PR 91*
Elder, Douglas Paul 1951- *WhoEmL 91*
Elder, Eldon 1921- *WhoAm 90*
Elder, Elliott Clay 1954- *WhoSSW 91*
Elder, Evelyn *TwCCr&M 91*
Elder, Fred Kingsley, Jr. 1921- *WhoAm 90*
Elder, Gary Michael 1939- *WhoWrEP 89*
Elder, Harvey Lynn 1934- *WhoSSW 91*
Elder, James H., Jr. 1924- *St&PR 91*
Elder, James Lanphere 1914- *WhoAm 90*
Elder, Janice Kay *BiDrAPA 89*
Elder, Jean Katherine 1941- *WhoAm 90, WhoAmW 91*
Elder, John N. 1930- *St&PR 91*
Elder, John Richard 1948- *St&PR 91*
Elder, Joseph Walter 1930- *WhoAm 90*
Elder, Joyce Elaine 1945- *WhoEmL 91*
Elder, Karl Curtis 1948- *WhoWrEP 89*
Elder, Leon *WhoWrEP 89*
Elder, Lonne, III 1931- *DrBlPA 90*
Elder, M.A. 1926- *St&PR 91*
Elder, Mark *BioIn 16*
Elder, Mark 1947- *PenDiMP*
Elder, Mark Philip 1947- *IntWWM 90, WhoE 91, WhoWor 91*
Elder, Muldoon 1935- *WhoAmA 91*
Elder, Paul G. 1917- *St&PR 91*
Elder, Peter Percival 1823-1914 *AmLegL*
Elder, R Bruce 1947- *WhoAmA 91*
Elder, Rex Alfred 1917- *WhoAm 90*
Elder, Robert Earnest 1934- *WhoSSW 91*
Elder, Robert George 1940- *St&PR 91*
Elder, Robert L. 1946- *St&PR 91*
Elder, Robert Laurie 1938- *WhoAm 90*
Elder, Robert Oscar 1941- *WhoSSW 91*
Elder, Samuel Adams 1929- *WhoAm 90*
Elder, Samuel Marshall 1847- *AmLegL*
Elder, Shirley 1931- *ConAu 132*
Elder, Stewart Taylor 1917- *WhoAm 90*
Elder, T.L. 1938- *St&PR 91*
Elder, William Hanna 1913- *WhoAm 90*
Elderfield, John 1943- *ConAu 132, WhoAmA 91*
Elderkin, Charles Edwin 1930- *WhoAm 90*
Elderkin, Dana Vance 1955- *WhoEmL 91*
Elderkin, Edwin Judge 1932- *WhoAm 90*
Elderkin, Noble S. 1810?-1875 *AmLegL*
Elders, Joycelyn *BioIn 16*
Elders, M. Joycelyn 1933- *WhoAm 90, WhoAmW 91*
Elders, Robert K. 1941- *St&PR 91*
Eldershaw, Flora 1897-1956 *FemiCLE*
Eldlitz, Doroth Meigs 1891-1976 *WhoAmA 91N*
Eldon, Elizabeth Jane *BiDrAPA 89*
Eldred, Charles *EncO&P 3*
Eldred, Dale 1934- *BioIn 16*
Eldred, Gerald Marcus 1934- *WhoAm 90*
Eldred, Jeffrey Laine 1956- *WhoEmL 91*
Eldred, Kenneth A. 1943- *BioIn 16*
Eldred, Kenneth McKechnie 1929- *St&PR 91, WhoAm 90, WhoWor 91*
Eldred, Stanley H *BiDrAPA 89*
Eldred, Willard G. 1928- *St&PR 91*
Eldredge, Adda 1864-1955 *BioIn 16*
Eldredge, Bruce B 1952- *WhoAmA 91*
Eldredge, Bruce Beard 1952- *WhoAm 90*
Eldredge, Charles Child, III 1944- *WhoAm 90, WhoAmA 91*
Eldredge, Hanford Wentworth 1909- *WhoAm 90*

Eldredge, James Henry 1920- *BiDrAPA 89*
Eldredge, John M. 1954- *St&PR 91*
Eldredge, Joseph Lippincott 1924- *WhoAm 90*
Eldredge, Mary Agnes 1942- *WhoAmA 91*
Eldredge, Stuart Edson 1902- *WhoAmA 91*
Eldredge, William Augustus, Jr. 1925- *WhoAm 90*
Eldridge, Anthony Ray 1955- *WhoSSW 91*
Eldridge, Charles Arthur 1949- *WhoSSW 91*
Eldridge, David Carlton 1949- *WhoAm 90*
Eldridge, Douglas Hilton 1916- *WhoAm 90*
Eldridge, Edward 1829-1892 *AmLegL*
Eldridge, Erwin James, III 1952- *WhoEmL 91*
Eldridge, Florence 1901- *NotWoAT*
Eldridge, Florence 1901-1988 *AnObit 1988, BioIn 16*
Eldridge, Frederic Louis 1924- *WhoAm 90*
Eldridge, George Thomas, Jr. 1942- *St&PR 91*
Eldridge, Henry Douglas 1935- *WhoE 91*
Eldridge, James F. 1946- *St&PR 91*
Eldridge, James Francis 1946- *WhoAm 90*
Eldridge, John Cole 1933- *WhoAm 90, WhoE 91*
Eldridge, Larry 1932- *WhoAm 90*
Eldridge, Marie Delaney 1926- *WhoAmW 91*
Eldridge, Richard Mark 1951- *WhoEmL 91*
Eldridge, Robert Coulter 1917- *WhoSSW 91*
Eldridge, Robert Huyck 1938- *WhoAm 90*
Eldridge, Robert J. 1944- *St&PR 91*
Eldridge, Roy 1911- *WorAlBi*
Eldridge, Roy 1911-1989 *AnObit 1989, BioIn 16, DrBIPA 90, OxCPMus*
Eldridge, Scott Anthony 1954- *WhoE 91*
Eleanor *WomWR*
Eleanor of Aquitaine 1122?-1204 *WomWR, WorAlBi*
Eleanor of Arborea *WomWR*
Eleazar of Garniza *EncO&P 3*
Electric Light Orchestra, The *EncPR&S 89*
Elefant, Bernard 1946- *St&PR 91*
Eleff, Michael Kay 1949- *BiDrAPA 89*
Elefterias-Kostakidis, Eleni 1957- *IntWWM 90*
Eleftheriades, Andreas Nicos 1956- *WhoWor 91*
Elegant, Robert 1928- *ConAu 30NR*
Elegant, Robert Sampson 1928- *WhoAm 90*
Elen, Gus 1862-1940 *OxCPMus*
Elena, Princess 1963- *BioIn 16*
Elenson, Joann 1952- *St&PR 91*
Elent, Roza 1944- *WhoAmW 91*
Eleonore of Austria 1433-1480 *EncCoWW*
Eleonore of Scotland *EncCoWW*
Elequin, Cleto, Jr. 1933- *WhoWor 91*
Eler, Marjorie Alt 1945- *BiDrAPA 89*
Elerding, John Ralph 1952- *St&PR 91*
Elers, David *PenDiDA 89*
Elers, John Philip *PenDiDA 89*
Elers, Karl E. 1938- *St&PR 91*
Elers, Karl Emerson 1938- *WhoAm 90*
Elestone, Sarah *BiDEWW*
Eleta, Graciela Quelquejeu de 1939- *WhoWor 91*
Elevation Express *NewAgMG*
Elevitch, Morton D. 1925- *WhoWrEP 89*
Elexner, Stuart B. 1928- *St&PR 91*
Elexpuru, Manuel 1930- *St&PR 91*
Eley, Elem Henry 1953- *IntWWM 90*
Eley, Geoff 1949- *ConAu 129*
Eley, Lynn W. 1925- *WhoAm 90*
Eley, Randall Robbi 1952- *WhoSSW 91*
Eley, Thomas Wendell 1953- *WhoE 91*
Elfbrandt, Barbara *BioIn 16*
Elfelt, James Sidle 1929- *WhoAm 90*
Elfenbein, Cherie I *BiDrAPA 89*
Elfenbein, Emanuel 1947- *BiDrAPA 89*
Elfenbein, Mickey 1947- *St&PR 91, WhoAm 90*
Elferdink, Terry Lee 1947- *WhoEmL 91*
Elfers, Lawrence Anthony 1938- *St&PR 91*
Elfers, William 1918- *St&PR 91, WhoAm 90*
Elfert, Donald Lee 1933- *WhoSSW 91*
Elfin, Mel 1929- *WhoAm 90*
Elfman, Eric Michael 1954- *WhoEmL 91*
Elfner, Albert H., III 1944- *St&PR 91*
Elfner, Albert Henry, III 1944- *WhoAm 90*
Elford, Catherine Williams 1951- *WhoAmW 91*
Elfrey, Priscilla 1930- *WhoAmW 91*
Elfstrom, Dorothy Lillian Bettencourt *WhoAm 90, WhoSSW 91*
Elftmann, Joel A. 1940- *St&PR 91*
Elfvin, John Thomas 1917- *WhoAm 90*
Elgabalawi, Fayez K. 1952- *BiDrAPA 89*
Elgar, Edward 1857-1934 *BioIn 16, PenDiMP A, WorAlBi*
Elgart, Beltran *BiDrAPA 89*
Elgart, Charlie *BioIn 16*
Elgart, Larry Joseph 1922- *WhoAm 90*
Elgart, Les 1918- *OxCPMus*
Elgart, Mervyn L. 1933- *WhoAm 90*
Elgavish, Ada 1946- *WhoAmW 91*
Elgee, D.J. 1943- *St&PR 91*
Elgee, Neil Johnson 1926- *WhoAm 90*
Elger, William Robert, Jr. 1950- *WhoEmL 91, WhoWor 91*
Elgin, Frank S *BiDrAPA 89*
Elgin, John Tom 1940- *WhoSSW 91*
Elgin, John Warren 1943- *St&PR 91*
Elgin, Joseph Clifford 1904-1988 *BioIn 16*
Elgin, Renee Kay 1953- *WhoEmL 91*
Elgin, Sarah Carlisle Roberts 1945- *WhoAmW 91*
Elgin, Suzette Haden 1936- *FemiCLE*
Elhoff, Charles Robert, Jr. 1946- *WhoSSW 91*
Elia, Hany Wadie 1955- *BiDrAPA 89*
Elia, Josephine *BiDrAPA 89*
Elia, Lee Constantine 1937- *WhoAm 90*
Elia, Michele 1945- *WhoWor 91*
Elia, Mumatz Hamid 1945- *WhoWor 91*
Eliachar, Haim S. *BioIn 16, NewYTBS 90*
Eliade, Mircea 1907- *EncO&P 3*
Eliade, Mircea 1907-1986 *BioIn 16, ConAu 30NR, EncPaPR 91, MajTwCW*
Eliahu, Mordechai 1928- *WhoWor 91*
Eliakim, Marcel 1921- *WhoWor 91*
Elias, Abigail 1952- *WhoEmL 91*
Elias, Al Munro 1872-1939 *Ballpl 90*
Elias, Amy P *ODwPR 91*
Elias, Arthur William 1927- *St&PR 91*
Elias, Blas, Jr. 1936- *WhoHisp 91*
Elias, Brian David 1948- *IntWWM 90*
Elias, David 1925- *St&PR 91*
Elias, Diana Linda 1955- *WhoAmW 91*
Elias, Ellen Victoria 1959- *WhoAmW 91*
Elias, Fred 1913- *St&PR 91*
Elias, Harold John 1920- *WhoAm 90, WhoAmA 91*
Elias, Irving 1899-1988 *BioIn 16*
Elias, John W. 1940- *WhoAm 90*
Elias, Julius Anthony 1925- *WhoAm 90*
Elias, Lee 1920- *EncACom*
Elias, Marisel 1956- *WhoHisp 91*
Elias, Norbert 1897-1990 *ConAu 132*
Elias, Paul S. 1926- *St&PR 91, WhoAm 90*
Elias, Peter 1923- *WhoAm 90*
Elias, Robert Henry 1914- *WhoAm 90*
Elias, Rosalind 1929- *IntWWM 90, PenDiMP*
Elias, Rosalind 1931- *WhoAm 90*
Elias, Samuel J. 1919- *St&PR 91*
Elias, Samy E. G. 1930- *WhoAm 90*
Elias, Sarah Davis 1934- *WhoAmW 91*
Elias, Sharon Louise 1941- *WhoAmW 91*
Elias, Sheila *WhoAmA 91*
Elias, T. O. 1914- *BioIn 16*
Elias, Taslim Olawale 1914- *BioIn 16*
Elias, Thomas Ittan 1947- *WhoEmL 91*
Elias, Thomas Sam 1942- *WhoAm 90*
Eliasberg, Jay 1919- *St&PR 91*
Eliasberg, Louis, Jr. 1929- *St&PR 91*
Eliasberg, Robert J. 1906-1989 *BioIn 16*
Eliasek, Thomas Gary 1951- *St&PR 91*
Eliasen, Reine *WhoWrEP 89*
Eliashof, Byron A 1935- *BiDrAPA 89*
Eliason, Edward Best 1940- *St&PR 91*
Eliason, James T., III 1926- *St&PR 91*
Eliason, Nancy Carol 1929- *WhoAmW 91*
Eliason, Norman Ellsworth 1907- *WhoAm 90*
Eliason, Robert Erwin 1933- *IntWWM 90*
Eliason, Shirley 1926-1988 *WhoAmA 91N*
Eliasoph, Paula 1895- *WhoAmA 91N*
Eliasoph, Philip *WhoAmA 91*
Eliassen, Frederick C. 1940- *WhoE 91*
Eliassen, Jon Eric 1947- *WhoAm 90*
Eliassen, Rolf 1911- *WhoAm 90*
Eliasson, Baldur 1937- *WhoWor 91*
Eliasson, Gunnar K. 1937- *WhoWor 91*
Eliasson, Jan K. 1940- *WhoWor 91*
Eliasson, Leif Sture Rudolf 1939- *WhoWor 91*
Eliasson, Sven Olaf 1933- *IntWWM 90*
Elick, Catherine Lilly 1953- *WhoWrEP 89*
Elicker, Gordon Leonard 1940- *WhoAm 90*
Elicker, Paul H. 1923- *St&PR 91, WhoAm 90*
Elie, Jean Andre 1943- *WhoAm 90*
Eliel, Ernest Ludwig 1921- *WhoAm 90*
Eliel, Stefan E. 1936- *St&PR 91*
Eliezar *EncO&P 3*
Elikann, Lawrence S. 1923- *WhoAm 90*
Elimimian, Isaac Irabor 1948- *WhoWor 91*
Elin, Caren Mindy 1950- *WhoAmW 91*
Elin, Ronald John 1939- *WhoAm 90*
Elina, Riccardo Anthony 1961- *WhoSSW 91*
Elins, Roberta 1955- *WhoAmW 91*
Elinski, Michael Joseph 1955- *BiDrAPA 89*
Elinson, Elaine 1947- *WhoAmW 91*
Elinson, Henry David 1935- *WhoWor 91*
Elinson, Jack 1917- *BioIn 16, WhoAm 90*
Elioff, Irma Mercado 1956- *WhoHisp 91*
Elion, Arthur S. 1918- *St&PR 91*
Elion, Gertrude B. 1918- *WorAlBi*
Elion, Gertrude Belle 1918- *BioIn 16, WhoAm 90, WhoAmW 91, WhoSSW 91, WhoWor 91*
Elion, Herbert A. 1923- *WhoAm 90, WhoWor 91*
Elion, Herbert Aaron 1923- *St&PR 91*
Eliot, Alexander 1919- *WhoAm 90*
Eliot, Charles W. *BioIn 16*
Eliot, Charles William 1834-1926 *WorAlBi*
Eliot, Charles William John 1928- *WhoAm 90*
Eliot, Dan *MajTwCW*
Eliot, George 1819-1880 *BioIn 16, EncPaPR 91, FemiCLE, WorAlBi, WrPh*
Eliot, Jared 1685-1763 *EncCRAm*
Eliot, John 1604-1690 *EncCRAm, WhNaAH, WorAlBi*
Eliot, Judi 1946- *WhoAmW 91*
Eliot, Lucy Carter *WhoAmA 91*
Eliot, Lucy Carter 1913- *WhoAm 90, WhoAmW 91, WhoE 91, WhoWor 91*
Eliot, Robert Salim 1929- *WhoAm 90*
Eliot, T. S. 1888-1965 *BioIn 16*
Eliot, T S 1888-1965 *MajTwCW*
Eliot, T. S. 1888-1965 *WorAlBi*
Eliot, T S 1888-1965 *WrPh*
Eliot, Theodore Lyman, Jr. 1928- *WhoAm 90*
Eliot, Thomas Stearns 1888-1965 *BioIn 16*
Eliot, Valerie *BioIn 16*
Elisa *EncCoWW*
Elisa Bonaparte 1777-1820 *WomWR*
Elisa Lucca 1777-1820 *WomWR*
Elisabeth of Nassau-Saarbrucken 1397?-1456 *EncCoWW*
Elisabeth of Schonau 1129-1164 *EncCoWW*
Elisar, Patricia Garside 1934- *WhoAm 90*
Elisaveta Ivanova Zirkowa 1888-1949 *EncCoWW*
Eliscu, Frank 1912- *WhoAmA 91*
Elise *EncCoWW*
Elish, Herbert *St&PR 91*
Elish, Herbert 1933- *WhoAm 90, WhoSSW 91*
Elisha, Walter Y. *St&PR 91*
Elisha, Walter Y. 1932- *WhoAm 90, WhoSSW 91*
Elisheva *EncCoWW*
Elisofon, Eliot 1911-1973 *WhoAmA 91N*
Elitzik, Paul 1945- *WhoWrEP 89*
Eliza *BiDEWW*
Elizabeth *WomWR*
Elizabeth 1866-1941 *BioIn 16*
Elizabeth 1900- *WhoWor 91*
Elizabeth I 1533-1603 *WomWR [port], WorAlBi*
Elizabeth I 1709-1762 *WomWR*
Elizabeth II 1926- *WhoAm 90, WhoWor 91, WomWR [port], WorAlBi*
Elizabeth, Empress of Russia 1709-1762 *BioIn 16*
Elizabeth of Bohemia, Queen 1596-1662 *BiDEWW*
Elizabeth of Gorlitz *WomWR*
Elizabeth of Luxembourg *WomWR*
Elizabeth of Poland *WomWR*
Elizabeth Petrovna 1709-1762 *BioIn 16*
Elizabeth, Princess of Toro *BioIn 16*
Elizabeth, Queen 1465-1503 *BioIn 16*
Elizabeth, Queen 1900- *BioIn 16*
Elizabeth, Queen of England 1533-1603 *BiDEWW*
Elizabeth I, Queen of England 1533-1603 *BioIn 16, FemiCLE*
Elizabeth II, Queen of Great Britain 1926- *BioIn 16*
Elizabeth, Ann *WhoWrEP 89*
Elizaitis, Gunther J. 1944- *St&PR 91*
Elizalde, Fred 1908-1969 *OxCPMus*
Elizondo, Ann Mock 1957- *WhoAmW 91, WhoEmL 91*
Elizondo, Edelmiro Bonifacio 1946- *WhoE 91*
Elizondo, Eduardo Luis 1935- *WhoE 91*
Elizondo, Hector 1936- *WhoAm 90, WhoHisp 91*
Elizondo, Patricia Irene 1955- *WhoHisp 91*
Elizondo, Raul 1948- *St&PR 91, WhoSSW 91*
Elizondo, Rey Soto 1940- *WhoHisp 91*
Elizondo, Sergio *ConAu 131, HispWr 90*
Elizondo, Sergio D. 1930- *BioIn 16, ConAu 131, HispWr 90, WhoHisp 91*
Elizondo, Virgil P. *WhoHisp 91*
Elizondo, Virgilio P. *BioIn 16*
Elkamel, Farag Mohamed 1952- *WhoWor 91*
Elkan, Gerald Hugh 1929- *WhoAm 90*
Elkan-Ho, Betty Yu-Lin 1930- *WhoWrEP 89*
Elkan-Moore, Brooke 1951- *WhoE 91*
Elkann, Alain *BioIn 16*
Elkashef, Ahmed Mohamed *BiDrAPA 89*
Elkema, Claudia Elise 1964- *WhoE 91*
Elkes, Anita 1924- *St&PR 91*
Elkes, Charmian 1919- *BiDrAPA 89*
Elkes, Elchanan 1879-1944 *BioIn 16*
Elkes, Joel J *BiDrAPA 89*
Elkes, Terrence Allen 1934- *WhoAm 90*
Elkhadem, Saad 1932- *ConAu 131*
Elkhadem, Saad Eldin Amin 1932- *WhoAm 90*
Elkies, Leonard 1924- *St&PR 91*
Elkies, William 1949- *St&PR 91*
Elkin, Benjamin 1911- *AuBYP 90*
Elkin, Bernice B *BiDrAPA 89*
Elkin, Beverly Dawn 1933- *WhoAmA 91*
Elkin, H V *ConAu 30NR*
Elkin, Irvin *WhoAm 90*
Elkin, Milton 1916- *WhoAm 90*
Elkin, Rowena Caldwell 1917- *WhoAmA 91*
Elkin, Scott Richard 1950- *BiDrAPA 89*
Elkin, Stanley 1930- *BioIn 16, WorAlBi*
Elkin, Stanley L 1930- *MajTwCW*
Elkin, Stanley Lawrence 1930- *WhoAm 90, WhoWrEP 89*
Elkind, David 1931- *WhoAm 90*
Elkind, Jerome Bernard 1939- *WhoWor 91*
Elkind, Mortimer Murray 1922- *WhoAm 90*
Elkind, Sue Nathanson 1943- *WhoAmW 91*
Elkind, Thomas I. 1951- *WhoAm 90*
Elkington, George Richard 1801-1865 *PenDiDA 89*
Elkington, Henry 1810?-1852 *PenDiDA 89*
Elkins, Aaron J. 1935- *TwCCr&M 91*
Elkins, Alan M 1930- *BiDrAPA 89*
Elkins, Albert Franklin 1943- *WhoE 91*
Elkins, Chris Charles 1929- *St&PR 91*
Elkins, David Earl 1954- *WhoEmL 91*
Elkins, David J. 1941- *WhoAm 90*
Elkins, Dov Peretz 1937- *AuBYP 90, ConAu 30NR*
Elkins, Francis Clark 1923- *WhoAm 90, WhoSSW 91*
Elkins, George W. 1899- *St&PR 91*
Elkins, Glen Ray 1933- *WhoAm 90*
Elkins, Hillard 1929- *WhoAm 90*
Elkins, James A., Jr. 1919- *St&PR 91*
Elkins, James Anderson, III 1952- *WhoSSW 91*
Elkins, James Anderson, Jr. 1919- *WhoAm 90, WhoSSW 91, WhoWor 91*
Elkins, James Andrew, Jr. 1940- *WhoSSW 91*
Elkins, Ken J. 1937- *WhoAm 90*
Elkins, Lane 1925- *WhoAmA 91*
Elkins, Lincoln Feltch 1918- *WhoAm 90*
Elkins, Lloyd Edwin, Sr. 1912- *WhoAm 90*
Elkins, Margreta 1932- *IntWWM 90*
Elkins, Merry Catherine 1948- *WhoWrEP 89*
Elkins, Mike *BioIn 16*
Elkins, Patricia A. 1941- *WhoAmW 91*
Elkins, Ronald Flagg, Jr. 1936- *WhoAm 90*
Elkins, Stanley Maurice 1925- *WhoAm 90*
Elkins, Stephen Benton 1841-1911 *BiDrUSE 89*
Elkins, Steven Paul 1949- *WhoWor 91*
Elkins, Stevens James 1958- *WhoEmL 91*
Elkins, Toni Marcus 1946- *WhoAmA 91*
Elkins, Wilson Homer 1908- *WhoE 91*
Elko, Nicholas Thomas 1909- *WhoAm 90*
Elkomoss, Sabry Gobran 1925- *WhoWor 91*
Elkon, Robert 1928-1983 *WhoAmA 91N*
Elkouri, Frank 1921- *WhoAm 90*
Elkowitz, Lloyd Kent 1936- *WhoE 91*
Elks, Hazel Hulbert 1916- *WhoAm 90*
Elks, William Chester, Jr. 1952- *WhoSSW 91*
Elksne, "rija 1928- *EncCoWW*
Elkun, Leonard David 1940- *BiDrAPA 89*
Elkus, Christopher J. *St&PR 91*
Elkus, Howard F. 1938- *St&PR 91*
Elkus, Howard Felix 1938- *WhoAm 90*
Elkus, Jonathan Britton 1931- *IntWWM 90*
Elkus, Philip 1926- *St&PR 91*
Elkus, Richard J. 1910- *WhoAm 90*
Elkus, Richard J., Jr. 1935- *WhoAm 90, WhoWor 91*
Ella, Istvan 1947- *IntWWM 90*
Ellacuria Beas Coechea, Ignacio *BioIn 16*
Ellard, Bret Lewis 1958- *WhoSSW 91*
Ellard, Stanley Mark 1953- *WhoSSW 91*
Ellard, Timothy Daniel 1934- *St&PR 91*
Ellebrecht, Mark Gerard 1954- *WhoEmL 91*
Elledge, Myles Fletcher *WhoE 91*
Elledge, Richard D. 1941- *WhoAm 90*
Elledge, Richard Douglas 1941- *St&PR 91*
Elledge, Scott Bowen 1914- *WhoAm 90, WhoWrEP 89*
Ellefson, James C. 1951- *WhoEmL 91*
Ellefson, Karen Ann 1943- *WhoSSW 91*
Ellegard, H. Alvar 1919- *WhoWor 91*
Ellegard, Sandra 1935- *St&PR 91*
Ellegood, Donald Russell 1924- *WhoAm 90*
Elleinstein, Jean 1927- *BiDFrPL*

Ellemann-Jensen, Uffe 1941- *WhoWor 91*
Ellemers, Jo Egbert 1930- *WhoWor 91*
Ellen *EncCoWW*
Ellen, Barbara 1938- *AuBYP 90*
Ellen, Roberta Doris 1944- *St&PR 91*
Ellenberg, Jack 1935- *BiDrAPA 89*
Ellenberg, Ludwig 1946- *WhoWor 91*
Ellenberger, Diane Marie 1946- *WhoAmW 91*
Ellenberger, Henri F *BiDrAPA 89*
Ellenberger, Jack Stuart 1930- *WhoAm 90*
Ellenberger-Thomas, Margaret Ann 1951- *WhoAmW 91*
Ellenbogen, George 1934- *WhoAm 90*
Ellenbogen, Leon 1927- *WhoAm 90*
Ellenbogen, Milton Joseph 1935- *WhoAm 90, WhoWrEP 89*
Ellenbogen, Tina Rochelle 1952- *WhoAmW 91*
Ellenbogen Handelsman, Joan 1954- *WhoEmL 91*
Ellenburg, Fred Carroll 1931- *WhoSSW 91*
Ellenburg, Laura Diane 1954- *WhoSSW 91*
Ellender, Patti Jean 1960- *WhoAmW 91*
Ellenis, Emmanuel *BioIn 16*
Ellenoff, Theodore 1924- *St&PR 91*
Ellens, J Harold 1932- *ConAu 31NR*
Ellentuch, Leonard I. 1938- *St&PR 91*
Ellentuck, Shan *AuBYP 90*
Ellenwood, Clayton John 1930- *St&PR 91*
Ellenzweig, Allen Bruce 1950- *WhoAmA 91, WhoE 91*
Eller, Brenda Ann 1959- *WhoAmW 91, WhoEmL 91*
Eller, Bruno 1936- *St&PR 91*
Eller, Charles Howe 1904- *WhoAm 90*
Eller, Charles Manning 1929- *St&PR 91*
Eller, David Gallaway 1938- *WhoSSW 91, WhoWor 91*
Eller, Evelyn 1933- *WhoAmA 91*
Eller, Hod 1894-1961 *Ballpl 90*
Eller, James E. 1931- *St&PR 91*
Eller, James Frederick 1956- *WhoEmL 91*
Eller, Joe Rodney, Jr. 1960- *WhoSSW 91*
Eller, Joseph Jordan 1896-1989 *BioIn 16*
Eller, Karl 1928- *WhoAm 90*
Eller, Leona Zigler 1910- *WhoAmW 91*
Eller, Leslie Robert 1949- *WhoEmL 91*
Eller, Scott *WhoWrEP 89*
Eller, Warren Bernson 1931- *WhoWor 91*
Eller, William Kyle 1934- *WhoSSW 91, WhoWor 91*
Eller, William Whitney, Jr. 1933- *St&PR 91*
Ellerbe, Frank 1895-1988 *Ballpl 90*
Ellerbe, Thomas Farr 1892-1987 *BioIn 16*
Ellerbe, Wilbur Spurgeon 1936- *WhoSSW 91*
Ellerbee, Garner McKenzie 1927- *St&PR 91*
Ellerbee, Linda *BioIn 16*
Ellerbee, Linda 1944- *WhoAm 90, WhoAmW 91*
Ellerbroek, Wallace C 1920- *BiDrAPA 89*
Ellerbrook, Niel Cochran 1948- *St&PR 91, WhoAm 90*
Ellerby, Alfred McKay 1911- *St&PR 91*
Ellerby, John H. 1939- *St&PR 91*
Ellerd, Gary L. 1950- *St&PR 91*
Ellerhorst, William J. 1929- *St&PR 91*
Ellerhusen, Florence Cooney *WhoAmA 91N*
Ellerhusen, Ulric H 1879-1957 *WhoAmA 91N*
Ellerin, Albert A. 1915- *St&PR 91*
Ellerin, Charles 1918- *St&PR 91*
Ellerman, Gene *WhoWrEP 89*
Ellerman, Winifred 1894-1983 *DcNaB 1981*
Ellers, Elizabeth Anne 1959- *WhoE 91, WhoEmL 91*
Ellert, Martha Schwandt 1940- *WhoAmW 91*
Ellerton, J.J. 1944- *St&PR 91*
Ellertson, Jaime 1957- *WhoE 91*
Ellery, John Blaise 1920- *WhoAm 90*
Ellery, William 1727-1820 *EncCRAm*
Elles, Frank Dee 1925- *St&PR 91*
Ellestad, David Elver 1940- *St&PR 91*
Ellet, Elizabeth 1812?-1877 *FemiCLE*
Ellett, Alan Sidney 1930- *St&PR 91, WhoAm 90*
Ellfeldt, Howard James 1937- *WhoAm 90*
Elli, Neal P. 1956- *St&PR 91*
Ellice, Douglas Vickers, Jr. 1947- *WhoWor 91*
Ellickson, Robert Chester 1941- *WhoAm 90*
Ellicott, John LeMoyne 1929- *WhoAm 90*
Ellicott, Thomas 1777-1859 *EncABHB 6*
Ellien, William George 1955- *BiDrAPA 89*
Elliff, John Eric 1961- *WhoEmL 91*
Ellig, Bruce Robert 1936- *St&PR 91, WhoAm 90, WhoE 91, WhoWor 91*
Elligett, Raymond Thomas, Jr. 1953- *WhoEmL 91*
Ellin, Leon R. 1943- *WhoAm 90*
Ellin, Marvin 1923- *WhoAm 90, WhoWor 91*
Ellin, Stanley 1916-1986 *MajTwCW, TwCCr&M 91*
Ellin, Sue *WhoE 91*
Ellingboe, Bradley Ross 1958- *IntWWM 90*
Ellingboe, James 1937- *WhoE 91*
Ellingboe, John Keith 1950- *WhoEmL 91*
Ellinger, Ilona E 1913- *WhoAmA 91*
Ellinger, Steven 1952- *WhoEmL 91*
Ellinghaus, William M. 1922- *St&PR 91, WhoAm 90*
Ellingsen, Kenneth J. 1956- *St&PR 91*
Ellingsen, Olav 1941- *WhoWor 91*
Ellingson, John Rostad 1938- *St&PR 91*
Ellingson, Linda Jeanne 1947- *IntWWM 90*
Ellingson, Richard A. 1936- *St&PR 91*
Ellingson, Steve 1910- *WhoAm 90*
Ellingson, William John 1933- *WhoAmA 91*
Ellingsworth, Marilyn L. 1947- *WhoAmW 91*
Ellington, Duke 1899-1974 *BioIn 16, DrBlPA 90, OxCPMus, PenDiMP A, WorAlBi*
Ellington, B. Kevin 1938- *St&PR 91*
Ellington, Charles Ronald 1941- *WhoAm 90*
Ellington, Howard W 1938- *WhoAmA 91*
Ellington, Jesse Thompson, Jr. 1931- *St&PR 91*
Ellington, John David 1935- *WhoSSW 91*
Ellington, John Stephen 1950- *WhoEmL 91*
Ellington, Mercer *BioIn 16*
Ellington, Mercer 1919- *DrBlPA 90*
Ellington, Mercer Kennedy 1919- *WhoAm 90*
Ellingwood, Bruce Russell 1944- *WhoAm 90*
Ellinor, Robert Allen 1939- *St&PR 91*
Ellinwood, Everett Hews, Jr. 1934- *BiDrAPA 89, WhoAm 90*
Ellinwood, Jeffrey G. 1940- *IntWWM 90*
Ellinwood, Leonard 1905- *IntWWM 90*
Elliot, Alistair 1932- *ConAu 129*
Elliot, Anne *FemiCLE*
Elliot, Bob 1923- *WorAlBi*
Elliot, Bruce *WhoWrEP 89*
Elliot, Cass 1941-1974 *ConMus 5 [port]*
Elliot, Catherine J 1947- *WhoAmA 91*
Elliot, Charlotte 1839-1880 *FemiCLE*
Elliot, David Clephan 1917- *WhoAm 90*
Elliot, David Hawksley 1936- *WhoAm 90*
Elliot, Douglas Gene 1941- *WhoSSW 91, WhoWor 91*
Elliot, Elisa Louise 1956- *WhoAmW 91*
Elliot, Harold Russell, Jr. 1927- *St&PR 91*
Elliot, Jackie *ODwPR 91*
Elliot, James Ludlow 1943- *WhoAm 90*
Elliot, Janet Lee 1955- *WhoAmW 91*
Elliot, Jared 1928- *WhoAm 90*
Elliot, Jeffrey M. 1947- *WhoAm 90, WhoWrEP 89*
Elliot, John H. 1927- *St&PR 91*
Elliot, John Murray 1927- *WhoAm 90*
Elliot, John T *WhoAm 90*
Elliot, John Theodore 1929- *WhoAmA 91*
Elliot, Michael Blake 1952- *WhoEmL 91*
Elliot, Ralph Gregory 1936- *WhoE 91*
Elliot, Robert *WhoWrEP 89*
Elliot, Sheila 1946- *WhoAmA 91*
Elliot, Sheila Hollihan 1946- *WhoEmL 91*
Elliot, William 1812-1893 *DcCanB 12*
Elliot, William Cater 1961- *WhoEmL 91*
Elliot, William Davis 1946- *St&PR 91*
Elliotson, John 1791-1868 *EncO&P 3*
Elliott, Miss *FemiCLE*
Elliott, A. Wright *WhoAm 90*
Elliott, A. Wright 1935- *St&PR 91*
Elliott, Albert Randle 1914- *WhoAm 90*
Elliott, Alfred M. 1905-1988 *BioIn 16*
Elliott, Anne 1944- *WhoAmA 91*
Elliott, Anson Wright 1935- *WhoAm 90*
Elliott, Anthony 1948- *IntWWM 90*
Elliott, Arlen R. 1928- *St&PR 91*
Elliott, Arthur James 1941- *WhoAm 90*
Elliott, Benjamin Paul 1920- *WhoAm 90*
Elliott, Bette G 1920- *WhoAmA 91*
Elliott, Bill *BioIn 16*
Elliott, Bill 1934-1983 *DrBlPA 90*
Elliott, Bill 1955- *WorAlBi*
Elliott, Billie W *BiDrAPA 89*
Elliott, Bob 1923- *BioIn 16*
Elliott, Boyce, III 1940- *BiDrAPA 89*
Elliott, Boyd Warren 1929- *St&PR 91*
Elliott, Brady Gifford 1943- *WhoSSW 91*
Elliott, Brig 1954- *WhoE 91*
Elliott, Byron Kauffman 1899- *WhoAm 90, WhoWor 91*
Elliott, C.L. 1910- *St&PR 91*
Elliott, Campbell Walter 1913- *St&PR 91*
Elliott, Candice K. 1949- *WhoAmW 91, WhoE 91, WhoEmL 91*
Elliott, Carl Hartley 1922- *WhoAm 90*
Elliott, Carol Harris 1950- *WhoAm 90, WhoEmL 91*
Elliott, Cass 1941-1974 *WorAlBi*
Elliott, Charles 1752-1832 *PenDiDA 89*
Elliott, Charles A. 1933- *St&PR 91*
Elliott, Charles Harold 1948- *WhoEmL 91*
Elliott, Charles W. 1932- *St&PR 91, WhoAm 90*
Elliott, Charles William 1953- *WhoEmL 91*
Elliott, Charlotte 1789-1871 *FemiCLE*
Elliott, Chris *BioIn 16*
Elliott, Constantine D 1925- *BiDrAPA 89*
Elliott, Corinne Adelaide *WhoWrEP 89*
Elliott, D. Stephen 1949- *St&PR 91*
Elliott, Daniel Robert, Jr. 1939- *St&PR 91, WhoAm 90*
Elliott, Daniel Whitacre 1922- *WhoAm 90*
Elliott, Darrell Kenneth 1952- *WhoWor 91*
Elliott, Darryl Lawrence 1961- *WhoSSW 91*
Elliott, David *ODwPR 91*
Elliott, David Duncan, III 1930- *WhoAm 90*
Elliott, David H. 1929- *St&PR 91*
Elliott, David John 1958- *IntWWM 90*
Elliott, David Joseph 1953- *WhoEmL 91*
Elliott, David LeRoy 1932- *WhoAm 90*
Elliott, David Mark 1959- *St&PR 91*
Elliott, David R. 1943- *St&PR 91*
Elliott, Deirdre Davina 1949- *BiDrAPA 89*
Elliott, Desiree 1966- *WhoAmW 91*
Elliott, Diana Beverly 1943- *WhoAmW 91*
Elliott, Diana Marie 1952- *WhoAmW 91*
Elliott, Don *MajTwCW*
Elliott, Donald Harrison 1932- *WhoAm 90*
Elliott, Doreen 1941- *WhoSSW 91*
Elliott, Dorothy Baden 1914- *WhoAmA 91*
Elliott, Dorothy Gale 1948- *WhoAmW 91*
Elliott, Douglas R. *ODwPR 91*
Elliott, Ebenezer 1781-1849 *BioIn 16, DcLB 96 [port]*
Elliott, Eddie Mayes 1938- *WhoAm 90*
Elliott, Edward 1915- *WhoAm 90*
Elliott, Edward Albert 1951- *BiDrAPA 89*
Elliott, Edward Procter 1916- *WhoAm 90*
Elliott, Edwin Donald, Jr. 1948- *WhoAm 90, WhoEmL 91*
Elliott, Edwin Oliver, Jr. 1954- *WhoEmL 91*
Elliott, Edwin Powers, Jr. 1947- *WhoWrEP 89*
Elliott, Elaine Sally 1951- *WhoAmW 91*
Elliott, Eleanor Thomas 1926- *WhoAm 90*
Elliott, Elizabeth Ann 1932- *WhoAmW 91*
Elliott, Emerson John 1933- *WhoAm 90*
Elliott, Emory Bernard 1942- *WhoAm 90*
Elliott, Eugenia L *BiDrAPA 89*
Elliott, Fleur Louise 1959- *IntWWM 90*
Elliott, Frank Nelson 1926- *WhoAm 90*
Elliott, Frank S. 1942- *St&PR 91*
Elliott, Frank Wallace 1930- *WhoAm 90, WhoSSW 91, WhoWor 91*
Elliott, G. H. 1884-1962 *OxCPMus*
Elliott, G Maurice 1883-1959 *EncO&P 3*
Elliott, George Arthur 1945- *WhoAm 90*
Elliott, George P. 1918-1980 *BioIn 16*
Elliott, George William 1933- *WhoAm 90*
Elliott, Gerald F. 1931- *WhoWor 91*
Elliott, Gerald M. 1928- *St&PR 91*
Elliott, Gordon Jefferson 1928- *WhoWor 91*
Elliott, Gordon Ray 1916- *WhoWor 91*
Elliott, Grace 1754-1823 *FemiCLE*
Elliott, Greg *ODwPR 91*
Elliott, Grover Sager 1940- *St&PR 91, WhoAm 90*
Elliott, H. Margaret 1925- *WhoAmW 91*
Elliott, H. Robert *ODwPR 91*
Elliott, Hal 1899-1963 *Ballpl 90*
Elliott, Harold Walker *BiDrAPA 89*
Elliott, Hayward Lee 1916- *St&PR 91*
Elliott, Herbert M. 1939- *St&PR 91*
Elliott, Howard, Jr. 1933- *WhoAm 90*
Elliott, J. Steve 1940- *St&PR 91*
Elliott, J. William 1936- *BiDrAPA 89*
Elliott, Jack 1931- *OxCPMus*
Elliott, Jack A. 1928- *WhoAm 90*
Elliott, James D. 1934- *St&PR 91*
Elliott, James Heyer 1924- *WhoAm 90, WhoAmA 91*
Elliott, James Lauriston 1943- *WhoSSW 91*
Elliott, James Robert 1910- *WhoAm 90*
Elliott, James Ward 1954- *WhoEmL 91*
Elliott, James William, Jr. 1950- *WhoWor 91*
Elliott, Janice *BioIn 16*
Elliott, Janice 1931- *FemiCLE*
Elliott, Jeanne Marie Koreltz 1943- *WhoAmW 91*
Elliott, Joan Elizabeth 1945- *WhoE 91*
Elliott, John 1713-1791 *PenDiDA 89*
Elliott, John, Jr. 1921- *WhoAm 90*
Elliott, John Cain, Jr. 1950- *WhoSSW 91*
Elliott, John Dorman 1941- *WhoWor 91*
Elliott, John F. 1958- *St&PR 91*
Elliott, John Frank 1920- *WhoAm 90*
Elliott, John Franklin 1915- *WhoSSW 91, WhoWor 91*
Elliott, John Gibson 1908- *WhoWrEP 89*
Elliott, John Gregory 1948- *WhoEmL 91*
Elliott, John J. 1935- *St&PR 91*
Elliott, John Michael 1941- *WhoAm 90*
Elliott, John W. 1944- *St&PR 91*
Elliott, Jon Victor 1954- *WhoEmL 91*
Elliott, Joseph Gordon, Jr. 1914- *WhoAm 90*
Elliott, Joyce Whitehead 1931- *WhoWrEP 89*
Elliott, Jumbo 1900-1970 *Ballpl 90*
Elliott, K. Charles 1924- *St&PR 91*
Elliott, Larry Paul 1931- *WhoAm 90*
Elliott, Larry Roger 1947- *WhoSSW 91*
Elliott, Lawrence 1924- *WhoAm 90, WhoWrEP 89*
Elliott, Lee Ann *WhoAm 90*
Elliott, Lee Ann 1923- *WhoAmW 91, WhoWor 91*
Elliott, Leonard *BioIn 16*
Elliott, Letha Elaine Cranford 1936- *WhoAmW 91*
Elliott, Lillian *WhoAmA 91*
Elliott, Linnea Constance 1948- *WhoAmW 91*
Elliott, Lois Lawrence 1931- *WhoAm 90*
Elliott, Margaret Johnson 1913- *WhoWrEP 89*
Elliott, Marianne 1948- *ConAu 132*
Elliott, Martin Alastair 1954- *IntWWM 90*
Elliott, Martin John 1951- *WhoWor 91*
Elliott, Maud 1854-1948 *FemiCLE*
Elliott, Maxine 1868-1940 *BioIn 16, NotWoAT*
Elliott, Maxine 1873-1940 *BioAmW*
Elliott, Melinda Jean 1958- *WhoAmW 91*
Elliott, Michael M. 1940- *St&PR 91*
Elliott, Milton J., III *ODwPR 91*
Elliott, Osborn 1924- *WhoAm 90, WhoE 91*
Elliott, Owen Basil 1922- *WhoSSW 91*
Elliott, Paul 1950- *IntWWM 90*
Elliott, Peggy Gordon 1937- *WhoAm 90, WhoAmW 91*
Elliott, Peter R. 1926- *WhoAm 90*
Elliott, Philip Clarkson 1903-1985 *WhoAmA 91N*
Elliott, R. Fraser 1921- *St&PR 91*
Elliott, R. Keith 1942- *St&PR 91, WhoAm 90*
Elliott, R Lance 1943- *WhoAm 90*
Elliott, Richard Aaron 1944- *St&PR 91*
Elliott, Richard Gibbons, Jr. 1940- *WhoE 91*
Elliott, Richard H. 1957- *St&PR 91*
Elliott, Richard Howard 1933- *WhoE 91*
Elliott, Richard L 1949- *BiDrAPA 89*
Elliott, Robbins Leonard 1920- *WhoAm 90*
Elliott, Robert B. 1923- *WhoAm 90*
Elliott, Robert Betzel 1926- *WhoWor 91*
Elliott, Robert Brown 1842-1884 *AmLegL, BlkAmsC [port]*
Elliott, Robert Burl 1919- *WhoSSW 91*
Elliott, Robert Conyers *IntWWM 90*
Elliott, Robert Edwin 1959- *BiDrAPA 89*
Elliott, Robert Francis 1947- *WhoWor 91*
Elliott, Robert J. *ODwPR 91*
Elliott, Robert John 1934- *WhoAm 90*
Elliott, Robert M. 1923- *St&PR 91*
Elliott, Robert N *BiDrAPA 89*
Elliott, Ronald Allen 1945- *WhoEmL 91*
Elliott, Ronald Paul 1958- *WhoEmL 91*
Elliott, Ronnie 1916- *WhoAmA 91*
Elliott, Roxanne Snelling 1954- *WhoWor 91*
Elliott, Roy Fraser 1921- *WhoAm 90*
Elliott, Sam 1944- *WhoAm 90, WorAlBi*
Elliott, Sarah B. 1848-1928 *BioAmW*
Elliott, Sarah Barnwell 1848-1928 *FemiCLE*
Elliott, Sarah McCarn 1930- *AuBYP 90*
Elliott, Scott Cameron 1941- *WhoAmA 91*
Elliott, Stephen Alan 1951- *St&PR 91*
Elliott, Stephen R. 1949- *St&PR 91*
Elliott, Stuart Jay 1952- *WhoE 91*
Elliott, Sumner Locke 1917- *WhoWrEP 89*
Elliott, Susan Jeannine 1954- *WhoSSW 91*
Elliott, Susan LaVerne 1955- *WhoAmW 91*
Elliott, Thomas L., Jr. 1937- *ODwPR 91*
Elliott, Thomas Lawrence 1940- *St&PR 91*
Elliott, Thomas Michael 1942- *WhoAm 90, WhoWor 91*
Elliott, Thomas Morrow 1939- *WhoWrEP 89*
Elliott, Tim 1948- *WhoAm 90*
Elliott, Vance Johnson, II 1961- *WhoSSW 91*
Elliott, Vernon Pelling 1912- *IntWWM 90*
Elliott, Vickie F. 1956- *WhoAmW 91*
Elliott, Walter Albert 1926- *WhoWor 91*
Elliott, Warren G. 1927- *WhoAm 90*
Elliott, Wilfred T 1918- *BiDrAPA 89*
Elliott, William 1816- *AmLegL*
Elliott, William 1920- *SmATA X [port]*
Elliott, William B. 1944- *St&PR 91*
Elliott, William H. 1932- *St&PR 91*
Elliott, William Hall 1932- *WhoAm 90*
Elliott, William Harrison 1941- *WhoSSW 91*

Elliott, William Homer, Jr. 1918- *WhoAm 90*
Elliott, William M. *NewYTBS 90*
Elliott, William M. 1903-1990 *BioIn 16*
Elliott, William M. 1922- *St&PR 91*
Elliott, William McBurney 1922- *WhoAm 90*
Elliott, William Robert 1944- *St&PR 91*
Elliott, William Trimble 1924- *WhoAm 90*
Elliott, Yancey Caldonia, Jr. 1935- *St&PR 91*
Elliott-Watson, Doris Jean 1932- *WhoAm 90, WhoWor 91*
Ellis, Albert 1913- *BioIn 16, WhoAm 90*
Ellis, Albert James 1929- *WhoWor 91*
Ellis, Alexander *BioIn 16*
Ellis, Alice *BiDEWW*
Ellis, Alice Thomas *BioIn 16*
Ellis, Alice Thomas 1932- *FemiCLE, WorAu 1980 [port]*
Ellis, Allison A. *ODwPR 91*
Ellis, Allison Allegra 1964- *WhoAmW 91*
Ellis, Alpheus Lee 1906- *St&PR 91*
Ellis, Andrew Jackson, Jr. 1930- *WhoWor 91*
Ellis, Anne Elizabeth 1945- *WhoAmW 91*
Ellis, Arleen Mary 1945- *WhoEmL 91*
Ellis, Arthur *BioIn 16*
Ellis, Arthur Baron 1951- *WhoAm 90*
Ellis, Arthur R. 1950- *WhoE 91*
Ellis, Arthur Stanwood 1926- *St&PR 91*
Ellis, Barbara Williams 1953- *WhoWrEP 89*
Ellis, Barnes Humphreys 1940- *WhoAm 90*
Ellis, Bernard H., Sr. 1925- *BiDrAPA 89*
Ellis, Bernice *WhoAmW 91, WhoE 91, WhoWor 91*
Ellis, Bernice Allred 1932- *WhoAmW 91*
Ellis, Bertram 1860-1920 *AmLegL*
Ellis, Brent 1946- *IntWWM 90*
Ellis, Brent E. 1946- *WhoAm 90*
Ellis, Bret Easton *BioIn 16*
Ellis, C. Douglas 1923- *WhoWrEP 89*
Ellis, Calvert N. 1904- *WhoAm 90*
Ellis, Carl Eugene 1932-1977 *WhoAmA 91N*
Ellis, Charles Calvert 1919- *WhoAm 90*
Ellis, Charles Warren 1927- *St&PR 91*
Ellis, Charlotte Honor 1942- *IntWWM 90*
Ellis, Cheryl Bonini 1951- *WhoAm 90*
Ellis, Clifford Wilson 1907-1985 *DcNaB 1981*
Ellis, Cynthia Elaine 1954- *WhoEmL 91*
Ellis, D. Rose Angela 1939- *WhoWrEP 89*
Ellis, David 1933- *IntWWM 90*
Ellis, David Dale 1952- *WhoEmL 91, WhoSSW 91*
Ellis, David M 1933- *BiDrAPA 89, WhoE 91*
Ellis, David Maldwyn 1914- *WhoAm 90*
Ellis, David W. 1923- *St&PR 91*
Ellis, David Wertz 1936- *WhoAm 90, WhoE 91*
Ellis, Debbie 1953- *St&PR 91*
Ellis, Deborah Hicks 1952- *WhoSSW 91*
Ellis, DeeAnn 1957- *WhoAmW 91*
Ellis, Denise Francine Thomas 1953- *WhoE 91*
Ellis, Denise Kay 1966- *WhoAmW 91*
Ellis, Denise Taylor 1946- *WhoEmL 91*
Ellis, Dock 1945- *Ballpl 90*
Ellis, Don 1934-1978 *BioIn 16, OxCPMus*
Ellis, Don Edwin 1908- *WhoAm 90*
Ellis, Donald Edwin 1939- *WhoAm 90*
Ellis, Donald Lee 1933- *WhoSSW 91*
Ellis, Donald Llewellyn 1926- *WhoE 91*
Ellis, Douglas E. 1946- *St&PR 91*
Ellis, Earl J. 1936- *St&PR 91*
Ellis, Edgar Heb, Jr. 1935- *WhoSSW 91*
Ellis, Edith 1861-1916 *FemiCLE*
Ellis, Edward B. 1937- *St&PR 91*
Ellis, Edward Prioleau 1929- *WhoWor 91*
Ellis, Edward Robb *BioIn 16*
Ellis, Edward W 1913- *BiDrAPA 89*
Ellis, Elizabeth Ann 1953- *BiDrAPA 89*
Ellis, Ella 1928- *AuBYP 90*
Ellis, Ella Thorp 1928- *WhoWrEP 89*
Ellis, Ellen E. 1829-1895 *FemiCLE*
Ellis, Elmer 1901-1989 *BioIn 16*
Ellis, Elmo Israel 1918- *WhoAm 90, WhoSSW 91*
Ellis, Elwood Addison, III 1947- *WhoAm 90*
Ellis, Emory Nelson, Jr. 1929- *WhoAm 90*
Ellis, Eva Lillian 1920- *WhoAmW 91, WhoWor 91*
Ellis, Evelyn 1894-1958 *DrBlPA 90*
Ellis, Felix *BiDrAPA 89*
Ellis, Florence Hawley 1906- *BioIn 16*
Ellis, Foster, Jr. 1958- *WhoSSW 91*
Ellis, Frances 1910-1989 *BioIn 16*
Ellis, Frank Everett 1928- *WhoE 91*
Ellis, Frank Hale 1916- *WhoAm 90*
Ellis, Franklin Henry, Jr. 1920- *WhoAm 90*
Ellis, Fred A. 1942- *WhoSSW 91*
Ellis, Fred Wilson 1914- *WhoAm 90*
Ellis, Fremont 1897-1985 *WhoAmA 91N*
Ellis, Gary Michael 1952- *WhoSSW 91*
Ellis, George Edward 1934- *WhoWrEP 89*
Ellis, George Edwin, Jr. 1921- *WhoWor 91*
Ellis, George Fitzallen, Jr. 1923- *WhoAm 90*
Ellis, George Hathaway 1920- *WhoAm 90, WhoE 91*
Ellis, George Richard 1937- *WhoAm 90, WhoAmA 91*
Ellis, Georgiann 1947- *WhoAmW 91*
Ellis, Giles Lambert, Jr. 1942- *St&PR 91*
Ellis, Glen Edward, Jr. 1960- *WhoSSW 91*
Ellis, Grace Carol 1935- *WhoAmW 91*
Ellis, Gregory Charles 1960- *IntWWM 90*
Ellis, Grover, Jr. 1920- *WhoAm 90*
Ellis, Harold A., Jr. 1931- *St&PR 91*
Ellis, Harold Bernard 1917- *WhoAm 90*
Ellis, Harold L. 1894-1989 *BioIn 16*
Ellis, Harry Bearse 1921- *AuBYP 90, WhoAm 90*
Ellis, Harry E. 1938- *St&PR 91*
Ellis, Havelock 1859-1939 *BioIn 16, WorAlBi*
Ellis, Henry Carlton 1927- *WhoAm 90*
Ellis, Henry M. 1929- *St&PR 91*
Ellis, Herbert Lee 1912- *WhoE 91*
Ellis, Herbert Wayne 1948- *WhoEmL 91*
Ellis, Howard Woodrow 1914- *WhoAm 90*
Ellis, Jack T 1930- *BiDrAPA 89*
Ellis, James Antony 1954- *IntWWM 90*
Ellis, James B. 1940- *St&PR 91*
Ellis, James David 1948- *WhoEmL 91*
Ellis, James Henry 1933- *WhoWor 91*
Ellis, James Jolly 1937- *WhoSSW 91*
Ellis, James Reed 1921- *WhoAm 90*
Ellis, James Theodore *BioIn 16*
Ellis, James Watson 1927- *WhoAm 90, WhoSSW 91*
Ellis, Jeanette Christine 1962- *WhoAmW 91*
Ellis, Jeffrey Warren 1947- *WhoEmL 91*
Ellis, Jerry L. 1947- *WhoWrEP 89*
Ellis, Joanne Hammonds 1946- *WhoEmL 91*
Ellis, Joel 1830- *BioIn 16*
Ellis, John 1912- *St&PR 91*
Ellis, John 1929- *WhoAm 90*
Ellis, John 1948- *Ballpl 90*
Ellis, John 1950- *WhoSSW 91*
Ellis, John B. 1924- *St&PR 91*
Ellis, John David 1949- *WhoEmL 91, WhoSSW 91*
Ellis, John Jay 1954- *WhoEmL 91*
Ellis, John Martin 1936- *WhoAm 90*
Ellis, John Thomas 1959- *WhoSSW 91*
Ellis, John Tracy 1905- *BioIn 16, CurBio 90 [port], WhoAm 90*
Ellis, John W. 1928- *St&PR 91, WhoAm 90*
Ellis, Joseph Bailey 1890- *WhoAmA 91N*
Ellis, Joseph H. *WhoAm 90*
Ellis, Joseph John Michael, III 1943- *WhoAm 90*
Ellis, Joseph N. 1928- *St&PR 91*
Ellis, Joseph Newlin 1928- *WhoAm 90*
Ellis, Joyce K. 1950- *WhoWrEP 89*
Ellis, Juanita *BioIn 16*
Ellis, Judith Kay 1939- *WhoAmW 91*
Ellis, Kathryn Purnell 1961- *WhoSSW 91*
Ellis, Kent 1921- *WhoAm 90*
Ellis, Kerri Anne 1964- *WhoAmW 91*
Ellis, Lakeal *BioIn 16*
Ellis, Landon *MajTwCW*
Ellis, Lawrence Dobson 1932- *WhoAm 90, WhoE 91, WhoWor 91*
Ellis, Leslie Lee, Jr. 1925- *WhoSSW 91*
Ellis, Linda Ann 1944- *WhoAmW 91*
Ellis, Lonnie Calvert 1945- *WhoSSW 91*
Ellis, Loren Elizabeth 1953- *WhoAmA 91*
Ellis, Lynn Webster 1928- *WhoAm 90*
Ellis, Margaret Boland 1925- *WhoWrEP 89*
Ellis, Mary *BioIn 16*
Ellis, Mary 1900- *OxCPMus*
Ellis, Mary Louise 1943- *WhoAm 90, WhoAmW 91*
Ellis, Maxine Ethel 1941- *WhoAmW 91*
Ellis, Melody Genneane 1952- *WhoEmL 91*
Ellis, Melvin Wilbur 1946- *St&PR 91*
Ellis, Michael 1917- *WhoAm 90*
Ellis, Michael David 1952- *WhoSSW 91*
Ellis, Michael Hudson 1944- *WhoSSW 91*
Ellis, Michael John 1946- *St&PR 91*
Ellis, Nan Jane 1956- *WhoSSW 91*
Ellis, Newton Cass 1934- *WhoAm 90*
Ellis, Osian Gwynn 1928- *IntWWM 90*
Ellis, Patricia Jasmine 1954- *WhoWor 91*
Ellis, Patrick 1928- *WhoAm 90*
Ellis, Penelope K 1926- *BiDrAPA 89*
Ellis, Perry *BioIn 16*
Ellis, Perry 1940-1986 *ConDes 90*
Ellis, Peter B.S. 1953- *St&PR 91*
Ellis, Peter Hudson 1944- *WhoAm 90*
Ellis, Ralph Joseph, Jr. 1939- *WhoSSW 91*
Ellis, Ray 1921- *WhoAmA 91*
Ellis, Raymond Clinton, Jr. 1921- *WhoE 91*
Ellis, Richard 1938- *WhoAmA 91, WhoE 91*
Ellis, Richard H. 1919-1989 *BioIn 16*
Ellis, Richard Lee 1940- *WhoAm 90*
Ellis, Richard Stephens 1934- *WhoAm 90*
Ellis, Robert Arthur 1926- *WhoAm 90*
Ellis, Robert Carroll 1923-1979 *WhoAmA 91N*
Ellis, Robert Charles 1954- *WhoEmL 91*
Ellis, Robert Griswold 1908- *WhoAm 90, WhoWor 91*
Ellis, Robert James 1943- *St&PR 91*
Ellis, Robert Lee 1938- *WhoE 91*
Ellis, Robert Lee 1949- *WhoEmL 91*
Ellis, Robert Leslie 1921- *WhoAm 90*
Ellis, Robert M 1922- *WhoAmA 91*
Ellis, Robert William 1939- *WhoAm 90*
Ellis, Rodney D. 1950- *St&PR 91*
Ellis, Ron 1946- *IntWWM 90*
Ellis, Ronald Kevin 1953- *WhoSSW 91*
Ellis, Rube 1885-1938 *Ballpl 90*
Ellis, Rudolph Lawrence 1911- *WhoAm 90*
Ellis, Sammy 1941- *Ballpl 90*
Ellis, Sarah *AuBYP 90*
Ellis, Sarah 1645-1695 *BiDEWW*
Ellis, Sarah 1799-1872 *FemiCLE*
Ellis, Sarah Stickney 1799-1882 *BioIn 16*
Ellis, Scott *TwCCr&M 91*
Ellis, Seymour *BioIn 16*
Ellis, Sophia Lugene 1927- *WhoAmW 91*
Ellis, Stacey Martin 1951- *WhoEmL 91, WhoSSW 91*
Ellis, Steven G. 1949- *ODwPR 91*
Ellis, Steven George 1949- *WhoAm 90*
Ellis, Susan Gottenberg 1949- *WhoAmW 91*
Ellis, Sydney 1917- *WhoAm 90*
Ellis, Terence *BioIn 16*
Ellis, Thelma C. 1936- *St&PR 91*
Ellis, Thomas Morgan 1930- *WhoSSW 91*
Ellis, Thomas Selby, III 1940- *WhoSSW 91*
Ellis, Todd *BioIn 16*
Ellis, Van Zandt *BioIn 16*
Ellis, Vivian 1904- *OxCPMus*
Ellis, Vivian Elizabeth *WhoAmW 91*
Ellis, Wayne Enoch 1945- *WhoSSW 91*
Ellis, Weldon Thompson, Jr. 1909- *WhoWor 91*
Ellis, William *BioIn 16*
Ellis, William B. 1940- *St&PR 91*
Ellis, William Ben 1940- *WhoAm 90*
Ellis, William Edward, Jr. 1948- *St&PR 91*
Ellis, William Elliott 1940- *WhoSSW 91*
Ellis, William Grenville 1940- *WhoWor 91*
Ellis, William Harold 1925- *WhoAm 90*
Ellis, William Hartshorne 1929- *WhoWor 91*
Ellis, William Leigh 1908- *WhoAm 90*
Ellis, Willis Hill 1927- *WhoAm 90*
Ellis Crawford Taylor, Emily 1898- *WhoWrEP 89*
Ellis-Fermor, Una Mary 1894-1958 *BioIn 16*
Ellis-Tracy, Jo *WhoAmA 91*
Ellis-Vant, Karen McGee 1950- *WhoEmL 91*
Ellisman, Roland Avery 1951- *WhoEmL 91*
Ellison, Alton Lynn, Jr. 1950- *WhoSSW 91*
Ellison, Arthur James 1920- *EncPaPR 91*
Ellison, Charles L. 1950- *St&PR 91*
Ellison, Cori Jean 1954- *WhoAmW 91*
Ellison, Cyril Lee 1916- *WhoAm 90*
Ellison, David Ernest 1921- *WhoAm 90*
Ellison, Diane Marie 1941- *WhoWor 91*
Ellison, Elaine 1926- *WhoAmW 91*
Ellison, Eugene Curtis 1949- *WhoAm 90*
Ellison, Floyd Earl, Jr. 1934- *St&PR 91*
Ellison, Fred Pittman 1922- *WhoAm 90*
Ellison, Glenn 1911- *WhoWrEP 89*
Ellison, Harlan 1934- *MajTwCW, RGTwCSF, WorAlBi*
Ellison, Harlan Jay 1934- *WhoAm 90, WhoWrEP 89*
Ellison, Herbert Jay 1929- *WhoAm 90*
Ellison, James M. 1952- *WhoE 91*
Ellison, James Michael *BiDrAPA 89*
Ellison, James Oliver 1929- *WhoAm 90*
Ellison, Jason *BioIn 16*
Ellison, Jeffrey L. 1948- *St&PR 91*
Ellison, Jeffrey Lynn 1948- *WhoE 91*
Ellison, Joan Audrey *IntWWM 90*
Ellison, Katherine Esther 1957- *WhoAmW 91*
Ellison, Katherine Ruffner White 1941- *WhoAmW 91*
Ellison, Leonard E 1928- *BiDrAPA 89*
Ellison, Lois Taylor 1923- *WhoAm 90*
Ellison, Lorin Bruce 1932- *WhoAm 90*
Ellison, Lucile Watkins *BioIn 16*
Ellison, Luther Frederick 1925- *St&PR 91, WhoWor 91*
Ellison, Martha French 1926- *St&PR 91*
Ellison, Pamela Jo 1956- *WhoAmW 91*
Ellison, Peter K. 1942- *St&PR 91*
Ellison, Ralph *BioIn 16*
Ellison, Ralph 1914- *MajTwCW, WhoAm 90, WorAlBi*
Ellison, Richard Arthur *BiDrAPA 89*
Ellison, Richard H. 1949- *St&PR 91*
Ellison, Richard Perham 1930- *St&PR 91*
Ellison, Robert Gordon 1916- *WhoAm 90*
Ellison, Robert W 1946- *WhoAmA 91*
Ellison, Roy J, Jr. 1925- *BiDrAPA 89*
Ellison, Samuel 1817-1889 *AmLegL*
Ellison, Samuel Porter, Jr. 1914- *WhoAm 90*
Ellison, Solon Arthur 1922- *WhoAm 90*
Ellison, Stephanie Elise 1962- *WhoAmW 91*
Ellison, Thorleif 1902- *WhoSSW 91, WhoWor 91*
Ellison, Virginia Howell 1910- *AuBYP 90*
Ellison, Waldo M *BiDrAPA 89*
Ellison, William 1927- *St&PR 91*
Ellman, Jon P *BiDrAPA 89*
Ellman, Neil Gilbert 1942- *WhoE 91*
Ellman, Roger Arnold 1952- *WhoEmL 91*
Ellmann, Douglas Stanley 1956- *WhoEmL 91*
Ellmann, Lucy 1956- *ConLC 61 [port]*
Ellmann, Maud 1954- *WhoWor 91*
Ellmann, Richard 1918-1987 *DcLB 103 [port], MajTwCW*
Ellmann, Sheila Frenkel 1931- *WhoAmW 91, WhoWor 91*
Ellmann, William Marshall 1921- *WhoAm 90, WhoWor 91*
Ellmer, Joseph Frank 1944- *WhoSSW 91*
Ellmore, Lewis Francis 1933- *St&PR 91*
Ellmyer, Virginia Ruth 1958- *WhoAmW 91*
Ellner, Carolyn Lipton 1932- *WhoAm 90, WhoAmW 91*
Ellner, Paul D. 1925- *WhoAm 90*
Elloian, Carolyn Autry *WhoAmA 91*
Elloian, Peter 1936- *WhoAmA 91*
Ellrod, Frederick Edward, III 1953- *WhoE 91*
Ellroy, James 1948- *BestSel 90-4 [port], TwCCr&M 91*
Ellsberg, Daniel 1931- *BioIn 16, WorAlBi*
Ellsberg, Edward 1891- *AuBYP 90*
Ellspermann, Stanley C. 1942- *St&PR 91*
Ellstein, Carol Gail 1951- *WhoAmW 91*
Ellstrom, Olof W., Jr. 1946- *St&PR 91*
Ellstrom-Calder, Annette 1952- *WhoAmW 91, WhoEmL 91, WhoWor 91*
Ellsweig, Phyllis Leah 1927- *WhoAmW 91*
Ellsworth, Arthur W. 1934- *St&PR 91*
Ellsworth, Arthur Whitney 1936- *WhoAm 90*
Ellsworth, Bruce Blake *WhoE 91*
Ellsworth, Clarence A 1885-1961 *WhoAmA 91N*
Ellsworth, Cynthia Ann 1950- *WhoWor 91*
Ellsworth, David John 1953- *WhoSSW 91*
Ellsworth, Dick 1940- *Ballpl 90*
Ellsworth, Duncan S., Jr. 1928- *St&PR 91*
Ellsworth, Duncan Steuart, Jr. 1928- *WhoAm 90*
Ellsworth, Frank L. 1943- *WhoAm 90*
Ellsworth, George A *BiDrAPA 89*
Ellsworth, John E. 1904- *St&PR 91*
Ellsworth, Joseph Cordon 1955- *WhoEmL 91, WhoSSW 91*
Ellsworth, Lincoln 1880-1951 *WorAlBi*
Ellsworth, Lucius Fuller 1941- *WhoAm 90*
Ellsworth, Maurice Owens 1948- *WhoAm 90*
Ellsworth, Michael J. 1943- *St&PR 91*
Ellsworth, Myrna Ruth 1948- *WhoWor 91*
Ellsworth, Oliver 1745-1807 *BioIn 16*
Ellsworth, Oliver Bryant 1940- *IntWWM 90*
Ellsworth, Robert Fred 1926- *WhoAm 90*
Ellsworth, Robert Malcolm 1928- *WhoAm 90*
Ellsworth, Samuel George 1916- *WhoAm 90*
Ellsworth, Stoughton Lathrop 1927- *St&PR 91*
Ellsworth, Thomas A. 1938- *St&PR 91*
Ellsworth, Warren 1954- *IntWWM 90*
Ellsworth, Whitney 1908-1980 *EncACom*
Ellul Vincenti, Michael 1958- *WhoWor 91*
Ellwanger, C. Scott 1947- *St&PR 91*
Ellwanger, J. David 1937- *WhoAm 90*
Ellwanger, Mike 1925- *WhoAm 90*
Ellwood, Kim *BioIn 16*
Ellwood, Mary 1623?-1708 *BiDEWW*
Ellwood, Scott 1936- *WhoAm 90*
Ellwood, William *NewAgMG*
Ellwood-Filkins, Lea Beatrice 1955- *WhoAmW 91*
Elly, Robert Arthur 1934- *St&PR 91*
Ellzey, Randal Edmond 1958- *WhoEmL 91*
Ellzy, Misha Therese 1962- *WhoAmW 91*
Elm, Clayton B. 1938- *St&PR 91*
Elmaghraby, Salah Eldin 1927- *WhoAm 90, WhoSSW 91*
Elmaleh, Joseph 1938- *St&PR 91, WhoWor 91*

Elmaleh, Lou *St&PR 91*
Elman, Gerry Jay 1942- *WhoAm 90, WhoE 91, WhoWor 91*
Elman, Howard Lawrence 1938- *WhoE 91*
Elman, Lynn *BiDrAPA 89*
Elman, Mischa 1891-1967 *PenDiMP, WorAlBi*
Elman, Naomi Geist *WhoAmW 91*
Elman, Philip 1918- *WhoAm 90*
Elman, Richard 1934- *WhoWrEP 89*
Elman, Robert 1930- *WhoE 91*
Elman, Ziggy 1914-1968 *OxCPMus*
Elmasry, Mohamed Ibrahim 1943- *WhoAm 90*
Elmburg, John Robert 1941- *St&PR 91*
Elmegreen, Debra Anne Meloy 1952- *WhoAmW 91*
Elmen, James W. 1932- *St&PR 91*
Elmen, Robert C. 1930- *St&PR 91*
Elmendorf, William Welcome 1912- *WhoAm 90*
Elmer, Bernard E. 1927- *St&PR 91*
Elmer, Brian Christian 1936- *WhoAm 90*
Elmer, Irene 1937- *AuBYP 90*
Elmer, Jean Radley 1946- *WhoAmW 91*
Elmer, Marilyn Ann 1931- *WhoSSW 91*
Elmer, William Morris 1915- *WhoAm 90*
Elmes, David Gordon 1942- *WhoAm 90*
Elmets, Craig Allan 1949- *WhoEmL 91*
Elmets, Harry Barnard 1920- *WhoAm 90*
Elmezzi, Thomas Damiano 1914- *WhoE 91*
Elmhirst, Thomas Walker 1895-1982 *DcNaB 1981*
Elmiligy, Ismail A. 1937- *St&PR 91*
Elmitt, Kate Mavis 1935- *IntWWM 90*
Elmitt, Martin 1944- *IntWWM 90*
Elmo, Cloe 1910-1962 *PenDiMP*
El'Mohammed, Ali Malik Bell 1944- *WhoWor 91*
Elmont, Stephen *BioIn 16*
Elmore, Carroll M *BiDrAPA 89*
Elmore, Cenieth Catherine 1930- *IntWWM 90*
Elmore, Edward Whitehead 1938- *St&PR 91, WhoAm 90*
Elmore, Eugene L. 1931- *St&PR 91*
Elmore, Garland Craft 1946- *WhoEmL 91*
Elmore, Geraldine Catharine 1936- *WhoAmW 91*
Elmore, James Bernard 1949- *WhoWrEP 89*
Elmore, James Hamilton 1946- *WhoEmL 91*
Elmore, James L 1933- *BiDrAPA 89*
Elmore, James Walter 1917- *WhoAm 90*
Elmore, John D 1922- *BiDrAPA 89*
Elmore, Matthew Bret 1951- *WhoEmL 91*
Elmore, Michael *BioIn 16*
Elmore, Parker Elliott 1963- *WhoAm 90*
Elmore, Paul Vincent 1962- *WhoEmL 91*
Elmore, Stancliff Churchill 1921- *WhoAm 90, WhoWor 91*
Elmore, Stanley McDowell 1933- *WhoSSW 91*
Elmore, Stephen A., Sr. 1952- *St&PR 91*
Elmore, Walter A. 1925- *WhoAm 90*
Elmquist, Ronald E. *WhoSSW 91*
Elms, James Cornelius, IV 1916- *WhoAm 90, WhoWor 91*
Elms, Roderick James Charles 1951- *IntWWM 90*
Elmslie, George Grant 1871-1952 *PenDiDA 89*
Elmslie, Kenward Gray 1929- *WhoAm 90*
Elmy, David A. 1941- *St&PR 91*
Elmy, Elizabeth Clark Wolstenholme- *BioIn 16*
Elnaggar, Samira M *BiDrAPA 89*
Elnekave, Sara Suchy 1939- *BiDrAPA 89*
Elody, Marta Stefania 1933- *BiDrAPA 89*
Elorriaga, John A. 1923- *St&PR 91*
Eloul, Kosso 1920- *WhoAmA 91*
Elowitch, Abraham B. 1917- *St&PR 91*
Elowitch, Annette 1942- *WhoAmA 91*
Elowitch, Robert Jason 1943- *WhoAmA 91*
Elowitch, Stanley J. 1942- *St&PR 91*
Elozua, Raymon 1947- *WhoAmA 91*
Elpers, John Richard 1938- *BiDrAPA 89*
Elphe, Thomas *PenDiDA 89*
Elphinstone, Francis *ConAu 30NR*
Elrafei, Mohamed Alaa *BiDrAPA 89*
Elrahman, Hassan A *BiDrAPA 89*
Elrefai, Alaa M 1955- *BiDrAPA 89*
Elrick, Stephen Thomas 1945- *St&PR 91*
Elrod, Ben Moody 1930- *WhoAm 90*
Elrod, Eugene Richard 1949- *WhoE 91, WhoEmL 91, WhoWor 91*
Elrod, Harold Glenn 1918- *WhoAm 90*
Elrod, James Lake, Jr. 1954- *St&PR 91*
Elrod, John William 1940- *WhoAm 90*
Elrod, Linda Ann 1949- *WhoAmW 91*
Elrod, Linda Diane Henry 1947- *WhoEmL 91*
Elrod, Margaret Ann 1919- *WhoAmW 91*
Elrod, Millard Eugene 1936- *WhoAm 90*
Elrod, Richard L. 1935- *St&PR 91*
Elrod, Robert Grant 1940- *WhoAm 90*
Elrod, Taylor Larue, Jr. 1933- *St&PR 91*
Elsaesser, Robert James 1926- *WhoAm 90*
Elsam, Elizabeth *BiDEWW*
Elsanusi, Ahmed Elnoman Abdella 1935- *WhoWor 91*
Elsas, Louis Jacob, II 1937- *WhoAm 90*
Elsasser, Albert B 1918- *WhoWrEP 89*
Elsasser, Walter Maurice 1904- *WhoAm 90*
Elsayed, Elsayed Mohamed 1944- *WhoWor 91*
Elsayed, Khalil Mohamad 1950- *WhoEmL 91*
Elsberg, John William 1945- *WhoWrEP 89*
Elsberg, Stuart Michael 1939- *WhoAm 90*
Elsbree, Gene 1933- *ODwPR 91*
Elsbree, John Francis 1912- *WhoAm 90*
Elsbree, William Earl, III 1945- *WhoSSW 91*
Elsbree, William Langdon 1958- *WhoE 91*
Elsdon, Margaret Buchanan 1949- *WhoAmW 91*
Else, Carolyn Joan 1934- *WhoAmW 91*
Else, Chas. W. 1911- *St&PR 91*
Else, Robert John 1918- *WhoAmA 91*
Else, Willis Irl 1931- *St&PR 91, WhoAm 90*
Elsea, Frederick J., III *St&PR 91*
Elsen, Albert Edward 1927- *WhoAm 90, WhoAmA 91*
Elsen, J.F. 1925- *St&PR 91*
Elsen, Sheldon Howard 1928- *WhoAm 90, WhoE 91, WhoWor 91*
Elsener, G. Dale 1951- *WhoEmL 91*
Elsener, James Edward 1943- *WhoAm 90*
Elsenhans, Virginia Delong 1947- *WhoAmW 91, WhoEmL 91*
Elser, Dan Ray 1953- *WhoEmL 91*
Elser, John Robert 1912- *WhoE 91*
Elser, Marco Maximilian 1958- *WhoWor 91*
Elsesser, James Richard 1944- *St&PR 91*
Elsey, George McKee 1918- *BioIn 16, WhoAm 90*
Elsey, John H. 1945- *St&PR 91*
Elsheimer, Adam 1578-1610? *IntDcAA 90, WorAlBi*
Elsheimer, Seth Robert 1952- *WhoSSW 91*
Elsie, Lily 1886-1962 *OxCPMus*
Elsila, David August 1939- *WhoAm 90*
Elsinger, George R. 1934- *St&PR 91*
Elsman, James Leonard, Jr. 1936- *WhoAm 90*
Elsner, Gisela 1937- *EncCoWW*
Elsner, James A. 1946- *St&PR 91*
Elsner, Larry Edward 1930- *WhoAm 90, WhoAmA 91*
Elsner, Sidney Edgar 1919- *WhoAm 90*
Elsner, William Joseph 1951- *WhoAm 90*
Elsom, Clint Gary 1946- *WhoEmL 91*
Elson, Abraham *BiDrAPA 89*
Elson, Alex 1905- *WhoAm 90*
Elson, Barry Russell 1941- *WhoSSW 91*
Elson, Charles 1909- *WhoAm 90*
Elson, Charles Myer 1959- *WhoEmL 91*
Elson, Eddie *BioIn 16*
Elson, Edward Elliott 1934- *WhoAm 90, WhoSSW 91, WhoWor 91*
Elson, Edward Lee Roy 1906- *WhoAm 90*
Elson, Gerald L. *St&PR 91*
Elson, Gerald W. 1922- *St&PR 91*
Elson, Mary 1623?-1706 *BiDEWW*
Elson, Norman W. *BioIn 16*
Elson, Ronald Lee 1943- *BiDrAPA 89*
Elson, Suzanne *BioIn 16*
Elson, Suzanne Goodman 1937- *WhoAmW 91*
Elsperman, Robert Pauly 1936- *St&PR 91*
Elssler, Fanny 1810-1884 *WorAlBi*
Elstad, Anne Karin 1938- *EncCoWW*
Elste, Charles E. 1941- *St&PR 91*
Elste, Rudolf Otto Martin 1952- *IntWWM 90*
Elstein, Stephen Edgar 1932- *St&PR 91*
Elster, Kevin 1964- *BioIn 16*
Elster, Kristian Mandrup 1841-1881 *DcScanL*
Elster, Leon 1926- *St&PR 91*
Elster, Samuel Kase 1922- *WhoAm 90*
Elstner, Richard Chesney 1924- *WhoAm 90*
Elstob, Elizabeth 1683-1756 *BiDEWW, BioIn 16, FemiCLE*
Elston, Andrew Stephen 1951- *WhoE 91*
Elston, Don 1929- *Ballpl 90*
Elston, Lloyd Warren 1926- *WhoAm 90*
Elston, Ralph Beckman 1937- *St&PR 91*
Elswit, Robert Alan 1951- *BiDrAPA 89*
Elterich, Joachim Gustav 1930- *WhoAm 90*
Eltgroth, Marlene Anne Bumgarner 1947- *WhoEmL 91*
Elthon, Donald Lee 1952- *WhoSSW 91*
Elting, Everett E. 1936- *WhoAm 90*
Elting, John R 1911- *ConAu 31NR*
Elting, Mary 1906- *AuBYP 90*
Elting, Victor, III 1938- *St&PR 91*
Eltinge, George M. 1918- *WhoAm 90*
Eltinge, Lamont 1926- *WhoAm 90*
Eltis, Walter 1933- *ConAu 131*
Eltis, Walter Alfred 1933- *WhoWor 91*
Elto, Patrick William 1947- *WhoEmL 91*
Elton, Antony 1935- *IntWWM 90*
Elton, Arnold 1920- *WhoWor 91*
Elton, Bruce Ferriday 1937- *St&PR 91*
Elton, Edmund Harry 1846-1920 *PenDiDA 89*
Elton, G R 1921- *ConAu 30NR*
Elton, Geoffrey Rudolph 1921- *WhoWor 91*
Elton, Howard *BioIn 16*
Elton, Michael John 1933- *WhoWor 91*
Elton, Milan Lee 1940- *St&PR 91*
Elton, Orville *BioIn 16*
Elton, William R. 1921- *WhoE 91*
Eltzroth, Carter Weaver 1952- *WhoEmL 91*
Eluard, Paul 1895-1952 *WorAlBi*
Elul, Rafael 1935- *BiDrAPA 89*
Elvenstar, Diane C. *ConAu 132*
Elverson, Devitt James *BiDrAPA 89*
Elverum, Gerard William, Jr. 1927- *WhoAm 90, WhoWor 91*
Elverum, H.D. 1925- *St&PR 91*
Elverum, Harvard Dea 1925- *WhoAm 90*
Elvet, Judith L *BiDrAPA 89*
Elvig, Merrywayne 1931- *WhoAmW 91*
Elvin, Peter Wayne 1955- *WhoE 91, WhoEmL 91*
Elvira, Pablo 1938- *IntWWM 90*
Elvira Delgado, Narciso D. 1967- *WhoHisp 91*
Elvire *EncCoWW*
Elvove, Carl X. 1919- *St&PR 91*
Elvove, Robert Morton 1941- *BiDrAPA 89*
Elvy, Cecelia Merritt 1940- *IntWWM 90*
Elwart, Nancy M. 1939- *WhoAmW 91*
Elway, John *BioIn 16*
Elway, John 1960- *CurBio 90 [port], News 90 [port], -90-3 [port], WorAlBi*
Elway, John Albert 1960- *WhoAm 90*
Elwell, Celia Candace 1954- *WhoEmL 91*
Elwell, Ellen C. 1945- *WhoAmW 91*
Elwell, Felicia Rosemary *AuBYP 90*
Elwell, Howard Andrew 1940- *WhoSSW 91*
Elwell, Richard Rhea 1926- *WhoAm 90*
Elwell, Rufus Newell 1862-1919 *AmLegL*
Elwes, Catherine 1952- *BiDWomA*
Elwes, Gervase 1866-1921 *PenDiMP*
Elwes, John 1946- *IntWWM 90*
Elwin, James William, Jr. 1950- *WhoEmL 91*
Elwing, Carl Magnus 1921- *WhoWor 91*
Elwonger, David Martin 1945- *BiDrAPA 89*
Elwood, Ann 1931- *BioIn 16*
Elwood, Anne Katharine *FemiCLE*
Elwood, Brian Clay 1958- *WhoEmL 91*
Elwood, David Michael 1935- *WhoAm 90*
Elwood, H. Philip 1946- *WhoEmL 91*
Elwood, Patricia 1941- *WhoE 91*
Elwood, Roger 1943- *AuBYP 90, BioIn 16*
Elwood, William Edward 1943- *WhoE 91*
Elwyn-Edwards, Dilys 1918- *IntWWM 90*
Elwyn-Jones, Lord 1909-1989 *AnObit 1989*
Elwyn-Jones, Frederick 1909-1989 *BioIn 16*
Elwyn-Jones of Llanelli & Newham, Baron 1909-1989 *BioIn 16*
Ely, Betty Jo 1947- *WhoEmL 91*
Ely, Bones 1863-1952 *Ballpl 90*
Ely, Bruce Peter 1955- *WhoEmL 91*
Ely, Donald Jean 1935- *WhoE 91, WhoWor 91*
Ely, Edward Marshall, II 1948- *St&PR 91*
Ely, Fanny G 1879-1961 *WhoAmA 91N*
Ely, George Melvin, Jr. 1927- *WhoSSW 91*
Ely, Joe *WhoNeCM [port]*
Ely, John Hart 1938- *WhoAm 90*
Ely, John Thomas Anderson 1923- *WhoWor 91*
Ely, Joseph Buell, II 1938- *St&PR 91, WhoAm 90, WhoE 91, WhoSSW 91*
Ely, Joy Wilson 1925- *BiDrAPA 89*
Ely, Lockhart *St&PR 91*
Ely, Marica McCann 1907- *WhoAmW 91, WhoWor 91*
Ely, Neal E *BiDrAPA 89*
Ely, Northcutt 1903- *WhoAm 90*
Ely, Paul C., Jr. 1932- *WhoAm 90*
Ely, Richard Theodore 1854-1943 *BioIn 16*
Ely, Robert Eugene 1949- *WhoEmL 91*
Ely, Robert Pollock, Jr. 1930- *WhoAm 90*
Ely, Timothy B. 1948- *St&PR 91*
Ely, Timothy Clyde 1949- *WhoAmA 91*
Ely, William H.H. 1943- *St&PR 91*
Elya, John Adel 1928- *WhoAm 90*
Elyachar, Jehiel R. *BioIn 16*
Elyan, Mohamed Ibrahim *BiDrAPA 89*
Elyasiani, Elyas 1949- *WhoE 91*
Elyea, Michael K. 1953- *St&PR 91*
Elymas the Sorcerer *EncO&P 3*
Elyn, Mark 1932- *WhoAm 90*
Elyse, Joy *WhoWrEP 89*
Elytis, Odysseus 1911- *EuWr 13, MajTwCW, WhoWor 91, WorAlBi*
Elzay, Richard Paul 1931- *WhoAm 90*
Elzea, Rowland Procter 1931- *WhoAmA 91, WhoE 91*
Elzinga, Donald Jack 1939- *WhoAm 90*
Elzinga, Peter 1944- *WhoAm 90*
Elzinga-Henry, Lynn Maree 1954- *WhoWor 91*
Em, David *BioIn 16*
Ema, Yasuo 1945- *WhoE 91, WhoWor 91*
Emad, Jamal 1931- *BiDrAPA 89, WhoE 91*
Emami, Mohsen 1945- *BiDrAPA 89*
Eman, Brenda Ethel 1947- *WhoWor 91*
Eman, Evelyn *ODwPR 91*
Eman, Henny *WhoWor 91*
Emans, Robert LeRoy 1934- *WhoAm 90*
Emants, Marcellus 1848-1923 *EncO&P 3*
Emanuel, Aaron *BioIn 16*
Emanuel, Diane Marie 1947- *WhoAmW 91*
Emanuel, Elise Anne 1938- *WhoSSW 91*
Emanuel, Herbert Leon 1930- *WhoAm 90*
Emanuel, Irvin 1926- *WhoAm 90*
Emanuel, Myron 1920- *ODwPR 91*
Emanuel, William Joseph 1938- *WhoAm 90*
Emanuele, Jack Anthony 1931- *St&PR 91*
Emanuele, Michael *BioIn 16*
Emanuelson, James Robert 1931- *St&PR 91, WhoAm 90*
Emanuelson, Karen Sue 1959- *WhoAmW 91, WhoSSW 91*
Emarthla, Charles *WhNaAH*
Emathla, Charley *WhNaAH*
Embach, James Thomas 1953- *WhoEmL 91*
Ember, Maria 1931- *EncCoWW*
Ember, Melvin Lawrence 1933- *WhoE 91*
Emberley, Edward Randolph 1931- *AuBYP 90*
Emblen, Frank J. *BioIn 16*
Embler, Stephen Frank 1952- *St&PR 91*
Embleton, Ron 1930-1988 *AnObit 1988*
Embleton, Tony Frederick Wallace 1929- *WhoAm 90*
Embody, Daniel Robert 1914- *WhoAm 90, WhoE 91, WhoWor 91*
Embody, Daniel Robert, Jr. 1954- *WhoEmL 91, WhoSSW 91*
Embree, A. S. 1877-1957 *EncAL*
Embree, Ainslie Thomas 1921- *WhoAm 90*
Embree, James Ray 1949- *WhoEmL 91, WhoSSW 91, WhoWor 91*
Embree, Lester Eugene 1938- *WhoE 91*
Embree, Norman R. 1943- *St&PR 91*
Embree, Red 1917- *Ballpl 90*
Embrey, Carl 1938- *BioIn 16*
Embrey, Carl Rice 1938- *WhoAmA 91*
Embrey, Cathy Graham 1956- *WhoAmW 91*
Embriachi, Antonio *PenDiDA 89*
Embriachi, Baldassare degli *PenDiDA 89*
Embriachi, Giovanni *PenDiDA 89*
Embry, Dianne C. 1932- *WhoAmW 91*
Embry, Jerry Jaggers *BiDrAPA 89*
Embry, Margaret Jacob 1919-1975 *AuBYP 90*
Embry, Michael Heard 1951- *WhoWor 91*
Embry, Norris 1921-1981 *WhoAmA 91N*
Embry, Stephen Creston 1949- *WhoEmL 91*
Embry, Susan Fleming 1954- *WhoAmW 91*
Embry, Wayne *BioIn 16*
Embry-Wardrop, Mary Rodriguez 1933- *WhoAmW 91*
Embury, Edward C. *BioIn 16, NewYTBS 90*
Embury, Emma 1806-1863 *FemiCLE*
Emch, Gerard Gustav 1936- *WhoAm 90, WhoSSW 91*
Emde, Robert N 1935- *BiDrAPA 89*
Emden, Jacob 1697?-1776 *BioIn 16*
Eme, Jim *BioIn 16*
Emecheta, Buchi *BioIn 16*
Emecheta, Buchi 1944- *FemiCLE, MajTwCW*
Emek, Sharon Helene 1945- *WhoAmW 91*
Emel, Thomas Jeffrey 1952- *WhoSSW 91*
Emelander, Ronald Lee 1961- *WhoEmL 91*
Emelity, David Clifford *BiDrAPA 89*
Emely, Charles Harry 1943- *WhoE 91, WhoWor 91*
Emen, Michael Stuart 1950- *St&PR 91*
Emenhiser, Jedon Allen 1933- *WhoAm 90*
Emens, Jan *PenDiDA 89*
Emerald Web *NewAgMG*
Emeric, Damaso 1921- *WhoHisp 91*
Emerich, Donald Warren 1920- *WhoAm 90, WhoSSW 91*
Emerick, Dale Alan Louis Edward 1951- *WhoSSW 91*
Emerick, David William 1945- *WhoSSW 91*
Emerick, James Edwin 1945- *St&PR 91*
Emerick, John P 1949- *BiDrAPA 89*

Emerick, Judson J 1941- *WhoAmA 91*
Emerick, Robert Twite 1950- *WhoE 91*
Emerine, Wendell R. 1939- *WhoSSW 91*
Emerine, Wendell Roger 1939- *St&PR 91*
Emering, Edward John 1945- *WhoWor 91*
Emering, Sandra Ann 1949- *WhoAmW 91*
Emerk, Kaya 1945- *WhoWor 91*
Emerling, Carol Frances 1930- *WhoAm 90, WhoAmW 91*
Emerling, Carol G. 1930- *St&PR 91*
Emerling, Stanley Justin 1926- *WhoSSW 91*
Emerson, Lake and Palmer *EncPR&S 89*
Emerson, Lake & Palmer/Powell *ConMus 5 [port]*
Emerson, Lake and Powell *EncPR&S 89*
Emerson, Alice Frey 1931- *WhoAm 90, WhoAmW 91, WhoE 91*
Emerson, Alton Calvin 1934- *WhoWor 91*
Emerson, Andi 1932- *WhoE 91, WhoWor 91*
Emerson, Andrew C. 1929- *St&PR 91*
Emerson, Andrew Craig 1929- *WhoAm 90*
Emerson, Ann Parker 1925- *WhoAmW 91*
Emerson, Anne Devereux 1946- *WhoAm 90, WhoEmL 91*
Emerson, Barbara Williams 1948- *WhoE 91*
Emerson, Cae Alexius 1950- *WhoEmL 91*
Emerson, Caroline Dwight 1891-1973 *AuBYP 90*
Emerson, Daniel Everett 1924- *St&PR 91, WhoAm 90*
Emerson, Danny G. 1947- *St&PR 91*
Emerson, David *BioIn 16*
Emerson, David Frederick 1926- *WhoAm 90*
Emerson, Deanna D 1939- *BiDrAPA 89*
Emerson, Donald Howard George 1939- *WhoWor 91*
Emerson, Duane E. 1937- *WhoAm 90*
Emerson, Earl W. 1948- *TwCCr&M 91*
Emerson, Edward James 194?- *WhoAm 90*
Emerson, Eleanor 1777-1808 *FemiCLE*
Emerson, Ellen T. 1809?-1831 *BioAmW*
Emerson, Everett Harvey 1925- *WhoWrEP 89*
Emerson, Frederick George 1933- *St&PR 91, WhoAm 90*
Emerson, Galo Putnam, Jr. 1932- *St&PR 91*
Emerson, Gloria *BioIn 16*
Emerson, Horace Mann, III 1914- *WhoAm 90*
Emerson, James Brownell 1937- *WhoSSW 91*
Emerson, James Larry 1938- *WhoSSW 91*
Emerson, Jerry Goodlett 1967- *WhoSSW 91*
Emerson, John Roy 1949- *WhoEmL 91*
Emerson, Kary Cadmus 1918- *WhoSSW 91, WhoWor 91*
Emerson, Kathy Lynn 1947- *SmATA 63 [port], WhoWrEP 89*
Emerson, Keith *ConMus 5 [port], EncPR&S 89*
Emerson, LeeAnne Rosenblum *WhoE 91*
Emerson, Lewis Cotesworth 1925- *WhoSSW 91*
Emerson, Lidian J. 1802-1892 *BioAmW*
Emerson, Madonna Sue 1942- *WhoAmW 91*
Emerson, Mark *WhoWrEP 89*
Emerson, Mark Forbush 1947- *WhoEmL 91*
Emerson, Paul Carlton 1923- *WhoAm 90*
Emerson, Ralph Waldo 1803-1882 *BioIn 16, WorAlBi, WrPh*
Emerson, Randall Allen 1948- *St&PR 91*
Emerson, Richard P *BiDrAPA 89*
Emerson, Roberta Shinn 1922- *WhoAmA 91*
Emerson, Rose 1945- *WhoAmW 91*
Emerson, Roy 1936- *WorAlBi*
Emerson, Ruth *BiDEWW*
Emerson, Sarae Susan 1947- *WhoAmW 91*
Emerson, Stephen Harold 1948- *IntWWM 90*
Emerson, Sylvia *BioIn 16*
Emerson, Thomas Edward, Jr. 1935- *WhoAm 90*
Emerson, Thomas Irwin 1907- *WhoAm 90*
Emerson, Tyra Kim 1957- *WhoAmW 91*
Emerson, Walter Caruth 1912- *WhoAm 90, WhoAmA 91, WhoWor 91*
Emerson, William 1938- *WhoAm 90*
Emerson, William Allen 1921- *WhoAm 90*
Emerson, William Harry 1928- *St&PR 91, WhoAm 90*
Emerson, William Keith 1925- *WhoAm 90*
Emerson, William R. *WhoAm 90*
Emerson, William Stevenson 1913- *WhoWor 91*
Emerson-Nelson, Diane Marie 1953- *WhoEmL 91*
Emerson-Smith, Luanne Bennett 1936- *WhoAmW 91*
Emery, Alan E. H. 1928- *WhoWor 91*
Emery, Alan Roy 1939- *WhoAm 90, WhoE 91*
Emery, Albion Bernard 1846-1894 *AmLegL*
Emery, Alden Hayes, Jr. 1925- *WhoAm 90*
Emery, Anne Eleanor McGuigan 1907- *AuBYP 90*
Emery, C.L., Jr. 1909- *St&PR 91*
Emery, Charles Christian, Jr. 1946- *WhoEmL 91*
Emery, Christine Vientiane 1957- *WhoAmW 91*
Emery, Dallas Truett John 1925- *St&PR 91*
Emery, Daniel Edward 1956- *WhoEmL 91*
Emery, Earl Eugene 1931- *St&PR 91*
Emery, Edwin 1914- *WhoAm 90*
Emery, Felice M *BiDrAPA 89*
Emery, Flora Mary *BiDrAPA 89*
Emery, Herschell Gene 1923- *WhoAm 90*
Emery, James L. 1931- *WhoAm 90*
Emery, James W. *St&PR 91*
Emery, James Woodward 1808-1891 *AmLegL*
Emery, Jill Houghton *WhoAm 90, WhoAmW 91*
Emery, John *BioIn 16*
Emery, John Colvin, Jr. 1924- *St&PR 91, WhoAm 90, WhoE 91*
Emery, Kenneth Orris 1914- *WhoAm 90*
Emery, Lavinia 1944- *St&PR 91*
Emery, Lin *WhoAmA 91*
Emery, Lynnda Joyce 1953- *WhoAmW 91*
Emery, Marc 1932- *ConAu 132*
Emery, Marcia Rose 1937- *WhoAmW 91, WhoWor 91*
Emery, Mary Alice 1924- *WhoAmW 91*
Emery, Mary Muhlenberg 1844-1927 *BioIn 16*
Emery, Oren Dale 1927- *WhoAm 90*
Emery, Paul E 1922- *BiDrAPA 89*
Emery, Paul Emile 1922- *WhoE 91*
Emery, Philip H., Jr. 1934- *St&PR 91*
Emery, Phyllis Helen Williams 1913- *WhoE 91*
Emery, Priscilla 1952- *WhoEmL 91*
Emery, Richard Gilbert 1915-1983 *DcNaB 1981*
Emery, Robert Firestone 1927- *WhoAm 90*
Emery, Robert J. 1937- *St&PR 91*
Emery, Ronald Howard 1944- *St&PR 91*
Emery, Russell Guy 1908- *AuBYP 90*
Emery, Sarah E.V. 1838-1895 *BioAmW*
Emery, Sherman R. *BioIn 16*
Emery, Sherman Raymond 1924- *WhoAm 90*
Emery, Sidney W., Jr. 1946- *St&PR 91*
Emery, Sue 1920- *WhoAm 90, WhoAmW 91*
Emery, Vince 1951- *WhoEmL 91*
Emes, John *PenDiDA 89*
Emes, Simon Nicholas 1959- *IntWWM 90*
Emick, William John 1931- *WhoSSW 91*
Emig, Donald Kenneth 1937- *St&PR 91*
Emig, Frank W. *BioIn 16*
Emig, Lois Irene 1925- *IntWWM 90*
Emigh, Donald C. 1927- *St&PR 91*
Emigh, Fonda Kay 1961- *WhoSSW 91*
Emil, Allan D 1898-1976 *WhoAmA 91N*
Emil, Arthur D 1924- *WhoAmA 91*
Emilian, Cornelia 1840-1910 *EncCoWW*
Emiliani, Andrea 1931- *WhoWor 91*
Emiliani, Cesare 1922- *WhoAm 90*
Emiliani, Nicholas Albert 1945- *BiDrAPA 89*
Emiliani, Vittorio 1935- *WhoWor 91*
Emilie *EncCoWW*
Emilita, Marie Bernadette 1945- *WhoAmW 91*
Emilson, C. Herbert *St&PR 91*
Emily, Dolores Jean 1952- *WhoWrEP 89*
Emin, Gevorg 1919- *WorAu 1980 [port]*
Eminescu, Mihai 1850-1889 *BioIn 16*
Emison, James W. 1930- *WhoAm 90*
Emistesigo 1752-1782 *WhNaAH*
Emken, Robert Allan 1929- *WhoAm 90*
Emken, Roy Lee *BiDrAPA 89*
Emlen, Stephen Thompson 1940- *WhoAm 90*
Emler, Jay Scott 1949- *WhoEmL 91*
Emlet, Harry Elsworth, Jr. 1927- *St&PR 91*
Emley, Suzanne Elaine 1949- *WhoAmW 91*
Emling, Jay 1955- *St&PR 91*
Emma *EncO&P 3, WomWR*
Emma, Arthur J. 1921-1989 *BioIn 16*
Emma, Robert J 1947- *BiDrAPA 89*
Emmanouilides, George Christos 1926- *WhoAm 90*
Emmanuel, Arghiri 1911- *WhoWor 91*
Emmanuel, Artemis 1923- *WhoWor 91*
Emmanuel, Daniel *NewAgMG*
Emmanuel, Hikmet N *BiDrAPA 89*
Emmanuel, Michel George 1918- *WhoAm 90*
Emmanuel, Naresh P *BiDrAPA 89*
Emmanuel, Pierre *ConAu 130*
Emmeline *EncCoWW*
Emmeluth, Bruce Palmer 1940- *WhoAm 90*
Emmen, Dennis R. 1933- *St&PR 91, WhoAm 90*
Emmens, Clifford Walter 1913- *WhoWor 91*
Emmens, David Peck 1948- *St&PR 91*
Emmer, Bradford Noel 1949- *WhoSSW 91*
Emmer, David M. 1954- *WhoEmL 91*
Emmer, Edward Z. 1946- *St&PR 91*
Emmer, John Richard 1940- *St&PR 91*
Emmer, Philip I. 1928- *St&PR 91*
Emmerich, Andre 1924- *WhoAm 90, WhoAmA 91, WhoE 91*
Emmerich, Anne-Catherine *EncCoWW*
Emmerich, Catherine 1774-1824 *EncO&P 3*
Emmerich, Irene Hillebrand *WhoAmA 91N*
Emmerich, Jo Ann *WhoAmW 91*
Emmerich, Jo Ann 1942- *St&PR 91*
Emmerich, John Patrick 1940- *St&PR 91*
Emmerich, Karol Denise 1948- *St&PR 91, WhoAm 90*
Emmerich, Klaus Rudolf 1928- *WhoWor 91*
Emmerich, Myron H. 1929- *St&PR 91*
Emmerich, Walter 1929- *WhoAm 90*
Emmerich, Werner Sigmund 1921- *WhoAm 90*
Emmerick, Anne-Catherine *EncCoWW*
Emmerling, Paul E. 1933- *St&PR 91*
Emmerman, Michael N 1945- *WhoAm 90*
Emmerson, Donald K. 1940- *ConAu 32NR*
Emmerson, J.O. 1920- *St&PR 91*
Emmerson, John Gregory 1950- *St&PR 91*
Emmerson, John Lynn 1933- *WhoAm 90*
Emmerson, Virginia Dillon 1929- *St&PR 91*
Emmert, Amor Charles, Jr. 1925- *St&PR 91*
Emmert, Gayle Evans 1938- *St&PR 91*
Emmert, Jeffrey Edward 1958- *IntWWM 90*
Emmert, Pauline Gore 1923- *WhoAmA 91*
Emmert, Richard Eugene 1929- *WhoAm 90, WhoE 91*
Emmert, Roy G. 1958- *St&PR 91*
Emmerton, William James 1947- *WhoAm 90*
Emmet, Christopher Temple 1943- *St&PR 91*
Emmet, E. *BiDWomA*
Emmet, Grenville Temple *BioIn 16*
Emmet, Herman Leroy *BioIn 16*
Emmet, Lydia Field 1866-1952 *BiDWomA*
Emmet, Lydia Field 1886-1952 *WhoAmA 91N*
Emmet, R *BiDWomA*
Emmet, Timothy Goodsmith 1958- *WhoEmL 91*
Emmett, Daniel Decatur 1815-1904 *OxCPMus, WorAlBi*
Emmett, Dorothy *BiDEWW*
Emmett, Frederick Joseph, Jr. 1945- *WhoAm 90*
Emmett, Martin F. C. 1934- *BioIn 16*
Emmett, Martin Frederick C. 1934- *St&PR 91*
Emmett, Michael 1945- *WhoSSW 91*
Emmett, Robert Addis, III 1943- *WhoAm 90*
Emmett, Walter Charles 1925- *WhoSSW 91, WhoWor 91*
Emmi, Michael J. 1942- *St&PR 91*
Emminger, David Wayne 1956- *WhoE 91*
Emmons, Beverly *BioIn 16*
Emmons, Beverly 1943- *NotWoAT*
Emmons, C. S. 1908- *WhoAm 90*
Emmons, Carl Willard, Jr. 1945- *BiDrAPA 89*
Emmons, Charles Wayne 1952- *WhoSSW 91*
Emmons, David Wayne 1954- *WhoAm 90*
Emmons, Delia McQuade 1947- *St&PR 91*
Emmons, Donn 1910- *WhoAm 90*
Emmons, Frederick E. 1907- *WhoAm 90*
Emmons, Guy W. 1947- *St&PR 91*
Emmons, Henry Carl 1958- *BiDrAPA 89, WhoEmL 91*
Emmons, Howard Wilson 1912- *WhoAm 90*
Emmons, Judith Crane 1954- *WhoAmW 91*
Emmons, Larry R. 1930- *St&PR 91*
Emmons, Larry Ralph 1930- *WhoAm 90*
Emmons, Linda Nye 1937- *WhoAmW 91*
Emmons, Lowell L *BiDrAPA 89*
Emmons, Marcus B 1915- *BiDrAPA 89*
Emmons, Marguerite Atteberry 1949- *WhoWrEP 89*
Emmons, Olin Neill 1917- *St&PR 91*
Emmons, Raymond Allen 1950- *St&PR 91, WhoAm 90*
Emmons, Robert Duncan 1932- *WhoAm 90*
Emmons, Robert John 1934- *WhoAm 90*
Emmons, Walter Franklin 1928- *St&PR 91*
Emmons, William Monroe, III 1959- *WhoE 91*
Emond, Douglas William 1960- *WhoE 91*
Emond, Edouard 1936- *St&PR 91*
Emond, Lionel Joseph 1932- *WhoE 91, WhoWor 91*
Emont, Milton David 1923- *WhoAm 90*
Emord, Jonathan Walker 1961- *WhoEmL 91*
Emorey, Howard O. 1928- *St&PR 91*
Emorey, Howard Omer 1928- *WhoAm 90*
Emory, Emerson 1925- *WhoWor 91*
Emory, John Brooks, III 1942- *WhoSSW 91*
Emory, John Druse 1938- *St&PR 91*
Emory, Kenneth Pike 1897- *BioIn 16*
Emory, Lee E. 1944- *BiDrAPA 89*
Emory, Martha Keller 1949- *WhoAmW 91*
Emory, Meade 1931- *WhoAm 90*
Emory, Samuel Thomas 1933- *WhoSSW 91*
Emory, Thomas M., Jr. 1940- *St&PR 91*
Emott, David T. 1944- *St&PR 91*
Empedocles 484?BC-424BC *WrPh P*
Empedocles 495?BC-435?BC *WorAlBi*
Emperado, Mercedes Lopez 1941- *WhoAm 90*
Emperor Akihito 1933- *WhoWor 91*
Empey, LaMar T 1923- *ConAu 30NR*
Empie, Hart Haller 1909- *WhoWor 91*
Emplit, Raymond Henry 1948- *WhoEmL 91, WhoWor 91*
Empson, William 1906-1984 *ConAu 31NR, DcNaB 1981, MajTwCW*
Empting-Koschorke, Larry D 1952- *BiDrAPA 89*
Emr, Stephen Thomas 1946- *St&PR 91*
Emrealp, Sadun Hasan 1954- *WhoWor 91*
Emrich, Duncan 1908-197-? *AuBYP 90*
Emrich, Edmund Michael 1956- *WhoEmL 91*
Emrich, Nancy Jones 1950- *WhoAmW 91*
Emrich, William Julius 1925- *St&PR 91*
Emrick, Michael Edward 1945- *WhoEmL 91*
Emrick, Terry Lamar 1935- *WhoAm 90*
Emry, C. Bruce 1946- *ODwPR 91*
Emry, Douglas Kriss 1938- *WhoWrEP 89*
Emshwiller, Carol Fries 1921- *WhoWrEP 89*
Emshwiller, Ed *NewYTBS 90*
Emshwiller, Ed 1925- *WhoAm 90*
Emslie, Bob 1859-1953 *Ballpl 90*
Emslie, Graham J 1950- *BiDrAPA 89*
Emslie-Smith, Donald 1922- *WhoWor 91*
Emson, Harry Edmund 1927- *WhoAm 90*
Emura, John K. 1935- *St&PR 91*
En Herdinna i Norden *EncCoWW*
Ena, Teruhiko *St&PR 91*
Enamurado Cuesta, Jose 1892- *HispWr 90*
Enaohwo, John Okpako 1950- *WhoWor 91*
Enarson, Harold L. 1919- *WhoAm 90*
Enatsu, Yutaka 1949- *Ballpl 90*
Enayat-Pour, Seyed Mohammad 1945- *BiDrAPA 89*
Enberg, Denis Alan *WhoWor 91*
Enberg, Dick *WhoAm 90*
Enberg, Henry Winfield 1940- *WhoE 91, WhoWor 91*
Encarnacao, Jose Luis 1941- *WhoWor 91*
Encarnacion-Kuilan, Eliseo *BiDrAPA 89*
Encausse, Gerard 1865-1916 *EncO&P 3*
Ench, Robert *WhoAm 90*
Enchi Fumiko 1905-1986 *ConAu 129*
Enchi, Fumiko 1905-1986 *WorAu 1980*
Encinias, John *BioIn 16*
Enciso, J. Raul 1954- *WhoEmL 91*
Enckell, Rabbe 1903-1974 *DcScanL*
Encle, Warren Charles 1948- *St&PR 91*
End, Henry 1915- *WhoAm 90, WhoWor 91*
End, John Michael 1946- *WhoEmL 91*
End, Ralph P. 1938- *St&PR 91, WhoAm 90*
End, William Thomas 1947- *WhoAm 90*
Endara, Guillermo *BioIn 16, WhoWor 91*
Ende, Michael 1929- *SmATA 61 [port], WorAu 1980 [port]*
Endecott, John 1588?-1665 *WhNaAH*
Endecott, John 1589?-1665 *EncCRAm*
Endell, August 1871-1925 *PenDiDA 89*
Endellion Quartet *PenDiMP*
Endelman, Sharon Jean 1948- *WhoEmL 91*
Endemann, Carl T. 1902- *WhoWrEP 89*
Ender, Clara Adams- *BioIn 16*
Ender, Elma Teresa Salinas 1953- *WhoHisp 91*
Ender, Jon T. 1942- *St&PR 91*
Ender, Jon Terry 1942- *WhoAm 90*
Enderle, Judith Ross 1941- *WhoWrEP 89*
Enderlein, Caspar 1560-1633 *PenDiDA 89*
Enderlin, Lee 1951- *WhoWrEP 89*
Enders, Allen Coffin 1928- *WhoAm 90*
Enders, Anthony Talcott 1937- *WhoAm 90*
Enders, August *EncCoWW*

Enders, Elizabeth McGuire 1939- *WhoAmA 91*
Enders, John F. 1897-1985 *WorAlBi*
Enders, Patrick D 1946- *BiDrAPA 89*
Enders, Richard *ConAu 32NR*
Enders, Thomas O. *BioIn 16*
Endich, Sylvan Victor 1945- *WhoE 91*
Endicott, David *ODwPR 91*
Endicott, Frank S 1904-1990 *ConAu 131*
Endicott, John 1588?-1665 *WhNaAH*
Endicott, Kenneth 1916- *BioIn 16*
Endicott, Noble A 1929- *BiDrAPA 89*
Endicott, William Crowninshield 1826-1900 *BiDrUSE 89*
Endicott, William F. 1935- *WhoAm 90*
Endieveri, Anthony Frank 1939- *WhoE 91, WhoWor 91*
Endlein, Kathryn Ann 1955- *WhoAmW 91*
Endler, Norman Solomon 1931- *WhoAm 90*
Endo Shusaku 1923- *EncJap*
Endo, Akira *PenDiMP*
Endo, Akira 1938- *IntWWM 90*
Endo, Shusaku 1923- *BioIn 16, MajTwCW, WhoWor 91*
Endon, Tace *BiDEWW*
Endore, Gita 1944- *WhoWrEP 89*
Endraske, Marilyn Joann 1947- *WhoAmW 91*
Endre, Laszlo 1896-1946 *BioIn 16*
Endrenyi, Janos 1927- *WhoAm 90*
Endres, Ernst Wolfgang 1943- *St&PR 91*
Endres, James Alfred 1951- *WhoSSW 91*
Endres, Peter 1939- *WhoWor 91*
Endres, Stephen Michael 1950- *St&PR 91*
Endresen, Endre, Jr. 1925- *St&PR 91*
Endress, Jay Wayne 1960- *WhoEmL 91*
Endrich, Thomas James Joseph 1942- *IntWWM 90*
Endries, John Michael 1942- *St&PR 91, WhoAm 90*
Endriss, James Wagner 1933- *WhoSSW 91*
Endruschat, Robert W. 1930- *St&PR 91*
Endsjo, Per-Christian 1941- *WhoWor 91*
Endsley, Gregory Howard 1949- *WhoEmL 91*
Endthoff, Gertrude Ellen 1918- *WhoAmW 91*
Endy, Melvin Becker, Jr. 1938- *WhoAm 90*
Endyke, Debra Joan 1955- *WhoAmW 91, WhoEmL 91*
Enebakk, Magnar Henry 1929- *WhoWor 91*
Enegren, Bradley 1947- *St&PR 91*
Enell, John Warren 1919- *WhoAm 90*
Enelow, Allen J 1922- *BiDrAPA 89*
Enelow, Allen Jay 1922- *WhoAm 90*
Enelow, Michael Ralph 1932- *WhoE 91*
Enelow, Morton L 1925- *BiDrAPA 89*
Eneme, Santiago Ovono 1958- *WhoWor 91*
Enenbach, David Edward 1959- *WhoEmL 91*
Enersen, Burnham 1905- *WhoAm 90*
Enesco, Georges 1881-1955 *PenDiMP*
Enescu, George 1881-1955 *PenDiMP*
Enfanto, Phyllis Anne 1958- *WhoE 91*
Enfield, Clifton Willis 1918- *WhoAm 90*
Enfield, Elizabeth Ann 1944- *WhoE 91*
Enfield, Franklin D. 1933- *WhoAm 90*
Enfield, Harry 1906-1958 *WhoAmA 91N*
Eng, Andrea *BioIn 16*
Eng, Anne Chin 1950- *WhoAmW 91*
Eng, Gloria 1951- *St&PR 91*
Eng, Ingrid Ong Lee 1962- *WhoAmW 91*
Eng, Joyce Frances 1946- *WhoWor 91*
Eng, Leonard K. *BiDrAPA 89*
Eng, Mamie 1954- *WhoEmL 91*
Eng, Steve 1940- *WhoWrEP 89*
Eng, William 1950- *WhoWor 91*
Enga, Richard J. *BioIn 16*
Engber, Michael Arthur 1942- *WhoE 91*
Engberg, Eric *BioIn 16*
Engberg, Robert Eugene 1937- *St&PR 91*
Engblom, Jarl Erik 1920- *WhoWor 91*
Engblom, Soeren Harry 1950- *WhoWor 91*
Engdahl, Horace 1948- *WhoWor 91*
Engdahl, Richard Alan 1941- *WhoSSW 91*
Engdahl, Richard Bott 1914- *WhoAm 90*
Engdahl, Sylvia Louise 1933- *AuBYP 90, BioIn 16*
Engebretsen, Arden Bernt *WhoAm 90*
Engebretsen, Arden Bernt 1931- *St&PR 91*
Engebretson, Charles K. 1950- *St&PR 91*
Engebretson, David J. 1951- *St&PR 91*
Engebretson, Terry *BioIn 16*
Engel, A. J. *ConAu 129*
Engel, Alan *ConAu 132*
Engel, Alan James 1947- *St&PR 91*
Engel, Albert Joseph 1924- *WhoAm 90*
Engel, Alfred Julius 1927- *WhoAm 90*
Engel, Andrew George 1930- *WhoAm 90*
Engel, Anne Rice 1963- *WhoAmW 91*
Engel, Arthur 1944- *ConAu 129*
Engel, Barbara Marcus 1946- *WhoAmW 91*
Engel, Bernard Theodore 1928- *WhoAm 90*
Engel, Beth Ann 1965- *WhoEmL 91*
Engel, Bob 1933- *Ballpl 90*
Engel, Brian Evan 1951- *WhoEmL 91*
Engel, Celeste G. *BioIn 16*
Engel, Charlene Stant 1946- *WhoAmW 91*
Engel, Charles Clifford, Jr. *BiDrAPA 89*
Engel, Charles Robert 1922- *WhoAm 90, WhoWor 91*
Engel, Conrad Albert 1943- *St&PR 91*
Engel, David Anthony 1951- *WhoE 91*
Engel, David Donald 1937- *St&PR 91*
Engel, David E. 1928- *WhoE 91*
Engel, David M. 1947- *St&PR 91*
Engel, David S. 1944- *St&PR 91*
Engel, David Wayne 1956- *WhoEmL 91*
Engel, Edward John 1948- *St&PR 91*
Engel, Eliot L. 1947- *BioIn 16, WhoAm 90, WhoE 91*
Engel, Frances Holiday 1915- *WhoAmW 91*
Engel, Francis Anton *BiDrAPA 89*
Engel, Frederik 1924- *St&PR 91*
Engel, George L *BiDrAPA 89*
Engel, George Larry 1947- *WhoEmL 91*
Engel, George Libman 1913- *WhoAm 90*
Engel, Harry 1901-1970 *WhoAmA 91N*
Engel, Herman A., Jr. 1915- *St&PR 91*
Engel, Howard 1931- *TwCCr&M 91*
Engel, Irving H. 1909- *St&PR 91*
Engel, Ivan J *BiDrAPA 89*
Engel, J.H. 1916- *St&PR 91*
Engel, James Joseph 1934- *St&PR 91*
Engel, Joan Marcia 1946- *WhoAmW 91*
Engel, Joe 1893-1969 *Ballpl 90*
Engel, Joel Stanley 1936- *WhoAm 90*
Engel, John Charles 1955- *WhoEmL 91*
Engel, John Jacob 1936- *WhoE 91*
Engel, Joseph Henry 1922- *WhoAm 90*
Engel, Juergen Kurt 1945- *WhoWor 91*
Engel, Karl 1923- *IntWWM 90*
Engel, Keith Curtiss 1948- *St&PR 91*
Engel, Lehman 1910-1982 *ConAu 31NR, OxCPMus*
Engel, Lenore *BiDrAPA 89*
Engel, Linda Jeanne 1949- *St&PR 91, WhoEmL 91*
Engel, Ludwig 1922- *WhoWor 91*
Engel, Madeline Helena 1941- *WhoE 91*
Engel, Marian 1933-1985 *FemiCLE*
Engel, Mary Grace 1924- *IntWWM 90*
Engel, Melissa Hale 1956- *WhoAmW 91*
Engel, Michael Francis *BiDrAPA 89*
Engel, Michael M 1896-1969 *WhoAmA 91N*
Engel, Michael Martin, II 1919- *WhoAmA 91, WhoE 91*
Engel, Milton 1935- *BiDrAPA 89, WhoE 91*
Engel, Monroe 1921- *WhoWrEP 89*
Engel, Nancy Lou *BiDrAPA 89, WhoE 91*
Engel, Nancy Sharts 1953- *WhoE 91*
Engel, Pamela Marie 1956- *WhoAmW 91*
Engel, Paul Bernard 1926- *WhoAm 90*
Engel, Peter H. *BioIn 16*
Engel, Ralph 1934- *WhoAm 90*
Engel, Ralph Manuel 1944- *WhoAm 90*
Engel, Robert 1952- *WhoE 91*
Engel, Robert Gehrels 1932- *WhoAm 90, WhoE 91*
Engel, Ronald Richard 1936- *St&PR 91*
Engel, Steen 1930- *WhoWor 91*
Engel, Stephanie 1952- *BiDrAPA 89*
Engel, Thomas 1942- *WhoAm 90*
Engel, Victor Boynton 1914- *WhoWor 91*
Engel, Walter *BioIn 16, NewYTBS 90*
Engel, Walter F 1908- *WhoAmA 91*
Engel, Werner H 1901- *BiDrAPA 89*
Engel, William Thomas, Jr. 1945- *WhoSSW 91*
Engel-Arieli, Susan Lee 1954- *WhoAmW 91, WhoEmL 91, WhoWor 91*
Engelbach, Florence 1872-1951 *BiDWomA*
Engelbardt, Robert Miles 1931- *St&PR 91, WhoAm 90*
Engelberg, Alan 1941- *ConAu 132*
Engelberg, Elaine A. 1930- *WhoAmW 91*
Engelberg, Steven James 1944- *BiDrAPA 89*
Engelberger, John K. 1930- *St&PR 91*
Engelberger, Joseph F. *BioIn 16*
Engelberger, Joseph F. 1925- *St&PR 91*
Engelberger, Joseph Frederick 1925- *WhoAm 90*
Engelberger, William V. 1938- *St&PR 91*
Engelbert, Arthur Ferdinand 1903- *WhoAm 90*
Engelbert, Roger Lee 1935- *BiDrAPA 89*
Engelbirn *EncCoWW*
Engelbrecht, Dale Robert 1959- *WhoEmL 91*
Engelbrecht, Eileen 1945- *IntWWM 90*
Engelbrecht, Hans-Juergen Alois Jakob 1956- *WhoWor 91*
Engelbrecht, Johann 1599-1642 *EncO&P 3*
Engelbrecht, Mary Lou 1954- *WhoE 91*
Engelbrecht, Richard Stevens 1926- *WhoAm 90*
Engelbrecht, Rudolf 1928- *WhoAm 90*
Engelbrecht, William Robert 1949- *St&PR 91*
Engelbretsdatter, Dorothe 1634-1716 *DcScanL*
Engelbretsdatter, Dorothe 1643-1716 *EncCoWW*
Engeleiter, Gerald H. 1951- *St&PR 91*
Engeleiter, Susan Shannon 1952- *WhoAmW 91*
Engeler, Margaret 1933- *IntWWM 90*
Engeler, William Ernest 1928- *WhoAm 90*
Engelhard, Diane Mary 1964- *WhoAmW 91*
Engelhard, Jack 1940- *ConAu 132*
Engelhard, Karl 1926- *WhoWor 91*
Engelhard, Magdalene Philippine 1756-1831 *EncCoWW*
Engelhardt, Albert George 1935- *WhoAm 90, WhoSSW 91*
Engelhardt, Cynthia Allison 1950- *WhoEmL 91*
Engelhardt, David M 1912- *BiDrAPA 89*
Engelhardt, Dean Lee 1940- *St&PR 91, WhoAm 90*
Engelhardt, Fred 1932- *St&PR 91*
Engelhardt, Hugo Tristram, Jr. 1941- *WhoAm 90, WhoWor 91*
Engelhardt, John Hugo 1946- *WhoEmL 91, WhoSSW 91, WhoWor 91*
Engelhardt, LeRoy A. 1924- *WhoAm 90*
Engelhardt, Mary Veronice 1912- *WhoAmW 91*
Engelhardt, Robert Joseph 1941- *St&PR 91*
Engelhardt, Rolf-Udo 1935- *WhoWor 91*
Engelhardt, Sara Lawrence 1943- *WhoAm 90*
Engelhardt, Susan Gay 1943- *WhoSSW 91*
Engelhardt, Thomas Alexander 1930- *WhoAm 90, WhoAmA 91*
Engelhart, Margaret 1924- *BioIn 16*
Engelhart, Michael Anthony 1945- *WhoAm 90*
Engelhart, Timothy Alan 1951- *St&PR 91*
Engelhorn, H Douglas 1937- *BiDrAPA 89*
Engelke, Kent Eric 1963- *WhoSSW 91*
Engelken, Edward Joseph 1939- *WhoSSW 91*
Engelkes, Donald John 1938- *St&PR 91, WhoAm 90*
Engelking, Ellen Melinda 1942- *WhoAmW 91, WhoWor 91*
Engelking, Henry Mark 1949- *WhoEmL 91*
Engelman, Donald Bertam 1948- *WhoEmL 91*
Engelman, Donald Max 1941- *WhoAm 90*
Engelman, Irwin 1934- *St&PR 91, WhoAm 90*
Engelman, Judith Carol *BiDrAPA 89*
Engelman, Karl 1933- *WhoAm 90*
Engelman, Melvin Alkon 1921- *WhoAm 90, WhoWor 91*
Engelman, Robert Mark 1951- *WhoE 91*
Engelman, Robert S. 1912- *WhoAm 90*
Engelman, Susan Phyllis 1948- *WhoE 91*
Engelmann, Folker 1931- *WhoWor 91*
Engelmann, Gunnar Asbjorn 1930- *WhoWor 91*
Engelmann, Hans Ulrich 1921- *IntWWM 90*
Engelmann, Hugo Otto 1917- *WhoAm 90*
Engelmann, Lothar Klaus 1926- *WhoAm 90*
Engelmann, Rudolf Jacob 1930- *WhoAm 90*
Engels, Frank A. 1936- *St&PR 91*
Engels, Friedrich 1820-1895 *WorAlBi*
Engels, Kathleen M. 1943- *St&PR 91*
Engels, Lawrence Arthur 1933- *St&PR 91, WhoAm 90*
Engels, Thomas J. 1958- *WhoEmL 91*
Engels, William D *BiDrAPA 89*
Engelson, Carol 1944- *WhoAmA 91*
Engelson, Carol Sue 1944- *WhoE 91*
Engelson, David 1920- *St&PR 91*
Engelstad, Ralph *BioIn 16*
Engeman, Jack, Mrs. 1912- *WhoAmW 91*
Engeman, John T. 1901- *AuBYP 90*
Engeman, William Knowles 1939- *WhoAm 90*
Engemann, Robert B. 1949- *St&PR 91*
Engen, D. Travis 1944- *St&PR 91*
Engen, Donald Davenport 1924- *WhoAm 90*
Engen, Donald Travis 1944- *WhoAm 90*
Engen, Keith 1925- *IntWWM 90, PenDiMP*
Enger, Carl Christian 1929- *WhoSSW 91*
Enger, Edward Henry, Jr. 1930- *WhoE 91*
Enger, Linda May 1955- *WhoEmL 91*
Enger, Walter Melvin 1914- *WhoAm 90*
Enger, Warren Jay 1940- *WhoE 91*
Engeran, Whitney John, Jr 1934- *WhoAmA 91*
Engerer, Brigitte 1952- *IntWWM 90*
Engerman, Stanley Lewis 1936- *WhoAm 90*
Engerrand, Doris Dieskow 1925- *WhoAmW 91, WhoSSW 91*
Engerrand, Kenneth G. 1952- *WhoWor 91*
Engers, John Albert, III *BiDrAPA 89*
Engert, Cornelius Van Hemert 1887-1985 *BioIn 16*
Engeswick, John Clifford 1934- *St&PR 91*
Engfer, Susan Marvel 1943- *WhoAm 90*
Enggaard, Knud 1929- *WhoWor 91*
Enggass, Robert 1921- *WhoAm 90, WhoAmA 91*
Engh, N. Rolf 1953- *WhoEmL 91*
Enghoff, Torben 1947- *IntWWM 90*
Engholm, Mary Korstad Mueller 1918- *WhoAmW 91, WhoWor 91*
Engibarov, Leonid G. 1935-1972 *BioIn 16*
Engineer, Madhubala F *BiDrAPA 89*
England, Anthony Wayne 1942- *WhoAm 90*
England, Arthur Jay, Jr. 1932- *WhoAm 90*
England, Brenda 1940- *WhoAmW 91*
England, C. McDonald 1916- *St&PR 91*
England, C. R. Bud *WhoSSW 91*
England, Dan Benjamin 1955- *WhoEmL 91, WhoSSW 91*
England, Daniel Eugene 1947- *St&PR 91*
England, Edward 1937- *St&PR 91*
England, Gary L. 1958- *St&PR 91*
England, Howard 1935- *St&PR 91*
England, Jack Ray 1921- *St&PR 91*
England, James W. 1938- *WhoAm 90*
England, John F.L. 1936- *St&PR 91*
England, Jonnie Lee 1949- *WhoSSW 91*
England, Joseph Walker 1940- *St&PR 91, WhoAm 90*
England, Lynne Lipton 1949- *WhoAmW 91, WhoEmL 91, WhoSSW 91, WhoWor 91*
England, Martha Winburn 1909-1989 *BioIn 16*
England, Mary Jane R *BiDrAPA 89*
England, Richard 1920- *St&PR 91, WhoAm 90*
England, Ruth Catherine 1955- *WhoAm 90*
England, Stephen James 1951- *WhoEmL 91*
England, Walter Gardner *BiDrAPA 89*
Englander, Benjamin H. 1907-1989 *BioIn 16*
Englander, Elliot Jordan 1931- *St&PR 91*
Englander, Gertrud 1904- *WhoAmA 91*
Englander, Joseph 1908- *St&PR 91*
Englander, Lester 1911- *IntWWM 90*
Englander, Ludwig 1859-1914 *OxCPMus*
Englander, Paula Tyo 1951- *WhoAmW 91, WhoEmL 91*
Englander, Robert L. 1933- *St&PR 91*
Englander, Roger Leslie 1926- *WhoAm 90*
Englander, Stanley, Mrs. *WhoE 91*
Englander, Tom 1946- *WhoSSW 91*
Englar, John David 1947- *St&PR 91, WhoAm 90*
Englard, Sara Fae 1959- *WhoEmL 91*
Engle, Adam S. 1963- *WhoE 91*
Engle, Almer Cabler, Jr. 1929- *WhoSSW 91*
Engle, Barbara Joanne 1933- *WhoE 91*
Engle, Benjamin J. 1941- *WhoWor 91*
Engle, Carole Ruth 1952- *WhoSSW 91*
Engle, Chet 1918- *WhoAmA 91*
Engle, Clyde 1884-1939 *Ballpl 90*
Engle, Clyde Wm. *St&PR 91*
Engle, Dave 1956- *Ballpl 90*
Engle, Donald Edward 1927- *WhoAm 90*
Engle, Harold Martin 1914- *WhoAm 90*
Engle, Jacob L. 1937- *ODwPR 91*
Engle, James Bruce 1919- *WhoAm 90*
Engle, Janet Patricia 1959- *WhoAmW 91*
Engle, Jeannette Cranfill 1941- *WhoAmW 91*
Engle, John D., Jr. 1922- *LiHiK*
Engle, John David, Jr. 1922- *WhoSSW 91*
Engle, Mark Tyler 1960- *WhoE 91*
Engle, Mary Allen English 1922- *WhoAm 90, WhoAmW 91*
Engle, Paul Hamilton 1908- *WhoWrEP 89*
Engle, Peggy Lorraine Smalling 1956- *WhoAmW 91*
Engle, Ralph Landis, Jr. 1920- *WhoAm 90*
Engle, Ralph P, Jr. 1932- *BiDrAPA 89*
Engle, Richard Carlyle 1934- *St&PR 91, WhoAm 90*
Engle, Robert Jackson 1922- *St&PR 91*
Engle, Robert V. *BioIn 16*
Engle, Sandra Louise 1949- *WhoAmW 91, WhoEmL 91*
Engledow, Frank Leonard 1890-1985 *DcNaB 1981*
Engledow, Jack Lee 1931- *WhoAm 90*
Englehart, Gerald F. 1927- *WhoAm 90*
Englehart, Harry 1947- *ODwPR 91*
Englehart, Joan Anne 1940- *WhoAmW 91, WhoWor 91*
Englehart, Richard Eric 1948- *IntWWM 90*
Englehart, Theodore M. 1920- *St&PR 91*

Englehaupt, William Myles 1918- WhoAm 90
Englehaupt, William Myles, III 1954- WhoEmL 91
Engleman, Charles Edward 1911- WhoSSW 91
Engleman, Dennis Eugene 1948- WhoSSW 91
Engleman, Donald James 1947- St&PR 91, WhoAm 90
Engleman, Ephraim Philip 1911- WhoAm 90
Engleman, Gene E. 1911- St&PR 91
Engleman, Patricia Lee 1952- WhoE 91
Engleman, Paul 1953- ConAu 131
Engleman, Reinhold 1918- St&PR 91
Engler, Frank Robert, Jr. 1947- WhoAm 90
Engler, Frederick Ernst 1928- St&PR 91
Engler, George Nichols 1944- WhoAm 90
Engler, Gideon 1936- WhoWor 91
Engler, Hans Philipp 1953- WhoE 91
Engler, Kathleen Girdler 1951- WhoAmA 91
Engler, Lilly 1918- BiDrAPA 89
Engler, Mark A. 1930- St&PR 91
Engler, Marky Ann 1956- WhoAmW 91
Engler, Michael BioIn 16
Engler, Robert 1922- WhoAm 90
Engler, W. Joseph, Jr. 1940- St&PR 91, WhoAm 90
Engler, William Dean, Jr. 1936- St&PR 91
Englert, Herbert Charles 1921- WhoE 91
Englert, Joseph S. 1918- St&PR 91
Englert, Roy Theodore 1922- WhoAm 90
Engles, Charles R. 1947- St&PR 91
Engles, Lily Lore BiDrAPA 89
Engles, Loretta Graham 1926- WhoSSW 91
Englesmith, Tejas 1941- WhoAm 90
Engley, Donald Brown 1917- WhoAm 90
Engli, Frank 1906-1977 EncACom
Engling, Robert John 1945- St&PR 91, WhoAm 90
English Beat, The EncPR&S 89
English, Alex 1954- WorAlBi
English, Alexander 1954- WhoAm 90
English, Arthur Vernon 1946- WhoSSW 91
English, Charles Brand 1924- WhoAm 90
English, Charles Royal 1938- WhoWor 91
English, Cindy Marie 1957- WhoAmW 91
English, Dale Lowell 1956- WhoEmL 91
English, David Floyd 1948- WhoE 91, WhoEmL 91
English, Donald Marvin 1951- WhoEmL 91
English, Edna Soraghan 1938- St&PR 91
English, Elizabeth Ann 1962- WhoEmL 91
English, Elizabeth Stacy 1959- WhoAmW 91
English, Ellen Darlene 1952- WhoAmW 91
English, Floyd Leroy 1934- St&PR 91, WhoAm 90
English, Francis Peter 1932- WhoWor 91
English, Gerald 1925- IntWWM 90
English, Gil 1909- Ballpl 90
English, Glenn 1940- WhoAm 90, WhoSSW 91
English, Helen Williams Drutt WhoAmA 91
English, Jack R. 1930- St&PR 91
English, James Duston 1941- St&PR 91
English, James Fairfield, Jr. 1927- WhoAm 90, WhoE 91
English, John Arbogast 1913- WhoAmA 91
English, John Wesley 1940- WhoWrEP 89
English, John Winfield 1933- WhoE 91
English, Joseph R. 1931- St&PR 91
English, Joseph T BiDrAPA 89
English, Joseph Thomas 1933- WhoAm 90
English, Kenneth Landford 1928- WhoSSW 91
English, Kevin W. 1953- St&PR 91
English, Lawrence Gregory 1948- St&PR 91
English, Lawrence William 1942- St&PR 91
English, Linda Ryan 1951- WhoAmW 91
English, Louis C BiDrAPA 89
English, Marlanda 1962- WhoEmL 91
English, Nicholas Conover 1912- WhoAm 90
English, Oliver S 1901- BiDrAPA 89
English, Paul Ward 1936- WhoAm 90, WhoSSW 91
English, Richard Allyn 1936- WhoAm 90
English, Richard D. 1948- WhoAm 90, WhoEmL 91
English, Robert Joseph 1932- WhoAm 90
English, Ruth Ann Cowder 1948- WhoAmW 91, WhoSSW 91
English, Ruth Hill 1904- WhoAmW 91, WhoE 91
English, Sally Ann 1946- WhoAmW 91
English, Sam BioIn 16
English, Stanley Fraser 1935- St&PR 91
English, Thomas James 1942- WhoAm 90
English, Walter 1904- St&PR 91
English, Wannell T. 1940- St&PR 91
English, Wayne Gordon 1922- St&PR 91
English, Wilke Denton 1949- WhoEmL 91
English, William Berkeley 1960- WhoE 91
English, William DeShay 1924- St&PR 91, WhoAm 90
English, William H 1902- BiDrAPA 89
English, William Hayden 1822-1896 AmLegL
English, William Hazen 1929- WhoAm 90
English, William N. 1950- St&PR 91
English, William Russell 1918- WhoE 91
English, Woodruff Jones 1909- WhoAm 90
English, Woody 1907- Ballpl 90
English, Zeborah Anita 1951- WhoEmL 91
Englund, Gage Bush 1931- WhoAm 90, WhoAmW 91, WhoSSW 91
Englund, Gregory Joseph 1956- WhoEmL 91
Englund, Gunnar Martin 1940- WhoWor 91
Englund, John Arthur 1926- St&PR 91, WhoAm 90
Englund, Lori Jean 1961- WhoAmW 91
Englund, Paul Theodore 1938- WhoAm 90
Englund, Robert BioIn 16
Englund, Robert 1949- ConTFT 8 [port], CurBio 90 [port]
Englund, Robert Derr 1947- St&PR 91
Englund, Sven Einer 1916- IntWWM 90
Engman, Gosta Einar 1945- WhoWor 91
Engman, John Robert 1949- WhoWrEP 89
Engman, Lewis August 1936- WhoAm 90, WhoWor 91
Engmann, Douglas Joe 1947- WhoEmL 91
Engo, Paul Bamela 1931- WhoWor 91
Engolia, Anthony Joseph 1960- WhoEmL 91
Engoren, Sampson Seymour 1929- WhoAm 90, WhoE 91
Engoron, Edward David 1946- WhoEmL 91, WhoWor 91
Engram, Beverly Leigh WhoAmW 91
Engram, Sara BioIn 16
Engstrom, Albert 1869-1940 DcScanL
Engstrom, Arne Vilhelm 1920- WhoWor 91
Engstrom, Bengt Olof 1926- IntWWM 90
Engstrom, Denton P BiDrAPA 89
Engstrom, Donald Elton 1934- BiDrAPA 89
Engstrom, Eric Gustaf 1942- WhoAm 90
Engstrom, Frederick W BiDrAPA 89
Engstrom, George F BiDrAPA 89
Engstrom, Karl William 1926- St&PR 91
Engstrom, Mark William 1955- WhoEmL 91
Engstrom, N. Daniel 1928- St&PR 91, WhoAm 90
Engstrom, Peter BioIn 16
Engum, Eric Stanley 1949- WhoSSW 91
Engver, Nikolai Nikolayevich BioIn 16
Engvick, William AuBYP 90
Engvold, Oddbjorn 1938- WhoWor 91
Enhorning, Constance Elisabet 1945- WhoWor 91
Enichen, Robert C. 1948- St&PR 91
Enis, Ben M 1942- WhoWrEP 89
Enis, Eva Marie WhoAmW 91
Enix, Agnes Lucille 1933- WhoAm 90
Enjeti, Mahesh Kumar 1953- WhoWor 91
Enke, Karin BioIn 16
Enloe, Cortez Ferdinand, Jr. 1910- WhoAm 90, WhoE 91, WhoWor 91
Enloe, Ed BioIn 16
Enloe, James A. 1938- St&PR 91
Enloe, Rebecca Lynn 1949- WhoSSW 91
Enloe, Robert Ted, III 1938- WhoAm 90, WhoSSW 91
Enloe, Ted 1938- St&PR 91
Enlow, Donald Hugh 1927- WhoAm 90
Enlow, Fred Clark 1940- WhoAm 90
Enlow, Larry Daniel 1947- St&PR 91
Enlund, E. Stanley 1917- St&PR 91
Enman, Tom Kenneth 1928- WhoAmA 91
Enmegahbowh WhNaAH
Enna, Salvatore Joseph 1944- WhoAm 90
Enna, Stephen Alexander 1946- St&PR 91
Ennedy, Bernard Peter Mel 1952- WhoWor 91
Ennemoser, Joseph 1787-1854 EncO&P 3
Ennes, Adylson De Albuquerque 1940- WhoWor 91
Ennest, John William 1942- St&PR 91
Ennevaara, Mikko Kyosti 1946- WhoWor 91
Enney, James Crowe 1930- WhoAm 90
Ennis, Bernice B 1911- BiDrAPA 89
Ennis, Billie Michael 1959- WhoEmL 91
Ennis, Billy Mack 1938- St&PR 91
Ennis, Brian R. St&PR 91
Ennis, C. Brady 1954- WhoEmL 91
Ennis, Del 1925- Ballpl 90
Ennis, Edward J. NewYTBS 90
Ennis, Edward J. 1907-1990 BioIn 16
Ennis, Elizabeth Farnum BiDrAPA 89
Ennis, Floyd R. 1928- St&PR 91
Ennis, George Elliott 1933- WhoSSW 91
Ennis, Gordon A. 1947- St&PR 91
Ennis, James Edward 1928- St&PR 91
Ennis, Jerome BiDrAPA 89
Ennis, Jerome 1924- WhoE 91
Ennis, Jonathan David BiDrAPA 89
Ennis, Kenneth Alan BiDrAPA 89
Ennis, Lamar Wallace 1954- WhoWrEP 89
Ennis, Leslie Frederick 1933- St&PR 91
Ennis, Lois 1945- WhoE 91
Ennis, Michael Don 1953- St&PR 91
Ennis, Ruth M. 1913- WhoWor 91
Ennis, Skinnay 1909-1963 OxCPMus
Ennis, Thomas Michael 1931- WhoAm 90, WhoWor 91
Ennis, William Pierce 1904-1989 BioIn 16
Ennis-Sutherland, Janine Marie 1958- WhoAmW 91
Ennosuke, Ichikawa 1939- BioIn 16
Enns, Mark Kynaston 1931- WhoAm 90
Enns, Rodrick John 1955- WhoEmL 91
Enntiere, Marie d' EncCoWW
Eno, Brian NewAgMG
Eno, Brian 1948- EncPR&S 89, WhoAm 90
Eno, James Lorne 1887-1952 WhoAmA 91N
Eno, Paul Frederick 1953- WhoE 91
Eno, Roger NewAgMG
Eno, William Phelps 1858-1945 BioIn 16
Enoch, Charles Johnson 1917- St&PR 91
Enoch, Jay Martin 1929- WhoAm 90
Enoch, Joan Ellen 1940- BiDrAPA 89, WhoE 91
Enoch, Leslie Blythe 1942- St&PR 91
Enoch, Leslie Blythe, II 1942- WhoSSW 91
Enoff, Louis D. 1942- WhoAm 90
Enos, Andrea Woronka 1940- WhoE 91
Enos, Paul 1934- WhoAm 90
Enos, Paul Richard 1931- St&PR 91
Enos, Randall 1936- WhoAm 90
Enos, Robert Warren 1932- St&PR 91
Enos, Ronald F. St&PR 91
Enouen, William Albert 1928- St&PR 91, WhoAm 90
Enowitch, Bennett I 1934- BiDrAPA 89
Enowitch, Bennett Irving 1934- WhoE 91
Enquist, Irving Fridtjof 1920- WhoAm 90
Enquist, Per Olof 1934- DcScanL
Enrico, Roger A. WhoE 91
Enright, Arthur Joseph 1932- WhoE 91
Enright, Daniel BioIn 16
Enright, Elizabeth 1909-1968 AuBYP 90
Enright, Gretchen Lorig 1960- BiDrAPA 89
Enright, James 1912-1982 Ballpl 90
Enright, James Peter 1941- St&PR 91
Enright, Joseph J. BioIn 16
Enright, Stephanie Veselich 1929- WhoAmW 91, WhoWor 91
Enright, Thomas Jones 1947- WhoAm 90
Enright, Valeria Jessie 1927- BiDrAPA 89
Enright, Vincent D. 1943- St&PR 91
Enright, William F. 1920- St&PR 91
Enright, William Fairleigh, Jr. 1920- WhoAm 90
Enrique Y Tarancon, Vicente 1907- WhoWor 91
Enriques, Edward R. 1940- St&PR 91
Enriquez, Camilo Ponce 1912-1976 BioIn 16
Enriquez, Carola Rupert 1954- WhoAm 90, WhoAmW 91
Enriquez, Domingo L, Jr. BiDrAPA 89
Enriquez, Gaspar 1942- WhoAmA 91
Enriquez, Jaime 1958- WhoHisp 91
Enriquez, Olga Lynette BiDrAPA 89
Enriquez, Oscar 1963- WhoHisp 91
Enriquez, Rene BioIn 16, NewYTBS 90 [port]
Enriquez, Rene 1931-1990 WhoHisp 91N
Enroth, Theresa Louise 1925- WhoWrEP 89
Enroth-Cugell, Christina Alma Elisabeth 1919- WhoAm 90, WhoAmW 91
Ensch, Jose 1942- EncCoWW
Ensch, Thomas J. 1938- St&PR 91
Ensenada, Marques de la 1702-1781 BioIn 16
Ensenat, Donald Burnham 1946- WhoEmL 91
Ensenat, Louis Albert 1916- WhoSSW 91, WhoWor 91
Ensenore WhNaAH
Enser, George 1890-1961 WhoAmA 91N
Ensey, Michael A. 1941- St&PR 91
Ensey, Wendell LeRoy 1940- St&PR 91
Ensign, D. Brent 1956- St&PR 91
Ensign, David James 1950- WhoEmL 91
Ensign, Richard L. 1925- St&PR 91
Ensign, Richard Papworth 1919- WhoAm 90
Ensign, William James 1924- WhoAm 90
Ensign, William Lloyd 1928- WhoAm 90
Ensinger, I.J. 1942- St&PR 91
Enslen, Mary Susan 1962- WhoSSW 91
Enslen, Richard Alan 1931- WhoAm 90
Ensley, Rodney Gene 1934- St&PR 91
Enslin, Jessie M BiDrAPA 89
Enslin, Theodore Vernon 1925- WhoAm 90, WhoWrEP 89
Enslinger, Gary Lee 1952- WhoEmL 91
Enslow, Ridley M., Jr. 1926- St&PR 91
Enslow, Ridley Madison, Jr. 1926- WhoAm 90
Enslow, Sam 1946- WhoSSW 91
Ensminger, Douglas 1910-1989 BioIn 16
Ensminger, Luther Glenn 1919- WhoAm 90
Ensminger, Marion Eugene 1908- WhoAm 90
Ensor, Gary Albert 1956- WhoEmL 91
Ensor, James 1860-1949 IntDcAA 90
Ensor, James Sydney 1860-1949 WorAlBi
Ensor, Patricia Lee 1959- WhoAmW 91
Ensroth, Jack F BiDrAPA 89
Ensroth, Kenneth Alan 1954- BiDrAPA 89
Ensrud, Wayne 1934- WhoAmA 91
Ensslin, Robert Frank, Jr. 1928- WhoAm 90
Enstice, Wayne 1943- WhoAmA 91
Enstine, Raymond Wilton, Jr. 1946- WhoE 91
Enstrom, James Eugene 1943- WhoAm 90, WhoWor 91
Enteen, Robert 1946- WhoE 91
Entel, Melvin Allen 1944- St&PR 91
Enteman, Willard Finley 1936- WhoAm 90
Entenberg, Herbert 1934- St&PR 91
Entenman, Alfred M., Jr. 1921- St&PR 91
Entenza, Ricardo 1921- BiDrAPA 89
Enterline, Sandra 1960- WhoAmA 91
Enters, Angna 1897?-1989 NotWoAT
Enters, Angna 1907-1989 BioIn 16
Entesari, Shopan 1951- WhoEmL 91
Enthoven, Adolf Jan Henri 1928- WhoSSW 91
Enthoven, Alain Charles 1930- WhoAm 90
Enthoven, Daco Jan Jacob 1955- WhoWor 91
Entin, Howard Jay 1950- BiDrAPA 89
Entin, Jonathan Lowe 1947- WhoEmL 91
Entine, Lynn Bergmann 1947- WhoAmW 91
Entley, Nancy Keller 1935- WhoSSW 91
Entmacher, Paul Sidney 1924- St&PR 91, WhoAm 90
Entman, Barbara Sue 1954- WhoAmW 91, WhoWor 91
Entman, Robert M. 1949- ConAu 130
Entner, Paul Dwight 1947- WhoEmL 91
Entorf, Richard Carl 1929- St&PR 91, WhoAm 90
Entrekin, Charles Edward, Jr. 1941- WhoWrEP 89
Entrekin, John Clay 1844-1905 AmLegL
Entrekin, Lang Moore 1943- WhoAmW 91
Entremont, Philippe 1934- IntWWM 90, PenDiMP, WhoAm 90, WhoWor 91
Entringer, Michel Andre 1937- WhoWor 91
Entwisle, Doris Roberts 1924- WhoAm 90
Entwisle, George 1922- WhoAm 90
Entwistle, Andrew John 1959- WhoEmL 91
Entwistle, Gordon Thomas 1942- St&PR 91
Entzeroth, Robert Elleard 1926- WhoAm 90
Entzminger, John Nelson, Jr. 1936- WhoAm 90, WhoSSW 91
Enver, Pasha 1881-1922 BioIn 16
Enya BioIn 16
Enyart, Paul WhoAm 90
Enyeart, James Lyle 1943- WhoAmA 91
Enyedy, Gustav, Jr. 1924- WhoAm 90
Enzensberger, Hans Magnus BioIn 16
Enzensberger, Hans Magnus 1929- WhoWor 91
Enzer, Charles Hart 1935- BiDrAPA 89
Enzer, Norbert B 1930- BiDrAPA 89
Enzer, Norbert Beverley 1930- WhoAm 90
Enzinger, Franz Michael 1923- WhoE 91
Eoff, Robert Grimshaw BioIn 16
Eosze, Laszlo 1923- IntWWM 90
Eotvos, Peter 1944- IntWWM 90, PenDiMP
Eovaldi, Marina Lucco 1940- WhoAmW 91
Epanow WhNaAH
Epcke, William Robert 1937- St&PR 91
Epel, David 1937- WhoAm 90
Ephelia BiDEWW, BioIn 16, FemiCLE
Ephraim, Charles 1924- WhoAm 90
Ephraim, Donald Morley 1932- WhoAm 90
Ephraim, Max, Jr. 1918- WhoAm 90
Ephremides, Anthony 1943- WhoAm 90
Ephron, Delia BioIn 16
Ephron, Harmon S BiDrAPA 89
Ephron, Nora BioIn 16
Ephron, Nora 1941- ConTFT 8, CurBio 90 [port], FemiCLE, WhoAm 90, WhoAmW 91, WorAlBi, WorAu 1980 [port]
Ephron, Phoebe W. 1916-1971 BioAmW

Ephross, Paul Hullman 1935- *WhoE 91*
Epich, Raymond John 1931- *St&PR 91*
Epictetus 50-130 *WrPh P*
Epictetus 50?-138? *WorAlBi*
Epicurus 341BC-270BC *WorAlBi, WrPh P*
Epifani, Richard I. 1937- *St&PR 91*
Epifano, Robert J. 1933- *St&PR 91*
Epinay, Louise-Florence-Petronille d' 1726-1783 *EncCoWW*
Epischofer, Hans *PenDiDA 89*
Eplett, William Samuel *St&PR 91N*
Epley, Deanna 1944- *WhoSSW 91*
Epley, Elton Lehman 1942- *St&PR 91*
Epley, Joe S. 1938- *ODwPR 91*
Epley, Lewis Everett, Jr. 1936- *WhoAm 90*
Epley, Marion Jay 1907- *WhoAm 90*
Epley, Marion Jay, III 1937- *WhoE 91*
Epley, Michael G. 1945- *St&PR 91*
Epley, Thomas Kerfoot, III 1947- *WhoEmL 91*
Epley-Shuck, Barbara Jeanne 1936- *WhoWrEP 89*
Epling, Gary Arnold 1945- *WhoE 91*
Epling, Richard Louis 1951- *WhoEmL 91*
Epner, Donald Bruce 1927- *St&PR 91*
Epner, Paul Lawrence 1950- *WhoEmL 91, WhoWor 91*
Epner, Steven Arthur *WhoAm 90*
Epp, Arthur Jacob 1939- *WhoAm 90*
Epp, Eldon Jay 1930- *WhoAm 90*
Epp, Mary Elizabeth 1941- *WhoAmW 91, WhoWor 91*
Epp, William H. 1929- *St&PR 91*
Eppel, Alan Brian 1950- *BiDrAPA 89*
Eppelmann, Rainer *WhoWor 91*
Eppen, Gary Dean 1936- *WhoAm 90*
Eppenstein, Louise 1892-1987 *BioIn 16*
Epper, Karl F. 1937- *St&PR 91*
Epperly, William Robert 1935- *WhoE 91*
Epperson, Aloise Barbour *HarlReB*
Epperson, Barbara 1921- *WhoSSW 91*
Epperson, Bradley Jay 1958- *WhoSSW 91*
Epperson, Charles Michael 1955- *WhoSSW 91*
Epperson, D. Mike 1944- *St&PR 91*
Epperson, David Ernest 1935- *WhoAm 90*
Epperson, Denise Lynn *BiDrAPA 89*
Epperson, Emory *ODwPR 91*
Epperson, Eric Robert 1949- *WhoEmL 91, WhoWor 91*
Epperson, Gordon 1921- *IntWWM 90*
Epperson, Jean Warner 1919- *WhoSSW 91*
Epperson, Joel Rodman 1945- *WhoEmL 91, WhoSSW 91, WhoWor 91*
Epperson, Kraettli Quynton 1949- *WhoEmL 91*
Epperson, Ralph Cameron, III 1943- *WhoSSW 91*
Epperson, Vaughn Elmo 1917- *WhoWor 91*
Eppes, Mavis 1937- *WhoAmW 91*
Eppes, Richard 1824-1896 *BioIn 16*
Eppes, Thomas E. 1952- *ODwPR 91*
Eppes, Thomas Jefferson *AmLegL*
Eppes, William David *WhoWrEP 89*
Eppich, Frank J. 1926- *St&PR 91*
Eppich, John L. 1934- *St&PR 91*
Eppich, Robert Edward 1938- *St&PR 91*
Eppinger, Josh *BioIn 16*
Eppinger, Mary Ann 1944- *BiDrAPA 89*
Epple, Dennis Norbert 1946- *WhoAm 90*
Epple, Kat *NewAgMG*
Epple, Kat 1952- *WhoEmL 91*
Epple, Kenneth Hall *BiDrAPA 89*
Eppler, Cecilia Maria 1951- *WhoEmL 91*
Eppler, David M. 1950- *St&PR 91*
Eppler, Jerome Cannon 1924- *WhoAm 90*
Eppler, Richard 1924- *WhoWor 91*
Eppler, Richard Andrew 1934- *WhoE 91*
Eppley, Frances Fielden 1921- *WhoAmW 91, WhoSSW 91*
Eppley, Perley E. *St&PR 91*
Eppley, Roland Raymond, Jr. 1932- *WhoAm 90, WhoE 91, WhoWor 91*
Eppley, Ronald L. 1943- *St&PR 91*
Eppley, Stephen Clyde 1949- *WhoAm 90*
Eppner, Gerald Allen 1939- *WhoAm 90, WhoWor 91*
Eppright, Thomas David *BiDrAPA 89*
Epps, Anna Cherrie 1930- *WhoAm 90*
Epps, Augustus Charles 1916- *WhoAm 90*
Epps, Charles H., Jr. 1930- *WhoAm 90*
Epps, James Haws, III 1936- *WhoSSW 91*
Epps, Richard Lee 1952- *WhoSSW 91*
Epps, Roselyn Elizabeth Payne 1930- *WhoAm 90, WhoWor 91*
Epps, Roselyn P. *BioIn 16*
Epps, Susie Rebecca Smith 1951- *WhoSSW 91*
Epps, William David 1951- *WhoWrEP 89*
Eppstein, Deborah Anne 1948- *WhoEmL 91*
Eppstein, Hans 1911- *IntWWM 90*
Eppstein, Paul 1901-1944 *BioIn 16*
Eppstein, Richard Tuteur 1947- *WhoEmL 91*
Eppstein, Ury 1925- *IntWWM 90*
Epright, Charles John 1932- *WhoSSW 91*
Epsilon *ConAu 33NR, MajTwCW*
Epsteen, Casper Morley 1902- *WhoAm 90, WhoWor 91*
Epstein, Abraham H. 1926- *WhoAm 90*
Epstein, Allan Cane 1937- *St&PR 91*
Epstein, Alvin 1925- *WhoAm 90*
Epstein, Ann Rachel 1955- *BiDrAPA 89*
Epstein, Arthur W 1923- *BiDrAPA 89*
Epstein, Arthur William 1923- *WhoAm 90*
Epstein, Barbara 1929- *WhoAm 90, WhoAmW 91*
Epstein, Barry R. 1942- *WhoAm 90*
Epstein, Beryl M. Williams 1910- *AuBYP 90*
Epstein, Brian 1934-1967 *BioIn 16, WorAlBi*
Epstein, Charles Joseph 1933- *WhoAm 90*
Epstein, Charles M. 1920- *St&PR 91*
Epstein, Clifford L. 1945- *St&PR 91*
Epstein, Cynthia Fuchs *BioIn 16, WhoAm 90*
Epstein, Dan *St&PR 91*
Epstein, Daniel Mark 1948- *WhoAm 90, WhoWrEP 89*
Epstein, David 1935- *WhoAm 90*
Epstein, David Gustav 1943- *WhoAm 90*
Epstein, David Lee 1947- *WhoEmL 91*
Epstein, David M. 1930- *IntWWM 90*
Epstein, David Mayer 1930- *WhoAm 90*
Epstein, David Stanley 1948- *WhoWor 91*
Epstein, Dena Julia 1916- *IntWWM 90*
Epstein, Donald Robert 1925- *St&PR 91*
Epstein, Edward Louis 1936- *WhoAm 90*
Epstein, Edward S. 1931- *WhoAm 90*
Epstein, Eleni Sakes 1925- *WhoAm 90*
Epstein, Eliahu 1903-1990 *CurBio 90N*
Epstein, Emanuel 1916- *WhoAm 90*
Epstein, Ethel S *WhoAmA 91N*
Epstein, Frances *BioIn 16*
Epstein, Franklin Harold 1924- *WhoAm 90*
Epstein, Gary Marvin 1946- *WhoAm 90, WhoEmL 91*
Epstein, George 1934- *WhoSSW 91*
Epstein, Gilbert M. 1927- *BioIn 16*
Epstein, Gilbert Michael 1942- *St&PR 91*
Epstein, Guita Eve *BiDrAPA 89*
Epstein, Harriet Pike *ODwPR 91, WhoAmW 91*
Epstein, Harry 1903- *BioIn 16*
Epstein, Harvey M. 1930- *ODwPR 91*
Epstein, Helen 1947- *BioIn 16*
Epstein, Helga Dreifuss 1924- *WhoAmW 91*
Epstein, Henry David 1927- *St&PR 91, WhoAm 90*
Epstein, Herbert 1922- *WhoAm 90*
Epstein, Herman *BioIn 16*
Epstein, Herman D. 1924- *WhoAm 90*
Epstein, Howard Michael 1927- *WhoAm 90*
Epstein, Jacob 1880-1959 *BioIn 16, IntDcAA 90*
Epstein, Jane Ingrid *BiDrAPA 89*
Epstein, Jane L. 1954- *St&PR 91*
Epstein, Jason *BioIn 16*
Epstein, Jason 1928- *CurBio 90 [port], News 91-1, WhoAm 90, WhoE 91, WorAlBi*
Epstein, Jaye Mark 1950- *WhoSSW 91*
Epstein, Jeffrey E. 1956- *St&PR 91*
Epstein, Jeffrey Emanuel 1956- *WhoAm 90, WhoE 91*
Epstein, Jeffrey Mark 1951- *WhoE 91*
Epstein, Jennifer Hillings 1954- *ODwPR 91*
Epstein, Jeremiah Fain 1924- *WhoAm 90*
Epstein, Jerome Michael 1943- *WhoE 91*
Epstein, Jerry A. *ODwPR 91*
Epstein, Joel L. 1946- *St&PR 91*
Epstein, John H. *St&PR 91N*
Epstein, John Howard 1926- *WhoAm 90*
Epstein, Jonathan Akiba 1963- *WhoEmL 91*
Epstein, Jose D. 1924- *St&PR 91*
Epstein, Joseph *BioIn 16*
Epstein, Joseph 1917- *WhoAm 90*
Epstein, Joseph 1937- *CurBio 90 [port], WhoAm 90, WhoWrEP 89, WorAu 1980 [port]*
Epstein, Joseph Hugo, Jr. 1931- *WhoSSW 91*
Epstein, Judith *BioIn 16*
Epstein, Julius J. 1909- *WhoAm 90*
Epstein, June *ConAu 30NR*
Epstein, Kenneth 1942- *St&PR 91*
Epstein, Kenneth Richard 1948- *WhoEmL 91*
Epstein, Laura 1914- *WhoAm 90*
Epstein, Lawrence J 1946- *ConAu 132*
Epstein, Lawrence Jeffrey 1946- *WhoE 91*
Epstein, Lee Joan 1958- *WhoSSW 91*
Epstein, Leon David 1919- *WhoAm 90*
Epstein, Leon J 1917- *BiDrAPA 89*
Epstein, Leon Joseph 1917- *WhoAm 90*
Epstein, Leslie *BioIn 16*
Epstein, Leslie 1938- *ConAu 12AS [port]*
Epstein, Leslie Donald 1938- *WhoWrEP 89*
Epstein, Lionel Charles 1924- *WhoAm 90*
Epstein, Lois Barth 1933- *WhoAm 90*
Epstein, Louis M. 1887-1949 *BioIn 16*
Epstein, Louis R. 1926- *St&PR 91*
Epstein, Louis Ralph 1926- *WhoAm 90*
Epstein, Lynn Chaikin *BiDrAPA 89*
Epstein, Mark *BiDrAPA 89*
Epstein, Marvin M. 1928- *St&PR 91*
Epstein, Matthew A. 1947- *IntWWM 90*
Epstein, Max *NewYTBS 90*
Epstein, Max 1925- *WhoAm 90*
Epstein, Melvin 1938- *WhoAm 90*
Epstein, Merrill H *BiDrAPA 89*
Epstein, Michael Alan 1954- *WhoEmL 91*
Epstein, Michael Anthony 1921- *WhoWor 91*
Epstein, Mike 1943- *Ballpl 90, BioIn 16*
Epstein, Mitch 1952- *WhoAmA 91*
Epstein, Morton Batlan 1921- *St&PR 91*
Epstein, Nathan B 1924- *BiDrAPA 89*
Epstein, Paul Martin *BiDrAPA 89*
Epstein, Paul Sophus 1883-1966 *DcScB S2*
Epstein, Perle 1938- *AuBYP 90*
Epstein, Philip Barry 1947- *WhoEmL 91*
Epstein, Phillip S *BiDrAPA 89*
Epstein, Raymond 1918- *St&PR 91, WhoAm 90*
Epstein, Richard A. 1943- *WhoAm 90*
Epstein, Richard S *BiDrAPA 89*
Epstein, Richard Saul *WhoE 91*
Epstein, Robert Alan 1946- *BiDrAPA 89*
Epstein, Robert Alan 1952- *St&PR 91*
Epstein, Robert Harry 1958- *WhoEmL 91*
Epstein, Robert Marvin 1928- *WhoAm 90*
Epstein, Samuel 1909- *AuBYP 90*
Epstein, Samuel 1919- *WhoAm 90*
Epstein, Samuel D. 1946- *WhoSSW 91*
Epstein, Samuel David 1946- *St&PR 91*
Epstein, Samuel H *BiDrAPA 89*
Epstein, Samuel Irving *BiDrAPA 89*
Epstein, Sara Ann *BiDrAPA 89*
Epstein, Scott *ODwPR 91*
Epstein, Selma 1927- *IntWWM 90, WhoAmW 91*
Epstein, Seymour 1917- *WhoWrEP 89*
Epstein, Shelley Jane *BiDrAPA 89*
Epstein, Sherwin Lewis 1930- *WhoWor 91*
Epstein, Sidney 1920- *WhoAm 90*
Epstein, Sidney 1923- *St&PR 91, WhoAm 90*
Epstein, Simon J 1934- *BiDrAPA 89*
Epstein, Simon Jules 1934- *WhoE 91*
Epstein, Steven 1949- *WhoEmL 91*
Epstein, Steven Alan 1960- *BiDrAPA 89*
Epstein, Stewart 1944- *St&PR 91*
Epstein, Thomas 1957- *St&PR 91, WhoEmL 91*
Epstein, William 1931- *WhoAm 90*
Epstein, William 1948- *WhoE 91*
Epstein, William Louis 1925- *WhoAm 90*
Epstein, William Stuart 1940- *St&PR 91, WhoAm 90, WhoE 91*
Epstein, Wilma *BioIn 16*
Epstein, Wilma Geller 1946- *WhoAm 90, WhoAmW 91*
Epstein, Wolfgang 1931- *WhoAm 90*
Epstein, Yale 1934- *WhoAmA 91, WhoE 91*
Epting, Cynthia Renee 1959- *WhoAmW 91*
Epting, Marion Austin 1940- *WhoAmA 91*
Epting, Rebecca Ann 1940- *WhoAmW 91*
Epton, Bernard *BioIn 16*
Epton, Delmar 1934- *St&PR 91*
Epton, Delmar F. 1934- *WhoAm 90*
Epton, Saul Arthur 1910- *WhoAm 90*
Equi, Marie D. 1872-1952 *EncAL*
Equiano, Olaudah 1745- *BioIn 16*
Equiluz, Kurt 1929- *IntWWM 90, PenDiMP*
Eraklis, Angelo John 1933- *WhoE 91*
Eramo, John Jeffrey 1954- *WhoEmL 91*
Eramu, Robert Peter 1948- *St&PR 91*
Erard, Barbara Hughes 1955- *WhoAmW 91*
Eras, Mustafa Erturk 1943- *WhoWor 91*
Erasmus, Charles John 1921- *WhoAm 90*
Erasmus, Desiderius 1466?-1536 *BioIn 16, WorAlBi*
Erasmus, John J. 1924- *St&PR 91*
Erath, George Snider 1927- *St&PR 91*
Eratosthenes 276?BC-195?BC *WorAlBi*
Erautt, Eddie 1924-1976 *Ballpl 90*
Erazmus, Walter Thomas 1947- *St&PR 91*
Erb, Clarence Leighton, Jr. 1917- *WhoE 91*
Erb, Donald 1927- *IntWWM 90, WhoAm 90*
Erb, Elke 1938- *EncCoWW*
Erb, Fred A. 1923- *St&PR 91*
Erb, Frederick Geist, III 1950- *WhoE 91, WhoSSW 91*
Erb, Jan Hal 1943- *WhoSSW 91*
Erb, Jane L. *BiDrAPA 89*
Erb, Karl 1877-1958 *PenDiMP*
Erb, Peter C. 1943- *ConAu 32NR*
Erb, Phyllis 1941- *WhoSSW 91*
Erb, Richard Louis Lundin 1929- *WhoAm 90, WhoWor 91*
Erb, Robert Allan 1932- *WhoAm 90*
Erbacher, Kathryn Anne 1947- *WhoAmW 91*
Erbe, Gary Thomas 1944- *WhoAmA 91, WhoE 91, WhoWor 91*
Erbe, Jack Rudolph 1926- *WhoWrEP 89*
Erbe, Joan 1926- *WhoAmA 91*
Erbe, Yvonne Mary 1947- *WhoWor 91*
Erbeck, Robert Nelson 1948- *WhoEmL 91*
Erben, Ralph 1931- *St&PR 91*
Erben, Valentin *PenDiMP*
Erber, James Edwin 1951- *IntWWM 90*
Erber, Les N. 1945- *St&PR 91*
Erber, Robert, Jr. 1931- *St&PR 91*
Erber, Thomas 1930- *WhoAm 90*
Erbes, Roslyn Maria *WhoAmA 91*
Erbes, William Tracy 1948- *WhoEmL 91*
Erbez, Elizabeth Anne 1963- *WhoAmW 91*
Erbse, Heimo 1924- *IntWWM 90*
Erbsen, Claude Ernest 1938- *St&PR 91, WhoAm 90*
Erbst, Fred Paul 1931- *St&PR 91*
Erburu, Robert F. 1930- *St&PR 91, WhoAm 90*
Erceg, Rose 1898- *MusmAFA*
Ercilla y Zuniga, Alonso de 1533-1584 *BioIn 16*
Erck, Jerome F. 1939- *St&PR 91*
Erck, Ruby Jewel 1928- *WhoAmW 91*
Erck, Theodore Augustus, Jr. 1949- *WhoEmL 91, WhoSSW 91, WhoWor 91*
Ercklentz, Alexander Tonio 1936- *WhoAm 90*
Ercklentz, Enno W., Jr. 1931- *St&PR 91*
Ercklentz, Enno Wilhelm, Jr. 1931- *WhoAm 90*
Ercolano, Thomas Francis 1944- *St&PR 91*
Ercole, Mario Anthony 1949- *BiDrAPA 89*
Ercole, Velia 1903-1978 *FemiCLE*
Ercum-Krasinski, Baiba 1942- *BiDrAPA 89, WhoE 91*
Erdahl, Leland Odell 1928- *St&PR 91*
Erdberg, Mindel Ruth *BiDrAPA 89*
Erdberg, Mindel Ruth 1916- *WhoE 91*
Erdel, Bert Paul 1943- *WhoE 91*
Erdelac, Joseph Mark *WhoAmA 91*
Erdeljac, Daniel Joseph 1932- *WhoAm 90*
Erdely, Stephen Lajos 1921- *WhoAm 90*
Erdelyi, Arthur 1908-1977 *DcScB S2*
Erdelyi, Csaba 1946- *IntWWM 90, PenDiMP*
Erdelyi, Miklos 1928- *IntWWM 90*
Erdem, Ismet Kaya 1928- *WhoWor 91*
Erden, Sybil Isolde 1950- *WhoAmW 91*
Erdim, Esim 1944- *WhoWor 91*
Erding-Swiridoff, Susanne 1955- *IntWWM 90*
Erdini Qoigyi Gyaincain 1937-1989 *BioIn 16*
Erdle, Rob 1949- *WhoAmA 91*
Erdman, Barbara 1936- *WhoAmW 91*
Erdman, Barry Richard 1952- *WhoEmL 91*
Erdman, Carl L. N. 1915- *WhoAm 90*
Erdman, Cindy Susan 1957- *WhoAmW 91*
Erdman, Daniel Gig 1955- *WhoSSW 91*
Erdman, Donald Seward 1919- *WhoWrEP 89*
Erdman, Ernie 1879-1946 *OxCPMus*
Erdman, George Emery 1928- *St&PR 91*
Erdman, Harold Richard, Jr. 1930- *St&PR 91*
Erdman, Howard Loyd 1935- *WhoAm 90*
Erdman, Joseph 1935- *WhoAm 90*
Erdman, Katherine M. *ODwPR 91*
Erdman, Kathleen Barry 1946- *BiDrAPA 89*
Erdman, Loula Grace *AuBYP 90*
Erdman, Lowell Paul 1926- *WhoAm 90*
Erdman, Michael H. *BioIn 16*
Erdman, Paul 1932- *WorAlBi*
Erdman, Paul E 1932- *TwCCr&M 91*
Erdman, Paul Emil 1932- *WhoAm 90, WhoWor 91*
Erdmann, Dallas Don *BiDrAPA 89*
Erdmann, Diane Carolyn 1939- *WhoE 91*
Erdmann, Edward Alexander, III 1947- *St&PR 91*
Erdmann, James Bernard 1937- *WhoE 91, WhoWor 91*
Erdmann, Kenneth John 1943- *BiDrAPA 89*
Erdmann, Paul Martin 1950- *BiDrAPA 89*
Erdmann, Robert Joseph 1937- *WhoWrEP 89*
Erdmann, William Louis 1928- *St&PR 91*
Erdogan, Selahaddin 1930- *BiDrAPA 89*
Erdonmez, Denise Elizabeth 1946- *IntWWM 90*
Erdos, John M *BiDrAPA 89*
Erdos, Linda M. *ODwPR 91*
Erdreich, Ben Leader 1938- *WhoAm 90, WhoSSW 91*
Erdreich, Stanley M., Jr. 1935- *St&PR 91*
Erdrich, Karen Louise 1954- *WhoAm 90, WhoAmW 91*
Erdrich, Louise *BioIn 16*
Erdrich, Louise 1954- *FemiCLE, MajTwCW, WorAu 1980 [port]*

Erdt, Hans Rudi 1883-1918 *BioIn 16*
Erdtmann, Elizabeth Terry 1961- *WhoAmW 91*
Erede, Alberto 1908- *IntWWM 90, PenDiMP*
Eremic, Kathleen Ann 1952- *WhoAmW 91, WhoE 91*
Erenberg, Eve Braun 1907- *St&PR 91*
Erenburg, Ilya 1891-1967 *BioIn 16*
Erenrich, Norman Henry 1952- *WhoSSW 91*
Erens, Jay Allan 1935- *WhoAm 90*
Erenstoft, David L. 1942- *St&PR 91*
Erera, Laurence E. 1940- *St&PR 91*
Eres, Eugenia 1928- *WhoAmA 91*
Erez, Chaim 1935- *WhoWor 91*
Erfani, Shervin 1948- *WhoE 91*
Erfe, Jose Asperin 1937- *BiDrAPA 89*
Ergas, Enrique 1938- *WhoAm 90, WhoE 91*
Ergas, Jean-Pierre M. 1939- *St&PR 91*
Ergas, Jean-Pierre Maurice 1939- *WhoAm 90*
Ergas, Martin *BioIn 16*
Ergas, Martin 1950- *St&PR 91*
Ergin, Umit C 1925- *BiDrAPA 89*
Erhard, Ludwig 1897-1977 *WorAlBi*
Erhard, Werner 1935?- *EncO&P 3, WhoAm 90, WorAlBi*
Erhardt, Henri S. 1943- *St&PR 91*
Erhardt, Warren Richard 1924- *WhoAm 90, WhoE 91*
Erhart, Charles H. 1925- *St&PR 91*
Erhart, Charles Huntington, Jr. 1925- *WhoAm 90*
Erhart, Shepard *BioIn 16*
Erhart, Thomas Robert 1953- *WhoEmL 91*
Eri, Vincent *WhoWor 91*
Eribal, Maria Corazon *BiDrAPA 89*
Eribes, Richard A. *WhoHisp 91*
Eric of the Windy Hat *EncO&P 3*
Eric the Red *EncCRAm*
Eric The Red 950?-1000? *WorAlBi*
Erichsen, Hans-Uwe 1934- *WhoWor 91*
Erichsen-Hubbard, Isabel Janice 1935- *WhoAmW 91*
Erick, Miriam A. 1948- *WhoWrEP 89*
Ericksen, Ephraim Edward 1882-1967 *BioIn 16*
Ericksen, Jerald Laverne 1924- *WhoAm 90*
Ericksen, Robert L. *St&PR 91*
Ericksen, Stephen E *BiDrAPA 89*
Ericksen, Wayne R. 1936- *St&PR 91*
Erickson, Alan Eric 1928- *WhoAm 90*
Erickson, Alice Lee Welcher *BioIn 16*
Erickson, Annmarie *ODwPR 91*
Erickson, Arthur 1924- *BioIn 16*
Erickson, Arthur Charles 1924- *WhoWor 91*
Erickson, Barden 1930- *St&PR 91*
Erickson, Brian Anthony 1960- *BiDrAPA 89*
Erickson, Brian F. 1936- *St&PR 91*
Erickson, Brian James 1950- *WhoSSW 91*
Erickson, C. Leonard 1912- *St&PR 91*
Erickson, Calvin Howard 1946- *WhoEmL 91*
Erickson, Carol Ann 1933- *WhoWor 91*
Erickson, Charles B. 1932- *St&PR 91*
Erickson, Charles Burton 1932- *WhoAm 90*
Erickson, Charles Edward 1947- *WhoE 91*
Erickson, Craig *BioIn 16*
Erickson, David Belnap 1951- *WhoEmL 91*
Erickson, David Burdette 1950- *WhoE 91, WhoWrEP 89*
Erickson, David Erick 1950- *WhoEmL 91*
Erickson, David L. 1948- *St&PR 91*
Erickson, Dennis *BioIn 16*
Erickson, Dennis D. 1938- *St&PR 91*
Erickson, Dennis Duane 1938- *WhoAm 90*
Erickson, Diane Quinn 1959- *WhoEmL 91*
Erickson, Don 1932-1988 *BioIn 16*
Erickson, Donald Alfred 1929- *St&PR 91*
Erickson, Donna Mary *WhoWrEP 89*
Erickson, Elaine Mae 1941- *IntWWM 90*
Erickson, Eric 1892-1965 *Ballpl 90*
Erickson, Florence Henrietta 1914- *WhoAm 90*
Erickson, Frank 1923- *IntWWM 90*
Erickson, Frank William 1923- *WhoAm 90*
Erickson, Gail 1934- *St&PR 91, WhoAm 90, WhoAmW 91*
Erickson, Garwood Elliott 1946- *WhoEmL 91, WhoWor 91*
Erickson, Gerald Meyer 1927- *WhoAm 90*
Erickson, Gertrude Victoria *BiDrAPA 89*
Erickson, Gordon Richard 1928- *St&PR 91*
Erickson, Harold M, Jr. 1936- *BiDrAPA 89*
Erickson, Homer Theodore 1925- *WhoAm 90*
Erickson, James Huston 1931- *WhoE 91*
Erickson, James Paul 1929- *WhoAm 90*
Erickson, James Warren 1935- *St&PR 91*
Erickson, Jeffrey Lee *BiDrAPA 89*
Erickson, John David 1933- *St&PR 91*
Erickson, John Duff 1933- *WhoAm 90*
Erickson, Joy M 1932- *WhoAmA 91*
Erickson, Joyce L 1930- *BiDrAPA 89*
Erickson, Kenneth Reed *BiDrAPA 89*
Erickson, Larry 1936- *St&PR 91*
Erickson, Lawrence Wilhelm 1915- *WhoAm 90*
Erickson, Lea Ella 1947- *WhoAmW 91*
Erickson, Leland John 1951- *WhoEmL 91*
Erickson, Lennart G. 1914- *St&PR 91*
Erickson, LeRoy Alexander 1921- *WhoAm 90*
Erickson, Linda Rae 1948- *WhoAmW 91*
Erickson, Luther Eugene 1933- *WhoAm 90*
Erickson, Margaret Jane *WhoAmA 91*
Erickson, Marilyn T. 1936- *WhoAmW 91*
Erickson, Mark D 1955- *WhoAmA 91*
Erickson, Mark Refell 1949- *St&PR 91*
Erickson, Mark Thomas 1953- *BiDrAPA 89*
Erickson, Marsha A 1945- *WhoAmA 91*
Erickson, Nancy Salome 1945- *WhoAm 90, WhoAmW 91*
Erickson, Neil Le Roy, II 1951- *WhoWrEP 89*
Erickson, Paul 1915- *Ballpl 90*
Erickson, Paul Joseph, Jr. 1953- *BiDrAPA 89, WhoE 91*
Erickson, Peter Brown 1945- *WhoWor 91*
Erickson, Philip Torry 1934- *St&PR 91*
Erickson, Phillip A. 1941- *St&PR 91*
Erickson, Phoebe *BioIn 16*
Erickson, Phoebe 1907- *AuBYP 90*
Erickson, Ralph Ernest 1928- *WhoAm 90, WhoWor 91*
Erickson, Ralph O. 1914- *BioIn 16, WhoAm 90*
Erickson, Raymond G. 1925- *St&PR 91*
Erickson, Raymond Leroy 1925- *WhoAm 90*
Erickson, Refell Leon 1912- *St&PR 91*
Erickson, Richard Ames 1923- *WhoAm 90*
Erickson, Richard Beau 1952- *WhoWor 91*
Erickson, Richard Carl 1937- *WhoAm 90*
Erickson, Richard John 1943- *WhoE 91*
Erickson, Richard L. 1942- *WhoAm 90*
Erickson, Richard Theodore 1932- *St&PR 91, WhoAm 90*
Erickson, Robert 1917- *IntWWM 90*
Erickson, Robert D. 1943- *St&PR 91*
Erickson, Robert Daniel 1943- *WhoAm 90*
Erickson, Robert Lewis 1929- *St&PR 91*
Erickson, Robert Orlando 1945- *St&PR 91*
Erickson, Roger 1956- *Ballpl 90*
Erickson, Roland Axel 1913- *WhoAm 90*
Erickson, Ronald K. 1938- *WhoE 91*
Erickson, Ronald Wilbur *WhoSSW 91*
Erickson, Roy Frederick, Jr. 1928- *WhoAm 90*
Erickson, Roy Lydeen 1923- *WhoAm 90*
Erickson, Russell E. 1932- *AuBYP 90*
Erickson, Scott Lee 1959- *WhoSSW 91*
Erickson, Stephen Emory 1945- *WhoAm 90*
Erickson, Stephen Michael 1950- *ConAu 129*
Erickson, Steve *ConAu 129*
Erickson, Steve 1950- *ConLC 64 [port]*
Erickson, Tamara Jo 1954- *St&PR 91*
Erickson, Thomas Franklin, Sr. 1918- *WhoSSW 91*
Erickson, Thomas Sherman 1932- *WhoAm 90*
Erickson, Virginia Bemmels 1948- *WhoEmL 91*
Erickson, Walter Bruce 1938- *WhoAm 90*
Erickson, William D 1935- *BiDrAPA 89*
Erickson, William G. *BioIn 16*
Erickson, William Hurt 1924- *WhoAm 90*
Erickson Williamson, Donna Constance 1952- *WhoAm 90, WhoAmW 91*
Erickstad, Ralph John 1922- *WhoAm 90*
Ericsdotter, Siw 1919- *IntWWM 90*
Ericson, Alvin Charles 1955- *WhoE 91, WhoEmL 91, WhoWor 91*
Ericson, Barbro 1930- *IntWWM 90*
Ericson, Beatrice *WhoAmA 91*
Ericson, Deborah Ruth 1949- *WhoWor 91*
Ericson, Ernest *WhoAmA 91N*
Ericson, James Donald 1935- *St&PR 91, WhoAm 90*
Ericson, John M., Jr. 1942- *St&PR 91*
Ericson, Jon Meyer 1928- *WhoAm 90*
Ericson, Leif 970?-1020? *WhNaAH*
Ericson, Leif 971-1015? *WorAlBi*
Ericson, Lester Lane 1927- *WhoSSW 91*
Ericson, Roger D. 1934- *St&PR 91*
Ericson, Roger Delwin 1934- *WhoAm 90, WhoSSW 91*
Ericson, Ruth A *BiDrAPA 89*
Ericson, Ruth Ann *WhoAmW 91, WhoSSW 91*
Ericson, Walter *AuBYP 90, ConAu 33NR, TwCCr&M 91*
Ericsson, Leif *BioIn 16*
Ericsson, Leif 970?-1020? *WhNaAH*
Ericsson, Samuel E 1931- *BiDrAPA 89*
Ericsson, Sven Torsten 1938- *WhoWor 91*
Ericsson, Volter *DcScanL*
Erijman, Mavricio Oscar 1944- *WhoWor 91*
Eriksen, Charles Walter 1923- *WhoAm 90*
Eriksen, Dennis A. 1939- *St&PR 91*
Eriksen, Gary 1943- *WhoAmA 91*
Eriksen, Gary L. 1943- *WhoE 91, WhoWor 91*
Eriksen, Jostein 1926- *IntWWM 90*
Eriksen, Otto Louis 1930- *WhoAm 90*
Eriksen, Poul Jakob 1925- *WhoWor 91*
Eriksen, Richard Eugene 1945- *WhoE 91, WhoEmL 91*
Eriksen, Rolf F. 1942- *St&PR 91*
Eriksen, Stein *BioIn 16*
Erikson, Ake *DcScanL*
Erikson, Erik H. 1902- *BioIn 16, ConAu 33NR, MajTwCW*
Erikson, Erik Homburger 1902- *WhoAm 90*
Erikson, George Emil 1920- *WhoAm 90, WhoWor 91*
Erikson, George William 1941- *St&PR 91*
Erikson, J. Lance 1943- *St&PR 91*
Erikson, Kai 1931- *WhoAm 90*
Erikson, Leif *BioIn 16*
Erikson, Leif 970?-1020? *WhNaAH*
Erikson, Mary J. 1930- *WhoAmW 91*
Erikson, Penny Lauren 1950- *WhoAmW 91*
Erikson, Raymond Leo 1936- *WhoAm 90*
Erikson, Robert Warren 1945- *St&PR 91*
Erikson, Roland E 1920- *BiDrAPA 89*
Erikson, Sheldon R. 1941- *St&PR 91, WhoAm 90*
Eriksson, Buntel *ConAu 33NR*
Eriksson, Erik 1917- *WhoWor 91*
Eriksson, Erik Alexander, Jr. 1953- *WhoEmL 91*
Eriksson, Larry John 1945- *St&PR 91, WhoEmL 91*
Eriksson, Lars David 1938- *WhoWor 91*
Eriksson, Leif 970?-1020? *EncCRAm, WhNaAH*
Eriksson, Nils Erik 1934- *WhoWor 91*
Eriksson, Ronald J. 1942- *St&PR 91*
Eriksson, Thorvald *EncCRAm*
Eriksson, Ulf Nils Erik 1958- *WhoWor 91*
Erill, Sergio 1938- *WhoWor 91*
Erim, Kenan T. 1929-1990 *NewYTBS 90 [port]*
Erim, Kenan Tevfik 1929- *WhoAm 90, WhoE 91, WhoWor 91*
Erim, Kenan Tevfik 1929-1990 *ConAu 132*
Erinna 370?BC- *EncCoWW*
Erisman, Fred Raymond 1937- *WhoSSW 91*
Erisman, Robert Dale 1942- *St&PR 91*
Erisman, Terrance Lee 1964- *WhoEmL 91*
Erith, Robert Felix 1938- *WhoWor 91*
Erk, Frank Chris 1924- *WhoE 91*
Erk, Robert Richard 1946- *WhoSSW 91*
Erkelens, Dirk Willem 1941- *WhoWor 91*
Erken, Ronald V 1929- *BiDrAPA 89*
Erkenbrack, Stephen Kenneth 1952- *WhoEmL 91*
Erkkila, Barbara Howell 1918- *WhoWrEP 89*
Erkkila, Kathleen Liisa 1947- *WhoAmW 91*
Erkkila, Paula Susan *BiDrAPA 89*
Erl, Gerhard Hans 1947- *St&PR 91*
Erla, Karen 1942- *WhoAm 90, WhoAmA 91*
Erlandson, David Alan 1936- *WhoAm 90*
Erlandson, Ray Sanford, Sr. 1893- *WhoAm 90, WhoSSW 91*
Erlandson, Sverker Erland 1939- *WhoWor 91*
Erlanger, Bernard Ferdinand 1923- *WhoAm 90*
Erlanger, David Kenneth 1953- *St&PR 91*
Erlanger, Elizabeth N 1901-1975 *WhoAmA 91N*
Erlanger, Ellen 1950- *BioIn 16, ConAu 32NR*
Erlanger, Ellen Renee 1953- *WhoAmW 91*
Erlanger, Joseph 1874-1965 *WorAlBi*
Erlanger, Martin S. 1916- *St&PR 91*
Erlanger, Steven Jay 1952- *WhoAm 90, WhoWor 91*
Erlanson, Deborah McFarlin 1943- *WhoAmW 91*
Erle, Joan B *BiDrAPA 89*
Erlebacher, Albert 1932- *WhoAm 90*
Erlebacher, Martha Mayer 1937- *WhoAmA 91*
Erlenbach, Gary L. 1945- *St&PR 91*
Erlenborn, John Neal 1927- *WhoAm 90*
Erlenmeyer-Kimling, L. *WhoAm 90, WhoAmW 91*
Erler, Fred C. 1945- *St&PR 91, WhoAm 90*
Erler, Ursula 1946- *EncCoWW*
Erlewine, Richard H. 1914- *St&PR 91*
Erlich, Henryk 1882-1942? *BioIn 16*
Erlich, Lawrence B *BiDrAPA 89*
Erlich, Lillian 1910- *AuBYP 90*
Erlich, Philip *BiDrAPA 89*
Erlich, Philip 1924- *WhoE 91*
Erlich, Richard Henry 1949- *WhoEmL 91*
Erlich, Victor 1914- *WhoAm 90*
Erlichman, Stanton Roy 1939- *WhoSSW 91*
Erlichson, Miriam 1948- *WhoAmW 91*
Erlicht, Lewis Howard 1939- *WhoAm 90*
Erlick, Everett Howard 1921- *WhoAm 90*
Erlien, Nancy Beth 1954- *WhoAmA 91*
Erlien, Rick *NewAgMG*
Erlih, Devy 1928- *PenDiMP*
Erline, N. T. *ConAu 130*
Erlingsson, Thorsteinn 1858-1914 *DcScanL*
Erlmann, Veit 1951- *IntWWM 90*
Erma, Reino Mauri 1922- *WhoWor 91*
Ermacora, Giovanni 1850-1898 *EncPaPR 91*
Ermacora, Giovanni Battista 1869-1898 *EncO&P 3*
Erman, Bruce 1945- *WhoAmA 91*
Erman, John 1935- *WhoAm 90*
Erman, Milton Karl 1948- *BiDrAPA 89*
Erman, Susan Reiner *BiDrAPA 89*
Ermann, Michael E. F. *WhoWor 91*
Ermel, Frederick C. 1942- *St&PR 91*
Ermenc, Joseph John 1912- *WhoAm 90*
Ermengarde *WomWR*
Ermengarde *WomWR*
Ermengarde, Viscountess of Narbonne *EncCoWW*
Ermensinde *WomWR*
Ermler, Mark 1932- *IntWWM 90, PenDiMP*
Ermolaev, Herman Sergei 1924- *WhoAm 90*
Ermolayeva, Vera Mikhailovna 1893-1938 *BiDWomA*
Ermutlu, Ilhan 1927- *BiDrAPA 89*
Ermutlu, Ilhan Mehmet 1927- *WhoSSW 91*
Ernest, Albert D., Jr. *St&PR 91*
Ernest, Albert Devery, Jr. 1930- *WhoAm 90, WhoSSW 91*
Ernest, C.S.C. *AuBYP 90*
Ernest, David J. 1929- *IntWWM 90*
Ernest, Judy 1939- *WhoAmW 91*
Ernest, Richard B. 1934- *St&PR 91*
Ernest, Robert Charles 1924- *St&PR 91*
Ernestine, Ida Cornelia *EncCoWW*
Erney, Thomas Allen 1947- *WhoSSW 91*
Erni, Hans 1909- *ConDes 90, WhoWor 91*
Ernsbarger, Rebecca Faye 1949- *WhoAmW 91*
Ernsberger, Donald Craig 1947- *WhoE 91*
Ernst, Albert A. 1926- *St&PR 91*
Ernst, Bruce Alan 1953- *WhoEmL 91*
Ernst, Calvin Bradley 1934- *WhoAm 90*
Ernst, Chad E. 1933- *St&PR 91*
Ernst, Chadwick Ellsworth 1933- *WhoWor 91*
Ernst, Chester Nelson 1948- *WhoEmL 91*
Ernst, Christina Miller 1949- *St&PR 91*
Ernst, Daniel Pearson 1931- *WhoWor 91*
Ernst, Douglas Ray 1950- *WhoEmL 91*
Ernst, Ed William 1950- *WhoEmL 91*
Ernst, Edward Willis 1924- *WhoAm 90*
Ernst, Franklin H, Jr. 1923- *BiDrAPA 89*
Ernst, Gerd Hans 1926- *St&PR 91*
Ernst, Heinrich 1814-1865 *PenDiMP*
Ernst, J.B. 1931- *St&PR 91*
Ernst, Janet Lee 1955- *WhoAmW 91, WhoEmL 91, WhoSSW 91*
Ernst, Jimmy 1920- *WhoAmA 91N*
Ernst, John Albert 1942- *WhoE 91*
Ernst, John Louis 1932- *WhoAm 90, WhoWor 91*
Ernst, Kathryn Fitzgerald 1942- *WhoE 91*
Ernst, Ken 1918-1985 *EncACom*
Ernst, Konrad 1903- *BiDrAPA 89*
Ernst, Lisa Campbell 1957- *BioIn 16*
Ernst, Lois Geraci 1933- *WhoAm 90*
Ernst, Ludwig 1928- *WhoWor 91*
Ernst, Marcia McCrory 1961- *WhoEmL 91*
Ernst, Mary Anne 1944- *WhoAmW 91*
Ernst, Max 1891-1976 *BioIn 16, IntDcAA 90, WhoAmA 91N, WorAlBi*
Ernst, Monique *BiDrAPA 89*
Ernst, Paul 1866-1933 *BioIn 16*
Ernst, Paul William 1939- *St&PR 91*
Ernst, Richard Dale 1951- *WhoEmL 91*
Ernst, Richard Edward 1942- *WhoE 91*
Ernst, Richard Robert 1933- *WhoWor 91*
Ernst, Rick C. 1955- *WhoSSW 91*
Ernst, Roger 1924- *WhoAm 90*
Ernst, Roger Charles 1914- *WhoAm 90*
Ernst, Thomas Albert 1941- *St&PR 91*
Ernst, Wallace Gary 1931- *WhoAm 90*
Ernst, William T. 1920- *St&PR 91*
Ernster, Jacquelyn 1939- *WhoAm 90, WhoAmW 91*
Ernstin, George K 1898- *BiDrAPA 89*
Ernsting, Eugene C. 1928- *St&PR 91*

Ernstrom, Adele Mansfield 1930- *WhoAmA 91*
Ernstrom, Edward Kenneth 1942- *WhoE 91*
Ernstthal, Henry L. 1940- *WhoAm 90*
Ernt, Bruce William 1942- *St&PR 91*
Eroglu, Hasan 1956- *WhoE 91*
Erokan, Dennis William 1950- *WhoAm 90*
Eron, Leonard David 1920- *WhoAm 90*
Eronen, Matti Juhani 1944- *WhoWor 91*
Eros, Peter 1936- *IntWWM 90*
Erosh, William Daniel 1956- *St&PR 91, WhoE 91*
Erp, Dirk van *PenDiDA 89*
Erp, Dirk van 1859-1933 *BioIn 16*
Erpenbeck, Mary-Lou Brockett 1961- *WhoWrEP 89*
Errante, F. Gerard 1941- *IntWWM 90*
Errazuriz, Hernan Felipe 1945- *WhoAm 90, WhoWor 91*
Errazuriz Echauren, Federico 1850-1901 *BioIn 16*
Errazuriz Zanartu, Federico 1825-1877 *BioIn 16*
Errecart, Joyce Hier 1950- *WhoEmL 91*
Errera, Paul 1928- *BiDrAPA 89, WhoE 91*
Errichetti, Anthony J 1925- *BiDrAPA 89*
Errickson, Barbara Bauer 1944- *WhoAmW 91, WhoWor 91*
Errickson, Dick 1914- *Ballpl 90*
Errico, Michael Edward 1920- *St&PR 91*
Errico, Vincent 1961- *WhoE 91*
Erro, Roger I *BiDrAPA 89*
Erroll, Josslyn Hay, Earl of 1901-1941 *BioIn 16*
Ersay, Ronald Emile *BiDrAPA 89*
Ersek, Bruce Andrew 1938- *St&PR 91*
Ersek, Gregory Joseph Mark 1956- *WhoEmL 91, WhoSSW 91, WhoWor 91*
Ersek, Robert Allen 1938- *WhoAm 90*
Erselius, Lynne Louise 1961- *WhoEmL 91*
Ersgaard, Ole Kristian 1948- *WhoWor 91*
Ershad, Hussain Muhammad 1930- *WhoWor 91*
Ershov, Ivan *PenDiMP*
Erskine, Alan L. *ODwPR 91*
Erskine, Albert Russel 1871-1933 *EncABHB 5 [port]*
Erskine, Bruce Alan 1947- *IntWWM 90*
Erskine, Carl 1926- *Ballpl 90*
Erskine, Charlene G. 1943- *WhoAmW 91*
Erskine, Dennis Wayne 1948- *WhoSSW 91*
Erskine, Frederick A *BiDrAPA 89*
Erskine, Harold Lester 1924- *WhoE 91*
Erskine, Harold Perry 1879-1951 *WhoAmA 91N*
Erskine, James Lorenzo 1942- *WhoAm 90*
Erskine, Jeffrey Allan 1960- *WhoEmL 91*
Erskine, John 1879-1951 *DcLB 102 [port]*
Erskine, John Morse 1920- *WhoAm 90, WhoWor 91*
Erskine, Margaret *TwCCr&M 91*
Erskine, Mary Cara 1947- *WhoAmW 91*
Erskine, Paul Anderson 1926- *St&PR 91*
Erskine, Ralph 1914- *WhoWor 91*
Erskine, Terry Michael 1943- *St&PR 91*
Erskine, William Robin 1943- *IntWWM 90*
Erskine Inglis, Frances 1804-1882 *BioIn 16*
Erslev, Allan Jacob 1919- *WhoAm 90*
Ersoz, Clara Jean 1937- *WhoAmW 91*
Erspamer, Michael Stephen 1949- *WhoWor 91*
Erstad, Leon Robert 1947- *WhoEmL 91, WhoWor 91*
Erstling, Christopher M 1947- *BiDrAPA 89*
Erstling, Christopher Michael 1947- *WhoE 91*
Erte *ConAu 131*
Erte 1892-1990 *BioIn 16, ConDes 90, CurBio 90N, NewYTBS 90 [port], News 90*
Ertegun, Ahmet M. *BioIn 16*
Ertegun, Ahmet Munir 1923- *WhoAm 90, WhoWor 91*
Ertegun, Mica *BioIn 16*
Ertegun, Nesuhi *BioIn 16*
Ertel, Allen Edward 1936- *WhoAm 90*
Ertel, Denise Marlene 1956- *WhoAmW 91*
Ertel, Gary Arthur 1954- *WhoEmL 91*
Ertel, Grace Roscoe 1921- *WhoAmW 91*
Ertel, Hans 1904-1971 *DcScB S2*
Ertel, Inta Janners 1932- *WhoAm 90*
Ertel, John Charles, IV *St&PR 91*
Ertell, Denise Dennis 1950- *ODwPR 91*
Erten, Mehmet Hayri 1920- *WhoAm 90*
Erteszek, Olga *BioIn 16*
Erth, Richard A. 1943- *St&PR 91*
Ertl, James Louis 1931- *St&PR 91*
Ertl, Richard D. 1939- *St&PR 91*
Ertman, Earl Leslie 1932- *WhoAmA 91*
Erto, Pasquale 1895- *EncO&P 3*
Ertz, Alexander Louis 1957- *WhoSSW 91*
Ertz, Carol Ann Ryan 1955- *WhoEmL 91*
Erumsele, Andrew Akhigbe 1944- *WhoE 91, WhoWor 91*
Erven, Eric Lynn 1965- *WhoEmL 91*
Ervin, Adele Quincy 1924- *WhoAmW 91*
Ervin, Billy Maxwell 1933- *WhoE 91, WhoWor 91*
Ervin, Connie Yvonne 1954- *WhoAmW 91*
Ervin, Donald Neal 1931- *St&PR 91*
Ervin, Janis 1953- *WhoAmW 91, WhoEmL 91*
Ervin, Joseph A. 1947- *St&PR 91*
Ervin, Kathey 1952- *WhoAmA 91*
Ervin, Klon Randol 1941- *St&PR 91*
Ervin, Lester *WhoSSW 91*
Ervin, Patrick Franklin 1946- *WhoEmL 91*
Ervin, Robert Marvin 1917- *WhoAm 90*
Ervin, Sam J. 1896-1985 *BioIn 16*
Ervin, Samuel J., Jr. 1896-1985 *WorAlBi*
Ervin, Samuel James, III 1926- *WhoAm 90, WhoSSW 91*
Ervin, Susan Chadwick 1951- *WhoAmW 91, WhoEmL 91*
Ervin, Thomas Marion 1953- *WhoEmL 91*
Ervine, Timothy DuWayne 1963- *WhoSSW 91*
Erving, Julius *BioIn 16*
Erving, Julius 1950- *WorAlBi*
Erving, Julius Winfield 1950- *WhoAm 90*
Erving, Turquoise *BioIn 16*
Ervolino, Joanne Marie 1959- *WhoAmW 91*
Erwig, Eric *BioIn 16*
Erwin, Alan R. 1945- *ODwPR 91*
Erwin, Albert Rich 1931- *WhoAm 90*
Erwin, Betty K. *AuBYP 90*
Erwin, Billie Sledge 1933- *WhoSSW 91*
Erwin, Cheryl Janette 1956- *WhoSSW 91*
Erwin, Douglas Homer 1954- *WhoEmL 91*
Erwin, Elizabeth Mae 1951- *WhoAmW 91*
Erwin, Elmer Louis 1926- *WhoAm 90*
Erwin, Frank W. 1931- *St&PR 91*
Erwin, Frank William 1931- *WhoAm 90*
Erwin, George Z. 1840-1894 *AmLegL*
Erwin, Henry Albert 1945- *WhoSSW 91*
Erwin, Jane Elizabeth 1960- *WhoAmW 91*
Erwin, Joseph Arnold 1956- *WhoEmL 91*
Erwin, Judith Ann 1939- *WhoAmW 91*
Erwin, Kate Morse 1951- *BiDrAPA 89*
Erwin, Maurice George 1937- *St&PR 91*
Erwin, Paul David 1935- *WhoSSW 91*
Erwin, Richard C. 1923- *WhoAm 90, WhoSSW 91*
Erwin, Robert Dean 1949- *St&PR 91*
Erwin, Steven P. 1943- *St&PR 91*
Erwin, Sue Carlanne 1950- *WhoEmL 91*
Erwin, Thomas Dary 1950- *WhoSSW 91*
Erwin, Thomas K. 1950- *St&PR 91*
Erwin, William J *BiDrAPA 89*
Erwin-Vallejo, Terry Ann 1952- *WhoAmW 91*
Erwine, Donald T. 1945- *St&PR 91*
Erwine, Stanford Wright 1956- *WhoEmL 91*
Erwitt, Elliott 1928- *BioIn 16*
Erwitt, Elliott Romano 1928- *WhoAm 90*
Erxleben, Albert Ernest 1921- *WhoSSW 91*
Erxleben, Dorothea von *EncCoWW*
Erzen, Robert F. *ODwPR 91*
Erzinger, Dennis Eugene, Sr. 1951- *WhoEmL 91, WhoWor 91*
Esak, J. Ronald 1944- *St&PR 91*
Esak, Joseph 1913- *St&PR 91*
Esaki, Leo 1925- *WhoAm 90, WhoE 91, WhoWor 91, WorAlBi*
Esaki, Yasuhiro 1941- *WhoAmA 91*
Esarey, Melvin M. 1910- *WhoWrEP 89*
Esasky, Nick 1960- *Ballpl 90*
Esau, Abraham 1865?-1901 *BioIn 16*
Esau, Erika 1949- *WhoAmA 91*
Esau, Katherine 1898- *WhoAm 90, WhoAmW 91*
Esau, Truman G 1926- *BiDrAPA 89*
Esau, Truman Gerald 1926- *WhoE 91*
Esaw, James Reginald 1956- *WhoSSW 91*
Esayag, Mery 1935- *WhoWor 91*
Esbensen, Barbara J 1925- *SmATA 62 [port]*
Esbensen, Barbara Juster *BioIn 16*
Esbensen, Barbara Juster 1925- *WhoWrEP 89*
Esbensen, Eric Thorvald 1939- *WhoAm 90*
Esbenshade, Kathryn Mitchell 1955- *WhoAmW 91*
Esber, Ed, Jr. *BioIn 16*
Esber, Edward Michael, Jr. 1952- *WhoAm 90*
Esbjornson, Robert Glendon 1918- *WhoAm 90*
Escala, Veronica *WhoHisp 91*
Escalada, Felipe *EncCoWW*
Escalada, Louis James 1940- *BiDrAPA 89*
Escalante, Barbara 1967- *WhoHisp 91*
Escalante, Francisco Silvestre Velez De 1745?-1780? *WhNaAH*
Escalante, Jaime *BioIn 16*
Escalante, Jaime 1930- *WhoHisp 91*
Escalante, Judson Robert 1930- *WhoE 91*
Escalante, Silvestre Velez De *EncCRAm*
Escalera, Albert D. 1943- *WhoHisp 91*
Escalera, Karen Weiner *ODwPR 91*
Escalera, Karen Weiner 1944- *WhoAmW 91*
Escalera, Nino 1929- *Ballpl 90*
Escalet, Edwin Michael 1952- *WhoHisp 91*
Escalet, Frank Diaz 1930- *WhoAmA 91*
Escalon Delgado, Clara Sue 1952- *WhoAmW 91*
Escalona, Daniel Maypa *BiDrAPA 89*
Escamilla, Gerardo M. 1958- *WhoHisp 91*
Escamilla, Manuel 1947- *WhoHisp 91*
Escandell, Noemi 1936- *WhoWrEP 89*
Escandon, Ralph 1928- *ConAu 33NR*
Escano, Merry Christine *BiDrAPA 89*
Escardot, L. *EncCoWW*
Escarraz, Enrique, III 1944- *WhoSSW 91*
Esce, Susan Nan 1961- *WhoEmL 91*
Esch, Martha *BioIn 16*
Esch, Robert Ernst 1932- *St&PR 91, WhoAm 90*
Esch, Robert Morley 1940- *WhoSSW 91*
Esch, Robin Ernest 1930- *WhoAm 90*
Eschbach, Eugenie Marie 1959- *BiDrAPA 89*
Eschbach, Jesse Ernest 1920- *WhoAm 90*
Eschbach, Pearl R. 1924- *St&PR 91*
Eschborn, Natalie 1836-1905 *BioIn 16*
Esche, Irena *BiDrAPA 89*
Escheikh, Abdelhamid 1935- *WhoWor 91*
Eschenbach, Christoph 1940- *BioIn 16, IntWWM 90, PenDiMP, WhoAm 90, WhoSSW 91*
Eschenbacher, Larry Watts 1965- *WhoEmL 91*
Eschenbrenner, Gunther Paul 1925- *WhoAm 90*
Eschenburg, Emil Paul 1915- *WhoWor 91*
Eschenburg, Johann Joachim 1743-1820 *DcLB 97 [port]*
Eschenlohr, John W. 1936- *St&PR 91, WhoAm 90*
Eschenmoser, Albert 1925- *WhoWor 91*
Eschenroeder, Alan Quade 1933- *WhoAm 90, WhoE 91, WhoWor 91*
Escher, Berend George 1885-1967 *DcScB S2*
Escher, M. C. 1898-1972 *WorAlBi*
Eschert, Erwin R. *St&PR 91*
Eschete, Mary Louise 1949- *WhoAmW 91*
Eschino, Robert P. 1940- *St&PR 91*
Eschiva of Ibelin *WomWR*
Eschmann, Jean Charles 1896-1961 *WhoAmA 91N*
Eschmann, Thomas A. 1936- *St&PR 91*
Eschmeyer, William Neil 1939- *WhoAm 90*
Eschner, Arthur Richard 1925- *WhoE 91*
Eschrich, Jane 1955- *IntWWM 90*
Eschstruth, Natalie von 1870-1939 *EncCoWW*
Eschweiler, Peter Quintus 1932- *WhoE 91*
Esco, Lois Oliver 1916- *WhoAmW 91*
Escobar, Carlos Enrique *BiDrAPA 89*
Escobar, Hilda Lopez 1929- *WhoAmW 91*
Escobar, J. Fernando 1954- *WhoSSW 91*
Escobar, Javier I 1943- *BiDrAPA 89, WhoE 91*
Escobar, Javier I., Sr. 1943- *WhoHisp 91*
Escobar, Jesus Ernesto 1948- *WhoHisp 91*
Escobar, M. *BiDWomA*
Escobar, Manuel G., Jr. 1953- *WhoEmL 91*
Escobar, Maria Luisa 1909- *IntWWM 90*
Escobar, Marisol *WhoAmA 91*
Escobar, Marisol 1930- *BioIn 16, WhoAm 90, WhoAmW 91*
Escobar, Pablo *BioIn 16*
Escobar, Roberto B. 1926- *IntWWM 90*
Escobar, Roberto E. *WhoHisp 91*
Escobar Cerda, Luis 1927- *WhoWor 91*
Escobar-Haskins, Lillian *WhoHisp 91*
Escobedo, Edmundo 1932- *WhoHisp 91*
Escobedo, Ernest 1948- *WhoEmL 91, WhoSSW 91*
Escobedo, Helen 1936- *WhoAmA 91*
Escobillo, Evangeline Crisostomo 1954- *WhoWor 91*
Escoffery, Gloria 1923- *FemiCLE*
Escoffier, Auguste *BioIn 16*
Escoffier, Georges Auguste 1846-1935 *WorAlBi*
Escolano, Mercedes 1964- *EncCoWW*
Escoll, Philip J 1928- *BiDrAPA 89*
Escombe, Edith 1865-1950 *FemiCLE*
Escondo, Gerson Z 1933- *BiDrAPA 89*
Escontrias, Manuel 1945- *WhoHisp 91*
Escorza, Monica Marie 1958- *WhoHisp 91*
Escot, Pozzi *WhoE 91*
Escot, Pozzi 1933- *IntWWM 90*
Escott, Bickham Aldred Cowan Sweet- 1907-1981 *DcNaB 1981*
Escott, Lloyd Harrison 1948- *St&PR 91*
Escott, Shoolah Hope 1952- *WhoAmW 91*
Escott, Susan Lee 1959- *WhoEmL 91*
Escovedo, Peter 1935- *BioIn 16*
Escribano-Alberca, Ignacio 1928- *WhoWor 91*
Escribano Iglesias, Francisco Javier 1951- *WhoWor 91*
Escriva, Charles 1924- *BiDrAPA 89*
Escriva de Balaguer y Albas, Jose Maria 1902-1975 *BioIn 16*
Escudero, Ernesto 1953- *WhoHisp 91*
Escudero, Gilbert 1945- *WhoHisp 91*
Escudero, Manuel M 1918- *BiDrAPA 89*
Esdaile, James 1808-1859 *EncO&P 3*
Esdorn, Richard L., III 1945- *St&PR 91*
Esecover, Harold B *BiDrAPA 89*
Esenberg, Franklyn 1933- *St&PR 91*
Esenin, Sergei 1895-1925 *WorAlBi*
Eseonu, Maxwell Obioma 1955- *WhoSSW 91*
Esfandiary, F M *ConAu 31NR*
Esfandiary, Mary Sadigh 1929- *WhoAmW 91, WhoWor 91*
Esgdaille, Elias 1953- *WhoHisp 91*
Esh, Dalia Regina 1950- *WhoAmW 91, WhoEmL 91*
Eshagian, Joseph 1951- *WhoEmL 91*
Esham, Faith 1950- *IntWWM 90*
Eshbach, Richard Earl 1932- *BiDrAPA 89*
Eshbach, Theresa Ann Cocklin 1940- *WhoE 91*
Eshbach, William Wallace 1917- *WhoAm 90*
Eshelbrenner, Gary C. 1942- *St&PR 91*
Eshelman, David Richard 1949- *WhoE 91, WhoEmL 91*
Eshelman, George C. 1952- *St&PR 91*
Eshelman, John *WhoAm 90*
Eshelman, John M. *St&PR 91*
Eshelman, Steven Dale 1952- *BiDrAPA 89*
Eshelman, Vicki Renee Walker 1959- *WhoEmL 91*
Eshelman, William Robert 1921- *WhoAm 90*
Eshenbaugh, William Arthur 1942- *WhoSSW 91*
Esherick, Joseph 1914- *BioIn 16, WhoAm 90*
Esherick, Joseph W. 1942- *AuBYP 90*
Esherick, Wharton *PenDiDA 89*
Esherick, Wharton 1887-1970 *WhoAmA 91N*
Eshkenazi, Azariah 1938- *BiDrAPA 89*
Eshkol, Levi 1895-1969 *PolLCME*
Eshleman, Clayton *BioIn 16*
Eshleman, Clayton 1935- *WhoWrEP 89*
Eshleman, Dennis Newcomer 1954- *WhoEmL 91*
Eshleman, J. Richard 1930- *St&PR 91*
Eshleman, James J. 1953- *St&PR 91*
Eshleman, S Kendrick, III 1928- *BiDrAPA 89*
Eshleman, Silas Kendrick, III 1928- *WhoE 91*
Eshoo, Barbara Anne Rudolph 1946- *WhoAmW 91, WhoE 91*
Eshoo, Robert 1926- *WhoAmA 91*
Eshpai, Andrey Yakoulevitch 1925- *IntWWM 90*
Eshugbayi, Ezekiel Aderogba *AuBYP 90*
Esiason, Boomer *BioIn 16*
Esiason, Boomer 1961- *News 91-1 [port], WhoAm 90, WorAlBi*
Esin, Numan Sabit 1929- *WhoWor 91*
Esipova, Anna *PenDiMP*
Eskaminzin 1825?-1890 *WhNaAH*
Eskandarian, Edward 1936- *St&PR 91, WhoAm 90*
Eskander, Hoda Selim *BiDrAPA 89*
Eskdale, George 1897-1960 *PenDiMP*
Eskes, Tom Kees 1933- *WhoWor 91*
Eskesen, Bennet Hallum, Jr. 1947- *WhoWrEP 89*
Eskesen, Lauritz B. 1940- *St&PR 91*
Eskesen, Ruth Ellen 1939- *WhoAmW 91*
Eskew, Carolyn Elizabeth 1942- *WhoAmW 91*
Eskew, Cathleen Cheek 1953- *WhoEmL 91*
Eskew, Rhea Taliaferro 1923- *St&PR 91, WhoAm 90*
Eskilson, Bengt V. 1932- *WhoWor 91*
Eskilson, Eskil T. 1905- *St&PR 91*
Eskilson, Thomas Talbot 1942- *St&PR 91*
Eskiminzin 1825?-1890 *WhNaAH*
Eskin, James A. 1953- *ODwPR 91*
Eskin, Jeffrey Laurence 1952- *WhoEmL 91*
Eskind, Norman Jo Andrew 1955- *WhoEmL 91*
Eskind, Steven Joseph 1951- *WhoSSW 91*
Eskoff, Richard Joseph 1936- *St&PR 91*
Eskola, Juhani Jyrki Altti 1951- *WhoWor 91*
Eskolin-Nurmesniemi, Vuokko 1930- *ConDes 90*
Eskow, Bonnie Michele 1966- *WhoAmW 91*
Eskow, Mary Ann 1946- *St&PR 91*
Eskow, Robert Norman 1942- *WhoE 91*
Eskreis, Naftali 1910- *BiDrAPA 89*
Eskridge, Albert Harold 1927- *St&PR 91*
Eskridge, Chauncey *BioIn 16*

Eskridge, James Arthur 1942- St&PR 91, WhoAm 90
Eskridge, John I. 1940- St&PR 91
Eskridge, Wayne 1942- St&PR 91
Eslami, Hossein Hojatol 1927- WhoAm 90
Eslami, Mahnoosh 1948- BiDrAPA 89
Eslava, Fernan Gonzalez de 1534-1601? BioIn 16
Esler, Anthony James 1934- WhoAm 90, WhoSSW 91, WhoWrEP 89
Esler, Erminda 1852?-1924 FemiCLE
Esler, John Kenneth 1933- WhoAm 90, WhoAmA 91
Esler, W. R. 1926- WhoSSW 91
Esler, William Christopher 1951- WhoWrEP 89
Eslick, Leonard James 1914- WhoAm 90
Eslinger, Troy Rhudy 1919- WhoSSW 91
Eslyn, Robert N. 1923- St&PR 91
Esmail, Mohamed Nabil 1942- WhoAm 90
Esmaili, Haydeh F 1950- BiDrAPA 89
Esman, Aaron H 1924- BiDrAPA 89, WhoE 91
Esman, Rosa 1927- WhoAmA 91
Esmay, Merle Linden 1920- WhoAm 90
Esmein, Jean 1923- ConAu 31NR
Esmilla, Sergio Zalamea, Jr. 1927- IntWWM 90
Esmond, Harriet TwCCr&M 91
Esmond, Jill NewYTBS 90
Esmond, Jimmy 1889-1949 Ballpl 90
Espada, Martin WhoHisp 91
Espada, Pedro, Jr. 1953- WhoHisp 91
Espaillat, Rhina Polonia 1932- WhoWrEP 89
Espaldon, Ernesto Mercader 1926- WhoAm 90
Espanca, Florbela de Alma da Conceicao 1894-1930 EncCoWW
Espanol, Rosemary 1948- WhoE 91
Espartero, Baldomero 1792?-1879 BioIn 16
Esparza, Jesus 1932- WhoHisp 91
Esparza, Lili V. 1937- WhoHisp 91
Esparza, Manuel, Jr. 1946- WhoHisp 91
Esparza, Moctesuma Diaz 1949- WhoEmL 91
Esparza, Phillip W. 1949- WhoHisp 91
Esparza, Thomas, Jr. 1952- WhoHisp 91
Espat, Roberto E. WhoHisp 91
Espe, David Ronald 1955- WhoE 91, WhoEmL 91
Espejo, Antonio De EncCRAm, WhNaAH
Espelage, John J. 1938- St&PR 91
Espeland, Pamela 1951- BioIn 16
Espenet 1920- WhoAmA 91
Espenlaub, Charles Fredrick, Jr. 1935- St&PR 91
Espenlaub, Sharon Kay Jury 1946- WhoSSW 91
Espenoza, Cecelia M. 1958- WhoHisp 91
Espenschied, Clyde WhoAmA 91
Espenshade, Edward Bowman 1910- AuBYP 90
Espenshade, Edward Bowman, Jr. 1910- WhoAm 90
Espenshade, Frederick Martin 1938- WhoE 91
Esper, William BioIn 16
Esper, William Joseph 1932- WhoE 91
Esperian, Kallen BioIn 16
Esperian, Kallen Rose 1961- WhoAm 90
Esperseth, Maurice H. 1925- St&PR 91
Espey, William M 1938- BiDrAPA 89
Espin, C. Elizabeth 1961- WhoE 91, WhoEmL 91
Espin, Orlando Oscar 1947- WhoHisp 91
Espinal, Luis BioIn 16
Espindola, Emilio G BiDrAPA 89
Espino, Fern R. WhoHisp 91
Espino, Fern Ruby WhoAmW 91
Espino, Hector 1939- Ballpl 90
Espinosa, Aurelio M. 1880-1958 BioIn 16, ConAu 131, HispWr 90
Espinosa, Aurelio M, Jr. 1907- ConAu 131
Espinosa, Aurelio M., Jr. 1907- HispWr 90
Espinosa, Aurelio Macedonio, Jr. 1907- WhoHisp 91
Espinosa, Carmen Luisa BiDrAPA 89
Espinosa, Fernando WhoHisp 91
Espinosa, Francisco C. WhoHisp 91
Espinosa, Francisco C. 1936- St&PR 91, WhoSSW 91
Espinosa, Hector WhoHisp 91
Espinosa, James 1938- WhoHisp 91
Espinosa, Jose Maria 1796-1883 ArtLatA
Espinosa, Juan B 1948- BiDrAPA 89
Espinosa, Maria Paz 1960- WhoWor 91
Espinosa, Nino 1953-1988 Ballpl 90
Espinosa, Paul 1950- WhoHisp 91
Espinosa, Rafael BiDrAPA 89
Espinosa-Araya, Soledad 1940- BiDrAPA 89
Espinosa y Almodovar, Juan 1941- WhoHisp 91
Espinoza, Alvaro 1962- WhoHisp 91
Espinoza, Elena Emilia 1960- WhoHisp 91
Espinoza, Eloisa 1960- WhoHisp 91
Espinoza, Francisco Teodoro 1932- WhoSSW 91
Espinoza, Laurie Edith 1943- WhoHisp 91
Espinoza, Mario Antonio 1962- WhoSSW 91
Espinoza, Michael Dan WhoHisp 91
Espinoza, Noe 1954- WhoHisp 91
Espinoza, Pete E., Jr. 1948- WhoHisp 91
Espirito-Santo, Manuel Ricardo 1933- WhoWor 91
Esplugues, Carlos Aurelio 1959- WhoWor 91
Esposito, Albert Charles 1912- WhoAm 90
Esposito, Alfred Lewis 1923- WhoAm 90
Esposito, Amedeo BiDrAPA 89
Esposito, Amy Sklar 1955- WhoAmW 91
Esposito, Andrea Marie 1957- St&PR 91
Esposito, Anthony F. 1935- St&PR 91
Esposito, Anthony Morris 1952- WhoEmL 91
Esposito, Bonnie Lou 1947- WhoAmW 91, WhoEmL 91
Esposito, Dennis Harry 1947- WhoEmL 91
Esposito, Donna J. 1954- WhoWrEP 89
Esposito, Eugene Henry 1940- St&PR 91
Esposito, Giancarlo 1958- DrBlPA 90
Esposito, Joseph C. 1950- WhoE 91
Esposito, Joseph John 1951- WhoAm 90
Esposito, Larry Wayne 1951- WhoEmL 91
Esposito, Maria Q BiDrAPA 89
Esposito, Marisa Lucia 1957- WhoEmL 91
Esposito, Michael 1956- St&PR 91
Esposito, Michael P., Jr. BioIn 16
Esposito, Michael P., Jr. 1939- St&PR 91
Esposito, Michael Patrick, Jr. 1939- WhoAm 90, WhoE 91
Esposito, Paulette 1945- WhoAmW 91, WhoEmL 91
Esposito, Phil 1942- WorAlBi
Esposito, Philip Anthony 1942- WhoE 91
Esposito, Robert Louis 1935- St&PR 91
Esposito, Rochelle Easton 1941- WhoAm 90
Esposito, Sammy 1931- Ballpl 90
Esposito, Thomas R. 1946- St&PR 91
Esposito, Tony ODwPR 91
Esposito, Valeria 1961- IntWWM 90
Esposito, Vincent 1957- WhoE 91
Espronceda, Jose de 1808-1842 BioIn 16
Espy, Charles Clifford 1910- WhoAm 90
Espy, James William 1948- WhoWor 91
Espy, Mary Susan 1952- St&PR 91, WhoAmW 91
Espy, Michael BioIn 16
Espy, Mike 1953- BlkAmsC [port], WhoAm 90, WhoSSW 91
Espy, Reynette Coats 1960- WhoAmW 91
Espy, Ronald Paul 1947- St&PR 91
Espy, Willard R. 1910- WhoWrEP 89
Espy, Willard Richard 1910- WhoAm 90
Esquibel, Augusto J 1926- BiDrAPA 89
Esquilache BioIn 16
Esquiros, Margarita 1945- WhoHisp 91
Esquivel, Agerico Liwag 1932- WhoAm 90
Esquivel, Alan de Souza 1946- WhoWor 91
Esquivel, Giselle Beatriz 1950- WhoEmL 91
Esquivel, Manuel 1940- BioIn 16, WhoWor 91
Esquivel, Rita WhoHisp 91
Esquivel, Roderick Lorenzo 1927- WhoWor 91
Esquivel, Ruben E. 1943- St&PR 91
Esrey, William Todd BioIn 16
Esrey, William Todd 1940- St&PR 91, WhoAm 90
Esry, Donald Howard 1940- WhoSSW 91
Essa, Lisa Beth 1955- WhoAmW 91
Essa, Mohsain 1945- BiDrAPA 89
Essack, Joosub Yusuf BiDrAPA 89
Essegian, Chuck 1931- Ballpl 90
Esselbeeck, Michiel PenDiDA 89
Esselstrom, Michael 1939- IntWWM 90
Essenberg, Jack R. 1938- St&PR 91
Essene, Virginia NewAgE 90
Essenwanger, Oskar Maximilian Karl 1920- WhoWor 91
Esser, Aristide H 1930- BiDrAPA 89
Esser, Aristide Henri 1930- WhoAm 90
Esser, Carl Eric 1942- WhoAm 90
Esser, Frank V. 1939- St&PR 91
Esser, Frank Vincent 1939- WhoAm 90
Esser, George Francis 1955- WhoEmL 91
Esser, Hermin 1928- IntWWM 90
Esser, Janet Brody WhoAmA 91
Esser, Richard M BiDrAPA 89
Esser, Robert A BiDrAPA 89
Esser, Steffen 1943- WhoWor 91
Essert, Gene Gordon 1917- BiDrAPA 89
Essex, Craig 1955- BiDrAPA 89
Essex, David 1947- OxCPMus
Essex, Harry J. 1912- BioIn 16
Essex, Harry J. 1915- WhoAm 90
Essex, Joseph Michael 1947- WhoAm 90
Essex, Judy Towne 1954- WhoAmW 91
Essex, Lewis W. 1932- St&PR 91
Essex, Michael Gilbert BiDrAPA 89
Essex, Myron Elmer 1939- WhoAm 90, WhoE 91, WhoWor 91
Essex, Robert Willson, Jr. 1945- WhoEmL 91
Essex, Stephen S. 1955- St&PR 91
Essian, Jim 1951- Ballpl 90
Essick, Bill 1881-1951 Ballpl 90
Essick, Samuel Coleman 1920- St&PR 91
Essig, Andrew Michael 1966- WhoE 91
Essig, Mitchell Neil 1950- WhoE 91
Essig, Nancy Claire 1939- WhoAm 90
Essig, Philip Martin 1939- St&PR 91
Essin, Emmett Mohammed, Jr. 1920- WhoSSW 91
Essinger, Giles F. 1934- St&PR 91
Essipoff, Anna Nicolayevna 1851-1914 BioIn 16
Essipova, Anna Nicolayevna 1851-1914 BioIn 16
Essler, Wilhelm Karl 1940- WhoWor 91
Essley, Roger Holmer 1949- WhoAmA 91
Esslin, Martin 1918- MajTwCW
Esslin, Martin Julius 1918- WhoAm 90
Esslinger, Anna Mae Linthicum 1912- WhoWor 91
Esslinger, Charlene Marie Dobbs 1945- WhoAmW 91
Esslinger, Dean Robert 1942- WhoE 91
Esslinger, Pat M ConAu 31NR
Esslinger, Tamra Jo 1959- WhoEmL 91
Essman, Douglas Jay 1956- WhoEmL 91
Essman, Elliot BioIn 16
Essman, Pansy Ellen 1918- WhoAmW 91
Essman, Robert Norvel 1937- WhoE 91
Essmann, Jeffrey BioIn 16
Essmyer, Michael Martin 1949- WhoEmL 91, WhoSSW 91, WhoWor 91
Essock, Cyd Pauline 1956- WhoWrEP 89
Essom, David Milnor 1932- BiDrAPA 89
Esson, J. Douglas 1940- St&PR 91
Esson, James Douglas 1940- WhoAm 90
Esson, Robert 1944- St&PR 91
Essrick, Abraham Joseph 1914- WhoWor 91
Esstman, Michael Brady 1946- St&PR 91
Essunger, Jan 1938- WhoWor 91
Esswood, Paul 1942- PenDiMP
Esswood, Paul Lawrence Vincent 1942- IntWWM 90
Estabrook, Alison 1951- WhoAmW 91
Estabrook, Evelyn Marie Basom 1908- WhoAmW 91
Estabrook, Leigh Stewart 1942- WhoAm 90
Estabrook, Michael Patrick 1963- WhoE 91
Estabrook, Reed 1944- WhoAm 90, WhoAmA 91
Estabrook, Robert Harley 1918- WhoAm 90
Estabrook, Ronald Winfield 1926- WhoAm 90
Estabrook, William Wallace, III 1942- BiDrAPA 89
Estabrooks, George Hoban 1895-1973 EncO&P 3
Estabrooks, George Hoben 1895-198-? EncPaPR 91
Estaing, Valery Giscard d' 1926- BioIn 16
Estalella, Bobby 1911- Ballpl 90
Estanislao WhNaAH
Estaris, Jovito Buada 1947- WhoAm 90
Estaugh, Elizabeth Haddon 1680-1762 EncCRAm
Este, Isabella d' 1475-1539 EncCoWW
Esteban 1500?-1539 WhNaAH
Esteban, Manuel A. 1940- WhoHisp 91
Estebanico the Moor 1500?-1539 WhNaAH
Estebany, Oskar EncPaPR 91
Estee, Charles Remington 1921- WhoAm 90
Estee, Morris M. 1833-1903 AmLegL
Estefan, Gloria BioIn 16
Estefan, Gloria 1958- WhoHisp 91
Estehghari, Mohamad Hassan 1950- WhoWor 91
Estenson, Noel Keith 1938- St&PR 91
Estenssoro, Victor Paz 1907- BioIn 16
Estep, Carolyn Benjamin 1947- WhoWrEP 89
Estep, Janet Olson 1956- WhoAmW 91
Estep, Leland 1945- WhoSSW 91
Estep, Sarah Virginia 1926- WhoE 91
Estep-Johnston, Megan Alexander 1957- WhoAmW 91
Estepa, Puruca Manuela BiDrAPA 89
Estepp, J. Mark BioIn 16
Esterbrook, Elizabeth WhoWrEP 89
Estergren, Eric D. 1944- St&PR 91
Esterhai, John Louis 1920- St&PR 91, WhoAm 90
Esterhazy, Ferdinand Walsin 1857-1923 BioIn 16
Esterhazy, Marie Charles 1847-1923 WorAlBi
Esterhill, Frank WhoE 91
Esterline, Shirley Jeanne 1936- WhoAmW 91
Esterly, Juliet King Bindt 1912- WhoAmW 91
Esterly, Nancy Burton 1935- WhoAm 90
Esterly, Randall Edward 1946- St&PR 91
Estern, Neil 1926- WhoAmA 91
Estern, Neil Carl 1926- WhoE 91
Esterow, David J. 1928- St&PR 91
Esterow, Gary 1957- ODwPR 91
Esterow, Milton 1928- WhoAmA 91
Esterquest, Peter 1946- St&PR 91
Esterson, Larry L. 1916- St&PR 91
Estes, Alexandra Haeger 1949- St&PR 91
Estes, Carl Lewis, II 1936- WhoAm 90, WhoSSW 91, WhoWor 91
Estes, Charles Byron 1946- IntWWM 90, WhoEmL 91
Estes, David Charles 1950- WhoSSW 91
Estes, Debra 1956- ODwPR 91
Estes, Donald W. 1930- St&PR 91
Estes, Donald Wayne 1930- WhoAm 90, WhoSSW 91
Estes, Edward Harvey, Jr. 1925- WhoAm 90
Estes, Edward Richard, Jr. 1925- WhoSSW 91
Estes, Elaine Rose Graham 1931- WhoAm 90, WhoAmW 91
Estes, Eleanor 1906- AuBYP 90
Estes, Eleanor 1906-1988 BioIn 16
Estes, Elliott M. 1916-1988 BioIn 16
Estes, Frank William 1940- St&PR 91, WhoAm 90
Estes, Gerald Walter 1928- St&PR 91, WhoAm 90
Estes, Glen BiDrAPA 89
Estes, Harper 1956- WhoEmL 91
Estes, Hubert R 1925- BiDrAPA 89
Estes, Jack WhoSSW 91
Estes, Jack Charles 1935- WhoSSW 91
Estes, Jacob Thomas, Jr. 1944- WhoSSW 91
Estes, James Russell 1937- WhoAm 90
Estes, Jeanne M BiDrAPA 89
Estes, Joan Ethel Peltier 1938- WhoAmW 91
Estes, John 1899-1977 OxCPMus
Estes, Jon Carleton 1944- St&PR 91
Estes, Joseph O. 1927- St&PR 91
Estes, Joseph Raymond 1945- WhoEmL 91
Estes, Linton H., Jr. 1920- St&PR 91
Estes, Lynda Sherryl 1945- WhoEmL 91
Estes, Marion M BiDrAPA 89
Estes, Moreau Pinckney, IV 1917- WhoSSW 91
Estes, Patricia Lynn 1950- WhoAmW 91
Estes, Richard 1932- WhoAm 90, WhoAmA 91
Estes, Richard 1948- IntWWM 90
Estes, Richard J. 1942- WhoE 91
Estes, Ronald Gene 1956- WhoEmL 91
Estes, Simon 1938- DrBlPA 90, IntWWM 90, PenDiMP
Estes, Simon Lamont 1938- WhoAm 90
Estes, Sylvia D. 1951- St&PR 91
Estes, William Kaye 1919- WhoAm 90
Estes-Simmons, Barbara 1938- St&PR 91
Estess, Floyd Merrill 1921- BiDrAPA 89
Estess, Michael E 1940- BiDrAPA 89
Estess, Sybil P. 1942- ConAu 129
Estevan 1500?-1539 WhNaAH
Estevanico EncCRAm
Estevanico 1500?-1539 WhNaAH
Estevanito 1500?-1539 WhNaAH
Esteve, Jean PenDiDA 89
Esteve, Pierre PenDiDA 89
Esteve, Yves 1943- WhoWor 91
Esteve-Coll, Elizabeth BioIn 16
Esteves, Antonio 1910-1983 MusmAFA
Esteves, Sandra Maria 1948- BioIn 16, WhoHisp 91
Estevez, Angel BiDrAPA 89
Estevez, Emilio 1962- WhoHisp 91
Estevez, Emilio 1963- BioIn 16
Estevez, Juan A., Jr. 1949- WhoHisp 91
Estevez, Linda Frances 1956- WhoHisp 91
Estey, Audree Phipps 1910- WhoAmW 91
Estey, John Sherman 1926- St&PR 91
Estey, Kendrick Allen 1940- St&PR 91
Estey, Willard Zebedee BioIn 16
Estey, Willard Zebedee 1919- WhoAm 90
Estienne, Nicole 1542?-1584? EncCoWW
Estigarribia, Jose Felix 1888-1940 BioIn 16
Estilette, Edward D. 1833- AmLegL
Estill, Donna Marie 1935- WhoAmW 91
Estill, John Staples, Jr. 1919- WhoSSW 91
Estill, Robert Whitridge 1927- WhoAm 90, WhoSSW 91
Estimauville, Josephine-Eleonore D' 1816-1893 DcCanB 12
Estime, Dumarsais 1900-1953 BioIn 16
Estin, Hans Howard 1928- St&PR 91, WhoAm 90, WhoE 91
Estin-Klein, Libbyada 1937- WhoAmW 91
Estis, Dennis Arnold 1947- WhoEmL 91

Estivill-Lorenz, Vincent 1925- *WhoHisp 91*
Estka Berding, Jean Theresa 1923- *WhoAmW 91*
Estleman, Loren D. *BioIn 16*
Estleman, Loren D 1952- *MajTwCW, TwCCr&M 91*
Estler, Harry Donald 1950- *WhoSSW 91*
Estock, Robert *BiDrAPA 89*
Eston, Robert *BiDrAPA 89*
Estorge, Gerald B., Jr. 1927- *St&PR 91*
Estoril, Jean *AuBYP 90*
Estrada, Angel 1958-1989 *BioIn 16*
Estrada, Anthony *WhoHisp 91*
Estrada, Carolina *BioIn 16*
Estrada, Chuck 1938- *Ballpl 90*
Estrada, Erik 1949- *WhoHisp 91*
Estrada, Ezequiel Martinez 1895-1964 *BioIn 16*
Estrada, Gabriel M. 1933- *WhoHisp 91*
Estrada, Jacquelyn Ann 1946- *WhoEmL 91*
Estrada, Jim 1943- *WhoHisp 91*
Estrada, Joan Arlene 1938- *WhoE 91*
Estrada, Jose Luis 1955- *WhoHisp 91*
Estrada, Jose Maria 1810?-1862 *BioIn 16*
Estrada, Jose Maria 1810?-1865 *ArtLatA*
Estrada, Leobardo 1945- *WhoHisp 91*
Estrada, Mar 1960- *WhoWor 91*
Estrada, Marc Napoleon 1965- *WhoHisp 91*
Estrada, Roberto 1938- *WhoHisp 91*
Estrada, Rodney Joseph 1937- *St&PR 91, WhoAm 90*
Estrada, Sergio D 1923- *BiDrAPA 89*
Estrada, Silvio J. *WhoHisp 91*
Estrada, Victoria Ocampo de 1891-1979 *BioIn 16*
Estrada Cabrera, Manuel 1857-1924 *BioIn 16*
Estrada Palma, Tomas 1835-1908 *BioIn 16*
Estreicher, Samuel 1948- *WhoEmL 91*
Estrella, Nicolas 1951- *WhoHisp 91*
Estrella, William A. 1953- *St&PR 91*
Estrella-Schultz, Hebe E *BiDrAPA 89*
Estrema, Louis Joseph 1954- *WhoE 91*
Estren, Mark James 1948- *St&PR 91, WhoAm 90*
Estrera, Annabella B *BiDrAPA 89*
Estrich, Susan *BioIn 16*
Estrich, Susan Rachel 1952- *WhoAmW 91*
Estridge, Robin *TwCCr&M 91*
Estrin family *BioIn 16*
Estrin, Eric Charles 1953- *WhoEmL 91*
Estrin, Gerald 1921- *WhoAm 90*
Estrin, Herbert Alvin 1925- *WhoAm 90*
Estrin, Herman A. 1915- *WhoWrEP 89*
Estrin, Herman Albert 1915- *WhoAm 90, WhoWor 91*
Estrin, Karen Judith 1940- *WhoE 91*
Estrin, Kari 1954- *WhoAmW 91, WhoEmL 91*
Estrin, Mitchell Stewart 1956- *IntWWM 90, WhoEmL 91*
Estrin, Morton 1923- *IntWWM 90*
Estrin, Richard William 1932- *WhoAm 90*
Estrin, Thelma Austern 1924- *WhoAm 90, WhoAmW 91*
Estroff, Todd Wilk *BiDrAPA 89*
Estrup, Peder Jan 1931- *WhoAm 90*
Estudillo, Jesus *BioIn 16*
Estupinan Bass, Nelson 1915- *HispWr 90*
Estwing, Norman E. 1921- *St&PR 91*
Esty, David Cameron 1932- *WhoAm 90, WhoE 91*
Esty, Fred R. 1915- *St&PR 91*
Esty, John Cushing, Jr. 1928- *WhoAm 90*
Eswein, Bruce James, II 1951- *WhoE 91, WhoEmL 91, WhoWor 91*
Eszterhas, Joe *ConAu 130*
Eszterhas, Joseph A. *ConAu 130*
Etchebarren, Andy 1942- *Ballpl 90*
Etchegaray, Roger 1922- *WhoWor 91*
Etchemendy, Jeanne Marie 1959- *WhoAmW 91*
Etcherelli, Claire 1934- *EncCoWW*
Etcheson, Warren Wade 1920- *WhoAm 90*
Etcheverry, Bernard 1921- *St&PR 91*
Etchison, Bruce 1918- *WhoAmA 91*
Etemad, Jacqueline G *BiDrAPA 89*
Etemadi, Azim Abdul *BiDrAPA 89*
Etemadi, Kasra 1949- *WhoE 91*
Eternal Wind *NewAgMG*
Etess, Edward 1937- *St&PR 91*
Etessami, Rambod 1960- *WhoEmL 91*
Etgen, Charles D. 1928- *St&PR 91*
Eth, Spencer 1950- *BiDrAPA 89*
Ethan, Carol Baehr 1920- *WhoAm 90, WhoAmW 91*
Ethans, Harry 1952- *St&PR 91*
Ethell, Donald *BioIn 16*
Etheredge, Charles E. 1937- *St&PR 91*
Etheredge, Forest DeRoyce 1929- *WhoAm 90*
Etheredge, Robert Foster 1920- *WhoAm 90*
Etheridge, Evelyn *BioIn 16*
Etheridge, J. Wayne 1946- *St&PR 91*
Etheridge, Jack Paul 1927- *WhoAm 90*
Etheridge, Jeff D., Jr. 1949- *St&PR 91*
Etheridge, Jeff David, Jr. 1949- *WhoAm 90*
Etheridge, Melissa *BioIn 16*
Etheridge, Melissa 1962?- *ConMus 4 [port]*
Etheridge, Richard Emmet 1929- *WhoAm 90*
Etherington, Edwin D. 1924- *St&PR 91*
Etherington, Edwin Deacon 1924- *WhoAm 90*
Etherington, Frank 1945- *BioIn 16*
Etherington, Geoffrey 1928- *St&PR 91*
Etherington, Geoffrey, II 1928- *WhoSSW 91, WhoWor 91*
Etherington, Roger B. 1923- *St&PR 91*
Etherington, Roger Bennett 1923- *WhoAm 90*
Ethern, Stella L. 1952- *WhoEmL 91*
Etherton, Gloria Elizabeth 1930- *WhoAmW 91*
Ethier, C. James *St&PR 91N*
Ethington, Ambrose, Jr. 1942- *WhoAm 90*
Ethington, James W. 1917- *St&PR 91*
Ethington, Raymond Lindsay 1929- *WhoAm 90*
Ethridge, D. Jean 1943- *IntWWM 90*
Ethridge, Deborah J. 1951- *St&PR 91*
Ethridge, E.W. 1931- *St&PR 91*
Ethridge, Edwin Clark 1950- *WhoEmL 91*
Ethridge, J.B. 1941- *St&PR 91*
Ethridge, James Merritt 1921- *WhoAm 90*
Ethridge, Larry Clayton 1946- *WhoEmL 91*
Ethridge, Leonard Carroll, Jr. 1935- *WhoSSW 91*
Ethridge, Mark Foster, III 1949- *WhoAm 90, WhoSSW 91*
Ethridge, Willie Snow 1900-1982 *LiHiK*
Etienne, Dirk *St&PR 91*
Etienne, Eugene Napoleon 1844-1921 *BiDFrPL*
Etienne, Jacobus Johannes 1939- *WhoWor 91*
Etienne, Jean-Louis *BioIn 16*
Etkind, Efim Grigorievich 1918- *WhoWor 91*
Etkind, Steven Mark 1961- *WhoE 91*
Etling, Howard F. 1914- *St&PR 91*
Etling, John Charles 1935- *WhoAm 90, WhoE 91*
Etling, Terry Douglas 1943- *WhoWor 91*
Etlinger, Joseph D. 1946- *WhoAm 90*
Etner, Stephen Morgan 1903- *WhoAmA 91N*
Eto, Fumio 1946- *WhoWor 91*
Eto, Jun 1932- *WhoWor 91*
Eto, Shinichi 1937- *Ballpl 90*
Eto, Susumu 1936- *St&PR 91*
Eto, Toshiya 1927- *PenDiMP*
Eton, Robert 1899-1989 *SmATA X*
Etowski, Earl John, Jr. 1942- *St&PR 91*
Etra, Blanche G. 1915- *WhoAmW 91*
Etra, Richard H. 1948- *St&PR 91*
Etris, Denise Eileen 1950- *WhoAmW 91*
Etris, Samuel Franklin 1922- *WhoAm 90*
Etrog, Sorel 1933- *WhoAmA 91*
Etrusca, Amarelli *EncCoWW*
Ets, Marie Hall 1893- *AuBYP 90*
Etsitty, Sylvia Mae 1957- *WhoAmW 91*
Ettari, Charles V *BiDrAPA 89*
Ettedgui, Eva Yvette *BiDrAPA 89*
Ettedgui, Joseph *BioIn 16*
Etteilla *EncO&P 3*
Ettelson, Charles David 1952- *WhoEmL 91*
Etten, Nick 1913- *Ballpl 90*
Ettenberg, Franklin Joseph 1945- *WhoAmA 91*
Ettensohn, Frank Robert 1947- *WhoSSW 91*
Ettenson, Mel W. 1933- *St&PR 91*
Etter, Constance Lynne 1943- *WhoAmW 91*
Etter, Dave 1928- *DcLB 105 [port], WhoWrEP 89*
Etter, David Pearson 1928- *WhoAm 90*
Etter, Gary Lee 1953- *BiDrAPA 89*
Etter, George, IV 1940- *St&PR 91, WhoSSW 91*
Etter, Howard Lee 1931- *WhoAmA 91*
Etter, Kevin McKelvey 1952- *BiDrAPA 89*
Etter, Robert M. 1932- *St&PR 91*
Etter, Robert Miller 1932- *WhoAm 90*
Etter, Steven M. 1946- *St&PR 91*
Etter, Thomas Clifton, Jr. 1938- *WhoE 91*
Etter, William D. 1940- *St&PR 91*
Etter, Zana Claire 1950- *WhoAmW 91*
Etterer, Sepp 1944- *WhoSSW 91*
Etterlin, Frido von Senger und 1891- *BioIn 16*
Etters, Ronald Milton 1948- *WhoE 91*
Ettigi, Prakash G 1947- *BiDrAPA 89*
Etting, Emlen 1905- *WhoAmA 91*
Etting, Ruth 1896-1978 *OxCPMus*
Etting, Ruth 1898-1978 *WorAlBi*
Ettinger, Alfred *BiDrAPA 89*
Ettinger, Anna Marie 1925- *WhoAm 90*
Ettinger, Blanche 1922- *WhoE 91*
Ettinger, Carolyn Ruth 1930- *BiDrAPA 89*
Ettinger, Charlotte 1930- *WhoWor 91*
Ettinger, George Harold 1896- *WhoAm 90*
Ettinger, Harry Joseph 1934- *WhoE 91*
Ettinger, Jean-Claude Georges 1947- *WhoWor 91*
Ettinger, Jeannette *BiDrAPA 89*
Ettinger, Joseph Alan 1931- *WhoWor 91*
Ettinger, Lawrence Jay 1947- *WhoAm 90*
Ettinger, Milton Gene 1930- *WhoAm 90*
Ettinger, Mort 1924- *WhoWor 91*
Ettinger, Richard Prentice 1922- *WhoAm 90*
Ettinger, S. Yona 1935- *WhoWor 91*
Ettinger, Susi Steinitz 1922- *WhoAmA 91*
Ettinghausen, Richard 1906-1979 *WhoAmA 91N*
Ettl, Dorothy Anne 1943- *WhoAmW 91*
Ettl, Georg 1931- *WhoAmA 91*
Ettl, Johanna Moselle 1964- *WhoAmW 91*
Ettling, Ruth 1910- *WhoAmA 91*
Ettlinger, L. D. *ConAu 129*
Ettlinger, Leopold D. *ConAu 129*
Ettlinger, Leopold David 1913-1989 *ConAu 129*
Ettlinger, Michael Pauw 1959- *WhoE 91*
Ettre, Leslie Stephen 1922- *WhoAm 90*
Ettrick, Marco Antonio 1945- *WhoE 91, WhoEmL 91, WhoWor 91*
Etu, Paul David 1954- *WhoE 91*
Etzel, Barbara Coleman 1926- *WhoAm 90, WhoAmW 91*
Etzel, James Edward 1929- *WhoAm 90*
Etzel, Michael A *BiDrAPA 89*
Etzel, Paul J. *BioIn 16*
Etzenbach, John William 1957- *WhoEmL 91*
Etzi, Susan *BiDrAPA 89*
Etzioni, Amitai 1929- *WorAu 1980 [port]*
Etzioni, Amitai Werner 1929- *WhoAm 90, WhoE 91*
Etzioni, Moshe 1908- *WhoWor 91*
Etzkorn, K. Peter *WhoAm 90*
Etzkorn, K. Peter 1932- *IntWWM 90*
Etzler, Marilynn Edith 1940- *WhoAmW 91*
Etzweiler, William David 1935- *St&PR 91*
Etzwiler, Donnell Dencil 1927- *WhoAm 90*
Eu, March Kong Fong 1922- *WhoAm 90, WhoAmW 91*
Eubank, Alvah Hovey, Jr. 1926- *WhoAm 90*
Eubank, J. Thomas 1930- *WhoAm 90*
Eubank, Ray H. 1927- *St&PR 91*
Eubank, Sandra K. 1958- *WhoEmL 91*
Eubanks, A. Benjamin 1946- *BiDrAPA 89*
Eubanks, Charles Aubrey *BiDrAPA 89*
Eubanks, Charles David 1940- *WhoSSW 91*
Eubanks, Eugene Emerson 1939- *WhoAm 90*
Eubanks, Gary Leroy, Sr. 1933- *WhoSSW 91*
Eubanks, Jackie Karen *WhoWrEP 89*
Eubanks, John R. 1939- *WhoSSW 91*
Eubanks, Philip D. 1952- *St&PR 91*
Eubanks, Rachel Amelia *IntWWM 90*
Eubanks, Robin *BioIn 16*
Eubanks, Ronald W. 1946- *WhoEmL 91, WhoSSW 91*
Eubanks, Steve *BioIn 16*
Eubanks, Tony *BioIn 16*
Eubanks, William Hunter, III 1945- *WhoEmL 91*
Eucheria *EncCoWW*
Eucken, Rudolph 1846-1926 *WorAlBi*
Euclid *WorAlBi*
Eudaly, Dick 1943- *WhoSSW 91*
Eudaly, Harold B, Jr. 1932- *BiDrAPA 89*
Eudaly, Nathan Hoyt, Jr. 1955- *WhoEmL 91*
Eudene, Stephen G. 1939- *St&PR 91*
Eudocia, Empress *BioIn 16*
Eudocia Macrembolitissa 1021-1096 *WomWR*
Eudokia 394-460 *EncCoWW*
Eudokia, Aelia 394-460 *EncCoWW*
Eudoxia *WomWR*
Eudoxia, Empress *BioIn 16*
Eudy, Judith F. 1942- *St&PR 91*
Eugene, Christie 1928- *St&PR 91*
Eugenia *BiDEWW, FemiCLE*
Eugenie-Marie 1826-1920 *WomWR*
Eugenio, Henry Almazan *BiDrAPA 89*
Euginie *EncCoWW*
Eugster, Ernest 1950- *WhoWor 91*
Eugster, Jack Wilson 1945- *St&PR 91, WhoAm 90*
Euille, William Darnell 1950- *WhoE 91*
Eula, Ernesto Giuseppe 1927- *WhoWor 91*
Eulau, Heinz 1915- *WhoAm 90*
Eulderink, Frits 1934- *WhoWor 91*
Eulenberg, Julia Neibuhr 1942- *WhoAmW 91*
Euler, Aline *WhoAmW 91*
Euler, Franz, III 1943- *St&PR 91*
Euler, Heinrich Gustav 1925- *WhoWor 91*
Euler, Leonhard 1707-1783 *BioIn 16, WorAlBi*
Euler, Ulf Svante Von 1905-1983 *WorAlBi*
Euler-Chelpin, Hans 1873-1964 *WorAlBi*
Eunice, Jan Ziglar 1962- *IntWWM 90*
Eunpu, Deborah Lee 1952- *WhoEmL 91*
Eunson, Roby *AuBYP 90*
Euphrosine *WomWR*
Euphrosyne *WomWR*
Eure, Barry Lynn 1955- *WhoSSW 91*
Eure, Charles Henry, Jr. 1928- *St&PR 91*
Eure, Thad 1899- *WhoSSW 91*
Eure, Thad, Jr. *BioIn 16*
Eureka Jubilee Singers *DcAfAmP*
Euren, Marcia Duke 1948- *WhoAmW 91*
Eurich, Nell 1919- *WhoAm 90*
Euripides 480?BC-406BC *WorAlBi*
Euro, Heikki 1940- *WhoWor 91*
Europe, James Reese 1881-1919 *BioIn 16, DrBlPA 90, OxCPMus*
Eurotea, Glacilla *EncCoWW*
Eury, Lynn Wade 1937- *St&PR 91, WhoAm 90*
Eurythmics *EncPR&S 89*
Eusden, John Dykstra 1922- *WhoAm 90*
Eusebio, Robert 1949- *St&PR 91*
Eusebio, Thomas Clifton 1952- *St&PR 91*
Eusebius, Bishop of Caesarea 260-340 *BioIn 16*
Eustace, Susan 1959- *WhoWor 91*
Eustache, Jean 1939-1981 *BioIn 16*
Euster, Joanne Reed 1936- *WhoAm 90, WhoAmW 91*
Eustice, Francis Joseph 1951- *WhoEmL 91*
Eustice, James Samuel 1932- *WhoAm 90*
Eustice, Russell Clifford 1919- *WhoE 91*
Eustis, Albert Anthony 1921- *WhoAm 90*
Eustis, Helen 1916- *TwCCr&M 91*
Eustis, James Biddle 1834-1899 *BioIn 16*
Eustis, Leola Barnhart 1920- *WhoAmW 91*
Eustis, Richmond Minor 1945- *WhoEmL 91*
Eustis, Robert Henry 1920- *WhoAm 90*
Eustis, Ruthild Panten 1929- *WhoAmW 91*
Eustis, William 1753-1825 *BiDrUSE 89*
Euteneuer, Ursula Brigitte 1949- *WhoAmW 91*
Euthymiou, Pavlos Nicolaos 1945- *WhoWor 91*
Euthymtou, Paraskevi 1923- *WhoWor 91*
Eutsler, Mark Leslie 1958- *WhoEmL 91*
Eutsler, Therese Anne 1959- *WhoEmL 91*
Eva C. *EncO&P 3*
Eva C 1886- *EncPaPR 91*
Eva Carriere 1886- *EncPaPR 91*
Evaldson, John Rune 1955- *BiDrAPA 89*
Evan, Cathy Emma 1958- *WhoAmW 91*
Evan, Charles 1905- *WhoE 91*
Evan, William Martin 1922- *WhoAm 90*
Evanbar, B. H. *WhoWrEP 89*
Evander, Per Gunnar Henning 1933- *DcScanL*
Evanega, George R. 1936- *St&PR 91*
Evangelakis, Miltiades G 1925- *BiDrAPA 89*
Evangelatos, Daphne 1952- *IntWWM 90*
Evangelista, Donato A. 1932- *St&PR 91, WhoAm 90*
Evangelista, Edward Michael 1961- *St&PR 91*
Evangelista, Florizel S *BiDrAPA 89*
Evangelista, Jesus Soriano 1946- *WhoE 91*
Evangelista, Leah Norona 1953- *BiDrAPA 89*
Evangelista, Osvaldo Jose 1949- *BiDrAPA 89*
Evangelista-Frakes, Paula *ODwPR 91*
Evanhoe, Clara May 1908- *WhoAmW 91*
Evanick, Robert Joseph 1952- *St&PR 91*
Evanko, Michelle Marianne 1960- *WhoAmW 91*
Evanoff, George C. 1931- *WhoAm 90*
Evanoff, Vlad 1916- *BioIn 16*
Evanoff-Morrison, Carolyn Yvonne 1955- *WhoAmW 91*
Evans, Abigail Rian 1937- *WhoE 91*
Evans, Abigail Winifred 1960- *WhoE 91*
Evans, Adeline Marie Lemelle 1939- *WhoAmW 91*
Evans, Al 1916-1979 *Ballpl 90*
Evans, Albert Leslie, Jr. 1939- *St&PR 91*
Evans, Alfred Lee, Jr. 1940- *WhoAm 90*
Evans, Alfred Lewis, Jr. 1928- *WhoSSW 91*
Evans, Alfred Spring 1917- *WhoAm 90*
Evans, Alice Catherine 1881-1975 *BioIn 16*
Evans, Alice Frazer 1939- *ConAu 30NR*
Evans, Alice McDonald 1940- *WhoWrEP 89*
Evans, Allen Donald 1956- *WhoSSW 91*
Evans, Amos Ray 1935- *BiDrAPA 89*
Evans, Angela Maria 1947- *WhoE 91*
Evans, Anne 1820-1870 *FemiCLE*
Evans, Anne 1939- *PenDiMP*
Evans, Anne 1941- *IntWWM 90*

Evans, Anthony Howard 1936- *WhoAm 90*
Evans, Anthony Ian 1966- *WhoWor 91*
Evans, Anthony John 1930- *WhoWor 91*
Evans, Anthony Maurice 1948- *WhoE 91*
Evans, Arthur R. 1939- *St&PR 91*
Evans, Audrey Elizabeth 1925- *WhoAm 90*
Evans, Augusta Jane 1835-1909 *FemiCLE*
Evans, Augustus O. 1831-1873 *AmLegL*
Evans, Austin James 1920- *WhoAm 90*
Evans, B. Ray 1943- *St&PR 91*
Evans, Barry 1956- *Ballpl 90*
Evans, Barry Roger 1932- *WhoE 91*
Evans, Barton, Jr. 1947- *St&PR 91, WhoAm 90*
Evans, Benjamin Hampton 1926- *WhoAm 90*
Evans, Bergen 1904-1978 *WorAlBi*
Evans, Bernard William 1934- *WhoAm 90*
Evans, Betty Louise 1930-1982 *BioIn 16*
Evans, Bill 1929-1980 *BioIn 16, OxCPMus*
Evans, Bill 1940- *WhoAm 90*
Evans, Bill 1958- *BioIn 16*
Evans, Billy 1884-1956 *Ballpl 90 [port]*
Evans, Blackwell Bugg 1927- *WhoAm 90*
Evans, Bob 1930- *BioIn 16*
Evans, Bob 1944- *WhoAmA 91*
Evans, Bob Overton 1927- *WhoAm 90*
Evans, Bradley D 1950- *BiDrAPA 89*
Evans, Bradley Dennis 1950- *WhoE 91*
Evans, Britt 1946- *St&PR 91*
Evans, Brock *BioIn 16*
Evans, Bruce Dwight 1934- *WhoAm 90*
Evans, Bruce Haselton 1939- *WhoAm 90, WhoAmA 91*
Evans, Bruce Max 1937- *WhoAm 90*
Evans, Burford Elonzo 1931- *WhoAmA 91*
Evans, Caren K. *ODwPR 91*
Evans, Carlos Elbert 1951- *St&PR 91*
Evans, Carole Lynn 1956- *WhoAmW 91*
Evans, Chad 1951- *ConAu 131*
Evans, Charles C. 1943- *St&PR 91*
Evans, Charles Hawes, Jr. 1940- *WhoAm 90, WhoE 91*
Evans, Charles Wayne, II 1929- *WhoSSW 91*
Evans, Charlotte Mortimer 1933- *WhoAmW 91*
Evans, Chester *St&PR 91*
Evans, Chreed Collier 1958- *WhoSSW 91*
Evans, Christmas 1766-1838 *BioIn 16*
Evans, Christopher 1931-1979 *EncO&P 3*
Evans, Christopher C. 1946- *St&PR 91*
Evans, Clifford Jessie 1923- *WhoAm 90, WhoWor 91*
Evans, Clifford Thomas 1948- *IntWWM 90*
Evans, Colin 1942- *IntWWM 90*
Evans, Colleen M. *ODwPR 91*
Evans, Cooper *BioIn 16*
Evans, Craig 1949- *WhoE 91, WhoEmL 91, WhoWor 91*
Evans, Craig A. 1952- *ConAu 129*
Evans, Craig N. 1947- *St&PR 91*
Evans, Cynthia Lynn 1955- *BiDrAPA 89*
Evans, D. John O. 1953- *IntWWM 90*
Evans, Dale 1912- *WorAlBi*
Evans, Damon 1950- *DrBIPA 90*
Evans, Daniel B. 1945- *St&PR 91*
Evans, Daniel E. 1936- *WhoAm 90*
Evans, Daniel Fraley 1922- *WhoAm 90*
Evans, Daniel Jackson 1925- *WhoAm 90*
Evans, Daniel Warren 1956- *WhoEmL 91*
Evans, Darrell 1947- *Ballpl 90 [port]*
Evans, Dave *BioIn 16*
Evans, Dave 1961- *BioIn 16*
Evans, David *BioIn 16*
Evans, David Alan 1952- *St&PR 91*
Evans, David Albert 1941- *WhoAm 90*
Evans, David Allan 1940- *ConAu 31NR, WhoWrEP 89*
Evans, David Bernard 1932- *WhoWor 91*
Evans, David C. 1924- *WhoAm 90*
Evans, David Cannon 1924- *St&PR 91*
Evans, David Gruffydd 1925- *IntWWM 90*
Evans, David Gwynne 1909-1984 *DcNaB 1981*
Evans, David Huhn, Jr. 1944- *IntWWM 90*
Evans, David J.D. 1944- *St&PR 91*
Evans, David Livingston 1948- *St&PR 91*
Evans, David Lloyd 1864-1929 *AmLegL*
Evans, David Lynn 1954- *WhoSSW 91*
Evans, David Stanley 1916- *WhoAm 90*
Evans, David Wainwright 1927- *WhoWor 91*
Evans, David William 1956- *St&PR 91*
Evans, Denise R *BiDrAPA 89*
Evans, Dennis Hyde 1939- *WhoAm 90*
Evans, Dennis Upshur *BiDrAPA 89*
Evans, Derek Thomas 1940- *WhoAm 90*
Evans, Dick 1941- *WhoAmA 91*
Evans, Dina Rees 1891-1989 *BioIn 16, NotWoAT*
Evans, Donald 1946-1977 *WhoAmA 91N*
Evans, Donald Durrell *BiDrAPA 89*
Evans, Donald Dwight 1927- *WhoAm 90, WhoWrEP 89*
Evans, Donald Frederick 1945- *WhoSSW 91*
Evans, Donald John 1926- *St&PR 91, WhoAm 90*
Evans, Donald Louis 1946- *St&PR 91*
Evans, Donna B. *WhoAm 90*
Evans, Donna Irene 1951- *WhoE 91*
Evans, Douglas C 1927- *BiDrAPA 89*
Evans, Douglas Gene 1953- *WhoEmL 91*
Evans, Douglas McCullough 1925- *WhoAm 90*
Evans, Douglas Raymond 1945- *St&PR 91*
Evans, Dwight 1951- *Ballpl 90 [port], WorAlBi*
Evans, Dwight Landis 1947- *BiDrAPA 89*
Evans, E Estyn 1905-1989 *ConAu 129*
Evans, E. Susan 1945- *St&PR 91*
Evans, Earl Alison, Jr. 1910- *WhoAm 90*
Evans, Edgar 1912- *IntWWM 90*
Evans, Edith 1888-1976 *BioIn 16, WorAlBi*
Evans, Edna 1913- *AuBYP 90*
Evans, Edward Nathaniel, II 1940- *St&PR 91*
Evans, Edward P. 1942- *St&PR 91*
Evans, Edward Parker 1942- *WhoAm 90, WhoE 91*
Evans, Edwin Charles 1910- *WhoAm 90*
Evans, Edwin Curtis 1917- *WhoAm 90*
Evans, Eli N. *BioIn 16*
Evans, Elizabeth Carpenter 1911- *WhoE 91*
Evans, Ellen Lovell 1930- *WhoSSW 91*
Evans, Ellis Dale 1934- *WhoAm 90*
Evans, Elmer Ellsworth 1921- *St&PR 91*
Evans, Elton E. 1932- *St&PR 91*
Evans, Elwood 1828-1898 *AmLegL*
Evans, Emory Gibbons 1928- *WhoAm 90*
Evans, Ephraim 1803-1892 *DcCanB 12*
Evans, Eric C. 1952- *St&PR 91*
Evans, Eric Charles 1952- *WhoEmL 91*
Evans, Eric W. 1956- *St&PR 91*
Evans, Ernestine D. 1917- *WhoHisp 91*
Evans, Ersel Arthur 1922- *WhoAm 90*
Evans, Essi H. 1950- *WhoE 91*
Evans, Estelle 1905?-1985 *DrBIPA 90*
Evans, Eva 1905- *AuBYP 90*
Evans, Farris 1925- *St&PR 91*
Evans, Francis Cope 1914- *WhoAm 90*
Evans, Franklin Bachelder 1922- *WhoAm 90*
Evans, Fred P. 1862- *EncO&P 3*
Evans, Frederick John 1937- *WhoAm 90*
Evans, G. Robert 1931- *St&PR 91*
Evans, Gail 1935- *WhoSSW 91*
Evans, Garen Lee 1946- *WhoEmL 91, WhoSSW 91*
Evans, Gareth 1944- *WhoWor 91*
Evans, Gary Cone 1957- *WhoEmL 91*
Evans, Gary Lee 1938- *WhoWor 91*
Evans, Gary Lee 1944- *WhoE 91*
Evans, George 1870-1915 *OxCPMus*
Evans, George 1920- *EncACom*
Evans, George Edward Charles 1930- *BiDrAPA 89, WhoE 91*
Evans, George Ewart 1909-1988 *BioIn 16*
Evans, George Henry 1805-1856 *BioIn 16*
Evans, George Monroe 1947- *St&PR 91*
Evans, George Robert, Jr. 1931- *WhoAm 90*
Evans, George Walton, Jr. 1954- *WhoEmL 91*
Evans, Geraint *BioIn 16*
Evans, Geraint 1922- *PenDiMP*
Evans, Geraint Llewellyn 1922- *IntWWM 90, WhoAm 90, WhoWor 91*
Evans, Gerald Johnson 1945- *WhoEmL 91*
Evans, Gil *BioIn 16*
Evans, Gil 1912-1988 *AnObit 1988, OxCPMus*
Evans, Godfrey B. 1954- *St&PR 91*
Evans, Gordon Ward 1932- *WhoE 91*
Evans, Gregory Thomas 1913- *WhoAm 90*
Evans, Griffith Conrad 1887-1973 *DcScB S2*
Evans, Grose 1916- *WhoAm 90, WhoAmA 91*
Evans, Harold 1911-1983 *ConAu 129*
Evans, Harold Edward 1927- *St&PR 91, WhoAm 90*
Evans, Harold J. 1921- *WhoAm 90*
Evans, Harold Matthew 1928- *WhoAm 90, WhoWrEP 89*
Evans, Harrison 1911- *BiDrAPA 89*
Evans, Harry *BioIn 16*
Evans, Harvey Allan *BiDrAPA 89*
Evans, Henry *BioIn 16*
Evans, Henry 1918- *WhoAmA 91*
Evans, Henry M 1942- *BiDrAPA 89*
Evans, Henry R. 1938- *St&PR 91*
Evans, Hilary 1929- *EncO&P 3*
Evans, Hiram Kraig 1953- *WhoEmL 91*
Evans, Howard Ensign 1919- *WhoAm 90*
Evans, Howard McTyiere 1927- *St&PR 91*
Evans, Howard Vernon 1922- *WhoAm 90*
Evans, Howell McKendree 1926- *St&PR 91*
Evans, Hubert 1892-1986 *BioIn 16, DcLB 92 [port]*
Evans, Hubert John Filmer 1904-1989 *ConAu 129*
Evans, Hugh E. 1934- *WhoAm 90*
Evans, Hugh Hinton, Jr. 1931- *WhoAm 90*
Evans, Idris 1925- *IntWWM 90*
Evans, Ifor 1899-1982 *DcNaB 1981*
Evans, Ira Hobart 1844-1923 *AmLegL*
Evans, Isham Harrison 1954- *BiDrAPA 89*
Evans, Jack Lewis *BiDrAPA 89*
Evans, Jack W. 1922- *St&PR 91*
Evans, Jack W., Sr. 1922- *WhoAm 90, WhoSSW 91*
Evans, Jacquelyn Faye 1947- *WhoEmL 91*
Evans, James 1927- *WhoE 91*
Evans, James Dominick 1922- *WhoAm 90*
Evans, James E. 1946- *WhoAm 90*
Evans, James Edmond 1946- *St&PR 91*
Evans, James Edward 1933- *St&PR 91*
Evans, James H. 1920- *St&PR 91*
Evans, James Hurlburt 1920- *WhoAm 90*
Evans, James L, III 1935- *BiDrAPA 89*
Evans, James L, Jr. *BiDrAPA 89*
Evans, James Stanley 1921- *St&PR 91, WhoSSW 91*
Evans, James William 1943- *WhoAm 90*
Evans, Jane *BioIn 16*
Evans, Jane 1944- *WhoAm 90, WhoAmW 91*
Evans, Janet *BioIn 16, NewYTBS 90 [port]*
Evans, Janet 1971- *WorAlBi*
Evans, Janet Ann 1936- *WhoAmW 91*
Evans, Janice Elizabeth *BiDrAPA 89*
Evans, Janice Weston 1946- *WhoAmW 91*
Evans, Jean Ellen 1950- *WhoAmW 91*
Evans, Jean Marie 1937- *WhoAmW 91*
Evans, Jerome Edward 1941- *BiDrAPA 89*
Evans, Jerry *WhoSSW 91*
Evans, Jerry B. 1928- *St&PR 91*
Evans, Jerry Lee 1931- *WhoAm 90*
Evans, Jerry Norman *WhoAm 90*
Evans, Jessica *ConAu 30NR*
Evans, Jessie Benton *WhoAmA 91*
Evans, Jim 1946- *Ballpl 90*
Evans, Jo Burt 1928- *WhoAmW 91, WhoSSW 91*
Evans, Jodie 1954- *WhoAmW 91*
Evans, Joe 1895-1953 *Ballpl 90*
Evans, Joel Michael 1952- *WhoE 91*
Evans, Joel Raymond 1948- *WhoEmL 91*
Evans, Johannes Sanao 1927- *WhoE 91, WhoWor 91*
Evans, John *TwCCr&M 91*
Evans, John 1814-1897 *WhNaAH*
Evans, John 1932- *WhoAm 90, WhoAmA 91*
Evans, John, Sr. 1884-1970 *EncABHB 7 [port]*
Evans, John Byron 1947- *WhoEmL 91*
Evans, John Colin 1945- *WhoWor 91*
Evans, John Davies 1925- *WhoWor 91*
Evans, John Dows 1930- *St&PR 91*
Evans, John Erik 1927- *WhoAm 90*
Evans, John Harvey 1914- *WhoAm 90*
Evans, John James 1923- *WhoAm 90*
Evans, John L. *St&PR 91N*
Evans, John Martin 1935- *WhoAm 90*
Evans, John Maurice 1936- *WhoAm 90*
Evans, John Mervin 1949- *WhoEmL 91*
Evans, John Millard 1918- *WhoE 91*
Evans, John Robert 1929- *WhoAm 90*
Evans, John Thomas, Jr. 1931- *St&PR 91*
Evans, John Vaughan 1933- *St&PR 91*
Evans, John Vaughn 1933- *WhoAm 90*
Evans, John Wainwright 1883- *EncO&P 3*
Evans, John Wainwright, Jr. 1909- *WhoAm 90*
Evans, John Westley 1909- *BiDrAPA 89*
Evans, John William 1943- *BiDrAPA 89*
Evans, Jon Hugh 1934- *WhoSSW 91*
Evans, Jonathan *TwCCr&M 91*
Evans, Joni 1942- *WhoAm 90, WorAlBi*
Evans, Joyce Gray 1941- *WhoAmW 91*
Evans, Judith *WhoAmA 91*
Evans, Judith Ann 1942- *WhoAmW 91*
Evans, Julia *AuBYP 90*
Evans, Karen 1958- *WhoEmL 91*
Evans, Karolyn E. 1953- *WhoWrEP 89*
Evans, Katharine Krieger 1952- *WhoAmW 91*
Evans, Katherine *BiDEWW, FemiCLE*
Evans, Katherine 1901-1964 *AuBYP 90*
Evans, Katherine Jeannine 1958- *St&PR 91*
Evans, Keith E. 1934- *ODwPR 91*
Evans, Kenneth Charles 1962- *WhoE 91*
Evans, Kenneth Eugene 1948- *St&PR 91*
Evans, Kim Denise 1953- *WhoSSW 91*
Evans, L.K. 1928- *St&PR 91*
Evans, Landon 1936- *St&PR 91*
Evans, Lane 1951- *WhoAm 90*
Evans, Larry *BioIn 16*
Evans, Larry 1932- *ConAu 129*
Evans, Larry 1939- *BiDrAPA 89*
Evans, Larry A. *St&PR 91*
Evans, Larry Fredric 1947- *WhoWrEP 89*
Evans, Larry Melvyn 1932- *WhoAm 90*
Evans, Lawrence Boyd 1934- *WhoAm 90*
Evans, Lawrence Jack, Jr. 1921- *WhoWor 91*
Evans, Lawrence Watt 1954- *ConAu 32NR*
Evans, Lena N. 1962- *St&PR 91*
Evans, Leon L 1950- *BiDrAPA 89*
Evans, Leslie R. 1934- *St&PR 91*
Evans, Linda 1942- *BioIn 16, WhoAm 90, WhoAmW 91*
Evans, Linda 1943- *WorAlBi*
Evans, Linda Perryman 1950- *WhoSSW 91*
Evans, Linda Youngman *BiDrAPA 89*
Evans, Lisbeth Clark 1953- *St&PR 91*
Evans, Lloyd I. 1927- *St&PR 91*
Evans, Lloyd R. 1932-1989 *BioIn 16*
Evans, Lloyd Ranney 1932- *WhoAm 90*
Evans, Lois Logan 1937- *WhoAm 90, WhoAmW 91*
Evans, Loren Kenneth 1928- *WhoAm 90*
Evans, Lori Waggener 1959- *WhoAmW 91*
Evans, Louise *WhoAm 90, WhoWor 91*
Evans, Lynne Smith 1947- *WhoAm 90*
Evans, Manuel John 1955- *WhoEmL 91*
Evans, Margaret 1938- *WhoAmW 91*
Evans, Margaret A. 1924- *WhoAmW 91*
Evans, Margarita Sawatzky 1930- *IntWWM 90*
Evans, Margiad 1909-1958 *BioIn 16, FemiCLE*
Evans, Mari *AuBYP 90, WhoAm 90, WhoWrEP 89*
Evans, Mari 1923- *BioIn 16, FemiCLE*
Evans, Mark *IntWWM 90*
Evans, Mark David J. 1955- *WhoEmL 91*
Evans, Mark Ira 1952- *WhoEmL 91*
Evans, Marvin W *BiDrAPA 89*
Evans, Mary Eileen 1942- *WhoE 91*
Evans, Mary Ellen 1936- *WhoAmW 91*
Evans, Mary Jane 1923- *BioIn 16*
Evans, Mary Jane Larson 1923- *NotWoAT*
Evans, Mary Johnston 1930- *WhoAm 90, WhoAmW 91*
Evans, Mary Tansey 1937- *WhoE 91*
Evans, Maurice 1901- *WorAlBi*
Evans, Maurice 1901-1989 *AnObit 1989, BioIn 16*
Evans, Max Jay 1943- *WhoAm 90*
Evans, Max T. 1924- *St&PR 91*
Evans, Melvin H. 1917-1984 *BioIn 16*
Evans, Melvin Herbert 1917-1984 *BlkAmsC [port]*
Evans, Merle 1891-1987 *BioIn 16*
Evans, Michael 1950?- *DrBIPA 90*
Evans, Michael Alan 1943- *BiDrAPA 89*
Evans, Michael Blake 1945- *WhoSSW 91*
Evans, Michael Dean 1953- *WhoSSW 91*
Evans, Michael K 1938- *ConAu 132*
Evans, Michael Kaye 1938- *WhoAm 90*
Evans, Michael P. 1953- *St&PR 91*
Evans, Milton Douglas 1945- *WhoWor 91*
Evans, Minnie 1892-1987 *MusmAFA, WhoAmA 91N*
Evans, N. Lyle, Mrs. 1921- *WhoAmW 91, WhoSSW 91*
Evans, Nancy 1915- *IntWWM 90, PenDiMP*
Evans, Nancy 1950- *WhoAm 90*
Evans, Nolly Seymour 1927- *WhoAm 90*
Evans, Norman Allen 1922- *WhoAm 90*
Evans, Oliver Norman *BiDrAPA 89*
Evans, Orinda D. 1943- *WhoAm 90, WhoAmW 91*
Evans, Pamela Roye 1957- *WhoAmW 91, WhoEmL 91*
Evans, Patricia Healy 1920- *AuBYP 90*
Evans, Patricia Margaret 1935- *IntWWM 90*
Evans, Paul M. 1954- *WhoEmL 91*
Evans, Pauline 1922- *WhoAmW 91*
Evans, Pauline Rush *AuBYP 90*
Evans, Peter *ConAu 131*
Evans, Peter 1950-1989 *BioIn 16*
Evans, Peter Angus 1929- *IntWWM 90*
Evans, Peter Geoffrey 1950- *IntWWM 90*
Evans, Philip Jay 1951- *WhoEmL 91*
Evans, Philip Morgan 1933- *WhoAm 90*
Evans, Ralph Aiken 1924- *WhoAm 90*
Evans, Ray 1915- *BioIn 16*
Evans, Rebecca Alexandria 1962- *WhoEmL 91*
Evans, Rees Thompson 1945- *WhoEmL 91*
Evans, Renee Yvonne 1965- *WhoAmW 91*
Evans, Richard 1923- *WhoAmA 91*
Evans, Richard, III 1933- *BiDrAPA 89*
Evans, Richard Aloysius 1923- *WhoAm 90*
Evans, Richard Andrew 1940- *St&PR 91*
Evans, Richard C 1932- *BiDrAPA 89*
Evans, Richard Gale, Jr. 1932- *St&PR 91*
Evans, Richard H. *ODwPR 91*
Evans, Richard H. 1944- *WhoE 91*
Evans, Richard I 1922- *ConAu 131*
Evans, Richard Kent 1923- *St&PR 91*
Evans, Richard L. 1952- *St&PR 91*
Evans, Richard Wayne 1942- *WhoSSW 91*
Evans, Rob *BioIn 16*
Evans, Robert, Jr. 1932- *WhoAm 90*
Evans, Robert A. 1952- *St&PR 91*
Evans, Robert Beverley 1906- *St&PR 91*

Evans, Robert Brown 1912- *WhoSSW 91*
Evans, Robert Carey 1955- *WhoE 91*
Evans, Robert D. 1947- *St&PR 91*
Evans, Robert E. 1940- *St&PR 91*
Evans, Robert George, Jr. 1953- *WhoWor 91*
Evans, Robert Graves 1944- *WhoAmA 91*
Evans, Robert J. 1930- *WhoAm 90*
Evans, Robert James 1914- *WhoAm 90*
Evans, Robert James 1937- *WhoWor 91*
Evans, Robert L 1917- *ConAu 32NR*
Evans, Robert Michael 1953- *St&PR 91*
Evans, Robert O. *BioIn 16*
Evans, Robert Sheldon 1944- *St&PR 91, WhoAm 90, WhoE 91*
Evans, Robert W W *BiDrAPA 89*
Evans, Robley D. 1957- *St&PR 91*
Evans, Robley Dunglison 1907- *WhoAm 90*
Evans, Roger 1951- *WhoWor 91*
Evans, Ronald A. 1940- *St&PR 91*
Evans, Ronald Allen 1940- *WhoAm 90*
Evans, Ronald D. 1944- *St&PR 91*
Evans, Ronald E. *NewYTBS 90 [port]*
Evans, Ronald E. 1933-1990 *BioIn 16*
Evans, Ronald E. 1938- *St&PR 91*
Evans, Rosaleen Malooly *WhoWor 91*
Evans, Rose Mary 1928- *WhoWrEP 89*
Evans, Rosemary Hall 1925- *WhoAmW 91, WhoE 91, WhoWor 91*
Evans, Rowland, Jr. 1921- *WhoAm 90*
Evans, Roxanne Romack 1952- *WhoSSW 91*
Evans, Roy 1874-1915 *Ballpl 90*
Evans, Rudulph 1879-1960 *WhoAmA 91N*
Evans, S. Clark 1938- *St&PR 91*
Evans, Sally Lees 1928- *WhoAmW 91*
Evans, Sandra Bernice 1955- *WhoEmL 91*
Evans, Sarah Anne 1665-1685 *FemiCLE*
Evans, Sarah Frances Hinton 1924- *WhoAmW 91*
Evans, Sharlene Kathryn 1951- *WhoE 91, WhoEmL 91*
Evans, Shirlee 1931- *BioIn 16*
Evans, Stanley Robert 1955- *WhoEmL 91*
Evans, Steve 1885-1943 *Ballpl 90*
Evans, Stuart 1934- *WorAu 1980 [port]*
Evans, Sue H. *ODwPR 91*
Evans, Suzanne Marie 1953- *WhoAmW 91*
Evans, Terence Thomas 1940- *WhoAm 90*
Evans, Thelma Jean Mathis 1944- *WhoAmW 91*
Evans, Thomas Chives Newton 1947- *WhoAm 90, WhoE 91, WhoEmL 91*
Evans, Thomas E. 1944- *St&PR 91*
Evans, Thomas Edgar, Jr. 1940- *WhoWor 91*
Evans, Thomas Mellon 1910- *St&PR 91*
Evans, Thomas Passmore 1921- *WhoSSW 91*
Evans, Thomas William 1930- *WhoAm 90, WhoE 91*
Evans, Timothy F. *ODwPR 91*
Evans, Timothy Monroe 1945- *St&PR 91*
Evans, Todd Edwin 1947- *WhoEmL 91*
Evans, Tolchard 1901-1978 *OxCPMus*
Evans, Tom R 1943- *WhoAmA 91*
Evans, Tommy Nicholas 1922- *WhoAm 90*
Evans, Travis G. 1933- *St&PR 91*
Evans, Trev Madoc 1953- *WhoE 91*
Evans, Trevor Heiser 1909- *WhoAm 90*
Evans, Trevor Maldwyn 1902-1981 *DcNaB 1981*
Evans, Trudy Jean 1954- *WhoSSW 91*
Evans, V. Bond 1934- *WhoAm 90*
Evans, Van Michael 1916- *WhoAm 90*
Evans, Victor M. 1939- *St&PR 91*
Evans, Victor Miles 1939- *WhoAm 90*
Evans, Virginia Parrish 1947- *WhoAmW 91*
Evans, W. H. 1877- *EncO&P 3*
Evans, W.R. 1955- *WhoSSW 91*
Evans, Walker 1903-1975 *BioIn 16*
Evans, Walter Cope 1948- *WhoEmL 91*
Evans, William Buell 1918- *WhoAm 90*
Evans, William E. *BioIn 16*
Evans, William E. 1930- *WhoAm 90*
Evans, William Earl, Jr. 1956- *WhoEmL 91, WhoSSW 91*
Evans, William Ellis 1952- *WhoEmL 91*
Evans, William Eugene, Jr. 1950- *BiDrAPA 89*
Evans, William Frederick 1957- *WhoAm 90*
Evans, William Halla 1950- *WhoEmL 91*
Evans, William James 1928- *WhoAm 90*
Evans, William John 1924- *St&PR 91, WhoAm 90*
Evans, William L. 1934- *St&PR 91*
Evans, William Lee 1924- *WhoAm 90*
Evans, William O. 1935- *St&PR 91*
Evans, William S, Jr. 1957- *BiDrAPA 89*
Evans, William Thomas 1941- *WhoWor 91*
Evans, William Wilson 1932- *WhoAm 90*
Evans, Winthrop Shattuck 1939- *WhoWor 91*
Evans, Yonynah Schub *BiDrAPA 89*
Evans-Charles, Marti *DrBlPA 90*
Evans-Freke, Stephen Ralfe 1952- *WhoAm 90*
Evans Kelly, Christine 1952- *St&PR 91*
Evans-Wentz, W Y 1878-1965 *EncO&P 3*
Evanson, Robert Verne 1920- *WhoAm 90*
Evanti, Lillian 1890-1967 *BioIn 16*
Evanturel, Francois 1821-1891 *DcCanB 12*
Evarts, Charles McCollister 1931- *WhoAm 90*
Evarts, Hal G. 1887-1934 *BioIn 16*
Evarts, Hal G. 1915- *AuBYP 90*
Evarts, Harry Franklin 1928- *St&PR 91, WhoAm 90*
Evarts, Helen Coleman 1928- *WhoAmW 91*
Evarts, M. Richard 1920- *St&PR 91*
Evarts, William Maxwell 1818-1901 *BiDrUSE 89, BioIn 16*
Evarts, William Maxwell, Jr. 1925- *WhoAm 90*
Evashwick, Connie Joann 1949- *WhoAmW 91*
Evatt, Herbert Vere 1894-1965 *BioIn 16*
Evaul, William H, Jr 1949- *WhoAmA 91*
Evaul, William Harper, Jr. 1949- *WhoE 91*
Evdokas, Takis 1928- *BiDrAPA 89*
Evdokimova, Eva 1948- *BioIn 16, WhoAm 90, WhoWor 91*
Eve, Rodney Ellis 1947- *St&PR 91*
Evearitt, Timothy Cedric 1942- *WhoSSW 91*
Eveillard, Elizabeth Mugar 1947- *St&PR 91*
Eveillard, Yves Serge *BiDrAPA 89*
Eveland, Winsor G. 1938- *St&PR 91*
Eveleigh, Virgil William 1931- *WhoAm 90*
Eveleth, Janet Stidman 1950- *WhoWrEP 89*
Evelson, Anatoly *BiDrAPA 89*
Evelyn, Douglas Everett 1941- *WhoAm 90*
Evelyn, John 1620-1706 *BioIn 16*
Evelyn, Judith 1913-1967 *OxCCanT*
Evelyn, Mary 1634?-1709 *FemiCLE*
Evelyn, Mary 1665-1685 *FemiCLE*
Evelyn, Mary, Jr. 1665-1685 *BiDEWW*
Evelyn, Mary, Sr. 1635?-1708? *BiDEWW*
Even Dozen Jug Band *OxCPMus*
Even, Francis Alphonse 1920- *WhoAm 90*
Even, Robert Lawrence 1929- *WhoAmA 91*
Even, Robert Lawrence 1932- *WhoAm 90*
Even, Uzi Jacob 1940- *WhoWor 91*
Even-Or, Mary 1939- *IntWWM 90*
Evenchik, Lynn Robin 1956- *WhoE 91*
Evens, Ronald Gene 1939- *WhoAm 90*
Evensen, David 1955- *St&PR 91*
Evensen, Norman A *BiDrAPA 89*
Evensmo, Sigurd 1912-1978 *DcScanL*
Evenson, Dean *NewAgMG*
Evenson, Dudley *NewAgMG*
Evenson, Elizabeth Anne 1961- *WhoAmW 91*
Evenson, Frederick Donald 1928- *St&PR 91*
Evenson, Martin L. 1951- *WhoSSW 91*
Evenson, Merle Armin 1934- *WhoAm 90*
Evenson, Russell Allen 1947- *St&PR 91, WhoEmL 91*
Evenson, S. Jeanne 1938- *WhoAmW 91*
Evera, Emily van *PenDiMP*
Everaert, Pierre Jean 1939- *WhoAm 90*
Everage, Dame Edna *ConAu 129*
Everall, John Dudley 1917- *WhoWor 91*
Everard, Margaret *BiDEWW*
Everbach, Otto George 1938- *WhoAm 90*
Everdell, William 1915- *WhoAm 90, WhoWor 91*
Everdell, William Romeyn 1941- *WhoAm 90*
Everding, August 1928- *IntWWM 90*
Evered, Donna R. 1955- *WhoEmL 91*
Everest, David *St&PR 91*
Everest, Richard James 1939- *St&PR 91*
Everett, Alexander Hill 1790-1847 *BioIn 16*
Everett, Anita Smith *BiDrAPA 89*
Everett, Bernard Jonathan 1943- *WhoWor 91*
Everett, Bill 1868-1938 *Ballpl 90*
Everett, Bill 1917-1973 *EncACom*
Everett, Bruce Edgar 1948- *WhoE 91*
Everett, C. Curtis 1930- *WhoAm 90*
Everett, Carl Bell 1947- *WhoEmL 91*
Everett, Chad 1937- *WorAlBi*
Everett, Curtis Lammar 1921- *St&PR 91*
Everett, Dan W 1922- *BiDrAPA 89*
Everett, Donald Edward 1920- *WhoAm 90*
Everett, Donna Raney 1939- *WhoAmW 91*
Everett, Dorothy A. 1917- *St&PR 91*
Everett, Durward R., Jr. 1925- *WhoAm 90*
Everett, Edward 1794-1865 *BiDrUSE 89, BioIn 16*
Everett, Ewing 1897-1990 *BioIn 16*
Everett, Francine 1921- *DrBlPA 90*
Everett, Gail *AuBYP 90*
Everett, George A. 1924- *WhoE 91*
Everett, Graham 1947- *WhoWrEP 89*
Everett, Henry C 1928- *BiDrAPA 89*
Everett, Jacquelin Brooks 1931- *WhoSSW 91*
Everett, James A. 1928- *ODwPR 91*
Everett, James H. 1916- *St&PR 91*
Everett, James LeGrand, III 1926- *St&PR 91, WhoAm 90*
Everett, James William, Jr. 1957- *WhoE 91*
Everett, Jeffrey Brent 1961- *WhoSSW 91*
Everett, Jessie Mary 1929- *WhoAmW 91*
Everett, Jim *BioIn 16*
Everett, Jim F. *WhoSSW 91*
Everett, Joann Marie 1950- *WhoWrEP 89*
Everett, Jonathan Jubal 1950- *WhoEmL 91*
Everett, Karen J. 1926- *WhoWor 91*
Everett, Karl Menoher, Jr. 1935- *WhoWor 91*
Everett, Laurie Ann 1956- *WhoAmW 91*
Everett, Len G *WhoAmA 91N*
Everett, Mark Allen 1928- *WhoAm 90*
Everett, Mary Elizabeth 1929- *WhoAmW 91*
Everett, Mary O 1876-1948 *WhoAmA 91N*
Everett, Michael 1949- *St&PR 91*
Everett, Pamela Irene 1947- *WhoAmW 91, WhoEmL 91*
Everett, Paul Joseph 1955- *IntWWM 90*
Everett, Percival *ConAu 129*
Everett, Percival L. 1956- *ConAu 129*
Everett, Peter 1931- *ConAu 31NR*
Everett, Ralph *BioIn 16*
Everett, Reynolds Melville, Jr. 1946- *WhoEmL 91*
Everett, Robert Nathan 1950- *WhoSSW 91*
Everett, Robert R. 1921- *St&PR 91*
Everett, Robert Rivers 1921- *WhoAm 90, WhoE 91*
Everett, Robinson Oscar 1928- *WhoAm 90*
Everett, Ronald Morton 1927- *St&PR 91*
Everett, Royice Bert 1946- *WhoSSW 91*
Everett, Rupert 1959- *ConTFT 8*
Everett, S. W. *WhoWrEP 89*
Everett, Samuel B. *ODwPR 91*
Everett, Thomas Gregory 1944- *IntWWM 90*
Everett, Vivian Denise 1958- *WhoAmW 91*
Everett, Warren Sylvester 1910- *WhoAm 90, WhoWor 91*
Everett, William Arlie 1962- *IntWWM 90*
Everett, William Carter 1935- *WhoE 91*
Everett, William Hume, III 1936- *St&PR 91*
Everett, William John 1956- *WhoE 91*
Everett, Woodrow Wilson 1937- *WhoAm 90, WhoWor 91*
Everett-Green, Evelyn 1856-1932 *FemiCLE*
Everett-Volgy, Sandra Sue 1946- *WhoAmW 91*
Everette, Sharon Esther McLeod 1949- *WhoEmL 91*
Evergettis, Barry P. 1936- *St&PR 91*
Evergon 1946- *WhoAmA 91*
Evergood, Philip 1901-1973 *EncAL, WhoAmA 91N*
Everhart, Don, II 1949- *WhoAmA 91*
Everhart, Edgar S. 1912- *St&PR 91*
Everhart, George Y. 1862-1946 *AmLegL*
Everhart, Kenneth Lee, Jr. 1954- *WhoE 91*
Everhart, Rex 1920- *WhoAm 90*
Everhart, Robert 1936- *IntWWM 90*
Everhart, Robert Lee 1951- *WhoSSW 91*
Everhart, Robert Phillip 1936- *WhoWrEP 89*
Everhart, Thomas Eugene 1932- *WhoAm 90, WhoWor 91*
Everidge, Foxene Lambert 1939- *WhoAmW 91*
Everill, Charles Henry 1943- *St&PR 91, WhoAm 90*
Everill, Richard Harold 1942- *WhoWor 91*
Everingham family *BioIn 16*
Everingham, Joyce Dubert 1929- *WhoAmW 91*
Everingham, Karen Sue 1946- *WhoAmW 91*
Everingham, Lyle J. 1926- *St&PR 91, WhoAm 90*
Everingham, Marilyn Marie 1952- *WhoEmL 91*
Everingham, Millard 1912- *WhoAmA 91N*
Everingham, Philip B. 1948- *St&PR 91*
Everist, R.A. 1925- *St&PR 91*
Everitt, Alice Lubin 1936- *WhoAmW 91*
Everitt, Betsy *BioIn 16*
Everitt, Byron F *EncABHB 4*
Everitt, Charles P. *St&PR 91*
Everitt, E. Glenn, Jr. 1944- *St&PR 91*
Everitt, George Bain 1914- *WhoAm 90*
Everitt, Leo Henry, Jr. 1931- *St&PR 91*
Everitt, Robert Henry 1939- *St&PR 91*
Everitt, Thomas, Mrs. 1825-1915 *EncO&P 3*
Everling, Lawrence J. 1941- *St&PR 91*
Everly Brothers *OxCPMus*
Everly Brothers, The *EncPR&S 89, WhoNeCM C [port], WorAlBi*
Everly, Albert Earl, III 1944- *WhoSSW 91*
Everly, Bradley S. 1951- *St&PR 91*
Everly, Don *BioIn 16*
Everly, Don 1937- *EncPR&S 89, OxCPMus, WorAlBi*
Everly, George Stotelmyer, Jr. 1950- *WhoEmL 91*
Everly, Jeannette 1908- *AuBYP 90*
Everly, Phil *BioIn 16*
Everly, Phil 1938- *WorAlBi*
Everly, Phil 1939- *EncPR&S 89, OxCPMus*
Everman, C. Robert 1936- *St&PR 91*
Everman, Paul Dawson 1932- *St&PR 91*
Evernden, Margery Elizabeth 1916- *WhoWrEP 89*
Evers, Alf 1905- *AuBYP 90*
Evers, Anne Bigelow 1954- *WhoAmW 91*
Evers, Bradley Wayne 1955- *St&PR 91, WhoEmL 91*
Evers, Charles K. 1928- *St&PR 91*
Evers, Helen *AuBYP 90*
Evers, Hoot 1921- *Ballpl 90*
Evers, James C. 1922- *WorAlBi*
Evers, Jean Graf 1917- *WhoE 91*
Evers, Johnny 1883-1947 *Ballpl 90 [port]*
Evers, Joyce Mary 1954- *WhoAmW 91*
Evers, Judith Ann 1939- *WhoAmW 91*
Evers, Kate 1948- *St&PR 91*
Evers, Mark Anthony 1953- *St&PR 91*
Evers, Medgar Wiley 1925-1963 *BioIn 16*
Evers, Myrlie *BioIn 16*
Evers, Robert N 1923- *BiDrAPA 89*
Evers, Sean Robert 1949- *WhoE 91*
Evers, Walter 1914-1990 *BioIn 16*
Evers, William Dohrmann 1927- *WhoAm 90*
Evers, William Henry 1930- *WhoE 91*
Evers, William Louis 1906- *WhoAm 90*
Evershed, Roger B. 1940- *St&PR 91*
Eversley, Frederick John 1941- *WhoAm 90, WhoAmA 91*
Eversman, George Harrison 1927- *St&PR 91*
Eversmann, Donald Frank 1945- *WhoAm 90*
Eversole, William Cromwell 1934- *St&PR 91*
Everson, Christine Ariail 1947- *WhoAmW 91*
Everson, Dale M. 1931- *St&PR 91*
Everson, David Beatty 1929- *St&PR 91*
Everson, Diane Louise 1953- *WhoAmW 91*
Everson, George A., Jr. 1943- *St&PR 91*
Everson, Jane McVicker 1958- *WhoAmW 91*
Everson, Kirke B., Jr. 1920- *St&PR 91*
Everson, Leonard Charles 1923- *WhoAm 90*
Everson, V. Hall *BioIn 16*
Everson, William 1912- *BioIn 16, MajTwCW*
Everson, William Keith 1929- *AuBYP 90*
Everson, William Oliver 1912- *WhoAm 90, WhoWor 91*
Eversull, Jack Wilson 1942- *St&PR 91*
Evert, Anghelos 1894-1970 *BioIn 16*
Evert, Chris *BioIn 16*
Evert, Chris 1954- *WorAlBi*
Evert, Christine Marie 1954- *WhoAm 90, WhoAmW 91, WhoWor 91*
Evert, Donald Thomas *BiDrAPA 89*
Evert, Patricia Ann 1962- *WhoAmW 91*
Evert, Ray Franklin 1931- *WhoAm 90*
Everton, Marta Ve 1926- *WhoAmW 91*
Everts, Connor 1926- *WhoAm 90, WhoAmA 91*
Everts, Delores Jean 1943- *WhoAmW 91*
Everts, Edward H. 1951- *St&PR 91*
Everts, Elizabeth B. 1948- *WhoSSW 91*
Everts, Kenneth V 1918- *BiDrAPA 89*
Everts, Philip Pelgrim 1938- *WhoWor 91*
Everts, William H *BiDrAPA 89*
Every, Martin Gaither 1939- *St&PR 91*
Every, Philip Cochrane *AuBYP 90*
Every, Richard W. 1942- *St&PR 91*
Every, Russel B. 1924- *St&PR 91, WhoAm 90*
Eves, Jeffrey Parvin 1946- *St&PR 91*
Eves, Walter Curtis 1925- *St&PR 91*
Evesham, Epiphanius 1570-1633? *BioIn 16*
Evett, Kenneth Warnock 1913- *WhoAmA 91*
Evey, Lois Reed 1925- *WhoE 91*
Evigan, Greg *BioIn 16*
Evilo *WhoAmA 91*
Evilsizer, Marjorie Joan 1961- *WhoAmW 91*
Evilsizor, Marvin Rex 1937- *WhoSSW 91*
Evinrude, Ole 1877-1934 *BioIn 16*
Evins, John C. 1912- *St&PR 91*
Evison, Herbert *BioIn 16*
Evitt, William Robert 1923- *WhoAm 90*
Evitt, William Thomas 1944- *WhoSSW 91*
Evnin, Anthony Basil 1941- *WhoAm 90*
Evola, Natuzza 1922- *EncPaPR 91*
Evold, Bent 1936- *ConAu 129*
Evoy, John Joseph 1911- *WhoAm 90*

Evoy, Martin 1902- *St&PR 91*
Evraiff, William 1924- *WhoAm 90*
Evrard, Janice Marie 1959- *WhoAmW 91*
Evren, Kenan 1918- *WhoWor 91*
Evseeff, George S 1919- *BiDrAPA 89*
Evslin, Bernard 1922- *AuBYP 90*
Evstatieva, Stefka 1950- *IntWWM 90*
Evyatar, Azriel 1926- *WhoWor 91*
Ewa, Joseph Francis *BiDrAPA 89*
Ewald, Earl 1908- *WhoAm 90*
Ewald, Elin Lake *WhoAmA 91*
Ewald, Elin Lake 1940- *WhoE 91*
Ewald, Henry Theodore, Jr. 1924- *WhoWor 91*
Ewald, Johannes 1743-1781 *DcScanL*
Ewald, Paul Peter 1888-1985 *DcScB S2*
Ewald, Randall Kim 1956- *WhoSSW 91*
Ewald, Rex Alan 1951- *WhoEmL 91*
Ewald, Robert H. 1947- *WhoAm 90*
Ewald, William Bragg, Jr. 1925- *WhoAm 90*
Ewaldz, Donald Baird 1933- *St&PR 91*
Ewalt, Jack R *BiDrAPA 89*
Ewan, George Thomson 1927- *WhoAm 90*
Ewan, James 1949- *St&PR 91*
Ewan, Joseph 1909- *WhoAm 90*
Ewanciw, Theodore M. 1958- *ODwPR 91*
Ewans, Michael 1946- *ConAu 129*
Ewart, Catherine Seaton *DcCanB 12*
Ewart, Charles D. *BioIn 16*
Ewart, Gavin 1916- *MajTwCW*
Ewart, Roberta Marie 1959- *WhoAmW 91*
Ewart-Biggs, Jane *BioIn 16*
Ewasko, Bernard Anthony 1934- *St&PR 91*
Ewbank, Thomas Peters 1943- *St&PR 91*
Ewbank, Weeb 1907- *WorAlBi*
Ewell, A. Ben, Jr. 1941- *WhoWor 91*
Ewell, Albert Hunter, Jr. 1925- *WhoAm 90*
Ewell, Charles Muse 1937- *WhoAm 90*
Ewell, Miranda Juan 1948- *WhoAm 90*
Ewell, Mona *BioIn 16*
Ewell, Tom 1909- *WorAlBi*
Ewell, Vincent Fletcher, Jr. 1943- *St&PR 91, WhoAm 90*
Ewen, Clark *WhoAm 90*
Ewen, David 1907-1985 *AuBYP 90, BioIn 16*
Ewen, David Paul 1944- *WhoWor 91*
Ewen, Frederic 1899-1988 *BioIn 16*
Ewen, Harold Irving 1922- *WhoAm 90, WhoWor 91*
Ewen, Pamela Binnings 1944- *WhoAmW 91*
Ewen, Paterson 1925- *WhoAmA 91*
Ewen, Paula Robey 1955- *WhoAmW 91*
Ewen, Robert W. 1931- *St&PR 91*
Ewers, John Canfield 1909- *WhoAm 90*
Ewers, R. Darrell 1933- *St&PR 91, WhoAm 90*
Ewert, Brita Louise 1929- *WhoWor 91*
Ewert, Russell Howard 1935- *WhoAm 90*
Ewick, Charles Ray 1937- *WhoAm 90*
Ewick, Richard Wayne 1945- *WhoSSW 91*
Ewing, Alton Parker, Jr. 1945- *WhoEmL 91*
Ewing, Bayard 1916- *St&PR 91, WhoAmA 91*
Ewing, Benjamin Baugh 1924- *WhoAm 90*
Ewing, Blair Gordon 1933- *WhoE 91*
Ewing, Bob 1873-1947 *Ballpl 90*
Ewing, Buck 1859-1906 *Ballpl 90 [port], BioIn 16*
Ewing, Catherine Ruth 1943- *WhoAmW 91*
Ewing, Channing Lester 1927- *WhoSSW 91*
Ewing, Charles Patrick 1949- *WhoEmL 91*
Ewing, David Gordon *BiDrAPA 89*
Ewing, Douglas Edwin *BiDrAPA 89*
Ewing, Eddie Ruth 1928- *St&PR 91*
Ewing, Edgar Louis 1913- *WhoAm 90, WhoAmA 91*
Ewing, Frank Crockett 1951- *WhoE 91*
Ewing, Frank Marion 1915- *WhoAm 90*
Ewing, Frederick R. *ConAu 32NR, MajTwCW*
Ewing, Geoffrey William 1949- *WhoWor 91*
Ewing, George B *BiDrAPA 89*
Ewing, George Edward 1933- *WhoAm 90*
Ewing, George H. 1925- *WhoAm 90*
Ewing, George Washington 1804-1866 *WhNaAH*
Ewing, George Wilmeth 1923- *WhoSSW 91*
Ewing, Jack 1945- *WhoWrEP 89*
Ewing, James D. 1917- *St&PR 91*
Ewing, James H *BiDrAPA 89*
Ewing, James L., III 1928- *ODwPR 91*
Ewing, James Ronald *BioIn 16*
Ewing, Jeanne Bunderson 1933- *WhoWrEP 89*
Ewing, Jerry L. 1930- *St&PR 91*
Ewing, Joan Ruth 1932- *WhoAmW 91*
Ewing, John A 1923- *BiDrAPA 89*
Ewing, John Alexander 1923- *WhoAm 90*
Ewing, John Arthur 1912- *WhoAm 90*
Ewing, John Isaac 1924- *WhoAm 90*
Ewing, John S., Jr. 1917- *BiDrAPA 89*
Ewing, Joseph Neff, Jr. 1925- *WhoE 91*
Ewing, Juliana 1841-1885 *FemiCLE*
Ewing, Juliana Horatia 1841-1885 *BioIn 16*
Ewing, Kathryn 1921- *AuBYP 90*
Ewing, Ky Pepper, Jr. 1935- *WhoAm 90*
Ewing, Laurence Lee 1943- *WhoAm 90*
Ewing, Lynn M., Jr. 1930- *St&PR 91*
Ewing, Lynn Moore, Jr. 1930- *WhoAm 90*
Ewing, Maria *BioIn 16*
Ewing, Maria 1950- *CurBio 90 [port], PenDiMP*
Ewing, Maria Louise *WhoAm 90*
Ewing, Maria Louise 1950- *IntWWM 90*
Ewing, Mark Jerome 1950- *St&PR 91*
Ewing, Martin Sipple 1945- *WhoEmL 91*
Ewing, Mary Arnold 1948- *WhoAmW 91*
Ewing, Michael *BioIn 16*
Ewing, Michael Delvin 1951- *WhoEmL 91*
Ewing, Michael E. 1944- *St&PR 91*
Ewing, Mike James *BiDrAPA 89*
Ewing, Montague 1890-1957 *OxCPMus*
Ewing, Nanine Ruth 1950- *WhoSSW 91*
Ewing, Noel E. 1935- *St&PR 91*
Ewing, Patrick *BioIn 16*
Ewing, Patrick 1962- *WhoAm 90, WorAlBi*
Ewing, Ralph Harold, Jr. 1947- *WhoSSW 91*
Ewing, Raymond C. 1936- *WhoAm 90, WhoWor 91*
Ewing, Raymond P. 1925- *ODwPR 91*
Ewing, Raymond Peyton 1925- *WhoWor 91*
Ewing, Richard Tucker 1918- *WhoAm 90*
Ewing, Robert 1922- *WhoAm 90, WhoE 91, WhoWor 91*
Ewing, Robert Clark 1957- *WhoEmL 91*
Ewing, Robert Edward 1921- *WhoAm 90*
Ewing, Robert Paul 1925- *St&PR 91, WhoAm 90*
Ewing, Samuel Daniel, Jr. 1938- *WhoAm 90*
Ewing, Sidney Alton 1934- *WhoAm 90*
Ewing, Skip *WhoNeCM [port]*
Ewing, Sondra Darlene 1948- *WhoWrEP 89*
Ewing, Tess *WhoWrEP 89*
Ewing, Thomas 1789-1871 *BiDrUSE 89*
Ewing, Vernon Richard 1948- *WhoEmL 91*
Ewing, Wayne T. 1933- *St&PR 91*
Ewing, Wayne Turner 1933- *WhoAm 90*
Ewing, William, Jr. 1912- *St&PR 91*
Ewing, William Griffith 1801-1854 *WhNaAH*
Ewing, William Henszey 1939- *WhoE 91*
Ewing, William M. 1906-1974 *WorAlBi*
Ewing, William Maurice 1906-1974 *DcScB S2*
Ewing-Taylor, Jacqueline Marie 1953- *WhoAmW 91*
Ewins, Maxie Staedtler 1936- *WhoAm 90, WhoE 91*
Ewoldt, Craig R. 1949- *St&PR 91*
Ewry, Ray 1873-1937 *WorAlBi*
Ewy, Gordon Allen 1933- *WhoAm 90*
Exarchou, Nicholas John *BiDrAPA 89*
Exchange *NewAgMG*
Exe, David Allen 1942- *WhoWor 91*
Exelbert, Lois Love 1948- *WhoAmW 91*
Exeter, Marquess of 1905-1981 *DcNaB 1981*
Exley, Charles E., Jr. *BioIn 16*
Exley, Charles E., Jr. 1929- *St&PR 91*
Exley, Charles Errol, Jr. 1929- *WhoAm 90*
Exley, Frederick *BioIn 16*
Exley, Mark King 1953- *WhoEmL 91*
Exline, John Kevin 1957- *WhoEmL 91*
Exline, Robert W. 1932- *St&PR 91*
Exner, Judith *BioIn 16*
Exner-Clayton, Katherine J. 1949- *St&PR 91*
Exon, John James 1921- *WhoAm 90, WhoWor 91*
Expose *ConMus 4 [port]*
Extein, Irl Lawrence 1948- *BiDrAPA 89*
Exter, Alexandra Alexandrovna 1882-1949 *BiDWomA*
Exton, William 1907-1988 *BioIn 16*
Exum, Frances Bell 1940- *WhoAmW 91*
Exum, Helen McDonald 1924- *St&PR 91*
Exum, James Gooden, Jr. 1935- *WhoAm 90, WhoSSW 91*
Exume, Claude 1949- *WhoWor 91*
Eyadema, Etienne Gnassingbe 1937- *WhoWor 91*
Eyberg, Donald Theodore, Jr. 1944- *WhoAm 90*
Eyck, Jan Van 1395?-1441 *WorAlBi*
Eycleshymer, Judith Lee 1943- *St&PR 91*
Eydoux, Henri-Paul 1907-1986 *BioIn 16*
Eye, Glen Gordon 1904- *WhoAm 90*
Eyen, Richard J 1930- *WhoAmA 91*
Eyer, Jerome Arlan 1934- *WhoSSW 91*
Eyer, John Geoffrey 1944- *St&PR 91*
Eyerman, Irwin R. 1944- *St&PR 91*
Eyerman, James David *BiDrAPA 89*
Eyerman, Linda Kathleen 1948- *WhoEmL 91*
Eyerman, Thomas Jude 1939- *WhoAm 90*
Eyers, Patrick Howard Caines 1933- *WhoWor 91*
Eyes, Raymond *WhoAm 90*
Eyestone *WhoWrEP 89*
Eygenstein, Willem F *BiDrAPA 89*
Eyk, Henriette van 1897-1980 *EncCoWW*
Eykhoff, Pieter 1929- *WhoWor 91*
Eyle, Felix *BioIn 16*
Eyler, Donald Neil 1931- *St&PR 91*
Eyles, Leonora 1889-1960 *FemiCLE*
Eyles, Marianne McGregor 1957- *St&PR 91*
Eyles, Thomas H. 1936- *St&PR 91*
Eyman, David Harry 1937- *WhoE 91*
Eyman, Earl 1891-1971 *MusmAFA*
Eyman, Earl Duane 1925- *WhoAm 90*
Eyman, Linda Mae 1945- *WhoAmW 91*
Eyman, Richard H. 1930- *St&PR 91*
Eyman, Richard Kenneth 1931- *WhoAm 90*
Eynhardt, Guillermo *ConAu 131, HispWr 90, MajTwCW*
Eynon, Richard Ries 1947- *St&PR 91*
Eynon, Stuart B. 1922- *St&PR 91*
Eynsford, Lord 1944- *WhoAm 90*
Eyre, Edward John 1815-1901 *BioIn 16*
Eyre, Elizabeth *BiDEWW*
Eyre, Frank 1910-1988 *SmATA 62*
Eyre, Ivan 1935- *WhoAm 90, WhoAmA 91*
Eyre, John Lamarche 1917- *WhoE 91*
Eyre, Pamela Catherine 1948- *WhoAmW 91, WhoEmL 91*
Eyre, Stephen Carstairs 1922- *St&PR 91*
Eyres, Lauren Marie *BiDrAPA 89*
Eyring, Anthony I. *St&PR 91N*
Eyring, Edward Marcus 1931- *WhoAm 90*
Eyring, Henry 1901-1981 *DcScB S2*
Eyring, LeRoy 1919- *WhoAm 90*
Eysel, Ulf 1944- *WhoWor 91*
Eysenck, H J 1916- *EncO&P 3*
Eysenck, Hans Jurgen 1916- *EncPaPR 91, WhoWor 91*
Eysenck, Michael 1944- *ConAu 131*
Eyser, Eberhard 1932- *IntWWM 90*
Eyskens, Erik Joannes 1935- *WhoWor 91*
Eyskens, Gaston 1905-1988 *AnObit 1988, BioIn 16*
Eyskens, Mark 1933- *WhoWor 91*
Eysler, Edmund 1874-1949 *OxCPMus*
Eysman, Harvey A. 1939- *WhoWrEP 89*
Eyster, Franklin S. 1941- *St&PR 91*
Eyster, James Parry 1952- *IntWWM 90*
Eyster, Mary Elaine 1935- *WhoAm 90, WhoE 91*
Eytan, Alice Auerbach *BiDrAPA 89*
Eytan, Serge *BiDrAPA 89*
Eytinge, Rose 1835-1911 *BioIn 16, NotWoAT*
Eyton, John Trevor 1934- *WhoAm 90*
Eyvindson, Peter 1946- *BioIn 16*
Eyzaguirre, Jaime 1935- *WhoWor 91*
Ezcurra, Andres Townsend 1915- *BioIn 16*
Eze, Augustine Okpu 1934- *WhoWor 91*
Eze, Emmanuel Ebelechukwu 1942- *BiDrAPA 89*
Ezeife, Chukwuemeka 1939- *WhoWor 91*
Ezekiel, Nissim 1924- *ConLC 61 [port]*
Ezekiel, Tish O'Dowd 1943- *ConAu 129*
Ezell, Annette Schram 1940- *WhoAmW 91*
Ezell, Carolyn Woltz 1949- *WhoWrEP 89*
Ezell, Howard Lee 1928- *WhoSSW 91*
Ezell, Kenneth Pettey, Jr. 1949- *WhoEmL 91*
Ezell, Kerry Moore 1935- *St&PR 91, WhoAm 90, WhoSSW 91*
Ezell, Margaret Prather 1951- *WhoEmL 91, WhoSSW 91*
Ezell, Reva Gross 1937- *WhoAmW 91*
Ezell, Shirley Dee 1938- *WhoAmW 91*
Ezelle, James Shumate, Jr. 1950- *BiDrAPA 89*
Ezelle, Robert Eugene 1927- *WhoAm 90*
Ezor, Sheldon D. 1924- *St&PR 91*
Ezra, Joseph 1945- *BiDrAPA 89*
Ezvan, Dominique Marie 1955- *WhoWor 91*
Ezzat, Emile Michel 1936- *WhoWor 91*
Ezzell, Lois Riggins 1939- *WhoAmW 91, WhoSSW 91*
Ezzell, Lois S. 1939- *WhoAm 90*

F

F Marion Crawford 1854-1909 EncO&P 3
F, Lisa Collado 1944- WhoAmA 91
F., Luis B. Prieto 1902- BioIn 16
Faa' Gonzaga, Camilla 1599-1662 EncCoWW
Faal, John J. BioIn 16
Faas, Ekbert 1938- ConAu 130
Faas, Larry Andrew 1936- WhoAm 90
Faatz, Jeanne Ryan 1941- WhoAmW 91
Fabacher, Jeffrey Everett 1953- BiDrAPA 89
Fabbri, Anne R WhoAmA 91
Fabbri, Brian John 1944- WhoAm 90
Fabbri, Franca 1935- IntWWM 90
Fabbri, Franco 1949- IntWWM 90
Fabbri, Remo, Jr. BiDrAPA 89
Fabbrini, Sergio 1949- WhoWor 91
Fabe, Robert 1917- WhoAmA 91
Fabel, Warren L. 1933- St&PR 91
Fabell, Walter C. AuBYP 90
Fabens, Andrew Lawrie, III 1942- WhoAm 90
Faber, Adele 1928- WhoAm 90
Faber, Betty Lane BioIn 16
Faber, Carol Antoinette 1937- WhoAmW 91
Faber, Charles Franklin 1926- WhoSSW 91
Faber, David Ray, II 1951- BiDrAPA 89
Faber, Doris 1924- AuBYP 90, ConAu 30NR
Faber, Eberhard 1936- St&PR 91
Faber, Edward Earl 1933- WhoAm 90
Faber, Elmer L. 1913- St&PR 91
Faber, Fred S., Jr. 1924- St&PR 91
Faber, Garold L 1923- BiDrAPA 89
Faber, Harold 1919- AuBYP 90
Faber, Harry Douglas 1942- BiDrAPA 89
Faber, Heije 1907- WhoWor 91
Faber, Heiko 1937- WhoWor 91
Faber, Horace B., Jr. 1931- St&PR 91
Faber, Inez McAlister 1897- WhoWrEP 89
Faber, Johann Ludwig PenDiDA 89
Faber, John Andrew 1958- BiDrAPA 89
Faber, John Henry 1918- WhoAm 90
Faber, Malte Michael 1938- WhoWor 91
Faber, Michael Warren 1943- WhoAm 90
Faber, Milton David 1909- St&PR 91
Faber, Peter Johannes 1924- WhoWor 91
Faber, Raymond A 1947- BiDrAPA 89
Faber, Red 1888-1976 Ballpl 90 [port]
Faber, Sandra Moore 1944- WhoAm 90, WhoAmW 91
Faber, Susan Fritsch 1949- WhoEmL 91
Faber, Vickie Lynn 1967- WhoEmL 91
Faber, William Joseph 1950- WhoEmL 91
Faberge, Peter Carl 1846-1920 PenDiDA 89, WorAlBi
Faberson, Paul 1926- ODwPR 91
Fabert, Jacques 1925- WhoAmA 91
Fabi, Bernard St&PR 91
Fabi, Mark Bernard BiDrAPA 89
Fabian AuBYP 90
Fabian 1943- ConMus 5 [port], EncPR&S 89, WorAlBi
Fabian, Alice E BiDrAPA 89
Fabian, Blaine F. 1930- ODwPR 91
Fabian, Blaine Frank 1930- WhoE 91
Fabian, Christopher A 1957- BiDrAPA 89
Fabian, Edward Leon, Jr. 1959- WhoWor 91
Fabian, F.G., Jr. 1915- St&PR 91
Fabian, Francis Gordon, Jr. 1915- WhoAm 90
Fabian, G. Leslie 1927- St&PR 91
Fabian, Jeanne 1946- WhoAmW 91
Fabian, John Andrew 1934- St&PR 91
Fabian, John M. WhoAm 90
Fabian, John McCreary 1939- St&PR 91
Fabian, Jose Luis BiDrAPA 89
Fabian, Joseph Vincent 1948- WhoSSW 91
Fabian, Judith A. 1947- St&PR 91
Fabian, Kenneth J BiDrAPA 89
Fabian, Larry Louis 1940- WhoAm 90
Fabian, Marta 1946- IntWWM 90, PenDiMP
Fabiani, Cesar A 1942- BiDrAPA 89
Fabiani, Dante C. 1917- St&PR 91
Fabiani, Dante Carl 1917- WhoAm 90
Fabiani, Mario J. 1923- St&PR 91
Fabiano, Diane Fabian 1952- WhoAmW 91
Fabiano, Marion Pinzotti 1937- WhoAmW 91
Fabiaschi, Michael Anthony 1955- St&PR 91
Fabick, Joseph G. 1927- St&PR 91
Fabila, Jose Andres 1955- WhoHisp 91
Fabilli, Mary 1914- WhoWrEP 89
Fabina, Susan Lynn 1960- WhoAmW 91
Fabius, Laurent BioIn 16
Fabius, Laurent 1946- BiDFrPL
Fabius Maximus Verrucosus, Quintus 265?BC-203BC WorAlBi
Fabray, Nanette 1920- WorAlBi
Fabre, Edouard-Charles 1827-1896 DcCanB 12
Fabre, Fred Ruffin 1939- WhoSSW 91
Fabre, Louis Fernand, Jr. BiDrAPA 89
Fabre, Pierre Jean 1590?-1650 EncO&P 3
Fabre, Raoul Francois 1925- WhoWor 91
Fabre, Ricardo Jose BiDrAPA 89
Fabre, Robert Charles Victor 1915- BiDFrPL
Fabrega, Horacio, Jr. BiDrAPA 89
Fabrega, Manuel BiDrAPA 89
Fabres, Oscar 1895-1961 WhoAmA 91N
Fabri, Ralph 1894-1975 WhoAmA 91N
Fabri, Zoltan 1917- BioIn 16
Fabricand, Burton Paul 1923- WhoAm 90
Fabricant, Arthur E. 1935- St&PR 91, WhoAm 90
Fabricant, Bruce 1942- WhoAm 90
Fabricant, Bruce J. 1942- ODwPR 91
Fabricant, Catherine Grenci 1919- WhoAmW 91
Fabricant, Solomon 1906-1989 BioIn 16, ConAu 129
Fabricio, Roberto C. 1946- WhoHisp 91
Fabricius, Sara DcScanL
Fabrick, Howard David 1938- WhoAm 90
Fabrikant, Craig Steven 1952- WhoEmL 91
Fabrikesi, Eugenia-Theodora 1950- WhoWor 91
Fabris, James A. 1938- WhoAm 90
Fabritiis, Oliviero De PenDiMP
Fabritius, Carel 1622?-1654 IntDcAA 90
Fabrizi, Aldo NewYTBS 90 [port]
Fabrizi, Aldo 1905-1990 BioIn 16
Fabrizio, Gerald James 1962- WhoEmL 91
Fabrizio, Margaret Mary 1954- WhoAmW 91
Fabro, Louis V. 1931- ODwPR 91
Fabros, Roberto Tancinco 1950- WhoE 91
Fabry, Laszlo Georg 1947- WhoWor 91
Fabry, Paul Andrew WhoSSW 91
Fabrycky, Wolter Joseph 1932- WhoAm 90
Fabrycy, Mark Zdzislaw 1922- WhoAm 90
Facchinetti, Nicola Antonio 1824-1900 ArtLatA
Facchini, Diane M. 1963- St&PR 91
Facci, Domenico 1916- WhoAmA 91
Facciano, Pauline Rose 1959- WhoAmW 91
Faccini, Ernest Carlo 1949- WhoWor 91
Faccinto, Victor Paul 1945- WhoAm 90, WhoAmA 91
Faccio, Franco 1840-1891 PenDiMP
Faccio, Rina EncCoWW
Faccioli-Licata, O. BiDWomA
Face, Philip Jon 1961- WhoEmL 91
Face, Roy 1928- Ballpl 90 [port]
Facenda, Albert Joseph 1947- St&PR 91
Facer, Eric Fouts 1953- WhoEmL 91
Facer, Nick BioIn 16
Faces, The EncPR&S 89, OxCPMus
Facey, John Abbott 1926- St&PR 91
Facey, John Abbott, III 1950- WhoEmL 91
Facey, Martin Kerr 1948- WhoAmA 91
Faches, William George 1928- WhoAm 90
Fachiri, Adela PenDiMP
Fachnie, Hugh Douglas 1952- WhoE 91
Fachrudin 1934- WhoWor 91
Facht-Ribbing, Marianne 1937- IntWWM 90
Faciana, Richard Angelo 1939- BiDrAPA 89
Facione, Peter Arthur 1944- WhoAm 90
Fackelman, Robert H. 1906- St&PR 91
Fackenheim, Emil L. BioIn 16
Facklam, Margery 1927- AuBYP 90, WhoWrEP 89
Fackler, Benjamine Lloyd 1926- St&PR 91, WhoAm 90
Fackler, Edwin John 1927- St&PR 91
Fackler, John Paul, Jr. 1934- WhoAm 90
Fackler, Martin Luther 1933- WhoAm 90
Fackler, Peter Coleman 1944- WhoE 91
Fackler, Walter David 1921- WhoAm 90
Fackler, William Marion 1938- WhoAm 90
Facos, James 1924- WhoWrEP 89
Factor, June AuBYP 90
Factor, Mallory 1950- ODwPR 91, St&PR 91
Factor, Max, III 1945- WhoAm 90
Factor, Morris BiDrAPA 89
Factor, Robert M 1946- BiDrAPA 89
Factor, Sidney 1916- St&PR 91
Faculak, Mary Helen 1960- WhoWrEP 89
Facundo, Jose R. 1938- WhoWor 91
Fadda, Mario 1948- WhoWor 91
Faddis, Wayne Allen 1960- WhoSSW 91
Fadeley, Brett Duane 1953- St&PR 91
Fadeley, Edward Norman 1929- WhoAm 90
Fadem, Lloyd Robert 1951- WhoSSW 91
Faden, Alan Ira 1945- WhoAm 90, WhoEmL 91
Faden, Lawrence Steven 1942- WhoAmA 91
Fader, Bruce Warren BiDrAPA 89
Fader, Daniel Nelson 1930- WhoAm 90
Fader, Ellen Strahs 1952- St&PR 91, WhoAmW 91, WhoE 91
Fader, Milton 1927- BiDrAPA 89
Fader, Seymour J. 1923- WhoE 91
Fader, Shirley Sloan WhoAm 90, WhoAmW 91, WhoE 91, WhoWor 91
Fader, William B. 1931- St&PR 91
Fader, William Benson Mann 1931- WhoAm 90
Fadial, John Murray 1965- IntWWM 90
Fadiman, Clifton WhoAm 90
Fadiman, Clifton 1904- WorAlBi
Fadlallah, Mohammed Hussein BioIn 16
Fadum, Ralph Eigil 1912- WhoAm 90
Fadyn, Joseph Nicholas 1947- WhoSSW 91
Faeder, Gustav S. 1921- WhoWrEP 89
Faedo, Len 1960- Ballpl 90
Faehn, Rhonda BioIn 16
Faehnle, Robert Kirkwood 1949- WhoEmL 91
Faerber, Donald Bartley 1935- WhoWrEP 89
Faerber, Jorg 1929- IntWWM 90, PenDiMP
Faerber, Tom Harold 1930- St&PR 91
Faerstein, Saul Jules 1943- BiDrAPA 89
Faesch, John Jacob 1729-1799 EncCRAm
Faetche, Jim Bruno 1943- WhoSSW 91
Fafian, Joseph, Jr. 1939- WhoAm 90, WhoE 91
Faflick, Carl E. 1922- St&PR 91
Fagal, William A. BioIn 16
Fagala, Gwen Eileen BiDrAPA 89
Fagaly, William Arthur 1938- WhoAm 90, WhoAmA 91
Fagan, Barney OxCPMus
Fagan, Billy BioIn 16
Fagan, Brian M 1936- ConAu 31NR
Fagan, Edward R. BioIn 16
Fagan, Eleanora 1915-1959 BioIn 16
Fagan, George Vincent 1917- WhoAm 90
Fagan, Gideon 1904-1980 PenDiMP
Fagan, James F. 1948- St&PR 91
Fagan, James Reynolds 1931- St&PR 91
Fagan, Joe Garrell BiDrAPA 89
Fagan, John Ernest 1949- WhoEmL 91
Fagan, John Paul 1930- St&PR 91, WhoAm 90
Fagan, Joseph Francis, III 1941- WhoAm 90
Fagan, Kate J. 1951- WhoEmL 91
Fagan, Maurice James, Jr. 1921- WhoAm 90
Fagan, Peter F. 1944- St&PR 91
Fagan, Peter Thomas 1948- WhoEmL 91
Fagan, Sheila ODwPR 91
Fagan, Sheila Fitzsimons 1942- St&PR 91
Fagan, Thomas A. 1935- St&PR 91
Fagan, Timothy Robert 1955- WhoEmL 91
Fagan, Wayne I. 1943- WhoSSW 91
Fagan, William E. 1945- St&PR 91
Fagan, William Francis 1941- St&PR 91
Fagan, William Thomas, Jr. 1923- WhoE 91
Fagans, Karl P. 1942- St&PR 91
Fage, Mary BiDEWW, FemiCLE
Fagelman, F Diane 1941- BiDrAPA 89
Fagen, Donald 1948- BioIn 16
Fagen, Richard Rees 1933- WhoAm 90, WhoWrEP 89
Fageol, Frank H EncABHB 4
Fageol, William B EncABHB 4
Fager, Charles Anthony 1924- WhoAm 90
Fager, Charles J 1936- WhoAmA 91

Fager, Joseph S 1916- *BiDrAPA 89*
Fagerberg, Jan Ernst 1951- *WhoWor 91*
Fagerberg, Roger Richard 1935- *WhoAm 90, WhoWor 91*
Fagerlund, Eric 1926- *St&PR 91*
Fageros, Karol *BioIn 16*
Fagersten, Barbara Jeanne 1924- *WhoAmW 91*
Fagerstone, Dennis E. 1949- *St&PR 91*
Fagerstrom, Per Olof 1946- *WhoWor 91*
Faget, Maxime Allan 1921- *WhoAm 90*
Faget, Otilia Miga *BiDrAPA 89*
Fagg, Bernard 1915-1987 *BioIn 16*
Fagg, Gary T. 1948- *St&PR 91*
Fagg, George Gardner 1934- *WhoAm 90*
Fagg, John Edwin 1916- *WhoAm 90*
Fagg, Kevin Stanley 1940- *WhoWor 91*
Fagg, Martha A. 1957- *WhoEmL 91*
Faggard, Phoebe 1956- *WhoAmW 91*
Faggi, John A. B. *BioIn 16*
Faggi, Virginia Xanthos *BioIn 16*
Faggin, Federico 1941- *WhoAm 90*
Faggioli, Justin Mark 1951- *WhoEmL 91*
Faggioni, Piero 1936- *IntWWM 90*
Fagher, Olof Erik Birger 1942- *WhoWor 91*
Faghin, Jack 1919- *BiDrAPA 89*
Fagin, Claire Mintzer *WhoAm 90, WhoAmW 91*
Fagin, David Kyle 1938- *WhoAm 90*
Fagin, Henry 1913- *WhoAm 90*
Fagin, Leonard Henry 1947- *WhoWor 91*
Fagin, Richard 1935- *St&PR 91, WhoAm 90*
Fagin, Ronald 1945- *WhoEmL 91*
Fagin, Terry 1944- *St&PR 91*
Fagnani, Michele Ann 1945- *WhoAmW 91*
Fago, Elizabeth Marie 1950- *WhoSSW 91*
Fagot, Joseph Burdell 1917- *WhoAm 90*
Fagot, Robert Frederick 1921- *WhoAm 90*
Faguet, Benjamin B *BiDrAPA 89*
Faguet, Robert A 1946- *BiDrAPA 89*
Fagundes, Jose Otavio 1941- *BiDrAPA 89*
Fagundes, Joseph Marvin, III 1953- *WhoEmL 91*
Fagundo, Ana Maria 1938- *WhoAm 90*
Fahad Ibn Abdul Aziz 1920- *WhoWor 91*
Fahberg, Antonia 1928- *IntWWM 90*
Fahd Bin Abd Al-Aziz Al Saud 1921- *PolLCME*
Fahd, King of Saudi Arabia 1922- *BioIn 16*
Faheem, Ahmed Daver 1948- *BiDrAPA 89*
Faherty, William Francis, Jr. 1926- *St&PR 91*
Fahey, Bill 1950- *Ballpl 90*
Fahey, Charles Joseph 1933- *WhoAm 90*
Fahey, Colleen Elizabeth 1950- *St&PR 91*
Fahey, David 1948- *ConAu 131*
Fahey, Joseph Francis, Jr. 1925- *WhoAm 90*
Fahey, Judell Spoering 1955- *WhoEmL 91*
Fahey, Michele Annette *BiDrAPA 89*
Fahey, Patricia Anne 1957- *WhoE 91*
Fahey, Philip M. 1940- *WhoAm 90*
Fahey, Walter John 1927- *WhoAm 90*
Fahien, Leonard August 1934- *WhoAm 90*
Fahim, Ayshe 1900- *WhoAmW 91*
Fahimi, H. Dariush 1933- *WhoWor 91*
Fahl, John 1936- *St&PR 91*
Fahlbeck, Reinhold Hans 1938- *WhoWor 91*
Fahlen, Charles C 1939- *WhoAmA 91*
Fahler, Jarl Ingmar 1925- *EncO&P 3*
Fahlgren, H. Smoot 1930- *St&PR 91*
Fahlgren, Herbert Smoot 1930- *WhoAm 90*
Fahlin, Roland 1938- *WhoWor 91*
Fahlman, Betsy Lee 1951- *WhoAmA 91*
Fahlstrom, Anders *PenDiDA 89*
Fahlstrom, Oyvind 1928-1976 *WhoAmA 91N*
Fahlund, Michael Jay 1949- *WhoE 91*
Fahmy, Randa 1964- *WhoAmW 91*
Fahn, Jay 1949- *WhoEmL 91*
Fahn, Stanley 1933- *WhoAm 90*
Fahnestock, Jean Howe 1930- *WhoAmW 91*
Fahnestock, Margaret 1952- *WhoEmL 91*
Fahrenbach, Jean Ridler 1924- *WhoE 91*
Fahrenbach, Jeri Lynn 1948- *WhoAmW 91*
Fahrenheit, Daniel Gabriel 1686-1736 *WorAlBi*
Fahrenkamp, Bettye M. *WhoAmW 91*
Fahrenkopf, Frank Joseph, Jr. 1939- *WhoAm 90*
Fahrenwald, William Edward 1955- *WhoEmL 91*
Fahrer, Rodolfo 1937- *BiDrAPA 89*
Fahringer, Catherine Hewson 1922- *WhoAm 90*
Fahringer, Herald Price 1930- *WhoAm 90*
Fahrion, Roland 1945- *WhoWor 91*
Fahrlander, Henry William, Jr. 1934- *WhoSSW 91*
Fahrner, Raymond Eugene 1951- *IntWWM 90*
Fahs, James Kenneth 1947- *St&PR 91*
Fahs, Jeffrey James 1952- *BiDrAPA 89*
Fahs, Raymond Ziegler *BioIn 16*
Fahs, Sophia Lyon 1876-1978 *BioAmW, BioIn 16*
Fahy, Charles Laurence 1947- *WhoSSW 91*
Fahy, Edward J. 1910-1989 *BioIn 16*
Fahy, Ellen T. *WhoAm 90*
Fahy, Everett *BioIn 16*
Fahy, Nancy Lee 1946- *WhoAmW 91, WhoEmL 91*
Fai, Leslie L 1919- *BiDrAPA 89*
Faiers, Ted 1908-1985 *WhoAmA 91N*
Faigen, Ivan M. 1926- *St&PR 91*
Faigin, Larry Bernard 1942- *WhoAm 90*
Faignant, John Paul 1953- *WhoEmL 91*
Faiks, Jan Ogozalek 1945- *WhoAmW 91*
Fail, Michelle Maxine 1953- *WhoAmW 91*
Failer, Raymond Victor 1933- *BiDrAPA 89*
Failey, George Leo 1928- *St&PR 91*
Failey, George Leo, Jr. 1928- *WhoAm 90*
Failing, Bruce F. *BioIn 16*
Failing, Craig Adam 1961- *WhoEmL 91*
Failing, George Edgar 1912- *WhoAm 90*
Failing, Henry 1834-1898 *EncABHB 6 [port]*
Failinger, Dianne Marie 1958- *WhoAmW 91*
Failla, Federico 1931- *WhoWor 91*
Failla, Frank Jerome, Jr. 1949- *St&PR 91*
Failla, Mark Edward 1962- *WhoEmL 91*
Failla, Patricia McClement 1925- *WhoAmW 91*
Faillace, Louis A 1932- *BiDrAPA 89*
Faillard, Hans 1924- *WhoWor 91*
Fails, Donna Gail 1958- *WhoAmW 91*
Faiman, Charles 1939- *WhoAm 90*
Faiman, Robert Neil 1923- *WhoAm 90*
Fain, Ferris 1921- *Ballpl 90 [port]*
Fain, Haskell 1926- *WhoAm 90*
Fain, Jay Lindsey 1950- *WhoEmL 91*
Fain, Joel Maurice 1953- *WhoEmL 91*
Fain, John Charles 1937- *St&PR 91*
Fain, John Nicholas 1934- *WhoAm 90*
Fain, John Wood 1953- *WhoAm 90*
Fain, Karen Kellogg 1940- *WhoAmW 91, WhoWor 91*
Fain, Raymond N. 1946- *St&PR 91*
Fain, Richard David 1947- *WhoAm 90, WhoWor 91*
Fain, Sammy 1902-1989 *AnObit 1989, BioIn 16, OxCPMus, WorAlBi*
Fainbairn, Ursula F. *St&PR 91*
Faini, Maria Luisa Teresa *WhoAm 90*
Fainlight, Ruth *BioIn 16*
Fainlight, Ruth 1931- *FemiCLE*
Fainman, Burt 1936- *St&PR 91*
Fainsbert, Amy 1962- *St&PR 91*
Fainsbert, Charles Mitchell 1932- *St&PR 91*
Fainsilber, Adrien 1932- *WhoWor 91*
Fainter, Robert A 1942-1978 *WhoAmA 91N*
Faintych, Max 1930- *BiDrAPA 89*
Fair, A. A. *MajTwCW, TwCCr&M 91*
Fair, C. James 1951- *ODwPR 91*
Fair, Ellis F 1915- *BiDrAPA 89*
Fair, Geraldine Ann 1927- *BiDrAPA 89*
Fair, Harold Lloyd 1924- *WhoAm 90*
Fair, Hudson Randolph 1953- *WhoEmL 91*
Fair, Ian Dennis 1948- *WhoWor 91*
Fair, J. Milton 1934- *St&PR 91*
Fair, James Richard 1950- *WhoEmL 91*
Fair, James Rutherford, Jr. 1920- *WhoAm 90*
Fair, Jean Everhard 1917- *WhoAm 90*
Fair, Jeremy George 1947- *St&PR 91*
Fair, John Douglas 1943- *WhoSSW 91*
Fair, Larry *BioIn 16*
Fair, Morris Harley 1929- *WhoAm 90*
Fair, Norma L. 1931- *St&PR 91*
Fair, Norman Arnold 1945- *St&PR 91*
Fair, Ray Clarence 1942- *WhoAm 90*
Fair, Rich Allen 1951- *WhoEmL 91*
Fair, Walter Russel 1936- *St&PR 91*
Fair, William R. *ODwPR 91*
Fair, William R. 1922- *St&PR 91*
Fair, William Robert 1935- *WhoAm 90*
Fairbairn, Clive Stuart 1946- *IntWWM 90*
Fairbairn, Robert H 1934- *BiDrAPA 89*
Fairbairn, Roger *TwCCr&M 91*
Fairbairn, W. Ronald D. *BioIn 16*
Fairbairn, William Ronald Dodds *BioIn 16*
Fairbairns, Zoe 1948- *FemiCLE*
Fairbank, Janet 1878-1951 *FemiCLE*
Fairbank, John King 1907- *WhoAm 90*
Fairbank, William M. 1917-1989 *AnObit 1989, BioIn 16*
Fairbanks, Charles Herron, Jr. 1944- *WhoAm 90*
Fairbanks, Charles Warren 1852-1918 *BiDrUSE 89*
Fairbanks, David C. 1937- *St&PR 91*
Fairbanks, Deborah Kay McGuire 1954- *WhoAmW 91*
Fairbanks, Douglas 1883-1939 *WorAlBi*
Fairbanks, Douglas 1909- *BioIn 16*
Fairbanks, Douglas, Jr. 1909- *WorAlBi*
Fairbanks, Douglas Elton, Jr. 1909- *WhoAm 90, WhoWor 91*
Fairbanks, Frank B. 1930- *St&PR 91, WhoE 91*
Fairbanks, Franklin 1828-1893? *AmLegL*
Fairbanks, Harold Vincent 1915- *WhoAm 90*
Fairbanks, J. Nelson *WhoSSW 91*
Fairbanks, Janet M *BiDrAPA 89*
Fairbanks, Jonathan Leo 1933- *WhoAm 90, WhoAmA 91*
Fairbanks, Karen Ann 1959- *WhoAmW 91*
Fairbanks, Mary Joanne 1939- *WhoAmW 91*
Fairbanks, Mary Lee *BioIn 16*
Fairbanks, Richard Monroe 1912- *WhoAm 90*
Fairbanks, Richard Monroe, III 1941- *WhoAm 90*
Fairbanks, Russell Norman 1919- *WhoAm 90*
Fairbanks, Tod Robert 1947- *WhoEmL 91*
Fairbanks, Virgil Fox 1930- *WhoAm 90*
Fairbourn, William T. *BioIn 16*
Fairbrother, Anne 1804?-1896 *DcCanB 12*
Fairbrother, Anne Elmore 1922- *WhoWrEP 89*
Fairburn, Robert Gordon 1911- *WhoAm 90*
Fairchild, Beatrice Magdoff 1916- *WhoAmW 91*
Fairchild, Charles Stebbins 1842-1924 *BiDrUSE 89*
Fairchild, David Lawrence 1946- *WhoAm 90*
Fairchild, Edgar W. B. 1905-1988 *BioIn 16*
Fairchild, Helen *EncO&P 3*
Fairchild, Hiram Orlando 1845-1925 *AmLegL*
Fairchild, James Delano 1942- *WhoAm 90*
Fairchild, John *BioIn 16*
Fairchild, John Burr 1927- *WhoAm 90*
Fairchild, Joseph Virgil, Jr. 1933- *WhoSSW 91*
Fairchild, Kentley Robert 1961- *WhoEmL 91*
Fairchild, Mahlon Lowell 1930- *WhoAm 90*
Fairchild, May 1872-1959 *WhoAmA 91N*
Fairchild, Morgan 1950- *WorAlBi*
Fairchild, Raymond Eugene 1923- *St&PR 91, WhoAm 90, WhoWor 91*
Fairchild, Raymond Francis 1946- *WhoWor 91*
Fairchild, Robert Charles 1921- *WhoAm 90*
Fairchild, Ronald B. 1957- *St&PR 91*
Fairchild, Thomas E. 1912- *WhoAm 90*
Fairchild, William Samuel 1947- *WhoSSW 91*
Faircloth, H. Lamar 1947- *WhoWrEP 89*
Faircloth, Joseph A. 1941- *WhoSSW 91*
Faircloth, Robert Frederick 1936- *St&PR 91*
Fairclough, Peter Donald 1946- *WhoWor 91*
Faires, Raymond Alan 1952- *WhoAm 90*
Faires, Ross N. 1934- *WhoSSW 91*
Fairey Aviation Band *OxCPMus*
Fairey, George Gage 1948- *BiDrAPA 89*
Fairey, Jim 1944- *Ballpl 90*
Fairey, Rebecca Lynn Olson 1958- *WhoAmW 91*
Fairfax, Beatrice *ConAu 131*
Fairfax, Charles Snowden 1829-1869 *AmLegL*
Fairfax, Edward *EncO&P 3*
Fairfax, Michael *BioIn 16*
Fairfax-Lucy, Brian 1898-1974 *AuBYP 90*
Fairfield, Betty Elaine Smith 1927- *WhoAmW 91*
Fairfield, Cicily Isabel 1892-1983 *DcNaB 1981*
Fairfield, John *WhoWrEP 89*
Fairfield, Lesley 1949- *ConAu 130*
Fairfield, Lory C. 1936- *St&PR 91*
Fairfield, Richard Thomas 1937- *WhoAmA 91*
Fairfield-Sonn, James Willed 1948- *WhoE 91*
Fairhurst, Charles 1929- *WhoAm 90*
Fairhurst, Thomas Milson 1955- *WhoEmL 91*
Fairlamb, Annie *EncO&P 3*
Fairlamb, David John 1949- *WhoWor 91*
Fairleigh, James Parkinson 1938- *IntWWM 90, WhoSSW 91, WhoWor 91*
Fairleigh, Marlane Paxson 1939- *WhoSSW 91*
Fairleigh, Runa *TwCCr&M 91*
Fairless, Michael 1869-1901 *BioIn 16, FemiCLE*
Fairley, E. Lee 1917- *IntWWM 90*
Fairley, Janet Christine 1949- *IntWWM 90*
Fairley, John 1939- *ConAu 131*
Fairley, Michael J. 1946- *St&PR 91*
Fairley, Nora Lou 1944- *BiDrAPA 89*
Fairlie, Gerald 1899-1983 *SpyFic*
Fairlie, Gerard 1899-1983 *TwCCr&M 91*
Fairlie, Henry *BioIn 16*
Fairlie, Henry *NewYTBS 90 [port]*
Fairlie, Henry 1924-1990 *ConAu 131*
Fairly, Ron 1938- *Ballpl 90 [port]*
Fairman, Joel Martin 1929- *WhoAm 90*
Fairman, Lydia *BiDEWW*
Fairman, Mary *BiDEWW*
Fairobent, Lynne Anne 1956- *WhoAmW 91*
Fairport Convention *OxCPMus*
Fairstein, Linda *BioIn 16, NewYTBS 90 [port]*
Fairstein, Linda 1948?- *News 91-1 [port]*
Fairweather, Charles Henry 1826-1894 *DcCanB 12*
Fairweather, Douglas A. 1934- *ODwPR 91*
Fairweather, George 1906-1986 *BioIn 16*
Fairweather, Howard Hessington 1938- *St&PR 91, WhoAm 90*
Fairweather, Robert Gordon Lee 1923- *WhoAm 90*
Fairweather, Sally H 1917- *WhoAmA 91*
Faisal 1906?-1975 *WorAlBi*
Faisal Bin Abd Al-Aziz Al Saud 1906-1975 *PolLCME*
Faisal, King of Saudi Arabia 1906-1975 *BioIn 16*
Faisal, Daniel Omar 1946- *BiDrAPA 89*
Faison, Edmund Winston, Jr. 1953- *WhoEmL 91*
Faison, Ferdinand Johnson 1934- *St&PR 91*
Faison, Frankie *ConTFT 8*
Faison, George 1946- *DrBlPA 90*
Faison, George 1947- *ConTFT 8*
Faison, Matthew *ConTFT 8*
Faison, Samson Lane, Jr 1907- *WhoAmA 91*
Faison, Sandy *ConTFT 8*
Faison, Seth Shepard 1924- *WhoAm 90*
Faison, Thomas G *BiDrAPA 89*
Fait, George A. 1926- *St&PR 91*
Faith, Adam 1940- *OxCPMus*
Faith, Carl Clifton 1927- *WhoAm 90, WhoE 91*
Faith, Mark David 1962- *WhoEmL 91*
Faith, Percy 1908-1976 *OxCPMus*
Faith-Ell, Age 1912- *ConDes 90*
Faithfull, Emily 1835-1895 *BioIn 16, FemiCLE*
Faithfull, Lucy 1910- *BioIn 16*
Faithfull, Marianne 1946?- *EncPR&S 89*
Faithorn, Eleanor Perry *BiDrAPA 89*
Fajack, D. James 1936- *St&PR 91*
Fajans, Jack 1922- *WhoAm 90*
Fajans, Kasimir 1887-1975 *DcScB S2*
Fajans, Stefan Stanislaus 1918- *WhoAm 90*
Fajardo, Demetrio P. *BiDrAPA 89*
Fajardo, Frederick J. 1935- *ODwPR 91*
Fajardo, Jorge Elias 1942- *WhoHisp 91*
Fajardo, Juan Ramon, Jr. 1958- *WhoHisp 91*
Fajardo, Katharine Lynn 1951- *WhoAmW 91, WhoE 91*
Fajardo, Robert A 1933- *BiDrAPA 89*
Fajerman, Leon 1943- *BiDrAPA 89*
Fajon, Etienne Louis-Henri 1906- *BiDFrPL*
Fajrajzen, Stefano *BiDrAPA 89*
Fakazis, Melvin D. 1948- *St&PR 91*
Fakes, Bonnie Marie 1945- *WhoEmL 91*
Fakes, Mary E. A. 1962- *WhoAmW 91*
Fakhruddin, A K M *BiDrAPA 89*
Faklaris, John Richard 1949- *St&PR 91*
Fako, Nancy Jordan 1942- *IntWWM 90*
Falahee, Patrick Joseph, Jr. 1961- *WhoEmL 91*
Falana, Lola *BioIn 16*
Falana, Lola 1942- *DrBlPA 90*
Falana, Lola 1946- *WorAlBi*
Falater, Scott Louis 1955- *WhoEmL 91*
Falb, John H. 1945- *St&PR 91*
Falb, Mark Charles 1947- *St&PR 91*
Falb, Peter Lawrence 1936- *WhoAm 90*
Falbe, Peter 1965- *WhoWor 91*
Falber, Harold Julius 1946- *WhoE 91*
Falbey, J. Wayne 1941- *WhoSSW 91*
Falceto, Olga Garcia *BiDrAPA 89*
Falchero, Piero *St&PR 91*
Falchetta, Stephen Louis 1936- *BiDrAPA 89*
Falci, Nina Lansky 1958- *WhoAmW 91*
Falci, Thomas Arthur 1950- *BiDrAPA 89*
Falcinelli, Rolande 1920- *IntWWM 90*
Falcini, Angiolo *PenDiDA 89*
Falcini, Luigi *PenDiDA 89*
Falck, Jacob L. 1953- *WhoWor 91*
Falcke, Caj Olof 1941- *WhoWor 91*
Falco *BioIn 16*
Falco, Charles Maurice 1948- *WhoEmL 91*
Falco, Edward 1948- *WhoWrEP 89*
Falco, JoAnn 1952- *WhoAmW 91, WhoWor 91*
Falco, Joao *EncCoWW*

Falco, Kathy Strickland 1958- *WhoSSW 91*
Falco, Louis 1942- *WhoAm 90, WhoE 91*
Falco, Maria Josephine 1932- *WhoAm 90*
Falco, Robert Anthony 1948- *WhoSSW 91*
Falco, Virgil J. 1928- *St&PR 91*
Falcomer, Marco Tullio *EncO&P 3*
Falcon, A Soledad M 1936- *BiDrAPA 89*
Falcon, Cornelie 1814-1897 *PenDiMP*
Falcon, Elise C *BiDrAPA 89*
Falcon, Hugo G 1934- *BiDrAPA 89*
Falcon, Juan Antonio 1959- *WhoWor 91*
Falcon, Juan Crisostomo 1820-1870 *BioIn 16*
Falcon, Juan Ramon *BiDrAPA 89*
Falcon, Lawrence Michael 1943- *St&PR 91*
Falcon, Lidia 1935- *IntvSpW [port]*
Falcon, Louis Albert 1932- *WhoAm 90*
Falcon, Raymond Jesus, Jr. 1953- *WhoE 91, WhoEmL 91, WhoWor 91*
Falcon, Ruth 1946- *IntWWM 90*
Falcon, Spencer Paul *BiDrAPA 89*
Falcon, Walter Phillip 1936- *WhoAm 90*
Falcon O'Neill, Lidia 1935- *EncCoWW*
Falconar, Harriet *FemiCLE*
Falconar, Maria *FemiCLE*
Falconbridge, Anna Maria *BioIn 16, FemiCLE*
Falcone, Anthony 1956- *St&PR 91*
Falcone, Carmine 1946- *WhoAm 90*
Falcone, Charles A. 1942- *St&PR 91*
Falcone, Donna Marie 1961- *WhoAmW 91*
Falcone, Emanuel John *BiDrAPA 89*
Falcone, Frank S. 1940- *WhoAm 90, WhoE 91*
Falcone, Leonard V. 1899-1985 *BioIn 16*
Falcone, Louis A. 1955- *WhoEmL 91*
Falcone, Lucille 1952- *WhoAmW 91*
Falcone, Nola Maddox 1939- *WhoAm 90, WhoAmW 91*
Falcone, Patricia Jeanne *WhoAmW 91*
Falcone, Pete 1953- *Ballpl 90*
Falcone, Peter 1936- *St&PR 91, WhoAm 90*
Falcone, Philip Francis 1929- *WhoWor 91*
Falcone, Richard Edward 1945- *WhoEmL 91*
Falconer, David Duncan 1940- *WhoAm 90*
Falconer, Elizabeth *BioIn 16*
Falconer, George 1932- *St&PR 91*
Falconer, Jacob Alexander 1869-1928 *AmLegL*
Falconer, Joan O. 1930- *IntWWM 90*
Falconer, Karen Ann 1948- *WhoEmL 91*
Falconer, Lanoe 1848-1908 *FemiCLE*
Falconer, Leslie Ann 1923- *WhoWor 91*
Falconer, Stanley *BioIn 16*
Falconer, William Bowman, Jr. 1926- *St&PR 91, WhoE 91*
Falconet, Etienne Maurice 1716-1791 *IntDcAA 90, PenDiDA 89*
Falconet, Noel 1644-1734 *EncO&P 3*
Falconieri, John V 1920- *ConAu 130*
Falconieri, John Vincent 1920- *WhoWor 91*
Falconio, Patrick E. 1941- *St&PR 91*
Faldbakken, Knut 1941- *DcScanL*
Faldini, Roberto 1948- *WhoWor 91*
Faldo, Nick *BioIn 16*
Falek, Ellen Bonnie 1951- *WhoE 91*
Falencki, William 1904- *WhoE 91*
Falender-Zohn, Carol Ann 1946- *WhoAmW 91*
Faleomavaega, Eni F. H. 1943- *WhoAm 90*
Fales, Catherine H *BiDrAPA 89*
Fales, Gregg Booth 1945- *WhoE 91*
Fales, Haliburton, II 1919- *WhoAm 90*
Fales, James M. 1943- *St&PR 91*
Fales, Susan *BioIn 16*
Faletti, Gerald P. 1924- *St&PR 91*
Faletti, Harold Everett 1952- *WhoEmL 91*
Faletti, Richard J. 1922- *St&PR 91*
Faletti, Richard Joseph 1922- *WhoAm 90*
Faley, Robert Lawrence 1927- *WhoWor 91*
Falfan, Alfredo 1936- *WhoAmA 91*
Falick, James 1936- *WhoAm 90, WhoSSW 91*
Falick, Mordecai L *BiDrAPA 89*
Falick, Paul 1944- *St&PR 91*
Falicov, Leopoldo Maximo 1933- *WhoAm 90*
Falik, Harold N. 1949- *St&PR 91*
Falise, Robert A. 1932- *St&PR 91, WhoAm 90*
Falit, Harvey Harris 1942- *BiDrAPA 89*
Falize, Lucien 1838-1897 *PenDiDA 89*
Falk, Alma Martha 1910- *WhoAmW 91, WhoWor 91*
Falk, Antoinette M *BiDrAPA 89*
Falk, Bernard Henry 1926- *WhoAm 90, WhoWor 91*
Falk, Bibb 1899- *Ballpl 90*
Falk, Bibb 1899-1989 *BioIn 16*
Falk, Burton Arthur 1936- *St&PR 91*
Falk, Carl Anton 1907- *WhoAm 90*
Falk, Diane M. 1947- *WhoWrEP 89*
Falk, Donald H 1955- *BiDrAPA 89*
Falk, Donna Joy 1963- *WhoAmW 91*
Falk, Edgar A. 1932- *ODwPR 91*
Falk, Edgar Alan 1932- *WhoAm 90, WhoE 91*
Falk, Edward Daniel 1925- *WhoAm 90*
Falk, Elizabeth Moxley 1942- *WhoAmW 91, WhoWor 91*
Falk, Eugene Hannes 1913- *WhoAm 90*
Falk, Eugene L. 1943- *WhoAm 90*
Falk, Ferdie Arnold 1928- *WhoAm 90, WhoWor 91*
Falk, Gary Lee 1942- *BiDrAPA 89*
Falk, Glenn Edward 1965- *WhoE 91*
Falk, James Harvey, Sr. 1938- *WhoAm 90, WhoE 91, WhoWor 91*
Falk, Janet Barbara 1937- *WhoE 91*
Falk, Janet L. *ODwPR 91*
Falk, Joan Frances 1936- *WhoE 91*
Falk, John C. 1946- *St&PR 91*
Falk, Julia S. 1941- *WhoAm 90*
Falk, Karl L. *BioIn 16*
Falk, Katherine 1944- *BiDrAPA 89, WhoE 91*
Falk, Lee H 1925- *BiDrAPA 89*
Falk, Lee Harrison *WhoAm 90, WhoWor 91*
Falk, Leon 1901-1988 *BioIn 16*
Falk, Lloyd David 1932- *St&PR 91*
Falk, Marshall A 1929- *BiDrAPA 89*
Falk, Marshall Allen 1929- *WhoAm 90, WhoWor 91*
Falk, Nina 1947- *IntWWM 90*
Falk, Norman 1928- *St&PR 91*
Falk, Peter *BioIn 16*
Falk, Peter 1927- *WhoAm 90, WorAlBi*
Falk, Richard S. 1941- *St&PR 91*
Falk, Richard Sands, Jr. 1941- *WhoAm 90*
Falk, Robert Hardy 1948- *WhoEmL 91, WhoWor 91*
Falk, Sigo 1934- *St&PR 91*
Falk, Theodore Carswell 1946- *WhoEmL 91*
Falk, Victor S., III 1945- *WhoEmL 91*
Falk, William Ellis 1945- *BiDrAPA 89*
Falkberget, Johan 1879-1967 *DcScanL*
Falke, Betty Louise Newman 1946- *WhoAmW 91, WhoEmL 91, WhoSSW 91*
Falkenberg, Anna Woytek 1946- *WhoEmL 91*
Falkenberg, Cy 1880-1961 *Ballpl 90*
Falkenberg, Edward 1940- *St&PR 91, WhoAm 90*
Falkenberg, Howard 1942- *ODwPR 91*
Falkenberg, John F. 1925- *St&PR 91*
Falkenberg, Mary Ann Theresa 1931- *WhoAmW 91*
Falkenberry, Joyce Knox 1955- *WhoSSW 91*
Falkenstein, Bruce Alan 1966- *WhoE 91*
Falkenstein, Claire *WhoAmA 91*
Falkenstein, Claire 1908- *BiDWomA, BioIn 16*
Falkenstein, Nancy Ann 1945- *WhoEmL 91*
Falkenstein, Richard Keith 1956- *IntWWM 90*
Falkenstein, Sheldon J 1938- *BiDrAPA 89*
Falker, John Richard 1940- *WhoAm 90*
Falkie, Thomas Victor 1934- *St&PR 91, WhoAm 90*
Falkingham, Donald Herbert 1918- *WhoSSW 91*
Falkirk, Richard *TwCCr&M 91*
Falkland, Elizabeth Cary 1585-1639 *BioIn 16, FemiCLE*
Falkman, Hans Fredrik 1927- *WhoWor 91*
Falkner, Frank Tardrew 1918- *WhoAm 90*
Falkner, Keith 1900- *IntWWM 90*
Falkner, Pandora Ilona 1958- *WhoEmL 91*
Falkoff, Milton 1915- *St&PR 91*
Falkowitz, Daniel 1936- *St&PR 91, WhoAm 90*
Falkowski, Patricia Ann 1947- *WhoAmW 91*
Fall, Albert B. 1861-1944 *WorAlBi*
Fall, Albert Bacon 1861-1944 *BiDrUSE 89*
Fall, Aminata Sow 1941- *BioIn 16*
Fall, Ibrahima 1942- *WhoWor 91*
Fall, John Alexander 1942- *St&PR 91*
Fall, Leo 1873-1925 *OxCPMus*
Fall, Medoune 1919- *WhoWor 91*
Fall, Steven Michael 1951- *WhoEmL 91*
Fall, Thomas 1917- *AuBYP 90*
Falla, Enrique C. 1939- *St&PR 91*
Falla, Enrique Crabb 1939- *WhoAm 90*
Falla, Manuel de 1876-1946 *BioIn 16, PenDiMP A, WorAlBi*
Falla y Matheu, Manuel de 1876-1946 *BioIn 16*
Fallaci, Oriana 1930- *EncCoWW, MajTwCW, WhoWor 91*
Fallada, Hans 1893-1947 *BioIn 16*
Fallarino, John 1941- *St&PR 91*
Fallding, Harold Joseph 1923- *WhoAm 90*
Falle, Daisy Carolyne 1940- *WhoAm 90*
Fallenstein, Judith Faye 1940- *WhoAmW 91*
Faller, Donald E. 1927- *WhoAm 90*
Faller, Dorothy Anderson 1939- *WhoWor 91*
Faller, Marion 1941- *WhoAmA 91, WhoE 91*
Faller, Susan Grogan 1950- *WhoEmL 91*
Fallesen, Gary David 1959- *WhoE 91*
Falletta, John Matthew 1940- *WhoAm 90*
Falletti, Michael Craig 1956- *WhoSSW 91*
Fallick, Edward *BiDrAPA 89*
Fallier, Jeanne Hanway 1920- *WhoWrEP 89*
Fallieres, Armand Clement 1841-1931 *BiDFrPL*
Fallin, Barbara Moore 1939- *WhoAmW 91*
Fallis, Albert Murray 1907- *WhoAm 90*
Fallis, Alexander Graham 1940- *WhoAm 90*
Fallon, Ann Louise 1953- *St&PR 91*
Fallon, Brett David 1961- *WhoEmL 91*
Fallon, Brian A. 1955- *BiDrAPA 89*
Fallon, Brian Anthony 1955- *WhoE 91*
Fallon, Daniel 1938- *WhoAm 90*
Fallon, Edward George 1941- *St&PR 91*
Fallon, Harold Joseph 1931- *WhoAm 90*
Fallon, Harry J. 1926- *St&PR 91*
Fallon, Irene Taylor 1866-1952 *BioIn 16*
Fallon, Ivan Gregory 1944- *WhoWor 91*
Fallon, John Golden 1946- *St&PR 91*
Fallon, Kristine K. 1949- *St&PR 91, WhoAmW 91, WhoEmL 91*
Fallon, Malachy 1961- *St&PR 91*
Fallon, Mark David 1955- *BiDrAPA 89*
Fallon, Martin *ConAu 33NR, MajTwCW, TwCCr&M 91*
Fallon, Mary 1951- *FemiCLE*
Fallon, Michael P. 1941- *WhoHisp 91*
Fallon, Michael Patrick 1942- *WhoWor 91*
Fallon, Patricia Anne 1951- *WhoAmW 91*
Fallon, Patricia Gayle 1945- *WhoAmW 91*
Fallon, Paul Anthony 1948- *BiDrAPA 89*
Fallon, Richard Gordon 1923- *WhoAm 90*
Fallon, Stephanie Keys *BiDrAPA 89*
Fallon, Tom 1936- *WhoWrEP 89*
Fallon, William Hume 1956- *WhoEmL 91*
Fallon, William M. 1946- *St&PR 91*
Fallows, David 1945- *IntWWM 90*
Fallows, James M. *BioIn 16*
Fallows, James Mackenzie 1949- *WhoAm 90, WhoWrEP 89*
Falls, Arthur GrandPre 1901- *WhoWor 91*
Falls, Charles Buckles 1874-1959 *WhoAmA 91N*
Falls, Charles Buckles 1874-1960 *AuBYP 90*
Falls, Edward Joseph 1920- *WhoAm 90*
Falls, Glen 1921- *St&PR 91*
Falls, Joe 1928- *Ballpl 90*
Falls, Joseph Francis 1928- *WhoAm 90*
Falls, Kathleene Joyce 1949- *WhoAmW 91, WhoWor 91*
Falls, Marilyn Lee 1949- *WhoE 91, WhoEmL 91*
Falls, O.B., Jr. 1913- *St&PR 91*
Falls, Olive Moretz 1934- *WhoSSW 91, WhoWor 91*
Falls, Ralph Lane, Jr. 1941- *St&PR 91*
Falls, Raymond Leonard, Jr. 1929- *WhoAm 90*
Falls, Richard Averett 1949- *WhoSSW 91*
Falls, Robert F. *ODwPR 91*
Falls, Robert Glenn 1921- *St&PR 91*
Falls, Waldtraut Margrete Goetze 1941- *WhoAmW 91*
Falls, William Wayne 1947- *WhoAm 90*
Falnes, Oscar J. 1898-1989 *BioIn 16*
Falo, Giovanni Battista Antonio 1942- *WhoWor 91*
Faloon, William Wassell 1920- *WhoAm 90*
Faloona, Michael Patrick 1961- *WhoEmL 91*
Falor, Marcia Hasek 1950- *WhoAmW 91*
Falquez-Certain, Miguel Angel 1948- *WhoHisp 91*
Falsetta, Vincent Mario 1949- *WhoAmA 91*
Falsetti, Christine Marie 1961- *WhoEmL 91*
Falsetto, Mario 1950- *WhoAmA 91*
Falsey, Edward F *BiDrAPA 89*
Falsgraf, William Wendell 1933- *WhoAm 90*
Falsini, Franco *NewAgMG*
Falstad, David B. 1936- *St&PR 91*
Falstad, David Bergfeld 1936- *WhoAm 90*
Falstein, Eugene I 1908- *BiDrAPA 89*
Falstein, Louis 1909- *WhoAm 90*
Falter, John 1910-1982 *WhoAmA 91N*
Falter, Paul Richard 1926- *St&PR 91*
Falter, Vincent Eugene 1932- *WhoAm 90*
Faltings, Gerd 1954- *WhoAm 90*
Faltus, Frank John 1946- *BiDrAPA 89*
Falu, Eduardo *BioIn 16*
Faludi, Andreas K.F. 1940- *WhoWor 91*
Faludy, George 1913- *BioIn 16*
Faluyi, Akinsola Olusegun 1934- *WhoWor 91*
Falvay, Attila 1958- *IntWWM 90*
Falvey, Rosemary 1929- *WhoE 91*
Falvo, Donna R. 1945- *WhoAmW 91*
Falvo, Janet V. *WhoAmW 91*
Falvy, Zoltan 1928- *IntWWM 90*
Falwell, David George 1943- *St&PR 91*
Falwell, Jerry *BioIn 16*
Falwell, Jerry L. 1933- *WhoAm 90, WorAlBi*
Falzarano, Jeffrey Mark 1960- *WhoEmL 91*
Falzo, Anthony *BioIn 16*
Falzone, Joseph Sam 1917- *WhoE 91, WhoWor 91*
Falzone, Nicholas 1945- *WhoEmL 91*
Fama, Maria 1951- *WhoWrEP 89*
Fama, Maureen Caroline 1957- *St&PR 91*
Famadas, Jose 1908- *WhoE 91, WhoWor 91*
Fambrough, William Louis, Jr. 1954- *WhoEmL 91*
Famchon, Mireille Isabelle *WhoWor 91*
Fame, Georgie 1943- *OxCPMus*
Famighetti, Robert Joseph 1947- *WhoE 91*
Famiglietti, Nancy Zima 1956- *WhoAmW 91, WhoE 91, WhoEmL 91, WhoWor 91*
Famke *BioIn 16*
Fan, Hung Y. 1947- *WhoAm 90*
Fan, Jesen C-S 1927- *BiDrAPA 89*
Fan, John C.C. 1943- *St&PR 91*
Fan, Ky 1914- *WhoAm 90*
Fan, Paula 1952- *IntWWM 90*
Fan, Susie Wu 1938- *WhoWor 91*
Fanaroff, Sheri Van Greenby 1955- *WhoEmL 91*
Fanburg, Walter H 1936- *BiDrAPA 89*
Fancher, Donald Alden 1943- *St&PR 91*
Fancher, George H., Jr. 1939- *WhoWor 91*
Fancher, Mary Frank 1912- *WhoAmW 91*
Fancher, Michael Reilly 1946- *WhoAm 90*
Fancher, Mollie 1848-1910 *EncO&P 3*
Fancher, Regenia Sue 1945- *WhoSSW 91*
Fancher, Robert Burney 1940- *St&PR 91, WhoAm 90*
Fancher, Ronald L. 1943- *St&PR 91*
Fanchi, Joseph B. 1936- *St&PR 91*
Fanciullo, John A. *St&PR 91*
Fandl, Helmuth R. 1926- *St&PR 91*
Fandrich, Lamont H. 1951- *WhoEmL 91*
Fane, Bron *ConAu 32NR*
Fane, Elizabeth *FemiCLE*
Fane, Frances *BiDEWW*
Fane, Lawrence 1933- *WhoAmA 91*
Fane, Violet 1843-1905 *BioIn 16, FemiCLE*
Fanella, Nicholas Robert 1936- *St&PR 91*
Fanella, Robert J. 1950- *St&PR 91*
Fanelli, Beverly Hanlin 1957- *WhoE 91*
Fanelli, Emil Joseph, Jr. 1942- *St&PR 91*
Fanelli, George Marion 1898-1989 *BioIn 16*
Fanelli, Irene Susan 1956- *WhoEmL 91*
Fanelli, Joseph G. *BiDrAPA 89*
Fanelli, Michael Francis 1943- *IntWWM 90*
Fanestil, Darrell Dean 1933- *WhoAm 90*
Faneuf, Leo J. 1925- *St&PR 91*
Fanfani, Amintore *BioIn 16*
Fanfani, Amintore 1908- *WhoWor 91*
Fang Lizhi *BioIn 16*
Fang Yi 1909- *WhoWor 91*
Fang, Ai Ding *BiDrAPA 89*
Fang, Bertrand Tien-Chueh 1932- *WhoAm 90*
Fang, Chih-min 1900-1935 *BioIn 16*
Fang, Frank Fu 1930- *WhoAm 90*
Fang, Irving E 1929- *ConAu 31NR*
Fang, Joong 1923- *WhoAm 90*
Fang, Li-chih *BioIn 16*
Fang, Pen Jeng 1931- *WhoE 91*
Fang, Russell Ju Fu 1940- *WhoAm 90*
Fangen, Ronald 1895-1946 *DcScanL*
Fanger, Donald Lee 1929- *WhoAm 90*
Fangohr, Patricia Ann *BiDrAPA 89*
Fangor, Voy 1922- *WhoAmA 91*
Fangzhou, Gu 1926- *WhoWor 91*
Fanizzi, Michael Vincent *BiDrAPA 89*
Fanjul, Juan Vasquez de Mella y 1861-1928 *BioIn 16*
Fank, Debora Lynn 1952- *WhoAmW 91*
Fann, Al 1925- *DrBlPA 90*
Fann, Jesse Ruey *BiDrAPA 89*
Fann, William Edwin 1930- *BiDrAPA 89*
Fanniere, Francois-Auguste 1818-1900 *PenDiDA 89*
Fanniere, Francois-Joseph-Louis 1820-1897 *PenDiDA 89*
Fannin, Cliff 1924-1966 *Ballpl 90*
Fannin, Heather Fay 1958- *BiDrAPA 89*
Fannin, Marianne Benjamin 1933- *WhoAmW 91*
Fannin, W. Raymond, Jr. *BiDrAPA 89*
Fanning, Barry Hedges 1950- *WhoAm 90, WhoEmL 91*
Fanning, Belinda J. 1952- *WhoAmW 91*
Fanning, Constance Mary *BiDrAPA 89*
Fanning, David John 1955- *IntWWM 90*
Fanning, Debra A. *ODwPR 91*
Fanning, Galen Duane 1949- *WhoE 91*
Fanning, John Charles 1931- *St&PR 91, WhoAm 90*

Fanning, John F NewYTBS 90
Fanning, John Harold NewYTBS 90 [port]
Fanning, Katherine BioIn 16
Fanning, Katherine Woodruff 1927- WhoAm 90, WhoAmW 91
Fanning, Louis Albert 1927- WhoAm 90
Fanning, Margaret Beverly 1937- WhoAmW 91
Fanning, Marjorie L. WhoAmW 91
Fanning, Mary Margaret 1945- WhoSSW 91
Fanning, Robbie 1947- ConAu 31NR
Fanning, Robert Allen 1931- WhoAm 90
Fanning, Samuel J. 1912-1988 BioIn 16
Fanning, William James 1927- WhoAm 90
Fannon, Adrian 1938- WhoE 91
Fannon, Diane WhoAmW 91
Fanny EncCoWW
Fano, Enzo BioIn 16
Fano, Robert Mario 1917- WhoAm 90
Fano, Ugo 1912- WhoAm 90
Fanoni, Roy Henry 1924- BiDrAPA 89
Fanovich, Frank 1922- Ballpl 90
Fanshaw, Mrs BiDEWW
Fanshaw, Margaret BiDEWW
Fanshawe, Ann 1625-1680 BiDEWW, FemiCLE
Fanshawe, Anne Harrison 1625-1680 BioIn 16
Fanshawe, Catherine 1765-1834 FemiCLE
Fanshawe, David Arthur 1942- IntWWM 90
Fanshel, David 1923- WhoAm 90
Fansler, Kevin Spain 1938- WhoE 91
Fant, Albert Edward, III BiDrAPA 89
Fant, Douglas Vernon 1952- WhoEmL 91
Fant, George C., Jr. 1926- St&PR 91
Fant, Joseph Lewis, III 1928- WhoAm 90
Fant, Patrick Joseph 1948- WhoAm 90
Fanta, Donald C. 1928- St&PR 91
Fanta, Donald Charles 1928- WhoAm 90
Fanta, Paul Edward 1921- WhoAm 90
Fantaci, Mary Kathryn 1962- WhoAmW 91
Fantasia, Tilia Joan 1936- WhoE 91
Fantastici, Agostino PenDiDA 89
Fantazzi, Nick 1949- St&PR 91
Fante, James Peter 1950- WhoEmL 91
Fante, John 1909-1983 BioIn 16, ConLC 60 [port]
Fantel, Ernest BiDrAPA 89
Fantel, Hans 1922- ConAu 31NR
Fanthorpe, R Lionel 1935- ConAu 32NR
Fanthorpe, U. A. 1929- FemiCLE
Fantin-Latour, Henri 1836-1904 WorAlBi
Fantini, Mario D. BioIn 16
Fantini, Mario D. 1927?-1989 ConAu 129
Fantini, Robert S. 1927- St&PR 91
Fantl, Kurt BiDrAPA 89
Fantl, Kurt 1914- EncO&P 3
Fantle, Jeffrey Morris 1948- WhoAm 90
Fantle, Sheldon W. 1923- WhoAm 90, WhoE 91
Fanton, Dolores Pfrengle 1952- WhoEmL 91
Fanton, Jonathan BioIn 16
Fanton, Jonathan Foster 1943- WhoAm 90, WhoE 91
Fanton, Roland Benjamin 1943- WhoWrEP 89
Fantone, Christine Lynn 1951- WhoAmW 91
Fantone, Emmanuel J BiDrAPA 89
Fantoni, Andrea 1699-1734 PenDiDA 89
Fantoni, Barry 1940- ConAu 129
Fantozzi, Peggy Ryone 1948- WhoAm 90
Fantozzi, Roberto 1947- WhoWor 91
Fantozzi, Umberto St&PR 91
Fantus, Robert A BiDrAPA 89
Fanucci, Jerome Benedict 1924- WhoAm 90
Fanuele, Michael Anthony 1938- WhoAm 90, WhoE 91, WhoWor 91
Fanuele, Vincent James 1950- WhoEmL 91
Fanus, Pauline Rife 1925- WhoAmW 91, WhoE 91, WhoWor 91
Fanwick, Ernest 1926- WhoAm 90
Fanzone, Carmen 1941- Ballpl 90
Faour, Anna Rose 1929- WhoAmW 91
Faqih, Asad Mansur al- 1909-1989 BioIn 16
Fara, John William 1942- St&PR 91, WhoAm 90
Farabee, Dale H 1926- BiDrAPA 89
Farabee, Ray 1932- WhoSSW 91
Farabee, Theodore Maurice 1950- WhoE 91
Farabow, Ford Franklin, Jr. 1938- WhoAm 90
Farace, Linda Diana 1948- WhoAmW 91
Farace-Epley, Diana Maria 1948- WhoAmW 91
Faraci, John Vincent, Jr. 1950- WhoAm 90
Faraday, Bruce John 1919- WhoSSW 91
Faraday, Michael 1791-1867 BioIn 16, EncO&P 3, EncPaPR 91, WorAlBi
Farady, John T. 1942- St&PR 91
Farag, Samir Fouad BiDrAPA 89
Faragasso, Jack 1929- WhoAmA 91, WhoE 91
Farage, Donald J. WhoAm 90, WhoWor 91
Faraghan, George Telford 1926- WhoE 91
Farago, Elena 1878-1954 EncCoWW
Farago, Margaret Ellen 1954- WhoAmW 91
Farago, Odon 1896-1935 PenDiDA 89
Farago-Fatma, Elena EncCoWW
Farah, Ardeshir NewAgMG
Farah, Benjamin Frederick 1956- WhoEmL 91
Farah, Caesar Elie 1929- WhoAm 90
Farah, Cynthia Weber 1949- WhoAmW 91
Farah, Hassan Noor 1950- WhoWor 91
Farah, James Clifton 1947- St&PR 91
Farah, Joseph Francis 1954- WhoAm 90
Farah, Madelain 1934- WhoWrEP 89
Farah, Moumin Bahdon 1939- WhoWor 91
Farah, Roger WhoAm 90, WhoSSW 91
Farah, Subhi Joseph 1903- St&PR 91
Faraldo, Anthony Robert 1941- WhoSSW 91
Farao, Lucia Victoria 1927- WhoHisp 91
Faraone, Ted 1956- WhoE 91
Faraoni, Melvin Ray 1944- St&PR 91
Fararo, Thomas John 1933- WhoAm 90
Faraut, Jean-Pierre 1944- WhoWor 91
Farb, Edith H. 1928- WhoAmW 91
Farb, Harry H BiDrAPA 89
Farb, Nathan BioIn 16
Farb, Peter 1929-1980 AuBYP 90
Farb, Susan ODwPR 91
Farb, Thomas Forest 1956- WhoE 91
Farbach, Carl Frederick 1901-1988 BioIn 16
Farbaky, Gezane Charlotte 1924- IntWWM 90
Farbar, Bernard BioIn 16
Farber, Amanda 1957- WhoAmA 91
Farber, Anne 1948- WhoEmL 91
Farber, Arthur David 1947- St&PR 91, WhoAm 90
Farber, Barry Leslie 1946- BiDrAPA 89
Farber, Barry M 1944- BiDrAPA 89
Farber, Bernard 1922- WhoAm 90
Farber, Bernard John 1948- WhoEmL 91, WhoWor 91
Farber, Daniel Alan 1950- WhoEmL 91
Farber, David J. BioIn 16
Farber, Deborah 1949- WhoAmA 91
Farber, Dennis H 1946- WhoAmA 91
Farber, Donald C ConAu 30NR
Farber, Emmanuel 1918- WhoAm 90
Farber, Eric S. 1961- WhoEmL 91
Farber, Evan Ira 1922- WhoAm 90
Farber, George Allan 1934- WhoSSW 91
Farber, Irving J 1926- BiDrAPA 89
Farber, Isadore E. 1917- WhoAm 90
Farber, Jack Lee 1946- BiDrAPA 89
Farber, Jackie 1927- WhoAm 90
Farber, Jay Joel 1932- WhoAm 90
Farber, John 1925- St&PR 91
Farber, John J. 1925- WhoAm 90
Farber, Martin Robert 1951- WhoE 91
Farber, Maurice 1911- St&PR 91
Farber, Maya M 1936- WhoAmA 91
Farber, Murray 1931- ODwPR 91
Farber, Norma BioIn 16
Farber, Norma 1909-1984 AuBYP 90
Farber, Paul Francis 1951- St&PR 91
Farber, Robert Holton 1914- WhoAm 90
Farber, Rosann Alexander 1944- WhoAmW 91
Farber, Saul Joseph WhoAm 90, WhoE 91
Farber, Seymour Morgan 1912- WhoAm 90
Farber, Thomas 1944- BioIn 16
Farber, Viola Anna 1931- WhoAm 90
Farberman, Harold 1929- IntWWM 90, PenDiMP
Farberman, Harold 1930- WhoAm 90
Farbstein, Burt BioIn 16
Farcot, Jean-Christian 1946- WhoWor 91
Fard, Kayoumars BiDrAPA 89
Fareed, Ahmed Ali 1932- WhoWor 91
Farell, H. Dan 1949- St&PR 91
Farella, Steven BioIn 16
Farenga, Patrick Lawrence 1957- WhoE 91
Farenthold, Frances Tarlton 1926- WhoAm 90, WhoAmW 91
Farentino, James 1938- WhoAm 90
Farer, Tom Joel 1935- WhoAm 90, WhoE 91
Fares, William O 1942- WhoAmA 91
Faretra, Gloria BiDrAPA 89
Farewell, Kelly BioIn 16
Farfan-Ramirez, Lucrecia WhoHisp 91
Farfar, Nermin BiDrAPA 89
Fargas, Antonio 1946- ConTFT 8, DrBlPA 90
Fargason, Rachel Epstein BiDrAPA 89
Fargis, Paul McKenna 1939- St&PR 91, WhoAm 90
Fargnoli, John A., Jr. 1946- St&PR 91
Fargo, Bronson Hart 1929- St&PR 91
Fargo, John Jay 1950- WhoEmL 91
Fargo, Louis James 1938- WhoAm 90
Fargo, Lucille Foster 1880- AuBYP 90
Fargo, William G. 1818-1881 WorAlBi
Fargo, William George 1818-1881 EncABHB 6 [port]
Farha, Alfred S. 1933- St&PR 91
Farha, Bryan 1957- WhoSSW 91
Farha, James Tannel 1941- St&PR 91
Farha, William Farah 1908- WhoAm 90
Farhad, Mohammad 1938-1987 BioIn 16
Farhi, Jean Claude 1940- WhoAmA 91
Faria, Gilberto 1942- WhoHisp 91
Faria, Luciano L. Oliveira 1921- WhoWor 91
Faria, Thomas George 1926- St&PR 91
Farian, Babette Sommerich 1916- WhoE 91
Farian, Barbette S 1916- WhoAmA 91
Farias, Ramiro, Jr. 1949- WhoHisp 91
Farias-Campero, Pablo Jose 1958- BiDrAPA 89
Farias-Daniels, Geraldine BiDrAPA 89
Faricy, Richard Thomas 1928- WhoAm 90
Farid, Basil M. 1959- BiDrAPA 89
Farida, Queen of Egypt 1921-1988 BioIn 16
Faridi, Tariq Mahmood 1948- BiDrAPA 89
Fariello, Frank Anthony 1934- St&PR 91
Faries, Belmont 1913- WhoAm 90
Faries, Charles E., Jr. 1933- St&PR 91
Farigoule, Louis MajTwCW
Farin, Lou Joseph 1943- St&PR 91
Farin Nepomechie, Susana 1959- WhoEmL 91
Farina DrBlPA 90
Farina, Almo 1950- WhoWor 91
Farina, Ana Beatriz 1950- WhoAmW 91, WhoEmL 91, WhoWor 91
Farina, Julie Lynn 1950- WhoEmL 91
Farina, Manuel BiDrAPA 89
Farina, Mark D. 1949- St&PR 91
Farina, Peter R. 1946- WhoE 91
Farina, Robert A. 1943- St&PR 91
Farina, Vincent M. 1953- St&PR 91
Farinacci, Jorge A. 1924- WhoHisp 91
Farinacci, Kathleen BiDrAPA 89
Farinas, Geronimo BiDrAPA 89
Farine, Cheryl Lee 1951- WhoAmW 91
Farinella, Donald Damian 1933- St&PR 91
Farinella, Paul James 1926- WhoAm 90, WhoE 91
Farinelli 1705-1782 PenDiMP
Farinelli, Jean L. ODwPR 91
Farinelli, Jean L. 1946- St&PR 91, WhoAm 90, WhoAmW 91
Farinha, Guilherme Manuel 1931- WhoWor 91
Farinholt, Larkin H. NewYTBS 90
Farinholt, Larkin Hundley 1905- WhoAm 90
Faris, Brunel De Bost 1937- WhoAmA 91
Faris, Corinne M. 1955- St&PR 91
Faris, Frank Edgar 1919- WhoE 91
Faris, George N. 1941- St&PR 91
Faris, Ingrid Barth 1951- WhoAmW 91
Faris, Lucile A. 1939- WhoAmW 91
Faris, Matthew Scott 1965- WhoSSW 91
Faris, Mustapha 1933- WhoWor 91
Faris, Peter Kinzie 1943- WhoAmA 91
Faris, Richard K. 1946- St&PR 91
Faris, Robert William 1958- WhoEmL 91
Faris, William 1728-1804 PenDiDA 89
Faris, William Elbert 1925- WhoSSW 91
Faris-Stockem, Debbie 1955- WhoAmW 91
Farisani, T. Simon BioIn 16
Farish, Blair BioIn 16
Farish, Charles Bernard 1947- St&PR 91
Farish, Charles Morrison 1946- WhoEmL 91
Farish, James Matthew 1946- WhoWor 91
Farish, Margaret K. 1918- IntWWM 90
Farish, Robert Edward, Jr. 1951- WhoSSW 91
Farish, Stephen Thomas, Jr. 1936- IntWWM 90
Farish, Teresa Irene 1953- WhoAmW 91
Farison, James Blair 1938- WhoAm 90
Fariss, Bruce Lindsay 1934- WhoAm 90
Fariss, James Lee, Jr. 1934- WhoAm 90
Farjeon, Benjamin Leopold 1838-1903 BioIn 16
Farjeon, Eleanor 1881-1965 BioIn 16, FemiCLE
Farjeon, Herbert 1887-1945 OxCPMus
Farkas, Andrew 1936- IntWWM 90
Farkas, Andrew E. 1947- St&PR 91
Farkas, Babette Frances BiDrAPA 89
Farkas, Edward Lewis 1953- BiDrAPA 89
Farkas, Emil 1946- ConAu 32NR
Farkas, Ferenc 1905- IntWWM 90
Farkas, Hazel D 1937- BiDrAPA 89
Farkas, Hazel Daphne Martin 1937- WhoE 91
Farkas, Israel 1948- St&PR 91
Farkas, James Paul 1947- WhoE 91, WhoWor 91
Farkas, John 1942- St&PR 91
Farkas, Mary E BiDrAPA 89
Farkas, Philip 1914- ConAu 31NR, IntWWM 90
Farkas, Philip Francis 1914- WhoAm 90
Farkas, Robin Lewis 1933- St&PR 91, WhoAm 90, WhoE 91
Farkas, Ruth Lewis 1906- WhoAm 90
Farkas, Stephen Gerard 1960- WhoE 91
Farkas, Walter M. 1935- WhoE 91
Farkas, Walter Morton BiDrAPA 89
Farland, Denise B. 1954- WhoEmL 91
Farland, Victor L BiDrAPA 89
Farley, Andrew Newell 1934- WhoAm 90, WhoE 91
Farley, Arthur John 1939- BiDrAPA 89
Farley, Carol 1936- AuBYP 90
Farley, Carole 1946- IntWWM 90, PenDiMP, WhoAm 90
Farley, Charles P. ODwPR 91
Farley, D. Stephen 1928- WhoE 91
Farley, Daniel William 1955- St&PR 91
Farley, Donald William 1943- WhoE 91
Farley, Edward R., Jr. 1918- St&PR 91
Farley, Edward Raymond, Jr. 1918- WhoAm 90
Farley, Eugene Joseph 1950- WhoE 91
Farley, Eugene Shedden, Jr. 1927- WhoAm 90
Farley, Frederick A. 1952- St&PR 91
Farley, Gail Conley 1936- WhoSSW 91
Farley, Genevieve Marie 1952- WhoAmW 91
Farley, Gilbert BioIn 16
Farley, Hugh T. WhoE 91
Farley, James A. 1888-1976 WorAlBi
Farley, James Alan BiDrAPA 89
Farley, James Aloysius 1888-1976 BiDrUSE 89, BioIn 16
Farley, James B. 1930- BioIn 16, St&PR 91
Farley, James Bernard 1930- WhoAm 90
Farley, James Duncan 1926- St&PR 91, WhoAm 90, WhoE 91, WhoWor 91
Farley, James Newton 1928- St&PR 91
Farley, James Parker 1924- WhoAm 90, WhoWor 91
Farley, James Patrick 1949- WhoEmL 91
Farley, James Thomas 1925- WhoAm 90
Farley, James Thompson 1829-1886 AmLegL
Farley, Jayne Dorothy BiDrAPA 89
Farley, Jennie 1932- ConAu 132
Farley, Jennie Tiffany Towle 1932- WhoAmW 91
Farley, John 1915-1990 BioIn 16
Farley, John Joseph 1920- WhoAm 90
Farley, John Michael 1930- WhoAm 90
Farley, John Wayne 1945- WhoSSW 91
Farley, Joseph 1961- WhoWrEP 89
Farley, Joseph J. 1923- St&PR 91
Farley, Joseph M. 1927- St&PR 91
Farley, Joseph McConnell 1927- WhoAm 90, WhoSSW 91
Farley, Laurence Joseph 1936- WhoAm 90
Farley, Lyle O. 1944- St&PR 91
Farley, Margaret M. 1952- WhoAm 90
Farley, Margaret Mary 1926- WhoAmW 91
Farley, Marian Diedre 1955- WhoAmW 91
Farley, Morgan 1901-1988 BioIn 16
Farley, Myron Foster 1921- WhoWrEP 89
Farley, Norvil Lee 1922- St&PR 91
Farley, Patricia B. ODwPR 91
Farley, Paul Emerson 1930- St&PR 91, WhoAm 90
Farley, Paul John, Jr. 1951- WhoE 91
Farley, Peggy Ann 1947- WhoAmW 91, WhoE 91, WhoEmL 91, WhoWor 91
Farley, Philip Judson 1916- WhoAm 90
Farley, Raymond Francis 1924- WhoAm 90
Farley, Robert C. 1946- St&PR 91
Farley, Robert D. 1941- St&PR 91
Farley, Robert Donald 1941- WhoAm 90
Farley, Robert John 1948- WhoSSW 91
Farley, Robert Joseph 1960- WhoEmL 91
Farley, Russell Clifford 1957- WhoEmL 91
Farley, Stacey Jeanne WhoWrEP 89
Farley, Stephen A. 1944- St&PR 91
Farley, Terrence Michael 1930- WhoAm 90, WhoE 91
Farley, Walter 1915-1989 AnObit 1989, BioIn 16
Farley, Walter 1916-1989 CurBio 90N
Farley, Walter 1920- AuBYP 90
Farley, Walter Lorimer 1925- WhoWrEP 89
Farley, William F. BioIn 16
Farley, William F. 1942- WhoAm 90
Farley-Villalobos, Robbie Jean 1953- WhoHisp 91
Farling, Robert J. 1936- St&PR 91, WhoAm 90
Farlo, Joseph P. BioIn 16
Farlow, Harry 1882-1956 WhoAmA 91N
Farlow, Lynne Ann 1960- WhoEmL 91
Farlow, Tal 1921- BioIn 16

Farm, Gerald E 1935- WhoAmA 91
Farmakides, John Basil WhoAm 90
Farmakis, George Leonard 1925- WhoWor 91
Farman, Allan George 1949- WhoEmL 91
Farman, Richard D. 1935- St&PR 91
Farman, Richard Donald 1935- WhoAm 90
Farmanfarmaian, Khodadad 1928- WhoWor 91
Farmar, George Edwin 1923- St&PR 91
Farmer, Art BioIn 16
Farmer, Beverley 1941- FemiCLE
Farmer, Carol Ann 1944- WhoAmW 91
Farmer, Catherine A. 1948- ODwPR 91
Farmer, Catherine Armbruster 1948- WhoEmL 91
Farmer, Catherine Schwallie 1959- WhoAmW 91
Farmer, Charles Albert 1930- St&PR 91
Farmer, Crofton Bernard 1931- WhoAm 90
Farmer, David Christopher 1945- WhoEmL 91
Farmer, David Lowell 1945- St&PR 91
Farmer, Deborah Lyn 1954- WhoEmL 91
Farmer, Donald Frederick 1944- St&PR 91
Farmer, Donald Jackson 1925- St&PR 91
Farmer, Ed 1949- Ballpl 90
Farmer, Elaine F. 1937- WhoAmW 91
Farmer, Fannie 1857-1915 WorAlBi
Farmer, Forest J. BioIn 16
Farmer, Frances 1914-1970 BioAmW, WorAlBi
Farmer, Gary BioIn 16
Farmer, Gary P. 1943- St&PR 91
Farmer, Guy 1912- St&PR 91
Farmer, Guy Otto, II 1941- WhoSSW 91
Farmer, H. Randolph 1939- St&PR 91
Farmer, Hallie BioIn 16
Farmer, Herbert Henry 1892-1981 DcNaB 1981
Farmer, J. Lloyd 1925- St&PR 91
Farmer, James BioIn 16
Farmer, James 1920- WhoAm 90
Farmer, James L. 1920- WorAlBi
Farmer, James Prentice, Jr. 1951- WhoEmL 91
Farmer, Janell Beth Hilton 1956- WhoAmW 91
Farmer, Janene Elizabeth 1946- WhoAmW 91
Farmer, Joe Sam 1931- WhoAm 90, WhoSSW 91
Farmer, John David 1939- WhoAm 90, WhoAmA 91
Farmer, John Martin 1934- WhoE 91
Farmer, John Quincy 1823-1904 AmLegL
Farmer, Josephus 1894- MusmAFA
Farmer, Kenneth Wayne 1938- St&PR 91
Farmer, Lenore 1943- BiDrAPA 89
Farmer, Lesley Suzanne 1949- WhoAmW 91
Farmer, Mabel McKibbin 1903- WhoAmA 91N
Farmer, Mary Bauder 1953- WhoAmW 91
Farmer, Norman Kittrell, Jr. 1934- WhoSSW 91
Farmer, Penelope 1939- AuBYP 90
Farmer, Philip Jose 1918- MajTwCW, RGTwCSF, WhoWrEP 89, WorAlBi
Farmer, Phillip W. 1938- St&PR 91
Farmer, Richard Carl 1950- WhoSSW 91
Farmer, Richard Gilbert 1931- WhoAm 90
Farmer, Richard T. 1934- WhoAm 90
Farmer, Robert Archie 1931- BiDrAPA 89
Farmer, Robert E. 1929- St&PR 91
Farmer, Robert Lindsay 1922- WhoAm 90
Farmer, Roy F. 1916- St&PR 91
Farmer, Scott David BiDrAPA 89
Farmer, Sharon Lee 1950- BiDrAPA 89
Farmer, Susan Baker 1953- WhoEmL 91
Farmer, Susan Lawson 1942- WhoAm 90
Farmer, Thomas Laurence 1923- WhoAm 90
Farmer, Thomas Shelby 1931- WhoSSW 91
Farmer, Thomas Wohlsen 1914- WhoAm 90
Farmer, Timothy David 1954- WhoEmL 91
Farmer, Virginia 1922- IntWWM 90
Farmer, Welford Stuart 1925- WhoAm 90
Farmer, Wendell AuBYP 90
Farmer, William A. 1953- St&PR 91
Farmer, William C. 1915- BioIn 16
Farmer, William Michael 1956- WhoE 91
Farmer-Dougan, Valeri Ann 1960- WhoAmW 91
Farmer-Patrick, Sandra BioIn 16
Farmer's Brother WhNaAH
Farnadi, Edith 1921-1973 PenDiMP
Farnagle, Alphaed E. WhoWrEP 89
Farnam, Anne 1940- WhoAm 90
Farnam, Walter Edward 1941- St&PR 91, WhoE 91
Farnan, D J 1919- ConAu 130
Farnan, Frank E. ODwPR 91
Farnborough, Mariabella, Jr. 1665- BiDEWW
Farnborough, Mariabella, Sr. 1626-1708 BiDEWW
Farncombe, Charles 1919- PenDiMP
Farncombe, Charles Frederick 1919- IntWWM 90
Farnel, Frank Jacques 1962- WhoWor 91
Farnell, Gerald William 1925- WhoAm 90
Farner, Donald S. 1915-1989 BioIn 16
Farner, Eleanor G. St&PR 91
Farner, Mark BioIn 16
Farner, Peter Worden 1954- WhoWor 91
Farnes, Gary William 1940- WhoAm 90
Farnetti, Giorgio 1923- WhoWor 91
Farney, Henry F. 1847-1916 WhNaAH
Farney, Thomas Patrick 1948- WhoEmL 91
Farnham, Alexander 1926- WhoAmA 91, WhoE 91
Farnham, Anthony Edward 1930- WhoAm 90
Farnham, Eliza 1815-1864 FemiCLE
Farnham, Eliza Wood Burhans 1815-1864 BioIn 16
Farnham, Emily 1912- WhoAmA 91, WhoE 91
Farnham, George Railton 1914- WhoAm 90
Farnham, Sally 1876-1943 BiDWomA
Farnham, Shawnee Lynn 1954- BiDrAPA 89
Farnham, Sherman Brett 1912- WhoAm 90
Farnham, Stanley Everett 1930- St&PR 91
Farnham, Wallace Dean 1928- WhoAm 90
Farnham, Willard Carlton 1937- St&PR 91
Farnham, William H. 1936- St&PR 91
Farnham-Diggory, Sylvia 1927- WhoAm 90
Farni, Susan Hazel 1949- WhoAmW 91
Farnie, H. B. 1820-1889 OxCPMus
Farnon, Robert 1917- OxCPMus, PenDiMP A
Farnon, Robert Joseph 1917- IntWWM 90
Farnow, Arthur D. 1916- St&PR 91
Farnow, Richard A. St&PR 91
Farnsley, Charles P. NewYTBS 90
Farnsworth, Alan H. 1952- St&PR 91
Farnsworth, Cherrill Kay 1948- WhoAmW 91
Farnsworth, Edward Allan 1928- WhoAm 90
Farnsworth, Ellen Jane 1943- WhoAmW 91
Farnsworth, Frank Albert WhoAm 90
Farnsworth, Helen Sawyer WhoAmA 91
Farnsworth, James Virgel 1951- St&PR 91
Farnsworth, Janice L. 1938- WhoAmW 91
Farnsworth, Jeffrey Earl 1959- WhoEmL 91
Farnsworth, Jerry 1895- WhoAmA 91N
Farnsworth, Julianne 1959- WhoSSW 91
Farnsworth, Ken BioIn 16
Farnsworth, Marjorie Anne Whyte 1921- WhoAmW 91
Farnsworth, Michael Gordon BiDrAPA 89
Farnsworth, Philip Richeson 1941- WhoAm 90
Farnsworth, Philo T. 1906-1971 BioIn 16
Farnsworth, Ralph 1935- St&PR 91
Farnsworth, Richard 1920- WhoAm 90
Farnsworth, Shorty WhoWrEP 89
Farnsworth, Susan Elizabeth 1955- WhoAmW 91
Farnsworth, Susan Steele Higgins 1949- WhoAmW 91
Farnsworth, T. Brooke 1945- WhoSSW 91, WhoWor 91
Farnsworth, William P. 1901-1989 BioIn 16
Farnum, Alexander 1830-1884 AmLegL
Farnum, Jonathan K. 1939- St&PR 91
Farnum, Jonathan Knight 1939- WhoE 91
Farnum, Mark 1923- St&PR 91
Farnum, Sylvia Arlyce 1936- WhoAmW 91
Farokhi, Elizabeth Dupree 1948- WhoAmW 91
Faron, John Frank 1933- WhoWor 91
Faron, Robert Steven 1947- WhoEmL 91
Farooq, Mohammed BioIn 16
Farooque, Rokeya Sultana BiDrAPA 89
Farouk 1920-1965 PolLCME
Farouky, Fawzia Husiene 1927- WhoWor 91
Farouq, Fadlullah 1934- WhoWor 91
Farquhar, David Andross 1928- IntWWM 90
Farquhar, Francis Peloubet 1887-1974 BioIn 16
Farquhar, George 1678-1707 WorAlBi
Farquhar, Gerald Blake 1949- WhoEmL 91, WhoSSW 91
Farquhar, James Allan BiDrAPA 89
Farquhar, John William 1927- WhoAm 90
Farquhar, Karen Lee 1958- WhoAmW 91
Farquhar, Marilyn Gist 1928- WhoAm 90, WhoAmW 91
Farquhar, Norman 1921- WhoAm 90
Farquhar, Paul George 1949- WhoWrEP 89
Farquhar, Peter Henry 1947- WhoE 91
Farquhar, Robin Hugh 1938- WhoAm 90
Farquhar, Thomas H. 1938- St&PR 91
Farquharson, Donald E. 1947- St&PR 91
Farquharson, Gordon MacKay 1928- WhoAm 90
Farr, Beverly Agnes 1928- WhoAmW 91
Farr, Caroline TwCCr&M 91
Farr, Charles Sims 1920- WhoAm 90, WhoE 91
Farr, David Donald 1948- IntWWM 90
Farr, David N. 1955- St&PR 91
Farr, Dennis Larry Ashwell 1929- WhoWor 91
Farr, Douglas Alan 1938- BiDrAPA 89
Farr, Finis King 1904- SpyFic
Farr, Florence 1860-1917 BioIn 16, FemiCLE
Farr, Fred 1914-1973 WhoAmA 91N
Farr, Fredrick Sharon 1910- WhoAm 90
Farr, H. Richard 1943- St&PR 91
Farr, Harvey A. ODwPR 91
Farr, Henry Bartow, Jr. 1921- WhoAm 90
Farr, Ivanne E. 1940- WhoAmW 91
Farr, Jack EncACom
Farr, James Francis 1911- WhoE 91, WhoWor 91
Farr, James Michael 1946- WhoWrEP 89
Farr, James Woodhull 1952- WhoE 91
Farr, Jamie WhoAm 90
Farr, Jamie 1934- WorAlBi
Farr, Jo-Ann Hunter 1936- WhoAmW 91, WhoE 91
Farr, John TwCCr&M 91
Farr, John Richard 1857-1933 AmLegL
Farr, Lona Mae 1941- WhoE 91
Farr, M. Paige 1945- WhoAmW 91
Farr, Mel 1944- St&PR 91
Farr, Morrill S. 1910- St&PR 91
Farr, Norman Nelson 1928- WhoAm 90
Farr, Patricia Hudak 1945- WhoAmW 91
Farr, Richard Claborn 1928- WhoAm 90
Farr, Richard Studley 1922- WhoAm 90
Farr, Rodger K BiDrAPA 89
Farr, Russell Mark 1955- BiDrAPA 89
Farr, Sidney Saylor 1932- WhoAmW 91
Farr, Steve 1956- Ballpl 90
Farr, Thomas Carey 1952- WhoEmL 91
Farr, Wallace J. 1921- St&PR 91
Farr, Walter Emil, Jr. 1945- WhoSSW 91
Farr, Walter Floy, Jr. 1939- BiDrAPA 89
Farr, Walter Greene, Jr. 1925- WhoAm 90
Farr, William Daven 1910- St&PR 91
Farr, William Joseph 1947- WhoE 91
Farr, William Robert 1939- St&PR 91
Farr, William Sharon 1903- St&PR 91
Farra, Chucri Ronald 1948- WhoE 91, WhoEmL 91, WhoWor 91
Farragut, David Glasgow 1801-1870 BioIn 16, WorAlBi
Farrah, Abdelkader 1926- ConDes 90
Farrakhan, Louis 1933- News 90 [port], WorAlBi
Farrales, Rodrigo L, Jr. 1943- BiDrAPA 89
Farrall, George William 1959- WhoE 91, WhoEmL 91, WhoWor 91
Farrall, Robert A. 1932- St&PR 91
Farrally, Betty 1915-1989 BioIn 16
Farrand, George Nixon, Jr. 1936- WhoE 91
Farrand, John 1944- BioIn 16
Farrant, Elizabeth 1914- WhoWrEP 89
Farrar, Beverly Jayne 1928- WhoAmW 91
Farrar, Clarence Raymond 1934- St&PR 91
Farrar, Donald Eugene 1931- WhoAm 90
Farrar, Donald Keith 1938- St&PR 91
Farrar, Douglas Evan 1957- WhoEmL 91
Farrar, Elaine Willardson 1929- WhoAmW 91, WhoWor 91
Farrar, Eleanor BioIn 16
Farrar, Elizabeth Grace Turrell 1957- WhoEmL 91
Farrar, Fletcher F. 1921- St&PR 91
Farrar, Frank Leroy 1929- WhoAm 90
Farrar, Geraldine 1882-1967 PenDiMP, WorAlBi
Farrar, Henry Cheairs 1926- WhoSSW 91
Farrar, James Jackson 1939- St&PR 91
Farrar, Janice M. 1933- ODwPR 91
Farrar, Joe Edmund 1947- St&PR 91
Farrar, John Edson, II 1938- WhoWor 91
Farrar, Marjorie S. 1922- St&PR 91
Farrar, Mark Edward 1958- WhoSSW 91
Farrar, Martha Carver BiDrAPA 89
Farrar, Pauline Elizabeth 1928- WhoAmW 91, WhoSSW 91
Farrar, Preston W. AmLegL
Farrar, Reginald Warren, Jr 1922- WhoSSW 91
Farrar, Ross William 1938- WhoE 91
Farrar, Stephen D. 1950- St&PR 91
Farre, Thomas R. 1946- WhoWrEP 89
Farrehi, Cyrus 1935- WhoAm 90
Farrell, Anne Van Ness 1935- WhoAmW 91
Farrell, B. A. ConAu 130
Farrell, Ben ConAu 30NR
Farrell, Brian ConAu 130
Farrell, Brian 1929- WhoWor 91
Farrell, Brian Anthony 1912- ConAu 130
Farrell, Brian J. 1954- St&PR 91
Farrell, Charles 1901-1990 BioIn 16, NewYTBS 90 [port]
Farrell, Charles F. 1930- St&PR 91
Farrell, Corinne BioIn 16
Farrell, David C. 1933- St&PR 91
Farrell, David Coakley 1933- WhoAm 90
Farrell, David J. 1950- St&PR 91
Farrell, Dennis BioIn 16
Farrell, Dennis Joseph 1962- WhoE 91
Farrell, Dick 1934-1977 Ballpl 90
Farrell, Doc 1901-1966 Ballpl 90
Farrell, Duke 1866-1925 Ballpl 90
Farrell, E. Joan 1925- WhoE 91
Farrell, Edgar Henry 1924- WhoE 91, WhoWor 91
Farrell, Edmund James 1927- WhoAm 90, WhoSSW 91, WhoWrEP 89
Farrell, Edward Joseph 1917- WhoAm 90, WhoWor 91
Farrell, Edward Vincent 1940- St&PR 91
Farrell, Edwin David 1941- WhoSSW 91
Farrell, Eileen 1920- IntWWM 90, PenDiMP, WorAlBi
Farrell, Eugene George 1905- WhoAm 90
Farrell, Frank A., Jr. 1938- St&PR 91
Farrell, Gaston Damian 1961- WhoEmL 91
Farrell, Gregory Alan 1942- WhoE 91
Farrell, Henry Moseley 1936- St&PR 91
Farrell, J G 1935-1979 MajTwCW
Farrell, J. Michael 1941- WhoAm 90
Farrell, James Andrew 1957- WhoEmL 91
Farrell, James E. 1940- St&PR 91
Farrell, James H. 1926- St&PR 91
Farrell, James Howden 1928- St&PR 91
Farrell, James Joseph 1949- WhoWrEP 89
Farrell, James P. 1903-1988 BioIn 16
Farrell, James T. 1904-1979 EncAL, MajTwCW, WorAlBi
Farrell, Jeremiah Edward 1937- WhoAm 90
Farrell, John 1876-1921 Ballpl 90
Farrell, John 1962- Ballpl 90
Farrell, John L., Jr. 1929- WhoAm 90
Farrell, John R. 1950- St&PR 91
Farrell, John S. 1938- St&PR 91
Farrell, John Stanislaus 1931- WhoWor 91
Farrell, John Timothy 1947- WhoAm 90
Farrell, Joseph 1935- WhoAm 90, WhoWor 91
Farrell, Joseph Christopher 1935- St&PR 91, WhoAm 90, WhoE 91
Farrell, Joseph David 1959- WhoEmL 91
Farrell, Joseph Michael 1922- WhoAm 90
Farrell, June Eleanor 1916- WhoAmW 91
Farrell, June Martinick 1940- WhoAm 90, WhoAmW 91
Farrell, Katherine L 1857- WhoAmA 91N
Farrell, Kathy St&PR 91
Farrell, Kerby 1913-1975 Ballpl 90
Farrell, Kevin John 1957- WhoE 91
Farrell, Larry Charles 1941- WhoSSW 91
Farrell, Louis G. 1955- St&PR 91
Farrell, M. J. BioIn 16, WorAu 1980
Farrell, Mairead BioIn 16
Farrell, Mary ODwPR 91
Farrell, Mary Cooney 1949- WhoAm 90
Farrell, Mike 1939- WhoAm 90, WorAlBi
Farrell, Naomi 1941- WhoAmW 91
Farrell, Neal Francis 1934- St&PR 91
Farrell, Neal J. 1932- St&PR 91
Farrell, Neal Joseph 1932- WhoAm 90
Farrell, Pamela Barnard WhoWrEP 89
Farrell, Pamela Barnard 1943- WhoAmW 91
Farrell, Patricia Ann 1945- WhoEmL 91
Farrell, Patricia Carolyn 1951- BiDrAPA 89
Farrell, Patrick Joseph 1939- St&PR 91
Farrell, Paul Edward 1926- WhoAm 90
Farrell, Paul Harry 1927- WhoAm 90
Farrell, Peter Snow 1924- IntWWM 90
Farrell, Raymond Maurice, Jr. 1940- WhoE 91
Farrell, Regis H. 1950- St&PR 91
Farrell, Richard J. 1943- St&PR 91
Farrell, Rita Ann 1955- WhoEmL 91
Farrell, Robert Edward 1946- WhoE 91
Farrell, Robert Steven 1960- WhoE 91
Farrell, Rodger Edward 1932- WhoAm 90
Farrell, Roger Hamlin 1929- WhoAm 90
Farrell, Ronald William 1951- WhoE 91
Farrell, Sandra Salem BioIn 16
Farrell, Sharon 1949- WhoAm 90
Farrell, Susan Florence 1952- WhoAmW 91
Farrell, Suzanne WhoAm 90, WhoAmW 91, WhoE 91
Farrell, Suzanne 1945- BioIn 16, WorAlBi
Farrell, Terrence 1950- IntWWM 90
Farrell, Thomas Dinan 1948- WhoEmL 91
Farrell, Thomas J. WhoSSW 91
Farrell, Thomas S. BioIn 16
Farrell, Timothy R. W. 1943- IntWWM 90

Farrell, William, Jr. 1922- *IntWWM 90*
Farrell, William Joseph 1936- *WhoAm 90, WhoE 91*
Farrell, William Patrick 1929- *St&PR 91*
Farrell-Logan, Vivian *WhoE 91*
Farrelly, Alexander 1923- *WhoSSW 91, WhoWor 91*
Farrelly, Cyril J., Jr. 1929- *St&PR 91*
Farrelly, Joseph William 1944- *St&PR 91*
Farrelly, Suzette L. 1964- *WhoAmW 91*
Farren, J. Michael 1952- *WhoAm 90*
Farren, Pat 1944- *WhoWrEP 89*
Farren, Richard M. *ConAu 33NR, MajTwCW*
Farren-Price, Ronald William 1930- *IntWWM 90*
Farrenc, Louise 1804-1875 *BioIn 16*
Farrens, Juanita G *WhoAmA 91*
Farrer, Claire Anne Rafferty 1936- *WhoAmW 91*
Farrer, Donald Nathanael 1935- *WhoSSW 91*
Farrer, Elizabeth Ann 1961- *WhoAmW 91*
Farrer, Franklin E. 1946- *St&PR 91*
Farrer, Katharine 1911- *TwCCr&M 91*
Farrer, Richard James 1941- *BiDrAPA 89*
Farrer, William Cameron 1922- *WhoAm 90, WhoWor 91*
Farres de Mieza, Carmen 1931-1976 *EncCoWW*
Farries, James F. 1940- *St&PR 91*
Farrigan, Julia Ann 1943- *WhoAmW 91, WhoE 91*
Farrimond, George Francis, Jr. 1932- *WhoWor 91*
Farrin, James Smith 1936- *St&PR 91*
Farringer, John Lee, Jr. 1920- *WhoSSW 91, WhoWor 91*
Farrington, Charles William 1940- *WhoSSW 91*
Farrington, Christopher Allan 1957- *WhoE 91, WhoEmL 91*
Farrington, D. P. *ConAu 130*
Farrington, David 1945- *WhoE 91*
Farrington, David P. 1944- *ConAu 130*
Farrington, Gene 1931- *ConAu 130*
Farrington, Helen Agnes 1945- *WhoE 91, WhoEmL 91*
Farrington, Hugh G. 1945- *WhoAm 90*
Farrington, James Francis 1926- *St&PR 91*
Farrington, Jerry S. 1934- *WhoAm 90, WhoSSW 91*
Farrington, John Peter 1933- *St&PR 91*
Farrington, Joseph Rider 1897-1954 *BioIn 16*
Farrington, Mary Elizabeth Pruett 1898- *BioIn 16*
Farrington, Michael H. 1940- *St&PR 91*
Farrington, Russell A., Jr. 1924- *St&PR 91*
Farrington, Selwyn Kip, Jr. 1904-1983 *AuBYP 90*
Farrington, Thomas Alex 1943- *WhoAm 90*
Farrington, Wallace Rider 1871-1933 *BioIn 16*
Farrington, William Benford 1921- *WhoAm 90*
Farrington-Hopf, Susan Kay 1940- *WhoAmW 91*
Farrior, Dianne Rodgers 1950- *WhoSSW 91*
Farrior, J. Rex, Jr. 1927- *WhoWor 91*
Farrior, Joseph Brown 1911- *WhoAm 90*
Farris, Alice Ward 1959- *St&PR 91*
Farris, Bain Joseph 1949- *WhoAm 90*
Farris, Charles Lowell 1910- *WhoAm 90*
Farris, David J. 1935- *St&PR 91*
Farris, Edward Thompson 1925- *WhoSSW 91, WhoWor 91*
Farris, Hansford White 1919- *WhoAm 90*
Farris, Ion L. 1878- *AmLegL*
Farris, Jack 1921- *ConAu 129*
Farris, Jack Brodie, Jr. 1935- *WhoAm 90*
Farris, Jefferson Davis 1927- *WhoAm 90*
Farris, Jerome 1930- *WhoAm 90*
Farris, John Adam 1933- *St&PR 91*
Farris, John Leo 1947- *WhoEmL 91*
Farris, John Wesley 1846-1915 *AmLegL*
Farris, Joseph 1924- *WhoAmA 91, WhoE 91*
Farris, Linda B 1944- *WhoAmA 91*
Farris, Louis Anthony, Jr. 1936- *WhoAm 90*
Farris, Marc 1947- *WhoEmL 91*
Farris, Marie Leazer *WhoAmW 91*
Farris, Martin Theodore 1925- *WhoAm 90*
Farris, Paul L. 1919- *BioIn 16*
Farris, Paul Leonard 1919- *WhoAm 90*
Farris, Robert Earl 1928- *WhoAm 90*
Farris, Robert Gene 1930- *WhoSSW 91*
Farris, Teresa Carolyn 1951- *WhoSSW 91*
Farris, Thomas Chad 1954- *WhoEmL 91*
Farris, Toby James 1945- *WhoEmL 91*
Farris, Trueman Earl, Jr. 1926- *WhoAm 90*
Farris, Vera King *WhoAm 90, WhoAmW 91*
Farris, William Harrison 1945- *WhoSSW 91*
Farris-Larson, Gail 1947- *WhoAmA 91*
Farrish, John R. 1945- *St&PR 91*
Farrish, Wanda Burruss *WhoAmW 91*
Farrissey, Francis Stack 1931- *St&PR 91*
Farrokh, Reza 1943- *WhoWor 91*
Farron, Robert 1947- *WhoE 91, WhoEmL 91*
Farrow, David John 1931- *St&PR 91*
Farrow, Jason 1939- *ODwPR 91*
Farrow, Jeffrey Lloyd 1951- *WhoE 91*
Farrow, Kenneth Ray 1947- *WhoSSW 91*
Farrow, Margaret Ann 1934- *WhoAmW 91*
Farrow, Mia *BioIn 16*
Farrow, Mia 1945- *WorAlBi*
Farrow, Mia Villiers 1945- *WhoAm 90, WhoAmW 91*
Farrow, Patrick Villiers 1942- *WhoAmA 91, WhoE 91*
Farrow, Robert Scott 1952- *WhoE 91*
Farrow, Theresa Sue *BiDrAPA 89*
Farrug, Eugene Joseph 1928- *WhoAm 90*
Farruggio, Remo Michael 1906- *WhoAmA 91*
Farrukh, Marwan Omar 1946- *WhoEmL 91, WhoWor 91*
Farry, Michael Allen 1957- *WhoEmL 91*
Farsetta, James Joseph 1947- *WhoAm 90*
Farson, Negley 1890-1960 *BioIn 16*
Farson, Richard Evans 1926- *WhoAm 90, WhoWor 91*
Farson, William Joseph 1932- *St&PR 91*
Farst, Don David 1941- *WhoAm 90*
Faruk 1920-1965 *WorAlBi*
Faruki, Charles Joseph 1949- *WhoEmL 91*
Faruki, Ghulam M Y 1934- *BiDrAPA 89*
Faruki, Mahmud T 1919- *BiDrAPA 89*
Farulli, Piero *PenDiMP*
Farulli, Piero 1920- *IntWWM 90*
Faruqi, Lois Ibsen al- 1927-1986 *BioIn 16*
Faruqi, Shamsur Rahman *WhoWor 91*
Farver, Mary Joan 1919- *WhoAm 90*
Farwell, Albert Edmond 1915- *WhoAm 90*
Farwell, Beatrice 1920- *WhoAmA 91*
Farwell, Byron Edgar 1921- *WhoAm 90, WhoWor 91, WhoWrEP 89*
Farwell, Charles *BiDrAPA 89*
Farwell, Charles, IV 1926- *WhoWor 91*
Farwell, Dorothy Anne 1936- *WhoAmW 91*
Farwell, Elwin D. 1919- *WhoAm 90*
Farwell, F. Evans 1906- *St&PR 91*
Farwell, Jill 1955- *ODwPR 91*
Farwell, Lloyd S. 1922- *WhoAm 90*
Farwell, Nancy L. *ODwPR 91*
Farwell, Peter *ODwPR 91*
Farwell, Peter 1943- *St&PR 91*
Fary, Debra Faye 1957- *WhoAmW 91*
Farzana, Farida *BiDrAPA 89*
Fasanella, Ralph 1914- *BioIn 16, EncAL, MusmAFA*
Fasanello, Sebastian S *BiDrAPA 89*
Fasanello, Vincent Joseph *BiDrAPA 89*
Fasang, Patrick Pad 1941- *WhoAm 90*
Fasano, Anthony John 1947- *WhoEmL 91, WhoSSW 91*
Fasano, Janette *WhoAmW 91*
Fasano, Kristine M. 1951- *St&PR 91*
Fasano, Renato 1902-1979 *PenDiMP*
Fasano N A, Clara *WhoAmA 91*
Fasbender, Clementine Marie Scully 1936- *WhoAmW 91*
Fascell, Dante B. 1917- *WhoAm 90, WhoSSW 91*
Fascett, Ernest Frank 1949- *St&PR 91*
Fascetta, Salvatore Charles 1940- *WhoE 91, WhoWor 91*
Fascia, Remo Mario 1922- *WhoAm 90*
Fasciani, John Guy 1955- *WhoE 91, WhoWor 91*
Fasciotti, Vittorio 1930- *WhoWor 91*
Fasel, Ida 1909- *WhoWrEP 89*
Fasel, Terry Lee 1946- *WhoSSW 91*
Fash, William Leonard 1931- *WhoAm 90*
Fashbaugh, Howard Dilts, Jr. 1922- *WhoWor 91*
Fasi, Allal Al- 1910?-1974 *PolLCME*
Fasi, Frank F. 1920- *WhoAm 90*
Fasi, Joseph Mario, II 1954- *WhoEmL 91*
Faske, Donna *WhoAmW 91*
Fasman, Gerald David 1925- *WhoAm 90*
Fasman, Zachary Dean 1948- *WhoEmL 91*
Fasnacht, Betty Beegle 1931- *WhoWrEP 89*
Fasnacht, Heide Ann 1951- *WhoAmA 91*
Fasoldt, Sarah Lowry 1950- *WhoAmA 91*
Fason, Fred Lanier *BiDrAPA 89*
Fasone, Donald, Sr. 1931- *St&PR 91*
Fasone, Lucille Geraldine 1954- *WhoAmW 91*
Fass, Alan D. *WhoE 91*
Fass, Barbara *WhoAm 90*
Fass, Jerome S 1928- *BiDrAPA 89*
Fass, Margot Lindsay *BiDrAPA 89*
Fass, Paula S. 1947- *ConAu 129*
Fass, Peter Michael 1937- *WhoAm 90*
Fass, Susan R. 1941- *WhoWrEP 89*
Fassak, Gary Thomas 1954- *WhoEmL 91*
Fassbaender, Brigitte 1939- *IntWWM 90, PenDiMP, WhoAm 90*
Fassbinder, Rainer Werner 1946-1982 *BioIn 16, ConAu 31NR*
Fassburg, T. A. 1947- *ODwPR 91*
Fassel, Velmer Arthur 1919- *WhoAm 90*
Fasser, Paul James, Jr. 1926- *WhoAm 90*
Fassett, Cornelia Adele 1831-1898 *BiDWomA*
Fassett, David Walter 1908- *WhoAm 90*
Fassett, Hugh Gardner 1927- *WhoSSW 91*
Fassett, John D. 1926- *WhoAm 90*
Fassihi, Theresa Carmela 1959- *WhoAmW 91*
Fassinger, Vicki Lee 1958- *WhoE 91*
Fassio, James S. 1955- *St&PR 91*
Fassio, Virgil 1927- *St&PR 91, WhoAm 90, WhoWor 91*
Fasske, Erhard Moritz Georg 1927- *WhoWor 91*
Fassler, Bernice 1930- *St&PR 91*
Fassler, Charles 1946- *WhoEmL 91, WhoSSW 91*
Fassler, Crystal G. 1942- *WhoAmW 91*
Fassler, David *BiDrAPA 89*
Fassler, Joseph K. 1942- *St&PR 91, WhoAm 90*
Fassler, Leon 1933- *St&PR 91*
Fassler, Leonard J. 1931- *St&PR 91*
Fassnacht, Debra Kerr *ODwPR 91*
Fassoulis, Satiris Galahad 1922- *WhoE 91, WhoWor 91*
Fast, Daniel E 1951- *BiDrAPA 89*
Fast, Diane K *BiDrAPA 89*
Fast, Elaine Clayton 1943- *WhoAmW 91*
Fast, Howard *TwCCr&M 91*
Fast, Howard 1914- *ConAu 33NR, EncAL, WhoWrEP 89, WorAlBi*
Fast, Howard Melvin 1914- *AuBYP 90, WhoAm 90*
Fast, Julius 1919- *WhoAm 90*
Fast, Larry *NewAgMG*
Faster, Walter W. 1933- *St&PR 91*
Fastert, Herbert P. 1936- *St&PR 91*
Fasthuber-Grande, Traudy 1950- *WhoEmL 91*
Fastiggi, Thomas *St&PR 91*
Fastove, Aaron 1898-1979 *WhoAmA 91N*
Fastovsky, Ivgenija J *BiDrAPA 89*
Fate, Martin E., Jr. 1933- *St&PR 91*
Fate, Martin Eugene, Jr. 1933- *WhoAm 90, WhoSSW 91*
Fate, Weldon Lee 1937- *St&PR 91*
Fateley, William Gene 1929- *WhoAm 90, WhoWrEP 89*
Fatemi, Nasrollah S. *NewYTBS 90 [port]*
Fatemi, Nasrollah S. 1910-1990 *BioIn 16, ConAu 131*
Fates, Joseph Gilbert 1914- *WhoAm 90*
Fath, Joan 1947- *St&PR 91*
Fathauer, Theodore Frederick 1946- *WhoEmL 91, WhoWor 91*
Fatheazam, Shahab 1950- *WhoE 91*
Father Divine 1874?-1965 *EncO&P 3*
Father Of Many Children *DcCanB 12*
Fathy, Hassan 1900-1989 *AnObit 1989, BioIn 16, ConAu 130*
Fatio, Louise 1904- *AuBYP 90*
Fatjo, Tom J., Jr. 1940- *St&PR 91*
Fatma *EncCoWW*
Fatma-Constanta *EncCoWW*
Fatmi, Mohammad Badrul 1954- *WhoSSW 91*
Fatouros, Georgios 1927- *WhoWor 91*
Fatovic, John 1932- *WhoE 91, WhoWor 91*
Fatse, George 1933- *St&PR 91*
Fatt, Amelia *BioIn 16*
Fatt, Irving 1920- *WhoAm 90*
Fattahi, Farro 1948- *St&PR 91*
Fattal, Irma Mary *BiDrAPA 89*
Fattell, Edward George 1934- *St&PR 91*
Fatten, Gerald F. 1941- *St&PR 91*
Fattman, George 1937- *WhoE 91*
Fattmann, Kenneth J 1955- *BiDrAPA 89*
Fattori, Giovanni 1825-1908 *BioIn 16, IntDcAA 90*
Fattorini *PenDiDA 89*
Fatzer, Harold R. 1910-1989 *BioIn 16*
Fatzinger, Walter R., Jr. 1942- *WhoE 91*
Fatzinger, Walter Robert, Jr. 1942- *St&PR 91*
Faubel, Nancy Caroline 1958- *WhoAmW 91*
Fauber, Joseph Everette, Jr. 1908- *WhoAm 90*
Fauber, Roy L. 1944- *St&PR 91*
Faubert, Jacques 1952- *IntWWM 90*
Faubert, Kathryn *ODwPR 91*
Faubion, Anne *WhoWrEP 89*
Faubion, Jno. J., Jr. 1915- *St&PR 91*
Faubion, S Michael 1952- *WhoAmA 91*
Faubus, Orval *BioIn 16*
Faubus, Orval 1910- *WorAlBi*
Faubus, Orval Eugene 1910- *WhoAm 90*
Faucett, Philip Matson, Jr. 1917- *WhoAm 90*
Faucett, Sam P. 1935- *St&PR 91*
Faucett, Thomas Richard 1920- *WhoAm 90*
Faucher, Albert 1915- *WhoAm 90, WhoWrEP 89*
Faucher, J.G. 1933- *St&PR 91*
Faucher De Saint-Maurice, N-H-E 1844-1897 *DcCanB 12*
Fauchier, Joseph *PenDiDA 89*
Fauci, Anthony S. *BioIn 16*
Fauci, Anthony Stephen 1940- *NewYTBS 90 [port], WhoAm 90*
Fauci, Lawrence Anthony 1929- *St&PR 91*
Fauci, Peter Anthony, Jr. 1933- *WhoE 91*
Fauconnier, Jacques-Henri 1776-1839 *PenDiDA 89*
Faude, Diane Elaine 1950- *WhoAmW 91*
Faude, William D. 1933- *St&PR 91*
Faude, Wilson Hinsdale 1946- *WhoAmA 91*
Faudie, Fred 1941- *WhoAmA 91, WhoE 91*
Fauerbach, George, Jr. 1946- *St&PR 91*
Faugeres, Margaretta 1771-1801 *FemiCLE*
Faught, Harold Franklin 1924- *St&PR 91, WhoAm 90*
Faul, Bill 1940- *Ballpl 90*
Faul, George Johnson 1918- *WhoAm 90*
Faul, John Charles 1931- *BiDrAPA 89*
Faul, June Patricia *WhoAmW 91*
Faulcon, Robert *ConAu 131*
Faulconer, Elizabeth M *BiDrAPA 89*
Faulconer, Mary *WhoAmA 91*
Faulconer, Robert Jamieson 1923- *WhoAm 90, WhoWor 91*
Faulconer, Thomas Pleasant 1912- *WhoWor 91*
Faulding, Gertrude Minnie 1875-1961 *FemiCLE*
Faulds, W Rod 1953- *WhoAmA 91*
Faulhaber, John Martin 1934- *St&PR 91*
Fauliso, Joseph J. 1916- *WhoAm 90, WhoE 91*
Faulk, Charles Edward, Jr. 1949- *BiDrAPA 89*
Faulk, Charles Johnson, Jr. 1916?-1990 *ConAu 131*
Faulk, Elizabeth Hammond 1925- *WhoAmW 91*
Faulk, John Henry *BioIn 16*
Faulk, John Henry *NewYTBS 90 [port]*
Faulk, John Henry 1913-1990 *ConAu 131*
Faulk, Richard Oran 1951- *WhoEmL 91*
Faulk, Suzanne H. 1949- *WhoAmW 91*
Faulkenberry, Charles V. 1935- *St&PR 91*
Faulkenbery, Monica Anne 1957- *WhoAmW 91*
Faulkner, Adele Lloyd 1911- *WhoAm 90*
Faulkner, Amanda 1953- *BiDWomA*
Faulkner, Anne Irvin *AuBYP 90*
Faulkner, Avery Coonley 1929- *WhoAm 90*
Faulkner, Barry 1881-1966 *WhoAmA 91N*
Faulkner, Benton H. 1930- *St&PR 91*
Faulkner, Brian 1921-1977 *BioIn 16*
Faulkner, Charles Herman 1937- *WhoSSW 91*
Faulkner, Charles James 1806-1884 *BioIn 16*
Faulkner, Claude Winston 1916- *WhoAm 90*
Faulkner, Edwin J. 1911- *St&PR 91*
Faulkner, Edwin Jerome 1911- *WhoAm 90, WhoWor 91*
Faulkner, Frank 1946- *WhoAmA 91*
Faulkner, Frank M. 1946- *WhoAm 90*
Faulkner, Georgene 1873- *AuBYP 90*
Faulkner, Gerald Dale 1932- *WhoAm 90*
Faulkner, Henry Lawrence 1924-1981 *BioIn 16*
Faulkner, Jack *WhoAm 90*
Faulkner, Jack Sherwood 1933- *St&PR 91*
Faulkner, James Hardin 1921- *WhoAm 90*
Faulkner, Joe Malcolm, Jr. 1951- *WhoSSW 91*
Faulkner, John Arthur 1923- *WhoAm 90*
Faulkner, John Samuel 1932- *WhoSSW 91*
Faulkner, Juanita Smith 1935- *WhoSSW 91, WhoWor 91*
Faulkner, Kady B 1901-1977 *WhoAmA 91N*
Faulkner, Larry Ray 1944- *WhoAm 90*
Faulkner, Larry Ray 1948- *BiDrAPA 89*
Faulkner, Lloyd C. 1926- *WhoAm 90*
Faulkner, Marilyn Hauch 1942- *WhoE 91*
Faulkner, Maurice Ervin 1912- *WhoWor 91*
Faulkner, Mike 1949- *WhoSSW 91*
Faulkner, Mikel D. 1949- *St&PR 91*
Faulkner, Nancy Irvin 1906- *AuBYP 90*
Faulkner, Patricia Ann 1961- *WhoAmW 91*
Faulkner, Phillip Gordon 1936- *St&PR 91*
Faulkner, Ray N 1906-1975 *WhoAmA 91N*
Faulkner, Ronnie Wayne 1952- *WhoEmL 91, WhoWrEP 89*
Faulkner, Sewell Ford 1924- *WhoAm 90*
Faulkner, Stanley 1909- *WhoE 91*
Faulkner, Walter Thomas 1928- *St&PR 91, WhoAm 90*

Faulkner, William 1897-1962 BioIn 16, ConAu 33NR, DcLB 102 [port], MajTwCW, WorAlBi, WrPh
Faulkner, William Ballard 1952- WhoSSW 91
Faulkner, Winthrop Waldron 1931- WhoAm 90
Faulknor, Harry Allen 1942- WhoE 91
Faulks, Sebastian 1953- ConAu 131
Faull, Ellen 1918- IntWWM 90
Faull, James Edward 1945- WhoEmL 91
Faulstich, Albert Joseph 1910- WhoAm 90, WhoWor 91
Faulstich, Gary George BiDrAPA 89
Faulstich, Louis J. WhoSSW 91
Faulwell, Gerald Edward 1942- St&PR 91, WhoAm 90
Fauman, Beverly Joyce 1943- BiDrAPA 89
Fauman, Michael A BiDrAPA 89
Faunce, Charles J., Jr. 1933- St&PR 91
Faunce, John Egner 1840- AmLegL
Faunce, Robert L. 1941- St&PR 91
Faunce, Robert Leroy 1941- WhoAm 90
Faunce, Sarah Cushing 1929- WhoAm 90, WhoAmA 91
Fauntleroy, Dort 1925- St&PR 91
FauntLeRoy, Jennifer Mary BiDrAPA 89
Fauntroy, Walter E. 1933- WhoAm 90, WhoE 91
Fauntroy, Walter Edward 1933- BlkAmsC [port]
Fauquez, Pierre-Joseph PenDiDA 89
Faure, Edgar 1908-1988 AnObit 1988, BioIn 16
Faure, Edgar Jean 1908-1988 BiDFrPL
Faure, Francois Felix 1841-1899 BiDFrPL
Faure, Gabriel 1845-1924 BioIn 16, PenDiMP A, WorAlBi
Faure, Gunter 1934- WhoAm 90
Faure, Jean-Baptiste 1830-1914 PenDiMP
Faure, Maurice Henri 1922- BiDFrPL
Faure, Michael Gerbert 1958- WhoWor 91
Faure, Paul 1878-1960 BiDFrPL
Faure, Sebastien 1858-1942 BiDFrPL
Faurer, Louis 1916- WhoAm 90, WhoAmA 91
Fauriol, Sandie 1949- WhoAmW 91
Faurot, Jeannette Louise 1943- WhoSSW 91
Faurre, Pierre Lucien 1942- WhoWor 91
Fausch, David A. 1935- ODwPR 91
Fausch, David Arthur 1935- St&PR 91
Fauset, Jessie Redmon 1882-1961 FemiCLE, HarlReB
Fauset, Jessie Redmon 1884?-1961 BioIn 16
Fausett, Dean 1913- WhoAmA 91
Fausett, Lynn 1894-1977 WhoAmA 91N
Fausold, Martin Luther 1921- WhoAm 90
Faust EncO&P 3
Faust, A. Donovan 1919- WhoAm 90
Faust, Allison Lee 1967- WhoAmW 91
Faust, Charles 1880-1915 BioIn 16
Faust, Charlie 1880-1915 Ballpl 90
Faust, E.F. 1925- St&PR 91
Faust, Elizabeth Ann 1958- BiDrAPA 89
Faust, Frederick 1892-1944 BioIn 16
Faust, Frederick Shiller 1892-1944 SpyFic
Faust, Harry Louis, Jr. BiDrAPA 89
Faust, Irvin 1924- WhoWrEP 89
Faust, Isabelle 1972- IntWWM 90
Faust, James 1949- WhoAmA 91
Faust, John Roosevelt, Jr. 1932- WhoAm 90
Faust, John William, Jr. 1922- WhoAm 90, WhoSSW 91
Faust, Joseph ODwPR 91
Faust, Leland Howard 1946- WhoEmL 91
Faust, Marcus G. 1953- WhoE 91
Faust, Marvin W BiDrAPA 89
Faust, Naomi Flowe WhoAmW 91, WhoE 91, WhoWor 91, WhoWrEP 89
Faust, Ray C., Jr. 1942- St&PR 91
Faust, Richard Alan, Jr. 1946- St&PR 91
Faust, Richard Edward 1927- WhoAm 90
Faust, Robert McNeer 1939- WhoAm 90
Faust, Roger Raymond 1942- St&PR 91
Faust, Victoria 1944- WhoAmA 91
Faust, William Marvin 1939- St&PR 91
Faustin I 1785?-1867? BioIn 16
Faustini, Joao Wilson 1931- IntWWM 90
Faustino, David BioIn 16
Faustino, Rui Antonio 1962- WhoWor 91
Fausto, Domenicantonio 1940- WhoWor 91
Fausto-Gil, Fidel 1955- WhoHisp 91
Fausz, James Lee Edward 1953- WhoSSW 91
Faut, Thierry Francois 1953- WhoWor 91
Fautrier, Jean 1898-1964 BioIn 16
Fautsko, Timothy Frank 1945- WhoEmL 91
Fauvel, Terence BiDrAPA 89
Fauvel, William Le Boutillier 1850-1897 DcCanB 12
Fauver, John William 1921- WhoAm 90
Fauvet, Jacques 1914- WhoWor 91
Fauvet, Jacques Jules Pierre Constant 1914- BiDFrPL
Faux, Eugene J 1922- BiDrAPA 89
Faux-Froidure, Eugenie Juliette 1876- BiDWomA
Fava, Giovanni Andrea 1952- BiDrAPA 89
Fava, Maria BioIn 16
Fava, Maurizio 1956- BiDrAPA 89
Favalora, John Clement 1935- WhoAm 90
Favaro, Dennis Ray 1961- WhoEmL 91
Favaro, Mary Kaye Asperheim 1934- WhoSSW 91
Favart, Marie-Justine-Benoite 1727-1772 PenDiMP
Favart, Vincent Jean 1939- WhoWor 91
Favazza, Armando R 1941- BiDrAPA 89
Favazza, Barbara S BiDrAPA 89
Favazza, Frank Wm BiDrAPA 89
Favazzo, Charles Nicholas 1941- St&PR 91
Favelukes, Hanne Else BiDrAPA 89
Favier, James Gordon, Jr. 1951- St&PR 91
Favier, Jean 1932- WhoWor 91
Favila, Rodolfo Gomez 1951- WhoHisp 91
Faville, Jeffrey James 1956- WhoE 91
Faville, Richard William 1930- WhoE 91
Favolora, John C. 1935- WhoSSW 91
Favorite, Felix 1925- WhoAm 90
Favorite, George Upton 1917- St&PR 91
Favorite, Paul Douglas 1948- St&PR 91
Favors, Malachi 1937- WhoAm 90
Favre, Alexandre Jean 1911- WhoWor 91
Favre, William BioIn 16
Favreau, Donald Francis 1919- WhoAm 90
Favreau, Jean-Philippe 1956- WhoE 91
Favreau, Susan Debra 1955- WhoAmW 91, WhoE 91, WhoEmL 91, WhoWor 91
Favro, K.D. 1936- St&PR 91
Favro, Murray 1940- WhoAmA 91
Favus, Mark Bernard 1946- WhoEmL 91
Faw, Bernadine C 1935- BiDrAPA 89
Faw, Duane Leslie 1920- WhoAm 90
Faw, Genevieve H. 1959- St&PR 91
Faw, Melvin Lee 1925- WhoAm 90
Fawcett, Charlotte Ann 1949- WhoEmL 91
Fawcett, Don Wayne 1917- WhoAm 90
Fawcett, Dwight Winter 1927- WhoAm 90
Fawcett, Farrah BioIn 16
Fawcett, Farrah 1947- WorAlBi
Fawcett, Farrah Leni 1947- WhoAm 90
Fawcett, Frank Conger 1934- WhoAm 90, WhoWor 91
Fawcett, George 1926- St&PR 91
Fawcett, Gerald A. 1933- St&PR 91
Fawcett, Harland Kent 1935- St&PR 91
Fawcett, Henry 1833-1884 BioIn 16
Fawcett, Howard Hoy 1916- WhoE 91, WhoWor 91
Fawcett, Howard Samuel 1877-1948 BioIn 16
Fawcett, Jan Alan 1934- BiDrAPA 89
Fawcett, John William, III 1920- WhoAm 90
Fawcett, Leslie Clarence, Jr. 1920- WhoSSW 91, WhoWor 91
Fawcett, Marie Ann Formanek 1914- WhoE 91
Fawcett, Michael James 1954- WhoWrEP 89
Fawcett, Millicent 1847-1929 FemiCLE
Fawcett, Millicent Garrett 1847-1929 BioIn 16
Fawcett, Ralph W 1943- BiDrAPA 89
Fawcett, Richard Steven 1948- WhoEmL 91
Fawcett, Robert 1903-1967 WhoAmA 91N
Fawcett, Robert Earl, Jr. 1931- St&PR 91, WhoAm 90
Fawcett, Robert George 1946- BiDrAPA 89
Fawcett, Sherwood Luther 1919- St&PR 91, WhoAm 90, WhoWor 91
Fawcett, Stancine Brenna WhoAmW 91
Fawell, Beverly Jean 1930- WhoAmW 91
Fawell, Harris W. 1929- WhoAm 90
Fawer, Martin S. 1933- St&PR 91
Fawkes, Guy 1570-1606 WorAlBi
Fawley, John Jones 1921- WhoAm 90
Fawley, Pamela Shelton BiDrAPA 89
Fawls, Joseph F. 1931- St&PR 91
Fawsett, Patricia C. 1943- WhoAmW 91
Fawver, Darlene Elizabeth 1952- IntWWM 90
Fawver, Jay Dee 1956- BiDrAPA 89
Fawzy, Fawzy Ibrahim 1942- BiDrAPA 89
Fax, Charles Samuel 1948- WhoE 91, WhoEmL 91
Fax, Elizabeth V. Murrell- BioIn 16
Fax, Elton 1909- BioIn 16
Fax, Elton Clay 1909- WhoAm 90, WhoAmA 91, WhoWrEP 89
Faxon, Alicia Craig 1931- WhoAmW 91
Faxon, Thomas Baker 1924- WhoAm 90
Faxton, James Fred 1932- St&PR 91
Fay, Albert Hill 1911- WhoAm 90
Fay, Allen 1934- BiDrAPA 89
Fay, Anitra Sharane 1954- WhoAmW 91
Fay, Annie Eva 1855?-1927 EncO&P 3, EncPaPR 91
Fay, Bette Berne 1922- WhoSSW 91
Fay, Carlyle Waldie 1926- St&PR 91
Fay, Charles Wilson, III 1946- WhoEmL 91
Fay, Darcy Hunt WhoAmW 91
Fay, David B. WhoAm 90
Fay, Eliza 1756-1816 BioIn 16, FemiCLE
Fay, Francis X. BioIn 16
Fay, Francois Michel 1944- WhoWor 91
Fay, Fred 1946- St&PR 91
Fay, Frederic Albert 1911- WhoAm 90
Fay, Gerald W. 1920-1988 BioIn 16
Fay, Gordon Hollis 1939- WhoE 91
Fay, H. B., Mrs. EncO&P 3
Fay, James Alan 1923- WhoAm 90
Fay, Jean-Baptiste PenDiDA 89
Fay, John C., Jr. 1937- St&PR 91
Fay, John Thomas, Jr. 1930- St&PR 91
Fay, Julie 1951- WhoWrEP 89
Fay, Julie Diane 1950- WhoAmW 91, WhoE 91, WhoEmL 91
Fay, Margaret F. 1949- WhoEmL 91
Fay, Mary Natalie 1952- WhoAmW 91
Fay, Maureen A. WhoAm 90, WhoAmW 91
Fay, Michael BioIn 16
Fay, Michael E. 1942- ODwPR 91
Fay, Ming G 1943- WhoAmA 91
Fay, Nancy Elizabeth 1943- WhoAmW 91
Fay, Paul Burgess, III 1949- St&PR 91
Fay, Peter Thorp 1929- WhoAm 90
Fay, Peter Ward 1924- WhoAm 90
Fay, Robert Clinton 1936- WhoAm 90
Fay, Robert Jesse 1920- WhoAm 90
Fay, Robert Marie WhoSSW 91
Fay, Robert W. 1946- St&PR 91
Fay, Robert Woods 1946- WhoAm 90, WhoEmL 91
Fay, Sandra Davis 1955- WhoSSW 91
Fay, Stephen 1938- ConAu 31NR
Fay, Thomas A. 1927- WhoAm 90
Fay, Thomas F. 1930- St&PR 91
Fay, Thomas Frederic 1940- WhoE 91
Fay, Thomas Holland 1926- WhoE 91
Fay, Thomas J. 1933- ODwPR 91
Fay, Toni Georgette 1947- WhoAmW 91
Fay, Wilbur M 1904-1959 WhoAmA 91N
Fay, William M. 1839- EncO&P 3
Fay, William Michael WhoAm 90
Fay, William North 1943- St&PR 91
Faye, Alice 1912- OxCPMus, WorAlBi
Faye, Alice 1915- BioIn 16
Faye, Lindsay Anton, Jr. 1932- St&PR 91
Fayed, Mohamed al- 1933- BioIn 16
Fayed, Ramzi 1938- WhoWor 91
Fayen, Maureen BiDrAPA 89
Fayer, Steve 1935- ConAu 132
Fayer, Steven Alan 1948- BiDrAPA 89
Fayermann, A. C. BiDWomA
Fayerweather, John 1922- WhoAm 90
Fayhee, Jerry 1948- St&PR 91
Fayne, Fred Albert BiDrAPA 89
Fayorsey, Clarence Bawa 1922- WhoWor 91
Fayyad, John Antoine BiDrAPA 89
Faz-Guevara, Eliud Aurelio 1947- BiDrAPA 89
Fazaluddin, Primla Hanif BiDrAPA 89
FazaludDin, Primla Hanif 1936- WhoE 91
Fazen, Marianne Fleming 1944- WhoSSW 91
Fazio, Anthony Lee 1937- WhoWor 91
Fazio, Evelyn M. WhoE 91
Fazio, Frank 1932- St&PR 91
Fazio, Gary J. 1954- St&PR 91
Fazio, Joseph F., Jr. 1957- St&PR 91
Fazio, Maria Lena 1951- WhoAmW 91
Fazio, Peter Victor, Jr. 1940- WhoAm 90
Fazio, Vic 1942- NewYTBS 90 [port], WhoAm 90
Fazio, Victor Warren 1940- WhoAm 90
Fazlur Rahman 1919-1988 BioIn 16
Fazzalari, Laura Sue 1962- WhoAmW 91
Fazzano, Henry W. 1931- St&PR 91
Fazzari, Anthony J. 1929- St&PR 91
Fazzari, Frank P. 1932- St&PR 91
Fazzini, Georgia Carol 1946- WhoAmW 91
Fazzini, John Richard 1937- St&PR 91
Fe-Bornstein, Marcos BiDrAPA 89
Feagan, John Frank 1922- St&PR 91
Feagins, Thomas Jackson, II 1938- WhoSSW 91
Feagins, Warren Douglas 1945- WhoWor 91
Feagler, Virginia Miller 1940- WhoAmW 91
Feagles, Anita MacRae 1927- AuBYP 90
Feagles, Robert West 1920- WhoAm 90
Feagley, Nathalie BioIn 16
Feaker, Darrell L. 1936- St&PR 91, WhoAm 90
Feamster, Elizabeth Susan 1958- WhoAmW 91
Fear, Arthur 1902- IntWWM 90
Fear, Daniel E 1949- WhoAmA 91
Fear, Douglass Durston 1913- WhoSSW 91
Fear, Geoffrey Charles 1928- St&PR 91
Fear, J.V.D. 1925- St&PR 91
Fear, Ypk van der EncCoWW
Fearey, Porter 1918- WhoSSW 91
Fearheiley, Nancy 1952- WhoE 91
Fearing, John M BiDrAPA 89
Fearing, Kenneth 1902-1961 BioIn 16, TwCCr&M 91, WorAlBi
Fearing, Sandra Dosch 1960- WhoEmL 91
Fearing, William Kelly 1918- WhoAmA 91, WhoSSW 91
Fearing, William L BiDrAPA 89
Fearnside, Philip Martin 1947- WhoWor 91
Fearon, Hilda 1878-1917 BiDWomA
Fearon, Jane 1655?-1737 BiDEWW
Fearon, Jane 1656?-1737 FemiCLE
Fearon, Robert Henry 1900- WhoAm 90
Fearon, Robert Henry, Jr. 1927- St&PR 91
Fears, Douglas Edwin 1949- St&PR 91
Fears, Louise Mathis 1935- WhoAmW 91
Feasel, Richard McDowell 1920- WhoSSW 91
Feasley, Charles Edward 1945- WhoEmL 91
Feaster, Mary Alliene 1952- WhoSSW 91
Feaster, Sandra Joan 1954- WhoAmW 91
Feather, Leonard BioIn 16
Feather, Leonard Geoffrey 1914- OxCPMus, WhoWrEP 89
Feather, Mark Randolph 1955- WhoEmL 91
Feather, Richard Keltz 1927- WhoAm 90
Feather, Roberta Brown 1942- WhoAmW 91
Feather, William, Jr. 1915- St&PR 91
Featherlin, Rebecca Lynn 1956- WhoEmL 91
Featherly, Walter Thomas, III 1955- WhoEmL 91
Featherman, Bernard 1929- WhoE 91, WhoWor 91
Featherman, Donald Oscar 1936- St&PR 91
Featherman, Sandra 1934- WhoAmW 91, WhoE 91, WhoWor 91
Featherston, C. Ronald 1938- St&PR 91
Featherston, Charles Ronald 1938- WhoSSW 91
Featherstone, David Byrum 1945- WhoAmA 91
Featherstone, David Edward 1930- St&PR 91
Featherstone, Harry Edwin 1929- St&PR 91
Featherstone, John Douglas Bernard 1944- WhoAm 90
Featherstone, Sarah BiDEWW
Featherstonhaugh, George William 1780-1866 BioIn 16
Feaver, Douglas David 1921- WhoAm 90
Feaver, George A. 1937- WhoAm 90
Feaver, John Clayton 1911- WhoAm 90
Feaver, Vicki 1943- ConAu 129
Feazel, Richard Michael 1950- WhoE 91
Feazell, Thomas Lee 1937- St&PR 91, WhoAm 90
Febbo, J.D. 1937- St&PR 91
Febbraio, Salvatore Michael Turlizzo 1935- IntWWM 90
Febland, Harriet WhoAmA 91, WhoE 91
Febo, Manuel Angel BiDrAPA 89
Febres-Cordero, Leon 1931- WhoWor 91
February, Vernie A. ConAu 129
February, Vernon Alexander 1938- ConAu 129
Fecamps, Elise MajTwCW
Fecher, Constance 1911- AuBYP 90
Fechhelm, Paul Leo 1959- WhoEmL 91
Fechner, Albert BiDrAPA 89
Fechner, Julius BiDrAPA 89
Fechner, Robert Eugene 1936- WhoAm 90
Fecho, Cecelia Hodges 1960- WhoAmW 91, WhoSSW 91
Fechter, Alan Edward 1934- WhoE 91
Fechter, George A. 1946- WhoEmL 91
Fechtner, Leopold BioIn 16
Feck, Luke Matthew 1935- WhoAm 90
Fecteau, Doris Beatrice 1939- St&PR 91
Fecteau, James R, Jr. BiDrAPA 89
Feczko, William Albert 1937- WhoE 91
Fedak, Edward 1943- St&PR 91
Fedak, Suzanne ODwPR 91
Fedchak, Gregg George 1956- WhoWrEP 89
Fedde, Elisabeth 1850-1921 BioIn 16
Fedde, Paul Andrew 1925- St&PR 91
Feddeck, Michael Brendan 1944- WhoE 91
Feddema, Leonard Jay 1955- St&PR 91
Fedder, Joel David 1931- WhoAm 90
Fedders, David Leo 1943- BiDrAPA 89
Fedders, John Michael 1941- WhoAm 90
Feddock, John Edward 1947- St&PR 91
Feddoes, Sadie Clothil 1931- WhoE 91
Fedele, Anthony V. 1936- WhoE 91
Fedele, Cassandra 1465-1558 EncCoWW
Fedele, Charles Robert 1942- WhoE 91
Fedele, Michael Christian 1955- WhoE 91
Fedele, Susan Marie 1949- WhoAmW 91, WhoEmL 91

Fedeli, Anthony Salvatore 1944- *St&PR 91*
Fedeli, Frederick 1931- *WhoAm 90*
Fedeli, Frederick 1931-1989 *BioIn 16*
Fedeli, Michael 1937- *St&PR 91*
Fedelle, Estelle *WhoAmA 91, WhoAmW 91*
Feder, Adriana *BiDrAPA 89*
Feder, Allan Appel 1931- *WhoAm 90*
Feder, Arthur A. 1927- *St&PR 91, WhoAm 90*
Feder, Ben 1923- *WhoAmA 91*
Feder, Bruce Stanley 1950- *WhoEmL 91*
Feder, Donn-Alexandre 1935- *IntWWM 90*
Feder, Gary Harold 1948- *WhoEmL 91*
Feder, Harold Abram 1932- *WhoAm 90*
Feder, Joseph 1932- *St&PR 91*
Feder, Joshua Daniel *BiDrAPA 89*
Feder, Leon A. 1920- *St&PR 91*
Feder, Marilyn 1934- *BiDrAPA 89*
Feder, Michael A. 1951- *St&PR 91*
Feder, Mike *BioIn 16*
Feder, Miklos 1954- *WhoWor 91*
Feder, Milton William *BiDrAPA 89*
Feder, Morris Louis 1917- *WhoAm 90*
Feder, Penny Joy 1949- *WhoAmA 91*
Feder, Robert 1930- *WhoE 91, WhoWor 91*
Feder, Robert Arthur *AuBYP 90*
Feder, Robert Elliot 1951- *WhoE 91*
Feder, Robert Elliott 1951- *BiDrAPA 89*
Feder, Samuel L 1915- *BiDrAPA 89*
Feder, Saul E. 1943- *WhoAm 90*
Feder, Stuart 1930- *BiDrAPA 89*
Feder, Susan 1953- *BiDrAPA 89*
Feder, Susan 1955- *IntWWM 90*
Federbush, Alexander Philip 1942- *St&PR 91*
Federe, Marion 1919- *WhoE 91*
Federe, Marion 1938- *WhoAmA 91*
Federer, Herbert 1920- *WhoAm 90*
Federhar, David Bernard 1951- *WhoEmL 91*
Federici, Dennis Carl 1950- *WhoEmL 91*
Federici, Marie Victoria 1962- *WhoAmW 91*
Federici, William Vito 1931- *WhoAm 90*
Federico, Gene 1918- *ConDes 90, WhoAm 90*
Federico, Gloria Cabralez 1953- *WhoHisp 91*
Federico, Ronald Charles 1941- *WhoE 91*
Federighi, Christine M 1949- *WhoAmA 91, WhoSSW 91*
Federighi, Renie Rideout 1932- *WhoAmW 91*
Federman, Harold Barrett 1922- *St&PR 91*
Federman, Joseph R. 1950- *St&PR 91*
Federman, Miles 1946- *St&PR 91*
Federman, Paula Rae 1958- *St&PR 91*
Federman, Raymond 1928- *WhoAm 90, WorAu 1980 [port]*
Federmann, Franklin Howard 1939- *WhoE 91, WhoWor 91*
Federow, Harold Louis 1949- *WhoEmL 91*
Federowich, Carmen 1939- *BiDrAPA 89*
Federspiel, Benedict 1941- *WhoWor 91*
Federspiel, Jurg 1931- *WorAu 1980 [port]*
Fedesna, Kenneth Joseph 1949- *St&PR 91*
Fedewa, Lawrence John 1937- *St&PR 91, WhoSSW 91, WhoWor 91*
Fedewa, Randy 1954- *St&PR 91*
Fedi, Peter Francis 1924- *WhoAm 90*
Fedi, Roberto 1947- *WhoWor 91*
Fedin, Konstantin 1892-1977 *WorAlBi*
Fedla, Mike *St&PR 91*
Fedor, Katherine Wusylko 1956- *WhoE 91*
Fedor, Lubica *BiDrAPA 89*
Fedor, Richard Thomas 1945- *St&PR 91*
Fedor-Joseph, Stephanie Rae 1956- *WhoSSW 91*
Fedorchik, Bette Joy Winter 1953- *WhoAm 90*
Fedorochko, Michael 1933- *St&PR 91*
Fedoroff, J. Paul 1958- *BiDrAPA 89*
Fedoroff, Nina Vsevolod 1942- *WhoAmW 91*
Fedoroff, Sergey 1925- *WhoAm 90*
Fedorov, Evgenii Konstantinovich 1910-1981 *DcScB S2*
Fedorovitch, Sophie 1893-1953 *BiDWomA*
Fedorowicz, J K 1949- *ConAu 130*
Fedors, John, Jr. 1953- *WhoEmL 91*
Fedoruk, Sylvia O. 1927- *WhoAm 90, WhoAmW 91*
Fedoseyev, Vladimir 1932- *PenDiMP*
Fedoseyev, Vladimir Ivanovich 1932- *IntWWM 90*
Fedotov, Georgii Petrovich 1886-1951 *BioIn 16*
Feduniewicz, Ken 1951- *WhoE 91*
Fee, Catherine Ann 1965- *WhoAmW 91*
Fee, Chong-Hwey 1959- *WhoEmL 91*
Fee, Elizabeth *WhoAmW 91*
Fee, Frank J. 1942- *St&PR 91*
Fee, Gerard Wayne Cowle 1933- *WhoWor 91*
Fee, John F. 1922- *St&PR 91*
Fee, Kevin T. 1949- *St&PR 91*
Fee, Margaret B. 1927- *St&PR 91*
Fee, Michael Charles 1961- *WhoE 91*
Fee, Paul Francis 1939- *St&PR 91*
Fee, Paul S. 1942- *St&PR 91*
Fee, Thomas 1928- *St&PR 91, WhoAm 90*
Feeder, William *ODwPR 91*
Feedore, Jeremy Randolph 1951- *WhoEmL 91*
Feege, Edward Henry 1934- *WhoAm 90*
Feehan, John Joseph 1953- *WhoEmL 91*
Feehan, Michael Joseph 1950- *WhoEmL 91*
Feehan, Thomas Joseph 1924- *WhoAm 90*
Feeheley, John J. 1927- *St&PR 91*
Feeks, J. Michael 1942- *St&PR 91*
Feeley, Elise Bernier 1946- *WhoE 91*
Feeley, G. Robert, Jr. 1939- *St&PR 91*
Feeley, Henry Joseph, Jr. 1940- *WhoAm 90*
Feeley, James Terence 1950- *WhoE 91*
Feeley, John Paul 1918- *WhoAm 90*
Feeley, Kathleen 1929- *WhoAmW 91*
Feeley, Mary Elizabeth 1960- *WhoAmW 91*
Feeley, Olivia Stadelman 1939- *WhoAmW 91, WhoE 91*
Feeley, Paul 1913-1966 *WhoAmA 91N*
Feeley, Sharon Denise 1949- *WhoAmW 91*
Feeley, Terence 1950- *St&PR 91*
Feelings, Muriel 1938- *BioIn 16*
Feelings, Tom 1933- *BioIn 16*
Feely, Guy A. 1875- *AmLegL*
Feely, Stephen J. 1948- *St&PR 91*
Feeman, Timothy George 1956- *WhoE 91*
Feenberg, Daniel Richard 1950- *WhoE 91*
Feeney, Charles Stoneham 1921- *WhoAm 90*
Feeney, David Wesley 1938- *WhoAm 90*
Feeney, Don Joseph, Jr. 1948- *WhoEmL 91, WhoWor 91*
Feeney, Floyd Fulton 1933- *WhoAm 90*
Feeney, Frank Michael 1928- *St&PR 91*
Feeney, Helen M. *BioIn 16*
Feeney, James P. 1936- *St&PR 91*
Feeney, John Robert 1950- *St&PR 91, WhoAm 90*
Feeney, Loretta 1961- *BioIn 16*
Feeney, Mark 1957- *WhoAm 90*
Feeney, Mary Rosalind 1951- *WhoAmW 91*
Feeney, Patrick Joseph 1952- *WhoEmL 91*
Feeney, Richard John 1953- *WhoE 91*
Feeney, Sandra Benedict 1936- *WhoAmA 91, WhoAmW 91*
Feenker, Cherie Diane 1950- *WhoAmW 91, WhoEmL 91*
Feer, Hans 1927- *WhoWor 91*
Feer, Mark Cecil Iselin 1928-1988 *BioIn 16*
Fees, James Richard 1931- *WhoWor 91*
Feese, Brenda 1959- *WhoAmW 91*
Feeser, Larry James 1937- *WhoAm 90*
Feeser, Patricia 1938- *WhoAmW 91*
Feeser, Robert Paxson 1932- *St&PR 91*
Feest, Ronald L. *St&PR 91*
Feezor-Stewart, Barbara Yvonne 1950- *WhoAmW 91*
Fefer, Leo 1921- *St&PR 91*
Feferman, Solomon 1928- *WhoAm 90*
Feffer, Gerald Alan 1942- *WhoAm 90*
Feffer, Paul Evan 1921- *WhoWor 91*
Fefferman, Charles Louis 1949- *WhoAm 90*
Fefferman, Hilbert 1913- *WhoE 91*
Fegan, Gerard E *BiDrAPA 89*
Fegelein, Hermann 1906-1945 *BioIn 16*
Feger, Clare Louise *WhoE 91*
Feghali, Charles Antoine 1954- *WhoE 91*
Feghali, Sylvie B. 1965- *WhoSSW 91*
Fegley, Kenneth Allen 1923- *WhoAm 90*
Fegley, Randall Arlin 1955- *WhoE 91*
Fegley, Robert LeRoy, Jr. 1919- *WhoAm 90*
Feher, George 1924- *WhoAm 90*
Feher, Joseph 1908-1987 *WhoAmA 91N*
Feher, Klara 1923- *EncCoWW*
Feher, Patri 1952- *WhoEmL 91*
Feher, Steve Joseph Kent 1950- *WhoEmL 91*
Fehl, Patricia Katherine 1927- *WhoAmW 91*
Fehl, Philipp P 1920- *WhoAmA 91*
Fehlberg, Robert Erick 1926- *WhoAm 90*
Fehle, Armin Gebhard 1932- *WhoWor 91*
Fehlig, Paul T. 1908- *St&PR 91*
Fehling, Jurgen Detlev 1929- *WhoWor 91*
Fehlinger, Irvin John 1924- *St&PR 91*
Fehm, Kurt 1939- *WhoWor 91*
Fehnel, Edward Adam 1922- *WhoAm 90*
Fehr, David S. 1935- *St&PR 91*
Fehr, Donald *BioIn 16*
Fehr, Ernest Ury 1936- *WhoWor 91*
Fehr, George D. 1917- *St&PR 91*
Fehr, J. Will 1926- *WhoAm 90*
Fehr, Kenneth Manbeck 1928- *St&PR 91, WhoAm 90*
Fehr, Peter J. 1957- *WhoWor 91*
Fehr, Randall W 1954- *BiDrAPA 89*
Fehr, Walter Ronald 1939- *WhoAm 90*
Fehrenbach, Elisabeth Maria 1937- *WhoWor 91*
Fehrenbach, Franz 1949- *St&PR 91*
Fehrenbach, William Edward 1926- *St&PR 91*
Fehrenbacher, Don Edward 1920- *WhoAm 90*
Fehribach, Joseph D. 1958- *WhoSSW 91*
Fehribach, Ronald Steven 1949- *WhoEmL 91*
Fehring, Raymond H. 1910- *St&PR 91*
Fehrle, Klaus Paul 1955- *WhoWor 91*
Fehrman, Carl Abraham 1915- *WhoWor 91*
Fehskens, Kenneth P. *BioIn 16*
Fei Xiaotong *BioIn 16*
Fei, Hsiao-t'ung *BioIn 16*
Fei, James Robert 1947- *WhoEmL 91*
Feibel, Ruth 1927- *BiDrAPA 89*
Feibelman, Nathan Donald *BiDrAPA 89*
Feibelman, Peter Julian 1942- *WhoAm 90*
Feiber, Ann Murray 1936- *WhoSSW 91*
Feibleman, Gilbert Bruce 1951- *WhoEmL 91*
Feibush, Eliot Alan 1956- *WhoEmL 91*
Feichtinger, Thomas Jacob 1963- *WhoEmL 91*
Feichtmayr, Johann Michael 1709?-1772 *PenDiDA 89*
Feichtmayr, Joseph Anton 1696-1770 *PenDiDA 89*
Feichtner, Jacob Martin 1937- *St&PR 91*
Feick, Carl W. 1923- *St&PR 91*
Feick, Fred L. 1939- *St&PR 91*
Feick, Ralph T. 1925- *St&PR 91*
Feick, Sheila D. *BioIn 16*
Feickert, Carl William 1906- *WhoAm 90*
Feidler, Robert Ernest 1950- *WhoEmL 91*
Feier, Stuart S. 1928- *St&PR 91*
Feierman, Jay *BiDrAPA 89*
Feierstein, Mark Errol 1948- *WhoEmL 91*
Feifarek, A.J. 1921- *St&PR 91*
Feifarek, Ellen Buckler *BiDrAPA 89*
Feifel, Herman *BioIn 16*
Feifel, Herman 1915- *WhoAm 90*
Feiffer, Jules *BioIn 16*
Feiffer, Jules 1929- *ConAu 30NR, ConLC 64 [port], EncACom, MajTwCW, SmATA 61 [port], WhoAm 90, WhoAmA 91, WhoE 91, WhoWrEP 89, WorAlBi*
Feig, Jerome H. 1920- *WhoAm 90*
Feig, Stephen Arthur 1937- *WhoAm 90*
Feigal, Cheryl Lee 1950- *BiDrAPA 89*
Feige, Hermann Albert Otto Maximilian *MajTwCW*
Feigel, Celeste Louise 1952- *WhoAmW 91, WhoEmL 91, WhoWor 91*
Feigelman, Theodor 1951- *WhoEmL 91*
Feigelson, Charles Isaac *BiDrAPA 89*
Feigelson, Eugene B 1930- *BiDrAPA 89*
Feigelson, Janet Lauren 1951- *BiDrAPA 89*
Feigelson, Philip 1925- *WhoAm 90*
Feigen, Brenda S. 1944- *WhoWor 91*
Feigen, Gerald M. 1912-1989 *BioIn 16*
Feigen, Irene 1944- *WhoAmW 91, WhoE 91*
Feigen, Richard L. 1930- *WhoAm 90, WhoAmA 91*
Feigenbaum, Armand Vallin 1920- *WhoAm 90, WhoE 91*
Feigenbaum, Edward Albert 1936- *WhoAm 90*
Feigenbaum, Edward D. 1958- *WhoEmL 91*
Feigenbaum, Elliott M 1921- *BiDrAPA 89*
Feigenbaum, Harriet 1939- *BioIn 16*
Feigenbaum, Harvey 1933- *WhoAm 90*
Feigenbaum, Joan 1958- *WhoE 91*
Feigenbaum, Joel Jay 1954- *WhoEmL 91*
Feigenbaum, Mitchell Jay 1944- *WhoAm 90*
Feigenbaum, Robert L. 1938- *St&PR 91*
Feigenbaum, Ruth I. 1944- *WhoE 91*
Feigenberg, Mitchell H. 1951- *WhoEmL 91*
Feiger, Alan David 1944- *BiDrAPA 89*
Feighan, Edward Farrell 1947- *WhoAm 90*
Feighan, John W. 1845-1898 *AmLegL*
Feighan, Lynne Rossen 1938- *WhoAmW 91*
Feighner, John Preston 1937- *BiDrAPA 89*
Feigin, Barbara S. 1937- *St&PR 91*
Feigin, Barbara Sommer 1937- *WhoAm 90, WhoAmW 91*
Feigin, Dorothy L 1904-1969 *WhoAmA 91N*
Feigin, Joel Stanley 1951- *WhoE 91*
Feigin, Judith Zobel 1941- *WhoAmW 91*
Feigin, Marsha 1948- *WhoAmA 91*
Feigin, Ralph David 1938- *WhoAm 90*
Feigin, Ronald Alan 1945- *BiDrAPA 89*
Feigin, Simeon L *BiDrAPA 89*
Feigl, Dorothy Marie 1938- *WhoAm 90*
Feigl, Hugo 1890-1961 *WhoAmA 91N*
Feigley, Charles Anderson 1925- *BiDrAPA 89*
Feigon, Elizabeth A *BiDrAPA 89*
Feigon, Judith Tova 1947- *WhoAmW 91, WhoWor 91*
Feigus, Jay *BioIn 16, NewYTBS 90*
Feijo, Diogo Antonio 1784-1843 *BioIn 16*
Feijoo, Julio A *BiDrAPA 89*
Feijoo y Montenegro, Benito Jeronimo 1676-1764 *BioIn 16*
Feikens, John 1917- *WhoAm 90*
Feil, Dina *BioIn 16*
Feil, Linda Mae 1948- *WhoEmL 91*
Feil, Thomas E. 1942- *St&PR 91*
Feild, James Rodney 1934- *WhoSSW 91*
Feilders, George Goldwin 1943- *WhoWor 91*
Feilding, Everard 1867-1936 *EncO&P 3, EncPaPR 91*
Feiler, Jo Alison 1951- *WhoAmW 91*
Feiler, Karen A. 1962- *WhoAmW 91*
Feilner, Simon *PenDiDA 89*
Feiman, David Maurice *BiDrAPA 89*
Feiman, Ronald Mark 1951- *WhoEmL 91*
Feiman, Thomas E. 1940- *WhoAm 90*
Feimster, Carolyn Jane 1954- *WhoEmL 91*
Fein, Adam Richard 1957- *WhoE 91*
Fein, Albert 1930-1989 *BioIn 16*
Fein, Arnold L. 1910-1989 *BioIn 16*
Fein, B R 1941- *WhoAmA 91*
Fein, Benjamin David 1946- *St&PR 91*
Fein, Bernard 1908- *St&PR 91, WhoAm 90*
Fein, Cheri 1950- *WhoWrEP 89*
Fein, Ethan 1948- *WhoEmL 91*
Fein, Harold Lenard 1913- *St&PR 91*
Fein, Harriet Kronman 1927- *WhoAmW 91*
Fein, Irving Ashley 1911- *WhoAm 90*
Fein, John Morton 1922- *WhoAm 90*
Fein, Lawrence Seth 1951- *WhoEmL 91*
Fein, Leah Gold 1910- *WhoAmW 91*
Fein, Leonard 1934- *WhoWrEP 89*
Fein, Leonard J. 1934- *WhoAm 90*
Fein, Linda Ann 1949- *WhoAmW 91*
Fein, Marvin Michael 1923- *WhoAm 90*
Fein, Melanie Lippincott 1949- *WhoEmL 91*
Fein, Mitchell Hunter 1966- *St&PR 91*
Fein, Rashi 1926- *WhoAm 90, WhoE 91*
Fein, Roger Gary 1940- *WhoAm 90*
Fein, Ronald David 1938- *St&PR 91*
Fein, Ronnie 1943- *WhoE 91*
Fein, Seymour Howard 1948- *WhoE 91*
Fein, Sherman Edward 1928- *WhoWor 91*
Fein, Sidney *BiDrAPA 89*
Fein, Stanley 1919- *WhoAmA 91*
Fein, Thomas Paul 1946- *WhoEmL 91*
Fein, William 1933- *WhoAm 90, WhoWor 91*
Feinbaum, George 1945- *WhoE 91*
Feinberg, Albert E. 1913- *St&PR 91*
Feinberg, Andrew G 1952- *BiDrAPA 89*
Feinberg, Barbara Jane 1938- *WhoWrEP 89*
Feinberg, Barbara Silberdick 1938- *BioIn 16*
Feinberg, Barry Lester *BiDrAPA 89*
Feinberg, Barton King 1952- *WhoE 91*
Feinberg, Bea *BioIn 16*
Feinberg, Bernard 1943- *BiDrAPA 89*
Feinberg, Charles E. *BioIn 16*
Feinberg, Daniel 1937- *BiDrAPA 89*
Feinberg, David Allen 1947- *WhoEmL 91*
Feinberg, David B 1956- *ConLC 59 [port]*
Feinberg, David Erwin 1922- *St&PR 91*
Feinberg, David Todd 1962- *BiDrAPA 89*
Feinberg, E Richard 1931- *BiDrAPA 89*
Feinberg, Eddie 1918-1986 *BioIn 16*
Feinberg, Edward Burton 1945- *WhoAm 90, WhoEmL 91*
Feinberg, Edward Richard 1947- *St&PR 91*
Feinberg, Elen *WhoAmA 91*
Feinberg, Eugene Alexander 1954- *WhoE 91*
Feinberg, Gerald 1933- *WhoAm 90*
Feinberg, Glenda Joyce 1948- *WhoAmW 91, WhoEmL 91*
Feinberg, Harry *St&PR 91*
Feinberg, Harvey B 1927- *BiDrAPA 89*
Feinberg, Hilda 1915- *WhoWrEP 89*
Feinberg, Irwin L. 1916- *St&PR 91, WhoAm 90*
Feinberg, Jean 1948- *WhoAmA 91*
Feinberg, Jill Leslie 1963- *WhoAmW 91*
Feinberg, Joel 1926- *WhoAm 90, WhoWrEP 89*
Feinberg, John David 1947- *WhoEmL 91*
Feinberg, Kenneth R. *BioIn 16*
Feinberg, Lawrence Bernard 1940- *WhoAm 90*
Feinberg, Leonard 1914- *WhoAm 90*
Feinberg, Louis 1887-1949 *BioIn 16*
Feinberg, Mark Ethan 1962- *WhoE 91*
Feinberg, Martin 1932- *WhoE 91*
Feinberg, Martin Robert 1942- *WhoAm 90*
Feinberg, Michael 1942- *WhoE 91*
Feinberg, Michael P 1942- *BiDrAPA 89*
Feinberg, Mortimer Robert 1922- *WhoAm 90*
Feinberg, Peter Fredric 1962- *WhoE 91*

Feinberg, Peter I. *BioIn 16*
Feinberg, Philip 1915- *BiDrAPA 89*
Feinberg, Richard Alan 1947- *WhoWor 91*
Feinberg, Richard B. 1945- *St&PR 91*
Feinberg, Richard Burt 1945- *WhoAm 90*
Feinberg, Robert Ira 1956- *WhoE 91, WhoEmL 91, WhoWor 91*
Feinberg, Robert Mark 1951- *WhoE 91*
Feinberg, Robert S. 1934- *WhoAm 90, WhoWor 91*
Feinberg, Robert Samuel 1940- *St&PR 91*
Feinberg, Rosa Castro 1939- *WhoHisp 91*
Feinberg, Samuel 1908- *WhoE 91*
Feinberg, Simeon Shalom 1954- *BiDrAPA 89*
Feinberg, Susan L. 1944- *WhoAmW 91*
Feinberg, Thomas Davis 1932- *St&PR 91*
Feinberg, Walter 1937- *WhoAm 90*
Feinberg, Wilfred 1920- *WhoAm 90, WhoE 91*
Feinblatt, Ebria *WhoAmA 91N*
Feindel, William Howard 1918- *WhoAm 90*
Feindt, Mary C. 1916- *WhoAmW 91*
Feine, Paul M. 1942- *ODwPR 91*
Feine, Paul Money 1942- *WhoWrEP 89*
Feinendegen, Ludwig Emil 1927- *WhoWor 91*
Feiner, Alexander 1928- *WhoAm 90*
Feiner, Arlene Marie 1937- *WhoAmW 91*
Feiner, Ava Sophia 1950- *WhoAmW 91, WhoE 91*
Feiner, Joel S 1938- *BiDrAPA 89, WhoE 91*
Feiner, Leon 1888-1945 *BioIn 16*
Feiner, Neil Frank *BiDrAPA 89*
Feiner, Ronald Ross 1938- *St&PR 91*
Feinerman, Leon Judah 1945- *WhoE 91*
Feinfeld, Linda Ellen 1947- *BiDrAPA 89*
Feinglas, Mitchel Alan 1948- *WhoEmL 91*
Feingold, David Sidney 1922- *WhoAm 90*
Feingold, Elisa Sharona *BiDrAPA 89*
Feingold, Henry L 1931- *ConAu 31NR*
Feingold, Henry Leo 1931- *WhoAm 90*
Feingold, Henry R 1925- *BiDrAPA 89*
Feingold, Marie 1919- *St&PR 91*
Feingold, Matthew Coleman 1945- *St&PR 91*
Feingold, Russell A. 1951- *WhoEmL 91*
Feingold, S Norman 1914- *ConAu 30NR*
Feingold, S. Norman 1914- *WhoAm 90*
Feingold, Victor 1912-1989 *BioIn 16*
Feinhandler, Edward Sanford 1948- *WhoEmL 91*
Feininger, Andreas 1906- *BioIn 16*
Feininger, Andreas B L 1906- *WhoAmA 91*
Feininger, Andreas Bernhard Lyonel 1906- *WhoAm 90*
Feininger, Lyonel *EncACom*
Feininger, Lyonel 1871-1956 *IntDcAA 90*
Feininger, T Lux 1910- *WhoAmA 91*
Feininger, Theodore Lux 1910- *WhoAm 90*
Feinleib, Manning 1935- *WhoAm 90*
Feinman, Stephen E 1932- *WhoAmA 91*
Feinman, Susan Margaret Ellmann 1930- *WhoAmW 91*
Feinschreiber, Selven F. 1912- *WhoWor 91*
Feinsilver, David B 1939- *BiDrAPA 89, WhoE 91*
Feinsilver, Donald Lee 1947- *BiDrAPA 89*
Feinsmith, Marvin P. 1937- *IntWWM 90*
Feinsod, Paul Martin 1955- *WhoEmL 91*
Feinstein, Alan Shawn 1931- *WhoAm 90*
Feinstein, Allen Lewis 1929- *WhoAm 90*
Feinstein, Alvan Richard 1925- *WhoAm 90*
Feinstein, Beverly 1943- *BiDrAPA 89*
Feinstein, Carl Bruce *BiDrAPA 89*
Feinstein, Dianne *BioIn 16, NewYTBS 90 [port]*
Feinstein, Dianne 1933- *WhoAm 90, WhoAmW 91, WorAlBi*
Feinstein, Elaine 1930- *BioIn 16, ConAu 31NR, FemiCLE, MajTwCW*
Feinstein, Elana Beth 1962- *WhoEmL 91*
Feinstein, Harris Elliot 1953- *BiDrAPA 89*
Feinstein, Howard M 1929- *BiDrAPA 89*
Feinstein, Irwin Keith 1914- *WhoAm 90*
Feinstein, Jack J. 1909- *St&PR 91*
Feinstein, Jeffrey E. 1957- *WhoEmL 91*
Feinstein, Jeffrey Mitchell 1946- *WhoEmL 91*
Feinstein, Jerald Lee 1943- *WhoSSW 91, WhoWor 91*
Feinstein, Jonathan Edward 1953- *WhoE 91*
Feinstein, Martin 1921- *WhoAm 90, WhoE 91*
Feinstein, Michael *BioIn 16*
Feinstein, Michael H. 1935- *St&PR 91*
Feinstein, Michael Jay 1956- *WhoAm 90, WhoE 91*
Feinstein, Moshe 1895-1986 *BioIn 16*
Feinstein, Neil Jeffrey 1939- *St&PR 91*
Feinstein, Paul Louis 1955- *WhoEmL 91*
Feinstein, Pratarnporn 1935- *BiDrAPA 89*
Feinstein, Robert Eric *BiDrAPA 89*
Feinstein, Robert N 1915- *WhoWrEP 89*
Feinstein, Ronald 1946- *St&PR 91*
Feinstein, Roni *WhoAmA 91*
Feinstein, Selwyn 1931- *WhoAm 90*
Feinstein, Sherman C *BiDrAPA 89*
Feinstein, Steven David 1940- *BiDrAPA 89, WhoE 91*
Feinstock, Toby G. 1937- *St&PR 91*
Feintuch, Henry P. *ODwPR 91*
Feintuch, Richard David 1952- *WhoEmL 91*
Feir, Dorothy Jean 1929- *WhoAm 90*
Feir, Gordon Douglas 1942- *WhoSSW 91*
Feir, Terence C *BiDrAPA 89*
Feirer, John Louis 1915- *WhoAm 90*
Feirstein, Frederick 1940- *WhoAm 90, WhoWrEP 89*
Feirstein, Ira D 1945- *BiDrAPA 89*
Feirstein, Janice 1942- *WhoAmW 91, WhoWor 91*
Feis, Herbert 1893-1972 *BioIn 16*
Feisel, Lyle Dean 1935- *WhoAm 90*
Feiss, Carl Lehman 1907- *WhoAm 90*
Feist, Fredric W *BiDrAPA 89*
Feist, Gene 1930- *ConAu 129, WhoAm 90*
Feist, Harold E 1945- *WhoAmA 91*
Feist, Joseph J. 1929- *St&PR 91*
Feist, Leonard 1910- *WhoAm 90*
Feist, Warner David 1909- *WhoAmA 91*
Feist-Fite, Bernadette 1945- *WhoAmW 91, WhoEmL 91*
Feit, Dudley 1906- *St&PR 91*
Feit, Evelyn Barbara 1932- *St&PR 91*
Feit, Theodore 1930- *WhoE 91*
Feitelson, Amy Sue 1955- *BiDrAPA 89, WhoE 91*
Feitelson, Dina 1926- *WhoWor 91*
Feitelson, Helen Lundeberg *WhoAmA 91*
Feitelson, Lorser 1898-1978 *WhoAmA 91N*
Feitler, Robert 1930- *St&PR 91, WhoWor 91*
Feito, Jose 1929- *WhoAm 90, WhoSSW 91*
Feitshans, Fred 1937- *St&PR 91*
Feitshans, Fred Rollin 1937- *WhoAm 90*
Feitshans, Theodore Alan 1956- *WhoEmL 91*
Feitsma, Anthonie 1928- *EncCoWW*
Feiwel, Jean Leslie 1953- *WhoWrEP 89*
Feiwel, Raphael Joseph 1907-1985 *ConAu 129*
Feiz, Reza 1939- *BiDrAPA 89*
Fejer, Andras *PenDiMP*
Fejes, Claire 1920- *BioIn 16, WhoAmA 91*
Fejes, Ernest 1954- *WhoWor 91*
Feke, Deborah Jo 1952- *WhoAmW 91*
Feke, Robert 1705?-1750? *EncCRAm*
Fekete, Brian 1955- *WhoAmA 91*
Fekete, George Otto *WhoWor 91*
Fekete, John 1946- *ConAu 129*
Fekkes, Harry J. *St&PR 91*
Fekula, Alexis P. *BioIn 16*
Fekula, Walter Peter 1936- *St&PR 91*
Felactu, Jim *BiDrAPA 89*
Felago, Ernest Michael 1944- *St&PR 91*
Feland, Armstead Milner, III 1921- *WhoAm 90, WhoSSW 91*
Felando, August J. 1929- *St&PR 91*
Felber, Bryan Coleman 1958- *WhoEmL 91*
Felber, John H 1917- *BiDrAPA 89*
Felber, Mathias John 1938- *WhoE 91*
Felber, Rene 1933- *WhoWor 91*
Felber, Richard J. 1928- *St&PR 91*
Felber, Ronald Jeffrey 1946- *WhoEmL 91*
Felberbaum, Carol Ann 1939- *WhoAmW 91*
Felch, William Campbell 1920- *WhoAm 90*
Felchlin, James Alois 1919- *St&PR 91*
Felchlin, Mary Kathleen Conroy 1951- *WhoAmW 91*
Felciano, Richard 1930- *IntWWM 90*
Feld, Alan David 1936- *WhoAm 90*
Feld, Alan Lewis 1940- *WhoAm 90*
Feld, Arthur Michael 1942- *WhoWor 91*
Feld, Augusta 1919- *WhoAmA 91*
Feld, Eliot 1942- *WhoAm 90, WhoE 91*
Feld, Frederick Albert, III 1947- *WhoSSW 91*
Feld, Fritz 1900- *WhoAm 90*
Feld, Jindrich 1925- *IntWWM 90*
Feld, Joseph 1919- *WhoE 91, WhoWor 91*
Feld, Judith Ann 1953- *BiDrAPA 89*
Feld, Karen Irma 1947- *WhoE 91*
Feld, Katherine Phoebe 1958- *WhoEmL 91*
Feld, Kenneth Jeffrey 1948- *BioIn 16, St&PR 91*
Feld, Leonard Bernard 1950- *WhoEmL 91*
Feld, Lipman Goldman 1914- *WhoAm 90*
Feld, Marian Parry *WhoAmA 91*
Feld, Michael Lee 1959- *BiDrAPA 89*
Feld, Michael Stephen 1940- *WhoAm 90*
Feld, Myron *BiDrAPA 89*
Feld, Nicholas 1915- *WhoAm 90*
Feld, Stephen 1947- *BiDrAPA 89*
Feld, Steve 1956- *WhoE 91*
Feld, Steven Alan 1955- *WhoEmL 91*
Feld, Steven Anatole 1945- *WhoEmL 91*
Feld, Stuart Paul 1935- *WhoAm 90, WhoAmA 91*
Feld, Thomas Robert 1944- *WhoAm 90*
Feld, Werner Joachim 1910- *WhoAm 90*
Feldbauer Jansen, Mary 1945- *WhoAmW 91*
Feldberg, Chester Ben 1939- *WhoAm 90*
Feldberg, Meyer 1942- *WhoAm 90*
Feldberg, Michael Svetkey 1951- *WhoEmL 91*
Feldberg, Sumner Lee 1924- *St&PR 91, WhoAm 90*
Feldberg, Theodore M 1919- *BiDrAPA 89*
Feldbrill, Victor 1924- *WhoAm 90*
Feldbrugge, Ferdinand Joseph Maria 1933- *WhoWor 91*
Feldbusch, Michael F. 1951- *WhoEmL 91*
Felde, Wayne *BioIn 16*
Felden, Victoria E. 1958- *WhoEmL 91*
Feldenkrais, Moshe 1904-1984 *NewAgE 90*
Feldenkreis, George 1935- *WhoSSW 91*
Felder, Andreas *BioIn 16*
Felder, B. Dell *WhoAm 90*
Felder, Diane Johnson 1957- *BiDrAPA 89*
Felder, Eleanor *AuBYP 90*
Felder, Frederick Joseph Daniel, Jr. 1952- *WhoSSW 91*
Felder, Jerome Solon 1925- *WhoE 91, WhoWor 91*
Felder, Louis 1960- *St&PR 91*
Felder, Mike 1961- *Ballpl 90*
Felder, Myrna *BioIn 16*
Felder, Pamela A *BiDrAPA 89*
Felder, Pamela Theresa 1956- *WhoSSW 91*
Felder, Raoul *BioIn 16*
Felder, Raoul Lionel 1934- *WhoE 91, WhoWor 91*
Felder, Richard E 1918- *BiDrAPA 89*
Felder, Sandra *BiDrAPA 89*
Felder, Warren Jay 1924- *St&PR 91*
Felderer, Bernhard 1941- *WhoWor 91*
Felderhof, Jan Reindent Adriaan 1907- *IntWWM 90*
Feldesman, Walter 1917- *St&PR 91*
Feldhammer, Tovita *BiDrAPA 89*
Feldhaus, Paul A 1926- *WhoAmA 91*
Feldheim, Deborah Lynne *BiDrAPA 89*
Feldheim, Deborah Lynne 1958- *WhoE 91*
Feldheim, Jack 1953- *St&PR 91*
Feldhof, Gerd 1931- *IntWWM 90*
Feldhorn, Earl I. 1938- *St&PR 91*
Feldhusen, Hazel J. 1928- *WhoAmW 91*
Feldhusen, John Frederick 1926- *WhoAm 90*
Feldkamp, Lynn Elmer 1955- *St&PR 91*
Feldman, Aileen 1953- *BiDrAPA 89*
Feldman, Albert 1926- *ODwPR 91*
Feldman, Allan Maurice 1943- *WhoE 91*
Feldman, Armin Ira 1949- *BiDrAPA 89*
Feldman, Arnold 1938- *BiDrAPA 89*
Feldman, Arthur I 1933- *BiDrAPA 89*
Feldman, Arthur Mitchell 1942- *WhoAmA 91*
Feldman, Barry Stewart 1940- *St&PR 91*
Feldman, Bella Tabak *WhoAmA 91*
Feldman, Ben 1912- *WhoSSW 91*
Feldman, Bernard Joseph 1946- *WhoEmL 91*
Feldman, Bernard Robert 1934- *WhoE 91*
Feldman, Bert 1874-1945 *OxCPMus*
Feldman, Brian C. 1942- *ODwPR 91*
Feldman, Bruce Alan 1959- *BiDrAPA 89*
Feldman, Bruce Allen 1941- *WhoE 91*
Feldman, Burton Gordon 1911- *WhoAm 90*
Feldman, Clarice Rochelle 1941- *WhoAm 90*
Feldman, Corey *BioIn 16*
Feldman, Corey 1971- *ConTFT 8*
Feldman, Daniel L 1949- *ConAu 131*
Feldman, David Borden 1956- *BiDrAPA 89*
Feldman, Debra Lynn 1955- *WhoAmW 91*
Feldman, Donald J 1940- *BiDrAPA 89*
Feldman, Edmund Burke 1924- *WhoAm 90, WhoAmA 91, WhoSSW 91*
Feldman, Edward I *BiDrAPA 89*
Feldman, Edward Steven 1947- *WhoEmL 91*
Feldman, Egal 1925- *WhoAm 90*
Feldman, Elaine Bossak 1926- *WhoAm 90*
Feldman, Ellen Kay *BiDrAPA 89*
Feldman, Elyse Carol *BiDrAPA 89*
Feldman, Franklin 1927- *St&PR 91, WhoAm 90, WhoAmA 91*
Feldman, Frederik 1937- *St&PR 91*
Feldman, Gary *ODwPR 91*
Feldman, Gary Jay 1942- *WhoAm 90*
Feldman, Gary Marc 1953- *WhoSSW 91*
Feldman, Gordon 1928- *WhoAm 90*
Feldman, H. Larry 1941- *WhoAm 90*
Feldman, Harold Raymond 1918- *St&PR 91*
Feldman, Harold S 1917- *BiDrAPA 89*
Feldman, Harold Samuel 1917- *WhoE 91*
Feldman, Harris Joseph 1942- *WhoWor 91*
Feldman, Harry 1919-1962 *Ballpl 90*
Feldman, Harry H. 1949- *WhoE 91*
Feldman, Herbert Franklin 1933- *WhoE 91*
Feldman, Herbert H. 1932- *St&PR 91*
Feldman, Hervey Allen 1937- *St&PR 91, WhoAm 90*
Feldman, Ira S. 1943- *WhoAm 90*
Feldman, Irving 1928- *WhoAm 90, WhoWrEP 89*
Feldman, Irwin Miles 1939- *WhoAm 90*
Feldman, Jacqueline Maus 1953- *BiDrAPA 89*
Feldman, James J. 1956- *BiDrAPA 89*
Feldman, Jamie Lynn *BiDrAPA 89*
Feldman, Janet Diane 1958- *WhoAmW 91*
Feldman, Jay N. 1936- *St&PR 91, WhoAm 90*
Feldman, Jeff 1955- *ODwPR 91*
Feldman, Jenat Levison 1951- *WhoEmL 91*
Feldman, Jerome Arthur 1938- *WhoAm 90*
Feldman, Jerome Howard *BiDrAPA 89*
Feldman, Jerome I. 1928- *St&PR 91*
Feldman, Jerome Ira 1928- *WhoAm 90*
Feldman, Jerome Myron 1935- *WhoAm 90*
Feldman, Jesse 1947- *WhoEmL 91*
Feldman, Joel Steven 1940- *St&PR 91*
Feldman, John Angelo 1939- *WhoE 91*
Feldman, Joseph David 1916- *WhoWrEP 89*
Feldman, Joseph H 1923- *BiDrAPA 89*
Feldman, Joseph Herbert 1923- *WhoE 91*
Feldman, Judith Levine 1944- *BiDrAPA 89*
Feldman, Larry Brian 1942- *BiDrAPA 89*
Feldman, Lauren 1961- *WhoAmW 91*
Feldman, Lawrence Herbert 1942- *WhoWor 91, WhoWrEP 89*
Feldman, Leon D. 1929- *St&PR 91*
Feldman, Lillian Maltz *WhoAmW 91*
Feldman, Louis Harry 1926- *WhoAm 90*
Feldman, Lynn Sonia *BiDrAPA 89*
Feldman, Lynn Sonia 1954- *WhoE 91*
Feldman, Marc David *BiDrAPA 89*
Feldman, Mark B. 1935- *WhoAm 90*
Feldman, Mark J. 1956- *ODwPR 91*
Feldman, Mark Russel 1949- *WhoAm 90*
Feldman, Marty 1933-1982 *WorAlBi*
Feldman, Marvin 1927- *WhoAm 90*
Feldman, Mary L. *ODwPR 91*
Feldman, Max 1923- *St&PR 91*
Feldman, Max 1935- *WhoE 91*
Feldman, Michael Harris 1949- *WhoEmL 91*
Feldman, Michael J 1944- *BiDrAPA 89*
Feldman, Michael Lloyd *BiDrAPA 89*
Feldman, Michael Sanford 1948- *WhoEmL 91*
Feldman, Miriam Ellin 1924- *WhoAmW 91*
Feldman, Mitchell Robert 1956- *WhoEmL 91*
Feldman, Morton *BioIn 16, NewAgMG*
Feldman, Morton 1926- *IntWWM 90*
Feldman, Myer 1917- *WhoAm 90*
Feldman, Nancy Beth 1960- *St&PR 91*
Feldman, Oscar Henry 1921- *St&PR 91*
Feldman, Paula Renee 1948- *WhoSSW 91*
Feldman, Philip M 1937- *BiDrAPA 89*
Feldman, Phyllis Sirotta *BiDrAPA 89*
Feldman, Raymond V. 1914- *St&PR 91*
Feldman, Richard N 1940- *BiDrAPA 89*
Feldman, Richard Warrren 1947- *WhoSSW 91*
Feldman, Robert C. 1956- *ODwPR 91*
Feldman, Robert George 1933- *WhoAm 90*
Feldman, Robert M. 1932- *St&PR 91*
Feldman, Roger Bruce 1939- *WhoAm 90*
Feldman, Roger David 1943- *WhoAm 90, WhoWor 91*
Feldman, Roger David 1945- *WhoAm 90*
Feldman, Roger Lawrence 1949- *WhoAmA 91*
Feldman, Roger Paul *BiDrAPA 89*
Feldman, Ronald *WhoAmA 91*
Feldman, Ronald Arthur 1938- *WhoAm 90*
Feldman, Rubin 1926- *St&PR 91*
Feldman, Russett 1951- *BiDrAPA 89*
Feldman, Ruth 1911- *ConAu 31NR, WhoWrEP 89*
Feldman, Ruth Duskin 1934- *WhoWrEP 89*
Feldman, Samuel Mitchell 1933- *WhoAm 90*
Feldman, Sandra 1939- *BioIn 16*
Feldman, Shelley 1926- *St&PR 91*
Feldman, Stanley George 1933- *WhoAm 90*
Feldman, Stanley Jay 1944- *WhoE 91*
Feldman, Stephen 1944- *WhoAm 90, WhoE 91*
Feldman, Stephen Aaron 1947- *St&PR 91*
Feldman, Stephen L. 1946-1990 *ConAu 132*
Feldman, Steven *BiDrAPA 89*
Feldman, Steven 1946- *WhoEmL 91*
Feldman, Susan Carol 1943- *WhoAmW 91*
Feldman, Vic 1934-1987 *OxCPMus*
Feldman, Victoria *ODwPR 91*

Feldman, Walter 1925- *WhoAmA 91*
Feldman, Walter S 1916- *BiDrAPA 89*
Feldman, Walter Sidney 1925- *WhoAm 90*
Feldman, Yael S. 1941- *WhoE 91*
Feldman-Gorn, Moises 1923- *BiDrAPA 89*
Feldmann, Edward George 1930- *WhoAm 90*
Feldmann, Erich 1929- *WhoWor 91*
Feldmann, Frank Neil 1954- *WhoEmL 91*
Feldmann, Harald 1925- *WhoWor 91*
Feldmann, Horst 1932- *WhoWor 91*
Feldmann, Peter 1945- *WhoEmL 91*
Feldmann, Shirley Clark 1929- *WhoAm 90*
Feldmann, Theodore Bruce 1951- *BiDrAPA 89*
Feldmann, Walther H. 1898-1988 *BioIn 16*
Feldmesser, Jeffrey A. 1954- *WhoE 91*
Feldon, Barbara 1941- *WorAlBi*
Feldon, Joan Sorge 1932- *WhoAmW 91*
Feldpausch, Sherry Miller 1961- *WhoEmL 91*
Feldschuh, Joseph 1935- *St&PR 91*
Feldshuh, Benjamin 1937- *BiDrAPA 89*
Feldshuh, Tovah 1953- *BioIn 16*
Feldsieper, Manfred Willi 1941- *WhoWor 91*
Feldstein, Albert B. 1925- *WhoAm 90, WhoWrEP 89*
Feldstein, Donald 1931- *WhoAm 90*
Feldstein, Joel R. 1942- *ODwPR 91*
Feldstein, Joel Robert 1942- *WhoAm 90*
Feldstein, Kathleen Foley 1941- *WhoE 91*
Feldstein, Martin E. 1939- *WorAlBi*
Feldstein, Martin Stuart 1939- *WhoAm 90, WhoWor 91*
Feldstein, Richard 1945- *BiDrAPA 89*
Feldstein, Richard Lawrence 1942- *St&PR 91*
Feldstein, Robert M 1933- *BiDrAPA 89*
Feldstein Soto, Luis A. 1960- *WhoHisp 91*
Feldt, John Harrell 1940- *WhoAm 90*
Feldt, Kjell-Olof 1931- *WhoWor 91*
Feldt, Robert Hewitt 1934- *WhoAm 90*
Feldtman, Henry Douglas 1928- *WhoWor 91*
Feldwisch, David Lewis 1952- *WhoEmL 91*
Feleciano, Paul, Jr. *WhoHisp 91*
Feledy, Charles Frank 1935- *WhoE 91*
Feles, Gust 1927- *St&PR 91*
Felfe, Peter Franz 1939- *WhoAm 90*
Felfe, Werner 1928-1988 *BioIn 16*
Felger, Hubert L *BiDrAPA 89*
Felger, Ralph William 1919- *WhoWor 91*
Felgran, Steven David 1953- *WhoE 91*
Felheim, Robert J. *BioIn 16*
Felice, Alex Emmanuel 1947- *WhoWor 91*
Felice Cardot, Carlos 1913-1986 *BioIn 16*
Felicella, Frank George 1946- *WhoE 91*
Felicetti, Armando L. 1933- *St&PR 91*
Felicetti, Daniel A. 1942- *WhoAm 90*
Felici, Angelo 1919- *WhoWor 91*
Feliciano, Donald Vincent 1952- *WhoSSW 91*
Feliciano, Jose 1945- *WhoHisp 91, WorAlBi*
Feliciano, Jose Celso 1950- *WhoEmL 91*
Feliciano, Miguel Angel 1947- *WhoE 91*
Feliciano, Nereida Iris *BiDrAPA 89*
Feliciano, Rebecca Acosta *BiDrAPA 89*
Feliciotti, Enio 1926- *St&PR 91*
Felicita, James Thomas 1947- *WhoWor 91*
Felinski, William Walter 1953- *WhoE 91, WhoEmL 91, WhoWor 91*
Felipe II, King of Spain 1527-1598 *BioIn 16*
Felipe IV, King of Spain 1605-1665 *BioIn 16*
Felipe V, King of Spain 1683-1746 *BioIn 16*
Felisky, Barbara Rosbe 1938- *WhoAmA 91*
Felisky, Catherine Anne 1958- *BiDrAPA 89*
Felitti, Dominick P. *BioIn 16*
Feliu, David Noel 1957- *WhoEmL 91*
Felix, Alan David *BiDrAPA 89*
Felix, Alan David 1957- *WhoE 91*
Felix, Allen O. *BioIn 16*
Felix, Anthony G., Jr. 1909- *WhoAm 90*
Felix, Arthur, Jr. 1945- *WhoHisp 91*
Felix, Charles Jeffrey 1921- *WhoSSW 91*
Felix, David 1918- *WhoAm 90*
Felix, Elaine Sawtelle 1958- *WhoEmL 91*
Felix, Gus 1895-1960 *Ballpl 90*
Felix, Hugo 1866-1934 *OxCPMus*
Felix, Jeanette Salzmann 1944- *WhoAmW 91*
Felix, Joseph F *BiDrAPA 89*
Felix, Junior Francisco 1967- *WhoHisp 91*
Felix, Lennie 1920-1981 *OxCPMus*
Felix, Luna *BioIn 16*
Felix, Patricia Jean 1941- *WhoAmW 91*
Felix, Richard James 1944- *WhoWor 91*
Felix, Richard Reid 1946- *BiDrAPA 89*
Felix, Robert H 1904- *BiDrAPA 89*
Felix, Robert H 1904-1990 *CurBio 90N, NewYTBS 90 [port]*
Felix, Robert Hanna 1904-1990 *BioIn 16*
Felix, Ted Mark 1947- *WhoE 91*
Felix, Vaclav 1928- *IntWWM 90*
Felix Mena, Jorge *WhoWor 91*
Felix-Tchicaya, Gerald *ConAu 129*
Felkenes, August Charles 1932- *St&PR 91*
Felker, Alex D. *BioIn 16*
Felker, Allyn C. 1962- *WhoAmW 91*
Felker, Bradford Laird *BiDrAPA 89*
Felker, David R. 1957- *WhoEmL 91, WhoWor 91*
Felker, Donald W. *WhoAm 90*
Felker, G. Stephen 1951- *St&PR 91*
Felker, George W., III 1915- *St&PR 91*
Felker, George Walton, III 1915- *WhoSSW 91*
Felker, James 1939- *St&PR 91*
Felker, James M. 1939- *WhoAm 90*
Felker, Kathleen Anne 1955- *WhoE 91*
Felker, Kelly A. 1961- *WhoSSW 91*
Felker, William H. 1953- *WhoEmL 91*
Felkins, Barbara Joyce *BiDrAPA 89*
Felknor, Bruce Lester 1921- *WhoAm 90*
Felknor, Laurie *WhoAmW 91*
Fell, Alison 1944- *FemiCLE*
Fell, Charles Francis 1939- *WhoWor 91*
Fell, Donald G. 1945- *WhoEmL 91, WhoSSW 91*
Fell, Donna Cyd *BiDrAPA 89*
Fell, Frederick Victor 1910- *WhoAm 90, WhoWrEP 89*
Fell, Gilbert Allen 1941- *St&PR 91*
Fell, Glen *St&PR 91*
Fell, Isaac 1758-1818 *PenDiDA 89*
Fell, John Louis 1927- *WhoAm 90*
Fell, Laurence T. 1937- *St&PR 91*
Fell, Lydia *BiDEWW*
Fell, Margaret 1614-1702 *BiDEWW, BioIn 16, FemiCLE*
Fell, Mary Elizabeth 1947- *WhoWrEP 89*
Fell, Robert *BioIn 16*
Fell, Robert S. 1931- *St&PR 91*
Fell, Roy Thomas 1933- *St&PR 91*
Fell, Sarah 1642-1714 *BiDEWW*
Fell, Sheila 1931-1980 *BiDWomA*
Fell, Stephen M. 1953- *St&PR 91*
Fell, Steven Louis 1950- *St&PR 91*
Fell, Thomas *PenDiDA 89*
Fellbaum, Jean Anne 1962- *WhoAmW 91*
Fellegi, Adam 1941- *IntWWM 90*
Fellegi, Ivan *BioIn 16*
Fellegi, Ivan Peter 1935- *WhoAm 90*
Fellenberg, William Y. 1948- *ODwPR 91*
Fellenberg, William Yukikazu 1948- *WhoE 91*
Fellendorf, George William 1925- *WhoAm 90*
Fellenstein, Cora Ellen Mullikin 1930- *WhoAmW 91*
Feller, Benjamin E. 1947- *WhoE 91*
Feller, Bob 1918- *Ballpl 90 [port]*
Feller, Carlos 1925- *IntWWM 90*
Feller, Christopher Adam 1952- *St&PR 91*
Feller, Dana Elizabeth 1963- *WhoE 91*
Feller, David E. 1916- *WhoAm 90*
Feller, David Scott 1958- *St&PR 91*
Feller, Harriet Burns 1942- *WhoAm 90*
Feller, Henrietta Odin 1800-1868 *BioIn 16*
Feller, Howard 1953- *WhoEmL 91*
Feller, John Douglas 1951- *WhoEmL 91*
Feller, Lawrence John C. 1957- *WhoE 91*
Feller, Mimi 1948- *ODwPR 91*
Feller, Richard Tabler 1919- *WhoE 91*
Feller, Robert 1918- *WorAlBi*
Feller, Robert L 1919- *WhoAmA 91*
Feller, Robert Livingston 1919- *WhoAm 90*
Feller, Robert William Andrew 1918- *AuBYP 90*
Feller, Roger L *BiDrAPA 89*
Feller, Sherm *BioIn 16*
Feller, Steven A. 1954- *St&PR 91*
Feller, William 1906-1970 *DcScB S2*
Fellerman, Linden Jan 1956- *WhoEmL 91*
Fellers, James Davison 1913- *WhoAm 90, WhoSSW 91*
Fellers, Rhonda Gay 1955- *WhoAmW 91*
Fellhauer, David E. 1939- *WhoAm 90, WhoSSW 91*
Fellheimer, Alan *BioIn 16*
Fellheimer, Alan S. 1943- *St&PR 91*
Fellin, Octavia Antoinette 1913- *WhoAmW 91*
Fellin, Phillip Alexander 1931- *WhoAm 90*
Felling, Albert Johan Alfons 1938- *WhoWor 91*
Fellinger, Imogen 1928- *IntWWM 90*
Fellingham, David Andrew 1937- *St&PR 91*
Fellingham, Steven V. *WhoSSW 91*
Fellini, Federico *BioIn 16*
Fellini, Federico 1920- *ConAu 33NR, WhoAm 90, WhoWor 91, WorAlBi*
Fellman, David 1907- *WhoAm 90*
Fellman, Malcolm Jay 1932- *WhoWor 91*
Fellman, Nelson M., Jr. *ODwPR 91*
Fellman, Richard Allen *BiDrAPA 89*
Fellman, Sandi 1952- *BioIn 16*
Fellman, William Stevens 1934- *St&PR 91*
Fellmeth, Scott Eugene 1955- *WhoEmL 91*
Fellner, Bernard Samuel 1947- *WhoEmL 91*
Fellner, Carl H *BiDrAPA 89*
Fellner, Michael Josef 1936- *WhoAm 90*
Fellner, Rudolph *AuBYP 90*
Fello, Bill *BioIn 16*
Fellowes, Frederick Gale, Jr. 1930- *WhoAm 90*
Fellowes, James Everett 1946- *St&PR 91*
Fellowes, Peter 1944- *WhoWrEP 89*
Fellows, Charles Robert 1950- *WhoSSW 91*
Fellows, Fred 1934- *WhoAmA 91*
Fellows, Fred H. 1918- *St&PR 91*
Fellows, Haynes Harold, Jr. 1919- *St&PR 91*
Fellows, Muriel H. *AuBYP 90*
Fellows, Oscar F. 1858-1921 *AmLegL*
Fellows, Robert Ellis 1933- *WhoAm 90*
Fellows, Robert Shaw 1947- *St&PR 91*
Fellows, Russell C. 1938- *St&PR 91*
Fellows, Russell Coleman 1938- *WhoAm 90, WhoSSW 91*
Fellows, Susan Marie 1964- *WhoAmW 91*
Fells, Robert Marshall 1950- *WhoEmL 91*
Felman, Alan B. *St&PR 91*
Felman, Leonard Stuart 1935- *WhoE 91*
Felman, Marc David 1954- *WhoSSW 91*
Felmlee, Vicki Patricia 1952- *WhoAmW 91*
Felmly, M Leslie *BiDrAPA 89*
Felmus, Laurence B. 1906-1989 *BioIn 16*
Felmy, Hellmuth 1885- *BioIn 16*
Felmy, John 1954- *St&PR 91*
Felner, Glenn Lawrence 1926- *WhoWor 91*
Felner, Theodore I. *BioIn 16, NewYTBS 90*
Felo, Matthew Francis, Jr. 1945- *St&PR 91*
Felous, Shahira Halim *BiDrAPA 89*
Felper, David Michael 1954- *WhoEmL 91*
Felqoise, Faye 1922- *St&PR 91*
Fels, C P 1912- *WhoAmA 91*
Fels, Charles Wentworth Baker 1943- *WhoSSW 91*
Fels, Gerald 1943- *St&PR 91*
Fels, Rendigs 1917- *WhoAm 90*
Fels, Robert Alan 1954- *WhoSSW 91*
Felsch, Happy 1891-1964 *Ballpl 90*
Felsen, Henry Gregor 1916- *AuBYP 90*
Felsen, Karl Edwin 1948- *WhoEmL 91, WhoWrEP 89*
Felsen, Leopold B. 1924- *WhoAm 90*
Felsen, Milt 1912- *BioIn 16*
Felsen, Rosamund 1934- *WhoAmA 91*
Felsenfeld, Gary 1929- *WhoAm 90*
Felsenthal, Bernard 1822-1908 *BioIn 16*
Felsenthal, Steven Altus 1949- *WhoWor 91*
Felske, Edwin Morgan 1934- *WhoE 91*
Felske, John 1942- *Ballpl 90*
Felski, Albina 1916- *MusmAFA*
Felson, Benjamin 1913-1988 *BioIn 16*
Felsted, Carla Martindell 1947- *WhoAmW 91*
Felt, Donald Kyle 1934- *WhoAm 90*
Felt, Irving Mitchell 1910- *St&PR 91, WhoAm 90*
Felt, William Breton 1927- *St&PR 91*
Feltch, Cynthia Anne 1955- *WhoE 91*
Felten, Donald L. 1938- *St&PR 91*
Felten, Edward Joseph 1938- *St&PR 91*
Felten, Ross Henry 1934- *St&PR 91*
Feltenstein, Harry David, Jr. 1920- *WhoAm 90*
Feltenstein, Mary Belle 1947- *St&PR 91*
Feltenstein, Paul Douglas 1947- *St&PR 91*
Felter, James Warren 1943- *WhoAmA 91*
Felter, John Kenneth 1950- *WhoEmL 91*
Felter, June Marie 1919- *WhoAmA 91*
Feltes, Charles Victor 1947- *WhoEmL 91*
Feltes, Marcia Duncan 1952- *WhoE 91*
Feltham, Ivan Reid 1930- *WhoAm 90*
Feltham, James E. 1930- *St&PR 91*
Feltham, Louise 1935- *WhoAmW 91*
Felthous, Alan Robert 1944- *BiDrAPA 89*
Felthouse, Patricia Mae Avrit 1924- *WhoAmW 91*
Feltman, David T. 1936- *St&PR 91*
Feltman, Lee 1918- *St&PR 91*
Feltmann, James Anthony 1925- *St&PR 91*
Felton, Bruce *ODwPR 91*
Felton, Carol 1947- *ODwPR 91*
Felton, Elaine Louise 1955- *WhoEmL 91*
Felton, Frank P., III 1928- *St&PR 91*
Felton, Geraldene *WhoAm 90*
Felton, Gordon H. 1925- *WhoAm 90*
Felton, Haleemon Shaik *EarBlAP*
Felton, Harold William 1902- *AuBYP 90*
Felton, Jean Spencer 1911- *WhoAm 90*
Felton, John Ross 1926- *WhoAm 90*
Felton, John W. 1929- *ODwPR 91, St&PR 91*
Felton, Judith R. 1942- *WhoAmW 91*
Felton, Jule Wimberly, Jr. 1932- *WhoAm 90*
Felton, Katherine C. 1873-1940 *BioAmW*
Felton, Nicholas G., Mrs. *EarBlAP*
Felton, Norman Francis 1913- *WhoAm 90*
Felton, Patricia Ann 1949- *WhoAmW 91*
Felton, Rebecca L. 1835-1930 *BioAmW*
Felton, Reginald McCoy 1947- *WhoEmL 91*
Felton, Richard *ODwPR 91*
Felton, Samuel Page 1919- *WhoWor 91*
Felton, Susann D. 1948- *St&PR 91*
Felton, Terry 1957- *Ballpl 90*
Felton, W. Sidney *St&PR 91N*
Felton, Warren Locker, II 1925- *WhoAm 90*
Felton, William Raymond 1956- *WhoEmL 91*
Felts, Barry S. *BiDrAPA 89*
Felts, Jeffrey E. 1944- *St&PR 91*
Felts, Joan April 1940- *WhoAmW 91*
Felts, Margaret Clemen 1950- *WhoAmW 91*
Felts, Margaret Davis 1917- *WhoAmW 91*
Felts, William Robert, Jr. 1923- *WhoAm 90*
Feltsman, Vladimir *BioIn 16*
Feltsman, Vladimir 1952- *IntWWM 90, PenDiMP*
Feltus, Alan Evan 1943- *WhoAmA 91*
Felty, James David 1947- *WhoEmL 91*
Felty, Kriss Delbert 1954- *WhoEmL 91*
Feltz, Ross C. 1948- *ODwPR 91*
Felzer, Jordan Wayne 1958- *WhoEmL 91*
Felzer, Lionel 1923- *St&PR 91*
Felzer, Lionel Herbert 1923- *WhoAm 90*
Felzer, Stanton Bernard 1928- *WhoE 91*
Femino, Jim 1952- *WhoEmL 91*
Femminella, Charles J., Jr. 1938- *WhoE 91*
Fen, Chang *BioIn 16*
Fenady, Andrew John 1928- *WhoWrEP 89*
Fenakel, Judit 1936- *EncCoWW*
Fenby, Barbara Lou 1938- *WhoE 91*
Fenby, Eric 1906- *PenDiMP*
Fenby, Eric William 1906- *IntWWM 90*
Fenci, Renzo 1914- *WhoAmA 91*
Fendell, Jonas J *WhoAmA 91*
Fendelman, Helaine 1942- *WhoAmW 91*
Fender, Christa D 1927- *BiDrAPA 89*
Fender, Christopher 1942- *St&PR 91*
Fender, Clarence Leo 1909- *WhoAm 90*
Fender, Freddy 1937- *WhoHisp 91*
Fender, Percy George Herbert 1892-1985 *DcNaB 1981*
Fenderson, Caroline Houston 1932- *WhoSSW 91*
Fenderson, Lewis Henry, Jr. *BioIn 16*
Fenderson, Maurice Linwood 1926- *St&PR 91*
Fendi *ConDes 90*
Fendi, Adele Casagrande *ConDes 90*
Fendi, Alda *BioIn 16*
Fendi, Alda 1940- *ConDes 90*
Fendi, Anna 1933- *ConDes 90*
Fendi, Carla 1937- *ConDes 90*
Fendi, Edoardo *ConDes 90*
Fendi, Franca 1935- *ConDes 90*
Fendi, Paola 1931- *ConDes 90*
Fendler, Janos Hugo 1937- *WhoAm 90*
Fendler, Oscar 1909- *WhoAm 90, WhoSSW 91*
Fendley, Michael Laymon 1950- *St&PR 91*
Fendrich, Charles Welles, Jr. 1924- *WhoAm 90*
Fendrich, Harry G. 1944- *St&PR 91*
Fendrich, Harry George 1944- *WhoAm 90*
Fendrick, Alan B. 1933- *St&PR 91*
Fendrick, Alan Burton 1933- *WhoAm 90*
Fenech-Adami, Edward 1934- *WhoWor 91*
Feneley, Roger Charles Leslie 1933- *WhoWor 91*
Fenello, Michael John 1916- *WhoAm 90*
Fenelon, Francois De Salignac DeLa Mothe 1651-1715 *WorAlBi*
Fenelon, Maurice 1834-1897 *DcCanB 12*
Feneon, Felix 1861-1944 *BioIn 16*
Fener, Gerald 1940- *St&PR 91*
Fenerty, Charles 1821-1892 *DcCanB 12*
Fenerty, Frank Burke 1927- *St&PR 91*
Fenety, George Edward 1812-1899 *DcCanB 12*
Feng Chi-Tsai 1942- *WorAu 1980*
Feng Jicai 1942- *WorAu 1980*
Feng Youlan 1895-1990 *NewYTBS 90*
Feng, Ling-ying 1944- *WhoWor 91*
Feng, Richard T. 1949- *St&PR 91*
Feng, Tse-yun 1928- *WhoAm 90*
Feng, Yen Tsai 1923- *WhoAm 90*
Feng, Zhi-Xiao 1938- *IntWWM 90*
Fenger, Manfred 1928- *WhoE 91*
Fengler, John Peter 1928- *WhoAm 90*
Fenical, Marlin E 1907-1983 *WhoAmA 91N*
Fenichel, Carol H. 1935- *WhoE 91*
Fenichel, Douglas M. *ODwPR 91*
Fenichel, Gladys Susan *BiDrAPA 89*
Fenichel, Norman Stewart 1924- *WhoAm 90*
Fenichel, Richard Lee 1925- *WhoAm 90*
Fenichel, Robert *BiDrAPA 89*
Fenick, Barbara Jean 1951- *WhoWrEP 89*
Fenig, Enrique Zvi 1945- *St&PR 91*
Feniger, Jerome Roland, Jr. 1927- *WhoAm 90, WhoE 91*

Fenimore, Edward L. 1922- *St&PR 91*
Fenimore, George Wiley 1921- *WhoAm 90*
Fenimore, William Gale 1939- *WhoE 91*
Feninger, Claude 1926- *St&PR 91, WhoAm 90*
Fenkart-Froschl, Wolfgang 1943- *WhoWor 91*
Fenkel, Morris Hal *St&PR 91N*
Fenkel, William Ralph 1952- *St&PR 91*
Fenker, John William 1926- *WhoAm 90*
Fenley, Joe Basil 1948- *WhoSSW 91*
Fenley, John David *BiDrAPA 89*
Fenlon, Thomas Bolger 1904- *WhoAm 90*
Fenn, Charles Van Orden 1908- *WhoAm 90*
Fenn, Elizabeth 1914- *WhoAmA 91*
Fenn, Eugene Henry 1930- *St&PR 91*
Fenn, Frank Alfred 1853-1927 *AmLegL*
Fenn, George Junior 1926- *WhoWor 91*
Fenn, Howard H 1946- *BiDrAPA 89*
Fenn, Jeffery William 1941- *WhoWor 91*
Fenn, Nicholas M. 1936- *WhoWor 91*
Fenn, Ormon William, Jr. 1927- *St&PR 91, WhoAm 90, WhoSSW 91*
Fenn, Raymond Wolcott, Jr. 1922- *WhoAm 90*
Fenn, Robert Sargent 1929- *WhoE 91*
Fenn, Stephen Southmyd 1820-1879 *AmLegL*
Fenn, Wallace Osgood 1893-1971 *DcScB S2*
Fennah, Ronald Gordon *BioIn 16*
Fennario, David *BioIn 16*
Fennario, David 1947- *OxCCanT*
Fennebresque, Kim S. 1950- *St&PR 91*
Fennebresque, Kim Samuel 1950- *WhoAm 90*
Fennell, David Karl *BiDrAPA 89*
Fennell, Diane Marie 1944- *WhoAmW 91*
Fennell, Dominic Joseph 1943- *St&PR 91*
Fennell, Donald Wayne 1952- *BiDrAPA 89*
Fennell, Francis 1944- *WhoE 91*
Fennell, Frederick 1914- *IntWWM 90, PenDiMP*
Fennell, John Romauld 1931- *St&PR 91*
Fennell, Rebekah Sue 1955- *WhoEmL 91*
Fennell, Thomas D B 1930- *BiDrAPA 89*
Fennell Robbins, Sally 1950- *WhoAmW 91, WhoE 91*
Fennelly, Brian 1937- *IntWWM 90*
Fennelly, Catherine Reynolds *BioIn 16*
Fennelly, Richard E. 1917- *St&PR 91*
Fennelly, Tony 1945- *WhoWrEP 89*
Fennema, Owen Richard 1929- *WhoAm 90*
Fenner, Burt L. 1929- *IntWWM 90*
Fenner, Derrick *BioIn 16*
Fenner, Don Gary *BiDrAPA 89*
Fenner, George G. 1934- *St&PR 91*
Fenner, George Gleason 1934- *WhoAm 90*
Fenner, Jack Ralph, Jr. 1947- *WhoEmL 91*
Fenner, James Harold 1944- *WhoSSW 91*
Fenner, Milton *BioIn 16*
Fenner, Peter D. 1936- *St&PR 91*
Fenner, Peter David 1936- *WhoAm 90*
Fenner, Phyllis Reid 1899-1982 *AuBYP 90*
Fenner, Richard Dean 1947- *WhoSSW 91*
Fenner, Suzan Ellen 1947- *WhoEmL 91*
Fennerty, Karen S. 1962- *WhoAmW 91*
Fennessey, Ann Marie 1945- *WhoAmW 91*
Fennessey, John Joseph, Jr. 1941- *WhoAm 90*
Fennessy, John James 1933- *WhoAm 90*
Fennessy, Marsha Beach Stewart 1952- *WhoAmW 91, WhoE 91, WhoEmL 91, WhoWor 91*
Fennimore, John W. *AmLegL*
Fenning, Andrew Robert Fenn 1950- *WhoWor 91*
Fenning, Lisa Hill 1952- *WhoAmW 91*
Fenninger, Leonard Davis 1917- *WhoAm 90*
Fenno, John 1751-1798 *BioIn 16*
Fenno, Nathan R. 1958- *St&PR 91*
Fenno, Richard Francis, Jr. 1926- *WhoAm 90*
Fennon, Victor J. 1942- *St&PR 91*
Fenoglio, Charles Henry 1946- *WhoSSW 91*
Fenoglio, William Ronald 1939- *St&PR 91*
Fenoglio-Preiser, Cecilia Mettler *WhoAm 90*
Fenollosa, Ernest Francisco 1853-1908 *EncJap*
Fensch, Charles Everette 1935- *WhoAmA 91*
Fenselau, Catherine Clarke 1939- *WhoAm 90*
Fenske, Charles Robert 1953- *WhoEmL 91*
Fenske, Elizabeth Deloris Wall 1929- *WhoE 91*
Fenske, Gail Gretchen 1954- *WhoE 91*
Fensler, Robert Kenneth, Sr. 1925- *St&PR 91*
Fenster, Albert J. 1918- *St&PR 91*
Fenster, Harold Alan 1944- *WhoSSW 91*
Fenster, Harvey 1941- *St&PR 91, WhoAm 90*
Fenster, Herbert Lawrence 1935- *WhoAm 90*
Fenster, Marvin 1918- *St&PR 91, WhoAm 90*
Fenster, Robert 1946- *ConAu 32NR*
Fenster, Robert David 1946- *WhoEmL 91*
Fenster, Saul 1933- *WhoAm 90, WhoE 91*
Fenstermacher, Thomas *BiDrAPA 89*
Fenstermaker, Nancy Ruth 1930- *WhoAmW 91*
Fenstermaker, Robin Joseph 1951- *WhoWor 91*
Fenstermaker, Sarah 1949- *WhoAmW 91*
Fensterstock, Blair Courtney 1950- *St&PR 91*
Fensterstock, Joyce Narins 1948- *St&PR 91, WhoWor 91*
Fensterstock, Lee 1947- *WhoAm 90*
Fenten, D. X. 1932- *AuBYP 90*
Fentener van Vlissingen, Rogier 1951- *WhoE 91*
Fenter, Felix West 1926- *WhoAm 90*
Fenton, Alan 1927- *WhoAm 90, WhoAmA 91, WhoWor 91*
Fenton, Alexander 1929- *ConAu 131*
Fenton, Anne Lobock 1951- *BiDrAPA 89*
Fenton, Arnold N. 1921- *WhoAm 90*
Fenton, Barry J 1948- *BiDrAPA 89*
Fenton, Beatrice 1887-1983 *WhoAmA 91N*
Fenton, Bruce Stuart 1946- *St&PR 91*
Fenton, Carroll Lane 1900-1969 *AuBYP 90*
Fenton, Catherine Scharfen 1954- *WhoAm 90*
Fenton, Charles E H 1943- *WhoAmA 91, WhoE 91*
Fenton, Christopher Webber *PenDiDA 89*
Fenton, David John 1944- *WhoWor 91*
Fenton, Don Alan 1951- *St&PR 91*
Fenton, Edward 1917- *AuBYP 90*
Fenton, Edward A. 1925- *WhoAm 90*
Fenton, Elizabeth *FemiCLE*
Fenton, Fred Robert 1940- *BiDrAPA 89*
Fenton, Howard Carter 1910- *WhoAmA 91*
Fenton, James 1949- *WorAu 1980 [port]*
Fenton, Jean Moyler 1934- *WhoSSW 91*
Fenton, John Nathaniel 1912-1977 *WhoAmA 91N*
Fenton, John William, Jr. 1940- *St&PR 91*
Fenton, Julia Ann 1937- *WhoAmA 91*
Fenton, Lawrence Jules 1940- *WhoAm 90*
Fenton, Lela Mae 1934- *WhoWrEP 89*
Fenton, Lewis Lowry 1925- *WhoAm 90*
Fenton, Maria Gambarelli *BioIn 16, NewYTBS 90*
Fenton, Marjorie 1935- *WhoAmW 91*
Fenton, Matthew Clark, IV 1951- *WhoE 91*
Fenton, Mildred Adams 1899- *AuBYP 90*
Fenton, Monica 1944- *WhoAmW 91*
Fenton, Noel John 1938- *WhoAm 90*
Fenton, Paula Blanche 1947- *WhoAmW 91*
Fenton, Ray W. *ODwPR 91*
Fenton, Robert Earl 1933- *WhoAm 90*
Fenton, Robert Leonard 1929- *WhoAm 90, WhoWor 91*
Fenton, Roger 1819-1869 *BioIn 16*
Fenton, Sally Douglas *BiDrAPA 89*
Fenton, Terry Lynn 1940- *WhoAm 90*
Fenton, Thomas Conner 1954- *WhoEmL 91*
Fenton, Thomas Trail 1930- *WhoAm 90*
Fenton, Timothy M. 1943- *WhoAm 90*
Fenton, Wayne S 1953- *BiDrAPA 89*
Fenton, William Nelson 1908- *WhoAm 90*
Fenton, William V., Jr. 1937- *ODwPR 91*
Fenton, Wilmer C. 1923- *St&PR 91*
Fentress, Charles *ODwPR 91*
Fentress, Gary William 1939- *WhoAm 90*
Fentress, Robert Houston *BioIn 16*
Fenves, Steven Joseph 1931- *WhoAm 90*
Fenvessy, Stanley John 1918- *WhoAm 90, WhoE 91, WhoWor 91*
Fenwick, Avril Hanning 1947- *WhoEmL 91*
Fenwick, Eliza *BioIn 16*
Fenwick, Eliza 176-?-184-? *FemiCLE*
Fenwick, Elizabeth 1920- *TwCCr&M 91*
Fenwick, George Edgeworth 1825-1894 *DcCanB 12*
Fenwick, Lynda Beck 1944- *WhoAmW 91*
Fenwick, Millicent Hammond 1910- *WhoAm 90, WhoAmW 91, WhoE 91*
Fenwick, Robert B. 1936- *St&PR 91*
Fenwick, Roly 1932- *WhoAmA 91*
Fenwick, William Augustus 1938- *WhoAm 90*
Fenwick-Owen, Roderic 1921- *ConAu 129*
Fenyes, Joseph Gabriel Egon 1925- *WhoSSW 91*
Fenyves, Alarich George 1945- *WhoEmL 91*
Fenza, William Joseph, Jr. 1929- *St&PR 91, WhoAm 90*
Fenzy, Albert Jean 1934- *WhoWor 91*
Feola, Eugene David 1948- *WhoEmL 91*
Feola, Jose M 1926- *EncO&P 3*
Feola, Jose Maria 1926- *EncPaPR 91*
Feraca, Jean Stephanie 1943- *WhoWrEP 89*
Ferand, Jean-Gaspard *PenDiDA 89*
Ferares, Kenneth 1957- *WhoE 91, WhoEmL 91*
Feravolo, Rocco Vincent 1922- *AuBYP 90*
Ferbel, Thomas 1937- *WhoAm 90*
Ferber, Albert 1911-1987 *PenDiMP*
Ferber, Arthur Henry 1922- *WhoE 91*
Ferber, Edna 1885-1968 *FemiCLE, NotWoAT*
Ferber, Edna 1887-1968 *BioAmW, BioIn 16, MajTwCW, WorAlBi*
Ferber, Herbert 1906- *WhoAm 90, WhoAmA 91*
Ferber, Jane S *BiDrAPA 89*
Ferber, Leon 1911- *BiDrAPA 89*
Ferber, Linda S. 1944- *WhoAm 90, WhoAmA 91, WhoE 91*
Ferber, Peter H 1932- *BiDrAPA 89*
Ferber, Roman 1933- *WhoE 91*
Ferber, Samuel 1920- *WhoAm 90*
Ferbert, Frederick Winzer, Jr. 1953- *St&PR 91*
Fercana, Terry Lynn 1962- *WhoAmW 91*
Ferchat, Robert Arthur 1934- *WhoAm 90*
Ferchland, William Thomas 1945- *WhoWor 91*
Fercho, Ivan H. 1948- *St&PR 91*
Ferd, Robert William 1927- *St&PR 91*
Ferden, Bruce 1949- *WhoAm 90*
Ferder, John Edward 1961- *WhoEmL 91*
Ferderber-Hersonski, Boris Constantin 1943- *WhoE 91*
Ferdinand V 1452-1516 *WorAlBi*
Ferdinand Albrecht 1636-1687 *BioIn 16*
Ferdinand VII, King of Spain 1784-1833 *BioIn 16*
Ferdinand, Frank 1923- *St&PR 91*
Ferdinand, William V. 1941- *St&PR 91*
Ferdinands, Ian S. 1936- *St&PR 91*
Ferdman, Alejandro Jose 1962- *WhoHisp 91*
Ferdman, Natacha Marie Mathilde 1944- *WhoWor 91*
Ferdon, Lee Monroe 1942- *WhoSSW 91*
Fereaud-Farber, Zulima V. 1944- *WhoHisp 91*
Ferebee, Gideon, Jr. 1950- *WhoWrEP 89*
Ferebee, John Spencer, Jr. 1947- *WhoAm 90*
Ferebee, Kim Louise 1966- *WhoEmL 91*
Ferebee, Stephen Scott, Jr. 1921- *WhoAm 90*
Ferekidis, Eleftherios 1941- *WhoWor 91*
Ferenbach, Richard Schooley 1928- *St&PR 91*
Ference, Cynthia *WhoAmA 91*
Ferenci, Luanne *BioIn 16*
Ferencik, G.M. *St&PR 91*
Ferencsik, Janos 1907-1984 *PenDiMP*
Ferencz, Charlotte 1921- *WhoAmW 91*
Ferencz, Judith Anne Maddock 1948- *IntWWM 90*
Ferencz, Robert Arnold 1946- *WhoEmL 91*
Ferenczi, Ilona 1949- *IntWWM 90*
Ferenczi, Ronald James 1950- *WhoWor 91*
Ferenczi, Sandor 1873-1933 *BioIn 16*
Ferenczy, Oto 1921- *IntWWM 90*
Ferens, Marcella *WhoAmW 91, WhoE 91, WhoWor 91*
Ferentchak, Linda Burleigh 1955- *WhoEmL 91*
Ferer, Harvey Dean 1926- *St&PR 91, WhoAm 90*
Fereres, Jose 1943- *WhoWor 91*
Feret, Adam Edward, Jr. 1942- *WhoE 91, WhoWor 91*
Feretic, Eileen Susan 1949- *WhoAm 90*
Fereydouni, Hamid Reza 1956- *WhoAm 90*
Ferger, Lawrence A. 1934- *St&PR 91*
Fergus, Allan 1932- *BiDrAPA 89*
Fergus, Patricia Marguerita 1918- *WhoAmW 91, WhoWor 91*
Ferguson, Alan Douglas *BioIn 16*
Ferguson, Alex 1897-1976 *Ballpl 90*
Ferguson, Alfred L. *BioIn 16*
Ferguson, Allen Richmond 1919- *WhoAm 90*
Ferguson, Amy Talley 1941- *WhoAmW 91*
Ferguson, Ann Jo 1952- *WhoEmL 91*
Ferguson, Anna Marie 1940- *WhoAmW 91*
Ferguson, Anne E. 1933- *WhoE 91*
Ferguson, Audri Dale 1954- *WhoAmW 91*
Ferguson, B.A. 1931- *St&PR 91*
Ferguson, Barbara Bess 1942- *BiDrAPA 89*
Ferguson, Barclay 1924- *WhoAmA 91*
Ferguson, Barry William Cammack 1942- *IntWWM 90*
Ferguson, Bernard J. *BioIn 16*
Ferguson, Betty Lou 1950- *WhoEmL 91*
Ferguson, Bob 1845-1894 *Ballpl 90*
Ferguson, Brooke Andrew 1954- *WhoSSW 91*
Ferguson, Bruce W. 1954- *WhoEmL 91*
Ferguson, C. David 1941- *WhoAm 90*
Ferguson, Carmela 1933- *WhoAmW 91*
Ferguson, Carolyn Sue 1935- *WhoAmW 91*
Ferguson, Charles Albert 1921- *WhoAm 90*
Ferguson, Charles Austin 1937- *WhoAm 90*
Ferguson, Charles B 1918- *WhoAmA 91*
Ferguson, Charles R. 1925- *St&PR 91*
Ferguson, Charles Ray 1925- *WhoAm 90*
Ferguson, Charles Winston 1913- *WhoAm 90*
Ferguson, Daniel C. 1927- *WhoAm 90*
Ferguson, Daniel Cuthbert 1927- *St&PR 91*
Ferguson, Daniel Wyatt 1924- *BiDrAPA 89*
Ferguson, David Michael 1947- *WhoEmL 91*
Ferguson, David Norman 1925- *St&PR 91*
Ferguson, David Robert 1949- *WhoAm 90, WhoEmL 91, WhoSSW 91*
Ferguson, Debora Louise *BiDrAPA 89*
Ferguson, Deborah Manning 1959- *WhoEmL 91*
Ferguson, Dee Ann 1947- *WhoAmW 91*
Ferguson, Dennis Lorne 1950- *WhoHisp 91*
Ferguson, Donald F. 1922- *St&PR 91*
Ferguson, Donald Guffey 1923- *WhoE 91, WhoWor 91*
Ferguson, Donald Jack 1936- *St&PR 91*
Ferguson, Donald John 1916- *WhoAm 90*
Ferguson, Donald L. 1940- *ODwPR 91, St&PR 91*
Ferguson, Doris Loper 1947- *WhoSSW 91*
Ferguson, Dorothy Margueritte *WhoWrEP 89*
Ferguson, Douglas Edward 1940- *WhoE 91*
Ferguson, E. C. 1833- *AmLegL*
Ferguson, E. Robert 1932- *WhoAm 90*
Ferguson, Earle Charles 1938- *WhoAm 90*
Ferguson, Edgar Robert 1932- *St&PR 91*
Ferguson, Edward Trevor, Jr. 1933- *WhoSSW 91*
Ferguson, Edwin Earle 1910- *WhoE 91*
Ferguson, Elizabeth 1737-1801 *FemiCLE*
Ferguson, Elizabeth Ann 1932- *WhoAmW 91*
Ferguson, Elizabeth Graeme 1737-1801 *EncCRAm*
Ferguson, Forest D. 1933- *St&PR 91*
Ferguson, Francis Eugene 1921- *St&PR 91, WhoAm 90*
Ferguson, Frank E. 1926- *St&PR 91*
Ferguson, Franklin Turner 1935- *WhoAm 90*
Ferguson, Fred J., Jr. 1940- *St&PR 91*
Ferguson, Frederic Gregory 1942- *St&PR 91*
Ferguson, Frederick Palmer 1916- *WhoAm 90*
Ferguson, G. Richard 1942- *St&PR 91*
Ferguson, Gary L. 1940- *St&PR 91*
Ferguson, Gary W. 1925- *ODwPR 91*
Ferguson, Gary Warren 1925- *WhoAm 90*
Ferguson, George 1886-1943 *Ballpl 90*
Ferguson, George Joseph *BiDrAPA 89*
Ferguson, George Wagoner, Jr. 1933- *St&PR 91*
Ferguson, Gerald 1937- *WhoAmA 91*
Ferguson, Gerald Paul 1951- *WhoEmL 91*
Ferguson, Glenn Walker 1929- *WhoAm 90*
Ferguson, Grace Renee *BiDrAPA 89*
Ferguson, Harley Robert 1936- *WhoAm 90*
Ferguson, Harold Vincent, Jr. 1956- *WhoEmL 91*
Ferguson, Helen *MajTwCW*
Ferguson, Helen Mott 1941- *WhoAmW 91, WhoSSW 91*
Ferguson, Henry 1927- *WhoAm 90*
Ferguson, Herman *BioIn 16*
Ferguson, Hill, III 1942- *St&PR 91*
Ferguson, Homer L. 1873-1953 *WorAlBi*
Ferguson, Howard 1908- *IntWWM 90*
Ferguson, James A. 1915- *WhoAm 90*
Ferguson, James Grant 1940- *WhoSSW 91*
Ferguson, James Joseph, Jr. 1926- *WhoAm 90*
Ferguson, James Karl 1942- *St&PR 91*
Ferguson, James L. *AmLegL*
Ferguson, James Larnard 1926- *St&PR 91*
Ferguson, James Mecham 1941- *BiDrAPA 89*
Ferguson, James Paul 1937- *WhoSSW 91*
Ferguson, James Peter 1937- *WhoAm 90*
Ferguson, Janice C *BiDrAPA 89*
Ferguson, Jeannette *ODwPR 91*
Ferguson, Jesse Babcock *EncO&P 3*
Ferguson, Jimmy Lee 1950- *WhoSSW 91*
Ferguson, Jo McCown 1915- *WhoAm 90*
Ferguson, Joan M. 1930- *WhoWrEP 89*
Ferguson, Joe 1946- *Ballpl 90*
Ferguson, John *BioIn 16*
Ferguson, John Cotter, II 1943- *St&PR 91*
Ferguson, John Henry 1907- *WhoAm 90*

Ferguson, John Hilton 1946- *WhoSSW 91*
Ferguson, John Lewis 1926- *WhoAm 90*
Ferguson, John Marshall 1921- *WhoAm 90*
Ferguson, John Patrick 1949- *WhoAm 90, WhoWor 91*
Ferguson, John Robert, Jr. 1915- *WhoAm 90*
Ferguson, John S. 1949- *St&PR 91*
Ferguson, John T., II *St&PR 91*
Ferguson, Joseph Gantt 1921- *WhoAm 90*
Ferguson, Julie Ann 1959- *WhoAmW 91*
Ferguson, Justin G. 1941- *St&PR 91*
Ferguson, Kate Joan 1959- *WhoEmL 91*
Ferguson, Katherine A 1946- *BiDrAPA 89*
Ferguson, Kathleen Elizabeth 1945- *WhoAmA 91*
Ferguson, Kathy E. *St&PR 91*
Ferguson, Kaye Irene 1939- *WhoAmW 91*
Ferguson, Kenneth Richmond 1924- *BiDrAPA 89*
Ferguson, Kenneth Wayne 1927- *St&PR 91*
Ferguson, Kingsley George 1921- *WhoAm 90*
Ferguson, Larry Scott 1954- *WhoAmA 91*
Ferguson, Lloyd Noel 1918- *WhoAm 90*
Ferguson, Lucy Carnegie *BioIn 16*
Ferguson, Lynn Douglas 1951- *WhoE 91*
Ferguson, M Carr, Jr. 1931- *ConAu 30NR*
Ferguson, Margaret Wallace 1914- *BiDrAPA 89*
Ferguson, Marilyn 1938- *EncO&P 3, NewAgE 90*
Ferguson, Mark Harmon 1953- *WhoAm 90*
Ferguson, Mark William James 1955- *WhoWor 91*
Ferguson, Mary Anne Heyward 1918- *WhoAm 90*
Ferguson, Mary Kay 1944- *St&PR 91*
Ferguson, Mary Virginia 1958- *WhoSSW 91*
Ferguson, Maynard 1928- *BioIn 16, DrBIPA 90, OxCPMus, WhoAm 90*
Ferguson, Melissa Renee *BiDrAPA 89*
Ferguson, Michael *BioIn 16*
Ferguson, Michael McVea 1951- *BiDrAPA 89*
Ferguson, Milton Carr, Jr. 1931- *WhoAm 90*
Ferguson, Miriam A. 1875-1961 *BioAmW*
Ferguson, Nancy Jean 1954- *WhoAmW 91*
Ferguson, Nancy Marie *BioIn 16*
Ferguson, Neil Taylor 1922- *WhoAm 90*
Ferguson, Oliver Watkins 1924- *WhoAm 90*
Ferguson, Pamela Anastacia 1943- *WhoAmW 91, WhoSSW 91*
Ferguson, Paul J. *St&PR 91*
Ferguson, Paul Wesley 1952- *WhoEmL 91, WhoSSW 91*
Ferguson, Perry 1901- *ConDes 90*
Ferguson, Peter Edwin 1946- *BiDrAPA 89*
Ferguson, R. D. *AmLegL*
Ferguson, Ramona 1954- *WhoEmL 91*
Ferguson, Robert 1937- *WhoE 91*
Ferguson, Robert A. 1942- *ConAu 131*
Ferguson, Robert Bury 1920- *WhoAm 90*
Ferguson, Robert D. 1905- *St&PR 91*
Ferguson, Robert Harry Munro 1937- *WhoAm 90*
Ferguson, Robert R., Jr. 1923- *St&PR 91, WhoAm 90, WhoE 91*
Ferguson, Robert Ray 1945- *WhoAm 90*
Ferguson, Robert S. 1915-1988 *BioIn 16*
Ferguson, Robert Stanley 1948- *IntWWM 90*
Ferguson, Robert Willi 1913- *WhoAm 90*
Ferguson, Ronald *BioIn 16*
Ferguson, Ronald Eugene 1942- *St&PR 91, WhoAm 90, WhoE 91*
Ferguson, Roy C., III 1946- *St&PR 91, WhoSSW 91*
Ferguson, Sanford Barnett 1947- *WhoEmL 91*
Ferguson, Sarah 1959- *BioIn 16, News 90 [port], -90-3 [port]*
Ferguson, Sharon Hermine 1953- *WhoAmW 91*
Ferguson, Sharon Sebastian 1950- *WhoAmW 91*
Ferguson, Shirley M 1923- *BiDrAPA 89*
Ferguson, Skitch 1949- *St&PR 91*
Ferguson, Susan Katharine Stover 1944- *WhoAmW 91*
Ferguson, Suzanne Carol 1939- *WhoAm 90*
Ferguson, Sybil 1934- *ConAu 129, WhoAm 90*
Ferguson, Theresa Lynn 1961- *WhoAmW 91*
Ferguson, Thomas C. 1933- *WhoAm 90*
Ferguson, Thomas George 1941- *WhoAm 90*
Ferguson, Thomas H. *BioIn 16, WhoAm 90*
Ferguson, Thomas K. *St&PR 91*
Ferguson, Thomas Marshall 1936- *WhoSSW 91*
Ferguson, Thomas Russell 1938- *St&PR 91*
Ferguson, Tom 1943- *WhoSSW 91*
Ferguson, Tracy Heiman 1910- *WhoAm 90*
Ferguson, Val *WhoAm 90*
Ferguson, Warren John 1920- *WhoAm 90*
Ferguson, Warren L. 1931- *St&PR 91*
Ferguson, Whitworth, III 1954- *WhoEmL 91*
Ferguson, William 1943- *ConAu 33NR*
Ferguson, William Chandler 1955- *WhoEmL 91*
Ferguson, William Charles 1930- *WhoAm 90*
Ferguson, William D 1941- *BiDrAPA 89*
Ferguson, William Emmett 1902- *WhoAm 90*
Ferguson, William McDonald 1917- *WhoAm 90*
Ferguson, William R. 1937- *St&PR 91*
Ferguson, William R. 1943- *WhoWrEP 89*
Ferguson, Yvonne B *BiDrAPA 89*
Ferguson Mann, Serena DeSantos 1957- *WhoAmW 91*
Ferguson-Pell, Margaret Alice 1951- *WhoAmW 91, WhoE 91*
Ferguson-Smith, Malcolm Andrew 1931- *WhoWor 91*
Ferguson-Wigerink, Margaretha 1920- *EncCoWW*
Fergusson, Donald Charles 1953- *St&PR 91*
Fergusson, Frances Daly 1944- *WhoAm 90, WhoAmW 91, WhoE 91*
Fergusson, Jeremy L. 1945- *ODwPR 91*
Fergusson, R Laurence *BiDrAPA 89*
Fergusson, Robert George 1911- *WhoAm 90*
Ferholt, Eleanore Heusser *WhoAmA 91*
Ferholt, Julian B 1942- *BiDrAPA 89*
Feria, Floridano 1937- *WhoHisp 91*
Ferin, Juraj 1925- *WhoE 91*
Ferino, Christopher Kenneth 1961- *WhoWor 91*
Feriola, James Philip 1925- *WhoAmA 91*
Ferkany, Edward A. 1937- *St&PR 91*
Ferkiss, Victor Christopher 1925- *WhoAm 90*
Ferko, Darly W. 1954- *St&PR 91*
Ferko, Frank Stephen 1950- *IntWWM 90*
Ferko, William Gerard 1954- *WhoEmL 91*
Ferland, Albert 1872-1943 *DcLB 92 [port]*
Ferland, Armand 1926- *IntWWM 90*
Ferland, Barbara 1919- *FemiCLE*
Ferland, Darlene Frances 1954- *WhoAmW 91, WhoEmL 91*
Ferland, E. James 1942- *St&PR 91, WhoAm 90, WhoE 91*
Ferlazzo, Ellen Lawson 1961- *WhoAmW 91*
Ferley, Lester J. 1911- *St&PR 91*
Ferlin, Nils Johan Einar 1898-1961 *DcScanL*
Ferling, Lawrence *MajTwCW*
Ferlinghetti, Lawrence 1919?- *MajTwCW, PoeCrit 1 [port], WhoAm 90, WorAlBi*
Ferlinghetti, Lawrence 1920- *WhoWrEP 89*
Ferlinz, Jack 1942- *WhoWor 91*
Ferlito, Andrew A. 1926- *St&PR 91*
Ferlov, Sonja *BiDWomA*
Ferm, Deane William 1927- *WhoAm 90*
Ferm, Lois Roughan 1918- *WhoAmW 91*
Ferm, Robert Livingston 1931- *WhoAm 90*
Ferm, Vergil Harkness 1924- *WhoAm 90*
Ferman, Allan S. 1941- *St&PR 91*
Ferman, Irving 1919- *WhoAm 90, WhoE 91, WhoWor 91*
Ferman, Johanna Lisa *BiDrAPA 89*
Fermat, Pierre de 1601-1665 *BioIn 16, WorAlBi*
Fermi, Enrico 1901-1954 *BioIn 16, WorAlBi*
Fermi, Laura Capon 1907-1977 *AuBYP 90*
Fermo, Joe Cruz, Jr. *BiDrAPA 89*
Fermo, Merli Gorospe *BiDrAPA 89*
Fermo, Victor Mendoza, Jr. *BiDrAPA 89*
Fermoile, Douglas Keith 1956- *WhoEmL 91*
Fermor, Patrick Leigh *MajTwCW*
Fermor, Una Mary Ellis- 1894-1958 *BioIn 16*
Fern, Alan Maxwell 1930- *WhoAm 90, WhoAmA 91, WhoE 91*
Fern, Benjamin R. 1921- *WhoSSW 91*
Fern, Carole L. 1958- *WhoAmW 91*
Fern, Eugene A. 1919-1987 *BioIn 16*
Fern, Fanny 1811-1872 *BioIn 16, FemiCLE*
Fern, Frederick Harold 1954- *WhoEmL 91*
Fern, Leon 1937- *St&PR 91*
Fern, Stewart A *BiDrAPA 89*
Fern, Tami Lynne 1945- *WhoAmW 91*
Fernald, Charles E., Jr. 1939- *St&PR 91*
Fernald, Charles Edward 1902- *WhoAm 90*
Fernald, David G. *NewYTBS 90*
Fernald, David G. 1923-1990 *BioIn 16*
Fernald, David Ralph 1940- *St&PR 91*
Fernald, George Herbert, Jr. 1926- *WhoAm 90*
Fernald, Harold Allen 1932- *WhoAm 90*
Fernald, Helen Elizabeth 1891-1964 *WhoAmA 91N*
Fernald, Linda Catherine 1943- *St&PR 91*
Fernald, Wayne Douglas 1947- *WhoE 91*
Fernan, Mary Brigid 1958- *WhoEmL 91*
Fernandes, Carlos Alberto da Silva 1938- *WhoWor 91*
Fernandes, Gary J. 1943- *St&PR 91*
Fernandes, Gary Joe 1943- *WhoAm 90*
Fernandes, Jeanne Mary 1948- *WhoE 91*
Fernandes, Joseph Edward 1923- *WhoWor 91*
Fernandes, Kathleen 1946- *WhoEmL 91*
Fernandes, Maria Helena Rosas 1933- *IntWWM 90*
Fernandes, Pedro Infante 1957- *WhoHisp 91*
Fernandes, Richard Louis 1931- *St&PR 91*
Fernandes, Stanislaw *BioIn 16*
Fernandes, Vasco Felipe 1954- *St&PR 91*
Fernandes, Zereen *BiDrAPA 89*
Fernandes Lopes, Jose Luis 1947- *WhoWor 91*
Fernandes Salling, Lehua 1949- *WhoAmW 91*
Fernandez, Adolfo, Jr. 1951- *WhoHisp 91*
Fernandez, Albert Bades *WhoHisp 91*
Fernandez, Alfonso 1951- *WhoHisp 91*
Fernandez, Alfred P. 1934- *WhoHisp 91*
Fernandez, Alfredo Jose 1957- *WhoEmL 91*
Fernandez, Antonio D 1936- *BiDrAPA 89*
Fernandez, Armand 1928- *BioIn 16*
Fernandez, Autonio J *BiDrAPA 89*
Fernandez, Belen Benito *BiDrAPA 89*
Fernandez, Benedict Joseph, III 1936- *WhoHisp 91*
Fernandez, Benjamin 1925- *BioIn 16*
Fernandez, Carlos Alejandro 1954- *WhoEmL 91*
Fernandez, Carlos Jesus 1951- *WhoHisp 91*
Fernandez, Castor A. *WhoHisp 91*
Fernandez, Celestino 1949- *WhoHisp 91*
Fernandez, Charles, Jr. 1931- *St&PR 91*
Fernandez, Charles M. *WhoHisp 91*
Fernandez, Chico *WhoHisp 91*
Fernandez, Chico 1932- *Ballpl 90*
Fernandez, Claude 1952- *St&PR 91*
Fernandez, Dolores M. 1944- *WhoHisp 91*
Fernandez, Doria Goodrich 1958- *WhoHisp 91*
Fernandez, Eduardo B. 1936- *WhoHisp 91*
Fernandez, Eduardo Buglioni 1936- *WhoSSW 91*
Fernandez, Erasto *WhoHisp 91*
Fernandez, Eugenia 1957- *WhoHisp 91*
Fernandez, Eustasio, Jr. 1919- *WhoAm 90, WhoHisp 91*
Fernandez, Fe 1953- *WhoAmW 91*
Fernandez, Felipe Nery 1930- *BiDrAPA 89*
Fernandez, Ferdinand Francis 1937- *WhoAm 90, WhoHisp 91*
Fernandez, Frances *WhoHisp 91*
Fernandez, Francisco *WhoHisp 91*
Fernandez, Francisco 1951- *BiDrAPA 89*
Fernandez, Frank 1943- *Ballpl 90*
Fernandez, Gaylen 1951- *WhoSSW 91*
Fernandez, Gigi 1964- *WhoHisp 91*
Fernandez, Gilbert, Jr. 1938- *WhoHisp 91*
Fernandez, Gilbert G. 1936- *WhoHisp 91*
Fernandez, Gustavo Antonio 1944- *WhoHisp 91*
Fernandez, Hector R. C. 1937- *WhoHisp 91*
Fernandez, Hermes 1920- *St&PR 91*
Fernandez, Ines Teresa 1952- *WhoE 91*
Fernandez, Iris Virginia *WhoAmW 91*
Fernandez, Iris Virginia 1955- *WhoHisp 91*
Fernandez, Isabel Lidia 1964- *WhoAmW 91, WhoEmL 91*
Fernandez, J. M. *WhoHisp 91*
Fernandez, Jenaro F 1938- *BiDrAPA 89*
Fernandez, John Anthony 1940- *WhoHisp 91*
Fernandez, John Victor *BiDrAPA 89*
Fernandez, Jorge A. 1944- *St&PR 91*
Fernandez, Jorge Antonio 1943- *WhoSSW 91*
Fernandez, Jorge Antonio 1944- *WhoHisp 91*
Fernandez, Jorge Enrique 1944- *WhoWor 91*
Fernandez, Jose *WhoHisp 91*
Fernandez, Jose Bartolome, Jr. 1923- *WhoWor 91*
Fernandez, Jose S 1893-1967 *EncO&P 3, EncPaPR 91*
Fernandez, Jose Walfredo 1955- *WhoEmL 91*
Fernandez, Joseph A. *BioIn 16, NewYTBS 90 [port]*
Fernandez, Joseph A. 1936- *WhoE 91, WhoHisp 91*
Fernandez, Juan *PenDiDA 89*
Fernandez, Juan Carlos *WhoHisp 91*
Fernandez, Juan Jose *BiDrAPA 89*
Fernandez, Julian, Jr. *WhoHisp 91*
Fernandez, Julio 1944- *BioIn 16*
Fernandez, Laura Bove 1915- *WhoAmW 91*
Fernandez, Leticia 1956- *WhoHisp 91*
Fernandez, Linda Ann 1947- *WhoAmW 91*
Fernandez, Linda Flawn 1943- *WhoAmW 91*
Fernandez, Liz 1959- *WhoHisp 91*
Fernandez, Louis Anthony 1939- *WhoHisp 91*
Fernandez, Luis F. 1951- *WhoHisp 91*
Fernandez, Luis Felipe 1958- *WhoHisp 91*
Fernandez, Lydia R *BiDrAPA 89*
Fernandez, Macedonio 1874-1952 *BioIn 16*
Fernandez, Magali 1935- *WhoAmW 91*
Fernandez, Manuel *St&PR 91*
Fernandez, Manuel B. 1925- *WhoHisp 91*
Fernandez, Manuel Felix 1789?-1843 *BioIn 16*
Fernandez, Manuel G. *WhoHisp 91*
Fernandez, Manuel Jose 1946- *WhoHisp 91*
Fernandez, Manuel Joseph 1939- *WhoHisp 91*
Fernandez, Manuela Duat *BiDrAPA 89*
Fernandez, Maria Isabel 1953- *WhoHisp 91*
Fernandez, Mariano Hugo 1939- *WhoAm 90*
Fernandez, Mark Antonio 1960- *WhoHisp 91*
Fernandez, Mary Joe 1971- *BioIn 16, WhoHisp 91*
Fernandez, Mildred *WhoHisp 91*
Fernandez, Moraima 1951- *WhoEmL 91*
Fernandez, Nanny 1918- *Ballpl 90*
Fernandez, Nestor A., Sr. *WhoHisp 91*
Fernandez, Nino J. *WhoHisp 91*
Fernandez, Nino J. 1941- *ODwPR 91, St&PR 91*
Fernandez, Nohema 1944- *IntWWM 90*
Fernandez, Nohema del Carmen 1944- *WhoHisp 91*
Fernandez, Norma Jocson *BiDrAPA 89*
Fernandez, Osberto B 1931- *BiDrAPA 89*
Fernandez, Prospero 1834-1885 *BioIn 16*
Fernandez, Rafael Ludovino 1948- *WhoHisp 91*
Fernandez, Ramiro A. 1951- *WhoHisp 91*
Fernandez, Ramon 1958- *WhoHisp 91*
Fernandez, Ramon S. 1934- *WhoHisp 91*
Fernandez, Raul A. 1945- *WhoHisp 91*
Fernandez, Reinaldo Julian 1941- *WhoSSW 91*
Fernandez, Rene 1961- *WhoEmL 91, WhoWor 91*
Fernandez, Ricardo 1940- *WhoHisp 91*
Fernandez, Ricardo, III 1970- *WhoHisp 91*
Fernandez, Ricardo J 1953- *BiDrAPA 89*
Fernandez, Ricardo Jesus 1953- *WhoHisp 91*
Fernandez, Robert C *BiDrAPA 89*
Fernandez, Roberto G. 1950- *BioIn 16*
Fernandez, Roberto G. 1951- *ConAu 131, HispWr 90, WhoHisp 91*
Fernandez, Rodney E. *WhoHisp 91*
Fernandez, Rodolfo 1940- *WhoHisp 91*
Fernandez, Roger Rodriguez 1934- *WhoHisp 91*
Fernandez, Rolando 1949- *BiDrAPA 89*
Fernandez, Roldan 1946- *St&PR 91*
Fernandez, Ruben D. 1949- *WhoHisp 91*
Fernandez, Ruben Mark 1954- *WhoHisp 91*
Fernandez, Ruben Omar 1958- *WhoWor 91*
Fernandez, Rudy M., Jr. 1948- *WhoHisp 91*
Fernandez, Sally Garza 1958- *WhoHisp 91*
Fernandez, Sid 1962- *Ballpl 90*
Fernandez, Thomas L. 1930- *WhoHisp 91*
Fernandez, Tony 1962- *Ballpl 90, WhoHisp 91*
Fernandez, Vicente Garcia Huidobro *ConAu 131, HispWr 90*
Fernandez, Waldo *BioIn 16*
Fernandez, Wilhelmenia *BioIn 16*
Fernandez, Wilhelmenia 1949- *PenDiMP*
Fernandez-Baca, David Fernando 1959- *WhoHisp 91*
Fernandez-Baca, Jaime A. 1954- *WhoHisp 91*
Fernandez Benlloch, Jose Vicente Carlos 1944- *WhoWor 91*
Fernandez-Bollo, Mariano Fermin 1919- *WhoWor 91*
Fernandez-Criado, Manuel 1952- *BiDrAPA 89*

Fernandez Cubas, Cristina 1945- *EncCoWW*
Fernandez de Lizardi, Jose Joaquin 1776-1827 *BioIn 16*
Fernandez de Mesa, Rafael 1942- *WhoSSW 91*
Fernandez de Oviedo y Valdes, Gonzalo 1478-1557 *BioIn 16*
Fernandez-Esteva, Frank 1931- *WhoHisp 91*
Fernandez-Franco, Sonia M. 1938- *WhoHisp 91*
Fernandez Haar, Ana Maria 1951- *WhoHisp 91*
Fernandez-Iznaola, Ricardo J. 1949- *IntWWM 90*
Fernandez-Iznaola, Ricardo Jaime 1949- *WhoEmL 91*
Fernandez-Jimenez, Juan 1946- *WhoHisp 91*
Fernandez Ledesma, Gabriel 1900-1983 *ArtLatA*, *BioIn 16*
Fernandez Luna, Manuel 1935- *WhoWor 91*
Fernandez-Madrid, Felix 1927- *WhoHisp 91*
Fernandez-Martinez, Jose 1930- *WhoSSW 91*, *WhoWor 91*
Fernandez Mendez, E. *HispWr 90*
Fernandez Mendez, Eugenio 1924- *HispWr 90*
Fernandez-Moran, Humberto 1924- *WhoAm 90*, *WhoWor 91*
Fernandez Moreno, Baldomero 1886-1950 *HispWr 90*
Fernandez Moreno, Cesar 1919- *ConAu 131*, *HispWr 90*
Fernandez-Morera, Dario *WhoHisp 91*
Fernandez Olmos, Margarite 1949- *WhoHisp 91*
Fernandez Ordonez, Francisco 1930- *WhoWor 91*
Fernandez-Pacheco, Ismael *WhoHisp 91*
Fernandez-Palmer, Lydia *WhoHisp 91*
Fernandez-Pol, Blanca Dora 1932- *BiDrAPA 89*, *WhoE 91*
Fernandez Retamar, Roberto 1930- *ConAu 131*, *HispWr 90*
Fernandez-Reyes, Emilio 1955- *WhoWor 91*
Fernandez-Rodriguez, Manuel-Nicolas 1938- *WhoWor 91*
Fernandez-Torriente, Gaston F. 1924- *WhoHisp 91*
Fernandez-Vazquez, Antonio A. 1949- *WhoHisp 91*
Fernandez-Velazquez, Juan R. 1936- *WhoHisp 91*
Fernandez-Velazquez, Juan Ramon 1936- *WhoAm 90*
Fernandez-Zayas, Marcelo R. 1938- *WhoHisp 91*
Fernandis, Sarah Collins 1863-1951 *HarlReB [port]*
Fernando, Anicetus 1959- *St&PR 91*
Fernando, Chitra 1935- *FemiCLE*
Fernando, Santhiapillai 1952- *BiDrAPA 89*
Fernando, Thomas Gamini 1945- *BiDrAPA 89*
Fernando, Tilak 1945- *WhoWor 91*
Fernandopulle, Gregory C *BiDrAPA 89*
Fernas, Edward William 1944- *WhoE 91*
Fernbach, Harvey 1944- *BiDrAPA 89*
Fernbach, Robert Dennis 1917- *WhoAm 90*
Fernea, Robert Alan 1932- *WhoAm 90*
Ferneau, Philip James 1962- *WhoE 91*
Ferner, F.J. *PenDiDA 89*
Ferner, Kathryn Eileen 1944- *WhoAmW 91*
Ferneyhough, Brian 1943- *IntWWM 90*, *PenDiMP A*
Ferneyhough, Charles Joseph, III 1949- *WhoSSW 91*
Ferng, Douglas Ming-Haw 1945- *WhoEmL 91*, *WhoWor 91*
Fernholz, Martin Anthony 1952- *WhoEmL 91*
Ferniani, Conte Annibale *PenDiDA 89*
Ferniany, Isaac William 1951- *WhoEmL 91*
Fernie, Bruce John 1952- *WhoE 91*
Fernie, John Chipman 1945- *WhoAmA 91*
Fernie, John Donald 1933- *WhoAm 90*
Ferniot, Jean 1918- *WhoWor 91*
Fernos, Antonio 1944- *WhoWor 91*
Fernous, Louis F., Jr. 1938- *St&PR 91*
Fernquist, Cyril L. 1921- *St&PR 91*
Ferns, Martin Allen 1921- *IntWWM 90*
Fernsler, John Ewig 1950- *WhoSSW 91*
Fernsler, John Paul 1940- *WhoAm 90*
Fernstrom, H. Allen 1939- *St&PR 91*
Fernstrom, Henry Allen 1939- *WhoAm 90*
Fernstrom, John Dickson 1947- *WhoE 91*
Fero, Bill *BioIn 16*
Fero, Merlin Bond 1928- *St&PR 91*
Feroe, Donald M. 1926- *St&PR 91*
Feroe, Paul James 1951- *WhoWrEP 89*
Ferolie, A. Joseph *BioIn 16*
Feron, David Snyder 1932- *WhoAm 90*
Feroz, Ehsan Habib 1952- *WhoEmL 91*
Ferra, Joan Miro 1893-1983 *BioIn 16*
Ferra, Max 1937- *WhoHisp 91*
Ferracci, Eraldo *BioIn 16*
Ferracci, Marie-Angele Vincenti 1948- *WhoWor 91*
Ferracuti, Franco 1927- *BiDrAPA 89*, *ConAu 30NR*
Ferradas, Renaldo 1932- *WhoHisp 91*
Ferraez, Martha Elizabeth 1937- *WhoAmW 91*
Ferragamo, Wanda *BioIn 16*
Ferragut, Rene *WhoHisp 91*
Ferraioli, Armando 1949- *WhoEmL 91*, *WhoWor 91*
Ferraiolo, Angela 1958- *WhoEmL 91*
Ferrales, Savino R. 1950- *St&PR 91*
Ferrall, Victor Eugene, Jr. 1936- *WhoAm 90*
Ferran, Ernesto, Jr. 1950- *BiDrAPA 89*
Ferran, Harry A. 1936- *St&PR 91*
Ferrand, Presidente 1657-1740 *EncCoWW*
Ferrand, Emma 1948- *IntWWM 90*
Ferrand, Jean Claude 1930- *WhoAm 90*
Ferrandino, Salvatore Anthony 1958- *WhoE 91*
Ferrando, Raymond 1912- *WhoWor 91*
Ferrang, Edward George 1950- *WhoEmL 91*
Ferrante, Anthony A 1938- *BiDrAPA 89*
Ferrante, David Anthony 1943- *St&PR 91*
Ferrante, J.F. 1925- *St&PR 91*
Ferrante, Jeffrey Anthony 1959- *WhoEmL 91*
Ferrante, Joan Marguerite 1936- *WhoAm 90*
Ferrante, Olivia Ann 1948- *WhoAmW 91*, *WhoEmL 91*
Ferrante, Robert L. 1937- *ODwPR 91*
Ferranti, Sebastian Ziani de 1864-1930 *BioIn 16*
Ferranti, Vince 1941- *WhoSSW 91*
Ferranty, Robert Johnson 1928- *St&PR 91*
Ferrao, Valeriano Inocencio 1939- *WhoAm 90*, *WhoWor 91*
Ferrar Family *FemiCLE*
Ferrar, Bathsheba *BiDEWW*
Ferrar, Mary 1550-1634 *FemiCLE*
Ferrara, Abel *BioIn 16*
Ferrara, Al 1939- *Ballpl 90*
Ferrara, Angelo Carmine 1931-1988 *BioIn 16*
Ferrara, Arthur Vincent 1930- *St&PR 91*, *WhoE 91*
Ferrara, Charles John 1939- *St&PR 91*
Ferrara, Dominick J., III 1939- *IntWWM 90*
Ferrara, Franco 1911- *PenDiMP*
Ferrara, Jackie *WhoAmA 91*
Ferrara, Joseph Patrick 1951- *WhoSSW 91*
Ferrara, Lawrence 1949- *IntWWM 90*
Ferrara, Mary F. 1960- *WhoAmW 91*
Ferrara, Peter Biagio, Jr. 1951- *WhoE 91*
Ferrara, Peter Joseph 1955- *WhoAm 90*
Ferrara, Roger C. 1943- *St&PR 91*
Ferrara, Salvatore S. 1931- *St&PR 91*
Ferrara, Salvatore Stephen 1931- *WhoAm 90*
Ferrara, Samuel Eugene 1957- *WhoSSW 91*
Ferrara, Stephen A. 1940- *St&PR 91*
Ferrara, Tony *BioIn 16*
Ferrara, V. Peter *BioIn 16*
Ferrara, V. Raymond 1947- *St&PR 91*
Ferrara, Vernon Peter *St&PR 91N*
Ferrara-Hazell, Catherine Lucille 1951- *WhoEmL 91*
Ferrara-Sherry, Donna Layne 1946- *WhoE 91*
Ferrare, Cristina *BioIn 16*
Ferrarese, Don 1929- *Ballpl 90*
Ferrarese Del Bene, Adriana 1755?-1799? *PenDiMP*
Ferrari, Domenico 1940- *WhoAm 90*
Ferrari, Donna Mae 1931- *WhoAmW 91*
Ferrari, Enzo 1898-1988 *AnObit 1988*, *BioIn 16*, *WorAlBi*
Ferrari, Febo 1865- *WhoAmA 91N*
Ferrari, Fulvio M 1931- *BiDrAPA 89*
Ferrari, Leon 1920- *ArtLatA*
Ferrari, Michael Richard, Jr. 1940- *WhoAm 90*
Ferrari, Michelle Marie *BiDrAPA 89*
Ferrari, Paul Francis 1930- *St&PR 91*
Ferrari, Pierre U. *BioIn 16*
Ferrari, Robert Joseph 1930- *St&PR 91*
Ferrari, Robert Joseph 1936- *WhoAm 90*
Ferrari, Virginio Luig 1937- *WhoAmA 91*
Ferrarin, Kimberly Lee Gardner 1961- *WhoEmL 91*
Ferrario, Joseph A. 1926- *WhoAm 90*
Ferrario, Marco 1953- *WhoWor 91*
Ferrarius *EncO&P 3*
Ferraro, Anthony Joseph 1946- *WhoAm 90*
Ferraro, Antonetta *BioIn 16*
Ferraro, Armando *BiDrAPA 89*
Ferraro, Arnaldo A. 1936- *WhoE 91*
Ferraro, Barbara *BioIn 16*
Ferraro, Bernadette A. 1952- *WhoWrEP 89*
Ferraro, Betty Ann 1925- *WhoAmW 91*
Ferraro, Charles A. 1953- *St&PR 91*
Ferraro, Charles John 1946- *St&PR 91*
Ferraro, Eugene T. 1913-1989 *BioIn 16*
Ferraro, Francis Stanley 1949- *St&PR 91*
Ferraro, Geraldine 1935- *BioAmW*
Ferraro, Geraldine A. *BioIn 16*
Ferraro, Geraldine Anne 1935- *WhoAm 90*, *WhoAmW 91*
Ferraro, Giovanni 1928- *WhoWor 91*
Ferraro, John Francis 1934- *WhoWor 91*
Ferraro, John Ralph 1918- *WhoAm 90*
Ferraro, Joseph L. 1922-1989 *BioIn 16*
Ferraro, Mike 1944- *Ballpl 90*
Ferraro, Niel Patrick 1931- *St&PR 91*
Ferrarotto, Louise Mary 1967- *WhoEmL 91*
Ferrars, Elizabeth 1907- *TwCCr&M 91*
Ferras, Christian 1933-1982 *PenDiMP*
Ferrat, Jacques Jean *ConAu 131*
Ferrat, Jean-Gaspard *PenDiDA 89*
Ferrater-Mora, Jose 1912- *HispWr 90*
Ferraz, Carlos Alberto Domingues 1945- *WhoWor 91*
Ferraz, Francisco Marconi 1951- *WhoE 91*, *WhoSSW 91*
Ferraz de Almeida Junior, Jose 1850-1899 *ArtLatA*
Ferre, Antonio Luis 1934- *WhoAm 90*, *WhoHisp 91*, *WhoSSW 91*, *WhoWor 91*
Ferre, Antonio R. *WhoHisp 91*
Ferre, Frederick Pond 1933- *WhoAm 90*
Ferre, Gianfranco *BioIn 16*
Ferre, Gianfranco 1944- *ConDes 90*, *WhoAm 90*, *WhoWor 91*
Ferre, John Yvan 1954- *WhoSSW 91*
Ferre, Luis A. 1904- *WhoHisp 91*
Ferre, Maurice *BioIn 16*
Ferre, Maurice Antonio 1935- *WhoHisp 91*
Ferre, Mercedes *BioIn 16*
Ferre, Richard C 1942- *BiDrAPA 89*
Ferre, Rosario *BioIn 16*
Ferre, Rosario 1942- *ConAu 131*, *HispWr 90*
Ferre, Susan Ingrid 1945- *IntWWM 90*
Ferre Aguayo, Luis Antonio 1904- *BioIn 16*
Ferree, Alberta Joyce 1930- *WhoAmW 91*
Ferree, H Lane 1937- *BiDrAPA 89*
Ferree, Mary Mericle 1938- *BiDrAPA 89*
Ferree, Myra Marx 1949- *WhoEmL 91*
Ferree, Patricia Ann 1947- *WhoSSW 91*
Ferreira, Antonio J *BiDrAPA 89*
Ferreira, Antonio Pedro 1936- *WhoWor 91*
Ferreira, Armando Thomas 1932- *WhoAm 90*, *WhoAmA 91*
Ferreira, Arthur David 1953- *WhoSSW 91*
Ferreira, Aurelio Buarque de Holanda *BioIn 16*
Ferreira, Carlos Trocado 1959- *WhoWor 91*
Ferreira, Edgar Mainardi 1956- *WhoWor 91*
Ferreira, Jack *WhoAm 90*
Ferreira, Jacqueline Lee 1958- *WhoAmW 91*
Ferreira, Jairo A. 1938- *St&PR 91*
Ferreira, Jose, Jr. 1956- *WhoAm 90*, *WhoE 91*
Ferreira, M. Jamie 1945- *WhoAmW 91*
Ferreira, Paulo Affonso De Moura 1940- *IntWWM 90*
Ferreira Aldunate, Wilson *BioIn 16*
Ferreira-Worth, Deirdre Charlyn 1958- *WhoWor 91*
Ferreiro, Claudio Eduardo 1939- *WhoHisp 91*
Ferrel, Cipriano *WhoHisp 91*
Ferrell, Anderson *BioIn 16*
Ferrell, Carl 1953- *WhoSSW 91*
Ferrell, Catherine 1947- *WhoAmA 91*
Ferrell, Catherine Klemann 1947- *WhoSSW 91*
Ferrell, Conchata 1943- *ConTFT 8*, *WhoHisp 91*
Ferrell, Conchata Galen 1943- *WhoAm 90*
Ferrell, David L. 1937- *ODwPR 91*
Ferrell, David Lee 1937- *WhoAm 90*
Ferrell, Donald Forrest 1929- *WhoAm 90*
Ferrell, Ernest E. 1944- *St&PR 91*
Ferrell, Frank *BioIn 16*
Ferrell, Gloria Louise 1948- *WhoAmW 91*
Ferrell, Jack L. 1927- *St&PR 91*
Ferrell, James E. 1939- *St&PR 91*
Ferrell, James Edwin 1939- *WhoAm 90*
Ferrell, James K. 1923- *WhoAm 90*
Ferrell, John Frederick 1942- *WhoAm 90*
Ferrell, Kelly Lynn 1962- *WhoAmW 91*
Ferrell, Mallory Hope 1935- *ConAu 30NR*
Ferrell, Michael D. 1941- *St&PR 91*, *WhoAm 90*
Ferrell, Michael Leslie 1957- *WhoEmL 91*
Ferrell, Milton Morgan, Jr. 1951- *WhoEmL 91*, *WhoWor 91*
Ferrell, Nancy Warren 1932- *WhoWrEP 89*
Ferrell, Otis C. 1920- *St&PR 91*
Ferrell, Ray Edward, Jr. 1941- *WhoAm 90*
Ferrell, Richard B 1943- *BiDrAPA 89*
Ferrell, Rick 1905- *Ballpl 90 [port]*
Ferrell, Robert Allen 1925- *St&PR 91*
Ferrell, Robert D 1917- *BiDrAPA 89*
Ferrell, Robert Hugh 1921- *WhoAm 90*, *WhoWrEP 89*
Ferrell, Robert Theodore 1950- *BiDrAPA 89*
Ferrell, Robert W., Jr. 1940- *BiDrAPA 89*
Ferrell, Sharon Legg 1951- *WhoAm 90*
Ferrell, Skip *WhoWrEP 89*
Ferrell, Stephanie Rene 1963- *WhoAmW 91*
Ferrell, Stephen W. 1951- *St&PR 91*
Ferrell, Trevor *BioIn 16*
Ferrell, Wes 1908-1976 *Ballpl 90 [port]*
Ferren, Bran 1954- *BioIn 16*
Ferren, John 1905-1970 *WhoAmA 91N*
Ferren, John Maxwell 1937- *WhoAm 90*, *WhoE 91*
Ferrendelli, James Anthony 1936- *WhoAm 90*
Ferrer, Adelardo M *BiDrAPA 89*
Ferrer, Betzaida 1943- *WhoHisp 91*
Ferrer, E.A. *St&PR 91*
Ferrer, Elizabeth Virginia 1955- *WhoEmL 91*
Ferrer, Fernando 1950- *WhoHisp 91*
Ferrer, Gloria M. Pagan *HispWr 90*
Ferrer, Jose 1912- *BioIn 16*, *WhoHisp 91*, *WorAlBi*
Ferrer, Jose Figueres 1906-1990 *BioIn 16*
Ferrer, Jose Vicente 1912- *WhoAm 90*
Ferrer, Marie Irene 1915- *WhoAm 90*
Ferrer, Mel 1917- *WorAlBi*
Ferrer, Miguel A 1932- *BiDrAPA 89*
Ferrer, Rafael 1933- *WhoAmA 91*
Ferrer, Rafael Douglas Paul 1957- *WhoEmL 91*
Ferrer, Rafael Gregory 1955- *WhoEmL 91*
Ferrer Bonsoms, Jose 1920- *WhoWor 91*
Ferrer Guardia, Francisco 1859-1909 *BioIn 16*
Ferrer-Meneses, Luis Manuel *BiDrAPA 89*
Ferrer Sala, Jose 1925- *WhoWor 91*
Ferrera, Alfred William 1924- *St&PR 91*, *WhoAm 90*
Ferrera, Arthur Rodney 1916- *WhoAm 90*
Ferrera, Kenneth Grant 1945- *St&PR 91*, *WhoAm 90*
Ferrera Torres, Raul 1942- *WhoWor 91*
Ferreri, Carl Albert 1928- *WhoE 91*
Ferreri, Joanne M. *WhoAmW 91*
Ferreri, Marco *BioIn 16*
Ferreri, Raymond N *BiDrAPA 89*
Ferreri, Samuel James 1955- *WhoEmL 91*
Ferreri, Vito Richard 1949- *WhoE 91*
Ferrero, Charles J. 1937- *St&PR 91*
Ferrero, Francoise P *BiDrAPA 89*
Ferrero, Guillermo E. 1954- *WhoHisp 91*
Ferrero, James J 1927- *BiDrAPA 89*
Ferrero, Louis Peter 1942- *St&PR 91*, *WhoAm 90*
Ferrero, Vittorio 1944- *BiDrAPA 89*
Ferretti, Bruno Raymond 1936- *St&PR 91*
Ferretti, D. *PenDiDA 89*
Ferretti, J. W. Todd *BioIn 16*
Ferretti, James John 1937- *BiDrAPA 89*
Ferretti, Julius J. *BioIn 16*
Ferretti, Lewis C. 1932- *St&PR 91*
Ferrey, E. E. 1920-1988 *BioIn 16*
Ferrey, Edgar Eugene 1920-1988 *BioIn 16*
Ferreyra, Beatriz Mercedes 1937- *IntWWM 90*
Ferrez, Marc 1843-1923 *ArtLatA*
Ferri, Alessandra *BioIn 16*
Ferri, Alessandra Maria 1963- *WhoAm 90*
Ferri, Everett Louis, Jr. 1945- *WhoE 91*
Ferri, James N. 1944- *ODwPR 91*
Ferri, Richard Stephen 1956- *WhoWrEP 89*
Ferri, Roger Cesare 1949- *WhoEmL 91*
Ferrick, Tom 1915- *Ballpl 90*
Ferrick, William J. 1926- *St&PR 91*
Ferriday, Carolyn Wolsey *BioIn 16*, *NewYTBS 90*
Ferrie, Gordon Hedley 1941- *St&PR 91*
Ferriell, Jeffrey Thomas 1953- *WhoEmL 91*
Ferrier, Andrew A. 1959- *St&PR 91*
Ferrier, Carole 1946- *WhoWor 91*
Ferrier, Kathleen 1912-1953 *PenDiMP*
Ferrier, Loretta Jean 1937- *WhoAmW 91*
Ferrier, Susan 1782-1854 *BioIn 16*, *FemiCLE*
Ferrieri, Anna Castelli *PenDiDA 89*
Ferries, John Charles 1937- *WhoAm 90*
Ferrigno, Dennis 1947- *St&PR 91*
Ferrigno, Lou *BioIn 16*
Ferrigno, Lou 1952- *ConTFT 8 [port]*
Ferril, W.C. 1931- *St&PR 91*
Ferrill, Arther 1938- *ConAu 129*
Ferrill, Harve Anthony 1932- *St&PR 91*
Ferrin, Allan Hogate 1951- *WhoEmL 91*

Ferrin, Allan Wheeler 1921- *WhoAm 90*
Ferrin, Robert Francis 1932- *St&PR 91*
Ferrini, Vincent 1913- *BioIn 16, WhoWrEP 89*
Ferriola, Joseph *BioIn 16*
Ferris, Barton Purdy, Jr. 1940- *WhoAm 90*
Ferris, Benjamin Greeley, Jr. 1919- *WhoAm 90*
Ferris, Charles Daniel 1933- *WhoAm 90*
Ferris, Charles J *BiDrAPA 89*
Ferris, Collins Hakes 1918- *St&PR 91*
Ferris, Dakin B. 1926- *St&PR 91*
Ferris, Dan George 1958- *WhoEmL 91*
Ferris, Daniel B 1947- *WhoAmA 91*
Ferris, Donald W 1942- *BiDrAPA 89*
Ferris, Elyse 1943- *WhoE 91*
Ferris, Frederick Joseph 1920- *WhoAm 90, WhoE 91*
Ferris, George Mallette 1894- *WhoAm 90*
Ferris, George Mallette, Jr. 1927- *St&PR 91, WhoAm 90*
Ferris, Helen Josephine 1890-1969 *AuBYP 90*
Ferris, Hobe 1877-1938 *Ballpl 90*
Ferris, James Peter 1932- *WhoAm 90*
Ferris, Jean 1939- *BioIn 16*
Ferris, John Charles 1933- *WhoWor 91*
Ferris, Keith 1929- *WhoAmA 91*
Ferris, Kent Robert 1953- *St&PR 91*
Ferris, Kimberlee Robin 1955- *WhoWrEP 89*
Ferris, Michael James 1944- *WhoAm 90*
Ferris, Peter Simon, Jr. 1929- *WhoE 91*
Ferris, Robert A. 1942- *St&PR 91*
Ferris, Robert Albert 1942- *WhoAm 90*
Ferris, Robert D. 1942- *ODwPR 91*
Ferris, Robert Edmund 1918- *WhoAm 90*
Ferris, Robert Michael 1944- *WhoSSW 91*
Ferris, Robert Nelson 1945- *WhoE 91*
Ferris, Roger Patrick 1952- *WhoE 91*
Ferris, Ronald Curry 1945- *WhoAm 90*
Ferris, Sean Daly 1948- *WhoE 91*
Ferris, Thomas Francis 1930- *WhoAm 90*
Ferris, Timothy 1944- *ConAu 30NR*
Ferris, Virginia Rogers *WhoAm 90*
Ferris, William Edward 1937- *IntWWM 90*
Ferris, William Michael 1948- *WhoEmL 91*
Ferris, William Reynolds 1942- *WhoSSW 91*
Ferriss, Abbott Lamoyne 1915- *WhoSSW 91, WhoWrEP 89*
Ferriss, Boo 1921- *Ballpl 90*
Ferriter, Clare 1913- *WhoAmA 91*
Ferritor, Daniel E. 1939- *WhoAm 90, WhoSSW 91*
Ferro, Benedict *WhoHisp 91*
Ferro, Deborah 1956- *WhoAmW 91*
Ferro, John Joseph 1961- *WhoE 91*
Ferro, Jorge 1948- *WhoHisp 91*
Ferro, Manuel, Jr. 1946- *WhoSSW 91*
Ferro, Matthew A. 1940- *St&PR 91*
Ferro, Maximilian Leonida 1942- *WhoAm 90*
Ferro, Ramon 1941- *WhoHisp 91*
Ferro, Ramon R. 1941- *St&PR 91*
Ferro, Robert 1941-1988 *BioIn 16*
Ferro, Simon *WhoHisp 91*
Ferro, Thomas Anthony 1954- *St&PR 91*
Ferro, Thomas Louis 1947- *WhoEmL 91*
Ferro, Walter *WhoAmA 91*
Ferro, Walter 1925- *WhoAm 90*
Ferro, William Ewart 1940- *St&PR 91*
Ferro-Nyalka, Ruth Rudys 1930- *WhoAmW 91*
Ferron, Frederick R 1951- *BiDrAPA 89*
Ferron, Jacques *BioIn 16*
Ferron, Jacques 1921-1985 *ConAu 129, OxCCanT*
Ferron, Patrick Lee 1933- *St&PR 91*
Ferrone, Soldano 1940- *WhoAm 90*
Ferrotti, Salvatore P. 1932- *St&PR 91*
Ferrucci, Gabriel 1936- *St&PR 91*
Ferrucci, Jeanne Marie 1940- *WhoE 91*
Ferrucci, Raymond Vincent 1926- *St&PR 91, WhoAm 90*
Ferruzza, Jeanne A. 1930- *St&PR 91*
Ferry, Andrew Peter 1929- *WhoAm 90*
Ferry, Bryan *BioIn 16, EncPR&S 89*
Ferry, Bryan 1945- *OxCPMus, WhoAm 90*
Ferry, Danny *BioIn 16*
Ferry, David Keane 1940- *WhoAm 90*
Ferry, George 1926- *St&PR 91*
Ferry, James Allen 1937- *St&PR 91, WhoAm 90*
Ferry, Joan Evans 1941- *WhoAmW 91, WhoE 91, WhoWor 91*
Ferry, John Douglass 1912- *WhoAm 90*
Ferry, Joseph Vincent, Jr. 1947- *WhoSSW 91*
Ferry, Jules Francois Camille 1832-1893 *BiDFrPL*
Ferry, Martha Morton 1945- *St&PR 91, WhoEmL 91*
Ferry, Michael James 1957- *WhoEmL 91*
Ferry, Miles Yeoman 1932- *WhoAm 90*
Ferry, Richard M. 1937- *St&PR 91*
Ferry, Richard Michael 1937- *WhoAm 90*
Ferry, Robert Dean 1937- *WhoAm 90, WhoE 91*
Ferry, Wilbur Hugh 1910- *WhoAm 90*
Fershtman, Julie Ilene 1961- *WhoAmW 91, WhoEmL 91, WhoWor 91*
Ferst, Albert F. 1919- *St&PR 91*
Ferstl, James H. *St&PR 91*
Fertel, Ruth *BioIn 16*
Fertell, Paul Adolph 1927- *WhoAm 90*
Fertig, Howard *WhoAm 90, WhoWrEP 89*
Fertig, John F. 1926- *St&PR 91*
Fertik, Ira J. 1940- *WhoAm 90*
Fertis, Demeter George 1926- *WhoAm 90*
Fertitta, Joseph Frank 1922- *St&PR 91*
Fertitta, Marian Boudreaux 1948- *WhoEmL 91*
Fertl, Mary Neese 1956- *WhoEmL 91*
Ferwerda, Anton 1945- *St&PR 91*
Ferwerda, Hedzer Adam 1933- *WhoWor 91*
Ferwerda, John Diedrich 1942- *IntWWM 90*
Fery, John B. *BioIn 16*
Fery, John Bruce 1930- *St&PR 91, WhoAm 90*
Ferzacca, William 1927- *WhoWor 91*
Feschotte, Pierre 1930- *WhoWor 91*
Fesen, Michael Robert 1957- *WhoEmL 91*
Fesenmaier, Helene 1937- *BiDWomA*
Feser, William Joseph 1925- *St&PR 91*
Feshbach, Herman 1917- *WhoAm 90*
Feshbach, Norma Deitch 1926- *WhoAm 90*
Feshbach, Seymour 1925- *WhoAm 90*
Feskoe, Gaffney Jon 1949- *WhoAm 90, WhoEmL 91*
Fesler, David Richard 1928- *WhoAm 90, WhoWor 91*
Fesler, F Anne *BiDrAPA 89*
Fesler, James Andrew 1938- *BiDrAPA 89*
Fesler, Robert L. 1937- *St&PR 91*
Fess, Marilynn Elaine Ewing 1944- *WhoWor 91*
Fess, Philip Eugene 1931- *WhoAm 90*
Fessenden, Benjamin 1797-1881 *AmLegL*
Fessenden, Hart 1927- *St&PR 91*
Fessenden, Samuel 1847-1908 *AmLegL*
Fessenden, William Pitt 1806-1869 *BiDrUSE 89, WorAlBi*
Fessenko, Tatiana 1915- *EncCoWW*
Fessier, Michael *BioIn 16*
Fessler, Ann Helene 1949- *WhoAmA 91*
Fessler, Denis Eugene 1949- *WhoEmL 91*
Fessler, Donald Francis 1931- *St&PR 91*
Fessler, William Andrew 1940- *WhoE 91*
Fest, Joachim 1926- *WhoWor 91*
Fest, Thorrel Brooks 1910- *WhoAm 90*
Festa, Roger Reginald 1950- *WhoEmL 91, WhoWor 91*
Fester, Gertrude *BioIn 16*
Festervan, Denise Campbell 1960- *WhoAmW 91*
Festinger, Leon 1919-1989 *BioIn 16, ConAu 31NR*
Fesus, George John 1942- *St&PR 91, WhoAm 90*
Fetch, Alan Michael 1953- *WhoEmL 91*
Fetchero, James V. 1920- *St&PR 91*
Fetchero, John Anthony, Jr. 1951- *WhoSSW 91*
Fetchit, Stepin 1892-1985 *DrBlPA 90*
Fetchko, Peter J. 1943- *WhoAm 90, WhoAmA 91, WhoE 91*
Feten, Douglas Leroy 1951- *WhoEmL 91*
Feth, Lawrence Lee 1943- *WhoAm 90*
Fetherolf, Joyce Wilson 1952- *WhoEmL 91*
Fetherstonhaugh, Maria 1847-1918 *FemiCLE*
Fetko, Paul 1931- *WhoWor 91*
Fetler, Andrew 1925- *WhoAm 90, WhoWrEP 89*
Fetler, Dan Gregor 1952- *WhoWor 91*
Fetler, Paul 1920- *WhoAm 90*
Fetner, Beverly 1928- *WhoE 91*
Fetner, Robert Henry 1922- *WhoAm 90*
Fetridge, Bonnie-Jean Clark 1915- *WhoAm 90, WhoWor 91*
Fetridge, Clark Worthington 1946- *St&PR 91, WhoAm 90*
Fetridge, William Harrison *St&PR 91N*
Fetridge, William Harrison 1906- *WhoAm 90*
Fetridge, William Harrison 1906-1989 *BioIn 16, ConAu 129*
Fetrow, John Edward 1939- *St&PR 91*
Fetscher, Paul George William 1945- *WhoE 91*
Fetske, Ruth Betty 1922- *WhoAmW 91*
Fett, Eugene Werner 1932- *WhoAm 90*
Fett, Robert H. 1932- *St&PR 91*
Fett, William F 1918- *WhoAmA 91*
Fetta, Frank Paul 1944- *IntWWM 90*
Fette, Lou 1907-1981 *Ballpl 90*
Fetter, Albert 1863-1949 *BioIn 16*
Fetter, Alexander Lees 1937- *WhoAm 90*
Fetter, Debora Kay 1956- *WhoE 91*
Fetter, Elizabeth Ann 1958- *WhoEmL 91*
Fetter, James Monroe, III 1953- *BiDrAPA 89*
Fetter, Jean Holmes 1937- *WhoAmW 91*
Fetter, John Branch 1951- *WhoE 91*
Fetter, Ralph R. 1943- *St&PR 91*
Fetter, Richard Elwood 1923- *WhoAm 90*
Fetter, Robert Barclay 1924- *WhoAm 90*
Fetter, Theodore Henry 1906- *WhoAm 90*
Fetter, Theodore Search 1913- *WhoAm 90*
Fetterhoff, Ira Lincoln 1928- *BiDrAPA 89*
Fetterly, Fred A. 1930- *ODwPR 91*
Fetterman, Allen Louis 1948- *WhoE 91*
Fetterman, James C. 1947- *WhoEmL 91*
Fetterman, Lynn K. 1947- *St&PR 91*
Fetterman, William Judd 1833?-1866 *WhNaAH*
Fetterolf, Charles E. 1932- *St&PR 91*
Fetterolf, Charles Frederick 1928- *St&PR 91, WhoAm 90, WhoE 91*
Fetteroll, Eugene Carl, Jr. 1935- *WhoE 91*
Fetters, Debra Ann 1959- *WhoAmW 91*
Fetters, Joan Frances 1939- *WhoAmW 91*
Fetters, Norman Craig, II 1942- *WhoAm 90*
Fetters, R. Thomas, Jr. *WhoSSW 91*
Fettes, Richard C *BiDrAPA 89*
Fetti, Domenico 1589?-1623 *IntDcAA 90*
Fetting, Fritz 1926- *WhoWor 91*
Fetting, Rainer 1949- *WhoAmA 91*
Fettinger, Laurie A. *WhoAmW 91*
Fettingis, Joseph *BioIn 16*
Fettman, Mark Samuel *BiDrAPA 89*
Fettweis, Alfred Leo Maria 1926- *WhoWor 91*
Fettweis, Yvonne Cache 1935- *WhoAmW 91, WhoE 91, WhoWor 91*
Fetzer, Edward Frank 1940- *WhoAm 90*
Fetzer, John 1901- *Ballpl 90*
Fetzer, John Charles 1949- *BiDrAPA 89*
Fetzer, John Charles 1953- *WhoEmL 91*
Fetzer, John E. 1901- *St&PR 91*
Fetzer, John Earl 1901- *WhoAm 90*
Fetzer, Wallace S. 1954- *St&PR 91*
Fetzner, Carl G. 1934- *St&PR 91*
Fetzner, James Frederick 1946- *St&PR 91*
Fetzner, Joseph John 1942- *St&PR 91*
Feuchere, Armand 1797-1860? *PenDiDA 89*
Feuchere, Jean-Jacques *PenDiDA 89*
Feuchere, Lucien-Francois *PenDiDA 89*
Feuchere, Pierre-Francois 1737-1823 *PenDiDA 89*
Feucht, Donald Lee 1933- *WhoAm 90*
Feucht, Robert W. 1934- *St&PR 91*
Feuchter, Robert 1926- *St&PR 91*
Feuchtmayer, Johann Michael *PenDiDA 89*
Feuchtwang, Thomas Emanuel 1930- *WhoAm 90*
Feuchtwanger, Lion 1884-1958 *BioIn 16, WorAlBi*
Feuchtwanger, Marta *BioIn 16*
Feuchtwanger, Rose A 1920- *BiDrAPA 89*
Feudale, Barry Francis 1946- *WhoEmL 91*
Feuer, Avrohom Chaim 1946- *ConAu 32NR*
Feuer, Cy 1911- *WhoAm 90*
Feuer, Ezra H 1949- *BiDrAPA 89*
Feuer, Henry 1912- *WhoAm 90*
Feuer, Lewis S. 1912- *WhoAm 90*
Feuer, Maria 1932- *IntWWM 90*
Feuer, Michelle H. *WhoAmW 91*
Feuer, Morris 1933- *St&PR 91*
Feuer, S.S. 1923- *St&PR 91*
Feuer, Stephanie 1955- *WhoEmL 91*
Feuerbach, Ludwig 1804-1872 *WorAlBi, WrPh P*
Feuerberg, Paul Richard 1946- *WhoEmL 91*
Feuerburgh, Joseph 1908- *WhoE 91*
Feuerherm, Kurt K 1925- *WhoAmA 91*
Feuerlein, Willy John Arthur 1911- *WhoAm 90*
Feuerman, Carole Jeane 1945- *WhoAmA 91*
Feuermann, Claudio A. *WhoHisp 91*
Feuermann, Emanuel 1902-1942 *PenDiMP*
Feuerstein, Claude 1951- *WhoWor 91*
Feuerstein, Donald M. 1937- *St&PR 91*
Feuerstein, Donald Martin 1937- *WhoAm 90*
Feuerstein, Gary Ray 1950- *WhoEmL 91*
Feuerstein, Georg 1947- *WhoWrEP 89*
Feuerstein, Herbert 1927- *St&PR 91*
Feuerstein, Howard M. 1939- *WhoAm 90*
Feuerstein, Marie Therese 1941- *WhoWor 91*
Feuerstein, Roberta 1950- *WhoAmA 91*
Feuerstein, Sheryl *ODwPR 91*
Feuerwerker, Albert 1927- *WhoAm 90, WhoWrEP 89*
Feuerzeig, Henry Louis 1938- *WhoAm 90*
Feuillatre, Eugene 1870-1916 *PenDiDA 89*
Feuille, Richard Harlan 1920- *WhoAm 90*
Feuless, Scott Charles 1960- *WhoEmL 91, WhoSSW 91*
Feuling, Jim *BioIn 16*
Feulner, Edwin John, Jr. 1941- *WhoAm 90, WhoE 91, WhoWor 91*
Feure, Georges de 1868-1943 *BioIn 16*
Feurey, Benita 1940- *WhoAmW 91*
Feurey, Benita S. *BioIn 16*
Feurey, Benita S. 1940?-1989 *ConAu 129*
Feurey, Claudia P. *ODwPR 91*
Feurey, Claudia Packer 1949- *WhoE 91*
Feurey, Monie Begley *ODwPR 91*
Feusner, Randy Bruce 1960- *WhoEmL 91*
Feuss, Charles D, Jr. 1921- *BiDrAPA 89*
Feusse, Thomas A. 1959- *St&PR 91*
Feussner, James Walter 1947- *BiDrAPA 89*
Feutre, Alain Philippe 1945- *WhoWor 91*
Fevang, Leroy Conrad 1936- *WhoAm 90*
Fever, Buck 1876-1941 *BioIn 16*
Fevola, Mario 1937- *WhoWor 91*
Fevrier, Jacques 1900-1979 *PenDiMP*
Fevurly, Keith Robert 1951- *WhoEmL 91*
Few, Catharine Nicholson 1764?- *BioIn 16*
Few, Daniel Lance 1944- *WhoE 91*
Few, Melinda Mulliniks 1938- *WhoAmW 91, WhoSSW 91*
Few, William 1748-1828 *BioIn 16*
Fewell, Rebecca Reid *WhoAm 90*
Fewell, Terry Glenn 1940- *WhoAm 90*
Fewin, Hugh Richard 1933- *St&PR 91*
Fewkes, Jesse Walter 1850-1930 *WhNaAH*
Fewster, Chick 1895-1945 *Ballpl 90*
Fey, David L. 1944- *St&PR 91*
Fey, Dorothy *WhoAm 90*
Fey, Harold E. *BioIn 16*
Fey, Harold E. *NewYTBS 90*
Fey, Harold E 1898-1990 *ConAu 130*
Fey, John Theodore 1917- *WhoAm 90*
Feydeau, Georges 1862-1921 *WorAlBi*
Feydy, Anne Lindbergh 1940- *AuBYP 90*
Feyerabend, Paul Karl 1924- *WhoAm 90*
Feyl, Renate 1944- *EncCoWW*
Feyler-Switz, Helen Shafter 1935- *WhoAmW 91*
Feynman, R. P. *ConAu 129, MajTwCW*
Feynman, Richard *ConAu 129, MajTwCW*
Feynman, Richard 1918-1988 *AnObit 1988*
Feynman, Richard P. *ConAu 129, MajTwCW*
Feynman, Richard P. 1918-1989 *WorAlBi*
Feynman, Richard Phillips *BioIn 16*
Feynman, Richard Phillips 1918- *WhoWrEP 89*
Feynman, Richard Phillips 1918-1988 *ConAu 129, MajTwCW*
Feys, Jean O *BiDrAPA 89*
Feyzioglu, Tarhan 1962- *WhoE 91*
Fezza, Andrew *BioIn 16*
Fezza, Anthony A. 1921- *St&PR 91*
Ffolkes, Michael 1925-1988 *AnObit 1988, BioIn 16*
Fforde, Arthur Frederic Brownlow 1900-1985 *DcNaB 1981*
Ffrangcon-Davies, David 1855-1919 *PenDiMP*
Fiacable, Joseph P 1934- *BiDrAPA 89*
Fiacco, Arthur J. *ODwPR 91*
Fiaccone, Hubert Novellino 1918- *WhoAm 90*
Fiad, Alfredo M *BiDrAPA 89*
Fiaich, Tomas O. 1923-1990 *NewYTBS 90 [port]*
Fiala, Brian Donald 1950- *WhoEmL 91*
Fiala, David Marcus 1946- *WhoEmL 91*
Fiala, George 1922- *IntWWM 90*
Fiala, Kenneth Richard 1932- *St&PR 91*
Fiala, Timothy D. *ODwPR 91*
Fialer, Philip Anthony 1938- *WhoAm 90*
Fialkov, Herman 1922- *St&PR 91, WhoAm 90, WhoWor 91*
Fialkov, Martin J 1944- *BiDrAPA 89*
Fialkov, Martin Jerome 1944- *WhoE 91*
Fialkow, Neil Joseph *BiDrAPA 89*
Fialkow, Philip Jack 1934- *WhoAm 90*
Fialkow, Steven 1943- *WhoE 91, WhoWor 91*
Fialkowski, Louise *BiDrAPA 89*
Fiallos-Montero, Denis *BiDrAPA 89*
Fialowski, Alice 1951- *WhoWor 91*
Fiamengo, Marya 1926- *FemiCLE*
Fiamingo, Nancy Anne 1949- *WhoAmW 91*
Fiandra, Orestes Alfredo 1921- *WhoWor 91*
Fiaush, John C. 1930- *St&PR 91*
Fibber McGee and Molly *WorAlBi*
Fibich, Howard Raymond 1932- *WhoAm 90*
Fibiger, John Andrew 1932- *St&PR 91, WhoAm 90, WhoE 91*
Fibiger, Mathilde Lucie 1830-1872 *EncCoWW*
Fibish, Nancy Connolly *WhoAmW 91*
Fibkins, Robert James 1936- *WhoAm 90*
Fibonacci, Leonardo 1170?-1240? *WorAlBi*
Fica, Juan 1949- *WhoE 91*
Ficarelli, Richard John, Jr. 1958- *WhoSSW 91*
Ficarra, Anthony M. 1942- *WhoE 91*
Ficarra, Dori Anne 1965- *WhoAmW 91*

Ficarra, Joseph Roman 1938- *BiDrAPA 89*
Ficarro, John Robert 1952- *WhoEmL 91*
Ficcaglia, Vince Paul 1946- *St&PR 91*
Fichandler, Zelda *BioIn 16*
Fichandler, Zelda Diamond 1924- *NotWoAT*
Fichenberg, Robert Gordon 1920- *WhoAm 90*
Fichera, Andrew J 1928- *BiDrAPA 89*
Fichte, Johann 1762-1814 *WorAlBi*
Fichte, Johann Gottlieb 1762-1814 *WrPh P*
Fichtel, Carl Edwin 1933- *WhoAm 90*
Fichtel, Mark Dilworth 1946- *St&PR 91*
Fichtel, Rudolph Robert 1915- *WhoAm 90*
Fichter, Gay Lloyd 1952- *WhoAmW 91*
Fichter, George S. *AuBYP 90*
Fichter, Herbert Francis 1920- *WhoAmA 91*
Fichter, Joseph H. 1908- *WhoAm 90*
Fichter, Robert W 1939- *WhoAmA 91*
Fichter, Thomas C. *NewYTBS 90*
Fichthorn, Luke Eberly, III 1941- *St&PR 91*
Ficino, Marsilio 1433-1499 *BioIn 16*
Fick, Bernard E. 1940- *St&PR 91*
Fick, Bradley Norman 1959- *WhoEmL 91*
Fick, E. Dean 1944- *St&PR 91*
Fick, Gary Warren 1943- *WhoAm 90*
Fick, Robert 1941- *St&PR 91*
Fickeisen, Cheryl L. 1946- *St&PR 91*
Ficken, Karen Valarie 1953- *WhoAmW 91*
Ficken, Millicent Sigler 1933- *WhoAmW 91*
Fickenwirth, Fred Iredale, Jr. 1956- *WhoEmL 91*
Ficker, Sarah Jane 1929- *WhoWrEP 89*
Fickert, Kurt J 1920- *ConAu 31NR*
Fickes, Jerry Wayne 1931- *St&PR 91*
Fickes, Marita Clark 1946- *WhoAmW 91*, *WhoEmL 91*
Fickes, Robert K. 1944- *ODwPR 91*
Fickey, Richard W. 1940- *St&PR 91*
Fickinger, Jan *ODwPR 91*
Fickinger, Wayne Joseph 1926- *WhoAm 90*
Fickinger, William Joseph 1934- *WhoAm 90*
Fickle, Marvin Dwane 1949- *BiDrAPA 89*
Ficklen, Jack Howells 1911-1980 *WhoAmA 91N*
Ficklen, James S., Jr. 1924- *St&PR 91*
Fickler, Yehuda 1925- *IntWWM 90*
Ficklin, Vickie J. 1955- *WhoEmL 91*
Fickling, Amy Leigh 1957- *WhoWrEP 89*
Fickling, William A., Jr. 1932- *St&PR 91*
Fickling, William Arthur, Jr. 1932- *WhoSSW 91*
Ficks, Robert L., Jr. 1919- *St&PR 91*
Ficorelli, Rick Thomas 1951- *WhoEmL 91*
Ficquette, Sharon Elaine 1956- *WhoEmL 91*
Ficurelli, Joseph P. 1939- *St&PR 91*
Ficzeri, Paul Daniel 1946- *WhoEmL 91*, *WhoSSW 91*
Fidaleo, Raymond A 1937- *BiDrAPA 89*
Fidanza, Gianni 1939- *St&PR 91*
Fidanzi, Mario A. 1951- *St&PR 91*
Fiddick, Paul William 1949- *WhoAm 90*, *WhoSSW 91*
Fiddler, Barbara Dillow 1940- *WhoE 91*
Fiddler, Sharon Ann 1950- *WhoSSW 91*
Fidel, Edward Allen 1914- *WhoE 91*
Fidel, Joseph A. 1923- *WhoHisp 91*
Fideldia, Vilma T *BiDrAPA 89*
Fidelia *FemiCLE*
Fidler, Donald Carl *BiDrAPA 89*
Fidler, Jay W. 1922- *St&PR 91*
Fidler, Jay W, Jr. 1917- *BiDrAPA 89*
Fidler, Jimmie 1900-1988 *BioIn 16*
Fidler, Mark W. 1952- *St&PR 91*
Fidler, Spencer D 1944- *WhoAmA 91*
Fidler, Steven E. 1943- *St&PR 91*
Fido, Franco 1931- *WhoAm 90*
Fidrych, Mark 1954- *Ballpl 90*
Fiducia, Benedict Anthony 1937- *WhoE 91*
Fiducia, Gene 1925- *St&PR 91*
Fie, Larry Eugene 1938- *St&PR 91*
Fiebach, H. Robert 1939- *WhoAm 90*
Fieber, Heribert 1927- *WhoWor 91*
Fiebert, Erik 1957- *St&PR 91*
Fiebert, Murray 1922- *St&PR 91*
Fiebig, Kurt 1908- *IntWWM 90*
Fiebig, Kurt S. 1947- *St&PR 91*
Fiebiger, Daniel Joseph 1951- *WhoEmL 91*
Fiedel, Roslyn *AuBYP 90*
Fiederlein, Gustav L. 1926- *St&PR 91*
Fiederlein, Thomas R. 1946- *St&PR 91*
Fiederowicz, Walter Michael 1946- *WhoAm 90*
Fiedler, Arthur 1894-1979 *PenDiMP*, *WorAlBi*
Fiedler, Edgar F. 1943- *St&PR 91*
Fiedler, Edward Henry, Jr. 1932- *St&PR 91*, *WhoAm 90*
Fiedler, Fred Edward 1922- *WhoAm 90*
Fiedler, Hans Karl 1955- *WhoSSW 91*
Fiedler, Harold Joseph 1924- *WhoAm 90*
Fiedler, Johann G. *PenDiDA 89*
Fiedler, Kurt R 1928- *BiDrAPA 89*
Fiedler, Leslie 1917- *WorAlBi*
Fiedler, Leslie A. *BioIn 16*
Fiedler, Leslie A 1917- *MajTwCW*
Fiedler, Leslie Aaron 1917- *WhoAm 90*, *WhoWrEP 89*
Fiedler, Marc 1955- *WhoEmL 91*
Fiedler, Michael Allen 1956- *WhoSSW 91*
Fiedler, Sally A. 1939- *WhoWrEP 89*
Fiedoral, Joseph Fletcher 1926- *St&PR 91*
Fiedorek, Eugene C. 1931- *St&PR 91*
Fieger, Addy Oppenheimer *BioIn 16*
Fiehn, Walter Dieter Wolfgang 1941- *WhoWor 91*
Fiehrer, R.A. 1934- *St&PR 91*
Fiel, David H. *WhoE 91*
Fiel, Maxine Lucille *WhoAm 90*, *WhoAmW 91*, *WhoWor 91*
Field, A. J. 1924- *WhoAm 90*
Field, Allen Wescott 1853-1915 *AmLegL*
Field, Andrea Bear 1949- *WhoE 91*
Field, Arthur N. 1905-1990 *BioIn 16*
Field, Arthur Norman 1935- *WhoAm 90*
Field, Barry Elliot 1947- *WhoE 91*, *WhoWor 91*
Field, Benjamin R. 1938- *St&PR 91*
Field, Charles Steven 1945- *WhoEmL 91*
Field, Corey 1956- *WhoEmL 91*
Field, Cyrus Adams 1902- *WhoAm 90*
Field, Cyrus W. 1819-1892 *WorAlBi*
Field, Dan *BioIn 16*
Field, Daniel Thomas 1947- *BiDrAPA 89*
Field, David Charles 1948- *St&PR 91*
Field, David Ellis 1953- *WhoEmL 91*
Field, Douglas Scott 1955- *WhoEmL 91*
Field, Edward 1924- *DcLB 105 [port]*, *WhoWrEP 89*
Field, Edwin Martin 1924- *WhoE 91*
Field, Elizabeth Farnham 1926- *St&PR 91*
Field, Eugene 1850-1895 *AuBYP 90*, *BioIn 16*, *WorAlBi*
Field, Francis Edward 1923- *WhoE 91*
Field, Frederick V. *ConAu 130*
Field, Frederick Vanderbilt 1905- *ConAu 130*
Field, Garrett 1954- *WhoEmL 91*
Field, George Brooks 1929- *WhoAm 90*
Field, George Franklin 1922- *St&PR 91*
Field, George Sydney 1905- *WhoAm 90*
Field, Hamilton Easter 1873-1922 *BioIn 16*
Field, Harold David, Jr. 1927- *WhoAm 90*
Field, Harold S. *St&PR 91*
Field, Harry J. 1896-1988 *BioIn 16*
Field, Harry Rush *WhoWrEP 89*
Field, Helen 1951- *IntWWM 90*
Field, Henry Augustus, Jr. 1928- *WhoAm 90*
Field, Henry Frederick 1941- *WhoAm 90*
Field, Hermann Haviland 1910- *WhoAm 90*
Field, Howard L 1928- *BiDrAPA 89*
Field, James Bernard 1926- *WhoAm 90*
Field, Joan Stuber 1934- *WhoAmW 91*
Field, John 1782-1837 *BioIn 16*
Field, John Louis 1930- *WhoAm 90*
Field, John W. 1914- *St&PR 91*
Field, Karen Ann 1936- *WhoAmW 91*
Field, Karen Lynn 1950- *St&PR 91*
Field, Kate 1838-1896 *BioAmW*, *BioIn 16*, *FemiCLE*
Field, Leslie *BioIn 16*
Field, Lyman 1914- *WhoAm 90*, *WhoAmA 91*
Field, M. Patricia 1958- *WhoEmL 91*
Field, Marcia Carole Kaplaw 1932- *WhoAmW 91*
Field, Marshall 1834-1906 *WorAlBi*
Field, Marshall 1941- *WhoAm 90*, *WhoWor 91*
Field, Marshall, III 1893-1956 *WorAlBi*
Field, Marshall, Jr. 1931- *St&PR 91*
Field, Martin Glenn, Jr. *BiDrAPA 89*
Field, Michael *FemiCLE*
Field, Nathan 1587-1620? *BioIn 16*
Field, Norman George 1944- *WhoWor 91*
Field, Norman J. 1922- *WhoE 91*
Field, Penny Shiffman 1960- *WhoEmL 91*
Field, Peter 1926- *St&PR 91*
Field, Philip Sidney 1942- *WhoAmA 91*
Field, R Patricia *BiDrAPA 89*
Field, Rachel 1894-1942 *ChlLR 21 [port]*, *WorAlBi*
Field, Rachel Lyman 1894-1942 *AuBYP 90*
Field, Richard Clark 1940- *WhoAm 90*
Field, Richard D. 1940- *St&PR 91*
Field, Richard Sampson 1931- *WhoAmA 91*
Field, Robert Bunten, Jr. 1943- *WhoE 91*
Field, Robert Edward 1945- *WhoEmL 91*
Field, Robert Steven 1949- *WhoEmL 91*
Field, Robert Warren 1944- *WhoAm 90*
Field, Ron *BioIn 16*
Field, Ron 1934-1989 *AnObit 1989*
Field, Ronald Emmett 1946- *WhoE 91*
Field, Sally *BioIn 16*
Field, Sally 1946- *WhoAm 90*, *WhoAmW 91*, *WorAlBi*
Field, Sandra Gusciora 1958- *WhoEmL 91*
Field, Saul 1912-1987 *WhoAmA 91N*
Field, Stanley *WhoWrEP 89*
Field, Stephen H. 1948- *St&PR 91*
Field, Steven David 1951- *BiDrAPA 89*
Field, Temple *TwCCr&M 91*
Field, Thomas C. 1942- *St&PR 91*
Field, Thomas Clark 1942- *WhoAm 90*
Field, Thomas Gordon 1957- *WhoEmL 91*
Field, Thomas Walter, Jr. 1933- *St&PR 91*
Field, William D. 1923- *St&PR 91*
Field, William Stephenson 1929- *WhoAm 90*
Field, William W. 1824-1907 *AmLegL*
Field-Hyde, Margaret 1905- *IntWWM 90*, *PenDiMP*
Fielden, C. Franklin, III 1946- *WhoEmL 91*
Fielder, Allyson Beth 1964- *WhoAmW 91*
Fielder, Cecil 1963- *Ballpl 90*
Fielder, Charles Robert 1943- *St&PR 91*, *WhoAm 90*, *WhoSSW 91*
Fielder, Donald Jerome 1945- *WhoSSW 91*
Fielder, Dorothy Robison 1944- *WhoSSW 91*
Fielder, Judy Parsons 1947- *WhoAmW 91*
Fielder, Virginia Dodge 1948- *St&PR 91*
Fieldhouse, Anthony 1944- *St&PR 91*
Fieldhouse, G.E. 1917- *St&PR 91*
Fielding, Allen Fred 1943- *WhoAm 90*
Fielding, David Alan 1953- *WhoWor 91*
Fielding, Elizabeth May 1917- *WhoAm 90*
Fielding, Fred Fisher 1939- *WhoAm 90*
Fielding, Henry 1707-1754 *BioIn 16*, *DcLB 101 [port]*, *WorAlBi*
Fielding, Ivor Rene 1942- *WhoAm 90*
Fielding, Lewis J 1909- *BiDrAPA 89*
Fielding, Morton D. 1928- *WhoE 91*
Fielding, Nigel G 1950- *ConAu 131*
Fielding, Peggy Lou Moss *WhoWrEP 89*
Fielding, Ronald H. 1949- *St&PR 91*
Fielding, Sarah 1710-1768 *BioIn 16*, *FemiCLE*
Fielding, Seth David 1942- *BiDrAPA 89*
Fielding, Tom Dennis 1940- *St&PR 91*
Fieldman, Leon 1926- *WhoAm 90*
Fieldman, Wayne Lyle 1944- *WhoWor 91*
Fields, Adam Amory 1955- *WhoEmL 91*
Fields, Annie 1834-1915 *BioIn 16*, *FemiCLE*
Fields, Annie A. 1834-1915 *BioAmW*
Fields, Barbara P. Linder 1950- *WhoAmW 91*
Fields, Becky Lynn 1963- *WhoAmW 91*
Fields, Bernard Nathan 1938- *WhoAm 90*
Fields, Bert 1929- *BioIn 16*
Fields, Bertram Harris 1929- *WhoAm 90*, *WhoWor 91*
Fields, Bessie Marie Williams 1940- *WhoAmW 91*
Fields, Brandon *BioIn 16*
Fields, Carl Victor 1951- *WhoEmL 91*
Fields, Charlie 1883-1966 *MusmAFA*
Fields, Christine G. 1952- *WhoAmW 91*
Fields, Cleo *BioIn 16*
Fields, Curtis Grey 1933- *St&PR 91*, *WhoAm 90*
Fields, Curtis Grey, Jr. 1958- *WhoSSW 91*
Fields, Daisy Bresley 1915- *WhoAmW 91*, *WhoE 91*
Fields, Darcey Ames 1950- *WhoEmL 91*
Fields, David C. 1937- *WhoAm 90*
Fields, David Charles 1937- *WhoWor 91*
Fields, Dawna Michelle 1961- *ODwPR 91*
Fields, Debbi *BioIn 16*
Fields, Debra Jane Sivyer 1956- *ConAmBL*
Fields, Dexter L 1944- *BiDrAPA 89*
Fields, Dorothy 1904-1974 *OxCPMus*
Fields, Dorothy 1905-1974 *BioIn 16*, *NotWoAT*, *WorAlBi*
Fields, Douglas Philip 1942- *St&PR 91*, *WhoAm 90*, *WhoWor 91*
Fields, Edgar M. 1939- *St&PR 91*
Fields, Edward 1913-1979 *ConDes 90*
Fields, Edward Lee 1943- *BiDrAPA 89*
Fields, Ellis Kirby 1917- *WhoAm 90*
Fields, Ernie 1904- *BioIn 16*
Fields, Freddie 1923- *WhoAm 90*
Fields, Fredrica H 1912- *WhoAmA 91*
Fields, Fredrica Hastings 1912- *WhoAmW 91*, *WhoE 91*
Fields, Garey Orlando 1958- *WhoEmL 91*
Fields, Garson R., Jr. 1949- *St&PR 91*
Fields, Gow Belton 1963- *WhoSSW 91*
Fields, Gracie 1898-1979 *OxCPMus*, *WorAlBi*
Fields, Harry 1924- *WhoAm 90*
Fields, Herbert 1897-1958 *OxCPMus*
Fields, Howard *BioIn 16*
Fields, Jack 1952- *WhoAm 90*, *WhoSSW 91*
Fields, James Edward, Jr. 1963- *WhoSSW 91*
Fields, Joan R. 1930- *WhoAmW 91*
Fields, Joe *BioIn 16*
Fields, Joel H 1931- *BiDrAPA 89*
Fields, Joseph 1885-1966 *OxCPMus*
Fields, Joyce M. 1947- *St&PR 91*, *WhoAm 90*
Fields, Karla Jo 1959- *WhoAmW 91*
Fields, Kathryn Patricia 1961- *WhoAmW 91*
Fields, Kathy Ann 1958- *WhoAmW 91*
Fields, Kim *BioIn 16*
Fields, Kim 1969- *DrBlPA 90*
Fields, Larry S. 1954- *WhoSSW 91*
Fields, Leo 1928- *St&PR 91*, *WhoAm 90*
Fields, Lew 1867-1941 *OxCPMus*
Fields, Lisa Gayle 1963- *WhoSSW 91*
Fields, Mary Durland 1930- *WhoSSW 91*
Fields, Meredith Ann *BiDrAPA 89*
Fields, Mitchell 1901-1966 *WhoAmA 91N*
Fields, Mitchell Andrew 1952- *WhoEmL 91*
Fields, Myrtice Elaine 1946- *WhoAmW 91*
Fields, Nancy Carlene 1952- *WhoWrEP 89*
Fields, Patricia L *BiDrAPA 89*
Fields, Paul Robert 1919- *WhoAm 90*
Fields, Ralph Raymond 1907- *WhoAm 90*
Fields, Randy 1947- *ConAmBL*
Fields, Richard Alan 1950- *BiDrAPA 89*
Fields, Rick D. 1942- *WhoWrEP 89*
Fields, Robert Charles 1920- *WhoAm 90*
Fields, Robert Lester 1940- *St&PR 91*
Fields, Robin Mae 1944- *WhoAmW 91*
Fields, Rona M. *BioIn 16*
Fields, Scott Michael 1957- *St&PR 91*
Fields, Shelia Rhonda 1953- *WhoAmW 91*, *WhoEmL 91*, *WhoSSW 91*
Fields, Shep 1910- *BioIn 16*
Fields, Stuart Howard 1943- *WhoE 91*
Fields, Susan Louise 1952- *WhoWrEP 89*
Fields, Suzanne 1936- *ConAu 129*
Fields, Suzanne Bregman 1936- *WhoE 91*
Fields, Theodore 1922- *WhoAm 90*
Fields, Virginia Mary 1952- *WhoAmW 91*
Fields, W. C. 1880-1946 *WorAlBi*
Fields, William Albert 1939- *WhoAm 90*
Fields, William Hudson, III 1934- *WhoAm 90*
Fields, William Jay 1936- *St&PR 91*
Fields, Zachary Russell 1946- *WhoSSW 91*
Fieldsteel, Robert Joseph 1922- *St&PR 91*
Fieleke, Norman S. 1932- *St&PR 91*
Fieleke, Norman Siegfried 1932- *WhoAm 90*
Fielo, Muriel Bryant 1921- *WhoAmW 91*, *WhoE 91*
Fielstra, Helen Adams 1921- *WhoAm 90*
Fienberg, Robert Littlewood 1939- *St&PR 91*
Fienberg, Stephen Elliott 1942- *WhoAm 90*, *WhoE 91*
Fiene, Alicia W 1919-1961 *WhoAmA 91N*
Fiene, Ernest 1894-1965 *WhoAmA 91N*
Fiene, Frank J. 1950- *St&PR 91*
Fienen, David Norman 1946- *IntWWM 90*
Fiennes, Celia 1662-1741 *BiDEWW*, *BioIn 16*, *FemiCLE*
Fiennes, Mark *BioIn 16*
Fiennes, Ranulph *BioIn 16*
Fiennes, Ranulph 1944- *News 90 [port]*, *-90-3 [port]*
Fiennes, Suzannah 1961- *BioIn 16*
Fier, Deborah *NewAgMG*
Fier, Elihu 1931- *WhoAm 90*
Fier, Morton 1932- *BiDrAPA 89*
Fierberg, Stephen Joel 1935- *St&PR 91*
Fierberg, Steven Edward 1954- *WhoEmL 91*
Fierce, Hughlyn F. *BioIn 16*
Fierce, Hughlyn Francis 1935- *WhoAm 90*
Fierce, Steven W. 1949- *St&PR 91*
Fierer, Joshua Allan 1937- *WhoAm 90*
Fierheller, George Alfred 1933- *WhoAm 90*, *WhoE 91*
Fiering, Norman 1935- *WhoAm 90*
Fierko, Edward J. 1941- *St&PR 91*
Fierle, Robert Joseph 1922- *St&PR 91*
Fierman, Daniel J. *St&PR 91*
Fierman, Eugene Joseph 1946- *BiDrAPA 89*
Fierman, Gerald Shea 1924- *St&PR 91*, *WhoE 91*, *WhoWor 91*
Fierman, Louis B 1922- *BiDrAPA 89*, *WhoE 91*
Fiero, Emilie L 1889-1974 *WhoAmA 91N*
Fiero, Gloria K 1939- *WhoAmA 91*
Fiero, Rollin P *BiDrAPA 89*
Fierro, Pancho 1810-1879 *ArtLatA*
Fierro, Robert John 1941- *WhoSSW 91*
Fierro Sanchez, Emilia Ana 1941- *WhoWor 91*
Fierros, Juan Enrique 1951- *WhoHisp 91*
Fierros, Ruth Victoria 1920- *WhoSSW 91*
Fiers, Alan D. 1939- *St&PR 91*
Fiers, Walter Charles 1931- *WhoWor 91*
Fierst, Bruce Philip 1951- *WhoEmL 91*
Fierstein, Harvey *BioIn 16*
Fierstein, Harvey 1954- *ConAu 129*
Fierstein, Harvey Forbes 1954- *WhoAm 90*
Fiery, Donald Ernst 1929- *St&PR 91*

Fies, Marie Joyce 1939- *WhoAmW 91*
Fieser, George Walter 1926- *WhoE 91*
Fieser, Louis Frederick 1899-1977 *DcScB S2*
Fiest, Frank E. 1938- *St&PR 91*
Fiester, Clark George 1934- *WhoAm 90*
Fiester, Susan Jean *BiDrAPA 89*
Fiete, Donald Jay 1934- *St&PR 91*
Fieve, Ronald R *BiDrAPA 89*
Fieve, Ronald Robert 1930- *WhoAm 90*
Fife, Alison *BiDrAPA 89*
Fife, Bernard 1915- *St&PR 91*
Fife, Bruce Fielding 1952- *WhoWrEP 89*
Fife, Dale 1901- *AuBYP 90*
Fife, David Joel 1950- *WhoE 91*
Fife, Dennis Jensen 1945- *WhoEmL 91*
Fife, Edward H. 1942- *WhoAm 90*
Fife, Eugene Vawter 1940- *WhoAm 90*
Fife, John Douglas, Jr. 1955- *WhoSSW 91*
Fife, Jonathan Donald 1941- *WhoE 91*
Fife, Kenneth Gordon 1945- *St&PR 91*
Fife, Lorin M. 1953- *St&PR 91*
Fife, Mary *WhoAmA 91*
Fife, W. Frank 1921- *St&PR 91*
Fife, William Franklin 1921- *WhoAm 90, WhoSSW 91*
Fife, William S *BiDrAPA 89*
Fife, Wilmer Krafft 1933- *WhoAm 90*
Fifer, Charles Norman 1922- *WhoAm 90*
Fifer, Julian *PenDiMP*
Fifer, Malcolm Stuart James 1943- *WhoSSW 91*
Fifer, Samuel 1950- *WhoEmL 91*
Fifer, William Ashworth 1932- *WhoAm 90*
Fifield, Cheryl Schneider 1955- *WhoAmW 91*
Fifield, Christopher G 1945- *ConAu 130*
Fifield, Russell Hunt 1914- *WhoAm 90*
Fifield, Samuel Stillman 1839-1915 *AmLegL*
Fifield, William 1916- *WhoWrEP 89*
Fifield, William Harry 1925- *WhoE 91*
Fiflis, Ted J. 1933- *WhoAm 90*
Fifth Dimension *EncPR&S 89*
Figari, Ernest Emil, Jr. 1939- *WhoWor 91*
Figari, Pedro 1861-1938 *ArtLatA*
Figarola, Carlos Jesus *BiDrAPA 89*
Figart, William Thomas 1926- *St&PR 91*
Fige, Sarah *BiDEWW*
Figen, I. Sevki 1924- *WhoWor 91*
Figen, Linda 1942- *BiDrAPA 89*
Figes, Eva *BioIn 16*
Figes, Eva 1932- *FemiCLE, WorAu 1980 [port]*
Figg, James Alfred, Jr. 1925- *WhoSSW 91*
Figg, Robert McCormick, Jr. 1901- *WhoAm 90, WhoSSW 91, WhoWor 91*
Figge, Charlene Elizabeth 1948- *WhoAmW 91*
Figge, F. J., II *WhoAm 90*
Figge, Frederick Henry, Jr. 1934- *WhoAm 90*
Figgie, Harry E. *BioIn 16*
Figgie, Harry E., Jr. 1923- *St&PR 91, WhoAm 90*
Figgins, David F. 1929- *St&PR 91*
Figgins, David Forrester 1929- *WhoAm 90*
Figgins, Letha Arlene 1916- *WhoAmW 91*
Figgis, Brian Norman 1930- *WhoWor 91*
Figgs, Carrie Law Morgan *HarlReB*
Figiel, Gary Steven *BiDrAPA 89*
Figilis, Karen 1954- *St&PR 91*
Figilis, William Murray 1940- *St&PR 91*
Figini, Michela *BioIn 16*
Figlar, Anita Wise 1950- *WhoAmW 91*
Figler, Alan Anthony 1948- *WhoEmL 91*
Figler, Byrnell Walter 1927- *IntWWM 90*
Figley, Melvin Morgan 1920- *WhoAm 90*
Figlioli, Lisa *ODwPR 91*
Figliozzi, John Philip 1946- *St&PR 91, WhoEmL 91*
Figliozzi, Robert J. 1938- *St&PR 91*
Fignar, Eugene Michael 1946- *WhoEmL 91*
Figner, Medea 1858-1952 *PenDiMP*
Figner, Nikolay 1857-1918 *PenDiMP*
Figner, Vera Nikolaevna 1852-1942 *EncCoWW*
Figucia, Joseph Charles, Jr. 1957- *WhoEmL 91*
Figueira, Servulo Augusto 1951- *WhoWor 91*
Figueiredo, Antonio Modesto 1943- *WhoWor 91*
Figueiredo, Hubert Fernandes 1958- *WhoEmL 91*
Figueiredo, Joao Baptista de Oliveira 1918- *BioIn 16*
Figuera, Henry Charles 1928- *St&PR 91*
Figueras, Jose M. 1928- *WhoWor 91*
Figueredo, Danilo H. 1951- *WhoHisp 91*
Figueredo, Nancy 1937- *BiDrAPA 89*
Figueredo Planchard, Reinaldo *WhoWor 91*
Figueres Ferrer, Jose 1906-1990 *BioIn 16, CurBio 90N, NewYTBS 90 [port]*
Figueroa, Angelo 1957- *WhoHisp 91*
Figueroa, Antonio *WhoHisp 91*
Figueroa, Benito, Jr. 1947- *WhoHisp 91*
Figueroa, Darryl Lynette 1959- *WhoHisp 91*
Figueroa, Ed 1948- *Ballpl 90*
Figueroa, Edduyn Ariel *BiDrAPA 89*
Figueroa, Edduynn Ariel 1945- *WhoEmL 91*
Figueroa, Howard G. 1930- *St&PR 91*
Figueroa, Howard George 1930- *WhoAm 90*
Figueroa, John 1949- *WhoHisp 91*
Figueroa, Jose *WhNaAH*
Figueroa, Jose-Angel 1946- *BioIn 16*
Figueroa, Juan A. 1953- *WhoHisp 91*
Figueroa, Julian 1943- *WhoHisp 91*
Figueroa, Liz 1951- *WhoHisp 91*
Figueroa, Loida 1917- *HispWr 90*
Figueroa, Manuel 1959- *WhoHisp 91*
Figueroa, Mario *WhoHisp 91*
Figueroa, Nicholas 1933- *WhoHisp 91*
Figueroa, Pablo 1938- *HispWr 90*
Figueroa, Pedro Jose 1780-1838 *ArtLatA*
Figueroa, Raul 1946- *WhoHisp 91*
Figueroa, Raymond 1947- *WhoHisp 91*
Figueroa, Sandra L. *WhoHisp 91*
Figueroa, Vicente *BiDrAPA 89*
Figueroa-Crawford, Diana Julie 1958- *WhoAmW 91*
Figueroa Larrain, Emiliano 1866-1931 *BioIn 16*
Figuier, Louis 1819-1894 *EncO&P 3*
Figuli, Margita 1909- *EncCoWW*
Figura, Phillip Michael 1949- *St&PR 91*
Figurelli, Francesco A *BiDrAPA 89*
Figurski, Gerald Anthony 1945- *WhoSSW 91*
Figurski, Robert John 1943- *St&PR 91*
Fihn, Jeffrey Glaser 1949- *WhoEmL 91*
Fike, Claude Edwin 1920- *WhoAm 90*
Fike, Edward Lake 1920- *WhoAm 90*
Fike, Elizabeth Smith 1960- *WhoAmW 91*
Fikejs, John Wayne 1939- *St&PR 91*
Fikes, Alan Lester 1938- *St&PR 91*
Fikes, Dennis Rae 1955- *WhoSSW 91*
Fikre-Selassie Wogderess *WhoWor 91*
Fikri, Errol 1964- *WhoWor 91*
Fiksdal, John P. 1949- *WhoEmL 91*
Fiksman, Irina 1953- *BiDrAPA 89*
Filak, Richard Joseph 1946- *St&PR 91*
Filali, Abdellatif 1928- *WhoWor 91*
Filandro, Anthony Salvatore 1930- *St&PR 91*
Filbert, John Schuyler 1924- *St&PR 91*
Filby, Percy William 1911- *WhoAm 90*
Filchock, E. *WhoWrEP 89*
Filchock, Ethel *WhoAmW 91*
Filderman, Robert Jay 1937- *WhoAm 90*
Filderman, Wilhelm 1882-1963 *BioIn 16*
Fildes, Paul Gordon 1882-1971 *DcScB S2*
Fildes, Robert Anthony 1938- *WhoAm 90*
File, Lucien Toney 1933- *ODwPR 91*
Filean, Arthur S. 1938- *St&PR 91*
Filek, Allan A. 1944- *St&PR 91*
Filene, Edward A. 1860-1937 *WorAlBi*
Filepp, George Edward 1949- *WhoE 91*
Filer, Elizabeth Ann 1923- *WhoAmW 91*
Filer, Emily Harkins 1936- *WhoSSW 91*
Filer, John H. 1924- *St&PR 91*
Filer, John Horace 1924- *WhoAm 90*
Filer, Lloyd Jackson, Jr. 1919- *WhoAm 90*
Filer, Randall Keith 1952- *WhoE 91*
Filer, Tom 1956- *Ballpl 90*
Filerman, Gary Lewis 1936- *WhoAm 90*
Filerman, Michael Herman 1938- *WhoAm 90*
Files, Evelyn June 1932- *WhoAmW 91*
Files, Gordon Louis 1912- *WhoWor 91*
Files, John T. 1918- *St&PR 91*
Files, Jon Mylne 1935- *St&PR 91*
Files, Lee Sid, III *BiDrAPA 89*
Files, Mark Willard 1941- *WhoSSW 91, WhoWor 91*
Files, Wilmer Robert 1931- *St&PR 91, WhoAm 90*
Filewood, Lewis Francis, Jr. 1931- *St&PR 91*
Filgas, James Frank 1934- *WhoAm 90*
Filiaci, Carlo 1939- *BiDrAPA 89*
Filiatrault, Edward J. 1938- *St&PR 91*
Filiatrault, Edward John, Jr. 1938- *WhoAm 90*
Filigno, Patricia Ann 1939- *WhoAmW 91*
Filimanov, Leonid Ivanovich *WhoWor 91*
Filion, Maurice *WhoAm 90, WhoE 91*
Filios, Louis A. 1905- *St&PR 91*
Filios, Vassilios 1952- *WhoWor 91*
Filipacchi, Daniel *BioIn 16*
Filipchenko, Iurii Aleksandrovich 1882-1930 *DcScB S2*
Filipi, Joan Leahy 1950- *WhoAmW 91*
Filipiak, Janusz 1952- *WhoWor 91*
Filipic, Peter 1948- *St&PR 91*
Filipov, Filip 1946- *St&PR 91*
Filipova, Elena 1957- *IntWWM 90*
Filipovic, Augustin 1931- *WhoAmA 91*
Filipowski, Richard E 1923- *WhoAmA 91*
Filipp, Carolyn Francine 1950- *WhoEmL 91*
Filipp, Mark Richard 1955- *WhoEmL 91*
Filippelli, Ann Marie 1961- *WhoAmW 91*
Filippelli, Ronald Lee 1938- *WhoAm 90*
Filippello, A. Nicholas 1942- *St&PR 91*
Filippi, Frank Joseph 1907- *WhoAm 90*
Filippi, Ronald K G 1930- *BiDrAPA 89*
Filippine, Edward Louis 1930- *WhoAm 90*
Filippo, Eduardo de *ConAu 132, MajTwCW*
Filippone, Ronald J 1937- *BiDrAPA 89*
Filippone, Vincent Anthony 1935- *St&PR 91*
Filipps, Frank Peter 1947- *St&PR 91, WhoAm 90*
Filips, Nicholas Joseph 1925- *WhoSSW 91*
Filitti, Martha *BiDrAPA 89*
Filizetti, Gary John 1945- *WhoAm 90*
Filkosky, Josefa 1933- *WhoAmA 91*
Fill, Clifford George 1950- *WhoSSW 91*
Fill, J Herbert *BiDrAPA 89*
Filla, Kimberly Marie 1966- *WhoAmW 91*
Filler, Robert 1923- *WhoAm 90*
Filler, Ronald Howard 1948- *WhoEmL 91*
Filler, Susan M. 1947- *IntWWM 90*
Filler, Susan Melanie 1947- *WhoEmL 91*
Filler-Morris, Hadassa 1946- *WhoAmW 91*
Fillerup, Mel 1924- *WhoAmA 91*
Fillet, Mitchell Harris 1948- *WhoAm 90, WhoE 91, WhoEmL 91, WhoWor 91*
Fillet, Toni Dee 1957- *WhoEmL 91*
Filleul Brothers *PenDiDA 89*
Filley, Bette Elaine 1933- *WhoAmW 91*
Filley, Dorothy McCracken 1915- *WhoAmW 91*
Filley, John P 1922- *BiDrAPA 89*
Fillie, Robert John 1947- *WhoE 91*
Fillingame, Sarah Ann 1946- *WhoAmW 91*
Fillingham, Patricia 1924- *WhoWrEP 89*
Fillingim, Dana 1893-1961 *Ballpl 90*
Fillion, Thomas John 1953- *WhoEmL 91*
Fillios, Louis Charles 1923- *WhoAm 90*
Fillip, Christine *ODwPR 91*
Fillips, Bruce Harold 1944- *St&PR 91*
Fillius, Milton Franklin, Jr. 1922- *WhoAm 90*
Fillmann, William Craig 1946- *St&PR 91*
Fillmore, Abigail Powers 1798-1853 *BioIn 16*
Fillmore, Caroline Carmichael McIntosh 1813-1881 *BioIn 16*
Fillmore, Henry 1881-1956 *OxCPMus*
Fillmore, Millard 1800-1871 *BiDrUSE 89*
Fillmore, Millard 1800-1874 *BioIn 16, WorAlBi*
Fillmore, Peter Arthur 1936- *WhoAm 90*
Fillo, Stephen W. *WhoE 91*
Fillon, Nick J. 1926- *St&PR 91*
Filmon, Gary *BioIn 16*
Filmon, Gary Albert 1942- *WhoAm 90*
Filmus, Michael 1943- *WhoE 91*
Filmus, Michael Roy 1943- *WhoAmA 91*
Filmus, Stephen I 1948- *WhoAmA 91*
Filmus, Tully 1908- *WhoAmA 91, WhoE 91*
Filo, William John 1946- *St&PR 91*
Filomena, William Anthony 1933- *WhoE 91*
Filon, Anna May 1911- *WhoE 91*
Filoramo, John Robert 1951- *WhoEmL 91*
Filoromo, Michael A. 1928- *St&PR 91*
Filosa, Gary Fairmont Randolph V., II 1931- *WhoAm 90, WhoSSW 91, WhoWor 91*
Filowitz, Mark S. 1951- *St&PR 91*
Filpus, Uno W. 1926- *St&PR 91*
Filskov, Susan B. 1950- *WhoAmW 91*
Filson, Pete 1958- *Ballpl 90*
Filson, Ronald Coulter 1946- *WhoAm 90*
Filson, Teresa Finch 1960- *WhoAmW 91*
Filston, Howard Church 1935- *WhoAm 90*
Filstrup, E. Christian 1942- *WhoAm 90*
Filstrup, Scott Hogenson 1942- *WhoWor 91*
Filteau, Marie-Josee *BiDrAPA 89*
Filter, Eunice M. 1940- *WhoAmW 91*
Filter, Terrance Anderson 1950- *WhoEmL 91*
Filtz, Regis F. 1937- *St&PR 91*
Filtzer, Hyman 1901-1967 *WhoAmA 91N*
Filutze, Barbara *BioIn 16*
Filzen, Daniel V. 1949- *St&PR 91*
Fimbres, Gabrielle M. 1963- *WhoHisp 91*
Fimbres, Martha M. 1948- *WhoHisp 91*
Fimian, Walter Joseph 1926- *WhoE 91*
Fimonoi *EncCoWW*
Fimrite, Ron *BioIn 16*
Finale, Frank Louis 1942- *WhoWrEP 89*
Finamore, Albert William 1927- *St&PR 91*
Finamore, Roy Edward 1953- *WhoE 91*
Finan, Ellen Cranston 1951- *WhoEmL 91*
Finberg, Alan Robert 1927- *St&PR 91, WhoAm 90*
Finberg, Barbara Denning 1929- *WhoAm 90, WhoAmW 91*
Finberg, Donald Richard 1931- *WhoE 91*
Finberg, Laurence 1923- *WhoAm 90*
Finburgh, Bert J. 1915- *St&PR 91*
Fincannon, L.N. *St&PR 91*
Fincanon, Bill Wayne 1950- *WhoSSW 91*
Finch, Alfred William 1854-1930 *PenDiDA 89*
Finch, Anne *BiDEWW*
Finch, Anne 1661-1720 *BiDEWW, BioIn 16, DcLB 95 [port], FemiCLE*
Finch, Annie Ridley Crane 1956- *WhoWrEP 89*
Finch, C. Herbert 1931- *WhoAm 90*
Finch, Caleb Ellicott 1939- *WhoAm 90, WhoWor 91*
Finch, Carolyn-Bogart 1938- *WhoAmW 91*
Finch, Charles B. 1920- *St&PR 91*
Finch, Charles Baker 1920- *WhoAm 90, WhoE 91*
Finch, Clarence Stewart 1939- *St&PR 91*
Finch, David 1950- *WhoE 91*
Finch, Debra Ann 1954- *WhoAmW 91*
Finch, Diane Shields 1947- *WhoAmW 91, WhoEmL 91*
Finch, E. C. Kip 1911-1988 *BioIn 16*
Finch, Earl Pierce 1828-1888 *AmLegL*
Finch, Edward Francis 1947- *WhoEmL 91*
Finch, Edward Ridley, Jr. 1919- *WhoAm 90, WhoE 91*
Finch, Eleanor Harrison 1908- *WhoE 91*
Finch, Elizabeth L 1951- *BiDrAPA 89*
Finch, Frank P. 1943- *St&PR 91*
Finch, George Danton, III 1946- *WhoEmL 91*
Finch, George Goode 1937- *St&PR 91*
Finch, Gordon L., Jr. 1934- *St&PR 91*
Finch, Harold Bertram, Jr. 1927- *St&PR 91, WhoAm 90*
Finch, Harold Curtis 1926- *WhoAm 90*
Finch, Herman Manuel 1914- *WhoAm 90, WhoWor 91*
Finch, James M., Jr. 1909- *St&PR 91*
Finch, James Nellis 1932- *WhoE 91*
Finch, Janet Mitchell 1950- *WhoSSW 91*
Finch, Jeremiah Stanton 1910- *WhoAm 90*
Finch, Judith Malone 1944- *WhoAm 90*
Finch, Leta CeCile 1948- *WhoAmW 91*
Finch, Michael David 1946- *St&PR 91*
Finch, Michael Paul 1946- *WhoWor 91*
Finch, Peter 1916-1977 *WorAlBi*
Finch, Randy Carl 1955- *WhoSSW 91*
Finch, Raymond Lawrence 1940- *WhoAm 90*
Finch, Robert David 1938- *WhoSSW 91*
Finch, Robert H 1925- *BiDrUSE 89*
Finch, Rogers Burton 1920- *WhoAm 90*
Finch, Ronald M., Jr. 1932- *WhoAm 90*
Finch, Ruth Woodward 1916- *WhoAmA 91*
Finch, Stuart M 1919- *BiDrAPA 89*
Finch, Stuart McIntyre 1919- *WhoAm 90*
Finch, Walter Goss Gilchrist 1918- *WhoAm 90, WhoWor 91*
Finch, William G. H. 1897-1990 *NewYTBS 90*
Finch, William George Harold 1897- *WhoAm 90, WhoWor 91*
Fincham, Laurie *BioIn 16*
Finchen, Jim 1952- *St&PR 91*
Fincher, Beatrice Gonzalez 1941- *WhoHisp 91*
Fincher, Cameron Lane 1926- *WhoAm 90*
Fincher, John Albert 1911- *WhoAm 90*
Fincher, John H 1941- *WhoAmA 91*
Fincher, Julian Hayes 1935- *WhoAm 90*
Fincher, Margaret Ann 1934- *WhoAmW 91*
Fincher, Robert C, Jr. *BiDrAPA 89*
Finck, Furman J 1900- *WhoAmA 91*
Finck, Herman 1872-1939 *OxCPMus*
Finck, Kevin William 1954- *WhoWor 91*
Finck, Peter Kevin 1951- *WhoEmL 91*
Fincke, Gary W. 1945- *WhoWrEP 89*
Fincke, Waring Roberts 1945- *WhoEmL 91*
Fincle, Louis P 1904- *BiDrAPA 89*
Finder, Alan *BioIn 16*
Finder, Alan Eliot 1952- *WhoE 91*
Finder, Frances Gould *BiDrAPA 89*
Finder, Jason Stuart 1959- *BiDrAPA 89*
Finder, Robert Andrew 1947- *WhoWor 91*
Finder, Theodore Roosevelt 1914- *WhoAm 90*
Findlater, Jane 1866-1946 *BioIn 16*
Findlater, Jane Helen 1866-1946 *FemiCLE*
Findlater, Mary 1865-1963 *BioIn 16, FemiCLE*
Findlay, David B. *BioIn 16*
Findlay, David B, Jr 1933- *WhoAmA 91*
Findlay, Eric Fraser 1926- *St&PR 91, WhoAm 90*
Findlay, Harald B. 1958- *St&PR 91*
Findlay, Helen T. 1909- *St&PR 91, WhoAmA 91*
Findlay, J. Arthur 1883-1964 *EncO&P 3*
Findlay, James Allen 1943- *WhoAmA 91*
Findlay, John Wilson 1915- *WhoAm 90*
Findlay, Michael Alistair 1945- *WhoAm 90*
Findlay, Roberta 1952- *WhoAmW 91*
Findlay, Ronald Edsel 1935- *WhoAm 90*
Findlay, S.H. 1943- *St&PR 91*
Findlay, Susan Halton 1943- *WhoAmW 91*

Findlay, Theodore Bernard 1939- *WhoAm 90*
Findlay, Walstein C., Jr. 1903- *St&PR 91, WhoAm 90*
Findlay-Shirras, Alasdair R. 1949- *St&PR 91*
Findler, Jean Kerch 1951- *WhoAmW 91*
Findley, Charles H. 1924- *WhoAm 90*
Findley, Danielle *BioIn 16*
Findley, John Allen, Jr. 1951- *WhoE 91, WhoEmL 91*
Findley, John Sidney 1942- *WhoSSW 91, WhoWor 91*
Findley, Mary Lou McBroom 1945- *WhoAmW 91*
Findley, Paul 1921- *WhoAm 90*
Findley, Russell Scott *BiDrAPA 89*
Findley, Susan 1943- *St&PR 91*
Findley, Timothy *BioIn 16*
Findley, Timothy 1930- *OxCCanT, WorAu 1980 [port]*
Findley, Timothy Irving 1930- *WhoAm 90, WhoWrEP 89*
Findley, William Edward, Jr. 1922- *St&PR 91*
Findley, William Nichols 1914- *WhoAm 90*
Findling, George Matthew 1942- *St&PR 91*
Findling, Robert Lawrence 1961- *BiDrAPA 89*
Findorff, Robert L. 1929- *St&PR 91*
Findorff, Robert Lewis 1929- *WhoAm 90*
Findur, Martin A. 1926- *St&PR 91*
Fine, Alan Selig 1953- *BiDrAPA 89*
Fine, Albert Samuel 1923- *WhoE 91*
Fine, Allan H. 1940- *St&PR 91*
Fine, Andrea Joiner 1950- *WhoWrEP 89*
Fine, Andrew Snyder 1936- *St&PR 91*
Fine, Arthur I. 1937- *WhoAm 90*
Fine, Barry 1931- *St&PR 91*
Fine, Barry Norton 1935- *BiDrAPA 89*
Fine, Benjamin 1948- *WhoE 91*
Fine, Bernard D *BiDrAPA 89*
Fine, Bernard David 1917- *WhoE 91*
Fine, Bernard J. 1926- *WhoAm 90*
Fine, Bob 1949- *WhoEmL 91*
Fine, Brewster William 1949- *WhoEmL 91*
Fine, Charles 1944- *St&PR 91*
Fine, Daniel Matthew 1959- *WhoEmL 91*
Fine, David 1912- *St&PR 91*
Fine, David Jeffrey 1950- *WhoWor 91*
Fine, Donald I. *BioIn 16*
Fine, Donald Irving 1922- *WhoAm 90*
Fine, Edward *BiDrAPA 89*
Fine, Elsa Honig 1930- *WhoWrEP 89*
Fine, Eric William 1936- *BiDrAPA 89*
Fine, Gary Martin 1950- *WhoEmL 91*
Fine, Harold Edward 1921- *St&PR 91*
Fine, Henri M. 1945- *St&PR 91*
Fine, Henry K 1943- *BiDrAPA 89*
Fine, Herman 1952- *St&PR 91*
Fine, Holly Katherine *BioIn 16*
Fine, Howard Alan 1941- *WhoAm 90, WhoSSW 91, WhoWor 91*
Fine, James *BiDrAPA 89*
Fine, James Allen 1934- *St&PR 91*
Fine, James Stephen 1946- *WhoEmL 91*
Fine, Jane 1958- *WhoAmA 91*
Fine, Jeffrey Scott *BiDrAPA 89*
Fine, Jim L. 1945- *St&PR 91*
Fine, Jo Renee 1943- *WhoAmW 91*
Fine, Joanna Lisa 1953- *BiDrAPA 89*
Fine, Joel Alan 1960- *BiDrAPA 89*
Fine, Jonathan 1954- *WhoAm 90*
Fine, Jud 1944- *WhoAmA 91*
Fine, Karen Jean 1944- *St&PR 91*
Fine, Kenneth Richard 1956- *WhoE 91, WhoSSW 91*
Fine, Leo 1914- *St&PR 91*
Fine, Leslie 1931- *BiDrAPA 89*
Fine, Lou 1915-1971 *EncACom*
Fine, Louis L 1940- *BiDrAPA 89*
Fine, Martin 1943- *BiDrAPA 89*
Fine, Max 1908-1989 *BioIn 16*
Fine, Max 1913- *St&PR 91*
Fine, Meredith Ann *BiDrAPA 89*
Fine, Michael B *BiDrAPA 89*
Fine, Michael Edward 1950- *IntWWM 90*
Fine, Michael Joseph 1937- *WhoAm 90, WhoE 91*
Fine, Miriam Brown 1913- *WhoE 91, WhoWor 91*
Fine, Neal Harvey 1944- *WhoE 91*
Fine, Norman David 1935- *WhoSSW 91*
Fine, Paul M 1933- *BiDrAPA 89*
Fine, Paul Ronald *BioIn 16*
Fine, Perle 1905-1988 *WhoAmA 91N*
Fine, Perry Scott 1962- *St&PR 91*
Fine, Phil David *NewYTBS 90 [port]*
Fine, Philip Russel 1945- *WhoAm 90*
Fine, Ralph 1928- *WhoE 91*
Fine, Rana Arnold 1944- *WhoAmW 91*
Fine, Richard Aaron 1929- *St&PR 91*
Fine, Richard Isaac 1940- *WhoAm 90, WhoWor 91*
Fine, Ruth E 1941- *WhoAmA 91*
Fine, Samuel 1925- *WhoAm 90*
Fine, Seymour H 1925- *ConAu 30NR*
Fine, Seymour Howard 1925- *WhoAm 90*
Fine, Sidney 1918- *BiDrAPA 89*
Fine, Sidney 1920- *WhoAm 90*
Fine, Stanley Sidney 1927- *St&PR 91, WhoAm 90*
Fine, Stephen Lewis 1940- *St&PR 91*
Fine, Sydney G 1906- *BiDrAPA 89*
Fine, Terrence Leon 1939- *WhoAm 90, WhoWor 91*
Fine, Timothy H. 1937-1990 *BioIn 16*
Fine, Timothy Herbert 1937- *WhoAm 90, WhoWor 91*
Fine, Vivian 1913- *IntWWM 90, WhoAm 90*
Fine, Wendy 1943- *IntWWM 90*
Fine, William Michael 1926- *WhoWor 91*
Fine, William Michael 1955- *WhoEmL 91*
Finebaum, Murray L. 1942- *St&PR 91*
Fineberg, Harvey Vernon 1945- *WhoAm 90*
Fineberg, Henry H 1913- *BiDrAPA 89*
Fineberg, Larry 1945- *OxCCanT*
Fineberg, Solomon Andhil 1896- *WhoAm 90*
Finegan, Bill 1917- *BioIn 16, OxCPMus*
Finegan, Gail Ann 1961- *WhoE 91*
Finegan, Patrick T'ung 1959- *WhoEmL 91*
Finegan, Thomas Aldrich 1929- *WhoAm 90*
Finegan, William Hugh 1946- *WhoSSW 91*
Finegold, Hyman B. 1934- *St&PR 91*
Finegold, Ronald 1942- *St&PR 91, WhoE 91*
Finegold, Sydney Martin 1921- *WhoAm 90*
Finelli, Gerard Peter 1947- *WhoE 91*
Finelli, Louise Stephania 1919- *WhoAmW 91*
Finello, Terry Lee 1947- *WhoAmW 91*
Fineman, Bayla T. 1932- *St&PR 91*
Fineman, David 1933- *St&PR 91*
Fineman, Evan Leslie 1951- *St&PR 91*
Fineman, Jo Ann *BiDrAPA 89*
Fineman, Joel *BioIn 16*
Fineman, Manuel Nathan 1920- *St&PR 91*
Fineman, Mark Elliott 1952- *WhoAm 90*
Fineman, Morton *AuBYP 90*
Fineman, Samuel M. 1930- *St&PR 91*
Fineout, Arthur John 1923- *WhoSSW 91*
Finer, Jeffry Keith 1955- *WhoEmL 91*
Finer, Michael Scott 1964- *WhoE 91, WhoEmL 91, WhoWor 91*
Finerty, Mary Ellen 1947- *WhoAmW 91*
Fines Fournier, Rebecca Eileen 1960- *WhoAmW 91*
Fineshriber, William H., Jr. 1909- *WhoAm 90*
Finesilver, Jay Mark 1955- *WhoEmL 91, WhoWor 91*
Finesilver, Sherman Glenn 1927- *WhoAm 90*
Finesman, Alvin B. *BioIn 16*
Finestein, Russell Mark 1956- *WhoEmL 91*
Finestone, Douglas Howard 1953- *BiDrAPA 89*
Finestone, Sheila 1927- *WhoAmW 91*
Finette, Florence 1906- *WhoAm 90*
Finfgeld, Richard K. 1931- *St&PR 91*
Finfrock, Ivan Ray 1929- *St&PR 91*
Fingar, Elmer Lee 1905-1989 *BioIn 16*
Fingarette, Herbert 1921- *WhoAm 90*
Finger, Avram C 1928- *BiDrAPA 89*
Finger, Bernard L. 1927- *St&PR 91*
Finger, Charles Joseph 1869?-1941 *AuBYP 90*
Finger, Diamon Lee 1927- *St&PR 91, WhoAm 90*
Finger, Eugene P. 1938- *St&PR 91*
Finger, Frank Whitney 1915- *WhoAm 90*
Finger, Harold B. 1924- *WhoAm 90, WhoE 91*
Finger, Jerry 1932- *St&PR 91*
Finger, John F. 1919- *St&PR 91*
Finger, John Holden 1913- *WhoAm 90*
Finger, Kenneth Franklin 1929- *WhoAm 90*
Finger, Mark Peter 1951- *BiDrAPA 89*
Finger, Peter Christian 1962- *WhoEmL 91*
Finger, Phyllis Thomas 1947- *WhoE 91, WhoEmL 91*
Finger, Seymour Maxwell 1915- *WhoAm 90*
Finger, Susan Pearl 1954- *IntWWM 90*
Finger, Thomas Emanuel 1949- *WhoEmL 91*
Fingerhut, Abe 1939- *WhoWor 91*
Fingerhut, Arden *BioIn 16*
Fingerhut, Karlheinz 1939- *WhoWor 91*
Fingerhut, Margaret 1955- *IntWWM 90*
Fingerle, Brian Earle 1934- *St&PR 91*
Fingerle, Lawrence Jay 1960- *St&PR 91*
Fingerle, Ralph Gustav 1930- *WhoE 91*
Fingerman, Milton 1928- *WhoAm 90, WhoSSW 91*
Fingeroth, Sharon L *BiDrAPA 89*
Fingers, Rollie 1946- *Ballpl 90 [port], WorAlBi*
Fingerson, Leroy Malvin 1932- *St&PR 91*
Fingert, Hyman H 1909- *BiDrAPA 89*
Fini, Leonor 1908?- *BiDWomA*
Finifter, Ada W 1938- *WhoWrEP 89*
Finigan, Jim 1928-1981 *Ballpl 90*
Finiguerra, Maso 1426-1464 *PenDiDA 89*
Finizzi, Marie Helene 1934- *WhoAmW 91*
Fink, Aaron 1916- *St&PR 91*
Fink, Aaron 1955- *WhoAmA 91*
Fink, Aaron Harlan 1956- *BiDrAPA 89*
Fink, Aaron Herman 1916- *WhoE 91, WhoWor 91*
Fink, Alan 1925- *WhoAmA 91*
Fink, Arthur Alan 1909- *St&PR 91*
Fink, Arthur Emil 1903- *WhoAm 90*
Fink, Barbara Arlene 1949- *WhoWrEP 89*
Fink, Charles Augustin 1929- *WhoAm 90, WhoSSW 91, WhoWor 91*
Fink, Conrad Charles 1932- *WhoAm 90, WhoSSW 91*
Fink, Daniel Julien 1926- *WhoAm 90, WhoE 91*
Fink, David Harvey 1942- *WhoE 91*
Fink, David Lee *BiDrAPA 89*
Fink, David Ream, Jr. 1928- *WhoAm 90*
Fink, Diane Joanne 1936- *WhoAm 90*
Fink, Donald Glen 1911- *WhoAm 90*
Fink, Donald Martin 1928- *St&PR 91*
Fink, Edward B 1944- *BiDrAPA 89*
Fink, Edward Laurence 1945- *WhoE 91*
Fink, Eugene Richard 1944- *WhoE 91*
Fink, Geraldine *BiDrAPA 89*
Fink, Gonthier Louis 1928- *WhoWor 91*
Fink, H. Bernerd 1909- *WhoAm 90*
Fink, Hans F 1922- *BiDrAPA 89*
Fink, Herbert Lewis 1921- *WhoAmA 91*
Fink, Herman 1911-1980 *Ballpl 90*
Fink, J. Theodore 1952- *WhoE 91*
Fink, James Brewster 1943- *WhoWor 91*
Fink, James Curtis 1944- *St&PR 91*
Fink, Jerold Albert 1941- *WhoAm 90*
Fink, Joanna Elizabeth 1958- *WhoAmA 91*
Fink, John 1926- *WhoAm 90*
Fink, John Francis 1931- *St&PR 91, WhoAm 90*
Fink, John W. 1949- *St&PR 91*
Fink, Jordan Norman 1934- *WhoAm 90*
Fink, Joseph Allen 1942- *WhoAm 90*
Fink, Joseph Leslie, III 1947- *WhoEmL 91*
Fink, Joseph Richardson 1940- *WhoAm 90*
Fink, Joyce Erleen 1930- *WhoAmW 91, WhoE 91*
Fink, Kenneth M *BiDrAPA 89*
Fink, Kerry Leif 1961- *WhoEmL 91*
Fink, L Jerome 1920- *BiDrAPA 89*
Fink, Larry *BioIn 16*
Fink, Larry 1941- *WhoAmA 91*
Fink, Lawrence Alfred 1930- *WhoAm 90*
Fink, Leo R. *BioIn 16*
Fink, Lester Harold 1925- *WhoAm 90*
Fink, Linda Marie 1959- *WhoAmW 91*
Fink, Lois Marie 1927- *WhoAm 90, WhoAmA 91*
Fink, Lorraine Julie 1931- *IntWWM 90*
Fink, Lou Anna *BiDrAPA 89*
Fink, Louis R 1925-1980 *WhoAmA 91N*
Fink, Lyman Roger 1912- *WhoAm 90*
Fink, Mark J. 1957- *WhoSSW 91*
Fink, Mary Alexander 1919- *WhoAmW 91*
Fink, Mary Virginia Daniel 1951- *WhoAmW 91*
Fink, Max 1923- *BiDrAPA 89, WhoAm 90*
Fink, Michael *BioIn 16*
Fink, Michael Armand 1939- *IntWWM 90*
Fink, Norman Stiles 1926- *WhoE 91, WhoWor 91*
Fink, Paul J. *BioIn 16*
Fink, Paul Jay 1933- *BiDrAPA 89*
Fink, Peter Mark 1947- *BiDrAPA 89*
Fink, Peter R. 1933- *St&PR 91*
Fink, R. Cullen 1955- *WhoWrEP 89*
Fink, Ray 1922- *WhoAmA 91*
Fink, Reginald H. 1931- *IntWWM 90*
Fink, Richard *BioIn 16*
Fink, Richard David 1936- *WhoAm 90*
Fink, Richard Merrill 1930- *St&PR 91*
Fink, Richard Robert 1947- *WhoEmL 91*
Fink, Robert 1905-1988 *BioIn 16*
Fink, Robert David *BiDrAPA 89*
Fink, Robert E. *WhoAm 90*
Fink, Robert Ivan 1948- *BiDrAPA 89*
Fink, Robert Louis 1958- *WhoEmL 91*
Fink, Robert Morgan 1915- *WhoAm 90*
Fink, Robert Russell 1933- *WhoAm 90*
Fink, Robert Steven 1943- *WhoAm 90*
Fink, Ronald Edward 1936- *St&PR 91*
Fink, Roy Warren 1933- *St&PR 91*
Fink, Ruth Garvey 1917- *WhoAm 90*
Fink, Samuel Donovan 1959- *WhoSSW 91*
Fink, Scott Alan 1953- *WhoEmL 91*
Fink, Sheldon Edwin 1925- *WhoE 91*
Fink, Stacey Marc 1950- *WhoSSW 91*
Fink, Stanley *BioIn 16*
Fink, Steven B. 1948- *ODwPR 91*
Fink, Stuart Simon 1934- *WhoAm 90*
Fink, Teri Ann 1955- *WhoEmL 91*
Fink, Tom *WhoAm 90*
Fink, Valerie Ann 1954- *WhoAmW 91*
Fink, William *MajTwCW*
Fink, William Louis 1948- *BiDrAPA 89*
Fink, William Samuel 1956- *WhoE 91*
Finkbeiner, Richard M. 1946- *St&PR 91*
Finkbinder, Thomas L. 1952- *WhoAm 90*
Finkbiner, Thomas L. 1952- *WhoSSW 91*
Finke, Blythe Foote 1922- *WhoAmW 91*
Finke, James *BioIn 16*
Finke, Jochen 1941- *ConDes 90*
Finke, Leonda Froehlich *WhoE 91*
Finke, Leonda Froelich *WhoAmA 91*
Finke, Martin 1948- *IntWWM 90*
Finke, Susanne Gail 1962- *WhoEmL 91*
Finkel, Alfred *BioIn 16*
Finkel, Alvin 1949- *ConAu 131*
Finkel, David 1945- *WhoE 91*
Finkel, Donald 1929- *WhoAm 90, WhoWrEP 89*
Finkel, Gerald Michael 1941- *WhoAm 90, WhoSSW 91*
Finkel, Harvey 1940- *St&PR 91*
Finkel, Janet Pearl 1961- *WhoE 91*
Finkel, Jay Alan 1952- *BiDrAPA 89*
Finkel, Jerry Bernard 1935- *BiDrAPA 89*
Finkel, Marcia Robin 1958- *WhoAmW 91*
Finkel, Marion Judith 1929- *WhoAm 90*
Finkel, Martin Howard 1952- *WhoEmL 91*
Finkel, Morris C. *BioIn 16*
Finkel, Nunjo *BiDrAPA 89*
Finkel, Sanford Irwin 1941- *BiDrAPA 89*
Finkel, Sheila Berg 1947- *WhoAmW 91*
Finkel, Sidney *BiDrAPA 89*
Finkel, Stuart Ira 1946- *WhoE 91*
Finkel, William Mark 1948- *WhoEmL 91*
Finkelday, John Paul 1943- *WhoSSW 91, WhoWor 91*
Finkelday, Karen Lynn 1944- *WhoAmW 91, WhoSSW 91, WhoWor 91*
Finkelhor, Dorothy Cimberg *BioIn 16*
Finkelhor, Howard B 1912- *BiDrAPA 89*
Finkelman, Isidore 1900- *BiDrAPA 89*
Finkelman, Jay Matthew 1945- *WhoEmL 91*
Finkelman, Michael Craig 1954- *IntWWM 90*
Finkelman, Roland Israel 1928- *St&PR 91*
Finkelmeier, Philip Renner 1914- *WhoAm 90*
Finkelor, Thomas Martin 1942- *BiDrAPA 89*
Finkelson, Allen *BioIn 16*
Finkelson, Susan Wexler *BioIn 16*
Finkelstein, Allen Lewis 1943- *WhoE 91*
Finkelstein, Barbara 1937- *WhoAm 90*
Finkelstein, Barry Marc 1954- *St&PR 91*
Finkelstein, Bernard 1930- *WhoAm 90*
Finkelstein, Caroline 1941- *WhoWrEP 89*
Finkelstein, David 1929- *WhoAm 90*
Finkelstein, Edward S. 1925- *St&PR 91*
Finkelstein, Edward Sydney 1925- *WhoAm 90, WhoE 91*
Finkelstein, Emily Anne *BiDrAPA 89*
Finkelstein, Frank Bennett 1942- *BiDrAPA 89*
Finkelstein, Henry D 1958- *WhoAmA 91*
Finkelstein, Herman *BioIn 16*
Finkelstein, Irwin S. 1934- *BiDrAPA 89*
Finkelstein, Jack, Jr. 1952- *WhoEmL 91*
Finkelstein, James 1930- *BiDrAPA 89*
Finkelstein, James Arthur 1952- *WhoEmL 91, WhoWor 91*
Finkelstein, James David 1933- *WhoAm 90*
Finkelstein, Joseph Simon 1952- *WhoEmL 91*
Finkelstein, Lionel 1926- *BiDrAPA 89*
Finkelstein, Louis 1895- *BioIn 16, WhoAm 90*
Finkelstein, Louis 1923- *WhoAmA 91*
Finkelstein, Marcia Lyn 1961- *WhoAmW 91*
Finkelstein, Mark Anderson 1959- *WhoSSW 91*
Finkelstein, Max 1915- *WhoAmA 91*
Finkelstein, Miriam 1928- *WhoWrEP 89*
Finkelstein, Nathan G. 1915-1989 *BioIn 16*
Finkelstein, Nisson Ascher 1925- *St&PR 91*
Finkelstein, Richard Alan 1930- *WhoAm 90*
Finkelstein, Seymour 1923- *St&PR 91, WhoAm 90*
Finkelstein, Susan Jane *BiDrAPA 89*
Finkelstein, William 1948- *St&PR 91*
Finken, Nancy Arndt 1934- *WhoSSW 91*
Finkenbrink, Ralph T. 1961- *St&PR 91*
Finkenstaedt, James C. 1921- *St&PR 91*
Finkes, John Richard 1940- *St&PR 91*
Finkl, Charles W. 1920- *St&PR 91*
Finkl, Charles William, II 1941- *WhoAm 90, WhoSSW 91, WhoWor 91*
Finkle, Beverly Arthur 1915- *WhoE 91*
Finkle, David *BioIn 16*
Finkle, Jeffrey Alan 1954- *WhoAm 90*
Finkle, Joseph Colls 1955- *BiDrAPA 89*
Finkle, Morton 1927- *St&PR 91*
Finklea, Tula Ellice 1923- *WhoAm 90*

Finkler, Robert Allan 1936- *WhoAmA 91*
Finks, James Edward 1927- *WhoAm 90, WhoSSW 91*
Finks, Jim *BioIn 16*
Finks, Perry David 1930- *WhoE 91*
Finks, Robert Melvin 1927- *WhoAm 90, WhoWor 91*
Finlay, Alex G. *St&PR 91*
Finlay, Ian Hamilton 1925- *BioIn 16*
Finlay, Jack *BioIn 16*
Finlay, James Campbell 1931- *WhoAm 90*
Finlay, John H. 1834-1916 *BioIn 16*
Finlay, John P. 1928- *St&PR 91*
Finlay, John W. 1923- *St&PR 91*
Finlay, Julie Aileen 1965- *WhoAmW 91*
Finlay, R. Derek 1932- *St&PR 91*
Finlay, Robert Derek 1932- *WhoAm 90*
Finlay, Roger 1952- *ConAu 132*
Finlay, Terence *WhoAm 90*
Finlay, Thomas Hiram 1938- *WhoE 91*
Finlay, Warren 1950- *St&PR 91*
Finlayson, A J Reid 1944- *BiDrAPA 89*
Finlayson, Bruce Alan 1939- *WhoAm 90*
Finlayson, Donald Lord 1897-1960 *WhoAmA 91N*
Finlayson, Geoffrey B A M 1934- *ConAu 131*
Finlayson, I.E. 1948- *St&PR 91*
Finlayson, Jock Kinghorn 1921- *St&PR 91*
Finlayson, Malcolm W *BiDrAPA 89*
Finlayson, Margaret 1859-1898 *DcCanB 12*
Finlayson, Niall Diarmid Campbell 1939- *WhoWor 91*
Finlayson, Richard Earl 1934- *BiDrAPA 89*
Finlayson, Roderick 1818-1892 *DcCanB 12*
Finler, Joel W 1938- *ConAu 32NR*
Finler, Joel Waldo 1938- *WhoWor 91*
Finley, Bernard L 1924- *BiDrAPA 89*
Finley, Carmen Joyce 1926- *WhoAm 90*
Finley, Charles *BioIn 16*
Finley, Charles Laughlin 1925- *St&PR 91*
Finley, Charles O. 1918- *Ballpl 90, WorAlBi*
Finley, Charles Oscar 1918- *WhoAm 90*
Finley, Chuck 1962- *Ballpl 90*
Finley, Constance 1952- *WhoAmW 91*
Finley, David Edward 1890-1977 *WhoAmA 91N*
Finley, Denise Michelle Byrd 1959- *WhoSSW 91*
Finley, Don Harris 1924- *St&PR 91*
Finley, Donny Lamenda 1951- *WhoAmA 91*
Finley, Elizabeth Adele *BiDrAPA 89*
Finley, Emogene 1926- *St&PR 91*
Finley, Frank Scott 1958- *WhoAm 90*
Finley, Fred W. 1920- *St&PR 91*
Finley, George Alvin, III 1938- *WhoSSW 91*
Finley, George Edward 1950- *WhoSSW 91*
Finley, Gerald Eric 1931- *WhoAmA 91*
Finley, Glenna 1925- *WhoAm 90, WhoWrEP 89*
Finley, Harold Marshall 1916- *St&PR 91, WhoAm 90*
Finley, James Bradley 1781-1856 *WhNaAH*
Finley, James David 1946- *WhoEmL 91*
Finley, James Edward 1922- *WhoAm 90*
Finley, John 1722?-1769 *EncCRAm*
Finley, John David 1953- *IntWWM 90*
Finley, John H., III 1936- *St&PR 91*
Finley, John M., II 1948- *St&PR 91*
Finley, Joseph Michael 1952- *WhoEmL 91*
Finley, Karen *BioIn 16*
Finley, Kathleen S. 1949- *WhoAmW 91*
Finley, Keith A. *St&PR 91*
Finley, Knox H 1904- *BiDrAPA 89*
Finley, Malcolm H *BiDrAPA 89*
Finley, Marion Jean 1940- *WhoAmW 91*
Finley, Martha 1828-1909 *FemiCLE, WorAlBi*
Finley, Mary L *WhoAmA 91N*
Finley, Michael Sherman 1948- *WhoSSW 91*
Finley, Murray Howard 1922- *WhoAm 90*
Finley, Nancy Newton 1942- *WhoAmW 91*
Finley, Patrick M. 1937- *St&PR 91*
Finley, Philip Bruce 1930- *WhoAm 90*
Finley, Robert Lawrence *BioIn 16*
Finley, Robert Van Eaton 1922- *WhoWor 91*
Finley, Ruth *BioIn 16*
Finley, Sara Crews 1930- *WhoAm 90*
Finley, Sarah Maude Merritt 1946- *WhoSSW 91*
Finley, Scott *BioIn 16*
Finley, Stephen A. *BioIn 16*
Finley, Wayne House 1927- *WhoAm 90*
Finman, Ted 1931- *WhoAm 90*
Finn, A. Michael 1929- *ODwPR 91, WhoAm 90*
Finn, Albert E. 1927- *St&PR 91*
Finn, Bobby *WhoWrEP 89*
Finn, Bruce Leon 1956- *WhoEmL 91*
Finn, Chester E. 1944- *BioIn 16*
Finn, Chester Evans 1918- *WhoAm 90*
Finn, Daniel Francis 1922- *WhoAm 90*
Finn, David 1921- *ODwPR 91, St&PR 91, WhoAm 90, WhoAmA 91*
Finn, Don William 1944- *WhoSSW 91*
Finn, Edwin E. 1936- *St&PR 91*
Finn, Frances M. 1937- *WhoAmW 91*
Finn, Frank 1928- *WhoAm 90, WhoSSW 91*
Finn, Gerald T. 1868-1936 *AmLegL*
Finn, Gilbert 1920- *WhoAm 90, WhoE 91*
Finn, Jacqueline Munley 1945- *WhoAmW 91*
Finn, James Francis 1924- *WhoAm 90*
Finn, James J. 1962- *ODwPR 91*
Finn, James Patrick 1947- *St&PR 91*
Finn, Joan L. *ODwPR 91*
Finn, Joan Lockwood *WhoAmW 91, WhoE 91, WhoWor 91*
Finn, John F. 1905-1988 *BioIn 16*
Finn, John Francis 1947- *St&PR 91*
Finn, John Thomas 1948- *WhoE 91*
Finn, Kenneth W. 1942- *St&PR 91*
Finn, M Richard 1925- *BiDrAPA 89*
Finn, Mary Catherine Murphy 1939- *IntWWM 90*
Finn, Michael Steven 1955- *St&PR 91*
Finn, Mickey 1904-1933 *Ballpl 90*
Finn, Murray E 1925- *BiDrAPA 89*
Finn, Patricia Ann *WhoAmW 91*
Finn, Patrick Matthew 1959- *WhoE 91*
Finn, Penelope Miller B. 1951- *WhoAmW 91*
Finn, Peter 1954- *ODwPR 91, WhoAm 90*
Finn, Peter Michael 1936- *WhoAm 90*
Finn, Philip A., Jr. *ODwPR 91*
Finn, Richard Henry 1934- *St&PR 91*
Finn, Robert 1930- *WhoAm 90*
Finn, Rolfe Baxter *BiDrAPA 89*
Finn, Sara *ODwPR 91*
Finn, Stephen Martin 1949- *WhoWor 91*
Finn, Steven Gerald 1946- *St&PR 91*
Finn, Thomas James 1940- *WhoAm 90*
Finn, Thomas Macy 1927- *WhoAm 90*
Finn, Tim *BioIn 16*
Finn, Timothy 1938- *ConAu 129*
Finn, Timothy John 1950- *WhoAm 90*
Finn, William Francis 1915- *WhoAm 90, WhoE 91, WhoWor 91*
Finn, William Lawrence 1945- *St&PR 91, WhoAm 90*
Finn, William Michael 1936- *St&PR 91*
Finnane, Daniel F. *WhoAm 90*
Finnbogadottir, Vigdis 1930- *WhoWor 91*
Finne, R. Michael *St&PR 91*
Finne, Robert W. *St&PR 91*
Finnebogadottir, Vigdis 1930- *WomWR*
Finneburgh, Morris Lewis 1900- *WhoAm 90*
Finnegan, Cyril Vincent 1922- *WhoAm 90*
Finnegan, George Bernard, Jr. 1903- *WhoWor 91*
Finnegan, James John, Jr. 1948- *WhoEmL 91*
Finnegan, John Robert, Sr. 1924- *WhoAm 90*
Finnegan, Joseph Daniel 1938- *WhoE 91*
Finnegan, Laurence P., Jr. 1937- *St&PR 91*
Finnegan, Laurence Patrick, Jr. 1937- *WhoAm 90*
Finnegan, Lawrence Joseph 1930- *St&PR 91*
Finnegan, Lawrence P. 1928- *St&PR 91*
Finnegan, Martha Ann 1953- *WhoEmL 91*
Finnegan, Mary Elizabeth O'Donnell 1907- *WhoE 91*
Finnegan, Neal F. 1938- *St&PR 91*
Finnegan, Neal Francis 1938- *WhoAm 90*
Finnegan, Patrick T. *BioIn 16*
Finnegan, Richard Paul 1950- *St&PR 91*
Finnegan, Rita Madonna 1933- *WhoAm 90*
Finnegan, Robert 1906-1947 *TwCCr&M 91*
Finnegan, Rose *WhoWrEP 89*
Finnegan, Sara A. 1939- *St&PR 91*
Finnegan, Sara Anne 1939- *WhoAm 90*
Finnegan, Sharyn Marie 1946- *WhoAmA 91*
Finnegan, Thomas Joseph 1900- *WhoWor 91*
Finnegan, Thomas Joseph, III 1951- *St&PR 91*
Finnegan, Thomas Joseph, Jr. 1935- *St&PR 91, WhoAm 90*
Finnegan, William *BioIn 16*
Finnell, Dallas Grant 1931- *WhoWor 91*
Finnell, Jack Stanley 1937- *St&PR 91*
Finnell, Leslie Burrow, Jr. 1939- *WhoSSW 91*
Finnell, Martin W. *WhoSSW 91*
Finnell, Michael Hartman 1927- *WhoAm 90*
Finnell, Robert Kirtley 1949- *WhoEmL 91*
Finnemore, Douglas Kirby 1934- *WhoAm 90*
Finnen, James F. 1932- *ODwPR 91*
Finneran, Adrian Paul 1957- *WhoEmL 91*
Finneran, Happy 1891-1942 *Ballpl 90*
Finneran, Susan Rogers 1947- *WhoEmL 91*
Finnerman, Gerald Perry *BioIn 16*
Finnerty, Adrian John 1961- *IntWWM 90*
Finnerty, Eileen 1928- *WhoAmW 91*
Finnerty, Linda *ODwPR 91*
Finnerty, Louise Hoppe 1949- *WhoAm 90*
Finnerty, Peter Joseph 1942- *St&PR 91*
Finney, Albert 1936- *WhoAm 90, WhoWor 91, WorAlBi*
Finney, Charles Grandison 1792-1875 *BioIn 16*
Finney, David John 1917- *WhoWor 91*
Finney, David Ross 1951- *WhoEmL 91*
Finney, Edward E. 1927- *St&PR 91*
Finney, Frederic N. 1937- *St&PR 91*
Finney, Gail Alexandria 1959- *WhoEmL 91*
Finney, Gertrude Elva 1892- *AuBYP 90*
Finney, Jack *WorAlBi*
Finney, Jack 1911- *RGTwCSF, TwCCr&M 91*
Finney, Joan Marie McInroy 1925- *WhoAm 90, WhoAmW 91*
Finney, Joseph C J *BiDrAPA 89*
Finney, Lou 1910-1966 *Ballpl 90*
Finney, Michael Peter 1943- *WhoSSW 91*
Finney, Paul Dustin 1920- *St&PR 91*
Finney, Paula Manning 1959- *WhoAmW 91*
Finney, Pete *WhoAm 90*
Finney, Ray Barron 1946- *St&PR 91*
Finney, Ray Council 1924- *St&PR 91*
Finney, Redmond Conyngham Stewart 1929- *WhoAm 90*
Finney, Robert Arthur 1906- *WhoAm 90*
Finney, Robert G. 1932- *St&PR 91, WhoAm 90*
Finney, Ross Lee 1906- *IntWWM 90, WhoAm 90*
Finney, Roy Pelham, Jr. 1924- *WhoWor 91*
Finney, Stephen T. 1949- *St&PR 91*
Finnie, Iain 1928- *WhoAm 90*
Finnie, Linda 1952- *IntWWM 90*
Finnie, Phillip Powell 1933- *WhoWor 91*
Finnigan, Claire Marie 1923- *WhoAmW 91*
Finnigan, John Julius, Jr. 1955- *WhoEmL 91*
Finnigan, Joseph T. 1944- *ODwPR 91*
Finnigan, Joseph Townsend 1944- *WhoAm 90*
Finnigan, Sheila Elizabeth 1942- *WhoAmW 91*
Finnila, Birgit 1931- *IntWWM 90, PenDiMP*
Finnis, Chera Millicent 1949- *WhoAmW 91*
Finnis, John Mitchell 1940- *WhoWor 91*
Finnissy, Michael 1946- *PenDiMP A*
Finnissy, Michael Peter 1946- *IntWWM 90*
Finocchiaro, Alfonso G. 1932- *WhoE 91*
Finocchiaro, Alfonso Giovanni 1932- *St&PR 91*
Finocchiaro, Maurice Anthony [illegible] *WhoAm 90*
Finore, Diane 1950- *WhoAmW 91, WhoEmL 91*
Finotti, J.S. 1948- *St&PR 91*
Finscher, Ludwig 1930- *IntWWM 90*
Finser, Siegfried Ernest 1932- *WhoE 91*
Finsinger, Joerg Eugen 1950- *WhoWor 91*
Finson, Hildred A 1910- *WhoAmA 91*
Finson, Lowell Wayne 1949- *WhoEmL 91*
Finstad, Donald Lee 1945- *St&PR 91*
Finstad, Suzanne 1955- *ConAu 131*
Finster, Howard *BioIn 16*
Finster, Howard 1916- *MusmAFA*
Finster, Robert Milton 1939- *WhoSSW 91*
Finsterwalder, Ulrich 1897-1988 *BioIn 16*
Finston, Peggy Anne *BiDrAPA 89*
Finta, Alexander 1881-1958 *WhoAmA 91N*
Fintel, Dan James 1953- *WhoEmL 91*
Fintel, Mark 1922- *WhoSSW 91*
Fintel, Norman Dale 1925- *WhoAm 90*
Finton, Timothy Christopher 1952- *WhoEmL 91*
Fintzy, Robert T 1934- *BiDrAPA 89*
Finucan, John Thomas 1930- *WhoAm 90*
Finucan, Karen J. 1960- *ODwPR 91*
Finucane, James *BioIn 16*
Finucane, Richard Daniel 1926- *WhoAm 90*
Finver, Mary 1948- *WhoEmL 91*
Finzel, Lilja Marie Tobie 1947- *WhoEmL 91*
Finzen, Bruce Arthur 1947- *WhoEmL 91*
Finzi, Bruno Vittorio 1918- *WhoWor 91*
Fiocco, M. J. K. 1953- *WhoAmW 91*
Fiock, Shari Lee 1941- *WhoAmW 91*
Fiondella, Jay *BioIn 16*
Fiondella, June Lea Bell 1941- *WhoAmW 91*
Fiondella, Robert William 1942- *St&PR 91, WhoAm 90, WhoE 91*
Fiorato, Hugo 1914- *WhoAm 90, WhoE 91*
Fioravante, Janice C. 1951- *WhoAmW 91*
Fioravanti, Leonardi *EncO&P 3*
Fiore, Alice M. 1949- *WhoAmW 91*
Fiore, Barbara Marie 1936- *WhoE 91*
Fiore, Carole Diane 1946- *WhoEmL 91*
Fiore, Cosmo Dominic 1932- *WhoE 91*
Fiore, David G. 1947- *St&PR 91*
Fiore, Ernest Dante, Jr. 1928- *St&PR 91*
Fiore, Joan De Wolfe 1924- *WhoAmW 91, WhoWor 91*
Fiore, Joseph A 1925- *WhoAmA 91*
Fiore, Joseph Albert 1925- *WhoAm 90*
Fiore, Melanie Ann 1956- *WhoEmL 91*
Fiore, Mike 1944- *Ballpl 90*
Fiore, Nicholas F. 1939- *St&PR 91*
Fiore, Nicholas Francis 1939- *WhoAm 90*
Fiore, Patrick M. *BioIn 16*
Fiore, Richard Francis Salvatore 1952- *WhoSSW 91*
Fiore, Rosario Russell 1908- *WhoAmA 91*
Fiore, Vicki M 1951- *BiDrAPA 89*
Fiore, William Francis, Jr. 1950- *WhoE 91*
Fiorella, Beverly Jean 1930- *WhoAmW 91*
Fiorelli, Joseph Stephen 1950- *WhoEmL 91*
Fiorello, Catherine A. 1959- *WhoSSW 91*
Fiorentini, Walter James 1937- *WhoAm 90*
Fiorentino, Imero *BioIn 16*
Fiorentino, Leon F. 1925- *St&PR 91*
Fiorentino, Leon Francis 1925- *WhoAm 90*
Fiorentino, Linda *BioIn 16*
Fiorentino, Mario Vincenzo 1927- *WhoWor 91*
Fiorentino, Quartetto *PenDiMP*
Fiorentino, Thomas Martin 1959- *WhoEmL 91, WhoSSW 91*
Fiorenza, Francis P. 1941- *WhoAm 90*
Fiorenza, Frank A. 1933- *St&PR 91*
Fiorenza, Joseph A. 1931- *WhoSSW 91*
Fiori, Michael A *BiDrAPA 89*
Fiori, Michael J. 1951- *WhoE 91*
Fiori, Pamela 1944- *WhoAm 90*
Fiori, Pamela Anne 1944- *WhoWrEP 89*
Fiorilli, Patrick R. *BioIn 16*
Fiorillo, David F. 1934- *St&PR 91*
Fiorillo, Elisa *BioIn 16*
Fiorini, Florio *BioIn 16*
Fiorini, Frank A. 1934- *St&PR 91*
Fiorito, Edward G. 1936- *St&PR 91*
Fiorito, Edward Gerald 1936- *WhoAm 90*
Fiorito, Ted 1900-1971 *BioIn 16, OxCPMus*
Fiorucci, Cesare 1941- *WhoWor 91*
Fiorucci, Elio 1935- *ConDes 90*
Fippinger, Grace J. 1927- *St&PR 91, WhoAm 90, WhoAmW 91*
Fippinger, Ronald Alan 1942- *WhoAm 90*
Fipps, Michael Wayne 1942- *St&PR 91*
Firack, David E. *St&PR 91*
Firbas, Wilhelm 1939- *WhoWor 91*
Firchow, Claus-Gerhard 1941- *St&PR 91*
Firchow, Evelyn Scherabon *WhoAm 90*
Firchow, Peter Edgerly 1937- *WhoAm 90, WhoWrEP 89*
Firdousi 941?-1020 *WorAlBi*
Fire, Rita *WhoAmW 91*
Firebaugh, Douglas Eric 1955- *WhoSSW 91*
Firebaugh, Francille Maloch 1933- *WhoAm 90*
Firebrace, Roy Charles 1889-1974 *EncO&P 3*
Firehammer, Richard Armin, Jr. 1957- *WhoEmL 91*
Fireman, Edward L. *NewYTBS 90*
Fireman, Edward L. 1922-1990 *BioIn 16*
Fireman, Joseph *BiDrAPA 89*
Fireman, Marian 1953- *BiDrAPA 89*
Fireman, Paul *BioIn 16, St&PR 91*
Fireman, Paul 1944- *ConAmBL, WhoAm 90, WhoE 91*
Fireman, Susan 1943- *WhoAm 90*
Fireovid, Robert Lynn 1951- *WhoE 91*
Firer, Ben Zion 1914- *SmATA X [port]*
Firer, Benzion 1914- *ConAu 131, SmATA 64 [port]*
Fires, Alan Jay 1950- *WhoSSW 91*
Fireside, Harvey Francis 1929- *WhoAm 90*
Firestein, Cecily Barth 1933- *WhoAmA 91, WhoE 91*
Firestein, Chester 1930- *WhoAm 90*
Firestein, Stephen K 1928- *BiDrAPA 89*
Firestone, Bruce Michael 1946- *WhoEmL 91*
Firestone, Charles Morton 1944- *WhoAm 90*
Firestone, David 1953- *St&PR 91*
Firestone, Debra Kay 1958- *WhoAmW 91*
Firestone, Edwin Ira 1921- *St&PR 91*
Firestone, Elaine Ruth 1959- *WhoAmW 91*
Firestone, Elizabeth Doran 1958- *WhoE 91*
Firestone, Esther Violet 1950- *WhoAmW 91*
Firestone, Evan R 1940- *WhoAmA 91*
Firestone, Evan Richard 1940- *WhoAm 90*
Firestone, Harvey S. 1868-1938 *WorAlBi*
Firestone, Judith Hall 1945- *WhoAmW 91*

Firestone, Lillian 1932- *ODwPR 91*
Firestone, Lynn Marie 1941- *WhoAmW 91*
Firestone, Marvin H *BiDrAPA 89*
Firestone, Melvin P 1929- *BiDrAPA 89*
Firestone, Morton H. 1935- *St&PR 91, WhoAm 90*
Firestone, Richard B. 1934- *St&PR 91*
Firestone, Richard Francis 1926- *WhoAm 90*
Firestone, Robert W. 1930- *ConAu 130*
Firestone, Susan Paul 1946- *WhoAmA 91*
Firetog, Theodore Warren 1950- *WhoE 91, WhoEmL 91*
Firfires, Nicholas Samuel 1917- *WhoAmA 91*
Firks, Robert F. 1927- *St&PR 91*
Firkusny, Rudolf 1912- *IntWWM 90, PenDiMP, WhoAm 90, WorAlBi*
Firlik, Russell James 1943- *WhoE 91*
Firling, Randall John *BiDrAPA 89*
Firman, A. H. *EncO&P 3*
Firman, A.H., Mrs. *EncO&P 3*
Firman, Gregory J 1943- *BiDrAPA 89*
Firman, Richard B. 1952- *St&PR 91*
Firmbach, Robert Paul 1942- *WhoE 91*
Firmin, Peter 1928- *BioIn 16*
Firmin, Peter Arthur, Jr. 1924- *WhoAm 90*
Firmin, Roxane Haefele 1949- *WhoEmL 91*
Firminger, Harlan Irwin 1918- *WhoAm 90*
Firnkas, Sepp 1925- *WhoE 91*
Firor, John William 1927- *WhoAm 90*
Firouz, Mozaffar *BioIn 16*
Firouz, Safiyeh *BioIn 16*
Firshein, Daniel Bruce 1952- *WhoE 91*
Firsova, Elena 1950- *IntWWM 90*
First, Harry 1945- *WhoAm 90*
First, Joseph Michael 1906- *WhoAm 90*
First, Mervin H. 1928- *St&PR 91*
First, Michael B. 1956- *BiDrAPA 89*
First, Michael Bruce 1956- *WhoE 91*
First, Ruth *BioIn 16*
First, Ruth 1925-1982 *FemiCLE*
First, Wesley 1920- *WhoAm 90, WhoE 91, WhoWor 91*
Firstenberg, Allen 1942- *St&PR 91*
Firstenberg, Jean 1936- *WhoAm 90*
Firstenberg, Paul B. 1933- *St&PR 91*
Firstenberg, Samuel 1950- *WhoEmL 91*
Firstenburg, Bruce Edward 1942- *St&PR 91*
Firstenburg, E.W. 1913- *St&PR 91*
Firstman, Eric Jacob 1957- *WhoEmL 91*
Firth, Anne Catherine 1947- *WhoAmW 91*
Firth, Colin *BioIn 16*
Firth, Everett Joseph 1930- *IntWWM 90, WhoAm 90*
Firth, Gary R. 1950- *St&PR 91*
Firth, James C. *St&PR 91*
Firth, Patsy Nerissa *BiDrAPA 89*
Firth, Paul Gerald 1953- *WhoSSW 91*
Firth, Raymond William 1901- *BioIn 16*
Firth, S Terry *BiDrAPA 89*
Firth, Tazeena 1935- *ConDes 90*
Firth, Violet Mary 1890-1946 *EncO&P 3*
Firvida, Francisco Jose *WhoSSW 91*
Fisbeck, Weldon Henry 1935- *St&PR 91*
Fiscella, Mary Ann 1960- *WhoAmW 91*
Fiscella, Robert Anthony 1944- *BiDrAPA 89*
Fisch, Alan *BiDrAPA 89*
Fisch, Arline *BioIn 16*
Fisch, Arline Marie *WhoAmA 91*
Fisch, Charles 1921- *WhoAm 90, WhoWor 91*
Fisch, Fredrick Lee 1955- *WhoEmL 91*
Fisch, Gerd 1942- *WhoWor 91*
Fisch, James M *BiDrAPA 89*
Fisch, Marcia E *BiDrAPA 89*
Fisch, Max Harold 1900- *WhoAm 90*
Fisch, Robert Otto 1925- *WhoAm 90*
Fisch, William Bales 1936- *WhoAm 90*
Fischbach, Ephraim 1942- *WhoAm 90*
Fischbach, Gerald Frederick 1942- *IntWWM 90*
Fischbach, Gerald Owen 1951- *BiDrAPA 89*
Fischbach, Joseph Franklin 1950- *St&PR 91*
Fischbach, Joseph W. *BioIn 16*
Fischbach, Leroy J. 1944- *St&PR 91*
Fischbach, Marc 1946- *WhoWor 91*
Fischbach, Marnin Eli *BiDrAPA 89*
Fischbarg, Jorge 1935- *WhoHisp 91*
Fischbeck, Helmut Johannes 1928- *WhoSSW 91*
Fischbein, Ellen Ruth 1945- *BiDrAPA 89*
Fischbein, Richard 1954- *BiDrAPA 89*
Fischberg, Bruce William 1930- *BiDrAPA 89*
Fischel, Daniel Norman 1922- *WhoAm 90*
Fischel, David 1936- *WhoAm 90*
Fischel, Edward Elliot 1920- *WhoAm 90*
Fischel, Robert Elliot 1948- *BiDrAPA 89*
Fischel, Shelley Duckstein 1950- *WhoEmL 91*
Fischel, William Alan 1945- *WhoAm 90*
Fischell, Robert Ellentuch 1929- *WhoAm 90*
Fischer, Adam 1949- *IntWWM 90, PenDiMP*
Fischer, Andre *BioIn 16*
Fischer, Andreas 1480?-1540? *BioIn 16*
Fischer, Annie 1914- *IntWWM 90, PenDiMP*
Fischer, Barbara Jean 1950- *WhoEmL 91*
Fischer, Bill 1891-1945 *Ballpl 90*
Fischer, Bill 1930- *Ballpl 90*
Fischer, Bobby 1943- *BioIn 16*
Fischer, Brent S. C. 1964- *WhoEmL 91*
Fischer, Bruce Alan 1951- *BiDrAPA 89*
Fischer, Bruce Elwood, Jr. 1951- *WhoEmL 91*
Fischer, Bruno 1908- *TwCCr&M 91*
Fischer, Carl 1905-1963 *Ballpl 90*
Fischer, Carl 1924- *WhoAm 90*
Fischer, Carl Robert 1939- *WhoAm 90, WhoSSW 91*
Fischer, Catherine Patricia 1947- *WhoEmL 91*
Fischer, Charles B., Jr. 1943- *St&PR 91*
Fischer, Charles Henry *BiDrAPA 89*
Fischer, Charles K. 1926- *St&PR 91*
Fischer, Charlotte G. 1949- *WhoAmW 91*
Fischer, Christian *PenDiDA 89*
Fischer, Craig 1947- *BiDrAPA 89*
Fischer, Craig Leland 1937- *WhoAm 90*
Fischer, Dale Arnold 1932- *WhoAm 90*
Fischer, Dale Susan 1951- *WhoAmW 91*
Fischer, Daniel Edward *BiDrAPA 89*
Fischer, Daniel Edward 1945- *WhoEmL 91, WhoSSW 91, WhoWor 91*
Fischer, David Charles 1948- *WhoAm 90*
Fischer, David John *BiDrAPA 89*
Fischer, David Jon 1952- *WhoEmL 91*
Fischer, David Seymour 1930- *WhoWor 91*
Fischer, Dennis James 1939- *WhoAm 90*
Fischer, Donald A. 1927- *ODwPR 91*
Fischer, Donald C 1951- *BiDrAPA 89*
Fischer, Donald Edward, Jr. 1941- *BiDrAPA 89*
Fischer, Donald J. 1940- *St&PR 91*
Fischer, Donald Sidney 1931- *St&PR 91*
Fischer, Douglas James 1943- *St&PR 91*
Fischer, Earl Bernard 1946- *St&PR 91*
Fischer, Edith 1935- *IntWWM 90*
Fischer, Edith Steinkraus 1923- *IntWWM 90*
Fischer, Edmond Henri 1920- *WhoAm 90*
Fischer, Edwin 1886-1960 *PenDiMP*
Fischer, Emanuel *BiDrAPA 89*
Fischer, Emil 1852-1919 *BioIn 16, WorAlBi*
Fischer, Eric Robert 1945- *St&PR 91, WhoAm 90, WhoE 91, WhoWor 91*
Fischer, Ernest L. 1922- *St&PR 91*
Fischer, Ernst Otto 1918- *WhoAm 90, WhoWor 91, WorAlBi*
Fischer, Eugene H. 1932- *WhoAm 90*
Fischer, Fayne Hirsh 1965- *WhoAmW 91*
Fischer, Floyd Brand 1916- *WhoAm 90*
Fischer, Frank E. 1933- *St&PR 91*
Fischer, Frank Ernest 1933- *WhoAm 90*
Fischer, Fritz 1908- *BioIn 16*
Fischer, George W. 1912- *St&PR 91*
Fischer, Glenn Edward 1942- *St&PR 91*
Fischer, Glenn M. 1950- *St&PR 91*
Fischer, Gregory W 1944- *BiDrAPA 89*
Fischer, Grete 1893-1977 *BioIn 16*
Fischer, Gyorgy 1935- *IntWWM 90, PenDiMP*
Fischer, H Keith 1916- *BiDrAPA 89*
Fischer, H Theodore 1901- *EncO&P 3*
Fischer, Hadwin Keith 1916- *WhoAm 90*
Fischer, Hal 1950- *WhoAmA 91*
Fischer, Hank 1940- *Ballpl 90*
Fischer, Hans 1881-1945 *WorAlBi*
Fischer, Harris E. 1922- *St&PR 91*
Fischer, Harry Arnold, Jr. 1926- *St&PR 91*
Fischer, Harry William 1921- *WhoAm 90*
Fischer, Henry George 1923- *WhoAm 90, WhoAmA 91, WhoE 91*
Fischer, Herman Christian *WhoSSW 91*
Fischer, Irene Kaminka 1907- *WhoAmW 91*
Fischer, Irvin Aaron 1949- *WhoE 91*
Fischer, Ivan 1951- *IntWWM 90, PenDiMP*
Fischer, James Adrian 1916- *WhoAm 90*
Fischer, James Louis 1948- *WhoEmL 91*
Fischer, Janet Jordan 1923- *WhoAm 90*
Fischer, Janet Lynn 1953- *St&PR 91*
Fischer, Joel 1939- *WhoAm 90*
Fischer, John Arthur 1929- *WhoSSW 91*
Fischer, John Clarence 1942- *St&PR 91*
Fischer, John Irwin 1940- *ConAu 129*
Fischer, John Robert *BiDrAPA 89*
Fischer, Josef E. 1937- *WhoAm 90*
Fischer, Joseph A. 1931- *St&PR 91*
Fischer, Joseph S *BiDrAPA 89*
Fischer, Karen Frances *BiDrAPA 89*
Fischer, Karoline Auguste Fernandine 1764-1842 *DcLB 94*
Fischer, Kenneth M. 1952- *St&PR 91*
Fischer, Kenneth R. 1918- *St&PR 91, WhoAm 90*
Fischer, Larry Lee 1936- *St&PR 91*
Fischer, Lawrence Joseph 1937- *WhoAm 90*
Fischer, Lee Alan 1946- *WhoSSW 91*
Fischer, Leonard Stephen 1949- *WhoSSW 91*
Fischer, LeRoy Henry 1917- *WhoAm 90*
Fischer, Lindsay Koehler *WhoAm 90, WhoE 91*
Fischer, Lorraine Claire 1963- *WhoEmL 91*
Fischer, Louis Theodore 1913- *WhoAm 90*
Fischer, Lucas C. 1915- *St&PR 91*
Fischer, Ludwig 1905-1947 *BioIn 16*
Fischer, Ludwig 1939- *WhoWor 91*
Fischer, Lynn Helen 1943- *WhoWrEP 89*
Fischer, Lynn Suzanne 1951- *WhoAmW 91*
Fischer, Manfred Manuel 1947- *WhoWor 91*
Fischer, Margaret Jane 1946- *WhoEmL 91*
Fischer, Margaret Thompson 1924- *WhoAm 90*
Fischer, Mark Alan 1961- *WhoEmL 91*
Fischer, Marsha Leigh 1955- *WhoAmW 91*
Fischer, Martin A *BiDrAPA 89*
Fischer, Martin S 1931- *BiDrAPA 89*
Fischer, Mary Dean Dunn 1928- *WhoAmW 91*
Fischer, Michael John 1942- *WhoAm 90*
Fischer, Michael Ludwig 1940- *WhoAm 90*
Fischer, Michael M. J. 1946- *WhoSSW 91*
Fischer, Michael Robert 1956- *WhoSSW 91*
Fischer, Michael Stanford 1949- *St&PR 91*
Fischer, Mildred 1907- *WhoAmA 91*
Fischer, Moritz *PenDiDA 89*
Fischer, Neil Jeffrey 1955- *St&PR 91, WhoEmL 91*
Fischer, Newell 1936- *BiDrAPA 89*
Fischer, Newton Duchan 1921- *WhoAm 90*
Fischer, Nora Barry 1951- *WhoEmL 91*
Fischer, Norman, Jr. 1924- *WhoSSW 91, WhoWor 91*
Fischer, Olga A *BiDrAPA 89*
Fischer, Oskar 1923- *WhoWor 91*
Fischer, Patrick Carl 1935- *WhoAm 90*
Fischer, Paul *PenDiMP*
Fischer, Paul G. 1946- *St&PR 91*
Fischer, Paula Kerins *BiDrAPA 89*
Fischer, Peter Anthony 1942- *St&PR 91, WhoAm 90*
Fischer, Peter Heinz 1942- *WhoSSW 91*
Fischer, Peter-Michael 1941- *WhoWor 91*
Fischer, Philip James *BiDrAPA 89*
Fischer, R M 1947- *WhoAmA 91*
Fischer, R. M. 1947- *WhoE 91*
Fischer, Raymond 1898-1988 *BioIn 16*
Fischer, Raymond P. 1900- *WhoAm 90*
Fischer, Richard 1935- *ConDes 90*
Fischer, Richard J 1941- *BiDrAPA 89*
Fischer, Richard L. 1936- *St&PR 91*
Fischer, Richard Lawrence 1936- *WhoAm 90*
Fischer, Richard Samuel 1937- *WhoAm 90, WhoWor 91*
Fischer, Rick 1946- *ODwPR 91*
Fischer, Robert 1943- *WorAlBi*
Fischer, Robert Andrew 1937- *WhoAm 90*
Fischer, Robert Blanchard 1920- *WhoAm 90*
Fischer, Robert Franklin *BiDrAPA 89*
Fischer, Robert George 1920- *WhoAm 90*
Fischer, Robert J. 1942- *St&PR 91*
Fischer, Robert Leo 1936- *BiDrAPA 89*
Fischer, Robert W. 1918- *St&PR 91*
Fischer, Robert William 1918- *WhoAm 90*
Fischer, Roger Adrian 1939- *WhoAm 90*
Fischer, Rube 1916- *Ballpl 90*
Fischer, Ruth Simons 1937- *BiDrAPA 89*
Fischer, Staci *BiDrAPA 89*
Fischer, Stanley 1943- *WhoAm 90, WhoE 91*
Fischer, Stephen E. 1937- *St&PR 91*
Fischer, Stephen Gary 1947- *WhoEmL 91*
Fischer, Steven Arthur 1945- *St&PR 91*
Fischer, Susan Lois 1947- *WhoEmL 91*
Fischer, Terence Joseph 1959- *WhoE 91*
Fischer, Therese Marie 1911- *WhoAmW 91*
Fischer, Thomas B. 1947- *St&PR 91*
Fischer, Thomas V. 1929- *St&PR 91*
Fischer, Victor *WhoAmA 91*
Fischer, Warren William 1943- *WhoE 91*
Fischer, William Austin 1943- *WhoE 91*
Fischer, William Donald 1928- *St&PR 91, WhoAm 90*
Fischer, William J. *BioIn 16*
Fischer, William Karl 1947- *St&PR 91*
Fischer, Wolfgang 1936- *WhoWor 91*
Fischer, Zoe Ann 1939- *WhoWor 91*
Fischer-Appelt, Peter 1932- *WhoWor 91*
Fischer-Dieskau, Dietrich 1925- *BioIn 16, PenDiMP, WhoAm 90, WhoWor 91, WorAlBi*
Fischer-Dieskau, Dietrich 1929- *IntWWM 90*
Fischer-Fabian, Siegfried 1922- *ConAu 130*
Fischer-Nagel, Andreas 1951- *BioIn 16*
Fischer-Nagel, Heiderose 1956- *BioIn 16*
Fischetti, John 1916-1980 *BioIn 16, WhoAmA 91N*
Fischetti, Michael 1940- *WhoE 91*
Fischetti, Robert James 1952- *WhoE 91*
Fischhoff, Baruch 1946- *WhoAm 90*
Fischhoff, Joseph 1924- *BiDrAPA 89*
Fischl, Alan Leslie 1955- *WhoEmL 91*
Fischl, Eric *BioIn 16*
Fischl, Eric 1948- *WhoAmA 91*
Fischl, Viktor *ConAu 30NR*
Fischler, Abraham Saul 1928- *WhoAm 90, WhoSSW 91*
Fischler, Barbara Brand 1930- *WhoAm 90*
Fischler, Bill *BioIn 16*
Fischler, Lori Faye 1956- *WhoE 91*
Fischler, Pamela Fran 1951- *WhoAmW 91, WhoE 91, WhoEmL 91*
Fischler, Shirley Balter 1926- *WhoAmW 91*
Fischlin, Mike 1955- *Ballpl 90*
Fischlowitz, Barbara Parker 1946- *WhoAmW 91*
Fischman, Bernard D. 1915- *St&PR 91, WhoAm 90*
Fischman, Edward Harold 1938- *WhoAm 90, WhoE 91*
Fischman, Gary Joseph *WhoE 91*
Fischman, Harold 1934- *St&PR 91*
Fischman, Harold Bernard 1953- *St&PR 91*
Fischman, Lawrence Gerson *BiDrAPA 89*
Fischman, Myrna Leah *WhoAmW 91, WhoE 91, WhoWor 91*
Fischman, Patricio 1957- *BiDrAPA 89*
Fischman, Paul 1945- *BiDrAPA 89*
Fischman, Stanley Edwin 1935- *BiDrAPA 89*
Fischman, Stanley Saul 1932- *St&PR 91*
Fischmann, Zdenka E. 1923- *IntWWM 90*
Fischmar, Richard Mayer 1938- *WhoWor 91*
Fischoff, Ephraim 1904- *WhoAm 90*
Fischoff, Gary Charles 1954- *WhoE 91*
Fischoff, Roger M. 1943- *St&PR 91*
Fischthal, Glenn Jay 1948- *WhoAm 90*
Fischtrom, Harvey *AuBYP 90*
Fiscina, Elizabeth Gladys 1944- *WhoAmW 91*
Fiscus, Richard Eugene 1930- *WhoSSW 91*
Fiscus, Robert L. 1937- *St&PR 91*
Fiser, David J. 1939- *St&PR 91*
Fiser, Lee *PenDiMP*
Fiset, Richard C. 1928- *St&PR 91*
Fish Carrier *WhNaAH*
Fish, A. Joe 1942- *WhoAm 90*
Fish, Aaron Max 1932- *St&PR 91*
Fish, Adrian Vernon 1956- *IntWWM 90*
Fish, Alice Gross *WhoAmA 91*
Fish, Andrew Joseph, Jr. 1944- *WhoE 91*
Fish, Barbara 1920- *BiDrAPA 89, WhoAm 90, WhoAmW 91*
Fish, Chet 1925- *WhoAm 90*
Fish, David E. 1936- *St&PR 91*
Fish, Donald Winston 1930- *St&PR 91, WhoAm 90*
Fish, Dorothy S 1906-1958 *WhoAmA 91N*
Fish, Frederick Samuel 1852-1936 *EncABHB 4 [port]*
Fish, Gary R. 1958- *St&PR 91*
Fish, George A *WhoAmA 91*
Fish, Hamilton 1808-1893 *BiDrUSE 89, BioIn 16, WorAlBi*
Fish, Hamilton 1849-1936 *AmLegL*
Fish, Hamilton, III 1951- *WhoE 91*
Fish, Hamilton, Jr. 1926- *WhoAm 90, WhoE 91*
Fish, Harry G., III 1950- *St&PR 91*
Fish, Helen Therese 1944- *WhoAmW 91*
Fish, Henry E. 1925- *St&PR 91*
Fish, Jacob E *BiDrAPA 89*
Fish, James Henry 1947- *WhoE 91*
Fish, James S. *ODwPR 91*
Fish, James Stuart 1915- *WhoAm 90*
Fish, Janet 1938- *BiDWomA*
Fish, Janet I 1938- *WhoAmA 91*
Fish, Janet Isobel 1938- *WhoAm 90*
Fish, Jeanne Spencer 1921- *WhoAmW 91*
Fish, Jefferson 1942- *WhoE 91*
Fish, Jerry R. 1949- *WhoEmL 91*
Fish, John Perry 1949- *WhoE 91*
Fish, Jonathan S. 1944- *St&PR 91*
Fish, Jonathon Kevin 1955- *WhoEmL 91*
Fish, June K. 1951- *St&PR 91*
Fish, Kathleen Ann 1956- *WhoEmL 91*
Fish, Laurence Harry 1926- *St&PR 91*
Fish, Lawrence Kingsbaker 1944- *WhoAm 90*
Fish, Leah 1814-1890 *EncO&P 3*
Fish, Lilian Mann 1901- *WhoAmW 91, WhoWrEP 89*

Fish, Mamie 1853-1915 *BioIn 16*
Fish, Marcus 1925- *St&PR 91*
Fish, Marie Poland 1902-1989 *BioIn 16*
Fish, Mary Ann Anthon 1853-1915 *BioIn 16*
Fish, Mary Martha 1930- *WhoAm 90*
Fish, Nicholas *BiDrAPA 89*
Fish, Paul Waring 1933- *WhoAm 90*
Fish, R. Talmage 1938- *St&PR 91*
Fish, Richard G 1925- *WhoAmA 91*
Fish, Robert Jay 1947- *WhoAm 90*
Fish, Robert L 1912-1981 *TwCCr&M 91*
Fish, Robert L. 1940- *St&PR 91*
Fish, Robert Richard 1942- *St&PR 91*
Fish, Ruby Mae Bertram 1918- *WhoAmW 91*
Fish, Seymour L. 1930- *St&PR 91*
Fish, Stanley *ConAu 132*
Fish, Stanley E. *ConAu 132*
Fish, Stanley Eugene 1938- *BioIn 16, ConAu 132, WhoAm 90, WhoWrEP 89*
Fish, Stephen P. 1952- *WhoE 91*
Fish, Stephen Richard 1953- *WhoE 91, WhoEmL 91*
Fish, Stewart Allison 1925- *WhoAm 90*
Fish, Susan Linda 1942- *WhoE 91*
Fish, Thomas C. 1933- *St&PR 91*
Fish, Thomas Edward, Jr. 1951- *WhoSSW 91*
Fish, Thomas Lee 1934- *St&PR 91*
Fish, Vera W *BiDrAPA 89*
Fishack, C. Edward 1942- *St&PR 91*
Fishack, Charles David, Jr. 1921- *St&PR 91*
Fishack, Charles Edward 1942- *St&PR 91*
Fishback, Timothy Michael 1959- *BiDrAPA 89*
Fishback, William Meade 1831-1903 *BioIn 16*
Fishbain, David Abraham 1943- *BiDrAPA 89*
Fishbain, Harold 1923- *BiDrAPA 89*
Fishbaugh, Franklin James 1943- *WhoAm 90*
Fishbein, Daniel Eli 1951- *WhoEmL 91*
Fishbein, Gershon William 1921- *WhoE 91*
Fishbein, I Leo 1907- *BiDrAPA 89*
Fishbein, Joseph H 1919- *BiDrAPA 89*
Fishbein, Martin 1936- *WhoAm 90*
Fishbein, Michael Claude 1946- *WhoEmL 91*
Fishbein, Peter Melvin 1934- *WhoAm 90*
Fishbein, Robert 1942- *St&PR 91*
Fishberg, Bruce 1949- *St&PR 91*
Fishberg, Gerard 1946- *WhoEmL 91*
Fishberger, Jeffrey *BiDrAPA 89*
Fishbone, Marie Lynn 1959- *WhoEmL 91*
Fishburn, Peter Clingerman 1936- *WhoAm 90*
Fishburn, Robert Nelson 1934- *WhoSSW 91*
Fishburne, F.B. *St&PR 91*
Fishburne, John Ingram, Jr. 1937- *WhoAm 90*
Fishburne, Larry *BioIn 16*
Fishburne, Laurence, III 1960?- *DrBIPA 90*
Fishburne, Mary W. 1917- *St&PR 91*
Fishburne, St Julian 1927- *WhoAmA 91*
Fishel, Bob 1914-1988 *Ballpl 90*
Fishel, David B *ODwPR 91*
Fishel, David B. 1948- *St&PR 91*
Fishel, David Burton 1948- *WhoAm 90*
Fishel, James David 1951- *WhoAm 90*
Fishel, James Dean 1953- *WhoEmL 91*
Fishel, James Joseph 1959- *WhoE 91*
Fishel, Joseph Donovan *BiDrAPA 89*
Fishel, Peter Livingston 1935- *WhoAm 90*
Fishel, Robert 1914-1988 *BioIn 16*
Fishel, Stanley Irvyng 1914- *WhoAm 90*
Fisher, Abigail 1649-1721 *BiDEWW*
Fisher, Agnew *BioIn 16*
Fisher, Aidan Hugh 1959- *IntWWM 90*
Fisher, Aileen Lucia 1906- *AuBYP 90*
Fisher, Alan 1922-1988 *AnObit 1988*
Fisher, Alan Washburn 1939- *WhoAm 90*
Fisher, Albert *EncABHB 4*
Fisher, Albert L 1920- *BiDrAPA 89*
Fisher, Alexander 1864-1936 *PenDiDA 89*
Fisher, Alfred Foster 1934- *WhoAm 90*
Fisher, Alice *ODwPR 91*
Fisher, Allan Campbell 1943- *WhoE 91, WhoWor 91*
Fisher, Allan Carroll, Jr. 1919- *WhoAm 90*
Fisher, Allan Herbert, Jr. 1922- *WhoAm 90*
Fisher, Alton Kindt 1905- *WhoAm 90*
Fisher, Alvan 1792-1863 *BioIn 16*
Fisher, Andrew 1920- *WhoAm 90*
Fisher, Andrew S. 1948- *St&PR 91*
Fisher, Andrew Somes 1948- *WhoEmL 91*
Fisher, Andrew Wilson 1945- *BiDrAPA 89*
Fisher, Anita Jeanne 1937- *WhoAmW 91, WhoSSW 91*
Fisher, Ann 1719-1778 *FemiCLE*
Fisher, Ann Katherine 1961- *WhoE 91*
Fisher, Anna L. *BioIn 16*
Fisher, Anna Lee 1949- *WhoAmW 91*
Fisher, Arthur 1931- *WhoAm 90, WhoWrEP 89*
Fisher, Barbara 1940- *ConAu 30NR*
Fisher, Barry William 1960- *BiDrAPA 89*
Fisher, Bart Steven 1943- *WhoE 91, WhoWor 91*
Fisher, Benjamin Chatburn 1923- *WhoAm 90*
Fisher, Benjamin Franklin, IV 1940- *ConAu 30NR*
Fisher, Bennett Lawson 1942- *St&PR 91*
Fisher, Bernard *BiDrAPA 89*
Fisher, Bernard 1918- *WhoAm 90*
Fisher, Bob 1887-1963 *Ballpl 90*
Fisher, Bob 1945- *WhoAm 90*
Fisher, Bonnie Lee Michaelson 1948- *WhoAmW 91*
Fisher, Brady Alan 1952- *WhoEmL 91*
Fisher, Brian 1962- *Ballpl 90*
Fisher, Brian Stanley 1950- *WhoWor 91*
Fisher, Bruce Cody *BiDrAPA 89*
Fisher, Bruce Dwight 1943- *WhoSSW 91*
Fisher, Bud 1884-1954 *EncACom*
Fisher, Calvin David 1926- *WhoAm 90*
Fisher, Carl Frederick 1924- *WhoAm 90*
Fisher, Carole Gorney *WhoAmA 91*
Fisher, Caroline MacFadyen 1947- *WhoSSW 91*
Fisher, Carrie *BioIn 16*
Fisher, Carrie 1956- *BestSel 90-4 [port], News 91-1 [port], WorAlBi*
Fisher, Carrie Frances 1956- *WhoAm 90*
Fisher, Catherine Ambrosiano 1946- *WhoEmL 91*
Fisher, Champe Andrews 1928- *WhoAm 90*
Fisher, Charles *BiDrAPA 89, EncABHB 4*
Fisher, Charles 1908-1988 *BioIn 16*
Fisher, Charles Frederick 1936- *WhoAm 90*
Fisher, Charles Harold 1906- *WhoAm 90, WhoSSW 91*
Fisher, Charles Page, Jr. 1921- *WhoAm 90*
Fisher, Charles Paul 1946- *BiDrAPA 89*
Fisher, Charles T. *BioIn 16*
Fisher, Charles T., III 1929- *St&PR 91*
Fisher, Charles Thomas, III 1929- *WhoAm 90*
Fisher, Charles Worley 1917- *WhoAm 90*
Fisher, Chauncey 1872-1939 *Ballpl 90*
Fisher, Chester Lewis, Jr. 1911- *WhoAm 90*
Fisher, Clara 1811-1889 *NotWoAT*
Fisher, Clara 1811-1898 *BioIn 16*
Fisher, Clarkson Sherman 1921- *WhoAm 90*
Fisher, Clarkson Sherman, Jr. 1952- *WhoEmL 91*
Fisher, Clay 1912- *BioIn 16*
Fisher, Craig Becker 1932- *WhoAm 90*
Fisher, D. Michael 1944- *WhoE 91*
Fisher, Dale Dunbar 1945- *WhoE 91, WhoEmL 91, WhoWor 91*
Fisher, Dale John 1925- *WhoAm 90*
Fisher, Daniel Billings 1943- *BiDrAPA 89*
Fisher, David *AuBYP 90*
Fisher, David Bruce 1954- *WhoE 91, WhoEmL 91*
Fisher, David I. 1939- *St&PR 91*
Fisher, David Judson 1936- *St&PR 91*
Fisher, David Woodrow 1927- *WhoAm 90*
Fisher, Dean L. 1940- *St&PR 91*
Fisher, Delbert Arthur 1928- *WhoAm 90, WhoWor 91*
Fisher, Donald 1949- *WhoEmL 91*
Fisher, Donald Edward 1928- *WhoAm 90*
Fisher, Donald G. 1928- *WhoAm 90*
Fisher, Donald R., Jr. 1943- *St&PR 91*
Fisher, Donald Roy 1927- *St&PR 91*
Fisher, Donald Wayne 1946- *WhoAm 90*
Fisher, Donald Wiener 1923- *WhoAm 90*
Fisher, Donne F. 1938- *St&PR 91*
Fisher, Donne Francis 1938- *WhoAm 90*
Fisher, Doris 1915- *OxCPMus*
Fisher, Dorothy 1879-1958 *FemiCLE*
Fisher, Dorothy Canfield 1879-1958 *AuBYP 90, BioAmW, DcLB 102 [port]*
Fisher, Douglas Arthur 1942- *St&PR 91*
Fisher, Duke De *BiDrAPA 89*
Fisher, Eddie *BioIn 16*
Fisher, Eddie 1928- *OxCPMus, WorAlBi*
Fisher, Eddie 1936- *Ballpl 90, BioIn 16*
Fisher, Edward F. 1939- *St&PR 91*
Fisher, Edward Francis 1939- *WhoE 91*
Fisher, Edward J 1945- *BiDrAPA 89*
Fisher, Edward Joseph 1913- *WhoAm 90*
Fisher, Ellena Allmond *WhoAmW 91*
Fisher, Eric O'Neill 1954- *WhoE 91*
Fisher, Erik Ward 1955- *BiDrAPA 89*
Fisher, Everett 1920- *WhoAm 90, WhoWor 91*
Fisher, F David 1929- *BiDrAPA 89*
Fisher, Fenimore 1926- *WhoAm 90, WhoWor 91*
Fisher, Florence Anna 1928- *WhoAmW 91*
Fisher, Frances *ConTFT 8*
Fisher, Franklin C., Jr. 1940- *St&PR 91*
Fisher, Franklin Marvin 1934- *WhoAm 90, WhoE 91*
Fisher, Fred 1875-1942 *BioIn 16, OxCPMus*
Fisher, Frederic J *EncABHB 4*
Fisher, Frederick 1939- *BiDrAPA 89*
Fisher, Frederick G. 1921-1989 *BioIn 16*
Fisher, Frederick Hendrick 1926- *WhoAm 90*
Fisher, Frederick Jack 1908-1988 *BioIn 16*
Fisher, Gail 1935?- *DrBIPA 90*
Fisher, Gary Alan 1951- *WhoAm 90*
Fisher, Gary Alan 1955- *WhoEmL 91*
Fisher, Gary N. 1955- *St&PR 91*
Fisher, Gene Jordan 1931- *WhoAm 90*
Fisher, George Andrew 1952- *WhoEmL 91*
Fisher, George Harold 1943- *WhoSSW 91*
Fisher, George M. 1925- *St&PR 91*
Fisher, George M. C. *BioIn 16*
Fisher, George Myles Cordell 1940- *WhoAm 90*
Fisher, George Ross, IV 1951- *WhoE 91*
Fisher, George Wescott 1937- *WhoAm 90*
Fisher, George William 1946- *WhoWrEP 89*
Fisher, Gerald Saul 1931- *WhoAm 90*
Fisher, Gillian *IntWWM 90*
Fisher, Hal Dennis 1948- *WhoWrEP 89*
Fisher, Ham 1901-1955 *EncACom*
Fisher, Harold Eugene 1939- *St&PR 91*
Fisher, Harold Leonard 1910- *WhoAm 90, WhoWor 91*
Fisher, Harold Manly 1940- *WhoSSW 91*
Fisher, Harold Wallace 1904- *WhoAm 90*
Fisher, Henry 1917- *St&PR 91*
Fisher, Henry 1936- *WhoWor 91*
Fisher, Herbert 1921- *St&PR 91, WhoAm 90*
Fisher, Herbert Franklin 1933- *WhoAm 90*
Fisher, Herbert Hirsh 1927- *WhoAm 90*
Fisher, Herbert O. *NewYTBS 90*
Fisher, Herbert R. 1910- *St&PR 91*
Fisher, Herman Guy 1898-1975 *ConAmBL*
Fisher, Irving 1867-1947 *BioIn 16*
Fisher, Isaac L. 1844?- *AmLegL*
Fisher, J Gregory 1962- *BiDrAPA 89*
Fisher, J. R. 1943- *WhoAmW 91*
Fisher, J. W. *NewYTBS 90*
Fisher, Jack 1919- *Ballpl 90*
Fisher, Jack Carrington 1932- *WhoAm 90*
Fisher, Jack J. 1925- *St&PR 91*
Fisher, Jack Robert 1948- *WhoE 91*
Fisher, James Abner, Jr. 1933- *WhoWrEP 89*
Fisher, James Aiken 1920- *WhoAm 90*
Fisher, James Burke 1932- *WhoAm 90*
Fisher, James Donald 1938- *WhoAmA 91*
Fisher, James McFarland 1932- *St&PR 91*
Fisher, James Selby 1913- *IntWWM 90*
Fisher, James Stevens 1938- *St&PR 91*
Fisher, James W., Jr. 1942- *WhoWor 91*
Fisher, James William 1925- *WhoAm 90*
Fisher, Jan Braddock 1951- *WhoEmL 91*
Fisher, Jeanette Nelson 1942- *WhoAmW 91*
Fisher, Jeffrey Barry 1949- *WhoEmL 91*
Fisher, Jerid Martin 1953- *WhoE 91*
Fisher, Jerome 1916- *WhoAm 90*
Fisher, Jerry Saul 1931- *WhoWrEP 89*
Fisher, Jewel T. 1918- *St&PR 91*
Fisher, Jewel Tanner 1918- *WhoAmW 91*
Fisher, Jimmie Lou 1941- *WhoAm 90, WhoAmW 91, WhoSSW 91*
Fisher, Jimmy Don 1947- *WhoSSW 91*
Fisher, Joan Margaret 1947- *WhoE 91*
Fisher, Joel A 1947- *WhoAmA 91*
Fisher, Joel Hilton 1918- *WhoAm 90*
Fisher, Joel Marshall 1935- *WhoAm 90*
Fisher, Johanna Marie *WhoAmW 91, WhoE 91*
Fisher, John 1469-1535 *BioIn 16*
Fisher, John Eastham 1926- *WhoSSW 91*
Fisher, John Edwin 1929- *St&PR 91, WhoAm 90, WhoWor 91*
Fisher, John Hurt 1919- *WhoAm 90*
Fisher, John J. *BioIn 16*
Fisher, John J., III 1951?-1990 *ConAu 131*
Fisher, John Jacob, III *NewYTBS 90*
Fisher, John James 1941- *WhoAm 90*
Fisher, John Joseph 1953- *WhoEmL 91*
Fisher, John Morris 1922- *WhoAm 90, WhoSSW 91, WhoWor 91*
Fisher, John Philip 1927- *St&PR 91, WhoAm 90*
Fisher, John Richard 1924- *WhoAm 90*
Fisher, John Sergio 1934- *WhoAm 90, WhoWor 91*
Fisher, John Wesley 1915- *St&PR 91, WhoAm 90*
Fisher, John William 1931- *WhoAm 90*
Fisher, Johnnie G *BiDrAPA 89*
Fisher, Jon Herbert 1947- *WhoEmL 91*
Fisher, Joseph Freiler 1955- *WhoEmL 91*
Fisher, Joseph Herbert 1936- *St&PR 91*
Fisher, Joseph Jefferson *WhoAm 90*
Fisher, Joseph Lyman 1914- *WhoAm 90*
Fisher, Joy Deborah 1952- *WhoAmW 91*
Fisher, Judith Ann *BiDrAPA 89*
Fisher, Judith Danelle 1951- *BiDrAPA 89*
Fisher, Jules 1937- *ConDes 90*
Fisher, Jules Edward 1937- *WhoAm 90*
Fisher, Kenneth Knight 1953- *WhoEmL 91*
Fisher, Kenneth L. 1944- *WhoAm 90*
Fisher, Kenneth Lee 1944- *WhoAmA 91*
Fisher, Kenneth Robinson 1906- *St&PR 91, WhoAm 90*
Fisher, Kevin Bruce 1959- *WhoEmL 91*
Fisher, King 1916- *St&PR 91, WhoSSW 91*
Fisher, Laddie Carter 1920- *WhoAmW 91, WhoSSW 91*
Fisher, Larry J. 1951- *St&PR 91*
Fisher, Larry N. 1944- *St&PR 91*
Fisher, Laura Burgher 1946- *BiDrAPA 89*
Fisher, Lawrence W. 1938- *ODwPR 91*
Fisher, Lee Elliott 1927- *WhoAm 90, WhoWor 91*
Fisher, Leon Harold 1918- *WhoAm 90*
Fisher, Leonard Albert 1921- *St&PR 91*
Fisher, Leonard Everett 1924- *AuBYP 90, BioIn 16, WhoAm 90, WhoAmA 91*
Fisher, Leonard Robert 1922- *St&PR 91, WhoE 91*
Fisher, Lester Emil 1921- *WhoAm 90*
Fisher, Lewis Webster 1931- *St&PR 91*
Fisher, Lloyd Edison, Jr. 1923- *WhoAm 90*
Fisher, Lola Janette 1949- *WhoSSW 91*
Fisher, Louis 1934- *WhoE 91*
Fisher, Louis McLane, Jr. 1938- *WhoAm 90*
Fisher, M. F. K. 1908- *BioIn 16*
Fisher, M. K. V. 1908- *FemiCLE*
Fisher, Marcia Ann 1957- *WhoAmW 91, WhoEmL 91, WhoWor 91*
Fisher, Margery 1913- *AuBYP 90*
Fisher, Margot *ConAu 31NR*
Fisher, Marion LeRoy, Jr. 1925- *WhoSSW 91*
Fisher, Marshall L 1911- *BiDrAPA 89*
Fisher, Marshall Lee 1944- *WhoAm 90*
Fisher, Mary 1623-1698 *BiDEWW, EncCRAm, FemiCLE*
Fisher, Mary Ann 1925- *WhoAm 90*
Fisher, Mary Ann 1926- *WhoWrEP 89*
Fisher, Mary Frances Kennedy 1908- *BioIn 16*
Fisher, Mary Maurine 1929- *WhoE 91*
Fisher, Max Martin 1908- *WhoAm 90*
Fisher, McLane 1938- *St&PR 91*
Fisher, Mel *BioIn 16*
Fisher, Michael Andrew 1953- *BiDrAPA 89*
Fisher, Michael Bruce 1945- *WhoAm 90, WhoWor 91*
Fisher, Michael Ellis 1931- *WhoAm 90*
Fisher, Milton Leonard 1922- *WhoAm 90*
Fisher, Mitchell Salem *NewYTBS 90*
Fisher, Mitchell Salem 1903-1990 *BioIn 16*
Fisher, Nancy *BioIn 16*
Fisher, Nancy 1941- *WhoAmW 91*
Fisher, Naomi Yasuda 1952- *WhoAmW 91*
Fisher, Neal Floyd 1936- *WhoAm 90*
Fisher, Ned Lawrence 1947- *WhoEmL 91*
Fisher, Nina Anne 1957- *WhoAmW 91*
Fisher, Norma 1940- *IntWWM 90*
Fisher, Oscar H., Jr. 1916- *St&PR 91*
Fisher, Patricia Sweeney 1954- *St&PR 91*
Fisher, Paul 1908- *WhoE 91*
Fisher, Paul C. 1913- *St&PR 91*
Fisher, Paul Gottshall 1922- *IntWWM 90*
Fisher, Paul L. 1923- *St&PR 91*
Fisher, Peggy Ann 1947- *WhoSSW 91*
Fisher, Perry M. 1939- *St&PR 91*
Fisher, Peter *BioIn 16*
Fisher, Peter Francis 1955- *WhoEmL 91*
Fisher, Philip 1941- *ConAu 33NR*
Fisher, Philip C 1930- *WhoAmA 91*
Fisher, Pierre James, Jr. 1931- *WhoAm 90*
Fisher, R.A. 1935- *St&PR 91*
Fisher, Randall Eugene 1949- *WhoEmL 91*
Fisher, Ray 1887-1982 *Ballpl 90*
Fisher, Raymond George 1911- *WhoAm 90*
Fisher, Raymond P. 1940- *St&PR 91*
Fisher, Rebecca Ann 1953- *St&PR 91*
Fisher, Reginald 1906-1966 *WhoAmA 91N*
Fisher, Richard Allen 1930- *St&PR 91*
Fisher, Richard B. *BioIn 16*
Fisher, Richard B. 1923- *St&PR 91*
Fisher, Richard B. 1936- *WhoAm 90*
Fisher, Richard E. *ODwPR 91*
Fisher, Richard Forrest 1941- *WhoAm 90*
Fisher, Richard Welton 1949- *WhoSSW 91*
Fisher, Richard Yale 1933- *St&PR 91*
Fisher, Ricky Dean 1963- *WhoSSW 91*
Fisher, Rob 1939- *WhoAmA 91*
Fisher, Robert 1926- *BiDrAPA 89*
Fisher, Robert 1943- *BioIn 16*
Fisher, Robert A *BiDrAPA 89*
Fisher, Robert Alan 1943- *WhoAm 90*
Fisher, Robert Allen 1951- *WhoAm 90*
Fisher, Robert Burton 1937- *BiDrAPA 89*
Fisher, Robert Charles 1930- *WhoAm 90*
Fisher, Robert Dale 1924- *WhoE 91*
Fisher, Robert Darryl 1939- *WhoSSW 91*

Fisher, Robert George 1917- *WhoAm 90*
Fisher, Robert Henry 1925- *St&PR 91*
Fisher, Robert Henry 1954- *WhoEmL 91*
Fisher, Robert I. 1939- *WhoAm 90*
Fisher, Robert J. 1942- *ODwPR 91*
Fisher, Robert J. 1947- *ODwPR 91*
Fisher, Robert Joseph 1940- *WhoE 91*
Fisher, Robert Lee 1929- *St&PR 91*
Fisher, Robert Lionel 1941- *BiDrAPA 89*
Fisher, Robert Norman 1939- *WhoE 91*
Fisher, Robert Scott 1960- *WhoEmL 91*
Fisher, Robert Warren 1952- *WhoEmL 91*
Fisher, Robert Wilson 1938- *St&PR 91*
Fisher, Robin Leeann 1955- *WhoAmW 91, WhoE 91, WhoEmL 91*
Fisher, Roger Anthony 1936- *IntWWM 90*
Fisher, Roger Dummer 1922- *WhoAm 90*
Fisher, Ronald 1950- *BiDrAPA 89, WhoE 91*
Fisher, Ronald Alymer 1890-1962 *EncPaPR 91*
Fisher, Rosalind Anita 1956- *WhoAmW 91*
Fisher, Roy 1930- *WorAu 1980 [port]*
Fisher, Roy Brent 1959- *St&PR 91*
Fisher, Roy Mac 1918- *WhoAm 90*
Fisher, Rudolph 1897-1934 *DcLB 102 [port], EarBlAP*
Fisher, Sallie Ann 1923- *WhoAmW 91*
Fisher, Sandra 1947- *WhoAmA 91*
Fisher, Sarah Lisbeth 1945- *WhoAmA 91*
Fisher, Saul H 1913- *BiDrAPA 89*
Fisher, Saul Harrison 1913- *WhoE 91*
Fisher, Seymour 1925- *WhoAm 90*
Fisher, Shirley Mahaley 1943- *WhoAmW 91*
Fisher, Stanley 1927- *WhoE 91*
Fisher, Stanley M. 1928- *St&PR 91*
Fisher, Stephen *BiDrAPA 89*
Fisher, Stephen Carey 1948- *IntWWM 90*
Fisher, Steve *BioIn 16*
Fisher, Steve 1912-1980 *TwCCr&M 91*
Fisher, Steven Robert 1949- *WhoSSW 91*
Fisher, Susan Grossman 1946- *WhoAm 90, WhoAmW 91*
Fisher, Susan Kay 1948- *WhoEmL 91*
Fisher, Susan Michal 1937- *BiDrAPA 89*
Fisher, Suzanne *ConAu 132*
Fisher, Sylvia 1910- *PenDiMP*
Fisher, Sylvia Gwendoline Victoria 1910- *IntWWM 90*
Fisher, Terry L. 1938- *ODwPR 91*
Fisher, Thomas D. 1952- *St&PR 91*
Fisher, Thomas George 1931- *St&PR 91, WhoAm 90*
Fisher, Thomas H. 1922- *St&PR 91*
Fisher, Thomas Joseph, Jr. 1954- *WhoSSW 91*
Fisher, Thomas L *BiDrAPA 89*
Fisher, Thomas Lee 1944- *St&PR 91*
Fisher, Thomas Michael 1951- *WhoWrEP 89*
Fisher, Thomas W. 1946- *WhoSSW 91*
Fisher, Todd Rogers 1949- *WhoSSW 91*
Fisher, Ulyss 1932- *St&PR 91*
Fisher, Vardis 1895-1968 *BioIn 16*
Fisher, Vernon *WhoAmA 91*
Fisher, Vicki Jo 1957- *WhoAmW 91*
Fisher, Virginia Zemp 1949- *WhoE 91*
Fisher, Walter Dummer 1916- *WhoAm 90*
Fisher, Walter Lowrie 1862-1935 *BiDrUSE 89*
Fisher, Walter Taylor 1892- *WhoAm 90*
Fisher, Wendy Astley-Bell 1944- *WhoAmW 91*
Fisher, Wesley Andrew 1944- *WhoE 91*
Fisher, Will Stratton 1922- *WhoAm 90*
Fisher, William A 1954- *BiDrAPA 89*
Fisher, William Lawrence 1932- *WhoAm 90*
Fisher, William P 1929- *BiDrAPA 89*
Fisher, William Thomas 1918- *WhoAm 90*
Fisher, Yale 1945- *St&PR 91*
Fisherkeller, Paul F. 1948- *St&PR 91*
Fisherkeller, Paul Francis 1948- *WhoSSW 91*
Fishkin, Howard S. 1946- *WhoWrEP 89*
Fishkin, Lana Prince 1942- *BiDrAPA 89*
Fishkin, Ralph Elliott 1940- *BiDrAPA 89*
Fishko, Bella *WhoAm 90, WhoAmA 91*
Fishko, Sol *BioIn 16*
Fishler, Bennett Hill, Jr. 1918- *St&PR 91*
Fishler, Lois A *BiDrAPA 89*
Fishler, Mary 1920- *AuBYP 90*
Fishley, George 1771-1865 *PenDiDA 89*
Fishlock, David 1932- *ConAu 130*
Fishman, Aaron Harry 1922- *St&PR 91*
Fishman, Alfred Paul 1918- *WhoAm 90*
Fishman, Barry Stuart 1943- *WhoSSW 91, WhoWor 91*
Fishman, Bernard 1920- *WhoAm 90*
Fishman, Charles 1942- *WhoWrEP 89*
Fishman, David Israel 1948- *WhoWor 91*
Fishman, Dorothy Janet *WhoAmW 91*
Fishman, Edward Marc 1946- *WhoEmL 91, WhoSSW 91, WhoWor 91*
Fishman, Erwin 1927- *WhoAm 90*
Fishman, Felix A. 1904- *St&PR 91*
Fishman, Fred Norman 1925- *WhoAm 90*
Fishman, Gary L *BiDrAPA 89*
Fishman, George Ganick 1945- *BiDrAPA 89*
Fishman, Gerald A 1949- *BiDrAPA 89*
Fishman, Gerald Alan 1949- *WhoE 91*
Fishman, Herbert B. 1928- *St&PR 91*
Fishman, Herman Charles *BiDrAPA 89*
Fishman, Howard H. 1930- *St&PR 91*
Fishman, Howard Stephen 1947- *WhoSSW 91*
Fishman, Jack 1930- *WhoAm 90*
Fishman, Jack Bradley 1961- *WhoEmL 91*
Fishman, Jacob R 1930- *BiDrAPA 89*
Fishman, Jacob Robert 1930- *WhoE 91, WhoWor 91*
Fishman, James Bart 1954- *WhoEmL 91*
Fishman, Joan Roslyn 1945- *WhoEmL 91*
Fishman, Joshua Aaron 1926- *WhoAm 90*
Fishman, Katharine Davis 1937- *ConAu 130*
Fishman, Kenneth Jay 1950- *WhoEmL 91*
Fishman, Lewis Warren 1951- *WhoEmL 91*
Fishman, Libby G. 1940- *WhoAm 90*
Fishman, Louis Yarrut 1941- *WhoSSW 91*
Fishman, Louise 1939- *WhoAm 90*
Fishman, Madeline Dotti 1942- *WhoAmW 91*
Fishman, Mark Alan 1954- *St&PR 91*
Fishman, Mark Brian 1951- *WhoEmL 91, WhoSSW 91, WhoWor 91*
Fishman, Marvin Allen 1937- *WhoAm 90*
Fishman, Merrill B. 1934- *St&PR 91*
Fishman, Michael E *BiDrAPA 89*
Fishman, Mitchell Steven 1948- *WhoEmL 91*
Fishman, Paul S. 1957- *BiDrAPA 89*
Fishman, Richard Glenn 1952- *WhoEmL 91*
Fishman, Robert Allen 1924- *WhoAm 90*
Fishman, Robert Michael 1953- *WhoEmL 91*
Fishman, Scott M 1959- *BiDrAPA 89*
Fishman, Seymour 1915- *WhoSSW 91*
Fishman, Sheila Marsha 1947- *WhoE 91*
Fishman, Stan David 1951- *WhoEmL 91*
Fishman, Steve *BioIn 16*
Fishman, Steven 1949- *WhoSSW 91*
Fishman, Sylvia C. 1920- *WhoE 91*
Fishman, Theodore David 1953- *BiDrAPA 89, WhoE 91*
Fishman, William Harold 1914- *WhoAm 90, WhoWor 91*
Fishter, Michael F *BiDrAPA 89*
Fishwick, John Palmer 1916- *WhoAm 90*
Fishwick, Nina Marie 1961- *WhoWrEP 89*
Fisk Jubilee Singers *DcAfAmP*
Fisk, Arthur G. 1867-1938 *AmLegL*
Fisk, Carlton 1947- *Ballpl 90 [port], BioIn 16*
Fisk, Carlton Ernest 1947- *WhoAm 90*
Fisk, Carol Fraser 1946- *WhoAmW 91*
Fisk, Carol Patricia 1948- *WhoSSW 91*
Fisk, Douglas Ray, Jr. 1948- *St&PR 91, WhoAm 90*
Fisk, Edward Ray 1924- *WhoAm 90, WhoWor 91*
Fisk, Eliot 1954- *IntWWM 90*
Fisk, Elizabeth Chester 1846- *BioIn 16*
Fisk, Erma J 1905?-1990 *ConAu 130*
Fisk, G W 1882-1972 *EncO&P 3*
Fisk, George William 1882-1972 *EncPaPR 91*
Fisk, Jack 1934- *ConTFT 8*
Fisk, Larry J. 1936- *St&PR 91*
Fisk, Lennard Ayres 1943- *WhoAm 90*
Fisk, Margaret Cronin 1946- *WhoWrEP 89*
Fisk, Norman Martin *BiDrAPA 89*
Fisk, Pamela House 1952- *WhoAmW 91*
Fisk, Richard L. 1944- *St&PR 91*
Fisk, Thomas Brian 1960- *WhoEmL 91*
Fiskaa, Haakon M. 1894-1987 *BioIn 16*
Fiske, Carol Ann 1956- *WhoSSW 91*
Fiske, Edward Bogardus 1937- *WhoAm 90*
Fiske, Fidelia 1816-1864 *BioAmW*
Fiske, Gertrude 1879-1961 *WhoAmA 91N*
Fiske, Guy Wilbur 1924- *WhoE 91*
Fiske, Irving L. *BioIn 16, NewYTBS 90*
Fiske, John 1842-1901 *BioIn 16*
Fiske, John, Jr. 1935- *St&PR 91*
Fiske, Minnie M. 1865-1932 *BioAmW*
Fiske, Minnie Maddern 1865-1932 *BioIn 16, NotWoAT*
Fiske, Richard Sewell 1932- *WhoAm 90*
Fiske, Robert Bishop, Jr. 1930- *WhoAm 90*
Fiske, Stephen Longfellow *NewAgMG*
Fiske, Terry Noble 1933- *WhoAm 90*
Fisken, Alexander McEwan 1922- *St&PR 91*
Fisketjon, Gary 1954- *BioIn 16, ConAu 129*
Fiskett, Anthony B. 1940- *ODwPR 91*
Fiskin, Judy 1945- *WhoAmA 91*
Fisler, John Chester 1949- *WhoEmL 91*
Fiss, Owen M. 1938- *WhoAm 90*
Fisseha, Desta 1941- *WhoWor 91*
Fissell, Lili Marlane 1944- *WhoAmW 91*
Fissell, William Henry 1931- *WhoE 91*
Fissinger, Edwin Russell 1920- *IntWWM 90, WhoAm 90*
Fistoulari, Anatole 1907- *IntWWM 90, PenDiMP*
Fiszbein, Abraham *BiDrAPA 89*
Fiszbin, Henri 1930- *BiDFrPL*
Fiszer, Janusz 1957- *WhoWor 91*
Fiszer-Szafarz, Berta 1928- *WhoAmW 91*
Fitall, Simon David 1956- *WhoWor 91*
Fitch, Alan *BioIn 16*
Fitch, Alva R. 1907-1989 *BioIn 16*
Fitch, Brian Thomas 1935- *WhoAm 90*
Fitch, Caribel Schuyler Sternbergh 1945- *WhoE 91*
Fitch, Charles Marden 1937- *WhoE 91, WhoWrEP 89*
Fitch, Clarke *AuBYP 90, MajTwCW*
Fitch, Coy Dean 1934- *WhoAm 90*
Fitch, David Robnett 1921- *WhoAm 90*
Fitch, Duane Douglas 1952- *WhoSSW 91*
Fitch, Florence Mary 1875-1959 *AuBYP 90*
Fitch, Frank Wesley 1929- *WhoAm 90*
Fitch, George Hopper 1909- *WhoAmA 91*
Fitch, Henry Delano 1799-1849 *BioIn 16*
Fitch, Howard Mercer 1909- *WhoAm 90, WhoSSW 91, WhoWor 91*
Fitch, Irene L. 1949- *WhoAmW 91*
Fitch, James Alexander 1931- *WhoAm 90*
Fitch, James Marston 1909- *WhoAm 90*
Fitch, John 1743-1798 *WorAlBi*
Fitch, John, IV *MajTwCW*
Fitch, Josefa Carrillo 1810-1893 *BioIn 16*
Fitch, Keith Leonard 1929- *St&PR 91*
Fitch, Linda Bauman 1947- *WhoAmW 91*
Fitch, Lyle Craig 1913- *WhoAm 90*
Fitch, Mary Killeen 1949- *WhoAmW 91, WhoEmL 91*
Fitch, Mary Virginia 1926- *St&PR 91*
Fitch, Morgan Lewis, Jr. 1922- *WhoAm 90*
Fitch, Nancy Elizabeth 1947- *WhoSSW 91*
Fitch, Rachel Farr 1933- *WhoAmW 91*
Fitch, Raymond William 1931- *WhoWor 91*
Fitch, Richard 1946- *St&PR 91*
Fitch, Rita LaVerne Pickens 1936- *WhoAmW 91*
Fitch, Robert McLellan 1928- *WhoAm 90*
Fitch, Sanford 1940- *St&PR 91*
Fitch, Stephen David *St&PR 91N*
Fitch, Steve 1949- *WhoAmA 91*
Fitch, Steven Joseph 1930- *WhoAm 90*
Fitch, Stona James 1931- *WhoAm 90*
Fitch, Timothy Michael 1952- *St&PR 91*
Fitch, Val L. 1923- *WorAlBi*
Fitch, Val Logsdon 1923- *WhoAm 90, WhoE 91, WhoWor 91*
Fitch, W. Chester 1916- *WhoAm 90*
Fitch, W.T.S. 1937- *St&PR 91*
Fitch, Walter Monroe 1929- *WhoAm 90*
Fitch, William C. 1934- *WhoAm 90, WhoE 91*
Fitch, William M. 1916- *St&PR 91*
Fitch, William Nelson 1941- *WhoWor 91*
Fitch, Worthie Gem Lenore 1934- *IntWWM 90*
Fitchen, Allen Nelson 1936- *WhoAm 90*
Fitchen, Douglas Beach 1936- *WhoAm 90*
Fitchen, Franklin Charles 1928- *WhoAm 90*
Fitcher, Manfred M *BiDrAPA 89*
Fitches, John Barrie 1934- *IntWWM 90*
Fitchet, Glenn R. 1947- *St&PR 91*
Fitchett, Vernon Harold 1927- *WhoWor 91*
Fite, Elwin 1913- *WhoAm 90*
Fite, Harvey 1903-1976 *BioIn 16, WhoAmA 91N*
Fite, Jack P. 1921- *St&PR 91*
Fite, James Robert 1925- *St&PR 91*
Fite, Kathleen Elizabeth *WhoAmW 91*
Fitelberg, Grzegorz 1879-1953 *PenDiMP*
Fiterman, Charles 1933- *BiDFrPL*
Fiterman, Dolly *WhoAmA 91*
Fites, Donald Vester 1934- *St&PR 91, WhoAm 90*
Fitgerald, Hugh, Captain *MajTwCW*
Fitilis, Theodore N. 1937- *WhoE 91*
Fitko, James 1952- *WhoEmL 91*
Fitler, Rachel *BioIn 16*
Fitt, Alfred Bradley 1923- *WhoAm 90*
Fitt, Benjamin Jones 1952- *WhoEmL 91*
Fitt, Mary 1897-1959 *TwCCr&M 91*
Fitt, Michael George 1931- *St&PR 91, WhoAm 90*
Fitterer, Richard Clarence 1946- *WhoEmL 91*
Fitteron, John J. 1941- *St&PR 91*
Fitteron, John Joseph 1941- *WhoAm 90*
Fitti, Charles John 1929- *WhoE 91*
Fitti, Regina M 1925- *BiDrAPA 89*
Fitti, Regina Mary 1925- *WhoE 91*
Fitting, Melinda Dell 1948- *WhoAmW 91*
Fitting-Gifford, Marjorie A. 1933- *WhoAmW 91*
Fittipaldi, Emerson *BioIn 16*
Fittipaldi, Frank Nicholas 1924- *WhoAm 90*
Fitton, David E. 1945- *St&PR 91*
Fitton, Harvey Nelson, Jr. *WhoSSW 91*
Fitton, James 1899-1982 *DcNaB 1981*
Fitton, Russell Patrick 1928- *St&PR 91*
Fitts, Bruce B. 1926- *St&PR 91*
Fitts, C. Austin 1950- *St&PR 91, WhoAm 90, WhoAmW 91, WhoE 91*
Fitts, Donald Dennis 1932- *WhoAm 90*
Fitts, Edward P., Jr. 1939- *St&PR 91*
Fitts, Elizabeth Anne 1951- *WhoAmW 91*
Fitts, Jay T. *St&PR 91*
Fitts, Jonathan Fairfield 1942- *WhoAm 90, WhoSSW 91*
Fitts, Martin Russell 1954- *WhoEmL 91*
Fitts, Robert Kenneth 1931- *St&PR 91*
Fitts, Thomas Allen 1966- *WhoEmL 91*
Fitz, Annette Elaine 1933- *WhoAm 90*
Fitz, David A. 1945- *St&PR 91*
Fitz, Guenther 1935- *WhoWor 91*
Fitz, Harold Carlton, Jr. 1926- *WhoE 91*
Fitz, Laurie J. 1955- *ODwPR 91*
Fitz, Raymond L. 1941- *WhoAm 90*
Fitzalan, Roger *TwCCr&M 91*
FitzAlan-Howard, Bennett-Thomas Henry R. 1955- *WhoE 91, WhoWor 91*
Fitzallan-Howard, R. F. *WhoWrEP 89*
Fitzenhagen, Wilhelm 1848-1890 *PenDiMP*
Fitzgeorge, Harold James 1924- *WhoAm 90*
Fitzgerald, Alan C. 1930- *St&PR 91*
Fitzgerald, Alice Louise 1874-1962 *BioIn 16*
Fitzgerald, Alton Leslie, Jr. 1954- *WhoSSW 91*
Fitzgerald, Astrid 1938- *WhoAmA 91*
FitzGerald, Barbara *ConAu 31NR*
Fitzgerald, Barbara Ann 1949- *BiDrAPA 89*
Fitzgerald, Barry 1888-1961 *WorAlBi*
Fitzgerald, Carol J. 1950- *WhoEmL 91*
FitzGerald, Cathleen 1932-1987 *BioIn 16*
Fitzgerald, Chicke W. 1957- *WhoAmW 91*
Fitzgerald, Clyde W. *BioIn 16*
Fitzgerald, Daniel J., III *BiDrAPA 89*
Fitzgerald, David 1813-1894 *DcCanB 12*
Fitzgerald, David Alan 1953- *St&PR 91*
Fitzgerald, Donal F. 1926- *St&PR 91*
Fitz Gerald, Ed 1924- *Ballpl 90*
Fitzgerald, Edith Jackson 1932- *WhoWor 91*
Fitzgerald, Edmund B. 1926- *St&PR 91*
Fitzgerald, Edmund Bacon 1926- *WhoAm 90, WhoWor 91*
Fitzgerald, Edmund J 1912-1989 *WhoAmA 91N*
FitzGerald, Edward 1809-1883 *BioIn 16*
Fitzgerald, Edward Earl 1919- *AuBYP 90, WhoAm 90*
Fitzgerald, Edwin Roger 1923- *WhoAm 90*
Fitzgerald, Ella *BioIn 16*
Fitzgerald, Ella 1918- *BioAmW, CurBio 90 [port], DrBlPA 90, IntWWM 90, OxCPMus, WhoAm 90, WhoAmW 91, WhoWor 91, WorAlBi*
Fitzgerald, Eric *TwCCr&M 91*
Fitzgerald, Ernest Abner 1925- *WhoAm 90, WhoSSW 91*
Fitzgerald, Eugene Francis 1925- *WhoAm 90*
Fitz-Gerald, F. Gregory 1941- *WhoAm 90*
Fitzgerald, F. Scott 1896-1940 *BioIn 16*
Fitzgerald, F Scott 1896-1940 *MajTwCW*
Fitzgerald, F. Scott 1896-1940 *ShSCr 6 [port], WorAlBi*
Fitzgerald, Frances *WhoWrEP 89*
FitzGerald, Frances 1940- *ConAu 32NR, WorAu 1980 [port]*
Fitzgerald, Francis Scott Key 1896-1940 *BioIn 16*
FitzGerald, Garret *BioIn 16*
FitzGerald, Garret 1926- *WhoWor 91*
Fitzgerald, Gerald 1932-1990 *BioIn 16, ConAu 131, NewYTBS 90*
Fitzgerald, Gerald Arthur 1899-1988 *BioIn 16*
Fitzgerald, Gerald Dennis 1939- *WhoAm 90*
Fitzgerald, Gerald Francis 1925- *WhoAm 90*
Fitzgerald, Gerald Richard 1936- *St&PR 91*
Fitzgerald, Geraldine 1913- *WhoAm 90, WorAlBi*
Fitzgerald, Geraldine 1914- *BioIn 16, ConTFT 8, NotWoAT*
Fitzgerald, Glenna Gibbs 1926- *WhoAmW 91*
Fitzgerald, Harold Kenneth 1921- *WhoE 91*
Fitzgerald, Harriet 1904- *WhoAmA 91*
Fitzgerald, J Edward 1923-1977 *WhoAmA 91N*
Fitzgerald, James Francis 1926- *WhoAm 90, WhoWor 91*
Fitzgerald, Janet Anne 1935- *WhoAm 90, WhoAmW 91*

Fitzgerald, Janet Marie 1943- *WhoAm 90*
Fitzgerald, Janice S. 1948- *WhoAmW 91, WhoEmL 91*
FitzGerald, Jay 1923- *WhoE 91*
Fitzgerald, Jerianne *ODwPR 91*
Fitzgerald, Jerry Dale 1959- *WhoEmL 91*
Fitzgerald, Jill Elaine 1952- *WhoEmL 91*
Fitzgerald, Joan Gallagher *ODwPR 91*
Fitzgerald, John 1863-1950 *WorAlBi*
Fitzgerald, John Bernard 1922- *St&PR 91*
Fitzgerald, John D. 1907- *AuBYP 90*
Fitzgerald, John D. 1907-1988 *BioIn 16*
Fitzgerald, John Edmund 1923- *WhoAm 90*
Fitzgerald, John Edward 1941- *WhoE 91*
FitzGerald, John Edward, III 1945- *WhoEmL 91*
Fitzgerald, John Joseph 1934- *St&PR 91*
Fitzgerald, John Robert 1939- *St&PR 91*
Fitzgerald, John Thomas, Jr. 1948- *WhoSSW 91*
Fitzgerald, John W. *WhoAm 90*
Fitzgerald, John Warner 1924- *WhoAm 90*
Fitzgerald, Jon Kevan 1945- *WhoEmL 91*
Fitz Gerald, Joseph A 1925- *BiDrAPA 89*
Fitzgerald, Joyce Isabel 1929- *WhoAmW 91*
Fitzgerald, Judith 1952- *ConAu 32NR*
Fitzgerald, Judith Klaswick 1948- *WhoAmW 91*
Fitzgerald, Kitty 1946- *ConAu 129*
Fitzgerald, Laurine Elizabeth 1930- *WhoAm 90*
Fitzgerald, Lee T. 1927- *St&PR 91*
Fitzgerald, Lou *BioIn 16*
Fitzgerald, Maria Kirsten *BiDrAPA 89*
Fitzgerald, Mark James 1906- *WhoAm 90*
Fitzgerald, Mary Catherine 1954- *WhoAmW 91*
Fitzgerald, Mary Elizabeth 1951- *WhoSSW 91*
Fitz-Gerald, Mary Jo Juneau 1954- *BiDrAPA 89*
Fitzgerald, Maura 1949- *ODwPR 91*
Fitzgerald, Maurice Patrick 1933- *St&PR 91*
Fitzgerald, Merni Ingrassia 1955- *BioIn 16*
Fitzgerald, Michael Anthony 1944- *WhoE 91*
Fitzgerald, Michael Francis 1946- *WhoWor 91*
Fitzgerald, Michael Garrett 1950- *WhoWor 91*
Fitzgerald, Michael Lee 1951- *WhoAm 90*
Fitzgerald, Michael Thomas 1948- *WhoEmL 91*
Fitzgerald, Mike 1960- *Ballpl 90*
Fitzgerald, Oscar P., IV 1943- *WhoAm 90, WhoE 91*
FitzGerald, Patricia Ann 1949- *WhoAmW 91*
Fitzgerald, Patrick T. 1945- *St&PR 91*
Fitzgerald, Patrick William 1953- *WhoWor 91*
Fitzgerald, Patrishya Anne 1952- *WhoEmL 91*
Fitzgerald, Paul J. *St&PR 91*
Fitzgerald, Pegeen *BioIn 16*
Fitzgerald, Pegeen 1910?-1989 *AnObit 1989*
Fitzgerald, Penelope *BioIn 16*
Fitzgerald, Penelope 1916- *ConLC 61 [port], FemiCLE*
Fitzgerald, Peter D. 1933- *St&PR 91*
Fitzgerald, Peter M. 1943- *St&PR 91*
Fitzgerald, R Vance *BiDrAPA 89*
Fitzgerald, Raymond Richard 1921- *WhoAm 90*
Fitzgerald, Richard Patrick 1950- *WhoEmL 91*
Fitzgerald, Robert 1910- *WhoWrEP 89*
Fitzgerald, Robert 1910-1985 *BioIn 16*
Fitzgerald, Robert Bernard 1911- *IntWWM 90*
Fitzgerald, Robert Drake 1932- *St&PR 91*
Fitzgerald, Robert Hannon, Jr. 1942- *WhoAm 90*
Fitzgerald, Robert Lee 1947- *WhoSSW 91*
Fitzgerald, Robert Maurice 1942- *St&PR 91, WhoAm 90*
Fitzgerald, Robert W. 1946- *St&PR 91*
Fitzgerald, Roger J. 1937- *WhoWrEP 89*
Fitz-Gerald, Roger Miller 1935- *WhoAm 90*
Fitzgerald, Rona Sonia 1951- *WhoE 91, WhoEmL 91*
Fitzgerald, Ronald Eugene 1946- *WhoE 91*
Fitzgerald, Ronald John 1941- *BiDrAPA 89*
Fitzgerald, Roy Gerald *BiDrAPA 89*
Fitzgerald, Sandra M 1955- *BiDrAPA 89*
Fitzgerald, Sandra Tucker 1955- *WhoAmW 91, WhoEmL 91*
Fitzgerald, Sheryl Cunningham 1955- *WhoAmW 91*
Fitzgerald, Stephen Patrick 1954- *WhoEmL 91*
Fitzgerald, Stuart *WhoWrEP 89*
Fitzgerald, Thomas Clifford 1939- *St&PR 91*
Fitzgerald, Thomas Francis Kelly 1959- *WhoE 91*
Fitzgerald, Thomas Rollins 1922- *WhoAm 90, WhoE 91*
Fitzgerald, Timothy Sean 1952- *WhoAm 90, WhoEmL 91*
Fitzgerald, Timothy Wall 1963- *WhoSSW 91*
Fitzgerald, Vincent James 1950- *WhoEmL 91*
Fitzgerald, Walter George 1936- *WhoE 91*
Fitzgerald, Warren Franklin 1955- *WhoEmL 91*
Fitzgerald, William Allingham 1937- *St&PR 91, WhoAm 90*
Fitzgerald, William F. 1908- *St&PR 91*
Fitzgerald, William Francis 1908- *WhoAm 90*
Fitzgerald, William H. *NewAgE 90*
Fitzgerald, William H. 1943- *St&PR 91*
Fitz Gerald, William Henry Gerald 1909- *WhoAm 90, WhoE 91*
Fitzgerald, William T. 1926- *WhoAm 90*
Fitzgerald, William Thomas 1926- *St&PR 91*
Fitzgerald, Zelda 1900-1948 *FemiCLE*
Fitzgerald, Zelda Sayre 1900-1948 *BioAmW*
Fitz Gerald-Bush, Frank Shepard 1925- *WhoWor 91*
Fitzgerald-Reddy, Kathleen April 1955- *WhoAmW 91*
FitzGibbon, Constantine 1919-1983 *DcNaB 1981*
Fitzgibbon, Donna Jean 1968- *WhoEmL 91*
FitzGibbon, Jane *WhoAmW 91*
Fitzgibbon, John Francis 1923- *WhoAm 90*
Fitzgibbon, John H. 1816?-1882 *WhNaAH*
Fitz Gibbon, L.J. 1913- *St&PR 91*
Fitzgibbon, Pierre 1954- *St&PR 91*
FitzGibbon, Scott Thomas 1945- *WhoEmL 91*
Fitzgibbon, Walter J., Jr. 1933- *St&PR 91*
Fitzgibbon, William Edward, III 1945- *WhoSSW 91*
Fitzgibbons, Ann 1951- *WhoEmL 91*
Fitzgibbons, David J. 1906-1988 *BioIn 16*
Fitzgibbons, David Lynn 1948- *St&PR 91*
Fitzgibbons, Donald R. 1951- *St&PR 91*
FitzGibbons, James Joseph 1958- *WhoEmL 91*
Fitzgibbons, James M. *WhoAm 90, WhoE 91*
Fitzgibbons, James M. 1934- *St&PR 91*
Fitzgibbons, John Murray 1950- *WhoEmL 91*
Fitzgibbons, Mark Francis 1948- *WhoSSW 91*
Fitzgibbons, Richard Peter *BiDrAPA 89*
Fitzhardinge, Joan Margaret 1912- *AuBYP 90*
Fitzharris, Timothy P. 1944- *WhoAm 90, WhoSSW 91*
Fitzhenry, Robert Irvine 1918- *WhoAm 90*
FitzHerbert, Margaret 1942-1986 *ConAu 130*
Fitzhugh, David Newby 1950- *WhoSSW 91*
Fitzhugh, Louise 1928-1974 *AuBYP 90*
Fitzhugh, Lynne Dennison 1942- *WhoE 91*
Fitzhugh, William Wyvill, Jr. 1914- *WhoAm 90, WhoE 91*
Fitz-James, Anna Maria *BiDWomA*
Fitzlar, Martin von *EncO&P 3*
Fitzmaurice, Gerald Gray 1901-1982 *DcNaB 1981*
Fitzmaurice, Laurence Dorset 1938- *WhoE 91*
Fitzmaurice, Robert John 1937- *St&PR 91*
Fitzmorris, Al 1946- *Ballpl 90*
Fitzmorris, Thomas Gerard 1951- *WhoSSW 91*
Fitzner, Kathryn Ethridge 1953- *WhoSSW 91*
Fitzpatrick, Barry Lane 1950- *WhoEmL 91*
Fitzpatrick, Blanche *WhoE 91*
Fitzpatrick, Carol Edna 1942- *St&PR 91*
Fitzpatrick, Charles R. 1938- *St&PR 91*
Fitzpatrick, Dana Gregory 1930- *St&PR 91*
Fitzpatrick, Daniel Robert 1891-1969 *BioIn 16*
Fitzpatrick, Daniel William 1947- *WhoEmL 91*
Fitzpatrick, Darleen A. 1941- *WhoAmW 91*
Fitzpatrick, David J. 1926- *St&PR 91*
Fitzpatrick, Denise Diane 1952- *WhoSSW 91*
Fitzpatrick, Donna Pearl 1930- *WhoSSW 91*
Fitzpatrick, Duross 1934- *WhoAm 90, WhoSSW 91*
Fitzpatrick, Elizabeth Floridis 1954- *WhoAmW 91*
Fitzpatrick, Ellen 1957- *WhoAmW 91*
FitzPatrick, Francis James 1916- *WhoE 91, WhoWor 91*
Fitzpatrick, Frank J., Jr. 1928- *St&PR 91*
Fitzpatrick, Frank P. 1934- *St&PR 91*
Fitzpatrick, Franklin Davidson 1952- *WhoSSW 91*
Fitzpatrick, George Austin 1934- *St&PR 91*
Fitzpatrick, Gerard J. 1928- *St&PR 91*
Fitzpatrick, Gilbert Lawrence 1930- *St&PR 91, WhoAm 90, WhoE 91*
Fitzpatrick, Gladys Eve *WhoAm 90*
Fitzpatrick, Harold Francis 1947- *WhoE 91, WhoEmL 91, WhoWor 91*
Fitzpatrick, James Charles 1940- *WhoE 91*
Fitzpatrick, James Daniel 1938- *St&PR 91*
Fitzpatrick, James Franklin 1933- *WhoAm 90*
Fitzpatrick, James G. 1931- *St&PR 91*
Fitzpatrick, James Ward, Jr. 1921- *WhoSSW 91*
Fitzpatrick, Jay W. 1941- *St&PR 91*
Fitzpatrick, Jeri Eileen *BiDrAPA 89*
Fitzpatrick, Joe Raymond, Jr. 1944- *WhoSSW 91*
Fitzpatrick, John Francis 1956- *WhoE 91*
Fitzpatrick, John Gregory 1953- *WhoEmL 91*
Fitzpatrick, John Henry 1956- *WhoAm 90*
Fitzpatrick, John J. 1918- *WhoAm 90, WhoSSW 91*
Fitzpatrick, John Malcolm 1924- *St&PR 91, WhoAm 90*
Fitzpatrick, John P. 1929- *ODwPR 91*
Fitzpatrick, John Patrick 1945- *WhoWor 91*
Fitzpatrick, Joseph Cyril 1909- *WhoAmA 91*
Fitzpatrick, Joseph Edward 1931- *WhoAm 90*
Fitzpatrick, Joseph William 1941- *St&PR 91*
Fitzpatrick, Karen *BiDrAPA 89*
Fitzpatrick, Martin Francis, Jr. 1952- *WhoAm 90*
Fitzpatrick, Michael Clifford 1953- *St&PR 91*
Fitzpatrick, Michael J. 1948- *St&PR 91*
Fitzpatrick, Morgan Cassius 1868-1908 *AmLegL*
Fitzpatrick, Paul J. *BioIn 16*
Fitzpatrick, Philip A. 1946- *St&PR 91*
Fitzpatrick, Richard M. 1953- *WhoAm 90*
Fitzpatrick, Robert 1945- *IntWWM 90*
Fitzpatrick, Robert F. 1931- *St&PR 91*
Fitzpatrick, Robert J. *ODwPR 91*
Fitzpatrick, Robert John 1940- *WhoAm 90*
Fitzpatrick, Sean Kevin 1941- *WhoAm 90, WhoWor 91*
Fitzpatrick, Stephen T. 1947- *St&PR 91*
Fitzpatrick, Thomas 1799?-1854 *WhNaAH*
Fitzpatrick, Thomas Bernard 1919- *WhoAm 90*
Fitzpatrick, Thomas Frank *BiDrAPA 89*
Fitzpatrick, Thomas Mark 1951- *WhoAm 90*
Fitzpatrick, Thomas Raymond 1930- *WhoWor 91*
Fitzpatrick, Tracy Elizabeth 1954- *WhoAmW 91*
Fitzpatrick, Vincent 1950- *ConAu 131*
Fitzpatrick, William Joseph 1941- *St&PR 91*
Fitzpatrick, William N 1920- *BiDrAPA 89*
Fitzpatrick-Davis, Judith 1941- *WhoAmW 91*
Fitz-Randolph, Jane *BioIn 16*
Fitzroy, Nancy deLoye 1927- *WhoAm 90*
Fitzroy, Robert 1805-1865 *BioIn 16*
Fitzsimmons, Edward J. 1932- *St&PR 91*
Fitzsimmons, Freddie 1901-1979 *Ballpl 90*
Fitzsimmons, James 1919-1985 *BioIn 16*
Fitzsimmons, James Albert 1937- *WhoAm 90*
Fitzsimmons, James Joseph 1908- *WhoAmA 91N*
Fitzsimmons, James R.B. 1939- *St&PR 91*
Fitzsimmons, John D. 1930- *St&PR 91*
Fitzsimmons, Joseph J. *St&PR 91*
Fitzsimmons, Joseph John 1934- *WhoAm 90*
Fitzsimmons, Keith Roberts 1952- *WhoEmL 91*
Fitzsimmons, Kevin Michael 1956- *WhoEmL 91*
Fitzsimmons, Lowell Cotton 1931- *WhoAm 90*
Fitzsimmons, Maureen *ConTFT 8*
Fitzsimmons, Michael P. 1949- *ConAu 129*
Fitzsimmons, Murray Charles 1932- *St&PR 91, WhoAm 90*
Fitzsimmons, Patrick Joseph *BiDrAPA 89*
Fitzsimmons, Richard *ODwPR 91*
FitzSimmons, Richard M. 1924- *WhoAm 90*
Fitzsimmons, Robert *AuBYP 90*
Fitzsimmons, Robert James 1940- *St&PR 91*
Fitzsimmons, Robert James 1946- *St&PR 91*
Fitzsimmons, Sophie Sonia 1943- *WhoAmW 91*
Fitzsimmons, Thomas 1926- *WhoWrEP 89*
Fitzsimonds, Carol Strause 1951- *WhoAmA 91*
Fitzsimonds, Roger Leon 1938- *St&PR 91, WhoAm 90*
Fitzsimons, Eleanor *ODwPR 91, WhoE 91*
Fitzsimons, Frederick William 1875- *EncO&P 3*
Fitzsimons, George K. 1928- *WhoAm 90*
Fitzsimons, John H. 1948- *St&PR 91*
Fitzsimons, John M. 1948- *St&PR 91*
Fitzsimons, Marjorie Fraser 1932- *WhoSSW 91*
FitzSimons, Sharon Russell 1945- *WhoAmW 91, WhoEmL 91*
Fitzsimons, Thomas 1741-1811 *BioIn 16*
Fitzsteward, Farmer *WhoWrEP 89*
Fitzwater, Bonnie 1923- *WhoAm 90*
Fitzwater, Marlin *BioIn 16*
Fitzwater, Marlin 1942- *WhoAm 90*
Fitzwater, Ronald Lee 1953- *St&PR 91*
Fitzwater, Sidney Allen 1953- *WhoAm 90*
Fitzwater-Heumann, Kathryn Anne 1951- *WhoAmW 91*
Fitzwilliam Quartet *PenDiMP*
Fiumara, Nicholas John 1912- *WhoE 91*
Fiumefreddo, Charles A. 1933- *St&PR 91, WhoAm 90*
Fiur, Henry M. *ODwPR 91*
Fiur, Henry Michael 1939- *St&PR 91*
Fiur, Merton 1932- *ODwPR 91*
Fiuzat, Abbas Ali 1947- *WhoSSW 91*
Fiveash, Don Pat 1956- *St&PR 91*
Fix, Alfred Harold 1930- *WhoAm 90*
Fix, James Douglas 1931- *WhoAm 90*
Fix, John Neilson 1937- *WhoAm 90*
Fix, John Robert 1934- *WhoAmA 91*
Fix, Meyer 1906- *WhoE 91*
Fix, Michael L. 1949- *St&PR 91*
Fix, Philippe *AuBYP 90*
Fix, Wilbur James 1927- *St&PR 91, WhoAm 90*
Fix-Romlow, Jeanne Kay 1947- *WhoAmW 91*
Fixell, Lester G. 1919- *WhoE 91*
Fixler, Allison Shira 1965- *WhoE 91*
Fixman, Ben 1925- *St&PR 91*
Fixman, Laura Beth *BiDrAPA 89*
Fixman, Marshall 1930- *WhoAm 90*
Fizdale, Richard *WhoAm 90*
Fizdale, Robert *PenDiMP*
Fjeldgaard, Kjeld 1946- *WhoEmL 91, WhoWor 91*
Fjeldstad, Oivin 1903- *PenDiMP*
Fjelstad, Paul 1954- *WhoEmL 91*
Fjelstad, Ralph Sylvester 1915- *WhoAm 90*
Fjord, Hilliard James 1924- *St&PR 91*
Flacco, Elaine Germano 1959- *WhoE 91*
Flaccus, Edward 1921- *WhoAm 90*
Flach, Frederic F 1927- *BiDrAPA 89*
Flach, Frederic Francis 1927- *WhoE 91*
Flach, Victor H. 1929- *WhoAm 90, WhoAmA 91*
Flacilla, Empress *BioIn 16*
Flack, Audrey *BioIn 16*
Flack, Audrey 1931- *BiDWomA*
Flack, Audrey L 1931- *WhoAmA 91*
Flack, David Bruce 1954- *St&PR 91*
Flack, Denise Ann 1966- *WhoEmL 91*
Flack, Dora D 1919- *WhoWrEP 89*
Flack, Duane Elliott 1935- *St&PR 91*
Flack, George R. 1949- *St&PR 91*
Flack, Harold E., II 1958- *St&PR 91*
Flack, James Monroe 1913-1989 *BioIn 16*
Flack, James Norton *BiDrAPA 89*
Flack, Jerry D 1943- *ConAu 131*
Flack, Joe Fenley 1921- *WhoAm 90*
Flack, Marjorie 1897-1958 *AuBYP 90*
Flack, Max 1890-1975 *Ballpl 90*
Flack, Michael Alan 1946- *St&PR 91*
Flack, Roberta *BioIn 16*
Flack, Roberta 1939- *EncPR&S 89, OxCPMus, WhoAm 90, WhoAmW 91, WorAlBi*
Flack, Roberta 1940- *ConMus 5 [port], DrBlPA 90*
Fladeland, Betty 1919- *WhoAm 90*
Flader, William W. 1948- *St&PR 91*
Flading, John Joseph 1960- *WhoSSW 91*
Fladmark, Lars 1935- *St&PR 91*
Fladung, Richard Denis 1953- *WhoEmL 91*
Flaer, Lorraine Florence 1935- *WhoAmW 91*
Flagan, Richard Charles 1947- *WhoAm 90, WhoEmL 91*
Flagel, Laverne Wayne 1934- *St&PR 91*
Flagel, Steven Alan 1950- *BiDrAPA 89*
Flagello, Ezio 1931- *PenDiMP*
Flagello, Ezio 1933- *IntWWM 90*
Flagello, Ezio Domenico 1932- *WhoAm 90*

Flagello, Nicolas 1928- *IntWWM 90*
Flagg, E. Alma Williams 1918- *WhoE 91, WhoWor 91*
Flagg, George V. 1941- *WhoAm 90*
Flagg, James Montgomery 1877-1960 *WhoAmA 91N*
Flagg, Jeanne Bodin 1925- *WhoAm 90*
Flagg, Josiah 1737-1794 *BioIn 16*
Flagg, Josiah 1737-1795? *EncCRAm*
Flagg, Laurie Anne 1963- *WhoE 91*
Flagg, Norman Lee 1932- *WhoWor 91*
Flagg, Raymond Osbourn 1933- *St&PR 91, WhoSSW 91*
Flagg, Robert Farrington 1924- *WhoSSW 91*
Flagg, Ronald Simon 1953- *WhoEmL 91*
Flagg, Vivian Annette 1960- *WhoSSW 91*
Flagle, Charles Denhard 1919- *WhoAm 90*
Flagler, Sheri Lee 1950- *WhoEmL 91*
Flagstad, Kirsten 1895-1962 *PenDiMP, WorAlBi*
Flagstead, Ira 1893-1940 *Ballpl 90*
Flaharty, Robert Richard 1948- *WhoEmL 91*
Flaherty, Daniel Leo 1929- *WhoAm 90*
Flaherty, David Thomas, Jr. 1953- *WhoEmL 91, WhoSSW 91, WhoWor 91*
Flaherty, Doug 1939- *WhoWrEP 89*
Flaherty, Dundas I. 1934- *St&PR 91*
Flaherty, Francis Xavier 1947- *WhoE 91*
Flaherty, G.S. 1938- *St&PR 91*
Flaherty, Gerald Stanley 1938- *WhoAm 90*
Flaherty, Gerlinde M. 1942- *WhoAmW 91*
Flaherty, Heidi Anne-Marie 1962- *WhoAmW 91*
Flaherty, Hugh E. 1931- *St&PR 91*
Flaherty, James Grant 1958- *WhoEmL 91*
Flaherty, James Robert 1946- *St&PR 91*
Flaherty, John Joseph 1932- *St&PR 91, WhoAm 90*
Flaherty, John P., Jr. 1931- *WhoAm 90, WhoE 91, WhoWor 91*
Flaherty, John Preston, Jr. 1942- *St&PR 91*
Flaherty, Joseph Allen 1946- *BiDrAPA 89*
Flaherty, Lee F. *St&PR 91*
Flaherty, Liz *BioIn 16*
Flaherty, Lois Talbot *BiDrAPA 89*
Flaherty, Marcia Kay 1951- *WhoEmL 91*
Flaherty, Marie Gloria *IntWWM 90*
Flaherty, Marilyn Elizabeth 1932- *WhoE 91*
Flaherty, Mary Pat 1955- *ConAu 132*
Flaherty, Michael Paul 1945- *WhoAm 90*
Flaherty, Pamela Potter 1944- *St&PR 91*
Flaherty, Patsy 1876-1968 *Ballpl 90*
Flaherty, Red 1918- *Ballpl 90*
Flaherty, Richard Alan 1952- *WhoEmL 91*
Flaherty, Robert Joseph 1884-1951 *AuBYP 90, BioIn 16*
Flaherty, Roberta D. 1947- *WhoAmW 91*
Flaherty, Tammy S. 1963- *St&PR 91*
Flaherty, Thomas J. 1924- *St&PR 91*
Flaherty, Tina S. *WhoAm 90, WhoAmW 91*
Flaherty, Tina Santi *ODwPR 91*
Flaherty, Tracy Ann 1958- *WhoEmL 91*
Flaherty, Vincent X. 1912-1977 *Ballpl 90*
Flaherty, William Edward 1933- *St&PR 91*
Flahiff, George Bernard 1905- *WhoWor 91*
Flaig, Paul Edward 1949- *WhoE 91, WhoEmL 91*
Flajser, Steven H. 1943- *St&PR 91*
Flake, David J. 1955- *St&PR 91*
Flake, Floyd Harold 1945- *BlkAmsC [port], WhoAm 90, WhoE 91*
Flake, John Joel 1948- *WhoEmL 91*
Flake, Joseph Anthony 1957- *WhoSSW 91*
Flake, L. Dickson 1938- *WhoSSW 91*
Flake, Robert A. 1929- *St&PR 91*
Flake, William Harold 1932- *St&PR 91*
Flakoll, Thomas Jerome 1944- *St&PR 91*
Flaksman, Michael 1946- *IntWWM 90*
Flam, Jack D 1940- *WhoAmA 91*
Flamand, Jean-Marie 1944- *WhoWor 91*
Flamberg, Daniel S. 1953- *ODwPR 91*
Flamberg, Morton 1920- *St&PR 91*
Flamberg, Richard A *BiDrAPA 89*
Flamel, Nicholas 1330?-1418 *EncO&P 3*
Flamm, Donald 1899- *WhoE 91, WhoWor 91*
Flamm, Donald L. 1943- *St&PR 91*
Flamm, Gerald H *BiDrAPA 89*
Flamman, Han 1934- *WhoWor 91*
Flammang, Donna M. 1951- *St&PR 91*
Flammang, Susann 1950- *WhoEmL 91*
Flammarion, Camille 1842-1925 *EncO&P 3*
Flammarion, Nicolas Camille 1842-1925 *EncPaPR 91*
Flamme, Arthur C. *St&PR 91*
Flammer, Josef 1948- *WhoWor 91*
Flammonde, Paris *WhoWrEP 89*
Flamson, Richard Joseph, III 1929- *St&PR 91, WhoAm 90, WhoWor 91*
Flamsteed, John 1646-1719 *WorAlBi*
Flanagan and Allen *OxCPMus*
Flanagan, Alvin George 1915- *WhoAm 90*
Flanagan, Anita Marie 1940- *WhoAmW 91, WhoE 91*
Flanagan, Barbara *WhoAm 90*
Flanagan, Barry 1941- *WhoAmA 91*
Flanagan, Bernice Mary 1958- *WhoE 91, WhoEmL 91*
Flanagan, Bob *BioIn 16*
Flanagan, Bud 1896-1968 *OxCPMus*
Flanagan, Charles Allen 1931- *WhoWor 91*
Flanagan, Christie Stephen 1938- *WhoAm 90*
Flanagan, Christopher Sean 1956- *St&PR 91*
Flanagan, Clyde H, Jr. 1939- *BiDrAPA 89*
Flanagan, Daniel George 1952- *St&PR 91*
Flanagan, David Francis *BiDrAPA 89*
Flanagan, David J. 1924- *St&PR 91*
Flanagan, David T. 1947- *St&PR 91*
Flanagan, Deborah Mary 1956- *WhoAmW 91*
Flanagan, Dennis 1919- *WhoAm 90*
Flanagan, Dennis Patrick 1948- *St&PR 91*
Flanagan, E Michael 1948- *WhoAmA 91*
Flanagan, Edward Charles 1927- *St&PR 91*
Flanagan, Edward J. 1886-1948 *WorAlBi*
Flanagan, Edward Michael, Jr. 1921- *WhoAm 90*
Flanagan, Edwin Wallace 1923- *WhoAm 90*
Flanagan, Eugene J.T. 1923- *St&PR 91*
Flanagan, Eugene John Thomas 1923- *WhoAm 90*
Flanagan, Fionnula 1941- *ConTFT 8*
Flanagan, Francis Dennis 1912- *WhoAm 90*
Flanagan, Gail Claire 1952- *WhoAmW 91*
Flanagan, Geraldine Lux *AuBYP 90*
Flanagan, Hallie 1890-1969 *BioAmW, BioIn 16, NotWoAT*
Flanagan, Harold Thomas, Jr. 1953- *WhoEmL 91*
Flanagan, James Henry, Jr. 1934- *WhoWor 91*
Flanagan, James Loton *WhoAm 90*
Flanagan, John Clemans 1906- *WhoAm 90, WhoWor 91*
Flanagan, John F 1898-1952 *WhoAmA 91N*
Flanagan, John Fortner 1944- *St&PR 91*
Flanagan, John Terrence 1929- *St&PR 91*
Flanagan, John Theodore 1906- *WhoAm 90*
Flanagan, Joseph Charles 1938- *WhoAm 90*
Flanagan, Joseph P. 1932- *St&PR 91*
Flanagan, Joseph Patrick 1938- *WhoAm 90, WhoWor 91*
Flanagan, Joseph Patrick, Jr. 1924- *WhoAm 90*
Flanagan, Judith Ann 1950- *WhoAmW 91*
Flanagan, Kathleen M. *ODwPR 91*
Flanagan, Kathy Christine *BiDrAPA 89*
Flanagan, Kathy Marie 1952- *WhoAmW 91*
Flanagan, Kenneth Jack 1940- *St&PR 91*
Flanagan, Lillian Lee Ann 1933- *WhoAmW 91*
Flanagan, Martha Lang 1942- *St&PR 91, WhoAm 90*
Flanagan, Michael 1943- *WhoAmA 91*
Flanagan, Michael Charles 1954- *WhoSSW 91*
Flanagan, Michael Joseph 1953- *WhoE 91*
Flanagan, Mike 1951- *Ballpl 90*
Flanagan, Natalie Smith 1913- *WhoAmW 91*
Flanagan, Paulette B. 1949- *St&PR 91*
Flanagan, Sean Patrick *BioIn 16*
Flanagan, Therese Ann 1955- *WhoAmW 91*
Flanagan, Thomas 1923- *MajTwCW, WorAu 1980 [port]*
Flanagan, Thomas A 1941- *BiDrAPA 89*
Flanagan, Van Kent 1945- *WhoAm 90*
Flanagan, Virginia *BiDrAPA 89*
Flanagan, Wayne 1955- *WhoE 91*
Flanagan, William B. 1924- *St&PR 91*
Flanagan, William Stanley, Jr. 1947- *WhoEmL 91*
Flanagan-Herstek, Katherine M. 1951- *WhoAmW 91, WhoE 91*
Flanagin, Harris 1817-1874 *BioIn 16*
Flanagin, Michele Diane 1959- *WhoEmL 91*
Flanagin, Neil 1930- *WhoAm 90*
Flanary, James Lee 1955- *WhoEmL 91*
Flanders, Allen F. 1945- *St&PR 91*
Flanders, Ann Elisabeth 1942- *WhoE 91*
Flanders, Charles 1907-1973 *EncACom*
Flanders, Deanne Bowman 1946- *WhoAmW 91*
Flanders, Donald H. 1924- *St&PR 91*
Flanders, Donald Hargis 1924- *WhoWor 91*
Flanders, Dudley Kennedy 1952- *St&PR 91*
Flanders, Dwight Prescott 1909- *WhoAm 90, WhoWor 91*
Flanders, Ed 1934- *WorAlBi*
Flanders, George James 1960- *WhoEmL 91*
Flanders, Helen Driver 1947- *WhoAmW 91*
Flanders, Henry Jackson, Jr. 1921- *WhoAm 90, WhoSSW 91, WhoWor 91*
Flanders, Howard Barrett, Jr. 1935- *St&PR 91*
Flanders, Michael 1922-1975 *AuBYP 90, OxCPMus*
Flanders, Peggy Sperber 1942- *WhoE 91*
Flanders, Stephen Lawrence 1942- *WhoAm 90*
Flanders, Walter E *EncABHB 4*
Flandin, Pierre-Etienne 1889-1958 *BiDFrPL*
Flandro, Paul Woods 1921- *St&PR 91*
Flanery, Gail 1947- *WhoAmA 91*
Flanigan, Jeanne Marie 1946- *WhoAmW 91*
Flanigan, John Pershing 1919- *St&PR 91*
Flanigan, Michael Cletus 1936- *WhoSSW 91*
Flanigan, Peter Magnus 1923- *St&PR 91, WhoAm 90*
Flanigan, Pierce John, III 1942- *St&PR 91*
Flanigan, Robert Daniel, Jr. 1949- *WhoEmL 91*
Flanigan, Susan Wilson 1946- *WhoAmW 91*
Flanigan, Vicki Karen 1954- *WhoAm 90*
Flanigan, William Joseph 1930- *WhoAm 90*
Flaniken, Forrest W. 1954- *St&PR 91*
Flannagan, Benjamin Collins, IV 1927- *WhoE 91*
Flannelly, Stephen John 1962- *WhoEmL 91*
Flanner, Janet 1892-1978 *BioIn 16, FemiCLE, WorAlBi*
Flanner, Joseph *Ballpl 90*
Flannery, Anne Catherine 1951- *WhoAmW 91*
Flannery, Caroline Olson 1942- *WhoAmW 91*
Flannery, Catherine Jean 1957- *BiDrAPA 89*
Flannery, Frank Travers 1947- *WhoE 91*
Flannery, Harry Audley 1947- *WhoEmL 91*
Flannery, John Charles 1932- *BiDrAPA 89*
Flannery, John Philip, II 1946- *WhoE 91*
Flannery, Joseph Patrick 1932- *St&PR 91, WhoAm 90*
Flannery, Rebecca R. 1952- *IntWWM 90*
Flannery, Robert Gene 1924- *St&PR 91*
Flannery, Robert James 1945- *St&PR 91*
Flannery, Thomas 1919- *WhoAmA 91*
Flannery, Tim *BioIn 16*
Flannery, Tim 1957- *Ballpl 90*
Flannery, Wilbur Eugene 1907- *WhoE 91, WhoWor 91*
Flannery, William Jackson, Jr. 1944- *WhoSSW 91*
Flannigan, Edward J. 1938- *St&PR 91*
Flannigan, James Patrick 1934- *WhoSSW 91*
Flannigan, Timothy E. 1948- *St&PR 91*
Flanningan, Wallace Benjamin *BiDrAPA 89*
Flansburg, James Sherman 1932- *WhoAm 90*
Flansburg, Leonard Doyce 1931- *WhoSSW 91*
Flansburg, Margaret Ann 1936- *WhoSSW 91*
Flansburgh, Earl Robert 1931- *WhoAm 90, WhoE 91, WhoWor 91*
Flansburgh, John *BioIn 16*
Flanzer, Robert Stephen 1934- *WhoE 91*
Flaschen, Evan Daniel 1957- *WhoE 91, WhoEmL 91, WhoWor 91*
Flaschen, Steward Samuel 1926- *St&PR 91, WhoAm 90, WhoWor 91*
Flashman, Alberta Rose 1934- *BiDrAPA 89*
Flashnick, Bruce Lloyd 1952- *WhoSSW 91*
Flaskamp, William Davidson 1924- *WhoAm 90*
Flaspoehler, Edward Paul, Jr. 1944- *WhoSSW 91*
Flaster, Karl West 1905-1965 *BioIn 16*
Flat Mouth 1774-1860? *WhNaAH*
Flatau, Carl R. 1924- *WhoE 91*
Flaten, Alfred N. 1934- *St&PR 91*
Flaten, Gunnar Arne 1956- *WhoWor 91*
Flaten, Steven James 1954- *WhoEmL 91*
Flathers, Judy Marlene 1952- *IntWWM 90*
Flathman, Richard Earl 1934- *WhoAm 90*
Flatley, Guy 1934- *WhoAm 90*
Flato, Franklin 1911- *St&PR 91*
Flato, Jud B. 1940- *St&PR 91, WhoE 91*
Flatow, Jeffrey H 1943- *BiDrAPA 89*
Flatow, Leslie 1954- *BiDrAPA 89*
Flatt And Scruggs *WhoNeCM C [port]*
Flatt, Adrian Ede 1921- *WhoAm 90*
Flatt, Ernest Orville 1918- *WhoAm 90*
Flatt, J. Ian *St&PR 91*
Flatt, Joanie L. 1948- *ODwPR 91*
Flatt, Lester 1914-1979 *OxCPMus, WorAlBi*
Flatt, Terry L. *IntWWM 90*
Flatt, William Perry 1931- *WhoAm 90, WhoSSW 91*
Flatte, Stanley Martin 1940- *WhoAm 90*
Flatten, Jeffrey Allan 1951- *WhoEmL 91*
Flattery, David Kevin 1960- *St&PR 91*
Flattery, Thomas Long 1922- *WhoAm 90, WhoWor 91*
Flattmann, Alan Raymond 1946- *WhoAmA 91, WhoSSW 91*
Flatz, Gebhard 1925- *WhoWor 91*
Flaubert, Gustave 1821-1880 *BioIn 16, WorAlBi*
Flaum, Joel Martin 1936- *WhoAm 90*
Flaum, Marshall Allen *WhoAm 90*
Flaum, Michael A 1953- *BiDrAPA 89*
Flaute, Richard Thomas 1935- *St&PR 91*
Flavell, John Hurley 1928- *WhoAm 90*
Flavin, Dan 1933- *WhoAmA 91*
Flavin, Daniel Kevin 1955- *BiDrAPA 89*
Flavin, John Joseph, Jr. 1956- *WhoE 91*
Flavin, Patrick Brian 1947- *St&PR 91*
Flavin, Richard Patrick 1936- *WhoE 91*
Flavin, Sonja 1936- *WhoAmA 91*
Flavio, John J. 1947- *St&PR 91*
Flax, Florence Roselin 1936- *WhoSSW 91*
Flax, Harold L. 1927- *St&PR 91*
Flax, James William 1948- *BiDrAPA 89*
Flax, Larry S. *BioIn 16*
Flax, Martin Howard 1928- *WhoAm 90*
Flax, Robert J. 1949- *St&PR 91*
Flax, Robert Leonard 1953- *WhoEmL 91*
Flax, Samuel Allan 1956- *WhoEmL 91*
Flax, Walter 1896-1982 *MusmAFA*
Flaxenburg, Gary Michael *BiDrAPA 89*
Flaxman, John 1755-1826 *BioIn 16, IntDcAA 90, PenDiDA 89*
Flay, Brian R. 1947- *WhoEmL 91*
Flayman, Jodi Beth 1966- *WhoSSW 91*
Flaysakier, J. Daniel 1951- *WhoWor 91*
Fleagle, John Gwynn 1948- *WhoE 91*
Fleagle, Robert Guthrie 1918- *WhoAm 90*
Flechner, Roberta Fay 1949- *WhoAmW 91, WhoEmL 91*
Flechner, Stuart Marc 1950- *WhoAm 90*
Flechtenmacher, Maria 1838-1888 *EncCoWW*
Flechtheim, Alfred 1878-1937 *BioIn 16*
Flechtner, Richard O. 1945- *St&PR 91*
Fleck, Alexander 1889-1968 *WorAlBi*
Fleck, Bela *BioIn 16*
Fleck, Betty *ConAu 31NR*
Fleck, Charles L. 1952- *St&PR 91*
Fleck, Elmer Earl 1926- *WhoAm 90*
Fleck, Florian Hans 1924- *WhoWor 91*
Fleck, George Morrison 1934- *WhoAm 90*
Fleck, Gustav Peter 1909- *WhoAm 90*
Fleck, Harold Ulrich 1935- *St&PR 91*
Fleck, Henry 1911-1990 *BioIn 16*
Fleck, Joanne Elizabeth Tuhkanen 1939- *WhoAmW 91*
Fleck, Mariann Bernice 1922- *WhoAmW 91*
Fleck, Paul Duncan 1934- *WhoAm 90, WhoAmA 91*
Fleck, Raymond Anthony, Jr. 1927- *WhoAm 90*
Fleck, Richard D. 1930- *St&PR 91*
Fleck, Richard Francis 1937- *WhoWrEP 89*
Fleck, Robert John 1947- *St&PR 91*
Fleck, Stephen 1912- *BiDrAPA 89, WhoE 91, WhoWor 91*
Fleck, Zachary Thomas 1961- *WhoEmL 91*
Fleckenstein, Opal R 1911- *WhoAmA 91*
Fleckenstein, Randall Craig 1952- *WhoWor 91*
Fleckenstein, William O. 1925- *WhoAm 90*
Flecker, Maurice Nathan 1940- *WhoAmA 91*
Fleckhaus, Willy 1925- *ConDes 90*
Fleckhaus, Willy 1925-1983 *BioIn 16*
Fleckles, Charles S *BiDrAPA 89*
Fledderjohn, Karl Ross 1935- *St&PR 91, WhoAm 90*
Fleddermann, Stephen Roy 1956- *WhoEmL 91*
Fleegal, Steven Arthur 1954- *WhoSSW 91*
Fleeger, Darrell Francis 1932- *WhoSSW 91*
Fleeger, Ron 1955- *WhoE 91, WhoEmL 91*
Fleeman, Douglas B. 1946- *WhoSSW 91*
Fleener, A.D. 1930- *St&PR 91*
Fleenor, James Lee 1942- *WhoE 91*
Fleenor, Michael Edward 1953- *WhoEmL 91*
Fleer, Marilyn June 1931- *WhoWrEP 89*
Fleeson, Doris 1901-1970 *BioIn 16*
Fleeson, William 1915- *BiDrAPA 89, WhoAm 90*
Fleet, Albert Zalman 1937- *WhoSSW 91*

Fleet, George Thurman, Jr. 1928- *St&PR 91*
Fleet, Jheri Chastain 1940- *WhoAmW 91, WhoSSW 91*
Fleet, Marlene Rose 1942- *IntWWM 90*
Fleet, Michael 1941- *ConAu 131*
Fleet, Reuben Hollis 1887-1975 *BioIn 16*
Fleet, Richard W. 1954- *St&PR 91*
Fleetwood Mac *ConMus 5 [port], EncPR&S 89, OxCPMus*
Fleetwood, M. Freile 1915- *WhoE 91*
Fleetwood, Maria Freile 1915- *BiDrAPA 89*
Fleetwood, Mick *EncPR&S 89*
Fleetwood, Mick 1942- *ConMus 5 [port], OxCPMus*
Fleetwood, Mick 1947- *WhoAm 90*
Fleetwood, Rex Allen 1951- *WhoE 91*
Fleetwood, Wallace W 1926- *BiDrAPA 89*
Fleetwoods, The *EncPR&S 89*
Fleezanis, Jorja Kay 1952- *WhoAm 90, WhoAmW 91*
Flegal, George Blair, Jr. 1927- *St&PR 91*
Flegal, Ralph Paul 1938- *WhoE 91*
Flege, John Blain, Jr. 1929- *WhoAm 90*
Flegeal-Kipp, Sonia Ruth 1949- *WhoAmW 91, WhoE 91*
Flegenheimer, Ernest 1927- *WhoAm 90*
Flegenheimer, Walter Victor 1931- *BiDrAPA 89*
Flegler, Joel B. 1941- *WhoWrEP 89*
Fleig, Fred 1908-1979 *Ballpl 90*
Fleisch, Herbert Andre 1933- *WhoWor 91*
Fleischaker, Jerry Jerome 1931- *BiDrAPA 89*
Fleischaker, Ted 1950- *WhoSSW 91*
Fleischauer, Emil A., Jr. 1927- *St&PR 91, WhoAm 90*
Fleischauer, Jack I. *WhoSSW 91*
Fleischauer, John Frederick 1939- *WhoAm 90*
Fleischer, Arthur, Jr. 1933- *WhoAm 90, WhoE 91*
Fleischer, Carl August 1936- *WhoWor 91*
Fleischer, Charlie *BioIn 16*
Fleischer, Debi 1950- *WhoEmL 91*
Fleischer, Denise M. 1958- *WhoWrEP 89*
Fleischer, Dorothy Ann 1957- *WhoAmW 91*
Fleischer, Edytha 1898- *IntWWM 90*
Fleischer, Everly Borah 1936- *WhoAm 90*
Fleischer, Gerald Albert 1933- *WhoAm 90*
Fleischer, Joseph A. 1924- *WhoWor 91*
Fleischer, Leonard T. 1911- *St&PR 91*
Fleischer, Leonore *BioIn 16*
Fleischer, Mary Susan 1956- *WhoAmW 91*
Fleischer, Mathew William 1944- *St&PR 91*
Fleischer, Max *EncACom*
Fleischer, Michael 1908- *WhoAm 90*
Fleischer, Nat 1887-1972 *WorAlBi*
Fleischer, Patricia Lee 1933- *WhoE 91*
Fleischer, Paul E. 1933- *WhoAm 90*
Fleischer, Richard Lee 1926- *WhoE 91*
Fleischer, Richard O. 1916- *WhoAm 90*
Fleischer, Robert 1941- *WhoWor 91*
Fleischer, Robert Louis 1930- *WhoAm 90*
Fleischer, Roland Edward 1928- *WhoAmA 91*
Fleischer, Scott Allan 1951- *BiDrAPA 89*
Fleischer, William Richard 1919- *WhoWor 91*
Fleischhauer, Kurt 1929- *WhoWor 91*
Fleischl, Maria F 1911- *BiDrAPA 89*
Fleischman, Aaron Isaac *BioIn 16*
Fleischman, Albert Sidney 1920- *AuBYP 90, BioIn 16, WhoAm 90, WhoWrEP 89*
Fleischman, Alexandra Wilbert 1941- *WhoE 91*
Fleischman, Barbara Greenberg 1924- *WhoAmW 91*
Fleischman, David Harold 1946- *St&PR 91*
Fleischman, Donald 1934- *St&PR 91*
Fleischman, Edward Hirsh 1932- *WhoAm 90*
Fleischman, Gail Robin 1959- *St&PR 91*
Fleischman, Herman Israel 1950- *WhoE 91, WhoWor 91*
Fleischman, Lawrence A 1925- *WhoAmA 91*
Fleischman, Lawrence Arthur 1925- *WhoAm 90*
Fleischman, Michael F. 1949- *St&PR 91*
Fleischman, Miguel 1949- *WhoEmL 91*
Fleischman, Paul *BioIn 16*
Fleischman, Paul 1952- *AuBYP 90*
Fleischman, Paul Robert 1945- *BiDrAPA 89*
Fleischman, Robert Werder 1937- *WhoE 91*
Fleischman, Sid 1920- *BioIn 16*
Fleischman, Sol Joseph 1910- *WhoSSW 91, WhoWor 91*
Fleischman, Virginia Muse 1946- *WhoEmL 91*
Fleischmann, Adolf R *WhoAmA 91N*
Fleischmann, Aloys Georg 1910- *IntWWM 90*
Fleischmann, C.W. *PenDiDA 89*
Fleischmann, E. Joseph 1936- *WhoSSW 91*
Fleischmann, Ernest Martin 1924- *IntWWM 90, WhoAm 90*
Fleischmann, Fred L. 1933- *St&PR 91*
Fleischmann, Gisela Ebert *BiDrAPA 89*
Fleischmann, Gisi 1894-1944 *BioIn 16*
Fleischmann, Glen Harvey 1909- *AuBYP 90*
Fleischmann, Hans Hermann Paul 1933- *WhoAm 90*
Fleischmann, John 1946- *WhoSSW 91*
Fleischmann, Julius *WhoAmA 91N*
Fleischmann, Konrad Anton 1812-1867 *BioIn 16*
Fleischmann, Martin *BioIn 16*
Fleischmann, Trude *NewYTBS 90*
Fleischmann, Trude 1895-1990 *BioIn 16*
Fleischner, Richard Hugh 1944- *WhoAmA 91*
Fleishell, John Raymond 1942- *St&PR 91*
Fleisher, Bernard 1926- *St&PR 91*
Fleisher, Bruce 1950- *St&PR 91*
Fleisher, Catherine Ellen Kate 1942- *WhoE 91*
Fleisher, David L. 1934- *WhoAm 90*
Fleisher, David Lee 1934- *St&PR 91*
Fleisher, Eric Wilfrid 1926- *WhoE 91*
Fleisher, Ernest M. *BioIn 16*
Fleisher, Gary Mitchell 1941- *WhoE 91, WhoWor 91*
Fleisher, Harold 1921- *WhoAm 90*
Fleisher, Jerrilyn 1952- *WhoAmW 91, WhoEmL 91, WhoWor 91*
Fleisher, Larry *BioIn 16*
Fleisher, Leon 1928- *IntWWM 90, PenDiMP*
Fleisher, Marcy Beth 1964- *WhoAmW 91*
Fleisher, Mark *BiDrAPA 89*
Fleisher, Pat *WhoAmA 91*
Fleisher, Robbin 1951-1977 *BioIn 16*
Fleisher, Steven M. 1945- *WhoEmL 91*
Fleisher, William Phillip 1950- *BiDrAPA 89*
Fleishman, Edwin Alan 1927- *WhoAm 90*
Fleishman, Ellen Marcy 1952- *WhoAmW 91*
Fleishman, Jay 1930- *St&PR 91*
Fleishman, Joel Lawrence 1934- *WhoAm 90*
Fleishman, Martin 1927- *BiDrAPA 89*
Fleishman, Morton Robert 1933- *WhoE 91*
Fleishman, Philip Robert 1935- *WhoAm 90, WhoE 91*
Fleishman, Stephen Baer 1948- *BiDrAPA 89*
Fleishman, Stewart B 1954- *BiDrAPA 89*
Fleisig, Ross 1921- *WhoAm 90*
Fleiss, Arthur N 1912- *BiDrAPA 89*
Fleisser, Marieluise 1901-1974 *BioIn 16, EncCoWW*
Flekovic, Petar 1932- *WhoWor 91*
Flemenbaum, Abraham 1942- *BiDrAPA 89*
Flemig, Ernest Robert 1937- *WhoSSW 91*
Fleming, A.D. 1939- *St&PR 91*
Fleming, Adrain W. 1948- *St&PR 91*
Fleming, Alexander 1881-1955 *WorAlBi*
Fleming, Alice 1928- *AuBYP 90*
Fleming, Alice Carew Mulcahey 1928- *WhoAmW 91*
Fleming, Alice Kipling 1868-1948 *EncO&P 3*
Fleming, Alice MacDonald 1868-1948 *EncPaPR 91*
Fleming, Alice May *WhoWor 91*
Fleming, Allan Robb 1929-1977 *ConDes 90, WhoAmA 91N*
Fleming, Amaryllis 1920- *IntWWM 90*
Fleming, Anthony Caldwell 1939- *WhoSSW 91, WhoWor 91*
Fleming, Arthur Ray, III 1951- *WhoSSW 91*
Fleming, Barbara Jean 1945- *WhoEmL 91*
Fleming, Berry 1899- *WhoWrEP 89*
Fleming, Berry 1899-1989 *BioIn 16, ConAu 129*
Fleming, Bill 1913- *Ballpl 90*
Fleming, Brian L. 1944- *St&PR 91*
Fleming, Brice Noel 1928- *WhoAm 90*
Fleming, Bruce E. 1949- *St&PR 91*
Fleming, Burton A 1925- *BiDrAPA 89*
Fleming, Charles 1916-1987 *BioIn 16*
Fleming, Charles Clifford, Jr. 1923- *WhoAm 90*
Fleming, Craig Alan 1947- *St&PR 91*
Fleming, D.G. 1930- *St&PR 91*
Fleming, Dan Barry 1931- *WhoSSW 91*
Fleming, David *St&PR 91*
Fleming, David Alan 1961- *WhoSSW 91*
Fleming, David Daniel 1948- *St&PR 91*
Fleming, David Francis 1953- *WhoSSW 91*
Fleming, Donald Charles 1949- *St&PR 91*
Fleming, Donald Harnish 1923- *WhoAm 90*
Fleming, Donald M 1905-1986 *ConAu 130*
Fleming, Douglas Riley 1922- *WhoAm 90, WhoSSW 91, WhoWor 91*
Fleming, Edward J. 1920- *WhoAm 90*
Fleming, Edward Stitt 1930- *WhoAm 90*
Fleming, Elizabeth Joyce 1959- *WhoEmL 91*
Fleming, Elizabeth P. 1888-1985 *AuBYP 90, BioIn 16*
Fleming, Everett R. 1928- *St&PR 91*
Fleming, Gail L. 1939- *St&PR 91*
Fleming, Gary G. 1937- *St&PR 91*
Fleming, George 1853-1938 *FemiCLE*
Fleming, George James *NewYTBS 90*
Fleming, George James 1904?-1990 *ConAu 132*
Fleming, George Robert 1947- *WhoEmL 91, WhoWor 91*
Fleming, Gladys Andrews *BioIn 16*
Fleming, Gordon Ballenger 1936- *St&PR 91*
Fleming, Graham Richard 1949- *WhoAm 90*
Fleming, Gus *WhoE 91*
Fleming, Harold Vincent 1922- *St&PR 91*
Fleming, Herbert John 1946- *WhoAm 90*
Fleming, Ian 1908-1964 *AuBYP 90, MajTwCW, TwCCr&M 91, WorAlBi*
Fleming, Ian Lancaster 1908-1964 *SpyFic*
Fleming, J. Michael 1934- *St&PR 91*
Fleming, J. Philip 1943- *St&PR 91*
Fleming, J. W. 1863?-1950 *BioIn 16*
Fleming, James Klein 1949- *WhoWrEP 89*
Fleming, James Lee 1953- *BiDrAPA 89*
Fleming, Jan Ellen 1954- *BiDrAPA 89*
Fleming, Jane Breed *BioIn 16*
Fleming, Joan 1908-1980 *TwCCr&M 91*
Fleming, John *BioIn 16*
Fleming, John 1919- *ConAu 129*
Fleming, John Gunther 1919- *WhoAm 90*
Fleming, John L 1949- *BiDrAPA 89*
Fleming, John Paul 1947- *WhoE 91*
Fleming, John Vincent 1936- *WhoAm 90*
Fleming, John William 1863?-1950 *BioIn 16*
Fleming, Jon Hugh 1941- *WhoWor 91*
Fleming, Jonathan A 1948- *BiDrAPA 89*
Fleming, Joseph Benedict 1919- *WhoAm 90*
Fleming, Julia Ann 1947- *WhoAmW 91*
Fleming, Julian Denver, Jr. 1934- *WhoAm 90*
Fleming, Kerry *BioIn 16*
Fleming, Larry A. 1949- *St&PR 91*
Fleming, Lee Virginia 1952- *WhoAmA 91*
Fleming, Les 1915-1980 *Ballpl 90*
Fleming, Lisa L. 1961- *WhoAmW 91*
Fleming, Louis K. 1925- *WhoWor 91*
Fleming, Louise Celestia 1862-1899 *BioIn 16*
Fleming, Mack Gerald 1932- *WhoAm 90*
Fleming, Margaret 1803-1811 *BioIn 16*
Fleming, Marjory 1803-1811 *BioIn 16, FemiCLE*
Fleming, Martin 1953- *WhoEmL 91*
Fleming, Martin L. 1930- *St&PR 91*
Fleming, May Agnes 1840-1880 *DcLB 99 [port], FemiCLE*
Fleming, Michael John 1938- *WhoAm 90*
Fleming, Michael R. *ODwPR 91*
Fleming, Nathan N. 1828-1864 *AmLegL*
Fleming, Ned N. *St&PR 91N*
Fleming, Ned N. *BioIn 16*
Fleming, Oliver *TwCCr&M 91*
Fleming, Oramenta Delores 1955- *WhoAmW 91*
Fleming, Patricia Ann 1955- *St&PR 91*
Fleming, Paula Ellen 1952- *WhoE 91, WhoEmL 91*
Fleming, Peggy *BioIn 16*
Fleming, Peggy 1948- *WorAlBi*
Fleming, Peggy Gale 1948- *WhoAm 90*
Fleming, Peter Emmet, Jr. 1929- *WhoAm 90*
Fleming, Philip Andrew 1930- *WhoAm 90, WhoE 91*
Fleming, Rex James 1940- *WhoAm 90*
Fleming, Rhonda *WhoAm 90*
Fleming, Rhonda 1923- *WorAlBi*
Fleming, Richard 1924- *WhoAm 90*
Fleming, Richard Allan 1943- *WhoSSW 91*
Fleming, Richard Carl Dunne 1945- *WhoAm 90*
Fleming, Richard Harrison 1947- *St&PR 91*
Fleming, Richard M 1920- *BiDrAPA 89*
Fleming, Robert Bradshaw 1953- *WhoSSW 91*
Fleming, Robert S, II *BiDrAPA 89*
Fleming, Robert T. 1923- *St&PR 91*
Fleming, Robert W. 1918- *St&PR 91*
Fleming, Robert William 1928- *WhoAm 90*
Fleming, Robert Wright 1918- *WhoAm 90*
Fleming, Robin 1955- *WhoE 91*
Fleming, Ronald Lee *BioIn 16*
Fleming, Ronald Lee 1941- *WhoAm 90, WhoAmA 91*
Fleming, Rose Ann 1932- *WhoAm 90*
Fleming, Russell 1938- *St&PR 91*
Fleming, Russell, Jr. 1938- *WhoAm 90*
Fleming, Samuel C. *BioIn 16*
Fleming, Samuel Crozier 1940- *St&PR 91*
Fleming, Samuel Crozier, Jr. 1940- *WhoAm 90, WhoE 91*
Fleming, Samuel M. 1908- *WhoAm 90*
Fleming, Sarah Lee Brown 1875-1963 *HarlReB*
Fleming, Scott 1923- *WhoAm 90*
Fleming, Scott T. 1955- *St&PR 91*
Fleming, Shirley 1931- *IntWWM 90*
Fleming, Sidney H *BiDrAPA 89*
Fleming, Solomon S. 1812- *AmLegL*
Fleming, Steven Robert 1951- *WhoE 91*
Fleming, Susan Alice 1949- *WhoEmL 91*
Fleming, Suzanne Marie 1927- *WhoAm 90*
Fleming, T Corwin 1932- *BiDrAPA 89*
Fleming, Thomas Crawley 1921- *WhoAm 90*
Fleming, Thomas F. 1946- *St&PR 91*
Fleming, Thomas James 1927- *AuBYP 90, WhoAm 90, WhoWrEP 89*
Fleming, Thomas Jeffrey 1955- *St&PR 91*
Fleming, Thomas Michael 1951- *WhoAmA 91*
Fleming, Timothy Woodbridge 1944- *IntWWM 90, WhoSSW 91*
Fleming, Victor Albert 1901- *IntWWM 90*
Fleming, Virginia Hesse 1959- *WhoAmW 91*
Fleming, W.R. 1923- *St&PR 91*
Fleming, Wendell Helms 1928- *WhoAm 90*
Fleming, William Adam 1921- *WhoAm 90*
Fleming, William Cary 1918- *WhoAm 90*
Fleming, William David 1910- *WhoAm 90*
Fleming, William H 1932- *BiDrAPA 89*
Fleming, William Harrison 1915- *WhoAm 90*
Fleming, William Henry 1856-1944 *AmLegL*
Fleming, William J. 1922- *St&PR 91*
Fleming, William Paul 1943- *St&PR 91*
Fleming, William Sloan 1937- *WhoAm 90, WhoE 91, WhoWor 91*
Fleming, William Wright, Jr. 1932- *WhoAm 90*
Fleming, Williamina Paton Stevens 1857-1911 *BioIn 16*
Flemister, Launcelot Johnson 1913- *WhoAm 90*
Flemister, Michael Gilbert 1957- *WhoEmL 91*
Flemke, Karl 1931- *WhoAm 90*
Flemma, Robert J. *NewYTBS 90*
Flemma, Robert J. 1935-1990 *BioIn 16*
Flemmer, Phyllis Rae 1933- *WhoAmW 91*
Flemming, Duchess *EncCoWW*
Flemming, Alex 1954- *WhoWor 91*
Flemming, Arthur Sherwood *BioIn 16*
Flemming, Arthur Sherwood 1905- *BiDrUSE 89*
Flemming, Brian 1939- *WhoE 91*
Flemming, Claire D. 1934- *St&PR 91*
Flemming, Edward John 1946- *St&PR 91*
Flemming, Paul Martin *St&PR 91*
Flemming, Timothy Clarence 1945- *St&PR 91*
Flemming, Walther 1843-1905 *WorAlBi*
Flemmons, Jerry 1936- *WhoSSW 91*
Flender, Harold 1924- *AuBYP 90*
Flenniken, Cecil Stephenson 1925- *St&PR 91, WhoAm 90*
Flenorl, Richard Lee 1955- *WhoSSW 91*
Flerlage, Stuart Q, Jr. *BiDrAPA 89*
Fles, Barthold 1902-1989 *BioIn 16*
Flesch, Carl 1873-1944 *PenDiMP*
Flesch, Robert Donald 1946- *WhoEmL 91*
Flesch, Sally Jane 1948- *WhoEmL 91*
Flescher, Sylvia Evelyn *BiDrAPA 89*
Fleschner, Marcia Harriet 1947- *WhoAmW 91, WhoWor 91*
Fleshel, Marcia Fran 1946- *WhoEmL 91*
Flesher, Dale Lee 1945- *WhoWrEP 89*
Flesher, Hubert Louis 1933- *WhoAm 90, WhoWor 91*
Fleshner, Mark Alvin 1956- *St&PR 91*
Flessel, Creig 1912- *EncACom*
Fletcher & Gardiner *PenDiDA 89*
Fletcher, Aaron 1934- *WhoWrEP 89*
Fletcher, Adrian 1943- *St&PR 91*
Fletcher, Alan 1931- *ConDes 90*
Fletcher, Alan Gordon 1925- *WhoAm 90*
Fletcher, Alan Mark 1928- *AuBYP 90*
Fletcher, Alice C. 1838-1923 *BioAmW*
Fletcher, Alice Cunningham 1838-1923 *BioIn 16, WhNaAH*
Fletcher, Angus 1930- *WhoAm 90*
Fletcher, Anthony L. 1935- *WhoAm 90*
Fletcher, Art 1885-1950 *Ballpl 90 [port]*
Fletcher, Arthur A. *WhoAm 90*
Fletcher, Arthur T. 1898- *St&PR 91*
Fletcher, Barbara Rainbow 1935- *WhoWrEP 89*
Fletcher, Beale *AuBYP 90*
Fletcher, Benjamin 1640-1703 *EncCRAm*
Fletcher, Betty B. 1923- *WhoAm 90, WhoAmW 91*

Fletcher, Brady Jones 1928- WhoE 91, WhoWor 91
Fletcher, Bramwell 1904-1988 BioIn 16
Fletcher, Carlos Alfredo 1959- WhoEmL 91
Fletcher, Catharine Anne 1961- WhoSSW 91
Fletcher, Cathy Ann 1949- WhoAmW 91, WhoEmL 91
Fletcher, Charlie May AuBYP 90
Fletcher, Christopher Wallace 1955- WhoEmL 91
Fletcher, Cliff 1935- WhoAm 90
Fletcher, Colin BioIn 16
Fletcher, Colin 1922- WhoAm 90
Fletcher, Curley 1892-1953 BioIn 16
Fletcher, D. Ed 1939- St&PR 91
Fletcher, David 1940-1988 TwCCr&M 91
Fletcher, David J. 1954- WhoEmL 91
Fletcher, David Ross 1959- WhoSSW 91
Fletcher, Denise K. 1948- St&PR 91
Fletcher, Denise Koen 1948- WhoAm 90, WhoEmL 91
Fletcher, Douglas B. 1925- St&PR 91
Fletcher, Douglas Baden 1925- WhoAm 90
Fletcher, Ed 1872-1955 BioIn 16
Fletcher, Edward Abraham 1924- WhoAm 90
Fletcher, Edward Taylor 1817-1897 DcCanB 12
Fletcher, Elbie 1916- Ballpl 90
Fletcher, Eliza 1770-1858 FemiCLE
Fletcher, Elizabeth 1638?-1658 BiDEWW
Fletcher, Elizabeth D 1909- BiDrAPA 89
Fletcher, Ellen BioIn 16
Fletcher, Eugene BioIn 16
Fletcher, Francis Marion, Jr. 1932- WhoSSW 91
Fletcher, Frank 1885-1973 WorAlBi
Fletcher, George Flynn 1947- St&PR 91
Fletcher, George P. 1939- WhoAm 90
Fletcher, H. Grant 1913- IntWWM 90
Fletcher, Harold J. 1950- St&PR 91
Fletcher, Harry George, III 1941- WhoAm 90, WhoWrEP 89
Fletcher, Helen Jill 1911- AuBYP 90
Fletcher, Henry Prather 1873-1959 BioIn 16
Fletcher, Herbert Roy 1928- St&PR 91
Fletcher, Homer Lee 1928- WhoAm 90
Fletcher, J S 1863-1935 TwCCr&M 91
Fletcher, James Andrew 1945- WhoAm 90, WhoEmL 91
Fletcher, James C., III 1938- St&PR 91
Fletcher, James Chipman 1919- WhoAm 90
Fletcher, James Holway 1947- St&PR 91
Fletcher, James Robert 1947- BiDrAPA 89
Fletcher, Jeffrey Edward 1948- WhoE 91
Fletcher, Jerald J. 1949- WhoSSW 91
Fletcher, Jerry Herbert 1954- BiDrAPA 89
Fletcher, Jesse Conrad 1931- WhoAm 90
Fletcher, Joanne Leslie 1950- WhoAmW 91
Fletcher, Joel Lafayette, III 1935- WhoSSW 91
Fletcher, John 1579-1625 BioIn 16, WorAlBi
Fletcher, John Caldwell 1931- WhoAm 90
Fletcher, John Capers BioIn 16
Fletcher, John Gould 1886-1950 BioIn 16
Fletcher, John William 1852-1913 EncO&P 3
Fletcher, Jonathan Moss 1914- WhoAm 90
Fletcher, Kay WhoWrEP 89
Fletcher, Kim 1927- St&PR 91, WhoAm 90
Fletcher, Laura Tristan 1965- WhoAmW 91
Fletcher, Leland Vernon 1946- WhoAm 90, WhoAmA 91
Fletcher, Leon 1921- ConAu 33NR
Fletcher, Leroy Stevenson 1936- WhoAm 90, WhoSSW 91, WhoWor 91
Fletcher, Lisa A. Brumbeloe ODwPR 91
Fletcher, Loren 1833-1919 AmLegL
Fletcher, Louise 1936- WhoAm 90, WhoAmW 91, WorAlBi
Fletcher, Lucille 1912- TwCCr&M 91
Fletcher, Marjorie Amos 1923- WhoAmW 91
Fletcher, Martin W. 1952- St&PR 91
Fletcher, Marvin Emil 1957- WhoEmL 91
Fletcher, Mary 1739-1815 FemiCLE
Fletcher, Mary Beth 1949- WhoE 91
Fletcher, Mary Lee WhoAmW 91, WhoWor 91
Fletcher, Mattie Ball 1888- BioIn 16
Fletcher, Max Ellis 1921- WhoAm 90
Fletcher, Norman Collings 1917- WhoAm 90
Fletcher, Oscar Jasper, Jr. 1938- WhoAm 90
Fletcher, Page Moss 1960- BiDrAPA 89
Fletcher, Pam BioIn 16
Fletcher, Paul D. 1959- St&PR 91, WhoSSW 91
Fletcher, Paul Litton, Jr. 1941- WhoSSW 91
Fletcher, Pauline Charlotte 1938- WhoWrEP 89
Fletcher, Percy E. 1879-1932 OxCPMus
Fletcher, Peter Caleb 1925- St&PR 91
Fletcher, Peyton B., III 1930- WhoE 91
Fletcher, Philip B. WhoAm 90
Fletcher, Philip Bernier 1933- St&PR 91
Fletcher, Phillip Douglas 1957- WhoE 91
Fletcher, Ray Weldon 1929- St&PR 91
Fletcher, Raymond Russwald, Jr. 1929- WhoAm 90
Fletcher, Riley Eugene 1912- WhoSSW 91, WhoWor 91
Fletcher, Robert BioIn 16
Fletcher, Robert 1920- WhoAm 90
Fletcher, Robert Blair 1948- St&PR 91
Fletcher, Robert Chipman 1921- WhoAm 90
Fletcher, Robert Hillman 1940- WhoAm 90
Fletcher, Robert L. 1930- St&PR 91
Fletcher, Ronald Darling 1933- WhoAm 90
Fletcher, Scott BioIn 16
Fletcher, Scott 1958- Ballpl 90
Fletcher, Sherry Lyn 1947- WhoAmW 91
Fletcher, Steven John 1951- St&PR 91
Fletcher, Stewart Gailey 1918- WhoAm 90
Fletcher, Suzanne Wright 1940- WhoAm 90, WhoAmW 91
Fletcher, Terry B. 1934- St&PR 91
Fletcher, Thomas PenDiDA 89
Fletcher, Valerie J 1951- WhoAmA 91
Fletcher, Wendy Ann 1955- WhoEmL 91
Fletcher, Willard Allen 1924- WhoAm 90
Fletcher, William Adrin 1948- WhoEmL 91
Fletcher, William Arthur 1947- St&PR 91
Fletcher, William Cameron 1944- St&PR 91
Fletcher, William Eric 1935- St&PR 91
Fletcher, William Wallace, Jr. 1947- WhoEmL 91
Fletcher, Winona Lee 1926- BioIn 16, NotWoAT
Fletcher-Smith, Claudia Ann 1948- WhoEmL 91
Flettner, Marianne 1933- WhoAm 90
Flettner, Peter PenDiDA 89
Fletzberger, Matthias 1965- IntWWM 90
Fleur, Paul MajTwCW
Fleurant, Gerdes 1939- WhoE 91
Fleurant, John Franklin 1948- WhoE 91
Fleurant, Lucien B 1931- BiDrAPA 89
Fleurat, Pierre PenDiDA 89
Fleuridas, Jack Andre 1930- St&PR 91
Fleuriet, Joseph Bernard, Jr. 1953- WhoEmL 91
Fleury, Andre 1903- IntWWM 90
Fleury, Leo A. 1930- St&PR 91
Fleury, Louis 1878-1926 PenDiMP
Fleury, Peg McCormick 1937- WhoAmW 91
Fleury, Robert Andre 1945- BiDrAPA 89
Fleury Durand-Greville, Alice Marie EncCoWW
Flew, Anthony Garrard Newton 1923- EncPaPR 91
Flew, Antony G N 1923- EncO&P 3
Flewelling, Diane Mae 1947- WhoAmW 91
Flexner, Ann Crawford 1874-1955 LiHiK
Flexner, Anne 1874-1955 FemiCLE
Flexner, Anne Crawford 1874-1955 BioIn 16, NotWoAT
Flexner, Helen T. BioAmW
Flexner, Hortense 1885-1973 LiHiK
Flexner, James Thomas 1908- WhoAm 90, WhoAmA 91
Flexner, Louis Barkhouse 1902- WhoAm 90
Flexner, Paul Arthur 1945- WhoE 91
Flexner, Stuart Berg 1928- WhoAm 90
Flexner, Stuart Berg 1928-1990 NewYTBS 90 [port]
Flick, Carl 1926- WhoAm 90
Flick, Elmer 1876-1971 Ballpl 90 [port]
Flick, Frederick Edward 1947- WhoAm 90
Flick, Gene Russell 1960- BiDrAPA 89
Flick, John Edmond 1922- WhoAm 90
Flick, Kent Roderick 1953- WhoEmL 91
Flick, Michael Albert 1948- St&PR 91
Flick, Paul John 1943- WhoAmA 91
Flick, Robbert 1939- WhoAmA 91
Flick, Sol E. 1915- St&PR 91, WhoAm 90
Flick, Thomas Michael 1954- WhoEmL 91
Flick, Willi Gerhard 1939- WhoWor 91
Flicker, David J BiDrAPA 89
Flicker, Dawn K. 1960- WhoAmW 91
Flicker, Eric L. 1949- St&PR 91
Flicker, Eric Lee 1949- WhoEmL 91
Flicker, Irving 1915- St&PR 91
Flicker, Marvin BiDrAPA 89
Flicker, Shanley E. 1917- St&PR 91
Flicker, Ted 1930- WhoAm 90
Flicker, Warren Louis 1943- St&PR 91
Flickinger, Allan L. 1929- St&PR 91
Flickinger, Burt P., Jr. 1926- WhoE 91
Flickinger, Burt Prentice, Jr. 1926- St&PR 91
Flickinger, Charles John 1938- WhoAm 90
Flickinger, Harry Harner 1936- WhoAm 90
Flickinger, Joe Arden 1949- WhoWor 91
Flickinger, Peter B. 1928- St&PR 91
Flickinger, Thomas L. 1939- WhoAm 90
Flickinger, Thomas Radcliffe 1932- St&PR 91
Flickinger, Wayne J. 1923- WhoSSW 91
Fliedner, Dietrich Karl Wilhelm 1929- WhoWor 91
Fliedner, Leonard J. BioIn 16
Fliegel, Frederick Martin 1956- WhoEmL 91
Fliegel, Leslie 1912-1968 WhoAmA 91N
Fliegel, Martin B BiDrAPA 89
Fliegelman, Avra Leah WhoAmW 91
Fliegelman, Stanley 1927- St&PR 91
Flieger, Howard Wentworth 1909- WhoAm 90
Flier, Michael S 1941- ConAu 32NR
Flier, Michael Stephen 1941- WhoAm 90
Fliermans, Carl Bernard 1944- WhoSSW 91
Fliess, Winston S., Jr. 1929- St&PR 91
Fliesser, Jeffrey Mark BiDrAPA 89
Flieth, Herbert 1911- IntWWM 90
Flietstra, R.R. 1949- St&PR 91
Fliger, Daniel James 1940- St&PR 91
Fligg, David Simon 1959- IntWWM 90
Fligg, Loren L. 1940- St&PR 91
Flight, Thomas PenDiDA 89
Fligsten, Kenneth E 1938- BiDrAPA 89
Flindell, Edwin Frederick 1926- IntWWM 90
Flinders, Matthew 1774-1814 BioIn 16
Flink, Edward B. 1951- WhoE 91
Flink, Jane Duncan 1929- WhoAmW 91
Flink, Peter Karl 1942- St&PR 91
Flink, Richard Allen 1935- St&PR 91, WhoAm 90
Flinkstrom, Henry Allan 1933- WhoE 91, WhoWor 91
Flinn, Charles Gallagher 1938- WhoSSW 91
Flinn, Don E 1923- BiDrAPA 89
Flinn, Lawrence, Jr. 1935- St&PR 91
Flinn, Michael Eugene 1946- WhoEmL 91
Flinn, Owen Ronald 1934- St&PR 91
Flinn, Roberta Jeanne 1947- WhoAmW 91, WhoWor 91
Flinn, Stephanie Strubing 1939- St&PR 91
Flinn, Thomas D. 1956- WhoEmL 91
Flinner, Charles Frederick 1920- WhoAm 90
Flinner, James C. 1956- St&PR 91
Flinner, Lyle Payson 1918- WhoSSW 91
Flint, Billa 1805-1894 DcCanB 12
Flint, Cynthia Marie 1956- WhoAmW 91
Flint, Daniel Waldo Boone 1926- WhoAm 90
Flint, Dennis F. 1943- St&PR 91
Flint, Emily Pauline Riedinger 1909- WhoAm 90
Flint, F. Harlan, Jr. 1930- St&PR 91
Flint, Garrett M. 1932- St&PR 91
Flint, George Graham 1929- St&PR 91
Flint, George Squire 1930- WhoAm 90
Flint, Janet Altic 1935- WhoAmA 91
Flint, Jeremy 1928-1989 BioIn 16, ConAu 130
Flint, Jerry S 1928- BiDrAPA 89
Flint, John E. 1930- WhoAm 90
Flint, Kathleen Patricia 1956- WhoAmW 91
Flint, Leslie 1911?- EncO&P 3
Flint, Leslie 1911-198-? EncPaPR 91
Flint, Mark Addison 1946- St&PR 91, WhoAm 90
Flint, Putnam P. 1918- St&PR 91
Flint, Randell Sherman 1955- WhoEmL 91
Flint, Richard Newell 1935- St&PR 91
Flint, Robert N. 1921- St&PR 91
Flint, Robert Nelson 1921- WhoAm 90
Flint, Roy K. 1928- BioIn 16
Flint, Susan Louise 1947- WhoAmW 91
Flint, Suzanne Elizabeth 1961- WhoAmW 91
Flippen, James Howard, III 1957- WhoEmL 91
Flippin, Gilmer Franklin 1947- WhoEmL 91
Flippin, Royce Norwood BioIn 16
Flippo, Leslie W. 1929- St&PR 91
Flippo, Ronnie Gene 1937- WhoAm 90, WhoSSW 91
Flippo, W. J. Bryan 1927- WhoSSW 91
Flipse, Eduard 1896-1972 PenDiMP
Flipse, John Edward 1921- WhoSSW 91
Flisher, Cynthia Dean 1961- WhoAmW 91
Flisi, Claudia Beth 1947- WhoEmL 91, WhoWor 91
Fliss, Raphael M. 1930- WhoAm 90
Flitcraft, Richard Kirby, II 1920- WhoAm 90
Flitner, Wilhelm 1889- BioIn 16
Flittie, Clifford Gilliland 1924- WhoAm 90
Flittie, John Howard 1936- WhoAm 90
Flo and Eddie EncPR&S 89
Floca, Frank Stewart 1950- BiDrAPA 89
Floch, Herve Alexander 1908- WhoWor 91
Floch, Joseph 1895-1977 WhoAmA 91N
Floch, Martin Herbert 1928- WhoAm 90
Floch-Baillet, Daniele Luce 1948- WhoWor 91
Flock, Henry H. 1935- St&PR 91
Flocke, Jenelle Louise 1949- WhoAmW 91
Flocken, John Murray 1926- St&PR 91
Flockhart, Sandra Layne 1950- WhoAmW 91
Flocks, Jay Stephen 1941- BiDrAPA 89
Flocks, Marcia Lea Hinds 1955- WhoAmW 91
Floda, Alfred Joseph 1955- WhoEmL 91
Floersheimer, Walter D. 1900-1989 BioIn 16
Floeter, Howard A. 1953- St&PR 91
Floeter, Kent 1937- WhoAmA 91
Floethe, Louise Lee 1913- AuBYP 90
Floethe, Richard 1901-1988 WhoAmA 91N
Flogstad, Kjartan 1944- DcScanL
Floherty, John Joseph 1882-1964 AuBYP 90
Flohn, Hermann Jerland 1912- WhoWor 91
Flohr, Daniel G., III 1942- St&PR 91
Flohr, Louis Michael BiDrAPA 89
Floissac, Vincent WhoWor 91
Flom, Edward Leonard 1929- St&PR 91, WhoAm 90, WhoSSW 91
Flom, Gerald Trossen 1930- WhoAm 90
Flom, Julia Mittle 1906- WhoAmW 91, WhoSSW 91
Flom, Reynold P BiDrAPA 89
Flomenhaft, Eleanor 1933- WhoAmA 91
Flonzaley Quartet PenDiMP
Flood, Bridget McDermott 1956- WhoEmL 91
Flood, Curt 1938- Ballpl 90 [port]
Flood, David Allan 1938- WhoE 91
Flood, Diane Lucy 1937- WhoAmW 91
Flood, Donald T. 1934- St&PR 91
Flood, Dorothy Garnett 1951- WhoAmW 91
Flood, Douglas James 1955- St&PR 91
Flood, Edward C 1944-1985 WhoAmA 91N
Flood, Francis Edward 1925- St&PR 91
Flood, Frank J. St&PR 91
Flood, Gay 1935- WhoAmW 91, WhoE 91
Flood, Howard Eaton 1930- St&PR 91
Flood, Howard L. 1934- St&PR 91, WhoAm 90
Flood, James Clair 1939- St&PR 91
Flood, James Joseph 1923- St&PR 91
Flood, James T. 1934- ODwPR 91
Flood, Joan Moore 1941- WhoAmW 91, WhoE 91, WhoWor 91
Flood, John A 1949- ConAu 129
Flood, John Etchells, Jr. 1929- St&PR 91
Flood, John W. 1930- St&PR 91
Flood, Kathleen Elizabeth 1962- WhoAmW 91
Flood, Randolph Gene 1950- WhoE 91, WhoEmL 91, WhoSSW 91
Flood, Richard Sidney 1943- WhoAmA 91
Flood, Robert E. BioIn 16
Flood, Theodore C. 1930- St&PR 91
Floody, C. Wallace BioIn 16
Floody, Wally 1918-1989 AnObit 1989
Flook, John C. 1947- St&PR 91
Floquet, Charles Thomas 1828-1896 BiDFrPL
Flor, Claus Peter 1953- IntWWM 90
Flora, Cornelia Butler 1943- WhoAmW 91
Flora, Edward Benjamin 1929- St&PR 91
Flora, Fletcher 1914-1968 TwCCr&M 91
Flora, George Claude 1923- WhoAm 90
Flora, Jairus Dale, Jr. 1944- WhoAm 90
Flora, James Royer 1914- AuBYP 90, WhoAmA 91
Flora, John Alan 1950- St&PR 91
Flora, John H. Ted 1919- St&PR 91
Flora, Joseph Martin 1934- WhoAm 90
Flora, Lacy Little 1960- WhoSSW 91
Flora, Philip Craig 1950- WhoEmL 91, WhoSSW 91
Flora, Sue Ann 1941- WhoAmW 91
Florance, Colden l'Hommedieu Ruggles 1931- WhoAm 90
Florance, Stanley Hunter 1939- St&PR 91
Florczyk-Matt, Sandra 1955- WhoAmW 91
Florea, Robert William 1947- WhoE 91, WhoEmL 91
Floren, Georgia B. 1931- WhoAmW 91
Floren, Myron 1919- ConAu 129
Floren, Roger C BiDrAPA 89
Florence, Anthony A. ODwPR 91
Florence, Donna Jean 1950- WhoE 91
Florence, Gerald P. 1933- St&PR 91
Florence, Jerry NewAgMG

Florence, Kenneth James 1943- *WhoWor 91*
Florence, Lella 1887-1966 *FemiCLE*
Florence, Lucy Mae 1942- *WhoAmW 91*
Florence, Malvina Pray 1830-1906 *BioIn 16*
Florence, Malvina Theresa Pray 1830-1906 *NotWoAT*
Florence, Mary Sargant 1857-1954 *BiDWomA*
Florence, Neal Richard *BiDrAPA 89*
Florence, Penny Jean Marsden 1948- *WhoWor 91*
Florence, Verena Magdalena 1946- *WhoAmW 91, WhoEmL 91*
Florence, Virginia Proctor Powell 1897- *BioIn 16*
Florence, William Herbert, Jr. 1933- *WhoSSW 91*
Florentin, Maria Corazon G Fernando *BiDrAPA 89*
Florenzano, Ramon Urzua 1944- *BiDrAPA 89*
Flores, Alberto Sierra 1956- *WhoHisp 91*
Flores, Alfonso J. 1949- *WhoHisp 91*
Flores, Alfredo Gonzalez 1877-1962 *BioIn 16*
Flores, Angel 1900- *ConAu 32NR, HispWr 90*
Flores, Antonio R. 1947- *WhoHisp 91*
Flores, Apolonio 1940- *WhoHisp 91*
Flores, Armando 1945- *St&PR 91*
Flores, Armando, Jr. 1945- *WhoHisp 91*
Flores, Aurora 1954- *WhoHisp 91*
Flores, Candida 1951- *WhoHisp 91*
Flores, Connie 1944- *WhoHisp 91*
Flores, Daniel Sanchez *NewYTBS 90*
Flores, Eduardo 1957- *WhoHisp 91*
Flores, Eileen *WhoHisp 91*
Flores, Eliezer 1959- *WhoHisp 91*
Flores, Enrique Antonio 1943- *WhoHisp 91*
Flores, Ernest Albert 1952- *BiDrAPA 89*
Flores, Ernie *WhoHisp 91*
Flores, Frank *WhoHisp 91*
Flores, Frank F. *St&PR 91*
Flores, Frank Fausto 1930- *WhoE 91, WhoWor 91*
Flores, Gerry *WhoHisp 91*
Flores, Hildegardo Edmundo 1942- *WhoSSW 91*
Flores, Ismael 1958- *WhoHisp 91*
Flores, Jesse 1914- *Ballpl 90*
Flores, Joe *WhoHisp 91*
Flores, John 1952- *WhoHisp 91*
Flores, John Ruben 1956- *WhoEmL 91*
Flores, Jose Obed 1954- *WhoWrEP 89*
Flores, Juan 1514-1575 *PenDiDA 89*
Flores, Juan Jose 1800-1864 *BioIn 16*
Flores, Juan M. *WhoHisp 91*
Flores, Juan Manuel 1951- *WhoHisp 91*
Flores, Kathryn A. 1954- *WhoAmW 91*
Flores, Laura Jane 1951- *WhoHisp 91*
Flores, Leonard Lopez, Jr. 1937- *WhoHisp 91*
Flores, Lito Tejada- *BioIn 16*
Flores, M. Betsi 1955- *WhoEmL 91*
Flores, Manuel, Jr. 1923- *WhoHisp 91*
Flores, Margarita Frances 1959- *WhoAmW 91*
Flores, Maria Carolina *WhoHisp 91*
Flores, Maria Teresa 1962- *WhoHisp 91*
Flores, Marion Thomas 1946- *WhoAm 90, WhoEmL 91*
Flores, Marjorie Joice 1937- *WhoAmW 91*
Flores, Matthew Gilbert 1962- *WhoHisp 91*
Flores, Orlando 1946- *WhoEmL 91, WhoHisp 91*
Flores, Patricio Fernandez 1929- *WhoHisp 91*
Flores, Patrick F. 1929- *WhoAm 90, WhoSSW 91*
Flores, Patrick Fernandez 1929- *BioIn 16*
Flores, Philip Joseph 1949- *WhoEmL 91*
Flores, Raymond Jose 1929- *WhoHisp 91*
Flores, Roberto J. 1935- *WhoHisp 91*
Flores, Robin Ann 1949- *WhoAmW 91*
Flores, Rosemary 1959- *WhoHisp 91*
Flores, Rosie *WhoNeCM [port]*
Flores, Ruben, Jr. 1954- *WhoHisp 91*
Flores, Rudy M. *WhoHisp 91*
Flores, Suzanne 1931- *WhoAmW 91*
Flores, Thomas R. 1937- *WhoAm 90*
Flores, Tom 1937- *BioIn 16, WhoHisp 91*
Flores, Venancio 1809-1868 *BioIn 16*
Flores, Wayne R. 1957- *WhoHisp 91*
Flores, William Hose 1954- *WhoEmL 91*
Flores de Apodaca, Roberto 1951- *WhoHisp 91*
Flores-Gallardo, Arturo 1922- *BiDrAPA 89*
Flores-Hughes, Grace 1946- *WhoHisp 91*
Flores Magon, Ricardo 1873-1922 *BioIn 16*
Flores Olea, Victor 1933- *BioIn 16*
Floresca, Felipe *WhoHisp 91*
Florescu, Ion Emanoil 1817-1893 *BioIn 16*
Florescue, Barry William 1943- *WhoAm 90*
Florestano, Patricia Sherer 1936- *WhoAmW 91*
Floreth, Frederick Dennis 1956- *WhoEmL 91*
Florey, Howard W. 1898-1968 *WorAlBi*
Florey, Klaus Georg 1919- *WhoAm 90*
Florey, Robert 1900- *BioIn 16*
Florez, Edward T. 1949- *WhoHisp 91*
Florez, Genaro A. 1907- *St&PR 91*
Florez, Juan B G 1931- *BiDrAPA 89*
Flori, Anna Marie DiBlasi LePoer 1940- *WhoWor 91*
Flori, Robert Donald 1927- *St&PR 91*
Florian, Daniel F. 1932- *St&PR 91*
Florian, Douglas 1950- *AuBYP 90, BioIn 16*
Florian, Frank L. 1933- *St&PR 91*
Florian, Frank Lee 1933- *WhoAm 90*
Florian, John S. 1947- *WhoWrEP 89*
Florian, Marianna Bolognesi *WhoAmW 91*
Florian, Olga Wisinger- 1844-1926 *BioIn 16*
Florida, Thomas Michael 1938- *WhoSSW 91*
Floridablanca, Conde de 1728-1808 *BioIn 16*
Florie, Terry Lynn 1956- *WhoEmL 91*
Florig, Robert R. 1940- *St&PR 91*
Florin, Cynthia Ann *BiDrAPA 89*
Florin, Peter 1921- *BioIn 16*
Florin, Robert Allan 1946- *BiDrAPA 89*
Florin, Sharon June 1952- *WhoAmA 91*
Florin, Wil Hermann 1955- *WhoWor 91*
Florine, Charlotte M *BiDrAPA 89*
Florio, Alba 1913- *EncCoWW*
Florio, Dominic Anthony 1946- *WhoEmL 91*
Florio, Emil L. 1946- *ODwPR 91*
Florio, Ermanno 1954- *WhoAm 90*
Florio, James 1937- *NewYTBS 90 [port]*
Florio, James J. *BioIn 16*
Florio, James J 1937- *CurBio 90 [port], News 91-2 [port], WhoAm 90, WhoE 91*
Florio, Maryanne J. 1940- *WhoAmW 91*
Florio, Steven T. 1949- *WhoAm 90, WhoE 91*
Florio, Steven Thomas 1949- *St&PR 91*
Florio, William A *BiDrAPA 89*
Florio, William Anthony, Jr. 1949- *BiDrAPA 89*
Floris, Cornelis *PenDiDA 89*
Floris, Frans 1519?-1570 *IntDcAA 90*
Floris, Jan 1514-1575 *PenDiDA 89*
Florit, Eugenio 1903- *BioIn 16, ConAu 32NR, HispWr 90*
Florit y Sanchez de Fuentes, Eugenio 1903- *ConAu 32NR, HispWr 90*
Florjancic, Frederick J. 1947- *St&PR 91*
Florjancic, Frederick Joseph, Jr. 1947- *WhoAm 90*
Florjancic, Ronald Merk 1936- *St&PR 91*
Florman, Jean Claire 1952- *WhoAmW 91*
Florman, Jonathan C 1958- *BiDrAPA 89*
Floros, Constantin 1930- *IntWWM 90*
Floros, Leo *ODwPR 91*
Florovsky, Georges 1893-1979 *BioIn 16*
Florsheim, Richard A 1916-1979 *WhoAmA 91N*
Florsheim, Stewart Jay 1952- *WhoEmL 91*
Florvall, Eskil Olof 1934- *WhoWor 91*
Flory, Arthur L 1914-1972 *WhoAmA 91N*
Flory, Daisy Parker 1915- *WhoAm 90*
Flory, Jane 1917- *AuBYP 90*
Flory, Joyce V. 1947- *WhoWrEP 89*
Flory, Lee J. 1926- *St&PR 91*
Flory, Robert Mikesell 1912- *WhoSSW 91, WhoWor 91*
Flory, Walter S., Jr. 1907- *WhoAm 90*
Flory, Wendy Stallard 1943- *ConAu 132*
Flory, William Evans Sherlock 1914- *WhoAm 90*
Floss, Heinz G. 1934- *WhoAm 90*
Flotner, Peter 1493-1546 *PenDiDA 89*
Flotow, Friedrich von 1812-1883 *PenDiMP A*
Flotsam and Jetsam *OxCPMus*
Flott, Andrew Frederick 1956- *St&PR 91*
Flott, Nancy Lee 1932- *WhoAmW 91*
Flottum, Kjersti 1953- *WhoWor 91*
Floum, B. Robert 1935- *St&PR 91*
Flournoy, Andra Brooks 1956- *WhoAmW 91*
Flournoy, August Woodridge 1810-1878 *AmLegL*
Flournoy, Dayl Jean 1944- *WhoSSW 91*
Flournoy, Houston Irvine 1929- *WhoAm 90*
Flournoy, Howard John, Jr. 1945- *WhoSSW 91*
Flournoy, Janie Davis 1950- *WhoAmW 91*
Flournoy, John Francis 1940- *St&PR 91*
Flournoy, Lucien 1919- *St&PR 91*
Flournoy, Nancy 1947- *WhoAmW 91*
Flournoy, Selwyn Lester, Jr. 1941- *WhoAm 90*
Flournoy, Theodore 1854-1920 *EncO&P 3, EncPaPR 91*
Flournoy, Thomas B. *AmLegL*
Flournoy, Thomas Neal 1922- *St&PR 91*
Flournoy, Valerie 1952- *BioIn 16*
Flowe, Benjamin Hugh, Jr. 1956- *WhoEmL 91*
Flowe, Carol Connor 1950- *WhoEmL 91*
Flower, Benjamin Orange 1858-1918 *BioIn 16*
Flower, Bernard *PenDiDA 89*
Flower, George Edward 1919- *WhoAm 90*
Flower, Joe *ConAu 130*
Flower, John Arnold 1921- *WhoAm 90*
Flower, Joseph Edward 1950- *ConAu 130*
Flower, Michael Lavin 1958- *WhoAmA 91*
Flower, Milton E 1910- *ConAu 129*
Flower, Robert E. 1937- *St&PR 91*
Flower, Walter Chew, III 1939- *WhoWor 91*
Flowerdew, Alice 1759-1830 *FemiCLE*
Flowerree, Robert E. 1921- *St&PR 91*
Flowerree, Robert Edmund 1921- *WhoAm 90*
Flowers, Amy Lee 1954- *WhoAmW 91*
Flowers, Ben 1927- *Ballpl 90*
Flowers, Betty Sue 1947- *WhoAmW 91, WhoWrEP 89*
Flowers, Brian Hilton 1924- *WhoWor 91*
Flowers, Carolyn Greene 1934- *WhoSSW 91*
Flowers, Charles V., Jr. 1926?-1990 *ConAu 130*
Flowers, Daniel Fort 1920- *St&PR 91*
Flowers, David Lee 1942- *St&PR 91*
Flowers, David R. *St&PR 91*
Flowers, Eugene Monroe, Jr. 1947- *WhoSSW 91*
Flowers, Francis Asbury, III 1955- *WhoEmL 91*
Flowers, Gayle Douglas 1934- *St&PR 91*
Flowers, Jack S. 1937- *St&PR 91*
Flowers, Jake 1902-1962 *Ballpl 90*
Flowers, James R. 1941- *St&PR 91*
Flowers, Judith Ann 1944- *WhoAmW 91*
Flowers, Kate *IntWWM 90*
Flowers, Kent Gordon, Jr. 1955- *WhoEmL 91*
Flowers, Langdon Strong 1922- *St&PR 91, WhoAm 90*
Flowers, Larry *BiDrAPA 89*
Flowers, Loma Kaye *BiDrAPA 89*
Flowers, Michael Edward 1953- *WhoEmL 91*
Flowers, Paul William 1952- *WhoEmL 91*
Flowers, Richard W. 1950- *St&PR 91*
Flowers, Richmond, Jr. *BioIn 16*
Flowers, Robert James 1943- *St&PR 91*
Flowers, Ronald Alan 1954- *WhoE 91*
Flowers, Sally A. 1954- *WhoAmW 91*
Flowers, Thomas Earl 1928- *WhoAmA 91*
Flowers, Virginia Anne 1928- *WhoAm 90, WhoAmW 91*
Flowers, W. Harold 1911-1990 *BioIn 16*
Flowers, Wayland *BioIn 16*
Flowers, William H. 1913- *St&PR 91*
Flowers, William Howard, Jr. 1913- *WhoAm 90*
Flowers-Chester, Phyllis Denise 1956- *WhoAmW 91*
Flowler, Robyn J. 1954- *St&PR 91*
Floy, Charles R. 1934- *St&PR 91*
Floyd, Alexander Graham 1947- *WhoSSW 91*
Floyd, Angeleita Stevens 1952- *IntWWM 90*
Floyd, Anita Louise 1930- *WhoAmW 91*
Floyd, Billy Wayne *BiDrAPA 89*
Floyd, Camille Maxine 1940- *WhoWrEP 89*
Floyd, Carl Leo 1936- *WhoAmA 91*
Floyd, Carlisle *BioIn 16*
Floyd, Carlisle 1926- *IntWWM 90, PenDiMP A*
Floyd, Charles 1901?-1934 *WorAlBi*
Floyd, Charles Arthur 1904-1934 *BioIn 16*
Floyd, Clark Alan 1940- *WhoWrEP 89*
Floyd, David Kenneth 1932- *WhoAm 90*
Floyd, Deborah Mae 1962- *WhoAmW 91*
Floyd, Edwin Earl 1924- *WhoAm 90*
Floyd, Fredrick Franklin 1933- *WhoSSW 91*
Floyd, Gareth 1940- *SmATA 62 [port]*
Floyd, Glen D. 1936- *St&PR 91*
Floyd, Glenn Leslie 1954- *St&PR 91*
Floyd, Gordon Carlson 1955- *WhoSSW 91*
Floyd, Jack William 1934- *WhoAm 90*
Floyd, James Eston, Jr. 1957- *WhoEmL 91*
Floyd, Joe, Jr. *BioIn 16*
Floyd, Joe, Sr. *BioIn 16*
Floyd, John Alex, Jr. 1948- *WhoSSW 91*
Floyd, John B., Jr. 1917- *WhoAm 90*
Floyd, John Buchanan 1806-1863 *BiDrUSE 89*
Floyd, John Taylor 1942- *WhoE 91*
Floyd, John Walker, Jr. 1946- *St&PR 91*
Floyd, Kay Cirksena 1943- *WhoSSW 91*
Floyd, Lillian Claire *WhoAmW 91*
Floyd, Malcolm John 1958- *IntWWM 90*
Floyd, Marguerite Marie 1924- *WhoAmW 91*
Floyd, Mark A. 1955- *St&PR 91*
Floyd, Melode Jo 1962- *WhoSSW 91*
Floyd, Michael Dennis 1953- *WhoEmL 91, WhoSSW 91*
Floyd, Otis L. *WhoAm 90, WhoSSW 91*
Floyd, Paul W. 1940- *St&PR 91*
Floyd, Pretty Boy 1904-1934 *BioIn 16*
Floyd, Raymond 1942- *WhoAm 90*
Floyd, Robert W. 1936- *WhoAm 90*
Floyd, Rodney Wayne 1938- *WhoWor 91*
Floyd, Samuel A. *BioIn 16*
Floyd, Samuel Alexander 1937- *IntWWM 90*
Floyd, Sara Jordon 1938- *WhoAmW 91*
Floyd, Walter Lawrence 1926- *WhoAm 90*
Floyd, Wayne 1930- *WhoWrEP 89*
Floyd, William 1734-1821 *EncCRAm*
Floyd, William Arthur 1946- *St&PR 91*
Floyd, William Clary, Jr. 1954- *WhoEmL 91*
Floyd, William Rodger 1944- *St&PR 91*
Floyd, William S., IV 1950- *St&PR 91*
Floyd, Wm. Carlton, Jr. *BiDrAPA 89*
Floyd-Teniya, Kathleen 1953- *WhoAmW 91, WhoEmL 91*
Flu-Allen, Barbara Carlock 1944- *WhoAmW 91*
Flubacher, Joseph Francis 1914- *WhoE 91*
Fluck, Diana Mary 1931-1984 *DcNaB 1981*
Fluck, Ekkehard Otto 1931- *WhoWor 91*
Fluck, George Louis 1941- *St&PR 91*
Fluck, Michele Marguerite 1940- *WhoAmW 91*
Fluck, Richard Conard 1938- *WhoSSW 91*
Fluck, Sandra Squire 1944- *WhoWrEP 89*
Fluckiger, Heinz 1939- *WhoWor 91*
Flud, Robert 1574-1637 *EncO&P 3*
Fludd, Reginald Joseph 1938- *WhoAmA 91*
Fludd, Robert 1574-1637 *EncO&P 3*
Fludernik, Monika 1957- *WhoWor 91*
Fludgate, Barrington J. 1946- *St&PR 91*
Flueckiger, Bryan Edward 1951- *BiDrAPA 89*
Fluegel, Elizabeth Leigh 1959- *WhoAmW 91*
Fluegel, John Ormond 1930- *BiDrAPA 89*
Fluegge, Robert Adolph 1934- *WhoSSW 91*
Fluegge, Ronald Marvin 1948- *WhoWor 91*
Fluehr, Darrell Krelle 1958- *WhoEmL 91*
Fluehr, Kuhlman 1931- *St&PR 91*
Fluek, Toby 1926- *WhoAmA 91*
Fluellen, Joel *DrBIPA 90*
Fluellen, Joel *BioIn 16, NewYTBS 90*
Fluellen, Shirley Ann 1952- *WhoAmW 91*
Fluet, Michelle L. 1960- *WhoAmW 91*
Flugelman, Maximo Enrique 1945- *WhoE 91, WhoWor 91*
Flugger, Penelope Ann 1942- *WhoAm 90, WhoAmW 91*
Flugsrud-Breckenridge, Marcia Reed *BiDrAPA 89*
Fluharty, James Robert 1943- *St&PR 91*
Fluhr, Frederick Robert 1922- *WhoE 91, WhoWor 91*
Fluhr, Howard 1943- *St&PR 91*
Fluhrer, David R. 1950- *ODwPR 91*
Fluk, Harold 1930- *WhoE 91*
Fluke, Lyla Schram *WhoAmW 91*
Flum, Jerry S. 1940- *WhoE 91*
Flume, David Lawrence *BiDrAPA 89*
Flume, Shiree Cecile *BiDrAPA 89*
Flume, Violet Sigoloff *WhoAmA 91*
Flumerfelt, John M *BiDrAPA 89*
Flummerfelt, Joseph 1937- *IntWWM 90*
Fluno, Jere D. 1941- *St&PR 91*
Fluno, Jere David 1941- *WhoAm 90*
Fluno, John Arthur 1914- *WhoSSW 91*
Fluor, John Robert, II 1945- *St&PR 91*
Fluor, Marjorie Letha Wade 1926- *WhoAmW 91, WhoWor 91*
Fluor, Peter J. 1947- *St&PR 91*
Fluss, Hella Ruth 1926- *BiDrAPA 89*
Flusser, Alan *BioIn 16*
Flussi, Harry Valentine 1918- *WhoAm 90*
Flute, Molly *ConAu 30NR*
Flutie, Doug *BioIn 16*
Fluty, Steven Jay 1957- *WhoWrEP 89*
Fly, Camillus S. 1849-1901 *BioIn 16*
Fly, Everett Lowell 1952- *WhoSSW 91*
Fly, Frederick George 1940- *St&PR 91*
Fly, Gale S. 1933- *St&PR 91*
Fly, James Douglas 1949- *WhoSSW 91*
Fly, James L. *BioIn 16*
Fly, James Lawrence, Jr. 1928- *WhoSSW 91*
Fly, William 1699?-1726 *BioIn 16*
Flye, M. Wayne 1942- *WhoAm 90*
Flye, William Mitchell 1948- *WhoSSW 91*
Flyer, Doris Moseley 1909- *St&PR 91*
Flyer, Jill S. 1942- *WhoAmW 91*
Flygare, Gordon Robert 1938- *WhoSSW 91*
Flygare, John Arnold 1933- *WhoSSW 91*

Flygare, Richard Watts 1955- WhoEmL 91
Flygare-Carlen, Emilie 1807-1892 EncCoWW
Flying Burrito Brothers, The EncPR&S 89, WhoNeCM A
Flying Hawk 1852-1931 WhNaAH
Flying Officer X MajTwCW
Flynn, Alva Anne Owen 1911- WhoAmW 91
Flynn, Anne Elizabeth 1928- WhoAmW 91
Flynn, Annette Theresa 1953- WhoAmW 91
Flynn, Anthony 1952- St&PR 91
Flynn, Arthur James 1926- St&PR 91
Flynn, Charles Everette 1912- St&PR 91
Flynn, Charles William 1935- St&PR 91
Flynn, Christopher F 1959- BiDrAPA 89
Flynn, Dana BioIn 16
Flynn, Daniel Joseph 1959- WhoEmL 91
Flynn, David Kevin 1954- WhoEmL 91
Flynn, David Paul 1940- WhoAm 90
Flynn, Dennis Patrick 1944- WhoAm 90
Flynn, Don ConAu 30NR
Flynn, Donald Edward 1940- St&PR 91
Flynn, Donald Francis 1939- St&PR 91, WhoAm 90
Flynn, Donald R 1928- ConAu 30NR
Flynn, Doug 1951- Ballpl 90
Flynn, Elizabeth Anne 1951- WhoAmW 91, WhoEmL 91
Flynn, Elizabeth G. 1890-1964 BioAmW
Flynn, Elizabeth Gurley 1890-1964 BioIn 16, EncAL, FemiCLE, WorAlBi
Flynn, Ellen F 1950- BiDrAPA 89
Flynn, Errol 1909-1959 BioIn 16, WorAlBi
Flynn, F. Patrick 1949- St&PR 91
Flynn, George ConAu 31NR
Flynn, George William 1937- IntWWM 90
Flynn, George William 1938- WhoAm 90
Flynn, Harry Joseph 1933- WhoAm 90
Flynn, Jackson Edward 1933- St&PR 91
Flynn, James Arthur, III 1940- WhoAm 90
Flynn, James Joseph 1911- AuBYP 90
Flynn, James L. 1934- St&PR 91
Flynn, James Leonard 1934- WhoAm 90
Flynn, James Peter 1961- WhoE 91
Flynn, James Rourke 1925- WhoAm 90
Flynn, Janet-Beth 1944- WhoAmW 91
Flynn, Jeffrey Paul 1959- WhoEmL 91
Flynn, Jo Ann 1946- WhoSSW 91
Flynn, John 1880-1951 BioIn 16
Flynn, John Francis St&PR 91
Flynn, John Michael 1940- WhoSSW 91
Flynn, John William 1939- St&PR 91, WhoAm 90
Flynn, Joseph Henry 1922- WhoE 91
Flynn, Judith A. 1937- ODwPR 91
Flynn, Judith Anne 1937- WhoAmW 91
Flynn, Judith C. 1944- WhoAmW 91
Flynn, Judith E. 1944- WhoAmW 91, WhoSSW 91
Flynn, Katherine Elizabeth 1959- WhoEmL 91
Flynn, Louis L, Jr. BiDrAPA 89
Flynn, Marie Cosgrove 1945- WhoAmW 91, WhoE 91
Flynn, Mary Ann 1959- WhoAmW 91
Flynn, Mary Margaret 1942- BiDrAPA 89
Flynn, Mary Veronica 1919- WhoAmW 91
Flynn, Matthew James 1929- St&PR 91
Flynn, Michael Harrington 1938- St&PR 91
Flynn, Michael James 1920- WhoE 91
Flynn, Monica Anne BiDrAPA 89
Flynn, Pat L 1954- WhoAmA 91
Flynn, Patricia M. 1950- WhoE 91
Flynn, Patrick J. St&PR 91
Flynn, Paul Bartholomew 1935- WhoAm 90, WhoE 91
Flynn, Paul M. 1953- St&PR 91
Flynn, Paul Michael 1949- WhoEmL 91
Flynn, Paul Michael 1953- WhoE 91
Flynn, Pauline T. 1942- WhoAm 90
Flynn, Peter Anthony 1942- WhoWor 91
Flynn, Peter E. 1959- St&PR 91
Flynn, Priscilla 1948- St&PR 91
Flynn, R. Marshall 1959- WhoEmL 91
Flynn, Ralph Melvin, Jr. 1944- WhoWor 91
Flynn, Raymond Leo 1939- WhoAm 90, WhoE 91
Flynn, Richard J. 1924- St&PR 91
Flynn, Richard James 1928- WhoAm 90, WhoE 91, WhoWor 91
Flynn, Richard Jerome 1924- WhoAm 90
Flynn, Richard McDonnell 1955- WhoWrEP 89
Flynn, Robert Emmett 1933- WhoAm 90
Flynn, Robert Warren 1943- WhoE 91
Flynn, Shaun Patrick 1955- St&PR 91
Flynn, Thomas 1852-1912 AmLegL
Flynn, Thomas Brown 1936- WhoAm 90
Flynn, Thomas Charles 1950- WhoWor 91
Flynn, Thomas G. ODwPR 91
Flynn, Thomas Joseph 1936- St&PR 91, WhoAm 90
Flynn, Thomas Joseph 1950- WhoEmL 91
Flynn, Thomas P. 1935- St&PR 91
Flynn, Thomas Patrick 1924- WhoAm 90
Flynn, Thomas T BiDrAPA 89
Flynn, Thomas William 1955- WhoE 91
Flynn, Walter BioIn 16
Flynn, William E 1931- BiDrAPA 89
Flynn, William Joseph 1926- WhoAm 90
Flynn, William R 1927- BiDrAPA 89
Flynt, Candace 1947- WhoWrEP 89
Flynt, Charles Homer, Jr. 1940- WhoSSW 91
Flynt, Drew R. 1946- WhoE 91
Flynt, James Edwin, Jr. 1950- WhoSSW 91
Flynt, John James, Jr. 1914- WhoAm 90
Flynt, Larry Claxton 1942- WhoAm 90
Flynt, Mark Alan 1955- WhoSSW 91
Flys, Carlos Ricardo 1963- WhoHisp 91
Flythe, Walter White 1930- St&PR 91
FM-2030 ConAu 31NR
Fo, Dario 1926- MajTwCW, WorAu 1980 [port]
Foa, Joseph Victor 1909- WhoAm 90, WhoE 91
Foa, Uriel G. 1916-1990 BioIn 16
Foan, John ConTFT 8
Foard, Susan Lee 1938- WhoAm 90
Foat, Lawrence M. 1946- St&PR 91
Fobbs, Joan Merna 1943- WhoAmW 91
Fobel, James M. 1946- ConAu 129
Fobel, Jim ConAu 129
Fobes, Donald Edwards 1910- WhoAm 90
Fobes, John Edwin 1918- WhoWor 91
Foccart, Jacques Guillaume Louis Marie 1913- BiDFrPL
Foch, Ferdinand 1851-1929 BiDFrPL, WorAlBi
Foch, Nina 1924- WhoAm 90, WhoAmW 91, WorAlBi
Fochler, Marcia BioIn 16
Focht, John A. BioIn 16
Focht, John Arnold, Jr. 1923- St&PR 91, WhoAm 90
Focht, Michael Harrison 1942- WhoAm 90
Fochtmann, Laura J BiDrAPA 89
Fock, Cornelia Willemina 1942- WhoWor 91
Fockler, Douglas D. 1942- WhoAm 90
Fockler, Herbert Hill 1922- WhoAm 90, WhoE 91, WhoWor 91
Fodden, Simon R. 1944- ConAu 131
Foden, Harry G. 1924- St&PR 91
Fodens Motor Works Band OxCPMus
Foderaro, Anthony Harolde 1926- WhoAm 90
Fodi, John 1944- IntWWM 90
Fodiman, Aaron Rosen 1937- WhoSSW 91, WhoWor 91
Fodor, Eugene 1905- WhoAm 90
Fodor, Eugene 1950- BioIn 16, IntWWM 90
Fodor, Frank 1924- BiDrAPA 89
Fodor, Gabor Bela 1915- WhoAm 90
Fodor, Janice Hoyer 1937- WhoAmW 91
Fodor, John 1929- St&PR 91
Fodor, Nandor 1895-1964 EncO&P 3, EncPaPR 91
Fodrea, Carolyn Wrobel 1943- WhoAmW 91
Fodrell, Pamela S. 1956- WhoSSW 91
Foege, Robert Louis 1938- WhoWor 91
Foege, Rose Ann Scudiero 1941- WhoAmW 91, WhoE 91
Foege, William Herbert 1936- WhoAm 90
Foehl, Edward Albert 1942- WhoAm 90
Foehner, Elvin M. 1902- St&PR 91
Foehrkolb, Susan Mary 1948- WhoAmW 91, WhoEmL 91, WhoWor 91
Foell, Earl William 1929- WhoAm 90, WhoWrEP 89
Foell, Lynn Waldo 1940- WhoE 91
Foell, Wesley Kay 1935- WhoAm 90
Foeller, George Paul 1931- IntWWM 90
Foelsch, Eckard Otto 1929- WhoWor 91
Foelster, Hans Juergen 1932- WhoWor 91
Foerch, Bruce Frederick 1949- WhoEmL 91
Foerder, Rudolf von Bennigsen- 1926-1989 BioIn 16
Foerst, John George, Jr. 1927- WhoE 91, WhoWor 91
Foerster, Bernd 1923- WhoAm 90
Foerster, Kathryn Stuever 1954- WhoEmL 91
Foerster, Mary Carson ODwPR 91
Foerster, Paul F. 1929- St&PR 91
Foerster, Paul Friedrich 1929- WhoAm 90
Foerster, Richard A. 1949- WhoWrEP 89
Foerster, Robin Stuart 1947- BiDrAPA 89
Foerster, Stephen Arthur 1941- St&PR 91
Foerster, Urban Michael, III 1952- WhoAm 90
Foertsch, James Gregory 1952- WhoEmL 91
Foffe, Maria Catherine 1948- WhoAmW 91
Fofonoff, Nicholas Paul 1929- WhoAm 90
Foft, John William 1928- WhoAm 90
Fogal, Ruth Ann Mallon 1952- WhoAmW 91
Fogarasi, Mariya Anne Toohey 1956- WhoWor 91
Fogarty, Dan ODwPR 91
Fogarty, David J. 1927- St&PR 91
Fogarty, Edward Michael 1948- WhoE 91, WhoEmL 91
Fogarty, Elizabeth Rummans 1916- WhoAmW 91
Fogarty, Finola Maeve BiDrAPA 89
Fogarty, Gerald Philip 1939- WhoAm 90
Fogarty, James E. 1913- St&PR 91
Fogarty, Jim BioIn 16
Fogarty, John F., Jr. 1921- St&PR 91
Fogarty, John Thomas 1929- St&PR 91, WhoAm 90
Fogarty, John Thomas 1940- WhoAm 90
Fogarty, Jonathan Titulescu MajTwCW
Fogarty, Kelly Patrick 1963- WhoEmL 91
Fogarty, M.G. 1933- St&PR 91
Fogarty, Michael Garrett 1933- WhoE 91
Fogarty, Robert Stephen 1938- WhoAm 90
Fogarty, Thomas BioIn 16
Fogarty, Thomas Michael BiDrAPA 89
Fogarty, Thomas Nilan 1936- WhoSSW 91
Fogarty, Walter Anthony 1936- St&PR 91
Fogarty, William Martin, Jr. 1935- WhoAm 90
Fogarty, William Thomas 1923- St&PR 91, WhoAm 90
Fogel, Adelaide Forst 1915- WhoAmW 91
Fogel, Barry Steven 1952- BiDrAPA 89, WhoEmL 91
Fogel, Belle 1924- St&PR 91
Fogel, Daniel Mark 1948- WhoWrEP 89
Fogel, Ernest James BiDrAPA 89
Fogel, Gerald Irving 1938- BiDrAPA 89
Fogel, Irving Martin 1929- WhoAm 90, WhoE 91, WhoWor 91
Fogel, Isaac K. 1943- St&PR 91
Fogel, Julius 1913- BiDrAPA 89
Fogel, Maurice 1911-1981 BioIn 16
Fogel, Meyer H. 1920- St&PR 91
Fogel, Neil 1954- WhoE 91
Fogel, Sander H 1927- BiDrAPA 89
Fogel, Sari Nussbaum BiDrAPA 89
Fogel, Seymour 1911-1984 WhoAmA 91N
Fogel, Wayne A., II 1941- WhoSSW 91
Fogelberg, Andrew 1732?-1793 PenDiDA 89
Fogelberg, Dan 1951- ConMus 4 [port]
Fogelberg, Daniel Grayling 1951- WhoAm 90
Fogelberg, Ernest Howard BiDrAPA 89
Fogelberg, Paul Alan 1951- WhoEmL 91
Fogelgrew, Stephen Walton 1947- St&PR 91
Fogelin, Russell J. 1919- St&PR 91
Fogelklou-Norlind, Emilia Maria 1878-1972 DcScanL
Fogell, Martin Maurice 1929- IntWWM 90
Fogelman, Avron BioIn 16
Fogelman, Hal David 1963- WhoSSW 91
Fogelman, Harold Hugo 1943- BiDrAPA 89, WhoE 91
Fogelman, John Aaron 1938- BiDrAPA 89
Fogelman, Mark Charles 1960- WhoEmL 91
Fogelman, Martin 1928- WhoAm 90
Fogelman, Mitchell Keith 1951- St&PR 91
Fogelman, Morris Joseph 1923- WhoAm 90
Fogelnest, Robert Craig 1946- WhoEmL 91
Fogelquist, Jan Elizabeth BiDrAPA 89
Fogelsanger, Allen 1962- WhoE 91
Fogelson, David 1903- WhoAm 90
Fogelson, David Leslie 1951- BiDrAPA 89
Fogelson, Nathan B. 1902-1989 BioIn 16
Fogelson, Raymond David 1933- WhoAm 90
Fogelsonger, Ned Raymond 1947- WhoE 91, WhoEmL 91
Fogerty, Arthur Joseph 1938- ODwPR 91, St&PR 91, WhoAm 90
Fogerty, John 1945- EncPR&S 89, WorAlBi
Fogerty, Patricia Marie 1943- WhoAmW 91
Fogg, Cynthia Ann 1956- WhoAmW 91
Fogg, Gordon Elliott 1919- WhoWor 91
Fogg, James Walter 1937- St&PR 91
Fogg, Joseph Graham, III 1946- WhoAm 90
Fogg, Monica WhoAmA 91
Fogg, Rebecca Snider 1949- WhoAmA 91
Fogg, Richard Lloyd 1937- St&PR 91, WhoAm 90
Fogg, Stephen Monroe 1952- St&PR 91
Fogg-Waberski, Joanna Halina 1956- BiDrAPA 89
Foggie, Charles Herbert 1912- WhoAm 90, WhoE 91
Foggie, Samuel Lewis 1927- St&PR 91
Foggini, Beppe 1938- WhoWor 91
Foggini, Giovanni Battista 1652-1725 PenDiDA 89
Foghat EncPR&S 89
Foght, James Loren 1936- WhoAm 90
Fogland, Dennis Johan 1951- WhoEmL 91
Fogle, Carole BioIn 16
Fogle, Edward Lawrence 1931- St&PR 91
Fogle, Fredric Dean 1936- St&PR 91
Fogle, James BioIn 16
Fogle, Joe Ann 1945- WhoAmW 91
Fogle, Richard Harter 1911- WhoAm 90
Fogleman, Harry Frank 1931- WhoAm 90
Fogleman, John Albert 1911- WhoAm 90
Fogleman, John Nelson 1956- WhoEmL 91
Fogleman, Julian Barton 1920- WhoAm 90
Fogleman, Ronald Robert 1942- WhoAm 90
Fogleman, Ross Lee, III 1955- WhoEmL 91
Fogler, Lloyd Stephen David 1933- St&PR 91
Foglesong, Marilee Ann 1936- WhoE 91
Foglia, Robert Donald 1929- WhoE 91
Foglietta, Thomas Michael 1928- WhoAm 90, WhoE 91
Fohl, Lee 1870-1965 Ballpl 90
Fohl, Timothy 1934- WhoAm 90
Fohn, Gerald Anthony 1945- WhoWor 91
Fohr, Jenny WhoAmA 91
Fohrmeister, Robert Charles 1945- WhoE 91
Foil, Jacqueline B. 1929- WhoAmW 91
Foil, Mary Beth 1954- WhoAmW 91
Foil, Robert Rodney 1934- WhoAm 90
Foiles, Hank 1929- Ballpl 90
Foillet, J. PenDiDA 89
Foisie, Jack 1919- WhoAm 90
Foisie, Philip Manning 1922- WhoAm 90
Foit, Franklin Frederick, Jr. 1942- WhoAm 90
Fojtik, John Patrick 1956- WhoSSW 91
Fok, Agnes Kwan 1940- WhoAmW 91
Fok, Thomas Dso Yun 1921- WhoAm 90, WhoWor 91
Fok, Vladimir Aleksandrovich 1898-1974 DcScB S2
Fokdal, Steffen 1939- WhoWor 91
Foke Luste Hajo WhNaAH
Foke-Lustee Hadjo WhNaAH
Fokine, Michel 1880-1942 WorAlBi
Fokstuen, Terge Sigbjorn 1924- BiDrAPA 89
Fol, Monique Eliane 1933- WhoAmW 91
Folberg, Harold Jay 1941- WhoAm 90
Folberth, William Mitchell, III 1944- WhoE 91
Folch-Pi, Diana Maria 1951- WhoEmL 91
Folda, Jaroslav, III 1940- WhoAmA 91
Folden, Virgil Alvis, III 1953- WhoEmL 91
Foldes, Andor 1913- IntWWM 90, PenDiMP
Foldes, Imre 1934- IntWWM 90
Foldes, Lawrence David 1959- WhoEmL 91
Foldi, Andrew Harry 1926- IntWWM 90, WhoAm 90
Folds, Charles Weston 1910- WhoAm 90
Folds, Thomas McKey 1908- WhoAmA 91, WhoE 91
Foldvari, Tibor L. 1936- St&PR 91
Foldvary, Fred E. 1946- WhoWrEP 89
Foley, Allan James PenDiMP
Foley, Anne Therese 1953- WhoEmL 91
Foley, Archie R BiDrAPA 89
Foley, Arthur James 1946- WhoEmL 91
Foley, Bernard James 1933- WhoE 91
Foley, Beverley B.L. 1945- WhoAmW 91
Foley, Brian Francis 1937- St&PR 91
Foley, C. Patrick 1933- WhoSSW 91
Foley, Carmel Anne BiDrAPA 89
Foley, Cecil B. 1933- St&PR 91
Foley, Daniel Joseph 1913- AuBYP 90
Foley, Daniel Ronald 1941- WhoAm 90, WhoWor 91
Foley, David Francis 1945- IntWWM 90
Foley, Dennis Donald 1923- St&PR 91
Foley, Dorothy Swartz WhoAmA 91
Foley, Edna Lois 1879-1943 BioIn 16
Foley, Edward Francis 1954- WhoEmL 91
Foley, Edward W. 1939- St&PR 91
Foley, Eileen Mary 1954- WhoAmW 91
Foley, Esther V. BioIn 16
Foley, Eugene P. St&PR 91
Foley, Gardner P.H. 1935- St&PR 91
Foley, Harold Cox 1939- St&PR 91
Foley, Helen 1917- FemiCLE
Foley, Helen Claiborne 1945- WhoAmW 91
Foley, James David 1942- WhoAm 90
Foley, James Francis 1946- St&PR 91
Foley, James Michael 1939- St&PR 91
Foley, James Thomas 1910- WhoAm 90
Foley, James Thomas 1910-1990 NewYTBS 90
Foley, Joan Coleman 1929- WhoAm 90
Foley, Joe L., III 1939- St&PR 91
Foley, John A. 1956- St&PR 91
Foley, John Daniel 1916- St&PR 91
Foley, John Francis 1936- St&PR 91
Foley, John J. St&PR 91
Foley, John Porter, Jr., Mrs. WhoAmW 91
Foley, John Samuel 1833-1918 BioIn 16

Foley, Joseph Bernard 1929- *WhoAm 90, WhoE 91*
Foley, Kathy Kelsey 1952- *WhoAmA 91*
Foley, Kevin 1953- *ODwPR 91*
Foley, Laurie Nell 1962- *WhoSSW 91*
Foley, Lewis Michael 1938- *WhoAm 90*
Foley, Louise Munro 1933- *AuBYP 90, BioIn 16*
Foley, Margaret 1827-1877 *BiDWomA*
Foley, Martin James 1946- *WhoEmL 91*
Foley, Mary Josephine 1936- *WhoAmW 91*
Foley, Maureen Frances 1946- *WhoAmW 91*
Foley, Michael C. 1944- *St&PR 91*
Foley, Michael Francis 1946- *WhoAm 90, WhoSSW 91*
Foley, Patricia Ann 1942- *St&PR 91*
Foley, Patricia Jean 1956- *WhoAmW 91*
Foley, Patricia M. *ODwPR 91*
Foley, Patrick J. 1930- *St&PR 91*
Foley, Patrick Joseph 1930- *WhoAm 90*
Foley, Patrick Martin 1930- *WhoAm 90*
Foley, Paul Allen 1934- *WhoWor 91*
Foley, Red 1910-1968 *OxCPMus, WorAlBi*
Foley, Richard K. 1941- *St&PR 91*
Foley, Robert Douglas 1954- *WhoEmL 91*
Foley, Robert Henry 1930- *St&PR 91*
Foley, Robert John Eugene 1942- *WhoWor 91*
Foley, Scott *AuBYP 90*
Foley, Stephen Bernard 1950- *WhoEmL 91*
Foley, Stephen J. 1951- *St&PR 91*
Foley, Sylvester Robert, Jr. 1928- *WhoAm 90*
Foley, Thomas 1942- *WhoAm 90*
Foley, Thomas C. 1952- *WhoAm 90*
Foley, Thomas Coleman 1952- *BioIn 16, St&PR 91*
Foley, Thomas L. 1942- *St&PR 91*
Foley, Thomas Michael 1943- *WhoE 91*
Foley, Thomas S *NewYTBS 90 [port]*
Foley, Thomas S. 1929- *BioIn 16, News 90 [port], WorAlBi*
Foley, Thomas Stephen 1929- *WhoAm 90*
Foley, Tom 1959- *Ballpl 90*
Foley, Vincent Paul 1947- *St&PR 91*
Foley, William Edward 1911- *WhoAm 90*
Foley, William P., II 1944- *St&PR 91*
Foley, William Thomas 1911- *WhoAm 90*
Folgate, Homer Emmett, Jr. 1920- *WhoAm 90*
Folger, Charles James 1818-1884 *BiDrUSE 89*
Folger, Henry Clay 1857-1930 *WorAlBi*
Folger, Thomas Duane 1944- *St&PR 91*
Foli, Signor 1835-1899 *PenDiMP*
Foli, Tim 1950- *Ballpl 90*
Folin, Otto 1867-1934 *BioIn 16*
Folino, Barbara Adele Schalk 1939- *WhoAmW 91*
Folinsbee, Marjory Cora 1925- *BiDrAPA 89*
Folinsbee, Robert Edward 1917- *WhoAm 90*
Folio, Lorenzo 1930- *WhoWor 91*
Foliot, Francois, I *PenDiDA 89*
Foliot, Francois, II 1748- *PenDiDA 89*
Foliot, Nicolas-Quinibert 1706-1776 *PenDiDA 89*
Folk, April Lynn 1960- *WhoAmW 91*
Folk, Barbara Theresa 1947- *WhoAmW 91*
Folk, Earl E. 1930- *St&PR 91*
Folk, James 1948- *WhoEmL 91*
Folk, James William, Jr. 1940- *BiDrAPA 89*
Folk, Mary Catherine 1947- *WhoEmL 91*
Folk, Norma H. *St&PR 91*
Folk, Richard Albert 1937- *WhoSSW 91*
Folk, Robert Louis 1925- *WhoAm 90*
Folk, Russell Harter 1947- *WhoSSW 91*
Folk, Sharon Lynn 1945- *WhoEmL 91*
Folk, Thomas Robert 1950- *WhoEmL 91*
Folkema, Judith Lynne *BiDrAPA 89*
Folkenflik, Max 1948- *WhoEmL 91*
Folkers, Cay 1942- *WhoWor 91*
Folkers, Karl August 1906- *WhoAm 90*
Folkers, Rich 1946- *Ballpl 90*
Folkert, David F. 1948- *St&PR 91*
Folkerts, James D. 1943- *St&PR 91*
Folkes, Marilyn Anita 1949- *WhoE 91*
Folkman, David H. 1934- *WhoAm 90*
Folkman, Georgia *WhoWrEP 89*
Folkman, Moses Judah 1933- *WhoAm 90*
Folkomer, John Hayward 1945- *WhoE 91*
Folks, David Gibson 1953- *BiDrAPA 89*
Folks, J. Leroy 1929- *WhoAm 90*
Folks, John M. 1948- *WhoAm 90*
Folkus, Dan 1946- *WhoAmA 91*
Folla, Paul Richard 1942- *St&PR 91*
Follain, Jean 1903-1971 *ConAu 130*
Folland, Edward F. 1916- *St&PR 91*
Folland, William Denton 1940- *St&PR 91*
Follansbee, Dorothy Leland 1911- *WhoAmW 91*
Follansbee, John Nathan 1936- *BiDrAPA 89*
Follesdal, Dagfinn 1932- *WhoAm 90*
Follet, John Sample 1944- *BiDrAPA 89*
Follett, Garth Benepe *BioIn 16*
Follett, Helen 1884?-1970 *AuBYP 90*
Follett, James 1939- *SpyFic*
Follett, Jean 1917- *BiDWomA*
Follett, Jean Frances 1917- *WhoAm 90, WhoAmA 91*
Follett, John Fassett 1831-1902 *AmLegL*
Follett, Ken 1949- *Au&Arts 6 [port], BioIn 16, ConAu 33NR, CurBio 90 [port], MajTwCW, TwCCr&M 91, WorAu 1980 [port]*
Follett, Kenneth 1949- *WorAlBi*
Follett, Kenneth Martin 1949- *SpyFic, WhoAm 90, WhoWor 91, WhoWrEP 89*
Follett, Kent Albert 1937- *St&PR 91*
Follett, Mary Parker 1868-1933 *BioIn 16*
Follett, Mary Vierling 1917- *WhoAmW 91*
Follett, Robert J.R. 1928- *St&PR 91*
Follett, Robert John Richard 1928- *WhoAm 90, WhoWrEP 89*
Follett, Ronald Francis 1939- *WhoAm 90*
Follett, Ross Charles 1940- *St&PR 91*
Follett, William S. *St&PR 91*
Follett, William W., III *BiDrAPA 89*
Follette, William Albert 1946- *WhoEmL 91*
Folley, Clyde H. 1927- *WhoAm 90*
Folley, Clyde Henry 1927- *St&PR 91*
Folley, Jarrett Harter 1913- *WhoAm 90*
Follezou, Jean-Yves 1948- *WhoWor 91*
Follick, Edwin Duane 1935- *WhoWor 91*
Follingstad, Carol Ann 1945- *WhoAmW 91*
Follini, Stefania *BioIn 16*
Follis, Cynthia A. 1941- *St&PR 91*
Follis, Harold W. 1945- *St&PR 91*
Follman, Dorothy Major 1932- *WhoAmW 91*
Follman, John Philip 1937- *St&PR 91*
Follman, Lazar *St&PR 91*
Follmann, Joseph Francis 1908-1989 *BioIn 16*
Follmer, John Scott 1951- *WhoEmL 91*
Follmer, Wilhelm Ferdinand 1908- *WhoWor 91*
Follot, Paul 1877-1941 *PenDiDA 89*
Follows, Jill Marilyn 1952- *WhoEmL 91*
Follweiler, Joanne Schaaf 1942- *WhoAmW 91*
Folman, E Erick *BiDrAPA 89*
Folmar, Jack Gordon 1931- *St&PR 91*
Folmsbee, Frank Arnold 1949- *St&PR 91*
Folon, Jean Michel 1934- *BioIn 16, ConDes 90*
Folonari, Francesco 1929-1990 *BioIn 16*
Folse, Parker Camile, III 1954- *WhoEmL 91*
Folsey, George 1898-1988 *AnObit 1988, BioIn 16*
Folsom, Burton Whitmore, Jr. 1947- *WhoSSW 91*
Folsom, David 1791-1847 *WhNaAH*
Folsom, Donald Lee 1933- *WhoSSW 91*
Folsom, Francis M. 1894-1970 *WorAlBi*
Folsom, Franklin 1907- *AuBYP 90*
Folsom, Franklin Brewster 1907- *WhoAm 90*
Folsom, Fred Gorham, III 1945- *WhoAmA 91, WhoE 91*
Folsom, Henry Richard 1913- *WhoAm 90*
Folsom, James, Jr. 1949- *WhoAm 90, WhoSSW 91*
Folsom, James C 1921- *BiDrAPA 89*
Folsom, James Cannon 1921- *WhoWor 91*
Folsom, James Elisha 1908-1987 *BioIn 16*
Folsom, John Roy 1918- *WhoAm 90*
Folsom, John W. 1950- *St&PR 91*
Folsom, Lauren Chenard 1957- *WhoEmL 91*
Folsom, Lowell Edwin 1947- *WhoEmL 91*
Folsom, Marion Bayard 1893- *BiDrUSE 89*
Folsom, Michael Brewster 1938- *AuBYP 90*
Folsom, Richard Gilman 1907- *WhoAm 90*
Folsom, Roger Lee 1952- *WhoSSW 91*
Folsom, Rose 1953- *WhoAmA 91*
Folsom, Thomas Lee 1954- *BiDrAPA 89*
Folsom, Willard V. 1936- *St&PR 91*
Folsom, Wynelle Stough 1924- *WhoAmW 91*
Folstein, Marshal Frank *BiDrAPA 89*
Folster, Bonnie *WhoAmW 91*
Folta, Carl *ODwPR 91*
Folts, David Jacob 1958- *WhoEmL 91*
Foltz, Clara Shortridge 1849-1934 *BioIn 16*
Foltz, Claude A. 1932- *St&PR 91*
Foltz, Forrest Lowell 1926- *St&PR 91*
Foltz, Richard Harry 1924- *WhoAm 90*
Foltz, Rodger Lowell 1934- *WhoAm 90*
Foltz, Shawn *BioIn 16*
Folwell, Samuel 1764?-1813 *BioIn 16*
Folwell, William Hopkins 1924- *WhoAm 90*
Folz, David Harold 1952- *WhoSSW 91*
Fombona, Rufino Blanco *HispWr 90*
Fombona, Rufino Blanco 1874-1944 *BioIn 16*
Fomenko, Joseph, Jr. 1932- *St&PR 91*
Fomenko, Witold 1905-1961 *BioIn 16*
Fomon, Robert M. 1925- *WhoAm 90*
Fomon, Samuel Joseph 1923- *WhoAm 90*
Fonash, Stephen Joseph 1941- *WhoAm 90*
Fonda, Bridget *BioIn 16*
Fonda, Bridget 1964?- *ConTFT 8*
Fonda, Henry 1905-1982 *WorAlBi*
Fonda, Jane 1937- *BioAmW, BioIn 16, WhoAm 90, WhoAmW 91, WhoWrEP 89, WorAlBi*
Fonda, Jean Pierre 1937- *IntWWM 90*
Fonda, Jere Williams 1929- *St&PR 91*
Fonda, John Day 1956- *St&PR 91*
Fonda, Peter 1939- *WorAlBi*
Fondahl, John Walker 1924- *WhoAm 90*
Fondaw, Ron 1954- *WhoAmA 91*
Fondelli, Andrea *PenDiDA 89*
Fondiller, Robert 1916- *WhoAm 90*
Fondiller, Shirley Hope Alperin *WhoE 91, WhoWor 91*
Fondren, Harold M 1922- *WhoAmA 91*
Fondren, Kervin 1963- *WhoWrEP 89*
Fondren, William M., Jr. 1940- *St&PR 91*
Fondren, William Merle, Jr. 1940- *WhoSSW 91*
Fondy, Dee 1924- *Ballpl 90*
Foner, Eric 1943- *WhoAm 90, WhoWrEP 89*
Foner, Naomi *BioIn 16*
Foner, Philip S. 1910- *WhoAm 90*
Foner, Philip Sheldon 1910- *EncAL*
Foner, Simon 1925- *WhoAm 90*
Fones, William Hardin Davis 1917- *WhoAm 90*
Fonfrias, Ernesto Juan 1909- *WhoWor 91*
Fong, Bernard W. D. 1926- *WhoAm 90*
Fong, David 1921- *BiDrAPA 89*
Fong, Francis Kam-Yuen 1956- *IntWWM 90*
Fong, Gifford *BioIn 16*
Fong, Harold Michael 1938- *WhoAm 90*
Fong, Hiram L. 1906- *WhoAm 90*
Fong, Joy C.Y. 1954- *WhoWor 91*
Fong, Peter 1924- *WhoSSW 91*
Fong, Peter C. K. 1955- *WhoEmL 91, WhoWor 91*
Fong, Quock Q. 1934- *St&PR 91*
Fong-Cornella, Jana Ree 1955- *WhoEmL 91*
Fonk, James R. *St&PR 91*
Fonkalsrud, Eric Walter 1932- *WhoAm 90*
Fonken, Gerhard Joseph 1928- *WhoAm 90*
Fons, Anthony L 1931- *BiDrAPA 89*
Fons, Gail Bassett 1961- *WhoAmW 91*
Fons, Russ 1944- *ODwPR 91*
Fonseca, Carlos *BioIn 16*
Fonseca, Lew 1899-1989 *Ballpl 90*
Fonseca, Manuel Deodoro Da 1827-1892 *BioIn 16*
Fonseca, Miguel Alberto *BiDrAPA 89*
Fonseca, Raymond J. *WhoAm 90*
Fonsh, Leslie Michele 1955- *WhoE 91*
Fontages *EncCoWW*
Fontaine, A. P. 1905-1989 *BioIn 16*
Fontaine, Andre Lucien 1921- *WhoWor 91*
Fontaine, Andre Lucien Georges 1921- *BiDFrPL*
Fontaine, Athanas Paul 1905-1989 *BioIn 16*
Fontaine, Bernard Leo, Jr. 1956- *WhoE 91*
Fontaine, Burt Caspar Maria 1928- *WhoWor 91*
Fontaine, Carla Joan 1952- *WhoAmW 91*
Fontaine, David Joseph *BiDrAPA 89*
Fontaine, E Joseph *WhoAmA 91*
Fontaine, Edward Paul 1936- *St&PR 91, WhoAm 90*
Fontaine, Eudore Joseph, Jr. 1929- *WhoE 91*
Fontaine, Frank 1920-1978 *WorAlBi*
Fontaine, Gilles 1948- *WhoAm 90*
Fontaine, Harvey L. 1948- *St&PR 91*
Fontaine, Jean de la *EncO&P 3*
Fontaine, Jean-Guy 1935- *BiDrAPA 89*
Fontaine, Jean-Paul 1943- *WhoWor 91*
Fontaine, Joan 1917- *BioAmW, WorAlBi*
Fontaine, Melissa Fay 1960- *IntWWM 90*
Fontaine, Pierre Francois Leonard 1762-1853 *BioIn 16, PenDiDA 89*
Fontaine, Rejean *BiDrAPA 89*
Fontaine, Remy Enrique 1947- *WhoWor 91*
Fontaine, Sue 1928- *WhoE 91*
Fontaine, Valerie Anne 1955- *WhoEmL 91*
Fontana, Aldo A. 1917- *St&PR 91*
Fontana, Annibale 1540?-1587 *PenDiDA 89*
Fontana, Bill Patrick 1947- *WhoAmA 91*
Fontana, Carl 1928- *BioIn 16*
Fontana, Flaminio *PenDiDA 89*
Fontana, Franco 1933- *WhoWor 91*
Fontana, Gabriele 1958- *IntWWM 90*
Fontana, Guido *PenDiDA 89*
Fontana, Louis Anthony 1951- *BiDrAPA 89*
Fontana, Lucio 1899-1968 *ArtLatA*
Fontana, Orazio *PenDiDA 89*
Fontana, Richard Alan 1953- *WhoE 91, WhoEmL 91*
Fontana, Robert Edward 1915- *WhoAm 90*
Fontana, Thomas M. 1950- *St&PR 91*
Fontana, Thomas M 1951- *ConAu 130*
Fontane, Henri Theodore 1819-1898 *BioIn 16*
Fontane, Theodor 1819-1898 *BioIn 16, WorAlBi*
Fontanet, Alvaro L. 1940- *WhoHisp 91*
Fontanez, Dale W. 1967- *WhoHisp 91*
Fontanez, Julio *BiDrAPA 89*
Fontanive, Karen M. *ODwPR 91*
Fontanne, Lynn 1887-1983 *BioIn 16, WorAlBi*
Fontanne, Lynn 1889?-1983 *NotWoAT*
Fontannini, Clare *WhoAmA 91N*
Fontayne, Cynthia L. *ODwPR 91*
Fonte, Moderata *EncCoWW*
Fonte, Morris *BioIn 16*
Fonte, Richard J *BiDrAPA 89*
Fontebasso, Andrea *PenDiDA 89*
Fontebasso, Giuseppe *PenDiDA 89*
Fontela, Emilio 1938- *WhoWor 91*
Fontenelle, Scuddy Francis, Jr. 1931- *St&PR 91*
Fontenette, Marvin Nathaniel 1957- *WhoEmL 91*
Fontenettes, Charles *EncO&P 3*
Fontenot, Albert E. 1946- *St&PR 91*
Fontenot, Elvina S. 1935- *St&PR 91*
Fontenot, Leonard Glynn 1937- *St&PR 91*
Fontenot, Mary Alice 1910- *ConAu 31NR*
Fontenot, Mary Ellen 1950- *WhoAmW 91*
Fontenot, Ray 1957- *Ballpl 90*
Fontes, Patricia J. 1936- *WhoAmW 91, WhoWor 91*
Fontes, Wayne 1939- *WhoAm 90*
Fonteyn, Margot 1919- *WorAlBi*
Fonteyn de Arias, Margot 1919- *WhoAm 90, WhoWor 91*
Fonteyne, Herman J. 1939- *St&PR 91*
Fonteyne, Jacques Emile 1937- *St&PR 91*
Fontheim, Claude G.B. 1955- *WhoE 91, WhoEmL 91, WhoWor 91*
Fontillas, Rico *BiDrAPA 89*
Fontinoy, Charles-Marie 1920- *WhoWor 91*
Fontyn, Jacqueline 1930- *IntWWM 90*
Fonvielle, William Harold 1943- *WhoE 91*
Fonville, Linda Jean 1949- *WhoAmW 91*
Foo, Annabella Sai-Yan 1956- *WhoEmL 91*
Fooden, Bart Lewis 1955- *St&PR 91*
Foody, Jan Petkus 1935- *WhoAmW 91*
Foody, Richard Edward 1950- *WhoEmL 91*
Fookes, Peter George 1933- *WhoWor 91*
Fooks, Roberta Hodges 1955- *WhoSSW 91*
Foolery, Tom 1947- *WhoAmA 91*
Fools Crow 1890?-1989 *BioIn 16*
Foon, Warren David 1956- *St&PR 91*
Foonberg, Jay G. 1935- *WhoWor 91*
Fooner, Michael *AuBYP 90*
Foor, John A. 1934- *St&PR 91*
Foos, David Charles 1945- *BiDrAPA 89*
Foos, Raymond Anthony 1928- *St&PR 91*
Foosaner, Judith 1940- *WhoAmA 91*
Foosaner, Samuel J. 1907-1988 *BioIn 16*
Foose, Richard Martin 1915- *WhoAm 90*
Foose, Robert James 1938- *WhoAmA 91*
Fooshee, Irb H. 1908-1989 *BioIn 16*
Fooshee, Malcolm 1898-1989 *BioIn 16*
Foot, Hugh 1907-1990 *CurBio 90N*
Foot, Katherine 1852- *BioIn 16*
Foot, Michael 1913- *BioIn 16*
Foot, Neal R. 1948- *St&PR 91*
Foot, Philippa Ruth 1920- *WhoAm 90*
Foot, S.B. 1947- *St&PR 91*
Foote, A. Peter 1941- *St&PR 91*
Foote, Andrea Davette 1946- *WhoEmL 91*
Foote, Barbara Austin 1918- *WhoAmW 91*
Foote, Barry 1952- *Ballpl 90*
Foote, Christopher Spencer 1935- *WhoAm 90*
Foote, David Kent 1947- *St&PR 91*
Foote, Dorothy Gargis 1942- *WhoAmW 91*
Foote, Edward Thaddeus, II 1937- *WhoAm 90, WhoSSW 91, WhoWor 91*
Foote, Emerson 1906- *WhoAm 90*
Foote, Emmerline 1955- *WhoEmL 91*
Foote, Evelyn Patricia 1930- *WhoAm 90, WhoAmW 91*
Foote, Frances Catherine 1935- *WhoAmW 91*
Foote, Frank W. 1911-1989 *BioIn 16*
Foote, Franklin Manley 1908- *WhoAm 90*
Foote, Horton 1916- *WhoAm 90, WhoWrEP 89*
Foote, Howard Reed 1936- *WhoAmA 91*
Foote, James Maxwell 1941- *WhoAm 90*
Foote, Joel Lindsley 1928- *WhoAm 90*
Foote, John, Jr *WhoAmA 91N*
Foote, Kay Janell 1938- *WhoSSW 91*
Foote, Linda Gass 1939- *WhoAmW 91*
Foote, Mark Charles *BiDrAPA 89*
Foote, Martha Louisa 1957- *WhoEmL 91*

Foote, Mary 1847-1938 FemiCLE
Foote, Mary Hallock 1847-1938 BioAmW
Foote, Merrill Newton 1888-1988 BioIn 16
Foote, Pamela McMurray 1952- ODwPR 91
Foote, Ray P., Jr. 1933- St&PR 91
Foote, Robert Hutchinson 1922- WhoAm 90
Foote, Robert Kenneth 1944- St&PR 91
Foote, Robert T. 1917- St&PR 91
Foote, Ruth Annette 1925- WhoWor 91
Foote, Shelby BioIn 16
Foote, Shelby 1916- News 91-2 [port], WhoAm 90, WhoWrEP 89
Foote, Sherrill Lynne 1940- WhoAmW 91, WhoWor 91
Foote, Timothy 1926- BioIn 16
Foote, Timothy Gilson 1926- WhoAm 90
Foote, W. David 1940- St&PR 91
Foote, Warren Edgar 1935- WhoE 91
Foote, Will Howe 1874-1965 WhoAmA 91N
Foote, William W BiDrAPA 89
Footer, Sheila 1938- WhoAmW 91
Footitt, Hilary 1948- ConAu 132
Footlik, Robert Barry 1946- WhoEmL 91
Footman, Gordon Elliott 1927- WhoWor 91
Footman, Robert Henry 1916- SpyFic
Footner, Hulbert 1879-1944 TwCCr&M 91
Foots, James William 1916- WhoWor 91
Foott, Mary Hannay 1846-1918 FemiCLE
Foott, Roger 1946- St&PR 91, WhoEmL 91
Fopeano, Stephan Mark 1963- WhoEmL 91
Foradori, Elizabeth Leary 1956- St&PR 91
Foraker, David Alan 1956- WhoEmL 91
Foran, Kenneth Lawrence 1941- WhoAm 90
Foran, Thomas Aquinas 1924- WhoAm 90
Forani, Madeleine Christine 1916- BiDWomA
Foraste, Roland 1938- BiDrAPA 89, WhoE 91
Forauer, Robert Richard 1946- WhoE 91
Foray, June ConTFT 8 [port]
Forberg, Ati 1925- AuBYP 90
Forberg, Beate Gropius AuBYP 90
Forbert, Steve 1954- BioIn 16
Forbes, Allan Louis 1928- WhoAm 90
Forbes, Bob F. 1933- St&PR 91
Forbes, Bryan 1926- BioIn 16, WhoAm 90
Forbes, Cabot L. AuBYP 90
Forbes, Charles R BiDrAPA 89
Forbes, Christopher BioIn 16
Forbes, Christopher 1950- WhoAm 90, WhoE 91, WhoEmL 91
Forbes, Colin TwCCr&M 91
Forbes, Colin 1928- ConDes 90
Forbes, Cynthia Ann 1951- WhoAmW 91
Forbes, Daniel BioIn 16, TwCCr&M 91
Forbes, Daniel Merrill 1954- WhoSSW 91
Forbes, David Craig 1938- WhoAm 90
Forbes, Donna Marie 1929- WhoAmA 91
Forbes, Edward Coyle 1915- WhoAm 90, WhoWor 91
Forbes, Edward W 1873-1969 WhoAmA 91N
Forbes, Elizabeth 1924- IntWWM 90
Forbes, Elizabeth Adela 1859-1912 BiDWomA
Forbes, Elliot 1917- IntWWM 90, WhoAm 90
Forbes, Eric G. BioIn 16
Forbes, Ernest Browning 1876-1966 BioIn 16
Forbes, Esther 1891-1967 FemiCLE
Forbes, Esther 1894-1967 AuBYP 90
Forbes, Eve-Lyn 1949- WhoAmW 91, WhoSSW 91
Forbes, Franklin Sim 1936- WhoAm 90
Forbes, George W., III 1946- St&PR 91
Forbes, Gilbert Burnett 1915- WhoAm 90
Forbes, Glenn S. 1947- WhoEmL 91
Forbes, Gordon 1934- BioIn 16
Forbes, Gordon Maxwell 1930- WhoAm 90
Forbes, Harland Clement 1898-1990 BioIn 16, NewYTBS 90 [port]
Forbes, Irvin Lynnell 1902-1987 BioIn 16
Forbes, James Wendell 1923- WhoAm 90
Forbes, John 1710-1759 EncCRAm
Forbes, John Alexander 1938- St&PR 91
Forbes, John Allison 1922- WhoAmA 91
Forbes, John Douglas 1910- WhoAm 90, WhoWor 91
Forbes, John Francis 1946- WhoE 91
Forbes, John Francis 1959- BiDrAPA 89
Forbes, John Kenneth 1956- WhoEmL 91
Forbes, John Murray 1813-1898 EncABHB 6 [port]
Forbes, John Ripley 1913- WhoAm 90, WhoWor 91
Forbes, Jon Ervin 1940- WhoAm 90
Forbes, Judie 1942- WhoAmW 91
Forbes, Justine S BiDrAPA 89
Forbes, Katherine AuBYP 90
Forbes, Kathryn 1909-1966 WorAlBi
Forbes, Kenneth Albert Faucher 1922- WhoWor 91
Forbes, Kenneth Paul 1943- St&PR 91
Forbes, Laurie Jane 1950- WhoAmW 91
Forbes, Lorna M 1921- BiDrAPA 89
Forbes, Lorna Miriam 1921- WhoAm 90
Forbes, Louis M. 1955- St&PR 91
Forbes, Malcolm 1919-1990 NewYTBS 90 [port], News 90
Forbes, Malcolm Holloway 1933- WhoAm 90
Forbes, Malcolm S 1919-1990 ConAu 131, CurBio 90N, News 90-3, WorAlBi
Forbes, Malcolm S., Jr. BioIn 16
Forbes, Malcolm S., Jr. 1947- St&PR 91
Forbes, Malcolm Stevenson BioIn 16
Forbes, Malcolm Stevenson St&PR 91N
Forbes, Malcolm Stevenson, Jr. 1947- WhoAm 90, WhoE 91
Forbes, Mary Gladys 1929- WhoAmW 91
Forbes, Paul S. 1929- ODwPR 91
Forbes, Peggy Marriott 1957- BiDrAPA 89
Forbes, Peter 1942- WhoAm 90, WhoE 91, WhoWor 91
Forbes, Peter Cairney 1945- St&PR 91
Forbes, Ramona Frances B. 1913- IntWWM 90
Forbes, Richard E. 1915- WhoAm 90
Forbes, Richard Mather 1916- WhoAm 90
Forbes, Robert F. 1941- St&PR 91
Forbes, Robert Stanard 1926- St&PR 91
Forbes, Ronald Omega 1948- BiDrAPA 89
Forbes, Rosita 1890-1967 BioIn 16, FemiCLE
Forbes, Samuel E. 1944- St&PR 91
Forbes, Samuel Emery 1944- WhoAm 90
Forbes, Sarah Elizabeth 1928- WhoAmW 91, WhoSSW 91
Forbes, Sebastian 1941- IntWWM 90
Forbes, Stanton 1923- TwCCr&M 91
Forbes, Steve BioIn 16
Forbes, Theodore McCoy, Jr. 1929- WhoAm 90
Forbes, Timothy Carter 1953- WhoAm 90, WhoWor 91
Forbes, Walter Alexander 1942- WhoAm 90
Forbes, Watson PenDiMP
Forbes, Watson 1909- IntWWM 90
Forbes, William, II 1924- WhoE 91
Forbes-Mosse, Irene 1864-1946 EncCoWW
Forbes-Richardson, Helen Hilda 1950- WhoAmW 91, WhoEmL 91, WhoWor 91
Forbin, Luc Jerome 1934- WhoWor 91
Forbis, Bryan Lester 1957- WhoEmL 91
Forbis, Jeff E. 1950- St&PR 91
Forbis, Oric L. Jr. 1922- BiDrAPA 89
Forbis, Richard George 1924- WhoAm 90
Forbush, Clifton Haskett, Jr. 1927- St&PR 91
Forcade, Emily Kukula 1947- BiDrAPA 89
Forcano, Xavier 1944- WhoWor 91
Force, Farid BiDrAPA 89
Force, Jack Keith 1946- WhoEmL 91
Force, Juliana BioIn 16
Force, Juliana R WhoAmA 91N
Force, Kenneth Richard 1940- IntWWM 90
Force, Maria Theresa 1958- WhoAmW 91
Force, Robert 1934- WhoAm 90
Force, Roland Wynfield 1924- WhoAm 90, WhoAmA 91, WhoE 91
Force, William M., Jr. 1939- St&PR 91
Forcellini, Lindbergh Charles 1928- St&PR 91
Forcese, Dennis Philip 1941- WhoAm 90
Forche, Carolyn FemiCLE
Forche, Carolyn 1950- WorAu 1980 [port]
Forcheskie, Carl S. 1927- WhoAm 90
Forchheimer, Otto L. 1926- St&PR 91
Forcier, Louise Maheux- 1929- BioIn 16
Forcier, Richard Charles 1941- WhoAm 90
Forcinio, Hallie Eunice 1952- WhoEmL 91
Forcione, Alban Keith 1938- WhoAm 90
Forcione, Antonio NewAgMG
Ford family BioIn 16
Ford, Allen H. 1928- St&PR 91
Ford, Allen Huntington 1928- WhoAm 90
Ford, Andrew 1957- IntWWM 90
Ford, Andrew Thomas 1944- WhoAm 90
Ford, Ann Suter 1943- WhoAmW 91
Ford, Anthony Dudley 1935- IntWWM 90
Ford, Arthur 1897-1971 EncPaPR 91
Ford, Arthur A 1897-1971 EncO&P 3
Ford, Ashley Lloyd 1939- St&PR 91, WhoAm 90
Ford, Barbara BioIn 16
Ford, Barbara A. 1952- WhoAmW 91
Ford, Barbara Hannon 1941- WhoAmW 91
Ford, Barbara Jean 1946- WhoAmW 91
Ford, Barbara Swicegood 1934- WhoSSW 91
Ford, Barry Wayne 1961- WhoSSW 91
Ford, Basil H. 1944- St&PR 91
Ford, Becky Lynn 1953- WhoEmL 91
Ford, Bernard R. 1943- St&PR 91
Ford, Betty BioIn 16
Ford, Betty 1912- BioIn 16
Ford, Betty Bloomer 1918- WhoAm 90, WhoAmW 91, WhoWor 91
Ford, Brian J. BioIn 16
Ford, Bridget 1636-1710 BiDEWW
Ford, Byron Milton 1939- WhoE 91
Ford, C. Michael BioIn 16
Ford, Carol BioIn 16
Ford, Carol Williams 1958- WhoAm 90
Ford, Cathy 1952- FemiCLE
Ford, Cathy Zoe 1953- WhoAmW 91
Ford, Charles BiDrAPA 89
Ford, Charles 1946- IntWWM 90
Ford, Charles Henri 1913- WhoAmA 91N
Ford, Charles Virgil 1937- WhoSSW 91
Ford, Charles Willard 1938- WhoAm 90, WhoE 91
Ford, Chris 1949- WhoAm 90, WhoE 91
Ford, Clarence Quentin 1923- WhoAm 90
Ford, Clebert 1932- DrBlPA 90
Ford, Clifford IntWWM 90
Ford, Clyde Michael 1938- St&PR 91
Ford, Cynthia Ann 1957- WhoAmW 91
Ford, Dale 1942- Ballpl 90
Ford, Dan 1952- Ballpl 90
Ford, Dave 1956- Ballpl 90
Ford, David Clayton 1949- WhoWor 91
Ford, David Mitchell 1950- WhoSSW 91
Ford, David Thurman 1950- WhoEmL 91
Ford, Debrah Sue 1958- WhoEmL 91
Ford, Denys Kensington 1923- WhoAm 90
Ford, Derek Clifford 1935- WhoAm 90
Ford, Dexter 1917- WhoAm 90
Ford, Donald Hainline 1906- WhoAm 90
Ford, Donald Herbert 1926- WhoAm 90
Ford, Donald James 1930- WhoAm 90
Ford, Donald Keith 1945- St&PR 91
Ford, E. B. 1901-1988 AnObit 1988
Ford, Earl William 1945- WhoEmL 91
Ford, Edna Akin BioIn 16
Ford, Edsel Bryant 1893-1943 EncABHB 5 [port], WorAlBi
Ford, Edwin Roe 1943- WhoSSW 91
Ford, Eileen Otte 1922- WhoAm 90, WhoAmW 91
Ford, Elaine 1938- WhoWrEP 89
Ford, Elbert S C 1914- BiDrAPA 89
Ford, Elbur TwCCr&M 91
Ford, Eleanor Clay 1896-1976 WhoAmA 91N
Ford, Elizabeth 1918- BioAmW, WorAlBi
Ford, Ellen Hodson 1913- WhoAmW 91, WhoWor 91
Ford, Emory A. 1940- WhoAm 90
Ford, Faith BioIn 16
Ford, Ford Barney 1922- WhoAm 90
Ford, Ford Madox 1873-1939 BioIn 16, ConAu 132, DcLB 98 [port], MajTwCW, TwCLC 39 [port], WorAlBi
Ford, Franklin Lewis 1920- WhoAm 90
Ford, Frederic Hugh 1939- IntWWM 90
Ford, Frederick R 1921- BiDrAPA 89
Ford, Gary Holloway 1945- WhoWor 91
Ford, George BioIn 16
Ford, George Albert, Jr. 1933- WhoE 91
Ford, George Burt 1923- WhoAm 90
Ford, George Harry 1914- WhoAm 90
Ford, George W. 1957- St&PR 91
Ford, Gerald R. 1913- BioIn 16, WorAlBi
Ford, Gerald Rudolph, Jr. 1913- BiDrUSE 89, WhoAm 90, WhoWor 91
Ford, Gertrude WhoWrEP 89
Ford, Gilbert 1931- St&PR 91
Ford, Glenn 1916- WhoAm 90, WorAlBi
Ford, Gordon Buell, Jr. 1937- WhoAm 90, WhoSSW 91, WhoWor 91
Ford, H. Charles 1935- St&PR 91
Ford, Hamilton F 1908- BiDrAPA 89
Ford, Harold Eugene 1945- BlkAmsC [port], WhoAm 90, WhoSSW 91
Ford, Harold V BiDrAPA 89
Ford, Harriet 1863?-1949 BioIn 16
Ford, Harriet French 1863?-1949 NotWoAT
Ford, Harrison BioIn 16
Ford, Harrison 1942- ConTFT 8 [port], News 90 [port], WhoAm 90, WorAlBi
Ford, Harry Eugene, III BiDrAPA 89
Ford, Harry McNamara 1932- St&PR 91
Ford, Harry Xavier 1921- WhoAmA 91
Ford, Henry EncABHB 5
Ford, Henry 1863-1947 BioIn 16, EncABHB 4 [port], WorAlBi
Ford, Henry 1917-1987 BioIn 16
Ford, Henry, II 1917-1987 EncABHB 5 [port], WorAlBi
Ford, Henry J 1929- BiDrAPA 89
Ford, Hilary 1922- BioIn 16
Ford, Hilary 1944- WhoE 91
Ford, Hod 1897-1977 Ballpl 90
Ford, Hugh 1913- WhoWor 91
Ford, Ita BioIn 16
Ford, J. Robert 1942- St&PR 91
Ford, James Andrew, Jr. 1942- WhoWor 91
Ford, James E. St&PR 91
Ford, James Francis 1942- St&PR 91
Ford, James Henry, Jr. 1931- WhoAm 90
Ford, James Stephen 1943- WhoSSW 91, WhoWor 91
Ford, James W. BioIn 16
Ford, Janet Marie 1941- WhoAmW 91
Ford, Jeffrey Duane 1949- WhoEmL 91
Ford, Jerry Lee 1940- WhoAm 90
Ford, Jesse Hill 1928- BioIn 16, WhoAm 90, WhoWrEP 89
Ford, Jimmie Richard 1936- WhoSSW 91
Ford, Joe T. 1937- St&PR 91
Ford, Joe Thomas 1937- WhoAm 90, WhoSSW 91
Ford, Johathan St&PR 91
Ford, John St&PR 91
Ford, John 1586-1640 BioIn 16, WorAlBi
Ford, John 1895-1973 WorAlBi
Ford, John 1950- WhoAmA 91
Ford, John Bailey 1934- WhoAm 90
Ford, John Charles 1929- WhoAmA 91
Ford, John Charles 1942- WhoE 91
Ford, John Gilmore WhoAm 90, WhoAmA 91
Ford, John Lawrence 1926- St&PR 91
Ford, John Stephen 1957- WhoEmL 91, WhoWor 91
Ford, John Suffern 1939- BiDrAPA 89
Ford, John T., Jr. 1953- WhoEmL 91, WhoWor 91
Ford, Johnny Lawrence 1942- BioIn 16
Ford, Jon Grant 1943- St&PR 91
Ford, Joseph 1914- WhoAm 90
Ford, Joseph Dillon 1952- IntWWM 90, WhoEmL 91, WhoSSW 91
Ford, Joseph Raymond 1949- St&PR 91, WhoE 91
Ford, Judith Ann 1935- WhoAm 90
Ford, Karrin Elizabeth 1951- IntWWM 90
Ford, Kathleen 1932- WhoAmW 91
Ford, Kathleen 1945- WhoWrEP 89
Ford, Kathryn 1950- BiDrAPA 89
Ford, Kay Louise 1944- WhoAmW 91
Ford, Kelly Jean 1957- WhoEmL 91
Ford, Kenneth William 1926- WhoAm 90
Ford, Lauren 1891- AuBYP 90
Ford, Lee Ellen 1917- WhoAmW 91, WhoWor 91
Ford, Leslie 1898-1983 TwCCr&M 91
Ford, Lewis Stanley 1933- WhoSSW 91
Ford, Linda Lou 1948- WhoAm 90
Ford, Linda Maria 1949- WhoEmL 91
Ford, Lisa Ann BiDrAPA 89
Ford, Lisa Ann 1956- WhoAmW 91, WhoSSW 91
Ford, Lisa Collado 1944- WhoE 91
Ford, Lita BioIn 16
Ford, Loretta C. 1920- WhoAm 90, WhoAmW 91
Ford, Lucille Garber 1921- WhoAm 90
Ford, M. Jane 1945- WhoEmL 91
Ford, Mari Jo H. WhoSSW 91
Ford, Mary Anne 1942- ODwPR 91
Ford, Maureen Morrissey 1936- WhoAmW 91
Ford, Merton Eugene 1925- St&PR 91
Ford, Michael H BiDrAPA 89
Ford, Michael Raye 1945- WhoSSW 91
Ford, Molly Flickinger 1956- WhoEmL 91
Ford, Morris Wesley, Jr. 1952- St&PR 91
Ford, Nancy Keffer 1906-1961 AuBYP 90
Ford, Nancy L. Steed 1944- WhoSSW 91
Ford, Nancy Leonard 1955- WhoEmL 91
Ford, Nancy Louise 1935- WhoAm 90
Ford, Naomi Ruth 1934- WhoSSW 91
Ford, Neal Carroll 1931- WhoSSW 91
Ford, Patricia Marie 1955- WhoE 91
Ford, Patrick ODwPR 91
Ford, Patrick Kildea 1935- WhoAm 90
Ford, Peter 1936- BioIn 16
Ford, Peter John 1946- IntWWM 90
Ford, Phyllis WhoWrEP 89
Ford, Phyllis M 1928- ConAu 30NR
Ford, R. A. D. 1915- BioIn 16
Ford, Richard 1944- BioIn 16, WorAu 1980 [port]
Ford, Richard Alan 1940- WhoE 91
Ford, Richard C. 1944- WhoWrEP 89
Ford, Richard Earl 1933- WhoAm 90
Ford, Richard Edmond 1927- WhoAm 90
Ford, Richard I. BioIn 16
Ford, Richard Irving 1941- WhoAm 90
Ford, Richard Michael 1955- WhoEmL 91
Ford, Robert WorAlBi
Ford, Robert Barney 1944- WhoAm 90
Ford, Robert Bruce 1931- BiDrAPA 89
Ford, Robert David 1956- WhoEmL 91
Ford, Robert Eustace Paul 1916- WhoWor 91
Ford, Robert MacDonald, III 1934- WhoSSW 91
Ford, Roger Hayes 1956- WhoSSW 91
Ford, Ronald Glen 1947- St&PR 91
Ford, Russ 1883-1960 Ballpl 90
Ford, Ruth BioIn 16
Ford, Ruth Elizabeth 1912?- NotWoAT
Ford, Sallie Rochester LiHiK
Ford, Sally BioIn 16
Ford, Sarah Ann 1951- WhoAmW 91
Ford, Sarah Litsey 1901- WhoWrEP 89

Ford, Sharon Ann *WhoAmW 91*
Ford, Sherri Ann 1960- *WhoEmL 91*
Ford, Stephen David 1946- *WhoAm 90*
Ford, Stephen M. 1952- *BiDrAPA 89*
Ford, Steven Milton 1954- *WhoEmL 91*
Ford, Steven Robert 1954- *WhoEmL 91*
Ford, T. Mitchell 1921- *St&PR 91*
Ford, Ted 1947- *Ballpl 90*
Ford, Tennessee Ernie 1919- *OxCPMus, WhoAm 90, WorAlBi*
Ford, Thomas E. 1929- *St&PR 91*
Ford, Thomas E., III 1939- *St&PR 91*
Ford, Thomas Jeffers 1930- *WhoSSW 91*
Ford, Thomas Joseph 1956- *WhoSSW 91*
Ford, Thomas Michael 1952- *WhoE 91*
Ford, Thomas Milton, Jr. 1943- *St&PR 91*
Ford, Thomas Patrick 1918- *WhoAm 90*
Ford, Thomas Robert 1923- *WhoAm 90*
Ford, Thomas Sparks 1944- *WhoSSW 91*
Ford, Timothy Alan 1951- *WhoSSW 91*
Ford, Timothy Joe 1954- *WhoSSW 91*
Ford, Trevor 1951- *IntWWM 90*
Ford, Trevor John 1931- *IntWWM 90*
Ford, Tsy 1957- *WhoAmW 91*
Ford, Vickie Lynn 1959- *WhoSSW 91*
Ford, Webster *MajTwCW*
Ford, Wendell Hampton 1924- *NewYTBS 90 [port], WhoAm 90, WhoSSW 91, WhoWor 91*
Ford, Whitey 1926- *Ballpl 90 [port]*
Ford, Whitey 1928- *WorAlBi*
Ford, William B. 1940- *St&PR 91*
Ford, William Clay 1925- *St&PR 91, WhoAm 90*
Ford, William Clay, Jr. *BioIn 16*
Ford, William David 1927- *WhoAm 90*
Ford, William F. 1925- *St&PR 91*
Ford, William F. 1936- *WhoAm 90*
Ford, William Francis 1925- *WhoAm 90*
Ford, William Kent, Jr. 1931- *WhoAm 90*
Ford, William Leslie 1942- *St&PR 91*
Ford, William S., Jr. 1934- *St&PR 91*
Ford, William Webster 1922- *St&PR 91*
Ford, Yancey William, Jr. 1940- *St&PR 91*
Ford-Choyke, Phyllis *WhoWrEP 89*
Ford-Coates, Barbara Williams 1948- *WhoAm 90*
Forde, Alvin Ralph 1933- *St&PR 91*
Forde, Dorothy Evadne 1952- *WhoWor 91*
Forde, Douglas Henderson 1945- *WhoE 91*
Forde, Florrie 1876-1940 *OxCPMus*
Forde, Harold McDonald 1916- *WhoWor 91*
Forde, Joyce P. 1950- *WhoWrEP 89*
Forde, Peter C. 1955- *St&PR 91*
Forde, Richard James 1949- *BiDrAPA 89*
Fordham, Benjamin Cleveland 1953- *WhoEmL 91*
Fordham, Christopher Columbus, III 1926- *WhoAm 90, WhoWor 91*
Fordham, Jefferson Barnes 1905- *WhoAm 90*
Fordham, Laurence Sherman 1929- *WhoAm 90*
Fordham, Sharon Ann 1952- *WhoAmW 91, WhoEmL 91*
Fordham, Sheldon Leroy 1919- *WhoAm 90*
Fordice, Daniel Kirkwood, III 1960- *St&PR 91*
Fordice, Daniel Kirkwood, Jr. 1934- *St&PR 91, WhoWor 91*
Fording, William G. 1939- *St&PR 91*
Fordrin, Louis *PenDiDA 89*
Fordtran, John Satterfield 1931- *WhoAm 90*
Fordyce, Barbara Ann 1955- *WhoAmW 91, WhoEmL 91*
Fordyce, Donald M. 1936- *St&PR 91*
Fordyce, Edward Winfield, Jr. 1941- *St&PR 91, WhoAm 90*
Fordyce, James Forrest 1953- *WhoEmL 91*
Fordyce, Phillip Randall 1928- *WhoAm 90*
Fordyce, Richard Eugene 1934- *St&PR 91*
Fore, Peter F 1955- *BiDrAPA 89*
Fore, William R. 1941- *St&PR 91*
Foreacre, John 1935- *WhoE 91*
Foregger, Lily Mae Lassiter *BioIn 16*
Forehand, Jennie Meador 1935- *WhoAmW 91*
Forehand, Margaret P. 1951- *WhoAm 90, WhoSSW 91*
Foreigner *EncPR&S 89*
Forell, David C. 1947- *St&PR 91*
Forell, David Charles 1947- *WhoAm 90*
Forell, George Wolfgang 1919- *WhoAm 90*
Forelle, Helen *WhoWrEP 89*
Forelli, Sam C. 1934- *St&PR 91*
Foreman, Anne N. 1947- *WhoAm 90, WhoAmW 91*
Foreman, Arlene Raina 1945- *WhoEmL 91*
Foreman, Carol Lee Tucker 1938- *WhoAm 90, WhoAmW 91*
Foreman, Clay Bertrand, Jr. 1933- *St&PR 91*
Foreman, Dale Melvin 1948- *WhoEmL 91*
Foreman, Dave 1947?- *News 90 [port], -90-3 [port]*
Foreman, Edward Rawson 1939- *WhoAm 90*
Foreman, Edwin Francis 1931- *WhoSSW 91, WhoWor 91*
Foreman, Ellen 1957- *ODwPR 91*
Foreman, Ellen S. 1957- *WhoEmL 91*
Foreman, Frank 1863-1957 *Ballpl 90*
Foreman, Gene Clemons 1934- *WhoAm 90, WhoE 91*
Foreman, George *BioIn 16*
Foreman, George 1949- *WorAlBi*
Foreman, Howard Wayne 1952- *WhoEmL 91*
Foreman, Jack P. *St&PR 91*
Foreman, James Davis 1925- *WhoAm 90*
Foreman, James Louis 1927- *WhoAm 90*
Foreman, Jeff 1951- *WhoEmL 91*
Foreman, John Richard 1952- *St&PR 91*
Foreman, Laura *BioIn 16, WhoAm 90, WhoAmA 91, WhoE 91*
Foreman, Michael 1938- *BioIn 16*
Foreman, Michael Marcellus 1941- *WhoSSW 91*
Foreman, Nancy Jean 1949- *WhoAmW 91*
Foreman, Nancy North 1938- *WhoAmW 91*
Foreman, Percy 1902-1988 *BioIn 16*
Foreman, Richard 1937- *BioIn 16, ConAu 32NR, WhoE 91*
Foreman, Ruth *BioIn 16*
Foreman, Spencer 1935- *WhoAm 90*
Foreman, Stephen 1807-1881 *WhNaAH*
Foreman, Thomas Alexander 1930- *WhoE 91, WhoWor 91*
Foremost Man *DcCanB 12*
Forer, Anne Ruth 1945- *WhoWrEP 89*
Forer, Arthur H. 1935- *WhoAm 90*
Forer, Bernard 1907- *WhoWrEP 89*
Forer, Margery Patricia 1922- *WhoAmW 91*
Forer, Morris L. 1912- *St&PR 91*
Forer, Raymond 1915- *WhoAm 90*
Forero, Enrique 1942- *WhoAm 90*
Forese, James J. 1935- *St&PR 91*
Forese, James John 1935- *WhoAm 90*
Foresman, Bruce Chalfin 1935- *WhoE 91*
Forest, Antonia *BioIn 16*
Forest, Charlene Lynn 1947- *WhoAmW 91*
Forest, Doris Elizabeth 1936- *WhoAm 90*
Forest, Georges *BioIn 16*
Forest, Harvey 1937- *St&PR 91, WhoE 91*
Forest, Herbert Leon 1910- *WhoAm 90*
Forest, Herman Silva 1921- *WhoAm 90*
Forest, Ira 1920- *St&PR 91*
Forest, James Hendrickson 1941- *WhoWor 91*
Forest, Kay Frances 1948- *WhoEmL 91*
Forest, Michael *BioIn 16*
Forest, Michael Franklin 1955- *St&PR 91*
Forest, Norman *TwCCr&M 91*
Forest, Philip Earle 1931- *WhoSSW 91*
Foresta, Anthony J. 1942- *St&PR 91*
Forester Sisters, The *WhoNeCM [port]*
Forester, Al *BioIn 16*
Forester, Bernard I. 1928- *St&PR 91, WhoAm 90*
Forester, Beth N. 1933- *WhoAmW 91*
Forester, Bruce M 1939- *BiDrAPA 89*
Forester, Bruce Michael 1939- *WhoWrEP 89*
Forester, C. S. 1899-1966 *WorAlBi*
Forester, David Lionel *BiDrAPA 89*
Forester, Erica Simms 1942- *WhoE 91*
Forester, Jean Martha Brouillette 1934- *WhoAmW 91, WhoSSW 91, WhoWor 91*
Forester, John E. 1913- *St&PR 91*
Forester, John Gordon, Jr. 1933- *WhoAm 90*
Forester, Russell 1920- *WhoAm 90, WhoAmA 91*
Foresti, Roy, Jr. 1925- *WhoAm 90*
Forestier, Etienne 1712?-1768 *PenDiDA 89*
Forestier, Etienne-Jean *PenDiDA 89*
Forestier, Pierre-Auguste 1755-1835 *PenDiDA 89*
Forestiere, Baldasare 1879-1946 *BioIn 16*
Foresythe, Reginald 1907-1958 *OxCPMus*
Foret, Allen James 1947- *St&PR 91*
Foret, Mickey Phillip 1945- *WhoAm 90*
Foretich, Eric A. *BioIn 16*
Foretich, Hilary *BioIn 16*
Forez *MajTwCW*
Forgacs, Eva Natalia 1947- *WhoWor 91*
Forgan, David Waller 1933- *WhoAm 90*
Forgason, Judy *BiDrAPA 89*
Forge, Andrew Murray 1923- *WhoAmA 91*
Forge, John E. 1947- *St&PR 91*
Forger, Robert Durkin 1928- *WhoAm 90*
Forget, Florent 1918-1985 *OxCCanT*
Forget, Paul Charles 1951- *WhoE 91*
Forgione, Michael John 1925- *St&PR 91*
Forgotson, Florence Frances 1908- *WhoAmW 91*
Forgotson, Judith H 1936- *BiDrAPA 89*
Forgue, Stanley Vincent 1916- *WhoAm 90*
Forinash, Bruce Alan 1942- *St&PR 91*
Forino, Enrichetta Caracciolo *EncCoWW*
Forissier, Marie-Jose 1948- *WhoWor 91*
Forizs, Lorant 1913- *BiDrAPA 89*
Fork, Donald Joseph 1938- *WhoE 91*
Fork, Richard Lynn 1935- *WhoAm 90*
Forkan, Patricia Ann 1944- *WhoAmW 91*
Forker, Lee R. 1906- *St&PR 91*
Forker, Lee Robinson 1906- *WhoE 91*
Forker, Olan Dean 1928- *WhoAm 90*
Forkin, Daniel 1942- *BiDrAPA 89*
Forkner, Donald Maxwell 1936- *St&PR 91*
Forkner, James L. 1922- *St&PR 91*
Forlani, Arnaldo 1925- *WhoWor 91*
Forlani, Roberto 1929- *WhoWor 91*
Forlano, Anthony 1936- *St&PR 91, WhoAm 90*
Forlano, Frederick Peter 1947- *WhoEmL 91*
Forlasto, Daniel A. 1940- *St&PR 91*
Forlines, John Arthur, Jr. 1918- *St&PR 91*
Forlini, Frank John, Jr. 1941- *WhoWor 91*
Form, Fredric Allan 1942- *WhoE 91, WhoWor 91*
Form, William H. 1917- *WhoAm 90*
Forman, Alice 1931- *WhoAmA 91*
Forman, Allen S. *BioIn 16*
Forman, Arthur Joel 1941- *BiDrAPA 89*
Forman, Barbara F 1945- *BiDrAPA 89*
Forman, Beth Rosalyne 1949- *WhoAmW 91*
Forman, Brenda 1936- *AuBYP 90*
Forman, Charles William 1916- *WhoAm 90*
Forman, Charlotte 1715-1787 *FemiCLE*
Forman, David C. 1936- *WhoAm 90*
Forman, Dayton M 1927- *BiDrAPA 89*
Forman, Donald T. 1932- *WhoAm 90*
Forman, Edgar Ross 1923- *WhoAm 90, WhoE 91*
Forman, Edward David 1931- *St&PR 91*
Forman, Frances Effie 1940- *BiDrAPA 89*
Forman, Frank Shane, III 1944- *WhoE 91*
Forman, George Whiteman 1919- *WhoAm 90*
Forman, Harrison 1904-1978 *AuBYP 90*
Forman, Henry Chandlee *WhoAm 90, WhoWor 91*
Forman, Herbert Michael 1950- *BiDrAPA 89*
Forman, Howard Irving 1917- *WhoAm 90, WhoWor 91*
Forman, I. Sanford 1936- *WhoE 91*
Forman, Irwin Harvey *BiDrAPA 89*
Forman, Jack David *BiDrAPA 89*
Forman, James 1928- *BioIn 16*
Forman, James Douglas 1932- *AuBYP 90, WhoE 91*
Forman, Jeanne Leach 1916- *WhoAmW 91*
Forman, Jeffrey J. 1949- *St&PR 91*
Forman, Jerome Scott 1957- *WhoE 91*
Forman, Joseph Charles 1931- *WhoAm 90*
Forman, Joseph James 1924- *St&PR 91*
Forman, Kenneth Howard 1947- *WhoE 91*
Forman, Kenneth Warner 1925- *WhoAmA 91*
Forman, Leonard *BioIn 16*
Forman, Leslie M 1947- *BiDrAPA 89*
Forman, Linda Eileen 1946- *St&PR 91*
Forman, Louis H 1912- *BiDrAPA 89*
Forman, Marc A 1935- *BiDrAPA 89*
Forman, Marjorie Lou *BiDrAPA 89*
Forman, Mark Leonard 1949- *WhoEmL 91*
Forman, Max *BiDrAPA 89*
Forman, Michael *BioIn 16*
Forman, Michael 1952- *ODwPR 91*
Forman, Milos *BioIn 16*
Forman, Milos 1932- *WhoAm 90, WhoWor 91*
Forman, Nancy *BiDrAPA 89*
Forman, Paula *WhoAm 90, WhoAmW 91*
Forman, Peter Gerald 1946- *WhoSSW 91*
Forman, Richard Allan 1939- *WhoE 91*
Forman, Richard T. T. 1935- *WhoAm 90, WhoE 91*
Forman, Saul Zundel 1942- *BiDrAPA 89*
Forman, Spencer Zalman 1949- *WhoE 91*
Forman, Stuart Marshall 1953- *BiDrAPA 89*
Forman, Sylvia Helen 1943- *WhoE 91*
Forman, Tamara 1947- *WhoAmW 91*
Forman, Thomas Michael 1945- *St&PR 91*
Forman, Wade K. 1913- *St&PR 91*
Forman, William Joel 1946- *WhoEmL 91*
Forman, William N. 1930- *WhoAm 90*
Forman, Willis M. 1925- *St&PR 91*
Formanek, Peter Raemin 1943- *St&PR 91, WhoAm 90*
Formant, Christopher Mathew 1951- *St&PR 91*
Formby, George 1877-1921 *OxCPMus*
Formby, George 1904-1961 *OxCPMus*
Formeister, Richard Bruno 1946- *WhoEmL 91*
Former, Fritz Herman *BiDrAPA 89*
Former, Tatjana T *BiDrAPA 89*
Formhals, Robert Willard Yates 1919- *WhoWor 91*
Formica, Gianni 1922- *WhoWor 91*
Formica Corsi, Mercedes 1918- *EncCoWW*
Formicola, John Joseph 1941- *WhoAmA 91*
Formigoni, Ugo C 1931- *BiDrAPA 89*
Formon, Julie Ann 1966- *WhoEmL 91*
Formoso, Esteban E. 1945- *St&PR 91*
Formwalt, Lee William 1949- *WhoSSW 91*
Formwalt, William Alexander 1951- *WhoEmL 91*
Fornaciari, Gilbert Martin 1946- *WhoEmL 91*
Fornaciari, Roberta 1947- *WhoWor 91*
Fornaess, John Erik 1946- *WhoE 91*
Fornal, Robert Earl 1943- *BiDrAPA 89*
Fornara, Charles William 1935- *ConAu 130, WhoAm 90*
Fornari, Harry David 1919- *St&PR 91*
Fornari, Ivo 1942- *WhoWor 91*
Fornari, Victor M *BiDrAPA 89*
Fornari, Victor Masliah *WhoE 91*
Fornas, Leander 1925- *WhoAmA 91*
Fornasetti, Piero 1913-1988 *BioIn 16, PenDiDA 89*
Fornasetti, Piero 1923-1988 *AnObit 1988*
Fornatto, Elio Joseph 1928- *WhoAm 90*
Fornay, Alfred Richard *WhoE 91*
Forndran, Erhard Adalbert G. 1938- *WhoWor 91*
Fornell, Martha Steinmetz 1920- *WhoAmW 91, WhoSSW 91*
Fornella, Norman G. 1948- *St&PR 91*
Fornelli, Joseph 1943- *WhoAmA 91*
Fornes, Maria Irene 1930- *BioIn 16, ConLC 61 [port], FemiCLE, HispWr 90, MajTwCW, NotWoAT, WhoAm 90, WhoHisp 91*
Forness, Steven Robert 1939- *WhoAm 90*
Forney, George David, Jr. 1940- *WhoAm 90*
Forney, John *BioIn 16*
Forney, Larry J. 1944- *WhoSSW 91*
Forney, Laurence Bruce 1925- *St&PR 91*
Forney, Mary Ann 1948- *WhoEmL 91*
Forney, Robert Clyde 1927- *St&PR 91, WhoAm 90*
Forney, Virginia Sue 1925- *WhoAmW 91*
Forni, Patricia Rose 1932- *WhoAm 90*
Fornieles, Mike 1932- *Ballpl 90*
Fornito, Anthony P *BiDrAPA 89*
Fornoff, Frank, Jr. 1914- *WhoE 91, WhoWor 91*
Fornshell, Dave Lee 1937- *WhoAm 90*
Fornuto, Donata Dominic 1931- *IntWWM 90*
Foronda, Elena Isabel 1947- *WhoAmW 91*
Forqueray, Antoine 1671?-1745 *PenDiMP*
Forqueray, Jean-Baptiste *PenDiMP*
Forr, Thomas Lee 1949- *WhoEmL 91*
Forrai, Miklos 1913- *IntWWM 90*
Forrellad, Luisa *EncCoWW*
Forrer, Gordon *BiDrAPA 89*
Forrer, Graydon R *BiDrAPA 89*
Forrest, Allen Wright 1941- *WhoSSW 91*
Forrest, Anne 1938- *ODwPR 91*
Forrest, Anthony *ConAu 130*
Forrest, Arlena Cornell 1940- *WhoAmW 91*
Forrest, Beth 1960- *WhoAmW 91*
Forrest, Christopher Patrick 1946- *WhoAmA 91*
Forrest, Dallah Anderson, Jr. 1959- *WhoSSW 91*
Forrest, David V 1938- *BiDrAPA 89*
Forrest, David Vickers 1938- *WhoE 91*
Forrest, Diane 1946- *St&PR 91*
Forrest, Edgar Hull 1916- *WhoE 91*
Forrest, Edward James 1949- *WhoSSW 91*
Forrest, Emmett 1927- *St&PR 91*
Forrest, Fred M *BiDrAPA 89*
Forrest, Gail 1955- *WhoEmL 91*
Forrest, Gary Gran 1943- *ConAu 32NR*
Forrest, George 1915- *OxCPMus*
Forrest, George William 1943- *St&PR 91*
Forrest, Hal 1892?-1959 *EncACom*
Forrest, Henry J. 1933- *WhoSSW 91*
Forrest, Herbert Emerson 1923- *WhoAm 90, WhoE 91, WhoWor 91*
Forrest, Hugh Sommerville 1924- *WhoAm 90*
Forrest, James E. 1949- *St&PR 91*
Forrest, James Taylor 1919- *WhoAmA 91*
Forrest, Katherine V 1939- *ConAu 131, TwCCr&M 91*
Forrest, Mabel 1872-1935 *FemiCLE*
Forrest, Marion Patricia 1935- *WhoAmW 91*
Forrest, Nathan Bedford 1821-1877 *WorAlBi*
Forrest, Othello C., Jr. 1928- *St&PR 91*
Forrest, Richard 1932- *TwCCr&M 91*
Forrest, Robert C. 1935- *St&PR 91*
Forrest, Roger Rodewald 1960- *WhoSSW 91*
Forrest, Sidney 1918- *IntWWM 90, WhoAm 90, WhoE 91*
Forrest, Stephen 1958- *WhoEmL 91*

Forrest, Steven David *WhoWrEP 89*
Forrest, Suzanne Sims 1926- *WhoAmW 91*
Forrest, Sybil *AuBYP 90*
Forrest, Victoria Kaufman 1944- *WhoAmW 91*
Forrest, William *BioIn 16*
Forrest, William E. 1939- *St&PR 91*
Forrest, Winston E. *BioIn 16*
Forrest-Richards, Frances M *BiDrAPA 89*
Forrest-Thomson, Veronica 1948-1975 *FemiCLE*
Forrestal, James V. 1892-1949 *WorAlBi*
Forrestal, James Vincent 1892-1949 *BiDrUSE 89*
Forrestal, Michael V. 1927-1989 *BioIn 16*
Forrestal, Robert Patrick 1931- *St&PR 91, WhoAm 90*
Forrestall, Thomas De Vany 1936- *WhoAmA 91*
Forrester, Alfred W 1953- *BiDrAPA 89*
Forrester, Alfred Whitfield 1953- *WhoEmL 91*
Forrester, Ann *WhoAmW 91*
Forrester, Charles Howard 1928- *WhoAmA 91*
Forrester, David Anthony 1954- *WhoE 91*
Forrester, David Mark 1946- *WhoEmL 91*
Forrester, Douglas Robert 1953- *WhoEmL 91*
Forrester, Duncan B 1933- *ConAu 131*
Forrester, Eleanor A. 1916- *St&PR 91*
Forrester, Eugene Priest 1926- *WhoWor 91*
Forrester, Fanny 1817-1854 *BioIn 16*
Forrester, Frank H. *BioIn 16*
Forrester, Frank H. 1919?-1986 *AuBYP 90*
Forrester, Harold C. 1908- *St&PR 91*
Forrester, Helen 1919- *BioIn 16, FemiCLE*
Forrester, Herb 1952- *St&PR 91*
Forrester, Herbert Glenn, Jr. 1952- *WhoSSW 91*
Forrester, J. Owen 1939- *WhoAm 90*
Forrester, Jay Wright 1918- *WhoAm 90, WhoE 91*
Forrester, Martyn 1952- *ConAu 129*
Forrester, Maureen 1930- *PenDiMP*
Forrester, Patricia Tobacco 1940- *WhoAmA 91*
Forrester, Patrick James, Jr. 1949- *WhoEmL 91*
Forrester, Stephen Cary 1954- *WhoEmL 91*
Forrester, Susan Annette 1962- *WhoWrEP 89*
Forrester, William D. 1931- *ODwPR 91*
Forrester, William Donald 1931- *WhoAm 90, WhoWor 91*
Forrette, John Elmer 1952- *WhoEmL 91*
Forristal, Dennis G. 1950- *ODwPR 91*
Forrow, Brian D. 1927- *St&PR 91*
Forrow, Brian Derek 1927- *WhoAm 90*
Forry, John Emerson 1920- *WhoAm 90*
Fors, Marc B. *WhoAm 90*
Forsbach, Jack Alan 1932- *WhoWor 91*
Forsberg, Carl Earl 1920- *IntWWM 90*
Forsberg, Charles Alton 1944- *WhoWor 91*
Forsberg, Dale John 1955- *St&PR 91*
Forsberg, Douglas L. 1945- *St&PR 91*
Forsberg, Edward C.A. 1920- *St&PR 91*
Forsberg, Franklin Sidney 1905- *WhoAm 90, WhoWor 91*
Forsberg, John Albert 1928- *St&PR 91*
Forsberg, Kevin John 1934- *WhoAm 90, WhoWor 91*
Forsberg, Roland 1939- *IntWWM 90*
Forsberg, Roy Walter 1937- *WhoAm 90*
Forsberg, Rudolf Percy, III 1950- *WhoEmL 91*
Forsberg, Susan Marie 1953- *WhoEmL 91*
Forsberg, Vivian *BioAmW*
Forsch, Bob 1950- *Ballpl 90*
Forsch, Frederick David 1915- *WhoE 91*
Forsch, Ken 1946- *Ballpl 90*
Forsdale, Louis 1922- *WhoAm 90*
Forse, Herbert E., Jr. 1932- *St&PR 91*
Forse, Ronald Erik 1956- *WhoE 91*
Forsee, Aylesa *AuBYP 90*
Forselius, Randall A. 1924- *St&PR 91*
Forsell, John 1858-1941 *PenDiMP*
Forsell, Ronald O. 1928- *WhoWrEP 89*
Forsen, Harold Kay 1932- *WhoAm 90*
Forsey, Chris 1950- *BioIn 16*
Forsgren, John H., Jr. 1946- *WhoAm 90*
Forsh, Ol'ga 1873-1961 *EncCoWW*
Forsha, Anita Louise 1950- *WhoAmW 91*
Forshaw, Robert L. 1938- *ODwPR 91*
Forshaw, Thelma 1923- *FemiCLE*
Forshay-Lunsford, Cin 1965- *SmATA 60 [port]*
Forshee, Ron *BioIn 16*
Forshey, William Osmond, III 1945- *WhoE 91*
Forslund, Per Gosta 1937- *WhoWor 91*
Forsman, Chuck 1944- *WhoAmA 91*
Forsman, John Vaino William 1924- *IntWWM 90*
Forson, Norman Ray 1929- *St&PR 91, WhoAm 90, WhoE 91*
Forssell, Lars 1928- *DcScanL*
Forssman, Bernhard Julius 1934- *WhoWor 91*
Forssmann, Werner 1904-1979 *WorAlBi*
Forssmann-Falck, Renate 1943- *BiDrAPA 89*
Forst, Alan Jay 1958- *WhoEmL 91*
Forst, Eric B. 1947- *St&PR 91*
Forst, Gilbert H. 1928- *St&PR 91*
Forst, Judith Doris 1943- *WhoAm 90*
Forst, Leland I. 1948- *St&PR 91*
Forst, Marion Francis 1910- *WhoAm 90*
Forst, Ralph 1921- *St&PR 91*
Forst, Sigmund 1904- *BioIn 16*
Forst, Thomas M. 1946- *St&PR 91*
Forstall, Edmond J 1794-1873 *EncABHB 6 [port]*
Forstall, Terrence Christopher 1945- *WhoEmL 91*
Forste, Norman Lee 1935- *WhoWor 91*
Forstein, Marshall *BiDrAPA 89*
Forster, Alan M. 1940- *St&PR 91*
Forster, Albert 1902-1948 *BioIn 16*
Forster, Arnold 1912- *BioIn 16, WhoAm 90, WhoWrEP 89*
Forster, Arthur Daniel 1931- *St&PR 91*
Forster, Bruce Alexander 1948- *WhoWor 91*
Forster, Cornelius Philip 1919- *WhoAm 90*
Forster, Denis 1941- *WhoAm 90*
Forster, E. M. 1879-1970 *BioIn 16*
Forster, E M 1879-1970 *DcLB 98 [port], MajTwCW*
Forster, E. M. 1879-1970 *WorAlBi*
Forster, E M 1879-1970 *WrPh*
Forster, Edward Morgan 1879-1970 *BioIn 16*
Forster, Eric Otto 1918- *WhoAm 90*
Forster, Eugene *BiDrAPA 89*
Forster, Francis Michael 1912- *WhoAm 90*
Forster, Georg 1754-1794 *DcLB 94 [port]*
Forster, Heinrich 1938- *IntWWM 90*
Forster, Henry 1889-1989 *BioIn 16*
Forster, Homer W. 1944- *WhoSSW 91*
Forster, James Francis 1956- *WhoEmL 91*
Forster, Julian 1918- *WhoAm 90*
Forster, Klaus 1945- *ConAu 131*
Forster, Kurt Walter 1935- *WhoAm 90*
Forster, Leslie Stewart 1924- *WhoAm 90*
Forster, Margaret 1938- *BioIn 16, FemiCLE, WorAu 1980 [port]*
Forster, Mary 1619-1686 *BiDEWW*
Forster, Mary 1620?-1687 *FemiCLE*
Forster, Merlin Henry 1928- *WhoAm 90*
Forster, Peter Hans 1942- *St&PR 91, WhoAm 90*
Forster, Peter Lloyd *BiDrAPA 89*
Forster, Robert 1926- *WhoAm 90*
Forster, Robert S. 1945- *St&PR 91*
Forster, Robert Sharp 1945- *WhoSSW 91*
Forster, Roy Philip 1911- *WhoAm 90*
Forster, Teresa Ann 1961- *WhoAmW 91*
Forster, Terry 1952- *Ballpl 90*
Forster, Therese Herbert- *BioIn 16*
Forster, Virginia L. 1953- *WhoAmW 91, WhoEmL 91*
Forster, W. E. 1818-1886 *BioIn 16*
Forster, William Daly 1946- *St&PR 91*
Forster, William Edward 1818-1886 *BioIn 16*
Forsthoefel, Frank Eugene *BiDrAPA 89*
Forsthoff, William Earle 1924- *St&PR 91*
Forsting, Lucy Theiler 1945- *WhoWor 91*
Forstman, Henry Jackson 1929- *WhoAm 90*
Forstmann, Julius Anthony 1938- *WhoAm 90*
Forsyth, Beverly *WhoWrEP 89*
Forsyth, Bill *BioIn 16*
Forsyth, Constance 1903-1987 *WhoAmA 91N*
Forsyth, E. Jardine 1943- *St&PR 91*
Forsyth, Elliott Christopher 1924- *WhoWor 91*
Forsyth, Eric Boyland 1932- *WhoAm 90*
Forsyth, Frederick 1938- *MajTwCW, SpyFic, TwCCr&M 91, WhoAm 90, WhoWor 91, WorAlBi*
Forsyth, George Alexander 1837-1915 *WhNaAH*
Forsyth, George Howard, Jr. 1901- *WhoAm 90*
Forsyth, Gloria *AuBYP 90*
Forsyth, Gordon, Jr. 1925- *St&PR 91*
Forsyth, Ilene H 1928- *WhoAmA 91*
Forsyth, Ilene Haering 1928- *WhoAm 90*
Forsyth, James William 1836-1906 *WhNaAH*
Forsyth, John 1780-1841 *BiDrUSE 89, BioIn 16*
Forsyth, John Emery 1954- *WhoEmL 91*
Forsyth, Joseph 1942- *WhoAm 90*
Forsyth, Malcolm Denis 1936- *IntWWM 90*
Forsyth, Raymond Arthur 1928- *WhoAm 90*
Forsyth, Rosemary 1944- *BioIn 16*
Forsyth, Steven E. 1947- *ODwPR 91*
Forsyth, Suzanne Mary 1943- *WhoAm 90*
Forsythe, Alan Barry 1940- *St&PR 91*
Forsythe, David John 1950- *BiDrAPA 89*
Forsythe, Donald G. 1938- *ODwPR 91, St&PR 91*
Forsythe, Donald John 1955- *WhoAmA 91*
Forsythe, Earl Andrew 1904- *WhoAm 90*
Forsythe, Edward James 1952- *WhoE 91*
Forsythe, Elizabeth M. 1951- *WhoAmW 91*
Forsythe, Eric 1947- *WhoEmL 91*
Forsythe, Frank S. 1932- *St&PR 91, WhoAm 90*
Forsythe, Henderson 1917- *WhoAm 90*
Forsythe, Janet W. 1957- *WhoEmL 91*
Forsythe, John *BioIn 16*
Forsythe, John 1918- *WhoAm 90, WorAlBi*
Forsythe, John G. 1947- *St&PR 91*
Forsythe, Lynn Maureen 1949- *WhoEmL 91*
Forsythe, Mary MacCornack 1920- *WhoAmW 91*
Forsythe, Patricia Hays *WhoAmW 91, WhoWor 91*
Forsythe, Peter Winchell 1937- *WhoAm 90*
Forsythe, Richard Hamilton 1921- *WhoAm 90*
Forsythe, Thomas Millard 1958- *WhoEmL 91*
Forsythe, Vic 1885-1962 *EncACom*
Fort, Arthur Tomlinson, III 1931- *WhoAm 90, WhoWor 91*
Fort, Arthur W. *WhoAm 90*
Fort, Catherine Foard 1927- *WhoAmW 91, WhoSSW 91*
Fort, Charles 1874-1932 *EncO&P 3*
Fort, Charles Hoy 1874-1932 *EncPaPR 91*
Fort, Denise Conlin 1943- *WhoAmW 91*
Fort, Domenico Giorgio 1946- *WhoWor 91*
Fort, Edward Bernard *WhoAm 90, WhoSSW 91*
Fort, Gary Watt 1956- *WhoWrEP 89*
Fort, James B. 1936- *St&PR 91*
Fort, James Tomlinson 1928- *WhoAm 90*
Fort, John Franklin 1941- *St&PR 91*
Fort, John Franklin, III 1941- *WhoAm 90, WhoE 91*
Fort, John P 1923- *BiDrAPA 89*
Fort, John Porter 1923- *WhoE 91*
Fort, Juliana Melody 1962- *BiDrAPA 89*
Fort, Lee Earthmon 1950- *WhoEmL 91, WhoWor 91*
Fort, Randall Martin 1956- *WhoAm 90*
Fort, Raymond Cornelius, Jr. 1938- *WhoAm 90*
Fort, Robert C. 1944- *ODwPR 91*
Fort, Syvilla 1917-1975 *DrBIPA 90*
Fort, Timothy Lyman 1958- *WhoEmL 91*
Fort, Tomlinson 1932- *WhoAm 90*
Fort-Brescia, Bernardo *BioIn 16, WhoHisp 91*
Fort-Brescia, Bernardo M 1951- *WhoAmA 91*
Fortabat, Amalia de *BioIn 16*
Fortado, Michael G. 1943- *St&PR 91*
Fortado, Michael George 1943- *WhoAm 90*
Fortanasce, Vincent M *BiDrAPA 89*
Fortas, Abe 1910-1982 *BioIn 16, WorAlBi*
Forte, Angelo 1938- *ODwPR 91*
Forte, Charles 1908- *WhoWor 91*
Forte, Chet *NewYTBS 90 [port]*
Forte, Chris Eric 1956- *WhoEmL 91*
Forte, Donald, Jr. 1942- *St&PR 91, WhoE 91*
Forte, Earl M., Jr. 1924- *St&PR 91*
Forte, James Peter 1936- *IntWWM 90*
Forte, Joseph Michael 1954- *WhoEmL 91*
Forte, Joseph P. 1944- *St&PR 91*
Forte, Stephen Forrest 1947- *WhoEmL 91, WhoSSW 91*
Forte, Vincent Joseph, Jr. 1956- *WhoEmL 91*
Forte, Wesley Elbert 1933- *St&PR 91, WhoAm 90*
Fortelka, Bruce P. *St&PR 91*
Fortenbach, Ray Thomas 1927- *WhoAm 90*
Fortenbaugh, Samuel B., III 1933- *St&PR 91*
Fortenbaugh, Samuel Byrod, III 1933- *WhoAm 90, WhoE 91, WhoWor 91*
Fortenbaugh, William Harvey *BioIn 16*
Fortenberry, Betty Dillard 1939- *WhoAmW 91*
Fortenberry, Carol Lomax 1959- *WhoSSW 91*
Fortenberry, Charles Nolan 1908- *WhoAm 90*
Fortes, Abraham R 1914- *BiDrAPA 89*
Fortes, Meyer 1906-1983 *BioIn 16, ConAu 129, DcNaB 1981*
Fortescue, Margaret L. 1940- *WhoAmW 91*
Fortescue-Brickdale, E. *BiDWomA*
Fortess, Karl E 1907- *WhoAmA 91*
Fortess, Karl Eugene 1907- *WhoAm 90*
Forteza, Mario Enrique 1927- *BiDrAPA 89*
Forth, Gerald Edward 1946- *St&PR 91*
Forth, Kevin Bernard 1949- *WhoAm 90*
Forth, Stuart 1923- *WhoAm 90*
Forthman, Mary *BioIn 16*
Forthuny, Pascal 1872-1962 *EncO&P 3, EncPaPR 91*
Forti, Corinne Ann 1941- *WhoAmW 91*
Fortier, D'Iberville *BioIn 16*
Fortier, D'Iberville 1926- *WhoAm 90*
Fortier, Jean-Marie 1920- *WhoAm 90*
Fortier, John Bertram 1942- *WhoAm 90*
Fortier, L. Yves 1935- *WhoAm 90, WhoWor 91*
Fortier, Normand Paul 1944- *St&PR 91*
Fortier, Richard Emery 1947- *BiDrAPA 89*
Fortier, Samuel John 1952- *WhoEmL 91*
Fortier, Skip Ernest 1954- *WhoSSW 91*
Fortin, Harold Paul 1932- *St&PR 91*
Fortin, Jean Noel *BiDrAPA 89*
Fortin, John J. 1922- *St&PR 91*
Fortin, Karen Ann 1936- *WhoSSW 91*
Fortin, Lucie *BiDrAPA 89*
Fortin, Luis Horacio 1920- *WhoAm 90*
Fortin, Martin Emerson, Jr. 1952- *WhoEmL 91*
Fortin, Michael James *BiDrAPA 89*
Fortin, Robert Joseph 1930- *WhoSSW 91*
Fortina, Antonio Formia 1952- *WhoWor 91*
Fortinberry, Glen W. 1927- *WhoAm 90*
Fortinberry, Glen Wood *BioIn 16*
Fortinberry, Glen Wood 1927- *St&PR 91*
Fortiner, Robert H 1934- *BiDrAPA 89*
Fortino, Anthony Peter 1928- *St&PR 91*
Fortino, Ron *St&PR 91*
Fortling, Jacob *PenDiDA 89*
Fortman, Edmund J. 1901-1990 *ConAu 130*
Fortman, Richard Allen 1936- *St&PR 91*
Fortna, Ira Curtis 1937- *IntWWM 90*
Fortna, Lixi 1913- *WhoAmW 91*
Fortner, Brand Irving 1955- *WhoEmL 91*
Fortner, Hueston Gilmore 1959- *WhoEmL 91*
Fortner, Joseph Gerald 1921- *WhoAm 90*
Fortner, Kathleen A. *BiDrAPA 89*
Fortner, Robert David 1949- *WhoSSW 91*
Fortner, Robert Steven 1948- *WhoWor 91*
Fortner, Wolfgang 1907-1987 *PenDiMP A*
Fortney, Diane Eline Osborn 1958- *WhoAmW 91*
Fortney, Judith A. 1938- *WhoAmW 91*
Fortney, Ray Arnold 1946- *St&PR 91*
Fortney, Wayne Hollis, Jr. 1941- *WhoSSW 91*
Fortson, Barksdale E 1932- *BiDrAPA 89*
Fortson, D. Eugene 1935- *St&PR 91*
Fortson, Edward Norval 1936- *WhoAm 90*
Fortson, Nicholas Keith 1957- *St&PR 91*
Fortson, Sanna 1944- *WhoWrEP 89*
Fortson, Sanna G. 1944- *WhoSSW 91*
Fortuin, Johannes Martinus H. 1927- *WhoWor 91*
Fortuin, Thomas Mark 1946- *WhoEmL 91*
Fortuna, J. Douglas 1958- *WhoEmL 91*
Fortuna, Julian Anthony 1956- *WhoSSW 91*
Fortuna, William Frank 1948- *WhoEmL 91, WhoWor 91*
Fortunato, Mark Anthony 1955- *WhoEmL 91*
Fortunato, Nancy 1941- *WhoAmA 91*
Fortunato, Roberta Ann 1936- *WhoAmW 91*
Fortune, Amos 1709?-1801 *BioIn 16*
Fortune, David Ramsay 1947- *WhoWor 91*
Fortune, Dion 1890-1946 *EncO&P 3*
Fortune, George 1935- *IntWWM 90*
Fortune, James Michael 1947- *WhoEmL 91, WhoWor 91*
Fortune, Janet Ellis 1945- *WhoEmL 91*
Fortune, Joanne C. 1941- *WhoWor 91*
Fortune, Lauren Susan Pitz 1948- *WhoAmW 91*
Fortune, Monique Joan 1961- *WhoWrEP 89*
Fortune, Patrick John 1947- *WhoAm 90*
Fortune, Philip Lee 1945- *WhoEmL 91*
Fortune, Philip Robert 1913- *WhoAm 90*
Fortune, Robert R. 1916- *St&PR 91*
Fortune, Robert Russell 1916- *WhoAm 90*
Fortune, Roberta *BioIn 16*
Fortune, Susan Elizabeth 1964- *WhoAmW 91*
Fortune, Timothy Thomas 1856-1928 *BioIn 16*
Fortune, William John 1946- *St&PR 91*
Fortune, William Lemcke 1912- *WhoAm 90, WhoWor 91*
Fortuno, Luis G. 1960- *WhoHisp 91*
Fortuno, Ramon Oscar 1958- *BiDrAPA 89*
Fortuny, Mariano 1871-1949 *PenDiDA 89*
Fortuny y Carbo, Mariano 1838-1874 *BioIn 16*

Fortuyn-Leenmans, Margaretha Droogleever *EncCoWW*
Fortwangler, Robert W. *St&PR 91*
Forty, Jean-Francois *PenDiDA 89*
Forwald, Haakon Gabriel 1897-1978 *EncO&P 3, EncPaPR 91*
Forward, David R. 1934- *WhoE 91*
Forward, Dorothy Elizabeth 1919- *WhoAmW 91*
Forward, Gordon E. *WhoSSW 91*
Forward, Robert Lull 1932- *WhoAm 90*
Forward, Susan *ConAu 130*
Forward, Walter 1786-1852 *BiDrUSE 89*
Fory, Jon Roger 1944- *WhoSSW 91*
Fory, Ronald Philip 1943- *WhoSSW 91*
Foryst, Carole *WhoAm 90*
Forzanti, Lionello *PenDiMP*
Forzley, Harold Helmar 1952- *St&PR 91*
Forzley, Paul Edward 1953- *WhoE 91*
Fosback, Norman George 1947- *WhoAm 90, WhoSSW 91*
Fosbroke, L. Lindley Powers 1926- *WhoWor 91*
Fosburg, Kenneth Robert 1925- *St&PR 91*
Fosburg, Richard Garrison 1930- *WhoAm 90*
Fosburgh, James Whitney 1910-1978 *WhoAmA 91N*
Fosburgh, Lacey 1942- *WhoWrEP 89*
Fosburgh, Liza 1930- *AuBYP 90, ConAu 30NR*
Fosbury, Dick 1947- *WorAlBi*
Foscante, Raymond Eugene 1942- *St&PR 91*
Foschini, Charles Joseph 1965- *WhoSSW 91*
Fosco, Angelo *WhoAm 90, WhoE 91*
Fosco, William N 1908- *BiDrAPA 89*
Fosdal, Frederick A 1938- *BiDrAPA 89*
Fosdick, Harry Emerson 1878-1969 *AuBYP 90, BioIn 16, WorAlBi*
Fosdick, Sina G *WhoAmA 91N*
Fosgate Heggli, Julie Denise 1954- *WhoAmW 91*
Foshag, William Frederick 1894-1956 *DcScB S2*
Foshage, Joseph Charles 1920- *St&PR 91*
Foshage, William F., Jr. 1924- *St&PR 91*
Foshay, Wilbur B. *BioIn 16*
Fosher, Donald Hobart 1935- *WhoWor 91*
Fosholt, Sanford Kenneth 1915- *WhoAm 90*
Foskett, Charles T. 1943- *St&PR 91*
Fosler, Gail D. 1947- *WhoAmW 91*
Fosmire, Fred Randall 1926- *WhoAm 90*
Fosmire, Frederick Randall 1926- *St&PR 91*
Fosnaught, Patricia S. 1943- *WhoAmW 91*
Fosnight, Alan D. 1961- *St&PR 91*
Fosnight, Dale Pennell 1923- *St&PR 91*
Foss, Brian Edwin 1953- *WhoE 91*
Foss, Charles R. 1945- *WhoEmL 91, WhoWor 91*
Foss, Clive 1939- *ConAu 132*
Foss, Clive Frank Wilson 1939- *WhoAm 90*
Foss, Daniel Karl *BiDrAPA 89*
Foss, David John 1956- *WhoEmL 91*
Foss, Donald G. 1929- *St&PR 91*
Foss, Donald John 1940- *WhoAm 90*
Foss, Edward S. 1950- *St&PR 91*
Foss, Ernestine V. 1939- *St&PR 91*
Foss, George B., Jr. 1924- *WhoSSW 91*
Foss, Harlan Funston 1918- *WhoAm 90*
Foss, Joe *BioIn 16*
Foss, Joe 1915- *News 90 [port], -90-3 [port], WhoAm 90*
Foss, John Frank 1938- *WhoAm 90*
Foss, John H. 1943- *St&PR 91*
Foss, Lukas 1922- *IntWWM 90, WhoAm 90, WhoWor 91*
Foss, Michelle Marie 1964- *WhoAmW 91*
Foss, Patricia Howland 1925- *WhoAmW 91*
Foss, Paulette D. 1952- *WhoEmL 91*
Foss, Phillip Oliver 1916- *WhoAm 90*
Foss, Ralph Scot 1945- *WhoSSW 91*
Foss, Richard F. 1917- *St&PR 91*
Foss, Ronald G. *St&PR 91*
Foss, Theodore Nicholas 1950- *WhoEmL 91*
Foss, Warren L. 1915- *St&PR 91*
Foss, William Francis 1917- *St&PR 91, WhoAm 90*
Foss, William Otto 1918- *AuBYP 90*
Fossati, Thomas 1957- *WhoEmL 91*
Fosse, Bob *BioIn 16*
Fosse, Bob 1927-1987 *OxCPMus, WorAlBi*
Fosse, Erwin Ray 1918- *WhoAm 90*
Fosse, Ray 1947- *Ballpl 90*
Fosseen, Neal Randolph 1908- *WhoWor 91*
Fossel, Jon S. 1942- *St&PR 91*
Fossella, Gregory 1933- *ConDes 90*
Fosselman, J.F. 1926- *St&PR 91*
Fosselman, Jacqueline Ann 1940- *WhoE 91*
Fossenkemper, Marius Emig 1902- *WhoWor 91*
Fossey, Andre-Julien-Eternel *PenDiDA 89*
Fossey, Brigitte 1946- *ConTFT 8*
Fossey, Dian *BioIn 16*
Fossey, Dian 1932-1985 *MajTwCW*
Fossey, Mark Douglas 1950- *BiDrAPA 89*
Fosshag, Bengt 1940- *BioIn 16*
Fossier, Ralph L., Jr. 1951- *St&PR 91*
Fossier, Ralph Laverne, Sr. 1914- *St&PR 91*
Fossland, Joeann Jones 1948- *WhoAmW 91, WhoEmL 91*
Fossum, Donna L. 1949- *WhoAmW 91, WhoEmL 91*
Fossum, Jerry George 1943- *WhoAm 90*
Fossum, Robert Merle 1938- *WhoAm 90*
Fossum, Theresa Welch 1957- *WhoAmW 91*
Fost, Dennis L. 1944- *St&PR 91*
Foster And Lloyd *WhoNeCM [port]*
Foster, Alan 1946- *Ballpl 90*
Foster, Alan Dean 1946- *WhoWrEP 89*
Foster, Alan Herbert 1925- *WhoAm 90*
Foster, Anthony 1926- *IntWWM 90*
Foster, April 1947- *WhoAmA 91*
Foster, Archibald McGhee 1915-1989 *BioIn 16*
Foster, Arlie O. 1918- *St&PR 91*
Foster, Arthur Eugene 1934- *St&PR 91*
Foster, Arthur L. 1947- *St&PR 91*
Foster, Arthur Rowe 1924- *WhoAm 90*
Foster, Barbara 1938- *WhoWrEP 89*
Foster, Barbara Anne 1955- *WhoEmL 91*
Foster, Bernard B 1939- *BiDrAPA 89*
Foster, Bill 1904-1978 *Ballpl 90*
Foster, Bobbie Dore 1938- *WhoAmW 91*
Foster, Bobby Lynn 1946- *St&PR 91*
Foster, Catherine Rierson 1935- *WhoAmW 91, WhoE 91, WhoWor 91*
Foster, Charles 1828-1904 *BiDrUSE 89*
Foster, Charles Allen 1941- *WhoSSW 91*
Foster, Charles H. 1838-1888 *EncO&P 3*
Foster, Charles Harman *BioIn 16, NewYTBS 90*
Foster, Charles Henry 1927- *WhoAm 90*
Foster, Charles William 1939- *WhoSSW 91*
Foster, Cheryl Ann 1943- *WhoE 91*
Foster, Conrad E. 1953- *St&PR 91*
Foster, Constance B. 1946- *WhoEmL 91*
Foster, Dale Warren 1950- *WhoSSW 91*
Foster, David Charles 1952- *WhoEmL 91*
Foster, David L. 1933- *St&PR 91*
Foster, David Lee 1933- *WhoAm 90*
Foster, David Mark 1932- *WhoAm 90*
Foster, David Ramsey 1920- *WhoWor 91*
Foster, David Scott 1938- *WhoAm 90*
Foster, David Smith 1927- *WhoAm 90*
Foster, David Vernon 1946- *BiDrAPA 89*
Foster, David William 1940- *WhoWrEP 89*
Foster, Deborah Jean 1952- *WhoEmL 91*
Foster, Dennis James 1952- *WhoEmL 91*
Foster, Dennis P. 1933- *WhoSSW 91*
Foster, Don 1932- *WhoAmA 91*
Foster, Don Parks 1951- *WhoE 91*
Foster, Donald Herbert 1934- *IntWWM 90*
Foster, Donald Isle 1925- *WhoAmA 91*
Foster, Donald Lee 1932- *WhoAm 90*
Foster, Donald W. 1950- *ConAu 132*
Foster, Douglas Allen 1952- *WhoSSW 91*
Foster, Douglas Goddard *BiDrAPA 89*
Foster, Douglas L 1931- *BiDrAPA 89*
Foster, Dudley Edwards, Jr. 1935- *IntWWM 90, WhoWor 91*
Foster, E. M., Mrs. *FemiCLE*
Foster, Eddie 1888-1937 *Ballpl 90*
Foster, Edson L. 1927- *WhoAm 90*
Foster, Edward E. 1939- *WhoAm 90*
Foster, Edward Mervyn 1933- *WhoAm 90*
Foster, Edwin Powell, Jr. 1942- *WhoSSW 91*
Foster, Edwin Thomas 1923- *St&PR 91*
Foster, Elaine Elizabeth 1934- *WhoAmW 91*
Foster, Eleazer Kingsbury 1813-1877 *AmLegL*
Foster, Elizabeth 1905-1963 *AuBYP 90*
Foster, Elizabeth C. 1902- *AuBYP 90*
Foster, Ellie *BioIn 16*
Foster, Eloise C. 1943- *BioIn 16*
Foster, Eric H. 1943- *WhoE 91*
Foster, Erin Maguire 1963- *ODwPR 91*
Foster, Estelle Ancrum 1887- *EarBlAP*
Foster, Esther Bond 1913-1963 *EncO&P 3*
Foster, Eugene Lewis 1922- *WhoAm 90*
Foster, Fern Allen 1921- *WhoAm 90*
Foster, Flynn Douglas 1967- *WhoSSW 91*
Foster, Frances 1924- *DrBlPA 90*
Foster, Frances Helen 1924- *WhoAm 90*
Foster, Fred G. 1946- *St&PR 91*
Foster, Frederick G *BiDrAPA 89*
Foster, Gary D. 1943- *St&PR 91*
Foster, Gary Dean 1944- *St&PR 91*
Foster, Genevieve 1893-1979 *AuBYP 90, WhoAmA 91N*
Foster, Genevieve Stump 1893-1979 *BioIn 16*
Foster, George *BioIn 16*
Foster, George 1948- *WorAlBi*
Foster, George 1949- *Ballpl 90 [port]*
Foster, George Allen 1907-1969 *AuBYP 90*
Foster, George Clark *BioIn 16*
Foster, George Everett 1939- *WhoE 91*
Foster, George McClelland, Jr. 1913- *WhoAm 90, WhoWor 91*
Foster, George Rainey 1943- *WhoAm 90*
Foster, George William, Jr. 1919- *WhoWor 91*
Foster, Gifford H. 1922- *St&PR 91*
Foster, Gloria 1936- *ConTFT 8, DrBlPA 90*
Foster, Golda Marie 1948- *WhoAmW 91, WhoEmL 91, WhoSSW 91*
Foster, Gordon Kay 1927- *St&PR 91*
Foster, Grace B. *ODwPR 91*
Foster, Grace Elizabeth 1928- *WhoWrEP 89*
Foster, H. Lincoln *BioIn 16*
Foster, Hal 1892-1982 *EncACom [port], WhoAmA 91N*
Foster, Hannah 1758-1840 *FemiCLE*
Foster, Harold Homer 1902-1986 *BioIn 16*
Foster, Harry *ConAu 31NR*
Foster, Helen Montague 1946- *BiDrAPA 89*
Foster, Henry H, Jr. *BiDrAPA 89*
Foster, Henry Hubbard 1911-1988 *BioIn 16*
Foster, Henry Louis 1925- *WhoAm 90*
Foster, Herbert Hastings *BioIn 16*
Foster, Herbert Lawrence 1928- *WhoE 91*
Foster, Holmes 1927- *WhoAm 90*
Foster, Howard E. 1944- *St&PR 91*
Foster, Howard Kennedy 1945- *BiDrAPA 89*
Foster, Idris Llewelyn 1911-1984 *DcNaB 1981*
Foster, Irene Parks 1927- *WhoAmW 91*
Foster, J A 1932- *ConAu 130*
Foster, J.B. 1934- *St&PR 91*
Foster, James Caldwell 1943- *WhoAm 90*
Foster, James Clifford 1950- *St&PR 91*
Foster, James H. *ODwPR 91*
Foster, James Henry 1930- *WhoAm 90*
Foster, James Henry 1933- *WhoAm 90*
Foster, James Howard 1947- *WhoSSW 91*
Foster, James Norton, Jr. 1954- *WhoEmL 91*
Foster, James Peter 1925- *St&PR 91*
Foster, James R. 1945- *St&PR 91*
Foster, James Vance 1934- *St&PR 91*
Foster, James W, Sr *WhoAmA 91N*
Foster, Jay W. 1957- *St&PR 91*
Foster, Jeffrey R *BiDrAPA 89*
Foster, Jesse G. 1938- *St&PR 91*
Foster, Joanna 1928- *AuBYP 90*
Foster, Joanne Leslie *BiDrAPA 89*
Foster, Jodie *BioIn 16*
Foster, Jodie 1962- *WhoAm 90, WhoAmW 91, WorAlBi*
Foster, Joe Anthony, Jr. 1950- *WhoSSW 91*
Foster, Joe C., Jr. 1925- *WhoAm 90*
Foster, John B 1863-1941 *Ballpl 90*
Foster, John B. 1928- *WhoAm 90*
Foster, John Galway 1903?-1982 *DcNaB 1981*
Foster, John Horace 1927- *WhoAm 90*
Foster, John McNeely 1949- *St&PR 91, WhoAm 90*
Foster, John Stanton 1921- *WhoAm 90*
Foster, John Stuart, Jr. 1922- *WhoAm 90*
Foster, John Thomas 1925- *AuBYP 90*
Foster, John Watson 1836-1917 *BiDrUSE 89, BioIn 16*
Foster, Joseph W. 1935- *St&PR 91*
Foster, Joseph Wayne 1961- *WhoSSW 91*
Foster, Joyce Geraldine 1951- *WhoAmW 91*
Foster, Judith Christine 1952- *WhoEmL 91, WhoWor 91*
Foster, Julian Francis Sherwood 1926- *WhoAm 90*
Foster, Julie Irene 1955- *WhoEmL 91*
Foster, Karen Leppert 1942- *WhoE 91*
Foster, Kathleen Hurley 1949- *WhoAmW 91*
Foster, Kathryn Carey 1955- *WhoAmW 91*
Foster, Kenneth E *WhoAmA 91N*
Foster, Kent B. *WhoAm 90*
Foster, Kevin Connell 1939- *St&PR 91*
Foster, Kimberly *BioIn 16*
Foster, Lafayette Lumpkin 1851-1901 *AmLegL*
Foster, Lafayette Sabine 1806-1880 *AmLegL*
Foster, Lanny Gordon 1948- *WhoE 91*
Foster, Laura 1957- *WhoEmL 91*
Foster, Laura Louise 1918- *AuBYP 90*
Foster, LaVerne Arnett 1930- *WhoAmW 91*
Foster, Lawrence 1941- *IntWWM 90, PenDiMP, WhoWor 91*
Foster, Lawrence 1947- *ConAu 131*
Foster, Lawrence G. 1925- *ODwPR 91*
Foster, Lawrence Gilmore 1925- *WhoAm 90*
Foster, Lawrence Gilmore 1927- *St&PR 91*
Foster, Lincoln Frank 1943- *WhoAm 90, WhoSSW 91*
Foster, Linda Lee 1947- *St&PR 91*
Foster, Linda Nemec 1950- *WhoWrEP 89*
Foster, Liz *WhoWrEP 89*
Foster, Lloyd Arthur 1933- *WhoE 91*
Foster, Louis W. 1913- *St&PR 91*
Foster, Lowell G 1935- *BiDrAPA 89*
Foster, Lowell Walter 1919- *WhoWor 91*
Foster, Lynn 1952- *ConAu 32NR*
Foster, Maelee Thomson 1932- *WhoAmA 91*
Foster, Marian Curtis 1909-1978 *AuBYP 90*
Foster, Mark Edward 1948- *WhoWor 91*
Foster, Marta 1941- *WhoHisp 91*
Foster, Martha Marshall 1935- *BiDrAPA 89*
Foster, Martha Tyahla 1955- *WhoAmW 91, WhoSSW 91*
Foster, Mary 1619-1686 *BiDEWW*
Foster, Mary 1951- *WhoAmA 91*
Foster, Mary Christine 1943- *WhoAm 90*
Foster, Mary Kathryn *BiDrAPA 89*
Foster, Maurice Brydon 1933- *WhoAm 90*
Foster, Maxie Elliott 1950- *WhoSSW 91*
Foster, Mayson H. 1946- *St&PR 91*
Foster, Melissa 1953- *WhoAmW 91*
Foster, Merritt Woodhull, Jr. 1920- *BiDrAPA 89*
Foster, Michael Joseph 1954- *St&PR 91*
Foster, Michael Paul 1947- *WhoSSW 91*
Foster, Michael Thomas 1951- *WhoEmL 91*
Foster, Michele Consigli 1956- *WhoAmW 91*
Foster, Milo George 1957- *WhoEmL 91*
Foster, Morgan Lawrence 1924- *WhoE 91*
Foster, Muriel 1877-1937 *PenDiMP*
Foster, Nancy Haston *WhoAmW 91, WhoWrEP 89*
Foster, Nicole Williams 1944- *St&PR 91*
Foster, Norman *PenDiDA 89*
Foster, Norman Robert 1935- *WhoWor 91*
Foster, Patricia Lynn *BiDrAPA 89*
Foster, Paul 1931- *WhoAm 90*
Foster, Paul Michael *BiDrAPA 89*
Foster, Paul Wesley, Jr. 1933- *St&PR 91*
Foster, Pauline Adele 1950- *WhoAmW 91*
Foster, Pearl Delphine 1922- *WhoAmW 91*
Foster, Philip Carey 1947- *WhoEmL 91*
Foster, Philip Ewing 1950- *WhoSSW 91*
Foster, Pop 1878-1944 *Ballpl 90*
Foster, R J 1929- *WhoWrEP 89*
Foster, Ralph B. 1928- *St&PR 91*
Foster, Randolph Courtney 1952- *WhoEmL 91*
Foster, Raymond C. 1919- *St&PR 91*
Foster, Reuben 1833-1898 *AmLegL*
Foster, Richard *TwCCr&M 91*
Foster, Richard *BioIn 16*
Foster, Richard 1930- *IntWWM 90*
Foster, Richard 1938- *WhoAm 90*
Foster, Richard Allen 1935- *St&PR 91*
Foster, Rita Dorn 1933- *WhoAm 90*
Foster, Robert Bruce 1950- *St&PR 91*
Foster, Robert Carmichael 1941- *St&PR 91, WhoAm 90*
Foster, Robert Francis 1926- *WhoAm 90*
Foster, Robert Ivan 1918- *IntWWM 90*
Foster, Robert Lawson 1925- *WhoAm 90*
Foster, Robert Watson 1926- *WhoAm 90*
Foster, Roger Sherman, Jr. 1936- *WhoAm 90*
Foster, Ronald H. 1944- *WhoSSW 91*
Foster, Roy 1945- *Ballpl 90*
Foster, Roy Wayne 1938- *St&PR 91*
Foster, Royce Porter 1928- *WhoAmW 91*
Foster, Rube 1878-1930 *Ballpl 90 [port]*
Foster, Rube 1889-1976 *Ballpl 90*
Foster, Ruth Mary 1927- *WhoAmW 91*
Foster, Sally 1937- *BioIn 16*
Foster, Scott Raymond 1932- *St&PR 91*
Foster, Sharon Lee 1949- *WhoAmW 91*
Foster, Stephen 1826-1864 *WorAlBi*
Foster, Stephen Anthony 1952- *WhoWor 91*
Foster, Stephen C 1941- *WhoAmA 91*
Foster, Stephen Collins 1825-1864 *LiHiK*
Foster, Stephen Collins 1826-1864 *OxCPMus*
Foster, Steven Douglas 1945- *WhoAmA 91*
Foster, Steven Raymond 1953- *WhoSSW 91*
Foster, Sumner J. 1930- *St&PR 91*
Foster, Susan Chandler 1949- *WhoAmW 91*
Foster, Susan Weltha 1946- *WhoAmW 91*
Foster, Sylvia Lee *BiDrAPA 89*
Foster, Tabatha 1984-1988 *BioIn 16*
Foster, Theda Ann *WhoSSW 91*
Foster, Theodore, II 1922- *St&PR 91*
Foster, Thomas A. 1938- *St&PR 91*
Foster, Thomas Elmore 1941- *WhoAm 90*

Foster, Thomas H. 1940- *St&PR 91*
Foster, Thomas Larry 1949- *WhoAm 90*
Foster, Thomas V 1920- *BiDrAPA 89*
Foster, Thomas Vernon, Jr. 1946- *BiDrAPA 89*
Foster, Tony *ConAu 130*
Foster, Vernon Keith 1961- *WhoSSW 91*
Foster, Vickie Lynn 1952- *WhoWrEP 89*
Foster, Vincent Stephen 1943- *WhoE 91*
Foster, Virginia 1914- *WhoAmW 91*
Foster, Virginia Highleyman 1935- *WhoAmW 91*
Foster, Virginia Lee 1929- *WhoAmW 91, WhoWor 91*
Foster, W. Douglas 1942- *WhoSSW 91*
Foster, Walter Herbert, Jr. 1919- *WhoE 91, WhoWor 91*
Foster, Walton Arthur 1927- *WhoWor 91*
Foster, Wanell Baize 1928- *WhoWor 91*
Foster, Wilbur Fisk 1841-1900 *AmLegL*
Foster, Willard Frank 1923- *St&PR 91*
Foster, William Austin, Jr. *St&PR 91*
Foster, William Bell, Jr. 1923- *St&PR 91*
Foster, William Edwin 1930- *WhoAm 90*
Foster, William Frederick 1961- *St&PR 91*
Foster, William James, III 1953- *WhoEmL 91*
Foster, William Z. 1881-1961 *EncAL*
Foster, William Zebulon 1881-1961 *BioIn 16, WorAlBi*
Fota, Frank George 1921- *WhoWor 91*
Foth, Joan *BioIn 16*
Foth, Joan B 1930- *WhoAmA 91*
Fothergill, Bob 1897-1938 *Ballpl 90*
Fothergill, Brian 1921-1990 *ConAu 132*
Fothergill, Caroline *FemiCLE*
Fothergill, Jessie 1851-1891 *BioIn 16, FemiCLE*
Fothergill, John *PenDiDA 89*
Fothergill, John Wesley, Jr. 1928- *WhoSSW 91*
Fotheringham, Allan 1932- *BioIn 16*
Foti, Anthony M 1937- *BiDrAPA 89*
Foti, Laurel Cohen 1943- *WhoAmW 91*
Foti, Margaret A. 1944- *WhoAm 90*
Foti, Mary Ellen *BiDrAPA 89*
Fotiades, George L. 1953- *St&PR 91*
Fotino, Elena *EncCoWW*
Fotinos, Katherine 1926- *WhoAmW 91*
Fotsch, Dan Robert 1947- *WhoEmL 91*
Fotsch, William G. 1903- *St&PR 91*
Fottrell, Eugene Joseph 1928- *WhoE 91*
Fou Ts'Ong 1934- *IntWWM 90, PenDiMP*
Foucault, Jean-Bernard-Leon 1819-1868 *WorAlBi*
Foucault, Jean Paul 1941- *WhoWor 91*
Foucault, Michel 1926-1984 *BioIn 16, EuWr 13, MajTwCW*
Foucault, Steve 1949- *Ballpl 90*
Fouch, David W. 1829-1901 *AmLegL*
Fouch, George Daniel 1948- *St&PR 91*
Fouch, Stephanie Saunders 1947- *WhoAm 90*
Fouchard, Joseph James 1928- *WhoE 91*
Fouche, Helen Strother 1939- *WhoAmW 91*
Fouche, Kathleen M *BiDrAPA 89*
Fouchek, Paula Trott 1951- *WhoAmW 91*
Foucher, Guy 1943- *WhoWor 91*
Fouchet, Christian 1911-1974 *BiDFrPL*
Foudree, Charles M. 1944- *St&PR 91*
Fougeron, Pierre Jacques 1927- *St&PR 91*
Fought, Stephen Oliver 1945- *WhoEmL 91*
Fougy, Ghislaine *BiDrAPA 89*
Foukal, Donald C. 1926- *St&PR 91*
Fouladgar-Mercer, Gita M *BiDrAPA 89*
Foulds, Donald Duane 1925- *WhoAm 90*
Foulet, Antoine 1710?-1775 *PenDiDA 89*
Foulk, David Lynn 1952- *St&PR 91*
Foulk, Malcolm 1937- *St&PR 91*
Foulke, Edwin Gerhart, Jr. 1952- *WhoEmL 91*
Foulke, Sarah B. 1955- *WhoAmW 91*
Foulke, William Green 1912- *WhoAm 90*
Foulke, William Green 1942- *WhoAm 90*
Foulkes, Llyn 1934- *WhoAm 90, WhoAmA 91*
Foulkes, William David 1935- *WhoSSW 91*
Foulkrod, Sarah Sutherland 1949- *WhoAmW 91*
Foulks, Edward F 1937- *BiDrAPA 89*
Foulks, Edward Francis 1937- *WhoAm 90*
Foullet, Antoine 1710?-1775 *PenDiDA 89*
Foulon, Didier Henri 1955- *WhoWor 91*
Found, J. Warren 1947- *St&PR 91*
Founds, Henry W. 1942- *St&PR 91*
Fountain, Albert Jennings 1838-1896 *AmLegL*
Fountain, Camille Christine 1961- *WhoAmW 91*
Fountain, Charles W 1926- *BiDrAPA 89*
Fountain, D. Ray 1938- *St&PR 91*
Fountain, Deward Green 1937- *St&PR 91*
Fountain, Frank Spratt 1929- *WhoE 91*
Fountain, Gerard *BiDrAPA 89*
Fountain, Henry Francis, Jr. 1924- *St&PR 91*
Fountain, James Ray, Jr. 1947- *WhoSSW 91*
Fountain, Kenneth Paul 1934- *St&PR 91*
Fountain, L. H. 1913- *WhoAm 90*
Fountain, Linda Kathleen 1954- *WhoAmW 91, WhoSSW 91*
Fountain, Lora Ellen 1944- *WhoWor 91*
Fountain, Peter Dewey, Jr. 1930- *WhoAm 90*
Fountain, Richard Maurice 1948- *WhoSSW 91*
Fountain, Robert Allen 1947- *WhoEmL 91*
Fountain, Robert Louis, Jr. 1946- *St&PR 91*
Fountain, Robert Roy, Jr. 1932- *WhoAm 90*
Fountain, Ronald Glenn 1939- *St&PR 91, WhoAm 90*
Fountaine, Margaret 1862-1940 *BioIn 16*
Fouquay, Nicolas *PenDiDA 89*
Fouquet, Jean 1420?-1477? *IntDcAA 90*
Four Bears *WhNaAH*
Four Freshmen, The *OxCPMus*
Four Harmony Kings *DcAfAmP*
Four Legs *WhNaAH*
Four Seasons, The *EncPR&S 89, OxCPMus*
Four Tops, The *EncPR&S 89, OxCPMus*
Fouraker, Lawrence Edward 1923- *WhoAm 90*
Fourastie, Jean Joseph Hubert 1907-1990 *ConAu 132*
Fourcade, Marie-Madeleine 1909-1989 *AnObit 1989, BiDFrPL, BioIn 16, ConAu 129*
Fourcard, Inez Garey *WhoAmA 91, WhoAmW 91*
Fourdinois, Alexandre-Georges 1799-1871 *PenDiDA 89*
Fourier, Charles 1772-1837 *WorAlBi, WrPh P*
Fourier, Jean-Baptiste-Joseph 1768-1830 *WorAlBi*
Fourmarier, Paul 1877-1970 *DcScB S2*
Fourmaux, George Marvin 1934- *St&PR 91*
Fournet, Claude Jacques 1942- *WhoWor 91*
Fournet, Jean 1913- *IntWWM 90, PenDiMP*
Fournet, Marilyn Michele 1949- *WhoAmW 91*
Fournet, Robert Louis 1928- *WhoSSW 91*
Fourney, Catherine Jo 1965- *WhoAmW 91*
Fourney, Michael E. 1936- *WhoAm 90*
Fournie, Raymond Richard 1951- *WhoEmL 91*
Fournie, Robert G. 1920- *WhoAm 90*
Fournier, Albert Edouard 1938- *WhoWor 91*
Fournier, Alexis Jean 1865-1948 *WhoAmA 91N*
Fournier, Bill *BioIn 16*
Fournier, Carol Sherman 1960- *WhoAmW 91*
Fournier, Christiane *BiDrAPA 89*
Fournier, Daniel S. 1947- *St&PR 91*
Fournier, Harold Nelson 1928- *St&PR 91*
Fournier, Henri 1886-1914 *BioIn 16*
Fournier, Jack 1892-1973 *Ballpl 90 [port]*
Fournier, Jean 1911- *PenDiMP*
Fournier, Jean-Pierre 1955- *BiDrAPA 89*
Fournier, Jennifer *BioIn 16*
Fournier, Keith Arthur 1954- *WhoEmL 91*
Fournier, Louis-Antoine 1720?-1786 *PenDiDA 89*
Fournier, N. Sue 1934- *St&PR 91*
Fournier, Pierre 1906-1986 *PenDiMP*
Fournier, Serge Raymond-Jean 1931- *WhoAm 90*
Fournier, Telesphore 1823-1896 *DcCanB 12*
Fournier, Winston C. 1920- *ODwPR 91*
Fourquet, Bernard Jean 1948- *WhoWor 91*
Fourroux, Melvin Ross 1944- *WhoE 91*
Fouse, Ron G. 1944- *St&PR 91*
Fousek, Frank Daniel 1913-1979 *WhoAmA 91N*
Fouss, James H. 1939- *WhoAm 90*
Fouss, James Helmer 1939- *St&PR 91*
Fousse, Jean-Louis Michel 1938- *WhoWor 91*
Foust, Ben S. 1923- *St&PR 91*
Foust, Charles William 1952- *WhoEmL 91*
Foust, Grace Naomi 1938- *WhoAmW 91*
Foust, Milton Jack 1958- *BiDrAPA 89*
Foust, Richard Duane, Jr. 1945- *WhoEmL 91, WhoWor 91*
Foust, Roscoe T. 1928- *St&PR 91*
Foust, Russel Eugene 1947- *WhoE 91*
Foust, Sharon Jeanette 1953- *WhoAmW 91*
Foust, William R. 1942- *St&PR 91*
Fout, George Douglas 1950- *WhoEmL 91*
Fouts, Donna Desti 1949- *WhoAmW 91*
Fouts, Elizabeth Browne 1927- *St&PR 91, WhoAmW 91, WhoSSW 91, WhoWor 91*
Fouts, Frank Richard 1947- *WhoEmL 91*
Fouts, James Fremont 1918- *St&PR 91, WhoSSW 91, WhoWor 91*
Fouts, James Ralph 1929- *WhoAm 90*
Fouts, Robert E. 1947- *St&PR 91*
Fouts, William P., III 1943- *St&PR 91*
Foutz, Dave 1856-1897 *Ballpl 90*
Foutz, Dell R. 1932- *WhoWrEP 89*
Foutz, Homer Ezra 1932- *WhoWor 91*
Foutz, Robert Vance 1948- *WhoSSW 91*
Fouvy, Charles Louis 1928- *IntWWM 90*
Fouwels, Ton John 1940- *WhoWor 91*
Fovall, Nettle L. 1921- *St&PR 91*
Fovenesi, John C. 1951- *WhoAm 90*
Fowble, William Franklin 1938- *St&PR 91, WhoAm 90*
Fowdar, Narud 1957- *WhoWor 91*
Fowinkle, Eugene W. 1934- *WhoAm 90*
Fowke, Edith Margaret Fulton 1913- *WhoAm 90, WhoAmW 91, WhoWrEP 89*
Fowke, Gerard 1855-1933 *WhNaAH*
Fowke, Martha *BiDEWW*
Fowke, Martha 1690-1736 *FemiCLE*
Fowke, Philip 1950- *PenDiMP*
Fowke, Philip Francis 1950- *IntWWM 90*
Fowkes, William Ivor 1950- *WhoEmL 91*
Fowle, Frank Fuller *BioIn 16*
Fowle, George D. 1924- *St&PR 91*
Fowle, Geraldine Elizabeth 1929- *WhoAmA 91*
Fowler, Alan Bicksler 1928- *WhoAm 90*
Fowler, Alfred 1889- *WhoAmA 91N*
Fowler, Anne Victoria 1945- *WhoAmW 91*
Fowler, Anthony Elton 1953- *WhoSSW 91*
Fowler, Arden Stephanie 1930- *WhoAmW 91*
Fowler, Art 1922- *Ballpl 90*
Fowler, Asa 1811-1885 *AmLegL*
Fowler, Audrian Huff 1940- *WhoAmW 91*
Fowler, Barbara Hughes 1926- *WhoAm 90*
Fowler, Beth 1940- *ConTFT 8 [port]*
Fowler, Betty *BioIn 16*
Fowler, Betty Janmae 1925- *WhoAmW 91*
Fowler, Betty Jo 1938- *WhoAmW 91*
Fowler, Bradley A. 1935- *St&PR 91*
Fowler, Bruce Andrew 1945- *WhoE 91, WhoWor 91*
Fowler, Caleb L. *WhoAm 90*
Fowler, Cecile Ann 1920- *WhoAmW 91, WhoE 91, WhoWor 91*
Fowler, Charles Albert 1920- *St&PR 91, WhoAm 90*
Fowler, Charles Allison Eugene 1921- *WhoAm 90, WhoWor 91*
Fowler, Charles Bruner 1931- *IntWWM 90*
Fowler, Christopher Gordon 1950- *WhoWor 91*
Fowler, Conrad Murphree 1918- *WhoAm 90, WhoSSW 91*
Fowler, Constance *BiDEWW, FemiCLE*
Fowler, Dan E. 1908- *St&PR 91*
Fowler, Daniel 1810-1894 *DcCanB 12*
Fowler, Dave *BioIn 16*
Fowler, David 1962- *St&PR 91*
Fowler, David Wayne 1937- *WhoAm 90*
Fowler, Deborah Lynn 1952- *WhoEmL 91*
Fowler, Delbert Marcom 1924- *WhoSSW 91*
Fowler, Dennis Lloyd 1944- *WhoE 91*
Fowler, Dick 1921-1972 *Ballpl 90*
Fowler, Don W. 1949- *WhoEmL 91*
Fowler, Dona Sylvia B. *WhoE 91*
Fowler, Donald Raymond 1926- *WhoWor 91*
Fowler, Donald Robert 1935- *BiDrAPA 89*
Fowler, Douglas R. 1940- *WhoWrEP 89*
Fowler, Earl Bealle 1925- *WhoWor 91*
Fowler, Earle Cabell 1921- *WhoAm 90*
Fowler, Edward P. *EncO&P 3*
Fowler, Elaine Wootten 1914- *WhoAm 90*
Fowler, Elizabeth Milton 1919- *WhoAmW 91*
Fowler, Ellen Thorneycroft 1860-1929 *FemiCLE*
Fowler, Eric Nicholas 1954- *WhoAmA 91, WhoE 91*
Fowler, Frank Eison 1946- *WhoAmA 91*
Fowler, Fred J. 1946- *St&PR 91*
Fowler, Frederick Victor, Jr. 1933- *St&PR 91, WhoE 91*
Fowler, Gene 1890-1960 *BioIn 16*
Fowler, Gene 1931- *WhoWrEP 89*
Fowler, George J., III 1950- *WhoHisp 91*
Fowler, George Selton, Jr. 1920- *WhoWor 91*
Fowler, Gilbert L. 1949- *WhoSSW 91*
Fowler, Hardy Booth, Jr. 1951- *WhoEmL 91*
Fowler, Harry Winthrop 1920- *St&PR 91*
Fowler, Henry H. 1908- *St&PR 91*
Fowler, Henry Hamill 1908- *BiDrUSE 89, WhoAm 90, WhoWor 91*
Fowler, Horatio Seymour 1919- *WhoAm 90*
Fowler, Howard *St&PR 91*
Fowler, Inez 1920- *BiDrAPA 89*
Fowler, Isaac Chapman 1831-1904 *AmLegL*
Fowler, J.W. 1944- *St&PR 91*
Fowler, James D., Jr. 1944- *WhoAm 90*
Fowler, James Daniel, Jr. 1944- *St&PR 91*
Fowler, James E. 1938- *ODwPR 91*
Fowler, James Edward 1931- *WhoAm 90*
Fowler, Jennifer 1939- *IntWWM 90*
Fowler, Joanna S. 1942- *WhoAmW 91*
Fowler, Joe Robert 1946- *WhoSSW 91*
Fowler, John A 1921- *BiDrAPA 89*
Fowler, John A. 1943- *St&PR 91*
Fowler, John Douglas 1931- *St&PR 91, WhoAm 90*
Fowler, John J. *BioIn 16*
Fowler, John Moore 1949- *WhoE 91*
Fowler, John Russell 1918- *St&PR 91, WhoAm 90*
Fowler, John Wellington 1935- *WhoAm 90*
Fowler, Jon Riggs 1938- *WhoSSW 91*
Fowler, Joseph Leon, Jr. 1943- *WhoSSW 91*
Fowler, Joseph William 1950- *WhoEmL 91*
Fowler, Julianne 1949- *WhoAmW 91*
Fowler, Karen Anne 1958- *St&PR 91*
Fowler, Kathleen Anne 1962- *WhoEmL 91*
Fowler, Keith 1928- *St&PR 91*
Fowler, Leslie *St&PR 91*
Fowler, Linda McKeever 1948- *WhoAmW 91*
Fowler, Lottie 1836-1899 *EncO&P 3*
Fowler, Mark Stapleton 1941- *WhoAm 90*
Fowler, Mark Thomas 1957- *WhoSSW 91*
Fowler, Marshall L *BiDrAPA 89*
Fowler, Mary Jean 1934- *WhoAmA 91*
Fowler, Mel 1921- *WhoAmA 91N*
Fowler, Mel 1922- *WhoAmA 91*
Fowler, Michael 1938- *WhoAm 90*
Fowler, Michael McSwain 1945- *WhoSSW 91*
Fowler, Nancy Crowley 1922- *WhoAmW 91, WhoWor 91*
Fowler, Nicholas P. 1952- *St&PR 91*
Fowler, Noble Owen 1919- *WhoAm 90*
Fowler, Patricia Cervantes Romero 1944- *WhoHisp 91*
Fowler, Patricia D. 1937- *St&PR 91*
Fowler, Paul *BioIn 16*
Fowler, Raymond David 1944- *WhoE 91*
Fowler, Richard Calvin 1940- *St&PR 91*
Fowler, Richard Cole *BiDrAPA 89*
Fowler, Richard Gildart 1916- *WhoAm 90, WhoWor 91*
Fowler, Richard Hindle 1910- *ConAu 130*
Fowler, Robert Archibald 1931- *WhoE 91*
Fowler, Robert Asa 1928- *WhoAm 90*
Fowler, Robert Glen 1930- *St&PR 91, WhoAm 90*
Fowler, Robert Howard 1926- *WhoAm 90*
Fowler, Robert K. 1944- *St&PR 91*
Fowler, Stephen Gillon 1938- *WhoWor 91*
Fowler, Stephen Leroy 1948- *WhoEmL 91*
Fowler, Stuart Athelstan 1930- *WhoWor 91*
Fowler, Susan Michele 1952- *WhoAmW 91*
Fowler, Talbert Bass, Jr. 1920- *WhoAm 90*
Fowler, Terri 1949- *WhoAmW 91, WhoEmL 91*
Fowler, Thomas Geoffrey 1924- *WhoWor 91*
Fowler, Thomas Kenneth 1931- *WhoAm 90*
Fowler, Virginia Christman 1949- *WhoSSW 91*
Fowler, Virginie *AuBYP 90*
Fowler, Vivian Delores 1946- *WhoAmW 91*
Fowler, Walton Berry 1946- *WhoWor 91*
Fowler, William A. 1911- *WorAlBi*
Fowler, William Alfred 1911- *WhoAm 90, WhoWor 91*
Fowler, William Carvel 1956- *WhoSSW 91*
Fowler, William Claybourne 1957- *WhoSSW 91*
Fowler, William Dix 1940- *WhoAm 90*
Fowler, William Morgan, Jr. 1944- *ConAu 31NR, WhoWrEP 89*
Fowler, William P *BiDrAPA 89*
Fowler, William Roy, Jr. 1950- *WhoSSW 91*
Fowler, William Wyche, Jr. 1940- *WhoAm 90, WhoSSW 91, WhoWor 91*
Fowler, Worth Blanding 1909-1988 *BioIn 16*
Fowler, Wyche, Jr. *NewYTBS 90 [port]*
Fowler, Wyman Beall 1937- *WhoAm 90*
Fowler-Losey, Ann *ODwPR 91*
Fowles, Dorothy Whaley *BiDrAPA 89*
Fowles, George Richard 1928- *WhoAm 90*
Fowles, John 1926- *AuBYP 90, BioIn 16, MajTwCW, WhoAm 90, WhoWor 91, WorAlBi, WrPh*
Fowles, William D. 1947- *St&PR 91*
Fowlie, Eldon Leslie 1928- *WhoAm 90*
Fowlkes, Albert R. 1930- *St&PR 91*
Fowlkes, Henry Pleasant 1843-1917 *AmLegL*
Fowlkes, Norman Eugene 1940- *WhoSSW 91*

Fowlkes, Yvonne Lampkin 1947- *WhoAmW 91*
Fowls, Don J *BiDrAPA 89*
Fox Sisters *EncO&P 3, EncPaPR 91*
Fox, Aileen Mary Henderson 1907- *BioIn 16*
Fox, Alexander 1919- *St&PR 91*
Fox, Alexander Sam 1946- *WhoSSW 91*
Fox, Allan 1935- *St&PR 91*
Fox, Andrea Nancy 1949- *WhoEmL 91*
Fox, Andrew Jay, Jr. 1930- *WhoWor 91*
Fox, Annette Joy 1951- *WhoAmW 91*
Fox, Arthur Charles 1926- *WhoAm 90*
Fox, Arthur J. *BioIn 16*
Fox, Arthur Joseph, Jr. 1923- *WhoAm 90*
Fox, Arturo Angel 1935- *WhoAm 90*
Fox, Barbara Figge 1940- *WhoE 91*
Fox, Bennett Louis 1938- *WhoAm 90*
Fox, Bernard *ConTFT 8*
Fox, Bernard 1915- *St&PR 91*
Fox, Bernard Hayman 1917- *WhoAm 90*
Fox, Bernard Michael 1942- *WhoAm 90*
Fox, Bill 1949- *St&PR 91*
Fox, Brad Steven 1957- *WhoEmL 91*
Fox, C. Fred 1937- *WhoAm 90*
Fox, C. Joseph, III 1947- *St&PR 91*
Fox, C. Wayne 1938- *St&PR 91*
Fox, Caroline 1819-1871 *FemiCLE*
Fox, Carolyn Elaine 1933- *WhoAmW 91, WhoSSW 91*
Fox, Carroll Lawson 1925- *St&PR 91, WhoAm 90*
Fox, Charles 1749-1806 *WorAlBi*
Fox, Charles Harold 1905-1979 *WhoAmA 91N*
Fox, Charles Ira 1940- *WhoAm 90*
Fox, Charles J. 1907- *St&PR 91*
Fox, Charles James 1749-1806 *EncCRAm*
Fox, Charles Lewis 1908-1989 *BioIn 16*
Fox, Charles S *BiDrAPA 89*
Fox, Charlie 1921- *Ballpl 90*
Fox, Colin L *BiDrAPA 89*
Fox, Connie T. 1932- *WhoWrEP 89*
Fox, Cyril A., Jr. 1937- *WhoAm 90*
Fox, Dana Alden 1960- *WhoEmL 91*
Fox, Daniel W. 1923-1989 *BioIn 16*
Fox, David 1941- *OxCCanT*
Fox, David Alan *BiDrAPA 89*
Fox, David Eliot 1960- *WhoEmL 91*
Fox, David Laurence *BiDrAPA 89*
Fox, David Martin 1948- *WhoEmL 91*
Fox, David Wayne 1931- *WhoAm 90*
Fox, Dean Frederick 1944- *WhoAm 90*
Fox, Derrick Sean 1964- *WhoWor 91*
Fox, Diane Wholley 1944- *WhoE 91*
Fox, Donald Melville 1942- *WhoSSW 91*
Fox, Donald Thomas 1929- *WhoAm 90, WhoE 91, WhoWor 91*
Fox, Dorothea M. *AuBYP 90*
Fox, Dorothy *AuBYP 90*
Fox, Douglas Allan 1927- *WhoAm 90*
Fox, Douglas Brian 1947- *St&PR 91*
Fox, Douglas Lee 1951- *WhoEmL 91*
Fox, Duke Melvin 1919- *WhoSSW 91*
Fox, E. *BiDWomA*
Fox, Edward A. 1936- *WhoAm 90, WhoE 91*
Fox, Edward Alan 1950- *WhoEmL 91*
Fox, Edward Inman 1933- *WhoAm 90, WhoWrEP 89*
Fox, Eleanor Mae Cohen 1936- *WhoAm 90, WhoWrEP 89*
Fox, Elizabeth Gordon 1884-1958 *BioIn 16*
Fox, Elizabeth Regina *WhoAmW 91*
Fox, Erika 1936- *IntWWM 90*
Fox, Erwin Joseph 1930- *St&PR 91*
Fox, Evan *BiDrAPA 89*
Fox, Flo 1945- *WhoAmA 91*
Fox, Fontaine 1884-1964 *EncACom*
Fox, Frances Barton 1887-1967 *LiHiK*
Fox, Francis Haney 1933- *WhoAm 90*
Fox, Francis Henry 1923- *WhoAm 90*
Fox, Frederick Gerald 1932- *St&PR 91*
Fox, Gail Strong 1943- *WhoAmW 91*
Fox, Gardner 1911-1986 *EncACom*
Fox, Gary 1939- *St&PR 91*
Fox, Gary Edwin 1950- *WhoEmL 91*
Fox, Genevieve May 1888-1959 *LiHiK*
Fox, Geoffrey Charles 1944- *WhoAm 90*
Fox, George 1624-1690 *EncPaPR 91*
Fox, George 1624-1691 *EncO&P 3, WorAlBi*
Fox, Gerald Julian 1927- *WhoE 91*
Fox, Gerald Lynn 1942- *WhoAm 90, WhoSSW 91*
Fox, Gerard F. 1923- *St&PR 91*
Fox, Geri 1954- *BiDrAPA 89*
Fox, Gerson I. 1927- *St&PR 91*
Fox, Graydon C. 1933- *St&PR 91*
Fox, Gretchen Hovemeyer 1940- *WhoAmW 91*
Fox, Helen Witkin 1927- *BiDrAPA 89*
Fox, Helene 1909- *WhoE 91*
Fox, Herbert 1939- *WhoE 91*
Fox, Herbert A *BiDrAPA 89*
Fox, Herbert Charles 1927- *St&PR 91*
Fox, Howard Neal 1946- *WhoAmA 91*
Fox, Howie 1921-1955 *Ballpl 90*
Fox, Hugh Bernard 1932- *WhoWrEP 89*
Fox, Hugh P. *BioIn 16*
Fox, Ira Leonard *BiDrAPA 89*
Fox, J Thomas, Jr. 1935- *BiDrAPA 89*
Fox, Jack Jay 1916- *WhoAm 90*
Fox, Jack Lawrence 1941- *WhoAm 90*
Fox, Jacob L. 1921- *St&PR 91*
Fox, Jacob Logan 1921- *WhoAm 90*
Fox, James 1939- *ConTFT 8*
Fox, James Carroll 1928- *WhoAm 90, WhoSSW 91*
Fox, James Erwin 1945- *WhoEmL 91*
Fox, James F. 1917- *ODwPR 91*
Fox, James Francis 1943- *St&PR 91*
Fox, James Frederick 1917- *WhoAm 90*
Fox, James Gahan 1943- *WhoAm 90*
Fox, James Harold, Jr. 1941- *WhoSSW 91*
Fox, James M. *TwCCr&M 91*
Fox, James Michael 1953- *IntWWM 90, WhoEmL 91*
Fox, James W. 1947- *St&PR 91*
Fox, Jean 1941- *WhoE 91*
Fox, Jeanne Marie 1952- *WhoAmW 91*
Fox, Jeffery Edward 1949- *WhoEmL 91*
Fox, Jeffrey 1951- *WhoE 91, WhoEmL 91, WhoWor 91*
Fox, Jimi 1946- *WhoWor 91*
Fox, Joan Marie 1948- *WhoE 91*
Fox, Joan Michelle 1947- *WhoAmW 91*
Fox, Joann Lewis 1931- *St&PR 91*
Fox, Joe *BioIn 16*
Fox, Joe M. 1915- *St&PR 91*
Fox, John 1927- *WhoAmA 91*
Fox, John 1952- *WhoWrEP 89*
Fox, John 1952-1990 *ConAu 132*
Fox, John, Jr. *LiHiK*
Fox, John Bayley, Jr. 1936- *WhoAm 90*
Fox, John Charles 1933- *St&PR 91*
Fox, John David 1929- *WhoAm 90*
Fox, John Duffell 1940- *WhoAm 90*
Fox, John Joseph, Jr. 1931- *WhoE 91*
Fox, John L. 1949- *St&PR 91*
Fox, John Patrick, Jr. 1918- *WhoAm 90*
Fox, Jonathan Randall 1958- *WhoWor 91*
Fox, Joseph Carter 1939- *St&PR 91, WhoSSW 91*
Fox, Joseph J. 1925- *St&PR 91*
Fox, Judith Hoos 1949- *WhoAmA 91, WhoEmL 91*
Fox, Judy Kay 1952- *WhoSSW 91*
Fox, Karen *BiDrAPA 89*
Fox, Karen 1949- *WhoAmW 91*
Fox, Karen Jean 1955- *WhoWrEP 89*
Fox, Karen Northridge 1956- *WhoEmL 91*
Fox, Karl August 1917- *WhoAm 90, WhoWor 91, WhoWrEP 89*
Fox, Kate 1836-1892 *EncO&P 3, EncPaPR 91*
Fox, Katherine 1839-1894 *BioAmW*
Fox, Kelly Diane 1959- *WhoAmW 91*
Fox, Kenneth 1929- *WhoAm 90*
Fox, Kenneth L. 1917- *WhoAm 90*
Fox, Kim Michael 1948- *WhoWor 91*
Fox, Kurt Lawrence 1946- *BiDrAPA 89*
Fox, Kymberly Covert 1960- *WhoAmW 91*
Fox, Lafe Palmer 1915- *St&PR 91*
Fox, Lamar M *BiDrAPA 89*
Fox, Larry *AuBYP 90*
Fox, Larry R. 1945- *WhoE 91*
Fox, Laurie Jo *BiDrAPA 89*
Fox, Lawrence, III 1947- *WhoAm 90*
Fox, Lawrence Martin 1946- *WhoWor 91*
Fox, Leah 1811?-1890 *EncPaPR 91*
Fox, Lee Barry 1952- *WhoEmL 91*
Fox, Leland Stanford 1931- *IntWWM 90*
Fox, Levi 1914- *ConAu 31NR*
Fox, Lincoln H 1942- *WhoAmA 91*
Fox, Lloyd Allan 1945- *WhoEmL 91, WhoSSW 91*
Fox, Louis 1917- *St&PR 91*
Fox, Luke 1586-1635 *EncCRAm*
Fox, M. Bradford 1961- *WhoEmL 91*
Fox, Malcolm 1946- *IntWWM 90*
Fox, Margaret *BiDEWW, BioIn 16*
Fox, Margaret 1833-1893 *EncO&P 3*
Fox, Margaret 1836-1893 *BioAmW*
Fox, Margaret Askew Fell 1614-1702 *BioIn 16*
Fox, Margaretta 1834?-1893 *EncPaPR 91*
Fox, Marian 1950- *WhoE 91*
Fox, Marietta Newton 1928- *EncO&P 3*
Fox, Martin 1935- *St&PR 91*
Fox, Mary Ann 1957- *WhoEmL 91*
Fox, Mary Ann Williams 1939- *WhoE 91*
Fox, Mary Ellen 1956- *WhoEmL 91*
Fox, Mary Virginia 1919- *AuBYP 90*
Fox, Marybeth *BiDrAPA 89*
Fox, Marye Anne 1947- *WhoAmW 91*
Fox, Matthew 1940- *NewAgE 90*
Fox, Matthew Ignatius 1934- *WhoAm 90*
Fox, Maurice Sanford 1924- *WhoAm 90*
Fox, Mem 1946- *AuBYP 90, BioIn 16, ChlLR 23 [port]*
Fox, Michael A. 1938- *St&PR 91*
Fox, Michael David 1937- *WhoAmA 91, WhoWor 91*
Fox, Michael Francis 1948- *WhoEmL 91*
Fox, Michael J. *BioIn 16*
Fox, Michael J. 1961- *WhoAm 90, WorAlBi*
Fox, Michael Joe 1945- *WhoEmL 91*
Fox, Michael Ross *BiDrAPA 89*
Fox, Michael Vass 1940- *WhoAm 90*
Fox, Michael Wilson 1937- *AuBYP 90, WhoAm 90, WhoWrEP 89*
Fox, Miles 1927- *WhoWor 91*
Fox, Milton D *BiDrAPA 89*
Fox, Milton S 1904-1971 *WhoAmA 91N*
Fox, Molly *BioIn 16*
Fox, Morris *BioIn 16*
Fox, Muriel 1928- *WhoAm 90, WhoAmW 91*
Fox, Neil Stewart 1945- *WhoAm 90*
Fox, Nellie 1927-1975 *Ballpl 90 [port], WorAlBi*
Fox, Olin Mackay *BiDrAPA 89*
Fox, Oliver 1885-1949 *EncO&P 3*
Fox, Patricia Anne 1951- *BiDrAPA 89*
Fox, Patricia Tucker 1951- *WhoSSW 91*
Fox, Patrick Bernard 1948- *WhoE 91*
Fox, Paul J., Jr. 1952- *St&PR 91*
Fox, Paul Raymond *BiDrAPA 89*
Fox, Paula *BioIn 16*
Fox, Paula 1923- *AuBYP 90, MajTwCW, SmATA 60 [port], WhoAm 90, WorAu 1980 [port]*
Fox, Pearl *WhoAmA 91*
Fox, Pete 1909-1966 *Ballpl 90*
Fox, Philip J. 1944- *St&PR 91*
Fox, Philip Stanley *BiDrAPA 89*
Fox, Phyllis Ann 1923- *WhoAmW 91*
Fox, R. Murdo *WhoWrEP 89*
Fox, Ralph W., II 1958- *WhoSSW 91*
Fox, Raymond Bernard 1926- *WhoAm 90*
Fox, Raymond C. 1930- *St&PR 91*
Fox, Raymond F. 1942- *St&PR 91*
Fox, Raymond Graham 1923- *WhoSSW 91*
Fox, Reeder Rodman 1934- *WhoAm 90*
Fox, Renee Claire 1928- *WhoAm 90, WhoAmW 91*
Fox, Richard Allen 1954- *St&PR 91*
Fox, Richard Gabriel 1939- *WhoSSW 91*
Fox, Richard Hilary 1928- *BiDrAPA 89*
Fox, Richard K. 1940- *St&PR 91*
Fox, Richard Paul *BiDrAPA 89*
Fox, Robert A. 1929- *St&PR 91*
Fox, Robert A. 1937- *St&PR 91*
Fox, Robert A, Jr. *BiDrAPA 89*
Fox, Robert Alan 1938- *WhoE 91*
Fox, Robert August 1937- *WhoAm 90*
Fox, Robert J. 1928- *St&PR 91*
Fox, Robert K. 1907- *St&PR 91*
Fox, Robert Kriegbaum 1907- *WhoAm 90*
Fox, Robert L. *St&PR 91N*
Fox, Robert R. 1943- *WhoWrEP 89*
Fox, Robert William 1934- *WhoAm 90*
Fox, Robin Lane *BioIn 16*
Fox, Rollo O., II 1951- *WhoSSW 91*
Fox, Ronald Barclay 1937- *WhoSSW 91*
Fox, Ronald Ernest 1936- *WhoAm 90*
Fox, Ronald Forrest 1943- *WhoAm 90*
Fox, Ronald Lee 1952- *WhoEmL 91, WhoWor 91*
Fox, Roy 1901-1982 *OxCPMus*
Fox, Roy W. 1920- *St&PR 91*
Fox, Ruth *BiDrAPA 89*
Fox, Ruth 1895-1989 *BioIn 16*
Fox, Ryburn Kenneth 1927- *St&PR 91*
Fox, Sam 1929- *WhoAm 90*
Fox, Samantha *BioIn 16*
Fox, Samuel 1905- *WhoAm 90*
Fox, Samuel Mickle, III 1923- *WhoAm 90*
Fox, Sara Jane 1955- *BiDrAPA 89*
Fox, Sheila 1947- *WhoAm 90*
Fox, Sherman Sol *BiDrAPA 89*
Fox, Sheryl Robin 1958- *WhoEmL 91*
Fox, Sidney Walter 1912- *WhoAm 90*
Fox, Simone Martha 1961- *WhoAmW 91*
Fox, Sonny 1925- *AuBYP 90*
Fox, Steven Phillip 1939- *St&PR 91*
Fox, Stuart Ira 1945- *WhoEmL 91*
Fox, Susan Christine 1943- *WhoWrEP 89*
Fox, Susan Rogan 1946- *WhoEmL 91*
Fox, Sylvan 1928- *WhoAm 90*
Fox, Terence J. 1938- *St&PR 91*
Fox, Terry *BioIn 16*
Fox, Terry 1935- *Ballpl 90*
Fox, Terry Alan 1943- *WhoAmA 91*
Fox, Thomas George 1942- *WhoAm 90*
Fox, Thomas L 1954- *BiDrAPA 89*
Fox, Thomas Michael *BiDrAPA 89*
Fox, Thomas South *BiDrAPA 89*
Fox, Thomas Walton 1923- *WhoAm 90*
Fox, Vernon Brittain 1916- *WhoAm 90, WhoSSW 91, WhoWrEP 89*
Fox, Virgil 1912-1980 *PenDiMP*
Fox, Virginia Gaines 1939- *WhoAmW 91*
Fox, W. Richard 1924- *St&PR 91*
Fox, W Walter 1924- *BiDrAPA 89*
Fox, Walter Henry 1914- *St&PR 91*
Fox, Wayne 1920- *St&PR 91*
Fox, Wendella Penister 1951- *WhoAmW 91*
Fox, William *ConTFT 8*
Fox, William Freeman 1840-1909 *BioIn 16*
Fox, William Joseph 1940- *St&PR 91*
Fox, William Lloyd 1921- *WhoE 91*
Fox, William T. R. 1912-1988 *BioIn 16*
Fox, William Templeton 1932- *WhoAm 90*
Fox, William Waring 1968- *WhoEmL 91*
Fox, William Wellington 1909- *AuBYP 90*
Fox-Biswell, Eileen Marie 1954- *WhoAmW 91*
Fox-Fenelon, Laura Michele 1962- *WhoAmW 91*
Fox-Freund, Barbara Susan 1949- *WhoAmW 91*
Fox-Penner, Peter Seth 1955- *WhoE 91*
Fox-Rosellini, Susan Eva 1956- *WhoAmW 91*
Foxcroft, Kenneth B. 1944- *St&PR 91*
Foxe, John 1516?-1587 *LitC 14 [port]*
Foxen, Bill 1884-1937 *Ballpl 90*
Foxen, Gene Louis 1936- *WhoAm 90, WhoWor 91*
Foxen, Lynne Anne 1950- *WhoAmW 91*
Foxen, Richard William 1927- *St&PR 91, WhoAm 90, WhoWor 91*
Foxhall, Kathryn 1950- *WhoWrEP 89*
Foxhoven, Michael John 1949- *WhoEmL 91*
Foxley, Alejandro 1939- *WhoAm 90*
Foxley, William Coleman 1935- *WhoAm 90*
Foxman, Bruce Mayer 1942- *WhoAm 90*
Foxman, Elliott *BiDrAPA 89*
Foxman, Eric 1951- *BiDrAPA 89*
Foxman, Stephen Mark 1946- *WhoE 91, WhoEmL 91*
Foxwell, Julia Elena 1944- *WhoE 91*
Foxworth, Charles Leonard 1932- *WhoSSW 91*
Foxworth, Jo *WhoAm 90*
Foxworth, John Edwin, Jr. 1932- *WhoAm 90*
Foxworth, John Michael *BiDrAPA 89*
Foxworth, Robert 1941- *WorAlBi*
Foxworth, Robert Heath 1941- *WhoAm 90*
Foxx, Inez 1942- *DrBlPA 90*
Foxx, Jack *ConAu 32NR, TwCCr&M 91*
Foxx, Jimmie 1907-1967 *Ballpl 90 [port], BioIn 16, WorAlBi*
Foxx, Redd *BioIn 16*
Foxx, Redd 1922- *DrBlPA 90, WorAlBi*
Foy, Allan B. 1929- *St&PR 91*
Foy, Catherine Anthony 1957- *WhoWrEP 89*
Foy, Deborah Sanford 1954- *WhoAmW 91*
Foy, Denise Colleen 1960- *St&PR 91, WhoEmL 91*
Foy, Eddie 1854-1928 *OxCPMus*
Foy, Eddie 1857-1928 *WorAlBi*
Foy, Eddie, Jr. 1905- *OxCPMus*
Foy, Edward A. 1917- *St&PR 91*
Foy, Herbert Miles, III 1945- *WhoEmL 91, WhoSSW 91*
Foy, Hjordis Elsa Mannbeck 1926- *WhoAmW 91*
Foy, James Edward 1944- *St&PR 91*
Foy, James L 1926- *BiDrAPA 89*
Foy, Joe 1943-1989 *Ballpl 90, BioIn 16*
Foy, Joe Hardeman 1926- *WhoAm 90*
Foy, John B. 1942- *St&PR 91*
Foy, Joseph Gerald 1910- *WhoAm 90*
Foy, Madeline *BioIn 16*
Foy, Marguerite Elisabeth 1952- *WhoAmW 91*
Foy, Peter *BioIn 16*
Foy, Richard Daniel 1929- *St&PR 91, WhoAm 90*
Foye, Jennifer Wilder 1959- *WhoAmW 91*
Foye, Laurance Vincent, Jr. 1925- *WhoAm 90*
Foye, Louis George 1930- *St&PR 91*
Foye, Patrick Joseph 1957- *WhoE 91*
Foye, Thomas Harold 1930- *WhoAm 90*
Foyes, Betty J. 1926- *WhoE 91*
Foyt, A. J. 1935- *WorAlBi*
Foyt, Anthony Joseph, Jr. 1935- *WhoAm 90*
Foyt, Arthur George 1937- *WhoAm 90*
Foytack, Paul 1930- *Ballpl 90*
Fozzati, Aldo 1950- *WhoEmL 91, WhoWor 91*
Fra, Dahli-Sterne 1901- *WhoAmA 91*
Fraasch, Douglas Roger 1946- *WhoEmL 91*
Frabel, Hans Godo 1941- *WhoAmA 91*
Fraber, John W., III 1947- *St&PR 91*
Frabutt, Peter J. 1932- *St&PR 91*
Fracalossi, Shelley Ann 1954- *WhoAmW 91*
Fracarossi, Joseph 1886-1970 *MusmAFA*
Fracassi, Michael A. 1957- *WhoEmL 91*
Fracci, Carla 1936- *WhoWor 91, WorAlBi*
Frace, Charles Lewis 1926- *WhoAmA 91*
Frachon, Benoit 1893-1975 *BiDFrPL*
Frackenpohl, Arthur 1924- *IntWWM 90*
Fracker, Robert Granger 1928- *WhoSSW 91, WhoWor 91*
Frackman, Noel 1930- *WhoAmA 91, WhoAmW 91, WhoE 91*
Frackman, Richard Benoit 1923- *WhoAm 90*

Frackmann, Margit Helga 1944- WhoWor 91
Frade, Peter Daniel 1946- WhoAm 90
Frader, Marc Andrew 1945- BiDrAPA 89
Fradkin, David Milton 1931- WhoAm 90
Fradkin, Hillel Gideon 1947- WhoAm 90
Fradkin, Howard Ross 1952- WhoEmL 91
Fradkin, Mindy Sue 1955- WhoAmW 91
Fradley, Frederick Macdonell 1924- WhoAm 90
Fradonnet, Catherine de EncCoWW
Frady, Marshall Bolton 1940- WhoWrEP 89
Fraedrich, Royal Louis 1931- WhoAm 90
Fraenkel, Dan Gabriel 1937- WhoAm 90
Fraenkel, Fred Steven 1949- WhoAm 90
Fraenkel, George Kessler 1921- WhoAm 90
Fraenkel, Gideon August 1932- WhoAm 90
Fraenkel, Jeffrey BioIn 16
Fraenkel, Jeffrey Andrew 1955- WhoAmA 91
Fraenkel, Michael 1896-1957 BioIn 16
Fraenkel, Stephen Joseph 1917- WhoAm 90
Fraga, Howard E. 1929- St&PR 91, WhoAm 90
Fraga, Juan R. 1924- WhoHisp 91
Fraga, Manuel 1922- BioIn 16
Fraga, Rosa WhoHisp 91
Fraga, Tina Antoinette 1965- WhoAmW 91
Fragala, M Richard 1943- BiDrAPA 89
Fragapane, Stephen A. 1949- St&PR 91
Frager, Albert S. 1922- St&PR 91, WhoAm 90
Frager, Malcolm 1935- IntWWM 90, PenDiMP
Frager, Marc Stephen 1949- WhoSSW 91
Frager, Norman 1936- WhoAm 90
Fragiacomo, Giorgio 1938- WhoWor 91
Fragola, Anthony Nicholas 1943- WhoWrEP 89
Fragomen, Austin Thomas 1919- WhoAm 90
Fragonard, Jean-Honore 1732-1806 BioIn 16, IntDcAA 90, WorAlBi
Fragson, Harry 1869-1913 OxCPMus
Fraguela, Rafael Jose 1955- WhoHisp 91
Frahm, August Wilhelm 1935- WhoWor 91
Frahm, Grechen Kai 1959- WhoAmW 91
Frahm, Sheila 1945- WhoAmW 91
Frahm, Sue Adele 1941- WhoAmW 91
Frahm, Toni Robinson 1947- WhoAmW 91
Fraiberg, Lawrence Phillip 1921- WhoAm 90, WhoE 91, WhoWor 91
Fraiche, Donna DiMartino 1951- WhoEmL 91
Fraidin, Stephen 1939- WhoAm 90, WhoWor 91
Fraier, Ronald Allen 1936- BiDrAPA 89
Fraile, Pedro 1946- WhoWor 91
Frailey, David C. 1921- ODwPR 91
Frailey, Stephen BioIn 16
Frailey, Stephen A 1957- WhoAmA 91
Frailing, Ken 1948- Ballpl 90
Fraim, William L. 1951- St&PR 91
Fraiman, Genevieve Lam 1928- WhoAm 90
Frain, Andrew Dennis 1936- WhoAm 90
Frain, James Lee 1953- WhoEmL 91
Frain, Joseph Carl 1943- WhoE 91
Fraina-Lewis Corey, Louis C. 1892?-1953 EncAL
Fraioli, Pamela Frances 1965- WhoEmL 91
Frair, Wayne Franklin 1926- WhoE 91
Fraiser, Gerald P. 1943- St&PR 91
Fraisse, Michel Marc 1950- WhoWor 91
Frajlich, Anna 1942- EncCoWW
Frake, Barbara Holliss 1945- WhoAmW 91
Frake, Charles Oliver 1930- WhoAm 90
Fraker, William A. 1923- WhoAm 90
Frakes, John Lewis 1934- WhoAm 90
Frakes, Lawrence Wright 1951- WhoAm 90, WhoSSW 91, WhoWor 91
Frakes, Rod Vance 1930- WhoAm 90
Frakes, Thomas Lee St&PR 91N
Fraknoi, Andrew 1948- WhoAm 90, WhoEmL 91
Fraleigh, John E. 1938- St&PR 91
Fraley, David K 1952- WhoAmA 91
Fraley, Elwin Eugene 1934- WhoAm 90
Fraley, Frederick William, III 1932- St&PR 91
Fraley, Henry M., Jr. 1927- St&PR 91
Fraley, John L. 1920- WhoAm 90, WhoSSW 91
Fraley, Jonathan David, Jr. 1941- WhoSSW 91
Fraley, Mark Thomas 1952- WhoEmL 91
Fralick, Richard Allston 1937- WhoE 91
Fram, David Hirsch 1937- BiDrAPA 89
Fram, Frederick Gordon 1962- WhoSSW 91
Framberg, Norman Stokes 1934- St&PR 91
Frame, Alistair 1929- WhoWor 91
Frame, Anne Parsons 1904- WhoAmW 91, WhoWor 91
Frame, Clarence George 1918- St&PR 91, WhoAm 90
Frame, Dorothy Elizabeth WhoAmW 91
Frame, E. Bartram, Jr. 1944- St&PR 91
Frame, Elizabeth 1820-1913 FemiCLE
Frame, Frank Riddell 1930- WhoWor 91
Frame, Helen Dunn 1939- WhoWrEP 89
Frame, J. Leonard 1924- WhoAm 90
Frame, Janet MajTwCW
Frame, Janet 1924- FemiCLE
Frame, John 1950- WhoAmA 91
Frame, John Timothy 1930- WhoAm 90
Frame, Paul 1914- SmATA 60 [port]
Frame, Paul Sutherland WhoAm 90
Frame, Peter WhoAm 90
Frame, Robert 1924- WhoAmA 91
Frame, Russell William 1929- WhoAm 90
Frame, William Douglas 1942- St&PR 91
Frame, William V. 1938- St&PR 91
Framel, John Edward 1935- WhoSSW 91
Framer, Walter H. 1908-1988 BioIn 16
Framme, Lawrence Henry, III 1949- WhoSSW 91
Frampton, George James 1860-1928 PenDiDA 89
Frampton, George Thomas 1917- St&PR 91, WhoAm 90
Frampton, George Thomas, Jr. 1944- WhoAm 90
Frampton, Hollis 1936-1984 WhoAmA 91N
Frampton, Larry G. 1939- St&PR 91
Frampton, Merle Elbert 1903- WhoAm 90
Frampton, Michael Frank BiDrAPA 89
Frampton, Paul Howard 1943- WhoAm 90
Frampton, Peter EncPR&S 89
Frampton, Peter 1950- OxCPMus, WhoAm 90, WorAlBi
Frampton, Walter Cobia 1948- WhoSSW 91
Framson, Joel 1947- WhoEmL 91
Franc, Maud Jeanne 1827-1886 FemiCLE
Franca, Celia 1921- WhoAm 90, WhoAmW 91, WorAlBi
Franca, Jose-Augusto 1922- WhoWor 91
Francaix, Jean 1912- IntWWM 90, PenDiMP A
France, Anatole MajTwCW
France, Anatole 1844-1924 WorAlBi
France, Bruce Eric, Sr. 1954- WhoEmL 91
France, Charles William Fearnley 1898- PenDiDA 89
France, Cheryl Ann BiDrAPA 89
France, Cheryl Lee BiDrAPA 89
France, Edward PenDiDA 89
France, Helen Way 1953- WhoAmW 91
France, Jacqueline Linda 1952- WhoEmL 91
France, James T. 1956- St&PR 91
France, John Lyons 1933- WhoAm 90
France, Johnny BioIn 16
France, Joseph David 1953- WhoE 91, WhoWor 91
France, Kenneth 1949- WhoE 91
France, Newell Edwin 1927- WhoAm 90, WhoSSW 91
France, Randal Dennis 1947- BiDrAPA 89
France, Richard E. 1926- St&PR 91
France, Richard William 1947- WhoEmL 91, WhoSSW 91
France, Richard Xavier 1938- WhoAm 90
France, Robert K. 1926- St&PR 91
France, Robert Rinehart 1921- WhoAm 90
France, Ruth 1913-1968 FemiCLE
France, W. DeWayne BioIn 16
France, William PenDiDA 89
France, William C. 1933- St&PR 91
Francella, John C., Jr. 1935- St&PR 91
Frances, Allen J 1942- BiDrAPA 89
Frances, Harriette Anton WhoAmA 91
Frances, Mary BioIn 16
Frances, Richard Joseph 1946- BiDrAPA 89, WhoE 91
Frances, Robert 1919- WhoWor 91
Frances, Sophia FemiCLE
Francesa, Doris Tina 1927- St&PR 91
Francescatti, Rene 1902- IntWWM 90
Francescatti, Zino 1902- PenDiMP
Francescatti, Zino Rene 1902- WhoAm 90
Franceschelli, Christopher 1955- St&PR 91
Franceschi, Ernest Joseph, Jr. 1957- WhoEmL 91, WhoWor 91
Franceschina, John Charles 1947- WhoSSW 91
Franceschini, Jose Antonio 1949- BiDrAPA 89
Francesco Di Giorgio 1439?-1501? IntDcAA 90
Francesco, di Giorgio Martini 1439-1501? BioIn 16
Francesco di Pieragnolo PenDiDA 89
Francesco Durantino PenDiDA 89
Francesco, Steven A. 1949- St&PR 91
Francesina, La PenDiMP
Francfort, Alfred John, Jr. 1939- WhoWor 91
Franch, Katherine A. 1959- BiDrAPA 89
Franch, Kenneth David 1950- WhoSSW 91
Franch, Richard Thomas 1942- WhoAm 90
Franchet d'Esperey, Louis Felix Marie F. 1856-1942 BiDFrPL
Franchetti, Arnold 1909- IntWWM 90
Franchi, Rafael L. 1927- WhoHisp 91
Franchi, Raoul Maurizio 1949- WhoWor 91
Franchi, Sergio BioIn 16, NewYTBS 90 [port]
Franchik, Carol Ann 1939- WhoAmW 91
Franchini, Girolamo PenDiDA 89
Franchini, R Gregory 1948- BiDrAPA 89
Franchini, Roxanne 1951- WhoAmW 91, WhoEmL 91
Franchomme, Auguste 1808-1884 PenDiMP
Francia, Jose Gaspar Rodriguez de 1766-1840 BioIn 16
Francione, Francesco di Giovanni PenDiDA 89
Franciosa, Anthony 1928- WhoAm 90, WorAlBi
Franciosa, Joseph Anthony 1936- WhoWor 91
Francis, de Sales 1567-1622 BioIn 16
Francis Ferdinand, Archduke 1863-1914 WorAlBi
Francis, of Assisi 1182-1226 BioIn 16
Francis of Assisi, Saint 1182-1226 EncPaPR 91, WorAlBi
Francis the Prophet WhNaAH
Francis Xavier, Saint 1506-1552 BioIn 16
Francis, Al BioIn 16
Francis, Albert John, II 1954- WhoEmL 91
Francis, Alexandria Stephanie 1952- WhoAmW 91
Francis, Andrew J, Jr. 1951- BiDrAPA 89
Francis, Anne 1738-1800 FemiCLE
Francis, Arlene 1908- WorAlBi
Francis, Betty Joe 1930- WhoWrEP 89
Francis, Bill Dean 1929- WhoAm 90, WhoAmA 91
Francis, Billy BioIn 16
Francis, Carol Jeanne 1958- WhoE 91
Francis, Carolyn Rae 1940- WhoAmW 91
Francis, Charles AuBYP 90, ConAu 132
Francis, Charles C. ODwPR 91
Francis, Charles Wesley, Jr. 1951- WhoSSW 91
Francis, Cheryl A. 1954- St&PR 91
Francis, Claude WhoAmW 91
Francis, Cleveland BioIn 16
Francis, Clyde Milton, Jr. 1925- WhoSSW 91
Francis, Connie 1938- EncPR&S 89, OxCPMus, WorAlBi
Francis, Dale Lyman 1917- WhoAm 90
Francis, Darryl Robert 1912- WhoAm 90
Francis, David Edward 1953- IntWWM 90
Francis, David Rowland 1850-1927 BiDrUSE 89, BioIn 16
Francis, Dee AuBYP 90
Francis, Dick 1920- Au&Arts 5 [port], MajTwCW, TwCCr&M 91, WhoAm 90, WorAlBi
Francis, Earl 1936- Ballpl 90
Francis, Edward WhoWrEP 89
Francis, Edward D. 1934- WhoAm 90
Francis, Elie Michael 1960- BiDrAPA 89
Francis, Emile Percy 1926- WhoAm 90, WhoE 91
Francis, Euclid Clyde 1925- WhoSSW 91
Francis, Eulalie Marie WhoAmW 91
Francis, Frank Chalton 1901-1988 BioIn 16
Francis, Frank J. 1948- St&PR 91
Francis, Freddie 1917- ConTFT 8, WhoAm 90, WhoWor 91
Francis, Harold Huyton 1928- WhoAm 90
Francis, Harry McDonald, Jr. 1933- St&PR 91, WhoAm 90
Francis, Henry S., Jr. 1925- AuBYP 90
Francis, Irving Alfred 1927- St&PR 91
Francis, James BioIn 16
Francis, James Delbert 1947- St&PR 91, WhoAm 90
Francis, Jean Thickens 1943- WhoAmA 91
Francis, Jeanne Lynne 1965- WhoEmL 91
Francis, John Darrell 1904- St&PR 91
Francis, John J 1916- BiDrAPA 89
Francis, Joseph A. 1923- WhoAm 90
Francis, Josiah WhNaAH
Francis, Kay 1903-1968 WorAlBi
Francis, Lee, Mrs. 1926- WhoAmW 91, WhoE 91
Francis, Livingston Le Stanley 1929- WhoE 91
Francis, Lloyd Cyril 1920- WhoAm 90
Francis, M. BiDWomA
Francis, M. E. 1858?-1930 FemiCLE
Francis, Madison Ke, Jr 1945- WhoAmA 91
Francis, Marion David 1923- WhoAm 90
Francis, Matthew 1956- ConAu 132
Francis, Merrill Richard 1932- WhoAm 90
Francis, Michael Lawrence, Jr. 1964- WhoE 91
Francis, Milly Hayo 1802-1848 WhNaAH
Francis, Norman C. 1931- WhoAm 90
Francis, Panama 1918- DrBIPA 90
Francis, Patricia B BiDrAPA 89
Francis, Patricia Lynn 1952- WhoE 91
Francis, Paul ConAu 131
Francis, Paul Raymond 1959- St&PR 91
Francis, Peggy Ann 1952- WhoAmW 91
Francis, Peter WhoAmA 91
Francis, Philip Hamilton 1938- WhoAm 90
Francis, Philip S., Jr. 1941- St&PR 91
Francis, Ray 1893-1934 Ballpl 90
Francis, Richard Haudiomont 1925- WhoAm 90
Francis, Richard L BiDrAPA 89
Francis, Robert J 1931- BiDrAPA 89
Francis, Roberta Williams 1943- WhoAmW 91
Francis, Sam 1923- BioIn 16, WhoAm 90, WhoAmA 91, WorAlBi
Francis, Samuel Todd 1947- WhoAm 90
Francis, Sarah Janet IntWWM 90
Francis, Spencer Lee 1943- St&PR 91
Francis, Sue Bryant 1940- WhoSSW 91
Francis, Susan C. 1873-1962 BioIn 16
Francis, Susan Gail 1957- WhoAmW 91
Francis, Sybil Eldridge 1947- WhoAmW 91
Francis, Timothy Duane 1956- WhoEmL 91, WhoWor 91
Francis, Tom 1951- WhoAmA 91
Francis, Virgil Walter, III 1938- St&PR 91
Francis-Vogelsang, Charee 1946- St&PR 91
Francisco NewAgMG
Francisco WhNaAH
Francisco Xavier 1506-1552 BioIn 16
Francisco, Charles Campbell 1937- St&PR 91
Francisco, Edgar Wiggin, III 1930- WhoSSW 91
Francisco, Lawrence R. 1931- St&PR 91
Francisco, Marcia Madora 1958- WhoAmW 91
Franciscovich, George 1954- WhoEmL 91
Franck, Bengt Erik Tomas 1958- IntWWM 90
Franck, Carol Eichert 1937- WhoAmW 91
Franck, Cesar 1822-1890 PenDiMP A, WorAlBi
Franck, David ODwPR 91
Franck, Donald G. 1935- St&PR 91
Franck, Frederick S 1909- WhoAmA 91
Franck, Frederick Sigfred 1909- WhoAm 90, WhoE 91
Franck, James 1882-1964 WorAlBi
Franck, Joanne Gross 1951- WhoEmL 91
Franck, John M. 1953- WhoSSW 91
Franck, Kaj 1911- ConDes 90, PenDiDA 89
Franck, Leonard J., Jr. 1932- St&PR 91
Franck, Martine 1938- BioIn 16
Franck, Michael 1932- WhoAm 90
Franck, Peter Goswyn 1913-1989 BioIn 16
Franck, Sebastian 1499?-1543? EncO&P 3
Franck, Thomas Martin 1931- WhoAm 90, WhoE 91
Franck, William Francis 1917- St&PR 91, WhoAm 90, WhoSSW 91
Francke, Master 1380?-1430? IntDcAA 90
Francke, Albert, III 1934- WhoAm 90
Francke, August Hermann 1663-1727 BioIn 16, WorAlBi
Francke, Bertold R 1940- BiDrAPA 89
Francke, Charles Frederick BiDrAPA 89
Francke, Christian 1549-1595? EncO&P 3
Francke, Donald Max 1929- IntWWM 90
Francke, Gloria Niemeyer 1922- WhoAmW 91
Francke, Linda Bird 1939- WhoAm 90
Francke, Lloyd Mortimer Hastings 1927-1988 BioIn 16
Franckle, Charles T. 1945- St&PR 91
Franco BioIn 16
Franco 1938-1989 AnObit 1989
Franco, Angel 1951- WhoHisp 91
Franco, Annemarie Woletz 1933- WhoAmW 91
Franco, Anthony M. 1933- BioIn 16, ODwPR 91, WhoAm 90
Franco, Armando 1935- St&PR 91
Franco, Barbara 1945- WhoAmA 91
Franco, Barbara Ann 1960- St&PR 91
Franco, Battista 1510?-1561 PenDiDA 89
Franco, Bettie Westervelt 1932- WhoAmW 91
Franco, Carole Ann 1948- WhoE 91, WhoWor 91
Franco, Dolores 1916- EncCoWW
Franco, Douglas Eugene 1948- WhoEmL 91
Franco, Eloise 1910- SmATA 62 [port]

Franco, Francisco 1892-1975 BioIn 16, WorAlBi
Franco, Giuseppe BioIn 16
Franco, Gloria Lopez WhoHisp 91
Franco, Harry 1932- St&PR 91
Franco, Howard 1952- St&PR 91
Franco, Itamar 1931- WhoWor 91
Franco, Johan 1908-1988 SmATA 62 [port]
Franco, John 1960- Ballpl 90, BioIn 16
Franco, John Albert 1942- St&PR 91, WhoAm 90
Franco, John J. 1944- St&PR 91
Franco, Jose, Jr. 1966- WhoHisp 91
Franco, Juan Roberto 1937- WhoSSW 91
Franco, Julio 1961- Ballpl 90, WhoHisp 91
Franco, Julio Cesar 1961- WhoAm 90
Franco, Kathleen Susan 1948- BiDrAPA 89
Franco, Kenneth Lawrence 1951- WhoE 91
Franco, Luis A 1962- BiDrAPA 89
Franco, Morris 1939- St&PR 91
Franco, Napoleon 1930- BiDrAPA 89
Franco, Pilar BioIn 16
Franco, Rafael 1897-1973 BioIn 16
Franco, Raymond M. 1937- St&PR 91
Franco, Robert 1941- WhoE 91
Franco, Robert J., II 1957- WhoEmL 91
Franco, Robert John 1932- WhoAmA 91N
Franco, Ruben 1947- WhoHisp 91
Franco, Veronica 1546-1591 EncCoWW
Franco, Victor 1937- WhoAm 90, WhoE 91
Franco, Yaacov 1946- WhoWor 91
Francoeur, Jacques G. 1925- St&PR 91
Francoeur, Leopold 1927- WhoAm 90
Francoeur, Robert T 1931- ConAu 31NR
Francois, Andre 1915- ConDes 90
Francois, Francis Bernard 1934- WhoAm 90, WhoE 91, WhoWor 91
Francois, Gregory 1946- St&PR 91
Francois, Guido Emile 1936- WhoWor 91
Francois, Joseph Francis 1961- WhoE 91
Francois, Michael Brian 1950- WhoEmL 91
Francois, Samson 1924-1970 PenDiMP
Francois, Simon 1924-1970 PenDiMP A
Francois, Terry A. 1921-1989 BioIn 16
Francois, William Armand 1942- St&PR 91, WhoAm 90
Francois-Marsal, Frederic 1874-1958 BiDFrPL
Francois-Poncet, Jean 1928- BiDFrPL
Francois-Poncet, Jean Andre 1928- WhoWor 91
Francoise 1863-1910 DcLB 92 [port]
Francoise, Marie Louise von 1817-1893 EncCoWW
Francoise, Sara Punirllo 1947- WhoAmA 91
Francolini, Geno F. 1931- St&PR 91
Francomano, George 1933- St&PR 91
Francomb, Lonnie Coleman 1953- WhoEmL 91
Francona, Terry 1959- Ballpl 90
Francona, Tito 1933- Ballpl 90
Francos, Alexis 1949- WhoEmL 91
Francy, Paul 1927- IntWWM 90
Frandsen, G. Kent 1927-1988 BioIn 16
Frandsen, John 1956- IntWWM 90
Franek, Bruno BiDrAPA 89
Franey, John Thomas 1949- St&PR 91
Frangella, Luis 1944- WhoAmA 91
Frangella, Luis 1944-1990 NewYTBS 90
Frangipane, Joseph R. 1936- St&PR 91
Frangopoulos, Victor Spiros 1935- St&PR 91
Frangos, James George 1934- WhoAm 90
Frangos, Nicholas Efstratios 1956- WhoE 91
Frangsmyr, Tore 1938- ConAu 129
Franjou, Marie-Helene 1946- WhoWor 91
Franju, Georges 1912-1987 BioIn 16
Frank, Agnes Theresa WhoAmW 91, WhoE 91
Frank, Alan 1922- BiDrAPA 89
Frank, Alan Clifford 1910- IntWWM 90
Frank, Alan I W 1932- WhoWor 91
Frank, Albert Eugene 1918- WhoAm 90
Frank, Alfred Louis 1922- WhoAm 90
Frank, Allan Dodds 1947- WhoAm 90, WhoE 91
Frank, Allison 1963- ODwPR 91
Frank, Andre Gunder 1929- WhoWor 91
Frank, Anne 1929-1945 BioIn 16, MajTwCW, WorAlBi
Frank, Anneliese 1929-1945 EncCoWW
Frank, Anthony M. BioIn 16
Frank, Anthony Melchior 1931- WhoAm 90
Frank, Arnold Jay 1934- BiDrAPA 89
Frank, Barbara Ann 1939- WhoAmW 91
Frank, Barney BioIn 16
Frank, Barney 1940- WhoAm 90, WhoE 91
Frank, Barry H. 1938- WhoWor 91
Frank, Bernard 1913- WhoAm 90, WhoWor 91
Frank, Bernard A. 1931- St&PR 91
Frank, Carla 1960- WhoAmW 91, WhoE 91
Frank, Caroline Kachura 1943- WhoAmW 91, WhoE 91, WhoWor 91
Frank, Cathrine 1951- BiDrAPA 89
Frank, Charles BioIn 16
Frank, Charles Raphael, Jr. 1937- WhoAm 90
Frank, Charles William, Jr 1922- WhoAmA 91
Frank, Claude 1925- IntWWM 90
Frank, Clinton Edward 1915- WhoAm 90
Frank, Courtenay WhoWrEP 89
Frank, Curtiss E. NewYTBS 90
Frank, Curtiss E. 1904-1990 BioIn 16
Frank, Daniel B. 1956- BioIn 16
Frank, Darlene 1946- WhoWrEP 89
Frank, David 1940- WhoAmA 91
Frank, David A. 1947- St&PR 91
Frank, David Abraham 1947- WhoAm 90
Frank, David Laurence 1956- BiDrAPA 89
Frank, Deane C. 1929- St&PR 91
Frank, Dieter 1930- WhoAm 90
Frank, Edgar Gerald 1931- WhoAm 90
Frank, Elizabeth 1945- WhoAm 90, WhoAmW 91, WhoE 91
Frank, Eric 1920- St&PR 91
Frank, Eugene 1934- BiDrAPA 89
Frank, Eugene Maxwell 1907- WhoAm 90
Frank, F. Alexander 1916- WhoAm 90
Frank, Floyd William 1922- WhoAm 90
Frank, Frederick 1932- St&PR 91
Frank, Frederick W BiDrAPA 89
Frank, Gary 1955- ODwPR 91
Frank, Geoffrey Edward 1955- WhoEmL 91
Frank, George C., Jr. 1936- St&PR 91
Frank, George Willard 1923- WhoAm 90
Frank, Gerald W. 1923- St&PR 91
Frank, Gerold 1907- WhoAm 90, WhoWrEP 89
Frank, Grace BiDrAPA 89
Frank, H. Alan 1930- St&PR 91
Frank, Halbert 1922- St&PR 91
Frank, Hans 1900-1946 BioIn 16
Frank, Harold Roy 1924- St&PR 91
Frank, Harvey 1944- St&PR 91, WhoSSW 91
Frank, Helen 1930- WhoAmA 91
Frank, Henry Jay WhoE 91
Frank, Herbert Lawrence 1932- WhoE 91
Frank, Hilda Rhea Kaplan 1939- WhoAmW 91
Frank, Howard 1941- WhoAm 90
Frank, Ilya 1908- WorAlBi
Frank, Ilya M. 1908-1990 NewYTBS 90
Frank, Ira Michel 1940- BiDrAPA 89
Frank, Irving BiDrAPA 89
Frank, Irwin Norman 1927- WhoAm 90, WhoE 91
Frank, Isaiah 1917- WhoAm 90
Frank, J. Louis 1936- WhoAm 90
Frank, Jacob 1936- St&PR 91
Frank, Jacquelyn A. 1941- WhoAmW 91
Frank, James Henry 1940- St&PR 91
Frank, Jay 1950 WhoSSW 91
Frank, Jerome B. 1934- WhoAm 90
Frank, Jerome D 1909- BiDrAPA 89
Frank, Jerome David 1909- WhoAm 90
Frank, Joanna BioIn 16
Frank, Joel I. 1956- St&PR 91
Frank, Joel J BiDrAPA 89
Frank, Joel Lawrence 1961- WhoEmL 91
Frank, Joele 1949- ODwPR 91
Frank, John BioIn 16
Frank, John Frederick 1925- St&PR 91
Frank, John Lewis 1939- BiDrAPA 89
Frank, John Nicholas 1953- WhoEmL 91
Frank, John Paul 1917- WhoAm 90, WhoWrEP 89
Frank, John R. 1955- St&PR 91
Frank, Joseph 1916- WhoAm 90
Frank, Joseph 1918- ConAu 32NR
Frank, Joseph Nathaniel 1918- WhoAm 90, WhoWrEP 89
Frank, Josette 1893- AuBYP 90
Frank, Josette 1893-1989 BioIn 16, ConAu 129, SmATA 63
Frank, Julia Bess 1951- BiDrAPA 89
Frank, Julie Ann 1953- WhoEmL 91
Frank, Karen Lee 1958- WhoE 91
Frank, Karl-Hermann 1898-1946 BioIn 16
Frank, Katherine Marie 1952- WhoEmL 91
Frank, Kenneth L. 1917- St&PR 91
Frank, Laura Jean 1945- WhoE 91
Frank, Laurie 1954- WhoEmL 91
Frank, Leonard C 1912- BiDrAPA 89
Frank, Leonhard 1882-1961 BioIn 16
Frank, Lloyd 1925- St&PR 91, WhoAm 90
Frank, Ludwig M BiDrAPA 89
Frank, Margit Van Leight- BioIn 16
Frank, Martha Steps 1939- WhoAmW 91
Frank, Martin 1947- WhoAm 90
Frank, Martin Harold 1941- St&PR 91
Frank, Marvin 1923- St&PR 91
Frank, Mary 1933- BiDWomA, WhoAm 90
Frank, Mary K. 1911-1988 BioIn 16
Frank, Mary Lou 1915- WhoAmW 91
Frank, Maurice PenDiMP
Frank, Melvin 1913-1988 AnObit 1988, BioIn 16
Frank, Melvin Porter 1841- AmLegL
Frank, Melvin S. 1925- St&PR 91
Frank, Michael M. 1937- WhoAm 90
Frank, Michael S. St&PR 91
Frank, Michael Sanford 1949- WhoEmL 91
Frank, Michael Victor 1947- WhoEmL 91
Frank, Michael William 1947- WhoE 91
Frank, Milton 1919- WhoAm 90, WhoWor 91
Frank, Mort 1912-1989 BioIn 16
Frank, Morton St&PR 91N
Frank, Morton 1912- WhoAm 90
Frank, Nancy Gillen 1943- WhoAmW 91
Frank, Natalie Susan 1963- WhoAmW 91
Frank, Neal S. ODwPR 91
Frank, Neil 1933- ODwPR 91
Frank, Pat 1907-1964 RGTwCSF
Frank, Paul Michael 1941- St&PR 91
Frank, Paula Feldman WhoAmW 91
Frank, Peter 1950- WhoWrEP 89
Frank, Peter Robert 1923- WhoWor 91
Frank, Peter Solomon 1950- WhoAm 90, WhoAmA 91
Frank, Philip J. 1930- St&PR 91
Frank, Philip Randall 1953- BiDrAPA 89
Frank, Randolph A 1925- BiDrAPA 89
Frank, Reuven 1920- WhoWrEP 89
Frank, Richard 1953- ConTFT 8 [port]
Frank, Richard Alan 1948- BiDrAPA 89
Frank, Richard Calhoun 1930- WhoAm 90
Frank, Richard Harvey 1942- WhoAm 90
Frank, Richard L BiDrAPA 89
Frank, Richard Lynn 1945- St&PR 91
Frank, Richard N. 1923- St&PR 91
Frank, Richard Sanford 1931- WhoAm 90
Frank, Robert 1924- BioIn 16
Frank, Robert Allen 1932- WhoE 91, WhoWor 91
Frank, Robert Allen 1950- WhoEmL 91
Frank, Robert E. 1949- St&PR 91
Frank, Robert G. 1918- St&PR 91
Frank, Robert George 1952- WhoEmL 91
Frank, Robert Joseph 1939- WhoWrEP 89
Frank, Robert Louis 1958- WhoEmL 91
Frank, Robert Worth, Jr. 1914- WhoAm 90
Frank, Roberta Vachss 1924- WhoE 91
Frank, Ronald Edward 1933- WhoAm 90
Frank, Ronald W. 1947- WhoEmL 91, WhoWor 91
Frank, Rosalind Claire BiDrAPA 89
Frank, Ross Delano 1939- BiDrAPA 89
Frank, Ruby Merinda 1920- WhoAmW 91
Frank, Rudolph J. BioIn 16
Frank, Sam Hager 1932- WhoAm 90
Frank, Sanders Thalheimer 1938- WhoAm 90, WhoWor 91
Frank, Sandra Kaye 1941- WhoAmW 91
Frank, Sarah Myers 1937- WhoAmW 91
Frank, Sebastian 1499?-1543? EncO&P 3
Frank, Sheldon M 1939- BiDrAPA 89
Frank, Sidney BioIn 16
Frank, Sidney W 1947- BiDrAPA 89
Frank, Stanley Donald 1932- WhoAm 90
Frank, Stephen Edward 1941- WhoAm 90
Frank, Stuart 1934- WhoAm 90
Frank, Thaisa 1943- WhoWrEP 89
Frank, Thomas 1922- BiDrAPA 89
Frank, Thomas Paul 1956- St&PR 91
Frank, Thomas V 1921- BiDrAPA 89
Frank, Tracy Steven Scott 1965- WhoWrEP 89
Frank, Victor H., Jr. 1927- St&PR 91, WhoWor 91
Frank, Waldo 1889-1967 EncAL
Frank, Waldo David 1889-1967 BioIn 16
Frank, Wally 1910- St&PR 91
Frank, Walter 1905-1945 BioIn 16
Frank, Werner L. 1929- St&PR 91
Frank, William Charles 1940- WhoAm 90
Frank, William Edward, Jr. 1943- WhoSSW 91
Frank, William Fielding 1944- WhoE 91
Frank, William G, Jr. 1926- BiDrAPA 89
Frank, William H. 1943- St&PR 91, WhoAm 90
Frank, William Nelson 1953- WhoWor 91
Frank, Yakira Hagalili 1923- WhoAmW 91
Frank, Zollie Sydney 1907- WhoAm 90
Frank Bayer, Ellen 1957- WhoAmW 91
Frankau, Pamela 1908-1967 BioIn 16, FemiCLE
Franke, Arnold Gene 1932- WhoWor 91
Franke, Cecelia Marie 1936- WhoSSW 91
Franke, Charles Henry 1933- WhoSSW 91
Franke, Eileen Diane 1956- WhoEmL 91
Franke, Frederick H. St&PR 91
Franke, Frederick Rahde 1918- WhoAm 90, WhoWor 91
Franke, Fritz Oswald 1941- BiDrAPA 89
Franke, Gunter 1944- WhoWor 91
Franke, Hans 1911- WhoWor 91
Franke, Herbert Max Wolfgang 1914- WhoWor 91
Franke, John Jacob, Jr. 1930- WhoAm 90
Franke, Kenneth A., Jr. 1958- St&PR 91
Franke, Maripat Kemps 1960- WhoAmW 91
Franke, Michael Wolfgang 1948- St&PR 91, WhoEmL 91
Franke, R.J. 1930- St&PR 91
Franke, Richard J. 1931- St&PR 91
Franke, Richard James 1931- WhoAm 90
Franke, Roger W. 1940- St&PR 91
Franke, Thomas E., Sr. 1961- St&PR 91
Franke, Thomas Stanley 1941- St&PR 91
Franke, Wayne Thomas 1950- WhoEmL 91
Franke, William Augustus 1937- St&PR 91, WhoAm 90
Frankeberger, Robert Russell 1937- WhoAm 90
Frankel, Alan David 1950- WhoE 91
Frankel, Alice K 1929- BiDrAPA 89
Frankel, Andrew J. 1932- St&PR 91
Frankel, Andrew Vance 1957- WhoE 91
Frankel, Anna 1949- WhoWor 91
Frankel, Arnold J. 1922- WhoAm 90
Frankel, Barry Roy 1950- WhoE 91
Frankel, Benjamin Harrison 1930- WhoAm 90
Frankel, Berdeen BiDrAPA 89
Frankel, Bernard 1929- St&PR 91
Frankel, Betty Sophia 1923- WhoAmW 91
Frankel, Bud BioIn 16
Frankel, C. David 1953- WhoSSW 91
Frankel, David Alexander 1943- WhoAm 90
Frankel, David Andrew BiDrAPA 89
Frankel, Dextra 1924- WhoAmA 91
Frankel, Donald Leon 1931- WhoAm 90
Frankel, Edward 1910- AuBYP 90
Frankel, Edward M. 1954- St&PR 91
Frankel, Eliot BioIn 16, NewYTBS 90
Frankel, Eliot 1922-1990 ConAu 130
Frankel, Ellen 1938- WhoE 91, WhoWrEP 89
Frankel, Ernest David 1924- St&PR 91
Frankel, Ernst Gabriel 1923- WhoAm 90
Frankel, Francine Ruth 1935- WhoAm 90
Frankel, Fred Harold 1924- BiDrAPA 89
Frankel, Gene 1923- WhoAm 90
Frankel, Glenn 1949- WhoAm 90, WhoE 91, WhoWor 91
Frankel, Harold O. N. 1904-1988 BioIn 16
Frankel, Herbert A. 1925- St&PR 91
Frankel, Joseph 1935- WhoAm 90
Frankel, Judith Jennifer Mariasha 1947- WhoAmW 91, WhoEmL 91
Frankel, Karen 1960- ODwPR 91
Frankel, Kenneth Mark 1940- WhoE 91, WhoWor 91
Frankel, Linda Kay BiDrAPA 89
Frankel, Linda Kay 1960- WhoE 91
Frankel, Marilyn Ellman 1942- WhoAmW 91
Frankel, Mark Henry BiDrAPA 89
Frankel, Martin Richard 1943- WhoAm 90, WhoE 91
Frankel, Marvin 1924- WhoAm 90
Frankel, Marvin E. 1920- WhoAm 90
Frankel, Max 1930- BioIn 16, WhoAm 90, WhoE 91, WhoWrEP 89, WorAlBi
Frankel, Merrell BioIn 16
Frankel, Michael 1951- BiDrAPA 89
Frankel, Morton Sedley 1924- St&PR 91
Frankel, Nancy Jean 1953- St&PR 91
Frankel, Ora BiDrAPA 89
Frankel, Otto Herzberg 1900- WhoWor 91
Frankel, Paul Warren WhoE 91
Frankel, Ronald A. 1929- ODwPR 91
Frankel, Russell E. 1943- St&PR 91
Frankel, Russell Edwin 1943- WhoAm 90
Frankel, Sandor 1943- WhoAm 90
Frankel, Saul Jacob 1917- WhoAm 90
Frankel, Sherman 1922- WhoAm 90
Frankel, Stanley A. 1918- ODwPR 91
Frankel, Stanley Arthur 1918- WhoAm 90
Frankel, Steven Alfred 1942- BiDrAPA 89
Frankel, Thomas H. 1943- St&PR 91
Frankel, Tracy BioIn 16
Frankel, Victor Hirsch 1925- WhoAm 90
Frankel, William Harry 1955- WhoEmL 91
Franken, Darrell 1930- WhoWrEP 89
Franken, Edmund Anthony, Jr. 1936- WhoAm 90
Franken, Franz Hermann 1926- WhoWor 91
Franken, Peter Alden 1928- WhoAm 90
Franken, Rose 1895?- FemiCLE
Franken, Rose 1895-1988 BioIn 16
Franken, Rose Dorothy Lewin 1895-1988 NotWoAT
Frankenberg, Robert Clinton 1911- WhoAmA 91
Frankenberger, Bertram, Jr. 1933- WhoAm 90
Frankenberger, Yoshiko Takagi 1946- IntWWM 90
Frankenburg, Frances R BiDrAPA 89

Frankenfeld, John William 1932- *WhoE 91*
Frankenheim, Samuel 1932- *St&PR 91, WhoAm 90*
Frankenheimer, John *BioIn 16*
Frankenheimer, John 1930- *WorAlBi*
Frankenheimer, John Michael 1930- *WhoAm 90*
Frankenhoff, William P. 1925- *St&PR 91*
Frankenstein, Alfred Victor 1906-1981 *WhoAmA 91N*
Frankenstein, George, IV 1935- *St&PR 91*
Frankenstein, Lester E. 1921- *St&PR 91*
Frankenthaler, Helen 1928- *BiDWomA, BioAmW, BioIn 16, News 90 [port], WhoAm 90, WhoAmA 91, WhoAmW 91, WorAlBi*
Franker, Stephen Grant 1949- *WhoEmL 91*
Frankforter, Weldon DeLoss 1920- *WhoAm 90*
Frankfother, Kent *ODwPR 91*
Frankfurt, Zvi Jehuda 1950- *BiDrAPA 89*
Frankfurter, Alfred *WhoAmA 91N*
Frankfurter, David 1909-1982 *BioIn 16*
Frankfurter, Felix 1882-1965 *BioIn 16, WorAlBi*
Frankfurter, Jack 1929- *WhoAmA 91*
Frankhouse, Fred 1904- *Ballpl 90*
Frankhouser, Homer Sheldon, Jr. 1927- *WhoSSW 91, WhoWor 91*
Frankhouser, Nancy Dobbs 1935- *WhoAmW 91*
Frankhouser, Nancy L. 1935- *St&PR 91*
Frankiewicz, Marcia Jean 1947- *WhoAmW 91*
Frankino, Steven P. 1936- *WhoAm 90*
Frankl, Daniel Richard 1922- *WhoAm 90*
Frankl, Karl H. 1933- *St&PR 91*
Frankl, Kenneth Richard 1924- *WhoAm 90*
Frankl, Paul Theodore 1876-1958 *WhoAmA 91N*
Frankl, Paul Theodore 1886-1958 *PenDiDA 89*
Frankl, Peter 1935- *IntWWM 90, PenDiMP*
Frankl, Spencer Nelson 1933- *WhoAm 90*
Frankl, Steven Kenneth 1944- *WhoE 91*
Frankl, Viktor E. 1905- *WhoAm 90*
Frankl, William Stewart 1928- *WhoAm 90, WhoE 91, WhoWor 91*
Frankl, Wolfe Julius 1920- *WhoE 91*
Frankland, Agnes Surriage 1726-1783 *EncCRAm*
Frankle, Barbara Stein 1940- *WhoSSW 91*
Frankle, Jerome H., Jr. 1928- *St&PR 91*
Frankle, Philip 1913-1968 *WhoAmA 91N*
Franklin, Adrian *BioIn 16*
Franklin, Alan James 1933- *WhoWor 91*
Franklin, Alfred Alton, Jr. 1947- *WhoSSW 91*
Franklin, Allan Ray 1945- *WhoSSW 91*
Franklin, Ann Smith 1696-1763 *BioIn 16*
Franklin, Ann Smith 1696-1765 *EncCRAm*
Franklin, Aretha *BioIn 16*
Franklin, Aretha 1942- *DrBlPA 90, EncPR&S 89, OxCPMus, WhoAm 90, WhoAmW 91, WorAlBi*
Franklin, Arthur J. 1928- *St&PR 91*
Franklin, Barbara Ann 1950- *WhoAmW 91*
Franklin, Barbara Hackman 1940- *WhoAmW 91*
Franklin, Barbara Kipp 1943- *WhoAmW 91*
Franklin, Ben T., Jr. 1944- *St&PR 91*
Franklin, Benjamin *ConAu 129, MajTwCW*
Franklin, Benjamin 1706-1790 *BioIn 16, EncCRAm [port], EncO&P 3, WhNaAH, WorAlBi*
Franklin, Benjamin, V 1939- *WhoSSW 91*
Franklin, Benjamin Barnum 1944- *WhoWor 91*
Franklin, Billy Joe 1940- *WhoAm 90, WhoSSW 91*
Franklin, Blair *ODwPR 91*
Franklin, Blake Timothy 1942- *WhoE 91*
Franklin, Bonnie 1944- *WorAlBi*
Franklin, Burton 1928- *BiDrAPA 89*
Franklin, C. L. *BioIn 16*
Franklin, Carl 1930?- *DrBlPA 90*
Franklin, Carol Bertha 1947- *WhoAmW 91*
Franklin, Carole R 1933- *WhoAmA 91*
Franklin, Carolyn *BioIn 16*
Franklin, Charles Dale 1931- *WhoAm 90*
Franklin, Charles Scothern 1937- *WhoAm 90*
Franklin, Churchill Gibson 1948- *WhoE 91*
Franklin, Clarence *WhoAmA 91N*
Franklin, Curtis Uvell, Jr. *BiDrAPA 89*
Franklin, Dale Helaine 1940- *WhoAmW 91*
Franklin, David *BioIn 16*
Franklin, David 1908-1973 *PenDiMP*
Franklin, David Jansen 1951- *WhoEmL 91*
Franklin, Dawson Cleveland, Jr. 1922- *St&PR 91*
Franklin, Deborah Read *EncCRAm [port]*
Franklin, Dennis Eugene *BiDrAPA 89*
Franklin, Donald Gene *BioIn 16*
Franklin, E. Thomas, Jr. 1944- *St&PR 91*
Franklin, Earl Robert 1943- *St&PR 91*
Franklin, Edward Ward 1926- *WhoAm 90*
Franklin, Frederick Russell 1929- *WhoWor 91*
Franklin, Freeman E. 183-?-1870 *AmLegL*
Franklin, Gene Farthing 1927- *WhoAm 90*
Franklin, George *BioIn 16*
Franklin, George S. 1913- *WhoAm 90, WhoWor 91*
Franklin, Gerald 1926- *WhoE 91*
Franklin, Gerald Saml 1936- *BiDrAPA 89*
Franklin, Gilbert Alfred 1919- *WhoAm 90, WhoAmA 91*
Franklin, Hannah 1937- *WhoAmA 91*
Franklin, Harriet Lewis 1938- *WhoAmW 91*
Franklin, Herbert H *EncABHB 4*
Franklin, Howard B. 1920- *St&PR 91*
Franklin, Hugh *BioIn 16*
Franklin, Hugh, Mrs. *WhoAmW 91*
Franklin, J E *DrBlPA 90*
Franklin, J.H. *St&PR 91*
Franklin, J. Manning *WhoWrEP 89*
Franklin, Jack Lee 1931- *WhoSSW 91*
Franklin, James 1697-1735 *BioIn 16*
Franklin, James M. 1943- *St&PR 91*
Franklin, James Nathan 1949- *St&PR 91*
Franklin, James Robert 1951- *WhoAm 90*
Franklin, James T. *EarBlAP*
Franklin, Jean 1941- *BiDrAPA 89, WhoE 91*
Franklin, Jerome H 1935- *BiDrAPA 89*
Franklin, Jill 1928-1988 *AnObit 1988*
Franklin, Joel Nicholas 1930- *WhoAm 90*
Franklin, John 1786-1847 *DcLB 99 [port], WorAlBi*
Franklin, John C. 1904-1989 *BioIn 16*
Franklin, John Hope 1915- *WhoAm 90, WhoWrEP 89*
Franklin, John Rankin 1820-1878 *AmLegL*
Franklin, Jon Daniel 1942- *WhoAm 90*
Franklin, Joseph Earl 1953- *WhoSSW 91*
Franklin, Jude Eric 1943- *WhoAm 90*
Franklin, Julian Harold 1925- *WhoAm 90*
Franklin, Kathleen Anna 1957- *WhoAmW 91*
Franklin, Kenneth Linn 1923- *WhoAm 90*
Franklin, Kerry *WhoWrEP 89*
Franklin, Lance 1952- *SmATA X [port]*
Franklin, Larry Daniel 1942- *St&PR 91*
Franklin, Leeann T. *St&PR 91*
Franklin, Lewis G. 1950- *St&PR 91*
Franklin, Linda Lawrence 1950- *WhoE 91*
Franklin, Lynn C. *BioIn 16*
Franklin, Lynne 1957- *ODwPR 91*
Franklin, Marc Adam 1932- *WhoAm 90*
Franklin, Margaret Lavona Barnum 1905- *WhoAmW 91, WhoWor 91*
Franklin, Margery Bodansky 1933- *WhoAm 90*
Franklin, Martha Minerva 1870-1968 *BioIn 16*
Franklin, Maud 1857-1941? *BioIn 16*
Franklin, Max *AuBYP 90, TwCCr&M 91*
Franklin, Michael Harold 1923- *WhoAm 90*
Franklin, Miles 1879-1954 *BioIn 16, FemiCLE*
Franklin, Miriam Anna 1894- *WhoWrEP 89*
Franklin, Murray Joseph 1922- *WhoAm 90*
Franklin, Oliver *BioIn 16*
Franklin, Omer White, Jr. 1914- *WhoAm 90*
Franklin, Pamela *BioIn 16*
Franklin, Pamela 1950- *ConTFT 8*
Franklin, Patricia O'Neill 1949- *WhoSSW 91*
Franklin, Patt 1941- *WhoAmA 91*
Franklin, Paul F *BiDrAPA 89*
Franklin, Paula Anne 1928- *WhoAmW 91*
Franklin, Peter Robert 1947- *IntWWM 90*
Franklin, Phyllis *BioIn 16*
Franklin, Phyllis 1932- *WhoAm 90*
Franklin, Ralph William 1937- *WhoAm 90*
Franklin, Rena Holt *ODwPR 91*
Franklin, Richard C. 1948- *St&PR 91*
Franklin, Richard Mark 1947- *WhoEmL 91*
Franklin, Richard Walter, Jr. 1955- *WhoEmL 91*
Franklin, Rita Sims 1943- *WhoSSW 91*
Franklin, Robert Brewer 1937- *WhoAm 90*
Franklin, Robert Charles 1936- *St&PR 91, WhoAm 90*
Franklin, Robert Drury 1935- *St&PR 91, WhoSSW 91*
Franklin, Robert J. 1928- *St&PR 91*
Franklin, Robert L *BiDrAPA 89*
Franklin, Robert McFarland 1943- *WhoWrEP 89*
Franklin, Roger Edwin, Jr. 1949- *WhoSSW 91*
Franklin, Rogers *WhoWrEP 89*
Franklin, Roland A. E. *BioIn 16*
Franklin, Roosevelt 1933- *WhoSSW 91*
Franklin, Rosalind *BioIn 16*
Franklin, Samuel Gregg 1946- *WhoE 91*
Franklin, Sheryl J. 1954- *WhoAmW 91*
Franklin, Shirley Clarke 1945- *WhoAm 90, WhoAmW 91*
Franklin, Sidney 1942- *WhoAm 90*
Franklin, Stanley Phillip 1931- *WhoAm 90*
Franklin, Stella Maria Miles Lampe 1879-1954 *BioIn 16*
Franklin, Sylvan L. 1934- *St&PR 91*
Franklin, Thomas Chester 1923- *WhoAm 90*
Franklin, Victoria Thompson 1951- *St&PR 91*
Franklin, Virginia Spiro 1915- *WhoE 91*
Franklin, Wallace G. 1926- *St&PR 91*
Franklin, Walt 1950- *WhoWrEP 89*
Franklin, Wendell James *DrBlPA 90*
Franklin, William 1731-1813 *EncCRAm*
Franklin, William A. 1946- *St&PR 91*
Franklin, William Emery 1933- *WhoAm 90*
Franklin, William Howard 1942- *WhoSSW 91*
Franklin, William P. *WhoSSW 91*
Franklin, William P. 1933- *St&PR 91*
Franklin, William P. 1953- *WhoEmL 91*
Franklin, William Warren 1915- *WhoAm 90*
Franklin-Lipsker, Eileen *BioIn 16*
Franklyn, Julian 1899-1970 *EncO&P 3*
Franknecht, Robert Howard 1955- *WhoAm 90*
Franko, Bernard Vincent 1922- *WhoAm 90*
Frankovich, George Richard 1920- *WhoAm 90*
Frankovich, Mary Jo 1954- *WhoAmW 91*
Frankovich, Mike J. 1910- *WhoAm 90*
Frankovich, Thomas Bernard 1951- *WhoEmL 91*
Frankowiak, James R. 1946- *ODwPR 91*
Franks, Charles Leslie 1934- *WhoAm 90*
Franks, Darrell Dean 1944- *BiDrAPA 89*
Franks, David A. 1929- *WhoE 91*
Franks, Donald Louis 1953- *WhoEmL 91*
Franks, Herbert Hoover 1934- *WhoWor 91*
Franks, Herman 1914- *Ballpl 90*
Franks, Hollis Berry 1916- *WhoSSW 91*
Franks, J. Robert 1937- *WhoAm 90*
Franks, James Byron 1949- *WhoSSW 91*
Franks, Jerry *BioIn 16*
Franks, Lawrence Albert 1933- *St&PR 91*
Franks, Leonard Maurice 1921- *WhoWor 91*
Franks, Lewis E. 1931- *WhoAm 90*
Franks, Lucinda Laura 1946- *WhoAm 90*
Franks, Martin Davis 1950- *WhoE 91*
Franks, Michael *BioIn 16*
Franks, Nanci Bernice 1951- *WhoEmL 91*
Franks, Richard M. 1945- *St&PR 91*
Franks, Richard Matthew 1945- *WhoAm 90*
Franks, Ronald Dwyer 1946- *BiDrAPA 89, WhoAm 90*
Franks, Thomas Matthew 1954- *WhoEmL 91*
Frankson, Harry Lawrence 1942- *St&PR 91*
Frankson-Kendrick, Sarah Jane 1949- *WhoAmW 91*
Frankston, Sherman 1945- *ODwPR 91*
Frankstone, Edward R. 1922- *St&PR 91*
Frankum, Carolyn Irene 1937- *WhoAmW 91*
Frankum, James Edward 1921- *WhoAm 90*
Frann, Mary *BioIn 16, WhoAmW 91*
Frano, Andrew Joseph 1953- *WhoEmL 91, WhoWor 91*
Fransen, Christine Irene 1947- *WhoAmW 91*
Fransioli, Thomas Adrian 1906- *WhoAmA 91*
Fransioli, Thomas Adrian, III 1933- *St&PR 91*
Fransman, Martin Jacques 1948- *WhoWor 91*
Franson, Donald R., Jr. 1952- *St&PR 91*
Franson, Marc Paul 1955- *WhoEmL 91*
Franson, Paul 1941- *ODwPR 91*
Franson, Paul Oscar, III 1941- *WhoAm 90*
Franson, William Alan 1943- *St&PR 91*
Frant, Jacqueline Louise 1953- *WhoE 91*
Franta, Rosalyn 1951- *St&PR 91, WhoAm 90*
Franta, William Roy 1942- *WhoAm 90*
Frantisak, Frank 1933- *WhoAm 90*
Frantum, Albert W., Jr. 1947- *St&PR 91*
Frantz, Andrew Gibson 1930- *WhoAm 90*
Frantz, Charles 1925- *WhoAm 90*
Frantz, Gerald J. 1938- *St&PR 91*
Frantz, Jack T. 1939- *St&PR 91*
Frantz, Jack Thomas 1939- *WhoAm 90*
Frantz, John C. 1953- *St&PR 91*
Frantz, John Corydon 1926- *WhoAm 90*
Frantz, John R *BiDrAPA 89*
Frantz, Justus 1944- *IntWWM 90*
Frantz, Katherine Barrett 1952- *BiDrAPA 89*
Frantz, Leroy, Jr. 1927- *St&PR 91*
Frantz, Marty Douglas 1951- *St&PR 91*
Frantz, Nanette Michelle 1955- *WhoAmW 91*
Frantz, Paul Lewis 1955- *WhoEmL 91*
Frantz, Ray William, Jr. 1923- *WhoAm 90*
Frantz, Robert Lewis 1925- *WhoAm 90*
Frantz, Robert Wesley 1950- *WhoEmL 91*
Frantz, Roger C. 1937- *St&PR 91*
Frantz, Stephen Richard 1958- *WhoEmL 91, WhoWor 91*
Frantz, Welby Marion 1912- *WhoAm 90*
Frantz, William E 1914- *BiDrAPA 89*
Frantze, David W. 1955- *WhoEmL 91*
Frantzen, Dirk Jozef 1951- *WhoWor 91*
Frantzen, Henry Arthur 1942- *St&PR 91, WhoAm 90*
Frantzve, Jerri Lyn 1942- *WhoAmW 91, WhoSSW 91*
Franyo, Richard Louis 1944- *WhoAm 90*
Franz Josef II, Prince 1906-1989 *AnObit 1989*
Franz Josef II, Prince of Liechtenstein 1906-1989 *BioIn 16*
Franz, Donald Eugene, Jr. 1944- *WhoE 91*
Franz, Frank Andrew 1937- *WhoAm 90*
Franz, Frederick William 1893- *WhoAm 90*
Franz, James Robert 1933- *St&PR 91*
Franz, Jeffrey Brian 1947- *WhoE 91, WhoWrEP 89*
Franz, Jennifer Danton 1949- *WhoEmL 91*
Franz, Jerry 1955- *ODwPR 91*
Franz, John E. 1929- *WhoAm 90*
Franz, John Matthias 1927- *WhoAm 90*
Franz, Juliana D *BiDrAPA 89*
Franz, Kurt 1914- *BioIn 16*
Franz, Lydia Millicent Truc 1924- *WhoAmW 91*
Franz, Robert W. 1924- *St&PR 91*
Franz, Sherman G 1937- *BiDrAPA 89*
Franzblau, David R *BiDrAPA 89*
Franzblau, Deborah Sharon 1957- *WhoE 91*
Franzblau, Michael 1935- *BiDrAPA 89*
Franzen, Barney L., III 1915- *St&PR 91*
Franzen, Bill *ConAu 129*
Franzen, Charles Rice 1957- *WhoWor 91*
Franzen, Earl Theodore 1915- *WhoAm 90*
Franzen, Frans Michael 1772-1847 *DcScanL*
Franzen, George Joseph 1940- *St&PR 91*
Franzen, Hans 1935- *IntWWM 90*
Franzen, Janice Marguerite Gosnell 1921- *WhoAm 90*
Franzen, Jonathan 1959- *ConAu 129*
Franzen, Olov Alfred 1946- *IntWWM 90*
Franzen, Richard B. 1946- *WhoWrEP 89*
Franzen, Stephen Edwards 1953- *WhoEmL 91*
Franzen, Ulrich J. 1921- *WhoAm 90*
Franzen, William Edward 1952- *ConAu 129*
Franzese, Bruce Joseph 1947- *St&PR 91*
Franzese, Michael *BioIn 16*
Franzetti, Joseph 1955- *St&PR 91*
Franzetti, Lillian Angelina 1925- *WhoE 91*
Franzheim, Barbara 1939- *WhoAmW 91*
Franzina, Giovanni F. 1932- *WhoWor 91*
Franzke, Allan 1930- *WhoAm 90*
Franzke, Andreas 1938- *ConAu 129*
Franzke, Hans-Hermann 1927- *WhoWor 91*
Franzke, Hermann Robert 1930- *WhoWor 91*
Franzke, Richard Albert 1935- *WhoAm 90*
Franzke, Roger Hume 1927- *St&PR 91*
Franzkowski, Rainer 1935- *WhoWor 91*
Franzman, A. Daniel 1934- *St&PR 91*
Franzmann, Albert Wilhelm 1930- *WhoAm 90*
Franzmeier, Alvin Henry 1933- *WhoSSW 91*
Franznick, Cathy 1957- *ODwPR 91*
Franzoni, Joseph D 1916- *BiDrAPA 89*
Franzoni, Lauryn L. 1957- *WhoAmW 91*
Frappier, Elizabeth Jane 1932- *WhoE 91*
Frappier, Gilles 1931- *WhoAm 90*
Frappier, Judy *BioIn 16*
Frappier, Lisa M *BiDrAPA 89*
Frary, Michael 1918- *WhoAmA 91*
Frary, Richard Spencer 1924- *WhoAm 90*
Frary, Richard Spencer, Sr. 1924- *St&PR 91*
Fras, Ivan 1936- *BiDrAPA 89*
Frasca, Robert 1933- *St&PR 91*
Frasca, Robert John 1933- *WhoAm 90*
Frascarelli, Sergio 1939- *WhoWor 91*
Frasch, Brian Bernard 1956- *WhoEmL 91*

Frasch, David E. 1947- *St&PR 91*
Frasch, David Edward 1947- *WhoAm 90*
Fraschilla, Ceaser 1936- *St&PR 91*
Fraschillo, Thomas V. 1946- *IntWWM 90*
Frascino, Edward *BioIn 16*
Frasconi, Antonio 1919- *AuBYP 90, BioIn 16, SmATA 11AS [port], WhoAmA 91*
Fraser, Lord 1911-1989 *AnObit 1989*
Fraser, Alvardo M *BiDrAPA 89*
Fraser, Andy *BioIn 16*
Fraser, Anthea *TwCCr&M 91*
Fraser, Antonia 1932- *BioIn 16, FemiCLE, MajTwCW, TwCCr&M 91, WhoAm 90, WorAlBi*
Fraser, Beatrice *AuBYP 90*
Fraser, Bill 1932- *BioIn 16*
Fraser, Bruce Austin 1888-1981 *DcNaB 1981*
Fraser, Bruce Douglas 1927- *St&PR 91*
Fraser, Bruce Wickersham 1941- *WhoWrEP 89*
Fraser, Bruce William 1947- *IntWWM 90*
Fraser, Campbell 1923- *St&PR 91, WhoAm 90*
Fraser, Charles Elbert 1929- *WhoAm 90*
Fraser, Chick 1871-1940 *Ballpl 90*
Fraser, Christopher Finlay 1839-1894 *DcCanB 12*
Fraser, Craig Wilson 1948- *St&PR 91*
Fraser, D. Ian 1931- *St&PR 91*
Fraser, David 1920- *BioIn 16, ConAu 129*
Fraser, David Ben 1926- *BiDrAPA 89*
Fraser, David John 1955- *WhoWor 91*
Fraser, David S. 1938- *St&PR 91*
Fraser, David Van 1930- *WhoSSW 91*
Fraser, David William 1944- *WhoAm 90, WhoE 91*
Fraser, Dawn 1937- *WorAlBi*
Fraser, Donald 1810?-1897 *DcCanB 12*
Fraser, Donald C. 1941- *WhoAm 90, WhoE 91*
Fraser, Donald MacKay 1924- *WhoAm 90*
Fraser, Douglas 1929-1982 *WhoAmA 91N*
Fraser, Douglas Andrew 1916- *EncABHB 5 [port]*
Fraser, Edie 1943- *ODwPR 91*
Fraser, Elisabeth G. 1962- *WhoSSW 91*
Fraser, Everett Mackay 1921- *St&PR 91*
Fraser, Ferrin *AuBYP 90*
Fraser, Frederick C. 1934- *St&PR 91*
Fraser, Geo. B. 1930- *St&PR 91*
Fraser, Georg Richard 1946- *WhoWor 91*
Fraser, George Broadrup 1914- *WhoAm 90*
Fraser, George Noel 1942- *WhoSSW 91*
Fraser, Gilly 1940- *FemiCLE*
Fraser, Glenn D 1912- *BiDrAPA 89*
Fraser, Greg *BioIn 16*
Fraser, Haddon S. 1929- *St&PR 91*
Fraser, Henry S. 1900- *WhoAm 90*
Fraser, Hugh Charles Patrick Joseph 1918-1984 *DcNaB 1981*
Fraser, Ian M. 1935- *St&PR 91*
Fraser, J.F. *St&PR 91*
Fraser, Jack Carlyle *St&PR 91N*
Fraser, James 1924- *TwCCr&M 91*
Fraser, James Cavender 1941- *WhoE 91*
Fraser, Jane *MajTwCW*
Fraser, John Allen 1931- *WhoAm 90*
Fraser, John Arthur 1838-1898 *DcCanB 12*
Fraser, John Foster 1930- *WhoAm 90*
Fraser, John J. 1951- *St&PR 91*
Fraser, John James 1829-1896 *DcCanB 12*
Fraser, John Keith 1922- *WhoAm 90*
Fraser, John Martin 1954- *WhoSSW 91*
Fraser, John Wayne 1944- *WhoSSW 91*
Fraser, Jon 1955- *WhoEmL 91*
Fraser, Joyce *BioIn 16*
Fraser, Julius Thomas 1923- *WhoE 91*
Fraser, Kathleen Joy 1937- *WhoAm 90*
Fraser, Kenneth William, Jr. 1937- *St&PR 91, WhoAm 90*
Fraser, Laura 1889-1966 *BiDWomA*
Fraser, Laura G 1889-1966 *WhoAmA 91N*
Fraser, Malcolm 1869-1949 *WhoAmA 91N*
Fraser, Malcolm 1930- *BioIn 16, WorAlBi*
Fraser, Malcolm Henry 1939- *IntWWM 90*
Fraser, Marjorie Alice 1914- *WhoAmW 91*
Fraser, Mary 1851-1922 *FemiCLE*
Fraser, Mary Edna 1952- *WhoAmA 91*
Fraser, Mary Karen 1946- *WhoE 91*
Fraser, Murray Judson 1930- *WhoAm 90*
Fraser, Patricia Lee 1944- *WhoAmW 91*
Fraser, Ray *ConAu 130*
Fraser, Raymond 1941- *ConAu 130*
Fraser, Renee 1952- *ODwPR 91*
Fraser, Renee White 1952- *WhoAmW 91*
Fraser, Richard Arnold 1943- *WhoAm 90*
Fraser, Robert Brown 1904-1985 *DcNaB 1981*
Fraser, Robert Carson 1925- *WhoE 91*
Fraser, Robert Gordon 1921- *WhoAm 90*
Fraser, Robert Murray 1930- *WhoAm 90*
Fraser, Robin 1933- *WhoWor 91*
Fraser, Ronald 1930- *ConAu 131*
Fraser, Russell Alfred 1927- *WhoAm 90, WhoWrEP 89*
Fraser, Scott 1958- *BioIn 16*
Fraser, Scott Alexander 1955- *WhoE 91*
Fraser, Shena Eleanor 1910- *IntWWM 90*
Fraser, Simon 1776-1862 *WhNaAH*
Fraser, Stanley Drew 1925- *St&PR 91*
Fraser, Stewart Erskine 1929- *ConAu 32NR*
Fraser, Sylvia *BioIn 16*
Fraser, Sylvia 1935- *ConLC 64 [port], FemiCLE*
Fraser, Thomas G. *St&PR 91*
Fraser, Thomas H. 1948- *St&PR 91*
Fraser, Tom 1911-1988 *AnObit 1988*
Fraser, William Lawrence 1929- *WhoAm 90*
Fraser, William Neil 1932- *WhoAm 90*
Fraser, Willie 1964- *Ballpl 90*
Fraser-Harris, David 1867-1937 *EncO&P 3*
Fraser-Reid, Bertram Oliver 1934- *WhoAm 90*
Fraser-Simson, Harold 1878-1944 *OxCPMus*
Fraser-Smith, Elizabeth Birdsey 1938- *WhoAmW 91*
Fraser-Tytler, Christiana 1848-1927 *FemiCLE*
Frasher, Thomas P. 1956- *St&PR 91*
Frashier, Gary E. 1936- *St&PR 91*
Frashure, James Marshal 1928- *St&PR 91*
Frasier, Ralph Kennedy 1938- *St&PR 91, WhoAm 90*
Frasier, Robin D'Arvin *BiDrAPA 89*
Frasier, Thomas Daniel 1938- *WhoWrEP 89*
Frasier, William Marshall 1946- *St&PR 91, WhoEmL 91*
Frassini, Natalie 1836-1905 *BioIn 16*
Frasure, William R. 1954- *St&PR 91*
Fratantoni, Kathleen Margaret 1959- *WhoEmL 91*
Fratcher, William Franklin 1913- *WhoAm 90*
Fratellini, Annie *BioIn 16*
Fratello, Michael Robert 1947- *WhoAm 90*
Frater, Hal 1909- *WhoAmA 91*
Frater, Robert William Mayo 1928- *WhoAm 90*
Frati, Luigi 1943- *WhoWor 91*
Fratianni, Joseph James 1932- *St&PR 91*
Fratini, Gina 1931- *ConDes 90*
Fratt, Gerald E. 1941- *St&PR 91*
Frattali, Rose Esther 1931- *St&PR 91*
Frattaroli, Carmen Aniello 1948- *WhoEmL 91*
Frattaroli, Elio John *BiDrAPA 89*
Fratti, Mario 1927- *WhoAm 90*
Frattini, Gianfranco 1926- *ConDes 90*
Fratz, Donald Douglas 1952- *WhoWrEP 89*
Frauchiger, Fritz A 1941- *WhoAmA 91*
Frauenfelder, Hans 1922- *WhoAm 90*
Frauenglas, Robert Alan 1950- *WhoWrEP 89*
Frauenhoffer, Gail Lynne 1958- *St&PR 91*
Fraughton, Edward James 1939- *WhoAmA 91*
Fraulo, Amadeo Andy 1920- *St&PR 91*
Fraumann, Timothy Alan 1951- *WhoE 91*
Fraunfelder, Frederick Theodore 1934- *WhoAm 90*
Fraunfelter, Brenda Lynn 1953- *WhoAmW 91*
Fraustino, Daniel Victor 1945- *WhoWrEP 89*
Frausto, Maria Christina 1952- *WhoAmW 91*
Frautschi, Dorothy Jones 1903- *St&PR 91*
Frautschi, Jack Russell 1954- *WhoSSW 91*
Frautschi, John Jones 1929- *St&PR 91*
Frautschi, Richard Lane 1926- *WhoE 91*
Frautschi, Steven Clark 1933- *WhoAm 90*
Frautschi, Timothy Clark 1937- *WhoAm 90*
Frautschi, Walter Albert 1901- *St&PR 91, WhoAm 90*
Fravala, George Michael 1951- *WhoEmL 91*
Fravel, Elizabeth Whitmore 1951- *WhoEmL 91*
Fravel, Steven Lee 1957- *WhoEmL 91*
Fravert, Colleen Mohnike 1951- *WhoEmL 91*
Frawley, Claire 1929- *WhoAmW 91*
Frawley, Daniel Seymour 1943- *WhoAm 90, WhoE 91*
Frawley, Patrick Joseph, Jr. 1923- *WhoAm 90*
Frawley, Thomas Francis 1919- *WhoAm 90*
Frawley, Timothy Joseph 1951- *WhoE 91*
Frawley, William 1887-1966 *WorAlBi*
Fraxedas, Ricardo 1953- *St&PR 91*
Fray, Earl Napoleon 1934- *St&PR 91*
Frayer, Dorothy Ann 1938- *WhoAmW 91*
Frayn, Douglas H 1936- *BiDrAPA 89*
Frayn, Michael *BioIn 16*
Frayn, Michael 1933- *ConAu 30NR, MajTwCW*
Fraze, Denny T 1940- *WhoAmA 91*
Fraze, Denny Turner 1940- *WhoSSW 91*
Fraze, Ermal Cleon *BioIn 16*
Frazee, Gerald Clifford 1958- *St&PR 91*
Frazee, Harry 1881-1929 *Ballpl 90*
Frazee, Harry H. 1930- *St&PR 91*
Frazee, Jane 1936- *IntWWM 90*
Frazee, John Powell, Jr. 1944- *St&PR 91, WhoAm 90*
Frazee, Rowland Cardwell 1921- *St&PR 91*
Frazee, Steve 1909- *BioIn 16*
Frazelle, Kenneth *BioIn 16*
Frazer, Andrew *AuBYP 90, TwCCr&M 91*
Frazer, Elizabeth Burgess 1937- *WhoAmW 91*
Frazer, Gregory James 1952- *WhoEmL 91*
Frazer, Ira 1954- *WhoEmL 91*
Frazer, J. Howard 1924- *St&PR 91*
Frazer, Jack Winfield 1924- *WhoAm 90*
Frazer, James 1854-1941 *WorAlBi*
Frazer, James, Jr 1949- *WhoAmA 91*
Frazer, James George 1854-1941 *BioIn 16*
Frazer, John Hamilton 1945- *WhoWor 91*
Frazer, John Howard 1924- *WhoAm 90*
Frazer, John Paul 1914- *WhoAm 90*
Frazer, John Thatcher 1932- *WhoAmA 91*
Frazer, John William 1917- *IntWWM 90*
Frazer, Joseph Washington 1892-1971 *EncABHB 5 [port]*
Frazer, Margaret Elspeth 1940- *WhoAm 90*
Frazer, Miriam K. *St&PR 91*
Frazer, Nathaniel Blevins 1949- *WhoSSW 91*
Frazer, Phyllis Seely 1953- *WhoAmW 91*
Frazer, Robert Caine *MajTwCW, TwCCr&M 91*
Frazer, Timothy Wayne 1957- *BiDrAPA 89*
Frazer, Wendy 1943- *WhoAmW 91*
Frazetta, Frank 1928- *BioIn 16, EncACom, WhoAm 90*
Frazier, A. D., Jr. 1944- *WhoAm 90*
Frazier, Alan D. 1951- *WhoEmL 91*
Frazier, Alice *BioIn 16*
Frazier, Allie Robert 1933- *WhoSSW 91*
Frazier, April *WhoWrEP 89*
Frazier, Brenda D. 1921-1982 *BioAmW*
Frazier, Carl *AuBYP 90*
Frazier, Charles Edwin 1943- *WhoSSW 91*
Frazier, Chet June 1924- *WhoAm 90*
Frazier, Claude A 1920- *ConAu 32NR*
Frazier, Cliff 1934- *DrBlPA 90*
Frazier, Donald 1924- *St&PR 91*
Frazier, Donald Tha, Sr. 1935- *WhoAm 90*
Frazier, Edward Clarence 1953- *WhoSSW 91*
Frazier, Edward Franklin 1894-1962 *BioIn 16*
Frazier, Ellen Elizabeth 1950- *WhoAmW 91, WhoEmL 91*
Frazier, Eugene Richard 1947- *WhoSSW 91*
Frazier, George 1911-1974 *BioIn 16*
Frazier, George 1954- *Ballpl 90*
Frazier, Gloria K. 1953- *St&PR 91*
Frazier, Gregory Craig 1950- *WhoSSW 91*
Frazier, Hal Hinton *BiDrAPA 89*
Frazier, Harold Leon 1939- *BiDrAPA 89*
Frazier, Henry Bowen, III 1934- *WhoAm 90*
Frazier, Howard *BioIn 16*
Frazier, Howard Stanley 1926- *WhoAm 90*
Frazier, Ian *BioIn 16*
Frazier, Ian 1951- *ConAu 130*
Frazier, J. Phillip 1939- *St&PR 91*
Frazier, James, Jr. 1940- *DrBlPA 90*
Frazier, Janice Dianne 1956- *WhoEmL 91*
Frazier, Jean Ann *BiDrAPA 89*
Frazier, Joe 1944- *WhoAm 90*
Frazier, John *ODwPR 91*
Frazier, John E., II 1940- *St&PR 91*
Frazier, John Lionel Devin 1932- *St&PR 91, WhoAm 90*
Frazier, John Mitchell 1828-1870 *AmLegL*
Frazier, John Phillip 1939- *WhoAm 90*
Frazier, John Richard *BiDrAPA 89*
Frazier, John Warren 1913- *WhoAm 90*
Frazier, John William 1944- *WhoSSW 91*
Frazier, Kendrick Crosby 1942- *WhoWrEP 89*
Frazier, Kenneth 1867-1949 *WhoAmA 91N*
Frazier, Kimberlee Gonterman 1953- *WhoAmW 91*
Frazier, Larry Elmer 1933- *WhoSSW 91*
Frazier, Larry G. 1952- *St&PR 91*
Frazier, Lawrence Alan 1936- *St&PR 91*
Frazier, LeRoy 1946- *WhoAm 90*
Frazier, Mack 1901- *St&PR 91*
Frazier, Neta 1890- *AuBYP 90*
Frazier, Neta Lohnes *NewYTBS 90*
Frazier, Neta Lohnes 1890-1990 *BioIn 16, ConAu 131*
Frazier, Owsley B. 1935- *St&PR 91, WhoAm 90*
Frazier, Pamela T *BiDrAPA 89*
Frazier, Patricia Bailey 1935- *St&PR 91*
Frazier, Paul D 1922- *WhoAmA 91*
Frazier, Paula Newby- *BioIn 16*
Frazier, Peter W. 1942- *St&PR 91*
Frazier, Richard R. 1946- *St&PR 91*
Frazier, Richard Williams 1922-1983 *WhoAmA 91N*
Frazier, Robert Edward 1943- *BiDrAPA 89*
Frazier, Robert G. 1923- *WhoAm 90*
Frazier, Rosalie *AuBYP 90*
Frazier, Ruth Mae 1944- *WhoAmW 91*
Frazier, Samuel Ramon 1927- *BiDrAPA 89*
Frazier, Sharon Rae 1965- *WhoSSW 91*
Frazier, Sheila 1948- *DrBlPA 90*
Frazier, Shervert 1921- *BioIn 16*
Frazier, Shervert H 1921- *BiDrAPA 89*
Frazier, Shervert Hughes, Jr. 1921- *WhoAm 90*
Frazier, Steven Carl 1954- *WhoEmL 91*
Frazier, Terry Francis 1953- *WhoSSW 91*
Frazier, Thomas G. 1943- *St&PR 91*
Frazier, Vic 1904-1977 *Ballpl 90*
Frazier, Walt 1945- *BioIn 16, WorAlBi*
Frazier, Walt, III *BioIn 16*
Frazier, Walter Ronald 1939- *WhoSSW 91, WhoWor 91*
Frazier, Warner C. 1932- *St&PR 91*
Frazier, Warner Carlisle 1932- *WhoAm 90*
Frazier, William Francis, Jr. 1957- *WhoEmL 91*
Frazier, William Henry 1943- *WhoSSW 91*
Frazier, William J. 1925- *St&PR 91*
Frazier, Winston Earle 1930- *WhoSSW 91*
Frazier-Tsai, Karen Lynne 1952- *WhoAmW 91*
Frazin, Bernard *BiDrAPA 89*
Frazza, George S. 1934- *St&PR 91, WhoAm 90*
Frazzetta, Thomas H. 1934- *WhoAm 90*
Freal, James Brendan 1962- *WhoSSW 91*
Fream, Anita Sue 1948- *WhoAmW 91*
Freaney, Diane M. 1943- *WhoAmW 91*
Frears, Stephen 1941- *BioIn 16, CurBio 90 [port]*
Frearson, Ann 1955- *WhoSSW 91*
Freas, Donald Hayes 1933- *St&PR 91*
Freas, Frank Kelly 1922- *WhoAm 90*
Freas, George Craig 1947- *WhoEmL 91*
Freas, Guy James 1962- *WhoEmL 91*
Frease, John Michael 1950- *WhoWor 91*
Freberg, Carl Roger 1916- *WhoAm 90*
Freberg, Stan *BioIn 16*
Freberg, Stanley 1926- *WhoAm 90*
Freccero, John 1931- *WhoAm 90*
Freccia, Massimo 1906- *IntWWM 90*
Frech, David Vincent, Sr. 1947- *WhoE 91*
Frech, Harry Edward, III 1946- *WhoEmL 91*
Frechen, Joseph G *BiDrAPA 89*
Frechen, Kathleen Ann *BiDrAPA 89*
Frechet, Rene Maurice 1878-1973 *DcScB S2*
Frechette, Alice Marie 1947- *WhoAmW 91*
Frechette, Claude J 1939- *BiDrAPA 89*
Frechette, Ernest Albert 1918- *WhoSSW 91*
Frechette, Louis-Honore 1839-1908 *DcLB 99 [port], OxCCanT [port]*
Frechette, Paul F 1933- *BiDrAPA 89*
Frechette, Peter *BioIn 16*
Frechette, Peter L. 1937- *St&PR 91*
Frechette, Peter Loren 1937- *WhoAm 90*
Frechette, Van Derck 1916- *WhoAm 90*
Freckelton, Sondra *BioIn 16*
Freckelton, Sondra 1936- *WhoAmA 91*
Fred, B. Alan 1927- *St&PR 91*
Freddie and the Dreamers *EncPR&S 89*
Freddo, Thomas Frank 1949- *WhoE 91*
Frede, Richard 1934- *ConAu 32NR*
Fredegond *WomWR*
Fredegund *WomWR*
Fredell, Jan Jacob Fabian 1937- *WhoWor 91*
Fredell, Patric Stig 1939- *WhoWor 91*
Fredenburg, David Marshall, Sr. 1932- *WhoWor 91*
Fredenthal, David 1914-1958 *WhoAmA 91N*
Fredenthal, Ruth Ann 1938- *WhoAmA 91*
Frederic, Francis J., Jr. 1926- *St&PR 91*
Frederic, Harold 1856-1898 *BioIn 16*
Frederic-Dupont, Edouard Frederic Dupont 1902- *BiDFrPL*
Frederich, Kathy W. 1953- *WhoAmW 91, WhoEmL 91*
Frederick II 1712-1786 *WorAlBi*
Frederick Augustus I 1670-1733 *PenDiDA 89*
Frederick III, German Emperor 1831-1888 *BioIn 16*
Frederick II, Holy Roman Emperor 1194-1250 *BioIn 16*
Frederick II, King of Prussia 1712-1786 *BioIn 16*

Frederick, the Great 1712-1786 *BioIn 16*
Frederick the Great 1712-1786 *LitC 14 [port]. PenDiMP*
Frederick, Bill *WhoSSW 91*
Frederick, Charlene J. 1951- *WhoAmW 91*
Frederick, Claire Cobb 1932- *BiDrAPA 89*
Frederick, Dawn Hildred Ruth 1956- *WhoWrEP 89*
Frederick, Deloras Ann 1942- *WhoAmA 91*
Frederick, Dolliver H. 1944- *WhoAm 90*
Frederick, Doyle Grimes 1935- *WhoAm 90*
Frederick, Earl James 1927- *WhoAm 90*
Frederick, Edward Charles 1930- *WhoAm 90*
Frederick, Elizabeth Ann 1954- *WhoAmW 91*
Frederick, Eugene Wallace 1927- *WhoAmA 91*
Frederick, Gary Donnell 1947- *WhoEmL 91*
Frederick, Ghislaine Renee 1933- *St&PR 91*
Frederick, Glenn *ODwPR 91*
Frederick, Helen 1945- *WhoAmA 91*
Frederick, Herbert Stanley 1930- *St&PR 91*
Frederick, Johnny 1902-1977 *Ballpl 90*
Frederick, Lafayette 1923- *WhoAm 90. WhoE 91*
Frederick, Linda Lenore 1949- *WhoWrEP 89*
Frederick, Linden *BioIn 16*
Frederick, Marijane 1953- *WhoAmW 91*
Frederick, Martin Barnett 1941- *St&PR 91*
Frederick, Michael Francis 1945- *St&PR 91*
Frederick, Pauline *BioIn 16. NewYTBS 90 [port]*
Frederick, Pauline 1885-1938 *BioAmW*
Frederick, Pauline 1906?-1990 *CurBio 90N*
Frederick, Pauline 1908-1990 *ConAu 131*
Frederick, Richard Andrew 1948- *WhoSSW 91*
Frederick, Robert L. 1939- *St&PR 91*
Frederick, Robert Lynn 1939- *WhoSSW 91*
Frederick, Rod *BioIn 16*
Frederick, Samuel Adams 1946- *WhoEmL 91*
Frederick, Saradell Ard *WhoAmA 91*
Frederick, Thomas S. 1945- *St&PR 91*
Frederick, Virginia Fiester 1916- *WhoAmW 91*
Frederick, William S. 1938- *St&PR 91*
Frederick, William Sherrad 1938- *WhoAm 90*
Frederick-Collins, Jana 1955- *WhoSSW 91*
Frederick-Mairs, Thyra Julie 1941- *WhoAmW 91*
Fredericks, Arnold *AuBYP 90*
Fredericks, Beverly Magnuson 1928- *WhoAmA 91*
Fredericks, Carlton 1910-1987 *BioIn 16*
Fredericks, Daniel Carl 1950- *WhoEmL 91*
Fredericks, David Michael 1950- *WhoEmL 91. WhoWor 91*
Fredericks, Fred 1929- *EncACom*
Fredericks, Henry Jacob 1925- *WhoWor 91*
Fredericks, James 1942- *St&PR 91*
Fredericks, Joan DeLanoy 1928- *WhoAmW 91*
Fredericks, Marshall Maynard 1908- *WhoAm 90. WhoAmA 91. WhoWor 91*
Fredericks, Norman J. 1914- *St&PR 91*
Fredericks, Norman J., Jr. 1940- *St&PR 91*
Fredericks, Norman John 1914- *WhoAm 90*
Fredericks, Sally O 1933- *BiDrAPA 89*
Fredericks, Tim *BioIn 16*
Fredericks, Vic *WhoWrEP 89*
Fredericks, Ward Arthur 1939- *WhoWor 91*
Fredericks, Wayne 1917- *WhoAm 90*
Fredericks, Wesley Charles, Jr. 1948- *WhoE 91. WhoEmL 91. WhoWor 91*
Fredericks, William Charles 1943- *St&PR 91*
Fredericks, William John 1924- *WhoSSW 91*
Fredericksen, Burton Baum 1934- *WhoAm 90*
Fredericksen, Gail Bergantino 1955- *WhoAmW 91*
Fredericksen, Jay A. 1945- *ODwPR 91*
Fredericksen, Paul H. 1945- *St&PR 91*
Frederickson, Arman Frederick 1918- *WhoAm 90*
Frederickson, Charles Richard 1938- *St&PR 91. WhoAm 90*
Frederickson, Horace George 1934- *WhoAm 90*
Frederickson, John Drew 1956- *WhoEmL 91*
Frederickson, Keith Alvin 1925- *WhoAm 90*
Frederics, Jocko *ConAu 32NR*
Frederics, Macdowell *ConAu 32NR*
Frederics, Richard 1949- *St&PR 91*
Frederiksen, Bjarne 1954- *WhoEmL 91*
Frederiksen, Henning 1924- *St&PR 91*
Frederiksen, Marilynn Elizabeth Conners 1949- *WhoAmW 91. WhoEmL 91*
Frederiksen, Patience Ann 1957- *WhoAmW 91*
Frederiksen, Paul Asger 1946- *WhoEmL 91*
Frederiksen, Robert G. 1925- *St&PR 91*
Frederiksen, William A. 1947- *St&PR 91*
Frederoel, Edna M. 1930- *St&PR 91*
Fredette, Barbara Wagner 1933- *WhoAmW 91*
Fredette, Diane Kaufman 1956- *WhoEmL 91*
Fredette, Jean Marie 1940- *WhoWrEP 89*
Fredette, Raymond David 1954- *WhoE 91*
Fredette, Richard C. 1934- *WhoAm 90. WhoE 91. WhoWor 91*
Fredette, Robert Francis 1952- *WhoE 91*
Fredga, Karl 1934- *WhoWor 91*
Frediani, Donald Joseph 1929- *St&PR 91*
Fredin, Leif Goran Reinhold 1945- *WhoSSW 91*
Fredine, Clarence Gordon 1909- *WhoAm 90*
Fredkin, Edward *BioIn 16*
Fredland, John Eric 1942- *WhoE 91*
Fredland, Kurt Roger 1948- *St&PR 91*
Fredland, Mio M *BiDrAPA 89*
Fredman, Daniel Joseph 1949- *BiDrAPA 89. WhoEmL 91*
Fredman, Faiya R 1925- *WhoAmA 91*
Fredman, Gerald S 1947- *BiDrAPA 89*
Fredman, Miriam I. *BioIn 16*
Fredman, Myer 1932- *IntWWM 90*
Fredman, Ralph 1914- *BiDrAPA 89*
Fredman, Susan Miriam 1950- *WhoAmW 91*
Fredmann, Martin 1943- *WhoAm 90*
Fredner, Randolph Mark 1955- *St&PR 91*
Fredner, Rolf 1913- *St&PR 91*
Fredrichsen, Richard Fredrick 1934- *St&PR 91*
Fredrick, Donald Arthur 1941- *St&PR 91*
Fredrick, Laurence William 1927- *WhoAm 90*
Fredrick, Nomi Judith *BiDrAPA 89*
Fredrick, Robert Frank 1948- *WhoEmL 91*
Fredrick, Susan Ray 1957- *BiDrAPA 89*
Fredrick, Susan Walker 1948- *WhoAmW 91*
Fredrick, Victoria M. 1950- *WhoAmW 91*
Fredricks, Richard 1933- *WhoAm 90*
Fredricks, Terry L. 1957- *WhoEmL 91*
Fredricksen, C.J. 1917- *St&PR 91*
Fredricksen, Cleve John 1917- *WhoAm 90*
Fredricksen, Cleve Laurance 1941- *WhoAm 90*
Fredrickson, Albert 1932- *St&PR 91*
Fredrickson, Arthur Allan 1923- *WhoAm 90*
Fredrickson, Bruce R., II 1943- *St&PR 91*
Fredrickson, Bryan Timothy 1956- *WhoEmL 91*
Fredrickson, Daniel Alan *WhoAmA 91*
Fredrickson, Donald Sharp 1924- *WhoAm 90*
Fredrickson, George Marsh 1934- *WhoAm 90*
Fredrickson, John Murray 1931- *WhoAm 90*
Fredrickson, John Wesley 1941- *St&PR 91*
Fredrickson, Lauralyn Gates *BiDrAPA 89*
Fredrickson, Lauralyn Gates 1961- *WhoEmL 91*
Fredrickson, Lawrence Thomas 1928- *WhoAm 90*
Fredrickson, Paul Austin *BiDrAPA 89*
Fredrickson, Robert Alan 1945- *WhoEmL 91*
Fredrickson, Roxanna Lynn 1952- *WhoEmL 91*
Fredrickson, Sharon Wong 1956- *WhoEmL 91*
Fredrik, Burry 1925- *WhoAm 90*
Fredriksen, Susan *BiDrAPA 89*
Fredrikson, Dennis Roy 1944- *St&PR 91*
Fredston, Arthur Howard 1929- *WhoAm 90*
Fredstrom, O'Ann Karin *BiDrAPA 89*
Free *MajTwCW*
Free, Ann Cottrell *WhoAmW 91*
Free, Betty Irene 1940- *WhoAmW 91*
Free, Dexter S. 1937- *St&PR 91. WhoAm 90*
Free, F. William *BioIn 16*
Free, John Martin 1923- *WhoAm 90*
Free, K K 1930- *WhoAmA 91*
Free, M. Virginia 1945- *St&PR 91*
Free, Mickey 1851-1913 *WhNaAH*
Free, Mike *St&PR 91*
Free, Noel Karl 1946- *BiDrAPA 89*
Free, Shirley *BioIn 16*
Free, Wendy Anne 1956- *WhoAmW 91*
Freeark, Robert James 1927- *WhoAm 90*
Freebairn, John William 1944- *WhoWor 91*
Freebeck, Robert Harry 1928- *St&PR 91*
Freeberg, Don 1924- *WhoAm 90*
Freeberg, Lawrence B. 1931- *St&PR 91*
Freeberg, Sarah Frances 1958- *WhoAmW 91*
Freeborn, Eric *BioIn 16*
Freeborough, Rita Vallino 1954- *WhoSSW 91*
Freeburg, Charles William 1946- *WhoEmL 91*
Freeburger, Thomas Oliver 1948- *WhoEmL 91*
Freebury, David Raymond *BiDrAPA 89*
Freed, Aaron David 1922- *WhoAm 90*
Freed, Alan 1922-1965 *BioIn 16. EncPR&S 89. OxCPMus. WorAlBi*
Freed, Alan David 1954- *WhoEmL 91*
Freed, Arthur 1894-1973 *OxCPMus*
Freed, Barry *MajTwCW*
Freed, Bert 1919- *WhoAm 90*
Freed, Charles Roger, Jr. 1955- *BiDrAPA 89*
Freed, David 1936- *WhoAmA 91*
Freed, David Clark 1936- *WhoAm 90*
Freed, Dean Winslow 1923- *St&PR 91. WhoAm 90*
Freed, DeBow 1925- *WhoAm 90*
Freed, Douglass Lynn 1944- *WhoAmA 91*
Freed, Erika 1957- *ODwPR 91*
Freed, Ernest Bradfield 1908- *WhoAmA 91N*
Freed, Fred 1920-1974 *BioIn 16*
Freed, Harvey M 1935- *BiDrAPA 89*
Freed, Hermine 1940- *WhoAmA 91*
Freed, Isidore 1910- *WhoE 91*
Freed, Jack Herschel 1938- *WhoAm 90*
Freed, James Ingo 1930- *WhoAm 90*
Freed, Joe Edward *BiDrAPA 89*
Freed, Joshua 1925- *St&PR 91*
Freed, K Wendy *BiDrAPA 89*
Freed, Karl Frederick 1942- *WhoAm 90*
Freed, Kenneth Alan 1957- *WhoEmL 91*
Freed, Leonard Alan 1947- *WhoEmL 91*
Freed, Lynn Ruth *WhoWrEP 89*
Freed, Marcia 1948- *BiDrAPA 89*
Freed, Murray Monroe 1924- *WhoAm 90*
Freed, Ray Forrest *WhoWrEP 89*
Freed, Richard 1928- *WhoE 91*
Freed, Richard D. 1928- *IntWWM 90*
Freed, Robert Leslie 1946- *WhoEmL 91*
Freed, Roger 1946- *Ballpl 90*
Freed, Roger Lee 1941- *BiDrAPA 89*
Freed, Russell William 1955- *St&PR 91*
Freed, Sam *BioIn 16*
Freed, Seymour 1929- *St&PR 91*
Freed, Stanley Arthur 1927- *WhoAm 90*
Freed, Susan 1954- *WhoEmL 91*
Freed, William 1902-1984 *WhoAmA 91N*
Freedberg, A. Stone 1908- *WhoAm 90*
Freedberg, Irwin Mark 1931- *WhoAm 90*
Freedberg, Leonard Earl *BiDrAPA 89*
Freedberg, Sydney Joseph 1914- *WhoAm 90. WhoAmA 91*
Freedenberg, Paul Herman 1943- *WhoAm 90*
Freedenburg, Daniel J 1943- *BiDrAPA 89*
Freedgood, Anne Goodman 1917- *WhoAm 90*
Freedland, Herbert Howard 1937- *St&PR 91*
Freedland, Jacob Berke 1913- *WhoSSW 91. WhoWor 91*
Freedland, Richard Allan 1931- *WhoAm 90*
Freedland, Sidney 1926- *St&PR 91*
Freedley, Vinton 1891-1969 *OxCPMus*
Freedman, Abraham 1914- *BiDrAPA 89*
Freedman, Alan Reinald 1935- *WhoE 91*
Freedman, Albert Zuro *WhoAm 90*
Freedman, Alfred M 1917- *BiDrAPA 89*
Freedman, Allen Royal 1940- *St&PR 91. WhoAm 90. WhoE 91*
Freedman, Andrew *Ballpl 90*
Freedman, Andrew 1860-1915 *BioIn 16*
Freedman, Anne Beller 1949- *WhoAmW 91*
Freedman, Anthony Stephen 1945- *WhoAm 90*
Freedman, Arnold Michael 1918- *WhoSSW 91*
Freedman, Arthur 1916- *St&PR 91*
Freedman, Bazil Eric 1942- *BiDrAPA 89*
Freedman, Ben 1906- *St&PR 91*
Freedman, Betty *WhoAmW 91*
Freedman, Bruce Howard 1948- *WhoEmL 91*
Freedman, Daniel X 1921- *BiDrAPA 89. WhoAm 90*
Freedman, David 1921- *St&PR 91*
Freedman, David A 1918- *BiDrAPA 89*
Freedman, David Amiel 1938- *WhoAm 90*
Freedman, David Noel 1922- *WhoAm 90. WhoWor 91*
Freedman, Deborah S 1947- *WhoAmA 91*
Freedman, Dennis Buch 1951- *WhoEmL 91*
Freedman, Donald P. 1939- *St&PR 91*
Freedman, Eric 1949- *WhoWrEP 89*
Freedman, Eugene M. 1932- *WhoAm 90*
Freedman, Frank Harlan 1924- *WhoAm 90*
Freedman, Gary K. 1952- *St&PR 91*
Freedman, Gary Richard 1947- *BiDrAPA 89*
Freedman, George Stephen 1941- *BiDrAPA 89*
Freedman, Harry 1922- *IntWWM 90. WhoAm 90*
Freedman, Helen Rosengren 1952- *WhoWrEP 89*
Freedman, Howard Joel 1945- *WhoWor 91*
Freedman, Jacqueline *WhoAmA 91*
Freedman, James Oliver 1935- *WhoAm 90. WhoE 91*
Freedman, Jay Michael 1939- *WhoWor 91*
Freedman, Jay Weil 1942- *WhoE 91*
Freedman, Jeffrey Bruce 1958- *BiDrAPA 89. WhoE 91*
Freedman, Jerome 1916- *WhoAm 90*
Freedman, Joan M. 1949- *WhoAmW 91*
Freedman, Jon Bruce 1959- *WhoEmL 91*
Freedman, Jonathan Andrew 1936- *WhoE 91*
Freedman, Jonathan Borwick 1950- *WhoAm 90*
Freedman, Joyce Beth 1945- *WhoEmL 91*
Freedman, Judith 1949- *BiDrAPA 89*
Freedman, Judith Greenberg 1939- *WhoAmW 91. WhoE 91*
Freedman, Kenneth David 1947- *WhoEmL 91. WhoWor 91*
Freedman, Larry A. 1943- *St&PR 91*
Freedman, Lawrence Z *BiDrAPA 89*
Freedman, Lawrence Zelic 1919- *WhoAm 90. WhoWor 91*
Freedman, Leon *BioIn 16*
Freedman, Marion Glickman 1922- *WhoAmW 91*
Freedman, Marvin *BiDrAPA 89*
Freedman, Maurice 1904- *WhoAmA 91N*
Freedman, Mervin Burton 1920- *WhoAm 90*
Freedman, Michael Hartley 1951- *WhoAm 90. WhoEmL 91*
Freedman, Michael Jay 1942- *BiDrAPA 89*
Freedman, Monroe Henry 1928- *WhoAm 90. WhoE 91. WhoWor 91*
Freedman, Neal 1964- *WhoE 91*
Freedman, Paul M. 1934- *BioIn 16*
Freedman, Penny Millicent 1941- *WhoAmW 91*
Freedman, Peter Eliot *BiDrAPA 89*
Freedman, Philip 1926- *WhoAm 90*
Freedman, Robert 1946- *BiDrAPA 89*
Freedman, Robert Louis 1940- *WhoAm 90*
Freedman, Ronald 1917- *WhoAm 90*
Freedman, Ronald D. 1949- *St&PR 91*
Freedman, Russell *BioIn 16*
Freedman, Russell 1929- *AuBYP 90*
Freedman, Samuel Orkin 1928- *WhoAm 90*
Freedman, Sandra Warshaw 1944- *WhoAm 90. WhoAmW 91. WhoSSW 91*
Freedman, Stanford William 1939- *St&PR 91*
Freedman, Stanley Arnold 1922- *WhoAm 90*
Freedman, Stanley Marvin 1923- *WhoAm 90*
Freedman, Steven Alan *BiDrAPA 89*
Freedman, Theodore *BioIn 16*
Freedman, Theodore Murray 1930- *St&PR 91*
Freedman, Walter 1914- *WhoAm 90*
Freedman, Walter S. 1925- *WhoAm 90*
Freedman, Wende Lee Pogust 1957- *WhoAmW 91*
Freedman, William 1929- *OxCCanT*
Freedom, John 1922- *WhoAm 90*
Freedson, Grace Elizabeth 1951- *WhoEmL 91*
Freedy, Amos 1938- *St&PR 91*
Freegard, Michael John 1933- *IntWWM 90*
Freeh, Edward James 1925- *WhoAm 90*
Freehafer, Alvin Arthur 1924- *WhoAm 90*
Freehan, Bill 1941- *Ballpl 90 [port]*
Freehan, Philip F. 1950- *St&PR 91*
Freehill, Maurice F. 1915- *WhoAm 90*
Freehill, Michael H. 1943- *St&PR 91*
Freehill, Patrick J 1940- *BiDrAPA 89*
Freehling, Deborah June 1955- *WhoEmL 91*
Freehling, Harold George, Jr. 1947- *WhoWor 91*
Freehling, Norman 1905- *St&PR 91. WhoAm 90*
Freehling, Paul Edward 1938- *WhoAm 90*
Freehling, Stanley M. 1924- *St&PR 91*
Freehling, Stanley Maxwell 1924- *WhoAm 90*
Freehling, Willard Maxwell 1913- *WhoAm 90*
Freehling, William Wilhartz 1935- *WhoAm 90. WhoWrEP 89*

Freehof, Solomon B. 1892-1990 BioIn 16, ConAu 131, NewYTBS 90 [port]
Freel, Charles William 1945- St&PR 91
Freel, James E. 1949- St&PR 91
Freeland, Claire Ann Bennett 1955- WhoEmL 91
Freeland, Colleen Louise 1957- WhoAmW 91
Freeland, James M. Jackson 1927- WhoAm 90
Freeland, Jerry M. 1936- St&PR 91
Freeland, Jesse Rae 1924- WhoWrEP 89
Freeland, John A. 1933- St&PR 91
Freeland, Judith Ann 1938- BiDrAPA 89
Freeland, Manning Corey 1925- St&PR 91
Freeland, Mark Sydnes 1943- WhoE 91
Freeland, Richard Alan 1952- BiDrAPA 89
Freeland, Sandra Tucker 1948- WhoAmW 91, WhoSSW 91, WhoWor 91
Freeland, William Lee 1929- WhoAmA 91
Freeland, William Thomas 1944- St&PR 91
Freeling, Nicolas 1927- ConAu 12AS [port], TwCCr&M 91, WorAlBi
Freeman, A.J. 1928- St&PR 91
Freeman, Adio A BiDrAPA 89
Freeman, Al, Jr. 1934- DrBlPA 90
Freeman, Alan Lyon 1951- WhoAm 90
Freeman, Albert E. 1931- WhoAm 90
Freeman, Alice Marie BiDrAPA 89
Freeman, Anita Nalini 1957- IntWWM 90
Freeman, Ann-Mary BiDEWW
Freeman, Anne Hobson 1934- WhoAmW 91, WhoWrEP 89
Freeman, Anthony L. BioIn 16
Freeman, Arthur 1925- WhoAm 90
Freeman, Arthur J. 1930- WhoAm 90
Freeman, Barbara 1951- St&PR 91
Freeman, Barbara Joyce 1953- WhoE 91
Freeman, Barbara M. 1947- ConAu 132
Freeman, Bee DrBlPA 90
Freeman, Benjamin Harrison, II 1936- St&PR 91
Freeman, Betty 1921- BioIn 16
Freeman, Betty N. 1940- WhoSSW 91
Freeman, Bob A. 1926- WhoAm 90
Freeman, Brian M. BioIn 16
Freeman, Bruce 1942- St&PR 91
Freeman, Buck 1871-1949 Ballpl 90 [port]
Freeman, Bud BioIn 16
Freeman, Bud 1906- OxCPMus
Freeman, Carl F. 1929- St&PR 91
Freeman, Carol Anne 1940- WhoAmW 91
Freeman, Carol Hart 1955- WhoAmW 91
Freeman, Carolyn Ruth 1950- WhoAm 90
Freeman, Carroll Benton 1951- IntWWM 90
Freeman, Cathy Lynn 1962- WhoSSW 91
Freeman, Charles W., Jr. 1943- WhoWor 91
Freeman, Claire E. WhoAm 90
Freeman, Clarence Calvin 1923- WhoAm 90
Freeman, Clifford Lee 1941- WhoAm 90
Freeman, Colenton Morgan 1955- WhoWor 91
Freeman, Corinne 1926- WhoAm 90
Freeman, Cynthia BioIn 16
Freeman, Cynthia 1915-1988 AnObit 1988
Freeman, Cynthia Jo 1947- WhoAm 90
Freeman, Daniel Moshe Avrom 1939- BiDrAPA 89
Freeman, Darlene Marie 1951- WhoHisp 91
Freeman, David 1944- WhoAm 90
Freeman, David 1947- OxCCanT [port]
Freeman, David E 1945- ConAu 131
Freeman, David F 1925- BiDrAPA 89
Freeman, David Forgan 1918- WhoAm 90
Freeman, David Franklin, Jr. 1959- WhoEmL 91
Freeman, David L 1937- WhoAmA 91
Freeman, David Lynn 1924- WhoAm 90
Freeman, Deborah Lynn 1955- WhoEmL 91
Freeman, Dennis Earl 1942- St&PR 91
Freeman, Dianne Mendoza 1947- WhoAmW 91, WhoWor 91
Freeman, Dick WhoAm 90
Freeman, Dirk Blair 1935- St&PR 91
Freeman, Don 1908-1978 AuBYP 90
Freeman, Don 1909-1978 WhoAmA 91N
Freeman, Donald Chester, Jr. 1930- WhoAm 90
Freeman, Donald K 1934- BiDrAPA 89
Freeman, Donald Wayne 1947- St&PR 91
Freeman, Donald Wilford 1929- WhoSSW 91, WhoWor 91
Freeman, Doris Branch 1925- WhoSSW 91
Freeman, Dorothy Dale 1909- WhoSSW 91
Freeman, Douglas Southall 1886-1953 BioIn 16
Freeman, Edward Livingston 1835-1907 AmLegL
Freeman, Edwin Armistead 1928- IntWWM 90
Freeman, Edwin N 1929- BiDrAPA 89
Freeman, Elaine Lavalle 1929- WhoAmW 91, WhoE 91
Freeman, Ellen S. ODwPR 91
Freeman, Elsie Joan BiDrAPA 89
Freeman, Emery W., II 1961- WhoE 91
Freeman, Ernest Lucier, III 1953- WhoSSW 91
Freeman, Ernest Robert 1933- WhoAm 90
Freeman, Eugene 1906- AuBYP 90
Freeman, Felix Joachim BioIn 16
Freeman, Florence Eleanor 1921- WhoAmW 91
Freeman, Floyd Mickel 1946- WhoSSW 91
Freeman, Frank S. BioIn 16
Freeman, Frankie Muse BioIn 16
Freeman, Fred BioIn 16
Freeman, Fred W. 1925- St&PR 91
Freeman, Gary W. 1948- St&PR 91
Freeman, Geoffrey E. 1949- WhoE 91
Freeman, George 1930- St&PR 91
Freeman, George Clemon, Jr. 1929- WhoAm 90
Freeman, George Lester 1928- WhoAm 90
Freeman, George Thomas 1930- WhoWor 91
Freeman, Gerald M. 1937- St&PR 91
Freeman, Gertrude 1927- WhoAmA 91
Freeman, Gillian 1929- FemiCLE
Freeman, Godfrey AuBYP 90
Freeman, Graham P. M. 1946- WhoAm 90
Freeman, Graydon LaVerne 1904- WhoAm 90
Freeman, Hal M. 1936-1988 BioIn 16
Freeman, Harold P. BioIn 16
Freeman, Harold Paul 1933- WhoAm 90
Freeman, Harrop Arthur 1907- WhoAm 90
Freeman, Harry Cole 1920- St&PR 91
Freeman, Harry Louis 1932- St&PR 91, WhoAm 90
Freeman, Harry Lynwood 1920- WhoAm 90
Freeman, Henry McCall 1947- WhoAm 90
Freeman, Herbert 1925- WhoAm 90
Freeman, Hersh 1928- Ballpl 90
Freeman, Horace L. 1922- St&PR 91
Freeman, Houghton 1921- St&PR 91
Freeman, Howard Edgar 1929- WhoAm 90
Freeman, Howard G. 1918- St&PR 91
Freeman, Howard Keith 1953- WhoE 91
Freeman, Howard L., Jr. 1935- St&PR 91
Freeman, Howard Lee, Jr. 1935- WhoAm 90
Freeman, Hugh James 1947- WhoAm 90
Freeman, Ira Henry 1906- WhoAm 90
Freeman, Ira Maximilian 1905-1987 BioIn 16
Freeman, Ira Maximillian 1905- AuBYP 90
Freeman, Jack St&PR 91
Freeman, Jack E. 1931- WhoAm 90
Freeman, James Darcy 1907- WhoWor 91
Freeman, James William 1928- St&PR 91
Freeman, Jane 1885-1963 WhoAmA 91N
Freeman, Jane Anne 1953- St&PR 91
Freeman, Jane Rosalie 1955- WhoAmW 91
Freeman, Janet Elizabeth 1956- WhoEmL 91
Freeman, Jennifer 1956- WhoEmL 91
Freeman, Jere Evans 1936- WhoAm 90
Freeman, Joe Bailey 1937- WhoAm 90, WhoSSW 91
Freeman, John Albert 1920- EncO&P 3
Freeman, John Mark 1933- WhoAm 90
Freeman, Joseph Morris 1925- St&PR 91
Freeman, Josh 1949- WhoEmL 91
Freeman, Kathleen TwCCr&M 91
Freeman, Kathryn 1956- WhoAmA 91
Freeman, Kenn DrBlPA 90
Freeman, Kenneth M. 1949- WhoEmL 91
Freeman, Kenneth W. 1950- St&PR 91
Freeman, Kester St. Clair, Jr. 1944- WhoAm 90
Freeman, Kim ODwPR 91
Freeman, L.L. St&PR 91N
Freeman, Larry S 1946- BiDrAPA 89
Freeman, Lee Allen, Jr. 1940- WhoAm 90
Freeman, Legh Richmond 1842-1915 BioIn 16
Freeman, Leisa 1955- WhoWor 91
Freeman, Leo C 1923- BiDrAPA 89
Freeman, Leonard Murray 1937- WhoAm 90
Freeman, Leslie Gordon 1935- WhoAm 90
Freeman, Linda 1951- WhoSSW 91
Freeman, Linda N 1950- BiDrAPA 89
Freeman, Linton Clarke 1927- WhoAm 90
Freeman, Louis McDaniel 1940- WhoSSW 91
Freeman, Louis S. 1940- WhoAm 90
Freeman, Lucy 1916- WhoAm 90
Freeman, Mae 1907- AuBYP 90
Freeman, Mallory Bruce 1938- WhoAmA 91
Freeman, Marcus A., Jr. 1934- WhoWrEP 89
Freeman, Mark WhoWrEP 89
Freeman, Mark 1908- WhoAm 90, WhoAmA 91
Freeman, Mark Leslie BiDrAPA 89
Freeman, Mark Price, Jr. 1930- WhoAm 90
Freeman, Mark William 1949- WhoEmL 91
Freeman, Marvin 1963- Ballpl 90
Freeman, Mary 1852-1930 FemiCLE
Freeman, Mary E. Wilkins 1852-1930 BioAmW
Freeman, Maurice Tracy 1904- WhoAm 90
Freeman, Max Herbert 1907- WhoAm 90
Freeman, Meredith Norwin 1920- WhoAm 90
Freeman, Michael A. BiDrAPA 89
Freeman, Michael G. 1938- St&PR 91
Freeman, Milton Malcolm Roland 1934- WhoAm 90
Freeman, Milton Victor 1911- WhoAm 90, WhoE 91, WhoWor 91
Freeman, Montine McDaniel 1915- WhoAm 90, WhoWor 91
Freeman, Morgan BioIn 16
Freeman, Morgan 1937- DrBlPA 90, News 90 [port], WhoAm 90
Freeman, Morgan 1939?- WorAlBi
Freeman, Morton S. 1912- WhoAm 90
Freeman, Myrna Faye 1939- WhoAmW 91
Freeman, Nancy 1932- SmATA 61 [port]
Freeman, Neal Blackwell 1940- WhoAm 90
Freeman, Neil 1948- WhoEmL 91
Freeman, Norman William 1933- St&PR 91
Freeman, Olen I, Jr. 1924- BiDrAPA 89
Freeman, Orville Lothrop 1918- BiDrUSE 89, WhoAm 90
Freeman, Palmer 1944- WhoSSW 91
Freeman, Pat S. 1943- WhoWrEP 89
Freeman, Patricia Elizabeth 1924- WhoAmW 91, WhoWor 91
Freeman, Paul 1936- BioIn 16, IntWWM 90, PenDiMP
Freeman, Paul Lamar 1907-1988 BioIn 16
Freeman, Paul Randolph 1957- WhoAm 90, WhoEmL 91
Freeman, Peter Craig 1956- WhoAm 90
Freeman, Peter J. WhoWrEP 89
Freeman, Philip Conrad, Jr. 1937- WhoAm 90
Freeman, Phillip S BiDrAPA 89
Freeman, Phyllis Therese 1928- WhoAmW 91, WhoWor 91
Freeman, R Austin 1862-1943 TwCCr&M 91
Freeman, R. B. 1915-1986 BioIn 16
Freeman, Ralph Douglas 1936- St&PR 91
Freeman, Ralph McKenzie NewYTBS 90
Freeman, Ralph McKenzie 1902-1990 BioIn 16
Freeman, Raymond L. 1920- St&PR 91
Freeman, Raymond Lee 1919- WhoAm 90
Freeman, Reino Samuel 1919- WhoAm 90
Freeman, Richard Benton 1931- WhoAm 90
Freeman, Richard Boyd 1947- WhoEmL 91
Freeman, Richard Broke 1915-1986 BioIn 16
Freeman, Richard C. 1926- WhoAm 90, WhoSSW 91
Freeman, Richard Francis 1934- WhoAm 90
Freeman, Richard Mark 1958- WhoE 91
Freeman, Richard Merrell 1921- WhoAm 90
Freeman, Richard Myron 1933- WhoAm 90
Freeman, Robert WhoAmA 91
Freeman, Robert Alan 1947- WhoEmL 91
Freeman, Robert John 1947- WhoEmL 91
Freeman, Robert Lee 1939- WhoAmA 91
Freeman, Robert M. WhoAm 90
Freeman, Robert Mallory BioIn 16
Freeman, Robert Mallory 1941- St&PR 91, WhoAm 90, WhoSSW 91
Freeman, Robert Mark 1942- WhoAm 90
Freeman, Robert Parke 1945- St&PR 91
Freeman, Robert Schofield 1935- IntWWM 90, WhoAm 90
Freeman, Robert Turner, Jr. 1918- WhoAm 90
Freeman, Roger Adolph 1904- WhoAm 90
Freeman, Roger John 1944- WhoWor 91
Freeman, Roland L. 1936- BioIn 16
Freeman, Ronald Larry 1947- WhoSSW 91
Freeman, Rowland Godfrey, III 1922- WhoAm 90
Freeman, Rudolf R. BioIn 16
Freeman, Rudolph, Jr. BiDrAPA 89
Freeman, Russell A. 1932- St&PR 91
Freeman, Russell Adams 1932- WhoAm 90
Freeman, Ruth B. 1906-1982 BioIn 16
Freeman, Samuel Ralph 1929- St&PR 91, WhoAm 90
Freeman, Scot Lewis 1958- WhoEmL 91
Freeman, Serge Herbert AuBYP 90
Freeman, Shelley 1958- WhoEmL 91
Freeman, Simon David 1926- WhoAm 90
Freeman, Stanislaw M BiDrAPA 89
Freeman, Stephan John 1956- WhoEmL 91
Freeman, Susan Swartzman 1957- WhoAmW 91, WhoEmL 91
Freeman, Susan Tax 1938- WhoAm 90
Freeman, Thomas E. 1930- St&PR 91
Freeman, Thomas J. 1924- ODwPR 91
Freeman, Thomas Lee 1951- St&PR 91
Freeman, Thomas Walter 1908-1988 BioIn 16
Freeman, Thomas Warren BiDrAPA 89
Freeman, Tina 1951- WhoAmA 91
Freeman, Val BioIn 16
Freeman, Victor J 1918- BiDrAPA 89
Freeman, Walter Coombs, Jr. 1941- WhoSSW 91
Freeman, William 1946- St&PR 91
Freeman, William A. 1943- St&PR 91
Freeman, William Bradford 1938- BioIn 16
Freeman, William Crawford BiDrAPA 89
Freeman, William David 1951- WhoEmL 91
Freeman, William Emmett 1957- WhoSSW 91
Freeman, William Ernest, Jr. 1913- WhoAm 90
Freeman, William M. 1913-1990 BioIn 16, ConAu 130, NewYTBS 90
Freeman, William M. 1919- St&PR 91
Freeman, William Peter 1949- WhoSSW 91
Freeman-Appelbaum, Margery WhoAmA 91
Freeman-Baraka, Rhonda Nichelle 1962- WhoAmW 91
Freeman-Longo, Robert Earl 1951- WhoEmL 91
Freeman Yeatts, Dorothy Elizabeth Butler 1925- WhoSSW 91
Freemantle, Brian 1936- TwCCr&M 91
Freemantle, Brian Harry 1936- SpyFic
Freemesser, George F 1933- BiDrAPA 89
Freemyer, Reginald Wayne 1960- WhoEmL 91
Freeny, Patrick Clinton 1942- WhoAm 90
Freer, Ada Goodrich EncO&P 3
Freer, Charles L. 1856-1919 WorAlBi
Freer, Coburn 1939- WhoAm 90
Freer, Howard Mortimer 1904-1960 WhoAmA 91N
Freer, John Herschel 1938- BiDrAPA 89, WhoAm 90
Freer, Lawrence Clayton BioIn 16
Freer, Robert Elliott, Jr. 1941- WhoAm 90, WhoWor 91
Freericks, Mary Avakian 1935- WhoWrEP 89
Freerksen, Deborah Lynne 1956- WhoAmW 91
Freerksen, Enno 1910- WhoWor 91
Freerksen, Gregory Nathan 1951- WhoWor 91
Freers, Theodore Frederick 1937- St&PR 91
Frees, Karen Ann 1962- WhoAmW 91
Freese, Ernst 1925-1990 BioIn 16
Freese, Frank Edward 1940- St&PR 91
Freese, Gene 1934- Ballpl 90
Freese, Howard L. 1941- St&PR 91
Freese, Melanie Louise 1945- WhoAmW 91
Freese, Peter 1939- WhoWor 91
Freese, Robert Gerard 1929- St&PR 91, WhoAm 90
Freesen, O. Robert 1925- St&PR 91
Freeston, Kenneth Russell 1950- WhoE 91
Freet, John F., Jr. 1949- St&PR 91
Freeth, Douglas D. 1935- St&PR 91
Freeth, Douglas Duncan 1935- WhoAm 90
Freeze, James Donald 1932- WhoAm 90
Freeze, Nancy Sue 1939- St&PR 91
Freeze, Thomas W. 1951- St&PR 91
Frega, Mark Richard 1961- WhoE 91
Fregeau, Jerome Heyde 1929- WhoAm 90
Fregetto, Eugene Fletcher 1947- WhoEmL 91
Fregosi, Claudia 1946- AuBYP 90
Fregosi, Jim 1942- Ballpl 90
Frei, Alphonse Emil 1938- St&PR 91
Frei, Emil, III 1924- WhoAm 90
Frei, Gebhard 1905-1967 EncO&P 3, EncPaPR 91
Frei, Hans W. 1922-1988 BioIn 16
Frei, John Karen 1936- WhoAmW 91
Frei, Norbert E. 1955- WhoWor 91
Frei, Robert Reed 1923- WhoAm 90
Frei, Rudolph John BiDrAPA 89
Frei Montalva, Eduardo 1911-1982 BioIn 16
Freiberg, Brenda Randall 1938- WhoAmW 91
Freiberg, Karen Louise 1944- WhoAmW 91
Freiberg, Lowell Carl 1939- St&PR 91, WhoAm 90

Freiberg, Stanley K 1923- *ConAu 31NR*
Freiberger, Fred *BioIn 16*
Freiberger, Walter Frederick 1924- *WhoAm 90, WhoWor 91*
Freibert, Lucy M. 1922- *WhoWrEP 89*
Freiburg, Magdalena von 1407?-1485 *EncCoWW*
Freiburger, Betsey *WhoWrEP 89*
Freid, Jacob *WhoAm 90*
Freidberg, Jill *BioIn 16*
Freidberg, Sidney 1914- *WhoAm 90, WhoWor 91*
Freidberg, Stephen P. 1939- *St&PR 91, WhoAm 90*
Freidel, Frank Burt, Jr. 1916- *WhoAm 90*
Freidenbergs, Ingrid 1944- *WhoAmW 91*
Freidheim, Cyrus F., Jr. 1935- *St&PR 91, WhoWor 91*
Freidin, Miriam Ross 1947- *BiDrAPA 89*
Freidinger, Arthur W 1916- *BiDrAPA 89*
Freidinger, Roger Merlin 1947- *WhoE 91*
Freidkin, George Jacob 1946- *WhoSSW 91*
Freidson, Eliot Lazarus 1923- *WhoAm 90*
Freidus, Bunny *BioIn 16*
Freidus-Katz, Lauren Sue *BiDrAPA 89*
Freier, Jerome Elden 1946- *WhoAm 90, WhoEmL 91*
Freier, Morton L 1915- *BiDrAPA 89*
Freier, Susan Marcie 1953- *WhoEmL 91*
Freiert, Donald Vincent, Jr. 1947- *WhoAm 90*
Freifeld, Charles Jay 1942- *WhoE 91*
Freifeld, Eric 1919- *WhoAmA 91N*
Freigang, Dietrich 1940- *St&PR 91*
Freigau, Howard 1902-1932 *Ballpl 90*
Freiheit, Clayton Fredric 1938- *WhoAm 90*
Freiherr von Aretin, Karl Otmar 1923- *WhoWor 91*
Freiherr von Handel, Norbert Erasmus 1942- *WhoWor 91*
Freiherr von Kleydorff, Ludwig Otto A. 1926- *WhoAm 90*
Freiherr Von Loe, Roderich 1958- *WhoWor 91*
Freiherr von Villiez, Hansjurgen 1927- *WhoWor 91*
Freihofer, Charles Christian 1941- *St&PR 91*
Freihofer, Hans Peter Michael 1937- *WhoWor 91*
Freiler, Frank Joseph 1955- *WhoEmL 91*
Freilich, Ann 1910- *WhoE 91*
Freilich, Jeff 1948- *WhoAm 90*
Freilich, Joan Sherman 1941- *WhoAmW 91*
Freilich, Judith Salzman *BiDrAPA 89*
Freilich, Michael L 1912-1975 *WhoAmA 91N*
Freilicher, Ira Lee 1937- *St&PR 91*
Freilicher, Jane *BioIn 16*
Freilicher, Jane 1924- *WhoAm 90, WhoAmA 91*
Freilicher, Melvyn S. 1946- *WhoWrEP 89*
Freilinger, Ida M. W. 1943- *WhoWrEP 89*
Freiman, Alvin Henry 1927- *WhoE 91, WhoWor 91*
Freiman, David Burl 1947- *WhoAm 90, WhoWor 91*
Freiman, David Galland 1911- *WhoAm 90*
Freiman, Gerald V *BiDrAPA 89*
Freiman, Herbert S. 1930- *WhoAm 90*
Freiman, Lela Kay 1939- *WhoAmW 91*
Freiman, Robert J 1917- *WhoAmA 91*
Freimarck, George Stephen Alfred 1917- *WhoE 91*
Freimark, Bob 1922- *WhoAmA 91*
Freimark, Jeffrey Philip 1955- *St&PR 91, WhoAm 90*
Freimark, Robert 1922- *WhoAm 90*
Freimer, Nelson B. *BiDrAPA 89*
Freimer, Susanna 1951- *BiDrAPA 89*
Freimuth, Joan Maria *BiDrAPA 89*
Freinhar, Jack P. *BiDrAPA 89*
Freinkel, Norbert 1926-1989 *BioIn 16*
Freinkel, Ruth Kimmelstiel 1926- *WhoAm 90*
Freire, Gloria Medonis 1929- *WhoAmW 91*
Freire, Jose R 1942- *BiDrAPA 89*
Freire, Manuel 1924- *BioIn 16*
Freire, Nelson 1944- *PenDiMP*
Freire, P. *ConAu 132*
Freire, Paulo 1921- *BioIn 16, ConAu 132*
Freire, Ramon 1787-1851 *BioIn 16*
Freire Falcao, Jose 1925- *WhoWor 91*
Freireich, Anna *BiDrAPA 89*
Freireich, Emil J 1927- *WhoAm 90*
Freirich, Ian Haskell 1958- *BiDrAPA 89*
Freirich, Jeff Robert 1946- *St&PR 91*
Freis, Edward David 1912- *WhoAm 90, WhoWor 91*
Freischlag, Paul H., Jr. 1954- *St&PR 91*
Freise, Bruce Harry 1935- *St&PR 91*
Freise, Kathryn Maria 1962- *WhoEmL 91*
Freiser, Ben Sherman 1951- *WhoAm 90*
Freisheim, James Harold 1937- *WhoAm 90*
Freisleben, Dave 1951- *Ballpl 90*
Freitag, Barbara Jo 1948- *WhoAmW 91*
Freitag, Erik 1940- *IntWWM 90*
Freitag, Frederick Gerald 1952- *WhoEmL 91, WhoWor 91*
Freitag, Harlow 1936- *WhoAm 90*
Freitag, Henry George 1932- *St&PR 91*
Freitag, James Milton 1953- *WhoEmL 91*
Freitag, Robert Frederick 1920- *WhoAm 90*
Freitag, Wolfgang Martin 1924- *WhoAm 90, WhoAmA 91*
Freitas, Cathryn Radin 1954- *WhoAmW 91*
Freitas, Joe A. 1926- *St&PR 91*
Freitas, Jose Pedro de *EncPaPR 91*
Freitas, Randall William 1951- *WhoE 91, WhoSSW 91*
Freitas, Tony 1908- *Ballpl 90*
Freitas Branco, Pedro de 1896-1963 *PenDiMP*
Freivalds, John 1944- *WhoWrEP 89*
Freiwald, Tani *BioIn 16*
Freizer, Louis A. 1931- *WhoAm 90, WhoE 91, WhoWor 91*
Frejacques, Claude Jacques 1924- *WhoWor 91*
Freke, Elizabeth 1641-1714 *BiDEWW, FemiCLE*
Freleng, Friz 1906- *ConTFT 8*
Freleng, I. *ConTFT 8*
Frelich, Phyllis 1944- *WhoAm 90*
Freligh, Helen Holcomb 1907- *WhoAmW 91*
Freling, Richard Alan 1932- *WhoAm 90*
Frelinger, Jeffrey Allen 1948- *WhoSSW 91*
Frelinghuysen, Frederick Theodore 1817-1885 *BiDrUSE 89, BioIn 16*
Frelinghuysen, Joseph Sherman 1941- *St&PR 91*
Frelinghuysen, Joseph Sherman, Jr. 1941- *WhoAm 90*
Frelinghuysen, Peter H. B. 1916- *WhoAm 90*
Frelinghuysen, Suzy 1912-1988 *BioIn 16*
Frelinghuysen, Theodore 1787-1862 *BioIn 16*
Frelinghuysen, Theodorus Jacobus 1691-1748? *EncCRAm*
Frell, Ellen Frances 1950- *WhoWrEP 89*
Frellsen, David Hugh 1941- *St&PR 91*
Frels, Bonita Marie Kozub 1949- *IntWWM 90*
Frels, William Bernard 1939- *St&PR 91*
Fremaux, Louis 1921- *PenDiMP*
Fremaux, Louis Joseph Felix 1921- *IntWWM 90*
Frembgen, Theodore Edward 1936- *St&PR 91*
Fremlin, Celia 1914- *TwCCr&M 91*
Fremon, Richard C. 1918- *WhoE 91*
Fremont, Ernest Hoar, Jr. 1925- *WhoWor 91*
Fremont, Jessie Benton 1824-1902 *BioAmW*
Fremont, John C. 1813-1890 *WorAlBi*
Fremont, John Charles 1813-1890 *BioIn 16, WhNaAH [port]*
Fremont-Smith, Marion R. 1926- *WhoAm 90*
Fremont-Smith, Richard 1935- *WhoE 91*
Fremont-Smith, Thayer 1931- *WhoAm 90*
Fremouw, Edward Joseph 1934- *WhoAm 90*
Fremstad, Olive 1871-1951 *PenDiMP*
Fremund, Zdenek Anthony 1946- *WhoE 91*
Frenay, Henri 1905-1988 *AnObit 1988, BioIn 16*
Frenaye, John Wray 1925- *St&PR 91*
French, A. P. 1920- *BioIn 16*
French, Alain Stanley 1948- *WhoSSW 91*
French, Alden, Jr. 1934- *St&PR 91*
French, Alexander Murdoch 1920-1987 *BioIn 16*
French, Alfred Porter 1941- *BiDrAPA 89*
French, Alfred W., Jr. 1903- *St&PR 91*
French, Alice *BioAmW*
French, Alvin Eugene 1927- *BiDrAPA 89, WhoE 91*
French, Anthony Philip 1920- *BioIn 16, WhoAm 90*
French, Arthur *DrBlPA 90*
French, Arthur Leeman, Jr. 1940- *WhoAm 90*
French, Benjamin B. 1800-1870 *BioIn 16*
French, Benjamin L., Jr. 1924- *ODwPR 91*
French, Bertram F. 1927- *St&PR 91*
French, Bevan Meredith 1937- *WhoAm 90*
French, Bruce Hartung 1915- *WhoAm 90*
French, Calvin Leonard 1934-1986 *BioIn 16*
French, Carol Ann 1944- *WhoAmW 91*
French, Carolyn J. 1946- *St&PR 91*
French, Catherine 1946- *WhoAm 90*
French, Charles Ezra 1923- *WhoAm 90*
French, Charles Ferris, Jr. 1918- *St&PR 91, WhoAm 90*
French, Charles Stacy 1907- *WhoAm 90*
French, Christopher W. *BioIn 16*
French, Christopher W. 1940?-1989 *ConAu 129*
French, Colin Val 1957- *WhoEmL 91*
French, Dainforth Baker 1940- *St&PR 91*
French, Daniel Chester 1850-1931 *BioIn 16, WorAlBi*
French, Daniel W. *BioIn 16*
French, David 1939- *BioIn 16, OxCCanT [port]*
French, David Heath 1918- *WhoAm 90*
French, Dolores *BioIn 16*
French, Donald Anthony 1955- *St&PR 91*
French, Dorothy Kayser 1926- *AuBYP 90*
French, E. J., Mrs. *EncO&P 3*
French, E Yulee 1926- *WhoWrEP 89*
French, Eleanor Clark *NewYTBS 90 [port]*
French, Elizabeth Irene 1938- *WhoSSW 91*
French, Emily S. 1830-1912 *EncO&P 3*
French, Eunice Pelafigue 1938- *WhoAm 90*
French, Everett Earl *BiDrAPA 89*
French, Glendon Everett, Jr. 1934- *WhoAm 90*
French, H. Louis 1940- *St&PR 91*
French, Harold Stanley 1921- *WhoE 91, WhoWor 91*
French, Henry Pierson, Jr. 1934- *WhoE 91, WhoWor 91*
French, Herbert Eliot 1912- *WhoAm 90*
French, Hollis, II 1927- *St&PR 91*
French, Jack Wm. 1917- *St&PR 91*
French, James T. 1931- *St&PR 91*
French, James William 1935- *St&PR 91, WhoAm 90*
French, Jameson Stevens 1954- *WhoE 91*
French, Jeffrey Stuart 1954- *WhoE 91*
French, Jim 1941- *Ballpl 90*
French, Joe F. 1926- *St&PR 91*
French, John Douglas 1911-1989 *BioIn 16*
French, John Dwyer 1933- *WhoAm 90, WhoWor 91*
French, John Henry, Jr. 1911- *WhoAm 90*
French, Judson Cull 1922- *WhoAm 90*
French, Larry 1907- *Ballpl 90 [port]*
French, Larry B. 1958- *St&PR 91*
French, Larry J. 1940- *St&PR 91*
French, Lew Daniel, III 1960- *WhoEmL 91*
French, Lexie Anne 1949- *WhoAmW 91*
French, Linda J. 1947- *St&PR 91*
French, Linda Jean 1947- *WhoAm 90*
French, Lisa 1953- *St&PR 91*
French, Lucy Virginia 1825-1881 *FemiCLE*
French, Lyle Albert 1915- *WhoAm 90*
French, M. DeVonne 1940- *BiDrAPA 89*
French, Marcus Emmett 1929- *WhoAm 90*
French, Margaret S 1918- *BiDrAPA 89*
French, Marilyn 1929- *ConAu 31NR, ConLC 60 [port], FemiCLE, MajTwCW, WhoAm 90, WhoWrEP 89*
French, Marion Flood *AuBYP 90*
French, Mark Dennis 1954- *WhoEmL 91*
French, Melvin Perry 1962- *WhoE 91*
French, Michael 1944- *BioIn 16*
French, Michael Bruce 1954- *WhoSSW 91*
French, Michael Harvey 1949- *WhoWrEP 89*
French, Nelson 1925- *St&PR 91*
French, Norma *BioIn 16*
French, Oliver 1921- *BiDrAPA 89, WhoE 91*
French, Patsy Ruth Jones 1936- *IntWWM 90*
French, Paul *AuBYP 90, MajTwCW*
French, Perrin Lindol 1943- *BiDrAPA 89*
French, Philip F. 1932- *St&PR 91*
French, Philip Franks 1932- *WhoAm 90*
French, Ray H 1919- *WhoAmA 91*
French, Raymond 1920- *St&PR 91, WhoAm 90*
French, Richard Frederic 1915- *IntWWM 90, WhoAm 90*
French, Richard Harry 1947- *WhoEmL 91*
French, Richard Noble, Jr. *BiDrAPA 89*
French, Robert Neil Hyde 1944- *WhoWor 91*
French, Robert Warren 1911- *WhoAm 90*
French, Sharon Marie 1952- *WhoSSW 91*
French, Shelby 1949- *WhoSSW 91*
French, Stanley George 1933- *WhoAm 90, WhoWrEP 89*
French, Stephanie 1951- *ODwPR 91*
French, Stephanie Taylor *WhoAmW 91*
French, Stephen Warren 1934- *WhoAmA 91*
French, Tania Gabrielle 1963- *IntWWM 90*
French, Thomas C. 1949- *St&PR 91*
French, Thomas Valpy 1825-1891 *BioIn 16*
French, Valerie *NewYTBS 90*
French, Vera V *BiDrAPA 89*
French, Victor *BioIn 16*
French, Virginia Lee 1939- *WhoAmW 91*
French, Walter 1899-1984 *Ballpl 90*
French, Warren Graham 1922- *WhoWor 91*
French, William Harold 1926- *WhoAm 90*
French, William Percy 1854-1920 *OxCPMus*
French-Christian, Lillian *EarBlAP*
Frenchak, Harry Nicholas 1939- *St&PR 91*
Frendt, Richard J. 1942- *St&PR 91*
Freneau, Philip 1752-1832 *BioIn 16, EncCRAm*
Freneau, Philip M. 1752-1832 *WorAlBi*
Frenette, Donald H. 1939- *ODwPR 91*
Frenger, Paul Fred 1946- *WhoEmL 91, WhoWor 91*
Frengut, Renee Hirsch 1945- *WhoAmW 91*
Freni, Mirella 1935- *IntWWM 90, PenDiMP, WhoAm 90, WhoWor 91*
Frenier, James Francis 1934- *St&PR 91*
Frenier, Thomas J. *St&PR 91*
Frenkel, Abraham Ramy *BiDrAPA 89*
Frenkel, David Scott 1953- *BiDrAPA 89*
Frenkel, Eugene Phillip 1929- *WhoAm 90*
Frenkel, Karen A. 1955- *WhoWrEP 89*
Frenkel, Michael 1936- *St&PR 91*
Frenkel, Nama Rachel 1951- *WhoE 91*
Frenkel, Rhoda S *BiDrAPA 89*
Frenkiel, Richard Henry 1943- *WhoAm 90*
Frenklach, Michael Yehoshua 1947- *WhoE 91*
Frenklova, Jana 1947- *IntWWM 90*
Frenn, Thomas Louis 1947- *WhoEmL 91*
Frenock, Larry 1956- *WhoEmL 91*
Frenois, Michel Albert 1939- *WhoWor 91*
Frentsos, Jeanne Marie 1958- *WhoEmL 91*
Frenyea, Melissa Mary 1968- *WhoEmL 91*
Frenyo, Zoltan 1955- *WhoWor 91*
Frenze, Robyn *ODwPR 91*
Frenzel, Bill 1928- *WhoAm 90*
Frenzel, Otto N., III 1930- *WhoAm 90*
Frenzel, Otto Nicholas, III *BioIn 16*
Frenzel, Otto Nicholas, III 1930- *St&PR 91*
Frenzer, Peter Frederick 1934- *St&PR 91, WhoAm 90*
Frere, Alexander Stuart 1892-1984 *DcNaB 1981*
Frere, John Edward 1947- *St&PR 91*
Frere, Mary Eliza 1845-1911 *FemiCLE*
Frerejean, Pierre Edward 1954- *WhoWor 91*
Freres, Ronald P. 1943- *St&PR 91*
Freret, Jean-Paul 1937- *WhoWor 91*
Frerichs, Ernest Sunley 1925- *WhoAm 90*
Frerichs, Ruth Colcord *WhoAmA 91*
Frerichs, Sarah Cutts *WhoE 91*
Freriks, Donald James 1944- *St&PR 91*
Freris, Andrew Francis 1945- *WhoWor 91*
Fresch, Marie Beth 1957- *WhoAmW 91, WhoWor 91*
Freschet, Berniece Louise 1927- *AuBYP 90*
Freschi, Bruno Basilio 1937- *WhoWor 91*
Fresco, Jacques Robert 1928- *WhoAm 90*
Frescobaldi, Fiammetta 1523-1586 *EncCoWW*
Frescobaldi, Girolamo 1583-1643 *BioIn 16*
Frescoln, Katharine Pitman 1917- *WhoAmW 91*
Frese, Millie Kay 1963- *WhoWrEP 89*
Frese, Walter Wenzel 1909- *WhoAm 90*
Freshwater, David 1950- *WhoE 91*
Freshwater, Michael Felix 1948- *WhoAm 90, WhoSSW 91*
Freske, Richard Clarence 1940- *St&PR 91*
Fresno Larrain, Juan Francisco 1914- *WhoWor 91*
Freso, Tibor 1918- *IntWWM 90*
Freson, Barbara D. 1942- *ODwPR 91*
Fresquez, Ernest C. 1955- *WhoHisp 91*
Fresquez, Ralph E. 1934- *WhoHisp 91*
Fressie, John 1939- *St&PR 91*
Freston, Thomas E. 1945- *WhoE 91*
Freston, Tom *BioIn 16*
Fret, Rosemarie 1935- *EncCoWW*
Freter, Lisa 1951- *WhoAmW 91, WhoEmL 91*
Freter, Mark Allen 1947- *WhoEmL 91, WhoWor 91*
Frets, Barbara J *WhoAmA 91*
Fretter, T. W. *WhoWrEP 89*
Fretter, William Bache 1916- *WhoAm 90*
Fretthold, Timothy J. 1949- *St&PR 91*
Fretts, Debra Rene 1955- *St&PR 91*
Fretwell, E.K., Jr. 1923- *St&PR 91*
Fretwell, Elbert Kirtley, Jr. 1923- *WhoAm 90, WhoSSW 91*
Fretwell, Elizabeth 1920- *IntWWM 90*
Fretwell, Francis Pearre 1926- *WhoSSW 91*
Fretz, Norman A *BiDrAPA 89*
Freuchen, Peter 1886-1957 *AuBYP 90*
Freud, Anna 1895-1982 *BioIn 16, DcNaB 1981, MajTwCW*
Freud, Arthur 1927- *WhoE 91*
Freud, Emma *BioIn 16*
Freud, Esti *BioIn 16*
Freud, John Milton 1946- *WhoEmL 91*
Freud, John Sigmund 1956- *WhoEmL 91*
Freud, Lucian *BioIn 16*
Freud, Lucian Michael 1922- *WhoWor 91*

Freud, Sigmund 1856-1939 *BioIn 16, EncO&P 3, EncPaPR 91, MajTwCW, WorAlBi, WrPh P*
Freud, Sophie 1924- *BioIn 16*
Freuden, Neal Barry 1945- *WhoE 91*
Freudenberg, Karl Johann 1886-1983 *DcScB S2*
Freudenberg, Reinhart 1932- *WhoAm 90*
Freudenberg, Timothy Bernard 1962- *WhoSSW 91*
Freudenberger, Herbert Justin 1926- *WhoAm 90, WhoE 91*
Freudenberger, Herman 1922- *WhoAm 90*
Freudenheim, Milton B. 1927- *WhoAm 90*
Freudenheim, Nina *WhoAmA 91*
Freudenheim, Tom Lippmann 1937- *WhoAm 90, WhoAmA 91*
Freudenstein, Ferdinand 1926- *WhoAm 90*
Freudenthal, Ernest G. 1920- *St&PR 91*
Freudenthal, Hugo David 1930- *WhoE 91*
Freudenthal, Nancy Ellen 1940- *WhoAmW 91*
Freudenthal, Otto 1934- *IntWWM 90*
Freudenthal, Peter C. *BioIn 16*
Freudenthal, Steven Franklin 1949- *WhoAm 90*
Freudiger, Fulop 1900-1976 *BioIn 16*
Freudmann, Axel Ivan 1946- *St&PR 91*
Freund, Bernard W 1933- *BiDrAPA 89*
Freund, Carol Louise 1933- *WhoWor 91*
Freund, Charles Gibson 1923- *WhoAm 90*
Freund, Eckhard 1940- *WhoWor 91*
Freund, Emma Frances 1922- *WhoAmW 91, WhoSSW 91, WhoWor 91*
Freund, Fred A. 1928- *WhoAm 90*
Freund, Gerald 1930- *WhoAm 90, WhoE 91, WhoWor 91*
Freund, Gisele 1912- *BioIn 16, WhoWor 91*
Freund, Harry Louis 1905- *WhoAmA 91*
Freund, Henry *BiDrAPA 89*
Freund, Hugh 1937- *St&PR 91*
Freund, Hugo Allen 1954- *WhoE 91*
Freund, J Dennis *BiDrAPA 89*
Freund, James Coleman 1934- *WhoAm 90*
Freund, Karl 1890-1969 *BioIn 16*
Freund, Lambert Ben 1942- *WhoAm 90, WhoE 91*
Freund, Marya 1876-1966 *PenDiMP*
Freund, Maxine B. 1946- *WhoE 91*
Freund, Mitchell David 1953- *WhoE 91*
Freund, Morton *BioIn 16*
Freund, Paul Abraham 1908- *WhoAm 90, WhoE 91*
Freund, Pepsi 1938- *WhoAmA 91*
Freund, Richard A. 1925-1989 *BioIn 16*
Freund, Richard L. 1921- *WhoAm 90*
Freund, Robert Michael 1953- *WhoE 91*
Freund, Ronald S. 1934- *WhoAm 90*
Freund, Sidney A. 1949- *WhoE 91*
Freund, Tibor 1910- *WhoAm 90, WhoAmA 91*
Freund, Will Frederick 1916- *WhoAmA 91*
Freund, William Curt 1926- *WhoAm 90, WhoE 91*
Freund-Klemperer, Margit *BiDrAPA 89*
Freundlich, August L 1924- *WhoAmA 91*
Freundlich, August Ludwig 1924- *WhoAm 90*
Freundlich, Lillian 1912- *IntWWM 90*
Freundlich, Peter *BioIn 16*
Freundlich, Richard L. 1937- *St&PR 91*
Frevert, Douglas James 1952- *WhoEmL 91*
Frevert, James Wilmot 1922- *WhoSSW 91, WhoWor 91*
Frevert, Richard Anton 1956- *WhoEmL 91*
Frew, Bud L. 1933- *WhoAm 90*
Frew, Charles Edward 1941- *St&PR 91*
Frew, James Shearer 1917- *WhoWor 91*
Frew, Robert Simpson 1940- *WhoE 91*
Frewer, Glyn 1931- *AuBYP 90*
Frewer, Matt *BioIn 16*
Frewer, Matt 1958- *ConTFT 8 [port]*
Frey, Albert 1903- *WhoAm 90*
Frey, Albert Wesley *BioIn 16*
Frey, Andrew Lewis 1938- *WhoAm 90*
Frey, Barbara Louise 1952- *WhoAmA 91*
Frey, Benny 1906-1937 *Ballpl 90*
Frey, Carl 1927- *WhoAm 90*
Frey, Charles Frederick 1929- *WhoAm 90, WhoWor 91*
Frey, Christian Miller 1923- *WhoAm 90*
Frey, Dale Franklin 1932- *St&PR 91, WhoAm 90*
Frey, David Gardner 1942- *St&PR 91, WhoAm 90*
Frey, Donald N. 1923- *St&PR 91*
Frey, Donald Nelson 1923- *WhoAm 90*
Frey, Elizabeth Bisnett 1926- *WhoE 91*
Frey, Emil Ferdinand 1927- *WhoAm 90*
Frey, Emma Margaret Moore 1923- *WhoAmW 91*
Frey, Erwin F 1892-1967 *WhoAmA 91N*
Frey, Frank William 1947- *WhoEmL 91*
Frey, Frederick August 1938- *WhoAm 90*
Frey, Gerard Louis 1914- *WhoSSW 91*
Frey, Gerhard 1915- *WhoWor 91*
Frey, Glenn 1948- *EncPR&S 89, WhoAm 90*
Frey, H. Garrett 1938- *St&PR 91*
Frey, Hans-Hasso 1927- *WhoWor 91*
Frey, Henry 1932- *BiDrAPA 89*
Frey, Henry Charles 1948- *WhoEmL 91*
Frey, Herman S. 1920- *WhoAm 90, WhoWor 91*
Frey, James G. 1931- *St&PR 91*
Frey, James Gottfried 1931- *WhoAm 90*
Frey, James McKnight 1932- *WhoAm 90*
Frey, Jan Paul 1942- *St&PR 91*
Frey, Jay J. 1932- *St&PR 91*
Frey, Jeffery Bryan 1943- *WhoSSW 91*
Frey, Jennifer N. *ODwPR 91*
Frey, Jerry McBride 1953- *St&PR 91*
Frey, Jim 1931- *Ballpl 90*
Frey, John A. 1920- *St&PR 91*
Frey, John M. 1928- *St&PR 91*
Frey, Joseph Charles 1941- *St&PR 91*
Frey, Kelly Leibert 1951- *WhoEmL 91*
Frey, Kiran 1950- *BiDrAPA 89*
Frey, Leon Harry 1933- *St&PR 91*
Frey, Leonard 1938-1988 *BioIn 16*
Frey, Linda Rachelle *BiDrAPA 89*
Frey, Linda Susan 1951- *WhoAmW 91*
Frey, Lonny 1910- *Ballpl 90*
Frey, Louis, Jr. 1934- *WhoAm 90*
Frey, Mark A. *St&PR 91*
Frey, Martin Alan 1939- *WhoSSW 91*
Frey, Nancy 1946- *WhoE 91*
Frey, Nicholas M. 1948- *WhoAm 90*
Frey, Otto-Herman 1929- *WhoWor 91*
Frey, Patti *ODwPR 91*
Frey, Philip, Jr. 1927- *St&PR 91*
Frey, Richard K. 1928- *St&PR 91*
Frey, Richard Lincoln 1905-1988 *BioIn 16*
Frey, Richelle M. 1961- *WhoAmW 91*
Frey, Robert Servetus 1930- *WhoSSW 91*
Frey, Roger 1913- *BiDFrPL*
Frey, Shaney *AuBYP 90*
Frey, Stuart M. 1925- *St&PR 91*
Frey, Stuart Macklin 1925- *WhoAm 90*
Frey, Timothy John 1955- *WhoEmL 91*
Frey, Viola 1933- *WhoAmA 91*
Frey, William Carl 1930- *WhoAm 90*
Frey-Rabine, Lia 1950- *IntWWM 90*
Freychet, Pierre Francois 1935- *WhoWor 91*
Freycinet, Charles-Louis de Saulces de 1828-1923 *BiDFrPL*
Freyd, Jennifer Joy 1957- *WhoAmW 91*
Freyd, Peter John 1936- *WhoAm 90*
Freyd, William Pattinson 1933- *WhoE 91, WhoWor 91*
Freyer, Achim 1934- *ConDes 90*
Freyer, Frederic *TwCCr&M 91*
Freyer, Hans 1887-1969 *BioIn 16*
Freyer, Victoria C. *WhoAmW 91*
Freyhan, Michael 1940- *IntWWM 90*
Freymond, Jacques 1911- *WhoWor 91*
Freymuth, G. Russell 1928- *St&PR 91, WhoAm 90*
Freymuth, Hans W *BiDrAPA 89*
Freyre, Ernesto, Jr. 1942- *WhoHisp 91*
Freyre, Gilberto 1900-1987 *BioIn 16*
Freyre, Ricardo Jaimes *HispWr 90*
Freyre, Ricardo Jaimes 1866-1933 *BioIn 16*
Freyse, Bill 1898-1969 *EncACom*
Freyss, David 1933- *WhoAm 90*
Freytag, Alfred Andrew 1929- *St&PR 91*
Freytag, Donald Ashe 1937- *WhoAm 90*
Freytag, Fredericka F *BiDrAPA 89*
Freytag, Sharon Nelson 1943- *WhoAmW 91, WhoWor 91*
Freytag Loeringhoff, Bettina von 1943- *WhoWor 91*
Freytag-Loringhoven, Elsa 1874-1927 *FemiCLE*
Freytag-Loringhoven, Else von 1874-1927 *BiDWomA*
Freytes Del Rio, Rodrigo *BiDrAPA 89*
Frezza, Andrea 1937- *WhoWor 91*
Frezza, Luciano Franco 1940- *WhoWor 91*
Fri, Robert Wheeler 1935- *WhoAm 90*
Friant, Ray J. 1931- *St&PR 91*
Friar, Christina 1948- *BiDrAPA 89*
Frias, Angelica Schilling 1941- *BiDrAPA 89*
Frias, Antonio 1939- *St&PR 91*
Frias, Carlos A *BiDrAPA 89*
Frias, Jaime Luis 1933- *WhoAm 90*
Frias, Joseph 1940- *St&PR 91*
Frias, Linda *WhoHisp 91*
Frias, Pepe 1948- *Ballpl 90*
Frias, Susan Louise 1957- *WhoSSW 91*
Friauf, Katherine Elizabeth 1956- *WhoAmW 91*
Fribance, Caroline E. 1945- *St&PR 91*
Friberg, Arnold 1913- *WhoAmA 91*
Friberg, Barney 1899-1958 *Ballpl 90*
Friberg, Justine Van Rensselaer Townsend *BioIn 16*
Fribolin, Carl William 1918- *St&PR 91*
Fribourg, Marjorie G. 1920- *AuBYP 90*
Fribourg, Michel *WhoAm 90*
Fribourgh, James Henry 1926- *WhoAm 90, WhoWor 91*
Fribush, Barry Ellis 1941- *WhoE 91*
Fricano, Marion 1923-1976 *Ballpl 90*
Fricano, Tom S 1930- *WhoAmA 91*
Fricano, Wayne R. 1944- *St&PR 91, WhoAm 90*
Fricchione, Gregory Lewis 1951- *BiDrAPA 89*
Frick, Arthur Charles *WhoAmA 91*
Frick, Donna Elliott *BiDrAPA 89*
Frick, Ford 1895-1978 *Ballpl 90 [port]*
Frick, Gary John 1940- *St&PR 91*
Frick, Gottlob 1906- *PenDiMP*
Frick, Gottlob 1908- *IntWWM 90*
Frick, Harvey Lee 1906- *EncO&P 3*
Frick, Henry Clay 1849-1919 *WorAlBi*
Frick, Ivan Eugene 1928- *WhoAm 90*
Frick, Joan 1942- *WhoAmA 91*
Frick, John William 1951- *WhoWor 91*
Frick, Joseph Francis 1930- *WhoAm 90*
Frick, Martin R. 1924- *St&PR 91*
Frick, Nancy Malinosky 1943- *WhoAmW 91*
Frick, Oscar Lionel 1923- *WhoAm 90*
Frick, Robert Burke *BiDrAPA 89*
Frick, Robert Oliver 1920- *WhoAmA 91*
Frick, Robert W *BiDrAPA 89*
Frick, Ronald Alan 1961- *WhoE 91*
Frick, Sidney Wanning 1915- *WhoAm 90*
Frick, Wilhelm 1877-1946 *BioIn 16*
Frick, William Avery 1943- *WhoSSW 91*
Fricke, Carolyn Marie 1951- *WhoEmL 91*
Fricke, Herbert H. 1939- *St&PR 91*
Fricke, Janie 1947- *WhoAm 90, WhoAmW 91*
Fricke, John W. 1945- *St&PR 91*
Fricke, Richard I. 1922- *St&PR 91*
Fricke, Richard Irvin 1922- *WhoAm 90, WhoSSW 91*
Fricker, Edward G. *EncO&P 3*
Fricker, Evan N. 1938- *St&PR 91*
Fricker, John Arthur 1931- *WhoAm 90*
Fricker, Peter Racine 1920- *IntWWM 90, PenDiMP A*
Frickert, E. M. *WhoWrEP 89*
Fricklas, Anita Alper 1937- *WhoAmW 91*
Fricks, Ernest Eugene 1948- *WhoEmL 91*
Fricks, William Peavy 1944- *WhoAm 90*
Fricsay, Ferenc 1914-1963 *PenDiMP*
Frid, Peter Albert 1947- *WhoEmL 91*
Friday, Elbert Walter, Jr. 1939- *WhoAm 90*
Friday, John Ernest, Jr. 1929- *WhoAm 90*
Friday, Nancy 1937- *MajTwCW, WhoWrEP 89*
Friday, Richard Harvey 1942- *St&PR 91*
Friday, William Clyde 1920- *WhoAm 90*
Fridegard, Jan 1897-1968 *DcScanL*
Fridenson, Patrick 1944- *ConAu 129*
Fridh, Kjell Tage 1944- *WhoWor 91*
Fridholm, George H. 1921- *WhoWor 91*
Fridholm, Roger Theodore 1941- *WhoAm 90*
Fridley, Robert Bruce 1934- *WhoAm 90*
Fridley, Saundra Lynn 1948- *WhoAmW 91, WhoEmL 91, WhoWor 91*
Fridling, David *ODwPR 91*
Fridling, David 1950- *St&PR 91*
Fridlington, John W. 1944- *St&PR 91*
Fridman, Esther D. 1958- *BiDrAPA 89*
Fridman, Josef Josel 1945- *WhoAm 90*
Fridman, Morton 1958- *BiDrAPA 89*
Fridovich, Irwin 1929- *WhoAm 90*
Frie, Diana Joan 1949- *WhoEmL 91*
Frieben, Lawrence Lee, Jr. 1944- *St&PR 91*
Fried, Albert, Jr. 1930- *St&PR 91, WhoAm 90*
Fried, Alexander 1902-1988 *BioIn 16*
Fried, Belle Warshavsky 1917- *WhoE 91*
Fried, Bernard 1928- *St&PR 91*
Fried, Bernard 1933- *WhoE 91*
Fried, Brenda Lynne 1956- *WhoAmW 91*
Fried, Burton David 1925- *WhoAm 90*
Fried, Burton Theodore 1940- *St&PR 91, WhoAm 90*
Fried, Charles 1935- *WhoAm 90, WhoE 91*
Fried, Charles A. 1945- *WhoAm 90*
Fried, David 1951- *WhoE 91*
Fried, Deborah 1956- *BiDrAPA 89*
Fried, Edward R. 1918- *WhoAm 90*
Fried, Elliot 1944- *WhoWrEP 89*
Fried, Erich 1921-1988 *AnObit 1988, BioIn 16*
Fried, Frederick E 1938- *BiDrAPA 89*
Fried, George H. 1926- *WhoE 91*
Fried, Gerald 1928- *BioIn 16*
Fried, Herbert Daniel 1928- *St&PR 91, WhoAm 90*
Fried, Howard Lee 1946- *WhoAmA 91*
Fried, Jeffrey Michael 1953- *WhoE 91, WhoEmL 91*
Fried, Joanne Bette 1955- *WhoAmW 91, WhoEmL 91, WhoSSW 91*
Fried, Joel Ethan 1954- *IntWWM 90*
Fried, John 1929- *St&PR 91*
Fried, John H. 1929- *WhoAm 90*
Fried, Jonathan Tear 1953- *WhoE 91*
Fried, Josef 1914- *WhoAm 90*
Fried, Joseph John 1897-1988 *BioIn 16*
Fried, Karen Joan 1962- *WhoAmW 91*
Fried, Lawrence Philip 1938- *WhoSSW 91*
Fried, Louis *BioIn 16*
Fried, Louis Lester 1930- *WhoWor 91*
Fried, Max 1932- *St&PR 91*
Fried, Miriam 1946- *IntWWM 90, PenDiMP*
Fried, Morton Herbert 1923-1986 *BioIn 16*
Fried, Nancy *BioIn 16*
Fried, Nancy Elizabeth 1948- *WhoEmL 91*
Fried, Oskar 1871-1941 *PenDiMP*
Fried, Philip Henry 1945- *WhoWrEP 89*
Fried, Philip P. 1933- *ODwPR 91*
Fried, Richard 1946- *St&PR 91*
Fried, Robert Franklin 1938- *WhoE 91*
Fried, Robert Nathan 1959- *St&PR 91*
Fried, Ronnee 1947- *WhoAmW 91*
Fried, Samuel 1951- *WhoAm 90*
Fried, Shari E. *ODwPR 91*
Fried, Stephen Mark 1950- *WhoEmL 91*
Fried, Suzanne R 1940- *BiDrAPA 89*
Fried, Walter Jay 1904- *WhoAm 90*
Fried, Walter Rudolf 1923- *WhoAm 90*
Fried, Walter S. 1907-1989 *BioIn 16*
Friedan, Betty *BioIn 16*
Friedan, Betty 1921- *FemiCLE, MajTwCW, WhoAm 90, WhoAmW 91, WhoWrEP 89, WorAlBi*
Friedberg, Barry Sewell 1941- *WhoAm 90*
Friedberg, Bernard 1938- *BiDrAPA 89*
Friedberg, Burton Steven 1942- *St&PR 91*
Friedberg, Eugene A *BiDrAPA 89*
Friedberg, Gertrude 1908?-1989 *ConAu 129*
Friedberg, Gertrude Tonkonogy *BioIn 16*
Friedberg, Harold David 1927- *WhoAm 90, WhoWor 91*
Friedberg, M. Paul 1931- *BioIn 16*
Friedberg, Martha A. 1916- *WhoWrEP 89*
Friedberg, Maurice 1929- *WhoAm 90*
Friedberg, Rachel 1929- *WhoAmA 91*
Friedberg, Richard S 1943- *WhoAmA 91*
Friedberg, Simeon Adlow 1925- *WhoAm 90*
Friedberg, Thomas Franklin 1958- *WhoEmL 91*
Friedberg, Thomas Harold 1939- *WhoAm 90, WhoSSW 91*
Friedberg, William David 1946- *WhoE 91*
Friede, Eleanor Kask 1920- *WhoAm 90*
Friede, Hans *BiDrAPA 89*
Friede, Jerzy George 1920- *WhoWor 91*
Friede, Reinhard L. 1926- *WhoAm 90, WhoWor 91*
Friedeberg, Pedro *BioIn 16*
Friedeberg, Pedro 1937- *WhoAm 90*
Friedel, Jacques 1921- *WhoWor 91*
Friedel, Michael Gerald 1948- *WhoEmL 91*
Friedel, Robert O 1936- *BiDrAPA 89*
Friedel, Robert Oliver 1936- *St&PR 91, WhoAm 90*
Friedell, Gilbert Hugo 1927- *WhoAm 90*
Friedell, Richard Alan 1946- *BiDrAPA 89*
Friedeman, Bert 1941- *St&PR 91*
Friedeman, Elliott M 1945- *BiDrAPA 89*
Friedemann *NewAgMG*
Friedemann, Elliott Kurt 1918- *IntWWM 90*
Frieden, Bernard Joel 1930- *WhoAm 90*
Frieden, Carl 1928- *WhoAm 90*
Frieden, Charles Leroy 1941- *WhoAm 90*
Frieden, Robert M. 1955- *WhoEmL 91*
Friedenberg, Amy Lynn *BiDrAPA 89*
Friedenberg, Daniel Meyer 1923- *WhoE 91*
Friedenberg, Karen Rosen 1949- *WhoAmW 91*
Friedenberg, Milton David 1923- *BiDrAPA 89*
Friedenberg, Richard Myron 1926- *WhoAm 90*
Friedensohn, Elias 1924- *WhoAmA 91*
Friedensohn, Elias Solomon 1924- *WhoAm 90*
Friedenson, Daniel Jacob 1944- *BiDrAPA 89*
Friedenthal, Jack H. 1931- *WhoAm 90*
Friedenthal, Steven Bruce 1961- *BiDrAPA 89*
Frieder, Barry Wayne 1944- *BiDrAPA 89*
Frieder, Bill *BioIn 16*
Frieder, Gideon 1937- *WhoAm 90*
Friederich, Jan 1944- *WhoAm 90*
Friederichs, Norman Paul 1936- *WhoWor 91*
Friederici, Hartmann H. R. 1927- *WhoAm 90*
Friedes, Peter Elliot 1941- *WhoAm 90*
Friedewald, William Frank 1912- *WhoAm 90*
Friedewald, William Thomas 1939- *WhoAm 90*
Friedgen, Christina J. 1943- *St&PR 91*
Friedheim, Arthur 1859-1932 *PenDiMP*
Friedheim, Eric Arthur 1910- *WhoAm 90*
Friedheim, Ernst A. H. 1899-1989 *BioIn 16*
Friedheim, Jerry Warden 1934- *WhoAm 90*

Friedheim, Michael 1943- *WhoAm 90*
Friedheim, Stephen Bailey 1934- *WhoSSW 91*
Friedhofer, Hugo 1902-1981 *BioIn 16*
Friedhofer, Hugo Wilhelm 1901-1981 *OxCPMus*
Friedhoff, Arnold J 1923- *BiDrAPA 89*, *WhoAm 90*
Friedkin, Don S. 1921- *St&PR 91*
Friedkin, Joseph Frank 1909- *WhoAm 90*
Friedkin, William *BioIn 16*
Friedl, Donald George 1932- *St&PR 91*
Friedl, Francis Peter 1917- *WhoAm 90*
Friedl, Friedrich 1944- *ConDes 90*
Friedl, Rick 1947- *WhoEmL 91*
Friedlaender, Ann Fetter 1938- *WhoAm 90*
Friedlaender, Bilge *WhoAmA 91*
Friedlaender, Fritz Josef 1925- *WhoAm 90*
Friedlaender, Gary Elliott 1945- *WhoAm 90*
Friedlaender, Israel 1876-1920 *BioIn 16*
Friedlaender, Walter *WhoAmA 91N*
Friedland, Alvin *BiDrAPA 89*
Friedland, Bernard 1930- *WhoAm 90*
Friedland, Billie Louise 1944- *WhoAmW 91*
Friedland, Ellen Beth 1958- *WhoEmL 91*
Friedland, Howard *BioIn 16*
Friedland, Jerold Arthur 1945- *WhoAm 90*
Friedland, Lew M. 1949- *WhoSSW 91*
Friedland, Lilli 1947- *WhoEmL 91*
Friedland, Louis N. 1913- *WhoAm 90*
Friedland, Paul Daniel 1954- *WhoEmL 91*
Friedland, Richard S. 1950- *St&PR 91*
Friedland, Richard Stewart 1950- *WhoAm 90*
Friedland, Robert M. *BioIn 16*
Friedland, Robert M. 1950- *St&PR 91*
Friedland, Seymour 1928- *WhoAmA 91*
Friedland, Steven Howard *BiDrAPA 89*
Friedland, Susan Helen 1947- *WhoWrEP 89*
Friedlander, Annekate Emma 1903- *IntWWM 90*
Friedlander, Carolee 1941- *WhoE 91*
Friedlander, Charles Douglas 1928- *WhoWor 91*
Friedlander, David Max 1941- *St&PR 91*
Friedlander, Edward Jay 1945- *WhoSSW 91*
Friedlander, Gerhart 1916- *WhoAm 90*
Friedlander, Herbert D. 1928- *St&PR 91*
Friedlander, Isac 1890-1968 *WhoAmA 91N*
Friedlander, James Stuart 1942- *WhoE 91*
Friedlander, Joanne K. 1930- *AuBYP 90*
Friedlander, Lee 1934- *BioIn 16*, *WhoAmA 91*
Friedlander, Leonard *BioIn 16*, *NewYTBS 90*
Friedlander, Malvin Elliott 1917- *WhoSSW 91*
Friedlander, Margaret *PenDiDA 89*
Friedlander, Mark Steven *BiDrAPA 89*
Friedlander, Michael Wulf 1928- *WhoAm 90*
Friedlander, Miles Herbert 1935- *WhoSSW 91*
Friedlander, Myrna Lois 1947- *WhoAmW 91*
Friedlander, Norman 1926- *St&PR 91*
Friedlander, Patricia Ann 1944- *WhoAmW 91*
Friedlander, Paul Josef Crost 1910- *WhoAm 90*
Friedlander, Paul Josef Crost 1910-1990 *NewYTBS 90 [port]*
Friedlander, Paul S. 1940- *St&PR 91*
Friedlander, Raymond Nathan 1926- *WhoAm 90*
Friedlander, Richard K *BiDrAPA 89*
Friedlander, Robert Lynn 1933- *WhoAm 90*, *WhoE 91*
Friedlander, Saul 1932- *ConAu 130*, *WorAu 1980 [port]*
Friedlander, Sheldon Kay 1927- *WhoAm 90*
Friedlander, Stephen Hale 1950- *WhoE 91*
Friedlander, William A. 1932- *St&PR 91*
Friedler, Egon 1932- *IntWWM 90*
Friedler, Eli 1954- *BiDrAPA 89*
Friedler, Frank, Jr. 1934- *WhoSSW 91*
Friedley, H. Herald 1927- *St&PR 91*
Friedli, Beat 1936- *WhoWor 91*
Friedli, Judy Alisa *BiDrAPA 89*
Friedlob, James Wesley 1946- *WhoSSW 91*
Friedly, John C. 1938- *WhoAm 90*
Friedman, Adam I. 1945- *ODwPR 91*
Friedman, Alan *WhoWrEP 89*
Friedman, Alan 1944- *WhoAmA 91*
Friedman, Alan H. 1946- *St&PR 91*
Friedman, Alan Herbert 1937- *WhoAm 90*, *WhoE 91*, *WhoWor 91*
Friedman, Alan Jacob 1942- *WhoAm 90*
Friedman, Alan Warren 1939- *WhoAm 90*
Friedman, Albert Barron 1920- *WhoAm 90*
Friedman, Alexander J 1909- *BiDrAPA 89*
Friedman, Alfred *St&PR 91*
Friedman, Alice Rosenberg 1941- *WhoSSW 91*
Friedman, Allan David 1950- *WhoEmL 91*
Friedman, Alvin 1931- *WhoAm 90*
Friedman, Alvin E. 1919- *St&PR 91*
Friedman, Alvin Edward 1919- *WhoAm 90*
Friedman, Alvin F. 1926- *St&PR 91*
Friedman, Arnold P *BiDrAPA 89*
Friedman, Arnold P. *NewYTBS 90*
Friedman, Arnold S. 1929- *WhoAm 90*, *WhoE 91*
Friedman, Arthur Daniel 1940- *WhoAm 90*, *WhoE 91*
Friedman, Arthur Leonard 1929- *St&PR 91*
Friedman, Arthur Meeker 1948- *WhoAm 90*
Friedman, B H 1926- *WhoAmA 91*, *WhoWrEP 89*
Friedman, Barbara Bernstein 1946- *WhoE 91*
Friedman, Barbara Glatt 1937- *WhoAmW 91*, *WhoE 91*
Friedman, Barry 1939- *BiDrAPA 89*
Friedman, Barry S. 1956- *WhoEmL 91*
Friedman, Barton Robert 1935- *WhoAm 90*
Friedman, Ben Ignatius 1926- *WhoAm 90*
Friedman, Benjamin Morton 1944- *WhoAm 90*, *WhoE 91*
Friedman, Benno 1945- *WhoAmA 91*
Friedman, Bernard 1932- *WhoE 91*
Friedman, Bernard Harper 1926- *WhoAm 90*
Friedman, Bernard Leonard 1922- *St&PR 91*
Friedman, Brian P. 1955- *St&PR 91*
Friedman, Brian Paul 1955- *WhoEmL 91*
Friedman, Bruce Jay 1930- *BioIn 16*
Friedman, Carl M 1914- *BiDrAPA 89*
Friedman, Cary D 1960- *BiDrAPA 89*
Friedman, Cathy J *BiDrAPA 89*
Friedman, Chad Isaac 1951- *WhoEmL 91*
Friedman, Charles J. 1941- *St&PR 91*
Friedman, Charles Stuart 1943- *WhoWor 91*
Friedman, Cherryl G *BiDrAPA 89*
Friedman, Dan 1945- *WhoAmA 91*
Friedman, Dana Elise 1951- *WhoE 91*
Friedman, Daniel Mortimer 1916- *WhoAm 90*
Friedman, Darlene 1955- *WhoAmW 91*
Friedman, David *NewAgMG*
Friedman, David 1938- *WhoAm 90*
Friedman, David B 1922- *BiDrAPA 89*
Friedman, David Leonard *BiDrAPA 89*
Friedman, Deborah H. *ODwPR 91*
Friedman, Deborah Leslie White 1950- *WhoSSW 91*
Friedman, Dena Seifer *BiDrAPA 89*
Friedman, Dennis Carl 1948- *WhoE 91*
Friedman, Donald Joseph 1929- *WhoAm 90*
Friedman, Dora Zucker *BioIn 16*
Friedman, Dorothy *WhoWrEP 89*
Friedman, Edward Alan 1935- *WhoAm 90*
Friedman, Edward David *WhoAm 90*
Friedman, Eli A. 1933- *WhoAm 90*
Friedman, Ellen G. 1944- *WhoAmW 91*
Friedman, Ellen S. 1954- *WhoEmL 91*
Friedman, Emanuel 1919- *WhoAm 90*
Friedman, Emanuel A. 1926- *WhoAm 90*
Friedman, Emerick 1910- *BiDrAPA 89*
Friedman, Emma Fleischman 1904- *WhoAm 90*
Friedman, Eric D. 1959- *St&PR 91*
Friedman, Erick 1939- *IntWWM 90*
Friedman, Ernest H 1931- *BiDrAPA 89*
Friedman, Ernest Harvey 1931- *WhoWor 91*
Friedman, Ernest J. *St&PR 91*
Friedman, Estelle 1920- *AuBYP 90*
Friedman, Eugene Warren 1919- *WhoAm 90*
Friedman, Frances 1928- *ODwPR 91*, *WhoAm 90*, *WhoAmW 91*
Friedman, Francine Ina *BiDrAPA 89*
Friedman, Frank Bennett 1940- *St&PR 91*, *WhoAm 90*
Friedman, Frank G. 1950- *St&PR 91*
Friedman, Frederick M. 1940- *St&PR 91*
Friedman, Fredrica Schwab 1939- *WhoAmW 91*
Friedman, Gary E. 1947- *St&PR 91*
Friedman, George *St&PR 91N*
Friedman, George H. 1954- *St&PR 91*
Friedman, George Henry 1954- *WhoEmL 91*
Friedman, George Jerry 1928- *WhoAm 90*
Friedman, Gerald Manfred 1921- *WhoAm 90*, *WhoE 91*, *WhoWor 91*
Friedman, Gloria Landsman 1925- *WhoAm 90*
Friedman, Gregg Lowell 1961- *BiDrAPA 89*
Friedman, H. Harold 1917- *WhoAm 90*
Friedman, Hans Adolf 1921- *WhoAm 90*
Friedman, Harold 1930- *St&PR 91*
Friedman, Harold B. 1904- *St&PR 91*
Friedman, Harold Edward 1934- *WhoAm 90*
Friedman, Harold S. 1937- *WhoE 91*
Friedman, Harris C. 1944- *St&PR 91*
Friedman, Harry 1907-1988 *BioIn 16*
Friedman, Harry Fred 1928- *St&PR 91*
Friedman, Harvey 1936- *St&PR 91*
Friedman, Harvey Martin 1948- *WhoAm 90*
Friedman, Helen Ruth 1951- *WhoEmL 91*
Friedman, Henry J *BiDrAPA 89*
Friedman, Herbert 1916- *WhoAm 90*, *WhoWor 91*
Friedman, Herbert 1931-1988 *BioIn 16*
Friedman, Herbert A. 1918- *WhoWor 91*
Friedman, Herman 1931- *WhoSSW 91*
Friedman, Howard J. *BioIn 16*
Friedman, Howard P *BiDrAPA 89*
Friedman, Howard W. 1925- *St&PR 91*, *WhoAm 90*
Friedman, Ignaz 1882-1948 *BioIn 16*, *PenDiMP*
Friedman, Ina 1926- *AuBYP 90*
Friedman, Ina R. *BioIn 16*
Friedman, Ira Hugh 1933- *WhoAm 90*
Friedman, Irving *BiDrAPA 89*
Friedman, Irving S 1915-1989 *ConAu 130*
Friedman, Irving Sigmund 1915- *WhoAm 90*
Friedman, Irving Sigmund 1915-1989 *BioIn 16*
Friedman, J. Roger 1933- *St&PR 91*
Friedman, Jack B. 1921- *St&PR 91*
Friedman, Jack J. 1939- *ODwPR 91*
Friedman, Jack Perry 1945- *WhoEmL 91*
Friedman, Jack Raphael 1950- *WhoE 91*
Friedman, Jacqueline 1937- *WhoWor 91*
Friedman, James Winstein 1936- *WhoAm 90*
Friedman, Jan Jacob 1952- *WhoWor 91*
Friedman, Janet Teri 1957- *WhoEmL 91*, *WhoWrEP 89*
Friedman, Janice Elaine *BiDrAPA 89*
Friedman, Jeffrey H. 1950- *WhoWrEP 89*
Friedman, Jeffrey Merl 1942- *WhoE 91*
Friedman, Jeffrey Robert 1956- *BiDrAPA 89*, *WhoE 91*
Friedman, Jerome Isaac 1930- *WhoAm 90*
Friedman, Jesse I. 1918- *St&PR 91*
Friedman, Jim 1955- *WhoEmL 91*
Friedman, Joan M. 1949- *WhoAm 90*
Friedman, Joel 1939- *St&PR 91*, *WhoAm 90*
Friedman, Joel Matthew 1942- *WhoE 91*
Friedman, Joel Stephen 1937- *St&PR 91*, *WhoAm 90*, *WhoE 91*
Friedman, Joel William 1951- *WhoAm 90*
Friedman, John Arthur 1952- *WhoEmL 91*
Friedman, Jon George 1951- *WhoE 91*, *WhoEmL 91*, *WhoWor 91*
Friedman, Jonathan Mark 1958- *WhoEmL 91*
Friedman, Joni Beth 1958- *WhoE 91*
Friedman, Joseph 1928- *WhoE 91*
Friedman, Joseph 1947- *WhoEmL 91*
Friedman, Joseph J 1907- *BiDrAPA 89*
Friedman, Joshua M. 1941- *WhoAm 90*
Friedman, Judi 1935- *BioIn 16*
Friedman, Judith Bryna 1950- *WhoAmW 91*
Friedman, K. Bruce 1929- *WhoAm 90*
Friedman, Katherine Emmich 1959- *WhoEmL 91*
Friedman, Ken 1949- *WhoAmA 91*
Friedman, Kinky *TwCCr&M 91*
Friedman, L. Jeanne 1951- *WhoAmW 91*
Friedman, Lawrence 1931- *BiDrAPA 89*
Friedman, Lawrence Andrew 1951- *WhoEmL 91*
Friedman, Lawrence Carl 1956- *WhoEmL 91*
Friedman, Lawrence M. 1930- *WhoAm 90*
Friedman, Lawrence P. 1943- *St&PR 91*
Friedman, Lee Richard 1952- *WhoEmL 91*
Friedman, Lenard R. 1942- *St&PR 91*
Friedman, Leonard J 1930- *BiDrAPA 89*
Friedman, Leonard M. 1943- *WhoE 91*
Friedman, Leonard Matthew 1930- *IntWWM 90*
Friedman, Leonard Robert 1936- *WhoE 91*
Friedman, Lesley 1953- *WhoAmW 91*
Friedman, Lester Herbert *BiDrAPA 89*
Friedman, Lester James 1951- *WhoEmL 91*
Friedman, Lieselotte J *BiDrAPA 89*
Friedman, Louis Frank 1941- *WhoAm 90*
Friedman, Lynn Kari *BiDrAPA 89*
Friedman, Malcolm 1936- *WhoAm 90*
Friedman, Marcel *BiDrAPA 89*
Friedman, Marcia *WhoE 91*
Friedman, Maria Andre 1950- *WhoAmW 91*, *WhoE 91*
Friedman, Marie R *BiDrAPA 89*
Friedman, Marion 1918- *WhoE 91*, *WhoWor 91*
Friedman, Mark F 1945- *BiDrAPA 89*
Friedman, Mark Steven 1949- *WhoSSW 91*
Friedman, Marna Wendy 1959- *WhoAmW 91*, *WhoEmL 91*
Friedman, Martin 1925- *WhoAm 90*, *WhoAmA 91*
Friedman, Martin Burton 1927- *St&PR 91*, *WhoAm 90*
Friedman, Martin David 1934- *WhoE 91*
Friedman, Martin Jay 1929- *WhoAm 90*
Friedman, Martin L. 1925- *BioIn 16*
Friedman, Marvin Ross *WhoAmA 91*
Friedman, Mary Brooks 1947- *WhoEmL 91*
Friedman, Matthew Emanuel 1923- *St&PR 91*
Friedman, Matthew Joel 1940- *BiDrAPA 89*, *WhoE 91*
Friedman, Matthew Roy 1944- *BiDrAPA 89*
Friedman, Maurice Stanley 1921- *WhoAm 90*
Friedman, Melvin 1930- *WhoAm 90*
Friedman, Melvin Jack 1928- *WhoAm 90*
Friedman, Meyer 1910- *WhoAm 90*
Friedman, Michael Elliot 1951- *WhoEmL 91*
Friedman, Michael Kent 1954- *BiDrAPA 89*
Friedman, Michael Phillip 1951- *WhoEmL 91*
Friedman, Michael Steven 1953- *WhoEmL 91*
Friedman, Michelle E 1954- *BiDrAPA 89*
Friedman, Mickey 1944- *WhoAm 90*
Friedman, Mildred S. *BioIn 16*
Friedman, Miles 1950- *WhoE 91*, *WhoEmL 91*, *WhoWor 91*
Friedman, Milton *BioIn 16*
Friedman, Milton 1912- *BioIn 16*, *EncABHB 7 [port]*, *MajTwCW*, *WhoAm 90*, *WhoWor 91*, *WorAlBi*
Friedman, Milton I. 1925- *St&PR 91*
Friedman, Morton 1927- *BiDrAPA 89*, *WhoE 91*
Friedman, Morton Lee 1932- *WhoAm 90*
Friedman, Murray 1926- *WhoAm 90*
Friedman, Myles Ivan 1924- *WhoAm 90*
Friedman, Naomi B. 1949- *WhoEmL 91*
Friedman, Nelson 1912- *St&PR 91*
Friedman, Nicholas R. 1946- *WhoEmL 91*
Friedman, Norman 1925- *St&PR 91*, *WhoWrEP 89*
Friedman, Orrie M. 1915- *St&PR 91*
Friedman, Orrie Max 1915- *WhoAm 90*
Friedman, Patricia Anne Hoffman 1943-1988 *BioIn 16*
Friedman, Paul *BioIn 16*
Friedman, Paul 1931- *WhoAm 90*
Friedman, Paul Alan 1937- *WhoWrEP 89*
Friedman, Paul Howard 1959- *WhoEmL 91*
Friedman, Paul Jay 1937- *WhoAm 90*
Friedman, Paul Lawrence 1944- *WhoAm 90*
Friedman, Penny 1951- *WhoAmW 91*
Friedman, Peter Charles 1958- *WhoEmL 91*
Friedman, Philip Scott 1954- *WhoEmL 91*
Friedman, Phillip L. 1947- *St&PR 91*
Friedman, Philmore H. 1925- *St&PR 91*
Friedman, Polly *ODwPR 91*
Friedman, Ralph 1904- *WhoAm 90*
Friedman, Ralph 1922- *St&PR 91*, *WhoE 91*
Friedman, Ralph David 1942- *WhoE 91*
Friedman, Raymond 1922- *WhoAm 90*
Friedman, Raymond J *BiDrAPA 89*
Friedman, Richard *BiDrAPA 89*
Friedman, Richard Alan 1956- *BiDrAPA 89*
Friedman, Richard C 1941- *BiDrAPA 89*
Friedman, Richard Everett 1942- *WhoAm 90*
Friedman, Richard N. 1941- *St&PR 91*
Friedman, Robert 1928- *WhoE 91*
Friedman, Robert 1947- *WhoAm 90*, *WhoEmL 91*
Friedman, Robert Alan 1941- *WhoAm 90*
Friedman, Robert Alan 1959- *BiDrAPA 89*
Friedman, Robert B. 1939- *St&PR 91*
Friedman, Robert Michael 1950- *WhoEmL 91*, *WhoSSW 91*, *WhoWor 91*
Friedman, Robert S. 1948- *WhoE 91*
Friedman, Robert Sidney 1927- *WhoAm 90*
Friedman, Rochelle Rame 1942- *BiDrAPA 89*
Friedman, Rodger 1951- *WhoE 91*
Friedman, Rohn Samuel 1952- *BiDrAPA 89*
Friedman, Ronald Jules 1946- *St&PR 91*
Friedman, Ronald Marvin 1930- *WhoAm 90*, *WhoE 91*, *WhoWor 91*
Friedman, Rose D *WhoWrEP 89*
Friedman, Roy Bennis 1934- *WhoWrEP 89*
Friedman, Sabra *WhoAmA 91*
Friedman, Sally Ceila 1932- *WhoAmA 91*
Friedman, Sally Celia 1932- *WhoE 91*

Friedman, Samuel H. *BioIn 16, NewYTBS 90 [port]*
Friedman, Samuel Selig 1935- *WhoAm 90, WhoE 91, WhoWor 91*
Friedman, Sandy *ODwPR 91*
Friedman, Sanford 1926- *St&PR 91*
Friedman, Seymour W 1917- *BiDrAPA 89*
Friedman, Shelly Arnold 1949- *WhoAm 90*
Friedman, Sidney A. 1935- *WhoAm 90*
Friedman, Sigmund 1938- *St&PR 91*
Friedman, Stanford J. 1927- *St&PR 91*
Friedman, Stanford Joseph 1927- *WhoSSW 91*
Friedman, Stanley 1925- *WhoAm 90*
Friedman, Stanley 1928- *WhoAm 90*
Friedman, Stanley M *BiDrAPA 89*
Friedman, Stanley Marcus 1925- *WhoE 91*
Friedman, Stanley P. 1925- *WhoWrEP 89*
Friedman, Stephen Belais 1945- *WhoEmL 91*
Friedman, Stephen F. 1946- *ODwPR 91*
Friedman, Stephen James 1938- *WhoE 91*
Friedman, Steve *BioIn 16*
Friedman, Steven A. 1950- *St&PR 91*
Friedman, Sue Tyler 1925- *WhoAmW 91, WhoWor 91*
Friedman, Susan Lynn Bell 1953- *WhoAmW 91*
Friedman, Sydney M. 1916- *WhoAm 90*
Friedman, Sylvia *BiDrAPA 89*
Friedman, Sylvia 1940- *WhoSSW 91*
Friedman, Theodore 1908- *BioIn 16*
Friedman, Thomas L. *BioIn 16*
Friedman, Thomas Loren 1953- *WhoAm 90, WhoE 91, WhoWor 91*
Friedman, Tobias T 1925- *BiDrAPA 89*
Friedman, Tully Michael 1942- *WhoWor 91*
Friedman, Victor 1938- *IntWWM 90*
Friedman, Victor Stanley 1933- *WhoAm 90*
Friedman, Walter 1930- *BiDrAPA 89*
Friedman, Warner 1934- *BioIn 16*
Friedman, Wilbur H. 1907- *St&PR 91*
Friedman, Wilbur Harvey 1907- *WhoAm 90*
Friedman, William Foster 1936- *WhoAm 90*
Friedman, William Hersh 1938- *WhoAm 90*
Friedman, William J. 1903- *St&PR 91*
Friedman, Yona 1923- *ConAu 130*
Friedmann, Arnold 1925- *ConDes 90*
Friedmann, Claude T H 1943- *BiDrAPA 89*
Friedmann, Emerich Imre 1921- *WhoAm 90*
Friedmann, Emily Maccaro 1949- *WhoAmW 91*
Friedmann, Herbert 1900-1987 *BioIn 16*
Friedmann, Norman E. 1929- *St&PR 91*
Friedmann, Paul 1933- *WhoE 91, WhoWor 91*
Friedmann, Peretz Peter 1938- *WhoAm 90, WhoWor 91*
Friedmann, Roseli Ocampo 1937- *WhoAmW 91, WhoSSW 91*
Friedmann, Rosemary Anne 1948- *WhoSSW 91*
Friedner, Jerry Franklin 1937- *St&PR 91*
Friedrich, Carl J. 1901-1984 *BioIn 16*
Friedrich, Carl Joachim 1901-1984 *ConAu 30NR*
Friedrich, Caspar David 1774-1840 *IntDcAA 90*
Friedrich, Charles William 1943- *St&PR 91*
Friedrich, Craig William 1946- *WhoE 91*
Friedrich, Eugene Victor *BiDrAPA 89*
Friedrich, Gloria Joy 1936- *WhoAmW 91*
Friedrich, Gotz 1930- *IntWWM 90*
Friedrich, James F. 1951- *St&PR 91*
Friedrich, Kathleen Rae 1950- *WhoE 91*
Friedrich, Margaret Wilson 1907- *WhoSSW 91*
Friedrich, Margit *EncCoWW*
Friedrich, Margret Cohen 1947- *WhoAmW 91, WhoE 91*
Friedrich, Otto Alva 1929- *WhoAm 90, WhoWrEP 89*
Friedrich, Paul 1927- *WhoAm 90*
Friedrich, Paul William 1927- *WhoWrEP 89*
Friedrich, Paula Jean 1965- *WhoE 91*
Friedrich, Peter 1936- *WhoWor 91*
Friedrich, Philip Francis 1941- *St&PR 91*
Friedrich, Philip Joseph 1947- *WhoE 91, WhoWor 91*
Friedrich, Robert Edmund 1918- *WhoAm 90*
Friedrich, Roman, III *St&PR 91*
Friedrich, Rose Marie 1941- *WhoAmW 91, WhoWor 91*
Friedrich, Stephen Miro 1932- *WhoAm 90*
Friedrich, Wayne H. 1928- *St&PR 91*
Friedrich, William Robert, Jr. 1949- *WhoE 91*
Friedrich-Freksa, Margarete *EncCoWW*
Friedrich-Patterson, Evelyn Beth 1953- *WhoAmW 91*
Friedrichs, Arthur Martin 1911- *WhoSSW 91*
Friedrichs, George Shelby 1911- *WhoAm 90*
Friedrichs, Robert Winslow 1923- *WhoAm 90*
Friedrichs, Wayne Lawrence 1940- *St&PR 91*
Friedrichsen, Rodney D. 1955- *St&PR 91*
Friedricks, Burton Lee 1928- *St&PR 91*
Friedricks, Larry 1937- *St&PR 91*
Friedsam, Ronald J. 1943- *St&PR 91*
Friedson, Belvin 1924- *St&PR 91*
Friehling, Arlene Dinnerstein *BioIn 16*
Friel, Brian *BioIn 16*
Friel, Brian 1929- *ConAu 33NR, ConLC 59 [port], MajTwCW, WhoAm 90*
Friel, Gerry *BioIn 16*
Friel, James Patrick 1935- *WhoE 91*
Friel, Karen Eileen 1957- *WhoEmL 91*
Friel, Margaret Anne *BiDrAPA 89*
Friel, Patricia Elizabeth 1956- *WhoAmW 91*
Friel, Patrick B 1925- *BiDrAPA 89*
Friel, Peter J. 1959- *WhoEmL 91*
Friel, Susan Noel 1945- *WhoE 91*
Friel, Thomas Patrick 1943- *WhoE 91*
Frieland, Alyce 1943- *WhoAmW 91*
Frieling, Barbara Johnston 1950- *WhoSSW 91*
Frieling, Gerald H., Jr. 1930- *St&PR 91*
Frieling, Gerald Harvey, Jr. 1930- *WhoAm 90*
Friels, Colin *ConTFT 8*
Frieman, Edward Allan 1926- *WhoAm 90*
Frieman, Hildegarde 1948- *WhoAmW 91, WhoE 91*
Frieman, Robert David 1940- *BiDrAPA 89*
Friemann, Robert Frederich 1947- *WhoE 91*
Frien D, David 1899-1978 *WhoAmA 91N*
Friend, Alexander Alan 1961- *St&PR 91*
Friend, Bob 1930- *Ballpl 90, BioIn 16*
Friend, Cliff 1893-1974 *OxCPMus*
Friend, Cynthia M. 1955- *WhoEmL 91*
Friend, David Lee 1951- *WhoEmL 91*
Friend, David Robert 1956- *WhoEmL 91*
Friend, David Wesley 1946- *St&PR 91*
Friend, Ed *TwCCr&M 91*
Friend, Edward Malcolm, III 1946- *WhoAm 90*
Friend, Edward Malcolm, Jr. *WhoAm 90*
Friend, Harold Charles 1946- *WhoSSW 91*
Friend, Irwin *BioIn 16*
Friend, Irwin 1915- *St&PR 91*
Friend, Jacqueline *BioIn 16*
Friend, Janice Katherine *BiDrAPA 89*
Friend, Linda Lee 1941- *BiDrAPA 89*
Friend, Lionel 1945- *IntWWM 90*
Friend, Mark Allen 1949- *WhoSSW 91*
Friend, Merril B 1923- *BiDrAPA 89*
Friend, Miriam Ruth 1925- *WhoAmW 91*
Friend, Olen Kent 1962- *WhoEmL 91*
Friend, Owen 1927- *Ballpl 90*
Friend, Patricia M 1931- *WhoAmA 91*
Friend, Patricia Montague 1931- *WhoE 91*
Friend, R Claire *BiDrAPA 89*
Friend, Richard E. 1950- *WhoEmL 91*
Friend, Robert London 1946- *BiDrAPA 89*
Friend, Ronald 1943- *WhoAm 90*
Friend, Theodore Wood, III 1931- *WhoAm 90*
Friend, Walter William 1920-1989 *BioIn 16*
Friend, William Benedict 1931- *WhoAm 90, WhoSSW 91*
Friend, William C *BiDrAPA 89*
Friend, William Kagay 1946- *St&PR 91, WhoAm 90*
Friendlich, Dick 1909- *AuBYP 90*
Friendlich, Richard J. *AuBYP 90*
Friendly, Alfred 1911-1983 *BioIn 16*
Friendly, Ed 1922- *ConTFT 8*
Friendly, Fred W. *BioIn 16*
Friendly, Fred W. 1915- *WhoAm 90, WorAlBi*
Friendly, Lynda E. *WhoAm 90*
Friends, Jalynn *WhoWrEP 89*
Frier, Sharon Boatwright 1942- *WhoAmW 91*
Friermood, Elisabeth 1903- *AuBYP 90*
Frierson, Andrew *DrBlPA 90*
Frierson, Daniel K. *BioIn 16*
Frierson, Daniel K. 1942- *WhoAm 90, WhoSSW 91*
Frierson, Pamela Arlene 1950- *WhoEmL 91*
Frierson, Paul Kruesi 1937- *St&PR 91*
Frierson, Richard Lesesne *BiDrAPA 89*
Frierson, Robert Lee, III *BiDrAPA 89*
Frierson, Virginia Wright- 1949- *BioIn 16*
Friery, Donna Elizabeth 1957- *WhoAmW 91*
Friery, John Joseph 1946- *WhoEmL 91*
Fries, Amy Rose 1958- *WhoWrEP 89*
Fries, Carl Elwood, Jr. 1946- *WhoEmL 91*
Fries, Charles W. *BioIn 16*
Fries, Donald E. 1943- *St&PR 91*
Fries, Donald Eugene 1943- *WhoAm 90*
Fries, Helen Sergeant Haynes *WhoAmW 91*
Fries, Herluf Beck 1915- *WhoWor 91*
Fries, Jack 1942- *St&PR 91*
Fries, James Lawrence 1932- *WhoAm 90*
Fries, James M *BiDrAPA 89*
Fries, Jay Robert 1954- *WhoEmL 91*
Fries, John Robert 1922- *St&PR 91*
Fries, John William 1953- *BiDrAPA 89*
Fries, Joseph Michael 1937- *WhoAm 90*
Fries, Maureen Holmberg 1931- *WhoAm 90*
Fries, Michael Thomas 1959- *WhoEmL 91*
Fries, Raymond Sebastian 1919- *WhoAm 90*
Fries, Robert Francis 1911- *WhoAm 90*
Fries Gardner, Lisa 1956- *WhoEmL 91*
Friese, George R. 1936- *St&PR 91*
Friese, George Ralph 1936- *WhoAm 90*
Friese, Helen Marie 1925- *WhoWrEP 89*
Friese, Robert Charles 1943- *WhoAm 90, WhoWor 91*
Friese, Wilhelm 1924- *WhoWor 91*
Friesecke, Raymond Francis 1937- *WhoAm 90*
Frieseke, Frances 1914- *WhoWrEP 89*
Friesem, Gus Daniel 1916- *St&PR 91*
Friesen, David *BioIn 16, NewAgMG*
Friesen, David R. 1943- *St&PR 91*
Friesen, Eugene *NewAgMG*
Friesen, Eugene Keith 1931- *St&PR 91*
Friesen, Gilbert Dean 1942- *St&PR 91*
Friesen, Gordon Arthur 1909- *WhoAm 90*
Friesen, Henry George 1934- *WhoAm 90*
Friesen, Michael Dean 1953- *IntWWM 90*
Friesen, Milo Eugene 1939- *WhoAm 90*
Friesen, Nancy Miller 1947- *WhoAmW 91*
Friesen, Patrick 1945- *ConAu 32NR*
Friesen, Susan Ruth Werner 1953- *IntWWM 90*
Friesen, Wesley *BioIn 16*
Friesen, Wesley Howard *BiDrAPA 89*
Frieser, Rudolf Gruenspan 1920- *WhoSSW 91*
Frieske, David A 1936- *BiDrAPA 89*
Friesland, James Max 1933- *WhoE 91*
Friesz, Donald Stuart 1929- *St&PR 91*
Friesz, Gerald Daniel 1941- *St&PR 91*
Friesz, Lynda M. 1960- *WhoAmW 91*
Frietze, Jose Victor 1943- *WhoHisp 91*
Frieze, Stanley B. *St&PR 91*
Frigerio, Alejandro 1955- *WhoSSW 91*
Frigerio, Charles Straith 1957- *WhoWor 91*
Frigerio, Ezio 1930- *BioIn 16*
Frigerio, Ismael 1955- *WhoHisp 91*
Frigerio, Rogelio Julio 1914- *WhoWor 91*
Frigo, Arthur Philip 1941- *St&PR 91*
Frigo, George G. 1940- *St&PR 91*
Frigoletto, Fredric David, Jr. 1933- *WhoAm 90*
Frigon, Henry Frederick 1934- *St&PR 91, WhoAm 90, WhoSSW 91, WhoWor 91*
Frigon, Judith Ann 1945- *WhoEmL 91*
Friis, Erik Johan 1913- *WhoAm 90*
Friis-Hansen, Bent Julius 1920- *WhoWor 91*
Frijsh, Povla 1881-1960 *PenDiMP*
Frijtom, Frederik van *PenDiDA 89*
Friley, William Alva 1917- *WhoAm 90*
Frilot, Bert Clark 1939- *WhoWor 91*
Frim, Rosalind S 1932- *BiDrAPA 89*
Friman, Alice 1933- *ConAu 129, WhoWrEP 89*
Frimerman, Leslie 1943- *WhoE 91*
Friml, Rudolf 1879-1972 *BioIn 16, OxCPMus, PenDiMP A, WorAlBi*
Frimmer, Isidore 1905- *BiDrAPA 89*
Frimmer, Paul Norman 1945- *WhoAm 90*
Frimmer, Steven 1928- *AuBYP 90*
Frimml, Jaymee Jo 1949- *WhoAmW 91, WhoWor 91*
Friner, Arlene Renee 1959- *WhoE 91*
Frings, Ketti *BioIn 16*
Frings, Ketti 1915?-1981 *NotWoAT*
Frink, Elizabeth 1930- *BiDWomA*
Frink, George Raymond 1918- *St&PR 91*
Frink, Peter Hill 1939- *WhoE 91*
Frink, Phillip F., Jr. 1938- *St&PR 91*
Frink, Tommie Shelby 1937- *St&PR 91*
Frinta, Mojmir Svatopluk 1922- *WhoAmA 91*
Frio, Kaze Utada *WhoWrEP 89*
Friou, Ann Wheelock 1953- *WhoAmW 91*
Friou, George Jacob 1919- *WhoAm 90*
Friou, James Samuel 1941- *WhoSSW 91*
Friou, Roger Patteson 1934- *St&PR 91*
Fripp, Robert 1946?- *EncPR&S 89*
Frisancho-Pineda, Ignacio *WhoWor 91*
Frisbee, Don C. 1923- *St&PR 91*
Frisbee, Don Calvin 1923- *WhoAm 90*
Frisbee, John Lee 1943- *WhoE 91*
Frisbee, Lucy Post *AuBYP 90*
Frisbee, William *PenDiDA 89*
Frisbie, F. Richard 1942- *St&PR 91*
Frisbie, Ronald Edgar 1922- *St&PR 91*
Frisbie, Steven James 1941- *St&PR 91*
Frisby, Gregory S. 1959- *St&PR 91*
Frisby, James Curtis 1930- *WhoAm 90*
Frisby, Jerry B. 1937- *St&PR 91*
Frisch, A. *ArtLatA*
Frisch, Alan J 1926- *BiDrAPA 89*
Frisch, August Wilbert 1940- *St&PR 91*
Frisch, Bertram 1931- *WhoWor 91*
Frisch, Frank 1898-1973 *BioIn 16*
Frisch, Frankie 1898-1973 *Ballpl 90 [port], WorAlBi*
Frisch, Fred I. 1935- *WhoWor 91*
Frisch, Glen Douglas *BiDrAPA 89*
Frisch, Harry David 1954- *WhoE 91, WhoEmL 91*
Frisch, Harry Lloyd 1928- *WhoAm 90*
Frisch, Henry Jonathan 1944- *WhoAm 90*
Frisch, Jack Aaron 1940- *WhoWor 91*
Frisch, Joseph 1921- *WhoAm 90*
Frisch, Karl Ritter Von 1886-1982 *DcScB S2*
Frisch, Karl Von 1886-1982 *WorAlBi*
Frisch, Max 1911- *ConAu 32NR, EuWr 13, MajTwCW, WorAlBi, WrPh*
Frisch, Max Rudolf 1911- *WhoWor 91*
Frisch, Michael Herbert 1942- *WhoAm 90*
Frisch, Otto Robert 1904- *AuBYP 90*
Frisch, Otto Robert 1904-1979 *BioIn 16, DcScB S2, WorAlBi*
Frisch, Robert A. 1928- *WhoAm 90*
Frisch, Robert Emile 1925- *WhoAm 90*
Frisch, Rose E. *AuBYP 90*
Frisch, Rose Epstein 1918- *WhoAmW 91*
Frisch, Walter M. 1951- *IntWWM 90*
Frisch, Wendi J. 1960- *WhoAmW 91*
Frischauf, Elisabeth C *BiDrAPA 89*
Frischenmeyer, Michael Leo 1951- *WhoEmL 91*
Frischenschlager, Friedhelm 1943- *WhoWor 91*
Frischer, Murray B. 1942- *St&PR 91*
Frischknecht, Hans Eugen 1939- *IntWWM 90*
Frischknecht, Jacqueline 1932- *WhoAmW 91*
Frischknecht, Lee Conrad 1928- *WhoAm 90*
Frischkorn, David Ephraim Keasbey, Jr. 1951- *WhoSSW 91*
Frischling, Carl 1937- *St&PR 91*
Frischmuth, Barbara 1941- *EncCoWW*
Frischnecht, Ruedi 1938- *St&PR 91*
Frisco, Louis Joseph 1923- *WhoAm 90*
Frisell, Bill *BioIn 16*
Frisell, Sonja *BioIn 16*
Frisell, Wilhelm Richard 1920- *WhoAm 90*
Frisell-Schroder, Sonja Bettie 1937- *WhoAm 90*
Frisella, Danny 1946-1977 *Ballpl 90*
Frishberg, Anatoly 1930- *BiDrAPA 89*
Frishberg, Dave 1933- *BioIn 16*
Frishberg, Tamara *BiDrAPA 89*
Frishman, Daniel 1919- *WhoE 91*
Frishman, Robert Joel 1940- *St&PR 91*
Frishmuth, Harriet Whitney 1880-1979 *WhoAmA 91N*
Frishmuth, Harriet Whitney 1880-1980 *BiDWomA*
Frisina, Robert Dana 1955- *WhoAm 90, WhoE 91, WhoEmL 91, WhoWor 91*
Frisina, Ruth M. 1950- *WhoAmW 91*
Frisk, Susan Jane 1936- *WhoAmW 91*
Friskberg, Kai Arthur 1942- *WhoWor 91*
Friskey, Margaret 1901- *AuBYP 90*
Frisman, Roger Lawrence 1952- *WhoEmL 91*
Frisoli, John E. *St&PR 91*
Frison, Nathaniel *BioIn 16*
Frison, Paul Maurice 1937- *WhoAm 90*
Frisque, Alvin Joseph 1923- *WhoAm 90*
Friss, Gabor 1926- *IntWWM 90*
Friss-Baastad, Babbis Ellinor 1921- *AuBYP 90*
Frissell, Toni 1907-1988 *BioIn 16*
Frist, Jane Elizabeth 1935- *WhoAmW 91*
Frist, Thomas Fearn, Jr. 1938- *WhoAm 90, WhoSSW 91*
Fristad, Kenneth Arthur 1941- *St&PR 91*
Fristad, Mark Robert 1953- *WhoEmL 91*
Fristedt, Hans 1943- *WhoAm 90, WhoE 91*
Fristedt, Sven 1940- *ConDes 90*
Friswold, Fred Ravndahl 1937- *WhoAm 90*
Fritchie, Hazel M. 1926- *WhoWrEP 89*
Fritchman, H. Vernon 1907- *St&PR 91*
Frith, Benjamin 1957- *IntWWM 90*
Frith, Mary *BiDEWW*
Frith, Michael Roger 1941- *IntWWM 90*
Frith, William Powell 1819-1909 *IntDcAA 90*
Fritkin, George 1938- *St&PR 91*
Frits, Godefridus P.F. 1947- *WhoWor 91*
Fritsch, Allen Joseph 1930- *St&PR 91*
Fritsch, Charles T. 1912-1989 *BioIn 16*
Fritsch, Cheryle Jean 1962- *WhoAmW 91*
Fritsch, Elisabeth *PenDiDA 89*
Fritsch, Karl 1903-1945 *BioIn 16*

Fritsche, Joellen Marie 1951- *WhoSSW 91*
Fritsche, Peter 1931- *WhoWor 91*
Fritsche, Richard Henry 1945- *St&PR 91*
Fritsche, Wolfgang 1928- *WhoWor 91*
Fritschler, A. Lee 1937- *WhoAm 90*
Fritsma, Darlene Kaye 1941- *WhoAmW 91*
Frittitta, Peter Anthony 1956- *WhoEmL 91*, *WhoWor 91*
Fritton, Karl Andrew 1955- *WhoEmL 91*
Fritts, Garland Gibson 1929- *St&PR 91*
Fritts, Harold Clark 1928- *WhoAm 90*
Fritts, Harry Washington, Jr. 1921- *WhoAm 90*
Fritts, Lillian Elizabeth 1923- *WhoAmW 91*
Fritts, Stewart Brooks 1932- *St&PR 91*
Fritz, Bruce Morrell 1947- *WhoAm 90*
Fritz, Carol Schweinforth 1944- *WhoSSW 91*
Fritz, Cecil M. 1921- *St&PR 91*
Fritz, Cecil Morgan 1921- *WhoAm 90*
Fritz, Charles Ladd 1925- *St&PR 91*
Fritz, David Tee 1953- *WhoSSW 91*
Fritz, Donald E. 1951- *St&PR 91*
Fritz, Donald Wayne 1929- *St&PR 91*
Fritz, Emanuel 1886-1988 *BioIn 16*
Fritz, Ernest F. 1930- *St&PR 91*
Fritz, Ethel Mae Hendrickson 1925- *WhoAmW 91*
Fritz, Gregory K 1945- *BiDrAPA 89*
Fritz, Gregory Robert 1948- *WhoEmL 91*
Fritz, Jack Wayne 1927- *WhoAm 90*
Fritz, James Sherwood 1924- *WhoAm 90*
Fritz, Jean 1915- *AuBYP 90*
Fritz, Jean Guttery 1915- *WhoAmW 91*
Fritz, Joanne Lee 1936- *WhoAmW 91*, *WhoSSW 91*
Fritz, Johann Paul 1940- *WhoWor 91*
Fritz, Marilyn Johnston 1937- *WhoAmW 91*
Fritz, Mary G. 1938- *WhoAmW 91*
Fritz, Maynard Eugene 1931- *St&PR 91*
Fritz, Michael Joseph 1942- *St&PR 91*
Fritz, Paul *BioIn 16*
Fritz, Paul Gerhard *BiDrAPA 89*
Fritz, Pelham *BioIn 16*
Fritz, Rene Eugene, Jr. 1943- *WhoAm 90*
Fritz, Roger Jay 1928- *WhoAm 90*
Fritz, Ruby M. 1928- *St&PR 91*
Fritz, Steven Edward 1960- *BiDrAPA 89*
Fritz, T.R. 1936- *St&PR 91*
Fritz, Terrence Lee 1943- *WhoWor 91*
Fritz, Thomas Clifford 1940- *WhoSSW 91*
Fritz, Thomas Vincent 1934- *WhoAm 90*
Fritz, William Warren 1943- *WhoAm 90*
Fritze, James Napier 1925- *St&PR 91*
Fritze, Julius Arnold 1918- *WhoSSW 91*, *WhoWor 91*
Fritze, Roger Laurence 1946- *WhoSSW 91*
Fritzhand, Marek 1913- *WhoWor 91*
Fritzke, Audrey Elmere 1933- *WhoAmW 91*
Fritzke, Paul Henry 1936- *St&PR 91*, *WhoAm 90*
Fritzler, Gerald J 1953- *WhoAmA 91*
Fritzsch, Harald 1943- *WhoWor 91*
Fritzsche, Hellmut 1927- *St&PR 91*, *WhoAm 90*
Fritzsche, Paul 1925- *St&PR 91*
Fritzsche, R. Wayne 1949- *WhoE 91*
Frizon, Maud *BioIn 16*
Frizzell, Kent 1929- *WhoAm 90*
Frizzell, Lefty *WhoNeCM C*
Frizzell, Lucille Bridgers 1925- *WhoAmW 91*, *WhoSSW 91*
Frizzell, Peter Graham *BiDrAPA 89*
Frizzell, William Kenneth 1928- *WhoAm 90*
Frizzell-Donner, Judith 1958- *WhoAmW 91*
Frobe, Gert 1913-1988 *AnObit 1988*, *BioIn 16*
Frobel, Doug 1959- *Ballpl 90*
Frobenius, Wolf 1940- *IntWWM 90*
Frobisher, Martin 1535?-1594 *EncCRAm*, *WorAlBi*
Frock, Edmond Burnell 1910- *WhoAm 90*
Frock, George 1938- *IntWWM 90*
Frock, John Daniel 1940- *WhoE 91*
Frock, Sam 1882-1925 *Ballpl 90*
Froding, Gustaf 1860-1911 *DcScanL*
Frodsham, Anthony Freer 1919- *WhoWor 91*
Frodsham, John David 1930- *WhoWor 91*
Froebe, Hans Albrecht 1931- *WhoWor 91*
Froebel, Friedrich Wilhelm 1782-1852 *WorAlBi*
Froehlich, Anna Ingrid 1956- *WhoAmW 91*
Froehlich, Clifford Wayne 1956- *WhoEmL 91*
Froehlich, Dean Alan 1950- *WhoEmL 91*
Froehlich, Fritz Edgar 1925- *WhoAm 90*
Froehlich, Harold Vernon 1932- *WhoAm 90*
Froehlich, Joachim William 1944- *WhoAm 90*, *WhoE 91*
Froehlich, John Francis 1948- *WhoSSW 91*
Froehlich, Josef Wolfgang 1935- *WhoWor 91*
Froehlich, Karlfried 1930- *WhoAm 90*
Froehlich, Kristi Lynn 1964- *WhoAmW 91*
Froehlich, Laurence Alan 1951- *WhoEmL 91*
Froehlich, Leonhard H. 1929- *St&PR 91*
Froehlich, Linda Ann 1947- *WhoAmW 91*
Froehlich, Margaret Walden 1930- *BioIn 16*
Froehlich, Ronald L. 1942- *ODwPR 91*
Froehlke, Robert Frederick 1922- *St&PR 91*, *WhoAm 90*
Froelich, Bernard John 1936- *St&PR 91*
Froelich, Frederick Karl 1946- *WhoE 91*, *WhoEmL 91*
Froelich, John Jacob *BiDrAPA 89*
Froelich, Paul 1897- *WhoAmA 91N*
Froelich, Ralph D 1936- *BiDrAPA 89*
Froelich, Wolfgang Andreas 1927- *WhoAm 90*
Froelicher, Andre 1959- *IntWWM 90*
Froemming, Bruce 1939- *Ballpl 90*, *BioIn 16*
Froemming, Herbert Dean 1936- *WhoAm 90*
Froemming, Karl-Heinz 1925- *WhoWor 91*
Froemming, Steve Craig 1946- *WhoE 91*
Froemsdorf, Donald Hope 1934- *WhoAm 90*
Froeschke, Linda Carol 1960- *WhoEmL 91*
Froeschle, Robert Edward 1918- *WhoAm 90*
Froese, Carol Ann *BiDrAPA 89*
Froese, Colleen Lynn *BiDrAPA 89*
Froese, Edgar *NewAgMG*
Froese, Leonhard 1924- *WhoWor 91*
Froese, Victor 1940- *WhoAm 90*
Froesel, David Wm. 1930- *St&PR 91*
Froesner, Gert G. 1942- *WhoWor 91*
Froessl, Horst Waldemar 1929- *WhoWor 91*
Froewiss, Kenneth Clark 1945- *WhoE 91*
Frogel, Marvin P *BiDrAPA 89*
Frogge, William Francis *WhoSSW 91*
Frohberg, Gunter 1935- *WhoWor 91*
Frohlich, Edward David 1931- *WhoAm 90*
Frohlich, Emil L. 1931- *St&PR 91*
Frohlich, Jack T. 1950- *WhoE 91*
Frohlich, Jurg Martin 1946- *WhoWor 91*
Frohlich, Kenneth R. 1945- *St&PR 91*
Frohlich, Marie A. 1905- *St&PR 91*
Frohlich, Moses M *BiDrAPA 89*
Frohling, Edward Sebastian 1924- *St&PR 91*
Frohman, Charles 1860-1915 *OxCPMus*
Frohman, Howard Loeb 1916- *WhoWrEP 89*
Frohman, Lawrence Asher 1935- *WhoAm 90*
Frohmann, Jules 1933- *St&PR 91*
Frohn, David Ross 1945- *WhoEmL 91*, *WhoSSW 91*
Frohne, Vincent Sauter 1936- *IntWWM 90*
Frohnmayer, David *BioIn 16*
Frohnmayer, David Braden 1940- *WhoAm 90*
Frohnmayer, John E. 1942- *BioIn 16*, *CurBio 90 [port]*
Frohnmayer, John Edward 1942- *WhoAm 90*
Frohnmayer, Katie *BioIn 16*
Frohnmayer, Kirsten *BioIn 16*
Frohnmayer, Lynn *BioIn 16*
Frohock, Fred Manuel 1937- *WhoAm 90*
Frohock, Joan 1939- *WhoAm 90*
Frohring, Paul Robert *WhoAm 90*
Frohwirth, Daniel Henry *BiDrAPA 89*
Frohwirth, Todd 1962- *Ballpl 90*
Froilan Gonzalez, Jose *BioIn 16*
Froke, Leo B *BiDrAPA 89*
Frolander, Ulf 1939- *WhoWor 91*
Frolich, B.D. 1940- *St&PR 91*
Frolich, Bruce Davison 1940- *WhoAm 90*
Frolio, Charles Michael 1950- *WhoE 91*
Frolov, Vadim 1913- *AuBYP 90*
Frolove, Ruth *BioIn 16*
Frolund, Hakon 1916- *WhoWor 91*
From, Harry *WhoE 91*
Fromageau, Jean-Baptiste 1726?-1781? *PenDiDA 89*
Froman, Ann *WhoAmW 91*
Froman, Ann 1942- *WhoAmA 91*
Froman, Charles A., Jr. 1929- *St&PR 91*
Froman, Michael Braverman 1962- *WhoEmL 91*
Froman, Ramon Mitchell 1908-1980 *WhoAmA 91N*
Froman, Robert 1917- *AuBYP 90*
Fromberg, Gerald 1925-1977 *WhoAmA 91N*
Fromberg, Kurt Christian 1934- *WhoWor 91*
Fromberg, Vivian *BiDrAPA 89*
Fromboluti, Sideo 1920- *BioIn 16*, *WhoAmA 91*, *WhoE 91*
Frome, David *TwCCr&M 91*
Frome, David Herman 1945- *WhoE 91*
Frome, Milton *BioIn 16*
Frome, R.L. *St&PR 91*
Frome, Simon J. 1928- *WhoSSW 91*
Froment, Louis de 1921- *PenDiMP*
Froment-Meurice, Emile 1837-1913 *PenDiDA 89*
Froment-Meurice, Francois-Desire 1802-1855 *PenDiDA 89*
Fromentin, Christine Anne 1953- *WhoAmA 91*
Fromer, Harvey S. 1941- *St&PR 91*
Fromery, Alex *PenDiDA 89*
Fromhagen, Carl, Jr. 1926- *WhoAm 90*
Fromkes, Saul *WhoAm 90*
Fromkin, Victoria Alexandria 1923- *WhoAm 90*
Fromm, Alfred 1905- *WhoAm 90*
Fromm, Arno Henry 1902- *WhoAm 90*
Fromm, Bernard 1935- *St&PR 91*
Fromm, Carolyn *ODwPR 91*
Fromm, David 1939- *WhoAm 90*
Fromm, Eli 1939- *WhoAm 90*
Fromm, Erich 1900-1980 *BioIn 16*, *EncAL*, *MajTwCW*, *WorAlBi*
Fromm, Erika 1910- *WhoAm 90*
Fromm, Erwin Frederick 1933- *WhoSSW 91*
Fromm, Hans 1919- *WhoWor 91*
Fromm, Henry Gordon 1911- *WhoAm 90*
Fromm, Janine Bergerac *BiDrAPA 89*
Fromm, Jeffery Bernard 1947- *WhoEmL 91*
Fromm, Joseph 1920- *WhoAm 90*
Fromm, Joseph L. 1930- *WhoWor 91*
Fromm, Laurentine A R 1948- *BiDrAPA 89*
Fromm, Paul Oliver 1923- *WhoAm 90*
Fromm, Winfield Eric 1918- *WhoAm 90*
Fromm-Kirsten, Rose 1913- *BiDrAPA 89*
Fromme, Arnold 1925- *IntWWM 90*
Fromme, Art 1883-1956 *Ballpl 90*
Fromme, Lynette 1948- *WorAlBi*
Fromme, William Raymond 1942- *WhoAm 90*
Frommell, James L. 1948- *St&PR 91*
Frommelt, Gayle Marie 1960- *WhoAmW 91*
Frommelt, Warren T. 1922- *St&PR 91*
Frommer, Henry 1943- *WhoE 91*
Frommer, Peter Leslie 1932- *WhoAm 90*
Frommer, Sara Hoskinson 1938- *WhoWrEP 89*
Frommeyer, Denise Li 1953- *WhoAmW 91*
Frommhold, Walter 1921- *WhoWor 91*
Fromont, Michel Jean 1940- *St&PR 91*
Fromowitz, Allen 1948- *WhoE 91*
Fromson, Antoinette Duval 1925- *WhoAmW 91*, *WhoE 91*
Fromson, Jeffrey 1944- *St&PR 91*
Fromson, John Adam 1953- *BiDrAPA 89*, *WhoE 91*
Fromstein, Mitchell S. *BioIn 16*
Fromstein, Stevie Ray *BioIn 16*
Fronabarger, Allen Kem 1948- *WhoAm 90*
Fronckiewicz, Robert Lawrence 1936- *St&PR 91*
Fronczek, Janusz *EncO&P 3*
Frondizi, Arturo 1908- *BioIn 16*
Fronduti, A. Rex 1926- *St&PR 91*
Fronek, Kitty 1925- *WhoAmW 91*
Fronheiser, James Joseph 1930- *St&PR 91*
Fronk, John D. 1954- *St&PR 91*
Fronk, Rhonda Beth 1956- *WhoEmL 91*
Fronk, Robert Steven 1959- *St&PR 91*
Fronk, William Joseph 1925- *WhoAm 90*
Frons, Aric *BioIn 16*
Front Man *DcCanB 12*
Front, Marshall Bernard 1937- *St&PR 91*
Front, Theodore 1909- *IntWWM 90*
Frontenac, Comte De Palluau Et De 1620-1698 *WhNaAH*
Frontenac, Louis De Buade, Comte De 1622-1698 *EncCRAm*
Frontera, Ernesto A *BiDrAPA 89*
Frontera, Miguel Antonio *BiDrAPA 89*
Frontiere, Georgia *WhoAm 90*, *WhoAmW 91*
Fronville, Claire Louise 1956- *WhoEmL 91*
Fronzoni, A G 1923- *ConDes 90*
Frooks, Dorothy *WhoAmW 91*
Froom, David 1951- *IntWWM 90*
Froom, William Watkins 1915- *WhoAm 90*
Froome, Marie Olive 1933- *WhoAmW 91*
Frosch, Aaron R. 1924- *WhoAm 90*
Frosch, Aaron R. 1924-1989 *BioIn 16*
Frosch, Emily J 1961- *BiDrAPA 89*
Frosch, James Peter 1949- *BiDrAPA 89*, *WhoE 91*
Frosch, John 1909- *BiDrAPA 89*
Frosch, Robert Alan 1928- *St&PR 91*, *WhoAm 90*
Frosch, William A 1932- *BiDrAPA 89*
Froschauer, Richard Alfred, Jr. 1963- *WhoE 91*
Froshaug, Anthony 1920-1984 *ConDes 90*
Frossard, Louis-Oscar 1889-1946 *BiDFrPL*
Frossi, Paolo 1921- *WhoWor 91*
Frost, A. Corwin 1934- *WhoE 91*
Frost, Allen Lee 1934- *St&PR 91*
Frost, Allison K. 1956- *WhoAmW 91*
Frost, Anne Breiding 1932- *WhoSSW 91*
Frost, Bobby Jean 1932- *WhoWor 91*
Frost, Brian Standish 1958- *WhoEmL 91*
Frost, Carl E. 1949- *WhoEmL 91*
Frost, Charles Estes, Jr. 1950- *WhoEmL 91*
Frost, Charles Harper 1920- *WhoSSW 91*
Frost, Charmaine L *BiDrAPA 89*
Frost, Cheryl Lynn 1961- *WhoSSW 91*
Frost, Chester Robert 1939- *St&PR 91*
Frost, Daniel Montague 1843- *BioIn 16*
Frost, Dave 1952- *Ballpl 90*
Frost, David 1939- *ConAu 31NR*, *WhoAm 90*, *WhoWor 91*, *WorAlBi*
Frost, Earle Wesley 1899- *WhoAm 90*
Frost, Elinor *BioIn 16*
Frost, Ellen Elizabeth 1947- *WhoE 91*
Frost, Ellen Louise 1945- *WhoAm 90*
Frost, F. Daniel 1922- *St&PR 91*
Frost, Faye Juanita 1927- *WhoWrEP 89*
Frost, Felicia Dodee 1956- *WhoAmW 91*
Frost, Herbert 1921- *WhoWor 91*
Frost, Herbert G., Jr. 1931- *St&PR 91*
Frost, Jacqueline Ford 1963- *WhoE 91*
Frost, James Arthur 1918- *WhoAm 90*
Frost, James Thomas 1929- *St&PR 91*
Frost, Janet I. 1935- *WhoAmW 91*
Frost, Jason *WhoWrEP 89*
Frost, Jerry William 1940- *WhoAm 90*
Frost, Joe Lindell 1933- *WhoAm 90*
Frost, John Eldridge 1917- *WhoE 91*, *WhoWor 91*
Frost, John Elliott 1924- *WhoSSW 91*, *WhoWor 91*
Frost, John Jared, Jr. 1954- *St&PR 91*
Frost, John K. *NewYTBS 90*
Frost, John Kingsbury 1922- *WhoAm 90*, *WhoE 91*
Frost, John Lawrence 1935- *St&PR 91*, *WhoAm 90*
Frost, John Orne Johnson 1852-1928 *MusmAFA*
Frost, John Sidney 1949- *St&PR 91*
Frost, John Wesley, II 1942- *WhoSSW 91*
Frost, Jonas Martin 1942- *WhoAm 90*, *WhoSSW 91*
Frost, Joni *ConAu 31NR*
Frost, Juanita Corbitt 1926- *WhoAmW 91*
Frost, Lane *BioIn 16*
Frost, Lawrence A 1907-1990 *ConAu 132*
Frost, Lawrence B. 1942- *St&PR 91*
Frost, Leopold 1926- *BiDrAPA 89*
Frost, Lloyd Howard *BiDrAPA 89*
Frost, Margaret Anne 1935- *WhoAmW 91*
Frost, Mark Edward 1948- *WhoE 91*
Frost, Mark Lynn *BiDrAPA 89*
Frost, Michael Lindsey 1961- *WhoSSW 91*
Frost, Monica McAsey 1959- *WhoAmW 91*
Frost, Nicholas R 1941- *BiDrAPA 89*
Frost, Norman Cooper 1923- *WhoAm 90*
Frost, Ormond 1927- *WhoAm 90*
Frost, Patricia *BioIn 16*
Frost, Paul *ConAu 32NR*
Frost, Phillip *BioIn 16*
Frost, Phillip 1936- *St&PR 91*
Frost, Reuben B. 1907-1989 *BioIn 16*
Frost, Richard George 1929- *WhoWrEP 89*
Frost, Richard Ray 1942- *WhoWor 91*
Frost, Robert 1874-1963 *BioIn 16*, *ConAu 33NR*, *MajTwCW*, *PoeCrit 1 [port]*, *WorAlBi*, *WrPh*
Frost, Robert 1939- *ODwPR 91*, *WhoAm 90*
Frost, Robert Edwin 1932- *WhoAm 90*
Frost, Ronald Watt 1945- *WhoEmL 91*
Frost, Rose Kobel 1950- *WhoAmW 91*
Frost, Russell, III 1921- *St&PR 91*
Frost, S. David 1930- *WhoAm 90*
Frost, Stuart Homer 1925- *WhoAmA 91*
Frost, Susan Ann 1945- *WhoAmW 91*
Frost, Susan Armor 1963- *WhoSSW 91*
Frost, T.C., Jr. 1927- *St&PR 91*
Frost, Terry 1915- *BioIn 16*
Frost, Thomas Clayborne 1927- *WhoAm 90*
Frost, William Lee 1926- *WhoAm 90*
Frost, Winston Lyle 1958- *WhoEmL 91*
Frost-Tucker, Vontell Delores 1951- *WhoE 91*
Frota-Pessoa, Oswaldo 1917- *WhoWor 91*
Frothingham, A. Michael 1921- *WhoAm 90*
Frothingham, Benjamin 1734-1809 *PenDiDA 89*
Frothingham, Benjamin, III *PenDiDA 89*
Frothingham, Louis Adams 1871-1928 *AmLegL*
Frothingham, Thomas Eliot 1926- *WhoAm 90*
Frotscher, Michael 1947- *WhoWor 91*

Frouchtben, Bernard 1878-1956 *WhoAmA 91N*
Froude, James Anthony 1818-1894 *BioIn 16*
Froula, James 1945- *WhoWrEP 89*
Frounberg, Ivar 1950- *IntWWM 90*
Frowen, Stephen Francis 1923- *WhoWor 91*
Frowick, Lawrence Harry 1920- *St&PR 91*
Frowick, Robert Holmes 1929- *WhoAm 90*
Frowick, Roy Halston *BioIn 16*
Fruchtenbaum, Edward 1948- *St&PR 91*
Fruchter, Jonathan Sewell 1945- *WhoEmL 91*
Fruchter, Scott Joseph 1951- *WhoEmL 91*
Fruchterman, James Robert, Jr. 1959- *WhoEmL 91*
Fruchthandler, Beatrice *BiDrAPA 89*
Fruchtman, Milton Allen *WhoAm 90*
Fruchtman, Shirley Millstein 1922- *WhoAmW 91*
Frudakis, Anthony P 1953- *WhoAmA 91*
Frudakis, Evangelos William 1921- *WhoAm 90, WhoAmA 91*
Frudakis, Gerd Hesness 1952- *WhoAmA 91*
Frudakis, Zenos 1951- *WhoAmA 91*
Frueauf, Wendy Holly 1953- *WhoEmL 91*
Fruechtel, Warren Bosset 1931- *WhoE 91*
Frueckert, Rolf Herbert 1945- *WhoWor 91*
Frueh, Joanna 1948- *WhoAmA 91*
Frueh, John Curt 1934- *St&PR 91*
Frueh, Lloyd W., II 1936- *St&PR 91*
Fruehan, Annette Shirley 1944- *WhoAmW 91*
Fruehauf, August Charles 1868-1930 *EncABHB 4*
Fruehauf, Harvey C. 1893-1968 *WorAlBi*
Fruehauf, Harvey C., Jr. 1929- *St&PR 91*
Fruehling, Carl R. 1935- *St&PR 91*
Fruehling, Donald Laverne 1931- *WhoAm 90, WhoE 91, WhoWor 91*
Fruehling, Rosemary T. 1933- *WhoAmW 91*
Frugoni, Orazio 1921- *BioIn 16, PenDiMP*
Fruhauf, Aline 1907-1978 *WhoAmA 91N*
Fruhauf, Louis 1897-1988 *BioIn 16*
Fruhbeck De Burgos, Rafael 1933- *IntWWM 90, PenDiMP, WhoAm 90, WhoWor 91*
Fruhling, Julian Lee 1953- *St&PR 91*
Fruhmann, Karen Anne *WhoAmW 91*
Fruin, Robert Cornelius 1925- *WhoAm 90*
Fruit, John A. 1939- *St&PR 91*
Fruit, Melvyn Herschel 1937- *WhoAm 90*
Fruit, Richard E. 1941- *St&PR 91*
Fruitman, Frederick Howard 1950- *WhoEmL 91*
Fruitt, Paul Nelson 1931- *St&PR 91*
Frulio, Francesco Paul 1939- *WhoSSW 91*
Frullini, Luigi 1839-1897 *PenDiDA 89*
Frum, Carlos M. 1945- *WhoHisp 91*
Frum, Elsie *BioIn 16*
Frumin, Morris 1922- *BiDrAPA 89*
Frumkes, Lewis Burke 1939- *WhoWrEP 89*
Frumkes, Melvyn Benjamin 1929- *WhoSSW 91*
Frumkes, Peter Jacob *BiDrAPA 89*
Frumkin, Aleksandr Naumovich 1895-1976 *DcScB S2*
Frumkin, Allan 1926- *WhoAm 90, WhoAmA 91*
Frumkin, Neil David 1939- *St&PR 91*
Frumkin, Victor Robert 1929- *St&PR 91*
Frunze, M. V. 1885-1925 *BioIn 16*
Frunze, Mikhail Vasil'evich 1885-1925 *BioIn 16*
Frush, James Carroll, Jr. 1930- *WhoWor 91*
Frushour, Susan Tydings 1947- *WhoSSW 91*
Frusinica *EncCoWW*
Fruth, Beryl Rose 1952- *WhoAmW 91, WhoEmL 91*
Frutiger, Adrian 1928- *ConDes 90*
Frux, Gregory William 1958- *WhoEmL 91*
Fruzzetti, Oreste Giorgio 1938- *WhoWor 91*
Fry, Albert Joseph 1937- *WhoAm 90*
Fry, Ann Lyons 1929- *WhoSSW 91*
Fry, Anne Evans 1939- *WhoAmW 91*
Fry, Barry James 1942- *WhoE 91*
Fry, C Brooks *BiDrAPA 89*
Fry, C George 1936- *ConAu 31NR*
Fry, C. Herbert 1926- *WhoAm 90*
Fry, Charles E., Jr. 1952- *St&PR 91*
Fry, Charles George 1936- *WhoWor 91*
Fry, Charles L. 1934- *St&PR 91*
Fry, Charles L. 1935- *ODwPR 91*
Fry, Christopher *BioIn 16*
Fry, Christopher 1907- *AuBYP 90, ConAu 30NR, MajTwCW, WorAlBi*
Fry, Cynthia Anne 1953- *WhoEmL 91*
Fry, Daniel 1908- *EncO&P 3*
Fry, David *ConAu 130*
Fry, David John 1929- *St&PR 91*
Fry, Donald Lewis 1924- *WhoAm 90*
Fry, Donald Owen 1921- *WhoAm 90*
Fry, Donna Marie 1947- *WhoAmW 91*
Fry, Doris Hendricks 1918- *WhoAm 90*
Fry, Edward 1935- *WhoAmA 91*
Fry, Edward Irad 1924- *WhoAm 90*
Fry, Edwin Maxwell 1899-1987 *BioIn 16*
Fry, Eldon Ervin 1946- *WhoE 91*
Fry, Elizabeth Gurney 1780-1845 *BioIn 16*
Fry, Harold H, Jr. *BiDrAPA 89*
Fry, Harry Wellman 1932- *St&PR 91*
Fry, Hayden 1929- *WhoAm 90*
Fry, Henry 1826-1896 *DcCanB 12*
Fry, J. Lee 1949- *St&PR 91*
Fry, James C. *St&PR 91*
Fry, James C. 1930- *WhoAm 90*
Fry, James Edward 1928- *WhoSSW 91*
Fry, James H 1923- *BiDrAPA 89*
Fry, James Wilson 1939- *WhoAm 90*
Fry, John 1930- *St&PR 91, WhoAm 90, WhoWrEP 89*
Fry, Keith A. 1955- *St&PR 91*
Fry, Laurel L. 1946- *ODwPR 91*
Fry, Leo Marcus, Jr. 1948- *WhoSSW 91*
Fry, Leolan Harold, Jr. 1949- *WhoSSW 91*
Fry, Linda Sue 1961- *WhoAmW 91*
Fry, Louis Edwin, Jr. 1928- *WhoAm 90*
Fry, M. Susanna *BioIn 16*
Fry, Malcolm Craig 1928- *WhoAm 90*
Fry, Marion Golda 1932- *WhoAmW 91*
Fry, Maxwell John 1944- *WhoAm 90*
Fry, Michael *BioIn 16*
Fry, Michael Graham 1934- *WhoAm 90*
Fry, Mildred Helen 1940- *WhoAmW 91*
Fry, Morton Harrison, II 1946- *WhoWor 91*
Fry, Nenah Elinor 1933- *WhoAm 90, WhoAmW 91*
Fry, Paul H. 1944- *ConAu 129*
Fry, Rabindranath *BiDrAPA 89*
Fry, Richard Newton 1938- *WhoSSW 91*
Fry, Robert Dean 1955- *St&PR 91*
Fry, Ronald William 1949- *WhoEmL 91*
Fry, Rosalie K. 1911- *SmATA 11AS [port]*
Fry, Rosalie Kingsmill 1911- *AuBYP 90*
Fry, Samuel Edwin, Jr. 1934- *WhoE 91*
Fry, Shanti Addison 1951- *WhoE 91*
Fry, Steve J. 1946- *St&PR 91*
Fry, Steven Edward 1945- *St&PR 91*
Fry, Thomas Richard 1948- *WhoEmL 91*
Fry, William F, Jr. *BiDrAPA 89*
Fry, William Frederick 1921- *WhoAm 90*
Fryar, Russell McKennie 1938- *St&PR 91*
Fryatt, Charles Algernon *BioIn 16*
Fryatt, Norma R. *AuBYP 90*
Fryback, Ronald D. 1936- *St&PR 91*
Fryberger, Amy Jo 1966- *WhoAmW 91*
Fryberger, Betsy G 1935- *WhoAmA 91*
Fryberger, H.B., Jr. 1906- *St&PR 91*
Fryburger, Vernon Ray, Jr. 1918- *WhoAm 90*
Fryczkowski, Andrzej Witold 1939- *WhoWor 91*
Frydenborg, Charles Arthur 1933- *St&PR 91*
Frydman, Roman 1948- *WhoE 91*
Frye, Billy Eugene 1933- *WhoAm 90*
Frye, Bobbie Sue 1937- *WhoAmW 91*
Frye, Dean *AuBYP 90*
Frye, Della Mae 1926- *WhoWrEP 89*
Frye, Don W. 1934- *St&PR 91*
Frye, Gilbert Bernard 1938- *St&PR 91*
Frye, Gilbert Chappelle 1924- *WhoAm 90*
Frye, Harvey R. *BioIn 16*
Frye, Helen Jackson 1930- *WhoAm 90, WhoAmW 91*
Frye, Henry E. 1932- *WhoAm 90*
Frye, Herbert David 1950- *WhoE 91*
Frye, John H., Jr. 1908- *WhoAm 90*
Frye, John William, III 1929- *WhoAm 90*
Frye, Joseph T. 1918- *St&PR 91*
Frye, Judith Eleen Minor *WhoAmW 91, WhoWor 91*
Frye, June Claire 1938- *BiDrAPA 89*
Frye, Keith Nale 1941- *WhoAm 90*
Frye, Leslie Legge Sarony 1897-1985 *DcNaB 1981*
Frye, Mauna 1947- *St&PR 91*
Frye, Newton Phillips, Jr. 1918- *WhoAm 90*
Frye, Northrop *BioIn 16*
Frye, Northrop 1912- *MajTwCW, WhoAm 90, WhoWor 91, WhoWrEP 89*
Frye, Paul Edward *BiDrAPA 89*
Frye, Richard Nelson 1920- *WhoAm 90*
Frye, Roland Mushat 1921- *WhoAm 90*
Frye, Roland Mushat, Jr. 1950- *WhoEmL 91*
Frye, Stephen H 1941- *BiDrAPA 89*
Frye, Thomas 1710-1762 *PenDiDA 89*
Frye, William Ruggles 1918- *WhoAm 90*
Frye Hoffman, Lois 1955- *WhoWrEP 89*
Fryer, Arlene Barbara 1931- *St&PR 91*
Fryer, Jack 1929- *IntWWM 90*
Fryer, Joan Cook 1952- *WhoAmW 91*
Fryer, John Ercel 1937- *BiDrAPA 89*
Fryer, John Stanley 1937- *WhoAm 90*
Fryer, Larry Anton *BiDrAPA 89*
Fryer, Minot Packer 1915- *WhoAm 90*
Fryer, Robert Sherwood 1920- *WhoAm 90, WhoWor 91*
Fryer, Simon John 1959- *IntWWM 90*
Fryer, Thomas Waitt, Jr. 1936- *WhoAm 90*
Fryer, Wendell F., Jr. 1934- *St&PR 91*
Fryer-McCulloch, Bronwyn 1954- *WhoAmW 91*
Fryet, Elizabeth *BiDEWW*
Frykberg, W. Randolph 1947- *WhoEmL 91*
Frykenberg, Robert Eric 1930- *WhoAm 90*
Fryland, Sonnich Jacob 1941- *WhoAm 90*
Frym, Gloria Lynn 1947- *WhoWrEP 89*
Fryman, Norman M. 1930- *WhoAm 90, WhoE 91*
Fryman, Woodie 1940- *Ballpl 90*
Frymer, Murry 1934- *WhoAm 90*
Frymier, Robert C 1931- *BiDrAPA 89*
Fryml, Martin Josef 1961- *St&PR 91*
Fryshdorf, Hannah *BioIn 16*
Fryt, Michael David 1955- *WhoEmL 91*
Frytom, Frederik van *PenDiDA 89*
Fryxell, David Allen 1956- *WhoAm 90*
Fryxell, Greta Albrecht 1926- *WhoAmW 91*
Fryxell, Regina Christina Holmen 1899- *IntWWM 90*
Fryz, Betty Farina 1930- *WhoE 91*
Fthenakis, Emanuel 1928- *St&PR 91*
Fthenakis, Emanuel John 1928- *WhoAm 90, WhoE 91, WhoSSW 91*
Fthenakis, Vasilis 1951- *WhoE 91*
Fu, Clara I-Hung 1964- *WhoE 91*
Fu, Karen King-Wah 1940- *WhoAm 90*
Fu, Monty Mong Chen 1946- *St&PR 91*
Fua, Giorgio 1919- *WhoWor 91*
Fubini, Eugene Ghiron 1913- *WhoAm 90*
Fuca, Juan De *EncCRAm*
Fucanan, Vilma D. *BiDrAPA 89*
Fucci, Elizabeth *BioIn 16*
Fucci, Joseph Leonard 1950- *WhoEmL 91*
Fucci, Linda D. 1947- *St&PR 91*
Fucci, Linda Dean 1947- *WhoAmW 91*
Fuchek, Robin Carol 1948- *WhoSSW 91*
Fuchs, Alfred Herman 1932- *WhoAm 90*
Fuchs, Anna-Riitta 1926- *WhoAm 90*
Fuchs, Anna Rupertina 1657-1722 *EncCoWW*
Fuchs, Anne Sutherland 1947- *WhoAm 90*
Fuchs, Bernard A. 1912- *St&PR 91*
Fuchs, Carl *PenDiMP*
Fuchs, Curtis Ray 1943- *WhoSSW 91, WhoWor 91*
Fuchs, D. Catherine *BiDrAPA 89*
Fuchs, Daniel 1909- *BioIn 16*
Fuchs, Edwin M *BiDrAPA 89*
Fuchs, Elaine V. 1950- *WhoAmW 91*
Fuchs, Frank Joseph 1954- *WhoEmL 91*
Fuchs, Fredica Ann 1949- *WhoEmL 91*
Fuchs, Fritz 1918- *WhoAm 90*
Fuchs, Hanno 1928- *WhoAm 90*
Fuchs, Helmuth Hans 1931- *WhoE 91, WhoWor 91*
Fuchs, Howard Bernard 1952- *WhoSSW 91*
Fuchs, Irvin J. 1926- *St&PR 91*
Fuchs, Jacob 1923- *IntWWM 90, WhoAm 90*
Fuchs, Jerome Herbert 1922- *WhoWor 91*
Fuchs, John M. *ODwPR 91*
Fuchs, Joseph *BioIn 16*
Fuchs, Joseph Louis 1931- *WhoAm 90*
Fuchs, Kathleen F. 1946- *WhoEmL 91*
Fuchs, Klaus 1911-1988 *AnObit 1988*
Fuchs, Klaus Emil Julius 1911-1988 *BioIn 16*
Fuchs, L. 1937- *St&PR 91*
Fuchs, Laurel Bernice 1935- *WhoWrEP 89*
Fuchs, Lawrence Howard 1927- *WhoAm 90*
Fuchs, Lucy 1935- *BioIn 16, ConAu 30NR*
Fuchs, Marc *St&PR 91*
Fuchs, Mary Allison 1926- *WhoAmW 91*
Fuchs, Mary Tharsilla 1912- *WhoAmA 91*
Fuchs, Michael *BioIn 16, NewYTBS 90*
Fuchs, Michael 1949- *WhoE 91*
Fuchs, Michael J. 1946- *WhoAm 90*
Fuchs, Michael Joseph *BioIn 16*
Fuchs, Morton S. 1932- *WhoAm 90*
Fuchs, Nancy Joan 1931- *WhoSSW 91*
Fuchs, Olivia Anne Morris 1949- *WhoEmL 91*
Fuchs, Owen George 1951- *WhoWor 91*
Fuchs, Pamela Marie 1964- *WhoAmW 91*
Fuchs, Patrick Eugene 1930- *WhoWor 91*
Fuchs, Renato 1942- *St&PR 91*
Fuchs, Roland John 1933- *WhoAm 90*
Fuchs, Ronnie Marion 1954- *BiDrAPA 89*
Fuchs, Ruth 1929- *BiDrAPA 89*
Fuchs, Ruth 1946- *BioIn 16*
Fuchs, Sam Lien 1963- *WhoAmW 91*
Fuchs, Susan *BiDrAPA 89*
Fuchs, Victor Robert 1924- *WhoAm 90*
Fuchs, Vivian 1908- *WhoWor 91*
Fuchs, William 1947- *WhoSSW 91*
Fuchsberg, Jacob David 1913- *WhoAm 90*
Fuchshuber, Annegert 1940- *AuBYP 90*
Fuchsin, Anna Rupertina 1657-1722 *EncCoWW*
Fuchsluger, Donna Jean 1952- *WhoEmL 91*
Fuchsteiner, Judith Agnes 1947- *WhoEmL 91*
Fucik, Donald Edward 1955- *WhoEmL 91*
Fucik, Frank M. 1917- *St&PR 91*
Fudalla, Marvin J. 1954- *St&PR 91*
Fudge, Dawn N. 1954- *St&PR 91*
Fudge, Dawn Natalie 1954- *WhoAmW 91*
Fudge, Deborah Ann 1961- *WhoAmW 91*
Fudge, Julie Lynne *BiDrAPA 89*
Fudold, Wallace A. 1944- *St&PR 91*
Fuduli, Robin Ann 1947- *WhoAmW 91*
Fudurich, Edward Charles 1944- *St&PR 91*
Fuechtmann, Kay Susan 1945- *WhoE 91*
Fueger, John Joseph 1955- *WhoSSW 91*
Fuegi, John 1936- *WhoAm 90*
Fuelberg, Bennie R. 1944- *St&PR 91*
Fuellgraf, Charles Louis, Jr. 1931- *St&PR 91*
Fuellhart, David Clark 1938- *WhoAm 90, WhoE 91, WhoWor 91*
Fuelling, Craig Alan *BiDrAPA 89*
Fuelling, Thomas Norton 1933- *WhoAm 90*
Fuenning, Esther Renate *WhoAmW 91*
Fuentealba, Gustavo Cifuentes 1947- *WhoWor 91*
Fuentealba, Victor William 1922- *WhoAm 90*
Fuentenebro, Filiberto 1950- *BiDrAPA 89*
Fuentes, Carlos *BioIn 16*
Fuentes, Carlos 1928- *ConAu 32NR, ConLC 60 [port], HispWr 90, MajTwCW, WhoAm 90, WhoWor 91, WorAlBi*
Fuentes, Elia Ivonne *WhoHisp 91*
Fuentes, Ernesto *WhoHisp 91*
Fuentes, Ernesto Venegas 1947- *WhoHisp 91*
Fuentes, Fernando Luis 1952- *WhoHisp 91*
Fuentes, Gregorio Lopez y *ConAu 131, HispWr 90*
Fuentes, Gus, Jr. 1953- *WhoSSW 91*
Fuentes, Humberto *WhoHisp 91*
Fuentes, John *WhoHisp 91*
Fuentes, Manuel 1955- *WhoHisp 91*
Fuentes, Martha Ayers 1923- *WhoAm 90, WhoWrEP 89*
Fuentes, Pete Acosta 1952- *WhoHisp 91*
Fuentes, R. Alan *WhoHisp 91*
Fuentes, Sonia Pressman 1928- *WhoAmW 91, WhoE 91*
Fuentes, Tina Guerrero 1949- *WhoHisp 91*
Fuentes, Tito 1944- *Ballpl 90*
Fuentes Blanco, Maria de los Reyes 1927- *EncCoWW*
Fuentevilla, Manuel Edward 1923- *WhoE 91*
Fuentez, Lucio 1944- *WhoHisp 91*
Fuerbringer, Alfred Ottomar 1903- *WhoAm 90*
Fueri, Maurice *PenDiMP*
Fuerniss, Gloria Villasana 1949- *WhoHisp 91*
Fueroghne, Dean Keith 1952- *WhoWor 91*
Fuerst, Beatrice Swancutt Wright *BioIn 16*
Fuerst, Harold T. *NewYTBS 90 [port]*
Fuerst, Harold T. 1909-1990 *BioIn 16*
Fuerst, Heinrich J R 1914- *BiDrAPA 89*
Fuerst, Shirley Miller 1928- *WhoAmA 91*
Fuerste, Frederick 1921- *WhoWor 91*
Fuerstenau, Douglas Winston 1928- *WhoAm 90*
Fuerstenberg, Gary J. 1943- *St&PR 91*
Fuerstenburg, Paul W 1875-1953 *WhoAmA 91N*
Fuertes, Carlos 1929- *WhoE 91*
Fuertes, Gloria 1918- *EncCoWW*
Fuess, Harold George 1910- *WhoAm 90*
Fuessel, Diana F. *St&PR 91*
Fuessel, Frederick Dennis *St&PR 91*
Fuessel, John Frederick *St&PR 91*
Fuessler, Rolf A. 1946- *ODwPR 91*
Fueyo, Antonio S 1920- *BiDrAPA 89*
Fufuka, Karama 1951- *BioIn 16*
Fugard, Athol *BioIn 16*
Fugard, Athol 1932- *ConAu 32NR, MajTwCW*
Fugard, Athol Harold 1932- *WhoWor 91*
Fugard, Sheila 1932- *FemiCLE*
Fugate, Douglas Brown 1906-1988 *WhoAm 90, WhoWor 91*
Fugate, Edward 1956- *WhoEmL 91*
Fugate, Ivan Dee 1928- *WhoAm 90*
Fugate, James K 1930- *BiDrAPA 89*
Fugate, Judith *WhoAm 90*
Fugate, Kendall Morgan 1937- *St&PR 91*
Fugate, Norman G. 1925- *St&PR 91*
Fugate, Robert A. 1946- *St&PR 91*
Fugate, Thomas Warren 1959- *WhoEmL 91*
Fugate, Virginia Kimbrough 1940- *WhoAmW 91*
Fugate-Wilcox, Terry 1944- *WhoAm 90*
Fugazy, William Denis *WhoAm 90*

Fugazzi, Paul Anthony 1959- *WhoSSW 91*
Fugelberg, Nancy Jean 1947- *WhoAmW 91*
Fugelle, Jacquelyn *IntWWM 90*
Fugere, Lucien 1848-1935 *PenDiMP*
Fugger, Jakob, II 1459-1525 *WorAlBi*
Fuggetta, Massimo 1961- *WhoWor 91*
Fuglestad, Judy Ellen 1948- *St&PR 91*
Fuhlrodt, Norman Theodore 1910- *WhoWor 91*
Fuhr, Grant *BioIn 16*
Fuhr, Grant 1962- *WorAlBi*
Fuhr, Jay A. *St&PR 91*
Fuhr, Theresa Marie 1964- *WhoAmW 91*
Fuhrer, Arthur K. 1926- *WhoE 91*
Fuhrer, David *BioIn 16*
Fuhriman, David H. 1947- *St&PR 91*
Fuhrman, Bruce L. 1936- *St&PR 91*
Fuhrman, Charles Andrew 1933- *WhoAm 90*
Fuhrman, David A. 1951- *St&PR 91*
Fuhrman, Edward J. 1935- *St&PR 91*
Fuhrman, Edward Joshua 1935- *WhoAm 90*
Fuhrman, Esther 1939- *WhoAmA 91, WhoAmW 91, WhoE 91*
Fuhrman, Frederick Alexander 1915- *WhoAm 90*
Fuhrman, Lawrence James 1949- *BiDrAPA 89*
Fuhrman, Ralph Edward 1909- *WhoAm 90*
Fuhrman, Robert Alexander 1925- *St&PR 91, WhoAm 90*
Fuhrmann, Charles J., II 1945- *WhoE 91*
Fuhrmann, Debora Josephine 1957- *WhoEmL 91*
Fuhrmann, Louis P. 1940- *WhoE 91*
Fuhrmann, Norbert 1940- *St&PR 91*
Fuhs, Allen Eugene 1927- *WhoAm 90*
Fuhs, Georg Wolfgang 1932- *WhoWor 91*
Fuino, Frank S., Jr. 1946- *St&PR 91*
Fuja, Abayomi *AuBYP 90*
Fujihira, Ikuko 1944- *WhoWor 91*
Fujii, Akio 1937- *WhoWor 91*
Fujii, June Seiko *BiDrAPA 89*
Fujii, Masayuki 1942- *WhoWor 91*
Fujii, Takashi 1929- *WhoWor 91*
Fujikawa, Eva 1958- *WhoAmW 91*
Fujikawa, Mayumi 1946- *IntWWM 90*
Fujimori, Alberto *BioIn 16*
Fujimori, Alberto 1938- *CurBio 90 [port], WhoWor 91*
Fujimori, Masamichi 1921- *WhoWor 91*
Fujimoto, Akira *BioIn 16*
Fujimoto, Hideo 1958- *WhoWor 91*
Fujimoto, Ichiro 1951- *WhoSSW 91*
Fujimoto, Patricia *AuBYP 90*
Fujimoto, Tetsuo 1930- *WhoWor 91*
Fujimoto, Tetsuya 1940- *WhoWor 91*
Fujimura, Tomio *Ballpl 90*
Fujioka, Masanobu Richard 1950- *WhoEmL 91*
Fujisawa, Norio 1925- *WhoWor 91*
Fujisawa, Tadashi 1931- *WhoWor 91*
Fujisawa, Tamotsu 1936- *WhoWor 91*
Fujita, Akio 1934- *WhoWor 91*
Fujita, Fujio 1907- *WhoWor 91*
Fujita, Fumiko 1937- *IntWWM 90*
Fujita, Kenji 1955- *WhoAmA 91*
Fujita, Masaaki 1922- *WhoWor 91*
Fujita, Milton T 1933- *BiDrAPA 89*
Fujita, S Neil 1921- *ConDes 90*
Fujita, Shigeji 1929- *WhoAm 90*
Fujita, Tetsuya Theodore 1920- *WhoAm 90*
Fujita, Tsuneo 1933- *WhoWor 91*
Fujita, Wayne Y. 1954- *St&PR 91*
Fujita, Yasuichiro 1931- *WhoWor 91*
Fujita, Yukio 1933- *WhoWor 91*
Fujiwara Clan *EncJap*
Fujiwara no Michinaga 966-1028 *EncJap*
Fujiwara no Teika 1162-1241 *EncJap*
Fujiwara, Elizabeth Jubin 1945- *WhoAmW 91*
Fujiwara, Hamao 1947- *WhoEmL 91*
Fujiwara, Hirofumi 1939- *WhoWor 91*
Fujiwara, Isao 1921- *WhoWor 91*
Fujiwara, Iwaichi 1908- *ConAu 132*
Fujiwara, Sakuhei 1884-1950 *EncPaPR 91*
Fukae, Kensuke 1926- *WhoE 91*
Fukai, Robert D. 1949- *St&PR 91*
Fukai, Yuh 1934- *WhoWor 91*
Fukami, Sucharu 1947- *PenDiDA 89*
Fukasawa, Tsutomu 1927- *WhoWor 91*
Fukazawa, Yoji 1933- *St&PR 91*
Fukita, Fumiaki 1926- *WhoWor 91*
Fuks, Zvi Yehiel 1936- *WhoAm 90, WhoE 91*
Fukuda Takeo 1905- *EncJap*
Fukuda, Hideko 1865-1927 *BioIn 16*
Fukuda, Michael K. 1949- *WhoEmL 91*
Fukuda, Michio 1930- *WhoWor 91*
Fukuda, Minoru 1945- *WhoEmL 91*
Fukuda, Shigeo 1932- *ConDes 90*
Fukuhara, Henry 1913- *WhoAmA 91*
Fukui, Hatsuaki 1927- *WhoAm 90, WhoWor 91*
Fukui, Kenichi 1918- *WhoAm 90, WhoWor 91, WorAlBi*
Fukui, Naoaki 1877-1963 *BioIn 16*
Fukui, Naotaka 1935- *IntWWM 90*
Fukui, Nobu 1942- *WhoAmA 91*
Fukui, Yasuhiro 1943- *WhoWor 91*
Fukumori, Yoshihiro 1952- *WhoWor 91*
Fukumoto, Joan Hanae *BiDrAPA 89*
Fukumoto, Leslie Satsuki 1955- *WhoEmL 91*
Fukumoto, Naoyuki 1939- *WhoWor 91*
Fukumoto, Yutaka 1947- *Ballpl 90*
Fukunaga, George Joji 1924- *St&PR 91, WhoAm 90*
Fukunaga, Keinosuke 1930- *WhoAm 90*
Fukunaga, Kenji *BioIn 16*
Fukurai, Tomobichi *EncO&P 3*
Fukurai, Tomokichi 1869-1952 *EncPaPR 91*
Fukushima, Akira 1936- *WhoWor 91*
Fukushima, Barbara Naomi 1948- *WhoAmW 91*
Fukushima, Keishiro 1946- *WhoWor 91*
Fukushima, Masanori 1948- *WhoWor 91*
Fukushima, Susan Naomi 1946- *BiDrAPA 89*
Fukushima, Tadamasa 1934- *WhoWor 91*
Fukushima, Tatsuhisa 1928- *WhoWor 91*
Fukutaki, Naren V. *BiDrAPA 89*
Fukuyama, Betty M. 1922- *WhoWrEP 89*
Fukuyama, Francis *BioIn 16*
Fukuyama, Tetsuo 1948- *WhoWor 91*
Fukuyama, Yukio 1928- *WhoWor 91*
Fukuzawa Yukichi 1835-1901 *EncJap*
Fukuzumi, Naoyoshi 1924- *WhoWor 91*
Fulani, Lenora *BioIn 16*
Fulbright, J. William *BioIn 16*
Fulbright, J. William 1905- *WorAlBi*
Fulbright, James William 1905- *WhoAm 90*
Fulcher, Carolyn Jean 1956- *WhoEmL 91*
Fulco, Armand John 1932- *WhoAm 90*
Fulco, Jose Roque 1927- *WhoAm 90*
Fuld, James Jeffrey 1916- *WhoAm 90*
Fuld, Richard S., Jr. 1946- *WhoAm 90*
Fuld, Stanley H. 1903- *WhoAm 90*
Fulda, Myron Oscar 1930- *WhoSSW 91*
Fuldauer, Ivan *ODwPR 91*
Fuldheim, Dorothy 1893-1989 *ConAu 130*
Fuldheim, Dorothy Snell *BioIn 16*
Fuldner, Christopher Terry 1951- *St&PR 91*
Fuldner, William Terry 1927- *St&PR 91*
Fule, Ofelia Almendral 1946- *BiDrAPA 89*
Fule, Vilma Garcia 1950- *WhoAmW 91*
Fulford, James A. 1937- *St&PR 91*
Fulford, Roger Thomas Baldwin 1902-1983 *DcNaB 1981*
Fulgham, Betty Reeves 1951- *WhoAmW 91*
Fulgham, John 1956- *Ballpl 90*
Fulgham, John Rawles, Jr. 1927- *St&PR 91*
Fulghum, Charles B, Jr. *BiDrAPA 89*
Fulghum, Robert *BioIn 16*
Fulginiti, Vincent 1931- *WhoAm 90*
Fulgoni, Gian Marc 1948- *WhoAm 90*
Fulgoni, Gian Mark 1948- *St&PR 91*
Fulgoni, Peter A. *St&PR 91*
Fulk, Roscoe Neal 1916- *WhoAm 90*
Fulk, Walter Lawrence 1951- *WhoSSW 91*
Fulkerson, Conrad Carnes 1942- *BiDrAPA 89*
Fulkerson, Conward Guard 1933- *WhoE 91*
Fulkerson, Gregory Locke 1950- *IntWWM 90*
Fulkerson, John Charles 1926- *WhoWor 91*
Fulkerson, John Rogers 1941- *WhoE 91*
Fulkerson, Richard Paul 1942- *WhoSSW 91*
Fulkerson, William Measey, Jr. 1940- *WhoAm 90*
Fulkes, Jean Aston *WhoWor 91*
Fulks, Bryan 1897- *AuBYP 90*
Fulks, Paula Jean 1954- *WhoEmL 91*
Fulks, Robert Grady 1936- *WhoE 91*
Fulks, Sarah Jane *WhoAmW 91*
Fulks, William B. 1932- *St&PR 91*
Full, Jerome K. 1926- *ODwPR 91*
Full, Jerome Kendrick 1926- *St&PR 91*
Full, Joanne N. *ODwPR 91*
Fullagar, Paul David 1938- *WhoAm 90*
Fullagar, Scott David 1960- *St&PR 91*
Fullagar, William Watts 1914- *WhoAm 90*
Fullam, John P. 1921- *WhoAm 90*
Fullam, Lisa L *ODwPR 91*
Fullan, Neil Patrick *BiDrAPA 89*
Fullbright, Wilbur D. 1926- *WhoWor 91*
Fuller, A Kenneth 1956- *BiDrAPA 89*
Fuller, Albert 1926- *IntWWM 90*
Fuller, Alfred C. 1885-1973 *WorAlBi*
Fuller, Alfred Worcester 1923- *WhoAm 90*
Fuller, Alice Cook *AuBYP 90*
Fuller, Allen Curtis 1822-1901 *AmLegL*
Fuller, Andrew 1754-1815 *BioIn 16*
Fuller, Anna 1853-1916 *FemiCLE*
Fuller, Anne *FemiCLE*
Fuller, Anne Edwards 1948- *WhoSSW 91*
Fuller, Anne Elizabeth Havens 1932- *WhoAm 90*
Fuller, Arthur D. 1944- *St&PR 91*
Fuller, Benjamin Franklin 1922- *WhoAm 90*
Fuller, Ber Karen Lackritz 1960- *WhoAmW 91*
Fuller, Blair Fairchild 1927- *WhoWrEP 89*
Fuller, Buckminster *MajTwCW*
Fuller, Buckminster 1895- *NewAgE 90*
Fuller, Caroline Case 1956- *WhoAmW 91*
Fuller, Cassandra Miller 1965- *WhoAmW 91*
Fuller, Charles *BioIn 16*
Fuller, Charles 1939- *MajTwCW, WhoAm 90, WorAlBi*
Fuller, Charles E. *BioIn 16*
Fuller, Charles Ellis 1933- *WhoSSW 91*
Fuller, Charles H., Jr. 1939- *DrBlPA 90*
Fuller, Christopher Robert 1953- *WhoEmL 91*
Fuller, Constance C. 1954- *ODwPR 91*
Fuller, Constance Crain 1947- *WhoAmW 91*
Fuller, Craig L. 1951- *ODwPR 91*
Fuller, Craig Lawrence 1951- *WhoAm 90*
Fuller, Curtis 1912- *EncO&P 3*
Fuller, Curtis 1934- *BioIn 16*
Fuller, Curtis G. 1912- *WhoAm 90*
Fuller, D. Ward 1945- *St&PR 91*
Fuller, David H, Jr. *BiDrAPA 89*
Fuller, David Lee *BiDrAPA 89*
Fuller, David Randall 1927- *IntWWM 90*
Fuller, David S 1930- *BiDrAPA 89*
Fuller, David William 1958- *WhoSSW 91*
Fuller, Derek Joseph Haggard 1917- *WhoAm 90*
Fuller, Diana 1931- *WhoAmA 91*
Fuller, Diana Lynn 1952- *WhoAmW 91*
Fuller, Dickie M. 1942- *WhoAmW 91*
Fuller, Donald Scott 1938- *St&PR 91*
Fuller, Dorothy 1930- *St&PR 91*
Fuller, Edmund 1914- *AuBYP 90*
Fuller, Edwin Daniel 1945- *WhoAm 90, WhoEmL 91, WhoWor 91*
Fuller, Elizabeth 1946- *ConAu 33NR*
Fuller, Emily Rutgers 1941- *WhoAmA 91*
Fuller, Ernie Cecil 1962- *WhoSSW 91*
Fuller, G. M. 1920- *WhoSSW 91*
Fuller, G. Robert 1938- *WhoE 91*
Fuller, Gail Elaine 1953- *WhoWor 91*
Fuller, Gail Marie *WhoAmW 91*
Fuller, George *WhoAm 90*
Fuller, Gilbert Amos 1941- *St&PR 91*
Fuller, Glenn Arthur 1940- *St&PR 91*
Fuller, Gloria Dawn 1953- *WhoWrEP 89*
Fuller, Gogo *BioIn 16*
Fuller, Gordon McIntosh 1957- *WhoE 91*
Fuller, Harold J, Jr. *BiDrAPA 89*
Fuller, Harry Laurance 1938- *WhoAm 90, WhoWor 91*
Fuller, Heidi *ODwPR 91*
Fuller, Herbert Harold 1946- *WhoEmL 91*
Fuller, Horace W. *BioIn 16*
Fuller, J F C 1878-1966 *EncO&P 3*
Fuller, Jack 1946- *ConAu 130*
Fuller, Jack Glendon, Jr. 1923- *WhoAm 90*
Fuller, Jack William 1946- *WhoAm 90*
Fuller, Jackson Franklin 1920- *WhoAm 90*
Fuller, James Chester Eedy 1927- *WhoAm 90*
Fuller, James Stanley 1947- *St&PR 91*
Fuller, Jane Hoffelt 1955- *WhoEmL 91*
Fuller, Jean 1915- *FemiCLE*
Fuller, Jean Overton 1915- *EncO&P 3*
Fuller, Jefferson Boyce 1926- *St&PR 91*
Fuller, Jeffrey P 1950- *WhoAmA 91*
Fuller, Jeffrey R. *St&PR 91*
Fuller, Jesse 1896-1976 *OxCPMus*
Fuller, Jewel Ladene Adams 1933- *WhoAmW 91*
Fuller, Jim *BioIn 16*
Fuller, John 1913-1990 *NewYTBS 90*
Fuller, John 1937- *ConLC 62 [port]*
Fuller, John Charles 1937- *WhoAmA 91, WhoE 91*
Fuller, John Chisholm 1932- *St&PR 91*
Fuller, John Frederick 1878-1966 *WorAlBi*
Fuller, John Frederick Charles 1878-1966 *BioIn 16*
Fuller, John Garsed Campbell 1930- *WhoAm 90*
Fuller, John Grant 1913- *WhoAm 90*
Fuller, John Joseph 1931- *WhoAm 90*
Fuller, John Langworthy 1910- *WhoAm 90*
Fuller, Joseph 1926- *St&PR 91*
Fuller, Joseph, Jr. 1947- *WhoE 91*
Fuller, Joseph D., III 1947- *WhoEmL 91*
Fuller, Juanita Faison 1927- *WhoAmW 91*
Fuller, Julia Pazdral 1945- *WhoAmW 91*
Fuller, Julia Ruth 1958- *WhoAmW 91*
Fuller, Justin 1926- *WhoSSW 91*
Fuller, Karen Ann 1947- *WhoAmW 91*
Fuller, Kenneth Roller 1913- *WhoAm 90*
Fuller, Kevin Douglas 1957- *WhoEmL 91*
Fuller, Lawrence Joseph 1914- *WhoAm 90*
Fuller, Lawrence Robert 1941- *WhoAm 90*
Fuller, Loie 1862-1928 *BioIn 16, NotWoAT*
Fuller, Lois B 1933- *BiDrAPA 89*
Fuller, Lois Hamilton 1915- *AuBYP 90*
Fuller, Lorenzo *EarBlAP*
Fuller, Lucia 1870-1924 *BiDWomA*
Fuller, Lucia Fairchild 1872-1924 *BioIn 16*
Fuller, Margaret 1810-1850 *BioAmW, BioIn 16, FemiCLE*
Fuller, Margaret Cathcart 1935- *WhoWrEP 89*
Fuller, Margaret Virginia 1948- *WhoAmW 91*
Fuller, Marilyn Rita 1957- *WhoSSW 91*
Fuller, Mark Adin, Jr. 1933- *St&PR 91, WhoAm 90*
Fuller, Mark Guthrie 1956- *BiDrAPA 89*
Fuller, Mary 1922- *WhoAmA 91*
Fuller, Mary Falvey 1941- *WhoWor 91*
Fuller, Mary Margaret Stiehm 1914- *WhoWrEP 89*
Fuller, Maxine Compton 1921- *WhoSSW 91, WhoWor 91*
Fuller, Melvin Stuart 1931- *WhoAm 90*
Fuller, Meta Vaux 1877-1968 *BiDWomA*
Fuller, Meta Vaux Warrick 1877-1968 *WhoAmA 91N*
Fuller, Michael David 1934- *WhoAm 90*
Fuller, Mike *BioIn 16*
Fuller, Mike Andrew 1964- *WhoWrEP 89*
Fuller, Millard *BioIn 16*
Fuller, Millard Dean 1935- *WhoAm 90*
Fuller, Mozelle James 1909- *WhoAmW 91*
Fuller, Myron F. *St&PR 91*
Fuller, Nancy J. 1949- *St&PR 91*
Fuller, Orville 1925- *St&PR 91*
Fuller, Paula G. 1949- *WhoAmW 91*
Fuller, Perry Lucian 1922- *WhoAm 90*
Fuller, Peter 1923- *St&PR 91*
Fuller, Peter 1947-1990 *BioIn 16*
Fuller, R. B. 1890-1963 *EncACom [port]*
Fuller, R Buckminster 1895-1983 *MajTwCW, WhoAmA 91N*
Fuller, R. Buckminster 1895-1983 *WorAlBi*
Fuller, Raymond Tifft 1889- *AuBYP 90*
Fuller, Reginald Horace 1915- *WhoAm 90*
Fuller, Richard 1804-1876 *BioIn 16*
Fuller, Richard Allen 1941- *WhoE 91*
Fuller, Richard Buckminster 1895-1983 *ConDes 90, PenDiDA 89*
Fuller, Richard Eugene 1897-1976 *WhoAmA 91N*
Fuller, Richard Harrison 1928- *WhoAm 90*
Fuller, Robert A. 1938- *St&PR 91*
Fuller, Robert Earl 1938- *BiDrAPA 89*
Fuller, Robert Ferrey 1929- *WhoAm 90*
Fuller, Robert Ray 1933- *WhoSSW 91*
Fuller, Robert Walker, III 1959- *WhoEmL 91*
Fuller, Roy 1912- *TwCCr&M 91*
Fuller, Russell Lee 1943- *WhoSSW 91*
Fuller, Ruth *ConAu 131*
Fuller, Ruth L *BiDrAPA 89*
Fuller, S. B. *BioIn 16*
Fuller, Sam *ConAu 129*
Fuller, Samuel *BioIn 16*
Fuller, Samuel 1911- *ConTFT 8*
Fuller, Samuel 1912- *ConAu 129, WhoAm 90*
Fuller, Samuel Ashby 1924- *WhoAm 90*
Fuller, Samuel Henry 1946- *St&PR 91*
Fuller, Samuel Henry, III 1946- *WhoAm 90, WhoE 91*
Fuller, Sarah Margaret 1810-1850 *WorAlBi*
Fuller, Sharon S. 1946- *WhoAmW 91, WhoEmL 91, WhoWor 91*
Fuller, Sherrilynne 1945- *WhoEmL 91*
Fuller, Stephen Herbert 1920- *St&PR 91, WhoAm 90*
Fuller, Steven Edward 1950- *WhoSSW 91*
Fuller, Steven Michael 1953- *WhoSSW 91*
Fuller, Sue *WhoAm 90, WhoAmA 91, WhoAmW 91*
Fuller, Sue 1914- *BiDWomA*
Fuller, Theodore 1918- *WhoAm 90*
Fuller, Theodore, Jr. 1937- *WhoSSW 91*
Fuller, Thomas 1823-1898 *DcCanB 12*
Fuller, Thomas Ashmead 1952- *WhoEmL 91*
Fuller, Thomas R. 1927- *St&PR 91*
Fuller, Thomas Ralph 1927- *WhoAm 90, WhoSSW 91*
Fuller, Tracy Annette 1962- *WhoAmW 91*
Fuller, Vern 1944- *Ballpl 90*
Fuller, Wallace Hamilton 1915- *WhoAm 90*
Fuller, Wanda Lou 1938- *WhoAmW 91*
Fuller, Warren O. 1951- *St&PR 91*
Fuller, Wayne Arthur 1931- *WhoAm 90*
Fuller, Willard 1915- *EncO&P 3*
Fuller, William Clark *BiDrAPA 89*
Fuller, William Henry *OxCCanT*
Fuller, William Miles 1938- *St&PR 91*
Fuller, William Norman 1948- *WhoSSW 91*
Fuller, William Samuel 1926- *WhoAm 90*

Fuller, William Sidney 1931- *WhoAm 90*
Fuller Levine, Janice Carol 1942- *WhoAmW 91*
Fuller-Rogers, Brenda Sue 1955- *WhoEmL 91*
Fullerton, Albert Louis, Jr. 1921- *WhoE 91*
Fullerton, Arthur King 1962- *WhoSSW 91*
Fullerton, Charles Gordon 1936- *WhoAm 90*
Fullerton, Charles William 1917- *WhoAm 90*
Fullerton, Curt 1898-1975 *Ballpl 90*
Fullerton, Dale A. 1930- *St&PR 91*
Fullerton, Donald T, Jr. 1932- *BiDrAPA 89*
Fullerton, Dorothy Mallan 1938- *WhoWor 91*
Fullerton, Fiona 1956- *ConTFT 8 [port]*
Fullerton, Gail Jackson 1927- *WhoAm 90, WhoAmW 91*
Fullerton, Gary Dodson 1939- *WhoAm 90*
Fullerton, Georgiana 1812-1885 *BioIn 16, FemiCLE*
Fullerton, Hugh S., Jr. 1904-1965 *Ballpl 90*
Fullerton, Hugh S., Sr. 1873-1935 *Ballpl 90*
Fullerton, James D. 1917- *St&PR 91*
Fullerton, James Gordon, III 1926- *St&PR 91*
Fullerton, Jymie Luie 1943- *WhoSSW 91*
Fullerton, Lawrence Rae 1952- *WhoEmL 91*
Fullerton, Mary 1868-1946 *FemiCLE*
Fullerton, Maryellen 1946- *WhoE 91*
Fullerton, Mollie Hays *WhoAmW 91, WhoE 91*
Fullerton, R. Donald 1931- *WhoAm 90, WhoWor 91*
Fullerton, Robert C. 1938- *St&PR 91*
Fullerton, Robert Victor 1918- *WhoAm 90*
Fullerton, Sally Ann 1934- *WhoAmW 91*
Fullerton, Susan Kathryn 1957- *WhoAmW 91*
Fullerton, William D. 1927- *WhoAm 90*
Fullerton, William Morton 1865-1952? *BioIn 16*
Fullilove, Mindy Thompson 1950- *BiDrAPA 89*
Fulling, Katharine Painter *WhoAmW 91, WhoWor 91*
Fullington, Richard Wayne 1942- *WhoAm 90*
Fullinwider, James W. *ODwPR 91*
Fullis, Chick 1904-1946 *Ballpl 90*
Fullman, Lynn Grisard 1949- *WhoAmW 91*
Fullmer, Daniel Warren 1922- *WhoAm 90*
Fullmer, Harold Milton 1918- *WhoAm 90*
Fullmer, Joseph A. 1943- *St&PR 91*
Fullmer, Paul *ODwPR 91*
Fullmer, Paul 1934- *St&PR 91, WhoAm 90*
Fulmer, Gary C. 1933- *St&PR 91*
Fulmer, Gary Creighton 1933- *WhoAm 90*
Fulmer, Hugh Scott 1928- *WhoAm 90, WhoWor 91*
Fulmer, Joe Jeff 1936- *St&PR 91, WhoAm 90*
Fulmer, Michael Clifford 1954- *WhoEmL 91, WhoWor 91*
Fulmer, Pruitt 1942- *St&PR 91*
Fulmer, Richard Warren 1930- *WhoAm 90*
Fulmer, Robert 1920- *St&PR 91*
Fulmer, Sandra Lee 1953- *WhoWrEP 89*
Fulmer, Thomas Earle 1925- *BiDrAPA 89*
Fulmer, Thomas Stephen 1934- *St&PR 91*
Fulmer, Vincent Anthony 1927- *WhoAm 90, WhoE 91*
Fulmer, Wanda 1939- *WhoSSW 91*
Fulmer, William B. 1948- *St&PR 91*
Fulop, Donald George 1950- *WhoSSW 91*
Fulop, George 1954- *BiDrAPA 89, WhoE 91*
Fulop, Michael Alain *BiDrAPA 89*
Fulop, Milford 1927- *WhoAm 90*
Fulp, James Alan 1951- *WhoEmL 91*
Fulrath, Irene 1945- *WhoAmW 91, WhoE 91*
Fulscher, Gary Vincent 1943- *St&PR 91*
Fulton, Albert E *BiDrAPA 89*
Fulton, Alice 1952- *WhoWrEP 89*
Fulton, Arthur Hawling 1929- *St&PR 91*
Fulton, Brian Thomas 1949- *BiDrAPA 89*
Fulton, Carl Lee *BiDrAPA 89*
Fulton, Chandler Montgomery 1934- *WhoAm 90*
Fulton, Cyrus James 1873-1949 *WhoAmA 91N*
Fulton, David Wilson 1947- *WhoSSW 91*
Fulton, Donald William, Jr. 1946- *St&PR 91*
Fulton, Dorothy Margaret Young 1926- *WhoWor 91*
Fulton, Edmund Davie 1916- *WhoAm 90*
Fulton, Eileen *BioIn 16*
Fulton, Fred Franklin 1920- *WhoAmA 91*
Fulton, George Pearman, Jr. 1914- *WhoAm 90*
Fulton, Hamish 1946- *WhoAmA 91*
Fulton, James 1930- *ConDes 90*
Fulton, James Franklin 1930- *WhoAm 90*
Fulton, James M. *BioIn 16*
Fulton, Jay David 1960- *WhoSSW 91*
Fulton, Joe Kirk, Jr. 1957- *WhoSSW 91, WhoWor 91*
Fulton, John J. 1928- *St&PR 91*
Fulton, Karen S. 1952- *St&PR 91*
Fulton, Katherine Nelson 1955- *WhoSSW 91*
Fulton, Len 1934- *WhoAm 90, WhoWrEP 89*
Fulton, Mark *BiDrAPA 89*
Fulton, Mary *FemiCLE*
Fulton, Paul 1934- *WhoAm 90*
Fulton, Richard 1921- *WhoAm 90*
Fulton, Richard Alsina 1926- *WhoAm 90*
Fulton, Richard F., Jr. 1954- *St&PR 91*
Fulton, Richard Harmon 1927- *WhoAm 90*
Fulton, Robert 1765-1815 *BioIn 16, WorAlBi*
Fulton, Robert Edward 1931- *WhoAm 90*
Fulton, Robert K. 1949- *St&PR 91*
Fulton, Robert Lester 1926- *WhoAm 90*
Fulton, Robin 1937- *WorAu 1980 [port]*
Fulton, Sandy M. 1943- *St&PR 91*
Fulton, Sandy Michael 1943- *WhoAm 90*
Fulton, Thomas 1949- *IntWWM 90*
Fulton, Thomas Benjamin 1918- *WhoAm 90*
Fulton, William A 1954- *BiDrAPA 89*
Fulton, William Kenneth, Jr. 1941- *IntWWM 90*
Fulton, Winthrop DeWolf 1946- *WhoEmL 91*
Fultz, Clair Ervin 1911- *WhoAm 90*
Fultz, Dave 1875-1959 *Ballpl 90*
Fultz, Dave 1921- *WhoAm 90*
Fultz, Kenneth R. 1935- *St&PR 91*
Fultz, Patrick E. 1959- *WhoEmL 91*
Fultz, William Joseph 1931- *St&PR 91*
Fulweiler, Howard Wells 1932- *WhoAm 90*
Fulweiler, Patricia Platt 1923- *WhoAmW 91, WhoE 91*
Fulweiler, Spencer Biddle 1913- *WhoWor 91*
Fulwiler, Robert Neal 1937- *WhoAm 90, WhoWor 91*
Fuma, John 1913- *BiDrAPA 89*
Fumagalli, Barbara Merrill 1926- *WhoAm 90, WhoAmA 91*
Fumaroli, Pierre Andre 1938- *WhoWor 91*
Fumelh, Madame de 1750?- *EncCoWW*
Fumero, Jose R *BiDrAPA 89*
Fumero, Luis R 1914- *BiDrAPA 89*
Fumero, Ricardo A *BiDrAPA 89*
Fumi, Fausto Gherardo 1924- *WhoWor 91*
Fumia, Dreama Fay 1953- *WhoE 91*
Fumihito, Prince of Japan 1965- *BioIn 16*
Fumo, Elvia *BioIn 16*
Funaba, Masatomi 1938- *WhoWor 91*
Funari, John H. 1929- *WhoAm 90*
Funaro, Dilson *BioIn 16*
Funches, Virginia *BioIn 16*
Funchess, Manley Lindsey 1942- *St&PR 91*
Fundaro, Frank Salvatore 1943- *St&PR 91*
Funderburg, I. Owen 1924- *St&PR 91*
Funderburg, Linda G *BiDrAPA 89*
Funderburk, Daniel C 1927- *BiDrAPA 89*
Funderburk, David B. 1944- *WhoAm 90*
Funderburk, Henry Hanly, Jr. 1931- *WhoAm 90, WhoSSW 91*
Funderburk, Mark 1957- *BioIn 16*
Funderburk, Morris Laney, Jr. 1938- *WhoSSW 91*
Fundingsland, O.M. 1943- *St&PR 91*
Fundingsland, Osmund T. *BioIn 16*
Funess, Richard *ODwPR 91*
Funesti, Julie Colette 1962- *WhoAmW 91*
Fung, Adrian Kin-Chiu 1936- *WhoAm 90*
Fung, Desmond S *BiDrAPA 89*
Fung, Frederick H.L. 1936- *St&PR 91*
Fung, Frederick Ho 1951- *WhoSSW 91*
Fung, Ho-Leung 1943- *WhoAm 90*
Fung, Kee-Ying 1948- *WhoEmL 91*
Fung, Kwok-King Victor 1945- *WhoWor 91*
Fung, Kwok Pui 1951- *WhoWor 91*
Fung, Lok-Nam 1918- *WhoWor 91*
Fung, Michael 1950- *St&PR 91*
Fung, Yuan-Cheng Bertram 1919- *WhoAm 90*
Fungai, Bernardino 1460-1516 *BioIn 16*
Funge, Robert 1931- *WhoWrEP 89*
Fungsang, Michael Wing 1951- *WhoEmL 91*
Funicello, Annette *BioIn 16*
Funicello, Annette 1942- *WorAlBi*
Funk, Albert Peter 1919- *St&PR 91*
Funk, Arthur W. 1930- *St&PR 91*
Funk, Arville Lynn 1929- *WhoAm 90*
Funk, Carole Ann 1942- *WhoSSW 91*
Funk, Charlotte M 1934- *WhoAmA 91*
Funk, Cyril Reed, Jr. 1928- *WhoAm 90*
Funk, Daniel Beat Ludwig 1726-1787 *PenDiDA 89*
Funk, David Albert 1927- *WhoAm 90, WhoWor 91*
Funk, David Leonard 1935- *WhoAm 90*
Funk, Donald Alan 1933- *St&PR 91*
Funk, Ella Frances 1921- *WhoAmW 91, WhoWor 91*
Funk, Frank 1935- *Ballpl 90*
Funk, Frank E. 1923- *WhoAm 90*
Funk, Gary Lloyd 1945- *WhoSSW 91*
Funk, Guenter W. 1928- *WhoWor 91*
Funk, Harald Franz 1917- *WhoWor 91*
Funk, Ian C *BiDrAPA 89*
Funk, Isaac Kauffman 1839-1912 *EncPaPR 91*
Funk, Isaac Kauffmann 1839-1912 *EncO&P 3*
Funk, James H. 1842- *AmLegL*
Funk, Johann Friedrich 1706-1775 *PenDiDA 89*
Funk, Johann Lorenz *PenDiDA 89*
Funk, John William 1937- *St&PR 91, WhoAm 90*
Funk, Joseph E., Jr. 1939- *St&PR 91*
Funk, Kathryn Marie *BiDrAPA 89*
Funk, Larry L. 1942- *St&PR 91*
Funk, Liz 1904-1968 *Ballpl 90*
Funk, Margaret J. 1930- *St&PR 91*
Funk, Martin Albert *BiDrAPA 89*
Funk, Mathaus 1697-1783 *PenDiDA 89*
Funk, Michelle *BioIn 16*
Funk, Morton 1923- *St&PR 91*
Funk, Paul Eugene 1920- *WhoAm 90*
Funk, Richard W. 1936- *St&PR 91*
Funk, Roger L 1934- *WhoAmA 91*
Funk, Sherman Maxwell 1925- *WhoAm 90*
Funk, Susan Ellen 1951- *WhoAmW 91*
Funk, Terry W. 1951- *St&PR 91*
Funk, Verne J 1932- *WhoAmA 91*
Funk, Vicki Jane 1951- *WhoEmL 91, WhoSSW 91*
Funk, Virginia B. 1923- *WhoWrEP 89*
Funk, Walter, Jr. 1916- *St&PR 91*
Funk, Walther 1890-1960 *BioIn 16*
Funk, Wayne A 1922- *BiDrAPA 89*
Funk, William Henry 1933- *WhoAm 90*
Funkadelic *EncPR&S 89*
Funke, Barbara Mary 1959- *BiDrAPA 89*
Funke, Friedrich Wilhelm 1921- *WhoWor 91*
Funke, Gerhard B. 1914- *WhoWor 91*
Funke, Ginny *WhoWrEP 89*
Funke, Klemens A. 1934- *St&PR 91*
Funke, Lewis Bernard 1912- *WhoAm 90*
Funke, Phyllis Ellen 1941- *WhoE 91*
Funke, Werner Ernst 1903- *WhoWor 91*
Funkenstein, Daniel H 1910- *BiDrAPA 89*
Funkenstein, H. Harris *BioIn 16, NewYTBS 90*
Funkhouser, A. Paul 1923- *St&PR 91*
Funkhouser, Bruce Bedford 1949- *WhoEmL 91*
Funkhouser, Deidra Ellen 1950- *WhoAmW 91*
Funkhouser, Eileen 1957- *WhoWrEP 89*
Funkhouser, Elmer Newton, Jr. 1916- *St&PR 91, WhoAm 90*
Funkhouser, Lawrence William 1921- *WhoAm 90*
Funkhouser, Richard Daniel Brunk 1935- *St&PR 91*
Funkhouser, Richard Nelson 1917- *WhoAm 90*
Funknouser, John W. 1944- *St&PR 91*
Funnell, John Francis 1925- *St&PR 91*
Funsch, Richard Henry 1931- *St&PR 91*
Funseth, Robert Lloyd Eric Martin 1926- *WhoAm 90*
Funston, Edward Hogue 1839-1911 *AmLegL*
Funston, Frederick 1865-1917 *BioIn 16*
Funt, Allen 1914- *WorAlBi*
Funtash, Paul A., Jr. 1943- *St&PR 91*
Fuqua, Gordon Andrew 1941- *BiDrAPA 89*
Fuqua, Harvey *EncPR&S 89*
Fuqua, J.B. 1918- *St&PR 91*
Fuqua, John Brooks 1918- *WhoAm 90, WhoSSW 91*
Fuqua, Paula Bills 1944- *BiDrAPA 89*
Furay, Catherine J. 1952- *WhoAmW 91*
Furbank, P N 1920- *WorAu 1980*
Furbay, John Harvey 1903- *WhoAm 90*
Furbee, Charles Wesley, III 1942- *WhoAm 90*
Furber, Edward Bixby 1929- *St&PR 91*
Furber, Edward Saxe 1927- *BiDrAPA 89*
Furber, Joseph W. 1814-1884 *AmLegL*
Furbish, Kate 1834-1931 *WomFie [port]*
Furbush, John 1937- *St&PR 91*
Furbush, Steven Dean 1958- *WhoEmL 91*
Furby, James R. 1936- *St&PR 91*
Furchtgott-Roth, Diana Elizabeth 1958- *WhoE 91*
Furchtgott-Roth, Harold Wilkes 1956- *WhoE 91*
Furcon, John Edward 1942- *WhoWor 91*
Furedy, Ronald L 1942- *BiDrAPA 89*
Furek, Robert M. 1942- *St&PR 91*
Furer, Manuel 1925- *BiDrAPA 89*
Furet, Charles-Joseph *PenDiMP*
Furey, Agnes 1937- *WhoAmW 91*
Furey, Joseph E. 1907- *BioIn 16*
Furey, Joseph Endicott 1906- *MusmAFA*
Furey, Laurence Thomas 1930- *WhoSSW 91*
Furey, Michael *TwCCr&M 91*
Furey, Raymond Joseph 1946- *WhoEmL 91*
Furey, Robert Joseph 1956- *WhoWrEP 89*
Furey, Thomas J. 1935- *St&PR 91*
Furey, Vincent E., Jr. 1939- *St&PR 91*
Furgason, Maiya Kathryn 1944- *WhoE 91*
Furgason, Mark Stephen 1957- *BiDrAPA 89*
Furgason, Robert Roy 1935- *WhoAm 90*
Furger, Andres 1948- *WhoWor 91*
Furger, Franz 1935- *WhoWor 91*
Furgison, Clifford Fredric 1948- *WhoEmL 91*
Furgiuele, Guy 1926- *St&PR 91*
Furgiuele, Margery Wood 1919- *WhoAmW 91*
Furgurson, Ernest Baker, Jr. 1929- *WhoAm 90*
Furht, Borivoje 1946- *WhoEmL 91*
Furie, Valerie Jayne 1960- *WhoE 91*
Furigay, Rodolfo Lazo 1938- *WhoE 91*
Furillo, Carl 1922- *Ballpl 90 [port]*
Furillo, Carl 1922-1989 *AnObit 1989, BioIn 16*
Furino, Antonio *WhoAm 90*
Furino, Nancy *BioIn 16*
Furlaud, Richard M. 1923- *St&PR 91*
Furlaud, Richard Mortimer 1923- *WhoAm 90, WhoE 91*
Furley, David John 1922- *WhoAm 90*
Furloh, Johan Hugo *PenDiDA 89*
Furlohg, Christopher 1737-1800? *PenDiDA 89*
Furlong, Alice 1875?- *FemiCLE*
Furlong, Brenda J. 1948- *St&PR 91*
Furlong, Charles Richard 1950- *WhoE 91*
Furlong, Dale Austin, Jr. 1929- *WhoSSW 91*
Furlong, Edward V., Jr. 1937- *St&PR 91, WhoAm 90*
Furlong, F. Wayne 1941- *BiDrAPA 89*
Furlong, George Morgan, Jr. 1931- *WhoAm 90*
Furlong, Gregory William 1947- *WhoEmL 91*
Furlong, James 1927- *ODwPR 91*
Furlong, Maurice B. 1909- *WhoWrEP 89*
Furlong, Monica 1930- *FemiCLE*
Furlong, Patrick David 1948- *WhoEmL 91, WhoWor 91*
Furlong, Philip J. 1892-1989 *BioIn 16*
Furlong, Raymond Bernard 1926- *WhoSSW 91*
Furlong, Stewart Sadler 1939- *St&PR 91*
Furlong, Suzanne 1956- *WhoAmW 91*
Furlong, Timothy James 1959- *BiDrAPA 89*
Furlong, William Edgar 1948- *St&PR 91*
Furlotte, Nicolas 1952- *WhoWrEP 89*
Furlow, Mack V., Jr. 1931- *St&PR 91*
Furlow, Mack Vernon, Jr. 1931- *WhoAm 90*
Furly, Anna, Jr. 1649- *BiDEWW*
Furly, Anna, Sr. 1624-1715 *BiDEWW*
Furmage, Ann Mason 1937- *WhoAmW 91*
Furman, Anthony Michael 1934- *WhoAm 90*
Furman, Arthur F *WhoAmA 91*
Furman, Arthur F, Mrs *WhoAmA 91*
Furman, Ashrita *BioIn 16*
Furman, Bernard 1929- *St&PR 91, WhoAm 90*
Furman, David Stephen 1945- *WhoAmA 91*
Furman, Deane Philip 1915- *WhoAm 90*
Furman, Donald M. 1918- *St&PR 91*
Furman, Eric Bertram 1934- *WhoSSW 91*
Furman, F. Foster 1911- *St&PR 91*
Furman, Gertrude Lerner Kerman 1909- *ConAu 31NR*
Furman, Gregory J. *ODwPR 91*
Furman, Harry Sutton 1947- *WhoAm 90*
Furman, Hezekiah Wyndol Carroll 1922- *WhoSSW 91*
Furman, Howard 1938- *WhoSSW 91*
Furman, James Merle 1932- *WhoAm 90*
Furman, John R. 1917- *St&PR 91*
Furman, Laura 1945- *ConAu 30NR, WhoWrEP 89*
Furman, Lucy 1870-1958 *LiHiK*
Furman, Mark Steven 1951- *WhoEmL 91*
Furman, Martin Julian 1949- *BiDrAPA 89, WhoE 91*
Furman, Morris *BioIn 16*
Furman, Richard 1755-1825 *BioIn 16*
Furman, Robert A 1924- *BiDrAPA 89*
Furman, Robert Howard 1918- *WhoAm 90*
Furman, Roger *DrBIPA 90*
Furman, Roy L. 1939- *St&PR 91*
Furman, Roy Lance 1939- *WhoAm 90*

Furman, Samuel Elliott 1932- *WhoE 91, WhoWor 91*
Furman, Thomas D., Jr. 1943- *St&PR 91*
Furman, Walter Laurie 1913- *WhoSSW 91*
Furman, William Stuart 1929- *WhoE 91*
Furmanski, Avishai 1935- *WhoWor 91*
Furmanski, Philip 1946- *WhoAm 90, WhoEmL 91*
Furmansky, Bert Sol 1945- *BiDrAPA 89*
Furmedge, Edyth *PenDiMP*
Furnas, David William 1931- *WhoAm 90, WhoWor 91*
Furnas, Howard Earl 1919- *WhoAm 90*
Furnas, J. C. 1905- *BioIn 16*
Furnas, Joseph Chamberlain 1905- *BioIn 16, WhoAm 90, WhoWrEP 89*
Furner, Raymond Lynn, Sr. 1943- *WhoSSW 91*
Furness, Alan 1949- *IntWWM 90*
Furness, Betty 1916- *WhoAm 90, WorAlBi*
Furness, Frank 1839-1912 *BioIn 16, PenDiDA 89*
Furness, Horace Howard 1833-1912 *BioIn 16*
Furness, Robyn Carole 1955- *WhoE 91*
Furney, Linda Jeanne 1947- *WhoAmW 91*
Furnier, Vincent *BioIn 16*
Furnish, Oliver Ray, Jr. 1932- *St&PR 91*
Furniss, Charles O *BiDrAPA 89*
Furniss, Tim *BioIn 16*
Furnival, George Mitchell 1908- *WhoAm 90*
Furnweger, Karen 1951- *WhoEmL 91*
Furr, Anthony Lloyd 1944- *St&PR 91*
Furr, Christine Marie 1960- *WhoAmW 91*
Furr, Jim 1939- *WhoAmA 91*
Furr, John H 1924- *BiDrAPA 89*
Furr, Quint Eugene 1921- *WhoE 91*
Furr, Warwick Rex, II 1940- *WhoAm 90, WhoE 91*
Furrer, James Douglas 1952- *WhoEmL 91*
Furrer, John Rudolf 1927- *WhoAm 90, WhoWor 91*
Furrer, Markus Julius 1955- *WhoWor 91*
Furrer, Ronald Walter 1934- *St&PR 91*
Furrey, Anne-Marie 1948- *WhoAmW 91*
Furrh, Chris *BioIn 16*
Furry, Mark Douglas 1947- *WhoE 91*
Furry, Richard L. 1938- *St&PR 91*
Furse, James Robert 1939- *St&PR 91, WhoAm 90*
Furse, Margaret 1911-1974 *ConDes 90*
Furse, Roger 1903-1972 *ConDes 90*
Fursland, Richard C. 1948- *ODwPR 91*
Furst, Alan 1941- *SpyFic*
Furst, Alex Julian 1938- *WhoSSW 91, WhoWor 91*
Furst, Ansgar Hermann 1930- *WhoWor 91*
Furst, Anton 1945?- *ConTFT 8*
Furst, Arthur 1914- *WhoAm 90, WhoWor 91*
Furst, Austin *BioIn 16*
Furst, Errol Kenneth 1946- *WhoAm 90, WhoE 91*
Furst, Gary Stuart 1951- *St&PR 91*
Furst, Henry Fairchild 1951- *WhoEmL 91*
Furst, Janos 1935- *IntWWM 90*
Furst, Joseph B *BiDrAPA 89*
Furst, Kenneth Errol 1946- *St&PR 91*
Furst, Lilian Renee 1931- *WhoAm 90*
Furst, Michael L *BiDrAPA 89*
Furst, Patricia Ann 1949- *St&PR 91*
Furst, Peter 1936- *WhoWor 91*
Furst, Rafael 1928- *St&PR 91*
Furst, Sidney Carl 1925- *WhoE 91*
Furst, Sidney S *BiDrAPA 89*
Furst, Sidney Selig 1921- *WhoE 91*
Furst, Stephen *BioIn 16*
Furst, Warren Arthur 1924- *St&PR 91*
Furst, William 1911- *BiDrAPA 89*
Furste, Wesley Leonard, II 1915- *WhoAm 90, WhoWor 91*
Furstenberg, Barbara Spar 1944- *WhoAmW 91*
Furstenberg, Maximilien de 1904-1988 *BioIn 16*
Furstman, Shirley Elsie Daddow 1930- *WhoAmW 91, WhoE 91*
Furtado, Stephen Eugene 1942- *WhoE 91*
Furtak, Hiroko 1953- *WhoAmW 91*
Furter, William Frederick 1931- *WhoAm 90*
Furth, Eugene David 1929- *WhoAm 90*
Furth, Frederick Paul 1934- *WhoAm 90*
Furth, George 1932- *WhoAm 90*
Furth, Harold Paul 1930- *WhoAm 90*
Furth, John Jacob 1929- *WhoAm 90*
Furth, Joseph Herbert 1899- *WhoE 91*
Furth, Mary Stang 1931- *BiDrAPA 89*
Furth, Peter David 1954- *WhoE 91*
Furth, Valerie Jakober *BioIn 16*
Furtwangler, Wilhelm 1886-1954 *PenDiMP, WorAlBi*
Furubotn, Eirik Grundtvig 1923- *WhoAm 90, WhoSSW 91*
Furukawa, Edward F 1924- *BiDrAPA 89*
Furukawa, Mitsuru 1932- *WhoWor 91*
Furukawa, Theodore Paul 1944- *WhoSSW 91*
Furukohri, Etsuko 1947- *WhoWor 91*
Furumoto, Horace 1931- *St&PR 91*
Furusaki, Shintaro 1938- *WhoWor 91*
Furuta Oribe 1544-1615 *EncJap*
Furuta, Takaaki 1953- *WhoSSW 91*
Furuto, Sharlene Bernice Choy Lin 1947- *WhoEmL 91*
Furuya, Shingo *BioIn 16*
Fury, Billy 1941-1983 *DcNaB 1981, OxCPMus*
Fusaro, Ramon Michael 1927- *WhoAm 90*
Fusaro, Sal *BiDrAPA 89*
Fuscaldo, Antonio Frank 1919- *WhoWor 91*
Fuschetti, Edward A. 1935- *St&PR 91*
Fusco, Andrew G. 1948- *WhoEmL 91, WhoSSW 91, WhoWor 91*
Fusco, Anthony Salvatore 1954- *WhoEmL 91*
Fusco, David Michael 1959- *WhoEmL 91*
Fusco, Denise 1957- *WhoEmL 91*
Fusco, Edmund J. 1924- *St&PR 91*
Fusco, Gabriel Paul 1933- *WhoAm 90, WhoE 91*
Fusco, Jacqueline Tecce 1956- *WhoAmW 91, WhoEmL 91*
Fusco, Laurie S 1941- *WhoAmA 91*
Fusco, Mario Louis 1946- *St&PR 91*
Fusco, Peter Richard 1945- *WhoAm 90, WhoAmA 91*
Fusco, Robert C 1950- *BiDrAPA 89*
Fusco, Yolanda 1922- *WhoAmA 91*
Fuseli, Henry 1741-1825 *IntDcAA 90, WorAlBi*
Fuselier, Louis Alfred 1932- *WhoAm 90*
Fuselier, Marilyn Monie 1931- *WhoSSW 91*
Fusfeld, Ira 1948- *St&PR 91*
Fushburne, Frank B. 1915- *St&PR 91*
Fusi, John C. 1955- *St&PR 91*
Fusi, Juan Pablo 1945- *ConAu 131, HispWr 90*
Fusi Aizpurua, Juan Pablo 1945- *WhoWor 91*
Fusillo, Michael 1948- *BiDrAPA 89*
Fusillo, Thomas Victor 1953- *WhoE 91*
Fusina, Alessandro Eugenio 1937- *WhoAm 90*
Fuson, Robert Henderson 1927- *WhoWrEP 89*
Fuss, Adam 1961- *BioIn 16*
Fuss, John M., Jr. 1930- *St&PR 91*
Fuss, Mark Anthony 1956- *WhoE 91*
Fuss, Peter S. 1933- *St&PR 91*
Fussell, Catharine Pugh 1919- *WhoAmW 91*
Fussell, Charles C. 1938- *IntWWM 90*
Fussell, Fred 1895-1966 *Ballpl 90*
Fussell, John Michael 1933- *IntWWM 90*
Fussell, Larry Wayne 1952- *WhoEmL 91*
Fussell, Louis 1925- *IntWWM 90*
Fussell, Norman Coldham 1937- *WhoWor 91*
Fussell, Paul 1924- *BioIn 16, MajTwCW, WhoAm 90, WhoWrEP 89*
Fussell, Ronald Moi 1956- *WhoEmL 91*
Fussenegger, Gary 1949- *St&PR 91*
Fussenegger, Gertrud 1912- *EncCoWW*
Fussiner, Howard 1923- *WhoAmA 91*
Fussler, Herman Howe 1914- *WhoAm 90*
Fussner, Liselotte Berthe 1941- *WhoWor 91*
Fuste, Damaso Berenguer y 1873-1953 *BioIn 16*
Fuster, Jaime B. 1941- *WhoAm 90, WhoHisp 91, WhoSSW 91*
Fuster, Joaquin 1930- *BiDrAPA 89*
Fuster, Mark 1947- *St&PR 91*
Fuster, Serge 1911-1988 *AnObit 1988*
Fuster, Valentin 1943- *WhoAm 90*
Futas, Elizabeth 1944- *WhoAm 90, WhoAmW 91*
Futas, George P. 1934- *St&PR 91*
Futch, Dennis William 1968- *WhoSSW 91*
Futch, Eddie *BioIn 16*
Futch, Tom R. 1951- *St&PR 91*
Futch, Tommy Ray 1951- *WhoAm 90, WhoEmL 91, WhoWor 91*
Futerman, Eli N. 1958- *St&PR 91*
Futerman, Mike 1927- *St&PR 91*
Futey, Bohdan A. 1939- *WhoAm 90*
Futia, Leo R. 1919- *St&PR 91*
Futia, Leo Richard 1919- *WhoAm 90*
Futral, Ronald Steven 1962- *WhoE 91*
Futrell, Basil Lee 1937- *WhoE 91, WhoWor 91*
Futrell, J. Richard, Jr. 1931- *St&PR 91*
Futrell, John William 1935- *WhoAm 90, WhoE 91*
Futrell, Jonas Richard, Jr. 1931- *WhoAm 90*
Futrell, Junius Marion 1870-1952 *BioIn 16*
Futrell, Mary Alice Hatwood 1940- *WhoAm 90, WhoAmW 91*
Futrell, Mary Hatwood *BioIn 16*
Futrell, Robert Frank 1917- *WhoSSW 91, WhoWor 91*
Futrelle, Jacques 1875-1912 *TwCCr&M 91*
Futter, Ellen Victoria 1949- *WhoAm 90, WhoAmW 91, WhoE 91*
Futter, Joan Babette 1921- *WhoE 91*
Futter, Thomas Marc 1921- *St&PR 91*
Futter, Victor 1919- *WhoAm 90*
Futterer, Edward 1831-1889 *BioIn 16*
Futterer, Edward Philip 1953- *WhoEmL 91*
Futterer, Karen Lehner 1953- *WhoSSW 91*
Futterknecht, James O. 1947- *St&PR 91*
Futterman, Edward H *BiDrAPA 89*
Futterman, Jack 1933- *St&PR 91*
Futterman, Samuel *BiDrAPA 89*
Futvoye, George 1808-1891 *DcCanB 12*
Fuwa, Tasuku 1915- *WhoWor 91*
Fuxa, James Roderick 1949- *WhoSSW 91*
Fuzak, Arthur Walter 1923- *St&PR 91*
Fuzek, Bettye Lynn 1924- *WhoAmW 91*
Fuzek, John Frank 1921- *WhoSSW 91*
Fuzesi, Stephen, Jr. 1948- *WhoAm 90, WhoEmL 91*
Fuzo, Frank John 1951- *WhoE 91*
Fyan, Loleta Dawson 1894-1990 *BioIn 16*
Fye, Paul McDonald 1912-1988 *BioIn 16*
Fye, Robert Floyd 1948- *St&PR 91*
Fyer, Abby Joy *BiDrAPA 89*
Fyer, Minna R *BiDrAPA 89*
Fyfe, Jo Suzanne 1941- *WhoAmA 91*
Fyfe, M.B. 1936- *St&PR 91*
Fyfe, William Sefton 1927- *WhoAm 90*
Fyffe, Will 1885-1947 *OxCPMus*
Fyge, Sarah *BiDEWW*
Fyge, Sarah 1670-1723 *FemiCLE*
Fyles, John Gladstone 1923- *WhoAm 90*
Fyock, James A. 1929- *ODwPR 91*
Fytche, Maria Amelia 1844-1926 *FemiCLE*
Fyvel, T. R. *ConAu 129*
Fyvel, Tosco Raphael *ConAu 129*

G

G, John Scott 1948- WhoEmL 91
G., Kenny BioIn 16
G.B.S. MajTwCW
G. de Zubiaurre, Leopoldo 1924- WhoWor 91
G.E.N.E. NewAgMG
Gaab, Michael Robert 1947- WhoWor 91
Gaab, Thomas Anthony 1953- IntWWM 90
Gaafar, Sayed Mohammed 1924- WhoAm 90
Gaal, Istvan 1933- BioIn 16
Gaal, Steven Alexander 1924- WhoAm 90
Gaalova, Barbara Kanzler 1953- WhoEmL 91
Gaar, Edwin Earl 1956- WhoEmL 91
Gaar, Marilyn A. Wiegraffe 1946- WhoAmW 91
Gaar, Norman Edward 1929- WhoWor 91
Gaar, William Charles 1941- St&PR 91
Gaard, David Reed 1949- St&PR 91
Gaardemo, Peter Michael 1956- WhoWor 91
Gaarder, Kenneth Ray BiDrAPA 89
Gaarder, Marie 1935- WhoAmW 91
Gaasch, Hubert Jean 1946- WhoWor 91
Gaasenbeek, Matthew 1930- St&PR 91, WhoAm 90
Gaastra, F S 1945- ConAu 132
Gaba, Barbara Blassingame 1947- WhoE 91
Gabain, Ethel Leontine 1883-1950 BiDWomA
Gabaldon, Julia K. 1947- WhoHisp 91
Gabaldon, Tony 1930- WhoHisp 91
Gabarro, John Joseph 1939- WhoAm 90
Gabatin, Jose Q 1930- BiDrAPA 89
Gabbard, Dana Chester 1962- WhoWrEP 89
Gabbard, Douglas, II 1952- WhoEmL 91
Gabbard, Glen Owens 1949- BiDrAPA 89, WhoAm 90, WhoEmL 91
Gabbard, Gregory Alan 1949- WhoEmL 91
Gabbard, Gregory N. 1941- WhoWrEP 89
Gabbard, Walter Ray 1936- St&PR 91
Gabbay, Marcel 1923- WhoWor 91
Gabbay, Sarah G. 1951- WhoEmL 91
Gabbe, Peter J. 1950- St&PR 91
Gabbe, Steven Glenn 1944- WhoAm 90
Gabbert, Donald H. 1917- St&PR 91
Gabbert, James Donald 1952- St&PR 91
Gabberty, James William 1959- WhoWor 91
Gabbour, Iskandar 1929- WhoAm 90
Gabby, James I 1926- BiDrAPA 89
Gabe, Caryl Jacobs 1949- WhoEmL 91
Gabe, Dora Petrova 1886-1983 EncCoWW
Gabe, Grace 1934- BiDrAPA 89
Gabe, Ron WhoAmA 91
Gabe, Sigmund BiDrAPA 89
Gabel, Allen Meredith 1943- St&PR 91
Gabel, Detlef 1946- WhoWor 91
Gabel, Gary Joseph 1949- WhoEmL 91
Gabel, George DeSaussure, Jr. 1940- WhoSSW 91, WhoWor 91
Gabel, Gerald R. 1950- IntWWM 90
Gabel, Harold Donald 1940- WhoSSW 91
Gabel, Hortense W 1912-1990 NewYTBS 90 [port]
Gabel, Katherine 1938- WhoAmW 91
Gabel, Krystal Leigh 1964- WhoAmW 91
Gabel, Richard Hugo 1950- BiDrAPA 89
Gabel, Stewart 1943- BiDrAPA 89
Gabel, Sukhreet BioIn 16
Gabel, W. Creighton 1931- WhoAm 90
Gabeler-Brooks, Jo 1931- WhoAmA 91
Gabelli, Mario BioIn 16
Gabellieri, F. Ralph 1929- St&PR 91
Gabelman, Irving Jacob 1918- WhoAm 90
Gabelman, James S. 1929- St&PR 91
Gabelmann, Hanus Friedrich Julius 1936- WhoWor 91
Gaberman, Harry 1913- WhoSSW 91
Gabert, Nori Lauren 1953- St&PR 91
Gabetti, Roberto 1925- PenDiDA 89
Gabin, George Joseph 1931- WhoAmA 91
Gable, Carl Irwin 1939- WhoAm 90
Gable, Carol Brignoli 1945- WhoAmW 91
Gable, Charles M BiDrAPA 89
Gable, Clark 1901-1960 BioIn 16, WorAlBi
Gable, Clark James BioIn 16
Gable, Dan BioIn 16
Gable, Dawn D'Amico 1951- BiDrAPA 89
Gable, Edward Brennan, Jr. 1929- WhoE 91, WhoWor 91
Gable, Fred Burnard 1929- WhoAm 90
Gable, G. Ellis 1905- WhoAm 90
Gable, Jeffrey Alan 1960- WhoEmL 91
Gable, Joanie Carole 1954- WhoEmL 91
Gable, John Clark BioIn 16
Gable, John Oglesby 1944- WhoAmA 91
Gable, Larry Dale 1942- WhoSSW 91
Gable, Leslie BiDrAPA 89
Gable, Martha Anne WhoAmW 91, WhoE 91, WhoWor 91
Gable, Richard Walter 1920- WhoAm 90
Gable, Robert E. 1934- St&PR 91
Gable, Robert Elledy 1934- WhoAm 90, WhoSSW 91
Gable, Robert L. 1930- St&PR 91
Gable, Thomas W 1937- BiDrAPA 89
Gable, Tom 1944- ODwPR 91
Gablehouse, Timothy Reuben 1951- WhoEmL 91
Gabler, Frank 1911-1967 Ballpl 90
Gabler, James Melvin 1945- WhoSSW 91
Gabler, John 1930- Ballpl 90
Gabler, Marilyn Ann 1954- WhoEmL 91
Gabler, Robert Earl 1927- WhoAm 90
Gables, Ken 1919-1960 Ballpl 90
Gablik, Suzi 1934- WhoAmA 91
Gabo, Naum 1890-1977 BioIn 16, IntDcAA 90, WhoAmA 91N
Gabor, Dennis 1900-1979 DcScB S2, WorAlBi
Gabor, Eva 1921- WorAlBi
Gabor, Georgia Miriam 1930- WhoWrEP 89
Gabor, Harvey 1934- WhoAm 90
Gabor, Ivan Robert 1938- BiDrAPA 89
Gabor, Jeffrey Alan 1942- WhoSSW 91
Gabor, Michael J. 1934- St&PR 91
Gabor, Peter Ivan 1946- St&PR 91
Gabor, Peter Reuven 1933- WhoWor 91
Gabor, Stanley C. WhoAm 90
Gabor, Zsa Zsa BioIn 16, WorAlBi
Gaboriau, Emile 1833-1873 TwCCr&M 91B
Gabos, Gabor 1930- IntWWM 90
Gabour, Jim 1947- WhoEmL 91
Gabovitch, Steven Alan 1953- WhoEmL 91
Gabria, Joanne Bakaitis 1945- WhoAmW 91, WhoEmL 91, WhoWor 91
Gabridge, Michael Gregory 1943- WhoAm 90
Gabriel, Achim Alfred 1931- WhoWor 91
Gabriel, Anthony Patrick 1944- WhoE 91
Gabriel, Anthony R BiDrAPA 89
Gabriel, Arthur N BiDrAPA 89
Gabriel, Astrik Ladislas 1907- WhoAm 90
Gabriel, Barbara Jamieson 1929- WhoAmW 91
Gabriel, Charles Alvin 1928- WhoAm 90
Gabriel, Earl A. 1925- WhoAm 90
Gabriel, Eberhard John 1942- St&PR 91
Gabriel, Edward Michael 1950- WhoAm 90
Gabriel, Gail Virginia 1946- WhoEmL 91
Gabriel, Georg 1928- St&PR 91
Gabriel, George Peter 1923- St&PR 91
Gabriel, Hannelore WhoAmA 91
Gabriel, Hugh Paul 1934- BiDrAPA 89
Gabriel, James BioIn 16
Gabriel, Jeffrey Nikolas 1940- St&PR 91
Gabriel, Jill A. 1958- St&PR 91
Gabriel, John 1874-1951 BioIn 16
Gabriel, Joseph Martin 1927- St&PR 91, WhoWor 91
Gabriel, Mark A. 1954- WhoWrEP 89
Gabriel, Mary Anne 1950- WhoEmL 91
Gabriel, Michael 1940- WhoAm 90
Gabriel, Mordecai Lionel 1918- WhoAm 90
Gabriel, Peter BioIn 16
Gabriel, Peter 1950- CurBio 90 [port], EncPR&S 89, WhoAm 90
Gabriel, Roger Eugene 1929- WhoSSW 91
Gabriel, Romano 1887?-1977 BioIn 16
Gabriel, Romano 1896-1977 MusmAFA
Gabriel, Rosalinda V 1939- BiDrAPA 89
Gabriel, William James BiDrAPA 89
Gabriel-Reyes, Asteria Masangkay 1933- WhoAmW 91
Gabriele, Charles 1921- IntWWM 90
Gabriele, Domenic J BiDrAPA 89
Gabriele, Orlando Frederick 1927- WhoAm 90
Gabriele, Vincenzo 1948- WhoSSW 91
Gabrieli Quartet PenDiMP
Gabrielle, Anthony F. 1927- St&PR 91
Gabrielle, Anthony Francis 1927- WhoSSW 91
Gabrielli BioIn 16
Gabrielli, Caterina 1730-1796 PenDiMP
Gabrielli, Thomas Robert 1947- WhoE 91
Gabrielli, William F, Jr. 1955- BiDrAPA 89
Gabrielsen, Jan Ernst 1945- WhoWor 91
Gabrielson, Ira Wilson 1922- WhoAm 90
Gabrielson, Len 1940- Ballpl 90
Gabrielson, Walter Oscar 1935- WhoAmA 91
Gabrielyants, Grigoriy Arkadyevich 1934- WhoWor 91
Gabriles, George Antonio 1926- St&PR 91
Gabrilove, Jacques Lester 1917- WhoAm 90
Gabrilowitsch, Ossip 1878-1936 BioIn 16, PenDiMP
Gabrino, Virginia V BiDrAPA 89
Gabron, Frank 1930- St&PR 91
Gabrovsek, Miran 1956- WhoWor 91
Gabroy, Jane R. 1949- St&PR 91
Gabry, Frank F. 1927- St&PR 91
Gabryella EncCoWW
Gabrynowicz, Joanne Irene 1949- WhoEmL 91
Gabrys, Gerard T. 1948- St&PR 91
Gaburro, Kenneth Louis 1926- IntWWM 90
Gaby, Daniel M. 1933- St&PR 91, WhoAm 90
Gaby, Nancy Sue BiDrAPA 89
Gacek, Walter Frank 1926- St&PR 91
Gach, Gary Gregory 1947- WhoWrEP 89
Gach, George 1909- WhoAmA 91
Gach, James Earl 1948- WhoE 91
Gach, John Paul 1946- WhoE 91
Gacha, Jose Gonzalo Rodriguez BioIn 16
Gachaw, Gabra S BiDrAPA 89
Gachman, Leon H. 1916- St&PR 91
Gachot, Charles A.J., Jr. 1931- St&PR 91
Gackenbach, Dick 1927- AuBYP 90, BioIn 16
Gackle, George D. 1925- St&PR 91
Gackowski, Dennis Edward 1948- WhoEmL 91
Gacon-Dufour, Madame 1762?- EncCoWW
Gad, Emma 1852-1921 EncCoWW
Gad, Robert K., III 1946- WhoEmL 91
Gad, Sarwat Morshed BiDrAPA 89
Gada, Manilal T 1947- BiDrAPA 89
Gadagila, Narahara Vishnu 1896-1966 BioIn 16
Gadaleta, Dominick C 1952- BiDrAPA 89
Gadamer, Hans-Georg 1900- WorAu 1980 [port]
Gadbois, Richard A., Jr. 1932- WhoAm 90
Gadd, William H. 1930- St&PR 91
Gaddarn, William James 1924- IntWWM 90
Gaddes, Richard 1942- IntWWM 90, WhoAm 90
Gaddi, Agnolo 1351?-1396? IntDcAA 90
Gaddi, Taddeo 1300?-1366 IntDcAA 90
Gaddie, David Michael 1947- St&PR 91
Gaddis, Denise Renea 1951- WhoAmW 91
Gaddis, John Lewis 1941- ConAu 30NR, WhoAm 90
Gaddis, Lois McFarland 1951- WhoSSW 91
Gaddis, Paul Otto 1924- WhoAm 90
Gaddis, Robert Smith 1931- St&PR 91
Gaddis, William 1922- MajTwCW, WhoAm 90, WhoWrEP 89, WorAlBi
Gaddis Rose, Marilyn 1930- WhoAm 90
Gaddy, David Winfred 1932- ConAu 129
Gaddy, James Leoma 1932- WhoAm 90
Gaddy, Oscar Lee 1932- WhoAm 90
Gaddy, Rodney Edwin 1955- WhoEmL 91
Gaddy, Steven Michael 1952- WhoAm 90
Gade, Karl 1939- WhoWor 91
Gade, Marvin Francis 1924- St&PR 91, WhoAm 90
Gade, Per 1944- IntWWM 90
Gade, Sandra Ann 1937- WhoAmW 91
Gaden, Barbara Joan 1954- WhoEmL 91
Gaden, Elmer Lewis, Jr. 1923- WhoAm 90, WhoSSW 91
Gadhafi, Muammar Muhammed 1942- WhoWor 91
Gadhia, Vinod Shamjibhai 1941- WhoE 91
Gadhoke, Sunil 1961- WhoWor 91
Gadient, Walter G. 1923- St&PR 91

Gadinsky, April Deanne 1963- *WhoAmW 91*
Gadish, Daniel B 1951- *BiDrAPA 89*, *WhoE 91*
Gadney, Reg 1941- *TwCCr&M 91*
Gadney, Reginald Bernard John 1941- *SpyFic*
Gado, Frank 1936- *ConAu 31NR*
Gadola, Paul V. 1929- *WhoAm 90*
Gadomski, Evelyn 1934- *WhoAmW 91*, *WhoWor 91*
Gadomski, Nina Marie 1960- *WhoEmL 91*
Gadomski, Robert Eugene 1947- *St&PR 91*
Gadon, Harold 1928- *St&PR 91*
Gadon, Steven Franklin 1931- *St&PR 91*, *WhoE 91*
Gadourek, Ivan 1923- *WhoWor 91*
Gadow, B. Curtis 1963- *St&PR 91*
Gadpaille, Warren J *BiDrAPA 89*
Gadra, Gerald John 1939- *St&PR 91*
Gadsby, Edward Northup, Jr. 1935- *WhoAm 90*
Gadsby, Gladstone *BiDrAPA 89*
Gadsby, Robin Edward 1939- *WhoAm 90*, *WhoE 91*
Gadsden, Christopher Henry 1946- *WhoEmL 91*
Gadsden, James 1788-1858 *BioIn 16*, *WhNaAH*
Gadsden, James Philip 1949- *WhoEmL 91*
Gadsden, Richard Hamilton 1925- *WhoAm 90*
Gadski, Johanna 1872-1932 *PenDiMP*
Gadson, Janice 1952- *WhoE 91*
Gadson, Michael Thomas *BiDrAPA 89*
Gady, Richard Lynn 1943- *St&PR 91*
Gadzheiv, Rauf Soltan Olgy 1922- *IntWWM 90*
Gaebelein, Frank Ely 1899-1983 *BioIn 16*
Gaede, Wolfgang 1878-1945 *DcScB S2*
Gaedel, Eddie 1925-1961 *Ballpl 90*
Gaehtgens, Thomas W. 1940- *WhoWor 91*
Gaeke, Harry Francis 1923- *St&PR 91*
Gaekwad, Fatesinghrao 1930-1988 *AnObit 1988*
Gael, J. S. *WhoWrEP 89*
Gaelen, Norbert 1926- *St&PR 91*
Gaeng, Paul Ami 1924- *WhoAm 90*
Gaer, Joseph 1897- *AuBYP 90*
Gaertner, Catherine Louise 1968- *WhoAmW 91*
Gaertner, Christopher Wolfgang 1962- *WhoAm 90*, *WhoWor 91*
Gaertner, Donell J. 1932- *WhoAm 90*
Gaertner, Johannes Alexander 1912- *WhoAm 90*
Gaertner, Kenneth Clark 1933- *WhoWrEP 89*
Gaertner, Richard Francis 1933- *WhoAm 90*
Gaertner, William Ronald 1952- *BiDrAPA 89*
Gaeta, Anthony R. *BioIn 16*
Gaeta, Gerald 1955- *WhoHisp 91*
Gaetano, Joyce Ann 1956- *WhoAmW 91*
Gaethe, George 1919- *WhoSSW 91*
Gaetti, Gary *BioIn 16*
Gaetti, Gary 1958- *Ballpl 90*
Gaev, Bennett Norman 1946- *BiDrAPA 89*
Gaff, Brian Michael 1962- *WhoWor 91*
Gaff, Frank W. 1941- *St&PR 91*
Gaff, Jerry Gene 1936- *WhoAm 90*
Gaff, William A. 1957- *St&PR 91*
Gaffey, F. Peter 1919- *St&PR 91*
Gaffey, Thomas Michael, Jr. 1934- *WhoAm 90*
Gaffga, Diane 1947- *WhoAmW 91*
Gaffigan, Michael 1936- *St&PR 91*
Gaffin, C. Harold 1939- *St&PR 91*
Gaffin, J. N. 1855-1906 *AmLegL*
Gaffney, Dorothea Finnen *WhoAmW 91*
Gaffney, Edward J. 1929- *WhoAm 90*
Gaffney, Gary Robert *BiDrAPA 89*
Gaffney, James *WhoAm 90*
Gaffney, James A. *Ballpl 90*
Gaffney, Janet DuVal *WhoSSW 91*
Gaffney, John *Ballpl 90*
Gaffney, Joseph M. 1946- *St&PR 91*
Gaffney, Mark William 1951- *WhoEmL 91*
Gaffney, Maureen 1943- *WhoAm 90*
Gaffney, Michael Scully 1928- *St&PR 91*, *WhoSSW 91*
Gaffney, Mo *BioIn 16*
Gaffney, Orville E. *St&PR 91*
Gaffney, Owen James 1935- *St&PR 91*
Gaffney, Patrick Joseph 1934- *WhoWor 91*
Gaffney, Paul Cotter 1917- *WhoAm 90*
Gaffney, Peter Charles 1912- *WhoAm 90*
Gaffney, Robert Joseph 1946- *St&PR 91*
Gaffney, Stiles 1954- *St&PR 91*
Gaffney, Terrence John 1949- *WhoEmL 91*
Gaffney, Thomas 1915- *WhoAm 90*
Gaffney, Thomas Edward 1930- *WhoAm 90*
Gaffney, Thomas Francis 1945- *St&PR 91*, *WhoAm 90*
Gaffney, Timothy Frank 1952- *WhoSSW 91*
Gaffney, Timothy R. *AuBYP 90*
Gaffney, William C. 1928- *St&PR 91*
Gafford, Charlotte Kelly *WhoWrEP 89*
Gafford, Mary May 1936- *WhoAmW 91*
Gafford, Nora N. 1924- *St&PR 91*
Gafford, W. Wade 1955- *St&PR 91*
Gafka, Sheila Kurlander 1939- *WhoAmW 91*
Gag, Flavia 1907-1979 *AuBYP 90*
Gag, Wanda 1893-1946 *BioAmW*
Gag, Wanda Hazel 1893-1946 *AuBYP 90*
Gagales, Anastassios 1952- *WhoWor 91*
Gagan, Richard D. 1936- *St&PR 91*
Gagarin, Yuri 1934-1968 *WorAlBi*
Gage, Andrew Arthur 1922- *WhoE 91*
Gage, Angela Waleeta 1958- *WhoEmL 91*
Gage, Bruce Carlson *BiDrAPA 89*
Gage, Calvin William 1929- *WhoAm 90*
Gage, Catherine *BiDEWW*
Gage, Charles S. *BioIn 16*
Gage, David Floyd 1945- *WhoEmL 91*, *WhoSSW 91*
Gage, Diane *BioIn 16*
Gage, Edwin C., III 1940- *WhoAm 90*
Gage, Faye Cauley 1937- *WhoE 91*
Gage, Frances 1808-1880 *FemiCLE*
Gage, Frances M 1924- *WhoAmA 91*
Gage, Fred Kelton 1925- *WhoAm 90*
Gage, Giuliana G. 1941- *BiDrAPA 89*
Gage, Gloria Ann *BiDrAPA 89*
Gage, Howard 1937- *WhoE 91*
Gage, Irwin 1939- *IntWWM 90*
Gage, John 1937- *WhoAm 90*
Gage, Kevin E. 1959- *St&PR 91*
Gage, Lyman Judson 1836-1927 *BiDrUSE 89*
Gage, Matilda 1826-1898 *FemiCLE*
Gage, Matilda Joslyn 1826-1898 *BioIn 16*
Gage, Maxwell *BiDrAPA 89*
Gage, Michael Eaton 1948- *WhoE 91*
Gage, Nancy Elizabeth 1947- *WhoAmW 91*, *WhoEmL 91*
Gage, Nathaniel Lees 1917- *WhoAm 90*
Gage, Nicholas *BioIn 16*
Gage, Nicholas 1939- *CurBio 90 [port]*, *WhoAm 90*
Gage, Nina Diadamia 1883-1946 *BioIn 16*
Gage, Patrick 1942- *WhoAm 90*
Gage, Samuel Wallace, II 1947- *WhoSSW 91*
Gage, Steven K. 1959- *WhoEmL 91*
Gage, Thomas 1721-1787 *EncCRAm*, *WorAlBi*
Gage, Tommy Wilton 1935- *WhoAm 90*
Gage, William James 1932- *WhoE 91*
Gage, Wilson *AuBYP 90*
Gage, Wilson 1922- *BioIn 16*
Gageby, Stephen L. 1940- *St&PR 91*
Gagel, Robert Francis 1946- *WhoSSW 91*
Gagge, Adolf Pharo 1908- *WhoAm 90*
Gaggini, Muriel Marguerite 1951- *WhoWor 91*
Gaggini, Nibilio *PenDiDA 89*
Gaggioli, Richard Arnold 1934- *WhoAm 90*
Gagliani, William Dennis 1959- *WhoWrEP 89*
Gagliano, Caren Calish 1950- *St&PR 91*
Gagliano, Frank Joseph 1931- *WhoAm 90*
Gagliano, Guido 1947- *St&PR 91*
Gagliano, Joseph W. 1924- *St&PR 91*
Gagliano, Louis Anthony 1941- *BiDrAPA 89*
Gagliano, Marco da 1582-1643 *PenDiMP A*
Gagliano, Nicholas Joseph 1926- *St&PR 91*
Gagliano, Phil 1941- *Ballpl 90*
Gagliano, Theodore E 1922- *BiDrAPA 89*
Gagliardi, Annette Jane 1950- *WhoWrEP 89*
Gagliardi, Anthony L. *BioIn 16*
Gagliardi, Elaine Hightower 1960- *WhoEmL 91*
Gagliardi, Francis A 1915- *BiDrAPA 89*
Gagliardi, Francis S *BiDrAPA 89*
Gagliardi, Frank Joseph 1933- *WhoAm 90*
Gagliardi, Joseph J. 1939- *St&PR 91*
Gagliardi, Lee Parsons 1918- *WhoAm 90*
Gagliardi, Michael J. 1940- *St&PR 91*
Gagliardi, Raymond Alfred 1922- *WhoAm 90*, *WhoWor 91*
Gagliardi, Ugo Oscar 1931- *WhoAm 90*
Gagliardo, Joseph 1925- *BiDrAPA 89*
Gagliardo, Reginald Saverio 1948- *WhoEmL 91*
Gagliardo, Ruth Garver 1895?-1980 *AuBYP 90*
Gaglione, Rae Ann 1962- *WhoAmW 91*
Gaglione, Robert J. 1958- *WhoEmL 91*
Gagne, Annmarie Paula 1955- *WhoE 91*
Gagne, Deborah *WhoAmW 91*
Gagne, George Francis 1952- *WhoE 91*
Gagne, Georgette Marie 1950- *WhoAmW 91*
Gagne, Greg 1961- *Ballpl 90*
Gagne, James L. 1954- *WhoEmL 91*
Gagne, Laura Lee 1959- *WhoE 91*
Gagne, Marc 1939- *IntWWM 90*
Gagne, Pamela Bashore 1955- *WhoAmW 91*, *WhoWor 91*
Gagne, Paul E. 1946- *St&PR 91*
Gagne, Paul Ernest 1946- *WhoAm 90*
Gagne, Pierre W 1942- *BiDrAPA 89*
Gagne, Robert Mills 1916- *WhoAm 90*
Gagne, Russell C. 1960- *St&PR 91*
Gagne, Walter Paul 1944- *WhoE 91*
Gagne, William Roderick 1955- *WhoE 91*, *WhoEmL 91*, *WhoWor 91*
Gagnebin, Albert Paul 1909- *WhoAm 90*
Gagner, Thomas Albert 1946- *WhoE 91*
Gagner, Wayne P. 1938- *WhoE 91*
Gagnere, Olivier *BioIn 16*
Gagneur, Marie-Louise 1832-1902 *EncCoWW*
Gagneux, Daniel Gerard 1940- *WhoAm 90*
Gagnier, Bruce 1941- *WhoAmA 91*
Gagnier, Charles E. 1934- *St&PR 91*
Gagnon, Alain 1938- *IntWWM 90*
Gagnon, Alfred Joseph 1914- *WhoAm 90*
Gagnon, Camille Alma 1955- *WhoE 91*
Gagnon, Cecile 1936- *BioIn 16*
Gagnon, Charles 1934- *WhoAmA 91*
Gagnon, Charles Eugene 1934- *WhoAmA 91*
Gagnon, Edith Morrison 1909- *WhoAmW 91*
Gagnon, Edouard 1918- *WhoWor 91*
Gagnon, Fabien 1953- *BiDrAPA 89*
Gagnon, Georges Z *BiDrAPA 89*
Gagnon, Janice M. 1955- *WhoAmW 91*
Gagnon, John H. 1931- *BioIn 16*
Gagnon, John Henry 1931- *WhoAm 90*
Gagnon, Lee A. 1937- *St&PR 91*
Gagnon, Lynne Marie 1951- *WhoAmW 91*
Gagnon, Madeleine 1938- *BioIn 16*, *FemiCLE*
Gagnon, Michael J. 1939- *St&PR 91*
Gagnon, Peter R. 1943- *St&PR 91*
Gagnon, Pierre Rene *BiDrAPA 89*
Gagnon, Rejean 1938- *St&PR 91*
Gagnon, Ria *BioIn 16*
Gagnon, Richard I. 1920- *St&PR 91*
Gagnon, Roger Joseph 1946- *WhoEmL 91*
Gagnon, Ronald J. 1939- *St&PR 91*
Gagnon, Salomon *BiDrAPA 89*
Gagnon, Yvonne 1946- *WhoAmW 91*, *WhoEmL 91*
Gagon, Eleanor Law 1950- *BiDrAPA 89*
Gagon, Terry Ersel *BiDrAPA 89*
Gagosian, Earl *BioIn 16*, *NewYTBS 90*
Gagosian, Larry *BioIn 16*
Gagosian, Robert B. 1944- *WhoAm 90*
Gagrat, Dinshah Dhun 1946- *BiDrAPA 89*
Gagrat, Shobha *BiDrAPA 89*
Gaguine, Benito 1912- *WhoAm 90*, *WhoE 91*
Gaha, Lotfi *BiDrAPA 89*
Gahagan, Hayes Edward 1947- *WhoEmL 91*
Gahagan, James, Jr 1927- *WhoAmA 91*
Gahagan, James Edward, Jr. 1927- *WhoAm 90*
Gahagen, Dennis L. 1945- *St&PR 91*
Gahan, William Patrick, III 1954- *WhoEmL 91*
Gahlen, Bernhard 1938- *WhoWor 91*
Gahm, George Irvin 1913- *BiDrAPA 89*
Gahmlich, Wilfried 1939- *IntWWM 90*
Gahona, Gabriel Vicente 1828-1899 *ArtLatA*
Gai, Eliezer 1944- *WhoE 91*
Gai, Paula Marchio 1943- *WhoAmW 91*
Gai, Pietro *PenDiDA 89*
Gaiber, Lawrence Jay 1960- *WhoEmL 91*
Gaich, Michael G. 1944- *WhoSSW 91*
Gaich, Sharon Denise 1961- *WhoWrEP 89*
Gaidano, Don Joseph 1948- *St&PR 91*
Gaige, Dorothy Dove 1945- *WhoWrEP 89*
Gaige, Mark Philip 1957- *WhoE 91*
Gail, Maxwell Trowbridge, Jr. 1943- *WhoAm 90*
Gailey, Edward David 1948- *WhoEmL 91*
Gailey, Franklin Bryan 1918- *WhoAm 90*
Gailey, Marguerite Henrietta 1917- *WhoAmW 91*
Gailey, Susan Coia 1954- *WhoEmL 91*
Gailhoustet, Renee 1929- *WomArch [port]*
Gailing, Walter 1930- *St&PR 91*
Gailis, Janis 1909-1975 *WhoAmA 91N*
Gailius, Gilbert Keistutis 1931- *St&PR 91*, *WhoAm 90*
Gaillard, Andre *BioIn 16*
Gaillard, Eugene 1862-1933 *PenDiDA 89*
Gaillard, Felix Achille d'Aime 1919-1970 *BiDFrPL*
Gaillard, John Palmer, Jr. 1920- *WhoAm 90*
Gaillard, Slim 1916- *DrBIPA 90*, *OxCPMus*
Gaillard, Thomas Ray 1947- *WhoEmL 91*, *WhoSSW 91*
Gaillard, Yvon Andre 1923- *WhoWor 91*
Gailys, John M. 1941- *St&PR 91*
Gaine, Hugh *BioIn 16*
Gainen, Susan Rose 1950- *WhoAmW 91*, *WhoEmL 91*
Gainer, Joseph Henry 1924- *WhoE 91*
Gainer, Leila Josephine 1948- *WhoAmW 91*
Gainer, Rhonda Hope 1956- *WhoEmL 91*
Gainer, Sandra Gertrude 1951- *WhoE 91*, *WhoEmL 91*
Gaines, Alan Jay 1942- *WhoAmA 91*
Gaines, Alan McCulloch 1938- *WhoAm 90*
Gaines, Alexander Pendleton 1910- *WhoAm 90*
Gaines, Alida Moira 1957- *WhoAmW 91*
Gaines, Anne Preston 1950- *WhoAmW 91*
Gaines, Barry Michael *BiDrAPA 89*
Gaines, Boyd 1953- *ConTFT 8*
Gaines, Charles Stephen 1947- *WhoEmL 91*
Gaines, Cheryl 1950- *BiDrAPA 89*
Gaines, Cristina E. 1946- *WhoHisp 91*
Gaines, David I. 1896-1989 *BioIn 16*
Gaines, Edmund Pendleton 1777-1849 *WhNaAH*
Gaines, Elizabeth Wolcott 1963- *WhoAmW 91*
Gaines, Ernest J. *WhoWrEP 89*
Gaines, Ernest J. 1933- *AuBYP 90*, *MajTwCW*
Gaines, Frank, Jr. 1918- *WhoE 91*
Gaines, Frank M, Jr. 1916- *BiDrAPA 89*
Gaines, Gail A 1915- *BiDrAPA 89*
Gaines, George Bernard 1921- *St&PR 91*
Gaines, Gerald William 1956- *St&PR 91*
Gaines, Gregory 1950- *WhoE 91*
Gaines, Howard C. 1940- *St&PR 91*
Gaines, Howard Clarke 1909- *WhoAm 90*
Gaines, J Arthur 1890?- *DcAfAmP*
Gaines, J. Donald 1936- *St&PR 91*
Gaines, Jack Weiss 1924- *BiDrAPA 89*
Gaines, James E 1928- *DrBIPA 90*
Gaines, James Edwin, Jr. 1938- *WhoAm 90*
Gaines, James Russell 1947- *WhoAm 90*
Gaines, Jeanie 1953- *WhoAmW 91*
Gaines, Joe 1936- *Ballpl 90*
Gaines, John Strother 1933- *WhoSSW 91*
Gaines, Joseph Allen 1924- *St&PR 91*
Gaines, Kendra Holly 1946- *WhoAmW 91*
Gaines, La Donna Adrian *WhoAmW 91*
Gaines, Leonard M. 1956- *WhoEmL 91*
Gaines, Lonnetta Marie 1946- *WhoE 91*
Gaines, Ludwell Ebersole 1927- *WhoAm 90*
Gaines, M. C. 1896-1947 *EncACom*
Gaines, Richard K *BiDrAPA 89*
Gaines, Robert Walker 1932- *St&PR 91*
Gaines, Sanford Ervin 1945- *WhoEmL 91*
Gaines, Thomas E. 1926- *St&PR 91*
Gaines, Thurston Lenwood, Jr. 1922- *WhoE 91*
Gaines, Tinsley Powell 1939- *WhoSSW 91*
Gaines, Weaver Henderson, Jr. 1943- *St&PR 91*, *WhoAm 90*
Gaines, William Chester 1933- *WhoAm 90*
Gaines, William M. 1922- *EncACom*
Gaines, William Maxwell 1922- *WhoAm 90*, *WhoE 91*, *WhoWor 91*
Gaines, William Robert 1927- *WhoAmA 91*
Gaines-Shelton, Ruth 1873- *EarBlAP*
Gaines Shelton, Ruth Ada 1872- *HarlReB*
Gainey, Bob 1953- *WorAlBi*
Gainey, Hugh Gerrard 1938- *St&PR 91*
Gainey, Robert Michael 1953- *WhoAm 90*, *WhoWor 91*
Gainey, Thomas P. 1925- *St&PR 91*
Gainham, Sarah 1922- *SpyFic*, *TwCCr&M 91*
Gainon, Jacqueline 1951- *BioIn 16*
Gainor, Del 1886-1947 *Ballpl 90*
Gainor, James Joseph 1931- *St&PR 91*
Gainor, Patricia Ann *BiDrAPA 89*
Gainor, Thomas Edward 1933- *St&PR 91*, *WhoAm 90*
Gainotti, Guido 1939- *WhoWor 91*
Gainsborough, Katherine N, Countess of 1665?-1704 *BiDEWW*
Gainsborough, Thomas 1727-1788 *IntDcAA 90*, *WorAlBi*
Gainsbourg, Serge 1928- *WhoWor 91*
Gainsley, Bruce Martin 1942- *BiDrAPA 89*
Gaintan, Alonso de Figueroa *PenDiDA 89*
Gair, Donald S *BiDrAPA 89*
Gair, Robert Marion 1929- *WhoE 91*
Gairdner, John Smith 1925- *WhoAm 90*
Gairy, Eric *BioIn 16*
Gaisberg, Frederick William *BioIn 16*
Gaiser, Charles Henry 1938- *WhoE 91*
Gaiser, Gary Vincent 1937- *St&PR 91*
Gaiser, William R. 1926- *St&PR 91*
Gaisford, Jana Sue 1952- *WhoAmW 91*
Gaisser, Hope Owren 1946- *St&PR 91*
Gaisser, James H. 1943- *St&PR 91*
Gaisser, Julia Haig 1941- *WhoAm 90*
Gaissert, George Brooks 1944- *St&PR 91*
Gait, Gary *BioIn 16*
Gait, Paul *BioIn 16*
Gaitan, Jorge Eliecer 1898-1948 *BioIn 16*
Gaitan, Jose E. 1951- *WhoEmL 91*
Gaite, Francis *TwCCr&M 91*
Gaitens, Larry Patrick 1938- *WhoE 91*
Gaither, Ann Heafner 1932- *WhoSSW 91*

Gaither, Edmund B 1944- WhoAmA 91
Gaither, Gary A. 1949- St&PR 91
Gaither, Gerald Henderson 1940- WhoSSW 91
Gaither, James C. 1937- WhoAm 90
Gaither, John F., Jr. WhoAm 90
Gaither, John F., Jr. 1949- St&PR 91
Gaither, John Francis 1918- WhoAm 90, WhoWor 91
Gaither, John Stokes 1944- St&PR 91
Gaither, O.D. 1927- St&PR 91
Gaither, R. Trent 1957- WhoEmL 91
Gaither, Robert Barker 1929- WhoAm 90
Gaither, Roger Dial 1955- WhoSSW 91
Gaither, William Samuel 1932- WhoAm 90
Gaitonde, Mangesh R 1925- BiDrAPA 89
Gaitskell, Lady 1901-1989 AnObit 1989
Gaitskell, Hugh 1906-1963 WorAlBi
Gaitskill, Kim BiDrAPA 89
Gaitz, Charles M 1922- BiDrAPA 89
Gajardo, Joel WhoHisp 91
Gajda, James Edward 1947- WhoEmL 91
Gajda, Patricia Ann 1941- WhoAmW 91
Gajda, Radola 1892-1948 BioIn 16
Gajdusek, Daniel Carleton 1923- WhoAm 90, WhoE 91, WhoWor 91
Gajdzik, David T. 1946- St&PR 91
Gajec, Lucile Cruz WhoHisp 91
Gajentaan, Johan Eduard 1931- WhoWor 91
Gajewski, Christine 1946- WhoAmW 91
Gajewski, Ferdinand John Vincent 1941- IntWWM 90
Gajewski, Henry Edward 1933- WhoAm 90
Gajewski, Patricia Louise 1959- WhoE 91
Gajwani, Ashok Kumar BiDrAPA 89
Gakwandi, Shatto Arthur 1943- ConAu 131
Gal, Laszlo 1933- BioIn 16, WhoAm 90
Gal, Veronica V BiDrAPA 89
Gal-Or, Esther 1951- WhoE 91
Gala, Andrew Roman 1959- WhoEmL 91
Galabert, Michel BioIn 16
Galaburda, Albert Mark 1948- WhoAm 90
Galainena, Mariano Luis 1922- WhoHisp 91
Galaly, Enan 1947- WhoWor 91
Galamba, Donald J. 1919- St&PR 91
Galambos, John Thomas 1921- WhoAm 90
Galambos, Theodore Victor 1929- WhoAm 90
Galamian, Ivan 1903-1981 PenDiMP
Galamison, Milton A. 1923-1988 BioIn 16
Galan, Augie 1912- Ballpl 90
Galan, Juan Arturo, Jr. 1944- WhoHisp 91
Galan, Nely 1964- WhoHisp 91
Galand, Rene 1923- WhoAm 90
Galane, Irma Adele Bereston 1921- WhoAmW 91, WhoWor 91
Galane, Morton Robert 1926- WhoAm 90, WhoWor 91
Galang, Mariano Abaya, III BiDrAPA 89
Galang-Feather, Nerissa V 1957- BiDrAPA 89
Galang-Jose, Aurora BiDrAPA 89
Galanis, Marian Monica 1918- St&PR 91
Galanis, Michael George 1955- BiDrAPA 89
Galanis, Terry S., Jr. 1947- St&PR 91
Galanis, Terry S., Sr. 1918- St&PR 91
Galanos, James 1924- ConDes 90, WhoAm 90
Galanos, Jimmy BioIn 16
Galant, Herbert Lewis 1928- WhoAm 90
Galante, Annamarie Lepore 1963- WhoE 91
Galante, Donna Lisa 1958- WhoE 91
Galante, Eugene J. 1925- St&PR 91
Galante, Gloria Myrtha BiDrAPA 89
Galante, Jane H. 1924- IntWWM 90
Galante, Jane Hohfeld 1924- ConAu 132
Galante, Jorge Osvaldo 1934- WhoAm 90
Galante, Nicholas Thomas, III 1955- WhoE 91
Galanter, Eugene 1924- WhoAm 90
Galanter, Lawrence ODwPR 91
Galanter, Marc 1941- BiDrAPA 89, WhoAm 90, WhoE 91
Galantin, I. J. 1910- BioIn 16
Galantine, Kathleen Patricia 1953- WhoWrEP 89
Galantuomini, Carol Brigida 1959- WhoAmW 91
Galardi, John N. 1938- St&PR 91
Galarnyk, Ihor A M BiDrAPA 89
Galarnyk, Timothy G. BioIn 16
Galarraga, Andres BioIn 16
Galarraga, Andres 1961- Ballpl 90
Galarraga, Andres Jose 1961- WhoHisp 91
Galarza, Ernest ConAu 131, HispWr 90
Galarza, Ernesto 1905-1984 BioIn 16, ConAu 131, HispWr 90
Galarza, Pedro A. St&PR 91
Galarza-Diaz, Nestor Jose 1945- BiDrAPA 89
Galas, Diamanda BioIn 16
Galas, Diamanda 1955- IntWWM 90
Galask, Rudolph Peter 1935- WhoAm 90, WhoWor 91
Galaskiewicz, Joseph James 1949- WhoEmL 91
Galassi, Jonathan 1949- WhoWrEP 89
Galassi, Peter 1951- BioIn 16, WhoAm 90
Galasso, Francis Salvatore 1931- WhoAm 90
Galasso, George John 1932- WhoE 91
Galati, Carmela Melso 1952- WhoE 91
Galati, Frank Joseph 1943- WhoAm 90
Galati, Gary M. ODwPR 91
Galati, Nikki BioIn 16
Galatianos, Gus Athanassios 1947- WhoEmL 91, WhoWor 91
Galatro, Vincent T. 1929- St&PR 91
Galatte-Howard, Gail Ann 1959- WhoAmW 91
Galatzer-Levy, Robert Milton 1944- BiDrAPA 89
Galay, Ted 1941- OxCCanT
Galazen, Kevin Paul 1962- WhoEmL 91
Galazka, Jacek Michal 1924- WhoAm 90
Galberaith, Richard O. 1939- St&PR 91
Galbis, Ricardo BiDrAPA 89
Galbis, Ricardo 1936- WhoE 91, WhoHisp 91
Galbo-Mangone, Roslyn 1954- WhoEmL 91
Galbraith, Bruce S. St&PR 91
Galbraith, Carol BioIn 16
Galbraith, Charles L. BioIn 16
Galbraith, Evan BioIn 16
Galbraith, Evan Griffith 1928- WhoAm 90
Galbraith, Harry Wilson 1918- St&PR 91
Galbraith, James C. 1912- St&PR 91
Galbraith, James Garber 1914- WhoAm 90
Galbraith, James K. 1952- ConAu 130
Galbraith, James Marshall 1942- WhoAm 90
Galbraith, James R. ODwPR 91
Galbraith, James Ronald 1936- WhoAm 90
Galbraith, John B. AmLegL
Galbraith, John Drummond, Jr. 1919- WhoWor 91
Galbraith, John Kenneth 1908- BioIn 16, MajTwCW, WhoAm 90, WhoWrEP 89, WorAlBi
Galbraith, John Semple 1916- WhoAm 90
Galbraith, John William 1921- WhoAm 90
Galbraith, Kirk 1942- St&PR 91
Galbraith, Matthew White 1927- St&PR 91, WhoAm 90
Galbraith, Paul 1964- IntWWM 90
Galbraith, Ruth Legg 1923- WhoAm 90
Galbraith, Ted Robert 1958- WhoSSW 91
Galbreath, J. Joseph 1935- St&PR 91
Galbreath, James H. St&PR 91
Galbreath, John W. 1898-1988 Ballpl 90
Galbreath, John Wilmer 1897-1988 BioIn 16
Galbreath, Joyce Dale Condray 1930- WhoAmW 91
Galbreath, Lizanne 1957- WhoEmL 91
Galbreath, Robert 1938- EncO&P 3
Galbreath, Robert Gerard 1937- WhoSSW 91
Galbreath, Terry Stephen 1950- WhoEmL 91
Galbreath, Theodore Ralph 1953- WhoEmL 91
Galbrun, Jean-Paul 1943- WhoWor 91
Galbut, Martin Richard 1946- WhoEmL 91
Galchick, Janet Mae 1951- WhoAmW 91
Galdi, Albert Peter, Jr. 1950- WhoEmL 91
Galdikas, Birute BioIn 16
Galdone, Paul 1914-1986 AuBYP 90, BioIn 16
Galdos, Benito Perez HispWr 90
Galdos, Benito Perez 1843-1920 BioIn 16
Galdos, Hugo Blanco 1934- BioIn 16
Galdston, Iago BiDrAPA 89
Galdston, Iago 1895-1989 BioIn 16
Galdston, Richard BiDrAPA 89
Gale, Augusta BioIn 16
Gale, Beresford EarBlAP
Gale, Charles G. 1916- St&PR 91
Gale, Connie 1946- St&PR 91
Gale, Connie Ruth 1946- WhoEmL 91
Gale, Elizabeth 1948- IntWWM 90
Gale, Eric BioIn 16
Gale, G. Donald 1933- St&PR 91
Gale, George Alexander 1906- WhoAm 90
Gale, John 1925-1974 BioIn 16
Gale, John Goddard, Jr. 1946- BiDrAPA 89
Gale, Melvin S 1945- BiDrAPA 89
Gale, Nancy Ann 1947- St&PR 91
Gale, Neil Jan 1960- St&PR 91, WhoEmL 91
Gale, Paula Jane 1946- WhoAmW 91
Gale, Peggy 1944- WhoAmA 91
Gale, Philip R 1920- BiDrAPA 89
Gale, Randall Glenn 1952- WhoEmL 91
Gale, Rich 1954- Ballpl 90
Gale, Richard Nelson 1896-1982 DcNaB 1981
Gale, Robert H 1935- BiDrAPA 89
Gale, Robert Lee 1919- WhoAm 90
Gale, Robert Peter BioIn 16
Gale, Robert Peter 1945- WhoAm 90
Gale, Stanley W 1947- BiDrAPA 89
Gale, Stanley William 1947- WhoE 91
Gale, Steven Hershel 1940- WhoSSW 91
Gale, Thomas Charles 1943- WhoAm 90
Gale, Thomas Martin 1926- WhoAm 90
Gale, Walter Rasin 1878-1959 WhoAmA 91N
Gale, William A. 1939- WhoWrEP 89
Gale, William Henry 1905- WhoAm 90
Gale, William Henry 1915- WhoAmA 91
Gale, Zona 1874-1938 BioAmW, BioIn 16, FemiCLE, NotWoAT
Galea, John Henry 1924- WhoAm 90
Galeana, Frank H. 1929- WhoHisp 91
Galeano, Eduardo 1940- ConAu 32NR, HispWr 90
Galeano, Eduardo H. 1940- BioIn 16
Galeano, Eduardo Hughes 1940- WhoWor 91
Galecio, Galo 1912- ArtLatA
Galeener, Frank Lee 1936- WhoAm 90
Galef, Andrew Geoffrey 1932- St&PR 91, WhoAm 90
Galef, Harold R 1928- BiDrAPA 89
Galef, Richard G. 1923- St&PR 91
Galehouse, Denny 1911- Ballpl 90, BioIn 16
Galehouse, Lawrence David 1946- WhoEmL 91
Galella, Joseph Peter 1956- WhoEmL 91
Galella, Ronald Edward 1931- WhoAm 90
Galen 130?-200 BioIn 16, WorAlBi
Galen, Clemens August von 1878-1946 BioIn 16
Galen, Elaine 1928- WhoAmA 91
Galeno, Joseph John 1946- WhoE 91
Galenson, Eleanor BiDrAPA 89
Galenson, Walter 1914- WhoAm 90
Galeos, Rowena Francisco BiDrAPA 89
Galeotti, Marzio 1440?-1494? EncO&P 3
Galeotti, Steven 1952- WhoE 91
Galerne, Andre 1926- St&PR 91
Gales, Joseph 1786-1860 BioIn 16
Gales, Mary E 1948- BiDrAPA 89
Gales, Michael Arthur 1943- BiDrAPA 89
Gales, Robert Sydney 1914- WhoAm 90
Galese, William 1931- St&PR 91
Galey, David Jonathan 1952- St&PR 91
Galey, Leon 1925- St&PR 91
Galey, Thomas S. 1955- St&PR 91
Galfo, Armand James 1924- WhoAm 90
Galgano, Victor Joseph 1943- St&PR 91
Galgoczi, Erzsebet 1930-1989 EncCoWW
Galian, Laurence Joseph Anthony Michael 1954- WhoEmL 91
Galiani, Ferdinando 1728-1787 BioIn 16
Galiano, Henry BioIn 16
Galiardo, John W. 1933- St&PR 91
Galiardo, John William 1933- WhoAm 90
Galiber, Joseph Lionel 1924- WhoE 91
Galie, Lawrence Pius 1952- WhoEmL 91
Galie, Louis Michael 1945- WhoE 91, WhoEmL 91, WhoWor 91
Galietta, Gerald Edward 1941- BiDrAPA 89
Galiev, M. S. Sultan- 1880?-1940? BioIn 16
Galigai, Leonora EncO&P 3
Galil, Uzia 1925- St&PR 91, WhoAm 90
Galilei, Celeste 1600-1634 EncCoWW
Galilei, Galileo 1564-1642 BioIn 16
Galileo 1564-1642 BioIn 16, WorAlBi
Galimi, Dominick Joseph 1945- WhoE 91
Galimir, Felix 1910- IntWWM 90, WhoAm 90
Galimore, Michael Oliver 1947- WhoWor 91
Galin, Julius L. 1924- St&PR 91
Galin, Miles A. 1932- WhoAm 90
Galin, Sofya G 1933- BiDrAPA 89
Galina, Lada EncCoWW
Galindez, Orlando F BiDrAPA 89
Galindez-Antelo, William BiDrAPA 89
Galindo, Beatriz EncCoWW
Galindo, Beatriz 1475-1534 EncCoWW
Galindo, Belisario August 1943- WhoE 91
Galindo, Conrado Gustavo, III 1947- WhoSSW 91
Galindo, Felipe BioIn 16
Galindo, Felipe 1957- WhoHisp 91
Galindo, Mazatl NewAgMG
Galindo, P. ConAu 131, HispWr 90
Galindo, P. 1929- WhoHisp 91
Galindo, Rafael WhoHisp 91
Galindo, Xiomara Inez 1961- WhoHisp 91
Galindo-Elvira, Carlos 1967- WhoHisp 91
Galinee, Rene De Brehant De EncCRAm
Galinsky, Andrew M. 1947- St&PR 91
Galinsky, Gotthard Karl 1942- WhoAm 90
Galinsky, Hans Karl 1909- WhoWor 91
Galinsky, Marsha Dee 1958- WhoEmL 91
Galinsky, Marvin D BiDrAPA 89
Galinsky, Morris D BiDrAPA 89
Galinsky, Norman 1942- WhoAmA 91
Galinsky, Raymond Ethan 1948- WhoEmL 91
Galioni, Elmer F 1924- BiDrAPA 89
Galioto, Frank Martin, Jr. 1942- WhoE 91
Galipo, Russell E. 1932- St&PR 91
Galitzin, Alvin L BiDrAPA 89
Galitzine, Georges Pierre 1931- WhoWor 91
Galitzine, Irene BioIn 16
Galkin, Elliott W. BioIn 16
Galkin, Elliott W. NewYTBS 90
Galkin, Elliott W. 1921- IntWWM 90
Galkin, Elliott W 1921-1990 ConAu 131
Galkin, Florence 1925- WhoAmW 91
Galkin, Robert Theodore 1926- St&PR 91
Galkin, Samuel Bernard 1933- WhoE 91, WhoWor 91
Galkovsky, Alexander PenDiMP
Gall 1840-1894 WhNaAH [port]
Gall, Adrienne Lynn 1960- WhoAmW 91
Gall, Alice AuBYP 90
Gall, Christian Franz 1927- WhoWor 91
Gall, David Anthony 1941- St&PR 91
Gall, Elizabeth Benson 1944- WhoAmW 91
Gall, Eric Papineau 1940- WhoAm 90
Gall, Francois 1922- WhoWor 91
Gall, Jeffrey Charles 1950- IntWWM 90
Gall, Jim BioIn 16
Gall, Joseph Grafton 1928- WhoAm 90
Gall, Lawrence Howard 1917- WhoAm 90
Gall, Lenore Rosalie 1943- WhoE 91
Gall, Lothar 1936- WhoWor 91
Gall, Mary Sheila WhoAm 90
Gall, Meredith Damien 1942- WhoAm 90, WhoWrEP 89
Gall, Robert Edward 1945- St&PR 91
Gall, Roxanne Bernadette 1954- WhoAmW 91
Gall, Sally Moore 1941- WhoWrEP 89
Gall, Sandy 1927- ConAu 130
Gall, Steve ODwPR 91
Gall, Suzanne Leigh 1959- WhoAmW 91
Gall, Yvonne 1885-1972 PenDiMP
Galla Placidia WomWR
Galla, Patrick P 1927- BiDrAPA 89
Gallacher, Calvin M. 1950- St&PR 91
Gallagher and Shean OxCPMus
Gallagher, Alan 1945- Ballpl 90
Gallagher, Alfred Kenneth 1936- WhoWor 91
Gallagher, Anne Porter 1950- WhoAmW 91, WhoEmL 91, WhoWor 91
Gallagher, Anne Timlin 1943- WhoAm 90
Gallagher, Anthony Reed 1949- WhoEmL 91
Gallagher, Bernard P. 1910-1989 BioIn 16
Gallagher, Carole 1950- WhoAmA 91
Gallagher, Cathy Louise 1948- WhoAmW 91
Gallagher, Charles Patrick 1938- St&PR 91
Gallagher, Cynthia WhoAmA 91
Gallagher, Daniel Joseph 1951- St&PR 91
Gallagher, Danny EncO&P 3
Gallagher, Dave BioIn 16
Gallagher, Dave 1960- Ballpl 90
Gallagher, Denise Connelly 1948- WhoE 91
Gallagher, Dennis Vincent 1952- WhoEmL 91
Gallagher, Donald Gerard 1948- WhoSSW 91
Gallagher, Ed OxCPMus
Gallagher, Edward J. 1929- St&PR 91
Gallagher, Eloise 1942- St&PR 91
Gallagher, F. Michael 1934- WhoAm 90
Gallagher, Frank W. 1925- St&PR 91
Gallagher, Gerald Raphael 1941- WhoAm 90
Gallagher, Gregory Allen 1953- St&PR 91
Gallagher, Hubert R. 1907- WhoAm 90
Gallagher, Idella Jane Smith 1917- WhoAmW 91
Gallagher, J Richard 1939- BiDrAPA 89
Gallagher, Jack B. 1947- IntWWM 90
Gallagher, Jack Burt 1947- WhoEmL 91
Gallagher, James 1904- Ballpl 90
Gallagher, James E. 1920- St&PR 91
Gallagher, James L 1950- BiDrAPA 89
Gallagher, James P. WhoAm 90
Gallagher, James P. 1948- ODwPR 91
Gallagher, James Paul 1948- St&PR 91
Gallagher, James Wes 1911- WhoAm 90
Gallagher, James William 1935- WhoAm 90
Gallagher, Jock 1938- ConAu 129
Gallagher, Joel Wayne 1945- WhoEmL 91
Gallagher, John Austin 1935- St&PR 91
Gallagher, John Francis WhoAm 90, WhoE 91
Gallagher, John Joseph 1943- WhoAm 90
Gallagher, John M BiDrAPA 89
Gallagher, John P. 1927- St&PR 91
Gallagher, John Patrick 1916- WhoAm 90
Gallagher, John Paul 1947- WhoEmL 91
Gallagher, John Pirie 1916- WhoAm 90

Gallagher, John Robert, Jr. 1941- *WhoWor 91*
Gallagher, John Sill, III 1947- *WhoAm 90*
Gallagher, John Thomas 1935- *St&PR 91*
Gallagher, John William 1948- *St&PR 91*
Gallagher, Joseph Francis 1926- *WhoAm 90*
Gallagher, Joseph Thomas 1936- *St&PR 91*
Gallagher, Julie Marie 1964- *WhoEmL 91*
Gallagher, Karen 1948- *WhoWrEP 89*
Gallagher, Katheleen C. 1922- *ODwPR 91*
Gallagher, Kathleen Ellen 1949- *WhoAmA 91*
Gallagher, Kathy Ann 1954- *WhoAmW 91*
Gallagher, Larry *BioIn 16*
Gallagher, Linda Parke 1944- *WhoE 91*
Gallagher, Lindy Allyn 1954- *WhoAmW 91, WhoE 91, WhoEmL 91*
Gallagher, Lorie Miller 1962- *WhoAmW 91*
Gallagher, Marian Gould 1914- *WhoAm 90*
Gallagher, Marjorie Curtis 1948- *BiDrAPA 89*
Gallagher, Martha Gavin 1955- *St&PR 91*
Gallagher, Mary Beth 1946- *WhoWrEP 89*
Gallagher, Mary Beth 1963- *WhoAmW 91*
Gallagher, Mary Jane *ODwPR 91*
Gallagher, Mary Patricia 1958- *WhoEmL 91*
Gallagher, Matthew G. 1932- *St&PR 91*
Gallagher, Matthew Philip, Jr. 1944- *WhoSSW 91*
Gallagher, Megan *BioIn 16*
Gallagher, Michael Clyde 1943- *WhoAm 90*
Gallagher, Michael Patrick 1958- *WhoEmL 91*
Gallagher, Michael Robert 1946- *WhoAm 90*
Gallagher, Michael Stephen 1948- *WhoEmL 91*
Gallagher, Nancy Anne 1952- *WhoAmW 91*
Gallagher, Olive 1943- *WhoAmW 91*
Gallagher, Owen 1943- *WhoE 91*
Gallagher, Pamela P 1947- *BiDrAPA 89*
Gallagher, Pat *BioIn 16*
Gallagher, Patricia Anne *BiDrAPA 89*
Gallagher, Patricia Cecilia *WhoWrEP 89*
Gallagher, Patricia Lynn *BiDrAPA 89*
Gallagher, Patrick *BioIn 16*
Gallagher, Patrick F. X. 1952- *ODwPR 91*
Gallagher, Patrick Ximenes 1935- *WhoAm 90*
Gallagher, Paul Thomas 1928- *St&PR 91*
Gallagher, Paula Marie 1964- *WhoAmW 91, WhoE 91*
Gallagher, Peter James 1935- *WhoE 91*
Gallagher, Peter Kevin 1951- *BiDrAPA 89*
Gallagher, R.R. *St&PR 91*
Gallagher, Richard *ConAu 31NR*
Gallagher, Richard Edward 1929- *St&PR 91*
Gallagher, Richard Eugene 1950- *BiDrAPA 89*
Gallagher, Richard F 1937- *BiDrAPA 89*
Gallagher, Richard Hugo 1927- *WhoAm 90, WhoE 91*
Gallagher, Robert C. 1938- *St&PR 91*
Gallagher, Robert Edmond 1923- *St&PR 91*
Gallagher, Robert Francis 1934- *St&PR 91, WhoAm 90*
Gallagher, Rollin M. III *BiDrAPA 89*
Gallagher, Rollin McCulloch, III 1943- *WhoE 91*
Gallagher, Rory 1949- *OxCPMus*
Gallagher, Sharon *ODwPR 91*
Gallagher, Susan Glockner 1958- *WhoEmL 91*
Gallagher, Terence Joseph 1934- *St&PR 91, WhoAm 90*
Gallagher, Terrence Vincent 1946- *WhoAm 90*
Gallagher, Tess *BioIn 16*
Gallagher, Tess 1943- *ConLC 63 [port], WhoWrEP 89, WorAu 1980 [port]*
Gallagher, Thomas Jordan, Jr. 1947- *WhoEmL 91*
Gallagher, Thomas Joseph 1949- *WhoE 91, WhoEmL 91*
Gallagher, Tom 1944- *WhoAm 90, WhoSSW 91*
Gallagher, Veronica Regina 1921- *St&PR 91*
Gallagher, Vicki Smith 1950- *WhoSSW 91*
Gallagher, Vincent Patrick 1945- *St&PR 91*
Gallagher, W. Kevin 1952- *ODwPR 91*
Gallagher, Walter B. 1912- *St&PR 91*
Gallagher, Walter Edward 1910- *WhoAm 90*
Gallagher, Wes 1911- *BioIn 16*
Gallagher, William 1932- *WhoE 91*
Gallagher, William Francis 1922- *WhoAm 90*
Gallagher, William Michael, Sr. 1952- *WhoSSW 91*
Gallagher, William P. 1940- *St&PR 91*
Gallaher, Art, Jr. 1925- *WhoAm 90*
Gallaher, Cynthia 1953- *WhoEmL 91, WhoWrEP 89*
Gallaher, Frank F. 1946- *St&PR 91*
Gallaher, G. Paige *BiDrAPA 89*
Gallaher, James A. 1947- *ODwPR 91*
Gallaher, Marian E 1929- *BiDrAPA 89*
Gallaher, Stuart William 1931- *WhoWor 91*
Gallaher, Walter Bryan 1931- *WhoSSW 91*
Gallahorn, George Edward *BiDrAPA 89*
Gallahue, David L 1943- *ConAu 30NR*
Gallalee, John Adams 1955- *BiDrAPA 89*
Gallamore, Betty Lou 1951- *WhoEmL 91*
Galland, Adolf 1912- *BioIn 16*
Galland, Frederick Lewis 1944- *St&PR 91*
Galland, R.I. 1916- *St&PR 91*
Gallander, Cathleen S 1931- *WhoAmA 91*
Gallant, Donald M 1929- *BiDrAPA 89*
Gallant, Edgar 1924- *WhoAm 90*
Gallant, Francis X. 1928- *St&PR 91*
Gallant, George William 1931- *WhoE 91*
Gallant, Gilles M. 1933- *St&PR 91*
Gallant, Herbert 1922- *St&PR 91*
Gallant, James T. 1937- *WhoWrEP 89*
Gallant, Judith S 1929- *BiDrAPA 89*
Gallant, Kenneth Stuart 1951- *WhoEmL 91*
Gallant, Lisa 1958- *WhoEmL 91*
Gallant, Mavis *BioIn 16*
Gallant, Mavis 1922- *CurBio 90 [port], FemiCLE, MajTwCW, WhoAm 90, WhoAmW 91*
Gallant, Neal *WhoSSW 91*
Gallant, Pamela L. 1942- *WhoWrEP 89*
Gallant, Roy Arthur 1924- *AuBYP 90*
Gallant, Sandra Kirkham 1933- *WhoWor 91*
Gallanty, Alan Todd 1959- *WhoEmL 91*
Gallanty, Julie Ann *WhoAmW 91*
Gallar, John Joseph 1936- *WhoWor 91*
Gallardo, Carlos 1944- *BioIn 16*
Gallardo, David Felipe 1958- *WhoHisp 91*
Gallardo, Dora Castillo 1947- *WhoHisp 91*
Gallardo, Edward *ConAu 131, HispWr 90*
Gallardo, Guadalupe 1962- *WhoHisp 91*
Gallardo, Jose Maria 1925- *WhoWor 91*
Gallardo, Juan 1947- *St&PR 91*
Gallardo, Ofelia E *BiDrAPA 89*
Gallardo, Ramon A. 1937- *WhoHisp 91*
Gallardo, Tony Ray 1941- *St&PR 91*
Gallarini, Luciano 1932- *WhoWor 91*
Gallarneau, John Bernard 1921- *St&PR 91*
Gallas, Daniel O. *WhoAm 90*
Gallas, Daniel Otis 1931- *St&PR 91*
Gallas, Helga 1940- *WhoWor 91*
Gallassero, Hilda Kilmer 1928- *WhoWrEP 89*
Gallastegui, Lynnette O *BiDrAPA 89*
Gallatin, Albert 1761-1849 *BiDrUSE 89, BioIn 16, EncABHB 6 [port], WhNaAH [port], WorAlBi*
Gallatin, Albert E. 1939- *St&PR 91*
Gallatin, Albert Eugene 1882-1952 *WhoAmA 91N*
Gallatin, James P. *St&PR 91*
Gallatin, Ronald L. 1945- *St&PR 91*
Gallatin, Sue Ann 1955- *St&PR 91*
Gallaudet, Denison 1944- *St&PR 91, WhoAm 90*
Gallaudet, Richard L. 1943- *St&PR 91*
Gallaudet, Thomas Hopkins 1787-1851 *WorAlBi*
Gallaugher, Barbara Alice 1950- *WhoAmW 91*
Gallaway, Lowell Eugene 1930- *WhoWor 91*
Gallay, Madeleine *BioIn 16*
Galle, Claude 1759-1815 *PenDiDA 89*
Galle, Emile 1846-1904 *PenDiDA 89*
Galle, Fred Charles 1919- *WhoAm 90*
Galle, Richard Lynn 1947- *WhoAm 90*
Galleani, Luigi 1861-1931 *EncAL*
Gallegly, Elton William 1944- *WhoAm 90*
Gallego, Laura 1924- *HispWr 90*
Gallego, Mike 1960- *WhoHisp 91*
Gallegos, Abigail Marquez 1952- *WhoHisp 91*
Gallegos, Albert V., Jr. *BioIn 16*
Gallegos, Andrew Lalo 1940- *WhoHisp 91*
Gallegos, Arnold Jose 1938- *WhoHisp 91*
Gallegos, Frederick 1947- *WhoEmL 91*
Gallegos, John Paul 1935- *WhoHisp 91*
Gallegos, Jose Guadalupe 1828-1867 *AmLegL*
Gallegos, Jose Manuel 1815-1875 *AmLegL, BioIn 16*
Gallegos, Jose Ramon *St&PR 91*
Gallegos, Larry A., Sr. 1944- *WhoHisp 91*
Gallegos, Larry Duayne 1951- *WhoEmL 91*
Gallegos, Laura Matilde 1924- *WhoHisp 91*
Gallegos, Leonardo Eufemio 1940- *WhoHisp 91*
Gallegos, Lou *WhoAm 90*
Gallegos, Lupe Leticia 1957- *WhoHisp 91*
Gallegos, Michael Sharon 1952- *WhoHisp 91*
Gallegos, Pete *WhoHisp 91*
Gallegos, Prudencio, Jr. 1959- *WhoHisp 91*
Gallegos, Robert C. 1940- *WhoHisp 91*
Gallegos, Romulo 1884-1969 *BioIn 16, ConAu 131, HispWr 90, MajTwCW*
Gallegos, Russell J. 1932- *St&PR 91*
Gallegos, Sandra Luz 1951- *WhoHisp 91*
Gallegos, Tony E. 1924- *WhoHisp 91*
Gallegos, Vincent *WhoHisp 91*
Gallegos-Chacon, Alvaro 1932- *BiDrAPA 89*
Gallemaert, Michel Gerard 1943- *WhoWor 91*
Gallemore, Johnnie L, Jr. *BiDrAPA 89*
Gallemore, Sandra Lucile 1942- *WhoSSW 91*
Gallen, Christopher C 1950- *BiDrAPA 89*
Gallen, David J. *St&PR 91*
Gallen, James M. 1952- *WhoEmL 91*
Gallen, Joel Andrew 1957- *WhoE 91*
Gallen, Sue S. 1931- *WhoAmW 91*
Gallenberger, Clara 1929- *St&PR 91*
Gallenkamp, Charles 1930- *ConAu 131*
Galleno, Anthony M. 1942- *St&PR 91*
Galleno, Anthony Massimo 1942- *WhoE 91*
Galleno, Humberto 1943- *WhoWor 91*
Gallensky, Neil Ellis 1959- *WhoEmL 91*
Gallent, Donald Gayle 1946- *WhoEmL 91*
Gallentine, Kathleen Anne 1949- *BiDrAPA 89*
Galler, Floyd B *BiDrAPA 89*
Galler, Janina Regina *BiDrAPA 89*
Gallerano, Andrew John 1941- *St&PR 91, WhoAm 90*
Gallery, Sharon Mendelson 1953- *WhoEmL 91, WhoWrEP 89*
Galles, Arie Alexander 1944- *WhoAmA 91*
Galles, Duane LeRoy Charles Mealman 1948- *WhoEmL 91*
Galletly, Alan D. *ODwPR 91*
Galletly, Alan David 1937- *WhoSSW 91*
Galletly, Donald *St&PR 91*
Galletta, Joseph Leo 1935- *WhoWor 91*
Galletti, Carl Andrew 1946- *WhoE 91*
Galletti, Pierre Marie 1927- *WhoAm 90*
Gallez-Neuman, Arlette 1928- *WhoWor 91*
Galli, Anthony P. 1926- *ODwPR 91*
Galli, Evelyn Diane 1954- *WhoAmW 91*
Galli, Filippo 1783-1853 *PenDiMP*
Galli, Robert G. 1933- *St&PR 91*
Galli, Stanley Walter *WhoAmA 91*
Galli-Curci, Amelita 1882-1963 *PenDiMP*
Galli-Marie, Celestine 1840-1905 *PenDiMP*
Gallia, Bert 1891-1976 *Ballpl 90*
Gallia, Thomas Nicolas 1921- *IntWWM 90*
Gallian, Russell Joseph 1948- *WhoWor 91*
Gallian, Virginia Anne 1933- *WhoAmW 91*
Galliano, Alina 1950- *WhoHisp 91*
Galliano, John *BioIn 16*
Gallicano, J. Robert 1935- *WhoE 91*
Gallick, Joseph James 1941- *St&PR 91*
Gallico, Paul 1897-1976 *AuBYP 90*
Gallico, Paul 1898-1976 *Ballpl 90*
Gallico, Paul William 1897-1976 *WorAlBi*
Gallien, Jean Christophe 1964- *WhoWor 91*
Gallien, Wrenda Baker *BiDrAPA 89*
Galliera, Alceo 1910- *IntWWM 90, PenDiMP*
Galliffet, Gaston Alexandre, Marquis de 1830-1909 *BiDFrPL*
Galligan, Edward B. 1946- *St&PR 91*
Galligan, Edward L. 1926- *WhoWrEP 89*
Galligan, James Edward 1934- *BiDrAPA 89*
Galligan, John Donald 1932- *WhoAm 90*
Galligan, Nancy *BioIn 16*
Galligan, Thomas Joseph, III 1944- *St&PR 91, WhoAm 90*
Galliher, Keith Edwin, Jr. 1947- *WhoWor 91*
Galliher, Mildred Joanna 1944- *WhoAmW 91*
Galliker, Franz 1926- *WhoWor 91*
Gallimard, Gaston 1881-1975 *BioIn 16*
Gallimore, David Alfred 1939- *St&PR 91*
Gallimore, Robert Stephenson 1920- *WhoAm 90*
Gallin, Sandy *BioIn 16*
Gallin, Thomas *BioIn 16*
Gallina, David Joseph 1940- *BiDrAPA 89*
Gallina, Guy King 1939- *WhoSSW 91*
Gallinal, Angel Vicente 1963- *WhoSSW 91*
Gallinaro, Nicholas Francis 1930- *St&PR 91*
Galliner, Peter 1920- *WhoWor 91*
Gallinger, Lois Mae 1922- *WhoAmW 91*
Gallinot, Ruth Maxine 1925- *WhoAmW 91, WhoWor 91*
Gallion, Michael Lewis 1942- *WhoWor 91*
Gallipo, James Joseph 1946- *St&PR 91, WhoEmL 91*
Gallivan, Gregory John 1938- *WhoWor 91*
Gallivan, John William 1915- *WhoAm 90*
Gallix, Franccois 1939- *WhoWor 91*
Gallman, C. Hunter 1922- *St&PR 91*
Gallman, Clarence Hunter 1922- *WhoAm 90*
Gallman, David Eugene 1939- *St&PR 91*
Gallman, John Gerry 1938- *WhoAm 90*
Gallman, Robert Emil 1926- *WhoAm 90*
Gallman, Waldemar J. 1899-1980 *BioIn 16*
Gallmeyer, Charles C. 1948- *St&PR 91*
Gallo, Arnold Joseph 1943- *BiDrAPA 89*
Gallo, Dean Anderson 1935- *WhoAm 90, WhoE 91*
Gallo, Dennis 1951- *St&PR 91*
Gallo, Diane 1949- *WhoWrEP 89*
Gallo, Donald Robert 1938- *WhoWrEP 89*
Gallo, Enzo D 1927- *WhoAmA 91*
Gallo, Ernest *BioIn 16*
Gallo, Ernest 1910- *ConAmBL*
Gallo, F. Alberto 1932- *IntWWM 90*
Gallo, Francis Carl 1943- *WhoE 91*
Gallo, Frank 1933- *WhoAmA 91*
Gallo, Frederick S. 1944- *St&PR 91*
Gallo, Gerald Peter 1952- *St&PR 91*
Gallo, Gloria Jean 1959- *WhoAmW 91*
Gallo, Joe 1954- *BioIn 16*
Gallo, Joyce Anne 1928- *WhoAmW 91*
Gallo, Judith Melita 1954- *WhoE 91*
Gallo, Julio *BioIn 16*
Gallo, Julio 1911- *ConAmBL*
Gallo, Louis Jacob 1945- *WhoWrEP 89*
Gallo, Louise Ann 1934- *WhoAmW 91*
Gallo, Mario Martin 1947- *WhoWor 91*
Gallo, Mary Ellen 1957- *WhoAmW 91*
Gallo, Nicholas A., III 1940- *St&PR 91*
Gallo, Richard Louis 1939- *WhoE 91*
Gallo, Robert 1937- *News 91-1 [port]*
Gallo, Robert Charles 1937- *WhoAm 90, WhoWor 91*
Gallo, Ross Alan *BiDrAPA 89*
Gallo, Sebastian John 1932- *WhoE 91*
Gallo, Teresa L. *WhoAmW 91*
Gallo, Vincent John 1943- *WhoSSW 91*
Gallo, William Victor 1922- *WhoAm 90, WhoAmA 91*
Gallob, Edward *AuBYP 90*
Gallof, Steven 1946- *St&PR 91*
Gallogly, James John 1948- *St&PR 91*
Gallon, Ray 1947- *WhoEmL 91*
Galloney, Frank H., III 1935- *St&PR 91*
Gallop, Jane 1952- *WhoAm 90*
Gallop, Jonathan David 1956- *WhoEmL 91*
Gallop, Richard C. 1938-1989 *BioIn 16*
Gallopoulos, Gregory Stratis 1959- *WhoEmL 91*
Galloway, Alene Marsha 1949- *WhoAmW 91*
Galloway, Allen Cem 1958- *WhoEmL 91*
Galloway, Barry George Duncan 1954- *WhoE 91, WhoEmL 91*
Galloway, Chick 1896-1969 *Ballpl 90*
Galloway, David Alexander 1943- *WhoAm 90*
Galloway, David John 1937- *IntWWM 90*
Galloway, Dock Roscoe 1915- *WhoSSW 91*
Galloway, Donald D G 1929- *EncPaPR 91*
Galloway, Douglas Scott *BiDrAPA 89*
Galloway, Ethan Charles 1930- *St&PR 91, WhoAm 90*
Galloway, George H. 1918- *St&PR 91*
Galloway, Grace *FemiCLE*
Galloway, Harry Patrick 1951- *WhoSSW 91*
Galloway, Harvey Scott, Jr. 1934- *St&PR 91, WhoAm 90*
Galloway, Hunter Henderson, III 1945- *WhoEmL 91*
Galloway, John William 1960- *WhoSSW 91*
Galloway, Joseph 1731-1803 *EncCRAm*
Galloway, Joseph Edward, Jr. 1928- *WhoSSW 91*
Galloway, Kenneth Franklin 1941- *WhoAm 90*
Galloway, Lillian Carroll 1934- *WhoAmW 91*
Galloway, Lois 1941- *WhoAmW 91*
Galloway, Marla Lynn 1961- *WhoAmW 91*
Galloway, Pat 1933- *OxCCanT*
Galloway, Patricia Denese 1957- *WhoE 91, WhoEmL 91*
Galloway, Patricia Kay 1945- *ConAu 30NR, WhoAm 90*
Galloway, Richard H. 1940- *WhoWor 91*
Galloway, Richard William 1954- *BiDrAPA 89*
Galloway, Robert Michael 1946- *WhoEmL 91*
Galloway, Robert Michael 1951- *WhoSSW 91*
Galloway, Robert Morton 1927- *St&PR 91*
Galloway, Stanley Auburn 1959- *WhoWrEP 89*

Galloway, Steve WhoAmA 91
Galloway, Thomas F. 1939- St&PR 91
Galloway, William J. 1924- BioIn 16
Galloway, William Jefferson 1922- WhoAm 90
Galloway, William Joyce 1924- WhoAm 90
Galloway-May, Diane Lenoir 1941- WhoWor 91
Gallucci, Gerard 1956- BiDrAPA 89
Gallun, Raymond Z. 1911- RGTwCSF
Gallup, Alan Francis 1953- St&PR 91
Gallup, David 1808-1883 AmLegL
Gallup, Dick 1941- WhoWrEP 89
Gallup, Donald Clifford 1913- WhoAm 90
Gallup, George H. 1901-1984 WorAlBi
Gallup, George Horace 1901-1984 BioIn 16
Gallup, Grant Morris 1932- WhoWrEP 89
Gallup, Jane Harrington 1949- WhoE 91
Gallup, Janet Louise 1951- WhoAmW 91
Gallup, John G. 1927- St&PR 91
Gallup, John Gardiner 1927- WhoAm 90
Gallup, Lawrence Calvin 1934- St&PR 91
Gallup, Ralph ConAu 132
Gallup, Shirley M 1923- BiDrAPA 89
Gallup, Stephen Edmonds 1950- WhoWrEP 89
Gallups, Vivian Lylay Bess 1954- WhoAmW 91, WhoEmL 91, WhoSSW 91
Gallusser, Werner Arnold 1929- WhoWor 91
Galluzzo, Camilla 1951- St&PR 91
Gallwey, Tim 1938- NewAgE 90
Gallwitz, Klaus 1930- ConAu 131
Galobart y Pujol, Xavier 1959- WhoWor 91
Galonski, Mary Sperlein BiDrAPA 89
Galoozis, George T. 1931- St&PR 91
Galos, Andrew John 1918- IntWWM 90
Galos, Ben WhoAmA 91N
Galotti, Donna 1955- WhoAmW 91
Galowich, Ronald H. 1936- St&PR 91
Galperin, Boris 1952- WhoSSW 91
Galperson, Julian 1926- St&PR 91
Galphin, Bruce Maxwell 1932- WhoAm 90, WhoWrEP 89
Galpine, Maurice David 1936- St&PR 91
Galston, Arthur William 1920- WhoAm 90, WhoE 91
Galston, Clarence Elkus 1909- WhoAm 90
Galston, Nancy Lee 1954- WhoAmW 91
Galston, Stephen G BiDrAPA 89
Galsworthy, John 1867-1933 DcLB 98 [port], EncPaPR 91, WorAlBi
Galt, Alexander Tilloch 1817-1893 DcCanB 12
Galt, Barry J. 1933- St&PR 91
Galt, John 1779-1839 DcLB 99 [port]
Galt, John Kirtland 1920- WhoAm 90
Galt, John William 1940- WhoAm 90
Galt, Thomas F., Jr 1908- WhoWrEP 89
Galt, Thomas M. 1921- St&PR 91
Galterio, Joseph Albert 1923- St&PR 91
Galterio, Lou 1942- IntWWM 90
Galterio, Robert John 1957- WhoE 91
Galtieri, Leopoldo Fortunato BioIn 16
Galton, Elizabeth 1941- BiDrAPA 89
Galton, Francis BioIn 16
Galton, Francis 1822-1911 WorAlBi
Galton, James Edward 1924- WhoAm 90
Galton, Paul H. 1924- St&PR 91
Galton, Valerie Anne 1934- WhoAm 90
Galun, Rachel 1926- WhoWor 91
Galusha, Bryant Leroy 1927- WhoAm 90
Galuszka, Frank Richard 1947- WhoAmA 91
Galuszka, Mary Helene 1945- WhoEmL 91
Galvan, Enrique Tierno 1918-1986 BioIn 16
Galvan, Jesus Gerrero WhoAmA 91N
Galvan, Manuel P. 1949- WhoHisp 91
Galvan, Noemi Ethel 1939- WhoHisp 91
Galvan, Robert A. 1923- WhoWrEP 89
Galvan, Robert J. 1921- WhoHisp 91
Galvani, Luigi 1737-1798 WorAlBi
Galvany, Marisa 1936- IntWWM 90
Galvarino, Mario Enrique 1943- BiDrAPA 89
Galvarriato, Eulalia 1905- EncCoWW
Galvez, Bernardo de 1746-1786 EncCRAm
Galvez, Javier V 1938- BiDrAPA 89
Galvez, Jose de 1720-1787 BioIn 16
Galvez, Juan Manuel 1887-1972 BioIn 16
Galvez, Manuel 1882-1962 BioIn 16, HispWr 90
Galvez, Maria Rosa 1768-1806 EncCoWW
Galvez, Mariano 1794-1862 BioIn 16
Galvez, Rodrigo Marcelo BiDrAPA 89
Galvez de Montalvo, Luis ConAu 32NR, HispWr 90
Galvin, Brendan 1938- ConAu 13AS [port]
Galvin, Brendan James 1938- WhoWrEP 89
Galvin, Charles O'Neill 1919- WhoAm 90
Galvin, Donald A. 1958- St&PR 91
Galvin, G. Alx BioIn 16
Galvin, James Norman 1947- St&PR 91
Galvin, James R. 1929- WorAlBi
Galvin, John BioIn 16
Galvin, John R 1929- News 90 [port]
Galvin, John Rogers 1929- WhoAm 90, WhoWor 91
Galvin, Joseph Mannion 1907- St&PR 91
Galvin, Madeline Sheila 1948- WhoWor 91
Galvin, Martin George 1937- WhoE 91
Galvin, Maryanne 1954- WhoWrEP 89
Galvin, Matthew Reppert 1950- BiDrAPA 89
Galvin, Paul V. 1895-1959 ConAmBL
Galvin, Pud 1856-1902 Ballpl 90 [port]
Galvin, Robert Kevin 1943- St&PR 91
Galvin, Robert W. 1922- St&PR 91, WhoAm 90
Galvin, Robert William 1922- ConAmBL
Galvin, Ruth Mehrtens 1922- WhoAm 90
Galvin, Thomas Francis 1926- WhoAm 90
Galvin, Thomas John 1932- WhoAm 90
Galvin, Thomas Joseph 1938- St&PR 91
Galvin, William W., III 1942- ODwPR 91
Galway, James 1939- IntWWM 90, PenDiMP, WhoAm 90, WhoWor 91, WorAlBi
Galway, Robert Conington TwCCr&M 91
Galya, Thomas Andrew 1947- WhoSSW 91
Galyas, Gary Alan 1950- WhoSSW 91
Galyean, George Ellsworth 1940- St&PR 91
Galyean, Howard J. 1930- St&PR 91
Galyean, Roy Allen 1942- St&PR 91
Galyon, James Raymond 1929- WhoSSW 91
Galzy, Jeanne 1883-1977 EncCoWW
Gama, Vasco Da 1460-1524 WorAlBi
Gama, Vasco Da 1469-1524 BioIn 16, EncCRAm
Gamache, R. Donald 1935- St&PR 91
Gamarra, Agustin 1785-1841 BioIn 16
Gamarra, Eduardo 1957- ConAu 131, HispWr 90
Gamarra, Jose 1934- ArtLatA
Gamba, Piero 1936- IntWWM 90, PenDiMP
Gambal, David 1931- WhoAm 90
Gambale, Amy Rose 1942- WhoAmW 91
Gambale, Anthony J. 1927- St&PR 91
Gamban, Dennis Laurinaria 1963- WhoEmL 91
Gambara, Veronica 1485-1550 EncCoWW
Gambardella, Rosemary WhoAmW 91
Gambaro, Griselda BioIn 16
Gambaro, Griselda 1928- ConAu 131, HispWr 90
Gambaro, Ralph BioIn 16
Gambaro, Thomas M. 1932- St&PR 91
Gambatese, John Francis 1937- St&PR 91
Gambee, Eleanor Brown 1904- WhoAmW 91
Gambee, Robert Rankin 1942- WhoAm 90
Gamber, Carol Esther BiDrAPA 89
Gamber, Gary Reese 1950- WhoE 91
Gamberini, Leopoldo 1922- IntWWM 90
Gambet, Daniel George 1929- WhoAm 90
Gambetta, Leon 1838-1882 WorAlBi
Gambetta, Leon Michel 1838-1882 BiDFrPL
Gambill, Ben S., Jr. 1945- St&PR 91
Gambill, Bethany Luella 1953- WhoAmW 91
Gambill, John Douglas 1941- BiDrAPA 89
Gambill, John R 1918- BiDrAPA 89
Gambill, John Randolph 1918- WhoAm 90
Gambill, Malcolm W. WhoAm 90, WhoE 91
Gambill, Malcolm W. 1930- St&PR 91
Gambill, Robert 1955- IntWWM 90
Gambill, Ted R. 1948- St&PR 91
Gambill, Ted Ronald 1948- WhoEmL 91
Gambill, Terry A. 1942- St&PR 91
Gambin, Jules PenDiDA 89
Gambini, Giulio PenDiDA 89
Gambino, Diane R. WhoWrEP 89
Gambino, Lorry 1942- WhoAmW 91
Gambino, Salvatore Raymond 1926- WhoAm 90, WhoE 91
Gambino, Thomas Dominic 1942- WhoE 91
Gamble, Alfred J. 1921- St&PR 91
Gamble, Bert Marr 1930- WhoSSW 91
Gamble, Charles W.K. 1932- St&PR 91
Gamble, David John 1949- St&PR 91
Gamble, Edward James 1929- WhoAm 90
Gamble, George Clinton 1910- WhoAm 90
Gamble, Guy Douglas 1950- WhoEmL 91
Gamble, James Frank, Jr. BiDrAPA 89
Gamble, James N. 1836-1932 WorAlBi
Gamble, John Lee 1958- WhoEmL 91
Gamble, Kamy Rayburn 1960- WhoAmW 91
Gamble, Kathryn Elizabeth 1915- WhoAmA 91
Gamble, Kenneth Gregory 1940- WhoE 91
Gamble, Kenny BioIn 16
Gamble, Kenny 1941- OxCPMus
Gamble, Mary Grace 1950- WhoEmL 91, WhoSSW 91
Gamble, Michael M 1942- BiDrAPA 89
Gamble, Oscar 1949- Ballpl 90
Gamble, Ross A. 1938- St&PR 91
Gamble, Theodore Robert, Jr. 1953- WhoE 91, WhoEmL 91, WhoWor 91
Gamble, Thomas Ranshaw 1942- St&PR 91
Gamble, Walter Randolph 1946- WhoEmL 91
Gamble, William Belser, Jr. 1925- WhoSSW 91, WhoWor 91
Gamble, William L. 1945- St&PR 91
Gamble, Winona Faye 1941- WhoSSW 91
Gambling, William Alexander 1926- WhoWor 91
Gamboa, Alejandro 1948- WhoHisp 91
Gamboa, Erasmo 1941- WhoHisp 91
Gamboa, Federico 1864-1939 BioIn 16
Gamboa, George Charles 1923- WhoAm 90
Gamboa, Harry, Jr. HispWr 90
Gamboa, Harry, Jr. 1951- WhoHisp 91
Gamboa, J. C. 1951- WhoAmW 91
Gamboa, John C. 1964- WhoHisp 91
Gamboa, Jose Caguiat, Jr. 1950- BiDrAPA 89
Gamboa, Manuel BioIn 16
Gamboa, Reymundo 1948- WhoWrEP 89
Gamboa-Bertrand, Maria 1922- BiDrAPA 89
Gambol, Donna J. 1949- WhoEmL 91
Gambon, Michael BioIn 16
Gambone, Joseph Robert, Jr. 1953- St&PR 91
Gambrell, David Henry 1929- WhoAm 90
Gambrell, James Bruton, III 1926- WhoAm 90
Gambrell, Luck Flanders 1930- WhoAmW 91
Gambrell, Richard Donald, Jr. 1931- WhoAm 90, WhoSSW 91, WhoWor 91
Gambrell, Sarah Belk 1918- WhoAmW 91
Gambro, Michael S. 1954- WhoWor 91
Gambs, Carl M. 1943- St&PR 91
Gambs, Gerard Charles 1918- WhoE 91
Gambuti, Gary 1937- WhoAm 90, WhoE 91
Game, David Aylward 1926- WhoWor 91
Gamel, Thomas W. 1940- St&PR 91
Gamel, Wendell W. 1929- St&PR 91
Gamel, Wendell Wesley 1929- WhoAm 90
Gamer, Carlton E. 1929- IntWWM 90
Gamer, Saul Richard 1906- WhoAm 90
Gameros, L. Ignacio 1939- WhoHisp 91
Games, Abram 1914- ConDes 90
Games, Donald W. 1924- St&PR 91
Games, Jack E 1931- BiDrAPA 89
Gamet, Donald Max 1916- St&PR 91, WhoAm 90, WhoWor 91
Gamewell, William T. 1949- St&PR 91
Gamey, Ronald Kenneth 1945- WhoAm 90
Gamez, Kathy Joe 1956- WhoHisp 91
Gamez, Raul Rodriguez 1945- WhoSSW 91
Gamez, Robert BioIn 16, NewYTBS 90 [port]
Gamez, Robert 1968- WhoHisp 91
Gaminitilake, Semage Donald Edmund 1950- WhoWor 91
Gamkrelidze, Thomas Valerian 1929- WhoWor 91
Gamm, Stanford R 1917- BiDrAPA 89
Gammage, Grady, Jr. 1951- WhoEmL 91
Gammelgard, Soren 1912- WhoWor 91
Gammell, Frances Allen Howland 1949- WhoEmL 91
Gammell, Frances Howland 1949- St&PR 91
Gammell, Gerald Henry 1937- BiDrAPA 89
Gammell, Gloria Ruffner 1948- WhoAmW 91, WhoEmL 91
Gammell, Stephen 1943- BioIn 16
Gammenthaler, Orville 1926- St&PR 91
Gammie, Anthony Petrie 1934- WhoAm 90
Gammill, Darryl Curtis 1950- WhoEmL 91
Gammill, Lee Morgan 1934- St&PR 91
Gammill, Lee Morgan, Jr. 1934- WhoAm 90, WhoWor 91
Gammill, William 1949- WhoWrEP 89
Gammino, Michael A., Jr. 1922- St&PR 91
Gammon, Daniel Tench BioIn 16
Gammon, George Davis 1947- BiDrAPA 89
Gammon, Glenna Jean 1951- WhoAmW 91
Gammon, James Alan 1934- WhoAm 90
Gammon, Juanita-La Verne WhoAmA 91
Gammon, Philip Greenway 1940- IntWWM 90
Gammon, Reginald Adolphus 1921- WhoAmA 91
Gammon, Samuel Rhea, III 1924- WhoAm 90
Gammond, Peter 1925- ConAu 31NR
Gammons, Robert C. 1945- St&PR 91
Gammons, Robert Franklin 1920- WhoAm 90
Gamoran, Abraham Carmi 1926- WhoAm 90
Gamota, George 1939- WhoAm 90
Gamow, George 1904-1968 WorAlBi
Gampell, Ralph J. 1916-1988 BioIn 16
Gamper, Albert R., Jr. 1942- WhoAm 90
Gamron, W. Anthony 1948- WhoAm 90
Gams, Andrija 1911- WhoWor 91
Gamsin, Sharon ODwPR 91
Gamso, Jeffrey Michael 1949- WhoEmL 91
Gamson, Bernard William 1917- WhoAm 90, WhoE 91
Gamson, William Anthony 1934- WhoAm 90
Gamson, Zelda Finkelstein 1936- WhoAmW 91
Gamwell, C.C. 1924- St&PR 91
Gamze, Jonathan Charles BiDrAPA 89
Gamzon, Robert 1905-1961 BioIn 16
Gamzon, Robert 1926- St&PR 91
Gan, Diwakar Govind 1942- WhoSSW 91
Gan, Elena 1814-1842 EncCoWW
Gan, Felisa So 1943- WhoWor 91
Gana, Alberto Blest 1830-1920 BioIn 16
Ganachaud, Bernard BioIn 16
Ganado Mucho 1809?-1893 WhNaAH
Ganas, Jane Andrew 1942- WhoWrEP 89
Ganas, Perry Spiros 1937- WhoAm 90
Ganaway, George K 1946- BiDrAPA 89
Ganay, Birgitte de BioIn 16
Ganc, Jaime 1939- BiDrAPA 89
Gancer, Donald Charles 1933- WhoAm 90
Gancher, David Arthur 1943- WhoAm 90
Ganchorre, Yolanda M L 1939- BiDrAPA 89
Ganci, James J. 1943- St&PR 91
Ganci, Paul J. 1938- St&PR 91
Ganczarczyk, Jerzy Jozef 1928- WhoAm 90
Gandal, Robert 1928- St&PR 91
Gandalac, Lennard MajTwCW
Gandara, Daniel 1948- WhoEmL 91
Gandee, Robert Lester 1947- WhoEmL 91
Gandek, Jean Davis 1931- WhoAmW 91
Gandel, Earl David 1934- WhoWor 91
Gandelman, Beth Iris 1955- WhoEmL 91
Gandelman, Mitchell Seth BiDrAPA 89
Gandelman, Richard 1919- St&PR 91
Gander, Forrest 1956- WhoWrEP 89
Gander, Frank Forest 1899-1976 BioIn 16
Gander, John Edward 1925- WhoAm 90
Gander, Sharon 1952- WhoEmL 91
Gandersheim, Hrotsvit of 935?-973? EncCoWW
Gandert, Miguel Adrian 1956- WhoAmA 91
Gandhi, Mahatma MajTwCW
Gandhi, Anil Kumar BiDrAPA 89
Gandhi, Arun BioIn 16
Gandhi, Asha Mahendra BiDrAPA 89
Gandhi, Ashok Thakorlal 1950- WhoEmL 91
Gandhi, Bhanu P BiDrAPA 89
Gandhi, Bharat 1942- St&PR 91
Gandhi, Bharat R. 1942- WhoAm 90
Gandhi, Hitendra A 1952- BiDrAPA 89
Gandhi, Indira 1917-1984 BioIn 16, WomWR [port], WorAlBi
Gandhi, Indira Priyadarshani 1917-1984 DcNaB 1981
Gandhi, Lajpat Rai 1952- BiDrAPA 89
Gandhi, M. K. ConAu 132, MajTwCW
Gandhi, Mahatma ConAu 132
Gandhi, Mahatma 1869-1948 BioIn 16
Gandhi, Mohandas K. 1869-1948 WorAlBi
Gandhi, Mohandas Karamchand 1869-1948 BioIn 16, ConAu 132, MajTwCW
Gandhi, Om Parkash 1934- WhoAm 90, WhoWor 91
Gandhi, Rajiv 1944- BioIn 16, WhoWor 91, WorAlBi
Gandhi, Ramesh Govindlal 1935- WhoWor 91
Gandhi, Sushma 1940- WhoE 91
Gandhy, Meera Pravin BiDrAPA 89
Gandhy, Pravin R BiDrAPA 89
Gandia, Aldo Ray 1958- WhoHisp 91
Gandia, Manuel Zeno 1855-1930 BioIn 16
Gandia, Nadine Ann 1941- WhoSSW 91
Gandil, Chick 1888-1970 Ballpl 90
Gandillon Family EncO&P 3
Gandillon, Antoinette EncO&P 3
Gandillon, Georges EncO&P 3
Gandillon, Perrenette EncO&P 3
Gandillon, Pierre EncO&P 3
Gandler, David Perry 1954- BiDrAPA 89
Gandois, Jean Guy 1930- WhoAm 90, WhoE 91, WhoWor 91
Gandolf, Raymond L. 1930- WhoAm 90
Gandolfo, Carlo 1946- WhoWor 91
Gandolfo, Giancarlo 1937- WhoWor 91
Gandolfo, Joseph John 1959- WhoEmL 91
Gandsey, Louis John 1921- WhoWor 91
Gandy, Bobby A. 1926- St&PR 91

Gandy, Charles David 1949- *WhoAm 90, WhoEmL 91*
Gandy, Dean Murray 1927- *WhoAm 90*
Gandy, Helen W. *BioIn 16*
Gandy, Joyce Ann 1937- *WhoAmW 91, WhoE 91, WhoWor 91*
Gandy, Richard N. 1939- *St&PR 91*
Gandy, Robert L., Jr. 1933- *St&PR 91*
Gandy, Sue Ann 1951- *WhoAmW 91*
Gane, Chris Peter 1938- *WhoE 91*
Gane, Roger Stuart 1946- *WhoWor 91*
Ganea, D. Andre 1924- *WhoE 91*
Ganea, Dinu Andre 1924- *BiDrAPA 89*
Ganek, Dorothy Skeados 1946- *WhoAmA 91*
Ganeles, David Joseph 1950- *BiDrAPA 89*
Ganeles, Jeffrey 1957- *WhoSSW 91*
Ganeles, Robert I *BiDrAPA 89*
Ganesan, Adayapalam Tyagarajan 1932- *WhoAm 90*
Ganesan, Ann Katharine 1933- *WhoAmW 91*
Ganesan, Soma 1950- *BiDrAPA 89*
Ganesbauer, Theodore John 1942- *BiDrAPA 89*
Ganesen, Karthigasoe 1932- *WhoWor 91*
Ganesh, Cherie Margaret 1950- *WhoAmW 91, WhoEmL 91*
Ganesh, Orekonde *BiDrAPA 89*
Ganesh, T S *BiDrAPA 89*
Ganet, A.S. 1925- *St&PR 91*
Gang, Carolyn Sue 1952- *WhoAmW 91, WhoSSW 91*
Gang, Stephen 1951- *St&PR 91*
Gang, Stephen R. 1951- *WhoE 91*
Gangavarapu, Sarath Babu 1954- *BiDrAPA 89*
Gange, Charles A. 1948- *St&PR 91*
Gange, Robert Allen 1936- *WhoE 91*
Gangemi, Kenneth 1937- *WhoWrEP 89*
Ganger, J. Harold 1934- *St&PR 91*
Gangi, Frank Joseph 1941- *St&PR 91*
Gangi, Guy Thomas 1950- *WhoEmL 91*
Gangi, Robert Curtis 1962- *WhoEmL 91*
Gangl, Kenneth Richard 1945- *St&PR 91*
Gangloff, Deborah 1952- *ConAu 130*
Gangloff, Linda Lee 1942- *WhoE 91*
Gangnes, A.V. 1920- *St&PR 91*
Gangopadhyay, Nirmal Kanti 1943- *WhoSSW 91*
Ganguli, Mary 1952- *BiDrAPA 89, WhoE 91*
Ganguli, Rohan 1950- *BiDrAPA 89*
Ganguly, Sachindra Nath 1932- *EncO&P 3*
Ganguly, Sukanta 1950- *WhoWor 91*
Ganguzza, Philip 1920- *St&PR 91*
Gangwal, Rakesh 1953- *St&PR 91*
Gangwere, Robert Lloyd 1952- *WhoEmL 91*
Gani, Joseph Mark 1924- *WhoAm 90*
Ganiere, Paul William 1922- *St&PR 91*
Ganiere, Robert C. 1936- *St&PR 91*
Ganilau, Penaia Kanatabatu 1918- *WhoWor 91*
Ganime, Peter David 1946- *BiDrAPA 89*
Ganin, Saul 1921- *St&PR 91*
Ganin, Steven L. 1952- *St&PR 91*
Ganina, Maiia Anatolievna 1927- *EncCoWW*
Ganis, Stephen Lane 1951- *WhoEmL 91*
Ganister, Ruth Eileen 1950- *WhoEmL 91*
Ganivet, Angel 1865-1898 *BioIn 16*
Ganley, Bob 1875-1945 *Ballpl 90*
Ganley, Gladys Dickens 1929- *WhoWrEP 89*
Ganley, James Francis 1935- *St&PR 91*
Ganley, James Joseph 1946- *WhoEmL 91*
Ganley, James Powell 1937- *WhoAm 90*
Ganley, Oswald Harold 1929- *WhoAm 90, WhoE 91*
Ganly, Helen 1940- *BioIn 16*
Gann, Barbara Marie 1962- *WhoSSW 91*
Gann, Ernest Kellogg 1910- *WhoAm 90, WhoWrEP 89*
Gann, Gregg 1948- *WhoEmL 91*
Gann, Jean Pope 1917- *WhoAmW 91*
Gann, Jo Rita 1940- *WhoAmW 91*
Gann, L H 1924- *ConAu 31NR*
Gann, Mark Stephen 1957- *WhoSSW 91*
Gann, Pamela Brooks 1948- *WhoAm 90*
Gann, Paul *BioIn 16*
Gann, Paul 1912-1989 *AnObit 1989*
Gann, Theresa Verlyn 1943- *WhoAmW 91*
Gannam, John 1907-1965 *WhoAmA 91N*
Gannatal, Joseph Paul 1955- *WhoEmL 91*
Gannaway, Gary *BioIn 16*
Gannaway, Joann Pickering 1930- *WhoAmW 91*
Ganne, Louis 1862-1923 *OxCPMus*
Gannello, Alfreda Mavis 1926- *WhoWrEP 89*
Gannett, Carrie S. 1934- *WhoE 91*
Gannett, Deborah Sampson 1760-1827 *BioIn 16*
Gannett, Frank Ernest 1876-1957 *BioIn 16*
Gannett, George Ashley 1948- *WhoEmL 91*
Gannett, Ruth Stiles 1923- *AuBYP 90*
Gannon, Ann Ida 1915- *WhoAm 90, WhoAmW 91*
Gannon, Anne Durney 1952- *WhoAmW 91*
Gannon, Barbara Charlotte 1934- *WhoWrEP 89*
Gannon, Carolyn 1945- *WhoAmW 91*
Gannon, David P. 1929- *St&PR 91*
Gannon, Dee 1953- *WhoWrEP 89*
Gannon, Francis C. *BioIn 16*
Gannon, Frederic L 1934- *BiDrAPA 89*
Gannon, J. Truett 1930- *WhoSSW 91*
Gannon, James Patrick 1939- *WhoAm 90*
Gannon, Jerome Aylward 1935- *WhoAm 90*
Gannon, John Patrick 1949- *WhoEmL 91*
Gannon, Lanie E *WhoAmA 91*
Gannon, Lola Fern 1932- *WhoAmW 91*
Gannon, Lucinda J. 1947- *St&PR 91*
Gannon, Lynette Marie 1948- *WhoAm 90, WhoSSW 91*
Gannon, Mary Carol 1944- *WhoAmW 91*
Gannon, Michael R. 1947- *St&PR 91*
Gannon, Patrick J *BiDrAPA 89*
Gannon, Robert Haines 1931- *WhoWrEP 89*
Gannon, Ronald F. 1950- *St&PR 91*
Gannon, Terrence S. *ODwPR 91*
Ganns, Karin Jonelle 1959- *WhoSSW 91*
Gano, John 1727-1804 *BioIn 16*
Gano, John 1924- *WhoAm 90, WhoSSW 91*
Ganodos Muchos 1809?-1893 *WhNaAH*
Ganoe, Charles Stratford 1929- *WhoAm 90*
Ganong, William Francis 1924- *WhoAm 90*
Ganong, William Francis, III 1951- *WhoAm 90*
Ganopole, Deidre Susan 1950- *WhoEmL 91*
Gans, Bruce Michael 1951- *WhoWrEP 89*
Gans, Carl 1923- *WhoAm 90*
Gans, David Ian 1963- *WhoE 91*
Gans, Dennis Joseph 1949- *WhoEmL 91*
Gans, Erna Irene *WhoAmW 91*
Gans, Erna Irene 1923- *St&PR 91*
Gans, Eugene Howard 1929- *WhoE 91*
Gans, Herbert J. *BioIn 16*
Gans, Herbert J. 1927- *WhoAm 90*
Gans, Jerome Samuel 1940- *BiDrAPA 89*
Gans, Leo 1926- *St&PR 91*
Gans, Lucy C 1949- *WhoAmA 91*
Gans, Marion Lois *WhoAmW 91*
Gans, Olivia *BioIn 16*
Gans, Robert W *BiDrAPA 89*
Gans, Roger Frederick 1941- *WhoAm 90*
Gans, Roma 1894- *AuBYP 90, ConAu 32NR*
Gans, Samuel Myer 1925- *WhoE 91, WhoWor 91*
Gans, Steven Lee 1963- *BiDrAPA 89*
Gans, Terry Alexander 1946- *St&PR 91*
Gansauer, Karl-Friedrich 1932- *WhoWor 91*
Gansch, Phillip Edward 1949- *St&PR 91*
Ganse, Jean Marie 1949- *WhoAmW 91*
Gansemans, Jos 1942- *IntWWM 90*
Ganser, Leonard J 1919- *BiDrAPA 89*
Gansloser, Wilbert Max *BiDrAPA 89*
Gansovsky, Sever 1918- *RGTwCSF*
Ganss, George Edward 1905- *ConAu 31NR*
Ganss, William E *BiDrAPA 89*
Gansz, Edgar Joseph, Jr. 1946- *WhoAm 90*
Gant, Charles Edward, Jr. 1950- *BiDrAPA 89*
Gant, Cynthia Eleanor 1948- *WhoAmW 91*
Gant, Donald R. 1928- *St&PR 91*
Gant, Donald Ross 1928- *WhoAm 90*
Gant, Duplain Rhodes 1924- *WhoE 91*
Gant, Elizabeth *AuBYP 90*
Gant, George Arlington Lee 1941- *WhoAm 90*
Gant, Harry T. 1942- *St&PR 91*
Gant, Horace Zed 1914- *WhoWor 91*
Gant, John William, Jr. 1955- *WhoEmL 91*
Gant, Katherine *AuBYP 90*
Gant, Norman Ferrell, Jr. 1939- *WhoAm 90*
Gant, Ron 1965- *Ballpl 90*
Gantenbein, Herbert B. 1912- *St&PR 91*
Ganter, Bernard J. 1928- *WhoAm 90, WhoSSW 91*
Ganter, Gladys Marie 1908- *WhoAmW 91*
Ganter, Pierre 1924- *WhoWor 91*
Gantin, Bernardin 1922- *WhoWor 91*
Gantley, Patrick Eugene 1944- *St&PR 91*
Gantner, Jim 1953- *Ballpl 90*
Gantner, Joseph C., III 1953- *ODwPR 91*
Gantner, Susan 1939- *SmATA 63 [port]*
Ganton, Thomas Richard *St&PR 91*
Gantos, Jack 1951- *AuBYP 90*
Gantos, John Bryan *AuBYP 90*
Gantos, L. Douglas 1931- *St&PR 91*
Gantos, LeRoy Douglas 1931- *WhoAm 90*
Gantschev, Ivan *AuBYP 90*
Gantsoudes, James G. 1942- *St&PR 91*
Gantt, Charles David 1956- *WhoEmL 91*
Gantt, Harvey *BioIn 16*
Gantt, Michael Eugene 1944- *St&PR 91*
Gantt, William Robert, III 1948- *St&PR 91*
Gantz, Ann Cushing 1935- *WhoAmA 91*
Gantz, Bruce Jay 1946- *WhoAm 90, WhoEmL 91*
Gantz, Charles V., Jr. 1932- *St&PR 91*
Gantz, David Alfred 1942- *WhoAm 90*
Gantz, Jack *BioIn 16, St&PR 91N*
Gantz, John G., Jr. 1948- *St&PR 91*
Gantz, Joseph 1947- *St&PR 91*
Gantz, Karen 1950- *WhoEmL 91*
Gantz, Nancy Rollins 1949- *WhoEmL 91*
Gantz, Robert Forrest 1925- *St&PR 91*
Gantz, Suzi Grahn 1954- *WhoAmW 91*
Gantz, Wilbur H. 1937- *St&PR 91*
Gantz, Wilbur Henry, III 1937- *WhoAm 90*
Gantzer, Mary Lou 1950- *WhoAmW 91, WhoEmL 91*
Ganus, Clifton Loyd, III 1945- *WhoSSW 91*
Ganus, Clifton Loyd, Jr. 1922- *WhoAm 90*
Ganz, Alice 1943- *WhoWrEP 89*
Ganz, Aura 1957- *WhoE 91*
Ganz, Bruno 1941- *ConTFT 8*
Ganz, Charles David 1946- *WhoEmL 91*
Ganz, David L. 1951- *WhoE 91, WhoEmL 91*
Ganz, Eileen *ODwPR 91*
Ganz, Erwin M. 1929- *St&PR 91, WhoAm 90*
Ganz, Gene 1935- *BiDrAPA 89*
Ganz, Isabelle Myra 1937- *IntWWM 90*
Ganz, Joseph 1929- *St&PR 91*
Ganz, Lowell 1948- *WhoAm 90*
Ganz, Mary Keohan 1954- *WhoEmL 91*
Ganz, Rudolph 1877-1972 *PenDiMP*
Ganz, Samuel 1911- *WhoAm 90, WhoE 91*
Ganz, Sylvia Squires *WhoAmA 91*
Ganz, Wilhelm 1833-1914 *PenDiMP*
Ganz, Yaffa 1938- *BioIn 16, SmATA 61 [port]*
Ganzarain, Ramon Cajiao 1923- *WhoSSW 91, WhoWor 91*
Ganzarolli, Wladimiro 1932- *IntWWM 90, PenDiMP*
Ganzel, John 1874-1959 *Ballpl 90*
Ganzenmuller, Albert 1905-1973? *BioIn 16*
Ganzerla, John Thomas 1955- *WhoEmL 91*
Ganzi, Victor Frederick 1947- *WhoE 91, WhoEmL 91*
Ganzini, Linda Kay *BiDrAPA 89*
Ganzoni, John Julian 1932- *WhoWor 91*
Gao Shiqi 1905-1989 *BioIn 16*
Gao, Min *BioIn 16*
Gaona, Tomas M. 1922- *WhoHisp 91*
Gaouette, Terry Allan 1955- *WhoEmL 91*
Gapen, Delores Kaye 1943- *WhoAm 90, WhoAmW 91*
Gaples, Harry S. 1935- *St&PR 91*
Gaples, Harry Seraphim 1935- *WhoAm 90*
Gapp, Paul John 1928- *WhoAm 90*
Gappa, Allison M. *BioIn 16*
Gappmayer, Richard B. 1936- *St&PR 91*
Gara, Aaron D. 1935- *St&PR 91*
Garabedian, Paul Roesel 1927- *WhoAm 90, WhoE 91*
Garabedian, Susan Mary 1957- *WhoAmW 91*
Garagiola, Joe 1926- *Ballpl 90 [port], BioIn 16, WhoAm 90*
Garahan, Peter Thomas 1946- *WhoAm 90*
Garahan, Peter Thomas 1948- *St&PR 91*
Garajalde, Fernando Alberto 1953- *WhoEmL 91*
Garakani, Houshang 1940- *BiDrAPA 89*
Garakani, Reza *BioIn 16*
Garakonke 1600?-1676 *WhNaAH*
Garakonthie 1600?-1676 *WhNaAH*
Garakontie, Daniel 1600?-1676 *WhNaAH*
Garam, Martha Jane 1947- *WhoAmW 91*
Garance, Dominick 1912- *WhoAm 90, WhoWor 91*
Garand, Bruce 1937- *St&PR 91*
Garand, Christopher Pierre 1947- *St&PR 91*
Garand, John C. 1888-1974 *WorAlBi*
Garand, Pierre Arthur 1954- *WhoWrEP 89*
Garant, Serge 1929- *IntWWM 90*
Garasanin, Ilija 1812-1874 *BioIn 16*
Garaud, Marie-Francoise 1934- *BiDFrPL*
Garaudy, Roger 1913- *BiDFrPL*
Garavaglia, Abdon Lewis 1915- *WhoAm 90*
Garavani, Valentino *BioIn 16*
Garavani, Valentino 1932- *WhoWor 91*
Garavelli, John Stephen 1947- *WhoAm 90*
Garay, Charles James 1939- *St&PR 91*
Garay, Epifanio 1849-1903 *ArtLatA*
Garay, Erica Blythe 1953- *WhoAmW 91, WhoEmL 91*
Garay, Val Christian 1942- *WhoHisp 91*
Garayua, Mary Isa 1945- *WhoHisp 91*
Garaza, Almario M 1936- *BiDrAPA 89*
Garazi, Ida Shwartz 1936- *WhoAmW 91*
Garazzi, Peyo 1937- *IntWWM 90*
Garb, Allan E. 1929- *St&PR 91*
Garb, Eslyn Teveth 1956- *BiDrAPA 89*
Garba, Edward Aloysius 1921- *WhoAm 90*
Garba, Joseph *BioIn 16*
Garbacz, Gerald George 1936- *St&PR 91, WhoAm 90, WhoE 91*
Garbaczewski, Daniel Frank 1950- *WhoEmL 91*
Garbarini, Edgar Joseph 1910- *WhoAm 90*
Garbarini, Robert F. 1918- *WhoAm 90*
Garbarino, Carol Ann 1950- *BiDrAPA 89*
Garbarino, J.C. 1952- *St&PR 91*
Garbarino, Joseph William 1919- *WhoAm 90*
Garbarino, Robert Paul 1929- *WhoWor 91*
Garbasso, Antonio Giorgio 1871-1933 *DcScB S2*
Garbaty, Eugene L *WhoAmA 91N*
Garbaty, Marie-Louise 1910- *WhoAmA 91, WhoAmW 91*
Garbayo, Alfonso 1929- *BiDrAPA 89*
Garbe, William 1948-1989 *BioIn 16, WhoAmA 91N*
Garbee, Richard E. 1937- *St&PR 91*
Garber, Anne Theresa 1946- *WhoEmL 91*
Garber, Benjamin 1937- *BiDrAPA 89*
Garber, Cynthia Ann 1956- *WhoWor 91*
Garber, Daniel 1880-1958 *WhoAmA 91N*
Garber, Darrell Henry 1949- *WhoEmL 91*
Garber, Donna Ann *BiDrAPA 89*
Garber, Earl S. 1932- *St&PR 91*
Garber, Floyd Wayne 1941- *WhoSSW 91*
Garber, Gene 1947- *Ballpl 90*
Garber, H Jordan 1954- *BiDrAPA 89*
Garber, Harry Douglas 1928- *St&PR 91, WhoAm 90*
Garber, Helen Kolikow 1954- *WhoEmL 91*
Garber, Jan 1897-1977 *BioIn 16*
Garber, John F., Jr. 1925- *St&PR 91*
Garber, Joseph R 1943- *ConAu 132*
Garber, Joyce S 1943- *BiDrAPA 89*
Garber, Joyce Steinhardt 1943- *WhoE 91*
Garber, Judith Ann 1949- *WhoAmW 91, WhoEmL 91*
Garber, Mary Beth 1946- *WhoEmL 91*
Garber, Miles Daniel, Jr. 1916- *BiDrAPA 89*
Garber, Norton S *BiDrAPA 89*
Garber, Paul *BioIn 16*
Garber, Raymond Alan 1951- *WhoEmL 91*
Garber, Richard P. 1943- *St&PR 91*
Garber, Robert Edward 1949- *St&PR 91, WhoAm 90, WhoEmL 91*
Garber, Robert Lloyd, Jr. 1944- *BiDrAPA 89*
Garber, Robert S 1912- *BiDrAPA 89*
Garber, Samuel B. 1934- *St&PR 91*
Garber, Samuel Baugh 1934- *WhoAm 90, WhoWor 91*
Garber, Stephen Meyer 1940- *St&PR 91*
Garber, Victor 1949- *BioIn 16*
Garberding, Larry Gilbert 1938- *WhoAm 90*
Garberi, Mercedes Precerutti 1927- *WhoWor 91*
Garbers, Christoph Friedrich 1929- *WhoWor 91*
Garbesi, Robert E. 1925- *St&PR 91*
Garbey, Barbaro 1956- *Ballpl 90*
Garbin, Albeno Patrick 1932- *WhoAm 90*
Garbini, Smaranda *EncCoWW*
Garbiniu, Smaranda *EncCoWW*
Garbis, Andrew Nicholas 1936- *WhoSSW 91*
Garbis, Michelle R. 1947- *St&PR 91*
Garbisch, Bernice Chrysler *WhoAmA 91N*
Garbisch, Edgar William 1899-1979 *WhoAmA 91N*
Garbo, Greta 1905-1990 *BioIn 16, CurBio 90N, NewYTBS 90 [port], News 90, -90-3, WorAlBi*
Garbo, Norman 1919- *WhoAm 90, WhoWrEP 89*
Garbo, Paul W. 1911- *St&PR 91*
Garborg, Arne 1851-1924 *DcScanL*
Garbose, S. Bernard 1929- *St&PR 91*
Garbousova, Raya 1905- *PenDiMP*
Garbrecht, Kurt 1932- *WhoWor 91*
Garbutt, Eugene James 1925- *WhoAm 90*
Garbutt, James Cameron 1949- *BiDrAPA 89*
Garbutt, Janice Lovoos *WhoAmA 91*
Garbutt, Jeremy 1950- *St&PR 91, WhoAm 90*
Garbuzova, Raya 1905- *PenDiMP*
Garceau, Albert Arthur 1945- *St&PR 91*
Garces, Dahlia Villaver 1942- *BiDrAPA 89*
Garces, Francisco 1738-1781 *EncCRAm*
Garcha, Jagnandan Singh 1945- *BiDrAPA 89*
Garchik, Leah Lieberman 1945- *WhoAm 90*
Garchik, Morton Lloyd 1929- *WhoAmA 91*

Garcia, Abalberto Carlos 1954- *WhoSSW 91*
Garcia, Abel 1949- *St&PR 91*
Garcia, Adalberto Moreno 1943- *WhoHisp 91*
Garcia, Adolfo Ramon 1948- *WhoEmL 91*
Garcia, Albert *WhoHisp 91*
Garcia, Albert B. 1944- *WhoHisp 91*
Garcia, Alberto 1930- *WhoHisp 91*
Garcia, Alberto A. 1945- *St&PR 91, WhoHisp 91*
Garcia, Alberto Ureta 1926- *WhoHisp 91*
Garcia, Alexander 1919- *WhoAm 90*
Garcia, Alfonso E., Sr. 1933- *WhoHisp 91*
Garcia, Alfonso Sanchez 1881-1953 *BioIn 16*
Garcia, Amando S., Sr. 1934- *WhoHisp 91*
Garcia, Andres 1948- *WhoHisp 91*
Garcia, Andy 1956- *ConTFT 8 [port], WhoHisp 91*
Garcia, Anthony Edward 1951- *WhoHisp 91*
Garcia, Antonio 1901- *BioIn 16*
Garcia, Antonio E. 1901- *WhoHisp 91*
Garcia, Antonio E. 1924- *WhoHisp 91*
Garcia, Antonio Jose 1959- *WhoHisp 91*
Garcia, Antonio M. 1946- *WhoHisp 91*
Garcia, Arcenio Arturo, Sr. 1947- *WhoHisp 91*
Garcia, Armando *WhoHisp 91*
Garcia, Arnulfo 1946- *WhoHisp 91*
Garcia, Arnulfo, Jr. 1948- *WhoHisp 91*
Garcia, Aron *BioIn 16*
Garcia, Bernardo Ramon 1956- *WhoHisp 91*
Garcia, Bienvenido C 1929- *BiDrAPA 89*
Garcia, Blanche 1946- *WhoHisp 91*
Garcia, Carlos *WhoHisp 91*
Garcia, Carlos A. 1935- *WhoHisp 91*
Garcia, Carlos E. *WhoHisp 91*
Garcia, Carlos Ernesto 1936- *WhoHisp 91*
Garcia, Carlos Fernando 1953- *WhoHisp 91*
Garcia, Carmen M. 1945- *WhoHisp 91*
Garcia, Carol Henderson 1956- *WhoEmL 91*
Garcia, Catalina Esperanza 1944- *WhoHisp 91*
Garcia, Cecilia Beatrice 1958- *BiDrAPA 89*
Garcia, Celso-Ramon 1921- *WhoAm 90, WhoE 91, WhoHisp 91*
Garcia, Chico *BioIn 16*
Garcia, Chico 1924- *Ballpl 90*
Garcia, Clara *WhoHisp 91*
Garcia, Conrad, Jr. *WhoHisp 91*
Garcia, Crispin, Jr. 1945- *WhoHisp 91*
Garcia, Damasco 1957- *Ballpl 90*
Garcia, Damaso Domingo 1957- *WhoHisp 91*
Garcia, Daniel Albert 1946- *WhoHisp 91*
Garcia, Dave 1920- *Ballpl 90*
Garcia, David 1956- *ODwPR 91*
Garcia, David H. 1949- *WhoHisp 91*
Garcia, David Joseph 1946- *WhoHisp 91*
Garcia, David M. 1956- *WhoHisp 91*
Garcia, David R. 1953- *WhoHisp 91*
Garcia, Dawn *BioIn 16*
Garcia, Dawn E. 1959- *WhoHisp 91*
Garcia, Delano J. *WhoHisp 91*
Garcia, Diane Lutz 1947- *WhoAmW 91*
Garcia, Domingo 1940- *WhoHisp 91*
Garcia, Edna I. 1951- *WhoAmW 91*
Garcia, Eduardo Alberto 1926- *BiDrAPA 89*
Garcia, Edward Harold 1942- *WhoSSW 91*
Garcia, Edward J. 1928- *WhoAm 90*
Garcia, Eleuterio M. 1943- *WhoHisp 91*
Garcia, Elizabeth 1961- *WhoAmW 91*
Garcia, Elizabeth Mildred 1956- *WhoHisp 91*
Garcia, Elsa Laura 1954- *WhoHisp 91*
Garcia, Elvira Elena 1938- *WhoHisp 91*
Garcia, Emanuel Ernest *BiDrAPA 89*
Garcia, Enildo Albert 1932- *WhoHisp 91*
Garcia, Ernest E. 1946- *BioIn 16*
Garcia, Ernest Eugene 1946- *WhoHisp 91*
Garcia, Esther 1945- *WhoHisp 91*
Garcia, Eugene Nicholas 1925- *WhoHisp 91*
Garcia, Eva 1950- *WhoHisp 91*
Garcia, Evangeline *BiDrAPA 89*
Garcia, Evelyn 1952- *WhoHisp 91*
Garcia, F. Chris 1940- *WhoAm 90, WhoHisp 91*
Garcia, Fernando *WhoHisp 91*
Garcia, Fernando Nunez 1944- *WhoHisp 91*
Garcia, Frances 1941- *WhoHisp 91*
Garcia, Frances Josephine 1938- *WhoHisp 91*
Garcia, Francisco Cesareo, III 1946- *WhoHisp 91*
Garcia, Francisco Goitia 1882-1960 *BioIn 16*
Garcia, Frank 1924- *WhoAmA 91*
Garcia, Gerald *BioIn 16*
Garcia, Guy D. 1955- *WhoHisp 91*
Garcia, Hector Gomez 1931- *WhoHisp 91*
Garcia, Hector Perez 1914- *BioIn 16, WhoHisp 91*
Garcia, Henry Frank 1943- *WhoSSW 91*
Garcia, Herlinda 1944- *WhoHisp 91*
Garcia, Hipolito Frank 1925- *WhoAm 90*
Garcia, Ignacio Molina 1950- *WhoWrEP 89*
Garcia, Iris Ana 1954- *WhoHisp 91*
Garcia, Isaac Vasquez *BioIn 16*
Garcia, Israel 1937- *WhoHisp 91*
Garcia, Iva *WhoHisp 91*
Garcia, Jane C. *WhoHisp 91*
Garcia, Jerry *BioIn 16*
Garcia, Jerry 1942- *ConMus 4 [port], CurBio 90 [port], WhoAm 90, WorAlBi*
Garcia, Jess *WhoHisp 91*
Garcia, Jesus 1941- *WhoHisp 91*
Garcia, Jesus G. *WhoHisp 91*
Garcia, Joaquin 1940- *WhoHisp 91*
Garcia, Joe Baldemar 1942- *WhoHisp 91*
Garcia, John 1917- *WhoHisp 91*
Garcia, John Anthony 1955- *WhoHisp 91*
Garcia, John F. 1964- *WhoHisp 91*
Garcia, John Martin 1949- *WhoHisp 91*
Garcia, Johnny *WhoHisp 91N*
Garcia, Jorge 1952- *WhoWor 91*
Garcia, Jorge Cruickshank *BioIn 16*
Garcia, Jorge Logan 1950- *WhoHisp 91*
Garcia, Jose *WhoHisp 91*
Garcia, Jose D., Jr. 1936- *WhoHisp 91*
Garcia, Jose F. 1928- *WhoHisp 91*
Garcia, Jose-Guadalupe Villarreal 1947- *WhoHisp 91*
Garcia, Jose Joel 1946- *WhoHisp 91*
Garcia, Jose Luis 1941- *BiDrAPA 89*
Garcia, Jose Luis 1943- *WhoE 91*
Garcia, Jose Zebedeo 1945- *WhoHisp 91*
Garcia, Josefina M. 1906- *WhoHisp 91*
Garcia, Josefina Margarita 1906- *WhoAmW 91*
Garcia, Joseph 1962- *WhoHisp 91*
Garcia, Joseph Antonio 1947- *WhoEmL 91*
Garcia, Joseph Charles 1931- *WhoE 91*
Garcia, Joseph E. 1950- *WhoHisp 91*
Garcia, Josie Alaniz 1946- *WhoHisp 91*
Garcia, Juan 1922- *BiDrAPA 89*
Garcia, Juan Castanon 1949- *WhoHisp 91*
Garcia, Juan Ignacio 1953- *BiDrAPA 89*
Garcia, Juan Pujol 1912?-1988 *AnObit 1988*
Garcia, Juan Ramon 1947- *WhoHisp 91*
Garcia, Juanita *WhoHisp 91*
Garcia, Julian S. 1950- *WhoWrEP 89*
Garcia, Julio H. *WhoHisp 91*
Garcia, Julio Hernan 1933- *WhoAm 90*
Garcia, Julio Ralph, Sr. 1932- *WhoHisp 91*
Garcia, Katherine Lee 1950- *WhoAmW 91*
Garcia, Kathleen J. 1949- *WhoWrEP 89*
Garcia, Kerry J. 1952- *WhoHisp 91*
Garcia, Kiko 1953- *Ballpl 90*
Garcia, Lauro *WhoHisp 91*
Garcia, Lauro, III *WhoHisp 91*
Garcia, Lawrence Dean 1936- *WhoHisp 91*
Garcia, Leo A. *WhoHisp 91*
Garcia, Leon M. N. *WhoHisp 91*
Garcia, Leonardo 1953- *WhoWor 91*
Garcia, Lino, Jr. 1934- *WhoHisp 91*
Garcia, Lionel G. 1935- *ConAu 131, HispWr 90*
Garcia, Lionel Gonzalo 1935- *WhoHisp 91*
Garcia, Loretta Jean 1955- *WhoEmL 91*
Garcia, Louie Joe 1954- *WhoHisp 91*
Garcia, Louis *WhoHisp 91*
Garcia, Louis J. 1927- *ODwPR 91*
Garcia, Louis Richard 1931- *St&PR 91*
Garcia, Luis Alonzo 1954- *WhoHisp 91*
Garcia, Luis M. *WhoHisp 91*
Garcia, Luis R. 1949- *WhoHisp 91*
Garcia, Magdalena *WhoHisp 91*
Garcia, Manuel 1775-1832 *PenDiMP*
Garcia, Manuel 1805-1906 *PenDiMP*
Garcia, Manuel, Jr. *WhoHisp 91*
Garcia, Manuel E 1947- *BiDrAPA 89*
Garcia, Manuel Orlando *BiDrAPA 89*
Garcia, Marc Anthony 1962- *WhoE 91*
Garcia, Margaret A. 1950- *WhoHisp 91*
Garcia, Margaret Louise 1963- *WhoHisp 91*
Garcia, Margarita *BiDrAPA 89*
Garcia, Maria 1955- *WhoHisp 91*
Garcia, Maria S. T. *WhoHisp 91*
Garcia, Mario T. 1944- *BioIn 16, WhoHisp 91*
Garcia, Marlene Linares 1956- *WhoHisp 91*
Garcia, Mary Ann 1937- *WhoHisp 91*
Garcia, Mary Jane *WhoHisp 91*
Garcia, Mary Jane Madrid 1936- *WhoAmW 91*
Garcia, Melva Ybarra 1950- *WhoHisp 91*
Garcia, Mercedes Maria 1958- *BiDrAPA 89*
Garcia, Michael *WhoHisp 91*
Garcia, Michael John 1948- *WhoHisp 91*
Garcia, Michael Patrick 1953- *WhoEmL 91*
Garcia, Miguel A., Jr. 1952- *WhoHisp 91*
Garcia, Miguel Angel 1938- *WhoHisp 91*
Garcia, Mike 1923-1986 *Ballpl 90*
Garcia, Mildred 1952- *WhoHisp 91*
Garcia, Myrna Aton 1956- *BiDrAPA 89*
Garcia, Nancy Yeatts 1947- *WhoAmW 91*
Garcia, Nestor 1953- *BiDrAPA 89*
Garcia, Nicolas Bruce 1961- *WhoHisp 91*
Garcia, Nora *WhoHisp 91*
Garcia, Norma G. 1950- *WhoHisp 91*
Garcia, Ofelia 1941- *WhoAmA 91*
Garcia, Olga Chaidez 1957- *WhoHisp 91*
Garcia, Olivia 1953- *WhoHisp 91*
Garcia, Orlando 1952- *WhoHisp 91*
Garcia, Orlando Jacinto 1954- *IntWWM 90*
Garcia, Oscar Nicolas 1936- *WhoAm 90, WhoHisp 91*
Garcia, Otto Luis 1947- *WhoHisp 91*
Garcia, Patricia A. 1956- *WhoEmL 91*
Garcia, Patricia Ann 1959- *WhoAmW 91*
Garcia, Pauline J. 1948- *WhoHisp 91*
Garcia, Pedro 1950- *Ballpl 90*
Garcia, Pedro 1954- *WhoSSW 91*
Garcia, Pedro F *BiDrAPA 89*
Garcia, Pedro Ignacio 1946- *BiDrAPA 89*
Garcia, Pedro Vasquez 1937- *WhoHisp 91*
Garcia, Pedro Vivino *BiDrAPA 89*
Garcia, Peter 1930- *WhoHisp 91*
Garcia, Peter C. *WhoHisp 91*
Garcia, Phyllis Josephine 1934- *WhoAmW 91*
Garcia, Rafael Erfe *BiDrAPA 89*
Garcia, Ramon Andres *BiDrAPA 89*
Garcia, Raul 1946- *WhoHisp 91*
Garcia, Raul A. 1949- *WhoHisp 91*
Garcia, Raul P., Jr. 1947- *WhoHisp 91*
Garcia, Rene 1939- *WhoHisp 91*
Garcia, Rene Luis 1945- *WhoHisp 91*
Garcia, Ricardo Alberto 1946- *WhoHisp 91*
Garcia, Ricardo J. 1947- *WhoHisp 91*
Garcia, Ricardo Romano 1938- *WhoHisp 91*
Garcia, Rich 1942- *Ballpl 90*
Garcia, Richard A. 1941- *HispWr 90*
Garcia, Richard Amado 1941- *WhoHisp 91*
Garcia, Robert L. 1948- *WhoHisp 91*
Garcia, Robert S. *WhoHisp 91*
Garcia, Roberto *WhoHisp 91*
Garcia, Roberto 1935- *BiDrAPA 89*
Garcia, Rod *WhoHisp 91*
Garcia, Roland, Jr. 1958- *WhoHisp 91*
Garcia, Roland B. *WhoHisp 91*
Garcia, Ron *WhoHisp 91*
Garcia, Rose *WhoHisp 91*
Garcia, Ruben *WhoHisp 91*
Garcia, Rudolph 1951- *WhoEmL 91*
Garcia, Rupert 1941- *BioIn 16, WhoAmA 91, WhoHisp 91*
Garcia, Sam *WhoHisp 91*
Garcia, Sam 1957- *HispWr 90, WhoHisp 91*
Garcia, Sandra Joanne Anderson 1939- *WhoAmW 91*
Garcia, Santos 1947- *WhoHisp 91*
Garcia, Sid 1959- *WhoHisp 91*
Garcia, Sylvia R. 1950- *WhoEmL 91*
Garcia, Teofilo 1942- *WhoHisp 91*
Garcia, Terry Donato 1953- *WhoEmL 91*
Garcia, Valerie Longval 1960- *WhoAmW 91*
Garcia, Vicente 1828?-1889 *AmLegL*
Garcia, Walter Manuel 1926- *WhoAm 90*
Garcia, Wanda *WhoHisp 91*
Garcia, William T. 1958- *WhoEmL 91*
Garcia, Yvette 1965- *WhoEmL 91*
Garcia, Yvonne 1949- *WhoHisp 91*
Garcia, Yvonne 1956- *WhoHisp 91*
Garcia-Ayvens, Francisco *WhoHisp 91*
Garcia-Barcena, Yanira E. 1950- *WhoHisp 91*
Garcia-Barrera, Gloria 1952- *WhoHisp 91*
Garcia Berlanga Marti, Luis 1921- *BioIn 16*
Garcia-Bosch, Jordi 1928- *WhoWor 91*
Garcia-Bunuel, Leonardo B *BiDrAPA 89*
Garcia Carbonell, Roberto Virgilio 1931- *WhoWor 91*
Garcia-Carrillo, Casimiro 1930- *WhoWor 91*
Garcia-Cruzado, Marcos 1939- *WhoWor 91*
Garcia-del-Solar, Lucio 1922- *WhoWor 91*
Garcia de Lujan, Alberto 1942- *WhoWor 91*
Garcia de Oteyza, Juan *WhoHisp 91*
Garcia-Diaz, Alberto 1945- *WhoHisp 91*
Garcia-Faure, Manuel Adolfo 1932- *BiDrAPA 89*
Garcia-Ferrer, Eduardo L 1954- *BiDrAPA 89*
Garcia-Ferrer, Magdalena Sofia 1956- *BiDrAPA 89*
Garcia-Fonseca, Maria D *BiDrAPA 89*
Garcia Fuste, Tomas *WhoHisp 91*
Garcia-Gomez, Jorge 1937- *WhoHisp 91*
Garcia Gonzalez, Rafael 1926- *WhoAm 90*
Garcia-Granados, Sergio Eduardo 1942- *WhoE 91*
Garcia Granados de Valdes, Sylvia 1946- *WhoWor 91*
Garcia-Granda, Bernardo Raul *BiDrAPA 89*
Garcia-Gray, Elizabeth A 1953- *BiDrAPA 89*
Garcia Iniguez, Calixto 1839-1898 *BioIn 16*
Garcia-Leyva, Gisela *BiDrAPA 89*
Garcia Lorca, Federico 1898-1936 *BioIn 16, ConAu 131, HispWr 90, MajTwCW, WorAlBi*
Garcia-Madrid, Jose M *BiDrAPA 89*
Garcia-Manzanedo, Hector 1926- *WhoHisp 91*
Garcia Marquez, Gabriel *BestSel 90-4 [port]*
Garcia Marquez, Gabriel 1928- *BioIn 16, HispWr 90, MajTwCW, WorAlBi*
Garcia Marquez, Gabriel Jose 1928- *WhoWor 91*
Garcia-Martinez, Antonio Hermes 1945- *WhoSSW 91*
Garcia Martos, Sofia 1963- *WhoWor 91*
Garcia Millan, Angel 1953- *WhoHisp 91*
Garcia Morales, Adelaida 1946- *EncCoWW*
Garcia-Moreno, Dolores *BiDrAPA 89*
Garcia Moreno, Gabriel 1821-1875 *BioIn 16*
Garcia-Oliveras, Ramon Luis *BiDrAPA 89*
Garcia Oller, Jose Luis 1923- *WhoAm 90, WhoHisp 91*
Garcia-Palmieri, Mario Ruben 1927- *WhoHisp 91*
Garcia-Paris, Carolina 1962- *WhoAmW 91*
Garcia Perez, Alan *BioIn 16*
Garcia Perez, Alan 1949- *WhoWor 91*
Garcia Pinto, Magdalena 1943- *WhoHisp 91*
Garcia Ponce, Juan 1932- *ConAu 131, HispWr 90*
Garcia-Prats, Joseph A. 1944- *WhoHisp 91*
Garcia-Rangel, Sara Marina 1939- *WhoHisp 91*
Garcia-Rios, Jose M. 1957- *WhoHisp 91*
Garcia Robles, Alfonso 1911- *WhoWor 91*
Garcia Rocha, Rina 1954- *HispWr 90*
Garcia-Rodriguez, Sergio 1961- *WhoHisp 91*
Garcia-Rosaly, Leticia 1949- *WhoHisp 91*
Garcia-Serrano, Maria Victoria 1959- *WhoHisp 91*
Garcia Silva, Nilda *BiDrAPA 89*
Garcia Terres, Jaime 1924- *WhoWor 91*
Garcia-Verdugo, Luisa 1960- *WhoHisp 91*
Garcilaso de la Vega, El Inca 1539-1616 *BioIn 16*
Garcin, Jules Auguste 1830-1896 *PenDiMP*
Garcisanz, Isabel 1934- *IntWWM 90*
Gard, Albert Wilson, III 1941- *St&PR 91*
Gard, Curtis Eldon 1921- *St&PR 91, WhoAm 90*
Gard, Janice *AuBYP 90*
Gard, Joyce 1911- *AuBYP 90*
Gard, Judy Richardson *BioIn 16*
Gard, Robert E 1910- *OxCCanT*
Gard, Robert Edward 1910- *AuBYP 90*
Gard, Roger Martin du 1881-1958 *BioIn 16*
Gard, Spencer Agassiz 1898- *WhoAm 90*
Gard, Wayne 1899-1986 *BioIn 16*
Garda, Robert Allen 1939- *WhoAm 90*
Gardam, Jane *BioIn 16*
Gardam, Jane 1928- *AuBYP 90, ConAu 33NR, MajTwCW*
Gardarsson, Thorsteinn 1952- *WhoWor 91*
Garde, Abraham 1926- *St&PR 91*
Garde, Betty 1905-1989 *BioIn 16*
Garde, Billie Pirner 1953- *WhoEmL 91*
Garde, Daniel Frederick 1940- *WhoE 91*
Garde, Herbert S. 1923- *St&PR 91*
Garde, Ira Batra *BiDrAPA 89*
Garde, John Charles 1961- *WhoWor 91*
Garde, Joseph L. 1929- *WhoAm 90*
Garde, Susan Reutershan 1953- *WhoAmW 91*
Gardea, Aili Tapio 1964- *WhoHisp 91*
Gardel, Carlos *BioIn 16*
Gardel, Carlos 1887-1935 *OxCPMus*
Gardella, Danny 1920- *Ballpl 90 [port], BioIn 16*
Gardella, Libero Anthony 1935- *WhoE 91*
Gardella, Robert R. 1934- *St&PR 91*
Gardella, Robert Rafti 1934- *WhoAm 90*
Gardella, Rose M. *BioIn 16*
Gardelli, Lamberto 1914- *IntWWM 90*
Gardelli, Lamberto 1915- *PenDiMP*
Garden, Domnern 1928- *WhoWor 91*
Garden, Judith *BioIn 16*
Garden, Mary 1874-1967 *BioIn 16, PenDiMP*
Garden, Nancy 1938- *AuBYP 90, ConAu 30NR*

Gardener, Andrew Todd 1958- *WhoSSW 91*
Gardener, Helen Hamilton 1853-1925 *FemiCLE*
Gardener, Ralph 1939- *BiDrAPA 89*
Gardenhire, Gary 1945- *WhoSSW 91*
Gardenhire, Ron 1957- *Ballpl 90*
Gardenhour, Eugene Charles 1932- *St&PR 91*
Gardenia, Vincent 1921- *WhoAm 90*
Gardenier, John Stark, II 1937- *WhoE 91*
Gardenier, Turkan Kumbaraci 1941- *WhoAm 90, WhoWor 91*
Gardin, Julius Markus 1949- *WhoEmL 91*
Gardin, T. Hershel 1947- *WhoEmL 91*
Gardine, Juanita Constantia Forbes 1912- *WhoSSW 91*
Gardiner, Arthur Zimmermann, Jr. 1935- *WhoAm 90*
Gardiner, Barbara *ODwPR 91*
Gardiner, Charles *AmLegL*
Gardiner, Charles Vere 1921- *St&PR 91*
Gardiner, Clarence I *BiDrAPA 89*
Gardiner, Donald Andrew 1922- *WhoAm 90*
Gardiner, Donald Kent 1939- *WhoAm 90*
Gardiner, E. Nicholas P. 1939- *WhoAm 90*
Gardiner, Eileen 1947- *WhoE 91*
Gardiner, Frances R. 1926- *St&PR 91*
Gardiner, Geoffrey Alexander, Jr. 1949- *WhoE 91*
Gardiner, George Clarke 1935- *BiDrAPA 89*
Gardiner, George R. 1917- *WhoAm 90*
Gardiner, Gerald *NewYTBS 90 [port]*
Gardiner, Gerald Austin 1900-1990 *BioIn 16*
Gardiner, Harry Walter 1938- *WhoWrEP 89*
Gardiner, Henry George, Jr. *BiDrAPA 89*
Gardiner, J.O. *St&PR 91*
Gardiner, Jennifer Ann 1950- *WhoWor 91*
Gardiner, John 1737-1793 *EncCRAm*
Gardiner, John Eliot *BioIn 16*
Gardiner, John Eliot 1943- *IntWWM 90, PenDiMP*
Gardiner, John Reynolds *AuBYP 90*
Gardiner, John Reynolds 1944- *BioIn 16, SmATA 64*
Gardiner, John W. 1931- *St&PR 91*
Gardiner, John William 1931- *WhoSSW 91*
Gardiner, Joseph William Fawsitt 1920- *WhoAm 90*
Gardiner, Keith Mattinson 1933- *WhoE 91*
Gardiner, Linda 1947- *WhoWrEP 89*
Gardiner, Lion Frederick 1938- *WhoE 91*
Gardiner, Margaret *BioIn 16*
Gardiner, Marguerite Power Farmer 1789-1849 *BioIn 16*
Gardiner, Michael Dean 1958- *WhoWor 91*
Gardiner, Michael James 1945- *St&PR 91*
Gardiner, Peter Alexander Jack 1935- *St&PR 91, WhoAm 90*
Gardiner, Peter Whitton 1934- *St&PR 91*
Gardiner, Piers Richard Rochfort 1940- *WhoWor 91*
Gardiner, Richard 1940- *BiDrAPA 89*
Gardiner, Richard Ernest 1951- *WhoEmL 91*
Gardiner, Robert *BioIn 16*
Gardiner, Robert M. 1922- *St&PR 91, WhoAm 90*
Gardiner, T Michael 1946- *WhoAmA 91*
Gardiner, Thomas G. 1957- *WhoEmL 91*
Gardiner, Thomas Joseph 1947- *St&PR 91*
Gardiner, Walter A. 1950- *St&PR 91*
Gardiner, Wayne Jay 1943- *WhoWrEP 89*
Gardiner, William Cecil, Jr. 1933- *WhoAm 90*
Gardiner, William Douglas Haig 1917- *St&PR 91, WhoAm 90*
Gardiner of Kittisford, Baron 1900-1990 *BioIn 16*
Gardini, Raul *BioIn 16*
Gardinier, David Elmer 1932- *WhoAm 90*
Gardinier, Glenn V. *ODwPR 91*
Gardino, Vincent Anthony 1953- *WhoE 91, WhoWor 91*
Gardis, Gilda J. 1944- *WhoAmW 91, WhoWor 91*
Gardissat, Jean-Louis 1949- *WhoWor 91*
Gardner, Abraham Brooks 1819-1881 *AmLegL*
Gardner, Alan Martin 1953- *WhoEmL 91*
Gardner, Alan Mathews *BiDrAPA 89*
Gardner, Alexander 1821-1882 *BioIn 16*
Gardner, Alvern K. 1934- *St&PR 91*
Gardner, Alvin Frederick 1920- *WhoAm 90*
Gardner, Amy *BiDrAPA 89*
Gardner, Andrew Bradford 1937- *WhoAmA 91*
Gardner, Anne *BiDEWW*
Gardner, Arnold Burton 1930- *WhoAm 90*
Gardner, Ava 1922- *BioAmW*
Gardner, Ava 1922-1990 *BioIn 16, CurBio 90N, NewYTBS 90 [port], News 90, WorAlBi*
Gardner, Barri Clare 1961- *WhoSSW 91*
Gardner, Beau *AuBYP 90*
Gardner, Beau 1941- *BioIn 16*
Gardner, Bernard 1931- *WhoAm 90*
Gardner, Bert Erwin 1928- *WhoAm 90*
Gardner, Bettiann *BioIn 16*
Gardner, Bettiann 1930- *WhoAmW 91*
Gardner, Billy 1927- *Ballpl 90*
Gardner, Booth *BioIn 16*
Gardner, Booth 1936- *WhoAm 90, WhoWor 91*
Gardner, Brenda Loyce 1954- *WhoSSW 91*
Gardner, Brian Collis 1959- *WhoEmL 91*
Gardner, Bruce Elwyn 1953- *WhoEmL 91*
Gardner, Bruce Lynn 1942- *WhoAm 90*
Gardner, Bruce William 1938- *St&PR 91*
Gardner, Burdett Harmon 1917- *WhoAm 90*
Gardner, Carol Robin 1956- *WhoAmW 91*
Gardner, Carole Jean 1942- *St&PR 91*
Gardner, Caryn Sue 1960- *WhoEmL 91*
Gardner, Charles Olda 1919- *WhoAm 90*
Gardner, Charles R. *WhoSSW 91*
Gardner, Charles Sperry *BiDrAPA 89*
Gardner, Charles Sperry 1949- *WhoE 91*
Gardner, Chester Stone 1947- *WhoAm 90*
Gardner, Clifford Speer 1924- *WhoAm 90*
Gardner, Clyde Edward 1931- *WhoWor 91*
Gardner, Colette Yvonne 1958- *WhoAmW 91*
Gardner, Colin R 1952- *WhoAmA 91*
Gardner, Dale Ray 1946- *WhoEmL 91*
Gardner, Daniel 1948- *BiDrAPA 89*
Gardner, David 1928- *OxCCanT*
Gardner, David Chambers 1934- *WhoE 91, WhoWor 91*
Gardner, David Edward 1923- *St&PR 91, WhoAm 90, WhoWor 91*
Gardner, David J 1936- *BiDrAPA 89*
Gardner, David John 1953- *WhoEmL 91*
Gardner, David Lance 1950- *BiDrAPA 89, WhoE 91*
Gardner, David Lee 1925- *St&PR 91*
Gardner, David P. 1933- *St&PR 91*
Gardner, David Pierpont 1933- *WhoAm 90, WhoWor 91*
Gardner, David Robert 1947- *St&PR 91*
Gardner, David Robert 1954- *WhoEmL 91*
Gardner, David Walton 1950- *WhoSSW 91*
Gardner, Den 1951- *ODwPR 91*
Gardner, Dennis Peter 1954- *WhoEmL 91*
Gardner, Dic 1931- *AuBYP 90*
Gardner, Donald LaVere 1930- *WhoAm 90*
Gardner, Dorsey Robertson 1942- *WhoAm 90*
Gardner, Douglas Frank 1943- *WhoWor 91*
Gardner, Edward B 1920- *BiDrAPA 89*
Gardner, Edward G. 1925- *ConAmBL*
Gardner, Eldon John 1909-1989 *BioIn 16*
Gardner, Elizabeth Jane 1837-1922 *BiDWomA*
Gardner, Erle Stanley 1889-1970 *MajTwCW, TwCCr&M 91, WorAlBi*
Gardner, Everette Shaw, Jr. 1944- *WhoSSW 91*
Gardner, F L 1857-1930? *EncO&P 3*
Gardner, Florence Cecelia 1913- *WhoWrEP 89*
Gardner, Francis *PenDiDA 89*
Gardner, Frank Harold 1923- *St&PR 91*
Gardner, Frank Webb, Jr. *BioIn 16*
Gardner, Frederick Boyce 1942- *WhoWor 91*
Gardner, G B 1884-1964 *EncO&P 3*
Gardner, Gail I. 1892- *BioIn 16*
Gardner, Gary David 1949- *IntWWM 90, WhoEmL 91*
Gardner, Gene Pritchard 1929- *St&PR 91*
Gardner, Geoffrey 1943- *WhoWrEP 89*
Gardner, George *BioIn 16*
Gardner, George P., Jr. 1917- *St&PR 91*
Gardner, George Peabody 1917- *WhoAm 90*
Gardner, Gerald B. 1884-1964 *NewAgE 90*
Gardner, Gerald Faye 1950- *WhoWrEP 89*
Gardner, Grace Daniel 1911- *WhoAmW 91*
Gardner, Grant Walter 1954- *WhoSSW 91*
Gardner, Guy S. *BioIn 16*
Gardner, Helen Louise 1908-1989 *BioIn 16*
Gardner, Henry Louis 1944- *WhoAm 90*
Gardner, Henry Robert 1921- *WhoSSW 91*
Gardner, Howard 1943- *WorAu 1980 [port]*
Gardner, Howard Alan 1920- *WhoAm 90*
Gardner, Howard Earl 1943- *WhoAm 90*
Gardner, Howard Garry 1943- *WhoWor 91*
Gardner, Howard Lane, Jr. 1919- *St&PR 91*
Gardner, Hugh 1910-1986 *BioIn 16*
Gardner, Hugh Willis *BiDrAPA 89*
Gardner, Hy 1908-1989 *AnObit 1989, BioIn 16*
Gardner, I. Leonard 1934- *St&PR 91*
Gardner, Isabella S. 1840-1924 *BioAmW*
Gardner, Isabella Stewart 1840-1924 *BioIn 16*
Gardner, Isabella Stewart 1915-1981 *FemiCLE*
Gardner, James 1907- *ConDes 90*
Gardner, James Albert 1943- *WhoAm 90*
Gardner, James Alston, Jr. 1949- *WhoSSW 91*
Gardner, James Bailey 1950- *WhoE 91*
Gardner, James Barrington 1934- *St&PR 91, WhoAm 90*
Gardner, James Carson 1933- *WhoAm 90, WhoSSW 91*
Gardner, James Earl 1953- *IntWWM 90*
Gardner, James Harkins 1943- *WhoAm 90*
Gardner, James M. 1931- *St&PR 91*
Gardner, James Richard 1944- *WhoE 91, WhoWor 91*
Gardner, Jane Carey 1951- *WhoEmL 91*
Gardner, Jelly 1895- *Ballpl 90*
Gardner, Jermaine *BioIn 16*
Gardner, Jill Christopher 1948- *WhoAmW 91, WhoE 91*
Gardner, Jim 1874-1905 *Ballpl 90*
Gardner, Joan A 1933- *WhoAmA 91*
Gardner, Joan M. 1954- *St&PR 91*
Gardner, Joel Robert 1942- *WhoE 91*
Gardner, John 1926- *MajTwCW, TwCCr&M 91*
Gardner, John 1933-1982 *AuBYP 90, ShSCr 7 [port], WorAlBi, WrPh*
Gardner, John 1939-1988 *BioIn 16*
Gardner, John, Jr. 1933-1982 *ConAu 33NR, MajTwCW*
Gardner, John B., III 1949- *St&PR 91*
Gardner, John Edmund 1926- *SpyFic*
Gardner, John Linton 1917- *IntWWM 90*
Gardner, John R. 1937- *St&PR 91*
Gardner, John W. 1912- *WorAlBi*
Gardner, John William 1912- *BiDrAPA 89, BiDrUSE 89, BioIn 16, WhoAm 90*
Gardner, Joseph C. 1942- *St&PR 91*
Gardner, Joseph L 1933- *ConAu 30NR*
Gardner, Joseph Lawrence 1933- *WhoAm 90, WhoWrEP 89*
Gardner, Joyce D. 1915- *WhoWrEP 89*
Gardner, Joyce Thresher 1922- *WhoSSW 91*
Gardner, Judith D *BiDrAPA 89*
Gardner, Kathleen D. 1947- *WhoAm 90*
Gardner, Kay *NewAgMG*
Gardner, Kay L. 1941- *IntWWM 90*
Gardner, Keith Hadrian 1930- *WhoAm 90, WhoWor 91*
Gardner, Keith Howard 1950- *WhoSSW 91*
Gardner, Keith Richard 1955- *WhoEmL 91*
Gardner, Kenneth Leroy 1941- *St&PR 91*
Gardner, Kirtland C. *St&PR 91*
Gardner, Larry 1886-1976 *Ballpl 90*
Gardner, Lee Robbins 1934- *BiDrAPA 89, WhoE 91*
Gardner, Leon Faye 1922- *St&PR 91*
Gardner, Leonard 1934- *St&PR 91*
Gardner, Leonard Burton, II 1927- *WhoAm 90*
Gardner, Lillian Soskin 1907- *AuBYP 90*
Gardner, Lloyd Calvin, Jr. 1934- *WhoAm 90*
Gardner, Lyndon 1954- *IntWWM 90*
Gardner, Lynn Sullivan 1957- *WhoAmW 91*
Gardner, M. Dozier 1933- *St&PR 91*
Gardner, Margaret Fenton 1932- *WhoAmW 91*
Gardner, Marjorie Hyer 1923- *WhoAm 90, WhoAmW 91*
Gardner, Mark S. 1953- *WhoEmL 91*
Gardner, Marshall Allen 1940- *St&PR 91*
Gardner, Martin 1914- *AuBYP 90, WhoSSW 91, WorAu 1980 [port]*
Gardner, Mary Ann *St&PR 91*
Gardner, Mary Bertha Hoeft Chadwick 1914- *WhoAmW 91*
Gardner, Mary Elizabeth 1945- *WhoEmL 91*
Gardner, Mary Sewall 1871-1961 *BioIn 16*
Gardner, Max L 1923- *BiDrAPA 89*
Gardner, Melvyn J *BiDrAPA 89*
Gardner, Murray Briggs 1929- *WhoAm 90*
Gardner, Nancy Bruff 1909- *WhoWrEP 89*
Gardner, Nancy Hazard 1949- *WhoAmW 91*
Gardner, Natalie Nellie Jaglom *WhoAmW 91, WhoE 91, WhoWor 91*
Gardner, Noel C. 1951- *BiDrAPA 89*
Gardner, Patrick Grant 1953- *IntWWM 90*
Gardner, Paul Allen 1947- *WhoEmL 91*
Gardner, Paul Allen 1950- *WhoWrEP 89*
Gardner, Paul Jay 1929- *WhoAm 90*
Gardner, Phyllis Ann 1946- *WhoEmL 91*
Gardner, R. H. 1918- *WhoAm 90*
Gardner, R. Hartwell 1934- *St&PR 91*
Gardner, Ralph David 1923- *WhoAm 90*
Gardner, Randy *BioIn 16*
Gardner, Randy Clyburn 1952- *IntWWM 90*
Gardner, Ray Dean, Jr. 1954- *WhoEmL 91*
Gardner, Richard A. 1931- *AuBYP 90, BiDrAPA 89*
Gardner, Richard Alan 1931- *WhoAm 90, WhoWrEP 89*
Gardner, Richard Barnum 1943- *St&PR 91*
Gardner, Richard Ernest 1942- *St&PR 91*
Gardner, Richard Hartwell 1934- *WhoAm 90*
Gardner, Richard Kent 1928- *WhoAm 90*
Gardner, Richard M. *AuBYP 90*
Gardner, Richard M. 1942- *WhoWrEP 89*
Gardner, Richard Newton 1927- *WhoAm 90*
Gardner, Richard W. 1913- *St&PR 91*
Gardner, Rob 1944- *Ballpl 90*
Gardner, Robert 1929- *AuBYP 90*
Gardner, Robert Abraham 1948- *WhoEmL 91*
Gardner, Robert Allen 1934- *St&PR 91*
Gardner, Robert Charles 1961- *WhoSSW 91*
Gardner, Robert D 1925- *BiDrAPA 89*
Gardner, Robert Earl 1919- *WhoAmA 91*
Gardner, Robert H. 1913- *ODwPR 91, St&PR 91*
Gardner, Robert Heys 1960- *WhoE 91, WhoWor 91*
Gardner, Robert Michael 1948- *WhoSSW 91*
Gardner, Robert Scott, Jr. 1958- *WhoEmL 91*
Gardner, Robert W 1933- *BiDrAPA 89*
Gardner, Robin Pierce 1934- *WhoAm 90*
Gardner, Ronald Bruce 1944- *WhoAm 90*
Gardner, Russell, Jr. 1938- *BiDrAPA 89*
Gardner, Russell Menese 1920- *WhoSSW 91, WhoWor 91*
Gardner, Sandra Lee 1946- *WhoAmW 91*
Gardner, Sarah *FemiCLE*
Gardner, Sheila 1933- *WhoAmA 91*
Gardner, Shirley Mae 1932- *WhoWor 91*
Gardner, Stanley Dwain 1956- *WhoEmL 91, WhoSSW 91*
Gardner, Stephen Leroy 1948- *WhoWrEP 89*
Gardner, Steven 1959- *WhoEmL 91*
Gardner, Stu *BioIn 16*
Gardner, Susan Ross 1941- *WhoAmA 91*
Gardner, Terry A. 1952- *St&PR 91*
Gardner, Thomas E. *WhoAm 90, WhoSSW 91*
Gardner, Thomas Earle 1938- *WhoAm 90, WhoE 91*
Gardner, Thomas Edward 1948- *WhoAm 90*
Gardner, Walter 1902- *WhoAm 90*
Gardner, Wanda Joyce 1950- *WhoEmL 91*
Gardner, Warner Winslow 1909- *WhoAm 90*
Gardner, Warren Edward, Jr. 1922- *WhoE 91*
Gardner, Wayne *BioIn 16*
Gardner, Wayne C. 1921- *St&PR 91*
Gardner, Wendell J. 1933- *St&PR 91*
Gardner, Wes 1961- *Ballpl 90*
Gardner, Wilford Robert 1925- *WhoAm 90*
Gardner, Wilfrid J *BiDrAPA 89*
Gardner, William A *BiDrAPA 89*
Gardner, William Albert, Jr. 1939- *WhoAm 90*
Gardner, William E., Jr. *WhoAm 90*
Gardner, William Earl 1928- *WhoAm 90*
Gardner, William George 1945- *St&PR 91, WhoAm 90*
Gardner, William Michael 1932- *WhoAm 90*
Gardner, William Michael 1948- *WhoAm 90, WhoE 91*
Gardner, Woodford Lloyd, Jr. 1945- *WhoEmL 91*
Gardner-Mayfield, Cinde Kae 1962- *WhoEmL 91*
Gardner-Sharpe, Laurene 1957- *WhoEmL 91*
Gardom, Garde Basil 1924- *WhoAm 90*
Gardons, S. S. *MajTwCW*
Gardos, George 1938- *BiDrAPA 89*
Gardos, Stephen 1945- *WhoE 91*
Gardose, Marietta Garcia *BiDrAPA 89*
Gardyne, Jock Bruce- 1930-1990 *BioIn 16*
Gare, Nene 1919- *FemiCLE*
Garebian, Keith 1943- *ConAu 129*
Garefino, Anello C. 1947- *St&PR 91*
Gareiss, Herbert, Jr. 1945- *St&PR 91*
Garel, Leo 1917- *WhoAmA 91*
Garelick, E. Lee 1934- *St&PR 91*
Garelick, Martin 1924- *WhoAm 90*
Garelick, May 1910- *AuBYP 90*
Garelick, May 1910-1989 *BioIn 16, ConAu 130*
Garell, Randy J. *St&PR 91*
Garet, Jedd 1955- *WhoAmA 91*

Garetz, Floyd K *BiDrAPA 89*
Garey, Charles Thomson 1947- *WhoEmL 91*
Garey, Donald Lee 1931- *WhoAm 90, WhoWor 91*
Garey, Jack 1930- *St&PR 91*
Garey, Pat 1932- *WhoAmA 91*
Garey, Patricia Martin 1932- *WhoAmW 91, WhoWor 91*
Garey, Roger W. 1921- *St&PR 91*
Garey, Terry A. 1948- *WhoWrEP 89*
Garfein, Arthur D 1942- *BiDrAPA 89*
Garfield, Allen 1939- *WhoAm 90*
Garfield, Bernard Howard 1924- *WhoAm 90*
Garfield, Bob *BioIn 16*
Garfield, Brian *BioIn 16*
Garfield, Brian 1939- *TwCCr&M 91*
Garfield, Brian Francis Wynne 1939- *SpyFic*
Garfield, Brian Wynne 1939- *WhoAm 90, WhoWrEP 89*
Garfield, David Anthony 1952- *BiDrAPA 89*
Garfield, David Crosby 1927- *St&PR 91, WhoAm 90*
Garfield, David Edward 1937- *WhoE 91*
Garfield, Eugene 1925- *WhoAm 90*
Garfield, Evelyn Picon 1940- *WhoAmW 91*
Garfield, Howard Robert 1933- *St&PR 91*
Garfield, Howard S., II 1947- *St&PR 91*
Garfield, James A. 1831-1881 *BioIn 16, WorAlBi*
Garfield, James Abram 1831-1881 *BiDrUSE 89*
Garfield, James Rudolph 1865-1950 *BiDrUSE 89*
Garfield, Joan Barbara 1950- *WhoAmW 91*
Garfield, John 1913-1952 *WorAlBi*
Garfield, John Samuel 1930- *WhoWor 91*
Garfield, Leon *BioIn 16*
Garfield, Leon 1921- *AuBYP 90, ChlLR 21 [port]*
Garfield, Leslie Jerome 1932- *WhoE 91, WhoWor 91*
Garfield, Lucretia Rudolph 1832-1918 *BioIn 16*
Garfield, Robert *BiDrAPA 89*
Garfield, Robert Edward 1955- *WhoAm 90*
Garfield, Robert Louis 1948- *WhoE 91*
Garfin, Louis 1917- *WhoAm 90*
Garfinkel, Alan 1941- *WhoWrEP 89*
Garfinkel, Barry David *BiDrAPA 89*
Garfinkel, Barry Herbert 1928- *WhoAm 90, WhoE 91*
Garfinkel, Fran Sylvia 1959- *WhoEmL 91*
Garfinkel, Harmon M. 1933- *St&PR 91*
Garfinkel, Harmon Mark 1933- *WhoAm 90*
Garfinkel, Herbert 1920- *WhoAm 90*
Garfinkel, Lawrence Saul 1932- *WhoWor 91*
Garfinkel, Marc Edward 1947- *BiDrAPA 89*
Garfinkel, Paul Earl 1946- *BiDrAPA 89*
Garfinkel, Philip 1926- *WhoAm 90*
Garfinkel, Renee Efra 1950- *WhoAmW 91*
Garfinkel, Simson L. 1965- *WhoE 91*
Garfinkel, Steven R. 1943- *St&PR 91*
Garfinkle, Barry David 1946- *WhoE 91*
Garfinkle, Caryn 1951- *WhoAmW 91*
Garfinkle, Louis Alan 1928- *WhoWor 91*
Garford, Arthur Lovett 1858-1933 *EncABHB 4*
Garfunkel, Art *BioIn 16*
Garfunkel, Art 1941- *ConMus 4 [port], EncPR&S 89, WhoAm 90, WorAlBi*
Garfunkel, Joseph M. 1926- *WhoWrEP 89*
Garg, Bimlesh *BiDrAPA 89*
Garg, Devendra Prakash 1934- *WhoAm 90, WhoSSW 91*
Garg, Kamlesh R. *BiDrAPA 89*
Garg, Prem Sagar 1945- *WhoWor 91*
Garg, Virendra Kumar 1949- *WhoWor 91*
Gargalli, Claire W. 1942- *St&PR 91, WhoAm 90, WhoAmW 91*
Gargan, Thomas Joseph 1952- *WhoEmL 91, WhoWor 91*
Gargan, William Michael 1950- *WhoWrEP 89*
Gargana, John J., Jr. 1931- *St&PR 91*
Gargana, John Joseph, Jr. 1931- *WhoAm 90*
Gargano, Charles Angelo 1934- *WhoAm 90, WhoWor 91*
Gargano, Pierfrancesco 1962- *WhoE 91*
Gargano, Richard Monte 1936- *WhoAm 90*
Garganta, Kevin James 1954- *WhoE 91*
Gargaro, Lynne Marie 1963- *WhoE 91*
Garges, Susan 1953- *WhoAmW 91*
Garges, Thomas W. *St&PR 91*
Gargill, Ann *FemiCLE*
Gargill, Anne 1634?- *BiDEWW*
Gargiulo, Andrea Weiner 1946- *WhoEmL 91*
Gargiulo, Frank X. *BioIn 16*
Gargiulo, Generio Thomas 1948- *St&PR 91*
Gargiulo-Kulikowski, Joan 1953- *WhoAmW 91*
Garhart, John Paul 1946- *WhoEmL 91*
Garhart, Martin J 1946- *WhoAmA 91*
Garibaldi, Giovanni *PenDiDA 89*
Garibaldi, Giuseppe 1807-1882 *BioIn 16, EncPaPR 91, WorAlBi*
Garibaldi, Marie Louise 1934- *WhoAm 90, WhoAmW 91, WhoE 91*
Garibay-Gutierrez, Luis 1916- *WhoAm 90, WhoSSW 91, WhoWor 91*
Garic, Harold N. 1946- *St&PR 91*
Garicano, Maria Fernanda *BiDrAPA 89*
Gariepy, Henry 1930- *WhoWrEP 89*
Garijo-Guembe, Miguel Maria 1935- *WhoWor 91*
Garin, Eugene 1922- *WhoWor 91*
Garin, Geoffrey Douglas 1953- *WhoAm 90*
Garinet, Jules 1797-1877? *EncO&P 3*
Garing, Ione Davis 1930- *WhoAmW 91*
Garing, John Seymour 1930- *WhoAm 90, WhoE 91*
Garinger, Louis Daniel *WhoAm 90*
Garippa, Joan 1945- *WhoAmW 91, WhoEmL 91*
Garison, Lynn Lassiter 1954- *WhoAmW 91*
Garitano, William Warren 1932- *BiDrAPA 89*
Garity, Joan Patricia 1944- *WhoAmW 91*
Garity, Mary Margaret 1950- *WhoAmW 91*
Garland, Augustus Hill 1832-1899 *BiDrUSE 89, BioIn 16*
Garland, Bennet 1939- *SpyFic*
Garland, Bennett *WhoWrEP 89*
Garland, Beverly 1926- *BioIn 16*
Garland, Carl Wesley 1929- *WhoAm 90*
Garland, Charles S., Jr. 1927- *St&PR 91*
Garland, Charles Stedman, Jr. 1927- *WhoAm 90*
Garland, David *BioIn 16*
Garland, Elspeth Jane *BiDrAPA 89*
Garland, Evelyn Claire 1952- *WhoEmL 91*
Garland, Floyd Richard 1938- *WhoE 91*
Garland, Hamlin 1860-1940 *EncO&P 3, WhNaAH, WorAlBi*
Garland, Hazel *BioIn 16*
Garland, James Wilson, Jr. 1933- *WhoAm 90*
Garland, Joan Bruder 1931- *WhoE 91*
Garland, Joanne Marie 1947- *WhoWrEP 89*
Garland, Joe 1903- *OxCPMus*
Garland, John W., III 1938- *BiDrAPA 89*
Garland, Joseph *BiDrAPA 89*
Garland, Judy *BioIn 16*
Garland, Judy 1922-1969 *BioAmW, OxCPMus, WorAlBi*
Garland, Kenneth 1929- *ConDes 90*
Garland, LaRetta Matthews *WhoAmW 91, WhoSSW 91*
Garland, Madge *NewYTBS 90*
Garland, Madge 1900?-1990 *ConAu 132*
Garland, Margie Y. 1937- *WhoAmW 91*
Garland, Merrick Brian 1952- *WhoEmL 91*
Garland, Patrick James 1931- *St&PR 91*
Garland, Peter Adams 1952- *IntWWM 90*
Garland, Phillip E. 1932- *St&PR 91*
Garland, Red 1923-1984 *BioIn 16*
Garland, Robert Field 1934- *WhoAm 90*
Garland, Sarah 1944- *SmATA 62*
Garland, Stephen B. 1946- *St&PR 91*
Garland, Sylvia Dillof 1919- *WhoAm 90*
Garland, Thomas J. 1934- *WhoSSW 91*
Garland, Wayne 1950- *Ballpl 90*
Garland, William James 1948- *WhoAm 90*
Garlets, Donovon G. 1938- *St&PR 91*
Garlette, William Henry Lee 1951- *WhoSSW 91*
Garley, R. Scott 1956- *WhoEmL 91*
Garlick, Andrew Mark 1951- *St&PR 91, WhoEmL 91*
Garlick, Antony 1927- *IntWWM 90*
Garlin, Linda Clayton 1937- *WhoAmW 91*
Garling, Carol Elizabeth 1939- *WhoSSW 91*
Garlinghouse, Bradley Kent 1941- *St&PR 91*
Garlington, Jack O'Brien 1917- *WhoWrEP 89*
Garlington, James Clarke 1908- *WhoAm 90*
Garlington, Robert J. 1939- *St&PR 91*
Garlisi, Laura *BiDrAPA 89*
Garlitz, Thomas Drake 1953- *WhoEmL 91*
Garlo, Olgierd C 1919- *BiDrAPA 89*
Garlock, Betty Blanche 1935- *St&PR 91*
Garlock, Richard Westley 1934- *St&PR 91*
Garlock, Steven Jay 1949- *WhoEmL 91*
Garlock, Tim A. 1959- *St&PR 91*
Garloff, Samuel John 1947- *WhoE 91*
Garlough, William Glenn 1924- *St&PR 91, WhoAm 90*
Garman, Arthur A. *St&PR 91*
Garman, Ed 1914- *WhoAmA 91*
Garman, Harry St. Clair 1945- *WhoE 91*
Garman, Karen Ann 1960- *WhoAmW 91*
Garman, Kathleen Ann 1956- *WhoAmW 91*
Garman, M. Lawrence 1943- *St&PR 91*
Garman, Mike 1949- *Ballpl 90*
Garman, Teresa Agnes 1937- *WhoAmW 91*
Garmendia, Anibal Pinto 1825-1884 *BioIn 16*
Garmer, William Robert 1946- *WhoEmL 91*
Garmezy, Norman 1918- *WhoAm 90*
Garmire, Elsa Meints 1939- *WhoAm 90*
Garmize, Sharon Marie 1950- *WhoAmW 91*
Garmon, Gregg Wesley 1948- *BiDrAPA 89*
Garmon, Henry B. 1943- *St&PR 91*
Garmon, J David 1957- *BiDrAPA 89*
Garmon, Philip B. 1944- *St&PR 91*
Garmon, William Norris 1950- *WhoSSW 91*
Garms, Debs 1908-1984 *Ballpl 90*
Garmus, David Paul 1940- *WhoE 91*
Garn, Doris Duenewald *BioIn 16*
Garn, Edwin Jacob 1932- *WhoAm 90, WhoWor 91*
Garn, Stanley Marion 1922- *WhoAm 90*
Garnand, Richard B 1927- *BiDrAPA 89*
Garneau, Francois-Xavier 1809-1866 *DcLB 99 [port]*
Garneau, Lucien Joseph 1931- *St&PR 91*
Garneau, Michel 1939- *OxCCanT*
Garneau, Raymond *BioIn 16*
Garneau, Richard *NewAgMG*
Garneau, Yvon 1946- *BiDrAPA 89*
Garneaux, Darlene Ann 1949- *WhoEmL 91*
Garner, Alan 1934- *AuBYP 90, BioIn 16, MajTwCW*
Garner, Alan 1950- *ConAu 132*
Garner, Albert Headden 1955- *WhoAm 90*
Garner, Alto Luther 1916- *WhoAm 90*
Garner, Archibald 1904-1970 *WhoAmA 91N*
Garner, Art 1952- *ODwPR 91*
Garner, Bennett Weil *BiDrAPA 89*
Garner, Bryan Andrew 1958- *WhoEmL 91*
Garner, C. Greene 1920- *St&PR 91*
Garner, Carlene Ann 1945- *WhoAmW 91*
Garner, Celeste Dixon 1934- *WhoSSW 91, WhoWor 91*
Garner, Charles Kent 1946- *St&PR 91, WhoAm 90, WhoSSW 91*
Garner, Charles William 1939- *WhoAm 90, WhoE 91*
Garner, Claud W. *AuBYP 90*
Garner, Dale Mark 1957- *WhoSSW 91*
Garner, Dan Reed 1944- *WhoAm 90*
Garner, Debra Williams 1957- *WhoWrEP 89*
Garner, Donald Glenn 1929- *St&PR 91*
Garner, Dorothy Ann 1959- *WhoAmW 91*
Garner, Edward Markley, II 1949- *WhoE 91*
Garner, Edwin Leon, Jr. 1959- *WhoEmL 91*
Garner, Erroll *BioIn 16*
Garner, Erroll 1921-1977 *WorAlBi*
Garner, Erroll 1923-1977 *DrBlPA 90, OxCPMus*
Garner, Frederick L. 1940- *St&PR 91*
Garner, G Josephine *BiDrAPA 89*
Garner, Gary Nelson 1935- *WhoSSW 91*
Garner, Harry Richard 1935- *St&PR 91*
Garner, Harvey 1926- *WhoE 91*
Garner, Harvey Louis 1926- *WhoAm 90*
Garner, Helen 1942- *FemiCLE*
Garner, Hugh 1913-1979 *ConAu 31NR*
Garner, J. Clayton 1936- *St&PR 91*
Garner, Jack *BioIn 16*
Garner, James 1928- *BioIn 16, WhoAm 90, WorAlBi*
Garner, James Parent 1923- *WhoAm 90*
Garner, Jo Ann Starkey 1934- *WhoAmW 91*
Garner, John C., Jr. 1947- *WhoSSW 91*
Garner, John Michael 1935- *St&PR 91, WhoAm 90*
Garner, John Nance 1868-1967 *BiDrUSE 89, WorAlBi*
Garner, John Patrick 1942- *St&PR 91*
Garner, LaForrest Dean 1933- *WhoWor 91*
Garner, Louis M. 1919- *St&PR 91*
Garner, Marcellus Craig, Jr. 1948- *WhoEmL 91*
Garner, Mary Jane 1916- *WhoAmW 91*
Garner, Mary Linhard 1953- *WhoSSW 91*
Garner, Michael Frederick 1937- *WhoWor 91*
Garner, Mildred Maxine 1919- *WhoAm 90*
Garner, Mousie 1909- *BioIn 16*
Garner, Ollie Belle 1928- *WhoAmW 91*
Garner, Paul Trantham 1951- *WhoEmL 91, WhoSSW 91*
Garner, Phil 1949- *Ballpl 90*
Garner, Richard Warren 1948- *St&PR 91*
Garner, Robert Edward Lee 1946- *WhoSSW 91*
Garner, Samuel Paul 1910- *WhoAm 90*
Garner, Saville 1908-1983 *DcNaB 1981*
Garner, Sharon Bush 1956- *WhoEmL 91*
Garner, Sharon Kay 1947- *WhoWrEP 89*
Garner, Stanley G 1934- *BiDrAPA 89*
Garner, Stanton Berry 1925- *WhoWrEP 89*
Garner, Stephen W. 1946- *IntWWM 90*
Garner, Stephen Warren 1946- *WhoSSW 91*
Garner, Sylvia Garrett 1958- *WhoEmL 91*
Garner, Thomas Joseph 1954- *WhoWor 91*
Garner, Wendell Richard 1921- *WhoAm 90*
Garner, William Darrell 1933- *WhoE 91*
Garner-Lipman, Karen Lee 1947- *WhoWrEP 89*
Garnes, Antoinette Elizabeth 1887-1938 *DcAfAmP*
Garnes, Delbert Franklin 1943- *WhoSSW 91*
Garnes, Ronald Vincent 1947- *WhoSSW 91, WhoWor 91*
Garnett, Alice 1903-1989 *BioIn 16*
Garnett, Barbara Jean Nichols 1953- *WhoSSW 91*
Garnett, Carla Renee *WhoAmW 91*
Garnett, Constance 1861-1946 *BioIn 16*
Garnett, Constance 1862-1946 *FemiCLE*
Garnett, David 1892-1981 *DcNaB 1981*
Garnett, Emmeline *AuBYP 90*
Garnett, Eve C. R. *AuBYP 90*
Garnett, Gerald 1944- *St&PR 91*
Garnett, John Sears 1945- *WhoE 91*
Garnett, Kathy B. *BioIn 16*
Garnett, Keith Jay 1938- *WhoAm 90*
Garnett, Michael Duane 1953- *BiDrAPA 89*
Garnett, Molly 1954- *ODwPR 91*
Garnett, Ramona Felarca 1953- *WhoEmL 91*
Garnett, Richard 1789-1850 *EncO&P 3*
Garnett, Richard 1835-1906 *BioIn 16*
Garnett, Richard W., Jr. *BiDrAPA 89*
Garnett, Roger *TwCCr&M 91*
Garnett, Stanley I., II 1943- *St&PR 91*
Garnett, Stanley Iredale, II 1943- *WhoAm 90*
Garnett, Stephen Hunter 1928- *St&PR 91*
Garnett, William 1916- *WhoAm 90*
Garnett, William Ashford 1916- *WhoAmA 91*
Garnevicus, Frank P. 1925- *St&PR 91*
Garney, Charles Arthur 1931- *St&PR 91*
Garnham, Alan 1954- *WhoWor 91*
Garnham, Percy Cyril Claude 1901- *WhoWor 91*
Garnier, Anton C. 1940- *St&PR 91*
Garnier, Constant 1816-1894 *DcCanB 12*
Garnier, Francois *PenDiDA 89*
Garnier, Gilles *EncO&P 3*
Garnier, Jacques *BioIn 16*
Garnier, Jean-Louis-Charles 1825-1898 *BioIn 16*
Garnier, John Hutchison 1823-1898 *DcCanB 12*
Garnier, Pierre *PenDiDA 89*
Garnier, Robert Charles 1916- *WhoAm 90, WhoWor 91*
Garns, John David Martin 1933- *St&PR 91*
Garnsey, Clarke Henderson 1913- *WhoAmA 91*
Garnsey, Walter Wood, Jr. 1945- *WhoEmL 91*
Garnsworthy, Lewis 1922-1990 *BioIn 16*
Garofalo, Denise Anne 1959- *WhoAmW 91, WhoE 91, WhoEmL 91*
Garofalo, John Gerard *BiDrAPA 89*
Garofalo, Joseph Anthony 1953- *WhoE 91*
Garofalo, Renee J. 1957- *WhoAmW 91*
Garofalo, Robert 1939- *IntWWM 90*
Garofalo, Rocca 1929- *BiDrAPA 89*
Garofalo, Roy Lawrence 1932- *St&PR 91*
Garofola, Anthony Charles 1954- *WhoEmL 91*
Garoian, Charles Richard 1943- *WhoAmA 91*
Garon, Gerald Stephen 1942- *St&PR 91*
Garon, Len 1945- *BioIn 16*
Garon, Richard Joseph, Jr. 1948- *WhoE 91*
Garonkonthie, Daniel 1600?-1676 *EncCRAm*
Garonzik, Sara E. 1951- *WhoAmW 91*
Garoufalis, Maria Elaine 1957- *WhoAmW 91*
Garouste, Elizabeth *BioIn 16*
Garouste, Gerard *BioIn 16*
Garoutte, Bill Charles 1921- *WhoAm 90, WhoWor 91*
Garoutte, P. J. 1937- *BioIn 16*
Garpestad, Renee Jeanette 1959- *WhoEmL 91*
Garpow, James E. 1944- *St&PR 91*
Garpow, James Edward 1944- *WhoAm 90*
Garr, Carl R. 1927- *St&PR 91*
Garr, Carl Robert 1927- *WhoAm 90*
Garr, Louis J., Jr. 1939- *WhoAm 90*

Garr, Louis Joseph, Jr. 1939- St&PR 91
Garr, Ralph 1945- Ballpl 90
Garr, Teri BioIn 16
Garr, Teri 1949- WorAlBi
Garr, Teri 1952- WhoAm 90, WhoAmW 91
Garra, Antonio BioIn 16
Garra, Antonio WhNaAH
Garrard, Christopher WhoWrEP 89
Garrard, Don 1929- IntWWM 90
Garrard, Don Edward Burdett WhoAm 90, WhoE 91
Garrard, Gardiner Wingfield, Jr. 1941- St&PR 91
Garrard, James 1939- OxCCanT
Garrard, Louis Ford 1847- AmLegL
Garrard, Mary Dubose 1937- WhoAmA 91
Garrard, Norma Lee 1945- WhoEmL 91
Garrard, Robert PenDiDA 89
Garrard, Robert 1793-1881 PenDiDA 89
Garrard, Robert L BiDrAPA 89
Garrard, Rose 1946- BiDWomA
Garrard, Timothy F 1943- ConAu 131
Garratt, Reg G. 1929- St&PR 91
Garratt, Sandra BioIn 16
Garraty, John Arthur 1920- WhoAm 90
Garraway, Brian Pattison 1931- WhoWor 91
Garre, John Michael 1949- St&PR 91
Garre, Walter J 1907- BiDrAPA 89
Garreau, Bruce John 1950- St&PR 91
Garreau, Joel 1948- WhoE 91
Garrels, Helen Ann 1940- WhoAmW 91
Garrels, John C., III 1940- St&PR 91
Garrels, Robert Minard 1916-1988 BioIn 16
Garrelts, Scott 1961- Ballpl 90
Garren, Kenneth Albert 1951- WhoEmL 91
Garren, Rebecca Smith 1952- WhoSSW 91
Garrenton, Vincent Trower, Jr. 1950- WhoAm 90
Garret, Merril D. 1935- St&PR 91
Garret, Paula Lyn 1951- WhoAm 90, WhoAmW 91, WhoEmL 91
Garreth, Ralph H. 1943- St&PR 91
Garreth, Ralph Hibbert 1943- WhoAm 90
Garretson, Ann Black 1955- WhoEmL 91
Garretson, Donald Everett 1921- WhoAm 90
Garretson, George Dalton 1925- WhoSSW 91
Garretson, Henry David 1929- WhoAm 90, WhoWor 91
Garretson, Kim K. 1950- ODwPR 91
Garretson, Robert L. 1920- IntWWM 90
Garrett, Andrea LeNaye 1962- WhoSSW 91
Garrett, Ann 1942- St&PR 91
Garrett, Barbara Jane 1950- WhoSSW 91
Garrett, Beatrice 1929- WhoWrEP 89
Garrett, Benjamin Caywood 1949- WhoEmL 91
Garrett, Brian K. St&PR 91
Garrett, Carlton Elonzo 1900- MusmAFA
Garrett, Caroline Kay 1952- WhoSSW 91
Garrett, Charlene Elizabeth 1960- WhoSSW 91
Garrett, Charles Geoffrey Blythe 1925- WhoAm 90, WhoWor 91
Garrett, Charles Hope 1953- WhoSSW 91
Garrett, Charles Leroy, Jr. 1940- WhoSSW 91
Garrett, Charles Thomasson 1954- WhoEmL 91
Garrett, David C., Jr. 1922- St&PR 91
Garrett, David Clyde, III 1948- WhoSSW 91
Garrett, David Clyde, Jr. 1922- WhoAm 90
Garrett, Davis Garland, Jr. BiDrAPA 89
Garrett, Deborra Elizabeth 1951- WhoEmL 91
Garrett, Duejean C. 1942- St&PR 91
Garrett, Echo Montgomery BioIn 16
Garrett, Echo Montgomery 1960- WhoEmL 91
Garrett, Edward Cortez 1948- WhoWrEP 89
Garrett, Edward Lee 1923- St&PR 91
Garrett, Eileen J 1892-1970 EncO&P 3, EncPaPR 91
Garrett, Eileen J. 1893-1970 BioAmW
Garrett, Eric 1933- IntWWM 90
Garrett, Floyd P BiDrAPA 89
Garrett, Foster Dale 1935- St&PR 91
Garrett, Franklin Miller 1906- WhoSSW 91
Garrett, Garet 1878-1954 BioIn 16
Garrett, George P. 1929- BioIn 16
Garrett, George Palmer, Jr. 1929- WhoAm 90, WhoWor 91, WhoWrEP 89
Garrett, Glenda Darlene 1963- WhoAmW 91
Garrett, Gloria Susan 1951- WhoAmW 91, WhoEmL 91
Garrett, Gordon ConAu 130
Garrett, Guy Thomas 1932- WhoAm 90
Garrett, Helen 1895- AuBYP 90
Garrett, Helen Marie WhoAmW 91
Garrett, Henry Lawrence, III 1939- WhoAm 90, WhoWor 91
Garrett, James Hardy 1932- WhoSSW 91
Garrett, James Leo, Jr. 1925- WhoWor 91
Garrett, Jerry Dale 1940- WhoSSW 91
Garrett, John B., Jr. St&PR 91
Garrett, John Keith 1957- WhoAm 90, WhoSSW 91
Garrett, John W., III 1930- St&PR 91
Garrett, John Work 1872-1942 BioIn 16
Garrett, Joseph B. 1936- St&PR 91
Garrett, Joseph Bernard 1936- WhoAm 90
Garrett, Joyce BioIn 16
Garrett, Kathryn Leigh 1958- WhoSSW 91
Garrett, Kenneth James 1953- WhoEmL 91
Garrett, Larry Carlton 1950- WhoSSW 91
Garrett, Laurel A. 1960- WhoAmW 91
Garrett, Lesley IntWWM 90
Garrett, Leslie 1932- WhoWrEP 89
Garrett, Luther Weaver, Jr. 1925- WhoAm 90
Garrett, Lynn 1946- WhoE 91
Garrett, Margaret L 1931- BiDrAPA 89
Garrett, Margaret Lucretia 1931- WhoE 91
Garrett, Maurice 1925- St&PR 91
Garrett, Melissa Jo 1956- WhoAmW 91
Garrett, Michael D BiDrAPA 89
Garrett, Nancy Roberts 1954- WhoAmW 91
Garrett, P.C. 1936- St&PR 91
Garrett, Panchita ODwPR 91
Garrett, Pat Thomas 1951- WhoEmL 91
Garrett, Patrick D. 1945- WhoSSW 91
Garrett, Paul Conrad 1946- WhoEmL 91
Garrett, Peter BioIn 16
Garrett, Peter John 1952- WhoWor 91
Garrett, Peter Todd 1947- WhoSSW 91
Garrett, Randall 1927-1987 ConAu 130, RGTwCSF
Garrett, Reginald Hooker 1939- WhoAm 90
Garrett, Richard W. 1944- St&PR 91
Garrett, Richard William 1925- WhoSSW 91
Garrett, Robert 1937- WhoAm 90
Garrett, Robert James 1951- WhoSSW 91
Garrett, Robert Stephens 1937- WhoWor 91
Garrett, Robert Wales BiDrAPA 89
Garrett, Roberta Kampschulte 1947- WhoSSW 91
Garrett, Ronald Doyle 1955- WhoEmL 91, WhoSSW 91
Garrett, Ruby Grant 1941- WhoAmW 91
Garrett, Ruby Joyce Burriss 1946- WhoAmW 91
Garrett, Shirley Duncan 1951- WhoSSW 91
Garrett, Shirley Gene 1944- WhoAmW 91
Garrett, Stephen 1922- WhoAmA 91
Garrett, Steven Lurie 1949- WhoEmL 91
Garrett, Stuart Grayson WhoAmA 91
Garrett, Susan Mary 1961- WhoWrEP 89
Garrett, Sylvester 1911- WhoAm 90
Garrett, Theodore Louis 1943- WhoAm 90
Garrett, Thomas PenDiDA 89
Garrett, Timothy Richard 1966- WhoSSW 91
Garrett, Wayne 1947- Ballpl 90
Garrett, Wilbur Eugene 1930- WhoAm 90, WhoWrEP 89
Garrett, William 1809-1875? AmLegL
Garrett, William Floyd, Jr. 1947- WhoEmL 91
Garrette, Marvin E. 1938- WhoAm 90
Garretto, Leonard Anthony, Jr. 1925- WhoWor 91
Garretto, Paolo 1903-1989 BioIn 16
Garrick, David 1717-1779 LitC 15 [port]
Garrick, Jan Dianne 1952- WhoEmL 91
Garrick, Joseph Daniel 1949- St&PR 91
Garrick, Laura Morris 1945- WhoAmW 91
Garrick, Marshall L 1950- BiDrAPA 89
Garrick, Michael IntWWM 90
Garrick, Thomas Robert 1950- BiDrAPA 89
Garrick, Tom, Jr. BioIn 16
Garrick, Tom, Sr. BioIn 16
Garrido, Angel E BiDrAPA 89
Garrido, Gil 1941- Ballpl 90
Garrido, Jorge L. WhoHisp 91
Garrido, Jorge Ramon BiDrAPA 89
Garrido, Jose A., Jr. 1953- WhoHisp 91
Garrido Atenas, Jorge 1940- WhoWor 91
Garrie, Stuart A 1943- BiDrAPA 89
Garriga, Erisbelia 1947- WhoAmW 91
Garriga, Julio 1955- WhoHisp 91
Garriga, Mariano Simon 1886-1965 BioIn 16
Garrigan, Richard Thomas 1938- WhoAm 90
Garrigan, Sean WhoWrEP 89
Garrigle, William Aloysius 1941- WhoE 91
Garrigo, Jose R. 1936- St&PR 91
Garrigue, Jean 1914-1972 FemiCLE
Garrigue, Sheila 1931- AuBYP 90, BioIn 16
Garriguenc, Pierre 1921- IntWWM 90
Garrigues, Suzanne 1945- WhoAmA 91
Garrigus, Harry Lucian 1876-1968 BioIn 16
Garrigus, Upson Stanley 1917- WhoAm 90
Garringer, Arthur W. 1926- St&PR 91
Garriott, Owen K. BioIn 16
Garriott, Owen K. 1930- WhoAm 90
Garriott, Richard BioIn 16
Garris, Emilie Ross 1947- WhoAmW 91
Garrish, Theodore John 1943- WhoAm 90
Garrison, Althea 1940- WhoAmW 91
Garrison, Ann Jardine 1938- WhoAmW 91
Garrison, Barbara 1931- WhoAmA 91
Garrison, Betty Bernhardt 1932- WhoAmW 91
Garrison, Brenda Joyce 1943- WhoAmW 91
Garrison, Burl Lourwood 1924- St&PR 91
Garrison, Carole Gozansky 1942- WhoAmW 91
Garrison, Clayton 1921- WhoAm 90
Garrison, Clifford Talmadge 1932- St&PR 91
Garrison, Dan 1949- St&PR 91
Garrison, David C. 1939- St&PR 91
Garrison, David Earl 1940- WhoAmA 91
Garrison, Denzil D. 1926- WhoAm 90
Garrison, Elizabeth Jane 1952- WhoAmA 91
Garrison, Ellen Barrier 1944- WhoSSW 91
Garrison, Eve 1908- WhoAmA 91
Garrison, Frederick AuBYP 90, MajTwCW
Garrison, Gary 1934- ODwPR 91, WhoSSW 91, WhoWor 91
Garrison, Gary Dean 1956- WhoEmL 91
Garrison, Gene K WhoAmA 91
Garrison, George Walker, Jr. 1939- WhoSSW 91
Garrison, Guy Grady 1927- WhoAm 90
Garrison, Harold 1923- MusmAFA
Garrison, Harry W. 1941- St&PR 91
Garrison, James Addison BiDrAPA 89
Garrison, James Wesley 1956- St&PR 91
Garrison, Jane Gayle 1951- WhoAmW 91
Garrison, Jesse Janes 1901- WhoAmA 91N
Garrison, Jim 1921- ConAu 132
Garrison, John Raymond 1938- WhoAm 90
Garrison, Jon 1944- IntWWM 90
Garrison, Jonathan Cross 1956- BiDrAPA 89
Garrison, Joseph M. 1944- ODwPR 91
Garrison, Karl C 1900-1980 ConAu 31NR
Garrison, Larry Richard 1951- WhoEmL 91
Garrison, Lindley Miller 1864-1932 BiDrUSE 89
Garrison, Mahala WhoWrEP 89
Garrison, Marion Ames 1907- WhoAm 90
Garrison, Mark Joseph 1930- WhoAm 90
Garrison, Michael Howard 1957- WhoSSW 91
Garrison, Michael William 1945- St&PR 91
Garrison, Mortimer, Jr. BioIn 16
Garrison, Neil Vincent 1960- WhoEmL 91
Garrison, Patricia ODwPR 91
Garrison, Paul Franklin 1929- St&PR 91
Garrison, Preston Jones 1942- WhoAm 90, WhoSSW 91
Garrison, Ray Harlan 1922- WhoAm 90, WhoWor 91
Garrison, Richard Christopher 1948- WhoAm 90
Garrison, Richard Hiles 1946- WhoEmL 91
Garrison, Robert A. 1941- St&PR 91
Garrison, Robert E. 1942- St&PR 91
Garrison, Robert Frederick 1936- WhoAm 90
Garrison, Robert Lawrence, Jr. 1945- St&PR 91
Garrison, Rodney Alan 1946- St&PR 91
Garrison, Roger L. 1943- St&PR 91
Garrison, Roy Gregory 1948- WhoEmL 91
Garrison, S. Olin BioIn 16
Garrison, Sara K. 1951- St&PR 91
Garrison, Stephen Allan 1940- St&PR 91, WhoAm 90
Garrison, Stuart Hugh 1945- WhoEmL 91
Garrison, Thomas Edmond 1922- WhoSSW 91
Garrison, Thomas S. 1952- WhoWrEP 89
Garrison, Truitt B. 1936- WhoAm 90
Garrison, Walter R. 1926- St&PR 91, WhoAm 90
Garrison, Wanda Brown 1936- WhoAmW 91
Garrison, Warren Baker BiDrAPA 89
Garrison, William Lloyd 1805-1879 BioIn 16, WorAlBi
Garrison, William Lloyd 1939- WhoWor 91
Garrison, William Louis 1924- WhoAm 90
Garrison, Zina BioIn 16
Garrison-Kilbourne, Clara Anne WhoWrEP 89
Garritson, Carrie BioIn 16
Garritson, Mike BioIn 16
Garrity, Donald Lee 1927- WhoAm 90
Garrity, Durwood James 1937- St&PR 91
Garrity, James Dart 1929- WhoWor 91
Garrity, John McCullough 1946- WhoSSW 91
Garrity, Keith R. WhoAm 90
Garrity, Keith Raymond 1931- St&PR 91
Garrity, Larry David 1948- St&PR 91
Garrity, Leo F. 1919- St&PR 91
Garrity, Norman C. 1941- St&PR 91
Garrity, Rodman Fox 1922- WhoAm 90
Garrity, Vincent Francis, Jr. 1937- WhoAm 90
Garrity, William L. 1924- St&PR 91
Garro, Alejandro Miguel 1950- WhoEmL 91
Garro, Elena 1920?- ConAu 131, HispWr 90
Garro, Samuel Joseph, Jr. 1954- WhoE 91
Garrod, Archibald Edward 1857-1936 DcScB S2
Garron de Doryan, Victoria 1920- WhoWor 91
Garrone, Gabriel Marie 1901- WhoWor 91
Garrott, Idamae T. 1916- WhoAmW 91, WhoE 91
Garrott, Thomas M. 1937- St&PR 91
Garrow, David Jeffries 1953- WhoAm 90
Garrow, Jack A. 1932- ODwPR 91, St&PR 91
Garrow, John Patrick 1928- St&PR 91
Garrow, William Casselman 1946- WhoE 91
Garroway, Dave 1913- WorAlBi
Garruto, John Anthony 1952- WhoEmL 91
Garry, Benjamin Thomas 1960- WhoEmL 91
Garry, Frederick Wilton 1921- WhoAm 90
Garry, Michael Joseph 1953- WhoEmL 91
Garry, Richard Leonard 1928- St&PR 91
Garry, William James 1944- WhoAm 90
Garsh, Fran 1951- WhoE 91
Garsh, Thomas Burton 1931- WhoAm 90
Garsha, Ronald J. 1946- St&PR 91, WhoEmL 91
Garshnek, Victoria 1957- WhoE 91
Garshol, Knut Finn 1944- WhoWor 91
Garside, Alice H. BioIn 16
Garside, Bettis Alston 1894-1989 BioIn 16
Garside, John Rushforth, II 1935- WhoAm 90
Garside, Marlene Elizabeth 1933- WhoAmW 91
Garside, Thomas Arthur BiDrAPA 89
Garske, Kathleen Agnes Gauthier 1946- WhoAmW 91, WhoSSW 91
Garson, Arthur 1914- St&PR 91
Garson, Dan 1920- St&PR 91
Garson, Eugenia AuBYP 90
Garson, Gary W. 1946- St&PR 91
Garson, Gary Wayne 1946- WhoEmL 91
Garson, Greer 1908- ConTFT 8, WorAlBi
Garson, Karin Best 1945- WhoAmW 91
Garson, Paul David 1940- BiDrAPA 89
Garson, Ronald Jay 1949- BiDrAPA 89
Garson, William J. 1917- WhoWor 91
Garst, Daniel Robert 1950- BiDrAPA 89
Garst, David Nelson 1959- WhoEmL 91
Garst, Doris Shannon 1894- AuBYP 90
Garst, Shannon AuBYP 90
Garstang, Roy Henry 1925- WhoAm 90
Garstang, Walter 1868-1949 DcScB S2
Garston, Gerald Drexler 1925- WhoAm 90, WhoAmA 91
Gart, John Jacob 1931- WhoE 91
Gart, Murray Joseph 1924- WhoAm 90
Gartel, Laurence M 1956- WhoAmA 91
Garten, Alan F.M. 1955- WhoE 91
Garten, Cliff 1954- WhoAmA 91
Garten, Jan AuBYP 90
Garten, Wayne Philip 1952- WhoAm 90
Gartenberg, Barry Felix 1956- St&PR 91
Gartenberg, Leo NewYTBS 90
Gartenberg, Seymour Lee 1931- WhoAm 90, WhoE 91, WhoWor 91
Gartenhaus, Solomon 1929- WhoAm 90
Garth NewAgMG
Garth, Bryant Geoffrey 1949- WhoAm 90
Garth, David 1930- WhoAm 90
Garth, John 1894-1971 WhoAmA 91N
Garth, Leonard I. 1921- WhoAm 90
Garth, Mathew WhoWrEP 89
Garth, Samuel 1661-1719 DcLB 95 [port]
Garthorne, Francis PenDiDA 89
Garthorne, George PenDiDA 89
Garthwaite, Anna Maria 1690-1763 PenDiDA 89
Garthwaite, Marion 1893- AuBYP 90
Garthwaite, Richard Loren 1950- St&PR 91
Gartlan, Eugene V. WhoAm 90, WhoE 91, WhoWor 91
Gartland, Frank Anthony 1946- St&PR 91
Gartland, J. Donald BioIn 16

Gartland, James J. 1954- *St&PR 91*
Gartland, James M. 1952- *St&PR 91*
Gartland, John Joseph 1918- *WhoAm 90*
Gartland, Robert *AuBYP 90*
Gartland, William Joseph 1944- *WhoWor 91*
Gartland, William Joseph, Jr. 1941- *WhoAm 90*
Gartler, Stanley Michael 1923- *WhoAm 90*
Gartley, Cheryle Blumberg 1947- *WhoAmW 91*
Gartman, Peter L. *St&PR 91*
Gartner, Alan P. 1935- *WhoAm 90*
Gartner, George, III 1954- *St&PR 91*
Gartner, Gideon I. 1935- *WhoAm 90*
Gartner, Harold Henry, III 1948- *WhoEmL 91*
Gartner, James J. 1941- *St&PR 91*
Gartner, Lawrence Mitchel 1933- *WhoAm 90*
Gartner, Leslie Paul 1943- *WhoE 91*
Gartner, Lillian Mary 1944- *WhoAmW 91*
Gartner, Michael 1938- *CurBio 90 [port]*
Gartner, Michael G. *BioIn 16*
Gartner, Michael Gay 1938- *WhoAm 90, WhoE 91*
Gartner, Murray 1922- *WhoAm 90*
Gartner, Scott Alan 1953- *WhoEmL 91*
Garton, Dennis Eugene 1950- *St&PR 91*
Garton, Gary K. 1941- *St&PR 91*
Garton, Graham 1929- *IntWWM 90*
Garton, Theresa Suzanne 1958- *BiDrAPA 89*
Garton, Vernon Keith 1931- *St&PR 91*
Gartrell, Carol Ann 1952- *IntWWM 90*
Gartrell, Douglas Mervyn *BiDrAPA 89*
Gartrell, Nanette K *BiDrAPA 89*
Gartrell, William George 1948- *WhoEmL 91*
Garts, James Rufus, Jr. 1949- *WhoSSW 91*
Gartshore, H L 1906- *BiDrAPA 89*
Gartz, Linda Louise 1949 *WhoAmW 91*
Gartzke, David G. 1943- *St&PR 91*
Garuffi, Mildred Brown 1934- *WhoE 91*
Garve, Andrew 1908- *TwCCr&M 91*
Garvens, Ellen *WhoAmA 91*
Garvens, James Arvine 1936- *St&PR 91*
Garvens, Kent Nashland 1936- *St&PR 91*
Garver, Bruce Allen 1939- *WhoE 91*
Garver, Fanny 1927- *WhoAmA 91*
Garver, Frederick Merrill 1945- *WhoEmL 91*
Garver, James Amos 1937- *WhoSSW 91*
Garver, Ned 1925 *Ballpl 90*
Garver, Richard Lloyd 1941- *St&PR 91*
Garver, Robert Vernon 1932- *WhoAm 90*
Garver, Theodore Meyer 1929- *St&PR 91, WhoAm 90*
Garver, Thomas H 1934- *WhoAmA 91*
Garver, Thomas Haskell 1934- *WhoAm 90*
Garver, Walter Raymond 1927- *WhoAmA 91*
Garvey, David 1922- *IntWWM 90*
Garvey, Ed *BioIn 16*
Garvey, Gerald Thomas 1935- *WhoAm 90*
Garvey, James Patrick *BioIn 16*
Garvey, James Sutherland 1922- *St&PR 91*
Garvey, James T 1924- *BiDrAPA 89*
Garvey, James Thomas 1932- *St&PR 91*
Garvey, Jane Roberts 1919- *WhoAmW 91*
Garvey, Joanne Marie 1935- *WhoAm 90*
Garvey, John Charles 1921- *WhoAm 90*
Garvey, John Cotton 1953- *WhoEmL 91*
Garvey, John Leo 1927- *WhoAm 90*
Garvey, Kenneth W. 1946- *St&PR 91*
Garvey, Marcus *EarBlAP*
Garvey, Marcus 1887-1940 *BioIn 16, WorAlBi*
Garvey, Michael J *BiDrAPA 89*
Garvey, Michelle K. 1958- *St&PR 91*
Garvey, Richard Anthony 1950- *WhoE 91*
Garvey, Richard Arthur 1948- *WhoEmL 91*
Garvey, Robert Robey, Jr. 1921- *WhoAm 90*
Garvey, Steve *BioIn 16*
Garvey, Steve 1948- *Ballpl 90 [port], WorAlBi*
Garvey, Virginia M. 1926- *ODwPR 91*
Garvey, William John 1952- *St&PR 91*
Garvick, Kenneth Ryan 1945- *WhoEmL 91*
Garvin, Andrew Paul 1945- *WhoAm 90*
Garvin, Clifton C., Jr. 1921- *St&PR 91*
Garvin, Florence Ward 1928- *WhoE 91*
Garvin, Jerry 1955- *Ballpl 90*
Garvin, Karen Sue 1958- *WhoE 91*
Garvin, Ned 1874-1908 *Ballpl 90*
Garvin, Noel Jack 1948- *St&PR 91*
Garvin, Richard W. 1940- *St&PR 91*
Garvin, Richard Wade 1940- *WhoAm 90*
Garvin, Robert P. 1921- *St&PR 91*
Garvin, Suzanne Marie 1953- *WhoEmL 91*
Garvin, Thomas Michael 1935- *St&PR 91, WhoAm 90*
Garvin, William Francis 1946- *WhoEmL 91*
Garwin, Richard *BioIn 16*
Garwin, Richard Lawrence 1928- *WhoAm 90*
Garwood, Audrey 1927- *WhoAmA 91*
Garwood, John Delvert 1915- *WhoAm 90*
Garwood, Lester Nugent 1948- *BiDrAPA 89*
Garwood, Margaret 1927- *IntWWM 90*
Garwood, Thomas Chason, Jr. 1944- *WhoSSW 91*
Garwood, Tirzah 1908-1951 *BiDWomA, BioIn 16*
Garwood, Victor Paul 1917- *WhoAm 90*
Garwood, William Lockhart 1931- *WhoAm 90*
Gary, Benjamin Walter, Jr. 1934- *WhoAm 90*
Gary, Charles Lester 1917- *WhoAm 90*
Gary, Deborah 1955- *WhoAmW 91*
Gary, Dorothy Hales 1917- *WhoAmA 91*
Gary, Elbert H. 1846-1927 *WorAlBi*
Gary, Frank Boyd 1860-1922 *AmLegL*
Gary, Gayle Harriet Margaret 1920- *WhoAmW 91*
Gary, James Albert 1833-1920 *BiDrUSE 89*
Gary, James Frederick 1920- *St&PR 91, WhoAm 90*
Gary, James Washington, Jr. 1943- *WhoSSW 91*
Gary, Jan 1925- *WhoAmA 91*
Gary, Jim 1905- *EncACom*
Gary, John 1932- *WhoAm 90*
Gary, Julia Thomas 1929- *WhoAmW 91*
Gary, Kathleen N. 1945- *ODwPR 91*
Gary, Madeleine Sophie 1923- *WhoWrEP 89*
Gary, Martin Neil 1948- *WhoSSW 91*
Gary, Nancy Elizabeth 1937- *WhoAm 90, WhoAmW 91, WhoE 91*
Gary, Richard David 1949- *WhoEmL 91*
Gary, Roger Vanstrom 1946- *WhoSSW 91*
Gary, Sharon Delight 1951- *WhoAmW 91*
Gary, Stephen *ODwPR 91*
Gary, William Fred 1950- *WhoEmL 91*
Gary, Wyndham Lewis 1916-1989 *BioIn 16*
Garyali, Veena *BiDrAPA 89*
Garza, Betty V. *WhoHisp 91*
Garza, Carlos, Jr. 1944- *WhoHisp 91*
Garza, Carmen Lomas *WhoHisp 91*
Garza, Catarino 1859-1902? *BioIn 16*
Garza, Cutberto 1947- *WhoHisp 91*
Garza, Cyndy 1956- *WhoHisp 91*
Garza, Edmund T. 1943- *WhoHisp 91*
Garza, Federico, Jr. 1958- *WhoHisp 91*
Garza, Francisco Xavier 1952- *WhoHisp 91*
Garza, Jaime Rene 1941- *WhoHisp 91*
Garza, Janet Lois 1939- *WhoAmW 91, WhoE 91*
Garza, Javier Joaquin 1955- *WhoHisp 91*
Garza, Juanita Elizondo 1939- *WhoHisp 91*
Garza, M. Antoinette 1939- *WhoHisp 91*
Garza, Marco *WhoHisp 91*
Garza, Margarito P. *WhoHisp 91*
Garza, Maria *WhoHisp 91*
Garza, Maria Luisa *WhoHisp 91*
Garza, Mary *WhoHisp 91*
Garza, Norma Perez 1962- *WhoSSW 91*
Garza, Oliver P. 1941- *WhoHisp 91*
Garza, Rachel Delores 1952- *WhoHisp 91*
Garza, Raynaldo T. 1957- *WhoHisp 91*
Garza, Reynaldo G. 1915- *WhoAm 90*
Garza, Roberto 1942- *WhoHisp 91*
Garza, Roberto J 1934- *HispWr 90*
Garza, Roberto Jesus 1934- *WhoHisp 91, WhoSSW 91*
Garza, Roberto Montes 1951- *WhoHisp 91*
Garza, Rudy A. 1952- *WhoEmL 91*
Garza, Salvador, Jr. 1955- *WhoHisp 91*
Garza, San Juanita 1955- *WhoHisp 91*
Garza, Thomas Jesus 1958- *WhoHisp 91*
Garza, William Alfred 1950- *WhoHisp 91*
Garza, Yolanda 1955- *WhoHisp 91*
Garza-Adame, Maria Dolores 1946- *WhoHisp 91*
Garza-Gongora, Sara R. *WhoHisp 91*
Garza T., Eduardo 1948- *WhoWor 91*
Garza-Trevino, Enrique S 1948- *BiDrAPA 89*
Garzarelli, Elaine *BioIn 16*
Garzarelli, Elaine M. 1951- *St&PR 91*
Garzarelli, Elaine Marie 1951- *WhoAm 90, WhoAmW 91*
Garzia, Samuel Angelo 1920- *WhoAm 90*
Garzio, Angelo C 1922- *WhoAmA 91*
Garzon-Blanco, Armando 1941- *WhoAmA 91*
Gasaway, Laura Nell 1945- *WhoAm 90, WhoAmW 91*
Gasbarre, George P. 1925- *St&PR 91*
Gasbarro, Louis Donald 1937- *WhoWor 91*
Gasca, Philip D. Ortega *ConAu 131*
Gasca, Philip D. Ortego y 1926- *BioIn 16*
Gasch, Bernd Karl 1941- *WhoWor 91*
Gasch-Cybyske, Nadine Marie 1951- *WhoEmL 91*
Gasche, Louis M. 1913- *St&PR 91*
Gaschen, Francis Allen 1950- *WhoE 91*
Gascoigne, Bamber 1935- *SmATA 62 [port]*
Gascoin, Leocadie 1818-1900 *DcCanB 12*
Gascon, Jean 1920-1988 *BioIn 16*
Gascon, Jean 1921-1988 *OxCCanT*
Gascoyne, David 1916- *MajTwCW*
Gascoyne-Cecil, Robert Arthur Talbot 1830-1903 *BioIn 16*
Gasdia, Cecilia 1960- *IntWWM 90*
Gash, Jeff David 1952- *St&PR 91*
Gash, Joe *ConAu 131, TwCCr&M 91*
Gash, Jonathan 1933- *TwCCr&M 91*
Gash, Mark Allen 1961- *WhoEmL 91*
Gasich, Welko Elton 1922- *St&PR 91, WhoAm 90*
Gasiorkiewicz, Eugene Anthony 1950- *WhoWor 91*
Gasiorowicz, Stephen George 1928- *WhoAm 90*
Gaska, Christine 1965- *WhoAmW 91*
Gaskell, Elizabeth 1810-1865 *FemiCLE, WorAlBi*
Gaskell, Elizabeth Cleghorn 1810-1865 *BioIn 16*
Gaskell, Robert Eugene 1912- *WhoAm 90*
Gaskell, Vernon Guy 1926- *St&PR 91*
Gaski, John Francis 1949- *WhoEmL 91*
Gaskill, Ada Perel *BiDrAPA 89*
Gaskill, Clarence 1892-1947 *OxCPMus*
Gaskill, Gudrun *BioIn 16*
Gaskill, Herbert S 1909- *BiDrAPA 89*
Gaskill, Jack Richard 1936- *St&PR 91*
Gaskill, Robert Clarence 1931- *WhoAm 90*
Gaskill, William Carlyle 1925- *St&PR 91*
Gaskin, Catherine 1929- *FemiCLE*
Gaskin, Fred Wayne *BiDrAPA 89*
Gaskin, Ina May 1940- *ConAu 129*
Gaskin, J C A 1936- *ConAu 131*
Gaskin, Jerry William 1940- *St&PR 91*
Gaskin, Lillian Bernice 1946- *WhoEmL 91*
Gaskin, Michael A. *St&PR 91N*
Gaskin, Stephen 1935- *ConAu 129*
Gaskin, Thomas Henry 1930- *St&PR 91*
Gaskin, W.M., Jr. 1932- *St&PR 91*
Gaskins, Douglas Kenneth 1951- *WhoSSW 91*
Gaskins, Fay Mary 1926- *BiDrAPA 89*
Gaskins, John L. 1852-1898 *AmLegL*
Gaskins, Larry Corbitt 1945- *WhoSSW 91*
Gaskins, Lee O. 1937- *St&PR 91*
Gaskins, Mary Anne *BiDrAPA 89*
Gaskins, Paul Thomas 1936- *WhoE 91*
Gaskins, Richard B. 1936- *WhoAm 90*
Gaskins-Clark, Patricia Renae 1959- *WhoSSW 91*
Gasko, Robert Charles 1930- *WhoSSW 91*
Gasman, David H 1934- *BiDrAPA 89*
Gasner, Anne 1927- *WhoWrEP 89*
Gasorek, Doretta Warden 1957- *WhoE 91*
Gaspar, Andrew 1948- *WhoE 91*
Gaspar, Anna Louise 1935- *WhoAmW 91*
Gaspar, George Jacob 1936- *St&PR 91*
Gaspar, Harry 1883-1940 *Ballpl 90*
Gaspar, Michele C. *ODwPR 91*
Gaspar, Peter Paul 1935- *WhoAm 90*
Gaspar, Pilo 1930- *Ballpl 90*
Gaspar-Guzman, Evangeline *BiDrAPA 89*
Gasparac, Philip John 1942- *St&PR 91, WhoAm 90*
Gasparetto, Ovidio 1928- *WhoWor 91*
Gaspari, Enzo *BioIn 16*
Gaspari, James A. 1956- *St&PR 91*
Gaspari, Joseph Donald 1953- *BiDrAPA 89*
Gaspari, Russell Arthur 1941- *WhoAm 90*
Gasparik, Frank 1938- *St&PR 91*
Gasparro, Frank 1909- *WhoAm 90, WhoAmA 91*
Gasparro, Madeline 1928- *WhoAmW 91*
Gasper, Jo Ann 1946- *WhoAm 90, WhoE 91*
Gasper, Ruth Eileen 1934- *WhoWor 91*
Gasper, William John 1950- *WhoE 91*
Gasperini, Elizabeth Carmela 1961- *WhoAmW 91*
Gasperini, Jim 1952- *BioIn 16*
Gasperoni, Ellen Jean Lias *WhoAmW 91, WhoSSW 91, WhoWor 91*
Gasperoni, Emil, Sr. 1926- *WhoSSW 91, WhoWor 91*
Gasque, Harrison 1958- *WhoSSW 91, WhoWor 91*
Gass, Clinton Burke 1920- *WhoAm 90*
Gass, David 1956- *WhoEmL 91*
Gass, Gertrude Zemon *WhoAmW 91*
Gass, Ian Graham 1926- *WhoWor 91*
Gass, Irene *AuBYP 90*
Gass, James *St&PR 91*
Gass, Judith Leah 1938- *St&PR 91*
Gass, Ken 1945- *OxCCanT*
Gass, Kurt E. 1957- *St&PR 91*
Gass, Manus M. 1928- *WhoAm 90*
Gass, Margery Stoops 1944- *WhoAmW 91*
Gass, Oscar J. *BioIn 16*
Gass, Paul S. 1938- *St&PR 91*
Gass, Raymond William 1937- *St&PR 91*
Gass, Robert *NewAgMG*
Gass, William H 1924- *ConAu 30NR, MajTwCW, WhoWrEP 89*
Gassel, Stuart P. *BioIn 16*
Gassen, Joseph Albert 1926- *WhoAm 90*
Gassendi, Pierre 1592-1655 *WorAlBi*
Gassenheimer, Eleanore *BioIn 16*
Gasser, Gary Lee 1950- *St&PR 91*
Gasser, Henry Martin 1909-1981 *WhoAmA 91N*
Gasser, Herbert S. 1888-1963 *WorAlBi*
Gasser, Randall William 1958- *WhoEmL 91*
Gasser, Robert Charles 1936- *St&PR 91, WhoAm 90*
Gasser, Thomas Peter 1933- *St&PR 91*
Gassere, Eugene Arthur 1930- *St&PR 91, WhoAm 90*
Gassert, Robert George 1921- *WhoAm 90*
Gasset, Jose Ortega y *ConAu 130, HispWr 90, MajTwCW*
Gasset, Jose Ortega y 1883-1955 *BioIn 16*
Gassler, Frank Henry 1951- *WhoWor 91*
Gassman, Jayne Dana 1957- *WhoWrEP 89*
Gassman, Paul George 1935- *WhoAm 90*
Gassman, Steven Jay 1962- *WhoWor 91*
Gassman, Victor A. 1935- *WhoE 91*
Gassman, Vittorio 1922- *ConTFT 8 [port], WhoWor 91*
Gassman, William G. 1926- *St&PR 91*
Gasste, Kerstin 1928- *WomArch [port]*
Gasstrom, Evald Herman 1912- *WhoE 91*
Gast, Carolyn Bartlett 1929- *WhoAmA 91*
Gast, Dwight V *WhoAmA 91*
Gast, Dwight V. 1951- *WhoE 91*
Gast, Jerome F. *ODwPR 91*
Gast, Michael Carl 1930- *WhoAmA 91*
Gast, Randall Todd 1961- *WhoAm 90, WhoEmL 91*
Gast, Richard Shaeffer 1956- *WhoEmL 91*
Gastall, Tommy 1932-1956 *Ballpl 90*
Gastambide, Daniel 1942- *WhoWor 91*
Gastel, Barbara Jean 1952- *WhoEmL 91*
Gaster, Harri Kay 1944- *WhoSSW 91*
Gaster, Orville Raymond, Jr. 1942- *WhoSSW 91*
Gasteyer, Carlin Evans 1917- *WhoAmW 91*
Gasteyer, Susan 1940- *BiDrAPA 89*
Gastfriend, David Robert 1954- *BiDrAPA 89, WhoE 91*
Gastil, Russell Gordon 1928- *WhoAm 90*
Gastineau, Clifford Felix 1920- *WhoAm 90*
Gastineau, Erin *BioIn 16*
Gastineau, Lisa *BioIn 16*
Gastineau, Mark *BioIn 16*
Gastler, Harold L. 1927- *St&PR 91*
Gastman, Theodore R. 1929- *St&PR 91*
Gaston, Cito *BioIn 16*
Gaston, Cito 1944- *WhoAm 90, WhoE 91*
Gaston, Clarence 1944- *Ballpl 90*
Gaston, Don F. *WhoAm 90, WhoE 91*
Gaston, Edwin Willmer, Jr. 1925- *WhoSSW 91, WhoWrEP 89*
Gaston, Gerald Nicholas 1932- *WhoAm 90*
Gaston, Hartley Russell 1938- *St&PR 91*
Gaston, Henry A. 1823- *AmLegL*
Gaston, Hugh Philip 1910- *WhoWor 91*
Gaston, John Oliver *BiDrAPA 89*
Gaston, Judith Ann 1950- *WhoAmW 91*
Gaston, Milt 1896- *Ballpl 90*
Gaston, Patrick David 1951- *WhoEmL 91*
Gaston, Peter F *BiDrAPA 89*
Gaston, Rebecca Lee 1952- *WhoAmW 91*
Gaston, W.W. 1926- *St&PR 91*
Gaston, Wendall Frank 1953- *WhoEmL 91*
Gaston, Wilbur B. 1924- *St&PR 91*
Gaston, William P. 1950- *St&PR 91*
Gaston, William W. 1926- *WhoAm 90, WhoSSW 91*
Gastwirth, Donald Edward 1944- *WhoE 91*
Gastwirth, Glenn Barry 1946- *WhoE 91*
Gastwirth, Joseph Lewis *WhoAm 90*
Gaswick, Carolyn Jean 1042- *WhoAmW 91*
Gaswirth, Ronald M. 1944- *WhoAm 90*
Gat, Azar 1959- *WhoWor 91*
Gat, Dimitri V 1936- *ConAu 31NR*
Gatch, Lee 1909-1968 *WhoAmA 91N*
Gatch, Milton McCormick, Jr. 1932- *WhoAm 90*
Gatchell, Seth Cole 1926- *St&PR 91*
Gate, Carl Oscar Simon *PenDiDA 89*
Gatell, Angelina 1926- *EncCoWW*
Gately, Arthur Thomas, Jr. 1927- *St&PR 91*
Gately, Frederick 1909-1988 *BioIn 16*
Gately, George 1928- *EncACom, WhoAm 90*
Gately, John C. 1923- *St&PR 91*
Gately, John J. 1947- *St&PR 91*
Gately, Robert Francis 1947- *WhoE 91*
Gatenby, Arthur Whitley 1933- *St&PR 91*
Gatens, John A. 1947- *WhoWor 91*
Gates, Anthony C. 1948- *St&PR 91*
Gates, Arthur Roland, II 1941- *St&PR 91*
Gates, Barbara Ann 1941- *WhoAmW 91*

Gates, Barbara Lynn 1954- *WhoAmW 91*
Gates, Brenda Lee 1958- *WhoAmW 91*
Gates, Charles Bradford 1921- *St&PR 91*
Gates, Charles Cassius 1921- *St&PR 91, WhoAm 90*
Gates, Charles R. 1948- *St&PR 91*
Gates, Chester Robert 1925- *St&PR 91*
Gates, Christopher C *BiDrAPA 89*
Gates, Crawford Marion 1921- *IntWWM 90, WhoAm 90*
Gates, Dale Merritt 1954- *WhoSSW 91*
Gates, Darryl Paul 1950- *WhoEmL 91*
Gates, Dillard Herbert 1925- *WhoAm 90*
Gates, Donald Dean 1930- *St&PR 91*
Gates, Donna *ODwPR 91*
Gates, Donna M. 1953- *WhoSSW 91*
Gates, Doris 1901- *AuBYP 90, BioIn 16*
Gates, Dorothy Louise 1926- *WhoAmW 91*
Gates, Earl J. 1918- *St&PR 91*
Gates, Edward Vernon *BioIn 16*
Gates, Elizabeth *BiDEWW*
Gates, Elmer D. 1929- *WhoAm 90, WhoE 91*
Gates, George *BioIn 16*
Gates, George Hamlin, Jr. 1936- *St&PR 91*
Gates, Gordon Doyle 1934- *WhoSSW 91*
Gates, Harry Irving 1934- *WhoAm 90, WhoAmA 91*
Gates, Henry Louis *BioIn 16*
Gates, Henry Louis, Jr. *NewYTBS 90 [port]*
Gates, Henry Louis, Jr. 1950- *WhoAm 90, WhoE 91, WhoWor 91*
Gates, Horatio 1728-1806 *EncCRAm, WorAlBi*
Gates, James Converse 1952- *WhoEmL 91*
Gates, James David 1927- *WhoAm 90*
Gates, James K., II 1944- *St&PR 91*
Gates, James Lloyd, Jr. 1957- *WhoEmL 91*
Gates, Jane Carol 1948- *WhoEmL 91*
Gates, Jay Rodney 1945- *WhoAmA 91*
Gates, Jerrol A. 1941- *St&PR 91*
Gates, John Charles 1948- *WhoEmL 91*
Gates, Jonathan Leland 1938- *St&PR 91*
Gates, Joycelyn 1936- *WhoAmW 91*
Gates, L. Patricia 1941- *WhoAmW 91*
Gates, Larry 1915- *WhoAm 90*
Gates, Leslie Clifford 1918- *WhoAm 90*
Gates, Louis W. *BioIn 16*
Gates, Madi 1938- *WhoAmW 91*
Gates, Mahlon Eugene 1919- *WhoAm 90*
Gates, Marilyn Taylor 1942- *WhoAmW 91*
Gates, Marshall DeMotte, Jr. 1915- *WhoAm 90*
Gates, Martina Marie 1957- *WhoAmW 91, WhoEmL 91*
Gates, Mary D. 1926- *WhoAmW 91*
Gates, Milo S. 1923- *St&PR 91*
Gates, Milo Sedgwick 1923- *WhoAm 90*
Gates, N. H. 1814-1889 *AmLegL*
Gates, Nancy Gotter 1931- *WhoWrEP 89*
Gates, Nathan H. 1910-1988 *BioIn 16*
Gates, Philip Don 1937- *WhoAm 90*
Gates, Phillip H *BiDrAPA 89*
Gates, Phyllis 1941- *ODwPR 91*
Gates, Reginald D. 1942- *WhoWrEP 89*
Gates, Richard Daniel 1942- *St&PR 91, WhoAm 90*
Gates, Robert M. *BioIn 16*
Gates, Rosemary Landow 1949- *WhoEmL 91*
Gates, Roy L. 1928- *St&PR 91*
Gates, Sheree Hunt 1958- *WhoSSW 91*
Gates, Signe Sandra 1949- *WhoAmW 91, WhoEmL 91*
Gates, Steven Leon 1954- *WhoSSW 91*
Gates, Susa 1856-1933 *FemiCLE*
Gates, Theodore Ross 1918- *WhoAm 90*
Gates, Theresa Ann 1959- *WhoAmW 91*
Gates, Thomas *EncCRAm*
Gates, Thomas Edward 1953- *WhoEmL 91*
Gates, Thomas J. 1950- *WhoEmL 91*
Gates, Thomas Paul 1941- *WhoAmA 91*
Gates, Thomas Sovereign, Jr. 1906- *BiDrUSE 89*
Gates, Timothy Joseph 1951- *St&PR 91*
Gates, Tood Jacob 1956- *BiDrAPA 89*
Gates, Walter B. 1931- *St&PR 91*
Gates, Walter Edward 1946- *St&PR 91, WhoAm 90*
Gates, William Allman, III 1949- *WhoEmL 91*
Gates, William Carl 1940- *St&PR 91*
Gates, William F. 1922- *St&PR 91*
Gates, William H. *BioIn 16*
Gates, William Henry 1955- *WhoAm 90*
Gates, William Henry, III 1955- *ConAmBL*
Gates, William S. 1944- *St&PR 91*
Gates-Cohen, Lisa 1955- *WhoAmW 91*
Gates-Spears, Lorene Cynthia 1952- *WhoAmW 91*
Gatesy, Carolyne Ilona 1950- *St&PR 91*
Gatewood, Aubrey 1938- *Ballpl 90*
Gatewood, Buford Echols 1913- *WhoAm 90*
Gatewood, D.M. 1948- *St&PR 91*
Gatewood, Diane Ridley 1951- *WhoEmL 91*
Gatewood, Lawrence E. 1945- *St&PR 91*
Gatewood, Leonard B. 1947- *St&PR 91, WhoAm 90*
Gatewood, Lottie *ODwPR 91*
Gatewood, Maud 1934- *WhoAmA 91*
Gatewood, Robert Payne 1923- *WhoWor 91*
Gatewood, Willard Badgett, Jr. 1931- *WhoAm 90*
Gath, Norman Clayton 1938- *St&PR 91*
Gath, Philip C. 1947- *St&PR 91*
Gathany, Van R. 1926- *WhoAm 90*
Gathard, Mary Paula 1939- *WhoAmW 91*
Gathercole, Patricia May 1920- *WhoSSW 91*
Gathercole, Virginia Carol 1947- *WhoSSW 91*
Gatheridge, R. Edward *WhoWrEP 89*
Gathers, Hank *BioIn 16*
Gathers, Hank *NewYTBS 90 [port]*
Gathers, Hank 1967?-1990 *News 90, -90-3*
Gathers, Patricia Kathleen 1964- *WhoAmW 91*
Gatherum, Gordon Elwood 1923- *WhoAm 90*
Gati, Istvan 1948- *IntWWM 90*
Gati, Norman Nandor 1924- *St&PR 91*
Gati, William Eugene *WhoE 91, WhoWor 91*
Gaticales, Maria Celia *BiDrAPA 89*
Gatinella, Wayne T. 1952- *St&PR 91*
Gatipon, Betty Becker 1931- *WhoAmW 91*
Gatje, Robert Frederick 1927- *WhoAm 90*
Gatland, Geoffrey H. *St&PR 91*
Gatlin, Eugene, Jr. 1935- *WhoSSW 91, WhoWor 91*
Gatlin, Larry Wayne 1948- *WhoAm 90*
Gatlin, Michael Gerard 1956- *WhoE 91, WhoEmL 91, WhoWor 91*
Gatlin, Richard Lamar 1953- *WhoSSW 91*
Gatling, Eva Ingersoll 1912- *WhoAmA 91*
Gatling, Richard J. 1818-1903 *WorAlBi*
Gatmaitan, Andres G. 1940- *WhoWor 91*
Gatner, Elliott S. M. 1914-1990 *BioIn 16*
Gatos, Harry Constantine 1921- *WhoAm 90*
Gatos, Nicolaos 1918- *WhoWor 91*
Gatrad, Abdul Rashid 1946- *WhoWor 91*
Gatrall, Jeffrey 1948- *WhoEmL 91*
Gatrell, Joselle Bernstein 1942- *WhoAmW 91*
Gatrell, Marion Thompson 1909- *WhoAmA 91N*
Gatrell, Robert Morris 1906-1982 *WhoAmA 91N*
Gatsch, Ted Stephen 1949- *WhoEmL 91, WhoSSW 91*
Gatschet, Timothy Paul *BiDrAPA 89*
Gatsik, Ronald Lee *BiDrAPA 89*
Gatski, Robert L 1919- *BiDrAPA 89*
Gatski, Robert Lawrence 1919- *WhoAm 90*
Gattas, Fred Patrick 1914- *St&PR 91*
Gattas, James Wood 1950- *St&PR 91*
Gattaz, Wagner Farid 1951- *WhoWor 91*
Gattegno, Caleb 1911-1988 *BioIn 16*
Gatter, Jeffery E. 1957- *St&PR 91*
Gatti, Attilio 1896- *AuBYP 90*
Gatti, Ellen *AuBYP 90*
Gatti, Frank R. 1947- *St&PR 91*
Gatti, Gabriele *WhoWor 91*
Gatti, Rosa M. 1950- *ODwPR 91*
Gattis, Jerry D. 1948- *St&PR 91*
Gattis, Samuel Mallette 1863-1931 *AmLegL*
Gattis, Sarah Brewer 1925- *WhoSSW 91*
Gatto, Barbara Anne 1949- *WhoEmL 91*
Gatto, Dominick J. 1947- *St&PR 91*
Gatto, Janice 1960- *WhoEmL 91*
Gatto, Louis Constantine 1927- *WhoAm 90*
Gatto, Rose Marie 1931- *WhoAmA 91*
Gatto, Victor Joseph 1893?-1965 *BioIn 16, MusmAFA*
Gatton, Danny *BioIn 16*
Gatty, Margaret 1809-1873 *BioIn 16, FemiCLE*
Gatus, Leandro Gulapa *BiDrAPA 89*
Gatwood, Elden 1926- *IntWWM 90*
Gatzek, Deborah R. 1948- *St&PR 91*
Gatzoyiannis, Eleni *BioIn 16*
Gaub, Margaret Luise *WhoAmW 91*
Gaubatz, Lynn Marie 1956- *WhoAmW 91*
Gaubert, Lloyd Francis 1921- *WhoSSW 91*
Gaubert, Philippe 1879-1941 *PenDiMP*
Gaubert, Rene Jean-Marie 1901- *BioIn 16*
Gaubert, Ronald Joseph 1946- *WhoEmL 91*
Gaubert, Thomas Merrill 1939- *St&PR 91*
Gaubis, Anthony *BioIn 16*
Gauch, Eugene William, Jr. 1922- *WhoAm 90*
Gauch, Patricia Lee 1934- *AuBYP 90, WhoWrEP 89*
Gaucher, Gerald Gaston 1944- *St&PR 91*
Gaucher, Yves 1934- *WhoAmA 91*
Gaudard, Pierre 1927- *WhoAmA 91*
Gaudeamus Quartet *PenDiMP*
Gaudens, Augustus Saint- 1848-1907 *BioIn 16*
Gauderer, Ernst Christian 1945- *BiDrAPA 89*
Gaudet, Belinda 1951- *St&PR 91*
Gaudet, Len *BioIn 16*
Gaudet, Lyne *BiDrAPA 89*
Gaudet, Venard J. *BioIn 16*
Gaudette, Henri Eugene 1932- *WhoAm 90*
Gaudi, Antoni 1852-1926 *BioIn 16*
Gaudi y Cornet, Antoni 1852-1926 *PenDiDA 89*
Gaudiani, Claire Lynn 1944- *WhoAm 90, WhoAmW 91*
Gaudier-Brzeska, Henri 1891-1915 *BioIn 16*
Gaudieri, Alexander V. J. 1940- *WhoAm 90*
Gaudieri, Alexander V J 1940- *WhoAmA 91*
Gaudieri, Alexander V. J. 1940- *WhoE 91, WhoWor 91*
Gaudieri, Millicent Hall 1941- *WhoAmW 91, WhoE 91, WhoEmL 91*
Gaudin, Dean R. 1933- *St&PR 91*
Gaudin, Marguerite 1909- *WhoAmA 91*
Gaudin, Nicolas Vincent 1959- *WhoWor 91*
Gaudino, Mario 1918- *WhoWor 91*
Gaudio, Maxine Diane 1939- *WhoAmW 91*
Gaudion, Donald Alfred 1913- *WhoAm 90*
Gaudlitz, William Arthur 1932- *St&PR 91*
Gaudreau, Antoine-Robert 1682?-1746 *PenDiDA 89*
Gaudreaux, Antoine-Robert 1682?-1746 *PenDiDA 89*
Gaudriot, Michele 1955- *BiDWomA*
Gaudry, Roger 1913- *WhoAm 90*
Gauen, Patrick Emil 1950- *WhoAm 90*
Gauer, Charlotte Edwina 1912- *WhoAm 90*
Gauerke, Mary *BioIn 16*
Gauff, Susan Tyrrell *ODwPR 91*
Gauff, Susan Tyrrell 1946- *WhoEmL 91*
Gaufridi, Louis *EncO&P 3*
Gauger, Charles H. 1944- *St&PR 91*
Gauger, John Hardy 1937- *WhoE 91*
Gauger, Joseph Frederick 1926- *St&PR 91*
Gauger, Michele Roberta 1949- *WhoAmW 91*
Gaugert, Richard K. *BioIn 16*
Gaugh, Harry F *WhoAmA 91*
Gaughan, Eugene Francis 1945- *WhoE 91, WhoWor 91*
Gaughan, Jack 1949- *WhoEmL 91*
Gaughan, Joanne Frances 1961- *WhoAmW 91*
Gaughan, Norbert F. 1921- *WhoAm 90*
Gaughan, Thomas Joseph *BiDrAPA 89*
Gaughan, Vincent Michael 1919- *WhoE 91*
Gaugler, Richard L. 1925- *St&PR 91*
Gauguin, Paul 1848-1903 *BioIn 16, IntDcAA 90, PenDiDA 89, WorAlBi*
Gauhar, Aruna 1940- *BiDrAPA 89*
Gauhar, Humayun Altaf 1949- *WhoWor 91*
Gauk, Alexander 1893-1963 *PenDiMP*
Gaul, Albro T. *AuBYP 90*
Gaul, Audrey Florine *WhoE 91*
Gaul, George B. 1916- *St&PR 91*
Gaul, George Brubaker 1916- *WhoAm 90*
Gaul, Kathleen Theresa 1960- *WhoAmW 91*
Gaul, Malinda Ann 1958- *WhoEmL 91*
Gaul, Randy 1959- *SmATA 63*
Gaul, Robert W. 1930- *St&PR 91*
Gauld, Alan *EncO&P 3*
Gauld, Alan 1932- *EncPaPR 91*
Gauldin, Diane Motley 1959- *WhoAmW 91*
Gauldin, Robert L. 1931- *IntWWM 90*
Gaulding, Jon Carlton 1953- *WhoSSW 91*
Gaulin, J. Guy 1927- *St&PR 91*
Gaulin, Jean *BioIn 16*
Gaulin, Jean 1942- *St&PR 91*
Gaulke, Mary Florence 1923- *WhoAmW 91*
Gaulke, Ramon George 1934- *WhoAm 90*
Gaull, Gerald Edward 1930- *WhoAm 90, WhoWor 91*
Gaulle, Charles Andre Marie Joseph de 1890-1970 *BiDFrPL*
Gaulle, Charles de 1890-1970 *BioIn 16*
Gaulli, Giovanni Battista 1639?-1709 *IntDcAA 90*
Gault, Alma Elizabeth 1891-1981 *BioIn 16*
Gault, Henri 1929- *ConAu 130*
Gault, Henry Jay 1945- *BiDrAPA 89*
Gault, Howard Harding 1917- *WhoSSW 91*
Gault, John Clifton 1945- *WhoWor 91*
Gault, John Franklin 1936- *St&PR 91, WhoAm 90*
Gault, N. L., Jr. 1920- *WhoAm 90*
Gault, Robert Kruger, Jr. 1944- *WhoAm 90*
Gault, Seth R. 1935- *WhoWrEP 89*
Gault, Stanley C. *BioIn 16*
Gault, Stanley C. 1926- *St&PR 91*
Gault, Stanley Carleton 1926- *WhoAm 90*
Gault, William Barry *BiDrAPA 89*
Gault, William Campbell 1910- *AuBYP 90, TwCCr&M 91*
Gault, Willie 1960- *News 91-2 [port]*
Gault, Willis M. 1908- *BioIn 16*
Gaultier, Denis 1600?-1672 *PenDiMP*
Gaultier, Ennemond 1575-1651 *PenDiMP*
Gaultier, Jean-Paul *BioIn 16*
Gaultier, Jean-Paul 1952- *ConDes 90*
Gaultney, John Orton 1915- *WhoAm 90*
Gaumer, Gary L. *St&PR 91*
Gaumond, George Raymond 1946- *WhoSSW 91*
Gaunaurd, Guillermo C. 1940- *WhoAm 90*
Gaunt, Elizabeth *BiDEWW, BioIn 16, FemiCLE*
Gaunt, Graham *TwCCr&M 91*
Gaunt, Mary 1861-1942 *FemiCLE*
Gauntlett, David Allan 1954- *WhoEmL 91*
Gauntt, William Amor 1926- *St&PR 91*
Gaupp, Andrew Christopher 1954- *WhoEmL 91, WhoSSW 91*
Gauquelin, Michel 1928- *ConAu 31NR, EncO&P 3*
Gauron, Eugene F. 1935- *WhoAm 90*
Gauron, Nicolas-Francois *PenDiDA 89*
Gaus, Michele Belinda 1964- *WhoEmL 91*
Gaus, Robert Eric 1966- *WhoE 91*
Gaus, William Thomas 1928- *St&PR 91*
Gauselman, Opal L. M. 1946- *WhoAmW 91*
Gausman, Edith Marie 1919- *WhoAm 90*
Gauss, Carl Friedrich 1777-1855 *BioIn 16*
Gauss, Clarence Edward 1887-1960 *BioIn 16*
Gauss, Karl Friedrich 1777-1855 *WorAlBi*
Gaussen, Robert Peter 1951- *WhoWor 91*
Gaustad, Edwin Scott 1923- *WhoAm 90, WhoWrEP 89*
Gaustad, John Eldon 1938- *WhoAm 90*
Gaut, C. Christopher 1956- *St&PR 91*
Gaut, Marvin Joseph 1911- *St&PR 91, WhoAm 90*
Gaut, Norman Eugene 1937- *St&PR 91, WhoAm 90*
Gautam, Shiv K. Sharma *BiDrAPA 89*
Gautam, Sunil Rashmikant 1954- *WhoWor 91*
Gauther, Agnes M. 1939- *St&PR 91*
Gauthier, Benoit *BiDrAPA 89*
Gauthier, Henry E. 1940- *St&PR 91*
Gauthier, Jean *EncO&P 3*
Gauthier, Joseph Delphis 1909- *WhoAm 90*
Gauthier, Joseph Stephen 1950- *WhoSSW 91*
Gauthier, Joseph W *BiDrAPA 89*
Gauthier, Marie-Angele 1828-1898 *DcCanB 12*
Gauthier, Russell John 1942- *St&PR 91*
Gauthier, Suzanne Anita 1948- *WhoAmA 91*
Gauthier, Victor Arthur, Jr. 1917- *WhoAm 90*
Gauthier, William P. 1929- *St&PR 91*
Gauthier, Yvan *BiDrAPA 89*
Gautier, Agnes M. 1939- *St&PR 91*
Gautier, Judith 1845?-1917 *EncCoWW*
Gautier, Norman Edward 1939- *St&PR 91*
Gautier, Theophile 1811-1872 *WorAlBi*
Gautney, George Ernest 1935- *St&PR 91*
Gautreau, Doc 1904-1970 *Ballpl 90*
Gautreaux, Marcelian Francis, Jr. 1930- *WhoAm 90*
Gautreaux, Tim Martin 1947- *WhoWrEP 89*
Gautschi, Walter 1927- *WhoAm 90*
Gautschoux, Daniel-Georges 1944- *WhoWor 91*
Gauvenet, Andre Jean 1920- *WhoWor 91*
Gauvey, Ralph Edward, Jr. 1947- *WhoWrEP 89*
Gauvin, Alvin L. 1947- *St&PR 91*
Gauvin, Claude E 1939- *WhoAmA 91*
Gauvreau, Claude 1925-1971 *OxCCanT*
Gauvreau, Emile Henry 1891-1956 *BioIn 16*
Gauvreau, Norman Paul 1948- *WhoE 91*
Gauvreau, Paul Richard 1939- *St&PR 91*
Gauvreau, Robert George 1948- *WhoAmA 91*
Gauvry, Isabelle *ODwPR 91*
Gava, Antonio 1930- *WhoWor 91*
Gavac, Donna Broderick 1926- *WhoWrEP 89*
Gavalas, Alexander Beary 1945- *WhoAmA 91, WhoE 91, WhoEmL 91, WhoWor 91*
Gavalas, George R. 1936- *WhoAm 90*
Gavali, Delsie B 1935- *BiDrAPA 89*
Gavalya, Alicia S *BiDrAPA 89*
Gavalya, Richard N 1931- *BiDrAPA 89*
Gavan, David Thomas *BiDrAPA 89*
Gavan, James Anderson 1916- *WhoAm 90*
Gavankar, Madhukar Laxman 1939- *WhoWor 91*

Gedge, Patrick 1949- *St&PR 91*
Gedge, Pauline 1945- *FemiCLE*
Gedin, Per 1928- *WhoWor 91*
Gedman, Rich 1959- *Ballpl 90*
Gedmin, Bruno Francis 1918- *St&PR 91*
Gedney, Richard 1948- *St&PR 91*
Gedney, William *BioIn 16*
Gedo, John E *BiDrAPA 89*
Gedraitis, John A. 1961- *St&PR 91*
Gedrick, Jason *BioIn 16*
Geduld, Emanuel E. 1943- *St&PR 91*
Geduld, Emanuel Edward 1943- *WhoAm 90*
Geduld, Irwin 1935- *St&PR 91*
Geduldig, Alfred 1936- *ODwPR 91*
Gee, Alvin Wong 1954- *WhoSSW 91*
Gee, Charles Daniel 1939- *WhoE 91*
Gee, Debbie Christine 1954- *BiDrAPA 89*
Gee, Elwood Gordon 1944- *WhoAm 90*
Gee, F. Denise 1965- *WhoWrEP 89*
Gee, George Duvall 1915- *WhoAm 90*
Gee, George L. Jr. 1922- *BiDrAPA 89*
Gee, Gregory Williams 1948- *WhoAm 90*
Gee, Harry Raglan 1924- *IntWWM 90*
Gee, Helen *WhoAmA 91*
Gee, Irene 1950- *WhoAmW 91*
Gee, James David 1934- *WhoAm 90*
Gee, Jean Marie *BioIn 16, NewYTBS 90*
Gee, Julie Beth 1962- *WhoEmL 91*
Gee, Karen S. 1962- *ODwPR 91*
Gee, Kenneth Allen 1933- *St&PR 91*
Gee, Li-Lan *WhoAmA 91*
Gee, Louis Stark 1922- *St&PR 91*
Gee, Maggie 1948- *ConAu 130, FemiCLE*
Gee, Maurine H. *AuBYP 90*
Gee, Nola Faye 1934- *WhoAmW 91, WhoSSW 91*
Gee, Norman D. 1930- *St&PR 91*
Gee, Robert E. 1925- *St&PR 91*
Gee, Robert LeRoy 1926- *WhoAm 90*
Gee, Robert Stark 1951- *St&PR 91*
Gee, Shirley 1932- *FemiCLE*
Gee, Thomas Gibbs 1925- *WhoAm 90, WhoSSW 91*
Gee, William R. 1940- *St&PR 91*
Gee, Yun 1906-1963 *WhoAmA 91N*
Geeding, Phillip Warren 1949- *WhoEmL 91*
Geehan, Robert William 1909- *WhoAm 90*
Geehl, Henry Ernest 1881-1961 *OxCPMus*
Geeker, Nicholas Peter 1944- *WhoAm 90*
Geekie, Thomas Anthony 1938- *St&PR 91*
Geelan, Peter Brian Kenneth 1929- *WhoWor 91*
Geen, Tim Dow 1944- *WhoSSW 91*
Geenans, Douglas Lee *BiDrAPA 89*
Geenen, William H. 1937- *St&PR 91*
Geentiens, Gaston Petrus, Jr. 1935- *WhoWor 91*
Geer, Abbot M. 1925- *ODwPR 91*
Geer, Emily Apt 1912- *WhoAmW 91*
Geer, Frances Pearl 1907- *WhoAmW 91*
Geer, Frank D 1923- *BiDrAPA 89*
Geer, Galen Lee 1949- *WhoWrEP 89*
Geer, Jack Charles 1927- *WhoAm 90*
Geer, James Hamilton 1924- *WhoAm 90*
Geer, James Hamilton, Jr. 1948- *WhoSSW 91*
Geer, James Henderson 1932- *WhoSSW 91*
Geer, John Farr 1930- *WhoAm 90*
Geer, John Mattison, Jr. 1945- *WhoSSW 91*
Geer, Johnny Glen 1938- *St&PR 91*
Geer, Roderick L. *BioIn 16*
Geer, Ronald Lamar 1926- *WhoAm 90*
Geer, Stephen DuBois 1930- *WhoAm 90*
Geer, Theodore Thurston 1851-1924 *AmLegL*
Geer, Thomas Lee 1951- *WhoEmL 91*
Geer, Timothy Andrew 1952- *WhoWor 91*
Geer, Will 1902-1978 *WorAlBi*
Geer, William Dudley 1922- *WhoAm 90*
Geerdes, James 1924- *WhoAm 90*
Geerdink, Henk F. 1944- *WhoWor 91*
Geerlings, Gerald Kenneth 1897- *WhoAm 90, WhoAmA 91*
Geerolf, Olivia *IntWWM 90*
Geers, Robert E. 1928- *St&PR 91*
Geers, Thomas Lange 1939- *WhoAm 90*
Geertgen tot Sint Jans 1455?-1495? *IntDcAA 90*
Geerts, Leo 1935- *WhoWor 91*
Geerts, Victor-Marcel Maria 1917- *WhoWor 91*
Geertsma, Robert Henry 1929- *WhoAm 90*
Geertz, Clifford *BioIn 16*
Geertz, Clifford 1926- *WorAu 1980 [port]*
Geertz, Clifford James 1926- *WhoAm 90*
Geertz, Hildred Storey 1927- *WhoAmW 91*
Geeseman, Deborah Beth 1953- *BiDrAPA 89*
Geeseman, Robert George 1944- *WhoE 91, WhoWor 91*
Geesey, Cynthia Jean 1954- *WhoAmW 91*
Geesey, Titus Cornelius 1893-1969 *WhoAmA 91N*
Geeslin, Campbell *BioIn 16*
Geeslin, Gene Smith 1927- *WhoSSW 91*
Geeslin, Lee Gaddis 1920- *WhoAmA 91*
Geeslin, Sara Chambers 1948- *WhoAmW 91, WhoEmL 91*
Geeson, Judy 1948- *ConTFT 8*
Geevarghese, Puthenpeedikayil Koshy 1933- *WhoSSW 91*
Geeze, Donald Stephan 1949- *BiDrAPA 89*
Gefen, Lisa J. 1960- *WhoEmL 91*
Gefert, Jerome T. 1954- *St&PR 91*
Geffen, Betty Ada 1911- *WhoAmW 91*
Geffen, David *BioIn 16*
Geffen, David 1943- *WhoAm 90*
Geffen, Frances Pearl 1919- *WhoAmW 91*
Geffen, Joel S. 1902-1988 *BioIn 16*
Geffen, Susan Rosenfield 1954- *IntWWM 90*
Geffen, Tobias *BioIn 16*
Geffert, Michael Andrew 1955- *St&PR 91*
Geffert, Paul H. 1945- *WhoE 91*
Geffken, Detlef 1943- *WhoWor 91*
Geffner, Donna Sue 1946- *WhoAmW 91*
Geffner, Nancy N. *St&PR 91*
Geffrard, Fabre Nicolas 1806-1879 *BioIn 16*
Gefke, Henry Jerome 1930- *WhoAm 90*
Gefors, Hans 1952- *IntWWM 90*
Gefrich, George Joseph, Jr. 1946- *WhoE 91*
Gefter, Judith Michelman *WhoAmA 91*
Gefter, William Irvin 1915- *WhoAm 90*
Gegenbach, Joseph *PenDiDA 89*
Gegenheimer, Harold W. 1910- *St&PR 91*
Geginat, Hartwig 1932- *WhoWor 91*
Gegios, Evan 1946- *WhoWor 91*
Geh, Cheng Hooi 1934- *WhoWor 91*
Geha, Alexander Salim 1936- *WhoAm 90*
Geha, Martha Sharon 1942- *WhoSSW 91*
Gehardt, Elena 1883-1961 *PenDiMP*
Gehl, Alice Elvira 1936- *WhoAmW 91*
Gehl, Danis Joyce 1952- *WhoEmL 91*
Gehl, Eugene Othmar 1923- *WhoAm 90*
Gehl, Gerald Andrew 1938- *BiDrAPA 89*
Gehl, Gerry Tolson 1955- *WhoEmL 91*
Gehl, John William 1941- *St&PR 91*
Gehl, Raymond H 1916- *BiDrAPA 89*
Gehl, Raymond Harold 1916- *WhoE 91*
Gehl, William D. 1946- *St&PR 91*
Gehlen, Joseph Peter 1955- *WhoEmL 91*
Gehlhoff, David A 1939- *BiDrAPA 89*
Gehling, John Adam 1920- *St&PR 91, WhoAm 90*
Gehling, Michael Paul 1962- *St&PR 91*
Gehlmann, Timothy Shawn 1960- *WhoWor 91*
Gehman, Christian 1948- *WhoWrEP 89*
Gehorsam, Elsbeth *BiDrAPA 89*
Gehorsam, Leon Albert 1924- *St&PR 91*
Gehr, James Benjamin 1930- *St&PR 91*
Gehr, Mary *WhoAm 90, WhoAmA 91*
Gehrels, Tom 1925- *BioIn 16*
Gehres, Ruth 1933- *WhoAmW 91*
Gehret, Joseph B. 1919- *St&PR 91*
Gehret, Thomas M. 1955- *St&PR 91*
Gehrig, Edward Harry 1925- *WhoAm 90*
Gehrig, Henry Louis 1903-1941 *BioIn 16*
Gehrig, Jule Lou 1935- *St&PR 91*
Gehrig, Leo Joseph 1918- *WhoAm 90*
Gehrig, Lou 1903-1941 *Ballpl 90 [port], BioIn 16, WorAlBi*
Gehring, David Austin 1930- *WhoE 91, WhoWor 91*
Gehring, Frederick William 1925- *WhoAm 90*
Gehring, John Gunter 1952- *WhoEmL 91*
Gehring, John V 1929- *BiDrAPA 89*
Gehring, Mary Ellen 1953- *WhoAmW 91, WhoEmL 91*
Gehring, Pamela Lauless 1950- *St&PR 91*
Gehring, Perry James 1936- *WhoAm 90*
Gehring, Richard Leo 1924- *WhoAm 90*
Gehring, Victor William 1961- *WhoEmL 91*
Gehringer, Charlie 1903- *Ballpl 90 [port]*
Gehringer, Michael Edward 1950- *WhoEmL 91*
Gehringer, Richard George 1949- *St&PR 91, WhoAm 90*
Gehrke, Allen Charles 1934- *WhoAm 90*
Gehrke, Charles William 1917- *WhoAm 90*
Gehrke, Fred C. 1935- *St&PR 91*
Gehrke, Karen Marie 1940- *WhoAmW 91*
Gehrt, Richard F. 1930- *St&PR 91*
Gehrt, Robert E. 1930- *ODwPR 91*
Gehry, Frank *BioIn 16*
Gehry, Frank O 1929- *WhoAmA 91*
Gehry, Frank Owen 1929- *WhoAm 90*
Gehrz, Robert Gustave 1915- *WhoAm 90*
Geib, Philip Oldham 1921- *WhoAm 90*
Geibel, Grace Ann 1937- *WhoAmW 91*
Geibel, Jeffrey Paul 1951- *WhoEmL 91*
Geiberger, Al *BioIn 16*
Geiduschek, Ernest Peter 1928- *WhoAm 90*
Geier, August F. 1929- *St&PR 91*
Geier, George 1918- *WhoAm 90*
Geier, James A.D. 1925- *St&PR 91*
Geier, James Aylward Develin 1925- *WhoAm 90*
Geier, Kathleen Ann 1956- *WhoAmW 91*
Geier, Mark Robin 1948- *WhoE 91*
Geier, Peter Jones 1951- *BiDrAPA 89*
Geier, Phil 1875-1967 *Ballpl 90*
Geier, Philip Henry, Jr. 1935- *St&PR 91, WhoAm 90*
Geier, Robert Morgan 1927- *St&PR 91*
Geigel, Kenneth Francis 1938- *WhoHisp 91*
Geigel Polanco, Vincente 1904-1979 *HispWr 90*
Geiger, Adam *NewAgMG*
Geiger, Alexander 1950- *WhoEmL 91*
Geiger, Brenda Houston *WhoAmW 91*
Geiger, Bryan Richard 1961- *WhoE 91*
Geiger, David H. *BioIn 16*
Geiger, Edith Lucile 1911- *IntWWM 90*
Geiger, Edith Rogers 1912- *WhoAmA 91*
Geiger, Edward R. 1942- *St&PR 91*
Geiger, Elizabeth De Chamisso *WhoAmA 91N*
Geiger, Erwin Paul 1930- *WhoSSW 91*
Geiger, Eugene Gregory 1949- *St&PR 91*
Geiger, Franklin C. 1928- *St&PR 91*
Geiger, Gary 1937- *Ballpl 90*
Geiger, Gene Edward 1928- *WhoAm 90*
Geiger, George Raymond 1903- *WhoAm 90*
Geiger, Hans 1920- *IntWWM 90*
Geiger, Hans Wilhelm 1882-1945 *WorAlBi*
Geiger, Helene R. 1950- *WhoWrEP 89*
Geiger, Henry *BioIn 16*
Geiger, James Norman 1932- *WhoSSW 91*
Geiger, John 1960- *ConAu 129*
Geiger, Joseph E. 1949- *St&PR 91*
Geiger, Karla Mary 1964- *WhoAmW 91*
Geiger, Kenneth C. 1954- *St&PR 91*
Geiger, Loren Dennis 1946- *IntWWM 90, WhoE 91, WhoEmL 91*
Geiger, Louis George 1913- *WhoAm 90, WhoWor 91*
Geiger, Lynn Ellen 1952- *WhoAmW 91*
Geiger, Mark Watson 1949- *WhoE 91*
Geiger, Mary E 1937- *BiDrAPA 89*
Geiger, Pat *BioIn 16*
Geiger, Peter Edward 1951- *St&PR 91*
Geiger, Phillip Neil 1956- *WhoAmA 91*
Geiger, Raymond A. 1910- *St&PR 91*
Geiger, Raymond Aloysius 1910- *WhoAm 90*
Geiger, Raymond James 1928- *St&PR 91*
Geiger, Richard Lawrence 1917- *WhoE 91*
Geiger, Robert Keith 1923- *WhoAm 90*
Geiger, Robert O. *BioIn 16*
Geiger, Ronald R. 1942- *St&PR 91*
Geiger, Ruth 1923- *IntWWM 90*
Geiger, Sharon Kay 1945- *WhoAmW 91*
Geiger, Teresa Marie 1964- *WhoAmW 91*
Geiger, Victor Alan 1948- *St&PR 91, WhoAm 90*
Geiger, Viva Ann 1964- *WhoAmW 91*
Geiger, William David 1950- *WhoEmL 91*
Geiger, William Harold 1947- *WhoEmL 91*
Geigerman, Michael Philip 1952- *WhoEmL 91*
Geigert, Daniel P. 1937- *St&PR 91*
Geigle, David Scott 1948- *WhoE 91*
Geijer, Erik Gustaf 1783-1847 *DcScanL*
Geil, Karl James 1957- *WhoEmL 91*
Geil, Kenneth P 1949- *BiDrAPA 89*
Geil, Wilma Jean 1939- *IntWWM 90*
Geilfuss, John Crittenden 1914- *St&PR 91*
Geils, J., Band *EncPR&S 89*
Geiman, J. Robert 1931- *WhoAm 90*
Geiman, Rodney Thomas 1937- *St&PR 91*
Geimer, Lawrence Paul 1951- *WhoSSW 91*
Gein, Edward 1906-1984 *BioIn 16*
Geingob, Hage Gottfried 1941- *WhoWor 91*
Geiringer, Karl 1899-1989 *BioIn 16*
Geis, Bernard 1909- *WhoAm 90*
Geis, Darlene Stern *AuBYP 90*
Geis, David M. 1950- *St&PR 91*
Geis, Duane Virgil 1923- *WhoAm 90*
Geis, Gilbert Lawrence 1925- *WhoAm 90*
Geis, Heather Kaye *BiDrAPA 89*
Geis, Heinz-Gunter 1936- *WhoWor 91*
Geis, Jerome Arthur 1946- *WhoEmL 91*
Geis, Milton Arthur 1926- *WhoAmA 91*
Geis, Norman Winer 1925- *WhoAm 90*
Geise, Norman A. 1918- *St&PR 91*
Geisel, C. Meade, Jr. 1937- *St&PR 91*
Geisel, Cameron Meade, Jr. 1937- *WhoAm 90*
Geisel, Dave 1955- *Ballpl 90*
Geisel, Harold Walter 1947- *WhoAm 90, WhoWor 91*
Geisel, Harry 1888-1966 *Ballpl 90*
Geisel, Helen *AuBYP 90*
Geisel, Henry Jules 1947- *WhoEmL 91*
Geisel, Martin Simon 1941- *WhoAm 90*
Geisel, Richard James 1946- *St&PR 91*
Geisel, Samuel George 1944- *WhoSSW 91*
Geisel, Theodor Seuss 1904- *AuBYP 90, BioIn 16, ConAu 32NR, MajTwCW, WhoAm 90, WhoAmA 91, WorAlBi*
Geiselman, Debra Ann 1955- *WhoAmW 91*
Geiselman, Paula Jeanne 1944- *WhoAmW 91*
Geisendorfer, Esther Lillian 1927- *WhoAmW 91*
Geisendorfer, James Vernon 1929- *WhoWor 91*
Geisenheimer, Emile J. 1947- *St&PR 91*
Geisenheimer, Emile Juan 1947- *WhoE 91*
Geiser, David F. 1952- *St&PR 91*
Geiser, Elizabeth Able 1925- *WhoAm 90*
Geiser, Frank M *BiDrAPA 89*
Geiser, J.W. 1925- *St&PR 91*
Geiser, James 1949- *WhoEmL 91*
Geiser, Max 1926- *WhoWor 91*
Geiser, Michael Thomas *BiDrAPA 89*
Geisert, Arthur *BioIn 16*
Geisert, Arthur Frederick 1941- *WhoAmA 91*
Geisert, Wayne Frederick 1921- *WhoAm 90, WhoSSW 91*
Geishecker, John Andrew, Jr. 1937- *WhoE 91*
Geishecker, John Andrew, Jr. 1938- *St&PR 91*
Geisinger, Kurt Francis 1951- *WhoE 91*
Geisinger, Robert Nelson 1925- *WhoAm 90*
Geisler, Carol Joy 1948- *WhoAmW 91*
Geisler, David Herbruck 1937- *WhoSSW 91*
Geisler, Ernest Keith, Jr. 1931- *WhoAm 90*
Geisler, George James, Jr. 1952- *WhoSSW 91*
Geisler, Gerhard 1927- *WhoWor 91*
Geisler, Hans Emanuel 1935- *WhoAm 90, WhoWor 91*
Geisler, Harlynne 1950- *WhoAmW 91*
Geisler, Herbert George, Jr. 1949- *WhoEmL 91*
Geisler, John Douglas 1933- *BiDrAPA 89*
Geisler, Jonathan David 1949- *WhoE 91*
Geisler, Linda Whitehead 1953- *WhoAmW 91*
Geisler, Robert Bailey 1949- *WhoSSW 91*
Geisler, Rosemary P. 1947- *St&PR 91*
Geisler, Stephen H. 1955- *BiDrAPA 89*
Geismar, Maxwell 1909-1979 *ConAu 33NR*
Geismar, Richard L. 1927- *St&PR 91*
Geismar, Richard Lee 1927- *WhoAm 90*
Geismar, Thomas H. 1931- *WhoAm 90*
Geismar, Thomas H 1932- *ConDes 90*
Geismer, Alan Stearn 1917- *WhoAm 90*
Geismer, Alan Stearn, Jr. 1948- *WhoEmL 91*
Geiss, Albert Edward 1920- *St&PR 91*
Geiss, David Richard 1953- *WhoEmL 91, WhoWor 91*
Geiss, Jacqueline Suzanne *St&PR 91*
Geissbuhler, Arnold 1897- *WhoAmA 91*
Geissbuhler, Steff 1942- *ConDes 90*
Geissbuhler, Stephan 1942- *WhoAm 90*
Geisse, John H. 1892-1988 *BioIn 16*
Geisser, Seymour 1929- *WhoAm 90*
Geissert, Katy 1926- *WhoAmW 91*
Geissinger, Frederick W. 1945- *St&PR 91*
Geissinger, John Blank 1906- *WhoAm 90*
Geissinger, Ladnor Dale 1938- *WhoSSW 91*
Geissler, Elmer E. 1929- *St&PR 91*
Geissler, Heiner 1930- *WhoWor 91*
Geissler, Heinrich 1814-1879 *WorAlBi*
Geissler, Rainer 1939- *WhoWor 91*
Geissler, Ursula 1931- *WhoWor 91*
Geist *NewAgMG*
Geist, Carl William, Jr. 1938- *St&PR 91*
Geist, Edgar John, Jr. 1920- *BiDrAPA 89*
Geist, Harold 1916- *WhoWrEP 89*
Geist, Jack E 1922- *BiDrAPA 89*
Geist, Jacob Myer 1921- *WhoAm 90*
Geist, James E. 1929- *St&PR 91*
Geist, Jerry Douglas 1934- *St&PR 91, WhoAm 90*
Geist, Karin Ruth Tammeus McPhail 1938- *WhoAmW 91, WhoWor 91*
Geist, Lester 1920- *St&PR 91*
Geist, Maggie Ann 1939- *WhoWrEP 89*
Geist, Sidney 1914- *WhoAmA 91*
Geister, Janet M. 1885-1964 *BioIn 16*
Geistfeld, Ronald Elwood 1933- *WhoAm 90, WhoWor 91*
Geistinger, Marie 1828-1903 *PenDiMP*
Geistinger, Marie 1833-1903 *OxCPMus*
Geisweidt, Lorilee Barrick 1960- *WhoAmW 91*
Geitgey, Doris Arlene 1920- *WhoAm 90*
Geithner, Edgar E. *ODwPR 91*
Geithner, Paul H., Jr. 1930- *St&PR 91*
Geithner, Paul Herman, Jr. 1930- *WhoAm 90, WhoSSW 91*
Geiwitz, Cynthia Ann 1955- *WhoAmW 91*
Gejdenson, Sam 1948- *WhoAm 90, WhoE 91*
Gekas, George William 1930- *WhoAm 90, WhoE 91*
Gekas, Paula Yvonne 1966- *WhoAmW 91*

Gekiere, Madeleine WhoAmA 91, WhoE 91
Gekker, Sofia BiDrAPA 89
Gekosky, Edward 1952- WhoEmL 91
Gela, George 1950- WhoEmL 91
Gelardin, Edward S 1934- BiDrAPA 89
Gelardin, Jacques P. WhoE 91
Gelato, Marie Catherine 1947- WhoE 91
Gelatt, Charles Daniel 1918- WhoAm 90
Gelatt, James Prentice 1944- WhoE 91
Gelatt, Philip Madison 1950- St&PR 91
Gelatt, Timothy Arthur 1955- WhoEmL 91
Gelb, Alan Michael 1938- WhoAm 90
Gelb, Arthur 1924- DcLB 103 [port], WhoAm 90, WhoE 91, WhoWrEP 89
Gelb, Arthur 1937- WhoAm 90
Gelb, Barbara 1926- DcLB 103 [port]
Gelb, Bruce S. 1927- St&PR 91, WhoAm 90
Gelb, Fritzi Gina 1949- WhoEmL 91
Gelb, Harold Seymour 1920- WhoAm 90
Gelb, Jan 1906-1978 WhoAmA 91N
Gelb, Joseph Donald 1923- WhoE 91, WhoWor 91
Gelb, Judith Anne 1935- WhoAm 90, WhoAmW 91, WhoE 91
Gelb, Leslie Howard 1937- WhoAm 90
Gelb, Lester A 1920- BiDrAPA 89
Gelb, Lester Arnold 1920- WhoE 91
Gelb, Max 1907- BioIn 16
Gelb, Norman 1929- ConAu 30NR
Gelb, Richard L. 1924- St&PR 91
Gelb, Richard Lee 1924- WhoAm 90, WhoE 91, WhoWor 91
Gelb, Victor 1926- WhoAm 90
Gelb-Libert, Joy Z. 1931- WhoAmW 91
Gelbach, Martha Harvey 1913- WhoAmW 91
Gelbach, Myron S., Jr. 1921- St&PR 91
Gelbach, W.H., Jr. 1921- St&PR 91
Gelband, Henry 1936- WhoAm 90
Gelbard, Robert Sidney 1944- WhoAm 90, WhoWor 91
Gelbart, Abe 1911- WhoAm 90, WhoWor 91
Gelbart, Larry BioIn 16
Gelbart, Larry 1923- ConLC 61 [port]
Gelbart, Larry 1925- WhoAm 90
Gelber, Arthur 1915- WhoAm 90
Gelber, Don Jeffrey 1940- WhoAm 90
Gelber, Gabriel 1921- St&PR 91
Gelber, Gail 1952- St&PR 91
Gelber, Gary Stephen 1936- BiDrAPA 89
Gelber, Herman 1935- BiDrAPA 89
Gelber, Jack 1932- WhoAm 90, WhoWrEP 89
Gelber, Linda Cecile 1950- WhoEmL 91
Gelber, Lionel 1907-1989 ConAu 129
Gelber, Lionel M. 1907-1989 BioIn 16
Gelber, Mark Howard 1951- WhoWor 91
Gelber, Samuel 1929- WhoAmA 91, WhoE 91
Gelber Rinaldo, Suzanne 1945- WhoAmW 91
Gelberman, Joseph H. 1912- NewAgE 90
Gelbert, Charley 1906-1967 Ballpl 90
Gelbman, Frank BiDrAPA 89
Gelboin, Harry Victor 1929- WhoAm 90
Gelbtuch, Howard Clarke 1950- St&PR 91
Gelburd, Diane Elizabeth 1952- WhoEmL 91
Gelburd, Gail Enid 1954- WhoAmA 91, WhoE 91
Gelbwasser, Frank Joseph 1949- WhoE 91
Gelci, Gianna Maria 1957- WhoAmW 91
Gelda, Steven Edward BiDrAPA 89
Geldart, Donald James Wallace 1938- WhoAm 90
Gelder, John William 1933- WhoAm 90
Gelder, Maurice David BiDrAPA 89
Gelder, Nick Van 1914- St&PR 91
Geldermann Hails, Barbara WhoAmA 91
Gelders, Ludo 1943- WhoWor 91
Geldhof, Alex R. 1920- St&PR 91
Geldmacher, Robert Carl 1917- WhoAm 90
Geldof, Bob BioIn 16, EncPR&S 89
Geldof, Bob 1952- OxCPMus
Geldon, Fred Wolman 1946- WhoEmL 91, WhoSSW 91
Geldorf, Bob 1953?- WorAlBi
Geldsetzer, Lutz Heinrich-Heine 1937- WhoWor 91
Gelehrter, Ann Gorris 1949- WhoEmL 91
Gelehrter, Thomas David 1936- WhoAm 90
Gelelemend 1722?-1811 WhNaAH
Gelenberg, Alan Jay 1944- BiDrAPA 89
Gelenger, Lorrie Ann 1958- WhoAmW 91
Gelernter, George J 1923- BiDrAPA 89
Gelernter, Joel Eli BiDrAPA 89
Geley, Gustav 1868-1924 EncO&P 3
Geley, Gustave 1868-1924 EncPaPR 91
Gelfand, Francine L 1939- BiDrAPA 89
Gelfand, Ivan 1927- WhoAm 90
Gelfand, Janice L BiDrAPA 89
Gelfand, Lawrence Emerson 1926- WhoAm 90
Gelfand, M. David 1949- WhoAm 90
Gelfand, Marilyn AuBYP 90
Gelfand, Marshall M. 1927- WhoAm 90
Gelfand, Michael Joseph 1957- WhoEmL 91
Gelfand, Morris Arthur 1908- WhoAm 90
Gelfand, Neal 1944- St&PR 91, WhoAm 90
Gelfand, Ronald 1948- BiDrAPA 89
Gelfand, Steven 1948- BiDrAPA 89
Gelfand, Steven B. 1948- WhoE 91
Gelfman, Robert William 1932- WhoAm 90
Gelfond, Joyce Jean BiDrAPA 89
Gelfond, Lawrence Peter WhoAm 90
Gelfond, Stephen David BiDrAPA 89
Gelhard, Nan Kevin 1955- WhoE 91
Gelinas, Charles J. 1903- St&PR 91
Gelinas, Gratien 1909- OxCCanT, WhoAm 90, WhoWrEP 89
Gelinas, John Gerald 1929- WhoAm 90
Gelinas, Marc Adrien 1947- WhoSSW 91
Gelinas, Paul Joseph 1914- WhoSSW 91
Gelinas, Raymond Gerald 1946- St&PR 91
Gelinas, Robert William 1931- WhoAmA 91
Gelineau, Louis Edward 1928- WhoAm 90, WhoE 91
Geliot, Michael 1933- IntWWM 90
Gelke, Ann BiDrAPA 89
Gelke, Kurt David 1957- WhoE 91
Gelker, Peter Alan 1946- BiDrAPA 89
Gell, Frank AuBYP 90
Gell, Wendy 1948- WhoAmW 91
Gell-Mann, Murray 1929- WhoAm 90, WhoWor 91, WorAlBi
Gellar, Richard 1944- BiDrAPA 89
Gellas, Bonnie ODwPR 91
Gellatly, David WhoSSW 91
Gellatly, Michael WhoAmA 91
Geller, A. Neal 1943- WhoAm 90
Geller, Andrew Michael 1924- WhoE 91
Geller, Barbara G 1939- BiDrAPA 89
Geller, Barbara Johnson 1958- WhoAmW 91
Geller, Eric Mitchell 1949- St&PR 91
Geller, Esther 1921- WhoAm 90, WhoAmA 91
Geller, Harold Arthur 1954- WhoE 91
Geller, Ian Barry 1950- BiDrAPA 89
Geller, Janice Grace 1938- WhoAmW 91, WhoE 91
Geller, Jeffrey Lee 1948- BiDrAPA 89
Geller, Joseph J BiDrAPA 89
Geller, Joseph Jerome 1917- WhoE 91
Geller, Leonard 1938- St&PR 91
Geller, Linda Berger 1944- WhoAmW 91
Geller, Louis M 1922- BiDrAPA 89
Geller, Margaret Joan 1947- WhoAmW 91
Geller, Martin Paul 1938- BiDrAPA 89
Geller, Matthew 1954- WhoAmA 91
Geller, Max 1930- BiDrAPA 89
Geller, Max A. 1899-1988 BioIn 16
Geller, Nancy Lorch 1944- WhoAmW 91
Geller, Robert James 1937- WhoAm 90, WhoE 91, WhoWor 91
Geller, Robert James 1952- WhoWor 91
Geller, Ronald Gene 1943- WhoAm 90
Geller, Seymour 1921- WhoAm 90
Geller, Stephanie 1940- BiDrAPA 89
Geller, Steven Anthony 1958- WhoEmL 91
Geller, Uri 1946- EncO&P 3, EncPaPR 91
Gellerman, Bruce Edward 1950- WhoE 91
Gellerman, Jay Michael 1938- St&PR 91
Gellermann, Henry 1912- WhoAm 90
Gellerstedt, Lawrence Love, Jr. 1925- St&PR 91
Gellerstedt, Marie Ada 1926- WhoAmW 91, WhoWor 91
Gellert, Alexander George 1964- WhoE 91
Gellert, Christian Furchtegott 1715-1769 DcLB 97 [port]
Gellert, George G. 1938- St&PR 91
Gellert, George Geza 1938- WhoAm 90
Gellert, Hugo 1892-1985 EncAL
Gellert, Martin Frank 1929- WhoAm 90
Gellert, Michael E. 1931- St&PR 91
Gellert, Michael Erwin 1931- WhoAm 90, WhoE 91
Gellert, Vance F WhoAmA 91
Gelles, Gerald 1931- St&PR 91
Gelles, Harry 1934- WhoAm 90
Gelles, Richard J. 1946- WhoWrEP 89
Gelles, Richard James 1946- WhoAm 90, WhoE 91
Gellhorn, Alfred 1913- WhoAm 90
Gellhorn, Ernest Albert Eugene 1935- WhoAm 90
Gellhorn, Martha BioIn 16
Gellhorn, Martha 1908- ConLC 60 [port], FemiCLE
Gellhorn, Martha E. 1908- BioAmW
Gellhorn, Peter 1912- IntWWM 90
Gellhorn, Walter 1906- WhoAm 90
Gellis, Barrie Fabian 1950- WhoEmL 91, WhoWrEP 89
Gellis, Roberta L 1927- WhoWrEP 89
Gellis, Sandy L WhoAmA 91
Gellis, Sandy L. 1946- WhoE 91
Gellis, Scott 1955- St&PR 91
Gellis, Sydney Saul 1914- WhoAm 90
Gellise, Mary Yvonne 1934- WhoAm 90
Gellman, Gloria Gae Seeburger Schick 1947- WhoAmW 91, WhoEmL 91, WhoWor 91
Gellman, Jerome I. 1927- St&PR 91
Gellman, Steven D. 1947- IntWWM 90
Gellman, Yale H. 1934- WhoAm 90
Gelman, Bernard 1933- WhoE 91, WhoWor 91
Gelman, Bernard 1940- WhoE 91
Gelman, Charles 1920- BioIn 16
Gelman, Charles 1931- St&PR 91
Gelman, Charles D. ODwPR 91
Gelman, David Graham 1926- WhoAm 90
Gelman, Dian D. 1938- St&PR 91
Gelman, Elaine Edith 1927- WhoAmW 91
Gelman, Jan 1963- BioIn 16
Gelman, Jon Leonard 1946- WhoEmL 91
Gelman, Juan 1930- HispWr 90
Gelman, Larry 1930- WhoAm 90
Gelman, Milton 1914- WhoAmA 91
Gelman, Milton S. BioIn 16
Gelman, Milton S. 1920?-1990 ConAu 131
Gelman, Norman Ira 1929- WhoE 91
Gelman, Renee L 1924- BiDrAPA 89
Gelman, Rita Golden 1937- BioIn 16, WhoAmW 91
Gelman, Steve 1934- AuBYP 90
Gelman, Warren Jay 1932- WhoAm 90
Gelmis, Joseph Stephan 1935- WhoAm 90
Gelnar, John 1943- Ballpl 90
Gelo, Daniel Joseph 1957- WhoSSW 91
Gelormino, Joan Ann 1939- WhoAmW 91
Geloso, Rosalia Ann 1962- WhoE 91
Gelperin, Jules BiDrAPA 89
Gelpi, Albert Joseph 1931- WhoAm 90
Gelpi, Barbara Charlesworth 1933- WhoAm 90
Gelpi, Jose Angel 1933- BiDrAPA 89, WhoE 91
Gelsey, Erwin S BioIn 16
Gelsey, Stephen Ian 1925- WhoAm 90
Gelsinger, Linda Mae 1950- WhoAmW 91, WhoEmL 91
Gelson, John Francis 1931- St&PR 91
Gelsted, Otto 1888-1968 DcScanL
Gelsthorpe, Joseph Dean 1943- WhoSSW 91
Gelt, Andrew Lloyd 1951- IntWWM 90
Geltman, Lily 1903- WhoAmA 91
Geltner, Sharon Fannie 1958- WhoEmL 91
Geltzer, Howard E. 1936- ODwPR 91, WhoAm 90
Geltzer, Robert Lawrence 1945- WhoAm 90
Geltzer, Sheila Simon ODwPR 91
Geltzer, Sheila Simon 1940- WhoAm 90
Gelvin, L. Millard 1928- St&PR 91
Gelwan, Eliot Marc 1952- BiDrAPA 89
Gely, L.-J.-J. PenDiDA 89
Gelzer, Helen 1950- St&PR 91
Gemayel, Amin BioIn 16
Gemayel, Amin 1942- WhoWor 91
Gemayel, Bashir 1948-1982 BioIn 16
Gemayel, Pierre 1905-1984 PolLCME
Gemballa, Eleanor F. 1928- WhoAmW 91
Gemberling, Roy D. 1940- St&PR 91
Gemberling, Stephen BioIn 16
Gemeinhardt, Charlie Clairborne 1947- WhoSSW 91
Gemelli, Ralph Joseph BiDrAPA 89
Gemelli, Thomas James 1940- St&PR 91
Gemelli-Carroll, Marie 1948- WhoEmL 91
Gemello, John Michael 1946- WhoAm 90
Gemery, Henry Albert 1930- WhoAm 90
Gemignani, Gino John, Jr. 1942- St&PR 91
Gemignani, Michael Caesar 1938- WhoAm 90, WhoSSW 91
Gemke, Pieter N.M. 1926- St&PR 91
Gemma, Joseph Grimaldi 1925- St&PR 91
Gemma, Peter Benedict, Jr. 1950- WhoSSW 91
Gemma, Steven Marc BiDrAPA 89
Gemmei-tenno 662-723 WomWR
Gemmel, Terry 1932- WhoAmW 91
Gemmell, Edgar Mills NewYTBS 90
Gemmell, Joseph Paul 1935- St&PR 91, WhoAm 90
Gemmell, Robert James 1932- St&PR 91
Gemmer, H. Robert 1923- WhoSSW 91, WhoWor 91
Gemmett, Robert James 1936- WhoAm 90
Gemmill, Elizabeth H. 1945- St&PR 91
Gemmill, John Kenneth 1943- WhoE 91
Gemmill, Kenneth W. 1910- St&PR 91
Gemmill, Robert Andrew 1911- WhoAm 90
Gempel, John Collins, Jr. 1953- WhoEmL 91
Gemper, Bodo Berno 1936- WhoWor 91
Gempler, Gregory James 1951- WhoEmL 91
Gems, Pam 1925- BioIn 16, FemiCLE
Gemson, Bennett 1920-1988 BioIn 16
Gemunder, Joel F. 1939- St&PR 91
Gemunder, Joel Frank 1939- WhoAm 90
Gen, Martin 1926- WhoE 91, WhoWor 91
Gen, Sam 1945- St&PR 91
Genabith, Richard Carl 1946- WhoE 91
Genack, Abraham BiDrAPA 89
Genader, Ann Marie 1932- WhoWrEP 89
Genaidy, Hannelore E 1923- BiDrAPA 89
Genain, Marc P. WhoWor 91
Genant, Harry Kenneth 1942- WhoAm 90
Genaro, Joseph M. 1930- WhoHisp 91
Genaro, Lorayne Edylyne 1949- WhoSSW 91
Genato, Vincent Michael 1946- WhoEmL 91
Genatossio, Francis Joseph 1956- WhoE 91
Genauer, Emanuel 1939- St&PR 91
Genauer, Emily WhoAmA 91
Genauer, Martin Jay 1949- WhoEmL 91
Gencer, Leyla 1924- IntWWM 90, PenDiMP
Genco, Michael T BiDrAPA 89
Genco, Robert Joseph 1938- WhoAm 90
Genda, Ellen Van Wagner 1942- WhoAmW 91
Genda, Minoru 1904-1989 AnObit 1989, BioIn 16
Gendein, Alvan R 1935- BiDrAPA 89
Gendel, Edward 1913- BiDrAPA 89
Gendel, Michael Himan 1948- BiDrAPA 89
Gendell, Gerald Stanleigh 1929- WhoAm 90
Gendelman, Sheldon 1930- St&PR 91
Gendernalik, David Robert BiDrAPA 89
Gendleman, Jill Marsha 1950- WhoE 91
Gendre, Francis Pierre 1935- WhoWor 91
Gendreau, Michael C. 1949- St&PR 91
Gendreau, Raymond Eugene 1936- WhoE 91
Gendron, Edward Charles 1928- St&PR 91, WhoAm 90
Gendron, Joseph L 1936- BiDrAPA 89
Gendron, Maurice 1920- IntWWM 90, PenDiMP
Gendron, Maurice 1920-1990 NewYTBS 90
Gendron, Odore Joseph 1921- WhoAm 90, WhoE 91
Gendron, Serge 1951- St&PR 91
Gendron, Yvon St&PR 91
Gendzel, Ivan B 1931- BiDrAPA 89
Genee, Richard 1823-1895 OxCPMus
Genel, Myron 1936- WhoAm 90, WhoE 91, WhoWor 91
Gener, Jose M. WhoHisp 91
General, Kathryn Elaine 1954- WhoAmW 91
Generale, Robert 1952- St&PR 91
Generales, Constantine D J 1908-1988 BioIn 16
Generes, Edwin Gerard 1949- St&PR 91
Genereux, Ann Marie 1960- WhoEmL 91
Genereux, Marc Richard 1957- WhoEmL 91
Genereux, Robert James 1930- WhoAm 90
Generous, Eric Yves Jacques 1960- WhoE 91
Genes, James St&PR 91
Genes, Janice St&PR 91
Genesen, Barry 1942- St&PR 91
Genesen, Judith Miriam 1932- WhoAm 90
Genesen, Louis 1926- St&PR 91
Geneser, Joseph Daniel 1937- St&PR 91
Genesis ConMus 4 [port], EncPR&S 89, OxCPMus
Genesse, Bryan BioIn 16
Genest, Francois J. 1950- St&PR 91
Genest, Jacques 1919- St&PR 91, WhoAm 90
Genest, Michel NewAgMG
Genet 1892-1978 BioIn 16
Genet, Jean 1910- WrPh
Genet, Jean 1910-1986 BioIn 16, EuWr 13, MajTwCW, WorAlBi
Genetet, Bernard 1931- WhoWor 91
Genetski, Robert James 1942- St&PR 91, WhoAm 90
Genevie, Michael 1951- WhoEmL 91
Genevoix, Maurice 1890-1980 BioIn 16
Genewich, Joe 1897-1985 Ballpl 90
Geng, Edward Joseph 1931- WhoAm 90
Geng, Karl H. 1941- St&PR 91
Geng, Veronica 1941- AuBYP 90
Genge, William Harrison 1923- St&PR 91, WhoAm 90
Gengenbach, Marianne S. 1956- WhoEmL 91
Genger, Marshall Allen 1951- St&PR 91
Genghis Khan 1162-1227 BioIn 16, WorAlBi
Gengler, M. Jeanne 1912- WhoAm 90
Gengler, Patrick Lee 1948- St&PR 91
Gengor, Virginia Anderson 1927- WhoAmW 91, WhoWor 91
Genheimer, J. Edward 1929- St&PR 91
Genheimer, Steven J 1952- BiDrAPA 89
Genier, Robert Arthur 1941- St&PR 91
Geniesse, Robert John 1929- WhoAm 90

Genillard, Robert Louis 1929- *WhoWor 91*
Genin, Roland 1927- *St&PR 91*
Genini, Ronald Walter 1946- *WhoEmL 91*
Genius, Garnet Lebeau 1919- *St&PR 91*
Geniusz, Robert Myles 1948- *WhoAmA 91*
Genji Clan *EncJap*
Genkin, Barry Howard 1949- *WhoEmL 91*
Genkin, Jonathan 1957- *WhoAmA 91*
Genkins, Gabriel 1928- *WhoAm 90*
Genlis, Stephanie-Felicite 1746-1830 *FemiCLE*
Genlis, Stephanie Felicite, comtesse de 1746-1830 *BioIn 16*
Genn, Nancy *WhoAm 90, WhoAmA 91*
Gennadios, Bishop 1924- *WhoAm 90*
Gennadios, His Grace Bishop 1924- *WhoWor 91*
Gennari, Francesco *BioIn 16*
Gennaro, Joseph 1924- *BioIn 16*
Gennaro, Peter 1924- *WorAlBi*
Gennet, Peter Robert 1947- *St&PR 91*
Gennis, Sylvia L *BiDrAPA 89*
Gennrich, Robert Paul, II 1950- *WhoAm 90, WhoEmL 91*
Geno, Paul W. 1957- *WhoSSW 91*
Genova, Anthony Charles 1929- *WhoAm 90*
Genova, Joseph Steven 1952- *WhoEmL 91*
Genova, Paul Arthur 1954- *BiDrAPA 89*
Genovese, C. Eleanor 1920- *WhoAmW 91*
Genovese, Eugene Dominick 1930- *WhoAm 90*
Genovese, Francis Charles 1921- *WhoAm 90, WhoE 91*
Genovese, Frank A. 1951- *St&PR 91*
Genovese, Peter J. 1946- *WhoAm 90*
Genovese, Philip William 1917- *WhoE 91*
Genovese, Richard 1947- *WhoAmA 91*
Genovese, Samuel Anthony 1948- *St&PR 91*
Genovese, Thomas Leonardo 1936- *St&PR 91, WhoAm 90*
Genovesi, Robert P. 1928- *St&PR 91*
Genoways, Hugh Howard 1940- *WhoAm 90*
Genrich, Willard Adolph 1915- *WhoE 91, WhoWor 91*
Gens, Helen Diane 1934- *WhoAmW 91*
Gens, Jacob 1905-1943 *BioIn 16*
Gens, Ralph Samuel 1924- *WhoAm 90*
Gens, Richard Howard 1929- *WhoWor 91*
Genscher, Hans Dietrich *BioIn 16*
Genscher, Hans-Dietrich 1927- *WhoWor 91, WorAlBi*
Genser, Sander Gary 1943- *BiDrAPA 89*
Gensert, Richard Michael 1922- *WhoAm 90, WhoWor 91*
Genshaft, Neil 1943- *WhoAm 90*
Gensheimer, Elizabeth Lucille 1955- *WhoEmL 91, WhoSSW 91*
Gensho-tenno *WomWR*
Gensinger, Raymond Albert 1941- *St&PR 91*
Gensler, Fredrick *BiDrAPA 89*
Gensler, John Calvin 1936- *St&PR 91*
Gensler, M. Arthur, Jr. 1935- *WhoAm 90*
Gent, Alan Neville 1927- *WhoAm 90*
Gent, Donald H 1926- *BiDrAPA 89*
Gent, Donald Herbert 1926- *WhoE 91*
Genter, David L. 1934- *St&PR 91*
Genth, Dean Alan 1949- *WhoEmL 91*
Genthe, William Klug 1931- *St&PR 91*
Gentile da Fabriano 1385?-1427? *IntDcAA 90*
Gentile, Anthony 1920- *WhoWor 91*
Gentile, Arlene Rose 1939- *WhoAmW 91*
Gentile, Arthur Christopher 1926- *WhoAm 90*
Gentile, Carmen Louis 1940- *WhoE 91*
Gentile, Dominick Edward 1932- *WhoAm 90*
Gentile, Edward Michael 1952- *BiDrAPA 89*
Gentile, Fred J. 1929- *St&PR 91*
Gentile, George Michael 1936- *St&PR 91, WhoAm 90*
Gentile, Gina Anne 1963- *WhoAmW 91*
Gentile, Gloria Irene *WhoAmA 91*
Gentile, Gloria Irene 1929- *WhoAm 90*
Gentile, Jack Vito 1950- *WhoWor 91*
Gentile, Jim 1934- *Ballpl 90*
Gentile, John S 1956- *ConAu 132*
Gentile, Joseph F. 1934- *WhoAm 90*
Gentile, Mark Joseph 1956- *WhoEmL 91*
Gentile, Patricia Marie 1960- *BiDrAPA 89*
Gentile, Regina Dominica 1951- *WhoAmW 91*
Gentile, Robert Henry 1944- *St&PR 91*
Gentile, Sharon Ann 1953- *WhoAmW 91*
Gentile, Tony 1920- *St&PR 91*
Gentile-Lange, Michele S. 1949- *WhoEmL 91*
Gentilesca, Franco J. 1943- *IntWWM 90*
Gentileschi, Artemisia 1593-1652? *IntDcAA 90 [port]*
Gentileschi, Artemisia 1597-1651 *BioIn 16*
Gentileschi, Orazio 1563-1639? *IntDcAA 90*
Gentili, Antonio 1519-1609 *PenDiDA 89*
Gentilin, Karen Eileen 1963- *WhoAmW 91*
Gentilz, Theodore 1819-1906 *WhNaAH*
Gentine, Lawrence John 1946- *WhoAm 90*
Gentine, Lee M. 1952- *St&PR 91*
Gentine, Lee Michael 1952- *WhoAm 90, WhoEmL 91*
Gentine, Louis P. 1947- *St&PR 91, WhoAm 90*
Gentle, Alfred Fernandez, Jr. 1953- *WhoSSW 91*
Gentle, Kenneth William 1940- *WhoAm 90*
Gentle, Mary 1956- *BioIn 16*
Gentle, Zana Alexander 1950- *WhoSSW 91*
Gentleman, Julia B. 1931- *WhoAmW 91*
Gentner, Russell Douglas 1954- *St&PR 91*
Gentry, Augustus, Jr 1927- *WhoAmA 91*
Gentry, Belynda 1952- *WhoAmW 91*
Gentry, Bern Leon, Sr. 1941- *WhoAm 90*
Gentry, Bobbie 1944- *OxCPMus*
Gentry, Carolyn Adele 1952- *WhoAmW 91*
Gentry, Cynthia Sue 1930- *WhoAmW 91*
Gentry, David Truett 1927- *St&PR 91*
Gentry, Gary 1946- *Ballpl 90*
Gentry, Grant C. 1924- *St&PR 91*
Gentry, Gregg Thornton 1957- *WhoSSW 91*
Gentry, Harold Wayne 1951- *WhoSSW 91*
Gentry, Helen 1897-1988 *BioIn 16*
Gentry, Herbert 1919- *WhoAmA 91*
Gentry, Hubert, Jr. 1931- *St&PR 91, WhoAm 90*
Gentry, Hugh E. *WhoSSW 91*
Gentry, Hugh E. 1929- *St&PR 91*
Gentry, James O'Conor 1926- *St&PR 91*
Gentry, Joanne Hester 1934- *WhoAmW 91*
Gentry, John N 1930-1989 *BioIn 16*
Gentry, Kevin Wayne 1952- *WhoEmL 91*
Gentry, Martha Imogen 1926- *WhoAmW 91*
Gentry, Minnie 1915- *DrBlPA 90*
Gentry, Patricia Webb 1947- *WhoAmW 91*
Gentry, Richard Ellsworth 1944- *St&PR 91*
Gentry, Robert Cecil 1916- *WhoAm 90, WhoSSW 91*
Gentry, Robert H, Jr. 1925- *BiDrAPA 89*
Gentry, Robert Vance 1933- *WhoAm 90*
Gentry, Rufe 1918- *Ballpl 90*
Gentry, Teddy *BioIn 16, WhoAm 90*
Gentry, Thomas H *BioIn 16*
Gentry, Warren Miller 1921- *WhoAmA 91*
Gentry, William C., Jr. 1935- *WhoSSW 91*
Gentry, William Norton 1908- *WhoSSW 91, WhoWor 91*
Gentsch, Henry W. 1904- *St&PR 91*
Genty, Richard Daniel 1926- *St&PR 91*
Gentz, William Howard 1918- *WhoWrEP 89*
Genung, Norman Bernard 1951- *WhoEmL 91*
Genyk, Ruth Bel 1955- *WhoAmW 91, WhoEmL 91*
Genz, Helen Doris 1944- *WhoAmW 91*
Genzabella, John Carmelo 1938- *St&PR 91*
Genzer, Stephen Bruce 1952- *WhoEmL 91*
Genzmer, Harold 1909- *IntWWM 90*
Geo-Karis, Adeline Jay 1918- *WhoAmW 91*
Geoffrey, Iqbal 1939- *WhoAm 90*
Geoffrion, Christophe-Alphonse 1843-1899 *DcCanB 12*
Geoffrion, Donald Robert 1936- *WhoSSW 91*
Geoffrion, Felix 1832-1894 *DcCanB 12*
Geoffroy, Charles Henry 1926- *WhoAm 90*
Geoffroy, Kevin Edward 1932- *WhoAm 90*
Geoffroy, Lloyd E., Sr. *St&PR 91N*
Geoga, Douglas Gerard 1955- *WhoEmL 91*
Geoghan, Joseph Edward 1937- *St&PR 91*
Geoghegan, Edward Joseph 1940- *St&PR 91*
Geoghegan, John Joseph 1917- *WhoAm 90*
Geoghegan, John W. 1945- *St&PR 91*
Geoghegan, Michel Henry 1937- *WhoE 91*
Geoghegan, Patricia 1947- *WhoEmL 91*
Geoghegan, Robert W, Jr. 1945- *BiDrAPA 89*
Geoghegan, Thomas *BioIn 16*
Geoghegan, William J. 1921- *St&PR 91*
Geoppinger, James Carl 1940- *WhoWor 91*
Geores, Ronald Joseph 1939- *WhoE 91*
Georgakas, Dan 1938- *WhoWrEP 89*
Georganas, Nicolas D. 1943- *WhoAm 90*
Georgantas, Aristides William 1943- *WhoAm 90*
Georgantas, Aristides William 1944- *St&PR 91*
Georgantzas, Nicholas Constantine 1958- *WhoEmL 91*
Georgas, John William 1928- *WhoAm 90, WhoSSW 91*
George, Duke of Kent 1902-1942 *BioIn 16*
George IV, King of Great Britain 1762-1830 *BioIn 16*
George V, King of Great Britain 1865-1936 *BioIn 16*
George VI, King of Great Britain 1895-1952 *BioIn 16*
George, Alan *PenDiMP*
George, Alan Norman 1949- *IntWWM 90*
George, Albert Richard 1938- *WhoAm 90*
George, Alex D., Jr. 1946- *St&PR 91*
George, Alexander Andrew 1938- *WhoWor 91*
George, Alexander Lawrence 1920- *WhoAm 90*
George, Alice Rose 1944- *WhoAm 90*
George, Ann Schipani *WhoEmL 91*
George, Anselm *BiDrAPA 89*
George, Barbara 1942- *WhoWrEP 89*
George, Barbara Ann 1932- *WhoAmW 91*
George, Barry Brian 1945- *WhoEmL 91*
George, Beauford James, Jr. 1925- *WhoAm 90*
George, Beth 1946- *WhoWrEP 89*
George, Carolyn Burke 1953- *WhoEmL 91*
George, Charles William 1914- *WhoAm 90*
George, Claude Swanson, Jr. 1920- *WhoAm 90*
George, Claudia K. 1949- *WhoAmW 91*
George, David A. 1942- *St&PR 91*
George, David Alan 1942- *WhoAm 90, WhoWor 91*
George, David C. 1921- *St&PR 91*
George, David Theodore *BiDrAPA 89*
George, David Webster 1922- *WhoAm 90*
George, Deveral D. 1939- *WhoAm 90*
George, Diane Elizabeth 1952- *WhoAmW 91*
George, Donald I 1921- *BiDrAPA 89*
George, E. T. *AmLegL*
George, Earl 1924- *IntWWM 90, WhoAm 90*
George, Edie 1940- *WhoAmW 91*
George, Edward H. 1955- *St&PR 91*
George, Edward Metcalf 1936- *St&PR 91*
George, Edwin Ordell 1905- *WhoAm 90*
George, Elizabeth 1949- *TwCCr&M 91*
George, Elizabeth Ann 1948- *WhoAmW 91*
George, Elwanda 1933- *WhoAmW 91*
George, Emery Edward 1933- *WhoAm 90*
George, Ernest Thornton, III 1950- *WhoEmL 91*
George, George Warren 1920- *WhoE 91*
George, Gerald William 1938- *WhoAm 90, WhoE 91*
George, Gwyneth *IntWWM 90*
George, Henry 1839-1897 *BioIn 16, WorAlBi*
George, Henry Hamilton 1934- *WhoE 91*
George, Jacob *BiDrAPA 89*
George, James A. 1932- *St&PR 91*
George, James Edward 1943- *WhoSSW 91*
George, James Henry Bryn 1929- *St&PR 91*
George, Jawad F. *NewYTBS 90*
George, Jean *PenDiDA 89*
George, Jean 1919- *FemiCLE*
George, Jean Craighead 1919- *AuBYP 90, BioIn 16, WhoAm 90, WhoWrEP 89*
George, Joey Russell 1963- *WhoE 91*
George, John 1936- *ConAu 132*
George, John Anthony 1948- *WhoEmL 91*
George, John C. 1954- *St&PR 91*
George, John Lothar 1916- *AuBYP 90*
George, John Martin, Jr. 1947- *WhoEmL 91*
George, Larry Wayne 1954- *WhoEmL 91*
George, Leslie *BioIn 16*
George, Lila-Gene Plowe Kennedy 1918- *IntWWM 90*
George, Llewellyn 1876-1954 *EncO&P 3*
George, Lloyd D. 1930- *WhoAm 90*
George, Louis D. 1922- *St&PR 91*
George, Lynda Day 1946- *ConTFT 8*
George, Mark Stork 1958- *BiDrAPA 89*
George, Mary Alice 1938- *WhoHisp 91*
George, Mary Carolyn Hollers 1930- *WhoSSW 91*
George, Mary Shannon 1916- *WhoAmW 91*
George, Maureen Rose 1951- *WhoEmL 91*
George, Melvin Douglas 1936- *WhoAm 90*
George, Merton Baron Tisdale 1920- *WhoAm 90*
George, Michael *IntWWM 90*
George, Michael J. 1947- *St&PR 91*
George, Myron Don 1931- *BiDrAPA 89*
George, N J *BiDrAPA 89*
George, Nathan *DrBlPA 90*
George, Nelson *BioIn 16*
George, Nicholas *WhoAm 90*
George, Nicholas 1952- *WhoEmL 91*
George, Norman *BioIn 16*
George, Norman 1946- *WhoWor 91*
George, Orlando John, Jr. 1945- *WhoAm 90*
George, Patrice Freeburger 1948- *WhoEmL 91*
George, Paula Louise 1952- *WhoAmW 91*
George, Pauline Horvath 1943- *WhoE 91*
George, Peter James 1941- *WhoAm 90*
George, Peter T. 1929- *WhoAm 90*
George, Phyllis *BioIn 16*
George, R. Warren, II 1947- *St&PR 91*
George, Rachel *BiDrAPA 89*
George, Raymond Ellis 1933- *WhoAmA 91*
George, Raymond Eugene, Jr. 1930- *WhoAm 90*
George, Reeba E. *BiDrAPA 89*
George, Richard Allan 1935- *WhoAmA 91*
George, Richard E., Jr. 1939- *St&PR 91*
George, Richard Lee 1950- *St&PR 91*
George, Richard Neill 1933- *WhoAm 90*
George, Robert A 1945- *BiDrAPA 89*
George, Robert D. 1942- *St&PR 91*
George, Robert Peter 1955- *WhoEmL 91*
George, Ronald Baylis 1932- *WhoAm 90*
George, Ross *St&PR 91*
George, Shirley H. 1938- *WhoAmW 91*
George, Stefan 1868-1935 *WorAlBi*
George, Stephan Anthony 1946- *WhoWor 91*
George, Stephen Michael 1945- *WhoE 91*
George, Steven Craig 1952- *WhoSSW 91*
George, Sue Ann 1948- *WhoSSW 91*
George, Susan 1934- *WhoWor 91*
George, Sylvia James 1921- *WhoAmA 91*
George, Thomas 1918- *WhoAm 90, WhoAmA 91*
George, Thomas Frederick 1947- *WhoAm 90*
George, Timothy Merrill 1960- *WhoE 91*
George, W.H. Krome 1918- *St&PR 91*
George, W. Peyton 1936- *WhoAm 90*
George, Walter Eugene, Jr. 1922- *WhoAm 90*
George, William Arthur 1910- *WhoAm 90*
George, William Brooks 1911- *St&PR 91*
George, William D. 1932- *St&PR 91*
George, William Douglas, Jr. 1932- *WhoAm 90*
George, William Francis 1927- *St&PR 91*
George, William Ickes 1931- *WhoAm 90*
George, William Leo, Jr. 1938- *WhoAm 90*
George, William Wallace 1942- *St&PR 91, WhoAm 90*
George, Yvonne C. 1945- *WhoSSW 91*
George-Alston, Myra Jewel 1962- *WhoSSW 91*
George-Brown, Baron 1914-1985 *DcNaB 1981*
George-Perry, Sharon Juanita 1938- *WhoAmW 91*
Georgeff, Edward Stephen 1927- *St&PR 91*
Georgehead, Christopher William 1912- *St&PR 91*
Georgehead, Christopher William 1942- *St&PR 91*
Georgel, Pierre 1943- *WhoWor 91*
Georgelas, Anthony J. 1953- *WhoE 91*
Georgelas, Anthony John 1953- *St&PR 91*
Georges, D. V. *AuBYP 90*
Georges, Georges Martin *ConAu 129, MajTwCW*
Georges, Jacques *PenDiMP*
Georges, John A. 1931- *St&PR 91, WhoAm 90, WhoE 91*
Georges, Paul G 1923- *WhoAmA 91*
Georges, Paul Gordon 1923- *WhoAm 90*
Georges, Peter John 1940- *WhoWor 91*
Georges, Richard Paul 1953- *WhoEmL 91*
Georgescu, Dan Corneliu 1938- *IntWWM 90*
Georgescu, Peter A. 1939- *St&PR 91*
Georgescu, Peter Andrew 1939- *WhoAm 90*
Georgescu, Vlad *BioIn 16*
Georgeson, Peter I. 1925- *St&PR 91*
Georghiou, Michael 1932- *WhoE 91*
Georghiou, Solon 1939- *WhoSSW 91*
Georgi, Rudolf 1943- *WhoWor 91*
Georgi, Walter 1925- *St&PR 91*
Georgia, Edward Henry, Jr. 1932- *BiDrAPA 89*
Georgiade, Nicholas George 1918- *WhoAm 90*
Georgiades, William Deen Hartog 1925- *WhoAm 90*
Georgiades, William Den Hartog 1925- *WhoSSW 91, WhoWor 91*
Georgiadesova, Johanka *EncCoWW*
Georgiadis, John *PenDiMP*
Georgian, Karine *BioIn 16, PenDiMP*
Georgiev, Dimiter Petrov 1947- *WhoWor 91*
Georgin, Michel Hubert 1947- *WhoWor 91*
Georgine, Robert *BioIn 16*
Georgine, Robert Anthony 1932- *WhoAm 90, WhoE 91*
Georgiou, Dimitrios C *BiDrAPA 89*
Georgiou, John Chrysostom 1946- *WhoWor 91*
Georgitis, John 1950- *WhoSSW 91*
Georgius, John R. 1944- *WhoAm 90*
Georgopapadakou, Nafsika Helen 1950- *WhoAmW 91*
Georgopoulos, Maria 1949- *WhoAmW 91, WhoE 91, WhoEmL 91*
Georgopulo, Panos *BioIn 16*

Georgotas, Anastasios 1946- BiDrAPA 89
Georgoulis, Stratton J. 1932- St&PR 91
Gephardt, Donald Louis 1937- IntWWM 90, WhoE 91
Gephardt, Jane BioIn 16
Gephardt, Richard A BioIn 16
Gephardt, Richard A. 1941- WorAlBi
Gephardt, Richard Andrew 1941- NewYTBS 90 [port], WhoAm 90
Gephardt, Thomas Steuber 1927- WhoAm 90
Gephardt, William Ellery, Jr. 1929- St&PR 91
Gepner, Abraham 1872-1943 BioIn 16
Gepner, Marsha Kay 1947- WhoAmW 91
Geppert, Kathryn Ann 1953- WhoAmW 91
Geppert, William A., Jr. 1923- St&PR 91
Gerace, Mary Alicia 1952- WhoWor 91
Gerace, Mary Kathryn 1958- WhoSSW 91
Gerace, Susan Terese 1950- WhoAmW 91
Geraci, Antonina Marie 1967- WhoAmW 91
Geraci, Carolyn 1960- WhoEmL 91
Geraci, Charles Frank 1967- WhoEmL 91
Geraci, Diane 1952- WhoAmW 91
Geraci, Lucian Arthur 1923- WhoAmA 91
Geraci, Michael Raleigh 1937- WhoE 91
Geraci, Philip Charles, Jr. 1929- WhoE 91
Geracioti, Thomas Dino, Jr. 1957- WhoE 91
Gerad, R. Peter 1937- St&PR 91
Geraghty, James Anthony 1947- WhoEmL 91
Geraghty, Kenneth George 1950- WhoAm 90
Geraghty, Margaret Karl 1947- WhoAmW 91
Gerald, Carolyn 1943- WhoWrEP 89
Gerald, Jeffrey Paul 1952- WhoEmL 91
Gerald, John Bart 1940- WhoWrEP 89
Gerald, Louis G. 1919- St&PR 91
Gerald, Michael Charles 1939- WhoAm 90
Gerald, Rex Ervin 1928- WhoAm 90
Geraldine, Queen 1916- BioIn 16
Geraldo 1904-1974 OxCPMus
Geraldson, Raymond I. 1911- WhoAm 90
Gerall, Arnold Abraham WhoAm 90
Geran, Joseph, Jr 1945- WhoAmA 91
Geran, Leonora Ann 1939- WhoAmW 91
Gerard, David E BioIn 16
Gerard, David E. 1945- WhoE 91
Gerard, Donald L 1923- BiDrAPA 89
Gerard, Dorothea 1855-1915 FemiCLE
Gerard, Emanuel 1932- St&PR 91, WhoAm 90
Gerard, Emily 1849-1905 FemiCLE
Gerard, Gary L. 1946- ODwPR 91
Gerard, Gil BioIn 16
Gerard, Hubert Edouard E.G. 1937- WhoWor 91
Gerard, James Watson 1867-1951 BioIn 16
Gerard, James Wilson 1935- WhoAm 90
Gerard, Jean Broward Shevlin 1938- WhoAm 90, WhoAmW 91, WhoWor 91
Gerard, Jules Bernard 1929- WhoAm 90
Gerard, Michel Marie 1934- WhoWor 91
Gerard, Paula 1907- WhoAmA 91
Gerard, Robert A BioIn 16
Gerard, Ronald Lynn 1950- IntWWM 90
Gerard, Roy Dupuy 1931- St&PR 91
Gerard, Roy Joseph 1924- WhoAm 90
Gerard, Stephen Stanley 1936- WhoWor 91
Gerard, Thomas Anthony 1948- WhoSSW 91
Gerard, Thomas H. 1928- St&PR 91
Gerard, Valrie Ann 1948- WhoAmW 91
Gerard, W. Gene 1932- WhoAm 90
Gerard, Whitney Ian 1934- WhoAm 90
Gerard-Sharp, Monica Fleur 1951- WhoAmW 91
Gerardi, Maryrose Acerra 1959- WhoAmW 91
Gerardia, Helen WhoAmA 91N
Gerardino, William Ernest 1933- WhoWrEP 89
Geras, Adele Daphne 1944- WhoWor 91
Geraschenko, Igor BioIn 16
Gerash, Helen P BiDrAPA 89
Gerasimides, Dionysios Nikolaos 1959- WhoWor 91
Gerasimov, Gennadi 1930- ConAu 32NR
Gerasimov, Irina 1937- BiDrAPA 89
Gerassi, John 1931- AuBYP 90
Gerathy, E. Carroll 1915- WhoAm 90
Geraty, Ronald D 1946- BiDrAPA 89
Gerault-Richard 1860-1911 BiDFrPL
Gerba, Charles Peter 1945- WhoEmL 91, WhoWor 91
Gerbarg, Darcy 1949- WhoAmA 91
Gerbarg, Patricia Lynn 1950- BiDrAPA 89
Gerbel, John Anthony 1931- St&PR 91
Gerber, Abraham 1925- WhoWor 91
Gerber, Albert B. 1913- WhoAm 90
Gerber, Alexander 1911-1988 BioIn 16
Gerber, Barbara Ann Witter 1934- WhoAm 90
Gerber, Barry Eldon 1942- WhoWor 91
Gerber, Bernard M 1947- BiDrAPA 89
Gerber, Carl Joseph 1934- BiDrAPA 89
Gerber, Charles A. 1942- St&PR 91
Gerber, Charles J., Jr. 1935- St&PR 91
Gerber, Charles Waas 1961- WhoE 91
Gerber, Dahlia Katz 1933- WhoAmW 91
Gerber, Daniel F 1898-1974 BioIn 16, WorAlBi
Gerber, Daniel Frank 1940- WhoWrEP 89
Gerber, Donald Stuart 1949- WhoE 91
Gerber, Dorothy Scott BioIn 16
Gerber, Douglas Earl 1933- WhoAm 90, WhoWrEP 89
Gerber, Eugene J. 1931- WhoAm 90
Gerber, Frank 1873-1952 WorAlBi
Gerber, Gaylon Edward 1963- WhoEmL 91
Gerber, Gwendolyn Loretta WhoAmW 91
Gerber, Harold Bruce 1925- St&PR 91
Gerber, Heinz Joseph 1924- St&PR 91, WhoAm 90
Gerber, Howard 1957- WhoEmL 91
Gerber, Isadore E 1903-1988 BioIn 16
Gerber, James L. 1928- St&PR 91
Gerber, Jayna BiDrAPA 89
Gerber, Joel 1940- WhoAm 90
Gerber, John Christian 1908- WhoAm 90, WhoWrEP 89
Gerber, John Jay 1914- WhoAm 90
Gerber, John P BiDrAPA 89
Gerber, John W. 1911- St&PR 91
Gerber, Joseph Newton 1910- WhoAm 90
Gerber, Linda Maxine 1953- WhoAmW 91
Gerber, Louis Emil 1930- WhoAm 90
Gerber, Lucille D. 1952- WhoAmW 91
Gerber, Merrill Joan 1938- SmATA 64
Gerber, Michael BioIn 16
Gerber, Michael H. 1944- St&PR 91
Gerber, Murray A. WhoAm 90
Gerber, Murray A. 1935- St&PR 91
Gerber, Randall Eric 1947- WhoEmL 91
Gerber, Robert Aluc 1927- St&PR 91
Gerber, Robert Evan 1947- WhoE 91
Gerber, Robert Mark 1957- BiDrAPA 89
Gerber, Robert Russell 1951- WhoAm 90
Gerber, Roger A. 1939- St&PR 91
Gerber, Roger Alan 1939- WhoAm 90
Gerber, Roman J. 1932- St&PR 91
Gerber, Ronald N. 1943- St&PR 91
Gerber, Sanford Edwin 1933- WhoAm 90
Gerber, Seymour 1920- WhoAm 90
Gerber, Stanley 1941- WhoE 91
Gerber, Steven Roy 1948- IntWWM 90
Gerber, Thomas William 1921- WhoAm 90
Gerber, Wally 1891-1951 Ballpl 90
Gerber, William 1908- WhoAm 90
Gerber, William Kenton 1954- St&PR 91, WhoAm 90, WhoEmL 91
Gerberding, Joan Elizabeth 1949- WhoAmW 91
Gerberding, Miles Carston 1930- WhoAm 90
Gerberding, William Passavant 1929- WhoAm 90, WhoWor 91
Gerberg, Judith Levine 1940- WhoAmW 91
Gerberg, Mort 1931- SmATA 64
Gerberich, Stephen J BioIn 16
Gerberich, William Warren 1935- WhoAm 90
Gerbie, Albert Bernard 1927- WhoAm 90
Gerbino, John 1941- WhoAm 90
Gerbner, George 1919- WhoAm 90
Gerbniono, Nicholas John 1966- WhoE 91
Gerbosi, William A. 1909- WhoAm 90
Gerbracht, Bob 1924- WhoAmA 91
Gerbracht, Richard Edwin 1932- WhoAm 90
Gerbracht, Terry Lynne 1955- WhoAmW 91
Gerchenson, Emile H. 1922- St&PR 91
Gerchick, Elias H 1915-1990 BioIn 16
Gerchick, Elias Herbert BiDrAPA 89
Gerchunoff, Alberto 1883-1950 HispWr 90
Gerckens, Laurence Conway 1934- WhoAm 90
Gerd, Steierwald 1929- WhoWor 91
Gerde, Carlyle Noyes 1946- WhoEmL 91
Gerdemann, James Wessel 1921- WhoAm 90
Gerdener, John Gerhard 1949- WhoEmL 91
Gerdes, Ingeborg 1938- WhoAmA 91
Gerdes, Larry Gene 1949- WhoAm 90
Gerdes, Michelle Ann 1961- WhoE 91
Gerdes, Neil Wayne 1943- WhoAm 90, WhoWor 91
Gerdes, Ralph Donald 1951- WhoEmL 91, WhoWor 91
Gerdes, Roberto Mauricio 1948- WhoE 91
Gerdes, Susan Taylor 1951- WhoWrEP 89
Gerdes, Thomas Robert 1948- St&PR 91
Gerdine, Leigh 1917- WhoAm 90
Gerding, Paul A. 1921- St&PR 91
Gerdis, Joyce Ellen BiDrAPA 89
Gerdis-Karp, Joyce Ellen 1961- WhoE 91
Gerdts, Abigail Booth 1937- WhoAmA 91
Gerdts, Elizabeth Kennedy 1950- WhoE 91
Gerdts, William H 1929- WhoAmA 91
Gere, James Monroe 1925- WhoAm 90
Gere, Richard 1949- WhoAm 90, WorAlBi
Gere, Terrence D. 1941- St&PR 91
Gereaue, Michael R. 1946- St&PR 91
Gereaux, Kathleen Margaret 1957- WhoAmW 91
Gereb, Daniel L. 1929- St&PR 91
Gerek, Terrence L. 1957- St&PR 91
Geremski, Terrence E. 1947- St&PR 91
Geremski, Terrence Eugene 1947- WhoEmL 91
Geren, Brenda L. 1950- WhoAmW 91
Geren, John Joseph BiDrAPA 89
Geren, Pete 1952- WhoAm 90, WhoSSW 91
Geren, Preston M 1952- BioIn 16
Geren, Preston Murdoch 1923- WhoAm 90
Gerencser, Michael Stephan 1955- WhoSSW 91
Gerend, John B. 1947- WhoEmL 91
Gerenday, Lacy Anthony De 1911- WhoAmA 91
Gerentz, Sven Thure 1921- WhoWor 91
Gerety, Doris W. St&PR 91
Gerety, Peter Leo 1912- WhoAm 90
Gerety, Tom 1946- WhoAm 90
Gerfen, Henry James 1940- WhoAm 90
Gerfin, Andrew Lotz, Jr. 1946- WhoSSW 91
Gergel, Randy Steven BiDrAPA 89
Gergelis, Richard Edward BiDrAPA 89
Gergely, Agnes 1933- EncCoWW
Gergely, Andrew Thomas 1959- BiDrAPA 89
Gergely, Arpad Jozsef 1938- WhoWrEP 89
Gergely, Tamas 1943- WhoWor 91
Gergely, Tibor 1900-1978 BioIn 16
Gergen, David Richmond 1942- WhoAm 90
Gergen, John Andrew 1932- BiDrAPA 89
Gerger, David Benjamin 1960- WhoEmL 91
Gergerian, Edmund L 1939- BiDrAPA 89
Gerges, Anwer Bernaba Attia 1926- WhoWor 91
Gergiev, Valery 1953- IntWWM 90
Gergis, Abdalla T. 1951- WhoE 91
Gergis, Samir Danial 1933- WhoAm 90
Gergo, Kathy BioIn 16
Gerhard, Anita Louise BiDrAPA 89
Gerhard, Earl Robert 1922- WhoAm 90
Gerhard, Edward NewAgMG
Gerhard, Harry E., Jr. 1925- WhoE 91, WhoWor 91
Gerhard, Herbert Fritz 1930- St&PR 91
Gerhard, J. Calvin 1938- WhoE 91
Gerhard, Lang Hallett 1945- WhoAm 90
Gerhard, Lee Clarence 1937- WhoAm 90
Gerhard, Roberto 1896-1970 PenDiMP A
Gerhardie, William 1895-1977 EncO&P 3
Gerhardstein, E. Michael 1923- St&PR 91
Gerhardstein, R P BiDrAPA 89
Gerhardt, Don John 1943- WhoSSW 91
Gerhardt, Glenn Rodney 1923- WhoSSW 91
Gerhardt, Greg Allen 1957- WhoEmL 91
Gerhardt, Ida G. M. 1905- EncCoWW
Gerhardt, Jon Stuart 1943- WhoAm 90
Gerhardt, Lillian Noreen 1932- WhoAm 90, WhoWrEP 89
Gerhardt, Philipp St&PR 91
Gerhardt, Philipp 1921- WhoAm 90
Gerhardt, Rosario Alejandrina 1953- WhoAmW 91
Gerhardt, Walter 1934- WhoWor 91
Gerhardts, Max Dieter 1932- WhoWor 91
Gerhardy, Louis P. 1934- St&PR 91
Gerhart, Ann 1955- St&PR 91
Gerhart, Dorothy Evelyn 1932- WhoAmW 91
Gerhart, Eugene Clifton 1912- St&PR 91, WhoAm 90
Gerhart, Glenna Lee 1954- WhoAmW 91, WhoEmL 91, WhoSSW 91
Gerhart, James Basil 1928- WhoAm 90
Gerhart, Ken 1961- Ballpl 90
Gerhart, Peter Milton 1945- WhoAm 90
Gerhart, Phil C. 1939- St&PR 91
Gerhart, Richard Stephen 1941- St&PR 91
Gerhart, Steven George 1948- WhoAm 90
Gerhart, Ursula Caroline 1927- WhoE 91
Gerhart, William Earle 1932- St&PR 91, WhoE 91
Gerheauser, Al 1917-1972 Ballpl 90
Gerhold, William Henry 1929- WhoAmA 91
Geri, Laurance Rudolph WhoE 91
Gericault, Theodore 1791-1824 IntDcAA 90, WorAlBi
Gericke, Otto L 1907- BiDrAPA 89
Gericke, Paul William 1924- WhoAm 90
Gerike, Ann Elizabeth 1933- WhoAmW 91
Gerike, Paul William 1956- WhoEmL 91
Gerima, Haile 1946- DrBlPA 90
Gerin, Winifred Eveleen 1901-1981 DcNaB 1981
Gerin-Lajoie, Antoine 1824-1882 DcLB 99 [port], OxCCanT [port]
Gerin-Lajoie, Guy 1928- WhoAmA 91
Gering, George S. 1932- St&PR 91
Gering, John P. 1953- St&PR 91
Gering, Joseph Michael 1958- WhoEmL 91
Gering, Travis Lee 1957- IntWWM 90
Gering, William J. 1945- St&PR 91
Geringas, David 1946- PenDiMP
Geringer, Edith Stateman BiDrAPA 89
Gerischer, Heinz 1919- WhoWor 91
Gerity, John E. 1955- WhoE 91
Gerjuoy, Edward 1918- WhoAm 90
Gerkan, Meinhard von WhoWor 91
Gerken, Henry J. 1940- St&PR 91
Gerken, Jeanne Lynn 1943- WhoAmW 91
Gerken, Roslyn Zuccarelli 1942- WhoE 91
Gerken, Walter Bland 1922- St&PR 91, WhoAm 90
Gerkin, Peter Ronald BiDrAPA 89
Gerking, Shelby Delos, Jr. 1918- WhoAm 90
Gerlach, Carol Danese 1955- WhoSSW 91
Gerlach, Christopher S 1952- WhoAmA 91
Gerlach, Clinton G. 1926- St&PR 91
Gerlach, Eckehart 1927- WhoWor 91
Gerlach, G. Donald 1933- WhoAm 90
Gerlach, Gary G. 1945- WhoAm 90, WhoSSW 91
Gerlach, Jeanne Elaine 1946- WhoAmW 91
Gerlach, John B. 1927- WhoAm 90
Gerlach, John J. 1902- St&PR 91
Gerlach, John Thomas 1932- St&PR 91
Gerlach, Klaus W. 1935- WhoWor 91
Gerlach, Lorenz F 1918- BiDrAPA 89
Gerlach, Luther Paul 1930- WhoAm 90
Gerlach, Manfred 1928- WhoWor 91
Gerlach, Otto B., III 1939- St&PR 91
Gerlach, Paul John 1933- St&PR 91
Gerlach, Richard D 1928- BiDrAPA 89
Gerlach, Richard G. 1934- St&PR 91
Gerlach, Robert A. 1927- St&PR 91
Gerlach, Robert Louis 1940- WhoAm 90
Gerlach, Roger Harold 1945- St&PR 91
Gerlach, Scott Borden 1948- St&PR 91
Gerlach, Sebastian Adam 1929- WhoWor 91
Gerlach, Thomas Bradfield 1926- St&PR 91
Gerle, Robert 1924- IntWWM 90
Gerler, William R. 1917- AuBYP 90, BioIn 16
Gerli, Karen Ann 1959- St&PR 91
Gerlich, Michael Anthony 1954- St&PR 91
Gerling, Paul J. 1947- St&PR 91
Gerling, Paul Joseph 1947- WhoEmL 91
Gerlits, Francis Joseph 1931- WhoAm 90
Gerlitz, Connie Marie 1943- St&PR 91, WhoAmW 91
Gerlitzki, Guenther Johannes 1924- WhoE 91
Gerlo, Ada EncCoWW
Gerloff, Hans 1887- EncO&P 3
Gerlough, Robert Tillman 1930- St&PR 91
Gerlt, Joseph Luther 1934- St&PR 91
Germain, Albert E. 1934- St&PR 91, WhoAm 90
Germain, Francois-Thomas 1726-1791 PenDiDA 89
Germain, Gerald 1942- St&PR 91, WhoAm 90
Germain, Jacques Pierre Bruny BiDrAPA 89
Germain, Jean-Claude 1939- OxCCanT [port]
Germain, Jeanette Eloise 1950- WhoWrEP 89
Germain, Louise BiDrAPA 89
Germain, Lucy D BioIn 16
Germain, Pierre 1645-1684 PenDiDA 89
Germain, Pierre, II 1720-1783 PenDiDA 89
Germain, Thomas 1673-1748 PenDiDA 89
Germain, Walter 1889-1962 EncO&P 3
Germain, William Leon 1940- St&PR 91
Germaine, George 1717-1785 EncCRAm
German, Bernard 1914- BiDrAPA 89, WhoE 91
German, Edward 1862-1936 OxCPMus, PenDiMP A
German, Edward Cecil 1921- WhoAm 90, WhoE 91, WhoWor 91
German, Jean Wesley 1931- WhoAmW 91
German, Joan W 1933- WhoWrEP 89
German, John George 1921- WhoAm 90
German, Katherine L. 1947- WhoAmW 91
German, Linda Lou BioIn 16
German, Michael BiDrAPA 89
German, Norman 1955- WhoWrEP 89
German, Ronald Stephen 1946- WhoAm 90, WhoSSW 91
German, Sandra Gwen 1954- WhoEmL 91
German, William 1919- WhoAm 90
Germane, Gayton Elwood 1920- WhoAm 90
Germani, Fernando 1906- PenDiMP
Germann, Albert George 1926- St&PR 91

Germann, Douglas Dean, Sr. 1946- WhoEmL 91
Germann, Richard Paul 1918- WhoAm 90
Germann-Audeoud, Helene-Lise 1937- WhoWor 91
Germano, Alan BiDrAPA 89
Germano, Martin C BioIn 16
Germano, Thomas 1963- WhoAmA 91
Germany, Daniel Monroe 1937- WhoAm 90
Germany, John Fredrick 1923- WhoAm 90
Germer, George Ernest 1868-1936 PenDiDA 89
Germer, Richard Eliason 1946- WhoAm 90
Germeshausen, Kenneth J. NewYTBS 90
Germeshausen, Kenneth J. 1907- St&PR 91
Germinario, John Anthony 1955- WhoEmL 91
Germine, Mark 1954- BiDrAPA 89
Germond, John Louis 1929- St&PR 91
Germonde EncCoWW
Germonio, Enrico-Alessandro 1944- WhoWor 91
Gerndt, Julie S 1957- BiDrAPA 89
Gerner, Raymond Edwin 1926- St&PR 91
Gerner, Robert Hugh 1946- BiDrAPA 89
Gernert, Dick 1928- Ballpl 90
Gernes, Sonia Grace 1942- WhoWrEP 89
Gernhardt, Henry Kendall 1932- WhoAmA 91
Gernhardt, Karen Kay 1949- WhoEmL 91
Gernon, George Owen, Jr. 1950- WhoSSW 91, WhoWor 91
Gernreich, Rudi 1922-1985 ConDes 90
Gernsback, Hugo 1884-1967 RGTwCSF
Gernsheim, Helmut Erich Robert 1913- WhoWor 91
Gerny, Harald 1946- WhoWor 91
Gero, Delmar Wade 1936- St&PR 91
Gero, James Farrington 1945- St&PR 91
Gerold, John Henry 1947- St&PR 91
Gerolimatos, Barbara 1950- WhoAmW 91, WhoE 91
Gerome MajTwCW
Gerome, Jean-Leon 1824-1904 BioIn 16, IntDcAA 90
Gerome, Nick Jerry 1944- St&PR 91
Geron, Ellen Hansman 1949- St&PR 91
Geronemus, Diann Fox 1947- WhoAmW 91
Geronimo 1825?-1909 WhNaAH [port]
Geronimo 1829-1909 BioIn 16, WorAlBi
Geronimo, Cesar 1948- Ballpl 90
Gerou, Emilie B BioIn 16
Gerould, Daniel C. 1928- ConAu 33NR
Gerould, Katharine 1879-1944 FemiCLE
Gerould, Ronald L. 1946- St&PR 91
Gerow, Edwin Mahaffey 1931- WhoAm 90
Gerow, Lynn Burdette, Jr. 1942- BiDrAPA 89
Gerowin, Mina WhoE 91
Gerra, Martin Jerome, Jr. 1927- WhoE 91
Gerra, Rosa A. WhoHisp 91
Gerrard, Connie BioIn 16
Gerrard, Jean 1933- BioIn 16
Gerrard, Jeffrey M BiDrAPA 89
Gerrard, Michael Burr 1951- WhoEmL 91
Gerrard, Robert W. 1927- St&PR 91
Gerrard, Robert Wilkin 1927- WhoAm 90
Gerrard, Roy 1935- BioIn 16, ChlLR 23 [port]
Gerraughty, Richard Gerard 1940- St&PR 91
Gerretsen, Reinder Willem 1925- WhoAm 90
Gerring, Joan Page 1943- BiDrAPA 89
Gerringer, Robert 1926-1989 BioIn 16
Gerringer, William F 1907- BiDrAPA 89
Gerringer-Busenbark, Elizabeth J. 1934- WhoAmW 91
Gerrish, Brian Albert 1931- WhoAm 90
Gerrish, Catherine R. 1911- St&PR 91
Gerrish, Catherine Ruggles 1911- WhoAmW 91, WhoE 91
Gerrish, Hollis G. 1907- St&PR 91, WhoE 91, WhoWor 91
Gerrish, Jeffrey Crane 1951- WhoEmL 91
Gerrish, Samuel BioIn 16
Gerritsen, Frans 1925- WhoWor 91
Gerritsen, Hendrik Jurjen 1927- WhoAm 90
Gerritsen, Jeroen 1951- WhoE 91
Gerritsen, Mary Ellen 1953- WhoAmW 91
Gerritsen, Paul S. 1945- St&PR 91
Gerrity, Edward J., Jr. 1924- ODwPR 91
Gerrity, Frank, II 1918- WhoAm 90
Gerrity, J. Frank 1918- St&PR 91
Gerrity, Richard Warren 1942- St&PR 91
Gerritz, Harrie Antonius 1940- WhoWor 91
Gerrold, David 1944- RGTwCSF
Gerry & the Pacemakers EncPR&S 89
Gerry and the Pacemakers OxCPMus
Gerry, Alan BioIn 16
Gerry, Albert Cleve 1943- St&PR 91
Gerry, Elbridge 1744-1814 BiDrUSE 89, BioIn 16, EncCRAm, WorAlBi
Gerry, Elbridge T. 1908- St&PR 91
Gerry, Elbridge Thomas 1908- WhoAm 90
Gerry, Elbridge Thomas, Jr. 1933- WhoAm 90
Gerry, Joseph John 1928- WhoAm 90
Gerry, Martin Hughes, IV 1943- WhoAm 90
Gerry, Roger Goodman 1916- WhoE 91, WhoWor 91
Gers, Harvey 1947- WhoEmL 91
Gers, Jerald 1947- WhoEmL 91
Gers, Seymour 1931- BiDrAPA 89, WhoE 91
Gersch, Harold Arthur 1922- WhoAm 90
Gersch, Seth J. 1947- St&PR 91
Gerschbacher, Corine Marie 1961- WhoAmW 91
Gerschefski, Edwin 1909- IntWWM 90
Gerschefski, Martha IntWWM 90
Gerschke, Elroy Louis 1919- St&PR 91
Gerscovich, Dolores R. 1942- WhoAmW 91
Gerscovich, Jose BiDrAPA 89
Gersdorf, Antoinette Graham 1952- WhoWrEP 89
Gersdorf, Robert 1933- WhoWor 91
Gersh, Bill 1943- WhoAmA 91
Gersh, Eugene 1924- BiDrAPA 89
Gersh, Richard Jay 1957- BiDrAPA 89
Gershanoff, Hal 1935- WhoE 91
Gershator, David 1937- WhoWrEP 89
Gershbein, Leon Lee 1917- WhoAm 90
Gershberg, Jack M 1924- BiDrAPA 89
Gershberg, Myron R BiDrAPA 89
Gershberg, Richard Louis 1954- WhoEmL 91
Gershel, George F., Jr. 1930- St&PR 91
Gershell, William Jay BiDrAPA 89
Gershen, Alvin E BioIn 16
Gershen, Barnett Leonard 1947- St&PR 91
Gershen, Bernard Jack 1931- WhoE 91
Gershengorn, Marvin Carl WhoAm 90
Gershenson, Harry 1902- WhoAm 90
Gershinowitz, Harold 1910- WhoAm 90
Gershman, Elizabeth Gibson 1927- WhoWrEP 89
Gershman, Ronald Allan BiDrAPA 89
Gershon, Daniel Erwin 1959- WhoEmL 91
Gershon, Elliot S BiDrAPA 89
Gershon, Elliot Sheldon WhoAm 90
Gershon, Fabianne W. 1941- ODwPR 91
Gershon, Ira Richard 1957- WhoEmL 91
Gershon, Karen 1923- FemiCLE
Gershon, Michael David 1938- WhoAm 90
Gershon, Michael Richard 1948- BiDrAPA 89
Gershon, Nina 1940- WhoAmW 91
Gershon, Samuel 1927- BiDrAPA 89, WhoE 91
Gershoni, Haim BioIn 16
Gershowitz, Harold 1938- St&PR 91
Gershoy, Eugenie 1901-1983 WhoAmA 91N
Gershunsky, Boris Semyonovich BioIn 16
Gershuny, Barry Michael 1957- BiDrAPA 89
Gershuny, Dianne Lynette 1952- WhoAmW 91
Gershuny, Seymour P. 1917- St&PR 91
Gershwin, George 1898-1937 BioIn 16, OxCPMus, PenDiMP A, WorAlBi
Gershwin, Ira 1896-1983 OxCPMus, WorAlBi
Gersin, Robert P BioIn 16
Gersin, Robert P 1929-1989 ConDes 90
Gersing, James Edward 1947- WhoSSW 91
Gerske, Janet Fay 1950- WhoAmW 91
Gersky, Robert H. 1935- St&PR 91
Gersman, Shawn Nathan 1963- BiDrAPA 89
Gerson, Alan H. 1946- St&PR 91
Gerson, Carol Roberts 1948- WhoEmL 91
Gerson, Gary Stanford 1945- WhoEmL 91
Gerson, Ines BiDrAPA 89
Gerson, Irwin Conrad 1930- WhoAm 90
Gerson, Jacki Ellen 1949- WhoAmW 91
Gerson, Jeffrey Scott BiDrAPA 89
Gerson, Jerome Howard 1928- WhoAm 90
Gerson, Lee L 1951- BiDrAPA 89
Gerson, Louis Lieb 1921- WhoE 91
Gerson, Mark David 1954- WhoWrEP 89
Gerson, Max 1881-1959 NewAgE 90
Gerson, Noel B 1914-1988 BioIn 16, SmATA 60
Gerson, Noel Bertram 1914- AuBYP 90, WhoWrEP 89
Gerson, Ralph J. 1949- St&PR 91
Gerson, Ralph Joseph 1949- WhoEmL 91, WhoWor 91
Gerson, Richard David BiDrAPA 89
Gerson, Robert Walthall 1935- WhoAm 90, WhoSSW 91
Gerson, Shoshana 1951- BiDrAPA 89
Gerson, Stephen N 1943- BiDrAPA 89
Gerson, Stephen Norman 1943- WhoE 91
Gerson, Steve 1947- St&PR 91
Gerson, Theodore S. 1915- St&PR 91
Gersoni-Edelman, Diane Claire 1947- WhoAmW 91
Gersons, Berthold P.R. 1945- WhoWor 91
Gersony, Welton Mark 1931- WhoAm 90
Gersovitz, Mark 1949- WhoE 91
Gersovitz, Sarah Valerie WhoAmA 91
Gerst, Elizabeth Carlsen 1929- WhoAmW 91, WhoE 91, WhoWor 91
Gerst, Hilde W WhoAmA 91
Gerst, Michael Dean 1951- WhoEmL 91
Gerst, Paul Howard 1927- WhoAm 90
Gerst, Steven Richard 1958- WhoSSW 91
Gerstbauer-Hill, LouAnn 1956- WhoAmW 91
Gerstein, David B. 1936- St&PR 91
Gerstein, David Brown 1936- WhoAm 90, WhoE 91
Gerstein, David Morris 1917- St&PR 91
Gerstein, David Steven 1951- WhoAmA 91
Gerstein, Doryne Shari 1960- WhoE 91
Gerstein, Edgar BiDrAPA 89
Gerstein, Esther 1924- WhoAmW 91, WhoE 91, WhoWor 91
Gerstein, Frank BioIn 16
Gerstein, Harvey S. 1935- St&PR 91
Gerstein, Irving R. 1942- WhoSSW 91
Gerstein, John Richard 1951- WhoEmL 91
Gerstein, Kurt 1905-1945 BioIn 16
Gerstein, Mel 1936- St&PR 91
Gerstein, Mordicai AuBYP 90
Gerstein, Mordicai 1935- BioIn 16
Gerstel, Else BioIn 16
Gerstel, Martin Stephen 1941- St&PR 91, WhoAm 90
Gerstell, A. Frederick 1938- St&PR 91, WhoAm 90
Gersten, Jerome William 1917- WhoAm 90
Gersten, Mark David 1950- St&PR 91
Gersten, S. William 1943- St&PR 91
Gersten, Steven Paul 1942- BiDrAPA 89
Gerstenberg, Alice 1885-1972 BioIn 16, FemiCLE, NotWoAT
Gerstenberg, Heinrich Wilhelm von 1737-1823 DcLB 97 [port]
Gerstenberg, Richard Charles 1909- EncABHB 5 [port]
Gerstenberger, Donna Lorine 1929- WhoAm 90
Gerstenberger, Walter 1915- WhoE 91
Gerstenengst, Iosif 1920- IntWWM 90
Gerstenzang, James Rose 1947- WhoE 91
Gerstenzang, Martin Louis BiDrAPA 89
Gerster, Etelka 1855-1920 PenDiMP
Gerster, Robert Gibson 1945- WhoAm 90
Gerstgrasser, Walter BioIn 16
Gersting, Judith Lee 1940- WhoAmW 91
Gerstl, Elfriede 1932- EncCoWW
Gerstley, Linda Jean 1955- WhoAmW 91
Gerstman, Henry 1938- St&PR 91
Gerstman, Sharon Stern 1952- WhoEmL 91
Gerstner, Alison Daugherty 1960- WhoEmL 91
Gerstner, John J. 1946- WhoWrEP 89
Gerstner, Karl 1930- ConDes 90
Gerstner, Lillian Polus 1951- WhoWrEP 89
Gerstner, Louis V., Jr. BioIn 16
Gerstner, Louis Vincent, Jr. 1942- WhoAm 90
Gerstner, Mary Ila 1950- St&PR 91
Gerstner, Richard Thomas 1939- St&PR 91, WhoAm 90
Gerstner, Robert William 1934- WhoAm 90
Gerstner, William L. 1939- St&PR 91
Gersuk, Lorraine 1949- WhoE 91
Gersz, Steven R. 1957- WhoEmL 91
Gert, Bernard 1934- WhoAm 90
Gert, Gerard Martin 1920- WhoAm 90
Gertel, Leon 1915- BiDrAPA 89
Gertenbach, Robert Frederick 1923- WhoAm 90
Gerth, Donald Rogers 1928- WhoAm 90
Gerth, Edwin Charles 1938- St&PR 91
Gerth, Hans Joachim Rudolf 1927- WhoWor 91
Gerth, Ruth WhoAmA 91N
Gertler, Alfred M. 1922- ODwPR 91
Gertler, Alfred Martin 1922- WhoAm 90
Gertler, Andre 1907- IntWWM 90, PenDiMP
Gertler, Menard M. 1919- WhoAm 90, WhoWor 91
Gertrud of Helfta 1256-1301? EncCoWW
Gertrud von Le Fort 1876-1971 EncCoWW
Gertrude, Katy 1928- WhoAmW 91
Gertsch, Max 1943- WhoWor 91
Gertsch, William Darrell 1940- WhoSSW 91
Gerty, Alvin V BiDrAPA 89
Gerty, Francis J BiDrAPA 89
Gertz, Alison BioIn 16
Gertz, Dwight Lyman 1951- WhoEmL 91
Gertz, Elizabeth BioIn 16
Gertz, Elmer 1906- WhoAm 90, WhoWrEP 89
Gertz, Geoffry BioIn 16
Gertz, Jami BioIn 16
Gertz, Raymond A. 1923- St&PR 91
Gerulaitis, Vitas Kevin 1954- WhoWor 91
Gerussi, Bruno 1928- OxCCanT
Gervais, Bishop EncO&P 3
Gervais, Barbara Elizabeth 1951- WhoE 91
Gervais, Carole BiDrAPA 89
Gervais, Cherie Nadine WhoAmW 91
Gervais, Generose 1919- WhoAm 90
Gervais, Heidi Dianne 1956- WhoAmW 91
Gervais, Henry Joseph 1928- St&PR 91
Gervais, Lucille Catherine Mayer WhoAmW 91
Gervais, Marcel Andre 1931- WhoAm 90
Gervais, Michel BiDrAPA 89
Gervais, Michel 1944- WhoAm 90, WhoWor 91
Gervais, Paul Nelson 1947- WhoE 91, WhoEmL 91, WhoWor 91
Gervais, Robert H 1929- BiDrAPA 89
Gervasi, Frank 1895-1986 BioIn 16
Gervasi, Frank 1906-1990 CurBio 90N
Gervasi, Frank 1908-1990 NewYTBS 90
Gervasi, Frank H 1908-1990 ConAu 130
Gervasi, Frank Henry 1908- AuBYP 90
Gervasi, Frank Henry 1908-1990 BioIn 16
Gervasi, Tom BioIn 16
Gervasio, Anthony Daniel, Sr. 1953- WhoSSW 91
Gerverot, Louis-Victor 1747-1829 PenDiDA 89
Gervers, Hilda F. 1909- IntWWM 90
Gervin, George 1952- WorAlBi
Gerwens, Joseph WhoSSW 91
Gerwick, Ben Clifford, Jr. 1919- WhoAm 90
Gerwick-Brodeur, Madeline Carol 1951- WhoEmL 91
Gerwig, Edgar C. 1941- St&PR 91
Gerwin, Brenda Isen 1939- WhoAmW 91
Gerwin, Edward F. 1926- St&PR 91
Gerwin, Leslie Ellen 1950- WhoEmL 91
Gerwin, Ronald Paul 1933- WhoE 91
Gery, Elizabeth H BiDrAPA 89
Gery, John Roy Octavius 1953- WhoWrEP 89
Gery, Paul Walter 1954- WhoWor 91
Gerye, Robert Allen 1953- WhoEmL 91
Geryol, Andrew J. 1942- St&PR 91
Gerz, Hans O 1926- BiDrAPA 89
Gerzina, John A. 1918- St&PR 91
Gerzso, Gunther 1915- WhoAmA 91
Geschwint, Ira 1931- St&PR 91, WhoAm 90, WhoE 91
Gesell, Arnold L. 1880-1961 WorAlBi
Gesell, Frederick John 1939- St&PR 91
Gesell, Gerhard BioIn 16
Gesell, Gerhard Alden 1910- WhoAm 90, WhoE 91
Geselowitz, David Beryl 1930- WhoAm 90
Gesensway, Daniel B 1932- BiDrAPA 89
Gesinski, Robert George 1951- St&PR 91
Geske, David Lyle 1946- BiDrAPA 89
Geske, Donald Charles 1947- St&PR 91
Geske, Larry D. 1939- St&PR 91
Geske, Norman Albert 1915- WhoAmA 91
Geskey, Ronald Dale 1942- St&PR 91
Geskin, Ernest Samuel 1935- WhoE 91
Gesmer, Henry 1912- WhoE 91
Gesner, Elsie Miller WhoWrEP 89
Gesriel, William F. St&PR 91
Gessa, Gian Luigi 1932- WhoWor 91
Gessay, Louis H 1919- BiDrAPA 89
Gessel, Arnold H 1932- BiDrAPA 89
Gessel, Ira Martin 1951- WhoE 91
Gessel, Stanley Paul 1916- WhoAm 90
Gessendorf, Mechthild IntWWM 90
Gessert, Autumn Roberta 1958- WhoAmW 91
Gessert, Lise Lynne 1954- WhoAmW 91
Gessler, Doc 1880-1924 Ballpl 90
Gessling, James Place 1954- WhoEmL 91
Gessner, Charles Herman 1938- WhoAm 90
Gessner, Harold B BioIn 16
Gessner, Salomon PenDiDA 89
Gessner, Salomon 1730-1788 DcLB 97 [port]
Gesso, Robert Joseph 1952- St&PR 91
Gessow, Alfred 1922- WhoAm 90, WhoE 91
Gest, Bernard 1924- St&PR 91
Gest, Howard 1921- WhoAm 90
Gest, Kathryn Waters 1947- WhoAm 90
Gest, Robert, III 1937- WhoE 91
Gestefeld, Ursula 1845-1921 FemiCLE
Gesteland, Robert Charles 1930- WhoAm 90
Gestetner, David 1937- WhoWor 91
Geston, Mark Symington 1946- WhoWrEP 89
Gestrin, B.V. 1935- St&PR 91
Gestur Palsson DcScanL
Gesumaria, Donna Beatrice 1955- WhoEmL 91
Geszty, Sylvia 1934- IntWWM 90, PenDiMP
Getchel, Nellie I. 1932- WhoAmW 91

Getchell, Charles Lawrence 1939- *WhoE 91*
Getchell, Charles Richard 1933- *St&PR 91*
Getchell, James Robert 1943- *WhoAm 90, WhoE 91*
Getgood, Susan Janet 1962- *WhoEmL 91*
Gethers, Peter 1953- *ConAu 31NR*
Gethers, Steven *BioIn 16*
Gethers, Steven 1922?-1989 *ConAu 130*
Gethin, Grace 1676-1697 *BiDEWW, FemiCLE*
Gethin, Grace Norton 1676-1697 *BioIn 16*
Gethmann, Jack B. 1937- *St&PR 91*
Gethmann, Kenneth W. 1913- *St&PR 91*
Getis, Arthur 1934- *WhoAm 90*
Getler, Helen 1925- *WhoAmA 91*
Getler, Michael 1935- *WhoAm 90, WhoE 91*
Getman, Ann *ODwPR 91*
Getman, Dennis Jon 1944- *St&PR 91*
Getman, Frank Newton 1910- *WhoAm 90*
Getman, Gerald Nathan 1914?-1990 *ConAu 131*
Getman, LaVerne W. 1922- *WhoE 91*
Getman, Morton J. *ODwPR 91*
Getman, Richard B *BiDrAPA 89*
Getman, Sheryl Marie 1947- *WhoAmW 91*
Getnick, Neil Victor 1953- *WhoEmL 91*
Getnick, Richard Alan 1943- *WhoE 91*
Geto, Ethan 1943- *ODwPR 91*
Getoff, Nikola 1922- *WhoWor 91*
Getoor, Richard C. 1930- *St&PR 91*
Getson, Lisa Marie 1962- *WhoEmL 91*
Gettel, Al 1917- *Ballpl 90*
Gettel, James Joseph 1959- *WhoEmL 91*
Gettelfinger, Nancy *WhoAmW 91*
Gettell, Linda Wong 1949- *WhoEmL 91*
Gettell, Richard Glenn 1912-1988 *BioIn 16*
Gettelman, Kenneth Milton 1925- *WhoAm 90*
Gettelman, Robin Claire 1952- *WhoAmW 91*
Getter, Elizabeth Valerie *BiDrAPA 89*
Getter, Keith Alan 1958- *WhoEmL 91*
Getter, Matylda *BioIn 16*
Gettier, Glenn Howard 1942- *WhoAm 90*
Gettier, Glenn Howard, Jr. 1942- *St&PR 91*
Gettig, Martin Winthrop 1939- *WhoE 91, WhoWor 91*
Gettig, Thomas E. 1945- *St&PR 91*
Getting, Ivan Alexander 1912- *WhoAm 90*
Gettinger, Lillian 1925- *St&PR 91*
Gettinger, Walter 1915- *St&PR 91*
Gettler, Benjamin 1925- *WhoAm 90, WhoWor 91*
Gettler, Benjamin 1927- *St&PR 91*
Getto, Carl Joseph *BiDrAPA 89*
Getto, Gary Allen 1948- *WhoEmL 91*
Getto, Michael Hutson 1934- *St&PR 91*
Getty, Ann *BioIn 16*
Getty, Benjamin H. *St&PR 91*
Getty, Carol Pavilack 1938- *WhoAmW 91*
Getty, Donald Ross 1933- *WhoAm 90*
Getty, Estelle *BioIn 16*
Getty, Estelle 1923- *CurBio 90 [port], WhoAm 90, WhoAmW 91*
Getty, Estelle 1924- *WorAlBi*
Getty, Ethel Salter 1921- *St&PR 91*
Getty, Gordon P. *BioIn 16*
Getty, Gordon Peter 1933- *WhoAm 90*
Getty, J. P. 1892-1976 *WorAlBi*
Getty, J. Paul 1892-1976 *BioIn 16*
Getty, J Paul 1892-1976 *WhoAmA 91N*
Getty, Jill E. 1959- *St&PR 91*
Getty, Nilda Fernandez 1936- *WhoAmA 91*
Getty, Paul Balthazar *BioIn 16*
Getty, Paul Merle 1951- *WhoSSW 91*
Getty, Susan 1946- *WhoE 91*
Getty, William Patton 1945- *WhoEmL 91*
Gettys, George Anderson 1948- *WhoAm 90*
Getu, Seyoum 1941- *WhoE 91*
Getz, Bert A. 1937- *St&PR 91*
Getz, Edwin Lee 1945- *St&PR 91*
Getz, Ernest John 1918- *WhoAm 90*
Getz, George F., Jr. 1908- *St&PR 91*
Getz, George Fulmer, Jr. 1908- *WhoAm 90*
Getz, George W *BiDrAPA 89*
Getz, Gus 1889-1969 *Ballpl 90*
Getz, Ilse 1917- *WhoAmA 91*
Getz, James Lawrence 1821-1891 *AmLegL*
Getz, Lorine M. 1942- *WhoSSW 91*
Getz, Lowell Lee 1931- *WhoAm 90*
Getz, Lowell Vernon 1932- *WhoSSW 91*
Getz, Malcolm 1945- *WhoAm 90*
Getz, Mike 1938- *WhoWrEP 89*
Getz, Morton Ernest 1930- *WhoSSW 91*
Getz, Richard Lee 1945- *St&PR 91*
Getz, Solomon 1936- *WhoE 91*
Getz, Stan 1927- *BioIn 16, IntWWM 90, OxCPMus, WhoAm 90, WorAlBi*
Getz, Wayne Marcus 1950- *WhoEmL 91*
Getzein, Charlie 1864-1932 *Ballpl 90*
Getzelman, John Chapell 1942- *St&PR 91, WhoAm 90*
Getzels, Jacob Warren 1912- *ConAu 30NR, WhoAm 90*
Getzendanner, Susan 1939- *WhoAm 90, WhoAmW 91*
Getzin, Paula Mayer 1941- *WhoAmW 91*
Getzler, Ezra 1962- *WhoE 91*
Geu, Thomas Earl 1957- *WhoEmL 91*
Geulincx, Arnold 1624-1669 *WrPh P*
Geupel, Carl Martin 1950- *WhoEmL 91*
Geupel, John C. 1927- *St&PR 91*
Geupel, John S. 1952- *St&PR 91*
Geurink, Terry Lee 1959- *WhoEmL 91*
Geuther, Carl F. 1945- *St&PR 91*
Gevaert, John Charles 1952- *WhoEmL 91*
Gevantman, Judith 1949- *WhoAmW 91, WhoE 91*
Gevantman, Lewis Herman 1921- *WhoAm 90*
Gevedon, Teresa Gaye *BiDrAPA 89*
Gever, Judith Pullman 1956- *WhoEmL 91*
Gevers, Jan Karel Maria 1944- *WhoWor 91*
Gevirtz, Don Lee 1928- *St&PR 91*
Gevirtz, Eliezer 1950- *BioIn 16*
Gewanter, Harry Lewis 1950- *WhoAm 90, WhoEmL 91*
Gewartowski, James Walter 1930- *WhoAm 90*
Gewe, Raddory *ConAu 30NR*
Geweily, Said M.H. 1938- *WhoWor 91*
Geweke, John Frederick 1948- *WhoAm 90*
Geweniger, Robert Arthur 1943- *St&PR 91*
Gewin, Joe Crawford 1942- *St&PR 91*
Gewirth, Alan 1912- *WhoAm 90*
Gewirtz, George Robert *BiDrAPA 89*
Gewirtz, Gerry 1920- *WhoAm 90, WhoAmW 91*
Gewirtz, Harold 1950- *WhoE 91*
Gewirtz, Jacob 1926- *WhoWor 91*
Gewirtz, Max *BioIn 16*
Gewirtzman, Garry Bruce 1947- *WhoSSW 91, WhoWor 91*
Gewolb, Eric Bank 1948- *BiDrAPA 89*
Gex, Walter Joseph, III 1939- *WhoAm 90, WhoSSW 91*
Geyelin, Anthony Allen 1945- *St&PR 91*
Geyelin, Frances Healy *BioIn 16*
Geyer, Donald H., Jr. *St&PR 91*
Geyer, Georgie Anne *BioIn 16*
Geyer, Georgie Anne 1935- *WhoAm 90, WhoAmW 91, WhoWrEP 89*
Geyer, Harold Carl 1905- *WhoAm 90*
Geyer, Kathy Van Ness 1954- *WhoSSW 91*
Geyer, Rube 1885-1962 *Ballpl 90*
Geyer, Steffi 1888-1956 *PenDiMP*
Geyer, William Richard 1948- *WhoEmL 91*
Geyger, Johann Caspar *PenDiDA 89*
Geylin, Michael 1954- *ODwPR 91*
Geylin, Michael Sola 1954- *WhoE 91*
Geyman, John Payne 1931- *WhoAm 90*
Geyser, Meryl Joyce 1943- *WhoAmW 91*
Gezella, Barbara Dantinne 1944- *St&PR 91*
Gezurian, Dorothy Ellen 1956- *WhoEmL 91*
Gfeller, Eduard 1937- *BiDrAPA 89*
Gfroehrer, Martin Timithy 1960- *St&PR 91*
Ghadiali, Dinshah Pestanji 1873-1966 *NewAgE 90*
Ghadirian, Abdu'L-Missagh 1936- *BiDrAPA 89*
Ghafar Baba, Abdul 1925- *WhoWor 91*
Ghaffar Khan *BioIn 16*
Ghaffar, Hussein Abdel 1940- *WhoWor 91*
Ghaffar Khan, Abdul 1890-1988 *AnObit 1988*
Ghahramani, Mahmood 1927- *BiDrAPA 89*
Ghai, Rajendra Durgaprasad 1943- *WhoE 91*
Ghali, Anwar Youssef 1944- *BiDrAPA 89, WhoE 91, WhoWor 91*
Ghaly, Hoda R F 1943- *BiDrAPA 89*
Ghaly, Nasri Naguib 1948- *BiDrAPA 89*
Ghambir, Ramesh Chander 1938- *WhoWor 91*
Ghammashi, Joseph 1949- *WhoSSW 91*
Ghandar, Ann 1943- *IntWWM 90*
Ghandhi, Sorab Khushro 1928- *WhoAm 90*
Ghandhistani, Abdullah Hassan 1920- *WhoWrEP 89*
Ghandour, Ziad 1961- *WhoEmL 91*
Ghanem, Hafez Mohamed Hafez 1957- *WhoE 91*
Ghani, Mohammed Abdul 1963- *St&PR 91*
Ghannam, Adel Nabih 1946- *WhoWor 91*
Ghanta, Supriya P. *BiDrAPA 89*
Ghantiwala, Pravin Ratilal 1951- *WhoEmL 91*
Gharagozlou-Hamadani, I *BiDrAPA 89*
Gharrett, Anthony John 1945- *WhoEmL 91*
Gharrity, Patsy 1892-1966 *Ballpl 90*
Gharse, Suresh 1948- *BiDrAPA 89*
Ghasemi, Seifollah 1944- *St&PR 91*
Ghaswala, Soli Kaikobad 1919- *WhoWor 91*
Ghatak, Ritwik 1926-1976 *BioIn 16*
Ghate, Vijay R *BiDrAPA 89*
Ghattas, Suhail E 1934- *BiDrAPA 89*
Ghausi, Mohammed Shuaib 1930- *WhoAm 90*
Ghazali, Al 1058?-1111 *WorAlBi*
Ghazarian, Sona 1945- *IntWWM 90*
Ghazinoor-Naini, Mehdi *BiDrAPA 89*
Ghaznavi, John J. 1935- *St&PR 91*
Ghebrehiwet, Berhane 1946- *WhoEmL 91*
Gheddo, Piero 1929- *WhoWor 91*
Ghegan, William S. 1948- *St&PR 91*
Ghelardi, Raymond Eusebius 1951- *WhoEmL 91*
Ghelelovitch, Sabbas 1911- *WhoWor 91*
Ghelfi, Alfred R. 1939- *St&PR 91*
Ghelfi-Sauthier, Fabrice Francois 1967- *WhoWor 91*
Ghenov, Paul Boiko 1942- *St&PR 91*
Ghent, Emmanuel R *BiDrAPA 89*
Ghent, Henri 1926- *WhoAmA 91*
Ghent, Henri Hermann 1926- *WhoE 91*
Ghent, Peer 1939- *St&PR 91*
Ghent, William J. *EncAL*
Ghenzer, Massimo 1943- *WhoWor 91*
Gheorghiu, Mihnea 1919- *WhoWor 91*
Gheorghiu, Virgil 1916- *ConAu 30NR*
Gherardi, Diane Paula 1941- *WhoAmW 91*
Gherardi, Piero 1909-1971 *ConDes 90*
Gherasim, Virgiliu *IntWWM 90*
Gherlein, Gerald Lee 1938- *WhoAm 90*
Gherlein, John Harlan 1926- *WhoAm 90*
Ghersi, Juan C *BiDrAPA 89*
Gherty, John E. 1944- *St&PR 91*
Ghetti, Bernardino Francesco 1941- *WhoAm 90*
Ghezzi, Grace Baranello 1955- *WhoEmL 91*
Ghezzo, Dinu 1941- *IntWWM 90*
Ghia *ConDes 90*
Ghiardi, James Domenic 1918- *WhoAm 90*
Ghiardi, John Felix Linus 1918- *WhoE 91*
Ghiaurov, Nicolai 1929- *IntWWM 90*
Ghiaurov, Nikolay *PenDiMP*
Ghiberti, Lorenzo 1378?-1455 *IntDcAA 90, WorAlBi*
Ghidella, Vittorio *BioIn 16*
Ghiglia, Oscar 1938- *IntWWM 90, PenDiMP*
Ghiglia, Oscar Alberto 1938- *WhoAm 90*
Ghiglieri, Dominick James 1940- *WhoE 91*
Ghiglione, Loren *BioIn 16*
Ghigna, Charles 1946- *WhoWrEP 89*
Ghignone, Albert A. 1942- *St&PR 91*
Ghikas, Panos George *WhoAmA 91*
Ghikas, Patience Haley *WhoAmA 91*
Ghilardi, Melinda Christina 1958- *WhoAmW 91, WhoEmL 91*
Ghileri, Sirleen Jean 1943- *WhoAmW 91*
Ghimire, Bishwa 1943- *St&PR 91*
Ghini, Massimo Iosa *BioIn 16*
Ghioldi, Americo 1899- *BioIn 16*
Ghiotto, Robert A. 1933- *St&PR 91*
Ghiraldini, Joan 1951- *WhoAmW 91, WhoE 91*
Ghirardelli, Cornelio *EncO&P 3*
Ghirardelli, Domenico 1817-1894 *BioIn 16*
Ghirlandaio 1449-1494 *IntDcAA 90*
Ghirlandaio, Domenico 1449-1494 *WorAlBi*
Ghiron, Giorgio 1933- *WhoWor 91*
Ghiselin, Brewster 1903- *WhoAm 90, WhoWrEP 89, WorAu 1980 [port]*
Ghitalla, Armando 1925- *IntWWM 90*
Ghiuselev, Nicola 1936- *IntWWM 90*
Ghiuselev, Nikolay *PenDiMP*
Ghiz, Joseph A. 1945- *WhoAm 90, WhoWor 91*
Ghnassia, Jill Dix 1947- *WhoAmW 91*
Ghobashy, Omar Zaki 1924- *WhoE 91*
Ghobrial, Claire Fahim 1933- *BiDrAPA 89*
Gholamasad, Dawud 1943- *WhoWor 91*
Gholson, Cecil Jack 1927- *WhoAm 90*
Gholson, Samuel Jackson 1808-1883 *AmLegL*
Ghomeshi, M. Mehdi 1956- *St&PR 91*
Ghoneim, Hussein Atta 1944- *WhoWor 91*
Ghorayeb, Bechara Youssef 1945- *WhoSSW 91*
Ghormley, Ralph McDougall 1927- *WhoAm 90*
Ghose, Aurobindo 1872-1950 *BioIn 16*
Ghose, Rabindra N. 1925- *St&PR 91*
Ghose, Rabindra Nath 1925- *WhoAm 90*
Ghose, Zulfikar 1935- *WorAu 1980 [port]*
Ghosh, Aparna *BiDrAPA 89*
Ghosh, Arun Kumar 1930- *WhoWor 91*
Ghosh, Asit Baran *BiDrAPA 89*
Ghosh, Kajal Kumar 1937- *WhoWor 91*
Ghosh, Nimai Kumar 1937- *WhoAm 90*
Ghosh, Ranendra Bhusan *BiDrAPA 89*
Ghosh, Tapobrata *BiDrAPA 89*
Ghoshal, Nani Gopal 1934- *WhoAm 90*
Ghosheh, Rajai Kamel *BiDrAPA 89*
Ghostagore, Srirupa Sen *BiDrAPA 89*
Ghostwriters *NewAgMG*
Ghougassian, Joseph 1944- *WhoWor 91*
Ghoz, E Hamdi 1951- *BiDrAPA 89*
Ghozali, Sid Ahmed 1937- *WhoWor 91*
Ghuman, Harinder Singh 1949- *BiDrAPA 89*
Ghuman, Jaswinder Kaur *BiDrAPA 89*
Ghunaym, Ghunaym Mahmoud 1940- *WhoSSW 91*
Ghussein, Jaweed al- *BioIn 16*
Ghylin, Clair 1929- *WhoAm 90*
Giacalone, Frank T. 1951- *WhoSSW 91*
Giacalone, Peter Paul 1962- *WhoSSW 91*
Giacalone, Rick *ODwPR 91*
Giacalone, Rick 1932- *St&PR 91*
Giacalone, Robert Augustine 1957- *WhoSSW 91*
Giacalone, Vito *WhoAmA 91, WhoE 91*
Giacchetti, Donald Joseph 1953- *St&PR 91*
Giacchi, Salvatore Anthony 1948- *WhoEmL 91*
Giaccio, Richard Gary *BiDrAPA 89*
Giacco, Alexander Fortunatus 1919- *St&PR 91, WhoAm 90*
Giacconi, Riccardo 1931- *WhoAm 90, WhoWor 91*
Giachello, Aida L. Maisonet 1945- *WhoHisp 91*
Giachetti, Edward John 1939- *St&PR 91*
Giacobbe, Nicholas Joseph, Jr. 1960- *WhoE 91*
Giacobello, James P. 1929- *WhoAm 90*
Giacoletto, Joseph Richard 1935- *WhoAm 90*
Giacoletto, Lawrence Joseph 1916- *WhoAm 90*
Giacolini, Earl L. *WhoAm 90*
Giacomazzi, Frank P. 1931- *St&PR 91*
Giacomazzi, Frank Paul 1931- *WhoAm 90*
Giacomelli, Francis Charles 1962- *WhoSSW 91*
Giacometti, Alberto 1901-1966 *BioIn 16, IntDcAA 90, ModArCr 1 [port], WorAlBi*
Giacometti, Donna *ODwPR 91*
Giacomin, Angelo Robert 1935- *St&PR 91*
Giacomini, Giuseppe 1940- *IntWWM 90, WhoAm 90*
Giacomini, Peter Donald 1955- *St&PR 91*
Giacomino, Bob *BioIn 16*
Giaconi, Luisa 1870-1908 *EncCoWW*
Giacontiere, Raymond Joseph, Jr. 1963- *WhoEmL 91*
Giacosa, Dante 1905- *ConDes 90*
Giaever, Ivar 1929- *WhoAm 90, WhoE 91, WhoWor 91, WorAlBi*
Giaimo, Thomas Vincent 1958- *WhoE 91*
Giakas, William John *BiDrAPA 89*
Gialanella, Donald G 1956- *WhoAmA 91*
Gialanella, Philip Thomas 1930- *St&PR 91, WhoAm 90, WhoWor 91*
Giallanza, Charles Philip 1950- *WhoEmL 91, WhoSSW 91*
Gialleonardo, Victor 1928- *St&PR 91, WhoE 91*
Giallonardo, Thomas Michael 1947- *St&PR 91*
Giallorenzi, Thomas Gaetano 1943- *WhoAm 90*
Giam, Choo-Seng 1931- *WhoAm 90*
Giamatti, A. Bartlett 1938-1989 *AnObit 1989, Ballpl 90, BioIn 16*
Giamatti, A Bartlett 1938-1989 *ConAu 129, News 90*
Giamatti, A. Bartlett 1938-1989 *WorAlBi*
Giambalvo, Anthony 1946- *St&PR 91*
Giambalvo, Vincent 1942- *WhoE 91*
Giambartolomei, Elvira 1934- *BiDrAPA 89*
Giambertone, Paul *WhoAmA 91*
Giambologna 1529-1608 *IntDcAA 90*
Giambrone, William, Jr. 1943- *WhoE 91*
Giambruni, Tio 1925-1971 *WhoAmA 91N*
Giammalvo, Peter John 1947- *WhoSSW 91*
Giammetti, Giancarlo *BioIn 16*
Giampalmi, Joseph John 1943- *WhoWrEP 89*
Giampetruzzi, Nicholas 1932- *BiDrAPA 89*
Giampietro, Isabel *WhoAmA 91*
Giampietro, Wayne Bruce 1942- *WhoWor 91*
Giana, James Joseph 1946- *WhoE 91*
Gianakon, Harry G 1924- *BiDrAPA 89*
Gianakos, Cristos 1934- *WhoAmA 91, WhoE 91*
Gianakos, John Angelo 1942- *St&PR 91*
Gianakos, John N. 1954- *St&PR 91*
Gianakos, Nicholas C. 1919- *St&PR 91*
Gianakos, Steve 1938- *WhoAmA 91*
Gianakoulis, Theodore *AuBYP 90*
Gianani, Felice 1936- *WhoWor 91*
Gianaras, Alex A. 1954- *St&PR 91*
Gianaris, Nicholas James 1963- *WhoE 91, WhoEmL 91*
Gianaris, Nicholas Vasil 1929- *WhoE 91*
Gianascol, Alfred Joseph *BiDrAPA 89*
Giancana, Sam *BioIn 16*

Giancarlo, Vaj 1922- WhoWor 91
Giancola, Dennis James 1952- WhoEmL 91
Giancola, Holly Harrington 1961- WhoAmW 91
Giancotti, Antonio 1927- BiDrAPA 89
Giancursio, Debra Ann WhoAmW 91
Gianelli, William Reynolds 1919- WhoAm 90
Gianetti, David BiDrAPA 89
Giangiacomo, Tosello O. WhoAm 90
Gianinno, Susan McManama 1948- WhoAm 90, WhoAmW 91
Gianino, Claude E. ODwPR 91
Gianino, Frank John 1927- St&PR 91
Gianino, John Joseph 1935- St&PR 91, WhoAm 90
Gianlorenzi, Nona Elena 1939- WhoAmA 91
Giannadrea, Paul Frank 1954- WhoE 91
Giannandrea, Paul Frank 1954- BiDrAPA 89
Giannaros, Demetrios Spiros 1949- WhoE 91
Giannasca, Barbara Lynn 1955- WhoEmL 91
Giannasio, Charles V BiDrAPA 89
Giannasio, Joseph Robert BiDrAPA 89
Giannattasio, Vincent A 1933- BiDrAPA 89
Giannetti, Louis Daniel 1937- WhoAm 90
Giannetti, Stephen J. 1949- St&PR 91
Gianni, Hector Daniel BiDrAPA 89
Gianni, Sebastian Joseph 1924- St&PR 91
Giannini, A James 1947- BiDrAPA 89
Giannini, A. James 1947- WhoWor 91
Giannini, A. P. 1870-1949 EncABHB 7 [port]
Giannini, Amadeo P. 1870-1949 WorAlBi
Giannini, Amadeo Peter 1870-1949 BioIn 16
Giannini, David 1948- WhoWrEP 89
Giannini, Dusolina 1900-1986 PenDiMP
Giannini, Ferruccio 1868-1948 PenDiMP
Giannini, Gabriel Maria 1905-1989 BioIn 16
Giannini, Gemma 1951- WhoEmL 91
Giannini, Giancarlo 1942- WorAlBi
Giannini, Lawrence M. 1894-1952 WorAlBi
Giannini, Matthew Carlo 1950- WhoEmL 91
Giannini, Valerio Louis 1938- WhoAm 90
Giannini, Vittorio 1903-1966 BioIn 16, PenDiMP A
Gianninoto, Francesco A BioIn 16
Gianninoto, Robert 1937- St&PR 91
Gianniny, Omer Allan, Jr. 1925- WhoAm 90
Giannitsis, Anastasios Constantine 1944- WhoWor 91
Giannizzero, Francis Kenneth 1946- WhoE 91
Giannou, Christopher BioIn 16
Giannukos, Nicholas John BiDrAPA 89
Giannuzzi, Frank James 1960- WhoSSW 91
Gianoli, Paul Louis 1943- WhoWrEP 89
Gianoukos, James Anthony 1955- WhoSSW 91
Gianturco, Daniel T 1934- BiDrAPA 89
Gianturco, Delio E. 1940- WhoAm 90
Gianturco, Maurizio Antonio 1928- St&PR 91, WhoAm 90
Gianturco, Paola 1939- WhoAmW 91
Giap, Hai Phuc BiDrAPA 89
Giap, Vo Nguyen 1912- BioIn 16
Giaquinto, Philip M. WhoAm 90
Giard, George Peter, Jr. 1938- St&PR 91
Giard, Joe 1898-1956 Ballpl 90
Giardina, Paul Anthony 1949- WhoAm 90, WhoEmL 91
Giardina, Salvatore 1921- St&PR 91
Giardini, Alessandro 1655- PenDiDA 89
Giardini, Angelo J.M. 1910- St&PR 91
Giardini, Carl P. 1935- St&PR 91
Giardini, Giovanni 1646-1721 PenDiDA 89
Giardini, Thomas M. 1947- St&PR 91
Giardino, Charles Andrew 1961- WhoE 91
Giarini, Orio 1936- WhoWor 91
Giarrano, Thomas 1953- WhoSSW 91
Giarrusso, Giovanni 1939- WhoAm 90
Giarrusso, John Robert, Jr. 1953- WhoSSW 91
Giasemedis, Frank Steve 1940- St&PR 91
Giasi, Ralph William 1940- St&PR 91
Giattini, Cheryl Heeke ODwPR 91
Giauque, William F. 1895-1982 WorAlBi
Giauque, William Francis 1895-1982 DcScB S2
Gibala, Louise 1897- WhoAmA 91
Gibala, Ronald 1938- WhoAm 90
Gibaldi, Milo 1938- WhoAm 90
Gibans, James David 1930- WhoAm 90
Gibas, Allen Henry 1945- WhoEmL 91
Gibb, Andy BioIn 16
Gibb, Andy 1958-1988 EncPR&S 89, WorAlBi
Gibb, Barry 1946- WorAlBi
Gibb, Beverly Jean 1963- WhoAmW 91
Gibb, Bill 1943-1988 AnObit 1988, ConDes 90
Gibb, David Fox 1934- St&PR 91
Gibb, Lee MajTwCW
Gibb, Lisa Jo Christenson 1961- WhoAmW 91, WhoEmL 91
Gibb, Maurice 1949- WorAlBi
Gibb, Richard Dean 1928- WhoAm 90
Gibb, Robert 1946- WhoWrEP 89
Gibb, Robin 1949- WorAlBi
Gibb, Ronald L. 1948- St&PR 91
Gibbard, Bruce Alexander BiDrAPA 89
Gibbens, Alfred Morton 1935- WhoAm 90
Gibbens, Margaret Louise 1933- WhoAmW 91
Gibberd, Frederick Ernest 1908-1984 DcNaB 1981
Gibbered, Eric Waters 1897-1972 WhoAmA 91N
Gibbes, Phebe FemiCLE
Gibbes, William Holman 1930- WhoWor 91
Gibbins, Malcolm George 1943- St&PR 91
Gibble, Kenneth L 1941- ConAu 130
Gibbon, C. Gilpin 1924- St&PR 91
Gibbon, Edward 1737-1794 BioIn 16, DcLB 104 [port], WorAlBi
Gibbon, Joe 1936- Ballpl 90
Gibbon, John 1827-1896 WhNaAH
Gibbon, John 1922- BiDrAPA 89
Gibbon, John Murray 1875-1952 DcLB 92 [port]
Gibbon, Robert, Jr. BiDrAPA 89
Gibboney, Marilyn Louise 1933- WhoAmW 91
Gibbons, Brenda Sue 1961- WhoSSW 91
Gibbons, Carroll 1903-1954 OxCPMus
Gibbons, Christopher 1615-1676 PenDiMP A
Gibbons, Cromwell AmLegL
Gibbons, Felton 1929-1990 BioIn 16
Gibbons, Felton L 1929-1990 ConAu 131
Gibbons, Floyd 1887-1939 BioIn 16
Gibbons, Gail BioIn 16
Gibbons, Gail 1944- AuBYP 90, SmATA 12AS [port]
Gibbons, Gregg Michael 1952- St&PR 91
Gibbons, Grinling 1648-1721 BioIn 16, PenDiDA 89
Gibbons, Hugh 1937- WhoAmA 91
Gibbons, James Anthony 1957- WhoEmL 91
Gibbons, James Franklin 1931- WhoAm 90
Gibbons, Jennifer BioIn 16
Gibbons, John H 1929- BioIn 16
Gibbons, John Howard 1929- WhoAm 90
Gibbons, John Joseph 1924- WhoAm 90
Gibbons, Joseph John 1906- WhoAm 90
Gibbons, Joseph Martin 1947- St&PR 91
Gibbons, Julia Smith 1950- WhoAm 90, WhoAmW 91, WhoSSW 91
Gibbons, June BioIn 16
Gibbons, Kathy BioIn 16
Gibbons, Mariko Uryu 1932- St&PR 91
Gibbons, Mary Peyser 1936- WhoAmW 91
Gibbons, Michael BioIn 16
Gibbons, Michael Eugene 1952- WhoEmL 91
Gibbons, Michael Francis, Jr. 1941- WhoE 91
Gibbons, Neal Nathan 1945- WhoEmL 91
Gibbons, O. Robert BioIn 16
Gibbons, P. Michael 1942- St&PR 91
Gibbons, Paul F. 1951- St&PR 91
Gibbons, Peter James 1937- WhoAm 90
Gibbons, Reginald 1947- WhoWrEP 89
Gibbons, Richard E. 1925- St&PR 91
Gibbons, Robert Alexander 1920- WhoSSW 91
Gibbons, Robert Ebbert 1940- WhoAm 90
Gibbons, Robert Edmund 1929- St&PR 91
Gibbons, Robert John 1943- St&PR 91, WhoAm 90
Gibbons, Ronald John 1932- WhoAm 90
Gibbons, Sam Melville 1920- WhoAm 90, WhoSSW 91
Gibbons, Sandra Lee 1942- WhoAmW 91
Gibbons, Sheila J. 1951- ODwPR 91
Gibbons, Sheila Marie 1931- St&PR 91, WhoAm 90, WhoAmW 91
Gibbons, Simon Thomas 1851-1896 DcCanB 12
Gibbons, Stella 1902-1989 AnObit 1989, BioIn 16, ConAu 130, FemiCLE
Gibbons, Steven Van 1955- WhoEmL 91
Gibbons, William Ernest 1943- WhoE 91
Gibbons, William H., Jr. 1945- ODwPR 91, St&PR 91
Gibbons, William John 1947- WhoEmL 91
Gibbons, William Reginald, Jr. 1947- WhoAm 90
Gibbs, A. Roger 1925- St&PR 91
Gibbs, Alonzo 1915- AuBYP 90
Gibbs, Anne B. 1949- St&PR 91
Gibbs, Barbara 1950- WhoAmA 91
Gibbs, Barbara Francesca 1912- WhoWrEP 89
Gibbs, Barbara Kennedy 1950- WhoAm 90
Gibbs, Beatrice Esther 1918- WhoAmW 91
Gibbs, Charles Frederick 1917- St&PR 91
Gibbs, David George 1925- WhoAm 90
Gibbs, Delbridge Lindley 1917- WhoAm 90
Gibbs, Denis Dunbar 1927- WhoWor 91
Gibbs, Donald C 1926- BiDrAPA 89
Gibbs, Donna 1960- ODwPR 91
Gibbs, Ezekiel 1889- MusmAFA
Gibbs, Frederick Winfield 1932- WhoAm 90
Gibbs, Henry TwCCr&M 91
Gibbs, Humphrey NewYTBS 90 [port]
Gibbs, Isaac L. 1824- AmLegL
Gibbs, Jack Porter 1927- WhoAm 90
Gibbs, Jake 1938- Ballpl 90
Gibbs, James 1938- BiDrAPA 89
Gibbs, James A. 1935- St&PR 91
Gibbs, James Alanson 1935- WhoAm 90, WhoSSW 91
Gibbs, James Howard 1929- WhoSSW 91
Gibbs, James J BiDrAPA 89
Gibbs, James R. 1944- St&PR 91
Gibbs, James Wenrich 1915- WhoWor 91
Gibbs, Jamie 1955- WhoWrEP 89
Gibbs, Jason A. 1933- St&PR 91
Gibbs, Jeffrey Neil 1953- WhoEmL 91
Gibbs, Joe BioIn 16
Gibbs, Joe 1940- WorAlBi
Gibbs, Joe Jackson 1940- WhoAm 90, WhoE 91
Gibbs, John LaPorte 1838-1908 AmLegL
Gibbs, John Patrick 1948- WhoEmL 91
Gibbs, Josiah W. 1839-1903 WorAlBi
Gibbs, June Nesbitt 1922- WhoAm 90, WhoAmW 91, WhoE 91
Gibbs, LaVeta Jane 1948- WhoAmW 91, WhoEmL 91
Gibbs, Lawrence B. 1938- WhoAm 90
Gibbs, Lippman Martin 1938- WhoAm 90
Gibbs, Marcus C. 1939- St&PR 91
Gibbs, Margaret Catherine 1914- WhoAmW 91
Gibbs, Marilyn Shisler 1948- WhoAmW 91
Gibbs, Marla BioIn 16
Gibbs, Marla 1931- WhoAm 90, WorAlBi
Gibbs, Marla 1946- DrBlPA 90
Gibbs, Martin 1922- WhoAm 90, WhoE 91
Gibbs, Mary Bramlett 1953- WhoAmW 91
Gibbs, May 1877-1969 FemiCLE
Gibbs, Mike 1937- OxCPMus
Gibbs, Norman Henry 1910-1990 ConAu 131
Gibbs, Phyllis Marilyn Yorke 1939- WhoSSW 91
Gibbs, Richard L. 1927- ODwPR 91
Gibbs, Richard L. 1947- St&PR 91
Gibbs, Robert H, Jr. BioIn 16
Gibbs, Robert Whysall 1965- IntWWM 90
Gibbs, Roger BioIn 16
Gibbs, Ronald Darnley 1904- WhoWor 91
Gibbs, Rose L. 1940- WhoAmW 91
Gibbs, Sarah Preble 1930- WhoAm 90
Gibbs, Sharon L. 1950- WhoAmW 91
Gibbs, Sheri Lynne 1949- WhoEmL 91
Gibbs, Stephen Mark 1955- WhoEmL 91
Gibbs, Tom 1942- WhoAmA 91
Gibbs, W.H. Holden 1932- St&PR 91
Gibbs, William Eugene 1930- WhoAm 90
Gibbs, William F 1920- BiDrAPA 89
Gibbs, William Harold 1950- WhoAm 90
Gibbs, William L. 1945- St&PR 91
Gibbs, William Lee 1945- WhoEmL 91
Gibbs-Fisher, Carole Ann 1937- St&PR 91
Gibby, Mabel Enid Kunce 1926- WhoAmW 91, WhoWor 91
Gibeau, Marie 1950- WhoAmW 91
Gibeau, Martin G. 1954- St&PR 91
Gibeon, Leonard 1945- WhoEmL 91
Giberga, Ulises 1932- St&PR 91
Giberne, Agnes 1845-1939 FemiCLE
Giberson, Kurt Alden 1953- WhoEmL 91
Giberson-Deane, Lydia BiDrAPA 89
Gibert, Gwendolyn 1938- St&PR 91
Gibert, Peter WhoHisp 91
Gibfried, James Paul 1946- BiDrAPA 89
Gibian, George 1924- WhoAm 90
Gibian, Gerald Zachary 1938- St&PR 91
Gibian, Marvin Paul 1927- St&PR 91
Gibian, Paul 1925- St&PR 91, WhoAm 90
Gibian, Thomas George 1922- WhoAm 90
Gibier, Paul 1851-1900 EncO&P 3
Giblett, Eloise Rosalie 1921- WhoAm 90, WhoAmW 91
Giblin, James 1933- BioIn 16
Giblin, James Cross 1933- AuBYP 90, SmATA 12AS [port]
Giblin, John J. 1943- St&PR 91
Giblin, Michael J. 1937- St&PR 91
Giblin, Patrick David 1932- St&PR 91, WhoAm 90
Giblin, Robert ODwPR 91
Giblin, Thomas Patrick 1947- WhoE 91
Giblon, Shirley T 1935- ConAu 131
Gibney, Charles W. 1949- St&PR 91
Gibney, Frank Bray 1924- WhoAm 90, WhoWor 91
Gibney, Kristen Elaine 1948- WhoAmW 91
Gibney, Sharon Ann 1953- WhoAmW 91
Gibney, Sherrie Groover 1954- WhoSSW 91
Gibney, Therese A. 1949- St&PR 91
Gibowicz, Charles Joseph 1934- WhoWor 91
Gibran, Kahlil 1883-1931 EncO&P 3, WorAlBi
Gibran, Kahlil 1922- WhoAm 90
Gibran, Kahlil George 1922- WhoAmA 91
Gibson, Aldred Darryl 1947- WhoWor 91
Gibson, Alexander 1926- PenDiMP
Gibson, Alexander Drummond 1926- IntWWM 90
Gibson, Althea 1927- BioIn 16, WhoAm 90, WhoAmW 91, WorAlBi
Gibson, Andrew John Gavan 1946- WhoWor 91
Gibson, Anne Reed 1947- WhoEmL 91
Gibson, Arthur 1943- ConAu 130
Gibson, Barry Joseph 1951- WhoAm 90
Gibson, Benedict S 1946- WhoAmA 91
Gibson, Benjamin F. 1931- WhoAm 90
Gibson, Bob 1935- Ballpl 90 [port], WorAlBi
Gibson, Bob 1957- Ballpl 90
Gibson, Bryan 1940- St&PR 91
Gibson, Buford, Jr. BiDrAPA 89
Gibson, C. Wayne 1943- St&PR 91
Gibson, Candler McGehee 1964- WhoE 91
Gibson, Carl Royce 1941- St&PR 91
Gibson, Carroll Allen, Jr. 1957- WhoEmL 91
Gibson, Charles 1943- BioIn 16
Gibson, Charles Colmery 1914- WhoAm 90
Gibson, Charles Dana 1867-1944 WorAlBi
Gibson, Charles Dana 1928- WhoE 91
Gibson, Charles DeWolf 1943- WhoAm 90
Gibson, Charles Reese 1842- AmLegL
Gibson, Charles Robert 1940- St&PR 91
Gibson, Count Dillon, Jr. 1921- WhoAm 90
Gibson, Dan NewAgMG
Gibson, Daryl Raymond 1954- WhoEmL 91
Gibson, David Argyle 1934- WhoAm 90
Gibson, David Bryan 1951- St&PR 91
Gibson, David Eugene 1940- St&PR 91
Gibson, David F. 1944- WhoE 91
Gibson, David Mark 1923- WhoAm 90
Gibson, De Marchia 1956- WhoWrEP 89
Gibson, Debbie BioIn 16
Gibson, Dennis James 1952- WhoEmL 91
Gibson, Dennis Leslie, Jr. 1935- WhoWor 91
Gibson, Derek Gair 1936- WhoWor 91
Gibson, Diane BioIn 16
Gibson, Dirk Cameron 1953- WhoSSW 91
Gibson, E. Bryan 1924- St&PR 91
Gibson, E. Martin 1938- St&PR 91
Gibson, Edmund P 1898-1961 EncO&P 3
Gibson, Edward Defield, Jr. BiDrAPA 89
Gibson, Edward Fergus 1937- WhoAm 90
Gibson, Edward G WhoAmA 91
Gibson, Eleanor Jack 1910- WhoAm 90, WhoAmW 91
Gibson, Elisabeth Jane 1937- WhoAmW 91, WhoWor 91
Gibson, Elizabeth BiDEWW
Gibson, Elizabeth Harris WhoAmW 91
Gibson, Elizabeth Hope BiDrAPA 89
Gibson, Ernest L., III 1945- WhoSSW 91
Gibson, Ernest Willard, III 1927- WhoAm 90, WhoE 91
Gibson, Eustace 1842-1900 AmLegL
Gibson, Everett Kay, Jr. 1940- WhoAm 90
Gibson, Floyd Robert 1910- WhoAm 90
Gibson, Frank 1890-1961 Ballpl 90
Gibson, Frank Andrew 1944- St&PR 91
Gibson, Fred D., Jr. 1927- St&PR 91
Gibson, Frederick Edward 1935- WhoAm 90
Gibson, Gary Wayne 1949- WhoEmL 91
Gibson, George 1880-1967 Ballpl 90
Gibson, George 1904- WhoAmA 91
Gibson, George M. 1934- WhoAm 90
Gibson, George R. 1905- St&PR 91
Gibson, Gerald John 1944- WhoWor 91
Gibson, Gertrude Montgomery 1929- St&PR 91
Gibson, Glynis L. 1962- ODwPR 91
Gibson, Graeme 1934- ConAu 130
Gibson, Guadelupe 1917- WhoHisp 91
Gibson, Hal Jean 1924- IntWWM 90
Gibson, Harvey BioIn 16
Gibson, Helena Christine 1937- WhoAmW 91
Gibson, Hoot BioIn 16
Gibson, Hugh 1883-1954 BioIn 16
Gibson, Hugh 1918- WhoAm 90
Gibson, Ian Bennett 1936- WhoWor 91
Gibson, J. Douglas 1928- WhoAm 90
Gibson, Jack BioIn 16
Gibson, James 1902- WhoAm 90

Gibson, James A *BiDrAPA 89*
Gibson, James D 1938- *WhoAmA 91*
Gibson, James Edwin 1941- *WhoAm 90*
Gibson, James Frederick 1943- *St&PR 91*
Gibson, James Glover 1927- *St&PR 91*
Gibson, James Isaac 1925- *St&PR 91*
Gibson, James John 1923- *WhoAm 90*
Gibson, James Michael 1949- *WhoSSW 91*
Gibson, James R. 1943- *St&PR 91*
Gibson, James Riley, Jr. 1944- *WhoWrEP 89*
Gibson, James Robert, Jr. 1951- *WhoEmL 91*
Gibson, James Thomas, Jr. 1921- *WhoAm 90*
Gibson, Janet Mayo 1939- *WhoSSW 91*
Gibson, Janice Thorne 1934- *WhoAm 90*
Gibson, Jeffrey Neal 1959- *WhoEmL 91*
Gibson, Jerry Leigh 1930- *WhoAm 90*
Gibson, Jim *ODwPR 91*
Gibson, Joan Marie 1945- *WhoE 91*
Gibson, John 1959- *WhoEmL 91*
Gibson, John Boyd 1931- *WhoSSW 91*
Gibson, John Egan 1926- *WhoAm 90*
Gibson, John Holden, II 1959- *St&PR 91*
Gibson, John L. 1933- *St&PR 91*
Gibson, John Robert 1925- *WhoAm 90*
Gibson, John Wheat 1946- *WhoEmL 91*
Gibson, Joseph Edwin 1923- *WhoAm 90*
Gibson, Joseph Whitton, Jr. 1922- *WhoAm 90*
Gibson, Josephine *AuBYP 90*
Gibson, Josh 1911-1947 *Ballpl 90 [port]*, *WorAlBi*
Gibson, Karon White 1946- *WhoAmW 91*
Gibson, Kathleen Rita 1942- *WhoAmW 91*
Gibson, Keiko Matsui 1953- *WhoWrEP 89*
Gibson, Keith Patrick 1953- *WhoEmL 91*
Gibson, Kenneth Trigg 1947- *St&PR 91*
Gibson, Kevin Thomas 1953- *WhoEmL 91*
Gibson, Kirk *BioIn 16*
Gibson, Kirk 1957- *Ballpl 90*, *WorAlBi*
Gibson, Kirk Harold 1957- *WhoAm 90*
Gibson, Linda Kay 1951- *WhoSSW 91*
Gibson, Lynn Allen 1955- *WhoEmL 91*, *WhoSSW 91*
Gibson, Margaret 1948- *FemiCLE*
Gibson, Margaret Ferguson 1944- *WhoWrEP 89*
Gibson, Martin Leroy, Jr. 1934- *WhoAm 90*
Gibson, Mary E. 1939- *WhoAmW 91*
Gibson, Mary Elizabeth G. 1924- *WhoWrEP 89*
Gibson, Mary Ellis 1952- *WhoSSW 91*
Gibson, McGuire 1938- *WhoAm 90*
Gibson, Mel *BioIn 16*
Gibson, Mel 1951- *WorAlBi*
Gibson, Mel 1956- *News 90 [port]*, *WhoAm 90*
Gibson, Melvin Roy 1920- *WhoAm 90*, *WhoWor 91*
Gibson, Michael Addison 1943- *WhoSSW 91*
Gibson, Michael Clay 1945- *St&PR 91*
Gibson, Michael L. 1953- *St&PR 91*
Gibson, Mitchell Earl *BiDrAPA 89*
Gibson, Mitchell Earl 1959- *WhoE 91*
Gibson, Morgan 1929- *WhoWrEP 89*
Gibson, Myrna Hawkins 1938- *WhoSSW 91*
Gibson, Nancy Jones 1955- *WhoAmW 91*
Gibson, Norwood 1877-1959 *Ballpl 90*
Gibson, Orville 1856-1918 *OxCPMus*
Gibson, Patricia Ann 1942- *WhoAmW 91*
Gibson, Paul 1960- *Ballpl 90*
Gibson, Paul Raymond 1924- *WhoAm 90*, *WhoWor 91*
Gibson, Paul Robert 1950- *WhoEmL 91*
Gibson, Peggy Kathryn 1936- *WhoAmW 91*
Gibson, Powell Willard 1875- *EarBlAP*
Gibson, Quentin Howieson 1918- *WhoAm 90*
Gibson, R Edward 1956- *BiDrAPA 89*
Gibson, R Lawrence 1937- *BiDrAPA 89*
Gibson, Ralph H 1939- *WhoAmA 91*
Gibson, Ralph Holmes 1939- *WhoAm 90*
Gibson, Randall Charles 1960- *WhoEmL 91*
Gibson, Rankin MacDougal 1916- *WhoAm 90*
Gibson, Raymond E. 1939- *St&PR 91*
Gibson, Raymond Eugene 1924- *WhoAm 90*
Gibson, Reginald Walker 1927- *WhoAm 90*
Gibson, Richard John 1945- *WhoSSW 91*
Gibson, Richard Stephen 1936- *WhoSSW 91*
Gibson, Robert 1935- *WhoAm 90*
Gibson, Robert Lee 1946- *BioIn 16*, *WhoAm 90*
Gibson, Robert N. 1941- *WhoAm 90*
Gibson, Robert Valentine 1921- *WhoAm 90*
Gibson, Robert W. *St&PR 91*
Gibson, Robert W 1924- *BiDrAPA 89*, *WhoE 91*
Gibson, Robert Wylie, Jr. *BiDrAPA 89*
Gibson, Roberta Maxine 1944- *WhoAmW 91*
Gibson, Roberta Suzanne 1950- *WhoAmW 91*
Gibson, Roger *BioIn 16*
Gibson, Roger Cass 1951- *WhoEmL 91*
Gibson, Roland 1902- *WhoAmA 91N*
Gibson, Roxanne Holly 1960- *WhoEmL 91*
Gibson, Roy N. 1941- *St&PR 91*
Gibson, Russ 1939- *Ballpl 90*
Gibson, Sam 1899-1983 *Ballpl 90*
Gibson, Sam Thompson 1916- *WhoAm 90*, *WhoE 91*, *WhoWor 91*
Gibson, Scott Carter 1959- *WhoE 91*
Gibson, Scott Wilbert 1948- *WhoEmL 91*
Gibson, Sharyn Delaine 1947- *WhoEmL 91*
Gibson, Stephen Brodie 1957- *IntWWM 90*
Gibson, Steven A. 1952- *WhoEmL 91*
Gibson, Sybil 1908- *MusmAFA*
Gibson, Teresa Dawn 1960- *WhoWrEP 89*
Gibson, Thomas Fenner, III 1955- *WhoAm 90*
Gibson, Thomas Joseph 1935- *St&PR 91*, *WhoAm 90*
Gibson, Thomas Richard 1942- *WhoAm 90*, *WhoE 91*
Gibson, Valerie 1957- *WhoAmW 91*
Gibson, Verna Kaye 1942- *WhoAm 90*
Gibson, Walter B. 1897-1985 *TwCCr&M 91*
Gibson, Walter Samuel 1932- *WhoAm 90*, *WhoAmA 91*
Gibson, Wanda D. 1948- *WhoAmW 91*
Gibson, Wayne Carlton 1958- *WhoSSW 91*
Gibson, Weldon Bailey 1917- *WhoAm 90*
Gibson, Wendy Joan 1953- *WhoEmL 91*
Gibson, Wilfred Ross, Jr. 1951- *WhoEmL 91*
Gibson, William *WhoSSW 91*
Gibson, William 1914- *WhoAm 90*, *WorAlBi*
Gibson, William 1948- *ConLC 63 [port]*
Gibson, William B. 1938- *WhoAm 90*
Gibson, William E *BioIn 16*
Gibson, William Edward 1944- *WhoAm 90*
Gibson, William Ford 1948- *RGTwCSF*
Gibson, William Francis 1952- *WhoE 91*
Gibson, William Lee 1949- *WhoE 91*, *WhoEmL 91*
Gibson, William M. 1945- *St&PR 91*
Gibson, William Michael 1960- *WhoSSW 91*
Gibson, William Shepard 1933- *St&PR 91*, *WhoAm 90*
Gibson, William Willard, Jr. 1932- *WhoAm 90*
Gibson-Harris, Sheree Lee 1956- *WhoSSW 91*
Gibson-Moore, David John 1943- *St&PR 91*
Gibu, Gary Kazuo 1954- *WhoEmL 91*
Gicking, Robert K. 1931- *St&PR 91*
Gicovate, Bernard 1922- *WhoAm 90*
Giczi, Gregory Joseph 1948- *WhoEmL 91*
Gidal, Nachum *AuBYP 90*
Gidal, Nachum Tim *WhoWor 91*
Gidal, Sonia 1922- *AuBYP 90*
Gidal, Tim 1909- *BioIn 16*
Gidal, Tim Nachum *AuBYP 90*
Giddens, Charles Edwin 1944- *WhoSSW 91*
Giddens, Don Peyton 1940- *WhoAm 90*
Giddens, Zelma Kirk *WhoAmW 91*
Giddings, Clifford Frederick 1936- *WhoE 91*
Giddings, Helen 1943- *WhoSSW 91*, *WhoWor 91*
Giddings, Lauren *WhoWrEP 89*
Giddings, Robert Killen 1928- *St&PR 91*
Giddins, Gary 1948- *ConAu 32NR*
Giddins, Gary Mitchell 1948- *WhoAm 90*
Giddon, Donald Bernard 1930- *WhoAm 90*, *WhoWor 91*
Giddon, Pamela 1951- *ODwPR 91*
Gide, Andre 1869-1951 *BioIn 16*, *MajTwCW*, *WorAlBi*, *WrPh*
Gide, Madeleine Louise Mathilde 1867?-1938 *BioIn 16*
Gidel, Robert Hugh 1951- *WhoWor 91*
Gideon, Clifton D. 1931- *St&PR 91*
Gideon, Donald L. 1928- *St&PR 91*
Gideon, Joyce *ODwPR 91*
Gideon, Kenneth Wayne 1946- *WhoAm 90*
Gideon, Miriam 1906- *IntWWM 90*, *WhoAm 90*
Gideon, Nancy Ann 1955- *WhoWrEP 89*
Gideon, Ruth Gandell 1945- *BiDrAPA 89*
Gideon, Sharon Lee 1955- *WhoAmW 91*
Gideon, William P. 1943- *WhoSSW 91*
Gideon-Hawke, Pamela Lawrence 1945- *WhoAmW 91*
Gidl, Guenter Norbert 1946- *WhoWor 91*
Gidley, Margaret Ann Devoe 1933- *IntWWM 90*
Gidley, William J. 1926- *St&PR 91*
Gidro-Frank, Lothar *BiDrAPA 89*
Gidseg, Glenn 1951- *WhoEmL 91*
Gidumal, Shyam Hira 1959- *WhoEmL 91*
Giduz, Thomas Tracy 1957- *BiDrAPA 89*
Gidwani, Bhagwan N. 1937- *St&PR 91*
Gidwani, Jagdish *BiDrAPA 89*
Gidwitz, Gerald 1906- *WhoAm 90*
Gidwitz, Gerald S. 1906- *St&PR 91*
Gidwitz, James Gerald 1946- *St&PR 91*
Gidwitz, John David 1941- *WhoE 91*
Gidwitz, Joseph L. 1905- *St&PR 91*
Gidwitz, Nancy 1948- *WhoAmW 91*
Gidwitz, Ronald J. 1945- *St&PR 91*, *WhoAm 90*
Giebel, Agnes 1921- *IntWWM 90*, *PenDiMP*
Giebel, Joseph L. 1930- *St&PR 91*
Giebel, Shirley F. 1934- *ODwPR 91*
Giebell, Floyd 1909- *Ballpl 90*
Giebisch, Gerhard Hans 1927- *WhoAm 90*
Giebler, Albert Cornelius 1921- *IntWWM 90*
Giedt, Bruce Alan 1937- *WhoAm 90*
Giedt, Warren Harding 1920- *WhoAm 90*
Giegerich-Schnurr, Jean Marie 1954- *WhoEmL 91*
Giel, Paul 1932- *Ballpl 90*
Giel, Robert Laurence 1947- *WhoE 91*
Gielen, Michael 1927- *PenDiMP*
Gielen, Michael Andreas 1927- *IntWWM 90*, *WhoWor 91*
Gielgud, John 1904- *BioIn 16*, *WhoAm 90*, *WhoWor 91*, *WorAlBi*
Gielgud, Maina 1945- *WhoWor 91*
Gielgud, Val 1900-1981 *TwCCr&M 91*
Gielgud, Val Henry 1900-1981 *DcNaB 1981*
Gielniak, Cary Frank 1957- *WhoEmL 91*
Gielow, Ronald W. 1952- *St&PR 91*
Gier, Audra May Calhoon 1940- *WhoAmW 91*
Gier, Karan Hancock 1947- *WhoAmW 91*
Gierczyk, James P. *St&PR 91*
Gierek, Edward 1913- *WorAlBi*
Gierer, Vincent A., Jr. 1947- *WhoAm 90*
Gierer, Vincent Andrew, Jr. 1947- *St&PR 91*
Gierhart, Douglas Mark 1956- *WhoEmL 91*
Giering, Richard Herbert 1929- *WhoWor 91*
Gieringer, Carl K. 1907- *St&PR 91*
Gierke, Herman Fredrick, III 1943- *WhoAm 90*
Gierl, Benedict Leo 1952- *BiDrAPA 89*
Gierlasinski, Kathy Lynn 1951- *WhoAmW 91*, *WhoEmL 91*
Gierlof, Christian *PenDiDA 89*
Giermak, Chester F. 1927- *St&PR 91*
Giersch, Herbert Hermann 1921- *WhoWor 91*
Gierster, Hans 1925- *IntWWM 90*
Giertz, J. Fred 1943- *WhoAm 90*
Gierz, Monika H. *BiDrAPA 89*
Gies, Carol 1947- *ODwPR 91*
Gies, David Thatcher 1945- *WhoAm 90*
Gies, Thomas Anthony 1930- *WhoAm 90*
Gies, W. Glenn 1936- *St&PR 91*
Giesbrecht, Penny Rosell *BioIn 16*
Gieschen, Martin John 1918- *WhoAmA 91*, *WhoE 91*, *WhoWor 91*
Giese, Alexis Anne 1955- *BiDrAPA 89*
Giese, Johann Ulrich *PenDiDA 89*
Giese, Lester John 1947- *WhoE 91*
Giese, Louis Bernhardt 1927- *St&PR 91*
Giese, Roger Kent 1942- *St&PR 91*
Giese, Tita 1942- *WhoWor 91*
Giese, William Herbert 1944- *WhoE 91*
Giesecke, Gustav Ernst 1908- *WhoAm 90*
Giesecke, Leonard Frederick 1937- *WhoSSW 91*
Giesecke, Mark Ernst 1948- *BiDrAPA 89*
Gieseke, Richard Wayne 1952- *IntWWM 90*
Gieseken, Carlos Adolfo *BiDrAPA 89*
Gieseking, Hal E. 1932- *ConAu 131*
Gieseking, Walter 1895-1956 *BioIn 16*, *PenDiMP*
Giesel, Robert L. 1916- *St&PR 91*
Gieseler, Walter J. *WhoWor 91*
Giesen, Dieter Joseph Heinrich Konrad 1936- *WhoWor 91*
Giesen, Heinrich 1938- *WhoWor 91*
Giesen, John William 1928- *WhoAm 90*
Giesen, Richard A. 1929- *St&PR 91*
Giesen, Richard Allyn 1929- *WhoAm 90*
Giesenhaus, William Frederick 1933- *St&PR 91*
Giesler, Gareth L. 1937- *St&PR 91*
Giesler, Janell Leigh *BiDrAPA 89*
Giesler, Jeanette Louise 1952- *WhoAmW 91*
Giesler, Luther Jackson 1949- *WhoEmL 91*
Giesler, Patric V 1950- *EncPaPR 91*
Giessinger, Lawrence Clyde 1946- *St&PR 91*
Gievers, Karen A. 1949- *WhoEmL 91*
Giff, Patricia Reilly 1935- *AuBYP 90*
Giffard, Ellen Hovde 1925- *EncO&P 3*
Giffard, Martha 1638-1722 *BiDEWW*, *FemiCLE*
Giffels, Donald James 1935- *St&PR 91*
Giffen, Daniel Harris 1938- *WhoAm 90*
Giffen, James Henry 1941- *WhoAm 90*
Giffen, John A. 1938- *St&PR 91*, *WhoAm 90*
Giffen, Lawrence Everett, Sr. 1923- *WhoWor 91*
Giffen, Martin B 1919- *BiDrAPA 89*
Giffhorn, Hans 1942- *WhoWor 91*
Giffin, Glenn Orlando, II 1943- *WhoAm 90*
Giffin, J. B. *AmLegL*
Giffin, Kenneth N. 1944- *St&PR 91*
Giffin, Margaret Ethel 1949- *WhoAmW 91*
Giffin, Mary 1919- *ConAu 130*
Giffin, Mary Elizabeth 1919- *WhoWrEP 89*
Giffin, Walter Charles 1936- *WhoAm 90*
Giffiths, Gregory 1951- *St&PR 91*
Gifford, Alfred T. 1918- *St&PR 91*
Gifford, Ann Gwynne 1937- *WhoE 91*
Gifford, Anthea 1949- *IntWWM 90*
Gifford, Barry 1946- *ConAu 30NR*
Gifford, Bernard R *BioIn 16*
Gifford, Bernard R. 1943- *WhoAm 90*
Gifford, Charles K. *St&PR 91*
Gifford, Charles Kilvert 1942- *WhoAm 90*
Gifford, Daniel Joseph 1932- *WhoAm 90*
Gifford, Don R. 1928- *St&PR 91*
Gifford, Ernest Milton 1920- *WhoAm 90*
Gifford, Frank *BioIn 16*
Gifford, Frank 1930- *WorAlBi*
Gifford, Frank Newton 1930- *WhoAm 90*
Gifford, Gary L. 1947- *St&PR 91*
Gifford, Gayle Lynn 1953- *WhoEmL 91*
Gifford, Gene 1908-1970 *OxCPMus*
Gifford, George E. 1924- *WhoSSW 91*
Gifford, Gerald Michael 1949- *IntWWM 90*
Gifford, Harry Cortland Frey 1919- *WhoAm 90*
Gifford, Helen 1935- *IntWWM 90*
Gifford, J Nebraska 1939- *WhoAmA 91*
Gifford, James Roy 1945- *WhoEmL 91*
Gifford, Jeanne D 1929- *BiDrAPA 89*
Gifford, Jeffrey Scott 1955- *St&PR 91*
Gifford, John Archer 1900-1989 *BioIn 16*
Gifford, Keith Austin 1955- *IntWWM 90*
Gifford, Michael F. 1948- *St&PR 91*
Gifford, Myron D. 1941- *St&PR 91*
Gifford, Nelson Sage 1930- *St&PR 91*, *WhoAm 90*, *WhoE 91*
Gifford, Porter William 1918- *WhoAm 90*
Gifford, Prosser 1929- *WhoAm 90*
Gifford, Ray Wallace, Jr. 1923- *WhoAm 90*, *WhoWor 91*
Gifford, Robert Marvin 1941- *IntWWM 90*
Gifford, Ronald Lynn 1955- *WhoSSW 91*
Gifford, Russell M. 1954- *St&PR 91*
Gifford, Samuel Lee, II 1935- *St&PR 91*
Gifford, Sanford R 1918- *BiDrAPA 89*
Gifford, Thomas 1937- *TwCCr&M 91*
Gifford, Virginia Snodgrass 1936- *WhoAmW 91*, *WhoE 91*
Gifford, Walter Sherman 1885-1966 *BioIn 16*
Gifford, Wendy Blythe 1949- *WhoEmL 91*
Gifford, William Leo 1930- *WhoAm 90*
Gifford, William Wallace 1928- *WhoAm 90*
Giffune, Magdalene Ann Pontolillo 1951- *WhoE 91*
Giffuni, Cathe 1949- *WhoEmL 91*, *WhoWrEP 89*
Giffuni, Flora Baldini *WhoAmA 91*
Giffuni, Joseph V *BioIn 16*
Gift, David Ayres 1953- *WhoEmL 91*
Gift, James Joseph 1942- *St&PR 91*
Gift, Roland *BioIn 16*
Gift, Roland 1960?- *News 90 [port]*
Gift, Thomas Edward 1946- *BiDrAPA 89*
Giftos, Dean A. 1942- *St&PR 91*
Giftos, P. Michael 1947- *St&PR 91*, *WhoAm 90*
Giftos, Peter Charles 1927- *St&PR 91*
Gigandet, Carl Francis 1940- *WhoAm 90*
Giger, Peter 1945- *WhoWor 91*
Gigerenzer, Gerd 1947- *WhoWor 91*
Gigerich, John L. 1942- *St&PR 91*
Giges, Burton *BiDrAPA 89*
Giges, Gerald 1923- *BiDrAPA 89*
Giggal, Kenneth *TwCCr&M 91*
Giggar-Johnson, Monya Marie 1957- *WhoAmW 91*
Giggey, James Walker 1931- *WhoAm 90*
Gigli, Beniamino 1890-1957 *PenDiMP*
Gigli, Irma 1931- *WhoAm 90*
Gigli, Rina 1916- *PenDiMP*
Gigli, Romeo *BioIn 16*
Giglietti, Patrice Ann 1964- *WhoAmW 91*
Giglio, Frank F. 1951- *St&PR 91*
Giglio, Harry Ronald 1950- *WhoEmL 91*
Giglio, Julie Jean *BiDrAPA 89*
Giglio, Mary Ann 1946- *WhoE 91*

Giglio, Ronald Joseph 1933- *St&PR 91*
Giglio, William P. 1929- *St&PR 91*
Gigliotti, Joanne Marie 1945- *WhoAmA 91*
Gigliotti, Richard Joseph 1945- *WhoE 91*
Gignac, Kenneth E. 1933- *St&PR 91*
Gignilliat, Arthur M., Jr. 1932- *St&PR 91*
Gignoux, Claude-Joseph 1890-1966 *BiDFrPL*
Gignoux, Dominique 1929- *St&PR 91*
Gignoux, Edward T 1916-1988 *BioIn 16*
Gignoux, Maurice 1881-1955 *DcScB S2*
Gigout, Eugene 1844-1925 *PenDiMP*
Giguere, Catherine *BiDrAPA 89*
Giguere, Eric *BiDrAPA 89*
Giguere, Roland 1929- *BioIn 16*
Gihwala, Ramesh *BiDrAPA 89*
Gijon y Robles, Rafael 1925- *WhoHisp 91*
Gikas, Carol Sommerfeldt 1950- *WhoAm 90, WhoAmW 91*
Gikas, Paul William 1928- *WhoAm 90*
Gikas, Rick Christopher 1957- *WhoEmL 91*
Gikow, Jacqueline Paula 1947- *WhoE 91*
Gikow, Louise *AuBYP 90*
Gikow, Ruth 1913-1982 *WhoAmA 91N*
Gil, Ana A 1957- *BiDrAPA 89*
Gil, Arthur *BioIn 16*
Gil, Avishai 1945- *WhoWor 91*
Gil, Federico Guillermo 1915- *WhoAm 90*
Gil, Francis Rene 1961- *WhoHisp 91*
Gil, Joseph Louis 1959- *WhoE 91*
Gil, Lourdes 1951- *WhoHisp 91*
Gil, Luis A. 1950- *WhoHisp 91*
Gil, William Joseph 1954- *WhoE 91*
Gil-Casares, Enrique 1946- *WhoWor 91*
Gil de Montes, Roberto 1950- *WhoHisp 91*
Gil-Montero, Martha 1940- *HispWr 90*
Gil-Recasens, Alejandro 1950- *WhoWor 91*
Gilashvili, Pavel Georgiyevich 1918- *WhoWor 91*
Gilb, Corinne Lathrop 1925- *WhoAmW 91*
Gilbane, Frank 1951- *WhoE 91*
Gilbane, Jean A. 1923- *St&PR 91*
Gilbane, Jean Ann 1923- *WhoAm 90, WhoAmW 91*
Gilbane, Thomas F., Jr. 1947- *WhoAm 90*
Gilbane, William James 1908- *WhoAm 90*
Gilberg, Arnold L 1936- *BiDrAPA 89, WhoAm 90*
Gilberg, Kenneth Roy 1951- *WhoE 91, WhoEmL 91*
Gilberg, Milton Joseph 1921- *St&PR 91*
Gilberg, Steven Michael 1962- *WhoEmL 91*
Gilbert and George *BioIn 16*
Gilbert and Sullivan *OxCPMus*
Gilbert, Alan D. 1929- *St&PR 91, WhoAm 90*
Gilbert, Albert Earl 1939- *WhoAmA 91*
Gilbert, Albert Francis 1937- *WhoAm 90*
Gilbert, Alfred 1854-1934 *PenDiDA 89*
Gilbert, Allan A. 1925- *St&PR 91*
Gilbert, Alvin Everett 1925- *WhoE 91*
Gilbert, Ann 1782-1866 *FemiCLE*
Gilbert, Anne 1772?-1834 *FemiCLE*
Gilbert, Anne Hluchan 1955- *BiDrAPA 89*
Gilbert, Anne Jane Hartley 1821-1904 *BioIn 16, NotWoAT*
Gilbert, Anne Wieland 1927- *WhoAm 90*
Gilbert, Anthony 1899-1973 *TwCCr&M 91*
Gilbert, Anthony Chapin 1937- *WhoAm 90*
Gilbert, Anthony John 1934- *IntWWM 90*
Gilbert, Arch Burton 1933- *St&PR 91*
Gilbert, Arnold 1933- *BiDrAPA 89*
Gilbert, Arnold Martin 1921- *WhoAmA 91*
Gilbert, Arthur Charles 1926- *WhoSSW 91*
Gilbert, Arthur Charles Francis 1929- *WhoAm 90, WhoE 91*
Gilbert, Arthur Dale 1953- *St&PR 91*
Gilbert, Arthur Lee 1939- *WhoE 91*
Gilbert, Arthur Lewis 1924- *St&PR 91*
Gilbert, Barbara *WhoWrEP 89*
Gilbert, Barry Lewis R *BiDrAPA 89*
Gilbert, Benjamin Franklin 1918- *WhoAm 90*
Gilbert, Bil *ConAu 129*
Gilbert, Billy 1876-1927 *Ballpl 90*
Gilbert, Brad *BioIn 16*
Gilbert, Brian David 1943- *WhoWor 91*
Gilbert, Bruce 1948- *BiDrAPA 89*
Gilbert, Bruce C. 1938- *St&PR 91*
Gilbert, Calvin Eugene 1926- *St&PR 91*
Gilbert, Carl Arthur 1942- *St&PR 91*
Gilbert, Carla Dilla 1953- *BiDrAPA 89*
Gilbert, Cass 1859-1934 *WorAlBi*
Gilbert, Celia 1932- *WhoWrEP 89*
Gilbert, Charles E., III 1949- *WhoEmL 91*
Gilbert, Charles Nelson 1951- *WhoEmL 91*
Gilbert, Charles Richard Alsop 1916- *WhoAm 90*
Gilbert, Charlie 1919-1983 *Ballpl 90*
Gilbert, Christina Ida 1950- *WhoWrEP 89*
Gilbert, Christopher 1949- *WhoWrEP 89*
Gilbert, Christopher Leslie 1947- *WhoWor 91*
Gilbert, Clyde Lingle 1898- *WhoAmA 91*
Gilbert, Creighton Eddy 1924- *WhoAm 90, WhoAmA 91, WhoWor 91*
Gilbert, Daniel Lee 1925- *WhoAm 90*
Gilbert, David 1945- *WhoE 91*
Gilbert, David Erwin 1939- *WhoAm 90*
Gilbert, David Evans 1951- *WhoSSW 91*
Gilbert, David Heggie 1932- *WhoAm 90*
Gilbert, E. L. *WhoSSW 91*
Gilbert, Edward 1937- *OxCCanT*
Gilbert, Elmer Grant 1930- *WhoAm 90*
Gilbert, Fabiola Cabeza de Baca 1895- *BioIn 16*
Gilbert, Felix 1905- *BioIn 16, ConAu 132, WhoAm 90*
Gilbert, Fred 1849-1903 *OxCPMus*
Gilbert, Fred Ivan, Jr. 1920- *WhoAm 90*
Gilbert, Geoffrey 1914-1989 *AnObit 1989*
Gilbert, George Seymour 1942- *St&PR 91*
Gilbert, Gerald Y. 1936- *WhoE 91*
Gilbert, Glenn Gordon 1936- *WhoAm 90*
Gilbert, Gwen B. 1938- *St&PR 91*
Gilbert, Harold Frederick 1916- *WhoWor 91*
Gilbert, Harold Stanley 1924- *WhoAm 90*
Gilbert, Harold Wendell 1939- *WhoAm 90*
Gilbert, Harriett Sarah 1948- *WhoWor 91*
Gilbert, Harry Ephraim, Jr. 1931- *WhoAm 90*
Gilbert, Helen Earle *AuBYP 90*
Gilbert, Helen Homans 1913-1989 *BioIn 16*
Gilbert, Helen Odell *WhoAmA 91*
Gilbert, Herb 1929- *WhoAmA 91*
Gilbert, Herman Cromwell 1923- *WhoWrEP 89*
Gilbert, Humphrey 1537?-1583 *WorAlBi*
Gilbert, Humphrey 1539?-1583 *EncCRAm*
Gilbert, Ian Richard 1942- *WhoE 91*
Gilbert, Ilsa 1933- *WhoWrEP 89*
Gilbert, Irwin Robert 1953- *WhoEmL 91*
Gilbert, Jack *WhoWrEP 89*
Gilbert, Jack Pittard 1925- *WhoE 91*
Gilbert, Jackson B. 1932- *WhoAm 90*
Gilbert, James B 1939- *ConAu 129*
Gilbert, James Cayce 1925- *WhoAm 90*
Gilbert, James Eastham 1929- *WhoAm 90*
Gilbert, James F. 1932- *St&PR 91*
Gilbert, James Melvin *BiDrAPA 89*
Gilbert, James Robert 1947- *WhoE 91*
Gilbert, Jarobin, Jr. *BioIn 16*
Gilbert, Jean 1879-1942 *OxCPMus*
Gilbert, Jeffrey M 1941- *BiDrAPA 89*
Gilbert, Jerome *BioIn 16*
Gilbert, Jerrold 1936- *St&PR 91*
Gilbert, Jerry Lon 1947- *WhoSSW 91*
Gilbert, Joan S. *ODwPR 91*
Gilbert, Joan Stulman 1934- *WhoAmW 91*
Gilbert, John 1817-1897 *BioIn 16*
Gilbert, John 1897-1936 *WorAlBi*
Gilbert, John B. 1921- *St&PR 91*
Gilbert, John Haspel 1959- *IntWWM 90*
Gilbert, John Humphrey Victor 1941- *WhoAm 90*
Gilbert, John Jordan 1907- *St&PR 91*
Gilbert, John Jouett 1937- *WhoAm 90*
Gilbert, John Neely, Jr. 1936- *St&PR 91*
Gilbert, John Oren 1942- *St&PR 91*
Gilbert, John R. 1946- *ODwPR 91*
Gilbert, Judith Arlene 1946- *WhoAm 90, WhoAmW 91*
Gilbert, Judith May 1934- *WhoAmW 91*
Gilbert, Kathie Simon 1943- *WhoAm 90*
Gilbert, Keith Duncan 1941- *St&PR 91, WhoAm 90*
Gilbert, Keith W. 1946- *St&PR 91*
Gilbert, Kenneth 1931- *IntWWM 90, PenDiMP*
Gilbert, Kenneth Albert 1931- *WhoAm 90*
Gilbert, Kenneth J. 1935- *St&PR 91*
Gilbert, Kenneth Paul 1952- *WhoE 91*
Gilbert, Kimberly Aileen 1961- *WhoEmL 91*
Gilbert, L. Wolfe 1886-1970 *OxCPMus*
Gilbert, Lawrence Irwin 1929- *WhoAm 90*
Gilbert, Lenore E. 1953- *IntWWM 90*
Gilbert, Leonard Harold 1936- *WhoAm 90*
Gilbert, Lewis 1920- *WhoWor 91*
Gilbert, Lewis Arms *BiDrAPA 89*
Gilbert, Lilian A. 1904-1989 *BioIn 16*
Gilbert, Linda Cheryl 1956- *WhoAmW 91*
Gilbert, Lionel 1912- *WhoAmA 91*
Gilbert, Louis J *BiDrAPA 89*
Gilbert, Louis J. 1914-1989 *BioIn 16*
Gilbert, Marie Rogers 1924- *WhoWrEP 89*
Gilbert, Mark Joseph 1959- *WhoEmL 91*
Gilbert, Martin 1936- *ConAu 31NR, WhoWor 91*
Gilbert, Martin 1954- *WhoEmL 91, WhoWor 91*
Gilbert, Maurice Daniel 1942- *St&PR 91*
Gilbert, Melissa *BioIn 16*
Gilbert, Melissa 1964- *WorAlBi*
Gilbert, Mercedes *EarBlAP*
Gilbert, Mercedes *DrBlPA 90*
Gilbert, Mercedes 1889-1952 *HarlReB [port]*
Gilbert, Michael 1912- *TwCCr&M 91, WorAlBi*
Gilbert, Michael 1919-1989 *BioIn 16*
Gilbert, Michael M 1915- *BiDrAPA 89*
Gilbert, Michael William 1954- *WhoEmL 91*
Gilbert, Mila *NewAgMG*
Gilbert, Milton Montague 1927- *St&PR 91*
Gilbert, Neil Robin 1940- *WhoAm 90*
Gilbert, Norman Sutcliffe 1919- *WhoSSW 91, WhoWor 91*
Gilbert, O. Rundle *BioIn 16*
Gilbert, Paul 1944- *BiDrAPA 89*
Gilbert, Perry Webster 1912- *WhoAm 90*
Gilbert, Peter *BioIn 16*
Gilbert, Phil Edward, Jr. 1915- *WhoAm 90, WhoWor 91*
Gilbert, Philip Henry 1939- *WhoSSW 91*
Gilbert, Phillip Noland 1949- *WhoEmL 91*
Gilbert, R A 1942- *EncO&P 3*
Gilbert, Rachel Shaw *WhoAmW 91*
Gilbert, Ralph Guyton 1926- *St&PR 91*
Gilbert, Ralph James 1929- *WhoAm 90*
Gilbert, Ray Wilson, Jr. 1951- *St&PR 91*
Gilbert, Rebecca 1952- *St&PR 91*
Gilbert, Richard G. 1920- *St&PR 91*
Gilbert, Richard Lee 1948- *WhoEmL 91*
Gilbert, Richard P. 1950- *St&PR 91*
Gilbert, Robert B. *WhoAm 90*
Gilbert, Robert Edward 1941- *WhoAm 90*
Gilbert, Robert Evan 1947- *WhoE 91, WhoEmL 91*
Gilbert, Robert Pettibone 1917- *WhoE 91*
Gilbert, Robert Wolfe 1920- *WhoWor 91*
Gilbert, Roberta M *BiDrAPA 89*
Gilbert, Ronald Rhea 1942- *WhoAm 90*
Gilbert, Roswell *BioIn 16*
Gilbert, Roy H.R. 1936- *St&PR 91*
Gilbert, Roy W., Jr. 1937- *WhoAm 90, WhoSSW 91*
Gilbert, Russell T. 1930- *St&PR 91*
Gilbert, Ruth 1917- *FemiCLE*
Gilbert, Sandra 1936- *FemiCLE*
Gilbert, Sandra M. 1936- *ConAu 33NR, MajTwCW*
Gilbert, Sara *BioIn 16*
Gilbert, Sara 1943- *AuBYP 90*
Gilbert, Sean *BioIn 16*
Gilbert, Selma L. 1936- *St&PR 91*
Gilbert, Seymour Parker 1892-1938 *BioIn 16*
Gilbert, Seymour Parker, Jr. 1892-1938 *EncABHB 7 [port]*
Gilbert, Sharon 1944- *WhoAmA 91*
Gilbert, Stephen Alan 1939- *St&PR 91*
Gilbert, Stephen L. 1943- *WhoWor 91*
Gilbert, Steven E. 1943- *IntWWM 90*
Gilbert, Steven Edward 1943- *IntWWM 90*
Gilbert, Steven P 1945- *BiDrAPA 89*
Gilbert, Suzanne Harris 1943- *WhoAmW 91*
Gilbert, Suzanne Harris 1948- *St&PR 91*
Gilbert, Terry 1932- *IntWWM 90*
Gilbert, Terry D. 1936- *St&PR 91*
Gilbert, Thomas Angus 1948- *WhoEmL 91*
Gilbert, Thomas James 1957- *WhoEmL 91*
Gilbert, Thomas Tibbals 1947- *WhoE 91*
Gilbert, Trimble Gwich'in *BioIn 16*
Gilbert, Virginia Lee 1946- *WhoWrEP 89*
Gilbert, W. S. 1836-1911 *OxCPMus*
Gilbert, Wally 1901-1958 *Ballpl 90*
Gilbert, Walter 1932- *WhoAm 90, WhoE 91, WhoWor 91, WorAlBi*
Gilbert, Walter F. 1926- *St&PR 91*
Gilbert, William 1544-1603 *WorAlBi*
Gilbert, William Henry 1938- *BiDrAPA 89*
Gilbert, William S. 1836-1911 *WorAlBi*
Gilbert, William Schwenck 1836-1911 *AuBYP 90*
Gilbert, Woodrow Keith 1946- *St&PR 91*
Gilbert, Xavier Francois 1943- *WhoWor 91*
Gilbert-Rolfe, Jeremy 1945- *WhoAmA 91*
Gilbertson, Alan Dale 1953- *WhoEmL 91*
Gilbertson, Arlan D. 1929- *St&PR 91*
Gilbertson, B Charlotte *WhoWrEP 89*
Gilbertson, Bernice Charlotte *WhoE 91*
Gilbertson, Charlotte *WhoAmA 91*
Gilbertson, Donald Edmund 1934- *WhoAm 90*
Gilbertson, Eric Raymond 1945- *WhoAm 90*
Gilbertson, Gene Roy 1949- *St&PR 91*
Gilbertson, Joel Warren 1949- *WhoEmL 91*
Gilbertson, John Raymond 1923- *St&PR 91*
Gilbertson, John S. 1943- *St&PR 91*
Gilbertson, Robert G. 1941- *WhoAm 90*
Gilbertson, Robert Gene 1941- *St&PR 91*
Gilbertson, Sherry Marie 1959- *WhoEmL 91*
Gilbey, Samuel *PenDiDA 89*
Gilbo, Anna-Carolyn 1940- *WhoWrEP 89*
Gilboa, Jacob 1920- *IntWWM 90*
Gilboa, Netta 1958- *WhoE 91, WhoEmL 91*
Gilbody, Robert Joseph 1928- *St&PR 91*
Gilboe, David Dougherty 1929- *WhoAm 90*
Gilborn, Craig Alfred 1934- *WhoE 91*
Gilboy, Margaretta 1943- *WhoAmA 91*
Gilboy, Michael Russell 1950- *WhoE 91*
Gilbreath, Freida Carol 1949- *WhoAmW 91*
Gilbreath, Rod 1952- *Ballpl 90*
Gilbreth, Edward S. 1933- *WhoAm 90*
Gilbreth, Frank Bunker, Jr. 1911- *WhoAm 90*
Gilbreth, Lillian M. 1878-1972 *BioAmW*
Gilbreth, Lillian Moller 1878-1972 *BioIn 16*
Gilbride, John Thomas, Jr. 1945- *WhoAm 90*
Gilbride, William Donald 1924- *WhoAm 90*
Gilby, John W.G. *St&PR 91*
Gilchrest, Thornton Charles 1931- *WhoAm 90*
Gilchriest, Lorenzo 1938- *WhoAmA 91*
Gilchrist, Agnes Addison 1907-1976 *WhoAmA 91N*
Gilchrist, Albert Waller 1858-1926 *AmLegL*
Gilchrist, Anne 1828-1885 *FemiCLE*
Gilchrist, Anne Marie 1960- *WhoAmW 91, WhoEmL 91*
Gilchrist, Barry D. 1947- *St&PR 91*
Gilchrist, David M. 1949- *St&PR 91*
Gilchrist, David Walter 1931- *St&PR 91*
Gilchrist, Elizabeth Brenda *WhoAmA 91*
Gilchrist, Ellen 1935- *FemiCLE, MajTwCW, WorAu 1980 [port]*
Gilchrist, Ellen Louise 1935- *WhoAm 90, WhoAmW 91*
Gilchrist, Forbes Daniel 1945- *WhoEmL 91*
Gilchrist, Frederick Charles 1859-1896 *DcCanB 12*
Gilchrist, Gerald Seymour 1935- *WhoAm 90*
Gilchrist, Henry 1924- *St&PR 91*
Gilchrist, James Austin 1953- *WhoE 91*
Gilchrist, James B. 1939- *St&PR 91*
Gilchrist, James Beardslee 1939- *WhoAm 90*
Gilchrist, Kenneth 1927- *St&PR 91*
Gilchrist, William G., III 1932- *St&PR 91*
Gilchrist, William McKenzie 1909- *St&PR 91*
Gilchrist, William Risque, Jr. 1944- *WhoSSW 91*
Gilcrease, Joy Victoria 1940- *St&PR 91*
Gilcrease, Richard 1937- *St&PR 91*
Gilcreast, James Everett, Jr. 1946- *WhoE 91*
Gilcrest, Roger W. 1937- *St&PR 91*
Gildart, Kevin P. 1949- *St&PR 91*
Gilday, Thomas John 1953- *WhoEmL 91*
Gildea, Brian Michael 1939- *WhoE 91*
Gildea, Edward J. 1951- *St&PR 91*
Gildea, Edward Joseph 1951- *WhoAm 90*
Gildea, John R. 1939- *St&PR 91*
Gildea, Margaret C L *BiDrAPA 89*
Gildehaus, Thomas Arthur 1940 *St&PR 91, WhoAm 90*
Gildemeister, Jerry 1934- *WhoWrEP 89*
Gilden, Anita 1938- *WhoAmA 91*
Gilden, David 1947- *St&PR 91*
Gilden, Mel *AuBYP 90*
Gildenberg, Philip Leon 1935- *WhoAm 90*
Gildenberg, Sanford R. 1942- *St&PR 91*
Gildenblatt, Stuart Alan 1950- *St&PR 91*
Gildenhorn, Joseph Bernard 1929- *WhoAm 90*
Gildenman, Moshe *BioIn 16*
Gilder, Charles Joseph 1934- *St&PR 91*
Gilder, David Austin *BiDrAPA 89*
Gilder, Eric 1911- *IntWWM 90*
Gilder, Helen 1848-1916 *BiDWomA*
Gilder, Richard Watson 1844-1909 *BioIn 16*
Gilder, Rodman 1918- *BiDrAPA 89*
Gilder, Rosamond 1891?-1986 *BioIn 16, NotWoAT*
Gilderhus, Mark Theodore 1941- *WhoAm 90*
Gildersleeve, Robert F. 1942- *St&PR 91*
Gildin, Herbert *St&PR 91*
Gildin, Joan Sandra 1953- *BiDrAPA 89*
Gilding, Elizabeth *FemiCLE*
Gildner, Gary 1938- *WhoWrEP 89*
Gildred, Theodore Edmonds 1935- *WhoAm 90, WhoWor 91*
Gildrie, Charles Arthur 1948- *WhoSSW 91*
Gildrie, Richard Peter 1945- *WhoSSW 91*
Gildzen, Alex 1943- *WhoAmA 91*
Gile, Mary Stuart 1936- *WhoAmW 91*
Gilels, Elena 1948- *PenDiMP*
Gilels, Emil 1916-1985 *BioIn 16, PenDiMP, WorAlBi*
Giles, Anne Diener 1948- *WhoAm 90*
Giles, Barbara 1912- *FemiCLE*
Giles, Brian 1960- *Ballpl 90*
Giles, Carl Howard 1935- *WhoSSW 91*
Giles, Clarence Alfred 1946- *WhoWor 91*

Giles, David M 1946- BiDrAPA 89
Giles, Donald Earl 1931- St&PR 91
Giles, Douglas J. 1942- St&PR 91
Giles, Eugene 1933- WhoAm 90
Giles, George 1909- Ballpl 90
Giles, Gerald Lynn 1943- WhoWor 91
Giles, Gordon A. AuBYP 90
Giles, Henry 1809-1882 BioIn 16
Giles, Henry 1916-1986 LiHiK
Giles, Homer Wayne 1919- WhoAm 90
Giles, James 1718-1780 PenDiDA 89
Giles, James Raymond 1932- WhoSSW 91
Giles, James S. 1836-1878 AmLegL
Giles, James Walter 1945- WhoEmL 91
Giles, Janice Holt 1909-1979 LiHiK
Giles, Jean Hall 1908- WhoAmW 91, WhoWor 91
Giles, Jeffry Alan 1964- WhoSSW 91
Giles, Judith Margaret 1939- WhoAmW 91
Giles, Karen Denise 1961- WhoAmW 91
Giles, Kenneth TwCCr&M 91
Giles, Lynda Fern 1943- WhoAmW 91
Giles, M. BiDWomA
Giles, Michael Peter 1941- WhoWor 91
Giles, Molly 1942- WhoWrEP 89
Giles, Nancy BioIn 16
Giles, Newell Walton, Jr 1928- WhoAmA 91
Giles, Norman Henry 1915- WhoAm 90
Giles, Peter 1938- St&PR 91, WhoAm 90
Giles, Phyllis Lenore 1912- WhoAmW 91
Giles, Richard W. 1930- St&PR 91
Giles, Robert Edward, Jr. 1949- WhoEmL 91
Giles, Robert H 1933- BioIn 16
Giles, Robert Hartmann 1933- WhoAm 90
Giles, Stephen Roy 1950- WhoWor 91
Giles, Thomas Foye 1947- WhoSSW 91
Giles, Warren 1896-1979 Ballpl 90 [port]
Giles, William Elmer 1927- WhoAm 90
Giles, William Jacob, Jr. 1948- WhoSSW 91
Giles, William Jefferson, IV 1958- WhoEmL 91
Giles, William Yale 1934- WhoAm 90, WhoE 91
Gilfillan, George William 1938- WhoAm 90
Gilfillan, John Thomas, Jr. BiDrAPA 89
Gilfillan, Ross W. 1926- WhoAm 90
Gilfoil, James Henry 1946- BiDrAPA 89
Gilfond, Edythe BioIn 16
Gilford, Jack 1907-1990 BioIn 16, NewYTBS 90 [port], News 90, WorAlBi
Gilford, Leon 1917- WhoE 91, WhoWor 91
Gilfrich, John Valentine 1927- WhoE 91
Gilgar, Arthur Emery 1944- St&PR 91
Gilger, Paul Douglass 1954- WhoWor 91
Gilgore, Sheldon Gerald 1932- WhoAm 90
Gilgun, John Francis 1935- WhoWrEP 89
Gilham, Robert Ernest 1943- WhoE 91
Gilhool, Thomas K BioIn 16
Gilhooley, Frank 1892-1959 Ballpl 90
Gilhooley, Jack ConAu 31NR
Gilhooley, John 1940- ConAu 31NR
Gilhooly, David James, III 1943- WhoAm 90, WhoAmA 91
Gilhooly, Kevin John 1960- WhoSSW 91
Gilhuley, Stephen E. 1944- St&PR 91
Gilhuly, Robert Thomas 1930- WhoAm 90
Gilhuys, Charles 1934- St&PR 91
Gili, Katherine 1948- BiDWomA
Gili, Paolo PenDiDA 89
Gilinsky, Stanley Ellis 1918- WhoAm 90, WhoE 91
Gilinsky, Victor 1934- WhoAm 90
Gilkerson, Robert E. 1922- MusmAFA
Gilkerson, Yancey Sherard 1919- WhoAm 90
Gilkerson-Daehnke, Cynthia Alexandra 1959- WhoEmL 91
Gilkes, Arthur G. 1915- St&PR 91
Gilkes, Arthur Gwyer 1915- WhoWor 91
Gilkes, Martha Jane Watkins 1953- WhoAmW 91
Gilkeson, Murray Mack 1922- WhoAm 90
Gilkeson, Robert Fairbairn 1917- WhoAm 90
Gilkey, Gordon Waverly 1912- WhoAm 90, WhoAmA 91, WhoWor 91
Gilkey, Herbert Talbot 1924- WhoSSW 91
Gilkey, John William 1956- BiDrAPA 89
Gilkey, Kenneth George 1942- St&PR 91
Gilkey, Langdon Brown 1919- BioIn 16, WhoAm 90
Gilkey, Richard Charles 1925- WhoAmA 91
Gilkyson, Eliza NewAgMG
Gill, Abigail Stanton 1945- St&PR 91, WhoEmL 91
Gill, Andrew Dunlap BiDrAPA 89
Gill, Anna Pietrangelo 1944- WhoAmW 91
Gill, Anton 1948- ConAu 130
Gill, Ardian C. 1929- WhoAm 90
Gill, B. M. ConAu 132
Gill, B. M. 1921- TwCCr&M 91
Gill, Baljit Singh 1956- BiDrAPA 89
Gill, Baltej Singh 1953- BiDrAPA 89
Gill, Bartholomew 1943- TwCCr&M 91
Gill, Becky Lorette 1947- BiDrAPA 89
Gill, Benjamin F 1917- BiDrAPA 89
Gill, Benjamin Franklin 1917- WhoAm 90
Gill, Bernard Ives 1921- WhoAm 90
Gill, Bhupinder Singh BiDrAPA 89
Gill, Bob 1931- ConDes 90
Gill, Brendan 1914- BioIn 16, MajTwCW, WhoAm 90, WhoWrEP 89
Gill, Carole O'Brien 1946- WhoAmW 91
Gill, Charles A T BiDrAPA 89
Gill, Charles B. 1938- St&PR 91
Gill, Claes 1910-1973 DcScanL
Gill, Clark Cyrus 1915- WhoAm 90
Gill, Daniel E. 1936- WhoAm 90, WhoE 91
Gill, David Brian 1957- WhoSSW 91
Gill, Deirdre BioIn 16
Gill, Diane L. 1948- WhoAmW 91
Gill, Donald Artley 1938- WhoSSW 91
Gill, Donald George 1927- WhoAm 90
Gill, Donald Joseph 1937- BiDrAPA 89
Gill, Ellen Wildy 1915- WhoAmW 91
Gill, Eric 1882-1940 BioIn 16, DcLB 98 [port]
Gill, Eunice 1958- BiDrAPA 89
Gill, Evalyn Pierpoint WhoAmW 91, WhoWor 91
Gill, Frank E 1925- BiDrAPA 89
Gill, Frederick James 1906-1974 WhoAmA 91N
Gill, Gail Stoorza 1943- ODwPR 91
Gill, Gene 1933- WhoAmA 91
Gill, George 1909- Ballpl 90
Gill, George K. 1939- St&PR 91
Gill, George Norman 1934- St&PR 91, WhoAm 90
Gill, Gerald Lawson 1947- WhoEmL 91, WhoSSW 91, WhoWor 91
Gill, Gregory William 1962- WhoEmL 91
Gill, Gurcharan P. S. 1953- WhoSSW 91
Gill, H.R. 1936- St&PR 91
Gill, Harbans Kaur BiDrAPA 89
Gill, Harlan 1922- St&PR 91
Gill, Harry S. 1945- St&PR 91
Gill, Harwant K BiDrAPA 89
Gill, Henry Clement 1927- St&PR 91
Gill, Henry Herr 1930- WhoAm 90
Gill, Howard B BioIn 16
Gill, Irving 1870-1936 BioIn 16
Gill, James C. 1843-1897 AmLegL
Gill, James Joseph BiDrAPA 89
Gill, Joan Huennekens 1961- BiDrAPA 89
Gill, Joanne Carlyne 1933- WhoAmW 91
Gill, John 1697-1771 BioIn 16
Gill, John Allen 1938- St&PR 91
Gill, John E. 1941- St&PR 91
Gill, John M. 1950- St&PR 91
Gill, John Welch, Jr. 1942- WhoAm 90
Gill, Jonathan B BiDrAPA 89
Gill, Jonathan Belding 1919- WhoE 91
Gill, Joseph Peter, Jr. 1928- St&PR 91
Gill, Kenneth Paul 1926- St&PR 91
Gill, Laurance Edward 1939- St&PR 91
Gill, Linda A. ODwPR 91
Gill, Linda Tracy 1951- WhoEmL 91
Gill, Lunda Lucinda 1959- WhoAmW 91
Gill, M Z I BiDrAPA 89
Gill, Madge EncO&P 3
Gill, Mark James 1956- St&PR 91
Gill, Mary Margaret 1956- WhoEmL 91
Gill, Merton 1914- BiDrAPA 89
Gill, Merwyn C. 1910- St&PR 91
Gill, Michael J BiDrAPA 89
Gill, Patricia Jane 1950- WhoEmL 91
Gill, Patrick MajTwCW
Gill, Peter L. 1942- St&PR 91
Gill, Raheela Safdar 1967- WhoAmW 91
Gill, Raymond Edward, Jr. 1950- WhoE 91
Gill, Raymond Joseph 1930- St&PR 91, WhoAm 90
Gill, Rebecca LaLosh 1944- WhoWor 91
Gill, Richard 1922-1989 BioIn 16
Gill, Richard Cochran 1901- AuBYP 90
Gill, Richard J. 1955- St&PR 91
Gill, Richard James 1941- IntWWM 90
Gill, Richard Thomas 1927- WhoAm 90
Gill, Robert 1911-1974 OxCCanT
Gill, Robert B. St&PR 91
Gill, Robert B. 1931- WhoAm 90
Gill, Robert Lewis 1911-1983 BioIn 16
Gill, Rockne 1931- WhoAm 90
Gill, Ronnie Joy 1949- WhoAmW 91
Gill, Roy G 1916- BiDrAPA 89
Gill, Sabra Hall ODwPR 91
Gill, Safdar Ali 1931- St&PR 91
Gill, Sam D. 1943- ConAu 130
Gill, Samuel Lafayette, Jr. 1936- WhoAm 90
Gill, Sandra Lee 1948- WhoEmL 91
Gill, Sarah 1728-1771 FemiCLE
Gill, Stanley Jensen 1929- WhoAm 90
Gill, Stephen 1932- SmATA 63 [port]
Gill, Stephen Paschall 1938- WhoAm 90
Gill, Steven Streatfield 1956- WhoWor 91
Gill, Thomas J. St&PR 91
Gill, Thomas James, III 1932- WhoAm 90
Gill, Thomas Michael 1941- St&PR 91
Gill, Tom EncACom
Gill, Vince WhoNeCM [port]
Gill, Virgil Lee 1934- WhoSSW 91
Gill, Walter Douglass 1950- WhoE 91
Gill, Wanda Kit-Wan 1955- WhoWor 91
Gill, Wilfred M 1906- BiDrAPA 89
Gill, William Albert, Jr. 1924- WhoAm 90
Gill, William Nelson 1928- WhoAm 90
Gill, Winifred M. 1958- WhoAmW 91
Gill Thompson, Norma N. 1920- WhoAmW 91
Gillam, James Kennedy 1922- WhoAm 90
Gillam, Jean Clare 1959- WhoAmW 91
Gillam, Max Lee 1926- WhoAm 90
Gillan, Allan Wayne 1946- WhoSSW 91
Gillan, John Terry 1937- WhoSSW 91
Gillan, Maria Mazziotti 1940- WhoWrEP 89
Gillan, William Thomas 1940- St&PR 91
Gillani, Fizza Syeda WhoE 91
Gillard, David Owen 1947- IntWWM 90
Gillars, Mildred 1900-1988 AnObit 1988
Gillars, Mildred Elizabeth 1900-1988 BioIn 16
Gillary, Randall Jay 1951- WhoEmL 91
Gillaspie, Athey Graves, Jr. 1938- WhoSSW 91
Gillaspie, Jon Alan 1950- IntWWM 90
Gillaspie, Richard C. WhoAm 90
Gillaugh, Raymond Dale 1930- St&PR 91
Gillberg, K. Gunnar 1942- St&PR 91
Gillberg, Rune Gunnar 1948- WhoWor 91
Gille, Isabelle Marie-Noolle Amelie 1959- WhoAmW 91
Gille, Lori-Jean 1952- St&PR 91
Gille, Marianne Birgitta 1944- WhoWor 91
Gillece, James Patrick, Jr. 1944- WhoAm 90
Gillelan, George Howard 1917- AuBYP 90
Gilleland, Brady Blackford 1922- WhoAm 90
Gilleland, Ken Orrin 1952- WhoEmL 91
Gillen, James Frederick John 1915- WhoAm 90
Gillen, James Robert 1937- St&PR 91, WhoAm 90
Gillen, John 1947- WhoAmA 91
Gillen, Stephen E. 1953- St&PR 91
Gillen, William Albert 1914- WhoAm 90
Gillens, Clara Belle 1954- WhoEmL 91
Gillenson, Mark Lee 1948- WhoSSW 91
Gillenwater, Carden 1918- Ballpl 90
Gillenwater, Chad Michie 1947- WhoEmL 91
Gillenwater, James E. 1931- St&PR 91
Gillenwater, Jay Young 1933- WhoAm 90
Giller, Earl L, Jr. 1943- BiDrAPA 89
Giller, Edward Bonfoy 1918- WhoAm 90
Giller, Howard M. 1956- St&PR 91
Giller, Martin BiDrAPA 89
Giller, Norman M. 1918- St&PR 91
Giller, Norman Myer 1918- WhoAm 90
Giller, Robert Maynard 1942- WhoE 91, WhoWor 91
Giller, Ruth Edna 1929- WhoAmW 91
Giller, Susan Ann 1946- WhoAmW 91
Gillerman, Dawn Iris 1956- WhoAmW 91
Gillert, Thomas Casey 1947- WhoSSW 91
Gilles de Laval 1404-1440 EncO&P 3
Gilles, Marie-Louise 1937- IntWWM 90
Gillespie, A.J., Jr. 1923- St&PR 91
Gillespie, Alastair William 1922- WhoAm 90
Gillespie, Alexander Joseph, Jr. 1923- WhoAm 90
Gillespie, Angus Kress 1942- ConAu 132
Gillespie, Anita Wright 1953- WhoAmW 91
Gillespie, Bob 1918- Ballpl 90
Gillespie, Bruce A. St&PR 91
Gillespie, Bryant W. 1922- St&PR 91
Gillespie, Carol Suzanne 1964- WhoSSW 91
Gillespie, Charles 1929-1989 BioIn 16
Gillespie, Charles Anthony, Jr. 1935- WhoAm 90, WhoWor 91
Gillespie, Claire Seybold 1947- St&PR 91
Gillespie, Colleen Patricia 1958- WhoEmL 91
Gillespie, Daniel Curtis, Sr. 1922- WhoAm 90
Gillespie, Daniel Joseph 1928- St&PR 91
Gillespie, Daniel P. St&PR 91
Gillespie, Daniel Paul 1941- WhoAm 90
Gillespie, David Ellis 1933- St&PR 91
Gillespie, Diane Filby 1943- ConAu 130
Gillespie, Dick BioIn 16
Gillespie, Dizzy 1917- BioIn 16, DrBIPA 90, OxCPMus, WhoAm 90, WorAlBi
Gillespie, Dorothy M. 1920- WhoE 91
Gillespie, Dorothy Merle 1920- BiDWomA
Gillespie, Dorothy Muriel 1920- WhoAmA 91
Gillespie, Douglas Grant 1946- WhoWor 91
Gillespie, Edward Malcolm 1935- WhoAm 90, WhoSSW 91
Gillespie, Floyd Harold 1924- St&PR 91
Gillespie, Frederick S. 1916- St&PR 91
Gillespie, Gale Sanson 1948- St&PR 91
Gillespie, George Joseph, III 1930- WhoAm 90
Gillespie, Gerald Ernest Paul 1933- WhoAm 90
Gillespie, Gregory Joseph 1936- WhoAmA 91
Gillespie, Gwain Homer 1931- WhoAm 90
Gillespie, Hal Gravley BiDrAPA 89
Gillespie, Harry Robinson 1922- WhoWor 91
Gillespie, Helen Davys 1954- WhoAmW 91
Gillespie, Helen Marie 1937- WhoSSW 91
Gillespie, Iain Erskine 1931- WhoWor 91
Gillespie, Ian 1946- WhoWor 91
Gillespie, Ian Andrew 1948- BiDrAPA 89
Gillespie, J. Martin 1949- WhoEmL 91
Gillespie, James Bennett 1905- WhoAm 90
Gillespie, James Davis 1955- WhoEmL 91, WhoSSW 91, WhoWor 91
Gillespie, James Howard 1917- WhoAm 90
Gillespie, James Trigg, Jr. BiDrAPA 89
Gillespie, John Birks 1917- BioIn 16, IntWWM 90
Gillespie, John T 1928- ConAu 31NR
Gillespie, John Thomas 1928- WhoAm 90
Gillespie, Joseph G. 1939- St&PR 91
Gillespie, Joseph Raymond 1950- WhoSSW 91
Gillespie, Luke O'Neil 1957- IntWWM 90
Gillespie, Marie F. BioIn 16
Gillespie, Mary Krempa 1941- WhoAmW 91
Gillespie, Mary Patrice BiDrAPA 89
Gillespie, Nan WhoWrEP 89
Gillespie, Nellie Redd WhoAmW 91
Gillespie, Ramon Edward 1928- St&PR 91
Gillespie, Ray Ballpl 90
Gillespie, Rhonda Marie 1941- IntWWM 90
Gillespie, Richard Roubaud 1930- St&PR 91
Gillespie, Robert Charles 1942- WhoAm 90
Gillespie, Robert J. 1942- St&PR 91
Gillespie, Robert James 1942- WhoAm 90
Gillespie, Robert T. E. 1931- WhoAm 90
Gillespie, Robert W. 1944- St&PR 91
Gillespie, Robert Wayne 1944- WhoAm 90
Gillespie, Rory Andrew 1956- WhoAm 90
Gillespie, Sarah Ashman 1953- WhoAm 90
Gillespie, Thomas James, III 1924- St&PR 91
Gillespie, Thomas Stuart 1938- St&PR 91, WhoAm 90
Gillespie, Thomas William 1928- WhoAm 90, WhoE 91, WhoWor 91
Gillespie, William A. 1924- St&PR 91
Gillespie, William Anthony 1950- WhoEmL 91, WhoWor 91
Gillespie, William Fulton 1931- WhoWor 91
Gillespie, William Hewitt 1905- EncO&P 3
Gillespie, William James, Jr. 1930- BiDrAPA 89
Gillet, Guillaume 1912-1988 BioIn 16
Gillet, Ronald A. 1941- St&PR 91
Gillett, Alistair James 1952- WhoEmL 91
Gillett, Charles 1915- WhoAm 90
Gillett, Edward 1915- ConAu 131
Gillett, Eric BiDrAPA 89
Gillett, George BioIn 16
Gillett, George Nield, Jr. 1938- WhoAm 90, WhoSSW 91
Gillett, Jonathan Newell 1941- WhoAm 90
Gillette, Anita 1938- WhoAm 90
Gillette, Bob WhoWrEP 89
Gillette, Carol May 1940- WhoAmW 91
Gillette, Constance J. 1948- WhoEmL 91
Gillette, Dean 1925- WhoAm 90
Gillette, Dennis 1939- St&PR 91
Gillette, E. Peter, Jr. 1934- St&PR 91
Gillette, Earle Peter, Jr. 1934- WhoAm 90
Gillette, Edward LeRoy 1932- WhoAm 90
Gillette, Edward Scranton 1898-1988 WhoAm 90
Gillette, Ethel Morrow 1921- WhoAmW 91
Gillette, Ethel Perry WhoWrEP 89
Gillette, Gary Melvin 1960- WhoEmL 91
Gillette, Gordon Edgar 1931- WhoSSW 91
Gillette, Gregory Mark 1949- BiDrAPA 89
Gillette, Halbert George 1926- WhoSSW 91
Gillette, Hyde 1906- WhoAm 90
Gillette, James R. 1943- St&PR 91
Gillette, John Albert 1958- WhoE 91
Gillette, John R BiDrAPA 89
Gillette, Joyce Lynne 1948- WhoEmL 91
Gillette, Kevin Mark 1955- WhoEmL 91
Gillette, King Camp 1855-1932 BioIn 16, WorAlBi
Gillette, Ned 1945- BioIn 16
Gillette, Paul 1938- WhoWrEP 89

Gillette, Paul Crawford 1942- *WhoAm 90*
Gillette, Robert S. 1913- *St&PR 91*
Gillette, Stanley C. *WhoAm 90*
Gillette, Susan Downs 1950- *WhoAmW 91*
Gillette, W. Michael 1941- *WhoAm 90*
Gillette, William 1933- *WhoAm 90*
Gillette, William Hooker 1853-1937 *BioIn 16*
Gilley, James R. 1934- *St&PR 91*
Gilley, Mickey Leroy 1936- *WhoAm 90, WorAlBi*
Gilleylen, Bruce C. 1946- *St&PR 91*
Gillham, John Kinsey 1930- *WhoAm 90*
Gillham, Nicholas Wright 1932- *WhoAm 90*
Gillham, Robert 1938- *WhoAm 90*
Gilliam, Carroll Lewis 1929- *WhoAm 90*
Gilliam, David Thomas *BiDrAPA 89*
Gilliam, Dennis Eugene 1945- *WhoEmL 91*
Gilliam, Elizabeth M. 1930- *WhoWrEP 89*
Gilliam, Florence *FemiCLE*
Gilliam, Jackson Earle 1920- *WhoAm 90*
Gilliam, James F. 1915-1990 *BioIn 16*
Gilliam, James H., Jr. 1945- *WhoAm 90*
Gilliam, James Howard, Jr. 1945- *St&PR 91*
Gilliam, James N. 1942- *St&PR 91*
Gilliam, Jim 1928-1978 *Ballpl 90 [port]*
Gilliam, John A. 1935- *WhoAm 90*
Gilliam, John Charles 1927- *WhoAm 90*
Gilliam, John Hilliard *BiDrAPA 89*
Gilliam, Lynda Faye 1949- *WhoAmW 91*
Gilliam, Mary 1928- *WhoAmW 91*
Gilliam, Melvin Randolph 1921- *WhoAm 90*
Gilliam, Paula Hutter *WhoAmW 91*
Gilliam, Robert Ballard 1805-1870 *AmLegL*
Gilliam, Sam 1933- *BioIn 16, WhoAmA 91, WhoE 91*
Gilliam, Stu 1943- *DrBlPA 90*
Gilliam, Terry *BioIn 16*
Gilliam, Terry Keith 1945- *St&PR 91*
Gilliam, Terry Vance 1940- *WhoAm 90*
Gilliam, William Michael 1966- *WhoSSW 91*
Gilliand, Harold 1932- *St&PR 91*
Gilliand, Merle E. 1921- *St&PR 91*
Gilliard, Debora J. 1956- *WhoEmL 91*
Gilliard, Judy Ann 1946- *WhoAmW 91*
Gilliatt, Neal 1917- *St&PR 91, WhoAm 90*
Gilliatt, Penelope *BioIn 16*
Gilliatt, Penelope 1932- *FemiCLE*
Gilliatt, Penelope 1933- *WorAlBi*
Gillibrand, Michael Gray 1948- *WhoWor 91*
Gillice, Sondra Jupin *WhoAmW 91, WhoE 91*
Gillice, Sondra Jupin 1936- *St&PR 91*
Gillick, Kimberly Ann 1960- *WhoE 91*
Gillick, Marvin 1944- *BiDrAPA 89*
Gillick, Patrick 1937- *WhoAm 90, WhoE 91*
Gillick, Victoria *BioIn 16*
Gillie, Annis Calder 1900-1985 *DcNaB 1981*
Gillies, Ann Steadry 1941- *WhoAmW 91*
Gillies, Donald Richard 1939- *WhoAm 90*
Gillies, George Thomas 1952- *WhoSSW 91*
Gillies, Hamish Grant 1936- *WhoWor 91*
Gillies, John F. *St&PR 91*
Gillies, Margaret 1803-1887 *BiDWomA*
Gillies, Mary Ann *WhoAmA 91N*
Gillies, Thomas Daniel 1920- *WhoAm 90*
Gillies, Valerie 1948- *FemiCLE*
Gillig, Paulette Marie *BiDrAPA 89*
Gillig, Stephen R. 1947- *St&PR 91*
Gilligan, Carol 1936- *BioIn 16*
Gilligan, Edward John 1938- *WhoE 91*
Gilligan, Harry E. 1931- *St&PR 91*
Gilligan, John Philip, III 1930- *WhoAm 90*
Gilligan, John R. 1927- *St&PR 91*
Gilligan, Martin Edward, Jr. 1938- *St&PR 91*
Gilligan, Michael Joseph Hilary 1943- *IntWWM 90*
Gilligan, Patrick Joseph 1927- *St&PR 91*
Gilligan, Roy 1923- *WhoWrEP 89*
Gillikin, Virginia 1952- *WhoAmW 91, WhoEmL 91*
Gillilan, James Palmer 1927- *St&PR 91*
Gillilan, John Vincent *BiDrAPA 89*
Gilliland, Denise Ellen 1961- *WhoE 91*
Gilliland, Dennis Crippen 1938- *WhoAm 90*
Gilliland, Eric Raymond 1962- *WhoEmL 91*
Gilliland, Hap 1918- *WhoWrEP 89*
Gilliland, Hope 1959- *WhoSSW 91*
Gilliland, J. Harold 1932- *St&PR 91*
Gilliland, John A. 1911- *St&PR 91*
Gilliland, John Knight 1960- *WhoSSW 91*
Gilliland, Larry Daniel 1938- *St&PR 91*
Gilliland, Marion Charlotte S. 1918- *WhoAmW 91*
Gilliland, Robert M 1921- *BiDrAPA 89*
Gilliland, Robert McMurtry, III *BiDrAPA 89*
Gilliland, Stanley Eugene 1940- *WhoSSW 91*
Gilliland, Theo T. 1924- *St&PR 91*
Gilliland, William Elton 1919- *WhoAm 90*
Gillilland, Thomas 1932- *WhoE 91, WhoWor 91*
Gillin, Edward Damien 1949- *WhoWor 91*
Gillin, Edward Francis 1913- *WhoWor 91*
Gillin, John Christian 1938- *BiDrAPA 89*
Gillin, Katy Elizabeth 1964- *WhoAmW 91*
Gillinder, James *PenDiDA 89*
Gillinder, Scott W. 1955- *St&PR 91*
Gillinder, William *PenDiDA 89*
Gillinder, William T. *PenDiDA 89*
Gilling, Lucille *WhoAmA 91*
Gillinger, Robert Wayne 1924- *St&PR 91*
Gillingham, Anna *BioIn 16*
Gillingham, Bryan R. 1944- *IntWWM 90*
Gillingham, Bryan Reginald 1944- *WhoAm 90*
Gillingham, James 1736- *PenDiDA 89*
Gillings, Daniel Andrew 1940- *St&PR 91*
Gillings, Joseph J. 1941- *St&PR 91*
Gillingwater, Denis Claude 1946- *WhoAmA 91*
Gillinson, Andrew Stuart 1948- *WhoE 91*
Gillio, Carolyn Irene 1931- *WhoAmW 91*
Gilliom, Judith Carr 1943- *WhoAm 90*
Gillis, Anne Therese *BiDrAPA 89*
Gillis, Antoine *PenDiDA 89*
Gillis, Bernard Thomas 1931- *WhoAm 90*
Gillis, Christine Diest-Lorgion *WhoAmW 91*
Gillis, Christopher *BioIn 16*
Gillis, Frank Lauren 1951- *WhoAm 90*
Gillis, James W. 1930- *St&PR 91*
Gillis, John Simon 1937- *WhoAm 90, WhoWor 91*
Gillis, Lynn S 1924- *BiDrAPA 89*
Gillis, Margaret Rose 1953- *WhoAm 90*
Gillis, Margie *BioIn 16*
Gillis, Marianne Edwards 1955- *WhoSSW 91*
Gillis, N. Scott 1953- *St&PR 91*
Gillis, Nelson Scott 1953- *WhoEmL 91*
Gillis, Paul Leonard 1953- *WhoAm 90*
Gillis, Robert Douglas 1955- *WhoSSW 91*
Gillis, Robert Patrick 1954- *BiDrAPA 89*
Gillis, Stephen Malcolm 1940- *WhoAm 90*
Gillis, Steven 1953- *WhoAm 90*
Gillis, Thomas G. 1955- *St&PR 91*
Gillis, William Freeman 1948- *WhoAm 90, WhoEmL 91*
Gillispie, Charles Coulston 1918- *WhoAm 90*
Gillispie, Charles Stephenson, Jr. 1942- *WhoAm 90*
Gilliss, Barbara Ellen 1938- *WhoAmW 91*
Gilliss, Catherine Lynch 1949- *WhoAmW 91*
Gilliss, Edward Johnson 1955- *WhoEmL 91*
Gilliss, Marcus R 1915- *BiDrAPA 89*
Gillman, Arthur E *BiDrAPA 89*
Gillman, Arthur Emanuel 1927- *WhoE 91*
Gillman, Barbara Baiyor 1956- *WhoEmL 91*
Gillman, Barbara Seitlin 1937- *WhoAmA 91*
Gillman, Donald O. 1930- *St&PR 91*
Gillman, Florence Morgan 1947- *WhoAmW 91*
Gillman, Leonard 1917- *WhoAm 90, WhoWor 91*
Gillman, Peter 1942- *ConAu 131*
Gillman, Robert D 1919- *BiDrAPA 89*
Gillman, Robert Edward 1943- *IntWWM 90*
Gillman, Robert N. 1930- *St&PR 91*
Gillmar, Stanley Frank 1935- *WhoAm 90*
Gillmer, Virginia 1949- *WhoEmL 91*
Gillmor, Charles Stewart 1938- *WhoAm 90*
Gillmor, John Edward 1937- *WhoAm 90*
Gillmor, Karen Lako 1948- *WhoAmW 91, WhoEmL 91*
Gillmor, Paul E. 1939- *BioIn 16, WhoAm 90*
Gillmore, Alver James 1947- *WhoEmL 91*
Gillmore, Robert 1946- *WhoAm 90*
Gillogly, Fred Dale 1918- *St&PR 91*
Gillogly, Terry Blake 1950- *St&PR 91*
Gillon, Arie Jan 1946- *WhoWor 91*
Gillon, John William 1900- *WhoAm 90*
Gillooly, Adrienne R. 1934- *WhoE 91*
Gillooly, Greg J. 1948- *St&PR 91*
Gillooly, Robert Bernard 1923- *St&PR 91*
Gillot, Claude *PenDiDA 89*
Gillow, Richard *PenDiDA 89*
Gillow, Robert *PenDiDA 89*
Gillow, Robert 1703-1772 *PenDiDA 89*
Gilloz, Andre-Pierre 1926- *WhoWor 91*
Gillson, Pauline Margaret 1943- *WhoAmW 91*
Gilluly, James 1896-1980 *DcScB S2*
Gillum, Elsie Felts 1930- *WhoAmW 91*
Gillum, Gary Wayne 1950- *WhoEmL 91*
Gillum, Keith Michael 1954- *St&PR 91*
Gillum, Ronald Lee 1938- *WhoSSW 91*
Gilly, Dinh 1877-1940 *PenDiMP*
Gilly, Michael 1952- *WhoEmL 91*
Gilman, Alan B. 1930- *WhoAm 90*
Gilman, Albert Franklin, III 1931- *WhoSSW 91*
Gilman, Alfred Goodman 1941- *WhoAm 90*
Gilman, Andrew D. 1951- *WhoEmL 91*
Gilman, Anne *BiDEWW, FemiCLE*
Gilman, Benjamin Arthur 1922- *WhoAm 90, WhoE 91*
Gilman, Bill 1945- *St&PR 91*
Gilman, Caroline 1794-1888 *FemiCLE*
Gilman, Charles Alan 1949- *WhoEmL 91*
Gilman, Charles Andrew 1833-1927 *AmLegL*
Gilman, Charlotte 1860-1935 *FemiCLE*
Gilman, Charlotte P. 1860-1935 *BioAmW*
Gilman, Charlotte Perkins 1860-1935 *EncAL, TwCLC 37 [port]*
Gilman, Cooper Lee 1928- *WhoAm 90*
Gilman, David Alan 1933- *WhoAm 90*
Gilman, Dorothy *AuBYP 90*
Gilman, Dorothy 1923- *ConAu 30NR, FemiCLE, SpyFic, TwCCr&M 91, WhoAm 90, WorAlBi*
Gilman, E Deborah 1940- *BiDrAPA 89*
Gilman, Ellen Deborah 1940- *WhoAmW 91, WhoE 91*
Gilman, Ernest Bernard 1946- *WhoE 91*
Gilman, Esther Morgenstern *BioIn 16*
Gilman, Ethan Henry 1937- *St&PR 91*
Gilman, Goodwin Orman 1936- *St&PR 91*
Gilman, Herbert *NewYTBS 90*
Gilman, Herbert 1924- *St&PR 91*
Gilman, Howard Eliot 1952- *BiDrAPA 89*
Gilman, Irvin Edward 1926- *IntWWM 90*
Gilman, Jane Piore 1945- *WhoE 91*
Gilman, Jerome Paul 1954- *WhoE 91*
Gilman, John Joseph 1925- *WhoAm 90*
Gilman, John William 1945- *WhoSSW 91*
Gilman, Julia M. 1942- *WhoWrEP 89*
Gilman, Julian D. 1947- *St&PR 91*
Gilman, Kenneth B. *WhoAm 90*
Gilman, Kenneth Bruce 1946- *St&PR 91*
Gilman, Leighton C. 1931- *ODwPR 91*
Gilman, Leonard H 1925- *BiDrAPA 89*
Gilman, Marvin Stanley 1922- *WhoAm 90*
Gilman, Neil Frederic 1954- *St&PR 91*
Gilman, Nicholas 1755-1814 *BioIn 16*
Gilman, Peter A. *WhoAm 90*
Gilman, Phoebe 1940- *BioIn 16*
Gilman, Richard 1925- *WhoAm 90, WhoWrEP 89*
Gilman, Richard Carleton 1923- *WhoAm 90*
Gilman, Robert H. 1942- *WhoE 91*
Gilman, Robert S. 1953- *St&PR 91*
Gilman, Ronald Lee 1942- *WhoAm 90*
Gilman, S.I. 1938- *St&PR 91*
Gilman, Sander Lawrence 1944- *WhoAm 90*
Gilman, Sari R. 1951- *BiDrAPA 89*
Gilman, Saul *BioIn 16*
Gilman, Sheldon Glenn 1943- *WhoWor 91*
Gilman, Shirley J. *St&PR 91, WhoAm 90*
Gilman, Sid 1932- *WhoAm 90*
Gilman, Steven Christopher 1952- *WhoE 91*
Gilman, Susan C 1948- *BiDrAPA 89*
Gilman, Susan Chernow 1948- *WhoE 91*
Gilmartin, F Thomas 1940- *WhoAmA 91*
Gilmartin, John A. 1942- *St&PR 91, WhoAm 90*
Gilmartin, Karen Baust 1961- *WhoAmW 91*
Gilmartin, Kevin Jarvus 1947- *WhoEmL 91*
Gilmartin, Patricia Purcell 1941- *WhoSSW 91*
Gilmartin, Raymond V. 1941- *St&PR 91, WhoAm 90, WhoE 91*
Gilmartin, William J., Jr. 1927- *St&PR 91*
Gilmer, Ann *ConAu 32NR*
Gilmer, B. von Haller 1909- *WhoAm 90, WhoWor 91*
Gilmer, Deborah Ann 1951- *WhoAmW 91*
Gilmer, Elizabeth 1861-1951 *WorAlBi*
Gilmer, Elizabeth Meriwether 1870?-1951 *BioIn 16*
Gilmer, Jimmy 1939- *EncPR&S 89*
Gilmer, Jimmy, and the Fireballs *EncPR&S 89*
Gilmer, La Jeanne Thompson 1934- *WhoWrEP 89*
Gilmer, Mary Elizabeth 1911- *WhoWrEP 89*
Gilmer, Penny Jane 1943- *WhoAmW 91*
Gilmer, Robert 1938- *WhoAm 90*
Gilmer, Thomas Edward, Jr. 1925- *WhoAm 90*
Gilmer, Thomas Walker 1802-1844 *BiDrUSE 89*
Gilmer, William Scott *BiDrAPA 89*
Gilmond, James Edward 1949- *WhoE 91*
Gilmont, Ernest Rich 1929- *WhoAm 90*
Gilmor, Jane E 1947- *WhoAmA 91*
Gilmor, Robert *BioIn 16*
Gilmor, Robert, Jr. 1935- *St&PR 91*
Gilmore, Art 1912- *WhoAm 90*
Gilmore, Artis 1949- *WorAlBi*
Gilmore, Barbara 1954- *WhoAmW 91*
Gilmore, Benjamin 1906- *St&PR 91*
Gilmore, Betty J. *St&PR 91*
Gilmore, Clarence Fielding 1922- *St&PR 91*
Gilmore, Clarence Percy 1926- *WhoAm 90, WhoWrEP 89*
Gilmore, Donald Brian 1955- *St&PR 91*
Gilmore, Elizabeth P *BiDrAPA 89*
Gilmore, F. Grant *EarBlAP*
Gilmore, Gail 1950- *IntWWM 90*
Gilmore, Gail P. 1948- *ODwPR 91*
Gilmore, Gordon Ray 1935- *WhoSSW 91*
Gilmore, H. William *WhoAm 90*
Gilmore, Helen R *BiDrAPA 89*
Gilmore, Henry Francis 1920- *WhoSSW 91*
Gilmore, Horace Herman 1903- *AuBYP 90*
Gilmore, Horace Weldon 1918- *WhoAm 90*
Gilmore, Howard N., Jr. 1933- *St&PR 91*
Gilmore, Hugh Redland 1916- *WhoSSW 91*
Gilmore, Iris 1900- *AuBYP 90*
Gilmore, J.F. 1927- *St&PR 91*
Gilmore, James A. 1870- *Ballpl 90*
Gilmore, James Stanley, Jr. 1926- *WhoAm 90, WhoWor 91*
Gilmore, Jerry Carl 1933- *WhoAm 90*
Gilmore, Jesse Lee 1920- *WhoAm 90*
Gilmore, Jimmie *WhoNeCM [port]*
Gilmore, John Allen Dehn 1947- *WhoEmL 91*
Gilmore, John F. 1940- *St&PR 91*
Gilmore, John Vaughn, Jr. 1948- *WhoEmL 91*
Gilmore, June Ellen 1927- *WhoAmW 91, WhoWor 91*
Gilmore, Karen J *BiDrAPA 89*
Gilmore, Kenneth O. 1930- *St&PR 91*
Gilmore, Kenneth Otto 1930- *WhoAm 90*
Gilmore, Kynna Lynnette 1956- *WhoEmL 91*
Gilmore, Lloyd M. 1925- *St&PR 91*
Gilmore, Lori Beth 1961- *WhoSSW 91*
Gilmore, Louisa Ruth 1930- *WhoAmW 91*
Gilmore, Margaret Mary 1946- *BiDrAPA 89*
Gilmore, Marjorie Havens 1918- *WhoAmW 91*
Gilmore, Mark Rand 1955- *WhoEmL 91*
Gilmore, Mary 1864-1962 *FemiCLE*
Gilmore, Mary 1865-1962 *BioIn 16*
Gilmore, Maurice Eugene 1938- *WhoE 91*
Gilmore, Michael 1952- *WhoWrEP 89*
Gilmore, Michael David 1950- *WhoEmL 91*
Gilmore, Mikal George 1951- *WhoEmL 91, WhoWor 91*
Gilmore, Millicent Jones 1920- *WhoAmW 91*
Gilmore, Patrick S. 1829-1892 *OxCPMus*
Gilmore, Patrick Sarsfield 1829-1892 *BioIn 16, PenDiMP*
Gilmore, Patrick Timothy 1928 *St&PR 91*
Gilmore, Richard G. 1927- *St&PR 91*
Gilmore, Rick Owen 1963- *WhoE 91*
Gilmore, Robert Eugene 1920- *St&PR 91, WhoAm 90*
Gilmore, Robert Karl 1927- *WhoAm 90*
Gilmore, Robert Noel 1948- *St&PR 91*
Gilmore, Robert Wallace *BioIn 16*
Gilmore, Roger 1932- *WhoAm 90, WhoAmA 91, WhoE 91*
Gilmore, Stephen Vincent 1952- *WhoEmL 91*
Gilmore, Stuart Irby 1930- *WhoAm 90*
Gilmore, Susan 1954- *BioIn 16*
Gilmore, Susan Astrid Lytle 1942- *WhoAmW 91*
Gilmore, Thomas Meyer 1942- *WhoE 91*
Gilmore, Timothy Jonathan 1949- *WhoEmL 91*
Gilmore, Voit 1918- *WhoAm 90*
Gilmore, William Gerard 1930- *St&PR 91*
Gilmore, William Harold 1932- *St&PR 91*
Gilmore-Galas, Veronica Anne 1949- *WhoEmL 91*
Gilmour, Allan 1816-1895 *DcCanB 12*
Gilmour, Allan D. *BioIn 16*
Gilmour, Allan Dana 1934- *St&PR 91, WhoAm 90*
Gilmour, Barbara *ConAu 132*
Gilmour, Cathryn A. 1945- *St&PR 91*
Gilmour, Edward E 1930- *BiDrAPA 89*
Gilmour, Edward Ellis 1930- *WhoAm 90*
Gilmour, Everett A. 1921- *St&PR 91*
Gilmour, J. Lowell 1928- *St&PR 91*
Gilmour, James H. 1942- *St&PR 91*
Gilmour, James H. Jr. *BiDrAPA 89*
Gilmour, Peter 1961?- *BioIn 16*
Gilmour, Robert Arthur 1944- *WhoE 91*
Gilner, Grace Marie 1961- *WhoAmW 91, WhoE 91*
Gilner, Samuel 1952- *St&PR 91*
Gilpatric, Chadbourne 1914-1989 *BioIn 16*

Gilpatric, Donald S. 1909-1989 BioIn 16
Gilpatric, Paula Melhado BioIn 16
Gilpatric, Roswell Leavitt 1906- St&PR 91, WhoAm 90
Gilpatrick, Dawn Michelle Curran 1963- WhoE 91
Gilpin, Charles 1878-1930 DrBlPA 90
Gilpin, Doris C W 1923- BiDrAPA 89
Gilpin, Glen Edwin 1923- St&PR 91
Gilpin, Henry Dilworth 1801-1860 BiDrUSE 89
Gilpin, Henry Edmund 1922- WhoAmA 91
Gilpin, John Bernard 1810-1892 DcCanB 12
Gilpin, Larry Vincent 1943- WhoAm 90
Gilpin, Laura 1891-1979 BioAmW, WhoAmA 91N
Gilpin, Richard William 1940- WhoE 91
Gilpin, Robert George, Jr. 1930- WhoAm 90
Gilpin, William 1724-1804 NinCLC 30 [port]
Gilrain, Gerard James 1929- St&PR 91
Gilrain, Ronald F. 1927- St&PR 91
Gilrane, James Joseph 1938- St&PR 91
Gilray, J. D. MajTwCW
Gilreath, Jerry Hollandsworth 1934- WhoE 91
Gilreath, Warren Dean 1920- WhoAm 90
Gilrin, Theodore H WhoAmA 91N
Gilroy, Beryl 1924- FemiCLE
Gilroy, Edwin Bernard 1923- St&PR 91
Gilroy, Frank 1925- WorAlBi
Gilroy, Frank D 1925- ConAu 32NR
Gilroy, Frank Daniel 1925- WhoAm 90
Gilroy, Hollie A. 1963- WhoAmW 91
Gilroy, John M. St&PR 91
Gilroy, Patricia Anne 1944- WhoAmW 91
Gilroy, Tracy Anne Hunsaker 1959- WhoEmL 91
Gilroy, William Francis 1936- St&PR 91
Gilroy, William Gerard 1954- WhoWrEP 89
Gilruth, Robert Rowe 1913- WhoAm 90
Gilsdorf, John B. St&PR 91
Gilsig, Toby 1940- St&PR 91
Gilsinan, James Francis, III 1945- WhoAm 90
Gilson, Arnold Leslie 1931- WhoWor 91
Gilson, Franklin L. 1846-1892 AmLegL
Gilson, Giles 1942- WhoAmA 91
Gilson, Goodwin Woodrow 1918- WhoE 91
Gilson, James Clayton 1926- WhoAm 90
Gilson, James R. 1917- St&PR 91
Gilson, James Russell 1951- WhoEmL 91
Gilson, Jamie 1933- AuBYP 90, BioIn 16
Gilson, Lottie BioIn 16
Gilson, Troy Daniel 1962- BiDrAPA 89
Gilson, William D BiDrAPA 89
Gilstad, June Russell 1928- WhoWrEP 89
Gilstein, Jacob Burrill 1923- WhoE 91
Gilstrap, Dennis Leon 1930- St&PR 91
Gilstrap, Suzanne T. 1950- St&PR 91
Giltinan, Alexander Smith 1925- St&PR 91
Giltinan, John A. 1956- St&PR 91
Giltner, Alyce Sharlene 1960- WhoAmW 91
Gilula, Marshall F 1939- BiDrAPA 89
Gilvar, Stephen Grant 1938- WhoE 91
Gilvary, James Joseph 1929- WhoAm 90
Gilvey, Edward Eugene 1926- St&PR 91
Gilway, Barry J. 1945- St&PR 91
Gilze, Johann Christoph PenDiDA 89
Gilze, Ludwig PenDiDA 89
Gimbel, Bernard F. 1885-1966 WorAlBi
Gimbel, Bruce 1951- BiDrAPA 89
Gimbel, Louis S., III 1929- St&PR 91
Gimbel, Madeleine Esther 1944- WhoSSW 91
Gimbel, Norman WhoAm 90
Gimbel, Patricia A. 1955- WhoAmW 91
Gimbel, William Thomas 1918- St&PR 91
Gimblett, Max 1935- WhoAmA 91
Gimbo, Angelo 1928- WhoWor 91
Gimbrone, Michael Anthony, Jr. 1943- WhoAm 90
Gimbutas, Marija 1921- WhoAm 90, WhoAmW 91
Gimenez, Blanca A BiDrAPA 89
Gimenez, Eduardo 1940- IntWWM 90
Gimenez, Florentin 1925- WhoWor 91
Gimenez, Jeronimo 1854-1923 OxCPMus
Gimenez, Jose Raul 1955- WhoHisp 91
Gimenez, Luis Enrique 1934- WhoWor 91
Gimenez, Luis Fernando 1952- WhoE 91
Gimenez-Gallego, Guillermo 1945- WhoWor 91
Gimenez-Porrata, Alfonso 1937- WhoHisp 91
Gimeno, Juan-Bosco 1956- WhoWor 91
Gimlett, James Irwin 1929- WhoAm 90
Gimma, Joseph 1907- St&PR 91
Gimma, Joseph A. NewYTBS 90 [port]
Gimma, Joseph A. 1907-1990 BioIn 16
Gimmaro, Steven Paul 1959- WhoEmL 91
Gimmy, Daniel Patrick 1946- WhoEmL 91
Gimpel, Bronislav 1911-1979 PenDiMP
Gimpel, Jack F. 1940- St&PR 91
Gimpel, Jakob 1906-1989 BioIn 16, PenDiMP
Gimpel, Rene BioIn 16
Gimpelson, Richard Joel 1946- WhoEmL 91
Gimpl, Martin Louis 1935- WhoWor 91
Gimson, Curtis S. 1955- St&PR 91
Gimson, Ernest William 1864-1919 PenDiDA 89
Gimstedt, Olle Gerhard 1914- WhoWor 91
Gina, Princess of Liechtenstein 1921-1989 BioIn 16
Ginader, John B. 1941- St&PR 91
Ginastera, Alberto 1916-1983 PenDiMP A
Ginchereau, Jacqueline E BiDrAPA 89
Gindel, Patricia Diane 1957- WhoSSW 91
Ginder, Michael Francis 1936- WhoSSW 91
Gindes, Marion E. 1939- WhoAmW 91
Gindi, Joseph M. 1925- St&PR 91
Gindy, Benjamin Lee 1929- WhoSSW 91
Ginepra, Alfred L., Jr. 1933- ODwPR 91
Giner de Los Rios, Francisco 1839-1915 BioIn 16
Ginesi, Edna 1902- BiDWomA
Ging, Rosalie J 1921- BiDrAPA 89
Gingell, Barry BioIn 16
Gingell, Patricia Jo 1946- WhoEmL 91
Ginger, Laura Ann 1954- WhoEmL 91
Ginger, Leonard George 1918- St&PR 91, WhoAm 90
Gingerella, David Anthony 1956- WhoEmL 91
Gingerich, Elizabeth M BiDrAPA 89
Gingerich, Florine Rose 1951- WhoAmW 91
Gingerich, John Charles 1936- St&PR 91
Gingerich, Owen Jay 1930- WhoAm 90
Gingerich, Philip Derstine 1946- WhoAm 90
Gingerich, Vernon Jason 1914- WhoAm 90
Gingery, Donald Edward, Jr. 1951- St&PR 91
Gingery, Gregory William 1946- St&PR 91
Gingery, James Montgomery 1958- St&PR 91
Gingery, Robben Raines 1951- BiDrAPA 89
Gingiss, Benjamin Jack 1911- WhoAm 90
Gingl, Manfred St&PR 91
Gingold, Dennis Marc 1949- WhoE 91, WhoEmL 91, WhoWor 91
Gingold, George Norman 1939- St&PR 91, WhoAm 90
Gingold, Helene 1874?-1926 FemiCLE
Gingold, Hermione 1897-1987 BioIn 16, OxCPMus, WorAlBi
Gingold, Josef 1909- BioIn 16, IntWWM 90
Gingold, Norbert 1902- IntWWM 90
Gingras, Bernard Arthur 1927- WhoAm 90
Gingras, Denis Georges 1960- WhoEmL 91
Gingras, Gerard G BiDrAPA 89
Gingras, Gustave 1918- WhoAm 90
Gingras, Luc 1954- BiDrAPA 89
Gingras, Michel Paul 1943- BiDrAPA 89
Gingrich, Harold WhoAm 90
Gingrich, Kay M. 1945- WhoAmW 91
Gingrich, Newell Shiffer 1906- WhoAm 90
Gingrich, Newt BioIn 16
Gingrich, Newt 1943- ConAu 131, News 91-1 [port]
Gingrich, Newton Leroy 1943- NewYTBS 90 [port], WhoAm 90, WhoSSW 91
Gingrich, Steven Bryan 1951- St&PR 91, WhoEmL 91
Gingrich-Petersen, Carolyn Ashcraft WhoAmW 91
Giniger, Kenneth Seeman 1919- WhoAm 90, WhoE 91
Ginley, Thomas J. 1938- WhoAm 90
Ginn, Angela Maria 1963- WhoWor 91
Ginn, Connie Mardean 1951- WhoSSW 91
Ginn, Greg BioIn 16
Ginn, John Charles 1937- St&PR 91, WhoAm 90, WhoWor 91
Ginn, Rawlins 1924- WhoSSW 91
Ginn, Robert M. 1924- St&PR 91
Ginn, Robert Martin 1924- WhoAm 90
Ginn, Ronn 1933- WhoAm 90
Ginn, Sam L. 1937- WhoAm 90
Ginn, Stephen Arnold 1915- BiDrAPA 89
Ginn, Susan B. 1950- WhoAmW 91
Ginn, Walter Pope 1948- WhoAm 90
Ginn, William Denton 1923- St&PR 91
Ginn-Paster, Sophie 1933- IntWWM 90
Ginna, William L., Jr. 1952- St&PR 91
Ginnane, Christopher Robert 1952- St&PR 91
Ginnever, Charles 1931- WhoAmA 91
Ginorio, Angela Beatriz 1947- WhoHisp 91
Ginos, James Zissis 1923- WhoE 91
Ginsberg, Alan Harvey 1942- WhoSSW 91
Ginsberg, Allen 1926- BioIn 16, MajTwCW, WhoAm 90, WhoE 91, WhoWor 91, WhoWrEP 89, WorAlBi
Ginsberg, Barry I BiDrAPA 89
Ginsberg, Benjamin 1923- St&PR 91
Ginsberg, Benjamin 1947- WhoE 91
Ginsberg, Bernardine Marilyn 1932- WhoE 91
Ginsberg, Craig Allan BiDrAPA 89
Ginsberg, David Lawrence 1932- WhoAm 90, WhoWor 91
Ginsberg, David Mark 1946- St&PR 91
Ginsberg, Donald Maurice 1933- WhoAm 90
Ginsberg, Edward 1917- WhoAm 90, WhoWor 91
Ginsberg, Emily Suzanne 1935- WhoAmW 91
Ginsberg, Ernest 1931- St&PR 91, WhoAm 90
Ginsberg, Errol 1956- St&PR 91
Ginsberg, Frank Charles 1944- WhoAm 90
Ginsberg, George L BiDrAPA 89
Ginsberg, Harold L. NewYTBS 90 [port]
Ginsberg, Harold Louis 1903- BioIn 16
Ginsberg, Harold Louis 1903-1990 ConAu 132
Ginsberg, Harold Nathan 1935- BiDrAPA 89
Ginsberg, Harold Samuel 1917- WhoAm 90
Ginsberg, Harvey 1930- St&PR 91
Ginsberg, Harvey Slom 1930- WhoAm 90
Ginsberg, Hersh Meier 1928- WhoAm 90
Ginsberg, Ira M. 1952- St&PR 91
Ginsberg, Ivy Robin 1961- WhoEmL 91
Ginsberg, James P BiDrAPA 89
Ginsberg, Jeffrey Scott 1962- WhoE 91
Ginsberg, Joe 1926- Ballpl 90, BioIn 16
Ginsberg, Judah Bennett 1942- WhoE 91
Ginsberg, Larry Floyd 1951- WhoEmL 91
Ginsberg, Lawrence David 1956- BiDrAPA 89
Ginsberg, Leon BiDrAPA 89
Ginsberg, Leon Herman 1936- WhoAm 90, WhoSSW 91
Ginsberg, Lewis Robbins 1932- WhoAm 90
Ginsberg, Marilyn Kaplan 1952- WhoAm 90
Ginsberg, Michael Isaac 1933- St&PR 91
Ginsberg, Morton A. 1919- St&PR 91
Ginsberg, Phillip Carl 1954- WhoE 91
Ginsberg, Robert I. 1933- St&PR 91
Ginsberg, Ronald Lawrence 1947- WhoE 91
Ginsberg, Seymour 1931- St&PR 91
Ginsberg, Stanley 1944- ODwPR 91
Ginsberg-Fellner, Fredda 1937- WhoAmW 91
Ginsburg, Ann 1932- WhoAmW 91
Ginsburg, Carl S. 1936- WhoWrEP 89
Ginsburg, Charles David 1912- WhoAm 90, WhoE 91, WhoWor 91
Ginsburg, Charles Pauson 1920- BioIn 16
Ginsburg, David Monroe 1930- St&PR 91
Ginsburg, Douglas Howard 1946- WhoAm 90, WhoE 91
Ginsburg, Ellin ODwPR 91
Ginsburg, Ellin Louis WhoAm 90
Ginsburg, Estelle 1924- WhoAmA 91
Ginsburg, Gerald J. 1930- WhoAm 90
Ginsburg, Gerald M. 1932- IntWWM 90
Ginsburg, Gerry Louis 1952- WhoEmL 91
Ginsburg, Iona H BiDrAPA 89
Ginsburg, Iona Horowitz 1931- WhoAmW 91, WhoE 91
Ginsburg, Jeannette Mirsky 1903-1987 BioIn 16
Ginsburg, Lee Robert 1942- WhoE 91
Ginsburg, Lucien 1928- WhoWor 91
Ginsburg, Marcus 1915- WhoAm 90, WhoSSW 91
Ginsburg, Mark Barry 1949- WhoE 91
Ginsburg, Marshall BiDrAPA 89
Ginsburg, Martin David 1932- WhoAm 90
Ginsburg, Matthew Meyer 1960- WhoE 91
Ginsburg, Max 1931- WhoAmA 91
Ginsburg, Mirra AuBYP 90, BioIn 16
Ginsburg, Norton Sydney 1921- WhoAm 90
Ginsburg, Robert H. 1942- St&PR 91
Ginsburg, Ruth Bader 1933- WhoAm 90, WhoE 91
Ginsburg, Seymour 1927- WhoAm 90
Ginsburg, Sigmund Gershen 1937- WhoAm 90
Ginsburg, Sybil Ann Yudin 1943- BiDrAPA 89
Ginsburgh, Robert Neville 1923- WhoAm 90
Ginsky, Marvin H. 1930- St&PR 91, WhoAm 90
Ginszanka, Zuzanna 1917-1944 EncCoWW
Gintel, Robert M. 1928- St&PR 91
Ginter, Dolores D. 1929- ODwPR 91
Ginter, Evelyn 1932- WhoAmW 91
Ginter, James Lee 1945- WhoAm 90
Ginter, Sally Ann 1944- WhoAmW 91
Ginter, Valerian Alexius 1939- WhoE 91, WhoWor 91
Ginters, August 1885-1944 BioIn 16
Ginther, Richie BioIn 16
Ginther, Richie 1930-1989 AnObit 1989
Gintis, Daniel 1923- WhoSSW 91
Ginwala, Kymus 1931- St&PR 91, WhoAm 90
Ginzberg, Eli BioIn 16
Ginzberg, Eli 1911- WhoAm 90
Ginzberg, Jeffrey David 1955- WhoE 91
Ginzberg, Louis 1873-1953 BioIn 16
Ginzberg, Michael Jay 1947- WhoEmL 91
Ginzberg, Sana EncCoWW
Ginzburg, Carlo 1939- WorAu 1980 [port]
Ginzburg, Harold M. 1945- WhoE 91
Ginzburg, Harold Myron 1945- BiDrAPA 89
Ginzburg, Leon 1898-1988 BioIn 16
Ginzburg, Lidiia 1902- EncCoWW
Ginzburg, Natalia BioIn 16, NewYTBS 90 [port]
Ginzburg, Natalia 1916- ConAu 33NR, CurBio 90 [port], EncCoWW, EuWr 13, MajTwCW
Ginzburg, Natalia Levi 1916- WhoWor 91
Ginzburg, Ralph 1929- WhoAm 90, WhoWrEP 89
Ginzburg, Rubin 1930- WhoAm 90
Ginzburg, Vitaly Lazarevich 1916- WhoWor 91
Ginzburg, Yankel 1945- WhoAm 90, WhoAmA 91
Ginzel, Andrew WhoAmA 91
Ginzel, Roland 1921- WhoAmA 91
Ginzig, Carol A. WhoAmW 91
Ginzton, Edward L. 1915- St&PR 91
Ginzton, Edward Leonard 1915- WhoAm 90
Gioannetti, Vittorio Amadeo PenDiDA 89
Gioannini, Theresa Lee 1949- WhoAmW 91
Giobbi, Edward Giacchino 1926- WhoAm 90
Giobbi, Edward Gioachino 1926- WhoAmA 91
Giocondi, Gino J. 1931- WhoAm 90
Gioello, Debbie 1935- WhoAmA 91
Gioia, Angelo Joseph 1951- WhoEmL 91
Gioia, Anthony 1948- St&PR 91
Gioia, Dana BioIn 16
Gioia, Dana 1950- ConAu 130, WhoWrEP 89
Gioia, Peter John 1955- BiDrAPA 89
Gioiella, Russell Michael 1954- WhoE 91, WhoEmL 91
Gioiello, John Leslie 1955- WhoEmL 91
Gioiosa, Margaret Mary BioIn 16
Gioioso, Joseph 1942- St&PR 91
Gioioso, Joseph Vincent 1939- WhoWor 91
Gioka, Tina P. 1936- WhoWor 91
Giokas, George 1951- WhoAm 90
Giolas, Dale 1953- BiDrAPA 89
Giolito, Julie D. St&PR 91
Giombi, Claudio 1937- IntWWM 90
Giometti, Paul Francis 1936- St&PR 91
Giomi, Thelma Anne 1947- WhoEmL 91
Gionfriddo, Al 1922- Ballpl 90
Gionis, Thomas BioIn 16
Giono, Jean 1895-1970 MajTwCW
Gior, Fino 1936- WhoE 91
Giordani, John E. 1942- St&PR 91
Giordano, Anne Shirley 1937- WhoAmW 91
Giordano, Anthony Bruno 1915- WhoAm 90
Giordano, Anthony Daniel 1948- WhoE 91
Giordano, Antoinette R. 1948- WhoAmW 91
Giordano, August Thomas 1923- WhoAm 90
Giordano, Dennis Nicholas 1945- WhoSSW 91
Giordano, Donald A. ODwPR 91
Giordano, Donald A. 1932- St&PR 91
Giordano, E. Lynn WhoAmW 91
Giordano, Frank L 1941- BiDrAPA 89
Giordano, Greg Joe 1960- WhoAmA 91
Giordano, John Vincent 1951- St&PR 91
Giordano, Joseph 1932- St&PR 91
Giordano, Joseph, Jr. 1953- WhoEmL 91
Giordano, Joseph Francis 1932- WhoAm 90
Giordano, Luca 1632-1705 IntDcAA 90
Giordano, Michael Francis 1943- St&PR 91
Giordano, Michele 1930- WhoWor 91
Giordano, Nicholas Anthony 1943- St&PR 91, WhoAm 90
Giordano, Patricia Schoppe 1947- WhoAmW 91, WhoE 91, WhoEmL 91
Giordano, Patrick Daniel 1930- St&PR 91
Giordano, Paul B BiDrAPA 89
Giordano, Paul Gregory 1956- WhoEmL 91
Giordano, Paul John 1931- St&PR 91
Giordano, Philip John 1947- St&PR 91

Giordano, Richard V. 1934- St&PR 91
Giordano, Richard Vincent 1934- WhoAm 90, WhoE 91, WhoWor 91
Giordano, Robert Michael 1948- WhoAm 90
Giordano, Salvatore 1910- St&PR 91
Giordano, Salvatore, Jr. 1938- St&PR 91, WhoAm 90
Giordano, Salvatore, Sr. 1910- WhoAm 90
Giordano, Saverio Paul 1943- WhoAm 90
Giordano, Serafino 1936- WhoE 91
Giordano, Toni Ann 1962- WhoAmW 91
Giordano, Tony 1939- WhoAm 90
Giordano, Umberto 1867-1948 PenDiMP A
Giorgi, Elsie Agnes 1911- WhoAm 90, WhoAmW 91
Giorgi, Lewis Ascentio 1919- WhoE 91
Giorgi, Robert James 1961- WhoEmL 91
Giorgianni, Albert J. 1945- St&PR 91
Giorgio, Maestro PenDiDA 89
Giorgio, Robert J. 1949- St&PR 91
Giorgio Martini, Francesco Di 1439-1501? BioIn 16
Giorgione 1477?-1510? IntDcAA 90, WorAlBi
Giorno, John 1936- WhoAmA 91, WhoE 91
Giorza, John C. 1950- WhoEmL 91
Gioscia, Nicolai BiDrAPA 89
Gioscia, Nicolai 1903- WhoE 91
Gioseffi, Daniela 1941- WhoAmW 91, WhoWrEP 89
Gioseffi, Linda M. 1950- St&PR 91
Giosta, Daniel 1955- WhoEmL 91
Giot, Richard PenDiDA 89
Giotto 1266?-1337 IntDcAA 90
Giotto 1267?-1337 WorAlBi
Giovacchini, Peter Louis 1922- BiDrAPA 89, WhoAm 90
Giovacchini, Philip BiDrAPA 89
Giovacchini, Robert Peter 1928- St&PR 91, WhoAm 90
Giovanelli, Riccardo 1946- WhoAm 90
Giovanetti, Michael Louis 1953- WhoEmL 91
Giovanisci, Stephen J. 1936- ODwPR 91
Giovanna I, Queen of Naples 1327?-1382 BioIn 16
Giovanna II, Queen of Naples 1371-1435 BioIn 16
Giovanni Da Milano IntDcAA 90
Giovanni da Udine PenDiDA 89
Giovanni da Verona, Fra 1457-1525 PenDiDA 89
Giovanni, di Paolo BioIn 16
Giovanni di Paolo 1395?-1482 IntDcAA 90
Giovanni, di Pietro BioIn 16
Giovanni Maria di Mariano PenDiDA 89
Giovanni, Benvenuto di 1436-1518? BioIn 16
Giovanni, Matteo Di 1430?-1495 BioIn 16
Giovanni, Nikki BioIn 16
Giovanni, Nikki 1943- AuBYP 90, ConLC 64 [port], FemiCLE, MajTwCW, WhoAm 90, WhoAmW 91, WhoWrEP 89
Giovanni, Paul NewYTBS 90
Giovanniello, Joseph, Jr. 1958- WhoEmL 91
Giovannini, Giovanni WhoWrEP 89
Giovannini, Pier Luigi 1946- WhoWor 91
Giovannitti, Arturo 1884-1959 EncAL
Giovannitti, Len 1920- WhoAm 90
Giovannucci, Daniel L. 1919- St&PR 91
Giovannucci, Livia A. 1922- St&PR 91
Giove, Barbara Ann Jean 1954- WhoEmL 91
Giove, Frank Carmen 1926- WhoE 91
Giove, Robert John 1923- St&PR 91
Giovenco, John V. 1936- St&PR 91, WhoAm 90
Giovetti, Alfred Charles 1948- WhoEmL 91, WhoWor 91
Giovetti, Paola 1938- EncPaPR 91
Giovi, Lawrence A. 1923- St&PR 91
Giovingo, Thomas Peter 1956- WhoEmL 91
Gipe, Lawrence 1962- WhoAmA 91
Gipp, George BioIn 16
Gippius, Zinaida 1869-1945 EncCoWW
Gipps, Bryan John 1952- IntWWM 90
Gipps, Ruth Dorothy Louisa 1921- IntWWM 90
Gips, C L Terry 1945- WhoAmA 91
Gips, Edward U. 1922- WhoAm 90
Gips, Walter F., Jr. 1920- St&PR 91
Gips, Walter Fuld, Jr. 1920- WhoAm 90
Gipson, Angela Christina 1954- WhoWrEP 89
Gipson, David G. 1946- St&PR 91
Gipson, Frederick Benjamin 1908-1973 AuBYP 90
Gipson, Gordon 1914- St&PR 91, WhoAm 90, WhoWrEP 89
Gipson, Hayward R., Jr. 1945- St&PR 91
Gipson, James Herrick 1912- WhoAm 90
Gipson, James Herrick, Jr. 1912- St&PR 91
Gipson, James William 1945- WhoSSW 91
Gipson, Ray 1938- St&PR 91
Gipson, Robert M. 1939- St&PR 91
Gipson, William Terry 1936- BiDrAPA 89
Gipstein, Brian Norman BiDrAPA 89
Giquinto, Marie Halina 1952- WhoE 91
Gira, Catherine Russell 1932- WhoAm 90
Giragos, John G 1937- BiDrAPA 89
Giral, Angela 1935- WhoHisp 91
Giraldi, Robert Nicholas 1939- WhoAm 90
Giraldi, Wanda Williamson 1943- WhoAmW 91
Girao, Jose Antonio Brito S. 1938- WhoWor 91
Girard, Alexander 1907- ConDes 90
Girard, Alexander Hayden 1907- WhoAm 90
Girard, Andrea Eaton 1946- WhoAmW 91
Girard, Carl Wilfred 1933- WhoSSW 91
Girard, Deborah Ann 1954- WhoAmW 91
Girard, Donald M. 1958- St&PR 91
Girard, Dorothy Rosenthal 1920- St&PR 91
Girard, Fernand St&PR 91
Girard, George BioIn 16
Girard, Jack 1951- WhoAmA 91
Girard, James Emery 1945- WhoAm 90
Girard, James Preston 1944- WhoWrEP 89
Girard, Jean-Baptiste 1680-1733 EncO&P 3
Girard, Jeffrey Charles 1947- St&PR 91
Girard, Joseph Bernard 1926- St&PR 91
Girard, Leonard A. 1942- St&PR 91
Girard, Leonard Arthur 1942- WhoAm 90
Girard, Linda Walvoord 1942- WhoAmW 91
Girard, Louis Joseph 1919- WhoAm 90
Girard, Marc-Amable 1822-1892 DcCanB 12
Girard, Mary Sabel 1912- WhoAmW 91
Girard, Narcisse 1797-1860 PenDiMP
Girard, Nettabell 1938- WhoAm 90, WhoAmW 91, WhoWor 91
Girard, Rene Noel 1923- WhoAm 90
Girard, Rodolphe 1879-1956 DcLB 92 [port], OxCCanT
Girard, Salli WhoWrEP 89
Girard, Stephen 1750-1831 EncABHB 6 [port]
Girard, Sylvie Marie 1956- BiDrAPA 89
Girard, Vincent St&PR 91
Girardeau, Marvin Denham 1930- WhoAm 90
Girardelli, Marc BioIn 16
Girardin, Carol Erickson 1957- St&PR 91
Girardon, Francois 1628?-1715 IntDcAA 90, WorAlBi
Giraud, Andre Louis Yves 1925- WhoWor 91
Giraud, Henri 1878-1949 BiDFrPL
Giraud, Raymond Dorner 1920- WhoAm 90
Giraudeau, Jean 1916- IntWWM 90
Giraudier, Antonio 1926- WhoAmA 91
Giraudier, Antonio A., Jr. 1926- WhoHisp 91
Giraudoux, Jean 1882-1944 BioIn 16, WorAlBi
Girault, Suzanne 1882-1973 BiDFrPL
Giray, Erol F BiDrAPA 89
Giray, Safa 1931- WhoWor 91
Giray, Saim 1927- BiDrAPA 89
Girbea, Smara EncCoWW
Girden, Eugene Lawrence 1930- WhoAm 90, WhoWor 91
Girden, Lisa Jan 1959- WhoAmW 91
Girdwood, William John 1936- St&PR 91
Gire, Michael Kent 1947- WhoEmL 91
Gire, Sharon Lee 1944- WhoAmW 91
Girello, Paul Vincent 1951- WhoEmL 91
Girga, Barbara Ann 1937- WhoAmW 91
Girgash, William J. 1926- ODwPR 91
Girgis, Mona Morad BiDrAPA 89
Girgis, Nina V. 1963- ODwPR 91
Girgis, Sabry BiDrAPA 89
Girgus, Joan Stern 1942- WhoAm 90
Giridhar, Sanjeevi 1952- BiDrAPA 89
Girion, Barbara 1937- BioIn 16
Girkins, David R. 1951- St&PR 91
Girlando, Regina Maria 1952- WhoAmW 91
Girling, Brough BioIn 16
Girling, Robert George William, III 1929- WhoSSW 91
Girls Next Door, The WhoNeCM [port]
Girod, Bernard A. 1942- St&PR 91
Girod, Frank Paul 1908- WhoWor 91
Girod, Susan Jane BiDrAPA 89
Girodias, Maurice NewYTBS 90
Girodias, Maurice 1919- ConAu 129
Girodias, Maurice 1919-1990 ConAu 132
Girola, Claudia 1923- ArtLatA
Girolamo, da Cremona BioIn 16
Girolamo, Maryanne M. 1945- WhoAmW 91
Giroldi, Adela Bonilla de BioIn 16
Giroldi Vega, Moises BioIn 16
Girombelli, Donatella BioIn 16
Giron PenDiMP
Giron, Aitala BiDrAPA 89
Giron, Andres BioIn 16
Giron, Arsenio 1932- IntWWM 90
Giron, Manuel Buendia Tellez 1926?-1984 HispWr 90
Giron, Vanessa O. 1962- WhoAmW 91
Gironda, R 1936- WhoAmA 91
Girondo, Oliverio 1891-1967 HispWr 90
Girone, Giovanni 1940- WhoWor 91
Girone, Joan Christine Cruse 1927- WhoAmW 91
Girone, Maria Elena 1939- WhoHisp 91
Girone, Vito Anthony 1910- WhoAm 90
Gironella, Alberto 1929- ArtLatA
Gironta, Michael 1941- St&PR 91
Girouard, Mark 1931- WorAu 1980
Girouard, Peggy Jo Fulcher 1933- WhoSSW 91
Girouard, Shirley Ann 1947- WhoAmW 91
Giroud, Francoise 1916- BiDFrPL
Giroux, Amy Susan 1960- WhoEmL 91
Giroux, Antoinette 1899-1978 OxCCanT
Giroux, E. X. 1924- TwCCr&M 91
Giroux, Germaine 1902-1975 OxCCanT
Giroux, Henry A 1943- ConAu 30NR
Giroux, Richard Leonard 1945- St&PR 91
Giroux, Robert BioIn 16
Giroux, Robert 1914- WhoAm 90
Giroux, Robert-Jean-Yvon 1939- WhoAm 90
Giroux, Stanley C. 1921- St&PR 91
Girri, A. HispWr 90
Girri, Alberto 1919- HispWr 90
Girsky, Howard ODwPR 91
Girsky, Joel H. 1939- St&PR 91
Girth, Marjorie Louisa 1939- WhoAm 90
Girtin, Thomas 1775-1802 IntDcAA 90
Girtman, William Lloyd 1943- WhoAm 90
Girton, Jack C. 1935- St&PR 91
Girton, Richard A., Jr. 1941- St&PR 91
Girty, Simon 1741-1818 EncCRAm, WhNaAH
Girvan, Brian J. 1955- St&PR 91
Girvan, Helen 1891- AuBYP 90
Girven, Joseph Francis 1934- WhoE 91
Girvigian, Raymond 1926- WhoAm 90
Girvin, Eb Carl 1917- WhoAm 90
Girvin, Gerald Thomas 1929- WhoE 91
Girvin, Richard Allen 1926- WhoWor 91
Girzone, Joseph F. BioIn 16
Girzone, Joseph F 1930- ConAu 130
Gisbert, Nelson 1946- WhoHisp 91
Gisborne, Frederic Newton 1824-1892 DcCanB 12
Gisca, Nicolae 1942- IntWWM 90
Giscard d'Estaing, Valery 1926- BiDFrPL, BioIn 16, WhoWor 91, WorAlBi
Gise, Leslie Hartley 1942- BiDrAPA 89, WhoE 91
Gisel, Pierre 1947- WhoWor 91
Gish, Alan 1941- St&PR 91
Gish, Dorothy 1898-1968 BioAmW, BioIn 16, NotWoAT, WorAlBi
Gish, Edward Rutledge 1908- WhoWor 91
Gish, Glenwood Littleton 1931- St&PR 91
Gish, Lillian WhoAm 90 WhoAmW 91
Gish, Lillian 1896- BioAmW, BioIn 16, WorAlBi
Gish, Lillian Diana 1896?- NotWoAT
Gish, Martin M BiDrAPA 89
Gish, Nancy K. 1942- ConAu 132
Gish, Norman Richard 1935- WhoAm 90
Gishler, Dara L. 1953- WhoAmW 91
Gislason, Eric Arni 1940- WhoAm 90
Gislason, Thorsteinn 1947- St&PR 91
Gismonoi, Paul Arthur 1955- WhoWor 91
Gisolfi, Anthony Maria 1909- WhoE 91
Gisolfi, Peter Anthony 1944- WhoAm 90
Gispert, Maria 1929- BiDrAPA 89
Giss, Vernon J. 1909- St&PR 91
Gissen, Aaron J. 1917-1989 BioIn 16
Gisser, Rivka 1939- St&PR 91
Gissing, George Robert 1857-1903 BioIn 16
Gissing, Vera BioIn 16
Gissler, Sigvard G. 1935- St&PR 91
Gissler, Sigvard Gunnar, Jr. 1935- WhoAm 90
Gist, Charles C BiDrAPA 89
Gist, Christopher 1705?-1759 EncCRAm
Gist, Christopher 1706?-1759 WhNaAH, WorAlBi
Gist, Howard Battle, Jr. 1919- WhoAm 90
Gist, Suzanne 1958- WhoAmW 91
Gistelinck, Daniel Marie Paul 1948- IntWWM 90
Gistelinck, David Nathan 1965- IntWWM 90
Gistelinck, Peter Herbert 1962- IntWWM 90
Gistenson, Donald E. 1932- St&PR 91
Gistrak, Allan B 1932- BiDrAPA 89
Gisvold, Kaare Moursund 1943- WhoWor 91
Gitana, Gertie 1888-1957 OxCPMus
Gitelle, Gene L 1923- BiDrAPA 89
Gitelson, Frances H 1905- BiDrAPA 89
Gitelson, Susan Aurelia WhoWor 91
Gitin, Herbert M. 1931- St&PR 91
Gitler, Bernard 1950- WhoE 91
Gitler, Samuel 1933- WhoAm 90
Gitles, Emanuel 1920- St&PR 91
Gitlin, Daniela Victorisz BiDrAPA 89
Gitlin, Irving Joseph 1918-1967 BioIn 16
Gitlin, Kevin Neal BiDrAPA 89
Gitlin, Martin ODwPR 91
Gitlin, Michael 1943- WhoAmA 91
Gitlin, Michael Jay 1950- BiDrAPA 89
Gitlin, Paul Jon 1953- BiDrAPA 89, WhoE 91
Gitlin, Todd BioIn 16
Gitlin, Todd 1943- WhoWrEP 89
Gitlis, Ivry 1922- IntWWM 90
Gitlitz, David Martin 1942- WhoAm 90
Gitlow, Abraham Leo 1918- WhoAm 90
Gitlow, Herman S. 1918- St&PR 91
Gitman, Paul 1940- WhoE 91
Gitman, Robert Charles 1958- WhoEmL 91
Gitner, Deanne 1944- WhoAmW 91
Gitner, Fred Jay 1951- WhoE 91
Gitner, Gerald L. 1945- WhoAm 90
Gitner, Maureen Murphy 1953- WhoE 91
Gits, John Robert 1933- St&PR 91
Gittell, Ross Jacobs 1957- WhoE 91
Gittelman, David Kalman 1958- BiDrAPA 89
Gittelman, Donald Henry 1929- WhoSSW 91
Gittelman, Marc Jeffrey 1947- St&PR 91, WhoAm 90
Gittelsohn, Roland Bertram 1910- BioIn 16
Gittelson, Abraham Jacob 1928- WhoSSW 91
Gittelson, Bernard 1918- WhoAm 90
Gittelson, Natalie Leavy 1929- WhoWrEP 89
Gittens, Chriss BioIn 16
Gittens, George Edward BiDrAPA 89
Gittens, Sheila Sledge 1948- WhoEmL 91
Gitterman, Alex 1938- WhoAm 90
Gitterman, Joseph L., III 1936- St&PR 91
Gitterman, Yitzhak 1889-1943 BioIn 16
Gittes, Ruben Foster 1934- WhoAm 90, WhoWor 91
Gittess, Franklin H 1938- BiDrAPA 89
Gittess, Ronald Marvin 1937- WhoSSW 91, WhoWor 91
Gittinger, Paul Allen 1959- St&PR 91
Gittings, Clare 1954- ConAu 130
Gittings, J.B. 1927- St&PR 91
Gittings, Jo Manton AuBYP 90
Gittins, Arthur Richard 1926- WhoAm 90
Gittis, Howard 1934- St&PR 91
Gittleman, Morris 1912- WhoWor 91
Gittleman, Sol 1934- WhoAm 90
Gittleman, Stanton C BiDrAPA 89
Gittler, Joseph Bertram 1912- WhoAm 90
Gittler, Norman 1931- WhoE 91
Gittlin, A. Sam 1914- WhoAm 90, WhoE 91, WhoWor 91
Gittlin, B. Morton 1922- St&PR 91
Gittman, Betty 1945- WhoAmW 91, WhoEmL 91
Giua, John Richard 1952- St&PR 91
Giudice, Gary ODwPR 91
Giudice, Patricia Ann 1942- WhoAmW 91
Giudice, William Anthony 1959- WhoSSW 91
Giuffra, Robert Joseph, Jr. 1960- WhoE 91
Giuffre, Jimmy BioIn 16
Giuffre, Victor M. 1955- St&PR 91
Giuffrida, Clare Gloria 1947- WhoE 91
Giuffrida, Giuseppe M. A. 1933- WhoWor 91
Giuffrida, Joseph 1927- St&PR 91
Giuffrida, Louis Onorato 1920- WhoAm 90
Giuffrida, Tom A. 1946- WhoSSW 91
Giuggio, John Peter 1930- St&PR 91
Giuggio, Ralph P. 1950- St&PR 91
Giugiaro, Giorgetto 1938- ConDes 90
Giuleanu, Victor 1914- IntWWM 90
Giuliani, Albert H. 1922- St&PR 91
Giuliani, Mauro 1781-1829 PenDiMP
Giuliani, Rudolph W. BioIn 16
Giuliani, Rudolph W. 1944- WhoAm 90, WhoE 91
Giuliani, Veronica 1660-1727 EncCoWW
Giuliano da Maiano 1432-1490 PenDiDA 89
Giuliano, Michael A 1944- BiDrAPA 89
Giuliano, Neil Gerard 1956- WhoEmL 91
Giuliano, Robert Paul 1943- WhoWor 91
Giuliano, Samuel J. 1926- St&PR 91
Giuliano, Sebastian R. 1931- St&PR 91
Giulianti, Mara Selena 1944- WhoAm 90, WhoAmW 91
Giulii, Joseph N. St&PR 91
Giulini, Carlo Maria 1914- IntWWM 90, PenDiMP, WhoWor 91
Giulio Giannuzzi 1492-1546 PenDiDA 89
Giulio Romano 1492-1546 PenDiDA 89
Giulio Romano 1499?-1546 IntDcAA 90
Giulio, Romano 1499?-1546 BioIn 16

Giumarra, John George, Jr. 1940- *St&PR 91*
Giumette, Joseph P. 1936- *ODwPR 91*
Giumette, Joseph Peter 1936- *WhoAm 90*
Giunta di Tugio *PenDiDA 89*
Giunta, Joseph 1951- *IntWWM 90*
Giuranna, Bruno 1933- *PenDiMP*
Giurgiu, Alexandra Maria 1958- *WhoAmW 91*
Gius, Julius 1911- *WhoAm 90*
Giusti, Dave 1939- *Ballpl 90, BioIn 16*
Giusti, George *WhoAm 90, WhoAmA 91*
Giusti, Gino Paul 1927- *St&PR 91, WhoAm 90*
Giusti, Joseph Paul 1935- *WhoAm 90*
Giusti, Robert George 1937- *WhoAm 90*
Giusti, William Roger 1947- *WhoE 91, WhoEmL 91*
Giustiniani, Biagio *PenDiDA 89*
Giustiniani, Michele *PenDiDA 89*
Giustiniani, Nicola 1736-1815 *PenDiDA 89*
Giustiniani, Vito Rocco 1916- *WhoWor 91*
Giusto, Joel 1954- *St&PR 91*
Giustra, Lawrence Joseph, Jr. 1950- *BiDrAPA 89*
Givan, Boyd Eugene *WhoAm 90*
Givan, Priscilla White 1942- *WhoAmW 91*
Givan, Richard Martin 1921- *WhoAm 90*
Givant, Philip Joachim 1935- *WhoWor 91*
Givaudan, Ben Trested, III 1936- *WhoAm 90*
Given, Charles Kemm, Jr. 1943- *WhoE 91*
Given, Kenna Sidney 1938- *WhoSSW 91*
Given, Leila Ione 1884-1959 *BioIn 16*
Givenchy *WhoWor 91*
Givenchy, Hubert de *BioIn 16*
Givenchy, Hubert De 1927- *WorAlBi*
Givens, Charles J 1942?- *BestSel 90-3 [port]*
Givens, Craig Lee 1949- *St&PR 91, WhoSSW 91*
Givens, David W. 1932- *St&PR 91, WhoAm 90*
Givens, Donna Neal 1947- *WhoAm 90*
Givens, Hurtis Lynn 1953- *WhoSSW 91*
Givens, Janet E 1932- *SmATA 60 [port]*
Givens, Janet Eaton 1932- *WhoAmW 91, WhoE 91*
Givens, Jean Frances 1948- *WhoEmL 91*
Givens, Jeanette Marlene 1948- *WhoEmL 91*
Givens, John Kenneth 1940- *WhoAm 90*
Givens, Judith Charlene 1923- *WhoAmW 91*
Givens, Paul Edward 1934- *WhoSSW 91*
Givens, Paul Ronald 1923- *WhoAm 90*
Givens, Robin *BioIn 16*
Givens, Sharon 1951- *WhoE 91*
Givens, Stephen Bruce 1941- *St&PR 91*
Givens, W. Mitchell 1934- *St&PR 91*
Givens, Walter Phillip 1941- *St&PR 91*
Givens, William P. *WhoAm 90*
Givens, William Phillip 1914- *St&PR 91*
Givens Julian, Leisa Irene 1959- *WhoAmW 91*
Giverink, Jack E. 1931- *St&PR 91*
Givhan, Steven Allen 1954- *WhoEmL 91*
Givi, Peyman 1958- *WhoE 91, WhoEmL 91, WhoWor 91*
Givirtz, Stanley *BioIn 16*
Givler, Diane Beryl 1953- *WhoAmW 91*
Givler, Michael E. 1955- *St&PR 91*
Givler, Walter M. 1933- *St&PR 91*
Givon, Bernd Shlomo 1932- *WhoWor 91*
Givonetti, John Alfred 1945- *WhoEmL 91*
Giza, Kathryn Alexandra 1963- *WhoEmL 91*
Gizbert Studnicka, Bogumila 1949- *IntWWM 90*
Gjellerup, Karl Adolf 1857-1919 *WorAlBi*
Gjellerup, Karl Adolph 1857-1919 *DcScanL*
Gjemre, Ken *BioIn 16*
Gjerde, Kristina Maria 1957- *WhoE 91, WhoEmL 91*
Gjerstad, Lidde Marie *WhoAmW 91*
Gjertsen, M. Falk 1847-1913 *BioIn 16*
Gjertson, Stephen Arthur 1949- *WhoAmA 91*
Gjevang, Anne 1948- *IntWWM 90*
Gjika, Elena 1828-1882 *EncCoWW*
Gkonos, James William 1924- *WhoAm 90*
Glaab, Charles Nelson 1927- *WhoAm 90*
Glab, John D. 1917- *St&PR 91*
Glabman, Andrew 1955- *WhoSSW 91*
Glabman, Richard J. 1945- *St&PR 91*
Glace, Beth Winifred 1960- *WhoAmW 91*
Glacel, Barbara Pate 1948- *WhoAmW 91, WhoEmL 91, WhoWor 91*
Glacken, Cynthia 1943- *WhoAmW 91*
Glacken, Michael F 1947- *BiDrAPA 89*
Glackens, Ira *NewYTBS 90*
Glackin, Caroline Elizabeth W. 1959- *WhoAmW 91, WhoEmL 91*
Glacking, Marjorie Joyce Straub 1936- *WhoAmW 91*
Glad, Edward Newman 1919- *WhoAm 90*
Glad, Lois Gayle 1931- *WhoWrEP 89*
Glad, Paul Wilbur 1926- *WhoSSW 91*
Gladchun, Lawrence L. 1950- *WhoAm 90*
Gladd, Neil Laurence 1955- *IntWWM 90*
Gladden, Carolan 1935- *WhoWrEP 89*
Gladden, Dan 1957- *Ballpl 90*
Gladden, Dean Robert 1953- *WhoEmL 91*
Gladden, James Walter, Jr. 1940- *WhoAm 90*
Gladden, Joseph R., Jr. 1942- *St&PR 91*
Gladden, Joseph Rhea, Jr. 1942- *WhoAm 90, WhoSSW 91*
Gladden, William Charles 1952- *IntWWM 90*
Gladding, Everett Bushnell 1917- *WhoSSW 91*
Gladding, Fred 1936- *Ballpl 90*
Gladding, Walter St. G. 1936- *St&PR 91*
Glade, Fred 1876-1934 *Ballpl 90*
Glade, John Frederick 1943- *St&PR 91*
Glade, Susan Klinger 1951- *BiDrAPA 89*
Glade, William Patton, Jr. 1929- *WhoAm 90*
Gladem, Martin D. 1923- *St&PR 91*
Gladen, Ralph G *BiDrAPA 89*
Gladieux, Bernard Louis 1907- *WhoAm 90*
Gladish, Donald P. 1926- *St&PR 91*
Gladkowska, Konstancja 1810-1889 *PenDiMP*
Gladman, Arthur E 1914- *BiDrAPA 89*
Gladson, Michael Bruce *BiDrAPA 89*
Gladstein, Sheldon *BiDrAPA 89*
Gladstone, Barbara *WhoAmA 91*
Gladstone, David John *St&PR 91*
Gladstone, Ernest 1931- *WhoE 91*
Gladstone, Henry A. 1940- *WhoAm 90*
Gladstone, Herbert Jack 1924- *WhoAm 90*
Gladstone, Herman P 1923- *BiDrAPA 89*
Gladstone, Joan 1953- *ODwPR 91*
Gladstone, Joyce Ann 1942- *WhoAmW 91*
Gladstone, Kim Diane 1957- *WhoAmW 91*
Gladstone, Lee *BiDrAPA 89*
Gladstone, Louis I. 1927- *St&PR 91*
Gladstone, M J 1923- *WhoAmA 91*
Gladstone, Richard Bennett 1924- *WhoAm 90*
Gladstone, Scott Bruce *BiDrAPA 89*
Gladstone, Suzanne Pink 1935- *WhoAmW 91*
Gladstone, W. E. 1809-1898 *BioIn 16*
Gladstone, William 1809-1898 *WorAlBi*
Gladstone, William Ewart 1809-1898 *BioIn 16, EncO&P 3, EncPaPR 91*
Gladstone, William Louis 1931- *WhoAm 90*
Gladstone, William Sheldon, Jr. 1923- *WhoAm 90*
Gladue, Philip J., Jr. 1930- *St&PR 91*
Gladwell, Graham Maurice Leslie 1934- *WhoAm 90*
Gladwin, Mary Elizabeth 1861-1939 *BioIn 16*
Gladwin, Walter H. 1902-1988 *BioIn 16*
Gladwin, William Joseph, Jr. 1946- *WhoEmL 91*
Glaefke, Deborah S. 1956- *WhoWrEP 89*
Glaenzer, Camille Henri 1932- *WhoWor 91*
Glaesel-Kohler, Kurt Joaquin 1936- *WhoWor 91*
Glaeser, William *St&PR 91*
Glaessmann, Doris Ann 1940- *WhoAmW 91, WhoE 91, WhoWor 91*
Glaessner, Philip Jacob Walk 1919- *WhoE 91*
Glagov, Seymour 1925- *WhoAm 90*
Glaid, Andrew Joseph, III 1923- *WhoAm 90*
Glaisner, Kurt F. 1946- *St&PR 91*
Glaister, Joseph W *BiDrAPA 89*
Glaman, Eugenie Fish 1872-1956 *WhoAmA 91N*
Glancy, Alfred R., III 1938- *St&PR 91*
Glancy, Diane 1941- *WhoWrEP 89*
Glancy, Dorothy Jean 1944- *WhoAmW 91*
Glancy, Mark Harold 1962- *WhoEmL 91*
Glancy, Michael 1950- *WhoAmA 91*
Glancy, Walter John 1942- *WhoAm 90*
Glanden, William Donald 1951- *WhoEmL 91*
Glander, Carlene Ann 1938- *WhoE 91*
Glander, William J. 1928- *St&PR 91*
Glang, Gabriele 1959- *WhoWrEP 89*
Glang, Reinhard 1929- *WhoSSW 91*
Glankoff, Peter P. 1944- *ODwPR 91*
Glann, Elizabeth Jane 1934- *WhoWrEP 89*
Glantz, Edward Joseph 1958- *WhoE 91*
Glantz, Gina 1943- *WhoAmW 91*
Glantz, Kalman 1937- *ConAu 132*
Glantz, Miles Maurice 1934- *St&PR 91*
Glantz, Richard G. 1931- *St&PR 91*
Glantz, Ronald A. 1941- *St&PR 91*
Glantz, Wendy Newman 1956- *WhoEmL 91*
Glantzman, Judy 1956- *WhoAmA 91*
Glanvil, Joseph 1636-1680 *EncPaPR 91*
Glanvill, Joseph 1636-1680 *EncO&P 3, EncPaPR 91*
Glanville, Brian Lester 1931- *AuBYP 90*
Glanville, Cecil E *BiDrAPA 89*
Glanville, Jerry *BioIn 16*
Glanville, Jerry 1941- *WhoAm 90, WhoSSW 91*
Glanville, Maxwell *EarBlAP*
Glanville, Maxwell 1918- *DrBlPA 90*
Glanville, Peter E. 1944- *St&PR 91*
Glanville, Robert Edward 1950- *WhoEmL 91*
Glanville-Hicks, Peggy 1912-1990 *NewYTBS 90*
Glanz, Andrea E 1952- *WhoAmA 91*
Glanzberg, Carol Jean *BiDrAPA 89*
Glanzel, Richard Kurt 1944- *WhoWor 91*
Glanzrock, Stephen Andrew 1948- *WhoEmL 91*
Glapa, Kathlene Macechak 1947- *St&PR 91*
Glapthorne, Henry 1610-1643? *BioIn 16*
Glarner, Fritz 1899-1972 *WhoAmA 91N*
Glasauer, Franz Ernst 1930- *WhoAm 90*
Glasberg, Alexandre 1902-1981 *BioIn 16*
Glasberg, Herbert Mark 1939- *BiDrAPA 89, WhoE 91, WhoWor 91*
Glasberg, Laurence Brian 1943- *WhoAm 90*
Glasberg, Paula Drillman 1939- *WhoAm 90, WhoAmW 91, WhoWor 91*
Glasby, Ian 1931- *WhoWor 91*
Glasco, Donald G 1929- *BiDrAPA 89*
Glasco, Joseph M 1925- *WhoAmA 91*
Glasco, Joseph Milton 1925- *WhoAm 90*
Glasco, Kimberly *BioIn 16, WhoAm 90*
Glascock, Anthony Philip, Jr. 1947- *WhoE 91*
Glascock, John Hays 1928- *St&PR 91*
Glascoe, Rosalyn B. 1944- *St&PR 91*
Glaser, Alvin 1932- *WhoE 91, WhoWor 91*
Glaser, Bruce 1933- *WhoAmA 91*
Glaser, Carol Groveman 1949- *WhoEmL 91*
Glaser, Christine Anne 1941- *IntWWM 90*
Glaser, Claude Edward, Jr. 1919- *WhoAm 90*
Glaser, Daniel 1918- *WhoAm 90*
Glaser, David *BioIn 16*
Glaser, David 1919- *WhoAmA 91, WhoE 91*
Glaser, Dianne E. 1937- *BioIn 16*
Glaser, Donald A. 1926- *WorAlBi*
Glaser, Donald Arthur 1926- *WhoAm 90, WhoWor 91*
Glaser, Edward Lewis 1929- *WhoAm 90*
Glaser, Elmer Eliot 1920- *WhoE 91*
Glaser, Frederick B 1935- *BiDrAPA 89*
Glaser, Gary A. 1944- *St&PR 91*
Glaser, Gilbert Herbert 1920- *WhoAm 90*
Glaser, Harold 1924- *WhoAm 90*
Glaser, Helen H 1924- *BiDrAPA 89*
Glaser, Herbert Otto 1927- *WhoAm 90*
Glaser, Horst Albert 1935- *WhoWor 91*
Glaser, Isabel Joshlin 1929- *WhoWrEP 89*
Glaser, Joseph Bernard 1925- *WhoAm 90*
Glaser, Joy Harriet 1941- *WhoAmW 91*
Glaser, Kurt 1914- *WhoAm 90*
Glaser, Kurt 1915- *BiDrAPA 89, WhoE 91*
Glaser, Louis F. 1933- *St&PR 91*
Glaser, Luis 1932- *WhoAm 90*
Glaser, Michael Lance 1939- *WhoAm 90*
Glaser, Michael S. 1943- *WhoWrEP 89*
Glaser, Milton 1929- *ConDes 90, WhoAm 90, WhoAmA 91*
Glaser, Nancy Ellen 1945- *WhoAmW 91*
Glaser, Paul Franklyn 1926- *St&PR 91*
Glaser, Peter Edward 1923- *St&PR 91, WhoAm 90*
Glaser, Robert 1921- *BioIn 16*
Glaser, Robert Edward 1935- *WhoAm 90*
Glaser, Robert Joy 1918- *St&PR 91, WhoAm 90*
Glaser, Robert Leonard 1929- *WhoAm 90*
Glaser, Ronald 1939- *WhoAm 90*
Glaser, Ruth Sass- 1919?- *BioIn 16*
Glaser, Vaughan 1872-1958 *OxCCanT*
Glaser, Vera Romans *WhoAm 90*
Glaser, Werner Wolf 1910- *IntWWM 90*
Glaser, William A 1925- *WhoWrEP 89*
Glaser, William Peter 1933- *St&PR 91*
Glaser, Wolfram *BiDrAPA 89*
Glasgall, Franklin 1932- *St&PR 91*
Glasgow, Agnes Jackie 1941- *WhoSSW 91*
Glasgow, Andrew *St&PR 91*
Glasgow, Ellen 1873-1945 *BioAmW, FemiCLE, WorAlBi*
Glasgow, Jean M 1911- *BiDrAPA 89*
Glasgow, Jesse Edward 1923- *WhoAm 90*
Glasgow, John Michael 1934- *WhoAm 90*
Glasgow, Ken Wallace 1948- *WhoEmL 91*
Glasgow, Lawrence Ervin 1957- *WhoEmL 91*
Glasgow, Lukman 1935-1988 *BioIn 16, WhoAmA 91N*
Glasgow, Norma Foreman *BioIn 16*
Glasgow, Norma Foreman 1927- *WhoAmW 91*
Glasgow, Thomas William, Jr. 1947- *St&PR 91, WhoAm 90*
Glasgow, Vaughn Leslie 1944- *WhoAm 90, WhoAmA 91*
Glasgow, Willene Graythen 1939- *WhoAmW 91*
Glasgow, William J. *St&PR 91*
Glasgow, William Jacob 1946- *WhoEmL 91*
Glashausser, Suellen 1945- *WhoE 91*
Glashow, Andrea Jean 1961- *WhoAmW 91*
Glashow, Sheldon L. *BioIn 16*
Glashow, Sheldon L. 1932- *WorAlBi*
Glashow, Sheldon Lee 1932- *WhoAm 90, WhoE 91, WhoWor 91*
Glasier, Alice Geneva *WhoAmA 91*
Glasier, Alice Geneva 1903- *WhoAm 90, WhoWor 91*
Glasier, Charles H. 1912- *St&PR 91*
Glasier, John 1809-1894 *DcCanB 12*
Glaske, Paul E. 1933- *St&PR 91*
Glaskey, Susan M. 1960- *WhoAmW 91*
Glaskin, Carol Lynne *BiDrAPA 89*
Glaskin, G M 1923- *EncO&P 3*
Glasmacher, Peter H. 1947- *WhoWor 91*
Glasmann, William 1858-1916 *AmLegL*
Glasner, Daniel Mayer 1940- *St&PR 91*
Glasner, David 1948- *WhoE 91*
Glasner, LeRoy A., Jr. 1928- *ODwPR 91*
Glasner, Saul *BiDrAPA 89*
Glaspell, Susan 1876-1948 *FemiCLE, NotWoAT*
Glaspell, Susan 1882-1948 *BioAmW, BioIn 16*
Glaspie, April Catherine 1942- *WhoAm 90, WhoAmW 91, WhoWor 91*
Glass, Alastair Malcolm 1940- *WhoAm 90*
Glass, Amanda *WhoWrEP 89*
Glass, Andrew *BioIn 16*
Glass, Andrew James 1935- *WhoAm 90*
Glass, Beaumont 1925- *IntWWM 90*
Glass, Brent D. 1947- *WhoAm 90*
Glass, Bryan Pettigrew 1919- *WhoAm 90*
Glass, Carolyn Bennion 1946- *WhoAmW 91*
Glass, Carson McElyea 1915- *WhoAm 90, WhoWor 91*
Glass, Carter 1858-1946 *BiDrUSE 89, EncABHB 7 [port], WorAlBi*
Glass, Cary Devin *BiDrAPA 89*
Glass, Charles *BioIn 16*
Glass, David Carter 1930- *WhoAm 90, WhoE 91*
Glass, David D. 1935- *St&PR 91, WhoAm 90, WhoSSW 91*
Glass, David Eugene *BiDrAPA 89*
Glass, David Vaughn 1955- *WhoE 91*
Glass, Dorothy F *WhoAmA 91*
Glass, Dorothy Finn *WhoE 91*
Glass, Douglas Alan 1954- *WhoEmL 91*
Glass, Elliott Michael 1934- *WhoAm 90*
Glass, Ernest J., Jr. 1937- *St&PR 91*
Glass, Frederick Marion 1913- *St&PR 91*
Glass, Gary 1947- *BiDrAPA 89*
Glass, Gary Michael 1948- *BiDrAPA 89, WhoE 91*
Glass, George Stuart 1941- *BiDrAPA 89, WhoSSW 91*
Glass, Guy Fredrick *BiDrAPA 89*
Glass, Harold A. 1919- *St&PR 91*
Glass, Henry Peter 1911- *WhoAm 90*
Glass, Herbert 1934- *WhoAm 90*
Glass, Holly P. 1955- *ODwPR 91*
Glass, Hugh 1785?-1833 *WhNaAH*
Glass, James R. 1933- *St&PR 91*
Glass, Jeffrey 1952- *BiDrAPA 89*
Glass, Jeffrey Craig *BiDrAPA 89*
Glass, Jeffrey Taylor 1959- *WhoSSW 91*
Glass, Joanna 1936- *FemiCLE, OxCCanT*
Glass, Joel Bennett 1942- *BiDrAPA 89, WhoE 91*
Glass, John Derek 1941- *WhoAm 90*
Glass, John P. *AmLegL*
Glass, John Sheldon 1936- *WhoE 91*
Glass, John Thomas 1935- *St&PR 91*
Glass, Joseph Hillard 1925- *WhoE 91*
Glass, Julie Kay 1960- *WhoEmL 91, WhoSSW 91*
Glass, Kenneth David 1951- *BiDrAPA 89*
Glass, Kenneth Edward 1940- *WhoWor 91*
Glass, Laurel 1923- *WhoAm 90*
Glass, Lawrence 1947- *BiDrAPA 89*
Glass, Lennin H. 1925- *WhoAm 90*
Glass, Leonard Liebes 1942- *BiDrAPA 89*
Glass, M. Milton 1906- *WhoAm 90*
Glass, Mark 1947- *WhoEmL 91*
Glass, Martha Daughtry 1944- *WhoAmW 91*
Glass, Mary Anne 1956- *WhoEmL 91*
Glass, Michael Gwinn 1938- *St&PR 91*
Glass, Michael L 1945- *WhoAmA 91*
Glass, Michael Robert 1933- *BiDrAPA 89*
Glass, Milton Louis 1929- *St&PR 91, WhoAm 90*
Glass, Molly 1925- *WhoWrEP 89*
Glass, Paul Eugene 1934- *IntWWM 90*
Glass, Paul F, Jr. *BiDrAPA 89*
Glass, Paul William Parsonnet 1945- *WhoAm 90*
Glass, Philip *BioIn 16*

Glass, Philip 1937- *IntWWM 90, PenDiMP A, WhoAm 90, WhoE 91, WorAlBi*
Glass, Richard E 1930- *BiDrAPA 89*
Glass, Richard M *BiDrAPA 89, BioIn 16*
Glass, Robert Davis 1922- *WhoAm 90, WhoE 91*
Glass, Ron 1945- *DrBlPA 90*
Glass, Ronald Lee 1946- *St&PR 91*
Glass, Ruth 1912-1990 *ConAu 131*
Glass, Sheldon D *BiDrAPA 89*
Glass, Simon David 1938- *BiDrAPA 89*
Glass, Steven Jerome 1950- *BiDrAPA 89*
Glass, Thomas Graham, Jr. 1926- *WhoSSW 91*
Glass, Torrey Allen 1952- *WhoSSW 91*
Glass, Walter 1909- *St&PR 91*
Glass, Wendy D 1925- *WhoAmA 91*
Glass, William E 1906- *BiDrAPA 89*
Glass, William Everett 1906- *WhoAm 90*
Glassberg, Stephen C 1945- *BiDrAPA 89*
Glassbrenner, Adolph 1810-1876 *BioIn 16*
Glassco, Bill 1935- *OxCCanT [port]*
Glassco, John 1909-1981 *BioIn 16*
Glassco, Robert B. 1917- *St&PR 91*
Glasscock, Amnesia *MajTwCW*
Glasscock, Bill 1938- *ODwPR 91*
Glasscock, Gary M. 1951- *WhoAm 90*
Glasscock, Jack 1859-1947 *Ballpl 90 [port]*
Glasscock, Larry C. 1948- *St&PR 91*
Glasscock, Larry Claborn 1948- *WhoAm 90*
Glasscock, Michael Emmanuel, III 1933- *WhoSSW 91*
Glasscock, Sarah 1952- *ConAu 130*
Glasscock, Susan Edelen 1962- *WhoSSW 91*
Glasse, Hannah 1708-1770 *BioIn 16, FemiCLE*
Glasse, John Howell 1922- *WhoAm 90*
Glassell, Alfred Curry, Jr. 1913- *WhoAm 90*
Glassenberg, Albert Bryant 1927- *St&PR 91*
Glasser, Harvey W *BiDrAPA 89*
Glasser, Herman 1924- *St&PR 91*
Glasser, Ira Saul 1938- *WhoAm 90*
Glasser, Israel Leo 1924- *WhoAm 90, WhoE 91*
Glasser, James J. 1934- *St&PR 91*
Glasser, Joseph 1925- *WhoAm 90*
Glasser, Leo George 1916- *WhoAm 90*
Glasser, Martin Evan *BiDrAPA 89*
Glasser, Marvin 1923- *St&PR 91*
Glasser, Matthew David 1952- *WhoEmL 91*
Glasser, Melvin Allan 1915- *WhoAm 90*
Glasser, Michael Alan *BiDrAPA 89*
Glasser, Michael E 1945- *BiDrAPA 89*
Glasser, Norma Penchansky 1941- *WhoAmA 91*
Glasser, Otto John 1918- *WhoAm 90*
Glasser, Paul Harold 1929- *WhoAm 90*
Glasser, Perry 1948- *WhoWrEP 89*
Glasser, Stephen Andrew 1943- *WhoE 91*
Glasser, Stephen Paul 1940- *WhoSSW 91*
Glasser, William 1925- *BiDrAPA 89*
Glassett, Jane 1960- *WhoAmW 91*
Glassett, Tim S. 1956- *St&PR 91*
Glassett, Tim Scott 1956- *WhoEmL 91*
Glassfield, Chris *NewAgMG*
Glassford, Russell Myles 1935- *St&PR 91*
Glassgold, Alfred Emanuel 1929- *WhoAm 90*
Glasshagel, Glenn E. 1945- *St&PR 91*
Glassick, Charles Etzweiler 1931- *WhoAm 90, WhoE 91*
Glassman, Alexander H 1934- *BiDrAPA 89*
Glassman, Armand Barry 1938- *WhoAm 90, WhoSSW 91*
Glassman, Barry Michael 1940- *BiDrAPA 89*
Glassman, Caroline Duby 1922- *WhoAm 90, WhoAmW 91, WhoE 91*
Glassman, Edward 1929- *WhoAm 90, WhoWor 91*
Glassman, Edwina 1939- *St&PR 91*
Glassman, Elizabeth Jane 1949- *WhoAmW 91*
Glassman, Gerald Seymour 1932- *St&PR 91, WhoAm 90*
Glassman, Geraldine Joan 1936- *WhoAmW 91*
Glassman, Herbert Haskel 1919- *WhoAm 90*
Glassman, Howard Theodore 1934- *WhoAm 90*
Glassman, Irvin 1923- *WhoAm 90*
Glassman, Jaga Nath Singh 1953- *BiDrAPA 89*
Glassman, James Kenneth 1947- *WhoAm 90*
Glassman, Jerome Martin 1919- *WhoAm 90*
Glassman, Jon David 1944- *WhoAm 90*
Glassman, Joyce *ConAu 129*
Glassman, Marvin 1935- *St&PR 91*
Glassman, Maureen Theresa 1948- *WhoE 91*
Glassman, Myra Lee 1945- *BiDrAPA 89*
Glassman, Peter Joel 1945- *WhoAm 90*
Glassman, Rita 1945- *ODwPR 91*
Glassman, Robert Alan 1946- *WhoEmL 91*
Glassman, Seth 1946- *WhoEmL 91*
Glassman, Wendi Gail 1955- *WhoEmL 91*
Glassmeyer, Edward 1915- *WhoAm 90*
Glassmeyer, James Milton 1928- *WhoWor 91*
Glassmoyer, Thomas Parvin 1915- *WhoAm 90, WhoE 91, WhoWor 91*
Glassner, Barry 1952- *WhoAm 90*
Glassock, Richard James 1934- *WhoAm 90*
Glasson, Jacques J. 1935- *St&PR 91*
Glasson, Lloyd 1931- *WhoAm 90, WhoAmA 91*
Glassow, Ruth Bertha *BioIn 16*
Glasspole, Florizel Augustus 1909- *WhoWor 91*
Glassy, Mark Charles 1952- *WhoEmL 91*
Glast, Celia Gellman 1945- *St&PR 91*
Glast, Robert Joel 1944- *St&PR 91*
Glastetter, Lori Jean *St&PR 91*
Glastris, Paul *BioIn 16*
Glatfelter, Charles Henry 1924- *WhoAm 90*
Glatfelter, Philip H., III 1916- *St&PR 91*
Glatfelter, Philip Henry, III 1916- *WhoAm 90*
Glathe, John P 1926- *BiDrAPA 89*
Glatman-Stein, Marcia 1944- *WhoAmW 91*
Glatt, David Allen 1960- *St&PR 91*
Glatt, Linnea 1949- *WhoAmA 91*
Glatt, Milton S *BiDrAPA 89*
Glatt, Mitchell Steven 1957- *WhoE 91*
Glattfelder, Calvin Fugard 1924- *WhoE 91*
Glatzer, Nahum N. 1903-1990 *NewYTBS 90 [port]*
Glatzer, Nahum Norbert 1903-1990 *BioIn 16, ConAu 131*
Glatzer, Robert Anthony 1932- *WhoWor 91*
Glatzer, Wolfgang P. W. 1944- *WhoWor 91*
Glatzmaier, Lisa Ann 1962- *WhoAmW 91*
Glaub, Kathleen Sereda 1953- *St&PR 91*
Glauber, Johann Rudolph 1604?-1670 *EncO&P 3*
Glauber, Michael A. 1943- *St&PR 91, WhoAm 90*
Glauber, Roy Jay 1925- *WhoAm 90*
Glauberman, Lionel 1930- *St&PR 91*
Glauberman, Murray 1927- *St&PR 91*
Glauberman, Stuart Craig 1953- *St&PR 91*
Glaubinger, Alan 1940- *WhoSSW 91*
Glaubinger, Lawrence D. 1925- *St&PR 91*
Glaubinger, Lawrence David 1925- *WhoWor 91*
Glaude, Stephen Anthony 1954- *WhoAm 90*
Glauner, Alfred William 1936- *WhoE 91*
Glauser, Friedrich 1896-1938 *BioIn 16*
Glauthier, T. James 1944- *WhoE 91*
Glavanovic, Pero Josip 1943- *WhoWor 91*
Glaviano, Tommy 1923- *Ballpl 90*
Glaviano, Vincent Valentino 1920- *WhoAm 90, WhoWor 91*
Glavickas, Joseph Albert 1939- *St&PR 91, WhoAm 90*
Glavin, James Edward 1923- *WhoAm 90*
Glavin, Richard J *BiDrAPA 89*
Glavin, William F. 1932- *BioIn 16*
Glavin, William Francis 1932- *WhoAm 90*
Glavine, Tom 1966- *Ballpl 90*
Glawe, Lloyd Neil 1932- *WhoSSW 91*
Glaz, Herta 1908- *IntWWM 90*
Glaza, Bryan K. 1954- *ODwPR 91*
Glazarova, Jarmila 1901-1977 *EncCoWW*
Glaze, Lawrence Clark 1956- *WhoEmL 91*
Glaze, Lynn Ferguson 1933- *WhoAmW 91*
Glaze, Max A *BiDrAPA 89*
Glaze, Michael 1935- *WhoWor 91*
Glaze, Ralph 1882-1968 *Ballpl 90*
Glaze, Robert A. 1942- *St&PR 91*
Glaze, Robert Howe 1952- *WhoEmL 91*
Glaze, Robert Pinckney 1933- *WhoAm 90*
Glaze, Thomas A. 1947- *St&PR 91*
Glazebrook, Ted James 1956- *St&PR 91*
Glazer, Charles T. 1951- *ODwPR 91*
Glazer, David 1913- *IntWWM 90*
Glazer, David Andrew 1953- *WhoE 91*
Glazer, Donald J. 1942- *St&PR 91*
Glazer, Donald Wayne 1944- *WhoAm 90*
Glazer, Esther *WhoAm 90*
Glazer, Frederic Jay 1937- *WhoAm 90, WhoSSW 91*
Glazer, George 1930- *ODwPR 91*
Glazer, Gesja *BioIn 16*
Glazer, Gilda *IntWWM 90*
Glazer, H. 1928- *St&PR 91*
Glazer, Ira S. 1937- *St&PR 91*
Glazer, Jack Henry 1928- *WhoWor 91*
Glazer, Jerome Sanford 1929- *St&PR 91*
Glazer, John Prescott 1945- *BiDrAPA 89*
Glazer, Larry Sylvester 1939- *WhoAm 90*
Glazer, Laurence Charles 1945- *St&PR 91, WhoAm 90*
Glazer, Mark Jonathan 1949- *WhoEmL 91*
Glazer, Nathan *BioIn 16*
Glazer, Nathan 1923- *WhoAm 90*
Glazer, Norman 1920- *WhoAm 90*
Glazer, Robert *IntWWM 90*
Glazer, Steven Mark 1951- *WhoEmL 91*
Glazer, Tom 1914- *AuBYP 90*
Glazer, Wendy 1959- *WhoEmL 91*
Glazer, William M 1947- *BiDrAPA 89*
Glazer, William Michael 1947- *WhoE 91*
Glazier, John 1809-1894 *DcCanB 12*
Glazier, Jonathan Hemenway 1949- *WhoEmL 91*
Glazier, Kenneth Charles 1949- *St&PR 91*
Glazier, Loss Pequeno *WhoHisp 91*
Glazier, Raymond Earl, Jr. 1941- *WhoE 91*
Glazier, Robert Carl 1927- *WhoAm 90*
Glazier-Seibel, Sharon Elaine *BiDrAPA 89*
Glazman, Josef 1913-1943 *BioIn 16*
Glazner, Whitey 1893- *Ballpl 90*
Glazunov, Aleksandr 1865-1936 *WorAlBi*
Glazunov, Alexander 1865-1936 *PenDiMP A*
Glazzard, Charles Donaldson 1928- *BiDrAPA 89*
Gleadell, Richard Eugene, Jr. 1950- *WhoEmL 91*
Gleasner, Diana 1936- *ConAu 33NR*
Gleasner, Diana Cottle 1936- *WhoWrEP 89*
Gleason, A. M. 1930- *WhoAm 90*
Gleason, Abbott 1938- *WhoAm 90, WhoWrEP 89*
Gleason, Alice Bryant 1940- *WhoAmW 91*
Gleason, Andrew Mattei 1921- *WhoAm 90*
Gleason, April Bridget 1949- *BiDrAPA 89*
Gleason, Arthur Stephen 1946- *St&PR 91*
Gleason, Bonnie J. 1929- *WhoAmW 91*
Gleason, C.B. *St&PR 91*
Gleason, Charles Thomas 1950- *WhoWor 91*
Gleason, Cynthia *ODwPR 91*
Gleason, Debora Rae 1957- *WhoEmL 91*
Gleason, Donald E *BiDrAPA 89*
Gleason, Douglas Renwick 1956- *WhoEmL 91*
Gleason, Edward Hinsdale, Jr. 1927- *WhoSSW 91*
Gleason, Edward M. 1940- *St&PR 91*
Gleason, Eliza Atkins 1909- *WhoAm 90*
Gleason, Elizabeth Hooper 1921- *WhoE 91*
Gleason, Frank J., Jr. 1930- *St&PR 91*
Gleason, G.W. 1952- *St&PR 91*
Gleason, George Donald 1920- *WhoWrEP 89*
Gleason, Harold Anthony 1945- *St&PR 91*
Gleason, J. Marne 1935- *St&PR 91*
Gleason, Jackie *BioIn 16*
Gleason, Jackie 1916-1987 *OxCPMus, WorAlBi*
Gleason, James Arthur 1905- *WhoAm 90*
Gleason, Jean Berko 1931- *WhoAm 90*
Gleason, Jean Wilbur 1943- *WhoAm 90*
Gleason, Joanna *BioIn 16*
Gleason, Joanna 1950- *WhoAmW 91*
Gleason, Joe Duncan 1879-1959 *WhoAmA 91N*
Gleason, John F. 1928- *St&PR 91*
Gleason, John Francis 1928- *WhoAm 90*
Gleason, John James 1941- *WhoAm 90*
Gleason, John Martin 1907- *WhoAm 90*
Gleason, John P., Jr. 1941- *St&PR 91*
Gleason, John Patrick, Jr. 1941- *WhoAm 90*
Gleason, John Scovil 1941- *WhoAm 90*
Gleason, Joseph B. *ODwPR 91*
Gleason, Kate 1865-1933 *BioIn 16*
Gleason, Kerry T. *ODwPR 91*
Gleason, Kid 1866-1933 *Ballpl 90*
Gleason, Lawrence David 1935- *St&PR 91, WhoAm 90*
Gleason, Leonard George 1954- *WhoEmL 91*
Gleason, Margaret *BiDrAPA 89*
Gleason, Norman Dale 1943- *WhoAm 90, WhoSSW 91*
Gleason, Peter Charles 1954- *BiDrAPA 89*
Gleason, Philip James 1954- *WhoSSW 91*
Gleason, Ralph Newton 1922- *WhoAm 90*
Gleason, Robert Michael 1929- *St&PR 91*
Gleason, Robert Willard 1932- *WhoAm 90*
Gleason, Stephen Charles 1946- *WhoEmL 91*
Gleason, Steve Anson 1949- *WhoAm 90*
Gleason, Thomas D. 1936- *St&PR 91*
Gleason-Baker, Eilene Ora 1951- *IntWWM 90*
Gleason-Fay, Helen Will 1940- *WhoAmW 91*
Gleaton, Frederick Neal 1952- *WhoEmL 91*
Gleaton, Jerry Don 1957- *Ballpl 90*
Gleaves, Edwin Sheffield 1936- *WhoAm 90, WhoSSW 91*
Gleaves, James L. 1952- *St&PR 91*
Gleaves, Leon Rogers 1939- *St&PR 91*
Gleazer, Edmund John, Jr. 1916- *WhoAm 90*
Gleba, Frank P., II 1955- *WhoEmL 91*
Gleberman, Jules Harvey 1922- *St&PR 91*
Gleckner, Donald Fowler 1903- *WhoE 91*
Gleckner, Robert Francis 1925- *WhoAm 90*
Gledhill, Russell William 1946- *St&PR 91*
Gleditsch, Scott Duane *BiDrAPA 89*
Glee, Glenna *WhoWrEP 89*
Gleed, George Clifford 1929- *St&PR 91*
Gleekel, Sherman Sherry 1930- *St&PR 91*
Gleeson, Austin Michael 1938- *WhoAm 90*
Gleeson, Jim 1912- *Ballpl 90*
Gleeson, Noel Martin 1934- *WhoWor 91*
Gleeson, Patrick *NewAgMG*
Gleeson, Paul Francis 1941- *WhoAm 90*
Gleich, Carol S. 1935- *WhoAmW 91*
Gleich, Gerald Joseph 1931- *WhoAm 90*
Gleichen, Feodora Georgina Maud 1861-1922 *BiDWomA*
Gleichen, Helena 1873-1947 *BiDWomA*
Gleichenhaus, Robert D. 1929- *St&PR 91*
Gleichert, Gregg Charles 1948- *St&PR 91*
Gleichman, John Alan 1944- *WhoWor 91*
Gleick, Beth Youman *AuBYP 90*
Gleick, James 1954- *ConAu 131*
Gleim, James Mac 1934- *WhoAm 90*
Gleim, Johann Wilhelm Ludwig 1719-1803 *DcLB 97 [port]*
Gleim, Michael Lee 1943- *St&PR 91*
Gleis, Linda Hood 1952- *WhoAmW 91*
Gleiss, Henry Weston 1928- *WhoWor 91*
Gleisser, Marcus David 1923- *WhoAm 90*
Gleissner, Friedrich Anton 1928- *WhoWor 91*
Gleitman, George 1928- *St&PR 91*
Gleitzman, Morris 1953- *ConAu 131*
Gleklen, Donald Morse 1936- *St&PR 91, WhoAm 90*
Glemann, Richard Paul 1949- *WhoEmL 91, WhoSSW 91*
Glemp, Jozef 1929- *WhoWor 91*
Glemser, Bernard 1908-1990 *BioIn 16, ConAu 131, NewYTBS 90*
Glemser, Oskar Max 1911- *WhoWor 91*
Glen, Alida Mixson 1930- *WhoAmW 91*
Glen, Emilie 1937- *WhoWrEP 89*
Glen, Eric Stanger 1934- *WhoWor 91*
Glen, John *BioIn 16*
Glen, Robert 1905- *WhoAm 90*
Glen, Robert S *BiDrAPA 89*
Glen, Robert Story 1920- *WhoAm 90*
Glenconner, Colin C Paget Tennant, Baron *BioIn 16*
Glencross, William Donald 1936- *St&PR 91*
Glenday, Graham 1949- *WhoE 91*
Glendening, Everett Austin 1929- *WhoAm 90*
Glendenning, Don Mark 1953- *WhoEmL 91*
Glendenning, Donn *ConAu 31NR*
Glendinning, Peter 1951- *WhoAmA 91*
Glendinning, Victoria *BioIn 16*
Glendinning, Victoria 1937- *WorAu 1980 [port]*
Glenesk, Gail Belle 1953- *WhoAmW 91*
Glenister, Brian Frederick 1928- *WhoAm 90*
Glenmullen, Joseph Peter *BiDrAPA 89*
Glenn, Abraham G 1916- *BiDrAPA 89*
Glenn, Albert H. 1922- *WhoAm 90, WhoSSW 91*
Glenn, Andrea Poutasse 1951- *WhoAmW 91*
Glenn, Belinda 1963- *WhoAmW 91*
Glenn, Clyde Albert, Jr. 1933- *St&PR 91*
Glenn, Constance White 1933- *WhoAmA 91*
Glenn, Debra Pahal 1953- *WhoAmW 91*
Glenn, Dennis Wayne 1952- *WhoSSW 91*
Glenn, Donald Taylor, Jr. 1948- *WhoSSW 91*
Glenn, Edward A 1925- *BiDrAPA 89*
Glenn, Elizabeth Conde 1859-1920 *BioIn 16*
Glenn, Ethel Chappell 1926- *WhoSSW 91*
Glenn, Gerald M. 1942- *St&PR 91*
Glenn, Gerald Marvin 1942- *WhoAm 90*
Glenn, Gordon S. 1948- *St&PR 91*
Glenn, James *ConAu 31NR*
Glenn, James 1937- *WhoAm 90*
Glenn, James Francis 1928- *WhoAm 90*
Glenn, Jerry Hosmer, Jr. 1938- *WhoAm 90*
Glenn, Joe Davis, Jr. 1921- *WhoSSW 91*
Glenn, John 1921- *BioIn 16*
Glenn, John H., Jr. 1921- *WorAlBi*
Glenn, John Herschel, Jr. 1921- *WhoAm 90, WhoWor 91*
Glenn, John M. 1931- *St&PR 91*
Glenn, Jules 1921- *BiDrAPA 89*
Glenn, Linda MacDonald 1955- *WhoAmW 91*
Glenn, Mark Dwight 1953- *BiDrAPA 89*
Glenn, Martha Anne 1946- *WhoEmL 91*
Glenn, Mary Stewart 1912- *WhoE 91*
Glenn, Mel 1943- *BioIn 16*
Glenn, Michael Douglas 1940- *WhoAm 90*

Glenn, Nancy Noyes 1953- WhoWrEP 89
Glenn, Norval Dwight 1933- WhoAm 90
Glenn, Patrick L. 1938- St&PR 91
Glenn, Paul Mitchell 1945- St&PR 91
Glenn, Peggy 1944- WhoWrEP 89
Glenn, Peter BioIn 16
Glenn, Richard Wray 1936- St&PR 91
Glenn, Robert Aubrey 1930- St&PR 91, WhoAm 90
Glenn, Robert Edward 1944- WhoAm 90
Glenn, Roy E 1914?-1971 DrBlPA 90
Glenn, Scott BioIn 16
Glenn, Scott 1942- WhoAm 90
Glenn, Shelia Campbell 1955- WhoSSW 91
Glenn, Stephen Charles 1945- St&PR 91
Glenn, Terry Kimball 1940- WhoAm 90
Glenn, Theodore J 1927- BiDrAPA 89
Glenn, Thomas Michael 1940- WhoAm 90
Glenn, Trevor D 1934- BiDrAPA 89
Glenn, Tyree 1912-1974 DrBlPA 90
Glenn, Wayne Eugene 1924- WhoAm 90
Glenn, William Allen 1925- WhoAm 90
Glenn, William Ellis BioIn 16
Glenn, William M. 1949- St&PR 91
Glenn, William Wallace Lumpkin 1914- WhoAm 90, WhoWor 91
Glenn, Willie L. 1936- St&PR 91
Glennen, Robert Eugene, Jr. 1933- WhoAm 90
Glenner, Richard Allen 1934- WhoWor 91
Glennie, Evelyn 1965- IntWWM 90, PenDiMP
Glennon, Charles Edward 1942- WhoWor 91
Glennon, Daniel C BiDrAPA 89
Glennon, Denis BioIn 16
Glennon, Harrison R., Jr. 1914- St&PR 91
Glennon, Harrison Randolph, Jr. 1914- WhoAm 90
Glennon, Joseph Anthony 1931- WhoSSW 91
Glenny, Lyman Albert 1918- WhoAm 90
Glenny, Michael Valentine 1927-1990 ConAu 132
Glenski, Joseph William 1961- WhoEmL 91
Glenwick, Henry BiDrAPA 89
Glerum, Rolf D. 1933- ODwPR 91
Gless, Sharon WhoAm 90, WhoAmW 91
Gless, Sharon 1943- WorAlBi
Glessner, Harry David 1960- WhoEmL 91
Glessner, Thomas Allen 1952- WhoEmL 91
Gleszer, Kenneth M. 1921- St&PR 91
Gleva, Karen J. 1952- WhoAmW 91
Glewwe, Paul William 1958- WhoE 91
Gley, Marcel-Eugene-Emile 1857-1930 DcScB S2
Glezer, Nechemia 1910- WhoAmA 91
Glezerman, Lois P. St&PR 91
Glezos, Matthews 1927- St&PR 91, WhoAm 90
Gliatta, Ronald 1950- WhoE 91, WhoWor 91
Glick, Allan H. 1938- WhoAm 90
Glick, Alvin Louis 1926- St&PR 91
Glick, Ana Berliant 1937- BiDrAPA 89
Glick, Andrew Justus 1948- WhoEmL 91
Glick, Barry 1949- St&PR 91
Glick, Carl 1921- St&PR 91
Glick, Cynthia Susan 1950- WhoAmW 91
Glick, Daniel M BiDrAPA 89
Glick, David 1908- WhoAm 90
Glick, Deborah Kelly 1953- WhoAmW 91, WhoEmL 91
Glick, Dennis R 1949- BiDrAPA 89
Glick, Eugene A 1931- BiDrAPA 89
Glick, Garland Wayne 1921- WhoAm 90
Glick, Gina Phillips Moran 1931- WhoAmW 91
Glick, Ira David 1935- BiDrAPA 89
Glick, Ira S. 1922- ODwPR 91
Glick, J. Leslie 1940- WhoAm 90
Glick, Jacob Ezra 1920- WhoAm 90
Glick, Jane Mills 1943- WhoAmW 91
Glick, John H. 1943- WhoAm 90
Glick, John P 1938- WhoAmA 91
Glick, Joseph 1935- WhoE 91
Glick, Karen Andrea 1962- WhoAmW 91
Glick, Kenneth Joel 1951- WhoE 91
Glick, Milton Don 1937- WhoAm 90
Glick, Muriel A. 1942- ODwPR 91
Glick, Nancy Joan 1932- WhoAmW 91
Glick, Nancy L. 1948- ODwPR 91
Glick, Paul Mitchell 1948- WhoEmL 91
Glick, Paula Florence WhoAmA 91, WhoE 91
Glick, Peter Allen 1947- St&PR 91
Glick, Philip Milton 1905- WhoAm 90
Glick, Richard Edwin 1927- WhoAm 90
Glick, Robert A. 1916- St&PR 91
Glick, Robert Alan 1941- BiDrAPA 89
Glick, Robert Dunn 1936- St&PR 91, WhoAm 90
Glick, Robert Ralph 1919- St&PR 91
Glick, Ronald M 1954- BiDrAPA 89
Glick, Ruth Burtnick 1942- WhoAm 90, WhoAmW 91
Glick, Srul Irving 1934- IntWWM 90
Glick, Todd W. 1962- WhoE 91
Glick, William Lee 1920- St&PR 91
Glick-Colquitt, Karen Lynne 1945- WhoAmW 91
Glicken, Howard Morten 1943- WhoAm 90, WhoSSW 91
Glicken, Howard Morton 1943- St&PR 91
Glickenhaus, James 1950- BioIn 16
Glickenhaus, Sarah Brody 1919- WhoAmW 91
Glicklich, Dana Natalia BiDrAPA 89
Glicklich-Rosenberg, Lucille B 1926- BiDrAPA 89
Glickman, A.B. 1937- St&PR 91
Glickman, Albert Seymour 1923- WhoAm 90
Glickman, Arthur 1923- WhoAmA 91
Glickman, Barbara 1947- WhoE 91
Glickman, Carl D. 1926- St&PR 91
Glickman, Carl Davis 1926- WhoAm 90
Glickman, Daniel Robert 1944- WhoAm 90
Glickman, Ernest Irwin 1940- St&PR 91
Glickman, Franklin Sheldon 1929- WhoAm 90
Glickman, Gerald Neal 1950- WhoSSW 91
Glickman, Harry 1924- WhoAm 90
Glickman, Joseph M BiDrAPA 89
Glickman, Laura Lee 1946- WhoAmW 91
Glickman, Lewis 1929- BiDrAPA 89
Glickman, Louis 1933- St&PR 91, WhoAm 90
Glickman, Mark Warren 1953- WhoSSW 91
Glickman, Marlene 1936- WhoAmW 91
Glickman, Marshall L. St&PR 91
Glickman, Marty BioIn 16
Glickman, Marty 1907- Ballpl 90
Glickman, Maurice 1906- WhoAmA 91
Glickman, Paula Rivlin WhoAmW 91, WhoE 91
Glickman, Rena BioIn 16
Glickman, Robert Jeffrey 1947- St&PR 91, WhoAm 90
Glickman, Robert Morris 1939- WhoAm 90
Glickman, Ronnie Carl 1956- WhoEmL 91
Glickman, Rosalind Helen 1937- WhoE 91
Glickman, Todd Scott 1956- WhoE 91
Glicksman, Arvin Sigmund 1924- WhoAm 90
Glicksman, Elliot Aaron 1954- WhoEmL 91
Glicksman, Martin Eden 1937- WhoAm 90
Glicksman, Maurice 1928- WhoAm 90
Glicksman, Michael Lewis 1941- WhoE 91
Glicksman, Russel Allen 1939- St&PR 91
Glicksman, Russell Allen 1939- WhoAm 90
Glickstein, Eileen Agard 1948- WhoAm 90
Glickstein, Neil Evans 1946- St&PR 91
Glidden, Allan H. 1920- St&PR 91
Glidden, Allan Hartwell 1920- WhoAm 90
Glidden, David Eric 1951- WhoWor 91
Glidden, Germain G. 1913- St&PR 91
Glidden, John Redmond 1936- WhoAm 90
Glidden, Lloyd Sumner, Jr. 1922- WhoAm 90
Glidden, Richard M. 1924- St&PR 91
Glidden, Robert Burr 1936- IntWWM 90, WhoAm 90
Glidden, Robert Littlefield, Jr. 1948- WhoE 91
Glidden, Robert Sterling 1944- St&PR 91
Glidden, Ronald C. 1939- St&PR 91, WhoAm 90
Glidewell, Alora Dawn 1960- WhoSSW 91
Glidewell, John Calvin 1919- WhoAm 90
Glieberman, Herbert Allen 1930- WhoAm 90
Gliedman, Marvin L. 1929- WhoAm 90
Gliege, John Gerhardt 1948- WhoEmL 91
Glier, Hans PenDiDA 89
Glier, Ingeborg Johanna 1934- WhoAm 90
Glier, Mike 1953- WhoAmA 91
Gligo, Niksa 1946- IntWWM 90
Gliha, John Lee 1953- WhoEmL 91, WhoWor 91
Glijansky, Alex 1948- BiDrAPA 89, WhoE 91
Glik, Hirsh 1922-1944 BioIn 16
Glik, Jeffrey Warren 1956- St&PR 91
Glik, Joseph 1926- St&PR 91
Glikes, Erwin Arno 1937- WhoAm 90
Glimcher, Arnold B. BioIn 16
Glimcher, Arnold B. 1938- WhoAm 90, WhoAmA 91
Glimcher, Melvin Jacob 1925- WhoAm 90
Glime, Garry Joseph 1942- St&PR 91
Glime, Rebecca Lee 1961- WhoAmW 91
Glimm, Adele 1937- WhoWrEP 89
Glimm, James Gilbert 1934- WhoAm 90, WhoE 91
Glimm, James Y 1942- ConAu 132
Glimmerveen, Ulco 1958- ConAu 132
Glimp, H. Earl 1943- St&PR 91
Glinberg, Tsilia BiDrAPA 89
Glindeman, Henry Peter, Jr. 1924- WhoAm 90
Glines, Alan Clair Edwin 1943- WhoWor 91
Glines, Carroll Vane, Jr. 1920- WhoAm 90
Glines, Ellen WhoAmA 91N
Glines, Stephen Ramey 1952- WhoE 91
Glink, Ilyce Renee 1964- WhoAmW 91
Glinka, Gleb 1948- WhoEmL 91
Glinka, Mikhail 1804-1857 WorAlBi
Glinka, Mikhail Ivanovich 1804-1857 BioIn 16, PenDiMP A
Glinski, David John 1946- WhoE 91
Glinski, Richard George, Jr. 1948- WhoEmL 91
Glinsky, Albert Vincent 1952- IntWWM 90
Glinsky, Vincent 1895-1975 WhoAmA 91N
Gliozzo, Christine A. ODwPR 91
Glismann, John D BiDrAPA 89
Glissant, Edouard Mathieu 1928- WhoAm 90
Glissman, Jean BiDrAPA 89
Glisson, Floyd W. 1947- St&PR 91
Glisson, Floyd Wright 1947- St&PR 91
Glisson, Jimmy Ray 1952- WhoSSW 91
Glisson, Myles Jon 1961- WhoE 91
Glitman, Karen Micque 1963- WhoAmW 91
Glitman, Maynard Wayne 1933- WhoAm 90, WhoWor 91
Glitter, Gary 1944- OxCPMus
Glitz, Debra Ann 1956- BiDrAPA 89
Glitz, Dohn George 1936- WhoAm 90
Gliwa, Denise Gorant ODwPR 91
Gliwa, Kevin Andrew 1956- WhoEmL 91
Glixon, David M 1908- WhoWrEP 89
Glixon, David Morris 1908- WhoAm 90
Gloag, Isabel Liliane 1865-1917 BiDWomA
Globerman, Linda Marilyn 1951- WhoAmW 91
Globig, David Phillip 1951- WhoEmL 91
Globke, Hans 1898-1973 BioIn 16
Globman, Richard Allen 1942- St&PR 91
Globocnik, Odilo 1904-1945 BioIn 16
Globokar, Andrea Rochelle 1946- WhoEmL 91
Globokar, Vinko 1934- PenDiMP
Globoke, Joseph Raymond 1955- WhoEmL 91
Globukar, Vinko 1934- IntWWM 90
Globus, Dorothy Twining WhoAmA 91
Globus, Gordon Gary 1934- BiDrAPA 89
Globus, Yoram WhoAm 90
Glocheski, Susan Kay BiDrAPA 89
Glock, Charles Young 1919- WhoAm 90
Glock, Earl Ferdinand 1924- WhoE 91
Glock, Marvin David 1912- WhoAm 90
Glock, William Frederick 1908- IntWWM 90
Glocker, Theodore Wesley, Jr. 1925- WhoAm 90
Glocker, Theodore William 1953- WhoSSW 91
Glockner, Maurice 1906- St&PR 91
Glockner, Peter G. 1929- WhoAm 90
Glod, Stanley Joseph 1936- WhoAm 90
Glodava, Milagros Garcia 1945- WhoWor 91
Glode, Leonard Michael 1947- WhoEmL 91
Glodny, Henry Felix 1959- WhoEmL 91
Glodowski, Shelley Jean 1950- WhoAmW 91
Glogowski, Dorothy Ann 1964- WhoAmW 91
Glomset, Daniel Anders 1913- WhoAm 90
Glomy, J.-B. PenDiDA 89
Gloor, Christopher Barta 1949- WhoEmL 91
Gloria, John Joseph 1930- St&PR 91
Glorie, Francis St&PR 91
Glorig, Ostor 1919- WhoAmA 91
Glos, Margaret Beach 1936- WhoAm 90, WhoE 91
Glosband, Daniel Martin 1944- WhoE 91
Gloss, Molly 1944- ConAu 132
Glosser, Caryle Rosen 1946- WhoAmW 91
Glosser, Diana Jean 1952- WhoEmL 91
Glosser, Ronald Dean 1933- St&PR 91
Glosser, William Louis 1929- WhoAm 90
Glossop, Al 1912- Ballpl 90
Glossop, Peter 1928- IntWWM 90, PenDiMP
Glossop, W. PenDiDA 89
Glosup, Lorene 1911- WhoAmW 91
Glotfelty, H Wayne 1923- BiDrAPA 89
Gloth, Alec Robert 1927- St&PR 91, WhoAm 90
Glotzbach, Louise Marie Deiter 1927- WhoAmW 91
Glotzbecker, Paul Gerald 1953- St&PR 91
Glotzer, Marilyn 1941- WhoE 91
Glotzer, Martin 1927- St&PR 91
Glotzner, Frank Ludwig 1938- WhoWor 91
Gloucester, Duchess of EncO&P 3
Gloudeman, Joseph Floyd 1935- St&PR 91
Gloudemans, Philip ODwPR 91
Glovach, David H. 1930- St&PR 91
Glovach, Linda 1947- AuBYP 90, ConAu 31NR
Glover, Arthur W. 1929- St&PR 91
Glover, Becky Jo 1958- WhoWor 91
Glover, Benjamin H, Jr. 1916- BiDrAPA 89
Glover, Catherine BioIn 16
Glover, Cato D. 1897-1988 BioIn 16
Glover, Cliff C. 1913- St&PR 91
Glover, Clifford Clarke 1913- WhoAm 90, WhoSSW 91
Glover, Danny BioIn 16
Glover, Danny 1947?- DrBlPA 90
Glover, Danny 1948- WorAlBi
Glover, David Carr 1925-1988 BioIn 16
Glover, Denis 1912-1980 ConAu 30NR
Glover, Donald Ellsworth 1933- WhoSSW 91
Glover, Durant Murrell 1951- WhoEmL 91
Glover, Edwin Eugene 1922- WhoWor 91
Glover, Elvira BioIn 16
Glover, Fred William 1937- WhoAm 90, WhoWor 91
Glover, Hilda Weaver 1933- WhoAmW 91
Glover, Imogene 1924- WhoAmW 91
Glover, James Edward 1925- WhoWor 91
Glover, James Edwin 1950- WhoSSW 91
Glover, James T. 1939- St&PR 91
Glover, Jane 1949- PenDiMP
Glover, Jane Alison 1949- IntWWM 90
Glover, Jerry Wayne 1949- WhoEmL 91
Glover, Jimmy 1861-1931 OxCPMus
Glover, Joe Charles 1944- WhoSSW 91
Glover, John 1732-1797 EncCRAm
Glover, Keith 1957- WhoAm 90
Glover, Keith Terrot 1950- WhoAm 90
Glover, Kenneth Dahnke 1932- WhoSSW 91
Glover, Kenneth W. 1927- St&PR 91
Glover, Kenneth Wadd 1927- WhoSSW 91
Glover, Laurice White 1930- WhoAmW 91, WhoE 91
Glover, Lyndia Ruth 1945- WhoWrEP 89
Glover, Marion Bellinger 1942- St&PR 91
Glover, Marty Anne 1958- WhoAmW 91
Glover, Norman James 1929- WhoAm 90, WhoE 91
Glover, R. Edward 1943- WhoAm 90
Glover, Ralph J. 1943- St&PR 91
Glover, Richard 1712-1785 DcLB 95 [port]
Glover, Robert 1936- WhoAmA 91
Glover, Ron K. 1940- WhoAm 90, WhoWor 91
Glover, Savion BioIn 16
Glover, Thomas EncJap
Glover, Vern L. 1935- St&PR 91
Glover, Walter 1922- St&PR 91
Glover, William Harper 1911- WhoAm 90, WhoE 91
Glover, William J., Jr. 1940- St&PR 91
Glovinsky, David Brian BiDrAPA 89
Glovka, Gerald Robert 1942- St&PR 91
Glovka, Richard Paul 1937- WhoAm 90
Glovsky, Alan WhoAmA 91
Glovsky, Susan G. L. 1955- WhoEmL 91
Glowac, Laurie Ann 1947- WhoAmW 91
Glowacki, Janusz BioIn 16
Glowacki, Janusz 1938- WorAu 1980 [port]
Glowacki, Jo Elaine 1948- WhoEmL 91
Glowacki, Peter BiDrAPA 89
Glowacki, Richard Chester 1932- WhoAm 90
Glowacki, Thomas Robert 1950- WhoEmL 91
Glower, Donald Duane 1926- WhoAm 90
Glowinski, Jerome James 1931- St&PR 91
Glowinski, Roland 1937- WhoAm 90
Glowitz, Charline Silvia 1951- WhoAmW 91
Gloyd, Lawrence Eugene 1932- WhoAm 90, WhoWor 91
Gloyd, Susan Vitali 1950- WhoAmW 91
Gloyna, Earnest Frederick 1921- WhoAm 90
Glozshteyn, Yakov 1936- St&PR 91
Glube, Constance Rachelle 1931- WhoAm 90, WhoE 91
Glubok, Shirley 1933- AuBYP 90
Glubrecht, Hellmut 1917- WhoWor 91
Gluch, Richard Philip, Jr. 1945- WhoEmL 91
Gluck 1895-1978 BiDWomA [port]
Gluck, Alma 1884-1938 PenDiMP
Gluck, Babette Elisabeth 1815-1894 EncCoWW
Gluck, Christoph 1714-1787 WorAlBi
Gluck, Christoph Willibald von 1714-1787 PenDiMP A
Gluck, Ernest BiDrAPA 89
Gluck, Frederick W. BioIn 16
Gluck, Heidi 1944- WhoAmA 91
Gluck, Herb 1925- ConAu 31NR
Gluck, Louise 1943- FemiCLE
Gluck, Louise Elisabeth 1943- WhoAm 90, WhoAmW 91, WhoWrEP 89
Gluck, Michael Irwin 1928- WhoE 91

Gluck, Richard Julian *BiDrAPA 89*
Gluck, Robert 1947- *ConAu 32NR*
Gluck, Stuart Ballon *BiDrAPA 89*
Gluckel of Hameln 1645-1724 *EncCoWW*
Gluckel, of Hameln 1646-1724 *BioIn 16*
Gluckman, Harold L. 1938- *St&PR 91*
Gluckman, Jack Louis 1945- *WhoEmL 91*
Gluckman, Robert M *BiDrAPA 89*
Gluckman, Simon *BioIn 16*
Gluckman, Thomas S. 1943- *St&PR 91*
Glucks, Richard 1889-1945 *BioIn 16*
Glucksman, David N. 1923- *St&PR 91*
Glucksman, Joyce Francine 1952- *WhoEmL 91*
Glucksman, Myron L 1935- *BiDrAPA 89*
Glucksman, Myron Samuel 1946- *WhoEmL 91*
Glucksman, Stephan Alan 1958- *WhoEmL 91*
Gluckson, Albert 1924- *WhoAm 90*
Gluckson, James Andrew 1956- *WhoWrEP 89*
Gluckstein, Fritz Paul 1927- *WhoAm 90*
Gluckstein, Hannah 1895-1978 *BiDWomA [port]*
Gluckstern, Henry Alan 1948- *WhoEmL 91*
Gluckstern, Robert Leonard 1924- *WhoAm 90*
Glueck, Bernard C *BiDrAPA 89*
Glueck, Helen Iglauer 1907- *WhoAmW 91*
Glueck, Sylvia Blumenfeld 1925- *WhoAmW 91, WhoSSW 91*
Glueck, Theodore P. 1934- *St&PR 91*
Gluhman, Joseph Walter 1934- *WhoAmA 91*
Gluhman, Margaret A *WhoAmA 91*
Glunt, William Kile 1959- *WhoSSW 91*
Glusac, Earl John 1959- *BiDrAPA 89*
Glusband, Steven Joseph 1947- *WhoE 91, WhoEmL 91*
Glushien, Anne Sorele Williams *BioIn 16*
Glushien, Morris P. 1909- *WhoAm 90, WhoWor 91*
Glushko, Valentin P. 1908-1989 *BioIn 16*
Gluska, Aharon *WhoAmA 91*
Gluski, Joseph Mathew 1959- *BiDrAPA 89*
Gluskin, Elliot Scott 1959- *WhoEmL 91*
Gluskin, Ludwig *BioIn 16*
Glusko, David Peter 1946- *WhoSSW 91*
Glusman, Murray *BiDrAPA 89*
Gluth, Robert C. 1924- *WhoAm 90*
Glutting, Robert V. 1934- *St&PR 91*
Gluzman, Semyon *BiDrAPA 89*
Glyde, Henry George 1906- *WhoAmA 91*
Glymour, Clark Noren 1942- *WhoAm 90*
Glymph, Dianne Tyler 1958- *WhoAmW 91*
Glymph, William E. 1950- *St&PR 91*
Glyn, Caroline 1947- *BioIn 16*
Glyn, Elinor 1864-1943 *BioIn 16, FemiCLE*
Glynn, Arthur Lawrence 1916- *WhoAm 90*
Glynn, Bill 1925- *Ballpl 90*
Glynn, Carlin 1940- *WhoAm 90*
Glynn, Ed 1953- *Ballpl 90*
Glynn, Edward 1935- *WhoAm 90, WhoE 91*
Glynn, Eugene D 1926- *BiDrAPA 89*
Glynn, Gary Allen 1946- *WhoE 91*
Glynn, J. Patrick 1946- *WhoEmL 91*
Glynn, James Vincent 1938- *St&PR 91*
Glynn, Jeffrey Thomas 1958- *St&PR 91*
Glynn, John Joseph 1933- *St&PR 91*
Glynn, Leonard M. 1948- *ConAu 130*
Glynn, Neil Held 1928- *WhoAm 90, WhoWor 91*
Glynn, Prudence 1935-1986 *ConAu 129*
Glynn, Robert D., Jr. 1942- *St&PR 91*
Glynn, Thomas Joseph 1927- *WhoAm 90*
Glynn, William C. 1944- *St&PR 91, WhoAm 90*
Gmach, Richard Eugene 1941- *St&PR 91*
Gmora, Kenneth N. 1930- *St&PR 91*
Gmuer, Cecilia Ann 1953- *WhoAmW 91*
Gmur, Peter 1939- *WhoWor 91*
Gnaedinger, John Phillip 1926- *St&PR 91*
Gnall, James Matthew 1945- *WhoEmL 91*
Gnam, Adrian 1940- *IntWWM 90*
Gnann, Alan J. 1949- *St&PR 91*
Gnann, John Wyatt, Jr. 1953- *WhoSSW 91*
Gnassi, Charles P 1931- *BiDrAPA 89*
Gnat, Raymond Earl 1932- *WhoAm 90*
Gnatzig, Bill *ODwPR 91*
Gnerlich, Rod Lawrence 1948- *WhoEmL 91*
Gnerre, William F. 1939- *St&PR 91*
Gnesin, Penelope Dara 1960- *WhoE 91*
Gneuss, Helmut Walter Georg 1927- *IntWWM 90, WhoWor 91*
Gniadek, Cheryl Lynn 1947- *WhoAmW 91*
Gnichtel, William Van Orden 1934- *WhoAm 90*
Gniewek, Raymond 1931- *IntWWM 90*
Gniewek, Raymond Louis 1947- *WhoAm 90*
Gnospelius, Richard Arthur 1939- *WhoAm 90*
Gnozzo, Nancy Ann 1945- *WhoAmW 91*
Go Bi *BioIn 16*
Go, Swie Hing *BiDrAPA 89*
Go-Daigo, Emperor 1288-1339 *EncJap*
Go-Go's *EncPR&S 89*
Go-Sakuramachi-tenno 1741-1814 *WomWR*
Goa, Hector H 1947- *BiDrAPA 89*
Goad, Barry Stephens 1930- *St&PR 91*
Goad, Carolyn Kay 1935- *WhoSSW 91*
Goad, Curtis Carl 1952- *St&PR 91*
Goad, Eric Warren *BiDrAPA 89*
Goad, Linda May 1948- *WhoAmW 91*
Goad, Rachell LaGuardia 1951- *WhoSSW 91*
Goad, Walter Benson, Jr. 1925- *WhoAm 90*
Goade, William Richard 1922- *WhoAm 90*
Goaley, Donald Joseph 1935- *St&PR 91*
Goans, Judy Winegar 1949- *WhoEmL 91, WhoSSW 91, WhoWor 91*
Goates, Delbert T 1932- *BiDrAPA 89*
Goates, Douglas Harold 1953- *WhoE 91*
Gobar, Alfred Julian 1932- *St&PR 91, WhoAm 90, WhoWor 91*
Gobar, Asad 1929- *BiDrAPA 89*
Gobar, Gail Tamara 1940- *WhoAmW 91*
Gobbato, Angelo Mario Giulio 1943- *IntWWM 90*
Gobbell, Ronald Vance 1948- *WhoSSW 91*
Gobbi, Tito 1913-1984 *PenDiMP*
Gobbi, Tito 1915-1984 *ConAu 129, WorAlBi*
Gobble, Harold Graves 1942- *St&PR 91*
Gobeil, Pierre 1938- *OxCCanT*
Gobeil, Ronald Charles *BiDrAPA 89*
Gobel, Jerry Walter 1943- *St&PR 91*
Gobel, John Henry 1926- *WhoAm 90*
Gobel, Reginald T *BiDrAPA 89*
Goben, Michael K. *St&PR 91*
Gober, Bruce Anthony 1945- *BiDrAPA 89*
Gober Cosgrove, Ritamae Adele 1950- *WhoEmL 91*
Gobhai, Mehlli *AuBYP 90*
Gobie, Henry Macaulay 1911- *WhoAm 90*
Gobind Singh, Guru 1666-1708 *BioIn 16*
Goble, Dorothy *AuBYP 90*
Goble, Frank G. 1917- *St&PR 91*
Goble, George G. 1929- *WhoAm 90*
Goble, Kimberly L. 1963- *St&PR 91*
Goble, Paul 1933- *AuBYP 90, ChlLR 21 [port], WhoAm 90, WhoWrEP 89*
Goble, Robert Thomas 1947- *WhoEmL 91, WhoSSW 91*
Goblet, Rene-Marie 1828-1905 *BiDFrPL*
Goblowsky, Michael 1962- *WhoEmL 91*
Gobright, Lawrence Augustus 1816-1879? *BioIn 16*
Gobris, Joseph J. 1936- *St&PR 91*
Gobuzas, Aldona M *WhoAmA 91*
Gocek, Matilda Arkenbout 1923- *WhoE 91*
Gocek, Matilda Arkensout 1923- *WhoWrEP 89*
Gochanour, George Gary 1959- *WhoEmL 91*
Gochberg, Thomas J. 1939- *St&PR 91*
Gochberg, Thomas Joel 1939- *WhoAm 90*
Gochenour, Douglas Allen 1962- *WhoSSW 91*
Gochenour, Theodore 1933- *WhoWrEP 89*
Gochfeld, Linda G 1939- *BiDrAPA 89*
Gochnauer, Richard Wallis 1949- *St&PR 91*
Gociar, Ferdinand *BiDrAPA 89*
Gocke, David Joseph 1933- *WhoAm 90*
Gocke, Neva Culley 1935- *WhoAmW 91*
Gockel, John Raymond 1947- *WhoEmL 91*
Gockel, Keith August *BiDrAPA 89*
Gockel, Michael Arthur 1936- *St&PR 91*
Gockley, Barbara Jean 1951- *WhoAmW 91*
Gockley, David 1943- *WhoSSW 91*
Gockley, David Woodrow 1918- *WhoAm 90*
Gockley, Gretchen Blaugher 1955- *WhoEmL 91*
Gockowski, Adam Stefan 1953- *St&PR 91*
Goda, Ellen Marie Killelea 1952- *WhoAmW 91, WhoEmL 91*
Goda, J. Joe 1943- *St&PR 91*
Godack, Christina Atkins 1956- *ODwPR 91*
Godar, Stephen Anthony 1959- *WhoEmL 91*
Godar, Thomas Paul 1955- *WhoEmL 91*
Godar, Vladimir 1956- *IntWWM 90*
Godard, Gwendolyn Annette 1961- *WhoSSW 91*
Godard, James McFate 1907- *WhoAm 90*
Godard, Jean Luc 1930- *BioIn 16, WhoAm 90, WhoWor 91, WorAlBi*
Godard, Randy Eugene 1952- *WhoEmL 91*
Godard, Sally L. 1954- *BiDrAPA 89*
Godbe, W. Bryan 1958- *ODwPR 91*
Godbey, Asa Lawrence, Jr. 1937- *BiDrAPA 89*
Godbey, Helen Kay 1946- *WhoAmW 91, WhoEmL 91*
Godbold, F.S. 1943- *St&PR 91*
Godbold, Francis Stanley 1943- *WhoAm 90, WhoSSW 91*
Godbold, John Cooper 1920- *WhoAm 90, WhoE 91*
Godbold, Nathan Terry 1948- *WhoSSW 91*
Godbold, Wilford, Jr. 1938- *St&PR 91*
Godbold, Wilford Darrington, Jr. 1938- *WhoAm 90*
Godbole, Anil G 1941- *BiDrAPA 89*
Godbolt, Jim 1922- *ConAu 129*
Godbout, Gregory J. 1946- *St&PR 91*
Godbout, Pamela Sue 1948- *WhoWrEP 89*
Godby, Carolyn Sue 1938- *WhoAmW 91*
Godchaux, Charles R. 1930- *St&PR 91*
Godchaux, Frank A., III 1927- *St&PR 91*
Goddard, A.B. 1943- *St&PR 91*
Goddard, Andrew William *BiDrAPA 89*
Goddard, Arabella 1836-1922 *BioIn 16, PenDiMP*
Goddard, Brent Lee 1954- *WhoEmL 91*
Goddard, Carol Ann 1941- *WhoAmW 91*
Goddard, Chris Ann *ODwPR 91*
Goddard, Donald 1934- *WhoAmA 91*
Goddard, Donald Letcher 1934- *WhoE 91*
Goddard, Hazel Idella 1911- *WhoWrEP 89*
Goddard, Henry Herbert 1866-1957 *BioIn 16*
Goddard, Jeremy Paul 1951- *WhoEmL 91*
Goddard, John 1723-1785 *PenDiDA 89*
Goddard, John, II *PenDiDA 89*
Goddard, Joseph Paul 1920- *WhoAm 90*
Goddard, Leon L. 1907- *St&PR 91*
Goddard, Lisa Ann 1960- *WhoE 91*
Goddard, M. Fay 1931- *WhoAmW 91*
Goddard, Mary Katherine 1738-1816 *EncCRAm*
Goddard, Morrill 1865-1937 *BioIn 16*
Goddard, Paulette 1905?-1990 *CurBio 90N*
Goddard, Paulette 1911- *BioAmW*
Goddard, Paulette 1911-1990 *BioIn 16, NewYTBS 90 [port]*
Goddard, Paulette 1915-1990 *WorAlBi*
Goddard, Ralph A *BiDrAPA 89*
Goddard, Richard Patrick 1952- *WhoEmL 91*
Goddard, Robert Hale Ives 1909- *WhoAm 90*
Goddard, Robert Hutchings 1882-1945 *BioIn 16, WorAlBi*
Goddard, Sandra Kay 1947- *WhoAmW 91, WhoEmL 91*
Goddard, Sarah Updike 1700?-1770 *BioIn 16, EncCRAm*
Goddard, Stanhope S., Jr. 1919- *St&PR 91*
Goddard, Stephen 1764-1804 *PenDiDA 89*
Goddard, Terry *WhoAm 90*
Goddard, Thomas 1765-1858 *PenDiDA 89*
Goddard, Thomas H. 1940- *St&PR 91*
Goddard, Vivian *WhoAmA 91*
Goddard, Wesley Rawdon 1915- *WhoAm 90*
Goddard, William 1740-1817 *BioIn 16*
Goddard, William Andrew, III 1937- *WhoAm 90*
Goddard, Winfred Baldwin, Jr. 1951- *WhoSSW 91*
Godden, Rumer 1907- *Au&Arts 6 [port], AuBYP 90, BioIn 16, FemiCLE, SmATA 12AS [port], WhoAm 90*
Goddess, Lynn Barbara 1942- *WhoAmW 91, WhoE 91*
Godding, George Arthur 1920- *WhoAm 90*
Goddu, Roland Jean-Berchmans 1936- *WhoSSW 91*
Gode, Richard O 1934- *BiDrAPA 89*
Godeau, Henry Francois Fernand 1920- *WhoWor 91*
Godeaux, Jean Eugene Auguste 1920- *WhoWor 91*
Godec, Maksimilijan 1937- *WhoE 91*
Godec, Max 1937- *St&PR 91*
Godec, Zdenko 1939- *WhoWor 91*
Godefroid de Claire 1145?-1173 *PenDiDA 89*
Godefroid de Huy 1145?-1173 *PenDiDA 89*
Godefroy, Scott P. Marchbank 1951- *WhoSSW 91*
Godek, Karen Denise 1956- *WhoAmW 91*
Godel, Kurt 1906-1978 *WorAlBi*
Godel, Kurt Friedrich 1906-1978 *DcScB S2*
Godenne, Ghislaine D *BiDrAPA 89*
Godenne, Ghislaine Dudley *WhoAm 90*
Goderich, Mario P. *WhoHisp 91*
Goderstad, Susan Grace 1959- *WhoAmW 91*
Goderwis, Jeffrey Michale 1965- *WhoSSW 91*
Godey, John 1912- *TwCCr&M 91*
Godey, Louis Antoine *BioIn 16*
Godey, Louis Antoine 1804-1878 *WorAlBi*
Godez, Susan Lynn 1953- *WhoAmW 91*
Godfrey *OxCPMus*
Godfrey *EncO&P 3*
Godfrey De Bouillon 1060?-1100 *WorAlBi*
Godfrey, Adolphus Frederick 1837-1882 *OxCPMus*
Godfrey, Arthur 1903-1983 *WorAlBi*
Godfrey, Arthur Eugene 1868-1939 *OxCPMus*
Godfrey, Bruce Lee, III 1951- *WhoEmL 91*
Godfrey, Charles 1790-1863 *OxCPMus*
Godfrey, Charles 1839-1919 *OxCPMus*
Godfrey, Charles 1851-1900 *OxCPMus*
Godfrey, Charles Brien *BiDrAPA 89*
Godfrey, Charles George 1866-1935 *OxCPMus*
Godfrey, Dan 1868-1939 *PenDiMP*
Godfrey, Dan Stuart 1893-1935 *OxCPMus*
Godfrey, Daniel 1831-1903 *OxCPMus*
Godfrey, Daniel Eyers 1868-1939 *OxCPMus*
Godfrey, Daniel Strong 1949- *IntWWM 90*
Godfrey, Dave 1938- *BioIn 16*
Godfrey, David 1938- *BioIn 16*
Godfrey, Donald W. 1934- *St&PR 91*
Godfrey, Edward Farley 1949- *St&PR 91*
Godfrey, Elizabeth 1854?-1918 *FemiCLE*
Godfrey, Francis 1788-1840 *WhNaAH*
Godfrey, Fred 1880-1953 *OxCPMus*
Godfrey, George Cheeseman, II 1926- *WhoE 91, WhoWor 91*
Godfrey, George Denton 1922- *WhoAm 90*
Godfrey, H.W. 1937- *St&PR 91*
Godfrey, Isidore 1900-1977 *OxCPMus, PenDiMP*
Godfrey, James B. 1909- *St&PR 91*
Godfrey, James Brown 1909- *WhoAm 90*
Godfrey, James Michael 1955- *WhoEmL 91*
Godfrey, James T, Jr. *BiDrAPA 89*
Godfrey, John Hector 1926- *WhoWor 91*
Godfrey, John Morrow 1912- *St&PR 91, WhoAm 90*
Godfrey, John Munro 1941- *WhoAm 90*
Godfrey, John S. 1937- *St&PR 91*
Godfrey, Joline Dudley 1950- *WhoAmW 91*
Godfrey, Joseph Lawrence 1945- *BiDrAPA 89*
Godfrey, Katherine Ann 1956- *BiDrAPA 89*
Godfrey, Kenneth E *BiDrAPA 89*
Godfrey, Kirk D. 1957- *St&PR 91*
Godfrey, Loren 1939- *St&PR 91*
Godfrey, Marjorie Ann *WhoWrEP 89*
Godfrey, Michael E. 1958- *WhoEmL 91*
Godfrey, Neale S. *BioIn 16*
Godfrey, Paul Victor 1939- *St&PR 91, WhoAm 90*
Godfrey, Peter David Hensman 1922- *IntWWM 90*
Godfrey, Robert 1941- *WhoAmA 91*
Godfrey, Robert Douglas 1948- *WhoEmL 91*
Godfrey, Robert Gordon 1927- *WhoAm 90*
Godfrey, Robert R. 1947- *WhoAm 90, WhoEmL 91, WhoWor 91*
Godfrey, Samuel Addison 1922- *WhoAm 90*
Godfrey, Thomas 1704-1749 *EncCRAm*
Godfrey, Thomas 1736-1763 *EncCRAm*
Godfrey, Thomas 1923- *St&PR 91*
Godfrey, Thomas Marvin, Jr. 1938- *WhoSSW 91*
Godfrey, Victor 1934- *IntWWM 90*
Godfrey, Walter P., Jr. 1944- *WhoSSW 91*
Godfrey, William Ashley 1938- *WhoAm 90, WhoWor 91*
Godfrey, William K. 1933- *St&PR 91*
Godfrey, Winnie 1944- *WhoAmA 91*
Godfroy, Francis 1788-1840 *WhNaAH*
Godie, Lee *MusmAFA*
Godin, H. Richard 1931- *ODwPR 91, WhoWrEP 89*
Godin, Jacques 1930- *OxCCanT*
Godin, Norman Joseph 1951- *WhoWor 91*
Godin, William N. 1936- *St&PR 91*
Godine, David Richard 1944- *WhoAm 90*
Godiner, Donald Leonard 1933- *St&PR 91, WhoAm 90*
Godinez, Hector G. *WhoHisp 91*
Godinez Flores, Ramon 1936- *WhoAm 90*
Goding, Charles A. 1934- *ODwPR 91*
Goding, James Watson 1946- *WhoWor 91*
Godino, Rino Lodovico 1925- *WhoE 91*
Godkin, Edwin Lawrence 1831-1902 *BioIn 16*
Godleski, Linda Susan 1956- *BiDrAPA 89*
Godlewski, James Bernard 1952- *WhoE 91*
Godley, Charlotte 1821-1907 *FemiCLE*
Godley, Nigel 1942- *St&PR 91*
Godmilow, Jill *BioIn 16*
Godofsky, Irvin David 1945- *BiDrAPA 89*
Godofsky, Stanley 1928- *WhoAm 90*
Godolphin, Margaret *BiDEWW*
Godolphin, Margaret 1652-1678 *FemiCLE*
Godonis, Thomas Gerald 1949- *WhoE 91*
Godowsky, Barry M. 1950- *St&PR 91*
Godowsky, Leopold 1870-1938 *BioIn 16, PenDiMP*
Godoy, Guillermo 1955- *WhoSSW 91*
Godoy, Julio *BioIn 16*
Godoy, Manuel de 1767-1851 *BioIn 16*
Godoy, Virgilio *WhoWor 91*

Godoy Alcayaga, Lucila 1889-1957 *BioIn 16, ConAu 131, HispWr 90, MajTwCW*
Godridge, Joseph Edward, Jr. 1926- *St&PR 91, WhoE 91*
Godschalk, David Robinson 1931- *WhoAm 90*
Godsey, Dwayne Erwin 1931- *St&PR 91*
Godsey, Glenn 1937- *WhoAmA 91*
Godsey, John Drew 1922- *WhoAm 90*
Godsey, Linda Ruth 1950- *WhoAmW 91*
Godsey, Raleigh Kirby 1936- *WhoAm 90*
Godsey, William C 1933- *BiDrAPA 89*
Godsey, William Cole 1933- *WhoSSW 91, WhoWor 91*
Godsey, William Lee 1933- *WhoAm 90*
Godshalk, David R. 1935- *St&PR 91*
Godshalk, Henry W. 1921- *St&PR 91*
Godshalk, James Bond 1914- *St&PR 91*
Godshall, Clark John 1954- *WhoE 91*
Godshall, Jonathan H. 1948- *St&PR 91*
Godsman, James Gillinder 1940- *St&PR 91*
Godsoe, P.C. 1938- *St&PR 91*
Godsoe, Peter Cowperthwaite 1938- *WhoAm 90*
Godson, Daphne 1932- *IntWWM 90*
Godson, Godfrey Nigel 1936- *WhoAm 90*
Goduco-Agular, Cesarea M *BiDrAPA 89*
Godunov, Alexander Boris 1949- *WhoAm 90*
Godunov, Boris 1552-1605 *WorAlBi*
Godwin, Andrew Charles *BiDrAPA 89*
Godwin, Carol Carey 1947- *WhoSSW 91*
Godwin, Charles Donald *BiDrAPA 89*
Godwin, David G. *St&PR 91N*
Godwin, Douglas Patrick 1951- *St&PR 91*
Godwin, Edward Arthur, Jr. 1922- *WhoSSW 91*
Godwin, Edward William 1833-1886 *PenDiDA 89*
Godwin, Elva Cockrell 1949- *WhoEmL 91*
Godwin, Frances Gray 1908-1979 *WhoAmA 91N*
Godwin, Frank 1889-1959 *EncACom*
Godwin, Gail 1937- *FemiCLE, MajTwCW, WorAlBi*
Godwin, Gail Kathleen 1937- *WhoAm 90, WhoAmW 91, WhoWrEP 89*
Godwin, Harold Norman 1941- *WhoAm 90*
Godwin, Harry 1901-1985 *DcNaB 1981*
Godwin, James Beckham 1918- *WhoAm 90*
Godwin, James Edward 1931- *St&PR 91*
Godwin, James William 1942- *WhoSSW 91*
Godwin, Jennie Floyd 1958- *WhoEmL 91*
Godwin, JoAn Massey 1931- *WhoAmW 91*
Godwin, Johnnie C. 1937- *St&PR 91*
Godwin, Joscelyn 1945- *IntWWM 90*
Godwin, Judith *WhoAmA 91*
Godwin, Karen L. 1957- *WhoEmL 91*
Godwin, Kathleen *BioIn 16*
Godwin, Kimberly Ann 1960- *WhoEmL 91*
Godwin, Lawrence 1934- *WhoAmA 91*
Godwin, Mary Jane 1766-1841 *BioIn 16*
Godwin, Mary Jo 1949- *WhoAmW 91*
Godwin, Nancy Elizabeth 1951- *WhoAmW 91, WhoEmL 91, WhoSSW 91*
Godwin, Parke 1816-1904 *BioIn 16*
Godwin, Paul Milton 1942- *IntWWM 90, WhoSSW 91*
Godwin, Phillip E 1954?-1989 *ConAu 130*
Godwin, Phyllis Elaine 1951- *WhoEmL 91*
Godwin, Pierce Monroe, Jr. 1964- *WhoSSW 91*
Godwin, R. Wayne 1941- *St&PR 91, WhoAm 90*
Godwin, Ralph Lee, Jr. 1954- *WhoE 91*
Godwin, Ralph Ray 1948- *WhoEmL 91*
Godwin, Richard Doyle 1953- *WhoSSW 91*
Godwin, Richard Jeffrey 1951- *WhoEmL 91*
Godwin, Sara 1944- *WhoAmW 91*
Godwin, William 1756-1836 *BioIn 16, DcLB 104 [port], TwCCr&M 91A, WorAlBi, WrPh P*
Godwin-Austen, Pamela 1952- *WhoAmW 91*
Goe, Gerald Lee 1942- *WhoAm 90*
Goebbels, Joseph 1897-1945 *BioIn 16, WorAlBi*
Goebbels, Paul Joseph 1897-1945 *BioIn 16*
Goebel, Barbara Leeper 1921- *WhoAmW 91*
Goebel, Bernard 1944- *St&PR 91*
Goebel, Chilton G., Jr. *ODwPR 91*
Goebel, Earle Stanwood 1930- *St&PR 91*
Goebel, John J. 1930- *WhoAm 90*
Goebel, Maristella 1915- *WhoAmW 91*
Goebel, Peter H. 1939- *St&PR 91*
Goebel, Reinhard 1952- *IntWWM 90*
Goebel, Richard Alan 1944- *WhoAm 90*
Goebel, Walther Frederick 1899- *WhoAm 90*
Goebel, William Douglas 1950- *WhoSSW 91*
Goebel, William Mathers 1922- *WhoAm 90*
Goebels, Franzpeter 1920- *IntWWM 90*
Goebert, Donald F.U. 1936- *St&PR 91*
Goebert, Robert J. 1941- *WhoAm 90*
Goebert, Robert Jeremy 1941- *St&PR 91*
Goecke, Floyd C. 1931- *St&PR 91*
Goecke, Jo *BioIn 16*
Goecks, James Ralph 1953- *WhoEmL 91*
Goedde, Alan George 1948- *WhoEmL 91, WhoWor 91*
Goedde, William Richard 1930- *St&PR 91*
Goedecke, Christopher John 1951- *WhoEmL 91*
Goedecke, Colin Edward 1958- *WhoE 91*
Goedecke, David Stewart 1929- *IntWWM 90*
Goedecke, Margret Anne 1907- *St&PR 91*
Goedecke, Otto 1906- *St&PR 91*
Goedeke, Nancy Lynn 1955- *WhoAmW 91*
Goedeker, Raymond Bernard 1923- *St&PR 91*
Goedert, John P. 1913- *St&PR 91*
Goedhuis, Daniel 1905- *WhoWor 91*
Goedicke, Hans 1926- *WhoAm 90*
Goedicke, Jean 1908- *WhoAmA 91*
Goedicke, Patricia 1931- *WhoWrEP 89*
Goedike, Shirl 1923- *WhoAmA 91*
Goedken, Florian H. 1929- *St&PR 91*
Goeglein, John B. 1922- *St&PR 91*
Goeglein, Richard John 1934- *WhoAm 90*
Goehlich, John Ronald 1934- *WhoAmA 91*
Goehner, Donna Marie 1941- *WhoAmW 91*
Goehr, Alexander 1932- *IntWWM 90, PenDiMP A*
Goehr, Walter 1903-1960 *PenDiMP*
Goehring, John Brown 1935- *WhoAm 90, WhoWor 91*
Goehring, Kenneth 1919- *WhoAm 90*
Goehring, Maude Cope 1915- *WhoAmW 91*
Goehring, Robert E. 1944- *St&PR 91*
Goehring, Robert L. *ODwPR 91*
Goehrke, Carsten 1937- *WhoWor 91*
Goeke, Klaus 1944- *WhoWor 91*
Goeke, Leo 1936- *IntWWM 90*
Goeken, John *BioIn 16*
Goel, Ameet Kumar *BiDrAPA 89*
Goel, Archana *BiDrAPA 89*
Goeld, Seymour *BioIn 16*
Goeldner, Charles Raymond 1932- *WhoAm 90*
Goeler, H. Timothy 1954- *WhoAm 90, WhoE 91, WhoEmL 91*
Goelet, Alexandra *BioIn 16*
Goelet, Robert *BioIn 16*
Goelet, Robert G. 1923- *WhoAm 90, WhoE 91*
Goell, Abby Jane *WhoAmA 91*
Goell, James Emanuel 1939- *WhoAm 90*
Goeller, Roger F. 1941- *St&PR 91*
Goellner, Jack Gordon 1930- *WhoAm 90*
Goeltz, Richard Karl 1942- *St&PR 91, WhoAm 90, WhoE 91*
Goelz, John Matthew 1957- *WhoWor 91*
Goelz, Paul Cornelius 1914- *WhoAm 90*
Goelzer, Daniel Lee 1947- *WhoAm 90, WhoEmL 91*
Goen, Bob *BioIn 16*
Goenjian, Armen Krikor *BiDrAPA 89*
Goenner, Judith Mary 1948- *WhoWrEP 89*
Goepfert, Eric Richard 1946- *WhoSSW 91*
Goepfert, Mary *BiDrAPA 89*
Goepfert, Richard W *BiDrAPA 89*
Goepp, Robert August 1930- *WhoAm 90*
Goeppert-Mayer, Maria 1906-1972 *BioIn 16*
Goeppert-Mayer, Marie 1906-1972 *WorAlBi*
Goeppinger, Susan *BioIn 16*
Goer, Alan Barry 1949- *St&PR 91*
Goerdt, Marcia Fae 1950- *WhoAmW 91*
Goergen, Anthony Joseph 1942- *St&PR 91*
Goergen, Jan Roger 1935- *WhoWor 91*
Goergen, Jerome James 1955- *WhoEmL 91*
Goergen, Robert B. 1938- *St&PR 91*
Goergens, Cathy *BioIn 16*
Goergens, Doug *BioIn 16*
Goering, Albert H. 1926- *St&PR 91*
Goering, Carroll E. 1934- *WhoAm 90*
Goering, George L. 1935- *St&PR 91*
Goering, Gordon David 1922- *WhoAm 90*
Goering, Hermann 1893-1946 *BioIn 16, WorAlBi*
Goering, Kenneth Justin 1913- *WhoAm 90*
Goeritz, Mathias 1915- *ArtLatA, WhoAmA 91*
Goerke, Annette Maureen 1938- *IntWWM 90*
Goerke, Robert F *BiDrAPA 89*
Goerler, Ronald B. 1925- *St&PR 91*
Goerler, Woldemar Ernst Heinrich 1933- *WhoWor 91*
Goerling, Heinrich Hans 1931- *WhoWor 91*
Goerner, Edward Alfred 1929- *WhoAm 90*
Goers, Melvin Armand 1918- *WhoAm 90*
Goertz, Augustus Frederick, III 1948- *WhoAm 90, WhoAmA 91*
Goertz, Gary Wayne 1952- *St&PR 91*
Goertz, Harald 1924- *IntWWM 90*
Goertzel, Bernard M *BiDrAPA 89*
Goes, Charles B. 1917- *St&PR 91*
Goes, Charles Berthold, IV 1947- *St&PR 91*
Goessel, William W. 1927- *WhoAm 90*
Goessel, William Warren 1927- *St&PR 91*
Goessling, John Gerald 1928- *St&PR 91*
Goetchius, Eugene Van Ness 1921- *WhoAm 90*
Goeth, Amon Leopold 1908-1946 *BioIn 16*
Goeth, Joe A. 1921- *St&PR 91*
Goethals, George R. 1944- *WhoAm 90*
Goethals, George Washington 1858-1928 *WorAlBi*
Goethals, Lucien Gustave Georges 1931- *IntWWM 90*
Goethals, Richard Bernard, Jr. 1950- *WhoEmL 91*
Goethe, Johann Wolfgang von 1749-1832 *DcLB 94 [port], EncO&P 3, EncPaPR 91, WorAlBi, WrPh*
Goethe, John William 1945- *BiDrAPA 89*
Goetsch, Gary Gordon 1938- *St&PR 91, WhoAm 90*
Goetsch, John Hubert 1933- *St&PR 91*
Goetschalckx, Marc 1954- *WhoSSW 91*
Goetschel, Franz Louis 1947- *WhoWor 91*
Goetschius, Herbert T. 1950- *St&PR 91*
Goette, Klaus H. W. 1932- *WhoWor 91*
Goettel, Gerard Louis 1928- *WhoAm 90, WhoE 91*
Goetter, Robert Walter 1947- *WhoAm 90*
Goettling-Krause, Gisela Erika W. 1926- *WhoAmW 91*
Goettsche, Roger Lyman *BiDrAPA 89*
Goetz, Bernhard *BioIn 16*
Goetz, Bernhard 1947- *WorAlBi*
Goetz, Betty Barrett 1943- *WhoAmW 91, WhoSSW 91*
Goetz, Cecelia Helen *WhoAmW 91*
Goetz, Charles Frederick 1956- *WhoSSW 91*
Goetz, Delia 1898- *AuBYP 90*
Goetz, Dennis William 1961- *WhoEmL 91*
Goetz, Diane M. *ODwPR 91*
Goetz, Donald Lee 1936- *St&PR 91*
Goetz, Douglas Neil 1953- *WhoEmL 91*
Goetz, Edith Jean 1918- *WhoAmA 91*
Goetz, John Bullock 1920- *WhoAm 90, WhoWrEP 89*
Goetz, Kenneth L 1958- *BiDrAPA 89*
Goetz, Larry 1900-1962 *Ballpl 90*
Goetz, Lionel John 1943- *St&PR 91*
Goetz, Maurice Harold 1924- *WhoAm 90*
Goetz, Maxwell *WhoWrEP 89*
Goetz, Oswald H 1896-1960 *WhoAmA 91N*
Goetz, Patricia L 1948- *BiDrAPA 89*
Goetz, Paul A. 1931- *St&PR 91*
Goetz, Paul C, Jr. *BiDrAPA 89*
Goetz, Peter Benedict 1934- *St&PR 91, WhoAm 90*
Goetz, Peter Henry 1917- *WhoAmA 91*
Goetz, Rainer 1930- *WhoWor 91*
Goetz, Richard Vernon 1915- *WhoAmA 91*
Goetz, Ruby Gail 1933- *WhoAmW 91*
Goetz, Rupert Rudolf 1951- *BiDrAPA 89*
Goetz, Ruth *BioIn 16*
Goetz, Scott Barry 1953- *BiDrAPA 89*
Goetz, Theodore 1947- *St&PR 91*
Goetz, William K. 1940- *St&PR 91*
Goetzberger, Adolf 1928- *WhoWor 91*
Goetze, David Wesley 1954- *WhoEmL 91, WhoSSW 91*
Goetze, Robert C. 1924- *St&PR 91*
Goetzel, Roger F. 1940- *St&PR 91*
Goetzinger, Germaine 1947- *EncCoWW*
Goetzke, Gloria Louise *WhoAmW 91, WhoWor 91*
Goetzke, Ronald Richard 1933- *St&PR 91*
Goetzl, Judith Chuckrow *WhoSSW 91*
Goetzl, Thomas Maxwell 1943- *WhoAmA 91*
Goetzman, John Robert 1949- *WhoSSW 91*
Goetzmann, Harry Edward, Jr. 1937- *WhoAm 90*
Goeudevert, Daniel *BioIn 16*
Goewey, Gordon Ira 1924- *WhoAm 90*
Goewey, James Arthur 1929- *St&PR 91*
Goez, Carlos R. *NewYTBS 90*
Goez, J. L. 1939- *WhoHisp 91*
Goff, Alvin H *BiDrAPA 89*
Goff, Barbara U 1933- *BiDrAPA 89*
Goff, Bradford M 1951- *BiDrAPA 89*
Goff, Christopher Wallick 1948- *WhoE 91*
Goff, Donald Charles 1953- *BiDrAPA 89*
Goff, Douglas Robert 1947- *WhoEmL 91*
Goff, Elbert Wayne 1935- *BiDrAPA 89*
Goff, Frederick E., Jr. *ODwPR 91*
Goff, G.A. *St&PR 91*
Goff, Harry Russell 1915- *WhoAm 90*
Goff, Hazel Avis 1892-1973 *BioIn 16*
Goff, J. Edward 1933- *St&PR 91*
Goff, Jan T 1936- *BiDrAPA 89*
Goff, Jerry K. 1952- *St&PR 91*
Goff, Kathleen Ann Murray 1960- *WhoAmW 91*
Goff, Kenneth W. 1928- *St&PR 91*
Goff, Kenneth Wade 1928- *WhoAm 90*
Goff, Kevin Michael 1961- *St&PR 91*
Goff, Lila Johnson 1944- *WhoAm 90, WhoAmW 91*
Goff, Michael Harper 1927- *WhoAm 90*
Goff, Nathan, Jr. 1843-1920 *BiDrUSE 89*
Goff, Orlando Scott 1843-1917 *WhNaAH*
Goff, Paul Alan 1941- *WhoAm 90*
Goff, Raymon Lee 1936- *St&PR 91*
Goff, Robert Burnside 1924- *St&PR 91, WhoAm 90*
Goff, Robert Edward 1952- *WhoE 91, WhoEmL 91*
Goff, Sharon Rose 1943- *WhoAmW 91*
Goff, Stanley Norman 1923- *St&PR 91*
Goff, Thomas Jefferson 1907- *WhoAmA 91*
Goff, Wayne B. 1938- *St&PR 91*
Goff, William Miller 1946- *WhoEmL 91*
Goffart, Walter Andre 1934- *WhoAm 90, WhoWrEP 89*
Goffaux, Pierre Eugene 1938- *St&PR 91*
Goffe, George Stanley 1926- *St&PR 91*
Goffe, Keith Alfonso *BiDrAPA 89*
Goffe, Thomas 1591-1629 *BioIn 16*
Goffe, Toni 1936- *SmATA 61 [port]*
Goffe, William Gregory 1949- *WhoE 91*
Goffen, Rona 1944- *WhoAm 90*
Goffin, Gerry 1939- *OxCPMus*
Goffin, Sumner 1919- *WhoWor 91*
Goffinet, Ray Frank 1929- *St&PR 91*
Goffman, Judy *WhoAmA 91*
Goffman, William 1924- *WhoAm 90*
Goffredo, Daniel Louis 1923- *St&PR 91*
Goffredo, R. Michael 1927- *St&PR 91*
Goffstein, M. B. *BioIn 16*
Goffstein, Marilyn Brooke 1940- *AuBYP 90*
Goforth, Brenda Kay 1960- *WhoEmL 91*
Goforth, Carolyn Mae 1931- *WhoAmW 91*
Goforth, Charles D. 1921- *St&PR 91*
Goforth, Eugene George *BiDrAPA 89*
Goforth, Joy 1921- *WhoSSW 91*
Goforth, William Clements 1937- *WhoSSW 91*
Gofrank, Catherine Ann 1951- *WhoEmL 91*
Gofrank, Frank L. 1918- *St&PR 91*
Gofrank, Frank Louis 1918- *WhoAm 90*
Goga, Octavian 1881-1938 *BioIn 16*
Gogan, James Wilson 1938- *WhoAm 90*
Gogek, Edward Burton *BiDrAPA 89*
Gogel, Timothy J. *St&PR 91*
Goggan, Celeste Roxanne 1950- *St&PR 91*
Goggan, John Patrick 1906- *LiHiK*
Goggans, Cathy Diane 1957- *WhoSSW 91*
Goggans, Frederick C 1950- *BiDrAPA 89*
Goggans, Roberta Daily 1926- *WhoAmW 91*
Goggin, Daniel A *BiDrAPA 89*
Goggin, Daniel Brendon 1935- *St&PR 91*
Goggin, John R. 1951- *WhoEmL 91*
Goggin, Joseph Robert 1926- *St&PR 91, WhoAm 90*
Goggin, Kathleen Mary 1956- *WhoAmW 91*
Goggin, Margaret Knox 1919- *WhoAm 90*
Goggin, Robert A. 1931- *ODwPR 91*
Goggin, William E. 1945- *St&PR 91*
Goggins, John Francis 1933- *WhoAm 90*
Goggins, William L. *St&PR 91N*
Gogh, Theo van 1857-1891 *BioIn 16*
Gogh, Vincent van 1853-1890 *BioIn 16, ModArCr 1 [port], WorAlBi*
Gogick, Kathleen Christine 1945- *WhoAm 90*
Gogineni, Rama Rao *BiDrAPA 89*
Gogisgi *WhoWrEP 89*
Goglia, Gennaro Louis 1921- *WhoAm 90*
Gogliettino, John Carmine 1952- *WhoE 91, WhoEmL 91*
Gogol, John Michael 1938- *WhoWrEP 89*
Gogol, Nikolai 1809-1852 *WorAlBi*
Gogol', Nikolai Vasil'evich 1809-1852 *BioIn 16*
Gogolewski, Bill 1947- *Ballpl 90*
Gogolin, Marilyn Tompkins 1946- *WhoAmW 91, WhoEmL 91*
Gogorza, Emilio de *PenDiMP*
Gogte, Sudheer Trimbak 1947- *WhoEmL 91*
Goguen, Paul Arthur 1929- *St&PR 91*
Goh Chok Tong 1941- *WhoWor 91*
Goh, Choo San *BioIn 16*
Goh, Guy 1945- *WhoWor 91*
Goh, Robert Eng-Huat 1950- *WhoWor 91*
Goh, Soonkhiang 1935- *WhoWor 91*
Goheen, Ellen Rozanne 1944- *WhoAmA 91*
Goheen, Richard C. 1936- *St&PR 91*
Goheen, Robert Francis 1919- *WhoAm 90, WorAlBi*
Gohil, Jivanlal P 1934- *BiDrAPA 89*

Gohil, Punit 1957- WhoEmL 91
Gohlke, Frank William 1942- WhoAm 90, WhoAmA 91
Gohmann, J. Michael 1945- St&PR 91
Gohmert, Louis Buller, Jr. 1953- WhoEmL 91
Goiburn, Gordon Henry 1938- St&PR 91
Goidell, Sheldon W. 1927- St&PR 91
Goin, Marcia K BiDrAPA 89
Goin, Michel 1951- WhoWor 91
Goines, Donald 1937-1974 TwCCr&M 91
Goines, Leonard 1934- WhoWor 91
Going, Jo WhoAmA 91
Going, Jonathan 1786-1844 BioIn 16
Going, William Thornbury 1915- WhoAm 90
Goings, James Arden 1941- St&PR 91
Goings, Ralph 1928- BioIn 16, ModArCr 1 [port], WhoAmA 91
Goins, Charlynn BioIn 16
Goins, Kenneth M., Jr. 1958- St&PR 91
Goins, Michael Edgar 1954- WhoSSW 91
Goiones, Doug St&PR 91
Goiri, Sabino de Arana 1865-1903 BioIn 16
Goisman, Robert M 1947- BiDrAPA 89
Goisman, Robert Michael 1947- WhoE 91
Goist, David Carl 1946- WhoEmL 91
Goitia, Francisco 1886-1969 ArtLatA
Goitia Garcia, Francisco 1882-1960 BioIn 16
Goizueta, Roberto C. BioIn 16
Goizueta, Roberto C. 1931- St&PR 91, WhoHisp 91
Goizueta, Roberto Crispulo 1931- ConAmBL, WhoAm 90, WhoSSW 91, WhoWor 91
Goizueta, Roberto Segundo 1954- WhoHisp 91
Gojawiczynska, Pola 1896-1963 EncCoWW
Gojkovich, Dusan 1931- WhoWor 91
Gojkovich, Dusan M 1935- BiDrAPA 89
Gojmerac-Leiner, Georgia 1949- WhoWrEP 89
Gojowy, Peter Lars Detlef 1934- IntWWM 90
Gokay, Fahrettin K BiDrAPA 89
Gokay, Michael Alan 1951- WhoE 91
Gokee, Marla A BiDrAPA 89
Gokel, George William 1946- WhoWor 91
Gokey, Vernon 1935- WhoE 91
Gokhale, Sudhir BiDrAPA 89
Gokharu, Surendra Sihna 1935- WhoWor 91
Goklaney, Ravi BiDrAPA 89
Goknar, Mehmet K BiDrAPA 89
Gokulan, Ajayan 1954- BiDrAPA 89
Gol, Jean 1942- WhoWor 91
Gola, Sandra Valentina 1955- WhoAmW 91, WhoEmL 91
Golan, Gila 1940?- BioIn 16
Golan, Menahem BioIn 16
Goland, Martin 1919- St&PR 91, WhoAm 90
Golani, Rivka 1946- PenDiMP
Golany, Gideon Salomon 1928- WhoAm 90
Golash, Terry Joseph 1949- BiDrAPA 89
Golashesky, Chrysa Zofia 1957- WhoAmW 91
Golaski, Walter Michael 1913- WhoAm 90, WhoE 91, WhoWor 91
Golaszewski, Thomas Jude 1948- WhoEmL 91
Golay, Alice EncCoWW
Golay, Frank Hindman 1915- WhoAm 90
Golay, Marcel J. E. 1902-1989 BioIn 16
Golbeck, Amanda Lorraine 1952- WhoEmL 91
Golberg, Martha 1907- AuBYP 90
Golberger, Norma Miller 1945- WhoEmL 91
Golbert, Gloria Esther 1940- WhoAmW 91
Golbey, Maurice BiDrAPA 89
Golbin, Alexander Zaler 1943- BiDrAPA 89
Golbin, Andree 1923- WhoAmA 91, WhoE 91
Golbitz, Patricia Cunningham 1927- WhoAm 90
Golboro, Alan S. 1930- St&PR 91
Golbranson, John Harris, Jr. 1934- WhoE 91
Golby, Ralph Wesley 1923- St&PR 91
Golchini-Shafa, Mehdi 1936- BiDrAPA 89
Golczewski, Frank 1948- WhoWor 91
Gold and Fizdale PenDiMP
Gold, Aaron A. 1919- St&PR 91
Gold, Aaron Alan 1919- WhoAm 90
Gold, Alan B. 1917- WhoAm 90
Gold, Albert 1916- WhoAm 90, WhoAmA 91
Gold, Allan Stuart BiDrAPA 89
Gold, Arnold Henry 1932- WhoAm 90
Gold, Arthur 1917- ConAu 132, PenDiMP
Gold, Arthur 1917-1990 BioIn 16, NewYTBS 90 [port]
Gold, Arthur Marvin 1941- BiDrAPA 89
Gold, Arthur Ralph BioIn 16
Gold, Bela 1915- WhoAm 90
Gold, Bernard Leon 1950- WhoEmL 91
Gold, Breena Fay 1956- WhoAmW 91
Gold, Carol Sapin WhoAm 90
Gold, David Marcus 1950- WhoEmL 91
Gold, Donald D, Jr. 1946- BiDrAPA 89
Gold, Doris Bauman 1919- WhoWrEP 89
Gold, Edgar 1934- WhoAm 90
Gold, Edward 1936- IntWWM 90
Gold, Edwin 1931- WhoWor 91
Gold, Eric Joseph 1962- WhoEmL 91
Gold, Erica Louise 1959- WhoAmW 91
Gold, Ernest 1921- IntWWM 90, OxCPMus
Gold, Eugene 1928- St&PR 91
Gold, Fay Helfand 1907- WhoAmA 91
Gold, Gerald Seymour 1931- WhoAm 90
Gold, Griffin BioIn 16
Gold, Harold Arthur 1929- WhoAm 90
Gold, Heidi J. 1963- WhoEmL 91
Gold, Herbert 1924- BioIn 16, WhoAm 90, WhoWrEP 89
Gold, Herbert Frank 1939- St&PR 91, WhoAm 90
Gold, I. Randall 1951- WhoEmL 91, WhoSSW 91, WhoWor 91
Gold, Ilene M 1949- BiDrAPA 89
Gold, Ivan 1932- WhoWrEP 89
Gold, Jay Charles 1950- BiDrAPA 89
Gold, Jeffrey M. 1945- St&PR 91
Gold, Jeffrey Mark 1945- WhoAm 90
Gold, Joe 1950- WhoWrEP 89
Gold, John Patrick 1940- St&PR 91
Gold, Joseph BiDrAPA 89
Gold, Joseph 1912- WhoE 91
Gold, Joseph 1930- WhoAm 90
Gold, Judith H 1941- BiDrAPA 89
Gold, Judith Hammerling 1941- WhoAm 90
Gold, Keith Dean 1956- WhoEmL 91
Gold, Kenneth Jay 1955- BiDrAPA 89
Gold, Kenneth Ray 1934- WhoSSW 91
Gold, Laurence Neil 1934- St&PR 91
Gold, Laurence Stephen 1936- WhoAm 90
Gold, Lee B 1926- BiDrAPA 89
Gold, Leonard 1910- BiDrAPA 89
Gold, Leonard C. 1926- St&PR 91
Gold, Leonard Singer 1934- WhoAm 90, WhoE 91
Gold, Leonard Steven 1954- St&PR 91
Gold, Liza Hannah 1958- BiDrAPA 89
Gold, Lonny 1951- St&PR 91
Gold, Lorne W. 1928- WhoAm 90
Gold, Lottie Stillerman 1906-1989 BioIn 16
Gold, Louis David 1940- BiDrAPA 89
Gold, Mari S. ODwPR 91
Gold, Mari S. 1940- WhoAm 90
Gold, Mark Stephen 1949- BiDrAPA 89, WhoEmL 91
Gold, Martha B 1938- WhoAmA 91
Gold, Martha Berman 1938- WhoE 91
Gold, Martin Alan 1947- WhoSSW 91
Gold, Martin Elliot 1946- WhoAm 90
Gold, Michael 1893-1967 EncAL
Gold, Michael Nathan 1952- WhoEmL 91, WhoWor 91
Gold, Ned Cooper, Jr. 1941- WhoWor 91
Gold, Norman Myron 1930- WhoAm 90
Gold, Patricia McManus 1934- WhoWrEP 89
Gold, Paul Nicholas 1953- WhoEmL 91
Gold, Peter Stephen 1941- St&PR 91
Gold, Philip William BiDrAPA 89
Gold, Phradie Kling 1933- WhoAmW 91
Gold, Richard Horace 1935- WhoAm 90, WhoWor 91
Gold, Richard L. 1925- St&PR 91
Gold, Richard L 1933- BiDrAPA 89
Gold, Richard N. 1945- WhoEmL 91, WhoWor 91
Gold, Risa Levenson 1956- BiDrAPA 89, WhoE 91
Gold, Robert Alan BiDrAPA 89
Gold, Robert C. 1955- ODwPR 91
Gold, Robert F. 1953- St&PR 91
Gold, Robert J. 1934- St&PR 91
Gold, Robert J. 1953- WhoEmL 91
Gold, Robert James 1932- St&PR 91
Gold, Robert S 1924- SmATA 63 [port]
Gold, Ronald Harvey BiDrAPA 89
Gold, Roslyn 1924- WhoE 91
Gold, Rozanne BioIn 16
Gold, Sandra Orenberg 1937- WhoAmW 91, WhoE 91
Gold, Seymour 1933- WhoWrEP 89
Gold, Sharon Cecile 1949- WhoAmA 91
Gold, Sheryl Ann Van Orden 1962- WhoAmW 91
Gold, Shirley Jeanne 1925- WhoAmW 91
Gold, Sidney BiDrAPA 89
Gold, Simon 1913- BiDrAPA 89
Gold, Stephen Howard 1947- WhoEmL 91
Gold, Steven Michael 1953- WhoEmL 91
Gold, Steven Neal 1953- WhoEmL 91
Gold, Stuart 1935- St&PR 91
Gold, Stuart M BiDrAPA 89
Gold, Stuart Walter 1949- WhoEmL 91
Gold, Susan Morrison 1949- WhoAmW 91
Gold, Thomas 1920- WhoAm 90
Gold, Tracey BioIn 16
Gold, Victoria 1943- WhoAmW 91
Gold, Warren Stuart 1946- BiDrAPA 89
Gold, Wendy Lee 1955- WhoEmL 91
Gold, Willard S 1932- BiDrAPA 89
Gold, William 1937- St&PR 91
Gold-Bikin, Lynne Z. 1938- WhoAmW 91
Gold Franke, Paula Christine 1952- WhoWrEP 89
Gol'danskii, Vitalii I. BioIn 16
Goldart, Jed Cory BiDrAPA 89
Golday, Jean 1948- BiDrAPA 89
Goldbach, Carol Closson 1926- WhoE 91
Goldbach, Hilda C 1905- BiDrAPA 89
Goldbach, Richard Albert 1936- St&PR 91
Goldbach, Scott Paxton 1960- WhoSSW 91
Goldbarg, Jeffrey Robbins 1948- BiDrAPA 89, WhoE 91
Goldbarth, Albert 1948- WorAu 1980 [port]
Goldbeck, Carl W. 1923- St&PR 91
Goldbeck, David M 1942- ConAu 30NR
Goldbeck, George 1925- St&PR 91
Goldbeck, Nikki 1947- ConAu 30NR
Goldberg, Abraham 1923- WhoWor 91
Goldberg, Alan 1942- WhoWrEP 89
Goldberg, Alan Eliot 1931- WhoAm 90
Goldberg, Alan Joel 1943- WhoWor 91
Goldberg, Alan M. 1930- St&PR 91
Goldberg, Alan Marvin 1939- WhoAm 90
Goldberg, Alan Michael BiDrAPA 89
Goldberg, Albert 1898-1990 ConAu 130
Goldberg, Albert Edward BiDrAPA 89
Goldberg, Alfred 1921- BiDrAPA 89
Goldberg, Allan 1937- BiDrAPA 89
Goldberg, Anatol 1910-1982 ConAu 131
Goldberg, Arnold Herbert 1933- WhoAmA 91
Goldberg, Arnold I 1929- BiDrAPA 89
Goldberg, Arthur Abba 1940- WhoAm 90, WhoE 91, WhoWor 91
Goldberg, Arthur H. 1942- WhoAm 90, WhoE 91
Goldberg, Arthur Henry NewYTBS 90 [port]
Goldberg, Arthur Henry 1905-1990 BioIn 16
Goldberg, Arthur Howard 1942- BioIn 16, St&PR 91
Goldberg, Arthur J. BioIn 16
Goldberg, Arthur J. 1908-1989 WorAlBi
Goldberg, Arthur J 1908-1990 ConAu 130, CurBio 90N, NewYTBS 90 [port]
Goldberg, Arthur Joseph 1908- BiDrUSE 89
Goldberg, Arthur Lewis 1939- WhoAm 90
Goldberg, Avram J. 1930- St&PR 91
Goldberg, Avram Jacob 1930- WhoAm 90, WhoE 91
Goldberg, Barbara Ann 1952- WhoEmL 91
Goldberg, Barbara June 1943- WhoWrEP 89
Goldberg, Barnet H. 1908- St&PR 91
Goldberg, Barry Stuart 1949- WhoEmL 91
Goldberg, Barton Sheldon 1933- St&PR 91
Goldberg, Bernard R BiDrAPA 89
Goldberg, Bertram J. 1942- WhoE 91
Goldberg, Beverli Sue 1952- BiDrAPA 89, WhoE 91
Goldberg, Bruce A 1951- BiDrAPA 89
Goldberg, Byron Wolfe 1928- BiDrAPA 89
Goldberg, Carol Rabb 1931- St&PR 91, WhoE 91
Goldberg, Caryn 1953- WhoAmW 91
Goldberg, Charles Barry 1955- WhoSSW 91
Goldberg, Charles E 1943- BiDrAPA 89
Goldberg, Charles Ned 1941- WhoWor 91
Goldberg, Dale Stephen 1954- WhoEmL 91
Goldberg, Daniel A BiDrAPA 89
Goldberg, Daniel Lewis 1939- St&PR 91
Goldberg, David Alan BiDrAPA 89
Goldberg, David Alan 1933- WhoAm 90
Goldberg, David Ben 1956- WhoEmL 91
Goldberg, David Charles 1940- WhoAm 90
Goldberg, David Charles 1957- WhoE 91
Goldberg, David Edward 1953- WhoSSW 91
Goldberg, David H. 1958- St&PR 91
Goldberg, David Meyer 1933- WhoAm 90
Goldberg, David S. 1960- ODwPR 91
Goldberg, Dennis 1942- St&PR 91
Goldberg, Dick 1947- WhoEmL 91
Goldberg, Donald 1934- BiDrAPA 89
Goldberg, Doretta Katzter 1955- WhoE 91
Goldberg, E. Susan 1937- St&PR 91
Goldberg, Edward 1929- WhoE 91
Goldberg, Edward Davidow 1921- WhoAm 90
Goldberg, Edward Jay 1950- WhoEmL 91, WhoSSW 91
Goldberg, Edwin 1937- WhoE 91
Goldberg, Elias 1887-1978 WhoAmA 91N
Goldberg, Elliott Marshall 1930- WhoAm 90
Goldberg, Estelle Maxine 1934- WhoAmW 91
Goldberg, Eugene L 1928- BiDrAPA 89
Goldberg, Faye Ruth 1957- WhoEmL 91
Goldberg, Fred Sellmann 1941- WhoAm 90
Goldberg, Fred T., Jr. WhoAm 90
Goldberg, Gary David 1944- WhoAm 90
Goldberg, Geraldine Elizabeth 1939- WhoAmW 91, WhoE 91, WhoWor 91
Goldberg, Gertrude 1906- St&PR 91
Goldberg, Glenn 1953- WhoAmA 91
Goldberg, Hannah Friedman 1933- WhoAm 90
Goldberg, Harold H. BioIn 16
Goldberg, Harold H 1922- BiDrAPA 89
Goldberg, Harold L 1936- BiDrAPA 89
Goldberg, Harold Seymour 1925- WhoAm 90
Goldberg, Harvey BioIn 16
Goldberg, Harvey Elliott 1945- WhoE 91
Goldberg, Herman Raphael 1915- WhoAm 90, WhoE 91
Goldberg, Hilary Tham 1946- WhoWrEP 89
Goldberg, Homer Beryl 1924- WhoAm 90
Goldberg, Honey Lynn 1957- WhoEmL 91
Goldberg, Howard Alan 1948- WhoEmL 91
Goldberg, Howard L. 1935- St&PR 91
Goldberg, Ian Simon BiDrAPA 89
Goldberg, Icchok Ignacy 1916- WhoAm 90
Goldberg, Irma Seeman BioIn 16
Goldberg, Irving H. 1905- St&PR 91
Goldberg, Irving Hyman 1926- WhoAm 90
Goldberg, Irving Loeb 1906- WhoAm 90
Goldberg, Irwin Charles 1957- BiDrAPA 89
Goldberg, Ivan Baer 1939- WhoSSW 91
Goldberg, Ivan D. 1934- WhoAm 90
Goldberg, Ivan K BiDrAPA 89
Goldberg, Jacob 1926- WhoAm 90
Goldberg, Jay Myron 1935- WhoAm 90
Goldberg, Jay Neal 1960- WhoEmL 91
Goldberg, Jean 1922- St&PR 91
Goldberg, Jeffrey 1955- BiDrAPA 89
Goldberg, Jeffrey L. 1936- St&PR 91
Goldberg, Jerold Martin 1938- WhoE 91
Goldberg, Jim WhoAmA 91
Goldberg, Jocelyn Hope Schnier 1953- WhoAmW 91, WhoEmL 91
Goldberg, Jodi Lynn 1961- WhoAmW 91
Goldberg, Joel Henry 1945- WhoWor 91
Goldberg, Jolande Elisabeth 1931- WhoE 91
Goldberg, Jon ODwPR 91
Goldberg, Joseph 1953- WhoE 91
Goldberg, Joseph Philip 1918- WhoE 91
Goldberg, Judith 1947- WhoAmA 91
Goldberg, Kenneth Jay 1953- WhoEmL 91
Goldberg, Kenneth Philip 1945- WhoE 91
Goldberg, Lawrence 1950- BiDrAPA 89
Goldberg, Lawrence Irwin 1940- WhoAm 90
Goldberg, Lawrence Roy 1954- WhoEmL 91
Goldberg, Lea BiDrAPA 89
Goldberg, Leah 1911-1970 EncCoWW
Goldberg, Lee Winicki 1932- WhoAmW 91, WhoWor 91
Goldberg, Leonard 1934- WhoAm 90
Goldberg, Les ODwPR 91
Goldberg, Leslie Rebecca 1959- WhoAmW 91
Goldberg, Marc David 1944- WhoSSW 91
Goldberg, Marc Evan 1957- WhoE 91, WhoEmL 91, WhoWor 91
Goldberg, Mark Steven 1952- St&PR 91
Goldberg, Martin 1924- BiDrAPA 89
Goldberg, Martin 1930- WhoAm 90
Goldberg, Marvin 1928- St&PR 91
Goldberg, Max 1920- BiDrAPA 89
Goldberg, Mayer S. 1923- St&PR 91
Goldberg, Mel J. 1944- St&PR 91
Goldberg, Melvin Arthur 1923- WhoAm 90
Goldberg, Michael 1924- WhoAmA 91
Goldberg, Michael Arthur 1941- WhoAm 90
Goldberg, Michael H. 1949- WhoE 91
Goldberg, Michael S. 1948- WhoSSW 91
Goldberg, Michael Sergio BiDrAPA 89
Goldberg, Milton D. 1914- St&PR 91
Goldberg, Mitchell 1957- St&PR 91
Goldberg, Moe A BiDrAPA 89
Goldberg, Montague Joshua 1924- WhoWor 91
Goldberg, Morton Edward 1932- WhoAm 90
Goldberg, Morton Falk 1937- WhoAm 90
Goldberg, Moses Haym 1940- WhoSSW 91
Goldberg, Murray M. 1929- St&PR 91
Goldberg, Myron Allen BiDrAPA 89
Goldberg, Myron Allen 1942- WhoE 91
Goldberg, Nolan Metz 1929- St&PR 91
Goldberg, Norman Albert 1918- WhoAm 90

Goldberg, Norman Lewis 1906-1982 WhoAmA 91N
Goldberg, Pamela Winer 1955- WhoAmW 91
Goldberg, Paul M. 1928- St&PR 91
Goldberg, Philip BiDrAPA 89
Goldberg, Ralph Steven 1949- WhoEmL 91
Goldberg, Ray Allan 1926- WhoAm 90, WhoWor 91
Goldberg, Reiner 1939- IntWWM 90, PenDiMP
Goldberg, Richard 1934- St&PR 91
Goldberg, Richard J 1949- BiDrAPA 89
Goldberg, Richard Jerome 1949- WhoE 91
Goldberg, Richard Lewis 1947- BiDrAPA 89
Goldberg, Richard R. 1941- St&PR 91
Goldberg, Richard Seth BiDrAPA 89
Goldberg, Richard Stuart 1951- BiDrAPA 89
Goldberg, Rita Maria 1933- WhoAm 90
Goldberg, Robert S. 1955- St&PR 91
Goldberg, Roger George 1942- WhoSSW 91
Goldberg, Ronald Howard 1941- BiDrAPA 89
Goldberg, Ronald Louis 1946- St&PR 91
Goldberg, Roselee WhoAmA 91, WhoE 91
Goldberg, Rube 1883-1970 EncACom
Goldberg, Salomea J 1925- BiDrAPA 89
Goldberg, Samuel 1925- WhoAm 90
Goldberg, Samuel 1928- WhoAm 90
Goldberg, Samuel Irving 1923- WhoAm 90
Goldberg, Samuel Theodore 1952- BiDrAPA 89
Goldberg, Sherman I. 1941- St&PR 91
Goldberg, Sherwood Dennis 1941- WhoE 91
Goldberg, Sidney 1931- St&PR 91, WhoAm 90, WhoE 91, WhoWor 91
Goldberg, Stanley Ira 1950- St&PR 91
Goldberg, Stanley Irwin 1934- WhoSSW 91
Goldberg, Stephanie Benson 1951- WhoAm 90
Goldberg, Stephen Floyd 1949- WhoEmL 91
Goldberg, Stephen Lyle 1952- WhoEmL 91
Goldberg, Steven Howard BiDrAPA 89
Goldberg, Steven Mark 1948- WhoEmL 91
Goldberg, Susan Fink 1950- St&PR 91
Goldberg, Susan Solomon 1944- WhoAmW 91
Goldberg, Szymon IntWWM 90
Goldberg, Szymon 1909- PenDiMP
Goldberg, Thomas Dunn 1954- WhoEmL 91
Goldberg, Vicki Belle 1945- WhoAmW 91
Goldberg, Victor Joel 1933- WhoAm 90
Goldberg, Vladislav Victorovich 1936- WhoE 91
Goldberg, Whoopi BioIn 16
Goldberg, Whoopi 1949- WorAlBi
Goldberg, Whoopi 1950?- DrBIPA 90
Goldberg, Whoopi 1955- WhoAmW 91
Goldberg, William Ralph 1911- WhoAm 90
Goldberg Goldrich, Judith Ilana 1962- WhoE 91
Goldberger, Alex BioIn 16
Goldberger, Alfred L. 1932- St&PR 91
Goldberger, Amy J. ODwPR 91
Goldberger, Arthur Stanley 1930- WhoAm 90
Goldberger, Barbara S BiDrAPA 89
Goldberger, Blanche Rubin 1914- WhoAmW 91
Goldberger, David 1925- IntWWM 90
Goldberger, George Stefan 1947- WhoE 91
Goldberger, Jack BioIn 16
Goldberger, Lawrence BioIn 16
Goldberger, Marianne R BiDrAPA 89
Goldberger, Marvin Leonard 1922- WhoAm 90, WhoE 91, WhoWor 91
Goldberger, Nancy Rule 1934- WhoAmW 91
Goldberger, Norma Miller 1945- WhoEmL 91
Goldberger, Paul 1950- ConAu 129
Goldberger, Paul Jesse 1950- WhoAm 90
Goldberger, Silim BiDrAPA 89
Goldberger, Stephen A. WhoE 91
Goldberger, William M. 1928- St&PR 91
Goldblatt, Barry Lance 1945- WhoE 91, WhoWor 91
Goldblatt, Eileen Witzman 1946- WhoEmL 91
Goldblatt, Gary 1943- BiDrAPA 89
Goldblatt, Hal Michael 1952- WhoWor 91
Goldblatt, Larry Stewart 1943- BiDrAPA 89
Goldblatt, Mark Joseph BiDrAPA 89
Goldblatt, Marvin Elijah 1922- St&PR 91
Goldblatt, Michael Lee 1949- WhoEmL 91
Goldblatt, Phillip Brian 1939- BiDrAPA 89
Goldblatt, Richard C. ODwPR 91
Goldblatt, Stanford Jay 1939- WhoAm 90
Goldblatt-Bond, Kathleen Boyle 1941- WhoAm 90
Goldblith, Samuel Abraham 1919- St&PR 91, WhoAm 90
Goldbloom, David Samuel 1953- BiDrAPA 89
Goldbloom, Richard Ballon 1924- WhoAm 90
Goldbloom, Theodore J 1933- BiDrAPA 89
Goldblum, Barbara Fran BiDrAPA 89
Goldblum, Jeff BioIn 16
Goldblum, Jeff 1952- WhoAm 90, WorAlBi
Goldby, Derek 1940- OxCCanT
Golde, David William 1940- WhoAm 90
Goldeen, Dorothy A 1948- WhoAmA 91
Goldeen, Dorothy Ann 1948- WhoEmL 91
Goldemberg, Isaac 1945- BioIn 16, ConAu 32NR, ConAu 12AS [port], HispWr 90, WhoHisp 91, WhoWrEP 89
Golden Gate Quartet OxCPMus
Golden, Arnold B 1934- BiDrAPA 89
Golden, Balfour Henry 1922- WhoE 91
Golden, Barbara Gilchrest 1946- WhoE 91
Golden, Beth Robinson 1959- WhoAmW 91
Golden, Bruce Paul 1943- WhoAm 90
Golden, Carole Ann 1942- WhoSSW 91
Golden, Christopher Anthony 1937- WhoAm 90
Golden, Clifford BiDrAPA 89
Golden, Dale Thomas 1952- St&PR 91
Golden, David Aaron 1920- WhoAm 90
Golden, David Edward 1932- WhoAm 90
Golden, Donald L. St&PR 91
Golden, Edward Scott 1955- WhoEmL 91, WhoWor 91
Golden, Edwin Harold 1931- WhoSSW 91, WhoWor 91
Golden, Ellen BioIn 16
Golden, Eunice WhoAmA 91
Golden, Gertrude BioIn 16
Golden, Gordon Ray 1952- WhoSSW 91
Golden, Gregg Hannan Stewart 1953- WhoE 91, WhoEmL 91
Golden, Harry 1902-1981 WorAlBi
Golden, Howard 1935- BiDrAPA 89
Golden, James John 1948- St&PR 91
Golden, Jim 1936- Ballpl 90
Golden, John F. 1949- WhoAm 90
Golden, John Frank 1915- St&PR 91
Golden, John J., Jr. 1943- WhoE 91
Golden, Joshua David 1955- BiDrAPA 89
Golden, Joshua Paul 1955- BiDrAPA 89
Golden, Joshua S 1931- BiDrAPA 89
Golden, Judith 1934- WhoAmA 91
Golden, Jules S 1922- BiDrAPA 89
Golden, Julius 1929- ODwPR 91
Golden, Kenneth Lacoy 1951- WhoSSW 91
Golden, Laurie Ruth 1945- WhoEmL 91
Golden, Leon 1930- WhoAm 90, WhoWor 91
Golden, Leslie Black 1955- WhoAmW 91
Golden, Libby WhoAmA 91
Golden, Louis M., Jr. 1919- St&PR 91
Golden, Marita BioIn 16
Golden, Marlene Patricia 1955- WhoAmW 91, WhoEmL 91
Golden, Max 1913- WhoAm 90
Golden, Michael F BiDrAPA 89
Golden, Michael Frank 1947- St&PR 91, WhoAm 90
Golden, Milton M. 1915- WhoAm 90
Golden, Morton J 1929- WhoAmA 91
Golden, Morton M BiDrAPA 89
Golden, Nancy Felice 1950- WhoAmW 91, WhoWor 91
Golden, Nat 1917- St&PR 91
Golden, Renata Michele 1952- WhoAmW 91
Golden, Renny BioIn 16
Golden, Richard Allen 1941- BiDrAPA 89
Golden, Robert Bennett 1948- St&PR 91, WhoEmL 91
Golden, Robert Charles 1946- WhoAm 90, WhoE 91
Golden, Robert M. 1920- St&PR 91
Golden, Robert Neal 1953- BiDrAPA 89
Golden, Rolland Harve 1931- WhoAmA 91
Golden, Roy Eugene 1941- WhoSSW 91
Golden, Seymour W. 1921- St&PR 91
Golden, Sheri Dianne 1960- WhoAmW 91
Golden, Terence C. 1944- WhoAm 90
Golden, William Brownell 1948- WhoE 91
Golden, William C. 1936- WhoAm 90
Golden, William T. 1909- St&PR 91
Golden, William Theodore 1909- BioIn 16, WhoAm 90
Golden, Wilson 1948- WhoEmL 91
Goldenberg, Andrew Avi 1945- WhoAm 90
Goldenberg, Barton Joshua 1955- WhoE 91
Goldenberg, David Milton 1938- WhoAm 90
Goldenberg, Debra Ann 1959- WhoAmW 91
Goldenberg, Edward 1953- BiDrAPA 89
Goldenberg, Eve A. 1926- St&PR 91
Goldenberg, George 1929- WhoAm 90, WhoSSW 91, WhoWor 91
Goldenberg, Gerald Joseph 1933- WhoAm 90
Goldenberg, Herbert J. 1939- St&PR 91
Goldenberg, Leslie Karp 1954- WhoSSW 91
Goldenberg, Melvyn Joel 1942- St&PR 91
Goldenberg, Perry B. 1935- St&PR 91
Goldenberg, Ronald Edwin 1931- WhoAm 90
Goldenberg, Samuel 1951- WhoWor 91
Goldenberg, Sherri Roberta 1964- WhoE 91
Goldenberg, Stephen Bernard 1943- WhoE 91
Goldensohn, Barry Nathan 1937- WhoWrEP 89
Goldensohn, Sidney S 1920- BiDrAPA 89
Goldensohn, Sidney S. 1920-1989 BioIn 16
Goldenson, Robert Myar 1908- WhoAm 90
Goldenweiser, Alexander 1875-1961 PenDiMP
Golder, Johann EncCoWW
Goldey, Harvey BiDrAPA 89
Goldey, James Mearns 1926- WhoAm 90
Goldfarb, Alan Steven 1939- WhoE 91
Goldfarb, Bernard Sanford 1917- WhoAm 90, WhoWor 91
Goldfarb, Charles 1931- BiDrAPA 89
Goldfarb, Clara A BiDrAPA 89
Goldfarb, Daniel David BiDrAPA 89
Goldfarb, David BioIn 16
Goldfarb, David NewYTBS 90 [port]
Goldfarb, David Barnett 1954- WhoEmL 91
Goldfarb, Donald 1941- WhoAm 90, WhoE 91
Goldfarb, Edward BiDrAPA 89
Goldfarb, Harry W 1928- BiDrAPA 89
Goldfarb, Herman NewYTBS 90
Goldfarb, Irene Dale 1929- WhoWor 91
Goldfarb, Joanne Jacob 1934- WhoAmW 91
Goldfarb, Marsha Geier 1942- WhoE 91
Goldfarb, Martin 1938- WhoAm 90
Goldfarb, Nancy ODwPR 91
Goldfarb, Phyllis 1955- WhoEmL 91
Goldfarb, Richard Marc 1953- WhoE 91
Goldfarb, Robert Stanley 1943- WhoAm 90
Goldfarb, Ronald Lawrence 1933- WhoAm 90
Goldfarb, Simon L 1912- BiDrAPA 89
Goldfarb, Warren 1949- WhoAm 90
Goldfarb, William 1915- BiDrAPA 89
Goldfeder, Fishel 1912-1981 BioIn 16
Goldfeder, Howard 1926- St&PR 91
Goldfein, Jerome Allen 1939- BiDrAPA 89
Goldfeld, Dorian 1947- WhoAm 90, WhoE 91
Goldfeld, Stephen Michael 1940- WhoAm 90
Goldfield, Alfred Sherman 1939- WhoAm 90
Goldfield, Burton Michael 1955- St&PR 91
Goldfield, Edward L 1930- WhoAmA 91
Goldfield, Edwin David 1918- WhoAm 90, WhoE 91
Goldfield, Michael David 1940- BiDrAPA 89
Goldfield, Robert S. 1927- St&PR 91
Goldfine, Howard 1932- WhoAm 90
Goldfine, Lee Mitchell BiDrAPA 89
Goldfine, Mel A. 1948- St&PR 91
Goldfine, Miriam ODwPR 91
Goldfine, Miriam 1933- WhoE 91
Goldfine, Peter Elliot BiDrAPA 89
Goldfinger, Andrew David 1945- WhoE 91
Goldfinger, Clarence S. 1923- St&PR 91
Goldfinger, Eliot 1950- WhoAmA 91
Goldfinger, Erno 1902-1987 BioIn 16, ConDes 90
Goldfinger, Michael Neil 1945- WhoE 91
Goldfinger, Solomon 1950- St&PR 91
Goldfinger, Stephen Mark 1951- BiDrAPA 89, WhoE 91
Goldfrank, Helen Colodny 1912- AuBYP 90
Goldfrank, Herbert J., Mrs. 1912- WhoAmW 91, WhoE 91, WhoWor 91
Goldfried, Marvin Robert 1936- WhoE 91
Goldfus, Donald Wayne 1934- St&PR 91, WhoAm 90
Goldgar, Bertrand Alvin 1927- WhoAm 90
Goldgraben, Gerald Robert 1940- WhoE 91
Goldhaber, F. I. WhoWrEP 89
Goldhaber, Gerald Martin 1944- WhoAm 90
Goldhaber, Gerson 1924- WhoAm 90
Goldhaber, Gertrude Scharff 1911- WhoAm 90, WhoAmW 91
Goldhaber, Jacob Kopel 1924- WhoAm 90
Goldhaber, Maurice 1911- WorAlBi
Goldhamer, Walter M. 1911- St&PR 91
Goldhammer, Henry N. 1943- St&PR 91
Goldhammer, Robert F. 1931- St&PR 91
Goldhammer, Robert Frederick 1931- WhoAm 90
Goldhawk, Norman Panter 1909- IntWWM 90
Goldhill, Paul M 1924- BiDrAPA 89
Goldhurst, William 1929- WhoAm 90, WhoWrEP 89
Goldiamond, Israel 1919- WhoAm 90
Goldie, Archibald Richardson 1925- WhoAm 90
Goldie, Celia BioIn 16
Goldie, Christine Mathews BioIn 16
Goldie, Dan BioIn 16
Goldie, George 1927- St&PR 91
Goldie, Ray Robert 1920- WhoWor 91
Goldie, Ron Robert 1951- WhoEmL 91, WhoWor 91
Goldie, Terrence William 1950- ConAu 32NR
Goldie, Terry ConAu 32NR
Goldie, Thomas 1850-1892 DcCanB 12
Goldin, Abraham 1911-1988 BioIn 16
Goldin, Alan Gary 1942- WhoAm 90
Goldin, Amy 1926-1978 WhoAmA 91N
Goldin, Barbara Diamond 1946- ConAu 132
Goldin, Claudia Dale 1946- WhoAmW 91, WhoE 91
Goldin, Gurston D 1930- BiDrAPA 89
Goldin, Gurston David 1930- WhoE 91
Goldin, Harrison J. BioIn 16
Goldin, Harrison Jacob 1936- WhoE 91
Goldin, Horace 1873-1939 BioIn 16
Goldin, Judah 1914- BioIn 16, WhoAm 90
Goldin, Leon 1923- WhoAm 90, WhoAmA 91
Goldin, Marion BioIn 16
Goldin, Melvin Lester 1950- BiDrAPA 89
Goldin, Michael R 1944- BiDrAPA 89
Goldin, Milton 1927- WhoAm 90
Goldin, Morris I BiDrAPA 89
Goldin, Sol 1909- WhoAm 90
Goldin, Victor 1927- BiDrAPA 89
Golding, Brage 1920- WhoAm 90
Golding, Carolyn May 1941- WhoAm 90
Golding, Cornelius Eugene 1947- St&PR 91
Golding, Elizabeth Bass 1902- WhoAm 90
Golding, George Theodore 1905-1990 BioIn 16
Golding, Irvin M 1928- BiDrAPA 89
Golding, Jay Harold 1945- St&PR 91
Golding, Leonard Sheldon 1935- WhoAm 90
Golding, Linda BioIn 16
Golding, Martin Philip 1930- WhoAm 90
Golding, Michael BioIn 16
Golding, Michael H.B. 1943- St&PR 91
Golding, Patricia Joyce Surratt 1948- WhoAmW 91
Golding, Robin Mavesyn 1928- IntWWM 90
Golding, Samuel Y. St&PR 91
Golding, William 1911- Au&Arts 5 [port], BioIn 16, ConAu 33NR, DcLB 100 [port], MajTwCW, WorAlBi
Golding, William Gerald 1911- WhoAm 90, WhoWor 91
Goldings, Carmen R BiDrAPA 89
Goldings, Herbert J 1929- BiDrAPA 89
Goldis, Sy 1928- WhoAm 90
Goldkette, Jean 1899-1962 BioIn 16, OxCPMus
Goldleaf, Steven 1953- WhoWrEP 89
Goldmacher, Steven M. 1945- ODwPR 91
Goldman family BioIn 16
Goldman, Aaron 1913- St&PR 91
Goldman, Abe A 1916- BiDrAPA 89
Goldman, Adila Sarah BiDrAPA 89
Goldman, Adolph 1927- BiDrAPA 89
Goldman, Alan Ira 1937- WhoAm 90
Goldman, Alan Stuart 1958- WhoE 91
Goldman, Albert Harry 1927- BioIn 16
Goldman, Alfred Emmanuel 1925- WhoAm 90
Goldman, Allan Bailey 1937- WhoAm 90
Goldman, Allan E. 1926- St&PR 91
Goldman, Allan Larry 1943- WhoSSW 91
Goldman, Allen Marshall 1937- WhoAm 90
Goldman, Alvin Lee 1938- WhoAm 90
Goldman, Arlene Leslie 1956- WhoAmW 91
Goldman, Arnold D 1933- BiDrAPA 89
Goldman, Arnold L. 1930- St&PR 91
Goldman, Arnold Melvyn 1936- WhoWor 91
Goldman, Arthur S. 1906-1989 BioIn 16
Goldman, Barbara BioIn 16
Goldman, Barbara Deren 1949- WhoAmW 91
Goldman, Barbara S. 1946- WhoAmW 91
Goldman, Benjamin Edward 1940- WhoAm 90
Goldman, Bernard 1928- St&PR 91, WhoAm 90
Goldman, Bert Arthur 1929- WhoAm 90

Goldman, Beth 1951- BiDrAPA 89
Goldman, Betsy Lee 1932- WhoWrEP 89
Goldman, Bo 1932- ConTFT 8
Goldman, Boleslaw 1938- WhoWor 91
Goldman, Brian Arthur 1946- WhoAm 90
Goldman, Brooks Calman 1936- WhoAm 90
Goldman, Bruce 1946- WhoEmL 91
Goldman, Carl A. 1934- St&PR 91
Goldman, Carl Lonny 1953- WhoEmL 91
Goldman, Charles N. 1932- St&PR 91
Goldman, Charles Norton 1932- WhoAm 90
Goldman, Charles R 1942- BiDrAPA 89
Goldman, Charles Remington 1930- WhoAm 90
Goldman, Charlotte R BiDrAPA 89
Goldman, Clifford Alan 1943- WhoE 91
Goldman, Clifford David BiDrAPA 89
Goldman, Clifford H. 1942- St&PR 91
Goldman, Dan C. 1943- WhoSSW 91
Goldman, Daniel C. 1943- St&PR 91
Goldman, Daniel Paul 1964- WhoE 91
Goldman, David L BiDrAPA 89
Goldman, David Philip BiDrAPA 89
Goldman, David S BiDrAPA 89
Goldman, Donald Howard 1942- WhoAm 90
Goldman, Edward Joseph 1938- St&PR 91
Goldman, Edwin Franko 1878-1956 OxCPMus, PenDiMP
Goldman, Eileen Kroll 1950- WhoEmL 91
Goldman, Elaine 1944- ODwPR 91
Goldman, Elliot 1935- WhoAm 90
Goldman, Emma 1869-1940 BioAmW, BioIn 16, EncAL [port], FemiCLE
Goldman, Eric 1915-1989 AnObit 1989
Goldman, Eric Frederick 1915-1989 BioIn 16
Goldman, Gail Meurice 1953- WhoEmL 91
Goldman, Gary Craig 1951- WhoEmL 91
Goldman, George D. BioIn 16
Goldman, George S 1906- BiDrAPA 89
Goldman, Gerald Hillis 1947- WhoAm 90
Goldman, Harold A. 1911- St&PR 91
Goldman, Harvey J. 1946- St&PR 91
Goldman, Henry Maurice 1911- WhoAm 90
Goldman, Herbert P 1939- BiDrAPA 89
Goldman, Howard Hirsch BiDrAPA 89
Goldman, Ilana Ruth 1960- BiDrAPA 89
Goldman, Ira Leon 1946- WhoE 91
Goldman, Ira Steven 1951- WhoE 91
Goldman, Irving BioIn 16
Goldman, Irving 1911- WhoAm 90
Goldman, Israel 1904-1979 BioIn 16
Goldman, Jacob E. 1921- St&PR 91
Goldman, James 1927- ConTFT 8 [port], WhoAm 90
Goldman, James A. 1955- St&PR 91
Goldman, James Adam 1962- WhoE 91
Goldman, James M. ODwPR 91
Goldman, Janet Parker 1958- WhoAmW 91, WhoEmL 91, WhoWor 91
Goldman, Jay 1930- WhoAm 90
Goldman, Jerome 1936- St&PR 91
Goldman, Jerry Alan 1956- WhoEmL 91
Goldman, Jerry Stephen 1951- WhoE 91
Goldman, Jill Minkoff 1953- WhoAmW 91
Goldman, Joel BioIn 16
Goldman, Joel J. 1940- WhoAm 90, WhoE 91, WhoWor 91
Goldman, Jonathan NewAgMG
Goldman, Jonathon D 1956- BiDrAPA 89
Goldman, Jordan ODwPR 91
Goldman, Joseph Bernard 1917- WhoAm 90
Goldman, Joseph Lawrence 1904- WhoWor 91
Goldman, Judith WhoAmA 91
Goldman, Kathryn Louise 1946- WhoAmW 91
Goldman, Larry Scott 1952- BiDrAPA 89
Goldman, Lawrence 1936- WhoE 91
Goldman, Lawrence Saul 1942- WhoE 91
Goldman, Leo 1920- WhoAm 90
Goldman, Leo Milton 1921- BiDrAPA 89
Goldman, Leonard B. 1907-1988 BioIn 16
Goldman, Leonard Manuel 1925- WhoAm 90
Goldman, Leonard W BiDrAPA 89
Goldman, Lester 1942- WhoAmA 91
Goldman, Lionel St&PR 91
Goldman, Louis Budwig 1948- WhoEmL 91
Goldman, Marcus Jacob 1960- BiDrAPA 89
Goldman, Margo Pfeffer 1952- BiDrAPA 89
Goldman, Marshall Irwin 1930- WhoAm 90, WhoE 91
Goldman, Martha Ann 1952- WhoEmL 91
Goldman, Martin 1945- St&PR 91
Goldman, Martin Raymond Rubin 1920- WhoAm 90, WhoWrEP 89
Goldman, Martyn Alan 1930- WhoSSW 91
Goldman, Marvin 1928- WhoAm 90
Goldman, Michael Lawrence 1961- WhoEmL 91
Goldman, Michael Paul 1936- WhoAm 90
Goldman, Milton 1914-1989 AnObit 1989, BioIn 16
Goldman, Moe BioIn 16
Goldman, Moises Julian 1949- WhoEmL 91
Goldman, Morris Benjamin 1953- BiDrAPA 89
Goldman, Morton Irwin 1926- St&PR 91
Goldman, Morton J. BioIn 16
Goldman, Murray Abraham 1937- St&PR 91, WhoAm 90
Goldman, Nancy Joan Kramer 1953- WhoAmW 91
Goldman, Nathan Carliner 1950- WhoSSW 91, WhoWor 91
Goldman, Neil Stephen 1943- BiDrAPA 89
Goldman, Norman Lewis 1933- WhoAm 90
Goldman, Patricia Ann 1942- WhoAm 90
Goldman, Paul 1950- ConAu 129
Goldman, Peter 1929- WhoAm 90
Goldman, Rachel Beth 1959- WhoEmL 91
Goldman, Rachel Bok 1937- WhoAmA 91
Goldman, Ralph Frederick 1928- WhoAm 90
Goldman, Renitta Librach 1938- WhoSSW 91
Goldman, Rhona Mednick 1945- WhoE 91
Goldman, Richard B. 1946- St&PR 91
Goldman, Richard Bruce 1946- WhoAm 90
Goldman, Richard Franko 1910-1980 PenDiMP
Goldman, Richard Paul 1935- WhoE 91
Goldman, Robert David 1939- WhoAm 90
Goldman, Robert Huron 1918- WhoAm 90, WhoWor 91
Goldman, Robert Irving 1932- St&PR 91, WhoAm 90
Goldman, Robert Joseph 1939- WhoE 91
Goldman, Robert N. 1949- St&PR 91
Goldman, Robert W. 1942- St&PR 91
Goldman, Roberta 1940- WhoE 91
Goldman, Ron G BiDrAPA 89
Goldman, Roslyn Bakst 1938- WhoAmW 91
Goldman, Ruth Oppenheim 1925- WhoE 91
Goldman, Samuel E 1948- BiDrAPA 89
Goldman, Sheldon 1939- WhoAm 90
Goldman, Sheldon T. St&PR 91
Goldman, Sherry Dale BiDrAPA 89
Goldman, Sherry R. 1958- ODwPR 91
Goldman, Sheryl Ann 1948- WhoEmL 91
Goldman, Siegmund 1924- St&PR 91
Goldman, Simon 1913- WhoAm 90
Goldman, Sol BioIn 16
Goldman, Solomon 1893-1953 BioIn 16
Goldman, Stan 1948- WhoEmL 91
Goldman, Stanford 1907- WhoAm 90
Goldman, Stephen Harris 1951- St&PR 91
Goldman, Stuart BioIn 16
Goldman, Stuart A. 1948- WhoEmL 91
Goldman, Stuart Jonathan BiDrAPA 89
Goldman, Stuart Jonathan 1951- WhoE 91
Goldman, Thomas Carl BiDrAPA 89
Goldman, William 1931- WorAlBi
Goldman, William Jay 1936- St&PR 91
Goldman, Zachary C. 1929- St&PR 91
Goldman-Sefton, Mindy Susanne 1959- WhoAmW 91
Goldmann, Allen A. 1919- St&PR 91
Goldmann, Kenneth Francis 1922- St&PR 91
Goldmann, Morton Aaron 1924- WhoAm 90
Goldmann, Nahum 1895-1982 BioIn 16
Goldmann, Thomas 1950- WhoWor 91
Goldmark, Carl 1909-1990 BioIn 16
Goldmark, Carl, Jr. NewYTBS 90
Goldmark, Karl 1830-1915 PenDiMP A
Goldmark, Peter C. BioIn 16
Goldmark, Peter C. 1906-1977 WorAlBi
Goldmark, Peter C. 1940- St&PR 91
Goldmark, Peter Carl 1940- WhoAm 90
Goldmuntz, Barry M BiDrAPA 89
Goldner, Bernard Burton 1919- St&PR 91
Goldner, David W. 1961- St&PR 91
Goldner, George Robert 1943- WhoAm 90
Goldner, Herman Wilson 1916- WhoAm 90
Goldner, Jane Schnuer 1949- WhoSSW 91
Goldner, Janet 1952- WhoAmA 91
Goldner, Leonard Howard 1947- WhoEmL 91
Goldner, Neal Richard 1946- St&PR 91
Goldner, Richard D 1924- BiDrAPA 89
Goldner, Ronald B. 1935- WhoAm 90
Goldner, Royston Maurice 1929- St&PR 91
Goldner, Sheldon Herbert 1928- WhoAm 90
Goldney, Kathleen M H EncO&P 3
Goldney, Kathleen Mary 1894- EncPaPR 91
Goldon, Jerry St&PR 91
Goldoni, Carlo 1707-1793 WorAlBi
Goldovsky, Boris 1908- IntWWM 90, PenDiMP, WhoAm 90
Goldowsky, Barbara 1936- WhoWrEP 89
Goldowsky, Noah 1909- WhoAmA 91N
Goldreich, Peter Martin 1939- WhoAm 90
Goldress, Jerry E. WhoAm 90, WhoSSW 91
Goldress, Jerry Edwin 1930- St&PR 91
Goldreyer, Daniel Robert 1927- WhoE 91
Goldrich, Laurie BioIn 16
Goldrich, S.N. 1950- St&PR 91
Goldrick, John Richard 1929- WhoAm 90
Goldring, Elizabeth 1945- WhoAmA 91, WhoE 91
Goldring, Harold Benjamin 1929- St&PR 91
Goldring, Malcolm David 1949- IntWWM 90
Goldring, Nancy Deborah 1945- WhoAmA 91, WhoE 91
Goldring, Norman Max 1937- WhoAm 90
Goldring, Winifred 1888-1971 DcScB S2
Goldsack, James F. 1930- St&PR 91
Goldsberry, Fred Lynn 1947- WhoSSW 91
Goldsberry, Gordon 1927- Ballpl 90
Goldsberry, Richard Eugene 1956- WhoEmL 91
Goldsberry, Ronald E. BioIn 16
Goldsberry, Steven WhoWrEP 89
Goldsberry, Steven 1949- ConAu 131
Goldsboro, Bobby 1944- WorAlBi
Goldsborough, Robert Gerald 1937- WhoAm 90
Goldsbrough, Arnold 1892-1964 PenDiMP
Goldscheider, Cecile 1902-1988 BioIn 16
Goldscheider, Sidney 1920- WhoAm 90
Goldschein, Max H. BioIn 16
Goldschein, Steven Marc 1946- St&PR 91
Goldschlag, William 1952- WhoAm 90
Goldschmid, Harvey Jerome 1940- WhoAm 90, WhoWor 91
Goldschmid, Mary Tait Seibert 1947- WhoEmL 91
Goldschmidt, Arnold Myron 1928- WhoE 91
Goldschmidt, Berthold 1903- IntWWM 90, PenDiMP, -A
Goldschmidt, Carel 1904-1989 BioIn 16
Goldschmidt, Charles 1921- WhoAm 90
Goldschmidt, Dietrich Hans Alfred 1914- WhoWor 91
Goldschmidt, Henny Otto 1920- WhoWor 91
Goldschmidt, Hubert Leopold WhoWor 91
Goldschmidt, Ib Jorgen 1926- WhoWor 91
Goldschmidt, Lothar 1928- BiDrAPA 89
Goldschmidt, Lucien 1912- WhoAmA 91
Goldschmidt, Lucien Camille 1912- WhoE 91
Goldschmidt, Lynn Harvey 1951- WhoEmL 91
Goldschmidt, Meir Aron 1819-1887 DcScanL
Goldschmidt, Millicent Edna 1926- WhoAmW 91
Goldschmidt, Neil E. 1940- BioIn 16
Goldschmidt, Neil Edward 1940- BiDrUSE 89, WhoAm 90, WhoWor 91
Goldschmidt, Nicholas BioIn 16
Goldschmidt, Oswald BioIn 16
Goldschmidt, Otto 1829-1907 PenDiMP
Goldschmidt, Pauline BiDrAPA 89
Goldschmidt, Robert Alphonse 1937- WhoAm 90
Goldschmidt, Thomas John BiDrAPA 89
Goldschmidt, Victor W. 1936- WhoHisp 91
Goldschmidt, Walter Rochs 1913- WhoAm 90
Goldschmied, Fabio Renzo 1919- WhoE 91
Goldsen, Rose Kohn 1918- ConAu 33NR
Goldshtein, Mosei Markovich 1891-1918 BioIn 16
Goldsleger, Cheryl 1951- WhoAmA 91
Goldsmith, A. Elaine 1935- WhoSSW 91
Goldsmith, Arlene Frances 1941- WhoAmW 91
Goldsmith, Arthur Austin 1926- WhoAm 90, WhoWrEP 89
Goldsmith, Barbara BioIn 16
Goldsmith, Barbara 1931- WhoAm 90, WhoAmA 91, WhoWrEP 89
Goldsmith, Benedict Isaac 1916- WhoAmA 91
Goldsmith, Billy Joe 1933- WhoAm 90
Goldsmith, Bram 1923- St&PR 91, WhoAm 90
Goldsmith, Caroline L. ODwPR 91
Goldsmith, Cathy Ellen 1947- WhoAmW 91
Goldsmith, Christopher C. 1947- WhoAm 90
Goldsmith, Claude Orville 1932- WhoAm 90
Goldsmith, Clifford Henry 1919- WhoAm 90
Goldsmith, Cornelia BioIn 16
Goldsmith, David L. St&PR 91
Goldsmith, Edwin M., III 1942- WhoAm 90
Goldsmith, Elizabeth ODwPR 91
Goldsmith, Elsa M 1920- WhoAmA 91
Goldsmith, Eric D BiDrAPA 89
Goldsmith, Gary 1954- BioIn 16
Goldsmith, Gary N 1948- BiDrAPA 89
Goldsmith, Gary Norman 1948- WhoE 91
Goldsmith, Harry Sawyer 1929- WhoAm 90
Goldsmith, Howard 1943- WhoAm 90
Goldsmith, Howard 1945- WhoWrEP 89
Goldsmith, Howard Michael 1942- WhoE 91
Goldsmith, Irving BioIn 16
Goldsmith, Jack Landman 1910- WhoAm 90
Goldsmith, James 1933- BioIn 16
Goldsmith, James Arthur 1955- WhoEmL 91
Goldsmith, Jeffrey Robert 1957- St&PR 91
Goldsmith, Jerry 1929- OxCPMus, WhoAm 90
Goldsmith, Jewett 1919- BiDrAPA 89
Goldsmith, Joel H. 1947- WhoE 91
Goldsmith, John Alan 1920- WhoAm 90
Goldsmith, John Arthur 1947- St&PR 91
Goldsmith, John H. BioIn 16
Goldsmith, John Herman Thorburn 1903-1987 BioIn 16
Goldsmith, Julian Royce 1918- WhoAm 90
Goldsmith, Karen Lee 1946- WhoEmL 91
Goldsmith, Kathleen Mawhinney 1957- WhoAmW 91
Goldsmith, Kenneth 1924- St&PR 91
Goldsmith, Larry Dean 1952- WhoWrEP 89
Goldsmith, Lawrence Charles 1916- WhoAmA 91
Goldsmith, Leda ODwPR 91
Goldsmith, Leda Carroll 1936- WhoE 91
Goldsmith, Lee Selig 1939- WhoAm 90
Goldsmith, Lowell Alan 1938- WhoAm 90, WhoWor 91
Goldsmith, Margaret 1894?- FemiCLE
Goldsmith, Marianne G. 1938- BiDrAPA 89
Goldsmith, Mark Edward BiDrAPA 89
Goldsmith, Martin H. 1947- WhoAm 90
Goldsmith, Marvin Fred 1941- St&PR 91
Goldsmith, Marvin L. 1925- WhoE 91
Goldsmith, Mary Ann 1952- WhoEmL 91
Goldsmith, Maxine Iris 1947- WhoAmW 91
Goldsmith, Melissa 1954- WhoWrEP 89
Goldsmith, Michael 1921-1990 NewYTBS 90
Goldsmith, Michael John 1932- WhoWor 91
Goldsmith, Morris BioIn 16
Goldsmith, Morton Ralph 1882-1971 WhoAmA 91N
Goldsmith, Nancy Carrol 1940- WhoAmW 91
Goldsmith, Oliver 1730?-1774 DcLB 104 [port], WorAlBi
Goldsmith, Oliver 1794-1861 DcLB 99 [port]
Goldsmith, Paul F. 1948- St&PR 91
Goldsmith, Paul Felix 1948- WhoAm 90
Goldsmith, Paul J. 1949- WhoAm 90
Goldsmith, Peter ConAu 33NR, MajTwCW
Goldsmith, Philip Robert 1945- WhoAm 90
Goldsmith, Raymond William 1904-1988 BioIn 16
Goldsmith, Richard BioIn 16
Goldsmith, Richard Jeffrey 1950- BiDrAPA 89
Goldsmith, Robert H. 1930- St&PR 91
Goldsmith, Robert Hillis 1911- WhoAm 90
Goldsmith, Robert Holloway 1930- WhoAm 90
Goldsmith, Robert Lewis 1928- WhoAm 90
Goldsmith, Ruth M 1919- SmATA 62 [port]
Goldsmith, Scott Jay BiDrAPA 89
Goldsmith, Shep 1928- St&PR 91
Goldsmith, Sidney 1930- WhoAm 90
Goldsmith, Stanley Joseph 1937- WhoAm 90
Goldsmith, Stephen R 1941- BiDrAPA 89
Goldsmith, Suzanne BioIn 16
Goldsmith, Sydney DrBlPA 90
Goldsmith, Ulrich Karl 1910- WhoAm 90
Goldsmith, Werner 1924- WhoAm 90
Goldsmith, William 1938- BiDrAPA 89
Goldsmith, William Glenn 1958- WhoEmL 91
Goldson, Amy Robertson 1953- WhoEmL 91
Goldson, Mary Funnye BioIn 16, NewYTBS 90
Goldspiel, Arnold Nelson 1949- WhoEmL 91

Goldspiel, Steven Ira 1946- *WhoAm 90*
Goldstaub, Mark *BioIn 16*
Goldstein, Abraham S. 1925- *WhoAm 90*
Goldstein, Abraham S 1933- *BiDrAPA 89*
Goldstein, Alan 1928- *St&PR 91*
Goldstein, Alan 1953- *WhoWrEP 89*
Goldstein, Alfred George 1932- *WhoAm 90*
Goldstein, Allan Leonard 1937- *WhoAm 90, WhoWor 91*
Goldstein, Alvin 1929- *WhoAm 90*
Goldstein, Arnold K. 1954- *St&PR 91*
Goldstein, Arthur L. 1935- *St&PR 91*
Goldstein, Avram 1919- *WhoAm 90*
Goldstein, B.B. 1919- *St&PR 91*
Goldstein, Barbara Block 1942- *WhoAmW 91*
Goldstein, Barbara Lee 1958- *BiDrAPA 89*
Goldstein, Barry 1935- *BiDrAPA 89*
Goldstein, Barry Bruce 1947- *WhoEmL 91*
Goldstein, Barry Howard 1953- *BiDrAPA 89*
Goldstein, Bernard 1929- *St&PR 91, WhoAm 90*
Goldstein, Bernard David 1939- *WhoAm 90*
Goldstein, Bernard Herbert 1907- *WhoAm 90*
Goldstein, Bertram *BiDrAPA 89*
Goldstein, Beth Lisa 1963- *WhoAmW 91*
Goldstein, Bonnie Joy 1949- *WhoEmL 91*
Goldstein, Burton J 1930- *BiDrAPA 89*
Goldstein, Burton Jack 1930- *WhoAm 90*
Goldstein, Carl 1938- *ConAu 130, WhoAmA 91*
Goldstein, Charles *BioIn 16*
Goldstein, Charles Arthur 1936- *WhoAm 90, WhoE 91, WhoWor 91*
Goldstein, Charles H. 1939- *WhoAm 90*
Goldstein, Charles Henry 1938- *WhoE 91*
Goldstein, Charles Irwin 1940- *WhoE 91*
Goldstein, Charlotte Lipson 1929- *WhoAmW 91*
Goldstein, Constance Sue 1931- *WhoAmW 91*
Goldstein, Daniel A. 1934- *ODwPR 91*
Goldstein, Daniel Joshua 1950- *WhoAmA 91*
Goldstein, Daniel L 1914- *BiDrAPA 89*
Goldstein, David *BioIn 16*
Goldstein, David Garson 1919- *St&PR 91*
Goldstein, David I. 1924-1987? *ConAu 130*
Goldstein, David Myron 1946- *BiDrAPA 89*
Goldstein, David Scott 1961- *WhoEmL 91*
Goldstein, Debra Edelson 1950- *WhoAmW 91*
Goldstein, Donald Aaron 1934- *WhoAm 90*
Goldstein, Donald E. 1946- *St&PR 91*
Goldstein, Donald Jay 1948- *WhoSSW 91*
Goldstein, Donald Maurice 1932- *WhoE 91, WhoWor 91*
Goldstein, Dora Benedict 1922- *WhoAm 90*
Goldstein, Doris *ODwPR 91*
Goldstein, Doris Mueller 1942- *WhoAmW 91*
Goldstein, E. Alexander 1951- *St&PR 91*
Goldstein, E. Ernest 1918- *WhoAm 90, WhoWor 91*
Goldstein, Edward David 1927- *WhoAm 90*
Goldstein, Edwin A *BiDrAPA 89*
Goldstein, Eleanor 1935- *WhoE 91, WhoWor 91*
Goldstein, Ellen *ODwPR 91*
Goldstein, Elliott 1915- *WhoAm 90, WhoWor 91*
Goldstein, Elliott J 1935- *BiDrAPA 89*
Goldstein, Emanuel V. 1914- *WhoE 91*
Goldstein, Ernest 1933- *BioIn 16*
Goldstein, Estelle Toby *BiDrAPA 89*
Goldstein, Evie Cara 1959- *WhoAmW 91*
Goldstein, Fern Beverley 1935- *WhoAmW 91*
Goldstein, Francie Lynn *BiDrAPA 89*
Goldstein, Francine Ellen 1952- *WhoAmW 91, WhoE 91*
Goldstein, Frank Robert 1943- *WhoAm 90*
Goldstein, Fred 1924- *WhoE 91*
Goldstein, Gary Bruce 1954- *WhoE 91*
Goldstein, George J. 1908- *St&PR 91*
Goldstein, George S. 1933- *St&PR 91*
Goldstein, Gerald 1931- *WhoE 91*
Goldstein, Gerald A *BiDrAPA 89*
Goldstein, Gladys *WhoAmA 91*
Goldstein, Gladys H. 1929- *WhoE 91*
Goldstein, Gregory Lee 1960- *WhoE 91*
Goldstein, Harold W. *St&PR 91*
Goldstein, Harris S 1934- *BiDrAPA 89*
Goldstein, Harris Sidney 1934- *WhoE 91*
Goldstein, Harry M. 1926- *St&PR 91*
Goldstein, Harvey A. 1939- *WhoAm 90*
Goldstein, Henry 1933- *ODwPR 91, WhoE 91*
Goldstein, Henry N *BiDrAPA 89*
Goldstein, Herbert S *BiDrAPA 89*
Goldstein, Howard 1933- *WhoAmA 91, WhoE 91*
Goldstein, Howard J. 1944- *St&PR 91*
Goldstein, Howard Mark 1952- *WhoE 91*
Goldstein, Howard Warren 1949- *WhoEmL 91*
Goldstein, Ira J. 1930- *St&PR 91*
Goldstein, Irving 1938- *St&PR 91, WhoAm 90*
Goldstein, Irving Robert 1916- *WhoE 91*
Goldstein, Irwin 1935- *BiDrAPA 89*
Goldstein, Irwin Melvin 1944- *WhoE 91*
Goldstein, Irwin Stuart 1947- *WhoSSW 91*
Goldstein, Israel 1896-1986 *BioIn 16*
Goldstein, Izzy 1908- *BioIn 16*
Goldstein, Jack 1938- *St&PR 91*
Goldstein, Jack 1945- *WhoAmA 91*
Goldstein, Jacob Herman 1915- *WhoAm 90*
Goldstein, Jan E. 1959- *ODwPR 91*
Goldstein, Jane 1944- *WhoSSW 91*
Goldstein, Janet Hollis Kirsh 1957- *WhoEmL 91*
Goldstein, Jeffrey 1949- *WhoEmL 91*
Goldstein, Jeffrey H 1942- *ConAu 32NR*
Goldstein, Jeremy S. 1962- *St&PR 91*
Goldstein, Jerome 1928- *WhoE 91*
Goldstein, Jerome Arthur 1941- *WhoAm 90, WhoSSW 91*
Goldstein, Jerome Charles 1935- *WhoAm 90*
Goldstein, Jerome J. 1922- *St&PR 91*
Goldstein, Jerome S. 1940- *WhoAm 90*
Goldstein, Jerry S. 1940- *St&PR 91*
Goldstein, Joel B *BiDrAPA 89*
Goldstein, Joel Neil 1960- *BiDrAPA 89*
Goldstein, Jonathan Amos 1929- *WhoAm 90*
Goldstein, Joseph 1923- *WhoAm 90*
Goldstein, Joseph E. 1946- *St&PR 91*
Goldstein, Joseph Irwin 1939- *WhoAm 90*
Goldstein, Joseph L 1910- *BiDrAPA 89*
Goldstein, Joseph L. 1940- *WorAlBi*
Goldstein, Joseph Leonard 1940- *WhoAm 90, WhoSSW 91, WhoWor 91*
Goldstein, Joyce *BioIn 16*
Goldstein, Judith Shelley 1935- *WhoAmW 91*
Goldstein, Julia Sonia 1923- *WhoSSW 91*
Goldstein, Julian Wade 1958- *St&PR 91*
Goldstein, Julius 1918- *WhoAmA 91*
Goldstein, June C. 1935- *WhoAmW 91*
Goldstein, K. Susanna 1951- *WhoE 91*
Goldstein, Larry Joel 1944- *WhoE 91*
Goldstein, Laurence Alan 1943- *WhoWrEP 89*
Goldstein, Laurence J *BiDrAPA 89*
Goldstein, Lawrence Jerome *St&PR 91*
Goldstein, Lee Harris 1946- *BiDrAPA 89*
Goldstein, Lee Scott *BioIn 16*
Goldstein, Leonard 1935- *WhoSSW 91*
Goldstein, Leonard Barry 1944- *WhoE 91*
Goldstein, Leonard D. 1921- *St&PR 91*
Goldstein, Leonard S 1946- *BiDrAPA 89*
Goldstein, Leonide 1914-1988 *BioIn 16*
Goldstein, Lester 1924- *WhoAm 90*
Goldstein, Lester S 1940- *BiDrAPA 89*
Goldstein, Lewis M. 1927- *St&PR 91*
Goldstein, Lisa Ilene *BiDrAPA 89*
Goldstein, Loren David 1955- *WhoEmL 91*
Goldstein, Louis Lazarus 1913- *WhoAm 90*
Goldstein, Louis R. 1947- *IntWWM 90*
Goldstein, Lynn E. 1932- *St&PR 91*
Goldstein, Malcolm 1925- *ConAu 32NR*
Goldstein, Manfred 1927- *WhoWor 91*
Goldstein, Marc *BioIn 16*
Goldstein, Marc Alan 1958- *WhoEmL 91*
Goldstein, Marc Steven 1945- *WhoAm 90*
Goldstein, Maria Isabel *BiDrAPA 89*
Goldstein, Marion Zucker *BiDrAPA 89*
Goldstein, Mark David 1947- *WhoAm 90*
Goldstein, Mark Kane 1938- *St&PR 91*
Goldstein, Marsha Feder 1945- *WhoAmW 91*
Goldstein, Martin 1919- *WhoAm 90*
Goldstein, Martin B 1933- *BiDrAPA 89*
Goldstein, Martin Barnet 1933- *WhoE 91*
Goldstein, Martin E. 1934- *WhoE 91*
Goldstein, Martin Joel 1954- *WhoSSW 91*
Goldstein, Martin S. 1933- *WhoE 91*
Goldstein, Melvyn C. *BioIn 16*
Goldstein, Melvyn C. 1938- *WhoAm 90*
Goldstein, Menek 1924- *WhoAm 90*
Goldstein, Michael *WhoAm 90*
Goldstein, Michael 1941- *St&PR 91*
Goldstein, Michael B. 1943- *WhoAm 90*
Goldstein, Michael Graham 1952- *BiDrAPA 89*
Goldstein, Michael H *BiDrAPA 89*
Goldstein, Michael Ross 1942- *WhoE 91, WhoWor 91*
Goldstein, Milton 1914- *WhoAmA 91*
Goldstein, Milton Houseman 1937- *WhoE 91*
Goldstein, Mitchell R *BiDrAPA 89*
Goldstein, Morris *BioIn 16*
Goldstein, Morris 1945- *WhoAm 90*
Goldstein, Murray 1925- *WhoAm 90*
Goldstein, Nancy Bernice 1954- *WhoAmW 91*
Goldstein, Nannette 1953- *BiDrAPA 89*
Goldstein, Naomi 1932- *BiDrAPA 89, WhoE 91*
Goldstein, Nathan 1927- *BioIn 16, WhoAmA 91, WhoE 91*
Goldstein, Nathan L. 1913- *St&PR 91*
Goldstein, Neal 1947- *WhoEmL 91*
Goldstein, Neil Howard 1952- *WhoE 91*
Goldstein, Neil Warren 1950- *WhoE 91*
Goldstein, Norman Philip 1921- *WhoAm 90*
Goldstein, Norman R. 1944- *St&PR 91, WhoAm 90*
Goldstein, Norman Robert 1928- *WhoAm 90*
Goldstein, Paul 1934- *St&PR 91*
Goldstein, Paul 1943- *WhoAm 90*
Goldstein, Paul Alan 1953- *WhoSSW 91*
Goldstein, Peggy R. 1921- *WhoAm 90, WhoWor 91*
Goldstein, Philip 1910- *AuBYP 90*
Goldstein, Phyllis Ann 1926- *WhoAmW 91*
Goldstein, Rhoda L *ConAu 30NR*
Goldstein, Richard Alan 1942- *St&PR 91*
Goldstein, Richard David 1957- *WhoEmL 91*
Goldstein, Richard Jay 1928- *WhoAm 90*
Goldstein, Robert *BioIn 16*
Goldstein, Robert 1924- *WhoAm 90*
Goldstein, Robert Arnold 1941- *WhoAm 90*
Goldstein, Robert Justin 1947- *ConAu 131*
Goldstein, Robert L *BiDrAPA 89*
Goldstein, Robert Lawrence 1931- *St&PR 91*
Goldstein, Robert Lee 1951- *WhoSSW 91*
Goldstein, Robert Lloyd 1938- *WhoE 91*
Goldstein, Robert S. 1932- *St&PR 91*
Goldstein, Robert Stanley 1936- *WhoE 91*
Goldstein, Robin 1955?-1989 *ConAu 129*
Goldstein, Robin Ellen 1958- *WhoAmW 91*
Goldstein, Rodney Louis 1952- *WhoEmL 91*
Goldstein, Ronald Erwin 1933- *WhoSSW 91*
Goldstein, Samuel Jack 1952- *WhoWor 91*
Goldstein, Samuel R. 1918- *WhoAm 90*
Goldstein, Sandra *WhoAmW 91*
Goldstein, Sheldon 1951- *WhoAmA 91*
Goldstein, Shirley Lila 1911- *St&PR 91*
Goldstein, Sidney 1927- *WhoAm 90*
Goldstein, Sol J *BiDrAPA 89*
Goldstein, Stanley P. 1934- *St&PR 91, WhoE 91*
Goldstein, Stanley Philip 1923- *WhoAm 90*
Goldstein, Stephen Barry 1947- *WhoAm 90*
Goldstein, Stephen Hillel 1951- *WhoEmL 91*
Goldstein, Stephen R 1938- *ConAu 30NR*
Goldstein, Steven *WhoAm 90*
Goldstein, Steven Jeffrey 1948- *WhoE 91*
Goldstein, Sumner I *BiDrAPA 89*
Goldstein, Susanna 1951- *BiDrAPA 89*
Goldstein, Sydney 1903-1989 *BioIn 16*
Goldstein, Sylvia Beatrice 1919- *WhoAmW 91*
Goldstein, Sylvia W. 1919- *St&PR 91*
Goldstein, Thomas 1944- *WhoSSW 91*
Goldstein, Vida 1869-1949 *FemiCLE*
Goldstein, William L. 1928- *St&PR 91*
Goldstein, William Marks 1935- *WhoAm 90*
Goldstein, William N 1943- *BiDrAPA 89*
Goldstein, William Steven 1941- *St&PR 91*
Goldstick, Thomas Karl 1934- *WhoAm 90*
Goldsticker, Ralph Philip 1952- *St&PR 91*
Goldstine, Abner D. 1929- *St&PR 91*
Goldstine, Herman Heine 1913- *WhoAm 90, WhoE 91*
Goldstine, Jonathan Heine 1959- *WhoSSW 91*
Goldstine, Sandra Dawn 1940- *WhoSSW 91, WhoWor 91*
Goldstine, Stephen Joseph 1937- *WhoAm 90*
Goldston, Barbara M. Harral 1937- *WhoAmW 91, WhoWor 91*
Goldston, Margaret Nell Stumpf 1932- *IntWWM 90*
Goldston, Mark *BioIn 16*
Goldston, Nathaniel R., III *BioIn 16*
Goldston, Robert Conroy 1927- *AuBYP 90*
Goldston, Stephen Eugene 1931- *WhoAm 90*
Goldston, William Frank 1947- *St&PR 91*
Goldstone, Allen Richard 1952- *St&PR 91*
Goldstone, Anthony Keith 1944- *IntWWM 90*
Goldstone, David Joseph 1929- *WhoWor 91*
Goldstone, Harmon Hendricks 1911- *WhoAm 90*
Goldstone, James 1931- *BioIn 16*
Goldstone, Jeffrey 1933- *WhoAm 90*
Goldstone, Lawrence A. *TwCCr&M 91*
Goldstone, Mark Lewis 1959- *WhoEmL 91*
Goldstone, Nancy Bazelon *BioIn 16*
Goldstone, Sanford 1926- *WhoAm 90*
Goldstrand, Dennis Joseph 1952- *WhoEmL 91*
Goldstrom, Donald *BioIn 16*
Goldsworthy, Earl E. 1934- *St&PR 91*
Goldszer, Bath-Sheba 1932- *WhoAmA 91*
Goldszmit, Henryk 1878-1942 *BioIn 16*
Goldthorpe, J.E. 1921- *ConAu 33NR*
Goldthorpe, John Clifford 1931- *WhoAm 90, WhoSSW 91*
Goldthorpe, Michael 1942- *IntWWM 90*
Goldthwait, John Turner 1921- *WhoAm 90*
Goldthwait, Sheldon F. 1938- *St&PR 91*
Goldthwaite, Anne Wilson 1869-1944 *BiDWomA*
Goldthwatt, Sheldon Forrest, Jr. 1938- *St&PR 91*
Goldwaser, Alberto Mario 1951- *BiDrAPA 89*
Goldwasser, Donald L. 1932- *St&PR 91*
Goldwasser, Eugene 1922- *WhoAm 90*
Goldwasser, Judith Wax 1944- *WhoWrEP 89*
Goldwasser, Ralph A. 1947- *St&PR 91*
Goldwasser, Robert Ellis 1945- *St&PR 91*
Goldwater, Allen *BiDrAPA 89*
Goldwater, Barry M. 1909- *BioIn 16, WorAlBi*
Goldwater, John L. 1916- *ConAu 131, WhoAm 90*
Goldwater, Leonard John 1903- *WhoAm 90*
Goldwater, Louise Isabel 1952- *BiDrAPA 89*
Goldwater, Richard 1946- *WhoAm 90*
Goldwater, Richard M. 1918-1989 *BioIn 16*
Goldwater, Richard P *BiDrAPA 89*
Goldwater, Robert 1907-1973 *WhoAmA 91N*
Goldwater, Robert 1952- *ODwPR 91*
Goldwater, Walter Eugene 1944- *BiDrAPA 89*
Goldwater, William Henry 1921- *WhoE 91*
Goldway, David *NewYTBS 90*
Goldwhite, Harold 1931- *WhoAm 90*
Goldwire, Sheila 1945- *BiDrAPA 89*
Goldwitz, Susan 1949- *WhoWrEP 89*
Goldwurm, Jean *NewYTBS 90*
Goldwyn, Craig D. 1949- *WhoE 91, WhoWrEP 89*
Goldwyn, Judith S. 1940- *WhoE 91*
Goldwyn, Ralph Norman 1925- *WhoAm 90, WhoWor 91*
Goldwyn, Robert M. 1930- *WhoWrEP 89*
Goldwyn, Samuel 1882-1974 *BioIn 16, WorAlBi*
Goldwyn, Samuel, Jr. *BioIn 16*
Goldwyn, Samuel, Jr. 1926- *ConTFT 8*
Goldwyn, Samuel John, Jr. 1926- *WhoAm 90*
Goldwyn, Sheree Diane 1955- *St&PR 91*
Goldzband, Melvin G 1929- *BiDrAPA 89*
Gole, Adriaan *PenDiDA 89*
Gole, Cornelius *PenDiDA 89*
Gole, Pierre 1620?-1684 *PenDiDA 89*
Golec, Janusz Stanislaw 1959- *WhoE 91*
Golec, Stanislaw 1956- *BiDrAPA 89*
Golechha, Gajraj R 1941- *BiDrAPA 89*
Goleizovsky, Kasyan *BioIn 16*
Golembeski, Jerome J. 1931- *St&PR 91*
Golembeski, Jerome John 1931- *WhoAm 90*
Golembieski, Michael Edward 1946- *WhoAm 90*
Golembiewski, Robert Thomas 1932- *WhoAm 90, WhoWrEP 89*
Golemme, Richard E. 1955- *St&PR 91*
Golemo, Stanley Michael, Jr. 1938- *St&PR 91*
Golemon, Albert Sidney 1904- *WhoAm 90*
Golenbock, Peter 1946- *Ballpl 90*
Goler, Karl Andrew 1950- *WhoSSW 91*
Goler, Robert 1956- *WhoAmA 91*
Goley, Frank Renfro 1933- *St&PR 91*
Goley, Mary Anne 1945- *WhoAmA 91, WhoE 91*
Golgi, Camillo 1843-1926 *WorAlBi*
Goli, Veeraindar 1954- *BiDrAPA 89*
Golia, Gerald E. 1945- *St&PR 91*
Golia, Mary Ann 1957- *WhoAmW 91*
Goliat, Mike 1925- *Ballpl 90*
Golieb, Howard A. *BioIn 16*
Goligher, Kathleen 1898- *EncPaPR 91*
Golightly, Cecelia King 1936- *WhoAmW 91*
Golightly, David Frederick 1948- *IntWWM 90*
Golightly, Donald Edward 1942- *WhoAm 90*
Golightly, Henry O. 1911- *St&PR 91*

Golightly, Lena Mills *WhoAm 90*
Golik, Donald Edward 1943- *St&PR 91*
Golikov, Filipp Ivanovich 1900-1980 *BioIn 16*
Golikov, Ivan Ivanovich 1735-1801 *BioIn 16*
Golin, Albert 1928- *BiDrAPA 89*
Golin, Alvin 1929- *ODwPR 91*
Golin, Gratsiana *BiDrAPA 89*
Golin, Milton 1921- *WhoWrEP 89*
Golinger, Ronald Clark 1942- *BiDrAPA 89*
Golinkin, Joseph Webster 1896-1977 *WhoAmA 91N*
Golinkin, Webster Fowler 1951- *St&PR 91*
Golino, Valeria *BioIn 16*
Golinski, Joseph John 1955- *St&PR 91*
Golitsyn, Georgiy 1935- *WhoWor 91*
Golitz, Loren Eugene 1941- *WhoAm 90*
Goll, Claire 1891-1977 *EncCoWW*
Goll, Reinhold Weimar 1897- *AuBYP 90*
Goll, Traugott Konrad Hans 1947- *WhoWor 91*
Gollan, Frank 1909-1988 *BioIn 16*
Gollancz, Victor 1893-1967 *BioIn 16*
Golland, John 1942- *IntWWM 90*
Gollberg, Harold R 1936- *BiDrAPA 89*
Golle, Adriaan *PenDiDA 89*
Golle, Cornelius *PenDiDA 89*
Golle, Pierre 1620?-1684 *PenDiDA 89*
Gollehon, Joe W. 1951- *ODwPR 91*
Goller, Norman James 1930- *St&PR 91*
Goller, Sue-Gray 1951- *WhoAmW 91*
Golley, Dean W *BiDrAPA 89*
Gollin, Albert Edwin 1930- *WhoAm 90*
Gollin, Joshua A 1905- *WhoAmA 91N*
Gollin, Stuart Allen 1941- *WhoAm 90*
Gollin, Susanne Merle 1953- *WhoAmW 91*
Gollings, Frank J. 1940- *St&PR 91*
Gollis, Elaine Sandra 1938- *WhoAmW 91*
Golliver, Robert Russell 1935- *St&PR 91*
Gollner, Marie Louise 1932- *IntWWM 90, WhoAm 90*
Gollner, Theodor 1929- *IntWWM 90*
Gollob, Herman *BioIn 16*
Gollob, Herman Cohen 1930- *WhoAm 90*
Gollob, Marvin E. 1931- *St&PR 91*
Gollobin, Leonard Paul 1928- *WhoAm 90*
Gollomb, Joseph 1881-1950 *AuBYP 90*
Gollon, Barbara Ann 1944- *WhoAmW 91*
Gollong, Paul Bernhard Werner 1916- *WhoAm 90*
Golloway, Glenn G 1925- *BiDrAPA 89*
Gollrad, Bette *ODwPR 91*
Gollub, Jerry *WhoAm 90*
Gollut, Christophe *BioIn 16*
Golman, Jeffrey A. 1955- *WhoAm 90*
Goloby, George William, Jr. 1949- *WhoSSW 91*
Golodner, Adam Marc 1959- *WhoEmL 91*
Golodner, Jack 1931- *WhoAm 90*
Golodner, Linda Fowler 1940- *WhoE 91, WhoWor 91*
Golomb, Claire 1928- *WhoAmW 91*
Golomb, David Leonard Dan 1921- *WhoAm 90*
Golomb, Frederick Martin 1924- *WhoAm 90, WhoWor 91*
Golomb, George Edwin 1947- *WhoEmL 91*
Golomb, Harvey Morris 1943- *WhoAm 90*
Golomb, Richard Moss 1958- *WhoE 91*
Golomb, Solomon Wolf 1932- *WhoAm 90*
Golomski, William Arthur J. *WhoAm 90*
Golonka, Sheila Lorraine 1958- *WhoAmW 91*
Golosow, Nikolas *BiDrAPA 89*
Golovchenko, Jene Andrew 1946- *WhoAm 90*
Golovinsky, Grigory 1923- *IntWWM 90*
Gols, A. George 1928- *St&PR 91*
Golschmann, Vladimir 1893-1972 *PenDiMP*
Golson, Benny 1929- *BioIn 16*
Golson, G. Barry 1944- *ConAu 33NR*
Golson, George Barry 1944- *WhoWrEP 89*
Goltare, Robert Brian 1949- *WhoEmL 91*
Golter, Harry 1924- *WhoAm 90*
Goltermann, Carl William 1952- *WhoEmL 91*
Goltra, David Dwight, Jr. 1954- *WhoSSW 91*
Goltz, Alan 1947- *WhoAm 90*
Goltz, Christel 1912- *IntWWM 90, PenDiMP*
Goltz, Dave 1949- *Ballpl 90*
Goltz, Robert William 1923- *WhoAm 90*
Goltzius, Hendrick 1558-1616? *IntDcAA 90*
Goltzman, David 1944- *WhoAm 90*
Golub, Alan 1939- *WhoAm 90*
Golub, Barbara Lewis *BioIn 16*
Golub, Bennett W. 1957- *St&PR 91*
Golub, David 1950- *IntWWM 90*
Golub, David S *BiDrAPA 89*
Golub, Gary E. 1943- *St&PR 91*
Golub, Gene Howard 1932- *WhoAm 90*
Golub, Harvey 1939- *WhoAm 90*
Golub, Howard V. 1945- *St&PR 91*
Golub, Howard Victor 1945- *WhoAm 90*
Golub, James Robert 1928- *WhoE 91*
Golub, Jeff *BioIn 16*
Golub, Lawrence Eric 1959- *WhoE 91*
Golub, Leon Albert 1922- *BioIn 16, WhoAm 90, WhoAmA 91*
Golub, Leon M *BiDrAPA 89*
Golub, Lewis 1931- *WhoAm 90*
Golub, Marcia Helene 1953- *WhoWrEP 89*
Golub, Neil *St&PR 91*
Golub, Rachelle Elias 1952- *St&PR 91*
Golub, Richard *BioIn 16*
Golub, Sharon Bramson 1937- *WhoAmW 91*
Golub, Sheldon 1937- *BiDrAPA 89, WhoE 91*
Golub, Stephen Bruce 1941- *WhoAm 90*
Golub, William 1904- *St&PR 91*
Golub, William Weldon 1914- *WhoAm 90*
Golubic, Theodore 1928- *WhoAmA 91*
Golubjatnikov, Ole 1930- *WhoE 91*
Golubkina, Anna Semionova 1864-1927 *BiDWomA*
Golubock, Harvey L. 1942- *St&PR 91*
Golubock, Harvey Lewis 1942- *WhoE 91*
Golumbeck, Carl Timothy *BiDrAPA 89*
Golusin, Millard R. 1947- *WhoEmL 91*
Goluskin, Norman Lewis 1938- *St&PR 91*
Golway, Thomas William 1956- *WhoEmL 91*
Golwyn, Daniel H *BiDrAPA 89*
Golz, James F. 1947- *St&PR 91*
Golz, Ronald A. 1934- *St&PR 91*
Golz, Ronald Alfred 1934- *WhoAm 90*
Golz, William C., Jr. 1947- *St&PR 91*
Golzadeh, Mohammad Mehdi 1949- *WhoWor 91*
Golzman, Ita Hass 1951- *WhoAmW 91*
Gom, Leona 1946- *FemiCLE*
Goman, Cynthia Marie 1957- *WhoEmL 91*
Gombach, Raymond 1937- *St&PR 91*
Gomberg, Edith S. Lisansky 1920- *WhoAm 90*
Gomberg, Ephraim R 1904- *BiDrAPA 89*
Gomberg, Henry Jacob 1918- *WhoAm 90*
Gomberg, Herbert L 1940- *BiDrAPA 89*
Gomberg, Ira A. 1943- *St&PR 91*
Gomberg, Jack Alan *BiDrAPA 89*
Gomberg, Ralph 1921- *IntWWM 90*
Gombert, Karl E. 1933- *IntWWM 90*
Gombo, Israel 1932- *WhoE 91*
Gombos, Bruce William 1950- *WhoE 91*
Gombos, Robert Steven 1943- *St&PR 91*
Gombosuren, Tserenpilyn 1943- *WhoWor 91*
Gombrich, E H 1909- *ConAu 32NR*
Gombrich, Ernst 1909- *WhoWor 91*
Gombrowicz, Witold *BioIn 16*
Gombrowicz, Witold 1904-1969 *EuWr 12*
Gomedella, Dominick George 1936- *WhoSSW 91*
Gomeldon, Jane *FemiCLE*
Gomer, Albert 1923- *St&PR 91*
Gomer, Richard Hans 1956- *WhoSSW 91*
Gomer, Robert 1924- *WhoAm 90*
Gomersall, Ann 1751?-1834? *FemiCLE*
Gomersall, Earl Raymond 1930- *WhoAm 90, WhoWor 91*
Gomery, Douglas 1945- *WhoE 91, WhoWrEP 89*
Gomes, Alair de Oliveira 1921- *EncO&P 3*
Gomes, Albert 1911-1978 *BioIn 16*
Gomes, Brian E. 1951- *St&PR 91*
Gomes, Jim A. 1940- *St&PR 91*
Gomes, Peter John 1942- *WhoAm 90*
Gomes, Richard David 1937- *St&PR 91*
Gomes, Wayne Reginald 1938- *WhoAm 90*
Gomes, Zachary 1955- *St&PR 91*
Gomez, Adalberto Palma 1951- *WhoWor 91*
Gomez, Adelina Marquez 1930- *WhoHisp 91*
Gomez, Adelina S. 1929- *WhoHisp 91*
Gomez, Agustin Alejo, Jr. 1942- *BiDrAPA 89*
Gomez, Alberto Perez *ConAu 130*
Gomez, Alfred *WhoHisp 91*
Gomez, Alfredo C. 1939- *WhoHisp 91*
Gomez, Alseny Rene *WhoWor 91*
Gomez, Andy Santiago 1954- *WhoHisp 91*
Gomez, Angel G 1931- *BiDrAPA 89*
Gomez, Antonio A. 1945- *WhoHisp 91*
Gomez, Armelio Juan 1947- *WhoHisp 91*
Gomez, Arturo A *BiDrAPA 89*
Gomez, Aurelia F. 1937- *WhoHisp 91*
Gomez, Ben *WhoHisp 91*
Gomez, Blanca M G A *BiDrAPA 89*
Gomez, Carlos F. 1958- *ConAu 129*
Gomez, Carol Vartuli 1950- *WhoAmW 91*
Gomez, Charles Lawrence 1934- *WhoHisp 91*
Gomez, Consuelo Nunez 1938- *BiDrAPA 89*
Gomez, Cynthia Ann 1958- *WhoHisp 91*
Gomez, Daniel B. 1936- *St&PR 91*
Gomez, Edward Casimiro 1938- *WhoAm 90, WhoHisp 91*
Gomez, Efrain A *BiDrAPA 89*
Gomez, Elena Rosa 1952- *BiDrAPA 89*
Gomez, Elias Galvan 1934- *WhoHisp 91*
Gomez, Elsa *WhoAm 90*
Gomez, Elsa 1938- *WhoHisp 91*
Gomez, Ernesto Alvarado 1946- *WhoHisp 91*
Gomez, Estevan *EncCRAm*
Gomez, Evaristo 1930- *BiDrAPA 89*
Gomez, Florangela 1947- *WhoWor 91*
Gomez, Francis D. 1941- *WhoHisp 91*
Gomez, Francis Dean 1941- *WhoAm 90, WhoWor 91*
Gomez, Gary B. 1947- *WhoSSW 91*
Gomez, George *WhoHisp 91*
Gomez, Glynn 1945- *BioIn 16*
Gomez, Guillermo G. 1933- *WhoHisp 91*
Gomez, Humberto 1929- *BiDrAPA 89*
Gomez, Isabel 1941- *WhoHisp 91*
Gomez, Jaime Armando *WhoHisp 91*
Gomez, Jairo 1944- *BiDrAPA 89*
Gomez, Jill 1942- *IntWWM 90, PenDiMP*
Gomez, John R., Sr. 1923- *WhoHisp 91*
Gomez, Jorge 1936- *BiDrAPA 89*
Gomez, Jose Felix 1949- *WhoHisp 91*
Gomez, Jose Francisco Pena *BioIn 16*
Gomez, Jose Miguel 1858-1921 *BioIn 16*
Gomez, Jose Pantaleon, III 1956- *WhoHisp 91*
Gomez, Juan Vicente 1857?-1935 *BioIn 16*
Gomez, Julian R 1933- *BiDrAPA 89*
Gomez, Julie 1946- *WhoAmW 91*
Gomez, Laureano *BiDrAPA 89*
Gomez, Laureano 1889-1965 *BioIn 16*
Gomez, Lawrence J. 1946- *WhoHisp 91*
Gomez, Lawrence T. 1940- *WhoHisp 91*
Gomez, Lefty 1908-1988 *Ballpl 90 [port]*
Gomez, Lefty 1908?-1989 *BioIn 16*
Gomez, Lefty 1909-1989 *AnObit 1989, WhoHisp 91N*
Gomez, Leonel, Jr. 1965- *WhoHisp 91*
Gomez, LeRoy Marcial 1934- *WhoHisp 91*
Gomez, Lloyd Edward 1933- *St&PR 91*
Gomez, Luis 1951- *Ballpl 90*
Gomez, Luis Oscar 1943- *WhoAm 90, WhoHisp 91*
Gomez, Madeleine *BiDrAPA 89*
Gomez, Madeleine Yvonne 1956- *WhoAmW 91*
Gomez, Manuel 1934-1988 *AnObit 1988*
Gomez, Manuel Rodriguez 1928- *WhoAm 90*
Gomez, Margaret Juarez 1944- *WhoHisp 91*
Gomez, Margarita 1940- *WhoHisp 91*
Gomez, Maria Cristina *BioIn 16*
Gomez, Mario J. 1956- *WhoHisp 91*
Gomez, Martin *BioIn 16*
Gomez, Martin J. 1951- *WhoHisp 91*
Gomez, Mary Louise 1950- *WhoHisp 91*
Gomez, Max *BioIn 16*
Gomez, Maximo 1836-1905 *BioIn 16*
Gomez, Medardo *BioIn 16*
Gomez, Michael 1942- *WhoE 91*
Gomez, Michael R. *ODwPR 91*
Gomez, Miguel Mariano 1890-1951 *BioIn 16*
Gomez, Orlando A. *WhoHisp 91*
Gomez, Oscar C. 1946- *St&PR 91, WhoHisp 91*
Gomez, Pedro Felix *BiDrAPA 89*
Gomez, Pedro Judas 1962- *WhoHisp 91*
Gomez, Pete *WhoHisp 91*
Gomez, Preston 1923- *Ballpl 90*
Gomez, Rafael 1946- *BiDrAPA 89*
Gomez, Rafael Leandro 1944- *WhoSSW 91*
Gomez, Ralph *NewYTBS 90*
Gomez, Raul Rocha *BiDrAPA 89*
Gomez, Raymond M. 1951- *ODwPR 91*
Gomez, Richard A., Sr. 1954- *WhoHisp 91*
Gomez, Richard Louis *BiDrAPA 89*
Gomez, Rod J. *WhoHisp 91*
Gomez, Rogelio Roberto 1950- *WhoWrEP 89*
Gomez, Rose 1946- *BiDrAPA 89*
Gomez, Roy Clement 1943- *WhoSSW 91*
Gomez, Ruben 1927- *Ballpl 90*
Gomez, Rudolph *WhoHisp 91*
Gomez, Rudolph 1930- *WhoAm 90*
Gomez, Rudolph Vasquez 1944- *WhoHisp 91*
Gomez, Ruth 1938- *WhoHisp 91*
Gomez, Sharon Jeanneene 1954- *WhoHisp 91*
Gomez, Tony *WhoHisp 91*
Gomez, Vernon Louis 1909-1989 *WhoHisp 91N*
Gomez, Victor J. 1941- *WhoHisp 91*
Gomez, Virginia 1934- *WhoAmW 91*
Gomez-Alba, Jose *BiDrAPA 89*
Gomez-Baisden, Gladys Esther 1943- *WhoHisp 91*
Gomez-Bezares, Fernando 1956- *WhoWor 91*
Gomez-Calderon, Javier 1948- *WhoHisp 91*
Gomez Carrillo, Enrique 1873-1927 *BioIn 16*
Gomez-Carrion, Patricia Jane *BiDrAPA 89*
Gomez de Avellaneda, Maria Gertrudis 1814-1873 *EncCoWW*
Gomez de Avellaneda y Arteaga, Gertrudis 1814-1873 *BioIn 16*
Gomez de la Serna, Ramon 1888-1963 *HispWr 90*
Gomez Gil, Alfredo 1936- *WhoHisp 91*
Gomez-Martinez, Jose Luis 1943- *WhoHisp 91, WhoSSW 91*
Gomez Ojea, Carmen 1945- *EncCoWW*
Gomez Palacio, Enrique 1947- *WhoHisp 91*
Gomez-Quinones, Juan *BioIn 16*
Gomez-Quinones, Juan 1940- *WhoHisp 91*
Gomez-Quinones, Juan 1942- *ConAu 131, HispWr 90*
Gomez-Quintero, Ela R. 1928- *WhoHisp 91*
Gomez-Quiroz, Juan 1939- *WhoAm 90, WhoHisp 91*
Gomez-Quiroz, Juan Manuel 1939- *WhoAmA 91*
Gomez-Rivera, Jose *BiDrAPA 89*
Gomez-Rodriguez, Manuel 1940- *WhoAm 90, WhoHisp 91*
Gomez Rosa, Alexis 1950- *HispWr 90, WhoHisp 91*
Gomez-Sicre, Jose 1916- *WhoAmA 91*
Gomez-Sicre, Jose Romualdo 1916- *WhoAm 90*
Gomez-Tumpkins-Preston, Cheryl Annette 1954- *WhoHisp 91*
Gomez-Vega, Ibis del Carmen 1952- *WhoHisp 91*
Gomezplata, Albert 1930- *WhoAm 90, WhoHisp 91*
Gomi, Taro 1945- *AuBYP 90, SmATA 64 [port]*
Gomide, Fernando de Mello 1927- *WhoWor 91*
Gomilak, Thomas A., Jr. 1932- *St&PR 91*
Gominger, Harry Douglas 1947- *WhoE 91, WhoEmL 91*
Gomm, Peter Albert 1931- *St&PR 91*
Gomm, Richard *PenDiDA 89*
Gomm, William 1698-1780 *PenDiDA 89*
Gomme, Donald 1916- *PenDiDA 89*
Gomme, Ebenezer *PenDiDA 89*
Gomolski, Thomas Frank 1947- *St&PR 91*
Gomory, Ralph E. *BioIn 16*
Gomory, Ralph Edward 1929- *St&PR 91, WhoAm 90*
Gompers, Paul *BioIn 16*
Gompers, Samuel 1850-1924 *BioIn 16, WorAlBi*
Gompers, William C. 1949- *St&PR 91*
Gompertz, Rolf 1927- *WhoWrEP 89*
Gompf, Arthur Milton 1909- *St&PR 91*
Gompf, Robert Ernest 1957- *WhoSSW 91*
Gomulka, Stanislaw 1940- *WhoWor 91*
Gomza, Alexander 1922- *WhoE 91*
Goncalves, Donald J. 1958- *ODwPR 91*
Goncalves, Fatima *WhoHisp 91*
Goncalves, Justino Mendes 1933- *WhoWor 91*
Gonce, Nancy Cummings 1939- *WhoAmW 91*
Goncebate, Rodolfo Sixto 1945- *WhoWor 91*
Gonchar, Joel 1943- *BiDrAPA 89*
Gonchar, Rosalie James 1927- *WhoAmW 91, WhoSSW 91*
Goncharoff, Jamie W. 1959- *WhoEmL 91*
Goncharov, Ivan 1812-1891 *WorAlBi*
Goncharov, Ivan Aleksandrovich 1812-1891 *BioIn 16*
Goncharova, Natalia Sergeevna 1881-1962 *BiDWomA*
Goncharova, Nataliia Sergeevna 1881-1962 *BioIn 16*
Goncher, Susan Ellen 1950- *WhoAmW 91*
Goncourt, Edmond Louis Antoine Huot De 1822-1896 *WorAlBi*
Goncourt, Jules Alfred Huot De 1830-1870 *WorAlBi*
Goncz, Arpad 1922- *WhoWor 91*
Gonda, Clara *BiDrAPA 89*
Gonda, Harry H 1915- *BiDrAPA 89*
Gonda, Janos 1932- *IntWWM 90*
Gonda, Louis Leslie 1948- *St&PR 91*
Gondek, Alyson *ODwPR 91*
Gondek, Janice Ruth 1934- *St&PR 91*
Gondek, Robert Joseph 1943- *St&PR 91*
Gondek, Therese Marie 1950- *WhoEmL 91*
Gondelach, Franz 1663-1717 *PenDiDA 89*
Gonder, Jesse 1936- *Ballpl 90*
Gondo, Hiroshi 1940- *Ballpl 90*
Gondo, Yasuo 1926- *WhoWor 91*
Gondoin, Jacques 1737-1818 *PenDiDA 89*
Gondos, Gordon Morris 1944- *BiDrAPA 89*
Gondosch, Linda 1944- *BioIn 16*
Gondosch, Linda Ann 1944- *WhoWrEP 89*
Gonella, Nat 1908- *OxCPMus*
Gong, Alice Kim 1954- *WhoSSW 91*
Gong, Dong 1850?-1900? *BioIn 16*
Gong, Edmond Joseph 1930- *WhoAm 90*
Gong, Pearl Jade *BiDrAPA 89*
Gongaware, Donald Francis 1935- *St&PR 91, WhoAm 90*
Gongora, Carlos de Siguenza y 1645-1700 *BioIn 16*
Gongora, Jaime 1939- *WhoWor 91*

Gongora, Leonel *WhoAmA 91*
Gongora, Maedale 1935- *WhoAmW 91*
Gongora-Trejos, Enrique 1931- *WhoWor 91*
Gongora Y Argote, Luis De 1561-1627 *WorAlBi*
Gongos, Laura *ODwPR 91*
Goni, Paul 1929- *WhoHisp 91*
Gonia, Charles 1925- *St&PR 91, WhoAm 90*
Gonick, Harvey Craig 1930- *WhoAm 90*
Gonick, Paul 1930- *WhoAm 90*
Gonior, Thomas H 1932- *BiDrAPA 89*
Gonne, Maud 1865?-1953 *FemiCLE*
Gonne, Maud 1866-1953 *BioIn 16*
Gonne, Maude 1866-1953 *WorAlBi*
Gonnella, Joseph Salvator 1934- *WhoAm 90*
Gonnella, Nina Celeste 1953- *WhoAmW 91*
Gonnerman, Charney Louise 1945- *WhoAmW 91*
Gonnerman, Mary F. 1927- *St&PR 91*
Gonnerman, Mary Frances 1927- *WhoAm 90*
Gonneville, Michel 1950- *IntWWM 90*
Gonnoud, Urban *BioIn 16, NewYTBS 90*
Gonos, Stephanie Suzanne 1956- *WhoEmL 91*
Gonring, Matthew P. *ODwPR 91*
Gonsalves, Donald John 1931- *St&PR 91*
Gonsalves, Gregory Jay 1968- *WhoE 91*
Gonsalves, Henry Edward 1953- *St&PR 91*
Gonsalves, Lenine Mark 1927- *WhoE 91*
Gonsalves, Paul G. 1959- *WhoE 91*
Gonsalves, Victor L. 1952- *St&PR 91*
Gonsalves-Ebrahim, Lilian Veronica *BiDrAPA 89*
Gonsalves-Wendt, Diana Lynn 1951- *WhoEmL 91*
Gonser, Thomas Howard 1938- *WhoAm 90*
Gonseth, Walter C. 1931- *St&PR 91*
Gonshak, Isabelle Lee 1932- *WhoSSW 91*
Gonshor, Harry 1928- *WhoE 91*
Gonson, S. Donald 1936- *WhoWor 91*
Gontcharova, Nathalie 1881-1962 *BioIn 16*
Gonthier, Charles Doherty 1928- *WhoAm 90*
Gontier, Jean Roger 1927- *WhoWor 91*
Gonul, Fusun Feride 1959- *WhoE 91*
Gonya, Patrice Yeager 1951- *WhoAmW 91*
Gonye, Peter Kallay 1955- *WhoE 91*
Gonyea, Edward Francis 1932- *WhoAm 90*
Gonzales, A. Nick 1946- *WhoHisp 91*
Gonzales, Alex D. 1927- *WhoHisp 91*
Gonzales, Alexis 1931- *WhoAm 90, WhoWor 91*
Gonzales, Alfred *WhoHisp 91*
Gonzales, Andre Agustine 1943- *WhoE 91*
Gonzales, Betty J. *WhoHisp 91*
Gonzales, Carlotta 1910- *WhoAmA 91*
Gonzales, Ciriaco *WhoHisp 91*
Gonzales, Corky 1929- *BioIn 16*
Gonzales, Diana Espana 1947- *WhoHisp 91*
Gonzales, Dorothy 1943- *WhoHisp 91*
Gonzales, Edward C. 1930- *St&PR 91*
Gonzales, Eloisa Aragon 1952- *WhoHisp 91*
Gonzales, Eugene 1925- *BioIn 16*
Gonzales, Eva 1849-1883 *BiDWomA, BioIn 16*
Gonzales, Farley Macam 1957- *WhoWor 91*
Gonzales, Francisco 1947- *WhoHisp 91*
Gonzales, Fred Patrick 1947- *St&PR 91*
Gonzales, Isabel *WhoHisp 91*
Gonzales, Jake, Jr. 1928- *WhoHisp 91*
Gonzales, Jeffrey Charles 1954- *WhoEmL 91*
Gonzales, Joe 1949- *WhoHisp 91*
Gonzales, Joe Anthony 1957- *WhoHisp 91*
Gonzales, John Edmond 1924- *WhoAm 90*
Gonzales, Jose *WhoHisp 91*
Gonzales, Juan Jose Torres 1921?-1976 *BioIn 16*
Gonzales, Juan L., Jr. 1945- *WhoHisp 91*
Gonzales, Junius John 1959- *BiDrAPA 89, WhoEmL 91*
Gonzales, Liz 1957- *WhoHisp 91*
Gonzales, Lucille Contreras 1937- *WhoAmW 91*
Gonzales, Marcia *WhoHisp 91*
Gonzales, Marie Guadalupe 1963- *WhoEmL 91*
Gonzales, Maya Bonoan *BiDrAPA 89*
Gonzales, Michael David 1951- *WhoHisp 91*
Gonzales, Mike 1890-1977 *Ballpl 90*
Gonzales, Pancho 1928- *BioIn 16, WhoHisp 91*
Gonzales, Patricia Buck 1940- *WhoAmW 91*
Gonzales, Paul Villareal 1952- *St&PR 91*
Gonzales, Pedro 1938- *Ballpl 90*
Gonzales, Philip Agustin 1951- *IntWWM 90*
Gonzales, Rebecca 1946- *WhoHisp 91*
Gonzales, Richard Alonzo 1928- *WhoHisp 91*
Gonzales, Richard Robert 1945- *WhoEmL 91*
Gonzales, Richard S. 1954- *WhoHisp 91*
Gonzales, Roberta Marie *WhoHisp 91*
Gonzales, Rodolfo 1929- *BioIn 16*
Gonzales, Romulo F 1925- *BiDrAPA 89*
Gonzales, Ron 1951- *WhoHisp 91*
Gonzales, Sylvia Alicia 1943- *HispWr 90*
Gonzales, Tomasa Calixta 1948- *WhoHisp 91*
Gonzales, Yolanda *WhoHisp 91*
Gonzales Martin, Marcelo 1918- *WhoWor 91*
Gonzales-Peralta, Carlos Ricardo 1951- *WhoWor 91*
Gonzales Rogers, Donna Jean 1959- *WhoHisp 91*
Gonzales-Thornell, Consuelo *WhoHisp 91*
Gonzalez, Abel Arturo *BiDrAPA 89*
Gonzalez, Aida Argentina 1940- *WhoHisp 91*
Gonzalez, Alberto 1952- *BiDrAPA 89*
Gonzalez, Alberto Luis 1955- *BiDrAPA 89*
Gonzalez, Alejandro 1960- *WhoHisp 91*
Gonzalez, Alex Ramon 1932- *WhoHisp 91*
Gonzalez, Alexander 1945- *WhoHisp 91*
Gonzalez, Alexander G. 1952- *WhoHisp 91*
Gonzalez, Alfonso, Jr. 1938- *WhoHisp 91*
Gonzalez, Andrew Manuel 1927- *St&PR 91, WhoHisp 91*
Gonzalez, Angel 1925- *BioIn 16*
Gonzalez, Angela 1947- *WhoHisp 91*
Gonzalez, Annabella Quintanilla 1941- *WhoHisp 91*
Gonzalez, Arleen Caballero 1957- *WhoHisp 91*
Gonzalez, Armando L. *WhoHisp 91*
Gonzalez, Arthur Padilla 1954- *WhoAmA 91*
Gonzalez, Arturo G 1924- *BiDrAPA 89*
Gonzalez, Avelino Juan 1951- *WhoSSW 91*
Gonzalez, Benancio, Sr. 1949- *WhoSSW 91*
Gonzalez, Bernardo Antonio 1950- *WhoE 91, WhoHisp 91*
Gonzalez, Caleb 1929- *WhoHisp 91*
Gonzalez, Candelario Leonel 1934- *WhoSSW 91*
Gonzalez, Carlos 1905- *ArtLatA*
Gonzalez, Carlos 1956- *BiDrAPA 89*
Gonzalez, Carlos Alberto 1958- *WhoHisp 91*
Gonzalez, Carlos Juan 1945- *WhoHisp 91*
Gonzalez, Carlos Manuel 1946- *St&PR 91, WhoHisp 91*
Gonzalez, Carlos Miguel 1941- *WhoSSW 91*
Gonzalez, Carmen 1939- *IntWWM 90*
Gonzalez, Celedonio 1923- *BioIn 16*
Gonzalez, Cesar A. *HispWr 90*
Gonzalez, Cesar Augusto 1931- *WhoHisp 91*
Gonzalez, Constantino Jose 1956- *WhoHisp 91*
Gonzalez, Crispin, Jr. 1936- *WhoHisp 91*
Gonzalez, Cristina 1951- *WhoHisp 91*
Gonzalez, Dalmacio 1945- *IntWWM 90*
Gonzalez, Daniel J. 1946- *WhoHisp 91*
Gonzalez, Dario R. 1953- *WhoHisp 91*
Gonzalez, David John 1951- *WhoHisp 91*
Gonzalez, David Lawrence 1957- *WhoHisp 91*
Gonzalez, Deena J. 1952- *WhoHisp 91*
Gonzalez, Diana 1946- *WhoHisp 91*
Gonzalez, Diane Kathryn 1947- *WhoAmW 91*
Gonzalez, Domingo Santa Maria 1825-1889 *BioIn 16*
Gonzalez, Edgar 1924- *WhoHisp 91*
Gonzalez, Edgar R. 1957- *WhoHisp 91*
Gonzalez, Eduardo *WhoHisp 91*
Gonzalez, Eduardo Oscar *BiDrAPA 89*
Gonzalez, Edulfo 1943- *BiDrAPA 89*
Gonzalez, Efren William 1929- *WhoAm 90*
Gonzalez, Elena Isabel 1965- *WhoHisp 91*
Gonzalez, Elma 1942- *WhoHisp 91*
Gonzalez, Elmo *WhoHisp 91*
Gonzalez, Emilio 1903- *WhoAm 90*
Gonzalez, Ernest Paul 1937- *WhoHisp 91*
Gonzalez, Eugene Robert *WhoAm 90, WhoHisp 91, WhoWor 91*
Gonzalez, Felipe *BioIn 16*
Gonzalez, Fernando 1950- *Ballpl 90*
Gonzalez, Fernando E 1938- *BiDrAPA 89*
Gonzalez, Fernando L. 1954- *WhoHisp 91*
Gonzalez, Francisco Thomas *BiDrAPA 89*
Gonzalez, Frank, Jr. 1948- *WhoHisp 91*
Gonzalez, Frank Woodward 1951- *WhoHisp 91*
Gonzalez, Frederick Andrew 1951- *WhoE 91*
Gonzalez, Fredrick J. 1949- *WhoHisp 91*
Gonzalez, Gaston Guerra 1956- *WhoWor 91*
Gonzalez, Genaro 1949- *WhoHisp 91*
Gonzalez, Genaro, Jr. 1957- *WhoHisp 91*
Gonzalez, Georgina S. *WhoHisp 91*
Gonzalez, Gerardo M. 1950- *WhoHisp 91*
Gonzalez, Gerardo P *BiDrAPA 89*
Gonzalez, Gisela Alexandra 1949- *WhoAmW 91*
Gonzalez, Gladys M. 1955- *WhoSSW 91*
Gonzalez, Graciela Maria *BiDrAPA 89*
Gonzalez, H. Bert 1954- *WhoSSW 91*
Gonzalez, Hector Hugo 1937- *WhoHisp 91*
Gonzalez, Hector R. 1933- *St&PR 91*
Gonzalez, Hector Xavier, Jr. 1956- *WhoHisp 91*
Gonzalez, Henry B. *BioIn 16*
Gonzalez, Henry Barbosa 1916- *WhoAm 90, WhoHisp 91, WhoSSW 91*
Gonzalez, Henry E., Jr. 1950- *WhoHisp 91*
Gonzalez, Henry William 1940- *IntWWM 90*
Gonzalez, Hernan 1949- *WhoSSW 91*
Gonzalez, Humberto Javier 1931- *BiDrAPA 89*
Gonzalez, James Raymond 1953- *WhoE 91*
Gonzalez, Jesse 1936- *St&PR 91*
Gonzalez, Jesus 1954- *BiDrAPA 89*
Gonzalez, Jim 1950- *WhoHisp 91*
Gonzalez, Joe Manuel 1950- *WhoWor 91*
Gonzalez, Joe Paul 1957- *WhoHisp 91*
Gonzalez, John E. *WhoHisp 91*
Gonzalez, Jorge A. 1952- *WhoHisp 91*
Gonzalez, Jorge Augusto 1932- *WhoHisp 91*
Gonzalez, Jose 1959- *WhoHisp 91*
Gonzalez, Jose Alejandro, Jr. 1931- *WhoAm 90, WhoHisp 91, WhoSSW 91*
Gonzalez, Jose Andrew 1953- *WhoEmL 91*
Gonzalez, Jose Antonio 1926- *BiDrAPA 89*
Gonzalez, Jose Antonio 1955- *BiDrAPA 89*
Gonzalez, Jose Froilan *BioIn 16*
Gonzalez, Jose Gamaliel 1933- *WhoAmA 91, WhoHisp 91*
Gonzalez, Jose Luis 1926- *ConAu 131, HispWr 90*
Gonzalez, Jose Luis 1939- *WhoHisp 91*
Gonzalez, Jose Manuel *BiDrAPA 89*
Gonzalez, Jose R. 1930- *WhoHisp 91*
Gonzalez, Jose Ramon 1951- *WhoE 91*
Gonzalez, Jose Victoriano 1887-1927 *BioIn 16*
Gonzalez, Joseph Frank 1941- *WhoHisp 91*
Gonzalez, Juan-Antonio 1950- *WhoHisp 91*
Gonzalez, Juan J 1945- *WhoAmA 91*
Gonzalez, Juan J. 1949- *WhoHisp 91*
Gonzalez, Juan Jesus 1951- *WhoSSW 91*
Gonzalez, Juan M *BiDrAPA 89*
Gonzalez, Juan Manuel, Sr. 1948- *WhoHisp 91*
Gonzalez, Juan Natalicio 1897-1966 *BioIn 16*
Gonzalez, Julio *BioIn 16*
Gonzalez, Julio 1876-1942 *IntDcAA 90*
Gonzalez, Julio 1935- *WhoSSW 91*
Gonzalez, Julio 1959- *Ballpl 90*
Gonzalez, Kenneth 1953- *WhoHisp 91*
Gonzalez, Kimberly Regina 1964- *WhoAmW 91, WhoEmL 91, WhoWor 91*
Gonzalez, Lauren Yvonne 1952- *WhoHisp 91*
Gonzalez, Lee *WhoHisp 91*
Gonzalez, Lino Isaac 1947- *WhoSSW 91*
Gonzalez, Lohr H. 1930- *WhoHisp 91*
Gonzalez, Lucas E. 1940- *WhoHisp 91*
Gonzalez, Luis Jorge 1936- *WhoHisp 91*
Gonzalez, Luis Jose 1942- *WhoHisp 91*
Gonzalez, Luis L. 1928- *WhoHisp 91*
Gonzalez, Luis Roberto *BiDrAPA 89*
Gonzalez, Luis Roberto 1952- *WhoE 91*
Gonzalez, Lynn Ammirato 1948- *WhoAmW 91*
Gonzalez, Macario Amador 1944- *WhoHisp 91*
Gonzalez, Manuel E. *WhoHisp 91*
Gonzalez, Margaret *WhoHisp 91*
Gonzalez, Margarita 1954- *WhoHisp 91*
Gonzalez, Maria Christina 1957- *WhoAmW 91*
Gonzalez, Maria Villar 1951- *WhoEmL 91*
Gonzalez, Mario 1936- *BiDrAPA 89*
Gonzalez, Mario J., Jr. 1941- *WhoHisp 91*
Gonzalez, Martha Alicia 1952- *WhoHisp 91*
Gonzalez, Martin 1929- *WhoHisp 91*
Gonzalez, Martin 1944- *WhoHisp 91*
Gonzalez, Martin Michael 1955- *WhoHisp 91*
Gonzalez, Mary Lou 1955- *WhoHisp 91*
Gonzalez, Mary Lou C. 1954- *WhoHisp 91*
Gonzalez, Mauricio Martinez 1945- *WhoAmA 91*
Gonzalez, Michael J. 1962- *WhoHisp 91*
Gonzalez, Mirta A. 1941- *WhoHisp 91*
Gonzalez, Mirza L. 1938- *WhoHisp 91*
Gonzalez, Nancie Loudon 1929- *WhoAm 90*
Gonzalez, Nicolas E. 1964- *WhoSSW 91*
Gonzalez, Nilda M 1957- *BiDrAPA 89*
Gonzalez, Nivia 1946- *BioIn 16, WhoHisp 91*
Gonzalez, Ondina Ester 1958- *WhoHisp 91*
Gonzalez, Orlando G. 1927- *St&PR 91*
Gonzalez, Pamela Louise 1946- *WhoEmL 91*
Gonzalez, Patricia 1958- *WhoAmA 91, WhoHisp 91*
Gonzalez, Paula 1932- *WhoAmW 91, WhoHisp 91*
Gonzalez, Pedro, Jr. 1945- *WhoHisp 91*
Gonzalez, Pedro J. 1895- *BioIn 16*
Gonzalez, Philip Albert 1946- *WhoE 91*
Gonzalez, Rafael C. 1942- *WhoHisp 91*
Gonzalez, Rafael Ceferino 1942- *WhoAm 90*
Gonzalez, Rafael Jesus 1935- *WhoHisp 91*
Gonzalez, Rafael Juvenal 1937- *BiDrAPA 89*
Gonzalez, Rafael Manuel *BiDrAPA 89*
Gonzalez, Ralph Edward 1961- *WhoHisp 91*
Gonzalez, Ralph P. 1955- *WhoHisp 91*
Gonzalez, Ramiro 1954- *WhoHisp 91*
Gonzalez, Ramon *BiDrAPA 89*
Gonzalez, Ramon Rafael, Jr. 1940- *WhoHisp 91*
Gonzalez, Raquel Maria 1952- *WhoEmL 91, WhoSSW 91*
Gonzalez, Raul A. 1940- *WhoHisp 91*
Gonzalez, Raul E *BiDrAPA 89*
Gonzalez, Raymond Emmanuel 1924- *BioIn 16, WhoHisp 91*
Gonzalez, Raymond L. 1939- *WhoHisp 91*
Gonzalez, Refugio A. 1947- *WhoHisp 91*
Gonzalez, Remigio G *BiDrAPA 89*
Gonzalez, Rene *BiDrAPA 89*
Gonzalez, Rene 1926- *BiDrAPA 89*
Gonzalez, Rene D. 1957- *WhoHisp 91*
Gonzalez, Ricardo A. 1946- *WhoHisp 91*
Gonzalez, Richard 1928- *WorAlBi*
Gonzalez, Richard Charles 1929- *WhoHisp 91*
Gonzalez, Richard D. 1932- *WhoHisp 91*
Gonzalez, Richard Peter 1942- *St&PR 91*
Gonzalez, Richard Rafael 1942- *WhoHisp 91*
Gonzalez, Robert J. *WhoHisp 91*
Gonzalez, Robert L. 1939- *WhoHisp 91*
Gonzalez, Roberto *BiDrAPA 89*
Gonzalez, Roberto 1951- *WhoHisp 91*
Gonzalez, Roberto-Juan 1953- *WhoHisp 91*
Gonzalez, Roberto Octavio 1950- *WhoHisp 91*
Gonzalez, Roger 1962- *WhoE 91*
Gonzalez, Romualdo 1947- *WhoHisp 91*
Gonzalez, Ronald 1952- *WhoAmA 91*
Gonzalez, Ronald Louis 1946- *WhoHisp 91*
Gonzalez, Rose T. 1934- *WhoHisp 91*
Gonzalez, Roseann Duenas 1948- *WhoHisp 91*
Gonzalez, Ruben *WhoAm 90*
Gonzalez, Ruben Earnest 1940- *BiDrAPA 89*
Gonzalez, Sandra Lynn 1955- *WhoHisp 91*
Gonzalez, Socorro Quinones 1954- *WhoHisp 91*
Gonzalez, Steve John 1958- *WhoHisp 91*
Gonzalez, Teofilo F. 1948- *WhoHisp 91*
Gonzalez, Tony 1936- *Ballpl 90*
Gonzalez, Victor R *BiDrAPA 89*
Gonzalez, Victoria Elena 1931- *WhoHisp 91*
Gonzalez, Wenceslao Jose 1957- *WhoWor 91*
Gonzalez, Wilfredo J. 1943- *WhoHisp 91*
Gonzalez, William G. 1940- *WhoAm 90*
Gonzalez, Wilma Sue Elcon 1945- *IntWWM 90*
Gonzalez, Xavier 1898- *WhoAmA 91, WhoHisp 91*
Gonzalez, Yolanda Martinez 1958- *WhoHisp 91*
Gonzalez-Acevedo, Alberto 1931- *BiDrAPA 89*
Gonzalez-Alexopoulos 1945- *WhoAm 90, WhoEmL 91*
Gonzalez Amezcua, Consuelo 1903- *BioIn 16*
Gonzalez-Avellanet, Ileana 1959- *WhoHisp 91*
Gonzalez-Aviles, Arnaldo 1959- *BiDrAPA 89, WhoEmL 91*
Gonzalez-Ayela, Antonio 1946- *WhoWor 91*
Gonzalez-Blanco, Mercedes 1940- *BiDrAPA 89*
Gonzalez Calvillo, Mayo Rafael 1948- *WhoWor 91*
Gonzalez-Calvo, Judith Teresa 1953- *WhoHisp 91*
Gonzalez-Carbo, Rafael *BiDrAPA 89*
Gonzalez Casanova, Pablo 1922- *WhoWor 91*
Gonzalez-Cawley, David 1953- *BiDrAPA 89*

Gonzalez Coiscou, Jose Luis 1926- *BioIn 16*
Gonzalez-Crussi, F 1936- *HispWr 90*
Gonzalez-Crussi, Francisco 1936- *WhoHisp 91*
Gonzalez-Cruz, Luis F. 1943- *BioIn 16, WhoHisp 91*
Gonzalez de Eslava, Fernan 1534-1601? *BioIn 16*
Gonzalez Del Valle, A D *BiDrAPA 89*
Gonzalez de Pesante, Anarda 1950- *WhoHisp 91*
Gonzalez de Rivera, Jose Luis 1944- *WhoWor 91*
Gonzalez de Santa Cruz, Roque 1576-1628 *BioIn 16*
Gonzalez-Dominguez, Olympia B. *WhoHisp 91*
Gonzalez-Durruthy, Diana Maria 1957- *WhoHisp 91*
Gonzalez-Echevarria, Roberto 1943- *WhoAm 90, WhoHisp 91*
Gonzalez Flores, Alfredo 1877-1962 *BioIn 16*
Gonzalez-Harvilan, Aida 1940- *WhoHisp 91*
Gonzalez-Levy, Sandra B. 1950- *WhoHisp 91*
Gonzalez-Lima, Francisco 1955- *WhoHisp 91*
Gonzalez-Maertens, Juan 1923- *BiDrAPA 89*
Gonzalez-Marin, Ludgardo F *BiDrAPA 89*
Gonzalez Marquez, Felipe 1942- *WhoWor 91*
Gonzalez Martinez, Enrique 1871-1952 *HispWr 90*
Gonzalez-Martinez, Ernesto 1938- *WhoHisp 91*
Gonzalez-Martinez, Merbil 1941- *WhoHisp 91*
Gonzalez-Mena, Janet 1937- *WhoWrEP 89*
Gonzalez-Novo, Enrique 1927- *WhoHisp 91*
Gonzalez Oyola, Ana Hilda 1948- *WhoHisp 91*
Gonzalez-Palacios, Alvar 1936- *BioIn 16*
Gonzalez Parsons, Lucia 1852?-1942 *BioIn 16*
Gonzalez-Pita, J. Alberto 1954- *WhoEmL 91*
Gonzalez Prada, Manuel 1844-1918 *BioIn 16, HispWr 90*
Gonzalez-Quevado, Oscar *EncO&P 3*
Gonzalez-Quevedo, Arnhilda 1947- *WhoHisp 91*
Gonzalez-Ramos, Gladys M. 1954- *WhoHisp 91*
Gonzalez Ruiz, Guillermo 1937- *ConDes 90*
Gonzalez-Santin, Edwin *WhoHisp 91*
Gonzalez-Sfeir, Javier Jose 1958- *WhoE 91*
Gonzalez-Soltero, Jose R 1952- *BiDrAPA 89*
Gonzalez-Suarez, Carlos Pedro 1954- *BiDrAPA 89*
Gonzalez T., Cesar A. 1931- *HispWr 90*
Gonzalez-Tornero, Sergio 1927- *WhoAmA 91*
Gonzalez-Vales, Luis Ernesto 1930- *WhoHisp 91, WhoSSW 91*
Gonzalez-Vaque, Luis 1944- *WhoWor 91*
Gonzalez-Velasco, Enrique Alberto 1940- *WhoHisp 91*
Gonzalez Videla, Gabriel 1898-1980 *BioIn 16*
Gonzalez-Villarreal, Esteban Alejandro 1955- *BiDrAPA 89*
Gonzalez Viquez, Cleto 1858-1937 *BioIn 16*
Gonzalez Zakarcheno, Jafet *BiDrAPA 89*
Gonzenbach, Jack Eugene 1950- *WhoEmL 91*
Gonzilez, Victor Hugo 1955- *WhoE 91*
Gonzlik, Pamela Joan 1948- *WhoAmW 91*
Goo, Abraham Meu Sen 1925- *St&PR 91, WhoAm 90*
Goo, Benjamin 1922- *WhoAmA 91*
Goo, Donald 1945- *St&PR 91*
Goo, Edward Kwock Wai 1956- *WhoEmL 91*
Gooch, Anthony Cushing 1937- *WhoAm 90, WhoE 91*
Gooch, Brad 1952- *ConAu 132*
Gooch, Daniel 1816-1889 *BioIn 16*
Gooch, Donald Burnette 1907- *WhoAmA 91*
Gooch, Donald Ray 1939- *WhoSSW 91*
Gooch, Edgar Eugene, III 1951- *WhoEmL 91*
Gooch, Elizabeth Sarah 1756- *FemiCLE*
Gooch, J. Glenn 1922- *St&PR 91, WhoAm 90*
Gooch, James A *BiDrAPA 89*
Gooch, James Oliver 1913- *WhoAm 90, WhoSSW 91, WhoWor 91*
Gooch, Johnny 1897-1975 *Ballpl 90*
Gooch, Lowell Thomas *St&PR 91*
Gooch, Nancy Jane 1941- *WhoAmW 91*
Gooch, Patricia Carolyn 1935- *WhoAm 90, WhoAmW 91, WhoSSW 91*
Gooch, Phillip W. 1943- *St&PR 91*
Gooch, Robert Miletus *WhoWrEP 89*
Gooch, Royce Lynn 1956- *WhoEmL 91*
Gooch, W. J. 1857-1917 *AmLegL*
Goocher, R.L. 1950- *St&PR 91*
Good Thunder 1790?-1863 *WhNaAH*
Good, Albert F. 1915- *St&PR 91*
Good, Anne Leeper 1923- *WhoAmW 91*
Good, Barbara Nissley 1953- *WhoE 91*
Good, Barry *BioIn 16*
Good, Betsey Sprei *WhoE 91*
Good, Celeste M *BiDrAPA 89*
Good, Charles E. 1948- *St&PR 91*
Good, Christopher H. 1955- *WhoE 91*
Good, Cynthia Annette 1951- *WhoAm 90*
Good, Daniel James 1940- *WhoAm 90, WhoE 91*
Good, David Allen 1954- *St&PR 91*
Good, David Michael 1954- *BiDrAPA 89*
Good, Donald W. 1956- *WhoSSW 91*
Good, Douglas Jay 1947- *WhoEmL 91*
Good, Edward K. 1931- *St&PR 91*
Good, Gail G. 1929- *St&PR 91*
Good, Gary Alan 1949- *WhoSSW 91*
Good, Gregory E. *ODwPR 91*
Good, Gregory Elmer, Jr. 1941- *WhoE 91*
Good, Henry H 1928- *BiDrAPA 89*
Good, Jack Duane 1936- *St&PR 91*
Good, James Robert 1947- *St&PR 91*
Good, James William 1866-1929 *BiDrUSE 89*
Good, Joan Duffey 1939- *WhoAmW 91*
Good, John Dudley 1928- *St&PR 91*
Good, John Leon, III 1943- *WhoE 91*
Good, John Scott 1957- *St&PR 91*
Good, Joseph R. 1911- *St&PR 91*
Good, Joseph Samuel 1939- *St&PR 91*
Good, Judith Marie 1955- *WhoAmW 91*
Good, Laurance Frederic 1932- *WhoAm 90*
Good, Laurence 1934- *WhoAm 90*
Good, Leonard 1907- *WhoAmA 91*
Good, Leonard Phelps 1907- *WhoAm 90, WhoWor 91*
Good, Linda Lou 1941- *WhoAmW 91*
Good, Lucy Swearingen 1920- *WhoSSW 91*
Good, Madelyn E. 1931- *WhoAmW 91*
Good, Mary L. 1931- *St&PR 91*
Good, Mary Lowe 1931- *WhoAm 90, WhoAmW 91*
Good, Michael Ian 1944- *BiDrAPA 89, WhoE 91*
Good, Nancy Susan 1940- *WhoAmW 91*
Good, Paul Joseph 1929- *WhoAm 90*
Good, Raphael S 1921- *BiDrAPA 89*
Good, Raymond F. 1928- *WhoAm 90*
Good, Richard A. *ODwPR 91*
Good, Robert Alan 1922- *WhoAm 90*
Good, Robert Gaylen 1953- *WhoEmL 91*
Good, Roland Hamilton, Jr. 1923- *WhoAm 90*
Good, Sheldon Fred 1933- *WhoWor 91*
Good, Terry R. 1944- *St&PR 91*
Good, Thomas Lindall 1943- *WhoAm 90, WhoWrEP 89*
Good, Virginia Johnson 1919- *WhoE 91*
Good, Walter Raymond 1924- *WhoAm 90, WhoE 91*
Good, Wealty W 1908- *BiDrAPA 89*
Good, Wilbur 1885-1963 *Ballpl 90*
Good, William Allen 1949- *WhoAm 90*
Good-Sept, Marcia Kay 1962- *WhoAmW 91*
Goodacre, Glenna 1939- *WhoAmA 91*
Goodale, Fairfield 1923- *WhoAm 90*
Goodale, James C. 1933- *BioIn 16*
Goodale, James Campbell 1933- *St&PR 91, WhoAm 90*
Goodale, Toni Krissel 1941- *WhoE 91*
Goodall, D. Mead 1950- *WhoEmL 91*
Goodall, Frances Louise 1915- *WhoAmW 91*
Goodall, H. L., Jr. 1952- *ConAu 132*
Goodall, Howard Lindsay 1958- *IntWWM 90*
Goodall, Jackson Wallace, Jr. *BioIn 16*
Goodall, Jackson Wallace, Jr. 1938- *St&PR 91, WhoAm 90*
Goodall, Jane *BioIn 16*
Goodall, Jane 1934- *MajTwCW, News 91-1 [port], WorAlBi*
Goodall, Leon S. 1925- *St&PR 91*
Goodall, Leon Steele 1925- *WhoAm 90*
Goodall, Leonard Edwin 1937- *WhoAm 90*
Goodall, Norman 1896-1985 *BioIn 16, DcNaB 1981*
Goodall, Reginald 1901- *IntWWM 90, PenDiMP*
Goodall, Reginald 1905-1990 *BioIn 16, NewYTBS 90 [port]*
Goodall, Valorie 1936- *IntWWM 90*
Goodarzy, Rahman 1924- *BiDrAPA 89*
Goodblatt, Morris S. 1901-1978 *BioIn 16*
Goodbody, Harold P. 1905-1988 *BioIn 16*
Goodbody, John Collett 1915- *WhoAm 90*
Goodbody, John Collett 1915-1990 *BioIn 16*
Goodbody, Slim 1949- *BioIn 16*
Goodbread, Bill *St&PR 91*
Goodbred, Ray Edward 1929- *WhoAmA 91*
Goodby, Donald Rhodes 1926- *St&PR 91*
Goodby, James Eugene 1929- *WhoAm 90*
Goodby, Richard W. 1917- *St&PR 91*
Goodchild, Anthony A. 1928-1988 *BioIn 16*
Goodchild, Heather Margaret 1957- *St&PR 91*
Goodchild, Jack 1950- *WhoEmL 91*
Goodchild, John Charles, Jr. 1945- *WhoAm 90*
Goodchild, Robert Marshall 1933- *St&PR 91, WhoE 91*
Goodchild, Stanley *BioIn 16*
Goode, Alexander David 1911-1943 *BioIn 16*
Goode, Bryan C. 1935- *St&PR 91*
Goode, Celia Ross 1950- *WhoSSW 91*
Goode, Clement Tyson 1929- *WhoAm 90*
Goode, Cynthia Baird 1957- *WhoE 91*
Goode, Daniel 1936- *IntWWM 90*
Goode, David Hurd 1902- *St&PR 91*
Goode, David John 1941- *BiDrAPA 89*
Goode, David Ronald 1941- *St&PR 91*
Goode, Diane 1949- *WhoE 91*
Goode, G. Stephen 1950- *WhoWor 91*
Goode, James Dennis 1951- *WhoSSW 91*
Goode, James Emory 1935- *St&PR 91*
Goode, James Moore 1939- *WhoAm 90*
Goode, Joe *BioIn 16*
Goode, Joe 1937- *WhoAmA 91*
Goode, John Martin 1934- *St&PR 91, WhoAm 90*
Goode, Martin 1928- *St&PR 91*
Goode, Michael Landers 1947- *WhoEmL 91*
Goode, Richard *BioIn 16*
Goode, Richard Benjamin 1916- *WhoAm 90, WhoE 91*
Goode, Richard Harris 1939- *WhoWor 91*
Goode, Richard Stephen 1943- *IntWWM 90, WhoAm 90*
Goode, S.M. 1943- *St&PR 91*
Goode, Seddon, Jr. 1932- *St&PR 91*
Goode, Stephen 1943- *BioIn 16*
Goode, Stephen Hogue 1924- *WhoAm 90*
Goode, Steven Lynn 1951- *WhoSSW 91*
Goode, W. Wilson 1938- *WhoAm 90, WhoE 91*
Goode, William Josiah 1917- *WhoAm 90, WhoE 91*
Goodell, Christina Marie 1959- *WhoAmW 91*
Goodell, George Sidney 1921- *WhoAm 90*
Goodell, Horace Grant 1925- *WhoAm 90*
Goodell, Larry 1935- *WhoWrEP 89*
Goodell, Peter Beasant 1952- *WhoEmL 91*
Goodell, Richard Lee 1956- *WhoWor 91*
Goodell, Robert Charles 1954- *St&PR 91*
Goodell, Robert P., Jr. 1928- *St&PR 91*
Goodell, Sol 1906- *WhoAm 90*
Goodell, Warren Franklin 1924- *WhoAm 90*
Goodelman, Aaron J 1891-1978 *WhoAmA 91N*
Goodelman, Alan Frank 1931- *St&PR 91*
Goodelman, Arthur Michael 1953- *St&PR 91*
Goodelman, Hilda 1931- *St&PR 91*
Goodelman, Ruth 1914- *WhoAmA 91*
Gooden, Dwight *BioIn 16*
Gooden, Dwight 1964- *Ballpl 90, WorAlBi*
Gooden, Dwight Eugene 1964- *WhoAm 90, WhoE 91*
Gooden, Glenda Stevens 1953- *WhoAmW 91*
Gooden, Lauretta Holman *HarlReB*
Gooden, Melinda Grady 1963- *WhoSSW 91*
Gooden, Reginald Heber 1910- *WhoAm 90*
Goodenough, Andrew Lewis 1955- *WhoE 91, WhoEmL 91*
Goodenough, John 1940- *WhoWor 91*
Goodenough, Judith B. 1942- *WhoWrEP 89*
Goodenough, Judith Beach 1942- *WhoAmW 91*
Goodenough, Judith Elizabeth 1948- *WhoAmW 91*
Goodenough, Mary 1652?-1692 *BiDEWW*
Goodenough, Walter H. 1939- *St&PR 91*
Goodenough, Ward Hunt 1919- *WhoAm 90*
Goodenow, Willis G *BiDrAPA 89*
Goodes, Melvin Russell 1935- *St&PR 91, WhoAm 90*
Goodey, Ila Marie *WhoWrEP 89*
Goodey, Ila Marie 1948- *WhoAmW 91, WhoEmL 91*
Goodfellow, Howard Douglas 1942- *WhoWor 91*
Goodfellow, James 1828-1898 *DcCanB 12*
Goodfellow, Joan Bennett 1928- *WhoAmW 91*
Goodfellow, Robin Irene 1945- *WhoAmW 91, WhoEmL 91, WhoWor 91*
Goodfellow, William Chester 1947- *WhoE 91*
Goodfriend, Arthur 1907- *BioIn 16, WhoAm 90*
Goodfriend, Barbara 1930- *WhoE 91*
Goodfriend, Gary 1951- *WhoEmL 91*
Goodfriend, Herbert Jay 1926- *WhoAm 90*
Goodfriend, Marlene Sally 1944- *BiDrAPA 89*
Goodfriend, Marvin S. 1950- *St&PR 91*
Goodfriend, Wendy Lee 1959- *WhoAmW 91*
Goodgame, Ronald Edward 1938- *St&PR 91*
Goodgame, Thomas LaFayette 1929- *WhoAm 90*
Goodger, John Verne 1936- *St&PR 91, WhoAm 90*
Goodgold, Jay Samuel 1954- *WhoEmL 91*
Goodgold, Joseph 1920- *WhoAm 90*
Goodgold, Lewis *BioIn 16*
Goodhart, A L *ConAu 31NR*
Goodhart, Al 1905-1955 *OxCPMus*
Goodhart, Arthur Lehman 1891-1978 *ConAu 31NR*
Goodhart, Karen Stephan 1947- *WhoAmW 91*
Goodhartz, Gerald 1938- *WhoE 91, WhoWor 91*
Goodheart, Barbara Jean 1934- *WhoWrEP 89*
Goodheart, Clyde Raymond 1931- *WhoAm 90*
Goodheart, Diane Louise 1962- *WhoAmW 91*
Goodheart, Karen 1958- *WhoAmW 91*
Goodhew, Howard R., Jr. 1923- *St&PR 91*
Goodhew, J. Mark 1955- *St&PR 91*
Goodhew, J. William, III 1937- *WhoSSW 91*
Goodhue, Benjamin 1748-1814 *BioIn 16*
Goodhue, Mary Brier 1921- *WhoAmW 91, WhoE 91*
Goodhue, Sarah 1641-1681 *FemiCLE*
Goodhue, William Walter, Jr. 1945- *WhoWor 91*
Goodier, J. Leslie 1920- *WhoAm 90*
Goodier, John Jefferis 1931- *St&PR 91*
Goodier, Robert 1912- *OxCCanT*
Goodin, Eileen Sue 1955- *WhoEmL 91*
Goodin, John Walter 1946- *St&PR 91*
Goodin, Julia C. 1957- *WhoAmW 91*
Goodin, Lyn Anderson *BiDrAPA 89*
Goodin, Michael Anthony 1951- *WhoWrEP 89*
Goodin, Robert Edward 1950- *WhoWrEP 89*
Goodin, Walker D 1934- *BiDrAPA 89*
Goodin, William Charles 1917- *WhoAm 90*
Goodin, William H, Jr. *BiDrAPA 89*
Goodin-Gautier, Sandia Joycelyn 1956- *WhoAmW 91*
Goodine, Francena White 1940- *WhoWrEP 89*
Goodine, Isaac Thomas 1932- *WhoWor 91*
Goodine, Julius 1954- *WhoEmL 91*
Goodine, Linda Adele 1958- *WhoAmA 91*
Gooding, Charles Arthur 1936- *WhoAm 90*
Gooding, Charles Thomas 1931- *WhoAm 90*
Gooding, David Eugene 1941- *WhoAm 90*
Gooding, Gladys 1893-1963 *Ballpl 90*
Gooding, Gretchen Ann Wagner 1935- *WhoAmW 91*
Gooding, Judson 1926- *WhoAm 90, WhoWrEP 89*
Gooding, Timothy James 1949- *St&PR 91*
Goodings, Allen 1925- *WhoAm 90*
Goodis, David 1917-1967 *TwCCr&M 91*
Goodison, Benjamin *PenDiDA 89*
Goodison, Lorna 1947- *FemiCLE*
Goodison, Nicholas 1934- *BioIn 16*
Goodkin, Deborah Gay 1951- *WhoAmW 91*
Goodkin, Karl *BiDrAPA 89*
Goodkin, Michael Jon 1941- *WhoAm 90*
Goodkind, Conrad George 1944- *WhoAm 90*
Goodkind, Louis William 1914- *WhoAm 90*
Goodkind, Robert H. 1921- *St&PR 91*
Goodlad, John Inkster 1920- *WhoAm 90*
Goodlin, Gary Russell 1953- *WhoSSW 91*
Goodling, William F. *WhoAm 90, WhoE 91*
Goodloe, John Duncan, IV 1935- *St&PR 91, WhoAm 90*
Goodloe, Robert 1936- *IntWWM 90*
Goodlund, Larry S 1946- *BiDrAPA 89*
Goodman, Abraham 1890-1988 *BioIn 16*
Goodman, Al 1890-1972 *OxCPMus*
Goodman, Alfred 1920- *IntWWM 90, WhoAm 90*
Goodman, Allen Charles 1947- *WhoAm 90*
Goodman, Alvin Irwin 1929- *WhoE 91*

Goodman, Alvin S. 1925- *WhoAm 90*
Goodman, Amy L 1957- *BiDrAPA 89*
Goodman, Andrew 1943-1964 *BioIn 16*
Goodman, Andrew David 1952- *WhoE 91*
Goodman, Arnold M. 1928- *BioIn 16*
Goodman, Aviel Li 1955- *BiDrAPA 89*
Goodman, Barbara Eason 1949- *WhoAmW 91*
Goodman, Benjamin 1904- *WhoAm 90, WhoAmA 91*
Goodman, Benny 1909-1986 *BioIn 16, ConMus 4 [port], OxCPMus, PenDiMP, WorAlBi*
Goodman, Bernard 1923- *WhoAm 90*
Goodman, Bernard 1926- *BiDrAPA 89*
Goodman, Bernard J. 1923- *WhoAm 90*
Goodman, Bernard Maurice 1914- *IntWWM 90*
Goodman, Berney 1935- *BiDrAPA 89*
Goodman, Bertram 1904- *WhoAmA 91*
Goodman, Beverly H *BiDrAPA 89*
Goodman, Billy 1926-1984 *Ballpl 90*
Goodman, Bonnie Ann 148- *WhoAmW 91*
Goodman, Bradley Sean *BiDrAPA 89*
Goodman, Brenda Joyce 1955- *WhoAmW 91*
Goodman, Bruce David 1945- *St&PR 91*
Goodman, Bruce Gerald 1948- *WhoEmL 91*
Goodman, Bruce K. 1926- *St&PR 91*
Goodman, Calvin Jerome 1922- *WhoAmA 91*
Goodman, Carol Roslyn 1950- *WhoAmW 91*
Goodman, Charles Morton 1906- *WhoAm 90*
Goodman, Charles Schaffner 1916- *WhoAm 90*
Goodman, Charles Schaffner, Jr. 1949- *WhoEmL 91, WhoWor 91*
Goodman, Constance Beth 1963- *WhoWrEP 89*
Goodman, Corey Scott 1951- *WhoAm 90*
Goodman, Craig Stephen 1957- *IntWWM 90, WhoEmL 91*
Goodman, David 1897-1989 *BioIn 16*
Goodman, David 1955- *BiDrAPA 89*
Goodman, David Barry Poliakoff 1942- *WhoAm 90*
Goodman, David Joel 1939- *WhoAm 90*
Goodman, David L. 1935- *ODwPR 91*
Goodman, David M. 1920- *St&PR 91*
Goodman, David Paul *BiDrAPA 89*
Goodman, David Richard, Jr. 1949- *St&PR 91*
Goodman, Deborah Lerme 1956- *BioIn 16*
Goodman, DeWitt Stetten 1930- *WhoAm 90*
Goodman, Donald C. 1927- *WhoAm 90*
Goodman, Elaine 1930- *AuBYP 90*
Goodman, Elaine I. *ODwPR 91*
Goodman, Elizabeth B. 1912- *AuBYP 90*
Goodman, Ellen 1941- *WorAu 1980 [port]*
Goodman, Ellen Holtz 1941- *WhoAm 90, WhoAmW 91*
Goodman, Elliot Raymond 1923- *WhoAm 90*
Goodman, Elliott Irvin 1934- *WhoAm 90*
Goodman, Ellis M. 1937- *St&PR 91*
Goodman, Emily Jane *BioIn 16*
Goodman, Erika *WhoAm 90*
Goodman, Florence Jeanne 1922- *WhoAmA 91*
Goodman, Frank H. 1947- *St&PR 91*
Goodman, G. D. Watson 1920- *WhoWor 91*
Goodman, Gail Busman 1953- *WhoAmW 91, WhoE 91*
Goodman, Garrison Kevin 1956- *WhoEmL 91*
Goodman, Gary Alan 1947- *WhoWor 91*
Goodman, George J W 1930- *ConAu 31NR*
Goodman, George Jerome Waldo 1930- *WhoAm 90*
Goodman, Gertrude Amelia 1924- *WhoAmW 91, WhoSSW 91*
Goodman, Gwendolyn Ann 1955- *WhoEmL 91*
Goodman, Hannah Grad *BioIn 16*
Goodman, Harold David 1948- *BiDrAPA 89*
Goodman, Harold S. 1937- *WhoAm 90*
Goodman, Harry 1907- *BiDrAPA 89*
Goodman, Helen 1939- *WhoAmA 91*
Goodman, Henry Maurice 1934- *WhoAm 90*
Goodman, Herbert Irwin 1923- *St&PR 91, WhoAm 90, WhoWor 91*
Goodman, Herman S *BiDrAPA 89*
Goodman, Howard M. 1938- *WhoAm 90*
Goodman, Hubert T 1933- *BiDrAPA 89*
Goodman, Ival 1908-1984 *Ballpl 90*
Goodman, Jack 1958- *ODwPR 91*
Goodman, James J 1922- *BiDrAPA 89*
Goodman, James Neil 1929- *WhoAmA 91*
Goodman, James S. 1951- *BiDrAPA 89*
Goodman, Janet Rebecca 1932- *BiDrAPA 89*
Goodman, Janis G 1951- *WhoAmA 91*
Goodman, Jean A. 1934- *St&PR 91*
Goodman, Jeremiah *BioIn 16*
Goodman, Jerome David 1933- *BiDrAPA 89*
Goodman, Jerry *NewAgMG*
Goodman, Jerry Alan 1946- *WhoEmL 91*
Goodman, Jerry Lynn 1939- *St&PR 91, WhoAm 90, WhoSSW 91*
Goodman, Joan E. 1950- *BioIn 16*
Goodman, Joel Barry 1948- *WhoWrEP 89*
Goodman, Joel Harry, Jr. 1944- *WhoAm 90*
Goodman, Joel Kopel 1935- *St&PR 91*
Goodman, Joel Warren 1933- *WhoAm 90*
Goodman, John *BioIn 16*
Goodman, John 1952- *News 90 [port], -90-3 [port]*
Goodman, John 1953- *WorAlBi*
Goodman, John Sefton 1934- *St&PR 91*
Goodman, John W 1930- *BiDrAPA 89*
Goodman, Jon P. *BioIn 16*
Goodman, Jordan Elliot 1954- *WhoE 91*
Goodman, Jory Frederic 1950- *BiDrAPA 89*
Goodman, Joseph Champion 1937- *WhoSSW 91*
Goodman, Joseph Magnus 1918- *IntWWM 90*
Goodman, Joseph Wilfred 1936- *WhoAm 90*
Goodman, Julia 1812-1906 *BiDWomA*
Goodman, Ken 1950- *WhoAmA 91*
Goodman, Kenneth Edward 1947- *St&PR 91*
Goodman, Kimberly Swain 1963- *WhoSSW 91*
Goodman, Lawrence Baron 1926- *WhoAm 90*
Goodman, Lawrence Judd 1935- *WhoSSW 91, WhoWor 91*
Goodman, Lee Hugh 1953- *WhoEmL 91*
Goodman, Leon 1920- *WhoAm 90*
Goodman, Leonard 1926- *WhoAm 90, WhoWor 91*
Goodman, Leonard S. 1921-1987 *BioIn 16*
Goodman, Leslie E. 1943- *St&PR 91*
Goodman, Leslie Eugene 1943- *WhoAm 90*
Goodman, Lila Vida 1934- *WhoAmW 91*
Goodman, Linda *WhoWor 91*
Goodman, Lowell I 1924- *BiDrAPA 89*
Goodman, Major Merlin 1938- *WhoAm 90*
Goodman, Malka L *BiDrAPA 89*
Goodman, Marci Levin 1960- *WhoEmL 91*
Goodman, Marguerite Ruth *WhoAmW 91*
Goodman, Marian 1928- *WhoAmA 91*
Goodman, Marianne 1949- *BiDrAPA 89*
Goodman, Mark 1946- *WhoAmA 91*
Goodman, Mark N. 1952- *WhoEmL 91, WhoWor 91*
Goodman, Martin M. 1938- *St&PR 91*
Goodman, Mary 1943- *WhoE 91*
Goodman, Marvin David 1933- *WhoWor 91*
Goodman, Mary Sheena 1923- *IntWWM 90*
Goodman, Max A. 1924- *WhoAm 90*
Goodman, Melvin B 1924- *BiDrAPA 89*
Goodman, Michael A. 1903- *WhoAm 90*
Goodman, Michael R *BiDrAPA 89*
Goodman, Morris *St&PR 91*
Goodman, N.N., Jr. 1925- *St&PR 91*
Goodman, Nicolas Daniels 1940- *WhoE 91*
Goodman, Noel C *BiDrAPA 89*
Goodman, Norman 1934- *WhoAm 90*
Goodman, Norton Victor 1936- *WhoAm 90*
Goodman, Patti Friedlander 1955- *WhoAmW 91*
Goodman, Paul 1911-1972 *EncAL, MajTwCW*
Goodman, Paul David 1942- *BiDrAPA 89*
Goodman, Percival 1904-1989 *BioIn 16, ConAu 129*
Goodman, Philip S. 1926- *WhoE 91*
Goodman, Phyllis L. 1946- *ODwPR 91*
Goodman, Ramona Lee 1960- *WhoEmL 91*
Goodman, Richard *ODwPR 91*
Goodman, Richard Edwin 1935- *IntWWM 90*
Goodman, Richard Eugene 1928- *WhoAm 90*
Goodman, Richard H. *WhoSSW 91*
Goodman, Robbin Schneider 1952- *ODwPR 91*
Goodman, Robert Mendel 1920- *WhoE 91*
Goodman, Robert Merwin 1945- *WhoAm 90*
Goodman, Robert Mitchell 1953- *WhoEmL 91*
Goodman, Robert Stewart 1951- *St&PR 91*
Goodman, Robin Fern 1955- *WhoAmW 91*
Goodman, Roland Alfred 1933- *WhoAm 90*
Goodman, Ronald 1920- *ODwPR 91*
Goodman, Ronald D. 1935- *St&PR 91*
Goodman, Ross Mathew 1958- *WhoEmL 91*
Goodman, Roy B. 1957- *St&PR 91*
Goodman, Roy M. 1930- *St&PR 91*
Goodman, Roy Matz 1930- *WhoAm 90, WhoE 91*
Goodman, Sam Leon 1942- *BiDrAPA 89*
Goodman, Sam R. 1930- *St&PR 91*
Goodman, Sam Richard 1930- *WhoAm 90*
Goodman, Seymour S. 1931- *WhoSSW 91*
Goodman, Sidney 1936- *WhoAmA 91*
Goodman, Stanley 1907- *WhoSSW 91*
Goodman, Stanley 1920- *BiDrAPA 89*
Goodman, Stanley 1931- *WhoAm 90*
Goodman, Stanley J. 1910- *St&PR 91*
Goodman, Stanley Joshua 1910- *WhoAm 90*
Goodman, Stanley Leonard 1920- *WhoAm 90*
Goodman, Stephen H. 1944- *WhoAm 90*
Goodman, Stephen Nathaniel 1932- *St&PR 91*
Goodman, Steven Mark 1959- *WhoEmL 91*
Goodman, Stuart F. 1943- *St&PR 91*
Goodman, Stuart Franklyn 1943- *WhoAm 90*
Goodman, Stuart Lauren 1938- *WhoAm 90*
Goodman, Sumner Harold *BiDrAPA 89*
Goodman, Susan D 1950- *BiDrAPA 89*
Goodman, Theodore Avram *BiDrAPA 89*
Goodman, Theodore Russell 1927- *St&PR 91*
Goodman, Thomas A. *ODwPR 91*
Goodman, Thomas Allen 1931- *BiDrAPA 89*
Goodman, Thomas Andrew 1954- *WhoAm 90*
Goodman, Thomas Leo 1929- *WhoAm 90*
Goodman, Tracey 1963- *BiDrAPA 89*
Goodman, Valerie Dawson 1948- *WhoAmW 91, WhoEmL 91*
Goodman, Velma C. 1901- *St&PR 91*
Goodman, Walter 1927- *AuBYP 90, WhoAm 90, WhoWrEP 89*
Goodman, Warren H. 1919- *ODwPR 91*
Goodman, Warren H 1935- *BiDrAPA 89*
Goodman, Wayne K *BiDrAPA 89*
Goodman, William Beehler 1923- *WhoAm 90, WhoWrEP 89*
Goodman, William David 1947- *WhoSSW 91*
Goodman, William E., IV 1932- *St&PR 91*
Goodman, William Eldridge 1946- *WhoSSW 91*
Goodman, William I. 1919- *WhoAm 90*
Goodman, William Jay 1942- *BiDrAPA 89*
Goodman, William Lee 1946- *WhoEmL 91*
Goodman, William Richard 1930- *WhoE 91*
Goodner, Dwight Benjamin 1913- *WhoAm 90*
Goodner, Homer Wade 1929- *WhoSSW 91*
Goodner, James Ernest 1926- *WhoAm 90*
Goodner, John Ross, Jr. 1927- *WhoAm 90*
Goodnick, Paul Joel 1950- *BiDrAPA 89, WhoSSW 91*
Goodnight, Fred Bryon 1949- *WhoSSW 91*
Goodnight, Marie Louise 1916- *WhoAmW 91*
Goodnough, Robert 1923- *WhoAmA 91*
Goodnow, Frank A 1923- *WhoAmA 91*
Goodnow, Minnie 1875-1952 *BioIn 16*
Goodnow, Wilma Elizabeth 1944- *WhoAmW 91*
Goodpaster, Andrew Jackson 1915- *WhoAm 90*
Goodpaster, Denzil 1908- *MusmAFA*
Goodpaster, William Van 1925- *St&PR 91*
Goodpastor, William E *BiDrAPA 89*
Goodpasture, Frank, Jr. 1923- *St&PR 91*
Goodpasture, James Dale 1942- *WhoAm 90*
Goodpasture, Jessie Carrol 1952- *WhoEmL 91*
Goodreau, Lou Ann 1955- *WhoEmL 91*
Goodreds, John Stanton 1934- *St&PR 91, WhoAm 90*
Goodrich, Alan Owens 1958- *WhoEmL 91, WhoSSW 91*
Goodrich, Anne W. 1866-1954 *BioAmW*
Goodrich, Annie Warburton 1866-1954 *BioIn 16*
Goodrich, Benjamin F. 1841-1888 *WorAlBi*
Goodrich, Bernard A. 1929- *ODwPR 91*
Goodrich, Bradley 1950- *St&PR 91*
Goodrich, D. Michael 1944- *St&PR 91*
Goodrich, D Wells 1924- *BiDrAPA 89*
Goodrich, David M. 1876-1950 *WorAlBi*
Goodrich, Dennis Keith 1954- *WhoEmL 91*
Goodrich, Donna Marie 1938- *WhoWrEP 89*
Goodrich, George Herbert 1925- *WhoAm 90, WhoE 91*
Goodrich, Glenn A. 1925- *St&PR 91*
Goodrich, Gloria Jean 1934- *WhoAmW 91*
Goodrich, Henry C. 1920- *St&PR 91*
Goodrich, Henry Calvin 1920- *WhoAm 90*
Goodrich, Isaac 1939- *WhoE 91*
Goodrich, James *BioIn 16*
Goodrich, James N. 1943- *St&PR 91*
Goodrich, James Tait 1946- *WhoE 91, WhoEmL 91, WhoWor 91*
Goodrich, James W 1939- *WhoAmA 91*
Goodrich, James William 1939- *WhoAm 90*
Goodrich, John Bernard 1928- *WhoAm 90*
Goodrich, John M. 1950- *St&PR 91*
Goodrich, Kenneth Paul 1933- *WhoAm 90*
Goodrich, Leland M. *NewYTBS 90*
Goodrich, Leon Raymond 1936- *WhoAm 90*
Goodrich, Lloyd *BioIn 16*
Goodrich, Lloyd 1897-1987 *ConAu 31NR*
Goodrich, Maurice Keith 1935- *St&PR 91, WhoAm 90, WhoWor 91*
Goodrich, Nathaniel Herman 1914- *WhoAm 90*
Goodrich, Norma Lorre 1917- *WhoAm 90*
Goodrich, Ronald Leonard 1934- *St&PR 91*
Goodrich, Samuel Melvin 1936- *WhoSSW 91*
Goodrich, Thomas Michael 1945- *WhoAm 90*
Goodrich, Warren Philip 1955- *BiDrAPA 89*
Goodrich, William Bruce 1926- *WhoSSW 91*
Goodrich-Freer, Ada 1857-1931 *EncO&P 3, EncPaPR 91*
Goodridge, Alan Gardner 1937- *WhoAm 90*
Goodridge, Allan D. 1936- *WhoAm 90*
Goodridge, Georgia Esther 1950- *WhoWrEP 89*
Goodridge, Harry *BioIn 16*
Goodridge, Lawrence Wayne 1941- *WhoAmA 91*
Goodridge, Noel Herbert Alan 1930- *WhoAm 90, WhoE 91*
Goodrum, Daniel Shepard 1926- *St&PR 91, WhoSSW 91*
Goodrum, Richard W. 1928- *St&PR 91*
Goodrum, Wayne Louis 1934- *WhoSSW 91*
Goodrum, William James 1958- *St&PR 91, WhoSSW 91*
Goodsell, Eugene H. 1953- *St&PR 91*
Goodsell, Jane *BioIn 16*
Goodsitt, Alan Martin 1937- *BiDrAPA 89*
Goodson, Carl Edward 1917- *WhoAm 90*
Goodson, Carole Edith McKissock 1946- *WhoAmW 91*
Goodson, Charles L. 1928- *WhoSSW 91*
Goodson, Ed 1948- *Ballpl 90*
Goodson, George Royden, III 1955- *St&PR 91*
Goodson, Linda Jane Kleckley 1942- *WhoAmW 91*
Goodson, Louie Aubrey, Jr. 1922- *St&PR 91, WhoAm 90*
Goodson, Mark 1915- *WhoAm 90, WhoE 91*
Goodson, Patricia Randolph 1954- *WhoEmL 91*
Goodson, R. Eugene 1935- *St&PR 91*
Goodson, Raymond Eugene 1935- *WhoAm 90*
Goodson, Richard Carle, Jr. 1945- *WhoE 91*
Goodson, Susan Gloria *BiDrAPA 89*
Goodson, Walter Kenneth 1912- *WhoAm 90*
Goodson, William H, Jr. 1936- *BiDrAPA 89*
Goodspeed, Barbara 1919- *WhoAmW 91*
Goodspeed, Edgar Johnson 1871-1962 *BioIn 16*
Goodspeed, Scott Winans 1954- *WhoE 91, WhoEmL 91*
Goodspeed, Stephen Spencer 1915- *WhoAm 90*
Goodspeed, Thomas Harper 1887-1966 *DcScB S2*
Goodstein, Barnett Maurice 1921- *WhoAm 90*
Goodstein, Charles 1937- *BiDrAPA 89*
Goodstein, Daniel Bela 1937- *WhoWor 91*
Goodstein, David Henry 1948- *WhoEmL 91*
Goodstein, David Louis 1939- *WhoAm 90*
Goodstein, Jacob *BioIn 16*
Goodstein, Jeanette Treat 1940- *WhoAmW 91*
Goodstein, Madeline Prager 1920- *WhoAmW 91*
Goodstein, Maurice Mac 1909- *St&PR 91*
Goodstein, Richard Edward 1953- *WhoSSW 91*
Goodstein, Richard Kuntz 1940- *BiDrAPA 89*
Goodstein, Sanders A. 1918- *St&PR 91*
Goodstein, Sanders Abraham 1918- *WhoWor 91*
Goodstein-Shapiro, F 1931- *WhoAmA 91*
Goodstone, Edward Harold 1934- *St&PR 91, WhoAm 90*

Goodstone, Rosemary Ann 1947- WhoAmW 91
Goodvich, Eugene Walter 1934- St&PR 91
Goodwill, Margaret 1950- WhoAmA 91
Goodwill, Margaret Jane 1950- WhoAmW 91, WhoEmL 91
Goodwillie, John Morley 1910-1987 BioIn 16
Goodwin, Alfred Theodore 1923- WhoAm 90
Goodwin, B. Terence 1932- St&PR 91
Goodwin, Barbara 1938- WhoAmW 91
Goodwin, Barbara Sue 1950- WhoSSW 91
Goodwin, Ben 1926- BiDrAPA 89
Goodwin, Bernard 1907- WhoAm 90, WhoWor 91
Goodwin, Bill 1942- WhoWrEP 89
Goodwin, Brenda Gayle 1954- WhoAmW 91
Goodwin, Bruce Kesseli 1931- WhoAm 90
Goodwin, Carl E. 1947- St&PR 91
Goodwin, Claude Elbert 1910- WhoAm 90
Goodwin, Craufurd David 1934- WhoAm 90
Goodwin, Dale E 1955- ODwPR 91
Goodwin, Daniel Robert 1953- WhoE 91
Goodwin, Danny 1953- Ballpl 90
Goodwin, Dianna Marylou 1953- WhoE 91
Goodwin, Donald G. 1927- St&PR 91
Goodwin, Donald W 1931- BiDrAPA 89
Goodwin, Donald William 1931- WhoAm 90
Goodwin, Douglas Ira 1946- WhoAm 90
Goodwin, E.L. 1899- St&PR 91
Goodwin, Elizabeth Tanner 1957- WhoAmW 91, WhoE 91
Goodwin, Francis Maurice 1956- WhoWrEP 89
Goodwin, Frederick K BiDrAPA 89
Goodwin, Frederick King 1936- WhoAm 90
Goodwin, George ODwPR 91
Goodwin, George Evans 1917- WhoAm 90
Goodwin, Glenn Arthur 1946- St&PR 91
Goodwin, Guy 1940- WhoAmA 91
Goodwin, H. Clark 1934- St&PR 91
Goodwin, Hal ConAu 131
Goodwin, Hal 1914-1990 BioIn 16
Goodwin, Harold L 1914-1990 ConAu 131
Goodwin, Harold Leland 1914-1990 BioIn 16
Goodwin, Harry Eugene 1922- WhoAm 90
Goodwin, James Barton 1947- WhoEmL 91
Goodwin, James Michael 1938- WhoSSW 91
Goodwin, Jan BioIn 16
Goodwin, Jean McClung 1946- WhoAmW 91, WhoEmL 91
Goodwin, Jean Patricia 1946- BiDrAPA 89
Goodwin, Jeffrey 1946- St&PR 91
Goodwin, Jesse Francis 1929- WhoAm 90
Goodwin, Joel Franklin, Sr. 1924- WhoSSW 91
Goodwin, John Abbot 1824-1884 AmLegL
Goodwin, John J, Jr. BiDrAPA 89
Goodwin, Joseph L 1926- St&PR 91
Goodwin, Kemper 1906- WhoAm 90
Goodwin, Ken 1934- ConAu 131
Goodwin, Lewis Billings 1957- St&PR 91
Goodwin, Louis 1906- St&PR 91
Goodwin, Louis Payne 1922- WhoAmA 91
Goodwin, Marcy 1948- WhoEmL 91
Goodwin, Marv 1893-1925 Ballpl 90
Goodwin, Mary BioIn 16
Goodwin, Maryellen 1964- WhoAmW 91
Goodwin, Mathew B BiDrAPA 89
Goodwin, Maud 1856-1935 FemiCLE
Goodwin, Mimi Kate Munroe 1956- WhoAmW 91
Goodwin, Nancy Lee 1940- WhoAm 90
Goodwin, Noel 1927- IntWWM 90
Goodwin, Paul 1919- St&PR 91
Goodwin, Paul Richard 1943- WhoAm 90
Goodwin, Peggy BioIn 16
Goodwin, Peggy Jane 1954- WhoAmW 91
Goodwin, Phillip Hugh 1940- WhoAm 90, WhoSSW 91
Goodwin, Ralph Roger 1917- WhoAm 90
Goodwin, Richard G. 1935- St&PR 91
Goodwin, Richard Hale 1910- WhoE 91
Goodwin, Richard N. BioIn 16
Goodwin, Richard T. 1953- St&PR 91
Goodwin, Robert Clare 1942- BiDrAPA 89
Goodwin, Robert Delmege 1920- WhoAm 90
Goodwin, Robert L DrBlPA 90
Goodwin, Robert L. 1924- St&PR 91
Goodwin, Rodney Keith Grove 1944- WhoAm 90
Goodwin, Ron 1925- OxCPMus
Goodwin, Ronald Alfred 1925- IntWWM 90
Goodwin, Rosanne 1954- WhoAmW 91
Goodwin, Ruby Berkley 1903- HarlReB
Goodwin, Samuel Dennis 1951- WhoSSW 91
Goodwin, Stephen 1943- WhoWrEP 89
Goodwin, Suzanne ConAu 31NR
Goodwin, Thomas Carl 1955- BiDrAPA 89
Goodwin, Todd 1931- WhoAm 90, WhoE 91
Goodwin, Tony McDaniel 1962- WhoSSW 91
Goodwin, Vernon Glenn, Jr. 1957- WhoEmL 91
Goodwin, Warren W BiDrAPA 89
Goodwin, Willard Elmer 1915- WhoAm 90
Goodwin, William Dean 1937- WhoSSW 91
Goodwyn, James Turner, Jr. 1928- St&PR 91
Goodwyn, Larry Don 1958- WhoEmL 91, WhoSSW 91
Goodwyn, Richard Blackwood 1939- St&PR 91
Goody, Joan 1935- News 90 [port]
Goody, Richard Mead 1921- WhoAm 90
Goodyear, Austin 1919- St&PR 91
Goodyear, Charles 1800-1860 BioIn 16, WorAlBi
Goodyear, E. Stephen, Jr. ODwPR 91
Goodyear, Frank H, Jr 1944- WhoAmA 91
Goodyear, Frank Henry, Jr. 1944- WhoAm 90, WhoE 91
Goodyear, Holly Sue 1942- WhoAmW 91
Goodyear, John L 1930- WhoAmA 91
Goodyear, John L. 1936- St&PR 91
Goodyear, John Lake 1930- WhoAm 90
Goodyear, Karen Anne 1959- BiDrAPA 89
Goodykoontz, Bess NewYTBS 90
Goodykoontz, Charles Alfred 1928- WhoAm 90
Gooel, Bert J. 1904- St&PR 91
Googasian, George Ara 1936- WhoAm 90
Googe, John Wesley 1925- WhoAm 90
Googin, Royane BioIn 16
Googins, Robert Reville 1937- WhoAm 90
Googins, Sonya Forbes 1936- WhoAmW 91
Goohs, Charles Alan 1956- WhoE 91
Goohya, Indrakumar P BiDrAPA 89
Gookin, Daniel 1612-1687 EncCRAm
Gookin, Thomas Allen Jaudon 1951- WhoEmL 91, WhoWor 91
Gookin, William Scudder 1914- WhoWor 91
Goolagong, Evonne 1951- BioIn 16
Goolagong, Evonne Cawley 1951- WorAlBi
Goolam Hoosen, Ismail 1949- BiDrAPA 89
Goold, Edmond J BiDrAPA 89
Goolkasian, Aram Richard 1924- WhoAm 90, WhoE 91
Goolkasian, Paula A. 1948- WhoAmW 91
Goolsbee, Charles Thomas 1935- St&PR 91, WhoAm 90
Goolsby, David Coleman 1944- WhoE 91
Goolsby, Jerry Randell 1951- WhoSSW 91
Goolsby, Kenneth Eugene, Jr. 1955- BiDrAPA 89
Goolsby, Philip Lane 1955- WhoSSW 91
Goon, Dickson Bing 1954- WhoE 91
Gooneratne, Yasmine 1935- FemiCLE
Goonetilleke, D C R A 1938- ConAu 130
Goor, Nancy 1944- ConAu 32NR
Goor, Ron 1940- ConAu 32NR
Goorey, Nancy Jane 1922- WhoAmW 91
Goorley, John Theodore 1907- WhoSSW 91
Goos, Robert Bruce BiDrAPA 89
Goos, Roger Delmon 1924- WhoAm 90
Goosman, Arlys N. 1932- St&PR 91
Goosman, Eleanor McKee 1917- WhoAmW 91
Goossen, Eugene Coons 1920- WhoAmA 91
Goossen, Jacob Frederic 1927- IntWWM 90, WhoSSW 91
Goossen, Lawrence BioIn 16
Goossens, Eugene 1867-1958 PenDiMP
Goossens, Eugene 1893-1962 PenDiMP, -A
Goossens, Jozef Elisa 1943- WhoE 91
Goossens, Leon 1897-1988 AnObit 1988, PenDiMP
Goossens, Marie 1894- PenDiMP
Goossens, Marie Henriette 1894- IntWWM 90
Goossens, Sidonie 1899- IntWWM 90, PenDiMP
Goossens, Willem Jozef Jan Maria 1943- WhoWor 91
Goostray, Stella 1886-1969 BioIn 16
Goostree, Robert Edward 1923- WhoAm 90
Gootgeld, Marla 1954- WhoAmW 91
Gootman, Gerald Martin 1937- St&PR 91
Gootman, Phyllis Myrna 1938- WhoAmW 91, WhoE 91
Gootnick-Bruce, Stephanie 1954- WhoWrEP 89
Goott, Daniel 1919- WhoAm 90
Gootzeit, Jack Michael 1924- WhoAm 90, WhoE 91, WhoWor 91
Gopal, Doddaiah BiDrAPA 89
Gopal, Sarvepalli 1923- WhoWor 91
Gopalakrishnan, Chennat 1936- ConAu 30NR
Gopalan, Ramanath 1951- BiDrAPA 89
Gopalani, Hanif A BiDrAPA 89
Gopen, George David 1945- WhoSSW 91
Gopfert, Michael J. 1947- BiDrAPA 89
Gopi Krishna, Pandit 1903-1984 EncO&P 3
Gopinath, Gopala 1937- WhoWor 91
Gopinath, Padmanabh 1939- WhoWor 91
Gopman, Glenn Henry 1955- WhoSSW 91
Goppelt, John W 1924- BiDrAPA 89
Goppers, Velta Maneks 1915- WhoAm 90
Gopu, Vijaya K.A. 1949- WhoSSW 91
Goralnick, Harvey A. 1950- St&PR 91
Goralnick, L. Arnold 1930- St&PR 91
Goran, Judith H. 1952- WhoAmW 91
Goran, Michael J BiDrAPA 89
Gorans, Gerald Elmer 1922- WhoAm 90
Goranson, Eric Edwin 1944- BiDrAPA 89
Goranson, Harold Theodore 1947- WhoSSW 91
Goranson, Lecy BioIn 16
Goray, Gerald Allen 1939- WhoSSW 91, WhoWor 91
Gorbachev, Mikhail BioIn 16
Gorbachev, Mikhail 1931- ConAu 132, MajTwCW, WorAlBi
Gorbachev, Mikhail Sergeyevich 1931- WhoWor 91
Gorbachev, Raisa Maksimovna BioIn 16
Gorbachev, Raisa Maximovna 1932- WhoWor 91
Gorban, Carol V 1944- BiDrAPA 89
Gorban, Stephen E 1942- BiDrAPA 89
Gorbanevskaya, Natal'ya 1936- EncCoWW
Gorbatenko, Margaret S BiDrAPA 89
Gorbett, David S. 1946- WhoEmL 91
Gorbunov, Anatoliy Valer'yanovich 1942- WhoWor 91
Gorcheff, Nick A. 1958- WhoEmL 91
Gorchels, Clarence Clifford 1916- WhoAm 90
Gorchov, Ron 1930- WhoAmA 91
Gorchynski, Orest BiDrAPA 89
Gorcyca, Raymond M. 1942- St&PR 91
Gord, Stuart Karl 1936- St&PR 91
Gordan, Andrew Leb 1923- WhoWor 91
Gordan, Gilbert Saul 1916- WhoAm 90
Gordan, Judith Allison 1956- WhoEmL 91
Gordan-Feller, Carla Janine 1936- WhoAmW 91
Gordeeva, Ekaterina BioIn 16
Gorden, Fred BioIn 16
Gorden, Gerald Niccola 1950- WhoSSW 91
Gorden, Nancy D. 1937- WhoWrEP 89
Gorden, Phillip WhoAm 90
Gordenker, Leon 1923- WhoAm 90
Gorder, Clayton J 1936-1987 WhoAmA 91N
Gorder, Herbert W. 1935- St&PR 91
Gorder, Wayne Douglas 1946- IntWWM 90
Gordesky, Morton 1929- WhoWor 91
Gordett, Marea Beth 1949- WhoWrEP 89
Gordevitch, Igor 1924- WhoWor 91
Gordien, Fortune BioIn 16
Gordier, Gerald Len 1948- WhoEmL 91
Gordievsky, Oleg BioIn 16
Gordillo, Manuel E 1930- BiDrAPA 89
Gordimer, Nadine 1923- BioIn 16, FemiCLE, MajTwCW, WhoWor 91, WorAlBi
Gordin, Dean Lackey 1935- WhoAm 90
Gordin, Misha 1946- WhoAmA 91
Gordin, Sidney 1918- WhoAmA 91
Gordine, Dora 1906- BiDWomA
Gordinier, Dean F. 1923- St&PR 91
Gordinier, Karl D., Jr. 1939- WhoE 91
Gordis, David Moses 1940- WhoAm 90
Gordis, Enoch 1931- WhoAm 90
Gordis, Leon 1934- WhoAm 90
Gordis, Robert 1908- BioIn 16, WhoAm 90
Gordley, Marilyn Classe 1929- WhoAmA 91, WhoSSW 91
Gordley, Metz Tranbarger 1932- WhoAmA 91
Gordon, Adoniram Judson 1836-1895 BioIn 16
Gordon, Alan Craig 1954- WhoEmL 91
Gordon, Alan Ira 1958- WhoE 91
Gordon, Alan L. 1935- St&PR 91
Gordon, Alan Lee BiDrAPA 89
Gordon, Alan Lester 1955- BiDrAPA 89
Gordon, Alan R. 1943- St&PR 91
Gordon, Albert F 1934- WhoAmA 91
Gordon, Albert H. 1901- St&PR 91
Gordon, Albert Hamilton 1901- WhoAm 90
Gordon, Albert Isaac 1903-1968 BioIn 16
Gordon, Alice Cleora Jordan 1912- WhoAmW 91
Gordon, Allan D. 1925- St&PR 91
Gordon, Allan S. 1942- St&PR 91
Gordon, Alvin J 1912-1989 ConAu 130
Gordon, Andrew Robertson 1851-1893 DcCanB 12
Gordon, Angela ConAu 31NR
Gordon, Angus Neal, Jr. 1919- WhoAm 90
Gordon, Anthony Robert 1959- WhoEmL 91
Gordon, Arlene ODwPR 91
Gordon, Aron Samuel 1911- St&PR 91, WhoSSW 91
Gordon, Arthur 1922- St&PR 91
Gordon, Audrey Kramen 1935- WhoAmW 91
Gordon, Barbara G BiDrAPA 89
Gordon, Baron Jack 1953- WhoWor 91
Gordon, Barry Joel 1945- St&PR 91, WhoAm 90, WhoE 91
Gordon, Barry Monroe 1947- WhoEmL 91
Gordon, Barton Jennings 1949- WhoAm 90, WhoSSW 91
Gordon, Basil 1932- WhoAm 90
Gordon, Bernard 1922- WhoAm 90
Gordon, Bernard John 1954- BiDrAPA 89
Gordon, Bernard Marshall 1927- St&PR 91
Gordon, Bernard S 1914- BiDrAPA 89
Gordon, Bert I. 1922- ConTFT 8
Gordon, Bonnie Heather 1952- WhoAmW 91
Gordon, Brenda Camp 1955- WhoAmW 91
Gordon, Brian Keith 1957- WhoEmL 91
Gordon, Bruce Joel 1931- WhoAm 90
Gordon, Bruce W. 1948- St&PR 91
Gordon, Cameron M. WhoAm 90
Gordon, Carl 1932- DrBlPA 90
Gordon, Caroline 1895-1981 BioAmW, BioIn 16, DcLB 102 [port], FemiCLE, LiHiK, MajTwCW
Gordon, Carolyn Elaine 1946- WhoEmL 91
Gordon, Cecil 1906-1960 BioIn 16
Gordon, Charles 1905- WhoAm 90
Gordon, Charles A. 1928- St&PR 91
Gordon, Charles G. 1833-1885 WorAlBi
Gordon, Charles George 1833-1885 BioIn 16
Gordon, Charles Thomas BiDrAPA 89
Gordon, Christopher D 1949- BiDrAPA 89
Gordon, Conrad J. 1937- St&PR 91, WhoE 91
Gordon, Constance Mary Brand 1956- WhoEmL 91
Gordon, Cyrus Herzl 1908- AuBYP 90, WhoAm 90
Gordon, Dale C. 1948- St&PR 91
Gordon, Dale Craig 1948- WhoAm 90
Gordon, Dane Rex 1925- WhoAm 90
Gordon, Daniel Bowman 1950- WhoEmL 91
Gordon, Daniel Paul 1941- St&PR 91
Gordon, Daniel Paul 1942- WhoSSW 91
Gordon, Daniel R. 1951- WhoEmL 91
Gordon, Darrell Roth 1926- St&PR 91
Gordon, Darryel BioIn 16
Gordon, David ConAu 130, NewAgMG
Gordon, David Edward 1945- WhoEmL 91
Gordon, David Eliot 1949- WhoEmL 91
Gordon, David Jamieson 1947- WhoAm 90, WhoE 91
Gordon, David Livingstone 1916- WhoE 91, WhoSSW 91
Gordon, David Michael 1944- WhoE 91
Gordon, Deborah Hannes 1946- ConAu 130
Gordon, Dexter BioIn 16
Gordon, Dexter 1923-1990 NewYTBS 90, News 90, OxCPMus
Gordon, Diana Russell 1938- WhoAm 90
Gordon, Don 1926- WhoAm 90
Gordon, Don 1959- Ballpl 90
Gordon, Donald Edward 1931- WhoAmA 91N
Gordon, Donald Ramsay 1929- ConAu 31NR
Gordon, Donna Grace 1934- WhoAmW 91
Gordon, Doreen ConAu 31NR
Gordon, Dorothy 1893-1970 AuBYP 90
Gordon, Edgar Bernard 1875-1961 BioIn 16
Gordon, Edward 1930- WhoAm 90
Gordon, Edward 1935- BiDrAPA 89
Gordon, Edward David 1919- St&PR 91
Gordon, Edward I. 1938- WhoAm 90
Gordon, Edward Larry NewAgMG
Gordon, Edythe Mae 1890?- HarlReB
Gordon, Ellen R. BioIn 16
Gordon, Ellen R. 1931- St&PR 91
Gordon, Ellen Rubin WhoAm 90, WhoAmW 91
Gordon, Elsa Leiter BiDrAPA 89
Gordon, Emmanuel 1896-1990 BioIn 16
Gordon, Eric A 1945- ConAu 132
Gordon, Eric Bruce 1961- WhoEmL 91
Gordon, Ernest 1916- WhoAm 90
Gordon, Eugene Andrew 1917- WhoAm 90
Gordon, Ezra 1921- WhoAm 90
Gordon, Felton Hays 1915- WhoSSW 91, WhoWor 91
Gordon, Francine E. 1948- WhoAmW 91
Gordon, Frank N., Jr. 1924- St&PR 91

Gordon, Frank Wallace 1935- *WhoAm 90*
Gordon, Fritz *WhoWrEP 89*
Gordon, G. Barry 1931- *St&PR 91*
Gordon, Gale 1906- *WorAlBi*
Gordon, Gary *AuBYP 90, ConAu 30NR*
Gordon, Gary Donald 1928- *WhoE 91*
Gordon, Gene 1922- *BiDrAPA 89*
Gordon, Gene Stephen *BiDrAPA 89*
Gordon, George Minot 1947- *WhoAm 90*
Gordon, George Stanley 1931- *WhoAm 90*
Gordon, George William 1820-1865 *BioIn 16*
Gordon, Gerard James 1941- *St&PR 91*
Gordon, Gerd Stray 1912- *WhoAmW 91*
Gordon, Gilbert 1911- *St&PR 91*
Gordon, Gilbert 1933- *WhoAm 90*
Gordon, Glen E. 1935- *WhoAm 90*
Gordon, Gordon 1906- *TwCCr&M 91*
Gordon, Gordon 1912- *AuBYP 90*
Gordon, Guanetta Stewart *WhoWrEP 89*
Gordon, Gustave G *BiDrAPA 89*
Gordon, Gyorgy 1924- *BioIn 16*
Gordon, Hal *ConAu 131*
Gordon, Hal 1914-1990 *BioIn 16*
Gordon, Harold *BioIn 16*
Gordon, Harris A. 1907- *WhoWrEP 89*
Gordon, Harry 1906-1988 *BioIn 16*
Gordon, Harry Bernard 1909- *WhoSSW 91*
Gordon, Henry C. *EncO&P 3*
Gordon, Herbert David 1938- *St&PR 91*
Gordon, Howard 1938- *WhoWor 91*
Gordon, Igor Michael 1952- *WhoEmL 91*
Gordon, Ivan H. 1934- *St&PR 91*
Gordon, J Berkeley *BiDrAPA 89*
Gordon, J. Douglas 1924- *WhoSSW 91*
Gordon, J.P. 1920- *St&PR 91*
Gordon, Jack A. 1959- *WhoEmL 91*
Gordon, Jack David 1922- *WhoAm 90, WhoSSW 91*
Gordon, Jack Leonard 1928- *St&PR 91, WhoAm 90*
Gordon, Jack Marshall 1949- *WhoWrEP 89*
Gordon, Jack R 1927- *BiDrAPA 89*
Gordon, Jacques Nicholas 1956- *WhoE 91*
Gordon, Jaimy 1944- *WhoWrEP 89*
Gordon, James Alan 1949- *WhoEmL 91*
Gordon, James Braund 1911- *WhoAm 90*
Gordon, James C. 1946- *WhoSSW 91*
Gordon, James Edward 1946- *WhoEmL 91*
Gordon, James Fleming *NewYTBS 90 [port]*
Gordon, James Fleming 1918-1990 *BioIn 16*
Gordon, James Harold 1941- *BiDrAPA 89*
Gordon, James Martin 1948- *WhoEmL 91*
Gordon, James Patrick 1950- *WhoEmL 91*
Gordon, James Samuel 1941- *BiDrAPA 89*
Gordon, Jan Baker 1941- *WhoWor 91*
Gordon, Jane Ellen 1946- *WhoEmL 91*
Gordon, Janet Jean 1956- *WhoAmW 91*
Gordon, Janine 1946- *BiDrAPA 89*
Gordon, Janine M. 1946- *ODwPR 91, St&PR 91, WhoAm 90, WhoAmW 91*
Gordon, Jeffie Ross *SmATA X, WhoWrEP 89*
Gordon, Jeffrey Mark 1952- *WhoE 91*
Gordon, Jeffrey Neil 1942- *St&PR 91*
Gordon, Jeffrey Neil 1949- *WhoEmL 91*
Gordon, Jerold James 1930- *St&PR 91*
Gordon, Jill *BioIn 16*
Gordon, Joan May 1946- *WhoEmL 91*
Gordon, Joe 1915-1978 *Ballpl 90*
Gordon, Joel 1927- *St&PR 91*
Gordon, Joel C. 1929- *St&PR 91*
Gordon, Joel Charles 1929- *WhoSSW 91*
Gordon, Joel Ethan 1930- *WhoAm 90*
Gordon, John 1912-1978 *WhoAmA 91N*
Gordon, John C. 1925- *St&PR 91*
Gordon, John Chalmers 1925- *WhoAm 90*
Gordon, John Charles 1939- *WhoAm 90*
Gordon, John Edward 1931- *WhoAm 90*
Gordon, John Leo 1933- *WhoAm 90*
Gordon, John N 1922- *BiDrAPA 89*
Gordon, John S 1946- *WhoAmA 91*
Gordon, Jonathan David 1949- *WhoAm 90*
Gordon, Jonathan W. 1820-1887 *AmLegL*
Gordon, Jose 1954- *BiDrAPA 89*
Gordon, Joseph *BiDrAPA 89*
Gordon, Joseph Elwell 1921- *WhoAm 90*
Gordon, Joseph H. 1909- *St&PR 91*
Gordon, Joseph Harold 1909- *WhoAm 90*
Gordon, Joseph K. 1925- *St&PR 91*
Gordon, Josephine *WhoAmA 91*
Gordon, Joy L 1933- *WhoAmA 91*
Gordon, Jule *BioIn 16*
Gordon, Julian M. 1930- *St&PR 91*
Gordon, Julie Peyton 1940- *WhoAm 90, WhoAmW 91*
Gordon, Julie Starkman 1957- *WhoEmL 91*
Gordon, June 1929- *WhoAmW 91*
Gordon, Katherine 1954- *WhoAmW 91*
Gordon, Keith *BioIn 16*
Gordon, Keith L *BiDrAPA 89*
Gordon, Kenneth H, Jr. 1924- *BiDrAPA 89*
Gordon, Kenneth Hickok 1924- *WhoE 91*
Gordon, Kenneth L 1948- *BiDrAPA 89*
Gordon, Kenneth Robert 1935- *St&PR 91*
Gordon, Kris Romstad 1945- *WhoAmW 91*
Gordon, Larry D. 1938- *WhoWor 91*
Gordon, Larry Jean 1926- *WhoAm 90*
Gordon, Lee E *BiDrAPA 89*
Gordon, Leonard 1935- *WhoAm 90*
Gordon, Leonard Abraham 1938- *WhoE 91*
Gordon, Leonard Victor 1917- *WhoAm 90*
Gordon, Lew *AuBYP 90*
Gordon, Lewis 1937- *St&PR 91*
Gordon, Lewis Francis 1918- *WhoSSW 91*
Gordon, Lincoln 1913- *WhoAm 90, WhoE 91*
Gordon, Linda Diane *BiDrAPA 89*
Gordon, Linnea Hammersten 1945- *WhoAmW 91*
Gordon, Lloyd Reid 1916- *St&PR 91*
Gordon, Lois Goldfein 1938- *WhoAm 90*
Gordon, Lonny Joseph 1942- *IntWWM 90, WhoWor 91*
Gordon, Lorne Bertram 1945- *WhoAm 90*
Gordon, Lucie Duff 1821-1869 *BioIn 16, FemiCLE*
Gordon, Lugenia J. *BioIn 16*
Gordon, Lynne A. 1939- *WhoAmW 91*
Gordon, Lynne Verdelle 1959- *WhoE 91*
Gordon, Mack 1904-1959 *OxCPMus*
Gordon, Mack 1915- *St&PR 91*
Gordon, Malcolm 1925- *BiDrAPA 89*
Gordon, Malcolm Stephen 1933- *WhoAm 90*
Gordon, Marcia L *BiDrAPA 89*
Gordon, Margaret H. 1957- *St&PR 91*
Gordon, Margaret Shaughnessy 1910- *WhoAm 90*
Gordon, Maria T. 1965- *WhoAmW 91*
Gordon, Marilyn Anita 1949- *WhoEmL 91*
Gordon, Marilyn Helen 1953- *IntWWM 90*
Gordon, Marjorie *IntWWM 90, ODwPR 91, WhoAm 90*
Gordon, Marshall 1937- *WhoAm 90*
Gordon, Martin 1939- *WhoAm 90, WhoAmA 91*
Gordon, Martin N *BiDrAPA 89*
Gordon, Marvin *BioIn 16*
Gordon, Marvin B. 1916- *St&PR 91*
Gordon, Mary 1949- *BioIn 16, FemiCLE, MajTwCW, WorAlBi*
Gordon, Mary Catherine 1949- *WhoAmW 91*
Gordon, Mary McDougall 1929- *ConAu 130*
Gordon, Maurice B *BiDrAPA 89*
Gordon, Max *BioIn 16*
Gordon, Max 1903-1989 *AnObit 1989, BioIn 16*
Gordon, Max 1931-1990 *NewYTBS 90*
Gordon, Maxwell 1910-1982 *WhoAmA 91N*
Gordon, Maxwell 1921- *WhoAm 90*
Gordon, Melvin J. 1919- *St&PR 91*
Gordon, Melvin Jay 1919- *WhoAm 90*
Gordon, Merrill Kern 1919- *St&PR 91*
Gordon, Michael 1909- *WhoAm 90*
Gordon, Michael 1923- *St&PR 91*
Gordon, Michael Herbert 1941- *WhoWor 91*
Gordon, Michael Owen 1944- *BiDrAPA 89*
Gordon, Michael R. 1951- *St&PR 91*
Gordon, Mike *ODwPR 91*
Gordon, Mildred 1905-1979 *TwCCr&M 91*
Gordon, Mildred 1912-1979 *AuBYP 90*
Gordon, Milton A. *NewYTBS 90*
Gordon, Milton A. 1908-1990 *BioIn 16*
Gordon, Milton G. 1922- *WhoAm 90*
Gordon, Milton Paul 1930- *WhoAm 90*
Gordon, Minita Elmira 1930- *WhoWor 91*
Gordon, Miriam Posey 1947- *WhoAmW 91*
Gordon, Mitchell Keith 1957- *WhoSSW 91*
Gordon, Monte J. *WhoAm 90*
Gordon, Monte J. 1923- *St&PR 91*
Gordon, Murray A 1941- *BiDrAPA 89*
Gordon, Nathan 1938- *St&PR 91*
Gordon, Neil R. 1948- *St&PR 91*
Gordon, Neil Roger 1948- *WhoEmL 91*
Gordon, Nicholas 1928- *WhoAm 90*
Gordon, Nicole Ann 1954- *WhoAm 90*
Gordon, Nina Marlene 1951- *WhoAmW 91*
Gordon, Nina Robin 1959- *WhoAmW 91*
Gordon, Norman Botnick 1921- *WhoAm 90*
Gordon, P S 1953- *WhoAmA 91*
Gordon, Patricia 1904- *AuBYP 90*
Gordon, Paul John 1921- *WhoAm 90, WhoWor 91*
Gordon, Paul Perry 1927- *WhoWrEP 89*
Gordon, Paul Wiley, Jr. *BiDrAPA 89*
Gordon, Paula Rossbacher 1953- *WhoAmW 91, WhoE 91*
Gordon, Peter H. 1948- *ConAu 130*
Gordon, Philip D. 1960- *WhoEmL 91*
Gordon, Philip Lynn 1960- *St&PR 91*
Gordon, Priscilla Ann 1938- *IntWWM 90*
Gordon, Ralph A. 1944- *St&PR 91*
Gordon, Ralph D. 1940- *St&PR 91*
Gordon, Randall Eugene 1949- *St&PR 91*
Gordon, Richard 1925- *BioIn 16*
Gordon, Richard E 1922- *BiDrAPA 89*
Gordon, Richard Edwards 1922- *WhoAm 90*
Gordon, Richard H. *BioIn 16*
Gordon, Richard Joseph 1933- *WhoAm 90*
Gordon, Richard Lewis 1934- *WhoAm 90*
Gordon, Richard M. Erik 1949- *WhoEmL 91*
Gordon, Rita Simon 1929- *WhoAmW 91*
Gordon, Robert Bailey *BiDrAPA 89*
Gordon, Robert Boyd 1929- *WhoAm 90*
Gordon, Robert Douglas 1948- *WhoAm 90*
Gordon, Robert Edward 1925- *WhoAm 90*
Gordon, Robert Frederick *WhoE 91*
Gordon, Robert James 1940- *WhoAm 90*
Gordon, Robert M. 1953- *WhoEmL 91*
Gordon, Robert P. 1935- *WhoWor 91*
Gordon, Robert Peter 1943- *BiDrAPA 89*
Gordon, Robert R., Jr. 1944- *St&PR 91*
Gordon, Robin Gail 1937- *WhoAmW 91*
Gordon, Rochelle H *BiDrAPA 89*
Gordon, Roger L. *WhoAm 90*
Gordon, Ronald Jay *BiDrAPA 89*
Gordon, Ronald John 1954- *WhoHisp 91*
Gordon, Rose Maria Elizabeth 1931- *WhoAmW 91*
Gordon, Roy Gerald 1940- *WhoAm 90*
Gordon, Roy Harris 1926- *St&PR 91*
Gordon, Russell Talbert 1936- *WhoAmA 91*
Gordon, Ruth 1896-1985 *BioIn 16, ConAu 31NR, FemiCLE, NotWoAT, WorAlBi*
Gordon, Ruth Evelyn 1910- *WhoE 91*
Gordon, Ruth Whitacre 1949- *WhoSSW 91*
Gordon, Samuel 1934- *WhoAm 90*
Gordon, Sandra Nitsch 1952- *WhoEmL 91*
Gordon, Sanford Daniel 1924- *WhoAm 90*
Gordon, Sanford R. 1924- *St&PR 91*
Gordon, Sara J. 1937- *WhoAmW 91*
Gordon, Sarah 1944- *ConAu 132*
Gordon, Scott 1949- *WhoE 91, WhoEmL 91*
Gordon, Scott Edward 1953- *WhoSSW 91*
Gordon, Selma *AuBYP 90*
Gordon, Shana *WhoE 91*
Gordon, Sheila 1927- *ConAu 132*
Gordon, Shirley 1921- *BioIn 16*
Gordon, Shirley Blom 1922- *WhoAm 90*
Gordon, Sid 1917-1975 *Ballpl 90*
Gordon, Sol 1923- *AuBYP 90*
Gordon, Spencer *BiDrAPA 89*
Gordon, Stephen Franklin 1945- *WhoEmL 91*
Gordon, Stephen M. 1942- *St&PR 91*
Gordon, Stephen Maurice 1942- *WhoAm 90*
Gordon, Steve *NewAgMG*
Gordon, Steven Eric 1960- *WhoEmL 91*
Gordon, Steven Robert *NewYTBS 90*
Gordon, Steven Stanley 1919- *WhoAm 90*
Gordon, Stewart *AuBYP 90*
Gordon, Stewart George 1937- *St&PR 91, WhoAm 90*
Gordon, Stewart Lynell 1930- *IntWWM 90*
Gordon, Stuart *BioIn 16*
Gordon, Ted Howard 1946- *WhoEmL 91*
Gordon, Teresa Peale 1948- *WhoAmW 91*
Gordon, Teresa Rosen *BioIn 16*
Gordon, Terry *ODwPR 91*
Gordon, Theodore 1924- *MusmAFA*
Gordon, Thomas Christian, Jr. 1915- *WhoAm 90*
Gordon, Tina *WhoAmA 91*
Gordon, Tom 1967- *Ballpl 90*
Gordon, Trina D. 1954- *St&PR 91*
Gordon, Violet 1907- *WhoAmA 91*
Gordon, Walter 1907- *WhoAm 90*
Gordon, Walter Kelly 1930- *WhoAm 90, WhoE 91*
Gordon, Ward Blake 1931- *St&PR 91*
Gordon, Wendell Chaffee 1916- *WhoAm 90*
Gordon, William Bernard 1935- *WhoE 91*
Gordon, William Donald 1858- *AmLegL*
Gordon, William E *BiDrAPA 89*
Gordon, William Edwin 1918- *WhoAm 90*
Gordon, William Livingston 1927- *WhoAm 90*
Gordon, William Richard 1913- *WhoAm 90*
Gordon-Bell, Ophelia 1915-1975 *BiDWomA*
Gordon-Fahn, Carin Rise *BiDrAPA 89*
Gordon-Hardy, Laurie Lloyd 1955- *WhoEmL 91*
Gordon-Kirsch, Mary T. 1957- *St&PR 91*
Gordon-Lathrop, Susan Marie 1950- *WhoEmL 91*
Gordon-Omelka, Judith Michele 1947- *WhoAmW 91*
Gordone, Charles 1925- *DrBlPA 90, MajTwCW*
Gordone, Charles 1927- *WhoAm 90*
Gordons *AuBYP 90*
Gordons, The *TwCCr&M 91*
Gordonsmith, John Arthur Harold 1942- *St&PR 91, WhoAm 90*
Gordonson, Robert Martin 1935- *St&PR 91, WhoAm 90, WhoWor 91*
Gordy, Adrienne Yvonne 1958- *WhoAmW 91*
Gordy, Berry 1929- *WhoAm 90, WorAlBi*
Gordy, Berry, Jr. *BioIn 16*
Gordy, Berry, Jr. 1929- *DrBlPA 90, EncPR&S 89, OxCPMus*
Gordy, Charlie Leon 1938- *WhoSSW 91*
Gordy, Denise Marie 1958- *WhoAmW 91*
Gordy, Michael A. 1947- *St&PR 91*
Gordy, Robert P 1933-1986 *WhoAmA 91N*
Gordy, Tracy R 1936- *BiDrAPA 89*
Gordy, Vaunda *St&PR 91*
Gore, Albert, Jr. *BioIn 16*
Gore, Albert, Jr. 1948- *WhoAm 90, WhoSSW 91, WhoWor 91, WorAlBi*
Gore, Albert A. 1907- *WorAlBi*
Gore, Altovise 1935- *DrBlPA 90*
Gore, Barry Maurice 1944- *WhoAm 90*
Gore, Brian H. 1951- *St&PR 91*
Gore, Catherine 1799-1861 *FemiCLE*
Gore, Catherine Grace Frances Moody 1799-1861 *BioIn 16*
Gore, Chadwick Rene 1949- *WhoE 91*
Gore, Christopher *BioIn 16*
Gore, Cynthia Dolores 1962- *WhoAmW 91*
Gore, David Curtiss 1964- *WhoEmL 91*
Gore, David Eugene 1935- *St&PR 91, WhoAm 90*
Gore, David Ormsby 1918-1985 *DcNaB 1981*
Gore, Genevieve Walton 1913- *St&PR 91*
Gore, George 1857-1933 *Ballpl 90 [port]*
Gore, George 1939- *WhoAm 90*
Gore, Howard Mason 1877-1947 *BiDrUSE 89*
Gore, Jeanne Guerrero 1945- *WhoWrEP 89*
Gore, Jefferson Anderson 1943- *WhoAmA 91*
Gore, Jerry Paul *BiDrAPA 89*
Gore, Ken 1911- *WhoAmA 91*
Gore, Lesley 1946- *WorAlBi*
Gore, Madhav Sadashiv 1921- *WhoWor 91*
Gore, Mary Elizabeth 1948- *BioIn 16*
Gore, Michael Edward John 1935- *WhoWor 91*
Gore, Patricia Louise 1942- *WhoSSW 91*
Gore, Patricia Lynn 1946- *WhoAmW 91*
Gore, Philip Larner 1911- *St&PR 91*
Gore, Richard Michael 1953- *WhoEmL 91*
Gore, Samuel Marshall 1927- *WhoAmA 91*
Gore, Thomas Orville *BiDrAPA 89*
Gore, Tipper 1948- *BioIn 16*
Gore, Tom 1946- *WhoAmA 91*
Gore, Tony Allen *BiDrAPA 89*
Gore, William Jay 1924- *WhoAm 90*
Gore-Booth, Eva 1870-1926 *FemiCLE*
Gore-Booth, Eva Selina 1870-1926 *BioIn 16*
Gore-Booth, Paul Henry 1909-1984 *DcNaB 1981*
Goreau, Angeline W. 1951- *WhoWrEP 89*
Gorecki, Henryk Mikolaj 1933- *IntWWM 90*
Gorecki, Jan 1926- *WhoAm 90*
Gorecki, Joseph F. 1953- *St&PR 91*
Gorecki, Stanley L. 1941- *St&PR 91*
Goree, Bea M. 1932- *WhoAmW 91*
Goree, Gary Paul 1951- *WhoAmA 91*
Goreham, B. Sheldon 1915- *St&PR 91*
Gorelick, Amy Sue *BiDrAPA 89*
Gorelick, David Alan 1947- *BiDrAPA 89*
Gorelick, Jamie Shona 1950- *WhoEmL 91*
Gorelick, Kenneth Paul 1942- *BiDrAPA 89, WhoE 91*
Gorelick, Kenny *BioIn 16*
Gorelick, Shelton 1929- *St&PR 91*
Gorelick, Shirley 1924- *WhoAmA 91, WhoE 91*
Gorelick, William 1934- *St&PR 91*
Gorelik, Asher Raphael 1957- *BiDrAPA 89, WhoSSW 91*
Gorelik, Mordecai 1899-1990 *BioIn 16, ConAu 131, ConDes 90*
Gorell, Wayne Cook 1948- *St&PR 91*
Goren, Alexander Mircea 1940- *WhoE 91*
Goren, Alvin 1927- *BiDrAPA 89*
Goren, Arnold Louis *WhoAm 90*
Goren, Bruce Neal 1956- *WhoEmL 91*
Goren, Charles H. 1901- *WorAlBi*
Goren, Eli *PenDiMP*
Goren, Eli 1923- *IntWWM 90*
Goren, Howard Joseph 1941- *WhoAm 90*
Goren, Marvin R. 1923- *St&PR 91*
Goren, William Hart 1946- *WhoEmL 91*
Gorenberg, Donald 1948- *St&PR 91*
Gorenflo, Rudolf 1930- *WhoWor 91*
Goreniuc, Mircea C Paul 1942- *WhoAmA 91*
Gorenko, Anna *EncCoWW*
Gorenstein, Edward 1936- *WhoE 91, WhoWor 91*

Gorenstein, Gabriel William 1957- *WhoEmL 91*
Gorenstein, Paul 1934- *WhoE 91*
Gorenstein, Shirley Slotkin 1928- *WhoAm 90*
Gorenstein-Fontetta, Diane 1955- *WhoE 91*
Gores, Joe 1931- *TwCCr&M 91*
Gores, Joseph Nicholas 1931- *WhoAm 90, WhoWrEP 89*
Gores, Landis 1919- *WhoAm 90*
Goresbeck, Clarence Jess 1934- *BiDrAPA 89*
Goresky, Walter Victor 1927- *BiDrAPA 89*
Goretta, Claude *BioIn 16*
Gorewitz, Rubin Leon 1924- *WhoE 91, WhoWor 91*
Gorey, Edward 1925- *BioIn 16, ConAu 30NR*
Gorey, Edward St. John 1925- *WhoAm 90, WhoWrEP 89*
Gorfine, Stephen Richard 1949- *WhoE 91*
Gorgas, Tamara Margaret 1959- *WhoEmL 91*
Gorgas, William C. 1854-1920 *WorAlBi*
Gorgas, William Crawford 1854-1920 *BioIn 16*
Gorges, Ferdinando 1568?-1647 *EncCRAm*
Gorges, Heinz August 1913- *WhoSSW 91*
Gorgi, Habib Y. 1956- *St&PR 91*
Gorgias 485?BC-380?BC *WrPh P*
Gorgues, Xavier 1958- *WhoWor 91*
Gorguze, V.T. 1916- *St&PR 91*
Gorham, David L. 1932- *St&PR 91, WhoAm 90, WhoE 91*
Gorham, Donald R. 1903- *WhoAm 90*
Gorham, Eville 1925- *WhoAm 90*
Gorham, Frank D., Jr. 1921- *St&PR 91*
Gorham, Frank DeVore, Jr. 1921- *WhoAm 90*
Gorham, Katherine L *BiDrAPA 89*
Gorham, Linda Joanne 1951- *WhoAmW 91*
Gorham, Michael *AuBYP 90*
Gorham, Nathaniel 1738-1796 *BiDrUSE 89, BioIn 16*
Gorham, Sally Mary 1945- *WhoSSW 91*
Gorham, Sidney 1870-1947 *WhoAmA 91N*
Gorham, William 1930- *WhoAm 90*
Gorham, William Hartshorne 1933- *WhoAm 90*
Gori, Lamberto Cristiano *PenDiDA 89*
Goria, Giovanni 1943- *WhoWor 91*
Gorigin, Eugene Boris 1919- *WhoAm 90*
Gorin, Barney Franklin 1945- *WhoE 91*
Gorin, Debra Sue *BiDrAPA 89*
Gorin, Ernest Bartley 1911-1989 *BioIn 16*
Gorin, George 1925- *WhoAm 90*
Gorin, Leonard Joseph 1917- *WhoWor 91*
Gorin, Michael 1941- *St&PR 91*
Gorin, Norbert Claude 1946- *WhoWor 91*
Gorin, Robert Murray, Jr. 1948- *WhoE 91, WhoEmL 91*
Gorin, Robert S. 1935- *St&PR 91*
Gorin, William 1908- *WhoAm 90*
Goring, Arthur William 1915- *WhoSSW 91*
Goring, David Arthur Ingham 1920- *WhoAm 90*
Goring, Hermann 1893-1946 *BioIn 16*
Goring, Peter Allan Elliott 1943- *WhoAm 90*
Gorinoviteh-Greenwich, Jurge Joan 1938- *WhoE 91, WhoWor 91*
Gorke, Thomas Peter 1948- *St&PR 91*
Gorkin, Jess 1913- *WhoWrEP 89*
Gorkin, Robert A *BiDrAPA 89*
Gorkuscha, Mischa 1946- *St&PR 91*
Gorky, Arshile 1904-1948 *IntDcAA 90*
Gorky, Arshile 1905-1948 *WorAlBi*
Gorky, Maksim 1868-1936 *BioIn 16*
Gorky, Maxim 1868-1936 *BioIn 16, WorAlBi*
Gorla, Carlo 1942- *St&PR 91*
Gorla, Michael Joseph 1952- *WhoEmL 91*
Gorlach, Manfred 1937- *WhoWor 91*
Gorland, Ronald K. 1944- *St&PR 91*
Gorland, Ronald Kent 1944- *WhoAm 90*
Gorlick, Alan E. 1948- *St&PR 91*
Gorlin, Rena Ann 1957- *WhoE 91, WhoEmL 91*
Gorlin, Richard 1926- *WhoAm 90*
Gorlin, Robert James 1923- *WhoAm 90*
Gorlitz, Axel 1935- *WhoWor 91*
Gorlitz, Samuel J. 1917- *WhoE 91*
Gorman, Aileen Patricia 1946- *St&PR 91*
Gorman, Alan Thomas 1952- *St&PR 91*
Gorman, Alvin L. 1933- *St&PR 91*
Gorman, Alvin Larry 1933- *WhoAm 90*
Gorman, Anne D. 1950- *WhoAmW 91*
Gorman, Arthur Pue 1839-1906 *AmLegL*
Gorman, Barry Charles *BiDrAPA 89*
Gorman, Beth *ConAu 31NR*
Gorman, Burton William 1907- *WhoAm 90*
Gorman, Charles Edmund 1844-1917 *AmLegL*
Gorman, Charles Paul 1956- *BiDrAPA 89*
Gorman, David H. 1946- *WhoAm 90*
Gorman, David Harlan 1946- *St&PR 91*
Gorman, Dennis Gregory Cates 1960- *WhoEmL 91, WhoSSW 91*
Gorman, Ed 1941- *TwCCr&M 91*
Gorman, Freddie *BioIn 16*
Gorman, Gerald Allen 1929- *St&PR 91*
Gorman, Gerald Warner 1933- *WhoAm 90*
Gorman, Harry *BioIn 16*
Gorman, Jack Matthew 1951- *BiDrAPA 89*
Gorman, James *AuBYP 90*
Gorman, James Carvill 1924- *St&PR 91*
Gorman, James Lou *WhoE 91*
Gorman, Jeff *BioIn 16*
Gorman, Jeffrey Scott 1952- *St&PR 91*
Gorman, John Andrew 1938- *WhoWrEP 89*
Gorman, John H. *St&PR 91*
Gorman, John William 1950- *WhoAm 90*
Gorman, Joseph Gregory, Jr. 1939- *WhoAm 90*
Gorman, Joseph P., Jr. 1943- *St&PR 91*
Gorman, Joseph Tolle 1937- *BioIn 16, St&PR 91, WhoAm 90*
Gorman, Joyce Johanna 1952- *WhoEmL 91*
Gorman, Judy 1942- *WhoWrEP 89*
Gorman, Karen Machmer 1955- *WhoAmW 91*
Gorman, Kenneth T. 1954- *St&PR 91*
Gorman, Kevin John *BiDrAPA 89*
Gorman, Kirk Edward 1950- *St&PR 91*
Gorman, Larry Edward 1954- *WhoEmL 91*
Gorman, Lauren K 1951- *BiDrAPA 89*
Gorman, Leon 1934- *BioIn 16*
Gorman, Leon A. 1934- *WhoAm 90*
Gorman, Leon Arthur 1934- *St&PR 91*
Gorman, Lynn R. 1942- *St&PR 91*
Gorman, Lynn Ray 1942- *WhoSSW 91, WhoWor 91*
Gorman, M Lorraine *BiDrAPA 89*
Gorman, Marcie Sothern 1949- *WhoAmW 91, WhoEmL 91, WhoSSW 91, WhoWor 91*
Gorman, Marvin 1928- *St&PR 91*
Gorman, Maureen V. *ODwPR 91*
Gorman, Michael Joseph 1941- *WhoAm 90*
Gorman, Michael Stephen 1951- *WhoEmL 91*
Gorman, Mike *BiDrAPA 89*
Gorman, Nancy J. 1948- *WhoEmL 91*
Gorman, Patricia Jane 1950- *WhoAm 90*
Gorman, Paul Francis 1923- *St&PR 91*
Gorman, Paul Joseph 1958- *WhoE 91*
Gorman, R. C. 1933- *BioIn 16*
Gorman, R C 1933- *WhoAmA 91*
Gorman, Robert A. 1937- *WhoAm 90*
Gorman, Robert Saul 1933- *WhoWor 91*
Gorman, Robin B. 1960- *ODwPR 91*
Gorman, Rudolph Carl 1933- *BioIn 16, WhoAm 90*
Gorman, Susan Marie 1946- *WhoAmW 91*
Gorman, Thomas D. *ODwPR 91*
Gorman, Thomas Francis Xavier 1913-1989 *BioIn 16*
Gorman, Thomas L 1947- *St&PR 91*
Gorman, Tom 1916-1986 *Ballpl 90*
Gorman, Tom 1925- *Ballpl 90*
Gorman, Tom 1957- *Ballpl 90*
Gorman, Warren F 1916- *BiDrAPA 89*
Gorman, William D 1925- *WhoAmA 91*
Gorman, William David 1925- *WhoAm 90*
Gorman, William Moore 1923- *WhoWor 91*
Gorman, William Thomas 1936- *St&PR 91*
Gorman, Wilma Rose 1923- *WhoAmW 91*
Gormandy, Winston *BiDrAPA 89*
Gorme, Eydie *WhoAm 90*
Gorme, Eydie 1932- *WorAlBi*
Gormezano, Keith Stephen 1955- *WhoEmL 91, WhoWor 91, WhoWrEP 89*
Gormley, Art *ODwPR 91*
Gormley, David P 1935- *BiDrAPA 89*
Gormley, Dennis James 1939- *St&PR 91, WhoAm 90*
Gormley, Edward Joseph 1928- *St&PR 91*
Gormley, Matthew J. *BioIn 16*
Gormley, Myra DeVee 1940- *WhoAm 90*
Gormley, Robert James 1921- *WhoAm 90*
Gormley, Robert John 1939- *WhoAm 90*
Gormley, William Paul 1926- *WhoE 91*
Gormly, Barbara Diesner 1943- *WhoAmW 91*
Gormly, John Matthew 1947- *St&PR 91*
Gormly, William W. *ODwPR 91*
Gormsen, Preben 1941- *WhoWor 91*
Gorn, Janet Marie 1938- *WhoAm 90*
Gornall, Glenn A. 1933- *St&PR 91*
Gorney, Henry S. 1942- *St&PR 91*
Gorney, Jay *NewYTBS 90*
Gorney, Jay 1896-1990 *BioIn 16, OxCPMus*
Gorney, Jay Philip 1952- *WhoAmA 91, WhoE 91*
Gorney, Roderic 1924- *BiDrAPA 89, WhoAm 90*
Gorney, Sondra K. 1918- *ODwPR 91*
Gorni, Yosef *ConAu 130*
Gorniak, Michael John 1953- *WhoEmL 91*
Gornichec, Roger F. 1949- *St&PR 91*
Gornick, Alan Lewis 1908- *WhoAm 90, WhoWor 91*
Gornick, Michael George 1947- *St&PR 91*
Gornick, Vivian *BioIn 16*
Gornicki, Hank 1911- *Ballpl 90*
Gornik, April *BioIn 16*
Gornik, April 1953- *WhoAmA 91*
Gornish, Gerald 1937- *WhoAm 90*
Gornish, Stanley Edward 1943- *WhoE 91*
Gornto, Albert B., Jr. 1929- *St&PR 91*
Gornto, Albert Brooks, Jr. 1929- *WhoAm 90, WhoSSW 91*
Gornto, Neil Brooks 1954- *St&PR 91*
Gorny, A-P 1950- *WhoAmA 91*
Gorny, Joseph *ConAu 130*
Gorny, Yosef 1933- *ConAu 130*
Goro, Cynthia A. 1955- *St&PR 91*
Gorodetsky, Galina M 1946- *BiDrAPA 89*
Gorodetzky, Charles W. *AuBYP 90*
Gorodetzky, Charles William 1937- *WhoAm 90*
Gorodnitzki, Sascha 1904-1986 *BioIn 16*
Gorog, William Francis 1925- *WhoAm 90*
Goroncy, John Anthony, III 1953- *WhoAm 90*
Goronkin, Herbert 1936- *WhoAm 90*
Goroo, Ramzan Mohd 1919- *WhoWor 91*
Gorostiza, Celestino *HispWr 90*
Gorostiza, Jose 1901-1973 *ConAu 131, HispWr 90*
Gorostiza, Jose 1901-1979 *BioIn 16*
Gorostiza-Tolod, Emelinda V *BiDrAPA 89*
Gorove, Margaret Joan 1935- *WhoAmA 91*
Gorovsky, Martin A. 1941- *WhoAm 90*
Gorowski, Mieczyslaw 1941- *ConDes 90*
Gorr, Ivan William *WhoAm 90*
Gorr, Ivan William 1929- *St&PR 91*
Gorr, Louis Frederick 1941- *WhoAm 90, WhoSSW 91*
Gorr, Rita 1926- *IntWWM 90, PenDiMP*
Gorrara, Riccardo 1964- *IntWWM 90*
Gorrell, Dena Ruth 1932- *WhoWrEP 89*
Gorrin, Eugene 1956- *WhoE 91, WhoEmL 91*
Gorry, F. Jack 1933- *St&PR 91*
Gorsch, Allen M 1928- *BiDrAPA 89*
Gorshkov, Sergei 1910-1988 *AnObit 1988*
Gorshkov, Sergei Georgievich 1910-1988 *BioIn 16*
Gorsica, Johnny 1915- *Ballpl 90*
Gorske, Robert H. 1932- *St&PR 91*
Gorske, Robert Herman 1932- *WhoAm 90*
Gorski, Ben 1930- *St&PR 91*
Gorski, Daniel Alexander 1939- *WhoAmA 91, WhoE 91*
Gorski, Jack 1931- *WhoAm 90*
Gorski, Jean Marilyn 1934- *WhoE 91*
Gorski, Jon Steven 1953- *WhoEmL 91*
Gorski, Karol 1903-1988 *BioIn 16*
Gorski, Paul Thomas 1940- *WhoSSW 91*
Gorski, Richard Kenny 1923- *WhoAmA 91*
Gorski, Roger Anthony 1935- *WhoAm 90*
Gorski, Walter Joseph 1943- *St&PR 91, WhoAm 90*
Gorski, William Edward 1950- *WhoWor 91*
Gorski-Simon, Kathleen M. 1958- *WhoEmL 91*
Gorsline, Douglas Warner 1913-1985 *WhoAmA 91N*
Gorsline, Russell Elvin 1943- *WhoWor 91*
Gorson, James Roy 1924- *WhoWor 91*
Gorson, S. Marshall 1924- *St&PR 91*
Gorst, Nina 1869-1926 *FemiCLE*
Gorst, Norma 1936- *WhoWrEP 89*
Gorsuch, John Wilbert 1930- *WhoAm 90*
Gorsuch, Norman Clifford 1942- *WhoAm 90*
Gort, Douglas Jon 1953- *St&PR 91*
Gort, Michael 1923- *WhoAm 90*
Gort, Seymour *St&PR 91*
Gortani, Michele 1883-1966 *DcScB S2*
Gortari, Carlos Salinas de *BioIn 16*
Gorter, James Polk 1929- *St&PR 91, WhoAm 90*
Gorth, William Phillip 1943- *WhoAm 90*
Gortner, Marjoe *BioIn 16*
Gortner, Susan Reichert 1932- *WhoAmW 91*
Gortner, Willis Alway 1913- *WhoAm 90*
Gorton, Arlene Elizabeth 1931- *WhoAm 90*
Gorton, Azita Bagheri 1961- *WhoEmL 91*
Gorton, Gregg Emmanuel 1953- *BiDrAPA 89, WhoE 91*
Gorton, Kaitlyn *WhoWrEP 89*
Gorton, Kaitlyn 1947- *SmATA X [port]*
Gorton, Lars 1939- *WhoWor 91*
Gorton, Roy E. 1936- *St&PR 91*
Gorton, Samuel 1592?-1677 *EncCRAm*
Gorton, Slade 1928- *WhoAm 90, WhoWor 91*
Gorton, Thomas Arthur 1910- *WhoAm 90*
Gortsema, Janet Phillips *WhoWrEP 89*
Gorup, Gregory James 1948- *WhoE 91, WhoWor 91*
Goryan, Sirak *ConAu 30NR, MajTwCW*
Goryl, Johnny 1933- *Ballpl 90*
Gorzegno, Walter Paul 1925- *St&PR 91*
Gorzynska, Barbara 1953- *IntWWM 90*
Gorzynski, Janusz G 1940- *BiDrAPA 89*
Gosa, James Jake 1947- *St&PR 91*
Gosch, David *BioIn 16*
Gosch, Johnny *BioIn 16*
Gosch, Noreen *BioIn 16*
Goschi, Nicholas Peter 1925- *WhoAm 90*
Gosciewski, Robert Louis 1957- *WhoE 91*
Goscinny 1926-1977 *BioIn 16*
Gosden, Freeman F. 1899-1982 *WorAlBi*
Gosden, Freeman F. 1928- *St&PR 91*
Gosden, Freeman F., Jr. 1928- *WhoAm 90*
Gose, Elliott Bickley 1926- *WhoAm 90*
Gose, Elliott Bickley, Jr. 1926- *WhoWrEP 89*
Gose, Wulf Achim 1938- *WhoAm 90*
Gosek, Ewa *BiDrAPA 89*
Gosen, Karen Mae *BiDrAPA 89*
Gosewehr, Carl Louis 1926- *St&PR 91*
Gosewich, Arnold 1934- *WhoAm 90*
Gosger, Jim 1942- *Ballpl 90*
Goshen, Charles E 1916- *BiDrAPA 89*
Goshen, Charles Ernest 1916-1989 *BioIn 16*
Goshen, Charles R *BiDrAPA 89*
Goshen-Gottstein, Moshe Henry 1925- *WhoWor 91*
Goshi, Keiichi 1927- *WhoWor 91*
Goshorn, Roy W *BiDrAPA 89*
Gosine, Raymond Francis 1934- *St&PR 91*
Goslee, James *BioIn 16*
Goslee, James Edward, III *NewYTBS 90*
Goslin, Goose 1900-1971 *Ballpl 90 [port]*
Goslin, John Alan 1947- *St&PR 91*
Goslin, Ruth Ella 1951- *WhoSSW 91*
Gosline, Ernest 1924- *BiDrAPA 89*
Gosline, Robert Bradley 1913- *WhoAm 90*
Gosline, William James, Jr. 1953- *WhoEmL 91*
Gosliner, Bertram J *BiDrAPA 89*
Gosling, John Albert 1948- *BiDrAPA 89, WhoE 91*
Gosling, Nigel 1909-1982 *ConAu 129*
Gosling, Paula 1939- *ConAu 30NR, TwCCr&M 91*
Gosman, Abraham D. 1928- *St&PR 91*
Gosman, Albert Louis 1923- *WhoAm 90*
Gosman, Lazar 1926- *IntWWM 90*
Gosnell, F. Laurence 1925- *WhoAm 90, WhoE 91*
Gosnell, Thomas Charles 1951- *WhoAm 90*
Gosney, Nora Katherine 1927- *St&PR 91*
Gosnold, Bartholomew 1572?-1607 *EncCRAm, WhNaAH*
Gospodinoff, Mario Luis 1937- *BiDrAPA 89*
Goss, A. Don 1943- *St&PR 91*
Goss, Adrian Cyril 1956- *IntWWM 90*
Goss, Arthur Burnett, II 1961- *WhoEmL 91*
Goss, Barbara Craig 1945- *WhoAmW 91*
Goss, Barry Andrew 1939- *WhoWor 91*
Goss, Charles Barry 1944- *BiDrAPA 89*
Goss, Charles H. 1930- *St&PR 91*
Goss, Charles Henry 1930- *WhoE 91*
Goss, Clay 1946- *DrBIPA 90*
Goss, Donna Richardson 1953- *WhoEmL 91*
Goss, Edwin J. 1926- *St&PR 91*
Goss, Eileen Abel 1942- *WhoAmW 91*
Goss, Frederick Daniel 1941- *WhoAm 90*
Goss, Georgia Bulman 1939- *WhoAmW 91, WhoWor 91*
Goss, Howard S. 1933- *St&PR 91*
Goss, Howard Simon 1933- *WhoAm 90*
Goss, Howie 1934- *Ballpl 90*
Goss, Irving Joseph 1943- *St&PR 91*
Goss, James Leslie 1930- *St&PR 91*
Goss, James Rockwell 1949- *WhoAm 90*
Goss, James Walter 1924- *WhoAm 90*
Goss, Jeffery Alan 1953- *WhoWor 91*
Goss, Jerome Eldon 1935- *WhoWor 91*
Goss, Joel Francis 1955- *WhoE 91, WhoEmL 91*
Goss, John 1800-1880 *PenDiMP*
Goss, John 1886- *WhoAmA 91N*
Goss, Joseph J 1920- *BiDrAPA 89*
Goss, Kenneth George 1922- *WhoAm 90*
Goss, Leonard George 1947- *WhoEmL 91*
Goss, Louise Chitwood 1918- *WhoSSW 91*
Goss, Luke *BioIn 16*
Goss, Mary E. Weber 1926- *WhoAm 90*
Goss, Matt *BioIn 16*
Goss, Porter 1938- *BioIn 16*
Goss, Porter J. 1938- *WhoAm 90, WhoSSW 91*
Goss, Richard Henry 1935- *WhoAm 90*
Goss, Richard Mathew *St&PR 91N*
Goss, Rita Jean 1952- *WhoEmL 91*
Goss, Robert Benedict 1928- *St&PR 91*
Goss, Robert Mitchell 1956- *St&PR 91*
Goss, Roland E. 1920- *St&PR 91*
Goss, Susan Marie 1964- *BiDrAPA 89*

Goss, Thomas Marks 1952- *WhoEmL 91*
Goss, William H. 1833- *PenDiDA 89*
Goss, William Krebs 1959- *WhoSSW 91*
Goss-Custard, Henry 1871-1964 *PenDiMP*
Goss-Custard, Reginald 1877-1956 *PenDiMP*
Goss-Moffitt, Nina Bess 1926- *BiDrAPA 89*
Gossaert, Jan 1476?-1532? *IntDcAA 90*
Gossage, Brett Neal 1955- *WhoSSW 91*
Gossage, E. Gene 1935- *St&PR 91*
Gossage, Goose 1951- *Ballpl 90 [port]*
Gossage, John R. 1946- *BioIn 16*
Gossage, John Ralph 1946- *WhoAm 90, WhoAmA 91*
Gossage, Rich 1951- *BioIn 16*
Gossage, Thomas Layton 1934- *St&PR 91, WhoAm 90, WhoWor 91*
Gossan, Brian Wesley 1954- *WhoWor 91*
Gossard, Arthur Charles 1935- *WhoAm 90*
Gossart, Robert M 1935- *BiDrAPA 89*
Gosse, Edmund 1849-1928 *BioIn 16*
Gosse, Nellie 1850- *BiDWomA*
Gosse, Sylvia 1881-1968 *BiDWomA*
Gosselin, Caroline *BiDrAPA 89*
Gosselin, Claude Alphonse Rene 1944- *WhoAm 90*
Gosselin, Jean-Yves 1929- *BiDrAPA 89*
Gosselin, Peter Gordon 1951- *WhoE 91*
Gosselin, Richard Pettengill 1921- *WhoAm 90*
Gosselin, Robert Edmond 1919- *WhoAm 90*
Gosselink, Jerry Dean 1943- *St&PR 91*
Gossen, Hermann Heinrich 1810-1858 *BioIn 16*
Gossens, Salvador Allende 1908-1973 *BioIn 16*
Gossett, Bruce 1947- *St&PR 91*
Gossett, Dalton Ray 1945- *WhoSSW 91*
Gossett, Donald Lance 1954- *WhoEmL 91*
Gossett, Earl Fowler, Jr. 1933- *WhoSSW 91*
Gossett, Harry A. 1939- *St&PR 91*
Gossett, Hattie 1942- *BioIn 16*
Gossett, Jon Kevin 1955- *WhoEmL 91*
Gossett, Kimberly A. 1960- *WhoAmW 91*
Gossett, Leigh Ann 1966- *WhoSSW 91*
Gossett, Lou 1936- *DrBlPA 90*
Gossett, Lou, Jr. 1936- *WorAlBi*
Gossett, Louis, Jr. *BioIn 16*
Gossett, Louis, Jr. 1936- *CurBio 90 [port], WhoAm 90*
Gossett, Margaret *AuBYP 90*
Gossett, Oscar Milton 1925- *WhoAm 90*
Gossett, Philip 1941- *IntWWM 90, WhoAm 90, WhoWor 91*
Gossett, Robert Francis, Jr. 1943- *WhoE 91*
Gossett, Robert M. 1938- *WhoAm 90*
Gossett, William H. 1930- *St&PR 91*
Gossick, Lee Van 1920- *WhoAm 90*
Gossinger, Gary Thomas 1945- *BiDrAPA 89*
Gossling, Harry Robert 1922- *WhoAm 90*
Gossman, Francis Joseph 1930- *WhoSSW 91*
Gossman, Lionel 1929- *WhoAm 90, WhoWrEP 89*
Gossman, Robert G. 1931- *St&PR 91*
Gossman, Wayne Thomas 1960- *BiDrAPA 89*
Gossmeyer, Melvin Leon 1951- *WhoEmL 91*
Gossner, Karl J F 1923- *BiDrAPA 89*
Gosstola, David John 1959- *St&PR 91*
Gossweiler, Robert Martin 1949- *WhoEmL 91*
Gostelow, Jonathan 1744-1795 *PenDiDA 89*
Gostelowe, Jonathan 1744-1795 *BioIn 16*
Gostin, Judson Jacob 1935- *WhoE 91*
Gostin, Lawrence 1949- *WhoEmL 91*
Gostkowski, Anthony James 1944- *St&PR 91*
Gostling, John 1650?-1733 *PenDiMP*
Goswami, Amit 1936- *ConAu 129*
Gotanda, Philip Kan *BioIn 16*
Gotay, Julio 1939- *Ballpl 90*
Gotch, Tarquin *BioIn 16*
Gotcher, Joan Elaine 1935- *WhoAmW 91*
Gotcher, Robert E L 1925- *BiDrAPA 89*
Gotchey, Shelley Smith 1951- *WhoSSW 91*
Gotchi, Iris 1933- *ConAu 132*
Got'e, IU. V. 1873-1943 *BioIn 16*
Got'e, IUrii Vladimirovich 1873-1943 *BioIn 16*
Gotfredson, James C. 1954- *St&PR 91*
Gotfryd, Alexander 1931- *WhoAm 90*
Gotfryd, Moyses Aron *BiDrAPA 89*
Goth, Amon Leopold 1908-1945? *BioIn 16*
Goth, Jorge Andres 1945- *WhoWor 91*
Goth, Miklos 1944- *WhoWor 91*
Gothard, Barbara *BioIn 16*
Gothard, Donita 1932- *WhoAmW 91*
Gothberg, Loren A. 1920- *St&PR 91*
Gothelf, Lou *BioIn 16*
Gotherman, John E. 1933- *WhoAm 90*
Gothers, Daniel Edward 1935- *St&PR 91*
Gotherson, Dorothea 1611-1680 *BiDEWW, FemiCLE*
Gotimer, Harry Albert 1947- *WhoE 91, WhoWor 91*
Gotkin, Michael Stanley 1942- *St&PR 91, WhoWor 91*
Gotkind, Lawrence *BiDrAPA 89*
Gotley, Paul 1925- *St&PR 91*
Gotlib, Lorraine 1931- *WhoAm 90*
Gotlib, Steven Lee *BiDrAPA 89*
Gotlieb, Calvin Carl 1921- *WhoAm 90*
Gotlieb, Irwin 1941- *BioIn 16*
Gotlieb, Irwin I. 1949- *WhoAm 90, WhoE 91*
Gotlieb, Jaquelin Smith 1946- *WhoAmW 91, WhoSSW 91*
Gotlieb, Phyllis 1926- *FemiCLE*
Gotlieb, Phyllis Fay Bloom 1926- *WhoAm 90, WhoWrEP 89*
Goto, Joseph 1920- *WhoAmA 91*
Goto, Ken 1952- *WhoWor 91*
Goto, Kimio 1926- *WhoWor 91*
Goto, Kunio 1930- *WhoWor 91*
Goto, Midori 1971- *BioIn 16*
Goto, Mitsuya 1929- *WhoWor 91*
Goto, Nobuo 1938- *WhoWor 91*
Goto, Sanehisa 1941- *WhoE 91*
Goto, Shigeru 1931- *WhoAm 90*
Goto, Toshio 1929- *WhoWor 91*
Goto, Wayne Kay *BiDrAPA 89*
Goto, Yoshio 1925- *WhoWor 91*
Gotoda, Masaharu 1914- *WhoWor 91*
Gotoff, Samuel Peter 1933- *WhoAm 90*
Gotoh, Hiroki 1937- *WhoWor 91*
Gotoh, Noboru 1916-1989 *BioIn 16*
Gots, Abram Rafailovich 1882-1940? *BioIn 16*
Gotsch, Allan E. *St&PR 91*
Gotsch, Richard Walter 1931- *St&PR 91*
Gotschall, George D. 1920- *St&PR 91*
Gotschall, Jeffrey P. 1948- *St&PR 91*
Gotschall, Thomas Edward 1961- *WhoSSW 91*
Gotshall, Mark Edward 1960- *WhoEmL 91*
Gotsopoulos, Barbara Lynn 1948- *WhoAmW 91*
Gotstein, Michael E. 1933- *St&PR 91*
Gott, Dorothy *FemiCLE*
Gott, James L. 1933- *St&PR 91*
Gott, Jim 1959- *Ballpl 90*
Gott, Susan Darnell 1946- *WhoEmL 91*
Gott, Vincent Lynn 1927- *WhoAm 90*
Gotta, Alexander Walter 1935- *WhoE 91, WhoWor 91*
Gottesman, Alexander Morey 1926- *WhoE 91*
Gottesman, David Marion 1940- *BiDrAPA 89*
Gottesman, David Sanford 1926- *WhoAm 90*
Gottesman, Howard Gerald *BiDrAPA 89*
Gottesman, Hyam 1953- *ODwPR 91*
Gottesman, Irving Isadore 1930- *WhoAm 90*
Gottesman, Ritva Anneli 1946- *WhoAmW 91*
Gottesman, Roy Tully 1928- *WhoAm 90*
Gottesman, S. D. *MajTwCW*
Gottesman, Walter *St&PR 91*
Gottesmann, Paul *PenDiMP*
Gottfeld, Gunther Max 1934- *WhoE 91*
Gottfredsen, Janet M. *ODwPR 91*
Gottfredson, Don Martin 1926- *WhoAm 90*
Gottfredson, Floyd 1907-1986 *EncACom*
Gottfried, Byron Stuart 1934- *WhoAm 90*
Gottfried, Deanne F 1932- *BiDrAPA 89*
Gottfried, Eugene Leslie 1929- *WhoAm 90, WhoWor 91*
Gottfried, Glenn Edward 1956- *WhoEmL 91*
Gottfried, Ira Sidney 1932- *WhoAm 90*
Gottfried, Kurt 1929- *WhoAm 90*
Gottfried, Leon Albert 1925- *WhoAm 90, WhoWrEP 89*
Gottfried, Lili Ann 1948- *BiDrAPA 89*
Gottfried, Mark Ellis 1953- *WhoEmL 91*
Gottfried, Martha A. *St&PR 91*
Gottfried, Martha Ann 1937- *WhoAmW 91*
Gottfried, Robert Lewis 1950- *WhoEmL 91*
Gottheil, Edward 1924- *BiDrAPA 89*
Gottheimer, Debra 1954- *ODwPR 91*
Gotthelf, Beth 1958- *WhoEmL 91*
Gotti, John *BioIn 16*
Gotti, Margaret R. *WhoAmW 91*
Gottier, Richard Chalmers 1918- *St&PR 91, WhoAm 90*
Gottlieb, A. Arthur 1937- *St&PR 91*
Gottlieb, Abraham Arthur 1937- *WhoAm 90, WhoSSW 91*
Gottlieb, Abraham Mitchell 1909- *WhoAm 90*
Gottlieb, Adolph 1903-1974 *WhoAmA 91N*
Gottlieb, Alex 1906-1988 *BioIn 16*
Gottlieb, Alexis *BiDrAPA 89*
Gottlieb, Allan 1945- *WhoE 91*
Gottlieb, Anthony A 1936- *BiDrAPA 89*
Gottlieb, Bernard *St&PR 91*
Gottlieb, Bernhardt S 1898- *BiDrAPA 89*
Gottlieb, Carla 1912- *WhoAmA 91*
Gottlieb, Daniel Seth 1954- *WhoEmL 91*
Gottlieb, David I 1929- *BiDrAPA 89*
Gottlieb, Diane Beth *BiDrAPA 89*
Gottlieb, Edward 1910- *ODwPR 91, WhoAm 90*
Gottlieb, Esther 1907-1988 *BioIn 16*
Gottlieb, Esther Hedberg *BiDrAPA 89*
Gottlieb, Felix I 1936- *BiDrAPA 89*
Gottlieb, Frank P. 1945- *WhoEmL 91*
Gottlieb, Fred 1934- *BiDrAPA 89*
Gottlieb, Gary Lloyd 1955- *BiDrAPA 89*
Gottlieb, Gerald 1923- *AuBYP 90*
Gottlieb, Gidon Alain Guy 1932- *WhoAm 90*
Gottlieb, Gordon 1948- *IntWWM 90*
Gottlieb, Henning Vincent 1926- *WhoWor 91*
Gottlieb, Howard Paul *BiDrAPA 89*
Gottlieb, Jane Ellen 1954- *IntWWM 90, WhoAm 90, WhoAmW 91, WhoEmL 91*
Gottlieb, Jay Mitchell 1952- *IntWWM 90*
Gottlieb, Jeffrey H *BiDrAPA 89*
Gottlieb, Jerome Irwin 1948- *BiDrAPA 89*
Gottlieb, Jerrold Howard 1946- *WhoAm 90*
Gottlieb, Joseph Abraham 1918- *WhoAm 90*
Gottlieb, Julius Judah 1919- *WhoE 91, WhoWor 91*
Gottlieb, Kenneth Ira 1942- *BiDrAPA 89*
Gottlieb, Lee 1925- *ODwPR 91*
Gottlieb, Leo *St&PR 91N*
Gottlieb, Leo 1896-1989 *BioIn 16*
Gottlieb, Leonard Solomon 1927- *WhoAm 90*
Gottlieb, Leslie E. 1944- *WhoAmW 91*
Gottlieb, Lester M. 1932- *St&PR 91, WhoE 91, WhoWor 91*
Gottlieb, Louis L. 1923- *St&PR 91*
Gottlieb, Lucille Montrose Fox 1929- *WhoAmW 91*
Gottlieb, Margaret Anne 1955- *WhoE 91*
Gottlieb, Marilyn 1942- *ODwPR 91*
Gottlieb, Marilyn Ann 1942- *WhoAm 90*
Gottlieb, Marise S. 1938- *St&PR 91*
Gottlieb, Marise Suss 1938- *WhoAmW 91*
Gottlieb, Martin *BioIn 16*
Gottlieb, Marvin E 1934- *BiDrAPA 89*
Gottlieb, Morton Edgar 1921- *WhoAm 90*
Gottlieb, Myron I. 1943- *St&PR 91*
Gottlieb, Paul 1935- *WhoAm 90*
Gottlieb, Paul 1936- *WhoWrEP 89*
Gottlieb, Paul Erwin 1935- *St&PR 91*
Gottlieb, Paul Mitchel 1954- *WhoEmL 91*
Gottlieb, Peter 1930- *IntWWM 90*
Gottlieb, Philip Daniel 1946- *BiDrAPA 89*
Gottlieb, Raymond L 1939- *BiDrAPA 89*
Gottlieb, Richard Douglas 1942- *St&PR 91, WhoAm 90*
Gottlieb, Richard Thomas *BiDrAPA 89*
Gottlieb, Robert 1931- *WorAlBi*
Gottlieb, Robert A 1931- *ConAu 129*
Gottlieb, Robert Adams 1931- *WhoAm 90, WhoE 91*
Gottlieb, Robert Erwin 1936- *St&PR 91*
Gottlieb, Robin 1928- *AuBYP 90*
Gottlieb, Sally Ann 1951- *WhoAmW 91*
Gottlieb, Sheldon Fred 1932- *WhoAm 90*
Gottlieb, Sidney Alan *WhoSSW 91*
Gottlieb, Stanley 1939- *BiDrAPA 89*
Gottlieb, William H. 1913- *ODwPR 91*
Gottlieb, William Paul 1917- *AuBYP 90*
Gottman, Jerome E. 1939- *St&PR 91*
Gottmann, Jean 1915- *WhoAm 90*
Gotto, Antonio Marion, Jr. 1935- *WhoAm 90, WhoSSW 91*
Gotto, Ray *EncACom*
Gottreich, Norman S *BiDrAPA 89*
Gottron, Francis Robert, III 1953- *WhoEmL 91*
Gottry, Karla Mae Styer 1951- *WhoAmW 91*
Gottry, Steven Roger 1946- *WhoEmL 91, WhoWor 91*
Gotts, Michael D 1952- *BiDrAPA 89*
Gottschalch, Hermann Wilfried 1929- *WhoWor 91*
Gottschalk And Ash International *ConDes 90*
Gottschalk, Alexander 1932- *WhoAm 90*
Gottschalk, Alfred 1930- *WhoAm 90, WhoWor 91*
Gottschalk, Arthur William 1947- *IntWWM 90*
Gottschalk, Arthur William 1952- *WhoEmL 91*
Gottschalk, Carl William 1922- *WhoAm 90*
Gottschalk, Charles Max 1928- *WhoAm 90*
Gottschalk, Fritz 1937- *ConDes 90, WhoAmA 91*
Gottschalk, Janice K. 1951- *WhoAmW 91*
Gottschalk, Jere Leroy 1924- *St&PR 91*
Gottschalk, John Simison 1912- *WhoAm 90*
Gottschalk, Lionel John, III *BiDrAPA 89*
Gottschalk, Louis A *BiDrAPA 89*
Gottschalk, Louis August 1916- *WhoAm 90*
Gottschalk, Louis Moreau 1829-1869 *BioIn 16, OxCPMus, PenDiMP*
Gottschalk, Mary Therese 1931- *WhoAm 90, WhoSSW 91*
Gottschalk, Max Jules 1909- *WhoAmA 91*
Gottschalk, Norman E., Jr. 1944- *St&PR 91*
Gottschalk, Robert Bruce, Jr. 1943- *BiDrAPA 89*
Gottschalk, Walter Helbig 1918- *WhoAm 90*
Gottschall, Edward Maurice 1915- *WhoAm 90, WhoWrEP 89*
Gottschall, Kenneth Lloyd 1946- *WhoEmL 91*
Gottschall, Victor Philippe 1941- *St&PR 91*
Gottsched, Johann Christoph 1700-1766 *DcLB 97 [port]*
Gottsched, Luise Adelgunde Victoria 1713-1762 *EncCoWW*
Gottschedinn *EncCoWW*
Gottsching, Manuel *NewAgMG*
Gottsegen, Gloria 1930- *WhoAm 90*
Gottshall, John F. 1947- *St&PR 91*
Gottsman, Jennifer Woods 1958- *WhoSSW 91*
Gottstein, Barnard Jacob 1925- *St&PR 91, WhoAm 90, WhoWor 91*
Gottstein, Karen 1946- *WhoWrEP 89*
Gottstein, Klaus Leo Ferdinand 1924- *WhoWor 91*
Gottwald, Bjorn A. 1937- *WhoWor 91*
Gottwald, Bruce C. 1933- *St&PR 91*
Gottwald, Bruce Cobb, Sr. 1933- *WhoAm 90, WhoSSW 91*
Gottwald, Floyd Dewey, Jr. 1922- *St&PR 91, WhoAm 90, WhoSSW 91*
Gottwals, Harry C. 1940- *WhoAm 90*
Gottwik, Gerda C 1939- *BiDrAPA 89*
Gotwals, Charles Place, Jr. 1917- *WhoAm 90*
Gotwals, Clayton K, II 1939- *BiDrAPA 89*
Gotwals, Vernon Detwiler, Jr. 1924- *WhoAm 90*
Gotwals, William Logan 1942- *St&PR 91*
Gotwalt, Norma Jean 1930- *WhoAmW 91*
Gotz, August Emil 1935- *WhoWor 91*
Gotz, Johann Nikolaus 1721-1781 *DcLB 97 [port]*
Gotz, Karl 1903- *BioIn 16*
Gotz, Werner 1934- *IntWWM 90*
Gotzkowsky, Johann Ernst *PenDiDA 89*
Goudard, Alain-Pierre 1938- *WhoWor 91*
Goudelock, Daniel S 1932- *BiDrAPA 89*
Goudey, Alice E. 1898- *AuBYP 90*
Goudge, Eileen *BioIn 16*
Goudge, Eileen 1950- *Au&Arts 6 [port]*
Goudge, Elizabeth 1900-1984 *AuBYP 90, BioIn 16, FemiCLE*
Goudge, Elizabeth De Beauchamp 1900-1984 *DcNaB 1981*
Goudia, Gayle Bastian 1951- *WhoSSW 91*
Goudie, Kenneth R. 1948- *St&PR 91*
Goudreau, Roland H. *St&PR 91*
Goudsmit, Samuel Abraham 1902-1978 *DcScB S2*
Goudy, Josephine Gray 1925- *WhoAmW 91*
Gouge, Pamela Carpousis 1949- *WhoE 91*
Gouge, Susan Cornelia Jones 1924- *WhoAm 90, WhoAmW 91, WhoWor 91*
Gouge, William M. 1796-1863 *EncABHB 6*
Gougelman, Paul Reina 1951- *WhoEmL 91*
Gougeon, Howard F. 1940- *St&PR 91*
Gougeon, Len Girard 1947- *WhoWrEP 89*
Gouger, Dale B. 1942- *BiDrAPA 89*
Gouger, Dale Bartlett 1942- *WhoE 91*
Gouges, Marie-Olympe de 1745-1793 *EncCoWW*
Gough, Barry Morton 1938- *ConAu 30NR*
Gough, Bill *ConAu 131*
Gough, Carolyn Harley 1922- *WhoAm 90*
Gough, Denis Ian 1922- *WhoAm 90*
Gough, Gary William 1942- *St&PR 91*
Gough, Georgia Belle 1920- *WhoAmA 91*
Gough, Harrison Gould 1921- *WhoWor 91*
Gough, Herbert Frederick, Mrs. *WhoAmW 91*
Gough, Jessie Post 1907- *WhoAmW 91, WhoSSW 91*
Gough, John 1957- *IntWWM 90*
Gough, John Bernard 1928- *WhoWor 91*
Gough, John Francis 1934- *WhoE 91*
Gough, Joseph M. 1927- *St&PR 91*
Gough, Judy S. 1945- *WhoAmW 91*
Gough, Kathleen 1925- *WhoAmW 91*
Gough, Lucille Doris 1947- *WhoE 91*
Gough, Pauline Bjerke 1935- *WhoAmW 91*

Gough, Phillip Alan 1955- St&PR 91
Gough, Piers 1946- BioIn 16
Gough, Robert Alan 1931- WhoAmA 91
Gough, Wilbert Donald 1946- WhoEmL 91
Gough, William 1945- ConAu 131
Gougher, Ronald Lee 1939- WhoE 91, WhoWor 91
Goughler, Donald H. 1945- WhoE 91
Goughnour, Roy Robert 1928- WhoSSW 91
Gougler, Charles Alan 1955- WhoEmL 91
Gouin, Jean Felix 1884-1977 BiDFrPL
Goujon, Jean 1510?-1568? IntDcAA 90
Gouker, Kim Patrick 1953- WhoEmL 91
Goulard, Guy Yvon 1940- WhoAm 90
Goulart, E. F. 1953- ODwPR 91
Goulart, Joao Belchior Marques 1918-1976 BioIn 16
Goulart, Ron 1933- TwCCr&M 91, WhoWrEP 89
Goulart, Ronald Joseph 1933- WhoAm 90
Goulazian, Peter BioIn 16
Goulazian, Peter Robert 1940- St&PR 91, WhoAm 90
Goulbourne, Donald Samuel, Jr. 1950- WhoE 91
Gould, Alan ODwPR 91
Gould, Alan Brant 1938- WhoAm 90
Gould, Alice Bache 1868-1953 EncCoWW
Gould, Allan 1944- ConAu 132
Gould, Alvin R. 1922- WhoAm 90, WhoWor 91
Gould, Ann 1609?-1699 BiDEWW
Gould, Beatrice Blackmar 1898-1989 BioIn 16
Gould, Bernard 1912- St&PR 91
Gould, Bonnie Marie 1947- WhoEmL 91
Gould, Bradley H 1948- BiDrAPA 89
Gould, Brian Stuart 1947- BiDrAPA 89
Gould, Bruce 1898-1989 BioIn 16, ConAu 129
Gould, Bruce Allan 1938- WhoSSW 91
Gould, Bruce Grant 1942- WhoWrEP 89
Gould, Charles L. 1942- St&PR 91
Gould, Charles Perry 1909- WhoAm 90, WhoWor 91
Gould, Chester 1900-1985 BioIn 16, ConAu 30NR, EncACom
Gould, Courtney A. 1915- St&PR 91
Gould, David I. 1930- St&PR 91
Gould, David Wilfred, III 1960- BiDrAPA 89
Gould, Deborah L. AuBYP 90
Gould, Dennis Jay 1942- WhoAm 90
Gould, Dirk Samuel 1933- WhoAm 90
Gould, Donald Everett 1932- WhoE 91, WhoWor 91
Gould, Donald William, Sr. 1942- St&PR 91
Gould, Edward M BiDrAPA 89
Gould, Edward P. 1931- St&PR 91
Gould, Edwin Sheldon 1926- WhoAm 90
Gould, Eileen Gordon 1948- WhoAmW 91
Gould, Elizabeth Davies 1904- IntWWM 90
Gould, Elliot 1938 BioIn 16
Gould, Elliott 1938- WhoAm 90, WorAlBi
Gould, Emil J. 1913- WhoSSW 91
Gould, Floyd Jerome 1936- WhoAm 90
Gould, Frank Horace 1856-1918 AmLegL
Gould, Frank Nelson 1926- St&PR 91
Gould, Frank Nelson, Jr. 1926- WhoAm 90
Gould, Fredric H. 1935- St&PR 91
Gould, Gary Robert 1951- WhoEmL 91
Gould, Gayle Mahoney 1955- WhoE 91
Gould, George AuBYP 90
Gould, Glenn 1932-1982 BioIn 16, PenDiMP, WorAlBi
Gould, Glenn Hunting 1949- WhoEmL 91, WhoSSW 91
Gould, Gordon BioIn 16
Gould, Gordon 1920- St&PR 91
Gould, Gregory 1920- St&PR 91
Gould, Hannah Flagg 1789-1865 FemiCLE
Gould, Harold 1923- ConTFT 8 [port], WhoAm 90
Gould, Harold Alton 1926- WhoAm 90
Gould, Harry Edward, Jr. 1938- St&PR 91, WhoAm 90, WhoE 91, WhoWor 91
Gould, Helen 1868-1938 BioAmW
Gould, Helen Grace 1904- WhoAmW 91
Gould, Howard BiDrAPA 89
Gould, Irving 1919- St&PR 91
Gould, James C. 1945- St&PR 91
Gould, James L. 1945- ConAu 130
Gould, James Spencer 1922- WhoAm 90, WhoWor 91
Gould, Jay 1836-1892 BioIn 16, WorAlBi
Gould, Jay 1940- St&PR 91
Gould, Jay Martin 1915- WhoAm 90
Gould, Jay S. 1947- St&PR 91
Gould, Jay Sheldon 1947- WhoEmL 91
Gould, Jean Rosalind 1919- AuBYP 90, WhoWrEP 89
Gould, Jeffrey Richard 1955- WhoSSW 91
Gould, Jennifer Jane BiDrAPA 89
Gould, Jodie E. 1957- ODwPR 91
Gould, John Edward 1944- WhoAm 90
Gould, John Howard 1929- WhoAmA 91
Gould, John Philip, Jr. 1939- WhoAm 90
Gould, John T. ODwPR 91
Gould, Karen Keel 1946- WhoAmA 91
Gould, Kenneth B. 1955- WhoEmL 91
Gould, Kenneth L. 1944- St&PR 91
Gould, Kenneth Lance 1938- WhoAm 90
Gould, Kenneth S 1927- BiDrAPA 89
Gould, Lewis Ludlow 1939- WhoAm 90
Gould, Linda Flewellen 1958- WhoEmL 91
Gould, Lois MajTwCW, WhoWrEP 89
Gould, Louis N 1901- BiDrAPA 89
Gould, Loyal Norman 1927- WhoAm 90
Gould, Marcia Rae 1937- WhoAmW 91
Gould, Marilyn 1928- AuBYP 90
Gould, Mark A BiDrAPA 89
Gould, Mark Allen 1930- WhoSSW 91
Gould, Mark R. 1949- ODwPR 91
Gould, Martha B. 1931- WhoAmW 91
Gould, Maxine Lubow 1942- WhoAmW 91, WhoWor 91
Gould, Milton S. 1909- St&PR 91
Gould, Milton Samuel 1909- WhoAm 90
Gould, Miriam 1925- BiDrAPA 89
Gould, Morley David 1936- WhoAm 90
Gould, Morton 1913- IntWWM 90, OxCPMus, WhoAm 90
Gould, Peter David 1952- IntWWM 90
Gould, Peter John 1941- St&PR 91
Gould, Peter Robin 1932- WhoAm 90
Gould, Philip 1922- WhoAmA 91
Gould, Phillip L. 1937- WhoAm 90
Gould, Phillips Brooks 1956- WhoEmL 91
Gould, R. Max 1939- St&PR 91
Gould, Ralph Albert, Jr. 1923- St&PR 91
Gould, Reuben R 1937- BiDrAPA 89
Gould, Richard Allan 1939- WhoAm 90
Gould, Richard Brent 1937- BiDrAPA 89
Gould, Robert A. 1951- St&PR 91
Gould, Robert E 1924- BiDrAPA 89
Gould, Robert J. ODwPR 91
Gould, Roberta 1941- WhoWrEP 89
Gould, Roberta Yvonne 1932- WhoAmW 91
Gould, Roger Louis 1935- BiDrAPA 89
Gould, Roy Walter 1927- WhoAm 90
Gould, Sam Charles 1941- BiDrAPA 89
Gould, Stanley Farrell 1949- WhoEmL 91
Gould, Stephen TwCCr&M 91
Gould, Stephen 1909- WhoAmA 91
Gould, Stephen H 1943- BiDrAPA 89
Gould, Stephen Jay 1941- BioIn 16, MajTwCW, WhoAm 90, WhoE 91
Gould, Stuart M, Jr. 1923- BiDrAPA 89
Gould, Stuart S. 1906- St&PR 91
Gould, Syd S. 1912- WhoSSW 91, WhoWor 91
Gould, Terri F. 1943- WhoAm 90
Gould, Toni S. AuBYP 90
Gould, Tony Madden 1939- St&PR 91
Gould, Walter Paul 1955- WhoSSW 91
Gould, Wesley Larson 1917- WhoAm 90
Gould, Will EncACom
Gould, William B 1936- ConAu 132
Gould, William Henry Mercur 1951- WhoE 91
Gould, William Richard 1919 St&PR 91, WhoAm 90
Gould, William Thomas 1946- St&PR 91
Goulden, Joseph C 1934- ConAu 31NR
Goulden, Joseph Chesley 1934- WhoAm 90, WhoWrEP 89
Goulder, Caroljean Hempstead 1933- WhoAmW 91, WhoE 91
Goulder, George V. 1914- St&PR 91
Goulder, Gerald Polster 1953- WhoEmL 91
Gouldey, Bruce K. 1952- St&PR 91
Gouldin, Frederick Caskey 1943- WhoE 91
Gouldin, Norman Hadley 1921- St&PR 91
Goulding, Fraser John 1947- IntWWM 90
Goulding, Jayne Marie 1957- WhoEmL 91
Goulding, Marrack Irvine 1936- WhoWor 91
Goulding, Nora WhoAmW 91
Goulding, Peter C. 1925- ODwPR 91
Goulding, Ray 1922-1990 BioIn 16, ConAu 131, CurBio 90N, NewYTBS 90 [port], WorAlBi
Goulding, Robert L 1917- BiDrAPA 89
Gouldner, Alvin W 1920-1980 MajTwCW
Goulds, Peter J 1948- WhoAmA 91
Gouldthorpe, Kenneth Alfred Percival 1928- WhoAm 90
Gouled Aptidon, Hassan 1916- WhoWor 91
Goulet, Brent BioIn 16
Goulet, Charles Rudolfe 1933- St&PR 91, WhoAm 90
Goulet, Charles Ryan 1927- WhoAm 90
Goulet, Claude 1925- WhoAmA 91
Goulet, Cynthia Wagner 1957- WhoAmW 91
Goulet, Denis Andre 1931- WhoAm 90
Goulet, Jean BiDrAPA 89
Goulet, Leon M. 1925- St&PR 91
Goulet, Lorrie 1925- WhoAmA 91, WhoAmW 91, WhoE 91
Goulet, Robert 1933- WorAlBi
Goulet, Robert Gerard 1933- WhoAm 90
Goulet, Suzanne Claire 1965- WhoAmW 91
Goulianos, Konstantin 1935- WhoAm 90
Goulston, Marilyn Gwen 1949- WhoAmW 91
Goulston, Mark Steven BiDrAPA 89
Gouma-Peterson, Thalia 1933- WhoAmA 91
Gounaris, Angela Francis WhoE 91
Gounaris, Anne Demetra 1924- WhoAm 90
Gouner, Farley A. 1941- St&PR 91
Gounod, Charles 1818-1893 PenDiMP A, WorAlBi
Gour, Betty 1914- WhoAmW 91, WhoWor 91
Gourad Hamadou, Barkat WhoWor 91
Gouran, Dennis Stephen 1941- WhoAm 90
Gourary, Samarious BioIn 16
Gouras, Mark Steven 1961- WhoEmL 91
Gouras, Peter 1930- WhoAm 90
Gouraud, Jackson S. 1923- WhoAm 90
Gourbin, Jean-Louis 1947- St&PR 91
Gourdeau, Jean-Guy 1964- St&PR 91
Gourdeau, Robert 1920- WhoAm 90
Gourdine, Simon Peter 1940- WhoAm 90, WhoWor 91
Gourevitch, Jacqueline 1933- WhoAmA 91
Gourevitch, Peter Alexis 1943- WhoAm 90
Gourevitch, Victor 1925- WhoAm 90
Gourgues, Harold Walter, Jr. 1937- WhoSSW 91
Gourlay, Elizabeth 1917- ConAu 30NR
Gourley, Desmond Robert Hugh 1922- WhoAm 90
Gourley, Dick R. 1944- WhoAm 90
Gourley, Fletcher A. 1912- WhoAm 90
Gourley, Fletcher A. 1913- St&PR 91
Gourley, James Leland 1919- WhoAm 90, WhoSSW 91, WhoWor 91
Gourley, Mary Margaret 1942- WhoAmW 91
Gourley, Ronald Robert 1919- WhoAm 90
Gourley, Willard BioIn 16
Gourlie, Rebecca Elizabeth 1948- WhoEmL 91
Gournay, La Damoiselle de EncCoWW
Gournay, Mademoiselle de EncCoWW
Gournay, Marie le Jars de 1565-1645 EncCoWW
Gouse, Andrew Tuck BiDrAPA 89
Gouse, S. William, Jr. 1931- WhoAm 90, WhoSSW 91
Gousha, Richard Paul 1923- WhoAm 90
Gousseland, Pierre 1922- St&PR 91
Goutallier, Philpe Bernard 1931- WhoWor 91
Gouterman, Martin Paul 1931- WhoAm 90
Gouthiere, Pierre 1732-1813 PenDiDA 89
Goutman, Dolya 1918- WhoAmA 91
Gouttama, Raymond BiDrAPA 89
Goutte, Rene 1935- St&PR 91
Gouveia, Judith Kathleen Blake 1944- WhoAmW 91
Gouveia, Lawrence J. 1951- St&PR 91
Gouyn, Charles PenDiDA 89
Gouyon, Paul 1910- WhoWor 91
Gouze, Victoria 1953- WhoEmL 91
Gouzenko, Igor Sergeievich 1919-1982 DcNaB 1981
Govan, Christine 1898- AuBYP 90
Govan, Francis Hawks 1916- WhoAmA 91
Govan, James Fauntleroy 1926- WhoAm 90
Gove, Gilbert English 1932- WhoAm 90
Gove, Harry Edmund 1922- WhoAm 90
Gove, John C. 1926- St&PR 91
Gove, Roger Madden 1914- BiDrAPA 89
Gove, Samuel Kimball 1923- WhoAm 90
Gove, William Hazeltine 1817-1876 AmLegL
Govekar, Paul Louis, Jr. 1945- WhoEmL 91
Govenar, Sidney A. 1918- St&PR 91
Gover, Alan Shore 1948- WhoEmL 91, WhoSSW 91
Gover, James Edwin 1940- WhoAm 90
Gover, Raymond Lewis 1927- St&PR 91, WhoAm 90
Goverman, Barry 1945- St&PR 91
Govich, Bruce Michael 1930- IntWWM 90
Govier, Gordon Oliver 1951- WhoEmL 91
Govier, Katherine 1948- FemiCLE
Govier, William Charles 1936- WhoAm 90
Govig, Valerie Cowls 1934- WhoAmW 91, WhoWrEP 89
Govil, Narendra Kumar 1940- WhoSSW 91
Govin, Mary-Jane C. 1943- WhoAmW 91
Govinda, Anagarika Brahmacari BioIn 16
Govindaiah, Sujatha G BiDrAPA 89
Govindan, Sadasivan 1932- BiDrAPA 89
Govindarajulu, Zakkala 1933- WhoSSW 91
Govindjee 1933- WhoAm 90
Govoni, Virginia Deliso 1934- St&PR 91
Govrin, Yosef 1930- WhoWor 91
Gow, David EncO&P 3
Gow, Ellen B. 1950- WhoWrEP 89
Gow, Jack F. 1920- ODwPR 91
Gow, James Gordon 1917- WhoWor 91
Gow, Nathaniel 1763-1831 OxCPMus, PenDiMP
Gow, Neil 1727-1807 PenDiMP
Gow, Niel 1727-1807 OxCPMus
Gow, Robert Haigh 1933- WhoAm 90
Gowac, John Joseph 1957- St&PR 91
Gowan, Arthur Mitchell 1910- WhoAm 90
Gowan, Elsie Park 1905- FemiCLE, OxCCanT
Gowan, Joseph Patrick, Jr. 1939- WhoAm 90, WhoWor 91
Gowan, Lawrence R, Sr. BiDrAPA 89
Gowan, Mary Olivia 1888-1977 BioIn 16
Gowan, William H., Jr. 1917- St&PR 91
Gowanlock, Theresa Mary DcCanB 12
Gowans, Alan 1923- WhoAmA 91
Gowans, Kathy Elizabeth 1948- WhoAmW 91
Gowans, William Rory, Mrs. WhoAmW 91
Gowaty, Frank Henry BiDrAPA 89
Gowda, Narasimhan Ramaiah 1949- WhoWor 91
Gowdy, Curt 1919- Ballpl 90, BioIn 16, WorAlBi
Gowdy, Curtis 1919- WhoAm 90
Gowdy, Hank 1889-1966 Ballpl 90
Gowdy, Miriam Betts 1928- WhoAmW 91
Gowen, Bradford Paul 1946- IntWWM 90
Gowen, Clarence William, Jr. 1952- WhoSSW 91
Gowen, Jerry Dale 1943- St&PR 91
Gowen, Paul H. 1925- St&PR 91
Gowen, Richard Joseph 1935- WhoAm 90
Gowen, Thomas Leo, Jr. 1949- WhoEmL 91
Gowen, William 1927- ODwPR 91
Gowens, Verneeta Viola 1913- WhoAmW 91
Gower, Elizabeth Ann 1957- WhoEmL 91
Gowin, Dixie Bob 1925- WhoE 91
Gowing, David 1933- BiDrAPA 89
Gowing, Nik 1951- SpyFic
Gowl, Colleen Butler WhoAmW 91
Gowland, Douglas R. 1942- WhoAm 90
Gowland, John Thomas 1947- St&PR 91
Gowland, Karen Elaine 1959- WhoEmL 91
Gowman, Lawrence Paul 1938- St&PR 91
Gowrie, Alexander Hore-Ruthven, Earl of 1939- BioIn 16
Goy, Pierre 1961- IntWWM 90
Goya, Donna BioIn 16
Goya, Francisco 1746-1828 BioIn 16, IntDcAA 90
Goya, Francisco De 1746-1828 WorAlBi
Goya y Lucientes, Francisco 1746-1828 IntDcAA 90
Goya y Lucientes, Francisco Jose de 1746-1828 BioIn 16
Goyak, Elizabeth 1922- ODwPR 91
Goyal, Raj Kumar 1937- WhoAm 90
Goyal, Rashmi 1937- BiDrAPA 89
Goyal, Saroj 1949- BiDrAPA 89, WhoE 91
Goyal, Subhash C BiDrAPA 89
Goyal, Vinod Kumar 1948- St&PR 91
Goyan, Michael D. 1938- St&PR 91
Goyan, Michael Donovan 1938- WhoAm 90
Goydan, Paul Alexander 1947- St&PR 91
Goydon, Raymond P. 1953- St&PR 91
Goyen, Jan van 1596-1656 IntDcAA 90
Goyeneche, Gabriel ConAu 32NR, HispWr 90
Goyeneche, Miguel de Muzquiz y 1719-1785 BioIn 16
Goyens, Alain Marie Sadi Andre 1945- WhoWor 91
Goyer, Francois PenDiDA 89
Goyer, Jean 1725?- PenDiDA 89
Goyer, Peter Francis 1943- WhoE 91
Goyer, Peter Francis, Jr. BiDrAPA 89
Goyer, Robert Andrew 1927- WhoAm 90
Goyer, Robert Stanton 1923- WhoAm 90
Goyert, Philip Renner, Jr. 1943- WhoSSW 91
Goyet, Jean-Marie 1945- St&PR 91
Goyette, John H. 1946- St&PR 91
Goyke, Louise Renee 1966- WhoAmW 91
Goynes, Roxie F. 1957- WhoAmW 91
Goytisolo, Agustin de 1924- WhoHisp 91
Goytisolo, Juan BioIn 16
Goytisolo, Juan 1931- ConAu 32NR, HispWr 90, IntvSpW [port], MajTwCW
Goza, Debbie Arlene 1956- WhoEmL 91
Goza, Kirk John 1957- WhoEmL 91
Goza, Marvella BioIn 16
Goza, Shirley Edmonds 1957- WhoEmL 91
Gozberk, Barbara Ann 1941- WhoAmW 91
Gozon, Felipe Lapus 1939- WhoWor 91
Gozon, Richard C. 1938- St&PR 91, WhoAm 90, WhoE 91
Gozonsky, Edwin S.P. 1930- St&PR 91
Gozzano, Francesco 1930- WhoWor 91
Gozzano, Guido 1883-1916 BioIn 16
Gozzard, Adrian BioIn 16

Gozzoli, Benozzo 1420?-1497 *IntDcAA 90*
Graae, Fleming Gomme *BiDrAPA 89*
Graae, Flemming Gomme 1948- *WhoE 91*
Graaskamp, Charles Fiske 1934- *St&PR 91*
Graaskamp, James *BioIn 16*
Grab, John M. 1946- *St&PR 91*
Grabach, John R 1880-1981 *WhoAmA 91N*
Grabar, Andre 1896-1990 *NewYTBS 90*
Grabar, Oleg 1929- *WhoAm 90*
Grabarkewitz, Billy 1946- *Ballpl 90*
Grabe, Hermann Friedrich 1900-1986 *BioIn 16*
Grabe, Nancy Elizabeth 1960- *WhoE 91*
Grabeel, Conrad L 1926- *BiDrAPA 89*
Grabek, James R. 1945- *St&PR 91*
Grabek, James Robert 1945- *WhoAm 90*
Grabel, Lawrence 1947- *WhoE 91, WhoEmL 91*
Grabel, Susan 1942- *WhoAmA 91*
Grabemann, Karl W. 1929- *WhoAm 90*
Graben, Roger Dale 1962- *WhoSSW 91*
Graber, Benjamin 1944- *BiDrAPA 89*
Graber, Donald Duane 1946- *BiDrAPA 89*
Graber, Doris Appel 1923- *WhoAm 90, WhoWrEP 89*
Graber, Edward Alex 1914- *WhoAm 90*
Graber, Eric Scarth 1940- *WhoE 91*
Graber, G. Thomas 1947- *WhoSSW 91*
Graber, Harris David 1939- *WhoE 91, WhoWor 91*
Graber, Hildegard K 1922- *BiDrAPA 89*
Graber, Kathleen Sue 1945- *WhoSSW 91*
Graber, Richard Allan 1933- *St&PR 91*
Graber, Sandra S *BiDrAPA 89*
Graber, Steve L. 1960- *St&PR 91*
Graber, Thomas M. 1917- *WhoAm 90*
Graber-Pastrone, Sylvia Lujean 1952- *WhoEmL 91*
Grabert, Garland Frederick 1923-1987 *BioIn 16*
Grabes, Herbert 1936- *ConAu 130*
Grabfield, Deborah Diller 1954- *WhoAmW 91*
Grabiel, Floyd E. 1946- *St&PR 91*
Grabill, Gloria Elizabeth 1938- *WhoE 91*
Grabill, James Roscoe, Jr. 1949- *WhoWrEP 89*
Grabko, Nicholas Wayne 1950- *WhoE 91*
Grable, Betty 1916-1973 *BioAmW, WorAlBi*
Grable, Betty 1918-1973 *OxCPMus*
Grable, Edward E. 1926- *WhoAm 90*
Grable-Wallace, Lisa Leonor 1953- *WhoEmL 91*
Grabner, George John 1918- *St&PR 91, WhoAm 90*
Grabo, Norman Stanley 1930- *WhoAm 90, WhoWrEP 89*
Graboff, Roy 1931- *St&PR 91*
Grabois, Lori Ann *BiDrAPA 89*
Grabois, Neil Robert 1935- *WhoAm 90, WhoE 91*
Grabon, Henry 1917- *St&PR 91*
Graboski, Thomas Walter 1947- *WhoAm 90*
Grabow, Barry G. 1943- *St&PR 91*
Grabow, John Charles 1956- *WhoE 91*
Grabow, Stephen Harris 1943- *WhoAm 90*
Grabowicz, George Gregory 1943- *WhoAm 90*
Grabowitz, Ellen Wail 1953- *BiDrAPA 89*
Grabowska, Arthur Joseph 1953- *WhoSSW 91*
Grabowski, Adam Stanislaw 1950- *BiDrAPA 89*
Grabowski, Chester Adam 1946- *WhoAm 90*
Grabowski, David Lawrence 1945- *WhoSSW 91*
Grabowski, Elizabeth 1940- *WhoAmW 91*
Grabowski, Janice Lynn 1948- *WhoAmW 91*
Grabowski, John *BiDrAPA 89*
Grabowski, John Francis 1947- *WhoWrEP 89*
Grabowski, Johnny 1900-1946 *Ballpl 90*
Grabowski, Marianne Cecilia 1958- *WhoEmL 91*
Grabowski, Raymond 1950- *St&PR 91*
Grabowski, Thomas Craig 1948- *WhoEmL 91*
Grabowski, Walter 1932- *BiDrAPA 89*
Grabowski, William J 1958- *WhoWrEP 89*
Grabowski, Zbigniew 1930- *WhoWor 91*
Grabowsky, Axel L. 1937- *St&PR 91*
Grabowsky, Max 1874-1946 *EncABHB 4*
Graboyes, Robert Francis 1954- *WhoEmL 91*
Graboys, George 1932- *WhoAm 90*
Grabscheid, William Henry 1931- *WhoWor 91*
Grabske, William John 1943- *WhoAm 90, WhoWor 91*
Grabski, Daniel A 1928- *BiDrAPA 89*
Grabski, Donald E. 1927- *St&PR 91*
Graburn, Nelson Hayes Henry 1936- *WhoAm 90*
Graca, Sandra Lynn 1965- *WhoE 91*
Grace, Princess of Monaco 1929-1982 *BioIn 16*
Grace, Bud *BioIn 16*
Grace, Candis Denise 1956- *BiDrAPA 89*
Grace, Catherine D. 1964- *WhoWrEP 89*
Grace, Charles Brown, Jr. 1934- *WhoE 91*
Grace, Charles Edward 1957- *WhoEmL 91*
Grace, Charles L. 1935- *St&PR 91*
Grace, Conan Terry 1932- *WhoE 91*
Grace, Corinne Bissette 1929- *WhoAmW 91, WhoWor 91*
Grace, David Joseph 1946- *WhoEmL 91*
Grace, Donald Ray 1937- *WhoSSW 91*
Grace, Earl 1907-1980 *Ballpl 90*
Grace, Edward *ConAu 129*
Grace, Eugene G. 1876-1960 *WorAlBi*
Grace, Eugene P. 1951- *St&PR 91*
Grace, Eugene Vernon 1927- *WhoWrEP 89*
Grace, H. David 1936- *WhoAm 90*
Grace, J Peter 1913- *News 90 [port]*
Grace, J. Peter 1913- *St&PR 91, WhoAm 90, WhoE 91, WorAlBi*
Grace, Jason Roy 1936- *St&PR 91, WhoAm 90, WhoE 91*
Grace, Jeffrey Jerome 1955- *BiDrAPA 89, WhoE 91*
Grace, Jerry L. 1941- *St&PR 91*
Grace, Joe 1914-1969 *Ballpl 90*
Grace, John Eugene 1931- *WhoAm 90*
Grace, John Kenneth 1945- *WhoE 91*
Grace, John Michael 1934- *BiDrAPA 89*
Grace, John Patrick 1942- *ConAu 31NR, WhoWor 91*
Grace, John Robert 1926- *St&PR 91*
Grace, John Ross 1943- *WhoAm 90*
Grace, John S. *BioIn 16*
Grace, John Wiliam 1927- *WhoAm 90*
Grace, Joseph Allain, Jr. 1958- *WhoE 91*
Grace, Judy Diane 1946- *WhoAmW 91*
Grace, Julianne Alice 1937- *St&PR 91, WhoAm 90, WhoAmW 91*
Grace, Kay Linda *BiDrAPA 89*
Grace, Lawrence A. 1945- *St&PR 91*
Grace, Lowell E. 1925- *St&PR 91*
Grace, Marcia Bell 1937- *WhoAm 90*
Grace, Mark 1964- *Ballpl 90*
Grace, Nancy O. 1936- *St&PR 91*
Grace, Oliver R. *BioIn 16*
Grace, Oliver R. 1909- *St&PR 91*
Grace, Oliver Russell 1909- *WhoAm 90*
Grace, Patricia *FemiCLE*
Grace, Richard Edward 1930- *WhoAm 90*
Grace, Robert Mitchell, Jr. 1947- *St&PR 91*
Grace, Roy 1936- *St&PR 91*
Grace, Thomas Edward 1954- *WhoEmL 91*
Grace, Thomas Lee 1955- *WhoE 91*
Grace, Wesley Gee, Jr. 1945- *WhoSSW 91*
Grace, William Gilbert 1848-1915 *BioIn 16*
Grace, William Russell 1832-1904 *BioIn 16*
Graceffo, Samuel A 1936- *BiDrAPA 89*
Gracen, Belinda Susan 1951- *WhoAmW 91*
Gracer, James Stephen 1952- *BiDrAPA 89*
Gracey, Dan J. 1948- *St&PR 91*
Gracey, Douglas Robert 1936- *WhoAm 90*
Gracey, James Steele 1927- *WhoAm 90*
Gracey, William Morgan 1953- *WhoEmL 91*
Gracia, Charles 1944- *WhoWor 91*
Gracia, Jorge J E 1942- *ConAu 30NR, HispWr 90*
Gracia, Jorge J. E. 1942- *WhoHisp 91*
Gracia, Jorge Jesus Emiliano 1942- *WhoAm 90*
Gracia, Luis 1926- *WhoHisp 91*
Gracia, Miguel F 1923- *BiDrAPA 89*
Gracia, Norma Elida 1940- *WhoHisp 91*
Gracia, Rafael I *BiDrAPA 89*
Gracia-Machuca, Rafael G. 1948- *WhoHisp 91*
Gracia-Pena, Idilio 1940- *WhoHisp 91*
Gracian y Morales, Baltasar 1601-1658 *LitC 15 [port]*
Gracida, Rene Henry 1923- *WhoAm 90, WhoSSW 91*
Gracie, Carolyn Nan *BiDrAPA 89*
Gracious, Barbara Lynn *BiDrAPA 89*
Gracis, Ettore 1915- *PenDiMP*
Gracy, David Bergen, II 1941- *WhoAm 90*
Gracy, Michael Lee 1962- *WhoEmL 91*
Gracza, Margaret Young 1928- *BioIn 16*
Graczyk, Alan Edward 1953- *WhoSSW 91*
Graczyk, David Charles 1955- *WhoSSW 91*
Grad, Bernard 1920- *EncO&P 3, EncPaPR 91*
Grad, Frank Paul 1924- *WhoAm 90*
Grad, Gary Jordan 1944- *BiDrAPA 89*
Grad, John J. 1938- *St&PR 91*
Grad, John Joseph 1938- *WhoAm 90*
Grad, Neil Elliott Marshall 1954- *WhoEmL 91*
Graddick, Charles Allen 1944- *WhoAm 90*
Graddick, Richard Adolph 1918- *WhoWrEP 89*
Grade, Lew 1906- *BioIn 16, WhoAm 90*
Grade, Lorna Jean 1954- *WhoEmL 91*
Gradel, Thomas J. *ODwPR 91*
Graden, John Joseph 1960- *WhoSSW 91*
Gradenwitz, Peter Werner Emanuel 1910- *IntWWM 90*
Grader, Charles Raymond 1931- *WhoE 91, WhoWor 91*
Grader, Jan Michael 1946- *WhoEmL 91*
Grader, Ralph Howard 1922- *St&PR 91*
Gradillas, Vicente 1936- *BiDrAPA 89*
Gradin, Anita 1933- *WhoWor 91*
Gradinger, J. Gary 1943- *St&PR 91*
Gradinger, Joseph F. *St&PR 91*
Gradinger, Stephanie Emory 1949- *WhoE 91*
Gradison, Heather Jane 1952- *WhoAm 90, WhoAmW 91*
Gradison, Willis David, Jr. 1928- *WhoAm 90*
Gradl, Johann Baptist 1904-1988 *BioIn 16*
Grado, Angelo John 1922- *WhoAm 90, WhoAmA 91*
Grado, John 1927- *St&PR 91*
Grado, John Angelo 1953- *St&PR 91*
Gradoville, Kathleen Evoy 1962- *WhoAmW 91*
Gradowski, Stanley J., Jr. 1938- *St&PR 91*
Gradowski, Stanley Joseph, Jr. 1938- *WhoAm 90*
Graduate of Oxford, A *ConAu 129*
Grady, Ann Jacqueline 1959- *WhoAmW 91*
Grady, Arey Wilson, Jr. 1949- *WhoSSW 91*
Grady, David F. 1938- *St&PR 91*
Grady, David J. 1941- *St&PR 91*
Grady, Denise *BioIn 16*
Grady, Duane G. 1936- *St&PR 91*
Grady, Edward F. 1936- *St&PR 91*
Grady, Gilbert Robidoux, Jr. 1936- *St&PR 91*
Grady, Harvell 1949- *St&PR 91*
Grady, Henry Francis 1882-1957 *BioIn 16*
Grady, Henry Woodfin 1850-1889 *BioIn 16*
Grady, Henry Woodfin, III 1962- *WhoSSW 91*
Grady, James 1949- *WhoWrEP 89*
Grady, James Thomas 1949- *SpyFic, WhoEmL 91*
Grady, John *NewYTBS 90*
Grady, John Edward, Jr. 1935- *WhoWor 91*
Grady, John F. 1929- *WhoAm 90*
Grady, John Francis 1902-1989 *BioIn 16*
Grady, John Francis 1934- *IntWWM 90, WhoAm 90*
Grady, John Joseph 1920- *WhoAm 90, WhoE 91*
Grady, John William 1951- *WhoE 91*
Grady, Kathryn Faber 1960- *WhoAmW 91*
Grady, Kenneth L *BiDrAPA 89*
Grady, Lee Timothy 1937- *WhoAm 90*
Grady, Maureen Frances 1960- *WhoAmW 91, WhoE 91, WhoEmL 91, WhoWor 91*
Grady, Mike 1869-1943 *Ballpl 90*
Grady, Robert A. 1925- *St&PR 91*
Grady, Robert Earl, Jr. 1955- *WhoSSW 91*
Grady, Ruby McLain 1944- *WhoAmA 91*
Grady, Sharon M. 1941- *St&PR 91*
Grady, Stafford Robert 1921- *St&PR 91*
Grady, Tana Annette 1962- *BiDrAPA 89*
Grady, Thomas J. 1914- *WhoAm 90, WhoSSW 91*
Graeb, Thelma Savard 1934- *WhoAmW 91*
Graebel, William Paul 1932- *WhoAm 90*
Graeber, Charlotte Towner *BioIn 16*
Graeber, Mike J. 1950- *WhoE 91*
Graebner, Eric Hans 1943- *IntWWM 90*
Graebner, James Herbert 1940- *WhoAm 90*
Graebner, Linda Susan 1950- *WhoEmL 91*
Graebner, Norman Arthur 1915- *WhoAm 90*
Graebner, William Sievers 1943- *ConAu 30NR*
Graedon, Sidney *BioIn 16*
Graef, Luther William 1931- *WhoAm 90, WhoWor 91*
Graef, Warren Donald, Jr. 1941- *WhoSSW 91*
Graefe, Ann Elizabeth 1935- *WhoAmW 91*
Graefe, Erhart 1943- *WhoWor 91*
Graefe, James Arthur *BioIn 16*
Graefe, Peter Ulrich 1942- *WhoE 91*
Graeff, David Wayne 1946- *WhoE 91, WhoEmL 91, WhoWor 91*
Graem, Niels 1945- *WhoWor 91*
Graeme, Bruce 1900-1982 *TwCCr&M 91*
Graeme, David *TwCCr&M 91*
Graeme, Peter 1921- *IntWWM 90*
Graeme, Roderic *TwCCr&M 91*
Graening, Orval 1910- *St&PR 91*
Graese, Clifford Ernest 1927- *WhoAm 90*
Graese, Judy 1940- *WhoAmA 91*
Graeser, Andreas 1942- *WhoWor 91*
Graessley, William Walter 1933- *WhoAm 90*
Graettinger, John Sells 1921- *WhoAm 90, WhoWor 91*
Graetz, Lynn H. *ODwPR 91*
Graetz, Saul M. 1910- *St&PR 91*
Graetzel, Michael 1944- *WhoWor 91*
Graf, Alan B. 1929- *St&PR 91*
Graf, Alan B., Jr. 1953- *St&PR 91*
Graf, Carol M 1946- *BiDrAPA 89*
Graf, Donald L. 1937- *St&PR 91*
Graf, Dorothy Ann 1935- *WhoAmW 91*
Graf, Edward Louis 1938- *St&PR 91*
Graf, Edward Louis, Jr. 1938- *WhoAm 90*
Graf, Engelbert Franz 1922- *WhoWor 91*
Graf, Ervin Donald 1930- *WhoWor 91*
Graf, Gary R. 1947- *WhoWrEP 89*
Graf, George N., Jr. 1933- *St&PR 91*
Graf, Hans *PenDiMP*
Graf, James E. 1947- *St&PR 91*
Graf, John A 1942- *BiDrAPA 89*
Graf, John C. 1948- *St&PR 91*
Graf, John C., Jr. 1948- *WhoE 91*
Graf, John Kenneth 1942- *St&PR 91*
Graf, Joseph Charles 1928- *WhoAm 90, WhoSSW 91*
Graf, Larry W. 1938- *St&PR 91*
Graf, Oskar Maria 1894-1967 *BioIn 16*
Graf, Paul Andrew 1956- *BiDrAPA 89*
Graf, Peter Gustav 1936- *WhoAm 90, WhoE 91, WhoWor 91*
Graf, Richard Karlem 1948- *WhoE 91*
Graf, Robert Arlan 1933- *St&PR 91, WhoAm 90*
Graf, Steffi *BioIn 16*
Graf, Steffi 1969- *WhoAm 90, WorAlBi*
Graf, Truman Frederick 1922- *WhoAm 90*
Graf, Uta 1915- *IntWWM 90*
Grafas, Van A. 1954- *WhoE 91*
Grafe, Ernst-Dieter 1938- *WhoWor 91*
Grafe, Warren Blair 1954- *WhoEmL 91, WhoWor 91*
Grafelman, Glenn Allen 1958- *WhoAmA 91*
Grafelman, Judy Rae 1953- *WhoAmW 91*
Graff, David Austin 1949- *WhoE 91, WhoEmL 91*
Graff, Donald Frederick 1928- *WhoAm 90*
Graff, Erik 1951- *WhoEmL 91*
Graff, George Stephen 1917- *WhoAm 90*
Graff, Gerald 1937- *ConAu 31NR*
Graff, Harold 1932- *BiDrAPA 89, WhoAm 90, WhoE 91, WhoWor 91*
Graff, Harry W 1931- *BiDrAPA 89*
Graff, Henry Franklin 1921- *WhoAm 90, WhoWor 91*
Graff, Herb *BioIn 16*
Graff, Ilene *BioIn 16*
Graff, J. William 1930- *WhoWrEP 89*
Graff, James R. 1933- *ODwPR 91*
Graff, John R. 1935- *St&PR 91*
Graff, Lawrence 1934- *St&PR 91*
Graff, Marc David 1948- *BiDrAPA 89, WhoEmL 91*
Graff, Mel 1907-1975 *EncACom*
Graff, Michael H. 1943- *St&PR 91*
Graff, Milton Arthur 1929- *St&PR 91*
Graff, Morris U. 1920- *St&PR 91*
Graff, Norman I 1921- *BiDrAPA 89*
Graff, Philip 1931- *St&PR 91*
Graff, Robert Alan 1953- *WhoEmL 91, WhoWor 91*
Graff, Roger David 1955- *St&PR 91*
Graff, S. Stewart 1908- *AuBYP 90*
Graff, Samuel Myron 1945- *WhoE 91*
Graff, Stephen Ney 1934- *WhoAm 90, WhoWor 91*
Graff, Stuart Leslie 1945- *WhoAm 90*
Graff, William 1925- *WhoAm 90*
Graff, William M. 1940- *St&PR 91*
Graffagnino, Paul N 1927- *BiDrAPA 89*
Graffenried, Christoph Von 1661-1743 *WhNaAH*
Graffenried, Christopher 1661-1743 *EncCRAm*
Graffeo, Anthony Salvatore 1938- *St&PR 91*
Graffin, Guillaume *WhoAm 90*
Graffis, Kathleen Ann 1953- *WhoAmW 91*
Graffman, Gary 1928- *IntWWM 90, PenDiMP, WhoAm 90*
Grafft, B.C. 1911- *St&PR 91*
Grafft, James 1950- *St&PR 91*
Grafke, Alfred G. 1940- *St&PR 91*
Graflund, Jeff L. 1949- *St&PR 91*
Grafman, Allan Irving 1953- *WhoEmL 91*
Grafstein, Bernice *WhoAm 90*
Grafton, C W 1909-1982 *TwCCr&M 91*
Grafton, Clive Llewellyn 1930- *WhoAm 90*
Grafton, Eugene S. 1930- *St&PR 91*
Grafton, Rick 1952- *WhoAmA 91*
Grafton, Sue *BioIn 16*
Grafton, Sue 1940- *BestSel 90-3 [port], ConAu 31NR, FemiCLE, TwCCr&M 91*
Grafton, Thurman Stanford 1923- *WhoAm 90*

Grafton, Tom Eugene 1955- *WhoEmL 91*
Gragasin, Jose Valliente 1900- *WhoWrEP 89*
Gragert, Steven Keith 1950- *WhoSSW 91*
Gragg, Bruce Moore 1951- *WhoEmL 91, WhoSSW 91*
Gragg, Gene Balford 1938- *WhoAm 90*
Gragg, Logan, Jr. *BiDrAPA 89*
Gragg, Rosa Slade *BioIn 16*
Gragg, Samuel *PenDiDA 89*
Gragg, Sara Elizabeth 1930- *WhoAmW 91*
Gragg, Thomas M *BiDrAPA 89*
Gragg, Thomas P. 1950- *St&PR 91*
Gragnola, John B. 1929- *St&PR 91, WhoAm 90*
Grah, Karen Elizabeth 1953- *WhoAmW 91*
Graham Central Station *EncPR&S 89*
Graham, Ada *AuBYP 90*
Graham, Al 1897- *AuBYP 90*
Graham, Albert Bruce 1919- *WhoAm 90*
Graham, Albert Darlington, Jr. 1948- *WhoE 91*
Graham, Alberta *AuBYP 90*
Graham, Alberta Newsome 1955- *WhoAmW 91*
Graham, Alexander John 1930- *WhoAm 90*
Graham, Alexander Steel 1917- *WhoAm 90*
Graham, Allister P. 1936- *St&PR 91*
Graham, Alsy *BioIn 16*
Graham, Amanda *AuBYP 90*
Graham, Angus Frederick 1916- *WhoAm 90*
Graham, Anna Regina 1947- *WhoAmW 91*
Graham, Anne 1949- *WhoAm 90, WhoAmW 91*
Graham, Arnold Harold 1917- *WhoAm 90*
Graham, Audrey 1953- *WhoAmW 91*
Graham, Augustus Washington 1848- *AmLegL*
Graham, Barbara Jeannette 1936- *WhoAmW 91*
Graham, Beardsley 1914- *WhoAm 90*
Graham, Benjamin *BioIn 16*
Graham, Bill 1884-1936 *Ballpl 90*
Graham, Bill 1931- *WhoAm 90, WorAlBi*
Graham, Billy 1918- *BioIn 16*
Graham, Bob *AuBYP 90*
Graham, Bob 1936- *BioIn 16, WhoWor 91*
Graham, Bob 1942- *SmATA 63 [port]*
Graham, Brenda J. 1944- *WhoAmW 91*
Graham, Bruce Douglas 1915- *WhoAm 90*
Graham, Carl Francis 1915- *WhoAm 90*
Graham, Carol Ethlyn 1941- *WhoAmW 91*
Graham, Caroline 1931- *TwCCr&M 91*
Graham, Catharine Macaulay 1731-1791 *BioIn 16*
Graham, Charles *OxCPMus*
Graham, Charles D. *BioIn 16*
Graham, Charles Danne, Jr. 1929- *WhoE 91*
Graham, Charles George 1946- *St&PR 91*
Graham, Charles J. 1929- *WhoSSW 91*
Graham, Charles John 1929- *WhoAm 90*
Graham, Charles Passmore 1927- *WhoAm 90*
Graham, Charles R *BiDrAPA 89*
Graham, Clarence R. 1907-1989 *BioIn 16*
Graham, Clarence Reginald 1907-1989 *AuBYP 90*
Graham, Clayton James 1942- *St&PR 91*
Graham, Clyde Benjamin, Jr. 1931- *WhoAm 90*
Graham, Coleman J. *BioIn 16*
Graham, Colin *WhoAm 90*
Graham, Colin 1931- *IntWWM 90*
Graham, Cora Joyce 1948- *WhoAmW 91*
Graham, Craig Edmund 1955- *WhoSSW 91*
Graham, Cynthia Armstrong 1950- *St&PR 91, WhoAm 90*
Graham, D. Richard 1944- *St&PR 91*
Graham, D. Robert 1936- *WhoAm 90, WhoSSW 91*
Graham, Daniel Arthur 1944- *WhoAm 90*
Graham, Daniel H 1942- *WhoAmA 91*
Graham, Daniel O 1925- *ConAu 132*
Graham, Daniel Orrin 1925- *WhoAm 90*
Graham, Daniel Robert 1936- *BioIn 16*
Graham, Darrell Jud 1939- *WhoSSW 91*
Graham, David Lynn 1947- *WhoSSW 91*
Graham, David Tredway 1917- *WhoAm 90*
Graham, David W. 1940- *St&PR 91*
Graham, Deborah Jane 1953- *WhoEmL 91*
Graham, Dee McDonald 1927- *WhoAm 90*
Graham, Dellas Ray 1934- *St&PR 91*
Graham, Denise Marie *BiDrAPA 89*
Graham, Donald B. 1940- *St&PR 91*
Graham, Donald E. 1945- *BioIn 16*
Graham, Donald Edward 1945- *St&PR 91*
Graham, Donald Paul 1957- *WhoEmL 91*
Graham, Douglas Bruce 1950- *WhoEmL 91*
Graham, Douglas J M *WhoAmA 91*
Graham, Douglas W. 1947- *St&PR 91*
Graham, Duncan *BioIn 16*
Graham, Duncan 1942- *WhoWor 91*
Graham, Elizabeth Peeler 1949- *IntWWM 90*
Graham, Elliott *BioIn 16*
Graham, Elmer Albert 1926- *St&PR 91*
Graham, Evarts Ambrose, Jr. 1921- *WhoAm 90*
Graham, Evelyne Moore 1929- *WhoSSW 91*
Graham, F. Joseph 1935- *WhoE 91*
Graham, Fiona *BiDrAPA 89*
Graham, Ford Mulford 1911- *WhoAm 90*
Graham, Frances Keesler 1918- *WhoAm 90, WhoAmW 91*
Graham, Frank, Jr. 1925- *AuBYP 90*
Graham, Fred *BioIn 16*
Graham, Fred Patterson 1931- *WhoAm 90*
Graham, Frederick Mitchell 1921- *WhoAm 90*
Graham, G. Edwin 1924- *WhoAm 90*
Graham, Garth Kinsey 1924- *WhoE 91*
Graham, Gene Steven 1951- *WhoEmL 91*
Graham, Geordie *BioIn 16*
Graham, George A. 1909- *St&PR 91*
Graham, George Adams 1904- *WhoAm 90*
Graham, George Gordon 1923- *WhoAm 90*
Graham, Gregory Dane 1947- *BiDrAPA 89*
Graham, Gwethalyn 1913-1965 *FemiCLE*
Graham, H. James 1946- *St&PR 91*
Graham, Hampton Davidson, Jr. 1945- *St&PR 91, WhoAm 90*
Graham, Hardy Moore 1912- *WhoSSW 91, WhoWor 91*
Graham, Harold Grove, Jr. 1929- *St&PR 91*
Graham, Harold Steven 1950- *WhoEmL 91*
Graham, Heather *BioIn 16*
Graham, Helen Holland *AuBYP 90*
Graham, Howard Barrett 1929- *St&PR 91, WhoAm 90*
Graham, Howard Holmes 1947- *WhoAm 90*
Graham, Howard Lee, Sr. 1942- *WhoSSW 91, WhoWor 91*
Graham, Howard O. 1957- *WhoSSW 91*
Graham, Hugh Davis 1936- *WhoAm 90*
Graham, Irene T. 1921- *St&PR 91*
Graham, Irwin Patton 1927- *WhoAm 90*
Graham, Isabella 1742-1814 *FemiCLE*
Graham, James *ConAu 33NR, MajTwCW, TwCCr&M 91*
Graham, James Cornelius Ruddell 1950- *WhoEmL 91*
Graham, James E. 1953- *St&PR 91*
Graham, James Elliot 1847-1899 *DcCanB 12*
Graham, James Gibbs 1946- *WhoSSW 91*
Graham, James Herbert 1921- *WhoAm 90, WhoWor 91*
Graham, James Jay 1945- *St&PR 91*
Graham, James L. 1818- *AmLegL*
Graham, James Patrick 1947- *WhoEmL 91*
Graham, James Robert, III 1943- *WhoAm 90*
Graham, Janelle Lear 1947- *WhoSSW 91*
Graham, Jarlath John 1919- *WhoAm 90*
Graham, Jennifer Cecile 1963- *WhoAmW 91, WhoEmL 91*
Graham, Jerry Lyle 1947- *WhoAm 90, WhoEmL 91*
Graham, Jim 1952- *St&PR 91*
Graham, JoAnn 1956- *WhoAmW 91*
Graham, Joe Michael 1952- *WhoWrEP 89*
Graham, John *BioIn 16*
Graham, John 1774-1820 *BioIn 16*
Graham, John 1867-1911 *BioIn 16*
Graham, John Alan 1949- *WhoEmL 91*
Graham, John Borden 1918- *WhoAm 90, WhoWor 91*
Graham, John D 1881-1961 *WhoAmA 91N*
Graham, John D. 1886-1961 *BioIn 16*
Graham, John D. 1937- *ODwPR 91*
Graham, John Dalby 1937- *WhoAm 90*
Graham, John E. 1938- *St&PR 91*
Graham, John E, III 1942- *BiDrAPA 89*
Graham, John Finlayson 1924- *WhoAm 90*
Graham, John Francis 1948- *WhoE 91*
Graham, John Gourlay 1938- *St&PR 91, WhoAm 90*
Graham, John Hamilton 1826-1899 *DcCanB 12*
Graham, John J. 1922- *St&PR 91*
Graham, John Joseph 1920- *WhoE 91*
Graham, John Joseph 1939- *St&PR 91*
Graham, John Louis 1955- *WhoEmL 91*
Graham, John Malcolm *BiDrAPA 89*
Graham, John Michael 1944- *St&PR 91*
Graham, John R 1934- *BiDrAPA 89*
Graham, John R. 1945- *St&PR 91*
Graham, John Robert, Jr. 1930- *WhoAm 90*
Graham, John Ruskin *NewYTBS 90*
Graham, John Ruskin 1909-1990 *BioIn 16*
Graham, John Webb 1912- *St&PR 91, WhoAm 90*
Graham, Jon Fredrick 1952- *WhoEmL 91*
Graham, Jorie 1951- *FemiCLE*
Graham, Joseph B 1882- *EncABHB 5*
Graham, Joseph P. 1935- *St&PR 91*
Graham, Jul Eliot 1953- *WhoEmL 91*
Graham, K M 1913- *WhoAmA 91*
Graham, Katharine *BioIn 16*
Graham, Katharine 1917- *WhoAm 90, WhoAmW 91, WhoE 91, WhoWor 91, WorAlBi*
Graham, Katharine M. 1917- *BioAmW*
Graham, Katherine Elizabeth 1964- *WhoAmW 91*
Graham, Kathleen Margaret 1913- *WhoAm 90*
Graham, Kathleen Murphy 1939- *WhoE 91*
Graham, Kenneth L. 1915- *WhoAm 90*
Graham, Kenneth Russell, II 1955- *BiDrAPA 89*
Graham, Kirsten R. 1946- *WhoAmW 91*
Graham, Kyle 1899-1973 *Ballpl 90*
Graham, Lanier 1940- *WhoAmA 91*
Graham, Larry 1946- *EncPR&S 89*
Graham, Larry 1962- *SmATA X [port]*
Graham, Larry A *BiDrAPA 89*
Graham, Laurie *BioIn 16*
Graham, Lawrence 1962- *SmATA 63 [port]*
Graham, Lawrence Edward 1936- *St&PR 91*
Graham, Lawrence Lee 1935- *WhoSSW 91*
Graham, Leslie A. 1959- *ODwPR 91*
Graham, Linda Diane 1953- *WhoAmW 91*
Graham, Linda Kay Edwards 1946- *WhoAm 90*
Graham, Lindsay A 1932- *BiDrAPA 89*
Graham, Lois 1930- *WhoAmA 91*
Graham, Lois Charlotte 1917- *WhoAmW 91*
Graham, Lola Amanda 1896- *WhoAmW 91, WhoWor 91*
Graham, Lola Amanda Beall 1896- *WhoWrEP 89*
Graham, Loren Raymond 1933- *WhoAm 90*
Graham, Lorenz 1902- *AuBYP 90*
Graham, Lorenz 1902-1989 *ConAu 129, SmATA 63*
Graham, Lorenz B. 1902-1989 *BioIn 16*
Graham, Malcolm Scott 1932- *St&PR 91*
Graham, Margaret Blandin 1949- *WhoSSW 91*
Graham, Margaret Helen 1923- *WhoAmW 91*
Graham, Marlon Anthony 1957- *BiDrAPA 89*
Graham, Martha *BioIn 16*
Graham, Martha 1893- *BioAmW*
Graham, Martha 1894- *ConAu 129, NotWoAT, WhoAm 90, WhoAmW 91, WhoE 91, WhoWor 91*
Graham, Martha 1895- *WorAlBi*
Graham, Mary Bertha 1934- *WhoHisp 91*
Graham, Maxene Oberman *WhoAmW 91*
Graham, Michael D. 1956- *St&PR 91*
Graham, Michael John 1951- *WhoEmL 91*
Graham, Nan Wood *NewYTBS 90 [port]*
Graham, Neil H. 1933- *St&PR 91*
Graham, Nicol G. 1952- *St&PR 91*
Graham, Norman Lewis 1934- *St&PR 91*
Graham, Oscar David 1935- *WhoSSW 91*
Graham, Otis Livingston, Jr. 1935- *WhoAm 90*
Graham, Ottie B. 1900- *EarBlAP*
Graham, Ottie Beatrice 1900- *HarlReB*
Graham, Otto 1921- *WorAlBi*
Graham, Otto Everett, Jr. 1921- *WhoAm 90*
Graham, Pamela Smith 1944- *WhoWor 91*
Graham, Patricia Albjerg 1935- *WhoAm 90, WhoWor 91*
Graham, Patricia M *BiDrAPA 89*
Graham, Patrick Francis 1940- *WhoAm 90*
Graham, Philip Leslie 1915-1963 *BioIn 16*
Graham, Polly A *BiDrAPA 89*
Graham, R. B. Cunninghame 1852-1936 *BioIn 16*
Graham, R B Cunninghame 1852-1936 *DcLB 98 [port]*
Graham, Ray A 1887-1932 *EncABHB 5*
Graham, Raymond J. *St&PR 91*
Graham, Rhea Lydia 1952- *WhoAmW 91*
Graham, Richard 1941- *WhoSSW 91*
Graham, Richard A. 1947- *St&PR 91*
Graham, Richard Harper 1911- *WhoAm 90*
Graham, Richard Marston 1939- *WhoAmA 91N*
Graham, Richard R. 1950- *St&PR 91*
Graham, Richard Zoll 1929- *St&PR 91*
Graham, Robert 1938- *WhoAmA 91*
Graham, Robert Arlington 1938- *WhoAm 90*
Graham, Robert C 1885- *EncABHB 5*
Graham, Robert C. 1925- *WhoAm 90*
Graham, Robert C, Jr 1941- *WhoAmA 91*
Graham, Robert Clare, III 1955- *WhoEmL 91*
Graham, Robert Claverhouse, Sr 1913- *WhoAmA 91*
Graham, Robert Grant 1931- *St&PR 91, WhoAm 90*
Graham, Robert Klark 1906- *WhoWor 91*
Graham, Robert Macdonald, Jr 1919- *WhoAmA 91*
Graham, Robert W. 1915-1990 *BioIn 16*
Graham, Robert William 1922- *WhoAm 90*
Graham, Robin Lee *BioIn 16*
Graham, Roger A 1928- *BiDrAPA 89*
Graham, Roger Craig *BiDrAPA 89*
Graham, Ronald Lewis 1935- *WhoAm 90*
Graham, Russell D. 1930- *St&PR 91*
Graham, Sam R. 1941- *St&PR 91*
Graham, Sarah Ann Wilkinson 1945- *WhoSSW 91*
Graham, Saxon 1922- *WhoAm 90*
Graham, Seymour C. 1914- *St&PR 91*
Graham, Sheilah *BioIn 16*
Graham, Sheilah 1904-1988 *AnObit 1988*
Graham, Sheilah 1905-1989 *WorAlBi*
Graham, Shelley Ann 1950- *WhoSSW 91*
Graham, Shirley 1906-1977 *BioIn 16*
Graham, Shirley 1907-1977 *AuBYP 90*
Graham, Stephen Arthur 1954- *WhoEmL 91*
Graham, Stephen Douglas Andrews 1955- *WhoAm 90*
Graham, Stephen Michael 1951- *WhoEmL 91*
Graham, Steve Howard 1945- *WhoAm 90*
Graham, Stuart Edward 1946- *St&PR 91*
Graham, Susan Lois 1942- *WhoAm 90*
Graham, Sylvia Swords 1935- *WhoAmW 91*
Graham, Thomas 1805-1869 *WorAlBi*
Graham, Thomas, Jr. 1933- *WhoAm 90*
Graham, Thomas C. 1927- *St&PR 91*
Graham, Thomas Carlisle 1927- *WhoAm 90*
Graham, Thomas Hardy 1945- *St&PR 91*
Graham, Thomas Richard 1942- *WhoE 91*
Graham, Thomas W 1951- *BiDrAPA 89*
Graham, Tom *MajTwCW*
Graham, Tommy, Jr. 1940- *WhoSSW 91*
Graham, Vernon Lee 1930- *St&PR 91*
Graham, Victor Ernest 1920- *WhoAm 90, WhoWrEP 89*
Graham, Vincent Gradford 1964- *WhoSSW 91*
Graham, Virginia 1912- *BioIn 16*
Graham, Walter 1903- *WhoAmA 91*
Graham, Walter Raleigh, Jr. 1944- *WhoSSW 91*
Graham, William 1918- *WorAlBi*
Graham, William Alexander 1804-1875 *BiDrUSE 89*
Graham, William Andrew 1939- *WhoAmA 91*
Graham, William Arthur 1921- *St&PR 91*
Graham, William Arthur Grover 1930- *WhoAm 90*
Graham, William Aubrey, Jr. 1930 *WhoSSW 91*
Graham, William B. 1911- *St&PR 91, WhoAm 90, WhoWor 91*
Graham, William Edgar, Jr. 1929- *St&PR 91, WhoAm 90*
Graham, William Franklin 1918- *WhoAm 90*
Graham, William Gordon 1920- *WhoWor 91*
Graham, William H 1938- *BiDrAPA 89*
Graham, William Hardin 1932- *WhoWor 91*
Graham, William James 1923- *WhoAm 90*
Graham, William Patton, III 1934- *WhoAm 90*
Graham, William Pierson 1935- *WhoWor 91*
Graham, William Robert 1937- *WhoAm 90*
Graham, William W. 1949- *St&PR 91*
Graham, Winston 1910- *TwCCr&M 91*
Graham-Cameron, Mike 1931- *BioIn 16*
Graham Du Bois, Shirley Lola 1896-1977 *HarlReB*
Graham-Henry, Diane Michelle 1946- *WhoWrEP 89*
Graham-Hurd, Melissa Ann 1956- *WhoEmL 91*
Graham-Jones, Ian 1937- *IntWWM 90*
Graham-Moore, Brian Edward 1935- *WhoSSW 91*
Grahame, Gloria 1925?-1981 *BioIn 16*
Grahame, Kenneth 1859-1932 *AuBYP 90, WorAlBi*
Grahame, Orville Francis Booth 1904- *WhoAm 90*
Grahame, Paula Easter Patton *WhoE 91*
Grahl, Timothy Galen 1948- *St&PR 91*
Grahl-Madsen, Atle 1922- *WhoWor 91*
Grahmann, Charles V. 1931- *WhoSSW 91*

Grahn, Barbara Ascher 1929- *WhoAmW 91*
Grahn, Judy 1940- *FemiCLE*
Grahn, Ulf 1942- *IntWWM 90*
Grahn, Ulf Ake Wilhelm 1942- *WhoSSW 91*
Grahner, Robert Earl 1927- *St&PR 91*
Grain, Corney 1844-1895 *OxCPMus*
Grainer, Ron 1922-1981 *OxCPMus*
Grainger, A. Jeffrey 1952- *WhoEmL 91*
Grainger, David Gregory 1953- *WhoSSW 91*
Grainger, David William 1927- *St&PR 91*
Grainger, Isaac B. 1895- *St&PR 91*
Grainger, Martin Allerdale 1874-1941 *DcLB 92 [port]*
Grainger, Nessa Posner *WhoAmA 91*
Grainger, Percy 1882-1961 *BioIn 16*
Grainger, Porter *DrBlPA 90, EarBlAP*
Grainger, Tom 1921- *OxCCanT*
Grainger, William *PenDiDA 89*
Grais, Edward 1920- *St&PR 91*
Grais, Sam S. 1906- *WhoWor 91*
Grala, Jane Marie *WhoAmW 91, WhoWor 91*
Gralen, Donald John 1933- *WhoAm 90*
Gralla, Arthur R. *St&PR 91*
Gralla, Eugene 1924- *St&PR 91, WhoAm 90*
Gralla, Lawrence 1930- *WhoAm 90*
Gralla, Milton 1928- *St&PR 91, WhoAm 90*
Graller, Jack L 1935- *BiDrAPA 89*
Gralley, Robert Emory 1926- *St&PR 91*
Grallo, Richard Martin 1947- *WhoE 91*
Gralnick, Alexander 1912- *BiDrAPA 89*
Gralnick, Marshall Larry 1940- *St&PR 91*
Gralnick, William J 1943- *BiDrAPA 89*
Gram, Harvey B., Jr. *St&PR 91N*
Gram, William Harold 1937- *St&PR 91*
Gramajo Morales, Hector Alejandro 1940- *WhoWor 91*
Gramatky, Hardie 1907-1979 *AuBYP 90, WhoAmA 91N ChlLR 22 [port]*
Grambau, Robert Fraser *BiDrAPA 89*
Gramberg, Liliana *WhoAmA 91*
Grambergu, Henry George, Jr. 1947- *WhoEmL 91*
Grambling, Jeffrey Arthur 1953- *WhoEmL 91*
Grambs, Jean D 1919-1989 *ConAu 129*
Grambs, Jean Dresden 1919-1989 *BioIn 16*
Gramelspacher, Glenn H. 1925- *St&PR 91*
Gramer, George Kerr, Jr. 1952- *WhoSSW 91*
Gramet, Charles *AuBYP 90*
Gramlich, Allan A. 1925- *St&PR 91*
Gramlich, James Vandle 1939- *WhoAm 90*
Gramlich, L. *St&PR 91*
Gramling, Frank Robert 1946- *WhoSSW 91*
Gramling, Nadine *BioIn 16*
Gramm, Wendy Lee *WhoAm 90, WhoAmW 91*
Gramm, William Philip 1942- *WhoAm 90, WhoSSW 91, WhoWor 91*
Gramman, E.G. 1922- *St&PR 91*
Grammas, Alex 1926- *Ballpl 90*
Grammaticas, W. *St&PR 91*
Grammatikakis, Miltos Dimitris 1962- *WhoSSW 91*
Grammenopoulos, Anthony Filios 1948- *WhoE 91*
Grammer, Elisa Joan 1952- *WhoEmL 91*
Grammer, Frank Clifton 1943- *WhoSSW 91*
Grammer, June Amos 1927- *BioIn 16*
Grammer, Kelsey *BioIn 16*
Grammer, Kelsey 19--?- *WorAlBi*
Grampp, William Dyer 1914- *WhoAm 90*
Grams, Ileana J. 1945- *WhoAmW 91*
Grams, William E. 1943- *St&PR 91*
Gramse, Richard G. 1935- *St&PR 91*
Gramza, Felix J. 1934- *St&PR 91*
Gran, Caroline Mary 1941- *WhoAmW 91*
Gran, Richard Joseph 1940- *WhoE 91*
Gran, Thorvald 1943- *WhoWor 91*
Grana, George F. 1939- *St&PR 91*
Grana, Michael J *BiDrAPA 89*
Granacher, Robert P, Jr. *BiDrAPA 89*
Granacki, Victoria Ann 1947- *WhoAmW 91*
Granada, Lemuel Orendain 1925- *BiDrAPA 89*
Granade, Callie Virginia Smith 1950- *WhoEmL 91*
Granado, Donald Casimir 1915- *WhoWor 91*
Granado, Elma Gonzales *BiDrAPA 89*
Granados, Candace Michele 1958- *WhoAmW 91*
Granados, Enrique 1867-1916 *BioIn 16, PenDiMP A*
Granados, Frank L. *WhoHisp 91*
Granados, Mimi I. 1946- *WhoHisp 91*
Granahan, James Charles 1965- *WhoEmL 91*
Granahan, Patrick John 1941- *St&PR 91*
Granat, Jay Paul 1952- *WhoEmL 91*
Granat, Juan Wolfgang 1918- *IntWWM 90*
Granat, Laurence Ronald 1938- *St&PR 91*
Granat, Robert *WhoWrEP 89*
Granata, Angela Rosaria 1960- *WhoEmL 91*
Granata, Robert John 1934- *St&PR 91*
Granath, Herbert A. 1928- *St&PR 91*
Granath, Kay Vivian 1949- *WhoAmW 91*
Granatir, William L *BiDrAPA 89*
Granatir, William Louis 1916- *WhoE 91*
Granato, F. Mark 1952- *ODwPR 91, St&PR 91*
Granato, James R. 1943- *St&PR 91*
Granato, Tony *BioIn 16*
Granatstein, Jack Lawrence 1939- *WhoAm 90, WhoWrEP 89*
Granberry, Clyde Wilfred 1928- *St&PR 91*
Granbery, Edwin Carleton, Jr. 1913- *WhoAm 90*
Grand Funk *OxCPMus*
Grand, Al *BioIn 16*
Grand, Bernard 1928- *St&PR 91*
Grand, Henry G 1910- *BiDrAPA 89*
Grand, Henry George 1910- *WhoE 91*
Grand, Milton J. 1904-1989 *BioIn 16*
Grand, Richard D. 1930- *WhoAm 90*
Grand, Sarah 1854-1943 *BioIn 16, FemiCLE*
Granda, Carlos 1961- *WhoHisp 91*
Grandberg, Gilbert Jason 1937- *WhoE 91, WhoWor 91*
Grandbois, Alain 1900-1975 *DcLB 92 [port]*
Grande Geule *WhNaAH*
Grande, B. Lynda 1957- *WhoEmL 91*
Grande, Charles W. 1940- *St&PR 91*
Grande, Frank A. 1923- *St&PR 91*
Grande, Luke F *BiDrAPA 89*
Grande, Paula Gail 1949- *WhoAmW 91, WhoEmL 91*
Grande, Peter Campbell 1951- *WhoEmL 91*
Grande, Sarina D'Amato 1910- *WhoE 91*
Grandee, Joe Ruiz 1929- *WhoAmA 91*
Grandestaff, Robert LaRoy 1943- *St&PR 91*
Grandey, George W. 1813-1893 *AmLegL*
Grandfield, Raymond Joseph 1931- *WhoE 91*
Grandi, Count 1895-1988 *AnObit 1988*
Grandi, Caterina 1933- *BiDrAPA 89*
Grandi, Dino 1895-1988 *BioIn 16*
Grandi, Hans 1904- *IntWWM 90*
Grandi, Margherita 1894- *IntWWM 90*
Grandier, Urbain *EncO&P 3*
Grandin, Glenn M. 1943- *St&PR 91*
Grandin, Temple 1947- *WhoAmW 91*
Grandin, Thomas Burnham 1907-1977 *BioIn 16*
Grandinetti, Carmin David 1957- *WhoEmL 91*
Grandinetti, Michael Lawrence 1960- *WhoEmL 91*
Grandis, Leslie Allan 1944- *WhoAm 90*
Grandjany, Marcel 1891-1975 *PenDiMP*
Grandle, Christopher Owen 1954- *WhoEmL 91*
Grandle, Ralph W. 1936- *St&PR 91*
Grandma Moses 1860-1961 *BioIn 16*
Grandmaison, J. Joseph 1943- *WhoAm 90*
Grandmaster Flash 1957?- *EncPR&S 89*
Grandmont, Eloi de 1921-1970 *OxCCanT*
Grandmont, Jean-Michel 1939- *WhoWor 91*
Grandolfo, Joe Frank 1947- *St&PR 91*
Grandone, Eugene 1948- *St&PR 91*
Grandone, Leo D. 1912- *St&PR 91*
Grandower, Elissa *TwCCr&M 91*
Grandpierre, Susan Morgana 1945- *WhoAmW 91, WhoE 91*
Grandstrand, Karen Louise 1955- *WhoEmL 91*
Grandval, Gilbert 1904-1981 *BiDFrPL*
Grandy, Charles C. 1928- *St&PR 91*
Grandy, Fred 1948- *WhoAm 90*
Grandy, James Frederick 1919- *WhoAm 90*
Grandy, Jay Franklin 1939- *St&PR 91*
Grandy, Leonard A. 1916- *WhoAm 90*
Grandy, Maria Clare 1937- *WhoAm 90*
Grandy, Nita Mary 1915- *WhoAmW 91, WhoWor 91*
Grandy, Walter Thomas, Jr. 1933- *WhoAm 90*
Granek, Iris Ann *BiDrAPA 89*
Granet, Lester *BioIn 16*
Granet, Lloyd 1958- *WhoSSW 91*
Granet, Roger B 1947- *BiDrAPA 89, WhoAm 90, WhoE 91*
Graney, Bernard John 1947- *WhoE 91*
Graney, Jack 1886-1978 *Ballpl 90*
Graney, Marshall John 1939- *WhoSSW 91*
Grangaard, Paul D. 1958- *St&PR 91*
Grange, Harold 1903- *WorAlBi*
Grange, Jacques *BioIn 16*
Grange, Janet B. 1944- *WhoAmW 91*
Grange, Jean-Daniel 1944- *WhoWor 91*
Grange, John *TwCCr&M 91*
Grange, Kenneth 1929- *ConDes 90*
Grange, Philip Roy 1956- *IntWWM 90*
Grange, Red *BioIn 16*
Grange, William Marshall 1947- *WhoEmL 91*
Granger, Beth 1962- *WhoE 91*
Granger, Bill *SpyFic*
Granger, Bill 1941- *ConAu 131, TwCCr&M 91, WhoAm 90, WhoWrEP 89*
Granger, David 1903- *St&PR 91, WhoAm 90, WhoWor 91*
Granger, David Mason 1952- *WhoSSW 91*
Granger, Dennis Lee 1938- *WhoWrEP 89*
Granger, Edward Brown 1937- *St&PR 91*
Granger, Farley 1925- *WorAlBi*
Granger, Francis 1792-1868 *BiDrUSE 89*
Granger, Gideon 1767-1822 *BiDrUSE 89*
Granger, Harvey, Jr. 1928- *St&PR 91, WhoAm 90, WhoSSW 91*
Granger, James Archibald 1931- *BiDrAPA 89*
Granger, Luc Andre 1944- *WhoAm 90*
Granger, Margaret Jane *AuBYP 90*
Granger, Marilyn 1957- *BiDrAPA 89*
Granger, Martha S *BiDrAPA 89*
Granger, Michel 1946- *BioIn 16*
Granger, Peg 1925?-1977 *AuBYP 90*
Granger, Raymond Earl, III 1948- *St&PR 91*
Granger, Stephen I 1930- *BiDrAPA 89*
Granger, Stewart 1913- *ConTFT 8, WorAlBi*
Granger, Wayne 1944- *Ballpl 90*
Granger, William Thiel, III 1942- *BiDrAPA 89*
Grangula *WhNaAH*
Granick, David 1926- *WhoAm 90*
Granick, Lois Wayne 1932- *WhoAm 90, WhoE 91*
Granieri, Michael Nicholas 1943- *WhoAm 90, WhoSSW 91*
Granieri, Vincent J. 1957- *St&PR 91*
Granieri, Vincent James 1957- *WhoEmL 91*
Graninger, Howard J. *St&PR 91*
Granirer, Edmond Ernest 1935- *WhoAm 90*
Granirer, Julius 1902-1990 *BioIn 16*
Granit, Ragnar Arthur 1900- *WhoAm 90, WhoWor 91*
Granito, Conrad Joseph *BiDrAPA 89*
Granitz, Marlene Ellen 1954- *WhoE 91*
Granlund, David John 1946- *WhoAm 90*
Granlund, Paul Theodore 1925- *WhoAmA 91*
Grann, Phyllis 1937- *WorAlBi*
Grann-O'Brien, Marcia Judith 1940- *WhoE 91*
Grannan, Robert J. 1952- *St&PR 91*
Granner, Daryl Kitley 1936- *WhoAm 90*
Granner, Nancy *BioIn 16*
Grannon, Charles Lee 1915- *St&PR 91*
Grannon-Devine, Debra Lynn 1959- *WhoAmW 91*
Grano, Joseph J. Jr., Jr. 1948- *WhoAm 90*
Grano, Olavi Johannes 1925- *WhoWor 91*
Granof, Michael H. 1942- *WhoAm 90*
Granoff, Abbot Lee 1945- *BiDrAPA 89*
Granoff, Gary Charles 1948- *WhoE 91, WhoWor 91*
Granoff, Jean Kessler 1926- *WhoAmW 91*
Granoff, Michael David 1958- *WhoE 91*
Granot, Eliazar *WhoWor 91*
Granovskii, T.N. 1813-1855 *BioIn 16*
Granovskii, Timofei Nikolaevich 1813-1855 *BioIn 16*
Granowetter, Linda 1951- *WhoAmW 91*
Granquist, Victor Martin 1955- *WhoEmL 91*
Granquist, Wayne George 1935- *St&PR 91*
Granqvist, Hakan Ragnar Axel 1935- *WhoWor 91*
Gransden, Antonia 1928- *ConAu 30NR*
Granstaff, William Boyd 1925- *WhoAmA 91*
Granston, David Wilfred 1939- *WhoE 91, WhoWor 91*
Granston, Larry R. 1938- *St&PR 91*
Granstrand, Sven Ove 1944- *WhoWor 91*
Granstrom, Marvin Leroy 1920- *WhoAm 90*
Grant, A Allison *BiDrAPA 89*
Grant, A. James 1940- *St&PR 91*
Grant, Adrian *BiDrAPA 89*
Grant, Alan J. 1925- *WhoAm 90*
Grant, Alberta 1946- *WhoSSW 91*
Grant, Alexander Marshall 1928- *WhoAm 90*
Grant, Alice Bacon *BioIn 16*
Grant, Alicia Brown 1945- *WhoAmW 91*
Grant, Allan Kerr 1924- *WhoWor 91*
Grant, Ambrose *TwCCr&M 91*
Grant, Amy 1961- *WhoAmW 91, WorAlBi*
Grant, Andrew Merritt 1943- *St&PR 91*
Grant, Anne 1755-1838 *FemiCLE*
Grant, Art *BioIn 16*
Grant, Art 1927- *WhoAmA 91*
Grant, Barbara Lee 1946- *WhoAmW 91, WhoSSW 91*
Grant, Barry Marvin 1936- *WhoAm 90*
Grant, Bernard Arthur 1945- *WhoEmL 91*
Grant, Bernie *BioIn 16*
Grant, Betty Ruth 1937- *WhoAmW 91*
Grant, Brian Lowell 1952- *BiDrAPA 89, WhoEmL 91*
Grant, Bruce 1893-1977 *AuBYP 90*
Grant, Carl N. 1939- *WhoAm 90*
Grant, Carol Phillips 1956- *WhoAmW 91*
Grant, Cary 1904-1986 *BioIn 16, WorAlBi*
Grant, Cathal Patrick *BiDrAPA 89*
Grant, Charles *Ballpl 90*
Grant, Charles Brasfield, III 1951- *St&PR 91*
Grant, Charles L. 1950- *St&PR 91*
Grant, Charles Truman 1946- *WhoAm 90*
Grant, Cheryl 1944- *WhoAm 90, WhoAmW 91*
Grant, Cheryn Lee 1947- *BiDrAPA 89*
Grant, Claude De Witt 1944- *WhoWrEP 89*
Grant, Clifford Scantlebury 1930- *IntWWM 90*
Grant, Cornelia Love 1932- *WhoSSW 91*
Grant, Courtney *BioIn 16*
Grant, Crislyn Jean 1951- *WhoEmL 91*
Grant, Cynthia Elizabeth 1948- *WhoAmW 91*
Grant, Dale Bezar 1942- *St&PR 91*
Grant, Daniel Angus 1944- *St&PR 91*
Grant, Daniel Gordon 1957- *WhoEmL 91*
Grant, Daniel Ross 1923- *WhoAm 90*
Grant, David B. 1915- *St&PR 91*
Grant, David James William 1937- *WhoAm 90*
Grant, David M. 1944- *ODwPR 91*
Grant, David Peabody 1952- *WhoE 91*
Grant, Debra Susan 1959- *WhoEmL 91*
Grant, Dennis Duane 1940- *WhoAm 90*
Grant, Dennis Henry 1942- *BiDrAPA 89*
Grant, Donald W. 1924- *St&PR 91*
Grant, Doris Leona 1915- *WhoAmW 91*
Grant, Duncan James Corrowr 1885-1978 *BioIn 16*
Grant, Eamonn Felix 1936- *WhoSSW 91*
Grant, Earl 1931-1970 *DrBlPA 90*
Grant, Earl Gilbert 1936- *St&PR 91*
Grant, Eddie 1883-1918 *Ballpl 90*
Grant, Edmund M. 1923- *St&PR 91*
Grant, Edward 1926- *WhoAm 90*
Grant, Edward Alexander 1950- *WhoAm 90*
Grant, Edwin R. 1943- *St&PR 91*
Grant, Elaine Elizabeth 1941- *WhoAmW 91*
Grant, Elizabeth 1797-1885 *FemiCLE*
Grant, Ellsworth S. 1917- *St&PR 91*
Grant, Elmer G. 1925- *St&PR 91*
Grant, Ethel *BioIn 16*
Grant, Eugene Lynn 1953- *WhoEmL 91*
Grant, Eva 1907- *AuBYP 90*
Grant, Felix *BioIn 16*
Grant, Frank 1868-1937 *Ballpl 90*
Grant, Franklin Dean 1941- *WhoSSW 91*
Grant, Frederick Anthony 1949- *WhoE 91, WhoEmL 91*
Grant, George 1903- *Ballpl 90*
Grant, George Monro 1835-1902 *DcLB 99 [port]*
Grant, George Parkin 1918-1988 *BioIn 16*
Grant, Gordon Hope 1875-1962 *WhoAmA 91N*
Grant, Gwen 1940- *BioIn 16*
Grant, H. Coleman, III 1938- *WhoSSW 91*
Grant, H Michael *BiDrAPA 89*
Grant, Harold Graham *BiDrAPA 89*
Grant, Harry 1906- *BiDrAPA 89*
Grant, Harry Johnston 1881-1963 *BioIn 16*
Grant, Henry J *BiDrAPA 89*
Grant, Horace Renshaw, Jr. 1924- *St&PR 91*
Grant, Hugh *ConTFT 8*
Grant, Hugh Mansfield 1936- *WhoAm 90*
Grant, Ian Stanley 1940- *WhoAm 90*
Grant, Igor 1942- *BiDrAPA 89*
Grant, Isabella Horton 1924- *WhoAmW 91*
Grant, J. B. 1940- *WhoWrEP 89*
Grant, J Jeffrey 1883-1960 *WhoAmA 91N*
Grant, James *BioIn 16*
Grant, James 1812-1891 *AmLegL*
Grant, James B. *St&PR 91N*
Grant, James Benton 1918-1989 *BioIn 16*
Grant, James Colin 1937- *WhoAm 90*
Grant, James D *BioIn 16*
Grant, James Deneale 1932- *WhoAm 90*
Grant, James Morgan 1943- *St&PR 91*
Grant, James Pineo 1922- *WhoAm 90, WhoWor 91*
Grant, James William 1943- *WhoAm 90, WhoSSW 91*
Grant, Jane Wentworth 1942- *WhoWor 91*
Grant, Janet Elizabeth 1957- *WhoWrEP 89*
Grant, Jedediah Morgan 1816-1856 *AmLegL*
Grant, Jeffrey Steven 1947- *WhoAm 90*

Grant, Jim 1940- WhoSSW 91
Grant, Joan 1907- EncO&P 3
Grant, Joan 1907-1989 AnObit 1989
Grant, Joanne Catherine 1940- WhoAmW 91
Grant, John Wallace 1942- WhoSSW 91
Grant, Joseph M. 1938- St&PR 91
Grant, Joseph Moorman 1938- WhoAm 90, WhoSSW 91
Grant, Joyce 1937- IntWWM 90
Grant, Juanita G. 1930- WhoAmW 91
Grant, Julia Dent 1826-1902 BioAmW, BioIn 16
Grant, Kathleen Susan 1949- WhoE 91
Grant, Kathryn Ann 1946- WhoAmW 91
Grant, Kenneth EncO&P 3
Grant, Kerry Scott 1945- IntWWM 90, WhoEmL 91
Grant, Lee BioIn 16
Grant, Lee 1931- ConTFT 8, WhoAm 90, WorAlBi
Grant, Leonard Tydings 1930- WhoAm 90
Grant, Lilias FemiCLE
Grant, M. Duncan 1950- WhoEmL 91
Grant, Madeleine Parker 1895- AuBYP 90
Grant, Margaret Davis 1944- WhoAmW 91
Grant, Margaret Ellen 1948- BiDrAPA 89
Grant, Margo BioIn 16
Grant, Maria 1845?- FemiCLE
Grant, Mark 1963- Ballpl 90
Grant, Mary Kathryn 1941- WhoAmW 91
Grant, Matthew AuBYP 90
Grant, Matthew 1934- St&PR 91
Grant, Maxwell TwCCr&M 91
Grant, Merrill Theodore 1932- WhoAm 90
Grant, Merwin Darwin 1944- WhoWor 91
Grant, Michael Donald, Jr. 1938- St&PR 91
Grant, Michael Peter 1936- WhoAm 90, WhoWor 91
Grant, Mickey Edward 1949- WhoEmL 91
Grant, Micki DrBlPA 90
Grant, Mimi 1948- WhoEmL 91
Grant, Miriam Rosenbloum WhoAmW 91
Grant, Mudcat 1935- Ballpl 90
Grant, Muir William 1923- St&PR 91
Grant, Nicholas John 1915- St&PR 91, WhoAm 90
Grant, Norman Howard 1927- WhoAm 90
Grant, Patrick 1941- ConAu 132
Grant, Patrick Alexander 1945- WhoEmL 91
Grant, Penny 1959- WhoAmW 91
Grant, Phyllis Hunt 1951- WhoAmW 91
Grant, R Peery 1939- BiDrAPA 89
Grant, Raymond Thomas 1957- WhoE 91
Grant, Rhoda 1902- WhoAmW 91
Grant, Richard 1937- ODwPR 91
Grant, Richard Evans 1927- WhoAm 90
Grant, Richard L 1933- BiDrAPA 89
Grant, Richard Lee 1955- St&PR 91, WhoSSW 91
Grant, Richard S. 1946- St&PR 91
Grant, Robert L. 1925- WhoWrEP 89
Grant, Robert McQueen 1917- WhoAm 90
Grant, Robert Nathan 1930- WhoAm 90
Grant, Robert Stephen 1942- WhoWrEP 89
Grant, Robert Ulysses 1929- WhoAm 90
Grant, Robert Wallace 1936- WhoAm 90
Grant, Robert Yearington 1913- WhoAm 90
Grant, Ronald Alfred 1938- BiDrAPA 89, WhoE 91
Grant, Ruby Jayne Johnson WhoAmW 91, WhoWor 91
Grant, Sandra E BiDrAPA 89
Grant, Sandra Milliken 1958- WhoAmW 91
Grant, Sandra Swearingen 1944- WhoAmW 91
Grant, Sara Catherine 1950- WhoAmW 91, WhoEmL 91
Grant, Shellie Evelyn 1951- BiDrAPA 89
Grant, Stanley Cameron 1931- WhoAm 90
Grant, Stephen Allen 1938- WhoE 91, WhoWor 91
Grant, Stephen R. 1939- St&PR 91
Grant, Steven C. 1942- St&PR 91
Grant, Surlene Georgette 1959- WhoEmL 91
Grant, Susan 1954- WhoAmW 91
Grant, Susan B. 1949- St&PR 91
Grant, Susan Irene 1953- WhoE 91, WhoEmL 91
Grant, Susan Pitt BiDrAPA 89
Grant, Sydney Robert 1926- WhoAm 90
Grant, Thomas James 1957- WhoE 91
Grant, Thomas Patrick 1954- WhoEmL 91
Grant, Tom NewAgMG
Grant, Tommy BioIn 16
Grant, Toni Gale BioIn 16
Grant, Ulysses S. 1822-1885 BioIn 16
Grant, Ulysses Simpson 1822-1885 BiDrUSE 89, WhNaAH, WorAlBi
Grant, Verne Edwin 1917- WhoAm 90
Grant, Vernon 1902-1990 NewYTBS 90
Grant, Virginia Annette 1941- WhoAm 90
Grant, W. Jack, III 1929- BiDrAPA 89
Grant, Walter Burton 1934- St&PR 91
Grant, Walter J BiDrAPA 89
Grant, Walter King, Sr. 1906- St&PR 91
Grant, Walter Matthews 1945- St&PR 91, WhoAm 90
Grant, William D. 1917- St&PR 91
Grant, William Downing 1917- WhoAm 90
Grant, William Frederick 1924- WhoAm 90
Grant, William H. 1954- St&PR 91
Grant, William Hurley BiDrAPA 89
Grant, William Packer, Jr. 1942- WhoE 91, WhoWor 91
Grant, William R. 1925- St&PR 91
Grant, William Robert 1925- WhoAm 90
Grant, William W., III 1932- St&PR 91
Grant, William West, III 1932- WhoAm 90
Grant-Adamson, Lesley 1942- TwCCr&M 91
Grant-Berger, Lynn 1950- WhoSSW 91
Grant Goldman, Pamela 1961- WhoEmL 91
Grant-Horrocks, Kelly Ann 1958- WhoE 91
Grant-Lynch, Carol Lee 1943- WhoAmW 91
Grantham, Charles Edward 1950- WhoSSW 91
Grantham, Dewey Wesley 1921- WhoAm 90
Grantham, Donald Frisbie 1933- WhoSSW 91
Grantham, George 1900-1954 Ballpl 90
Grantham, George Leighton 1920- WhoAm 90
Grantham, Harry BiDrAPA 89
Grantham, Joseph Michael, Jr. 1947- WhoEmL 91
Grantham, Richard Robert 1927- St&PR 91, WhoAm 90
Grantham, Robert William 1931- St&PR 91
Grantham, Thomas 1634-1692 BioIn 16
Grantier, Barry Murdock 1942- St&PR 91
Grants, Andris 1943- St&PR 91
Grants, Valdis 1942- WhoWor 91
Grantuskas, Patricia Mary 1952- WhoAmW 91
Grantz, A Irwin BiDrAPA 89
Granum, Robert Marion 1924- St&PR 91
Granville, Bonita 1923-1988 AnObit 1988, BioIn 16
Granville, Charles Strecker 1951- WhoE 91
Granville, M.F. 1915- St&PR 91
Granvold, Naomi Wagner 1949- BiDrAPA 89
Granz, Norman BioIn 16
Granz, Norman 1918- OxCPMus
Granzer, Friedrich Leo 1926- WhoWor 91
Granzier, Paul A. 1927- St&PR 91
Granzow, A.W. St&PR 91
Granzow, Gary W. St&PR 91
Granzow, Paul H. 1927- WhoAm 90
Grapes, Marcus Jack 1942- WhoWrEP 89
Graphia, Anthony V. 1938 St&PR 91
Graphos, Gerald G. 1937- St&PR 91
Grapin, Jacqueline G. 1942- WhoE 91
Grapp, Wesley Gleason 1918- WhoWor 91
Grappe, Ronald E. 1953- St&PR 91
Grappelli, Stephane BioIn 16
Grappelli, Stephane 1908- IntWWM 90, OxCPMus, PenDiMP
Grappelly, Stephane 1908- PenDiMP
Grappo, Gary Anthony 1950- WhoE 91
Grapski, Ladd Raymond 1942- WhoAm 90
Grasbeck, Ralph Gustaf Armas 1930- WhoWor 91
Grasberger, Joseph Cook 1912- BiDrAPA 89
Graser, Harold P 1918- BiDrAPA 89
Graser, Lyle Richard 1948- WhoAm 90
Graser, Merle Lawrence 1929- St&PR 91, WhoAm 90
Grashel, David Scott 1954- WhoSSW 91
Grashof, August Edward 1932- WhoAm 90
Grashow, James Bruce 1942- WhoAmA 91
Grasley, Michael Howard 1937- St&PR 91
Grasmick, Joseph Christian 1949- WhoE 91
Grass, Alex 1927- St&PR 91
Grass, Alexander 1927- WhoAm 90, WhoE 91
Grass, Charla Elaine 1949- WhoEmL 91, WhoSSW 91
Grass, Guenter 1927- MajTwCW
Grass, Gunter 1927- BioIn 16, EuWr 13, WhoWor 91, WorAlBi
Grass, Henry James 1945- BiDrAPA 89
Grass, John 1837?-1918 WhNaAH
Grass, Martin L. 1954- St&PR 91
Grass, Martin Lehrman 1954- WhoAm 90
Grass, Patty Patterson WhoAmA 91
Grassby, George Edward 1954- WhoEmL 91
Grasse, Donald Anthony 1929- St&PR 91
Grasse, Francois, Comte De 1722-1788 WorAlBi
Grasse, John M., Jr. 1927- BiDrAPA 89
Grassel, Nancy Louise 1957- WhoEmL 91
Grasselli, Jeanette Gecsy 1928- WhoAm 90, WhoAmW 91
Grasser, Emil Josef 1927- WhoWor 91
Grasser, George Robert 1939- WhoAm 90
Grasser, William Jackman 1943- WhoSSW 91
Grasset, Bernard 1933- WhoWor 91
Grasshoff, Alex WhoAm 90
Grassi, Angela 1826-1883 EncCoWW
Grassi, Anthony Prentice 1944- WhoAm 90
Grassi, Anton PenDiDA 89
Grassi, Giorgio 1935- BioIn 16
Grassi, Joseph F. 1949- WhoE 91, WhoEmL 91
Grassi, Joseph Gerald 1919- WhoAm 90
Grassi, Maggi Lidchi ConAu 132
Grassi, Marco 1934- WhoAmA 91
Grassi, Mario 1927- St&PR 91
Grassi, Michael O A 1913- BiDrAPA 89
Grassia, Thomas Charles 1946- WhoEmL 91, WhoWor 91
Grassian, Stuart Edwin 1946- BiDrAPA 89
Grassini, Lawrence Patrick 1945- WhoEmL 91
Grassl, Hartmut 1940- WhoWor 91
Grassle, Karen WhoAm 90
Grassley, Charles Ernest 1933- WhoAm 90, WhoWor 91
Grassmick, Eugene R. 1928- St&PR 91, WhoAm 90
Grassmuck, George Ludwig 1919- WhoAm 90
Grasso, Alfred 1958- WhoE 91
Grasso, Benjamin Cesare BiDrAPA 89
Grasso, Carmine John 1950- WhoE 91
Grasso, Christopher Anthony 1950- WhoEmL 91
Grasso, Doreen Marie 1955- WhoAmW 91
Grasso, Doris 1914- WhoAmA 91
Grasso, Ella 1919-1980 BioIn 16
Grasso, Jack 1927- WhoAmA 91
Grasso, James Anthony 1954- WhoEmL 91
Grasso, Mary Ann 1952- WhoAm 90
Grasso, Mickey 1920-1975 Ballpl 90
Grasso, Patrick St&PR 91
Grasso, Ralph J 1939- BiDrAPA 89
Grasso, Richard A. WhoAm 90
Grasso, Salvatore Fortunato 1945- WhoAmA 91
Grasso, William D. 1930- St&PR 91
Grasty, Charles H. 1863-1924 BioIn 16
Gratch, Serge 1921- WhoAm 90
Grate, Isaac 1952- WhoSSW 91
Grate, Marshall Warren 1955- WhoEmL 91
Grateful Dead OxCPMus
Grateful Dead, The ConMus 5 [port], EncPR&S 89
Grater, Michael 1923- BioIn 16
Grates, Carole Marie 1939- WhoAmW 91
Grates, Gary F 1959- ODwPR 91
Grathwohl, Joseph A. 1937- St&PR 91
Grathwohl, Thomas Judd 1955- St&PR 91
Gratovich, Eugene Alexis 1941- WhoSSW 91
Grattan, George H. 1923- St&PR 91
Grattan, John L. 1830-1854 WhNaAH
Grattan, Patricia E. 1944- WhoAm 90
Grattan, Robert T BiDrAPA 89
Grattan, Susan Amy 1957- WhoEmL 91
Grattan-Guiness, Ivor 1941- EncPaPR 91
Grattan-Guinness, Ivor 1941- EncO&P 3
Gratto, Sandra Ann 1962- WhoE 91
Gratton, John Bernard 1950- WhoSSW 91
Gratton, Patrick John Francis 1933- WhoWor 91
Gratwick, Barbara Burnett BioIn 16
Gratwick, John 1923- WhoAm 90
Gratz, Irwin Leonard 1957- WhoE 91
Gratz, Loren William 1945- WhoEmL 91
Gratz, Norman Gerald 1925- WhoWor 91
Gratz, Pauline 1924- WhoAm 90
Gratz, Rebecca 1781-1869 BioAmW
Gratz, Reed Howe 1950- WhoEmL 91
Gratz, Samuel 1920- St&PR 91
Gratz, Silvia Sarah 1945- BiDrAPA 89
Gratz, Stanley D. 1954- St&PR 91
Gratzer, George Andrew 1936- WhoAm 90
Grau, Conrad 1932- WhoWor 91
Grau, John Michael 1952- WhoAm 90
Grau, Juan WhoHisp 91
Grau, Marcy Beinish 1950- WhoAmW 91, WhoWor 91
Grau, Shirley Ann 1929- BioAmW, FemiCLE, MajTwCW, WhoAm 90, WhoAmW 91, WhoWrEP 89, WorAlBi
Grau, Wilfried 1943- St&PR 91
Grau San Martin, Ramon 1887-1969 BioIn 16
Graubard, Ann Wolfe WhoAmA 91
Graubard, Seymour 1911- WhoAm 90
Graubard, Stephen Richards 1924- WhoAm 90
Graubart, Michael 1930- IntWWM 90
Graubert, John David 1956- WhoEmL 91
Graue, Donna Marie 1963- WhoAmW 91
Graue, Fremont David 1926- WhoAm 90
Grauer, Allan L. 1930- St&PR 91
Grauer, Douglas Dale 1956- WhoEmL 91
Grauer, Eva Marie 1925- WhoSSW 91
Grauer, Frederick Lee Albert 1947- WhoAm 90
Grauer, Frederick Miller, Jr. 1942- St&PR 91
Grauer, Gladys 1923- WhoAmA 91
Grauer, Sherry 1939- WhoAmA 91
Graugnard, F.A., Jr. 1916- St&PR 91
Graugnard, Sharon ODwPR 91
Graul, David M. 1941- WhoSSW 91
Graul, Emil Heinz 1920- WhoWor 91
Graul, Lonnie Milton 1952- St&PR 91
Graule, Raymond Siegfried 1932- WhoSSW 91
Grauley, Stephen O. 1879-1958 Ballpl 90
Graulich, Sherri Marcia 1960- WhoSSW 91
Graumann, William Albert 1932- St&PR 91
Graunke, Kurt 1915- IntWWM 90
Graupe, Daniel 1934- WhoAm 90
Graupe-Pillard, Grace WhoAmA 91
Graupe-Pillard, Grace 1941- WhoE 91
Graupmann, Thomas L. 1957- St&PR 91
Graupner, Kenneth Carl 1941- BiDrAPA 89
Grausman, Philip 1935- BioIn 16, WhoAmA 91
Grauzam, Roland 1943- WhoWor 91
Grava, Alfred H. St&PR 91
Grava, Donald Walter, Jr. 1955- WhoE 91, WhoEmL 91
Grave, Frederick D., Jr. 1926- St&PR 91
Grave, Jean 1854-1939 BiDFrPL
Grave, Katherine Ann 1945- WhoAmW 91
Gravel, Camille Francis, Jr. 1915- WhoWor 91
Gravel, David Charles 1956- St&PR 91
Gravel, James 1943- St&PR 91
Gravel, Keith 1929- St&PR 91
Gravel, Nancy 1946- WhoEmL 91
Gravel, Tina Marie 1960- WhoSSW 91
Gravelet, Jean-Francois 1824-1897 DcCanB 12
Graveline, Daniel Anthony 1941- WhoSSW 91
Gravelle, Pierre 1941- WhoAm 90
Gravely, Edward Martin 1945- St&PR 91
Gravely, Elbert Richard 1966- WhoEmL 91
Gravem, Hamish Forrest 1934- St&PR 91
Graven, Timothy M. 1951- St&PR 91
Gravenstein, Joachim Stefan 1925- WhoAm 90
Graver, David Lee 1939- BiDrAPA 89
Graver, Jack Edward 1935- WhoAm 90
Graver, Lawrence Stanley 1931- WhoAm 90
Graverol, Jeanne 1907- BiDWomA
Graves, Alan Scott 1957- WhoSSW 91
Graves, Anne Carol Finger 1933- WhoAmW 91
Graves, Bari Cordia 1947- WhoAmW 91
Graves, Ben E. 1925- WhoSSW 91
Graves, Benjamin Barnes 1920- WhoAm 90
Graves, Bradford 1939- WhoAmA 91
Graves, Calvin 1844?-1924 BioIn 16
Graves, Caroline McCall 1947- WhoSSW 91
Graves, Catherine ODwPR 91
Graves, Charles Allen 1941- St&PR 91
Graves, Charles C 1901- BiDrAPA 89
Graves, Charles C, III 1925- BiDrAPA 89
Graves, Charles Hinman 1839-1928 AmLegL
Graves, Charles Parlin 1911-1972 AuBYP 90
Graves, Clo. 1863-1932 FemiCLE
Graves, Curtis Matthew 1938- WhoE 91
Graves, Daniel BioIn 16
Graves, Daryl Lynn 1950- WhoEmL 91
Graves, Douglas E. BioIn 16
Graves, Earl G. 1935- St&PR 91
Graves, Earl G., Jr. BioIn 16
Graves, Earl Gilbert 1935- WhoAm 90
Graves, Eben M. 1903- St&PR 91
Graves, Edward S., Mrs. 1937- WhoAmW 91
Graves, Eleanor MacKenzie 1926- BioIn 16
Graves, Ernest, Jr. 1924- WhoAm 90
Graves, F. Charles 1936- ODwPR 91
Graves, Frank X. BioIn 16
Graves, Frank X., Jr. NewYTBS 90 [port]
Graves, Fred Hill 1914- WhoAm 90
Graves, G.T., III 1949- St&PR 91
Graves, Garrett Van A, Jr. 1944- BiDrAPA 89
Graves, Gregory Allen 1948- WhoSSW 91
Graves, H. Brice 1912- WhoAm 90
Graves, Harry Hammond 1956- WhoWor 91

Graves, Harry M., Jr. 1953- *St&PR 91*
Graves, Jacqueline Carolyn 1948- *WhoE 91*
Graves, James H, Jr. 1924- *BiDrAPA 89*
Graves, James Robinson 1820-1893 *BioIn 16*
Graves, James Thomas 1934- *St&PR 91*
Graves, James Warren 1949- *WhoEmL 91*
Graves, John Alexander 1920- *WhoWrEP 89*
Graves, John Sheldon 1943- *BiDrAPA 89*
Graves, John W *WhoAmA 91N*
Graves, John William 1942- *WhoSSW 91*
Graves, Judy Twiehaus 1947- *WhoEmL 91*
Graves, Ka *WhoAmA 91*
Graves, Kenneth Martin 1943- *WhoSSW 91*
Graves, Kenneth Robert 1942- *WhoAmA 91*
Graves, Kenny Max 1949- *St&PR 91*
Graves, Lawrence Lester 1917- *WhoAm 90*
Graves, Lorraine Elizabeth 1957- *WhoAm 90*
Graves, Maitland 1902- *WhoAmA 91N*
Graves, Malcolm J. 1932- *St&PR 91*
Graves, Mark R. 1941- *WhoE 91*
Graves, Mary Ware 1925- *WhoAmW 91*
Graves, Matthew C. 1956- *St&PR 91*
Graves, Matthew Carl 1956- *WhoEmL 91*
Graves, Maureen Ann 1946- *WhoAmW 91, WhoWor 91*
Graves, Max D 1918- *BiDrAPA 89*
Graves, Maxine Elizabeth 1962- *WhoAmW 91*
Graves, Meheko Akiba *BiDrAPA 89*
Graves, Michael *BioIn 16*
Graves, Michael 1934- *BioIn 16, ConDes 90, PenDiDA 89, WhoAm 90, WhoAmA 91, WhoE 91*
Graves, Michael A R 1933- *ConAu 131*
Graves, Michael Wesley, Sr. 1953- *WhoSSW 91*
Graves, Morris 1910- *WhoAmA 91*
Graves, Nancy 1940- *BiDWomA, BioIn 16*
Graves, Nancy Stevenson *WhoAmW 91*
Graves, Nancy Stevenson 1940- *WhoAmA 91*
Graves, Nathan Alan 1957- *WhoEmL 91*
Graves, Newton Abbott 1931- *St&PR 91*
Graves, Patrick Lee 1945- *WhoWor 91*
Graves, Peter 1925- *WorAlBi*
Graves, Peter 1926- *WhoAm 90*
Graves, Pirkko Maija-Leena 1930- *WhoAm 90*
Graves, R. Danner 1943- *ODwPR 91*
Graves, Ralph *BioIn 16*
Graves, Ralph Huntington 1926- *St&PR 91*
Graves, Ray 1924- *WhoAm 90*
Graves, Richard Gordon 1933- *WhoAm 90*
Graves, Richard Perrin *BioIn 16*
Graves, Robert 1895-1985 *AuBYP 90, BioIn 16, DcLB 100 [port], MajTwCW, WorAlBi, WrPh*
Graves, Robert Edward 1929- *WhoAmA 91*
Graves, Robert Jackson 1913- *St&PR 91*
Graves, Robert Lawrence 1926- *WhoAm 90*
Graves, Robert Ranke 1895-1985 *DcNaB 1981*
Graves, Robert Roy 1930- *St&PR 91, WhoAm 90*
Graves, Ronald Norman 1942- *St&PR 91, WhoAm 90*
Graves, Roy Neil 1939- *WhoWrEP 89*
Graves, Roy Stanley 1951- *St&PR 91*
Graves, Rupert *BioIn 16*
Graves, Rupert 1963- *ConTFT 8*
Graves, Stuart McLaren 1946- *BiDrAPA 89, WhoE 91*
Graves, Theresa 1949?- *DrBIPA 90*
Graves, Thomas Ashley, Jr. 1924- *WhoE 91*
Graves, Valerie *BioIn 16*
Graves, Valerie Jo 1950- *WhoEmL 91*
Graves, Wallace B. 1931- *St&PR 91*
Graves, Wallace Billingsley 1922- *WhoAm 90*
Graves, Walter Albert 1920- *WhoAm 90*
Graves, William *AuBYP 90*
Graves, William H.B. 1928- *St&PR 91*
Graves, William Lester 1915- *IntWWM 90*
Graves, William M. 1937- *St&PR 91*
Graves, William P. E. *WhoAm 90*
Graves, William Preston 1953- *WhoAm 90*
Graves, William T. 1934- *WhoSSW 91*
Graves, William Terrell 1934- *St&PR 91*
Gravesen, Ernst 1941- *WhoWor 91*
Gravett, Dale P. *BioIn 16*
Gravett, Linda Sue 1950- *WhoAmW 91*
Gravgaard, Miles A. 1946- *St&PR 91*
Gravier, Jacques 1651-1708 *EncCRAm*
Graville, Anne Malet de 1490?-1543? *EncCoWW*
Gravina, John 1930- *St&PR 91*
Gravink, Philip Ton 1935- *St&PR 91*
Gravino, Nelson 1951- *WhoWor 91*
Gravlee, Grace Downing 1913- *WhoWrEP 89*
Gravley, Ernestine Hudlow *WhoWrEP 89*
Gravley, Nancy Carroll 1940- *WhoAmW 91*
Grawitz, Ernst Robert 1899-1945 *BioIn 16*
Gray, Alasdair 1934- *MajTwCW, WorAu 1980*
Gray, Alexia 1606-1640 *BiDEWW*
Gray, Alfred M. 1928- *WhoAm 90*
Gray, Alfred Orren 1914- *WhoAm 90*
Gray, Alice *AuBYP 90, BioIn 16*
Gray, Alice Wirth 1934- *WhoWrEP 89*
Gray, Allen Gibbs 1915- *WhoAm 90, WhoWor 91*
Gray, Allen Samuel 1934- *WhoAm 90*
Gray, Alvin L. 1928- *St&PR 91, WhoAm 90*
Gray, Ann Maynard 1945- *St&PR 91, WhoAm 90, WhoAmW 91*
Gray, Anne Cameron 1937- *WhoSSW 91*
Gray, Anthony Rollin 1939- *WhoSSW 91*
Gray, Arthur, Jr. 1922- *WhoAm 90*
Gray, Asa 1810-1888 *BioIn 16, WorAlBi*
Gray, Aurum 1935- *St&PR 91*
Gray, Barbara L. *WhoAmW 91*
Gray, Barry Lyndon 1942- *St&PR 91*
Gray, Barry Sherman 1916- *WhoAm 90, WhoE 91*
Gray, Barry W. 1931- *St&PR 91*
Gray, Bartley 1952- *St&PR 91*
Gray, Basil 1904-1989 *BioIn 16*
Gray, Beatriz Fenix *BiDrAPA 89*
Gray, Billy *BioIn 16*
Gray, Bob *BioIn 16*
Gray, Boyden *NewYTBS 90 [port]*
Gray, Bradley Allen 1948- *WhoSSW 91*
Gray, Braley 1941- *St&PR 91*
Gray, Brian Mark 1939- *WhoWor 91*
Gray, Bruce M *BiDrAPA 89*
Gray, Bruce William 1944- *WhoAm 90*
Gray, Burton Craige *BioIn 16*
Gray, C. Boyden *BioIn 16*
Gray, C.C. Howard 1949- *St&PR 91*
Gray, C. Jackson 1947- *St&PR 91*
Gray, Candace Jean 1948- *WhoEmL 91*
Gray, Carl Ralph *BiDrAPA 89*
Gray, Carol Hickson 1958- *WhoAmW 91, WhoEmL 91, WhoSSW 91, WhoWor 91*
Gray, Carol Joyce *WhoAm 90*
Gray, Carol Lippert 1950- *WhoWrEP 89*
Gray, Catherine Darlene 1948- *WhoWrEP 89*
Gray, Cecil 1895-1951 *BioIn 16*
Gray, Charles 1928- *ConTFT 8 [port]*
Gray, Charles Augustus 1928- *WhoE 91, WhoWor 91*
Gray, Charles Elmer 1919- *WhoAm 90*
Gray, Charles Lawrence 1941- *St&PR 91*
Gray, Charles Montgomery 1928- *WhoAm 90*
Gray, Charlinda Davis 1962- *WhoSSW 91*
Gray, Chester L. 1932- *St&PR 91*
Gray, Christian 1772- *FemiCLE*
Gray, Christopher Donald 1951- *WhoEmL 91, WhoWor 91*
Gray, Clarence Jones 1908- *WhoSSW 91, WhoWor 91*
Gray, Clayland Boyden 1943- *WhoAm 90*
Gray, Cleve 1918- *WhoAm 90, WhoAmA 91*
Gray, Colin Antony 1964- *IntWWM 90*
Gray, Constance Ann 1937- *WhoAmW 91*
Gray, Crystal Grace 1954- *WhoEmL 91*
Gray, Dahli 1948- *WhoAmW 91, WhoEmL 91, WhoWor 91*
Gray, Daniel Farnum 1963- *WhoSSW 91*
Gray, Darlene Agnes 1957- *WhoAmW 91*
Gray, David 1932- *IntWWM 90*
Gray, David Judson 1944- *WhoE 91*
Gray, David Lawrence 1930- *WhoAm 90*
Gray, David Ross 1940- *St&PR 91*
Gray, Dawn *ODwPR 91*
Gray, Dawn Plambeck 1957- *WhoAmW 91, WhoEmL 91*
Gray, Diane 1941- *WhoAm 90*
Gray, Dolly 1878-1956 *Ballpl 90*
Gray, Dolores 1924- *OxCPMus*
Gray, Don 1935- *WhoAmA 91, WhoE 91*
Gray, Donald Eugene, Jr. 1949- *WhoEmL 91*
Gray, Donald Lyman 1929- *WhoSSW 91*
Gray, Donna Mae 1933- *WhoAmW 91*
Gray, Dorothy Landis 1922- *IntWWM 90*
Gray, Dorothy Stephens *WhoE 91*
Gray, Dulcie 1920- *FemiCLE, TwCCr&M 91*
Gray, Duncan Montgomery, Jr. 1926- *WhoAm 90, WhoSSW 91*
Gray, D'Wayne 1931- *WhoAm 90*
Gray, Dwight Elder 1903- *WhoE 91, WhoWor 91*
Gray, Ed H *BiDrAPA 89*
Gray, Edman Lowell 1939- *WhoAm 90*
Gray, Edward Barton, Jr. 1924- *WhoE 91*
Gray, Edward C. *BioIn 16*
Gray, Edward John 1930- *WhoAm 90*
Gray, Edwin John 1935- *WhoAm 90*
Gray, Eileen 1879-1976 *BioIn 16, ConDes 90, PenDiDA 89*
Gray, Elise N 1936- *WhoAmA 91*
Gray, Elizabeth Janet 1902- *AuBYP 90*
Gray, Enid Maurine 1943- *WhoAm 90*
Gray, Eula 1912- *EncAL*
Gray, Eunice Sullivan 1907- *WhoAmW 91*
Gray, Fay Beth 1943- *WhoAmW 91*
Gray, Festus Gail 1943- *WhoWor 91*
Gray, Frances M. 1910- *WhoAm 90*
Gray, Francine 1930- *FemiCLE*
Gray, Francine du Plessix 1930- *BestSel 90-3 [port], ConAu 33NR, MajTwCW, WhoAm 90, WhoWrEP 89*
Gray, Francis Campbell 1940- *WhoAm 90*
Gray, Frank George 1942- *St&PR 91, WhoAm 90*
Gray, Frank Truan 1920- *WhoAm 90*
Gray, Franklin Dingwall 1904- *WhoAm 90*
Gray, Fred 1942- *St&PR 91*
Gray, Fred L. 1938- *St&PR 91*
Gray, Frederick Thomas, Jr. 1951- *WhoAm 90*
Gray, Gary 1952- *Ballpl 90*
Gray, Gary Michael 1933- *WhoAm 90*
Gray, Gary Michael · *WhoSSW 91*
Gray, George 1907- *WhoAm 90, WhoWor 91*
Gray, George W. 1940- *St&PR 91*
Gray, Gilda 1901-1959 *WorAlBi*
Gray, Gloria Jean 1948- *WhoAmW 91, WhoSSW 91*
Gray, Gordon Joseph 1910- *WhoWor 91*
Gray, Gordon L. 1924- *WhoAm 90*
Gray, Gordon R. *St&PR 91*
Gray, Grattan 1925- *St&PR 91*
Gray, Gregory Edward 1954- *BiDrAPA 89*
Gray, Gwen Cash 1943- *WhoAmW 91*
Gray, Hanna Holborn 1930- *WhoAm 90, WhoAmW 91, WhoWor 91, WorAlBi*
Gray, Harold 1894-1968 *EncACom, WhoAmA 91N*
Gray, Harold Edward 1952- *WhoEmL 91*
Gray, Harry Barkus 1935- *WhoAm 90*
Gray, Harry Jack 1919- *WhoAm 90, WhoE 91*
Gray, Harry Joshua 1924- *WhoAm 90*
Gray, Helen M 1925- *BiDrAPA 89*
Gray, Henry David 1908- *WhoAm 90, WhoWor 91*
Gray, Henry F. *BioIn 16*
Gray, Howard *WhoWrEP 89*
Gray, Jabez *WhoAmA 91N*
Gray, Jack 1927- *OxCCanT*
Gray, Jack Borland, Jr. 1942- *WhoSSW 91*
Gray, Jack Kenneth, Jr. 1943- *BiDrAPA 89*
Gray, James 1923- *WhoAm 90*
Gray, James A., III 1948- *ODwPR 91*
Gray, James Alexander 1920- *WhoAm 90*
Gray, James Gordon 1919- *St&PR 91*
Gray, James L. *BioIn 16*
Gray, James P., II 1953- *St&PR 91*
Gray, James Patrick 1958- *St&PR 91, WhoEmL 91*
Gray, James Peyton 1943- *WhoAm 90*
Gray, James R. *BioIn 16*
Gray, James Thomas, Jr. *BiDrAPA 89*
Gray, James William 1945- *WhoEmL 91*
Gray, James William, Jr. 1928- *St&PR 91*
Gray, Jan Charles 1947- *WhoEmL 91, WhoWor 91*
Gray, Jason Stephen 1943- *St&PR 91*
Gray, Jeffrey Huston 1950- *St&PR 91*
Gray, Jeffrey T 1956- *BiDrAPA 89*
Gray, Jennifer Ann *WhoAmW 91*
Gray, Jerry 1915-1976 *OxCPMus*
Gray, Jesse *BioIn 16*
Gray, Jessie Benton Evans *WhoAmA 91*
Gray, Jim 1932- *WhoAmA 91*
Gray, Joanne Maria 1958- *WhoAmW 91, WhoEmL 91*
Gray, John 1916- *WhoSSW 91*
Gray, John 1927- *Ballpl 90*
Gray, John 1946- *BioIn 16, OxCCanT*
Gray, John Archibald 1918- *WhoWor 91*
Gray, John Bullard 1927- *St&PR 91, WhoAm 90, WhoE 91*
Gray, John C. 1943- *St&PR 91*
Gray, John Carter Stewart 1953- *WhoEmL 91*
Gray, John D. 1919- *St&PR 91*
Gray, John Delton 1919- *WhoAm 90*
Gray, John Douglas 1945- *St&PR 91, WhoAm 90, WhoEmL 91*
Gray, John Edmund 1922- *WhoAm 90, WhoWor 91*
Gray, John F., Jr. 1913- *BiDrAPA 89*
Gray, John H. 1939- *St&PR 91*
Gray, John Lathrop, III 1931- *WhoAm 90*
Gray, John S *EncABHB 5*
Gray, John S. 1841-1906 *EncABHB 4 [port]*
Gray, John Stephens 1910- *WhoAm 90*
Gray, John Walker 1931- *WhoAm 90*
Gray, John Walton David 1936- *WhoWor 91*
Gray, John Wylie 1935- *WhoSSW 91*
Gray, Jonathan *TwCCr&M 91*
Gray, Juanita Hamilton 1928- *WhoWor 91*
Gray, Judith Neapolitan 1945- *WhoAmW 91*
Gray, Judy Marie 1964- *WhoAmW 91*
Gray, Kathryn Lynn *BiDrAPA 89*
Gray, Kenneth D. 1940- *St&PR 91*
Gray, Kenneth Eugene 1930- *WhoAm 90*
Gray, Kenneth Fairbanks 1954- *WhoEmL 91*
Gray, Kenneth J. 1924- *WhoAm 90*
Gray, Kenneth John 1919- *WhoAm 90*
Gray, Kenneth Wayne 1944- *WhoSSW 91*
Gray, Kermit Victor 1958- *WhoSSW 91*
Gray, Kevin Franklin *BiDrAPA 89*
Gray, Kim *BioIn 16*
Gray, Kimi *BioIn 16*
Gray, Larry 1944- *WhoAmA 91*
Gray, Laurie Davis 1956- *WhoE 91*
Gray, Lawrence Clarke, Jr. 1942- *St&PR 91*
Gray, Lawrence W. 1948- *St&PR 91*
Gray, Lee Kathleen 1949- *WhoSSW 91*
Gray, Lee Learner 1924- *AuBYP 90*
Gray, Linda *BioIn 16, WhoAm 90*
Gray, Linda Esther 1948- *IntWWM 90, PenDiMP*
Gray, Liz *WhoWrEP 89*
Gray, Lois Howard 1920- *St&PR 91*
Gray, Louise Ann 1953- *WhoAmW 91*
Gray, Lydia E. *ODwPR 91*
Gray, Lynn Zuckerman 1949- *St&PR 91*
Gray, Malcolm *ConAu 30NR, TwCCr&M 91*
Gray, Margaret Ann 1950- *WhoAmW 91*
Gray, Marie Elise *WhoAmA 91*
Gray, Martha Hyndman 1939- *WhoAmW 91*
Gray, Martin David *BiDrAPA 89*
Gray, Marvin Lee, Jr. 1945- *WhoAm 90*
Gray, Mary Anne 1812-1845 *FemiCLE*
Gray, Mary Ellen 1948- *WhoAmW 91*
Gray, Mary Wheat 1939- *WhoAm 90*
Gray, Maurine *WhoSSW 91*
Gray, Maurisse Taylor 1954- *St&PR 91*
Gray, Maxwell 1847-1923 *FemiCLE*
Gray, Melvin 1932- *St&PR 91*
Gray, Michael Robert 1958- *BiDrAPA 89*
Gray, Michelle Lee 1963- *WhoAmW 91, WhoEmL 91*
Gray, Milner 1899- *ConDes 90*
Gray, Milton H. 1910- *St&PR 91*
Gray, Milton Hefter 1910- *WhoAm 90*
Gray, Miriam Mary 1905- *WhoWor 91*
Gray, Mitchel Robert 1946- *WhoE 91*
Gray, Morris 1921- *St&PR 91*
Gray, Myles McClure 1932- *WhoAm 90*
Gray, Nancy Ann Oliver 1951- *WhoAmW 91*
Gray, Neil Harold 1952- *WhoEmL 91*
Gray, Nicholas Stuart 1922-1981 *AuBYP 90*
Gray, Noel 1898-1983 *BioIn 16*
Gray, Oliver *ConTFT 8*
Gray, Olwen Leigh *WhoWrEP 89*
Gray, Oriel 1920- *FemiCLE*
Gray, Oscar Shalom 1926- *WhoAm 90*
Gray, Pamela 1940- *WhoAmW 91*
Gray, Pamela Ann 1948- *WhoAmW 91*
Gray, Patricia *AuBYP 90*
Gray, Patricia Ellen 1939- *WhoAmW 91*
Gray, Patrick Worth 1937- *WhoWrEP 89*
Gray, Patsey *AuBYP 90*
Gray, Paul 1918- *BiDrAPA 89*
Gray, Paul E. 1932- *BioIn 16*
Gray, Paul Edward 1932- *WhoAm 90, WhoE 91, WhoWor 91*
Gray, Paulette Styles 1943- *WhoE 91*
Gray, Penelope Parsons *WhoAmW 91*
Gray, Pete 1915- *BioIn 16*
Gray, Pete 1917- *Ballpl 90*
Gray, Peter 1954- *St&PR 91*
Gray, Philip Elza 1937- *St&PR 91*
Gray, Philip Howard 1926- *WhoAm 90, WhoWor 91*
Gray, Phyllis Anne 1926- *WhoAm 90*
Gray, Ralph 1915- *WhoAm 90*
Gray, Richard 1928- *WhoAmA 91*
Gray, Richard Alexander, Jr. 1927- *WhoAm 90*
Gray, Richard Edwin, III 1950- *WhoSSW 91*
Gray, Richard Michael 1932- *St&PR 91*
Gray, Richard S. *ODwPR 91*
Gray, Robert *AuBYP 90*
Gray, Robert 1755-1806 *WhNaAH, WorAlBi*
Gray, Robert Alexander 1941- *WhoE 91*
Gray, Robert C. 1906- *St&PR 91*
Gray, Robert Edmond 1938- *St&PR 91*
Gray, Robert Howard 1937- *WhoAm 90*
Gray, Robert Hugh 1931- *WhoAmA 91*
Gray, Robert K. 1925- *ODwPR 91*
Gray, Robert Keith 1923- *St&PR 91, WhoAm 90*
Gray, Robert M. 1904-1989 *BioIn 16*
Gray, Robert Molten 1943- *WhoAm 90*
Gray, Robert Perry 1926- *St&PR 91*
Gray, Robert Steele 1923- *WhoAm 90, WhoWor 91*

Gray, Robert Ward 1916- WhoAmA 91
Gray, Roger Harold 1945- BiDrAPA 89
Gray, Roland B. 1938- ODwPR 91
Gray, Roland William 1947- WhoSSW 91
Gray, Ronald Kent BiDrAPA 89
Gray, Ronald P. 1939- St&PR 91
Gray, Ross E.S. 1954- St&PR 91
Gray, Russell TwCCr&M 91
Gray, Russell Orton, Sr. 1920- WhoE 91
Gray, Sam 1897-1953 Ballpl 90
Gray, Samuel Braley, III 1941- St&PR 91
Gray, Sarah Ann 1956- WhoAmW 91
Gray, Sarah Virginia 1934- WhoSSW 91
Gray, Scotty Wayne 1934- IntWWM 90
Gray, Seymour 1911- ConAu 130, WhoAm 90
Gray, Sheila Hafter BiDrAPA 89
Gray, Sheila Hafter 1930- WhoAm 90, WhoAmW 91, WhoE 91, WhoWor 91
Gray, Sheldon W. 1938- St&PR 91
Gray, Sidney John 1942- WhoWor 91
Gray, Simon 1936- ConAu 32NR, MajTwCW
Gray, Simon James Holliday 1936- BioIn 16, WhoWor 91
Gray, Skip 1955- IntWWM 90
Gray, Spalding 1941- WhoWrEP 89
Gray, Stanley F. BioIn 16
Gray, Stephen BioIn 16
Gray, Stephen T. 1950- St&PR 91
Gray, Ted 1924- Ballpl 90
Gray, Thaddeus Ives 1959- WhoE 91
Gray, Thelma 1924- ODwPR 91
Gray, Thomas 1716-1771 PoeCrit 2 [port], WorAlBi
Gray, Thomas Alexander 1943- WhoSSW 91
Gray, Thomas Alexander 1948- WhoAmA 91
Gray, Thomas M. ODwPR 91
Gray, Thomas Stephen 1950- WhoAm 90
Gray, Virginia Anne 1955- WhoEmL 91
Gray, Virginia Hickman 1945- WhoAm 90
Gray, Walter Franklin 1929- St&PR 91, WhoAm 90
Gray, Wardell 1921-1955 BioIn 16
Gray, Wellington Burbank 1919-1977 WhoAmA 91N
Gray, William 1917- BiDrAPA 89, WhoE 91
Gray, William Allan 1950- WhoEmL 91
Gray, William G BiDrAPA 89
Gray, William H., III BioIn 16
Gray, William H., III 1941- WhoAm 90, WhoE 91
Gray, William H., Jr. 1927- WhoSSW 91
Gray, William Herbert, III 1941- BlkAmsC [port]
Gray, William J., Jr. 1953- St&PR 91
Gray, William Kelly, Jr. 1949- WhoE 91
Gray, William L. 1946- St&PR 91
Gray, William Percival 1912- WhoAm 90
Gray, William Scott, III 1927- WhoAm 90
Gray-Farmer, Christal Lynn 1959- WhoAmW 91
Gray-Little, Bernadette 1944- WhoAmW 91
Gray-Nix, Elizabeth W. 1956- WhoAmW 91
Graybeal, Sidney Norman 1924- WhoAm 90
Graybiel, Ashton 1938- WhoSSW 91
Graybill, David Lowell BiDrAPA 89
Graybill, David Wesley 1949- WhoAm 90, WhoEmL 91
Graybill, James B. 1938- St&PR 91
Graybill, Wallie Dee 1949- WhoSSW 91
Graybill, Wesley James 1942- WhoAm 90
Graybow, Marvin 1925- St&PR 91
Grayce, Paul A 1939- BiDrAPA 89
Grayck, Marcus Daniel 1927- WhoAm 90
Grayden, Thomas John 1954- BiDrAPA 89
Graydon, Augustus Tompkins 1916- WhoAm 90
Graye, Gerard Edward 1952- WhoEmL 91
Grayer, Jeff BioIn 16
Grayhack, John Thomas 1923- WhoAm 90
Graylow, Richard Vernon 1940- WhoWor 91
Graysmith, Robert 1942- WhoAm 90
Grayson, Albert Kirk 1935- WhoAm 90
Grayson, C. Jackson St&PR 91
Grayson, Cassandra WhoAmA 91
Grayson, Charles Jackson, Jr. 1923- WhoAm 90
Grayson, Clifford Prevost 1857-1951 WhoAmA 91N
Grayson, Dave BioIn 16
Grayson, David 1870-1946 BioIn 16
Grayson, David D. 1920- St&PR 91
Grayson, David Edward 1943- St&PR 91
Grayson, Donald Kenneth 1945- WhoEmL 91
Grayson, Donald Ross 1937- BiDrAPA 89
Grayson, Edward Davis 1938- St&PR 91
Grayson, G. W. 1843-1920 BioIn 16
Grayson, Garry Sandlin 1951- BiDrAPA 89
Grayson, Gene 1928- St&PR 91
Grayson, George Washington 1843-1920 BioIn 16
Grayson, Gerald Herbert 1940- WhoAm 90
Grayson, Grace Riethmuller 1917- WhoAmW 91
Grayson, Harry M. 1894-1968 Ballpl 90
Grayson, Jessie DrBlPA 90
Grayson, Joel 1938- St&PR 91
Grayson, John Allan 1930- WhoAm 90
Grayson, John R. 1925- St&PR 91
Grayson, Kathryn 1922- OxCPMus, WorAlBi
Grayson, Lawrence Peter 1937- WhoAm 90
Grayson, Lisa Jeanne 1961- WhoEmL 91
Grayson, Marion 1906-1976 AuBYP 90
Grayson, Mark Edward 1950- ODwPR 91
Grayson, Richard 1951- ConAu 31NR, WhoWrEP 89
Grayson, Richard E. 1929- St&PR 91
Grayson, Richard Ethan 1948- WhoEmL 91
Grayson, Richard Steven 1944- WhoAm 90
Grayson, Robert Allen 1927- WhoAm 90
Grayson, Robert S 1928- BiDrAPA 89
Grayson, Stanley Edward 1950- BioIn 16
Grayson, Susan Cubillas 1946- WhoAm 90, WhoEmL 91, WhoSSW 91
Grayson, Susan Lois BiDrAPA 89
Grayson, Walton George, III 1928- St&PR 91, WhoAm 90
Grayson, William Curtis, Jr. 1929- WhoE 91
Grayson, William Jackson, Jr. 1930- St&PR 91
Grayson, William John 1788-1863 BioIn 16
Grayston, J. Thomas 1924- WhoAm 90
Grayzel, John Aron 1943- WhoE 91
Graz, Charles M 1934- BiDrAPA 89
Grazda, Ed 1947- WhoAmA 91
Grazevich, Lawrence Carl 1923- St&PR 91
Grazi, Abraham V. St&PR 91
Grazi, Jack V. St&PR 91
Grazi, Maurice V. St&PR 91
Graziadei, Frank M. 1953- WhoEmL 91
Graziadei, William Daniel, III 1943- WhoAm 90
Graziadio, George L. 1919- WhoAm 90
Graziani, Augusto 1933- WhoWor 91
Graziani, N. Jane 1958- WhoSSW 91
Graziani, Sante 1920- WhoAmA 91
Graziano, Anthony Walter, Jr. 1941- WhoAm 90
Graziano, Bonny Gayle 1951- WhoEmL 91
Graziano, Frank D. 1933- St&PR 91
Graziano, Gary Calvin 1956- WhoEmL 91
Graziano, Lawrence M. 1921-1990 BioIn 16
Graziano, Lisa Baker BiDrAPA 89
Graziano, Paul S. 1918-1988 BioIn 16
Graziano, Rocky NewYTBS 90 [port]
Graziano, Rocky 1921-1990 BioIn 16
Graziano, Rocky 1922-1990 News 90, WorAlBi
Graziano, Thomas Anthony 1943- St&PR 91
Graziano, Vincent James 1933- St&PR 91
Grazie, Marie Eugenie delle 1864-1931 EncCoWW
Grba, Eli 1934- Ballpl 90
Grcevich, Stephen 1961- BiDrAPA 89
Greacen, Edmund 1877-1949 WhoAmA 91N
Gread, Joel J. 1956- WhoEmL 91
Greaney, Dennis Michael 1946- WhoAm 90
Greaney, James M. 1941- St&PR 91
Greaney, Patrick Joseph 1939- St&PR 91, WhoAm 90
Greanias, George Constantine 1948- WhoEmL 91
Greanias, Stanley Louis 1949- WhoAm 90
Grear, J Malcolm 1931- ConDes 90
Grear, James Malcolm 1931- WhoAmA 91
Grear, Joseph Anthony 1959- WhoEmL 91
Greaser, Constance Udean 1938- WhoAmW 91, WhoWor 91
Greaser, Marion Lewis 1942- WhoAm 90
Greaser, Maylin H. 1909- WhoAm 90, WhoWor 91
Greason, Arthur LeRoy, Jr. 1922- WhoAm 90, WhoE 91
Greason, D. M. BioIn 16
Greason, David M. BioIn 16
Greason, Frances Crawford BiDrAPA 89
Greason, Thomas L BiDrAPA 89
Great Sun WhNaAH
Great, Don Charles 1951- WhoWor 91
Greatbach, William 1735-1813 PenDiDA 89
Greatbatch, Wilson 1919- WhoAm 90
Greathouse, Patricia Dodd 1935- WhoAmW 91
Greathouse, Richard Francis 1923- WhoSSW 91
Greathouse, Terrence Ray 1932- WhoSSW 91
Greathouse, Walser S WhoAmA 91N
Greatorex, David Samuel 1933- WhoWor 91
Greatorex, Eliza 1820-1897 BiDWomA
Greatrakes, Valentine 1629-1683 EncO&P 3
Greatrex, Toni S BiDrAPA 89
Greaver, Hanne 1933- WhoAmA 91
Greaver, Harry 1929- WhoAm 90, WhoAmA 91
Greaver, Joanne Hutchins 1939- WhoAmW 91, WhoSSW 91
Greaver, Maurice F., II 1951- St&PR 91
Greaver, Paul NewAgMG
Greaves, Brian L. 1943- St&PR 91
Greaves, Clive Walter 1936- WhoAm 90
Greaves, Denise Davidson 1957- IntWWM 90
Greaves, James L 1943- WhoAmA 91
Greaves, James Louis 1943- WhoAm 90
Greaves, Margaret 1914- AuBYP 90
Greaves, Marguerite BiDrAPA 89
Greaves, Susan F. BioIn 16
Greaves, Thomas Guy, Jr. 1918- WhoAm 90
Greaves, William 1926- DrBlPA 90
Greaves, William Garfield WhoAm 90
Greb, Gordon Barry 1921- WhoAm 90
Greb, Jacqueline Kay 1944- WhoAmW 91
Grebanier, Michael Peter 1937- WhoAm 90
Grebb, Jack Alan 1953- BiDrAPA 89
Grebe, David C. 1939- St&PR 91
Grebe, Henry L. 1932- St&PR 91
Grebe, Thomas William 1934- St&PR 91
Greben, Stanley E BiDrAPA 89
Greben, Stanley Edward 1927- WhoAm 90
Grebene, Alan Bekir 1939- WhoAm 90
Grebenshikov, Boris BioIn 16
Grebenshikov, Boris 1953- News 90 [port], WhoWor 91
Greblo, Zorislav BiDrAPA 89
Grebner, Bernice May Prill WhoWrEP 89
Grebner, Dennis William 1932- WhoAm 90
Grebner, Georg Friedrich PenDiDA 89
Grebow, Edward 1949- St&PR 91, WhoAm 90
Grebstein, Sheldon Norman 1928- WhoAm 90, WhoE 91
Grech Orr, Charles 1927- WhoWor 91
Grechaninov, Alexander Tikhonovich 1864-1956 PenDiMP A
Grecian, Phil Douglas 1948- WhoEmL 91
Grecina, Trine EncCoWW
Greck, Linda 1962- ODwPR 91
Grecky, Joseph M. 1939- St&PR 91
Greco, El 1541-1614 BioIn 16, IntDcAA 90, WorAlBi
Greco, Albert Nicholas 1945- WhoE 91, WhoEmL 91
Greco, Anna Maria 1958- WhoEmL 91
Greco, Anthony Joseph 1937- WhoAmA 91
Greco, Barbara Ruth Gomez 1938- WhoAmW 91
Greco, Frank J. 1951- St&PR 91
Greco, Joann 1960- WhoWrEP 89
Greco, Jose 1918- WhoAm 90
Greco, Joseph Dominic, Jr. 1955- WhoEmL 91
Greco, Judy Wong 1950- WhoAmW 91
Greco, Juliette 1927- OxCPMus
Greco, Mary Cebulski 1952- WhoAmW 91
Greco, Michael S. 1942- WhoAm 90
Greco, Patricia Mary 1954- WhoE 91
Greco, Philip Scot 1946- BiDrAPA 89
Greco, Robert WhoAmA 91N
Greco, Vito Louis 1943- St&PR 91
Grecsek, Matthew Thomas 1963- WhoEmL 91
Grecu, Grant Allen 1950- WhoEmL 91
Grede, Fred Charles 1935- St&PR 91
Grede, William J. 1897-1989 BioIn 16
Greden, John Francis 1942- BiDrAPA 89
Greditor, Alan S. BioIn 16
Greditzer, Arthur S BiDrAPA 89
Gredys, Keith J. 1955- St&PR 91
Greece, Michael Norman 1942- WhoE 91
Greece, Mike 1942- ODwPR 91
Greef, Arthur de PenDiMP
Greehey, William Eugene 1936- St&PR 91, WhoAm 90, WhoSSW 91
Greek, Darold I. 1909- WhoAm 90
Greeley, Andrew M. 1928- BioIn 16, MajTwCW, TwCCr&M 91, WorAlBi
Greeley, Andrew Moran 1928- WhoWrEP 89
Greeley, Charles Matthew 1941- WhoAmA 91
Greeley, Gale Elisabeth 1944- BiDrAPA 89
Greeley, Horace 1811-1872 BioIn 16, EncO&P 3, EncPaPR 91, WorAlBi
Greeley, John Edward 1961- WhoE 91
Greeley, Joseph May 1902- WhoAm 90
Greeley, Michael H. St&PR 91
Greeley, Paul David 1957- WhoEmL 91
Greeley, Sean McGovern 1961- WhoE 91, WhoWor 91
Greeley, Walter Franklin 1931- St&PR 91, WhoAm 90
Greeley-Smith, Nixola 1880-1919 BioIn 16
Greely, Adolphus W. 1844-1935 WorAlBi
Greely, Michael Truman 1940- WhoAm 90
Green, A. C. BioIn 16
Green, Adele C. 1938- WhoAmW 91
Green, Adolph 1915- ConAu 130, OxCPMus, WorAlBi
Green, Al 1946- DrBlPA 90, EncPR&S 89, WhoAm 90
Green, Alan, Jr. 1925- WhoWor 91
Green, Alan Colby BioIn 16, NewYTBS 90
Green, Alan Ivan BiDrAPA 89
Green, Alan Ivan 1943- WhoE 91
Green, Alan Jay 1947- WhoE 91
Green, Alexander C 1942- BiDrAPA 89
Green, Alfred G BiDrAPA 89
Green, Alfred J. BioIn 16
Green, Allen Russell 1949- St&PR 91
Green, Allison Anne 1936- WhoAmW 91, WhoWor 91
Green, Alvin 1931- St&PR 91, WhoAm 90
Green, Amy BiDrAPA 89
Green, Andrew William 1960- WhoEmL 91
Green, Andrew Wilson 1923- WhoAm 90
Green, Ann ODwPR 91
Green, Anna 1933- IntWWM 90
Green, Anna Katharine 1846-1935 TwCCr&M 91
Green, Anna Katherine 1846-1935 BioIn 16, FemiCLE
Green, Anne 1899- FemiCLE
Green, Anne Canevari 1943- SmATA 62 [port]
Green, Anne Catharine BioIn 16
Green, Anne Catherine Hoof 1720?-1775 EncCRAm
Green, Anthony Raymond 1930- St&PR 91
Green, Anthony Robert 1946- IntWWM 90
Green, Aron 1950- BiDrAPA 89
Green, Art 1941- WhoAmA 91
Green, Arthur George 1911- WhoAm 90
Green, Arthur H BiDrAPA 89
Green, Arthur Nelson 1941- WhoAm 90
Green, Asa Norman 1929- WhoAm 90
Green, Ashbel 1928- WhoAm 90, WhoWrEP 89
Green, Barbara AuBYP 90
Green, Barbara Strawn 1938- WhoAmW 91
Green, Barry 1945- IntWWM 90
Green, Barry 1948- WhoEmL 91
Green, Barry Steven 1957- WhoEmL 91, WhoWor 91
Green, Barton Clark 1935- WhoE 91
Green, Benjamin Edwards 1822-1907 BioIn 16
Green, Benjamin Louis 1951- WhoAm 90
Green, Benjamin Paul 1950- BiDrAPA 89
Green, Benson Arthur WhoWor 91
Green, Bernard WhoAm 90
Green, Bernard 1887-1951 WhoAmA 91N
Green, Bernard 1917- St&PR 91
Green, Bert Franklin, Jr. 1927- WhoAm 90
Green, Beverly Diane Hillyer 1948- WhoE 91
Green, Brian MajTwCW
Green, Bruce Quinton 1934- BiDrAPA 89
Green, Bunky BioIn 16
Green, Burton R. 1940- ODwPR 91
Green, Carl Jay 1939- WhoWor 91
Green, Carol H. 1944- WhoAm 90, WhoAmW 91, WhoE 91
Green, Carol Harriet BiDrAPA 89
Green, Cecil Howard 1900- BioIn 16, WhoAm 90, WhoWor 91
Green, Celia 1935- EncPaPR 91
Green, Celia Elizabeth 1935- EncO&P 3
Green, Charles K. 1943- St&PR 91
Green, Charles L. 1955- St&PR 91
Green, Charles LaVerne 1932- WhoSSW 91
Green, Claire Magidovitch 1953- WhoAmW 91
Green, Cliff 1934- ConAu 131
Green, Clifford Scott 1923- WhoAm 90
Green, Coppie 1946- WhoWrEP 89
Green, Curtis H. 1925- St&PR 91
Green, Cyril K. 1931- St&PR 91
Green, Cyril Kenneth 1931- WhoAm 90
Green, Dale Monte 1922- WhoAm 90
Green, Dallas BioIn 16
Green, Dallas 1934- Ballpl 90, WhoE 91
Green, Dan 1935- WhoAm 90
Green, Daniel 1907- WhoSSW 91
Green, Daniel G. 1937- WhoAm 90
Green, Danny 1876-1914 Ballpl 90
Green, David 1899- WhoAm 90
Green, David 1922- WhoWor 91
Green, David 1960- Ballpl 90

Green, David Alfred George 1930- WhoWor 91
Green, David C. 1933- ODwPR 91
Green, David Charles 1929- WhoE 91
Green, David E. 1938- St&PR 91
Green, David Henry 1921- WhoAm 90
Green, David O. 1923- WhoAm 90
Green, David Oliver 1908- WhoAmA 91
Green, David Wedgwood BiDrAPA 89
Green, Deborah Lynn 1951- WhoEmL 91
Green, Debra Lynn 1961- WhoAmW 91
Green, Denise G 1946- WhoAmA 91
Green, Dennis Eugene 1959- WhoEmL 91
Green, Dennis Joseph 1941- St&PR 91, WhoAm 90
Green, Dick 1941- Ballpl 90
Green, Dixie J. 1950- WhoSSW 91
Green, Don Wesley 1932- WhoAm 90
Green, Donald Chickford 1928- WhoSSW 91
Green, Donald Edward 1936- WhoSSW 91
Green, Donald Joseph 1953- WhoEmL 91
Green, Donald M. 1932- St&PR 91
Green, Donald Webb 1944- WhoE 91
Green, Douglas Alvin 1925- WhoSSW 91
Green, Douglas Brant 1931- St&PR 91
Green, Douglas Carson 1945- St&PR 91
Green, Douglas O 1942- BiDrAPA 89
Green, Duff 1791-1875 BioIn 16
Green, E.F. 1918- St&PR 91
Green, Eddie EarBlAP
Green, Eddie 1901?-1950 DrBlPA 90
Green, Edmon Lee BiDrAPA 89
Green, Edward BiDrAPA 89
Green, Edward Crocker 1944- WhoE 91
Green, Edward Rodman BiDrAPA 89
Green, Edward Thomas, Jr. 1921- WhoSSW 91
Green, Elaine K. 1932- WhoAmW 91, WhoSSW 91
Green, Elaine Reeves 1947- BiDrAPA 89
Green, Eliot I. 1935- St&PR 91
Green, Elizabeth A. H. BioIn 16
Green, Elizabeth A. H. 1906- IntWWM 90
Green, Elizabeth Adine Herkimer 1906- WhoWrEP 89
Green, Erika Ana 1928- WhoAmW 91
Green, Eugene W 1907- BiDrAPA 89
Green, F. Ray 1938- St&PR 91
Green, Fitzhugh NewYTBS 90
Green, Fitzhugh 1917- WhoAm 90
Green, Fitzhugh 1917-1990 ConAu 132
Green, Flora Hungerford 1941- WhoAmW 91
Green, Frances Marian 1945- WhoEmL 91
Green, Francis E., Jr. 1939- St&PR 91
Green, Francis J. 1906- WhoAm 90
Green, Francis William 1920- WhoWor 91
Green, Freddie 1933- Ballpl 90
Green, Gail Teresa 1953- WhoAmW 91
Green, Gareth Montraville 1931- WhoAm 90
Green, Gaylon Wayne 1947- St&PR 91
Green, Gene 1933-1981 Ballpl 90
Green, Gene S. ODwPR 91
Green, George 1793-1841 BioIn 16
Green, George Calvin 1925- St&PR 91
Green, George D 1943- WhoAmA 91
Green, George Dallas 1934- WhoE 91
Green, George Everitt 1880-1895 DcCanB 12
Green, George Joseph 1938- WhoAm 90, WhoE 91
Green, George Preston 1932- St&PR 91
Green, Gerald 1922- WhoAm 90, WhoWrEP 89
Green, Gerald Walker 1945- WhoEmL 91, WhoSSW 91
Green, Gerard Leo 1928- WhoE 91
Green, Gertrude Dorsey 1949- WhoAmW 91
Green, Gil 1906- EncAL
Green, Gilbert Bruce 1941- BiDrAPA 89
Green, Gloria B BiDrAPA 89
Green, Gordon Jay 1957- WhoAm 90
Green, Gordon Ralph 1924- WhoSSW 91
Green, Grant S., Jr. 1938- WhoAm 90
Green, Guy Mervin Charles WhoAm 90
Green, H. Kermit BioIn 16
Green, Hamilton WhoWor 91
Green, Hannah ConAu 32NR
Green, Hannah 1932- BioIn 16
Green, Harriette Denice BiDrAPA 89
Green, Harry Joyce, Jr. 1930- WhoSSW 91
Green, Harry Western, II 1940- WhoAm 90
Green, Harry William 1932- St&PR 91
Green, Harvey 1946- WhoE 91
Green, Harvey Joel BiDrAPA 89
Green, Havious BioIn 16
Green, Heidi Choate 1961- WhoE 91
Green, Henrietta 1834-1916 WorAlBi
Green, Henry Joseph 1950- BiDrAPA 89
Green, Hetty 1834-1916 BioAmW, BioIn 16, EncABHB 6 [port]
Green, Hilton A. 1929- WhoAm 90
Green, Holcombe Tucker, Jr. 1939- WhoAm 90
Green, Hope Stuart 1944- WhoE 91
Green, Howard S BiDrAPA 89
Green, Ida M. BioIn 16
Green, Irene Martha 1928- WhoAmW 91
Green, Irving D. 1922- St&PR 91
Green, J Cliff 1940- BiDrAPA 89
Green, J. Ed EarBlAP
Green, Jack BiDrAPA 89
Green, Jack Allen 1945- WhoAm 90
Green, Jack Peter 1925- WhoAm 90
Green, Jacquelyn Kay BiDrAPA 89
Green, James Alan 1953- WhoSSW 91
Green, James Arthur, III 1958- WhoSSW 91
Green, James Craig 1955- WhoSSW 91
Green, James D 1921- BiDrAPA 89
Green, James Francis 1948- WhoWor 91
Green, James Harry 1932- WhoWrEP 89
Green, James L. 1920-1990 BioIn 16
Green, James Leonard 1926- St&PR 91
Green, James Lewis 1944- St&PR 91
Green, James R 1944- ConAu 130
Green, James Weston 1913- WhoAm 90
Green, James Wilder 1927- WhoAm 90
Green, James Wyche 1915- WhoAm 90
Green, Jana Elaine 1954- WhoSSW 91
Green, Jane 1937- AuBYP 90
Green, Jane Burden 1950- WhoAmW 91
Green, Janet 1939- ConAu 30NR
Green, Janina 1944- WhoWor 91
Green, Jay M. WhoAm 90
Green, Jay M. 1948- ODwPR 91
Green, Jay Marc 1948- WhoAm 90
Green, Jay Martin 1947- St&PR 91
Green, Jean Susanne 1949- WhoWrEP 89
Green, Jedd H 1934- BiDrAPA 89
Green, Jeffrey A. 1957- WhoEmL 91
Green, Jeffrey Emanuel 1954- WhoE 91
Green, Jeffrey Harris 1956- BiDrAPA 89, WhoE 91
Green, Jerome Frederic 1928- WhoAm 90
Green, Jerome George 1929- WhoAm 90
Green, Jerome Keith 1936- St&PR 91
Green, Jerry Howard 1930- WhoWor 91
Green, Jerry Richard 1946- WhoAm 90
Green, Jersey Michael-Lee 1952- WhoEmL 91
Green, Jesse BioIn 16
Green, Joe C. 1941- St&PR 91
Green, John PenDiDA 89
Green, John 1908-1989 BioIn 16, OxCPMus
Green, John A. 1949- WhoWor 91
Green, John Alden 1925- WhoAm 90
Green, John Arnold 1946- St&PR 91
Green, John Cawley 1910- WhoAm 90
Green, John Clancy 1949- WhoSSW 91
Green, John Cleve 1800-1875 BioIn 16
Green, John Hampson 1932- WhoE 91
Green, John Joseph 1931- St&PR 91, WhoAm 90
Green, John Lafayette, Jr. 1929- WhoWrEP 89
Green, John Lafayette, Jr. 1933- WhoAm 90, WhoWor 91
Green, John Michael 1965- WhoE 91
Green, John Orne 1922- WhoAm 90
Green, John Richard 1837-1883 BioIn 16
Green, John Root 1920- WhoAm 90
Green, John T. 1937- St&PR 91
Green, Johnny 1908-1989 AnObit 1989
Green, Jonathan D. 1946- St&PR 91
Green, Joseph Barnet 1928- WhoAm 90
Green, Joseph M 1925- BiDrAPA 89
Green, Joshua 1869-1975 EncABHB 7 [port]
Green, Joshua, III 1936- EncABHB 7 [port], St&PR 91
Green, Joshua, Jr. 1908-1985 EncABHB 7 [port]
Green, Joyce 1928- WhoWor 91
Green, Joyce Hens 1928- WhoAm 90, WhoAmW 91, WhoE 91
Green, Judi Barbara 1951- WhoEmL 91
Green, Judith WhoE 91
Green, Judith Gibson 1941- WhoE 91
Green, Judith Maxine 1947- WhoAmW 91
Green, Judy 1943- WhoAmW 91
Green, Julia BioIn 16
Green, Julian 1900- ConAu 33NR
Green, Julie Jayne WhoAmW 91
Green, Julien ConAu 33NR
Green, Julien 1900- BioIn 16, MajTwCW
Green, June Lazenby 1914- WhoAm 90, WhoAmW 91
Green, Karen ODwPR 91
Green, Karen Bleier 1945- WhoAmW 91
Green, Karen Ina Margulies 1939- WhoAmW 91
Green, Karl Walter 1940- WhoSSW 91
Green, Kathleen AuBYP 90
Green, Ken BioIn 16
Green, Kenneth Norton 1938- WhoWor 91
Green, LaQuita Stephens 1957- WhoAmW 91
Green, Larry A. 1948- WhoSSW 91
Green, Larry Allen 1947- WhoWrEP 89
Green, Lauralee Maynard 1959- WhoAmW 91
Green, Lawrence Jamalian 1945- WhoEmL 91
Green, Leah M 1949- BiDrAPA 89
Green, Lenny 1934- Ballpl 90
Green, Leo E. WhoE 91
Green, Leon 1888-1979 BioIn 16
Green, Leon, Jr. 1922- WhoAm 90
Green, Leon Morton 1949- BiDrAPA 89, WhoE 91
Green, Leon William 1925- WhoAm 90
Green, Leonard I. 1933- St&PR 91
Green, Leslie Claude 1920- WhoAm 90
Green, Lester Duane 1925- St&PR 91
Green, Lewis 1946- WhoWrEP 89
Green, Linda Lou 1946- WhoAmW 91, WhoEmL 91, WhoSSW 91
Green, Linda Terry Promo 1956- WhoAmW 91
Green, Lisa Michele 1957- WhoE 91
Green, Lydia Ann 1953- WhoE 91
Green, Lynne 1944- WhoAmW 91, WhoWor 91
Green, M Joan BiDrAPA 89
Green, Margaret 1926- AuBYP 90
Green, Margaret Dell 1952- WhoAmW 91
Green, Margaret Ellen BiDrAPA 89
Green, Marguerite 1922- WhoAm 90
Green, Maria Antoinette 1964- WhoAmW 91
Green, Maria del Rosario ConAu 130, HispWr 90
Green, Marian 1940- IntWWM 90
Green, Marjorie 1943- WhoAmW 91
Green, Mark Alan 1956- WhoEmL 91
Green, Mark David 1951- BiDrAPA 89
Green, Mark J. BioIn 16
Green, Mark Joseph 1945- WhoAm 90
Green, Mark William 1949- BiDrAPA 89
Green, Marshall 1916- BioIn 16, WhoAm 90
Green, Martin Leonard 1936- WhoAmA 91
Green, Martyn 1899-1975 OxCPMus
Green, Marvin Howe, Jr. 1935- St&PR 91
Green, Mary Hester 1941- WhoAmW 91, WhoSSW 91, WhoWor 91
Green, Mary Jo 1952- ODwPR 91
Green, Mary McBurney 1896- AuBYP 90
Green, Maurice 1926- WhoAm 90
Green, Maurice R 1922- BiDrAPA 89, WhoE 91
Green, Maurice Warner 1927- St&PR 91
Green, Meyer H. 1917- WhoAm 90
Green, Meyra Jeanne 1946- WhoAmW 91, WhoEmL 91
Green, Michael 1920- BiDrAPA 89
Green, Michael D. 1944- St&PR 91
Green, Michael Ian 1958- WhoEmL 91
Green, Michael Jeffrey 1942- WhoE 91
Green, Monica BioIn 16
Green, Morris 1922- WhoAm 90
Green, Nancy Elizabeth 1955- WhoAmA 91, WhoE 91
Green, Nancy L. 1947- St&PR 91
Green, Nancy Loughridge 1942- WhoAmW 91
Green, Nancy W. BioIn 16
Green, Nancye BioIn 16
Green, Nancye Lewis 1947- WhoE 91
Green, Neil Harold George BioIn 16
Green, Neil Lyle 1952- WhoEmL 91
Green, Nelson F. 1929- St&PR 91
Green, Nicholas A BiDrAPA 89
Green, Norma 1925- AuBYP 90
Green, Norma Ruth 1944- BiDrAPA 89
Green, Norman Bayard 1905-1988 BioIn 16
Green, Norman H. 1929- St&PR 91
Green, Norman Kenneth 1924- WhoAm 90
Green, Ole-Carsten 1922- IntWWM 90
Green, Oliver Francis, Jr. 1924- WhoAm 90
Green, Orville Cronkhite, III 1926- WhoAm 90
Green, Pamela BioIn 16
Green, Patricia Ann 1950- WhoEmL 91
Green, Patricia L BiDrAPA 89
Green, Paul Andrew 1957- WhoEmL 91
Green, Paul Eliot, Jr. 1924- WhoAm 90
Green, Paul Warren 1926- St&PR 91
Green, Paula 1927- WhoAm 90
Green, Paula Ann 1953- WhoAmW 91
Green, Paulette Leczek 1957- WhoEmL 91
Green, Peggy BioIn 16
Green, Peggy Ellen 1949- WhoSSW 91
Green, Peggy Meyers 1943- WhoAmW 91
Green, Peter L. 1939- St&PR 91
Green, Peter Morris 1924- WhoAm 90
Green, Philip Bevington 1933- WhoAm 90
Green, Phillip Dale 1954- WhoAm 90, WhoEmL 91
Green, Phillip E 1931- BiDrAPA 89
Green, Pumpsie 1933- Ballpl 90
Green, R. Keith 1951- St&PR 91
Green, Rachael Paulette 1953- WhoSSW 91
Green, Raleigh E., II 1951- WhoWrEP 89
Green, Raymond Bert 1929- WhoAm 90, WhoE 91, WhoWor 91
Green, Raymond Ferguson St. John 1950- WhoE 91
Green, Raymond Robert 1946- WhoE 91
Green, Raymond Silvernail 1915- WhoAm 90, WhoE 91, WhoWor 91
Green, Rayna 1942- FemiCLE
Green, Rhonda Beverly 1958- WhoEmL 91
Green, Richard 1936- BiDrAPA 89
Green, Richard Alan 1926- WhoAm 90
Green, Richard C. 1957- St&PR 91
Green, Richard Calvin, Jr. 1954- WhoAm 90
Green, Richard Donald 1946- St&PR 91
Green, Richard G. 1913- St&PR 91
Green, Richard James 1928- WhoAm 90
Green, Richard John 1944- WhoAm 90
Green, Richard Lancelyn 1953- WhoAm 90
Green, Richard R. BioIn 16
Green, Richard S 1928- BiDrAPA 89
Green, Richard Stedman 1914- WhoE 91
Green, Robert Charles 1956- WhoEmL 91
Green, Robert Edward 1921- WhoAm 90, WhoE 91, WhoWor 91
Green, Robert Edward 1953- St&PR 91
Green, Robert Edward, Jr. 1932- WhoAm 90
Green, Robert Glenn 1950- WhoEmL 91
Green, Robert L, Jr. 1921- BiDrAPA 89
Green, Robert Lamar 1914- WhoAm 90
Green, Robert Lamar, Jr. 1951- WhoEmL 91
Green, Robert Leonard 1931- St&PR 91, WhoAm 90
Green, Robert Louis 1942- WhoSSW 91
Green, Robert Lynn 1955- WhoE 91
Green, Robert S. 1927- WhoAm 90
Green, Robert T. 1943- WhoAm 90
Green, Roberta J. 1943- St&PR 91
Green, Roger Curtis 1932- WhoWor 91
Green, Roger Gilbert Lancelyn 1918- AuBYP 90
Green, Roger J. 1944- BioIn 16, WhoAmA 91
Green, Roger Lancelyn 1918-1987 BioIn 16
Green, Ronald Lloyd 1943- BiDrAPA 89
Green, Ronald Michael 1942- WhoAm 90
Green, Rory Eric BiDrAPA 89
Green, Rose Basile 1914- WhoAm 90, WhoAmW 91, WhoE 91, WhoWor 91
Green, Russell M. 1938- St&PR 91
Green, RuthAnn 1935- WhoAmW 91
Green, Samuel Edward BiDrAPA 89
Green, Samuel Leonard 1948- WhoWrEP 89
Green, Samuel Marvin BiDrAPA 89
Green, Sara Edmond 1954- WhoAmW 91
Green, Sarah FemiCLE
Green, Saul 1925- WhoAm 90
Green, Scott E. 1951- ConAu 132
Green, Sharon Jordan 1948- WhoEmL 91
Green, Sheila Ellen AuBYP 90
Green, Shia Toby Riner 1937- WhoAmW 91
Green, Shirley Moore 1933- WhoAmW 91
Green, Stanley NewYTBS 90
Green, Stephen Alan 1945- BiDrAPA 89
Green, Stephen J 1940- ConAu 131
Green, Stephen Joel 1940- WhoE 91
Green, Steven J. 1952- St&PR 91
Green, Susan P. 1947- St&PR 91
Green, Susan Ruth 1957- WhoAmW 91
Green, Sydney H 1907- BiDrAPA 89
Green, Sylvia Ann 1958- WhoSSW 91
Green, Terence F. BioIn 16
Green, Theo 1956- WhoWrEP 89
Green, Theodore, III 1938- WhoAm 90
Green, Thomas Edward 1938- WhoE 91
Green, Thomas Edward 1948- WhoSSW 91
Green, Thomas George 1931- WhoAm 90
Green, Timothy Haskell 1948- WhoE 91
Green, Tom 1942- WhoAmA 91
Green, Walter Luther 1934- WhoAm 90
Green, Wanda Lorio 1954- WhoAmW 91
Green, Warren Harold 1915- WhoAm 90, WhoWor 91
Green, Wayne Hugo 1941- BiDrAPA 89
Green, Wilder 1927- WhoAmA 91
Green, William 1870-1952 BioIn 16
Green, William 1929- WhoAm 90, WhoE 91
Green, William 1942- St&PR 91
Green, William A. 1951- WhoSSW 91
Green, William Anthony 1951- WhoE 91
Green, William Edward 1943- WhoE 91
Green, William F 1906- BiDrAPA 89
Green, William H 1948- BiDrAPA 89
Green, William J BiDrAPA 89
Green, William L. 1941- St&PR 91
Green, William Porter 1920- WhoAm 90, WhoWor 91
Green, William Scott 1946- WhoAm 90
Green, William Tate, III 1948- WhoEmL 91

Green, William Wells 1911- *WhoSSW 91*
Green, Willie Harold 1940- *WhoSSW 91*
Green-Field, Albert *WhoAmA 91N*
Greenacre, Phyllis *BiDrAPA 89*
Greenacre, Phyllis 1894-1989 *BioIn 16*
Greenage, Julie Ann Calloway 1960- *WhoSSW 91*
Greenagel, John 1941- *ODwPR 91*
Greenamyer, George Mossman 1939- *WhoAmA 91*
Greenan, Frank Joseph 1920- *St&PR 91*
Greenawald, William F. 1934- *St&PR 91*
Greenawalt, David Franklin 1933- *St&PR 91, WhoAm 90*
Greenawalt, Karen Louise 1951- *WhoSSW 91*
Greenawalt, Nancy Putnam 1945- *WhoSSW 91*
Greenawalt, Peggy Tomarkin 1942- *WhoAmW 91, WhoE 91*
Greenawalt, Robert Kent 1936- *WhoAm 90*
Greenawalt, Ruth Marjorie 1942- *WhoAmW 91*
Greenawalt, William Sloan 1934- *WhoE 91, WhoWor 91*
Greenaway, Catherine *AuBYP 90*
Greenaway, Emerson 1906-1990 *BioIn 16, CurBio 90N*
Greenaway, Kate 1846-1901 *AuBYP 90, BiDWomA, BioIn 16*
Greenaway, Roger 1938- *OxCPMus*
Greenbacker, John Everett 1917- *WhoAm 90*
Greenbain, Mark *BiDrAPA 89*
Greenbank, Percy 1878-1968 *OxCPMus*
Greenbank, Richard Kelly 1924- *EncO&P 3*
Greenbaum, Carol Ann 1947- *WhoAmW 91*
Greenbaum, Daniel Wolf 1926- *St&PR 91*
Greenbaum, Donald Reuben 1951- *St&PR 91*
Greenbaum, Dorothea Schwarcz 1893-1986 *WhoAmA 91N*
Greenbaum, Esther *BiDrAPA 89*
Greenbaum, Esther 1909-1989 *BioIn 16*
Greenbaum, Henry *BiDrAPA 89*
Greenbaum, Hyam 1901-1942 *PenDiMP*
Greenbaum, James R. 1933- *St&PR 91*
Greenbaum, James Richard 1933- *WhoAm 90*
Greenbaum, Jeffrey Philip *BiDrAPA 89*
Greenbaum, Kyla 1922- *PenDiMP*
Greenbaum, Lowell Marvin 1928- *WhoAm 90*
Greenbaum, Marty 1934- *WhoAmA 91*
Greenbaum, Maurice C. 1918- *WhoAm 90*
Greenbaum, Philip S 1908- *BiDrAPA 89*
Greenbaum, Sidney 1929- *ConAu 33NR*
Greenbaum, Stuart I. 1936- *WhoAm 90*
Greenbaum, Theodore 1926- *BiDrAPA 89*
Greenbaum, William Ivan 1950- *WhoE 91*
Greenberg, Aaron R. 1932- *WhoE 91*
Greenberg, Alan C. *BioIn 16*
Greenberg, Alan C. 1927- *St&PR 91*
Greenberg, Alan Courtney 1927- *WhoAm 90, WhoE 91*
Greenberg, Albert 1924- *WhoAm 90, WhoE 91*
Greenberg, Alfred H. *NewYTBS 90*
Greenberg, Alfred H. 1924-1990 *BioIn 16*
Greenberg, Alfred Henry 1924- *WhoWrEP 89*
Greenberg, Alfred Henry 1924-1990 *ConAu 131*
Greenberg, Allan 1917- *WhoAm 90*
Greenberg, Allan David 1945- *St&PR 91*
Greenberg, Allan E. 1942- *St&PR 91*
Greenberg, Allen 1931- *WhoE 91*
Greenberg, Alvin David 1932- *WhoWrEP 89*
Greenberg, Ann Mathis 1936- *BiDrAPA 89*
Greenberg, Arline Francine *WhoAmW 91*
Greenberg, Arnold C. 1933- *St&PR 91*
Greenberg, Arnold Chaim 1933- *WhoAm 90*
Greenberg, Arthur A. *WhoAm 90*
Greenberg, Arthur Wayne 1953- *WhoEmL 91*
Greenberg, Barbara L *BiDrAPA 89*
Greenberg, Barbara Levenson 1932- *WhoWrEP 89*
Greenberg, Ben S. 1925- *St&PR 91*
Greenberg, Benjamin S. 1922- *ODwPR 91*
Greenberg, Bernard 1922- *WhoAm 90*
Greenberg, Blu 1936- *WhoAmW 91*
Greenberg, Blue 1926- *WhoAmA 91*
Greenberg, Bonnie Shirlee 1961- *WhoEmL 91*
Greenberg, Bradley Sander 1934- *WhoAm 90*
Greenberg, Bruce Charles 1943- *WhoE 91*
Greenberg, Byron Stanley 1919- *WhoAm 90*
Greenberg, Carl 1934- *WhoAm 90*
Greenberg, Charles *BiDrAPA 89*
Greenberg, Charles Steven 1950- *WhoSSW 91*
Greenberg, Clement 1909- *BioIn 16*
Greenberg, Daniel Herbert 1919- *WhoE 91*
Greenberg, Daniel M. 1952- *WhoSSW 91*
Greenberg, David A. 1936- *St&PR 91*
Greenberg, David Bernard 1928- *WhoAm 90*
Greenberg, David I. 1954- *ODwPR 91*
Greenberg, David Lewis 1956- *WhoAm 90*
Greenberg, Edward Alan 1941- *St&PR 91*
Greenberg, Edward Seymour 1942- *WhoAm 90*
Greenberg, Elinor Miller 1932- *WhoAmW 91*
Greenberg, Frank S. 1929- *WhoSSW 91*
Greenberg, Frank Stanford 1929- *St&PR 91*
Greenberg, Gary Howard 1948- *WhoEmL 91*
Greenberg, Gloria 1932- *WhoAmA 91*
Greenberg, Hank 1911-1986 *Ballpl 90 [port], BioIn 16, WorAlBi*
Greenberg, Harold 1926- *WhoAm 90*
Greenberg, Harold A 1921- *BiDrAPA 89*
Greenberg, Harvey Herman 1948- *WhoEmL 91*
Greenberg, Harvey R 1935- *BiDrAPA 89*
Greenberg, Harvey Roy 1935- *WhoE 91*
Greenberg, Herbert Marvin 1929- *WhoAm 90*
Greenberg, Heywood Lazar 1941- *WhoSSW 91*
Greenberg, Howard *WhoAm 90*
Greenberg, Irwin 1922- *WhoAmA 91*
Greenberg, Irwin E. *St&PR 91*
Greenberg, Irwin M 1930- *BiDrAPA 89*
Greenberg, Jack 1924- *WhoAm 90*
Greenberg, Jack M. 1942- *WhoAm 90*
Greenberg, Jacob 1929- *WhoAm 90, WhoE 91, WhoWor 91*
Greenberg, Jan 1942- *BioIn 16, SmATA 61 [port]*
Greenberg, Jane Diane 1947- *BiDrAPA 89*
Greenberg, Jeanne LeCrann 1935- *WhoAm 90*
Greenberg, Jeffrey W. *St&PR 91*
Greenberg, Jerome 1936- *WhoAm 90*
Greenberg, Jerome Mayo 1922- *WhoWor 91*
Greenberg, Jerrold Selig 1942- *WhoAm 90*
Greenberg, Joan 1934- *WhoE 91*
Greenberg, Joanne 1932- *BioIn 16, ConAu 32NR, WhoWrEP 89*
Greenberg, Joel S. 1931- *WhoE 91*
Greenberg, John Leonard 1945- *WhoWor 91*
Greenberg, Jonathan 1950- *WhoSSW 91*
Greenberg, Jonathan David 1958- *WhoEmL 91*
Greenberg, Jonathan S 1952- *BiDrAPA 89*
Greenberg, Joseph H. 1915- *WhoAm 90*
Greenberg, Joshua F. 1933- *WhoAm 90*
Greenberg, Judith *BiDrAPA 89*
Greenberg, Judith Horovitz 1947- *WhoAmW 91*
Greenberg, Keith Elliot *AuBYP 90*
Greenberg, Kenneth 1933- *ODwPR 91*
Greenberg, Larrie Warren 1940- *WhoE 91*
Greenberg, Larry *BioIn 16*
Greenberg, Larry 1937- *St&PR 91*
Greenberg, Lawrence Bruce *BiDrAPA 89*
Greenberg, Lawrence Howard *BiDrAPA 89*
Greenberg, Lawrence M 1935- *BiDrAPA 89*
Greenberg, Lenore *ODwPR 91*
Greenberg, Linn Turner *BiDrAPA 89*
Greenberg, Lon R. 1950- *St&PR 91*
Greenberg, Louis 1893?-1946 *BioIn 16*
Greenberg, Margaret H. 1935- *WhoWrEP 89*
Greenberg, Marilyn Werstein 1937- *WhoWrEP 89*
Greenberg, Mark E. 1946- *ODwPR 91*
Greenberg, Marshall G. 1935- *St&PR 91*
Greenberg, Marshall Gary 1935- *WhoAm 90*
Greenberg, Martin *BiDrAPA 89*
Greenberg, Martin Gary 1941- *BioIn 16*
Greenberg, Martin J. 1945- *ConAu 131*
Greenberg, Martin Stephen 1940- *WhoAm 90*
Greenberg, Marvin *BiDrAPA 89*
Greenberg, Maurice R. 1925- *St&PR 91*
Greenberg, Maurice Raymond 1925- *WhoAm 90, WhoE 91, WhoWor 91*
Greenberg, Maxwell Elfred 1922- *WhoAm 90*
Greenberg, Melvin Nathaniel 1928- *WhoAm 90*
Greenberg, Michael Jay 1958- *WhoEmL 91*
Greenberg, Michael John 1931- *WhoAm 90*
Greenberg, Milton 1918- *WhoAm 90*
Greenberg, Milton 1927- *WhoAm 90, WhoE 91*
Greenberg, Morris *WhoWor 91*
Greenberg, Morton Ira 1933- *WhoAm 90*
Greenberg, Moshe 1928- *WhoWor 91*
Greenberg, Myron Silver 1945- *WhoWor 91*
Greenberg, Nancy Jean 1947- *WhoWrEP 89*
Greenberg, Nat 1918- *WhoAm 90*
Greenberg, Nathan 1919- *WhoAm 90, WhoWor 91*
Greenberg, Nathan Abraham 1928- *WhoAm 90*
Greenberg, Neville Geoffrey 1943- *St&PR 91*
Greenberg, Noah 1919-1966 *PenDiMP*
Greenberg, Norman 1945- *ConAu 129*
Greenberg, Oscar Wallace 1932- *WhoAm 90*
Greenberg, Paul 1937- *WhoAm 90, WhoWrEP 89*
Greenberg, Pearl Katz 1927- *WhoAmW 91*
Greenberg, Peter Martin *BiDrAPA 89*
Greenberg, Philip Alan 1948- *WhoEmL 91*
Greenberg, Philip M 1920- *BiDrAPA 89*
Greenberg, Polly 1932- *AuBYP 90, BioIn 16*
Greenberg, Ramon M 1930- *BiDrAPA 89*
Greenberg, Raphael 1912- *BiDrAPA 89*
Greenberg, Reuben M. 1944- *BioIn 16*
Greenberg, Richard *BioIn 16*
Greenberg, Richard A. 1931- *St&PR 91, WhoE 91*
Greenberg, Richard Adam 1958- *WhoEmL 91*
Greenberg, Richard Alan 1931- *BiDrAPA 89*
Greenberg, Richard Allen 1946- *WhoE 91*
Greenberg, Richard Davis 1946- *BiDrAPA 89*
Greenberg, Richard M *BiDrAPA 89*
Greenberg, Richard S. 1960- *WhoE 91*
Greenberg, Robbie *BioIn 16*
Greenberg, Robert Arthur 1930-1989 *BioIn 16, ConAu 129*
Greenberg, Robert B 1941- *BiDrAPA 89*
Greenberg, Robert I. 1930- *WhoAm 90*
Greenberg, Robert M 1916- *BiDrAPA 89*
Greenberg, Robert Michael *BiDrAPA 89*
Greenberg, Robert Milton 1916- *WhoE 91*
Greenberg, Roger David 1944- *IntWWM 90*
Greenberg, Roger P 1941- *ConAu 131*
Greenberg, Ronald David 1939- *WhoAm 90*
Greenberg, Ronald K 1937- *WhoAmA 91*
Greenberg, Rosalie *BiDrAPA 89*
Greenberg, Samuel I 1912- *BiDrAPA 89*
Greenberg, Sanford David 1940- *WhoAm 90*
Greenberg, Scott Lee 1949- *WhoEmL 91*
Greenberg, Scott Neil 1956- *WhoAm 90*
Greenberg, Sheldon Burt 1948- *WhoE 91*
Greenberg, Sheldon S 1944- *BiDrAPA 89*
Greenberg, Sidney 1917- *BioIn 16*
Greenberg, Simon 1901- *BioIn 16, WhoAm 90*
Greenberg, Stanley *BiDrAPA 89*
Greenberg, Stephen Jay 1941- *WhoAm 90*
Greenberg, Stephen Michael 1944- *WhoAm 90*
Greenberg, Stephen Rollin 1945- *BiDrAPA 89*
Greenberg, Steven *BioIn 16*
Greenberg, Steven Morey 1949- *WhoE 91, WhoEmL 91, WhoWor 91*
Greenberg, Suzanne Gabrielle Schlichtman 1961- *WhoEmL 91*
Greenberg, Sylvia 1955- *IntWWM 90*
Greenberg, William Ephraim *BiDrAPA 89*
Greenberg, William M 1946- *BiDrAPA 89*
Greenberg, William Michael 1946- *WhoE 91*
Greenberg-Englander, Susan B 1952- *BiDrAPA 89*
Greenberger, Bette Jo 1937- *WhoAmW 91*
Greenberger, Ellen 1935- *WhoAm 90*
Greenberger, Ernest 1923- *WhoAm 90*
Greenberger, Evelyn Barish *ConAu 132*
Greenberger, George 1912- *St&PR 91*
Greenberger, Howard Leroy 1929- *WhoAm 90*
Greenberger, I. Michael 1945- *WhoAm 90, WhoEmL 91, WhoWor 91*
Greenberger, Lanie *BioIn 16*
Greenberger, Marsha Moses 1943- *WhoAmW 91*
Greenberger, Martin 1931- *WhoAm 90*
Greenberger, Norton Jerald 1933- *WhoAm 90*
Greenberger, Paul Allen 1947- *WhoEmL 91*
Greenberger, Raymond Stuart 1945- *St&PR 91*
Greenberger, Steven Robert 1954- *WhoEmL 91*
Greenblat, Arleigh Charles 1936- *WhoE 91*
Greenblatt, Arthur E 1942- *WhoAmA 91*
Greenblatt, Deana Charlene 1948- *WhoAmW 91*
Greenblatt, Eugene Newton 1923-1989 *BioIn 16*
Greenblatt, James Mark 1957- *BiDrAPA 89*
Greenblatt, Kenneth D. 1946- *St&PR 91*
Greenblatt, Maurice Theodore 1928- *St&PR 91*
Greenblatt, Milton 1914- *BiDrAPA 89, WhoAm 90*
Greenblatt, Miriam *WhoAmW 91*
Greenblatt, Ray Harris 1931- *WhoAm 90*
Greenblatt, Richard 1952- *ConAu 130*
Greenblatt, Seth Alan 1960- *WhoE 91*
Greenblatt, Sherwin 1941- *St&PR 91, WhoAm 90*
Greenblatt, Stuart L. 1950- *ODwPR 91*
Greenblum, David Nathan 1950- *BiDrAPA 89*
Greenblum, Lucie S *BiDrAPA 89*
Greenburg, Dan 1936- *WhoAm 90, WhoWrEP 89*
Greenburg, David Julius 1925- *WhoAm 90*
Greenbury, Richard 1936- *WhoAm 90*
Greendale, Robert Allan 1942- *BiDrAPA 89*
Greene, Abe J. *BioIn 16*
Greene, Adele S. *WhoAmW 91, WhoE 91*
Greene, Alan I. 1929- *St&PR 91*
Greene, Alan S. 1930- *St&PR 91*
Greene, Albert Lawrence 1949- *WhoAm 90, WhoEmL 91*
Greene, Alexander Plunket *BioIn 16, NewYTBS 90*
Greene, Allen Earl 1929- *WhoWor 91*
Greene, Allen Steven 1946- *WhoE 91, WhoEmL 91*
Greene, Alvin 1932- *WhoAm 90*
Greene, Alvin Carl 1923- *WhoAm 90*
Greene, Balcomb 1904-1990 *WhoAmA 91N NewYTBS 90*
Greene, Bancroft Farrar 1941- *WhoSSW 91*
Greene, Barbara Ann Mary 1945- *WhoAmW 91*
Greene, Barry Steven 1946- *St&PR 91*
Greene, Belle Da Costa 1887?-1950 *BioIn 16*
Greene, Benjamin 1932- *St&PR 91*
Greene, Benjamin Carroll 1937- *WhoSSW 91*
Greene, Bernard Harold 1925- *WhoAm 90*
Greene, Bernard L 1910- *BiDrAPA 89*
Greene, Betsy Katherine 1957- *WhoAmW 91*
Greene, Bette 1934- *AuBYP 90, BioIn 16, WhoWrEP 89*
Greene, Beverly Ann 1950- *WhoAmW 91, WhoE 91*
Greene, Bob 1947- *WhoAm 90*
Greene, Bruce Howard *BiDrAPA 89*
Greene, Bruce Howard 1958- *WhoE 91*
Greene, Bruce Wilkie 1939- *St&PR 91*
Greene, Carl William 1935- *St&PR 91, WhoE 91, WhoWor 91*
Greene, Carla 1916- *AuBYP 90, WhoAm 90, WhoWrEP 89*
Greene, Carol *AuBYP 90*
Greene, Carolyn B. 1948- *WhoAmW 91*
Greene, Catherine Antoinette 1958- *WhoAmW 91*
Greene, Catherine Littlefield 1755-1814 *BioIn 16*
Greene, Catherine Morton *BiDrAPA 89*
Greene, Charles A. 1935- *St&PR 91*
Greene, Charles Abraham 1933- *WhoE 91*
Greene, Charles Busch *BiDrAPA 89*
Greene, Charles Cassius 1897- *WhoAm 90*
Greene, Charles E., III *WhoWrEP 89*
Greene, Charles Michael 1956- *WhoSSW 91*
Greene, Charles Nelson 1937- *WhoE 91, WhoWor 91*
Greene, Charles Reed 1950- *WhoEmL 91*
Greene, Charles Sumner 1868-1957 *BioIn 16, PenDiDA 89*
Greene, Cheryl 1946- *BiDrAPA 89*
Greene, Constance C. *BioIn 16*
Greene, Constance C. 1924- *AuBYP 90, SmATA 11AS [port]*
Greene, Dale E. 1946- *St&PR 91*
Greene, Dallas Whorton, Jr. 1923- *WhoAm 90*
Greene, David Elsworth 1949- *WhoAm 90*
Greene, David Gorham 1915- *WhoAm 90, WhoE 91*
Greene, David L, Jr. *BiDrAPA 89*
Greene, David Lee 1938- *WhoAm 90*
Greene, David Mason 1920- *WhoAm 90*
Greene, David Paul 1941- *St&PR 91*
Greene, Deborah 1951- *WhoWrEP 89*
Greene, Deborah Lyn 1955- *WhoAmW 91*
Greene, Donald Johnson 1916- *WhoAm 90, WhoWrEP 89*
Greene, Donald Richard 1947- *WhoEmL 91*
Greene, Donna Sue 1956- *WhoSSW 91*
Greene, Edward Allen 1926- *WhoE 91*
Greene, Edward Forbes 1922- *WhoAm 90*

Greene, Edward Hampton 1947- *WhoEmL 91*
Greene, Edward L *BiDrAPA 89*
Greene, Elaine F. 1940- *WhoAmW 91*
Greene, Elinore Aschah 1928- *WhoAmW 91*
Greene, Elizabeth Ivory 1929- *WhoAmW 91*
Greene, Ellen *BioIn 16*
Greene, Ellin 1927- *AuBYP 90*
Greene, Elmer Westley, Jr 1907-1964 *WhoAmA 91N*
Greene, Emily Boykin 1954- *WhoAmW 91*
Greene, Ethel Maud 1912- *WhoAmA 91*
Greene, F. Colman 1922-1988 *BioIn 16*
Greene, Fayal *ODwPR 91*
Greene, Ford 1952- *WhoEmL 91*
Greene, Francis M. *BioIn 16*
Greene, Francis Thornton 1908- *WhoAm 90*
Greene, Frank J 1935- *BiDrAPA 89*
Greene, Frank Sullivan, Jr. 1938- *WhoAm 90*
Greene, Freda 1929- *WhoAmW 91*
Greene, Frederick, II 1927- *WhoAm 90*
Greene, Gary 1952- *IntWWM 90*
Greene, George Benjamin, Jr. 1914- *WhoAm 90*
Greene, George E., III 1935- *WhoAm 90*
Greene, George H. 1938- *St&PR 91*
Greene, Gertrude 1904-1956 *BiDWomA, WhoAmA 91N*
Greene, Gordon K. 1927- *IntWWM 90*
Greene, Graham 1904- *AuBYP 90, BioIn 16, DcLB 100 [port], MajTwCW, SpyFic, TwCCr&M 91, WhoAm 90, WhoWor 91, WorAlBi, WrPh*
Greene, Graham Carleton 1936- *WhoWor 91*
Greene, Harold H. *BioIn 16*
Greene, Harold H. 1923- *WhoAm 90, WhoE 91*
Greene, Harris 1921- *WhoWor 91*
Greene, Harris Carl 1921- *SpyFic*
Greene, Harry Plunket 1865-1936 *PenDiMP*
Greene, Henry Mather 1870-1954 *PenDiDA 89*
Greene, Herbert Bruce 1934- *St&PR 91, WhoAm 90*
Greene, Howard 1931- *ODwPR 91*
Greene, Howard Paul 1931- *WhoAm 90*
Greene, Ira S. 1946- *WhoEmL 91*
Greene, J Barry 1895-1966 *WhoAmA 91N*
Greene, Jack Phillip 1931- *WhoAm 90*
Greene, Jacqueline Holly 1960- *WhoAmW 91*
Greene, James Allen 1939- *BiDrAPA 89*
Greene, James Bert 1946- *WhoAm 90*
Greene, James C. 1915- *St&PR 91*
Greene, James R. 1929- *St&PR 91*
Greene, Janelle L. 1940- *St&PR 91*
Greene, Janelle Langley 1940- *WhoAmW 91*
Greene, Jeffrey Bryan 1956- *WhoEmL 91*
Greene, Jerry George 1937- *WhoAm 90*
Greene, Joe 1911- *Ballpl 90*
Greene, Joe 1946- *WorAlBi*
Greene, John *PenDiDA 89*
Greene, John Burkland 1939- *WhoAm 90*
Greene, John Frederick 1940- *WhoAm 90, WhoSSW 91*
Greene, John Joseph 1946- *WhoAm 90, WhoWor 91*
Greene, John Lee 1940- *St&PR 91*
Greene, John Lee 1963- *WhoSSW 91*
Greene, John Thomas, Jr. 1929- *WhoAm 90*
Greene, Jonathan 1943- *LiHiK*
Greene, Joseph Byron 1947- *BiDrAPA 89*
Greene, Joseph Nathaniel, Jr. 1920- *WhoAm 90*
Greene, Joshua Eli 1951- *WhoE 91*
Greene, Jule Blounte 1922- *WhoAm 90*
Greene, Karen Annette Helms 1961- *WhoSSW 91*
Greene, Karen Sandra 1942- *WhoAmW 91, WhoE 91*
Greene, Kermit 1925- *St&PR 91*
Greene, Lancaster M. 1901- *St&PR 91*
Greene, Lauren Ann *BiDrAPA 89*
Greene, Lawrence M. 1911- *St&PR 91*
Greene, Leonard Michael 1918- *WhoAm 90*
Greene, Leslie Speed 1949- *WhoEmL 91*
Greene, Liliane 1928- *WhoAm 90*
Greene, Linda Kay 1943- *WhoAmW 91*
Greene, Loretta *DrBIPA 90*
Greene, Lori *BiDrAPA 89*
Greene, Lorna *WhoWrEP 89*
Greene, Lorne 1915-1987 *OxCCanT [port], WorAlBi*
Greene, Louise Weaver 1953- *WhoAmA 91*
Greene, Lynne Jeannette 1938- *WhoAmW 91, WhoE 91*
Greene, Margaret Cicely Langton 1913- *WhoWor 91*
Greene, Margaret Lyford 1942- *St&PR 91*
Greene, Marilyn *BioIn 16*
Greene, Mark 1942- *St&PR 91*
Greene, Marshall A 1931- *BiDrAPA 89*
Greene, Marva Rosalee 1951- *WhoAmW 91*
Greene, Mary Cooper *BioIn 16*
Greene, Michael Edward 1935- *WhoE 91*
Greene, Michele *BioIn 16*
Greene, Mildred Sarah 1929- *WhoAmW 91*
Greene, Milton Anthony 1938- *WhoAm 90*
Greene, Murray A. 1927- *WhoE 91*
Greene, Nancy Ellen 1947- *WhoAmW 91, WhoEmL 91*
Greene, Nathanael 1742-1786 *BioIn 16, EncCRAm [port], WorAlBi*
Greene, Nathanael 1935- *WhoAm 90*
Greene, Norvin R. 1902- *St&PR 91*
Greene, Oscar, III 1948- *St&PR 91*
Greene, Pamela 1961- *WhoE 91*
Greene, Pat Ryan 1930- *WhoWrEP 89*
Greene, Patricia Clark *BioIn 16*
Greene, Patricia Leonard 1946- *WhoSSW 91*
Greene, Paul Irving 1933- *St&PR 91*
Greene, Peter A. 1946- *WhoAm 90*
Greene, Phyllis H. *BioIn 16*
Greene, Raleigh William, Jr. 1927- *WhoAm 90*
Greene, Raleigh Williams 1927- *St&PR 91*
Greene, Randall B *BiDrAPA 89*
Greene, Randall Frederick 1949- *St&PR 91, WhoWor 91*
Greene, Reuben 1938- *DrBIPA 90*
Greene, Richard 1948- *St&PR 91*
Greene, Richard D. 1950- *WhoEmL 91*
Greene, Richard E. 1938- *St&PR 91*
Greene, Richard Francis 1956- *WhoEmL 91*
Greene, Richard James 1957- *WhoE 91*
Greene, Richard Myron 1953- *WhoE 91*
Greene, Richard Tucker 1941- *St&PR 91*
Greene, Robert 1558?-1592 *BioIn 16*
Greene, Robert Allan 1931- *WhoAm 90*
Greene, Robert Bernard, Jr. 1947- *WhoAm 90, WhoWrEP 89*
Greene, Robert Edward Lee, Jr. 1941- *St&PR 91*
Greene, Robert Everett 1936- *WhoE 91*
Greene, Robert Michael 1945- *WhoEmL 91*
Greene, Robert Warren 1928- *WhoE 91*
Greene, Robert William 1929- *WhoAm 90*
Greene, Roberta *BioIn 16, ODwPR 91*
Greene, Sarah 1856-1935 *FemiCLE*
Greene, Sarah Carey 1941- *WhoAmW 91*
Greene, Sarah Elizabeth 1956- *WhoSSW 91*
Greene, Sarah Laschinger 1929- *WhoSSW 91*
Greene, Sarah Louise 1952- *WhoAmW 91*
Greene, Sharon Louise 1960- *WhoAmW 91*
Greene, Sheldon L. 1934- *ConAu 132*
Greene, Stanley 1911-1981 *DrBIPA 90*
Greene, Stefanie K 1937- *BiDrAPA 89*
Greene, Stephanie Harrison 1950- *WhoAmW 91, WhoEmL 91*
Greene, Stephen 1917- *WhoAm 90, WhoE 91*
Greene, Stephen 1918- *WhoAmA 91*
Greene, Steven *TwCCr&M 91*
Greene, Stuart Crane 1949- *BiDrAPA 89*
Greene, Susan 1955- *IntWWM 90*
Greene, Theodore J. 1934- *St&PR 91*
Greene, Thomas Alan 1934- *St&PR 91*
Greene, Thomas Lee 1939- *St&PR 91*
Greene, Thomas McLernon 1926- *WhoAm 90*
Greene, Vernon 1908-1965 *EncACom*
Greene, Vernon Van Atta *WhoAmA 91N*
Greene, Virginia Carvel 1934- *WhoAmW 91*
Greene, Wade 1933- *AuBYP 90*
Greene, Walter Skinner 1951- *WhoE 91*
Greene, Warren K. 1936- *St&PR 91*
Greene, Warren Keeler 1936- *WhoAm 90*
Greene, Wendy Segal 1929- *WhoAmW 91*
Greene, William Henry L'Vel 1943- *WhoAm 90*
Greene, Yvonne *BioIn 16*
Greene-Curtis, Sally Jane 1953- *WhoAmW 91*
Greene-Mercier, Marie Zoe 1911- *WhoAmA 91, WhoWor 91*
Greenebaum, James Eugene, II 1927- *St&PR 91*
Greenebaum, Leonard Charles 1934- *WhoE 91, WhoWor 91*
Greener, Douglas Lawrence 1943- *WhoWor 91*
Greener, Jack *BiDrAPA 89*
Greener, Jay Leslie 1959- *WhoEmL 91*
Greener, Judith Robin 1953- *St&PR 91*
Greener, William I., III 1950- *ODwPR 91*
Greener, William I., Jr. 1925- *ODwPR 91*
Greenes, Rhoda 1926-1979 *WhoAmA 91N*
Greenes, Robert B. 1921- *St&PR 91*
Greenewalt, Crawford H. 1902- *St&PR 91*
Greeney, Laura Anne 1961- *WhoAmW 91*
Greenfeld, David George *BiDrAPA 89*
Greenfeld, Howard *AuBYP 90*
Greenfeld, Josh 1928- *SmATA 62 [port]*
Greenfeld, Norman 1925- *WhoE 91*
Greenfeld, William P. 1906-1960 *BioIn 16*
Greenfield, Amy 1940- *WhoAmA 91*
Greenfield, Anne Louise 1953- *WhoEmL 91*
Greenfield, Arthur Aaron *BiDrAPA 89*
Greenfield, Bruce Harold 1917- *WhoAm 90*
Greenfield, Carol Nathan 1942- *WhoAmW 91*
Greenfield, Charles *BioIn 16*
Greenfield, Craig Bennett 1962- *WhoE 91*
Greenfield, D. Cornelius 1932- *BioIn 16*
Greenfield, Daniel Paul 1945- *BiDrAPA 89*
Greenfield, Darby *ConAu 30NR*
Greenfield, David W. 1940- *WhoAm 90*
Greenfield, Edward Harry 1928- *IntWWM 90*
Greenfield, Elaine 1942- *IntWWM 90*
Greenfield, Elizabeth Taylor *BioIn 16*
Greenfield, Elliot 1926- *St&PR 91*
Greenfield, Eloise 1929- *BioIn 16, SmATA 61 [port]*
Greenfield, Eloise Little 1929- *WhoWrEP 89*
Greenfield, George B. 1928- *WhoAm 90*
Greenfield, Gerald 1939- *WhoAm 90*
Greenfield, Gordon Kraus 1915- *WhoAm 90*
Greenfield, Harry William 1945- *WhoEmL 91*
Greenfield, Helen Meyers 1908- *WhoAm 90, WhoAmW 91, WhoE 91*
Greenfield, Helen Muehl 1910- *WhoAmW 91*
Greenfield, Holly Fern *BiDrAPA 89*
Greenfield, Irwin Gilbert 1929- *WhoAm 90*
Greenfield, James *BioIn 16*
Greenfield, James Robert 1926- *WhoAm 90*
Greenfield, Jay 1932- *WhoAm 90*
Greenfield, Jeff *BioIn 16*
Greenfield, Jerome Francis 1959- *BiDrAPA 89*
Greenfield, Joan 1932- *WhoAmW 91*
Greenfield, Joan Beatrice 1931- *WhoAmA 91*
Greenfield, John Charles 1945- *WhoAm 90*
Greenfield, Kenneth Darwin 1927- *St&PR 91*
Greenfield, Kent 1902-1978 *Ballpl 90*
Greenfield, Lazar John 1934- *WhoAm 90*
Greenfield, Lois *BioIn 16*
Greenfield, Louise Stern 1917- *IntWWM 90*
Greenfield, Lucille Jean 1929- *IntWWM 90*
Greenfield, Maurice H. 1942- *St&PR 91*
Greenfield, Meg 1930- *BioIn 16, WhoAm 90, WhoAmW 91, WhoE 91*
Greenfield, Michael *BiDrAPA 89*
Greenfield, Nancy L 1936- *BiDrAPA 89*
Greenfield, Norman Samuel 1923- *WhoAm 90*
Greenfield, Robert K. 1915- *St&PR 91*
Greenfield, Robert Kauffman 1915- *WhoAm 90*
Greenfield, Ronald H. 1944- *ODwPR 91*
Greenfield, Sanford Raymond 1926- *WhoAm 90*
Greenfield, Seymour Stephen 1922- *St&PR 91, WhoAm 90*
Greenfield, Shelly F *BiDrAPA 89*
Greenfield, Stanley Marshall 1927- *WhoAm 90*
Greenfield, Sue McClain 1941- *WhoAmW 91, WhoSSW 91*
Greenfield, Taylor Hatton 1905- *WhoAm 90, WhoWor 91*
Greenfield, Val Shea 1932- *WhoAm 90, WhoE 91*
Greenfield, W. M 1944- *WhoAmW 91*
Greenfield, William *BiDrAPA 89*
Greenfield-Sanders, Timothy 1952- *WhoAmA 91, WhoE 91*
Greengard, Paul 1925- *WhoAm 90*
Greenglass, Bertram *BioIn 16*
Greengold, Bonnie Blum 1955- *WhoAmW 91*
Greengrass, Jim 1927- *Ballpl 90*
Greengus, Samuel 1936- *WhoAm 90*
Greenhalgh, Frederick A. 1942- *St&PR 91*
Greenhalgh, Jo Lynn *St&PR 91*
Greenhalgh, Marion Lee 1954- *WhoAmW 91*
Greenhalgh, Paul 1955- *ConAu 130*
Greenhalgh, Terry L. 1950- *WhoSSW 91*
Greenhalgh, Thomas J. 1949- *St&PR 91*
Greenhaus, Thelma Nurenberg *AuBYP 90*
Greenhaw, Dale 1921- *St&PR 91*
Greenhaw, Wayne 1940- *BioIn 16*
Greenhill, Amy M. *ODwPR 91*
Greenhill, Diane Marie 1960- *WhoAmW 91*
Greenhill, Laurence Lee 1941- *BiDrAPA 89*
Greenhill, Richard Harry 1939- *St&PR 91*
Greenhill, Robert Foster 1936- *BioIn 16*
Greenhough, John Hardman 1939- *WhoAm 90*
Greenhouse, Bernard 1916- *IntWWM 90, WhoAm 90*
Greenhouse, Brian Baruch 1952- *St&PR 91*
Greenhouse, Linda Joyce 1947- *WhoAmW 91*
Greenhouse, Lloyd 1923- *St&PR 91*
Greenhow, Rose O. 1815?-1864 *BioAmW*
Greenhut, Deborah Schneider 1951- *WhoAmW 91*
Greenhut, Melvin Leonard 1921- *WhoAm 90, WhoSSW 91*
Greenhut, Robert *ConTFT 8*
Greenia, George Daniel 1950- *WhoSSW 91*
Greeniaus, H. John *WhoAm 90, WhoE 91*
Greenidge, Edwin *AuBYP 90*
Greening, Anthony John 1940- *IntWWM 90*
Greenish, Patrick R. 1948- *St&PR 91*
Greenkorn, Robert Albert 1928- *WhoAm 90*
Greenland, Gregory Lance 1945- *St&PR 91*
Greenland, Leo 1920- *St&PR 91, WhoAm 90*
Greenland, Steven *St&PR 91*
Greenlea, Sam *BioIn 16*
Greenleaf, Cynthia 1947- *WhoE 91*
Greenleaf, Daniel Edward 1951- *WhoWrEP 89*
Greenleaf, Esther 1905-1989 *WhoAmA 91N*
Greenleaf, Esther Hargrave *BioIn 16*
Greenleaf, James Fowler 1942- *WhoAm 90*
Greenleaf, Katherine Maxim 1948- *St&PR 91*
Greenleaf, Ken 1945- *WhoAmA 91*
Greenleaf, Margery *AuBYP 90*
Greenleaf, Ray *WhoAmA 91N*
Greenleaf, Richard Edward 1930- *WhoAm 90*
Greenleaf, Robert K. *NewYTBS 90*
Greenleaf, Robert T. 1926- *St&PR 91*
Greenleaf, Stephen 1942- *TwCCr&M 91*
Greenleaf, Virginia *WhoAmA 91*
Greenlease, Robert Cosgrove *BioIn 16*
Greenlee, Billy C. 1930- *St&PR 91*
Greenlee, Bruce Carleton 1931- *St&PR 91*
Greenlee, George Thomas 1953- *WhoE 91*
Greenlee, Gus 1897-1952 *Ballpl 90*
Greenlee, Herbert Breckenridge 1927- *WhoAm 90*
Greenlee, Howard Scott 1919- *WhoAm 90*
Greenlee, John Alden 1911- *WhoAm 90*
Greenlee, Richard Wesley 1954- *WhoSSW 91*
Greenlee, Robert L 1922- *BiDrAPA 89*
Greenlee, Stewart David 1950- *WhoEmL 91*
Greenlees, Thomas William 1926- *WhoE 91*
Greenleigh, Lawrence F *BiDrAPA 89*
Greenler, Robert *BioIn 16*
Greenler, Robert George 1929- *WhoAm 90*
Greenlick, Merwyn Ronald 1935- *WhoAm 90*
Greenly, Colin 1928- *WhoAm 90, WhoAmA 91*
Greenly, Lewis Allen *BiDrAPA 89, WhoE 91*
Greenman, Deborah *BiDrAPA 89*
Greenman, Frederic Edward 1936- *St&PR 91, WhoAm 90*
Greenman, George W *BiDrAPA 89*
Greenman, Jill D. *ODwPR 91*
Greenman, Lawrence A *BiDrAPA 89*
Greenman, Martin Allen 1917- *WhoAm 90*
Greenman, Norman Lawrence 1923- *St&PR 91, WhoAm 90*
Greenman, W. Frank *St&PR 91*
Greeno, J. Ladd 1949- *St&PR 91*
Greeno, John Ladd 1949- *WhoE 91, WhoEmL 91, WhoWor 91*
Greenop, David C. 1932- *St&PR 91*
Greenough, Carol Boyer 1930- *WhoAmW 91*
Greenough, Peter B., Mrs. *WhoAmW 91, WhoWor 91*
Greenough, William Bates, III 1932- *WhoE 91*
Greenough, William C. 1914-1989 *BioIn 16*
Greenough, William Croan 1914-1989 *ConAu 130*
Greenough, William Edward, Jr. 1942- *St&PR 91*
Greenough, William Tallant 1944- *WhoAm 90*
Greenquist, Thomas Alfred 1928- *St&PR 91*

Greensfelder, Harry, III 1949- *St&PR 91*
Greenslade, Brian 1930- *St&PR 91*
Greenslade, David Leslie 1957- *WhoEmL 91*
Greenslade, Forrest Charles 1939- *WhoAm 90*
Greensmith, John Brian 1929- *IntWWM 90*
Greenson, Daniel Peter 1937- *BiDrAPA 89*
Greenspan, Alan *BioIn 16*
Greenspan, Alan 1926- *EncABHB 7 [port], WhoAm 90, WhoE 91, WhoWor 91, WorAlBi*
Greenspan, Arnold Michael 1938- *St&PR 91, WhoE 91*
Greenspan, Brad Kirby *BiDrAPA 89*
Greenspan, Bud 1926- *WhoAm 90*
Greenspan, David Ian 1955- *BiDrAPA 89*
Greenspan, Donald 1928- *WhoAm 90*
Greenspan, Douglas Howard 1951- *WhoEmL 91*
Greenspan, Francis S. 1920- *WhoAm 90*
Greenspan, Gail Sandra 1957- *BiDrAPA 89*
Greenspan, George 1900- *WhoAmA 91*
Greenspan, George, Mrs *WhoAmA 91*
Greenspan, Harvey Philip 1933- *WhoAm 90*
Greenspan, Herbert S 1915- *BiDrAPA 89*
Greenspan, Jeffrey Dov 1954- *WhoEmL 91*
Greenspan, Joseph 1930- *St&PR 91*
Greenspan, Kenneth 1938- *BiDrAPA 89*
Greenspan, Leon Joseph 1932- *WhoE 91, WhoWor 91*
Greenspan, Martin *BioIn 16*
Greenspan, Nancy 1936- *WhoE 91*
Greenspan, Ruth 1931- *WhoAm 90*
Greenspan, Stanley Ira 1941- *BiDrAPA 89*
Greenspan, Stephen Barry 1941- *WhoWor 91*
Greenspan, Steven Barry 1945- *WhoEmL 91*
Greenspan-Birns, Robin Lisa 1958- *WhoEmL 91*
Greenspan-Margolis, June E 1934- *BiDrAPA 89*
Greenspan-Margolis, June Rita Edelman 1934- *WhoAmW 91*
Greenspon, Herbert Mitchell 1917- *St&PR 91*
Greenspon, Joshua E. 1928- *BioIn 16*
Greenspon, Robert Alan 1947- *WhoEmL 91*
Greenspoon, Leonard J 1945- *ConAu 30NR*
Greenspun, H M 1909-1989 *ConAu 129*
Greenspun, Hank *ConAu 129*
Greenspun, Hank 1909-1989 *BioIn 16*
Greenstadt, Melvin 1918- *WhoAm 90*
Greenstein, Abraham Jacob 1949- *WhoE 91*
Greenstein, Albert *ODwPR 91*
Greenstein, Alvin 1928- *St&PR 91*
Greenstein, Fred Irwin 1930- *WhoAm 90*
Greenstein, George 1940- *ConAu 130*
Greenstein, Harold *BioIn 16*
Greenstein, Ilise 1928- *WhoAmA 91N*
Greenstein, Jack 1915- *ConAu 130*
Greenstein, James F. 1924- *St&PR 91*
Greenstein, Jesse Leonard 1909- *WhoAm 90*
Greenstein, Joel Robert 1937- *WhoE 91*
Greenstein, Julius Sidney 1927- *WhoAm 90*
Greenstein, Marla Nan 1957- *WhoEmL 91*
Greenstein, Martin Richard 1944- *WhoAm 90*
Greenstein, Michael Steven 1949- *WhoE 91*
Greenstein, Neil David 1954- *WhoEmL 91*
Greenstein, Rita Rappoport 1928- *WhoAmW 91*
Greenstein, Robert Alan 1941- *BiDrAPA 89, WhoE 91*
Greenstein, Robert Irwin 1929- *WhoE 91*
Greenstein, Robert Stanley 1955- *WhoEmL 91*
Greenstein, Ruth Louise 1946- *WhoAm 90*
Greenstein, Yakov 1950- *BiDrAPA 89*
Greenstone, J. David *NewYTBS 90*
Greenstone, J. David 1937-1990 *BioIn 16*
Greenstone, James Lynn 1943- *WhoAm 90*
Greenstone, Julius Hillel 1873-1955 *BioIn 16*
Greenstone, Marion 1925- *WhoAmA 91*
Greenstreet, Robert Charles 1952- *WhoEmL 91*
Greenstreet, Sydney 1879-1954 *WorAlBi*
Greenswag, Richard Alan 1954- *WhoEmL 91*
Greentree, Jonathan Princenthal 1951- *WhoEmL 91*
Greenwade, George Dennis 1956- *WhoSSW 91*
Greenwade, Tom 1904-1986 *Ballpl 90*
Greenwald, Alan Frank 1944- *WhoE 91*
Greenwald, Alice 1952- *WhoAmA 91*
Greenwald, Blaine Stuart *BiDrAPA 89*
Greenwald, Burton Jay 1929- *WhoE 91*
Greenwald, Carol Schiro 1939- *WhoAm 90*
Greenwald, Caroline Meyer 1936- *WhoAm 90*
Greenwald, Daniel Jack, III 1949- *WhoWor 91*
Greenwald, Daniel Maier 1943- *BiDrAPA 89*
Greenwald, Dennis Harold 1925- *St&PR 91*
Greenwald, Dorothy I. 1920- *WhoE 91*
Greenwald, Gerald *BioIn 16*
Greenwald, Gerald 1935- *St&PR 91, WhoAm 90, WhoWor 91*
Greenwald, Gerald Bernard 1929- *WhoAm 90*
Greenwald, Gilbert Saul 1927- *WhoAm 90*
Greenwald, Hank *BioIn 16*
Greenwald, Harry R. 1930- *St&PR 91*
Greenwald, Herbert 1910- *WhoE 91*
Greenwald, James L. 1927- *St&PR 91*
Greenwald, Jerry 1946- *St&PR 91*
Greenwald, John Edward 1942- *WhoAm 90, WhoSSW 91*
Greenwald, Jules 1943- *St&PR 91*
Greenwald, Martin 1942- *WhoAm 90*
Greenwald, Mathew Henry 1946- *WhoEmL 91*
Greenwald, Michael 1939- *WhoE 91*
Greenwald, Peter *BioIn 16*
Greenwald, Peter 1936- *WhoAm 90*
Greenwald, Phyllis Louise *BiDrAPA 89*
Greenwald, R Lila *BiDrAPA 89*
Greenwald, Robert 1927- *ODwPR 91, WhoAm 90*
Greenwald, Robert A. 1947- *St&PR 91*
Greenwald, Sheila 1934- *AuBYP 90*
Greenwald, Sheila Ellem 1934- *WhoE 91*
Greenwald, Sidney Fuld 1921- *St&PR 91*
Greenwald, Stephen M 1933- *BiDrAPA 89*
Greenwalt, Clifford Lloyd 1933- *St&PR 91, WhoAm 90*
Greenwalt, Lynn Adams 1931- *WhoAm 90*
Greenwalt, Sandra Joyce 1962- *WhoAmW 91*
Greenwalt, Tibor Jack 1914- *WhoAm 90*
Greenway, Francis *BiDEWW*
Greenway, Hugh Davids Scott 1935- *WhoAm 90*
Greenway, John Selmes 1924- *WhoAm 90*
Greenway, Margaret *BiDEWW*
Greenway, Patsy Jo 1937- *WhoWrEP 89*
Greenway, Rebecca Marie Kimball 1951- *WhoEmL 91*
Greenway, William Henry, Jr. 1947- *WhoWrEP 89*
Greenwell, Arnold 1956- *WhoSSW 91*
Greenwell, Dora 1821-1882 *BioIn 16, FemiCLE*
Greenwell, Karen Dawn 1955- *WhoEmL 91*
Greenwell, Mike 1963- *Ballpl 90*
Greenwell, Paul Clellan Dale 1935- *WhoSSW 91*
Greenwell, Richard L. 1947- *ODwPR 91*
Greenwell, Roger Allen 1941- *WhoWor 91*
Greenwell, Ronald Everett 1938- *WhoAm 90*
Greenwich, Ellie 1940- *EncPR&S 89, OxCPMus*
Greenwold, Douglas Jay 1942- *St&PR 91*
Greenwold, Warren Eldon 1923- *WhoAm 90*
Greenwood, Albert *BiDrAPA 89*
Greenwood, Albert Leon 1934- *WhoE 91*
Greenwood, Allan N. *WhoAm 90*
Greenwood, Anita Rurka 1956- *WhoSSW 91*
Greenwood, Arthur William James 1911-1982 *DcNaB 1981*
Greenwood, Audrey Gates 1917- *WhoAmW 91, WhoE 91*
Greenwood, Barrie Leck 1934- *IntWWM 90*
Greenwood, Bill *BioIn 16*
Greenwood, C. Ramon 1927- *ODwPR 91*
Greenwood, Donald Theodore 1923- *WhoAm 90*
Greenwood, Edward Alister 1930- *ConAu 30NR*
Greenwood, Frank 1924- *WhoE 91, WhoWor 91*
Greenwood, Frans 1680-1762 *PenDiDA 89*
Greenwood, Gaynol Dewane 1935- *WhoSSW 91*
Greenwood, Glenda S. 1955- *WhoEmL 91*
Greenwood, Gordon Edward 1935- *WhoSSW 91*
Greenwood, Grace 1823-1904 *BioIn 16, FemiCLE*
Greenwood, Harriet Lois 1950- *WhoAmW 91*
Greenwood, Hugh John 1931- *WhoAm 90*
Greenwood, Ivan Anderson 1921- *WhoWor 91*
Greenwood, James Charles 1951- *WhoE 91*
Greenwood, James Gregory 1947- *WhoEmL 91*
Greenwood, Jane *BioIn 16*
Greenwood, Jane 1934- *NotWoAT*
Greenwood, Janet Kae Daly 1943- *WhoAm 90, WhoAmW 91, WhoE 91*
Greenwood, Joen Elizabeth 1934- *WhoAmW 91*
Greenwood, John *TwCCr&M 91*
Greenwood, John Edson 1927- *WhoWrEP 89*
Greenwood, John Malcolm 1941- *St&PR 91*
Greenwood, Joseph A. *BioIn 16*
Greenwood, Joseph Albert 1906- *EncO&P 3*
Greenwood, Joseph Albert 1906-1988 *EncPaPR 91*
Greenwood, Laurence Joseph 1943- *BiDrAPA 89*
Greenwood, Lawrence George 1921- *St&PR 91, WhoAm 90*
Greenwood, M. R. C. 1943- *WhoAm 90*
Greenwood, Marion 1909-1970 *BiDWomA, WhoAmA 91N*
Greenwood, Michael Richard 1939- *WhoE 91*
Greenwood, Myrtle Rae 1950- *WhoEmL 91*
Greenwood, Norman Neill 1925- *WhoWor 91*
Greenwood, Pat M. 1906- *St&PR 91*
Greenwood, Richard Edwin 1938- *St&PR 91*
Greenwood, Richard M. 1947- *St&PR 91*
Greenwood, Robert L. 1930- *WhoSSW 91*
Greenwood, Roger K. 1943- *St&PR 91*
Greenwood, Steven Matlin 1950- *WhoEmL 91*
Greenwood, Ted *ConAu 30NR*
Greenwood, Teresa *BiDEWW*
Greenwood, Thomas S. 1921- *St&PR 91*
Greenwood, Tim S. 1949- *St&PR 91*
Greenwood, Virginia Maxine McLeod 1930- *WhoSSW 91*
Greenwood, William Edward 1938- *St&PR 91*
Greenwood, William Warren 1942- *WhoAm 90*
Greenwood, Wilson 1923- *St&PR 91*
Greenzang, Ted R 1952- *BiDrAPA 89*
Greer, Albert E. *St&PR 91*
Greer, Alexander Hugh Courtney 1926- *WhoWor 91*
Greer, Allen Curtis, II 1951- *WhoAm 90, WhoEmL 91*
Greer, Ann Bolling 1957- *WhoSSW 91*
Greer, Barbara DeGaster 1957- *WhoEmL 91*
Greer, Bettejane *ConTFT 8*
Greer, Brian Frederick *BiDrAPA 89*
Greer, Carl C. 1940- *St&PR 91*
Greer, Carl Crawford 1940- *WhoAm 90*
Greer, Charles Eugene 1945- *WhoEmL 91*
Greer, Cynthia Kay *BiDrAPA 89*
Greer, Dabbs 1917- *ConTFT 8 [port]*
Greer, David *BioIn 16*
Greer, David Clive 1937- *IntWWM 90*
Greer, David S. 1925- *WhoAm 90*
Greer, Dennis L. 1945- *St&PR 91*
Greer, Dennis Lynn 1945- *WhoAm 90*
Greer, Diane Cecilia *BiDrAPA 89*
Greer, Ed *BioIn 16*
Greer, Edward 1924- *WhoAm 90*
Greer, Ellen *BioIn 16*
Greer, Eric Reginald 1904-1983 *BioIn 16*
Greer, Evelyn Langlieb 1950- *WhoEmL 91*
Greer, Gary LaVerne 1935- *WhoAm 90*
Greer, Gayle 1956- *WhoWor 91*
Greer, George C. 1932- *St&PR 91*
Greer, George R 1950- *BiDrAPA 89*
Greer, George W., III 1939- *St&PR 91*
Greer, Germaine 1939- *BioIn 16, ConAu 33NR, FemiCLE, MajTwCW, WhoAm 90*
Greer, Gina 1954- *ODwPR 91*
Greer, Gordon Bruce 1932- *WhoAm 90, WhoWor 91*
Greer, Harold Eugene 1958- *WhoAm 90*
Greer, Harry A *BiDrAPA 89*
Greer, Harvey Franklin 1935- *St&PR 91*
Greer, Herschel Lynn, Jr. 1941- *WhoSSW 91*
Greer, Howard Earl 1921- *WhoAm 90*
Greer, J. Wayne 1942- *St&PR 91*
Greer, Jack P. 1928- *St&PR 91*
Greer, James Alexander, II 1932- *WhoAm 90*
Greer, James Bradford 1934- *WhoSSW 91*
Greer, James Edward 1951- *BiDrAPA 89*
Greer, Jana Waring *ODwPR 91*
Greer, Jane 1924- *ConTFT 8 [port]*
Greer, Jane H. 1938- *St&PR 91*
Greer, Jane Ruth 1941- *WhoAmA 91*
Greer, Jeanette Mulder 1924- *WhoAmW 91*
Greer, Joanne Marie Greer 1937- *WhoAmW 91*
Greer, Joel Thomas Soorholtz 1953- *WhoEmL 91*
Greer, John Henry 1922- *St&PR 91*
Greer, John J. 1942- *St&PR 91*
Greer, John Sydney 1944- *WhoAmA 91*
Greer, Joseph Epps 1923- *WhoAm 90, WhoWor 91*
Greer, Leonard W. 1934- *St&PR 91*
Greer, Linda Jean 1950- *WhoAmW 91*
Greer, Meg *BioIn 16*
Greer, Melvin 1929- *WhoAm 90*
Greer, Michael Reed 1951- *St&PR 91*
Greer, Monte Arnold 1922- *WhoAm 90, WhoWor 91*
Greer, Patric Robert 1954- *St&PR 91*
Greer, Paul W. 1951- *St&PR 91*
Greer, Pedro Jose, Jr. 1956- *WhoHisp 91*
Greer, Randall Dewey 1951- *St&PR 91, WhoAm 90*
Greer, Raymond White 1954- *WhoSSW 91*
Greer, Reg 1904-1983 *BioIn 16*
Greer, Richard *ConAu 130, MajTwCW*
Greer, Richard Alden *BiDrAPA 89*
Greer, Richard R. 1952- *St&PR 91*
Greer, Rita Gilbert 1948- *WhoSSW 91*
Greer, Robert J *BiDrAPA 89*
Greer, Robert Sim 1951- *WhoEmL 91*
Greer, Roberta Leslie 1935- *WhoAmW 91*
Greer, Ronny Lloyd 1954- *WhoSSW 91*
Greer, Rowan A., III 1934- *WhoAm 90*
Greer, S. Allan 1903- *St&PR 91*
Greer, Sonny 1895-1982 *BioIn 16*
Greer, Theresa Whelan *BiDrAPA 89*
Greer, Thomas Francis, Jr. 1944- *WhoWor 91*
Greer, Thomas H. 1916- *IntWWM 90*
Greer, Thomas Hoag 1914- *WhoAm 90*
Greer, Thomas Upton 1928- *WhoAm 90*
Greer, Thomas Vernon 1932- *WhoAm 90*
Greer, Walter 1920- *WhoAmA 91*
Greer, Wayne 1942- *St&PR 91*
Greer, Wesley Dwaine 1937- *WhoAmA 91*
Greer, William C *BiDrAPA 89*
Greer, William Jackson *BioIn 16*
Greer, William Joseph 1947- *WhoEmL 91*
Greer, William Thomas 1960- *WhoWor 91*
Greer, William Wayne 1942- *St&PR 91*
Greeraerts, Frans L *BiDrAPA 89*
Greeson, Janet Rosemary 1943- *WhoAmW 91*
Greet, Norman Roy 1947- *St&PR 91*
Greever, William St. Clair 1916- *WhoAm 90*
Greeves, R V 1935- *WhoAmA 91*
Greevy, Bernadette 1940- *IntWWM 90*
Gref, Robert 1939- *St&PR 91*
Grefe, Richard 1945- *WhoAm 90*
Grefe, Rolland Eugene 1920- *WhoAm 90*
Greff, Gunter 1947- *WhoWor 91*
Greg, Mother *BiDEWW*
Grega, Stephen Paul, Jr. 1941- *WhoSSW 91*
Gregan, John Patrick 1947- *WhoE 91, WhoEmL 91*
Greganti, Mac Andrew 1947- *WhoAm 90*
Greger, Debora 1949- *ConAu 31NR*
Greger, Mark Allan 1962- *WhoEmL 91*
Greger-Holt, George Patrick 1955- *WhoSSW 91*
Gregersen, Erik 1935- *WhoWor 91*
Gregersen, Gunnar 1929- *WhoWor 91*
Gregersen, Kenneth A. 1931- *St&PR 91*
Gregerson, Rebecca Ostar 1955- *WhoAmW 91, WhoEmL 91*
Gregerson, Robert Louis 1938- *St&PR 91*
Gregg, Candace Carlene 1961- *WhoSSW 91*
Gregg, Charles Thornton 1927- *WhoAm 90*
Gregg, David, III 1933- *WhoWor 91*
Gregg, Davis Weinert 1918- *WhoAm 90*
Gregg, Donald *BioIn 16*
Gregg, Donald B. *WhoE 91*
Gregg, Donald Phinney 1927- *WhoAm 90*
Gregg, Dorothy *ODwPR 91*
Gregg, Dorothy Elizabeth 1919- *WhoAmW 91*
Gregg, Elinor 1889-1970 *BioIn 16*
Gregg, Eric 1951- *Ballpl 90*
Gregg, Gloria E. 1924- *St&PR 91*
Gregg, Hal 1921- *Ballpl 90*
Gregg, Hubert 1914- *OxCPMus*
Gregg, Hugh 1917- *WhoAm 90*
Gregg, Jamie V. 1953- *St&PR 91*
Gregg, Joe Neely 1961- *WhoE 91*
Gregg, John Franklin 1943- *WhoAm 90*
Gregg, John Nathan 1934- *WhoAm 90, WhoWor 91*
Gregg, John T. 1848-1910 *AmLegL*
Gregg, Josiah 1806-1850 *WhNaAH*
Gregg, Judd 1947- *WhoAm 90, WhoE 91, WhoWor 91*
Gregg, Kevin David 1961- *BiDrAPA 89*
Gregg, Mark Vaughan 1945- *WhoEmL 91*
Gregg, Michael 1953- *BioIn 16*
Gregg, Michael B. 1930- *WhoAm 90*
Gregg, Michael W. 1935- *St&PR 91, WhoAm 90*
Gregg, Raymond Harry 1930- *St&PR 91*
Gregg, Richard Alexander 1927- *WhoAm 90*
Gregg, Richard Leo 1944- *WhoAm 90*

Gregg, Richard Nelson 1926-1986 *WhoAmA 91N*
Gregg, Robert Baxter 1948- *WhoSSW 91*
Gregg, Robert E. 1960- *WhoHisp 91*
Gregg, Robert Eckler 1949- *WhoSSW 91*
Gregg, Susan J. *WhoAmW 91*
Gregg, Tommy 1963- *Ballpl 90*
Gregg, Vean 1885-1964 *Ballpl 90*
Gregg, Walter E., Jr. 1941- *St&PR 91*
Gregga, Bruce A. *BioIn 16*
Greggains, Joanie Catherine 1944- *WhoAmW 91*
Greggs, Elizabeth May Bushnell 1925- *WhoWor 91*
Grego, Claudio 1947- *St&PR 91*
Grego, Michael Francis 1951- *WhoEmL 91*
Grego, Michael Joseph 1945- *WhoEmL 91*
Gregoire, Dennis James 1954- *St&PR 91*
Gregoire, Gaspard 1751-1846 *PenDiDA 89*
Gregoire, Mathieu A 1953- *WhoAmA 91*
Gregoire, Michael J. *WhoAm 90*
Gregoire, Michel Fernand *BiDrAPA 89*
Gregoire, Michel R. 1946- *WhoWor 91*
Gregoire, Paul 1911- *WhoAm 90, WhoE 91, WhoWor 91*
Gregor, Andrew *St&PR 91*
Gregor, Andrew, Jr. 1948- *WhoAm 90*
Gregor, Arthur 1923- *WhoAm 90, WhoWrEP 89, WorAu 1980 [port]*
Gregor, Bohumil 1926- *IntWWM 90*
Gregor, Dorothy Deborah 1939- *WhoAmW 91*
Gregor, Harold Laurence 1929- *WhoAmA 91*
Gregor, Howard Frank 1920- *WhoAm 90*
Gregor, Lee *MajTwCW*
Gregor, Mary Jeanne 1928- *WhoAmW 91*
Gregor, Tibor Philip 1919- *WhoAm 90*
Gregor-Smith, Bernard *PenDiMP*
Gregoratti, Guillermo Jesus *BiDrAPA 89*
Gregori, Mina *BioIn 16*
Gregori, Theodore Joseph 1950- *St&PR 91*
Gregorian, Rouben 1915- *IntWWM 90*
Gregorian, Vartan *BioIn 16*
Gregorian, Vartan 1934- *News 90 [port], -90-3 [port], WhoAm 90, WhoE 91, WhoWor 91*
Gregorie, Henry Baker, III 1955- *WhoSSW 91*
Gregorio, Frank Michael 1948- *St&PR 91*
Gregorio, Louis J.L. 1929- *St&PR 91*
Gregorio, Luis Justino Lopes 1929- *WhoAm 90*
Gregorio, Peter Anthony 1916- *WhoSSW 91, WhoWor 91*
Gregorius, Beverly June 1915- *WhoAmW 91*
Gregorius, Hans Henry 1947- *BiDrAPA 89*
Gregoropoulos, John 1921- *WhoAmA 91*
Gregorski, Peggy Wilk 1959- *WhoAmW 91*
Gregory XIII 1502-1585 *WorAlBi*
Gregory, Lady 1852-1932 *BioIn 16*
Gregory Thaumaturgus, Saint 213?-270 *EncPaPR 91*
Gregory the Seventh, Pope 1023?-1085 *EncO&P 3*
Gregory, Alfred William 1928- *St&PR 91*
Gregory, Angela 1903-1990 *WhoAmA 91N*
Gregory, Anita 1925-1984 *EncO&P 3, EncPaPR 91*
Gregory, Ann Young 1935- *WhoAmW 91, WhoSSW 91*
Gregory, Anne 1939- *WhoAmA 91*
Gregory, Arthur Robert 1925- *WhoAm 90*
Gregory, Arthur Stanley 1914- *WhoAm 90*
Gregory, Augusta 1852-1932 *FemiCLE*
Gregory, Barbara Jean 1954- *WhoEmL 91*
Gregory, Bettina Louise 1946- *WhoAm 90*
Gregory, Bobby Lee 1938- *WhoAm 90*
Gregory, Bonita Belinda 1956- *WhoAmW 91*
Gregory, Bonnie Jo *BiDrAPA 89*
Gregory, Bruce 1917- *WhoAmA 91*
Gregory, Calvin 1942- *WhoWor 91*
Gregory, Carolyn Holmes 1950- *WhoWrEP 89*
Gregory, Charles Coleman, III 1955- *WhoSSW 91*
Gregory, Clive C. L. *EncPaPR 91*
Gregory, Cynthia *BioIn 16*
Gregory, Cynthia 1946- *News 90 [port], WorAlBi*
Gregory, Cynthia Kathleen 1946- *WhoAmW 91*
Gregory, Daniel Kevin 1958- *WhoEmL 91, WhoSSW 91*
Gregory, Dennis Edward 1949- *WhoSSW 91*
Gregory, Dennis Leander 1956- *St&PR 91, WhoEmL 91*
Gregory, Diana 1933- *BioIn 16*
Gregory, Dick *BioIn 16, NewAgE 90*
Gregory, Dick 1932- *DrBlPA 90, News 90 [port], -90-3 [port], WorAlBi*
Gregory, Donald Munson 1897- *WhoAm 90*
Gregory, Douglas P 1926- *BiDrAPA 89*
Gregory, E. John 1919- *WhoHisp 91*
Gregory, Edward Meeks 1922- *WhoSSW 91*
Gregory, Fletcher Harrison, Jr. 1919- *St&PR 91*
Gregory, Garold Fay 1926- *WhoSSW 91*
Gregory, George 1917- *St&PR 91*
Gregory, George G. 1932- *WhoAm 90*
Gregory, George Martin 1934- *St&PR 91*
Gregory, George Tillman, Jr. 1921- *WhoAm 90, WhoSSW 91*
Gregory, Gus 1940- *WhoSSW 91*
Gregory, Hardy, Jr. 1936- *WhoAm 90, WhoSSW 91*
Gregory, Henry C. 1935-1990 *BioIn 16*
Gregory, Henry C., III *NewYTBS 90*
Gregory, Herold La Mar 1923- *WhoAm 90*
Gregory, Holly Wanda Januszkiewicz 1956- *WhoAmW 91*
Gregory, Ian 1926- *BiDrAPA 89*
Gregory, Isabella Augusta 1852-1932 *WorAlBi*
Gregory, Isabella Augusta Persse, Lady 1852-1932 *BioIn 16*
Gregory, Jack 1925- *St&PR 91*
Gregory, James 1911- *WhoAm 90*
Gregory, James M. 1947- *ODwPR 91*
Gregory, James Michael 1935- *WhoAm 90*
Gregory, Jane Thurmond 1930- *St&PR 91*
Gregory, Jean Winfrey 1947- *WhoAmW 91, WhoEmL 91, WhoSSW 91*
Gregory, Jerry Glen 1943- *BiDrAPA 89*
Gregory, Joan 1930- *WhoAmA 91*
Gregory, John 1879-1958 *WhoAmA 91N*
Gregory, John B. 1924- *St&PR 91*
Gregory, John Harry 1950- *WhoE 91*
Gregory, John Leonard 1931- *WhoE 91*
Gregory, John R. *ODwPR 91*
Gregory, Joseph Tracy 1914- *WhoAm 90*
Gregory, Josephine Lane 1955- *WhoWrEP 89*
Gregory, Julia P. 1952- *St&PR 91*
Gregory, Kathrine Patricia 1952- *WhoEmL 91*
Gregory, Lewis Dean 1953- *WhoEmL 91*
Gregory, Linda Susan *St&PR 91*
Gregory, Lydia May Jencks 1903- *WhoE 91, WhoWor 91*
Gregory, Marian Frances 1919- *WhoAmW 91*
Gregory, Marion F. 1933- *St&PR 91*
Gregory, Marion F., Jr. 1933- *WhoAm 90*
Gregory, Martha Ann 1942- *WhoAmW 91*
Gregory, Mel Hyatt, Jr. 1936- *WhoAm 90*
Gregory, Michael *BioIn 16*
Gregory, Michael 1940- *WhoWrEP 89*
Gregory, Michael Alfred 1955- *WhoEmL 91*
Gregory, Michael Strietmann 1929- *WhoAm 90*
Gregory, Myra May 1912- *WhoE 91*
Gregory, Nelson Bruce 1933- *WhoWor 91*
Gregory, Norman Wayne 1920- *WhoAm 90*
Gregory, Patricia Diane 1952- *WhoWrEP 89*
Gregory, Paul 1908- *Ballpl 90*
Gregory, Paul Eugene 1929- *St&PR 91*
Gregory, Paul G *BiDrAPA 89*
Gregory, Philippa 1954- *ConAu 131*
Gregory, Richard Claxton *BioIn 16*
Gregory, Richard Thomas 1948- *WhoE 91*
Gregory, Rick Dean 1954- *WhoEmL 91, WhoSSW 91*
Gregory, Robert D. 1929- *St&PR 91*
Gregory, Robert E., Jr. 1942- *St&PR 91*
Gregory, Robert Earle, Jr. 1942- *WhoAm 90, WhoE 91*
Gregory, Robert George 1939- *WhoWor 91*
Gregory, Ross 1933- *WhoAm 90*
Gregory, Ruth Wilhelmene 1910- *WhoAm 90*
Gregory, Stan 1948- *WhoAmA 91*
Gregory, Ted Walter 1933- *St&PR 91*
Gregory, Thomas Bradford 1944- *WhoWor 91*
Gregory, Thomas L. 1926- *St&PR 91*
Gregory, Thomas L. 1935- *St&PR 91*
Gregory, Thomas Lang 1935- *WhoAm 90*
Gregory, Thomas Watt 1861-1933 *BiDrUSE 89, BioIn 16*
Gregory, Victor 1918- *BiDrAPA 89*
Gregory, Vincent L., Jr. 1923- *St&PR 91*
Gregory, Virgie Mae *WhoAmW 91*
Gregory, Walter R. 1945- *St&PR 91*
Gregory, Wanda Jean 1925- *WhoAmW 91*
Gregory, Waylande 1905-1971 *WhoAmA 91N*
Gregory, Wayne Wilson 1932- *St&PR 91*
Gregory, William David 1947- *WhoSSW 91*
Gregory, William Edward 1958- *WhoEmL 91*
Gregory, William George 1957- *WhoEmL 91*
Gregory, William King 1876-1970 *DcScB S2*
Gregory, Wilton D. 1947- *WhoAm 90*
Gregory-Goodrum, Ellna Kay 1943- *WhoAmA 91*
Gregotti, Vittorio 1927- *ConDes 90*
Gregson, Brian DeLynn 1931- *WhoAm 90*
Gregson, Dana Alan 1955- *St&PR 91*
Gregson, Edward 1945- *IntWWM 90*
Gregus, Linda Anna 1956- *WhoAmW 91*
Gregus, Shellie Lynn 1961- *WhoAmW 91*
Gregware, James Murray 1956- *WhoE 91, WhoEmL 91*
Grehan, Harold Simon, Jr. 1927- *St&PR 91*
Greicar, Conrad J. 1937- *St&PR 91*
Greider, Clarence Edwin 1922- *WhoSSW 91*
Greidinger, B. Bernard 1906- *WhoAm 90*
Greie-Cramer, Johanna 1864- *EncAL*
Greif, Bill 1950- *Ballpl 90*
Greif, Ed 1909- *ODwPR 91*
Greif, Edward Louis 1909- *WhoAm 90*
Greif, Jim 1948- *ODwPR 91*
Greif, Mortimer 1926- *St&PR 91*
Greif, Robert 1938- *WhoAm 90, WhoE 91*
Greifeld, Julia Considine 1957- *WhoAmW 91*
Greifer, Gerald I. 1943- *St&PR 91*
Greifer, Ira 1931- *WhoAm 90*
Greifer, Julian L. 1901-1989 *BioIn 16*
Greiff, Barrie S *BiDrAPA 89*
Greiff, Barrie Sanford 1935- *WhoE 91*
Greiff, Constance Mann 1929- *WhoAmW 91*
Greiffenberg, Catharina Regina von 1633-1694 *EncCoWW*
Greifner, Roni B *BiDrAPA 89*
Greig, Brian Strother 1950- *WhoEmL 91*
Greig, John Augus 1941- *St&PR 91*
Greig, Russell G. 1952- *WhoE 91*
Greig, Thomas Currie 1931- *WhoAm 90*
Greig, William Harold 1951- *WhoEmL 91*
Greig, William Taber, Jr. 1924- *WhoAm 90*
Greigg, Ronald Edwin 1946- *WhoEmL 91*
Greiling, James A. 1957- *St&PR 91*
Greiling, Paul Theodore 1939- *WhoAm 90*
Greilsheimer, James Gans 1937- *WhoAm 90*
Greim, Helmut 1935- *WhoWor 91*
Greim, Robert, Ritter von 1892-1945 *BioIn 16*
Greiman, April 1948- *BioIn 16, ConDes 90, WhoAm 90, WhoAmW 91*
Greimas, A. J. *ConAu 132*
Greimas, Algirdas Julien 1917- *ConAu 132*
Grein, Richard F. 1932- *BioIn 16*
Grein, Richard Frank 1932- *WhoAm 90*
Greindl, Josef 1912- *IntWWM 90, PenDiMP*
Greiner, Carl Bruce 1950- *BiDrAPA 89*
Greiner, Christian Daniel *PenDiDA 89*
Greiner, David Lee 1964- *WhoSSW 91*
Greiner, Gordon Gary 1934- *WhoAm 90*
Greiner, Gotthelf *PenDiDA 89*
Greiner, Harold Fredric 1922- *St&PR 91*
Greiner, Jeffrey Peter 1958- *WhoEmL 91*
Greiner, Johann Friedrich *PenDiDA 89*
Greiner, Johann Georg *PenDiDA 89*
Greiner, John Hammond, Jr. 1935- *WhoSSW 91*
Greiner, Ludwig *BioIn 16*
Greiner, Mary Louise 1949- *WhoEmL 91*
Greiner, Morris Esty, Jr. 1920- *WhoAm 90*
Greiner, Paul Calvin 1926- *St&PR 91*
Greiner, Peter Charles 1938- *WhoAm 90*
Greiner, Theodore H 1924- *BiDrAPA 89*
Greiner, Walter Albin Erhard 1935- *WhoWor 91*
Greiner, William Robert 1934- *WhoAm 90*
Greinke, Everett Donald 1929- *WhoAm 90*
Greis, Howard Arthur 1925- *St&PR 91*
Greis, Wayne Raymond 1942- *WhoWor 91*
Greisen, Kenneth Ingvard 1918- *WhoAm 90*
Greiser, Arthur 1897-1946 *BioIn 16*
Greisiger, Arthur Eugene, Jr. 1954- *WhoEmL 91*
Greisler, Howard Parker 1950- *WhoAm 90*
Greisman, Harvey W. 1948- *ODwPR 91*
Greisman, Harvey William 1948- *WhoEmL 91*
Greissle, Hermann A 1925- *WhoAmA 91*
Greist, John Howard 1906- *BiDrAPA 89*
Greist, John Huth 1939- *BiDrAPA 89*
Greist, Mary Coffey 1947- *WhoAmW 91*
Greiter, W.D. 1954- *St&PR 91*
Greitzer, Betty F. 1951- *ODwPR 91*
Greitzer, Edward Marc 1941- *WhoAm 90, WhoE 91*
Greitzer, Herman S. 1919- *WhoAm 90*
Greitzer, Robert Warren 1946- *St&PR 91*
Greitzer, Sol 1925-1989 *BioIn 16*
Greiwe, John Robert 1960- *WhoEmL 91*
Grekin, Paul M *BiDrAPA 89*
Grekova, I. *EncCoWW*
Grele, Milton Drummer 1925- *St&PR 91*
Grelle, Francis Gerard 1948- *St&PR 91*
Grelle, Martin Glen 1954- *WhoAmA 91*
Greller, Martin Michael 1950- *WhoEmL 91*
Gremban, Joe Lawrence 1920- *WhoAm 90*
Grembowski, Eugene 1938- *WhoWor 91*
Gremeaux, Paul M. 1940- *St&PR 91*
Gremetz, Maxime 1928- *BiDFrPL*
Gremillion, Curtis Lionel, Jr. 1924- *WhoAm 90, WhoWor 91*
Gremillion, Denise 1955- *WhoAmW 91*
Gremillion, F. Marcel 1940- *St&PR 91*
Gremley, Robert C. 1929- *St&PR 91*
Gremm, Judye Dyan 1953- *WhoEmL 91*
Gremmels, Marion Chapman 1924- *AuBYP 90*
Gremminger, Ed 1874-1942 *Ballpl 90*
Gren, Joann Martha 1956- *WhoAmW 91*
Grenald, Raymond 1928- *WhoAm 90*
Grenander, M. E. 1918- *WhoAm 90*
Grenard, Nancy Carole 1946- *WhoEmL 91*
Grenawalt, Mychal J. 1955- *WhoSSW 91*
Grenda-Lukas, John Michael 1945- *WhoWrEP 89*
Grendell, Timothy Joseph 1953- *WhoEmL 91*
Grendey, Giles 1693-1780 *PenDiDA 89*
Grendi, Ernest W. *WhoAm 90*
Grendi, Ernest Walter 1946- *St&PR 91*
Grendler, Paul Frederick 1936- *WhoAm 90*
Grendon, Stephen *AuBYP 90*
Greneker, Lillian Lidman *BioIn 16, NewYTBS 90*
Grenell, Barbara 1944- *WhoAmA 91*
Grenell, James Henry 1924- *WhoAm 90*
Grenert, Beverly Diane 1938- *WhoE 91*
Grenesko, Donald C. 1948- *St&PR 91*
Grenfell, Clarine Coffin 1910- *WhoWrEP 89*
Grenfell, Edward Charles 1870-1941 *BioIn 16*
Grenfell, Joyce 1910-1979 *OxCPMus*
Grenfell, Thomas Nicholas 1940- *St&PR 91*
Grenfell, Wilfred Thomason 1865-1940 *DcLB 92 [port]*
Grenga, Helen Eva 1938- *WhoAm 90*
Grengg, Marie *EncCoWW*
Grenier, Donald P. 1931- *St&PR 91*
Grenier, Edward Joseph, Jr. 1933- *WhoAm 90*
Grenier, Pasquier *PenDiDA 89*
Greninger, Edwin Thomas 1918- *WhoSSW 91*
Grenley, Philip 1912- *WhoWor 91*
Grenn-Scott, Debbi *ODwPR 91*
Grennan, Jim 1933- *WhoSSW 91*
Grennell, Robert Lovell 1910- *WhoE 91*
Grenon, Rene Eugene 1934- *WhoWor 91*
Grenquist, Peter Carl 1931- *WhoAm 90*
Grensing, Linda Leigh 1959- *WhoAmW 91, WhoEmL 91, WhoWrEP 89*
Grenvik, Christer Jan *BioIn 16*
Grenville, George 1712-1770 *EncCRAm*
Grenville, Kate 1950- *ConLC 61 [port], FemiCLE*
Grenville, Pelham *ConAu 33NR, MajTwCW*
Grenville, Richard 1541?-1591 *EncCRAm*
Grenzke, Norman Frederick, Jr. 1946- *St&PR 91*
Grenzke, Richard A. 1946- *St&PR 91*
Greppin, John Aird Coutts 1937- *WhoAm 90*
Gres, Madame 1899- *ConDes 90*
Gres, Alfred D. 1923- *St&PR 91*
Gres, Alix 1899?- *BioIn 16*
Gresalfi, Thomas John, Jr. *BiDrAPA 89*
Greschler, Ira Emmanuel 1956- *WhoEmL 91*
Greshake, Gisbert 1933- *WhoWor 91*
Gresham, Ann Elizabeth 1933- *WhoWor 91*
Gresham, David Melvin 1956- *WhoAm 90*
Gresham, Douglas H. 1945- *BioIn 16*
Gresham, Gary Stuart 1951- *WhoAm 90*
Gresham, Glen Edward 1931- *WhoAm 90*
Gresham, James Arthur 1928- *WhoAm 90*
Gresham, Karen Craig 1961- *WhoAmW 91*
Gresham, Perry Epler 1907- *WhoAm 90, WhoWor 91*
Gresham, Phyllis Kilmer 1934- *WhoAmW 91*
Gresham, Robert Coleman 1917- *WhoAm 90*
Gresham, Robert Lee 1942- *St&PR 91*
Gresham, Robert M. 1943- *St&PR 91*
Gresham, Rupert N., Jr. 1922- *St&PR 91*
Gresham, Stephen Deane 1960- *WhoE 91*
Gresham, Thomas Andrew 1953- *WhoSSW 91, WhoWor 91*
Gresham, Walter Quintin 1832-1895 *BiDrUSE 89, BioIn 16*
Gresko, Bernetta Lieser 1938- *WhoAmW 91*
Gresla, Jack F. 1920- *St&PR 91*
Gresov, Boris 1914- *St&PR 91, WhoAm 90*
Gress, Ann Maria 1955- *WhoAm 90*

Gress, Elsa 1919- EncCoWW
Gress, Gary L. 1944- St&PR 91
Gress, Gerald L. 1944- St&PR 91
Gress, Rose Marie 1930- WhoE 91
Gressak, Anthony Raymond, Jr. 1947- WhoAm 90
Gressel, Michael L 1902- WhoAmA 91
Gressel, Michael Ludwig 1902- WhoE 91
Gresser, Lawrence T. BioIn 16
Gresser, Seymour Gerald 1926- WhoAmA 91
Gressette, Lawrence M., Jr. 1932- WhoSSW 91
Gressitt, Stevan Edward 1950- BiDrAPA 89
Gressman, Eugene 1917- WhoAm 90, WhoE 91
Gressner, Axel Max 1943- WhoWor 91
Gretener, Claus 1942- WhoWor 91
Grether, David Maclay 1938- WhoAm 90
Gretsch, Judith Constance 1963- WhoAmW 91
Gretsch, Richard F. 1908- St&PR 91
Grettenberger, John O. BioIn 16
Grettenberger, John O. 1937- St&PR 91
Gretter, Lystra 1858-1951 BioIn 16
Gretton, Elizabeth BiDEWW
Gretz, Stephen Randolph 1948- WhoE 91
Gretzinger, Ralph Edwin, III 1948- WhoEmL 91, WhoSSW 91
Gretzky, Wayne BioIn 16
Gretzky, Wayne 1961- WhoAm 90, WorAlBi
Greubel, Joseph E. 1937- St&PR 91
Greule, Alan L. 1956- WhoEmL 91
Greulich, Richard Curtice 1928- WhoAm 90
Greulich, Richard E. 1926- St&PR 91
Greuze, Jean Baptiste 1725-1805 IntDcAA 90
Grevatt, Wallace 1925- ConAu 129
Greve, Bertrand Joseph 1923- St&PR 91
Greve, Douglas W 1934- BiDrAPA 89
Greve, Gerald V. 1948- St&PR 91
Greve, J. William 1929- St&PR 91
Greve, John Henry 1934- WhoAm 90
Greve, Lucius, II 1915- WhoWor 91
Greve, Marilyn J. 1943- WhoAmW 91
Greve, Peter 1949- WhoWor 91
Grevelle, Robin 1959- WhoSSW 91
Greves, Larry Allen 1947- St&PR 91
Greville, Frances 1726-1789 BioIn 16, FemiCLE
Greville, Frances Evelyn Maynard 1861-1933 BioIn 16
Greville, Fulke 1554-1628 BioIn 16
Greville, Henry 1842-1902 EncCoWW
Greville, Nicholas A. 1943- St&PR 91
Greville, T N E 1910- EncO&P 3
Greville, Thomas Nall Eden 1910- EncPaPR 91
Grevy, Francois Judith Paul 1807-1891 BiDFrPL
Grew, James 1929- WhoWor 91
Grew, Joseph C. 1880-1965 BioIn 16
Grew, Kimberly Ann 1962- WhoEmL 91
Grew, Robert Ralph 1931- WhoE 91, WhoWor 91
Grew, William TwCCr&M 91
Grewal, Amarjit Singh 1944- BiDrAPA 89
Grewal, Harpal S. 1951- WhoSSW 91
Grewal, Rajdev Kaur 1938- BiDrAPA 89
Grewdead, Roy ConAu 30NR
Grewe, Arthur H. 1926- St&PR 91
Grewe, John Mitchell 1938- WhoE 91
Grewell, Judith Lynn 1945- WhoEmL 91
Grewelle, Larry Allan 1937- WhoSSW 91
Grex, Leo TwCCr&M 91
Grey Owl 1888-1938 BioIn 16, DcLB 92 [port]
Grey, Alan Lewis 1919- WhoAm 90
Grey, Charles 1764-1845 WorAlBi
Grey, Clifford 1887-1941 OxCPMus
Grey, Deborah Cleland 1952- WhoAmW 91
Grey, Earle 1892-1978 OxCCanT
Grey, Elizabeth 1917- AuBYP 90
Grey, Elizabeth Caroline 1798-1869 FemiCLE
Grey, Francis Joseph 1931- WhoE 91
Grey, Henry 1954- St&PR 91, WhoAm 90
Grey, Jane 1537-1554 FemiCLE, WomWR [port], WorAlBi
Grey, Jennifer BioIn 16
Grey, Jerry 1926- WhoAm 90, WhoE 91
Grey, Joel 1932- BioIn 16, OxCPMus, WhoAm 90, WorAlBi
Grey, Leslie BiDrAPA 89, WhoWrEP 89
Grey, Louis TwCCr&M 91
Grey, Madeleine 1896- PenDiMP
Grey, Margery Lynn 1960- WhoAmW 91
Grey, Maria 1816-1906 FemiCLE
Grey, Maria Georgina 1816-1906 BioIn 16
Grey, Paul BioIn 16
Grey, Peter Munson 1943- BiDrAPA 89
Grey, Robert Constantine 1928- St&PR 91
Grey, Robert Dean 1939- WhoAm 90
Grey, Sylvan NewAgMG
Grey, William H 1923- BiDrAPA 89
Grey, William L. 1916-1988 BioIn 16
Grey, Zane 1872-1939 BioIn 16, ConAu 132, MajTwCW
Grey, Zane 1875-1939 Ballpl 90, WorAlBi
Greyson, Charles Bruce 1946- BiDrAPA 89, WhoE 91
Greytak, Gil Guy 1941- St&PR 91
Greytak, Thomas John 1940- WhoAm 90
Greze, Jean-Louis 1931- St&PR 91, WhoWor 91
Grib, Boris F. 1924- St&PR 91
Gribben, Alan 1941- WhoSSW 91
Gribben, James Joseph 1942- St&PR 91
Gribbins, Richard James 1944- St&PR 91
Gribble, Carole L. 1940- WhoAmW 91
Gribble, Gordon Wayne 1941- WhoAm 90
Gribble, Leonard 1908- TwCCr&M 91
Gribbon, Daniel McNamara 1917- WhoAm 90
Gribbs, Paula Rewald 1955- WhoEmL 91
Gribbs, Roman S. 1925- WhoAm 90
Gribelin, Simon 1661-1731 PenDiDA 89
Gribetz, Michael D BiDrAPA 89
Gricc, Giuseppe 1700-1770 PenDiDA 89
Gricci, Giuseppe 1700-1770 PenDiDA 89
Grice, George Daniel 1929- WhoAm 90
Grice, Ian Eric 1937- WhoWor 91
Grice, Richard Lee 1946- St&PR 91
Grice, Wayne DrBIPA 90
Grich, Bobby 1949- Ballpl 90 [port]
Grider, George William 1912- WhoAm 90
Grider, Joseph Kenneth 1921- WhoAm 90
Grider, Warren Lee 1948- WhoSSW 91
Gridle, Mary BiDEWW
Gridley, Daila Sefers 1944- WhoWor 91
Gridley, Henry Meeker 1933- St&PR 91
Gridley, Marion E. 1906-1974 AuBYP 90
Grieb, George A. 1935- St&PR 91
Grieb, R.W. 1930- St&PR 91
Grieb, Robert Frederick 1945- St&PR 91
Griebe, Mark Henry 1942- St&PR 91
Griebel, Pamela Dawn 1953- WhoEmL 91
Griebel, Richard P. 1937- ODwPR 91
Grieben, Leo R J 1932- BiDrAPA 89
Griebling-Long, Karen Jean 1957- IntWWM 90
Griech, Fred George 1944- St&PR 91
Grieco, Gary James 1941- WhoSSW 91
Grieco, Jessica BioIn 16
Grieco, Paul Anthony 1944- WhoAm 90
Grieco, Richard BioIn 16
Grieder, Elmer Moery 1909-1989 BioIn 16
Grieder, Jerome B. 1932- ConAu 130
Grieder, Karen Suzanne 1957- WhoAmW 91
Grieder, Terence 1931- WhoAmA 91
Grieder, Thomas Arthur 1959- BiDrAPA 89
Griefen, John Adams 1942- WhoAm 90, WhoAmA 91
Grieg, Edvard 1843-1907 PenDiMP A, WorAlBi
Grieg, Johan Nordahl Brun 1902-1943 DcScanL
Grieger, Pauline J. 1938- ODwPR 91
Griego, Jose Sabino 1938- WhoHisp 91
Griego, Linda 1935- WhoHisp 91
Griego, Phillip Joseph 1951- WhoEmL 91
Griego, Vincent E. 1940- WhoHisp 91
Griem, John Michael 1945- St&PR 91, WhoWor 91
Griem, Melvin Luther 1925- WhoAm 90
Griem, Sylvia Fudzinski 1929- WhoAmW 91
Grieman, John Joseph 1944- St&PR 91
Griemert, Hubert 1905- PenDiDA 89
Griendling, Robert ODwPR 91
Grieniger, Johann Georg PenDiDA 89
Griep, Clifford M. 1951- St&PR 91
Griepp, Randall Bertram 1940- WhoAm 90
Grier, Barbara G. 1933- WhoAmW 91, WhoWrEP 89
Grier, Baxter 1919- St&PR 91
Grier, Charles F. 1951- St&PR 91
Grier, Charles Paul 1930- St&PR 91
Grier, David Allen 1956- DrBIPA 90
Grier, Dorothy Ann Pridgen 1936- WhoE 91
Grier, Hardy Cannon 1950- WhoE 91
Grier, Harry Dobson Miller 1914-1972 WhoAmA 91N
Grier, Herbert E. 1911- St&PR 91
Grier, Herbert Earl 1911- WhoAm 90
Grier, Hugh Christopher 1922- IntWWM 90
Grier, James R., III 1938- St&PR 91
Grier, John BioIn 16
Grier, Joseph Williamson, Jr. 1915- WhoAm 90
Grier, Katherine C. 1953- ConAu 132
Grier, Margot Edmands 1946- WhoAmA 91
Grier, Pam BioIn 16
Grier, Pam 1950?- DrBIPA 90
Grier, Phillip Michael 1941- WhoAm 90, WhoE 91
Grier, Roger Dale 1961- WhoSSW 91
Grier, Roosevelt 1932- DrBIPA 90
Grier, Sydney C. 1868-1933 FemiCLE
Grier, Wayne WhoSSW 91
Grier, William H BiDrAPA 89
Grierson, Benjamin Henry 1826-1911 WhNaAH
Grierson, Constantia 1704?-1732 FemiCLE
Grierson, Constantia 1706?-1733 BioIn 16
Grierson, Edward 1914-1975 TwCCr&M 91
Grierson, Francis 1848-1927 BioIn 16
Grierson, Philip 1910- ConAu 129
Gries, David Joseph 1939- WhoAm 90
Gries, George Alexander 1917- WhoAm 90
Gries, John Paul 1911- WhoAm 90
Gries, Philip R. 1943- WhoWor 91
Gries, Thomas 1960- WhoWor 91
Griesa, Thomas Poole 1930- WhoAm 90
Griese, Bob 1945- WorAlBi
Griesedeck, Edward Joseph, III 1958- WhoEmL 91
Griesedieck, Ellen 1948- WhoAmA 91
Griesemer, John N. 1930- WhoAm 90
Griesse, Paul D. 1943- St&PR 91
Griesser, Kurt William 1955- WhoSSW 91
Griessler, Franz Anton 1897-1974 WhoAmA 91N
Griest, Debra Lynn 1959- WhoAmW 91
Grieve, Bill 1900-1979 Ballpl 90
Grieve, Bruce Brogan 1954- WhoEmL 91
Grieve, C.M. 1892-1978 ConAu 33NR, MajTwCW
Grieve, Christopher Murray 1892-1978 BioIn 16
Grieve, Harold Walter 1901- WhoAm 90
Grieve, Leona Lee 1954- WhoWrEP 89
Grieve, Pierson M. 1927- St&PR 91
Grieve, Pierson MacDonald 1927- WhoAm 90
Grieve, Thomas Alan 1948- WhoAm 90, WhoSSW 91
Grieve, Tom 1948- Ballpl 90
Grieves, Carolyn Ann 1947- WhoEmL 91
Grieves, Robert Belanger 1935- WhoAm 90
Grifalconi, Ann 1929- AuBYP 90
Griff, Bernard Matthew 1935- WhoWrEP 89
Griff, David Phillip 1940- WhoWor 91
Griff, Merle Dawn 1948- WhoEmL 91
Griffel, Kay 1940- IntWWM 90
Griffel, Margaret D BiDrAPA 89
Griffen, Clyde Chesterman 1929- WhoAm 90
Griffen, Elizabeth AuBYP 90
Griffen, Lucille 1954- WhoAmW 91
Griffen, Vanessa FemiCLE
Griffen, Ward O., Jr. 1928- WhoAm 90
Griffenhagen, George Bernard 1924- WhoAm 90
Griffeth, Paul Lyman 1919- WhoAm 90
Griffey, Dick 1943- ConAmBL
Griffey, Eric Clark 1943- BiDrAPA 89
Griffey, Ken, Jr. BioIn 16
Griffey, Ken, Jr. 1967- Ballpl 90
Griffey, Ken, Sr. BioIn 16
Griffey, Ken, Sr. 1950- Ballpl 90
Griffin, Adrian Mark 1944- BiDrAPA 89
Griffin, Alan Gary 1952- WhoSSW 91
Griffin, Albert Bruce 1946- WhoSSW 91
Griffin, Alfredo 1957- Ballpl 90, WhoHisp 91
Griffin, Anne McLean BiDrAPA 89
Griffin, Annie BioIn 16
Griffin, Archie 1954- BioIn 16
Griffin, Arthur Marsh 1959- BiDrAPA 89
Griffin, Barbara Jane 1935- WhoAmW 91
Griffin, Ben Hill, Jr. BioIn 16
Griffin, Ben Hill, Jr. NewYTBS 90 [port]
Griffin, Bessie BioIn 16
Griffin, Billy L. 1930- WhoAm 90
Griffin, Billy Loyd 1930- St&PR 91
Griffin, Bob Franklin 1935- WhoAm 90
Griffin, Byron Kent 1942- St&PR 91
Griffin, Campbell Arthur, Jr. 1929- WhoAm 90
Griffin, Carleton Hadlock 1928- WhoAm 90
Griffin, Chris A WhoAmA 91
Griffin, Claibourne Eugene 1929- WhoAm 90
Griffin, Clayton Houstoun 1925- WhoAm 90
Griffin, Cornelius F. 1939- St&PR 91
Griffin, Cyrus 1748-1810 BiDrUSE 89
Griffin, Darrell Alton BiDrAPA 89
Griffin, David Ray 1952- WhoSSW 91
Griffin, David W. 1951- St&PR 91
Griffin, Dawn Kathleen 1965- WhoEmL 91
Griffin, Deborah Seltzer 1949- WhoEmL 91
Griffin, DeWitt James 1914- WhoAm 90, WhoWor 91
Griffin, Diane 1940- WhoE 91
Griffin, Diane Edmund 1940- WhoAmW 91
Griffin, Donald Kenneth 1941- WhoSSW 91
Griffin, Donald Redfield 1915- BioIn 16, WhoAm 90, WhoE 91
Griffin, Donald W. 1937- St&PR 91
Griffin, Donald Wayne 1937- WhoAm 90
Griffin, Doug 1947- Ballpl 90
Griffin, Edward D. 1940- St&PR 91
Griffin, Edward Michael 1937- WhoAm 90
Griffin, Elizabeth BiDEWW
Griffin, Ella AuBYP 90
Griffin, Emilie Russell Dietrich 1936- WhoWrEP 89
Griffin, Emmett G. 1926- St&PR 91
Griffin, Eugene F. 1926- St&PR 91
Griffin, F. O'Neil 1926- St&PR 91, WhoAm 90
Griffin, Fred Long 1948- BiDrAPA 89
Griffin, G. Lee St&PR 91
Griffin, G. Lee 1938- WhoAm 90, WhoSSW 91
Griffin, Gale Lockhart 1943- WhoE 91
Griffin, Gary A. 1937- St&PR 91
Griffin, Gerald F. 1934- St&PR 91
Griffin, Gerard R. 1941- ODwPR 91
Griffin, Gillett Good 1928- AuBYP 90
Griffin, Gilroye Alfred, Jr. 1938- WhoAm 90
Griffin, Gladys Bogues 1937- WhoSSW 91
Griffin, Gregory 1770-1827 BioIn 16
Griffin, Henry E. 1943- St&PR 91
Griffin, Henry Ludwig 1916- WhoAm 90
Griffin, Herman A. 1932- St&PR 91
Griffin, Herman Talmadge 1948- WhoSSW 91
Griffin, Herschel Emmett 1918- WhoAm 90
Griffin, J. William 1939- WhoWrEP 89
Griffin, James Anthony 1934- WhoAm 90
Griffin, James Bennett 1905- WhoAm 90
Griffin, James C. St&PR 91
Griffin, James Donald 1929- WhoAm 90, WhoE 91
Griffin, James Edwin 1927- St&PR 91, WhoAm 90
Griffin, James Howard, III 1940- WhoE 91
Griffin, James M. 1934- St&PR 91
Griffin, James Michael 1941- WhoE 91
Griffin, James Philip 1932- St&PR 91
Griffin, Jane Flanigen 1933- WhoAmW 91
Griffin, Jasper 1937- WhoWor 91
Griffin, Jean 1931- WhoAmW 91
Griffin, Jeffrey Thomas 1944- St&PR 91
Griffin, Jo Ann Thomas 1933- WhoAmW 91, WhoE 91
Griffin, Joan Solomon 1958- WhoAmW 91, WhoEmL 91
Griffin, John B BiDrAPA 89
Griffin, John Charles 1954- WhoSSW 91
Griffin, John D BiDrAPA 89
Griffin, John Douglas 1906- WhoAm 90
Griffin, John Fredrick, Jr. 1963- WhoE 91
Griffin, John Howard 1920-1980 BioIn 16
Griffin, John Joseph 1943- BiDrAPA 89
Griffin, John Lee 1943- WhoSSW 91
Griffin, John R. 1942- St&PR 91
Griffin, Johnny BioIn 16
Griffin, Jonathan ConAu 129
Griffin, Joseph 1932- St&PR 91
Griffin, Joseph Edward 1947- WhoEmL 91
Griffin, Joseph F., III BiDrAPA 89
Griffin, Joseph J. 1932- WhoAm 90
Griffin, Joseph Parker, Jr. 1944- WhoE 91
Griffin, Joyce Marie 1955- WhoEmL 91
Griffin, Judith Ann 1948- WhoE 91
Griffin, Judith Berry AuBYP 90, BioIn 16
Griffin, Judson 1951- IntWWM 90
Griffin, Julius BiDrAPA 89
Griffin, Karen E. 1957- WhoE 91
Griffin, Keith Broadwell 1938- WhoAm 90
Griffin, Keith Henry BiDrAPA 89
Griffin, Kenneth Patrick 1930- St&PR 91
Griffin, Larry Don 1951- WhoSSW 91
Griffin, Larry Paul 1947- WhoSSW 91
Griffin, Laura M. 1925- WhoAmW 91
Griffin, Lee Martin 1929- BiDrAPA 89
Griffin, Leland Milburn 1920- WhoAm 90
Griffin, Linda Claire 1950- WhoEmL 91
Griffin, Linda Suzzanne 1954- WhoEmL 91
Griffin, Louis Austin 1931- St&PR 91
Griffin, Mark Adam 1960- WhoEmL 91
Griffin, Mark Edward St&PR 91
Griffin, Marvin Anthony 1923- WhoAm 90
Griffin, Mary 1916- WhoAm 90
Griffin, Mary Frances 1925- WhoAmW 91
Griffin, Melanie Hunt 1949- WhoAmW 91, WhoEmL 91, WhoSSW 91
Griffin, Merv 1925- BioIn 16, ConAu 130, WorAlBi
Griffin, Merv Edward 1925- WhoAm 90
Griffin, Mervyn Edward, Jr. 1925- ConAmBL
Griffin, Michael Daniel 1939- WhoAm 90
Griffin, Michael Jay 1961- WhoSSW 91
Griffin, Michael Vincent 1953- WhoE 91
Griffin, Mike 1865-1908 Ballpl 90
Griffin, Mike 1957- Ballpl 90
Griffin, Norris Samuel 1931- WhoAm 90

Griffin, O. Daniel, Jr. 1960- WhoEmL 91, WhoSSW 91, WhoWor 91
Griffin, Oscar O'Neal, Jr. 1933- WhoAm 90
Griffin, P.G. 1946- St&PR 91
Griffin, Patricia Anne 1941- WhoAmW 91
Griffin, Patricia Lee 1958- WhoSSW 91
Griffin, Patrick, Jr. ODwPR 91
Griffin, Patrick Joseph 1956- WhoEmL 91
Griffin, Peni Rae 1961- WhoWrEP 89
Griffin, Peter J. 1943- WhoAm 90
Griffin, Phillip Stone 1938- St&PR 91
Griffin, Phillip Stone, I 1938- WhoAm 90
Griffin, Priscilla Loring 1930- WhoE 91
Griffin, R.H. St&PR 91N
Griffin, Rachael S WhoAmA 91N
Griffin, Rachel 1917- WhoWrEP 89
Griffin, Ralph 1925- MusmAFA
Griffin, Richard G 1933- BiDrAPA 89
Griffin, Robert A BiDrAPA 89
Griffin, Robert C. 1948- St&PR 91
Griffin, Robert Emmett 1935- St&PR 91
Griffin, Robert G. 1951- St&PR 91
Griffin, Robert John Thurlow 1906- ConAu 129
Griffin, Robert P. 1923- WhoAm 90, WorAlBi
Griffin, Robert Thomas 1917- WhoAm 90
Griffin, Robert Wooten 1952- WhoEmL 91
Griffin, Rosalind Elaine BiDrAPA 89
Griffin, Rutledge Avalon 1944- St&PR 91
Griffin, Samuel BioIn 16
Griffin, Samuel M. 1951- St&PR 91
Griffin, Scott 1938- St&PR 91
Griffin, Sharon L. 1939- WhoAmW 91
Griffin, Sheila 1951- WhoEmL 91
Griffin, Sherry Lumbert 1937- WhoAmW 91
Griffin, Simon Goodell 1824-1902 AmLegL
Griffin, Somsri BiDrAPA 89
Griffin, Susan 1943- FemiCLE
Griffin, Susan Ann 1946- WhoAmW 91
Griffin, Susan Elizabeth Cilley 1851-1926 BioIn 16
Griffin, Suzanne Elizabeth 1963- WhoAmW 91
Griffin, Suzanne J 1951- BiDrAPA 89
Griffin, Sylvia Gail 1935- WhoAmW 91
Griffin, Tamira 1959- WhoEmL 91
Griffin, Terry Lee 1955- WhoSSW 91
Griffin, Terry Monroe 1956- WhoSSW 91
Griffin, Thomas A. 1931- St&PR 91
Griffin, Thomas Aquinas, Jr. 1927- St&PR 91
Griffin, Thomas E., Jr. 1946- ConAu 131
Griffin, Thomas H. 1931- St&PR 91
Griffin, Thomas McLean 1922- WhoAm 90
Griffin, Thomas W. 1945- WhoAm 90
Griffin, Tom ConAu 131
Griffin, Tom 1926- WhoAm 90
Griffin, Tom 1948- Ballpl 90
Griffin, Tommy 1948- WhoSSW 91
Griffin, Velma AuBYP 90
Griffin, Vicki Ann 1953- WhoAmW 91
Griffin, Villard Stuart, Jr. 1937- WhoAm 90
Griffin, W.L. Hadley 1918- St&PR 91
Griffin, Walter 1937- WhoWrEP 89
Griffin, Walter Wanzel 1926- WhoSSW 91
Griffin, William Henry 1812-1900 DcCanB 12
Griffin, William Leonard, Jr. 1948- St&PR 91
Griffin, William Lester Hadley 1918- WhoAm 90
Griffin, William M. 1926- St&PR 91
Griffin, William Ralph 1943- WhoAm 90
Griffin, William Ray, Jr. BiDrAPA 89
Griffin, William Russell, Jr. 1938- WhoSSW 91
Griffin, William Thomas 1905- WhoAm 90, WhoWor 91
Griffin, William V, III BiDrAPA 89
Griffin, Yvonne Marie 1952- WhoAmW 91
Griffin-George, Jamilia Ann 1952- WhoEmL 91
Griffin-Holst, Jean 1943- WhoAmW 91, WhoWor 91
Griffing, Joseph Bruce 1919- WhoAm 90
Griffing, Richard Gary BioIn 16
Griffins, Herbert R. 1938- St&PR 91
Griffis, Anthony Eric 1950- WhoEmL 91
Griffis, David R. 1939- St&PR 91
Griffis, James D. 1932- St&PR 91
Griffis, Jane Jetton 1923- WhoSSW 91
Griffis, Katherine Millicent 1954- WhoAmW 91, WhoEmL 91
Griffis, Roy A. 1936- St&PR 91
Griffis, Sandra Lee 1957- WhoAmW 91
Griffis, Stanton 1887-1974 BioIn 16
Griffis, William Elliot 1843-1928 BioIn 16
Griffiss, James E 1928- ConAu 132
Griffith, A. Wayne 1938- St&PR 91
Griffith, Alan R. 1941- St&PR 91
Griffith, Alan Richard 1941- WhoAm 90
Griffith, Aline BioIn 16
Griffith, Alvin P 1960- BiDrAPA 89
Griffith, Andy 1926- BioIn 16, WhoAm 90, WorAlBi
Griffith, Bezaleel Herold 1925- WhoAm 90
Griffith, Bill ConAu 131, TwCCr&M 91
Griffith, Bill 1944- ConAu 129
Griffith, C. Wayne 1933- St&PR 91
Griffith, Carl David 1937- WhoWor 91
Griffith, Cecil FemiCLE
Griffith, Charles R. 1931- St&PR 91
Griffith, Clark 1869-1955 Ballpl 90 [port]
Griffith, Clark Calvin, II 1941- WhoAm 90
Griffith, D. W. 1875-1948 WorAlBi
Griffith, Daniel Allen 1951- WhoEmL 91
Griffith, Daniel Boyd 1934- St&PR 91, WhoAm 90
Griffith, David Crockett 1928- St&PR 91
Griffith, David Dahlberg 1936- BiDrAPA 89
Griffith, David Edwin 1958- WhoSSW 91
Griffith, David J. St&PR 91
Griffith, David Jackson 1946- St&PR 91
Griffith, David M. 1943- St&PR 91
Griffith, David Wark 1875-1948 LiHiK
Griffith, Don Montague 1943- St&PR 91
Griffith, Donald Kendall 1933- WhoAm 90
Griffith, Dotty 1949- WhoEmL 91
Griffith, E Clay BiDrAPA 89
Griffith, Edward David 1944- WhoWor 91
Griffith, Edwin Claybrook 1915- WhoAm 90
Griffith, Elizabeth 1727-1793 BioIn 16, FemiCLE
Griffith, Elizabeth Ann 1955- WhoAmW 91
Griffith, Elwin Jabez 1938- WhoAm 90
Griffith, Emile 1938- WorAlBi
Griffith, Emlyn Irving 1923- WhoAm 90, WhoE 91, WhoWor 91
Griffith, Ernest Ralph 1928- WhoAm 90
Griffith, Ezra E H BiDrAPA 89
Griffith, Ezra Edward Holman 1942- WhoE 91
Griffith, F. Lee, III 1947- WhoE 91
Griffith, Field AuBYP 90
Griffith, G. Larry 1937- WhoAm 90
Griffith, Garth Ellis 1928- WhoAm 90
Griffith, Gary Ernest 1948- WhoEmL 91
Griffith, Geraline Moeller 1916- WhoWrEP 89
Griffith, Gregory Wood 1952- WhoWor 91
Griffith, Helen V. BioIn 16
Griffith, Helen V. 1934- WhoWrEP 89
Griffith, Henry E. BioIn 16
Griffith, Hugh 1912-1980 WorAlBi
Griffith, Jack William 1929- WhoAm 90
Griffith, James Clifford 1948- WhoSSW 91, WhoWor 91
Griffith, James Joseph 1927- WhoE 91
Griffith, James Lamont 1950- BiDrAPA 89
Griffith, James Leigh 1951- WhoEmL 91
Griffith, James Lewis 1940- WhoE 91
Griffith, James M. 1942- ODwPR 91
Griffith, James Paul BiDrAPA 89
Griffith, James William 1922- WhoAm 90
Griffith, Janice Clare 1940- WhoE 91
Griffith, Jay Michael BiDrAPA 89
Griffith, Jerry Dice 1933- WhoAm 90, WhoWor 91
Griffith, Joel Harold BiDrAPA 89
Griffith, John Dorland 1931- BiDrAPA 89
Griffith, John E. 1930- St&PR 91
Griffith, John Francis 1934- WhoAm 90
Griffith, John H. 1925- St&PR 91
Griffith, John Keith 1946- St&PR 91
Griffith, John V. WhoAm 90
Griffith, Katherine Scott 1942- WhoAmW 91
Griffith, Ladd Ray 1930- WhoAm 90
Griffith, Leah Marie 1956- WhoAmW 91
Griffith, Louis Oscar 1875-1956 WhoAmA 91N
Griffith, Madlynne Veil 1951- WhoE 91
Griffith, Marshall 1953- IntWWM 90
Griffith, Martha H. 1945- WhoAmW 91, WhoEmL 91
Griffith, Mary Lavinia WhoSSW 91
Griffith, Mary Louise Kilpatrick 1926- WhoAmW 91, WhoE 91
Griffith, Melanie BioIn 16
Griffith, Melanie 1957- CurBio 90 [port], WhoAm 90, WorAlBi
Griffith, Melvin Eugene 1912- WhoSSW 91, WhoWor 91
Griffith, Michael Ted 1949- IntWWM 90
Griffith, Nanci BioIn 16, WhoNeCM [port]
Griffith, Osbie Hayes 1938- WhoAm 90
Griffith, P. Leroy 1908- St&PR 91
Griffith, Patricia Browning WhoWrEP 89
Griffith, Patricia King 1925- WhoAmW 91
Griffith, Ralph Franklin, Jr. 1940- WhoSSW 91
Griffith, Richard C. 1941- ODwPR 91
Griffith, Richard Edward, Jr. 1956- WhoEmL 91
Griffith, Richard L. 1931- WhoAm 90
Griffith, Richard Robert 1947- St&PR 91
Griffith, Robert Charles 1939- WhoWor 91
Griffith, Robert Kenaston 1917- WhoAm 90
Griffith, Robert Rhys 1952- WhoEmL 91
Griffith, Robert W. 1930- St&PR 91
Griffith, Roberta 1937- WhoAmA 91, WhoAmW 91
Griffith, Ronald L. 1934- St&PR 91
Griffith, Sima L. 1960- ODwPR 91
Griffith, Stephen R 1943- BiDrAPA 89
Griffith, Steve C., Jr. 1933- St&PR 91
Griffith, Steve Campbell, Jr. 1933- WhoAm 90
Griffith, Steven Franklin, Sr. 1948- WhoEmL 91, WhoSSW 91, WhoWor 91
Griffith, Thomas 1915- WhoAm 90
Griffith, Thomas Jefferson 1923- WhoSSW 91
Griffith, Tommy 1889-1967 Ballpl 90
Griffith, W Brooks 1929- BiDrAPA 89
Griffith, Walter G, Jr. BiDrAPA 89
Griffith, Wayland Coleman 1925- WhoAm 90
Griffith, William Alexander 1922- St&PR 91, WhoAm 90
Griffith, William Dunbar BioIn 16
Griffith, William Edgar 1920- WhoAm 90
Griffith, William Schuler 1949- WhoSSW 91
Griffith, William Victor 1953- WhoSSW 91
Griffith Joyner, Florence BioIn 16
Griffith Joyner, Florence 1959- WorAlBi
Griffith-Joyner, Florence Delores WhoAm 90
Griffith-Smith, Bella IntWWM 90
Griffiths, Anthony F. 1930- WhoAm 90
Griffiths, Anthony Frear 1930- St&PR 91
Griffiths, Barclay H. 1942- St&PR 91
Griffiths, Bede 1906- BioIn 16
Griffiths, Bill BioIn 16
Griffiths, Charles Robert 1941- WhoSSW 91
Griffiths, Daniel Edward 1917- WhoAm 90
Griffiths, David 1945- WhoEmL 91
Griffiths, David Neil 1935- St&PR 91, WhoAm 90
Griffiths, Debbie Wright 1956- WhoEmL 91
Griffiths, Donald P., Sr. 1919- St&PR 91
Griffiths, Douglas Howard BiDrAPA 89
Griffiths, Frank A. WhoAm 90
Griffiths, Gareth Lloyd 1954- WhoWor 91
Griffiths, Georgia Dorothy 1951- WhoAmW 91
Griffiths, Georgia Gregory 1939- St&PR 91
Griffiths, Helen 1939- AuBYP 90, BioIn 16
Griffiths, Iorwerth David Ace WhoAm 90
Griffiths, James Watters 1927- St&PR 91
Griffiths, John Brittain 1937- WhoAm 90
Griffiths, L. Gene 1940- St&PR 91
Griffiths, Linda 1953- OxCCanT
Griffiths, Linda 1956- ConAu 132
Griffiths, Lloyd Joseph 1941- WhoAm 90
Griffiths, Lynn Christopher 1940- WhoAm 90
Griffiths, Martha 1912- WhoAm 90, WhoAmW 91, WorAlBi
Griffiths, Michael C 1928- ConAu 31NR
Griffiths, Paul 1947- IntWWM 90
Griffiths, Peter Boyd 1956- WhoE 91
Griffiths, Philip John 1948- St&PR 91
Griffiths, Phillip A. WhoAm 90
Griffiths, Richard Reese 1931- WhoAm 90
Griffiths, Robert Budington 1937- WhoAm 90
Griffiths, Robert P. 1949- St&PR 91
Griffiths, Stephen Gareth 1949- ConAu 131
Griffiths, Steve ConAu 131
Griffiths, Sylvia Preston 1924- WhoAm 90
Griffiths, William Perry 1937- WhoAmA 91
Griffitts, Hannah 1727-1817 FemiCLE
Griffo, James Vincent, Jr. 1928- WhoAm 90
Griffo, John Thomas 1948- St&PR 91
Griffo, Lynn Jennifer 1957- WhoWrEP 89
Griffon, Joseph P. 1914- St&PR 91
Griffuelhes, Jean Victor 1874-1922 BiDFrPL
Griffy ConAu 129
Griffy, Thomas Alan 1936- WhoAm 90
Griga, Frank 1962- WhoSSW 91
Grigalonis, Mary Lou 1962- WhoE 91
Grigaut, Paul L WhoAmA 91N
Grigereit, Hugh Reeves, Jr. 1930- WhoSSW 91
Grigg, Betty Ann Carpenter 1932- WhoAmW 91, WhoE 91
Grigg, Carol BioIn 16
Grigg, Jon Richard 1955- BiDrAPA 89
Grigg, Kenneth A 1933- BiDrAPA 89
Grigg, Mary Monica 1922- BiDrAPA 89
Grigg, W Randolph 1944- BiDrAPA 89
Grigg, William 1934- WhoWrEP 89
Grigg, William Humphrey 1932- St&PR 91, WhoAm 90
Griggs, Art 1883-1938 Ballpl 90
Griggs, Benjamin Glyde, Jr. 1928- St&PR 91, WhoAm 90
Griggs, Bobbie June 1938- WhoSSW 91
Griggs, Daniel John 1959- WhoEmL 91
Griggs, Debra Jane 1953- WhoEmL 91
Griggs, Douglas Meriwether, Jr. 1928- WhoAm 90
Griggs, Graham Peter Lloyd 1955- IntWWM 90
Griggs, Hal 1928- Ballpl 90
Griggs, Henry ODwPR 91
Griggs, John Alavan 1941- WhoE 91
Griggs, John Robert 1949- WhoEmL 91
Griggs, John Wilbur 1948- WhoEmL 91
Griggs, John William 1849-1927 BiDrUSE 89
Griggs, Katharine Miller 1943- WhoWor 91
Griggs, Laurin Baker 1933- St&PR 91
Griggs, Leonard LeRoy, Jr. 1931- WhoAm 90
Griggs, Maitland Lee BioIn 16
Griggs, Maitland Lee 1902-1989 WhoAmA 91N
Griggs, Mary ConAu 131
Griggs, Phyllis Kay 1937- WhoAmW 91
Griggs, Robert Charles 1939- WhoAm 90
Griggs, Ron 1940- St&PR 91
Griggs, Stephen P. 1957- St&PR 91
Griggy, Kenneth Joseph 1934- St&PR 91, WhoAm 90
Grignani, Franco 1908- ConDes 90
Grignard, Victor 1871-1935 WorAlBi
Grigor, Margaret Christian 1912-1981 WhoAmA 91N
Grigorcea, Adrian Gabriel 1965- WhoE 91
Grigoriadis, Mary 1942?- BiDWomA, WhoAmA 91
Grigorian, Haikaz M 1927- BiDrAPA 89
Grigorian, Meline 1958- WhoAmW 91
Grigoriu, Theodor 1926- IntWWM 90
Grigsbay, Charles T. 1939- St&PR 91
Grigsby, Chester Poole, Jr. 1929- St&PR 91, WhoSSW 91, WhoWor 91
Grigsby, Daryl Russell 1955- WhoWrEP 89
Grigsby, Della 1950- IntWWM 90
Grigsby, E.K. 1939- St&PR 91
Grigsby, Gordon 1927- WhoWrEP 89
Grigsby, Henry Jefferson, Jr. 1930- WhoAm 90
Grigsby, Jack Webster 1923- St&PR 91
Grigsby, James Alfred A. 1942- St&PR 91
Grigsby, Jefferson Eugene, Jr. 1918- WhoAm 90, WhoAmA 91
Grigsby, John Lee 1951- WhoSSW 91
Grigsby, John Lynn 1924- WhoAm 90
Grigsby, Lonnie Oscar 1939- WhoAm 90
Grigsby, Margaret Elizabeth 1923- WhoAm 90, WhoAmW 91
Grigsby, Marshall C. 1946- WhoAm 90
Grigsby, Richard Paul 1954- St&PR 91
Grigsby-Stephens, Klaron 1952- WhoAmW 91
Grigson, Geoffrey 1905-1985 AuBYP 90, ConAu 33NR, MajTwCW
Grigson, Geoffrey Edward Harvey 1905-1985 DcNaB 1981
Grigson, James P. 1932- BioIn 16
Grigson, James Paul 1932- BiDrAPA 89
Grigson, Jane 1928- SmATA 63
Grigson, Jane 1928-1990 BioIn 16, ConAu 131
Grijalva, Michelle Armijo 1953- WhoHisp 91
Grijpink, Johannes Henricus A.M. 1946- WhoWor 91
Griles, J. Steven 1947- WhoAm 90
Griley, Theodore D. 1932- St&PR 91
Griliches, Zvi 1930- WhoAm 90
Grilikhes, Michel BioIn 16
Grill, Andries PenDiDA 89
Grill, Anthony 1600-1675 PenDiDA 89
Grill, Donald A. 1932- St&PR 91
Grill, Johannes 1614-1678 PenDiDA 89
Grill, Lawrence J. 1936- WhoAm 90
Grill, Linda 1938- WhoHisp 91
Grill, Magnus 1945- WhoWor 91
Griller Quartet PenDiMP
Griller, David 1948- WhoAm 90
Griller, Sidney 1911- PenDiMP
Griller, Sidney Aaron 1911- IntWWM 90
Grillet, Alain Robbe- 1922- BioIn 16
Grillet, Pierre Antoine 1941- WhoSSW 91
Grilli, Chloe Lenore WhoWrEP 89
Grilli, Steve 1949- Ballpl 90
Grilliot, Mary I. 1954- St&PR 91
Grilliot, William Lawrence 1949- St&PR 91
Grillis, Lucas Chris 1931- St&PR 91
Grillo, Cecilia Meireles 1901-1964 BioIn 16
Grillo, Esther Angela 1954- WhoAmA 91

Grillo, Hermes Conrad 1923- *WhoAm 90*
Grillo, J. Ed 1870-1920 *Ballpl 90*
Grillo, James Thomas 1950- *WhoEmL 91*
Grillo, Janet *St&PR 91*
Grillo, Joann 1939- *IntWWM 90*
Grillo, Joseph M. 1949- *ODwPR 91*
Grillo, Louis Vincent 1951- *WhoE 91*
Grillo, Robert Alfred, Jr. *BiDrAPA 89*
Grillos, John J. 1947- *St&PR 91*
Grillparzer, Franz 1791-1872 *WorAlBi*
Grills, George B. 1940- *St&PR 91*
Grim, Bob 1930- *Ballpl 90*
Grim, Eugene Donald 1922- *WhoAm 90*
Grim, J. Lawrence, Jr. 1933- *St&PR 91*
Grim, Kathleen M. 1952- *ODwPR 91*
Grim, Patricia Ann 1940- *WhoAmW 91*
Grim, Samuel Oram 1935- *WhoAm 90*
Grim, Shelle K. 1955- *St&PR 91*
Grim, William Edward 1955- *IntWWM 90*
Grimaila, Patricia Perpetua 1928- *WhoAmW 91*
Grimaldi, Alberto 1927- *ConTFT 8*
Grimaldi, Andrew C. 1935- *St&PR 91*
Grimaldi, Anthony Eugene 1950- *WhoAmA 91*
Grimaldi, Anthony Julio 1933- *St&PR 91*
Grimaldi, Edmond Anthony 1948- *WhoE 91*
Grimaldi, James Thomas 1928- *WhoSSW 91*
Grimaldi, Jean-Marie de 1796-1874 *BioIn 16*
Grimaldi, John A R, Jr. 1952- *BiDrAPA 89*
Grimaldi, John P. 1944- *ODwPR 91*
Grimaldi, Juan de 1796-1874 *BioIn 16*
Grimaldi, Nicholas Lawrence 1950- *WhoAm 90*
Grimaldi, Nicolo *PenDiMP*
Grimaud, Maurice 1913- *BiDFrPL*
Grimaud, Michel 1945- *ConAu 129*
Grimball, Caroline Gordon 1946- *WhoSSW 91*
Grimball, Edward B. 1944- *St&PR 91*
Grimball, William Heyward 1917- *WhoAm 90*
Grimble, Charles James *MajTwCW*
Grimes, Burleigh 1893-1985 *Ballpl 90 [port]*
Grimes, Burton Piper 1909- *BiDrAPA 89*
Grimes, Connie Carr 1960- *WhoAmW 91*
Grimes, Dale Mills 1926- *WhoAm 90*
Grimes, David Lynn 1947- *WhoAm 90, WhoSSW 91*
Grimes, Don W. 1944- *St&PR 91*
Grimes, Donald Joe 1936- *WhoE 91*
Grimes, Ev 1947- *IntWWM 90*
Grimes, Frances T 1869-1963 *WhoAmA 91N*
Grimes, Frank 1891-1961 *BioIn 16*
Grimes, Geoffrey C. 1946- *WhoEmL 91*
Grimes, Howard Ray 1918- *St&PR 91, WhoAm 90*
Grimes, Howard Warren 1922- *WhoE 91*
Grimes, Hugh Gavin 1929- *WhoAm 90*
Grimes, J. William *BioIn 16*
Grimes, James Alan 1948- *St&PR 91*
Grimes, John Frank, III 1947- *WhoSSW 91*
Grimes, Joseph Edward 1941- *WhoWor 91*
Grimes, Joseph Rudolph 1923- *WhoWor 91*
Grimes, Katherine E *BiDrAPA 89*
Grimes, Kathleen Josephine *WhoE 91*
Grimes, Lenna Juanita 1928- *WhoAmW 91*
Grimes, Leonard Eugene 1938- *WhoSSW 91*
Grimes, Lloyd 1916-1989 *BioIn 16*
Grimes, Lloyd Malcolm, Jr. 1914- *WhoSSW 91*
Grimes, Margaret Katherine 1955- *WhoAmW 91*
Grimes, Margaret W *WhoAmA 91*
Grimes, Martha *MajTwCW, TwCCr&M 91, WhoAmW 91, WorAlBi*
Grimes, Mary Anne 1936- *WhoAmW 91*
Grimes, Mary Catherine *WhoE 91*
Grimes, Mary Loftin 1933- *WhoSSW 91*
Grimes, Mary Phyllis 1946- *WhoSSW 91*
Grimes, Melissa *BioIn 16*
Grimes, Michael Duane 1946- *WhoSSW 91*
Grimes, Nikki *BioIn 16*
Grimes, Nikki 1950- *WhoWrEP 89*
Grimes, Oscar 1915- *Ballpl 90*
Grimes, Patricia Strahota 1951- *WhoAmW 91*
Grimes, Paul Lonsdale 1917- *IntWWM 90*
Grimes, Peter 1938- *WhoSSW 91*
Grimes, Ray 1893-1953 *Ballpl 90*
Grimes, Richard Allen 1929- *WhoSSW 91*
Grimes, Robert C. 1923- *St&PR 91*
Grimes, Robert O. 1920- *St&PR 91*
Grimes, Russell Newell 1935- *WhoAm 90, WhoSSW 91*
Grimes, Ruth Elaine 1949- *WhoAmW 91, WhoWor 91*
Grimes, Sandra Ruth *BiDrAPA 89*
Grimes, Stephen Henry 1927- *WhoAm 90, WhoSSW 91*
Grimes, William 1905-1988 *AnObit 1988*
Grimes, William Alvan 1911- *WhoAm 90*
Grimke, Angelina E. 1805-1879 *BioAmW*
Grimke, Angelina Emily 1805-1879 *BioIn 16, FemiCLE, WorAlBi*
Grimke, Angelina Weld 1880-1958 *EarBlAP, FemiCLE, HarlReB [port]*
Grimke, Charlotte 1837-1914 *FemiCLE*
Grimke, Sarah M. 1792-1873 *BioAmW*
Grimke, Sarah Moore 1792-1873 *BioIn 16, FemiCLE, WorAlBi*
Grimland, John Martin, Jr. 1917- *WhoSSW 91*
Grimley, Cynthia Patrizi 1958- *WhoAmW 91*
Grimley, Jeffrey Michael 1957- *WhoEmL 91*
Grimley, Liam Kelly 1936- *WhoAm 90*
Grimley, Oliver Fetterolf 1920- *WhoAmA 91*
Grimley, Robert G. 1940- *St&PR 91*
Grimley, Slater Samuel 1921- *WhoAm 90*
Grimm, Ben Emmet 1924- *WhoAm 90*
Grimm, Billy Charles 1938- *WhoSSW 91*
Grimm, Charles E. 1943- *St&PR 91*
Grimm, Charlie 1898-1983 *Ballpl 90 [port]*
Grimm, Dan K. 1949- *WhoAm 90*
Grimm, Donald E. 1930- *St&PR 91*
Grimm, Edgar C. *ODwPR 91*
Grimm, Goetz 1928- *St&PR 91*
Grimm, Hans 1875-1959 *BioIn 16*
Grimm, Jacob 1785-1863 *BioIn 16*
Grimm, Jacob Ludwig Carl 1785-1863 *WorAlBi*
Grimm, Jakob Ludwig Karl 1785-1863 *AuBYP 90*
Grimm, James R. 1935- *WhoAm 90*
Grimm, James Timothy *BiDrAPA 89*
Grimm, James Timothy 1956- *WhoE 91*
Grimm, Jay Vaughn 1926- *St&PR 91*
Grimm, John Francis 1939- *St&PR 91*
Grimm, Kathleen 1946- *WhoAmW 91*
Grimm, Kurt Ross 1953- *WhoEmL 91*
Grimm, Lloyd Richard 1934- *St&PR 91*
Grimm, Louis John 1933- *WhoAm 90*
Grimm, Lucille Davis 1929- *WhoAmA 91*
Grimm, Nancy Beth 1955- *WhoEmL 91*
Grimm, Nancy R *BiDrAPA 89*
Grimm, Paul Edward 1931- *St&PR 91*
Grimm, Paula 1950- *WhoAmW 91*
Grimm, Peter Michael 1942- *St&PR 91*
Grimm, Raymond Max 1924- *WhoAmA 91*
Grimm, Reinhold 1931- *WhoAm 90*
Grimm, Robert 1915- *St&PR 91*
Grimm, Roland D. 1926- *St&PR 91*
Grimm, Roland DuBois 1926- *WhoAm 90*
Grimm, Rolf 1936- *WhoWor 91*
Grimm, Rudi Friedrich Wilhelm 1947- *WhoWor 91*
Grimm, Thomas L. *St&PR 91*
Grimm, Victor E. 1937- *WhoAm 90*
Grimm, Walter B. 1945- *St&PR 91*
Grimm, Wilhelm 1786-1859 *BioIn 16*
Grimm, Wilhelm Carl 1786-1859 *WorAlBi*
Grimm, Wilhelm Karl 1786-1859 *AuBYP 90*
Grimm, Willard T. 1902- *St&PR 91*
Grimm, William Arthur 1939- *St&PR 91*
Grimm-Richardson, Anna Louise 1927- *WhoWrEP 89*
Grimmeiss, Hermann Georg 1930- *WhoWor 91*
Grimmell, Karen Ethel *BiDrAPA 89*
Grimmer, Jerome *BioIn 16*
Grimmer, John C. *St&PR 91*
Grimmer, Margot 1944- *WhoAmW 91*
Grimmer, Mineko 1949- *WhoAmA 91*
Grimmett, Gerald Glen 1942- *WhoWrEP 89*
Grimmett, Howard Hill 1949- *WhoEmL 91*
Grimmig, Robert John 1928- *St&PR 91*
Grims-Land, Ebbe B. V. 1915- *IntWWM 90*
Grimshaw, Donald Harvey 1923- *WhoWor 91*
Grimshaw, James Albert, Jr. 1940- *WhoSSW 91*
Grimshaw, Thomas Drysdale 1933- *WhoWrEP 89*
Grimsley, James Alexander, Jr. 1921- *WhoAm 90, WhoSSW 91*
Grimsley, James Edward 1927- *WhoAm 90*
Grimsley, Ross 1950- *Ballpl 90*
Grimsley, Will Henry 1914- *WhoAm 90, WhoWrEP 89*
Grimsley, William Elmer, Jr. 1943- *WhoSSW 91*
Grimson, Todd 1952- *ConAu 129*
Grimsrud, Lars Gudmund 1956- *WhoEmL 91*
Grimsson, Stefan Hordur 1920- *DcScanL*
Grimston, Elizabeth *BioIn 16*
Grimur Thorgrimsson Thomsen *DcScanL*
Grimwade, R. Reed 1929- *St&PR 91*
Grin, S. Spencer 1928- *WhoAm 90, WhoWor 91*
Grina, Kenneth Ivreson 1923- *WhoE 91*
Grinager, Alexander 1865-1949 *WhoAmA 91N*
Grinberg, Meyer Stewart 1944- *WhoE 91, WhoWor 91*
Grinberg, Michael Mark 1950- *BiDrAPA 89*
Grinblat, Joseph Alfred 1944- *WhoE 91*
Grinde, Kjell 1929- *WhoWor 91*
Grinde, Nils 1927- *IntWWM 90*
Grinde, Ralph Wayne 1943- *St&PR 91*
Grindea, Carola *IntWWM 90*
Grindea, Daniel 1924- *St&PR 91, WhoAm 90, WhoWor 91*
Grindea, Nadia Myra 1943- *IntWWM 90*
Grindinger, Lawrence Lee, Sr. 1943- *WhoSSW 91*
Grindlay, Jonathan Ellis 1944- *WhoAm 90*
Grindle, Barbara S. 1955- *WhoAmW 91*
Grindle, Robert Gail 1924- *St&PR 91*
Grindle, Vernon Fred 1955- *WhoEmL 91*
Grindley, Mitchell P. 1959- *St&PR 91*
Grindley, Robert B. 1929- *St&PR 91*
Grindlinger, Jonathan Levi *BiDrAPA 89*
Grindstaff, Douglas *BioIn 16*
Grine, Donald Reaville 1930- *WhoAm 90*
Grinell, Sheila 1945- *WhoAm 90*
Griner, Dan 1888-1950 *Ballpl 90*
Griner, Jimmy Wayne 1949- *WhoSSW 91*
Griner, Kenneth Edward 1948- *WhoSSW 91*
Griner, Ned H 1928- *WhoAmA 91*
Griner, Norman 1932- *WhoE 91*
Griner, Paul Francis 1933- *WhoAm 90*
Griner, Terry Wyn 1947- *St&PR 91*
Gring, David M. 1945- *WhoAm 90*
Gringer, Donald 1933- *St&PR 91*
Gringhuis, Dirk *AuBYP 90*
Gringhuis, Richard H. 1918-1974 *AuBYP 90*
Grings, William 1918- *WhoAm 90*
Grinke, Frederick 1911-1987 *PenDiMP*
Grinker, Morton 1928- *WhoWrEP 89*
Grinker, Roy R, Jr. 1927- *BiDrAPA 89*
Grinker, Roy R, Sr. 1900- *BiDrAPA 89*
Grinker, Roy Richard, Jr. 1927- *WhoAm 90*
Grinker, Roy Richard, Sr. 1900- *WhoAm 90*
Grinker, Susan Ann 1948- *St&PR 91*
Grinker, William Stephen 1934- *St&PR 91, WhoE 91*
Grinkmeyer, Kerry John 1944- *WhoSSW 91*
Grinko, Sigmund John 1924- *St&PR 91*
Grinkov, Sergei *BioIn 16*
Grinnan, Richardson 1940- *St&PR 91*
Grinnell, Alan Dale 1936- *WhoAm 90*
Grinnell, David *AuBYP 90*
Grinnell, Gary Shawn 1952- *WhoWor 91*
Grinnell, George Bird 1849-1938 *BioIn 16, WhNaAH, WorAlBi*
Grinnell, John 1936- *St&PR 91*
Grinnell, Laurence M. *ODwPR 91*
Grinnell, Sheldon W 1928- *BiDrAPA 89*
Grinney, Jay 1951 *WhoSSW 91*
Grinols, Donald R *BiDrAPA 89*
Grinspoon, Lester 1928- *BiDrAPA 89*
Grinstead, David Alan 1921- *St&PR 91*
Grinstead, Eugene Andrews 1923- *WhoAm 90*
Grinstead, Michele R. 1961- *St&PR 91*
Grinstead, William Carter, Jr. 1930- *WhoAm 90*
Grinstein, Alberto *BiDrAPA 89*
Grinstein, Alexander 1918- *BiDrAPA 89*
Grinstein, Gerald 1932- *St&PR 91, WhoAm 90, WhoSSW 91*
Grinstein Richman, Louise Sonia 1929- *WhoE 91*
Grioni, John Sergio 1938- *WhoWor 91*
Grip, Carl Manfred, Jr. 1921- *WhoAm 90*
Gripari, Pierre 1925- *ConAu 31NR*
Gripe, Maria K. 1923- *AuBYP 90*
Gripenberg, Bertil 1878-1947 *DcScanL*
Gripon, Edward Brown 1943- *BiDrAPA 89*
Grippe, Florence 1912- *WhoAmA 91*
Grippe, Florence Berg 1912- *WhoE 91*
Grippe, Peter 1912- *WhoAmA 91*
Gripper, Norma Jean 1940- *WhoSSW 91*
Grippi, Salvatore William 1921- *WhoAm 90, WhoAmA 91*
Grippin, Eugene W. 1931- *St&PR 91*
Gris, Charles Edouard Jeanneret- 1887-1965 *BioIn 16*
Gris, Juan 1887-1927 *BioIn 16, IntDcAA 90*
Grisanti, Anthony F. 1949- *St&PR 91*
Grisanti, Eugene Philip 1929- *St&PR 91, WhoAm 90*
Griscom, Frank Norris, III 1946- *WhoEmL 91*
Griscom, Lloyd Carpenter 1872-1959 *BioIn 16*
Griscom, Nina *BioIn 16*
Griscom, Thomas C. *ODwPR 91*
Griscom, Thomas Cecil 1949- *WhoAm 90*
Grise, Wilma Marie 1937- *WhoAmW 91, WhoWor 91*
Griseuk, Gail Gentry 1948- *WhoAmW 91, WhoEmL 91*
Grisez, Germain G. 1929- *WhoWrEP 89*
Grisham, Edith Pearl Moles 1926- *WhoAmW 91*
Grisham, Joe Wheeler 1931- *WhoAm 90, WhoWor 91*
Grisham, Judith Ann 1949- *WhoAmW 91, WhoSSW 91*
Grisham, Richard Bond 1945- *WhoSSW 91*
Grisham, Sandra Ann 1949- *WhoEmL 91*
Grishchenko, Anatoly *NewYTBS 90*
Grisi, Arthur John 1952- *St&PR 91*
Grisi, Giuditta 1805-1840 *PenDiMP*
Grisi, Giulia 1811-1869 *PenDiMP*
Griskey, Richard George 1931- *WhoAm 90*
Grismer, Joseph F *BiDrAPA 89*
Grismer, William J. 1929- *St&PR 91*
Grisolia, Beatriz *BiDrAPA 89*
Grispino, Maria Genevieve 1954- *WhoAmW 91*
Grissinger, James Adams *WhoAm 90*
Grissom, Beverly McMurtry 1946- *WhoAmW 91*
Grissom, Charles Austin, Jr. 1954- *WhoEmL 91*
Grissom, Eugene Edward 1922- *WhoAmA 91*
Grissom, Freda Gill *WhoAmA 91*
Grissom, Garth Clyde 1930- *WhoAm 90*
Grissom, Hubert 1942- *BioIn 16*
Grissom, J. David 1938- *St&PR 91*
Grissom, J. David 1939- *WhoAm 90*
Grissom, Joseph Carol 1931- *WhoAm 90*
Grissom, Kimberly Diane 1963- *WhoAmW 91*
Grissom, Lee 1907- *Ballpl 90*
Grissom, Lee Alan 1942- *WhoAm 90*
Grissom, Marv 1918- *Ballpl 90*
Grissom, Patsy Coleen 1934- *WhoAmW 91*
Grissom, Stephen David 1952- *St&PR 91*
Grissom, Steven Edward 1949- *WhoWrEP 89*
Grissom, Virgil I. 1926-1967 *WorAlBi*
Grist, Bill M. 1946- *WhoSSW 91*
Grist, Reri *DrBlPA 90*
Grist, Reri 1932- *BioIn 16, IntWWM 90, PenDiMP*
Griswold, Benjamin H., III 1911- *St&PR 91*
Griswold, Denny *WhoAm 90, WhoE 91*
Griswold, Erwin Nathaniel 1904- *WhoAm 90, WhoWor 91*
Griswold, Francis Hopkins 1904-1989 *BioIn 16*
Griswold, Frank Tracy, III 1937- *WhoAm 90*
Griswold, Frederick Daniel 1929- *St&PR 91*
Griswold, Gary Norris 1947- *WhoE 91, WhoEmL 91*
Griswold, George *ConAu 130*
Griswold, George 1919- *WhoSSW 91*
Griswold, James Francis 1940- *BiDrAPA 89*
Griswold, Jerome 1947- *ConAu 130*
Griswold, Kent Carrier 1958- *WhoEmL 91*
Griswold, Laura *ODwPR 91*
Griswold, Norman H. 1929- *St&PR 91*
Griswold, Richard Bruce 1947- *St&PR 91, WhoEmL 91*
Griswold, Richard Merle 1931- *St&PR 91*
Griswold, Robert L 1924- *BiDrAPA 89*
Griswold, Rufus Wilmot 1815-1857 *BioIn 16*
Griswold, Valerie Anne 1962- *WhoAmW 91*
Griswold, Wait R 1912- *BiDrAPA 89*
Griswold, William G. 1949- *St&PR 91*
Griswold, William Tudor, II 1921- *St&PR 91*
Griswold del Castillo, Richard A. 1942- *WhoHisp 91*
Gritse-Milliex, Tatiana *EncCoWW*
Gritsi-Milliex, Tatiana 1920- *EncCoWW*
Gritter, Gordon W 1927- *BiDrAPA 89*
Gritti, Francesco Martino 1937- *WhoWor 91*
Grittman, Ronald 1933- *St&PR 91*
Gritton, Eugene Charles 1941- *WhoAm 90*
Gritton, Patricia Bauman 1916- *WhoAmW 91*
Gritton, Robin William Langford 1939- *IntWWM 90*
Gritz, Elliott 1961- *BiDrAPA 89*
Gritz, Louis 1925- *St&PR 91*
Gritzmann, Peter 1943- *WhoWor 91*
Grivalsky, Eleanor Ann 1944- *WhoAmW 91*
Grivas, Theodore 1922- *WhoAm 90*
Grivna, Howard Walter 1934- *St&PR 91*
Grizi, Samir Amine 1942- *WhoWor 91*
Grizo, Aleksander 1920- *WhoWor 91*
Grizzard, Lewis *BioIn 16*

Grizzard, Lewis 1946- *ConAu 129, MajTwCW, NewYTBS 90 [port]*
Grizzell, June Laverne 1937- *WhoSSW 91*
Grizzle, J. David 1954- *St&PR 91*
Grizzle, James Ennis 1930- *WhoAm 90*
Grizzle, Jerry W. 1953- *St&PR 91*
Grizzle, Mary R. 1921- *WhoAmW 91, WhoSSW 91*
Grizzle, Rhonda Mewborn 1952- *WhoAmW 91*
Groah, Linda Kay 1942- *WhoAmW 91*
Groark, David P. 1946- *St&PR 91*
Groark, Thomas J., Jr. 1937- *WhoAm 90*
Groat, Dick 1930- *Ballpl 90 [port]*
Groat, Hall Pierce 1932- *WhoAmA 91*
Groat, Hall Pierce, II 1967- *WhoAmA 91*
Groat, Linda Noel 1946- *WhoEmL 91*
Groat, Robin R. 1930- *WhoAmW 91*
Groat, Ronald Douglas 1951- *BiDrAPA 89*
Grob, Bruce Russell 1951- *WhoSSW 91*
Grob, Charles Stephen 1950- *BiDrAPA 89*
Grob, Gerald N. 1931- *WhoAm 90, WhoWrEP 89*
Groban, Mark David 1941- *BiDrAPA 89*
Grobe, Albert A. *BioIn 16, NewYTBS 90 [port]*
Grobe, Charles Stephen 1935- *WhoAm 90*
Grobe, Kenneth A. 1927- *St&PR 91*
Grobe, William Howard 1916- *WhoWor 91*
Grobel, Lawrence 1947- *ConAu 131*
Grobelny, Julian 1893-1944 *BioIn 16*
Grobelny, Lori Jo-Ann 1954- *WhoAmW 91*
Groberg, James J. 1928- *St&PR 91*
Groberg, James Jay 1928- *WhoAm 90*
Grobety, Anne-Lise 1949- *EncCoWW*
Groble, Robert Edward 1943- *BiDrAPA 89*
Grobman, Arnold Brams 1918- *WhoAm 90*
Grobman, Hulda Gross 1920- *WhoAm 90*
Grobman, Jerald *BiDrAPA 89*
Grobois, Brian S *BiDrAPA 89*
Grobois, Brian Saul 1957- *WhoE 91*
Grobowsky, George Erwin 1934- *St&PR 91*
Grobstein, Clifford 1916- *ConAu 130, WhoAm 90*
Groce, Ashleigh *BioIn 16*
Groce, Herbert Monroe, Jr. 1929- *WhoE 91*
Groce, James Freelan 1948- *WhoSSW 91*
Groce, Julie Carithers 1960- *WhoSSW 91*
Groce, Leroy 1927- *St&PR 91*
Groce, Steven Fred 1956- *WhoEmL 91*
Groce, William John 1947- *St&PR 91*
Groch, Judith 1929- *AuBYP 90*
Grochmal, Chuck *BioIn 16*
Grochoski, Gregory Thomas 1946- *St&PR 91*
Grocock, Robert 1925- *IntWWM 90*
Grodberg, Marcus Gordon 1923- *WhoE 91*
Grodd, Clifford 1924- *St&PR 91*
Grode, Redway *ConAu 30NR*
Grodecki, George 1930- *St&PR 91*
Grodecki, Mary Reginella 1912- *WhoAm 90, WhoSSW 91*
Groden, Gerald 1931- *WhoE 91*
Groden, Michael 1947- *ConAu 131*
Grodensky, Samuel 1894-1974 *WhoAmA 91N*
Grodhaus, Greg R. 1947- *St&PR 91*
Grodi, Michael Edward 1951- *WhoEmL 91*
Grodin, Charles *BioIn 16*
Grodin, Charles 1935- *WhoAm 90, WorAlBi*
Grodin, Douglas M 1942- *BiDrAPA 89*
Grodin, Joseph R. *BioIn 16*
Grodinsky, Jack 1923- *St&PR 91*
Grodnik, Daniel 1952- *St&PR 91*
Grodsky, David 1939- *BiDrAPA 89*
Grodsky, Gerold Morton 1927- *WhoAm 90*
Grody, Donald 1927- *WhoAm 90*
Grody, Mark S. 1938- *ODwPR 91*
Grody, Mark Stephen 1938- *WhoAm 90*
Groe, Antoinette Dianne 1949- *WhoEmL 91*
Groebel, Jo 1950- *WhoWor 91*
Groeber, David Paul 1935- *St&PR 91*
Groeber, Ronald Xavier 1949- *WhoEmL 91*
Groebli, Werner Fritz 1915- *WhoAm 90*
Groebner, Edgar F 1922- *BiDrAPA 89*
Groedel, Burt Jay 1937- *WhoAmA 91, WhoE 91*
Groefsema, Bruce Kenneth 1950- *St&PR 91*
Groeger, Joseph Herman 1925- *WhoAm 90*
Groeger, Lynne Ann 1960- *WhoEmL 91*
Groeger, Phyllis J. 1940- *St&PR 91*
Groell, Theophil 1932- *WhoAmA 91, WhoE 91*
Groemling, Robert Max 1930- *WhoSSW 91*
Groen, Frances K. *BioIn 16*
Groendyke, John *BioIn 16*
Groene, Beatrice M *BiDrAPA 89*
Groener, Harry 1951- *ConTFT 8 [port]*
Groeneveld, Wolf-Hinrich 1937- *WhoWor 91*
Groenewold, Hilbrand Johannes 1910- *WhoWor 91*
Groenewold, Kenneth Gene 1946- *St&PR 91*
Groening, Gert D. 1944- *WhoWor 91*
Groening, Matt *BioIn 16*
Groening, Matt 1954- *CurBio 90 [port], EncACom*
Groening, Matt 1955?- *News 90 [port]*
Groening, Matthew Akbar 1954- *WhoAm 90*
Groening, William Andrew, Jr. 1912- *WhoAm 90*
Groenink, Rijkman Willem Johan 1949- *WhoWor 91*
Groenke, Theodore A. 1921- *WhoAm 90*
Groennert, Charles Willis 1937- *St&PR 91, WhoAm 90*
Groennings, Sven Ole 1934- *WhoAm 90*
Groer, Hans Herrmann 1919- *WhoWor 91*
Groer, Maureen Wimberly 1944- *WhoSSW 91*
Groesbeck, Elise de Branges de Bourica 1936- *WhoAmW 91, WhoSSW 91, WhoWor 91*
Groeschel, August H. 1908-1989 *BioIn 16*
Groesschen, Heribert Johannes 1943- *WhoWor 91*
Groethe, Reed 1952- *WhoEmL 91*
Grof, Stanislav 1932- *EncPaPR 91*
Grofe, Ferde 1892-1972 *OxCPMus*
Grofe, Jerrold G 1927- *BiDrAPA 89*
Groff, Henry Clay 1957- *BiDrAPA 89*
Groff, Janet Yvonne 1954- *WhoEmL 91*
Groff, Jim *St&PR 91*
Groff, JoAnn 1956- *WhoAmW 91*
Groff, John *NewYTBS 90*
Groff, Jon P. 1939- *St&PR 91*
Groff, Kenelm A. 1929- *St&PR 91*
Groff, Pamela Joanne 1961- *WhoWrEP 89*
Groff, Raymond David 1933- *St&PR 91, WhoE 91*
Groff, Stephen Henry 1933- *BiDrAPA 89*
Groff, Wilhelm 1680?-1742 *PenDiDA 89*
Groft, Mary LaRue 1947- *WhoEmL 91*
Grogan, Alice Washington 1956- *WhoAmW 91, WhoEmL 91, WhoSSW 91*
Grogan, Bette Lowery 1931- *WhoAmW 91*
Grogan, Bob *BioIn 16*
Grogan, Donald W. 1947- *St&PR 91*
Grogan, Donald Wayne 1953- *BiDrAPA 89*
Grogan, Earlean Stanley 1922- *WhoWrEP 89*
Grogan, Hugh 1923- *WhoAm 90*
Grogan, James Tillman, Jr. 1938- *WhoSSW 91*
Grogan, John J. *St&PR 91*
Grogan, Kenneth Augustine 1924- *WhoAm 90*
Grogan, Kevin 1948- *WhoAm 90, WhoAmA 91*
Grogan, Michael John 1938- *WhoSSW 91*
Grogan, Rae 1954- *WhoAmW 91*
Grogan, Regina Louise 1949- *WhoE 91*
Grogan, Robert Edward 1914- *St&PR 91*
Grogan, Robert Harris 1933- *WhoSSW 91*
Grogan, Steven James 1953- *WhoAm 90*
Grogan, William Robert 1924- *WhoAm 90*
Grogg, James Royer 1934- *St&PR 91*
Grogg, R. C. 1967- *WhoWrEP 89*
Grogg, William Ross 1950- *WhoE 91*
Grogger, Paula 1892-1984 *EncCoWW*
Groh, Clifford John 1926- *WhoAm 90*
Groh, Heinie 1889-1968 *Ballpl 90 [port]*
Groh, Lucille Sider 1946- *WhoAmW 91*
Groh, Robert H 1913- *BiDrAPA 89*
Groh, Susan 1947- *WhoE 91*
Grohe, Guillaume 1808-1885 *PenDiDA 89*
Groher, Leslie 1952- *WhoE 91*
Grohman, Paul William, Jr. 1954- *WhoAm 90, WhoEmL 91*
Grohmann, Eckhart George 1936- *St&PR 91*
Grohne, Bob *BioIn 16*
Grohne, Douglas E. 1955- *WhoEmL 91*
Grohnke, Susan Kay 1944- *WhoAmW 91*
Grohol, Robert M. 1932- *St&PR 91*
Groholski, John S. 1939- *St&PR 91*
Grohs, Saul Ernest 1937- *St&PR 91*
Grohse, Edward William 1915- *WhoE 91*
Grohskopf, Bernice *WhoWrEP 89*
Grohskopf, Bernice 1921- *AuBYP 90*
Groiss, Fred George 1936- *WhoAm 90*
Grojsman, Sophia *BioIn 16*
Grold, L James 1932- *BiDrAPA 89*
Grolier, Jean 1479-1565 *PenDiDA 89*
Groll, Gary Steven 1954- *WhoE 91*
Groller, Richard 1955- *WhoSSW 91*
Grollmes, Eugene Edward 1931- *WhoWrEP 89*
Grolnick, Herbert Norman 1932- *St&PR 91, WhoAm 90*
Grolnick, Lawrence Ely 1933- *BiDrAPA 89*
Grolnick, Simon A 1930- *BiDrAPA 89*
Grom, Bogdan 1918- *WhoAmA 91*
Grom, George W. 1931- *St&PR 91*
Groman, Arthur 1914- *WhoAm 90*
Groman, Janice *BioIn 16*
Groman, Neal Benjamin 1921- *WhoAm 90*
Gromek, Steve 1920- *Ballpl 90*
Gromelski, Stanley John 1942- *WhoAm 90*
Gromen, Richard John 1930- *WhoAm 90*
Gromer, Frank Joseph, Jr. 1925- *WhoAm 90*
Gromfin, Herbert 1930- *St&PR 91*
Grommesh, Donald Joseph 1931- *St&PR 91, WhoAm 90*
Grommet, Allen Norman 1954- *WhoSSW 91*
Gromov, Boris *BioIn 16*
Gromyko, Andrei 1909-1989 *AnObit 1989, News 90*
Gromyko, Andrei Andreevich 1909-1989 *BioIn 16*
Gronauer, Clifford R. 1958- *WhoEmL 91*
Gronbach, Robert Charles 1928- *WhoE 91*
Gronbech, Vilhelm Peter 1873-1948 *DcScanL*
Gronbeck, Bruce E 1941- *ConAu 132*
Gronberg, John Eric 1955- *WhoSSW 91*
Gronborg, Erik 1931- *WhoAmA 91*
Groncki, Paul John 1949- *WhoAm 90, WhoEmL 91*
Gronda, Richard F. 1941- *St&PR 91*
Grondal, Benedikt Sveinbjarnarson 1826-1907 *DcScanL*
Grondin, Conrad A. 1926- *St&PR 91*
Grondin, Mary L. 1941- *WhoAmW 91*
Grondin, Robert J. 1936- *St&PR 91*
Grondine, Robert Francis 1952- *WhoWor 91*
Grone, James A. 1945- *St&PR 91*
Gronemeier, R. Gary 1935- *St&PR 91*
Groner, Beverly Anne 1922- *WhoAm 90, WhoWor 91*
Groner, David William 1955- *WhoEmL 91*
Groner, Michael Case *BiDrAPA 89*
Groner, Pat Neff 1920- *WhoAm 90*
Groner, Samuel Brian 1916- *WhoAm 90, WhoE 91, WhoWor 91*
Gronick, Patricia Ann Jacobsen 1931- *WhoAmW 91*
Groninger, Donald L. 1941- *St&PR 91*
Gronk 1954- *WhoAmA 91*
Gronlier, Juan F. 1951- *WhoHisp 91*
Gronlier, Juan Francisco 1951- *WhoSSW 91*
Gronniger, Kimberly Newton 1960- *WhoAmW 91*
Gronning, Lloyd Joseph 1951 *WhoEmL 91*
Gronningsater, Eric Anton 1952- *WhoE 91*
Gronon, Rose *EncCoWW*
Gronouski, John A. 1919- *BiDrUSE 89*
Gronowicz, Antoni 1913-1985 *AuBYP 90*
Gronowitz, Salo Schmul 1928- *WhoWor 91*
Gronquist, Richard A. 1935- *ODwPR 91*
Gronski, Robert L. 1950- *WhoE 91*
Gronvall, John A. *NewYTBS 90*
Groobert, David 1965- *ODwPR 91*
Groody, Louise 1897-1961 *OxCPMus*
Groom, Bob 1884-1948 *Ballpl 90*
Groom, Dale 1912- *WhoAm 90*
Groom, Denis J. 1932- *WhoAm 90*
Groom, Donald Joseph 1947- *WhoE 91*
Groom, Gary L. 1946- *St&PR 91*
Groom, Gary Lee 1946- *WhoAm 90*
Groom, John Miller 1936- *WhoAm 90*
Groom, Joseph Douglas 1934- *WhoSSW 91*
Groom, Lester Herbert 1929- *IntWWM 90*
Groom, Winston 1944- *BioIn 16*
Groombridge, Walter Stanley 1913- *WhoAmA 91*
Groome, L.D. 1908- *St&PR 91*
Groome, Reginald K. 1927- *St&PR 91, WhoAm 90*
Groome, Sally Lucynthia 1936- *WhoAmW 91*
Groomer, Cindy Lee 1956- *WhoSSW 91*
Groomer, Vera MacKinnon 1915- *BioIn 16*
Grooms, Harlan Hobart 1900- *WhoAm 90*
Grooms, Jack D. 1934- *St&PR 91*
Grooms, Mary Ella Hicks 1926- *WhoAmW 91, WhoE 91*
Grooms, Red 1937- *WhoAm 90, WhoAmA 91*
Grooms, Suzanne Simmons 1945- *WhoAmW 91, WhoEmL 91, WhoSSW 91*
Grooms, Vickie Lynn 1955- *WhoSSW 91*
Groos, Arthur Bernhard, Jr. 1943- *WhoAm 90*
Groos, Richard T. 1929- *St&PR 91*
Groosman, Ernest Florimond 1917- *WhoWor 91*
Groot, Candice Beth 1954- *WhoAmA 91*
Groot, Maria de 1937- *EncCoWW*
Groote, Philip de *PenDiMP*
Groothof, William A *BiDrAPA 89*
Groothuis, Douglas Richard 1957- *WhoEmL 91*
Groothuis, Richard Bernard 1937- *St&PR 91*
Grootveld, John E. *St&PR 91*
Groover, Jan 1943- *WhoAmA 91*
Gropius, Walter 1883-1969 *BioIn 16, PenDiDA 89, WorAlBi*
Gropp, Louis Oliver 1935- *WhoAm 90, WhoWrEP 89*
Gropp, Walter Edward 1930- *St&PR 91*
Gropp, William 1914- *WhoWor 91*
Groppa, Carlos G. 1931- *WhoWrEP 89*
Gropper, Allan Louis 1944- *WhoAm 90*
Gropper, Cathy 1949- *WhoAmA 91*
Gropper, Edward 1920- *St&PR 91*
Gropper, William 1897-1977 *EncAL, WhoAmA 91N*
Groppi, James E. 1930-1985 *BioIn 16*
Gros, Daniel 1955- *WhoWor 91*
Gros Louis, Kenneth Richard Russell 1936- *WhoAm 90, WhoWor 91*
Grosbard, Ulu *BioIn 16*
Grosbard, Ulu 1929- *WhoAm 90*
Grosby, Herbert Leon 1919- *St&PR 91*
Grosch, Herbert Reuben John 1918- *WhoWor 91*
Grosch, Laura 1945- *WhoAmA 91*
Grosch, William Neil 1944- *BiDrAPA 89*
Grose, B. Donald 1943- *WhoAm 90, WhoWrEP 89*
Grose, David E. 1952- *St&PR 91*
Grose, Donald Gene 1935- *St&PR 91*
Grose, Robert Freeman 1924- *WhoAm 90*
Grose, Robert Warfield 1941- *WhoAm 90*
Grose, Thomas Lucius Trowbridge 1924- *WhoAm 90*
Grose, William Rush 1939- *WhoAm 90*
Groseclose, Everett Harrison 1938- *WhoAm 90*
Groseclose, Jay C. 1951- *WhoWor 91*
Groseclose, Kel 1940- *ConAu 32NR*
Groseclose, William H. 1930- *St&PR 91*
Groseilliers, Medard Chouart, Sieur Des 1618?-1697? *WhNaAH*
Groseilliers, Medart Chouart, Sieur De 1625?-1697? *EncCRAm*
Grosenbaugh, Clare Henry *BiDrAPA 89*
Grosfeld, Jay Lazar 1935- *WhoAm 90*
Grosh, Doris Lloyd 1924- *WhoAmW 91*
Groshans, Werner 1913-1986 *WhoAmA 91N*
Groshek, Michael Dean 1932- *WhoAm 90*
Groshner, Maria Star 1961- *WhoAmW 91*
Groshong, Claudia Clark 1949- *WhoAmW 91*
Grosklaus, James G. 1935- *WhoAm 90, WhoSSW 91*
Grosland, Emery Layton 1929- *WhoAm 90*
Groslier, Bernard Philippe 1926-1986 *BioIn 16*
Grosman, Haika 1919- *BioIn 16*
Gross, Abraham 1928- *WhoAm 90*
Gross, Al 1918- *WhoAm 90*
Gross, Alan 1947- *BioIn 16*
Gross, Alice *WhoAmA 91*
Gross, Anthony 1905-1984 *DcNaB 1981*
Gross, Arthur J 1926- *BiDrAPA 89*
Gross, Arye *ConTFT 8*
Gross, Barbara Elizabeth Rudd *WhoAmW 91*
Gross, Barry M. 1941- *WhoE 91*
Gross, Benjamin L *BiDrAPA 89*
Gross, Carey Clayton *BiDrAPA 89*
Gross, Carol Cott 1942- *WhoWrEP 89*
Gross, Carol Jane 1949- *WhoWrEP 89*
Gross, Caroline Lord 1940- *WhoAmW 91, WhoE 91*
Gross, Chaim 1904- *WhoAmA 91*
Gross, Charles Gordon 1936- *WhoAm 90*
Gross, Charles H. *BioIn 16*
Gross, Charles Meridith 1952- *WhoEmL 91*
Gross, Charles Merrill 1935- *WhoAmA 91*
Gross, Charles Wayne 1930- *WhoAm 90*
Gross, David Andrew 1954- *WhoEmL 91*
Gross, David Arlen 1947- *BiDrAPA 89*
Gross, David Danforth 1949- *St&PR 91, WhoEmL 91*
Gross, David E. 1937- *St&PR 91*
Gross, David Earl *BiDrAPA 89*
Gross, David J. 1958- *WhoE 91*
Gross, David Jonathan 1941- *WhoAm 90*
Gross, David Lee 1943- *WhoAm 90*
Gross, David P 1922- *BiDrAPA 89*
Gross, David R. 1950- *St&PR 91*
Gross, David Richard 1950- *WhoAm 90*
Gross, Dennis S. 1958- *St&PR 91*
Gross, Don 1931- *Ballpl 90*
Gross, Don Hargrave 1923- *EncO&P 3*
Gross, Donald 1947- *WhoE 91*
Gross, Douglas H. 1943- *St&PR 91*
Gross, Earl 1899- *WhoAmA 91*
Gross, Edmund Samuel 1950- *WhoEmL 91*
Gross, Edward *WhoAm 90*
Gross, Elissa Frances 1954- *WhoAmA 91*
Gross, Eric T. B. 1901-1988 *BioIn 16*
Gross, Ernest Arnold 1906- *WhoAm 90*
Gross, Estelle Shane *WhoAmA 91*
Gross, Esther Moneysmith 1936- *WhoWrEP 89*

Gross, Evelyn Rosenberg 1926- *WhoAmW 91*
Gross, Feliks 1906- *WhoE 91, WhoWor 91*
Gross, Fritz A. 1910- *WhoAm 90*
Gross, George A 1923- *BiDrAPA 89*
Gross, George Raymond Farrow 1956- *WhoEmL 91*
Gross, Greg 1952- *Ballpl 90*
Gross, Gregory M. 1952- *St&PR 91*
Gross, Hal Raymond 1914- *WhoAm 90*
Gross, Harriet P. Marcus 1934- *WhoAmW 91, WhoSSW 91*
Gross, Harriet Sharon *BiDrAPA 89*
Gross, Harriet Sharon 1958- *WhoEmL 91*
Gross, Harvey 1922- *St&PR 91*
Gross, Henry 1949- *WhoE 91, WhoEmL 91*
Gross, Herbert S 1933- *BiDrAPA 89*
Gross, Herbert S 1935- *BiDrAPA 89*
Gross, Howard Alan 1944- *BiDrAPA 89*
Gross, Irwin 1934- *WhoE 91*
Gross, Irwin Lee 1943- *WhoE 91*
Gross, Jack 1910- *St&PR 91*
Gross, James Dehnert 1929- *WhoAm 90*
Gross, James Paul 1949- *WhoAm 90*
Gross, Jeanne Bilger 1925- *WhoAmW 91, WhoWor 91*
Gross, Jenard Morris 1929- *WhoWor 91*
Gross, Jerome 1917- *WhoAm 90*
Gross, Jerry *BioIn 16*
Gross, Jerry M. 1935- *St&PR 91*
Gross, Joan S *BiDrAPA 89*
Gross, Joan S. 1936- *WhoE 91*
Gross, Joel 1951- *ConAu 31NR*
Gross, Joel Edward 1939- *WhoE 91, WhoWor 91*
Gross, John Birney 1924- *WhoAm 90*
Gross, John E. 1936- *St&PR 91*
Gross, John F. 1942- *St&PR 91*
Gross, John Jacob 1935- *WhoWor 91*
Gross, John Richard 1931- *St&PR 91*
Gross, Jonathan Light 1941- *WhoAm 90, WhoE 91*
Gross, Jonothon Ezra *BiDrAPA 89*
Gross, Joseph H. 1934- *WhoWor 91*
Gross, Joseph Nathan 1951- *WhoEmL 91*
Gross, Julia Ann 1957- *WhoAmW 91*
Gross, Julie 1959- *WhoE 91*
Gross, Kathleen Ann *BiDrAPA 89*
Gross, Kathy Ann 1951- *WhoEmL 91*
Gross, Kenneth A. 1946- *St&PR 91*
Gross, Kenneth Andrew 1951- *WhoE 91, WhoEmL 91*
Gross, Kenneth Irwin 1938- *WhoE 91*
Gross, Kenneth J. 1944- *St&PR 91*
Gross, Kevin 1961- *Ballpl 90*
Gross, Larry Paul 1942- *WhoAm 90*
Gross, Laura Ann 1948- *WhoAmW 91*
Gross, Laurie Carol 1953- *St&PR 91*
Gross, Laurie Sue 1964- *WhoAmW 91*
Gross, Lawrence Robert 1941- *St&PR 91*
Gross, Lawrence Stuart *BiDrAPA 89*
Gross, Leo 1903- *WhoE 91*
Gross, Leon Jay 1945- *WhoEmL 91*
Gross, Leonard 1928- *SpyFic*
Gross, Leonard 1930- *WhoE 91*
Gross, Leonard 1935- *St&PR 91*
Gross, Leroy 1926- *WhoAm 90*
Gross, Leslie Pamela 1952- *WhoAmW 91*
Gross, Lillian 1932- *BiDrAPA 89*
Gross, Linda Beth *BiDrAPA 89*
Gross, Liza Elisa 1957- *WhoHisp 91*
Gross, Louis 1930- *St&PR 91*
Gross, Louis Ernest 1953- *IntWWM 90*
Gross, Ludwik 1904- *WhoAm 90*
Gross, Marcy Sharon 1963- *WhoAmW 91*
Gross, Marie M *BiDrAPA 89*
Gross, Marilyn Agnes 1937- *WhoWrEP 89*
Gross, Martin Arnold 1934- *WhoE 91*
Gross, Max Menachem 1951- *WhoE 91*
Gross, Meir 1936- *BiDrAPA 89*
Gross, Melanie B. 1946- *St&PR 91*
Gross, Melanie Belman 1946- *WhoEmL 91*
Gross, Merryl Jane 1963- *WhoAmW 91*
Gross, Michael *BiDrAPA 89, BioIn 16*
Gross, Michael 1947- *WorAlBi*
Gross, Michael 1948- *BioIn 16*
Gross, Michael James 1952- *WhoWor 91*
Gross, Michael M. 1936- *St&PR 91*
Gross, Michael Paul 1943- *BiDrAPA 89*
Gross, Milt 1895-1953 *EncACom*
Gross, Milt 1912-1973 *Ballpl 90*
Gross, Milton Oliver *BioIn 16*
Gross, Mortimer D 1921- *BiDrAPA 89*
Gross, Morton 1923- *St&PR 91*
Gross, Murray *St&PR 91*
Gross, Nathan 1933- *WhoE 91*
Gross, Nelson Boon 1929- *St&PR 91*
Gross, Patrick Walter 1944- *St&PR 91, WhoAm 90, WhoWor 91*
Gross, Paul 1902- *WhoAm 90*
Gross, Paul A. 1937- *St&PR 91*
Gross, Paul Allan 1937- *WhoAm 90, WhoSSW 91*
Gross, Paul Kenneth *BiDrAPA 89*
Gross, Paul Randolph 1928- *WhoAm 90, WhoSSW 91*
Gross, Peter Alan 1938- *WhoAm 90, WhoE 91, WhoWor 91*
Gross, Philip *BioIn 16*
Gross, Philip 1934- *BiDrAPA 89*
Gross, Philip 1952- *ConAu 131*
Gross, Philip James 1952- *WhoEmL 91*
Gross, Priva Baidaff 1911- *WhoAmW 91, WhoE 91, WhoWor 91*
Gross, Richard Charles 1939- *St&PR 91*
Gross, Richard Edmund 1920- *WhoAm 90*
Gross, Richard L 1934- *BiDrAPA 89*
Gross, Richard Warren 1945- *St&PR 91*
Gross, Richard Wilson 1948- *WhoEmL 91*
Gross, Robert Alan 1945- *WhoAm 90*
Gross, Robert Alfred 1927- *WhoAm 90*
Gross, Robert E. 1897-1961 *WorAlBi*
Gross, Robert E. 1905-1988 *BioIn 16*
Gross, Robert E. 1911- *St&PR 91*
Gross, Robert Hadley *BiDrAPA 89*
Gross, Robert John *BiDrAPA 89*
Gross, Rochelle 1949- *WhoAmW 91*
Gross, Ronald Martin *WhoAm 90, WhoE 91*
Gross, Ronald Martin 1933- *St&PR 91*
Gross, Rudolph A 1940- *BiDrAPA 89*
Gross, Ruth Belov 1929- *AuBYP 90*
Gross, Ruth Taubenhaus 1920- *WhoAm 90, WhoAmW 91*
Gross, Samson Richard 1926- *WhoAm 90*
Gross, Sandra Lerner *WhoAmA 91*
Gross, Seymour Lee 1926- *WhoAm 90*
Gross, Shelley *WhoWrEP 89*
Gross, Shelly 1921- *WhoAm 90*
Gross, Shirley Marie 1917- *WhoAmW 91*
Gross, Sidney W. 1904- *WhoAm 90, WhoWor 91*
Gross, Solomon *BioIn 16*
Gross, Stanley C. 1938- *WhoWor 91*
Gross, Stephen Mark 1938- *WhoAm 90, WhoE 91*
Gross, Stephen Randolph 1947- *WhoSSW 91, WhoWor 91*
Gross, Terry *BioIn 16*
Gross, Theodore Lawrence 1930- *WhoAm 90, WhoWrEP 89*
Gross, Timothy Scott 1956- *St&PR 91*
Gross, Walter Robert 1903-1974 *DcScB S2*
Gross, Wayne 1952- *Ballpl 90*
Gross, Wendy *ODwPR 91*
Gross, Wilfried 1949- *WhoWor 91*
Gross, William Frederick 1956- *WhoEmL 91*
Gross, William H. *BioIn 16*
Gross, William Harvey 1950- *WhoE 91*
Gross, Willis Charles, Jr. 1924- *WhoWor 91*
Grossbard, Arthur S. 1958- *WhoEmL 91*
Grossberg, David Burton 1956- *WhoE 91*
Grossberg, George Thomas 1948- *BiDrAPA 89*
Grossberg, Jake 1932- *WhoAmA 91*
Grossberg, Kenneth Alan 1946- *WhoE 91*
Grossberg, Rami P. 1954- *WhoEmL 91*
Grossberg, Sidney Edward 1929- *WhoAm 90*
Grosschmid-Zsogod, Geza Benjamin 1918- *WhoAm 90*
Grosscup, Bryan D. 1950- *St&PR 91*
Grosscup, Fred Paul 186-?- *AmLegL*
Grosse, C 1931- *WhoAmA 91*
Grosse, Eduard 1928- *St&PR 91*
Grosse, Edward Ralph 1940- *WhoSSW 91*
Grosse, Jacqueline Weaver 1926- *WhoAmW 91*
Grosse, Richard R. 1942- *St&PR 91*
Grosse, Robert M. *BioIn 16*
Grossekettler, Heinz Georg 1939- *WhoWor 91*
Grossen, Francoise 1943- *WhoAmA 91*
Grossenbacher, Rene 1953- *WhoWor 91*
Grossenbacher, Rudolf 1943- *WhoWor 91*
Grosser, Bernard I 1929- *BiDrAPA 89*
Grosser, Bernard Irving 1929- *WhoAm 90*
Grosser, Frank Thomas 1946- *WhoEmL 91*
Grosset, Jessica Ariane 1952- *WhoAmW 91, WhoEmL 91*
Grosseteste, Robert 1175?-1253 *EncO&P 3*
Grossetete, Ginger Lee 1936- *WhoAmW 91*
Grossfeld, Stan *BioIn 16*
Grossfeld, Stanley 1951- *WhoAm 90*
Grossfield, Rena *ODwPR 91*
Grossi, Edward James 1949- *WhoE 91, WhoEmL 91*
Grossi, Giovanni Francesco 1653-1697 *PenDiMP*
Grossi, Margaret Thorne 1928- *WhoAmW 91*
Grossi, Olindo 1909- *WhoAm 90*
Grossi, Philip Albert *BiDrAPA 89*
Grossi, Richard J. 1935- *WhoAm 90*
Grossich, Mark Chris 1950- *WhoEmL 91*
Grossinger, Jennie 1892-1972 *BioAmW, WorAlBi*
Grossinger, Paul 1915-1989 *BioIn 16*
Grossinger, Richard Selig 1944- *WhoAm 90*
Grossinger, Tania Seifer 1937- *WhoWrEP 89*
Grosskopf, Barry 1945- *BiDrAPA 89*
Grosskopf, Dean Alan 1949- *St&PR 91*
Grosskreutz, Joseph Charles 1922- *WhoAm 90*
Grosslight, Joseph H. *BioIn 16*
Grossman, Allen Richard 1932- *WhoAm 90*
Grossman, Andrew C. 1951- *St&PR 91*
Grossman, Andrew Joseph 1958- *WhoWrEP 89*
Grossman, Bernard D. 1917- *St&PR 91*
Grossman, Bernard I. *St&PR 91*
Grossman, Carl M 1914- *BiDrAPA 89*
Grossman, Carl Stuart 1949- *St&PR 91*
Grossman, Chaika *BioIn 16*
Grossman, David *BioIn 16*
Grossman, David Benjamin 1951- *WhoEmL 91*
Grossman, David Z. 1938- *St&PR 91*
Grossman, Deena 1955- *IntWWM 90*
Grossman, Earl Martin 1958- *WhoEmL 91*
Grossman, Edgar 1919- *St&PR 91*
Grossman, Elizabeth Korn 1923- *WhoAm 90, WhoAmW 91*
Grossman, Elmer Roy 1929- *WhoAm 90*
Grossman, Frances Kaplan 1929- *WhoAmW 91*
Grossman, Fred *BiDrAPA 89*
Grossman, Fred 1958- *WhoE 91*
Grossman, Garry S. 1950- *WhoEmL 91*
Grossman, Gordon William 1932- *St&PR 91*
Grossman, H. Philip 1955- *WhoEmL 91*
Grossman, Hal J. 1948- *WhoEmL 91*
Grossman, Harold Allan 1946- *BiDrAPA 89*
Grossman, Harry 1911-1989 *BioIn 16*
Grossman, Helene Dubrow 1936- *WhoE 91*
Grossman, Herbert 1923- *St&PR 91*
Grossman, Herbert J *BiDrAPA 89*
Grossman, Herbert Maxim *BiDrAPA 89*
Grossman, Herschel I. 1939- *WhoAm 90*
Grossman, Hillel T *BiDrAPA 89*
Grossman, Hyman C. 1935- *St&PR 91*
Grossman, Jack 1925- *St&PR 91, WhoAm 90*
Grossman, Jacob 1916- *WhoAm 90*
Grossman, Jacob S. 1930- *WhoAm 90*
Grossman, Jeffrey W. 1963- *St&PR 91*
Grossman, Jerome Barnett 1919- *St&PR 91, WhoAm 90*
Grossman, Jerome Harvey 1939- *WhoAm 90*
Grossman, Jerome Kent 1953- *WhoEmL 91*
Grossman, Jerrold Wayne 1948- *WhoEmL 91*
Grossman, Joan Delaney 1928- *WhoAm 90*
Grossman, Joanne Barbara 1949- *WhoEmL 91*
Grossman, Joel Barry 1936- *WhoAm 90*
Grossman, John Henry 1914- *WhoWor 91*
Grossman, John Henry, III 1945- *WhoAm 90*
Grossman, Karl 1942- *ConAu 130*
Grossman, Karl H. 1942- *WhoAm 90*
Grossman, Larry *BioIn 16*
Grossman, Lawrence 1924- *WhoAm 90*
Grossman, Lawrence K. *BioIn 16*
Grossman, Lawrence Kugelmass 1931- *WhoAm 90*
Grossman, Lawrence Morton 1922- *WhoAm 90*
Grossman, Lee Paul *BiDrAPA 89*
Grossman, Leonard Albert 1926- *St&PR 91*
Grossman, Leonard E. 1935- *St&PR 91*
Grossman, Leslie *ODwPR 91*
Grossman, Lisa *BioIn 16*
Grossman, Loomis J. *BioIn 16*
Grossman, Louis 1914- *St&PR 91*
Grossman, Louis Irwin 1901-1988 *BioIn 16*
Grossman, Louis Joseph 1951- *WhoE 91*
Grossman, Manny 1927- *St&PR 91*
Grossman, Mark Jay 1952- *WhoE 91, WhoEmL 91*
Grossman, Marshall Bruce 1939- *WhoAm 90*
Grossman, Martin Allen 1943- *WhoWrEP 89*
Grossman, Marvin 1927- *St&PR 91*
Grossman, Matthew Rodney 1948- *WhoSSW 91*
Grossman, Maurice 1907- *BiDrAPA 89*
Grossman, Maurice 1922- *St&PR 91, WhoAm 90*
Grossman, Maurice Kenneth 1927- *WhoAmA 91*
Grossman, Maurice O *BiDrAPA 89*
Grossman, Melvyn L 1935- *BiDrAPA 89*
Grossman, Mendel 1917-1945 *BioIn 16*
Grossman, Michael 1941- *St&PR 91*
Grossman, Michael 1942- *WhoAm 90*
Grossman, Michael D. 1954- *ODwPR 91*
Grossman, Michael J. 1939- *WhoAm 90*
Grossman, Miriam 1955- *St&PR 91*
Grossman, Mitchell 1954- *St&PR 91*
Grossman, Morton 1926- *WhoAmA 91*
Grossman, Moses 1921- *WhoAm 90*
Grossman, N. Bud 1921- *St&PR 91, WhoAm 90*
Grossman, Nancy *WhoAm 90*
Grossman, Nancy 1940- *WhoAmA 91*
Grossman, Nancy 1942- *BiDWomA*
Grossman, Nancy Perkins *BiDrAPA 89*
Grossman, Paula Lynn *BiDrAPA 89*
Grossman, Peter Frost 1954- *WhoSSW 91*
Grossman, Peter J. 1956- *St&PR 91*
Grossman, Richard Leslie 1948- *WhoE 91*
Grossman, Richard Parker 1934- *St&PR 91*
Grossman, Robert Allen 1941- *St&PR 91*
Grossman, Robert George 1933- *WhoAm 90*
Grossman, Robert Mayer 1934- *WhoAm 90*
Grossman, Rodney Charles 1938- *WhoSSW 91*
Grossman, Ronald 1936- *St&PR 91*
Grossman, Samuel 1897- *WhoWor 91*
Grossman, Sanford *BioIn 16*
Grossman, Sanford 1929- *WhoAm 90*
Grossman, Sanford Jay 1953- *WhoAm 90, WhoE 91*
Grossman, Sebastian Peter 1934- *WhoAm 90*
Grossman, Seymour 1933- *BiDrAPA 89*
Grossman, Sheldon 1940- *WhoAmA 91*
Grossman, Sol C 1907- *BiDrAPA 89*
Grossman, Stanley *BiDrAPA 89*
Grossman, Stefan *NewAgMG*
Grossman, Steven A. *ODwPR 91*
Grossman, Steven J. 1942- *St&PR 91*
Grossman, Steven Jay 1945- *WhoEmL 91*
Grossman, Vasily 1905-1964 *ConAu 130, MajTwCW, WorAu 1980 [port]*
Grossman, William 1940- *WhoAm 90*
Grossman, William I *BiDrAPA 89*
Grossman, William King 1945- *WhoE 91*
Grossmann, David Michael 1944- *BiDrAPA 89*
Grossmann, Edith 1863-1931 *FemiCLE*
Grossmann, Ignacio Emilio 1949- *WhoAm 90*
Grossmann, John Richard 1951- *WhoEmL 91*
Grossmann, Ralph L. 1939- *St&PR 91*
Grossmann, Robert Horst 1960- *WhoEmL 91*
Grossmann, Ronald Stanyer 1944- *WhoAm 90*
Grossmann, Siegfried Karl F. 1930- *WhoWor 91*
Grossmann, Walter 1918- *WhoAm 90*
Grossmith, George 1847-1912 *OxCPMus*
Grossmith, George, Jr. 1874-1935 *OxCPMus*
Grossniklaus, Albert H. 1953- *WhoEmL 91*
Grosso, Anthony Joseph 1926- *St&PR 91*
Grosso, George D. 1941- *St&PR 91*
Grosso, Gerard Shaw 1943- *WhoAm 90*
Grosso, Gino 1948- *WhoE 91*
Grosso, Gino J *BiDrAPA 89*
Grosso, John 1946- *St&PR 91*
Grosso, Joseph Xavier 1939- *BiDrAPA 89*
Grosso, Michael 1937- *EncPaPR 91*
Grosso, Niccolo *PenDiDA 89*
Grosso, Patrick F. 1937- *St&PR 91*
Grosso, Rubina Irene 1929- *St&PR 91*
Grosso, Salvador *BioIn 16*
Grosso, Sonny *BioIn 16*
Grosso, Vincent Anthony 1934- *WhoE 91*
Grosswasser, Leonora Maria 1961- *WhoAmW 91*
Grossweiner, Leonard Irwin 1924- *WhoAm 90, WhoWor 91*
Grosswiler, Ed 1942- *ODwPR 91*
Grostick, Sara Stanford 1946- *WhoAmW 91*
Grosvenor, Charles Henry 1833-1917 *AmLegL*
Grosvenor, Edwin Stuart 1951- *WhoWrEP 89*
Grosvenor, Gerald Cavendish 1951- *BioIn 16, WhoWor 91*
Grosvenor, Gilbert Hovey *BioIn 16*
Grosvenor, Gilbert Melville 1931- *WhoAm 90, WhoWrEP 89*
Grosvenor, Melville Bell 1901-1982 *BioIn 16*
Grosvenor, Robert 1937- *WhoAmA 91*
Grosvenor, Wayne Lee 1926- *St&PR 91*
Grosz, Barbara Jean 1948- *WhoAm 90*
Grosz, Daniel 1952- *BiDrAPA 89*
Grosz, Franz Joseph 1909- *WhoAmA 91*
Grosz, George 1893-1959 *BioIn 16, IntDcAA 90, WhoAmA 91N*
Grosz, Hanus J *BiDrAPA 89*
Grosz, Karoly *BioIn 16*
Grosz, Karoly 1930- *WhoWor 91*
Groszek, William Alexander 1935- *St&PR 91*

Grot, Anton 1884-1974 ConDes 90
Grot, John B. 1943- St&PR 91
Grote, C. Nelson WhoSSW 91
Grote, Claus 1927- WhoWor 91
Grote, David 1945- ConAu 130
Grote, Jerry 1941- Ballpl 90
Grote, Robert E., III 1943- St&PR 91
Grote, Stephen Henry 1942- WhoAm 90
Grote, Walter F. 1901- St&PR 91
Grote, William AuBYP 90
Grote, William Dominic 1939- St&PR 91
Grotell, Maija 1899-1973 ConDes 90, WhoAmA 91N
Groteluschen, David 1953- St&PR 91
Groten, Barnet 1933- WhoAm 90
Groten, Dallas 1951- SmATA 64
Grotenfelt, Sten 1939- WhoWor 91
Grotenrath, Ruth 1912-1988 WhoAmA 91N
Groth, A. Nicholas 1937- WhoSSW 91
Groth, Alexander Jacob 1932- WhoAm 90
Groth, Betty WhoWor 91
Groth, Brian Joseph 1960- WhoWrEP 89
Groth, Bruno 1905- WhoAmA 91
Groth, John 1908-1988 BioIn 16
Groth, Johnny 1926- Ballpl 90
Groth, Joyce Lorraine 1935- WhoAmW 91
Groth, Klaus 1923- WhoWor 91
Groth, Larry Dale 1952- WhoEmL 91
Groth, Leon BiDrAPA 89
Groth, Patricia Celley 1932- WhoWrEP 89
Groth, Raymond Clarence 1947- St&PR 91
Groth, William I. 1927- St&PR 91
Grothaus, Pamela Sue 1958- WhoEmL 91
Grothe, Dale F. 1930- St&PR 91
Grothkopf, Chad 1914- EncACom
Grothusen, Klaus-Detlev 1928- WhoWor 91
Grotius, Hugo 1583-1645 WorAlBi
Grotjahn, Martin 1904- BiDrAPA 89, BioIn 16, WhoWor 91
Grotjahn, Martin 1904-1990 ConAu 132
Grotjahn, Michael 1935- BiDrAPA 89
Groton, James Purnell 1927- WhoAm 90, WhoSSW 91
Grotowski, Jerzy 1933- WhoWor 91
Grotsky, Harold W. 1942- WhoWor 91
Grotstein, James S BiDrAPA 89
Grotta, Louis William 1933- St&PR 91
Grotta, Sandra Brown 1934- WhoAmW 91
Grottendieck, Virginia Randolph 1945- WhoAmW 91
Grotterod, Knut 1922- WhoAm 90
Grotz, Dorothy Rogers WhoAmA 91
Grotzinger, Laurel Ann 1935- WhoAm 90, WhoAmW 91
Grotzinger, Randolph Harrison 1942- St&PR 91
Grouard, Frank 1850-1905 WhNaAH
Grouchy de Condorcet, Sophie de 1766-1822 EncCoWW
Groueff, Lil BioIn 16
Groult, Andre 1884-1967 PenDiDA 89
Groult, Benoite 1920- EncCoWW
Groult, Flora 1924- EncCoWW
Ground, Mary BioIn 16
Groussard, Serge Hariton 1921- WhoWor 91
Groussman, Ray G. 1935- St&PR 91
Groussman, Raymond G. 1935- WhoAm 90
Grout, Josiah 1842-1925 AmLegL
Grout, Stuart 1924- WhoE 91
Groux, Guy Marc 1945- WhoWor 91
Groux, Peter John 1960- WhoSSW 91
Grove, Alfred Frank, Jr. 1939- St&PR 91
Grove, Andrew S. St&PR 91
Grove, Andrew S. 1936- ConAu 130, WhoAm 90
Grove, Brandon Hambright, Jr. 1929- WhoAm 90
Grove, Charlotte BioIn 16
Grove, Cheryl Wade 1946- WhoAmW 91
Grove, David Lawrence 1918- WhoAm 90
Grove, E.L., Jr. 1924- St&PR 91
Grove, Edward Ryneal 1912- WhoAm 90, WhoAmA 91
Grove, Fred 1913- BioIn 16
Grove, Frederick Philip 1879-1948 DcLB 92 [port]
Grove, Garth Walden 1945- WhoSSW 91
Grove, Helen Harriet WhoAmW 91, WhoWor 91
Grove, Henry S. 1933- St&PR 91
Grove, Jack F. 1953- St&PR 91
Grove, Jack Stein 1951- WhoEmL 91
Grove, James W. 1929- St&PR 91
Grove, Janet Elaine 1951- St&PR 91
Grove, Jean Donner 1912- WhoAm 90, WhoAmA 91, WhoAmW 91
Grove, John Landis 1921- St&PR 91
Grove, John Whitaker 1954- WhoE 91
Grove, Kalvin Myron 1937- WhoAm 90
Grove, Lefty 1900-1975 Ballpl 90 [port], BioIn 16, WorAlBi
Grove, Lester W. 1944- St&PR 91
Grove, Marvin H. BioIn 16
Grove, Myrna Jean 1949- WhoAmW 91, WhoEmL 91
Grove, Nancy Carol WhoE 91
Grove, Orval 1919- Ballpl 90
Grove, Richard Martin 1950- WhoEmL 91, WhoWor 91
Grove, Russell Sinclair, Jr. 1939- WhoAm 90
Grove, Samuel Harold 1925- WhoAmA 91
Grove, Sheryl Ann BiDrAPA 89
Grove, Ted Russell 1961- WhoSSW 91
Grove, Thomas K. 1929- St&PR 91
Grove, Vallejo Marmaduke 1879-1954 BioIn 16
Grove, William A., Jr. 1932- ODwPR 91
Grove, William Boyd 1929- WhoSSW 91
Grove, William Johnson 1920- WhoAm 90
Grovenstein, Erling, Jr. 1924- WhoAm 90
Grover, Brent R. 1950- St&PR 91
Grover, Brent Richard 1950- WhoEmL 91
Grover, Eulalie Osgood 1873- AuBYP 90
Grover, Eve Ruth 1929- WhoE 91
Grover, James Robb 1928- WhoE 91
Grover, John Henry 1927- St&PR 91
Grover, LaFayette 1823-1911 AmLegL
Grover, Lee BioIn 16
Grover, Michael Barry BiDrAPA 89
Grover, Myron Robert BiDrAPA 89
Grover, Neal 1950- St&PR 91
Grover, Norman LaMotte 1928- WhoAm 90
Grover, Phyllis Florence Bradman 1924- WhoAmW 91
Grover, Ray BioIn 16
Grover, Robert John 1942- WhoAm 90
Grover, Robert Lawrence 1910- WhoAm 90
Grover, Rosalind Redfern 1941- WhoAmW 91, WhoSSW 91, WhoWor 91
Grover, Sherwood 1912-1986 BioIn 16
Grover, Susan Kay 1957- BiDrAPA 89
Grover, Thomas David 1953- WhoEmL 91
Grover, William Herbert 1938- WhoAm 90, WhoE 91
Grover, William L 1919- BiDrAPA 89
Grover-Haskin, Kim Arleen 1960- WhoAmW 91
Groves, Barbara Jane 1934- WhoSSW 91
Groves, Charles 1915- PenDiMP
Groves, Charles Barnard 1915- IntWWM 90, WhoWor 91
Groves, David Dwight Arthur 1952- WhoSSW 91
Groves, David Updegraff 1926- WhoWor 91
Groves, Franklin Nelson 1930- St&PR 91, WhoAm 90
Groves, George H. 1944- St&PR 91
Groves, George L., Jr. St&PR 91
Groves, George L., Jr. 1928- WhoAm 90
Groves, Gerald BioIn 16
Groves, Gerald A BiDrAPA 89
Groves, Gordon Capron 1930- St&PR 91
Groves, Hannah Cutier 1868-1952 WhoAmA 91N
Groves, Hurst Kohler 1941- WhoE 91
Groves, J. Randall 1939- St&PR 91
Groves, James Elton 1946- BiDrAPA 89
Groves, John Taylor, III 1943- WhoAm 90
Groves, Leslie Richard 1896-1970 WorAlBi
Groves, Lindell Griffith 1939- WhoAmW 91
Groves, Michael 1936- St&PR 91, WhoAm 90
Groves, Nancy Ann 1950- WhoEmL 91
Groves, Naomi Jackson WhoAmA 91
Groves, Olive PenDiMP
Groves, Ray John 1935- WhoAm 90
Groves, Richard A. 1931- St&PR 91
Groves, Richard Melvin 1929- St&PR 91
Groves, Rockwell M. 1934- St&PR 91
Groves, Rosalind Ganzel 1934- WhoAmW 91, WhoSSW 91, WhoWor 91
Groves, Sharon Darlene 1951- WhoSSW 91
Groves, Sheridon Hale 1947- WhoEmL 91, WhoSSW 91, WhoWor 91
Groves, Stephen Peterson, Sr. 1956- WhoEmL 91
Groves, Theodore Francis, Jr. 1941- WhoAm 90
Groves-Raines, Nicholas BioIn 16
Groves-Raines, Ralph Gore Antony 1913- AuBYP 90
Grovier, Mireille M. 1939- WhoAmW 91
Grow, Ann Elizabeth 1950- WhoEmL 91
Grow, Buel K, Jr. BiDrAPA 89
Grow, David Parnell 1951- WhoEmL 91
Grow, Galusha Aaron 1823-1907 BioIn 16
Growdon, Marcia Cohn 1945- WhoAmA 91
Growe, Colleen Marie 1959- WhoE 91
Growe, Joan Anderson 1935- WhoAm 90, WhoAmW 91
Growney, James Patrick 1939- WhoE 91
Groza, Alex 1926- BioIn 16
Groza, Lou 1924- BioIn 16
Grua, Rudolph 1928- St&PR 91
Grub, Phillip D. 1932- ConAu 32NR
Grub, Phillip Donald 1931- WhoAm 90
Grubar, Francis Stanley 1924- WhoAmA 91
Grubaugh, Steven Jack 1946- WhoSSW 91
Grubb, Albany Delmer 1942- St&PR 91
Grubb, Charles Carr 1946- WhoEmL 91
Grubb, David Alan 1950- WhoEmL 91
Grubb, David George 1945- BiDrAPA 89
Grubb, David H. 1936- St&PR 91, WhoAm 90
Grubb, Donald H. 1924- St&PR 91
Grubb, Donald Hartman 1924- WhoAm 90
Grubb, Donald James 1946- BiDrAPA 89
Grubb, Edgar Harold 1939- WhoAm 90
Grubb, Eric A. 1936- St&PR 91
Grubb, Farley Ward 1954- WhoE 91
Grubb, Johnny 1948- Ballpl 90
Grubb, Larry Keith 1947- BiDrAPA 89
Grubb, Lewis Craig 1954- WhoEmL 91
Grubb, Linda Fern 1944- WhoAmW 91
Grubb, Pat Pincombe 1922-1977 WhoAmA 91N
Grubb, Phyllis Bowman 1934- WhoAmW 91
Grubb, Robert Lynn 1927- WhoSSW 91, WhoWor 91
Grubb, Stephen Bunyan 1945- WhoSSW 91
Grubb, William Francis X. 1944- WhoAm 90
Grubb, Wilson Lyon 1910- WhoAm 90
Grubbe, Kenneth S. 1935- St&PR 91
Grubbs, Donald Ray 1947- WhoSSW 91
Grubbs, Donald Shaw, Jr. 1929- St&PR 91, WhoAm 90, WhoWor 91
Grubbs, Elven Judson 1930- WhoAm 90
Grubbs, Geoffrey Hilton 1951- WhoAm 90
Grubbs, Gerald Reid 1947- St&PR 91
Grubbs, James Holt 1948- BiDrAPA 89
Grubbs, Robert H. 1942- WhoAm 90
Grubbs, Shelby Russell 1949- WhoEmL 91
Grubbs, Stephen BioIn 16
Grubbs, Wilbur Charles 1929- St&PR 91
Grubbstrom, Karl Robert William 1941- WhoWor 91
Grube, Bruce F. WhoAm 90
Grube, Frank 1905-1945 Ballpl 90
Grube, Gerald G. 1919- St&PR 91
Grube, James Richard 1947- WhoEmL 91
Grube, Lewis Blaine 1917- St&PR 91
Grube, Michael 1954- IntWWM 90
Grube, Rebecca Sue 1945- WhoAmW 91
Grubea, John M BiDrAPA 89
Gruber, Aaronel Deroy WhoAmA 91
Gruber, Alan Richard 1927- St&PR 91, WhoAm 90, WhoE 91
Gruber, Charles WhoSSW 91
Gruber, David Paul 1941- St&PR 91
Gruber, David Steven 1948- WhoEmL 91
Gruber, Debra R. 1951- St&PR 91
Gruber, Douglas Lloyd 1920- WhoE 91
Gruber, Frank 1904-1969 TwCCr&M 91
Gruber, Fred 1947- St&PR 91
Gruber, Fredric Francis 1931- WhoAm 90
Gruber, H K 1943- PenDiMP A
Gruber, Heinz Karl 1943- IntWWM 90
Gruber, Helen Elizabeth 1946- WhoAmW 91
Gruber, Ira Dempsey 1934- WhoAm 90
Gruber, J. Richard 1948- WhoAm 90
Gruber, J Richard 1948- WhoAmA 91
Gruber, Jacques 1871-1936 PenDiDA 89
Gruber, John Ballpl 90
Gruber, John Balsbaugh 1935- WhoAm 90
Gruber, Karl 1881-1927 EncO&P 3
Gruber, Kelly 1962- Ballpl 90
Gruber, Louis Nover 1938- BiDrAPA 89
Gruber, Marion Elizabeth 1945- WhoAmW 91
Gruber, Mark Stephen 1951- WhoEmL 91
Gruber, Max 1921- WhoWor 91
Gruber, Nelson Peter BiDrAPA 89
Gruber, Peter Felix 1946- WhoWor 91
Gruber, Randall Paul 1963- WhoEmL 91
Gruber, Robert BiDrAPA 89
Gruber, Robert S. ODwPR 91
Gruber, Robert Stuart 1932- St&PR 91
Gruber, Seymour 1920- BiDrAPA 89
Gruber, Sheldon 1930- WhoAm 90
Gruber, Sylvia E. St&PR 91
Gruber, William Lloyd 1918- WhoSSW 91
Gruber, William Paul 1932- WhoAm 90
Gruber, William Stewart 1963- WhoEmL 91
Gruberg, Cy 1928- WhoAm 90
Gruberg, Kermit H 1917- BiDrAPA 89
Gruberg, Martin 1935- WhoAm 90
Gruberova, Edita 1946- IntWWM 90, PenDiMP
Grubert, Carl Alfred 1911-1979 WhoAmA 91N
Grubiak, Jim Frank 1938- St&PR 91
Grubin, Arnold 1929- St&PR 91
Grubisich, Thomas James 1936- WhoE 91
Grubman, Herman Joseph 1927- St&PR 91
Grubman, Wallace Karl 1928- St&PR 91, WhoAm 90
Grucci, Felix 1905- BioIn 16
Grucci, Jimmy BioIn 16
Gruchacz, Robert S. 1929- WhoAm 90
Gruchalla, Michael Emeric 1946- WhoEmL 91, WhoWor 91
Gruchy, Allan Garfield 1906-1990 BioIn 16
Grucza, Leo 1935- WhoAmA 91
Grucza, Nancy Marceca 1955- WhoAmW 91
Grude, Wanda A. 1948- WhoEmL 91
Grudzinski, Sigmund S. 1955- WhoE 91
Grue, Aurelio 1699-1743 PenDiDA 89
Grue, Carlantonio 1655-1723 PenDiDA 89
Grue, Francesco Antonio 1618-1673 PenDiDA 89
Grue, Francesco Antonio Xaverio 1686-1746 PenDiDA 89
Grue, Howard W. 1927- St&PR 91
Grue, Lee Meitzen WhoWrEP 89
Grue, Liborio PenDiDA 89
Grue, Saverio 1731-1799 PenDiDA 89
Grueber, Cynthia Marie 1957- WhoAmW 91
Grueby, William Henry BioIn 16
Grueby, William Henry 1867-1925 PenDiDA 89
Gruel, Steven Francis 1956- WhoEmL 91
Gruelle, Johnny 1880-1938 EncACom
Gruen, David Henry 1929- WhoAm 90
Gruen, Erich S 1935- ConAu 131
Gruen, Erich Stephen 1935- WhoAm 90
Gruen, G. John 1945- St&PR 91
Gruen, Gerald Elmer 1937- WhoAm 90
Gruen, John 1926- WhoAmA 91
Gruen, Mary Hoagland 1918- WhoAmW 91
Gruen, Michael Stephan 1942- WhoWor 91
Gruen, Peter H 1939- BiDrAPA 89, WhoAm 90
Gruen, Robert 1913- St&PR 91
Gruen, Shirley Schanen 1923- WhoAmA 91
Gruenbaum, Gerald Carlton 1944- WhoSSW 91
Gruenbaum, Itzhak 1879-1970 BioIn 16
Gruenberg, Alan Mark 1952- BiDrAPA 89
Gruenberg, Don 1942- St&PR 91
Gruenberg, Elliot Lewis 1918- WhoE 91, WhoWor 91
Gruenberg, Erich PenDiMP
Gruenberg, Erich 1924- IntWWM 90
Gruenberg, Ernest M BiDrAPA 89
Gruenberg, John, II 1918- ODwPR 91, WhoE 91
Gruenberg, Kenneth M 1948- BiDrAPA 89
Gruenberg, Louis 1884-1964 PenDiMP A
Gruenberg, Mark Jonathan 1953- WhoE 91
Gruenberg, Peter Barnard 1935- BiDrAPA 89
Gruenberg, Robert 1922- WhoAm 90
Gruenberg, Sidonie 1881-1974 AuBYP 90
Gruenberger, Peter 1937- WhoAm 90
Gruener, Johann M BiDrAPA 89
Gruener, Robert D 1925- BiDrAPA 89
Gruenewald, Carl William, II 1933- St&PR 91
Gruenfeld, Lee 1950- WhoEmL 91
Gruenhut, Egon 1922- St&PR 91
Gruening, Ernest 1887-1974 WorAlBi
Gruenling, Edwin H. 1939- St&PR 91
Gruenspecht, Manfred 1924- St&PR 91
Gruenthaler, Rudolf Erich 1922- WhoWor 91
Gruenther, Sue Cory WhoAmA 91N
Gruentzig, Andreas R. 1939-1985 BioIn 16
Gruenwald, George Henry 1922- WhoAm 90, WhoWor 91, WhoWrEP 89
Gruenwald, Gerald 1929- WhoWor 91
Gruenwald, Mark Eugene 1953- WhoE 91
Grueske, Karl-Dieter 1946- WhoWor 91
Gruetter, Richard Allen 1946- WhoEmL 91
Gruetzmacher, Cheryl K. 1955- St&PR 91
Gruetzner, Peter Georg A. 1925- WhoWor 91
Gruger, Frederick R 1871-1953 WhoAmA 91N
Gruhl, Andrea Morris 1939- WhoAmW 91, WhoE 91, WhoWor 91
Gruhl, James 1945- WhoWor 91
Gruhl, Robert H. 1945- St&PR 91
Gruhl, Robert Herbert 1945- WhoAm 90
Gruhl, William Wagner 1941- St&PR 91
Gruhn, Joel D. 1947- St&PR 91
Gruhn, Nora 1905- IntWWM 90
Gruidl, Thomas G. 1937- St&PR 91
Grulke, James Max, Jr. 1954- WhoEmL 91
Grulkowski, Ray A. 1937- St&PR 91
Grum, Clifford J. 1934- St&PR 91, WhoAm 90, WhoSSW 91

Grumbach, Argula von 1492?-1554? *EncCoWW*
Grumbach, Doris 1918- *ConLC 64 [port], WhoAm 90, WhoWrEP 89, WorAu 1980 [port]*
Grumbach, Madeleine F *BiDrAPA 89*
Grumbach, Melvin Malcolm 1925- *WhoAm 90*
Grumbine, David Allen 1949- *WhoEmL 91*
Grumbine, E. Evalyn 1900- *AuBYP 90*
Grumbles, Lynnelle Dahlgren 1959- *WhoEmL 91*
Grumer, Elliott Henry *BiDrAPA 89*
Grumer, Lawrence Charles 1952- *WhoE 91*
Grumer, Robert George *BiDrAPA 89*
Grumet, Gerald W 1937- *BiDrAPA 89*
Grumet, Gerald Warren 1937- *WhoE 91*
Grumet, Priscilla Hecht 1943- *WhoAmW 91*
Grumet, Robert Steven 1949- *WhoE 91*
Grumet, Ross F *BiDrAPA 89*
Grumiaux, Arthur 1921-1986 *PenDiMP*
Grumman, Leroy R. 1895-1982 *WorAlBi*
Grummann, Paul H *WhoAmA 91N*
Grummer, Arnold E. 1923- *BioIn 16*
Grummer, Brenda Kennedy *BioIn 16*
Grummer, Elisabeth 1911-1986 *PenDiMP*
Grummer, Paul *PenDiMP*
Grummon, Phyllis Haight 1951- *WhoEmL 91*
Grun, Bernard 1901-1972 *OxCPMus*
Grun, Otto *BioIn 16*
Grunau, Charles Frederick Von 1943- *WhoE 91*
Grunau, Paul E. 1911- *St&PR 91*
Grunbaum, Adolf 1923- *WhoAm 90*
Grunbaum, Norbert *BiDrAPA 89*
Grunberg, Frederic *BiDrAPA 89*
Grunberg, Robert Leon Willy 1940- *WhoAm 90, WhoE 91, WhoWor 91*
Grunberger, Dezider 1922- *WhoAm 90*
Grund, Carl Henry, Jr. 1947- *WhoE 91*
Grund, Joseph Richard 1929- *St&PR 91*
Grund, Walter James, Jr. 1927- *WhoAm 90*
Grundbacher, Frederick John 1926- *WhoAm 90*
Grundberg, Andy 1947- *WhoAmA 91*
Grunder, Paul E. 1931- *St&PR 91*
Grunder, Paul Edwin 1931- *WhoAm 90*
Grundfast, Kenneth Martin 1944- *WhoE 91*
Grundfest, Joseph A. *BioIn 16*
Grundfest, Joseph Alexander 1951- *WhoAm 90*
Grundheber, Franz 1937- *IntWWM 90*
Grundhofer, Jerry A. 1944- *St&PR 91*
Grundhofer, John Francis 1939- *St&PR 91*
Grundig, Lea 1906-1977 *BiDWomA*
Grundig, Max 1908-1989 *AnObit 1989, BioIn 16*
Grundland, Barry *BiDrAPA 89*
Grundlehner, Conrad Ernest 1942- *WhoSSW 91*
Grundman, Robert Alan 1948- *WhoEmL 91*
Grundmann, Christoph Johann 1908- *WhoAm 90*
Grundmann, Volker Robert 1931- *St&PR 91*
Grundmeyer, Douglas Lanaux 1948- *WhoEmL 91, WhoSSW 91, WhoWor 91*
Grundner, Thomas Michael 1945- *WhoEmL 91*
Grundstein, Nathan David 1913- *WhoAm 90*
Grundtvig, Nikolaj Frederik Severin 1783-1872 *DcScanL*
Grundy, Betty Lou Bottoms 1940- *WhoAmW 91*
Grundy, Felix 1777-1840 *BiDrUSE 89*
Grundy, J 1911-1985 *WhoAmA 91N*
Grundy, Jess W. 1918- *St&PR 91*
Grundy, Kenneth William 1936- *WhoAm 90*
Grune, George Vincent 1929- *St&PR 91, WhoAm 90*
Gruneau, Richard S 1948- *ConAu 30NR*
Grunebaum, Ernest Michael 1934- *WhoAm 90*
Grunebaum, Henry U 1926- *BiDrAPA 89*
Gruneich, Kevin Ross 1958- *St&PR 91*
Gruner, Charles Ralph 1931- *WhoWrEP 89*
Gruner, Erich 1915- *WhoWor 91*
Gruner, Richard Steven 1953- *WhoEmL 91*
Grunert, Ingo 1942- *WhoWor 91*
Grunes, David Leon 1921- *WhoAm 90*
Grunes, Jerome M *BiDrAPA 89*
Grunewald, Bjorn Mikael 1940- *WhoWor 91*
Grunewald, Donald 1934- *WhoAm 90, WhoWor 91*
Grunewald, Fritz *EncO&P 3*
Grunewald, Fritz 1885-1925 *EncPaPR 91*
Grunewald, Gary Lawrence 1937- *WhoAm 90*
Grunewald, John H. 1936- *St&PR 91*
Grunewald, Katharine Klevesahl 1952- *WhoAmW 91*
Grunewald, Mathis 1445?-1528? *IntDcAA 90*
Grunewald, Matthias 1470?-1528 *WorAlBi*
Grunfeld, Ernst *WhoAm 90*
Grunfeld, Rudy 1919- *St&PR 91*
Grunhaus, Leon Jacobo 1948- *BiDrAPA 89*
Grunhof, Natalie von 1836-1905 *BioIn 16*
Grunhut, Isidoro 1862-1896 *BioIn 16*
Grunig, James Elmer 1942- *WhoAm 90, WhoE 91*
Grunik, Sally Ann 1955- *WhoE 91*
Gruninger, Paul 1891-1972 *BioIn 16*
Grunke, Mary Ellen 1950- *WhoAmW 91*
Grunke, Richard John 1951- *WhoEmL 91*
Grunland, Paul Allen 1924- *St&PR 91*
Grunnah, Robert James 1944- *WhoSSW 91*
Grunnah, S. Thomas 1936- *St&PR 91*
Grunner, Jocelyn Sari 1958- *WhoAmW 91*
Grunow, Richard Frederick 1945- *IntWWM 90*
Grunschlag, Martin *BiDrAPA 89*
Grunseth, Jon Rieder 1945- *St&PR 91*
Grunsfeld, Ernest Alton, III 1929- *WhoAm 90*
Grunsten, Robert 1945- *BiDrAPA 89*
Grunt, Jerome Alvin 1923- *WhoAm 90*
Gruntz, George *BioIn 16*
Grunwald, Ernest Max 1923- *WhoAm 90*
Grunwald, Henry Anatole 1922- *WhoAm 90, WhoWor 91*
Grunwald, John J. 1929- *WhoAm 90, WhoWor 91*
Grunwaldt, Constance Jean 1963- *WhoAmW 91*
Grupas, Angela Kathryn 1964- *WhoEmL 91*
Grupe, Amy Elizabeth 1958- *WhoAmW 91*
Grupe, Warren Edward 1933- *WhoAm 90*
Grupka, Richard Allen 1952- *St&PR 91*
Grupp, Carl Alf 1939- *WhoAmA 91*
Gruppe, Charles 1928- *WhoAmA 91*
Gruppe, Emil Albert 1896-1978 *WhoAmA 91N*
Gruppe, Karl Heinrich 1893-1982 *WhoAmA 91N*
Gruschka, Heinz Dieter 1934- *WhoWor 91*
Grusensky, Marc Harris *BiDrAPA 89*
Grush, Mary Ellen 1947- *WhoAmW 91, WhoWor 91*
Grush, Paul Lee 1961- *WhoEmL 91, WhoSSW 91*
Grushka, Donald J. 1945- *WhoEmL 91*
Grushkin, Philip 1921- *St&PR 91, WhoAmA 91*
Grusin, Dave *BioIn 16*
Grusin, Dave 1934- *WhoAm 90*
Gruskin, Felice Rhoda 1928- *WhoAmW 91*
Gruskin, Mary J. *WhoAm 90*
Gruskin, Mary Josephine *WhoAmA 91*
Gruson, Hiroko Tsubota 1940- *WhoE 91*
Gruson, Sydney 1916- *St&PR 91*
Gruss, Joseph *BioIn 16*
Gruss, Peter 1949- *WhoWor 91*
Grussendorf, Benjamin Franklin, Jr. 1942- *WhoAm 90*
Gruszecka, Aniela 1884-1976 *EncCoWW*
Grutka, Andrew G. 1908- *WhoAm 90*
Grutman, David Stanley 1908- *St&PR 91*
Gruttadaro, Michele Marie 1964- *WhoE 91*
Grutzmacher, Friedrich 1832-1903 *PenDiMP*
Grutzmacher, June Edith 1956- *WhoAmW 91*
Gruver, C. Robert *ODwPR 91*
Gruver, Daryl Lee 1945- *WhoEmL 91*
Gruver, James David 1947- *WhoEmL 91*
Gruver, Nancy *BioIn 16, NewYTBS 90*
Gruver, William Rolfe 1944- *WhoAm 90*
Gruverman, Irwin J. 1933- *St&PR 91*
Gruy, Henry Jones 1915- *St&PR 91, WhoAm 90*
Gruy, Robert H. 1942- *St&PR 91*
Gruys, Erik 1944- *WhoWor 91*
Gruzenski, William Paul 1941- *BiDrAPA 89*
Gruzleski, Thomas Floyd 1945- *WhoE 91*
Gruzlewski, Bernard J. 1934- *St&PR 91*
Gryce, David Conrad 1955- *WhoE 91*
Gryden, Harry E. 1840-1884 *BioIn 16*
Gryder, Rosa Meyersburg 1926- *WhoAm 90*
Grygiel, James Richard 1958- *WhoEmL 91*
Grygiel, John Andrew 1926- *St&PR 91*
Gryglas, Ronald J. 1945- *St&PR 91*
Gryglas, Stephen 1915- *St&PR 91*
Gryglas, Steven E. 1943- *St&PR 91*
Grygotis, Dennis C 1942- *BiDrAPA 89*
Grygutis, Barbara 1946- *WhoAmA 91*
Gryka, George Edwin 1932- *WhoWor 91*
Gryler, Roy B *BiDrAPA 89*
Grymeston, Elizabeth *BioIn 16*
Grymeston, Elizabeth 1563?-1602? *FemiCLE*
Grymeston, Elizabeth 1563?-1603? *BiDEWW*
Gryna, Frank Michael 1928- *WhoE 91*
Grynberg, Elizabeth W *BiDrAPA 89*
Gryniuk, Kathleen Dianne 1957- *WhoAmW 91*
Grynszpan, Herschel 1921-1943? *BioIn 16*
Gryp, Firmin A. 1927- *St&PR 91*
Grypma, Jane Patricia 1960- *WhoAmW 91*
Gryski, Camilla *AuBYP 90*
Gryson, Joseph Anthony 1932- *WhoAm 90*
Gryte, Rolf Edward 1945- *WhoWor 91*
Grzanka, Leonard 1947- *WhoWrEP 89*
Grzenda, Joe 1937- *Ballpl 90*
Grzesik, Tadeusz 1933- *WhoWor 91*
Grzinic, Marina 1958- *WhoWor 91*
Grzybowski, Kazimierz 1911- *WhoAm 90*
Grzybowski, Walter T. *St&PR 91*
Gschneidner, Karl Albert, Jr. 1930- *WhoAm 90*
Gschwend, Ralf Detlev 1959- *WhoSSW 91*
Gschwendtner, Alfred Benedict 1936- *WhoE 91*
Gschwind, A. Edward 1932- *St&PR 91*
Gschwind, Donald 1933- *WhoAm 90*
Gschwind, John K. 1934- *St&PR 91*
Gschwind, John Karl 1934- *WhoAm 90*
Gsell, Jay Alvin, Jr. 1951- *WhoE 91*
Gstrein, Rainer Johannes 1960- *IntWWM 90*
GTO *ArtLatA*
Gu Mu *WhoWor 91*
Gu Xiulian 1935- *WhoWor 91*
Guadagni, Gaetano 1725?-1792 *PenDiMP*
Guadagno, Anton 1925- *IntWWM 90, PenDiMP*
Guadagnoli, Nello T 1929- *WhoAmA 91*
Guadalajara, Diego De *EncCRAm*
Guadalupe, Robert 1942- *WhoHisp 91*
Guajardo, Francetta 1960- *WhoEmL 91*
Guajardo, Larry 1943- *WhoHisp 91*
Gual, Jordi 1957- *WhoWor 91*
Gual, Peter Gatkuoth 1938- *WhoWor 91*
Gualandi, Louis D. *BioIn 16*
Gualda, Sylvio 1939- *PenDiMP*
Gualde, Norbert 1943- *WhoWor 91*
Gualtieri, C Thomas *BiDrAPA 89*
Gualtieri, Joseph P 1916- *WhoAmA 91*
Gualtieri, Joseph Peter 1916- *WhoAm 90, WhoE 91*
Guan Sushuang *BioIn 16*
Guan, Bo 1958- *WhoE 91*
Guancione, Karen Ann 1957- *WhoE 91*
Guanciroli *PenDiDA 89*
Guanco, Gema Aguilar 1940- *BiDrAPA 89*
Guandolo, John 1919- *WhoAm 90*
Guandolo, Joseph 1906- *WhoAm 90*
Guante, Cecilio 1960- *Ballpl 90*
Guaraldo, Rosalind Joan 1946- *WhoE 91*
Guarasci, Carin Marie 1946- *WhoE 91*
Guard, Mary Beth 1955- *WhoAmW 91, WhoSSW 91*
Guardi, Francesco 1712?-1793 *IntDcAA 90*
Guardia, David King 1952- *WhoEmL 91*
Guardia, Ernesto de la 1904-1983 *BioIn 16*
Guardia, Francisco Ferrer 1859-1909 *BioIn 16*
Guardia, Rafael Angel Calderon 1900-1970 *BioIn 16*
Guardia, Ricardo Adolfo de la 1899-1970 *BioIn 16*
Guardia, Tomas 1832-1882 *BioIn 16*
Guardineer, Fred 1913- *EncACom*
Guardino, Harry 1925- *WhoAm 90*
Guardo, Carol J. 1939- *WhoAm 90, WhoAmW 91*
Guare, John *BioIn 16*
Guare, John 1938- *ConTFT 8, MajTwCW, WhoAm 90, WorAlBi*
Guarini, Frank J. 1924- *WhoAm 90, WhoE 91*
Guarini, Richard Anthony 1945- *St&PR 91*
Guarino, Brad Lawrence 1957- *WhoE 91*
Guarino, Carl Anthony 1957- *St&PR 91*
Guarino, Edward Joseph 1947- *WhoE 91*
Guarino, John Ralph 1915- *WhoAm 90*
Guarino, Martin Vincent 1939- *WhoSSW 91*
Guarino, Pasquale 1953- *WhoE 91*
Guarino, Ralph J. 1946- *St&PR 91*
Guarino, Robert L. 1940- *WhoE 91*
Guarino, Roger Charles 1929- *WhoAm 90, WhoSSW 91*
Guarino, Salvatore Frank 1937- *WhoAm 90*
Guarino, Thomas V. 1953- *St&PR 91*
Guarino, Walter Cesar *BiDrAPA 89*
Guarino, Walter F. 1942- *St&PR 91*
Guarnaschelli, Maria DiBenedetto 1941- *WhoAm 90*
Guarneri Quartet *PenDiMP*
Guarneschelli, Philip George 1932- *St&PR 91*
Guarnieri, Johnny 1917-1985 *OxCPMus*
Guarnieri, Michael Stephen 1962- *WhoE 91*
Guarrera, Frank 1923- *IntWWM 90*
Guastafero, Angelo 1932- *WhoAm 90*
Guastafeste, Al *BioIn 16*
Guastella, C Dennis 1947- *WhoAmA 91*
Guastella, Frank Phillip *BiDrAPA 89*
Guay, Edward 1943- *WhoAm 90*
Guay, Georgette 1952- *BioIn 16, ConAu 132*
Guay, Gordon Hay 1948- *WhoEmL 91*
Guay, Kathi Lynn 1958- *WhoE 91*
Guay, Marie Ann *BiDrAPA 89*
Guayasamin, Oswaldo 1919- *ArtLatA*
Guazzo, Eugene 1929- *WhoE 91*
Guba, Egon Gotthold 1924- *WhoAm 90*
Gubaidulina, Sofia 1931- *IntWWM 90*
Gubaidulina, Sofya 1931- *PenDiMP A*
Gubala, Jack J. 1938- *WhoE 91*
Gubanich, Andrew Joseph, Jr. 1950- *WhoE 91*
Gubar, Susan 1944- *MajTwCW*
Gubbins, Keith Edmund 1937- *WhoAm 90, WhoE 91*
Guber, Lee 1920-1988 *BioIn 16*
Guber, Peter *BioIn 16*
Guberman, David Aaron 1949- *WhoEmL 91*
Guberman, Robert Paul 1945- *WhoSSW 91*
Guberman, Sidney Thomas 1936- *WhoAmA 91*
Gubicza, Mark 1962- *Ballpl 90*
Gubiotti, Ross Anthony 1948- *WhoEmL 91*
Gubisch, Robert Aloysius 1928- *St&PR 91*
Gubser, Lyn M. 1939- *WhoE 91*
Gucci, Aldo *NewYTBS 90*
Gucci, Aldo 1905?-1990 *BioIn 16*
Gucci, Maurizio *BioIn 16*
Guccio di Mannaia *PenDiDA 89*
Guccione, Anthony Joseph, II 1961- *WhoE 91*
Guccione, Juanita *WhoAmA 91*
Guccione, Piero 1935- *BioIn 16*
Guccione, Robert 1930- *ConAmBL*
Guccione, Robert Charles Joseph Edward S 1930- *WhoAm 90*
Guchemand, Margaret Kelso 1939- *IntWWM 90*
Guchkov, Aleksandr Ivanovich 1862-1936 *BioIn 16*
Guckenheimer, Daniel Paul 1943- *WhoWor 91*
Gucker, Jane Gleason 1951- *WhoAmW 91*
Guckert, Harry J. 1934- *St&PR 91*
Guckes, William Ruhland, Jr. 1944- *WhoE 91*
Guda, Harry Eugene 1931- *BiDrAPA 89*
Gudbergur Bergsson *DcScanL*
Gude, Gilbert 1923- *WhoE 91*
Gude, William Morgan 1934- *St&PR 91*
Gudegast, Hans *ConTFT 8*
Gudel, Joachim Felix 1927- *IntWWM 90*
Gudelis, Drasutis 1933- *St&PR 91*
Gudeman, Jon E 1936- *BiDrAPA 89*
Gudeman, Stephen Frederick 1939- *WhoAm 90*
Guden, Paul Alexander 1944- *St&PR 91*
Gudenberg, Baron von *PenDiDA 89*
Gudenberg, Harry Richard 1933- *WhoAm 90, WhoE 91*
Guderian, Heinz 1888-1954 *WorAlBi*
Gudev, Vladimir 1940- *WhoWor 91*
Gudger, William Dillard 1947- *WhoSSW 91*
Gudiksen, Karen S 1939- *BiDrAPA 89*
Gudinas, Donald Jerome 1933- *WhoAm 90*
Gudis, Malcolm J. 1941- *St&PR 91, WhoAm 90*
Gudis, Matthew Allan 1947- *BiDrAPA 89*
Gudjonsson, Halldor *DcScanL*
Gudjonsson, Hermann 1952- *WhoWor 91*
Gudmundsen-Holmgreen, Pelle 1932- *IntWWM 90*
Gudmundson, Shirley M. *AuBYP 90*
Gudmundsson, Finnbogi 1924- *WhoWor 91*
Gudmundsson, Kristmann 1901-1983 *DcScanL*
Gudmundsson, Ormar Thor 1935- *WhoWor 91*
Gudmundsson, Sigurdur Elimundur 1932- *WhoWor 91*
Gudmundsson, Thorir 1960- *WhoWor 91*
Gudmundsson, Tomas 1901-1983 *DcScanL*
Gudmundur Bodvarsson *DcScanL*
Gudmundur Gislason Hagalin *DcScanL*
Gudmundur Kamban *DcScanL*
Gudmundur Magnusson *DcScanL*
Gudorf, Kenneth Francis 1939- *St&PR 91, WhoAm 90*
Gudwer, Roseanne Denig 1936- *WhoAmW 91*
Gudyka, Louis Carl 1930- *St&PR 91*
Gudzak, Scott Andrew 1959- *WhoSSW 91*

Gudzak, Shelley Overholt 1958- *WhoSSW 91*
Gudzent, Dietrich Eberhard 1926- *WhoWor 91*
Guebhard, Adrien, Mme *EncCoWW*
Guecia, Albert Joseph 1940- *WhoSSW 91*
Guedel, John Bimel 1913- *WhoAm 90*
Gueden, Hilde 1917-1988 *PenDiMP*
Guedes, Amancio d'Alpoim Miranda 1925- *WhoWor 91*
Guedes, Antonio *WhoHisp 91*
Guedes-Vieira, Manuel Jose 1943- *WhoWor 91*
Guedry, James Walter 1941- *WhoAm 90*
Guedry, Leo J. 1940- *WhoAm 90*
Gueguen, Pierre-Gilles 1946- *WhoWor 91*
Guehl, John J 1919- *BiDrAPA 89*
Guelda, Arthur Francis, III 1934- *St&PR 91*
Gueldner, Helmar 1939- *St&PR 91*
Gueldner, Robert F., III 1950- *St&PR 91*
Guelfi, Giangiacomo 1924- *IntWWM 90*
Guelfi, Giovanni Battista *BioIn 16*
Gueli, Nicolo 1952- *WhoWor 91*
Guelich, Robert *BioIn 16*
Guelich, Robert V. 1917- *ODwPR 91*
Guelich, Robert Vernon 1917- *WhoAm 90*
Guendel, Thomas Joseph 1927- *St&PR 91*
Guendelsberger, Robert Joseph 1950- *WhoEmL 91*
Guenette, Francoise 1951- *WhoAm 90*
Guengerich, Gary David 1945- *St&PR 91*
Guenst, Rodney S. 1956- *St&PR 91*
Guenter, Gail Marie 1961- *WhoAmW 91*
Guenter, Raymond Albert 1932- *St&PR 91*
Guenther, Arthur Henry 1931- *WhoAm 90*
Guenther, Charles 1920- *WhoWrEP 89*
Guenther, Charles John 1920- *WhoAm 90*
Guenther, Frederick Oliver 1919- *WhoSSW 91*
Guenther, George C. 1931- *St&PR 91*
Guenther, George Carpenter 1931- *WhoAm 90*
Guenther, Jack Donald 1929- *WhoAm 90*
Guenther, Jack Egon 1934- *WhoAm 90*
Guenther, John S. 1942- *St&PR 91*
Guenther, Karl Heinz 1947- *WhoSSW 91*
Guenther, Kenneth Allen *WhoAm 90*
Guenther, Paul B. 1940- *St&PR 91*
Guenther, Paul Bernard 1940- *WhoAm 90, WhoE 91*
Guenther, Peter W 1920- *WhoAmA 91*
Guenther, Ralph Russell 1914- *IntWWM 90*
Guenther, Robert Anthony 1942- *St&PR 91, WhoWor 91*
Guenther, Robert Stanley, II 1950- *WhoEmL 91*
Guenther, Robert Wallace 1929- *WhoAm 90*
Guenther, Thomas P. 1932- *St&PR 91*
Guenther, Timothy Eric 1955- *IntWWM 90*
Guenzel, Frank Bernhard 1938- *WhoAm 90*
Guenzel, Paul Walter 1910- *WhoAm 90*
Guenzel, Rudolf Paul 1940- *St&PR 91, WhoAm 90*
Guequierre, John Phillip 1946- *St&PR 91*
Guequirre, John Phillip 1946- *WhoEmL 91*
Guerard, Albert Joseph 1914- *WhoAm 90, WhoWrEP 89*
Guerci, Louis J. 1944- *St&PR 91*
Guercino 1591?-1666 *IntDcAA 90*
Guercio, Gregory Joseph 1948- *WhoE 91*
Guererro, Barbara 1900?-1979 *EncPaPR 91*
Gueret Wardle, David Francis 1943- *WhoWor 91*
Guerette, Robert Charles *BiDrAPA 89*
Guericke, Otto Von 1602-1686 *WorAlBi*
Guerin, Camille A. 1938- *St&PR 91*
Guerin, Christian Jean Marie 1947- *WhoWor 91*
Guerin, Daniel 1904-1988 *BiDFrPL*
Guerin, Dava *ODwPR 91*
Guerin, Dean P. 1922- *St&PR 91*
Guerin, Dean Patrick 1922- *WhoAm 90*
Guerin, Didier 1950- *WhoWor 91*
Guerin, Eugenie-Henriette-Augustine de 1805-1848 *EncCoWW*
Guerin, Herve Bernard 1941- *WhoWor 91*
Guerin, Jean 1938- *WhoWor 91*
uerin, Joel F. 1948- *St&PR 91*
uerin, John J. 1926- *St&PR 91*
uerin, John William 1920- *WhoAm 90, WhoAmA 91*
uerin, Kenneth Joseph 1948- *WhoE 91*
uerin, Philip Joseph, Jr. *BiDrAPA 89*
uerin, Whitcomb Halsey 1951- *WhoEmL 91*
uerin De Neco, Judy 1935- *ODwPR 91*
uerindon, Pierre Claude 1927- *WhoAm 90*
ierine, Morton 1934- *St&PR 91*
ierisse, Albert *BioIn 16*
ierisse, Albert 1911-1989 *AnObit 1989*
eritey, Harold Charles, Jr. 1939- *St&PR 91*

Guernica, Antonio Jose 1951- *WhoHisp 91*
Guernsey, Bruce Argyle *BiDrAPA 89*
Guernsey, David Michael 1948- *WhoEmL 91*
Guernsey, Janet B. *BioIn 16*
Guernsey, Janet Brown 1913- *WhoAmW 91*
Guernsey, Joseph Shedd 1918- *WhoAm 90*
Guernsey, Louis Harold 1923- *WhoAm 90*
Guernsey, Nancy Patricia 1955- *WhoEmL 91, WhoWrEP 89*
Guernsey, Otis Love, Jr. 1918- *WhoAm 90*
Guernsey, Peter E. 1921- *St&PR 91*
Guernsey, Valerie Dee *BiDrAPA 89*
Guernsey, William Arnold, Jr. 1951- *WhoEmL 91*
Guernswey, Anthony H. 1936- *St&PR 91*
Gueron, Jules *NewYTBS 90*
Guerra, Alicia R. 1960- *WhoHisp 91*
Guerra, Armando J. 1951- *WhoSSW 91*
Guerra, Arturo 1948- *WhoHisp 91*
Guerra, Arturo Gregorio 1927- *WhoHisp 91*
Guerra, Berto *WhoHisp 91*
Guerra, Charles A. 1960- *WhoHisp 91*
Guerra, Charles Albert 1960- *WhoEmL 91, WhoSSW 91, WhoWor 91*
Guerra, Daniel J. 1955- *WhoHisp 91*
Guerra, Emma Maria 1956- *WhoAmW 91, WhoEmL 91*
Guerra, Fernando J. 1958- *WhoHisp 91*
Guerra, Frank 1945- *BiDrAPA 89*
Guerra, Fred Richard, Jr. 1955- *WhoEmL 91*
Guerra, Jorge Rolando 1926- *BiDrAPA 89*
Guerra, Marcelo Ernesto *BiDrAPA 89*
Guerra, Marcos Antonio 1940- *St&PR 91*
Guerra, Mark 1918-1989 *WhoHisp 91N*
Guerra, Mauro Rene 1958- *WhoSSW 91*
Guerra, Mike 1912- *Ballpl 90*
Guerra, Rene A. 1945- *WhoHisp 91*
Guerra, Rolando, Jr. 1965- *WhoHisp 91*
Guerra, Stella *WhoHisp 91*
Guerra, Stella Garcia 1945- *WhoAm 90*
Guerra, Tonino 1920- *ConTFT 8*
Guerra, Victor Javier 1949- *WhoHisp 91*
Guerra-Castro, Jorge 1952- *WhoHisp 91*
Guerra Gonzalez, Alfonso 1940- *WhoWor 91*
Guerra-Hanson, Imelda Celine 1953- *WhoHisp 91*
Guerra-Vela, Claudio 1945- *WhoHisp 91*
Guerrant, David Edward 1919- *WhoAm 90*
Guerrant, Edward Owings 1911- *WhoAm 90*
Guerreiro, Antonio Manuel Afonso 1952- *WhoWor 91*
Guerrera, Eugene Rocco 1940- *WhoE 91*
Guerrera, Nicholas Stephen 1960- *WhoE 91*
Guerrero, Anthony R., Jr. 1945- *St&PR 91*
Guerrero, Eduardo 1917- *BioIn 16*
Guerrero, Epy *BioIn 16*
Guerrero, Gonzalo *BioIn 16*
Guerrero, Guillermo E. 1946- *WhoHisp 91*
Guerrero, James Samuel *BiDrAPA 89*
Guerrero, Jose 1914- *WhoAm 90, WhoAmA 91*
Guerrero, Jose Miguel 1958- *WhoHisp 91*
Guerrero, Juan N. 1946- *WhoHisp 91*
Guerrero, Lalo 1917- *BioIn 16*
Guerrero, Lena 1957- *WhoHisp 91*
Guerrero, Manuel Amador 1833-1909 *BioIn 16*
Guerrero, Mario 1949- *Ballpl 90*
Guerrero, Martin *BiDrAPA 89*
Guerrero, Pedro *BioIn 16*
Guerrero, Pedro *WhoHisp 91N*
Guerrero, Pedro 1956- *Ballpl 90, WhoAm 90, WhoHisp 91, WorAlBi*
Guerrero, Pedro W. *BioIn 16*
Guerrero, Raul 1945- *WhoAmA 91*
Guerrero, Raul Jaime *BiDrAPA 89*
Guerrero, Roberto *BioIn 16*
Guerrero, Roberto 1958- *WhoHisp 91*
Guerrero, Steven E. 1949- *WhoSSW 91*
Guerrero, Xavier 1896-1974 *ArtLatA*
Guerrero Galvan, Jesus 1910-1973 *ArtLatA*
Guerrero-Martinez, Agustin 1934- *BiDrAPA 89*
Guerri, Sergio 1905- *WhoWor 91*
Guerri, William Grant 1921- *WhoAm 90*
Guerrier, Edmond *WhNaAH*
Guerrieri, Michael Anthony 1946- *St&PR 91*
Guerrise, Patrick P. 1943- *St&PR 91, WhoE 91*
Guerry, Alex, Jr. *St&PR 91N*
Guerster, Rene L. 1938- *St&PR 91, WhoAm 90*
Guertin, Donald L. 1930- *WhoE 91*
Guertin, Robert G. 1947- *St&PR 91*
Guertin, Robert Powell 1939- *WhoAm 90*
Guesde, Jules 1845-1922 *WorAlBi*
Guesde, Mathieu Bazile 1845-1922 *BiDFrPL*

Gueson, Emerita Torres 1942- *WhoAmW 91*
Guess Who, The *EncPR&S 89*
Guess, Cecil Willard, Jr. 1954- *WhoSSW 91*
Guess, Charles Anthony 1950- *WhoEmL 91*
Guess, James Edgar 1945- *WhoSSW 91*
Guess, Paul Richard 1945- *WhoEmL 91*
Guest, Barbara *WhoWrEP 89*
Guest, Barbara 1920- *FemiCLE, WhoAm 90*
Guest, C. Z. *BioIn 16*
Guest, Charlotte Bertie Elizabeth 1812-1895 *BioIn 16*
Guest, Cornelia *BioIn 16*
Guest, Donald Britnor 1929- *WhoSSW 91, WhoWor 91*
Guest, Douglas 1916- *PenDiMP*
Guest, Douglas Albert 1916- *IntWWM 90*
Guest, Edgar A. 1881-1959 *WorAlBi*
Guest, Elizabeth Polk 1910-1990 *BioIn 16*
Guest, George 1924- *PenDiMP*
Guest, George Hywel 1924- *IntWWM 90*
Guest, Howard Brandon 1959- *WhoEmL 91*
Guest, James Alfred 1940- *WhoAm 90*
Guest, Judith 1936- *MajTwCW*
Guest, Judith Ann 1936- *WhoAm 90, WhoWrEP 89*
Guest, Karl Macon 1915- *WhoAm 90*
Guest, Lynn 1939- *ConAu 131*
Guest, Maurice Mason 1906- *WhoAm 90*
Guest, Rita Carson 1950- *WhoWor 91*
Guest, Robert Henry 1916- *WhoAm 90*
Guest, William F. 1931- *St&PR 91*
Gueth, Thomas Franklin 1950- *WhoE 91*
Guettel, Henry Arthur 1928- *WhoAm 90*
Guetterman, Lee 1958- *Ballpl 90*
Guetterman, Stephanie Ann 1969- *WhoAmW 91*
Guetz, Burton Walter 1951- *WhoEmL 91*
Guetzkow, Daniel 1949- *St&PR 91*
Guetzkow, Daniel Steere 1949- *WhoE 91, WhoEmL 91*
Guetzkow, Diana 1947- *WhoEmL 91*
Guevara, Che *HispWr 90*
Guevara, Che 1928-1967 *BioIn 16, WorAlBi*
Guevara, Ernesto 1928-1967 *BioIn 16, HispWr 90*
Guevara, Gilberto 1942- *WhoHisp 91*
Guevara, Gustavo, Jr. 1949- *WhoHisp 91*
Guevara, Walter *BiDrAPA 89*
Guevara, Yingo 1931- *WhoHisp 91*
Guevara Alvarado, Rolando Anibal 1960- *WhoWor 91*
Guevara Arze, Walter 1911- *BioIn 16*
Guevara-Lacki, Nanette Rose 1953- *WhoAmW 91*
Guevara Pinero, Jose Luis 1931- *WhoHisp 91*
Guevara-Ramos, Luz Minerva *BiDrAPA 89*
Guevremont, Jacques 1932- *St&PR 91*
Guffey, George *ConAu 132*
Guffey, George R. *ConAu 132*
Guffey, George Robert 1932- *ConAu 132*
Guffey, James Roger 1929- *St&PR 91, WhoAm 90*
Guffey, John W. 1938- *St&PR 91*
Guffey, Joseph F. 1870-1959 *WorAlBi*
Guffey, Leo Wesley 1955- *WhoE 91*
Guffin, Gilbert L. 1906- *WhoAm 90*
Gugas, Chris 1921- *WhoWor 91*
Gugel, Craig Thomas 1954- *WhoE 91, WhoEmL 91, WhoWor 91*
Gugel, Paul Edward 1956- *WhoEmL 91*
Gugelot, Hans *PenDiDA 89*
Gugelot, Piet Cornelis 1918- *WhoAm 90*
Guggenheim, Alan Andre Albert Paul E. 1950- *WhoWor 91*
Guggenheim, Barbara Meyer 1834-1900 *BioIn 16*
Guggenheim, Benjamin 1865-1912 *BioIn 16*
Guggenheim, Charles E. 1924- *WhoAm 90*
Guggenheim, Daniel 1856-1930 *BioIn 16, WorAlBi*
Guggenheim, Daniel 1938- *BioIn 16*
Guggenheim, Edmond Alfred 1888-1972 *BioIn 16*
Guggenheim, Eleanor May 1898- *BioIn 16*
Guggenheim, Frederick G 1935- *BiDrAPA 89*
Guggenheim, Harry Frank 1890-1971 *BioIn 16, WhoAmA 91N*
Guggenheim, Hazel 1903- *BioIn 16*
Guggenheim, Isaac 1854-1922 *BioIn 16*
Guggenheim, Janet Goodman 1938- *IntWWM 90*
Guggenheim, M. Robert 1885-1959 *BioIn 16*
Guggenheim, M. Robert 1910- *BioIn 16*
Guggenheim, Marguerite 1898-1979 *BioAmW, BioIn 16*
Guggenheim, Martin 1946- *ConAu 129*
Guggenheim, Meyer 1828-1905 *BioIn 16, WorAlBi*

Guggenheim, Murry 1858-1939 *BioIn 16*
Guggenheim, Peggy 1898-1979 *BioIn 16, WhoAmA 91N, WorAlBi*
Guggenheim, Richard E. 1913- *WhoAm 90*
Guggenheim, Simon 1867-1941 *BioIn 16*
Guggenheim, Solomon Robert 1861-1949 *BioIn 16*
Guggenheim, William 1868-1941 *BioIn 16*
Guggenheim, William 1907-1947 *BioIn 16*
Guggenheim, William 1939- *BioIn 16*
Guggenheimer, Elinor 1912- *WhoAmW 91*
Guggenheimer, Heinrich Walter 1924- *WhoAm 90*
Guggenheimer, Minnie 1882-1966 *BioAmW*
Guggenheimer, Randolph, Jr. 1935- *St&PR 91*
Guggenheimer, Richard Henry 1906-1977 *WhoAmA 91N*
Guggenhime, Richard Johnson 1940- *WhoAm 90, WhoWor 91*
Gugino, Carmelo, Jr. 1915- *St&PR 91*
Gugler, Adolf Emil 1929- *WhoWor 91*
Gugler, Anne Tonetti *BioIn 16, NewYTBS 90*
Guglielmi, Frank A. 1951- *St&PR 91*
Guglielmi, Frank J. 1963- *ODwPR 91*
Guglielmi, Louis O 1906-1956 *WhoAmA 91N*
Guglielmi, Peter Anthony 1942- *WhoAm 90*
Guglielmi, Robert Vincent 1936- *St&PR 91*
Guglielminetti, Amalia 1885-1941 *EncCoWW*
Guglielmino, Paul Joseph 1942- *WhoSSW 91*
Gugliott, P.J. 1957- *St&PR 91*
Gugliotta, Bobette 1918- *ConAu 31NR*
Gugliuzza, Kristene Koontz 1956- *WhoAmW 91*
Guha, Subhendu 1942- *St&PR 91*
Guhleman, Henry V, Jr. *BiDrAPA 89*
Gui, Henry 1926- *IntWWM 90*
Gui, James Edmund 1928- *WhoAm 90, WhoE 91*
Gui, Vittorio 1885-1975 *PenDiMP*
Guia, Romana N I 1929- *BiDrAPA 89*
Guiard, Adelaide Labille- 1749-1803 *BioIn 16*
Guibert, Elisabeth 1725-1787? *EncCoWW*
Guibert, Honore 1720?-1791 *PenDiDA 89*
Guice, Don W. 1950- *St&PR 91*
Guice, John Thompson 1923- *WhoAm 90*
Guice, Leslie Kieth 1954- *WhoSSW 91*
Guichard, Johann Philipp *PenDiDA 89*
Guichard, Olivier-Marie Maurice 1920- *BiDFrPL*
Guicharnaud, June 1922-1989 *BioIn 16, ConAu 129*
Guichet, Melody 1949- *WhoAmA 91*
Guida, Dominick 1946- *WhoAmA 91*
Guida, F.A. 1934- *St&PR 91*
Guida, Frank J. 1922- *IntWWM 90*
Guida, Pat 1929- *WhoAmW 91*
Guida, Peter Matthew 1927- *WhoAm 90*
Guidacci, Margherita 1921- *EncCoWW*
Guidano, Vittorio Filippo 1944- *WhoWor 91*
Guide, Robert George 1933- *St&PR 91*
Guidebeck, Ronald Patrick 1936- *St&PR 91*
Guidera, Brian M. 1939- *St&PR 91*
Guidette, Elizabeth *St&PR 91*
Guidette, Jeffrey G. 1941- *WhoE 91*
Guidi, Doris Fraser 1934- *WhoAm 90, WhoAmW 91*
Guidi, Nedda 1927- *BiDWomA*
Guiditta, Thomas Anthony 1944- *St&PR 91*
Guido Durantino *PenDiDA 89*
Guido, Beatriz 1924-1988 *HispWr 90*
Guido, Diana Lydia 1954- *WhoEmL 91*
Guido, Jo Ann 1952- *WhoWrEP 89*
Guido, John A 1922- *BiDrAPA 89*
Guido, Judith Cooper *WhoAmW 91, WhoE 91*
Guido, Michael Frank 1952- *St&PR 91*
Guido, Shareon Christine 1946- *WhoAmW 91, WhoEmL 91, WhoWor 91*
Guidoboni, Thomas Anthony 1946- *WhoEmL 91*
Guidoni, T. Lee 1946- *WhoAmW 91*
Guidotti, Guido 1933- *WhoAm 90*
Guidry, Don D. 1937- *WhoSSW 91*
Guidry, Karen Louise 1956- *WhoAmW 91*
Guidry, Krisandra Ann 1963- *WhoSSW 91*
Guidry, Rodney-Lee Joseph 1935- *WhoSSW 91*
Guidry, Ron *BioIn 16*
Guidry, Ron 1950- *Ballpl 90, WorAlBi*
Guidry, Steven Anthony 1956- *WhoEmL 91*
Guidry, Susan Diane Arnold 1953- *WhoEmL 91*
Guidugli, Piero Angelo 1952- *St&PR 91*
Guie, E. Heister 1867- *AmLegL*
Guiffre, Jean Ellen 1942- *WhoAmW 91*

Guignard, Jacques Marcel 1941- *WhoWor 91*
Guignard, Jean-Louis Marie Joseph 1931- *WhoWor 91*
Guigon, John V. 1929- *St&PR 91*
Guihan, J. Lawrence 1952- *St&PR 91*
Guiher, James Morford, Jr. 1927- *WhoAm 90*
Guijarro, Antonio Aparisi y 1815-1872 *BioIn 16*
Guijarro-Morales, Antonio 1943- *WhoWor 91*
Guikema, Dale J. 1940- *St&PR 91*
Guilbault, Lawrence James 1940- *St&PR 91*
Guilbault, Pierre 1954- *St&PR 91*
Guilbeault, Luce 1935- *OxCCanT*
Guilbert, Jamee Becker *BioIn 16*
Guilbert, Yvette 1865-1944 *OxCPMus, PenDiMP*
Guilboa, Amos 1912- *WhoHisp 91*
Guild, Alden 1929- *St&PR 91, WhoAm 90*
Guild, Carol Elizabeth *WhoE 91*
Guild, Clark Joseph, Jr. 1921- *WhoAm 90*
Guild, Donald C 1946- *BiDrAPA 89*
Guild, Donald George 1927- *St&PR 91*
Guild, Emma Marie Cadwalader 1843-1912? *BiDWomA*
Guild, Henry Rice, Jr. 1928- *St&PR 91*
Guild, Nelson Prescott 1928- *WhoAm 90*
Guild, Nicholas M 1944- *SpyFic*
Guild, Richard Samuel 1925- *WhoE 91, WhoWor 91*
Guilelmus, Archbishop of Tyre 1130?-1190? *BioIn 16*
Guilet, Daniel 1899-1990 *NewYTBS 90*
Guilevitch, Daniel *PenDiMP*
Guilford, Andrew John 1950- *WhoEmL 91*
Guilford, J. Paul 1897-1987 *BioIn 16*
Guilford, Morgan B. 1935- *St&PR 91*
Guilford, Nanette 1903-1990 *BioIn 16, NewYTBS 90*
Guilfoyle, David *St&PR 91*
Guilfoyle, George H. 1913- *WhoE 91*
Guilfoyle, John W. *BioIn 16*
Guilfoyle, Marion Irene 1920-1989 *BioIn 16*
Guiliano, Mireille *ODwPR 91*
Guillame, Raymond Kendrick 1943- *St&PR 91*
Guillaume de Carpentras *EncO&P 3*
Guillaume de Paris 1180?-1249 *EncO&P 3*
Guillaume, Charles E. 1861-1938 *WorAlBi*
Guillaume, Edith 1943- *IntWWM 90*
Guillaume, Germaine Gabrielle 1949- *WhoAmW 91*
Guillaume, Gilbert 1930- *WhoWor 91*
Guillaume, Jacquette *EncCoWW*
Guillaume, Lionel *BiDrAPA 89*
Guillaume, Marnix L.K. 1938- *St&PR 91*
Guillaume, Marnix Leo Karl 1938- *WhoAm 90*
Guillaume, Raymond Kendrick 1943- *WhoAm 90*
Guillaume, Robert 1927- *DrBlPA 90*
Guillaume, Robert 1939- *WorAlBi*
Guillaumin, Denis Marie 1952- *WhoWor 91*
Guillaumont, Patrick 1939- *WhoWor 91*
Guillebeau, Julie Graves 1948- *WhoWrEP 89*
Guillelma de Rosers *EncCoWW*
Guillem, Sylvie *BioIn 16*
Guillemette, A. Roger 1934- *St&PR 91*
Guillemette, Eugene Joseph 1956- *WhoEmL 91*
Guillemette, Gloria Vivian 1929- *WhoAmW 91*
Guillemette, Roger Gerard 1959- *WhoE 91*
Guillemin, Roger 1924- *WhoAm 90, WhoWor 91, WorAlBi*
Guillen, Ana Magda *WhoHisp 91*
Guillen, Francisco 1946- *WhoWor 91*
Guillen, Jorge 1893-1984 *HispWr 90, WorAlBi*
Guillen, Nicolas 1902-1989 *AnObit 1989, BioIn 16, ConAu 129, HispWr 90*
Guillen, Ozzie 1964- *Ballpl 90, WhoHisp 91*
Guillen, Tomas 1949- *WhoHisp 91*
Guillen Y Batista, Nicolas 1902-1989 *HispWr 90*
Guillermin, Armand Pierre 1936- *WhoSSW 91*
Guillermit, Jean-Paul 1937- *WhoWor 91*
Guillermo, Linda Sue 1951- *WhoAmW 91*
Guillery, Rainer Walter 1929- *WhoAm 90*
Guillet *DcCanB 12*
Guillet, James Edwin 1927- *WhoAm 90*
Guillet, Pernette du 1520?-1545 *EncCoWW*
Guilli, Franco 1926- *PenDiMP*
Guillibaud, Jean-Baptiste *PenDiDA 89*
Guilliouma, Larry Jay, Jr. 1950- *WhoSSW 91*
Guillory, Elbert Lee 1944- *WhoSSW 91*
Guillory, Linda 1950- *WhoAmW 91*
Guillory, Vivian Broussard 1953- *WhoEmL 91*
Guillot, Gerard 1947- *WhoWor 91*
Guillot, Rene 1900-1969 *AuBYP 90, ChlLR 22 [port]*
Guillot, Robert Miller 1922- *WhoSSW 91*
Guillot, Walter L *BiDrAPA 89*
Guillotte, Preston J. 1938- *St&PR 91*
Guillum Scott, John Arthur 1910-1983 *DcNaB 1981*
Guilmain, Jacques 1926- *WhoAmA 91, WhoE 91*
Guilmant, Alexandre 1837-1911 *PenDiMP*
Guilmartin, Judith Ohr 1939- *WhoAmW 91*
Guiloff, Andres 1954- *WhoWor 91*
Guiloff, Jorge Francisco 1952- *WhoHisp 91*
Guimaraes, Dona *BioIn 16*
Guimaraes, Dona 1926?-1989 *ConAu 129*
Guimaraes, Eduardo Pereira 1941- *WhoWor 91*
Guimaraes, Johnny 1966- *WhoSSW 91*
Guimard, Hector 1867-1942 *PenDiDA 89*
Guimond, Gary Albert 1941- *WhoE 91*
Guimond, John Patrick 1927- *WhoAm 90*
Guimond, Olivier 1914-1971 *OxCCanT*
Guimond, Richard *BioIn 16*
Guimond, Richard Joseph 1947- *WhoAm 90*
Guimorva Moreira, Airto 1941- *BioIn 16*
Guin, David Jonathan 1960- *WhoEmL 91, WhoSSW 91*
Guin, Debra Mauriece 1953- *WhoSSW 91*
Guin, Don Lester 1940- *WhoSSW 91*
Guin, James Patrick 1946- *St&PR 91*
Guin, Junius Foy, Jr. 1924- *WhoAm 90, WhoSSW 91*
Guin, Marilyn Potts- *BioIn 16*
Guin, Winford Harold 1926- *WhoAm 90*
Guinan, James M. *St&PR 91*
Guinan, James Martin 1932- *WhoAm 90*
Guinan, John Grange 1945- *WhoE 91*
Guinan, Mary Elizabeth 1939- *WhoAmW 91*
Guinan, Mary Louise 1951- *WhoE 91*
Guinan, Texas 1884-1933 *WorAlBi*
Guindon, Kurt Roberts 1959- *BiDrAPA 89*
Guinee, William T. 1932- *St&PR 91*
Guiney, Louise 1861-1920 *FemiCLE*
Guiney, Louise I. 1861-1920 *BioAmW*
Guinier, Ewart *NewYTBS 90*
Guinier, Ewart 1910-1990 *BioIn 16*
Guinivan, Thomas W. 1922- *St&PR 91*
Guiniven, John E. 1941- *ODwPR 91*
Guinn, Al F. 1928- *IntWWM 90, WhoWor 91*
Guinn, David Crittenden 1926- *WhoAm 90, WhoSSW 91*
Guinn, Dorothy C. *EarBlAP*
Guinn, Gary Mark 1948- *WhoWrEP 89*
Guinn, Geoffrey Kyle 1948- *St&PR 91*
Guinn, Janet Martin 1942- *WhoAmW 91*
Guinn, Jerry Hill 1929- *St&PR 91*
Guinn, Kenny C. 1934- *WhoAm 90*
Guinn, Kenny C. 1936- *St&PR 91*
Guinn, Norma Joanne *WhoAmW 91*
Guinn, Stanley Willis 1953- *WhoEmL 91, WhoWor 91*
Guinness, Alec *BioIn 16*
Guinness, Alec 1914- *ConTFT 8 [port], WhoAm 90, WhoWor 91, WorAlBi*
Guinness, Bryan *BioIn 16*
Guinness, Loel 1906-1988 *BioIn 16*
Guinness, Mariga 1932-1989 *AnObit 1989*
Guinness, Matthew 1942- *ConTFT 8*
Guinot, Herve Marie Camille 1955- *WhoWor 91*
Guinter, John Robert 1922- *St&PR 91*
Guinther, Fred E. *ODwPR 91*
Guinther, Frederick E. 1932- *St&PR 91*
Guintu, Arthur Yambao *BioIn 16*
Guintu, Generosa G *BiDrAPA 89*
Guinup, Linda L. 1954- *WhoEmL 91*
Guinzburg, Frederick 1897-1978 *WhoAmA 91N*
Guinzburg, Thomas H. *BioIn 16*
Guiol, Patrice Roland 1954- *WhoEmL 91*
Guion, Owen H. 1861- *AmLegL*
Guion, Robert Morgan 1924- *WhoAm 90*
Guion-Shipley, Joyce 1946- *WhoWrEP 89*
Guiora, Susie Nira 1932- *WhoWor 91*
Guiot, Andrea 1928- *IntWWM 90*
Guiot, Jean 1956- *IntWWM 90*
Guiot-Bordoni, Lorenza 1954- *IntWWM 90*
Guipago *WhNaAH*
Guira, Jorge M. 1959- *WhoEmL 91*
Guiraldes, Ricardo 1886-1927 *BioIn 16, ConAu 131, HispWr 90, MajTwCW, TwCLC 39 [port]*
Guirdham, Arthur 1905- *EncO&P 3*
Guirguis, Ezzat F 1938- *BiDrAPA 89*
Guirlinger, Richard B. 1953- *St&PR 91*
Guirma, Frederic *BioIn 16*
Guirnalda, Nemesia *BiDrAPA 89*
Guise, David Earl 1931- *WhoAm 90, WhoWor 91*
Guise, Thomas James 1944- *St&PR 91*
Guisewite, Cathy *BioIn 16*
Guisewite, Cathy 1950- *EncACom*
Guisewite, Cathy Lee 1950- *WhoAmW 91*
Guiss, Russell L *BiDrAPA 89*
Guist, Carl G. 1946- *St&PR 91*
Guist, Fredric Michael 1946- *WhoAm 90*
Guitar Slim, Jr. *BioIn 16*
Guitart, Jorge Miguel 1937- *WhoHisp 91*
Guitart, Michael Horacio 1935- *WhoSSW 91, WhoWor 91*
Guitart Ferre, Francisco 1944- *WhoWor 91*
Guite, Jean Charles Michel 1945- *WhoE 91*
Guiterman Freund, Laura Mayer 1925- *WhoAmW 91*
Guith, Deanna Marie *BiDrAPA 89*
Guithues, Denise Michele 1954- *WhoEmL 91*
Guiton, Bonnie F. 1941- *WhoAm 90, WhoAmW 91*
Guiton, John H. 1929- *St&PR 91*
Guiton, Theresa Anne 1962- *WhoAmW 91*
Guittar, Lee J. 1931- *St&PR 91*
Guittarr, Dennis C. 1947- *St&PR 91*
Guiver, Abby Bernstein 1942- *WhoAmW 91*
Guiver, Dennis L. 1938- *ODwPR 91*
Guiyab, Maria Uy 1941- *BiDrAPA 89*
Guizar, Ricardo Diaz 1933- *WhoAm 90*
Guizzetti, Joe Dale 1951- *St&PR 91*
Gujavarty, Krishnareddy S *BiDrAPA 89*
Gujral, Inder Kumar 1919- *WhoWor 91*
Guju, John G. 1924- *WhoAm 90*
Gula, Robert J. 1941-1989 *BioIn 16*
Gulacsy, Iren 1894-1945 *EncCoWW*
Gulamerian, Claire S. 1930- *St&PR 91*
Gulan, Bonnie *BioIn 16*
Gulas, Edward John 1932- *St&PR 91*
Gulas, Theodore Constantine 1950- *WhoSSW 91*
Gulasekaram, Bala *BiDrAPA 89*
Gulati, Anil 1959- *WhoE 91*
Gulbadan, Princess 1523?-1603 *FemiCLE*
Gulbenkian, Paul 1927- *WhoAm 90*
Gulbicki, William Thomas 1937- *WhoSSW 91*
Gulbin, John George 1935- *St&PR 91*
Gulbinowicz, Henryk Roman 1928- *WhoWor 91*
Gulbrandsen, Nora *PenDiDA 89*
Gulbrandson, L. C. 1922- *WhoAm 90*
Gulbransen, Capron R. 1923- *St&PR 91*
Gulbransen, Margery Elizabeth *WhoWrEP 89*
Gulbranson, Ellen 1863-1947 *PenDiMP*
Gulcher, Robert Harry 1925- *WhoAm 90*
Gulda, Edward James 1945- *WhoAm 90*
Gulda, Friedrich 1930- *IntWWM 90, PenDiMP*
Guldberg, Tatiana 1913- *WhoWor 91*
Guldborg, Soren 1943- *WhoWor 91*
Gulden, Frank *BioIn 16*
Gulden, Simon 1938- *St&PR 91, WhoAm 90*
Gulden, Vern Theodore 1948- *St&PR 91*
Guldenstern, David L. 1943- *St&PR 91*
Guldenstubbe, L von 1820-1873 *EncO&P 3*
Guldimann, Till M. 1949- *WhoE 91*
Guldner, Mary Ellen *WhoWrEP 89*
Guleke, James O., II 1948- *WhoEmL 91*
Gulesian, Susan *BiDrAPA 89*
Gulevich, George D *BiDrAPA 89*
Gulian, Jo-Anne 1943- *WhoAmW 91*
Gulick, Betty 1929- *St&PR 91*
Gulick, Bill 1916- *BioIn 16*
Gulick, Donald E. 1942- *St&PR 91*
Gulick, Donna Marie 1956- *WhoAmW 91*
Gulick, Henry Thomas 1872-1964 *MusmAFA*
Gulick, Jack A. 1929- *St&PR 91*
Gulick, John 1924- *WhoAm 90*
Gulick, John Thomas 1832-1923 *DcScB S2*
Gulick, Luther Halsey 1892- *WhoAm 90*
Gulick, Paul Irving 1935- *WhoSSW 91*
Gulick, Peggy 1918- *AuBYP 90*
Gulick, Roy M. 1934- *St&PR 91*
Gulick, Sidney Lewis 1860-1945 *BioIn 16*
Gulick, Walter Lawrence 1927- *WhoAm 90*
Gulin, Angeles 1943- *IntWWM 90*
Gulino, Ateo Louis 1917- *WhoAm 90*
Gulis, Dean Alexander 1955- *WhoEmL 91*
Gulka, John Matthew 1953- *WhoEmL 91, WhoSSW 91*
Gulker, Myron 1939- *St&PR 91*
Gulkin, Harry 1927- *WhoAm 90*
Gulko, Edward 1950- *WhoEmL 91*
Gulko, Kathleen 1943- *WhoAmW 91*
Gulko, Paul Michael 1944- *WhoAm 90*
Gullace, Carmelo 1928- *BiDrAPA 89*
Gullahorn, Genevieve *AuBYP 90*
Gullan, Richard Wilson 1953- *WhoWor 91*
Gullander, Werner Paul 1908- *WhoAm 90*
Gullans, Charles 1929- *WhoWrEP 89*
Gullapalli, S.M. 1936- *St&PR 91*
Gullattee, Alyce *BiDrAPA 89*
Gullberg, Hjalmar Robert 1898-1961 *DcScanL*
Gullberg, William Karl 1925- *WhoWor 91*
Gulledge, A Dale 1932- *BiDrAPA 89*
Gulledge, Jack 1924- *WhoAm 90*
Gulledge, Karen Stone 1941- *WhoAmW 91*
Gulledge, Sidney Loy, Jr. 1921- *St&PR 91*
Guller, Irving Bernard 1932- *WhoWor 91*
Guller, Youra 1895-1981 *PenDiMP*
Gullett, Don 1951- *Ballpl 90*
Gullett, John E. 1941- *ODwPR 91*
Gullett, John Estes 1941- *St&PR 91*
Gullette, Irene D. 1906- *WhoSSW 91*
Gulley, Don R. 1940- *St&PR 91*
Gulley, Joan L. 1947- *St&PR 91*
Gulley, Judie 1942- *BioIn 16*
Gulley, Lawrence Rucker *BiDrAPA 89*
Gulley, Leona Grace 1935- *WhoSSW 91*
Gulley, Marcus M *BiDrAPA 89*
Gulley, Ralph Grady 1902-1990 *BioIn 16*
Gulley, W. L. 1922- *WhoAm 90*
Gulley, Wilbur Paul 1948- *WhoSSW 91*
Gulley, Wilbur Paul, Jr. 1923- *WhoAm 90*
Gulli, Franco 1926- *IntWWM 90*
Gullickson, Bill 1959- *Ballpl 90*
Gullickson, Glenn, Jr. 1919- *WhoAm 90*
Gullickson, William Dean 1924- *St&PR 91*
Gullino, Frank *BioIn 16*
Gulliver, John William 1951- *WhoEmL 91*
Gulliver, Suzy Bird 1961- *WhoAmW 91*
Gullixson, Craig Alan 1956- *WhoEmL 91*
Gullo, Johnni Lee 1962- *WhoE 91*
Gullo, Paula Maria 1957- *WhoE 91*
Gullo, Stephen Pernice 1950- *WhoWor 91*
Gullotte, Stephanie Deran Wiggins 1956- *WhoEmL 91*
Gully, Anthony Lacy 1938- *WhoAmA 91*
Gully, Chester *WhoWrEP 89*
Gulmi, James Singleton 1946- *St&PR 91, WhoAm 90, WhoEmL 91*
Gulotta, Frank A. *BioIn 16*
Gulotta, Victor 1954- *WhoE 91*
Gulpen, J.C. 1955- *St&PR 91*
Gulski, Nelson Joseph 1906- *St&PR 91*
Gultekin, Muharrem *BiDrAPA 89*
Gulvin, David H. 1934- *St&PR 91*
Gulyas, Denes 1954- *IntWWM 90*
Gulyas, Gyorgy 1916- *IntWWM 90*
Gulyn, Bohdan E *BiDrAPA 89*
Gulzar, Sikander 1958- *WhoWor 91*
Gum, Dawn Alicia 1956- *WhoAmW 91*
Guma, Greg 1947- *WhoWrEP 89*
Guma, Greg William 1947- *WhoAm 90, WhoEmL 91*
Gumaer, Elliott Wilder, Jr. 1933- *WhoAm 90*
Gumas, John George 1959- *WhoEmL 91*
Gumb, Dana Frederic 1924- *St&PR 91*
Gumbaridze, Givi G. *WhoWor 91*
Gumbel, Bryant 1948- *BioIn 16, DrBlPA 90, NewYTBS 90 [port], News 90 [port]*
Gumbel, Bryant C. 1948- *WorAlBi*
Gumbel, Bryant Charles 1948- *WhoAm 90, WhoE 91*
Gumbert, Harry 1909- *Ballpl 90*
Gumberts, William A 1912- *WhoAmA 91N*
Gumbiner, Anthony Joseph 1945- *St&PR 91*
Gumbiner, Kenneth Jay 1946- *WhoEmL 91*
Gumbinner, Paul S. 1942- *WhoE 91*
Gumble, Arthur Robert 1920- *WhoWor 91*
Gumbleton, Thomas J. 1930- *WhoAm 90*
Gumer, Alan Austin *BiDrAPA 89*
Gumerson, Jean Gilderhus 1923- *WhoAm 90, WhoAmW 91*
Gumfory, Thomas Mac 1948- *WhoEmL 91*
Gumienny, Helen L. 1939- *WhoAmW 91*
Gumilev, Nikolai 1886-1921 *WorAlBi*
Gumley, James *PenDiDA 89*
Gumley, John 1691-1727 *PenDiDA 89*
Gumm, Ernest Frank 1930- *St&PR 91*
Gummattira, Pushpa K *BiDrAPA 89*
Gummel, Hermann Karl 1923- *WhoAm 90*
Gummelt, Samuel 1944- *WhoAmA 91*
Gummer, Charles L. *St&PR 91*
Gummer, Don 1946- *WhoAmA 91*
Gummere, Jerry D. 1932- *St&PR 91*
Gummere, John 1928- *St&PR 91*
Gummere, Samuel Rene 1849-1920 *BioIn 16*
Gummere, Walter Cooper 1917- *WhoAm 90*
Gummert, David D. 1957- *WhoEmL 91*
Gump, Judith Louise 1944- *WhoAmW 91*
Gump, Richard Anthony 1917- *WhoAm 90*
Gumpel, Hugh 1926- *WhoAmA 91*
Gumpel, Karl-Werner 1930- *IntWWM 90*
Gumpert, Dave 1958- *Ballpl 90*
Gumpert, Gunther 1919- *WhoAm 90, WhoAmA 91*
Gumpert, Randy 1918- *Ballpl 90*
Gumpertz, Bob 1925- *AuBYP 90*
Gumpertz, Werner Herbert 1917- *St&PR 91, WhoAm 90*
Gumperz, John J 1922- *ConAu 132*
Gumport, Stephen L. 1913-1989 *BioIn 16*
Gumucio, Marcelo A. 1937- *St&PR 91*

Gumucio, Marcelo Andres 1937- *WhoAm 90*
Gunasekera, Jay Sarath 1946- *WhoEmL 91*
Gunasinghe, Siri 1925- *WhoAmA 91*
Gunawardhana, Hemachandra *BiDrAPA 89*
Gunby, Bjorn Ove 1932- *BiDrAPA 89*
Gunby Kelly, Carolyn 1954- *WhoSSW 91*
Gunckel, Stuart Squier 1936- *WhoAm 90*
Gund, Gordon 1939- *WhoAm 90*
Gund, Graham *BioIn 16*
Gundarev, Victor *BioIn 16*
Gundelfinger, Genevieve May 1956- *WhoWor 91*
Gundelfinger, John Andre 1937- *WhoAmA 91*
Gundelfinger, Margaret Ellen 1956- *WhoEmL 91*
Gunderia, Dhruvkumar V 1951- *BiDrAPA 89*
Gunderman, Karen M 1951- *WhoAmA 91*
Gunderrode, Karoline von 1780-1806 *EncCoWW*
Gundersen, Alice Marshall 1934- *WhoAmW 91*
Gundersen, Allison Maureen 1959- *WhoAmW 91*
Gundersen, Egil Arnt 1941- *IntWWM 90*
Gundersen, Robert Alexander 1954- *WhoEmL 91*
Gundersen, Wayne Campbell 1936- *WhoAm 90*
Gundersheimer, Herman 1903- *WhoAmA 91*
Gundersheimer, Karen 1939- *BioIn 16*
Gundersheimer, Werner Leonard 1937- *WhoAm 90, WhoE 91*
Gunderson, Barry L 1945- *WhoAmA 91*
Gunderson, Charles H., Jr. 1939- *St&PR 91*
Gunderson, Clark Alan 1948- *WhoSSW 91*
Gunderson, Elmer Millard 1929- *WhoAm 90*
Gunderson, Eric *BioIn 16*
Gunderson, Gerald Axel 1940- *WhoAm 90*
Gunderson, Joanna 1932- *WhoWrEP 89*
Gunderson, John Brooks 1931- *St&PR 91*
Gunderson, John Gunder 1942- *BiDrAPA 89*
Gunderson, Judith Keefer 1939- *WhoAmW 91*
Gunderson, Karen 1943- *WhoAmA 91*
Gunderson, Leif Kingsley 1958- *WhoSSW 91*
Gunderson, Norman Gustav 1917- *WhoAm 90*
Gunderson, Richard L. 1933- *St&PR 91*
Gunderson, Robert Vernon, Jr. 1951- *WhoEmL 91, WhoWor 91*
Gunderson, Steve Craig 1951- *WhoAm 90*
Gunderson, Steven Alan 1949- *WhoEmL 91*
Gundesen, Hans 1946- *WhoWor 91*
Gundlach, Heinz L. 1937- *St&PR 91*
Gundlach, Heinz Ludwig 1937- *WhoAm 90*
Gundlach, Helen Fuchs 1892-1959 *WhoAmA 91N*
Gundlach, Herman 1913- *St&PR 91*
Gundlach, Kathryn Eggen 1952- *WhoEmL 91*
Gundlach, Skip 1945- *WhoSSW 91*
Gundlach, T.F. 1924- *St&PR 91*
Gundle, Michael J 1944- *BiDrAPA 89*
Gundle, Sigmund 1915- *BiDrAPA 89*
Gundling, Beulah O. 1916- *BioIn 16*
Gundrum, Brad William 1956- *St&PR 91*
Gundrum, James Richard 1929- *WhoAm 90*
Gundrum, Lawrence Joseph 1943- *St&PR 91*
Gundrum, Russell Fred 1948- *St&PR 91*
Gundry, Inglis 1905- *IntWWM 90*
Gundry, Rachel K *BiDrAPA 89*
Guner, Hitay 1936- *WhoWor 91*
Guner, Mehmet Irfan 1931- *WhoWor 91*
Gunerman, Penny Ann 1953- *WhoE 91*
Guney, Yilmaz *BioIn 16*
Gungaadorj, Sharavyn 1935- *WhoWor 91*
Gungl, Josef 1810-1889 *OxCPMus*
Gungor, Ogan Denis 1956- *WhoSSW 91*
Gungwu, Wang 1930- *WhoWor 91*
Gunja, Donald Edward 1949- *WhoEmL 91*
Gunja, Sakina Zahir *BiDrAPA 89*
Gunji, Hiromi 1939- *St&PR 91*
Gunkel, Debra Marie 1958- *WhoAmW 91*
Gunkler, Carl Andrew, Jr. 1920- *WhoAm 90*
Gunlock, William L. 1928- *St&PR 91*
Gunn, Alan 1940- *WhoAm 90*
Gunn, Albert Edward 1933- *WhoAm 90*
Gunn, Bill *BioIn 16*
Gunn, Bill 1934-1989 *ConTFT 8*
Gunn, Bill 1939-1989 *DrBlPA 90*
Gunn, Christy Howard 1954- *WhoAmW 91*
Gunn, David W. 1960- *St&PR 91*
Gunn, Edgar Lindsey 1950- *WhoSSW 91*
Gunn, Ellen 1951- *WhoAmA 91*
Gunn, Gaylia Gunn 1947- *WhoEmL 91, WhoWor 91*
Gunn, George F., Jr. 1927- *WhoAm 90*
Gunn, George R., Jr. *ODwPR 91*
Gunn, George R., Jr. 1939- *WhoAm 90*
Gunn, Giles Buckingham 1938- *WhoAm 90*
Gunn, Guy Greg 1958- *WhoE 91*
Gunn, James Edwin 1923- *WhoWrEP 89*
Gunn, Janet Penelope 1954- *WhoAmW 91*
Gunn, Jeannie 1870-1961 *FemiCLE*
Gunn, Jennifer H 1954- *BiDrAPA 89*
Gunn, John Battiscombe 1928- *WhoAm 90*
Gunn, John Reginald 1943- *WhoAm 90, WhoWor 91*
Gunn, Karen Sue 1951- *WhoAmW 91*
Gunn, Kay Lee 1932- *WhoAmW 91*
Gunn, Kenneth David 1940- *WhoSSW 91*
Gunn, Kenneth Milton, Jr. 1958- *WhoEmL 91, WhoSSW 91, WhoWor 91*
Gunn, Kenneth T. 1936- *St&PR 91*
Gunn, Lawrence Eugene 1951- *WhoE 91*
Gunn, M. Walker 1939- *IntWWM 90*
Gunn, Mary Elizabeth 1914- *WhoAmW 91*
Gunn, Michael William 1945- *St&PR 91, WhoAm 90*
Gunn, Michela F 1940- *BiDrAPA 89*
Gunn, Morey Walker, Jr. 1939- *WhoSSW 91, WhoWor 91*
Gunn, Moses 1929- *DrBlPA 90, WhoAm 90*
Gunn, Paul James 1922- *WhoAmA 91*
Gunn, Robert Burns 1939- *WhoAm 90*
Gunn, Robert Dewey 1928- *WhoAm 90*
Gunn, Robert Murray 1927- *WhoAm 90*
Gunn, Robert Norman 1925- *WhoWor 91*
Gunn, Roderick James 1945- *WhoAm 90*
Gunn, Thom *BioIn 16*
Gunn, Thom 1929- *ConAu 33NR, MajTwCW, WhoWrEP 89*
Gunn, Thomas Allen, Jr. 1931- *St&PR 91*
Gunn, Thomson 1929- *WhoAm 90*
Gunn, Wendell Lavelle 1932- *St&PR 91*
Gunn, William John 1920- *WhoE 91*
Gunnar Gunnarsson *DcScanL*
Gunnars, Kristjana 1948- *BioIn 16, FemiCLE*
Gunnarson, John A. 1925- *St&PR 91*
Gunnarson, Lynn Marie 1964- *WhoEmL 91*
Gunnarsson, Bengt-Ove 1940- *IntWWM 90*
Gunnarsson, Gunnar 1889-1975 *DcScanL*
Gunnell, John A. 1947- *WhoWrEP 89*
Gunnell, Kenneth A. 1946- *St&PR 91*
Gunnels, Lawrence 1931- *St&PR 91*
Gunner, Frances *EarBlAP*
Gunnersen, Uwe 1935- *WhoWor 91*
Gunnerson, Robert M. 1949- *St&PR 91*
Gunnerson, Robert Mark 1949- *WhoAm 90*
Gunness, Robert Charles 1911- *WhoAm 90*
Gunning, Adrian Paul Courtenay 1956- *IntWWM 90*
Gunning, Elizabeth 1769-1823 *FemiCLE*
Gunning, Francis Patrick 1923- *St&PR 91, WhoAm 90*
Gunning, James P. 1948- *St&PR 91*
Gunning, James R. 1933- *St&PR 91*
Gunning, John Thaddeus 1917- *WhoAm 90*
Gunning, Laurie Froydis 1950- *WhoEmL 91*
Gunning, Michael Anthony 1958- *WhoEmL 91*
Gunning, Robert Clifford 1931- *WhoAm 90*
Gunning, Susannah 1740?-1800 *FemiCLE*
Gunning, Susannah Minifie 1740-1800 *BioIn 16*
Gunnison, Douglas 1944- *WhoAm 90*
Gunnoe, Nancy Lavenia 1921- *WhoSSW 91*
Gunsalus, Carolyn Kristina 1957- *WhoEmL 91*
Gunsalus, Irwin C. 1912- *WhoAm 90*
Gunsalus, Robert Philip 1947- *WhoEmL 91*
Gunshor, Ruth *WhoAmA 91*
Gunson, Ameral *IntWWM 90*
Gunson, Diane Lee 1947- *WhoEmL 91*
Gunsser, John Daniel 1939- *WhoE 91*
Gunst, Morgan A., Jr. 1918- *St&PR 91*
Gunst, Robert A. 1948- *St&PR 91*
Gunst, Robert Allen 1948- *WhoAm 90*
Gunston, William Tudor 1927- *AuBYP 90*
Gunstream, Robby D. 1951- *IntWWM 90*
Gunsul, Brooks R. W. 1928- *WhoAm 90*
Guntensperger, Wilfried *BioIn 16*
Gunter, Cornell *BioIn 16, NewYTBS 90*
Gunter, Daniel Cornelius, Jr. 1926- *WhoSSW 91*
Gunter, Dawn Ellen *BiDrAPA 89*
Gunter, Emily Diane 1948- *WhoEmL 91*
Gunter, Frank Delano 1933- *St&PR 91*
Gunter, Frank Elliott 1934- *WhoAm 90, WhoAmA 91*
Gunter, Franklin Delano 1933- *WhoAm 90*
Gunter, Gordon 1909- *WhoWor 91*
Gunter, Horst 1913- *IntWWM 90*
Gunter, John B. 1919- *St&PR 91*
Gunter, John Brown, Jr. 1919- *WhoAm 90*
Gunter, John L. *St&PR 91*
Gunter, John Richmond 1941- *WhoAm 90*
Gunter, Karen Johnson 1948- *WhoAmW 91*
Gunter, Katherine Ann Stough 1956- *WhoAmW 91*
Gunter, Lisa Ann 1967- *WhoAmW 91*
Gunter, Martin J 1919- *BiDrAPA 89*
Gunter, Michael Donwell 1947- *WhoSSW 91*
Gunter, Michael Martin 1943- *WhoSSW 91*
Gunter, Prentis R 1946- *BiDrAPA 89*
Gunter, Rickey Van 1944- *WhoSSW 91*
Gunter, Russell Allen 1950- *WhoSSW 91*
Gunter, Teresa Dianne 1963- *WhoAmW 91*
Gunter, Wilkin Jacob 1948- *WhoSSW 91*
Gunter, William Dawson, Jr. 1934- *WhoAm 90*
Gunter, William Dayle, Jr. 1932- *WhoWor 91*
Gunter, William Joseph 1942- *St&PR 91*
Gunter-Gore, Ava Elaine 1952- *WhoAmW 91, WhoEmL 91*
Guntharp, Grady Elvis 1942- *WhoSSW 91*
Gunther, Agnes 1863-1911 *EncCoWW*
Gunther, Charles F 1933- *WhoAmA 91*
Gunther, Conrad J., Jr. 1946- *St&PR 91*
Gunther, George Lackman 1919- *WhoE 91*
Gunther, Gerald 1927- *WhoAm 90*
Gunther, Jack Disbrow 1908-1990 *BioIn 16*
Gunther, Jane Perry 1916- *WhoAm 90*
Gunther, John 1901-1970 *AuBYP 90, BioIn 16, WorAlBi*
Gunther, John A. 1947- *St&PR 91*
Gunther, Karl Michael 1952- *WhoSSW 91*
Gunther, Leon 1939- *WhoAm 90*
Gunther, Marc 1951- *ConAu 129, WhoAm 90*
Gunther, Meyer Samuel *BiDrAPA 89*
Gunther, Timothy 1957- *WhoAm 90*
Gunther-Sprecher, William 1924- *IntWWM 90*
Guntheroth, Warren Gaden 1927- *WhoAm 90*
Gunthorp, John Desbrow 1913- *St&PR 91*
Gunthorpe, Stacey *BioIn 16*
Guntrum, Suzanne Simmons 1946- *WhoWrEP 89*
Gunyou, John Mark 1948- *WhoEmL 91*
Gunzberg, Guy Walter 1940- *St&PR 91*
Gunzburger, Gerard J. 1931- *St&PR 91*
Gunzenhauser, Gerard Ralph, Jr. 1936- *St&PR 91, WhoAm 90*
Gunzenhauser, Keith 1933- *St&PR 91, WhoAm 90*
Gunzenhauser, Rul 1933- *WhoWor 91*
Gunzenhauser, Stephen 1942- *IntWWM 90*
Gunzenhauser, Stephen Charles 1942- *WhoAm 90*
Guo Moruo 1892-1978 *BioIn 16*
Guo Zurong *BioIn 16*
Guo, Zhong-heng 1933- *WhoWor 91*
Guokas, Matt 1944- *WhoAm 90*
Guowei, Tu 1928- *WhoWor 91*
Gup, Benton Eugene 1936- *WhoAm 90, WhoSSW 91*
Gup, Theodore Samuel 1950- *WhoE 91*
Guppy, Agnes *EncPaPR 91*
Guppy, Paul William 1960- *WhoEmL 91*
Guppy, Samuel, Mrs. *EncO&P 3*
Guppy, Samuel, Mrs. *EncO&P 3*
Gupta, Anil 1948- *WhoEmL 91*
Gupta, Anil Kumar 1946- *WhoWor 91*
Gupta, Anil Kumar 1949- *WhoE 91*
Gupta, Arun Kuman *BiDrAPA 89*
Gupta, Ashok Kumar *BiDrAPA 89*
Gupta, Ashwani Kumar 1948- *WhoAm 90, WhoE 91*
Gupta, Bal Krishan *BiDrAPA 89*
Gupta, Bhupendra K *BiDrAPA 89*
Gupta, Bimleshwar Prasad 1946- *WhoEmL 91*
Gupta, Dham K 1953- *BiDrAPA 89*
Gupta, Dham Krishan 1953- *WhoE 91*
Gupta, Goutam 1945- *WhoEmL 91*
Gupta, Kishore Kumar 1951- *WhoWor 91*
Gupta, Krishan Kumar *BiDrAPA 89*
Gupta, Krishna *BiDrAPA 89*
Gupta, Krishna Chandra 1948- *WhoAm 90*
Gupta, Kul Bhushan 1952- *BiDrAPA 89*
Gupta, Kuldip Chand 1940- *WhoAm 90, WhoWor 91*
Gupta, Mahabir Prashad 1942- *WhoWor 91*
Gupta, Narayan C *BiDrAPA 89*
Gupta, Neera Rani *BiDrAPA 89*
Gupta, Nirmal Kumar 1934- *WhoWor 91*
Gupta, P. S. 1933- *WhoWor 91*
Gupta, Parmeshwari Lal 1914- *WhoWor 91*
Gupta, Prafulla Chandra 1944- *St&PR 91*
Gupta, Raj Kumar 1936- *WhoWor 91*
Gupta, Rajendra 1943- *WhoSSW 91*
Gupta, Rakesh Kumar 1948- *WhoWor 91*
Gupta, Ramlal Prasad *BiDrAPA 89*
Gupta, Ratan Mala 1930- *WhoWor 91*
Gupta, Sarv K 1930- *BiDrAPA 89*
Gupta, Sat P. 1940- *WhoE 91*
Gupta, Satish Kumar 1942- *WhoSSW 91*
Gupta, Subhash Chandra 1941- *WhoE 91*
Gupta, Suraj Narayan 1924- *WhoAm 90, WhoWor 91*
Gupta, Vijay Kumar 1941- *WhoAm 90*
Gupta, Virendra Kumar 1941- *St&PR 91*
Guptan, Narayanan C *BiDrAPA 89*
Guptill, James Daniel 1951- *WhoEmL 91*
Guptill, Leighton 1920- *WhoAm 90*
Gupton, Marcia Walker 1954- *WhoAmW 91*
Guptrushi, Balbir Krishanan 1941- *WhoWor 91*
Gur, Raquel E *BiDrAPA 89*
Gura, Jerry W. 1949- *ODwPR 91*
Gura, Judith 1935- *ODwPR 91*
Gura, Larry 1947- *Ballpl 90*
Gurak, Kathleen Theresa 1943- *WhoAmW 91*
Gurak, Randall B 1958- *BiDrAPA 89*
Guralnick, Sidney Aaron 1929- *WhoAm 90*
Guralnik, David Bernard 1920- *WhoAm 90*
Gurash, John Thomas 1910- *St&PR 91, WhoE 91*
Gurawski, Jerzy 1935- *ConDes 90*
Gurbacs, John Joseph 1947- *WhoAmA 91*
Gurczynski, Ronald Raymond 1953- *WhoE 91*
Gurdian Moreno, Rodolfo Alberto 1949- *WhoWor 91*
Gurdjieff, Georgei Ivanovitch 1877?-1949 *EncO&P 3*
Gurdziel, Gloria Kreis *BiDrAPA 89*
Gure, Steven V. 1935- *BioIn 16*
Gureasko, Michael Allan 1942- *BiDrAPA 89*
Gureck, William Alexander 1929- *WhoAm 90*
Guren, Sheldon B. 1924- *St&PR 91*
Gurevich, David *BiDrAPA 89*
Gurevich, Mikhail *BiDrAPA 89*
Gurevitch, Arnold William 1936- *WhoAm 90*
Gurevitz, Howard 1930- *BiDrAPA 89*
Gurewitz, Barton I. 1941- *St&PR 91*
Gurewitz, Thomas Mark 1949- *WhoEmL 91*
Gurfein, Richard Alan 1946- *WhoE 91*
Gurfein, Stuart James 1947- *WhoE 91*
Gurganus, Allan *BioIn 16*
Gurgin, Vonnie Ann 1940- *WhoAm 90*
Gurguis, George N M *BiDrAPA 89*
Gurguis, George Nazmy Messiha 1953- *WhoE 91*
Gurian, Harvey 1926- *BiDrAPA 89*
Gurian, Jeffrey Lee *WhoE 91*
Gurian, Mal 1926- *WhoE 91*
Gurian, Stanley 1930- *St&PR 91*
Gurieva, Diana *BioIn 16*
Gurijala, Lalitha *BiDrAPA 89*
Gurijala, Vidyasagar R *BiDrAPA 89*
Gurik, Diane Green 1949- *WhoAmW 91, WhoEmL 91*
Gurik, Robert 1932- *BioIn 16, ConAu 129, OxCCanT [port]*
Gurin, Arnold 1917- *WhoAm 90*
Gurin, Maurice G. *NewYTBS 90*
Gurin, Maurice Gilbert 1911- *WhoE 91*
Gurin, Richard S. 1940- *St&PR 91*
Gurin, Richard Stephen 1940- *WhoAm 90*
Gurin, Samuel 1905- *WhoAm 90*
Gurion, David Ben- 1886-1973 *BioIn 16*
Guritz, Karen Noreen 1950- *WhoEmL 91*
Gurka, Allen S. 1939- *St&PR 91, WhoE 91*
Gurke, Sharon McCue 1949- *WhoAmW 91, WhoWor 91*
Gurkin, Kathryn Bright 1934- *WhoWrEP 89*
Gurklis, John Anthony, Jr. *BiDrAPA 89*
Gurko, Miriam *BioIn 16*
Gurkoff, Jon Buch 1951- *St&PR 91*
Gurland, David Barry 1939- *BiDrAPA 89*
Gurland, Joseph 1923- *WhoAm 90*
Gurler, Aziz 1925- *BiDrAPA 89*
Gurley, Clair E. 1907- *St&PR 91*
Gurley, Franklin Louis 1925- *WhoAm 90, WhoWor 91*
Gurley, Gail C. 1942- *WhoAmW 91*
Gurley, Geraldine Marie 1947- *WhoAmW 91, WhoEmL 91*
Gurley, James A. 1933- *St&PR 91*
Gurley, Michael Edward 1947- *WhoEmL 91*
Gurley, Steven Harrison 1957- *WhoSSW 91*

Gurley, Victoria Irene 1950- WhoEmL 91
Gurlitz, Judith 1936- WhoE 91
Gurman, Ina Ruth 1944- WhoE 91
Gurmankin, Alan E. 1935- St&PR 91
Gurmendi, Gonzalo Gabriel BiDrAPA 89
Gurne, Patricia Dorothy 1941- WhoAmW 91
Gurnee, Robert Francis 1927- WhoAm 90
Gurnett, Donald Alfred 1940- WhoAm 90
Gurney, A. R. 1930- BioIn 16
Gurney, A. R., Jr. 1930- ConAu 32NR, WorAu 1980 [port]
Gurney, Albert Ramsdell 1930- BioIn 16, WhoAm 90
Gurney, Albert Ramsdell, Jr. 1930- WhoWrEP 89
Gurney, Anna 1795-1857 FemiCLE
Gurney, Brian Jeffrey 1949- WhoE 91
Gurney, Daniel Sexton 1931- WhoAm 90
Gurney, Edmund 1847-1888 EncO&P 3, EncPaPR 91
Gurney, Edward John 1914- WhoAm 90
Gurney, Elizabeth Tucker Guice 1941- WhoAmW 91
Gurney, George 1939- WhoAmA 91
Gurney, J. Eric 1910- AuBYP 90
Gurney, James Thomas 1901- WhoAm 90, WhoWor 91
Gurney, Lee A. 1933- St&PR 91
Gurney, Nancy AuBYP 90
Gurney, Pamela Kay 1948- WhoEmL 91
Gurney, Patrick Joseph 1952- WhoSSW 91
Gurney, Peter ConAu 32NR
Gurney, Robert James 1951- WhoE 91
Gurney, Susan Lee 1958- WhoAmW 91
Gurney, Susan Rothwell 1951- WhoAmA 91
Gurnham, Robert F. 1951- St&PR 91
Gurnitz, Robert N. 1938- St&PR 91
Gurnitz, Robert Ned 1938- WhoE 91
Gurnsey, Avery L. 1954- WhoEmL 91
Gurnsey, Kathleen Wallace WhoAmW 91
Guro, Elena EncCoWW
Gurpegui, Manuel 1951- BiDrAPA 89
Gurr, David 1936- ConAu 132
Gurr, Ted Robert 1936- WhoAm 90
Gurrera, Ronald Joseph BiDrAPA 89
Gurri, Joseph N BiDrAPA 89
Gurrola, Augustine E. WhoHisp 91
Gurry, Francis Gerard 1951- WhoEmL 91, WhoWor 91
Gurry, William Patrick 1947- WhoWor 91
Gursey-Owen, Deha 1924- BiDrAPA 89
Gursky, Alvin 1919- St&PR 91
Gursky, Elliot James 1945- BiDrAPA 89
Gursky, Herbert 1930- WhoAm 90
Gursoy, Ahmet 1929- WhoAmA 91
Gurstel, Norman Keith 1939- WhoWor 91
Gurtin, Morton Edward 1934- WhoAm 90
Gurtner, Heinrich 1924- IntWWM 90
Guru Bawa EncO&P 3
Guru Ma BioIn 16
Guru Maharaj Ji 1957- EncO&P 3
Guru Nanak 1469-1538 BioIn 16
Gurubasavaraj, Kottur Hallukotrappanavar 1951- WhoEmL 91
Gurudeva, Srila NewAgMG
Gururajan, Krishnamurthy BiDrAPA 89
Gurusinghe, Nihal Trevor 1946- WhoWor 91
Gur'vich, Fedor Il'ich 1871-1947 BioIn 16
Gurvich, Philip Bernard 1926- WhoE 91
Gurvis, Sandra Jane 1951- WhoWrEP 89
Gurvitch, Geraldine Wilma 1942- WhoAmW 91
Gurvits, Tamara Victor 1936- BiDrAPA 89
Gurvitz, Milton Solomon 1919- WhoAm 90
Gurwitch, Arnold Andrew 1925- WhoAm 90
Gurwitsch, Aron 1901-1973 BioIn 16
Gurwitt, Alan R BiDrAPA 89
Gurwitt, Alan Richard 1936- WhoE 91
Gury, David J. 1938- St&PR 91
Gury, Jeremy 1913- WhoAm 90, WhoWrEP 89
Gurzi, William Robert 1947- WhoEmL 91
Gusberg, Saul Bernard 1913- WhoAm 90
Guschlbauer, Theodor 1939- IntWWM 90, PenDiMP
Guschwan, Andrew F 1937- BiDrAPA 89
Guscott, Kenneth Irvin 1925- St&PR 91
Gusdon, John Paul, Jr. 1931- WhoSSW 91
Guse, Carl Edward 1929- St&PR 91
Gusella, Ernest 1941- WhoAmA 91
Gusev, Pyotr Andreievich BioIn 16
Gusewelle, C. W. 1933- WhoWrEP 89
Gusewelle, Charles Wesley 1933- WhoAm 90
Gusfield, Joseph R. 1923- BioIn 16
Gusfield, Joseph Robert 1923- WhoAm 90
Gushard, Keith Lee 1958- WhoE 91
Gushee, Allison Taylor 1962- WhoAmW 91
Gushee, Charles H. 1903- St&PR 91
Gushee, John W.H. 1932- St&PR 91
Gushiken, Elson Clyde 1950- WhoEmL 91
Gushin, Stephen R 1932- BiDrAPA 89
Gushman, John Louis 1912- WhoAm 90
Gushue, Edward Joseph 1933- St&PR 91
Gushue, John Joseph 1951- WhoEmL 91
Gushue, John Michael 1945- WhoE 91
Guske, Jack Dean 1951- WhoEmL 91
Guske, Lawrence Arthur 1944- St&PR 91
Guskin, Alan E. 1937- WhoAm 90
Guskin, Joel Craig 1951- WhoEmL 91
Gusmer, John H. 1932- St&PR 91
Gusmer, William E. 1934- St&PR 91
Gusmorino, Paul 1948- BiDrAPA 89, WhoE 91
Gusnard, Raymond Thomas 1926- WhoAm 90
Gusnard, Raymond Thomas 1927- St&PR 91
Guss, Jeffery Richard 1953- BiDrAPA 89
Gussak, Elizabeth Emmons 1919- WhoAmW 91
Gussenhoven, John W. 1946- St&PR 91
Gussin, Robert Zalmon 1938- WhoAm 90
Gussman, Lawrence 1915- WhoAm 90
Gussow, Alan 1931- WhoAm 90, WhoAmA 91
Gussow, David Alan BiDrAPA 89
Gussow, Don 1907- ConAu 132, WhoAm 90
Gussow, John Andrew 1946- WhoE 91
Gussow, Mel 1933- WhoAm 90
Gussow, Michelle Denise 1963- WhoAmW 91
Gussow, Roy 1918- WhoAm 90, WhoAmA 91
Gussow, Sue Ferguson 1935- WhoAmA 91
Gussow, William Carruthers 1908- WhoAm 90
Gussow-Gross, Nancy E. ODwPR 91
Gust, Alfred C. 1932- St&PR 91
Gust, Anne Baldwin 1958- WhoEmL 91
Gust, Joan Marie 1937- WhoE 91
Gust, LeRoy Charles 1941- St&PR 91
Gust, Lysle A. 1931- St&PR 91
Gustaf II Adolf, King of Sweden 1594-1632 BioIn 16
Gustaferro, William R. 1929- WhoAm 90
Gustafson, Albert Katsuaki 1949- WhoEmL 91, WhoWor 91
Gustafson, Alice Fairleigh 1946- WhoEmL 91
Gustafson, Barbara Ann Helton 1948- WhoAmW 91
Gustafson, C. Donald 1930- St&PR 91
Gustafson, Dale R. BioIn 16
Gustafson, David Alan 1949- WhoEmL 91
Gustafson, David Earl 1950- WhoEmL 91
Gustafson, Deborah Lee 1948- WhoE 91
Gustafson, Dwight Leonard 1930- IntWWM 90, WhoAm 90
Gustafson, Elton T. AuBYP 90
Gustafson, Frances Decker 1928- WhoSSW 91
Gustafson, Frances Goodwin 1917- St&PR 91
Gustafson, Glendon Davis 1938- St&PR 91
Gustafson, James M. 1925- WhoAm 90
Gustafson, Jeanne 1946- WhoAmW 91
Gustafson, John Alfred 1925- WhoAm 90
Gustafson, Karl Erik 1950- St&PR 91
Gustafson, Marjorie AuBYP 90
Gustafson, Nancy 1956- IntWWM 90
Gustafson, Norman C. 1938- St&PR 91
Gustafson, Paul Edward 1946- WhoE 91
Gustafson, Paula 1941- WhoWrEP 89
Gustafson, Philip Edward 1916- St&PR 91
Gustafson, Philip Felix 1924- WhoAm 90
Gustafson, Pier WhoAmA 91
Gustafson, Ralph Barker 1909- WhoAm 90, WhoWrEP 89
Gustafson, Randall Lee 1947- WhoWor 91
Gustafson, Rebecca Susanne 1962- WhoAmW 91
Gustafson, Richard Alrick 1941- WhoAm 90, WhoE 91
Gustafson, Richard Charles 1942- WhoAm 90
Gustafson, Richard Paul 1957- WhoEmL 91, WhoWor 91
Gustafson, Robert L. St&PR 91
Gustafson, Ronald Eric 1934- St&PR 91
Gustafson, William L, Jr. 1928- BiDrAPA 89
Gustafson, William Robert 1943- St&PR 91
Gustafson, Winthrop Adolph 1928- WhoAm 90
Gustafsson, Bengt Harald WhoWor 91
Gustafsson, Borje Karl 1930- WhoAm 90
Gustafsson, Lars 1936- DcScanL
Gustafsson, Madeleine 1937- WhoWor 91
Gustafsson, Sten BioIn 16
Gustainis, John Edward 1958- WhoSSW 91
Gustav, Karl WhoWrEP 89
Gustavson, Carl Gustav 1915- WhoAm 90, WhoWor 91
Gustavson, Dean Leonard 1924- WhoAm 90
Gustavson, Joan Ellen Carlson 1947- WhoAmW 91
Gustavson, Leland WhoAmA 91N
Gustavson, Paul 1917-1977 EncACom
Gustavson, Warner H. 1933- St&PR 91
Gustavus II 1594-1653 WorAlBi
Gustavus Adolphus 1594-1632 BioIn 16
Guste, Roy Francis, Jr. 1951- WhoWrEP 89
Guste, William Joseph, Jr. 1922- WhoAm 90, WhoSSW 91
Gustenhover EncO&P 3
Gustilo, Maria Merma BiDrAPA 89
Gustilo, Rose Marie BiDrAPA 89
Gustin, Christopher WhoAmA 91
Gustin, John Craig 1952- BiDrAPA 89
Gustin, Lawrence R. 1933- St&PR 91
Gustin, Thomas A 1933- BiDrAPA 89
Gustine, Dixie Lee Alms 1952- WhoEmL 91
Gustine, Frankie 1920- Ballpl 90
Gustke, Constance Anne 1951- WhoEmL 91
Gustkey, Earl 1940- AuBYP 90
Gustlin, Philip Raymond 1934- WhoAm 90
Gustloff, Wilhelm 1895-1936 BioIn 16
Gustman, Alan Leslie 1944- WhoAm 90, WhoE 91
Guston, David H. 1965- WhoWrEP 89
Guston, Philip 1913-1980 BioIn 16, WhoAmA 91N
Gut, Gary Frederick 1948- WhoAm 90
Gut, Gom ConAu 129, MajTwCW
Gut, Rainer E. 1932- St&PR 91
Gutberg, Ingrid Maria IntWWM 90
Gutberg, Karin IntWWM 90
Gutche, Gene 1907- IntWWM 90, WhoAm 90, WhoWor 91
Gutek, Gerald Lee 1935- WhoAm 90
Gutekanst, William P. St&PR 91
Gutekunst, Richard Ralph 1926- WhoAm 90
Gutelius, Edward Warner 1922- WhoSSW 91
Gutelius, Josepha Sophia Debra 1952- WhoE 91
Gutenberg, Johannes 1398?-1468 WorAlBi
Gutenberg, Rhonda Lynn 1957- WhoAmW 91, WhoEmL 91
Gutenkunst, Richard Laacke 1933- St&PR 91
Gutenstein, Robert G. 1933- St&PR 91
Guterbock, Hans Gustav 1908- WhoAm 90
Guterman, Burte 1918- BiDrAPA 89
Guterman, James Hans 1952- WhoEmL 91
Gutermann, Paul Eric 1956- WhoE 91
Gutermuth, Blaine Earl 1930- St&PR 91
Gutermuth, Scott Alan 1953- WhoWor 91
Guterson, David 1956- ConAu 132
Gutfeld, Norman E. 1911- WhoAm 90
Gutfreund, John BioIn 16
Gutfreund, John H. 1929- St&PR 91, WhoAm 90, WhoE 91, WhoWor 91
Gutfreund, Susan BioIn 16
Guth, Alan H. BioIn 16
Guth, Alan Harvey 1947- WhoAm 90
Guth, Deborah 1950- WhoWor 91
Guth, DeLloyd J. 1938- ConAu 129
Guth, Donald John 1916- WhoAm 90
Guth, Gary Robert 1944- WhoAm 90
Guth, James Edward 1955- WhoEmL 91
Guth, Marshall C. 1955- St&PR 91
Guth, Mary Anne 1954- WhoEmL 91
Guth, Paul 1910- WhoWor 91
Guth, Paul C. 1922- WhoAm 90, WhoE 91
Guth, Paul David 1932- WhoAm 90, WhoWor 91
Guth, Raymond Charles 1921- WhoAm 90
Guth, Scott Charles BiDrAPA 89
Guth, Sherman Leon 1932- WhoAm 90
Guthans, Robert Anthony 1929- St&PR 91
Guthart, Leo 1937- St&PR 91
Guthary, Barry Curtis 1944- WhoE 91
Gutheil, Dawn Miriam 1963- WhoAmW 91
Gutheil, John Gordon 1944- WhoAm 90
Gutheil, Thomas Gordon BiDrAPA 89
Gutheil-Schroder, Marie 1874-1935 PenDiMP
Gutheim, Allen Herman 1945- WhoWor 91
Gutheim, Frederick 1908- WhoAm 90
Gutheim, Robert Julius 1911- WhoAm 90
Gutherie, Melvin Charles, III 1959- St&PR 91
Gutherie, William Thomas 1963- St&PR 91
Guthke, Karl Siegfried 1933- WhoAm 90
Guthke, Wilmot WhoSSW 91
Guthman, Jack 1938- WhoAm 90
Guthman, Leo S WhoAmA 91
Guthmann, Louis B., Jr. 1923- St&PR 91
Guthrey, George Henry 1921- BiDrAPA 89
Guthrie, A. B. 1901- BioIn 16
Guthrie, A.B., Jr. 1901- LiHiK, SmATA 62 [port]
Guthrie, Alastair 1929- BiDrAPA 89
Guthrie, Alfred Bertram 1901- BioIn 16
Guthrie, Alfred Bertram, Jr. 1901- WhoAm 90
Guthrie, Anne 1890-1979 AuBYP 90
Guthrie, Arlo 1947- OxCPMus, WorAlBi
Guthrie, Bill Ballpl 90
Guthrie, Bill M. 1933- St&PR 91
Guthrie, Carlton BioIn 16
Guthrie, Catherine S. Nicholson WhoAmW 91
Guthrie, Debora Allen BioIn 16
Guthrie, Diana Fern 1934- WhoAmW 91
Guthrie, Donna AuBYP 90
Guthrie, Donna W 1946- SmATA 63 [port]
Guthrie, Edward A. 1944- St&PR 91
Guthrie, Edward Everett 1941- WhoAm 90
Guthrie, Eleanor Y. 1915- St&PR 91
Guthrie, Elisabeth Benson BiDrAPA 89
Guthrie, Florence Ann BiDrAPA 89
Guthrie, Francis J., Jr. 1937- St&PR 91
Guthrie, Frank Albert 1927- WhoAm 90
Guthrie, Frank Edwin 1923- WhoAm 90
Guthrie, G. Ralph 1928- St&PR 91
Guthrie, Gary Patterson 1950- WhoSSW 91
Guthrie, George Ralph 1928- WhoAm 90, WhoSSW 91, WhoWor 91
Guthrie, George Wilkins 1848-1917 BioIn 16
Guthrie, Gerald Ray 1934- St&PR 91
Guthrie, Harvey Henry, Jr. 1924- WhoAm 90
Guthrie, Helen A. 1925- WhoAm 90, WhoAmW 91
Guthrie, Isobel ConAu 33NR, MajTwCW
Guthrie, J. Lee 1952- WhoEmL 91
Guthrie, James 1792-1869 BiDrUSE 89
Guthrie, James Bryan 1957- WhoEmL 91
Guthrie, James Martin 1953- IntWWM 90
Guthrie, James Williams 1936- WhoAm 90
Guthrie, Janet 1938- WhoAm 90, WorAlBi
Guthrie, Jerry Ralph 1949- WhoEmL 91
Guthrie, John F., Jr. 1943- St&PR 91
Guthrie, John Gilkeson 1936- St&PR 91
Guthrie, John R. 1940- ODwPR 91
Guthrie, John Reiley 1921- WhoAm 90
Guthrie, John Robert 1942- WhoSSW 91
Guthrie, Julie Ann 1962- BiDrAPA 89
Guthrie, Keith 1906-1981 DcNaB 1981
Guthrie, M. Philip 1945- St&PR 91
Guthrie, Mark Claude 1955- WhoEmL 91
Guthrie, Marshal Beck 1919-1989 BioIn 16
Guthrie, Mary Lee 1965- WhoAmW 91
Guthrie, Mearl Raymond, Jr. 1922- WhoAm 90
Guthrie, Michael BioIn 16
Guthrie, Michael Beck 1946- BiDrAPA 89
Guthrie, Norman David BiDrAPA 89
Guthrie, Patricia Sue 1958- WhoAm 90
Guthrie, Randee Rae 1960- WhoAmW 91
Guthrie, Randolph H. 1905-1989 BioIn 16
Guthrie, Randolph Hobson 1905- WhoAm 90
Guthrie, Randolph Hobson, Jr. 1934- WhoAm 90, WhoWor 91
Guthrie, Ray 1934- St&PR 91
Guthrie, Richard Alan 1935- WhoAm 90
Guthrie, Richard Y. 1944- St&PR 91
Guthrie, Robert Lillard 1936- WhoSSW 91
Guthrie, Robert Val 1930- WhoAm 90
Guthrie, Russell Allen 1954- WhoEmL 91
Guthrie, Sally Record 1929- WhoWrEP 89
Guthrie, Steven ODwPR 91
Guthrie, Thomas Lee 1928- St&PR 91
Guthrie, Tyrone 1900-1971 OxCCanT [port], WorAlBi
Guthrie, Wayne E. 1919- St&PR 91
Guthrie, William N. 1929- St&PR 91
Guthrie, Woody WhoNeCM C [port]
Guthrie, Woody 1912-1967 BioIn 16, EncAL, OxCPMus, WorAlBi
Gutierrez, Alberto F. WhoHisp 91
Gutierrez, Alvaro Mario BiDrAPA 89
Gutierrez, Anthony 1961- WhoHisp 91
Gutierrez, Armando A BiDrAPA 89
Gutierrez, Carlos WhoHisp 91
Gutierrez, Carlos Jose 1927- WhoWor 91
Gutierrez, Cesar 1943- Ballpl 90
Gutierrez, Daniel BiDrAPA 89
Gutierrez, David G. WhoHisp 91
Gutierrez, David Gregory 1954- WhoHisp 91
Gutierrez, Donald Kenneth 1932- WhoHisp 91
Gutierrez, Elia Garza 1932- WhoAmW 91
Gutierrez, F. Jerry BioIn 16
Gutierrez, Felix Frank 1943- WhoHisp 91
Gutierrez, Gayle V BiDrAPA 89
Gutierrez, George Armando 1932- WhoHisp 91
Gutierrez, Gerard V. 1924- WhoHisp 91
Gutierrez, German BiDrAPA 89
Gutierrez, Guillermo 1946- WhoHisp 91
Gutierrez, Guillermo Tirona 1924- WhoWor 91
Gutierrez, Gustavo ConAu 130, HispWr 90

Gutierrez, Gustavo 1928- WhoWor 91
Gutierrez, H Omar 1937- BiDrAPA 89
Gutierrez, Hector, Jr. 1947- WhoHisp 91
Gutierrez, Henry Florentino 1948- WhoHisp 91
Gutierrez, Horacio BioIn 16
Gutierrez, Horacio 1948- IntWWM 90
Gutierrez, Horacio Tomas 1948- WhoWor 91
Gutierrez, Irma Guadalupe 1951- WhoHisp 91
Gutierrez, Jack Allen 1951- WhoHisp 91
Gutierrez, Jackie 1960- Ballpl 90
Gutierrez, Jaime P. 1949- WhoHisp 91
Gutierrez, Jay Jose 1951- WhoHisp 91
Gutierrez, Jesus 1928- WhoHisp 91
Gutierrez, John David BioIn 16
Gutierrez, John R. 1952- WhoHisp 91
Gutierrez, Jose WhoHisp 91
Gutierrez, Jose Angel BioIn 16
Gutierrez, Jose Angel 1944- WhoHisp 91
Gutierrez, Jose Asuncion 1941- BiDrAPA 89
Gutierrez, Juan A. WhoHisp 91
Gutierrez, Juan Francisco, Jr. 1947- WhoSSW 91
Gutierrez, Juan J. WhoHisp 91
Gutierrez, Leonel Guadalupe 1953- WhoSSW 91
Gutierrez, Leonidas Plaza 1865?-1932 BioIn 16
Gutierrez, Linda 1955- WhoAmW 91, WhoHisp 91
Gutierrez, Lisa Jean 1962- WhoHisp 91
Gutierrez, Lorraine Padilla 1925- WhoHisp 91
Gutierrez, Luden A BiDrAPA 89
Gutierrez, Luis BiDrAPA 89
Gutierrez, Luis Carlos 1936- BiDrAPA 89
Gutierrez, Luis V. 1953- WhoHisp 91
Gutierrez, M. BiDWomA
Gutierrez, Max, Jr. 1930- WhoAm 90, WhoWor 91
Gutierrez, Nemesio Emilio S 1952- BiDrAPA 89
Gutierrez, Nicasio BiDrAPA 89
Gutierrez, Nicasio Sanchez, Jr. 1953- BiDrAPA 89
Gutierrez, Norma B 1929- BiDrAPA 89
Gutierrez, Octavio BiDrAPA 89
Gutierrez, Orlando WhoHisp 91
Gutierrez, Orlando A. WhoHisp 91
Gutierrez, Oscar BiDrAPA 89
Gutierrez, Pamela Jean Holbrook 1956- WhoWor 91
Gutierrez, Peter Luis 1939- WhoHisp 91
Gutierrez, Rafael H 1945- BiDrAPA 89
Gutierrez, Ralph 1931- WhoHisp 91
Gutierrez, Ralph Joseph 1945- WhoHisp 91
Gutierrez, Ramon Arturo 1951- WhoHisp 91
Gutierrez, Rene 1936- WhoSSW 91
Gutierrez, Robert P. WhoHisp 91
Gutierrez, Rosie Maria 1949- WhoHisp 91
Gutierrez, Rudolfo C., Jr. 1947- WhoHisp 91
Gutierrez, Sally Valencia 1918- WhoHisp 91
Gutierrez, Sergio BioIn 16
Gutierrez, Sidney M. WhoHisp 91
Gutierrez, Sonia I. 1939- WhoHisp 91
Gutierrez, Ted A. 1940- WhoHisp 91
Gutierrez, Victor Asaldo 1951- BiDrAPA 89
Gutierrez, Yezid 1936- WhoHisp 91
Gutierrez-Agramonte, E A BiDrAPA 89
Gutierrez Alea, Tomas BioIn 16
Gutierrez-Andrade, Guillermo 1938- WhoSSW 91
Gutierrez-Girardot, Rafael 1928- WhoWor 91
Gutierrez Lozano, Jaime Manuel 1925- WhoWor 91
Gutierrez M., Gustavo ConAu 130, HispWr 90
Gutierrez Merino, Gustavo 1928- ConAu 130, HispWr 90
Gutierrez Najera, Manuel 1859-1895 BioIn 16
Gutierrez-Revuelta, Pedro 1949- WhoHisp 91
Gutierrez-Santos, Luis Emiliano 1945- WhoAm 90, WhoEmL 91
Gutierrez-Spencer, Maria E. 1919- WhoHisp 91
Gutierrez Torrero, Concepcion EncCoWW
Gutierrez-Witt, Laura 1941- WhoHisp 91
utin, Irving 1932- St&PR 91, WhoAm 90
utjahr, H.C. 1930- St&PR 91
utkin, Peter 1944- WhoAmA 91
utknecht, James Evan 1950- St&PR 91
utkoski, Joe BioIn 16
utkowski, Mitch BioIn 16
utkowski, Robert Michael BioIn 16
utmacher, Elijah 1796?-1874 BioIn 16
utman, Alberto 1959- WhoHisp 91
utman, Alfred Elihu 1916- St&PR 91, WhoE 91
Gutman, Bill AuBYP 90
Gutman, D. Milton 1933- WhoWor 91
Gutman, E Michael 1935- BiDrAPA 89
Gutman, Gary Sander 1948- WhoSSW 91
Gutman, Herbert EncAL
Gutman, Herbert George 1928-1985 BioIn 16
Gutman, I. Cyrus 1912- WhoE 91, WhoWor 91
Gutman, Mindi S. 1958- St&PR 91
Gutman, Natalia 1942- IntWWM 90
Gutman, Richard Edward 1944- WhoE 91
Gutman, Robert William 1925- WhoAm 90
Gutman, Roy 1944- ConAu 131
Gutman, Semion 1950- WhoSSW 91
Gutman, Stephen J. 1943- St&PR 91
Gutmann, Cheryl Monica BiDrAPA 89
Gutmann, David Leo 1925- WhoAm 90
Gutmann, Francis BioIn 16
Gutmann, James 1897-1988 BioIn 16
Gutmann, Joan Marie 1955- WhoEmL 91
Gutmann, John 1905- WhoAmA 91
Gutmann, Joseph 1923- WhoAm 90, WhoAmA 91
Gutmann, Leonard M. 1930- St&PR 91
Gutmann, Max 1922- St&PR 91, WhoAm 90
Gutmann, Miriam Bette BiDrAPA 89
Gutmann, Natalia 1942- PenDiMP
Gutmann, Reinhart Bruno 1916- WhoAm 90
Gutmann, Ronald J. 1940- WhoE 91
Gutmann, William C. 1927- St&PR 91
Gutner, Kim Allison 1956- BiDrAPA 89
Gutnik, Bruce David 1946- BiDrAPA 89
Gutnisky, Griselda Renedo BiDrAPA 89
Gutowski, Michael Francis 1950- WhoEmL 91
Gutowski, Raymond Joel 1940- St&PR 91
Gutowsky, Herbert Sander 1919- WhoAm 90
Gutrath, Gordon C. 1937- St&PR 91
Gutridge, David S. 1947- St&PR 91
Gutsch, William Anthony, Jr. 1946- WhoAm 90, WhoE 91
Gutsche, Carl David 1921- WhoAm 90, WhoSSW 91
Gutshall, Arthur Robert 1948- WhoEmL 91
Gutshall, Priscilla Jean 1944- WhoAmW 91
Gutshall, Richard Brice, Jr. 1938- WhoAm 90
Gutshall, Thomas L. 1938- WhoAm 90
Gutstadt, Joseph P 1923- BiDrAPA 89
Gutstein, Ernst 1924- IntWWM 90
Gutstein, Morris Aaron 1905-1986 BioIn 16
Gutt, Camille A. 1884-1971 WorAlBi
Gutt, Daniel Z. 1948- St&PR 91
Guttay, Andrew John Robert 1924- WhoAm 90
Guttell, Steven Michael 1947- WhoEmL 91
Guttenberg, Albert Ziskind 1921- WhoAm 90
Guttenberg, John Paul, Jr. 1936- WhoE 91
Guttenberg, Steve 1958- WhoAm 90, WorAlBi
Guttenplan, Harold E. 1924- St&PR 91
Guttenplan, Harold Esau 1924- WhoAm 90
Guttentag, Gilbert 1940- St&PR 91
Guttentag, Jack Mark 1923- WhoAm 90
Guttentag, Joseph Harris 1929- WhoAm 90
Gutter, Robert Harold 1938- WhoAm 90, WhoSSW 91
Gutteridge, Don 1912- Ballpl 90
Gutterman, Bernard 1926- St&PR 91
Gutterman, Diane Flora BiDrAPA 89
Gutterman, Gary Stuart BiDrAPA 89
Gutterman, Gerald S. 1929- St&PR 91, WhoAm 90
Gutterman, Marvin 1922- St&PR 91
Gutterman, Robert B BiDrAPA 89
Gutterman, Scott 1958- St&PR 91
Gutterman-Reinfeld, Debra Ellen 1948- WhoAmW 91
Gutterres, Cheryl Scofield 1933- WhoAmW 91
Gutterson, Gerald 1930- St&PR 91
Gutterson, Janet Miriam 1939- WhoAmW 91
Gutting, James M. 1952- WhoEmL 91
Guttler, Ludwig 1943- IntWWM 90
Guttmacher, Alan F. 1898-1974 WorAlBi
Guttmacher, Jonathan A BiDrAPA 89
Guttmacher, Leonore Gidding BioIn 16
Guttman, Albert 1937- IntWWM 90
Guttman, Alicia J 1949- BiDrAPA 89
Guttman, Dena Ann 1934- WhoWrEP 89
Guttman, Egon 1927- WhoAm 90, WhoE 91
Guttman, Helene Nathan 1930- WhoAm 90, WhoAmW 91
Guttman, Herta Ann BiDrAPA 89
Guttman, Irving Allen 1928- WhoAm 90
Guttman, Louis 1916-1987 BioIn 16
Guttman, Samuel A 1914- BiDrAPA 89
Guttman, Steven J. 1946- St&PR 91
Guttman, Zoltan Lou 1949- WhoAm 90
Guttmann, H. Peter 1919- St&PR 91
Guttosch, Thomas James 1950- St&PR 91
Guttuso, Lisa BiDrAPA 89
Gutwirth, Marcel Marc 1923- WhoAm 90
Gutzeit, Fred WhoAmA 91
Gutzke, Karl Norbert 1933- WhoSSW 91
Gutzman, Richard Dean 1932- WhoSSW 91
Gutzmann, Gordon Keith 1932- St&PR 91
Gutzmer, Peter Esmond 1953- WhoEmL 91
Gutzwiller, Frank William 1926- WhoAm 90
Guy, Barry 1947- PenDiMP
Guy, Barry John 1947- IntWWM 90
Guy, Buddy 1936?- ConMus 4
Guy, C.W. 1948- St&PR 91
Guy, Carol Ann 1943- WhoWrEP 89
Guy, Clarence Caldwell 1932- St&PR 91
Guy, Donald Russell 1945- St&PR 91
Guy, E Samuel 1953- BiDrAPA 89
Guy, Eleanor Bryenton 1930- WhoAmW 91
Guy, Fraser BiDrAPA 89
Guy, James M 1910-1983 WhoAmA 91N
Guy, Jasmine BioIn 16, DrBIPA 90
Guy, Jean 1940- OxCCanT
Guy, Karen Louise 1946- WhoSSW 91
Guy, Leona Ruth 1913- WhoAmW 91
Guy, Louis L., Jr. 1938- St&PR 91
Guy, Matthew Joel 1945- WhoEmL 91
Guy, Michel NewYTBS 90
Guy, Mildred Dorothy 1929- WhoAmW 91
Guy, Ralph B., Jr. 1929- WhoAm 90
Guy, Ray 1939- BioIn 16
Guy, Richard BioIn 16
Guy, Richard Henry 1954- WhoEmL 91
Guy, Robert Dean 1934- WhoAm 90
Guy, Rosa BioIn 16
Guy, Rosa 1925- FemiCLE, SmATA 62 [port]
Guy, Rosa 1928- WorAu 1980 [port]
Guy, Ruth Maureen 1932- IntWWM 90
Guy, Sharon Kaye 1958- WhoAmW 91
Guyan, Cheryl Ann 1964- WhoEmL 91
Guyard, Marius-Francois 1921- WhoWor 91
Guyart, Marie 1599-1672 EncCoWW, WhNaAH
Guyashusta 1725?-1794? WhNaAH
Guyasuta 1725?-1794? WhNaAH
Guyden, Thomas E BiDrAPA 89
Guyer, Dan G BiDrAPA 89
Guyer, David L. 1925-1988 BioIn 16
Guyer, Joe E. 1924- St&PR 91
Guyer, Paul David 1948- WhoAm 90
Guyer, Raymond L. 1944- St&PR 91
Guyer, Walter Albert 1937- St&PR 91
Guyett, Robert Losee 1937- St&PR 91, WhoAm 90
Guyette, James M. 1945- St&PR 91
Guyker, William Charles, Jr. 1933- WhoAm 90
Guymer, Mary 1909- BioIn 16
Guymon, Gary LeRoy 1935- WhoAm 90
Guyn, Lew James 1953- WhoEmL 91
Guynes, Karen Lea 1960- WhoAmW 91
Guynn, Jack 1942- St&PR 91
Guynn, Robert W 1942- BiDrAPA 89
Guynn, Robert William 1942- WhoAm 90
Guyon, Madame 1648-1717 EncO&P 3
Guyon, Mme 1648-1717 EncCoWW
Guyon, Eugene Lamar 1954- WhoSSW 91
Guyon, Joe 1892-1971 Ballpl 90
Guyon, John Carl 1931- WhoAm 90
Guyon, Maximilienne 1868-1903 BiDWomA
Guyon, Stephen A. 1948- St&PR 91
Guyot, James Alfred 1928- St&PR 91
Guyot, Lawrence BioIn 16
Guyot, Philippe Adelin 1950- St&PR 91
Guyre, David C. ODwPR 91
Guyre, William H. 1942- St&PR 91
Guyse, Sheila DrBIPA 90
Guyton, Arthur Clifton 1919- WhoAm 90
Guyton, Joseph L 1923- BiDrAPA 89
Guyton, Richard Lent 1941- St&PR 91
Guyton, Robert P. 1937- St&PR 91
Guyton, Robert Pool 1937- WhoAm 90
Guyton, Samuel Percy 1937- WhoAm 90
Guyton, William J. 1922- St&PR 91
Guzak, Karen W 1939- WhoAmA 91
Guze, Barry Hobart 1956- BiDrAPA 89
Guze, Samuel B 1923- BiDrAPA 89
Guze, Samuel Barry 1923- WhoAm 90
Guzevich-Sommers, Kreszenz 1923- WhoAmA 91
Guzewicz, Henry Joseph BioIn 16
Guziec, Frank Stanley, Jr. 1946- WhoEmL 91
Guzikow, Michal Jozef 1806-1837 PenDiMP
Guzman, Aida BiDrAPA 89
Guzman, Antonio Leocadio 1801-1884 BioIn 16
Guzman, Corazon Banez BiDrAPA 89
Guzman, Debra Lynne 1951- WhoAmW 91
Guzman, Dominic de 1170-1221 BioIn 16
Guzman, Enrique Gonzales 1944- WhoHisp 91
Guzman, Gemma A BiDrAPA 89
Guzman, Herman F 1939- BiDrAPA 89
Guzman, J Eduardo 1951- BiDrAPA 89
Guzman, Jacobo Arbenz 1913-1971 BioIn 16
Guzman, Jesse M. WhoHisp 91
Guzman, Jose 1963- Ballpl 90, WhoHisp 91
Guzman, Juanita Elizabeth 1961- WhoAmW 91
Guzman, Manuel 1927- BiDrAPA 89
Guzman, Martin Luis 1887-1976 BioIn 16, HispWr 90
Guzman, Paschal WhoHisp 91
Guzman, Ralph C. 1924-1985 BioIn 16
Guzman, Ramiro WhoHisp 91
Guzman, Ruben Joseph 1957- WhoHisp 91
Guzman, Suzanna 1955- WhoHisp 91
Guzman Berrios, Andrea 1929- WhoHisp 91
Guzman Blanco, Antonio 1828-1899 BioIn 16
Guzman de Garcia, Lily 1952- WhoHisp 91
Guzman de Luna, Vickie BioIn 16
Guzman-Forbes, Robert 1929- WhoAmA 91
Guzman Reynoso, Abimael 1934- BioIn 16
Guzman y de la Cerda, Maria Isidra Q 1768-1803 EncCoWW
Guzowski, Bruce Thomas 1953- St&PR 91
Guzowski, Lawrence F. 1942- St&PR 91
Guzowski, Lawrence T. 1944- St&PR 91
Guzowski, Robert James 1962- WhoSSW 91
Guzy, Marguerita Linnes 1938- WhoWor 91
Guzyk, Jan 1875-1928 EncO&P 3
Guzzetta, Salvatore Joseph 1936- WhoSSW 91
Guzzetti, Louis A. BioIn 16
Guzzetti, Louis A., Jr. 1939- St&PR 91
Guzzetti, William Louis 1943- St&PR 91
Guzzi, Frank Charles 1933- St&PR 91
Guzzi, Paul 1942- St&PR 91
Guzzle, Timothy L. 1936- WhoAm 90, WhoSSW 91
Guzzman, Freddy 1939- WhoHisp 91
Guzzo, Sandra Elizabeth 1941- WhoWrEP 89
Gwai-Gu-Unlthin DcCanB 12
Gwaltney, Corbin 1922- WhoAm 90, WhoWor 91
Gwaltney, Donald Marvin 1936- WhoAm 90
Gwaltney, E.C. 1918- St&PR 91
Gwaltney, Eugene C. 1918- WhoAm 90, WhoSSW 91
Gwaltney, Jack Merrit, Jr. 1930- WhoAm 90
Gwaltney, John Langston 1928- WhoAm 90
Gwartney, Stephen W. 1949- St&PR 91
Gwathmey, Charles 1938- BioIn 16
Gwathmey, Robert 1903-1988 AnObit 1988, BioIn 16, WhoAmA 91N
Gwenn, Edmund 1875-1959 WorAlBi
Gwiazda, Stanley John 1922- WhoAm 90
Gwilliam, Gilbert Franklin 1925- WhoAm 90
Gwillim, Russell Adams 1922- St&PR 91, WhoAm 90
Gwin, Anne 1692-1715 BiDEWW
Gwin, Daniel Monroe 1953- IntWWM 90
Gwin, Dorothy Jean Bird 1934- WhoSSW 91
Gwin, James Ellsworth 1947- WhoSSW 91
Gwin, John Michael 1949- WhoEmL 91
Gwin, Robert H., Jr. 1930- St&PR 91
Gwin, Shannon BiDrAPA 89
Gwinn, Geraldine B. 1952- WhoE 91
Gwinn, John C. 1929- St&PR 91
Gwinn, Linda C. ODwPR 91
Gwinn, Mary Ann 1951- WhoAm 90
Gwinn, Naomi Jean 1952- WhoAmW 91
Gwinn, Robert P. 1907- St&PR 91, WhoAm 90
Gwinn, William Dulaney 1916- WhoAm 90
Gwinner, Robert Fred, Jr. 1935- WhoAm 90
Gwinnett, Button 1735?-1777 EncCRAm, WorAlBi
Gwinup, Kimberly Sue 1965- WhoAmW 91
Gwirtsman, Harry Edward BiDrAPA 89
Gwosdz, Marilyn Marie 1951- WhoSSW 91
Gwyer, Fred V BiDrAPA 89
Gwyn, Douglas Allan 1948- WhoE 91
Gwyn, Nell 1650-1687 BioIn 16, WorAlBi

Gwynn, Albinia *FemiCLE*
Gwynn, Anthony Keith 1960- *WhoAm 90*
Gwynn, Chris *BioIn 16*
Gwynn, David Wayne 1960- *WhoEmL 91*
Gwynn, Kay Sue 1917- *WhoAmW 91*
Gwynn, R. S. 1948- *WhoWrEP 89*
Gwynn, Tony *BioIn 16*
Gwynn, Tony 1960- *Ballpl 90, WorAlBi*
Gwynne, Arthur V. 1936- *St&PR 91*
Gwynne, Fred 1926- *ConTFT 8, WhoAm 90*
Gwynne, John Harold 1899- *AuBYP 90*
Gwynne-Jones, Allan 1892-1982 *DcNaB 1981*
Gyarmati, Ernest Erno 1916- *BiDrAPA 89*
Gyaurov, Nikolay 1929- *PenDiMP*
Gyenes, Alexandre 1934- *WhoWor 91*
Gyenes, Lawrence Andrew 1950- *WhoEmL 91*
Gyermek, Stephen A 1930- *WhoAmA 91*
Gyetvan, Angela Wilson 1962- *WhoAmW 91*
Gyftopoulos, Elias Panayiotis 1927- *WhoAm 90*
Gyger, John Thomas, Jr. *St&PR 91N*
Gygi, Karen Maurine 1934- *IntWWM 90*
Gyi, Maung Maung *BioIn 16*
Gyimah, Albert *BiDrAPA 89*
Gyles, Henry 1645-1709 *PenDiDA 89*
Gyles, John 1680-1755 *DcLB 99*
Gylfason, Thorvaldur 1951- *WhoWor 91*
Gylfe, Carl E. 1925- *St&PR 91*
Gyllander, Nikki K. 1946- *WhoAmW 91*
Gyllembourg, Thomasine 1773-1856 *DcScanL, EncCoWW*
Gyllembourg-Ehrensvard, Thomasine 1773-1856 *DcScanL*
Gyllenborg, Gustaf Fredrik 1731-1808 *DcScanL*
Gyllenhammar, Pehr G. *BioIn 16*
Gyllenhammar, Pehr Gustaf 1935- *WhoWor 91*
Gyllensten, Lars 1921- *DcScanL*
Gyllensten, Lars Johan Wictor 1921- *WhoWor 91*
Gyllstrom, Hans Christer 1944- *WhoSSW 91*
Gynt, Kaj *EarBlAP*
Gyohten, Toyoo *BioIn 16*
Gyorfi, Roberta *BioIn 16*
Gyorgyi, Albert Szent- 1893-1986 *BioIn 16*
Gyp *EncCoWW*
Gyra, Francis Joseph, Jr 1914- *WhoAmA 91*
Gysbers, Norman Charles 1932- *WhoAm 90*
Gyselynck, Jean-Baptiste 1946- *IntWWM 90*
Gysi, Charles L., III 1957- *WhoWrEP 89*
Gysi, Gregor 1948- *WhoWor 91*
Gysin, Fritz Rudolf 1937- *WhoWor 91*
Gyulai, Laszlo *BiDrAPA 89*
Gyulai, Laszlo 1949- *WhoE 91*
Gyulay, Jo-Eileen 1941- *WhoAmW 91*
Gyume Tibetan Monks *NewAgMG*
Gyuricsko, Holly Ann 1964- *WhoAmW 91*
Gyuzelev, Nikolay 1936- *PenDiMP*
Gzowski, Casimir Stanislaus 1813-1898 *DcCanB 12*

H

H. EncCoWW
H.A.N. EncCoWW
H. D. BioAmW, MajTwCW
H. D. 1886-1961 BioIn 16
H.D. 1886-1961 FemiCLE
H.D.S. EncCoWW
Ha, Chong Wan 1938- WhoWor 91
Ha, Christine C BiDrAPA 89
Ha, Hector Chang BiDrAPA 89
Ha, Sang-Tai 1937- BiDrAPA 89
Ha, Yong Soo BiDrAPA 89
Ha-Levi, Judah ben Samuel 1085?-1140? EncO&P 3
Ha-Ngoc, Tuan 1952- St&PR 91
Ha-So-De 1918- WhoAmA 91
Haab, Fred C., Jr. St&PR 91
Haab, Larry D. 1937- St&PR 91
Haab, Larry David 1937- WhoAm 90
Haab, Peter William 1931- St&PR 91
Haack, Cynthia R WhoAmA 91
Haack, David Wilford 1945- WhoEmL 91
Haack, Richard Wilson 1935- WhoWor 91
Haack, Robert William 1917- St&PR 91
Haack, William B. 1925- St&PR 91
Haacke, Hans Christoph 1936- WhoAmA 91, WhoE 91
Haacke, Lorraine ODwPR 91
Haacke, Wilmont 1911- WhoWor 91
Haag, Carol A ODwPR 91
Haag, Carol Ann 1947- WhoAmW 91
Haag, Carol Ann Gunderson WhoAmW 91
Haag, David E. 1946- St&PR 91
Haag, Everett Keith 1928- WhoAm 90
Haag, Jacqueline Vera 1951- WhoEmL 91
Haag, Richard BioIn 16
Haag, Ron 1937- St&PR 91
Haag, Walter Monroe, Jr. 1940- WhoAm 90
Haag, William George 1910- WhoAm 90
Haaga, Agnes 1916- BioIn 16
Haaga, Agnes Marie 1916- NotWoAT
Haaga, Candice Ann Fogel 1960- WhoAmW 91
Haagen, Elaine K BiDrAPA 89
Haagensen, Cushman D. NewYTBS 90
Haagensen, Cushman D 1900-1990 ConAu 132
Haahr, Jane May 1948- WhoEmL 91
Haak, Alex Johan Henri 1930- WhoWor 91
Haak, Daniel H. 1944- St&PR 91
Haak, Harold Howard 1935- WhoAm 90
Haake, Catharine Ann 1954- WhoEmL 91
Haake, Daniel Joseph 1951- WhoEmL 91
Haake, F. Peter 1934- St&PR 91
Haake, Jed Alfred BiDrAPA 89
Haake, Paul 1932- WhoAm 90
Haake, Robert A., Jr. 1946- St&PR 91
Haakenstad, Dale Leonard 1928- St&PR 91
Haaland, Gordon Arthur 1940- WhoAm 90
Haaland, John Edward 1935- St&PR 91
Haaland, Kathleen York 1946- WhoEmL 91
Haan, Carolina Lea de 1881-1932 EncCoWW
Haan, Charles Thomas 1941- WhoAm 90
Haan, G. James 1928- St&PR 91
Haan, Raymond Henry 1938- IntWWM 90
Haan, Roelf Leendert 1938- WhoWor 91
Haanes, Merle A BiDrAPA 89
Haanpaa, Pentti 1905-1955 DcScanL
Haanstra, Bert 1916- BioIn 16
Haar, Ana Maria Fernandez 1951- WhoAmW 91, WhoWor 91
Haar, Francis 1908- WhoAmA 91
Haar, James 1929- IntWWM 90
Haar, Jay D 1940- BiDrAPA 89
Haar, Paul Saul 1953- WhoEmL 91
Haar, Tom 1941- WhoAmA 91
Haarde, Geir Hilmar 1951- WhoWor 91
Haarer, John G 1919- BiDrAPA 89
Haarlander, John R. 1936- St&PR 91
Haarmann, Bruce Donald 1952- WhoEmL 91
Haars, Neil Wayne 1939- WhoSSW 91, WhoWor 91
Haas Family ConAmBL
Haas, Andreas Martin 1963- WhoWor 91
Haas, Antonio 1923- ConAu 131
Haas, Bert 1914- Ballpl 90
Haas, Bruce Randy 1952- St&PR 91
Haas, Carl Christian 1947- St&PR 91
Haas, Carolyn Buhai 1926- WhoAmW 91
Haas, Carroll St&PR 91
Haas, Charles David 1941- WhoSSW 91
Haas, David Charles 1950- BiDrAPA 89
Haas, David Henry 1955- WhoEmL 91
Haas, David Jean 1939- WhoE 91
Haas, David Robert 1941- St&PR 91
Haas, David Robert 1957- IntWWM 90
Haas, Dorothy F. AuBYP 90, BioIn 16
Haas, Edward Lee 1935- WhoAm 90, WhoWor 91
Haas, Eleanor A. 1932- WhoAmW 91, WhoE 91, WhoWor 91
Haas, Ellen Roberta 1942- WhoAmW 91
Haas, Ernst Bernard 1924- WhoAm 90
Haas, Felix 1921- WhoAm 90
Haas, Frank J 1914- BiDrAPA 89
Haas, Frank Joseph 1911- St&PR 91
Haas, Frederick Carl 1936- St&PR 91, WhoAm 90
Haas, Frederick Peter 1911- WhoAm 90
Haas, George Aaron 1919- WhoAm 90
Haas, George C O 1883- EncO&P 3
Haas, George William, Jr. 1924- St&PR 91
Haas, Gilbert Miller BioIn 16
Haas, Gregory George 1949- WhoSSW 91
Haas, Harold 1917- WhoAm 90
Haas, Harold Murray 1925- WhoAm 90
Haas, Howard Green 1924- WhoAm 90
Haas, Ingrid Elizabeth 1953- WhoAmW 91
Haas, John F. 1949- St&PR 91
Haas, John William 1931- BiDrAPA 89
Haas, Joseph Marshall 1927- St&PR 91, WhoAm 90
Haas, Karen Jean 1952- WhoEmL 91
Haas, Karl 1900-1970 PenDiMP
Haas, Kenneth 1943- IntWWM 90
Haas, Kenneth Gregg 1943- WhoAm 90, WhoE 91
Haas, Lester Carl 1913- WhoAm 90
Haas, Lukas 1976- ConTFT 8 [port]
Haas, M Randall ODwPR 91
Haas, Marc NewYTBS 90 [port]
Haas, Marc 1908- St&PR 91, WhoAm 90
Haas, Mark Richard 1954- WhoEmL 91
Haas, Melvyn Robert 1938- BiDrAPA 89
Haas, Merrill Wilber 1910- WhoAm 90
Haas, Miriam Levien 1921- WhoWor 91
Haas, Monique 1906-1987 PenDiMP
Haas, Moose 1956- Ballpl 90
Haas, Mule 1903-1974 Ballpl 90
Haas, Neil Bernard 1941- BiDrAPA 89
Haas, Paul Arnold 1929- WhoSSW 91
Haas, Paul R. 1915- St&PR 91
Haas, Paul Raymond 1915- WhoAm 90, WhoWor 91
Haas, Peter 1929- ODwPR 91
Haas, Peter E. 1918- ConAmBL, St&PR 91, WhoAm 90
Haas, Ralph Arthur 1916- St&PR 91
Haas, Richard Allen 1951- WhoE 91
Haas, Richard John 1936- WhoAmA 91
Haas, Robert D. 1942- St&PR 91
Haas, Robert Donnell 1953- WhoEmL 91, WhoSSW 91, WhoWor 91
Haas, Robert Douglas 1942- ConAmBL, WhoAm 90
Haas, Robert Terry 1947- WhoE 91
Haas, Ronald BioIn 16
Haas, Sandra Fruit 1942- WhoE 91
Haas, Sonja BioIn 16
Haas, Theodore John, Jr. 1946- WhoSSW 91
Haas, Thomas Craig 1943- St&PR 91
Haas, Tracy L. 1958- St&PR 91
Haas, Vinton Benjamin, Jr. 1923- WhoAm 90
Haas, Walter 1928- WhoWor 91
Haas, Walter A. 1889-1979 ConAmBL, WorAlBi
Haas, Walter A., Jr. 1916- ConAmBL, St&PR 91, WhoAm 90
Haas, Ward John 1921- WhoAm 90
Haas, Warren James 1924- WhoAm 90
Haas, Wayne Paul 1950- St&PR 91
Haas, William Paul 1927- WhoAm 90
Haas, Yvette Renee 1963- WhoAmW 91
Haas-Wolfson, Jody Marie 1952- WhoAmW 91
Haase, Ashley Thomson 1939- WhoAm 90
Haase, David Glen 1948- WhoSSW 91
Haase, Donald Wyman 1948- WhoEmL 91
Haase, Gretchen Elizabeth 1951- WhoAmW 91
Haase, Harley Dean 1946- St&PR 91
Haase, Jacquelyn 1947- WhoEmL 91
Haase, Otto Wolfgang 1936- WhoWor 91
Haase, Richard Henry 1924- WhoAm 90
Haase, Susanne ODwPR 91
Haase, William Edward 1943- WhoAm 90, WhoWor 91
Haasen, Peter 1927- WhoWor 91
Haaser, Richard C BiDrAPA 89
Haaseth, Ronald Carl 1952- WhoEmL 91
Haass, Erwin Herman 1904- St&PR 91, WhoAm 90
Haass, Richard Nathan 1951- WhoEmL 91
Haasse, Hella 1918- EncCoWW
Haavardsholm, Espen 1945- DcScanL
Haavelmo, Trygve BioIn 16, WorAlBi
Haavelmo, Trygve 1911- WhoWor 91
Haavikko, Paavo 1931- DcScanL, WorAu 1980 [port]
Haavikko, Paavo Juhani 1931- WhoWor 91
Haavio, Martti Henrikki DcScanL
Haayen, Richard Jan 1924- WhoAm 90
Haba, Leonard Allen WhoAm 90
Haba, Leonard Allen 1931- St&PR 91
Haba, Michele Lynn 1956- WhoAmW 91
Habakkuk, John Hrothgar 1915- WhoWor 91
Habal, Mutaz Billah 1938- WhoSSW 91
Habalewsky, Martin J. ODwPR 91
Haban, Tom 1948- WhoEmL 91
Habarta, Joseph George 1947- WhoEmL 91
Habash, George 1925- BioIn 16
Habash, George 1926- PolLCME
Habbas, Kelly Atwa 1931- St&PR 91
Habbe, Donald Edwin 1931- WhoAm 90
Habberton, William AuBYP 90
Habbestad, Kathryn Louise 1949- WhoAmW 91
Habbick, Brian Ferguson 1939- WhoAm 90
Habbu, Ranganath S 1951- BiDrAPA 89
Habeck, Frederic Harvey 1933- WhoE 91
Habecker, Eugene Brubaker 1946- WhoAm 90
Habeeb, Alfred, Jr. BiDrAPA 89
Habeeb, Onsi Abadir BiDrAPA 89
Habeeb, Patricia Ann 1947- WhoAmW 91
Habeeb, Virginia Thabet WhoAm 90
Habegger, Alfred 1941- ConAu 131
Habel, Arthur A. ODwPR 91
Habel, Kathleen Marilyn 1945- WhoEmL 91
Habel, Robert Earl 1918- WhoAm 90
Habel, Ronald Douglas 1938- St&PR 91
Haben, Mary Kay 1956- WhoAmW 91
Habeneck, Francois-Antoine 1781-1849 PenDiMP
Habenicht, Wenda 1956- WhoAmA 91
Habenstreit, Abraham I ODwPR 91
Habenstreit, Barbara 1937- AuBYP 90
Haber, Allan BioIn 16
Haber, Bruce J. 1952- St&PR 91
Haber, Calvin Harvy 1932- BiDrAPA 89
Haber, Danielle A 1957- BiDrAPA 89
Haber, Edgar 1932- St&PR 91, WhoAm 90, WhoE 91
Haber, Francis Colin 1920-1990 ConAu 131
Haber, Fred 1925- St&PR 91
Haber, Fred 1928- St&PR 91
Haber, Fritz BioIn 16
Haber, Gary Mark 1953- St&PR 91
Haber, George 1944- ODwPR 91
Haber, Geri ODwPR 91
Haber, Heinz 1913- AuBYP 90
Haber, Henry 1922- St&PR 91
Haber, Ira Joel 1947- WhoAm 90, WhoAmA 91
Haber, Jack Jacob 1952- WhoEmL 91
Haber, Jane Victoria 1949- WhoEmL 91
Haber, Jerome 1941- St&PR 91
Haber, Joseph 1911- BiDrAPA 89
Haber, Joyce 1932- WhoAm 90, WhoWor 91
Haber, Lina Levit 1956- BiDrAPA 89
Haber, Martin David 1946- St&PR 91
Haber, Meryl Harold 1934- WhoAm 90
Haber, Norman 1929- St&PR 91
Haber, Ralph Norman 1932- WhoAm 90
Haber, Richard Maurice 1959- BiDrAPA 89
Haber, Robert Keith 1956- WhoE 91
Haber, Samuel S. BioIn 16
Haber, Seymour 1929- WhoE 91
Haber, Shari ODwPR 91
Haber, Sidney A BiDrAPA 89

Haber, Warren H. 1941- St&PR 91, WhoAm 90, WhoE 91
Haber, William 1899-1988 BioIn 16
Haberecht, Rolf R. 1929- WhoAm 90
Haberfeld, Bert John 1930- St&PR 91
Habergritz, George Joseph 1909- WhoAmA 91
Haberkern, Roy C 1943- BiDrAPA 89
Haberkorn, Margaret DcCanB 12
Haberkorn, William Edward 1935- St&PR 91
Haberl, Valerie Elizabeth 1947- WhoAmW 91
Haberland, David Lee 1960- WhoSSW 91
Haberle, Charles A 1919- BiDrAPA 89
Haberle, Joan Baker WhoAm 90, WhoAmW 91, WhoE 91
Haberle, Susan E. 1948- ODwPR 91
Haberman, Daniel 1933- WhoWrEP 89
Haberman, E. Patrick 1950- WhoSSW 91
Haberman, Frederick William 1908- WhoAm 90
Haberman, Irwin L. 1946- St&PR 91
Haberman, Maurice 1951- BiDrAPA 89
Haberman, Shelby Joel 1947- WhoAm 90
Haberman, Wiliam E. St&PR 91
Habermann, Franz Xaver 1721-1796 PenDiDA 89
Habermann, Helen Margaret 1927- WhoAm 90, WhoE 91
Habermann, Michael Robert 1950- IntWWM 90
Habermann, Norman 1933- WhoAm 90
Habermann, Norman Neil 1933- St&PR 91
Habermas, Jurgen BioIn 16
Habermas, Ronald Thomas 1951- WhoEmL 91
Habermehl, Karl-Heinz 1921- WhoWor 91
Habermehl, Lawrence LeRoy 1937- WhoE 91
Habermeier, Hanns Ulrich 1945- WhoWor 91
Habersham, James 1712-1775 EncCRAm
Habersham, Joseph 1751-1815 BiDrUSE 89
Haberstock, Peter 1934- St&PR 91
Haberstroh, James Howard 1948- St&PR 91
Haberstroh, Jon A. 1940- St&PR 91
Habetha, Klaus Otto Paul 1932- WhoWor 91
Habgood, Anthony John 1946- WhoAm 90
Habgood, John Stapylton 1927- WhoWor 91
Habib, Asadullah 1941- WhoWor 91
Habib, David Peter 1921- St&PR 91
Habib, Nadia Elias BiDrAPA 89
Habib, Philip Charles BioIn 16
Habib, Philip Charles 1920- WhoAm 90, WhoWor 91
Habib, William Anthony 1957- WhoEmL 91
Habib Abdelsayed, Habib Adly 1955- WhoWor 91
Habibi, Hassan Ebrahim 1937- WhoWor 91
Habibiyya, The NewAgMG
Habibollahzadeh, Dariush 1953- WhoEmL 91
Habic, Frank Joseph 1939- St&PR 91
Habicht, Allen R. 1946- St&PR 91
Habicht, Christian Herbert 1926- WhoAm 90
Habicht, Frank H. 1920- St&PR 91
Habicht, Frank Henry 1920- WhoAm 90
Habicht, Frank Henry, II 1953- WhoAm 90
Habicht, Jean-Pierre 1934- WhoAm 90
Habicht, Werner 1930- WhoWor 91
Habie, Lissie 1954- BioIn 16
Habif, David Valentine WhoAm 90
Habif, Robert Alan 1950- WhoSSW 91
Habig, Anthony P. 1925- St&PR 91
Habig, Arnold Frank 1907- St&PR 91
Habig, Douglas Arnold 1946- St&PR 91
Habig, John Basil 1933- St&PR 91
Habig, Thomas L. 1928- St&PR 91
Habig, Thomas Louis 1928- WhoAm 90
Hablutzel, Margo Lynn 1961- WhoAmW 91, WhoEmL 91
Hablutzel, Philip Norman 1935- WhoWor 91
Haborak, George E. 1936- WhoSSW 91
Habovstiak, Alojz 1932- WhoWor 91
Habraken, J.J. 1936- St&PR 91
Habre, Hissene WhoWor 91
Habre, Samer Said 1963- WhoE 91
Habsbourg, Charles de 1887-1922 BioIn 16
Habsburgo, Inmaculada WhoHisp 91
Habsburgo-Lorena, Inmaculada de BioIn 16
Habschmidt, James J. 1955- St&PR 91
Habush, Robert Lee 1936- WhoWor 91
Haby, Rene-Jean 1919- BiDFrPL
Haby, Vincent Andrew 1940- WhoSSW 91
Habyan, John 1964- Ballpl 90
Habyarimana, Juvenal 1937- WhoWor 91
Haczla, Joseph R. BioIn 16
Hacault, Antoine Joseph Leon 1926- WhoAm 90
Haccoun, David 1937- WhoAm 90
Hach, Clifford Charles St&PR 91N
Hach, Robert William 1917- St&PR 91
Hachar, Edward Charles 1956- St&PR 91
Hachar, George L. 1931- St&PR 91
Hache, Juste 1823-1895 DcCanB 12
Hache, Reginald W. 1932- IntWWM 90
Hachen, Hans Juerg 1936- WhoWor 91
Hachette, Jean-Louise 1925- WhoWor 91
Hachey, Thomas Eugene 1938- WhoAm 90, WhoWrEP 89
Hachfeld, Douglas Armin 1952- BiDrAPA 89
Hachida, Howard Mitsugi 1953- WhoE 91
Hachiya, Kiyoshi G BiDrAPA 89
Hachmeister, Hugh Gregory 1959- WhoEmL 91
Hachtel, Gary H. 1951- St&PR 91
Hachten, William Andrews 1924- WhoAm 90
Hack, Carole Mae 1942- WhoAmW 91
Hack, John Tilton 1913- WhoAm 90
Hack, Lillian A. 1935- WhoAmW 91
Hack, Patricia Y 1926- WhoAmA 91
Hack, Phillip S 1916- WhoAmA 91
Hack, Raymond L 1916- BiDrAPA 89
Hack, Robert Jefferson 1937- St&PR 91
Hack, Ronald Lee 1955- WhoEmL 91
Hack, Stan 1909-1979 Ballpl 90 [port]
Hackam, Reuben 1936- WhoAm 90
Hackathorn, Don Lee 1942- St&PR 91
Hackbarth, Elizabeth Margaret 1957- WhoAmW 91
Hackeborn, Mechtild von 1241-1299 EncCoWW
Hackel, Emanuel 1925- WhoAm 90
Hackel-Sims, Stella Bloomberg 1926- WhoAm 90
Hackeman, Calvin Leslie 1953- WhoEmL 91
Hacken, Emanuel BiDrAPA 89
Hackenberg, Audrey Susanna 1960- WhoEmL 91, WhoSSW 91
Hackenbroch, Yvonne Alix 1912- WhoAmA 91
Hackenbrock, Charles R. 1929- WhoAm 90
Hacker, Alan 1938- PenDiMP
Hacker, Alan Ray 1938- IntWWM 90
Hacker, Andrew 1929- WhoAm 90
Hacker, Benjamin Thurman 1935- WhoAm 90
Hacker, David PenDiDA 89
Hacker, Elaine S 1928- BiDrAPA 89
Hacker, Frederick 1914-1989 AnObit 1989
Hacker, Frederick J 1914- BiDrAPA 89
Hacker, Frederick J. 1914-1989 BioIn 16, ConAu 129
Hacker, Hans H. 1919- St&PR 91
Hacker, Hilary Baumann 1913- WhoAm 90
Hacker, J. Edward 1923- IntWWM 90
Hacker, John F BiDrAPA 89
Hacker, Jon Christopher 1950- WhoE 91
Hacker, Joseph 1932- WhoSSW 91
Hacker, Karen Kay 1958- WhoEmL 91
Hacker, Lisa Marie BiDrAPA 89
Hacker, Marilyn 1942- FemiCLE
Hacker, Robert William 1923- WhoWor 91
Hacker, Sabina Ann Gonzales 1957- WhoHisp 91
Hacker, Timothy J. 1952- WhoEmL 91
Hacker, Warren 1924- Ballpl 90
Hackerman, Norman 1912- WhoAm 90
Hackert, Marvin LeRoy 1944- WhoSSW 91
Hackes, Peter Sidney 1924- WhoAm 90
Hackett, Albert 1900- AuBYP 90
Hackett, Anthony Patrick 1939- WhoWor 91
Hackett, Bobby 1915-1976 BioIn 16, OxCPMus, WorAlBi
Hackett, Bruce Clayton 1938- WhoAm 90
Hackett, Buddy 1924- ConTFT 8, WhoAm 90, WorAlBi
Hackett, Carol Ann Hedden 1939- WhoAmW 91
Hackett, Charles 1950- WhoEmL 91
Hackett, Cheryl Lynn 1956- WhoEmL 91
Hackett, David Kramer 1948- WhoSSW 91
Hackett, Dwight Vernon 1945- WhoAmA 91
Hackett, Earl J. 1941- St&PR 91
Hackett, Earl Randolph 1932- WhoAm 90
Hackett, Ellen-Mary ODwPR 91
Hackett, Frances AuBYP 90
Hackett, George Whitehouse 1949- WhoEmL 91
Hackett, James E. 1942- St&PR 91
Hackett, James T. 1954- St&PR 91
Hackett, Janice Claire 1953- WhoAmW 91
Hackett, Jean Bates 1943- WhoAmW 91, WhoWor 91
Hackett, Jean Marie 1956- WhoE 91
Hackett, Jeffrey Eugene 1956- WhoEmL 91
Hackett, John Byron 1933- WhoAm 90
Hackett, John Desmond 1926- BiDrAPA 89
Hackett, John Edward 1938- St&PR 91
Hackett, John Francis NewYTBS 90
Hackett, John Francis 1911- WhoAm 90
Hackett, John Francis 1911-1990 BioIn 16
Hackett, John Peter 1942- WhoAm 90
Hackett, John Thomas 1932- St&PR 91, WhoAm 90
Hackett, John Winthrop 1910- BioIn 16
Hackett, Lee Philip 1939- St&PR 91
Hackett, Louise 1933- WhoAmW 91
Hackett, Luther Frederick 1933- St&PR 91, WhoAm 90
Hackett, Lynn Hunter 1949- BiDrAPA 89
Hackett, Mary 1908-1987 BioIn 16
Hackett, Mickey WhoAmA 91
Hackett, Nora Ann 1943- WhoAmW 91
Hackett, Norbert Allen 1934- WhoAm 90
Hackett, Patricia 1932- IntWWM 90
Hackett, Randall Winslow 1935- WhoAm 90
Hackett, Richard Cecil 1949- WhoAm 90, WhoSSW 91
Hackett, Roger Fleming 1922- WhoAm 90
Hackett, Stanley Hailey 1945- WhoSSW 91
Hackett, Suzanne Frances 1961- WhoWrEP 89
Hackett, Timothy Clark 1950- WhoE 91
Hackett, Timothy Duncan 1956- WhoSSW 91
Hackett, Winifred Mary 1908-1987 BioIn 16
Hackey, Doris Plummer 1928- WhoE 91
Hackhl, Joseph PenDiDA 89
Hacking, Ian Macdougall 1936- WhoWrEP 89
Hacking, Rulon 1949- BioIn 16
Hackinson, Robert Ralph 1936- St&PR 91
Hackl, A.J. 1925- St&PR 91
Hackl, Alphons J. 1917- WhoAm 90
Hackl, Alphons John 1917- St&PR 91
Hackl, Donald John 1934- WhoAm 90
Hackl, Muriel Forster 1924- WhoAmW 91
Hackler, John Byron, III 1925- WhoAm 90
Hackler, Michael Lewis 1960- WhoSSW 91
Hackler, Wallace Leroy 1926- St&PR 91
Hackley, E Azalia 1867-1922 BioAmW
Hackley, Emma Azalia BioIn 16
Hackley, Jerry R. 1929- St&PR 91
Hacklin, Allan Dave 1943- WhoAmA 91
Hackman, Gene 1930- WhoAm 90, WorAlBi
Hackman, Gene 1931- BioIn 16
Hackman, Helen Anna Henriette 1908- WhoAmW 91, WhoWor 91
Hackman, John Clement 1947- WhoSSW 91
Hackman, John Edward 1940- WhoSSW 91
Hackman, Karen Lee 1956- WhoEmL 91
Hackman, Roger 1930- St&PR 91
Hackman, Roger L. 1930- St&PR 91
Hackman, Vicki Lou 1952- WhoAmW 91
Hackmann, Glen F. 1941- St&PR 91
Hackney, Anita Jo 1962- WhoEmL 91
Hackney, Clinton Rudolph, III 1953- WhoEmL 91
Hackney, David Charles 1944- WhoE 91
Hackney, David Russell 1954- St&PR 91
Hackney, Francis Sheldon 1933- WhoAm 90, WhoWor 91
Hackney, Hoyt M. 1938- St&PR 91
Hackney, James Acra, III 1939- St&PR 91, WhoAm 90
Hackney, James Acra, Jr. 1917- St&PR 91
Hackney, John Grant, Jr. 1952- WhoEmL 91
Hackney, Keith D. 1948- St&PR 91
Hackney, Ki ODwPR 91
Hackney, Ralph Hodges 1941- St&PR 91
Hackney, Ray Wesley 1934- St&PR 91
Hackney, Thomas Maury 1954- WhoEmL 91
Hackney, William P. 1924- St&PR 91
Hackney, William Pendleton 1924- WhoAm 90
Hackstedt, C.E. 1950- St&PR 91
Hackwood, Susan 1955- WhoAm 90, WhoEmL 91
Hackwood, William PenDiDA 89
Hackworth, David H. BioIn 16
Hackworth, David H. 1931- ConAu 130
Hackworth, Donald E. 1937- WhoAm 90
Hackworth, Gary N. 1949- St&PR 91
Hacon, Catherine BiDEWW
Hacthoun, Augusto 1945- WhoWrEP 89
Hada 1936- WhoAmA 91
Hadad, Herb ODwPR 91
Hadad Strittmatter, Kathleen Mary 1951- WhoSSW 91
Hadar, Mary 1945- WhoAm 90
Hadari, Omri 1941- IntWWM 90
Hadas, Elizabeth Chamberlayne 1946- WhoAm 90, WhoAmW 91
Hadas, Gershon 1896-1980 BioIn 16
Hadas, Julia Ann 1947- WhoEmL 91
Hadas, Pamela White 1946- WhoWrEP 89
Hadas, Rachel 1948- WhoWrEP 89
Hadaway, Deborah Lorraine 1952- WhoEmL 91
Hadaway, Eileen 1949- WhoEmL 91
Haddad, Abraham Herzl 1938- WhoAm 90
Haddad, Alain Nessim 1941- WhoWor 91
Haddad, Anees Adib 1931- WhoAm 90
Haddad, Elias Mtanis 1945- BiDrAPA 89
Haddad, Ernest Mudarri 1938- WhoE 91, WhoWor 91
Haddad, Fred 1946- WhoWor 91
Haddad, George Ilyas 1935- WhoAm 90
Haddad, George Richard 1918- IntWWM 90, WhoAm 90, WhoWor 91
Haddad, Heskel Marshall 1930- WhoAm 90
Haddad, Jamil Raouf 1923- WhoAm 90
Haddad, Jerrier Abdo 1922- WhoAm 90
Haddad, Linda 1951- WhoEmL 91
Haddad, Nabil St&PR 91
Haddad, Rolando I 1928- BiDrAPA 89
Haddad, Thurayya Hanna 1939- WhoE 91
Haddad, Wadi Dahir 1941- WhoWor 91
Haddaway, James D. 1933- St&PR 91
Hadden, Alexander Hawthorne 1924- WhoAm 90
Hadden, E.M. 1955- St&PR 91
Hadden, Jeffrey Bell 1947- WhoAm 90
Hadden, Jeffrey Keith 1936- WhoAm 90, WhoSSW 91
Hadden, John A, Jr. BiDrAPA 89
Hadden, Mayo Addison 1943- WhoWor 91
Hadden, Samuel B BiDrAPA 89
Haddie WhoWrEP 89
Haddix, Carol Ann 1946- WhoAm 90
Haddix, Harvey 1925- Ballpl 90
Haddock, Aubura Glen 1935- WhoAm 90
Haddock, Bradley Eugene 1955- WhoEmL 91
Haddock, Fred Theodore 1919- WhoAm 90
Haddock, George 1866-1926 Ballpl 90
Haddock, Harold, Jr. 1932- WhoAm 90, WhoSSW 91
Haddock, Hoyt S. BioIn 16
Haddock, James N 1920- BiDrAPA 89
Haddock, John Wolcott 1904- WhoWor 91
Haddock, Richard Marshall 1951- St&PR 91
Haddock, Robert Lynn 1945- WhoE 91, WhoEmL 91
Haddock, Robert M. 1945- St&PR 91
Haddock, Ron W. 1940- St&PR 91
Haddock, Ronald Wayne 1940- WhoAm 90, WhoSSW 91
Haddon, Beverly Jeanne 1941- St&PR 91, WhoAm 90
Haddon, Celia 1944- ConAu 130
Haddon, Christopher TwCCr&M 91
Haddon, Dayle BioIn 16
Haddon, Harold Alan 1940- WhoAm 90
Haddon, Harvey L. 1938- St&PR 91
Haddon, James Francis 1954- WhoAm 90
Haddon, Phoebe Anniese 1950- WhoAmW 91
Haddon, Robert Cort 1943- WhoE 91
Haddon, Sam Ellis 1937- WhoAm 90
Haddon, Timothy J. 1948- St&PR 91
Haddow, David Forbes 1953- WhoSSW 91
Haddox, Benjamin Edward 1923- WhoAm 90
Haddox, Charles Edward 1951- WhoSSW 91
Haddox, James David 1952- BiDrAPA 89
Haddox, James H. 1948- St&PR 91
Haddy, Francis John 1922- WhoAm 90
Haden, Charles H., II 1937- WhoSSW 91
Haden, Charlie BioIn 16
Haden, Clovis Roland 1940- WhoAm 90
Haden, E.D. 1929- St&PR 91
Haden, Eunice 1901- WhoAmA 91
Haden, Richard Max 1939- St&PR 91
Haden, Walter Darrell 1931- WhoSSW 91
Hader, Berta 1890?-1976 AuBYP 90
Hader, Elmer 1889-1973 WhoAmA 91N
Hader, Elmer Stanley 1889-1973 AuBYP 90
Hader, Rodney N. BioIn 16
Haderer, Edward George 1931- WhoE 91
Hadermann, Andre Joseph 1935- WhoWor 91
Hadewijch EncCoWW
Hadfield, Debra S. 1953- WhoAmW 91
Hadfield, Frederick William 1936- St&PR 91
Hadfield, Gillian Kereldena 1961- WhoEmL 91
Hadfield, James Irvine Havelock 1930- WhoWor 91
Hadfield, James L. 1941- St&PR 91
Hadfield, Michael James 1934- WhoWor 91

Hadfield, Robert Franklin 1944- WhoWor 91
Hadfield, Ronald C. 1940- St&PR 91
Hadfield, Ted Lee 1950- WhoAmA 91
Hadges, Thomas Richard 1948- WhoWor 91
Hadid, Mohamed BioIn 16
Hadida, Paul Joseph 1931- WhoWor 91
Hadidian, Dikran Yenovk 1920- WhoAm 90
Hadik, Robert Edward 1932- St&PR 91
Hadinata, Rudy Bambang 1940- WhoWor 91
Hadipriono, Fabian Christy 1947- WhoEmL 91, WhoWor 91
Hadithi, Mwenye AuBYP 90
Hadithi, Mwenye 1950- SmATA X
Hadjidakis, Manos 1925- OxCPMus
Hadjinikos, George 1923- IntWWM 90
Hadley, Arthur Twining 1924- WhoE 91
Hadley, Bump 1904-1963 Ballpl 90
Hadley, Candice Ann 1957- WhoAmW 91
Hadley, Carmer 1919- BiDrAPA 89
Hadley, Carolyn Beth 1945- WhoAmW 91
Hadley, Charles A. 1931- St&PR 91
Hadley, Charles D, Jr. 1942- ConAu 31NR
Hadley, Charles O. BioIn 16
Hadley, Cornelia Q. 1930- WhoAmW 91
Hadley, David Price 1952- WhoE 91
Hadley, Donald Hale, II 1951- St&PR 91
Hadley, Garland Ray 1936- WhoSSW 91
Hadley, Henry PenDiMP
Hadley, Henry Lee 1922- WhoAm 90
Hadley, J.L. 1926- St&PR 91
Hadley, Jane Byington 1929- WhoAmW 91, WhoE 91
Hadley, Jerry 1952- IntWWM 90, WhoAm 90
Hadley, Joan TwCCr&M 91
Hadley, June L BiDrAPA 89
Hadley, Lee 1934- BioIn 16
Hadley, Leila 1925- AuBYP 90
Hadley, Leila Eliott-Burton 1925- WhoAmW 91, WhoWor 91
Hadley, Leonard A. 1934- St&PR 91
Hadley, Leonard Anson 1934- WhoAm 90
Hadley, Mark James 1950- WhoEmL 91
Hadley, Marlin LeRoy 1931- WhoAm 90
Hadley, Paul Ervin 1914- WhoAm 90
Hadley, Peter Starr 1928- St&PR 91
Hadley, Ralph Vincent, III 1942- WhoSSW 91
Hadley, Rebekah Lynn 1961- WhoSSW 91
Hadley, Robert James 1938- WhoAm 90
Hadley, Rollin Van Nostrand 1927- WhoAm 90, WhoAmA 91, WhoWor 91
Hadley, Samuel Trevor 1916- WhoE 91
Hadley, Stanton Thomas 1936- St&PR 91, WhoAm 90
Hadley, Susan Jane 1919- WhoAm 90
Hadley, Theodore D. 1928- St&PR 91
Hadlock, John M. 1937- WhoAm 90
Hadlock, Wendell Stanwood 1911-1978 WhoAmA 91N
Hadlow, David Moore 1928- St&PR 91
Hadlow, Earl B. 1924- St&PR 91
Hadlow, Earl Bryce 1924- WhoAm 90
Hadorn, Ernst 1902-1976 DcScB S2
Hadow, Katharine Lunsford 1963- WhoAmW 91
Hadreas, James Demetrios 1910- WhoWor 91
Hadrian 76-138 WorAlBi
Hadrill, Michael Wallace- 1916-1985 DcNaB 1981
Hadwiger, Don Frank 1930- WhoAm 90
Hadzi, Dimitri 1921- WhoAm 90, WhoAmA 91
Hadzima, Joseph George, Jr. 1951- WhoEmL 91
Haebel, Robert Edward 1927- WhoAm 90
Haeberle, Bernadette A BiDrAPA 89
Haeberle, Frederick Roland 1919- WhoWor 91
Haeberlin, John Benjamin, Jr. 1909-1988 WhoAm 90
Haeberlin, Peter 1947- WhoWor 91
Haebler, Ingrid 1926- IntWWM 90, PenDiMP
Haeckel, Ernst 1834-1919 WorAlBi
Haeckel, Ernst Heinrich 1834-1919 WrPh P
Haeckel, Gerald B. 1929- St&PR 91
Haeckel, Gerald Burseth 1929- WhoAm 90
Haedo, Jorge Alberto 1945- WhoE 91, WhoHisp 91
Haedrich, Thomas W. St&PR 91
Haefele, Edwin Theodore 1925- WhoAm 90
Haefele, Gary R. 1942- St&PR 91
Haefliger, Arthur Robert 1919- WhoWor 91
Haefliger, Ernst 1919- IntWWM 90, PenDiMP
Haeflinger, Sharon Kay 1949- WhoAmW 91
Haefner, George 1932- WhoSSW 91
Haefner, Heinz F. 1926- WhoWor 91
Haefner, James C. 1956- St&PR 91
Haefner, Mickey 1912- Ballpl 90
Haeg, Lawrence P., Jr. ODwPR 91
Haegele, John Ernest 1941- WhoAm 90
Haegele, Patricia 1950- WhoAm 90
Haeger, M.R. 1936- St&PR 91
Haeger, Mats Fredrik 1954- WhoWor 91
Haeger, Phyllis Marianna 1928- WhoAm 90, WhoAmW 91
Haehl, John George 1922- St&PR 91
Haehl, John George, Jr. 1922- WhoAm 90
Haehnel, William Otto, Jr. 1924- WhoAm 90
Haelterman, Edward Omer 1918- WhoAm 90
Haelwaeters, Frans Nathalia 1937- WhoWor 91
Haemer, Jim B. 1946- St&PR 91
Haemmel, William Gordon 1924- WhoSSW 91
Haemmerlie, Frances Montgomery 1948- WhoAmW 91
Haen, Victor Raymond 1938- St&PR 91
Haendel, Ida 1923- PenDiMP
Haendel, Ida 1928- IntWWM 90
Haenel, Louis Charles, III 1942- WhoE 91
Haenicke, Diether Hans 1935- WhoAm 90
Haenigsen, Harry 1900- EncACom
Haenlein, George Friedrich Wilhelm 1927- WhoAm 90
Haenninen, Osmo Otto 1939- WhoWor 91
Haensel, William B. 1945- St&PR 91
Haenszel, William Manning 1910- WhoAm 90
Haentjens, Richard Peter St&PR 91
Haentjens, W.D. 1921- St&PR 91
Haentzschel, Lester E BiDrAPA 89
Haerer, Carol 1933- WhoAm 90, WhoAmA 91, WhoE 91
Haerer, Deane N. ODwPR 91
Haerer, Deane Norman 1935- WhoWor 91
Haerian, Mohammad 1943- BiDrAPA 89
Haering, Edwin Raymond 1932- WhoAm 90
Haering, Rudolph Roland 1934- WhoAm 90
Haerle, Paul Raymond 1932- WhoAm 90
Haerle, Wilfried 1941- WhoWor 91
Haerther, Daniel P. 1925- St&PR 91
Haesaert, Clara 1924- EncCoWW
Haeseler, John A. NewYTBS 90
Haeseler, William, III 1930- WhoWor 91
Haeske, Horst 1925- WhoAm 90
Haessle, Jean-Marie Georges 1939- WhoAm 90, WhoAmA 91
Haessler, Gregory David 1950- St&PR 91
Haessler, John F. 1936- St&PR 91
Haessler, Walter T 1940- BiDrAPA 89
Haessly, Jacqueline 1937- WhoAmW 91, WhoWrEP 89
Haeuser, Jamie Leonhard 1953- WhoEmL 91
Haeuser, John H. 1957- WhoEmL 91
Haeusler, Eberhard Ludwig 1926- WhoWor 91
Haeussler, William B 1929- BiDrAPA 89
Hafeez, Abdul BiDrAPA 89
Hafeman, Lyle R. 1930- St&PR 91
Hafemann, William C. 1928- St&PR 91
Hafen, Ann W. 1893-1970 BioAmW
Hafen, Bruce Clark 1940- WhoAm 90
Hafenbreidel, Louis B. 1937- St&PR 91
Hafer, Duane R. 1933- St&PR 91
Hafer, Frederick Douglass 1941- St&PR 91, WhoAm 90
Hafer, Henry M. 1917- St&PR 91
Hafer, Mark Curtis 1952- WhoEmL 91
Haferbecker, Gordon Milton 1912- WhoAm 90
Haferkamp, H.J. 1927- St&PR 91
Hafesh, Joseph W. 1942- WhoE 91
Hafey, Chick 1903-1973 Ballpl 90 [port]
Hafez, Hisham 1952- BiDrAPA 89
Haff, Barbara J E WhoAmA 91
Haff, Deborah Rose 1950- WhoE 91
Haff, Richard W. 1945- St&PR 91
Haffke, Ernest Arthur 1936- BiDrAPA 89
Haffner, Alden Norman 1928- WhoAm 90, WhoE 91
Haffner, Alfred Loveland, Jr. 1925- WhoAm 90
Haffner, C.C., III 1928- St&PR 91
Haffner, Charles Christian, III 1928- WhoAm 90
Haffner, Jeannine Marie 1966- WhoAmW 91
Haffner, Joel J BiDrAPA 89
Haffner, Johan Fredrik Wilhelm 1940- WhoWor 91
Haffner, Karl Henry 1948- St&PR 91
Haffner, Marlene Elisabeth 1941- WhoAmW 91, WhoE 91
Haffner, Oscar Harvey 1926- St&PR 91
Hafford, Patricia Ann 1947- WhoAmW 91, WhoEmL 91
Hafid, Ali BioIn 16
Hafif, Marcia 1929- WhoAmA 91
Hafif, Marcia Woods 1929- WhoE 91
Hafiz BioIn 16
Hafiz 1320?-1390? WorAlBi
Hafiz, Ali Abdel-Qadir 1907-1988 AnObit 1988
Hafiz, Mahmooda BiDrAPA 89
Hafiz, Syeda Nasreen R BiDrAPA 89
Hafken, Louis 1947- BiDrAPA 89
Hafkenschiel, Joseph Henry, Jr. 1916- WhoE 91
Hafley, Michael Kendrick 1952- WhoEmL 91
Hafner, Arthur Wayne 1943- WhoAm 90
Hafner, Dudley H. 1935- WhoAm 90
Hafner, John Henry 1938- WhoSSW 91
Hafner, John Michael 1967- WhoEmL 91
Hafner, Joseph A., Jr. 1944- WhoAm 90
Hafner, Joseph Albert, Jr. 1944- St&PR 91
Hafner, Lawrence Erhardt 1924- WhoSSW 91
Hafner, Marylin 1925- BioIn 16
Hafner, Theodore BioIn 16, NewYTBS 90
Hafner, Thomas Mark 1943- WhoAm 90
Hafner, Volker W. 1936- St&PR 91
Hafner, Warren Grimm 1955- WhoE 91
Haft, Howard S. 1929- St&PR 91
Haft, Jay Stuart 1927-1990 BioIn 16
Haft, Marilyn Geisler 1943- WhoAmW 91, WhoE 91
Haft, Robert Stephen 1929- St&PR 91
Haft, Steven BioIn 16
Haftek, Stanley R. 1942- St&PR 91
Haftel, Howard W. 1925- St&PR 91
Haftendorn, Helga 1933- WhoWor 91
Hafter, Martin 1923- St&PR 91
Hafter, Robert 1951- St&PR 91
Hagalin, Gudmundur Gislason 1898- DcScanL
Hagaman, Scott Dennis 1956- BiDrAPA 89, WhoE 91
Hagamen, Mary B BiDrAPA 89
Hagan, Brian Thomas 1963- WhoEmL 91
Hagan, Charles F. 1923- WhoAm 90
Hagan, Darian BioIn 16, NewYTBS 90 [port]
Hagan, Donald Kieth 1949- St&PR 91
Hagan, Eileen 1930- WhoE 91
Hagan, Epsie Lewis 1927- WhoAmW 91
Hagan, Frank M. 1918- St&PR 91
Hagan, Frederick 1918- WhoAmA 91
Hagan, James A. 1946- St&PR 91
Hagan, James Garrison 1936- WhoAmA 91
Hagan, Jeannette 1906-1988 BioIn 16
Hagan, John Aubrey 1936- St&PR 91, WhoAm 90
Hagan, Joseph Henry 1935- WhoAm 90, WhoE 91
Hagan, Joseph L. 1942- St&PR 91
Hagan, Juanice M. 1949- St&PR 91
Hagan, Katherine Ellen 1959- WhoAmW 91
Hagan, Michael 1831?-1896 DcCanB 12
Hagan, Peter Anthony 1947- WhoEmL 91
Hagan, Randall Lee 1945- St&PR 91, WhoEmL 91
Hagan, Robert Leslie 1923- WhoAm 90
Hagan, Sarah 1960- WhoE 91
Hagan, Timothy P. 1942- St&PR 91
Hagan, Wallace Woodrow 1913- WhoAm 90
Hagan, William E. St&PR 91
Hagan, William John St&PR 91N
Hagan, William Thomas 1918- WhoAm 90
Hagans, Jonathan BioIn 16
Hagans, Marjean BioIn 16
Hagans, Robert Frank 1926- St&PR 91, WhoAm 90
Hagar, Al 1930- St&PR 91
Hagar, Alice 1894-1969 AuBYP 90
Hagar, Joanne Lee BiDrAPA 89
Hagar, Judith ConAu 129
Hagar, Sammy BioIn 16
Hagar, Sammy 1947- EncPR&S 89
Hagar, William Scott 1943- WhoE 91
Hagarty, John Hawkins 1816-1900 DcCanB 12
Hagauer, Richard William 1928- WhoSSW 91
Hagberg, Chris Eric 1949- WhoE 91
Hagberg, Jeff Leigh 1951- St&PR 91
Hagberg, Lars Goran 1939- WhoWor 91
Hagberg, Nils Arne 1919- WhoWor 91
Hagberg, Viola Wilgus 1952- WhoAmW 91
Hage, Raymond Joseph 1943- WhoAmA 91
Hagedorn, Donald James 1919- WhoAm 90
Hagedorn, Dorothy Louise 1929- WhoAm 90, WhoAmW 91
Hagedorn, Fred B. 1928- WhoSSW 91
Hagedorn, Raymond Thomas 1947- St&PR 91
Hagegard, Erland 1944- IntWWM 90, PenDiMP
Hagegard, Hakan 1945- IntWWM 90, PenDiMP, WhoWor 91
Hagel, John, III 1950- WhoWor 91
Hagel, Raymond Charles 1916- WhoAm 90
Hagele, Glenn Fred, Jr. 1957- St&PR 91
Hagelgans, John Michael 1961- WhoEmL 91
Hagelman, Charles William, Jr. 1920- WhoAm 90
Hagelstein, Peter BioIn 16
Hagelstein, Robert P. 1942- St&PR 91
Hagelstein, Robert Philip 1942- WhoAm 90
Hageman, Charles Lee 1935- WhoAmA 91
Hageman, Gilbert Robert 1947- WhoSSW 91
Hageman, Howard Garberich 1921- WhoAm 90
Hageman, Richard Harry 1917- WhoAm 90
Hageman, Richard Philip, Jr. 1941- WhoE 91, WhoWor 91
Hageman, Thomas BioIn 16
Hagemann, Dolores Ann 1935- WhoAmW 91
Hagemann, Douglas Lee 1936- St&PR 91
Hagemann, Philip Henry 1932- IntWWM 90
Hagemeister, George 1925- St&PR 91
Hagemeyer, Loren A. 1934- St&PR 91
Hagen, Arthur Ainsworth 1933- WhoAm 90
Hagen, Carsten 1942- St&PR 91
Hagen, Celeste Lynne 1956- WhoAmW 91
Hagen, Charles William St&PR 91N
Hagen, Charles William, Jr. 1918- WhoAm 90
Hagen, Daron Aric 1961- IntWWM 90
Hagen, Deb ODwPR 91
Hagen, Donald Floyd 1938- WhoAm 90
Hagen, Duane Quentin 1935- BiDrAPA 89
Hagen, Elizabeth K. 1948- ODwPR 91
Hagen, George Leon 1924- St&PR 91, WhoAm 90
Hagen, Glenn W. 1948- WhoEmL 91
Hagen, Harold Alfred 1926- St&PR 91
Hagen, James A. 1932- BioIn 16, St&PR 91
Hagen, James Alfred 1932- WhoAm 90
Hagen, John P. NewYTBS 90
Hagen, John P 1908-1990 CurBio 90N
Hagen, John William 1940- WhoAm 90
Hagen, Kathryn Eileen 1952- WhoAmW 91
Hagen, Larry William 1945- WhoEmL 91
Hagen, Mark Eric 1963- WhoEmL 91
Hagen, Michael E. 1947- St&PR 91
Hagen, Nicholas Stewart 1942- WhoWor 91
Hagen, Oliver H. 1932- St&PR 91
Hagen, Paul Beo 1920- WhoAm 90
Hagen, Per Rolf 1927- WhoWor 91
Hagen, R. E. 1933- WhoAm 90
Hagen, Ralph Leslie 1942- BiDrAPA 89
Hagen, Stephen Close 1942- St&PR 91
Hagen, Stuart Martin 1950- St&PR 91
Hagen, Susan Hirt 1935- WhoAmW 91
Hagen, Teunis 1945- WhoWor 91
Hagen, Thomas Bailey 1935- St&PR 91, WhoE 91
Hagen, Uta 1919- BioIn 16, NotWoAT, WorAlBi
Hagen, Uta Thyra 1919- WhoAm 90, WhoAmW 91
Hagen, Walter 1892-1969 BioIn 16, WorAlBi
Hagen-Groll, Walter 1927- PenDiMP
Hagenah, Elizabeth Artman 1935- IntWWM 90
Hagenah, William John, Jr. 1920- WhoAm 90
Hagenau, Steven E. 1951- St&PR 91
Hagenauer, Fedor BiDrAPA 89
Hagenbuch, John Jacob 1951- WhoWor 91
Hagenbuch, Lynn Way 1952- WhoEmL 91
Hagenbuch, William H. 1918- St&PR 91
Hagenbuchle, Roland 1932- WhoWor 91
Hagendorn, William 1925- WhoAm 90
Hagenfeldt, Jan Arthur 1931- WhoWor 91
Hagenlocker, Edward E. BioIn 16
Hagenlocker, Edward E. 1939- WhoAm 90
Hagenstad, M. Thomas 1938- WhoE 91
Hagenstein, Perry Reginald 1931- WhoE 91
Hagenstein, William David 1915- WhoAm 90
Hager, Bob BioIn 16
Hager, Bronson Q. 1959- St&PR 91
Hager, Charles Read 1937- WhoAm 90
Hager, Douglas Eugene 1947- WhoEmL 91
Hager, E.B. 1931- St&PR 91
Hager, Edward Paul 1948- WhoE 91
Hager, Elizabeth Sears 1944- WhoAmW 91
Hager, Frederick H. 1957- St&PR 91
Hager, Fritz-Peter P. 1939- WhoWor 91
Hager, Gary BioIn 16
Hager, George Philip 1916- WhoAm 90
Hager, George W, Jr. 1917- BiDrAPA 89
Hager, Hellmut W 1926- WhoAmA 91

Hager, Hellmut Wilhelm 1926- *WhoAm 90*
Hager, Henry Brandebury 1926- *WhoWrEP 89*
Hager, Jimmy Nelson 1947- *WhoWrEP 89*
Hager, John Patrick 1936- *WhoAm 90*
Hager, Kathy Elaine 1951- *WhoAmW 91, WhoEmL 91, WhoWor 91*
Hager, Larry Stanley 1942- *WhoAm 90, WhoWrEP 89*
Hager, Laurence Michael 1938- *WhoWor 91*
Hager, Leopold 1935- *IntWWM 90, PenDiMP, WhoWor 91*
Hager, Louis Busch *BioIn 16*
Hager, Lowell Paul 1926- *WhoAm 90*
Hager, Nathaniel Ellmaker, Jr. 1922- *WhoE 91, WhoWor 91*
Hager, Nina 1950- *WhoWor 91*
Hager, P Elisabeth *BiDrAPA 89*
Hager, Paul Calvin 1931- *WhoSSW 91*
Hager, Robert *WhoAm 90*
Hager, Robert L. 1947- *St&PR 91*
Hager, Robert Worth 1928- *St&PR 91, WhoAm 90*
Hager, Sterling *ODwPR 91*
Hager, Thomas Arthur 1953- *WhoEmL 91*
Hager, Werner 1900- *WhoWor 91*
Hager, William Ward 1948- *WhoSSW 91*
Hagerman, Allen Reid 1951- *WhoAm 90*
Hagerman, Edward 1939- *ConAu 130*
Hagerman, George E. 1933- *St&PR 91*
Hagerman, John David 1941- *WhoSSW 91, WhoWor 91*
Hagerman, Peter Stanley 1939- *WhoAm 90*
Hagerman, Rip 1888-1930 *Ballpl 90*
Hagerman, Theodore Frederick 1908- *St&PR 91*
Hagerson, John David 1966- *WhoEmL 91, WhoWor 91*
Hagerson, Lawrence John 1931- *WhoWor 91*
Hagerstrand, Martin Alan 1911- *WhoAmA 91*
Hagerth, Steven Alvar 1938- *St&PR 91*
Hagerty, Father *EncAL*
Hagerty, Betty Lee *St&PR 91, WhoAmW 91, WhoE 91*
Hagerty, Herbert George 1932- *WhoE 91*
Hagerty, James C. 1909-1981 *BioIn 16, ConAu 129*
Hagerty, James J. 1941- *St&PR 91*
Hagerty, John Brady 1951- *WhoEmL 91*
Hagerty, Laurence J. 1953- *St&PR 91*
Hagerty, Polly Martiel 1946- *WhoAmW 91, WhoEmL 91*
Hagerup, Inger 1905-1985 *EncCoWW*
Hagerup, Inger Halsor 1905-1985 *DcScanL*
Hagerup, Richard H. 1952- *WhoEmL 91*
Hages, Michelle Marie *BiDrAPA 89*
Hageseth, Christian N M, III 1941- *BiDrAPA 89*
Hagey, Steven Lee 1946- *WhoSSW 91*
Hagey, Walter Rex 1909- *WhoE 91, WhoWor 91*
Hagfors, Tor 1930- *WhoAm 90*
Haggai, Thomas Stephens 1931- *St&PR 91*
Haggander, Mari Anne 1956- *IntWWM 90*
Haggar, Sara Thompson 1963- *WhoAmW 91*
Haggard, David Eugene 1934- *St&PR 91*
Haggard, Forrest Deloss 1925- *WhoAm 90*
Haggard, Geraldine Langford 1929- *WhoAmW 91*
Haggard, H. Rider 1856-1925 *BioIn 16*
Haggard, Henry Rider 1856-1925 *BioIn 16, EncPaPR 91*
Haggard, James C. 1945- *WhoEmL 91*
Haggard, Merle *BioIn 16, WhoNeCM C [port]*
Haggard, Merle 1937- *OxCPMus, WorAlBi*
Haggard, Paul Wintzel 1933- *WhoSSW 91*
Haggard, Tamara C. 1949- *St&PR 91*
Haggard, William 1907- *SpyFic, TwCCr&M 91*
Haggarty, Donna M. *ODwPR 91*
Haggbom, Nils-Ake 1940- *WhoWor 91*
Haggen, Donald Edmund 1931- *St&PR 91*
Haggen, Richard R. 1945- *St&PR 91*
Haggerty, Brian A 1943- *ConAu 32NR*
Haggerty, David M. 1942- *St&PR 91*
Haggerty, Frederick *St&PR 91*
Haggerty, James Joseph 1920- *WhoE 91, WhoWor 91*
Haggerty, James Joseph 1936- *WhoAm 90, WhoE 91*
Haggerty, John Edward 1918- *WhoAm 90*
Haggerty, John J, Jr. 1945- *BiDrAPA 89*
Haggerty, John Richard 1935- *St&PR 91, WhoAm 90*
Haggerty, Lawrence G. 1916- *St&PR 91*
Haggerty, Lawrence George 1916- *WhoAm 90*
Haggerty, Mary Ann 1945- *WhoAmW 91*
Haggerty, Mary Ellen 1920- *St&PR 91*
Haggerty, Mick *BioIn 16*
Haggerty, Richard Paul 1939- *St&PR 91*
Haggerty, Robert Henry 1919- *WhoAm 90*
Haggerty, Robert Johns 1925- *WhoAm 90*
Haggerty, Robert V.J. 1937- *St&PR 91*
Haggerty, Roger E. *St&PR 91*
Haggerty, Ronda 1960- *WhoSSW 91*
Haggerty, Stephanie Murch 1944- *WhoSSW 91*
Haggerty, William J. 1930- *St&PR 91*
Haggett, William *St&PR 91*
Haggh, Barbara Helen 1955- *IntWWM 90*
Haggh, Raymond Herbert 1920- *IntWWM 90*
Haggin, Ben Ali 1882-1951 *WhoAmA 91N*
Haggis, Arthur George, Jr. 1924- *WhoSSW 91, WhoWor 91*
Haggis, Paul Edward 1953- *WhoAm 90, WhoEmL 91*
Hagglund, Clarance Edward 1927- *WhoAm 90, WhoWor 91*
Hagin, Joseph Whitehouse, II 1956- *WhoAm 90*
Hagin, Nancy 1940- *WhoAmA 91*
Hagio, Kunio *BioIn 16*
Hagis, Peter, Jr. 1926- *WhoAm 90, WhoE 91*
Hagiwara, Kokichi 1924- *St&PR 91, WhoE 91*
Hagland, Mark Martin *WhoWrEP 89*
Hagle, Dios C. *AmLegL*
Hagle, George Herbert, Jr. 1936- *WhoAm 90*
Hagleitner, Diane J. 1951- *St&PR 91*
Haglelgam, John Richard 1949- *WhoWor 91*
Hagler 1690?-1763 *WhNaAH*
Hagler, Christine Louise 1963- *WhoSSW 91*
Hagler, Erwin Harrison 1947- *WhoAm 90*
Hagler, Jon Lewis 1936- *WhoAm 90*
Hagler, Lillie Mae 1916- *WhoAmW 91*
Hagler, Marion Otho 1939- *WhoAm 90*
Hagler, Marvin 1954- *WhoAm 90, WhoE 91*
Hagler, Robert John 1939- *St&PR 91*
Hagler, Samuel Henry 1940- *St&PR 91*
Haglund, David Roy 1951- *WhoEmL 91*
Haglund, Gerhard Oscar, Sr. 1916- *WhoAm 90*
Haglund, Marlene Linda 1959- *WhoAmW 91*
Hagmaier, Craig Owen 1960- *WhoE 91*
Hagman, George R. 1931- *St&PR 91*
Hagman, Harlan Lawrence 1911- *WhoAm 90*
Hagman, Jean Cassels 1947- *WhoAmA 91*
Hagman, Jennifer Ona *BiDrAPA 89*
Hagman, Larry *BioIn 16*
Hagman, Larry 1931- *WhoAm 90, WorAlBi*
Hagmann, Peter 1950- *IntWWM 90*
Hagmann, Rainer 1938- *WhoWor 91*
Hagmeir, Thomas Edmiston 1933- *WhoE 91*
Hagn, George Hubert 1935- *WhoAm 90*
Hagner, Arthur Feodor 1911- *WhoAm 90*
Hagner, Samuel B 1925- *BiDrAPA 89*
Hagner, Samuel Benedict 1925- *WhoE 91*
Hagni, Richard Davis 1931- *WhoAm 90*
Hagood, Annabel Dunham 1924- *WhoAm 90*
Hagood, Bo L. 1949- *St&PR 91*
Hagood, Gary Steve 1958- *WhoSSW 91*
Hagood, Patricia Carr 1943- *WhoE 91*
Hagood, Robert B 1914- *BiDrAPA 89*
Hagood, Susan Stewart Hahn 1953- *WhoSSW 91*
Hagoort, Thomas Henry 1932- *WhoAm 90*
Hagopian, Berge Kipling 1941- *St&PR 91*
Hagopian, Gloria Ann 1938- *WhoE 91*
Hagopian, Harry H. 1930- *St&PR 91*
Hagopian, Larry S. 1947- *St&PR 91*
Hagopian, Louis Thomas 1925- *St&PR 91*
Hagopian, Michael Richard 1961- *WhoEmL 91*
Hagrup, Knut 1913- *WhoWor 91*
Hagseth, Paul Eugene 1956- *WhoEmL 91*
Hagson, Carl Allan 1921- *WhoWor 91*
Hagstram, W. R. 1946- *WhoAm 90*
Hagstrom, Barbara Barbat 1946- *WhoEmL 91*
Hagstrom, Jon 1939- *St&PR 91*
Hagstrom, Tony Gunnar 1936- *WhoWor 91*
Hagstrum, Homer Dupre 1915- *WhoAm 90*
Hagstrum, Jean Howard 1913- *WhoAm 90*
Hague, Albert 1920- *OxCPMus*
Hague, Albert Frederick 1947- *WhoE 91*
Hague, James D *BiDrAPA 89*
Hague, Jane Frances 1946- *WhoAmW 91*
Hague, Joe 1944- *Ballpl 90*
Hague, John Ross 1907- *BiDrAPA 89*
Hague, John William, Jr. 1943- *WhoAm 90*
Hague, Kathleen 1949- *BioIn 16*
Hague, Michael 1948- *BioIn 16*
Hague, Raoul 1905- *WhoAm 90, WhoAmA 91*
Hague, Robert W. 1926- *St&PR 91*
Hague, Roger S. 1928- *St&PR 91*
Hague, Roger Sampson 1928- *St&PR 91*
Hague, William 1952- *WhoE 91*
Hague, William Edward 1919- *WhoAm 90, WhoWrEP 89*
Hague, William H *BiDrAPA 89*
Hagura, Nobuya 1919- *St&PR 91*
Hagy, James William 1936- *WhoSSW 91*
Hagy, Susan Hall Winstead 1960- *WhoAmW 91*
Hagy, Teresa Jane 1950- *WhoAmW 91*
Hagye, Melissa Marie 1952- *WhoAmW 91*
Hahl, Neil M. 1948- *St&PR 91*
Hahlbeck, Karen J. 1950- *WhoEmL 91*
Hahm, David Edgar 1938- *WhoAm 90*
Hahn, A William *BiDrAPA 89*
Hahn, Alexander *BioIn 16*
Hahn, Arthur W. 1944- *WhoAm 90*
Hahn, Bessie King 1939- *WhoAm 90, WhoAmW 91*
Hahn, Betty 1940- *WhoAm 90, WhoAmA 91*
Hahn, Beverly Sue 1954- *WhoWor 91*
Hahn, Bradley D. 1942- *St&PR 91*
Hahn, Carl Horst 1926- *WhoAm 90, WhoWor 91*
Hahn, Carol Barnes Griffith 1941- *IntWWM 90*
Hahn, Cathy Clifford 1947- *WhoSSW 91*
Hahn, Daniel Brase 1949- *WhoEmL 91*
Hahn, David Bennett 1945- *WhoEmL 91*
Hahn, David Michael 1953- *WhoE 91*
Hahn, Dean LuVerne 1933- *St&PR 91*
Hahn, Don 1948- *Ballpl 90*
Hahn, Donna G. 1957- *ODwPR 91*
Hahn, Earl R 1925- *BiDrAPA 89*
Hahn, Ed 1875-1941 *Ballpl 90*
Hahn, Edward Lorenz 1937- *St&PR 91*
Hahn, Elizabeth F. 1914- *WhoAmW 91*
Hahn, Elliot Frank 1944- *WhoSSW 91*
Hahn, Emanuel Otto 1881-1957 *WhoAmA 91N*
Hahn, Emily 1905- *AuBYP 90, FemiCLE, WhoAm 90*
Hahn, Erwin Louis 1921- *WhoAm 90*
Hahn, Eugene Richard 1938- *St&PR 91*
Hahn, F. E. *ConAu 129*
Hahn, Frank Horace 1925- *WhoWor 91*
Hahn, Fred 1906- *WhoE 91*
Hahn, Fred E. *ConAu 129*
Hahn, Fred Ernest *ConAu 129*
Hahn, Frederic Louis 1941- *WhoAm 90*
Hahn, Friedrich Ernest 1916-1989 *ConAu 129*
Hahn, Gene *St&PR 91*
Hahn, George LeRoy 1934- *WhoAm 90*
Hahn, George Thomas 1930- *WhoAm 90*
Hahn, Gilbert, Jr. 1921- *WhoAm 90*
Hahn, Harlan Dean 1939- *WhoAm 90*
Hahn, Harold Thomas 1924- *WhoWor 91*
Hahn, Helen L. 1920- *St&PR 91*
Hahn, J. Jacob 1902-1990 *BioIn 16*
Hahn, Jack Albert Louis 1922- *WhoAm 90*
Hahn, James C. *St&PR 91*
Hahn, James Maglorie 1936- *WhoAm 90*
Hahn, Jane Meehae *BiDrAPA 89*
Hahn, Jeffrey P. 1944- *St&PR 91*
Hahn, Jerome P. 1924- *St&PR 91*
Hahn, Jessica *BioIn 16*
Hahn, Jhynelda Mae B. 1942- *WhoAmW 91*
Hahn, Joan Christensen 1933- *WhoAmW 91, WhoWor 91*
Hahn, John W. 1932- *St&PR 91*
Hahn, John William 1940- *WhoE 91*
Hahn, Karen Virginia 1947- *WhoAmW 91*
Hahn, Karl 1937- *WhoWor 91*
Hahn, Kenneth H. 1922- *St&PR 91*
Hahn, Kent S. 1955- *St&PR 91*
Hahn, Kurt Robert *BiDrAPA 89*
Hahn, Laura L. 1959- *St&PR 91, WhoEmL 91*
Hahn, Lewis Edwin 1908- *WhoAm 90, WhoWor 91*
Hahn, Lithia B. 1951- *WhoAmW 91*
Hahn, Lloyd C. 1919- *St&PR 91*
Hahn, Lloyd Edward 1925- *St&PR 91, WhoAm 90*
Hahn, Lucille Denise 1940- *WhoAmW 91*
Hahn, Ludwig 1908- *BioIn 16*
Hahn, Mary Downing 1937- *BioIn 16, SmATA 12AS [port]*
Hahn, Maurice *WhoAmA 91*
Hahn, Michael 1830-1886 *AmLegL*
Hahn, Nicholas George, Jr. 1960- *WhoEmL 91*
Hahn, Noodles 1879-1960 *Ballpl 90*
Hahn, Norman Jacob 1965- *WhoE 91*
Hahn, Oscar 1938- *ConAu 131, HispWr 90*
Hahn, Oswald 1928- *WhoWor 91*
Hahn, Otto 1879-1968 *WorAlBi*
Hahn, Paul Frederick 1930- *St&PR 91*
Hahn, Reynaldo 1874-1947 *PenDiMP A*
Hahn, Reynaldo 1875-1947 *OxCPMus*
Hahn, Rhoda K *BiDrAPA 89*
Hahn, Richard Christian 1939- *St&PR 91*
Hahn, Richard Ferdinand 1909- *WhoAm 90*
Hahn, Richard Leonard 1934- *WhoE 91*
Hahn, Richard Ray 1930- *WhoAm 90*
Hahn, Richard S. 1951- *St&PR 91*
Hahn, Robert E. 1957- *St&PR 91*
Hahn, Robert G. 1928- *St&PR 91*
Hahn, Roger 1932- *WhoAm 90*
Hahn, Roger C 1933- *BiDrAPA 89*
Hahn, Roslyn *WhoAmA 91*
Hahn, Samuel Wilfred 1921- *WhoAm 90*
Hahn, Sandra Elaine 1964- *WhoSSW 91*
Hahn, Sang Joon 1921- *WhoWor 91*
Hahn, Sharon Lee 1939- *WhoAmW 91*
Hahn, Stanley Robert, Jr. 1946- *WhoSSW 91*
Hahn, Stephen 1921- *WhoAmA 91*
Hahn, Suk Jeong 1932- *BiDrAPA 89*
Hahn, Sung-Up *BiDrAPA 89*
Hahn, Theodore Thomas 1942- *St&PR 91*
Hahn, Thomas Marshall, Jr. 1926- *St&PR 91, WhoAm 90, WhoSSW 91*
Hahn, Vera *BioIn 16, NewYTBS 90*
Hahn, Werner 1912- *WhoWor 91*
Hahn, William Harry 1946- *St&PR 91, WhoEmL 91*
Hahn, William M. 1933- *St&PR 91*
Hahn, Wonsam 1941- *BiDrAPA 89*
Hahn, Young Soo *BiDrAPA 89*
Hahn, Yukap 1932- *WhoE 91*
Hahn-Hahn, Countess von 1805-1880 *EncCoWW*
Hahn-Sporzynski, Jadwiga *BiDrAPA 89*
Hahn-Vogel, Colette Camille 1961- *WhoEmL 91*
Hahne, C. E. 1940- *WhoSSW 91*
Hahne, Henry Victor 1924- *WhoAm 90*
Hahne, Robert Louis 1938- *WhoAm 90*
Hahneman, Samuel 1755- *NewAgE 90*
Hahnke, Timothy J. *BioIn 16*
Hahon, Nicholas 1924- *WhoSSW 91*
Hahs, Dale E. 1963- *St&PR 91*
Hai, Carol Sue 1938- *WhoAmW 91*
Haich, George Donald 1928- *WhoSSW 91*
Haid, Charles M. 1943- *WhoAm 90*
Haidar, Amer Sleiman 1944- *BiDrAPA 89*
Haidar, Salim Mohammad 1958- *WhoE 91*
Haider, Jorg 1950- *WhoWor 91*
Haider, Syed Ikram 1945- *WhoWor 91*
Haider, Ursula 1413-1498 *EncCoWW*
Haidet, George Charles 1951- *WhoEmL 91*
Haidis, John Fotios 1963- *WhoWor 91*
Haidt, Harold 1926- *WhoAm 90, WhoWor 91*
Haies, Pirjo 1946- *BiDrAPA 89*
Haig, Alexander 1924- *WorAlBi*
Haig, Alexander M., Jr. 1914- *WorAlBi*
Haig, Alexander Meigs 1924- *BioIn 16*
Haig, Alexander Meigs, Jr. 1924- *BiDrUSE 89, WhoAm 90, WhoWor 91*
Haig, Douglas 1861-1928 *BioIn 16, WorAlBi*
Haig, Fenil *ConAu 132, MajTwCW*
Haig, Frank Rawle 1928- *WhoAm 90*
Haig, Patigian 1876-1950 *WhoAmA 91N*
Haig, Robert Leighton 1947- *WhoE 91, WhoEmL 91, WhoWor 91*
Haig, Theodor 1913- *WhoWor 91*
Haig, Thomas *PenDiDA 89*
Haigh, Andrew Wilfred 1954- *IntWWM 90*
Haigh, George Whylden 1931- *WhoAm 90*
Haigh, John C. 1930- *St&PR 91*
Haigh, John Richard 1953- *St&PR 91*
Haigh, Robert William 1926- *WhoAm 90, WhoWor 91*
Haigh, Ronald K. 1934- *St&PR 91*
Haight, Anna Louise 1958- *WhoAmW 91*
Haight, Barbara Kavanagh 1937- *WhoSSW 91*
Haight, Carol Barbara 1945- *WhoAmW 91*
Haight, Charles 1838-1891 *AmLegL*
Haight, Charles Sherman, Jr. 1930- *WhoAm 90*
Haight, Edward Allen 1910- *WhoAm 90, WhoWor 91*
Haight, Ehrick Kilner, Jr. 1960- *WhoEmL 91*
Haight, Gilbert Pierce, Jr. 1922- *WhoAm 90*
Haight, Gordon S. 1901-1985 *DcLB 103 [port]*
Haight, James Theron 1924- *St&PR 91, WhoAm 90*
Haight, Jay Dale 1952- *WhoEmL 91*
Haight, Kenneth Lee 1955- *WhoE 91*
Haight, Peter V. 1937- *St&PR 91*
Haight, Thomas Charles 1948- *WhoEmL 91*
Haight, Warren Gazzam 1929- *WhoAm 90, WhoWor 91*
Haiglar 1690?-1763 *WhNaAH*
Haigler 1690?-1763 *WhNaAH*
Haigler, Theodore E., Jr. 1924- *St&PR 91*
Haigler-Mills, Eunice Estelle Young 1950- *WhoAmW 91*
Haigler Ramirez, Esteban Jose 1953- *WhoHisp 91*

Haigley, Harry 1943- *ODwPR 91*
Haigood, Lyndell Wayne 1949- *St&PR 91*
Haik, Joseph 1930- *St&PR 91*
Haikal, Walid Hassan 1942- *WhoWor 91*
Haikalis, Susan Williams 1941- *WhoAmW 91*
Haiken, Leatrice Brown 1934- *WhoAm 90*
Haiko, Geraldine Mae 1940- *WhoAmW 91, WhoWor 91*
Hail, Anthony *BioIn 16*
Hail, Barbara Andrews 1930- *WhoE 91*
Hail, Gerry *ODwPR 91*
Hail, John Wesley 1930- *WhoSSW 91*
Hail, Kenneth E. 1930- *St&PR 91*
Haile Selassie 1892-1975 *WorAlBi*
Haile Selassie I, Emperor of Ethiopia 1891-1975 *BioIn 16*
Haile, H. G. 1931- *WhoAm 90, WhoWrEP 89*
Haile, James Francis 1920- *WhoAm 90*
Haile, Kenneth W. 1942- *St&PR 91*
Haile, L. John, Jr. 1945- *WhoAm 90*
Haile, Lawrence Barclay 1938- *WhoAm 90, WhoWor 91*
Haile, Leroy Yellott, Jr. 1929- *WhoWor 91*
Haile, Martha Helen 1947- *BiDrAPA 89*
Haile, Raymond Alderson, Jr. 1930- *WhoAm 90*
Haile, Sam *BioIn 16*
Haile Giorgis, Workneh 1930- *WhoWor 91*
Hailes, Julia 1961- *ConAu 130*
Hailey, Arthur 1920- *BestSel 90-3 [port], MajTwCW, WhoAm 90, WhoWor 91, WhoWrEP 89, WorAlBi*
Hailey, Chenault William 1932- *WhoSSW 91*
Hailey, James L. *WhoSSW 91*
Hailey, Louie William, Jr. 1935- *WhoSSW 91*
Hailey, Richard A. 1949- *WhoSSW 91*
Hailparn Ledeen, Lydia Rosen 1938- *IntWWM 90*
Hailperin, Herman 1899-1973 *BioIn 16*
Hails, Jean *BioIn 16*
Hails, Kevin Charles 1950- *BiDrAPA 89*
Hails, Robert Emmet 1923- *WhoAm 90, WhoWor 91*
Hailsham of St. Marylebone, Baron 1907- *BioIn 16*
Hailsham of St. Marylebone, Quintin M H 1907- *WhoWor 91*
Hailu, Abaferda Yilma 1930- *WhoWor 91*
Hailwood, Michael 1940-1981 *DcNaB 1981*
Haim, Corey *BioIn 16*
Haim, Corey 1972- *ConTFT 8*
Haim, Paul Ben- 1897-1984 *BioIn 16*
Haim, Ruth 1952- *St&PR 91*
Haiman, Franklyn Saul 1921- *WhoAm 90*
Haiman, Irwin Sanford 1916- *WhoAm 90*
Haiman, Robert James 1936- *WhoAm 90, WhoSSW 91*
Haiman, Todd *BioIn 16*
Haimann, Theo 1911- *WhoAm 90*
Haimbaugh, George Dow, Jr. 1916- *WhoAm 90, WhoWor 91*
Haimes, Yacov Yosseph 1936- *WhoAm 90*
Haimo, Deborah Tepper 1921- *WhoAm 90*
Haimovitz, Jules 1950- *St&PR 91, WhoAm 90*
Haimovitz, Matt *BioIn 16*
Haimovitz, Matt 1970- *IntWWM 90*
Haimowitz, Benjamin 1939- *ODwPR 91*
Haims, Anna *St&PR 91*
Haimsohn, Michael Anthony *NewYTBS 90*
Hain, Anthony Michael 1948- *St&PR 91*
Hain, Charles R. 1942- *St&PR 91*
Hain, Denise Marie 1959- *WhoE 91*
Hain, Douglas Keith 1956- *WhoEmL 91*
Hain, Peggy Suzanne 1962- *WhoAmW 91*
Hain, Peter 1950- *ConAu 131*
Haine, Robert E. 1930- *ODwPR 91*
Haine, Robert Edward 1930- *St&PR 91*
Hainer, John Linton 1929- *St&PR 91*
Haines, Albert E. 1944- *WhoAm 90*
Haines, Barry Gordon 1961- *WhoE 91*
Haines, Bruce Shoemaker 1955- *WhoEmL 91*
Haines, C. Robert 1910-1990 *BioIn 16*
Haines, Charles 1928- *AuBYP 90*
Haines, Daniel Webster 1937- *WhoE 91*
Haines, David Clark 1942- *WhoE 91*
Haines, Diana Copeland 1950- *WhoAmW 91*
Haines, Elijah Middlebrook 1822-1889 *AmLegL*
Haines, Francis X 1947- *BiDrAPA 89*
Haines, Frank S. 1921- *St&PR 91*
Haines, Frederick H 1869-1944 *EncO&P 3*
Haines, Gail Kay 1943- *AuBYP 90, ConAu 31NR*
Haines, Henry H *BiDrAPA 89*
Haines, Hinkey 1898-1979 *Ballpl 90*
Haines, Jacqueline Irene 1933- *WhoE 91*
Haines, James S., Jr. 1946- *St&PR 91*
Haines, Jeffrey Mark *BiDrAPA 89*
Haines, Jesse 1893-1978 *Ballpl 90 [port]*
Haines, Jim Allen 1946- *WhoEmL 91*
Haines, John M. 1924- *WhoWrEP 89*
Haines, Jordan L. 1927- *St&PR 91*
Haines, Lawrence Archibald 1928- *St&PR 91*
Haines, Lee Mark, Jr. 1927- *WhoAm 90*
Haines, Lewis Francis 1907- *WhoAm 90, WhoWor 91*
Haines, Linda Jane *BiDrAPA 89*
Haines, Lisbeth Anne *BiDrAPA 89*
Haines, Martha Mahan 1952- *WhoEmL 91*
Haines, Mary June 1932- *WhoWrEP 89*
Haines, Michael Lee 1948- *WhoSSW 91*
Haines, Perry Vansant 1944- *St&PR 91, WhoAm 90*
Haines, Philip C. 1936- *St&PR 91*
Haines, Philip C 1947- *BiDrAPA 89*
Haines, Richard 1906-1984 *WhoAmA 91N*
Haines, Richard Foster 1937- *WhoAm 90*
Haines, Robert Earl 1929- *WhoAm 90*
Haines, Robert Henry 1920- *WhoE 91*
Haines, Ronald *St&PR 91*
Haines, Stephen John 1949- *WhoEmL 91*
Haines, Thomas W. W. 1941- *WhoAm 90*
Haines, Walter Wells 1918- *WhoAm 90*
Haines, William Henry, IV 1948- *St&PR 91*
Haines, William J. 1919- *WhoAm 90*
Haines, William Stokes 1921- *St&PR 91*
Haines, William Wister 1908-1989 *BioIn 16, ConAu 130*
Hainfeld, Frederick, Jr. 1909- *WhoAm 90*
Haing S. Ngor *BioIn 16*
Hainhofer, Philipp *PenDiDA 89*
Haining, James Howard 1950- *WhoWrEP 89*
Haining, Peter 1940- *EncO&P 3*
Hainline, Forrest Arthur, Jr. 1918- *WhoAm 90, WhoSSW 91, WhoWor 91*
Hainline, Ross L 1919- *BiDrAPA 89*
Haino, Edward Donald 1939- *St&PR 91*
Hainsworth, David Roger 1931- *WhoWor 91*
Hainsworth-Straus, Christine Louise 1962- *WhoAmW 91*
Hainy, Keith W. 1951- *St&PR 91*
Hair, Catherine S *BiDrAPA 89*
Hair, Danny G. 1949- *St&PR 91*
Hair, Don B. 1950- *St&PR 91*
Hair, Donald W. 1938- *St&PR 91*
Hair, Jay Dee 1945- *WhoAm 90*
Hair, Kittie Ellen 1948- *WhoEmL 91*
Hair, Marcia Elizabeth 1948- *WhoAmW 91, WhoEmL 91, WhoSSW 91*
Hair, Mattox Strickland 1938- *WhoSSW 91*
Hair, Paul E. 1928- *St&PR 91*
Hairald, Mary Payne 1936- *WhoAmW 91*
Haire, Bill Martin 1936- *WhoAm 90*
Haire, Douglas MacArthur 1944- *WhoSSW 91*
Haire, James 1938- *WhoAm 90*
Haire, John R. 1925- *St&PR 91*
Haire, John Russell 1925- *WhoAm 90*
Haire, Michael Joseph 1947- *WhoEmL 91*
Hairell, Melvin Lloyd 1938- *St&PR 91*
Hairgrove, Robert Dale 1952- *WhoWor 91*
Hairs, Hugh Michael 1940- *WhoWrEP 89*
Hairston, Brenda C. 1947- *St&PR 91*
Hairston, J.T. 1934- *St&PR 91*
Hairston, Jerry 1952- *Ballpl 90*
Hairston, Jester 1901- *BioIn 16, DrBlPA 90*
Hairston, Nelson George 1917- *WhoAm 90*
Hairston, William 1928- *DrBlPA 90*
Hairston, William Burton, Jr. 1924- *WhoWor 91*
Hairston, William Michael 1947- *WhoSSW 91*
Hairston, William Russell, Jr. 1928- *WhoAm 90, WhoSSW 91*
Haisch, Bernhard Michael 1949- *WhoEmL 91*
Haiser, Gary Martin 1945- *WhoSSW 91*
Haiser, Karl Francis, Jr. 1942- *WhoWor 91*
Haisley, Fay Beverley 1933- *WhoAm 90*
Haislip, David Craig 1962- *WhoEmL 91*
Haislmaier, Robert Joseph 1929- *WhoAm 90*
Haist, Dean Woodward 1953- *WhoEmL 91*
Hait, Gershon 1927- *WhoAm 90*
Hait, Richard Scott 1926- *WhoAm 90*
Haitink, Bernard 1929- *PenDiMP, WorAlBi*
Haitink, Bernard J.H. 1929- *WhoWor 91*
Haitink, Bernard Johan Herman 1929- *IntWWM 90*
Haitko, Deborah Ann 1951- *WhoAmW 91*
Haizlip, Ellis 1929- *DrBlPA 90*
Haizlip, Henry H., Jr. 1913- *St&PR 91*
Haizlip, Henry Hardin, Jr. 1913- *WhoAm 90*
Haizlip, Shirlee Anne Morris Taylor 1937- *WhoAmW 91*
Haizlip, Thomas M 1932- *BiDrAPA 89*
Hajal, Fady 1944- *BiDrAPA 89*
Hajariwala, Dilip C *BiDrAPA 89*
Hajdu, Lorant 1937- *IntWWM 90*
Haje, Khrystyne *BioIn 16*
Haje, Peter Robert 1934- *WhoAm 90*
Hajec, Richard George 1935- *St&PR 91*
Hajek, Albert Joseph 1928- *St&PR 91, WhoAm 90*
Hajek, Francis Paul 1958- *WhoEmL 91, WhoWor 91*
Hajek, Joseph C. 1942- *St&PR 91*
Hajek, Lubor 1921- *BioIn 16*
Hajek, Otomar 1930- *WhoAm 90*
Hajek, Philip Thomas *BiDrAPA 89*
Hajela, Prabhat 1956- *WhoSSW 91*
Hajian, Gerald 1940- *WhoSSW 91*
Hajinian, Nazar 1925- *St&PR 91*
Hajivassiliou, Vassilis Argyrou 1957- *WhoE 91*
Hajj, Edward A. 1950- *ODwPR 91*
Hajjar, Jeanette 1927- *WhoAmW 91*
Hajra, Monowara *BiDrAPA 89*
Haka, Clifford Hughey 1949- *WhoEmL 91*
Hakanson, Sten Einar 1939- *WhoWor 91*
Hakansson, Lars-Ove 1937- *WhoWor 91*
Hake, Jean Harris *BiDrAPA 89*
Hake, William M. 1953- *St&PR 91*
Hakeem, Michael 1916- *WhoAm 90*
Hakel, Milton Daniel, Jr. 1941- *WhoAm 90*
Haken, Wolfgang 1928- *WhoAm 90*
Hakensen, David R. *ODwPR 91*
Haker, Franklin Arthur 1951- *WhoEmL 91*
Hakes, John Earl 1932- *St&PR 91*
Hakes, Nell Beth 1961- *WhoAmW 91*
Hakim, Iqbal R 1945- *BiDrAPA 89*
Hakim, Louise Zalta 1922- *WhoWor 91*
Hakim, Masud 1936- *St&PR 91, WhoAm 90*
Hakim, Omar *BioIn 16*
Hakim, Safaa Shafik *BiDrAPA 89*
Hakim, Seymour 1933- *WhoWor 91*
Hakim, Tawfiq al- 1898-1987 *WorAu 1980*
Hakim-Elahi, Enayat 1934- *WhoE 91, WhoWor 91*
Hakimi, Fraidoun *BiDrAPA 89*
Hakimi, S. Louis 1932- *WhoAm 90*
Hakimi, Yosef 1937- *BiDrAPA 89*
Hakimoglu, Ayhan 1927- *St&PR 91, WhoAm 90*
Hakimoglu, Geraldine A. 1950- *St&PR 91*
Hakimoglu, Geraldine Ann 1950- *WhoAmW 91, WhoEmL 91, WhoWor 91*
Hakki, Ahmed *BiDrAPA 89*
Hakkinen, Raimo Jaakko 1926- *WhoAm 90*
Hakli, Esko Antero 1936- *WhoWor 91*
Hakluyt, Richard 1552?-1616 *EncCRAm*
Hakola, Hannu Panu Aukusti 1932- *WhoWor 91*
Hakola, John Wayne 1932- *WhoE 91*
Hakomori, Sen-itiroh 1929- *WhoWor 91*
Haksteen, John Jacob 1931- *BiDrAPA 89*
Hakuin Ekaku 1686-1769 *EncJap*
Halabi, Mohamed K 1949- *BiDrAPA 89*
Halaby, Henry Joseph 1928- *St&PR 91*
Halaby, Najeeb E. 1915- *WhoAm 90*
Halaby, Samia Asaad 1936- *WhoAm 90, WhoAmA 91, WhoE 91*
Halacy, Daniel Stephen, Jr. 1919- *AuBYP 90*
Haladej, M. Andrew 1927- *St&PR 91*
Halahmy, Oded 1938- *WhoAmA 91, WhoE 91*
Halamandaris, Harry 1938- *WhoAm 90*
Hal'amova, Masa 1908- *EncCoWW*
Halan, John Paul 1928- *WhoAm 90*
Halapin, Philip Thomas *BiDrAPA 89*
Halaris, Angelos 1942- *WhoAm 90*
Halaris, Angelos E 1942- *BiDrAPA 89*
Halarnakar, Vasant G *BiDrAPA 89*
Halas, Cynthia Ann 1961- *WhoAmW 91*
Halas, Edward J. 1943- *St&PR 91*
Halas, Evan J 1922- *BiDrAPA 89*
Halas, George 1895-1983 *Ballpl 90, WorAlBi*
Halasi-Kun, George Joseph 1916- *WhoAm 90*
Halaska, Howard E. 1919- *St&PR 91*
Halaska, Robert H. 1940- *WhoAm 90*
Halaska, Thomas Edward 1945- *WhoSSW 91*
Halasz, George 1949- *WhoWor 91*
Halasz, John E 1920- *BiDrAPA 89*
Halasz, Laszlo 1905- *IntWWM 90*
Halasz, Marilynn Jean 1937- *WhoAmW 91*
Halasz, Nicholas Alexis 1931- *WhoAm 90*
Halasz, Piri 1935- *WhoAmA 91, WhoE 91*
Halbach, David Allen 1931- *WhoAmA 91*
Halbach, Edward Christian, Jr. 1931- *WhoAm 90*
Halbach, Gustav Krupp von Bohlen Und 1870-1950 *BioIn 16*
Halben, Robert Arthur 1931- *St&PR 91*
Halberg, Charles John August, Jr. 1921- *WhoAm 90*
Halberg, G. Peter 1915- *WhoAm 90*
Halberstadt, Harvey 1924- *BiDrAPA 89*
Halberstadt, Paul Edward, Jr. 1944- *WhoSSW 91*
Halberstadt, Robert Bilheimer 1918- *WhoE 91, WhoWor 91*
Halberstadt, Victor 1939- *WhoWor 91*
Halberstam, David 1934- *WhoAm 90, WhoWrEP 89, WorAlBi*
Halberstam, Heini 1926- *WhoAm 90*
Halberstam, Malvina 1937- *WhoAm 90*
Halberstein, Joseph L. 1915- *St&PR 91*
Halbert, Helen E *BiDrAPA 89*
Halbert, John Thomas 1935- *BiDrAPA 89*
Halbert, Larry Jack 1944- *St&PR 91*
Halbig, Michael Thomas 1963- *WhoEmL 91*
Halbouty, Manah Robert 1914- *WhoSSW 91, WhoWor 91*
Halbouty, Michel T. 1909- *St&PR 91*
Halbouty, Michel Thomas 1909- *WhoAm 90, WhoWor 91*
Halbreich, Harry Leopold 1931- *IntWWM 90*
Halbreich, Kathy *BioIn 16*
Halbreich, Uriel 1943- *BiDrAPA 89, WhoE 91*
Halbritter, Marc Alan 1955- *St&PR 91*
Halbrook, Anne-Mieke Platt *WhoAmA 91*
Halbrook, Rita Robertshaw 1930- *WhoAmA 91*
Halbrooks, Darryl Wayne 1948- *WhoAmA 91*
Halby, William Grandjean 1931- *St&PR 91*
Halco, Ann Marie 1936- *WhoAmW 91*
Halcolm *WhoWrEP 89*
Hald, Niels Tove Edward *PenDiDA 89*
Haldane, J. B. S. 1892-1964 *BioIn 16*
Haldane, John Burdon 1892-1964 *WorAlBi*
Haldane, John Burdon Sanderson 1892-1964 *BioIn 16*
Haldeman, Charles Edgar, Jr. 1948- *WhoEmL 91*
Haldeman, H. R. 1926- *WorAlBi*
Haldeman, Harry R. 1926- *WhoAm 90*
Haldeman, Joe 1943- *ConLC 61 [port], RGTwCSF*
Haldeman, Joe William 1943- *WhoAm 90, WhoWrEP 89*
Haldeman, Robert B. 1934- *St&PR 91*
Haldeman-Julius, Emanuel 1889-1951 *BioIn 16*
Haldemann, Helmut 1935- *WhoWor 91*
Halden, Walter O 1922- *BiDrAPA 89*
Halder, Franz 1884-1972 *BioIn 16*
Halder, Ras Mohun 1905?-1990 *ConAu 131*
Halderman, John R 1946- *BiDrAPA 89*
Haldimand, Frederick 1718-1791 *WhNaAH*
Haldimann, Martha Marian 1940- *WhoWor 91*
Haldipur, Chaitanya V *BiDrAPA 89*
Hale, A. Dean 1929- *WhoWrEP 89*
Hale, Adrian Spencer 1946- *WhoSSW 91*
Hale, Alan 1918-1990 *BioIn 16*
Hale, Alan, Jr. *NewYTBS 90 [port]*
Hale, Alice Ann 1951- *BiDrAPA 89*
Hale, Allean Lemmon 1914- *ConAu 30NR, WhoWrEP 89*
Hale, Arlene *AuBYP 90*
Hale, Arlene 1924-1982 *BioIn 16*
Hale, Arnold Wayne 1934- *WhoSSW 91, WhoWor 91*
Hale, Bernard Joseph 1937- *St&PR 91, WhoAm 90*
Hale, Binnie 1899-1984 *OxCPMus*
Hale, Bob 1933- *Ballpl 90*
Hale, Carl Dennis 1949- *WhoEmL 91*
Hale, Cecil Harrison 1919- *St&PR 91*
Hale, Charles 1831-1882 *AmLegL*
Hale, Charles F. 1931- *St&PR 91*
Hale, Charles H 1936- *BiDrAPA 89*
Hale, Charles Martin 1936- *WhoAm 90, WhoWor 91*
Hale, Charles Russell 1916- *WhoAm 90, WhoWor 91*
Hale, Charles W. 1948- *ODwPR 91*
Hale, Charlotte *ConAu 130*
Hale, Charlotte 1928- *WhoAmW 91*
Hale, D. Curtis 1951- *WhoAm 90, WhoEmL 91, WhoSSW 91*
Hale, Danny Lyman 1944- *St&PR 91, WhoAm 90*
Hale, David 1791-1849 *BioIn 16*
Hale, David Glen 1952- *WhoEmL 91*
Hale, Dennis Gene 1948- *WhoEmL 91*
Hale, Donald J. 1937- *St&PR 91*
Hale, Edward Joseph 1839-1922 *BioIn 16*
Hale, Ellen Day 1855-1940 *BiDWomA*
Hale, Ford R., Jr. 1918- *WhoSSW 91*
Hale, Francis Joseph 1922- *WhoSSW 91*
Hale, Frank Abram 1910- *BiDrAPA 89*
Hale, Gary A. 1954- *WhoE 91*

Hale, George E. 1868-1938 *WorAlBi*
Hale, Gerald Albert 1927- *WhoAm 90*
Hale, Gerald Michael 1947- *WhoEmL 91*
Hale, Gina LaStelle 1959- *WhoAmW 91*
Hale, H. David 1944- *St&PR 91*
Hale, Hamilton Orin 1906- *WhoAm 90*
Hale, Harvey Gene 1934- *WhoSSW 91*
Hale, Helen *AuBYP 90*
Hale, Hilton Ingram 1956- *WhoEmL 91, WhoWor 91*
Hale, Hope *WhoWrEP 89*
Hale, Horatio Emmons 1817-1896 *DcCanB 12, WhNaAH*
Hale, Jack K. 1928- *WhoAm 90*
Hale, James Otis 1959- *WhoEmL 91*
Hale, James Pierce 1928- *WhoSSW 91*
Hale, James Randolph 1951- *St&PR 91*
Hale, James Russell 1918- *WhoAm 90*
Hale, James Russell 1955- *WhoSSW 91*
Hale, James Thomas 1940- *WhoAm 90*
Hale, Janet Campbell 1947- *AuBYP 90*
Hale, Joe Michael 1933- *WhoSSW 91*
Hale, John 1953- *Ballpl 90*
Hale, John Alexander 1930- *WhoWor 91*
Hale, John Dewey 1937- *WhoAm 90*
Hale, John L. 1940- *St&PR 91*
Hale, John Rigby 1923- *WhoWor 91*
Hale, Joseph Rice 1935- *WhoAm 90*
Hale, Judson D. 1933- *St&PR 91*
Hale, Judson Drake 1933- *WhoWrEP 89*
Hale, Katherine 1878-1956 *FemiCLE*
Hale, Katherine Lee 1951- *St&PR 91*
Hale, Kaycee 1947- *WhoEmL 91*
Hale, Lance Mitchell 1956- *WhoEmL 91*
Hale, Laurence Swart 1925- *WhoAm 90*
Hale, Leslie C. *WhoAm 90*
Hale, Lilian 1881-1963 *BiDWomA*
Hale, Lillian Westcott 1881-1963 *WhoAmA 91N*
Hale, Lucretia Peabody 1820-1900 *FemiCLE*
Hale, Mahlon S *BiDrAPA 89*
Hale, Margaret Smith 1945- *WhoAmW 91, WhoE 91*
Hale, Marilyn Carlene 1951- *WhoAmW 91*
Hale, Martha *FemiCLE*
Hale, Martin De Mora 1941- *St&PR 91*
Hale, Mary Carter 1928- *WhoAmW 91*
Hale, Mary Helen Parker 1920- *WhoAmW 91*
Hale, Mary Lou *BiDrAPA 89*
Hale, Mason E. 1928-1990 *BioIn 16, ConAu 131*
Hale, Michael L. 1946- *ODwPR 91*
Hale, Nancy 1908- *FemiCLE*
Hale, Nancy 1908-1988 *BioIn 16*
Hale, Nathan 1755-1776 *EncCRAm, WorAlBi*
Hale, Nathan Cabot 1925- *WhoAmA 91*
Hale, Nathan Kelly 1942- *IntWWM 90*
Hale, Odell 1908-1980 *Ballpl 90*
Hale, Oron James 1902- *WhoAm 90*
Hale, Owen Thomas 1950- *WhoEmL 91*
Hale, R. Walter, III 1943- *St&PR 91*
Hale, Ralph G. 1923- *IntWWM 90*
Hale, Ralph Webster 1935- *WhoAm 90*
Hale, Rebecca Hendricks 1959- *WhoEmL 91*
Hale, Richard Lee 1930- *WhoAm 90, WhoSSW 91, WhoWrEP 89*
Hale, Richard Thomas, Jr. 1945- *WhoAm 90, WhoE 91*
Hale, Robert 1933- *IntWWM 90*
Hale, Robert Beverly 1901- *WhoAmA 91N*
Hale, Roger Loucks 1934- *St&PR 91, WhoAm 90*
Hale, Russell Thomas 1939- *St&PR 91*
Hale, Ruth Ann 1956- *WhoAmW 91*
Hale, Sammy 1896-1974 *Ballpl 90*
Hale, Samuel Edward 1934- *WhoSSW 91*
Hale, Sarah Josepha *BioIn 16*
Hale, Sarah Josepha 1788-1879 *BioAmW, FemiCLE*
Hale, Sheila B. 1944- *St&PR 91*
Hale, Sherrie Jane 1961- *WhoSSW 91*
Hale, Sina Kaye 1951- *WhoAmW 91*
Hale, Sonnie 1902-1959 *OxCPMus*
Hale, Truman W. 1953- *St&PR 91*
Hale, William Bayard 1869-1924 *BioIn 16*
Hale, William Robert 1952- *BiDrAPA 89*
Hale O'Connor, Diann 1934- *WhoAm 90*
Hale-Robinson, Lorraine Augusta 1948- *WhoAmW 91*
Halecky, Benedicta Martha 1958- *WhoEmL 91*
Halegua, Alfredo 1930- *WhoAmA 91*
Halek, Mark F. 1959- *WhoE 91*
Halem, Robert Gordon 1933- *BiDrAPA 89*
Halem, Victor von 1940- *IntWWM 90*
Haleman, Laura Rand 1946- *WhoAmA 91, WhoE 91*
Halemane, Thirumala Raya 1953- *WhoWor 91*
Halen, Walter John 1930- *IntWWM 90*
Hales, Ada Matilda Mary 1878-1957 *FemiCLE*
Hales, Alfred Washington 1938- *WhoAm 90*
Hales, Daniel B. 1941- *WhoAm 90*
Hales, Deborah 1951- *BiDrAPA 89*
Hales, Duke C. 1941- *St&PR 91*
Hales, Lisa Linn Herman 1961- *WhoAmW 91*
Hales, Peter Bacon 1950- *ConAu 132*
Hales, Robert E 1948- *BiDrAPA 89*
Hales, Roberta Louise 1962- *WhoAmW 91*
Halevi, Yacov 1946- *WhoWor 91*
Halevie-Goldman, Brian D 1954- *BiDrAPA 89*
Halevy, Abraham Hayim 1927- *WhoWor 91*
Halevy, Hilda Maria *WhoWor 91*
Halevy, Jacques Francois 1799-1862 *PenDiMPA*
Halevy, Ludovic 1834-1908 *OxCPMus*
Halevy, Simon 1929- *WhoAm 90*
Haley, Alex *BioIn 16*
Haley, Alex 1921- *MajTwCW, WorAlBi*
Haley, Alex Palmer 1921- *WhoWrEP 89*
Haley, Arthur H. 1912- *BioIn 16*
Haley, Benton Fairfield *St&PR 91N*
Haley, Bill 1925-1981 *EncPR&S 89, OxCPMus, WorAlBi*
Haley, Brian Paul 1945- *WhoEmL 91*
Haley, C. James, Jr. 1942- *St&PR 91*
Haley, Charles Frederick 1945- *WhoEmL 91*
Haley, Clifton E. 1931- *St&PR 91*
Haley, Clifton Edward 1931- *WhoAm 90*
Haley, Dianne Rae 1944- *St&PR 91*
Haley, Frederick Thomas 1912- *St&PR 91*
Haley, Gail E 1939- *ChlLR 21 [port], WhoAmA 91*
Haley, George 1929- *WhoAm 90*
Haley, Jack *NewYTBS 90 [port]*
Haley, Jack 1899-1979 *WorAlBi*
Haley, James Evetts, Jr. 1931- *WhoSSW 91*
Haley, Jane Gosiger 1930- *St&PR 91*
Haley, John Charles 1905- *WhoAmA 91*
Haley, John Charles 1929- *WhoAm 90*
Haley, John David 1924- *WhoWor 91*
Haley, John J. 1958- *St&PR 91*
Haley, Johnetta Randolph *WhoAmW 91, WhoWor 91*
Haley, Lyodene Branham 1935- *WhoAmW 91*
Haley, Mark Tyler 1951- *St&PR 91*
Haley, Neale *BioIn 16*
Haley, Nedom Angier 1943- *WhoSSW 91*
Haley, P. Edward *ConAu 130*
Haley, Patience E *WhoAmA 91*
Haley, Priscilla J 1926- *WhoAmA 91*
Haley, Priscilla Jane 1926- *WhoAm 90*
Haley, Richard Charles 1942- *WhoSSW 91*
Haley, Robert A *BiDrAPA 89*
Haley, Robert D 1893-1959 *WhoAmA 91N*
Haley, Roy W. 1946- *St&PR 91, WhoSSW 91*
Haley, Russell John 1931- *St&PR 91*
Haley, Sally 1908- *WhoAmA 91*
Haley, Susan Carol *BiDrAPA 89*
Haley, Vanessa Leigh 1954- *WhoWrEP 89*
Haley, Vincent Peter 1931- *WhoAm 90*
Haley, Wallace F 1921- *BiDrAPA 89*
Haley, Warren Jay 1934- *WhoSSW 91*
Haley, William Francis 1952- *WhoEmL 91*
Haley, William Patrick 1955- *WhoEmL 91*
Half, Robert 1918- *WhoAm 90, WhoWor 91*
Half-King *WhNaAH*
Half-King 1700?-1754 *WhNaAH*
Halfant, Gary D. 1953- *WhoEmL 91, WhoWor 91*
Halfen, David 1924- *WhoAm 90*
Halff, Alex Hart 1931- *St&PR 91*
Halff, Bro 1946- *WhoWrEP 89*
Halff, Robert H 1908- *WhoAmA 91*
Halffter, Cristobal 1930- *IntWWM 90*
Halfin, Aron 1956- *BiDrAPA 89*
Halfin, Preston Richard 1937- *St&PR 91*
Halfin, Vivian P *BiDrAPA 89*
Halfon, Peter B. 1938- *St&PR 91*
Halford, Allan 1838-1888 *OxCCanT*
Halford, Donna LaNelle 1942- *WhoAmW 91*
Halford, Keith *BioIn 16*
Halfpenny, James C. 1947- *WhoEmL 91, WhoWor 91*
Halfpenny, Thomas Patrick, Jr. 1944- *WhoAm 90*
Halfpenny, William *PenDiDA 89*
Halfvarson, Lucille Robertson 1919- *WhoAmW 91*
Halgrimson, Kenneth W 1926- *BiDrAPA 89*
Haliassos, Michael 1959- *WhoE 91*
Haliburton, Susanna Lucy Anne 1817?-1899 *DcCanB 12*
Haliburton, Thomas Chandler 1796-1865 *DcLB 99 [port]*
Halicka, Alice 1889-1975 *BiDWomA*
Halicke, Philip V *BiDrAPA 89*
Halicki, Ed 1950- *Ballpl 90*
Halicki, John *BiDrAPA 89*
Halicki, Toby *BioIn 16*
Halicky, John P. 1950- *St&PR 91*
Haliczer, James Solomon 1952- *WhoEmL 91, WhoSSW 91, WhoWor 91*
Halifax, Earl of 1881-1959 *WorAlBi*
Halik, Nancy Lickerman 1954- *WhoAmW 91*
Halikas, James A 1941- *BiDrAPA 89*
Halim, Eduardus *BioIn 16*
Halin, Rudolf Johann Georg 1934- *WhoWor 91*
Halinen, Hannu Tapio 1947- *WhoWor 91*
Haling, Thomas Parsons 1953- *WhoEmL 91*
Halio, Jay Leon 1928- *WhoAm 90*
Halir, Karel 1859-1909 *PenDiMP*
Halischuk, Grant Frederick 1957- *BiDrAPA 89*
Halitzki, Roman 1952- *WhoWor 91*
Halivni, David *BioIn 16*
Haliw, Andrew Jerome, III 1946- *WhoEmL 91*
Halka, Kathleen Grace 1953- *WhoAmW 91*
Halket, Anne 1623-1699 *BiDEWW*
Halket, Thomas D. 1948- *WhoE 91*
Halkett, Alan Neilson 1931- *WhoAm 90*
Halkett, Anne 1623-1699 *FemiCLE*
Halkett, Anne Murray 1622-1699 *BioIn 16*
Halki, John Joseph 1926- *WhoAm 90*
Halkias, John T *BiDrAPA 89*
Halkin, Abraham S. *NewYTBS 90*
Halkin, Abraham S. 1903-1990 *BioIn 16, ConAu 131*
Halkin, Adele Diane 1931- *WhoAmW 91*
Halkin, Hubert 1936- *WhoAm 90*
Halkin, John 1927- *SpyFic*
Halkin, Theodore 1924- *WhoAmA 91*
Halko, Joe 1940- *BioIn 16, WhoAmA 91*
Halkyard, Edwin Milton 1934- *St&PR 91, WhoAm 90*
Halkyard, Robert C. 1935- *St&PR 91*
Hall & Oates *EncPR&S 89*
Hall, Adam 1920- *TwCCr&M 91*
Hall, Adelaide 1909- *OxCPMus*
Hall, Adelaide 1910- *DrBlPA 90*
Hall, Adele 1910- *AuBYP 90*
Hall, Adrian *BioIn 16*
Hall, Adrian 1927- *WhoWrEP 89*
Hall, Adrienne Ann *WhoAm 90, WhoAmW 91*
Hall, Alan *ODwPR 91*
Hall, Alan Eugene 1945- *WhoAm 90*
Hall, Albert 1937- *DrBlPA 90*
Hall, Albert 1958- *Ballpl 90*
Hall, Albert Carruthers 1914- *WhoAm 90*
Hall, Albert Leander 1926- *WhoAm 90*
Hall, Albert R. 1842-1905 *AmLegL*
Hall, Alden Barker 1927- *WhoE 91*
Hall, Alfred Watne 1947- *WhoEmL 91*
Hall, Alice May *BioIn 16*
Hall, Allison Yeakel *BiDrAPA 89*
Hall, Almon C. 1946- *St&PR 91*
Hall, Alvin Stewart, Jr. 1942- *St&PR 91*
Hall, Amanda McFarland 1940- *WhoAmW 91*
Hall, Amelia 1916?-1984 *OxCCanT [port]*
Hall, Andrew Clifford 1944- *WhoSSW 91*
Hall, Andrew Douglass 1910- *WhoAm 90*
Hall, Andrew J. *WhoE 91*
Hall, Ann Louise 1946- *WhoWrEP 89*
Hall, Anna Christene 1946- *WhoAmW 91*
Hall, Anna Maria 1800-1881 *BioIn 16, FemiCLE*
Hall, Anne *BiDEWW*
Hall, Anne Schleiger 1956- *WhoEmL 91*
Hall, Anthony Robert 1938- *St&PR 91, WhoAm 90*
Hall, Aristides 1936- *WhoWor 91*
Hall, Arnold Alexander 1915- *WhoAm 90, WhoWor 91*
Hall, Arsenio *BioIn 16*
Hall, Arsenio 1955- *News 90 [port]*
Hall, Arsenio 1958?- *DrBlPA 90, WorAlBi*
Hall, Arthur Eugene, Jr. 1955- *WhoEmL 91*
Hall, Arthur Perry, Jr. 1955- *WhoEmL 91*
Hall, Arthur Raymond, Jr. 1922- *WhoAm 90*
Hall, Arthur W. 1943- *St&PR 91*
Hall, Asaph Hale 1933- *WhoAm 90*
Hall, Audrey Morrison 1958- *WhoEmL 91*
Hall, Benjamin Downs 1932- *WhoAm 90*
Hall, Benjamin Lambert, Jr. 1959- *WhoEmL 91*
Hall, Bernard 1925- *WhoAm 90*
Hall, Bernard Joseph 1955- *WhoSSW 91*
Hall, Beth S. 1946- *St&PR 91*
Hall, Betty Kathleen 1908- *WhoWrEP 89*
Hall, Beverly Adele 1935- *WhoAm 90*
Hall, Beverly Elaine 1957- *WhoAmW 91, WhoEmL 91*
Hall, Bill *BioIn 16*
Hall, Blanche Barbara 1928- *WhoSSW 91*
Hall, Bob *BioIn 16*
Hall, Bob 1923-1983 *Ballpl 90*
Hall, Bradley Clarke 1941- *St&PR 91*
Hall, Brenda Yvonne 1957- *WhoAmW 91*
Hall, Brett Gerard 1954- *WhoEmL 91*
Hall, Brian H. 1947- *St&PR 91*
Hall, Brian Keith 1941- *WhoAm 90*
Hall, Brinley Morgan 1912- *WhoAm 90*
Hall, Brooks 1921- *St&PR 91*
Hall, Cameron *MajTwCW*
Hall, Carl Alvin 1921- *WhoAmA 91*
Hall, Carl William 1924- *WhoAm 90*
Hall, Carlyle Washington, Jr. 1943- *WhoAm 90*
Hall, Carolyn Vosburg 1927- *AuBYP 90*
Hall, Carrie May 1873-1963 *BioIn 16*
Hall, Caryl R. 1949- *WhoAmW 91, WhoEmL 91*
Hall, Cathy Jayne Wright 1951- *WhoAmW 91*
Hall, Charles Adams 1949- *WhoEmL 91*
Hall, Charles Allan 1941- *WhoAm 90*
Hall, Charles Allen 1933- *WhoAm 90*
Hall, Charles Douglas 1948- *WhoSSW 91*
Hall, Charles F. 1924- *St&PR 91*
Hall, Charles Frederick 1920- *WhoAm 90*
Hall, Charles John 1925- *IntWWM 90*
Hall, Charles M. 1863-1914 *WorAlBi*
Hall, Charles Martin 1949- *WhoEmL 91*
Hall, Charles Potter, Jr. 1932- *WhoE 91*
Hall, Charles Richard 1934- *WhoE 91*
Hall, Charles W. 1944- *St&PR 91, WhoAm 90*
Hall, Charles Washington 1930- *WhoAm 90*
Hall, Charles William 1922- *WhoAm 90*
Hall, Charley 1885-1943 *Ballpl 90*
Hall, Charlotte Hauch 1945- *WhoAm 90*
Hall, Cheryl Ann 1954- *WhoAmW 91*
Hall, Cheryl Lee 1947- *WhoSSW 91*
Hall, Christie Lea 1958- *WhoWrEP 89*
Hall, Christine Ann 1958- *WhoEmL 91*
Hall, Christopher George Longden 1956- *WhoE 91*
Hall, Christopher Patrick 1954- *WhoEmL 91*
Hall, Clarence Albert, Jr. 1930- *WhoAm 90*
Hall, Claude Hampton 1922- *WhoAm 90*
Hall, Clyde Eugene 1959- *WhoEmL 91*
Hall, Conrad 1926- *WhoAm 90*
Hall, Conrad Mercer 1943- *St&PR 91*
Hall, Cornelia 1898- *BioIn 16*
Hall, Cynthia Holcomb 1929- *WhoAm 90, WhoAmW 91*
Hall, D. Elaine 1949- *WhoWrEP 89*
Hall, Dale Ray 1932- *WhoSSW 91*
Hall, Daniel 1819-1895 *AmLegL*
Hall, Daniel G. 1946- *St&PR 91*
Hall, Daniel Ray Acomb 1927- *WhoAm 90, WhoE 91*
Hall, Daryl 1948- *EncPR&S 89, OxCPMus*
Hall, Daryl 1949- *WhoAm 90, WorAlBi*
Hall, Daryl, and Oates, John *OxCPMus*
Hall, David 1916- *IntWWM 90, WhoAm 90*
Hall, David 1943- *WhoE 91*
Hall, David Alvin *BiDrAPA 89*
Hall, David Arthur 1948- *WhoEmL 91*
Hall, David Charles 1944- *WhoAm 90*
Hall, David Connolly 1946- *BiDrAPA 89*
Hall, David Dean 1950- *BiDrAPA 89*
Hall, David E. 1937- *St&PR 91*
Hall, David Edward *BioIn 16*
Hall, David N. 1939- *St&PR 91*
Hall, David Spencer 1929- *St&PR 91*
Hall, David William 1962- *WhoEmL 91*
Hall, Deidre *BioIn 16*
Hall, Dennis A. 1946- *WhoAm 90, WhoSSW 91*
Hall, Dennis J. 1941- *St&PR 91*
Hall, Dennis William 1956- *WhoEmL 91*
Hall, Derek Harry 1945- *WhoAm 90*
Hall, Dewey Eugene 1932- *WhoWor 91*
Hall, Dick 1930- *Ballpl 90, BioIn 16*
Hall, Don Alan 1938- *WhoAm 90*
Hall, Donald 1928- *Ballpl 90, BioIn 16, ConLC 59 [port], WhoAm 90, WhoWrEP 89*
Hall, Donald Andrews, Jr. 1928- *AuBYP 90*
Hall, Donald Keith 1931- *St&PR 91*
Hall, Donald Norman Blake 1944- *WhoAm 90*
Hall, Donald Perry 1927- *St&PR 91, WhoAm 90*
Hall, Donald S. 1940- *WhoAm 90*
Hall, Donna Ann 1962- *St&PR 91*
Hall, Donna F. 1927- *St&PR 91*
Hall, Dorothy Gay Nell 1941- *St&PR 91, WhoAm 90*
Hall, Dorsey G. 1961- *WhoSSW 91*
Hall, Doug 1957?- *BioIn 16*
Hall, Douglas Lee 1947- *WhoSSW 91*
Hall, Drew 1963- *Ballpl 90*
Hall, Dwayne Allen 1958- *WhoSSW 91*
Hall, E. Eugene 1932- *WhoAm 90*
Hall, E. Raymond 1902-1986 *BioIn 16*
Hall, Ed 1931- *DrBlPA 90*
Hall, Edmond *BioIn 16*
Hall, Edmund Joseph, Jr. 1930- *St&PR 91*

Hall, Edward H., Jr. 1935- *St&PR 91*
Hall, Edward Marshall- 1858-1927 *BioIn 16*
Hall, Edward Twitchell 1914- *WhoAm 90*
Hall, Edwin Bacon *BiDrAPA 89*
Hall, Edwin K. *ODwPR 91*
Hall, Elizabeth 1929- *AuBYP 90, ConAu 31NR, WhoAmW 91*
Hall, Elizabeth Cornelia 1898-1989 *BioIn 16*
Hall, Ellen Wood *WhoAm 90*
Hall, Elliott Sawyer 1938- *St&PR 91*
Hall, Elvajean 1910- *AuBYP 90*
Hall, Ernest L. 1940- *WhoAm 90*
Hall, Ernst Paul 1925- *WhoAm 90*
Hall, Esther Greenacre *AuBYP 90*
Hall, Esther Jane Wood 1911- *WhoAm 90*
Hall, Eugene Raymond 1902-1986 *BioIn 16*
Hall, F. McKamy 1942- *St&PR 91*
Hall, Floyd 1938- *WhoE 91*
Hall, Francoise *BiDrAPA 89*
Hall, Francoise Puvrez 1932- *WhoAmW 91*
Hall, Frank K. 1942- *St&PR 91*
Hall, Frank Kennedy 1942- *WhoAm 90*
Hall, Freddie Lee, Jr. 1943- *WhoSSW 91*
Hall, Frederic 1939- *BiDrAPA 89*
Hall, Frederick Keith 1930- *WhoAm 90*
Hall, Frederick Leonard 1899- *WhoAm 90*
Hall, G. Stanley 1844-1924 *BioIn 16*
Hall, Gaines Bruce 1938- *WhoAm 90*
Hall, Gary Leroy 1950- *WhoE 91*
Hall, Georganna Mae 1951- *WhoSSW 91*
Hall, George Atwater 1925- *St&PR 91, WhoAm 90*
Hall, George F. 1908- *WhoWrEP 89*
Hall, George Kennedy, Jr. 1946- *WhoEmL 91*
Hall, George L *BiDrAPA 89*
Hall, George L. 1928- *St&PR 91*
Hall, George Peyton, Jr. 1951- *WhoEmL 91*
Hall, George Vincent 1915 *WhoWor 91*
Hall, Gimone 1940- *ConAu 33NR*
Hall, Gordon Langley *AuBYP 90*
Hall, Gordon R. 1926- *WhoAm 90*
Hall, Graeme Edison 1937- *IntWWM 90*
Hall, Granville Stanley 1844-1924 *BioIn 16, EncPaPR 91, WorAlBi*
Hall, Gregory J. *St&PR 91*
Hall, Gus 1910- *EncAL, WhoAm 90*
Hall, Guy Charles 1958- *WhoEmL 91*
Hall, H Gaston 1931- *ConAu 131*
Hall, Halsey 1899-1978 *Ballpl 90*
Hall, Harold Emile 1916- *WhoAm 90*
Hall, Harold G. 1922- *St&PR 91*
Hall, Harold Lloyd, II 1945- *WhoSSW 91*
Hall, Harry A., III 1928- *St&PR 91*
Hall, Harry H. 1934- *WhoSSW 91*
Hall, Heather M *BiDrAPA 89*
Hall, Helen Norton 1911- *WhoSSW 91*
Hall, Henry 1898-1989 *AnObit 1989, OxCPMus*
Hall, Henry B. 1933- *St&PR 91*
Hall, Henry Kingston, Jr. 1924- *WhoAm 90*
Hall, Henry Lawrence 1940- *St&PR 91*
Hall, Henry Lee 1949- *WhoSSW 91*
Hall, Henry Lyon, Jr. 1931- *WhoAm 90*
Hall, Homer James 1911- *WhoAm 90*
Hall, Howard E. 1930- *St&PR 91*
Hall, Howard Henry 1939- *St&PR 91*
Hall, Howard J. 1931- *ODwPR 91, St&PR 91*
Hall, Howard L., Jr. 1934- *WhoAm 90*
Hall, Howard Tracy 1919- *WhoAm 90*
Hall, Hugh David 1931- *WhoAm 90*
Hall, Huntz 1920- *BioIn 16*
Hall, Ira D. *BioIn 16*
Hall, Irv 1918- *Ballpl 90*
Hall, Jack Gilbert 1927- *WhoAm 90*
Hall, Jacqueline 1955- *WhoEmL 91*
Hall, James 1793-1868 *WhNaAH*
Hall, James 1887-1951 *WorAlBi*
Hall, James A 1934- *EncO&P 3*
Hall, James A. 1942- *St&PR 91*
Hall, James Alan 1949- *WhoEmL 91*
Hall, James Albert 1934- *BiDrAPA 89*
Hall, James Alexander 1920- *WhoAm 90*
Hall, James Alexander 1946- *WhoEmL 91*
Hall, James B 1918- *ConAu 12AS [port]*
Hall, James Baker 1935- *LiHiK*
Hall, James Bryan 1946- *WhoSSW 91*
Hall, James Byron 1918- *WhoAm 90, WhoWrEP 89*
Hall, James Curtis 1926- *WhoAm 90*
Hall, James Edward 1933- *St&PR 91*
Hall, James Fay, Jr. 1916- *WhoAm 90*
Hall, James Frederick 1921- *WhoAm 90*
Hall, James Gordon *BiDrAPA 89*
Hall, James Granville, Jr. 1917- *WhoSSW 91*
Hall, James Henry 1939- *WhoAm 90, WhoWor 91*
Hall, James Leo, Jr. 1936- *WhoAm 90, WhoWor 91*
Hall, James Norman 1887-1951 *AuBYP 90*
Hall, James Parker 1906- *WhoAm 90*
Hall, James Stanley 1930- *WhoAm 90*
Hall, James William 1937- *WhoAm 90, WhoE 91*
Hall, James William 1953- *WhoSSW 91*
Hall, Jane Anna 1959- *WhoAmW 91, WhoE 91, WhoEmL 91, WhoWor 91*
Hall, Jane Dory 1944- *WhoAmW 91*
Hall, Jay 1932- *WhoAm 90, WhoWrEP 89*
Hall, Jeannine D. 1973- *WhoWrEP 89*
Hall, Jeffrey S. 1951- *St&PR 91*
Hall, Jeffrey Stuart 1951- *WhoAm 90*
Hall, Jennifer *BioIn 16*
Hall, Jennifer Loie Pray 1951- *WhoEmL 91*
Hall, Jerald Culver 1931- *St&PR 91*
Hall, Jerome 1901- *WhoAm 90, WhoWrEP 89*
Hall, Jerome William 1943- *WhoAm 90*
Hall, Jerry *BioIn 16*
Hall, Jesse *AuBYP 90*
Hall, Jesse Seaborn 1929- *WhoAm 90*
Hall, Jill Watkins 1946- *WhoEmL 91*
Hall, Jim 1930- *BioIn 16*
Hall, Jimmie 1938- *Ballpl 90*
Hall, Jimmy Dwain, Sr. 1929- *St&PR 91*
Hall, Joan 1939- *WhoE 91*
Hall, Joan Joffe 1936- *WhoWrEP 89*
Hall, Joan M. 1939- *WhoAm 90*
Hall, Joe E. 1938- *WhoAm 90*
Hall, Joel Allen 1934- *St&PR 91*
Hall, John *PenDiDA 89, St&PR 91*
Hall, John 1943- *WhoAmA 91*
Hall, John A 1914- *WhoAmA 91*
Hall, John Allen 1914- *WhoAm 90*
Hall, John C. 1936- *St&PR 91*
Hall, John Daniel, II 1947- *WhoSSW 91*
Hall, John Emmett 1925- *WhoAm 90*
Hall, John Frederick 1941- *St&PR 91*
Hall, John Fry 1919- *WhoAm 90*
Hall, John Herbert 1942- *WhoE 91*
Hall, John Hopkins 1925- *WhoAm 90, WhoSSW 91, WhoWor 91*
Hall, John Lee 1940- *BiDrAPA 89*
Hall, John Lewis 1934- *WhoAm 90*
Hall, John Manning 1841-1905 *AmLegL*
Hall, John Marshall 1935- *WhoAm 90*
Hall, John Michael *BiDrAPA 89*
Hall, John Noble, III 1945- *WhoEmL 91*
Hall, John R. 1932- *St&PR 91*
Hall, John Randolph, Jr. 1913- *WhoSSW 91*
Hall, John Richard 1932- *WhoAm 90, WhoSSW 91, WhoWor 91*
Hall, John S. 1949- *St&PR 91*
Hall, John Thomas 1938- *WhoSSW 91*
Hall, John Wesley, Jr. 1948- *WhoEmL 91, WhoWor 91*
Hall, John Whitling 1934- *WhoSSW 91*
Hall, Josef Washington 1894-1960 *BioIn 16*
Hall, Joseph A. 1931- *St&PR 91*
Hall, Joseph E. 1914- *St&PR 91*
Hall, Joslyn R. 1961- *WhoEmL 91*
Hall, Joy Louise 1954- *WhoAmW 91*
Hall, Joyce C. 1891-1982 *WorAlBi*
Hall, Joyce Turner 1948- *WhoAmW 91*
Hall, Juanita 1902-1968 *DrBIPA 90*
Hall, Juanita D. 1919- *St&PR 91*
Hall, Judith Kay 1943- *St&PR 91*
Hall, Julia Brainerd 1859-1925 *BioIn 16*
Hall, Karen 1956?- *BioIn 16*
Hall, Katherine Ann 1963- *WhoAmW 91*
Hall, Kathleen Ann 1948- *WhoSSW 91*
Hall, Kathryn Colby 1960- *BiDrAPA 89*
Hall, Kathryn Evangeline *WhoAmW 91, WhoWor 91*
Hall, Katie Beatrice 1938- *BlkAmsC [port]*
Hall, Katy 1947- *BioIn 16*
Hall, Keith Lynn 1964- *WhoEmL 91*
Hall, Keith Martin 1957- *WhoSSW 91*
Hall, Kenneth D. 1942- *St&PR 91*
Hall, Kenneth Eugene 1930- *WhoAm 90*
Hall, Kenneth F. 1952- *St&PR 91*
Hall, Kenneth Marion 1926- *St&PR 91*
Hall, Kenneth Richard 1939- *WhoAm 90*
Hall, Kenneth Robbins 1953- *BiDrAPA 89*
Hall, Kenneth W 1929- *BiDrAPA 89*
Hall, Kevin Peter *BioIn 16*
Hall, Larry D. 1942- *St&PR 91, WhoAm 90*
Hall, Larry Wayne, Sr. 1937- *WhoSSW 91*
Hall, Laurence B 1919- *BiDrAPA 89*
Hall, Lawrence W., Jr. 1940- *St&PR 91*
Hall, Lawrence Wilbur, Jr. 1940- *WhoAm 90*
Hall, Lee 1934- *WhoAm 90, WhoAmA 91, WhoAmW 91, WhoE 91*
Hall, Lee Boaz 1928- *St&PR 91, WhoAm 90, WhoWor 91*
Hall, Leo E. 1917- *St&PR 91*
Hall, Leon W. *BioIn 16*
Hall, Leslie Carlton 1952- *WhoAmW 91, WhoEmL 91*
Hall, Loren Oklan 1928- *WhoSSW 91*
Hall, Loretta J. 1932- *WhoAmW 91*
Hall, Louisa Jane 1802-1892 *FemiCLE*
Hall, Luther Egbert, Jr. 1926- *WhoAm 90*
Hall, Lydia Eloise 1906-1969 *BioIn 16*
Hall, Lyman 1724-1790 *EncCRAm*
Hall, Lynn 1937- *AuBYP 90, BioIn 16*
Hall, Madelon Carol Syverson 1937- *WhoAmW 91*
Hall, Malcolm 1945- *AuBYP 90*
Hall, Mamie Barton 1928- *WhoAmW 91, WhoSSW 91*
Hall, Manly Palmer 1901- *EncO&P 3, NewAgE 90*
Hall, Manly Palmer 1901-1990 *ConAu 132*
Hall, Marc 1887-1915 *Ballpl 90*
Hall, Marcel Scott 1926- *WhoSSW 91*
Hall, Marcia Joy 1947- *WhoAmW 91, WhoE 91, WhoEmL 91*
Hall, Margaret O'Connor 1940- *WhoAmW 91*
Hall, Marian Ella 1920- *WhoAmW 91, WhoWor 91*
Hall, Marie 1884-1956 *PenDiMP*
Hall, Marie 1942- *WhoAmW 91*
Hall, Marion Austin 1931- *IntWWM 90*
Hall, Marion Trufant 1920- *WhoAm 90*
Hall, Marjory 1908- *AuBYP 90*
Hall, Mark Walter 1941- *WhoAm 90*
Hall, Marshall, Jr. 1910- *WhoAm 90*
Hall, Martin C. 1950- *IntWWM 90*
Hall, Mary Fields 1934- *WhoAmW 91*
Hall, Mary-jo 1947- *WhoAmW 91*
Hall, Maximilian John Bettles 1953- *WhoWor 91*
Hall, Mel 1960- *Ballpl 90*
Hall, Michael *PenDiMP*
Hall, Michael Alan 1950- *WhoEmL 91*
Hall, Michael David 1941- *WhoAmA 91*
Hall, Michael Garibaldi 1926- *WhoSSW 91*
Hall, Michael James 1944- *St&PR 91*
Hall, Michael Lee 1946- *WhoE 91*
Hall, Miles Lewis, Jr. 1924- *WhoAm 90, WhoWor 91*
Hall, Millard Frank, Jr. 1945- *WhoAm 90, WhoSSW 91*
Hall, Milton Reese 1932- *WhoAm 90*
Hall, Molly J *BiDrAPA 89*
Hall, Monica 1938- *IntWWM 90*
Hall, Monty 1923- *WorAlBi*
Hall, Monty 1925- *BioIn 16, WhoAm 90*
Hall, Myra *BioIn 16*
Hall, N John 1933- *ConAu 31NR*
Hall, Nancy *BioIn 16*
Hall, Nancy Atkins 1942- *WhoE 91*
Hall, Nancy Christensen 1946- *WhoAm 90*
Hall, Nathan Kelsey 1810-1874 *BiDrUSE 89*
Hall, Nechie Tesitor 1946- *WhoEmL 91*
Hall, Newell J. 1932- *St&PR 91, WhoAm 90*
Hall, Newman A. 1913- *WhoAm 90*
Hall, O. Glen 1929- *WhoAm 90*
Hall, Ogden Henderson 1922- *WhoAm 90*
Hall, Oliver Morgan, Jr. 1947- *St&PR 91*
Hall, Owen 1853-1907 *OxCPMus*
Hall, Pamela S. 1944- *WhoAm 90, WhoAmW 91, WhoWor 91*
Hall, Patricia Dean 1958- *WhoEmL 91*
Hall, Paul L. *ODwPR 91*
Hall, Peggie Ann 1947- *WhoAmW 91*
Hall, Perry 1895- *BioIn 16*
Hall, Peter Francis 1924- *WhoAm 90*
Hall, Peter John 1940- *IntWWM 90*
Hall, Peter Reginald Frederick 1930- *IntWWM 90, WhoWor 91*
Hall, Phil 1964- *WhoWrEP 89*
Hall, Philip 1904-1982 *DcNaB 1981*
Hall, Philip Adam 1964- *WhoE 91*
Hall, Philip Layton 1940- *WhoSSW 91*
Hall, Philip McCloy 1944- *St&PR 91*
Hall, Phillip A. 1927- *St&PR 91*
Hall, Phoebe Poulterer 1941- *WhoAmW 91*
Hall, Prescott F 1868-1921 *EncO&P 3, EncPaPR 91*
Hall, Preston Winship 1932- *St&PR 91*
Hall, R Janet 1936- *BiDrAPA 89*
Hall, R. Martin *St&PR 91*
Hall, R. Vance 1928- *WhoAm 90*
Hall, Radclyffe 1880-1943 *FemiCLE*
Hall, Radclyffe 1886-1943 *BioIn 16*
Hall, Ralph Corbin 1899- *WhoWor 91*
Hall, Ralph Frederick 1940- *WhoWor 91*
Hall, Ralph Macon 1941- *St&PR 91*
Hall, Ralph Moody 1923- *WhoAm 90, WhoSSW 91*
Hall, Ramsay Fuller 1954- *WhoSSW 91*
Hall, Ray C. 1944- *St&PR 91*
Hall, Rex Earl 1924- *WhoAmA 91*
Hall, Rex Elliot 1952- *WhoSSW 91*
Hall, Richard A. 1932- *IntWWM 90*
Hall, Richard Allan 1940- *WhoAm 90*
Hall, Richard C W 1942- *BiDrAPA 89*
Hall, Richard C. W. 1942- *WhoSSW 91*
Hall, Richard Clayton 1931 *WhoE 91*
Hall, Richard Leland 1923- *WhoAm 90*
Hall, Richard S. 1944- *St&PR 91*
Hall, Ridgway Macy, Jr. 1941- *WhoAm 90*
Hall, Robert Alan 1958- *WhoEmL 91, WhoWor 91*
Hall, Robert B. 1924-1988 *BioIn 16*
Hall, Robert Carlton 1915- *WhoAm 90*
Hall, Robert Chambers 1931- *St&PR 91*
Hall, Robert E 1924- *BiDrAPA 89*
Hall, Robert Ernest 1943- *WhoAm 90*
Hall, Robert Givin 1953- *WhoSSW 91*
Hall, Robert Grayson 1964- *WhoSSW 91*
Hall, Robert Howell 1921- *WhoAm 90, WhoSSW 91*
Hall, Robert James 1956- *WhoEmL 91*
Hall, Robert Joseph 1926- *WhoAm 90*
Hall, Robert L *WhoAmA 91*
Hall, Robert Leicester 1905- *WhoAm 90*
Hall, Robert Lynn 1945- *St&PR 91*
Hall, Robert MacLaren 1934- *WhoSSW 91*
Hall, Robert McClellan 1942- *WhoAm 90*
Hall, Robert Turnbull, III 1945- *WhoWor 91*
Hall, Robert William 1928- *WhoAm 90*
Hall, Roger Dale 1955- *St&PR 91*
Hall, Roger Fisher, Jr. 1951- *WhoEmL 91*
Hall, Roger Lee 1942- *IntWWM 90*
Hall, Ronald E. *WhoSSW 91*
Hall, Ronald William 1929- *St&PR 91*
Hall, Rosalys Haskell 1914- *AuBYP 90*
Hall, Roxanne Kay 1957- *WhoSSW 91*
Hall, Ryland James 1936- *WhoSSW 91*
Hall, Sally Lawrence *BiDrAPA 89*
Hall, Sam Blakeley, Jr. 1924- *WhoAm 90*
Hall, Samuel Carter 1800-1889 *BioIn 16*
Hall, Sandra Jean 1958- *WhoWrEP 89*
Hall, Sara Finney 1937- *WhoAmW 91*
Hall, Sarah 1761-1830 *FemiCLE*
Hall, Scott Michael 1950- *WhoEmL 91*
Hall, Scott Michael 1966- *WhoE 91*
Hall, Sharlot M. 1870-1943 *BioAmW*
Hall, Sherrill Gray 1933- *St&PR 91*
Hall, Shirley *BioIn 16*
Hall, Stanley Eckler 1934- *St&PR 91*
Hall, Stephen Austin 1942- *WhoSSW 91*
Hall, Stephen M. 1921- *St&PR 91*
Hall, Stephen Pudney 1950- *WhoAm 90*
Hall, Steven Craig 1948- *WhoAm 90, WhoSSW 91*
Hall, Stewart Kent 1947- *St&PR 91*
Hall, Susan *WhoAm 90*
Hall, Susan 1943- *WhoAmA 91*
Hall, Susan Bartholomew 1943- *WhoAmW 91*
Hall, Susan Laurel 1943- *WhoE 91*
Hall, Telka Mowery Elium 1936- *WhoAmW 91*
Hall, TennieBee May 1940- *WhoAmW 91*
Hall, Theodore Dana 1943- *WhoWrEP 89*
Hall, Theodore Thomas 1940- *St&PR 91*
Hall, Thomas Durand 1939- *St&PR 91*
Hall, Thomas J. 1923- *St&PR 91*
Hall, Thomas Louis 1952- *WhoEmL 91*
Hall, Thomas William 1921- *WhoAm 90*
Hall, Thor 1927- *WhoAm 90*
Hall, Tina Ann 1957- *WhoAmW 91*
Hall, Tom 1947- *Ballpl 90*
Hall, Tom 1955- *IntWWM 90*
Hall, Tom T. *BioIn 16*
Hall, Tom T 1936- *ConMus 4 [port], OxCPMus, WhoAm 90*
Hall, Tony P. 1942- *WhoAm 90*
Hall, Trevor H 1910- *EncO&P 3*
Hall, Trevor Henry 1910- *EncPaPR 91*
Hall, Victoria Ellen 1944- *WhoSSW 91*
Hall, W. Reginald 1936- *WhoAm 90*
Hall, Wade 1934- *LiHiK*
Hall, Wade Henry 1934- *WhoSSW 91*
Hall, Walter 1933- *St&PR 91*
Hall, Walter G. *BioIn 16*
Hall, Warren F. 1937- *St&PR 91*
Hall, Warren Nesbitt 1949- *WhoEmL 91*
Hall, Warren Seiyu 1957- *WhoEmL 91*
Hall, Wayne L. 1953- *WhoSSW 91*
Hall, Wendell Woods 1896-1969 *OxCPMus*
Hall, Wendy Julia 1951- *WhoAmW 91*
Hall, Wilbur Dallas, Jr. 1938- *WhoAm 90*
Hall, Wilbur Sheridan 1925- *WhoE 91*
Hall, William Austin 1945- *WhoAm 90*
Hall, William Carroll 1937- *St&PR 91*
Hall, William Darlington 1914- *WhoAm 90*
Hall, William Edward 1940- *St&PR 91*
Hall, William Edward, Jr. 1951- *WhoEmL 91*
Hall, William G. 1929- *St&PR 91*
Hall, William Jackson 1929- *WhoAm 90*
Hall, William Joel 1926- *WhoAm 90*
Hall, William King 1943- *St&PR 91, WhoAm 90*
Hall, William Lloyd 1925- *WhoSSW 91*
Hall, William Norman 1915-1974 *AuBYP 90*
Hall, William Pudney 1923- *St&PR 91*
Hall, William Reginald 1870-1943 *BioIn 16*
Hall, William Robert, Jr. 1953- *WhoSSW 91*
Hall, William S *BiDrAPA 89*
Hall, William Smith, Jr. 1941- *WhoE 91*
Hall, William Stone 1915- *WhoAm 90*
Hall, William Tompie, III 1946- *WhoEmL 91, WhoWor 91*
Hall, William Wendell 1956- *WhoEmL 91*

Hall, Willis 1929- MajTwCW
Hall, Yong Ok 1950- WhoAmW 91
Hall Brault, Phyllis 1941- WhoAmW 91
Hall-Davis, Jacquelyn BiDrAPA 89
Hall-Ewig, Leona Maxine 1934- WhoAmW 91
Hall-McDermott, Kimberly Ann 1962- WhoSSW 91
Hall-Quest, Edna Olga 1899-1986 AuBYP 90
Hall-Quest, Olga W. 1899-1986 BioIn 16
Hall-Sheedy, Leslee 1955- St&PR 91
Halla, Robert Christian 1949- WhoWrEP 89
Hallack, John James 1938- St&PR 91
Halladay, Laurie Ann 1945- WhoAm 90
Halladay, Robert T., Jr. 1931- WhoSSW 91
Hallahan, Bill 1902-1981 Ballpl 90
Hallahan, Gerard Joseph 1959- WhoEmL 91
Hallahan, Kirk ODwPR 91
Hallahan, William H. TwCCr&M 91
Hallahan, William Henry SpyFic
Hallam, Beverly 1923- WhoAm 90, WhoAmA 91
Hallam, Eliza Tuke 1764?-1806? BioIn 16, NotWoAT
Hallam, Lewis, Jr. 1740?-1808 EncCRAm
Hallam, Lewis, Mrs. BioIn 16, EncCRAm
Hallam, Lewis, Sr., Mrs. NotWoAT
Hallam, Robert Gaston 1941- St&PR 91
Hallanan, Elizabeth V. 1925- WhoAm 90, WhoAmW 91
Hallanan, Sharon Margaret 1961- WhoEmL 91
Hallard, Wayne Bruce 1951- WhoE 91, WhoEmL 91, WhoWor 91
Hallas, Henry 1924- St&PR 91
Hallauer, Alan Douglas 1953- WhoEmL 91
Hallauer, Arnel Roy 1932- WhoAm 90
Hallauer, Jay M 1923- BiDrAPA 89
Hallawell, Kent Harry 1932- WhoAm 90
Hallawell, Philip Charles 1951- WhoWor 91
Hallbauer, Robert E. 1930- St&PR 91
Hallbauer, Robert Edward 1930- WhoAm 90
Hallbauer, Rosalie Carlotta 1939- WhoAmW 91
Hallberg, Garth Ragnar 1944- WhoAm 90
Hallberg, Nancy Levy 1951- WhoAmW 91
Hallberg, Owen Kenneth 1923- WhoAm 90
Hallberg, Rudolph John 1928- BiDrAPA 89
Hallbom, Harold Raymond, Jr. 1951- WhoEmL 91
Hallborg, Robert B BiDrAPA 89
Halldor Gudjonsson DcScanL
Halldor Kiljan Laxness DcScanL
Halldorsson, Skuli 1914- IntWWM 90
Halldorsson, Theodor Skuli 1951- WhoWor 91
Halle, Aloys Jean 1934- WhoWor 91
Halle, Charles 1819-1895 BioIn 16, PenDiMP
Halle, James 1916- St&PR 91
Halle, John Joseph 1947- WhoEmL 91
Halle, Louis 1908- BiDrAPA 89
Halle, Louis Joseph 1910- WhoAm 90
Halle, Marilyn Anne 1933- WhoAmW 91
Halle, Mark 1951- WhoWor 91
Halle, Mark Thomas BiDrAPA 89
Halle, Morris 1923- WhoAm 90
Halle Keyloun, Susan Anne 1952- WhoAmW 91
Halleck, Charles A. 1900-1986 WorAlBi
Halleck, Charles White 1929- WhoAm 90
Halleck, Fitz-Greene 1790-1867 WorAlBi
Halleck, Henry Wager 1815-1872 WorAlBi
Halleck, Seymour L BiDrAPA 89
Hallee, Neal David 1943- WhoE 91
Halleen, Otis H. St&PR 91
Halleen, Owen Paul 1934- St&PR 91
Hallen, E. Donald 1930- St&PR 91
Hallen, Lars Gunnar 1946- WhoWor 91
Hallen, Philip Burgh BiDrAPA 89
Hallen, Philip Burgh 1930- WhoAm 90
Hallenbeck, Alfred Madison 1930- WhoAm 90
Hallenbeck, Pomona Juanita 1938- WhoAmA 91
Hallenbeck, Wilbur Chapman 1892-1986 BioIn 16
Hallenberg, Nancy Lee 1941- WhoAmW 91, WhoSSW 91
Hallenborg, Bruce BiDrAPA 89
Hallene, Alan Montgomery 1929- WhoAm 90, WhoWor 91
Haller, Adolf 1897- AuBYP 90
Haller, Albrecht Von 1708-1777 WorAlBi
Haller, Amelia Jane 1927- WhoWrEP 89
Haller, Archibald Orben 1926- WhoAm 90, WhoWor 91
Haller, Bill 1935- Ballpl 90
Haller, Calvin John 1925- WhoAm 90
Haller, Charles Edward 1924- WhoAm 90
Haller, Donna Lou 1956- WhoEmL 91
Haller, Ellen 1958- BiDrAPA 89
Haller, Emanuel 1927- WhoAmA 91, WhoE 91
Haller, Harlan Thomas 1924- St&PR 91
Haller, Hayden Abney 1950- WhoAmW 91
Haller, Heinz 1914- WhoWor 91
Haller, Hermann 1914- IntWWM 90
Haller, Howard Edward 1947- WhoWor 91
Haller, John C. 1945- WhoAm 90
Haller, John Charles 1950- St&PR 91
Haller, John Edward 1954- WhoEmL 91
Haller, Jordan Daniel 1932- WhoE 91
Haller, Lee Higdon 1947- BiDrAPA 89, WhoE 91
Haller, Robert T. 1930- WhoE 91, WhoWor 91
Haller, Russell W. 1923- St&PR 91
Haller, Terry 1934- WhoWrEP 89
Haller, Terry Lyndon 1948- St&PR 91
Haller, Tom 1937- Ballpl 90
Haller, Tracy ODwPR 91
Halleran, Arthur Joseph 1947- St&PR 91
Halleran, Richard Carroll 1941- St&PR 91
Hallet, Jack 1913-1982 Ballpl 90
Hallett, Carol B NewYTBS 90 [port]
Hallett, Carol Boyd 1937- WhoAm 90, WhoAmW 91, WhoWor 91
Hallett, Charles Arthur, Jr. 1939- WhoAm 90
Hallett, Fred N. 1938- St&PR 91
Hallett, Frederick Howard 1929- St&PR 91
Hallett, Lewellyn 1953- WhoWrEP 89
Hallett, Mark 1943- WhoAm 90
Hallett, Pat Jessop BioIn 16
Hallett, Thomas Vance 1941- St&PR 91
Hallett, William 1707?-1781 PenDiDA 89
Hallett, William Jared 1923- WhoAm 90
Halleux, Albert Martin Julien 1920- WhoWor 91
Halleux, Laurent PenDiMP
Halley, Edmond 1656-1742 BioIn 16
Halley, Edmund 1656-1742 WorAlBi
Halley, James Harvey 1926- WhoAm 90
Halley, James Woods, Jr. 1938- WhoAm 90
Halley, Paul NewAgMG
Halley, Peter 1953- WhoAmA 91
Halley, Shawn Ellen 1957- WhoSSW 91
Hallgren, Hugh Ralph 1947- WhoSSW 91
Hallgren, Richard Edwin 1932- WhoAm 90
Hallgrimsson, Geir 1925- WhoWor 91
Hallgrimsson, Hflidi 1941- IntWWM 90
Hallgrimsson, Jonas 1807-1845 DcScanL
Hallgrimur Petursson DcScanL
Halliburton, Alan D. 1945- St&PR 91
Halliburton, Gus G. 1911- St&PR 91
Halliburton, John Robert 1934- WhoWor 91
Halliburton, Lloyd 1934- WhoSSW 91
Halliburton, Richard BioIn 16
Halliburton, William Dobinson 1860 1931 DcScB S2
Halliday, Brett TwCCr&M 91
Halliday, Brett 1904-1977 TwCCr&M 91
Halliday, Dorothy TwCCr&M 91
Halliday, Edward Irvine 1902-1984 DcNaB 1981
Halliday, Harriet Hudnut 1941- WhoAmW 91
Halliday, Ian 1928- WhoAm 90
Halliday, John Meech 1936- WhoAm 90, WhoWor 91
Halliday, Michael MajTwCW, TwCCr&M 91
Halliday, Nancy R 1936- WhoAmA 91
Halliday, R. Michael 1955- St&PR 91
Halliday, Rene Bruton 1955- St&PR 91
Halliday, Robert Lee 1931- St&PR 91
Halliday, Stephen M. 1927- St&PR 91
Halliday, Thomas Carlisle 1924- St&PR 91
Halliday, Walter John 1907- WhoAm 90
Halliday, William R. 1926- BioIn 16
Halliday, William R. 1952- St&PR 91
Halliday, William Ross 1926- WhoAm 90, WhoWor 91
Hallier, Gerard Edouard 1941- WhoAm 90
Hallier, Hans-Joachim 1930- WhoWor 91
Halligan, Howard Ansel 1937- WhoAm 90
Halligan, James Edmund 1936- WhoAm 90
Halligan, John T. 1941- ODwPR 91
Halligan, Marion 1940- FemiCLE
Halligan, Roger John, Jr. 1948- WhoEmL 91
Halligan, Susan Claire 1938- IntWWM 90
Halligan, T.W. 1922- St&PR 91
Halligan, Thomas Walsh 1922- WhoAm 90
Hallila, Bruce Allan 1950- WhoSSW 91
Halliley, John Elton 1912-1983 DcNaB 1981
Hallin, David Anthony 1945- WhoSSW 91
Hallin, Gayle Annette 1948- WhoAmW 91
Hallin, Margareta 1931- IntWWM 90
Hallinan, Maureen T. WhoAm 90
Hallinan, Paul J. BioIn 16
Halling, Hal P. 1937- St&PR 91
Halling, Leonard William 1927- WhoAm 90
Hallingby, Paul, Jr. 1919- St&PR 91, WhoAm 90, WhoE 91
Hallisey, John Francis 1906- St&PR 91
Hallisey, Michael Joseph 1929- St&PR 91
Hallisey, Paul Michael 1947- St&PR 91
Hallissey, Michael 1943- WhoWor 91
Hallissy, Margaret Mary 1945- WhoE 91
Halliwell, David 1936- ConAu 31NR
Halliwell, Leslie 1929-1989 AnObit 1989, BioIn 16
Halliwell, Walter G. 1953- St&PR 91
Hallman, Bill 1867-1920 Ballpl 90
Hallman, Bill 1876-1950 Ballpl 90
Hallman, Bob Everett 1952- WhoSSW 91
Hallman, Eugene Sanborn 1919- WhoAm 90
Hallman, Gary L. 1940- WhoAm 90
Hallman, Gary Lee 1940- WhoAmA 91
Hallman, Grady Lamar, Jr. 1930- WhoAm 90
Hallman, H Theodore, Jr 1933- WhoAmA 91
Hallman, Henry Theodore, Jr. 1933- WhoAm 90
Hallman, Ludlow Boyd 1941- IntWWM 90
Hallman, Robert ODwPR 91
Hallman, Stanley P. St&PR 91
Hallman, Ted WhoAmA 91
Hallmark, Donald Parker 1945- WhoAmA 91
Hallmark, Sandra Wallach 1955- WhoEmL 91
Hallmundsson, Hallberg 1930- WhoWrEP 89
Hallo, William Wolfgang 1928- WhoAm 90
Hallock, C. Wiles, Jr. 1918- WhoAm 90
Hallock, David Duncan, Sr. 1938- WhoSSW 91
Hallock, Gerard 1800-1866 BioIn 16
Hallock, Helen L 1919- BiDrAPA 89
Hallock, James Anthony 1942- WhoAm 90
Hallock, Keith Richard BiDrAPA 89
Hallock, Paul L. 1948- St&PR 91
Hallock, Robert Bruce 1943- WhoAm 90
Hallock, Robert Wayne 1944- WhoAm 90
Hallock-Muller, Pamela 1948- WhoAmW 91
Halloran, Bernard Francis 1944- WhoSSW 91
Halloran, Bernard Thorpe 1931- WhoAm 90
Halloran, Clifford P. 1930- St&PR 91
Halloran, Daniel Edward 1939- St&PR 91
Halloran, Daniel F. 1926- WhoWrEP 89
Halloran, Daniel J. BioIn 16
Halloran, David G. 1932- St&PR 91
Halloran, John J. 1942- St&PR 91
Halloran, John M. 1952- St&PR 91
Halloran, Kathleen L. 1952- St&PR 91, WhoAm 90, WhoEmL 91
Halloran, Leo Augustine 1931- WhoE 91
Halloran, Michael Kevin 1948- WhoSSW 91
Halloran, Richard Colby 1930- WhoAm 90
Halloran, Richard Francis 1922- St&PR 91
Halloran, Thomas Giuld 1949- WhoEmL 91
Halloran, William Frank 1934- WhoAm 90
Hallowell, Burton Crosby 1915- St&PR 91, WhoAm 90
Hallowell, Edward McKey BiDrAPA 89
Hallowell, H. Thos., Jr. St&PR 91N
Hallowell, John Hamilton 1913- WhoAm 90
Hallowell, Robert Edward 1918- WhoAm 90
Hallowell, Roger H. 1910-1989 BioIn 16
Hallowell, Walter H. 1943- St&PR 91
Hallowell, Walter Henry 1943- WhoAm 90
Hallows, Michael C.L. 1941- St&PR 91
Hallows, Michael Colin Lloyd 1941- WhoAm 90
Hallquist, William Dean 1949- WhoEmL 91
Halls, Geraldine TwCCr&M 91
Halls, James Arnett 1928- WhoAm 90
Hallstead, William Finn 1924- AuBYP 90
Hallstead, William Finn, III 1924- WhoWrEP 89
Hallstein, Ingeborg 1937- IntWWM 90
Hallsten Mc Garry, Susan Joan 1948- WhoWrEP 89
Hallstrom, Arne Per 1931- WhoWor 91
Hallstrom, Judith BiDrAPA 89
Hallstrom, Lasse BioIn 16
Hallstrom, Tore 1935- WhoWor 91
Halluin, Albert P. 1939- St&PR 91
Halluin, Albert Price 1939- WhoWor 91
Hallums, Burgess Nathaniel 1958- WhoEmL 91
Hallward, M.B. 1955- St&PR 91
Halm, Klaus 1929- WhoSSW 91
Halma, John Robert 1935- WhoE 91
Halman, Talat Sait 1931- WhoAm 90
Halmi, Katherine A 1939- BiDrAPA 89
Halmi, Robert 1924- WhoAm 90
Halmos, Imre Hubertus 1946- WhoE 91
Halmos, Peter Anthony 1943- WhoAm 90
Halmrast, Lynn James 1949- WhoEmL 91
Halo, Hugo Hona 1930- BiDrAPA 89
Halonen, Marilyn Jean 1941- WhoAmW 91
Halonen, Yrjo Esa 1929- WhoWor 91
Halper, Anita Solovy 1935- WhoAmW 91
Halper, Emanuel Barry 1933- WhoAm 90, WhoE 91
Halper, Ira S 1935- BiDrAPA 89
Halper, James Paul BiDrAPA 89
Halper, Jaroslava 1953- WhoAmW 91, WhoSSW 91
Halper, June Ann 1949- WhoAmW 91, WhoEmL 91
Halper, Mitchell Reid BiDrAPA 89
Halper, Sam 1916-1989 BioIn 16
Halper, Thomas 1942- WhoAm 90
Halperin, Alexander BiDrAPA 89
Halperin, Bertrand Israel 1941- WhoAm 90
Halperin, Corrine Sandra 1936- WhoAmW 91
Halperin, David A 1934- BiDrAPA 89
Halperin, David Avrohm 1934- WhoE 91
Halperin, Donald Marc 1945- WhoE 91
Halperin, Edward N 1937- BiDrAPA 89
Halperin, Eric Brian 1959- WhoEmL 91
Halperin, Esther Waitz 1925- WhoAmW 91
Halperin, George Bennett 1926- WhoE 91
Halperin, H. Gary 1947- St&PR 91
Halperin, Jerome Yale 1930- WhoAm 90
Halperin, John Stephen 1942- WhoAm 90
Halperin, John William 1941- WhoAm 90
Halperin, Jonathan L. 1949- ConAu 132
Halperin, Joseph 1922- WhoWor 91
Halperin, Marian Ragan 1924- WhoE 91
Halperin, Mark David 1950- WhoE 91
Halperin, Mark Warren 1940- WhoWrEP 89
Halperin, Morton H. 1938- WhoAm 90
Halperin, Peter Jonathan BiDrAPA 89
Halperin, Rebecca L 1959- BiDrAPA 89
Halperin, Richard E. 1954- WhoAm 90
Halperin, Richard George 1948- WhoEmL 91
Halperin, Robert M. 1928- St&PR 91
Halperin, Robert Milton 1928- WhoAm 90
Halperin, Samuel 1930- WhoAm 90
Halperin, Thomas Charles 1941- St&PR 91
Halperin, William Paul 1945- WhoAm 90
Halpern, Abraham E. 1891-1962 BioIn 16
Halpern, Abraham L 1925- BiDrAPA 89
Halpern, Abraham Leon 1925- WhoAm 90, WhoE 91
Halpern, Alexander 1948- WhoEmL 91
Halpern, Alvin Michael 1938- WhoAm 90
Halpern, Ben 1912-1990 BioIn 16, ConAu 131
Halpern, Betsy 1943- ODwPR 91
Halpern, Bruce Peter 1933- WhoAm 90
Halpern, Burton 1941- St&PR 91
Halpern, Charles Robert 1939- WhoAm 90, WhoWrEP 89
Halpern, Daniel 1945- WhoAm 90, WhoWrEP 89
Halpern, Dinah BioIn 16
Halpern, Emily Alyssa 1960- BiDrAPA 89
Halpern, Frances Joy WhoAmW 91
Halpern, Frederick Michael 1948- WhoE 91
Halpern, Georges Maurice 1935- WhoWor 91
Halpern, Harry 1899-1981 BioIn 16
Halpern, Isidore 1901-1990 BioIn 16
Halpern, Jack 1925- WhoAm 90, WhoWor 91
Halpern, James Bladen 1936- WhoAm 90
Halpern, Jeffrey 1959- ODwPR 91
Halpern, Jeffrey Kim BiDrAPA 89
Halpern, Jodi Lauren BiDrAPA 89
Halpern, Keith Stacy 1956- WhoEmL 91
Halpern, Kevin Gregg 1948- WhoAm 90
Halpern, Larry J. 1941- WhoSSW 91
Halpern, Lea WhoAmA 91
Halpern, Linda Ann 1954- WhoEmL 91
Halpern, Manfred 1924- WhoAm 90
Halpern, Nathan L 1914- WhoAmA 91
Halpern, Nathan Loren 1914- WhoAm 90, WhoWor 91
Halpern, Parker P. 1915- St&PR 91
Halpern, Philip Morgan 1956- WhoEmL 91
Halpern, Ralph Lawrence 1929- WhoAm 90

Halpern, Samuel Joseph 1946- *WhoEmL 91*
Halpern, Sidney 1927- *WhoE 91, WhoWor 91*
Halpern, Sol *BioIn 16*
Halpern, Stanton David 1949- *WhoE 91, WhoWor 91*
Halpern, Steven *NewAgE 90, NewAgMG*
Halpern, Steven Jay 1959- *WhoSSW 91*
Halpern, Steven Lon 1951- *WhoE 91*
Halpern, Werner I 1924- *BiDrAPA 89*
Halpern, Werner Israel 1924- *WhoE 91*
Halperson, Michael Allen 1946- *St&PR 91, WhoE 91, WhoEmL 91*
Halpert, Debra *ODwPR 91*
Halpert, E Stephen *BiDrAPA 89*
Halpert, Eugene 1931- *BiDrAPA 89*
Halpert, Leonard S. 1922- *St&PR 91*
Halpert, Leonard Walter 1924- *WhoAm 90, WhoE 91*
Halpert, Stephen A. 1935- *St&PR 91*
Halpin, Anna Marie 1923- *WhoAm 90*
Halpin, Brooke 1949- *IntWWM 90*
Halpin, Charles Aime 1930- *WhoAm 90*
Halpin, Daniel William 1938- *WhoAm 90*
Halpin, Edmond Howard 1922- *WhoE 91*
Halpin, Lisa Schmid 1947- *WhoEmL 91*
Halpin, Patricia 1935- *IntWWM 90*
Halpin, Patricia Ann 1940- *WhoE 91*
Halpin, Robert E., Jr. 1946- *WhoSSW 91*
Halpin, Steven Edward 1948- *WhoEmL 91*
Halpin, William Gerard 1936- *WhoE 91*
Halporn, James Werner 1929- *WhoAm 90*
Halprin, Anna 1920- *BioIn 16*
Halprin, Anna Schuman 1920- *WhoAm 90*
Halprin, Lawrence 1916?- *BioIn 16*
Hals, Frans 1580?-1666 *BioIn 16, IntDcAA 90*
Hals, Frans 1581?-1666 *WorAlBi*
Halsband, Frances 1943- *WhoAm 90, WomArch [port]*
Halsband, Robert *BioIn 16*
Halsband, Robert 1914-1989 *ConAu 130*
Halse, Emmeline 1856-1930 *BiDWomA*
Halseide, Philip J. 1952- *St&PR 91*
Halsell, Grace 1923- *AuBYP 90*
Halsell, Grace Eleanor 1923- *WhoAm 90*
Halsell, James Donald 1928- *St&PR 91*
Halsey, Betty Lou 1950- *St&PR 91*
Halsey, Brenton Shaw 1927- *St&PR 91, WhoAm 90, WhoSSW 91*
Halsey, Brian Elliott 1942- *WhoAmA 91*
Halsey, Franklin McTier 1939- *St&PR 91*
Halsey, Gregory Steven 1958- *WhoEmL 91*
Halsey, James Albert 1930- *WhoAm 90, WhoWor 91*
Halsey, Jewel F. 1922- *St&PR 91*
Halsey, Martha Taliaferro 1932- *WhoE 91*
Halsey, Philip 1928- *BioIn 16*
Halsey, Richard Sweeney 1929- *WhoAm 90*
Halsey, Robert Clark 1938- *WhoE 91*
Halsey, Simon Patrick 1958- *IntWWM 90*
Halsey, Thomas Lloyd 1776?-1855 *BioIn 16*
Halsey, Wesley Eugene 1939- *St&PR 91*
Halsey, William Darrach 1918- *WhoWrEP 89*
Halsey, William F., Jr. 1882-1959 *WorAlBi*
Halsey, William Frederick 1882-1959 *BioIn 16*
Halsey, William Lanier, Jr. 1920- *St&PR 91*
Halsey, William Melton 1915- *WhoAmA 91*
Halsman, Philippe 1906-1979 *AuBYP 90, WhoAmA 91N*
Halsor, Richard L. 1927- *St&PR 91*
Halsor, Richard R. 1937- *St&PR 91*
Halstead, Bruce Walter 1920- *WhoAm 90*
Halstead, Burnett A. 1930- *St&PR 91*
Halstead, Dirck S. 1936- *WhoAm 90*
Halstead, Edward George 1949- *BiDrAPA 89*
Halstead, Fred 1927-1988 *EncAL*
Halstead, Fred W. *BioIn 16*
Halstead, Georgia 1915- *WhoAm 90*
Halstead, Harry Moore 1918- *WhoAm 90*
Halstead, John G. H. 1922- *WhoAm 90*
Halstead, Lester Mark, Jr. 1950- *WhoWor 91*
Halstead, Murat 1829-1908 *BioIn 16*
Halstead, Peter David 1955- *WhoSSW 91*
Halstead, Ronald 1927- *WhoWor 91*
Halstead, William Byron 1949- *St&PR 91*
Halsted, Donald M., Jr. 1927- *St&PR 91*
Halsted, Fred O. 1945- *St&PR 91*
Halsted, James A. 1905-1984 *BioIn 16*
Halsted, John Burt 1926- *WhoAm 90*
Halsted, John Mac Harg 1905- *WhoAm 90*
Halsted, Richard Lent 1939- *St&PR 91*
Halsted, William S. 1852-1922 *WorAlBi*
Halsted, William Stewart 1852-1922 *BioIn 16*
Halston *BioIn 16*
Halston 1932-1990 *ConDes 90, CurBio 90N, NewYTBS 90 [port], News 90, -90-3, WorAlBi*
Halston, Daniel William 1960- *WhoEmL 91*
Halston, Julie 1954- *ConTFT 8 [port]*
Halt, Marie Robert 1849-1908 *EncCoWW*
Halter, Edmund John 1928- *WhoSSW 91*
Halter, H. James, Jr. 1947- *WhoSSW 91, WhoWor 91*
Halter, Jon C. 1941- *AuBYP 90*
Halter, Jon Charles 1941- *WhoAm 90*
Halter, Kevin B. 1935- *St&PR 91*
Halter, Marek *BioIn 16*
Haltiner, George Joseph 1918- *WhoAm 90*
Haltiwanger, Robert Sidney, Jr. 1923- *WhoAm 90*
Haltiwanger, Steven George *BiDrAPA 89*
Haltom, Elbert Bertram, Jr. 1922- *WhoAm 90, WhoSSW 91*
Haltom, Gary Allen 1944- *St&PR 91*
Halton, Richard J. 1934- *St&PR 91*
Halton, Rosalind 1951- *IntWWM 90*
Haluczak, Ronald Douglas 1960- *WhoEmL 91*
Halula, John R. 1940- *St&PR 91*
Haluza-Harriston, Karen 1957- *St&PR 91*
Halva, Allen Keith 1913- *WhoWor 91*
Halver, John Emil 1922- *WhoAm 90*
Halversen, Thomas A 1929- *BiDrAPA 89*
Halverson, Duane A. 1945- *St&PR 91*
Halverson, Ellen Joan 1960- *BiDrAPA 89*
Halverson, George Clarence 1914- *WhoAm 90*
Halverson, Lawrence H. 1930- *St&PR 91*
Halverson, Norm Edward 1946- *St&PR 91*
Halverson, Paul Kenneth 1959- *WhoEmL 91*
Halverson, Richard Christian 1916- *WhoAm 90*
Halverson, Richard Paul 1941- *WhoAm 90*
Halverson, Ronald Charles 1943- *St&PR 91*
Halverson, Steven Thomas 1954- *WhoEmL 91*
Halverson, Susan Emilie 1948- *WhoSSW 91*
Halverson, Wendell Quelprud 1916- *WhoAm 90*
Halverstadt, Donald Bruce 1934- *WhoAm 90, WhoSSW 91*
Halverstadt, Robert D. 1920- *St&PR 91*
Halverstadt, Robert Dale 1920- *WhoE 91*
Halvorsen, Andrew Christian 1946- *St&PR 91*
Halvorsen, Elspeth Colette 1929- *WhoAmA 91*
Halvorsen, F.H. 1942- *St&PR 91*
Halvorsen, Gail *BioIn 16*
Halvorsen, Gladys C *BiDrAPA 89*
Halvorsen, Lisa 1953- *WhoWrEP 89*
Halvorsen, Morrie Edward 1931- *WhoAm 90*
Halvorsen, Robert Carl 1932- *WhoAm 90*
Halvorsen, Susan Marie 1955- *WhoAmW 91*
Halvorson, Eric Christian 1958- *WhoEmL 91*
Halvorson, George Charles 1947- *WhoEmL 91*
Halvorson, Harlyn Odell 1925- *WhoAm 90*
Halvorson, Judith Anne 1943- *WhoAmW 91*
Halvorson, Marilyn 1948- *ConAu 132*
Halvorson, Newman Thorbus, Jr. 1936- *WhoAm 90*
Halvorson, Robert Michael 1953- *WhoE 91*
Halwig, J. Michael 1954- *WhoEmL 91, WhoSSW 91*
Halwig, Nancy Diane 1954- *WhoSSW 91*
Halyard, Rebecca Anne 1944- *WhoAmW 91*
Halzel, Michael Harris 1941- *WhoSSW 91*
Ham, Bette 1929- *St&PR 91*
Ham, Charles H., Jr. 1937- *BiDrAPA 89*
Ham, Debra Newman 1948- *WhoE 91*
Ham, Elizabeth 1783-1852? *FemiCLE*
Ham, George Eldon 1939- *WhoWor 91*
Ham, Inyong 1925- *WhoAm 90*
Ham, James Francis 1925- *St&PR 91*
Ham, James Milton 1920- *WhoAm 90*
Ham, Joe Strother, Jr. 1928- *WhoAm 90*
Ham, Lee Edward 1919- *WhoAm 90*
Ham, Leslie Gilmer 1930- *WhoAm 90*
Ham, Norman Douglas 1929- *WhoAm 90*
Ham, Ronald Edgar 1945- *WhoSSW 91*
Ham, Sok-hon 1901-1989 *BioIn 16*
Ham, Tibor *NewYTBS 90*
Hama, Mary Yoshiko 1945- *WhoE 91*
Hamachek, Ross Frank 1942- *WhoAm 90*
Hamachek, Tod Russell 1946- *St&PR 91, WhoAm 90*
Hamad bin Isa Al-Khalifa, Sheikh 1950- *WhoWor 91*
Hamad ibn Muhammad Al-Sharqi, Sheikh 1949- *WhoWor 91*
Hamada Shoji 1894-1978 *EncJap*
Hamada, Fumimasa 1931- *WhoWor 91*
Hamada, Keinosuke 1924- *WhoWor 91*
Hamada, Robert Seiji 1937- *WhoAm 90*
Hamada, Shoji 1894-1978 *PenDiDA 89*
Hamadani, Houshang G 1936- *BiDrAPA 89*
Hamadou, Barkat Gourad *WhoWor 91*
Hamady, Dan R. 1915- *WhoE 91*
Hamady, Jack Ameen 1909- *WhoAm 90*
Hamady, Sally A. *ODwPR 91*
Hamady, Walter Samuel 1940- *WhoAmA 91*
Hamaguchi, Yozo 1909- *WhoAmA 91*
Hamai, James Yutaka 1926- *WhoWor 91*
Hamalainen, Helvi 1907- *EncCoWW*
Hamalainen, Marja-Liisa *BioIn 16*
Hamalainen, Pekka Kalevi 1938- *WhoAm 90*
Haman, Jerry Lee 1947- *WhoEmL 91*
Hamana, Masamichi 1950- *WhoWor 91*
Hamani, Abdou 1942- *WhoWor 91*
Hamann, Bente *AuBYP 90*
Hamann, Carl H *BiDrAPA 89*
Hamann, Donald Lee 1949- *IntWWM 90*
Hamann, Donald Robert 1939- *WhoAm 90*
Hamann, Johann Georg 1730-1788 *DcLB 97 [port]*
Hamann, Jose G *BiDrAPA 89*
Hamann, Marilyn D 1945- *WhoAmA 91*
Hamann Wolfe, Marcia Joanne 1945- *WhoEmL 91*
Hamar, Duane Sheldon 1952- *WhoEmL 91*
Hamar, Michael John 1946- *WhoEmL 91*
Hamari, Julia 1942- *IntWWM 90, PenDiMP*
Hamarneh, Sami Khalaf 1925- *WhoAm 90, WhoWrEP 89*
Hamasaki, Sharry 1947- *BiDrAPA 89*
Hamati, Fawwaz Ibrahim 1960- *BiDrAPA 89*
Hambartsumjan, Victor Hamazaspi 1908- *WhoWor 91*
Hamber, Deborah 1963- *ODwPR 91*
Hamberg, Daniel 1924- *WhoAm 90*
Hamberger, Larry Kevin 1953- *WhoEmL 91*
Hambidge, Douglas Walter 1927- *WhoAm 90*
Hamblen, Clyde Mack 1929- *St&PR 91*
Hamblen, John Wesley 1924- *WhoAm 90*
Hamblen, Karen A *WhoAmA 91*
Hamblen, Lapsley Walker, Jr. 1926- *WhoAm 90*
Hamblen, Stuart 1908-1989 *BioIn 16*
Hamblet, Newman 1914- *WhoAm 90*
Hambleton, Chalkley Jay 1912- *WhoAm 90*
Hambleton, George Blow Elliott 1929- *WhoE 91, WhoWor 91*
Hambleton, Jack *AuBYP 90*
Hambleton, Richard A 1954- *WhoAmA 91*
Hambleton, Thomas Edward 1911- *WhoAm 90*
Hambleton, Tom *BioIn 16*
Hamblett, Stephen 1934- *St&PR 91, WhoAm 90, WhoE 91*
Hamblett, Theora 1895- *WhoAmA 91N*
Hamblett, Theora 1895-1977 *MusmAFA*
Hambley, Douglas Frederick 1950- *WhoEmL 91*
Hambley, Mark G. 1948- *WhoWor 91*
Hamblin, Dora Jane 1920- *AuBYP 90*
Hamblin, Jacob 1819-1886 *BioIn 16*
Hamblin, James D. 1937- *St&PR 91*
Hamblin, Robert W 1938- *ConAu 131*
Hambling, Maggi 1945- *BiDWomA*
Hambly, Frederick Jean 1942- *BiDrAPA 89*
Hambly, Loveday 1604-1682 *BiDEWW*
Hambourg, Boris 1884-1954 *PenDiMP*
Hambourg, Jan 1882-1947 *PenDiMP*
Hambourg, Maria Morris 1949- *ConAu 130*
Hambourg, Mark 1879-1960 *PenDiMP*
Hambraeus, Bengt 1928- *IntWWM 90, WhoAm 90*
Hambraeus, Gunnar Axel 1919- *WhoWor 91*
Hambric, Donna 1944- *St&PR 91*
Hambrick, George Walter, Jr. 1922- *WhoAm 90*
Hambrick, Jackson Reid 1917- *WhoAm 90*
Hambrick, Marvin K. 1921- *WhoAm 90*
Hambrick, Peggy Joan 1936- *St&PR 91*
Hambright, James William 1952- *WhoEmL 91*
Hambright, Robert Benjamin 1947- *St&PR 91*
Hambro, Robin *BioIn 16*
Hambrook, Ernest C. 1937- *St&PR 91*
Hambrusch, Heinz 1941- *WhoWor 91*
Hamburg, Beatrix Ann 1923- *WhoAm 90, WhoAmW 91*
Hamburg, Charles Bruce 1939- *WhoAm 90*
Hamburg, David A *BiDrAPA 89*
Hamburg, Doris Alice 1951- *WhoE 91*
Hamburg, Joseph 1922- *WhoAm 90*
Hamburg, Marian V. *BioIn 16*
Hamburg, Marian Virginia 1918- *WhoAm 90*
Hamburg, Otto 1924- *IntWWM 90*
Hamburg, Paul 1945- *BiDrAPA 89, WhoE 91*
Hamburg, Steve Jack 1952- *WhoEmL 91*
Hamburgen, Mary Elizabeth *BiDrAPA 89*
Hamburger, Edmund Anthony 1927- *WhoAm 90*
Hamburger, Ernest *BiDrAPA 89*
Hamburger, Jean 1909- *WhoWor 91*
Hamburger, Mary Ann 1939- *WhoAmW 91, WhoE 91, WhoWor 91*
Hamburger, Michael Wile 1953- *WhoEmL 91*
Hamburger, Paul 1920- *IntWWM 90*
Hamburger, Philip 1914- *WhoAm 90*
Hamburger, Richard James 1937- *WhoAm 90, WhoWor 91*
Hamburger, Sydney K 1935- *WhoAmA 91*
Hamburger, Viktor 1900- *WhoAm 90*
Hamburger, Werner 1910- *BiDrAPA 89*
Hamburgh, Max 1922-1989 *BioIn 16*
Hamby, A. Garth 1938- *WhoSSW 91*
Hamby, Alonzo Lee 1940- *WhoAm 90*
Hamby, Carolynn Sue 1938- *WhoAmW 91*
Hamby, George Russell 1935- *St&PR 91*
Hamby, J.W. 1925- *St&PR 91*
Hamby, James A. 1943- *WhoWrEP 89*
Hamby, Jeannette 1933- *WhoAmW 91*
Hamby, John Holden, Jr. 1938- *St&PR 91*
Hamby, Robert E., Jr. 1946- *St&PR 91*
Hamcke, William R. 1924-1988 *BioIn 16*
Hamdan ibn Muhammad Al-Nahayan, Sheikh 1930- *WhoWor 91*
Hamdan ibn Rashid Al-Maktum, Sheikh 1945- *WhoWor 91*
Hamdan-Allen, Ghada Ali *BiDrAPA 89*
Hamdoon, Nizar Said 1944- *WhoWor 91*
Hamed, Martha Ellen 1950- *WhoAmW 91*
Hameenniemi, Eero Olavi 1951- *IntWWM 90*
Hameister, Lavon Louetta 1922- *WhoAmW 91, WhoWor 91*
Hameka, Hendrik Frederik 1931- *WhoAm 90*
Hamel, Aldona Mary 1946- *WhoAmW 91, WhoEmL 91*
Hamel, Dana Bertrand 1923- *WhoAm 90*
Hamel, Elizabeth Cecil 1918- *WhoAmW 91*
Hamel, Emilienne M. 1919- *St&PR 91*
Hamel, Gilles 1945- *St&PR 91*
Hamel, Jean-Louis 1942- *St&PR 91*
Hamel, Jean-Marc 1925- *WhoAm 90*
Hamel, Louis Reginald 1945- *WhoEmL 91*
Hamel, Marion Dexter 1942- *WhoSSW 91*
Hamel, Mark Edwin 1953- *WhoEmL 91*
Hamel, Matthew Edward 1960- *WhoEmL 91, WhoWor 91*
Hamel, Peter Michael *NewAgE 90, NewAgMG*
Hamel, Reginald 1931- *WhoAm 90*
Hamel, Rodolphe 1929- *St&PR 91, WhoAm 90, WhoE 91*
Hamel, Veronica 1943- *WhoAm 90, WhoAmW 91*
Hamel, Vicki Otto 1947- *WhoAmW 91*
Hamelberg, William 1925- *WhoAm 90*
Hamelfarb, Rena M. *ODwPR 91*
Hamelin, Jean-Guy 1925- *WhoAm 90*
Hamelin, Louis-Edmond 1923- *WhoAm 90*
Hamelin, Marcel 1937- *WhoAm 90*
Hamelink, Crystal Mary 1947- *WhoAmW 91*
Hamengkubuwono IX, Sultan 1912-1988 *BioIn 16*
Hament, Joel I. 1950- *St&PR 91*
Hameon, Brigitte *BiDrAPA 89*
Hamer, Charles James 1931- *WhoAmA 91*
Hamer, Edward Stephen 1948- *BiDrAPA 89*
Hamer, Fannie Lou 1917-1977 *WorAlBi*
Hamer, Harold Alec *BiDrAPA 89*
Hamer, Harold Alec 1939- *WhoE 91*
Hamer, James M. 1951- *St&PR 91*
Hamer, Jean Jerome 1916- *WhoWor 91*
Hamer, Jeffrey Michael 1949- *WhoWor 91*
Hamer, Joseph 1925- *IntWWM 90*
Hamer, Marilyn A. *ODwPR 91*
Hamer, Marilyn Sue *BiDrAPA 89*
Hamer, Robert E. 1951- *St&PR 91*
Hamer, Rusty *BioIn 16*
Hamer, William *WhoSSW 91*
Hamerman, Esther 1886-1977 *MusmAFA*
Hamermesh, Daniel Selim 1943- *WhoAm 90*
Hamermesh, Lawrence Abraham 1952- *WhoEmL 91*
Hamermesh, Morton 1915- *WhoAm 90*
Hamerow, Theodore Stephen 1920- *WhoAm 90*
Hamerslag, Rudolf 1931- *WhoWor 91*
Hamerton, John Laurence 1929- *WhoAm 90*
Hames, Carl Martin 1938- *WhoAmA 91*
Hames, Clifford M. 1926- *St&PR 91*

Hames, Clifford Moffett 1926- *WhoAm 90*
Hames, Curtis Gordon 1920- *WhoAm 90*
Hames, John Foster 1928- *St&PR 91*
Hames, Martin *BioIn 16*
Hames, Richard *ODwPR 91*
Hames, Richard C *BiDrAPA 89*
Hames, Richard David 1945- *IntWWM 90*
Hames, Robert William 1953- *WhoSSW 91*
Hames, William Lester 1947- *WhoEmL 91*
Hamid, Michael 1934- *WhoAm 90*
Hamil, Thomas Arthur 1928- *AuBYP 90*
Hamil, Wade Lee 1964- *WhoEmL 91*
Hamilburg, Daniel M. *St&PR 91N*
Hamilburg, Joseph Daniel 1948- *St&PR 91*
Hamilburg, Maurice Joseph 1946- *St&PR 91*
Hamill, James E 1920- *BiDrAPA 89*
Hamill, John 1946- *ODwPR 91*
Hamill, John Mark 1959- *BiDrAPA 89*
Hamill, John P. 1940- *St&PR 91*
Hamill, John Ransom 1946- *WhoEmL 91*
Hamill, Judith Ellen 1953- *WhoAmW 91, WhoEmL 91*
Hamill, Mark 1951- *WhoAm 90, WorAlBi*
Hamill, Mary Kay 1956- *WhoAmW 91*
Hamill, Nancy Lynn 1957- *WhoEmL 91*
Hamill, Paul J. 1943- *WhoWrEP 89*
Hamill, Pete *BioIn 16*
Hamill, Pete 1935- *WhoWrEP 89*
Hamill, Richard D. 1939- *St&PR 91*
Hamill, Thomas A. 1934- *ODwPR 91*
Hamill, Tim J 1942- *WhoAmA 91*
Hamill, William Henry Baldwin 1946- *St&PR 91*
Hamilton, A. Lamar 1930- *St&PR 91*
Hamilton, Albert Charles 1921- *WhoAm 90*
Hamilton, Albert Garland 1927- *St&PR 91*
Hamilton, Albert Hyde 1925- *WhoE 91*
Hamilton, Alexander 1755-1804 *EncABHB 6 [port], EncCRAm [port], WorAlBi*
Hamilton, Alexander 1757-1804 *BiDrUSE 89, BioIn 16*
Hamilton, Alice *BioIn 16*
Hamilton, Alice 1869-1970 *BioAmW*
Hamilton, Allan Corning 1921- *WhoAm 90*
Hamilton, Andrew 1676-1741 *EncCRAm*
Hamilton, Angela L. 1955- *WhoAmW 91*
Hamilton, Anne Linnea 1949- *WhoAmW 91*
Hamilton, Anthony R. *BioIn 16*
Hamilton, Barbara 1921- *OxCCanT*
Hamilton, Barbara 1943- *WhoAmW 91*
Hamilton, Barbara 1944- *St&PR 91*
Hamilton, Beatrice 1947- *WhoAmW 91*
Hamilton, Bernie *DrBlPA 90*
Hamilton, Beverly Lannquist *ODwPR 91*
Hamilton, Beverly Lannquist 1946- *St&PR 91*
Hamilton, Bill *BioIn 16*
Hamilton, Billy 1866-1940 *Ballpl 90 [port]*
Hamilton, Bobby Wayne 1946- *WhoEmL 91, WhoSSW 91*
Hamilton, Bruce Bucknam 1936- *WhoAm 90*
Hamilton, Bruce E. *St&PR 91*
Hamilton, Calvin Sargent 1924- *WhoAm 90*
Hamilton, Carol Jean 1935- *WhoWrEP 89*
Hamilton, Carrie 1964- *BioIn 16*
Hamilton, Charles 1913- *AuBYP 90*
Hamilton, Charles Henry 1903- *WhoAm 90*
Hamilton, Charlotte S *BiDrAPA 89*
Hamilton, Chico 1921- *BioIn 16, DrBlPA 90*
Hamilton, Cicely 1872-1952 *BioIn 16, FemiCLE*
Hamilton, Clive *AuBYP 90, ConAu 33NR, MajTwCW*
Hamilton, Clyde Henry 1934- *WhoAm 90, WhoSSW 91*
Hamilton, Constance Bette 1933- *WhoAmW 91*
Hamilton, Cynthia S 1951- *BiDrAPA 89*
Hamilton, D.D. 1920- *St&PR 91*
Hamilton, Dagmar Strandberg 1932- *WhoAmW 91*
Hamilton, Daniel Stephen 1932- *WhoAm 90*
Hamilton, Dave 1947- *Ballpl 90*
Hamilton, David 1922- *WhoSSW 91*
Hamilton, David 1935- *IntWWM 90*
Hamilton, David John 1956- *WhoE 91*
Hamilton, David Mike 1951- *WhoEmL 91*
Hamilton, David Peter 1935- *WhoAm 90*
Hamilton, David R. 1939- *St&PR 91*
Hamilton, David Wendell 1953- *WhoAm 90, WhoWor 91*
Hamilton, Denis 1918-1988 *AnObit 1988, BioIn 16*
Hamilton, Dennis James 1945- *WhoSSW 91*
Hamilton, Diane *AuBYP 90*
Hamilton, Diane Bronkema 1946- *WhoAmW 91*
Hamilton, Don Reed 1947- *WhoE 91*
Hamilton, Donald 1916- *SpyFic, TwCCr&M 91*
Hamilton, Donald Bengtsson 1916- *WhoAm 90, WhoWrEP 89*
Hamilton, Donald Curtis 1951- *WhoSSW 91*
Hamilton, Donald Emery 1938- *WhoAm 90*
Hamilton, Doris Jean *WhoWrEP 89*
Hamilton, E. Haden, Jr. 1942- *St&PR 91*
Hamilton, Earl 1891-1968 *Ballpl 90*
Hamilton, Earle Grady, Jr. 1920- *WhoAm 90*
Hamilton, Edith 1867-1963 *BioAmW*
Hamilton, Edmond 1904-1977 *RGTwCSF*
Hamilton, Edsel Poston, III 1949- *WhoSSW 91*
Hamilton, Edward Jackson, Jr. 1947- *St&PR 91, WhoEmL 91*
Hamilton, Edward Marsh 1941- *WhoWor 91*
Hamilton, Edwin 1936- *WhoE 91*
Hamilton, Eleanor Leigh 1909- *WhoAmW 91*
Hamilton, Elissa Lynn Alkoff 1958- *WhoWrEP 89*
Hamilton, Elizabeth 1758-1816 *BioIn 16, FemiCLE*
Hamilton, Elizabeth, Duchess of 1616?-1659 *BiDEWW*
Hamilton, Emily Rebecca 1938- *WhoAmW 91*
Hamilton, Emma 1761?-1815 *BioIn 16*
Hamilton, Ernest *MajTwCW*
Hamilton, Eugenia Elizabeth 1949- *WhoAmW 91*
Hamilton, Frank Moss 1930- *WhoAmA 91*
Hamilton, Frank Roy 1945- *St&PR 91*
Hamilton, Franklin *MajTwCW*
Hamilton, Frederic Crawford 1927- *St&PR 91*
Hamilton, Gail *AuBYP 90*
Hamilton, Gail 1833-1896 *BioIn 16*
Hamilton, Gale Wayne 1944- *WhoWor 91*
Hamilton, Gary Glen 1943- *WhoAm 90*
Hamilton, George *BioIn 16*
Hamilton, George 1915- *WhoSSW 91*
Hamilton, George 1939- *WorAlBi*
Hamilton, George E., Jr. 1895- *WhoAm 90*
Hamilton, George Earl 1934- *WhoAmA 91*
Hamilton, George Heard 1910- *WhoAm 90*
Hamilton, Gordon Brown 1922- *St&PR 91*
Hamilton, Grant Matthew 1947- *WhoE 91*
Hamilton, Guy 1922- *ConTFT 8*
Hamilton, Hamish 1900-1988 *AnObit 1988, BioIn 16*
Hamilton, Harold Philip 1924- *WhoAm 90*
Hamilton, Helen *FemiCLE*
Hamilton, Henry 1734-1796 *WhNaAH*
Hamilton, Henry N *BiDrAPA 89*
Hamilton, Horace George 1925- *WhoAm 90*
Hamilton, Howard Britton 1923- *WhoAm 90*
Hamilton, Howard Laverne 1916- *WhoAm 90, WhoWor 91*
Hamilton, Hugh Alexander 1929- *WhoAm 90*
Hamilton, Hugh B., Jr. 1946- *St&PR 91*
Hamilton, Hughbert Clayton 1903- *WhoAm 90*
Hamilton, Iain 1920-1986 *ConAu 130*
Hamilton, Iain 1922- *PenDiMPA*
Hamilton, Iain Ellis 1922- *IntWWM 90, WhoAm 90*
Hamilton, Ian 1938- *BioIn 16*
Hamilton, J. Stephen 1948- *St&PR 91*
Hamilton, Jack 1938- *Ballpl 90*
Hamilton, Jack Reese 1945- *WhoSSW 91*
Hamilton, Jackson Douglas 1949- *WhoEmL 91*
Hamilton, Jacqueline 1942- *WhoAmW 91, WhoSSW 91*
Hamilton, James 1810-1896 *DcCanB 12*
Hamilton, James 1938- *WhoAm 90, WhoWrEP 89*
Hamilton, James A 1907- *BiDrAPA 89*
Hamilton, James Andrew 1930- *St&PR 91*
Hamilton, James B. 1949- *St&PR 91*
Hamilton, James Charles 1952- *WhoEmL 91*
Hamilton, James Lynn 1943- *WhoAm 90*
Hamilton, James Marvie 1950- *WhoAm 90*
Hamilton, Janet 1795-1873 *FemiCLE*
Hamilton, Janet Virginia 1936- *WhoAmW 91, WhoSSW 91*
Hamilton, Jay W. 1927- *St&PR 91*
Hamilton, Jean Ann 1950- *BiDrAPA 89*
Hamilton, Jeff 1964- *Ballpl 90*
Hamilton, Jeffrey Scott 1956- *WhoEmL 91*
Hamilton, Jerald 1927- *IntWWM 90, WhoAm 90*
Hamilton, Joe 1929- *ConTFT 8*
Hamilton, John Alfred 1929- *WhoAm 90*
Hamilton, John Bruce 1943- *WhoE 91*
Hamilton, John David 1944- *BiDrAPA 89*
Hamilton, John Dayton, Jr. 1934- *WhoAm 90*
Hamilton, John Frederick 1945- *WhoEmL 91*
Hamilton, John Kent 1945- *WhoSSW 91*
Hamilton, John L. Jack 1918- *St&PR 91*
Hamilton, John M *BiDrAPA 89*
Hamilton, John Maxwell *BioIn 16*
Hamilton, John Ross 1924- *WhoAm 90*
Hamilton, John Taylor 1843-1925 *AmLegL*
Hamilton, Joseph Devance 1947- *BiDrAPA 89*
Hamilton, Joseph E. 1951- *St&PR 91*
Hamilton, Joseph Hants, Jr. 1932- *WhoAm 90*
Hamilton, Joyce Kay 1950- *WhoAmW 91, WhoEmL 91*
Hamilton, Juan B 1945- *WhoAmA 91*
Hamilton, Judy Elizabeth 1964- *WhoSSW 91*
Hamilton, Karen Jude 1962- *WhoAmW 91*
Hamilton, Katherine Louise 1957- *WhoAmW 91*
Hamilton, Kay *AuBYP 90*
Hamilton, Kim *DrBlPA 90*
Hamilton, Kimberly Darlene 1960- *WhoAmW 91*
Hamilton, Laura Ann 1939- *WhoAmW 91*
Hamilton, Laura Frances 1958- *WhoWor 91*
Hamilton, Lee H. *BioIn 16*
Hamilton, Lee Herbert 1931- *WhoAm 90*
Hamilton, Leona 1915- *WhoWrEP 89*
Hamilton, Leonard Derwent 1921- *WhoAm 90*
Hamilton, Lillias *FemiCLE*
Hamilton, Linda *BioIn 16*
Hamilton, Linda Kay 1945- *WhoWrEP 89*
Hamilton, Lois Ann 1939- *WhoE 91*
Hamilton, Lyman Critchfield, Jr. 1926- *WhoAm 90*
Hamilton, Lynn 1930- *DrBlPA 90*
Hamilton, M. Raymond 1953- *WhoSSW 91*
Hamilton, Madison Hayne 1932- *St&PR 91, WhoAm 90, WhoSSW 91*
Hamilton, Malcolm Cowan 1938- *WhoAm 90*
Hamilton, Marcella Denise 1954- *WhoWrEP 89*
Hamilton, Margaret *BiDEWW*
Hamilton, Margaret Lawrence 1948- *WhoEmL 91*
Hamilton, Margaret Letitia *St&PR 91*
Hamilton, Marian Eloise 1931- *WhoAmW 91, WhoSSW 91*
Hamilton, Mark *ODwPR 91*
Hamilton, Mark F. *BioIn 16*
Hamilton, Mary 1739-1818? *FemiCLE*
Hamilton, Mary 1884-1962 *FemiCLE*
Hamilton, Mary 1927- *BioIn 16*
Hamilton, Mary K. 1926- *St&PR 91*
Hamilton, Mary Lucia Kerr 1926- *WhoAmW 91*
Hamilton, Maura Anne 1957- *WhoEmL 91*
Hamilton, Max 1912-1988 *AnObit 1988*
Hamilton, Mel *BioIn 16*
Hamilton, Melvin Charles 1950- *St&PR 91*
Hamilton, Michael 1927- *ConAu 30NR*
Hamilton, Michael Scott 1953- *WhoAm 90, WhoWor 91*
Hamilton, Michaela Ann 1948- *St&PR 91*
Hamilton, Milton Earle 1952- *WhoEmL 91*
Hamilton, Milton Holmes, Sr. 1925- *WhoAm 90*
Hamilton, Milton Wheaton 1901-1989 *BioIn 16*
Hamilton, Mollie *MajTwCW*
Hamilton, Mollie 1908- *SmATA X [port]*
Hamilton, Mykol Cecilia 1952- *WhoAmW 91*
Hamilton, Nancy 1908- *OxCPMus*
Hamilton, Nancy Beth 1948- *WhoAmW 91, WhoEmL 91, WhoWor 91*
Hamilton, Nancy Jeanne 1959- *WhoEmL 91*
Hamilton, Norman Blom 1933- *BiDrAPA 89*
Hamilton, Norman Gregory 1945- *BiDrAPA 89*
Hamilton, O. F. *BioIn 16*
Hamilton, Pamela Gerie 1955- *BiDrAPA 89*
Hamilton, Patricia Rose 1948- *WhoAmA 91, WhoE 91*
Hamilton, Patricia Wardley 1930- *WhoWrEP 89*
Hamilton, Patrick 1904-1962 *TwCCr&M 91*
Hamilton, Patti 1958- *WhoSSW 91*
Hamilton, Paul 1762-1816 *BiDrUSE 89*
Hamilton, Paul Mason *BiDrAPA 89*
Hamilton, Perrin C. 1921- *WhoWor 91*
Hamilton, Peter Bannerman 1946- *St&PR 91, WhoAm 90, WhoEmL 91*
Hamilton, Peter Boris 1928- *WhoWor 91*
Hamilton, Peter M. *ODwPR 91*
Hamilton, Peter Stevens 1826-1893 *DcCanB 12*
Hamilton, Philip R. 1945- *St&PR 91*
Hamilton, Rachel *BiDrAPA 89*
Hamilton, Ralph West 1933- *WhoE 91*
Hamilton, Rhoda Lillian Rosen 1915- *WhoAmW 91*
Hamilton, Richard *BioIn 16*
Hamilton, Richard B. 1943- *St&PR 91*
Hamilton, Richard Daniel 1928- *WhoAm 90*
Hamilton, Richard Frederick 1930- *WhoAm 90, WhoWrEP 89*
Hamilton, Richard Lee 1939- *WhoAm 90*
Hamilton, Richard Parker 1931- *WhoAm 90*
Hamilton, Robert 1937- *IntWWM 90*
Hamilton, Robert A. 1917- *St&PR 91*
Hamilton, Robert Morrison 1936- *WhoAm 90*
Hamilton, Robert Newell 1925- *St&PR 91*
Hamilton, Robert Thomas, III 1943- *WhoAm 90*
Hamilton, Robert William 1939- *WhoAm 90*
Hamilton, Robert William 1958- *BiDrAPA 89*
Hamilton, Robin Michael 1955- *BiDrAPA 89*
Hamilton, Ronald E. 1945- *WhoSSW 91*
Hamilton, Ronald T. *EarBlAP*
Hamilton, Ronnie Edward 1957- *WhoEmL 91*
Hamilton, Rosemary Ann *WhoWrEP 89*
Hamilton, Roy 1929-1969 *BioIn 16, DrBlPA 90*
Hamilton, Russel *AuBYP 90*
Hamilton, Russell George, Jr. 1934- *WhoAm 90*
Hamilton, S Sutton 1935- *BiDrAPA 89*
Hamilton, Samuel Stephen 1960- *WhoEmL 91*
Hamilton, Sandra 1959- *WhoAmW 91*
Hamilton, Sarah Tucker 1944- *WhoAmW 91*
Hamilton, Scott 1958- *WorAlBi*
Hamilton, Scott Lee 1951- *WhoEmL 91*
Hamilton, Scott Scovell 1958- *WhoAm 90*
Hamilton, Scott W. 1954- *St&PR 91*
Hamilton, Sheryl Lynn 1955- *WhoSSW 91*
Hamilton, Shirley Siekmann 1928- *WhoAmW 91*
Hamilton, Steve 1935- *Ballpl 90*
Hamilton, Steven G. 1939- *St&PR 91*
Hamilton, Stuart 1929- *IntWWM 90*
Hamilton, Susan Owens 1951- *WhoSSW 91*
Hamilton, T. Earle 1905- *WhoAm 90*
Hamilton, T Glen 1873-1935 *EncO&P 3*
Hamilton, Thomas *St&PR 91*
Hamilton, Thomas Allen 1947- *WhoEmL 91, WhoSSW 91*
Hamilton, Thomas Michael 1947- *WhoE 91, WhoEmL 91*
Hamilton, Thomas Stewart 1911- *WhoAm 90*
Hamilton, Thomas Stuart 1959- *WhoE 91*
Hamilton, Thomas Woolman 1948- *WhoEmL 91, WhoWor 91*
Hamilton, Virginia 1926- *AuBYP 90*
Hamilton, Virginia 1936- *BioIn 16, MajTwCW, WhoAm 90, WhoAmW 91, WhoWrEP 89*
Hamilton, W Paul C 1938- *WhoAmA 91*
Hamilton, Warren Bell 1925- *WhoAm 90*
Hamilton, Weston Thomas 1944- *BiDrAPA 89*
Hamilton, William 1788-1856 *BioIn 16*
Hamilton, William 1924- *BioIn 16*
Hamilton, William 1930- *IntWWM 90*
Hamilton, William 1939- *WhoAm 90*
Hamilton, William Berry, Jr. 1929- *WhoAm 90*
Hamilton, William Douglas, II 1948- *WhoSSW 91*
Hamilton, William Frank 1939- *WhoAm 90, WhoE 91*
Hamilton, William G. 1936- *St&PR 91*
Hamilton, William Howard 1918- *WhoAm 90*
Hamilton, William L. 1941- *St&PR 91*
Hamilton, William Milton 1925- *St&PR 91, WhoAm 90*
Hamilton, William Pinkney, IV 1950- *WhoE 91*
Hamilton, William R. 1805-1865 *WorAlBi*
Hamilton, William Rowan 1805-1865 *BioIn 16*
Hamilton, William T. 1939- *WhoAm 90*
Hamilton, William Thomas 1822-1908 *WhNaAH*
Hamilton, Winthrop W. 1941- *St&PR 91*
Hamilton-Finlay, Ian 1925- *BioIn 16*
Hamilton-Kemp, Thomas Rogers 1942- *WhoSSW 91, WhoWor 91*
Hamilton-Paterson, James *AuBYP 90*
Hamington, Armand 1933- *St&PR 91*
Hamister, Donald Bruce 1920- *St&PR 91, WhoAm 90*

Hamister, Mark Edward 1951- *WhoEmL 91*
Hamiter, Allen H. 1867-1933 *AmLegL*
Hamlar, Portia Yvonne Trenholm *WhoAmW 91*
Hamlet, Gordon Edward 1940- *St&PR 91*
Hamlet, James Frank 1921- *WhoAm 90*
Hamlet, Joseph Frank 1934- *St&PR 91, WhoAm 90*
Hamlet, Kenneth Bruce 1944- *WhoAm 90*
Hamlet, Ova 1935- *SmATA X*
Hamlet, Susan H 1954- *WhoAmA 91*
Hamlet, Sybil E. 1913?-1989 *ConAu 129*
Hamlett, Curtis 1949- *IntWWM 90*
Hamlett, Dale Edward 1921- *WhoAmA 91*
Hamlett, Robert Barksdale 1949- *WhoSSW 91*
Hamlin, A.H. 1934- *St&PR 91*
Hamlin, Allen C. 1949- *WhoSSW 91*
Hamlin, Arthur Tenney 1913- *WhoAm 90*
Hamlin, Carole Adrienne 1938- *WhoAmW 91*
Hamlin, Cary Lee 1949- *BiDrAPA 89*
Hamlin, Charles 1837-1911 *AmLegL*
Hamlin, Charles Borden 1947- *WhoE 91*
Hamlin, Dan William 1947- *WhoSSW 91*
Hamlin, Edmund Martin, Jr. 1949- *WhoEmL 91*
Hamlin, Hannibal 1809-1891 *BiDrUSE 89, WorAlBi*
Hamlin, Harry *BioIn 16*
Hamlin, Harry 1951- *WorAlBi*
Hamlin, Harry Robinson 1951- *WhoAm 90*
Hamlin, Hatti *ODwPR 91*
Hamlin, Henry Allen 1930- *St&PR 91*
Hamlin, James Turner, III 1929- *WhoAm 90*
Hamlin, Jefferson Davis 1932- *WhoSSW 91*
Hamlin, Ken 1935- *Ballpl 90*
Hamlin, Kenneth Eldred, Jr. 1917- *WhoAm 90*
Hamlin, Louise 1949- *WhoAmA 91*
Hamlin, Luke 1906-1978 *Ballpl 90*
Hamlin, Percy G *BiDrAPA 89*
Hamlin, Richard Eugene 1925- *WhoAm 90*
Hamlin, Robert Henry 1923- *WhoAm 90*
Hamlin, Roger Eugene 1945- *WhoAm 90, WhoEmL 91*
Hamlin, Sonya B. *WhoAmW 91*
Hamlin, Thomas Allen 1950- *BiDrAPA 89*
Hamlin, Tim Allen 1960- *St&PR 91*
Hamlin, Vincent T. 1900- *EncACom*
Hamlin, William C. 1949- *St&PR 91*
Hamling, Ana Marie 1950- *WhoEmL 91*
Hamling, James L. 1941- *St&PR 91*
Hamlisch, Marvin 1944- *IntWWM 90, OxCPMus, WhoAm 90*
Hamlisch, Robert E 1928- *BiDrAPA 89*
Hamlyn, Adrian Noel 1944- *WhoWor 91*
Hamlyn, D W 1924- *ConAu 132*
Hamlyn, Harry Ward 1958- *BiDrAPA 89*
Hamlyn, Richard L. 1950- *St&PR 91*
Hamm, Albert 1860-1891 *DcCanB 12*
Hamm, Barbara Lois *BiDrAPA 89*
Hamm, Beth Creevy 1885-1958 *WhoAmA 91N*
Hamm, Charles 1925- *IntWWM 90*
Hamm, Charles J. 1937- *St&PR 91*
Hamm, Charles John 1937- *WhoAm 90*
Hamm, Charles R. 1933- *WhoAm 90*
Hamm, Coleman Durden, Jr. 1947- *WhoEmL 91*
Hamm, David Bernard 1948- *WhoEmL 91*
Hamm, David Robert 1957- *WhoEmL 91*
Hamm, Deborah S 1951- *BiDrAPA 89*
Hamm, Donald George, Jr. 1954- *St&PR 91*
Hamm, Donald Ivan 1928- *WhoAm 90*
Hamm, Frances Jayne 1935- *WhoAmW 91*
Hamm, Henry Stevens 1921- *WhoE 91*
Hamm, John Edward 1946- *BiDrAPA 89*
Hamm, Manfred Ruediger 1952- *WhoWor 91*
Hamm, Michael 1934- *IntWWM 90*
Hamm, Norma Beth 1945- *WhoEmL 91*
Hamm, Robert B. 1940- *St&PR 91*
Hamm, Ronald John 1946- *WhoE 91*
Hamm, Rose Condon 1939- *WhoSSW 91*
Hamm, Suzanne Margaret 1943- *WhoAmW 91*
Hamm, Thomas Michael 1944- *WhoE 91*
Hamm, William Gerald 1931- *St&PR 91, WhoAm 90, WhoE 91*
Hamm, William Joseph 1910- *WhoAm 90*
Hamm, William Robert 1952- *St&PR 91*
Hammack, Charles Joseph 1923- *St&PR 91*
Hammack, Henry Edgar 1928- *WhoSSW 91*
Hammaker, Atlee 1958- *Ballpl 90*
Hammaker, David M.G. 1938- *St&PR 91*
Hammaker, Paul M. 1903- *WhoAm 90*
Hammalian, Stephen John 1941- *St&PR 91*
Hammam, M. Shawky 1919- *WhoAm 90*
Hamman, Robert J. 1914- *St&PR 91*
Hamman, Thomas Arthur 1957- *WhoEmL 91*
Hammann, Johann Wolfgang *PenDiDA 89*
Hammann, Kenneth Robert 1947- *WhoEmL 91*
Hammans, Charles Erle, Jr. 1926- *St&PR 91*
Hammar, Lester E. 1927- *St&PR 91*
Hammarberg, Thomas Viktor Asmund 1942- *WhoWor 91*
Hammargren, Sten-Peter 1923- *WhoWor 91*
Hammarskjold, Dag 1905-1961 *BioIn 16, WorAlBi*
Hammas, Refik 1935- *WhoWor 91*
Hamme, Robert K. 1942- *St&PR 91*
Hammega, Erik Jan 1950- *WhoE 91*
Hammel, Charles Louis 1925- *St&PR 91*
Hammel, Eugene Alfred 1930- *WhoAm 90*
Hammel, George F. 1930- *St&PR 91*
Hammel, Robert Edward 1935- *St&PR 91*
Hammel, Robert F. 1956- *St&PR 91*
Hammel, Susan Marie 1964- *WhoWor 91*
Hammel-Geiger, Mary Celeste 1956- *WhoAmW 91*
Hammele, Joseph F. 1929- *St&PR 91*
Hammell, Grandin Gaunt 1945- *WhoEmL 91, WhoWor 91*
Hammell, Randall W. 1944- *St&PR 91*
Hammer, Alfred Emil 1925- *WhoAm 90, WhoAmA 91*
Hammer, Armand *St&PR 91*
Hammer, Armand 1898- *BioIn 16, WhoAm 90, WhoWor 91, WorAlBi*
Hammer, Armand 1898-1990 *NewYTBS 90 [port], WhoAmA 91N*
Hammer, Carl *BiDrAPA 89*
Hammer, Carl 1914- *WhoAm 90*
Hammer, Charles *BioIn 16*
Hammer, Charles Lawrence 1922- *WhoAm 90*
Hammer, Cheryl Lynn 1960- *WhoEmL 91*
Hammer, Daniel William 1932- *WhoAm 90*
Hammer, David Andrew 1943- *WhoE 91*
Hammer, David Eugene 1947- *St&PR 91, WhoEmL 91*
Hammer, David Lindley 1929- *WhoWor 91*
Hammer, David P. *ODwPR 91*
Hammer, Dennis Glen 1953- *St&PR 91*
Hammer, Diane Bennett *BiDrAPA 89*
Hammer, Donald Price 1921- *WhoAm 90*
Hammer, Eileen 1953- *WhoEmL 91*
Hammer, Elizabeth B *WhoAmA 91*
Hammer, Emanuel Frederick 1926- *WhoAm 90*
Hammer, Frances *BioIn 16*
Hammer, Hali Diane 1948- *WhoAmW 91*
Hammer, Harold Harlan 1920- *St&PR 91, WhoAm 90, WhoE 91*
Hammer, Harvey M 1935- *BiDrAPA 89*
Hammer, Herman N. 1924- *St&PR 91*
Hammer, Ireene Wicker 1900-1987 *BioIn 16*
Hammer, Jacob 1950- *WhoSSW 91*
Hammer, Jacob Myer 1927- *WhoAm 90*
Hammer, Jan *BioIn 16, NewAgMG*
Hammer, Jeffrey S 1941- *BiDrAPA 89*
Hammer, Joel 1943- *St&PR 91*
Hammer, John Gregory 1949- *WhoSSW 91*
Hammer, John Richard 1922- *WhoSSW 91*
Hammer, John William 1952- *St&PR 91*
Hammer, Karol Elizabeth 1962- *WhoE 91*
Hammer, Laurie Paula 1953- *BiDrAPA 89*
Hammer, Leon I *BiDrAPA 89*
Hammer, Louis Zelig 1931- *WhoWrEP 89*
Hammer, M.C. *ConMus 5 [port], News 91-2 [port]*
Hammer, Mark 1943- *St&PR 91*
Hammer, Meredith Fuchs *ODwPR 91*
Hammer, N. Robert 1942- *St&PR 91*
Hammer, Norbert Francis, III 1949- *WhoSSW 91*
Hammer, Otto Robert 1946- *WhoEmL 91*
Hammer, Roger A. 1934- *WhoWrEP 89*
Hammer, Roger Harry 1931- *WhoAm 90*
Hammer, Ronald Page, Jr. 1953- *WhoEmL 91*
Hammer, Roy Armand 1934- *WhoAm 90*
Hammer, Russell Jeffrey 1953- *St&PR 91*
Hammer, Sanford S. *BioIn 16, NewYTBS 90*
Hammer, Susan Berman 1950- *WhoAmW 91*
Hammer, Theodore S. 1945- *St&PR 91*
Hammer, Thomas John 1949- *WhoEmL 91*
Hammer, Tor Amund 1935- *WhoWor 91*
Hammer, Victor Karl *WhoAmA 91N*
Hammer, Victor Karl 1882-1967 *BioIn 16*
Hammer, Wade Burke 1932- *WhoAm 90*
Hammer, William A. 1962- *ODwPR 91*
Hammer, William Austin 1953- *WhoEmL 91*
Hammer, William Charles 1929- *St&PR 91*
Hammerbeck, Carol Marie 1960- *BiDrAPA 89*
Hammerbeck, Wanda Lee 1945- *WhoAmA 91*
Hammerle, Fredric Joseph 1944- *WhoAm 90*
Hammerli, Angela Mitchell 1950- *WhoEmL 91*
Hammerlund, Jeffrey Bryan 1956- *WhoEmL 91*
Hammerly, David L. 1941- *St&PR 91*
Hammerly, Harry Allan 1934- *St&PR 91, WhoAm 90*
Hammerly, Mary Leverenz 1952- *WhoEmL 91*
Hammerman, Irving Harold, II 1920- *WhoWor 91*
Hammerman, Jeffrey Lee 1942- *BiDrAPA 89*
Hammerman, Kenneth Carl 1945- *WhoEmL 91*
Hammerman, Pat Jo 1953- *WhoAmA 91*
Hammerman, Pat Jo 1954- *WhoE 91*
Hammerman, Steven *BiDrAPA 89*
Hammers, Colleen Romick 1962- *WhoEmL 91*
Hammers, Oliver Bertrand 1924- *WhoAm 90*
Hammerschick, Joseph 1937- *WhoWor 91*
Hammerschlag, Carl A. *BioIn 16*
Hammerschmidt, John Paul 1922- *WhoAm 90, WhoSSW 91*
Hammersley, Donald W 1925- *BiDrAPA 89*
Hammersley, Frederick 1919- *WhoAmA 91*
Hammersmith, Gary S. 1960- *WhoEmL 91*
Hammersmith, Jack Leonard 1941- *WhoSSW 91*
Hammerstein, Jurgen U. G. D. 1925- *WhoWor 91*
Hammerstein, Oscar 1847-1919 *WorAlBi*
Hammerstein, Oscar 1895-1960 *BioIn 16*
Hammerstein, Oscar, II 1895-1960 *OxCPMus, WorAlBi*
Hammerstrom, Donald E. *ODwPR 91*
Hammes, Gordon G. 1934- *WhoAm 90*
Hammes, Lynn F. 1951- *St&PR 91*
Hammes, Michael Noel 1941- *WhoAm 90*
Hammes, Sara Elizabeth 1964- *WhoAmW 91*
Hammes, Terry Marie 1955- *WhoAmW 91, WhoEmL 91*
Hammesfahr, James Frederick 1951- *WhoSSW 91*
Hammesfahr, Robert Winter 1954- *WhoEmL 91*
Hammett, Dashiell 1894-1961 *MajTwCW, TwCCr&M 91, WorAlBi*
Hammett, Earl Donald 1928- *St&PR 91*
Hammett, Edward Harold 1956- *WhoEmL 91*
Hammett, Elliot Brian 1936- *BiDrAPA 89*
Hammett, Ellis Theodore 1920- *WhoWrEP 89*
Hammett, Floyd E. 1930- *St&PR 91*
Hammett, John R. 1948- *St&PR 91*
Hammett, Polly Horton 1930- *WhoAmA 91*
Hammett, Roy 1933- *St&PR 91*
Hammett, Theresa Clair Hoy 1946- *WhoSSW 91*
Hammett, Warren Eugene 1954- *WhoSSW 91*
Hammett, William M. H. 1944- *WhoAm 90*
Hammill, John Roberts 1931- *St&PR 91*
Hamming, Richard Wesley 1915- *WhoAm 90*
Hammink, Niles H. 1911- *St&PR 91*
Hammitt, Harry Andrew 1953- *WhoE 91*
Hammitt, John Michael 1943- *St&PR 91*
Hammitt, Karleen B 1941- *BiDrAPA 89*
Hammock, H. Rex 1954- *WhoEmL 91*
Hammock, Joseph Culver 1926- *WhoAm 90*
Hammock, Raymond Leslie, Jr. 1951- *WhoSSW 91*
Hammock, Virgil Gene 1938- *WhoAmA 91*
Hammon, Ann Lucinda *BiDrAPA 89*
Hammon, Arthur Christopher 1951- *WhoWrEP 89*
Hammon, Jupiter 1711-1806? *EncCRAm*
Hammon, Patricia Jane 1946- *WhoAmW 91*
Hammon, William McDowell 1904-1989 *BioIn 16*
Hammond, Allen Lee 1943- *WhoAm 90*
Hammond, Anna Dean 1940- *WhoAmW 91*
Hammond, Arthur 1904- *IntWWM 90*
Hammond, Barbara *BioIn 16*
Hammond, Benjamin Franklin 1934- *WhoAm 90*
Hammond, Bennett *NewAgMG*
Hammond, Bennett *BioIn 16*
Hammond, C. Dean, III 1947- *St&PR 91*
Hammond, Caleb D. 1915- *St&PR 91*
Hammond, Caleb Dean 1915- *WhoAm 90*
Hammond, Carol Anne 1940- *WhoAmW 91*
Hammond, Catherine Currin 1953- *WhoEmL 91*
Hammond, Charles Ainley 1933- *WhoAm 90*
Hammond, Charles Bessellieu 1936- *WhoAm 90*
Hammond, Charles Taylor 1923- *WhoAm 90*
Hammond, Chester *BioIn 16*
Hammond, Christopher Fitzsimons, III 1939- *St&PR 91*
Hammond, David Alan 1948- *WhoAm 90, WhoSSW 91*
Hammond, David Anthony 1948- *WhoEmL 91*
Hammond, David Bramson *BiDrAPA 89*
Hammond, David Greene 1913- *WhoAm 90*
Hammond, DeAnna 1945- *WhoEmL 91*
Hammond, Deanna Lindberg 1942- *WhoAm 90, WhoAmW 91*
Hammond, Denise Whitehead 1951- *WhoWor 91*
Hammond, Doris Blersch 1933- *WhoSSW 91*
Hammond, Dorothy Lee 1924- *WhoAmW 91*
Hammond, E. Cuyler 1912-1986 *BioIn 16*
Hammond, Edward Cuyler 1912-1986 *BioIn 16*
Hammond, Edward H. 1944- *WhoAm 90*
Hammond, Edwin Hughes 1919- *WhoAm 90*
Hammond, Frank Joseph 1919- *WhoAm 90*
Hammond, Gale Thomas 1939- *WhoAmA 91*
Hammond, George Denman 1923- *WhoAm 90*
Hammond, George Simms 1921- *WhoAm 90*
Hammond, Gerald 1926- *TwCCr&M 91*
Hammond, Gilbert Palmer, Jr. 1944- *St&PR 91*
Hammond, Glen R. 1937- *St&PR 91*
Hammond, Glenn Barry, Sr. 1947- *WhoEmL 91*
Hammond, Guyton Bowers 1930- *WhoAm 90*
Hammond, Harmony 1944- *BiDWomA, WhoAmA 91, WhoE 91*
Hammond, Harold Francis 1908- *WhoAm 90*
Hammond, Harold Logan 1934- *WhoAm 90*
Hammond, Henry 1914-1989 *BioIn 16*
Hammond, Howard David 1924- *WhoE 91*
Hammond, J. D. 1933- *WhoWrEP 89*
Hammond, J. Emmett 1938- *WhoAm 90*
Hammond, J. R. 1933- *ConAu 130*
Hammond, Jack Arnold 1938- *St&PR 91*
Hammond, Jack Lansford 1953- *BiDrAPA 89*
Hammond, James Gerald 1943- *St&PR 91*
Hammond, James Henry 1807-1864 *BioIn 16*
Hammond, James Wilson 1951- *WhoEmL 91*
Hammond, Jane 1950- *WhoAmA 91*
Hammond, Jane Laura *WhoAm 90*
Hammond, Jerome Jerald 1942- *WhoAm 90, WhoWor 91*
Hammond, Jerrold E 1923- *BiDrAPA 89*
Hammond, Jesse Charles 1948- *WhoSSW 91*
Hammond, Joan 1912- *IntWWM 90, PenDiMP*
Hammond, JoAnn 1957- *WhoAmW 91*
Hammond, Joe Phil 1922- *WhoAm 90*
Hammond, John 1910-1987 *OxCPMus*
Hammond, John Arlen 1937- *St&PR 91*
Hammond, John Payne 1913- *WhoAm 90*
Hammond, John William 1946- *WhoEmL 91*
Hammond, Joseph M. 1928- *St&PR 91*
Hammond, Judy McLain 1956- *WhoEmL 91*
Hammond, Judy Oliver 1946- *WhoAmW 91, WhoSSW 91*
Hammond, Karen Smith 1954- *WhoAmW 91, WhoEmL 91, WhoSSW 91*
Hammond, Kathleen Doorish 1950- *St&PR 91*
Hammond, Kenric W 1947- *BiDrAPA 89*
Hammond, Kevin W. 1960- *St&PR 91*
Hammond, Lee Roger *BiDrAPA 89*
Hammond, Leslie King 1944- *WhoAmA 91*
Hammond, Lou Rena *ODwPR 91*
Hammond, Lou Rena Charlotte 1939- *WhoE 91*
Hammond, Margaret Ann 1947- *WhoAmW 91, WhoEmL 91*
Hammond, Marjorie Woodford 1936- *WhoAmW 91*

Hammond, Mary Elizabeth 1942- *WhoAmW 91*
Hammond, Michael Peter 1932- *WhoAm 90*
Hammond, Michael W. 1938- *St&PR 91*
Hammond, Natalie Hays 1904- *WhoAmA 91N*
Hammond, Nicholas *ConTFT 8*
Hammond, Ogden Haggerty 1869-1956 *BioIn 16*
Hammond, Patricia Flood 1948- *WhoAmW 91*
Hammond, Paul Young 1929- *WhoAm 90, WhoE 91*
Hammond, Phyllis Baker 1930- *WhoAmA 91*
Hammond, Phyllis Baker 1936- *WhoE 91*
Hammond, R. Philip 1916- *WhoAm 90*
Hammond, Ralph *AuBYP 90, BioIn 16*
Hammond, Ralph Charles 1916- *WhoSSW 91*
Hammond, Raymond William 1944- *WhoSSW 91*
Hammond, Red 1947- *WhoAmA 91*
Hammond, Rex D 1917- *BiDrAPA 89*
Hammond, Richard Howard 1948- *WhoSSW 91*
Hammond, Richard M. 1934- *St&PR 91*
Hammond, Richard P. 1820-1891 *AmLegL*
Hammond, Richard W. 1946- *St&PR 91*
Hammond, Robert Alexander, III 1930- *WhoAm 90*
Hammond, Robert Lee 1926- *WhoAm 90*
Hammond, Robert Tracy 1944- *St&PR 91*
Hammond, Roger Stuart 1942- *WhoSSW 91*
Hammond, Rose Marie 1949- *WhoAmW 91*
Hammond, Roy Joseph 1929- *St&PR 91, WhoAm 90*
Hammond, Ruth Elizabeth 1954- *WhoWrEP 89*
Hammond, S. Katharine 1949- *WhoE 91*
Hammond, Stuart Lindsley 1922- *St&PR 91*
Hammond, Teresa Lynn 1961- *WhoAmW 91*
Hammond, Thomas L. 1936- *St&PR 91*
Hammond, Thomas T. 1938- *St&PR 91*
Hammond, Timothy Scott 1963- *WhoSSW 91*
Hammond, William *WhoE 91*
Hammond, William Rogers 1920-1990 *WhoAm 90*
Hammond, William Thomas, Jr. 1945- *WhoEmL 91*
Hammond, Wilton N. 1927- *St&PR 91*
Hammond, Winifred 1899- *AuBYP 90*
Hammond-Chambers, Robert Alexander 1942- *St&PR 91*
Hammond Innes, Ralph *TwCCr&M 91*
Hammond-Innes, Ralph 1913- *AuBYP 90, BioIn 16, WhoWor 91*
Hammond-Kominsky, Cynthia Cecelia 1957- *WhoAmW 91*
Hammond-Stroud, Derek 1926- *IntWWM 90, WhoWor 91*
Hammond-Stroud, Derek 1929- *PenDiMP*
Hammonds, George Hamilton 1930- *St&PR 91, WhoAm 90*
Hammonds, Timothy Merrill 1944- *WhoWor 91*
Hammons, Allen James, Jr. 1958- *WhoEmL 91*
Hammons, Brian Kent 1958- *St&PR 91, WhoEmL 91*
Hammons, David *BioIn 16*
Hammons, James Hutchinson 1934- *WhoAm 90*
Hammons, Kenneth Russell 1945- *WhoSSW 91*
Hammons, Stanley *BiDrAPA 89*
Hammontree, R. James 1933- *St&PR 91*
Hammurabi *EncO&P 3*
Hammurabi 1792?BC-1750BC *WorAlBi*
Hamner, Carol 1942- *WhoAmW 91*
Hamner, Granny 1927- *Ballpl 90*
Hamner, Homer Howell 1915- *WhoAm 90, WhoWor 91*
Hamner, Mark Benjamin *BiDrAPA 89*
Hamner, Patrick F. 1955- *St&PR 91*
Hamner, Ralph 1916- *Ballpl 90*
Hamner, Sharon Boone 1939- *WhoSSW 91*
Hamner, Suzanne Leath 1940- *WhoAmW 91*
Hamner, W. Easley 1937- *St&PR 91*
Hamnet, Nina 1890-1956 *FemiCLE*
Hamnett, Nina 1890-1956 *BiDWomA*
Hamod, Sam 1936- *WhoWrEP 89*
Hamolsky, Milton William 1921- *WhoAm 90*
Hamon, Louis 1866-1936 *EncO&P 3*
Hamon, Richard Grady 1937- *WhoAm 90*
Hamor, Tibor 1910- *St&PR 91*
Hamori, Jozsef *WhoWor 91*
Hamori, Ruth E *BiDrAPA 89*
Hamovitch, William 1922- *WhoAm 90*
Hamowy, Albert 1923- *St&PR 91*
Hamp, Eric Pratt 1920- *WhoAm 90*
Hamparson, George Crosby 1924- *St&PR 91*
Hampe, Henry Theodore 1934- *St&PR 91*
Hampe, Michael 1935- *IntWWM 90*
Hampe, Warren W, Jr. *BiDrAPA 89*
Hampe Martinez, Teodoro 1960- *WhoWor 91*
Hampel, Alfred H. 1926- *St&PR 91*
Hampel, Alvin 1927- *WhoAm 90*
Hampel, Robert Edward 1941- *St&PR 91, WhoAm 90*
Hamper, Robert Joseph 1956- *WhoEmL 91, WhoWor 91*
Hampl, Patricia 1946- *WhoWrEP 89*
Hample, Stephen R. 1947- *WhoEmL 91*
Hampleman, Richard Allen 1946- *WhoEmL 91*
Hampshire, Alan Curtis *BiDrAPA 89*
Hampshire, John K 1914- *BiDrAPA 89*
Hampshire, Susan 1938- *WorAlBi*
Hampshire, Susan 1942- *ConAu 129, WhoAm 90, WhoWor 91*
Hampson, Ferdinand Charles 1947- *WhoAmA 91*
Hampson, Frank 1918-1985 *DcNaB 1981*
Hampson, Joan G 1922- *BiDrAPA 89*
Hampson, John L 1922- *BiDrAPA 89*
Hampson, Mary Joan 1947- *WhoE 91*
Hampson, Richard Kenneth 1942- *St&PR 91*
Hampson, Sherbie Rose Jared 1957- *IntWWM 90*
Hampson, Thomas *BioIn 16*
Hampson, Thomas 1955- *IntWWM 90*
Hampson, Thomas Lee 1948- *WhoE 91*
Hampson, William 1854-1926 *BioIn 16*
Hampsten, Andy *BioIn 16*
Hampton Institute Singers *DcAfAmP*
Hampton, Ambrose Gonzales, Jr 1926- *WhoAmA 91*
Hampton, Archibald S *BiDrAPA 89*
Hampton, Barbara Elaine 1961- *WhoSSW 91*
Hampton, Benjamin Bertram 1925- *WhoAm 90*
Hampton, Bill 1925-1977 *WhoAmA 91N*
Hampton, Calvin J. 1950- *WhoEmL 91*
Hampton, Carol McDonald 1935- *WhoAmW 91*
Hampton, Christopher 1946- *MajTwCW, WorAu 1980 [port]*
Hampton, Christopher James 1946- *WhoWor 91*
Hampton, Clark W. 1934- *St&PR 91*
Hampton, Colin *PenDiMP*
Hampton, D.J. 1945- *St&PR 91*
Hampton, Dan *BioIn 16*
Hampton, Daniel Oliver 1957- *WhoAm 90*
Hampton, Delon 1933- *WhoAm 90, WhoE 91*
Hampton, Derrinita La Shun 1964- *WhoSSW 91*
Hampton, Duane *BioIn 16*
Hampton, E. Lynn 1947- *WhoAm 90, WhoEmL 91*
Hampton, Eddie, Jr. 1943- *WhoE 91*
Hampton, Edward John 1952- *WhoWor 91*
Hampton, Gena Faye 1959- *WhoSSW 91*
Hampton, George Patrick 1958- *WhoE 91, WhoEmL 91*
Hampton, Glen Richard 1948- *WhoWor 91*
Hampton, Gordon Francis 1912- *WhoAm 90*
Hampton, Grace 1937- *WhoAmA 91*
Hampton, Henry Eugene, Jr. 1940- *WhoAm 90*
Hampton, James 1909-1964 *MusmAFA*
Hampton, James R. 1924- *St&PR 91*
Hampton, Jean Elizabeth 1954- *WhoAmW 91*
Hampton, John Lewis 1935- *WhoAm 90*
Hampton, John N. 1944- *St&PR 91*
Hampton, John W 1918- *WhoAmA 91*
Hampton, Joseph L. 1949- *WhoSSW 91*
Hampton, Judi *ODwPR 91*
Hampton, Leroy 1927- *WhoAm 90*
Hampton, Lionel *BioIn 16*
Hampton, Lionel 1909- *OxCPMus*
Hampton, Lionel 1913- *DrBlPA 90, WorAlBi*
Hampton, Louis R. 1920- *St&PR 91*
Hampton, Lucile Paquin Smith 1904- *WhoAmW 91*
Hampton, Mabel *BioIn 16*
Hampton, Margaret Frances 1947- *St&PR 91*
Hampton, Margaret Josephine 1935- *WhoAmW 91*
Hampton, Maria Hopp 1949- *WhoAmW 91*
Hampton, Mark *BioIn 16*
Hampton, Mark Garrison 1923- *WhoAm 90*
Hampton, Michael Douglas 1954- *WhoSSW 91*
Hampton, Morgan C. 1938- *St&PR 91*
Hampton, Oscar P., III 1933- *St&PR 91*
Hampton, Philip McCune 1932- *St&PR 91, WhoAm 90*
Hampton, Phillip Jewel 1922- *WhoAmA 91*
Hampton, Phillip Michael 1932- *WhoAm 90*
Hampton, Ralph Clayton, Jr. 1934- *WhoAm 90*
Hampton, Raymond Oliver 1936- *St&PR 91*
Hampton, Rex H. 1918- *St&PR 91*
Hampton, Rex Herbert 1918- *WhoAm 90*
Hampton, Robert Edward 1922- *WhoAm 90*
Hampton, Robert Lester, III 1945- *BiDrAPA 89*
Hampton, Robert Norris 1927- *St&PR 91*
Hampton, Robert S. 1919- *St&PR 91*
Hampton, Robert Wayne 1953- *WhoEmL 91*
Hampton, Slide 1932- *BioIn 16*
Hampton, Susan 1949- *FemiCLE*
Hampton, Suzanne Harvey 1934- *WhoAmW 91*
Hampton, Thomas Edward 1943- *WhoSSW 91*
Hampton, Trevor Allan *WhoAm 90*
Hampton, Verne C., II 1934- *St&PR 91*
Hampton, Verne Churchill, II 1934- *WhoAm 90*
Hampton, Wade 1818-1902 *BioIn 16, WorAlBi*
Hampton, William Christopher 1954- *WhoEmL 91*
Hampton, William H 1925- *BiDrAPA 89*
Hampton, William J. *ODwPR 91*
Hampton, William J. *BioIn 16*
Hampton-Kauffman, Margaret Frances 1947- *WhoAmW 91*
Hamra, Badri Joseph *BiDrAPA 89*
Hamrell, Sven Bertil 1928- *WhoWor 91*
Hamren, Nancy Van Brasch 1947- *WhoEmL 91*
Hamri, Thorsteinn fra *DcScanL*
Hamric, Frederick Leonidas 1923- *WhoAm 90*
Hamrick, Allen Willard *BiDrAPA 89*
Hamrick, C. Page 1944- *WhoSSW 91*
Hamrick, C. Rush, Jr. 1921- *St&PR 91*
Hamrick, C. Wake 1941- *St&PR 91*
Hamrick, Cindy Rector 1954- *WhoEmL 91*
Hamrick, David Oliver 1924- *St&PR 91*
Hamrick, Gordon Grice 1930- *St&PR 91*
Hamrick, J.M. 1939- *St&PR 91*
Hamrick, John M. 1913- *St&PR 91*
Hamrick, Joseph Eugene, Jr. 1954- *WhoEmL 91*
Hamrick, Joseph Thomas 1921- *WhoSSW 91*
Hamrick, Joseph Thomas, Jr. 1960- *WhoEmL 91*
Hamrick, Karen Susan 1955- *WhoEmL 91*
Hamrick, Kenneth Edison 1923- *WhoAm 90*
Hamrick, Richard Minor, III 1956- *WhoSSW 91*
Hamrick, Samuel J 1929- *SpyFic*
Hamrick, Vaughn Martin 1960- *WhoEmL 91*
Hamrouche, Mouloud *WhoWor 91*
Hamsa, Bobbie 1944- *BioIn 16*
Hamstra, Sietse 1934- *WhoWor 91*
Hamsun, Knut *MajTwCW*
Hamsun, Knut 1859-1952 *DcScanL, WorAlBi*
Hamsun, Marie 1881-1969 *EncCoWW*
Hamsund, Knut Pedersen *MajTwCW*
Hamvas, Lewis 1919- *IntWWM 90*
Hamway, Edward George, Jr. 1942- *St&PR 91*
Hamway, Michael C. 1946- *St&PR 91*
Hamwi, Richard Alexander 1947- *WhoAmA 91*
Hamzaee, Reza Gholi 1951- *WhoEmL 91, WhoWor 91*
Hamzaoui, Abdelaziz 1935- *WhoAm 90, WhoWor 91*
Han *PenDiDA 89*
Han Leran 1898-1947 *BioIn 16*
Han Meilin *BioIn 16*
Han Suyin 1917- *FemiCLE*
Han, Ba *BiDrAPA 89*
Han, Chien-Pai 1936- *WhoAm 90*
Han, Edward Soobong 1942- *BiDrAPA 89*
Han, Francoise 1928- *EncCoWW*
Han, Ittah 1939- *WhoWor 91*
Han, Jaok 1930- *WhoAm 90*
Han, Ki Soo *BiDrAPA 89*
Han, Lit S. 1925- *WhoAm 90*
Han, Moo-Young 1934- *WhoAm 90*
Han, Peter *BioIn 16*
Han, Qi Zhi 1932- *WhoWor 91*
Han, Sangwoon *BiDrAPA 89*
Han, Soo Woong *BiDrAPA 89*
Han, Thwan Ham *BiDrAPA 89*
Han, Weimin 1963- *WhoE 91*
Han, Young Jo 1956- *WhoSSW 91*
Hanache, Jeanne Anne 1937- *BiDrAPA 89*
Hanae Mori *EncJap*
Hanafi, Moustafa Ahmed 1935- *WhoWor 91*
Hanafin, Bernard M. 1954- *St&PR 91*
Hanafin, Marcella Griffin *St&PR 91*
Hanafusa, Hidesaburo 1929- *WhoAm 90*
Hanagan, Eva 1923- *FemiCLE*
Hanahan, Donald James 1919- *WhoAm 90*
Hanahan, James Lake 1932- *WhoSSW 91*
Hanak-Hall, Elaine Cheryl 1945- *WhoAmW 91*
Hanamirian, Varujan 1952- *WhoEmL 91, WhoWor 91*
Hanan, Jane McKahen 1957- *WhoEmL 91*
Hanan, Patrick Dewes 1927- *WhoAm 90*
Hanani, Yehuda 1943- *IntWWM 90*
Hanappi, Gerhard 1951- *WhoWor 91*
Hanas, Sven Ragnar 1951- *WhoWor 91*
Hanau, Kenneth John, Jr. 1927- *WhoAm 90*
Hanau, Peter Wolfgang 1935- *WhoWor 91*
Hanauer, Joe Franklin 1937- *WhoAm 90*
Hanawalt, Philip Courtland 1931- *WhoAm 90*
Hanaway, Donald John 1933- *WhoAm 90*
Hanback, Christopher Brecht 1950- *St&PR 91*
Hanback, Hazel Marie Smallwood 1918- *WhoAmW 91*
Hanbidge, R. Walter D. 1925- *St&PR 91*
Hanbury, George Lafayette, II 1943- *WhoAm 90*
Hanby, Robert M. Butch 1940- *St&PR 91*
Hanby, Walter Dana 1944- *WhoSSW 91*
Hance, James H., Jr. 1944- *St&PR 91*
Hance, Laconla Hinson 1923- *WhoAm 90*
Hance, Margaret T. *BioIn 16, NewYTBS 90*
Hance, William Adams 1916- *WhoAm 90*
Hancey, James Orlo 1948- *BiDrAPA 89*
Hanchey, Janet Lynn 1956- *WhoAmA 91*
Hanchuk, Hilary Theodore *BiDrAPA 89*
Hanckel, Allan Robertson 1930- *WhoSSW 91*
Hancock *WhNaAH*
Hancock, Alexander DiGiulio 1952- *WhoWrEP 89*
Hancock, Allyson Butler 1966- *WhoSSW 91*
Hancock, Arthur Boyd 1910-1972 *BioIn 16*
Hancock, Arthur Boyd, III *BioIn 16*
Hancock, Arthur Stewart 1926- *St&PR 91*
Hancock, Benjamin Wesley 1928- *St&PR 91*
Hancock, Brent H. 1942- *St&PR 91*
Hancock, Bull 1910-1972 *BioIn 16*
Hancock, Butch *WhoNeCM [port]*
Hancock, Carol Brooks 1941- *St&PR 91*
Hancock, Charles Cavanaugh, Jr. 1935- *WhoAm 90*
Hancock, Charles E. 1874- *BioIn 16*
Hancock, Charles Wilbourne 1924- *WhoAm 90*
Hancock, Clenric Guy 1948- *WhoSSW 91*
Hancock, Cynthia Chapman 1936- *WhoAmW 91, WhoSSW 91*
Hancock, Dain Michael 1941- *St&PR 91*
Hancock, Daryl Delano, Jr. 1961- *WhoSSW 91*
Hancock, Diana Ison 1937- *WhoAm 90*
Hancock, Don *St&PR 91*
Hancock, Ellen M. *BioIn 16*
Hancock, Ellen M. 1943- *St&PR 91*
Hancock, Ellen Marie 1943- *WhoAm 90, WhoAmW 91*
Hancock, Emily Stone 1945- *WhoAmW 91*
Hancock, Ernest William 1927- *WhoAm 90*
Hancock, Garry 1954- *Ballpl 90*
Hancock, Geoffrey White 1946- *WhoAm 90*
Hancock, George Louis, Jr. 1953- *WhoEmL 91*
Hancock, Gerre Edward 1934- *IntWWM 90, WhoAm 90*
Hancock, Herbert Jeffrey 1940- *WhoAm 90*
Hancock, Herbie 1940- *BioIn 16, ConTFT 8 [port], DrBlPA 90, EncPR&S 89, OxCPMus, WorAlBi*
Hancock, Ian Francis 1942- *WhoAm 90*
Hancock, Jack L. 1930- *WhoAm 90*
Hancock, James C, Jr. 1931- *BiDrAPA 89*
Hancock, John 1737-1793 *BiDrUSE 89, BioIn 16, EncCRAm [port], WorAlBi*
Hancock, John Allan 1940- *WhoAm 90*
Hancock, John Coulter 1929- *St&PR 91, WhoAm 90*
Hancock, John D. 1939- *WhoAm 90*
Hancock, John Shonk 1914- *WhoAm 90*
Hancock, John W. 1937- *St&PR 91*
Hancock, John Walker, III 1937- *WhoAm 90*
Hancock, Joseph *PenDiDA 89*
Hancock, Judith Duffield Eckerman 1934- *IntWWM 90*
Hancock, Kathleen Marie 1962- *WhoAmW 91*

Hancock, Keith 1898-1988 *AnObit 1988*
Hancock, Langley George 1909- *WhoWor 91*
Hancock, Loni 1940- *WhoAmW 91*
Hancock, Marion Donald 1939- *WhoAm 90*
Hancock, Mary Louise *BioIn 16*
Hancock, Mel 1929- *WhoAm 90*
Hancock, Melton D. 1929- *BioIn 16*
Hancock, Monte Floyd, Jr. 1953- *WhoSSW 91*
Hancock, Paul 1952- *IntWWM 90*
Hancock, Paul Byron 1951- *WhoSSW 91*
Hancock, Peter Adrian 1953- *WhoEmL 91*
Hancock, Priscilla Tedesco 1938- *WhoAmW 91*
Hancock, Robert 1730-1817 *PenDiDA 89*
Hancock, S. Dale 1952- *WhoEmL 91*
Hancock, S. Lee 1955- *WhoWor 91*
Hancock, Sandra Olivia 1947- *WhoAmW 91*
Hancock, Seth *BioIn 16*
Hancock, Sheila 1933- *BioIn 16*
Hancock, Stewart F. 1950- *St&PR 91*
Hancock, Thomas 1913- *WhoAm 90*
Hancock, Virgil Iverson, III *BiDrAPA 89*
Hancock, Walker 1901- *BioIn 16, WhoAmA 91*
Hancock, Walker Kirtland 1901- *WhoAm 90*
Hancock, Wayne Mitchell 1931- *St&PR 91*
Hancock, William 1794- *PenDiDA 89*
Hancock, William Frank, Jr. 1942- *WhoWor 91*
Hancock, William Glenn 1950- *St&PR 91, WhoAm 90*
Hancock, William Henry, Jr. 1942- *St&PR 91*
Hancock, Winfield Scott 1824-1886 *BioIn 16, WhNaAH, WorAlBi*
Hancox, Ralph 1929- *St&PR 91, WhoAm 90*
Hancox, Robert Ernest 1943- *WhoAm 90, WhoE 91, WhoWor 91*
Hancox, Susan Caroline 1950- *WhoAmW 91*
Hancq, Paul David 1957- *WhoEmL 91*
Hand, Bethlyn Jean *St&PR 91*
Hand, Brian Edward 1963- *WhoE 91, WhoWor 91*
Hand, Bruce Eugene 1934- *BiDrAPA 89*
Hand, Cadet Hammond, Jr. 1920- *WhoAm 90*
Hand, Charles T. 1928- *St&PR 91*
Hand, Colin 1929- *IntWWM 90*
Hand, Colton *BiDrAPA 89*
Hand, Donald Edmund 1925- *St&PR 91*
Hand, Elbert O. 1939- *WhoAm 90*
Hand, George H. 1837-1891 *AmLegL*
Hand, Herbert Hensley 1931- *WhoSSW 91, WhoWor 91*
Hand, John 1926- *WhoAm 90*
Hand, John Oliver 1941- *WhoAm 90, WhoAmA 91*
Hand, Judson *BioIn 16*
Hand, Kathleen Margaret 1947- *WhoAmW 91*
Hand, Kerry Wayne 1952- *St&PR 91*
Hand, Lawrence L. *BioIn 16*
Hand, Lloyd W. *ODwPR 91*
Hand, Marcus Vernon 1937- *WhoSSW 91*
Hand, Molly Williams 1892-1951 *WhoAmA 91N*
Hand, Paul Edgar 1931- *WhoE 91*
Hand, Peter James 1937- *WhoAm 90*
Hand, Rich 1948- *Ballpl 90*
Hand, Robert Frank 1939- *St&PR 91*
Hand, Robert G. *BioIn 16*
Hand, Roger 1938- *WhoAm 90*
Hand, Sallie Catherine 1964- *WhoAmW 91*
Hand, Sally Carolyn 1959- *WhoAmW 91*
Hand, Samuel Patton *BiDrAPA 89*
Hand, Scott M. 1942- *St&PR 91*
Hand, Scott McKee 1942- *WhoAm 90*
Hand, Susan *WhoWrEP 89*
Hand, Thomas Millet 1930- *WhoE 91*
Hand, Wayland Debs 1907-1986 *BioIn 16*
Hand, William Brevard 1924- *WhoAm 90, WhoSSW 91*
Handahl, Donald H. 1924- *St&PR 91*
Handal, Paul Oscar 1961- *WhoWor 91*
Handberg, Irene Deak *WhoAm 90, WhoAmW 91*
Handberg, Ronald 1938- *St&PR 91*
Handel, Bernard 1926- *WhoE 91*
Handel, David Jonathan 1946- *WhoAm 90*
Handel, George 1685-1759 *WorAlBi*
Handel, George Frideric 1685-1759 *BioIn 16, PenDiMP A*
Handel, Luis *BiDrAPA 89*
Handel, Maximo *BiDrAPA 89*
Handel, Michael I. 1942- *ConAu 131*
Handel, Morton E. 1935- *St&PR 91*
Handel, Morton Emanuel 1935- *WhoAm 90*
Handel, Nancy H. 1951- *St&PR 91*
Handel, Peter H. 1937- *WhoAm 90*
Handel, Philip J. *PenDiDA 89*
Handel-Mazzetti, Enrica von 1871-1955 *EncCoWW*
Handell, Albert George 1937- *WhoAmA 91*
Handelman, Alice Roberta 1943- *WhoAmW 91*
Handelman, Benjamin 1924- *St&PR 91*
Handelman, David E. 1950- *WhoAm 90*
Handelman, David Y. 1938- *St&PR 91*
Handelman, Karen 1954- *WhoAmW 91*
Handelman, Lester J. 1911- *St&PR 91*
Handelman, Neil J. 1935- *St&PR 91*
Handelman, Stephen 1947- *WhoWor 91*
Handelman, William Alan 1948- *WhoE 91*
Handelsman, Harold S. 1946- *WhoAm 90*
Handelsman, Harold Samuel 1946- *St&PR 91*
Handelsman, Lawrence Marc 1945- *WhoEmL 91*
Handelsman, Leonard 1946- *BiDrAPA 89*
Handelsman, M. Gene 1923- *WhoAm 90*
Hander, O. Benjamin 1918- *WhoAm 90*
Handford, H Allen 1930- *BiDrAPA 89*
Handford, Martin 1956- *ChILR 22 [port], SmATA 64 [port]*
Handforth, Thomas S 1897-1948 *WhoAmA 91N*
Handforth, Thomas Schofield 1897-1948 *AuBYP 90*
Handin, Irving L *BiDrAPA 89*
Handin, John Walter 1919- *WhoAm 90*
Handke, Peter 1942- *ConAu 33NR, MajTwCW*
Handl, Irene 1901-1987 *FemiCLE*
Handl, Max *PenDiMP*
Handlan, Allen Layman 1947- *WhoEmL 91*
Handlan, John B., II 1928- *St&PR 91, WhoAm 90*
Handleman, David 1915- *St&PR 91*
Handleman, Marshall J *BiDrAPA 89*
Handler, Adam Michael 1959- *WhoEmL 91*
Handler, Alan B. 1931- *WhoE 91*
Handler, Arlene Frances 1943- *WhoAmW 91*
Handler, Audrey 1934- *WhoAmA 91*
Handler, Barbara Hershey 1939- *WhoAmW 91*
Handler, Diane Helen 1942- *WhoE 91*
Handler, Douglas Perry 1957- *WhoE 91*
Handler, Elisabeth *ODwPR 91*
Handler, Elisabeth Helen 1944- *WhoAmW 91*
Handler, Elliot 1916- *ConAmBL*
Handler, Evelyn Erika 1933- *WhoAm 90, WhoAmW 91, WhoE 91, WhoWor 91*
Handler, Harold Robert 1935- *WhoAm 90*
Handler, Ira Scott *BiDrAPA 89*
Handler, Jerome Sidney 1933- *WhoAm 90*
Handler, Ken *BioIn 16*
Handler, Lawrence David 1945- *WhoAm 90*
Handler, Mark S. 1933- *St&PR 91, WhoAm 90, WhoE 91*
Handler, Milton 1903- *WhoAm 90*
Handler, Milton E. 1926- *St&PR 91*
Handler, Mimi 1934- *WhoAm 90*
Handler, Robert Isaac 1952- *BiDrAPA 89*
Handler, Ruby Ann *WhoAmW 91*
Handler, Ruth 1916- *ConAmBL*
Handler, Sidney 1932- *WhoE 91*
Handler, Thomas John 1956- *WhoEmL 91*
Handler, Wendy 1963- *ODwPR 91*
Handlery, Paul R. 1920- *St&PR 91*
Handlery, Paul Robert 1920- *WhoAm 90*
Handley, Alan *BioIn 16, NewYTBS 90*
Handley, Anthony James 1942- *WhoWor 91*
Handley, Eric Walter 1926- *WhoWor 91*
Handley, Jean M. 1926- *WhoAmW 91*
Handley, Lee 1913-1970 *Ballpl 90*
Handley, Leon Hunter 1927- *WhoAm 90, WhoSSW 91, WhoWor 91*
Handley, Margie Lee 1939- *WhoAmW 91*
Handley, Roger Patrick 1945- *WhoAm 90*
Handley, Vernon 1930- *PenDiMP*
Handley, Vernon George 1930- *IntWWM 90*
Handlin, Joseph Jason 1952- *WhoEmL 91*
Handlin, Oscar 1915- *WhoAm 90, WorAlBi*
Handlir, David Y. 1947- *St&PR 91*
Handly, Earl John 1922- *St&PR 91*
Handmaker, Stuart Allen 1930- *St&PR 91*
Handman, Louis A. 1894-1956 *BioIn 16*
Handren, Maura *BioIn 16*
Handrup, Theodore B, Jr. *BiDrAPA 89*
Hands, Bill 1940- *Ballpl 90*
Hands, Elizabeth *FemiCLE*
Hands, Steven Michael 1959- *WhoEmL 91*
Hands, Terence David 1941- *WhoWor 91*
Hands, William Arthur 1917- *WhoAm 90*
Handsaker, Morrison 1907- *WhoAm 90*
Handschin, Edmund Johannes 1941- *WhoWor 91*
Handschumacher, Albert G. 1918- *St&PR 91*
Handschumacher, Albert Gustave 1918- *WhoAm 90, WhoWor 91*
Handscomb, Charles Wesley 1867-1906 *OxCCanT*
Handsome Lake 1735?-1815 *WhNaAH*
Handspicker, Brian DeWitt 1957- *WhoE 91*
Handt, Herbert 1926- *IntWWM 90*
Handville, Robert T 1924- *WhoAmA 91*
Handville, Robert Tompkins 1924- *WhoAm 90*
Handwerger, Ellen 1947- *WhoEmL 91*
Handwerker, A. M. 1928- *WhoWor 91*
Handwerker, Earl Howard 1946- *WhoSSW 91*
Handwerker, Kevin 1956- *WhoEmL 91*
Handwerker, Murray 1921- *St&PR 91*
Handwerker, Sy 1933- *ODwPR 91*
Handy, Alice Warner 1948- *WhoAm 90, WhoAmW 91, WhoSSW 91*
Handy, Catherine Marie 1932- *WhoAmW 91*
Handy, Charles Brooks 1924- *WhoAm 90*
Handy, Charlotte C. *BioIn 16*
Handy, David G. 1939- *WhoAm 90*
Handy, Drucilla 1924- *ODwPR 91*
Handy, Edward O., Jr. 1929- *St&PR 91, WhoAm 90*
Handy, John *BioIn 16*
Handy, Lyman Lee 1919- *WhoAm 90*
Handy, Mary Nixeon Civille 1909- *WhoWrEP 89*
Handy, Paul Brooks 1958- *WhoEmL 91*
Handy, Randall Crieghton, Jr. 1943- *WhoE 91*
Handy, Richard Lincoln 1929- *WhoAm 90*
Handy, Richard Y. *BioIn 16*
Handy, Robert Maxwell 1931- *WhoAm 90*
Handy, Robert Truman 1941- *WhoSSW 91*
Handy, Rollo Leroy 1927- *WhoAm 90, WhoE 91, WhoWor 91*
Handy, W C 1873-1958 *DrBlPA 90*
Handy, W. C. 1873-1958 *OxCPMus, WorAlBi*
Handy, William Henry 1927- *St&PR 91*
Handy, William Russell 1950- *WhoEmL 91*
Handy, William Talbot, Jr. 1924- *WhoAm 90*
Handzel, Henry James, Jr. 1947- *WhoEmL 91*
Hane, Antonio C.P. 1939- *St&PR 91*
Hane, Mikiso 1922- *WhoAm 90*
Haneborg, Linda C *WhoAmW 91*
Hanek, Donald John 1957- *WhoEmL 91*
Hanek, Patricia Ann 1951- *WhoAmW 91*
Hanel, Lewis Sterling 1916- *St&PR 91*
Haneline, Richard L. 1944- *St&PR 91*
Haneman, Dan *WhoWor 91*
Hanemann, Ardley R., Jr. 1943- *ODwPR 91*
Hanemann, James, Jr. 1935- *WhoWor 91*
Hanen, Marsha *WhoAm 90*
Hanen, Samuel R. 1839- *AmLegL*
Hanenkrat, Frank Thomas 1939- *WhoSSW 91*
Hanes, Andrew Guy 1929- *St&PR 91*
Hanes, Constance Margo *BiDrAPA 89*
Hanes, Darlene Marie 1956- *WhoAmW 91*
Hanes, David Gordon 1941-1991 *WhoAm 90*
Hanes, DeWitt Chatham *BioIn 16*
Hanes, Donald Keith 1933- *St&PR 91, WhoE 91*
Hanes, Elson C. 1924- *St&PR 91*
Hanes, Frank Borden 1920- *WhoAm 90, WhoWrEP 89*
Hanes, Hugh D. 1935- *St&PR 91*
Hanes, James 1924- *WhoAmA 91*
Hanes, James Albert 1924- *WhoE 91*
Hanes, James Henry 1922- *WhoAm 90*
Hanes, John Grier 1936- *St&PR 91*
Hanes, Lee D 1927- *BiDrAPA 89*
Hanes, Patrick Dennis 1949- *WhoEmL 91*
Hanes, Ralph Philip, Jr. 1926- *St&PR 91, WhoAm 90*
Hanes, Robert G. 1936- *St&PR 91*
Hanes-Jenkins, Debra Lee Blaylock 1947- *WhoEmL 91*
Hanesian, Deran 1927- *WhoAm 90*
Hanesworth, Daniel J. 1944- *St&PR 91*
Hanex, Taylor Anne 1953- *WhoAmW 91*
Haney, Carol 1924-1964 *WorAlBi*
Haney, Charles Earl 1919- *St&PR 91*
Haney, David P. 1938- *WhoWrEP 89*
Haney, Erene Cheki *AuBYP 90*
Haney, Fred 1898-1977 *Ballpl 90*
Haney, Helen Marie E. 1959- *WhoEmL 91*
Haney, Hoyt A. 1933- *St&PR 91*
Haney, J. Terrence 1933- *WhoAm 90*
Haney, John Benjamin 1931- *WhoE 91*
Haney, John F B 1938- *BiDrAPA 89*
Haney, John Frederick Brown 1938- *WhoE 91*
Haney, Joseph Donald 1936- *St&PR 91*
Haney, Julia Jamison 1942- *WhoSSW 91*
Haney, Larry 1942- *Ballpl 90*
Haney, Lucie Renee *BiDrAPA 89*
Haney, Marcella Helen 1922- *WhoAmW 91*
Haney, Paul Dunlap 1911- *WhoAm 90*
Haney, R. Lee 1939- *St&PR 91*
Haney, Robert Elmer 1932- *St&PR 91*
Haney, Robert Joseph 1946- *WhoE 91*
Haney, Roger A. 1938- *St&PR 91*
Haney, Sharon 1950- *WhoWrEP 89*
Haney, Steven Thomas 1951- *BiDrAPA 89*
Haney, Sue Ellen 1945- *WhoAmW 91*
Haney, William J. 1907- *St&PR 91*
Haney, William Keith *BiDrAPA 89*
Haney, William V. *ODwPR 91*
Haney, William V. 1936- *St&PR 91*
Hanff, Helene 1916- *WhoWrEP 89*
Hanfield, Genevieve R. *BioIn 16*
Hanfling, Robert Irwin 1938- *WhoAm 90*
Hanfmann, George M A 1911-1986 *WhoAmA 91N*
Hanford, Agnes Rutledge 1927- *WhoSSW 91*
Hanford, Aubrey L., III 1939- *St&PR 91*
Hanford, Craig Bradley 1953- *WhoE 91*
Hanford, George Hyde 1920- *WhoAm 90, WhoE 91*
Hanford, Grail Stevenson 1932- *WhoSSW 91*
Hanford, Timothy Lloyd 1955- *WhoEmL 91*
Hanft, Ruth S. Samuels 1929- *WhoAm 90, WhoAmW 91*
Hanga, Fred, Jr. 1931- *WhoAm 90*
Hange, Donald Wayne, Jr. 1959- *WhoEmL 91*
Hangen, Bruce 1947- *IntWWM 90*
Hanger, Clifford *WhoWrEP 89*
Hanger, James Marshall 1833-1912 *AmLegL*
Hanger, Robert Edwin 1934- *WhoSSW 91*
Hanger, Wallace Carlton, Jr. 1955- *WhoE 91*
Hangin, John Gombojab 1921-1989 *BioIn 16*
Hangley, William Thomas 1941- *WhoE 91, WhoWor 91*
Hangstefer, James B. 1927- *St&PR 91*
Hanhart, Jan 1931- *WhoWor 91*
Hani, Antoine G 1925- *BiDrAPA 89*
Hani, Martin Thembisile *BioIn 16*
Hanick, Jack M. 1950- *WhoEmL 91*
Hanify, Edward B. 1912- *St&PR 91*
Hanig, Lynn 1946- *WhoEmL 91*
Hanigan, Lawrence 1925- *WhoAm 90*
Hanigan, Marvin Frank 1931- *St&PR 91*
Hanigan, Thomas E. 1922- *St&PR 91*
Hanigan, Thomas Edward, Jr. 1922- *WhoAm 90*
Hanin, Edward 1932- *BiDrAPA 89, WhoE 91*
Hanin, Israel 1937- *WhoAm 90*
Hanin, Leda Toni 1940- *WhoAmW 91*
Haning, Charles Robert 1934- *St&PR 91*
Haninger, Elsie Blalock 1934- *WhoAmW 91*
Hanington, Paula Kay 1956- *WhoAmW 91*
Hank, Bernard J., Jr. 1929- *St&PR 91*
Hanke, Byron Reidt 1911- *WhoAm 90*
Hanke, Dode M *BiDrAPA 89*
Hanke, Douglas Pierson 1948- *WhoEmL 91*
Hanke, Karl William, III 1958- *WhoEmL 91*
Hanke, Lewis *BioIn 16*
Hanke, Lewis Ulysses 1905- *WhoAm 90*
Hanke, Maria Ecaterina 1952- *IntWWM 90*
Hanke, Nancy *BiDrAPA 89*
Hanke, Wilfried 1927- *WhoWor 91*
Hanken, James Carl 1939- *WhoAm 90*
Hanken, Shannon D. 1961- *WhoEmL 91*
Hankenson, Edward Craig, Jr. 1935- *WhoAm 90*
Hankerson, Joseph Lester *BioIn 16*
Hanket, Mark J. 1943- *St&PR 91*
Hankey, Muriel 1895-1978 *EncPaPR 91*
Hankey, Muriel W Arnold 1895-1978 *EncO&P 3*
Hankey, Paul V. 1931- *St&PR 91*
Hankey, Robert E 1931- *WhoAmA 91*
Hankin, Bernard Jacob 1913- *WhoAm 90*
Hankin, C A 1937- *ConAu 131*
Hankin, Elaine Krieger 1938- *WhoAmW 91*
Hankin, Errol Patrick 1942- *WhoAm 90*
Hankin, Irving E. *BioIn 16*
Hankin, Jerry Dean 1956- *WhoEmL 91*
Hankin, Joseph Nathan 1940- *WhoAm 90*
Hankin, Leonard J. 1917- *WhoAm 90*
Hankin, Noel N. *ODwPR 91*
Hankin, Noel N. 1946- *WhoEmL 91*
Hankin, William H 1946- *BiDrAPA 89*
Hankin, William Henry 1946- *WhoE 91*
Hankins, Alton Benton, Jr. *BiDrAPA 89*
Hankins, E. Candice 1966- *WhoAmW 91*
Hankins, Gale William 1955- *WhoEmL 91*
Hankins, Gary Colfax 1941- *BiDrAPA 89*
Hankins, George B. 1927- *St&PR 91*
Hankins, Hugh Walter 1933- *St&PR 91*
Hankins, Melissa M *BiDrAPA 89*

Hankins, Mitchell Dale 1957- WhoEmL 91
Hankins, Priscilla B BiDrAPA 89
Hankins, Roy Dewayne BiDrAPA 89
Hankins, Shirley 1931- WhoAmW 91
Hankins, Timothy Howard 1956- WhoEmL 91
Hankinson, Alan 1926- ConAu 130
Hankinson, James F. 1943- WhoAm 90
Hankinson, Michael 1946- IntWWM 90
Hankinson, Phyllis 1961- St&PR 91
Hankinson, Risdon William 1938- WhoSSW 91
Hankla, Cathryn 1958- WhoWrEP 89
Hankla, Cathy Anne 1958- WhoSSW 91
Hankoff, Leon D 1927- BiDrAPA 89
Hankoff, Leon Dudley 1927- WhoE 91
Hanks, Alan R. 1939- WhoAm 90
Hanks, David Allen 1940- WhoAmA 91
Hanks, Don B. 1937- St&PR 91
Hanks, Grace Mary 1954- WhoAmW 91
Hanks, James Judge, Jr. 1943- WhoAm 90
Hanks, John Donald 1920- St&PR 91
Hanks, Kenneth R. 1954- St&PR 91
Hanks, Marshall Bernard 1884-1948 BioIn 16
Hanks, Nancy 1927-1983 BioAmW, BioIn 16, NotWoAT, WhoAmA 91N
Hanks, Richard Duff 1960- WhoE 91
Hanks, Robert Jack 1923- WhoAm 90
Hanks, Stephen Grant 1950- WhoEmL 91
Hanks, Tom BioIn 16
Hanks, Tom 1956- WhoAm 90, WorAlBi
Hanks, William Bruce 1954- St&PR 91
Hanks, William Vilas 1929- St&PR 91
Hanle, Paul Arthur 1947- WhoAm 90
Hanle, William Scott 1948- St&PR 91
Hanlen, John 1922- WhoAmA 91
Hanlen, John Garrett 1922- WhoAm 90
Hanley, Anne BiDEWW
Hanley, Charles 1920- WhoAm 90
Hanley, Charles E. St&PR 91
Hanley, Daniel Thomas 1930- WhoE 91
Hanley, David Burris 1954- WhoEmL 91
Hanley, Edward John 1941- WhoAm 90
Hanley, Frank 1930- WhoAm 90
Hanley, Gerald Stephen 1943- WhoWor 91
Hanley, Jack 1952- WhoAmA 91
Hanley, James 1901-1985 MajTwCW
Hanley, James A. 1931- St&PR 91
Hanley, James Eugene 1946- WhoEmL 91
Hanley, James F. 1892-1942 OxCPMus
Hanley, James Frederick 1892-1942 BioIn 16
Hanley, John Gerald 1907- WhoAm 90
Hanley, Joseph A. 1922- St&PR 91
Hanley, Keith Graham 1954- WhoEmL 91
Hanley, Liam 1933- BioIn 16
Hanley, Mary Ann IntWWM 90
Hanley, Michael J. 1948- St&PR 91
Hanley, Michael Joseph 1940- WhoSSW 91
Hanley, Peter Christopher 1948- WhoSSW 91
Hanley, Peter R. 1939- St&PR 91
Hanley, Peter Ronald 1939- WhoAm 90
Hanley, Philip M. 1945- St&PR 91
Hanley, Priscilla E. St&PR 91
Hanley, Robert 1933- St&PR 91
Hanley, Robert Francis 1924- WhoAm 90
Hanley, Robert Lee, Jr. 1956- WhoEmL 91
Hanley, Rochelle Marie 1952- WhoEmL 91
Hanley, Susan K. 1948- ODwPR 91
Hanley, T Edward WhoAmA 91N
Hanley, Thomas BioIn 16
Hanley, Thomas Patrick 1951- WhoEmL 91
Hanley, Thomas Richard 1945- WhoAm 90, WhoSSW 91
Hanley, W. Lee, Jr. 1940- St&PR 91
Hanley, Wayne S. 1945- St&PR 91
Hanley, William J, Sr. BiDrAPA 89
Hanley, William T. 1947- St&PR 91
Hanley-Hackenbruck, Peggy BiDrAPA 89
Hanlin, Hugh Carey 1925- WhoAm 90, WhoSSW 91
Hanlin, R.L. 1932- St&PR 91
Hanlon, Betty Ellen 1935- WhoAmW 91
Hanlon, David Patrick 1944- WhoAm 90
Hanlon, Emily 1945- AuBYP 90, BioIn 16, WhoWrEP 89
Hanlon, Everett 1930- St&PR 91
Hanlon, James Allison 1937- St&PR 91, WhoAm 90
Hanlon, Janet Moore 1954- WhoEmL 91
Hanlon, John J. 1912-1988 BioIn 16
Hanlon, John L. 1935- St&PR 91
Hanlon, John William 1937- St&PR 91
Hanlon, Ned 1857-1937 Ballpl 90 [port]
Hanlon, Pamela 1946- ODwPR 91
Hanlon, Pamela Irene 1948- WhoAmW 91
Hanlon, Patricia Mary 1956- WhoSSW 91
Hanlon, Robert, Jr. 1946- WhoEmL 91
Hanlon, Robert J., Jr. 1946- St&PR 91
Hanlon, Robert Timothy 1937- WhoAm 90
Hanlon, Susan Deasy 1941- WhoAmW 91
Hanlon, Timothy Joseph, Jr. 1949- WhoEmL 91
Hanly, Brian Vaughan 1940- IntWWM 90
Hanman, Gary Edwin 1934- WhoAm 90
Hanmer, Davina ConAu 32NR
Hanmer, Rebecca W. 1941- WhoAmW 91
Hann, Barbara JoAnn 1946- WhoAmW 91
Hann, Elmer L. BioIn 16, NewYTBS 90
Hann, George Charles 1924- WhoAm 90
Hann, J. David 1931- St&PR 91
Hann, James David 1931- WhoAm 90
Hann, Marek J 1939- BiDrAPA 89
Hann, Morag 1939- ODwPR 91
Hann, Robert Kenneth 1945- St&PR 91
Hann, Roy William, Jr. 1934- WhoAm 90
Hanna, Archibald, Jr. 1916- WhoAm 90
Hanna, Betty Elliott 1921- WhoAmW 91
Hanna, Bill 1862-1930 Ballpl 90
Hanna, Daniel C. BioIn 16
Hanna, Dennis Donald 1955- WhoEmL 91
Hanna, Eduardo Zacarias 1941- WhoE 91
Hanna, Edward Aloysius 1958- WhoEmL 91
Hanna, Frank Joseph 1939- WhoSSW 91
Hanna, Geneva R. AuBYP 90
Hanna, Geoffrey Chalmers 1920- WhoAm 90
Hanna, George Verner, III 1943- WhoSSW 91
Hanna, Gordon 1920- WhoAm 90
Hanna, Harry Adolphus 1940- WhoAm 90
Hanna, Hoda Zaki 1949- BiDrAPA 89
Hanna, Irene Anneli 1959- BiDrAPA 89
Hanna, Jack BioIn 16
Hanna, Jack Bushnell 1947- WhoAm 90
Hanna, James W. AmLegL
Hanna, John A. 1942- St&PR 91, WhoAm 90
Hanna, Judith Lynne BioIn 16
Hanna, Katherine 1913-1988 WhoAmA 91N
Hanna, Katherine Merritt 1953- WhoEmL 91
Hanna, Louis Benjamin 1942- St&PR 91
Hanna, Lourdes A BiDrAPA 89
Hanna, Marcus S. 1837-1904 WorAlBi
Hanna, Martin Shad 1940- WhoAm 90
Hanna, Melvin Wesley 1932- WhoAm 90
Hanna, Michael George, Jr. 1936- WhoAm 90
Hanna, Michael Stephen 1939- WhoSSW 91
Hanna, Milad Mikhail 1940- BiDrAPA 89
Hanna, Nell 1908- BioIn 16
Hanna, Nessim 1938- WhoAm 90
Hanna, Nora Clare 1959- WhoAmW 91
Hanna, Paul Dean, Jr WhoAmA 91
Hanna, Paul Johnston 1915- St&PR 91
Hanna, Paul Robert 1902-1988 BioIn 16
Hanna, Peggy Ann 1931- WhoAmW 91
Hanna, Preston 1954- Ballpl 90
Hanna, Pricie 1948- St&PR 91
Hanna, Ralph, III 1942- WhoAm 90
Hanna, Richard W. 1930- St&PR 91
Hanna, Richard Whitman 1930- WhoE 91
Hanna, Robert Clyde 1928- St&PR 91
Hanna, Roberta Jones 1925- WhoAmW 91, WhoSSW 91
Hanna, Rose Elizabeth 1934- WhoAmW 91
Hanna, Ruth Ellen 1944- WhoSSW 91
Hanna, Stanley G 1934- BiDrAPA 89
Hanna, Thomas King WhoAmA 91N
Hanna, Thomas Louis WhoWrEP 89
Hanna, Thomas Louis 1928- WhoAm 90
Hanna, Warren L 1898- ConAu 130
Hanna, Wassfy M BiDrAPA 89
Hanna, William 1910- BioIn 16, ConTFT 8
Hanna, William Brian 1939- St&PR 91
Hanna, William Brooks 1936- WhoAm 90
Hanna, William Denby 1910- WhoAm 90
Hanna, William Johnson 1922- WhoAm 90
Hanna, William Royal 1950- WhoEmL 91
Hannafin, James D. 1946- St&PR 91
Hannafin, Laurence L. 1940- WhoE 91
Hannaford, D.C. 1930- St&PR 91
Hannaford, David Carlyle 1959- WhoEmL 91
Hannaford, Peter 1932- ConAu 130
Hannaford, Peter D. 1932- ODwPR 91
Hannaford, Peter Dor 1932- WhoAm 90
Hannah, Barry 1942- MajTwCW, WhoSSW 91, WorAu 1980 [port]
Hannah, Connie Jean 1950- WhoSSW 91
Hannah, Darryl 1961- WorAlBi
Hannah, Daryl BioIn 16
Hannah, Daryl 1961- CurBio 90 [port], WhoAm 90
Hannah, David H. 1951- St&PR 91
Hannah, Duncan 1952- WhoAmA 91
Hannah, Hamner, III 1939- WhoAm 90
Hannah, John Junior 1923- WhoAmA 91
Hannah, John Robert, Sr. 1939- WhoSSW 91, WhoWor 91
Hannah, Martin John 1926- St&PR 91
Hannah, Mary-Emily 1936- WhoAm 90, WhoE 91
Hannah, Mosie R. 1949- St&PR 91
Hannah, Norman Britton 1919- WhoAm 90
Hannah, Paul BiDrAPA 89
Hannah, Paul F. 1905- St&PR 91
Hannah, Ray Eugene 1936- St&PR 91
Hannah, Thomas 1831?- AmLegL
Hannah, Wayne Robertson, Jr. 1931- WhoAm 90
Hannallah, Raafat Samy 1944- WhoE 91
Hannam, Anne BioIn 16
Hannam, Charles 1925- BioIn 16
Hannan, Bradley 1935- WhoAmW 91
Hannan, Carol Elizabeth 1927- St&PR 91
Hannan, Cecil James 1925- WhoWor 91
Hannan, Diane 1950- ODwPR 91
Hannan, Edward Lees 1943- WhoWor 91
Hannan, J. R. 1937- ODwPR 91
Hannan, Jane Freeman 1954- WhoSSW 91
Hannan, Jim 1940- Ballpl 90
Hannan, John Thomas 1942- WhoE 91
Hannan, Joseph Edward, Jr. 1947- BiDrAPA 89
Hannan, Michael Francis 1949- IntWWM 90
Hannan, Myles 1936- St&PR 91
Hannan, Robert W. St&PR 91
Hannan, Robert William 1939- WhoAm 90
Hannawalt, Willis Dale 1928- WhoAm 90
Hannaway, Patricia Hinman 1929- WhoAmW 91
Hannay, Alastair 1932- ConAu 130
Hannay, Janneka 1933- WhoAmA 91
Hannay, Janneka Evans 1933- WhoE 91
Hannay, Margaret Patterson 1944- WhoWrEP 89
Hannay, Norman Bruce 1921- WhoAm 90
Hannay, Roger Durham 1930- IntWWM 90
Hanneborg, Knut 1929- WhoWor 91
Hannegan, Robert Emmet 1903-1949 BiDrUSE 89
Hanneken, John William 1949- WhoSSW 91
Hanneman, Elaine Esther 1928- WhoAmW 91
Hanneman, Rodney E. 1936- St&PR 91
Hanneman, Rodney Elton 1936- WhoAm 90
Hannen, Ada Lorelei 1942- WhoAmW 91
Hannen, John Edward 1937- WhoAm 90
Hanner, Dawna Melanson 1947- WhoAmW 91
Hanner, Emil Joseph 1929- St&PR 91
Hanners, David WhoSSW 91
Hannes Petursson DcScanL
Hannes Sigfusson DcScanL
Hannes, James A. 1943- St&PR 91
Hannes, Peter John 1942- St&PR 91
Hannesson, John D. 1952- St&PR 91
Hannesson, Paul Edward 1940- St&PR 91
Hanni, John W 1922- BiDrAPA 89
Hanni, R.B. 1928- St&PR 91
Hannibal 247BC-183BC WorAlBi
Hannibal, Edward L. 1936- WhoWrEP 89
Hannibal, Joseph Harry 1945- WhoAmA 91
Hannibalsson, Jon Baldvin 1939- WhoWor 91
Hannigan, Eugene Joseph 1939- WhoE 91
Hannigan, Frank 1931- WhoAm 90
Hannigan, Gregory Stewart 1950- St&PR 91
Hannigan, John David 1947- WhoE 91
Hannigan, John Joseph 1947- St&PR 91
Hannigan, Joseph Clyde 1945- WhoEmL 91
Hannigan, Jud BioIn 16
Hannigan, Richard James Patrick 1933- WhoAm 90
Hannigan, Vera Simmons 1932- WhoAm 90
Hannikainen, Ann-Elise 1946- IntWWM 90
Hannikainen, Pekka 1854-1924 PenDiMP
Hannikainen, Tauno 1896-1968 PenDiMP
Hanninen, Pentti Tapani 1930- WhoWor 91
Hanning, Gary William 1942- WhoSSW 91, WhoWor 91
Hannity, Vince 1944- ODwPR 91
Hannity, Vincent Thomas 1944- St&PR 91
Hannley, Patricia Jean 1950- St&PR 91
Hanno, Marshall 1945- St&PR 91
Hannock, Stephen BioIn 16
Hannon, Beverly A. 1932- WhoAmW 91
Hannon, Brian Owens 1959- WhoWrEP 89
Hannon, Bruce M. 1934- WhoAm 90
Hannon, Byron L. 1951- St&PR 91
Hannon, Daniel Leroy 1934- WhoSSW 91
Hannon, Debra Sue 1960- WhoE 91
Hannon, Donald F. 1927- St&PR 91
Hannon, Ezra MajTwCW
Hannon, F. Robert 1951- WhoEmL 91
Hannon, Farrell BioIn 16
Hannon, James E. 1949- St&PR 91
Hannon, James I 1935- BiDrAPA 89
Hannon, John Robert 1945- WhoE 91, WhoEmL 91
Hannon, John W. 1920- St&PR 91
Hannon, Kathy Maley 1954- St&PR 91
Hannon, Kitty Sue 1954- WhoAmW 91
Hannon, Michael 1947- WhoE 91
Hannon, Michael Stewart-Moore 1942- WhoWor 91
Hannon, Norman Leslie 1923- WhoWor 91
Hannon, Raymond 1935- ODwPR 91
Hannon, Raymond E. 1938- St&PR 91
Hannon, Thomas Michael 1939- WhoWrEP 89
Hannon, Timothy Patrick 1948- WhoEmL 91
Hannon, William Evans 1932- WhoSSW 91
Hannon, William M. WhoAm 90
Hannong, Charles-Francois 1669-1739 PenDiDA 89
Hannong, Joseph PenDiDA 89
Hannong, Paul-Antoine 1700-1760 PenDiDA 89
Hannong, Pierre-Antoine 1739-1794? PenDiDA 89
Hannsmann, Margarete 1921- EncCoWW
Hannum, John N BiDrAPA 89
Hannum, Richard Lee 1936- St&PR 91
Hannum, Sara AuBYP 90
Hannum, William Y C BiDrAPA 89
Hannum-Cox, Susan Michelle 1956- WhoWrEP 89
Hannum-McPherson, Melissa Ann 1946- WhoAm 90
Hano, Arnold 1922- AuBYP 90
Hano, Frank E. 1933- St&PR 91
Hano, George 1929- St&PR 91
Hanold, Terrance 1912- WhoAm 90
Hanon, David I. 1940- St&PR 91
Hanotaux, Albert Auguste Gabriel 1853-1944 BiDFrPL
Hanover, Marc J. 1950- St&PR 91
Hanrahan, Barbara 1939- FemiCLE
Hanrahan, Edward Stephenson 1929- WhoAm 90
Hanrahan, Gorman E BiDrAPA 89
Hanrahan, John Joseph 1932- WhoE 91
Hanrahan, Kip BioIn 16
Hanrahan, Patrick Jude 1954- WhoSSW 91
Hanrahan, Peter F. St&PR 91
Hanrahan, Robert Joseph 1932- WhoAm 90, WhoSSW 91
Hanrath, David Allen 1935- St&PR 91
Hanrath, Linda Carol 1949- WhoEmL 91
Hanratty, Carin Gale 1953- WhoAmW 91
Hanratty, Lawrence Charles 1935- St&PR 91
Hanratty, Thomas Joseph 1926- WhoAm 90
Hanretta, Allan G 1930- BiDrAPA 89
Hanretty, Julie Claire 1950- WhoEmL 91
Hans von Reutlingen PenDiDA 89
Hans, Harry L. 1933- WhoAm 90
Hans, Paul BiDrAPA 89
Hans, Paul Charles 1946- St&PR 91, WhoEmL 91
Hans, Peter Edgar 1954- WhoEmL 91
Hans-Adam 1945- WhoWor 91
Hansalik, Kathryn ODwPR 91
Hansard, Deborah Ingram BiDrAPA 89
Hansard, James William 1936- WhoAm 90
Hansard, Luke 1752-1828 BioIn 16
Hansbarger, Larry DeFord 1921- St&PR 91
Hansberger, Allan P. 1924- St&PR 91
Hansberger, Robert Vail 1920- WhoAm 90
Hansberry, Lorraine 1930-1965 BioAmW, BioIn 16, ConLC 62 [port], DrBlPA 90, EncAL, FemiCLE, MajTwCW, NotWoAT, WorAlBi
Hansburg, Freda 1950- WhoEmL 91
Hansburg, Henry G. 1910-1989 BioIn 16
Hansbury, Stephan Charles 1946- WhoEmL 91
Hansch, Corwin Herman 1918- WhoAm 90
Hansch, Paul A BiDrAPA 89
Hansch, Theodor Wolfgang 1941- WhoWor 91
Hanschu, Lisa D. 1960- WhoAmW 91
Hanscom, Andrew Jackson 1828-1907 AmLegL
Hanscom, Robert James BiDrAPA 89
Hansel, C E M 1917- EncO&P 3
Hansel, Charles Edward 1917- EncPaPR 91
Hansel, Paul George 1917- WhoAm 90
Hansel, Richard Walter 1943- WhoE 91
Hansel, Stephen Arthur 1947- St&PR 91, WhoAm 90
Hansell, David Alan 1953- WhoEmL 91
Hansell, Edgar Frank 1937- WhoAm 90
Hansell, Freya WhoAmA 91
Hansell, Haywood S. 1903-1988 BioIn 16

Hansell, Heidi Nerwin 1953- *WhoAmW 91*
Hansell, Howard W *BiDrAPA 89*
Hansell, John Royer 1931- *WhoAm 90*
Hansell, Kathleen Amy Kuzmick 1941- *IntWWM 90*
Hansell, Nils *BioIn 16*
Hansell, Norris 1931- *BiDrAPA 89*
Hansell, Saul Henry 1962- *WhoEmL 91*
Hansell, William Howard, Jr. 1937- *WhoAm 90*
Hanselman, Orlando B. 1959- *St&PR 91*
Hanselman, Richard Wilson 1927- *St&PR 91*, *WhoAm 90*
Hanselmann, Fredrick Charles 1955- *WhoEmL 91*
Hanseman, Dennis J. 1950- *St&PR 91*
Hansen, A Victor, Jr. *BiDrAPA 89*
Hansen, Aase 1893-1981 *EncCoWW*
Hansen, Aimee Isaacs 1961- *WhoAmW 91*
Hansen, Alfred G. 1933- *WhoAm 90*
Hansen, Andrew Marius 1929- *WhoAm 90*
Hansen, Andy 1924- *Ballpl 90*
Hansen, Ann Natalie 1927- *WhoWrEP 89*
Hansen, Anne *BioIn 16*
Hansen, Anne Lyon 1878-1938 *BioIn 16*
Hansen, Armin Carl 1886-1957 *WhoAmA 91N*
Hansen, Arne Rae 1940- *WhoAm 90*, *WhoAmA 91*
Hansen, Arthur G. 1947- *St&PR 91*
Hansen, Arthur Gene 1925- *WhoAm 90*
Hansen, Arthur Magne 1946- *St&PR 91*, *WhoAm 90*
Hansen, Arvid R. 1920- *St&PR 91*
Hansen, Barbara Caleen 1941- *WhoAm 90*, *WhoAmW 91*
Hansen, Barbara J. 1947- *St&PR 91*
Hansen, Bernard F 1917- *BiDrAPA 89*
Hansen, Bobby J. 1926- *WhoSSW 91*
Hansen, Bobby Jean 1926- *WhoWor 91*
Hansen, Bonnie Jo 1950- *WhoAmW 91*
Hansen, Brooks 1965- *ConAu 132*
Hansen, Bruce Elwood 1962- *WhoE 91*
Hansen, Bryan C. 1943- *St&PR 91*
Hansen, Carl 1860-1916 *DcScanL*
Hansen, Carl Richard, Jr. *BiDrAPA 89*
Hansen, Carol *BioIn 16*
Hansen, Carol Dianne 1948- *WhoEmL 91*
Hansen, Cecil *ConAu 131*
Hansen, Cecil Dan *ConAu 131*
Hansen, Charles 1926- *St&PR 91*, *WhoAm 90*
Hansen, Charles W. 1930- *St&PR 91*
Hansen, Christian Andreas, Jr. 1926- *WhoAm 90*
Hansen, Claire V. 1925- *WhoAm 90*
Hansen, Clifford Peter 1912- *WhoAm 90*
Hansen, Coral June 1950- *WhoEmL 91*
Hansen, David E. 1940- *St&PR 91*
Hansen, David L. 1961- *St&PR 91*
Hansen, Deborah A. 1957- *WhoAmW 91*
Hansen, Deborah Ann 1950- *WhoAmW 91*, *WhoEmL 91*
Hansen, Donald 1909- *St&PR 91*
Hansen, Donald D. 1928- *St&PR 91*
Hansen, Donald John 1947- *WhoE 91*
Hansen, Donald W. 1924- *WhoAm 90*
Hansen, Donald W. 1927- *St&PR 91*
Hansen, Doris Anne 1937- *WhoAmW 91*
Hansen, Douglas B 1929- *BiDrAPA 89*
Hansen, Edward Allen 1929- *WhoAm 90*
Hansen, Edward L. *ODwPR 91*
Hansen, Edward W. 1956- *St&PR 91*
Hansen, Elisa Marie 1952- *WhoAmW 91*
Hansen, Elizabeth J. 1930- *WhoWrEP 89*
Hansen, Eric *BioIn 16*
Hansen, Eric Peter 1951- *WhoEmL 91*
Hansen, Eric R. 1918- *St&PR 91*
Hansen, Erik Denslow 1940- *WhoSSW 91*
Hansen, Everett Mathew 1946- *WhoEmL 91*
Hansen, F. C. C. *EncO&P 3*
Hansen, Florence Marie Congiolosi 1934- *WhoAmW 91*
Hansen, Frances *BioIn 16*
Hansen, Frances Frakes *WhoAmA 91*
Hansen, Francis Eugene 1925- *WhoAm 90*
Hansen, Gary B. 1935- *WhoWrEP 89*
Hansen, Gary Lee 1951- *WhoSSW 91*
Hansen, Gary Vaughn 1962- *WhoEmL 91*
Hansen, Gaylen Capener 1921- *WhoAmA 91*
Hansen, George K. 1935- *St&PR 91*
Hansen, George P. 1951- *EncPaPR 91*
Hansen, George R. 1923- *St&PR 91*
Hansen, Glenn Charles 1947- *WhoEmL 91*
Hansen, Grant Lewis 1921- *WhoAm 90*
Hansen, Gregg Allan 1946- *St&PR 91*
Hansen, Gunnar 1947- *WhoEmL 91*, *WhoWrEP 89*
Hansen, Gustav 1924- *WhoWor 91*
Hansen, H. Jack 1922- *WhoWor 91*
Hansen, Hans Bertil Harald 1921- *WhoWor 91*
Hansen, Hans Edwin 1949- *IntWWM 90*
Hansen, Hans Robert 1941- *WhoWor 91*
Hansen, Harold D. 1921- *St&PR 91*
Hansen, Harold John 1942- *WhoAmA 91*
Hansen, Harry 1884-1977 *AuBYP 90*
Hansen, Herbert Edwin 1920- *WhoAm 90*
Hansen, Herbert H. 1925- *WhoAm 90*
Hansen, Herbert W. 1935- *WhoAm 90*
Hansen, Herman W. 1854-1924 *WhNaAH*
Hansen, Hobart G 1923- *BiDrAPA 89*
Hansen, Hobart Garfield 1923- *WhoAm 90*
Hansen, Howard E *BiDrAPA 89*
Hansen, Howard Louis 1915- *St&PR 91*
Hansen, Hugh 1927- *St&PR 91*
Hansen, Hugh Justin 1923- *WhoAm 90*
Hansen, Irene A. *ODwPR 91*
Hansen, James Bernard 1934- *St&PR 91*
Hansen, James Elbert 1944- *WhoSSW 91*
Hansen, James Hans 1952- *WhoEmL 91*
Hansen, James L. 1930- *St&PR 91*
Hansen, James Lee 1925- *WhoAm 90*, *WhoAmA 91*
Hansen, James V. 1932- *WhoAm 90*
Hansen, James Vernon 1936- *WhoWor 91*
Hansen, Janine Sue 1962- *WhoAmW 91*
Hansen, Jens Alfred Martin *DcScanL*
Hansen, Jessie Lynn 1938- *WhoE 91*
Hansen, Jo-Ida Charlotte 1947- *WhoAmW 91*
Hansen, John Arthur 1930- *WhoWor 91*
Hansen, John H. 1919- *St&PR 91*
Hansen, John Herbert 1945- *WhoEmL 91*
Hansen, John Paul 1928- *WhoAm 90*
Hansen, Jorgen Hartmann 1936- *St&PR 91*, *WhoAm 90*
Hansen, Jorgen Lindberg 1947- *WhoEmL 91*
Hansen, Joseph 1923- *TwCCr&M 91*
Hansen, Joyce *BioIn 16*
Hansen, Joyce 1942- *ChlLR 21 [port]*
Hansen, Joyce Kay 1946- *WhoAmW 91*
Hansen, Judith Evelyn 1947- *WhoEmL 91*
Hansen, Julia 1934- *IntWWM 90*
Hansen, Karen L. 1958- *St&PR 91*
Hansen, Karen Lee 1958- *WhoEmL 91*
Hansen, Karen Thornley 1945- *WhoAmW 91*
Hansen, Karen V. 1955- *WhoAmW 91*
Hansen, Karsten 1911- *WhoAm 90*
Hansen, Kathleen Ann 1954- *WhoAmW 91*
Hansen, Kathryn Ann 1957- *WhoAmW 91*
Hansen, Kathryn Gertrude 1912- *WhoAmW 91*
Hansen, Kendell G *BiDrAPA 89*
Hansen, Kent E. 1947- *St&PR 91*
Hansen, Kent Forrest 1931- *WhoAm 90*
Hansen, Kermit Read 1917- *WhoAm 90*
Hansen, Kurt Paul 1938- *St&PR 91*
Hansen, Larry E. 1949- *St&PR 91*
Hansen, Larry Keith 1940- *St&PR 91*
Hansen, Lars Peter 1952- *WhoAm 90*
Hansen, Laura Ann 1959- *WhoEmL 91*
Hansen, Laurie Jo 1960- *WhoAmW 91*, *WhoWor 91*
Hansen, Lawrence Leroy 1937- *WhoSSW 91*
Hansen, Leland Joe 1944- *WhoWor 91*
Hansen, Leonard Joseph 1932- *WhoWor 91*
Hansen, Leroy E. 1932- *St&PR 91*
Hansen, LeRoy John 1922- *WhoAm 90*
Hansen, Leroy John 1922-1990 *ConAu 132*
Hansen, Lisa Young 1957- *WhoAmW 91*
Hansen, Lois M. 1931- *St&PR 91*
Hansen, Marie Ruth 1946- *WhoAm 90*
Hansen, Mark Douglas 1956- *WhoEmL 91*
Hansen, Mark Raymond *BiDrAPA 89*
Hansen, Marleen Berry 1945- *WhoAmW 91*
Hansen, Martin A. 1909-1955 *DcScanL*
Hansen, Mary Susan *BiDrAPA 89*
Hansen, Max Arthur 1949- *WhoEmL 91*
Hansen, Maynard Lawrence 1931- *St&PR 91*
Hansen, Mindee 1957- *ODwPR 91*
Hansen, Morris Howard 1910- *WhoAm 90*
Hansen, Nancy Ruth 1963- *WhoAmW 91*
Hansen, Nancy Siegfried 1946- *St&PR 91*
Hansen, Neil William 1932- *WhoAm 90*
Hansen, Nick Dane 1938- *St&PR 91*, *WhoAm 90*
Hansen, Niles M 1937- *ConAu 30NR*
Hansen, Niles Maurice 1937- *WhoAm 90*
Hansen, Orval 1926- *WhoAm 90*
Hansen, Patrick David 1958- *WhoEmL 91*
Hansen, Per Brinch 1938- *WhoAm 90*, *WhoWor 91*
Hansen, Per Kristian 1932- *WhoE 91*
Hansen, Peter 1917- *IntWWM 90*
Hansen, Peter F. 1925- *St&PR 91*
Hansen, Peter Jeffrey 1945- *WhoEmL 91*
Hansen, Peter Sijer 1911- *WhoAm 90*
Hansen, Phyllis Jean 1934- *WhoAmW 91*
Hansen, Preben 1908-1989 *BioIn 16*
Hansen, Ralph Holm 1923- *WhoAm 90*
Hansen, Reimer 1937- *WhoWor 91*
Hansen, Richard Arthur 1941- *WhoAm 90*
Hansen, Richard Fred 1932- *WhoAm 90*
Hansen, Richard Paul 1947- *St&PR 91*
Hansen, Richard W. 1919- *WhoAm 90*
Hansen, Richard W. 1937- *St&PR 91*
Hansen, Rick *BioIn 16*
Hansen, Robert 1924- *WhoAmA 91*
Hansen, Robert Arnold 1950- *WhoEmL 91*
Hansen, Robert Bruce 1930- *St&PR 91*, *WhoAm 90*
Hansen, Robert Clinton 1926- *WhoAm 90*
Hansen, Robert H., Jr. 1952- *WhoSSW 91*
Hansen, Robert Howard 1951- *IntWWM 90*
Hansen, Robert Joseph 1918- *WhoAm 90*
Hansen, Robert Suttle 1918- *WhoAm 90*
Hansen, Roger B. 1943- *St&PR 91*
Hansen, Roger Towner 1934- *St&PR 91*
Hansen, Ron *BioIn 16*
Hansen, Ron 1938- *Ballpl 90*
Hansen, Ron 1947- *AuBYP 90*
Hansen, Royal Ivory 1948- *WhoEmL 91*
Hansen, Sarah Eveleth 1917- *WhoAmA 91*, *WhoE 91*
Hansen, Sigvard Theodore, Jr. 1935- *WhoAm 90*
Hansen, Soeren Halling 1946- *St&PR 91*
Hansen, Soren Viktor 1943- *WhoWor 91*
Hansen, Stanley F 1916- *BiDrAPA 89*
Hansen, Stephen Christian 1940- *WhoAm 90*
Hansen, Steven Alan 1949- *WhoEmL 91*
Hansen, Steven Mark 1957- *WhoEmL 91*
Hansen, Steven V 1934- *BiDrAPA 89*
Hansen, Susana 1943- *WhoAmW 91*
Hansen, Theodore Carl 1935- *IntWWM 90*
Hansen, Theodore L. 1911- *St&PR 91*
Hansen, Thomas 1956- *WhoE 91*
Hansen, Thomas Edward *BiDrAPA 89*
Hansen, Thomas R 1953- *BiDrAPA 89*
Hansen, Thomas W 1946- *BiDrAPA 89*
Hansen, Thorkild 1927-1989 *DcScanL*
Hansen, Troels Mork 1943- *WhoWor 91*
Hansen, W.E. 1921- *St&PR 91*
Hansen, W. Lee 1928- *WhoAm 90*
Hansen, Walter Eugene 1929- *WhoWor 91*
Hansen, Wendell Jay 1910- *WhoWor 91*
Hansen, William F 1941- *ConAu 30NR*
Hansen, William Webster 1909-1949 *BioIn 16*
Hansen, Zenon C. R. *NewYTBS 90 [port]*
Hansen-Flaschen, John Hyman 1950- *WhoEmL 91*
Hansen-Hochstadt, Sven S. 1946- *WhoWor 91*
Hanser, Richard Frederick 1909-1981 *AuBYP 90*
Hanseth, George L. 1944- *St&PR 91*
Hansford Johnson, Pamela 1912-1981 *DcNaB 1981*
Hanshaw, Annette 1910- *OxCPMus*
Hanshaw, James Barry 1928- *WhoAm 90*
Hanshew, Thomas W. 1857-1914 *TwCCr&M 91*
Hansler, George E. 1921- *IntWWM 90*
Hanslin, Tony 1943- *St&PR 91*
Hanslip, Edward Robert 1930- *WhoAm 90*
Hansma, Georges J.J. 1915- *WhoWor 91*
Hansman, Robert John, Jr. 1954- *WhoE 91*
Hansmann, Ralph Emil 1918- *WhoAm 90*
Hansmeier, Ralph Henry 1912- *St&PR 91*
Hansmeier, Wanda Violet 1917- *St&PR 91*
Hanson, A.L. 1913- *St&PR 91*
Hanson, Albert LeRoy 1952- *WhoE 91*
Hanson, Alice Marie 1949- *IntWWM 90*
Hanson, Allan Morris 1934- *WhoAm 90*
Hanson, Allen Dennis 1936- *WhoAm 90*
Hanson, Angus Alexander 1922- *WhoAm 90*
Hanson, Anne Coffin 1921- *WhoAm 90*, *WhoAmA 91*
Hanson, Arnold Philip 1924- *WhoAm 90*
Hanson, Arthur M *BiDrAPA 89*
Hanson, Avarita Laurel 1953- *WhoEmL 91*, *WhoSSW 91*
Hanson, Betty Lucile *WhoAmW 91*
Hanson, Bruce Eugene 1942- *WhoWor 91*
Hanson, Charles G. 1912- *St&PR 91*
Hanson, Dale *BioIn 16*
Hanson, Dale S. 1938- *WhoAm 90*
Hanson, Dale Sven 1938- *St&PR 91*
Hanson, Dale William 1949- *WhoSSW 91*
Hanson, Daniel Ralph 1947- *BiDrAPA 89*
Hanson, Darcy Chris 1959- *WhoEmL 91*
Hanson, David B. 1946- *WhoE 91*
Hanson, David Jon 1955- *WhoEmL 91*
Hanson, Diane Charske 1946- *WhoAmW 91*
Hanson, Dick Vincent 1925- *WhoWrEP 89*
Hanson, Donald Burnett 1938- *WhoE 91*
Hanson, Donald Norman 1918- *WhoAm 90*
Hanson, Duane 1925- *WhoAmA 91*
Hanson, Duane Elwood 1925- *WhoAm 90*
Hanson, Durwin Melford 1915- *WhoAm 90*
Hanson, Dwain 1925- *ODwPR 91*
Hanson, Earl Dorchester 1927- *WhoAm 90*, *WhoE 91*
Hanson, Earl T. 1934- *St&PR 91*
Hanson, Elizabeth *FemiCLE*
Hanson, Elizabeth Ann 1961- *WhoE 91*
Hanson, Eric Alan 1953- *WhoEmL 91*, *WhoWor 91*
Hanson, Erik 1965- *Ballpl 90*
Hanson, Eugene Nelson 1917- *WhoAm 90*
Hanson, Floyd Bliss 1939- *WhoAm 90*
Hanson, Gary A. 1954- *WhoEmL 91*
Hanson, Gary Douglas 1943- *BiDrAPA 89*
Hanson, Gaylord Heber 1936- *St&PR 91*
Hanson, Geoffrey 1939- *IntWWM 90*
Hanson, George Fulford 1916- *WhoAm 90*
Hanson, George Victor 1908- *St&PR 91*
Hanson, Gilbert Nikolai 1936- *WhoAm 90*
Hanson, Graeme 1935- *BiDrAPA 89*
Hanson, Gregg W. *St&PR 91*
Hanson, Hans J. 1955- *St&PR 91*
Hanson, Harold B 1901- *BiDrAPA 89*
Hanson, Harold Palmer 1921- *WhoAm 90*
Hanson, Hilary 1963- *ODwPR 91*
Hanson, Howard 1896-1981 *BioIn 16*, *PenDiMP A*, *WorAlBi*
Hanson, J B 1946- *WhoAmA 91*
Hanson, James Arthur 1940- *ConAu 30NR*
Hanson, James Austin 1947- *WhoAm 90*
Hanson, James Eric 1946- *St&PR 91*
Hanson, James Freeman 1944- *WhoSSW 91*
Hanson, James Henry 1918- *St&PR 91*
Hanson, Janet Lundstrom 1961- *WhoEmL 91*
Hanson, Jean M. 1958- *St&PR 91*
Hanson, Jeanne Carol 1947- *WhoAmW 91*
Hanson, Jeanne Sutley 1946- *WhoSSW 91*
Hanson, Jill Alane 1949- *WhoAmW 91*
Hanson, Jo *WhoAm 90*, *WhoAmA 91*
Hanson, John 1715-1783 *BiDrUSE 89*
Hanson, John 1721-1783 *WorAlBi*
Hanson, John 1921- *OxCPMus*
Hanson, John Eugene 1934- *St&PR 91*
Hanson, John J. 1922- *WhoAm 90*
Hanson, John K. 1913- *St&PR 91*
Hanson, John L. 1933- *St&PR 91*
Hanson, John M. 1932- *WhoAm 90*
Hanson, John Melvin 1932- *St&PR 91*
Hanson, John Randall 1952- *WhoEmL 91*
Hanson, John W. *BioIn 16*
Hanson, Jon Gregory 1956- *WhoEmL 91*
Hanson, Joseph E. *BioIn 16*
Hanson, Joseph J. 1930- *WhoAm 90*
Hanson, Judy *WhoAmA 91*
Hanson, Karl H 1912- *BiDrAPA 89*
Hanson, Kenneth L. 1935- *St&PR 91*
Hanson, Kent Bryan 1954- *WhoEmL 91*
Hanson, Kermit Osmond 1916- *WhoAm 90*
Hanson, Kirk L. 1938- *St&PR 91*
Hanson, Larry K. 1932- *St&PR 91*
Hanson, Larry Keith 1932- *WhoAm 90*
Hanson, Lawrence 1936- *WhoAmA 91*
Hanson, Lee 1937- *WhoAmW 91*
Hanson, Leila Fraser 1942- *WhoAm 90*, *WhoAmW 91*
Hanson, Lloyd Eldred 1945- *WhoEmL 91*
Hanson, Lyle Eugene 1920- *WhoAm 90*
Hanson, Marla *BioIn 16*
Hanson, Martha Annette 1946- *BiDrAPA 89*
Hanson, Mary Jane Shirar 1953- *WhoAmW 91*
Hanson, Mary-Jean 1948- *St&PR 91*
Hanson, Mary Kaye 1956- *WhoEmL 91*
Hanson, Maurice Francis 1907- *WhoAm 90*
Hanson, Miles Norman 1919- *St&PR 91*
Hanson, Monte R. 1956- *WhoEmL 91*
Hanson, Morgan Alfred 1930- *WhoSSW 91*
Hanson, Norman Jack 1938- *St&PR 91*
Hanson, Norman Peter *BiDrAPA 89*
Hanson, Patricia W *BiDrAPA 89*
Hanson, Paul David 1939- *WhoAm 90*
Hanson, Paul Gerhard, III 1953- *WhoEmL 91*
Hanson, Paul Nathan 1946- *St&PR 91*
Hanson, Pauline *WhoAm 90*
Hanson, Peg 1946- *WhoE 91*
Hanson, Philip Holton 1943- *WhoAmA 91*
Hanson, Philip Llewellyn 1961- *WhoE 91*
Hanson, Randy Gale 1959- *WhoEmL 91*
Hanson, Raymond Lester 1912- *WhoAm 90*
Hanson, Richard Arthur 1936- *WhoAm 90*
Hanson, Richard Edwin 1931- *WhoSSW 91*
Hanson, Richard Wayne 1946- *St&PR 91*
Hanson, Robert A. 1924- *St&PR 91*
Hanson, Robert Arthur 1924- *WhoAm 90*
Hanson, Robert Carl 1926- *WhoAm 90*
Hanson, Robert DeLolle 1916- *WhoE 91*, *WhoWor 91*
Hanson, Robert Duane 1935- *WhoAm 90*
Hanson, Robert Ernest 1948- *WhoEmL 91*
Hanson, Robert Eugene 1947- *WhoAm 90*
Hanson, Robert Frederic 1948- *IntWWM 90*
Hanson, Robert L. 1946- *WhoEmL 91*

Hanson, Robert Leonard 1937- St&PR 91
Hanson, Robin Elaine 1956- WhoAmW 91, WhoSSW 91
Hanson, Roger James 1927- WhoAm 90
Hanson, Roger Kvamme 1932- WhoAm 90
Hanson, Roger Wayne 1922- WhoAm 90
Hanson, Ronald Lee 1949- St&PR 91
Hanson, Ronald Windell 1947- WhoEmL 91, WhoWor 91
Hanson, Rosalind Putney 1914- WhoE 91
Hanson, Roy BioIn 16
Hanson, Roy Carl 1938- St&PR 91
Hanson, Rudolph A. 1924- St&PR 91
Hanson, Russell Fredric 1947- WhoEmL 91
Hanson, Sandra D. 1946- St&PR 91
Hanson, Sandra J. McKenzie 1949- WhoAmW 91
Hanson, Shirley Ann 1934- WhoE 91
Hanson, Stephen Raymond 1949- WhoEmL 91
Hanson, Sue Margaret 1962- St&PR 91
Hanson, Susan D. BioIn 16, NewYTBS 90
Hanson, Susan E BiDrAPA 89
Hanson, Susan Easton 1943- WhoAm 90
Hanson, Susan Jane 1958- WhoAmW 91
Hanson, Susan Ruth 1953- WhoAmW 91
Hanson, Thomas E. St&PR 91
Hanson, Thomas Jeffrey 1950- WhoEmL 91
Hanson, Thomas L. 1953- St&PR 91
Hanson, Thomas Michael 1947- WhoSSW 91
Hanson, Thor 1928- WhoAm 90
Hanson, Timothy Miles 1953- St&PR 91
Hanson, Victor Henry, II 1930- St&PR 91, WhoAm 90, WhoSSW 91
Hanson, Walter Edmund 1916- WhoAm 90
Hanson, Walter Edward 1925- WhoAm 90
Hanson, Wayne Roger 1928- St&PR 91
Hanson, Wendi Kay 1964- WhoSSW 91
Hanson, William Carl 1954- St&PR 91
Hanson, William Herbert 1936- WhoAm 90
Hansotia, Behram Jehanbux 1948- WhoEmL 91
Hansotia, Hooty Noshir 1949- WhoAmW 91
Hansraj, Prakash Hassanand 1945- WhoWor 91
Hanssen, Carl Alf 1927- BiDrAPA 89
Hanssen, Gary Michael 1938- St&PR 91
Hanssen, Kenneth Ralph 1945- WhoEmL 91
Hanssen, Tora M BiDrAPA 89
Hanssens, Francis Joseph, Jr. 1950- WhoE 91
Hanssmann, Dennett John 1941- BiDrAPA 89
Hansson, Gun Carita 1947- WhoWor 91
Hansson, Gunilla 1939- SmATA 64 [port]
Hansson, Inge Leif Herbert 1949- WhoWor 91
Hansson, Margaret Sutherland St&PR 91
Hansson, Ola 1860-1925 DcScanL
Hanstein, Penelope 1948- WhoSSW 91
Hansuld, John A. St&PR 91
Hansum, Richard Valentine 1946- WhoSSW 91
Hantgan, Richard Selden 1956- WhoE 91
Hantho, Charles St&PR 91
Hantho, Charles Harold 1931- WhoAm 90
Hantke, Terri Lee Cain 1951- WhoAmW 91
Hantman, David Lewis 1957- WhoE 91
Hanton, E. Michael WhoE 91, WhoWor 91
Hantoot, Mark Steven BiDrAPA 89
Hantzschel, Walter Helmut 1904-1972 DcScB S2
Hanus, Frank Jay, III 1949- St&PR 91
Hanus, Steven Howard BiDrAPA 89
Hanus, Thomas Joel 1940- St&PR 91
Hanuschak, George Alan 1949- WhoAm 90
Hanuschak, Lee Nicholas 1947- WhoE 91
Hanuschak, Michael S. 1944- WhoSSW 91
Hanuse, Elena J. BioIn 16
Hanushek, Eric Alan 1943- WhoAm 90
Hanussen, Erik Jan EncO&P 3
Hanussen, Erik Jan 1889-1933 EncPaPR 91
Hanuszewska-Schaeffer, Mieczyslawa 1929- IntWWM 90
Hanuszkiewicz, Adam 1924- WhoWor 91
Hanvey, Jan Eugene 1947- WhoEmL 91
Hanwacker, Daniel Anthony 1951- St&PR 91
Hanwacker, Patricia Aileen Ludwig 1951- WhoAmW 91
Hanway, Donald Grant 1918- WhoAm 90
Hanway, Jonas BioIn 16
Hanway, Mary Ann BioIn 16, FemiCLE
Hanysak, Denny Paul 1944- St&PR 91
Hanzalek, Astrid Teicher 1928- WhoAmW 91
Hanzel, John Francis 1949- St&PR 91
Hanzl, Jiri PenDiMP
Hanzlicek, Charles George 1942- WhoWrEP 89
Hanzlik, Alan Edward 1947- St&PR 91, WhoAm 90
Hanzlik, Cheryl Ann 1955- WhoE 91
Hanzlik, Donald George, Jr. 1951- WhoE 91
Hanzlik, Rayburn DeMara 1938- WhoAm 90
Hanzlik, Stephen John 1957- WhoE 91
Hao, I-Min 1919- BiDrAPA 89
Hapala, Milan Ernest 1919- WhoAm 90
Hapgood, Norman 1868-1937 BioIn 16
Hapgood, Robert Derry 1928- WhoAm 90
Hapgood, Susan T 1957- WhoAmA 91
Hapke, Daniel Super, Jr. 1946- WhoEmL 91
Hapke, Joyce Zellinger 1932- WhoAmW 91
Hapke, Paul Frederick 1922-1984 WhoAmA 91N
Hapner, Isak Eisig BiDrAPA 89
Happ, Harvey Heinz 1928- WhoAm 90
Happel, Henry W. BioIn 16
Happel, John 1908- WhoAm 90, WhoWor 91
Happel, Marvin H. 1939- St&PR 91
Happer, William, Jr. 1939- WhoAm 90
Happoncourt, Francoise d'Issembourg d' 1695-1758 EncCoWW
Hapunda, Fredrick Shumba 1945- WhoWor 91
Hapworth, William Emery BiDrAPA 89
Haq, Kaiser Mohamed Hamidul 1950- WhoWor 91
Haque, Fareed BioIn 16
Haque, Inam Ul BiDrAPA 89
Haque, Malika Hakim WhoAmW 91, WhoWor 91
Haque, Shamsul M 1937- BiDrAPA 89
Haque, Waheedul 1940- BiDrAPA 89
Har-Esh, Edith BiDrAPA 89
Har-Even, Reuven 1948- WhoE 91
Hara, Akira 1935- St&PR 91
Hara, Ernest Hideo 1909- WhoAm 90
Hara, George 1952- WhoEmL 91
Hara, Keiko WhoAmA 91
Hara, Kenzaburo 1907- WhoWor 91
Hara, Minoru 1930- WhoWor 91
Hara-Isa, Nancy Jeanne 1961- WhoAmW 91
Harache, Pierre PenDiDA 89
Haracznak, Stephen R. ODwPR 91
Harad, George Jay 1944- St&PR 91, WhoAm 90
Harada, Koichiro PenDiMP
Harada, Sadao PenDiMP
Harada, Takashi 1939- WhoWor 91
Harada, Yukio 1938- WhoWor 91
Haragan, Donald Robert 1936- WhoAm 90
Harakal, Concetta 1923- WhoAmW 91
Harakal, Eileen ODwPR 91
Harakas, Stanley Samuel 1932- WhoWrEP 89
Haralambidis, Maroula 1959- WhoAmW 91
Haralambopoulos, Ioannis 1919- WhoWor 91
Harald, Eric AuBYP 90
Haraldsson, Erlendur 1931- EncO&P 3, EncPaPR 91
Haraldsson, Ingthor Gudmundur 1932- WhoWor 91
Haralick, Robert Martin 1943- WhoAm 90
Haralson, Carol Louise 1948- WhoWrEP 89
Haralson, Jeremiah 1846-1916? BlkAmsC [port]
Haralson, Linda Jane 1959- WhoAmW 91
Haralson, Mary Elaine 1961- WhoSSW 91
Haramundanis, Katherine Leonora 1937- WhoAmW 91
Haran, Christopher James 1955- WhoE 91
Haran, Judith Ann 1954- BiDrAPA 89
Haran, Mary Cleere BioIn 16
Harari, Hananiah 1912- WhoAm 90, WhoAmA 91
Harary, Donald Keith 1953- WhoEmL 91
Harary, Frank 1921- WhoAm 90
Harary, Joseph Maurice 1961- WhoEmL 91
Harary, Keith 1953- EncO&P 3, EncPaPR 91
Harasevych, Maria S. 1918- WhoWor 91
Harasty, Zoltan A. 1930- St&PR 91
Harasym, Myron BiDrAPA 89
Haraszthy de Mokcsa, Agoston 1812-1869 BioIn 16
Haraszti, Joseph Sandor 1944- BiDrAPA 89
Haratunian, Michael 1933- St&PR 91
Harb, Charlene Alice WhoAmW 91
Harb, Larry E. 1953- St&PR 91
Harbach, Barbara 1946- IntWWM 90
Harbach, Barbara Carol 1946- WhoAmW 91
Harbach, Otto 1873-1963 OxCPMus
Harbage, Alfred B. TwCCr&M 91
Harbar, Ludmila BiDrAPA 89
Harbart, Gertrude Felton 1908- WhoAmA 91
Harbater, David 1952- WhoE 91
Harbaugh, Carl Ray 1939- WhoE 91
Harbaugh, Daniel Paul 1948- WhoEmL 91
Harbaugh, George Milton 1930- WhoAm 90
Harbaugh, Jane Worth 1930- WhoAm 90
Harbaugh, John W 1926- ConAu 30NR
Harbaugh, John Warvelle 1926- WhoAm 90
Harbaugh, William L. 1940- St&PR 91
Harbeck, William James 1921- WhoAm 90, WhoWor 91
Harber, Harley Joe 1950- BiDrAPA 89
Harber, Loretta Michele 1954- WhoAmW 91
Harberger, Arnold Carl 1924- WhoAm 90
Harberman, Michael Allen 1947- BiDrAPA 89
Harbers, Susan Ethel 1944- WhoAmW 91
Harbert, Bill Lebold 1923- St&PR 91, WhoAm 90, WhoSSW 91
Harbert, Edward Wesley, III 1955- St&PR 91
Harbert, Guy Morley, Jr. 1929- WhoAm 90
Harbert, John Murdoch, III 1921- St&PR 91
Harbert, Kenneth Ray 1947- WhoE 91
Harbert, Norman C. 1933- St&PR 91
Harbert, Pamela Annett 1963- WhoAmW 91
Harbert, Terry Lee 1947- WhoEmL 91
Harbert, Tyrus G. 1924- St&PR 91
Harbert, Virgil BioIn 16
Harbeson, William Byrd, III 1933- WhoSSW 91
Harbin, Buford Goodwin 1945- WhoSSW 91
Harbin, Carlton Dennis 1959- St&PR 91
Harbin, Charles C 1922- BiDrAPA 89
Harbin, Henry T 1946- BiDrAPA 89
Harbin, James Anthony 1950- WhoSSW 91
Harbin, Lyle D. 1934- St&PR 91
Harbin, Robert 1909-1978 BioIn 16
Harbinson, Robert 1928- BioIn 16
Harbison, Diana BiDrAPA 89
Harbison, Earle Harrison, Jr. 1928- St&PR 91, WhoAm 90, WhoWor 91
Harbison, G. Richard 1941- WhoSSW 91
Harbison, John 1938- IntWWM 90, WhoAm 90
Harbison, John R. 1953- St&PR 91
Harbison, Lawrence Roehm 1951- St&PR 91
Harbison, Lillian V. Gray 1914- WhoAmW 91
Harbison, Robert Gene 1939- St&PR 91
Harbison, W. 1922- St&PR 91
Harbison, William James 1923- WhoAm 90, WhoSSW 91
Harbo, Nils 1956- IntWWM 90
Harbolt, James G. 1933- St&PR 91
Harboort, Julien Jean 1926- WhoWor 91
Harbor, Robert Neal 1931- St&PR 91
Harbour, Jeanne Dulas BiDrAPA 89
Harbour, Nancy Caine 1949- WhoAmW 91, WhoEmL 91
Harbour, Robert L. 1929- St&PR 91
Harbour, Tracy Ray 1963- WhoSSW 91
Harbrant, Robert Francis 1942- WhoAm 90
Harbrecht, Joseph William 1944- St&PR 91
Harbuck, Edwin Charles 1934- WhoSSW 91
Harburg, E. Y. 1896-1981 WorAlBi
Harburg, E. Y. 1898-1981 OxCPMus
Harburg, Edgar Y. 1898-1981 EncAL
Harburger, James Steven 1942- BiDrAPA 89
Harbury, Henry Alexander 1927- WhoAm 90
Harbutt, Charles 1935- WhoAm 90, WhoAmA 91
Harcleroad, Fred Farley 1918- WhoAm 90, WhoWrEP 89
Harclerode, Howard Charles, II 1947- WhoEmL 91
Harclerode, Jack Edgar 1935- WhoAm 90
Harcourt, Anne 1602?- BiDEWW
Harcourt, Mary 1750?-1833 FemiCLE
Harcourt, Michel BioIn 16
Harcourt, Palma ConAu 31NR, SpyFic
Harcourt, Richard Douglas 1939- St&PR 91
Harcus, Portia Gwen WhoAmA 91
Hard, Curtis V. 1845-1917 BioIn 16
Hard, Elizabeth Jackson 1908- WhoAmW 91
Hard, William 1878-1962 BioIn 16
Hardach, Karl 1936- ConAu 130
Hardage, Page Taylor 1944- WhoAmW 91
Hardart, Augustin Stephen, Jr. 1922- St&PR 91
Hardart, Thomas R. 1918-1988 BioIn 16
Hardaway, Beverly Lynne 1961- WhoAmW 91
Hardaway, Robert Morris, III 1916- WhoAm 90
Hardaway, Thomas Gray, II 1953- BiDrAPA 89
Hardbeck, George William 1925- WhoAm 90
Hardberger, Phillip Duane 1934- WhoAm 90
Hardcastle, Heather Sheila BiDrAPA 89
Hardcastle, John B. 1936- St&PR 91
Hardcastle, Keith Stewart 1950- WhoSSW 91
Hardcastle, Kenneth Lloyd 1934- St&PR 91, WhoAm 90
Hardcastle, Michael 1933- BioIn 16
Hardcastle, Robert Thomas 1949- WhoEmL 91
Hardee, Alvin J., Jr. 1942- WhoSSW 91
Hardee, Evelyn Rocker 1921- WhoAmW 91
Hardee, Laurance Ashley 1950- WhoEmL 91
Hardee, Ray McKay 1961- WhoSSW 91
Hardee, William Covington 1919- WhoAm 90
Hardegree, Carol 1949- WhoSSW 91
Hardegree, David Louis, Jr. 1951- WhoSSW 91
Hardeland, Rudiger Hermann Horst 1943- WhoWor 91
Hardelot, Guy d' 1858-1936 OxCPMus
Hardeman, Donald Watson 1947- WhoEmL 91
Hardeman, Thomas, Jr. 1825-1891 AmLegL
Harden, Acheson Adair, Jr. 1921- WhoSSW 91
Harden, Alice V. 1948- WhoAmW 91
Harden, Anita Joyce 1947- WhoEmL 91
Harden, Arthur 1865-1940 WorAlBi
Harden, Blaine Charles 1952- WhoAm 90
Harden, David E. 1927- St&PR 91
Harden, Douglas W. 1948- St&PR 91
Harden, Doyle Benjamin 1935- WhoSSW 91, WhoWor 91
Harden, Elmer Hilton, Jr. BiDrAPA 89
Harden, Ernest, Jr. DrBlPA 90
Harden, Gary Martin 1955- WhoEmL 91
Harden, Harold W M, III 1947- BiDrAPA 89
Harden, Herman Lee 1953- WhoSSW 91
Harden, Jeffrey Calvin BiDrAPA 89
Harden, Jimmie Leigh 1946- WhoSSW 91
Harden, Joan Piper 1947- WhoAmW 91
Harden, Jon BioIn 16
Harden, Jon Bixby 1944- WhoAm 90
Harden, Kirk B. 1951- St&PR 91
Harden, Marvin WhoAm 90, WhoAmA 91
Harden, Michael Duane 1957- WhoSSW 91
Harden, Michael Patrick 1952- WhoEmL 91, WhoWrEP 89
Harden, Michele Louise 1958- WhoWrEP 89
Harden, N.E. 1934- St&PR 91
Harden, Oleta Elizabeth 1935- WhoAm 90
Harden, Patrick Alan 1936- WhoAm 90
Harden, Richard Lee 1946- St&PR 91
Harden, Robert James BiDrAPA 89
Harden, Robert Lawson 1945- St&PR 91
Harden-Hickey, James Aloysius 1854-1898 BioIn 16
Hardenberger, Hakan 1961- IntWWM 90, PenDiMP
Hardenbrook, Yvonne Imogene 1928- WhoWrEP 89
Hardenburg, Lina 1949- WhoAmW 91
Hardenburg, Wes 1958- St&PR 91
Harder, Charles Mabry 1899-1959 WhoAmA 91N
Harder, F. William 1904-1989 BioIn 16
Harder, Frederick Lee 1940- WhoE 91, WhoSSW 91
Harder, Gary Ray 1944- St&PR 91
Harder, Heather Anne 1948- WhoEmL 91
Harder, Jane Daniels 1950- St&PR 91
Harder, John E. 1930- WhoAm 90
Harder, Kelsie Brown 1922- WhoAm 90
Harder, Kristine 1949- WhoEmL 91
Harder, Lewis B. 1918- St&PR 91
Harder, Lewis Bradley 1918- WhoAm 90
Harder, Lloyd 1925- WhoSSW 91
Harder, Marilyn Anne 1951- WhoAmW 91
Harder, Mark Allen 1960- WhoEmL 91
Harder, Martin David 1940- St&PR 91
Harder, Mel 1909- Ballpl 90 [port]
Harder, Robert Clarence 1929- WhoAm 90
Harder, Rolf 1929- ConDes 90
Harder, Rolf Peter 1929- WhoAm 90, WhoAmA 91
Harder, Ronald R. 1943- St&PR 91
Harder, Sarah Snell 1937- WhoAmW 91
Harder, Virgil Eugene 1923- WhoAm 90

Harder, William Ewald 1932- *St&PR 91*
Harder-Bernier, Catherine Gail 1962- *WhoE 91*
Hardester, Royce Dean 1952- *WhoWrEP 89*
Hardesty, C. Howard, Jr. 1922- *WhoAm 90*
Hardesty, Edward F. *BioIn 16*
Hardesty, Egbert Railey 1915- *WhoAm 90*
Hardesty, Hiram Haines 1914- *WhoAm 90*
Hardesty, James Dunn 1946- *St&PR 91*, *WhoAm 90*
Hardesty, Margie Anne *WhoSSW 91*
Hardesty, Robert Lynch 1940- *WhoAm 90*
Hardesty, Sarah *ODwPR 91*
Hardey, Mary A. 1809-1886 *BioAmW*
Hardey, Mathew W. 1952- *St&PR 91*
Hardgrave, Robert Lewis, Jr. 1939- *WhoAm 90*
Hardgrove, Thomas J 1905- *BiDrAPA 89*
Hardie, Dee *BioIn 16*
Hardie, Frank 1911-1989 *AnObit 1989*
Hardie, George Graham 1933- *WhoAm 90*
Hardie, Gwen 1962- *BiDWomA*
Hardie, James Hiller 1929- *WhoAm 90*
Hardie, Keir 1856-1915 *BioIn 16*
Hardie, Michael C. 1946- *St&PR 91*
Hardie, William Francis Ross 1902-1990 *ConAu 132*
Hardiek, Bernard L. 1940- *St&PR 91*
Hardig, Mark Nelson 1955- *WhoEmL 91*
Hardigg, James Sutton 1922- *St&PR 91*
Hardigree, Randolph Stephen 1938- *St&PR 91*
Hardiman, Joseph Raymond 1937- *St&PR 91*, *WhoAm 90*
Hardiman, Therese Anne 1956- *WhoAmW 91*, *WhoE 91*
Hardin, Adlai S. 1901-1989 *BioIn 16*
Hardin, Adlais 1901-1989 *WhoAmA 91N*
Hardin, Charles M 1908- *ConAu 30NR*
Hardin, Charles Roe, Jr. 1921- *WhoAm 90*
Hardin, Clifford Morris 1915- *BiDrUSE 89*, *WhoAm 90*
Hardin, Daniel R. 1953- *WhoSSW 91*
Hardin, Earl D 1933- *BiDrAPA 89*
Hardin, Edwin Milton 1926- *St&PR 91*
Hardin, Elizabeth Ann 1959- *WhoAmW 91*
Hardin, Eugene B., Jr. 1930- *St&PR 91*
Hardin, Eugene Brooks, Jr. 1930- *WhoAm 90*
Hardin, Fred A. 1918- *WhoAm 90*
Hardin, George Cecil, Jr. 1920- *WhoAm 90*
Hardin, Hal D. 1941- *WhoAm 90*
Hardin, Hal S. 1922- *St&PR 91*
Hardin, Helen *WhoWrEP 89*
Hardin, Herschel 1936- *OxCCanT*
Hardin, Hilliard Frances 1917- *WhoAmW 91*
Hardin, James Michael 1956- *WhoSSW 91*
Hardin, James Neal 1939- *WhoAm 90*
Hardin, James Neal, Jr. 1939- *WhoWrEP 89*
Hardin, Jim 1943- *Ballpl 90*
Hardin, John 1957- *St&PR 91*
Hardin, John Alexander 1911- *WhoAm 90*
Hardin, Joseph 1921-1989 *MusmAFA*
Hardin, Joseph S. 1945- *St&PR 91*
Hardin, Kenneth Lee 1916- *WhoWrEP 89*
Hardin, Lloyd T., Jr. 1949- *St&PR 91*
Hardin, Louis *BioIn 16*
Hardin, Lowell Stewart 1917- *WhoAm 90*
Hardin, Michael J. 1947- *St&PR 91*
Hardin, Paul 1931- *WhoAm 90*, *WhoSSW 91*, *WhoWor 91*
Hardin, Richard V. 1939- *St&PR 91*
Hardin, Russell 1940- *WhoAm 90*
Hardin, Sherrie Ann 1950- *WhoAmW 91*
Hardin, Shirley G 1920- *WhoAmA 91*
Hardin, Sondra Higdon 1958- *WhoAmW 91*
Hardin, Terri Lynn 1950- *WhoAmW 91*
Hardin, William Downer 1926- *WhoAm 90*
Hardin, William Samuel 1946- *St&PR 91*
Hardin-Cheung, Judy Ann 1945- *WhoAmW 91*
Harding, Field Marshal Lord 1896-1989 *AnObit 1989*
Harding, Ann 1942- *WhoAmA 91*
Harding, Anne Raikes 1781-1858 *FemiCLE*
Harding, Benjamin Franklin 1823-1899 *AmLegL*
Harding, Boyd Wesley 1926- *WhoAm 90*
Harding, Charles F. 1947- *St&PR 91*
Harding, Charles Malim 1911- *WhoAm 90*
Harding, Charles Tayloe 1959- *IntWWM 90*
Harding, Clifford Vincent, III 1957- *WhoEmL 91*
Harding, Conrad 1946- *St&PR 91*
Harding, Darlene Carol 1945- *WhoE 91*
Harding, Douglas E. 1909- *EncO&P 3*
Harding, Elizabeth *FemiCLE*
Harding, Enoch, Jr. 1931- *WhoE 91*
Harding, Ethel M. 1927- *WhoAmW 91*
Harding, Eva Victoria 1913- *WhoWrEP 89*
Harding, Fann 1930- *WhoAm 90*, *WhoAmW 91*
Harding, Florence Kling de Wolfe 1860-1924 *BioIn 16*
Harding, Francis James 1944- *St&PR 91*
Harding, Frank Fountain 1934- *St&PR 91*
Harding, Frank I. 1944- *WhoAm 90*
Harding, Frank I., III 1944- *St&PR 91*
Harding, Fred H. 1931- *St&PR 91*
Harding, Fred R. 1943- *St&PR 91*
Harding, George *WhoAmA 91N*
Harding, George Tryon, IV 1929- *BiDrAPA 89*
Harding, Glenn William 1928- *WhoSSW 91*
Harding, Harry 1946- *WhoAm 90*
Harding, Henry W. 1910- *St&PR 91*
Harding, Herndon P *BiDrAPA 89*
Harding, Herndon P, Jr. 1955- *BiDrAPA 89*
Harding, Hurshel Rudolph 1929- *WhoAm 90*
Harding, J. A. *AmLegL*
Harding, James 1929- *ConAu 32NR*
Harding, James George 1949- *WhoEmL 91*, *WhoWor 91*
Harding, James Warren 1918- *WhoAm 90*
Harding, Janice Kay 1956- *WhoAmW 91*, *WhoEmL 91*
Harding, John 1896-1989 *BioIn 16*
Harding, John C., III 1937- *St&PR 91*
Harding, John David 1944- *St&PR 91*
Harding, John Hibbard 1936- *St&PR 91*, *WhoAm 90*
Harding, Khit 1942- *WhoWrEP 89*
Harding, Louis Thomas 1929- *WhoE 91*
Harding, Mark Mayens 1947- *WhoEmL 91*
Harding, Noel Robert 1945- *WhoAmA 91*
Harding, Owen B. 1926- *St&PR 91*
Harding, Peter John Martin 1953- *St&PR 91*
Harding, Prudence *BiDEWW*
Harding, Ray Murray, Jr. 1953- *WhoEmL 91*
Harding, Raymond James 1948- *IntWWM 90*
Harding, Richard Kent 1945- *BiDrAPA 89*, *WhoSSW 91*
Harding, Richard Merrick 1950- *WhoSSW 91*
Harding, Robert Charles 1939- *WhoE 91*
Harding, Robert E. 1935- *St&PR 91*
Harding, Robert Linn 1942- *WhoSSW 91*
Harding, Sandra Ellen 1944- *WhoAmW 91*
Harding, Sheila Ann 1940- *WhoAmW 91*
Harding, Thomas Lynn 1927- *St&PR 91*
Harding, Thomas Robert *BiDrAPA 89*
Harding, Tim *WhoAmA 91*
Harding, Vicki Ruth 1954- *WhoEmL 91*
Harding, Victor Mathews 1908- *WhoAm 90*
Harding, Walter 1917- *WhoE 91*, *WhoWrEP 89*
Harding, Warren G. 1865-1923 *BioIn 16*, *WorAlBi*
Harding, Warren Gamaliel 1865-1923 *BiDrUSE 89*
Harding, Wayne Edward, III 1954- *WhoEmL 91*
Harding, William Malcolm 1933- *St&PR 91*
Harding of Petherton, Baron 1896-1989 *BioIn 16*
Hardinge, Henry 1785-1856 *BioIn 16*
Hardinge, Thomas Hunt 1924- *St&PR 91*
Hardinger, Rowena Adaline 1926- *WhoAmW 91*
Hardis, Stephen Roger 1935- *St&PR 91*, *WhoAm 90*
Hardish, Patrick Michael 1944- *IntWWM 90*
Hardison, Donald Leigh 1916- *WhoAm 90*
Hardison, Kadeem *BioIn 16*
Hardison, Leslie C. 1929- *St&PR 91*
Hardison, O B 1928-1990 *ConAu 132*
Hardison, O. B., Jr. *NewYTBS 90 [port]*
Hardison, Osborne Bennett, Jr. 1928- *WhoAm 90*, *WhoWrEP 89*
Hardison, Ruth Inge *WhoAm 90*
Hardister, Darrell Edward 1934- *WhoSSW 91*
Hardisty, Donald Mertz 1932- *IntWWM 90*
Hardjo Prakoso, Mastini 1923- *WhoWor 91*
Hardman, Daniel Clarke 1954- *WhoSSW 91*
Hardman, Harold Francis 1927- *WhoAm 90*
Hardman, James Charles 1931- *WhoAm 90*
Hardman, James Felix 1941- *St&PR 91*
Hardman, Joel Griffeth 1933- *WhoAm 90*
Hardman, John 1811-1867 *PenDiDA 89*
Hardman, John 1940- *WhoWor 91*
Hardman, John Barnett *BiDrAPA 89*
Hardman, Katherine Elizabeth 1955- *WhoEmL 91*
Hardman, Kathleen Goldie 1915- *WhoE 91*
Hardman, Lamartine Griffin, III 1939- *St&PR 91*
Hardoby, William Joseph 1946- *BiDrAPA 89*
Hardon, John Anthony 1914- *WhoAm 90*
Hardoon, Laurence Eric 1950- *WhoEmL 91*
Hardrick, Maria Darshell 1966- *WhoAmW 91*
Hards, Robert George 1954- *WhoEmL 91*
Hardstaff, Maurice 1922-1986 *BioIn 16*
Hardt, Athia Lee 1948- *WhoEmL 91*
Hardt, Barbara A *BiDrAPA 89*
Hardt, Gunther 1920- *WhoWor 91*
Hardt, Hanno Richard Eduard 1934- *WhoAm 90*
Hardt, Robert Miller 1945- *WhoAm 90*
Hardway, Wendell Gary 1927- *WhoAm 90*
Hardwick, B Randol *BiDrAPA 89*
Hardwick, Cathy *BioIn 16*
Hardwick, Cathy 1933- *ConDes 90*
Hardwick, Charles L. 1941- *BioIn 16*
Hardwick, Charles Leighton 1941- *WhoAm 90*
Hardwick, David Francis 1934- *WhoAm 90*
Hardwick, Elizabeth *BioIn 16*
Hardwick, Elizabeth 1916- *ConAu 32NR*, *FemiCLE*, *LiHiK*, *MajTwCW*, *NotWoAT*, *WhoAm 90*, *WhoWrEP 89*
Hardwick, Jack Newton 1955- *WhoEmL 91*
Hardwick, Karen Lee 1952- *WhoEmL 91*
Hardwick, Todd *BioIn 16*
Hardwicke, Cedric 1893-1964 *WorAlBi*
Hardwicke, Edward 1932- *ConTFT 8 [port]*
Hardwicke, James Ernest 1924- *St&PR 91*
Hardwicke, Robert A *ODwPR 91*
Hardwig, Jeffrey Thomas *BiDrAPA 89*
Hardy, A. B. C. 1869-1946 *EncABHB 4 [port]*
Hardy, Alice Joan 1949- *WhoEmL 91*
Hardy, Alister 1896-1985 *EncPaPR 91*
Hardy, Alister Clavering 1896-1985 *DcNaB 1981*, *EncO&P 3*
Hardy, Anne Dunlap 1910- *WhoAmW 91*, *WhoWor 91*
Hardy, Annie 1839-1934 *BiDWomA*
Hardy, Archie 1936- *WhoSSW 91*
Hardy, Arthur B 1913- *BiDrAPA 89*
Hardy, Barbara Nathan 1924- *BioIn 16*
Hardy, Benson B. 1920- *WhoWor 91*
Hardy, Billy Eugene 1925- *WhoSSW 91*
Hardy, Bruce Blondel 1930- *St&PR 91*
Hardy, C. Colburn 1910- *WhoWrEP 89*
Hardy, Carroll 1933- *Ballpl 90*
Hardy, Cherryl 1952- *WhoEmL 91*
Hardy, Cyril G *BiDrAPA 89*
Hardy, Daniel Weir 1943- *BiDrAPA 89*
Hardy, David 1924- *WhoAm 90*
Hardy, David Gordon 1940- *WhoWor 91*
Hardy, David Walter 1942- *WhoE 91*
Hardy, David Whittaker, III 1929- *WhoAmA 91*
Hardy, Deborah Welles 1927- *WhoAm 90*
Hardy, Dewitt 1940- *WhoAmA 91*
Hardy, Donald J. 1935- *St&PR 91*
Hardy, Dorcas Ruth 1946- *WhoAm 90*, *WhoAmW 91*
Hardy, Duane Horace 1931- *WhoWor 91*
Hardy, Earl M. *St&PR 91*
Hardy, Edward Clark 1934- *St&PR 91*
Hardy, Elizabeth *ODwPR 91*
Hardy, Ellen Marie 1964- *WhoAmW 91*
Hardy, Evan Alan 1890-1963 *BioIn 16*
Hardy, Gene M. 1937- *St&PR 91*
Hardy, George *NewYTBS 90*
Hardy, Gordon Alfred 1918- *WhoAm 90*
Hardy, Gyme Dufault 1952- *WhoAmW 91*
Hardy, Henry Reginald, Jr. 1931- *WhoE 91*
Hardy, Howard 1900-1988 *WhoAmA 91N*
Hardy, Hugh 1932- *BioIn 16*
Hardy, Hugh Gelston 1932- *WhoAm 90*
Hardy, Jack S. *ODwPR 91*
Hardy, James Chester 1930- *WhoAm 90*
Hardy, James Deane 1929- *St&PR 91*
Hardy, Jane Elizabeth 1930- *WhoAmW 91*, *WhoE 91*
Hardy, Jerome S. 1918- *St&PR 91*
Hardy, Joelle Louise *BiDrAPA 89*
Hardy, John *WhoAmA 91*
Hardy, John Christopher 1941- *WhoAm 90*
Hardy, John Edward 1922- *WhoAm 90*, *WhoWrEP 89*
Hardy, Jon 1958- *BioIn 16*
Hardy, Joseph 1918- *WhoAm 90*
Hardy, June Dorflinger 1929- *WhoAmW 91*, *WhoE 91*
Hardy, Kenneth Reginald 1929- *WhoE 91*
Hardy, Larry 1948- *Ballpl 90*
Hardy, Leland *BioIn 16*
Hardy, Linda B 1954- *BiDrAPA 89*
Hardy, Lois Lynn 1928- *WhoAmW 91*, *WhoWor 91*
Hardy, Margaret Antoinette Kumko 1949- *WhoSSW 91*
Hardy, Mark Gary 1956- *WhoSSW 91*
Hardy, Mary Anne Duffus 1825?-1891 *FemiCLE*
Hardy, Mary Lynn 1941- *WhoAmW 91*
Hardy, Mary M. *EncO&P 3*
Hardy, Oliver 1892-1957 *BioIn 16*, *WorAlBi*
Hardy, Paul Jude 1942- *WhoSSW 91*
Hardy, Phillip Michael 1948- *St&PR 91*
Hardy, Ralph W. F. 1934- *WhoAm 90*, *WhoE 91*, *WhoWor 91*
Hardy, Richard B. 1932- *St&PR 91*
Hardy, Richard Earl 1938- *WhoAm 90*
Hardy, Robert 1938- *WhoAmA 91*
Hardy, Robert Gerald 1944- *WhoAm 90*
Hardy, Robert Orgain 1950- *BiDrAPA 89*
Hardy, Susan Narina 1957- *WhoEmL 91*
Hardy, Thomas 1840-1928 *BioIn 16*, *MajTwCW*, *WorAlBi*
Hardy, Thomas 1921- *WhoAmA 91*
Hardy, Thomas Austin 1921- *WhoAm 90*
Hardy, Thomas B 1840-1928 *WrPh*
Hardy, Thomas C *BiDrAPA 89*
Hardy, Thomas Cresson 1942- *St&PR 91*, *WhoAm 90*
Hardy, Thomas G. 1945- *St&PR 91*
Hardy, Tiziana *BioIn 16*
Hardy, Tom Charles, Jr. 1945- *WhoAm 90*
Hardy, Victoria Elizabeth 1947- *WhoAmW 91*
Hardy, Walter Newbold 1940- *WhoAm 90*
Hardy, William Everett, III 1949- *WhoEmL 91*
Hardy, William Robinson 1934- *WhoAm 90*, *WhoWor 91*
Hardymon, James 1934- *St&PR 91*
Hardymon, James F. 1934- *WhoAm 90*
Hare, Cyril 1900-1958 *TwCCr&M 91*
Hare, David *BioIn 16*
Hare, David 1917- *WhoAm 90*, *WhoAmA 91*
Hare, David 1947- *MajTwCW*, *WhoAm 90*, *WhoWor 91*, *WorAu 1980 [port]*
Hare, Delores Pritchard 1944- *WhoAmW 91*
Hare, Donald Eustis 1929- *St&PR 91*
Hare, Frederick Kenneth 1919- *WhoAm 90*
Hare, Glenn F. 1931- *St&PR 91*
Hare, Henry P., Jr. 1925- *BiDrAPA 89*
Hare, Henry Phillip, Jr. 1925- *WhoSSW 91*
Hare, Ian Christopher 1949- *IntWWM 90*
Hare, J. Patrick 1953- *St&PR 91*
Hare, J. William 1929- *St&PR 91*
Hare, John 1844-1921 *BioIn 16*
Hare, John Hugh 1911-1982 *DcNaB 1981*
Hare, John Weldon 1961- *WhoE 91*
Hare, Maria 1798-1870 *FemiCLE*
Hare, Maud Cuney 1874-1936 *HarlReB*
Hare, Michael Meredith 1909-1968 *WhoAmA 91N*
Hare, Nathan 1933- *WhoAm 90*
Hare, Nicholas John Knyvett 1940- *IntWWM 90*
Hare, Peter Hewitt 1935- *WhoAm 90*
Hare, R M 1919- *ConAu 31NR*
Hare, Raymond Arthur 1901- *BioIn 16*
Hare, Richard 1938- *St&PR 91*
Hare, Robert 1781-1858 *EncO&P 3*, *EncPaPR 91*
Hare, Robert Lewis 1923- *WhoAm 90*
Hare, Robert Yates 1921- *IntWWM 90*, *WhoAm 90*
Hare, Sandra Florence 1952- *WhoAmW 91*
Hare, Susan A. 1962- *WhoEmL 91*
Hare, W. H. 1853- *AmLegL*
Hare, Walter W. 1947- *St&PR 91*
Hare, William Richard 1957- *WhoEmL 91*, *WhoSSW 91*
Hare, Wm John 1944- *WhoE 91*
Harel, Aron 1922- *BiDrAPA 89*
Harel, Claude Albert 1932- *WhoWor 91*
Harel, Ezra 1950- *St&PR 91*, *WhoAm 90*
Hareld, Gail Beverly 1954- *WhoE 91*
Harelick, Marjorie Alma 1943- *BiDrAPA 89*
Harelson, Hugh 1930- *WhoAm 90*
Haren, Charles Wells, Jr. 1933- *St&PR 91*
Haren, Nathalie S. 1932- *St&PR 91*
Harenchar, Michael J. 1926- *St&PR 91*
Harer, Frederick W 1879-1949 *WhoAmA 91N*
Harer, Kathleen Frances 1947- *WhoSSW 91*
Hares, William Joseph 1949- *WhoE 91*
Hareven, Tamara K 1937- *ConAu 30NR*
Harewood, The Earl of 1923- *IntWWM 90*
Harewood, Dorian 1950?- *DrBlPA 90*
Harewood-Jones, Wanda Lorrainne 1946- *WhoEmL 91*
Harezlak, Walter John 1954- *St&PR 91*
Harff, Charles H. 1929- *St&PR 91*

Harff, Charles Henry 1929- *WhoAm 90*
Harff, James Warren 1940- *ODwPR 91*
Harford, James Joseph 1924- *WhoAm 90*
Harford, Lesbia 1891-1927 *FemiCLE*
Harford, Madeline W 1948- *BiDrAPA 89*
Hargadon, Bernard Joseph, Jr. 1927- *WhoAm 90*
Hargan, Alison 1950- *IntWWM 90*
Hargan, Steve 1942- *Ballpl 90*
Hargens, William Garman 1943- *WhoAm 90*
Harger, Catherine L 1949- *BiDrAPA 89*
Harger, Gary Donald 1949- *WhoEmL 91*
Harger, Mark Alan 1954- *WhoEmL 91*
Harger, Robert Owens 1932- *WhoAm 90*
Hargesheimer, Alan 1956- *Ballpl 90*
Hargett, Billy Howell 1928- *WhoAm 90*
Hargett, Donald Edward 1945- *St&PR 91*
Hargett, Paul Glenn 1954- *St&PR 91*
Hargis, Billy James 1925- *WhoAm 90, WhoWor 91*
Hargis, Darel Edwin 1955- *WhoSSW 91*
Hargiss, James Leonard 1921- *WhoAm 90*
Hargitt, Rollin Jerry 1931- *St&PR 91*
Hargous, Dominique Jean Maurice 1945- *WhoWor 91*
Hargrave, Alexander D. 1920- *St&PR 91*
Hargrave, Alexander Davidson 1920- *WhoAm 90*
Hargrave, Bubbles 1892-1969 *Ballpl 90*
Hargrave, Cecille Terry 1917- *WhoAmW 91*
Hargrave, Irvin P.H. 1935- *St&PR 91*
Hargrave, John Gordon 1894-1982 *DcNaB 1981*
Hargrave, Joseph James 1841-1894 *DcCanB 12*
Hargrave, Lawrence 1850-1915 *BioIn 16*
Hargrave, Leonie *AuBYP 90, MajTwCW*
Hargrave, Pinky 1896-1942 *Ballpl 90*
Hargrave, R.W. 1920- *St&PR 91*
Hargrave, Rita Rozanne 1951- *BiDrAPA 89*
Hargrave, Robert Larson 1941- *St&PR 91*
Hargrave, Robert Love 1931- *BiDrAPA 89*
Hargrave, Robert Warren 1944- *WhoSSW 91*
Hargrave, Robert Webb 1920- *WhoAm 90*
Hargrave, Sarah Quesenberry 1944- *WhoAm 90, WhoAmW 91*
Hargrave, Victoria Elizabeth 1913- *WhoAm 90*
Hargraves, Dalton Douglas 1942- *WhoSSW 91*
Hargraves, Gordon Sellers 1932- *WhoE 91*
Hargreave, Timothy Bruce 1944- *WhoWor 91*
Hargreaves, Alec G 1948- *ConAu 131*
Hargreaves, Charlie 1896-1979 *Ballpl 90*
Hargreaves, David William 1943- *WhoE 91*
Hargreaves, George Henry 1916- *WhoAm 90*
Hargreaves, Kenneth L. 1948- *St&PR 91*
Hargreaves, Norman Creighton 1939- *WhoSSW 91*
Hargreaves, Robert 1914- *WhoAm 90*
Hargreaves, Roger *BioIn 16*
Hargreaves, Roger 1935-1988 *AnObit 1988*
Hargroder, Charles Merlin 1926- *WhoSSW 91*
Hargrove, Barbara W. *BioIn 16*
Hargrove, Cheryl M. *ODwPR 91*
Hargrove, Dean *BioIn 16*
Hargrove, G. Thomas 1939- *St&PR 91*
Hargrove, George Matthew 1951- *St&PR 91*
Hargrove, Gregor Hazen 1947- *WhoEmL 91*
Hargrove, James Lee 1946- *WhoEmL 91*
Hargrove, James Ward 1922- *WhoAm 90*
Hargrove, Jim 1947- *BioIn 16*
Hargrove, John R. 1923- *WhoAm 90*
Hargrove, John Russell 1947- *WhoAm 90, WhoSSW 91*
Hargrove, Joseph Leonard, Jr. 1949- *WhoEmL 91*
Hargrove, Laurie Elizabeth 1927- *WhoSSW 91*
Hargrove, Mary Julia 1950- *WhoSSW 91*
Hargrove, Michael B. 1941- *WhoE 91*
Hargrove, Mike 1949- *Ballpl 90*
Hargrove, R.L., Jr. 1932- *St&PR 91*
Hargrove, William Gregory 1947- *WhoEmL 91*
Hargus, Vicky Lyn 1962- *WhoAmW 91*
Hari, Kenneth 1947- *WhoAmA 91*
Hari, Kenneth Stephen 1947- *WhoAm 90*
Haribhakti, Shailesh Vishnubhai 1956- *WhoWor 91*
Haribhakti, Vishnubhai Bhagwandas 1929- *WhoWor 91*
Harig, Bernhardt Peter Gold 1926- *St&PR 91*
Harigan, John D. 1934- *St&PR 91*
Harik, Issam Elias 1952- *WhoSSW 91*
Harika, Jopindar Pal 1953- *BiDrAPA 89*
Harimoto, Isao 1935- *Ballpl 90*
Harinck, Emmanuel 1934- *WhoWor 91*
Harindran, Usha J *BiDrAPA 89*
Haring, Bernard 1912- *WorAlBi*
Haring, Ellen Stone 1921- *WhoAm 90*
Haring, Eugene Miller 1927- *WhoAm 90*
Haring, Gene Frances 1940- *BiDrAPA 89*
Haring, Howard Jack 1924- *WhoAm 90*
Haring, Joseph Emerick 1931- *WhoWor 91*
Haring, Keith 1958-1990 *BioIn 16, CurBio 90N, NewYTBS 90 [port], News 90, -90-3, WhoAmA 91N*
Haring, Olga Munk 1917- *WhoAm 90*
Harington, Charles Richard 1933- *WhoAm 90*
Harington, Charles Robert 1897-1972 *DcScB S2*
Harington, Donald *BioIn 16*
Harington, Lucy 1581-1627 *BiDEWW*
Hariot, Thomas 1560-1621 *EncCRAm*
Haririan, Mehdi 1950- *WhoE 91*
Harisdangkul, Valee 1941- *WhoAm 90*
Harish-Chandra 1923-1983 *DcScB S2*
Harisis, T.G. 1930- *St&PR 91*
Haritatos, George M. 1959- *WhoWor 91*
Haritatos, James Stephen 1948- *WhoEmL 91*
Hariton, Gerry *BioIn 16*
Haritov, Bogdan *EncCoWW*
Haritun, Rosalie Ann 1938- *IntWWM 90*
Harivel, Jean Henri 1946- *WhoWor 91*
Harjo, Benjamin 1945- *BioIn 16*
Harjo, Benjamin, Jr 1945- *WhoAmA 91*
Harjo, Joy 1951- *FemiCLE, WhoWrEP 89*
Harjung, Kurt Stephen 1950- *WhoE 91*
Harkabi, Yehoshafat 1921- *BioIn 16*
Harkavy, Abraham I. 1907- *St&PR 91*
Harkavy, Jack Z. 1939- *St&PR 91*
Harkavy, Robert E 1936- *ConAu 30NR*
Harkema, Steven J. 1963- *St&PR 91*
Harker, Clifford *IntWWM 90*
Harker, Howard R. 1933- *St&PR 91*
Harker, John V. 1934- *St&PR 91*
Harker, Joseph Edward 1936- *WhoAm 90*
Harker, Robert Ian 1926- *WhoAm 90*
Harker, William C. 1938- *St&PR 91*
Harkey, Ira Brown, Jr. 1918- *WhoAm 90*
Harkey, John Norman 1933- *WhoAm 90*
Harkey, Mike 1966- *Ballpl 90*
Harkey, Verna Rae 1928- *IntWWM 90, WhoWor 91*
Harkhani, Jethalal S *BiDrAPA 89*
Harkin, Thomas Richard 1939- *WhoAm 90, WhoWor 91*
Harkin, Tom 1939- *BioIn 16*
Harkins, C. Patrick 1950- *St&PR 91*
Harkins, Daniel Conger 1960- *WhoEmL 91*
Harkins, Dennis Richter 1950- *WhoAmA 91*
Harkins, Edwin L. 1940- *WhoAm 90*
Harkins, George *BioIn 16*
Harkins, George C, Jr 1934- *WhoAmA 91*
Harkins, George Frederick 1913- *WhoAm 90*
Harkins, Herbert Perrin 1912- *WhoE 91*
Harkins, Ignatius John, III 1936- *WhoE 91*
Harkins, John Graham, Jr. 1931- *WhoAm 90*
Harkins, Joseph Francis 1938- *WhoAm 90*
Harkins, Joseph James *St&PR 91*
Harkins, Kimberly Kay 1959- *WhoAmW 91*
Harkins, Lida E. 1944- *WhoAmW 91*
Harkins, Lucretia Lee 1957- *WhoEmL 91*
Harkins, Michael E. 1941- *WhoAm 90, WhoE 91*
Harkins, Peter Bowers 1941- *WhoSSW 91*
Harkins, Philip 1912- *AuBYP 90*
Harkins, Philip Joseph 1945- *St&PR 91*
Harkins, Philip Joseph 1946- *WhoE 91*
Harkins, William D. 1873-1951 *WorAlBi*
Harkins, William Daniel 1943- *WhoAm 90*
Harkins, William Edward 1921- *WhoAm 90*
Harkins, William Holliday 1942- *St&PR 91*
Harkleroad, William Derryl 1938- *St&PR 91*
Harkley, Alfred Leon *BiDrAPA 89*
Harkna, Eric 1940- *St&PR 91, WhoAm 90*
Harkness, Bruce 1923- *WhoAm 90*
Harkness, Donald Ray 1921- *WhoWrEP 89*
Harkness, Donald Richard 1932- *WhoAm 90*
Harkness, James Linwood 1931- *St&PR 91*
Harkness, James Willard 1941- *St&PR 91*
Harkness, John C. 1916- *St&PR 91*
Harkness, Lucetta *BioIn 16*
Harkness, M. Stephen 1948- *St&PR 91*
Harkness, Mabel Gleason 1913- *WhoAmW 91*
Harkness, Madden 1948- *WhoAmA 91*
Harkness, Margaret 1861?-1921 *FemiCLE*
Harkness, Margaret Elise 1861-1923 *BioIn 16*
Harkness, Mary Lou 1925- *WhoAm 90*
Harkness, R. Kenneth 1949- *WhoSSW 91*
Harkness, Rebekah 1915-1982 *BioAmW*
Harkness, Rebekah West 1915-1982 *BioIn 16*
Harkness, Scott J. 1955- *St&PR 91*
Harkness, Tim 1937- *Ballpl 90*
Harkness, William Leonard 1934- *WhoAm 90*
Harknett, Richard F. 1938- *St&PR 91*
Harkow, Jaye Fredrica 1959- *WhoSSW 91*
Harkrader, Carleton Allen 1917- *WhoAm 90*
Harkrader, Carol Elizabeth 1951- *BiDrAPA 89*
Harkrader, Charles Johnston, Jr. 1913- *WhoAm 90*
Harkrader, Milton K., Jr. 1938- *St&PR 91*
Harkrader, Milton Keene, Jr. 1937- *WhoAm 90*
Harkrader, Sue Robertson 1941- *WhoSSW 91*
Harkrider, David Garrison 1931- *WhoAm 90*
Harkrider, Harold G. 1928- *St&PR 91*
Harl, Neil Eugene 1933- *WhoAm 90*
Harlacher, Beth Ann 1962- *WhoAmW 91*
Harlacher, Meredith I. 1942- *St&PR 91*
Harlam, Dean B 1947- *BiDrAPA 89*
Harlan, Andrew Jackson 1815-1907 *AmLegL*
Harlan, Brenda Kay *BiDrAPA 89*
Harlan, Bruce Lovell 1959- *WhoEmL 91*
Harlan, Christoph 1952- *IntWWM 90*
Harlan, David C. 1950- *St&PR 91*
Harlan, Donald Michael, Jr. 1956- *WhoEmL 91*
Harlan, Estle Mae 1939- *WhoAmW 91*
Harlan, Glen *ConAu 30NR*
Harlan, Irma *WhoSSW 91*
Harlan, Jack Rodney 1917- *WhoAm 90*
Harlan, James 1820-1899 *BiDrUSE 89*
Harlan, James C. 1928- *St&PR 91*
Harlan, James Kenneth 1951- *WhoWor 91*
Harlan, Jane Ann 1947- *WhoAmW 91*
Harlan, Jean Durgin 1924- *WhoAmW 91*
Harlan, John G. *BioIn 16, NewYTBS 90*
Harlan, John M. 1833-1911 *WorAlBi*
Harlan, John Marshall 1933- *St&PR 91*
Harlan, Leonard Morton 1936- *WhoE 91, WhoWor 91*
Harlan, Louis Rudolph 1922- *WhoAm 90*
Harlan, Martha *BioIn 16*
Harlan, Nathan V. 1846-1911 *AmLegL*
Harlan, Neil Eugene *BioIn 16*
Harlan, Neil Eugene 1921- *St&PR 91, WhoAm 90*
Harlan, Norman Ralph 1914- *WhoWor 91*
Harlan, Robert Dale 1929- *WhoAm 90*
Harlan, Robert Ernest 1936- *WhoAm 90*
Harlan, Robert Warren 1921- *WhoAm 90*
Harlan, Roma Christine *WhoAm 90, WhoAmA 91, WhoAmW 91, WhoWor 91*
Harlan, Ross 1919- *WhoWrEP 89*
Harlan, Ross Edgar 1919- *WhoAm 90, WhoSSW 91*
Harlan, Stephen Donald 1933- *WhoAm 90*
Harlan, Susan Negley 1949- *WhoAmW 91, WhoEmL 91*
Harlan, Thomas C. 1931- *St&PR 91*
Harlan, W. Glen 1912- *WhoAm 90*
Harland, Barbara Ferguson 1925- *WhoAmW 91, WhoE 91*
Harland, Marion 1830-1922 *FemiCLE*
Harland, Mary Kathryn Holtan 1946- *WhoAmW 91*
Harland, Sydney Cross 1891-1982 *DcNaB 1981*
Harland, William Bryce 1931- *WhoWor 91*
Harlass, Sherry Ellen Pool 1961- *WhoAmW 91*
Harle, John 1956- *PenDiMP*
Harlech, Baron 1918-1985 *DcNaB 1981*
Harlem, Susan Lynn 1950- *WhoAm 90*
Harleman, Ann 1945- *WhoWrEP 89*
Harleman, Donald Robert Fergusson 1922- *WhoAm 90*
Harless, Byron Brittingham 1916- *WhoAm 90*
Harless, Joe *BioIn 16*
Harless, Kathryn Frances 1946- *WhoWor 91*
Harless, Robert Lee 1940- *St&PR 91*
Harless, Susan Ettinger 1947- *WhoEmL 91*
Harleston, Bernard Warren 1930- *WhoAm 90, WhoE 91*
Harley, Al Boyce, Jr. 1932- *BiDrAPA 89*
Harley, Alexander Medard 1894- *IntWWM 90*
Harley, Brilliana 1600-1643 *BiDEWW, BioIn 16, FemiCLE*
Harley, Colin Kent 1953- *WhoEmL 91*
Harley, Dick 1872-1952 *Ballpl 90*
Harley, Edward Thomas 1927- *St&PR 91*
Harley, Martha *FemiCLE*
Harley, Naomi Hallden 1932- *WhoAm 90, WhoAmW 91*
Harley, Ned Richard *BiDrAPA 89*
Harley, Philip B. 1918- *St&PR 91*
Harley, Robert 1661-1724 *BioIn 16*
Harley, Robison Dooling 1911- *WhoAm 90*
Harley, Steve 1863-1947 *MusmAFA*
Harley, Wayne Chapin 1947- *St&PR 91*
Harley, William Gardner 1911- *WhoAm 90*
Harley, William Wallace, II 1951- *WhoE 91*
Harlin, Marilyn Miler 1934- *WhoAmW 91, WhoE 91*
Harlin, Robert Ray 1932- *WhoAm 90*
Harlin, Sam H. 1939- *St&PR 91*
Harlin, Vivian Krause 1924- *WhoAm 90*
Harline, Leigh 1907-1969 *OxCPMus*
Harling, Per Gunnar 1948- *IntWWM 90*
Harling, Robert 1910- *BioIn 16, TwCCr&M 91*
Harling, Robert 1951- *BioIn 16*
Harlinghausen, Martin 1902- *BioIn 16*
Harllee, JoAnn Towery 1951- *WhoEmL 91*
Harllee, John Thomas 1935- *WhoWrEP 89*
Harloff, Robert C. 1943- *St&PR 91*
Harlos, Steven Chapman 1953- *IntWWM 90*
Harlow, Alvin Fay 1875- *AuBYP 90*
Harlow, Ann 1951- *WhoAmA 91*
Harlow, Bonnie *BioIn 16*
Harlow, Bryce L. 1949- *WhoAm 90*
Harlow, Chris *BioIn 16*
Harlow, David Michael 1956- *WhoEmL 91*
Harlow, Eugene Marchand, Sr. 1957- *WhoEmL 91*
Harlow, Gary Lee 1945- *St&PR 91*
Harlow, Harold Eugene 1925- *WhoAm 90*
Harlow, James Gindling, Jr. 1934- *St&PR 91, WhoAm 90, WhoSSW 91*
Harlow, Jean 1911-1937 *BioAmW, WorAlBi*
Harlow, John Gronbech 1944- *St&PR 91*
Harlow, Jules 1931- *BioIn 16*
Harlow, Larry 1951- *Ballpl 90*
Harlow, LeRoy Francis 1913- *WhoAm 90, WhoWor 91*
Harlow, Lisa Lavoie 1951- *WhoAmW 91*
Harlow, Robert *BioIn 16*
Harlow, Robert Dean 1938- *St&PR 91, WhoAm 90*
Harlow, Steven Michael 1963- *WhoSSW 91*
Harlowe, Diane Marie 1947- *WhoEmL 91*
Harm, Duane R. 1939- *St&PR 91*
Harma, Laurence E. 1944- *St&PR 91*
Harman, Beulah *BioIn 16*
Harman, Billie C 1942- *BiDrAPA 89*
Harman, Carter 1918- *IntWWM 90*
Harman, Charles A. 1942- *St&PR 91*
Harman, Charles Michael 1947- *St&PR 91, WhoSSW 91*
Harman, Charles Morgan 1929- *WhoAm 90*
Harman, David E. 1933- *St&PR 91*
Harman, David Rex 1948- *IntWWM 90*
Harman, Donald Lee 1948- *WhoEmL 91, WhoWor 91*
Harman, Dudley M. 1935- *St&PR 91*
Harman, Fred *EncACom*
Harman, G. Don 1949- *St&PR 91*
Harman, George Gibson 1924- *WhoAm 90*
Harman, Gilbert Helms 1938- *WhoAm 90*
Harman, Jane 1945- *WhoEmL 91*
Harman, Jeanne Perkins *WhoSSW 91*
Harman, John Robert, Jr. 1921- *WhoAm 90*
Harman, John Royden 1921- *WhoAm 90*
Harman, Jonathan William 1954- *WhoE 91*
Harman, Julie Ann 1958- *WhoAmW 91*
Harman, Marla Zelene 1957- *WhoAmW 91*
Harman, Maryann Whittemore 1935- *WhoAmA 91*
Harman, Patt Claude, III 1947- *St&PR 91*
Harman, Samuel Bickerton 1819-1892 *DcCanB 12*
Harman, Thomas Scott 1957- *WhoEmL 91*
Harman, Willard Nelson 1937- *WhoAm 90*
Harman, William Boys, Jr. 1930- *WhoAm 90*
Harman, William Rittenhouse 1941- *WhoAm 90*
Harmar, Fairlie 1876-1945 *BiDWomA*
Harmar, Josiah 1753-1813 *WhNaAH*
Harmata, Al *BioIn 16*
Harmatuk, Frances A *BiDrAPA 89*
Harmatz, Fred Mark 1954- *St&PR 91*
Harmel, Hilda Herta *WhoAmW 91*
Harmel, Merel Hilber 1917- *WhoAm 90*
Harmelin, Stephen Joseph 1939- *WhoAm 90, WhoE 91, WhoWor 91*

Harmelink, Herman, III 1933- *WhoWor 91*
Harmell, Pamela Hersh 1947- *WhoAmW 91*
Harmen, Wendy Susan 1960- *WhoAmW 91, WhoE 91*
Harmening, Denise M. 1952- *WhoAmW 91*
Harmening, Thomas E. 1946- *ODwPR 91*
Harmening, Thomas Edward 1946- *WhoEmL 91*
Harmer, Alexander 1856-1925 *WhNaAH*
Harmer, Bertha 1885-1934 *BioIn 16*
Harmer, Clive Lucas 1940- *WhoWor 91*
Harmer, David G. 1943- *St&PR 91*
Harmer, Juliet *AuBYP 90*
Harmeson, Greg 1946- *St&PR 91*
Harmet, A. Richard 1932- *WhoWrEP 89*
Harmeyer, MaryEllen 1965- *WhoAmW 91*
Harmon, Alfred 1929- *St&PR 91*
Harmon, Allen D. 1951- *St&PR 91*
Harmon, Amy Catherine 1962- *WhoSSW 91*
Harmon, Artice Ward 1940- *WhoAmW 91*
Harmon, Barbara Nelle 1944- *WhoAmW 91*
Harmon, Barbara Sayre 1927- *WhoAmA 91*
Harmon, Benjamin Franklin, IV 1953- *WhoEmL 91*
Harmon, Bob 1887-1961 *Ballpl 90*
Harmon, Carolyn Kirkman 1942- *WhoSSW 91*
Harmon, Charlotte Buchwald 1916- *WhoAmW 91*
Harmon, Chuck 1926- *Ballpl 90*
Harmon, Claude 1916-1989 *BioIn 16*
Harmon, Cliff Franklin 1923- *WhoAmA 91*
Harmon, Cynthia Ann 1956- *WhoAmW 91*
Harmon, Dale Lynn 1931- *WhoSSW 91*
Harmon, Daniel Patrick 1938- *WhoAm 90*
Harmon, David Edward 1953- *WhoAmA 91*
Harmon, David Lynn 1958- *WhoEmL 91*
Harmon, Debbie *BioIn 16*
Harmon, Douglas Alexander 1946- *St&PR 91*
Harmon, Eli Beller *BiDrAPA 89*
Harmon, Emma Lee 1939- *WhoAmW 91*
Harmon, Florence Marion 1880-1936 *HarlReB*
Harmon, Foster 1912- *WhoAm 90, WhoAmA 91, WhoSSW 91, WhoWor 91*
Harmon, Gail McGreevy 1943- *WhoAmW 91*
Harmon, Gary G. 1937- *St&PR 91*
Harmon, Gary Lee 1935- *WhoAm 90*
Harmon, Gene L. *BioIn 16*
Harmon, George Marion 1934- *WhoAm 90, WhoSSW 91*
Harmon, Harry William 1918- *WhoAm 90*
Harmon, Jacqueline Baas 1934- *WhoSSW 91*
Harmon, James Allen 1935- *St&PR 91, WhoAm 90, WhoE 91*
Harmon, James Roderick 1952- *WhoAmA 91*
Harmon, Judith Trivette 1938- *WhoAmW 91*
Harmon, Judson 1846-1927 *BiDrUSE 89*
Harmon, Judy T. *ODwPR 91*
Harmon, Keith Hanna 1952- *WhoSSW 91*
Harmon, Lee Estabrook 1952- *WhoEmL 91*
Harmon, Leon G. 1925- *WhoAm 90*
Harmon, Lily 1912- *WhoAm 90, WhoAmA 91*
Harmon, Lynn Adrian 1944- *St&PR 91, WhoAm 90*
Harmon, Mark *BioIn 16*
Harmon, Mark 1951- *WhoAm 90, WorAlBi*
Harmon, Mark Nelson 1953- *WhoWor 91*
Harmon, Merle Reid, Sr. 1927- *WhoAm 90*
Harmon, Merrilee Lafferty 1952- *WhoAmW 91*
Harmon, Mont Judd 1917- *WhoAm 90*
Harmon, Patrick 1916- *WhoAm 90*
Harmon, Paul A. 1957- *St&PR 91*
Harmon, Phillip Louis 1954- *WhoEmL 91*
Harmon, Raymond William 1925- *St&PR 91*
Harmon, Richard L. 1923- *ODwPR 91*
Harmon, Robert E. 1939- *St&PR 91*
Harmon, Robert Gerald 1944- *WhoAm 90*
Harmon, Robert John 1946- *BiDrAPA 89*
Harmon, Robert Lee 1926- *St&PR 91, WhoAm 90*
Harmon, Robert Lon 1938- *WhoWor 91*
Harmon, Robert Lynn 1941- *WhoSSW 91*
Harmon, Robert Wayne 1929- *WhoAm 90*
Harmon, Ronald Lee 1943- *BiDrAPA 89*
Harmon, Ronald Paul 1952- *WhoAm 90*
Harmon, Terry 1944- *Ballpl 90*
Harmon, Tom *NewYTBS 90 [port]*
Harmon, Tom 1919-1990 *BioIn 16, News 90, -90-3*
Harmon, Tommy Allison, Jr. 1956- *WhoEmL 91*
Harmon, Victoria Tham 1956- *WhoAmW 91*
Harmon, W. David 1943- *WhoE 91*
Harmon, Wende Lyn 1960- *WhoEmL 91*
Harmon, William 1938- *ConAu 32NR*
Harmon, William Henry, Jr. 1943- *BiDrAPA 89*
Harmon Brown, Valarie Jean 1948- *WhoAmW 91*
Harmon-Pugh, Deborah 1956- *WhoEmL 91*
Harmonay, Maureen 1950- *WhoAmW 91*
Harmonic Choir *NewAgMG*
Harmoning, H. David 1938- *St&PR 91*
Harmony, Marlin Dale 1936- *WhoAm 90*
Harmony, Terrence *WhoWrEP 89*
Harms, Barbara J. 1947- *St&PR 91*
Harms, Carol J. 1953- *St&PR 91*
Harms, Douglas John 1951- *WhoEmL 91*
Harms, Elizabeth 1924- *WhoAmA 91*
Harms, Elizabeth Louise 1924- *WhoAm 90*
Harms, Fred D. 1946- *St&PR 91*
Harms, Gregory Martin 1949- *WhoSSW 91*
Harms, Henry B.C. 1919- *WhoWor 91*
Harms, Herbert Martin 1937- *WhoE 91*
Harms, John Kevin 1960- *WhoEmL 91*
Harms, Judy Ann 1949- *WhoEmL 91*
Harms, Lynn Roe 1951- *WhoEmL 91*
Harms, Robert Thomas 1932- *WhoAm 90*
Harms, Steven Alan 1949- *WhoEmL 91*
Harms, Valerie 1940- *WhoWrEP 89*
Harms, Warren *BioIn 16*
Harms, Wolfgang 1936- *WhoWor 91*
Harmsen, Harlan F. 1927- *St&PR 91*
Harmsen, Ricardo Eduardo 1955- *WhoHisp 91*
Harmsen, Tyrus George 1924- *WhoAm 90*
Harmsworth, Alfred Charles William 1865-1922 *BioIn 16*
Harnack, Curtis 1927- *WhoWrEP 89*
Harnack, Curtis, Mrs. *WhoAmW 91, WhoWor 91*
Harnack, Don Steger 1928- *WhoAm 90*
Harnack, Robert Spencer 1918- *WhoAm 90*
Harnage, Burnis E. *WhoSSW 91*
Harnden, Ruth Peabody *AuBYP 90*
Harned, David Baily 1932- *WhoAm 90*
Harned, Herbert Spencer, Jr. 1921- *WhoSSW 91*
Harned, Robert Glenn *BiDrAPA 89*
Harned, Roger Kent 1934- *WhoAm 90*
Harnedy, Edmund Richard 1930- *St&PR 91, WhoAm 90*
Harner, Michael *NewAgMG*
Harner, Michael James 1929- *WhoAm 90*
Harner, Paul B. 1909- *WhoAm 90*
Harner, Robert Harold 1927- *WhoAm 90*
Harnesk, Priscilla Ann 1955- *WhoAmW 91*
Harness, Gerry *BioIn 16*
Harness, Hugh Gregory 1930- *St&PR 91*
Harness, John Parker 1937- *St&PR 91*
Harness, Robert L. *St&PR 91*
Harness, William Edward 1940- *WhoAm 90*
Harness, William Walter 1945- *WhoSSW 91*
Harnest, Grant Hopkins 1916- *WhoAm 90*
Harnett, Carol Ann 1958- *WhoE 91*
Harnett, Cynthia Mary 1893-1981 *AuBYP 90*
Harnett, Daniel Joseph 1930- *WhoAm 90*
Harnett, David S *BiDrAPA 89*
Harnett, David S. 1951- *WhoE 91*
Harnett, Donald Lee 1937- *WhoAm 90*
Harnett, James Francis 1921- *WhoAm 90*
Harnett, Joel William 1925- *WhoAmA 91*
Harnett, Joel William, Mrs *WhoAmA 91*
Harnett, Joseph Durham 1917- *WhoAm 90*
Harnett, Lila 1926- *WhoAmW 91*
Harnett, Thomas Aquinas 1924- *WhoAm 90*
Harney, Ben 1871-1938 *OxCPMus*
Harney, Ben 1948- *DrBIPA 90*
Harney, Charles F. 1951- *St&PR 91*
Harney, Charles Francis 1951- *WhoAm 90*
Harney, David Moran 1924- *WhoWor 91*
Harney, Debra Ann 1962- *WhoAmW 91*
Harney, George Julian 1817-1897 *BioIn 16*
Harney, Kenneth Robert 1944- *WhoAm 90, WhoWrEP 89*
Harney, William John 1932- *St&PR 91*
Harney, William Selby 1800-1889 *WhNaAH*
Harnick, Robert Steven 1946- *BiDrAPA 89*
Harnick, Sheldon 1924- *OxCPMus*
Harnick, Sheldon Mayer 1924- *WhoAm 90*
Harnik, Peter Jonathan 1949- *WhoEmL 91*
Harning, Daniel Thomas 1935- *St&PR 91*
Harnish, Jay Dewey 1898- *WhoAm 90*
Harnish, Stephen Norman 1948- *BiDrAPA 89, WhoE 91*
Harnly, Caroline Day 1951- *WhoEmL 91*
Harnois, Gaston Paul 1943- *BiDrAPA 89*
Harnois, L. Paul 1931- *St&PR 91*
Harnois, Michael David 1956- *WhoEmL 91*
Harnoncourt, Nikolaus 1929- *IntWWM 90, PenDiMP, WhoWor 91, WorAlBi*
Harnoy, Ofra 1965- *IntWWM 90, PenDiMP*
Harnsberger, Therese Coscarelli *WhoAmW 91, WhoWor 91*
Haro *WhoAmA 91*
Haro, Jess D. *WhoHisp 91*
Haro, John Calvin 1928- *St&PR 91*
Haro, Sid 1931- *WhoHisp 91*
Haroian, Gary E. 1951- *St&PR 91*
Harold II 1020?-1066 *WorAlBi*
Harold, Georg 1947- *BioIn 16*
Harold, John Gordon 1955- *WhoAm 90, WhoWor 91*
Harold, John Thomas 1950- *St&PR 91*
Harold, Vincent John 1941- *St&PR 91*
Haroldson, Jeffrey David 1957- *WhoEmL 91*
Haroon, Abdullah Hussain 1950- *WhoWor 91*
Haroon-Ahmed, Syed 1931- *WhoWor 91*
Harootunian, Berj Avedis 1928- *WhoE 91*
Harootunian, Claire M 1930- *WhoAmA 91*
Haroun, Ansar M 1947- *BiDrAPA 89*
Harowitz, Charles Lichtenberg 1926- *WhoSSW 91*
Harp, Dana L. 1950- *WhoWor 91*
Harp, Donald Leon 1928- *St&PR 91*
Harp, Emile Francis 1928- *St&PR 91*
Harp, Paul Lindsey 1948- *St&PR 91*
Harp, Rufus William 1923- *WhoAm 90, WhoWor 91*
Harp, Steven Ray 1952- *St&PR 91*
Harp, William Lee 1949- *BiDrAPA 89*
Harpaz, Amos 1928- *WhoWor 91*
Harpe, Bernard De La *EncCRAm*
Harpe, Carol Ann 1955- *BiDrAPA 89*
Harpe, Winfield Scott 1937-1988 *BioIn 16*
Harper, Alfred E. *BioIn 16*
Harper, Alfred John, II 1942- *WhoAm 90*
Harper, Alison 1964- *BiDWomA*
Harper, Andrew *BioIn 16*
Harper, Andrew Henry 1935- *IntWWM 90*
Harper, Ashby Taylor 1916- *WhoAm 90*
Harper, Brian 1959- *Ballpl 90*
Harper, Carey Davis, III 1945- *St&PR 91*
Harper, Charles Little 1930- *WhoSSW 91*
Harper, Charles Michael 1926- *ConAmBL*
Harper, Charles Michael 1927- *St&PR 91*
Harper, Charles Michel 1927- *WhoAm 90, WhoWor 91*
Harper, Clyde Maurice 1931- *St&PR 91*
Harper, Conrad Kenneth 1940- *WhoAm 90*
Harper, Cornelia 1944- *WhoSSW 91*
Harper, David Edwin 1939- *St&PR 91*
Harper, David Michael 1953- *WhoSSW 91*
Harper, Dean Harrison 1929- *WhoAm 90*
Harper, Dean Owen 1934- *WhoSSW 91*
Harper, Deborah Ann Flammer 1953- *WhoAmW 91, WhoEmL 91*
Harper, Deborah Morse 1954- *WhoAmW 91*
Harper, Denise C. 1955- *WhoAmW 91*
Harper, Diane 1950- *WhoWor 91*
Harper, Dianne Sweat 1949- *WhoAmW 91*
Harper, Donald Jack 1928- *St&PR 91, WhoAm 90, WhoE 91*
Harper, Donald Victor 1927- *WhoAm 90*
Harper, Douglas C. 1934- *WhoWrEP 89*
Harper, Douglas M 1938- *BiDrAPA 89*
Harper, Dyan 1942- *WhoAmW 91*
Harper, Edward 1941- *PenDiMPA*
Harper, Edward J. 1910- *WhoAm 90*
Harper, Edwin L. 1941- *St&PR 91*
Harper, Edwin Leland 1941- *WhoAm 90*
Harper, Eleanor O'Neil 1919- *WhoAmA 91, WhoE 91*
Harper, Elisabeth 1957- *WhoAmW 91*
Harper, Emery Walter 1936- *WhoAm 90*
Harper, Ernest Bouldin, Jr. 1924- *St&PR 91*
Harper, Frances Ellen Watkins 1825-1911 *FemiCLE*
Harper, Fred Partick, Jr. 1951- *WhoEmL 91*
Harper, G.K. 1927- *St&PR 91*
Harper, George 1892-1978 *Ballpl 90*
Harper, George Coburn 1887-1962 *WhoAmA 91N*
Harper, George Mills 1914- *WhoAm 90*
Harper, Gerald 1945- *St&PR 91*
Harper, Gladys Coffey *WhoAmW 91*
Harper, Gordon P 1942- *BiDrAPA 89*
Harper, Gregory Livingston 1956- *WhoEmL 91*
Harper, Hal Dishon 1950- *WhoEmL 91*
Harper, Harlan, Jr. 1928- *WhoAm 90*
Harper, Harry 1895-1963 *Ballpl 90*
Harper, Harry Clifford 1939- *St&PR 91*
Harper, Heather 1930- *IntWWM 90, PenDiMP*
Harper, Heather Mary 1930- *WhoAm 90, WhoWor 91*
Harper, Henry H. 1934- *WhoAm 90*
Harper, Howard Fyfe 1930- *WhoWor 91*
Harper, Howard M., Jr. 1930- *WhoWrEP 89*
Harper, Ida 1851-1931 *FemiCLE*
Harper, Jack *BioIn 16*
Harper, Jack 1878-1950 *Ballpl 90*
Harper, James Allie, Jr. 1929- *WhoAm 90*
Harper, James Earl, III 1948- *WhoEmL 91, WhoSSW 91*
Harper, James Thomas 1949- *WhoSSW 91*
Harper, James William 1944- *St&PR 91*
Harper, James Winsmore 1939- *WhoSSW 91*
Harper, Janet Sutherlin Lane 1940- *WhoAmW 91*
Harper, Jean Marilyn 1952- *IntWWM 90*
Harper, Jeanne *ODwPR 91*
Harper, Jeff *BioIn 16*
Harper, Jene 1910- *WhoAm 90*
Harper, Jene Paul 1910- *St&PR 91*
Harper, Jewel Benton 1925- *WhoSSW 91, WhoWor 91*
Harper, Joe Steven 1947- *WhoSSW 91*
Harper, John Lander 1925- *WhoWor 91*
Harper, John R. 1931- *St&PR 91*
Harper, John Russell 1914-1983 *WhoAmA 91N*
Harper, Joseph Stanway 1953- *WhoEmL 91*
Harper, Josephine Cook 1929- *IntWWM 90*
Harper, Judson Morse 1936- *WhoAm 90*
Harper, Ken 1939?- *DrBIPA 90*
Harper, Laura Jane 1914- *WhoAmW 91*
Harper, Linda *WhoWrEP 89*
Harper, Linda Sue *BiDrAPA 89*
Harper, Lyndus E. 1905- *St&PR 91*
Harper, Marion 1916-1989 *BioIn 16*
Harper, Marion, Jr. 1916-1989 *CurBio 90N*
Harper, Marjory 1956- *ConAu 129*
Harper, Mary Sadler 1941- *St&PR 91, WhoAmW 91*
Harper, Michael John Kennedy 1935- *WhoSSW 91*
Harper, Mitchell Raymond 1958- *WhoSSW 91*
Harper, Norman Arthur James 1952- *IntWWM 90*
Harper, Norman Bernard 1923- *St&PR 91*
Harper, Owen Howe 1937- *WhoAm 90*
Harper, Patricia Ann 1957- *WhoAmW 91, WhoEmL 91*
Harper, Patricia Louise Hornberger 1942- *IntWWM 90*
Harper, Patricia N *BiDrAPA 89*
Harper, Ralph Champlin 1916- *WhoAm 90*
Harper, Ramey Wilson 1920- *WhoAm 90*
Harper, Richard Barnard 1949- *WhoEmL 91*
Harper, Richard Henry 1950- *WhoEmL 91, WhoWor 91*
Harper, Richard Russell 1944- *St&PR 91*
Harper, Robert *St&PR 91*
Harper, Robert Alexander 1924- *WhoAm 90*
Harper, Robert Allan 1915- *WhoAm 90*
Harper, Robert Andrew 1954- *WhoEmL 91*
Harper, Robert James 1940- *WhoWor 91*
Harper, Robert L. *ODwPR 91*
Harper, Robert Leslie 1939- *WhoAm 90*
Harper, Robert N 1922- *BiDrAPA 89*
Harper, Robert Ramsey 1936- *WhoSSW 91*
Harper, Robin Kelly 1961- *WhoAmW 91*
Harper, S. Birnie 1944- *St&PR 91, WhoAm 90*
Harper, Scott Peter 1962- *WhoE 91*
Harper, Stephen Coale 1947- *WhoSSW 91*
Harper, Sylvia K. 1949- *St&PR 91*
Harper, Terrell Ray 1908- *WhoAm 90*
Harper, Terry 1955- *Ballpl 90*
Harper, Thomas Buckman, III 1955- *WhoEmL 91*
Harper, Thomas S *BiDrAPA 89*
Harper, Tommy 1940- *Ballpl 90*
Harper, Valerie *BioIn 16*
Harper, Valerie 1940- *WhoAm 90, WorAlBi*
Harper, Walter Joseph 1947- *WhoAm 90, WhoEmL 91*
Harper, Wilhelmina 1884-1973 *AuBYP 90*
Harper, William 1944- *WhoAmA 91*
Harper, William Curtis 1942- *St&PR 91*
Harper, William Dana 1948- *WhoEmL 91*
Harper, William H. 1934- *St&PR 91*
Harper, William Rainey 1856-1906 *BioIn 16, WorAlBi*
Harper, William Thomas, III 1956- *WhoSSW 91*

Harper, Wyatt Eugene, III 1946- *WhoSSW 91*
Harpin, Lorna Rae 1958- *WhoAmW 91*
Harpole, B.C. 1934- *St&PR 91*
Harpole, Jerry Lee 1928- *WhoAm 90, WhoSSW 91*
Harpole, Murray J. 1921- *St&PR 91*
Harpool, Robert Thomas, Jr. 1918- *St&PR 91*
Harpprecht, Klaus Christoph 1927- *WhoWor 91*
Harpstead, Dale Douglas 1926- *WhoAm 90*
Harpster, James Erving 1923- *WhoSSW 91, WhoWor 91*
Harr, Clair H. 1939- *St&PR 91*
Harr, Donald L 1923- *BiDrAPA 89*
Harr, Gale Ann 1955- *WhoEmL 91*
Harr, Karl Gottlieb, Jr. 1922- *WhoAm 90*
Harr, Lawrence Francis 1938- *St&PR 91, WhoAm 90*
Harr, Lucy *ODwPR 91*
Harr, Lucy Loraine 1951- *WhoAm 90, WhoEmL 91*
Harr, Michael Edward 1951- *WhoEmL 91*
Harraden, Beatrice 1864-1936 *BioIn 16, FemiCLE*
Harrah, Robert E. 1916- *St&PR 91*
Harrah, Robert Eugene 1916- *WhoAm 90*
Harrah, Toby 1948- *Ballpl 90, BioIn 16*
Harral, Harriet Briscoe 1944- *WhoAmW 91*
Harral, John Menteith 1948- *WhoSSW 91*
Harran, Don 1936- *IntWWM 90*
Harrap, Julian *BioIn 16*
Harrar, George E. 1949- *WhoE 91*
Harrawood, Paul 1928- *WhoAm 90*
Harre, Alan Frederick 1940- *WhoAm 90*
Harreld, J. Bruce 1950- *St&PR 91*
Harreld, James Bruce 1950- *WhoAm 90*
Harreld, Kemper 1885-1971 *DcAfAmP*
Harreld, Michael Neal 1944- *St&PR 91*
Harrell, Anne *ConAu 30NR*
Harrell, Arthur Lee 1940- *WhoSSW 91*
Harrell, Barbara Fowler 1961- *WhoEmL 91*
Harrell, Brett Alexander 1961- *WhoSSW 91*
Harrell, Charles Lydon, Jr. 1916- *WhoSSW 91, WhoWor 91*
Harrell, Charles M. 1928- *St&PR 91*
Harrell, David Edwin, Jr. 1930- *WhoAm 90*
Harrell, Eileen *ODwPR 91*
Harrell, Everett Richard, Jr. 1922- *WhoAm 90*
Harrell, Gilbert D. *St&PR 91*
Harrell, Henry Howze 1939- *St&PR 91, WhoAm 90, WhoSSW 91*
Harrell, Horace William 1947- *WhoSSW 91*
Harrell, Irene Burk 1927- *WhoWrEP 89*
Harrell, Jackson J. 1944- *ODwPR 91*
Harrell, John M. 1828- *AmLegL*
Harrell, Linda Darlyn 1949- *WhoEmL 91*
Harrell, Lloyd Vernell 1944- *WhoSSW 91*
Harrell, Lyman Christian, III 1937- *St&PR 91*
Harrell, Lynn 1944- *IntWWM 90, PenDiMP*
Harrell, Lynn Morris 1944- *WhoAm 90*
Harrell, Mack 1909-1960 *PenDiMP*
Harrell, Martha Lynn Blackwell 1948- *WhoEmL 91*
Harrell, Matt *BioIn 16*
Harrell, Melton L. 1940- *St&PR 91*
Harrell, Phil *BioIn 16*
Harrell, Ray 1912-1984 *Ballpl 90*
Harrell, Ray Evans 1941- *IntWWM 90*
Harrell, Rebecca Ann Cobb 1960- *WhoSSW 91*
Harrell, Redin Paul 1932- *St&PR 91*
Harrell, Roy Alvin, Jr. 1936- *WhoE 91*
Harrell, Roy Harrison, Jr. 1928- *WhoSSW 91*
Harrell, Samuel Delargy 1958- *St&PR 91*
Harrell, Samuel M. 1931- *St&PR 91*
Harrell, Samuel Macy 1931- *WhoAm 90*
Harrell, Theresa Ann 1953- *WhoAmW 91*
Harrell, Walter Stanton, Jr. 1958- *WhoEmL 91*
Harrell, Wanda Faye 1942- *WhoSSW 91*
Harrell, William Edward, Jr. 1948- *WhoSSW 91*
Harrelson, Bud 1944- *Ballpl 90, WhoE 91*
Harrelson, Ken 1941- *Ballpl 90*
Harrelson, Ken 1942- *WhoAm 90*
Harrelson, Teresa Lynn 1950- *WhoAmW 91*
Harrelson, Walter Joseph 1919- *WhoAm 90, WhoWor 91*
Harrelson, Woody *BioIn 16*
Harrelson, Woody 19--?- *WorAlBi*
Harrer, Gustave Adolphus 1924- *WhoAm 90*
Harrer, Heinrich 1912- *ConAu 31NR*
Harreys, John Fisher 1933- *St&PR 91*
Harrhy, Eiddwen 1949- *IntWWM 90*
Harriau, Robert Raymond 1929- *St&PR 91*
Harribance, Lalsingh 1940- *EncPaPR 91*
Harrice, Nicholas Cy 1915- *WhoE 91*
Harridge, Will 1883-1971 *Ballpl 90 [port]*
Harries, Clive 1951- *IntWWM 90*
Harries, Gruffydd John 1954- *IntWWM 90*
Harries, Karsten 1937- *WhoAm 90*
Harries, Kathryn *IntWWM 90*
Harries, Mags 1945- *WhoAmA 91*
Harries, Susan Ann 1946- *WhoEmL 91*
Harriff, Suzanna Elizabeth 1953- *WhoAmW 91, WhoEmL 91*
Harrigan and Hart *OxCPMus*
Harrigan, Anthony Hart 1925- *WhoAm 90*
Harrigan, Arthur Washington 1919- *WhoAm 90, WhoE 91*
Harrigan, Edward 1844-1911 *OxCPMus*
Harrigan, Gail Labruzza 1951- *St&PR 91*
Harrigan, John Frederick 1925- *WhoAm 90*
Harrigan, John Thomas, Jr. 1929- *WhoAm 90, WhoE 91, WhoWor 91*
Harrigan, Kenneth W. 1927- *St&PR 91*
Harrigan, Kenneth William J. 1927- *WhoAm 90, WhoWor 91*
Harrigan, William Sweetser 1943- *St&PR 91, WhoAm 90*
Harriger, Gary Carl 1940- *St&PR 91*
Harrigian, Harold 1935- *St&PR 91*
Harrill, Donald L. 1950- *St&PR 91*
Harrill, Robert W. 1941- *WhoE 91*
Harriman, Averell 1891-1986 *BioIn 16*
Harriman, Constance Bastine *WhoAm 90*
Harriman, Edward H. 1848-1909 *WorAlBi*
Harriman, Florence Jaffray Hurst 1870-1967 *BioIn 16*
Harriman, Gerald Eugene 1924- *WhoAm 90*
Harriman, John Howland 1920- *WhoAm 90*
Harriman, Lucy L. 1951- *WhoAmW 91*
Harriman, Malcolm Bruce 1950- *WhoEmL 91, WhoSSW 91*
Harriman, Pamela *BioIn 16*
Harriman, Pamela Digby Churchill 1920- *WhoAm 90, WhoAmW 91*
Harriman, W. Averell 1891-1986 *WorAlBi*
Harriman, William Averell 1891-1986 *BiDrUSE 89*
Harriman-Kumor, Lisa Jayne 1959- *WhoAmW 91*
Harring, Barbara Allen 1933- *WhoAmW 91*
Harring, Dean Kenneth 1951- *WhoE 91*
Harringer, Olaf Carl 1919- *WhoAm 90*
Harrington, Anthony Ross 1958- *WhoSSW 91*
Harrington, Arnold Whitman 1931- *St&PR 91*
Harrington, Arthur John 1950- *WhoEmL 91*
Harrington, Bart, Jr. 1951- *WhoSSW 91*
Harrington, Basil Scott *BiDrAPA 89*
Harrington, Benjamin Davis 1924- *St&PR 91*
Harrington, Benjamin Davis, Jr. 1952- *St&PR 91*
Harrington, Benjamin Franklin, III 1922- *WhoAm 90*
Harrington, Bill 1927- *Ballpl 90*
Harrington, Bruce Michael 1933- *WhoAm 90*
Harrington, Bryan Rulison 1953- *WhoAmA 91*
Harrington, Chestee Marie 1941- *WhoAmA 91*
Harrington, Cornelius Daniel, Jr. 1927- *St&PR 91, WhoE 91*
Harrington, Craig James 1957- *WhoEmL 91*
Harrington, Daniel Phillip 1932- *BiDrAPA 89*
Harrington, David *BioIn 16, PenDiMP*
Harrington, Dean Butler *WhoAm 90*
Harrington, Deborah Jackson *BiDrAPA 89*
Harrington, Deborah Jane 1949- *WhoE 91*
Harrington, Diane Gail 1963- *WhoAmW 91, WhoWor 91*
Harrington, Donald C. 1912- *WhoAm 90*
Harrington, Donald James 1945- *WhoAm 90*
Harrington, Elizabeth Dallas *St&PR 91*
Harrington, Evelyn Davis *AuBYP 90*
Harrington, Francis Emile 1935- *BiDrAPA 89*
Harrington, Francis L. 1913- *St&PR 91*
Harrington, Frank L., Jr. 1928- *St&PR 91*
Harrington, Fred Harvey 1912- *WhoAm 90*
Harrington, Gary Burnes 1934- *WhoSSW 91*
Harrington, George F. *AmLegL*
Harrington, George Fred 1923- *WhoSSW 91*
Harrington, George L 1916- *BiDrAPA 89*
Harrington, George William 1929- *WhoAm 90*
Harrington, Gerald E. 1945- *St&PR 91*
Harrington, Gerard, III 1956- *WhoE 91*
Harrington, Geri *WhoWrEP 89*
Harrington, Glenn Lewis 1942- *St&PR 91, WhoWor 91*
Harrington, Harold E. 1929- *St&PR 91*
Harrington, J. P. 1865-1939 *OxCPMus*
Harrington, James V. 1939- *St&PR 91*
Harrington, Jean Patrice *WhoAm 90*
Harrington, Jeremiah J. 1936- *St&PR 91*
Harrington, Jeremy Thomas 1932- *WhoAm 90*
Harrington, Jerry *ODwPR 91*
Harrington, Jesse Moye, III 1940- *St&PR 91*
Harrington, Joanna 1845-1895 *DcCanB 12*
Harrington, John Charles 1955- *WhoE 91*
Harrington, John F. 1940- *ODwPR 91*
Harrington, John L 1928- *BiDrAPA 89*
Harrington, John Leonard, Jr. 1955- *WhoEmL 91*
Harrington, John Michael, Jr. 1921- *WhoAm 90*
Harrington, John Norris 1939- *WhoSSW 91*
Harrington, John Timothy 1921- *WhoAm 90*
Harrington, John Vincent 1919- *WhoAm 90*
Harrington, John W 1918-1986 *ConAu 132*
Harrington, Joseph 1939- *St&PR 91*
Harrington, Joseph John 1937- *WhoAm 90*
Harrington, Joyce *ODwPR 91, TwCCr&M 91*
Harrington, Joyce Gay 1939- *WhoE 91*
Harrington, Kathy *WhoAmW 91*
Harrington, Kevin B. 1929- *WhoE 91*
Harrington, LaMar 1917- *WhoAm 90, WhoAmA 91*
Harrington, Lee K. 1946- *St&PR 91*
Harrington, Louis Frank 1935- *WhoAm 90*
Harrington, Lyn Davis 1911- *AuBYP 90*
Harrington, Marguerite A. 1949- *St&PR 91*
Harrington, Marguerite Ann 1949- *WhoEmL 91*
Harrington, Marion Ray 1924- *WhoAm 90*
Harrington, Marjorie Elaine 1928- *WhoAmW 91*
Harrington, Matthew Jerome 1962- *WhoE 91*
Harrington, Michael 1928- *WhoWrEP 89*
Harrington, Michael 1928-1989 *AnObit 1989, BioIn 16, ConAu 129, EncAL, WorAlBi*
Harrington, Michael Ballou 1940- *WhoE 91*
Harrington, Michael Francis 1916- *WhoAm 90*
Harrington, Michael P. 1936- *St&PR 91*
Harrington, Michaele Mary 1946- *WhoE 91*
Harrington, Nancy Elaine 1955- *WhoSSW 91*
Harrington, Nora 1921- *WhoAmW 91*
Harrington, Pat, Jr. *WhoAm 90*
Harrington, Paul Charles 1939- *WhoAm 90*
Harrington, Peter N. *ODwPR 91*
Harrington, Peter Tyrus 1951- *WhoEmL 91*
Harrington, Rex *BioIn 16*
Harrington, Robert William 1950- *WhoEmL 91*
Harrington, Roger Fuller 1925- *WhoAm 90*
Harrington, Ronald George 1940- *St&PR 91*
Harrington, Ronald Rice 1937- *BiDrAPA 89*
Harrington, Roy V. 1928- *St&PR 91*
Harrington, Russell Doyne, Jr. 1944- *WhoSSW 91*
Harrington, Shaun Donald 1949- *St&PR 91*
Harrington, Sherman B. 1948- *WhoEmL 91*
Harrington, Susan Diane 1949- *WhoAmW 91*
Harrington, T.P. 1923- *St&PR 91*
Harrington, Theodore J. 1937- *St&PR 91*
Harrington, Thomas Daniel 1952- *WhoSSW 91*
Harrington, Thomas Joseph 1935- *WhoAm 90*
Harrington, Timothy J. 1918- *WhoAm 90, WhoE 91*
Harrington, Travers Rountree, Jr. 1949- *WhoEmL 91*
Harrington, Walter Joel 1916- *WhoAm 90*
Harrington, William 1931- *TwCCr&M 91, WhoE 91*
Harrington, William Charles 1942- *WhoAmA 91*
Harrington, William D. 1930- *St&PR 91*
Harrington, William David 1930- *WhoAm 90*
Harrington, William Fields 1920- *WhoAm 90*
Harrington-Connors, Erin 1959- *WhoWrEP 89*
Harrington-Hughes, Kathryn 1955- *WhoWrEP 89*
Harrington-Lloyd, Jeanne Leigh 1946- *WhoWor 91*
Harriott, Peter 1927- *WhoAm 90*
Harris, Aaron 1930- *WhoAm 90*
Harris, Adrian Llewellen 1950- *WhoWor 91*
Harris, Agnes *AuBYP 90*
Harris, Alan Jay 1950- *WhoAm 90*
Harris, Alan Michael 1953- *WhoSSW 91*
Harris, Albert Edward 1932- *St&PR 91*
Harris, Albert J 1908-1990 *ConAu 132*
Harris, Alfred 1919- *WhoAm 90*
Harris, Alfred Gene 1939- *St&PR 91*
Harris, Alfred Peter 1932- *WhoAmA 91, WhoE 91*
Harris, Alice *BioIn 16*
Harris, Alice Eaton 1924- *IntWWM 90, WhoAmW 91*
Harris, Alicia Lynne 1958- *WhoAmW 91*
Harris, Allan E. 1908- *St&PR 91*
Harris, Allen 1929- *WhoAm 90, WhoE 91, WhoWor 91*
Harris, Allen, Jr. 1906- *St&PR 91*
Harris, Allen Will *BioIn 16*
Harris, Andre *BioIn 16*
Harris, Anita Louise 1952- *WhoAmW 91*
Harris, Ann Birgitta Sutherland 1937- *WhoAm 90*
Harris, Ann Marie 1959- *WhoAmW 91*
Harris, Ann Noble 1947- *WhoEmL 91*
Harris, Ann S. *WhoAm 90*
Harris, Ann Sutherland 1937- *WhoAmA 91*
Harris, Anne Singer 1928- *WhoAmW 91*
Harris, Arthur James 1932- *St&PR 91*
Harris, Arthur Leon 1939- *BiDrAPA 89*
Harris, Arthur Travers 1892-1984 *DcNaB 1981*
Harris, Audrey Ellen 1916- *WhoWrEP 89*
Harris, Aurand 1915- *WhoAm 90*
Harris, Austin Francis 1928- *St&PR 91*
Harris, B. Clare 1937- *WhoAm 90*
Harris, B. Meyer 1910- *St&PR 91*
Harris, Barbara *ODwPR 91*
Harris, Barbara 1935- *WhoAm 90, WorAlBi*
Harris, Barbara Anne 1945- *WhoEmL 91*
Harris, Barbara Beck Czika 1942- *WhoAmW 91*
Harris, Barbara C. *BioIn 16*
Harris, Barbara Clementine 1930- *WhoAmW 91*
Harris, Barbara Jane 1953- *WhoAmW 91*
Harris, Barbara Thomas 1951- *WhoEmL 91*
Harris, Barry Lee 1939- *St&PR 91*
Harris, Basil 1918-1989 *BioIn 16*
Harris, Belinda Kay 1952- *WhoAmW 91*
Harris, Ben Jorj 1904-1957 *WhoAmA 91N*
Harris, Ben Maxwell 1923- *WhoAm 90*
Harris, Benjamin *BioIn 16*
Harris, Benjamin 1673?-1716 *EncCRAm*
Harris, Benjamin P., III 1936- *St&PR 91*
Harris, Bernard David 1956- *St&PR 91*
Harris, Bernard P. 1918- *St&PR 91*
Harris, Bernice 1893-1973 *FemiCLE*
Harris, Bernice Eisen 1927- *WhoE 91*
Harris, Bertha 1937- *FemiCLE*
Harris, Betsy Lee 1937- *WhoAmW 91*
Harris, Beverly Lorraine 1945- *WhoAmW 91*
Harris, Beverly Moore *BiDrAPA 89*
Harris, Bill *ConAu 30NR*
Harris, Bill 1900-1965 *Ballpl 90*
Harris, Bill 1923-1988 *BioIn 16*
Harris, Bill J. 1924- *St&PR 91*
Harris, Boaz 1926- *BiDrAPA 89*
Harris, Bob *ODwPR 91*
Harris, Bob 1916- *Ballpl 90*
Harris, Bob 1916-1976 *Ballpl 90*
Harris, Brian *BioIn 16*
Harris, Brian Craig 1941- *WhoWor 91*
Harris, Bruce Eugene 1950- *WhoEmL 91, WhoWor 91*
Harris, Bruce S. 1938- *WhoAm 90*
Harris, Bryan 1961- *ODwPR 91*
Harris, Bucky 1896-1977 *Ballpl 90 [port]*
Harris, Burt Irving 1922- *WhoAm 90*
Harris, Burton Henry 1941- *WhoE 91*
Harris, Burton M. 1938- *WhoAm 90*
Harris, C Glenn *BiDrAPA 89*
Harris, C. Philip 1949- *St&PR 91*
Harris, Calvin Jerome *BiDrAPA 89*
Harris, Carl Matthew 1940- *WhoE 91*
Harris, Carl R. 1951- *St&PR 91*
Harris, Carl Vernon 1922- *WhoAm 90*
Harris, Carmon Coleman 1904- *WhoAm 90*
Harris, Cassandra *BioIn 16*
Harris, Catherine Gardrine 1958- *WhoAmW 91*

Harris, Cecil 1919- BiDrAPA 89
Harris, Charles Edgar 1915- WhoAm 90, WhoSSW 91, WhoWor 91
Harris, Charles Edison 1946- WhoAm 90, WhoEmL 91
Harris, Charles Elmer 1922- WhoAm 90
Harris, Charles Frederick 1934- WhoAm 90
Harris, Charles Jewett 1949- WhoEmL 91
Harris, Charles K. 1865-1930 BioIn 16
Harris, Charles K. 1867-1930 OxCPMus
Harris, Charles Leon 1943- WhoE 91
Harris, Charles Robert BiDrAPA 89
Harris, Charles Thomas 1943- WhoAm 90
Harris, Charles Upchurch 1914- WhoWor 91
Harris, Charles Ward 1926- WhoAm 90
Harris, Charlie 1926- Ballpl 90
Harris, Charney Anita WhoAmA 91
Harris, Chauncy Dennison 1914- WhoAm 90, WhoWor 91
Harris, Cheryl Montgomery 1949- WhoWor 91
Harris, Chester 1938- WhoSSW 91
Harris, Christie 1907- AuBYP 90
Harris, Christie Lucy 1907- WhoAm 90
Harris, Christopher 1933- WhoAm 90
Harris, Christy Franklin 1945- WhoEmL 91
Harris, Claire 1937- FemiCLE
Harris, Claude 1940- WhoAm 90, WhoSSW 91
Harris, Clinton Page 1947- WhoEmL 91
Harris, Colin Cyril 1928- WhoAm 90
Harris, Colin George Scott 1944- WhoWor 91
Harris, Colver AuBYP 90
Harris, Conley 1943- WhoAmA 91
Harris, Coralee 1954- St&PR 91
Harris, Corra 1869-1935 FemiCLE
Harris, Corra May 1869-1935 BioAmW
Harris, Curtis B., Jr. 1944- St&PR 91
Harris, Cynthia O 1923- BiDrAPA 89
Harris, Cyril Manton WhoAm 90
Harris, D. Alan 1949- WhoEmL 91
Harris, D. George 1933- WhoAm 90
Harris, Dale Anne 1953- BiDrAPA 89
Harris, Dale Benner 1914- WhoAm 90
Harris, Dale Hutter 1932- WhoAmW 91
Harris, Dale Ray 1937- WhoAm 90
Harris, Daniel Paul 1959- WhoEmL 91
Harris, Darryl Wayne 1941- WhoAm 90
Harris, Dave 1900-1973 Ballpl 90
Harris, David B. 1946- WhoEmL 91
Harris, David Ford 1931- WhoE 91
Harris, David Henry 1924- WhoAm 90
Harris, David J. St&PR 91N
Harris, David Jack 1948- WhoAmA 91
Harris, David Marshall 1949- WhoSSW 91
Harris, David Mayer 1944- St&PR 91
Harris, David Nelson 1954- WhoE 91
Harris, David P. 1937- St&PR 91
Harris, David Scott 1958- WhoEmL 91
Harris, Debra BiDrAPA 89
Harris, Debra Lynne 1956- WhoAmW 91
Harris, Deena R 1951- BiDrAPA 89
Harris, Del William WhoAm 90
Harris, Denise Koppelman 1953- WhoE 91
Harris, Dian Helms 1951- WhoSSW 91
Harris, Diana Clelland 1952- WhoAmW 91, WhoE 91
Harris, Diana Koffman 1929- WhoAmW 91
Harris, Diane 1947- WhoAmW 91
Harris, Diane Barbara BiDrAPA 89
Harris, Diane Carol 1942- St&PR 91, WhoAm 90, WhoAmW 91
Harris, Diane Feuillan 1932- WhoWrEP 89
Harris, Dolores Ashley WhoAmA 91
Harris, Dolores M. 1930- WhoAmW 91
Harris, Don Victor, Jr. 1921- WhoAm 90
Harris, Donald 1931- IntWWM 90, WhoAm 90
Harris, Donald George 1932- St&PR 91
Harris, Donald Paul 1931- BiDrAPA 89
Harris, Donald S. ODwPR 91
Harris, Donna Lee 1949- WhoAmW 91
Harris, Dorothy Clark 1949- WhoAmW 91
Harris, Dorothy D 1935- WhoAmA 91
Harris, Dorothy Dierks 1935- WhoAmW 91
Harris, Dorothy Vilma 1936- WhoHisp 91
Harris, Douglas Clay 1939- St&PR 91, WhoAm 90
Harris, Douglas J. 1955- St&PR 91
Harris, E. Edward 1931- WhoAm 90
Harris, Earl Douglas 1947- WhoSSW 91
Harris, Earl F. 1921- St&PR 91
Harris, Ed 1950- WorAlBi
Harris, Eddie 1934- DrBlPA 90
Harris, Edna Mae 1914?- DrBlPA 90
Harris, Edna Mae 1950- WhoWrEP 89
Harris, Edward Allen 1950- WhoAm 90
Harris, Edward D., Jr. 1937- WhoAm 90
Harris, Edward S. 1928- St&PR 91
Harris, Edward Sawyer 1928- WhoE 91
Harris, Eldon Dwayne 1938- St&PR 91
Harris, Elizabeth Ann 1957- WhoAmW 91
Harris, Elizabeth Holder 1944- WhoAmW 91
Harris, Ella Mae 1930- WhoAmW 91
Harris, Ellen Gandy 1910- WhoAm 90
Harris, Ellen Schwartz 1949- WhoAmA 91
Harris, Elliot Albert 1925- BiDrAPA 89
Harris, Elliott Stanley 1922- WhoAm 90
Harris, Elmer Beseler 1939- WhoAm 90
Harris, Emily 1947- WorAlBi
Harris, Emily Katharine WhoWrEP 89
Harris, Emily Marion 1844?-1900 FemiCLE
Harris, Emily Stella BiDrAPA 89
Harris, Emma Earl 1936- WhoAmW 91
Harris, Emmylou BioIn 16, WhoNeCM A [port]
Harris, Emmylou 1947- ConMus 4 [port], WhoAm 90, WhoAmW 91, WorAlBi
Harris, Emmylou 1949- OxCPMus
Harris, Eric Nathan 1959- WhoEmL 91
Harris, Everett 1916- St&PR 91
Harris, F. Edward WhoSSW 91
Harris, Frances Alvord 1909- WhoAmW 91
Harris, Frances Ann 1950- WhoSSW 91
Harris, Francesca Treppeda 1958- WhoAmW 91, WhoE 91
Harris, Francis 1957- ConAu 130
Harris, Franco 1950- WorAlBi
Harris, Frank 1851-1931 BioIn 16
Harris, Frank 1856-1931 WorAlBi
Harris, Frank, III BioIn 16
Harris, Frank, III 1956- WhoWrEP 89
Harris, Frank H BiDrAPA 89
Harris, Frank Richard 1931- ODwPR 91
Harris, Fred R. 1930- WhoAm 90
Harris, Fred Scott 1942- St&PR 91
Harris, Frederick George 1922- WhoAm 90
Harris, Gail 1931- Ballpl 90
Harris, Gary Brooks 1955- WhoSSW 91
Harris, Gayle Thomas 1938- WhoAmW 91
Harris, Geneva Duke 1946- WhoAmW 91
Harris, George A. 1950- ConAu 130
Harris, George C BiDrAPA 89
Harris, George Clinton 1925- WhoAm 90
Harris, George Daniel 1954- WhoEmL 91
Harris, Geraldine 1951- BioIn 16
Harris, Gladys Bailey 1947- WhoEmL 91
Harris, Glen Alan 1960- WhoEmL 91
Harris, Glenn Ferguson 1949- BiDrAPA 89
Harris, Gloriane 1947- WhoAmA 91
Harris, Grace Salzman 1929- WhoAmW 91
Harris, Grant Anderson 1914- WhoAm 90
Harris, Greg 1955- Ballpl 90
Harris, Greg 1963- Ballpl 90
Harris, Gregory Scott 1955- WhoAm 90
Harris, Guy D. 1943- St&PR 91
Harris, Gypsy Joe BioIn 16
Harris, H A 1902-1974 ConAu 30NR
Harris, H S 1926- ConAu 130
Harris, Hannah E 1938- BiDrAPA 89
Harris, Harold 1915- ConAu 132
Harris, Harold Daniel 1942- St&PR 91
Harris, Harold Joseph 1920- BiDrAPA 89
Harris, Harold R. 1895-1988 AnObit 1988
Harris, Harold Ross 1895-1988 BioIn 16
Harris, Harriet Louise 1950- WhoEmL 91
Harris, Harry 1919- WhoAm 90
Harris, Harvey Sherman 1915- WhoAmA 91
Harris, Harwell Hamilton NewYTBS 90
Harris, Harwell Hamilton 1903- WhoAm 90
Harris, Helen Webb EarBlAP
Harris, Hendon M. 1916-1981 BioIn 16
Harris, Henry Hiter, Jr. 1922- WhoAm 90
Harris, Henry U., Jr. 1926- St&PR 91
Harris, Henry Upham, Jr. 1926- WhoAm 90
Harris, Henry William 1919- WhoAm 90
Harris, Henry Wood 1938- WhoAm 90
Harris, Herbert 1911- TwCCr&M 91
Harris, Herbert I 1905- BiDrAPA 89
Harris, Herbert Irwin 1926- WhoWor 91
Harris, Herbert Michael 1950- WhoSSW 91
Harris, Hiawatha 1929- BiDrAPA 89
Harris, Hilda BioIn 16
Harris, Hollis Loyd 1931- St&PR 91, WhoAm 90, WhoSSW 91
Harris, Howard E. 1929- St&PR 91
Harris, Howard Elliott 1943- WhoAm 90
Harris, Howard Frank 1923- St&PR 91
Harris, Howard Hunter 1924- WhoAm 90
Harris, Hoyt Clark 1920- WhoSSW 91
Harris, Hubert L. BioIn 16
Harris, Hunter P BiDrAPA 89
Harris, Irving 1927- WhoAm 90, WhoWor 91
Harris, Irving Brooks 1910- St&PR 91, WhoAm 90
Harris, Irving D BiDrAPA 89
Harris, Isaac Henson 1912- WhoAm 90
Harris, Isaac Ron 1954- WhoEmL 91
Harris, J. Ira BioIn 16
Harris, J. Roy 1901- St&PR 91
Harris, J. Warren WhoSSW 91
Harris, Jack H. BioIn 16
Harris, Jack Howard, II 1945- WhoEmL 91, WhoSSW 91, WhoWor 91
Harris, Jacke Curtis 1929- WhoE 91
Harris, Jacob 1924- BiDrAPA 89
Harris, Jacob George 1938- WhoAm 90
Harris, Jacqueline Ann 1955- BiDrAPA 89
Harris, Jacqueline L 1929- SmATA 62 [port]
Harris, James, III BioIn 16
Harris, James B. 1925- St&PR 91
Harris, James Carol Overton, Jr. 1940- WhoE 91
Harris, James Carroll 1940- BiDrAPA 89
Harris, James Carroll, II 1951- WhoSSW 91
Harris, James Dexter 1919- WhoAm 90
Harris, James Franklin 1941- WhoAm 90
Harris, James Herman 1942- WhoWor 91
Harris, James Howard 1961- WhoEmL 91
Harris, James Martin 1928- WhoAm 90
Harris, James R 1924- BiDrAPA 89
Harris, James Stewart, Jr. 1942- WhoAm 90
Harris, James T. 1951- ODwPR 91
Harris, James Thomas 1851-1931 BioIn 16
Harris, Jana N. 1947- WhoWrEP 89
Harris, Janet 1932-1979 AuBYP 90
Harris, Janet Young 1952- WhoEmL 91
Harris, Jay BioIn 16
Harris, Jay H. St&PR 91
Harris, Jay Stephen 1938- WhoE 91
Harris, Jay Terrence 1948- WhoAm 90
Harris, Jean BioIn 16
Harris, Jean C. 1927-1988 BioIn 16
Harris, Jean Louise 1931- WhoAm 90
Harris, Jean Noton 1934- IntWWM 90
Harris, Jean Witt 1924- BioAmW
Harris, Jed Gilbert, Jr. 1954- WhoSSW 91
Harris, Jeffery 1936- IntWWM 90
Harris, Jeffrey 1944- WhoAm 90
Harris, Jeffrey Sherman 1944- WhoAm 90
Harris, Jerome Estese 1953- WhoEmL 91
Harris, Jerome Sylvan 1909- WhoAm 90
Harris, Jessie G. 1909- WhoAmW 91
Harris, Jessie Moffat 1937- WhoE 91
Harris, Joan Bernstein WhoAmW 91
Harris, Joan Patricia 1930- St&PR 91
Harris, Joe 1882-1966 Ballpl 90
Harris, Joe 1891-1959 Ballpl 90
Harris, Joe Allen BiDrAPA 89
Harris, Joe Eugene 1958- WhoSSW 91
Harris, Joe Frank 1936- WhoAm 90, WhoSSW 91, WhoWor 91
Harris, Joe Newton 1946- WhoEmL 91
Harris, Joel Bruce 1941- WhoAm 90
Harris, Joel Chandler 1848-1908 AuBYP 90, BioIn 16, WorAlBi
Harris, Joellen Cotten 1944- WhoSSW 91
Harris, John AuBYP 90, TwCCr&M 91
Harris, John 1931- BioIn 16
Harris, John A. 1932- St&PR 91
Harris, John Bunyan, III 1952- WhoE 91
Harris, John Charles 1943- WhoAm 90
Harris, John Corydon 1947- St&PR 91
Harris, John Edward 1936- WhoAm 90
Harris, John J 1934- BiDrAPA 89
Harris, John Kenneth 1948- WhoE 91
Harris, John Leonard 1833-1898 DcCanB 12
Harris, John N. 1939- St&PR 91
Harris, John Patrick 1942- WhoE 91
Harris, John Randall, IV BiDrAPA 89
Harris, John William 1920- WhoAm 90
Harris, John William 1949- WhoAm 90
Harris, John Woods 1893- WhoWor 91
Harris, Jonathan 1921- BioIn 16
Harris, Jonathan Beryl 1958- WhoEmL 91
Harris, Jonathan M. 1947- St&PR 91
Harris, Jonathan Mark 1948- WhoE 91
Harris, Joseph 1835-1899 DcCanB 12
Harris, Joseph 1918- WhoWrEP 89
Harris, Joseph H BiDrAPA 89
Harris, Joseph Lamar 1951- WhoSSW 91
Harris, Joseph P. 1935- St&PR 91
Harris, Joya Renee 1961- WhoAmW 91, WhoWor 91
Harris, Joyce A. 1954- WhoSSW 91
Harris, Judith Ann White 1939- WhoWor 91
Harris, Judith Hill 1949- WhoAmW 91
Harris, Jules Eli 1934- WhoAm 90
Harris, Julian 1896-1988 ConAu 31NR
Harris, Julie BioIn 16
Harris, Julie 1925- AuBYP 90, ConTFT 8 [port], NotWoAT, WhoAm 90, WorAlBi
Harris, Julius 1924?- DrBlPA 90
Harris, Jullian Hoke 1906-1987 WhoAmA 91N
Harris, June Starkey 1932- St&PR 91
Harris, Junius J. 1834- AmLegL
Harris, K. David 1927- WhoAm 90
Harris, Karen H. 1934- WhoWrEP 89
Harris, Karen Kostock 1942- St&PR 91, WhoAmW 91
Harris, Katherine Kirby BiDrAPA 89
Harris, Katherine Leidel 1954- WhoAmW 91
Harris, Kathy Jean 1951- WhoEmL 91
Harris, Keith David 1949- IntWWM 90
Harris, Keith Dwain 1938- St&PR 91
Harris, Keith Lloyd BiDrAPA 89
Harris, Kenneth 1919- ConAu 129
Harris, Kevin J. 1953- WhoWrEP 89
Harris, Kim Sutherland 1952- St&PR 91
Harris, Kimberly Anne 1965- WhoSSW 91
Harris, King W. 1943- St&PR 91
Harris, King William 1943- WhoAm 90
Harris, Lara 1962- WhoE 91
Harris, Larry 1939- BioIn 16
Harris, Lavinia ConAu 32NR
Harris, Lawrence Peyton, Jr. 1947- WhoEmL 91
Harris, Lawrence Thomas 1873-1960 AmLegL
Harris, Lenore Zobel 1944- WhoAmW 91
Harris, Leon A., Jr. 1926- AuBYP 90, WhoAm 90
Harris, Leon A, Jr 1926- WhoAmA 91
Harris, Leon Martin 1934- BiDrAPA 89
Harris, Leonard 1927- BiDrAPA 89, St&PR 91
Harris, Leonard R. ODwPR 91
Harris, Leonard Richard 1922- WhoAm 90
Harris, Leslie 1929- WhoAm 90
Harris, Lily Marjorie 1956- WhoAmA 91
Harris, Linda Faye Bates 1939- WhoAmW 91
Harris, Linda Kay 1947- WhoAmW 91
Harris, Lisa Campbell 1961- WhoAmW 91
Harris, Llywela Vernon 1931- IntWWM 90
Harris, Lolita Pazant 1947- WhoSSW 91
Harris, Louis 1921- WhoAm 90
Harris, Louis A. 1932- St&PR 91
Harris, Louis William 1939- WhoAm 90
Harris, Louise IntWWM 90, ODwPR 91
Harris, Louise 1903- WhoAmW 91, WhoE 91, WhoWor 91
Harris, Lucille S 1914-1984 WhoAmA 91N
Harris, Lum 1915- Ballpl 90
Harris, Lynne Stallings 1943- WhoAmW 91
Harris, Lyttleton Tazwell, IV 1940- WhoSSW 91
Harris, M Jackuelyn 1957- BiDrAPA 89
Harris, M.M. 1916- St&PR 91
Harris, M Robert 1919- BiDrAPA 89
Harris, Mac Donald 1921- WhoWrEP 89
Harris, Madalene Ruth 1925- WhoWrEP 89
Harris, Major BioIn 16
Harris, Margaret 1943- WhoAmW 91, WhoE 91, WhoWor 91
Harris, Margaret Rosezarian 1943- IntWWM 90
Harris, Margie Coleman 1891- WhoAmA 91N
Harris, Marie 1943- WhoWrEP 89
Harris, Marie-Therese 1939- WhoWrEP 89
Harris, Marilyn 1931- BioIn 16
Harris, Marion Hopkins 1938- WhoAmW 91
Harris, Marion Rose 1925- ConAu 30NR
Harris, Marjorie Fields 1964- WhoEmL 91
Harris, Mark 1922- Ballpl 90, WhoAm 90, WhoWrEP 89
Harris, Mark Hugh 1932- WhoE 91
Harris, Mark Jonathan 1941- WhoWrEP 89
Harris, Mark Wayne 1950- WhoEmL 91
Harris, Markham 1907- WhoAm 90
Harris, Martha G. 1943- WhoWrEP 89
Harris, Martha Jane 1926- WhoAmW 91
Harris, Martin 1944- BioIn 16
Harris, Martin Harvey 1932- WhoAm 90
Harris, Martin Seymour 1935- WhoE 91
Harris, Martyn 1952- ConAu 132
Harris, Marvin 1927- WhoWrEP 89
Harris, Marvin 1932- BiDrAPA 89
Harris, Mary BiDEWW
Harris, Mary 1830-1930 BioIn 16
Harris, Mary B. 1933- WhoAmW 91
Harris, Matthew 1956- IntWWM 90
Harris, Matthew Jeffrey 1959- St&PR 91
Harris, Max 1918- IntWWM 90, OxCPMus
Harris, Mel BioIn 16
Harris, Mel 1942- BioIn 16
Harris, Melanie Gause 1949- WhoWrEP 89
Harris, Melba Iris 1945- WhoSSW 91
Harris, Melvin 1940- EncO&P 3
Harris, Merle Wiener 1942- WhoE 91
Harris, Merry WhoWrEP 89
Harris, Micalyn Shafer 1941- WhoAmW 91, WhoE 91, WhoWor 91

Harris, Michael Alan 1937- *BiDrAPA 89*
Harris, Michael Robert 1943- *WhoE 91*
Harris, Mickey 1917-1971 *Ballpl 90*
Harris, Milton 1906- *WhoAm 90*
Harris, Milton E. 1927- *WhoAm 90*
Harris, Milton Lanier, Jr. 1956- *BiDrAPA 89*
Harris, Milton M. 1916- *WhoAm 90*
Harris, Miriam 1834-1925 *FemiCLE*
Harris, Morgan 1916- *WhoAm 90*
Harris, Morgan Hovey, Jr. 1932- *WhoWor 91*
Harris, Muriel 1925- *BiDrAPA 89*
Harris, Natholyn Dalton 1939- *WhoAmW 91*
Harris, Neil 1938- *WhoAm 90*
Harris, Neil Patrick *BioIn 16*
Harris, Neison 1915- *St&PR 91, WhoAm 90*
Harris, Nell H. *WhoAm 90*
Harris, Nelson G. 1926- *St&PR 91*
Harris, Nelson George 1926- *WhoAm 90*
Harris, Nicholas George 1939- *WhoAm 90*
Harris, Nick G. 1927- *St&PR 91*
Harris, Oren 1903- *WhoAm 90*
Harris, Orville Jeff 1937- *WhoSSW 91*
Harris, Owen L. 1942- *St&PR 91*
Harris, Patricia Lea 1952- *WhoAmW 91*
Harris, Patricia Roberts 1924-1985 *BiDrUSE 89, WorAlBi*
Harris, Paul 1925- *WhoAm 90, WhoAmA 91*
Harris, Paul Charles 1953- *WhoEmL 91*
Harris, Paul David 1956- *IntWWM 90*
Harris, Paul G. *ODwPR 91*
Harris, Paul Lynwood, Jr. 1945- *WhoAm 90*
Harris, Paul Rogers 1933- *WhoAmA 91*
Harris, Paul Stewart 1906- *WhoAm 90, WhoAmA 91*
Harris, Penny Smith 1941- *WhoE 91*
Harris, Peter Charles 1923- *WhoWor 91*
Harris, Peter Christopher 1942- *WhoAm 90*
Harris, Peter Quincy *BiDrAPA 89*
Harris, Peter Quincy 1947- *WhoE 91*
Harris, Phil 1904- *OxCPMus*
Harris, Phil 1906- *WorAlBi*
Harris, Philip John 1926- *WhoAm 90*
Harris, Philip Robert 1926- *WhoAm 90*
Harris, R. Eleanor M. 1936- *WhoAmW 91*
Harris, Ralph N *BiDrAPA 89*
Harris, Randy *WhoAm 90*
Harris, Randy Hayes 1956- *WhoEmL 91*
Harris, Raymond 1919-1989 *BioIn 16, ConAu 129*
Harris, Raymond Jesse 1916- *WhoE 91, WhoWor 91*
Harris, Reese H., Jr. 1911- *St&PR 91*
Harris, Reta Loreen 1953- *BiDrAPA 89*
Harris, Rhonda K. 1957- *St&PR 91*
Harris, Rhonda Kidd 1957- *St&PR 91*
Harris, Richard 1928?-1987 *ConAu 129*
Harris, Richard 1933- *WhoAm 90, WorAlBi*
Harris, Richard Carter 1946- *St&PR 91, WhoAm 90*
Harris, Richard Colebrook 1936- *WhoAm 90*
Harris, Richard Eugene Vassau 1945- *WhoEmL 91*
Harris, Richard Foster, III 1942- *WhoSSW 91*
Harris, Richard Foster, Jr. 1918- *WhoAm 90, WhoSSW 91, WhoWor 91*
Harris, Richard Franklin 1940- *St&PR 91*
Harris, Richard Hayden 1928- *St&PR 91*
Harris, Richard John 1936- *St&PR 91, WhoAm 90*
Harris, Richard Lee 1928- *WhoAm 90*
Harris, Richard Leigh 1956- *IntWWM 90*
Harris, Richard Mallaby *WhoAm 90*
Harris, Richard Max 1935- *WhoAm 90*
Harris, Richard Michael 1941- *WhoAm 90, WhoSSW 91*
Harris, Richard Philip 1951- *BiDrAPA 89*
Harris, Richard Steven 1949- *WhoEmL 91*
Harris, Robert *BioIn 16*
Harris, Robert *BioIn 16*
Harris, Robert 1952- *WhoAm 90*
Harris, Robert A. 1928- *IntWWM 90*
Harris, Robert Allen 1938- *WhoAm 90*
Harris, Robert Allison 1939- *WhoAm 90*
Harris, Robert Bruce 1931- *St&PR 91*
Harris, Robert Bruce 1945- *WhoEmL 91*
Harris, Robert C. 1916- *St&PR 91*
Harris, Robert E. 1928- *St&PR 91*
Harris, Robert George 1911- *WhoAmA 91*
Harris, Robert Glen 1933- *St&PR 91*
Harris, Robert Jennings 1907- *WhoAm 90*
Harris, Robert Laird 1911- *WhoAm 90*
Harris, Robert Mark 1948- *BiDrAPA 89*
Harris, Robert N. *St&PR 91*
Harris, Robert Norman 1920- *WhoAm 90*
Harris, Robert Oberndoerfer 1929- *WhoE 91*
Harris, Roberta Lucas 1916- *WhoAmW 91*
Harris, Roberta Stuart 1937- *WhoAmW 91*
Harris, Robie H. *BioIn 16*
Harris, Robin *NewYTBS 90*
Harris, Robin 1953-1990 *BioIn 16*
Harris, Rod D. 1955- *WhoEmL 91*
Harris, Rodger Craig 1949- *WhoEmL 91*
Harris, Rodney 1947- *WhoEmL 91*
Harris, Roger Clark 1938- *BiDrAPA 89, WhoE 91*
Harris, Roger Clyde 1940- *IntWWM 90*
Harris, Ronald David 1938- *WhoAm 90*
Harris, Ronald Harvey 1947- *St&PR 91*
Harris, Ronald Lee 1942- *St&PR 91*
Harris, Ronald Paul 1955- *WhoEmL 91*
Harris, Ronell F. 1934- *St&PR 91*
Harris, Ronnie Charles 1953- *WhoEmL 91*
Harris, Rosalie Shonfeld *ODwPR 91*
Harris, Rosemary *AuBYP 90, BioIn 16, ConAu 30NR*
Harris, Rosemary Ann 1930- *NotWoAT, WhoAm 90*
Harris, Roy 1898-1979 *PenDiMP A*
Harris, Roy Hartley 1928- *WhoAm 90*
Harris, Rue M. 1931- *St&PR 91*
Harris, Rufus C. 1897-1988 *BioIn 16*
Harris, Russell E. 1942- *St&PR 91*
Harris, Ruth Bates *WhoAm 90*
Harris, Ruth Berman 1916- *IntWWM 90, WhoAmW 91*
Harris, Ruth Cameron 1916- *WhoAmW 91*
Harris, Ruth Morrison *WhoAmW 91*
Harris, Sandra Arrington 1951- *WhoAmW 91*
Harris, Sandy Ellen 1956- *WhoAmW 91*
Harris, Sharon Joy 1953- *WhoEmL 91*
Harris, Sharon Mae 1957- *WhoAmW 91*
Harris, Shelley Follansbee 1949- *WhoAmW 91*
Harris, Shelly A. *St&PR 91*
Harris, Shereen Nina 1961- *WhoAmW 91*
Harris, Sherri Kay 1960- *WhoEmL 91*
Harris, Sherwin J *BiDrAPA 89*
Harris, Sidon, V 1935- *WhoSSW 91*
Harris, Silas G. *AmLegL*
Harris, Sophia Bracy *BioIn 16*
Harris, Spence 1900-1982 *Ballpl 90*
Harris, Stacy *WhoAmW 91, WhoWrEP 89*
Harris, Stanley Earl 1952- *BiDrAPA 89*
Harris, Stanley S. 1927- *WhoAm 90*
Harris, Stephen E. 1943- *St&PR 91*
Harris, Stephen Ernest 1936- *WhoAm 90*
Harris, Stephen James 1954- *WhoEmL 91*
Harris, Stephen M 1929- *BiDrAPA 89*
Harris, Stephen Russell 1951- *WhoEmL 91*
Harris, Steven Jay 1945- *WhoEmL 91*
Harris, Steven M. 1964- *St&PR 91*
Harris, Steven Michael 1957- *BioIn 16*
Harris, Steven P. 1936- *St&PR 91*
Harris, Steven Zoltan 1953- *WhoEmL 91*
Harris, Stuart *ConAu 129*
Harris, Susan *BioIn 16, WhoAm 90, WhoAmW 91*
Harris, Susan Adele *BiDrAPA 89*
Harris, Susan Hunt 1959- *WhoAmW 91*
Harris, Susan Rose 1957- *WhoEmL 91*
Harris, Susan Straw *BioIn 16*
Harris, Susannah *EncO&P 3*
Harris, Suzanne Straight 1944- *WhoAm 90*
Harris, Sydney Malcolm 1917- *WhoAm 90*
Harris, T. George 1924- *WhoAm 90, WhoWrEP 89*
Harris, Temple W. 1948- *St&PR 91*
Harris, Thelissa A *BiDrAPA 89*
Harris, Theodore 1912-1988 *BioIn 16*
Harris, Theodore Edward 1919- *WhoAm 90*
Harris, Theodore Wilson 1921- *BioIn 16*
Harris, Theresa *DrBlPA 90*
Harris, Thomas 1940- *TwCCr&M 91*
Harris, Thomas A *BiDrAPA 89*
Harris, Thomas Everett 1912- *WhoAm 90*
Harris, Thomas Harold 1933- *WhoAm 90*
Harris, Thomas L. 1931- *ODwPR 91, St&PR 91, WhoAm 90*
Harris, Thomas Lake 1823-1906 *EncO&P 3*
Harris, Thomas Orville 1935- *WhoSSW 91*
Harris, Thomas R., Jr. 1931- *St&PR 91*
Harris, Thomas Raymond 1937- *WhoAm 90*
Harris, Thomas Sarafen 1947- *WhoEmL 91, WhoWor 91*
Harris, Thomas Stuart 1941- *BiDrAPA 89*
Harris, Tim *BioIn 16*
Harris, Timothy 1946- *TwCCr&M 91*
Harris, Timothy Francis 1948- *St&PR 91*
Harris, Tom P. 1951- *St&PR 91*
Harris, Townsend 1804-1878 *BioIn 16, EncJap*
Harris, Traci Alane 1961- *WhoAmW 91*
Harris, Tracy 1958- *WhoAmA 91*
Harris, Valerie Coleman 1957- *WhoAmW 91*
Harris, Vera Evelyn 1932- *WhoAmW 91*
Harris, Vic 1905-1978 *Ballpl 90*
Harris, Vic 1950- *Ballpl 90*
Harris, Victoria Louise *BiDrAPA 89*
Harris, Vincent Crockett 1913- *WhoAm 90*
Harris, W. Alden 1932- *St&PR 91*
Harris, W. Gibson 1916- *St&PR 91*
Harris, Wade Allen *BiDrAPA 89*
Harris, Walter Edgar 1915- *WhoAm 90*
Harris, Walton Bryan 1949- *WhoSSW 91*
Harris, Warren Louis 1952- *WhoEmL 91*
Harris, Wayne Manley 1925- *WhoAm 90, WhoWor 91*
Harris, Weston J. *BioIn 16*
Harris, Whitney Robson 1912- *WhoAm 90, WhoWor 91*
Harris, Wiley Lee 1949- *WhoE 91*
Harris, William 1945- *WorAlBi*
Harris, William C. *WhoSSW 91*
Harris, William Cecil 1913- *WhoAm 90*
Harris, William E.B. 1919- *St&PR 91*
Harris, William F., Jr. 1933- *ConAu 30NR*
Harris, William Franklin 1951- *WhoSSW 91*
Harris, William G. 1952- *St&PR 91*
Harris, William Hamilton 1927- *WhoAm 90*
Harris, William Hamilton 1944- *WhoAm 90, WhoSSW 91*
Harris, William J. 1942- *WhoWrEP 89*
Harris, William James, Jr. 1918- *WhoAm 90*
Harris, William John 1928- *WhoAm 90*
Harris, William Lee 1948- *WhoSSW 91*
Harris, William Lewarne Capes 1929- *IntWWM 90*
Harris, William M 1919- *BiDrAPA 89*
Harris, William Merl 1931- *WhoAm 90*
Harris, William Myrick 1919- *WhoE 91*
Harris, William Norman 1952- *WhoE 91*
Harris, William North 1938- *WhoSSW 91*
Harris, William R. 1922- *St&PR 91*
Harris, William Robert *BiDrAPA 89*
Harris, William S. 1938- *St&PR 91*
Harris, William Stanworth 1950- *WhoSSW 91*
Harris, William T. 1948- *WhoEmL 91*
Harris, William Thomas *BioIn 16*
Harris, William Torrey 1835-1909 *WorAlBi*
Harris, William Vernon 1938- *WhoAm 90*
Harris, William Wadsworth, II *WhoAmA 91*
Harris, William Warren 1956- *WhoE 91*
Harris, Wilson 1921- *BioIn 16, MajTwCW*
Harris, Yvonne Leigh 1945- *WhoAmW 91*
Harris-Bain, Amy L. 1937- *WhoAmW 91*
Harris-Crouthers, Rebecca Louise 1959- *WhoEmL 91*
Harris-Holoway, Geraldine 1958- *WhoAmW 91*
Harris-Smith, Joan A. 1933- *WhoAmW 91*
Harrisberger, Edgar Lee 1924- *WhoAm 90*
Harrison, Alan V. 1952- *St&PR 91*
Harrison, Albert Vale 1924- *BiDrAPA 89*
Harrison, Alexandra M *BiDrAPA 89*
Harrison, Aline M. 1940- *WhoAmW 91*
Harrison, Allan 1911- *WhoAmA 91N*
Harrison, Allen 1940- *St&PR 91*
Harrison, Anna Jane 1912- *WhoAm 90, WhoAmW 91*
Harrison, Anna Symmes 1775-1864 *BioIn 16*
Harrison, Anne Elizabeth 1941- *WhoAmW 91*
Harrison, Anthony R. *ODwPR 91*
Harrison, Antony H. 1948- *ConAu 132*
Harrison, Barbara Grizzuti 1934- *WhoAm 90*
Harrison, Barry 1935- *ConAu 129*
Harrison, Beatrice 1892-1965 *PenDiMP*
Harrison, Beatrice Marie 1958- *WhoAmW 91, WhoWor 91*
Harrison, Benjamin 1833-1901 *BiDrUSE 89, BioIn 16, WorAlBi*
Harrison, Benjamin 1910- *St&PR 91*
Harrison, Benjamin Leslie 1928- *WhoAm 90*
Harrison, Betty Carolyn Cook 1939- *WhoAmW 91*
Harrison, Bruce Raymond 1947- *WhoAm 90*
Harrison, Burgess Antonio 1957- *WhoEmL 91*
Harrison, C. William, Jr. 1913- *AuBYP 90*
Harrison, Carl W. 1936- *St&PR 91*
Harrison, Carla Isley 1948- *WhoAmW 91*
Harrison, Carlos Enrique 1956- *WhoHisp 91*
Harrison, Carole 1933- *WhoAmA 91*
Harrison, Caroline Scott 1832-1892 *BioIn 16*
Harrison, Carter Henry 1935- *St&PR 91, WhoAm 90*
Harrison, Charles Edgar 1926- *St&PR 91*
Harrison, Charles Edward 1923- *WhoWrEP 89*
Harrison, Charles Maurice 1927- *WhoAm 90*
Harrison, Charles Philip 1948- *St&PR 91*
Harrison, Charles Wagner, Jr. 1913- *WhoAm 90, WhoWor 91*
Harrison, Charles William 1940- *St&PR 91*
Harrison, Chip *TwCCr&M 91*
Harrison, Christine Delane 1947- *WhoAmW 91*
Harrison, Chuck 1941- *Ballpl 90*
Harrison, Claire 1934- *ODwPR 91*
Harrison, Clifford Joy, Jr. 1925- *WhoAm 90*
Harrison, Constance 1843-1920 *FemiCLE*
Harrison, Craig Donald 1956- *WhoEmL 91, WhoWor 91*
Harrison, Dandridge L. 1953- *ODwPR 91*
Harrison, David Lee 1937- *St&PR 91*
Harrison, David Livingstone 1933- *WhoAm 90*
Harrison, David Wesley 1954- *WhoSSW 91*
Harrison, Deborah Ann 1957- *WhoAmW 91*
Harrison, Derek Birch 1947- *IntWWM 90*
Harrison, Donald 1928- *WhoAm 90*
Harrison, Donald Carey 1934- *WhoAm 90*
Harrison, Donald Gilmour 1920- *St&PR 91*
Harrison, Dorothy L. 1916-1989 *BioIn 16*
Harrison, Douglas Edwin 1937- *St&PR 91*
Harrison, Douglas Patrick 1937- *WhoSSW 91*
Harrison, E. Bruce 1932- *ODwPR 91*
Harrison, Earl David 1932- *WhoAm 90, WhoE 91, WhoWor 91*
Harrison, Earle 1903- *WhoAm 90*
Harrison, Edna Brigham 1902- *WhoWrEP 89*
Harrison, Edward Robert 1919- *WhoAm 90*
Harrison, Edwin Thomas, III 1949- *WhoEmL 91*
Harrison, Elizabeth *FemiCLE*
Harrison, Elizabeth Pittman 1948- *WhoSSW 91*
Harrison, Emmett Bruce, Jr. 1932- *WhoAm 90*
Harrison, Ernest 1926- *WhoWor 91*
Harrison, Ernest Franklin 1929- *WhoAm 90*
Harrison, Evelyn Byrd 1920- *WhoAm 90*
Harrison, Frances Marie 1934- *WhoAmW 91*
Harrison, Frank 1913- *WhoAm 90*
Harrison, Frank E., IV 1950- *St&PR 91*
Harrison, Frank Joseph 1919- *WhoWor 91*
Harrison, Frank Llewelyn 1905-1987 *BioIn 16*
Harrison, Frank Randall 1953- *WhoEmL 91*
Harrison, Frank Russell, III 1935- *WhoAm 90*
Harrison, Fred *ConAu 31NR*
Harrison, Frederic 1831-1923 *BioIn 16*
Harrison, George *BioIn 16, PenDiMP*
Harrison, George 1943- *ConTFT 8, EncPR&S 89, OxCPMus, WhoAm 90, WhoWor 91, WorAlBi*
Harrison, George Braxton 1941- *WhoSSW 91*
Harrison, George L. 1887-1958 *EncABHB 7 [port]*
Harrison, Gerald 1929- *St&PR 91, WhoAm 90*
Harrison, Gilbert Warner 1940- *WhoE 91*
Harrison, Glennon Joseph 1952- *WhoE 91*
Harrison, Gloria Gimma 1928- *WhoAmW 91*
Harrison, Gordon Ray 1931- *WhoAm 90*
Harrison, Gregory 1950- *WhoAm 90*
Harrison, Gregory Arnold 1944- *WhoE 91*
Harrison, Gretchen Steiner 1957- *WhoEmL 91*
Harrison, H. Duane 1930- *ODwPR 91*
Harrison, Harry 1925- *RGTwCSF, WhoWrEP 89*
Harrison, Harry Max 1925- *AuBYP 90*
Harrison, Helen Amy 1943- *WhoAmA 91*
Harrison, Helen Eileen Connolly 1949- *WhoAmW 91*
Harrison, Helen Mayer *WhoAmA 91*
Harrison, Henry Baldwin 1821-1901 *AmLegL*
Harrison, Henry Starin 1930- *WhoAm 90, WhoE 91*
Harrison, Herman A. 1932- *St&PR 91*
Harrison, Horace Hawes 1924- *WhoAm 90*
Harrison, Howard F 1947- *BiDrAPA 89*
Harrison, Hubert H. 1883-1927 *EncAL*
Harrison, Ira Enell 1933- *WhoSSW 91*
Harrison, Irving B *BiDrAPA 89*
Harrison, Irwin J. 1930- *WhoAm 90*
Harrison, J. Frank, Jr. 1930- *WhoAm 90, WhoSSW 91*
Harrison, J. Smith 1925- *St&PR 91*
Harrison, Jackita 1947- *WhoAmW 91*

Harrison, James C. 1931- *WhoSSW 91*
Harrison, James C., IV 1947- *St&PR 91*
Harrison, James G 1925- *BiDrAPA 89*
Harrison, James J., Jr. 1936- *St&PR 91*
Harrison, James Joshua, Jr. 1936- *WhoAm 90*
Harrison, James Martin 1951- *St&PR 91*
Harrison, James Merritt 1915- *WhoAm 90*
Harrison, James Thomas 1937- *WhoAm 90, WhoWrEP 89*
Harrison, James Wilburn 1918- *WhoSSW 91*
Harrison, Jane 1850-1928 *FemiCLE*
Harrison, Jane Ellen 1850-1928 *BioIn 16*
Harrison, Janet Leah 1944- *WhoAmW 91*
Harrison, Jeffrey Standish 1958- *WhoSSW 91*
Harrison, Jeffrey Woods 1957- *WhoWrEP 89*
Harrison, Jeremy Thomas 1935- *WhoAm 90*
Harrison, Jerry *BioIn 16*
Harrison, Jim 1937- *BioIn 16*
Harrison, Jimmie 1952- *WhoAmA 91*
Harrison, Joan Shirley 1934- *WhoAmW 91*
Harrison, John *PenDiDA 89*
Harrison, John 1924- *ConAu 129*
Harrison, John Alexander 1944- *WhoAm 90*
Harrison, John Armstrong 1915- *WhoAm 90*
Harrison, John Arthur 1936- *WhoAm 90*
Harrison, John Brown 1944- *WhoSSW 91*
Harrison, John Clement 1913-1989 *BioIn 16*
Harrison, John Conway 1913- *WhoAm 90*
Harrison, John Devereux, Jr. 1955- *WhoWrEP 89*
Harrison, John H. 1928- *St&PR 91*
Harrison, John Marc 1945- *WhoE 91*
Harrison, John Mark 1958- *WhoEmL 91*
Harrison, John Ray 1930- *WhoAm 90, WhoSSW 91*
Harrison, John Raymond 1933- *WhoAm 90*
Harrison, John Robert 1923- *WhoAm 90*
Harrison, John Whately 1931- *BiDrAPA 89*
Harrison, Jonty 1952- *IntWWM 90*
Harrison, Joseph Gillis, Jr. 1950- *WhoHisp 91*
Harrison, Joseph Glenn *BiDrAPA 89*
Harrison, Joseph Heavrin 1929- *WhoWor 91*
Harrison, Joseph Robert, Jr 1918- *WhoAmA 91*
Harrison, Juanita 1891?- *HarlReB*
Harrison, Judy Coffin 1939- *WhoAmW 91*
Harrison, Keith Patrick 1938- *St&PR 91*
Harrison, Ken L. 1942- *St&PR 91, WhoAm 90*
Harrison, Laura Colvin- *BioIn 16*
Harrison, Lawrence V *BiDrAPA 89*
Harrison, Leisa Dione 1962- *WhoAmW 91*
Harrison, Leland 1883-1951 *BioIn 16*
Harrison, Lois Cowles 1934- *WhoAmW 91*
Harrison, Lois Smith 1924- *WhoAmW 91, WhoE 91*
Harrison, Lou *NewAgMG*
Harrison, Lou 1917- *IntWWM 90*
Harrison, Lynde 1837-1906 *AmLegL*
Harrison, Lynn Henry, Jr. 1944- *WhoSSW 91*
Harrison, Marcie Anne 1946- *WhoEmL 91*
Harrison, Margaret Maud 1899- *IntWWM 90*
Harrison, Marguerite 1879-1970 *BioAmW*
Harrison, Maria 1823?-1904 *BiDWomA*
Harrison, Marion Edwyn 1931- *WhoAm 90, WhoE 91, WhoWor 91*
Harrison, Marjorie Jeanne 1923- *WhoAmW 91, WhoWor 91*
Harrison, Mark Alan 1931- *St&PR 91*
Harrison, Mark I. 1934- *WhoAm 90*
Harrison, Mark Robert 1819-1894 *DcCanB 12*
Harrison, Mark Scott 1945- *WhoAm 90*
Harrison, Marshall 1933- *BioIn 16*
Harrison, Martha Elaine 1962- *WhoAmW 91*
Harrison, Mary 1788-1875 *BiDWomA*
Harrison, Mary Anne 1944- *WhoAmW 91*
Harrison, Mary Elizabeth 1938- *IntWWM 90*
Harrison, Mary Frances Nall 1918- *WhoAmW 91*
Harrison, Mary Kathryn 1952- *WhoAmW 91*
Harrison, Mary Lu 1942- *WhoAmW 91*
Harrison, Mary Scott Lord Dimmick 1858-1948 *BioIn 16*
Harrison, Mary St. Leger Kingsley 1852-1931 *BioIn 16*
Harrison, Maxwell 1912-1990 *BioIn 16*
Harrison, May 1891-1959 *PenDiMP*
Harrison, Merritt Neel 1934- *St&PR 91*
Harrison, Michael *BioIn 16, NewAgMG*
Harrison, Michael 1907- *TwCCr&M 91*
Harrison, Michael Jay 1932- *WhoAm 90*
Harrison, Michelle 1942- *BiDrAPA 89*
Harrison, Monika Edwards 1949- *WhoAm 90*
Harrison, Nelsine Frances 1941- *WhoAmW 91*
Harrison, Newton A 1932- *WhoAmA 91*
Harrison, Orrin Lea, III 1949- *WhoEmL 91*
Harrison, Otis Gene 1929- *St&PR 91*
Harrison, Patricia *BiDrAPA 89*
Harrison, Patricia Greenwood 1937- *WhoAmW 91*
Harrison, Patricia S. *ODwPR 91*
Harrison, Patrick Woods 1946- *WhoEmL 91*
Harrison, Paul Carter 1936- *DrBIPA 90*
Harrison, Peter 1716-1775 *EncCRAm*
Harrison, Phil *ODwPR 91*
Harrison, Philip Lewis 1945- *WhoEmL 91, WhoWrEP 89*
Harrison, Phyllis 1934- *WhoAmW 91*
Harrison, Phyllis A *BiDrAPA 89*
Harrison, R.D. 1923- *St&PR 91*
Harrison, R.S. 1931- *St&PR 91*
Harrison, Ray 1928- *TwCCr&M 91*
Harrison, Raymond Patrick 1949- *WhoEmL 91*
Harrison, Rebecca Fay 1949- *WhoSSW 91*
Harrison, Reginald Carey 1908-1990 *ConAu 131*
Harrison, Rex *BioIn 16, ConAu 131*
Harrison, Rex 1908-1990 *CurBio 90N, NewYTBS 90 [port], News 90, OxCPMus, WorAlBi*
Harrison, Richard 1864-1935 *DrBIPA 90*
Harrison, Richard 1920- *WhoWor 91*
Harrison, Richard Donald 1923- *WhoAm 90, WhoSSW 91*
Harrison, Richard L *BiDrAPA 89*
Harrison, Richard Norris 1949- *WhoSSW 91*
Harrison, Robert Arthur 1926- *St&PR 91*
Harrison, Robert Castleman 1800?-1868 *AmLegL*
Harrison, Robert Charles 1933- *St&PR 91*
Harrison, Robert Drew 1923- *WhoAm 90*
Harrison, Robert Edwin 1944- *WhoSSW 91*
Harrison, Robert H *BiDrAPA 89*
Harrison, Robert J. 1931- *BioIn 16*
Harrison, Robert Joseph 1931- *WhoAm 90*
Harrison, Robert Lee 1930- *St&PR 91*
Harrison, Robert Sattler 1931- *WhoAm 90*
Harrison, Robert Stephen 1932- *WhoSSW 91*
Harrison, Robert Vernon McElroy 1935- *WhoAm 90*
Harrison, Robert Wayne 1950- *WhoEmL 91*
Harrison, Robert William 1915- *WhoE 91, WhoWor 91*
Harrison, Robert William 1927- *St&PR 91*
Harrison, Roberta Francine 1942- *WhoSSW 91*
Harrison, Roger Gran 1943- *WhoAm 90*
Harrison, Roric 1946- *Ballpl 90*
Harrison, Rosalie Thornton 1917- *WhoAmW 91*
Harrison, S. David 1930- *WhoAm 90*
Harrison, Samuel Hughel 1956- *WhoEmL 91, WhoSSW 91*
Harrison, Sarah 1946- *SmATA 63*
Harrison, Saul I 1925- *BiDrAPA 89*
Harrison, Selig Seidenman 1927- *WhoAm 90*
Harrison, Shelley Brown 1951- *WhoAmW 91*
Harrison, Sidney 1903-1986 *PenDiMP*
Harrison, Simon M. 1954- *WhoEmL 91*
Harrison, Stanley Earl 1930- *WhoAm 90*
Harrison, Stephen Andrew 1941- *St&PR 91*
Harrison, Stephen Coplan 1943- *WhoAm 90*
Harrison, Stephen Earle 1941- *St&PR 91*
Harrison, Stephen Ray 1943- *BiDrAPA 89*
Harrison, Steven Dale 1958- *WhoEmL 91*
Harrison, Steven R. 1951- *St&PR 91*
Harrison, Susan 1859-1935 *FemiCLE*
Harrison, Susan Frances 1859-1935 *DcLB 99 [port]*
Harrison, Susanna 1752-1784 *FemiCLE*
Harrison, Ted 1926- *BioIn 16*
Harrison, Teresa Harshman 1953- *WhoEmL 91*
Harrison, Thomas A. 1953- *ODwPR 91*
Harrison, Thomas E. *WhoAm 90*
Harrison, Thomas Gene 1949- *WhoEmL 91*
Harrison, Thomas James 1935- *WhoAm 90*
Harrison, Tillson Lever 1888-1946 *BioIn 16*
Harrison, Timothy Stone 1927- *WhoAm 90*
Harrison, Tony 1931- *WhoAmA 91*
Harrison, Tony 1937- *MajTwCW, WorAu 1980 [port]*
Harrison, Utta Karin 1936- *St&PR 91*
Harrison, Vickie Elaine 1959- *WhoEmL 91*
Harrison, Virginia Budd 1927- *WhoSSW 91*
Harrison, W. Allen 1932- *St&PR 91*
Harrison, Wallace K. 1895-1981 *WorAlBi*
Harrison, Wallace Kirkman 1895-1981 *BioIn 16*
Harrison, Warren 1951- *WhoEmL 91*
Harrison, Warren 1956- *WhoEmL 91*
Harrison, Wayne L 1951- *BiDrAPA 89*
Harrison, Whit *TwCCr&M 91*
Harrison, William *PenDiMP*
Harrison, William B. 1943- *St&PR 91*
Harrison, William Burwell, Jr. 1943- *WhoAm 90*
Harrison, William Henry 1773-1841 *BiDrUSE 89, BioIn 16, WhNaAH, WorAlBi*
Harrison, William Loring 1936- *St&PR 91*
Harrison, William Neal 1933- *WhoAm 90, WhoWrEP 89*
Harrison, William Oliver, Jr. 1945- *WhoSSW 91*
Harrison, William Wright 1915- *WhoAm 90*
Harrison, Wilma Marcia *BiDrAPA 89*
Harrison, Yola G. 1947- *WhoSSW 91*
Harrison-Clark, Anne 1938- *WhoAmW 91*
Harrison-Hinds, Sharlene Mavis 1951- *WhoEmL 91*
Harrison-Johnson, Yvonne E. 1939- *WhoAmW 91*
Harrison-McClafferty, Monica Regina 1964- *WhoAmW 91*
Harriss, Clement Lowell 1912- *WhoE 91*
Harriss, Don *NewAgMG*
Harriss, Herbert Lynch 1943- *St&PR 91*
Harriss, Lucas Edward 1934- *St&PR 91*
Harriss, R. P. 1902-1989 *BioIn 16*
Harriss, R P 1902-1989 *ConAu 129*
Harriss, Robert Preston 1902-1989 *BioIn 16*
Harriss, Slim 1896-1963 *Ballpl 90*
Harrist, Earl 1919- *Ballpl 90*
Harriton, Abraham 1893-1986 *WhoAmA 91N*
Harritt, Norman L. 1941- *St&PR 91*
Harro, Barbara Leigh 1928- *WhoAmW 91*
Harrod, Billy Joe 1933- *WhoAm 90, WhoWor 91*
Harrod, Delton Vernal 1949- *WhoE 91*
Harrod, Donald Joseph 1944- *St&PR 91*
Harrod, Frances 1866-1956 *FemiCLE*
Harrod, Jeffrey William 1935- *WhoWor 91*
Harrod, Lawrence Wayne 1950- *WhoEmL 91*
Harrod, Scott 1910- *WhoAm 90*
Harrod's Jubilee Singers *DcAfAmP*
Harroff, Jerry Marlin 1932- *St&PR 91*
Harrold, Bernard 1925- *WhoAm 90*
Harrold, Dennis Edward 1947- *WhoEmL 91*
Harrold, Gordon Coleson 1906- *WhoSSW 91, WhoWor 91*
Harrold, James Sammuel, Jr. 1950- *BiDrAPA 89*
Harrold, Orville Robert 1932- *St&PR 91*
Harrold, Pamela Kay 1947- *WhoEmL 91*
Harrold, Ronald Thomas 1933- *WhoAm 90*
Harrold, William Eugene 1936- *WhoWrEP 89*
Harron, Donald 1924- *OxCCanT*
Harron, Gerald A. 1943- *St&PR 91*
Harrop, Daniel Smith, III 1954- *BiDrAPA 89, WhoE 91*
Harrop, Robert Daniel 1950- *WhoEmL 91*
Harrop, William Caldwell 1929- *WhoAm 90, WhoWor 91*
Harroun, Dorothy Sumner 1935- *WhoAmA 91*
Harrover, Roy Perkins 1928- *WhoAm 90*
Harrow, Gustave *NewYTBS 90*
Harrow, Lisa *ConTFT 8*
Harrow, Rachel Sarah *BiDrAPA 89*
Harrower, Angeline A. 1937- *WhoAmW 91*
Harrower, Elizabeth 1928- *FemiCLE*
Harrower, George Alexander 1924- *WhoAm 90*
Harry, Bruce Edgar 1949- *BiDrAPA 89*
Harry, Deborah 1945- *ConMus 4 [port], ConTFT 8 [port], News 90 [port], WorAlBi*
Harry, Deborah Ann 1945- *ConAu 129, WhoAm 90*
Harry, Jackee *BioIn 16*
Harry, Robert Hayden 1918- *WhoAm 90*
Harry, Roy Thomas 1953- *BiDrAPA 89*
Harry, Susan Elaine 1961- *WhoAmW 91*
Harry, William, III 1955- *WhoAm 90, WhoE 91, WhoWor 91*
Harryhausen, Ray 1920- *ConTFT 8*
Harryvan, Jacobus Franciscus 1949- *WhoWor 91*
Harsaghy, Fred Joseph, Jr. 1916- *WhoE 91, WhoWor 91*
Harsanyi, Charles 1905-1973 *WhoAmA 91N*
Harsanyi, Fruzsina M. *ODwPR 91*
Harsanyi, Fruzsina M. 1942- *St&PR 91*
Harsanyi, Janice 1929- *IntWWM 90, WhoAm 90*
Harsanyi, John Charles 1920- *WhoAm 90*
Harsanyi, Nicholas 1913- *IntWWM 90*
Harsch, Harold H *BiDrAPA 89*
Harsch, Joseph C. 1905- *WhoAm 90*
Harsch, Steven Merrill 1947- *WhoEmL 91*
Harsdorf, Sheila Eloise 1956- *WhoAmW 91*
Harsen, Edward Charles 1958- *WhoWrEP 89*
Harsh, Donald Ramon, Jr. 1946- *St&PR 91*
Harsh, Griffith Rutherford, III 1924- *WhoAm 90*
Harsh, Levi H. 1826- *AmLegL*
Harsha, Jacqueline Gayle 1946- *WhoEmL 91*
Harshaw, David Hare 1904- *WhoAm 90*
Harshaw, Margaret 1909- *IntWWM 90, PenDiMP*
Harshaw, Nannie M. 1932- *St&PR 91*
Harshaw, Ruth Hetzel 1890-1968 *AuBYP 90*
Harshawat, Paras 1948- *BiDrAPA 89*
Harshaway, Bobby Lee 1954- *St&PR 91*
Harshbarger, Dwight 1938- *WhoAm 90*
Harshbarger, Richard B. 1934- *WhoAm 90*
Harshbarger, Sam Ross 1928- *WhoAm 90*
Harshfield, Edward G. 1937- *St&PR 91*
Harshman, Amy *WhoSSW 91*
Harshman, Jack 1927- *Ballpl 90*
Harshman, Morton Leonard 1932- *WhoAm 90*
Harshman, Terry Webb *AuBYP 90*
Harsney, Johanna Marie Offner 1914- *WhoAmW 91*
Harson, Sley *MajTwCW*
Harsono 1939- *WhoWor 91*
Harsoyo, Raden *BioIn 16*
Harstad, Clifford Allen 1947- *St&PR 91*
Harston, Robert Gordon 1932- *St&PR 91, WhoAm 90*
Hart, Agnes *WhoAmA 91N*
Hart, Alden Sherburne, Jr. 1956- *WhoE 91*
Hart, Alex Way 1940- *St&PR 91, WhoAm 90, WhoE 91*
Hart, Alfred A. 1816-1908 *BioIn 16*
Hart, Alison Ann 1963- *WhoAmW 91*
Hart, Allen M 1925- *WhoAmA 91*
Hart, Alvin Leroy 1925- *WhoAm 90*
Hart, Ann Weaver 1948- *WhoEmL 91*
Hart, Arthur Alvin 1921- *WhoAm 90*
Hart, Augustin Snow, Jr. 1915- *WhoAm 90*
Hart, Barbara Lane 1941- *WhoSSW 91*
Hart, Betty Miller 1918- *WhoAmA 91*
Hart, Bill 1865-1936 *Ballpl 90*
Hart, Bobby Sidna 1954- *WhoWrEP 89*
Hart, Boots Dale 1954- *WhoAmW 91*
Hart, Bruce 1938- *BioIn 16*
Hart, C. Allan 1909- *WhoAm 90*
Hart, Carl Kiser, Jr. 1955- *WhoEmL 91*
Hart, Carole 1943- *BioIn 16*
Hart, Carole Urcell 1955- *WhoAmW 91*
Hart, Carolyn G. 1936- *TwCCr&M 91*
Hart, Carroll Joseph 1931- *WhoSSW 91*
Hart, Cecil William Joseph 1931- *WhoAm 90, WhoWor 91*
Hart, Charles 1940- *BioIn 16*
Hart, Charles E. 1925- *WhoAm 90, WhoSSW 91*
Hart, Charles Edwin, III 1919- *WhoE 91*
Hart, Charles H. *St&PR 91*
Hart, Charles Richard *St&PR 91*
Hart, Christine E. 1950- *WhoAmW 91*
Hart, Christopher Hyams 1958- *IntWWM 90*
Hart, Claudia 1955- *WhoAmA 91*
Hart, Claudia Mary 1953- *WhoE 91*
Hart, Cynthia Louise 1948- *WhoAmW 91*
Hart, Daniel Anthony 1927- *WhoAm 90*
Hart, Daniel Martin 1961- *WhoEmL 91*
Hart, David *BioIn 16*
Hart, David A. 1947- *St&PR 91*
Hart, David Churchill 1940- *WhoAm 90*
Hart, David Floyd 1949- *WhoEmL 91*
Hart, Deborah *ODwPR 91*
Hart, Deborah JoAnn 1958- *BiDrAPA 89*
Hart, Debra A. *ODwPR 91*
Hart, Dolores 1938?- *BioIn 16*
Hart, Dominick Joseph 1942- *WhoSSW 91*
Hart, Donald Avery 1936- *St&PR 91*
Hart, Donald John 1917- *WhoAm 90*
Hart, Donald L. 1933- *St&PR 91*
Hart, Donald Purple 1937- *WhoAm 90*
Hart, Dorothy *WhoAm 90*
Hart, Dorothy Lea Cramer 1940- *St&PR 91*

Hart, Edward LeRoy 1916- *WhoAm 90, WhoWrEP 89*
Hart, Edwin James 1910- *WhoAm 90*
Hart, Edwin Robert, Jr. 1953- *WhoSSW 91*
Hart, Eileen Kelly 1947- *WhoAmW 91*
Hart, Ellis *MajTwCW*
Hart, Elsie Faye 1920- *WhoAmW 91*
Hart, Eric M. 1925- *St&PR 91*
Hart, Eric Mullins 1925- *WhoAm 90*
Hart, Evelyn *BioIn 16*
Hart, Evelyn 1956- *WhoAm 90*
Hart, Frances Noyes 1890-1943 *TwCCr&M 91*
Hart, Francis *ConAu 31NR*
Hart, Fred Clinton 1940- *WhoAm 90*
Hart, Frederick Donald 1915- *WhoAm 90*
Hart, Frederick Michael 1929- *WhoAm 90*
Hart, Gary 1936- *BioIn 16*
Hart, Gary W. 1936- *WhoAm 90*
Hart, Gary Warren 1936- *SpyFic*
Hart, George E. 1951- *St&PR 91*
Hart, George M. 1932-1989 *BioIn 16*
Hart, George Philip Parleyns 1935- *WhoAm 90*
Hart, Gerald E. 1931- *St&PR 91*
Hart, Grace *BiDrAPA 89*
Hart, Gurnee Fellows 1929- *WhoE 91, WhoWor 91*
Hart, Hal 1926- *ODwPR 91*
Hart, Harry James 1918- *WhoWor 91*
Hart, Harvey 1928-1989 *BioIn 16*
Hart, Helen P. 1927- *WhoAmW 91*
Hart, Henry Walker 1954- *WhoWrEP 89*
Hart, Herbert Michael 1928- *WhoAm 90, WhoE 91, WhoWor 91*
Hart, Hornell 1888-1967 *EncO&P 3*
Hart, Hornell Norris 1888-1967 *EncPaPR 91*
Hart, Jack 1909- *WhoAm 90*
Hart, Jack Robert 1946- *WhoEmL 91*
Hart, James *BioIn 16*
Hart, James D. *NewYTBS 90*
Hart, James D 1911-1990 *ConAu 132*
Hart, James Francis 1948- *St&PR 91*
Hart, James Lee 1933- *BiDrAPA 89*
Hart, James Robert *BiDrAPA 89*
Hart, James W. 1953- *WhoAm 90*
Hart, James W., Jr. *ODwPR 91*
Hart, James W., Jr. 1953- *St&PR 91*
Hart, James Warren 1944- *WhoAm 90*
Hart, Jane 1948- *WhoAmW 91*
Hart, Jay Albert Charles 1923- *St&PR 91*
Hart, Jeanne 1906- *WhoWrEP 89*
Hart, Jerome Anthony 1933- *St&PR 91*
Hart, Jill Alison 1948- *WhoWrEP 89*
Hart, Jim Ray 1941- *Ballpl 90*
Hart, John 1711?-1779 *EncCRAm*
Hart, John 1948- *WhoWrEP 89*
Hart, John Clifton 1945- *WhoEmL 91*
Hart, John Edward 1937- *St&PR 91*
Hart, John Francis 1868- *WhoAmA 91N*
Hart, John Fraser 1924- *WhoAm 90*
Hart, John Herd 1931- *BiDrAPA 89*
Hart, John Joseph 1930- *WhoE 91*
Hart, John Lewis 1931- *WhoAm 90, WhoAmA 91*
Hart, John Mason 1935- *ConAu 132*
Hart, John Maynard 1947- *WhoAm 90*
Hart, Johnny 1931- *EncACom*
Hart, Joseph H. 1931- *WhoAm 90*
Hart, Juanita T *BiDrAPA 89*
Hart, Julia Catherine 1796-1867 *DcLB 99 [port], FemiCLE*
Hart, Karl Vance 1937- *WhoSSW 91*
Hart, Katherine M. 1908-1988 *BioIn 16*
Hart, Kenneth Nelson 1930- *WhoAm 90*
Hart, Kenneth Wayne 1939- *IntWWM 90*
Hart, Kent Butler 1942- *BiDrAPA 89*
Hart, Kitty Carlisle *BioIn 16*
Hart, Kitty Carlisle 1917- *WhoAm 90, WhoAmW 91*
Hart, Larry A. 1912- *St&PR 91*
Hart, Larry Edward 1945- *WhoE 91*
Hart, Lauren L. 1952- *WhoEmL 91*
Hart, Lenie 't *BioIn 16*
Hart, Lewis Justice, Jr. 1945- *WhoE 91*
Hart, Lois Borland 1941- *WhoWrEP 89*
Hart, Lorenz 1895-1943 *BioIn 16, OxCPMus, WorAlBi*
Hart, Loring Edward 1924- *WhoAm 90*
Hart, Lynn Patricia 1954- *WhoAmW 91*
Hart, Marian Griffith 1929- *WhoAmW 91*
Hart, Marie D. 1932- *St&PR 91*
Hart, Marion G 1935- *BiDrAPA 89*
Hart, Marion Rice *NewYTBS 90 [port]*
Hart, Marion Rice 1892?-1990 *ConAu 132*
Hart, Mark *ODwPR 91*
Hart, Mark Carlisle 1921- *St&PR 91*
Hart, Martin *ConAu 129*
Hart, Martin B. 1950- *St&PR 91*
Hart, Martin J. 1924- *St&PR 91*
Hart, Martin V 1934- *BiDrAPA 89*
Hart, Marvin C. 1938- *St&PR 91*
Hart, Mary *BioIn 16*
Hart, Mary 1951- *WorAlBi*
Hart, Maurice Arthur 1927- *WhoAm 90*
Hart, Maxine Barton 1934- *WhoSSW 91*
Hart, Mel 1938- *St&PR 91*
Hart, Michael A. 1953- *St&PR 91*
Hart, Michael David 1951- *WhoEmL 91*
Hart, Michelle A. 1961- *WhoAmW 91*
Hart, Mickey 1944?- *News 91-2 [port]*
Hart, Milledge A., III 1934- *St&PR 91*
Hart, Morgan Drake 1899- *WhoAmA 91N*
Hart, Moss 1904-1961 *OxCPMus, WorAlBi*
Hart, N. Berne 1930- *St&PR 91, WhoAm 90*
Hart, Nancy 1735?-1830 *EncCRAm*
Hart, Nathaniel Irwin 1930- *WhoAm 90*
Hart, Nelson S. 1926- *St&PR 91*
Hart, Neva Jones 1947- *WhoSSW 91*
Hart, Oliver 1723-1795 *BioIn 16*
Hart, Oliver D'Arcy 1948- *WhoE 91*
Hart, Orson H. 1913- *WhoAm 90*
Hart, Patrick Joseph 1925- *WhoAm 90, WhoWrEP 89*
Hart, Philip A. 1912-1976 *WorAlBi*
Hart, Ralph A. 1904- *St&PR 91*
Hart, Ray Lee 1929- *WhoAm 90*
Hart, Raymond Kenneth 1928- *WhoSSW 91*
Hart, Richard Banner 1932- *WhoAm 90*
Hart, Richard Nevel, Jr. 1940- *St&PR 91, WhoAm 90, WhoE 91*
Hart, Richard Oliver 1949- *WhoE 91, WhoWor 91*
Hart, Richard V. 1927- *St&PR 91*
Hart, Robert Camillus 1934- *WhoAm 90*
Hart, Robert Carmon 1926- *WhoAm 90*
Hart, Robert George 1926- *WhoAm 90*
Hart, Robert Gordon 1921- *WhoAm 90, WhoAmA 91, WhoE 91*
Hart, Robert John Kirland 1916- *St&PR 91*
Hart, Robert Joseph 1937- *WhoAm 90*
Hart, Robert Leonard 1927- *WhoE 91*
Hart, Robert Raymond 1943- *BiDrAPA 89*
Hart, Roderick P. 1945- *WhoAm 90*
Hart, Ronald E. 1930- *ODwPR 91*
Hart, Ronald Wilson 1942- *WhoAm 90*
Hart, Rosana L. 1942- *WhoWrEP 89*
Hart, Rosemary Anne 1953- *WhoAm 90*
Hart, Sally Millner 1953- *WhoAmW 91*
Hart, Sandra Hile 1947- *WhoEmL 91, WhoSSW 91*
Hart, Sidney 1939- *BiDrAPA 89*
Hart, Stanley Robert 1935- *WhoAm 90*
Hart, Steven Weber 1956- *St&PR 91, WhoAm 90*
Hart, Susan *BioIn 16*
Hart, Susan Renee 1961- *WhoAmW 91*
Hart, Sylvia E. 1928- *WhoAmW 91*
Hart, Terry Jonathan 1946- *WhoAm 90*
Hart, Thomas Daniel 1939- *WhoE 91*
Hart, Thomas E. 1943- *St&PR 91*
Hart, Thomas F. 1929- *St&PR 91*
Hart, Thomas Judson 1958- *WhoEmL 91*
Hart, Thomas R. 1925- *WhoAm 90*
Hart, Timothy Ray 1942- *WhoWor 91*
Hart, Vincent J. 1899-1990 *BioIn 16*
Hart, Wayne *BiDrAPA 89*
Hart, Wayne Douglas 1950- *WhoEmL 91*
Hart, Will *BioIn 16*
Hart, William Gardner 1921- *St&PR 91, WhoE 91*
Hart, William L. 1917- *St&PR 91*
Hart, William Levata 1924- *WhoAm 90*
Hart, William S. 1870?-1946 *BioIn 16, WorAlBi*
Hart, William Sebastian 1920- *IntWWM 90*
Hart, William T 1921- *BiDrAPA 89*
Hart, William Thomas 1929- *WhoAm 90*
Hart-Kelly, Lesly Margarita 1949- *WhoHisp 91*
Hartack, Bill 1932- *WorAlBi*
Hartal, Paul 1936- *WhoAmA 91*
Hartal, Paul Zev 1936- *WhoE 91*
Hartdegen, Stephen J. 1907-1989 *BioIn 16, ConAu 130*
Harte, Andrew Dennis 1946- *WhoE 91, WhoEmL 91, WhoWor 91*
Harte, Bernice Joan *BiDrAPA 89*
Harte, Bret 1836?-1902 *AuBYP 90, BioIn 16, WorAlBi*
Harte, Christopher M. 1947- *St&PR 91*
Harte, Edward Holmead 1922- *WhoSSW 91*
Harte, Houston 1893-1972 *BioIn 16*
Harte, Houston Harriman 1927- *St&PR 91, WhoAm 90, WhoSSW 91*
Harte, James Richard 1928- *BiDrAPA 89*
Harte, John 1927- *WhoAmA 91*
Harte, John Henderson, III 1949- *WhoEmL 91*
Harte, John Joseph Meakin 1914- *WhoAm 90*
Harte, John Michael 1944- *St&PR 91*
Harte, Joseph Michael 1940- *St&PR 91*
Harte, Lisa R. 1966- *St&PR 91*
Harte, Thomas Michael 1959- *WhoE 91*
Hartel, Stephen Allen 1957- *WhoEmL 91*
Hartelius, Margaret A. *AuBYP 90*
Hartell, John 1902- *WhoAmA 91*
Hartenstein, Chuck 1942- *Ballpl 90*
Hartenstine, Warren Richard 1945- *WhoE 91*
Harter, Alvin Adam 1927- *St&PR 91*
Harter, Carol C. *WhoAm 90*
Harter, David John 1942- *WhoWor 91*
Harter, Donald Harry 1933- *BiDrAPA 89, WhoAm 90, WhoE 91, WhoWor 91*
Harter, Donald Scott 1950- *WhoEmL 91*
Harter, Duane L. 1932- *St&PR 91*
Harter, Frieda J *BiDrAPA 89*
Harter, Georges 1942- *WhoWor 91*
Harter, Hugh Anthony 1922- *WhoAm 90*
Harter, Jean Ann 1959- *WhoAmW 91*
Harter, John Burton 1940- *WhoAmA 91*
Harter, Lafayette George, Jr. 1918- *WhoAm 90, WhoWor 91*
Harter, Lawrence D 1929- *BiDrAPA 89*
Harter, Michael Thomas 1942- *WhoAm 90*
Harter, Penny 1940- *WhoWrEP 89*
Harter, Richard Morton 1936- *WhoAm 90*
Harter, Robert Hugh 1915- *WhoAm 90*
Harter, Steven John 1946- *WhoEmL 91*
Hartfield, Elizabeth Ann 1950- *WhoAm 90, WhoSSW 91*
Hartford, Huntington 1911- *WhoAm 90*
Hartford, James Thomas 1947- *BiDrAPA 89*
Hartford, Jane Davis 1927- *WhoAmA 91*
Hartford, John *AuBYP 90*
Hartford, John Cowan 1937- *WhoAm 90*
Hartford, Madelon *BiDrAPA 89*
Hartford, Thomas James, III 1959- *WhoEmL 91*
Hartford, William H. 1938- *WhoAm 90*
Hartgen, Vincent Andrew 1914- *WhoAm 90, WhoAmA 91*
Hartgraves, Al L. 1944- *WhoSSW 91*
Hartgrove, Beverly Newman 1944- *WhoAmW 91*
Harth, Erica *WhoAm 90*
Harth, Kathleen 1960- *ODwPR 91*
Harth, Phillip 1926- *WhoAm 90*
Harth, Robert James 1956- *WhoAm 90*
Harth, Sidney 1929- *IntWWM 90, WhoAm 90*
Harthun, Luther A. 1935- *St&PR 91*
Harthun, Luther Arthur 1935- *WhoAm 90*
Hartig, Elmer Otto 1923- *WhoAm 90*
Hartig, Judith Martin 1938- *WhoAmW 91*
Hartig, Michael Andrew 1954- *WhoE 91*
Hartig, Paul 1898- *WhoWor 91*
Hartigan, Grace 1922- *BiDWomA, WhoAm 90, WhoAmA 91*
Hartigan, James J. 1924- *WhoAm 90*
Hartigan, Lynda Roscoe 1950- *WhoAmA 91, WhoEmL 91*
Hartigan, MaryEllen 1957- *WhoEmL 91*
Hartigan, Neil F. 1938- *WhoAm 90*
Hartigan, Stephen C. *BioIn 16*
Hartin, Robert Marvin 1949- *WhoEmL 91, WhoSSW 91*
Harting, Emilie Clothier 1942- *WhoWrEP 89*
Harting, G. Robert 1927- *St&PR 91*
Hartinger, Albert F. 1946- *IntWWM 90*
Hartje, Judy Ann 1964- *WhoWrEP 89*
Hartje, Keith Douglas 1950- *St&PR 91*
Hartje, Robert Wayne, Sr. 1938- *WhoE 91*
Hartje, Thomas 1949- *WhoWor 91*
Hartke, Stephen 1952- *ConMus 5*
Hartke, Stephen Paul 1952- *IntWWM 90*
Hartke, Vance 1919- *WorAlBi*
Hartl, Albert Victor 1911- *WhoAm 90*
Hartl, Charles *St&PR 91*
Hartl, Daniel Lee 1943- *WhoAm 90*
Hartl, Leon 1889- *WhoAmA 91N*
Hartl, Richard James 1937- *St&PR 91*
Hartl, Wilbur Michael 1916- *St&PR 91*
Hartl, William P. 1935- *ODwPR 91*
Hartl, William Parker 1935- *WhoE 91*
Hartlage, James A. 1938- *St&PR 91*
Hartlage, Lawrence Clifton 1934- *WhoAm 90*
Hartlage, Thomas Joseph 1951- *WhoSSW 91*
Hartland, Michael 1941- *SpyFic*
Hartlaub, Felix 1913-1945 *BioIn 16*
Hartlaub, Genoveva 1915- *EncCoWW*
Hartlaub, Gustav Friedrich 1884-1963 *EncO&P 3*
Hartlaud, George H 1930- *BiDrAPA 89*
Hartle, Robert Wyman 1921- *WhoAm 90*
Hartle, William George 1948- *St&PR 91*
Hartleb, David Frederick 1944- *WhoAm 90*
Hartleb, Emil A. 1938- *St&PR 91*
Hartleben, Faye Pearl 1940- *WhoWrEP 89*
Hartlep, Ralph Q. 1946- *St&PR 91*
Hartley, Baron Manning 1924- *WhoE 91*
Hartley, Bonalyn J. 1944- *St&PR 91*
Hartley, Brian Selby 1926- *WhoWor 91*
Hartley, Cecil Glenn, Sr. 1932- *WhoSSW 91*
Hartley, Craig Hilliard 1953- *WhoSSW 91*
Hartley, Dale Allison 1952- *WhoEmL 91*
Hartley, David 1705-1757 *WrPh P*
Hartley, David Paul 1946- *BiDrAPA 89*
Hartley, Domenic G. 1947- *St&PR 91*
Hartley, Donald, Sr. 1941- *WhoSSW 91*
Hartley, Felton William, Jr. 1939- *WhoSSW 91*
Hartley, Fred *BioIn 16*
Hartley, Fred 1905- *OxCPMus*
Hartley, Fred L. *NewYTBS 90 [port]*
Hartley, Fred L. 1917- *St&PR 91*
Hartley, Fred Lloyd 1917- *WhoAm 90*
Hartley, Grace Van Tine 1916- *WhoAmW 91*
Hartley, Grover 1888-1964 *Ballpl 90*
Hartley, James Michaelis 1916- *WhoWor 91*
Hartley, Jean Ayres 1914- *WhoWrEP 89*
Hartley, John Bryan 1953- *WhoE 91*
Hartley, John Clark 1945- *WhoSSW 91*
Hartley, John T., Jr. 1930- *St&PR 91, WhoAm 90, WhoSSW 91*
Hartley, Joseph Wayman, Jr. 1933- *St&PR 91, WhoAm 90*
Hartley, Karen Jeanette 1950- *WhoAmW 91*
Hartley, Kirk T. 1957- *WhoEmL 91*
Hartley, L.P. 1895-1972 *ConAu 33NR, MajTwCW*
Hartley, Mariette 1940- *WhoAm 90, WhoAmW 91*
Hartley, Marsden 1877-1943 *BioIn 16*
Hartley, Paul Jerome 1943- *WhoAmA 91*
Hartley, Richard Glendale 1926- *WhoAm 90*
Hartley, Robert E. 1936- *ConAu 130*
Hartley, Robert Frank 1927- *WhoAm 90*
Hartley, Sara Lynn 1947- *BiDrAPA 89*
Hartley, Stuart Leslie 1938- *WhoAm 90*
Hartley, Terry L. 1947- *WhoEmL 91*
Hartley, Thomas 1748-1800 *BioIn 16*
Hartley, Travis *ConAu 31NR*
Hartley, Vernon L 1923- *BiDrAPA 89*
Hartley, W Douglas 1921- *WhoAmA 91*
Hartley, Walter Joseph, Jr. 1952- *WhoSSW 91*
Hartley, Walter Sinclair 1927- *WhoE 91*
Hartley, William *NewAgE 90*
Hartley, William A. 1935- *St&PR 91*
Hartley, William H. 1926- *St&PR 91*
Hartley-Leonard, Darryl *WhoAm 90*
Hartley-Linse, Bonnie Jean 1923- *WhoAmW 91, WhoWor 91*
Hartley-Urquhart, William Roland 1958- *WhoE 91*
Hartline, Haldan Keffer 1903-1983 *WorAlBi*
Hartling, Peter 1933- *WhoWor 91*
Hartling, Poul 1914- *WhoWor 91*
Hartlove, Michele Denise 1959- *WhoSSW 91*
Hartly, Michelle Jeannette 1959- *WhoAmW 91*
Hartman, Alan Roy 1955- *WhoEmL 91*
Hartman, Alexander S *BiDrAPA 89*
Hartman, Ann 1948- *St&PR 91*
Hartman, Arthur *BioIn 16*
Hartman, Arthur A. 1926- *WhoAm 90*
Hartman, Ashley Powell 1922- *WhoAm 90*
Hartman, Bertram 1882- *WhoAmA 91N*
Hartman, Betty G. *BioIn 16*
Hartman, Boyd Kent *BiDrAPA 89*
Hartman, Brenda Alane 1952- *WhoEmL 91*
Hartman, Burton Arthur 1924- *WhoAm 90*
Hartman, Carl 1917- *WhoAm 90*
Hartman, Catherine Rudisill 1916- *WhoAmW 91*
Hartman, Charles Henry 1933- *WhoAm 90*
Hartman, Christopher C. *ODwPR 91*
Hartman, Clark Edward 1949- *WhoE 91*
Hartman, David *BioIn 16*
Hartman, David 1935- *WorAlBi*
Hartman, David 1955- *St&PR 91*
Hartman, David Downs 1935- *WhoAm 90*
Hartman, David Elliott 1954- *WhoEmL 91*
Hartman, David G. 1942- *St&PR 91*
Hartman, David Gardiner 1942- *WhoAm 90*
Hartman, David Gene 1951- *St&PR 91*
Hartman, David James 1948- *WhoE 91*
Hartman, David William 1949- *BiDrAPA 89*
Hartman, Deborah Stanton 1956- *WhoAmW 91*
Hartman, Diana Marie 1953- *WhoE 91*
Hartman, Domenica Nicolette Samargin 1960- *WhoAmW 91, WhoEmL 91*
Hartman, Don Burton 1955- *WhoEmL 91*
Hartman, Douglas Arthur 1938- *St&PR 91*
Hartman, Edith D *BiDrAPA 89*
Hartman, Elizabeth Ann 1959- *WhoWrEP 89*
Hartman, Ellen W. 1952- *ODwPR 91*
Hartman, Emily Lou 1932- *WhoAmW 91*
Hartman, Ena *DrBIPA 90*
Hartman, Frank R *BiDrAPA 89*
Hartman, Fred 1868-1938 *Ballpl 90*
Hartman, Fred George 1905- *WhoE 91*
Hartman, Gary Michael 1959- *WhoEmL 91*

Hartman, Geoffrey H. BioIn 16
Hartman, Geoffrey H. 1929- WhoAm 90
Hartman, George Eitel 1936- WhoAm 90, WhoE 91
Hartman, George Solomon 1921- WhoE 91
Hartman, Gerald Charles 1936- St&PR 91
Hartman, Gregory Calvin 1946- WhoEmL 91
Hartman, Harold Richard 1920- WhoE 91
Hartman, Harry Ballpl 90
Hartman, Harry Sebastian, IV 1949- WhoSSW 91
Hartman, Henry A. 1929- St&PR 91
Hartman, Herbert Arthur, Jr. 1947- WhoEmL 91
Hartman, Howard Levi 1924- WhoAm 90
Hartman, Imre PenDiMP
Hartman, James Le-Roy 1940- WhoWor 91
Hartman, James O. 1947- St&PR 91
Hartman, James Theodore 1925- WhoAm 90
Hartman, Jane E. 1928- BioIn 16, WhoWrEP 89
Hartman, Janice Ann 1950- WhoEmL 91
Hartman, Jeannette Marie 1952- WhoAmW 91
Hartman, Jennifer Weaver 1947- WhoE 91
Hartman, Joan Edna 1930- WhoAmW 91
Hartman, John Kenneth 1945- WhoEmL 91
Hartman, John W. 1943- ODwPR 91
Hartman, John Wheeler 1922- WhoAm 90, WhoSSW 91
Hartman, Johnny 1923?-1983 DrBlPA 90
Hartman, Joseph John 1924- St&PR 91, WhoAm 90
Hartman, Joy C. 1948- St&PR 91
Hartman, Keith Edward 1941- BiDrAPA 89
Hartman, Lee Ann Walraff 1945- WhoAmW 91
Hartman, Lisa Ellen 1962- WhoSSW 91
Hartman, Margaret J. 1943- WhoAm 90
Hartman, Mark Lawrence BiDrAPA 89
Hartman, Mark William 1937- St&PR 91
Hartman, Mary S. 1941- WhoAm 90
Hartman, Melanie Ann 1960- WhoEmL 91
Hartman, Nancy Lee 1951- WhoAmW 91
Hartman, Neil 1947- BiDrAPA 89
Hartman, Nicholas J. 1930- St&PR 91
Hartman, Patricia Yunker 1950- WhoEmL 91
Hartman, Paul Arthur 1926- WhoAm 90
Hartman, Paul T BiDrAPA 89
Hartman, Philip Emil 1926- WhoAm 90
Hartman, R.S. 1914- St&PR 91
Hartman, Ralph D. WhoHisp 91
Hartman, Richard E. 1940- St&PR 91
Hartman, Richard Leon 1937- WhoAm 90
Hartman, Richard Russell 1926- WhoAm 90
Hartman, Richard Thomas 1921- WhoAm 90
Hartman, Robert F. 1947- St&PR 91
Hartman, Robert James 1937- St&PR 91
Hartman, Robert L. 1930- St&PR 91
Hartman, Robert Leroy 1926- WhoAm 90, WhoAmA 91
Hartman, Robert S. 1914- WhoAm 90
Hartman, Russell BioIn 16
Hartman, Ruth Ann 1938- WhoAmW 91
Hartman, Sherry W. 1946- ODwPR 91
Hartman, Stephen Jennings, Jr. 1945- WhoAm 90, WhoE 91
Hartman, Stewart Eugene, Jr. 1931- WhoAm 90
Hartman, Thomas Jeffery 1966- WhoE 91
Hartman, Timothy P. 1939- St&PR 91
Hartman, Timothy Patwill 1939- WhoAm 90
Hartman, William Arthur 1955- WhoAm 90
Hartman, William Vernon 1922- WhoAm 90
Hartman-Abramson, Ilene 1950- WhoAmW 91
Hartman-Goldsmith, Joan 1933- WhoAm 90, WhoAmW 91
Hartmanis, Juris 1928- WhoAm 90
Hartmann, Darlene Marie 1963- WhoAmW 91
Hartmann, Donald Conrad 1954- IntWWM 90
Hartmann, E. Jan 1929- St&PR 91
Hartmann, Eduard von 1842-1906 EncO&P 3
Hartmann, Edward George 1912- WhoAm 90
Hartmann, Edward H. 1940- St&PR 91
Hartmann, Edward Scott BiDrAPA 89
Hartmann, Ernest L 1934- BiDrAPA 89
Hartmann, Franz 1838-1912 EncO&P 3
Hartmann, Frederick Howard 1922- WhoAm 90
Hartmann, Frederick William 1928- WhoAm 90
Hartmann, Georg Theo 1894-1976 WhoAmA 91N
Hartmann, George Herman 1927- WhoAm 90
Hartmann, Judy Anne 1955- WhoAmW 91
Hartmann, Jurgen Heinrich 1945- WhoWor 91
Hartmann, Klaus 1925- WhoWor 91
Hartmann, Klaus 1944- BiDrAPA 89
Hartmann, Lawrence 1937- BiDrAPA 89, WhoWor 91
Hartmann, Peter Claus 1940- WhoWor 91
Hartmann, Richard J. 1933- St&PR 91
Hartmann, Robert Carl 1919- WhoAm 90
Hartmann, Robert E. 1926- St&PR 91
Hartmann, Robert Elliott 1926- WhoAm 90
Hartmann, Robert S. 1948- ODwPR 91
Hartmann, Robert Sankey 1948- WhoE 91
Hartmann, Robert Trowbridge 1917- WhoAm 90, WhoE 91
Hartmann, Robert Walter BiDrAPA 89
Hartmann, Rose S BiDrAPA 89
Hartmann, Ruth Annemarie 1936- WhoAmW 91
Hartmann, Steven James 1955- BiDrAPA 89
Hartmann, Svend E. 1931- St&PR 91
Hartmann, William Edward 1916- WhoAm 90
Hartmann, William Herman 1931- WhoAm 90
Hartmann, William Kenneth 1939- WhoAm 90
Hartmann-Downing, Nancy L. St&PR 91
Hartmann-Johnsen, Olaf Johan 1924- WhoWor 91
Hartnack, Carl Edward 1916- WhoAm 90
Hartnagel, Betty Carolyn 1951- WhoAmW 91
Hartnagel, William R BiDrAPA 89
Hartness, James Larry 1946- WhoSSW 91
Hartness, Sandra Jean 1944- WhoAmW 91, WhoWor 91
Hartness, Thomas Signor 1918- St&PR 91
Hartnett, Anna E BiDrAPA 89
Hartnett, Bernard Michael, Jr. 1929- WhoAm 90
Hartnett, Edward Francis 1931- WhoAm 90
Hartnett, Gabby 1900-1972 Ballpl 90 [port], BioIn 16
Hartnett, James Patrick 1924- WhoAm 90, WhoWor 91
Hartnett, Jennifer Lynne 1964- WhoAmW 91
Hartnett, John A. 1936- St&PR 91
Hartnett, John F. 1937- WhoE 91
Hartnett, John F. 1947- WhoE 91
Hartnett, Katherine 1951- WhoAmW 91
Hartnett, Michael 1941- ConAu 130
Hartnett, Thomas D 1933- BiDrAPA 89
Hartnett, Thomas J., Jr. 1942- St&PR 91
Hartnett, Thomas Patrick 1942- St&PR 91
Hartnett, Thomas Robert, III 1920- WhoSSW 91, WhoWor 91
Hartnett, Will Ford 1956- WhoEmL 91, WhoSSW 91
Hartnett, William Edward 1925- WhoE 91
Hartoch, Kenneth 1927- St&PR 91
Hartocollis, Peter 1922- BiDrAPA 89
Hartog, Albert Staal 1930- WhoE 91
Hartog, Diana 1942- FemiCLE
Hartog, Jack Byron 1927- St&PR 91, WhoAm 90
Hartog, Jan de 1914- BioIn 16
Hartog, Joseph BiDrAPA 89
Hartogensis, Stephen 1931- St&PR 91
Hartom-Boze, Barbara Cheslene 1953- WhoAmW 91
Harton, Ernest H. 1936- St&PR 91
Harton, John James 1941- St&PR 91, WhoAm 90
Harton, Thomas Dean 1945- St&PR 91
Harton, Thomas Gordon 1909- WhoSSW 91
Hartong, Hendrik Johan 1939- St&PR 91
Hartono, Michael Bambang 1939- WhoWor 91
Hartono, Setya Budi 1941- WhoWor 91
Hartsaw, William O. 1921- WhoAm 90
Hartsel, Donald Ralph, Jr. 1947- WhoSSW 91
Hartsel, Topsy 1874-1944 Ballpl 90
Hartsfield, Charles B. 1928- St&PR 91
Hartsfield, Henry Warren, Jr. 1933- WhoAm 90
Hartsfield, Roy 1925- Ballpl 90
Hartsfield, Stephanie Laverne 1962- WhoAmW 91
Hartsfield, William E. 1950- WhoEmL 91
Hartshorn, Mary A BiDrAPA 89
Hartshorn, W.T. 1944- St&PR 91
Hartshorn, Willis E 1950- WhoAmA 91
Hartshorne, Charles 1897- WhoAm 90
Hartsock, Linda Sue 1940- WhoAm 90, WhoAmW 91
Hartsock, Robert Lawrence 1939- WhoAm 90
Hartson, Susan Belt 1958- WhoE 91
Hartsook, Larry D. 1943- St&PR 91, WhoAm 90
Hartsough, Walter Douglas 1924- WhoAm 90
Hartstein, Jacob I. 1912- WhoAm 90
Hartstein, Norman B 1947- BiDrAPA 89
Hartstein, Sam 1921- WhoE 91
Hartstone, Barry 1942- St&PR 91
Hartsuck, Jean Ann 1939- WhoAmW 91
Hartt, Andrew Douglas 1947- St&PR 91
Hartt, Charles Franklin 1925- St&PR 91
Hartt, Frederick 1914- WhoAm 90, WhoAmA 91
Hartt, Julian N 1911- ConAu 132
Hartt, Julian Norris 1911- WhoAm 90
Hartt, Susan Kay 1948- WhoEmL 91
Hartung, Clint 1922- Ballpl 90
Hartung, Ernest William, Jr. 1917- WhoAm 90
Hartung, Glenn J. 1935- St&PR 91
Hartung, Hans 1904-1989 AnObit 1989, BioIn 16, ConAu 130, CurBio 90N
Hartung, Lorraine E. 1944- WhoHisp 91
Hartung, Margaret Ursula 1941- WhoAmW 91
Hartung, Mary WhoAmW 91
Hartung, Paul William, Jr. 1927- St&PR 91
Hartung, Richard L. 1956- WhoWor 91
Hartung, Robert Leonard 1931- St&PR 91
Hartung, Roderick Lee 1935- WhoAm 90
Hartung, Ronald Frederick 1952- WhoSSW 91
Hartung, Steven Lee 1946- St&PR 91
Hartung, Walter Magnus 1907- WhoAm 90
Hartung, Willi A. 1930- St&PR 91
Hartung, Wolfgang 1937- St&PR 91
Hartvig-Nielsen, Niels 1956- WhoEmL 91
Hartweg, Dale S. 1933- St&PR 91
Hartwell, Constance G 1912- BiDrAPA 89
Hartwell, Dan J. 1948- St&PR 91
Hartwell, George Kenneth 1891-1949 WhoAmA 91N
Hartwell, Hamilton 1926- St&PR 91
Hartwell, Hugh Kenneth 1945- IntWWM 90
Hartwell, Jane Barry 1956- WhoEmL 91
Hartwell, John M. 1916- St&PR 91
Hartwell, Karen Jane BiDrAPA 89
Hartwell, Leland Harrison 1939- WhoAm 90
Hartwell, Margaret Carroll 1937- St&PR 91
Hartwell, Nancy AuBYP 90
Hartwell, Patricia Lochridge 1916- WhoAmA 91
Hartwell, Philip Alan 1946- WhoEmL 91
Hartwell, Robert van Laer 1956- WhoE 91
Hartwell, Samuel A. 1930- St&PR 91
Hartwell, Stephen 1915- St&PR 91
Hartwell, Stephen 1916- WhoAm 90
Hartwick, Elbert Stuart 1903-1990 WhoAm 90
Hartwick, Nanci J. 1945- WhoAmW 91
Hartwick, Randall Lenis 1952- WhoEmL 91
Hartwig, Clayton Michael BioIn 16
Hartwig, Cleo 1911-1988 BioIn 16
Hartwig, Daniel J. 1949- WhoEmL 91
Hartwig, Edgar Emerson 1913- WhoAm 90
Hartwig, Eugene Lawrence 1933- WhoAm 90
Hartwig, Heinie 1939- WhoAmA 91
Hartwig, Karl Hans August 1948- WhoWor 91
Hartwig, Karl Theodore, Jr. 1946- WhoSSW 91
Hartwig, Larry D. 1940- St&PR 91
Hartwig, M. A. 1944- ODwPR 91
Hartwig, Thomas Leo 1952- WhoE 91
Hartwig, Thomas Roger 1936- St&PR 91
Hartwigsen, Nelson Leroy 1941- WhoWor 91
Harty, Hamilton 1879-1941 PenDiMP, -A
Harty, James D. 1929- St&PR 91, WhoAm 90
Harty, James Quinn 1925- WhoAm 90
Harty, John Richard 1940- St&PR 91
Harty, Roger Philip 1916- St&PR 91
Harty, Russell 1934-1988 AnObit 1988, BioIn 16
Harty, Sheila Therese 1948- WhoAm 90
Hartz, Bradley Scott 1955- WhoEmL 91
Hartz, Brendan Thomas 1956- WhoEmL 91
Hartz, Charles A. 1938- St&PR 91
Hartz, Fred Robert 1933- WhoSSW 91
Hartz, Holly 1954- ODwPR 91
Hartz, John Ernest, Jr. 1935- St&PR 91
Hartz, Louis 1919-1986 BioIn 16
Hartz, Luetta Bertha 1947- WhoAmW 91
Hartz, Renee Semo 1946- WhoAmW 91
Hartz, Robert K BiDrAPA 89
Hartzel, David M. 1948- St&PR 91
Hartzell, Andrew Cornelius, Jr. 1927- WhoAm 90
Hartzell, Charles R. 1941- WhoAm 90
Hartzell, David Edward 1946- St&PR 91
Hartzell, Frank Carlisle 1925- St&PR 91
Hartzell, George Turner 1920- WhoE 91
Hartzell, Irene Janofsky 1938- WhoAmW 91
Hartzell, James R. 1934- St&PR 91
Hartzell, Lawrence William 1942- IntWWM 90
Hartzell, Paul 1953- Ballpl 90
Hartzell, Robert L. 1934- St&PR 91
Hartzell, Roy 1881-1961 Ballpl 90
Hartzell, William Alan 1951- WhoSSW 91
Hartzler, Cheryl Elaine 1945- WhoAmW 91, WhoEmL 91, WhoWor 91
Hartzler, Susan Frances 1958- WhoAmW 91
Hartzog, Annabeth BioIn 16
Haruke, Yukihiro 1939- WhoE 91
Harun, Joseph Stanley 1925- St&PR 91
Haruna, Kazuo 1920- WhoWor 91
Harunobu 1725?-1770 EncJap
Haruo, Okabe 1933- WhoWor 91
Haruta, Mako Emily 1962- WhoE 91
Harvanek, Robert Francis 1916- WhoAm 90
Harvard, Beverly Joyce Bailey 1950- WhoAmW 91
Harvard, John 1607?-1638 WorAlBi
Harvard, Stephen 1948-1988 BioIn 16
Harvatin, Anthony Christopher 1951- WhoE 91
Harvell, Cecil C. 1927- St&PR 91
Harvell, Diane Lynn 1957- WhoAmW 91
Harvell, Grady E. 1949- St&PR 91
Harvest, Jan Monberg 1942- WhoWor 91
Harvester, Simon 1910-1975 SpyFic, TwCCr&M 91
Harvey, Abner McGehee 1911- WhoAm 90
Harvey, Alan Christopher 1951- WhoEmL 91
Harvey, Alexander, II 1923- WhoAm 90, WhoE 91
Harvey, Alexander E 1915- BiDrAPA 89
Harvey, Andre 1941- WhoAmA 91
Harvey, Andrew 1952- ConAu 132
Harvey, Anthony BioIn 16
Harvey, Anthony Kesteven 1931- WhoAm 90, WhoWor 91
Harvey, Arthur Herbert 1931- WhoAm 90
Harvey, Arthur Wallace 1939- IntWWM 90
Harvey, Bernard S. 1941- St&PR 91
Harvey, Bertha Bowen 1957- BiDrAPA 89
Harvey, Bessie 1929- MusmAFA
Harvey, Brett BioIn 16
Harvey, Brett 1936- SmATA 61 [port]
Harvey, Brian 1926- St&PR 91
Harvey, Bruce Dewolfe 1928- St&PR 91
Harvey, Bruce Kenyon 1946- WhoEmL 91
Harvey, Bryan 1963- Ballpl 90
Harvey, Bryan Laurence 1937- WhoAm 90
Harvey, Calvin Rea 1943- WhoAm 90, WhoE 91
Harvey, Charles A. St&PR 91
Harvey, Charles Barnet 1900- BioIn 16
Harvey, Charles Ernest 1963- WhoE 91
Harvey, Colin Edwin 1944- WhoAm 90
Harvey, Curran W. 1928- St&PR 91
Harvey, Curran Whitthorne, Jr. 1928- WhoAm 90
Harvey, Cynthia WhoAm 90
Harvey, David Christopher 1959- St&PR 91
Harvey, David R M 1922- BiDrAPA 89
Harvey, Dermot 1941- WhoAmA 91
Harvey, Don BioIn 16
Harvey, Donald 1930- WhoAm 90, WhoAmA 91
Harvey, Donald Angus 1948- WhoE 91
Harvey, Donald Gilbert 1947- WhoAmA 91
Harvey, Donald Joseph 1922- WhoAm 90
Harvey, Donald Phillips 1924- WhoAm 90
Harvey, Doris Cannon 1930- WhoAmW 91
Harvey, Dorothy May 1922- WhoWrEP 89
Harvey, Doug 1924-1989 BioIn 16
Harvey, Doug 1930- Ballpl 90
Harvey, Douglass Coate 1917- WhoAm 90
Harvey, Edmund Huxley, Jr. 1934- WhoAm 90, WhoWrEP 89
Harvey, Edmund Newton 1887-1959 DcScB S2
Harvey, Edward J. 1936- St&PR 91
Harvey, Edward James 1936- WhoAm 90
Harvey, Edward Thomas 1948- St&PR 91, WhoAm 90
Harvey, Edwin Malcolm 1928- WhoAm 90, WhoSSW 91
Harvey, Edythe P 1956- BiDrAPA 89
Harvey, Elinor B 1912- BiDrAPA 89
Harvey, Enid Mary WhoAmW 91
Harvey, Ethel Browne 1885-1965 BioIn 16
Harvey, F. Barton, Jr. 1921- WhoAm 90
Harvey, F. Reese 1941- WhoAm 90
Harvey, Frank M. 1939- WhoE 91

Harvey, Frank W. 1931- *St&PR 91, WhoAm 90*
Harvey, Fred 1932- *St&PR 91*
Harvey, Frederick Parker 1920- *WhoAm 90*
Harvey, Frederick Wilfred, Jr. 1929- *WhoWor 91*
Harvey, George 1864-1928 *BioIn 16*
Harvey, George Burton 1931- *St&PR 91, WhoAm 90, WhoE 91*
Harvey, George E. 1945- *St&PR 91*
Harvey, George Edwin 1938- *WhoAm 90*
Harvey, Gerald Joseph 1925- *St&PR 91*
Harvey, Gina Cantoni 1922- *ConAu 33NR*
Harvey, Glenn F. 1940- *WhoAm 90*
Harvey, Gregory Alan 1949- *WhoEmL 91, WhoWor 91*
Harvey, Guy *BioIn 16*
Harvey, Herschel A., Jr. 1929- *St&PR 91*
Harvey, Herschel Ambrose, Jr. 1929- *WhoSSW 91, WhoWor 91*
Harvey, Irwin M. 1931- *St&PR 91*
Harvey, J. R. 1937- *WhoAm 90*
Harvey, James 1922- *WhoAm 90*
Harvey, James Douglas 1929- *WhoAm 90*
Harvey, James Martin, Jr. 1956- *WhoEmL 91*
Harvey, James Neal 1925- *WhoAm 90*
Harvey, James R. 1934- *St&PR 91*
Harvey, James Ross 1934- *WhoAm 90*
Harvey, James V *WhoAmA 91N*
Harvey, Jane 1776- *FemiCLE*
Harvey, Jane R. 1945- *WhoAmW 91*
Harvey, Jean 1932- *IntWWM 90*
Harvey, Joan C. 1948- *ConAu 132*
Harvey, Joanne H. 1932- *WhoAmW 91*
Harvey, Joe Alan 1960- *WhoEmL 91*
Harvey, John 1742-1807 *EncCRAm*
Harvey, John Adriance 1930- *WhoAm 90*
Harvey, John Anthony 1935- *WhoWor 91*
Harvey, John Christopher 1943- *WhoE 91*
Harvey, John Collins 1923- *WhoAm 90, WhoE 91*
Harvey, John Douglas 1960- *WhoE 91*
Harvey, John Frederick 1921- *WhoWor 91*
Harvey, John Grover 1934- *WhoAm 90*
Harvey, John Stewart 1932- *WhoE 91*
Harvey, John W. 1952- *WhoE 91*
Harvey, Jonathan 1939- *PenDiMP A*
Harvey, Jonathan Dean 1939- *IntWWM 90*
Harvey, Joseph Harold *BiDrAPA 89*
Harvey, Joseph Paul, Jr. 1922- *WhoAm 90*
Harvey, Joseph S. 1920- *WhoAm 90*
Harvey, Joseph Seep 1920- *St&PR 91*
Harvey, Julia *WhoWrEP 89*
Harvey, Karen Kay 1950- *WhoAmW 91*
Harvey, Katherine Abler 1946- *WhoAmW 91*
Harvey, Keith *PenDiMP*
Harvey, Kenneth Ricardo 1956- *WhoWrEP 89*
Harvey, Kit Hesketh- *BioIn 16*
Harvey, L. James 1930- *WhoE 91*
Harvey, Laurence 1928-1973 *WorAlBi*
Harvey, Leonard A. 1925- *St&PR 91, WhoAm 90*
Harvey, Lynne Cooper *WhoAmW 91*
Harvey, Malcolm 1936- *WhoAm 90*
Harvey, Marc Sean 1960- *WhoEmL 91, WhoWor 91*
Harvey, Michelle Mauthe 1954- *WhoAmW 91, WhoEmL 91, WhoSSW 91*
Harvey, Milton E 1910- *BiDrAPA 89*
Harvey, Nigel 1916- *ConAu 30NR*
Harvey, Norman Ronald 1933- *WhoAm 90*
Harvey, Pat Dotson 1939- *BiDrAPA 89*
Harvey, Patricia Jean 1931- *WhoAmW 91, WhoWor 91*
Harvey, Paul 1918- *WhoAm 90*
Harvey, Paul Henry 1911- *WhoAm 90*
Harvey, Paul Milton 1935- *IntWWM 90*
Harvey, Peter James 1941- *WhoAm 90*
Harvey, Pierre *BioIn 16*
Harvey, Ralph G. 1937- *St&PR 91*
Harvey, Raymond *BioIn 16*
Harvey, Raymond Curtis 1950- *IntWWM 90, WhoAm 90*
Harvey, Richard Allen 1953- *IntWWM 90*
Harvey, Richard Cleveland 1936- *St&PR 91*
Harvey, Richard Henry, Jr. 1957- *WhoEmL 91*
Harvey, Richard Lee 1942- *St&PR 91*
Harvey, Robert D.H. 1920- *St&PR 91*
Harvey, Robert Duncan 1919- *WhoAm 90*
Harvey, Robert Martin 1924- *WhoAmA 91, WhoWor 91*
Harvey, Robert Wilson 1920- *WhoAm 90*
Harvey, Rodney *BioIn 16*
Harvey, Ronald Gilbert 1927- *WhoAm 90*
Harvey, Stewart Alexander, II 1962- *WhoEmL 91*
Harvey, Thomas W. 1946- *St&PR 91*
Harvey, Timothy L *BiDrAPA 89*
Harvey, Timothy R. 1951- *St&PR 91*
Harvey, Van Austin 1926- *WhoAm 90*
Harvey, William 1578-1657 *BioIn 16, WorAlBi*
Harvey, William A *BiDrAPA 89*
Harvey, William Brantley, Jr. 1930- *WhoAm 90*
Harvey, William Burnett 1922- *WhoAm 90*
Harvey, William Morris 1942- *WhoE 91*
Harvey, William Robert 1941- *WhoAm 90, WhoSSW 91*
Harvey-Jones, John *BioIn 16*
Harvey-Jones, John Henry 1924- *WhoWor 91*
Harvie, Donald Southam 1924- *St&PR 91*
Harvie, James 1933- *St&PR 91*
Harvie, John 1742-1807 *EncCRAm*
Harvie, Peggy Ann 1936- *WhoAmW 91*
Harvie, Wilson Burwell 1955- *WhoSSW 91*
Harvieux, Anne Marie 1945- *WhoAmW 91*
Harvill, Howard Louis 1946- *WhoSSW 91*
Harville, James M. 1940- *WhoSSW 91*
Harvin, Charles Alexander, III 1950- *WhoEmL 91*
Harvin, David Tarleton 1945- *WhoAm 90*
Harvin, Lucius H., III 1938- *WhoAm 90, WhoSSW 91*
Harvin, William Charles 1919- *WhoAm 90*
Harvin-Welch, Virginia Raines 1919- *WhoAm 90*
Harvith, John Dana 1946- *WhoEmL 91*
Harvith, Susan Edwards 1946- *WhoEmL 91*
Harvuot, Clifford 1912-1990 *NewYTBS 90*
Harward, Brisco Lynn 1957- *WhoSSW 91*
Harward, Donald *WhoAm 90*
Harward, Gary John 1941- *St&PR 91, WhoAm 90*
Harward, Vernon J. 1922-1989 *BioIn 16*
Harway, Michele 1947- *WhoAmW 91*
Harwell, Anne L. 1963- *WhoAmW 91*
Harwell, Aubrey Biggs 1942- *WhoSSW 91*
Harwell, David Walker 1932- *WhoAm 90*
Harwell, Eddy G. 1952- *St&PR 91*
Harwell, Edwin Whitley 1929- *WhoAm 90*
Harwell, Ernie 1918- *Ballpl 90*
Harwell, Gary Winston 1951- *WhoEmL 91*
Harwell, John Monroe 1947- *St&PR 91*
Harwell, Paul Lafayette 1930- *WhoSSW 91*
Harwell, Robert C. 1945- *St&PR 91*
Harwell, Ron 1948- *WhoSSW 91*
Harwell, Rupert Alfred, Jr. 1938- *WhoSSW 91*
Harwell, William Earnest 1918- *WhoAm 90*
Harwell, William J. 1932- *St&PR 91*
Harwick, James Melvin 1946- *WhoEmL 91*
Harwin, Brian *AuBYP 90*
Harwin, Sherry Broadwater 1948- *WhoAmW 91*
Harwit, Martin Otto 1931- *WhoAm 90, WhoWor 91*
Harwith, Ronald Morgan 1942- *St&PR 91*
Harwitt, Carla Schiller 1954- *WhoEmL 91*
Harwood, Bernice *WhoAmA 91*
Harwood, Brian Dennis 1932- *WhoAm 90*
Harwood, Daniel H. 1953- *St&PR 91*
Harwood, David Dewey *BiDrAPA 89*
Harwood, Douglas Amend 1912- *WhoAm 90, WhoWor 91*
Harwood, Eleanor Cash 1921- *WhoAmW 91, WhoWor 91*
Harwood, Elizabeth *NewYTBS 90*
Harwood, Elizabeth 1938- *PenDiMP*
Harwood, Elizabeth Jean 1938- *IntWWM 90*
Harwood, Gwen 1920- *FemiCLE*
Harwood, Hugh *St&PR 91N*
Harwood, Isabella 1838?-1888 *FemiCLE*
Harwood, Ivan Richmond 1939- *WhoAm 90*
Harwood, J. Graham 1940- *St&PR 91*
Harwood, J. Keith *BioIn 16*
Harwood, James Taylor 1860-1940 *BioIn 16*
Harwood, Jerry 1926- *WhoAm 90*
Harwood, Jim 1939- *St&PR 91*
Harwood, Julius J. 1918- *St&PR 91*
Harwood, Lowell Richard 1929- *St&PR 91*
Harwood, Michael *BioIn 16*
Harwood, Michael 1934?-1989 *ConAu 130*
Harwood, Paul H, Jr. *BiDrAPA 89*
Harwood, Pearl Augusta 1903- *AuBYP 90*
Harwood, Richard Lee 1925- *WhoAm 90*
Harwood, Richard Roberts, Jr. 1921- *WhoAm 90*
Harwood, Richard Soper 1946- *WhoEmL 91*
Harwood, Ronald 1934- *ConTFT 8*
Harwood, Sanford E. 1924- *St&PR 91*
Harwood, Stephanie M. 1951- *ODwPR 91*
Harwood, Vanessa Clare 1947- *WhoAm 90*
Harwood, Virginia Ann 1925- *WhoAmW 91, WhoWor 91*
Harwood, William Bradford 1925- *WhoE 91*
Harwood, Willis B. 1924- *St&PR 91*
Harz, Christopher R. 1944- *St&PR 91*
Has, Wojciech 1925- *BioIn 16*
Hasan, Harris 1956- *WhoWor 91*
Hasan, Mahmudul 1936- *WhoWor 91*
Hasan, Syed Shabihul 1944- *WhoWor 91*
Hasan, Waqar 1963- *WhoEmL 91*
Hasan, Zainab *BiDrAPA 89*
Hasanfatta, Umar Salehmohmed 1950- *WhoWor 91*
Hasani, Sinan 1922- *WhoWor 91*
Hasbrook, William George, Jr. 1959- *WhoEmL 91*
Hasbrouck, Kenneth E, Sr. 1916- *ConAu 31NR*
Hasbrouck, Norman Gene 1952- *WhoE 91*
Hasbrouck, Stephen J. 1940- *St&PR 91*
Hasbrouck, Wilbert Roland 1931- *WhoAm 90*
Hascall, James George 1938- *St&PR 91*
Hasch, Jack J. 1922- *WhoE 91*
Hasche, Bruce A. 1953- *St&PR 91*
Haschek-Hock, Wanda Maria 1949- *WhoEmL 91*
Haschke, Bernadette Devers 1945- *WhoEmL 91*
Hasdeu, Iulia 1869-1888 *EncCoWW*
Hase, David John 1940- *WhoAm 90*
Hase, Donald A. 1928- *St&PR 91*
Hasebroock, Margaret E. *BioIn 16*
Hasegawa, Akira 1934- *WhoAm 90*
Hasegawa, Alan Akira *BiDrAPA 89*
Hasegawa, Itsuko 1941- *WomArch*
Hasegawa, Keiko *PenDiDA 89*
Hasegawa, Lee Patton 1951- *WhoEmL 91*
Hasegawa, Norishige 1907- *St&PR 91*
Hasegawa, Tomohiro 1962- *WhoE 91*
Hasegawa, Tony Seisuke 1941- *WhoWor 91*
Hasegawa, Yoshinobu 1930- *WhoWor 91*
Hasek, Jaroslav 1883-1923 *ConAu 129, MajTwCW, WorAlBi*
Hasek, Joseph Karel 1911- *WhoE 91*
Hasel, Norman L. 1932- *St&PR 91*
Haselden, Catherine Anderson 1957- *WhoSSW 91*
Haselden, Clyde LeRoy 1914- *WhoAm 90*
Haselden, John *ConAu 129*
Haseley, Dennis 1950- *BioIn 16*
Haselkorn, Robert 1934- *WhoAm 90*
Haselmann, John Philip 1940- *WhoAm 90, WhoWor 91*
Haselmayer, Louis August 1911- *WhoAm 90*
Haselow, John H. *ODwPR 91*
Haseltine, Florence Pat 1942- *WhoAm 90, WhoAmW 91*
Haseltine, Herbert 1877-1962 *WhoAmA 91N*
Haseltine, James Lewis 1924- *WhoAmA 91*
Haseltine, Maury 1925- *WhoAmA 91*
Haseltine, Oran L. 1925- *St&PR 91*
Haselton, William Raymond 1925- *WhoAm 90*
Hasen, Burt Stanly 1921- *WhoAmA 91*
Hasen, Burton Stanly 1921- *WhoAm 90*
Hasen, Irwin 1918- *EncACom*
Hasenclever, Peter 1716-1793 *EncCRAm*
Hasenour, Lee 1936- *WhoSSW 91*
Hasenpflug, Jerome Francis 1955- *WhoE 91*
Haser, Michael Wayne *BiDrAPA 89*
Haserick, John Roger 1915- *WhoAm 90*
Hasford, Gustav *BioIn 16*
Hash, Cecil Jackson 1942- *WhoSSW 91*
Hash, John Frank 1944- *WhoAm 90*
Hashagen, John D. 1941- *St&PR 91*
Hashem, Tufie *Ballpl 90*
Hashemi, Seyed M N *BiDrAPA 89*
Hashemi-Rafsanjani, Ali Akbar 1935- *WhoWor 91*
Hashiguchi, Yasugo 1924- *WhoWor 91*
Hashim, Elinor M. 1933- *WhoAm 90*
Hashim, Junaid *BiDrAPA 89*
Hashimi, Mir Habibullah *BiDrAPA 89*
Hashimoto, Akira 1936- *St&PR 91*
Hashimoto, Dean Masaru 1954- *WhoEmL 91*
Hashimoto, Eiji 1931- *IntWWM 90*
Hashimoto, Frances Kazuko 1943- *WhoWor 91*
Hashimoto, Ryutaro 1937- *WhoWor 91*
Hashimoto, Takuji 1934- *WhoWor 91*
Hashimoto, Tomisaburo *NewYTBS 90*
Hashimoto, Tomisaburo 1901-1990 *BioIn 16*
Hashimoto, Tooru 1925- *WhoWor 91*
Hashimoto, Yoshio 1928- *WhoWor 91*
Hashiura, Haruko 1898-1975 *BioIn 16*
Hashmi, Alamgir 1951- *WhoWor 91*
Hashmi, Sajjad Ahmad 1933- *WhoAm 90*
Hashmi, Syed Haseen 1935- *WhoWor 91*
Hasija, Om P. 1943- *St&PR 91*
Haskell, Arthur E. 1919- *St&PR 91*
Haskell, Arthur J. 1926- *St&PR 91*
Haskell, Arthur Jacob 1926- *WhoAm 90*
Haskell, Barbara 1946- *WhoAm 90, WhoAmA 91, WhoAmW 91*
Haskell, Barry Geoffry 1941- *WhoAm 90*
Haskell, Blanton Winship 1920- *WhoAm 90*
Haskell, Brian Merwin 1952- *WhoEmL 91*
Haskell, Charles Thomson, III 1948- *WhoEmL 91*
Haskell, David Lincoln 1948- *WhoE 91*
Haskell, David Saks 1934- *BiDrAPA 89*
Haskell, Dudley Chase 1842-1883 *AmLegL*
Haskell, Edward N. 1920- *St&PR 91*
Haskell, Franklin Aretas 1828-1864 *BioIn 16*
Haskell, Harry 1954- *ConAu 129*
Haskell, Helen Beaumont Park 1916- *WhoWor 91*
Haskell, John Henry Farrell, Jr. 1932- *St&PR 91, WhoAm 90*
Haskell, Kim Shopp 1953- *WhoAmW 91*
Haskell, Molly *BioIn 16*
Haskell, Paul Gershon 1927- *WhoAm 90*
Haskell, Paul Heger 1934- *WhoWor 91*
Haskell, Paul S. 1938- *St&PR 91*
Haskell, Peter Abraham 1934- *WhoAm 90*
Haskell, Preston Hampton 1938- *St&PR 91*
Haskell, Preston Hampton, III 1938- *WhoAm 90*
Haskell, Raymond Hilbert 1930- *St&PR 91*
Haskell, Robert H *BiDrAPA 89*
Haskell, Robert Steven 1947- *WhoSSW 91*
Haskell, Thomas Langdon 1939- *WhoAm 90*
Haskell, William H 1875-1952 *WhoAmA 91N*
Haskell-Robinson, Patricia Corbin 1931- *WhoSSW 91*
Haskett, Roger F 1944- *BiDrAPA 89*
Haskew, George M. 1927- *St&PR 91*
Haskew, Joyce Annette 1942- *WhoAmW 91*
Haskil, Clara 1895-1960 *PenDiMP*
Haskin, David Warren 1933- *St&PR 91*
Haskin, Donald Lee 1945- *WhoE 91*
Haskin, Donald Marcus 1920- *WhoAmA 91*
Haskin, John James, Jr. 1951- *BiDrAPA 89*
Haskin, Larry Allen 1934- *WhoAm 90*
Haskin, Marvin Edward 1930- *WhoAm 90*
Haskin, Sandra Lynn *BiDrAPA 89*
Haskins, Barbara Gay 1951- *BiDrAPA 89*
Haskins, Caryl Parker 1908- *WhoAm 90, WhoE 91, WhoWor 91*
Haskins, Don 1930- *BioIn 16*
Haskins, George Lee 1915- *WhoAm 90*
Haskins, Jack Lionel 1935- *St&PR 91*
Haskins, James 1941- *AuBYP 90, BioIn 16, WhoAm 90, WhoE 91*
Haskins, Jim *AuBYP 90*
Haskins, John Franklin 1919- *WhoAmA 91*
Haskins, Kittredge 1836-1860 *AmLegL*
Haskins, Linda M. 1954- *St&PR 91*
Haskins, Luther Granville, III 1951- *WhoEmL 91*
Haskins, Patrick Dean 1956- *WhoEmL 91*
Haskins, Richard Earl 1927- *St&PR 91*
Haskins, Robert William 1923- *St&PR 91*
Haskins, Sandra L. 1944- *St&PR 91*
Haskins, Susan Marie 1954- *WhoE 91*
Haskins, Terry Edward 1955- *WhoEmL 91*
Haskins, Theresa Joan 1945- *WhoAmW 91*
Haskins, Thomas Marston 1950- *WhoWor 91*
Haskins, Todd *BioIn 16*
Haskins, Victoria Jean 1953- *WhoSSW 91*
Haskins, Walter Dewey 1956- *WhoEmL 91*
Haskit, Roberta Tefft 1944- *St&PR 91*
Hasko, Peter 1957- *WhoWor 91*
Haslam, Douglas Frank 1941- *St&PR 91*
Haslam, Gerald Peter 1945- *WhoAm 90*
Haslam, Gerald William 1937- *WhoWrEP 89*
Haslam, Nicholas *BioIn 16*
Haslam, Patricia Ann 1947- *WhoSSW 91*
Haslem, Jane N 1934- *WhoAmA 91, WhoE 91*
Hasler, Arthur Davis 1908- *WhoAm 90*
Hasler, E.A. 1949- *St&PR 91*
Hasler, Eveline *EncCoWW*
Hasler, Joseph William 1934- *St&PR 91*
Hasler, William Albert 1941- *WhoAm 90, WhoWor 91*
Haslerud, George M. *NewYTBS 90*
Haslerud, George M. 1906-1990 *BioIn 16*
Haslett, Nancy Rose 1937- *BiDrAPA 89*
Hasley, Michael James 1946- *St&PR 91*
Haslin, Mickey 1910- *Ballpl 90*
Hasling, Jill Freeman 1952- *WhoAmW 91*
Hasling, Robert John 1929- *St&PR 91*
Haslinger, Kenneth Robert 1940- *St&PR 91*
Haslund, Ebba 1917- *DcScanL, EncCoWW*

Hasnas, Sandra G. 1962- *WhoAmW 91*
Hasner, Rolf K. 1919- *St&PR 91*
Hasner-Scharf, Mary Frances 1953- *BiDrAPA 89*
Haspel, Arthur Carl 1945- *WhoAm 90, WhoEmL 91*
Haspel, David K. 1949- *WhoEmL 91, WhoWor 91*
Haspel, Stanley Joel 1931- *WhoAm 90*
Haspeslagh, Philippe Cyriel 1950- *WhoWor 91*
Hass, Anthony 1923- *WhoAm 90*
Hass, E. A. *AuBYP 90*
Hass, Hyman 1934- *St&PR 91*
Hass, Joseph Monroe 1955- *WhoEmL 91*
Hass, Richard Warren 1944- *IntWWM 90*
Hass, Robert 1941- *ConAu 30NR, DcLB 105 [port]*
Hass, Sabine 1949- *IntWWM 90*
Hassall, Joan 1906- *BioIn 16*
Hassall, Joan 1906-1988 *AnObit 1988*
Hassam, Childe 1859-1935 *WorAlBi*
Hassan II 1929- *PolLCME, WhoWor 91, WorAlBi*
Hassan bin Talal 1947- *WhoWor 91*
Hassan, Aftab Syed 1952- *WhoE 91, WhoWor 91*
Hassan, Faisal Abboud 1964- *WhoE 91*
Hassan, Farooq Azim 1941- *WhoAm 90*
Hassan, Fred 1945- *WhoAm 90*
Hassan, Giulio 1940- *WhoWor 91*
Hassan, Ihab 1925- *ConAu 12AS [port]*
Hassan, Ihab Habib 1925- *WhoWrEP 89*
Hassan, Kamal Yousif 1958- *WhoWor 91*
Hassan, Khan Mamnoon 1941- *WhoSSW 91*
Hassan, Mohammad K 1942- *BiDrAPA 89*
Hassan, Mohammed Samir 1941- *BiDrAPA 89*
Hassan, Salah Salem 1953- *WhoEmL 91*
Hassan, Tariq Ibrahim *BiDrAPA 89*
Hassan, William Ephriam, Jr. 1923- *WhoAm 90*
Hassan, Yassin Abdel 1945- *WhoSSW 91*
Hassan, Zia Mohammad 1933- *WhoAm 90*
Hassanal Bolkiah, Sultan of Brunei 1946- *BioIn 16*
Hassanal Bolkiah, Mui'zzaddin Waddaulah 1946- *WhoWor 91*
Hassanali, Noor Mohamed 1918- *WhoWor 91*
Hassanein, Khatab M. 1926- *WhoAm 90*
Hassani, Jay Jalil 1920- *St&PR 91*
Hassani, Tamara 1928-1988 *AnObit 1988*
Hassard, Howard 1910- *St&PR 91, WhoAm 90*
Hassberger, Richard Lord 1949- *St&PR 91*
Hasse, Arthur A. 1940- *St&PR 91*
Hasse, Glenn Warren, Jr. 1941- *St&PR 91*
Hasse, Helmut 1898-1979 *DcScB S2*
Hasse, Johann Adolf 1699-1783 *PenDiMP A*
Hasse, John Edward 1948- *IntWWM 90*
Hasse, Marquard *BioIn 16*
Hasse, Rolf Helmut 1940- *WhoWor 91*
Hassebrock, Steve Allen 1945- *St&PR 91*
Hassebroeck, Johannes 1910- *BioIn 16*
Hassebroek, Jerry Cox 1945- *WhoSSW 91*
Hassel, David John 1923- *ConAu 32NR*
Hassel, R. Chris, Jr. 1939- *ConAu 129*
Hasselbacher, Frank 1919- *BiDrAPA 89*
Hasselbalch, Marilyn Jean 1930- *WhoAmW 91*
Hasselberg-Olsson, Elisabet 1932- *ConDes 90*
Hasselbring, Bruce A. 1955- *St&PR 91*
Hasselbring, Jane R. 1931- *St&PR 91*
Hasselgren, Kristina 1920- *EncCoWW*
Hasselgren, Robert William 1949- *St&PR 91*
Hassell, Aarno A. 1939- *St&PR 91*
Hassell, Fey von *BioIn 16*
Hassell, Gerald L. 1951- *WhoAm 90*
Hassell, Jon *NewAgMG*
Hassell, Martin 1927- *St&PR 91*
Hassell, Michael Patrick 1942- *WhoWor 91*
Hassell, Morris William 1916- *WhoSSW 91, WhoWor 91*
Hassell, Peggy L *BiDrAPA 89*
Hassell, Stephen P. 1949- *St&PR 91*
Hassell, Ulrich von 1881-1944 *BioIn 16*
Hasselle, James Eugene, III 1935- *BiDrAPA 89*
Hasselman, Richard B. 1926- *WhoAm 90*
Hasselmeier, A. Gale 1944- *St&PR 91*
Hasselmeyer, Eileen Grace 1924- *WhoAm 90*
Hasselmo, Nils 1931- *WhoAm 90, WhoWor 91*
Hasselquist, M.B. 1919- *St&PR 91*
Hasselquist, Maynard Burton 1919- *WhoAm 90, WhoWor 91*
Hasselstrom, Linda M. *BioIn 16*
Hasselstrom, Linda M. 1943- *WhoWrEP 89*
Hasselwander, Alan C. *WhoAm 90*
Hassenfeld, Alan Geoffrey 1948- *St&PR 91, WhoAm 90, WhoE 91*
Hassenfeld, Harold 1916- *St&PR 91*
Hassenfeld, Irwin N 1932- *BiDrAPA 89*
Hassenfeld, John Eliot 1957- *St&PR 91*
Hassenfeld, Stephen David *BioIn 16*
Hassenfeld, Stephen David 1942-1989 *ConAmBL*
Hasser, Michael D. 1946- *St&PR 91*
Hassett, Buddy 1911- *Ballpl 90*
Hassett, Carol Alice 1947- *WhoAmW 91, WhoE 91, WhoWor 91*
Hassett, Joseph Malk 1943- *WhoWrEP 89*
Hassett, Joseph Mark 1943- *WhoAm 90*
Hassett, Raymond Michael 1932- *St&PR 91*
Hassett, Robert Emmett 1932- *St&PR 91*
Hassey, Ron 1953- *Ballpl 90*
Hassib, Mahmoud Zaki 1914- *WhoWor 91*
Hassibi, Mahin 1937- *BiDrAPA 89*
Hassid, Sami 1912- *WhoAm 90*
Hassinger, Karl William 1947- *WhoE 91*
Hassinger, Mark Alan 1956- *WhoEmL 91, WhoWor 91*
Hassiotis, Nicholas Daniel 1926- *St&PR 91*
Hasslacher, Elizabeth A *BiDrAPA 89*
Hasslein, George Johann 1917- *WhoAm 90*
Hassler, Andy 1951- *Ballpl 90*
Hassler, Bonnie Barham 1932- *WhoAmW 91*
Hassler, Donald M 1937- *ConAu 31NR*
Hassler, Donald Mackey, II 1937- *WhoAm 90, WhoWrEP 89*
Hassler, Ferdinand R *BiDrAPA 89*
Hassler, Howard E. 1929- *St&PR 91*
Hassler, John Mathias 1942- *BiDrAPA 89*
Hassler, Jon 1933- *WhoWrEP 89*
Hassler, Paul Mark, Sr. 1927- *St&PR 91*
Hassler, Thomas Andrew 1937- *WhoSSW 91*
Hassner, Martin I. *ODwPR 91*
Hasso, Signe Eleonora Cecilia 1915- *WhoAm 90*
Hasson, Esther Voorhees 1868-1942 *BioIn 16*
Hasson, Haskia 1951- *WhoWor 91*
Hasson, Herbert 1923- *St&PR 91*
Hasson, Maurice 1934- *PenDiMP*
Hasson, Nathan 1945- *St&PR 91*
Hasson, Raymond I. 1950- *St&PR 91*
Hasson, Vester Maxwell, III 1947- *WhoSSW 91*
Hassouna, Fred 1918- *WhoWor 91*
Hassrick, Peter H 1941- *WhoAmA 91*
Hassuk, Bruce Michael *BiDrAPA 89*
Hast, Adele 1931- *WhoAm 90*
Hast, Herbert H., Jr. 1938- *St&PR 91*
Hast, Joan Eileen 1955- *WhoAmW 91, WhoEmL 91*
Hast, Malcolm Howard 1931- *WhoAm 90, WhoWor 91*
Hasted, John B 1921- *EncO&P 3*
Hasten, Michael Alan 1955- *St&PR 91*
Hastenteufel, Dieter 1939- *WhoAmA 91*
Hastert, Dennis 1942- *WhoAm 90*
Hastie, K. Larry 1942- *WhoAm 90*
Hastie, Reid 1916-1987 *WhoAmA 91N*
Hastie, Rod *BioIn 16*
Hastings, A. Baird 1895-1987 *BioIn 16*
Hastings, Alice L. *BioIn 16*
Hastings, Anthea Esther 1924-1981 *DcNaB 1981*
Hastings, Arthur 1935- *EncPaPR 91*
Hastings, Arthur Claude 1935- *EncO&P 3*
Hastings, Baird 1919- *IntWWM 90*
Hastings, Brooke *ConAu 130*
Hastings, Catherine Manson 1959- *WhoWrEP 89*
Hastings, Cora *BioIn 16*
Hastings, Deborah 1959- *WhoAmW 91, WhoEmL 91*
Hastings, Donald Francis 1934- *WhoAm 90*
Hastings, Edward Walton 1931- *WhoAm 90*
Hastings, Evelyn Grace 1938- *WhoAmW 91, WhoSSW 91*
Hastings, George Sands 1899-1990 *BioIn 16*
Hastings, Graham *TwCCr&M 91*
Hastings, Harold 1946- *WhoWor 91*
Hastings, Ian 1912- *SmATA 62 [port]*
Hastings, Joel Prescott 1948- *WhoWrEP 89*
Hastings, John Woodland 1927- *WhoAm 90*
Hastings, Joseph H. 1949- *St&PR 91*
Hastings, Julianne *ODwPR 91*
Hastings, Julianne Francesca 1946- *WhoE 91, WhoEmL 91*
Hastings, Kathleen Agnes 1947- *WhoEmL 91*
Hastings, Kevin Lee 1937- *St&PR 91*
Hastings, Lawrence Vaeth 1919- *WhoAm 90, WhoWor 91*
Hastings, Lois Jane 1928- *WhoAm 90*
Hastings, Lucy *BiDEWW*
Hastings, Lynn Courtlandt 1942- *WhoWor 91*
Hastings, March *ConAu 31NR*
Hastings, Matthew Tate 1952- *WhoSSW 91*
Hastings, Michael 1938- *SpyFic*
Hastings, Philip Kay 1922- *WhoAm 90*
Hastings, Richard G., III 1941- *St&PR 91*
Hastings, Robert D. 1940- *St&PR 91*
Hastings, Robert Eugene 1932- *WhoWor 91*
Hastings, Robert Pusey 1910- *WhoAm 90*
Hastings, Robert William, II 1946- *WhoEmL 91*
Hastings, Robin Hood William Stewart 1917-1990 *ConAu 131*
Hastings, Roderic *TwCCr&M 91*
Hastings, Susan Ann 1955- *WhoAmW 91*
Hastings, Susan Kay 1952- *WhoAmW 91*
Hastings, Thomas 1860-1929 *BioIn 16*
Hastings, Victoria S. *ODwPR 91*
Hastings, Warren 1732-1818 *WorAlBi*
Hastings, Warren Ray 1965- *WhoSSW 91*
Hastings, William Charles 1921- *WhoAm 90*
Hastings, William H. 1913- *St&PR 91*
Hastings, Wilmot Reed 1935- *WhoAm 90*
Haston, Jack Steve 1946- *WhoSSW 91*
Haston, Richard Thomas 1946- *WhoSSW 91*
Hastorf, Albert Herman 1920- *WhoAm 90*
Hastreiter, Joe *ODwPR 91*
Hastrich, Jerome Joseph 1914- *WhoAm 90*
Hasty, Bob 1896-1972 *Ballpl 90*
Hasty, Curtis Bush 1921- *St&PR 91*
Hasty, Gerald Richard 1926- *WhoWor 91*
Hasty, Jack *St&PR 91*
Haswell, Carleton Radley 1939- *WhoAm 90*
Haswell, Ernest Bruce 1889-1965 *WhoAmA 91N*
Haswell, Hollee 1948- *WhoAmA 91*
Haszard, Patricia Moyes 1923- *SmATA X [port]*
Hat, Martha *BiDEWW*
Hata Clan *EncJap*
Hatada, Kazuyuki 1951- *WhoWor 91*
Hatanaka, Hiroshi 1932- *WhoWor 91*
Hatanaka, Thomas Toby 1926- *St&PR 91*
Hatano, Daryl Glen 1958- *WhoEmL 91*
Hatasu *WomWR*
Hataway, Louis Grady 1929- *St&PR 91*
Hatch, Albert Ruyter 1817-1882 *AmLegL*
Hatch, Alden 1898-1975 *AuBYP 90*
Hatch, Anthony P. 1937- *ODwPR 91*
Hatch, Arthur A. 1930- *St&PR 91*
Hatch, Charles Ray 1943- *WhoAm 90*
Hatch, David Lincoln 1910- *WhoAm 90*
Hatch, Denison Hurlbut, Jr. 1949- *WhoEmL 91*
Hatch, Dorothy L. 1920- *WhoWrEP 89*
Hatch, Edwin I. 1913- *St&PR 91*
Hatch, Emily Nichols 1871-1959 *WhoAmA 91N*
Hatch, George Clinton 1919- *St&PR 91, WhoAm 90*
Hatch, Gerald Gordon 1922- *WhoWor 91*
Hatch, Gordon Lee 1933- *St&PR 91*
Hatch, H. Clifford 1916- *St&PR 91*
Hatch, Harold Arthur 1924- *WhoAm 90*
Hatch, Harold Eugene 1935- *St&PR 91*
Hatch, Henry Albert 1927- *St&PR 91*
Hatch, James Alfred 1939- *WhoAm 90*
Hatch, James Henry, III 1922- *St&PR 91*
Hatch, James Stokes 1943- *St&PR 91*
Hatch, Jami McCowan 1960- *WhoAmW 91*
Hatch, Jeffrey B. *BioIn 16*
Hatch, Jennifer Seyler 1947- *WhoEmL 91*
Hatch, John B. 1933- *ODwPR 91*
Hatch, John Davis 1907- *WhoAm 90, WhoAmA 91, WhoWor 91*
Hatch, John W 1919- *WhoAmA 91*
Hatch, Lynda Sylvia 1950- *WhoAmW 91*
Hatch, Marshall 1918- *WhoAmA 91*
Hatch, Marshall, Mrs 1918- *WhoAmA 91*
Hatch, Mary 1848-1935 *FemiCLE*
Hatch, Mary 1935- *WhoAmA 91*
Hatch, Mary Gies 1913- *WhoAm 90, WhoSSW 91*
Hatch, Mary Wendell Vander Poel 1919- *WhoAmW 91, WhoE 91, WhoWor 91*
Hatch, Michael Francis 1947- *St&PR 91*
Hatch, Monroe W., Jr. 1933- *WhoAm 90*
Hatch, Nancy R. 1958- *WhoEmL 91*
Hatch, Nathan O 1946- *ConAu 129*
Hatch, Norman S. 1950- *St&PR 91*
Hatch, Orrin Grant 1934- *WhoAm 90, WhoWor 91*
Hatch, Patricia M. 1953- *WhoWrEP 89*
Hatch, Peter J. 1949- *BioIn 16*
Hatch, Rebecca Blackmon 1955- *WhoAmW 91, WhoEmL 91*
Hatch, Richard 1948- *WhoEmL 91*
Hatch, Robert Alan 1948- *WhoEmL 91*
Hatch, Robert Allen 1947- *St&PR 91*
Hatch, Robert Norris 1914- *WhoAm 90*
Hatch, Robert Norris, Jr. 1952- *St&PR 91*
Hatch, Robert Walter 1929- *WhoE 91*
Hatch, Robert Winslow 1938- *St&PR 91, WhoAm 90*
Hatch, Sandra Lee 1948- *WhoAmW 91*
Hatch, Sinclair 1906-1989 *BioIn 16*
Hatch, Stephan Lavor 1945- *WhoEmL 91*
Hatch, T. Brad 1924- *St&PR 91*
Hatch, Tony 1939- *OxCPMus*
Hatch, Tracy Soper 1960- *WhoE 91*
Hatch, W A S 1948- *WhoAmA 91*
Hatcher, Allen Edward 1944- *WhoAm 90*
Hatcher, Betty Francis 1932- *St&PR 91*
Hatcher, Billy 1960- *Ballpl 90*
Hatcher, Charles 1939- *WhoAm 90, WhoSSW 91*
Hatcher, Charles Ross, Jr. 1930- *WhoAm 90*
Hatcher, Daphne *BioIn 16*
Hatcher, David E. 1923- *St&PR 91*
Hatcher, E. Kennette 1952- *St&PR 91*
Hatcher, Elizabeth Roberta 1945- *BiDrAPA 89*
Hatcher, Everett *BioIn 16*
Hatcher, Gary C. *BioIn 16*
Hatcher, Harlan H. 1898- *LiHiK*
Hatcher, Jak P. 1928- *WhoAm 90*
Hatcher, James A. 1952- *St&PR 91*
Hatcher, James Donald 1923- *WhoAm 90*
Hatcher, James Mitchell 1950- *WhoSSW 91*
Hatcher, Jeffrey French *WhoE 91*
Hatcher, Joe Branch 1936- *WhoAm 90*
Hatcher, Kenneth Wayne 1943- *St&PR 91*
Hatcher, LeAnna Jepson 1954- *WhoE 91*
Hatcher, Marilyn Ann 1950- *WhoAmW 91*
Hatcher, Martha Olivia Taylor 1920- *WhoAmW 91, WhoWor 91*
Hatcher, Mickey *BioIn 16*
Hatcher, Mickey 1955- *Ballpl 90*
Hatcher, Milford Burriss 1909- *WhoAm 90*
Hatcher, Paul Graham 1954- *WhoEmL 91*
Hatcher, Paula Braniff 1947- *IntWWM 90*
Hatcher, Ray F. 1939- *St&PR 91*
Hatcher, Richard G. 1933- *WorAlBi*
Hatcher, Robert Douglas 1924- *WhoAm 90*
Hatcher, Robin Lee 1951- *WhoWrEP 89*
Hatcher, Stanley Ronald 1932- *WhoAm 90*
Hatcher, Stephen Randolph 1942- *St&PR 91*
Hatcher, Thomas Fountain 1931- *WhoWor 91*
Hatcher, Tina Simpson 1958- *WhoEmL 91*
Hatcher, William Claude 1922- *St&PR 91*
Hatcher, William Julian, Jr. 1935- *WhoAm 90, WhoSSW 91*
Hatcher, William Spottswood 1935- *WhoAm 90*
Hatchett, Duayne 1925- *WhoAmA 91*
Hatchett, Edward Earl 1923- *WhoAm 90*
Hatchett, Joseph Woodrow 1932- *WhoAm 90*
Hatem, Frederick Joseph, Jr. 1956- *WhoEmL 91*
Hatem, George 1910-1988 *BioIn 16*
Hatfield, A. Richard, Jr. 1942- *St&PR 91*
Hatfield, Charles Donald 1935- *WhoAm 90*
Hatfield, Charles H. 1937- *St&PR 91*
Hatfield, Charles Lee 1953- *WhoEmL 91*
Hatfield, Charles Mallory 1876-1958 *BioIn 16*
Hatfield, David Underhill 1940- *WhoAm 90, WhoAmA 91*
Hatfield, Donald Gene 1932- *WhoAmA 91*
Hatfield, Elaine Catherine 1937- *WhoAm 90*
Hatfield, Eloise Janette 1947- *WhoWrEP 89*
Hatfield, Fred 1925- *Ballpl 90*
Hatfield, Harry Maxwell 1947- *WhoEmL 91*
Hatfield, Jack Kenton 1922- *WhoWor 91*
Hatfield, James Walker 1942- *St&PR 91*
Hatfield, Jane Stauff 1911- *WhoAmW 91*
Hatfield, Jerry Lee 1949- *WhoAm 90*
Hatfield, Julie Stockwell 1940- *WhoAm 90*
Hatfield, Leonard Fraser 1919- *WhoAm 90*
Hatfield, Mark O. 1922- *WhoAm 90, WhoWor 91, WorAlBi*
Hatfield, Michael 1936- *IntWWM 90*
Hatfield, Paul Gerhart 1928- *WhoAm 90*
Hatfield, Paul Harold 1936- *St&PR 91*
Hatfield, Phillip L. 1945- *St&PR 91*
Hatfield, Richard Bennett 1931- *WhoAm 90*
Hatfield, Robert Sherman 1916- *WhoAm 90*
Hatfield, W.C. 1926- *St&PR 91*
Hatfield, W. C. 1926- *WhoAm 90*
Hatfield, William Emerson 1937- *WhoAm 90*

Hatfield, William Walter 1913- *WhoE 91*
Hatgil, Paul 1921- *WhoAmA 91*
Hathaway, Alden Moinet 1933- *WhoAm 90, WhoE 91*
Hathaway, Amos Townsend 1913- *WhoSSW 91*
Hathaway, Calvin S *WhoAmA 91N*
Hathaway, Carl Emil 1933- *WhoAm 90*
Hathaway, Carmrid Glaston 1922- *WhoE 91*
Hathaway, Cheryl Kaye 1947- *WhoEmL 91*
Hathaway, Donny 1945-1979 *BioIn 16, EncPR&S 89*
Hathaway, Harold Grant 1927- *St&PR 91, WhoAm 90*
Hathaway, Joan Boyette 1935- *WhoAmW 91*
Hathaway, John David 1934- *St&PR 91*
Hathaway, John Wallace 1906-1987 *BioIn 16*
Hathaway, John Whitcomb 1926- *WhoE 91*
Hathaway, Kathy R. Moore 1953- *WhoWrEP 89*
Hathaway, Lovering 1898-1949 *WhoAmA 91N*
Hathaway, Marvin L. 1926- *St&PR 91*
Hathaway, Michael Jerry 1961- *WhoWrEP 89*
Hathaway, Michael Manning 1946- *WhoEmL 91*
Hathaway, Paul L., Jr. 1934- *WhoAm 90*
Hathaway, Paul Lawrence 1934- *St&PR 91*
Hathaway, Raeburn B., Jr. 1934- *St&PR 91*
Hathaway, Raeburn Burton, Jr. 1934- *WhoAm 90*
Hathaway, Richard Dean 1927- *WhoAm 90*
Hathaway, Robert Lawton 1932- *WhoAm 90*
Hathaway, Roger 1933- *St&PR 91*
Hathaway, Stanley K. 1924- *BiDrUSE 89*
Hathaway, William Kitchen 1944- *WhoWrEP 89*
Hathcoat, Ronald Andrew 1949- *WhoEmL 91, WhoSSW 91*
Hathcock, Cathy Lynn 1959- *WhoAmW 91*
Hathcox, VaLinda 1947- *WhoEmL 91*
Hatheway, Jane M 1918- *BiDrAPA 89*
Hatheway, John Harris 1926- *WhoAm 90*
Hathorn, Paula *BioIn 16*
Hatie, George Daniel 1910- *WhoAm 90*
Hatke, Walter Joseph 1948- *WhoAmA 91*
Hatleberg, James L 1925- *BiDrAPA 89*
Hatlelid, John Michael 1948- *WhoEmL 91*
Hatlen, Burton Norval 1936- *WhoAm 90*
Hatley, Bobby Gene 1937- *St&PR 91*
Hatley, Von Devin 1959- *WhoSSW 91*
Hatley-Brickey, Lael Ann 1956- *WhoEmL 91*
Hatling, John Allen 1955- *WhoEmL 91*
Hatlo, James 1898-1963 *WhoAmA 91N*
Hatlo, Jimmy 1898-1963 *EncACom*
Hatmaker, Michael William 1942- *St&PR 91*
Hatoff, Howard Ira 1931- *WhoAm 90*
Hatoum, Mona 1952- *BiDWomA*
Hatrik, Juraj 1941- *IntWWM 90*
Hatry, Paul A. 1929- *WhoWor 91*
Hatschek, Rudolf Alexander 1918- *WhoWor 91*
Hatshepsut *WomWR*
Hatsopoulos, G. N. *BioIn 16*
Hatsopoulos, George N. *BioIn 16*
Hatsopoulos, George N. 1927- *St&PR 91*
Hatsopoulos, George Nicholas 1927- *WhoAm 90*
Hatsopoulos, John Nicholas 1934- *St&PR 91, WhoAm 90*
Hatt, Hannah *BiDEWW*
Hatta, Mohammad 1902- *BioIn 16*
Hattab, Fawzi J F 1940- *BiDrAPA 89*
Hattab, Helen Gergis *BiDrAPA 89*
Hattabaugh, Aaron Eugene 1964- *WhoSSW 91*
Hattabaugh, Fred Lee 1942- *WhoSSW 91*
Hattal, Alvin M. *ODwPR 91*
Hattal, Tacey Thomas 1955- *WhoAmW 91*
Hattan, Marie Candice 1951- *WhoWor 91*
Hattan, Richard F 1930- *BiDrAPA 89*
Hattangadi, Sunder 1935- *BiDrAPA 89*
Hatteberg, Larry Merle 1944- *WhoAm 90*
Hattem, Albert Worth 1951- *WhoSSW 91*
Hattem, Robert Paul 1952- *St&PR 91*
Hattemer, Theresa Ida 1954- *BiDrAPA 89*
Hatten, Anita Marie 1940- *WhoSSW 91*
Hatten, Joe 1916-1988 *Ballpl 90*
Hatten, William Seward 1917- *WhoAm 90*
Hattendorf, Joseph Mark 1950- *St&PR 91*
Hatter, Lou 1920-1988 *Ballpl 90*
Hatter, Terry Julius, Jr. 1933- *WhoAm 90*
Hatteras, Amelia *MajTwCW*
Hatteras, Owen *MajTwCW*
Hatterer, Julie A. *BiDrAPA 89*
Hatterer, Lawrence J 1925- *BiDrAPA 89*
Hatterer, Myra S *BiDrAPA 89*
Hattersley, Robert Sherwood 1931- *WhoSSW 91*
Hattersley-Smith, Geoffrey Francis 1923- *WhoAm 90*
Hattervig, Robin Lynn 1958- *WhoEmL 91*
Hattery, Robert R. 1939- *WhoAm 90*
Hatti, Shivkumar S 1952- *BiDrAPA 89*
Hattin, Donald Edward 1928- *WhoAm 90*
Hattink, Odo 1927- *WhoWor 91*
Hatton, Aiden Emmet, Jr. 1933- *St&PR 91*
Hatton, Alice E. 1675?- *BiDEWW*
Hatton, Ann 1764-1838 *FemiCLE*
Hatton, Candace Lee 1948- *St&PR 91*
Hatton, Carl Edward 1945- *St&PR 91*
Hatton, Carolyn Marie 1942- *WhoE 91*
Hatton, Elizabeth 1578-1646 *BiDEWW*
Hatton, Frances *BiDEWW*
Hatton, Frank 1846-1894 *BiDrUSE 89, BioIn 16*
Hatton, Frederick L. 1943- *St&PR 91, WhoAm 90*
Hatton, Gaylen A. 1928- *IntWWM 90*
Hatton, Grady 1922- *Ballpl 90*
Hatton, John Ernest 1938- *WhoWor 91*
Hatton, John Liptrot 1809-1886 *OxCPMus*
Hatton, Lloyd W *BiDrAPA 89*
Hatton, Mary 1630?- *BiDEWW*
Hatton, Richard L. *St&PR 91*
Hatton, Robert Wayland 1934- *WhoWrEP 89*
Hattori, Akira 1949- *WhoWor 91*
Hattori, Noriyasu 1943- *St&PR 91*
Hattori, Shoji 1937- *St&PR 91, WhoAm 90*
Hattox, Brock Alan 1948- *St&PR 91, WhoAm 90*
Hattox, Patsy Leeth 1949- *St&PR 91*
Hatvani, Balazs Imre 1953- *BiDrAPA 89*
Hatvary, George Egon 1921- *WhoWrEP 89*
Hatwalkar, Shrikant M. 1938- *BiDrAPA 89*
Hatwood, Josephine *BioIn 16*
Hatz, Elizabeth 1953- *WomArch*
Hatzai, Glen A. 1946- *ODwPR 91*
Hatzai, Glen Alan *WhoEmL 91*
Hatzakis, Michael 1928- *WhoAm 90*
Hatzel, Richard F. 1924- *St&PR 91*
Hatzenbeler, Lawrence J *BiDrAPA 89*
Hatzlerin, Klara 1450?-1476? *EncCoWW*
Hau Pei-tsun 1919- *WhoWor 91*
Hau, Pei-tsun *BioIn 16*
Hau, Steen 1947- *WhoWor 91*
Hau, Suk Kei Simon 1954- *WhoWor 91*
Hau, Theodor Friedrich 1924- *WhoWor 91*
Haub, Erivan Karl 1932- *WhoWor 91*
Hauben, Robert *BiDrAPA 89*
Haubenreich, George R., Jr. 1948- *St&PR 91*
Haubenstoch, Alfred B. 1916- *St&PR 91*
Haubenstock-Ramati, Roman 1919- *IntWWM 90, PenDiMP A*
Hauber, Eclea Zugman 1933- *WhoWor 91*
Hauber, Louis Kenneth 1949- *BiDrAPA 89*
Hauber, Patricia Anne 1953- *WhoAmW 91, WhoE 91*
Hauber, Peter John *BiDrAPA 89*
Hauber, William M. 1929- *St&PR 91*
Hauberg, Allen Bernard 1937- *St&PR 91*
Hauberg, John H. 1916- *St&PR 91*
Haubrichs, Wolfgang 1942- *WhoWor 91*
Hauch, Frederikke Elisabeth Brun Juul 1811-1896 *EncCoWW*
Hauck, C. Peter 1930- *St&PR 91*
Hauck, Charles Francis 1912- *WhoAm 90*
Hauck, Christine Claire Kraus 1951- *WhoAmW 91, WhoEmL 91*
Hauck, Dennis William 1945- *WhoEmL 91*
Hauck, Donald F. 1943- *WhoAm 90*
Hauck, Donna Joanne 1960- *WhoAmW 91*
Hauck, Elaine Marie 1950- *WhoAmW 91*
Hauck, Frederick A. 1894- *St&PR 91*
Hauck, Frederick Hamilton 1941- *BioIn 16, WhoAm 90*
Hauck, John M. 1926- *St&PR 91*
Hauck, Joseph George 1947- *WhoEmL 91*
Hauck, Marguerite Hall 1948- *WhoAm 90, WhoAmW 91*
Hauck, Roger Paul 1936- *St&PR 91*
Hauck, Stephanie *ODwPR 91*
Hauck, Steven Barry 1951- *St&PR 91*
Haudenschild, Christian Charles 1939- *WhoE 91*
Haueisen, Anthony Joseph 1945- *St&PR 91*
Hauenstein, Christina Marie 1964- *WhoAmW 91*
Hauenstein, Henry William 1924- *WhoAm 90*
Hauenstein, Julia Pledger 1948- *BiDrAPA 89*
Hauenstein, Nancy Dean 1961- *WhoAmW 91*
Hauenstein, Thomas G. 1933- *St&PR 91*
Hauer, Bonaventura Gottlieb 1710-1782 *PenDiDA 89*
Hauer, Dave 1937- *St&PR 91*
Hauer, Jeanne T. 1951- *WhoAmW 91*
Hauerslev, Lars Steen Randel 1940- *WhoWor 91*
Haueter, Eric D. 1925- *St&PR 91*
Hauff, Wilhelm *AuBYP 90*
Hauffe, Frederica 1801-1829 *EncO&P 3*
Haufler, Christopher Hardin 1950- *WhoAm 90*
Haufler, George J. 1932- *St&PR 91*
Haufrecht, Herbert *AuBYP 90*
Hauft, Amy *WhoAmA 91*
Haug, Charles James 1946- *WhoSSW 91*
Haug, Dale E. 1946- *St&PR 91*
Haug, Donald Raymond 1925- *WhoAmA 91*
Haug, Elsie L *BiDrAPA 89*
Haug, Kay Denise 1962- *WhoEmL 91*
Haug, Nancy G. 1944- *WhoAmW 91*
Haug, Richard Leo 1939- *St&PR 91*
Haug, Scott Erik 1958- *WhoEmL 91*
Haugaard, Erik Christian 1923- *AuBYP 90, SmATA 12AS [port]*
Haugaard, Johannes Dag 1951- *WhoWor 91*
Haugaard, Niels 1920- *WhoAm 90*
Haugaard Pedersen, Nils Bo 1944- *WhoWor 91*
Haugan, Richard D. 1944- *St&PR 91*
Hauge, Alfred 1915- *DcScanL*
Hauge, Denise B. 1949- *St&PR 91*
Hauge, Keith A. 1938- *St&PR 91*
Hauge, Olav Hakonson 1908- *DcScanL*
Hauge, Sharon Kaye 1943- *WhoE 91*
Haugen, David William 1942- *St&PR 91*
Haugen, Einar Ingvald 1906- *WhoAm 90*
Haugen, Gerald Alan 1940- *St&PR 91, WhoAm 90*
Haugen, Marilyn Anne 1932- *WhoAmW 91*
Haugen, Rolf Eugene 1936- *WhoAm 90*
Haugen, Susan Dawn 1951- *WhoAmW 91*
Hauger, Leslie Starr 1904- *WhoWrEP 89*
Hauger, Richard Lynn 1949- *WhoEmL 91*
Haugh, Barbara Ann 1950- *WhoWrEP 89*
Haugh, Cherie Dawn 1949- *WhoEmL 91*
Haugh, Clarence Gene 1936- *WhoAm 90*
Haugh, John Richard 1940- *WhoE 91*
Haugh, Robert C. 1920- *St&PR 91*
Haugh, Robert Cyril 1920- *WhoAm 90, WhoSSW 91*
Haugh, Robert J. 1926- *St&PR 91*
Haugh, Robert James 1926- *WhoAm 90*
Haughey, Betty Ellen *AuBYP 90*
Haughey, Carlos Harold 1928- *St&PR 91*
Haughey, Charles *BioIn 16*
Haughey, Charles James 1925- *WhoWor 91*
Haughey, James M 1914- *WhoAmA 91*
Haughey, James McCrea 1914- *WhoAm 90*
Haughey, Sheila Cowles 1952- *WhoEmL 91*
Haught, Daniel Deforest 1932- *St&PR 91*
Haught, James Albert, Jr. 1932- *WhoAm 90*
Haught, William Dixon 1939- *WhoAm 90*
Haughton, Bill 1923-1986 *WorAlBi*
Haughton, Charles Steele *BiDrAPA 89*
Haughton, Dominique Marie Annick 1955- *WhoE 91*
Haughton, James Gray 1925- *WhoAm 90*
Haughton, Rosemary 1927- *AuBYP 90*
Haughton-Denniston, Pamela Gail 1951- *WhoAmW 91*
Haugland, Aage 1944- *IntWWM 90, PenDiMP*
Haugland, Brynhild 1905- *WhoAmW 91*
Haugland, John Clarence 1929- *WhoAm 90*
Haugland, Loren Andrew 1941- *St&PR 91*
Haugland, Richard C. 1935- *St&PR 91*
Hauhart, Robert Charles 1950- *WhoEmL 91*
Hauk, A. Andrew 1912- *WhoAm 90*
Hauk, Carol Ann 1943- *BiDrAPA 89*
Hauk, Donald B. 1944- *St&PR 91*
Hauk, Donald Benjamin 1944- *WhoAm 90*
Hauk, Minnie 1851-1929 *PenDiMP*
Hauke, Adolph Covel 1920- *IntWWM 90*
Hauke, Gary Richard 1942- *WhoWor 91*
Hauke, Mary Elizabeth 1911- *WhoAmW 91*
Haukebo, Noel W 1932- *BiDrAPA 89*
Haukeness, Helen Liza 1938- *WhoWrEP 89*
Haukohl, Mark Fehrs 1951- *WhoSSW 91*
Haulbrook, Lester Craig 1953- *WhoSSW 91*
Haulman, Harry Lindsay 1917- *St&PR 91*
Haulton, Dean M. 1935- *St&PR 91*
Haumschild, Mark James 1951- *WhoSSW 91*
Haun, Eloise Clymer 1936- *BiDrAPA 89*
Haun, James William 1924- *WhoAm 90*
Haun, John Daniel 1921- *WhoAm 90*
Haun, L. Maxine Sharpe 1926- *WhoAmW 91*
Haun, Robert Dee, Jr. 1930- *WhoE 91*
Haunschild, Willard Marion 1922- *St&PR 91*
Haupt, Adrienne Lynn 1948- *WhoAmW 91*
Haupt, Alma Cecelia 1893-1956 *BioIn 16*
Haupt, Charles V. 1939- *WhoAm 90*
Haupt, Donald Norman 1948- *BiDrAPA 89*
Haupt, Georg 1741-1784 *PenDiDA 89*
Haupt, Paul Andrew 1949- *WhoEmL 91*
Hauptfleisch, Louis Alois 1918- *WhoAm 90*
Hauptfuhrer, George Jost, Jr. 1926- *WhoAm 90*
Hauptfuhrer, Robert P. 1931- *St&PR 91*
Hauptfuhrer, Robert Paul 1931- *WhoAm 90, WhoSSW 91, WhoWor 91*
Hauptli, Barbara Beatrice 1953- *WhoAmW 91*
Hauptly, Denis J. 1945- *BioIn 16*
Hauptly, Denis James 1945- *WhoEmL 91*
Hauptman, Bruce *BiDrAPA 89*
Hauptman, Herbert A. 1917- *WorAlBi*
Hauptman, Herbert Aaron 1917- *WhoAm 90, WhoE 91, WhoWor 91*
Hauptman, Michael 1933- *St&PR 91, WhoAm 90*
Hauptman, Theodore 1952- *WhoE 91*
Hauptmann, Bruno Richard 1900-1936 *WorAlBi*
Hauptmann, Carl 1858-1921 *BioIn 16*
Hauptmann, Gerhart 1862-1946 *BioIn 16, WorAlBi*
Haure, Jean *PenDiDA 89*
Haury, Emil W. 1904- *BioIn 16*
Haury, Emil Walter 1904- *WhoAm 90*
Haury, John Carroll 1948- *WhoEmL 91*
Haury, Richard A. 1929- *St&PR 91*
Haus, Hermann Anton 1925- *WhoAm 90*
Hausammann, Beverly Ann 1934- *WhoAmW 91*
Hausch, Mary Ellen 1949- *WhoAmW 91*
Hauschild, Douglas Carey 1955- *WhoEmL 91, WhoSSW 91, WhoWor 91*
Hauschild, Thomas B 1920- *BiDrAPA 89*
Hauschild, Thomas John 1954- *WhoEmL 91*
Hauschildt, Juergen 1936- *WhoWor 91*
Hauschka, Carol Spaeth 1883-1948 *WhoAmA 91N*
Hauschka, Stephen Denison 1940- *WhoAm 90*
Hauschka, Theodore Spaeth 1908- *WhoAm 90, WhoWor 91*
Hause, Edith Collins 1933- *WhoAmW 91*
Hause, Edward Earle *BiDrAPA 89*
Hause, Jesse Gilbert 1929- *WhoAm 90*
Hauseman, Cass *WhoWrEP 89*
Hauser, Abe *BiDrAPA 89*
Hauser, Alexis 1947- *IntWWM 90*
Hauser, Arnold 1888-1966 *Ballpl 90*
Hauser, Bruce H. 1943- *St&PR 91*
Hauser, Carl 1949- *WhoE 91*
Hauser, Charles F 1940- *BiDrAPA 89*
Hauser, Charles Newland McCorkle 1929- *WhoAm 90, WhoE 91*
Hauser, Christopher George 1954- *WhoE 91, WhoEmL 91*
Hauser, Crane Cheshire 1923- *WhoAm 90*
Hauser, Donald Edwin 1957- *BiDrAPA 89*
Hauser, Fred Paul 1937- *St&PR 91*
Hauser, Gary Curtis *BiDrAPA 89*
Hauser, Gregory Francis 1954- *WhoEmL 91*
Hauser, Gustave M. 1929- *WhoAm 90*
Hauser, Gwen 1944- *FemiCLE*
Hauser, Harris M 1932- *BiDrAPA 89*
Hauser, Harry Raymond 1931- *WhoAm 90*
Hauser, Hillary 1944- *ConAu 30NR*
Hauser, Joe 1899- *Ballpl 90*
Hauser, John Reid 1938- *WhoAm 90*
Hauser, Joseph Martin 1954- *WhoSSW 91*
Hauser, Joyce Roberta *WhoAmW 91, WhoE 91, WhoWor 91*
Hauser, Kaspar 1812?-1833 *EncO&P 3*
Hauser, Katrina Curdy 1960- *IntWWM 90*
Hauser, Lawrence Allen 1955- *BiDrAPA 89*
Hauser, Mark Jeffrey 1955- *BiDrAPA 89*
Hauser, Martin 1934- *St&PR 91*
Hauser, Matthew Joseph 1955- *WhoEmL 91*
Hauser, Michael George 1939- *WhoAm 90*
Hauser, Michael Leon 1930- *IntWWM 90*
Hauser, Michele Ann *BiDrAPA 89*
Hauser, Norbert A. 1935- *St&PR 91*
Hauser, Paul J. 1942- *St&PR 91*
Hauser, Peter *BiDrAPA 89*
Hauser, Peter Paul 1955- *WhoE 91*
Hauser, Philip Morris 1909- *WhoAm 90*
Hauser, Richard Alan 1943- *WhoAm 90*
Hauser, Richard Lee *BiDrAPA 89*
Hauser, Rita E. *BioIn 16*

Hauser, Rita Eleanore Abrams 1934- *WhoAm 90, WhoAmW 91, WhoE 91*
Hauser, Robert Eugene 1948- *WhoEmL 91*
Hauser, Robert I 1933- *BiDrAPA 89*
Hauser, Robert Mason 1942- *WhoAm 90*
Hauser, Ronald Joseph *BiDrAPA 89*
Hauser, Stephen T. 1956- *ODwPR 91*
Hauser, Stuart T 1938- *BiDrAPA 89*
Hauser, Victor LaVern 1929- *WhoAm 90*
Hauser, Walter 1924- *WhoAm 90*
Hauser, Walter A *BiDrAPA 89*
Hauser, William Barry 1939- *WhoAm 90*
Hauser, Wings *ConTFT 8 [port]*
Hauserman, W.F. 1919- *St&PR 91*
Hauserman, William Foley 1919- *WhoAm 90*
Hausey, Robert Michael 1949- *WhoAmA 91*
Haushalter, Mary Ann 1906- *WhoE 91*
Hausherr, Rosmarie *AuBYP 90*
Haushofer, Marlen 1920-1970 *EncCoWW*
Hauske, Thomas John 1936- *St&PR 91*
Hauskens, Allan 1949- *St&PR 91*
Hauslein, R.E. 1929- *St&PR 91*
Hausler, William John, Jr. 1926- *WhoAm 90*
Hausman, Arthur H. 1923- *St&PR 91*
Hausman, Arthur Herbert 1923- *WhoAm 90*
Hausman, Bruce 1930- *St&PR 91, WhoAm 90*
Hausman, Fred S 1921- *WhoAmA 91*
Hausman, Gerald Andrews 1945- *WhoWrEP 89*
Hausman, Helen M. 1924- *WhoAmW 91*
Hausman, Howard 1945- *WhoE 91, WhoEmL 91, WhoWor 91*
Hausman, Jerome Joseph 1925- *WhoAmA 91*
Hausman, Jerry Allen 1946- *WhoAm 90*
Hausman, Keith Lynn 1949- *WhoEmL 91*
Hausman, Leo 1909- *St&PR 91*
Hausman, Louis *BioIn 16*
Hausman, Samuel 1897- *St&PR 91*
Hausman, Tom 1953- *Ballpl 90*
Hausman, William 1925- *BiDrAPA 89*
Hausman, William Ray 1941- *WhoAm 90*
Hausmann, Albert Charles 1932- *WhoSSW 91*
Hausmann, Clem 1919-1972 *Ballpl 90*
Hausmann, Frank William, Jr. 1914- *WhoAm 90*
Hausmann, Franz Josef 1943- *WhoWor 91*
Hausmann, George 1916- *Ballpl 90*
Hausmann, Klaus Wilhelm 1947- *WhoWor 91*
Hausmann, Marianne Pisko *WhoAmA 91N*
Hausmann, Robert 1852-1909 *PenDiMP*
Hausmann, Ronald Lee 1949- *St&PR 91*
Hausmann, Werner Karl 1921- *WhoAm 90*
Hausner, Albert R. 1931- *St&PR 91*
Hausner, Gideon *NewYTBS 90 [port]*
Hausner, Gideon 1915- *BioIn 16*
Hausner, Melvin 1928- *WhoE 91*
Hauspurg, Arthur 1925- *St&PR 91, WhoE 91*
Hausrath, Jan *ODwPR 91*
Hausrath, Joan W 1942- *WhoAmA 91*
Hausrath, Ralph Allan 1918- *WhoWrEP 89*
Hauss, Deborah 1955- *ODwPR 91, WhoWrEP 89*
Hausser, Gerald Arthur 1931- *St&PR 91, WhoAm 90*
Hausser, Robert Louis 1914- *WhoAm 90*
Haussermann, Oscar William, Jr. 1921- *WhoAm 90*
Hausten, Lisa Anne 1956- *WhoAmW 91*
Hausvater, Alexander 1948- *ConAu 130*
Hausvater, Alexandre 1949- *OxCCanT*
Hauswald, Jeananne Kay 1944- *St&PR 91, WhoAm 90*
Hauswaldt, Juan Federico *BiDrAPA 89*
Hauswirth, Robert J. 1923- *St&PR 91*
Hauswirth, William Frederic 1949- *WhoE 91*
Haut, Claire *WhoAmA 91*
Hautala, Judith Ann 1945- *St&PR 91*
Hautekiet, Jan 1955- *IntWWM 90*
Hauth, Willard Ellsworth, III 1948- *WhoEmL 91*
Hautval, Adelaide 1906- *BioIn 16*
Hautzig, Esther 1930- *AuBYP 90, ChlLR 22 [port]*
Hautzig, Walter 1921- *IntWWM 90*
Hautzinger, James Edward 1936- *WhoAm 90*
Hauver, Constance Longshore 1938- *WhoAm 90*
Hauver, Larry King 1945- *WhoE 91*
Hauver, Terence Lee 1947- *WhoEmL 91*
Hauzinger, Heinz-Hellmuth 1944- *WhoWor 91*
Havas, John M. 1928- *ODwPR 91*
Havas, Kato 1920- *IntWWM 90*
Havasy, Edward Stephen 1925- *St&PR 91*
Havdala, Henri Salomon 1931- *WhoAm 90*
Havekes, Gerard Wilhelm 1925- *WhoWor 91*
Havekost, Daniel John 1936- *WhoAm 90*
Havel, Jean Eugene Martial 1928- *WhoAm 90, WhoWrEP 89*
Havel, Joseph G 1954- *WhoAmA 91*
Havel, Olga *BioIn 16*
Havel, Richard Joseph 1925- *WhoAm 90*
Havel, Stanislav 1930- *WhoWor 91*
Havel, Thomas Earl, Jr. *BiDrAPA 89*
Havel, Vaclav *BioIn 16*
Havel, Vaclav 1936- *MajTwCW, News 90 [port], -90-3 [port], WhoWor 91, WorAlBi*
Havelaar, Charles Eduard 1908- *IntWWM 90*
Haveliwala, Yoosuf A *BiDrAPA 89*
Havelka, Thomas Edward 1947- *IntWWM 90, WhoEmL 91, WhoWor 91*
Havelock, Christine Mitchell 1924- *WhoAm 90, WhoAmA 91*
Havelock, Henry 1795-1857 *BioIn 16*
Havelos, Sam George 1915- *WhoSSW 91*
Havemann, Hans August 1912- *WhoWor 91*
Havemeyer, Henry Osborne 1847-1907 *BioIn 16, WorAlBi*
Havemeyer, Horace 1914-1990 *BioIn 16*
Havemeyer, Horace, Jr. *NewYTBS 90*
Havemeyer, Louisine Waldron Elder 1855-1929 *BioIn 16*
Havemeyer, Robert G. 1927- *St&PR 91*
Haven, Alice B. 1827-1863 *BioAmW, FemiCLE*
Haven, Granville James 1927- *St&PR 91*
Haven, Mary Clare 1939- *WhoAmW 91*
Haven, Miles Jonathan 1945- *St&PR 91*
Haven, Thomas Edward 1920- *WhoAm 90*
Haven, Thomas Kenneth 1906- *WhoAm 90*
Havener, Marlin R. 1942- *St&PR 91*
Havener, Robert Dale 1930- *WhoAm 90*
Havenick, Fred Stanley 1943- *St&PR 91*
Havens, Brad 1959- *Ballpl 90*
Havens, Candace Jean 1952- *WhoAmW 91, WhoEmL 91*
Havens, Candace Sherwood 1957- *WhoAmW 91*
Havens, Charles W., III 1936- *WhoAm 90, WhoE 91*
Havens, Glen Harold *BiDrAPA 89*
Havens, James Dexter 1900-1960 *WhoAmA 91N*
Havens, Jan 1948- *WhoAmA 91*
Havens, Jennifer Falk *BiDrAPA 89*
Havens, John F. 1927- *St&PR 91*
Havens, John Franklin 1927- *WhoAm 90*
Havens, Leston L 1924- *BiDrAPA 89*
Havens, Leston Laycock 1924- *WhoAm 90, WhoE 91*
Havens, Murray Clark 1932- *WhoAm 90*
Havens, Murry P *WhoAmA 91N*
Havens, Oliver Hershman 1917- *WhoAm 90*
Havens, Pamela Ann 1956- *WhoAmW 91*
Havens, Richie 1941- *DrBIPA 90*
Havens, Suzanne Jean Harman 1952- *WhoEmL 91*
Havens, Thomas R 1915- *BiDrAPA 89*
Havens, Timothy Markle 1945- *WhoE 91, WhoWor 91*
Havens, Walter Paul, Jr. 1911- *WhoAm 90*
Havens, Woodrow W, II *BiDrAPA 89*
Haver, Jack Richard 1931- *St&PR 91*
Haver, Richard Leonhardt 1945- *WhoE 91*
Havergal, Frances Ridley 1836-1879 *BioIn 16, FemiCLE*
Haverkampf, Kathleen Lea 1959- *WhoAmW 91*
Haverly, John Gordon 1937- *BiDrAPA 89*
Haverly, Paul F. 1934- *St&PR 91*
Haverly, Robert J. 1954- *WhoEmL 91*
Haveron, Patrick J. 1961- *St&PR 91*
Havers, Alice Mary 1850-1890 *BiDWomA*
Havers, Mandy 1953- *BiDWomA*
Haversat, Lillian Kerr 1938- *WhoAmA 91*
Haverstock, James Edward 1925- *St&PR 91*
Haverstock, Mary Sayre 1932- *AuBYP 90*
Haverstock, Susan Louise 1958- *BiDrAPA 89*
Haverstock, Van Dusen 1953- *WhoSSW 91*
Haverty, Harold V. 1930- *WhoAm 90*
Haverty, John Rhodes 1926- *WhoAm 90*
Haverty, Rawson 1920- *St&PR 91, WhoAm 90, WhoSSW 91*
Haves, Valorie 1957- *BiDrAPA 89*
Haveson, Alan Michael 1937- *WhoE 91*
Havey, Elizabeth A. 1947- *WhoWrEP 89*
Havey, I. Malinde 1887-1938 *BioIn 16*
Havey, Rosemary J. *BiDrAPA 89*
Haviaras, Stratis 1935- *WhoWrEP 89*
Havice, Christine *BioIn 16*
Havice, James F. 1938- *St&PR 91*
Havighurst, Clark Canfield 1933- *WhoAm 90*
Havighurst, Marion *AuBYP 90*
Havighurst, Robert J. 1900- *WhoAm 90*
Havighurst, Walter Edwin 1901- *AuBYP 90*
Haviland, Bancroft Dawley 1925- *WhoAm 90*
Haviland, Camilla Klein 1926- *WhoAmW 91*
Haviland, David Sands 1942- *WhoAm 90*
Haviland, Frederick *BioIn 16*
Haviland, James West 1911- *WhoAm 90*
Haviland, Laura S. 1808-1898 *BioAmW*
Haviland, Leona 1916- *WhoAmW 91*
Haviland, Morrison Chandler 1915- *WhoE 91, WhoWor 91*
Haviland, Robert Paul 1913- *WhoAm 90*
Haviland, Thomas Heath 1822-1895 *DcCanB 12*
Haviland, Virginia 1911-1988 *AuBYP 90, BioIn 16*
Havill, Juanita *AuBYP 90*
Havill, Nancy Ches 1945- *WhoEmL 91*
Havilland, Ben 1924- *WhoE 91*
Havinden, Ashley 1903-1973 *ConDes 90*
Havinden, John 1909-1987 *BioIn 16*
Havir, Bryan Thomas 1963- *WhoE 91, WhoEmL 91*
Havir, Darrell David 1929- *St&PR 91*
Havira, R. Mark 1944- *St&PR 91*
Havist, Marjorie Victoria 1931- *WhoAmW 91*
Havlicek, Franklin J. 1947- *WhoAm 90, WhoE 91, WhoEmL 91*
Havlicek, Hondo 1940- *BioIn 16*
Havlicek, John 1940- *BioIn 16, WhoAm 90, WorAlBi*
Havner, Galen Clifford 1949- *WhoSSW 91*
Havner, Ronald L., Jr. 1957- *St&PR 91*
Havoc, June 1916- *BioIn 16, NotWoAT, WhoAm 90*
Havran, Geary A. 1953- *WhoSSW 91*
Havran, Martin Joseph 1929- *WhoSSW 91*
Havrevold, Finn 1905- *AuBYP 90*
Haw, Cecile Elaine 1953- *St&PR 91*
Haw, George Gordon 1939- *St&PR 91*
Hawawini, Gabriel Alfred 1947- *WhoWor 91*
Hawbaker, Diana Sue 1953- *WhoAmW 91, WhoEmL 91*
Hawcroft, Francis W. 1925-1988 *BioIn 16*
Hawe, David Lee 1938- *WhoWor 91*
Haweeli, John David 1950- *St&PR 91*
Haweis, Stephen 1879-1969 *BioIn 16*
Hawekotte, Robert S. 1925- *St&PR 91*
Hawerchuk, Dale 1963- *WorAlBi*
Hawes, Alexander Boyd, Jr. 1947- *WhoAm 90*
Hawes, Charles Boardman 1889-1923 *AuBYP 90*
Hawes, Douglas Wesson 1932- *St&PR 91, WhoAm 90*
Hawes, Elizabeth 1903-1971 *BioAmW, BioIn 16, EncAL*
Hawes, Herbert Hiram 1939- *WhoE 91*
Hawes, Jack Richards 1916- *IntWWM 90*
Hawes, Josiah Johnson 1808-1901 *BioIn 16*
Hawes, Kenneth Monroe 1937- *St&PR 91*
Hawes, Louis 1931- *WhoAmA 91*
Hawes, Louise 1943- *SmATA 60 [port]*
Hawes, Lynne Gusikoff Salop 1931- *WhoWrEP 89*
Hawes, Ralph Edgar, Jr. 1930- *WhoAm 90*
Hawes, Robert Dowell 1937- *WhoSSW 91*
Hawes, Robert E. 1943- *St&PR 91*
Hawes, Warren George 1928- *St&PR 91*
Hawes, William Dale 1935- *WhoSSW 91*
Hawk, Alan B. *BiDrAPA 89*
Hawk, Alex 1926- *BioIn 16*
Hawk, Arthur W. 1932- *St&PR 91*
Hawk, Carmen *BioIn 16*
Hawk, Charles R. *St&PR 91*
Hawk, Donald Lee 1947- *St&PR 91, WhoAm 90*
Hawk, George Wayne 1928- *St&PR 91, WhoAm 90*
Hawk, Mary Ruth 1963- *WhoAmW 91*
Hawk, Phillip Michael 1939- *WhoAm 90*
Hawk, Robert M. 1938- *ODwPR 91*
Hawk, Robert Steven 1949- *WhoAm 90*
Hawk, Samuel Silas 1954- *WhoSSW 91, WhoWor 91*
Hawke, Bernard Ray 1946- *WhoAm 90*
Hawke, Cassandra 1746-1813 *FemiCLE*
Hawke, Ethan *BioIn 16*
Hawke, John Daniel, Jr. 1933- *WhoAm 90*
Hawke, Robert 1929- *WorAlBi*
Hawke, Robert James Lee 1929- *WhoWor 91*
Hawke, Roger Jewett 1935- *WhoAm 90*
Hawke, Rose Lagman 1931- *WhoWrEP 89*
Hawken, Janet Sarita 1954- *WhoWor 91*
Hawken, Patty Lynn 1932- *WhoAmW 91*
Hawkens, Edward Roy 1953- *WhoEmL 91*
Hawker, George Wiley 1943- *St&PR 91*
Hawker, Robert A. 1915- *St&PR 91*
Hawkes, Carol A. *WhoAm 90*
Hawkes, Elizabeth H 1943- *WhoAmA 91*
Hawkes, Elizabeth Lawrence 1944- *WhoAmW 91*
Hawkes, Gerald 1943- *MusmAFA*
Hawkes, Glenn Rogers 1919- *WhoAm 90*
Hawkes, Gloria Dawn 1934- *WhoWor 91*
Hawkes, Hester 1900- *AuBYP 90*
Hawkes, Jacquetta Hopkins 1910- *BioIn 16*
Hawkes, Jim 1944- *ODwPR 91*
Hawkes, John 1925- *MajTwCW, WhoAm 90, WhoWrEP 89, WorAlBi*
Hawkes, Judith 1949- *ConAu 132*
Hawkes, Peter H R 1923- *BiDrAPA 89*
Hawkes, Richard N. 1917- *St&PR 91*
Hawkes, Robert Howie 1930- *St&PR 91*
Hawkes, Sidney Gerard 1933- *St&PR 91*
Hawkes, Terence Frederick 1932- *WhoWor 91*
Hawkesworth, Eric 1921- *AuBYP 90*
Hawkesworth, John 1920- *ConTFT 8 [port]*
Hawkey, G. Michael 1941- *WhoAm 90*
Hawkey, Penelope J. 1942- *WhoAmW 91*
Hawkey, Philip A. 1946- *WhoAm 90*
Hawking, S. W. *BioIn 16, ConAu 129*
Hawking, Stephen 1942- *WorAlBi*
Hawking, Stephen W. *BioIn 16*
Hawking, Stephen W 1942- *ConAu 129, ConLC 63 [port], News 90 [port], WhoWor 91*
Hawkins, Albert Douglas, Jr. 1947- *St&PR 91*
Hawkins, Allan *BioIn 16*
Hawkins, Altonnette Denise 1958- *WhoAmW 91*
Hawkins, Andy 1960- *Ballpl 90*
Hawkins, Annie Lucy 1955- *WhoAmW 91*
Hawkins, Armis Eugene 1920- *WhoAm 90*
Hawkins, Arthur Michael 1942- *WhoAm 90, WhoWor 91*
Hawkins, Ashton 1937- *WhoAm 90*
Hawkins, Augustus Freeman 1907- *BlkAmsC [port], NewYTBS 90 [port], WhoAm 90*
Hawkins, Barbara 1947- *WhoAmA 91*
Hawkins, Benjamin 1754-1816 *WhNaAH*
Hawkins, Benjamin Sanford 1909- *WhoSSW 91*
Hawkins, Brett William 1937- *WhoAm 90*
Hawkins, Brian 1936- *IntWWM 90*
Hawkins, Brian 1944- *WhoWor 91*
Hawkins, Carmen Doloras 1955- *WhoEmL 91*
Hawkins, Charles Arthur 1960- *WhoEmL 91*
Hawkins, Coleman *BioIn 16*
Hawkins, Coleman 1901-1969 *OxCPMus*
Hawkins, Coleman 1904-1969 *DrBIPA 90, WorAlBi*
Hawkins, Dale Louis 1945- *St&PR 91*
Hawkins, Dallas E. 1923- *St&PR 91*
Hawkins, David 1927- *BiDrAPA 89*
Hawkins, David Frederick 1933- *WhoAm 90*
Hawkins, David H. 1940- *St&PR 91*
Hawkins, David Miller 1940- *BiDrAPA 89*
Hawkins, David R 1923- *BiDrAPA 89*
Hawkins, David Rollo 1923- *WhoAm 90*
Hawkins, David Rollo, Jr. *BiDrAPA 89*
Hawkins, Deborah 1665-1750 *BiDEWW*
Hawkins, Deborah Louise 1954- *St&PR 91*
Hawkins, Dixie Lee 1950- *ODwPR 91*
Hawkins, Donald 1931- *St&PR 91*
Hawkins, Donald Lee 1941- *St&PR 91*
Hawkins, Donald Merton 1921- *WhoAm 90*
Hawkins, Dorisula Wooten 1941- *WhoSSW 91*
Hawkins, Dwight 1938- *BioIn 16*
Hawkins, Edward Jackson 1927- *WhoAm 90, WhoE 91*
Hawkins, Elinor Dixon 1927- *WhoAmW 91, WhoSSW 91*
Hawkins, Eliot Dexter 1932- *WhoAm 90*
Hawkins, Ellis Delano 1941- *WhoWor 91*
Hawkins, Erick *BioIn 16, WhoAm 90*
Hawkins, Erskine 1914- *BioIn 16, DrBIPA 90, OxCPMus*
Hawkins, Eugene Palmer 1904- *WhoAm 90*
Hawkins, Falcon Black, Jr. 1927- *WhoAm 90, WhoSSW 91*
Hawkins, Francis Glenn 1917- *WhoAm 90*
Hawkins, Frank Nelson 1940- *St&PR 91*
Hawkins, Fred Hopka, Jr. 1949- *St&PR 91*
Hawkins, Frederick Campbell, Jr. 1937- *WhoWor 91*
Hawkins, Gene Russell 1928- *St&PR 91*
Hawkins, Geri Sue 1940- *WhoAmW 91*
Hawkins, Gina Gayle 1963- *WhoAmW 91*
Hawkins, Hannah Arnold 1962- *WhoE 91*
Hawkins, Hersey *BioIn 16*
Hawkins, Howard Gresham, Jr. 1916- *WhoAm 90*
Hawkins, Howard John 1918- *St&PR 91*
Hawkins, Hugh 1929- *ConAu 31NR*
Hawkins, Hugh Willis, Jr. 1948- *WhoEmL 91*
Hawkins, Hunt 1943- *WhoWrEP 89*
Hawkins, Ida Faye 1928- *WhoAmW 91, WhoWor 91*

Hawkins, Ira 1944?- DrBlPA 90
Hawkins, Jack 1910-1973 WorAlBi
Hawkins, Jack, Jr. 1945- WhoAm 90
Hawkins, Jack Milton 1935- BiDrAPA 89
Hawkins, Jack Wade 1934- WhoAm 90, WhoSSW 91
Hawkins, Jacquelyn 1943- WhoAmW 91
Hawkins, James Alexander, II 1929- WhoE 91
Hawkins, James Dale 1944- St&PR 91
Hawkins, James Gregory 1951- St&PR 91
Hawkins, James Leo, Jr. 1954- WhoSSW 91
Hawkins, James M. 1924- St&PR 91
Hawkins, James Robert BiDrAPA 89
Hawkins, James Victor 1936- WhoAm 90
Hawkins, James William BiDrAPA 89
Hawkins, Jasper Stillwell, Jr. 1932- WhoAm 90
Hawkins, Joellen Margaret 1941- WhoAmW 91
Hawkins, John 1532-1595 WorAlBi
Hawkins, John 1719-1789 DcLB 104 [port]
Hawkins, John 1944- IntWWM 90
Hawkins, John Donald, Jr. 1956- WhoEmL 91
Hawkins, John S. 1956- St&PR 91
Hawkins, Joseph Elmer 1914- WhoAm 90
Hawkins, Joseph Gailyard 1956- WhoEmL 91
Hawkins, Karen Frances 1947- WhoEmL 91
Hawkins, Katherine Ann 1947- WhoAmW 91
Hawkins, Kim Michael 1954- St&PR 91
Hawkins, Laetitia Matilda 1759-1835 BioIn 16, FemiCLE
Hawkins, Linda L BiDrAPA 89
Hawkins, Linda Parrott 1947- WhoAmW 91, WhoSSW 91
Hawkins, Malcolm 1944- IntWWM 90
Hawkins, Margaret Albright 1951- WhoEmL 91
Hawkins, Marilyn ODwPR 91
Hawkins, Mary Ellen 1923- WhoAmW 91
Hawkins, Mary Ruth Reynolds 1944- WhoAmW 91
Hawkins, Mason BioIn 16
Hawkins, Merrill Morris 1914- WhoAm 90
Hawkins, Michael Daly 1945- WhoAm 90
Hawkins, Michael William 1952- St&PR 91
Hawkins, Mylan Barin 1940- WhoAmW 91
Hawkins, Myrtle H WhoAmA 91
Hawkins, Norval Abiel 1867-1936 EncABHB 4 [port]
Hawkins, Osie 1913- IntWWM 90
Hawkins, Osie Penman, Jr. 1913- WhoAm 90
Hawkins, Paula WhoAm 90, WhoAmW 91
Hawkins, Phillip Lee 1926- WhoSSW 91
Hawkins, Phyllis BiDrAPA 89
Hawkins, Quail AuBYP 90
Hawkins, Ralph W. 1938- St&PR 91
Hawkins, Regina Annette Keener W. 1955- WhoSSW 91
Hawkins, Richard 1938- ConAu 129
Hawkins, Richard C. 1940- St&PR 91
Hawkins, Richard Michael 1949- WhoEmL 91, WhoWor 91
Hawkins, Richard Spencer Daddow 1943- WhoWor 91
Hawkins, Rita Sue 1946- WhoEmL 91
Hawkins, Robert 1930- St&PR 91
Hawkins, Robert F. 1921- St&PR 91
Hawkins, Robert Garvin 1936- WhoAm 90
Hawkins, Robert L. 1922- St&PR 91
Hawkins, Robert Lewis, III 1951- WhoEmL 91
Hawkins, Roger Leonard 1947- WhoE 91
Hawkins, Ronald Harris 1932- St&PR 91
Hawkins, Ronnie 1935- BioIn 16
Hawkins, Ronnie 1937?- EncPR&S 89
Hawkins, Russell Walker, Jr. 1953- WhoEmL 91
Hawkins, Sabe Warren 1933- St&PR 91
Hawkins, Sally Cain 1883-1959 BioIn 16
Hawkins, Sean Christopher 1955- WhoEmL 91
Hawkins, Shirley Maynard 1939- St&PR 91
Hawkins, Thomas, Jr. WhoSSW 91
Hawkins, Thomas Cleve 1949- St&PR 91, WhoEmL 91
Hawkins, Thomas Steven 1956- WhoAm 90
Hawkins, Thomas Wilson, Jr 1941- WhoAmA 91
Hawkins, Tommy 1936- BioIn 16
Hawkins, Virgil D. 1906-1988 BioIn 16
Hawkins, Walter Lincoln 1911- WhoAm 90
Hawkins, Whitley BioIn 16
Hawkins, William F. 1931- St&PR 91, WhoAm 90
Hawkins, William Grant 1945- WhoE 91
Hawkins, William Lawrence 1895-1990 MusmAFA
Hawkins, Willis E., Jr. 1928- St&PR 91
Hawkins, Willis M. 1913- St&PR 91
Hawkins, Willis Moore 1913- WhoAm 90
Hawkins, Wilton A. 1922- St&PR 91
Hawkins, Wynn 1936- Ballpl 90
Hawkinson, Gary M. 1948- St&PR 91
Hawkinson, Gary Michael 1948- WhoAm 90, WhoEmL 91
Hawkinson, John 1912- St&PR 91
Hawkinson, John Samuel 1912- AuBYP 90
Hawkinson, Leona A. 1944- St&PR 91
Hawkinson, Lucy 1924-1971 AuBYP 90
Hawkinson, Nellie Xenia 1886-1971 BioIn 16
Hawkinson, Robert W. 1920- St&PR 91
Hawkinson, Thomas Edwin 1952- WhoEmL 91, WhoWor 91
Hawkinson, Tim BioIn 16
Hawkrigg, Melvin Michael 1930- WhoAm 90
Hawks, Carol Pitts 1958- WhoAmW 91
Hawks, Denise Marie BiDrAPA 89
Hawks, Howard 1896-1977 WorAlBi
Hawks, Kitty BioIn 16
Hawksworth, Donald 1930- IntWWM 90
Hawksworth, Paul David 1934- St&PR 91
Hawlett, Mark K. St&PR 91
Hawley, Alan 1950- WhoEmL 91
Hawley, Anne 1943- WhoAm 90, WhoAmW 91
Hawley, Beatrice 1944-1985 FemiCLE
Hawley, Carol Ann 1951- WhoEmL 91
Hawley, Christine 1949- WomArch
Hawley, Donald Springer 1928- WhoWrEP 89
Hawley, Ellis Wayne 1929- WhoAm 90
Hawley, Frank Jordan, Jr. 1927- WhoAm 90, WhoE 91
Hawley, Frank K. 1937- St&PR 91
Hawley, Frederick William, III 1931- WhoE 91
Hawley, James Leeper, II 1939- WhoSSW 91
Hawley, Jean Gannett 1924- WhoAm 90, WhoAmW 91, WhoE 91
Hawley, Jeffrey Lance 1948- St&PR 91
Hawley, Linda Donovan 1946- WhoEmL 91
Hawley, Margaret Foote 1880-1963 WhoAmA 91N
Hawley, Michael Christopher 1938- St&PR 91
Hawley, Nanci Elizabeth 1942- WhoAmW 91
Hawley, Philip Metschan 1925- St&PR 91, WhoAm 90, WhoWor 91
Hawley, Phillip Eugene 1940- WhoWor 91
Hawley, Pink 1872-1938 Ballpl 90
Hawley, Robert B. 1955- St&PR 91
Hawley, Robert C. 1933- WhoWrEP 89
Hawley, Robert Coit 1933- WhoE 91
Hawley, Ronald I. St&PR 91
Hawley, Samuel Waller 1910- WhoAm 90
Hawley, Sandra Sue 1948- WhoAmW 91
Hawley, Steve 1950- WhoAmA 91
Hawley, Susan 1622-1706 BiDEWW
Hawley, Timothy John 1944- IntWWM 90
Hawley, Todd Bryan 1961- WhoEmL 91
Hawley, Wendell Charles 1930- St&PR 91
Hawley, William Lee 1954- WhoEmL 91
Hawley, William Palmer 1950- IntWWM 90
Hawn, Gates Helms 1948- WhoAm 90
Hawn, Goldie BioIn 16
Hawn, Goldie 1945- WhoAm 90, WhoAmW 91, WorAlBi
Hawn, James F. 1927- St&PR 91
Hawn, Patti BioIn 16
Hawn, Van Zandt 1945- St&PR 91
Hawn, Virginia Shuford 1928- WhoSSW 91
Haworth, Arlene Wilkinson 1959- WhoAmW 91
Haworth, B Coquill 1904- WhoAmA 91N
Haworth, Charles Ray 1943- WhoAm 90, WhoSSW 91
Haworth, Charles Taylor 1937- WhoSSW 91
Haworth, Dale Keith 1924- WhoAm 90
Haworth, Daniel Thomas 1928- WhoAm 90
Haworth, Danny Earl 1950- WhoEmL 91
Haworth, Donald Robert 1928- WhoAm 90
Haworth, Gerrard W. 1911- St&PR 91
Haworth, James Chilton 1923- WhoAm 90
Haworth, Joan Gustafson 1938- WhoAmW 91
Haworth, Kayle Merl 1947- WhoEmL 91
Haworth, Lawrence Lindley 1926- WhoAm 90, WhoWrEP 89
Haworth, Leslie W. 1943- St&PR 91
Haworth, Leslie William 1943- WhoAm 90
Haworth, Mary 1918- IntWWM 90
Haworth, Michael Elliott, Jr. 1928- WhoAm 90
Haworth, Patricia Anne 1951- WhoAmW 91
Haworth, Peter 1889- WhoAmA 91N
Haworth, Richard G. 1942- St&PR 91
Haworth, Steven Clay 1950- St&PR 91
Haworth, Thomas Howard 1940- St&PR 91
Haworth, Trevor 1947- St&PR 91
Haworth, Walter N. 1883-1950 WorAlBi
Hawpe, David Vaughn 1943- WhoAm 90
Hawpe, Nancy Thomas 1946- WhoAmW 91
Hawran, Paul William 1952- St&PR 91
Hawrylyshyn, Bohdan W. 1926- WhoWor 91
Hawrylyshyn, Leslie Michael 1954- WhoWor 91
Haws, David Virgil BiDrAPA 89
Haws, Howard D. 1932- St&PR 91
Haws, John Philip 1935- BiDrAPA 89
Haws, L. Edward, Jr. 1933- ODwPR 91
Hawthorn, Leslie R. 1902-1989 BioIn 16
Hawthorn, Pam 1939- OxCCanT
Hawthorne, David Madison 1946- WhoEmL 91
Hawthorne, Dent, Jr. 1922- St&PR 91
Hawthorne, Donald Bruce 1955- WhoEmL 91
Hawthorne, Douglas Lawson 1942- St&PR 91, WhoAm 90
Hawthorne, Elizabeth 1802-1883 FemiCLE
Hawthorne, Frank Howard 1923- WhoAm 90
Hawthorne, George Duncan 1947- WhoWor 91
Hawthorne, H. Bagley 1949- St&PR 91
Hawthorne, Henry Wilson 1937- St&PR 91
Hawthorne, Hildegarde AuBYP 90
Hawthorne, Jack Gardner 1921- WhoAmA 91
Hawthorne, James Burns 1930- WhoWor 91
Hawthorne, Jewell Ann 1952- WhoAmW 91, WhoEmL 91
Hawthorne, Jimmie D 1931- BiDrAPA 89
Hawthorne, John William 1941- WhoAm 90, WhoWor 91
Hawthorne, Joyce LaBossiere ODwPR 91
Hawthorne, Karen M. 1956- St&PR 91
Hawthorne, Marion Frederick 1928- WhoAm 90
Hawthorne, Nathaniel 1804-1864 AuBYP 90, BioIn 16, WorAlBi, WrPh
Hawthorne, Rose 1851-1926 BioIn 16
Hawthorne, Sophia P. 1809-1871 BioAmW
Hawthorne, Victor Morrison 1921- WhoAm 90
Hawthorne, William B 1940- BiDrAPA 89
Hawtrey, Charles 1914-1988 AnObit 1988, BioIn 16
Hawtrey, Valentina FemiCLE
Hawver, Karl Derek 1936- BiDrAPA 89
Hawver, Mary Anne 1957- WhoEmL 91
Hax, Arnoldo Cubillos 1936- WhoAm 90
Hax, Herbert 1933- WhoWor 91
Haxby, W. EncO&P 3
Haxo, Francis Theodore 1921- WhoAm 90
Haxthausen, Bruce C. ODwPR 91
Haxton, David 1943- WhoAm 90, WhoAmA 91
Hay, A John 1938- WhoAmA 91
Hay, Allan Stuart 1929- WhoAm 90
Hay, Austin 1915- WhoWrEP 89
Hay, Betty Jo 1931- WhoAmW 91
Hay, Beverly Reed 1943- IntWWM 90
Hay, Charles Richard 1950- WhoEmL 91
Hay, Dick 1942- WhoAmA 91
Hay, Donald Peter 1944- BiDrAPA 89
Hay, Edward James 1937- St&PR 91
Hay, Elizabeth 1936- ConAu 131
Hay, Elizabeth Dexter 1927- WhoAm 90, WhoAmW 91
Hay, Eloise Knapp 1926- WhoAm 90
Hay, Eugene G. St&PR 91
Hay, George Austin 1915- WhoAm 90, WhoAmA 91, WhoE 91, WhoWor 91
Hay, Helen Scott 1869-1932 BioIn 16
Hay, Henry G. BioIn 16
Hay, Ike 1944- WhoAmA 91
Hay, Jack Lee 1925- WhoWrEP 89
Hay, James D. 1940- St&PR 91
Hay, James Miller 1929- WhoAm 90
Hay, Jess Thomas 1931- St&PR 91, WhoAm 90, WhoSSW 91
Hay, John BioIn 16
Hay, John 1838-1905 WorAlBi
Hay, John A. 1931- St&PR 91
Hay, John Milton 1838-1905 BiDrUSE 89, BioIn 16
Hay, Judy Thompson 1932- WhoAmW 91
Hay, Leland Glen 1927- St&PR 91
Hay, Louise Schmir 1935-1989 BioIn 16
Hay, Lucy 1599-1660 BiDEWW
Hay, Mark H. 1944- St&PR 91
Hay, Nelson Edward 1945- WhoWrEP 89
Hay, Pamela Camp 1954- WhoAmW 91
Hay, Peter Heinrich 1935- WhoAm 90
Hay, Peter M. 1921- St&PR 91
Hay, Raymond A. 1928- WhoAm 90, WhoSSW 91
Hay, Raymond Alexander 1928- St&PR 91
Hay, Richard Laurence 1929- WhoAm 90
Hay, Richard Le Roy 1926- WhoAm 90
Hay, Robert Dean 1921- WhoAm 90
Hay, Robert John 1926- St&PR 91
Hay, Ronald L. 1942- St&PR 91
Hay, Roy 1910-1989 AnObit 1989
Hay, Timothy AuBYP 90
Hay, Timothy 1910-1952 BioIn 16
Hay, Virgil Kenton 1943- St&PR 91
Hay, William J. 1937- WhoAm 90
Hay, William Winn 1934- WhoAm 90
Hay-Messick, Velma WhoAmA 91
Haya de la Torre, Victor Raul 1895-1979 BioIn 16
Hayaishi, Osamu 1920- WhoWor 91
Hayakawa Sesshu 1886-1973 EncJap
Hayakawa, Kan-Ichi 1931- WhoAm 90, WhoWor 91
Hayakawa, Milton 1928- St&PR 91
Hayakawa, Norio 1958- WhoSSW 91
Hayakawa, Samuel I. 1906- WorAlBi
Hayakawa, Samuel Ichiye 1906- WhoAm 90
Hayakawa, Sessue 1890-1973 WorAlBi
Hayakawa, Yoshio 1917- ConDes 90
Hayasaka, Taijiro 1923- WhoWor 91
Hayaseca y Eizaguirre, Jorge ConAu 32NR, HispWr 90, MajTwCW
Hayashi Razan 1583-1657 EncJap
Hayashi, Fujio 1954- WhoEmL 91
Hayashi, Hajime 1925- WhoWor 91
Hayashi, Joji 1939- WhoAm 90
Hayashi, Kenjiro 1925- WhoWor 91
Hayashi, Leslie Ann 1954- WhoAmW 91, WhoEmL 91
Hayashi, Masumi 1945- WhoAmA 91
Hayashi, Mitsuhiko 1930- WhoWor 91
Hayashi, Shizuo 1922- WhoWor 91
Hayashi, Tadao WhoWor 91
Hayashi, Teru 1914- WhoAm 90
Hayashi, Teruo Terry 1921- WhoAm 90
Hayashi, Tetsumaro 1929- WhoAm 90, WhoWrEP 89
Hayashi, Toshihiko 1941- WhoWor 91
Hayashi, Yasuko 1943- PenDiMP
Hayashi, Yasuko 1948- IntWWM 90
Hayashi, Yoshihiro 1940- WhoWor 91
Hayashi, Yoshimi 1922- WhoAm 90
Hayashi, Yutaro 1935- St&PR 91
Hayashida, Motoi BiDrAPA 89
Hayashida, Motoi 1960- WhoE 91
Hayasi, Nisiki 1929- WhoE 91
Hayat, Suzanne 1947- ODwPR 91
Haycock, Kathryn Proffitt 1951- WhoAmW 91, WhoWor 91
Haycox, Ernest 1931- ODwPR 91
Haycox, Ernest J. 1931- St&PR 91
Haycox, James Arthur 1925- BiDrAPA 89
Haycraft, Anna WorAu 1980
Haycraft, Howard AuBYP 90
Haydanek, Ronald Edward 1932- WhoAm 90
Haydarzadeh, Goudarz 1946- St&PR 91
Hayde, Daniel Francis 1942- St&PR 91
Haydee, Marcia 1939- WhoWor 91
Hayden, Alden H 1925- BiDrAPA 89
Hayden, Alvin Lee 1943- St&PR 91
Hayden, Anne Elizabeth 1948- WhoAmW 91
Hayden, Benjamin F. AmLegL
Hayden, C. E. 1866- AmLegL
Hayden, Carl 1877-1972 WorAlBi
Hayden, Charles Ross 1960- BiDrAPA 89
Hayden, Constance Nelson 1952- BiDrAPA 89
Hayden, Dan BioIn 16
Hayden, David Evans 1958- WhoE 91
Hayden, David Lawrence 1954- WhoEmL 91
Hayden, Dolores 1945- WhoWrEP 89
Hayden, Donald Eugene 1915- WhoAm 90
Hayden, Donna-Ann P. ODwPR 91
Hayden, Donna-Ann Patricia 1955- St&PR 91
Hayden, Ferdinand Vandeveer 1829-1887 WhNaAH
Hayden, Gerald F. 1924- St&PR 91
Hayden, Huguette S BiDrAPA 89
Hayden, J. Page, Jr. 1929- St&PR 91
Hayden, James Francis 1954- WhoEmL 91
Hayden, Jay ConAu 31NR
Hayden, Jerry L. 1933- St&PR 91
Hayden, John Kenneth 1960- WhoEmL 91
Hayden, John Michael 1944- WhoAm 90, WhoWor 91
Hayden, John Olin 1932- WhoAm 90
Hayden, Joseph A., Jr. 1944- WhoE 91
Hayden, Joseph Page, Jr. 1929- WhoAm 90
Hayden, Julian Dodge 1911- BioIn 16
Hayden, Maria B EncO&P 3
Hayden, Marna 1938- St&PR 91, WhoE 91
Hayden, Martin Scholl 1912- WhoAm 90

Hayden, Melissa 1923- *WorAlBi*
Hayden, Michael Joseph 1964- *WhoE 91*
Hayden, Mildred S. 1944- *St&PR 91*
Hayden, Neil Steven 1937- *WhoE 91*
Hayden, Norman Lee 1926- *St&PR 91*
Hayden, Palmer C 1893-1973 *WhoAmA 91N*
Hayden, Pamela Monaco 1956- *WhoEmL 91*
Hayden, Ralph Frederick 1922- *WhoAm 90*
Hayden, Raymond Paul 1939- *WhoAm 90*
Hayden, Richard M. 1945- *St&PR 91*
Hayden, Richard Michael 1945- *WhoAm 90*
Hayden, Robert C. 1937- *BioIn 16*
Hayden, Robert E. 1913-1980 *EarBlAP, MajTwCW*
Hayden, Robert Earl 1913-1980 *AuBYP 90*
Hayden, Robert Russell 1934- *WhoE 91*
Hayden, Ruth Marie 1951- *WhoE 91*
Hayden, Sterling 1916-1986 *BioIn 16*
Hayden, Steven Charles 1946- *St&PR 91*
Hayden, Thomas A. *St&PR 91*
Hayden, Tom *BioIn 16, EncAL*
Hayden, Tom 1939- *WhoAm 90, WhoWrEP 89, WorAlBi*
Hayden, Virgil O. 1921- *WhoAm 90*
Hayden, William *BioIn 16*
Hayden, William George 1933- *WhoWor 91*
Hayden, William Hughes 1940- *St&PR 91*
Hayden, William Joseph 1929- *St&PR 91, WhoAm 90*
Hayden-Wing, Larry Dean 1935- *WhoWor 91*
Haydn, Joseph 1732-1809 *BioIn 16, PenDiMP A, WorAlBi*
Haydn, Lili *BioIn 16*
Haydock, Eleanor *BiDEWW*
Haydock, Eleanor *BiDEWW*
Haydon, Benjamin Robert 1786-1846 *BioIn 16*
Haydon, Edward Eliot 1940- *St&PR 91*
Haydon, Harold 1909- *WhoAmA 91*
Haydon, Harold Emerson 1909- *WhoAm 90*
Haydon, Julie 1910- *BioIn 16, NotWoAT*
Haydu, Juan B. 1930- *St&PR 91*
Haye, Henry T *BiDrAPA 89*
Haye, Mark Richard 1956- *WhoEmL 91*
Haye, Mary Teressa 1953- *WhoEmL 91*
Hayeck, Alphonse 1950- *BiDrAPA 89*
Hayek, Carolyn Jean 1948- *WhoAmW 91*
Hayek, F A 1899- *MajTwCW*
Hayek, Friedrich A. von 1899- *BioIn 16*
Hayek, Friedrich August 1899- *WhoWor 91*
Hayek, Friedrich August Von 1899- *WorAlBi*
Hayek, Grace Molly 1962- *WhoAmW 91, WhoEmL 91*
Hayek, Lee-Ann Collins 1943- *WhoAmW 91*
Hayek, William Edward 1947- *WhoE 91*
Hayen, William Joseph 1948- *St&PR 91*
Hayes, Aaron O'Neal 1948- *WhoSSW 91*
Hayes, Alberta Phyllis Wildrick 1918- *WhoAmW 91*
Hayes, Alexandria Lynn 1957- *WhoAmW 91*
Hayes, Alfred 1910-1989 *BioIn 16, CurBio 90N*
Hayes, Alfred Jackson 1944- *St&PR 91*
Hayes, Alice 1657-1720 *BiDEWW, FemiCLE*
Hayes, Alice Bourke 1937- *WhoAm 90, WhoAmW 91*
Hayes, Allene Valerie Farmer 1958- *WhoAmW 91*
Hayes, Alton Odis 1936- *WhoSSW 91*
Hayes, Andrew Wallace, II 1939- *WhoAm 90, WhoSSW 91*
Hayes, Ann Carson 1941- *WhoSSW 91, WhoWor 91*
Hayes, Ann Louise 1924- *WhoAm 90, WhoWrEP 89*
Hayes, Anne Marie 1931- *BiDrAPA 89*
Hayes, Arthur Chester 1918- *WhoWor 91*
Hayes, Arthur Hull, Jr. 1933- *WhoAm 90*
Hayes, Arthur Michael 1915- *WhoAm 90*
Hayes, Ben 1957- *Ballpl 90*
Hayes, Benjamin Holt 1934- *St&PR 91*
Hayes, Bernard Lewis 1956- *WhoE 91*
Hayes, Bernardine Frances 1939- *WhoAmW 91*
Hayes, Bobby K. 1930- *St&PR 91*
Hayes, Bree Audrey 1945- *WhoAmW 91*
Hayes, Byron Jackson, Jr. 1934- *WhoWor 91*
Hayes, Carl Richard 1945- *St&PR 91*
Hayes, Carl Steven 1948- *WhoSSW 91*
Hayes, Carlton Joseph Huntley 1882-1964 *BioIn 16*
Hayes, Carol J. 1940- *WhoE 91*
Hayes, Charles 1950- *WhoWor 91*
Hayes, Charles A. 1918- *WhoAm 90*
Hayes, Charles A. 1935- *WhoAm 90, WhoSSW 91*
Hayes, Charles Albert 1934- *St&PR 91*
Hayes, Charles Arthur 1918- *BlkAmsC [port]*
Hayes, Charles Austin 1946- *WhoSSW 91*
Hayes, Charles Herbert 1934- *WhoAm 90*
Hayes, Charles Lawton 1927- *WhoAm 90*
Hayes, Charles Leonard 1940- *WhoWrEP 89*
Hayes, Charles Robert *BiDrAPA 89*
Hayes, Clarence B *EncABHB 4*
Hayes, Claude Quinten Christopher 1945- *WhoEmL 91, WhoWor 91*
Hayes, Cynthia Lela 1949- *WhoEmL 91*
Hayes, Daniel Peter *BiDrAPA 89*
Hayes, David *BioIn 16, NewAgMG*
Hayes, David John Arthur, Jr. 1929- *WhoAm 90, WhoWor 91*
Hayes, David M. 1943- *St&PR 91*
Hayes, David Matthew 1959- *WhoEmL 91, WhoSSW 91*
Hayes, David Michael 1943- *WhoAm 90*
Hayes, David Ryan 1937- *WhoE 91*
Hayes, David Vincent 1931- *WhoAm 90, WhoAmA 91*
Hayes, Dean Robert, Jr. 1966- *WhoEmL 91*
Hayes, Deborah 1939- *IntWWM 90*
Hayes, Delbert J. 1935- *WhoAm 90*
Hayes, Denis *NewYTBS 90 [port]*
Hayes, Denis A 1944- *ConAu 132*
Hayes, Denis Allen 1944- *WhoAm 90*
Hayes, Dennis 1952- *ConAu 130*
Hayes, Dennis Edward 1938- *WhoAm 90*
Hayes, Dennis Joseph 1934- *WhoAm 90, WhoE 91*
Hayes, Derek Cumberland 1936- *WhoAm 90*
Hayes, Don A. 1938- *WhoSSW 91*
Hayes, Donald Horace 1931- *St&PR 91*
Hayes, Donald J. 1933- *St&PR 91*
Hayes, Donald Paul 1945- *WhoSSW 91*
Hayes, Donald Powell 1948- *St&PR 91*
Hayes, Dorothy Damon 1950- *St&PR 91, WhoEmL 91*
Hayes, Dorothy Earline Lorraine 1935- *WhoWor 91*
Hayes, Douglas Martin 1943- *WhoWor 91*
Hayes, Edgar 1904-1979 *BioIn 16*
Hayes, Edward J. 1924- *St&PR 91*
Hayes, Edward James 1924- *WhoAm 90*
Hayes, Edwin Junius, Jr. 1932- *WhoAm 90*
Hayes, Edwin Keith 1956- *WhoWrEP 89*
Hayes, Eileen Patricia 1946- *IntWWM 90, WhoAmW 91*
Hayes, Elvin 1945- *WorAlBi*
Hayes, Florence 1895- *AuBYP 90*
Hayes, Francis Wingate, Jr. 1914- *WhoE 91*
Hayes, Frank J. 1930- *St&PR 91*
Hayes, Frank N. 1938- *St&PR 91*
Hayes, Frank W 1934- *BiDrAPA 89*
Hayes, Frankie 1914-1955 *Ballpl 90*
Hayes, Gabby 1885-1969 *WorAlBi*
Hayes, Gary J. 1948- *IntWWM 90*
Hayes, Gaynelle Hasselmeier 1943- *WhoSSW 91*
Hayes, Geoff *BioIn 16*
Hayes, Gerald 1940- *WhoAmA 91*
Hayes, Gerald Joseph 1950- *WhoEmL 91, WhoWor 91*
Hayes, Gladys Lucille Allen 1913- *WhoAmW 91*
Hayes, Gordon Glenn 1936- *WhoWor 91*
Hayes, Grace *BioIn 16*
Hayes, Gregory Dean *BioIn 16*
Hayes, H. David 1944- *St&PR 91*
Hayes, Harold *BioIn 16*
Hayes, Harold 1926-1989 *AnObit 1989*
Hayes, Harold T.P. 1926- *WhoWrEP 89*
Hayes, Helen 1900- *BioAmW, BioIn 16, NotWoAT, WhoAm 90, WhoAmW 91, WorAlBi*
Hayes, Henry 1842-1928 *FemiCLE*
Hayes, Henry P. *BioIn 16*
Hayes, Herman Lee 1923- *MusmAFA*
Hayes, Hobe *AuBYP 90*
Hayes, Howard Randolph 1935- *St&PR 91*
Hayes, Hugh Joseph 1946- *WhoEmL 91*
Hayes, Isaac 1942- *DrBlPA 90, EncPR&S 89, OxCPMus, WhoAm 90, WorAlBi*
Hayes, Jack Dee 1940- *St&PR 91*
Hayes, Jackie 1906-1983 *Ballpl 90*
Hayes, Jacqueline Crement 1941- *WhoAmW 91*
Hayes, James A. 1930- *St&PR 91*
Hayes, James Alison 1946- *WhoAm 90, WhoSSW 91*
Hayes, James B. *WhoAm 90*
Hayes, James Brinson 1945- *WhoSSW 91*
Hayes, James Edward 1928- *WhoAm 90*
Hayes, James L. 1914-1989 *BioIn 16*
Hayes, James Robert 1946- *St&PR 91*
Hayes, James W., III 1948- *St&PR 91*
Hayes, Janet Gray 1926- *WhoAm 90*
Hayes, Janice Cecile Osgard 1941- *WhoSSW 91*
Hayes, Jeffrey Charles 1954- *WhoEmL 91*
Hayes, Jennifer Lynn 1965- *WhoAmW 91*
Hayes, Jerralynn Estelle 1941- *WhoSSW 91*
Hayes, Joe Ben 1939- *BiDrAPA 89*
Hayes, John B *BiDrAPA 89*
Hayes, John Bruton, Jr. 1942- *WhoE 91*
Hayes, John Calvin, III 1945- *WhoSSW 91*
Hayes, John Chandler *BiDrAPA 89*
Hayes, John Coleman 1937- *WhoSSW 91*
Hayes, John Edward 1941- *WhoSSW 91*
Hayes, John Francis 1919- *WhoAm 90*
Hayes, John Freeman 1926- *WhoAm 90*
Hayes, John J. 1930- *St&PR 91*
Hayes, John P. 1921- *St&PR 91*
Hayes, John Patrick 1921- *WhoAm 90, WhoSSW 91*
Hayes, John Patrick 1944- *WhoAm 90*
Hayes, John Patrick, Jr. 1949- *WhoAm 90*
Hayes, John Robert *BiDrAPA 89*
Hayes, John Stanley 1932- *WhoAm 90*
Hayes, John Trevor 1929- *WhoWor 91*
Hayes, Joseph 1918- *ConAu 30NR, TwCCr&M 91, WhoAm 90, WhoWrEP 89*
Hayes, Joseph 1920- *IntWWM 90*
Hayes, K. William 1943- *WhoSSW 91*
Hayes, Kate E. 1856-1945 *FemiCLE*
Hayes, Kathe Penney 1949- *WhoAmW 91*
Hayes, Kathleen Zimmerman 1944- *WhoAmW 91*
Hayes, Kirk Monroe 1936- *St&PR 91*
Hayes, Larry D. 1938- *St&PR 91*
Hayes, Laura M 1927- *WhoAmA 91*
Hayes, Lisa Sanders 1960- *WhoAmW 91*
Hayes, Lisabeth Ann 1958- *WhoAmW 91*
Hayes, Lucy Webb 1831-1889 *BioAmW, BioIn 16*
Hayes, Malcolm Lionel Fitzroy 1951- *IntWWM 90*
Hayes, Marc Philip 1950- *WhoSSW 91*
Hayes, Margaret Mary 1957- *WhoEmL 91*
Hayes, Margaret T 1926- *BiDrAPA 89*
Hayes, Maria Ferraro 1951- *WhoEmL 91*
Hayes, Maria Mitchell *WhoWrEP 89*
Hayes, Marian Mercer 1963- *WhoAmW 91*
Hayes, Marjorie 1916- *BiDrAPA 89*
Hayes, Mark Allan 1914- *WhoAm 90*
Hayes, Mark Harrison 1960- *WhoEmL 91*
Hayes, Marshall Anderson 1914- *St&PR 91*
Hayes, Mary Ann G *BiDrAPA 89*
Hayes, Mary Eshbaugh 1928- *WhoAmW 91*
Hayes, Mary Jane 1948- *WhoEmL 91*
Hayes, Mary P. 1921- *St&PR 91*
Hayes, Mary Phyllis 1921- *WhoAmW 91, WhoWor 91*
Hayes, Mary Regina 1953- *WhoAmW 91*
Hayes, Matthew B. *ODwPR 91*
Hayes, Maurice L 1917- *BiDrAPA 89*
Hayes, Max *EncAL*
Hayes, Melinda Kay 1953- *WhoEmL 91*
Hayes, Michael Charles 1946- *WhoEmL 91*
Hayes, Myra Nell 1943- *WhoAmW 91*
Hayes, Nancy Victoria 1952- *WhoEmL 91*
Hayes, Neville A. 1936- *St&PR 91*
Hayes, Nicholas 1947- *WhoEmL 91*
Hayes, Norman Robert, Jr. 1948- *WhoE 91, WhoEmL 91*
Hayes, Patricia Ann 1944- *WhoAm 90, WhoAmW 91*
Hayes, Paul Gordon 1934- *WhoAm 90, WhoWrEP 89*
Hayes, Paul W 1911- *BiDrAPA 89*
Hayes, Peter J. 1942- *St&PR 91*
Hayes, Peter Lind 1915- *WhoAm 90*
Hayes, Randal Allan 1959- *WhoEmL 91*
Hayes, Randy 1944- *WhoAmA 91*
Hayes, Ray H *BiDrAPA 89*
Hayes, Rebecca Anne 1950- *WhoWor 91*
Hayes, Richard Alan 1957- *WhoWrEP 89*
Hayes, Richard Edward 1932- *St&PR 91*
Hayes, Richard J. 1932-1989 *BioIn 16*
Hayes, Richard Johnson 1933- *WhoAm 90, WhoWor 91*
Hayes, Richard L. 1941- *St&PR 91*
Hayes, Richard L. 1946- *WhoSSW 91*
Hayes, Richard P. *BioIn 16*
Hayes, Rob *ODwPR 91*
Hayes, Robert *BioIn 16*
Hayes, Robert B. 1942- *ODwPR 91, St&PR 91*
Hayes, Robert Bruce 1925- *WhoAm 90*
Hayes, Robert Emmet 1920- *WhoAm 90*
Hayes, Robert Herrick 1936- *WhoAm 90*
Hayes, Robert James 1947- *WhoEmL 91*
Hayes, Robert Mac 1945- *WhoSSW 91*
Hayes, Robert Mayo 1926- *WhoAm 90*
Hayes, Robert Patrick 1939- *WhoSSW 91*
Hayes, Robert Randal 1927- *St&PR 91*
Hayes, Roland 1887-1976 *DrBlPA 90*
Hayes, Roland 1887-1977 *DcAfAmP [port], PenDiMP*
Hayes, Ron 1956- *St&PR 91*
Hayes, Ronald George 1936- *WhoAm 90, WhoWor 91*
Hayes, Roy *St&PR 91*
Hayes, Rutherford B. 1822-1893 *BioIn 16, WorAlBi*
Hayes, Rutherford Birchard 1822-1893 *BiDrUSE 89*
Hayes, Samuel Banks, III 1936- *St&PR 91, WhoAm 90*
Hayes, Samuel Linton, III 1935- *WhoAm 90, WhoWor 91*
Hayes, Samuel Perkins 1910- *WhoAm 90, WhoE 91*
Hayes, Sandra Echols 1944- *WhoAmW 91*
Hayes, Sarah *AuBYP 90*
Hayes, Sarah Hall 1934- *WhoAm 90, WhoWrEP 89*
Hayes, Sarah Jane 1948- *WhoEmL 91*
Hayes, Scott Birchard 1926- *WhoAm 90*
Hayes, Scott M. 1947- *St&PR 91*
Hayes, Sheila 1937- *AuBYP 90, BioIn 16, WhoWrEP 89*
Hayes, Shelley Alene *BiDrAPA 89*
Hayes, Stephen Gregory *BiDrAPA 89*
Hayes, Stephen Kurtz 1949- *WhoWor 91*
Hayes, Steven C 1948- *ConAu 31NR*
Hayes, Steven Douglas 1949- *St&PR 91*
Hayes, Thelma Ann 1918- *WhoAmW 91*
Hayes, Thomas Anthony 1943- *St&PR 91*
Hayes, Thomas Burke 1912- *WhoAm 90*
Hayes, Thomas Jay, III 1914- *WhoAm 90*
Hayes, Thomas Patrick 1940- *St&PR 91*
Hayes, Thomas William *WhoAm 90*
Hayes, Timothy Joseph 1951- *BiDrAPA 89*
Hayes, Timothy Michael 1955- *WhoEmL 91*
Hayes, Tua *WhoAmA 91*
Hayes, Tua Huger 1916- *WhoE 91*
Hayes, Vertis Clemon 1911- *WhoAm 90*
Hayes, Von 1958- *Ballpl 90*
Hayes, Wayland Jackson, Jr. 1917- *WhoAm 90, WhoWor 91*
Hayes, Wayne 1913-1987 *WorAlBi*
Hayes, Webb Cook, III 1920- *WhoAm 90*
Hayes, Wilbur Frank 1936- *WhoE 91*
Hayes, William Aloysius 1920- *WhoAm 90*
Hayes, William Christopher *WhoAmA 91N*
Hayes, William Dimitty 1913- *AuBYP 90*
Hayes, William Ellie, Jr. 1930- *St&PR 91*
Hayes, William Patrick, Jr. 1954- *BiDrAPA 89*
Hayes, Wingate 1823-1877 *AmLegL*
Hayes, Woody *BioIn 16*
Hayflick, Leonard 1928- *WhoAm 90*
Hayford, Gladys May Casely 1904-1950 *HarlReB*
Hayford, John Sargent 1940- *St&PR 91, WhoAm 90*
Hayford, John Taylor *St&PR 91N*
Hayford, Mary Regina *BioIn 16*
Haygreen, John Grant 1930- *WhoAm 90*
Hayhurst, James Frederick Palmer 1941- *WhoAm 90*
Hayhurst, John Blake 1948- *WhoEmL 91*
Haykal, Radwan Faysal 1950- *BiDrAPA 89*
Haykin, Martin D 1928- *BiDrAPA 89*
Hayko, Dianne 1949- *WhoAmW 91*
Hayko, Leonard J. 1942- *St&PR 91*
Hayle, Edmond Hermenentons 1949- *WhoSSW 91*
Haylett, Clarice H 1922- *BiDrAPA 89*
Haylett, Margaret Wendy 1953- *WhoAmW 91*
Hayley, Barbara 1938- *ConAu 131*
Hayley, Eliza 1750-1797 *FemiCLE*
Hayley, William 1745-1820 *DcLB 93 [port]*
Hayllar, Edith 1860-1948 *BiDWomA*
Hayllar, Jessica 1858-1940 *BiDWomA*
Hayllar, Kate *BiDWomA*
Hayllar, Mary *BiDWomA*
Haymaker, Douglas James 1957- *WhoE 91*
Haymaker, Gideon Timberlake 1958- *St&PR 91*
Haymaker, Timothy L. 1947- *WhoSSW 91*
Hayman, Carol Bessent 1927- *WhoAm 90*
Hayman, Diane W. 1961- *St&PR 91*
Hayman, Fred *BioIn 16*
Hayman, Gale *BioIn 16*
Hayman, Harry 1917- *WhoAm 90*
Hayman, James Alexander 1920- *St&PR 91*
Hayman, LeRoy 1916- *AuBYP 90*
Hayman, Lester Linton, Jr. 1958- *WhoSSW 91*
Hayman, Lillian *DrBlPA 90*
Hayman, Martin Arthur 1929- *BiDrAPA 89*
Hayman, Max 1908- *BiDrAPA 89*
Hayman, Richard Warren Joseph 1920- *IntWWM 90, WhoAm 90*
Hayman, Robert 1575-1629 *DcLB 99*
Hayman, Robyne Marie 1961- *WhoAmW 91*
Hayman, Seymour 1914- *WhoAm 90*
Hayman, Terry Mitchell 1962- *WhoWrEP 89*

Haymes, Dick 1916-1980 OxCPMus
Haymes, Dick 1918-1980 BioIn 16, WorAlBi
Haymes, Harmon Hayden 1927- WhoAm 90
Haymes, James Burch 1931- St&PR 91
Haymes, Joseph A., Jr. 1925- St&PR 91
Haymes, Malcolm Douglas 1955- WhoSSW 91
Haymes, Robert C. 1931- WhoAm 90
Haymes, Robert William BioIn 16
Haymon, S. T. ConAu 131
Haymon, S T 1918- TwCCr&M 91
Haymon, Sylvia 1918?- ConAu 131
Haymond, David Ruel 1936- BiDrAPA 89
Haymond, Edward Owen, Jr. 1936- St&PR 91
Haymond, Paula J. 1949- WhoAmW 91
Haymond, Phillip M. 1934- WhoAm 90
Haymour, Eddy BioIn 16
Haynam, Harvey H. 1910- St&PR 91
Haynau, E. von BiDWomA
Hayne, Arminius N. BioIn 16
Hayne, C. Peck 1934- St&PR 91
Hayne, Carole Hixson 1942- WhoAmW 91
Hayne, David Mackness 1921- WhoAm 90
Hayne, Harriet Ann 1922- WhoAmW 91
Hayne, Paul Hamilton 1830-1886 BioIn 16
Hayne, Thomas Arthur 1937- WhoAm 90
Hayner, Donald Joseph 1930- WhoE 91
Hayner, George Oliver 1945- WhoSSW 91
Hayner, Herman Henry 1916- WhoWor 91
Hayner, Jeannette Clare 1919- WhoAmW 91
Hayner, Kimerick F. 1941- St&PR 91
Hayner, Linda Kay 1946- WhoSSW 91
Haynes, Alfred C. BioIn 16
Haynes, Arden R. WhoAm 90, WhoWor 91
Haynes, Arden Ramon 1927- St&PR 91
Haynes, B. Thomas 1937- WhoAm 90
Haynes, Barton F. WhoAm 90
Haynes, Benn A 1942- BiDrAPA 89
Haynes, Betsy 1937- BioIn 16
Haynes, Boyd Withers, Jr. 1917- WhoAm 90
Haynes, Buren Thomas 1937- St&PR 91
Haynes, Bythell AmLegL
Haynes, C. D. FemiCLE
Haynes, Christy Ray 1939- St&PR 91
Haynes, Daniel L 1894-1954 DrBlPA 90
Haynes, Deborah Sue 1956- BiDrAPA 89
Haynes, Donald 1934-1988 BioIn 16
Haynes, Douglas H 1936- WhoAmA 91
Haynes, Douglas Martin 1922- WhoAm 90
Haynes, Eleanor Louise 1929- WhoE 91
Haynes, Elizabeth BiDEWW
Haynes, Elizabeth Sterling 1897-1957 OxCCanT
Haynes, Elmer 1902- BiDrAPA 89
Haynes, Elwood 1857-1925 EncABHB 4 [port]
Haynes, Eugene, Jr. IntWWM 90
Haynes, F. Jay 1853-1921 BioIn 16
Haynes, Frank Jay 1853-1921 BioIn 16
Haynes, Frank L 1944-1990 BioIn 16
Haynes, Frank L. Jr. NewYTBS 90
Haynes, Frederick Leslie 1934- WhoWor 91
Haynes, Gary Allen 1936- WhoAm 90, WhoE 91
Haynes, George E. 1880-1960 WorAlBi
Haynes, George Edward 1910- WhoAmA 91
Haynes, George S. 1943- St&PR 91
Haynes, Gwendolyn Mary Duhon 1963- WhoAmW 91
Haynes, Herbert C 1920- BiDrAPA 89
Haynes, Hilda 1912-1986 DrBlPA 90
Haynes, James Almand 1933- ConAu 131, WhoWor 91
Haynes, James Darwin 1940- WhoSSW 91
Haynes, James Earl, Jr. 1943- WhoAm 90
Haynes, James Edward 1943- WhoE 91
Haynes, Janice Beheler 1955- WhoAmW 91
Haynes, Jean Reed 1949- WhoAm 90, WhoAmW 91, WhoEmL 91, WhoWor 91
Haynes, Jim ConAu 131
Haynes, Jim 1937- ODwPR 91
Haynes, Jimmy Lee 1936- WhoSSW 91, WhoWor 91
Haynes, Jimmy Ray 1946- WhoSSW 91
Haynes, Jo Ann BiDrAPA 89
Haynes, Joan Spinner 1942- BiDrAPA 89
Haynes, Joe 1917-1967 Ballpl 90
Haynes, John 1594?-1654 EncCRAm
Haynes, John Jackson 1925- WhoAm 90
Haynes, John Lenneis 1934- WhoSSW 91
Haynes, John Mabin 1928- WhoAm 90
Haynes, John Scott 1962- WhoSSW 91
Haynes, Josiah Manchester 1839-1906 AmLegL
Haynes, Karen Sue 1946- WhoAm 90
Haynes, Keith Edward 1941- BiDrAPA 89
Haynes, Kenneth George 1925- WhoAm 90
Haynes, Kenneth W. 1942- St&PR 91
Haynes, Landon Carter 1816-1875 AmLegL
Haynes, Leonard L. 1923- WhoAm 90
Haynes, Lincoln Murray 1924- WhoWrEP 89
Haynes, Linda Estes 1948- WhoSSW 91
Haynes, Lloyd 1934-1986 DrBlPA 90
Haynes, Marcia Margaret 1931- WhoAmW 91
Haynes, Mark BioIn 16
Haynes, Martha Patricia 1951- WhoAmW 91
Haynes, Marti 1947- WhoAmW 91, WhoSSW 91
Haynes, Mary L. 1942- WhoAmW 91
Haynes, Mary Rapstine 1945- WhoAmW 91
Haynes, Michael James Heflin 1953- WhoAm 90
Haynes, Moses Alfred 1921- WhoAm 90
Haynes, Nancy 1947- WhoAmA 91
Haynes, Nelma AuBYP 90
Haynes, Norman Ray 1936- WhoAm 90
Haynes, Peter L. 1939- St&PR 91
Haynes, R 1934- WhoAmA 91
Haynes, R. Michael 1940- WhoAm 90
Haynes, Renee 1906- EncO&P 3, EncPaPR 91
Haynes, Richard Terry 1946- WhoEmL 91
Haynes, Robert Hall 1931- WhoAm 90, WhoWor 91
Haynes, Robert Vaughn 1929- WhoAm 90
Haynes, Roy 1926- BioIn 16
Haynes, S. Janice 1940- WhoAmW 91
Haynes, Sherwood Kimball 1910- WhoAm 90
Haynes, Stanley 1950- IntWWM 90
Haynes, Stephen Howard 1949- WhoE 91
Haynes, Susan Henlein 1962- WhoAmW 91
Haynes, Thomas Joseph 1947- WhoEmL 91
Haynes, Thomas Morris 1918- WhoAm 90
Haynes, Tiger 1907- DrBlPA 90
Haynes, Ulric St. Clair, Jr. 1931- WhoAm 90
Haynes-Jones, Patricia 1949- WhoAmW 91
Haynie, B. Don 1947- St&PR 91
Haynie, Carolyn R BiDrAPA 89
Haynie, Fred Hollis 1932- WhoSSW 91
Haynie, Hiram G, Jr. 1926- BiDrAPA 89
Haynie, Howard Edward 1928- WhoAm 90
Haynie, Hugh 1927- WhoAmA 91
Haynie, L. Morris 1942- St&PR 91
Haynie, Mary Elizabeth 1923- WhoWor 91
Haynie, Robert Morris 1915- St&PR 91
Haynie, Thomas Powell, III 1932- WhoAm 90
Haynie, Tony Wayne 1955- WhoEmL 91
Haynor, Patricia Manzi WhoAmW 91
Haynos, Marilyn Sadie 1949- WhoE 91
Haynos, Robert Alex 1932- St&PR 91
Haynsworth, Clement 1912-1989 AnObit 1989
Haynsworth, Clement F., Jr. BioIn 16
Haynsworth, Harry Jay, IV 1938- WhoAm 90
Hayon, Elie M. 1932- WhoAm 90
Hayre, Ruth Wright BioIn 16
Hayry, Pekka Juha 1939- WhoWor 91
Hays, Bonnie Linn 1950- WhoEmL 91
Hays, Charles Francis 1946- St&PR 91
Hays, David Arthur 1930- WhoAm 90
Hays, David S 1920- BiDrAPA 89
Hays, David Thomas 1953- WhoSSW 91
Hays, Dennis Edward 1951- WhoEmL 91
Hays, Diana Joyce Watkins 1945- WhoAmW 91, WhoE 91, WhoEmL 91
Hays, Donald 1947- ConAu 132
Hays, Donald Osborne 1907- WhoAm 90
Hays, Elizabeth ODwPR 91
Hays, Ethel EncACom
Hays, Gary Palmer 1945- St&PR 91
Hays, George Waight Secrest 1954- WhoEmL 91
Hays, George Washington 1863-1927 BioIn 16
Hays, Glenn Koble 1922- WhoSSW 91
Hays, H R 1904-1980 ConAu 31NR
Hays, Harrison Lowe, III 1930- St&PR 91
Hays, Harry Sanders 1935- St&PR 91
Hays, Herschel Martin 1920- WhoSSW 91, WhoWor 91
Hays, Holly Mary 1952- WhoAmW 91
Hays, Howard H. 1917- WhoAm 90
Hays, Howard H., Jr. 1917- St&PR 91
Hays, James A. 1936- St&PR 91
Hays, James Fred 1933- WhoAm 90
Hays, James S. 1901-1989 BioIn 16
Hays, John Coffee 1817-1883 WhNaAH
Hays, John Edward 1948- St&PR 91
Hays, Kathryn WhoAm 90
Hays, Larry Weldon 1936- WhoSSW 91
Hays, Lee 1914-1981 BioIn 16
Hays, Lewis W. 1914- WhoAm 90
Hays, Lon Roberts BiDrAPA 89
Hays, Marcia Lee BiDrAPA 89
Hays, Marguerite Thompson 1930- WhoAm 90
Hays, Marilyn Patricia 1935- WhoAmW 91, WhoWor 91
Hays, Mary 1760-1843 BioIn 16, FemiCLE
Hays, Mary Katherine Jackson WhoAmW 91, WhoWor 91
Hays, Matilda 1820-1866? FemiCLE
Hays, Patrick Gregory 1942- WhoAm 90
Hays, Patrick Henry 1947- WhoEmL 91
Hays, Peggy Ann 1948- WhoEmL 91
Hays, Peter BiDrAPA 89
Hays, Peter L. 1938- WhoAm 90
Hays, Randy Kurt 1953- St&PR 91
Hays, Richard Joseph 1947- WhoEmL 91
Hays, Richard M. 1927- St&PR 91
Hays, Richard T. 1928- St&PR 91
Hays, Robert BioIn 16
Hays, Robert 1947- WorAlBi
Hays, Robert William 1925- WhoSSW 91, WhoWor 91
Hays, Ronald Jackson 1928- WhoAm 90
Hays, Ronnie Dale 1946- St&PR 91
Hays, S. Robert St&PR 91
Hays, Seth M. 1811-1873 BioIn 16
Hays, Sidney Brooks 1931- WhoSSW 91
Hays, Sorrel Doris 1941- IntWWM 90
Hays, Steele 1925- WhoAm 90
Hays, Thomas A. 1932- St&PR 91
Hays, Thomas Alan 1953- BiDrAPA 89
Hays, Thomas Anthony 1957- WhoWrEP 89
Hays, Thomas Chandler 1935- WhoAm 90, WhoE 91, WhoWor 91
Hays, Thomas Clyde 1951- WhoEmL 91
Hays, Thomas R. 1915- WhoAm 90, WhoE 91, WhoWor 91
Hays, Treva Nadeja 1937- WhoAmW 91
Hays, Wayne L. 1911-1989 AnObit 1989
Hays, Wayne Levere 1911-1989 BioIn 16
Hays, Will S. 1837-1907 LiHiK
Hays, William Alton, Jr. 1941- BiDrAPA 89
Hays, William Harrison 1879-1954 BiDrUSE 89
Hays, William Jacob 1830-1875 WhNaAH
Hays, William L. WhoAm 90
Hays, William Paul 1929- IntWWM 90
Hays, Wilma Pitchford 1909- AuBYP 90
Haysbert, Raymond V., Sr. 1920- St&PR 91
Haysbert, Reginald 1948- St&PR 91
Hayslett, John Paul 1935- WhoAm 90
Hayslett, Roderick James 1945- St&PR 91, WhoAm 90
Hayslip, Le Ly BioIn 16
Haysom, Ian Richard 1949- WhoAm 90
Haysom, Simon David Leybourne 1945- WhoEmL 91
Haystead, Wesley 1942- WhoWrEP 89
Hayt, John T. 1938- St&PR 91
Haytayan, Harry M. St&PR 91
Hayter, Adrian 1914-1990 ConAu 131
Hayter, Karen Johnson 1943- WhoAmW 91
Hayter, S. W. 1901-1988 AnObit 1988
Hayter, Stanley William 1901-1988 BioIn 16
Haythe, Winston McDonald 1940- WhoE 91
Haythorne, Robert Poore 1815-1891 DcCanB 12
Haythornthwaite, Robert Morphet 1922- WhoAm 90
Haytin, Harold A. 1918- St&PR 91
Hayton, Jacob William 1926- WhoAm 90
Hayton, Lori Jeanne 1959- WhoEmL 91
Hayton, Richard Neil 1916- WhoWrEP 89
Hayum, George Theodore 1945- WhoEmL 91
Hayutin, David Lionel 1930- WhoAm 90
Hayward, A E 1885-1939 EncACom
Hayward, Amey BiDEWW, FemiCLE
Hayward, Austin L. 1924- St&PR 91
Hayward, Charles E. BioIn 16
Hayward, Charles W. 1927- St&PR 91
Hayward, Charles William 1937- WhoE 91
Hayward, Charles Winthrop 1927- WhoAm 90
Hayward, Gary Van 1936- St&PR 91
Hayward, Graham George 1938- WhoWor 91
Hayward, Harold 1920- WhoE 91
Hayward, James 1943- WhoAmA 91
Hayward, Jane 1918- WhoAm 90, WhoAmA 91
Hayward, Jean 1924- BiDrAPA 89
Hayward, John L. 1927- St&PR 91
Hayward, John Tucker 1910- WhoAm 90
Hayward, Leland 1902-1971 WorAlBi
Hayward, Margaret McGee 1959- WhoAmW 91
Hayward, Merle A. 1924- St&PR 91
Hayward, Peter 1905- WhoAmA 91
Hayward, Richard TwCCr&M 91
Hayward, Ronald Hamilton 1927- WhoAm 90
Hayward, Sally Jane 1960- WhoAmW 91
Hayward, Sarah 1620?- BiDEWW
Hayward, Susan 1917-1975 WorAlBi
Hayward, Susan 1919-1975 BioAmW
Hayward, Teresa Calcagno 1907- WhoAmW 91, WhoE 91, WhoWor 91
Hayward, Thomas Zander, Jr. 1940- St&PR 91, WhoAm 90
Hayward, Troy E. 1939- St&PR 91
Hayward, William Robert St&PR 91
Hayward-Surry, Jeremy Keith 1942- St&PR 91
Haywood, Anne Mowbray 1935- WhoAmW 91
Haywood, Barbara Smith 1951- WhoSSW 91
Haywood, Betty Jean 1942- WhoAmW 91
Haywood, Big Bill 1869-1928 BioIn 16
Haywood, Bruce 1925- WhoAm 90
Haywood, Carolyn NewYTBS 90 [port]
Haywood, Carolyn 1898-1990 AuBYP 90, BioIn 16, ChILR 22 [port], ConAu 130, SmATA 64
Haywood, Charles 1904- WhoAm 90
Haywood, Charles Anthony 1956- WhoEmL 91
Haywood, Charles Richard 1940- St&PR 91
Haywood, Clarence Robert 1921- WhoAm 90
Haywood, Donald 1900-1951 EarBlAP
Haywood, Edmund Burke 1953- WhoEmL 91
Haywood, Eliza 1690?-1756? FemiCLE
Haywood, Eliza 1693?-1756 BiDEWW
Haywood, Eliza Fowler 1693?-1756 BioIn 16
Haywood, H. Carl 1931- BioIn 16
Haywood, Harry 1898-1985 EncAL
Haywood, Herbert Carlton 1931- WhoAm 90
Haywood, L. Julian 1927- WhoAm 90
Haywood, Lorna Marie 1939- IntWWM 90
Haywood, Mary Carolyn 1898-1990 BioIn 16
Haywood, Oliver Garfield 1911- WhoAm 90
Haywood, Robert Alton 1959- WhoSSW 91
Haywood, Robert Carroll 1950- WhoEmL 91
Haywood, Spencer BioIn 16
Haywood, Theodore Joseph 1929- WhoAm 90
Haywood, William D. 1869-1928 EncAL
Haywood, William Dudley 1869-1928 BioIn 16
Haywood, William Thomas, III 1955- WhoEmL 91
Hayworth, Ray 1904- Ballpl 90
Hayworth, Ray Milton 1937- BiDrAPA 89
Hayworth, Rita 1918-1987 BioAmW, BioIn 16, WorAlBi
Hayworth, Robert Wilson, III 1963- WhoSSW 91
Haza, Ofra BioIn 16
Hazama, Hidebumi 1928- WhoWor 91
Hazan, Marcella BioIn 16
Hazan, Marcella Maddalena 1924- WhoAm 90
Hazan, Martin 1928- St&PR 91
Hazan, Toby BiDrAPA 89
Hazard, Ebenezer 1744-1817 EncCRAm
Hazard, Gary M. 1951- St&PR 91
Hazard, Geoffrey Cornell, Jr. 1929- WhoAm 90
Hazard, James Arthur 1935- WhoWrEP 89
Hazard, John N 1909- ConAu 31NR
Hazard, John Newbold 1909- WhoAm 90, WhoE 91, WhoWor 91
Hazard, John Wharton 1912- WhoAm 90
Hazard, Merle Pabst 1935- WhoAmW 91
Hazard, Neil Livingstone 1952- WhoE 91, WhoEmL 91
Hazard, Robert Culver, Jr. 1934- WhoAm 90
Hazard, Roberta Louise 1934- WhoAmW 91
Hazard, Warren B. 1937- St&PR 91
Hazarian, Tina Lola Rebecca WhoAmW 91, WhoE 91, WhoWor 91
Hazel, Carol BioIn 16
Hazel, Diane Hunter 1949- WhoAmW 91
Hazel, Gerald Vernon 1931- St&PR 91
Hazel, Joseph Ernest 1933- WhoAm 90
Hazel, Palpu BiDrAPA 89
Hazel, Robert 1921- LiHiK
Hazel, William Augustus BioIn 16
Hazelip, Herbert Harold 1930- WhoAm 90
Hazelkorn, David 1948- WhoEmL 91
Hazell, Frank 1883- WhoAmA 91N
Hazelman, Donald Frederick 1930- St&PR 91
Hazelrig, Jane B. 1937- WhoAmW 91
Hazelrig, Paul Edward, Sr. 1916- St&PR 91
Hazelrigg, Charles Richard 1933- WhoAm 90
Hazelrigg, Charles Tabb 1915- WhoAm 90

Hazelrigg, George Arthur, Jr. 1939- *WhoE 91*
Hazelrigg, Meredith Kent 1942- *WhoWor 91*
Hazeltine, Alice Isabel 1878- *AuBYP 90*
Hazeltine, Barrett 1931- *WhoAm 90*
Hazeltine, Herbert S., Jr. 1908- *St&PR 91*
Hazeltine, Herbert Samuel, Jr. 1908- *WhoAm 90*
Hazeltine, Joyce *WhoAm 90, WhoAmW 91*
Hazeltine, Mark Steven 1952- *WhoEmL 91*
Hazeltine, Sherman 1907- *St&PR 91*
Hazelton, Elizabeth Baldwin *AuBYP 90*
Hazelton, Jon G. 1938- *St&PR 91*
Hazelton, Nancy Toler 1949- *WhoAmW 91*
Hazelton, Nika *BioIn 16*
Hazelton, Paul Vernon 1919- *WhoAm 90*
Hazelton, Warren J. *ODwPR 91*
Hazelwood, Carroll T. 1941- *St&PR 91*
Hazelwood, Christina Lee 1961- *WhoEmL 91*
Hazelwood, John Arthur 1938- *WhoAm 90*
Hazelwood, Joseph J. *BioIn 16*
Hazelwood, Keith William 1947- *WhoEmL 91*
Hazelwood, Lee 1929- *OxCPMus*
Hazen, Barbara Shook 1930- *BioIn 16, WhoAmW 91, WhoWrEP 89*
Hazen, Elizabeth Lee 1885-1975 *BioAmW*
Hazen, Joseph H *WhoAmA 91*
Hazen, Paul 1941- *St&PR 91*
Hazen, Paul Mandeville 1941- *WhoAm 90*
Hazen, Richard *NewYTBS 90*
Hazen, Richard 1911-1990 *BioIn 16*
Hazen, Robert Blyth 1932- *St&PR 91*
Hazen, Robert Miller 1948- *IntWWM 90, WhoAm 90*
Hazen, Stanley Phillip 1924- *WhoAm 90*
Hazen, Thomas N. 1935- *St&PR 91*
Hazen, Wallace Richard 1934- *St&PR 91, WhoAm 90*
Hazen, William Babcock 1830-1887 *WhNaAH*
Hazen, William H. 1931- *St&PR 91*
Hazen, William Harris 1931- *WhoAm 90*
Hazenfield, Phillip A. 1945- *St&PR 91*
Hazer, Melvin *BioIn 16*
Hazewinkel, Michiel 1943- *WhoWor 91*
Hazle, Bob 1930- *Ballpl 90*
Hazlehurst, Franklin Hamilton 1925- *WhoAmA 91*
Hazlehurst, John Livingston 1931- *WhoSSW 91*
Hazlehurst, Robert Purviance, Jr. 1919- *WhoAm 90*
Hazleton, Lesley *BioIn 16*
Hazleton, Lloyd W. 1911- *St&PR 91*
Hazlett, D. Marlene 1948- *WhoAmW 91*
Hazlett, Donald Arthur 1936- *BiDrAPA 89*
Hazlett, Edward Everett 1892- *AuBYP 90*
Hazlett, James Arthur 1917- *WhoAm 90*
Hazlett, James Stephen 1940- *WhoAm 90*
Hazlett, John R. 1939- *St&PR 91*
Hazlewood, Mark Philip 1953- *St&PR 91*
Hazlewood, Robert E 1939- *BiDrAPA 89*
Hazlitt, Don 1948- *WhoAmA 91*
Hazlitt, Henry 1894- *WhoAm 90*
Hazlitt, Joan Quiter 1936- *WhoAmW 91*
Hazlitt, William 1778-1830 *NinCLC 29 [port]*
Hazo, Samuel 1928- *ConAu 31NR*
Hazoume, Guy Landry 1940- *WhoWor 91*
Hazouri, Louis Abraham, Jr. 1948- *St&PR 91, WhoAm 90*
Hazouri, Thomas L. 1944- *WhoAm 90, WhoSSW 91*
Hazra, B.K. 1946- *St&PR 91*
Hazra, Bilas Kumar 1946- *WhoEmL 91*
Hazrat Mahal *WomWR*
Hazuchova, Nina 1926- *IntWWM 90*
Hazy, James Kent 1955- *WhoE 91*
Hazzard, Alvira *EarBlAP*
Hazzard, Alvira 1899-1953 *HarlReB*
Hazzard, Dorothy *BiDEWW*
Hazzard, Mary Dwight 1928- *WhoWrEP 89*
Hazzard, Shirley 1931- *BioIn 16, FemiCLE, MajTwCW, WhoAm 90, WhoAmW 91, WhoWrEP 89*
H'Doubler, Francis Todd, Jr. 1925- *WhoAm 90*
He Haixia *BioIn 16*
He Zhen *BioIn 16*
He, Lu-Ting 1903- *IntWWM 90*
Heaberlin, David A. 1949- *St&PR 91*
Heacker, Terrill Dyanne 1957- *WhoSSW 91*
Heacock, Don R *BiDrAPA 89*
Heacock, Donald Dee 1934- *WhoSSW 91*
Heacock, Grace Anne 1943- *WhoAmW 91*
Heacock, Steven Robert 1956- *WhoEmL 91*
Heacock, Walter Judson 1921- *WhoAm 90*
Heacox, Edwin Paul 1939- *WhoAm 90*
Head, Albert 1838- *AmLegL*
Head, Albert Lee, III 1952- *WhoSSW 91*
Head, Antony Henry 1906-1983 *DcNaB 1981*
Head, Asbury J. 1914- *St&PR 91*
Head, Bessie 1937-1986 *FemiCLE, MajTwCW*
Head, Charles T. 1942- *St&PR 91*
Head, Christopher Alan 1951- *WhoEmL 91*
Head, Ed 1918-1980 *Ballpl 90*
Head, Edith 1897-1981 *ConDes 90*
Head, Edith 1907-1981 *WorAlBi*
Head, Edward Dennis 1919- *WhoAm 90, WhoE 91*
Head, Evelyn Harris-Shields 1944- *WhoWrEP 89*
Head, George Bruce 1931- *WhoAmA 91*
Head, Haskell Lee 1946- *BiDrAPA 89*
Head, Hayden Wilson, Jr. 1944- *WhoSSW 91*
Head, Holman 1926- *WhoAm 90*
Head, Howard 1914- *WhoAm 90*
Head, Ivan Leigh 1930- *WhoAm 90*
Head, James Crawford 1943- *WhoSSW 91*
Head, James Franklin 1935- *WhoE 91*
Head, John Douglas 1927- *WhoAm 90*
Head, John Francis, Jr. 1920- *St&PR 91*
Head, Jonathan Frederick 1949- *WhoSSW 91*
Head, Marie Doss 1956- *WhoEmL 91*
Head, Marsha Marie 1951- *WhoAmW 91*
Head, Matthew *WhoWrEP 89*
Head, Matthew 1907-1985 *TwCCr&M 91*
Head, Michael D. 1946- *St&PR 91*
Head, Mitch 1955- *ODwPR 91*
Head, Mitchell Ernest 1955- *WhoSSW 91*
Head, Patrick J. 1932- *St&PR 91*
Head, Patrick James 1932- *WhoAm 90*
Head, Richard Louis 1931- *St&PR 91*
Head, Robert 1942- *WhoWrEP 89*
Head, Robert G 1915- *BiDrAPA 89*
Head, Robert William 1941- *WhoAmA 91*
Head, Thomas Clarke 1956- *WhoEmL 91*
Head, Thomas F., III 1929- *St&PR 91*
Head, Thomas James 1934- *WhoE 91*
Head, Violet Beryl 1922- *WhoAmW 91*
Head, William Carl 1951- *WhoEmL 91, WhoWor 91*
Head, William Iverson, Sr. 1925- *WhoSSW 91, WhoWor 91*
Head, Yvonne 1948- *WhoWrEP 89*
Headden, Laura Benson 1950- *WhoEmL 91*
Headding, Lillian Susan 1944- *WhoAmW 91*
Headings, Ronald Lynn 1960- *WhoEmL 91*
Headington, Christopher 1930- *AuBYP 90*
Headington, Christopher John Magenis 1930- *IntWWM 90*
Headland, J.P. *St&PR 91*
Headlee, Raymond 1917- *BiDrAPA 89, WhoAm 90*
Headlee, Richard Harold 1930- *St&PR 91, WhoAm 90*
Headlee, Rolland Dockeray 1916- *WhoAm 90*
Headley, Anne Renouf 1937- *WhoAm 90, WhoE 91*
Headley, Barbara Joan 1946- *WhoEmL 91*
Headley, David Allen 1946- *WhoAmA 91*
Headley, Elizabeth *AuBYP 90*
Headley, James Jerald, Jr. 1947- *WhoSSW 91*
Headley, John M. 1929- *ConAu 130*
Headley, Shari *BioIn 16*
Headly, Glenne *BioIn 16*
Headly, Glenne 1955- *ConTFT 8*
Headly, Jay Rutherford 1930- *WhoE 91*
Headrick, George O. *ODwPR 91*
Headrick, John Anderson 1931- *WhoWor 91*
Headrick, Jon C. 1943- *St&PR 91*
Headrick, Roger L. 1936- *St&PR 91*
Headrick, Samuel Philip 1952- *IntWWM 90*
Headrick, Stirman Russell 1951- *WhoEmL 91*
Headrick, Thomas Edward 1933- *WhoAm 90*
Headstrom, Birger Richard 1902- *AuBYP 90*
Heady, Eleanor B 1917-1979 *ConAu 31NR*
Heady, Eleanor Butler 1917- *AuBYP 90*
Heady, Ferrel 1916- *WhoAm 90*
Heady, Harold F 1916- *ConAu 31NR*
Heady, Harold Franklin 1916- *WhoAm 90*
Heafey, Edwin Austin, Jr. 1930- *WhoAm 90*
Heafey, Thomas Robert 1948- *WhoEmL 91*
Heagarty, Margaret Caroline 1934- *WhoAm 90, WhoAmW 91*
Heagy, Lorraine Mary 1935- *WhoAmW 91*
Heagy, Thomas Charles 1945- *WhoAm 90*
Heal, Ambrose 1872-1959 *PenDiDA 89*
Heal, Jane 1946- *ConAu 132*
Heal, Kenneth Lee 1942- *St&PR 91*
Heal, Richard Albert 1945- *St&PR 91*
Heald, Anthony 1944- *ConTFT 8*
Heald, Bruce Day 1935- *WhoE 91, WhoWor 91*
Heald, Darrel Verner 1919- *WhoAm 90, WhoE 91*
Heald, David L. 1943- *St&PR 91*
Heald, Emily Eastham 1917- *WhoAmW 91*
Heald, James C 1937- *BiDrAPA 89*
Heald, James Eudean 1929- *WhoAm 90*
Heald, Jane Dewey 1931- *WhoWrEP 89*
Heald, Kala Donna 1943- *WhoSSW 91*
Heald, Mark Aiken 1929- *WhoAm 90*
Heald, Melinda Merle 1962- *WhoAmW 91*
Heald, Milton Tidd 1919- *WhoAm 90*
Heald, Morrell 1922- *WhoAm 90*
Heald, Phillip P. 1939- *St&PR 91*
Heald, Suzette 1943- *ConAu 132*
Heald, Tim 1944- *ConAu 30NR, TwCCr&M 91*
Heald, Timothy Villiers 1944- *SpyFic*
Heald-Smith, Geoffrey 1930- *IntWWM 90*
Healey, Andrew Edward 1955- *WhoE 91*
Healey, Ann Ruston 1939- *WhoAmW 91*
Healey, Arthur H. 1920- *WhoAm 90, WhoE 91*
Healey, Ben *TwCCr&M 91*
Healey, Brooks *WhoWrEP 89*
Healey, Christopher K 1948- *BiDrAPA 89*
Healey, David Clayton 1946- *St&PR 91*
Healey, David Lee 1950- *WhoEmL 91, WhoSSW 91*
Healey, Denis *BioIn 16*
Healey, Derek Edward 1936- *WhoAm 90, WhoWor 91*
Healey, Donald M. 1898-1988 *BioIn 16*
Healey, Dorothy 1914- *EncAL*
Healey, Edward Hopkins 1925- *WhoAm 90*
Healey, Francis Xavier 1938- *WhoE 91*
Healey, Frank Henry 1924- *WhoAm 90*
Healey, Jack 1938?- *News 90 [port]*
Healey, James C 1930- *BiDrAPA 89*
Healey, James Francis 1920- *St&PR 91*
Healey, James Stewart 1931- *WhoAm 90*
Healey, Jeff *BioIn 16*
Healey, Jeff 1966?- *ConMus 4*
Healey, John G. 1938- *WhoAm 90, WhoWor 91*
Healey, Lois Ann 1958- *WhoAmW 91, WhoEmL 91*
Healey, Louis P. 1950- *St&PR 91*
Healey, Lynne Kover *WhoAmW 91*
Healey, Marie 1936- *WhoSSW 91*
Healey, Patricia 1950- *ODwPR 91*
Healey, Ralph Joseph, Jr. 1935- *St&PR 91*
Healey, Richard *BioIn 16*
Healey, Robert Joseph 1925- *WhoAm 90*
Healey, Robert Kenneth 1925- *St&PR 91*
Healey, Robert William 1947- *WhoEmL 91*
Healey, Walter James 1949- *BiDrAPA 89*
Healion, Mary Stephen *BioIn 16*
Healton, Donald Carney 1930- *WhoAm 90*
Healy, Alice Fenvessy 1946- *WhoAm 90*
Healy, Anne Laura 1939- *WhoAmA 91*
Healy, Arthur K D 1902-1978 *WhoAmA 91N*
Healy, Barbara Anne 1951- *WhoAmW 91, WhoWor 91*
Healy, Bernadine P. 1944- *WhoAm 90, WhoAmW 91*
Healy, Charles B. 1937- *St&PR 91*
Healy, Daniel James 1959- *St&PR 91*
Healy, David *BioIn 16*
Healy, Deborah Ann *WhoAmA 91*
Healy, Edward John, Jr. 1935- *St&PR 91*
Healy, Fran 1946- *Ballpl 90*
Healy, Francis Patrick 1932- *St&PR 91*
Healy, George William, III 1930- *WhoAm 90, WhoWor 91*
Healy, Gerry 1913-1989 *AnObit 1989*
Healy, Harold Harris, Jr. 1921- *WhoAm 90*
Healy, James B. 1930- *WhoE 91, WhoWor 91*
Healy, James Bruce 1947- *WhoEmL 91, WhoWor 91*
Healy, James Casey 1956- *WhoE 91, WhoEmL 91, WhoWor 91*
Healy, James Joseph 1948- *St&PR 91, WhoE 91*
Healy, Jane Elizabeth 1949- *WhoAm 90, WhoAmW 91, WhoSSW 91*
Healy, Jeremiah 1948- *TwCCr&M 91*
Healy, Jeremiah Francis, III 1948- *WhoEmL 91*
Healy, John David 1945- *WhoEmL 91*
Healy, John J. 1936- *St&PR 91*
Healy, John P. *ODwPR 91*
Healy, John Russell 1951- *WhoWor 91*
Healy, Joseph Francis, Jr. 1930- *WhoAm 90, WhoSSW 91, WhoWor 91*
Healy, Joyce A. 1947- *St&PR 91*
Healy, Joyce Ann Kury 1947- *WhoAm 90*
Healy, Julia Schmitt 1947- *WhoAmA 91*
Healy, Justin D. 1949- *St&PR 91*
Healy, Kenneth C. 1905- *St&PR 91*
Healy, Kent Allen 1932- *WhoAm 90*
Healy, Kieran John Patrick 1957- *WhoWor 91*
Healy, M. Brian 1943- *St&PR 91*
Healy, Martin J., Jr. *BioIn 16*
Healy, Mary 1918- *WhoAm 90*
Healy, Mary Jacqueline 1952- *WhoEmL 91*
Healy, Maureen Winifred 1953- *WhoE 91*
Healy, Nanci A. 1944- *ODwPR 91*
Healy, Nicholas Joseph 1910- *WhoAm 90, WhoWor 91*
Healy, Otis McDowell 1927- *St&PR 91*
Healy, Patricia 1951- *WhoEmL 91*
Healy, Patricia A. 1932- *St&PR 91*
Healy, Patricia Ann 1951- *WhoE 91*
Healy, Paul Michael 1914- *St&PR 91*
Healy, Robert Danforth 1939- *WhoE 91, WhoWor 91*
Healy, Robert Edward 1904- *WhoAm 90*
Healy, Robert Edwin 1950- *WhoE 91*
Healy, Stephen Francis 1955- *WhoSSW 91*
Healy, Steven Michael 1949- *WhoEmL 91, WhoWor 91*
Healy, Theresa Ann 1932- *WhoAm 90*
Healy, Thomas B., Jr. 1928- *St&PR 91*
Healy, Thomas Martin 1921- *WhoAm 90*
Healy, Timothy S 1923- *News 90 [port]*
Healy, Timothy Stafford 1923- *BioIn 16, WhoAm 90, WhoE 91, WhoWor 91*
Healy, Walter F. X. 1941- *WhoWor 91*
Healy, William Kent 1930- *St&PR 91, WhoE 91*
Healy Eige, Sharon Janet 1946- *WhoEmL 91*
Heaney, Dorothy Phelps 1963- *WhoEmL 91*
Heaney, James A. 1928- *ODwPR 91*
Heaney, Joe 1947- *St&PR 91*
Heaney, John E. 1927- *ODwPR 91*
Heaney, Joseph A 1929- *BiDrAPA 89*
Heaney, Patrick G. 1938- *St&PR 91*
Heaney, Robert Proulx 1927- *WhoAm 90*
Heaney, Seamus *BioIn 16*
Heaney, Seamus 1939- *MajTwCW*
Heaney, Seamus Justin 1939- *WhoAm 90, WhoWor 91*
Heaney, Thomas Edward 1921- *St&PR 91*
Heany, Donald Francis 1918-1990 *ConAu 132*
Heap, Alan Franklin *BiDrAPA 89*
Heap, Frank K. 1941- *WhoAm 90*
Heap, James Clarence *WhoWor 91*
Heap, Jane 1887-1964 *FemiCLE*
Heap, Sylvia Stuber 1929- *WhoAmW 91*
Heaphy, Edward T. 1938- *St&PR 91*
Heaphy, Eileen Michele 1945- *WhoAmW 91*
Heaphy, James Cullen, III 1952- *WhoWrEP 89*
Heaphy, John Merrill 1927- *WhoAm 90*
Heaphy, Thomas M. 1931- *St&PR 91*
Heaps, Harry D. 1922- *St&PR 91*
Heaps, Marvin Dale 1932- *WhoAm 90*
Heaps, Willard Allison 1908- *AuBYP 90*
Heard, Alexander 1917- *WhoAm 90*
Heard, Anthony *BioIn 16*
Heard, Arthur Bernard 1924- *WhoAm 90*
Heard, Chauncy Lee 1950- *WhoAmW 91*
Heard, Cheryl Vyette 1956- *WhoAmW 91*
Heard, Craig P. 1945- *St&PR 91*
Heard, D. Dennis 1940- *St&PR 91*
Heard, David Dennis 1940- *WhoAm 90*
Heard, Delano R *BiDrAPA 89*
Heard, Drayton 1941- *St&PR 91*
Heard, Edwin Anthony 1926- *St&PR 91, WhoAm 90*
Heard, George 1940- *St&PR 91*
Heard, Gerald *TwCCr&M 91*
Heard, Gerald 1889-1971 *EncO&P 3, EncPaPR 91, RGTwCSF*
Heard, Gordon 1939- *IntWWM 90*
Heard, H F 1889-1971 *TwCCr&M 91*
Heard, J. C. 1917-1988 *BioIn 16*
Heard, James Charles 1917-1988 *BioIn 16*
Heard, John Beaton 1929- *WhoAm 90*
Heard, John G. 1922- *WhoAm 90*
Heard, John McDonald 1939- *St&PR 91*
Heard, Johny Carol 1942- *WhoAmW 91*
Heard, Lawrence M. 1950- *St&PR 91*
Heard, Lawrence Milton 1950- *WhoAm 90*
Heard, Mary Frances Suffecool 1948- *WhoAmW 91*
Heard, Patricia Loader 1930- *WhoAmW 91*
Heard, Prudence Jensen 1941- *WhoSSW 91*
Heard, Stephanie Lynne *BiDrAPA 89*
Heard, Wilbur Wright 1905- *WhoAm 90*
Heard, William R. 1925- *St&PR 91*
Heard, William Robert 1925- *WhoWor 91*
Hearding, David Warren 1950- *WhoEmL 91*
Hearey Taffet, Michele 1959- *WhoAmW 91*
Hearin, Annie Laurie *BioIn 16*
Hearin, Joe 1912- *St&PR 91*

Hearin, Robert M. *BioIn 16*
Hearin, William J. 1909- *St&PR 91*
Hearin, William Jefferson 1909- *WhoAm 90, WhoSSW 91*
Hearle, Douglas G. 1933- *ODwPR 91*
Hearle, Douglas Geoffrey 1933- *WhoAm 90*
Hearle, Edward F.R. 1931- *St&PR 91*
Hearn, Albert Amsden 1928- *St&PR 91*
Hearn, Bunny 1891-1959 *Ballpl 90*
Hearn, David W., Jr. 1930- *St&PR 91*
Hearn, Edell Midgett 1929- *WhoAm 90*
Hearn, Emily *BioIn 16*
Hearn, George Henry 1927- *WhoAm 90*
Hearn, James Woodrow 1931- *WhoAm 90*
Hearn, Jim 1921- *Ballpl 90*
Hearn, John 1827-1894 *DcCanB 12*
Hearn, Joyce Camp *WhoAmW 91*
Hearn, Kathleen K. 1947- *WhoAmW 91*
Hearn, Lafcadio 1850-1904 *BioIn 16, EncJap*
Hearn, Leo Charles, Jr. 1959- *WhoSSW 91*
Hearn, M F, Jr 1938- *WhoAmA 91*
Hearn, Paula Clarice 1955- *WhoAmW 91*
Hearn, Richard E. 1936- *St&PR 91*
Hearn, Rosamond Ernst 1924- *WhoAmW 91, WhoE 91*
Hearn, Rosemary 1929- *WhoAmW 91*
Hearn, Ruby Puryear 1940- *WhoAmW 91*
Hearn, Sharon Sklamba 1956- *WhoAmW 91*
Hearn, Thomas K., Jr. 1937- *WhoAm 90, WhoSSW 91*
Hearn, Wendy Lee 1958- *WhoEmL 91*
Hearne, Betsy Gould *BioIn 16*
Hearne, Carl N. *WhoSSW 91*
Hearne, Elizabeth G. *BioIn 16*
Hearne, George Archer 1934- *WhoAm 90*
Hearne, Gerardette A. 1957- *WhoAmW 91*
Hearne, John 1926- *MajTwCW*
Hearne, John William 1942- *WhoSSW 91*
Hearne, Larry Steven 1959- *WhoEmL 91*
Hearne, Mary *BiDEWW, FemiCLE*
Hearne, Nikki Jo 1951- *WhoAmW 91*
Hearne, Samuel 1745-1792 *DcLB 99 [port], EncCRAm, WhNaAH*
Hearne, Stephen Zachary 1952- *WhoSSW 91*
Hearne, Thomas M. 1943- *St&PR 91*
Hearnes, Warren Eastman 1923- *WhoAm 90*
Hearns, John Burton, II 1959- *WhoWor 91*
Hearns, Thomas *BioIn 16*
Hearon, Shelby 1931- *ConLC 63 [port], WhoWrEP 89*
Hearons, James Searle 1932- *St&PR 91*
Hearsey, Marguerite Capen *BioIn 16*
Hearst, Austine McDonnell 1928- *WhoAm 90, WhoAmW 91*
Hearst, Bella Rachael *WhoAm 90, WhoAmW 91, WhoWor 91*
Hearst, Earl David 1944- *BiDrAPA 89*
Hearst, Edward D. 1960- *WhoEmL 91*
Hearst, George Randolph, Jr. 1927- *WhoAm 90*
Hearst, Gladys Whitley Henderson *WhoAmW 91*
Hearst, John Eugene 1935- *WhoAm 90*
Hearst, Patricia 1954- *WorAlBi*
Hearst, Patricia C. 1954- *BioAmW*
Hearst, Patricia Campbell *BioIn 16*
Hearst, Phoebe A. 1842-1919 *BioAmW*
Hearst, Randolph A. 1915- *St&PR 91*
Hearst, Randolph Apperson 1915- *WhoAm 90*
Hearst, William Randolph 1863-1951 *BioIn 16, EncACom, WorAlBi*
Hearst, William Randolph, III 1949- *WhoAm 90*
Hearst, William Randolph, Jr. 1908- *St&PR 91, WhoAm 90, WhoWor 91*
Heart *EncPR&S 89*
Heartney, Eleanor 1954- *WhoAmA 91*
Heartt, Charlotte Beebe 1933- *WhoE 91*
Heartt, Jonas Coe 1793-1874 *AmLegL*
Heartz, Daniel Leonard 1928- *IntWWM 90, WhoAm 90*
Heasley, Katharine Ziegler 1909- *WhoAmW 91*
Heasley, Ross Edward 1939- *St&PR 91*
Heaslip, Joy Gail 1953- *St&PR 91*
Heaslip, William A. *WhoAm 90*
Heaslip, William R. 1944- *St&PR 91*
Heaster, Arlene Louise 1958- *WhoAmW 91*
Heasty, Alfred R, Sr. 1926- *BiDrAPA 89*
Heater, Claude 1930- *IntWWM 90*
Heater, Floyd Raymond 1959- *WhoE 91*
Heater, Kurt Duane 1957- *WhoEmL 91*
Heater, William Joseph 1954- *WhoAm 90*
Heath, Adam G. 1962- *WhoEmL 91*
Heath, Alan Frank 1943- *St&PR 91*
Heath, Benjamin W. 1914- *St&PR 91*
Heath, Betsy Robbins 1953- *WhoAmW 91*
Heath, Carl Ernest 1930- *WhoE 91*
Heath, Catherine 1924- *ConAu 30NR*
Heath, Charles Dickinson 1941- *WhoWor 91*
Heath, Charles Thomas *BiDrAPA 89*
Heath, Christopher *PenDiDA 89*
Heath, Cynthia Marie 1947- *WhoAmW 91*
Heath, David C 1940- *WhoAmA 91*
Heath, David Clay 1942- *WhoE 91*
Heath, David Martin 1931- *WhoAmA 91*
Heath, Desmond P S *BiDrAPA 89*
Heath, Dianne Gay 1948- *WhoEmL 91*
Heath, Donald Read 1894-1981 *BioIn 16*
Heath, Douglas Hamilton 1925- *WhoAm 90*
Heath, Dwight Braley 1930- *WhoAm 90*
Heath, E Sheldon 1931- *BiDrAPA 89*
Heath, Edward 1916- *BioIn 16, WorAlBi*
Heath, Edward Richard George 1916- *WhoWor 91*
Heath, Frank Bradford 1938- *WhoSSW 91, WhoWor 91*
Heath, George Ross 1939- *WhoAm 90*
Heath, Gilbert A. 1936- *St&PR 91*
Heath, Gloria Whitton 1922- *WhoAm 90*
Heath, Gordon 1918- *DrBlPA 90*
Heath, Gordon Adair 1938- *BiDrAPA 89*
Heath, H. Ellis 1912- *St&PR 91*
Heath, James Albert 1912- *St&PR 91*
Heath, James Lee 1939- *WhoAm 90*
Heath, Jane Ellen *BiDrAPA 89*
Heath, Jeff 1915-1975 *Ballpl 90*
Heath, Jeffrey 1950- *WhoE 91*
Heath, Jim N. 1942- *St&PR 91*
Heath, Jimmy 1926- *BioIn 16*
Heath, Joel 1941- *St&PR 91*
Heath, John *PenDiDA 89*
Heath, John C. 1939- *St&PR 91*
Heath, John Charles 1947- *WhoEmL 91*
Heath, John F *BiDrAPA 89*
Heath, John L. 1935- *St&PR 91*
Heath, Lyn Barrett 1934- *WhoWrEP 89*
Heath, Malcolm 1957- *ConAu 130*
Heath, Mariwyn Dwyer 1935- *WhoAmW 91, WhoWor 91*
Heath, Michael H. 1941- *WhoAm 90, WhoSSW 91*
Heath, Mike 1955- *Ballpl 90*
Heath, Milton Weeks, Jr. 1929- *St&PR 91*
Heath, Richard Murray 1927- *WhoAm 90*
Heath, Richard Raymond 1929- *WhoAm 90*
Heath, Robert Dennis 1959- *IntWWM 90*
Heath, Robert Everett 1941- *St&PR 91*
Heath, Robert G 1915- *BiDrAPA 89*
Heath, Robert Galbraith 1915- *WhoAm 90*
Heath, Roger C. 1943- *St&PR 91*
Heath, Roger Charles 1943- *WhoE 91*
Heath, Roy A. K. 1926- *ConAu 33NR*
Heath, Roy A K 1926- *MajTwCW*
Heath, Russ 1926- *EncACom*
Heath, S. Rollie, Jr. *WhoAm 90*
Heath, Ted 1900-1969 *OxCPMus*
Heath, William 1929- *ConAu 31NR*
Heath, William Henry 1944- *St&PR 91*
Heath, William Otto 1960- *WhoEmL 91*
Heath-Davies, Valerie 1940- *IntWWM 90*
Heathcoat Amory, Derick 1899-1981 *DcNaB 1981*
Heathcock, Clayton Howell 1936- *WhoAm 90*
Heathcock, Jeff 1959- *Ballpl 90*
Heathcock, John Herman 1943- *WhoSSW 91, WhoWor 91*
Heathcote, Caleb 1666-1721 *EncCRAm*
Heathcote, Cliff 1898-1939 *Ballpl 90*
Heathcote, Robert E. *BioIn 16*
Heatherington, J. Scott 1919- *WhoAm 90*
Heatherley, Nelda Harris 1945- *WhoSSW 91*
Heatherly, David Alan 1950- *St&PR 91, WhoAm 90*
Heatherly, Henry Edward 1936- *WhoSSW 91*
Heatherton, Joey *BioIn 16*
Heathorn, Jennifer Ives 1943- *IntWWM 90*
Heatley, Connie F. 1942- *ODwPR 91*
Heatley, Connie Frances 1942- *WhoAmW 91, WhoE 91*
Heatley, Sidney M. 1928- *St&PR 91*
Heatly, Danny J. 1955- *St&PR 91*
Heaton, Andrew Patrick 1946- *St&PR 91*
Heaton, Clement 1824-1882 *PenDiDA 89*
Heaton, Clement J. 1861-1940 *PenDiDA 89*
Heaton, Clifford O. 1939- *St&PR 91*
Heaton, Donald Slade 1946- *St&PR 91*
Heaton, Eric F. *St&PR 91*
Heaton, Eugene Edward, Jr. 1934- *St&PR 91*
Heaton, Fritz Charles 1954- *WhoEmL 91*
Heaton, Gwendolyn 1954- *BiDrAPA 89*
Heaton, Hannah 1721-1794 *BioIn 16*
Heaton, Maurice 1900- *PenDiDA 89*
Heaton, Melinda Ann 1960- *WhoAmW 91*
Heaton, Neal 1960- *Ballpl 90*
Heaton, Robert C. 1933- *St&PR 91*
Heaton, William Sutcliffe, Jr. 1925- *St&PR 91*
Heatter, Gabriel 1890-1972 *BioIn 16*
Heatter, Maida *BioIn 16*
Heatwole, Mark M. 1948- *WhoEmL 91*
Heatwole, Milton *St&PR 91*
Heatwole, Thomas Cromer 1948- *WhoE 91*
Heaven, Constance *AuBYP 90*
Heavener, David E. 1947- *St&PR 91*
Heavenrich, Andreas Robert 1955- *St&PR 91*
Heavenrich, Robert Maurice 1913- *WhoAm 90*
Heaver, Lynwood *BiDrAPA 89*
Heaverlo, Dave 1950- *Ballpl 90*
Heavilin, Jay *AuBYP 90*
Heaviside, Oliver 1850-1925 *BioIn 16, WorAlBi*
Heavner, Ann Denise 1956- *WhoE 91*
Heavrin, Daniel William 1950- *WhoE 91*
Heavysege, Charles 1816-1876 *DcLB 99 [port], OxCCanT*
Heazel, Francis James, Jr. 1920- *St&PR 91, WhoSSW 91*
Hebald, Carol 1934- *WhoWrEP 89*
Hebald, Milton Elting 1917- *WhoAm 90, WhoAmA 91*
Hebalkar, Prakash Gurunath 1844- *WhoWor 91*
Hebard, Christopher Learned 1952- *WhoEmL 91*
Hebard, Emory A. 1917- *WhoAm 90*
Hebard, Robert R. 1953- *St&PR 91*
Hebb, Caroline Raut 1919- *WhoAmW 91*
Hebb, Donald Bruce, Jr. *WhoAm 90*
Hebb, George Sanford, Jr. 1921- *St&PR 91*
Hebb, Joseph Stephen 1948- *St&PR 91*
Hebb, Malcolm Hayden 1910- *WhoAm 90*
Hebb, Peter Harvey 1938- *St&PR 91*
Hebbard, Neysa Stanley *WhoWrEP 89*
Hebbelinck, Marie-Jeanne Chartrain- 1909-1987 *BioIn 16*
Hebble, Jacob G, III *BiDrAPA 89*
Hebble, W.J. *St&PR 91N*
Hebblethwaite, Margaret 1951- *ConAu 129*
Hebda, Edwin Thomas 1935- *St&PR 91*
Hebda, Lawrence John 1954- *WhoEmL 91*
Hebden, Mark 1916- *TwCCr&M 91*
Hebden, William Ernest 1934- *St&PR 91*
Hebeka, Elias Khalil 1936- *St&PR 91*
Hebeker, Fritz Herman 1931- *St&PR 91*
Hebel, Anthony Jerome 1928- *WhoAm 90*
Hebel, Friedrich 1813-1863 *WorAlBi*
Hebeler, Henry Koester 1933- *WhoAm 90*
Hebeler, Joan Rochelle *BiDrAPA 89*
Hebenstreit, Jean Estill Stark *WhoAmW 91*
Hebenstreit, Richard Henry 1925- *St&PR 91*
Heber, Carl A 1885-1956 *WhoAmA 91N*
Heber, Gordon Eric 1952- *WhoSSW 91*
Heberer, James H. 1955- *St&PR 91*
Heberlein, Garrett Thomas 1939- *WhoAm 90*
Heberling, Glen Austin 1915- *WhoAmA 91*
Heberling, Peter D.W. 1951- *St&PR 91*
Heberling, Phyllis McMillan 1926- *WhoSSW 91*
Hebert, Anne 1916- *FemiCLE, MajTwCW, OxCCanT [port]*
Hebert, Archille William 1909- *WhoWor 91*
Hebert, Bliss 1930- *IntWWM 90*
Hebert, Bliss Edmund 1930- *WhoAm 90*
Hebert, Clifford Joseph 1940- *WhoAm 90*
Hebert, Frederick B 1942- *BiDrAPA 89*
Hebert, Frederick William 1946- *St&PR 91*
Hebert, Guy 1949- *St&PR 91*
Hebert, Harold R. 1940- *St&PR 91*
Hebert, Howard Neil 1928- *St&PR 91*
Hebert, Jean *BiDrAPA 89*
Hebert, John P. *ODwPR 91*
Hebert, Leon P. 1931- *St&PR 91*
Hebert, Leonard Bernard, Jr. 1924- *St&PR 91*
Hebert, Maria Darene 1956- *WhoEmL 91*
Hebert, Mary Olivia 1921- *WhoAmW 91*
Hebert, Nick P. 1947- *St&PR 91*
Hebert, Pamela 1946- *IntWWM 90*
Hebert, Paul 1924- *OxCCanT*
Hebert, Richard F. *ODwPR 91*
Hebert, Richard K. 1951- *St&PR 91*
Hebert, Richard Leo 1940- *WhoAm 90*
Hebert, Robert D. 1938- *WhoAm 90, WhoSSW 91*
Hebert, Ronald A. 1946- *IntWWM 90*
Hebert, Stephen W *BiDrAPA 89*
Hebert, Steven Douglas 1960- *WhoSSW 91*
Hebert, Thomas William 1947- *WhoE 91*
Hebert, Victor A. 1937- *St&PR 91*
Hebert, Wally 1907- *Ballpl 90*
Heberton, William Baily 1931- *St&PR 91*
Hebertson, Val M. 1935- *WhoAm 90*
Hebner, Paul C. 1919- *St&PR 91*
Hebner, Paul Chester 1919- *WhoAm 90*
Hebner, Richie 1947- *Ballpl 90*
Hebra, Alexius Johannes 1919- *WhoSSW 91*
Hebrank, Roger Adolph 1932- *St&PR 91*
Hebron, Fe Pambid *BiDrAPA 89*
Hebson, Ann 1925- *LiHiK, WhoAm 90*
Heceta, Bruno 1751-1807 *EncCRAm*
Heceta, Estherbelle Aguilar 1935- *WhoAm 90*
Hechinger, Fred Michael 1920- *WhoAm 90*
Hechinger, John W., Jr. 1950- *WhoAm 90*
Hechinger, John Walter 1920- *WhoAm 90*
Hechler, Arthur William 1938- *WhoE 91*
Hechler, Ken 1914- *WhoAm 90, WhoSSW 91*
Hechler, Robert Lee 1936- *St&PR 91, WhoAm 90*
Hecht, Abraham Berl 1922- *WhoAm 90*
Hecht, Alan Dannenberg 1918- *WhoAm 90*
Hecht, Anita Gessler 1938- *WhoAmW 91*
Hecht, Anthony Evan 1923- *WhoAm 90, WhoWrEP 89*
Hecht, Ben 1894-1964 *BioIn 16, WorAlBi*
Hecht, Carl E. 1925- *St&PR 91*
Hecht, Chic 1928- *WhoAm 90*
Hecht, Daniel *NewAgMG*
Hecht, Eli C. 1921- *St&PR 91*
Hecht, Emil 1924- *St&PR 91, WhoAm 90*
Hecht, Ethel Morell *WhoAmW 91*
Hecht, Eva Crossman- *BioIn 16*
Hecht, Frederick 1930- *WhoAm 90*
Hecht, Gary M. 1943- *ODwPR 91*
Hecht, George Max 1943- *BiDrAPA 89*
Hecht, Harvey E. 1939- *WhoWrEP 89*
Hecht, Horst 1943- *WhoWor 91*
Hecht, Howard A. 1928- *St&PR 91*
Hecht, Irene 1949- *WhoAmA 91, WhoE 91*
Hecht, Irene Winchester D. 1932- *WhoAmW 91*
Hecht, Jeff 1947- *ConAu 131*
Hecht, Joshua 1929- *IntWWM 90*
Hecht, Kevin Walker 1953- *WhoEmL 91*
Hecht, Lee 1942- *St&PR 91*
Hecht, Lee Martin 1942- *WhoAm 90*
Hecht, Louis A. 1944- *St&PR 91*
Hecht, Louis Alan 1944- *WhoAm 90*
Hecht, Marie Bergenfeld 1918- *WhoAmW 91*
Hecht, Michael Allen 1945- *St&PR 91*
Hecht, Myron Jay 1954- *WhoEmL 91*
Hecht, Nathan Lincoln 1949- *WhoAm 90, WhoEmL 91*
Hecht, Norman Bernard 1940- *WhoAm 90*
Hecht, Norman F. *St&PR 91*
Hecht, Paul 1909-1989 *BioIn 16*
Hecht, Paul 1941- *ConTFT 8 [port]*
Hecht, Robert Earl, Sr. 1925- *WhoAm 90*
Hecht, Roger D. 1945- *St&PR 91*
Hecht, Tannia Rubiano *BioIn 16*
Hecht, Zoltan 1890-1968 *WhoAmA 91N*
Hecht-Meyer, Goldee 1945- *WhoE 91*
Hechtel, Florence May Marguerite 1939- *IntWWM 90*
Hechtel, Johann Richard 1913- *WhoAm 90*
Hechter, Rebecca H 1920- *BiDrAPA 89*
Hecimovich, John Richard 1939- *St&PR 91*
Heck, Albert Frank 1932- *WhoAm 90*
Heck, Alfons 1928- *ConAu 131*
Heck, Barbara 1734-1804 *WorAlBi*
Heck, Barbara Ruckle 1734-1804 *EncCRAm*
Heck, David Joseph 1952- *BiDrAPA 89*
Heck, James Baker 1930- *WhoAm 90*
Heck, Jeffrey M. 1948- *St&PR 91*
Heck, Kathleen 1954- *WhoAmW 91*
Heck, L. Douglas 1918- *WhoAm 90*
Heck, Paul D. 1928- *St&PR 91*
Heck, R.J. 1933- *St&PR 91*
Heck, Richard Joseph 1947- *WhoEmL 91*
Heck, Rita Zenzen *ODwPR 91*
Heck, Robert E. 1925- *St&PR 91*
Heck, Walter Philip, Jr. 1931- *St&PR 91*
Heckadon, Robert Gordon 1933- *WhoWor 91*
Heckaman, Curtis R. *St&PR 91*
Heckaman, David F. *St&PR 91*
Heckaman, Patricia A. *St&PR 91*
Heckart, Eileen 1919- *BioIn 16, WhoAm 90, WhoAmW 91, WorAlBi*
Heckathorn, Glen James 1946- *St&PR 91*
Heckathorn, William Gary 1946- *WhoEmL 91*
Heckathorne, Donald Frank 1948- *St&PR 91*
Heckel, John Louis 1931- *St&PR 91, WhoAm 90*
Heckel, Richard Wayne 1934- *WhoAm 90*
Heckelmann, Charles N 1913- *ConAu 30NR*
Heckelmann, Charles Newman 1913- *WhoAm 90, WhoWrEP 89*
Heckelmann, Dieter 1937- *WhoWor 91*
Hecken, Rudolf Peter 1931- *WhoE 91*
Heckenbach, David William 1954- *WhoEmL 91*
Heckendorf, Glenn 1942- *WhoE 91*
Heckendorn, John Glenn 1947- *WhoE 91*
Heckendorn, Paul Lee 1950- *St&PR 91*

Hecker, Anne 1924- *WhoAmW 91*
Hecker, Bruce Albert 1919- *WhoAm 90*
Hecker, Burton Glenn 1932- *St&PR 91*
Hecker, Carlos Metsch 1937- *BiDrAPA 89*
Hecker, Debra Ann 1963- *WhoAmW 91*
Hecker, George Sprake 1922- *WhoAm 90*
Hecker, Guy 1856-1938 *Ballpl 90*
Hecker, Guy Leonard, Jr. 1932- *WhoAm 90*
Hecker, Helen Jean *WhoWrEP 89*
Hecker, Isaac Thomas 1819-1888 *BioIn 16*
Hecker, Richard 1930- *WhoSSW 91, WhoWor 91*
Hecker, Sharon Ruth 1958- *WhoAmW 91*
Hecker, Siegfried Stephen 1943- *WhoAm 90*
Hecker, William Fulham 1936- *WhoSSW 91*
Heckerling, Amy *BioIn 16, WhoAmW 91*
Heckerman, Jerry D. 1938- *St&PR 91*
Heckert, Paul Andrew 1953- *WhoEmL 91*
Heckert, Paul Charles 1929- *WhoAm 90, WhoE 91*
Heckert, Richard Edwin *BioIn 16*
Heckert, Richard Edwin 1924- *St&PR 91, WhoE 91*
Heckert, Winfield W. 1902-1988 *BioIn 16*
Heckethorn, John E. 1917- *St&PR 91*
Heckewelder, John Gottlieb Ernestus 1743-1823 *WhNaAH*
Heckhausen, Jutta 1957- *WhoWor 91*
Hecking, Erwin Hans 1943- *WhoWor 91*
Hecking, Klaus C.A. 1941- *WhoWor 91*
Heckler, Charles Victor 1945- *WhoE 91*
Heckler, Edward Eugene 1946- *WhoSSW 91*
Heckler, George Earl 1920- *WhoAm 90*
Heckler, Gloryanne 1945- *WhoE 91*
Heckler, John Maguire 1927- *WhoE 91, WhoWor 91*
Heckler, Jonellen Beth 1943- *WhoWrEP 89*
Heckler, Margaret Mary 1931- *BiDrUSE 89, WhoAmW 91, WhoWor 91*
Heckler, Paul Scott 1954- *St&PR 91*
Heckler, Sheryl Bills 1945- *WhoAm 90*
Heckler, Walter Tim 1942- *WhoSSW 91*
Heckman, Carey E. 1954- *St&PR 91*
Heckman, Carol A. 1944- *WhoAmW 91*
Heckman, H. Edward 1950- *St&PR 91*
Heckman, Harold Klein *BiDrAPA 89*
Heckman, Henry Trevennen Shick 1918- *WhoWor 91*
Heckman, James Franklin *WhoAm 90*
Heckman, James Joseph 1944- *WhoAm 90, WhoE 91*
Heckman, James R. 1931- *St&PR 91*
Heckman, Jerome Harold 1927- *WhoE 91*
Heckman, JoAnn 1950- *WhoAmW 91, WhoE 91, WhoEmL 91, WhoWor 91*
Heckman, Lynn Geringer *BiDrAPA 89*
Heckman, Mary Anne 1957- *WhoEmL 91*
Heckman, Norman Eugene 1947- *WhoE 91*
Heckman, Richard Ainsworth 1929- *WhoWor 91*
Heckman, Stephen Paul 1939- *St&PR 91*
Heckman, William Guy 1925- *St&PR 91*
Heckman, William Joseph 1909- *WhoWor 91*
Heckmann, Harald 1924- *IntWWM 90*
Heckmann, Irvin Lee 1925- *WhoAm 90*
Heckmann, James Michael 1953- *WhoEmL 91*
Heckmann, Richard Carl 1953- *BiDrAPA 89*
Heckrodt, Frank H. 1926- *St&PR 91*
Heckroth, Hein 1901-1970 *ConDes 90*
Heckscher, August 1913- *WhoE 91*
Heckscher, Morrison Harris 1940- *WhoAm 90*
Heckscher, William Sebastian 1904- *WhoAmA 91*
Hecksher, Henry D. *BioIn 16, NewYTBS 90*
Hecktman, Jerold Allen 1937- *St&PR 91*
Heckwelder, John Gottlieb 1743-1823 *EncCRAm*
Hector, Annie French 1825-1902 *BioIn 16*
Hector, Bruce John 1950- *WhoEmL 91*
Hector, Louis Julius 1915- *WhoAm 90*
Hector-Harris, Carol Ann 1950- *WhoAmW 91*
Hectus, Charles Thomas 1949- *WhoEmL 91*
Hed, Kenneth A. 1931- *St&PR 91*
Heda, William Claesz 1594?-1680? *IntDcAA 90*
Hedahl, Gorden Orlin 1946- *WhoEmL 91*
Hedahl, Richard Neil 1950- *St&PR 91*
Hedaya, Robert Joseph 1952- *BiDrAPA 89, WhoE 91*
Hedback, Brenda Lee 1940- *WhoAmW 91*
Hedberg, Bo Lage Torsten 1944- *WhoWor 91*
Hedberg, David L 1931- *BiDrAPA 89*
Hedberg, Gregory Scott 1946- *WhoAmA 91, WhoE 91*
Hedberg, Hans 1917- *BioIn 16*
Hedberg, Hollis Dow 1903-1988 *BioIn 16*
Hedberg, Mildred Elaine Pons 1929- *WhoAm 90*
Hedberg, Paul Clifford 1939- *WhoAm 90*
Hedberg, Robert Daniel 1922- *WhoAm 90*
Hedberg, Steven Michael 1958- *WhoEmL 91*
Hedblom, Lawrence James 1955- *St&PR 91*
Heddaeus, David R. 1944- *St&PR 91*
Hedden, David K *BiDrAPA 89*
Hedden, Gregory Dexter 1919- *WhoAm 90*
Hedden, Kenneth Forsythe 1941- *WhoSSW 91*
Hedden, Lucy Margaret 1949- *WhoAmW 91*
Hedden, Monty Scott *St&PR 91*
Hedden, Russell A. 1918- *St&PR 91*
Hedden, Willard Laing 1928- *St&PR 91*
Hedden-Sellman, Zelda *WhoAmA 91*
Heddens, Karen Rae 1954- *WhoEmL 91*
Heddens, Robert D. 1938- *St&PR 91*
Heddesheimer, Walter Jacob 1910- *WhoAm 90*
Hedeman, Robert J. 1954- *St&PR 91*
Hedeman, Robert M. 1919- *St&PR 91*
Hedeman, William M. 1936- *St&PR 91*
Hedemark, N. Charles 1942- *St&PR 91*
Heder, Leopold 1918- *BioIn 16*
Hederman, H. Henry 1920- *St&PR 91, WhoSSW 91*
Hederman, James Joseph *BiDrAPA 89*
Hedewig, Roland 1936- *WhoWor 91*
Hedfwig, Douglas Frederick 1951- *IntWWM 90*
Hedge, Arthur Joseph, Jr. 1936- *WhoAm 90*
Hedge, Frederic Henry 1805-1890 *BioIn 16*
Hedge, George Albert 1939- *WhoAm 90*
Hedge, Jeanne Colleen 1960- *WhoAmW 91, WhoE 91, WhoEmL 91, WhoWor 91*
Hedge, Jeffrey George *BiDrAPA 89*
Hedge, Mary Gelhaus 1952- *WhoAmW 91, WhoEmL 91*
Hedgecock, Dixie Lee 1962- *WhoAmW 91*
Hedgeman, Anna Arnold *BioIn 16*
Hedgeman, Anna Arnold 1899-1990 *ConAu 130*
Hedgepeth, Richard L. 1928- *St&PR 91*
Hedger, Alison Claire 1946- *IntWWM 90*
Hedges, Anthony John 1931- *IntWWM 90*
Hedges, Carl Devon 1924- *WhoWor 91*
Hedges, Carl Edward 1920- *St&PR 91*
Hedges, Charles F., Jr. 1951- *St&PR 91*
Hedges, Dan 1951- *WhoWrEP 89*
Hedges, Donald W. 1921- *WhoAm 90*
Hedges, Doris 1900- *FemiCLE*
Hedges, Harry George 1923- *WhoAm 90*
Hedges, Harry Slicer 1945- *WhoAm 90*
Hedges, James 1938- *WhoWrEP 89*
Hedges, Jean Kyle 1930- *WhoAmW 91*
Hedges, Lorrette Jean *WhoAmW 91*
Hedges, Marylynn Jarrard 1951- *WhoAmW 91*
Hedges, Michael *NewAgMG*
Hedges, Mollie Ellen 1952- *WhoAmW 91*
Hedges, Pat *BioIn 16*
Hedges, Robert W. 1945- *St&PR 91*
Hedges, Steven Douglas 1955- *WhoEmL 91*
Hedges, Thomas D. 1949- *St&PR 91*
Hedges, William A. 1941- *St&PR 91*
Hedges, Wyllys A. 1857- *AmLegL*
Hedgespeth, Joanne 1954- *WhoAmW 91*
Hedgpeth, Harding Brent 1947- *WhoEmL 91*
Hedgpeth, Joe 1941- *WhoAm 90*
Hedicker, Marianne 1946- *WhoAmW 91*
Hedien, Wayne Evans 1934- *St&PR 91*
Hediger, Gary Roddey 1944- *St&PR 91*
Hediger, Gary Roddy 1944- *WhoAm 90*
Hedin, Andrea L 1949- *BiDrAPA 89*
Hedine, Kristian Einar 1956- *WhoEmL 91*
Hedison, Al *ConTFT 8*
Hedison, David 1928- *ConTFT 8*
Hedland, Robert W. 1928- *St&PR 91*
Hedley, David Van Houten 1945- *WhoAm 90*
Hedley, Leslie Woolf 1921- *WhoWrEP 89*
Hedley, Robert Peveril 1937- *St&PR 91, WhoAm 90*
Hedley-Whyte, Elizabeth Tessa 1937- *WhoAmW 91*
Hedley-Whyte, John 1933- *WhoAm 90*
Hedling, Susan Eckstrom 1946- *WhoAmW 91*
Hedlund, Douglas A 1935- *BiDrAPA 89*
Hedlund, Gunnar 1900-1989 *BioIn 16*
Hedlund, James Lane 1928- *WhoAm 90*
Hedlund, Marilou 1937- *ODwPR 91*
Hedlund, Mike 1946- *Ballpl 90*
Hedlund, Richard Peter *BiDrAPA 89*
Hedlund, Ronald 1939- *WhoAm 90*
Hedman, Dale Eugene 1935- *WhoAm 90*
Hedman, Frederick Alvin 1937- *WhoE 91*
Hedman, Janice Lee 1938- *WhoAmW 91*
Hedman, Jonathan W. 1943- *St&PR 91*
Hedman, Teri Jo 1944- *WhoAmA 91*
Hedquist, Jeffrey Paul 1945- *WhoEmL 91*
Hedric, Lisa Robinette 1959- *WhoSSW 91*
Hedrick, Basil Calvin 1932- *WhoAm 90, WhoWrEP 89*
Hedrick, Bonnie Lee 1940- *WhoSSW 91*
Hedrick, Charles Lynnwood 1934- *St&PR 91*
Hedrick, David E. 1929- *St&PR 91*
Hedrick, David Warrington 1917- *WhoSSW 91*
Hedrick, Donald Ward 1917- *WhoAm 90*
Hedrick, Floyd Dudley 1927- *WhoAm 90*
Hedrick, Gary R. 1954- *St&PR 91*
Hedrick, Gary Read 1954- *WhoSSW 91*
Hedrick, Hal C., Jr. 1945- *St&PR 91*
Hedrick, Jerry Leo 1936- *WhoAm 90*
Hedrick, John Warrington 1955- *WhoEmL 91*
Hedrick, Larry Willis 1939- *WhoAm 90*
Hedrick, Mary Sasser 1963- *WhoSSW 91*
Hedrick, Robert Kenny, Jr. 1949- *WhoE 91*
Hedrick, Steve Brian 1958- *WhoSSW 91*
Hedrick, Wally Bill 1928- *WhoAmA 91*
Hedstrom, Ana Lisa *WhoAmA 91*
Hedstrom, Mitchell Warren 1951- *WhoE 91*
Hedstrom, Ruth Elaine 1925- *IntWWM 90*
Hedtke, Barbara Ann 1956- *WhoAmW 91*
Hedwall, Lennart 1932- *IntWWM 90*
Hedwig, Queen of Poland 1371?-1399 *BioIn 16*
Hedwig, St. *WomWR*
Hedyle 3--?BC- *EncCoWW*
Hee, Harold S.Y. 1925- *St&PR 91*
Hee, Hon-Chew 1906- *WhoAmA 91*
Hee, Thomas Wah Sung 1955- *WhoEmL 91*
Heeb, Camille Storey 1944- *WhoWor 91*
Heeb, Louis F. 1930- *St&PR 91*
Heebe, Frederick Jacob Regan 1922- *WhoAm 90, WhoSSW 91*
Heebner, Albert Gilbert 1927- *WhoAm 90, WhoE 91*
Heebner, David Richard 1927- *St&PR 91, WhoAm 90*
Heebner, Kenneth *BioIn 16*
Heefner, John David 1941- *BiDrAPA 89*
Heefner, William Frederick 1922- *WhoAm 90*
Heege, Hermann J. 1931- *WhoWor 91*
Heeger, Alan Jay 1936- *WhoAm 90*
Heeger, Jack J. 1930- *ODwPR 91*
Heekin, James R., Jr. *BioIn 16*
Heekin, Valerie Anne 1953- *WhoAmW 91*
Heeks, Willy 1951- *WhoAmA 91*
Heel, Johann 1637-1709 *PenDiDA 89*
Heelan, Patrick Aidan 1926- *WhoAm 90*
Heeley, Desmond *BioIn 16*
Heeley, Desmond 1930- *OxCCanT*
Heeley, Desmond 1931- *ConDes 90, IntWWM 90*
Heem, Jan Davidsz. de 1606?-1683? *IntDcAA 90*
Heemskerck, Jacoba Berendina van Beest v 1876-1923 *BiDWomA*
Heemskerck, Maerten van 1498-1574 *IntDcAA 90*
Heemskerk, William Jacobsz van 1613-1692 *PenDiDA 89*
Heenan, Ashley David Joseph 1925- *IntWWM 90*
Heenan, Edward J. 1947- *St&PR 91*
Heenan, Greg Stephen 1950- *WhoSSW 91*
Heenan, William Patrick 1954- *WhoWrEP 89*
Heeney, Gwen *BioIn 16*
Heeney, Walter J. 1941- *St&PR 91*
Heep, Danny 1957- *Ballpl 90*
Heer, David Macalpine 1930- *WhoAm 90*
Heer, Edwin Le Roy 1938- *St&PR 91*
Heer, Ewald 1930- *WhoWor 91*
Heer, Hans De 1927- *IntWWM 90*
Heer, Nicholas Lawson 1928- *WhoAm 90*
Heer, Paul Edward 1936- *St&PR 91*
Heer, William 1921- *St&PR 91*
Heeramaneck, Nasil M 1902-1971 *WhoAmA 91N*
Heere, Karen R. 1944- *WhoAmW 91*
Heeren, Reid L. *St&PR 91*
Heerens, Robert Edward 1915- *WhoAm 90*
Heering, Peter Frederik Suhm 1934- *WhoWor 91*
Heeringa, George D. 1914- *St&PR 91*
Heersema, Philip H *BiDrAPA 89*
Heertje, Arnold 1934- *ConAu 131, WhoWor 91*
Heerwagen, Herbert Alfred 1910- *WhoE 91, WhoWor 91*
Heerwagen, Louie M. 1935- *St&PR 91*
Hees, George *BioIn 16*
Hees, George Harris 1910- *WhoAm 90*
Heesacker, Mary Agnes 1927- *WhoE 91*
Heeschen, David Sutphin 1926- *WhoAm 90*
Heeseler, Richard Carlton 1946- *WhoE 91*
Heeseman, Rex 1942- *WhoAm 90*
Heestand, Diane Elissa 1945- *WhoEmL 91*
Heesterbeek, Yvan Joseph 1934- *WhoWor 91*
Heezen, Bruce C 1924-1977 *DcScB S2*
Heffelbower, Dwight Earl 1925- *St&PR 91, WhoAm 90*
Heffer, Janet Cassandra 1947- *WhoAmW 91*
Heffer, Reuben George 1908-1985 *DcNaB 1981*
Hefferan, Colien Joan 1949- *WhoE 91*
Hefferlin, Gladys *EncO&P 3*
Heffern, Gordon E. 1924- *St&PR 91*
Heffern, Gordon Emory 1924- *WhoAm 90*
Heffernan, Carol Gamble *WhoAmW 91*
Heffernan, Donald P. 1945- *St&PR 91*
Heffernan, Gerard E. 1937- *St&PR 91*
Heffernan, Helen 1896-1987 *BioIn 16*
Heffernan, James *BioIn 16*
Heffernan, James Dannehl, Jr. 1953- *WhoE 91*
Heffernan, James Scott 1953- *WhoEmL 91*
Heffernan, James Vincent 1926- *WhoAm 90*
Heffernan, Marion C. *BioIn 16*
Heffernan, Michael Joseph 1942- *WhoWrEP 89*
Heffernan, Michele Olga 1949- *WhoEmL 91*
Heffernan, Nathan Stewart 1920- *WhoAm 90*
Heffernan, Patricia Conner 1946- *WhoAmW 91*
Heffernan, Peter John 1945- *WhoE 91*
Heffernan, Phillip Thomas, Jr. 1922- *WhoAm 90*
Heffernan, Richard Joseph 1951- *WhoAm 90*
Heffernan, Roger Leonard 1946- *St&PR 91*
Heffernan, Stuart DeBell 1943- *WhoSSW 91*
Heffernan, Thomas 1939- *WhoWrEP 89*
Heffernan, Wilbert Joseph 1932- *WhoAm 90*
Heffernan, William Joseph, II 1935- *St&PR 91*
Heffernan, William Patrick 1939- *St&PR 91*
Heffernan-Shrimpton, Patricia Marie 1962- *WhoE 91*
Heffernen-Smothers, Sheryl A *BiDrAPA 89*
Hefferon, Jenny L. *ODwPR 91*
Heffinck, Paul 1942- *WhoWor 91*
Heffington, Jack Grisham 1944- *WhoSSW 91*
Heffler, Paul Mark 1953- *WhoEmL 91*
Heffner, Benjamin 1909-1988 *BioIn 16*
Heffner, Bob 1938- *Ballpl 90*
Heffner, Daniel Jason 1956- *WhoEmL 91, WhoWor 91*
Heffner, Don 1911- *Ballpl 90*
Heffner, Don 1911-1989 *BioIn 16*
Heffner, Grover Chester 1919- *WhoAm 90*
Heffner, H. Michael *ODwPR 91*
Heffner, Laurie J. *ODwPR 91*
Heffner, Leland Grant *BiDrAPA 89*
Heffner, Phyllis Jean 1958- *BiDrAPA 89, WhoEmL 91*
Heffner, Ralph H. 1938- *WhoAm 90*
Heffner, Richard Douglas 1925- *WhoAm 90*
Heffner, Timothy Douglas 1949- *St&PR 91*
Heffner, William Joseph 1928- *St&PR 91*
Heffron, Howard A. 1927- *WhoAm 90*
Heffron, Jonathon Kenneth 1952- *St&PR 91*
Heffron, Robert Norman 1935- *St&PR 91*
Heffron, William M *BiDrAPA 89*
Hefler, Herbert H. 1923- *St&PR 91*
Hefley, Joel M. *WhoAm 90*
Heflin, E. Neil 1951- *WhoSSW 91*
Heflin, Howell Thomas 1921- *NewYTBS 90, WhoAm 90, WhoSSW 91, WhoWor 91*
Heflin, Jett Christopher 1959- *WhoSSW 91*
Heflin, Martin Ganier 1932- *WhoAm 90*
Heflin, Tom Pat 1934- *WhoAmA 91*
Heflin, Van 1910-1971 *WorAlBi*
Hefner, Christie *BioIn 16*
Hefner, Christie 1952- *St&PR 91*
Hefner, Christie Ann 1952- *WhoAm 90, WhoAmW 91*
Hefner, Christine Ann 1952- *ConAmBL*
Hefner, Donald Bryan 1931- *St&PR 91, WhoAm 90*
Hefner, Harry Simon 1911- *WhoAmA 91*
Hefner, Hugh *BioIn 16*
Hefner, Hugh 1926- *WorAlBi*
Hefner, Hugh M. 1926- *St&PR 91*
Hefner, Hugh Marston 1926- *ConAmBL, WhoAm 90*
Hefner, James A. *WhoAm 90, WhoSSW 91*
Hefner, Jerrie Lou 1957- *WhoAmW 91*

Hefner, Philip James 1932- *WhoAm 90*
Hefner, Raymond H., Jr. 1927- *St&PR 91, WhoSSW 91*
Hefner, Robert Alan 1929- *WhoAm 90*
Hefner, Robert Eugene 1927- *WhoSSW 91*
Hefner, Stanley Vas 1946- *WhoSSW 91*
Hefner, Terry Thomas 1949- *WhoEmL 91, WhoSSW 91*
Hefner, W. G. Bill 1930- *WhoAm 90, WhoSSW 91*
Heft, David Yule Marchbank 1943- *IntWWM 90*
Heft, James Lewis 1943- *WhoAm 90*
Hefter, Benjamin Richard 1916- *St&PR 91*
Hefter, Daniel S. 1956- *WhoEmL 91*
Hefter, Gilbert M 1932- *BiDrAPA 89*
Hefter, Harry Oscar 1929- *St&PR 91*
Hefter, Laurence Roy 1935- *WhoAm 90*
Hefter, Wilfred Roy 1937- *St&PR 91*
Hefti, Neal 1922- *OxCPMus*
Heftman, Kurt 1928- *WhoWor 91*
Hefton, John M. *BioIn 16*
Hegaard, Lars 1950- *IntWWM 90*
Hegamin, Lucille *BioIn 16*
Hegan, Alice Caldwell 1870-1942 *SmATA X*
Hegan, Jim 1920-1984 *Ballpl 90 [port]*
Hegan, Mike 1942- *Ballpl 90*
Hegan, Robert S. 1928- *St&PR 91*
Hegan, William P. 1926- *St&PR 91*
Hegarty, Angela Mary *BiDrAPA 89*
Hegarty, James Daniel 1962- *BiDrAPA 89*
Hegarty, James P. 1935- *St&PR 91*
Hegarty, Jo Ann M. 1945- *St&PR 91*
Hegarty, Judith I 1942- *BiDrAPA 89*
Hegarty, Mary Frances 1950- *WhoEmL 91, WhoWor 91*
Hegarty, Michael J. 1939- *St&PR 91*
Hegarty, Reginald Beaton 1906-1973 *AuBYP 90*
Hegarty, Thomas Joseph 1935- *WhoAm 90*
Hegarty, Timothy F., Jr. 1948- *St&PR 91*
Hegarty, William Edward 1926- *WhoAm 90*
Hegarty, William Kevin 1926- *WhoAm 90*
Hege, Darvin Lee 1947- *BiDrAPA 89*
Hegedus, L. Louis 1941- *WhoAm 90*
Hegedus, Olga 1920- *IntWWM 90*
Hegedusich, William 1960- *WhoEmL 91*
Hegel, Carolyn Marie 1940- *WhoAmW 91*
Hegel, Garrett R. 1950- *St&PR 91*
Hegel, Georg W. 1770-1831 *WorAlBi*
Hegel, Georg Wilhelm 1770-1831 *WrPh P*
Hegel, Paul Thomas 1947- *St&PR 91*
Hegelmann, Julius 1921- *WhoAm 90*
Hegeman, Irene Marion *BiDrAPA 89*
Hegeman, James Alan 1943- *WhoE 91, WhoWor 91*
Hegenderfer, Jonita Susan 1944- *WhoAm 90, WhoAmW 91*
Hegenderfer, Jonni *ODwPR 91*
Heger, Carl James 1937- *St&PR 91*
Heger, Frank J. 1927- *St&PR 91*
Heger, Herbert Krueger 1937- *WhoAm 90*
Heger, Kyle *ODwPR 91*
Heger, Robert 1886-1978 *PenDiMP*
Heger, Ulrich W. 1953- *St&PR 91*
Hegg, Arlene Patricia *BiDrAPA 89*
Hegg, George Lennart 1930- *St&PR 91*
Hegg, John Peter 1925- *St&PR 91*
Hegge, Per Egil 1940- *WhoWor 91*
Heggeland, Robert A. *St&PR 91*
Heggem, Mark Francis 1958- *WhoEmL 91*
Heggen, Almar 1933- *IntWWM 90*
Heggen, Arthur William 1945- *St&PR 91*
Heggestad, Robert E. 1939- *St&PR 91*
Heggie, Robah Gray, Jr. 1929- *St&PR 91*
Heggie, Robert James 1913- *WhoAm 90*
Heggie, Steven Wayne 1962- *WhoEmL 91*
Heggoy, Alf Andrew 1938-1987 *BioIn 16*
Heghinian, Elizabeth Alban Trumbower 1917- *WhoAmW 91, WhoE 91*
Hegi, Ursula Johanna 1946- *WhoWrEP 89*
Heginbotham, Erland Howard 1931- *WhoAm 90*
Heginbotham, Jan Sturza 1954- *WhoAmW 91*
Heginbotham, Stanley Jay 1938- *WhoE 91*
Hegji, Charles Edward 1945- *WhoSSW 91*
Hegler, Jean Anne 1959- *WhoEmL 91*
Heglin, Richard Theodore 1936- *St&PR 91*
Hegrenes, Jack Richard 1929- *WhoWor 91*
Hegstad, Roland Rex 1926- *WhoAm 90*
Hegstrom, Gary Clifford 1946- *WhoEmL 91*
Hegstrom, Robert Arthur 1942- *St&PR 91*
Hegstrom, William Jean 1923- *WhoSSW 91, WhoWor 91*
Hegyeli, Ruth Ingeborg Elisabeth J. 1931- *WhoWor 91, WhoWrEP 89*
Hegyi, Albert Paul 1944- *WhoAm 90, WhoE 91*
Hegyi, Erzsebet 1927- *IntWWM 90*
Hegyi, Julius 1923- *WhoAm 90*
Hegyvary, Csaba 1938- *BiDrAPA 89*
Heh, Chen-Wen Chris 1958- *BiDrAPA 89*
Hehir, Michael K. 1947- *St&PR 91*
Hehir, Michael Kevin 1947- *WhoAm 90*
Hehmeyer, Alexander 1910- *WhoAm 90*
Hehmeyer, Philip *BioIn 16*
Hehn, Barry 1949- *St&PR 91*
Hehn, Lorne Frederick 1936- *WhoAm 90*
Heibel, Anthony Edward 1956- *WhoE 91*
Heiber, Robert Jay 1951- *WhoEmL 91*
Heiberg, Elisabeth 1945- *WhoEmL 91*
Heiberg, Gunnar Edvard Rode 1857-1929 *DcScanL*
Heiberg, Harold Willard 1922- *IntWWM 90, WhoSSW 91*
Heiberg, Jens 1939- *WhoWor 91*
Heiberg, Johan Ludvig 1791-1860 *DcScanL*
Heiberg, Johanne Luise 1812-1890 *EncCoWW*
Heiberg, Robert Alan 1943- *WhoAm 90*
Heichele, Hildegard 1948- *IntWWM 90*
Heid, Bill *BioIn 16*
Heid, Konrad *St&PR 91*
Heid, Markham Alexander 1949- *St&PR 91*
Heidbreder, Warren W. 1946- *St&PR 91*
Heidbrink, Virgil Eugene 1925- *WhoSSW 91*
Heide, Christopher 1951- *OxCCanT*
Heide, Florence Parry 1919- *AuBYP 90, WhoWrEP 89*
Heidebrecht, Arthur C. *WhoAm 90*
Heidebrecht, John Stanley 1938- *St&PR 91*
Heidebrecht, Norman 1938- *St&PR 91*
Heidecker, Stephen C. 1942- *St&PR 91*
Heidegger, Martin 1889-1976 *BioIn 16, MajTwCW, WorAlBi, WrPh P*
Heidel, Frederick 1915- *WhoAmA 91*
Heidel, Stephen Hunt *BiDrAPA 89*
Heidelberg, Helen Susan Hatvani 1957- *WhoAmW 91, WhoEmL 91*
Heidelberg, Stephanie M 1944- *BiDrAPA 89*
Heidelberger, Cheryl E *BiDrAPA 89*
Heidelberger, Kathleen Patricia 1939- *WhoAm 90*
Heidelberger, Michael 1888- *BioIn 16, WhoAm 90*
Heidelberger, Michael 1947- *ConAu 130*
Heideloff, William R. 1940- *St&PR 91*
Heideman, Richard Dennis 1947- *WhoAm 90, WhoEmL 91, WhoWor 91*
Heideman, Richard Oliver 1948- *St&PR 91*
Heidemann, Else Gertrud 1947- *WhoWor 91*
Heidemann, Jack 1949- *Ballpl 90*
Heidemann, Marilyn Cummins 1959- *ODwPR 91*
Heidemann, Robert Albert 1936- *WhoAm 90*
Heiden, Bernhard 1910- *IntWWM 90*
Heiden, Charles Kenneth 1925- *WhoAm 90*
Heiden, Eric 1958- *WorAlBi*
Heiden, Jeri McManus 1959- *WhoEmL 91*
Heiden, William Mark 1952- *WhoEmL 91*
Heidenheim, Roger Stewart 1909- *WhoAm 90*
Heidenheimer, Arnold Joseph 1929- *WhoWor 91*
Heidenreich, Douglas Robert 1932- *WhoAm 90*
Heidenreich, James R. *St&PR 91*
Heidenstam, Carl Gustaf Verner von 1859-1940 *DcScanL*
Heidenstam, Verner Von 1859-1940 *WorAlBi*
Heider, David Arthur 1941- *St&PR 91*
Heider, Fritz 1868- *PenDiDA 89*
Heider, Fritz 1896-1988 *BioIn 16*
Heider, Hans 1867-1952 *PenDiDA 89*
Heider, Jon V. 1934- *St&PR 91*
Heider, Jon Vinton 1934- *WhoAm 90*
Heider, Karl G 1935- *ConAu 132*
Heider, Karl Gustav 1935- *WhoAm 90*
Heider, Katherine Trapp 1956- *WhoEmL 91*
Heider, Maximilian von 1839- *PenDiDA 89*
Heider, Rudolph 1870- *PenDiDA 89*
Heider, Tony Karl 1948- *WhoEmL 91*
Heider, Wally *BioIn 16*
Heiderstadt, Dorothy 1907- *AuBYP 90*
Heidig, Elizabeth Anne 1959- *WhoEmL 91*
Heidingsfield, Myron S 1914-1969 *ConAu 31NR*
Heidkamp, Patricia Jean 1951- *WhoEmL 91*
Heidkamp, Walter Gerald 1936- *St&PR 91*
Heidke, Ronald Lawrence 1937- *WhoAm 90*
Heidmann, Jean 1923- *ConAu 130*
Heidorn, Fred Robert 1941- *St&PR 91*
Heidrich, Arthur G., Jr. 1920- *St&PR 91*
Heidrich, James K., Jr. 1944- *St&PR 91*
Heidrick, Emmet 1876-1916 *Ballpl 90*
Heidrick, Gardner W. 1911- *St&PR 91*
Heidrick, Gardner Wilson 1911- *WhoAm 90*
Heidrick, Robert Lindsay 1941- *WhoAm 90*
Heidrick, Virginia Louise 1951- *WhoWrEP 89*
Heidt, Carl Elmer 1928- *WhoE 91*
Heidt, Herbert Francis 1915- *WhoAm 90*
Heidt, James Robert 1951- *WhoEmL 91*
Heidt, John Harry 1939- *WhoE 91*
Heidt, John M. 1931- *St&PR 91*
Heidtman, Martin Carl 1924- *St&PR 91*
Heidweiller, Henricus A. F. 1929-1989 *BioIn 16*
Heiens, Richard Allen 1940- *WhoSSW 91*
Heier, David Scott 1953- *WhoEmL 91*
Heier, Thomas Eugene 1948- *St&PR 91*
Heiferman, Marvin 1948- *BioIn 16, WhoAmA 91*
Heifetz, Alan William 1943- *WhoAm 90*
Heifetz, Benar *PenDiMP*
Heifetz, Daniel 1948- *IntWWM 90*
Heifetz, Jascha 1901-1987 *BioIn 16, PenDiMP, WorAlBi*
Heifetz, Paul 1927- *St&PR 91*
Heifetz, Ronald *BioIn 16*
Heifetz, Sonia 1929- *WhoAmW 91*
Heifetz, Susan 1950- *WhoEmL 91*
Heiges, Donald Russel 1910-1990 *WhoAm 90*
Heiges, Jesse Gibson 1914- *WhoAm 90*
Heigham, James Crichton 1930- *WhoAm 90*
Height, Dorothy Ephrates 1950- *WhoAmW 91*
Heighton, Gladys Ehrenreich 1932- *WhoAmW 91*
Heighway, James Edward 1946- *St&PR 91, WhoEmL 91*
Heigl, James John, Jr. 1940- *St&PR 91, WhoSSW 91*
Heijmen, Ton Cornelis Maria 1944- *St&PR 91*
Heijn, Cornelis, Jr. *BiDrAPA 89*
Heike Clan *EncJap*
Heikel, Karin Alice *DcScanL*
Heiken, Jay Paul 1952- *WhoEmL 91*
Heikensten, Lars Johan 1950- *WhoWor 91*
Heiker, Vince E. 1942- *St&PR 91*
Heikkila, Antti Yrjana 1946- *WhoWor 91*
Heikkila, Simo 1943- *ConDes 90*
Heikkinen, Dale Wayne 1944- *St&PR 91*
Heikoff, Joseph Meyer 1917- *WhoAm 90*
Heil, Jeffrey E. 1953- *St&PR 91*
Heil, Julius Peter 1876-1949 *EncABHB 5*
Heil, Karl Wayne 1947- *WhoEmL 91*
Heil, Mark S. 1961- *St&PR 91*
Heil, Paul Samuel 1947- *WhoE 91, WhoEmL 91*
Heil, Peter Friedrich 1949- *WhoWor 91*
Heil, Roland Lee 1933- *St&PR 91*
Heil, Russell Howard *BioIn 16*
Heil, Russell Howard 1942- *St&PR 91*
Heil, Wolfgang Heinrich 1940- *WhoSSW 91*
Heiland, Juanita Marie 1942- *WhoHisp 91*
Heilberg, David Leonard 1953- *WhoEmL 91*
Heilberg, Robert *WhoE 91*
Heilborn, George H. 1935- *St&PR 91*
Heilbron, David Michael 1936- *WhoAm 90*
Heilbron, Gail 1951- *WhoEmL 91*
Heilbron, Ian Morris 1886-1959 *DcScB S2*
Heilbron, John L. 1934- *WhoAm 90*
Heilbron, Louis Henry 1907- *WhoAm 90*
Heilbron, Susan M. 1945- *WhoAm 90, WhoAmW 91, WhoE 91, WhoWor 91*
Heilbron, Valerie Johnson 1948- *IntWWM 90*
Heilbroner, Joan 1922- *SmATA 63*
Heilbroner, Joan Knapp 1922- *AuBYP 90*
Heilbroner, Robert L. 1919- *WhoAm 90, WorAu 1980 [port]*
Heilbronn, Hans Arnold 1908-1975 *DcScB S2*
Heilbronn, W. Michael 1946- *St&PR 91*
Heilbronner, Edgar 1921- *WhoWor 91*
Heilbronner, Hans 1926- *WhoE 91*
Heilbrun, Carolyn 1926- *FemiCLE*
Heilbrun, Carolyn G. *TwCCr&M 91*
Heilbrun, Carolyn G. 1926- *BioIn 16*
Heilbrun, Carolyn Gold 1926- *WhoAm 90, WhoAmW 91, WhoWrEP 89*
Heilbrun, James 1924- *WhoAm 90*
Heilbrun, Lois Hussey *BioIn 16*
Heilbrunn, Jeffrey 1950- *WhoAm 90, WhoWor 91*
Heilbrunn, Paul *BioIn 16*
Heilbrunn, Richard *BioIn 16*
Heiler, Alfred G. 1938- *St&PR 91*
Heiles, Carl Eugene 1939- *WhoAm 90*
Heilferty, Henry W. 1930- *St&PR 91*
Heilig, Margaret Cramer 1914- *WhoAmW 91, WhoWor 91*
Heilig, Paul T. *ODwPR 91*
Heilig, William Wright 1940- *WhoAm 90*
Heiligenstein, Christian E. 1929- *WhoWor 91*
Heiligenstein, Eric 1955- *BiDrAPA 89*
Heiligenstein, John Harrison 1945- *BiDrAPA 89*
Heiliger, Wilbur David 1946- *St&PR 91*
Heiligman, Richard 1928- *St&PR 91*
Heiller, Anton 1923-1979 *PenDiMP*
Heilman, Carl Edwin 1911- *WhoAm 90, WhoE 91, WhoWor 91*
Heilman, Dan 1924-1965 *EncACom*
Heilman, Earl Bruce 1926- *WhoAm 90*
Heilman, Joan Rattner *BioIn 16, WhoWrEP 89*
Heilman, M. Grant 1919- *WhoWrEP 89*
Heilman, Pamela Davis 1948- *WhoEmL 91*
Heilman, Richard Dean 1937- *WhoSSW 91*
Heilman, Robert Bechtold 1906- *WhoAm 90*
Heilman, Robert Leo 1952- *WhoWrEP 89*
Heilman, Roger Harvey 1943- *BiDrAPA 89*
Heilmann, Christian Flemming 1936- *WhoE 91*
Heilmann, Harry 1894-1951 *Ballpl 90 [port]*
Heilmann, Leroy W. 1932- *St&PR 91*
Heilmeier, George Harry 1936- *St&PR 91, WhoAm 90*
Heilner, David P., Jr. *BiDrAPA 89*
Heilner, Irwin 1908- *IntWWM 90*
Heiloms, May *WhoAm 90, WhoAmA 91*
Heilpern, Philip S 1932- *BiDrAPA 89*
Heilprin, Laurence Bedford 1906- *WhoAm 90*
Heilprin, Mary Ann Hardy 1948- *WhoEmL 91*
Heilshorn, John William 1926- *WhoAm 90*
Heilweil, Marc Stephen 1945- *WhoSSW 91*
Heim, Bruce Jay *BioIn 16, NewYTBS 90*
Heim, Bruce Kennedy 1941- *WhoE 91*
Heim, Bruno Bernard 1911- *WhoWor 91*
Heim, Carol Elizabeth 1955- *WhoE 91*
Heim, Donald John 1927- *St&PR 91, WhoAm 90*
Heim, Elsbeth 1917- *IntWWM 90*
Heim, Frederic A. 1926- *St&PR 91*
Heim, John W. 1902-1988 *BioIn 16*
Heim, Kathleen McEntee *WhoAm 90*
Heim, Kathryn Marie 1952- *WhoAmW 91*
Heim, Leo Edward 1913- *WhoAm 90*
Heim, Michael Ronald 1947- *WhoEmL 91*
Heim, Norman Michael 1929- *IntWWM 90*
Heim, Oliver M. *St&PR 91*
Heim, Paul 1939- *BiDrAPA 89*
Heim, Ray Vincent 1920- *WhoSSW 91*
Heim, Roger 1900- *EncO&P 3*
Heim, Ross Cornell 1947- *WhoEmL 91*
Heim, Tonya Sue 1948- *WhoAmW 91*
Heimach, Fred 1901-1973 *Ballpl 90*
Heiman, David Gilbert 1945- *WhoAm 90*
Heiman, Elliott M 1938- *BiDrAPA 89*
Heiman, Gary L. 1951- *St&PR 91*
Heiman, Grover George, Jr. 1920- *WhoAm 90*
Heiman, Jarvin R 1926- *BiDrAPA 89*
Heiman, John Charles 1947- *WhoSSW 91*
Heiman, Mark J. 1954- *St&PR 91*
Heiman, Marvin Stewart 1945- *WhoEmL 91*
Heiman, Maxwell 1932- *WhoAm 90*
Heiman, Michael F 1945- *BiDrAPA 89*
Heiman, Paul L. 1926- *St&PR 91*
Heiman, Peter Lynd 1942- *BiDrAPA 89, WhoE 91*
Heimann, Edward A. 1937- *St&PR 91*
Heimann, Gail *ODwPR 91*
Heimann, Janet Barbara 1931- *WhoAmW 91*
Heimann, John G. *BioIn 16*
Heimann, John Gaines 1929- *WhoAm 90, WhoE 91*
Heimann, Joshua Gaines 1959- *WhoEmL 91*
Heimann, Robert Alvin 1942- *St&PR 91*
Heimann, Robert Karl *NewYTBS 90 [port]*
Heimann, Robert Karl 1918-1990 *BioIn 16, ConAu 130*
Heimann, Sandra Anne 1943- *St&PR 91*
Heimann, William Emil 1928- *WhoAm 90*
Heimarck, Gregory J 1935- *BiDrAPA 89*
Heimbach, David Tucker 1950- *WhoEmL 91*
Heimbach, Sidney B 1929- *BiDrAPA 89*
Heimbaugh, James Ross 1918- *WhoAm 90*
Heimberg, Alice Rose 1956- *BiDrAPA 89*
Heimberg, Carolyn 1959- *BiDrAPA 89, WhoEmL 91*
Heimberg, Eugene B. 1933- *St&PR 91*
Heimberg, Marilyn Markham *ConAu 31NR*
Heimberg, Murray 1925- *WhoAm 90, WhoSSW 91*
Heimbinder, Isaac 1943- *St&PR 91, WhoAm 90, WhoSSW 91*
Heimbold, Charles Andreas, Jr. 1933- *WhoAm 90*

Heimbold, Margaret Byrne 1946- *WhoAmW 91, WhoWor 91*
Heimburger, Donald James 1947- *WhoWrEP 89*
Heimburger, Elizabeth M 1932- *BiDrAPA 89*
Heimdal, Georg 1943- *WhoAmA 91*
Heimerl, Richard Charles 1943- *St&PR 91*
Heimers, Patricia A. 1959- *ODwPR 91*
Heimert, Alan Edward 1928- *WhoAm 90*
Heimes, Joseph C. 1928- *St&PR 91*
Heimlich, Barry N. 1941- *St&PR 91*
Heimlich, Ellen Kramer 1942- *WhoAmW 91*
Heimlich, Henry Jay 1920- *WhoAm 90*
Heimlich, Ralph Edward 1948- *WhoEmL 91*
Heimlich, Richard Allen 1932- *WhoAm 90*
Heimowitz, Daniel N. 1953- *St&PR 91*
Heimpel, Hermann 1901-1988 *AnObit 1988*
Heims, Steve J 1926- *ConAu 131*
Heims, Steve Paul *ConAu 131*
Heimsch, Charles 1914- *WhoAm 90*
Heimsch, Richard David 1953- *St&PR 91*
Heimsoeth, Hans-Jurgen 1953- *WhoWor 91*
Hein, August Henry 1931- *WhoE 91*
Hein, Cheryl 1945- *WhoSSW 91*
Hein, Christoph *BioIn 16*
Hein, David Leon 1939- *St&PR 91*
Hein, Edgar W 1954- *BiDrAPA 89*
Hein, Gerhardt A 1933- *BiDrAPA 89*
Hein, Glen Orville 1945- *St&PR 91*
Hein, John William 1920- *WhoAm 90*
Hein, Jurgen 1942- *WhoWor 91*
Hein, Leonard William 1916- *WhoAm 90*
Hein, Lucille Eleanor 1915- *AuBYP 90*
Hein, Margaret Allyce 1952- *St&PR 91*
Hein, Max 1943- *WhoAmA 91*
Hein, Peter Leo, Jr. 1930- *BiDrAPA 89*
Hein, Piet 1905- *DcScanL*
Hein, Pieter 1938- *ConDes 90*
Hein, Robert E. 1929- *St&PR 91*
Hein, Todd Jonathan 1960- *WhoEmL 91*
Hein, Walter C. 1930- *St&PR 91*
Heinbach, Eric Scott 1964- *WhoE 91*
Heinbecker, Peter Papin *BiDrAPA 89*
Heindel, Max 1865-1919 *EncO&P 3, NewAgE 90*
Heindel, Ned Duane 1937- *WhoAm 90*
Heindl, Clifford Joseph 1926- *WhoAm 90*
Heindl, Dennis Duane 1942- *WhoE 91*
Heindl, Phares Matthews 1949- *WhoEmL 91*
Heindl, Warren Anton 1922- *WhoAm 90*
Heine, Alan Louis 1946- *BiDrAPA 89*
Heine, Andrew N. 1928- *St&PR 91*
Heine, Edward J., Jr. 1925- *St&PR 91*
Heine, Edward Joseph, Jr. 1925- *WhoAm 90*
Heine, Frederick Ernest 1944- *St&PR 91*
Heine, Gunter Karl 1941- *WhoWor 91*
Heine, Harry 1928- *WhoAmA 91*
Heine, Heinrich 1797-1856 *BioIn 16, WorAlBi*
Heine, Helme *BioIn 16*
Heine, Leonard M., Jr. 1924- *WhoE 91, WhoWor 91*
Heine, Mary Elizabeth 1961- *WhoAmW 91*
Heine, Peter Johannes 1955- *WhoWor 91*
Heine, Raymond Arnold Carl 1922- *WhoAm 90*
Heine, Richard Walter 1918- *WhoAm 90*
Heine, Spencer H. 1942- *WhoAm 90*
Heine, Ursula Ingrid 1926- *WhoAmW 91*
Heine, Willi Otto Paul 1930- *WhoWor 91*
Heine-Baux, Manfred 1940- *WhoAmA 91*
Heinecke, Walter Herman 1926- *St&PR 91*
Heinecken, Robert Friedli 1931- *WhoAm 90, WhoAmA 91*
Heineken, Alfred Henry 1923- *WhoWor 91*
Heineman, Andrew David 1928- *WhoAm 90*
Heineman, Ben Walter 1914- *WhoAm 90*
Heineman, Benjamin W., Jr. 1944- *St&PR 91*
Heineman, Benjamin Walter, Jr. 1944- *WhoAm 90*
Heineman, Fred K. *WhoSSW 91*
Heineman, Harry Francis 1920- *St&PR 91*
Heineman, Heinz 1913- *WhoAm 90*
Heineman, Herbert A., Jr. 1932- *St&PR 91*
Heineman, Jacklyn Kay 1939- *WhoWor 91*
Heineman, Natalie *WhoAm 90*
Heineman, Paul Lowe 1924- *WhoAm 90*
Heineman, Ronald E. 1957- *St&PR 91*
Heineman, William Arthur 1924- *WhoAm 90*
Heineman Ransom, Karen Benvin 1953- *WhoAmW 91*
Heinemann, Edward H. 1908- *WhoAm 90*
Heinemann, Katherine 1918- *WhoAmW 91*
Heinemann, Kirsten S. 1959- *St&PR 91*
Heinemann, Larry 1944- *ConAu 31NR*
Heinemann, Peter 1931- *WhoAmA 91, WhoE 91*
Heinen, Gloria Jean 1942- *WhoAmW 91*
Heinen, James Albin 1943- *WhoAm 90*
Heinen, Paul A. 1930- *St&PR 91*
Heinen, Paul Abelardo 1930- *WhoAm 90*
Heinen, Peter H. 1944- *St&PR 91*
Heiner, Clyde Mont 1938- *St&PR 91, WhoAm 90*
Heiner, Dennis Grant 1943- *St&PR 91, WhoAm 90*
Heiner, Earl W. 1935- *St&PR 91*
Heiner, George M. 1922- *St&PR 91*
Heiner, Jay R 1932- *BiDrAPA 89*
Heiner, Lawrence E. 1938- *St&PR 91*
Heiner, Lawrence Elden 1938- *WhoAm 90*
Heiner, Robert T. 1925- *WhoAm 90*
Heines, Danny *NewAgMG*
Heines, Jack Jay 1935- *St&PR 91*
Heines, Molly Kathleen 1953- *WhoEmL 91*
Heinesen, William 1900- *DcScanL*
Heiney, J.W. 1913- *St&PR 91*
Heiney, John Weitzel 1913- *WhoAm 90*
Heiney, Sue Porter 1950- *WhoEmL 91*
Heinhold, Josef Martin 1912- *WhoWor 91*
Heinichen, Jeffrey Kirk 1952- *WhoEmL 91*
Heinicke, Janet L Hart *WhoAmA 91*
Heininen, Paavo 1938- *IntWWM 90*
Heininger, Erwin Carl 1921- *WhoAm 90*
Heininger, Peter *ODwPR 91*
Heininger, S. Allen 1925- *St&PR 91*
Heininger, Samuel Allen 1925- *WhoAm 90*
Heinio, Mikko 1948- *IntWWM 90*
Heinisch, James R. 1931- *St&PR 91*
Heinitz, Eva Maria 1907- *IntWWM 90*
Heink, Ernestine Schumann- 1861-1936 *BioIn 16*
Heinkel, Don 1959- *Ballpl 90*
Heinle, Robert Alan 1933- *WhoE 91, WhoWor 91*
Heinle, Robert G. 1946- *St&PR 91*
Heinlein, Robert 1907- *WorAlBi*
Heinlein, Robert 1907-1988 *AnObit 1988*
Heinlein, Robert A. 1907-1988 *BioIn 16, MajTwCW, RGTwCSF*
Heinlein, Robert Anson 1907-1988 *AuBYP 90*
Heinlein, Robert Anthony 1953- *WhoSSW 91*
Heinlen, Ronald Eugene 1937- *WhoAm 90*
Heino, Gregory Lee 1957- *WhoEmL 91*
Heino, Jukka Rafael 1930- *WhoWor 91*
Heinol, Dennis *St&PR 91*
Heinold, Rosemary Elizabeth 1948- *WhoEmL 91*
Heinonen, Keijo Gunnar 1923- *WhoWor 91*
Heinonen, Olavi Ensio 1938- *WhoWor 91*
Heinonen, Reijo Jorma 1939- *WhoWor 91*
Heinrich, Adel Verna 1926- *IntWWM 90*
Heinrich, Bernd 1940- *WhoAm 90*
Heinrich, Bonnie *WhoAmW 91*
Heinrich, Donna Trauscht 1960- *WhoAmW 91*
Heinrich, Dori 1958- *BiDrAPA 89*
Heinrich, Dorothea Josephine 1917- *WhoAmW 91*
Heinrich, Edwin C. 1925- *St&PR 91*
Heinrich, Elmer G. 1934- *WhoSSW 91*
Heinrich, Gerald 1950- *St&PR 91*
Heinrich, Helen Herron 1936- *WhoE 91*
Heinrich, John E. 1944- *St&PR 91*
Heinrich, Peggy 1929- *WhoWrEP 89*
Heinrich, Raymond Lawrence 1911- *WhoSSW 91*
Heinrich, Richard L 1944- *BiDrAPA 89*
Heinrich, Ross Raymond 1915- *WhoAm 90*
Heinrich, Siegfried 1935- *IntWWM 90*
Heinrichs, Daniel John 1929- *BiDrAPA 89*
Heinrichs, Douglas W *BiDrAPA 89*
Heinrichs, Mary Ann 1930- *WhoAmW 91*
Heinrichs, William LeRoy 1932- *WhoAm 90*
Heinrici, Johann Martin 1711-1786 *PenDiDA 89*
Heinroth, Oskar August 1871-1945 *DcScB S2*
Heins, Albert Edward 1912- *WhoAm 90*
Heins, Arnold Hermann 1928- *WhoWor 91*
Heins, Arthur James 1931- *WhoAm 90*
Heins, Ernst Lodewijk 1937- *IntWWM 90*
Heins, Ethel L. 1918- *WhoAm 90*
Heins, Gordon Lawrence 1929- *St&PR 91*
Heins, James Edward 1930- *St&PR 91*
Heins, Marilyn 1930- *WhoAm 90*
Heins, Maurice Haskell 1915- *WhoEmL 91*
Heins, Paul N. 1919- *St&PR 91*
Heins, Robert Louis 1924- *BiDrAPA 89*
Heinse, Wilhelm 1746-1803 *DcLB 94 [port]*
Heinselman, James L. 1935- *WhoAm 90*
Heinselman, Miron Lee 1920- *WhoAm 90*
Heinsohn, Carmel Reid *BiDrAPA 89*
Heinsohn, Tommy 1934- *BioIn 16*
Heinsohn, Walter L. 1954- *WhoEmL 91*
Heinssen, Robert Kenneth 1957- *WhoE 91*
Heintel, Carl C., Jr. 1944- *St&PR 91*
Heintschel, Thomas William 1952- *WhoEmL 91*
Heintz, Ann *BioIn 16*
Heintz, Carolinea Cabaniss 1920- *WhoAmW 91*
Heintz, Edward Allein 1931- *WhoE 91*
Heintz, Gerald Christopher 1961- *BiDrAPA 89*
Heintz, Jack 1907- *WhoAm 90*
Heintz, Mary Ann 1956- *WhoAmW 91*
Heintz, Norman V *BiDrAPA 89*
Heintz, Paul Norman 1958- *St&PR 91*
Heintz, Roger Lewis 1937- *WhoAm 90*
Heintz, Ronald Terrance *BiDrAPA 89*
Heintz-Stritzinger, Jennifer Anne 1963- *WhoEmL 91*
Heintze, Johann Georg 1707?- *PenDiDA 89*
Heintze, Juliette C. 1947- *St&PR 91*
Heintzelman, Arthur W 1890-1965 *WhoAmA 91N*
Heintzelman, Carol Ann 1942- *WhoAmW 91*
Heintzelman, Donald Shaffer 1938- *WhoE 91*
Heintzelman, Ken 1915- *Ballpl 90*
Heintzleman, Mary Strickler 1921- *WhoAmW 91*
Heintzman, Theodor August 1817-1899 *DcCanB 12*
Heinz, Brian James 1946- *WhoWrEP 89*
Heinz, Don J. 1931- *WhoAm 90*
Heinz, Donald James 1949- *WhoEmL 91*
Heinz, Elise Brookfield 1935- *WhoAm 90*
Heinz, Hanspeter 1939- *WhoWor 91*
Heinz, Henry John 1844-1919 *WorAlBi*
Heinz, Henry John 1908-1987 *BioIn 16*
Heinz, Henry John, II 1908-1987 *WorAlBi*
Heinz, Henry John, III 1938- *WhoAm 90, WhoE 91, WhoWor 91*
Heinz, James Joseph 1941- *St&PR 91*
Heinz, John F. *ODwPR 91*
Heinz, John Peter 1936- *WhoAm 90*
Heinz, Joy Marie 1964- *WhoAmW 91*
Heinz, Manfred Raimund 1947- *WhoWor 91*
Heinz, Susan *WhoAmA 91*
Heinz, Susan Louise *WhoE 91*
Heinz, Walter Ernst Edward 1920- *WhoAm 90*
Heinz, Walter Richard 1939- *WhoWor 91*
Heinze, Bernard 1894-1982 *PenDiMP*
Heinze, Frank R. *BioIn 16*
Heinze, Gerhard *BiDrAPA 89*
Heinze, Harold C. 1942- *WhoAm 90*
Heinze, Karl Godfried 1929- *St&PR 91*
Heinze, Linda Holli 1939- *WhoAmW 91, WhoWor 91*
Heinze, Peter R. 1942- *St&PR 91, WhoE 91*
Heinzelman, Fred 1914- *St&PR 91*
Heinzen, Bernard George 1930- *WhoE 91, WhoWor 91*
Heinzerling, Larry Edward 1945- *WhoAm 90, WhoEmL 91*
Heinzman, Gail E.D. 1955- *St&PR 91*
Heinzman, Patricia Ann 1957- *WhoAmW 91*
Heiple, James Dee 1933- *WhoAm 90*
Heiple, Loren Ray 1918- *WhoAm 90*
Heiple, Robert Jay 1947- *St&PR 91*
Heipp, Richard Christian 1952- *WhoAmA 91*
Heir, Douglas 1960- *WhoWor 91*
Heir, Kal M. 1919- *WhoSSW 91*
Heiremans, Luis Alberto *BioIn 16*
Heires, John Hopkins 1918-1988 *BioIn 16*
Heirman, Aime Gustaaf 1937- *WhoWor 91*
Heirman, Donald N. 1940- *WhoAm 90, WhoWor 91*
Heironimus, Robert A. 1922- *St&PR 91*
Heirs, Ben J. *BioIn 16*
Heisch, James A. 1943- *St&PR 91*
Heise, Bob 1947- *Ballpl 90*
Heise, George Armstrong 1924- *WhoAm 90*
Heise, John Frederick 1926- *St&PR 91*
Heise, John I. 1952- *WhoEmL 91*
Heise, Keith A. 1955- *St&PR 91*
Heise, Marilyn 1935- *ODwPR 91*
Heise, Marilyn Beardsley 1935- *WhoAmW 91*
Heise, Myron Robert 1934- *WhoAmA 91, WhoE 91*
Heisel, J Stephen 1947- *BiDrAPA 89*
Heisel, Ralph Arthur 1935- *WhoE 91, WhoWor 91*
Heisenberg, Werner Karl 1901-1976 *DcScB S2, WorAlBi*
Heiser, Arnold Melvin 1933- *WhoAm 90*
Heiser, Charles Bixler, Jr. 1920- *WhoAm 90*
Heiser, James S. 1956- *St&PR 91*
Heiser, John David 1929- *St&PR 91*
Heiser, John Edward 1931- *St&PR 91*
Heiser, Joseph Miller, Jr. 1914- *WhoAm 90*
Heiser, Rolland Valentine 1925- *WhoSSW 91, WhoWor 91*
Heiser, Scott Thomas 1949- *WhoAmA 91*
Heiser, T. Walter 1955- *WhoEmL 91*
Heiserer, Albert, Jr. 1937- *WhoE 91*
Heiserman, Hewitt 1930- *St&PR 91*
Heisey, W. Lawrence 1930- *WhoAm 90*
Heisey, Walter F. 1919- *St&PR 91*
Heisig, Kenneth Joseph 1950- *WhoEmL 91*
Heisinger, Harold Brent 1937- *IntWWM 90*
Heisinger, James Gordon, Jr. 1952- *WhoEmL 91*
Heiskanen, Weikko Aleksanteri 1895?-1971 *DcScB S2*
Heiskell, Diana *WhoAmA 91*
Heiskell, Diana 1910- *WhoE 91*
Heiskell, John Netherland 1872-1972 *BioIn 16*
Heiskell, William 1788-1871 *AmLegL*
Heisler, Albert 1924- *St&PR 91*
Heisler, Clifford Budd 1918- *WhoAm 90*
Heisler, Elwood Douglas 1935- *WhoWor 91*
Heisler, Faye *BiDrAPA 89*
Heisler, Friedy B *BiDrAPA 89*
Heisler, James T. 1946- *St&PR 91*
Heisler, Jeanne Michelle 1954- *WhoAmW 91*
Heisler, John Charles 1960- *WhoEmL 91*
Heisler, John Columbus 1926- *WhoAm 90*
Heisler, Norman Tony 1955- *BiDrAPA 89*
Heisler, Philip S. 1915-1988 *BioIn 16*
Heisler, Quentin George, Jr. 1943- *WhoAm 90*
Heisler, Robert B., Jr. 1948- *St&PR 91*
Heisler, Sidney Earl *BiDrAPA 89*
Heisler, Stanley Dean 1946- *WhoAm 90, WhoE 91, WhoWor 91*
Heisler, Stephen 1942- *BiDrAPA 89*
Heisley, Judith F. 1966- *ODwPR 91*
Heismeyer, Fred Charles, III 1955- *WhoSSW 91*
Heisner, Laura Jean 1958- *WhoEmL 91*
Heiss, Arthur Henry 1944- *WhoE 91*
Heiss, John 1938- *IntWWM 90*
Heiss, Michael Harris 1949- *WhoEmL 91*
Heiss, Paul Kenneth 1948- *St&PR 91*
Heiss, Richard Walter 1930- *St&PR 91, WhoAm 90*
Heiss, Wolf-Dieter 1939- *WhoWor 91*
Heissenbuttel, Walter John 1947- *St&PR 91*
Heisserman, Theresa Ann 1951- *WhoAmW 91*
Heist, Charles Henry 1950- *St&PR 91*
Heist, L.C. 1931- *St&PR 91*
Heist, Lewis Clark 1931- *WhoAm 90, WhoE 91*
Heistand, Coleen Renee 1948- *WhoE 91*
Heistand, Donald Lee 1935- *St&PR 91*
Heistand, Joseph Thomas 1924- *WhoAm 90*
Heistand, Paul Kenneth 1949- *WhoSSW 91*
Heistein, Josef 1925- *WhoWor 91*
Heisten, Gaellan M *BiDrAPA 89*
Heister, Robert John, Jr. 1953- *WhoE 91*
Heit, Daniel S. 1947- *WhoEmL 91*
Heit, Ivan 1946- *WhoEmL 91, WhoSSW 91*
Heit, James Richard 1961- *WhoEmL 91*
Heit, Robert *AuBYP 90*
Heit, Steven Robert 1943- *WhoAmA 91*
Heithaus, Walter D. 1934- *ODwPR 91*
Heithoff, Ronald Elmer 1936- *St&PR 91*
Heiting, Thomas A. 1941- *St&PR 91*
Heitkamp, Marie 1924- *WhoAmW 91*
Heitkamp, Mary Kathryn 1955- *WhoAmW 91*
Heitkamper, Peter 1943- *WhoWor 91*
Heitler, George 1915- *WhoAm 90*
Heitler, Walter Heinrich 1904-1981 *DcNaB 1981*
Heitman, Frederick C. 1936- *St&PR 91*
Heitman, Hubert, Jr. 1917- *WhoAm 90*
Heitman, Richard Edgar 1930- *St&PR 91*
Heitman, Warren P. 1920- *St&PR 91*
Heitmann, Adair Wilson 1953- *WhoEmL 91*
Heitmann, Fred W., Jr. 1918- *St&PR 91*
Heitmann, George Joseph 1933- *WhoAm 90*
Heitmann, John A. 1948- *WhoEmL 91*
Heitmann, Klaus 1930- *WhoWor 91*
Heitner, Kenneth Howard 1948- *WhoEmL 91*
Heitner, Mark Andrew 1955- *BiDrAPA 89*
Heitner, Paul *BioIn 16*
Heitner, Robert Richard 1920- *WhoAm 90*
Heitsch, Ernst 1928- *WhoWor 91*
Heitz, Glenn Edward 1924- *WhoAm 90*
Heitz, John Gregory 1943- *St&PR 91*
Heitz, Raymond J. 1932- *St&PR 91*
Heitz, Walter 1932- *WhoWor 91*
Heitzer, Donald Alfred 1925- *St&PR 91*

Heitzman, George Richard *BiDrAPA 89*
Heitzman, Gregory Paul 1959- *WhoEmL 91*
Heitzman, Robert E. 1927- *St&PR 91*
Heitzman, Robert Edward 1927- *WhoAm 90*
Heitzman, William Ray 1948- *WhoWrEP 89*
Heivilin, Fred G. 1941- *St&PR 91*
Heizer, Edgar Francis, Jr. 1929- *WhoAm 90, WhoWor 91*
Heizer, Ida Ann 1919- *WhoAmW 91*
Hejazi, Masoud S 1952- *BiDrAPA 89*
Hejduk, John 1929- *BioIn 16*
Hejduk, John Quentin 1929- *WhoAm 90*
Hejinian, John Paull 1941- *BiDrAPA 89*
Hejl, James George 1939- *WhoSSW 91*
Hejtmancik, Milton Rudolph 1919- *WhoSSW 91*
Hejtmanek, Danton Charles 1951- *WhoEmL 91, WhoWor 91*
Helaakoski, Aaro *DcScanL*
Helander, Bruce Paul 1947- *WhoAmA 91, WhoSSW 91*
Helander, Robert Charles 1932- *WhoAm 90*
Helander, Robert E. 1930- *St&PR 91*
Helber, Larry Charles 1947- *St&PR 91*
Helberg, Barbara Anne 1946- *WhoWrEP 89*
Helberg, Shirley Adelaide Holden *WhoAmW 91*
Helbert, Clifford L. 1920- *WhoAm 90*
Helbich, Wolfgang Johannes 1935- *WhoWor 91*
Helbig, James R. *ODwPR 91*
Helbing, Emil G. 1926- *St&PR 91*
Helbling, Paul Arthur 1953- *St&PR 91*
Helbling, Robert Eugene 1923- *WhoAm 90*
Helbronner, Jacques 1873-1943 *BioIn 16*
Helburn, Isadore B. 1938- *WhoAm 90*
Helburn, Nicholas 1918- *WhoAm 90*
Helburn, Stephen 1946- *St&PR 91*
Helburn, Theresa 1887-1959 *BioIn 16, NotWoAT*
Helcher, Regina 1964- *IntWWM 90*
Helchis, Jacobus *PenDiDA 89*
Helck, Peter *BioIn 16*
Helck, Peter 1893-1988 *WhoAmA 91N*
Held, Al 1928- *BioIn 16, WhoAm 90, WhoAmA 91*
Held, Alan H. 1936- *St&PR 91*
Held, Alma M *WhoAmA 91N*
Held, Anna 1865?-1918 *BioIn 16, NotWoAT*
Held, Anna 1873-1918 *OxCPMus*
Held, Claude C., II 1943- *St&PR 91*
Held, John, Jr. 1889-1958 *EncACom, WhoAmA 91N*
Held, Jonathan, Jr 1947- *WhoAmA 91*
Held, Julius S 1905- *WhoAmA 91*
Held, K. Lars 1946- *St&PR 91*
Held, Lila M. 1925- *WhoAmW 91*
Held, Martin W 1947- *BiDrAPA 89*
Held, Matthew 1929- *St&PR 91*
Held, Peter *BioIn 16, MajTwCW, TwCCr&M 91*
Held, Peter Allen 1949- *WhoSSW 91*
Held, Philip 1920- *WhoAm 90, WhoAmA 91*
Held, Robert Paul 1939- *WhoE 91*
Held, Virginia 1929- *WhoAm 90*
Held, Walter George 1920- *WhoAm 90*
Held, Woodie 1932- *Ballpl 90*
Heldenbrand, Marilyn Louise 1939- *WhoAmW 91*
Heldenfels, Frederick William, Jr. 1911- *WhoAm 90*
Helder, Bruce Alan 1953- *WhoEmL 91*
Helder, David Ernest 1947- *WhoAmA 91*
Heldermon, Donna Kae 1951- *WhoEmL 91*
Helders, Han 1938- *St&PR 91*
Helding, Phillip G 1955- *BiDrAPA 89*
Heldman, Alan Wohl 1936- *WhoAm 90*
Heldman, Dennis R. 1938- *WhoAm 90*
Heldman, Louis Marc 1949- *WhoSSW 91*
Heldman, Patricia F *BiDrAPA 89*
Heldman, Thomas S. 1923- *St&PR 91*
Heldmann, Walter T. 1904-1990 *BioIn 16*
Heldreth, Joseph B. 1955- *St&PR 91*
Heldreth, Leonard Guy 1939- *WhoWrEP 89*
Heldrich, Eleanor Maar 1929- *WhoAmW 91*
Heldt, Carl Randall 1925- *WhoAmA 91*
Heldt, Sharon Dorothea 1957- *WhoEmL 91*
Heldt, W.D. 1936- *St&PR 91*
Helemish, Mohamed Abdelwahab 1936- *WhoWor 91*
Helena Lecapena *WomWR*
Helene, Claude Michel 1938- *WhoWor 91*
Helenek, Mary Jane 1960- *WhoEmL 91*
Helenius, Ester 1875-1955 *BiDWomA*
Helesfay, Andrea 1948- *IntWWM 90*
Helewicz, Joseph S. 1945- *ODwPR 91*
Helf, Gary L. 1946- *St&PR 91*
Helf, Judith 1951- *WhoAmW 91*
Helf, Marvin M. 1919- *St&PR 91*
Helf, Steven *St&PR 91*
Helfand, Arthur E. 1935- *WhoAm 90*
Helfand, David *BioIn 16*
Helfand, Eugene 1934- *WhoAm 90*
Helfant, Art 1898-1971 *EncACom*
Helfer, Al 1912-1975 *Ballpl 90*
Helfer, Herman Lawrence 1929- *WhoAm 90*
Helfer, Jeffrey Joseph 1943- *St&PR 91*
Helfer, John *BiDrAPA 89*
Helfer, Michael Stevens 1945- *WhoAm 90*
Helfer, Wayne C. 1941- *St&PR 91*
Helfert, David Low 1945- *WhoSSW 91*
Helfert, Erich Anton 1931- *WhoAm 90*
Helffer, Claude 1922- *IntWWM 90, PenDiMP*
Helfferich, Friedrich G. 1922- *WhoAm 90*
Helfgott, Daniel 1952- *WhoWrEP 89*
Helfgott, Roy B. 1925- *WhoAm 90, WhoE 91*
Helfing, Saul Herschel *BiDrAPA 89*
Helfinstein, Bert Ira 1933- *WhoAm 90*
Helfinstine, Kelly Ann 1957- *WhoAmW 91, WhoEmL 91*
Helfman, Barbara Brook 1941- *WhoAmW 91*
Helfman, Elizabeth 1911- *AuBYP 90*
Helfman, Harry 1910- *AuBYP 90*
Helfman, Joel 1929- *St&PR 91*
Helfond, Riva *WhoAmA 91*
Helford, Irwin 1934- *St&PR 91*
Helford, Paul Quinn 1947- *WhoEmL 91*
Helforth, John *MajTwCW*
Helfrecht, Donald J. 1922- *St&PR 91*
Helfrecht, Donald John 1922- *WhoAm 90*
Helfrich, Paul Michael 1955- *IntWWM 90, WhoEmL 91*
Helfrich, Roger William 1951- *BiDrAPA 89*
Helfrich-Miller, Kathleen *BioIn 16*
Helft, Claudine 1937- *EncCoWW*
Helft, Michael R. 1941- *St&PR 91*
Helgason, Dean Eugene 1940- *WhoWor 91*
Helgason, Hallgrimur 1914- *IntWWM 90*
Helgason, Haukur 1936- *WhoWor 91*
Helgason, Pall Bergsson 1938- *WhoWor 91*
Helgason, Sigurdur 1921- *WhoWor 91*
Helgason, Sigurdur 1927- *WhoAm 90, WhoE 91, WhoWor 91*
Helgeland, David Lee 1951- *WhoEmL 91*
Helgeland, Walter 1935- *St&PR 91*
Helgerson, John Walter 1938- *WhoAm 90*
Helgeson, Eunice May 1947- *WhoEmL 91*
Helgeson, Peter Loren 1933- *WhoE 91*
Helgesson, Lars-Ake 1941- *WhoAm 90*
Helgesson, Uno H *BiDrAPA 89*
Helias, Mark *BioIn 16*
Helie, Claude 1943- *St&PR 91*
Heliker, John 1909- *WhoAm 90*
Heliker, John Edward 1909- *WhoAmA 91*
Helin, Jacquelyn 1951- *IntWWM 90*
Helin, James Dennis 1942- *WhoAm 90*
Heline, Corinne S. *NewAgE 90*
Helinger, Michael Green 1947- *WhoE 91*
Hellinski, Donald Raymond 1933- *WhoAm 90*
Helioff, Anne Graile *WhoAmA 91, WhoAmW 91, WhoWor 91*
Helion, Jean 1904-1987 *BioIn 16*
Helis, William G. *BioIn 16*
Helitzer, Florence 1928- *WhoE 91*
Helke, Cinda Jane 1951- *WhoAmW 91*
Hell, Richard 194-?- *EncPR&S 89*
Hellaakoski, Aaro 1893-1952 *DcScanL*
Hellams, Alfred Allen 1912- *BiDrAPA 89*
Helland, George Archibald, Jr. 1937- *WhoAm 90*
Helland, Patricia Anne 1964- *WhoAmW 91*
Helland, Richard Erling 1931- *St&PR 91*
Helland-Hansen, Bjorn 1877-1957 *DcScB S2*
Hellauer, James Carroll 1939- *St&PR 91*
Hellawell, Piers 1956- *IntWWM 90*
Hellawell, Robert 1928- *WhoAm 90*
Hellberg, Clifford William 1925- *St&PR 91*
Hellbusch, Jay Jay 1939- *WhoWrEP 89*
Helldorfer, M. C. 1954- *ConAu 129*
Helle, Eeva *DcScanL*
Helle, Wim 1926- *WhoWor 91*
Helleiner, Gerald Karl 1936- *WhoAm 90*
Hellekson, Carla *BiDrAPA 89*
Hellems, Harper Keith 1920- *WhoAm 90*
Hellen, Marie Evoline 1950- *WhoWor 91*
Hellenbach, Lazar De Baczolay 1827-1887 *EncO&P 3*
Hellenbrand, Curtis Marvin, Jr. 1957- *WhoEmL 91*
Hellenbrand, Samuel Henry 1916- *St&PR 91, WhoAm 90*
Hellenbrand, Vernon John 1933- *St&PR 91*
Hellendale, Robert 1917- *WhoAm 90*
Hellenhofferu, Vojtech Kapristian z *ConAu 129, MajTwCW*
Hellenthal, S. Ronald 1949- *WhoEmL 91*
Heller, Abraham *BiDrAPA 89*
Heller, Adam 1933- *WhoAm 90*
Heller, Alfred 1930- *WhoAm 90*
Heller, Alfred 1931- *IntWWM 90*
Heller, Amy Anne 1957- *WhoAmW 91*
Heller, Aniko Nagy *St&PR 91*
Heller, Arthur 1930- *WhoAm 90*
Heller, Barbara Ruth 1931- *WhoAmW 91*
Heller, Ben 1925- *WhoAmA 91*
Heller, Boris *BiDrAPA 89*
Heller, Charles Andrew, Jr. 1929- *WhoAm 90*
Heller, Cheryl *BioIn 16*
Heller, Cheryl Christine 1950- *WhoAmW 91*
Heller, Clarence E. 1926- *St&PR 91*
Heller, Donald *St&PR 91*
Heller, Dorothy *WhoAmA 91*
Heller, Dorothy 1926- *WhoE 91*
Heller, Doug *BioIn 16*
Heller, Douglas Max 1918- *WhoAm 90*
Heller, Duane L. 1951- *IntWWM 90*
Heller, E. Michael 1958- *St&PR 91*
Heller, Edward Lincoln 1912- *WhoE 91*
Heller, Edward M. 1926- *St&PR 91*
Heller, Edwin 1929- *WhoAm 90*
Heller, Ellen Distiller 1942- *WhoAmW 91*
Heller, Erich 1911- *WhoAm 90*
Heller, Erich 1911-1990 *ConAu 132, NewYTBS 90 [port]*
Heller, Francis H 1917- *ConAu 31NR*
Heller, Francis Howard 1917- *WhoAm 90*
Heller, Fred 1924- *St&PR 91, WhoAm 90, WhoE 91*
Heller, Fred 1925- *WhoE 91*
Heller, Fred Ira 1945- *WhoEmL 91*
Heller, Frederick 1932- *WhoAm 90*
Heller, George 1922- *St&PR 91*
Heller, George N. 1941- *IntWWM 90*
Heller, George William 1926- *St&PR 91*
Heller, Gerald 1936- *WhoSSW 91*
Heller, Goldie *WhoAmA 91*
Heller, Harry *BioIn 16*
Heller, Hartmut 1941- *WhoWor 91*
Heller, Heinz Robert 1940- *WhoAm 90, WhoWor 91*
Heller, Herbert A. 1930- *St&PR 91*
Heller, Horace Craig 1943- *WhoAm 90*
Heller, Ira I. 1954- *St&PR 91*
Heller, J. Roderick, III 1937- *St&PR 91*
Heller, J Ronald 1947- *BiDrAPA 89*
Heller, Jack Isaac 1932- *WhoAm 90*
Heller, Jack Joseph 1932- *IntWWM 90*
Heller, Jacqueline *BiDrAPA 89*
Heller, James Bradley 1946- *WhoEmL 91*
Heller, James John 1921- *WhoAm 90*
Heller, James R. 1914- *St&PR 91*
Heller, James Stephen 1950- *WhoEmL 91*
Heller, Janet A *BiDrAPA 89*
Heller, Janet Ruth 1949- *WhoWrEP 89*
Heller, Janis *BioIn 16*
Heller, Jeffrey Alan 1958- *WhoEmL 91*
Heller, Jeffrey Merwin 1939- *St&PR 91*
Heller, Jenny Fanny *BiDrAPA 89*
Heller, Joan 1944- *IntWWM 90*
Heller, John 1949- *St&PR 91*
Heller, John Herbert 1921- *WhoAm 90*
Heller, John L., II 1953- *WhoEmL 91*
Heller, John R. 1905-1989 *AnObit 1989*
Heller, John Roderick 1905-1989 *BioIn 16*
Heller, John Roderick, III 1937- *WhoAm 90*
Heller, Joseph *BiDrAPA 89, BioIn 16*
Heller, Joseph 1923- *ConLC 63 [port], MajTwCW, WhoWrEP 89, WorAlBi*
Heller, Jules 1919- *WhoAm 90, WhoAmA 91*
Heller, Karen Lenore 1961- *WhoAmW 91*
Heller, Lois Jane 1942- *WhoAmW 91*
Heller, Marc *WhoWrEP 89*
Heller, Mark 1955- *WhoEmL 91, WhoWor 91*
Heller, Marlene Ann 1953- *WhoWrEP 89*
Heller, Max M. 1919- *WhoWor 91*
Heller, Maxwell 1881-1963 *WhoAmA 91N*
Heller, Melvin S 1922- *BiDrAPA 89*
Heller, Meryl A. 1952- *WhoAmW 91*
Heller, Mitchell Thomas 1948- *WhoAm 90*
Heller, Naomi B 1935- *BiDrAPA 89*
Heller, Neil Andrew 1951- *WhoE 91*
Heller, Norman 1927- *St&PR 91*
Heller, Otto *BioIn 16*
Heller, Pamela 1954- *WhoAmA 91*
Heller, Paul 1914- *WhoAm 90*
Heller, Paul Michael 1927- *WhoAm 90*
Heller, Peter 1920- *ConAu 32NR*
Heller, Philip 1910- *St&PR 91*
Heller, Philip Henri 1919- *WhoAm 90*
Heller, Preston B., Jr. 1929- *St&PR 91*
Heller, Reinhold August 1940- *WhoAm 90, WhoAmA 91*
Heller, Richard 1954- *IntWWM 90*
Heller, Richard H. *WhoAm 90*
Heller, Robert 1932- *ConAu 132*
Heller, Robert H. 1940- *St&PR 91*
Heller, Robert James 1934- *WhoSSW 91*
Heller, Robert Leo 1919- *WhoAm 90*
Heller, Robert Martin 1942- *WhoAm 90*
Heller, Ronald Gary 1946- *WhoAm 90*
Heller, Ronald Ian 1956- *WhoEmL 91*
Heller, Ruth M. 1924- *ConAu 130*
Heller, Stanley S 1936- *BiDrAPA 89*
Heller, Steven *BioIn 16*
Heller, Susanna 1956- *WhoAmA 91*
Heller, Theodore F. 1942- *St&PR 91*
Heller, Walter W. *BioIn 16*
Heller-Nemzoff, Jeanette June 1924- *BiDrAPA 89*
Hellerman, F. Stokes 1945- *St&PR 91*
Hellerman, Fred 1927- *WhoAm 90*
Hellerman, Gerald 1937- *WhoE 91*
Hellerman, Marvin Lawrence 1927- *WhoE 91*
Hellermann, LaReine Otten 1921- *IntWWM 90*
Hellermann, William David 1939- *IntWWM 90, WhoAmA 91*
Hellerson, Robert Keith 1944- *St&PR 91*
Hellerstein, Alvin Kenneth 1933- *WhoAm 90*
Hellerstein, David Joel 1953- *BiDrAPA 89, WhoE 91*
Hellerstein, Simon 1931- *WhoAm 90*
Hellew, Joyce Virginia 1949- *WhoWrEP 89*
Helley, William P. 1931- *St&PR 91*
Hellickson, Dean Robert 1962- *WhoSSW 91*
Hellickson, Martin Leon 1945- *WhoEmL 91*
Hellie, Richard 1937- *WhoAm 90, WhoWor 91, WhoWrEP 89*
Hellier, Odile *BioIn 16*
Helliker, Steven A. 1948- *WhoE 91*
Helling, Dennis Keith 1948- *WhoAm 90*
Helling, Dorothy Luise 1950- *WhoEmL 91*
Hellinga, Lotte 1932- *ConAu 129*
Hellinger, Bernard S 1925- *BiDrAPA 89*
Hellinger, Douglas A. 1948- *WhoWrEP 89*
Hellinger, Gary Lloyd 1940- *St&PR 91*
Hellinger, Marilyn 1941- *St&PR 91*
Hellinger, Mark 1903-1947 *BioIn 16*
Hellinger, Stephen H. 1948- *WhoWrEP 89*
Helliwell, Clifton 1907- *IntWWM 90*
Helliwell, David Leedom 1935- *WhoAm 90*
Helliwell, Geoffrey Ernest 1951- *WhoAm 90*
Helliwell, Thomas McCaffree 1936- *WhoAm 90*
Hellman, Arthur David 1942- *WhoAm 90*
Hellman, Bruce 1942- *St&PR 91*
Hellman, Dennis I. 1946- *WhoEmL 91*
Hellman, Donna Lee 1958- *WhoWrEP 89*
Hellman, F. Warren 1934- *St&PR 91*
Hellman, Frederick Warren 1934- *WhoAm 90, WhoWor 91*
Hellman, Geoffrey T 1907-1977 *ConAu 30NR*
Hellman, George Edward 1958- *WhoEmL 91*
Hellman, Glen 1955- *WhoE 91*
Hellman, Glenn M. 1952- *St&PR 91*
Hellman, Hal 1927- *WhoWrEP 89*
Hellman, Harold 1927- *AuBYP 90*
Hellman, Herbert M. 1943- *St&PR 91*
Hellman, Herbert Martin 1943- *WhoAm 90*
Hellman, Isaias 1842-1920 *EncABHB 6 [port]*
Hellman, Jack M. 1931- *St&PR 91*
Hellman, Jay M. 1941- *St&PR 91*
Hellman, Jesse M 1942- *BiDrAPA 89*
Hellman, John 1940- *ConAu 129*
Hellman, Lillian 1905-1984 *BioAmW, FemiCLE, WorAlBi*
Hellman, Lillian 1906-1984 *BioIn 16, ConAu 33NR, MajTwCW*
Hellman, Lillian 1907-1984 *EncAL*
Hellman, Lillian Florence 1905?-1984 *NotWoAT*
Hellman, Louis M. *NewYTBS 90 [port]*
Hellman, Louis M. 1908- *WhoAm 90*
Hellman, Monte 1932- *BioIn 16*
Hellman, Murray 1934- *St&PR 91*
Hellman, Patrick D. 1941- *St&PR 91*
Hellman, Peter S. 1949- *St&PR 91*
Hellman, Ronald Edwin 1948- *BiDrAPA 89, WhoE 91*
Hellman, Samuel 1934- *WhoAm 90*
Hellman, Sheila Almer 1928- *WhoWrEP 89*
Hellman, William 1920- *St&PR 91*
Hellmann, Donald Charles 1933- *WhoAm 90*
Hellmann, Gail Marie *BiDrAPA 89*
Hellmann, Norma Janelle 1949- *WhoAmW 91*
Hellmann, Robert Alvin 1927- *WhoE 91*
Hellmann, Selden Stuart, Jr. 1930- *St&PR 91*
Hellmesberger, Ferdinand 1863-1940 *PenDiMP*
Hellmesberger, Georg 1800-1873 *PenDiMP*

Hellmesberger, Joseph 1828-1893 *PenDiMP*
Hellmuth, George Francis 1907- *WhoAm 90, WhoWor 91*
Hellmuth, James G. 1923- *St&PR 91*
Hellmuth, William Frederick, Jr. 1920- *WhoAm 90*
Hellot, Jean *PenDiDA 89*
Hellriegel, Raymond J. *BioIn 16*
Hellstrom, Eva Backstrom 1898- *EncO&P 3*
Hellstrom, Gunnar Sten 1947- *WhoWor 91*
Hellstrom, Gustaf 1882-1953 *DcScanL*
Hellstrom, John G. 1929- *St&PR 91*
Hellums, Bonnie Crane 1943- *WhoAmW 91*
Hellums, Jesse David 1929- *WhoAm 90*
Hellwarth, Robert Willis 1930- *WhoAm 90*
Hellweg, M. John 1932- *St&PR 91*
Hellwig, Frank Zielinski 1959- *WhoEmL 91*
Helly, Eduard 1884-1943 *DcScB S2*
Helly, Walter Sigmund 1930- *WhoAm 90*
Hellyer, Clement David 1914- *WhoAm 90*
Hellyer, Constance Anne 1937- *WhoAmW 91*
Hellyer, Paul Theodore 1923- *WhoAm 90*
Hellyer, Timothy Michael 1954- *WhoWor 91*
Helm, Anne 1938?- *BioIn 16*
Helm, Buck *BioIn 16*
Helm, Carole Ann 1943- *WhoAmW 91*
Helm, Charles John 1817-1868 *BioIn 16*
Helm, David Arthur *BiDrAPA 89*
Helm, DeWitt Frederick, Jr. 1933- *WhoAm 90, WhoE 91, WhoWor 91*
Helm, Donald Cairney 1937- *WhoAm 90*
Helm, E. Eugene 1928- *IntWWM 90*
Helm, F.D. 1930- *St&PR 91*
Helm, Frederick 1926- *WhoAm 90*
Helm, George Neville, III 1954- *WhoEmL 91*
Helm, Hans 1934- *IntWWM 90*
Helm, Hugh Barnett 1914- *WhoSSW 91, WhoWor 91*
Helm, James M. 1947- *St&PR 91*
Helm, Janet *ODwPR 91*
Helm, Joan Mary 1934- *WhoAmW 91*
Helm, John F. Jr 1900-1972 *WhoAmA 91N*
Helm, June 1924- *WhoAm 90*
Helm, Juta *BiDrAPA 89*
Helm, Karl 1938- *IntWWM 90*
Helm, Lewis Marshall 1931- *WhoAm 90*
Helm, Marjorie M. 1949- *WhoEmL 91*
Helm, Mark Douglas *BiDrAPA 89*
Helm, Mike 1942- *WhoWrEP 89*
Helm, P. Ralph 1926- *St&PR 91*
Helm, Robert Meredith 1917- *WhoAm 90*
Helm, Rudy *NewAgMG*
Helm, Sherrell 1935- *St&PR 91*
Helman, Alfred Blair 1920- *WhoAm 90*
Helman, Andrea Jean 1946- *WhoWrEP 89*
Helman, Barry Saul 1939- *St&PR 91*
Helman, Carol Lynn *BiDrAPA 89*
Helman, Eve L *WhoAmA 91*
Helman, Gerald Bernard 1932- *WhoAm 90*
Helman, Phoebe 1929- *WhoAmA 91*
Helman, Robert Alan 1934- *WhoAm 90*
Helman, William Wilson 1928- *St&PR 91*
Helman, Zofia 1937- *IntWWM 90*
Helmbold, Nancy Pearce 1918- *WhoAm 90*
Helmbold, William Ross 1947- *WhoEmL 91, WhoWor 91*
Helmchen, Hanfried *BiDrAPA 89*
Helmcke, Hans 1922- *WhoWor 91*
Helmcken, James Douglas 1927- *St&PR 91*
Helme, Edward Alfred 1947- *WhoE 91*
Helme, Elizabeth *FemiCLE*
Helmecke, Monika 1943- *EncCoWW*
Helmer, Adam 1754-1830 *WhNaAH*
Helmer, David Alan 1946- *WhoEmL 91, WhoWor 91*
Helmer, Hamilton Wright 1947- *WhoE 91*
Helmer, Paul John 1926- *St&PR 91*
Helmer, Star 1950- *WhoWrEP 89*
Helmer, Thomas Jay 1949- *WhoEmL 91*
Helmerich, Hans Christian 1958- *WhoAm 90*
Helmerich, W.H., III 1923- *St&PR 91*
Helmerich, Walter Hugo, III 1923- *WhoAm 90, WhoSSW 91*
Helmericks, Harmon 1917- *WhoAm 90*
Helmers, Carl 1948- *St&PR 91*
Helmes, L. Scott 1945- *WhoWrEP 89*
Helmetag, Carl 1948- *WhoE 91*
Helmetag, Charles Hugh 1935- *WhoAm 90*
Helmfrid, Staffan 1927- *WhoWor 91*
Helmhack, Abraham 1654-1724 *PenDiDA 89*
Helmholdt, Gerald Richard 1934- *WhoAm 90*
Helmholdt, Thomas Dean 1957- *WhoEmL 91*
Helmholtz, Herman von 1821-1894 *EncPaPR 91*
Helmholtz, Hermann 1821-1894 *WorAlBi*
Helmholz, August Carl 1915- *WhoAm 90*
Helmholz, Richard Henry 1940- *WhoAm 90*
Helmick, Aileen Barnett 1930- *WhoWor 91*
Helmick, Charles Gardiner, III 1950- *WhoSSW 91*
Helmick, Katharina 1941- *WhoE 91*
Helmick, L.G., Jr. 1920- *St&PR 91*
Helmick, Susan Taylor 1945- *St&PR 91*
Helming, C.T. 1906- *St&PR 91*
Helming, Scott Bryon 1953- *WhoE 91*
Helminger, Paul Andrew 1941- *WhoSSW 91*
Helminski, Camille Adams 1951- *WhoAmW 91*
Helminski, Edmund Richard 1947- *WhoWrEP 89*
Helminski, Francis 1957- *WhoEmL 91*
Helmkamp, Elmer J. 1929- *St&PR 91*
Helmkamp, John G. 1938- *WhoAm 90*
Helmken, Charles Michael 1932-1989 *BioIn 16*
Helmond, Katherine 1934- *WhoAm 90, WorAlBi*
Helmreich, Ernst Johann Michael 1922- *WhoWor 91*
Helmreich, Jonathan Ernst 1936- *WhoAm 90*
Helmreich, Robert Louis 1937- *WhoAm 90*
Helmrich, Eberhard *BioIn 16*
Helms, Bennett Lyon 1930- *St&PR 91*
Helms, Charles A. 1953- *St&PR 91*
Helms, Christine Moss *ConAu 129*
Helms, David Alonzo 1934- *WhoWor 91*
Helms, Erwin Bruno 1913- *WhoWor 91*
Helms, Fletcher B., Jr. 1940- *St&PR 91*
Helms, Fred Bryan 1896- *WhoAm 90, WhoWor 91*
Helms, George Frank 1930- *St&PR 91*
Helms, Helen Rutherford 1930- *St&PR 91*
Helms, J. Lynn 1925- *WhoAm 90*
Helms, Jerry Wayne 1940- *WhoAm 90*
Helms, Jesse 1921- *NewYTBS 90 [port], WhoAm 90, WhoSSW 91, WhoWor 91*
Helms, Jesse A. *BioIn 16*
Helms, Jesse A. 1921- *WorAlBi*
Helms, John Alvin 1935- *St&PR 91*
Helms, Kenneth William 1958- *WhoEmL 91*
Helms, Lawrence Stephen 1938- *St&PR 91*
Helms, Luther Sherman, III 1943- *St&PR 91*
Helms, Martin Ronald 1942- *St&PR 91*
Helms, Mary Ann 1935- *WhoAmW 91*
Helms, Paul Maben, Jr. *BiDrAPA 89*
Helms, Richard *BioIn 16*
Helms, Richard McGarrah 1913- *WhoAm 90*
Helms, Robert Brake 1940- *WhoAm 90*
Helms, Robert W. 1947- *St&PR 91*
Helms, Ronald Gene 1945- *WhoEmL 91*
Helms, Ronald Nelson 1939- *WhoAm 90*
Helms, Thomas H. 1937- *St&PR 91*
Helms, Thomas Joseph 1939- *WhoAm 90*
Helms, Tommy 1941- *Ballpl 90*
Helms, W. Richard 1929- *WhoAm 90*
Helms-VanStone, Mary Wallace 1938- *WhoAmW 91*
Helmsin, Elizabeth Poth 1925- *WhoAmW 91*
Helmsing, Frederick George 1940- *WhoAm 90*
Helmsley, Grace *BiDEWW*
Helmsley, Harry B. *St&PR 91*
Helmsley, Harry B. 1909- *BioIn 16, WhoAm 90, WhoE 91*
Helmsley, Leona *BioIn 16*
Helmsley, Leona Mindy *WhoAmW 91*
Helmsley, Sherman 1938- *WorAlBi*
Helmstetter, Charles Edward 1933- *WhoAm 90*
Helmuth, Dennis Osborn 1956- *BiDrAPA 89*
Heloise 1089?-1164 *WorAlBi*
Heloise 1098?-1164 *EncCoWW*
Heloise 1100?-1163? *FemiCLE*
Heloise 1101-1164 *BioIn 16*
Heloise 1951- *WhoAm 90, WhoAmW 91*
Heloreth, Joseph Brown 1955- *St&PR 91*
Helou, Anissa *BioIn 16*
Helpap, John Frederick 1940- *WhoAm 90*
Helper, Alexandra *BiDrAPA 89*
Helpern, David Moses 1917- *WhoAm 90*
Helpern, Herman 1909-1990 *BioIn 16*
Helphand, Ben J. 1915- *WhoAm 90*
Helphingstine, Cynthia Jeanette Goodson 1949- *WhoAmW 91*
Helprin, Lisa Kennedy 1950- *WhoEmL 91*
Helprin, Mark 1947- *MajTwCW, WhoAm 90*
Helps, Racey 1913-1971 *AuBYP 90*
Helps, Robert 1928- *IntWWM 90*
Helrich, Martin 1922- *WhoAm 90*
Helsel, David Shafer 1954- *BiDrAPA 89*
Helsel, Jess F. 1924- *St&PR 91*
Helsell, Robert M. 1937- *WhoAm 90*
Helsen, Kristiaan 1961- *WhoE 91*
Helsinger, Marc Howard 1948- *WhoAm 90*
Helsley, Grover Cleveland 1926- *WhoAm 90*
Helsmoortel, Daniel Paul 1930- *WhoWor 91*
Helsmoortel, Robert *WhoAmA 91*
Helson, Henry Berge 1927- *WhoAm 90*
Helstad, Orrin LaVerne 1922- *WhoAm 90*
Helsten, Charles Thomas 1933- *WhoSSW 91*
Helt, Chester LeRoy 1936- *St&PR 91*
Heltay, Laszlo 1930- *PenDiMP*
Heltay, Laszlo Istvan 1930- *IntWWM 90*
Heltne, Paul Gregory 1941- *WhoAm 90*
Helton, Ann 1947- *BiDrAPA 89*
Helton, Bill D. 1938- *St&PR 91*
Helton, Glenn S. 1951- *ODwPR 91*
Helton, Harry Vinsant 1934- *St&PR 91*
Helton, Jack Alan, II 1952- *WhoEmL 91*
Helton, Karen Elizabeth Johnson 1962- *WhoEmL 91*
Helton, Lucille Henry Hanrattie 1942- *WhoAmW 91*
Helton, Max Edward 1940- *WhoSSW 91*
Helton, Melanie Harder 1958- *WhoAmW 91*
Helton, Sandra Lynn 1949- *WhoEmL 91*
Heltzel, Marlene Sue 1934- *WhoAmW 91*
Heltzel, Roy Franklin, Jr. 1961- *WhoSSW 91*
Helveston, Eugene McGillis 1934- *WhoAm 90*
Helvetius, John Friedrich 1625-1709 *EncO&P 3*
Helvey, Edward Douglas 1956- *WhoEmL 91, WhoWor 91*
Helvey, Julius Louis 1931- *St&PR 91*
Helvey, Julius Louis, II 1931- *WhoAm 90*
Helvick, Allen K. 1943- *St&PR 91*
Helvig, Amalie von 1776-1831 *EncCoWW*
Helweg, Hans H. 1917- *BioIn 16*
Helwig, Arthur Louis 1899-1976 *WhoAmA 91N*
Helwig, Arthur Woods 1929- *St&PR 91, WhoAm 90*
Helwig, David 1938- *BioIn 16*
Helwig, Elson Bowman 1907- *WhoAm 90*
Helwig, George J. 1935- *St&PR 91*
Helwig, Gilbert John 1918- *WhoAm 90*
Helwig, Hans *BioIn 16*
Helwig, Maggie *ConAu 130*
Helwig, Ralph Daniel 1946- *WhoE 91*
Helwig, Sarah Magdalen 1961- *ConAu 130*
Helwys, Thomas 1550?-1616? *BioIn 16*
Helz, Jean Werner 1946- *BiDrAPA 89*
Helzer, James Dennis 1938- *WhoAm 90*
Helzer, John Earl 1941- *BiDrAPA 89*
Helzer, Richard Brian 1943- *WhoAmA 91*
Hemachandra, M G Sarath 1941- *BiDrAPA 89*
Hemala, Katherine Gojztonyi *BiDrAPA 89*
Hemann, Dan *BioIn 16*
Hemann, Raymond Glenn 1933- *WhoAm 90, WhoWor 91*
Hemans, Felicia 1793-1835 *DcLB 96 [port], FemiCLE, NinCLC 29 [port]*
Hemans, Felicia Dorothea Browne 1793-1835 *BioIn 16*
Hemaya, Rizk Mishriky *BiDrAPA 89*
Hembel, Joy Ann 1948- *WhoEmL 91*
Hemberg, Bengt Sven Eskil 1938- *WhoWor 91*
Hemberg, Eskil 1938- *IntWWM 90*
Hemberger, Harold Joseph 1953- *WhoE 91*
Hembling, Donald C. 1918- *St&PR 91*
Hembree, Charles R. 1925- *St&PR 91*
Hembree, George Hunt 1930- *WhoAm 90*
Hembree, Gregory Mark 1954- *WhoSSW 91*
Hembree, Hugh L. 1931- *St&PR 91*
Hembree, Hugh Lawson, III 1931- *WhoAm 90*
Hembree, James D. 1929- *WhoAm 90*
Hembree, Kent Douglas 1960- *WhoSSW 91*
Hembrick, Anthony *BioIn 16*
Hemby, Dorothy Jean 1940- *WhoAmW 91*
Hemby, James B., Jr. 1934- *WhoAm 90*
Hemdal, Hakan Olof 1930- *WhoE 91*
Hemedinger, Lauren 1934- *WhoSSW 91*
Hemelrike, Corneille Yvon 1944- *WhoE 91*
Hemelt, William J. 1954- *St&PR 91*
Hemens, Henry John 1913- *WhoAm 90*
Hemenway, David 1945- *WhoE 91*
Hemenway, Jack B. 1935- *St&PR 91*
Hemenway, Robert E. 1941- *WhoAm 90*
Hemenway, Robert P. 1937- *St&PR 91*
Hemeyer, Terry *ODwPR 91*
Hemeyer, Terry 1938- *St&PR 91*
Hemeze *ConAu 132*
Hemeze, Sebastian *HispWr 90*
Heming, Charles E. 1926- *WhoAm 90*
Heming, George *PenDiDA 89*
Heming, Thomas 1722?-1801 *PenDiDA 89*
Heminger, Edwin L. 1926- *St&PR 91*
Hemington, Judith 1949- *ConAu 129*
Hemingway, Angie 1955- *WhoSSW 91*
Hemingway, Beth Rowlett 1913- *WhoAmW 91*
Hemingway, Ernest 1898-1961 *WrPh*
Hemingway, Ernest 1899-1961 *BioIn 16, ConLC 61 [port], DcLB 102 [port], MajTwCW, WorAlBi*
Hemingway, George F. 1947- *St&PR 91*
Hemingway, Gerry *BioIn 16*
Hemingway, Grace Hall 1872-1951 *BioAmW*
Hemingway, Hadley 1891-1979 *BioAmW*
Hemingway, Jack Wilson 1920- *WhoSSW 91*
Hemingway, Margaux 1955- *BioIn 16*
Hemingway, Mariel *BioIn 16*
Hemingway, Mary 1908-1986 *BioIn 16*
Hemingway, Mary Welsh 1908- *BioAmW*
Hemingway, Pauline Pfeiffer 1895-1951 *BioAmW*
Hemingway, Richard William 1927- *WhoAm 90, WhoWor 91*
Hemingway, W. David 1947- *St&PR 91*
Heminway, John Hylan *BioIn 16*
Hemion, Dwight 1926- *ConTFT 8*
Hemion, Dwight Arlington 1926- *WhoAm 90*
Hemke, Frederick L. 1935- *IntWWM 90*
Hemlepp, Catherine Braden *ODwPR 91*
Hemler, Elizabeth Ann 1956- *WhoAmW 91*
Hemley, Judith Kemp 1941- *WhoAmW 91*
Hemley, Robin 1958- *ConAu 130*
Hemlock, Camille *BiDrAPA 89*
Hemlow, Joyce 1906- *WhoAm 90*
Hemm, Anton *BioIn 16*
Hemmelgarn, Richard Arthur 1947- *St&PR 91*
Hemmer, James Paul 1942- *WhoAm 90*
Hemmer, Jarl Robert 1893-1944 *DcScanL*
Hemmer, Paul Edward 1944- *WhoAm 90*
Hemmerdinger, H. Dale 1944- *WhoE 91, WhoEmL 91, WhoWor 91*
Hemmerdinger, Lyn *BioIn 16*
Hemmerdinger, William John 1951- *WhoAm 90*
Hemmerdinger, William John, III 1951- *WhoAmA 91*
Hemmerick, Ed Paul 1956- *St&PR 91*
Hemmerlin, Albert Joseph 1938- *WhoWor 91*
Hemmerly, Thomas Ellsworth 1932- *WhoSSW 91*
Hemmes, Michael 1958- *WhoWrEP 89*
Hemmeter, Christopher Bagwell 1939- *WhoAm 90*
Hemming, Brian *ODwPR 91*
Hemming, Charles 1950- *ConAu 132*
Hemming, George Fred 1937- *WhoWrEP 89*
Hemming, James E. 1937- *St&PR 91*
Hemming, Roy G. 1928- *WhoAm 90, WhoWrEP 89*
Hemming, Walter William 1939- *WhoAm 90, WhoE 91*
Hemming, Wayne J. 1948- *St&PR 91*
Hemminghaus, Roger Roy 1936- *St&PR 91, WhoAm 90, WhoSSW 91*
Hemmings, David 1941- *WorAlBi*
Hemmings, David Leslie Edward 1941- *WhoWor 91*
Hemmings, Madeleine Blanchet 1942- *WhoAmW 91*
Hemmings, Peter William 1934- *IntWWM 90*
Hemmingsen, Barbara Bruff 1941- *WhoAmW 91*
Hemon, Louis 1880-1913 *DcLB 92*
Hemond, Roland 1929- *Ballpl 90*
Hemond, Roland A. 1929- *WhoAm 90, WhoE 91*
Hemp, Ralph Clyde 1936- *WhoAm 90*
Hempel, Amy *BioIn 16*
Hempel, Anouska *BioIn 16*
Hempel, Dean J 1926- *BiDrAPA 89*
Hempel, Frieda 1885-1955 *PenDiMP*
Hempel, Gotthilf 1929- *WhoWor 91*
Hempel, Kathleen J. 1950- *St&PR 91*
Hempel, Kathleen Jane 1950- *WhoAm 90, WhoAmW 91*
Hempel, Valdemar 1919- *WhoAm 90*
Hempel, William J. 1933- *WhoAm 90*
Hempen, Lorraine 1931- *St&PR 91*
Hempfling, Gregory Jay 1961- *WhoSSW 91*
Hempfling, Linda Lee 1947- *WhoAmW 91*
Hemphill, A Marcus *DrBIPA 90*
Hemphill, Alan Polk 1933- *WhoWor 91*
Hemphill, Charlie 1876-1953 *Ballpl 90*
Hemphill, Frederick Harold, Jr. 1939- *St&PR 91*
Hemphill, Gary Brian 1947- *WhoEmL 91, WhoSSW 91*

Hemphill, Helen Berneta 1912- WhoAmW 91
Hemphill, Herbert Waide 1929- BioIn 16
Hemphill, Herbert Waide, Jr 1929- WhoAmA 91
Hemphill, Jo 1930- WhoAmW 91
Hemphill, Kenneth John 1940- St&PR 91
Hemphill, Marlin R. 1916- St&PR 91
Hemphill, Maureen Lucille 1937- WhoAmW 91
Hemphill, Pamela 1927- WhoAmA 91
Hemphill, Paul 1936- AuBYP 90
Hemphill, Robert B. 1936- St&PR 91
Hemphill, Robert Davis 1947- WhoSSW 91
Hemphill, Shirley DrBlPA 90
Hemphill, Teresa G. 1955- St&PR 91
Hemphill, William Alfred, III 1949- WhoEmL 91
Hemphill, William Howard 1916- St&PR 91
Hemphill-Hammond, Betty 1911- WhoWor 91
Hempler, Orval F 1915- WhoAmA 91
Hempler, Orval Frederick 1915- WhoAm 90
Hempling, Randall 1945- WhoSSW 91
Hempstead, George H., III 1943- WhoAm 90
Hempstead, Harry 1869-1938 Ballpl 90
Hempstone, Smith, Jr. 1929- WhoAm 90, WhoWor 91
Hempt, Gerald Leonard 1945- St&PR 91
Hempton, Gordon BioIn 16
Hemry, Jerome Eldon 1905- WhoAm 90
Hemsath, Randolph Heinrich BiDrAPA 89
Hemschemeyer, Judith 1935- AuBYP 90, WhoWrEP 89
Hemsing, Albert E. 1921- WhoAm 90, WhoWrEP 89
Hemsing, Josephine Claudia 1953- WhoE 91, WhoEmL 91
Hemsley, Estelle 1887-1968 DrBlPA 90
Hemsley, Grace BiDEWW
Hemsley, Maarten D. 1949- WhoAm 90
Hemsley, Rollie 1907-1972 Ballpl 90
Hemsley, Sherman 1938- DrBlPA 90, WhoAm 90
Hemsley, Thomas 1927- IntWWM 90, PenDiMP
Hemsley, Winston Dewitt DrBlPA 90
Hemsworth, Kathleen Garrigan 1961- WhoAmW 91, WhoE 91
Hemsworth, Martin Carl 1918- WhoAm 90
Hemus, Solly 1923- Ballpl 90
Hemyng, Bracebridge 1841-1901 BioIn 16
Henabery, Jeanne ODwPR 91
Henahan, Donal 1921- IntWWM 90, WhoAm 90
Henao, Sergio E 1940- BiDrAPA 89
Henao, Wanda J W 1935- BiDrAPA 89
Henard, Elizabeth Ann 1947- WhoAmW 91
Henares-Levy, Lourdes 1945- BiDrAPA 89
Henault, Mary Beth Berie- BioIn 16
Henault, Ralph 1944- St&PR 91
Henbest, Nigel BioIn 16
Henbest, Robert LeRoy 1923- WhoE 91
Henbest, William Harrison 1955- WhoEmL 91, WhoWor 91
Hench, John B 1943- ConAu 131
Hench, Philip Kahler 1930- WhoAm 90, WhoWor 91
Hench, Philip S. 1896-1965 WorAlBi
Hendarto, Hendarmin 1937- WhoWor 91
Henday, Anthony EncCRAm, WhNaAH
Hendee, Ellen Jackson 1925- WhoWor 91
Hendee, John Clare 1938- WhoAm 90
Hendee, John Hollister, Jr. 1926- WhoAm 90
Hendee, William Richard 1938- WhoAm 90
Hendel, Frank Joseph 1918- WhoAm 90
Hendel, Gregory Arthur 1947- WhoAm 90
Hendeles, Frieda R BiDrAPA 89
Hendelman, Beverly Ilene BiDrAPA 89
Henderiks, Joy-Corine 1953- WhoWor 91
Henderly, William G. 1953- St&PR 91
Henders, Orma L., Jr. 1928- St&PR 91
Henders, Sharlene Carol 1950- St&PR 91
Hendershot, Carol Miller 1959- WhoAmW 91
Hendershot, Delores Anne 1931- St&PR 91
Hendershot, Ingrid Reardon 1957- St&PR 91
Hendershot, J L 1941- WhoAmA 91
Hendershot, Judith AuBYP 90
Hendershot, Judith 1940- BioIn 16
Hendershot, June Norman 1930- St&PR 91
Hendershot, William Fred 1930- WhoAm 90
Hendershott, Phillip Leroy 1937- WhoAm 90
Hendershott Love, Arles June 1956- WhoAmW 91
Henderson, Alastair Colin 1940- WhoWor 91
Henderson, Albert 1938- WhoAm 90
Henderson, Albert John 1920- WhoAm 90
Henderson, Alexander BioIn 16
Henderson, Algo D. 1897-1988 BioIn 16
Henderson, Allen L. 1948- St&PR 91
Henderson, Archibald 1877-1963 DcLB 103 [port]
Henderson, Archibald 1916- WhoWrEP 89
Henderson, Arnold Glenn 1934- WhoAm 90
Henderson, Arthur 1863-1935 BioIn 16
Henderson, Arthur P., Jr. 1943- St&PR 91
Henderson, Arthur R 1922- BiDrAPA 89
Henderson, Arvis Burl 1943- WhoSSW 91, WhoWor 91
Henderson, Barbara ODwPR 91
Henderson, Barbara B. 1935- WhoAmW 91
Henderson, Bernard Levie, Jr. 1950- WhoAm 90
Henderson, Bernard R. 1933- ODwPR 91
Henderson, Bertha Roberts 1940- WhoAmW 91
Henderson, Betty W. 1933- St&PR 91
Henderson, Bill DrBlPA 90
Henderson, Brian Edmond 1937- WhoAm 90
Henderson, Bruce Doolin 1915- WhoAm 90, WhoWor 91
Henderson, Bruce Raymond 1948- WhoWrEP 89
Henderson, C. R. 1911-1989 BioIn 16
Henderson, Carlesta 1925- IntWWM 90
Henderson, Carol Lee 1957- WhoAmW 91
Henderson, Charles Brooke 1929- WhoAm 90
Henderson, Charles R. 1911-1989 BioIn 16
Henderson, Claude B 1925- BiDrAPA 89
Henderson, Clement Robert 1937- WhoSSW 91
Henderson, Conway Wilson 1942- WhoSSW 91
Henderson, D James 1940- BiDrAPA 89
Henderson, Dan Fenno 1921- WhoAm 90
Henderson, Daniel Gregory 1953- WhoEmL 91
Henderson, Dave 1958- Ballpl 90
Henderson, Deirdre Healy 1942- WhoAmW 91
Henderson, Denise Laureen 1952- WhoAmW 91
Henderson, Denys 1932- St&PR 91
Henderson, Diana Elizabeth 1957- WhoAmW 91
Henderson, Donald 1938- WhoAm 90
Henderson, Donald Ainslie 1928- WhoAm 90
Henderson, Donald Blanton 1949- WhoEmL 91, WhoSSW 91
Henderson, Donna Jean 1956- WhoEmL 91
Henderson, Dorland John 1898- WhoAm 90
Henderson, Douglas Boyd 1935- WhoAm 90, WhoE 91
Henderson, Dwight Franklin 1937- WhoAm 90, WhoSSW 91
Henderson, Edward Hugh 1939- WhoSSW 91
Henderson, Edward Mark 1956- St&PR 91
Henderson, Edward Shelton 1932- WhoAm 90
Henderson, Edwin Harold 1927- WhoAm 90
Henderson, Ernest, III 1924- St&PR 91, WhoAm 90
Henderson, Erskine D. 1949- WhoWrEP 89
Henderson, Eugene Leroy 1925- WhoAm 90
Henderson, F. C. MajTwCW
Henderson, Fletcher 1897-1952 OxCPMus
Henderson, Fletcher 1898-1952 BioIn 16, DrBlPA 90, WorAlBi
Henderson, Florence 1934- WhoAm 90, WorAlBi
Henderson, Frank Ellis 1928- WhoAm 90
Henderson, Frederic Lee 1946- BiDrAPA 89
Henderson, Frederick B. 1941- St&PR 91
Henderson, Frederick Bishop 1941- WhoAm 90
Henderson, Gary L. 1952- St&PR 91
Henderson, George 1932- WhoAm 90
Henderson, George Ervin 1947- WhoEmL 91
Henderson, Gerald Barnett 1928- St&PR 91
Henderson, Geraldine Thomas 1924- WhoAmW 91
Henderson, Gloria Mason 1936- WhoSSW 91
Henderson, Gordon BioIn 16
Henderson, Gordon 1950- BioIn 16
Henderson, Gordon Desmond 1930- WhoAm 90
Henderson, Greer Francis 1932- St&PR 91
Henderson, Gregory BioIn 16
Henderson, Gregory Benson 1953- WhoSSW 91
Henderson, H. Harry 1926- ODwPR 91, St&PR 91
Henderson, Harold L. 1935- WhoAm 90, WhoSSW 91
Henderson, Harold Lawrence 1935- St&PR 91
Henderson, Harold R. 1942- St&PR 91
Henderson, Harold Richard, Jr. 1942- WhoAm 90, WhoE 91
Henderson, Harriet 1949- WhoSSW 91
Henderson, Harry Brinton, Jr. 1914- WhoAm 90, WhoWrEP 89
Henderson, Harry Convery, Jr. 1921- BiDrAPA 89
Henderson, Hazel 1933- ConAu 129
Henderson, Horace 1904-1988 BioIn 16
Henderson, Horace Edward WhoAm 90
Henderson, Howard Bart 1957- WhoSSW 91
Henderson, Hubert Platt 1918- WhoAm 90
Henderson, Hugh Richard 1943- BiDrAPA 89
Henderson, Ian Hamilton 1925- IntWWM 90
Henderson, Ian William 1941- WhoWor 91
Henderson, Jack James 1955- WhoEmL 91
Henderson, Jack W 1931- WhoAmA 91
Henderson, James A. 1934- St&PR 91
Henderson, James A., Jr. 1938- WhoAm 90
Henderson, James Alan 1934- WhoAm 90
Henderson, James Alexander 1921- WhoAm 90
Henderson, James Allen 1948- WhoEmL 91
Henderson, James Brooke 1926- WhoAm 90
Henderson, James Gary 1954- WhoEmL 91
Henderson, James H. 1944- ODwPR 91
Henderson, James Harold 1948- WhoEmL 91, WhoWor 91
Henderson, James L. 1921- St&PR 91
Henderson, James Marvin 1921- St&PR 91, WhoAm 90
Henderson, James McInnes 1911-1989 BioIn 16
Henderson, James Robert 1947- WhoSSW 91
Henderson, James Walter 1960- WhoSSW 91
Henderson, Jana L. 1944- WhoAmW 91, WhoE 91
Henderson, Jane Whalen 1913- WhoAmW 91
Henderson, Jim 1947- ODwPR 91
Henderson, Jo 1934-1988 BioIn 16
Henderson, John Brown 1918- WhoAm 90
Henderson, John Drews 1933- WhoAm 90
Henderson, John Harold, Jr. 1931- BiDrAPA 89
Henderson, John Hope 1929- BiDrAPA 89
Henderson, John L. WhoAm 90
Henderson, John Mc Innes 1940- BiDrAPA 89
Henderson, John Richard 1953- WhoEmL 91
Henderson, John Robert 1950- WhoWor 91
Henderson, John Woodworth 1916- WhoAm 90
Henderson, Jon Loren 1951- St&PR 91
Henderson, Joseph Welles 1920- WhoAm 90
Henderson, Joyce Ball 1954- WhoSSW 91
Henderson, Julie K. 1950- WhoWrEP 89
Henderson, Karen 1954- WhoE 91
Henderson, Karen LeCraft 1944- WhoAmW 91
Henderson, Kathleen Hayden 1919- WhoWrEP 89
Henderson, Kathleen Susan 1952- WhoWrEP 89
Henderson, Kathy BioIn 16
Henderson, Kathy Lynn 1954- BiDrAPA 89
Henderson, Kaye N. BioIn 16
Henderson, Kaye Neil 1933- WhoAm 90, WhoSSW 91
Henderson, Ken 1946- Ballpl 90
Henderson, Kenneth Atwood 1905- WhoE 91, WhoWor 91
Henderson, Kenneth Lee 1954- WhoEmL 91
Henderson, Kenneth Reed 1935- WhoWor 91
Henderson, Larry Ray 1950- WhoSSW 91
Henderson, Lawrence W BiDrAPA 89
Henderson, Le Grand 1905-1965 AuBYP 90
Henderson, Lenneal Joseph, Jr. 1946- WhoAm 90, WhoWor 91
Henderson, Leona Harriette 1934- WhoAmW 91
Henderson, Leonard William 1921- IntWWM 90
Henderson, Lester Klerstead 1906- WhoAmA 91N
Henderson, Lillian Milbra 1945- WhoEmL 91
Henderson, Linda Dalrymple 1948- WhoAmA 91
Henderson, Linda Shlatz 1946- WhoAmW 91
Henderson, Louis Clifton, Jr. 1937- St&PR 91, WhoAm 90
Henderson, Louise Elaine 1947- WhoEmL 91
Henderson, Loy Wesley 1892-1986 BioIn 16
Henderson, Luther, Jr. 1919- DrBlPA 90
Henderson, Luther A. 1920- St&PR 91
Henderson, Lynne BioIn 16
Henderson, Lynnie 1952- WhoEmL 91
Henderson, Madeline Mary 1922- WhoAm 90
Henderson, Marc C. 1959- St&PR 91
Henderson, Marcia Irene 1947- WhoE 91
Henderson, Marilyn Ann 1949- WhoAmW 91, WhoEmL 91
Henderson, Marion Easley 1941- WhoSSW 91
Henderson, Mark William 1951- WhoEmL 91
Henderson, Marshall Deane 1935- WhoSSW 91
Henderson, Mary Catherine 1933- WhoSSW 91
Henderson, Mary Lynn Crawford 1955- WhoAmW 91
Henderson, Maureen McGrath 1926- WhoAm 90, WhoAmW 91
Henderson, Maurice Brian 1961- WhoWrEP 89
Henderson, Maxine Olive Book 1924- WhoAmW 91
Henderson, Maxwell 1908- ConAu 132
Henderson, Melford J. 1950- WhoEmL 91, WhoWor 91
Henderson, Melody Lynn 1954- WhoAmW 91
Henderson, Michael Douglas 1932- WhoWrEP 89
Henderson, Michael K. 1954- St&PR 91
Henderson, Michael Lynn 1962- WhoEmL 91
Henderson, Mike WhoAmA 91
Henderson, Mildred 1931- WhoWrEP 89
Henderson, Mildred K. 1931- WhoWrEP 89
Henderson, Milton Arnold 1922- WhoAm 90
Henderson, Mitchel Lee 1952- WhoSSW 91
Henderson, Monika 1954- ConAu 129
Henderson, Nancy Grace 1947- WhoAmW 91, WhoEmL 91
Henderson, Neil M. 1942- St&PR 91
Henderson, Nicholas BioIn 16
Henderson, Nicholas 1919- ConAu 132
Henderson, Patricia McGovern 1940- WhoAmW 91
Henderson, Paul Audine 1925- WhoAm 90
Henderson, Paul Bargas, Jr. 1928- WhoAm 90
Henderson, Peter Ben 1936- St&PR 91
Henderson, Phillip Theodore 1945- St&PR 91
Henderson, Ralph B. 1926- WhoAm 90
Henderson, Ralph B. 1926-1989 BioIn 16
Henderson, Ralph Ernest 1899-1989 BioIn 16
Henderson, Ralph Hale 1937- WhoAm 90, WhoWor 91
Henderson, Ray 1896-1970 BioIn 16, OxCPMus
Henderson, Richard 1735-1785 EncCRAm
Henderson, Richard 1928- St&PR 91
Henderson, Richard Cleveland, III 1948- St&PR 91
Henderson, Richard L 1935- BiDrAPA 89
Henderson, Rickey BioIn 16
Henderson, Rickey 1957- Ballpl 90 [port]
Henderson, Rickey 1958- CurBio 90 [port], WorAlBi
Henderson, Rickey Henley 1958- WhoAm 90
Henderson, Robbin Legere 1942- WhoAmA 91
Henderson, Robbye Robinson 1937- WhoAm 90
Henderson, Robert Arthur 1925- WhoAm 90
Henderson, Robert C. 1940- St&PR 91
Henderson, Robert Cameron 1940- WhoAm 90
Henderson, Robert Dean 1916- WhoAm 90
Henderson, Robert Douglas, Jr. 1952- WhoSSW 91
Henderson, Robert Earl 1935- WhoAm 90
Henderson, Robert Floyd, Jr. 1951- WhoSSW 91

Henderson, Robert Jules 1943- *WhoAm 90*
Henderson, Robert Morton 1931- *WhoSSW 91*
Henderson, Robert W. 1925- *St&PR 91*
Henderson, Robert Waugh 1920- *WhoAm 90*
Henderson, Robin Claude Lee 1951- *St&PR 91*
Henderson, Robin Gregory 1943- *BiDrAPA 89*
Henderson, Rodney James 1946- *St&PR 91*
Henderson, Roger C. 1931- *St&PR 91*
Henderson, Roger C. 1938- *WhoAm 90*
Henderson, Ronald Wilbur 1933- *WhoAm 90*
Henderson, Rosa 1896-1968 *BioIn 16*
Henderson, RoseMary Miller 1940- *WhoAmW 91*
Henderson, Ross 1928- *WhoWor 91*
Henderson, Roy 1899- *IntWWM 90, PenDiMP*
Henderson, Ruth Watson 1932- *IntWWM 90*
Henderson, Safiya 1950- *WhoWrEP 89*
Henderson, Schuyler Kent 1945- *WhoEmL 91*
Henderson, Scott *BioIn 16*
Henderson, Skitch 1918- *WhoAm 90*
Henderson, Sonya *BioIn 16*
Henderson, Stanley Dale 1935- *WhoAm 90*
Henderson, Steve 1952- *Ballpl 90*
Henderson, Steven Lee 1948- *WhoEmL 91*
Henderson, Susan *ODwPR 91*
Henderson, Susan Lee 1952- *WhoEmL 91*
Henderson, Suzanne 1943- *WhoAmW 91*
Henderson, Sylvia *MajTwCW*
Henderson, T.J. *St&PR 91*
Henderson, Tammy Jean 1961- *WhoWrEP 89*
Henderson, Thelton Eugene 1933- *WhoAm 90*
Henderson, Thomas 1955- *WhoEmL 91*
Henderson, Thomas Henry, Jr. 1939- *WhoAm 90*
Henderson, Thomas James 1931- *WhoAm 90*
Henderson, Thomas K. 1940- *St&PR 91*
Henderson, Thomas Shields 1932- *St&PR 91*
Henderson, Tommye Corley 1950- *WhoSSW 91*
Henderson, Ty *DrBlPA 90*
Henderson, Ursula E *BiDrAPA 89*
Henderson, Victor 1939- *WhoAmA 91*
Henderson, Victor Maurice 1924- *WhoWrEP 89*
Henderson, W.W. 1927- *St&PR 91*
Henderson, Walter G. 1930- *St&PR 91, WhoAm 90*
Henderson, Wiley Joseph 1934- *WhoSSW 91*
Henderson, William Boyd 1928- *WhoAm 90, WhoE 91*
Henderson, William Boyd 1936- *WhoAm 90*
Henderson, William Charles 1941- *WhoAm 90, WhoWrEP 89*
Henderson, William H 1946- *BiDrAPA 89*
Henderson, William Lee 1929- *St&PR 91*
Henderson, William Wendel 1906- *St&PR 91*
Henderson, William Wilmot 1926- *St&PR 91*
Henderson, Zenna 1917-1983 *RGTwCSF*
Henderson-Dawson, Michelle *BioIn 16*
Henderson-Hudson, Brenda Dianne 1964- *WhoEmL 91*
Henderson-Pierce, Shirley Anne 1943- *WhoAmW 91*
Hendery, Robert 1814-1897 *DcCanB 12*
Hendig, Klaus G. 1939- *St&PR 91*
Hendin, David 1945- *St&PR 91*
Hendin, David Bruce 1945- *WhoAm 90*
Hendin, Gerald A. 1944- *ODwPR 91*
Hendin, Herbert 1926- *ConAu 129*
Hendin, Herbert M 1926- *BiDrAPA 89*
Hendizadeh, Yousef 1951- *BiDrAPA 89*
Hendl, Walter 1917- *IntWWM 90, WhoAm 90*
Hendler, Gary *BioIn 16*
Hendler, Gordon Lee 1946- *WhoEmL 91*
Hendler, Mark Stephen 1948- *WhoSSW 91*
Hendler, Maury Harworth, Jr. 1938- *WhoE 91*
Hendler, Nelson Howard 1944- *BiDrAPA 89*
Hendler, Samuel 1946- *BiDrAPA 89*
Hendler, Samuel I. 1922- *St&PR 91, WhoAm 90*
Hendler, Yehudi Leon 1944- *St&PR 91*
Hendley, Bob 1939- *Ballpl 90*
Hendley, Dan Lunsford 1938- *St&PR 91, WhoAm 90, WhoSSW 91*
Hendley, Edith Di Pasquale 1927- *WhoAmW 91*
Hendley, Essie Kirkland *WhoAmW 91*
Hendley, James C. 1908- *St&PR 91*
Hendon, Betty Joyce 1935- *WhoSSW 91*
Hendon, Lea Alpha 1953- *WhoAmW 91*
Hendon, Robert Caraway 1912- *WhoAm 90*
Hendra, Barbara J. 1938- *ODwPR 91*
Hendra, Jill Lynne 1953- *BiDrAPA 89*
Hendrawan, Frans 1936- *WhoWor 91*
Hendren, Jo Ann 1935- *WhoSSW 91*
Hendren, Merlyn Churchill 1926- *WhoAmW 91*
Hendren, Robert Lee 1930- *WhoSSW 91*
Hendren, Robert Lee 1949- *BiDrAPA 89*
Hendren, Robert Lee, Jr. 1925- *WhoAm 90, WhoWor 91*
Hendrey, George Rummens 1940- *WhoE 91*
Hendrick 1680?-1755 *EncCRAm, WhNaAH*
Hendrick, Clyde 1936- *WhoAm 90*
Hendrick, Edward Joseph, Jr. 1941- *WhoE 91*
Hendrick, George 1929- *WhoAm 90*
Hendrick, George 1949- *Ballpl 90*
Hendrick, Gerald P. 1949- *St&PR 91*
Hendrick, Gerald Paul 1949- *WhoAm 90*
Hendrick, Harvey 1897-1941 *Ballpl 90*
Hendrick, Howard H. 1954- *WhoSSW 91*
Hendrick, Irving Guilford 1936- *WhoAm 90*
Hendrick, James Pomeroy 1901- *WhoAm 90*
Hendrick, John Preston 1954- *BiDrAPA 89*
Hendrick, Jozef Octave Marie 1942- *WhoWor 91*
Hendrick, Kate Marie 1957- *WhoAmW 91*
Hendrick, Keith Coleman 1926- *WhoAm 90*
Hendrick, Kingsley Monroe 1935- *WhoSSW 91*
Hendrick, Lynn D. 1937- *WhoSSW 91*
Hendrick, Rick *BioIn 16*
Hendrick, Ronald L. 1946- *St&PR 91*
Hendrick, Victoria 1963- *BiDrAPA 89*
Hendricks, A Ross 1914- *BiDrAPA 89*
Hendricks, Angela Tutone 1944- *WhoAmW 91*
Hendricks, Anne Lowrey 1946- *BiDrAPA 89*
Hendricks, Barbara *BioIn 16*
Hendricks, Barbara 1948- *IntWWM 90, PenDiMP, WhoAm 90, WhoAmW 91, WhoWor 91*
Hendricks, Barkley Leonnard 1945- *WhoAmA 91*
Hendricks, Bob 1925- *WhoSSW 91*
Hendricks, Carolyn Sue 1935- *WhoAmW 91*
Hendricks, Charles Durrell, Jr. 1926- *WhoAm 90*
Hendricks, Charles Francis 1943- *St&PR 91*
Hendricks, Charles Henning 1917- *WhoAm 90*
Hendricks, David Charles 1948- *WhoAmA 91*
Hendricks, Donald Duane 1931- *WhoAm 90*
Hendricks, Donna Darlene Denney 1951- *WhoAmW 91*
Hendricks, Ed Jerald 1935- *WhoAm 90*
Hendricks, Edward Lee 1952- *WhoAmA 91*
Hendricks, Elizabeth *BiDEWW*
Hendricks, Ellie 1940- *Ballpl 90*
Hendricks, Geoffrey 1931- *WhoAm 90, WhoAmA 91*
Hendricks, Gertrude Elizabeth 1907- *WhoAmW 91*
Hendricks, Jack 1875-1943 *Ballpl 90*
Hendricks, James 1938- *WhoAmA 91*
Hendricks, James Edwin 1935- *WhoAm 90*
Hendricks, James Powell 1938- *WhoAm 90*
Hendricks, John Aloysius 1940- *St&PR 91*
Hendricks, John Samuel *BioIn 16*
Hendricks, Jon *BioIn 16*
Hendricks, Joseph Avery 1942- *St&PR 91*
Hendricks, Kathleen 1939- *WhoWrEP 89*
Hendricks, M. Lavelle 1961- *WhoSSW 91*
Hendricks, Mark Kenneth 1952- *WhoEmL 91*
Hendricks, Nancy Ann 1960- *St&PR 91*
Hendricks, Paige Kelly 1949- *WhoAmW 91*
Hendricks, Paulette Jane 1941- *WhoAmW 91*
Hendricks, Randal 1945- *BioIn 16*
Hendricks, Rayman Michael 1937- *WhoAm 90*
Hendricks, Robert Bruce 1934- *St&PR 91*
Hendricks, Robert John 1950- *WhoEmL 91*
Hendricks, Robert Michael 1943- *WhoWor 91*
Hendricks, Roger C *BiDrAPA 89*
Hendricks, S. Kenneth 1941- *St&PR 91*
Hendricks, Stacy Ann 1960- *WhoAmW 91*
Hendricks, Stanley Marshall, II 1952- *WhoEmL 91*
Hendricks, Thomas Andrews 1819-1885 *BiDrUSE 89*
Hendricks, Thomas L. 1940- *St&PR 91*
Hendricks, Thomas M. 1935- *St&PR 91*
Hendricks, Thomas Manley 1949- *WhoWrEP 89*
Hendricks, Thomas Vernon 1942- *St&PR 91*
Hendricks, William H. 1932- *St&PR 91*
Hendricks, William Hulin 1932- *WhoAm 90*
Hendricks, William Lawrence 1929- *WhoSSW 91*
Hendricks-Verdejo, Carlos Doel, Sr. 1959- *WhoHisp 91*
Hendrickse, William Alfred 1949- *BiDrAPA 89*
Hendricksen, Holmes G. 1933- *WhoAm 90*
Hendrickson, Alan Bryce 1945- *St&PR 91*
Hendrickson, Bruce Carl 1930- *WhoAm 90*
Hendrickson, Candace Sue 1959- *WhoEmL 91*
Hendrickson, Carol Follmuth 1920- *WhoWrEP 89*
Hendrickson, Charles John 1950- *St&PR 91, WhoAm 90*
Hendrickson, Constance Marie M. 1949- *WhoAmW 91, WhoSSW 91*
Hendrickson, Gary Lee 1949- *WhoEmL 91*
Hendrickson, Helen E *BiDrAPA 89*
Hendrickson, J. Wilbur, Jr. 1919- *St&PR 91*
Hendrickson, Jack Reynold, Jr. 1953- *WhoEmL 91*
Hendrickson, James Norman 1945- *WhoEmL 91*
Hendrickson, Jeffrey Thomas 1944- *WhoAm 90*
Hendrickson, Jerome Orland 1918- *WhoAm 90*
Hendrickson, Jo Ann Elizabeth 1944- *WhoWrEP 89*
Hendrickson, Kate M 1946- *BiDrAPA 89*
Hendrickson, L. Bruce 1945- *St&PR 91*
Hendrickson, Magnus 1864-1944 *EncABHB 4*
Hendrickson, Marshall D. 1935- *St&PR 91*
Hendrickson, Marshall David 1935- *WhoAm 90*
Hendrickson, Melissa Batka 1955- *WhoEmL 91*
Hendrickson, Mona Lynn 1951- *WhoAmW 91*
Hendrickson, Robert 1924- *St&PR 91*
Hendrickson, Robert Augustus 1923- *WhoAm 90, WhoWor 91*
Hendrickson, Robert Charles 1952- *WhoEmL 91*
Hendrickson, Robert Frederick 1933- *WhoAm 90*
Hendrickson, Robert M. 1929- *St&PR 91*
Hendrickson, Robert Meland 1929- *WhoAm 90*
Hendrickson, Roland M. 1923- *St&PR 91*
Hendrickson, Steven Eric 1951- *WhoAm 90*
Hendrickson, Thomas N. 1942- *St&PR 91*
Hendrickson, Timothy Paul, Jr. 1946- *WhoEmL 91*
Hendrickson, Tom Allen 1935- *St&PR 91*
Hendrickson, Vanessa M. 1959- *WhoAmW 91*
Hendrickson, Willard James 1916- *BiDrAPA 89*
Hendrickson, William Frenzel 1917- *St&PR 91*
Hendrickson, William George 1918- *WhoWor 91*
Hendrickson, William Wilson 1945- *WhoEmL 91*
Hendrickx, Andrew George 1933- *WhoAm 90*
Hendrie, Elaine *WhoAmW 91*
Hendrie, Gerald Mills 1935- *IntWWM 90*
Hendrie, Hugh Curtis 1936- *BiDrAPA 89*
Hendrie, Joseph Mallam 1925- *WhoAm 90*
Hendriks, Paul *PenDiMP*
Hendrikse, George W. 1958- *WhoWor 91*
Hendrikson, Lisa A. 1960- *St&PR 91*
Hendriksz, Anton Rene 1948- *St&PR 91*
Hendrikx, Louis 1927- *IntWWM 90*
Hendrix, Bill Gene, Jr. 1952- *WhoSSW 91*
Hendrix, Claude 1889-1944 *Ballpl 90*
Hendrix, Connie 1942- *WhoAmA 91*
Hendrix, Dennis Ralph 1940- *St&PR 91, WhoAm 90, WhoSSW 91*
Hendrix, Harville 1935- *ConAu 130*
Hendrix, James Lee 1961- *WhoEmL 91*
Hendrix, James Madison, II 1934- *WhoSSW 91*
Hendrix, James Robert 1905- *WhoSSW 91*
Hendrix, James Walter 1930- *WhoAm 90*
Hendrix, Jimi *BioIn 16*
Hendrix, Jimi 1942-1970 *DrBlPA 90, EncPR&S 89, OxCPMus, WorAlBi*
Hendrix, Jon Richard 1938- *WhoAm 90*
Hendrix, Loren Ervin 1942- *WhoE 91*
Hendrix, Louise Butts 1911- *WhoWor 91*
Hendrix, Lynn Parker 1951- *WhoEmL 91*
Hendrix, Mark Jacob 1957- *WhoEmL 91*
Hendrix, Marvin L. 1942- *St&PR 91*
Hendrix, Michael 1937- *St&PR 91*
Hendrix, Randy Lee 1956- *WhoSSW 91*
Hendrix, Robert Allen 1951- *WhoSSW 91*
Hendrix, Robert E. 1946- *St&PR 91*
Hendrix, Stephen Joseph 1956- *WhoEmL 91*
Hendrix, Sue 1959- *WhoSSW 91*
Hendrix, Susan Clelia Derrick 1920- *WhoAmW 91*
Hendrix, Walter Newton, Jr. 1955- *WhoSSW 91*
Hendrix-Ward, Nancy Katherine 1944- *WhoAmW 91, WhoE 91, WhoSSW 91*
Hendry, Aaron W. 1936- *St&PR 91*
Hendry, Charles H 1936- *BiDrAPA 89*
Hendry, George Orr 1937- *St&PR 91*
Hendry, George Stuart 1904- *WhoAm 90*
Hendry, Gloria 1949- *DrBlPA 90*
Hendry, Iain Wilson Menzies 1927- *WhoAm 90*
Hendry, James E. 1912- *WhoSSW 91*
Hendry, Jean Sharon 1947- *WhoAmW 91*
Hendry, Lloyd G. 1922- *St&PR 91*
Hendry, Robert Ryon 1936- *WhoSSW 91*
Hendry, Tom 1929- *OxCCanT*
Hendry, William Forbes 1938- *WhoWor 91*
Hendryx, Nona *BioIn 16*
Hendryx, Tim 1891-1957 *Ballpl 90*
Hendy, Valerie H. *ODwPR 91*
Hene, Sonya Johanna 1962- *WhoAmW 91*
Heneault, Robert Edmond 1926- *WhoAm 90*
Heneberry, David Arthur 1931- *WhoAm 90*
Henegan, John Clark 1950- *WhoSSW 91*
Henegan, William B *ODwPR 91*
Heneghan, Francis Michael 1932- *St&PR 91*
Heneghan, James 1930- *BioIn 16, ConAu 129*
Heneghan, John J. *BioIn 16*
Heneghan, John James 1940- *St&PR 91*
Heneker, David 1906- *OxCPMus*
Henel, Rolf Heinrich 1937- *WhoAm 90*
Henely, Joann Housh 1928- *WhoAmW 91*
Henes, Donna 1945- *WhoAmA 91, WhoWrEP 89*
Henes, Samuel Ernst 1937- *WhoAm 90*
Heney, Helen 1907- *FemiCLE*
Heney, Joseph Edward 1927- *St&PR 91, WhoAm 90*
Heng Samrin 1934- *WhoWor 91*
Heng, Donald James, Jr. 1944- *WhoAm 90*
Heng, Frankie Fook Kow 1949- *WhoWor 91*
Heng, Siang Gek 1960- *WhoAmW 91, WhoEmL 91*
Heng, Stanley Mark 1937- *WhoAm 90*
Heng, William E. 1945- *St&PR 91*
Hengel, Martin 1926- *WhoWor 91*
Hengemuhle, Joseph F. *BioIn 16*
Hengen, William Lincoln 1914- *WhoAm 90*
Hengsbach, Franz 1910- *WhoWor 91*
Hengstschlaeger, Johannes Franz 1940- *WhoWor 91*
Henican, Caswell Ellis 1905- *WhoAm 90, WhoSSW 91*
Henick, Steven T. 1942- *St&PR 91*
Henie, Sonja 1912-1969 *WorAlBi*
Heniff, Marilyn Rose 1939- *WhoAmW 91*
Henigan, Mark Hamilton 1953- *BiDrAPA 89*
Heniger, Alice Minnie Herts 1870?-1933 *BioIn 16, NotWoAT*
Henighan, Violet Alfreda 1947- *BiDrAPA 89*
Henike, Barbara J *BiDrAPA 89*
Henikoff, Leo M., Jr. 1939- *WhoAm 90*
Hening, Keith 1947- *BiDrAPA 89*
Heninger, George R 1934- *BiDrAPA 89*
Heninger, Owen E 1929- *BiDrAPA 89*
Heninger, Owen P *BiDrAPA 89*
Heninger, Simeon Kahn, Jr. 1922- *WhoAm 90*
Heninger, Wendy Marie *BiDrAPA 89*
Henington, David Mead 1929- *WhoAm 90, WhoSSW 91*
Henion, David L. 1944- *St&PR 91*
Henion, Nancy Frank 1930- *WhoE 91*
Henissart, Paul Henri 1923- *SpyFic*
Henisz, Jerzy Emil 1937- *BiDrAPA 89, WhoE 91*
Henize, Karl Gordon 1926- *WhoAm 90*
Henke, Ana Mari 1954- *WhoAmW 91, WhoEmL 91*
Henke, Emerson Overbeck 1916- *WhoAm 90*
Henke, Eugenio *BioIn 16*
Henke, Janice Carine 1938- *WhoAmW 91, WhoWor 91*
Henke, Michael John 1940- *WhoAm 90*

Henke, Patricia Norris 1950- WhoE 91
Henke, Raymond Lange 1953- WhoEmL 91
Henke, Sue Ellen 1951- WhoAmW 91
Henke, Tom 1957- Ballpl 90
Henkel, Arthur John 1945- St&PR 91
Henkel, Arthur John, Jr. 1945- WhoE 91
Henkel, David R. 1946- St&PR 91
Henkel, David Richard 1951- WhoSSW 91
Henkel, Eloise Elizabeth 1923- WhoAmW 91
Henkel, Kathryn G. 1952- WhoEmL 91
Henkel, Konrad Karl 1954- St&PR 91
Henkel, Mary McKenzie 1910- St&PR 91
Henkel, Oliver Carl, Jr. 1936- WhoAm 90
Henkel, William 1941- WhoAm 90
Henkel, Zane Grey 1937- WhoSSW 91, WhoWor 91
Henkelman, Frank William 1922- St&PR 91
Henkels, Paul M. 1924- St&PR 91
Henkels, Paul MacAllister 1924- WhoAm 90
Henken, Deborah Lynn 1958- WhoEmL 91
Henken, Morris 1919- IntWWM 90
Henken, Willard John 1927- WhoAm 90
Henker, Fred O, III 1922- BiDrAPA 89
Henkes, Kevin 1960- AuBYP 90, BioIn 16, ChlLR 23 [port]
Henkhaus, James David 1944- St&PR 91
Henkin, Hilary BioIn 16
Henkin, Leon Albert 1921- WhoAm 90
Henkin, Louis 1917- WhoAm 90, WhoE 91
Henkin, Minerva Salzman BioIn 16
Henkin, Patricia 1947- WhoAmW 91
Henkin, Robert Irwin 1930- WhoAm 90
Henkin, Roxanne Lee 1951- WhoAmW 91
Henkin, Stephen Morgan 1947- WhoEmL 91
Henkin-Bookman, Jean Patricia 1948- WhoWrEP 89
Henkle, Herman Henry 1900-1987 BioIn 16
Henkle, James Lee 1927- WhoAmA 91
Henkle, Roger B. 1935- ConAu 129
Henkle, Roger Black 1935- WhoAm 90, WhoWrEP 89
Henkle, Teresa 1955- WhoAmW 91
Henkus, Ira 1949- St&PR 91
Henle, Fritz 1909- WhoAmA 91
Henle, Guy 1920- WhoAm 90
Henle, Mary 1913- WhoAmW 91
Henle, Peter 1919- WhoAm 90
Henle, Robert A. 1924-1989 BioIn 16
Henle, Robert John 1909- WhoAm 90
Henlein, Peter PenDiDA 89
Henley, Arthur 1921- WhoAm 90, WhoWrEP 89
Henley, Arthur Boyden, Jr. 1933- St&PR 91
Henley, Beth BioIn 16, ConAu 32NR, MajTwCW
Henley, Beth 1952- FemiCLE, WhoAm 90, WhoAmW 91, WorAu 1980 [port]
Henley, Bruce Frazier 1953- WhoSSW 91
Henley, Cheryl Chris 1948- WhoAmW 91
Henley, Don BioIn 16
Henley, Don 1947- EncPR&S 89
Henley, Earle Burr, Jr. 1915- WhoAm 90
Henley, Elizabeth Becker 1952- ConAu 32NR, MajTwCW
Henley, Ernest Mark 1924- WhoAm 90
Henley, Gail 1950- WhoWrEP 89
Henley, Henry Howard, Jr. 1921- St&PR 91, WhoAm 90
Henley, Joseph Oliver 1949- WhoE 91, WhoEmL 91, WhoWor 91
Henley, Joseph P. 1926- St&PR 91
Henley, Karen Melinda BiDrAPA 89
Henley, Lee Ann 1949- WhoEmL 91
Henley, Lila Mary 1926- WhoAmW 91
Henley, Mary Beth 1952- NotWoAT
Henley, Melvin Brent 1935- WhoSSW 91
Henley, Nixon Carr 1936- St&PR 91
Henley, Richard James 1956- WhoEmL 91
Henley, Richard Merle 1952- WhoEmL 91
Henley, Rudolph 1949- WhoSSW 91
Henley, Terry Lew 1940- WhoWor 91
Henley, Thomas F 1912- BiDrAPA 89
Henley, Thomas Ladd 1942- BiDrAPA 89
Henley, Thomas W. 1932- St&PR 91
Henley, Vernard William 1929- St&PR 91, WhoAm 90
Henley, Weldon 1880-1960 Ballpl 90
Henley, William Ernest 1849-1903 BioIn 16
Henline, Butch 1894-1957 Ballpl 90
Henline, Florence IntWWM 90
Henman, Graham BioIn 16
Henn, Barbara Jeanne 1936- WhoAmW 91
Henn, Catherine Emily Campbell 1942- St&PR 91
Henn, Fritz A 1941- BiDrAPA 89
Henn, Fritz Albert 1941- WhoE 91
Henn, Harry George 1919- WhoAm 90
Henn, John Howard 1942- WhoAm 90
Henn, Mary Ann 1930- WhoWrEP 89
Henn, Ralph Frank 1947- BiDrAPA 89
Hennby, Bo Albert 1930- WhoWor 91
Henne, Dagmar BioIn 16
Henne, Frank R 1902- BiDrAPA 89
Henne, Nancy Diane 1955- WhoWrEP 89
Hennebach, Ralph L. 1920- St&PR 91
Henneberger, Lawrence Francis 1938- WhoAm 90
Hennecy, Bobbie Bobo 1922- WhoAmW 91, WhoSSW 91
Hennefer, David A. 1948- St&PR 91
Hennefer, Nancy White 1958- WhoAmW 91
Hennegan, John Owen 1947- WhoEmL 91
Henneke, David Charles 1955- WhoEmL 91
Hennekens, Candace Anne 1948- WhoEmL 91
Hennell, David 1712-1785 PenDiDA 89
Hennell, David 1767- PenDiDA 89
Hennell, Robert 1741-1811 PenDiDA 89
Hennell, Robert 1769- PenDiDA 89
Hennell, Robert 1794-1868 PenDiDA 89
Hennell, Robert 1826?-1892 PenDiDA 89
Hennell, Robert George PenDiDA 89
Hennell, Samuel 1778-1837 PenDiDA 89
Hennell, Thomas 1903-1945 BioIn 16
Hennelly, Edmund Paul 1923- WhoE 91, WhoWor 91
Henneman, Dorothy Hughes 1923- WhoAm 90
Henneman, Elwood 1915- WhoAm 90
Henneman, John Bell, Jr. 1935- ConAu 31NR, WhoAm 90
Henneman, Mike 1961- Ballpl 90
Henneman, Richard Lewis 1958- WhoSSW 91
Henneman, Stephen Charles 1949- WhoEmL 91
Hennemeyer, Robert Thomas 1925- WhoAm 90
Hennenhoefer, Gerald J. 1947- St&PR 91
Hennepin, Louis 1640-1701? EncCRAm, WhNaAH
Henner, Daniel Jacques 1941- WhoWor 91
Henner, Egon 1923- WhoE 91
Henner, Marilu BioIn 16
Henner, Peter William 1952- WhoEmL 91
Hennerova, Marie EncCoWW
Hennes, Harvey 1947- St&PR 91, WhoEmL 91
Hennes, Peter Michael 1954- WhoEmL 91
Hennes, Robert T. 1955- St&PR 91
Hennes, Robert Taft 1930- WhoAm 90
Hennessee, Manassa Nixon 1930- St&PR 91, WhoSSW 91
Hennessey, Alice Elizabeth 1936- WhoAmW 91
Hennessey, Audrey Kathleen 1936- WhoAmW 91
Hennessey, Carol Ludwick 1949- WhoAmW 91
Hennessey, Daniel F. 1942- St&PR 91
Hennessey, David Charles 1949- WhoEmL 91
Hennessey, David Patrick 1950- WhoEmL 91
Hennessey, Edward Francis 1919- WhoE 91
Hennessey, John Philip 1937- St&PR 91
Hennessey, John William, Jr. 1925- WhoAm 90
Hennessey, Patrick Lee 1950- St&PR 91
Hennessey, Patrick Leo 1934- St&PR 91
Hennessey, Ralph Edward 1916- St&PR 91
Hennessey, Raymond Frank 1925- WhoE 91
Hennessey, Robert J. 1941- St&PR 91
Hennessey, Robert John 1941- WhoAm 90
Hennessey, William John 1948- WhoAm 90, WhoAmA 91
Hennessy, Anne Dominica 1955- BiDrAPA 89
Hennessy, Charlene Koehler 1945- WhoAmW 91
Hennessy, Charles W. 1926- St&PR 91
Hennessy, Colleen M. 1961- WhoEmL 91
Hennessy, Daniel Kraft 1941- WhoAm 90
Hennessy, Dean McDonald 1923- St&PR 91, WhoAm 90
Hennessy, Debra 1959- St&PR 91
Hennessy, Edward Lawrence, Jr. 1928- St&PR 91, WhoAm 90, WhoE 91, WhoWor 91
Hennessy, Hugh J. 1917- St&PR 91
Hennessy, James Ernest 1933- WhoAm 90
Hennessy, John Francis 1928-1989 BioIn 16
Hennessy, John Francis, III 1955- WhoE 91
Hennessy, John Francis, Jr. 1928- St&PR 91
Hennessy, John M. 1936- St&PR 91
Hennessy, John Pope- BioIn 16
Hennessy, Joseph John 1953- St&PR 91
Hennessy, Madeleine Joyce 1948- WhoWrEP 89
Hennessy, Margaret B. 1952- WhoAmW 91
Hennessy, Mary Margaret BiDrAPA 89
Hennessy, Paul Raymond 1925- St&PR 91
Hennessy, Robert Bruce 1934- St&PR 91
Hennessy, Susan Margaret 1961- WhoAmW 91
Hennessy, Thomas Christopher 1916- WhoAm 90
Hennessy, Wesley Joseph 1914- WhoAm 90
Hennesy, Dale 1926-1981 ConDes 90
Hennesy, Gerald Craft 1921- WhoAm 90, WhoAmA 91, WhoSSW 91
Henney, Dagmar Renate WhoAmW 91
Hennig, Emil Hans Willi 1913-1976 DcScB S2
Hennig, Frederick E. WhoAm 90
Hennig, Frederick E. 1932- St&PR 91
Hennig, G. Karen 1941- WhoSSW 91
Hennig, Jeffrey Carlton 1944- St&PR 91
Hennig, Wolfgang Hans Gunter 1941- WhoWor 91
Hennigan, Leo P BiDrAPA 89
Hennigan, Patrick John 1945- WhoE 91
Hennigan, Phil 1946- Ballpl 90
Hennigar, Curtis Alan 1959- WhoSSW 91
Hennigar, Dana E. 1933- St&PR 91
Hennigar, David J. 1939- WhoAm 90
Hennigar, Harold Frank, Jr. 1953- WhoSSW 91
Hennigar, William Grant, Jr. 1947- WhoEmL 91
Henniger, David Thomas 1936- WhoSSW 91
Henniker, Florence 1855-1923 FemiCLE
Henning, Alyson Balfour 1955- WhoEmL 91
Henning, Barbara J. 1948- WhoWrEP 89
Henning, Basil Duke BioIn 16
Henning, Basil Duke NewYTBS 90
Henning, Basil Duke 1910-1990 ConAu 130
Henning, Charles Nathaniel 1915- WhoAm 90
Henning, Dan 1942- WhoAm 90
Henning, Daniel C. BioIn 16
Henning, David Richard 1943- St&PR 91
Henning, Donna Eileen 1952- WhoE 91
Henning, Doug 1947- WhoAm 90
Henning, Edward Burk 1922- WhoAm 90, WhoAmA 91
Henning, Emilie Anne 1930- WhoAmW 91
Henning, Gary 1951- St&PR 91
Henning, George A. 1947- St&PR 91
Henning, George Thomas, Jr. 1941- WhoAm 90
Henning, Harold O. 1924- St&PR 91
Henning, Harold W. 1919-1988 BioIn 16
Henning, Harold Walter 1919- WhoAm 90
Henning, Heinz-Dieter Richard 1943- WhoWor 91
Henning, Joel Frank 1939- WhoAm 90
Henning, John F., Jr. 1923- St&PR 91
Henning, John J. 1941- St&PR 91
Henning, John R. 1934- St&PR 91
Henning, Michael D. 1944- St&PR 91
Henning, Michael Fredrick 1963- WhoSSW 91
Henning, Paul 1911- BioIn 16
Henning, Paul Francis, Jr. 1932- St&PR 91
Henning, Pete 1887-1939 Ballpl 90
Henning, Rachel 1826-1914 FemiCLE
Henning, Robert V. 1916- St&PR 91
Henning, Ronda Regina 1957- WhoAmW 91, WhoEmL 91
Henning, Rudolf Ernst 1923- WhoAm 90, WhoSSW 91
Henning, Susan June 1946- WhoAmW 91
Henning, Thomas E. 1953- St&PR 91
Henning, William Clifford 1918- WhoWor 91
Henning, William Wilson 1946- St&PR 91
Henninger, Ann Louise 1946- WhoAmW 91
Henninger, John G. 1916- St&PR 91
Henninger, Kenneth Alan 1938- St&PR 91
Hennings, Deirdre Ellen 1951- WhoAmW 91
Hennings, Emmy 1885- BiDWomA
Hennings, Emmy 1885-1948 EncCoWW
Hennings, Frederick Louis 1931- St&PR 91
Hennings, Leah K. 1967- WhoEmL 91
Hennings, Nancy NewAgMG
Hennings, Roger Charles 1932- WhoSSW 91
Hennings, William M. 1950- St&PR 91
Hennings-Ball, Emmy 1885- BiDWomA
Henningsen, Agnes Kathinka Malling 1868-1962 EncCoWW
Henningsen, Peter, Jr. 1926- St&PR 91, WhoAm 90
Henningsen, Poul 1894-1967 PenDiDA 89
Henningsen, Victor William, Jr. 1924- St&PR 91, WhoE 91
Hennion, Carolyn Laird 1943- WhoAmW 91
Hennion, Reeve Lawrence 1941- WhoAm 90
Hennum, Laura Alferd 1964- WhoAmW 91
Hennum, Susanna S. 1928- WhoAmW 91
Henny, George Christian 1899-1988 BioIn 16
Henquinet, Wayne K. St&PR 91
Henreid, Paul WhoAm 90
Henreid, Paul 1908- WorAlBi
Henri, Adrian 1932- MajTwCW
Henri, Lise Marie 1962- WhoAmW 91
Henri, Louie PenDiMP
Henri, Robert 1865-1929 WorAlBi
Henri, Victor 1872-1940 DcScB S2
Henrich, Biff 1953- WhoAmA 91
Henrich, Christopher John 1942- WhoE 91
Henrich, Jean MacKay 1909- WhoE 91
Henrich, LeAnn Jean 1957- WhoAmW 91
Henrich, Stephen Brown 1950- WhoEmL 91
Henrich, Tommy 1913- Ballpl 90, BioIn 16
Henrich, William Joseph, Jr. 1929- WhoAm 90
Henrichs, Albert Maximinus 1942- WhoAm 90
Henrichs, Roy Beddow 1953- WhoEmL 91
Henrichs, Susan Margaret 1952- WhoEmL 91
Henrick, Joanne B. 1953- ODwPR 91
Henricks, Jerry Arnold 1934- St&PR 91
Henricks, Lorraine Eleanor BiDrAPA 89
Henricks, Steven Carl BiDrAPA 89
Henricksen, Anne E. WhoAmW 91
Henricksen, Bruce Conley 1941- WhoWrEP 89
Henricksen, Ralf Christian 1907-1975 WhoAmA 91N
Henrickson, Charles Henry 1938- WhoSSW 91
Henrickson, Eiler Leonard 1920- WhoAm 90
Henrickson, Martha 1942- WhoAmA 91
Henrickson, Pamela Quigg 1958- WhoEmL 91
Henrickson, Paul Robert WhoAmA 91
Henrickson, Richard Ralph 1948- WhoE 91, WhoWor 91
Henrickson, Thomas 1944- WhoAmA 91
Henrie, Betty Collins 1922- WhoE 91
Henriet, Raoul Robert 1927- WhoWor 91
Henrietta Maria 1609-1669 BiDEWW
Henrietta Maria, Queen 1609-1669 BioIn 16
Henriette de Cleves WomWR
Henriksen, Alicia Jeanne 1955- WhoEmL 91
Henriksen, David L. 1954- St&PR 91
Henriksen, Lance ConTFT 8
Henriksen, Mary Jo 1954- WhoWrEP 89
Henriksen, Melvin 1927- WhoAm 90
Henriksen, Niel Christian 1960- WhoEmL 91
Henriksen, Thomas Hollinger 1939- WhoAm 90
Henrikson, Arthur A 1921- ConAu 130
Henrikson, Katherine Pointer 1939- WhoAmW 91
Henrikson, Lennart Karl Nils 1935- WhoWor 91
Henrikson, Lois Elizabeth 1921- WhoAmW 91, WhoWor 91
Henrikson, Steven Thomas 1946- WhoEmL 91
Henriksson, Anders Goran 1937- WhoWor 91
Henriksson, Jan Hugo Lennart 1933- WhoWor 91
Henriod, Lorraine 1925- AuBYP 90
Henrion, F H K 1914- ConDes 90
Henrion, Jean Paul Guillaume 1932- WhoWor 91
Henriot, Philippe 1889-1944 BiDFrPL
Henriques, Adolfo 1953- St&PR 91
Henriques, Diana Blackmon 1948- WhoE 91
Henriques, Donald Andrew 1957- IntWWM 90
Henriques, Patricia Ann 1949- WhoAmW 91, WhoWor 91
Henriquez, Nelson 1941- WhoHisp 91
Henriquez, Norma BiDrAPA 89
Henriquez-Freeman, Hilda Josefina 1938- WhoAmW 91
Henriquez Gaztanondo, Antonio Santos 1936- WhoWor 91
Henriquez Urena, Pedro 1884-1946 BioIn 16
Henritze, Thomas King 1932- St&PR 91
Henru, Charles 1923-1990 BiDFrPL
Henry IV 1553-1610 WorAlBi
Henry VII 1457-1509 WorAlBi
Henry VIII 1491-1547 WorAlBi
Henry, Infante of Portugal 1394-1460 BioIn 16
Henry V, King of England 1387-1422 BioIn 16
Henry VIII, King of England 1491-1547 BioIn 16

Henry III, King of France 1551-1589 *BioIn 16*
Henry IV, King of France 1553-1610 *BioIn 16*
Henry, of Navarre 1553-1610 *BioIn 16*
Henry, Prince of Great Britain 1984- *BioIn 16*
Henry, the Navigator 1394-1460 *BioIn 16*
Henry the Navigator 1394-1460 *EncCRAm, WorAlBi*
Henry, Aaron *BioIn 16*
Henry, Alan Pemberton 1949- *WhoAm 90*
Henry, Alan Ray 1941- *WhoAm 90*
Henry, Alexander 1739-1824 *DcLB 99, WhNaAH*
Henry, Alice 1857-1943 *FemiCLE*
Henry, Allan Francis 1925- *WhoAm 90*
Henry, Andrew 1775?-1833 *WhNaAH*
Henry, Ann 1914- *OxCCanT*
Henry, Ann Rainwater 1939- *WhoSSW 91*
Henry, Anne Marshall 1944- *WhoAmW 91*
Henry, Barbara A. 1952- *WhoAmW 91, WhoE 91*
Henry, Bill 1927- *Ballpl 90*
Henry, Bill W. 1934- *St&PR 91*
Henry, Blondy Sewell 1915- *WhoSSW 91*
Henry, Bruce *St&PR 91*
Henry, Bruce Edward 1952- *WhoEmL 91*
Henry, Bruce Gordon 1943- *BiDrAPA 89*
Henry, Buck *WhoAm 90*
Henry, Carl Ferdinand Howard 1913- *WhoAm 90*
Henry, Charles E. 1930- *St&PR 91*
Henry, Charles Joseph 1936- *WhoAm 90*
Henry, Charles L. *BioIn 16*
Henry, Charles Robert 1937- *WhoAm 90*
Henry, Charles Wolcott 1926- *St&PR 91*
Henry, Claudette 1947- *WhoAmW 91*
Henry, Clifford Hugh, Jr. 1928- *WhoSSW 91*
Henry, Colin Samuel 1950- *WhoEmL 91*
Henry, Daniel John, Jr. 1960- *WhoEmL 91*
Henry, David Howe, II 1918- *WhoAm 90, WhoSSW 91, WhoWor 91*
Henry, De Witt P. 1941- *WhoWrEP 89*
Henry, DeLysle Leon 1935- *WhoWor 91*
Henry, Desmond Paul 1921- *ConAu 132*
Henry, DeWitt 1941- *ConAu 131*
Henry, DeWitt Pawling, II 1941- *WhoAm 90*
Henry, Donna Edwards 1949- *WhoAmW 91*
Henry, Dutch 1902-1968 *Ballpl 90*
Henry, Dwayne 1962- *Ballpl 90*
Henry, Edward A. 1910- *St&PR 91*
Henry, Edward Frank 1923- *WhoWor 91*
Henry, Edward LeRoy 1921- *WhoAm 90*
Henry, Edward Oscar 1941- *IntWWM 90*
Henry, Elizabeth *BioIn 16*
Henry, Eric Timothy 1939- *St&PR 91*
Henry, Frances Ann 1939- *WhoAmW 91*
Henry, Francis Bradford *St&PR 91*
Henry, Franklyn L *BiDrAPA 89*
Henry, Garth W. *St&PR 91*
Henry, Geoffrey Arama 1940- *WhoWor 91*
Henry, George M 1937- *BiDrAPA 89*
Henry, Gerrit Van Keuren 1950- *WhoAmA 91*
Henry, Harold Robert 1928- *WhoAm 90*
Henry, Herman Luther, Jr. 1918- *WhoAm 90*
Henry, Homer C. 1950- *WhoEmL 91*
Henry, Hugh Fort 1916- *WhoAm 90*
Henry, Hunter Woods 1928- *WhoAm 90*
Henry, Hunter Woods, Jr. 1928- *St&PR 91*
Henry, Ismay E *BiDrAPA 89*
Henry, James Brian 1938- *WhoAm 90*
Henry, James C., Jr. 1926- *St&PR 91*
Henry, James Searcy 1902- *St&PR 91*
Henry, Jane Stinnett 1952- *WhoAmW 91*
Henry, Jay Edward 1950- *WhoEmL 91*
Henry, Jean *WhoAmA 91*
Henry, Jean Shelley Jennings 1913- *WhoAmW 91*
Henry, Joe E. 1933- *St&PR 91*
Henry, John 1889-1941 *Ballpl 90*
Henry, John B. 1948- *St&PR 91*
Henry, John Bernard 1928- *WhoAm 90*
Henry, John Case 1905-1990 *ConAu 132*
Henry, John Frederick 1931- *WhoAm 90*
Henry, John P., Jr. 1935- *St&PR 91*
Henry, John Philip 1927- *WhoE 91*
Henry, John Porter, Jr. 1911- *WhoAm 90*
Henry, John Raymond 1943- *WhoAmA 91*
Henry, John T. 1933- *St&PR 91*
Henry, John Thomas 1933- *WhoAm 90*
Henry, Jon William 1942- *WhoAm 90*
Henry, Jonathan G A 1954- *BiDrAPA 89*
Henry, Joseph 1797-1878 *BioIn 16, WorAlBi*
Henry, Joseph C. 1952- *St&PR 91*
Henry, Joseph Louis 1924- *WhoAm 90*
Henry, Judy Garretson 1931- *WhoSSW 91*
Henry, Judy Marlowe 1948- *WhoAmW 91, WhoEmL 91*
Henry, Justin Worthington 1971- *WhoEmL 91*
Henry, Katherine Savage 1944- *WhoSSW 91*
Henry, Kathleen Marie 1950- *WhoAmW 91, WhoEmL 91*
Henry, Katrina Deloris 1945- *WhoE 91*
Henry, Laurin Luther 1921- *WhoAm 90*
Henry, Lawrence C. 1944- *St&PR 91*
Henry, Lesa M. *ODwPR 91*
Henry, Lorene H *BiDrAPA 89*
Henry, Margaret 1914- *WhoAm 90*
Henry, Marguerite *WhoAm 90, WhoWrEP 89*
Henry, Marguerite 1902- *AuBYP 90*
Henry, Marion *MajTwCW*
Henry, Marshall Webster, Jr. 1946- *St&PR 91*
Henry, Martha 1938- *OxCCanT*
Henry, Martin Daniel 1940- *WhoAm 90*
Henry, Mary Ellen 1948- *WhoE 91*
Henry, Milton Lyman, Jr. 1945- *WhoEmL 91*
Henry, Miriam Jennings 1942- *WhoSSW 91*
Henry, Nancy Rose 1938- *WhoAmW 91*
Henry, Nicholas Llewellyn 1943- *WhoAm 90, WhoSSW 91*
Henry, O. *AuBYP 90, ConAu 131, MajTwCW*
Henry, O. 1862-1910 *WorAlBi*
Henry, Oliver *ConAu 131, MajTwCW*
Henry, Ormond Lee 1937- *St&PR 91, WhoAm 90*
Henry, Patrick 1736-1799 *BioIn 16, WorAlBi*
Henry, Patrick 1739-1799 *EncCRAm [port]*
Henry, Patrick G. 1939- *WhoAm 90*
Henry, Paul *St&PR 91*
Henry, Paul Brentwood 1942- *WhoAm 90*
Henry, Paul Raleigh 1928- *St&PR 91*
Henry, Paul Shala 1944- *WhoAm 90*
Henry, Peter York 1951- *WhoEmL 91, WhoSSW 91, WhoWor 91*
Henry, Philip Clark 1932- *St&PR 91*
Henry, Phillip Francis 1952- *IntWWM 90*
Henry, Ragan *BioIn 16*
Henry, Ralph S. 1921- *St&PR 91*
Henry, Randolph Marshall 1946- *WhoEmL 91, WhoSSW 91*
Henry, Ray *St&PR 91*
Henry, Regina *ODwPR 91*
Henry, Rene A., Jr. 1933- *ODwPR 91*
Henry, Rene Arthur, Jr. 1933- *WhoAm 90, WhoE 91*
Henry, Rene Paul, Sr. 1917- *WhoSSW 91*
Henry, Richard Charles 1925- *WhoAm 90*
Henry, Richard Conn 1940- *WhoAm 90*
Henry, Robert *TwCCr&M 91*
Henry, Robert 1933- *WhoAmA 91*
Henry, Robert Fillmore 1934- *St&PR 91*
Henry, Robert H. 1953- *WhoAm 90, WhoSSW 91*
Henry, Robert J. 1950- *St&PR 91*
Henry, Robert Joseph 1946- *St&PR 91*
Henry, Ronald George 1949- *WhoEmL 91*
Henry, Ronald James Whyte 1940- *WhoAm 90*
Henry, Roseann 1958- *WhoAmW 91*
Henry, Roxann Elizabeth 1953- *WhoEmL 91*
Henry, Samuel P. 1838- *AmLegL*
Henry, Sandra Kednocker *WhoAmW 91, WhoWor 91*
Henry, Sara Lynn 1942- *WhoAmA 91*
Henry, Sarah Winston 1710-1784 *BioAmW*
Henry, Shirley Ann 1937- *WhoWor 91*
Henry, Stephen Allen 1949- *WhoE 91*
Henry, Stephen Lewis 1953- *WhoEmL 91*
Henry, Steven Carl 1948- *WhoAm 90*
Henry, Susan Armstrong 1946- *WhoAm 90*
Henry, Thomas J., Jr. 1943- *St&PR 91*
Henry, Thomas Joseph 1934- *St&PR 91*
Henry, W. Lester, Jr. *BioIn 16*
Henry, Walter L. 1941- *WhoAm 90*
Henry, Walter Lester, Jr. 1915- *WhoAm 90*
Henry, Warner W. 1938- *St&PR 91*
Henry, Wayne Burton 1945- *WhoEmL 91*
Henry, Wayne Edward 1932- *St&PR 91*
Henry, Will 1912- *AuBYP 90, BioIn 16*
Henry, William 1729-1786 *EncCRAm*
Henry, William A., III 1950- *ConAu 130*
Henry, William Abbott 1939- *St&PR 91*
Henry, William Alfred, III 1950- *WhoAm 90*
Henry, William Aloysius 1956- *WhoE 91*
Henry, William Earl 1917- *WhoAm 90*
Henry, William Keith 1953- *WhoEmL 91*
Henry, William Oscar Eugene 1927- *WhoAm 90*
Henry, William Ray 1925- *WhoAm 90*
Henry, Zachary Adolphus 1930- *WhoSSW 91*
Henry-John, Emmanuel Sylvester 1949- *WhoEmL 91*
Henry Schoen, Janice Lu 1946- *WhoEmL 91*
Henry-Thiel, Lois Hollender 1941- *WhoAmW 91*
Henryon, Dominique 1951- *WhoWor 91*
Henrys *BioIn 16*
Hensala, John David *BiDrAPA 89*
Hensche, Ada Rayner *WhoAmA 91*
Hensche, Henry 1901- *WhoAmA 91*
Henschel, David Frank 1950- *WhoEmL 91*
Henschel, George 1850-1934 *PenDiMP*
Henschel, Georgie *BioIn 16*
Henschel, Helen *PenDiMP*
Henschel, John James 1954- *WhoEmL 91*
Henschel, Leonard P *BiDrAPA 89*
Henschell, Todd Edward 1954- *WhoEmL 91*
Henschen, Gary Mayes 1948- *BiDrAPA 89*
Henschke, Alfred 1890-1928 *BioIn 16*
Hensel, Cornelius Leroy 1936- *St&PR 91*
Hensel, Fanny Cecile Mendelssohn 1805-1847 *BioIn 16*
Hensel, Friedrich 1933- *WhoWor 91*
Hensel, Georg 1923- *WhoWor 91*
Hensel, H. Struve 1901- *WhoAm 90*
Hensel, Karen Astrid 1944- *WhoE 91*
Hensel, Katherine Ruth 1959- *WhoEmL 91*
Hensel, Luise Maria 1798-1876 *EncCoWW*
Hensel, Paul Joseph 1948- *WhoEmL 91*
Hensel, Robin Ann Morgan 1960- *WhoEmL 91*
Hensel, Steven James 1956- *WhoSSW 91*
Hensel, Witold 1917- *WhoWor 91*
Henseler, Gerald A. 1940- *St&PR 91*
Henseler, Gerald Anthony 1940- *WhoAm 90*
Henselmann, Caspar 1933- *WhoAmA 91*
Henselmeier, Sandra Nadine 1937- *WhoAmW 91*
Henselt, Adolf von 1814-1889 *BioIn 16*
Hensen, Deirdre Munisteri 1954- *WhoAmW 91*
Henshall, Dalwyn James 1957- *IntWWM 90*
Henshall, James Arthur, Jr. 1941- *St&PR 91*
Henshall, Russell George 1958- *WhoEmL 91*
Henshaw, Anne *BiDEWW*
Henshaw, David 1791-1852 *BiDrUSE 89*
Henshaw, Edgar Cummings 1929- *WhoAm 90*
Henshaw, Jonathan Cook 1922- *St&PR 91, WhoAm 90*
Henshaw, Marion Updike 1945- *WhoSSW 91*
Henshaw, Roy 1911- *Ballpl 90*
Henshaw, William M. *St&PR 91*
Henshaw, William Raleigh 1932- *WhoSSW 91*
Henshel, Harry B. 1919- *St&PR 91*
Henshel, Harry Bulova 1919- *WhoAm 90*
Henshell, Mort 1926- *St&PR 91*
Henshilwood, Donald Keith 1930- *IntWWM 90*
Hensing, John Andrew 1947- *WhoEmL 91*
Hensinger, Janet Paula Maupin 1944- *WhoAmW 91*
Hensinger, Margaret Elizabeth 1950- *WhoAmW 91, WhoSSW 91, WhoWor 91*
Henske, John M. *BioIn 16*
Henske, John McClanahan *NewYTBS 90*
Hensleigh, Sarah Esther 1911- *WhoWrEP 89*
Hensler, Guenter Manfred 1939- *WhoAm 90, WhoE 91*
Hensley, Allan Lance 1944- *WhoSSW 91*
Hensley, Annette Elaine 1964- *WhoAmW 91*
Hensley, Betty Austin 1923- *IntWWM 90*
Hensley, Dwayne Scott 1961- *WhoSSW 91*
Hensley, Edward Randolph 1933- *St&PR 91*
Hensley, Elizabeth Catherine 1921- *WhoAm 90*
Hensley, Eugene Benjamin 1918- *WhoAm 90*
Hensley, Jackson Morey 1940- *WhoAmA 91*
Hensley, Joe L 1926- *ConAu 31NR, TwCCr&M 91, WhoWrEP 89*
Hensley, Jon 1966- *BioIn 16*
Hensley, Joseph 1824-1894 *DcCanB 12*
Hensley, Kathleen Noelle 1960- *WhoE 91, WhoEmL 91*
Hensley, Louis Samuel, Jr. 1926- *WhoWor 91*
Hensley, Margaret Ann 1941- *WhoAmW 91*
Hensley, Mary Lynne Floyd 1952- *WhoAmW 91, WhoEmL 91*
Hensley, Michael Wayne 1956- *WhoEmL 91*
Hensley, Robert T., Jr. 1932- *St&PR 91*
Hensley, Robert Thornton, Jr. 1932- *WhoAm 90*
Hensley, Roger Boyd 1949- *BiDrAPA 89*
Hensley, Ronald Verne 1936- *BiDrAPA 89*
Hensley, Sharon Quan 1947- *WhoSSW 91*
Hensley, Sophia Margaretta 1866-1946 *FemiCLE*
Hensley, Sophie Almon 1866-1946 *DcLB 99*
Hensley, Stephen Allan 1950- *WhoSSW 91*
Hensley, Tom *ODwPR 91*
Hensley, William Andrew 1946- *WhoAm 90*
Hensley-Jones, Constance Irene 1950- *WhoEmL 91*
Henslow, George 1834-1925 *EncO&P 3*
Henson, Anna Miriam Morgan 1935- *WhoAmW 91*
Henson, Arnold 1931- *St&PR 91, WhoAm 90*
Henson, C. Ward 1940- *WhoAm 90*
Henson, Claudia E. *BiDrAPA 89*
Henson, Cynthia Lynn 1958- *WhoAmW 91*
Henson, Daniel P., III 1943- *St&PR 91*
Henson, Donald Lentz, Jr. *BiDrAPA 89*
Henson, E. Eddie 1936- *St&PR 91*
Henson, Frank Herman 1938- *St&PR 91*
Henson, Franklin Shannon 1955- *WhoEmL 91*
Henson, Gene Ethridge 1924- *WhoAmW 91*
Henson, Henry Paul 1931- *WhoSSW 91*
Henson, James Bond 1933- *WhoAm 90*
Henson, James H. 1933- *WhoAm 90*
Henson, James Maury 1936-1990 *ConAu 131*
Henson, Jeffery Weldon 1958- *WhoSSW 91*
Henson, Jim *BioIn 16, ConAu 131*
Henson, Jim *NewYTBS 90 [port]*
Henson, Jim 1936-1990 *CurBio 90N, News 90, WorAlBi*
Henson, John 1929- *BioIn 16*
Henson, John Clark, Sr. 1945- *St&PR 91*
Henson, John Ely 1947- *WhoSSW 91*
Henson, Ken Levon 1933- *WhoSSW 91*
Henson, L. Luton 1906- *St&PR 91*
Henson, Leslie 1891-1957 *OxCPMus*
Henson, Matthew A. 1866-1955 *WorAlBi*
Henson, Matthew Alexander 1866-1955 *BioIn 16*
Henson, Paul Harry 1925- *St&PR 91, WhoAm 90*
Henson, Ray David 1924- *WhoAm 90*
Henson, Reid M. 1939- *WhoAm 90*
Henson, Richard Lay 1946- *St&PR 91*
Henson, Robert Frank 1925- *WhoAm 90*
Henson, Robert W., Sr. 1914- *St&PR 91*
Henson, Steven Ralph *BiDrAPA 89*
Henson-Conant, Deborah *BioIn 16*
Henss, Phillip S. 1933- *St&PR 91*
Henstell, Bruce 1945- *ConAu 131*
Henstell, Bruce Michael 1945- *WhoEmL 91*
Henstock, Barry A. 1939- *St&PR 91*
Hentges, Edward Joel 1931- *St&PR 91*
Hentges, Richard Joseph 1938- *St&PR 91*
Henthorne, Patricia M. *St&PR 91*
Hentoff, Margot 1930- *WhoAm 90, WhoWrEP 89*
Hentoff, Nat *BioIn 16*
Hentoff, Nat Irving 1925- *AuBYP 90*
Hentoff, Nathan Irving 1925- *WhoAm 90, WhoWrEP 89*
Henton, Willis Ryan 1925- *WhoAm 90, WhoSSW 91*
Hentschel, David A. 1934- *St&PR 91, WhoAm 90, WhoSSW 91*
Hentschel, Julius Konrad *PenDiDA 89*
Hentschel, Uwe 1940- *WhoWor 91*
Henty, G. A. 1832-1902 *BioIn 16*
Henty, G A 1832-1902 *SmATA 64 [port]*
Henty, George Alfred 1832-1902 *BioIn 16*
Hentz, Ann Louise 1921- *WhoAmW 91*
Hentz, Caroline Lee 1800-1856 *FemiCLE*
Hentz, Marie Eva 1920- *WhoAmW 91*
Hentzen, Herbert D., Jr. 1927- *St&PR 91*
Hentzen, William R. 1932- *St&PR 91*
Henwood, Douglas Francis 1952- *WhoE 91*
Henwood, Sheila Patricia 1947- *WhoWor 91*
Henych, Ivo 1935- *WhoWor 91*
Henyey, James Frederick 1951- *St&PR 91*
Henz, Donald John 1937- *St&PR 91*
Henze, Calvin Rudolph 1924- *WhoAm 90*
Henze, Hans Werner 1926- *IntWWM 90, PenDiMP A, WhoWor 91*
Henze, Paul Bernard 1924- *WhoAm 90, WhoWrEP 89*
Henze, Raymond F., III *WhoAm 90*
Henzell-Lopez, Holly 1957- *St&PR 91*
Heong, Ng Toh 1953- *WhoWor 91*
Hepburn, A. Barton 1846-1922 *EncABHB 6 [port]*
Hepburn, Audrey 1929- *BioIn 16, WhoAm 90, WorAlBi*
Hepburn, Brian Matthew *BiDrAPA 89*
Hepburn, David 1924-1985 *DrBlPA 90*

Hepburn, Irene Maria Wilson 1920- WhoE 91
Hepburn, Katharine 1909- BioAmW, BioIn 16, News 91-2 [port], WorAlBi
Hepburn, Katharine Houghton BioIn 16
Hepburn, Katharine Houghton 1907- NotWoAT
Hepburn, Katharine Houghton 1909- WhoAm 90, WhoAmW 91, WhoWor 91
Hepburn, Philip 1941?- DrBlPA 90
Hepburn, Tracy L. 1962- WhoAmW 91
Hepfer, John William, Jr. 1924- WhoAm 90
Hepfer, Penrod G 1915- BiDrAPA 89
Hepler, Donald Eugene 1928- WhoAm 90
Hepler, Ernest M. 1930- St&PR 91
Hepler, Kenneth Russel 1926- WhoWor 91
Hepler, Martin Eugene 1949- WhoEmL 91, WhoWor 91
Hepler, Robert Sidney 1934- WhoAm 90
Hepler, Thomas E. 1932- St&PR 91
Hepler-Smith, Elizabeth 1954- BiDrAPA 89
Hepner, Michael Jules 1952- WhoEmL 91
Hepner, Ruth BiDrAPA 89
Hepp, Peter S. 1929- St&PR 91
Heppa, Douglas Van 1945- WhoE 91
Heppe, David L. 1950- St&PR 91
Heppe, Ralph Richard 1923- St&PR 91
Heppel, Leon Alma 1912- WhoAm 90
Heppenheimer, Thomas Adolph 1947- WhoEmL 91
Heppenheimer, William Christian 1860-1933 AmLegL
Heppenstall, Barry 1946- St&PR 91
Hepper, Carol 1953- BioIn 16, WhoAmA 91, WhoE 91
Heppermann, Donald C. 1943- St&PR 91
Hepplewhite, David Wilson 1951- WhoEmL 91
Hepplewhite, George PenDiDA 89, WorAlBi
Hepplewhite, Lionel Karl 1936- IntWWM 90
Heppner, Frank Henry 1940- WhoE 91
Heppner, Gloria Hill 1940- WhoAmW 91
Hepps, Robert B 1941- BiDrAPA 89
Heptinstall, Debra Lou 1952- WhoEmL 91
Heptinstall, Robert Hodgson 1920- WhoAm 90
Hepworth, Barbara 1903-1975 BiDWomA, BioIn 16, IntDcAA 90, WorAlBi
Hepworth, Dorothy BiDWomA
Hepworth, Kenneth 1931- St&PR 91
Hera 1940- WhoAmA 91
Heraclitus 500?BC- WrPh P
Heraclitus 540?BC-480?BC WorAlBi
Herald, Beverly Taylor 1946- WhoSSW 91
Herald, Cherry Lou 1940- WhoAmW 91
Herald, Christopher E. St&PR 91
Herald, George William 1911- WhoWor 91
Herald, John Patrick 1947- WhoEmL 91
Herald, Kathleen ConAu 32NR
Herald, Kathleen 1929- SmATA X [port]
Herald-Sowers, Anita Ann 1939- WhoAmW 91
Herard, Marvin T 1929- WhoAmA 91
Herasimchuk, David Alexander 1942- St&PR 91
Herath, Adolph Jamnalal 1939- BiDrAPA 89
Herath, Barbara Daun 1946- WhoSSW 91
Heraud, Javier 1942-1963 ConAu 131, HispWr 90
Herauf, William Anton 1957- WhoEmL 91
Herb, Elizabeth Ann 1945- BiDrAPA 89
Herb, Frank Steven 1949- WhoEmL 91
Herb, Jerome Bruce 1940- St&PR 91
Herb, Patricia Lynn 1955- WhoSSW 91
Herb, Raymond G. 1908- WhoAm 90
Herb, Raymond George 1908- St&PR 91
Herbart, Johann Friedrich 1776-1841 WorAlBi
Herbeck, Johann 1831-1877 PenDiMP
Herbein, Bonnie Fleming 1955- WhoAmW 91
Herbein, John Giles 1938- St&PR 91
Herbel, Bryon Lee 1959- BiDrAPA 89
Herbel, Ron 1938- Ballpl 90
Herbelin, Jeanne Mathilde 1820-1904 BiDWomA
Herbener, Patricia Wendy 1945- WhoAmW 91, WhoEmL 91
Herbener, Suzanne Elizabeth BiDrAPA 89
Herbenick, Bernard M. 1944- St&PR 91
Herber, Steven Carlton 1960- WhoEmL 91
Herberg, Will BioIn 16
Herberger, G. Robert 1904- WhoAm 90
Herberich, Frederick D. 1925- St&PR 91
Herberich, Frederick David 1925- WhoAm 90
Herbers, John Andrew 1957- WhoEmL 91
Herbers, Tod Arthur 1948- WhoAm 90, WhoEmL 91
Herbert, Adam William, Jr. 1943- WhoAm 90
Herbert, Albert Edward, Jr. 1928- WhoAm 90
Herbert, Anne BiDEWW
Herbert, April H 1934- WhoAmA 91
Herbert, Bob BioIn 16
Herbert, Chesley C 1943- BiDrAPA 89
Herbert, Claire Donaldson 1960- WhoAmW 91
Herbert, Don 1917- AuBYP 90, ConAu 30NR
Herbert, Dorothea 1770-1829 FemiCLE
Herbert, Edward F. 1946- ODwPR 91
Herbert, Eugene Forrest 1932- WhoWor 91
Herbert, Frank BioIn 16
Herbert, Frank 1920- WorAlBi
Herbert, Frank 1920-1986 MajTwCW, RGTwCSF
Herbert, Gary Bruce 1941- WhoSSW 91
Herbert, Gavin S. 1932- St&PR 91
Herbert, Gavin Shearer, Jr. 1932- WhoAm 90
Herbert, George 1539-1633 WorAlBi
Herbert, George 1593-1633 BioIn 16
Herbert, George R. 1922- St&PR 91
Herbert, George Richard 1922- WhoAm 90
Herbert, Helen 1947- BioIn 16
Herbert, Hilary Abner 1834-1919 BiDrUSE 89
Herbert, Ira C. 1927- St&PR 91, WhoAm 90, WhoSSW 91
Herbert, James Arthur 1938- WhoAm 90, WhoAmA 91
Herbert, James Charles 1941- WhoE 91
Herbert, James Keller 1938- WhoAm 90
Herbert, James Paul 1941- WhoAm 90
Herbert, James Wesley 1939- IntWWM 90
Herbert, Jocelyn 1917- ConDes 90, IntWWM 90
Herbert, John 1926- OxCCanT
Herbert, John Andrew 1943- St&PR 91
Herbert, John Campbell 1950- WhoSSW 91
Herbert, John Goss 1939- BiDrAPA 89
Herbert, John Louis BiDrAPA 89
Herbert, John Warren 1924- St&PR 91, WhoAm 90
Herbert, Kevin Barry John 1921- WhoAm 90
Herbert, LeRoy James 1923- WhoAm 90
Herbert, Lucy 1669-1744 FemiCLE
Herbert, Marian 1899-1960 WhoAmA 91N
Herbert, Marilynne 1944- WhoAmW 91
Herbert, Mary E. 1945- WhoAmW 91
Herbert, Mary Eliza 1832?-1872 FemiCLE
Herbert, Mary Katherine Atwell 1945- WhoAmW 91
Herbert, Mary Sidney 1561-1621 BioIn 16
Herbert, Michael Kinzly 1942- WhoAm 90, WhoWrEP 89
Herbert, Peter Noel 1941- WhoAm 90
Herbert, Philip Sidney, Jr. 1923- BiDrAPA 89
Herbert, Pinkney 1954- WhoAmA 91
Herbert, Ray 1929- Ballpl 90
Herbert, Richard D. 1935 St&PR 91
Herbert, Robert J BiDrAPA 89
Herbert, Robert L. 1929- WhoAm 90, WhoAmA 91
Herbert, Robert Michael 1954- WhoE 91
Herbert, Sally Mary 1948- WhoEmL 91
Herbert, Sandra 1942- ConAu 130
Herbert, Sarah 1824-1846 FemiCLE
Herbert, Sarah E 1945- BiDrAPA 89
Herbert, Stephen W. 1941- WhoAm 90
Herbert, Theodore Terence 1942- WhoSSW 91
Herbert, Victor BioIn 16
Herbert, Victor 1859-1924 OxCPMus, PenDiMP A, WorAlBi
Herbert, Victor James 1917- WhoAm 90
Herbert, Walter William 1934- WhoWor 91
Herbert, Xavier 1901-1984 WorAu 1980 [port]
Herbert, Zbigniew 1924- MajTwCW, WorAlBi
Herbert-Forster, Therese BioIn 16
Herberts, Mary FemiCLE
Herbich, John Bronislaw 1922- WhoAm 90
Herbig, George Howard 1920- WhoAm 90
Herbig, Gunther 1931- IntWWM 90, PenDiMP, WhoAm 90, WhoWor 91
Herbin, Reece A. 1946- WhoAmW 91
Herbine, Lois Lorraine 1961- IntWWM 90
Herbison, John 1939- WhoAm 90
Herbison, John Stephen 1939- St&PR 91
Herbison, Robin J. 1961- WhoAmW 91
Herbits, Stephen E. 1942- ODwPR 91, St&PR 91
Herbits, Stephen Edward 1942- WhoAm 90
Herblock 1909- BioIn 16, WhoAm 90, WhoE 91
Herbold-Wootten, Heidi 1936- WhoAmW 91
Herbolsheimer, Robert Tilton 1954- WhoEmL 91
Herbranson, Kai Wold 1935- WhoAm 90
Herbruck, W. Gibbs 1923- St&PR 91
Herbst, Arthur Lee 1931- WhoAm 90
Herbst, Curt Alfred 1866-1946 DcScB S2
Herbst, Della 1935- WhoAmW 91
Herbst, Douglas James 1955- St&PR 91
Herbst, Hartwig Martin 1945- WhoWor 91
Herbst, Joachim 1928- St&PR 91
Herbst, John Anthony 1952- WhoE 91
Herbst, Josephine 1892-1969 EncAL, FemiCLE
Herbst, Josephine Frey 1897-1969 BioAmW
Herbst, Jurgen 1928- WhoAm 90
Herbst, Margaret Mary 1917- WhoE 91
Herbst, Marie Antoinette WhoAmW 91, WhoE 91
Herbst, Robert LeRoy 1935- WhoAm 90, WhoSSW 91
Herbst, Thomas James 1964- BiDrAPA 89
Herbst, Todd Leslie 1952- WhoWor 91
Herbst, Walter Joseph 1942- WhoE 91
Herbster, David Parke 1941- St&PR 91, WhoAm 90
Herbster, James Richard 1941- St&PR 91, WhoAm 90
Herbster, William Gibson 1933- WhoAm 90
Herch, Frank Alan 1949- WhoEmL 91
Herchenefreda 5--?-6--? EncCoWW
Herchenroether, Peter Young 1954- WhoEmL 91
Hercher, Jo Maria 1966- St&PR 91
Herchmer, William Macauley 1844-1892 DcCanB 12
Hercules, Costas BiDrAPA 89
Hercules, David Michael 1932- WhoAm 90
Hercus, Luise Anna 1926- WhoWor 91
Herd, Charmian June 1930- WhoAmW 91
Herd, Harold Shields 1918- WhoAm 90
Herd, Shirley WhoWrEP 89
Herda, Hans-Heinrich 1938- WhoE 91
Herda, Ralph Edward 1953- St&PR 91
Herdan, Johannes EncCoWW
Herdan-Zuckmayer, Alice BioIn 16
Herdeg, Howard Brian 1929- WhoWor 91
Herdeg, Klaus 1937- ConAu 130
Herdeman, James Robert 1957- WhoEmL 91
Herdemian, Gregory John 1954- St&PR 91
Herder, Gary Alan 1947- St&PR 91
Herder, Gerhard 1928- WhoAm 90, WhoE 91, WhoWor 91
Herder, Johann G. 1744-1803 WorAlBi
Herder, Johann Gottfried 1744-1803 DcLB 97 [port]
Herder, Stephen Rendell 1928- WhoAm 90
Herdina, Eileen C. 1927- St&PR 91
Herdle, William Bruce 1947- WhoE 91
Herdman, John Mark Ambrose 1932- WhoWor 91
Herdrich, Norman Wesley 1942- WhoAm 90
Heredia, Alberto Urista 1947- WhoHisp 91
Heredia, Jose Maria 1803-1839 BioIn 16, WorAlBi
Heredia, Luis 1951- WhoHisp 91
Hereford, Frank Loucks, Jr. 1923- WhoAm 90
Hereford, Laura 1831-1870 BiDWomA
Hereford, Robert A. 1902- AuBYP 90
Heremans, Dirk Paul Marie Florent 1943- WhoWor 91
Herendeen, Sherrie Lynn 1952- BiDrAPA 89
Herenstein, Ira 1937- St&PR 91
Herer, Gilbert R. BioIn 16
Herfield, Phyllis 1947- WhoAmA 91
Herfindahl, Lloyd Manford 1922- WhoWor 91
Herfkens, Kristine Marie 1962- WhoEmL 91
Herford, Henry 1947- IntWWM 90
Herford, Laura 1831-1870 BiDWomA
Herford, Oliver 1863-1935 AuBYP 90
Herford, Robert David 1938- WhoSSW 91
Herforth, Sandra Lee 1951- WhoAmW 91
Herfst, Jan Fred 1921- WhoWor 91
Herge ConAu 31NR
Herge, Henry Curtis, Jr. 1950- WhoAm 90
Herge, Henry Curtis, Sr. 1905- WhoAm 90, WhoSSW 91
Herge, J. Curtis 1938- WhoAm 90
Hergenhan, Joyce 1941- ODwPR 91, St&PR 91, WhoAm 90, WhoAmW 91
Hergenrather, Edmund Richard 1917- St&PR 91
Hergenrather, K.M. 1918- St&PR 91
Hergenrather, Richard Ames 1949- St&PR 91
Herger, Wally W., Jr. 1945- WhoAm 90
Hergert, David Evan 1955- St&PR 91
Hergert, Louis George, Jr. 1927- St&PR 91, WhoAm 90
Hergesheimer, Joseph 1880-1954 DcLB 102 [port]
Herguner, Umit 1957- WhoWor 91
Herguth, Robert John 1926- WhoAm 90
Herholz, Karl 1952- WhoWor 91
Herias, Miguel Angel 1962- WhoWor 91
Heric, Blaine Richard 1956- WhoWor 91
Heric, John F 1942- WhoAmA 91
Hericourt, Jenny P. d' 1809-1875 EncCoWW
Herincx, Raimund 1927- IntWWM 90, PenDiMP
Hering, Charles D., Jr. 1927- St&PR 91
Hering, Doris Minnie 1920- WhoAm 90
Hering, Grant Barnitz 1936- WhoAm 90
Hering, Gunther E. 1936- St&PR 91
Hering, Harry 1887-1967 WhoAmA 91N
Hering, Henry 1874-1949 WhoAmA 91N
Hering, Karl-Josef 1929- IntWWM 90
Hering, Robert Gustave 1934- WhoAm 90
Herington, Cecil John 1924- WhoAm 90
Herington, Thomas Michael 1954- WhoEmL 91
Herink, Richie 1932- WhoE 91
Heriot, Richard Morrison 1932- WhoSSW 91
Herip, Walter Michael 1947- WhoEmL 91
Heris, Toni 1932- WhoAmW 91
Heritage, Robert 1927- ConDes 90
Heritage, Sharon K. 1955- WhoAmW 91
Heritier, Charles Andre 1931- WhoWor 91
Heritte-Viardot, Louise Pauline Marie 1841-1919 BioIn 16
Herjanic, Marijan 1931- BiDrAPA 89
Herjulfson, Bjarni EncCRAm
Herke, Robert, Sr. 1932- WhoSSW 91
Herkimer, Lawrence Russell 1925?- AuBYP 90
Herkimer, Nicholas 1728-1777 WhNaAH, WorAlBi
Herkness, Lindsay Coates, III 1943- WhoAm 90
Herkomer, Hubert von 1849-1914 BioIn 16
Herlache, Thomas L. 1942- St&PR 91
Herlihy, Charles E 1924- BiDrAPA 89
Herlihy, Charles E, Jr. 1949- BiDrAPA 89
Herlihy, David Joseph 1930- WhoAm 90
Herlihy, Francis Bond WhoAm 90
Herlihy, James E. 1942- St&PR 91
Herlihy, James Edward 1942- WhoAm 90
Herlihy, James Leo 1927- WhoAm 90
Herlihy, Jim 1953- ODwPR 91
Herlihy, Robert Edward 1931- WhoAm 90
Herlihy, Thomas 1958- St&PR 91
Herlihy, Thomas Mortimer 1953- WhoEmL 91
Herlihy, Walter C. 1951- St&PR 91
Herling, John 1905- WhoAm 90, WhoE 91
Herling, Michael WhoAm 90
Herling, Michael James 1957- WhoEmL 91
Herlong, D. C. WhoSSW 91
Herlow, Erik 1913- ConDes 90
Herluf, Claus Robert 1941- WhoWor 91
Hermach, Francis Lewis 1917- WhoAm 90
Herman, Alan David 1947- WhoAmA 91
Herman, Alan John 1943- St&PR 91
Herman, Allen Ian 1950- WhoE 91, WhoEmL 91
Herman, Andrea Bettina 1960- WhoE 91
Herman, Andrea Maxine 1938- WhoAm 90, WhoAmW 91
Herman, August C 1917- BiDrAPA 89
Herman, Babe 1903-1987 Ballpl 90 [port]
Herman, Barbara F. 1941- WhoAmW 91
Herman, Barry Keith 1950- BiDrAPA 89
Herman, Bernard BioIn 16
Herman, Bernard 1927- St&PR 91
Herman, Bernard Albert 1910- St&PR 91, WhoE 91, WhoWor 91
Herman, Billy 1909- Ballpl 90 [port]
Herman, Brett P. 1955- WhoEmL 91
Herman, Burton BioIn 16
Herman, Carl A. 1930- St&PR 91
Herman, Carl D 1931- BiDrAPA 89
Herman, Carl David 1931- WhoE 91
Herman, Carol Korngut 1952- WhoAm 90, WhoAmW 91
Herman, Charles Jacob 1937- WhoAm 90
Herman, Charles Robert 1925- IntWWM 90, WhoAm 90
Herman, Chester Joseph 1941- WhoAm 90
Herman, Chloe Anna 1937- WhoAmW 91
Herman, David 1917- St&PR 91
Herman, David Jay 1954- WhoSSW 91
Herman, Edith Carol 1944- WhoAm 90, WhoAmW 91
Herman, Edward Lee 1932- BiDrAPA 89
Herman, Edward Richard BiDrAPA 89
Herman, Edward Roy 1928- St&PR 91
Herman, Elizabeth BiDrAPA 89
Herman, Frances BioIn 16
Herman, Frank 1926- WhoAm 90
Herman, Fred L. 1950- WhoWor 91
Herman, Georg Nicholas 1954- WhoEmL 91
Herman, George Edward 1920- WhoAm 90, WhoE 91

Herman, Grace G. 1926- WhoWrEP 89
Herman, Grace Gales 1926- WhoAmW 91
Herman, Greta BiDrAPA 89
Herman, Hank Lewis 1949- WhoAm 90
Herman, Herbert 1934- WhoAm 90
Herman, Irving Leonard 1920- WhoAm 90
Herman, Jeffrey A. BiDrAPA 89
Herman, Jeffrey Hal 1958- WhoEmL 91
Herman, Jeffry Bernard 1951- WhoE 91
Herman, Jerry WhoAm 90
Herman, Jerry 1932- WorAlBi
Herman, Jerry 1933- OxCPMus
Herman, Joan E. 1953- St&PR 91
Herman, Joan Elizabeth 1953- WhoEmL 91
Herman, John Benjamin 1951- BiDrAPA 89
Herman, Josef 1911- BioIn 16
Herman, Judith Lewis BiDrAPA 89
Herman, Judith Lewis 1942- WhoE 91
Herman, Kenneth 1927- WhoE 91
Herman, Kenneth Neil 1954- WhoAm 90
Herman, Lail Lewis 1934- WhoAmW 91
Herman, Lawrence 1924- WhoAm 90
Herman, Lloyd Eldred 1936- WhoAmA 91
Herman, Louis BiDrAPA 89
Herman, Louis M. BioIn 16
Herman, Lydia Beatrice 1959- WhoAmW 91
Herman, Malcolm Jay 1930- St&PR 91
Herman, Mario Luis 1958- WhoE 91
Herman, Mary Margaret 1935- WhoAmW 91, WhoSSW 91
Herman, Melvin Duaine 1925- St&PR 91
Herman, Merrill Scot 1957- BiDrAPA 89
Herman, Michael Edward 1941- St&PR 91
Herman, Michael Lee 1947- WhoSSW 91
Herman, Michelle 1955- WhoEmL 91, WhoWrEP 89
Herman, Morris 1906- BiDrAPA 89
Herman, Nadine 1954- IntWWM 90
Herman, Pee-wee BioIn 16
Herman, R. Dixon NewYTBS 90
Herman, R. Dixon 1911-1990 BioIn 16
Herman, Reuben A. 1931- St&PR 91
Herman, Richard Blair 1955- WhoEmL 91
Herman, Robert 1914- WhoAm 90
Herman, Robert Alan 1957- BiDrAPA 89, WhoE 91
Herman, Robert Lewis 1927- St&PR 91, WhoE 91
Herman, Robert M BiDrAPA 89
Herman, Robert S. 1919- WhoAm 90
Herman, Rochelle BiDrAPA 89
Herman, Roger 1947- WhoAmA 91
Herman, Ronald S 1933- BiDrAPA 89
Herman, Ruth Fay BiDrAPA 89
Herman, Ruth Fay 1962- WhoE 91
Herman, Samuel 1928- St&PR 91
Herman, Samuel J. 1936- PenDiDA 89
Herman, Sarah Andrews 1952- WhoEmL 91
Herman, Sol 1933- BiDrAPA 89
Herman, Stan BioIn 16
Herman, Stephen 1942- St&PR 91
Herman, Stephen Gerald 1939- WhoSSW 91, WhoWor 91
Herman, Stephen Paul 1946- BiDrAPA 89
Herman, Steven Roger 1952- WhoEmL 91
Herman, Sumner Wilfred 1928- WhoE 91
Herman, Theodore L. 1936- St&PR 91
Herman, Valerie J BiDrAPA 89
Herman, Vasile 1929- IntWWM 90
Herman, Vic WhoAmA 91
Herman, Walter ConAu 33NR
Herman, Walter 1945- WhoAm 90
Herman, William, III 1938- St&PR 91
Herman, William Hickey 1948- St&PR 91
Herman, William John 1942- WhoE 91
Herman, William Sparkes 1931- WhoAm 90
Herman, Witold Walenty 1932- IntWWM 90
Herman, Woody BioIn 16
Herman, Woody 1913-1987 OxCPMus, WorAlBi
Herman, Zelek Seymour 1945- WhoEmL 91
Hermance, Richard Thomas 1928- St&PR 91
Hermand, Jost 1930- ConAu 31NR
Hermanies, John Hans 1922- WhoAm 90, WhoWor 91
Hermaniuk, Maxim 1911- WhoAm 90, WhoWor 91
Hermann, Allan Jacob 1937- BiDrAPA 89
Hermann, Allen Max 1938- WhoAm 90
Hermann, Arthur W. 1944- St&PR 91, WhoAm 90
Hermann, Carol 1937- BiDrAPA 89
Hermann, Edward Robert 1920- WhoAm 90, WhoWor 91
Hermann, Frederick A., Jr. 1924- St&PR 91
Hermann, Gabrielle J. WhoAmW 91
Hermann, Gerald W. 1934- St&PR 91
Hermann, Harland T, Sr. BiDrAPA 89
Hermann, Harold B. 1900-1988 BioIn 16
Hermann, Horst 1930- WhoWor 91
Hermann, Irene Irma 1914- WhoAmW 91
Hermann, Jacob 1615?-1685 PenDiDA 89
Hermann, Jane Pomerance 1935- WhoAm 90
Hermann, Lawrence Shepley 1952- St&PR 91
Hermann, M L WhoAmA 91
Hermann, Margaret Gladden 1938- WhoAmW 91
Hermann, Naomi Basel 1918- WhoAmW 91
Hermann, Paul David 1925- WhoAm 90
Hermann, Philip J. 1916- WhoAm 90
Hermann, Robert J. 1933- St&PR 91
Hermann, Robert J. 1944- St&PR 91
Hermann, Robert Jay 1933- WhoAm 90
Hermann, Robert John 1944- WhoAm 90
Hermann, Robert R. 1923- St&PR 91
Hermann, Robert Ringen 1923- WhoAm 90
Hermann, Roland 1936- IntWWM 90
Hermann, Steven Istvan 1934- WhoE 91
Hermann, Wilfred Leroy 1933- St&PR 91
Hermann, William Henry 1924- WhoAm 90
Hermanns, Fritz 1925- WhoWor 91
Hermannsson, Steingrimur 1928- WhoWor 91
Hermanoff, Sandra M. ODwPR 91
Hermanoff, Sandra Marlene WhoAmW 91
Hermanovski, Egils P. WhoAm 90
Hermanowicz, Henry Joseph 1928- WhoAm 90
Hermanowski, Robert W 1965- BiDrAPA 89
Herman's Hermits ConMus 5 [port], EncPR&S 89, OxCPMus
Hermans, Kathy BioIn 16
Hermans, Reginald Boydell, Jr. 1937- St&PR 91
Hermansen, Bruce Allen 1954- BiDrAPA 89
Hermansen, Lars 1950- WhoWor 91
Hermanski, Gene 1920- Ballpl 90
Hermanson, Ake Oscar Werner 1923- IntWWM 90
Hermanson, Carol Diane 1951- WhoAmW 91
Hermanson, Eliza Louise Williams 1942- WhoSSW 91
Hermanson, William Francis 1947- St&PR 91
Hermanson Ogilvie, Judith 1945- WhoE 91
Hermele, Jules Joseph 1951- St&PR 91
Hermele, Noel S 1948- BiDrAPA 89
Hermelin, Victor M. 1914- St&PR 91
Hermenet, Eugene W. 1936- St&PR 91
Hermens, Ferdinand Aloys 1906- WhoE 91
Hermens, Willem Theodor 1940- WhoWor 91
Hermes, Frank J. 1943- St&PR 91
Hermes, Gertrude 1902- BiDWomA
Hermes, Gertrude Anna Bertha 1901-1983 DcNaB 1981
Hermes, Johann Timotheus 1738-1821 DcLB 97 [port]
Hermes, Juanita H. 1943- St&PR 91
Hermes, Julia Christine BiDrAPA 89
Hermes, Nancy Jean BiDrAPA 89
Hermes, Patricia 1936- BioIn 16
Hermesch, Alan L. 1946- WhoEmL 91
Hermesdorf, James E. 1943- St&PR 91
Hermida, Carlos Lorenzo 1942- WhoSSW 91
Hermida, Manuel E 1925- BiDrAPA 89
Herminghouse, Patricia Anne 1940- WhoAm 90
Hermo, Alfonso Davila 1931- WhoHisp 91
Hermodsson, Elisabet 1927- DcScanL
Hermogenes CIMLC 6
Hermon-Taylor, John 1936- WhoWor 91
Hermosillo, Danny James 1962- WhoHisp 91
Hermoso-Kramer, Josefina BiDrAPA 89
Herms, Joyce E. 1937- St&PR 91
Herms, Thomas Christian 1946- WhoEmL 91
Hermsen, Gail Marie 1951- WhoAmW 91
Hermstedt, Simon 1778-1846 PenDiMP
Hermus, Rudolph Joseph 1941- WhoWor 91
Hern, Carol 1954- WhoAm 90
Hern, George L., Jr. 1924- ODwPR 91
Hern, John Robert 1953- St&PR 91
Hern, Karen Sue 1949- WhoAmW 91
Hernadi, Paul 1936- WhoAm 90, WhoWrEP 89
Hernandez, Abilio A BiDrAPA 89
Hernandez, Albert L. 1924- WhoHisp 91
Hernandez, Albert P. 1948- WhoHisp 91
Hernandez, Alexander BiDrAPA 89
Hernandez, Alexander E BiDrAPA 89
Hernandez, Alexander James 1948- WhoE 91
Hernandez, Alfonso A BiDrAPA 89
Hernandez, Alfonso V. 1937- WhoHisp 91
Hernandez, Alfredo Luis BiDrAPA 89
Hernandez, Andrew WhoHisp 91
Hernandez, Angel Alberto 1938- BiDrAPA 89
Hernandez, Anna Maria 1960- St&PR 91
Hernandez, Anthony Louis 1947- WhoAmA 91
Hernandez, Antonia 1948- WhoAmW 91, WhoHisp 91
Hernandez, Antonio 1938- WhoHisp 91
Hernandez, Augustin 1937- WhoHisp 91
Hernandez, Avelino 1944- WhoWor 91
Hernandez, Benigno Cardenas 1862-1954 BioIn 16
Hernandez, Benigno Carlos 1917- BioIn 16, WhoHisp 91
Hernandez, Benito BiDrAPA 89
Hernandez, Braulio Nicolas BiDrAPA 89
Hernandez, C. Lynn BiDrAPA 89
Hernandez, Caridad Ana BiDrAPA 89
Hernandez, Celida Alcaraz 1953- WhoAmW 91
Hernandez, Cesar Augusto 1932- BiDrAPA 89
Hernandez, Christine 1951- WhoHisp 91
Hernandez, Cirilo C. 1929- WhoHisp 91
Hernandez, Concepcion G BiDrAPA 89
Hernandez, Consuelo 1952- WhoHisp 91
Hernandez, Daniel Arthur 1945- WhoSSW 91
Hernandez, David P. 1936- WhoHisp 91
Hernandez, Diego Edyl 1934- WhoHisp 91
Hernandez, Dolores F BiDrAPA 89
Hernandez, Edward 1946- WhoHisp 91
Hernandez, Elena Marisa BiDrAPA 89
Hernandez, Elia 1969- WhoHisp 91
Hernandez, Elise Ann 1945- WhoEmL 91
Hernandez, Encarnacion 1946- WhoHisp 91
Hernandez, Enrique 1951- WhoE 91, WhoEmL 91, WhoHisp 91
Hernandez, Enzo 1949- Ballpl 90
Hernandez, Ernest G. 1931- WhoHisp 91
Hernandez, Evelyn 1958- WhoHisp 91
Hernandez, Evelyn Irma 1954- WhoE 91
Hernandez, Francis Xavier 1965- WhoHisp 91
Hernandez, Gary J. 1953- WhoHisp 91
Hernandez, George S. WhoHisp 91
Hernandez, Gladys 1951- WhoHisp 91
Hernandez, Gonzalez Jose Maria 1927- WhoAm 90
Hernandez, Graciela Emilia BiDrAPA 89
Hernandez, Guillermo BiDrAPA 89
Hernandez, Guillermo Villanueva 1954- WhoHisp 91
Hernandez, Gustavo G 1937- BiDrAPA 89
Hernandez, Hector Rene BioIn 16
Hernandez, Henry O., Jr. 1956- WhoHisp 91
Hernandez, Hilda 1947- WhoHisp 91
Hernandez, Irene Beltran 1945- WhoHisp 91
Hernandez, Irene R. St&PR 91
Hernandez, Isabel C. 1959- WhoHisp 91
Hernandez, Ivan Antonio 1961- BiDrAPA 89, WhoE 91
Hernandez, Jackie 1940- Ballpl 90
Hernandez, Jacqueline Charmaine 1960- WhoE 91, WhoEmL 91, WhoWor 91
Hernandez, James, Jr. 1942- WhoHisp 91
Hernandez, Jo Farb 1952- WhoAmA 91
Hernandez, John R. 1955- WhoHisp 91
Hernandez, John Stephen 1945- WhoHisp 91
Hernandez, Jose 1834-1886 BioIn 16
Hernandez, Jose Antonio 1951- WhoHisp 91
Hernandez, Jose E. 1957- WhoHisp 91
Hernandez, Jose Guillermo 1945- St&PR 91
Hernandez, Jose Manuel BiDrAPA 89
Hernandez, Jose Manuel 1853-1919? BioIn 16
Hernandez, Jose Manuel 1925- WhoHisp 91
Hernandez, Joseph Anthony 1950- WhoHisp 91
Hernandez, Juan Belulia 1913- WhoWor 91
Hernandez, Juan Donaldo 1933- WhoHisp 91
Hernandez, Juan Miguel BiDrAPA 89
Hernandez, Juana Amelia WhoHisp 91
Hernandez, Juano 1896-1970 DrBlPA 90
Hernandez, Julio, Jr. 1920- WhoHisp 91
Hernandez, Keith 1953- Ballpl 90 [port], BioIn 16, WhoAm 90, WhoHisp 91, WorAlBi
Hernandez, Leodoro 1930- WhoHisp 91
Hernandez, Librada 1955- WhoHisp 91
Hernandez, Linda Louise 1952- WhoAmW 91
Hernandez, Louis Fernando 1952- WhoHisp 91
Hernandez, Louis Robert 1947- St&PR 91
Hernandez, Luis Garcia 1941- WhoHisp 91
Hernandez, Luz Corpi 1945- WhoHisp 91
Hernandez, Mack Ray 1944- WhoHisp 91
Hernandez, Manuel, Jr. 1951- WhoHisp 91
Hernandez, Manuel O BiDrAPA 89
Hernandez, Maria L. BioIn 16
Hernandez, Marjorie Ray 1927- WhoAmW 91
Hernandez, Martha Florence 1953- BiDrAPA 89
Hernandez, Michael BiDrAPA 89
Hernandez, Michael Bruington 1960- WhoHisp 91
Hernandez, Miguel Angel, Jr. 1941- WhoHisp 91
Hernandez, Mike A. WhoHisp 91
Hernandez, Minerva 1959- WhoAmW 91
Hernandez, Nicolas, Jr. 1953- WhoHisp 91
Hernandez, Noel WhoHisp 91
Hernandez, Onesimo 1925- WhoHisp 91
Hernandez, Oscar M BiDrAPA 89
Hernandez, Paul F. 1954- WhoHisp 91
Hernandez, Ramon 1935- BioIn 16
Hernandez, Ramon 1940- Ballpl 90
Hernandez, Randal J. 1959- WhoHisp 91
Hernandez, Raoul Emilio 1955- WhoHisp 91
Hernandez, Raul Antonio 1962- WhoHisp 91
Hernandez, Richard G. 1953- WhoHisp 91
Hernandez, Rita Rios 1953- WhoHisp 91
Hernandez, Robert Louis 1947- WhoHisp 91
Hernandez, Robert M. 1944- St&PR 91
Hernandez, Robert Michael 1945- WhoHisp 91
Hernandez, Roberto F. 1948- WhoHisp 91
Hernandez, Roberto Perales BioIn 16
Hernandez, Roberto Reyes 1950- WhoEmL 91, WhoSSW 91, WhoWor 91
Hernandez, Rodolfo BiDrAPA 89
Hernandez, Roger Emilio 1955- WhoHisp 91
Hernandez, Ronald J. WhoHisp 91
Hernandez, Sam 1948- WhoAmA 91, WhoHisp 91
Hernandez, Santiago 1947- WhoHisp 91
Hernandez, Sergio Anthony 1946- WhoHisp 91
Hernandez, Sigfredo Augusto 1954- WhoHisp 91
Hernandez, Sonia Caridad 1954- WhoAmW 91
Hernandez, Susan 1960- WhoHisp 91
Hernandez, Tabare BiDrAPA 89
Hernandez, Teme Paul 1919- WhoHisp 91
Hernandez, Thomas Joseph 1955- WhoEmL 91
Hernandez, Tony WhoHisp 91
Hernandez, Vicar F. 1954- WhoSSW 91
Hernandez, Victoria 1948- WhoHisp 91
Hernandez, Wanda Grace 1942- WhoAmW 91
Hernandez, Wilbert Eduardo 1916- WhoWor 91
Hernandez, William Franklin 1943- WhoE 91
Hernandez, William Hector, Jr. 1930- WhoAm 90, WhoE 91, WhoHisp 91
Hernandez, Willie 1954- Ballpl 90
Hernandez-Agosto, Miguel Angel 1927- WhoHisp 91, WhoSSW 91
Hernandez Alvarez, Jose 1948- WhoWor 91
Hernandez Aquino, Luis 1907?- HispWr 90
Hernandez-Avila, Manuel Luis 1935- WhoHisp 91
Hernandez-Chernys, Griselle Claudia 1953- WhoAmW 91, WhoSSW 91
Hernandez-Colon, Rafael BioIn 16
Hernandez Colon, Rafael 1936- WhoHisp 91, WhoSSW 91, WhoWor 91
Hernandez-Cruz, Luis WhoAmA 91
Hernandez Cruz, Victor 1949- BioIn 16
Hernandez de Lopez, Ana Maria 1930- WhoHisp 91
Hernandez-G., Manuel de Jesus 1949- WhoHisp 91
Hernandez Martinez, Maximiliano 1882-1966 BioIn 16
Hernandez-Miyares, Julio Enrique 1931- WhoE 91, WhoHisp 91
Hernandez Montis, Vicente 1925- EncO&P 3
Hernandez-Morales, Roberto Eduardo 1931- WhoHisp 91
Hernandez-Pinero, Sally WhoHisp 91
Hernandez-Rivera, Andres 1935- WhoHisp 91
Hernandez-Serna, Isabel 1945- WhoHisp 91
Hernandez-Serrano, Ruben J 1924- BiDrAPA 89
Hernandez Toledo, Rene Antonio 1943- WhoHisp 91
Hernandez Torres, Zaida WhoHisp 91
Hernandez-Trujillo, Juan Manuel 1944- WhoE 91
Hernandis, John A. 1937- ODwPR 91
Herndon, Albert Arbie, Jr. 1940- WhoE 91
Herndon, Angelo EncAL

Herndon, Bradley J. 1957- *WhoEmL 91*
Herndon, Charles Harbison 1915- *WhoAm 90*
Herndon, Claude Nash 1916- *WhoAm 90*
Herndon, D.A., Jr. 1908- *St&PR 91*
Herndon, D. Alton *St&PR 91*
Herndon, James E. 1925- *WhoAm 90*
Herndon, James Francis 1929- *WhoAm 90*
Herndon, James Henry 1938- *WhoAm 90*
Herndon, John Joyce Carter 1931- *WhoAm 90*
Herndon, Lance H. *BioIn 16*
Herndon, Larry 1953- *Ballpl 90*
Herndon, Leonard Randolph 1951- *WhoSSW 91*
Herndon, Mark *WhoAm 90*
Herndon, Noah Twist 1932- *St&PR 91*
Herndon, Rhonda Dianne 1960- *WhoSSW 91*
Herndon, Robert G. 1934- *St&PR 91*
Herndon, Robert McCulloch 1935- *WhoAm 90*
Herndon, Rosemary Van Vleet 1931- *WhoAmW 91*
Herndon, Terry 1939- *ConAu 130*
Herndon, Terry Eugene 1939- *WhoAm 90*
Herndon, Thomas Glenn 1920- *WhoSSW 91*
Herndon, Thomas J 1831-1893 *OxCCanT*
Herndon, Venable 1927- *ConAu 32NR*
Herndon, Vernon Edward 1907- *WhoAm 90*
Herndon, William Cecil 1932- *WhoAm 90*
Herndon, William E. *NewYTBS 90*
Herne, Chrystal 1882?-1950 *BioIn 16*
Herne, Chrystal Katharine 1882-1950 *NotWoAT*
Herne, Frank *EncO&P 3*
Herne, Frank 1850?- *EncPaPR 91*
Herne, Katharine Corcoran 1856-1943 *NotWoAT*
Herne, Katherine Corcoran 1857?-1943 *BioIn 16*
Hernes, Seymour Irwin 1927- *St&PR 91*
Hernke, Richard R. 1954- *St&PR 91*
Hernmarck, Helena *BioIn 16*
Hernmarck, Helena 1941- *ConDes 90*
Hernon, Joseph Martin, Jr. 1936- *WhoAm 90*
Hernon, Richard Francis 1940- *WhoE 91*
Hernquist, Karl Gerhard 1922- *WhoAm 90*
Hernstadt, Judith Filenbaum 1942- *WhoAm 90, WhoWor 91*
Hernton, Calvin C. 1934- *WhoWrEP 89*
Hernu, Charles *BioIn 16*
Hernu, Charles 1923-1990 *NewYTBS 90 [port]*
Hernz, William Joseph *BiDrAPA 89*
Hero, Byron A. 1950- *WhoAm 90*
Hero, Gregory Sophocles 1956- *WhoE 91*
Hero, Numa Charles, III 1942- *BiDrAPA 89*
Hero, Peter Decourcy 1942- *WhoAmA 91*
Herod The Great 73?BC-4BC *WorAlBi*
Herod, Catherine Lynn *BiDrAPA 89*
Herodotus *BioIn 16*
Herodotus 485?BC-430?BC *WorAlBi*
Herold, Charles W., Jr. 1929- *St&PR 91*
Herold, Christian Friedrich 1700?-1779? *PenDiDA 89*
Herold, Edward William 1907- *WhoAm 90*
Herold, Jiri *PenDiMP*
Herold, Johann Gregor *PenDiDA 89*
Herold, Joseph Herman 1936- *WhoE 91*
Herold, Karl Guenter 1947- *WhoEmL 91, WhoWor 91*
Herold, Robert Daniel 1953- *WhoEmL 91*
Herold, Ronald Joseph 1939- *St&PR 91*
Herold, William J. 1930- *St&PR 91*
Heroldt, Christian Friedrich 1700?-1779? *PenDiDA 89*
Heroman, Donald T. 1951- *St&PR 91*
Heron Family, The *OxCCanT*
Heron, Antoinette Tomai 1947- *St&PR 91*
Heron, David Winston 1920- *WhoAm 90*
Heron, Duncan, Jr. 1926- *WhoAm 90*
Heron, Geoffrey B *BiDrAPA 89*
Heron, Hilary 1923-1976 *BiDWomA*
Heron, Jacqueline Brenda 1949- *WhoWrEP 89*
Heron, Jane Dattaro *WhoAmW 91*
Heron, Jean Ellen 1942- *WhoAmW 91*
Heron, Joanne Elizabeth 1944- *WhoAmW 91*
Heron, Mary *FemiCLE*
Heron, Matilda 1830-1877 *NotWoAT*
Heron, Matilda Agnes 1830-1877 *BioIn 16*
Heron, Nye Brian 1952- *WhoE 91*
Heron, Patrick 1920- *WhoWor 91*
Heron, Robert Methven *PenDiDA 89*
Heron, William B. 1940- *St&PR 91*
Heron, William J., Jr. 1941- *St&PR 91*
Heronemus, Richard Cadmus 1932- *St&PR 91*
Herophilus, of Chalcedon 335?BC-280?BC *BioIn 16*
Heroy, William Bayard, Jr. 1915- *WhoAm 90*
Herpel, George Lloyd 1921- *WhoAm 90*
Herpich, Susan 1947- *WhoEmL 91*
Herpst, Martha Jane 1911- *WhoAmA 91N*
Herpst, Robert Dix 1947- *WhoE 91, WhoWor 91*
Herr, Beth Shelly 1957- *WhoEmL 91*
Herr, Betty Ellen 1946- *BiDrAPA 89*
Herr, Bonita Louise Bower 1945- *WhoAmW 91*
Herr, Dan 1917- *WhoAm 90, WhoWor 91*
Herr, Dan 1917-1990 *ConAu 132*
Herr, David Fulton 1950- *WhoEmL 91*
Herr, Earl Binkley, Jr. 1928- *WhoAm 90*
Herr, Eddie 1872-1943 *Ballpl 90*
Herr, Eric B. 1948- *St&PR 91*
Herr, Judy Ann 1941- *WhoAmW 91*
Herr, Kenneth Julian 1927- *WhoAm 90*
Herr, Lucien Charles 1864-1926 *BiDFrPL*
Herr, Mark Charles 1952- *WhoEmL 91*
Herr, Martha 1952- *IntWWM 90*
Herr, Michael *BioIn 16*
Herr, Michael 1940?- *MajTwCW*
Herr, Ober Samuel, Jr. 1927- *St&PR 91*
Herr, Philip Michael 1955- *WhoE 91*
Herr, Richard 1922- *WhoAm 90*
Herr, Robert C. 1939- *St&PR 91*
Herr, Ruth Smith 1965- *WhoAmW 91*
Herr, Stanley Sholom 1945- *WhoEmL 91*
Herr, Terry Edward 1959- *WhoE 91*
Herr, Tom 1956- *Ballpl 90*
Herrad of Hohenberg 1130?-1195 *EncCoWW*
Herran, Manuel A. *WhoHisp 91*
Herrbold, William Philip 1945- *St&PR 91*
Herre, Michael F. 1948- *St&PR 91*
Herregat, Guy-Georges Jacques 1939- *WhoE 91, WhoWor 91*
Herrell, Steve *BioIn 16*
Herrell, Wallace Edgar 1909- *WhoAm 90*
Herrema, Donald J. 1952- *St&PR 91*
Herrema, Robert Dale 1941- *IntWWM 90*
Herren, Lloyd Kendall 1922- *IntWWM 90*
Herren, William Richard 1946- *St&PR 91*
Herrera, Albert A. 1950- *WhoHisp 91*
Herrera, Alfred J. *WhoHisp 91*
Herrera, Amilcar Oscar 1920- *WhoWor 91*
Herrera, Anibal P 1926- *BiDrAPA 89*
Herrera, Carmen 1915- *WhoAmA 91*
Herrera, Carolina *BioIn 16, WhoHisp 91*
Herrera, Eduardo Antonio 1953- *WhoHisp 91*
Herrera, Edward A 1937- *BiDrAPA 89*
Herrera, Efren 1951- *BioIn 16*
Herrera, Enrique Olaya 1881-1937 *BioIn 16*
Herrera, Estela Maris 1943- *WhoHisp 91*
Herrera, Fidel Michael 1939- *WhoHisp 91*
Herrera, Frank G. 1943- *WhoHisp 91*
Herrera, George 1957- *WhoHisp 91*
Herrera, Georgina Del Carmen *BiDrAPA 89*
Herrera, Henry Richard *BiDrAPA 89*
Herrera, Herman Richard 1940- *WhoHisp 91*
Herrera, Irma Dolores 1951- *WhoEmL 91*
Herrera, Ismael 1931- *WhoAm 90*
Herrera, John *WhoAm 90*
Herrera, Joseph Q. *WhoHisp 91*
Herrera, Juan Felipe 1948- *ConAu 131, HispWr 90*
Herrera, Juan Ramon 1948- *WhoWor 91*
Herrera, Lorenzo, Jr. 1948- *WhoHisp 91*
Herrera, Luis Alberto de 1873-1959 *BioIn 16*
Herrera, Marina A. 1942- *WhoHisp 91*
Herrera, Mary Cardenas 1938- *WhoAmW 91*
Herrera, Monica Maria 1944- *WhoHisp 91*
Herrera, Omar Torrijos 1929-1981 *BioIn 16*
Herrera, Pancho 1934- *Ballpl 90*
Herrera, Paul Fredrick 1948- *WhoE 91*
Herrera, Peter 1953- *WhoHisp 91*
Herrera, Rafael C. 1934- *WhoHisp 91*
Herrera, Rene Justo 1953- *WhoSSW 91*
Herrera, Renee J. 1953- *WhoHisp 91*
Herrera, Rodimiro, Jr. 1944- *WhoHisp 91*
Herrera, Rosalinda 1948- *WhoHisp 91*
Herrera, Sandra Johnson 1944- *WhoAmW 91*
Herrera, Shirley Mae 1942- *WhoAmW 91*
Herrera, Steve 1949- *WhoHisp 91*
Herrera, William Trinidad 1949- *WhoEmL 91*
Herrera Campins, Luis 1925- *BioIn 16*
Herrera-Lavan, Mario Antonio 1931- *WhoHisp 91*
Herrera-Muraida, JoLynn J *BiDrAPA 89*
Herrera-Sobek, Maria *ConAu 131, HispWr 90*
Herrera y Reissig, Julio 1875-1910 *BioIn 16, HispWr 90*
Herrerias, Catalina 1948- *WhoAmW 91*
Herrero Grande *WhNaAH*
Herrero, Carmen A. 1960- *WhoHisp 91*
Herrero, Jose-Miguel Melchor 1954- *WhoWor 91*
Herrero, Julio H *BiDrAPA 89*
Herrero, Luis Arturo 1943- *BiDrAPA 89*
Herrero Rodriguez de Minon, Miguel 1940- *WhoWor 91*
Herres, Phillip Benjamin 1941- *St&PR 91*
Herres, Robert T. 1932- *WorAlBi*
Herres, Robert Tralles 1932- *WhoAm 90*
Herreshoff, Halsey Chase 1933- *St&PR 91, WhoE 91*
Herrhausen, Alfred *BioIn 16*
Herrhausen, Alfred 1930-1989 *AnObit 1989*
Herrick, Bruce Hale 1936- *WhoAm 90*
Herrick, Charles Robert *BiDrAPA 89*
Herrick, Clarence J. 1907- *St&PR 91*
Herrick, David Fraser 1947- *WhoEmL 91*
Herrick, Donald T. 1943- *St&PR 91*
Herrick, Genevieve Forbes 1894-1962 *BioIn 16*
Herrick, George Moulton 1918- *St&PR 91*
Herrick, Gregory Evans 1951- *WhoEmL 91*
Herrick, Howard D 1925- *BiDrAPA 89*
Herrick, Jeanne Mellin *AuBYP 90*
Herrick, John Berne 1919- *WhoAm 90*
Herrick, John D. 1932- *St&PR 91*
Herrick, John Dennis 1932- *WhoAm 90, WhoWor 91*
Herrick, Kathleen Magara 1943- *WhoAmW 91*
Herrick, Kenneth Gilbert 1921- *WhoAm 90*
Herrick, Kristine Ford 1947- *WhoE 91*
Herrick, Myron Timothy 1854-1929 *BioIn 16*
Herrick, Paul 1949- *St&PR 91*
Herrick, Peter 1926- *St&PR 91, WhoAm 90, WhoE 91*
Herrick, Robert 1591-1674 *LitC 13 [port], WorAlBi*
Herrick, Robert Ford 1912- *WhoAm 90*
Herrick, Robert H *BiDrAPA 89*
Herrick, Sheila M. 1943- *St&PR 91*
Herrick, Sonja Jane 1949- *WhoAmW 91*
Herrick, Stephen G. 1909- *St&PR 91*
Herrick, Susan Lynn 1959- *WhoAmW 91*
Herrick, Todd W. 1942- *WhoAm 90*
Herrick, Todd Wesley 1942- *St&PR 91*
Herrick, William 1915- *WhoWrEP 89*
Herrick, William Duncan 1941- *WhoSSW 91*
Herrick, Wm. Gregory 1945- *St&PR 91*
Herridge, Peter Lamont 1951- *BiDrAPA 89, WhoE 91*
Herriford, Robert Levi, Sr. 1931- *WhoAm 90*
Herrigel, Howard Ralph 1924- *St&PR 91*
Herriman, George 1880-1944 *EncACom [port]*
Herrin, Moreland 1922- *WhoAm 90*
Herrin, Rebecca D 1944- *BiDrAPA 89*
Herrin, Steve Johnson *BiDrAPA 89*
Herring, Allen Victor 1944- *St&PR 91*
Herring, Alvan A., Jr. 1943- *St&PR 91*
Herring, Anne *BiDEWW*
Herring, Art 1907- *Ballpl 90*
Herring, Carolyn Leigh 1959- *WhoAmW 91*
Herring, Charlanne Fields 1947- *WhoWrEP 89*
Herring, Christina Lee 1946- *BiDrAPA 89*
Herring, David Lawrence 1946- *WhoE 91*
Herring, Elizabeth Boleman 1951- *WhoWor 91*
Herring, Frances Elizabeth 1851-1916 *FemiCLE*
Herring, Glenn Anthony 1953- *WhoSSW 91*
Herring, Gregory 1950- *St&PR 91, WhoSSW 91*
Herring, Jack Herman 1922- *WhoAm 90*
Herring, Jack William 1925- *WhoAm 90*
Herring, Jan 1923- *WhoAmA 91*
Herring, Jerone Carson 1938- *St&PR 91, WhoAm 90*
Herring, John 1818-1896 *DcCanB 12*
Herring, John R. 1931- *St&PR 91*
Herring, Judith Teel 1960- *WhoSSW 91*
Herring, Kay *ODwPR 91*
Herring, Leonard G. 1927- *St&PR 91*
Herring, Leonard Gray 1927- *WhoAm 90, WhoSSW 91*
Herring, Nancy L. 1956- *WhoAmW 91*
Herring, Patricia LeBlanc 1944- *WhoAmW 91*
Herring, Phil *BioIn 16*
Herring, Reuben 1922- *WhoAm 90*
Herring, Robert H. 1938- *WhoWrEP 89*
Herring, Shirley Macklin 1954- *St&PR 91*
Herring, Susan Weller 1947- *WhoAmW 91*
Herring, Tyrone E. 1946- *WhoSSW 91*
Herring, Victoria L. 1947- *WhoEmL 91*
Herring, William Arthur 1945- *WhoWor 91*
Herring, William Conyers 1914- *WhoAm 90*
Herringer, Frank C. 1942- *St&PR 91*
Herringer, Frank Casper 1942- *WhoAm 90*
Herrington, Arthur W 1891-1970 *WhoAmA 91N*
Herrington, James Benjamin, Jr. 1953- *WhoSSW 91*
Herrington, John 1939- *BiDrUSE 89*
Herrington, John David, III 1934- *WhoAm 90*
Herrington, John Stewart 1939- *WhoAm 90, WhoSSW 91, WhoWor 91*
Herrington, Lester Clyde 1944- *WhoSSW 91*
Herrington, Mark Bruce 1959- *WhoSSW 91*
Herrington, Nell Ray *WhoAmA 91N*
Herrington, Raymond F. *St&PR 91*
Herrington, Terri 1957- *WhoWrEP 89*
Herrington-Borre, Frances June 1935- *WhoAmW 91*
Herrinton, Dan Bruce 1938- *WhoSSW 91*
Herrinton, John Peter 1943- *WhoAm 90*
Herriot, Edouard 1872-1957 *BiDFrPL*
Herriot, James *BioIn 16*
Herriot, James 1916- *AuBYP 90, WhoWor 91, WorAlBi*
Herriott, Bernadine Shriver 1948- *WhoAmW 91*
Herriott, Donald Richard 1928- *WhoAm 90*
Herriott, Michael Gordon *BiDrAPA 89*
Herriott, Scott H. 1945- *St&PR 91*
Herritt, David Michael 1957- *St&PR 91*
Herrling, Anthony C. *ODwPR 91*
Herrman, Augustine 1605?-1686 *EncCRAm*
Herrman, James R. 1950- *St&PR 91*
Herrmann, Alexander 1844-1896 *BioIn 16*
Herrmann, Arthur Dominey 1926- *WhoAm 90*
Herrmann, Barbara H. 1946- *St&PR 91*
Herrmann, Benjamin Edward 1919- *WhoAm 90*
Herrmann, Bernard 1911-1975 *OxCPMus*
Herrmann, Bryan Louis 1935- *St&PR 91*
Herrmann, Carol 1944- *WhoAmW 91*
Herrmann, Charles West 1947- *WhoSSW 91*
Herrmann, Christian, Jr. 1921- *WhoAm 90*
Herrmann, Daniel Lionel 1913- *WhoAm 90*
Herrmann, Donald Joseph 1915- *WhoAm 90*
Herrmann, Douglas J. 1941- *WhoAm 90*
Herrmann, Duane Lawrence 1951- *WhoWrEP 89*
Herrmann, Ed 1943- *WorAlBi*
Herrmann, Ed 1946- *Ballpl 90*
Herrmann, Edward Kirk 1943- *WhoAm 90*
Herrmann, Frederick 1941- *St&PR 91*
Herrmann, Garry 1859-1931 *Ballpl 90*
Herrmann, George 1921- *WhoAm 90*
Herrmann, Gretchen Mary 1948- *WhoEmL 91*
Herrmann, John 1931- *WhoSSW 91, WhoWrEP 89*
Herrmann, John A., Jr. 1935- *St&PR 91*
Herrmann, John J, Jr 1937- *WhoAmA 91*
Herrmann, John Robert 1928- *St&PR 91*
Herrmann, Karl-Ernst 1936- *ConDes 90*
Herrmann, Katherine Scott 1959- *WhoAmW 91*
Herrmann, Kenneth James 1962- *BiDrAPA 89*
Herrmann, Kenneth John, Jr. 1943- *WhoE 91, WhoWor 91*
Herrmann, Lacy Bunnell 1929- *WhoAm 90, WhoE 91, WhoWor 91*
Herrmann, Ned *BioIn 16*
Herrmann, Norbert 1926- *St&PR 91*
Herrmann, Paul N. 1929- *St&PR 91*
Herrmann, Raymond R. 1920- *St&PR 91*
Herrmann, Roland 1952- *WhoWor 91*
Herrmann, Ronee 1929- *BiDrAPA 89*
Herrmann, Thomas Francis 1951- *WhoEmL 91*
Herrmann, Thomas Leo 1951- *BiDrAPA 89*
Herrmann, William E. 1922- *WhoSSW 91*
Herrmann, William J. 1919- *St&PR 91*
Herrmann, William Joseph 1951- *WhoE 91*
Herrmanns, Ralph 1933- *AuBYP 90*
Herrnstadt, Richard Lawrence 1926- *WhoAm 90*
Herrnstein, Richard Julius 1930- *WhoAm 90*
Herrnstein, William Henry 1936- *St&PR 91*
Herro, John Joseph 1945- *WhoSSW 91*
Herrold, Kenneth Frederick 1913- *WhoAm 90*
Herrold, Russell Phillips, Jr. 1924- *WhoAm 90*
Herron, B Bernie 1931- *BiDrAPA 89*
Herron, Carolivia 1947- *WhoAmW 91*
Herron, David William 1940- *St&PR 91*
Herron, Donald Patrick 1954- *WhoEmL 91*
Herron, Drew Jonathan 1956- *WhoEmL 91*

Herzog, Chaim 1918- *BioIn 16, WhoWor 91*
Herzog, David Anthony 1942- *BiDrAPA 89*
Herzog, David Brandeis 1946- *BiDrAPA 89, WhoE 91*
Herzog, E. *MajTwCW*
Herzog, Emile Solomon Wilhelm *AuBYP 90*
Herzog, Ernest 1934- *St&PR 91*
Herzog, Forest Edward 1951- *St&PR 91*
Herzog, Fred F. 1907- *WhoAm 90*
Herzog, Harold Kenneth 1924- *St&PR 91*
Herzog, Jacob Hawley 1911- *St&PR 91, WhoWor 91*
Herzog, James Michael *BiDrAPA 89*
Herzog, Joan Dorothy 1938- *WhoAmW 91*
Herzog, John A. 1928- *St&PR 91*
Herzog, John E. 1936- *WhoAm 90*
Herzog, Kathryn Rose 1955- *WhoAmW 91*
Herzog, Lester Barry 1953- *WhoEmL 91*
Herzog, Norbert Karl 1955- *WhoSSW 91*
Herzog, Peter Emilius 1925- *WhoAm 90*
Herzog, Philippe Albert Robert 1940- *BiDFrPL*
Herzog, Renee Barbara 1947- *WhoAmW 91*
Herzog, Richard Barnard 1939- *WhoAm 90*
Herzog, Richard Dennis 1950- *WhoE 91*
Herzog, Robert I. *BioIn 16, NewYTBS 90*
Herzog, Teri Nelson 1962- *WhoSSW 91*
Herzog, Todd A. 1944- *St&PR 91*
Herzog, Volker 1939- *WhoWor 91*
Herzog, Werner 1942- *BioIn 16*
Herzog, Whitey *BioIn 16*
Herzog, Whitey 1931- *Ballpl 90 [port], WhoAm 90, WorAlBi*
Herzstein, Robert Erwin 1931- *WhoAm 90*
Hes, Jozef Philip 1925- *BiDrAPA 89*
Hesburgh, Theodore M. 1917- *WorAlBi*
Hesburgh, Theodore Martin *BioIn 16*
Hesburgh, Theodore Martin 1917- *WhoAm 90*
Heschel, Abraham Joshua 1907-1972 *BioIn 16*
Hesdorf, Hans 1921- *WhoWor 91*
Heseltine, Gilbert F *BiDrAPA 89*
Heseltine, Michael *BioIn 16*
Heseltine, Philip 1894-1930 *BioIn 16*
Heselton, H. Murray 1925- *St&PR 91*
Hesford, Michael Bryan 1930- *IntWWM 90*
Heshler, Marlene Joyce 1948- *St&PR 91*
Hesiod *WorAlBi*
Hesiod 750?BC- *ClMLC 5 [port]*
Heskes, Irene 1928- *IntWWM 90*
Hesketh *WhoAmA 91N*
Hesketh, Howard Edward 1931- *WhoAm 90*
Hesketh, Joe 1959- *Ballpl 90*
Hesketh, Phoebe 1909- *FemiCLE*
Hesketh-Harvey, Kit *BioIn 16*
Heskett, James Lee 1933- *WhoAm 90*
Heslin, Cathleen Jane 1929- *WhoWor 91*
Heslin, James D. *BioIn 16*
Heslin, James J. 1916- *WhoAm 90*
Hesling, Donald Mills 1914- *WhoAm 90*
Heslop, Maura *BioIn 16*
Heslop, Terence Murray 1942- *WhoAm 90*
Hespos, Richard Franklin 1934- *WhoAm 90*
Hesprich, Steven Francis 1951- *WhoEmL 91*
Hess Family *PenDiDA 89*
Hess, Alan Marshall 1942- *WhoE 91*
Hess, Alison Lee 1958- *WhoEmL 91*
Hess, Andrea Megaery 1954- *IntWWM 90*
Hess, Armand Melvin 1935- *St&PR 91*
Hess, Arthur 1927- *WhoAm 90*
Hess, August 1924- *St&PR 91*
Hess, Bartlett Leonard 1910- *WhoWor 91*
Hess, Bernard Andes, Jr. 1940- *WhoAm 90*
Hess, Ceferina Gayo 1939- *WhoSSW 91*
Hess, Charles Edward 1931- *WhoAm 90*
Hess, Charles W. 1917- *St&PR 91*
Hess, Cheryl D. 1947- *St&PR 91*
Hess, Dale Francis 1929- *St&PR 91*
Hess, David Willard 1933- *WhoAm 90*
Hess, Dean Austin, Jr. 1941- *WhoE 91*
Hess, Debra 1953- *WhoAmW 91*
Hess, Dennis John 1940- *St&PR 91, WhoAm 90, WhoE 91*
Hess, Dianne Martin 1943- *WhoSSW 91*
Hess, Donald Fallis 1928- *St&PR 91*
Hess, Donald K. 1930- *WhoAm 90*
Hess, Earl Hollinger 1928- *WhoAm 90*
Hess, Edward John 1936- *St&PR 91*
Hess, Edwin John 1933- *WhoAm 90*
Hess, Eugene Lyle 1914- *WhoAm 90*
Hess, Evelyn Victorine 1926- *WhoAm 90*
Hess, Geoffrey LaVerne 1949- *WhoE 91*
Hess, George Kellogg, Jr. 1922- *WhoAm 90*
Hess, George Paul 1926- *WhoAm 90*
Hess, George Robert 1941- *WhoAm 90*
Hess, H. Jurgen 1961- *ODwPR 91*
Hess, Hans Ober 1912- *WhoAm 90*
Hess, Harriet Schneider 1927- *WhoAmW 91*
Hess, Harry Hammond 1906-1969 *BioIn 16, DcScB S2*
Hess, Hazel Elizabeth 1929- *WhoAmW 91*
Hess, Henry Richard 1936- *St&PR 91*
Hess, Howard *BiDrAPA 89*
Hess, Irma 1939- *WhoAmW 91*
Hess, James T. 1945- *St&PR 91*
Hess, Joan *TwCCr&M 91*
Hess, Johann *PenDiDA 89*
Hess, Johann Benedikt, I 1636?-1674 *PenDiDA 89*
Hess, Johann Benedikt, II 1672-1736 *PenDiDA 89*
Hess, Joyce *WhoAmA 91*
Hess, Karen E. 1944- *WhoE 91*
Hess, Karen Jo Matison 1939- *WhoWrEP 89*
Hess, Karen Matison 1939- *WhoAmW 91*
Hess, Karl 1945- *WhoAm 90*
Hess, Karsten 1930- *St&PR 91, WhoAm 90*
Hess, Lawrence Eugene, Jr. 1923- *WhoE 91, WhoWor 91*
Hess, Lee Howard 1947- *St&PR 91, WhoAm 90*
Hess, Leon 1914- *ConAmBL, WhoAm 90, WhoE 91*
Hess, Leonard G. 1930- *St&PR 91*
Hess, Leonard Wayne 1949- *WhoSSW 91*
Hess, Lilo 1916- *AuBYP 90*
Hess, Lincoln Robert 1956- *BiDrAPA 89*
Hess, Loretta Rooney *WhoWrEP 89*
Hess, Lucy *St&PR 91*
Hess, Marcia Wanda 1934- *WhoAmW 91*
Hess, Margaret Johnston 1915- *WhoAmW 91, WhoWor 91*
Hess, Marshall 1927- *St&PR 91*
Hess, Mary Barbara 1953- *WhoWrEP 89*
Hess, Melvin Harold 1960- *BiDrAPA 89*
Hess, Merrill R. 1923- *St&PR 91*
Hess, Milton Siegmund 1941- *WhoAm 90*
Hess, Moses 1812-1875 *BioIn 16*
Hess, Myra 1890-1965 *PenDiMP, WorAlBi*
Hess, Nigel John 1953- *IntWWM 90*
Hess, Orvan W. *WhoAm 90, WhoWor 91*
Hess, Otto 1878-1926 *Ballpl 90*
Hess, P. Gregory 1946- *WhoE 91*
Hess, Patrick Henry 1931- *WhoAm 90*
Hess, Peter 1709-1782 *PenDiDA 89*
Hess, Philip K. 1960- *WhoE 91*
Hess, Randall Duane 1954- *WhoSSW 91*
Hess, Robert A. 1946- *ODwPR 91*
Hess, Robert B. 1959- *WhoE 91*
Hess, Robert C. 1947- *St&PR 91*
Hess, Robert Daniel 1920- *WhoAm 90*
Hess, Robert John 1937- *St&PR 91*
Hess, Robert Lee 1932- *WhoAm 90, WhoE 91*
Hess, Robert Pratt 1942- *WhoWor 91*
Hess, Robert W. 1930- *IntWWM 90*
Hess, Rolf Paul 1946- *WhoWor 91*
Hess, Ronald L. 1942- *St&PR 91*
Hess, Rudolf 1894-1987 *BioIn 16*
Hess, Sebastian *PenDiDA 89*
Hess, Sidney J., Jr. 1910- *WhoAm 90*
Hess, Sidney Wayne 1932- *WhoAm 90*
Hess, Sol *EncACom*
Hess, Stanley William 1939- *WhoAmA 91*
Hess, Stephen 1933- *ConAu 30NR, WhoAm 90, WhoWrEP 89*
Hess, Thomas B 1920-1978 *WhoAmA 91N*
Hess, W.J. 1937- *St&PR 91*
Hess, Walter Otto 1918- *WhoWor 91*
Hess, Wanda Jean 1949- *WhoE 91*
Hess, Wheeler Herdman 1931- *St&PR 91, WhoAm 90*
Hess, William Curtis 1948- *WhoSSW 91*
Hess, William E. 1936- *St&PR 91*
Hess, Wilmot Norton 1926- *WhoAm 90*
Hess-Luttich, Ernest Walter Bernhard 1949- *WhoWor 91*
Hessayon, David Gerald 1928- *WhoWor 91*
Hessberg, Rufus R. 1921- *WhoAm 90*
Hessburg, Arthur J. 1929- *St&PR 91*
Hesse, Axel Ernst 1935- *IntWWM 90*
Hesse, Christian August 1925- *St&PR 91*
Hesse, Eva 1936-1970 *BiDWomA, BioIn 16*
Hesse, Eva 1936-1972 *WhoAmA 91N*
Hesse, Grete Anna Erna 1933- *WhoAmW 91*
Hesse, Helmut Siegfried 1934- *WhoWor 91*
Hesse, Hermann 1877-1962 *BioIn 16, EncO&P 3, MajTwCW, WorAlBi, WrPh*
Hesse, James D. 1938- *St&PR 91*
Hesse, John Walter 1949- *St&PR 91*
Hesse, Martha 1942- *ODwPR 91*
Hesse, Martha O. 1942- *WhoAm 90, WhoAmW 91*
Hesse, Paul A. 1941- *ODwPR 91*
Hesse, Ruth 1936- *IntWWM 90*
Hesse, Stephen Bradley 1941- *St&PR 91*
Hesse, Stephen M. 1948- *WhoAm 90*
Hesse, William R. 1914- *WhoE 91, WhoWor 91*
Hessel, Andrea M *BiDrAPA 89*
Hessel, Andrea Michele 1952- *WhoEmL 91*
Hessel, Helena 1949- *St&PR 91*
Hessel, Susan Lee 1961- *WhoSSW 91*
Hesselbach, Bruce William 1950- *WhoWrEP 89*
Hesselbach, Charles F *BiDrAPA 89*
Hesselbein, Frances Richards *St&PR 91, WhoAm 90, WhoAmW 91*
Hesselberg, Erik *AuBYP 90*
Hesselink, Lambertus 1948- *WhoEmL 91*
Hesselius, John 1728-1778 *EncCRAm*
Hesselroth, Warren 1926- *St&PR 91*
Hesseltine, William H., Jr. 1932- *St&PR 91*
Hesseman, Howard 1940- *WhoAm 90, WorAlBi*
Hessen, Beatrice Minkus *BioIn 16*
Hesser, Danielle Elan 1949- *WhoAmW 91*
Hesser, E. Grant 1919- *St&PR 91*
Hesser, Grant V. 1947- *St&PR 91*
Hesser, Melanie Jean 1962- *WhoAmW 91*
Hessing, Valjeam McCarty 1934- *BioIn 16*
Hession, Eileen Melia *WhoWrEP 89*
Hession, Jeanne M. 1930- *St&PR 91*
Hession, Joseph Michael 1955- *WhoWrEP 89*
Hesske, Daniel J. 1943- *St&PR 91*
Hessler, Curtis Alan 1943- *WhoAm 90*
Hessler, David William 1932- *WhoAm 90*
Hessler, Gary Lee 1943- *WhoWor 91*
Hessler, Robert Roamie 1918- *WhoAm 90*
Hesslund, Bradley Harry 1958- *WhoEmL 91, WhoWor 91*
Hessol, Gail I. 1953- *St&PR 91*
Hest, Amy *BioIn 16*
Hestad, Bjorn Mark 1926- *WhoWor 91*
Hestand, Cynthia Ann 1955- *WhoAmW 91*
Hestehave, Borge Tage 1923- *St&PR 91*
Hestehave, Marianne 1924- *St&PR 91*
Hestenes, Roberta *BioIn 16*
Hestenes, Roberta Rae 1939- *WhoAmW 91*
Hester, Albert Lee 1932- *WhoSSW 91*
Hester, Betty Parrish 1936- *WhoAmW 91*
Hester, Bob Drerve 1928- *St&PR 91*
Hester, Carolyn LaVar 1948- *WhoAmW 91*
Hester, Donnie Phil 1950- *St&PR 91*
Hester, Douglas Benjamin 1927- *WhoAm 90*
Hester, Elizabeth James 1963- *WhoAmW 91*
Hester, Eugene 1944- *St&PR 91*
Hester, Eugene Alfred 1932- *WhoSSW 91*
Hester, Gina Loraine 1961- *WhoSSW 91*
Hester, Harris Ryland 1942- *WhoAm 90*
Hester, James Edward 1931- *WhoSSW 91*
Hester, James Francis, Jr. *St&PR 91N*
Hester, James Lynn 1939- *WhoAm 90*
Hester, James McNaughton 1924- *WhoAm 90*
Hester, James Stephen 1952- *WhoEmL 91*
Hester, Karlton Edward 1949- *WhoE 91*
Hester, Linda Hunt 1938- *WhoSSW 91*
Hester, M Thomas 1941- *ConAu 131*
Hester, Marcus Baxter 1937- *WhoSSW 91*
Hester, Mark Bowman 1956- *IntWWM 90*
Hester, Martin Luther 1947- *WhoWrEP 89*
Hester, Marylee Babendreier 1935- *WhoAmW 91*
Hester, Nancy Elizabeth 1950- *WhoAmW 91*
Hester, Norman Eric 1946- *WhoAm 90*
Hester, Randolph Thompson, Jr. 1944- *WhoAm 90*
Hester, Raymond Bernreuter 1943- *WhoSSW 91*
Hester, Ross Wyatt 1924- *WhoSSW 91*
Hester, Terry L. 1954- *St&PR 91*
Hester, Thomas P. 1937- *St&PR 91*
Hester, Thomas R 1946- *ConAu 32NR*
Hester, Thomas Roy 1946- *WhoAm 90*
Hester, Thomas William 1951- *BiDrAPA 89*
Hester, Timothy Uel 1956- *WhoSSW 91*
Hester, William *ConAu 129*
Hester, William C. 1934- *ConAu 129*
Hester-Lunt, Jean 1953- *WhoEmL 91*
Hester-Mitich, Louis John 1929- *WhoWrEP 89*
Hestler, Ralph 1930- *St&PR 91*
Heston, Charlton *BioIn 16*
Heston, Charlton 1923- *WorAlBi*
Heston, Charlton 1924- *WhoAm 90, WhoWor 91*
Heston, Fraser *BioIn 16*
Heston, Joan *WhoAmA 91, WhoE 91*
Heston, Leonard Lancaster 1930- *WhoAm 90*
Heston, W. Craig 1935- *St&PR 91*
Heston, William May 1922- *WhoAm 90*
Heth, Diana Sue 1948- *WhoEmL 91*
Heth, Meir 1932- *St&PR 91*
Hetherington, Charles Ray 1919- *WhoAm 90*
Hetherington, David L. 1943- *St&PR 91*
Hetherington, Edwin S. 1949- *St&PR 91*
Hetherington, Gordon Scott 1960- *WhoSSW 91*
Hetherington, James Richard 1931- *St&PR 91*
Hetherington, Jerre *BioIn 16*
Hetherington, John Warner 1938- *St&PR 91, WhoAm 90*
Hetherington, Mary Elizabeth 1962- *WhoAmW 91*
Hetherly, Katheryn Johnson 1928- *WhoSSW 91*
Hetherly, Vroni *BiDrAPA 89*
Hetherwick, Frederic Matthew 1952- *St&PR 91*
Hetkaemper, Robert 1949- *WhoWor 91*
Hetki, Johnny 1922- *Ballpl 90*
Hetland, James Lyman, Jr. 1925- *WhoAm 90, WhoWor 91*
Hetland, Janice Elizabeth 1950- *WhoEmL 91*
Hetland, Jerry E. 1947- *St&PR 91*
Hetland, John Robert 1930- *WhoAm 90, WhoWor 91*
Hetman, Nicholas Wayne 1950- *WhoEmL 91*
Hetnal, Mieczyslaw J 1955- *BiDrAPA 89*
Hetnarski, Leokadia E *BiDrAPA 89*
Hetrick, Bruce K. *ODwPR 91*
Hetrick, Charles Brady 1932- *WhoSSW 91*
Hetrick, Christopher Jon 1958- *St&PR 91*
Hetrick, Dawn Barbara *BiDrAPA 89*
Hetrick, Demaris K. 1947- *ODwPR 91*
Hetrick, Jack G. 1955- *WhoSSW 91*
Hetrick, Michelle 1958- *WhoAmW 91*
Hetrick, Suzanne H. 1943- *WhoAmW 91*
Hetsch, Gustav Friedrich *PenDiDA 89*
Hetsko, Cyril Francis 1911- *WhoAm 90, WhoE 91, WhoWor 91*
Hettich, Arthur *St&PR 91*
Hettich, Arthur Matthias 1927- *WhoAm 90, WhoE 91*
Hettich, Michael 1953- *WhoWrEP 89*
Hettiger, Lorin J. 1956- *WhoAmW 91*
Hettinga, Donald Roy 1953- *WhoEmL 91*
Hettinger, J *EncO&P 3*
Hettinger, John 1880- *EncPaPR 91*
Hettinger, Steve *WhoSSW 91*
Hettleman, Michael Kalman 1936- *St&PR 91*
Hettler, Madeline Therese 1949- *WhoAmW 91*
Hettmansberger, James Darrell 1945- *WhoEmL 91*
Hettrick, James Parkinson 1958- *St&PR 91*
Hettrick, John L. 1934- *St&PR 91*
Hettrick, John Lord 1934- *WhoAm 90*
Hettrick, William Eugene 1939- *IntWWM 90*
Hetu, Helene *BiDrAPA 89*
Hetu, Herbert E. 1929- *ODwPR 91*
Hetu, Jacques 1938- *IntWWM 90*
Hetzel, C. Charles 1941- *St&PR 91*
Hetzel, Carl Paul 1929- *St&PR 91*
Hetzel, Donald Stanford 1941- *St&PR 91*
Hetzel, Frederick Armstrong 1930- *WhoAm 90, WhoWor 91*
Hetzel, Fredrick William 1946- *WhoEmL 91*
Hetzel, Glenn Braith 1955- *St&PR 91*
Hetzel, Ralph Dorn, Jr. 1912- *WhoAm 90*
Hetzel, William Gelal 1933- *WhoAm 90*
Hetzendorfer, Simon *PenDiDA 89*
Hetzer, Richard Michael 1941- *St&PR 91*
Hetzler, Hans Wilhelm 1929- *WhoWor 91*
Hetzler, Kenneth Alf 1949- *BiDrAPA 89*
Hetznecker, William *BiDrAPA 89*
Hetzron, Robert 1937- *WhoAm 90*
Heubaum, William Lincoln 1938- *WhoAm 90*
Heuberger, Oscar 1924- *WhoAm 90*
Heuberger, Richard 1850-1914 *OxCPMus*
Heuchling, Theodore Paul 1925- *St&PR 91*
Heuck, Roger William 1939- *St&PR 91*
Heuer, Dieter Otto 1938- *WhoAm 90*
Heuer, Gerald Arthur 1930- *WhoAm 90*
Heuer, Helmut Herbert 1932- *WhoWor 91*
Heuer, Kenneth John 1927- *ConAu 30NR, WhoAm 90*
Heuer, Margaret B. 1935- *WhoAmW 91*
Heuer, Martin 1934- *WhoSSW 91*
Heuer, Marvin Arthur 1947- *WhoE 91*
Heuer, Michael Alexander 1932- *WhoAm 90*
Heuer, Otto H. 1904-1988 *BioIn 16*
Heuer, Robert Maynard, II 1944- *WhoAm 90*
Heuerman, Richard Arnold 1930- *St&PR 91*
Heuermann, Magda 1868- *WhoAmA 91N*
Heuermann, Patricia Calhoun 1936- *IntWWM 90*

Heuertz, Sarah Jane 1950- *WhoAmW 91*
Heuglin, Johann Erhard, I 1652-1712 *PenDiDA 89*
Heuglin, Johann Erhard, II 1687-1757 *PenDiDA 89*
Heule, Michael John 1955- *WhoEmL 91*
Heule, Robert Kneeland 1925- *WhoAm 90*
Heuler, Walter Kenneth 1949- *BiDrAPA 89*
Heuman, D.H. 1951- *St&PR 91*
Heuman, Donna Rena 1949- *WhoAmW 91*
Heuman, Warner J. 1924- *St&PR 91*
Heuman, William 1912-1971 *AuBYP 90*
Heumann, Karl Fredrich 1921- *WhoAm 90*
Heumann, Klemens Richard 1931- *WhoWor 91*
Heumann, Roger Jay 1954- *St&PR 91*
Heumann, Scott Fredric 1951- *WhoAm 90*
Heumann, Stephen Michael 1941- *St&PR 91*
Heupel, Donald Dean 1947- *St&PR 91*
Heureaux, Ulises 1845-1899 *BioIn 16*
Heurich, Charles Richard 1925- *St&PR 91*
Heuring, Rickey Lynn 1951- *WhoEmL 91*
Heurtaut, Nicolas 1702-1771 *BioIn 16*
Heurtaut, Nicolas 1720- *PenDiDA 89*
Heurtaux, Andre 1898-1983 *BioIn 16*
Heurtematte, Roberto 1908- *St&PR 91*
Heusch, Robert W. *St&PR 91*
Heuschele, Sharon Jo 1936- *WhoAmW 91*
Heuschele, Werner Paul 1929- *WhoAm 90*
Heuscher, Julius E 1918- *BiDrAPA 89*
Heusde, Sarah Cornelius de *BiDEWW*
Heusdens, Christian Roger 1953- *WhoWor 91*
Heusel, Gary Lee 1947- *WhoSSW 91*
Heuser, Henry Vogt 1914- *St&PR 91*
Heusi, Joe Duane 1942- *WhoAm 90*
Heusler, Anton F *BiDrAPA 89*
Heuss, Ernst 1922- *WhoWor 91*
Heusser, Calvin John 1924- *WhoAm 90*
Heusser, Ed 1900-1956 *Ballpl 90*
Heusser, Eleanore Elizabeth *WhoAmA 91*
Hevel, David Roger 1950- *WhoEmL 91*
Hevelius, Johannes 1611-1687 *WorAlBi*
Hevener, Barbara Cooley 1945- *WhoAmW 91*
Hevener, Fillmer, Jr. 1933- *WhoSSW 91*
Heveran, Ronald D. 1932- *St&PR 91*
Heverin, Edward John 1946- *WhoSSW 91*
Heverly, Nancy Eleanor 1954- *WhoEmL 91*
Heverly, Richard Charles 1928- *St&PR 91*
Hevesy, Georg 1885-1966 *WorAlBi*
Hevesy, Joseph W. 1945- *St&PR 91*
Hevey, Richard C. 1941- *St&PR 91*
Hevia, David Rene 1943- *St&PR 91*
Hevia, Modesto F 1921- *BiDrAPA 89*
Heving, Joe 1900-1970 *Ballpl 90*
Heving, Johnnie 1896-1968 *Ballpl 90*
Hevner, Alan Raymond 1950- *WhoE 91*
Hevner, Vernon Lewis 1928- *St&PR 91*
Hevrdejs, Richard Jerome 1933- *St&PR 91*
Hewa, Cynthia Lynne 1966- *WhoAmW 91*
Heward, Leslie 1897-1943 *PenDiMP*
Hewat, William Brian 1936- *WhoAm 90*
Hewelke, Maria Dorothea *PenDiDA 89*
Hewelke, Nathaniel Friedrich *PenDiDA 89*
Hewell, James R., Jr. 1930- *St&PR 91*
Hewell, Jimmie Carl 1945- *WhoSSW 91*
Hewerdine, Boo *BioIn 16*
Hewes, Agnes 1874-1963 *AuBYP 90*
Hewes, Henry 1917- *WhoAm 90*
Hewes, Joseph 1750-1779 *EncCRAm*
Hewes, Laurence I. 1902-1989 *BioIn 16*
Hewes, Laurence Ilsley, III 1933- *WhoAm 90*
Hewes, Phillip A. 1929- *St&PR 91*
Hewes, Tucker F. *ODwPR 91*
Hewes, William H *BiDrAPA 89*
Hewett, Anita 1918- *AuBYP 90*
Hewett, Arthur Edward 1935- *WhoAm 90, WhoWor 91*
Hewett, Charles Earle 1950- *WhoEmL 91*
Hewett, Christopher Benjamin 1958- *WhoAm 90*
Hewett, Dorothy 1923- *FemiCLE*
Hewett, Dwight Cecil 1959- *WhoSSW 91*
Hewett, Ed Albert 1942- *WhoAm 90*
Hewett, Edward Osborne 1835-1897 *DcCanB 12*
Hewett, Emily Lorraine 1951- *WhoSSW 91*
Hewett, Joan *AuBYP 90*
Hewett, JoAnne Lea 1960- *WhoAmW 91*
Hewett, Peter John 1936- *St&PR 91*
Hewett, Thomas Charles 1948- *WhoSSW 91*
Hewish, Antony 1924- *WhoWor 91, WorAlBi*
Hewit, Benjamin Lightner 1833-1894 *AmLegL*
Hewit, Russell Lyle 1952- *WhoEmL 91*
Hewitt, Abram S. 1822-1903 *WorAlBi*
Hewitt, Carl Herbert 1952- *WhoAm 90*
Hewitt, Charles Cary 1939- *BioIn 16*
Hewitt, Dean J. 1929- *ODwPR 91*
Hewitt, Deborah Lynn 1969- *WhoE 91*
Hewitt, Dennis Edwin 1944- *WhoAm 90*
Hewitt, Dickie M. 1938- *WhoAmW 91*
Hewitt, Don 1922- *BioIn 16*
Hewitt, Don S. 1922- *WhoAm 90*
Hewitt, Donald O. 1943- *WhoAm 90*
Hewitt, Duncan Adams 1949- *WhoAmA 91*
Hewitt, Edwin 1920- *WhoAm 90*
Hewitt, Francis Ray 1936- *WhoAmA 91*
Hewitt, Frank Seaver 1941- *St&PR 91, WhoAm 90*
Hewitt, Frankie Lea 1931- *WhoE 91*
Hewitt, Gerald 1920- *BiDrAPA 89*
Hewitt, Harry Donald 1921- *IntWWM 90*
Hewitt, Hugh 1956- *WhoAm 90*
Hewitt, James J. 1933- *WhoAm 90*
Hewitt, James Lester 1948- *BiDrAPA 89*
Hewitt, Jerene Cline 1917- *WhoWrEP 89*
Hewitt, Jess Paul, III 1957- *WhoSSW 91*
Hewitt, John 1907-1987 *WorAu 1980 [port]*
Hewitt, John Marshall 1841-1887 *AmLegL*
Hewitt, John Napoleon Brinton 1859-1937 *WhNaAH*
Hewitt, Karen Renee 1950- *WhoSSW 91*
Hewitt, Lawrence Lee 1953- *WhoEmL 91*
Hewitt, Marilyn Patricia 1947- *WhoAmW 91*
Hewitt, Marsha A. 1945- *St&PR 91*
Hewitt, Maurice *PenDiMP*
Hewitt, Michael Earling 1936- *WhoWor 91*
Hewitt, Nicholas 1945- *ConAu 132*
Hewitt, Ralph Clement, Jr. 1942- *WhoSSW 91*
Hewitt, Robert C. 1945- *St&PR 91*
Hewitt, Robert Lee 1934- *WhoAm 90*
Hewitt, Robert T 1909- *BiDrAPA 89*
Hewitt, Susan M E *ODwPR 91*
Hewitt, Thomas Edward 1939- *WhoAm 90*
Hewitt, Vivian Ann Davidson *WhoAm 90*
Hewitt, William Joseph 1939- *WhoE 91*
Hewitt, William Lane 1916- *WhoAm 90*
Hewitt, William M. 1946- *St&PR 91*
Hewko, Alan Robert 1960- *WhoEmL 91*
Hewko, Eric 1955- *WhoEmL 91*
Hewko, Walter J *BiDrAPA 89*
Hewlett, Cecil James 1923- *WhoAm 90*
Hewlett, Horace Wilson 1915- *WhoAm 90*
Hewlett, James *DrBlPA 90*
Hewlett, Louise R *BiDrAPA 89*
Hewlett, Richard Greening 1923- *WhoAm 90*
Hewlett, Sylvia Ann 1946- *BioIn 16*
Hewlett, Valerie Balcik 1963- *WhoAmW 91*
Hewlett, William 1913- *WhoAm 90*
Hewlett, William A *BiDrAPA 89*
Hewlett, William R. *BioIn 16*
Hewlett, William Redington 1913- *ConAmBL*
Hewlett-Kierstead, Nancy Carrick 1927- *WhoWor 91*
Hewson, Anne *BiDEWW*
Hewson, Donna Walters 1947- *WhoAmW 91, WhoEmL 91, WhoSSW 91, WhoWor 91*
Hewson, John 1744-1821 *PenDiDA 89*
Hewson, Martin Gerard 1929- *WhoE 91*
Hewson, Paul *BioIn 16*
Hewson, Robert Emmet 1955- *WhoE 91*
Hewytt, Mary *BiDEWW*
Hexamer, Eleanor Anne 1946- *WhoAm 90*
Hexberg, Karin 1945- *WhoEmL 91*
Hext, Harrington *TwCCr&M 91*
Hext, Kathleen Florence 1941- *WhoAmW 91*
Hextall, Ron *BioIn 16*
Hextall, Ron 1964- *WorAlBi*
Hexter, George F *BiDrAPA 89*
Hexter, Jack H. 1910- *WhoAm 90*
Hexter, Maurice B. *NewYTBS 90 [port]*
Hexter, Maurice Beck 1891- *WhoAm 90*
Hexter, Robert Maurice 1925- *WhoAm 90*
Hey, Angela Margaret 1953- *WhoEmL 91*
Hey, John Charles 1935- *WhoAm 90*
Hey, John Denis 1944- *WhoWor 91*
Hey, Robert Pierpont 1935- *WhoAm 90*
Hey, Thomas H. 1947- *St&PR 91*
Heybach, John Peter 1950- *WhoEmL 91, WhoWor 91*
Heyborne, Robert Linford 1923- *WhoAm 90*
Heyburn, Weldon Brinton 1852-1912 *BioIn 16*
Heyck, Gertrude Paine Daly 1910- *WhoAmW 91, WhoSSW 91, WhoWor 91*
Heyck, Theodore Daly 1941- *WhoWor 91*
Heyd, David 1945- *WhoWor 91*
Heyde, James Wallace 1933- *St&PR 91*
Heyde, Lalla J. 1933- *St&PR 91*
Heyde, Martha Bennett 1920- *WhoAmW 91, WhoE 91*
Heydebrand, Wolf Von 1930- *WhoAm 90*
Heyden, Gary Franklin 1938- *WhoSSW 91*
Heyder, Dietrich W 1926- *BiDrAPA 89*
Heydler, John A. 1869-1956 *Ballpl 90*
Heydon, John 1629-1668? *EncO&P 3*
Heydrich, Reinhard 1904-1942 *BioIn 16, WorAlBi*
Heydron, Vicki Ann 1945- *ConAu 131*
Heydt, Erich *BiDrAPA 89*
Heyduk, Daniel 1944- *WhoE 91*
Heye, Jacqueline Vito Cooper 1940- *WhoAmW 91*
Heyel, Carl 1908- *WhoWrEP 89*
Heyen, Aileen Mahoney 1947- *WhoEmL 91*
Heyen, William H. 1940- *WhoWrEP 89*
Heyer, Anna Harriet 1909- *WhoAmW 91, WhoSSW 91*
Heyer, Carol 1950- *ConAu 130*
Heyer, Carol Ann 1950- *WhoEmL 91*
Heyer, Georgette 1902-1974 *BioIn 16, FemiCLE, MajTwCW, TwCCr&M 91*
Heyer, John Hajdu 1945- *WhoEmL 91*
Heyer, John Whitefoord 1916- *WhoWor 91*
Heyer, Marilee 1942- *SmATA 64*
Heyer, Paul Otto 1936- *WhoAm 90*
Heyer, Terrence E. 1945- *St&PR 91*
Heyerdahl, Thor *BioIn 16*
Heyerdahl, Thor 1914- *MajTwCW, WhoWor 91, WorAlBi*
Heyert, Martin David 1934- *WhoAm 90*
Heyes, Gerald Bernard 1954- *WhoEmL 91*
Heying, Theodore Louis 1927- *WhoAm 90*
Heyl, Allen Van, Jr. 1918- *WhoWor 91*
Heyl, Bernard Chapman 1905-1966 *WhoAmA 91N*
Heyl, Bruce Anthony *BiDrAPA 89*
Heyl, Donald C. 1921- *St&PR 91*
Heyl, Larry Gerald 1947- *WhoSSW 91*
Heyler, Grover Ross 1926- *WhoAm 90*
Heyliger, William 1884- *AuBYP 90*
Heylin, Michael 1930- *WhoAm 90*
Heylyn, Edward *PenDiDA 89*
Heym, Gerard *EncO&P 3*
Heymair, Magdalena 1530?-1586? *EncCoWW*
Heymairin, Magdalena 1530?-1586? *EncCoWW*
Heyman, Arlene Nancy 1942- *BiDrAPA 89*
Heyman, David 1935- *St&PR 91*
Heyman, David John 1922- *WhoAm 90*
Heyman, Flavel Josef 1957- *WhoEmL 91*
Heyman, George Harrison, Jr. 1916- *WhoAm 90*
Heyman, Ira Michael 1930- *WhoAm 90, WhoWor 91*
Heyman, Joseph Martin 1942- *WhoE 91*
Heyman, Judith Ann 1938- *WhoAmW 91*
Heyman, Juliane Marion 1925- *WhoAmW 91*
Heyman, Ken 1930- *BioIn 16*
Heyman, Lawrence Murray 1932- *WhoAm 90, WhoAmA 91*
Heyman, Leonard J. 1925- *St&PR 91*
Heyman, Marsha Ruth *BiDrAPA 89*
Heyman, Matthew David 1961- *WhoEmL 91*
Heyman, Ralph Edmond 1931- *WhoAm 90*
Heyman, Robert Louis 1941- *WhoAm 90*
Heyman, Samuel J. 1939- *WhoAm 90, WhoE 91*
Heyman, Stephen J. 1939- *St&PR 91*
Heyman, Steven 1952- *WhoAmA 91*
Heyman, Therese Thau *WhoAmA 91*
Heymann, C. David *ConAu 129, WhoWrEP 89*
Heymann, Clemens Claude 1945- *ConAu 129, WhoWrEP 89*
Heymann, Clemens David 1945- *WhoAm 90*
Heymann, Donald L. 1952- *ODwPR 91*
Heymann, E. Donald 1928- *St&PR 91*
Heymann, Monica Golda 1959- *WhoAmW 91, WhoEmL 91*
Heymann, Paul F. 1926- *St&PR 91*
Heymann, Philip B. 1932- *WhoAm 90*
Heymann, Stephen Timothy 1940- *WhoAm 90*
Heymans, G. 1857-1930 *EncO&P 3*
Heymans, Gerardus 1857-1930 *EncPaPR 91*
Heymont, George 1947- *WhoWrEP 89*
Heymont, George Adam 1947- *WhoEmL 91*
Heyn, Anton Nicolaas J. 1906- *WhoSSW 91*
Heyn, Arno Harry Albert 1918- *WhoAm 90*
Heyn, Eileen Leone 1945- *WhoAmW 91*
Heyn, Ernest V. 1904- *WhoAm 90*
Heyn, F A 1910- *EncO&P 3*
Heyn, Rudolf Frans 1944- *WhoWor 91*
Heyn, William Carveth *WhoE 91*
Heyndrickx, Aubin Marie Achille Cesar 1927- *WhoWor 91*
Heyne, Herbert Barthel 1940- *St&PR 91*
Heyne, Roswitha *WhoWor 91*
Heyneker, Herbert Louis 1944- *WhoAm 90*
Heyneman, Donald 1925- *WhoAm 90*
Heyneman, Ellen Katherine *BiDrAPA 89*
Heyneman, Ellen Katherine 1958- *WhoE 91*
Heynes, William 1903-1989 *AnObit 1989*
Heyninck, Jean-Marie 1944- *WhoWor 91*
Heynis, Aafje 1924- *IntWWM 90*
Heyns, Kurt Fritz 1908- *WhoWor 91*
Heyns, Roger William 1918- *WhoAm 90*
Heyrend, F Lamarr 1927- *BiDrAPA 89*
Heyrick, Elizabeth 1769-1831 *FemiCLE*
Heys, Edward Scarborough 1935- *St&PR 91*
Heyse, Richard Paul 1965- *WhoE 91*
Heyse, Warren John 1923- *St&PR 91, WhoAm 90*
Heyssel, Robert Morris 1928- *WhoAm 90*
Heyting, Arend 1898-1980 *DcScB S2*
Heyum, Renee 1917- *WhoAmW 91*
Heyward, Andrew John 1950- *WhoE 91*
Heyward, Andy 1949- *WhoAm 90*
Heyward, Carter *BioIn 16*
Heyward, Charles Edward 1933- *St&PR 91*
Heyward, Craig *BioIn 16*
Heyward, Donald 1900-1951 *EarBlAP*
Heyward, George Harry 1947- *St&PR 91*
Heyward, Thomas 1746-1809 *EncCRAm*
Heywood, Colin 1947- *ConAu 130*
Heywood, Donald 1900-1951 *EarBlAP*
Heywood, Eddie *DrBlPA 90*
Heywood, Eddie 1915-1989 *AnObit 1989, BioIn 16, OxCPMus*
Heywood, Ezra 1829-1893 *EncAL*
Heywood, Ezra H. 1829-1893 *BioIn 16*
Heywood, George H., Jr. 1920- *St&PR 91*
Heywood, J C 1941- *WhoAmA 91*
Heywood, James D. 1928- *St&PR 91*
Heywood, John Benjamin 1938- *WhoAm 90, WhoE 91*
Heywood, Joseph T. 1943- *ODwPR 91*
Heywood, Karen 1946- *BioIn 16*
Heywood, Peter 1943- *WhoWrEP 89*
Heywood, Philip Crane 1929- *WhoAm 90*
Heywood, Robert Gilmour 1949- *WhoEmL 91*
Heywood, Robert Wales 1933- *WhoAm 90*
Heywood, Rosalind 1895-1980 *EncO&P 3, EncPaPR 91*
Heywood, Stanley John 1925- *WhoAm 90*
Heywood, Thomas 1574?-1641 *BioIn 16*
Heyworth, Anthony A. 1944- *St&PR 91*
Heyworth, James O. 1942- *WhoAm 90*
Heyworth, Peter Lawrence Frederick 1921- *IntWWM 90*
Hiaasen, Carl 1953- *TwCCr&M 91, WhoWrEP 89*
Hiam, Peter *BioIn 16*
Hiaring, Robert Dale 1941- *WhoAm 90*
Hiatt, Arnold 1927- *WhoAm 90*
Hiatt, Arnold S. 1927- *St&PR 91*
Hiatt, Barry Alan *BiDrAPA 89*
Hiatt, David Ellis *BiDrAPA 89*
Hiatt, Duane Evan 1937- *WhoWrEP 89*
Hiatt, Florence Ellen 1928- *IntWWM 90*
Hiatt, Harold 1921- *BiDrAPA 89*
Hiatt, Howard H. 1925- *WhoAm 90*
Hiatt, Jack 1942- *Ballpl 90*
Hiatt, John *BioIn 16*
Hiatt, John David 1949- *WhoSSW 91*
Hiatt, Marjorie McCullough 1923- *WhoAm 90*
Hiatt, Paul F. 1927- *St&PR 91*
Hiatt, Peter 1930- *WhoAm 90*
Hiatt, Randy Eugene 1955- *WhoSSW 91*
Hiatt, Robert Burritt *NewYTBS 90*
Hiatt, Robert Burritt 1917-1990 *BioIn 16*
Hiatt, Robert Nelson 1936- *WhoAm 90*
Hiatt, Robert Worth 1913- *WhoAm 90*
Hiatt, Wood Coleman *BiDrAPA 89*
Hiawatha *WhNaAH*
Hibbard, Aldro Thompson 1886-1972 *WhoAmA 91N*
Hibbard, Dwight H. 1923- *St&PR 91*
Hibbard, Howard 1928-1984 *WhoAmA 91N*
Hibbard, Irving E. 1939- *St&PR 91*
Hibbard, J.W. Kearny 1937- *St&PR 91*
Hibbard, John Winslow 1949- *WhoEmL 91*
Hibbard, Mary Eugenie 1856-1946 *BioIn 16*
Hibbard, Richard Paul 1923- *WhoWor 91*
Hibbard, Robert A. 1937- *St&PR 91*
Hibbard, Robert W 1924- *BiDrAPA 89*
Hibbard, Walter Rollo, Jr. 1918- *WhoAm 90*
Hibbeln, Joseph Raymond *BiDrAPA 89*
Hibben, Randolph Moulding 1957- *St&PR 91*
Hibberd, Roy Wayne 1952- *WhoEmL 91*
Hibberd, Stuart 1893-1983 *DcNaB 1981*
Hibbert, Alun 1949- *ConAu 130*
Hibbert, Eleanor 1906- *WhoWor 91*
Hibbert, Gary Francis 1948- *St&PR 91*
Hibbert, Peggy Barnes 1950- *WhoSSW 91*
Hibbert, William Andrew, Jr. 1932- *WhoSSW 91, WhoWor 91*
Hibbett, Howard Scott 1920- *WhoAm 90*
Hibbler, Al 1915- *DrBlPA 90*
Hibbs, Ben 1901-1975 *BioIn 16*
Hibbs, David Reed 1938- *WhoSSW 91*

Hibbs, Glen H. 1940- St&PR 91
Hibbs, John David 1948- WhoEmL 91, WhoWor 91
Hibbs, John J. 1936- St&PR 91
Hibbs, John Stanley 1934- WhoAm 90
Hibbs, Leon 1930- WhoAm 90
Hibbs, Loyal Robert 1925- WhoAm 90
Hibbs, Richard Guythal 1922- WhoAm 90
Hibbs, William Ernest, III 1950- WhoWor 91
Hibdon, James Edward 1924- WhoAm 90
Hibel, Bernard 1916- WhoAm 90
Hibel, Edna 1917- WhoAmA 91
Hibler, Douglas Harry 1935- WhoAm 90
Hibner, Barbara L BiDrAPA 89
Hibner, Don Telfer, Jr. 1934- WhoAm 90
Hibner, Geoffrey 1949- St&PR 91
Hibner, Geoffrey John 1949- WhoAm 90
Hibner, Rae Anne 1956- WhoAmW 91
Hibschweiler, Barbara Mary 1945- WhoAmW 91
Hibshman, Norbert K. 1915- St&PR 91
Hice, Joseph S., Jr. 1952- ODwPR 91
Hichar, Joseph Kenneth 1928- WhoAm 90
Hick, John Harwood 1922- WhoAm 90, WhoWrEP 89
Hick, Kenneth William 1946- WhoEmL 91, WhoWor 91
Hick, Wallace Leonard, Jr. 1935- WhoAm 90
Hickam, Nancy Dixon 1955- WhoAmW 91
Hickcox, Curtiss Bronson 1913- WhoAm 90
Hickel, Walter J. 1919- BiDrUSE 89
Hickel, Walter Joseph 1919- BioIn 16, WhoAm 90
Hicken, Philip Burnham 1910-1985 WhoAmA 91N
Hicken, Victor 1921- WhoAm 90
Hickerson, Glenn Lindsey 1937- WhoAm 90
Hickerson, John Dewey 1898-1989 BioIn 16
Hickerson, Otrie B BiDrAPA 89
Hickerson, Robin Lea 1956- BiDrAPA 89
Hickey, Barbara Standish 1946- WhoWor 91
Hickey, Bonnie Anne 1945- WhoAmW 91
Hickey, Brian Edward 1945- St&PR 91, WhoAm 90
Hickey, Charles Louis 1930- St&PR 91
Hickey, Constance Sue 1958- WhoEmL 91
Hickey, Dennis Walter 1914- WhoAm 90
Hickey, Edward Joseph, Jr. 1912- WhoAm 90
Hickey, Elizabeth Louise 1958- WhoE 91, WhoEmL 91
Hickey, Emily 1845-1924 FemiCLE
Hickey, Frank G. St&PR 91
Hickey, Frank G. 1927- WhoAm 90
Hickey, George R. BioIn 16
Hickey, Howard Wesley 1930- WhoAm 90
Hickey, James 1920- WhoAm 90, WhoE 91
Hickey, James Aloysius 1920- WhoWor 91
Hickey, James Aloysius Harden- 1854-1898 BioIn 16
Hickey, James Joseph 1930- St&PR 91
Hickey, John Heyward 1954- WhoEmL 91
Hickey, John T. 1934- St&PR 91
Hickey, John Thomas 1925- St&PR 91, WhoAm 90
Hickey, John W. 1916- St&PR 91
Hickey, John William 1938- WhoAm 90
Hickey, Joseph A. St&PR 91
Hickey, Joseph James 1907- WhoAm 90
Hickey, Joseph Michael, Jr. 1940- WhoAm 90
Hickey, Kevin 1956- Ballpl 90
Hickey, Leo Joseph 1940- WhoAm 90
Hickey, Leonard Edward 1929- St&PR 91
Hickey, Margaret A. 1902- WhoAm 90
Hickey, Mary Agnes 1874-1954 BioIn 16
Hickey, Mary Louise BioIn 16
Hickey, Michael A 1932- BiDrAPA 89
Hickey, Patrick Joseph 1938- St&PR 91
Hickey, Raymond 1949- St&PR 91
Hickey, Robert Cornelius 1917- WhoAm 90
Hickey, Robert Nelson 1941- WhoAm 90
Hickey, Rose Van Vrancken WhoAmA 91
Hickey, Ruth Cecelia 1914- WhoAm 90
Hickey, Terry Lee 1945- WhoAm 90
Hickey, Theresa Carole 1949- WhoEmL 91
Hickey, Thomas Joseph 1934- WhoAm 90
Hickey, Timothy Andrew 1945- WhoEmL 91
Hickey, Walter B. D. BioIn 16
Hickey, Walter B.D., Jr. 1937- St&PR 91
Hickey, William BioIn 16
Hickey, William A. WhoAm 90
Hickey, William Vincent, Jr. 1944- St&PR 91
Hickey, Winifred Espy WhoAmW 91
Hickey-Pellizzoni, Margarita 1753-1791? EncCoWW
Hickinbotham, Alan David 1925- WhoWor 91
Hickinbotham, Donald Eugene 1933- St&PR 91
Hickland, Edward Lee 1948- WhoEmL 91
Hickley, Robert C. 1947- St&PR 91
Hicklin, Marcia 1958- WhoSSW 91
Hickling, Alan Micklem 1936- EncO&P 3
Hickling, Frederick W 1944- BiDrAPA 89
Hickman, Anita M. 1937- ODwPR 91
Hickman, Annie BioIn 16
Hickman, Bert George, Jr. 1924- WhoAm 90
Hickman, Bertram Raymond 1946- St&PR 91
Hickman, Bryan D. 1945- St&PR 91
Hickman, Cleveland Pendleton, Jr. 1928- WhoAm 90
Hickman, Clifton Claude 1948- WhoSSW 91
Hickman, Darcy J. 1955- WhoAmW 91
Hickman, Darryl 1931- BioIn 16
Hickman, David Gordon 1953- WhoSSW 91
Hickman, David Scott 1940- St&PR 91
Hickman, Dwayne BioIn 16
Hickman, Edna L. 1944- WhoAmW 91
Hickman, Frederic W. 1927- WhoAm 90
Hickman, Gail Morgan 1948- WhoEmL 91
Hickman, Grace Marguerite 1921- WhoAmW 91
Hickman, Halbert I. 1939- St&PR 91
Hickman, Harold E. 1920- St&PR 91
Hickman, Irene WhoWrEP 89
Hickman, J. Kenneth 1928- WhoAm 90
Hickman, James Blake 1921- WhoAm 90
Hickman, James Charles 1927- WhoAm 90
Hickman, James Harry 1933- BiDrAPA 89
Hickman, Jeannine Frances 1944- WhoWrEP 89
Hickman, Jim 1937- Ballpl 90, BioIn 16
Hickman, John 1827-1877 AmLegL
Hickman, John Bibb 1935- St&PR 91
Hickman, John C. 1927- St&PR 91
Hickman, John Fredrick BiDrAPA 89
Hickman, John Hampton, III 1937- St&PR 91, WhoAm 90, WhoWor 91
Hickman, Jolene Kay 1954- WhoAmW 91
Hickman, Leon Edward 1900- WhoAm 90
Hickman, Linda Marie 1953- WhoAmW 91
Hickman, Lucille 1949- WhoAmW 91
Hickman, Marjorie Ruth 1918- WhoAmW 91
Hickman, Martha Whitmore 1925- WhoWrEP 89
Hickman, Norman G. BioIn 16
Hickman, Paul Thomas 1945- WhoEmL 91
Hickman, Paula Diane 1947- WhoAmW 91, WhoSSW 91
Hickman, Paula Hazelrig 1950- WhoEmL 91
Hickman, Peter James 1931- WhoE 91
Hickman, Piano Legs 1876-1934 Ballpl 90
Hickman, Richard H. 1942- St&PR 91
Hickman, Richard Lonnie 1950- WhoEmL 91, WhoWor 91
Hickman, Robert Alan 1944- St&PR 91
Hickman, Robert Harrison 1953- WhoAm 90
Hickman, Robert J. 1946- St&PR 91
Hickman, Robert Norman 1935- St&PR 91
Hickman, Rose 1527?-1613 FemiCLE
Hickman, Stephen Lee 1942- St&PR 91
Hickman, Traphene Parramore 1933- WhoAm 90
Hickman, Waymon Logan 1934- St&PR 91
Hickman, William Albert 1877-1957 DcLB 92
Hickman, William Holly 1943- WhoSSW 91
Hickok, David Keith 1936- WhoWor 91
Hickok, Floyd A. 1907- WhoWrEP 89
Hickok, Gloria Vando 1934- WhoWrEP 89
Hickok, James Butler 1837-1876 WhNaAH, WorAlBi
Hickok, Lorena A. 1892?-1968 AuBYP 90, BioAmW
Hickok, Lorena A. 1893-1968 BioIn 16
Hickok, Raymond T. 1918- St&PR 91
Hickok, Richard Sanford 1925- WhoAm 90
Hickok, Robert Lyman, Jr. 1929- WhoAm 90
Hickok, Will AuBYP 90
Hickox, Richard 1948- PenDiMP
Hickox, Richard Sidney 1948- IntWWM 90, WhoWor 91
Hickox, William Horace, III 1941- WhoWor 91
Hickrod, George Alan Karnes Wallis 1930- WhoWor 91
Hicks, Alec, Jr. 1941- St&PR 91
Hicks, Alice Blackmore 1946- WhoAmW 91
Hicks, Allen Morley 1928- WhoAm 90
Hicks, Arthur Wesley, Jr. 1958- St&PR 91
Hicks, Audrey Marion Grabfield 1957- WhoAmW 91
Hicks, Bethany Gribben 1951- WhoAmW 91, WhoEmL 91, WhoWor 91
Hicks, Brenda Joy 1943- WhoAmW 91
Hicks, Bruce E. ODwPR 91
Hicks, Charles Robert 1920- WhoAm 90
Hicks, Charles S. 1937- WhoSSW 91
Hicks, Charles William, III BiDrAPA 89
Hicks, Chas. E. 1919- St&PR 91
Hicks, Clair Lloyd 1945- WhoEmL 91
Hicks, Clifford B. 1920- AuBYP 90, BioIn 16
Hicks, Clifford Byron 1920- WhoAm 90, WhoWrEP 89
Hicks, Daniel Joseph BiDrAPA 89
Hicks, Daniel W 1950- BiDrAPA 89
Hicks, David 1929- BioIn 16, ConDes 90
Hicks, David Earl 1931- WhoWor 91
Hicks, David Lee 1954- WhoEmL 91
Hicks, Donald W. 1943- St&PR 91
Hicks, Donovan Blake 1937- WhoAm 90
Hicks, E.M. 1915- St&PR 91
Hicks, Edward 1780-1849 WorAlBi
Hicks, Edward L 1943- BiDrAPA 89
Hicks, Edwin Hugh 1932- WhoAm 90
Hicks, Ele Wyatte 1926- WhoAm 90
Hicks, Eleanor B. AuBYP 90
Hicks, Frances Ross 1900- WhoAmW 91
Hicks, Frederick Gilbert 1955- BiDrAPA 89
Hicks, George Alvin, Jr. 1951- WhoSSW 91
Hicks, Gilbert, IV 1945- St&PR 91
Hicks, Glen Thomas 1951- WhoE 91
Hicks, Granville BioIn 16
Hicks, Granville 1901-1982 EncAL
Hicks, Gregory Steven 1959- WhoEmL 91
Hicks, Gregory Tyler 1948- WhoEmL 91
Hicks, H. Mason 1904-1989 BioIn 16
Hicks, Helen Anne 1962- WhoEmL 91
Hicks, Henry Davies 1915- WhoAm 90
Hicks, Hilly 1950- DrBIPA 90
Hicks, Howard Randall 1947- BiDrAPA 89
Hicks, Irle Raymond 1928- WhoAm 90
Hicks, J. C. 1922- WhoSSW 91
Hicks, Jack Morgan 1930- WhoWrEP 89
Hicks, James Bradley 1959- WhoEmL 91
Hicks, James Earl 1951- WhoEmL 91
Hicks, James Leon 1922- WhoSSW 91
Hicks, James Robert 1929- St&PR 91
Hicks, James Robert 1946- BiDrAPA 89
Hicks, James Thomas 1924- WhoWor 91
Hicks, Janet Kelty 1949- WhoSSW 91
Hicks, Janet Marie 1955- WhoAmW 91
Hicks, John 1904-1989 AnObit 1989
Hicks, John Darwin 1923- St&PR 91, WhoAm 90
Hicks, John Mark 1957- WhoSSW 91
Hicks, John Richard 1904-1989 BioIn 16
Hicks, John Trimmer 1946- WhoWor 91
Hicks, John V 1907- ConAu 30NR
Hicks, John Victor 1907- WhoWrEP 89
Hicks, Joseph Robert 1922- WhoAm 90
Hicks, Julie Brasel 1950- WhoAmW 91
Hicks, June Tucker 1932- WhoSSW 91
Hicks, Karen Kay 1953- WhoAmW 91
Hicks, Ken C. 1953- St&PR 91
Hicks, Ken Carlyle 1953- WhoAm 90, WhoEmL 91
Hicks, Kenneth William 1923- WhoAm 90
Hicks, Kima Rene 1960- WhoAmW 91
Hicks, L. Westcott 1920- St&PR 91
Hicks, Larry E. BioIn 16
Hicks, Lawrence Robert 1944- St&PR 91
Hicks, Lawrence Wayne 1940- St&PR 91
Hicks, Leon Nathaniel 1933- WhoAmA 91
Hicks, Les 1943- St&PR 91
Hicks, Leslie Hubert 1927- WhoAm 90
Hicks, Linda Joyce 1946- WhoAmW 91
Hicks, Lonnie EarBlAP
Hicks, Lucile P. 1938- WhoAmW 91
Hicks, M. Elizabeth 1944- WhoAmW 91
Hicks, Margaret Ann 1954- WhoAmW 91
Hicks, Marlyn L. 1929- St&PR 91
Hicks, Maryellen Whitlock 1949- WhoAmW 91
Hicks, Mercer, III 1940- St&PR 91
Hicks, Mildred Walker WhoAmW 91
Hicks, Nancy J. ODwPR 91
Hicks, Nicola 1960- BiDWomA
Hicks, Orton Havergal 1900- WhoAm 90
Hicks, Paul B., Jr. 1925- ODwPR 91, WhoAm 90, WhoE 91
Hicks, Paul Burton, III 1956- WhoE 91
Hicks, Paul Burton, Jr. 1925- St&PR 91
Hicks, Paul William 1937- St&PR 91
Hicks, Pauline Ellis 1947- WhoAmW 91
Hicks, Philip S 1928- BiDrAPA 89
Hicks, Ray BioIn 16
Hicks, Richard E 1929- BiDrAPA 89
Hicks, Robert S BiDrAPA 89
Hicks, Sandy Lee 1959- WhoAmW 91
Hicks, Seymour 1871-1954 OxCPMus
Hicks, Sheila PenDiDA 89
Hicks, Sheila 1934- WhoAmA 91
Hicks, Shelby Leon 1921- BiDrAPA 89
Hicks, Steven Wells 1950- WhoEmL 91
Hicks, Susan Lynn Bowman 1952- WhoAmW 91
Hicks, Taylor M., Jr. 1944- WhoAm 90
Hicks, Terry Ray 1948- BiDrAPA 89
Hicks, Thomas 1936- ConAu 129
Hicks, Thomas H. 1946- St&PR 91
Hicks, Thomas Howard 1946- WhoAm 90
Hicks, Timothy Gerald 1952- WhoEmL 91
Hicks, Tyler Gregory 1921- WhoAm 90
Hicks, Vernon O. 1932- St&PR 91
Hicks, Vicki Jean 1955- WhoEmL 91
Hicks, W. Wesley BioIn 16
Hicks, Wayland R. 1942- St&PR 91
Hicks, William Albert, III 1942- WhoAm 90
Hicks, William Hampton 1956- WhoEmL 91, WhoWor 91
Hicks, William Henry 1817?-1899 DcCanB 12
Hicks, William Joynson- 1865-1932 BioIn 16
Hicks, William R 1935- BiDrAPA 89
Hicks-Moore, Peggy Ann 1959- WhoAmW 91
Hickson, Eileen Hassett 1916- WhoAmW 91
Hickson, Joan Bogle 1906- WhoAm 90
Hickson, Joseph 1830-1897 DcCanB 12
Hickson, Robert Comins, Jr. 1955- WhoEmL 91
Hickson, Robin Julian 1944- WhoSSW 91
Hickson, Shirley Ann 1944- WhoSSW 91
Hida, Kinzo 1922- WhoWor 91
Hidaki, Makoto BioIn 16
Hidalgo, Alberto 1935- WhoHisp 91
Hidalgo, Diego 1942- WhoWor 91
Hidalgo, Edward 1912- BioIn 16, WhoAm 90
Hidalgo, Elvira de 1888-1980 PenDiMP
Hidalgo, Horacio Augusto 1929- WhoE 91
Hidalgo, James Michael 1951- WhoHisp 91
Hidalgo, Joy Faye 1950- WhoWrEP 89
Hidalgo, Liverson WhoWrEP 89
Hidalgo, Nelson D 1948- BiDrAPA 89
Hidalgo y Costilla, Miguel 1753-1811 BioIn 16
Hidas, Frigyes 1928- IntWWM 90
Hidayatallah, Munawar Hussain 1944- St&PR 91
Hidden, James Clifford 1813-1889 AmLegL
Hide, Peter Nicholas 1944- WhoAmA 91
Hide, Raymond 1929- WhoWor 91
Hiden, Charles Edward 1926- St&PR 91
Hiden, Robert Battaile, Jr. 1933- WhoAm 90, WhoWor 91
Hideo, Kuroda 1917- WhoWor 91
Hider, William Oliver 1946- WhoEmL 91
Hideyoshi Toyotomi EncJap
Hidore, John Junior 1932- WhoAm 90
Hidvegi, Gabor 1956- WhoWor 91
Hidy, David Eugene 1946- WhoE 91
Hidy, George Martel 1935- WhoAm 90
Hieatt, Allen Kent 1921- WhoAm 90, WhoWrEP 89
Hieatt, Constance Bartlett 1928- WhoAm 90, WhoAmW 91, WhoWrEP 89
Hieb, LeRoy Martin 1948- St&PR 91
Hieb, Marianne 1946- WhoEmL 91
Hieber, George Frederick 1911- WhoSSW 91
Hiebert, Alvin Leroy 1918- WhoAm 90
Hiebert, Elizabeth Blake 1910- WhoAmW 91, WhoWor 91
Hiebert, Paul Gerhardt 1892-1987 BioIn 16
Hiebert, Ray E. 1932- ODwPR 91
Hiebert, Ray Eldon 1932- WhoAm 90
Hiebert, Thomas Nels 1955- IntWWM 90
Hiegel, Jerry M. 1927- St&PR 91
Hielscher, Robert A. 1948- St&PR 91
Hielscher, Robert Allen 1948- WhoAm 90
Hiemenz, Robert Dale 1947- WhoEmL 91
Hiemstra, R.J.J. 1941- St&PR 91
Hiemstra, Roger 1938- WhoAm 90, WhoE 91
Hiemstra, Stephen Wayne 1953- WhoE 91
Hiendlmayr, Richard 1924- St&PR 91
Hienke, John D. St&PR 91
Hienton, Diane DeBrosse 1948- WhoAmW 91
Hienton, James Robert 1951- WhoEmL 91
Hier, Mark 1948- ODwPR 91
Hierhoizer, Klaus Hermann 1929- WhoWor 91
Hierholzer, Robert Wayne 1955- BiDrAPA 89
Hieronymus, Clara Booth Wiggins 1913- WhoAm 90
Hieronymus, Edward Whittlesey 1943- WhoAm 90

Hieronymus, Eusebius BioIn 16
Hierro, Jose 1922- BioIn 16
Hiers, Lois 1910- LiHiK
Hierstein, Paul Michael 1948- WhoEmL 91, WhoSSW 91
Hiesiger, Emile Milton 1949- WhoE 91
Hiesserer, Dieter 1939- WhoWor 91
Hiestand, Ernst 1935- ConDes 90
Hiestand, Jean Carter 1922- St&PR 91
Hiestand, Ursula 1936- ConDes 90
Hiestermann, Horst 1934- IntWWM 90
Hietanen, Seppo Olavi 1945- WhoWor 91
Hiett, Edward Emerson 1922- WhoAm 90
Hiett, Helen 1913-1961 BioIn 16
Higa 1938- WhoAmA 91
Higa, Lori Reiko 1955- ODwPR 91
Higa, Matthew BioIn 16
Higa, Scott BioIn 16
Higashi, Elizabeth Mary 1952- St&PR 91
Higashikuni, Naruhiko NewYTBS 90
Higashikuni, Naruhiko 1887-1990 BioIn 16
Higbe, Kirby 1915-1985 Ballpl 90
Higbee, Ann G. ODwPR 91
Higbee, David John 1940- IntWWM 90
Higbee, David M. 1944- St&PR 91
Higbee, Florence Salick WhoAmW 91
Higbee, James L. 1942- St&PR 91
Higbee, Joan Florence 1945- WhoAmW 91
Higbee, Ronald Wayne 1947- St&PR 91
Higbie, Barbara NewAgMG
Higbie, Leslie Wilson 1914- WhoE 91
Higbie, Ruth Griggs 1909- WhoWrEP 89
Higby, Edward Julian 1939- WhoSSW 91, WhoWor 91
Higby, James Harland 1946- WhoAm 90
Higby, John H. St&PR 91
Higby, Wayne 1943- BioIn 16, WhoAmA 91
Higdon, Barbara J. 1930- WhoAm 90, WhoAmW 91
Higdon, Bernice Cowan 1918- WhoAmW 91, WhoWor 91
Higdon, Charles E. 1941- St&PR 91
Higdon, David Leon 1939- WhoAm 90, WhoWrEP 89
Higdon, E. G. 1909-1988 BioIn 16
Higdon, Emerson Granville 1909-1988 BioIn 16
Higdon, Gregory Thurman 1952- WhoEmL 91
Higdon, Jerry L. 1930- St&PR 91
Higdon, Norris Bruce 1950- WhoEmL 91, WhoSSW 91
Higdon, Polly Susanne 1942- WhoAmW 91
Higdon, Roger D. 1941- St&PR 91
Higgens, William John, III 1951- WhoEmL 91
Higger, Michael 1898-1952 BioIn 16
Higges, Susan BiDEWW
Higginbotham, A. Leon, Jr. 1928- WhoAm 90, WhoE 91
Higginbotham, Anthony Simyon 1944- WhoSSW 91
Higginbotham, Arnold Lee, Jr. 1940- WhoSSW 91
Higginbotham, J. C. 1906-1973 BioIn 16, OxCPMus
Higginbotham, Jay C. 1906-1973 WorAlBi
Higginbotham, Marcus H. 1940- St&PR 91
Higginbotham, Patrick Errol 1938- WhoAm 90, WhoSSW 91
Higginbotham, Richard Alan 1947- St&PR 91
Higginbotham, W.R. BioIn 16
Higginbotham, William Lynn, Jr. 1945- WhoSSW 91
Higginbottom, Edward 1946- IntWWM 90
Higginbottom, Samuel Logan 1921- WhoAm 90
Higgins, A. Lawrence 1922- WhoAm 90
Higgins, Andrew G. 1947- WhoAm 90
Higgins, Andrew Jackson 1886-1952 WorAlBi
Higgins, Anthony Paul 1940- St&PR 91
Higgins, Barbara Louisa 1945- WhoAmW 91
Higgins, Billy BioIn 16
Higgins, Bryan Ralph 1949- WhoEmL 91
Higgins, Carlisle Wallace, Jr. 1918- St&PR 91
Higgins, Charles Tyng 1940- WhoSSW 91
Higgins, Clare 1957?- ConTFT 8
Higgins, Clark Worthen 1944- St&PR 91
Higgins, Colin 1941-1988 BioIn 16, ConAu 30NR
Higgins, D S 1938- ConAu 132
Higgins, Daryl Clyde 1948- WhoSSW 91
Higgins, David C. 1948- St&PR 91
Higgins, David L. 1945- St&PR 91
Higgins, David Wayne 1954- WhoEmL 91
Higgins, Dennis 1939- Ballpl 90
Higgins, Dick 1938- WhoAm 90, WhoAmA 91, WhoE 91
Higgins, Donald Stone 1932- WhoE 91
Higgins, Dorothy Marie 1930- WhoAmW 91
Higgins, Edward 1930- WhoAmA 91
Higgins, Edward Aloysius 1931- WhoAm 90
Higgins, Edward Ferdinand WhoAmA 91
Higgins, Edward Koelling 1926- WhoAmA 91
Higgins, Eugene 1875-1958 WhoAmA 91N
Higgins, Frederick Benjamin, Jr. 1936- WhoAm 90
Higgins, Geoffrey Trevor 1932- WhoAm 90
Higgins, George A. 1946- St&PR 91
Higgins, George Edward 1930- WhoAm 90
Higgins, George V. 1939- BioIn 16, MajTwCW, TwCCr&M 91, WorAlBi
Higgins, George Vincent 1939- WhoAm 90, WhoWrEP 89
Higgins, Godfrey 1772-1833 EncO&P 3
Higgins, Harold Bailey 1922- WhoAm 90
Higgins, Harriet Pratt 1950- WhoEmL 91
Higgins, Irwin Raymond 1919- WhoSSW 91
Higgins, Isabelle Jeanette 1919- WhoAmW 91
Higgins, J.M. 1941- St&PR 91
Higgins, Jack ConAu 33NR, MajTwCW
Higgins, Jack 1929- TwCCr&M 91, WorAlBi
Higgins, Jack 1954- WhoAm 90
Higgins, Jack Kirby 1928- St&PR 91
Higgins, James C. 1940- St&PR 91
Higgins, James Charles, III 1947- WhoE 91
Higgins, James F. WhoE 91
Higgins, James Henry, III 1940- WhoE 91
Higgins, James Thaddeus 1954- WhoEmL 91
Higgins, Janine Audrey 1953- WhoEmL 91
Higgins, Jay F. 1945- St&PR 91
Higgins, Jay Francis 1945- WhoAm 90
Higgins, Joan Marie WhoAmW 91
Higgins, John A. 1947- ODwPR 91
Higgins, John C 1934- ConAu 132
Higgins, John J. 1943- St&PR 91
Higgins, John Joseph 1934- WhoAm 90
Higgins, John R. BioIn 16, NewYTBS 90
Higgins, Joseph Wayne 1949- WhoSSW 91
Higgins, Kenneth Raymond 1915- WhoAm 90
Higgins, L. Boyd 1927- St&PR 91
Higgins, Leo Michael, III 1950- WhoSSW 91
Higgins, Marguerite 1920-1966 BioIn 16, WorAlBi
Higgins, Martin V. 1954- WhoE 91
Higgins, Mary Celeste 1943- WhoWor 91
Higgins, Mary Lou 1926- WhoAmA 91
Higgins, Matthew Joseph 1938- WhoAm 90
Higgins, Michael Joseph 1951- WhoE 91
Higgins, Patricia BioIn 16
Higgins, Patricia Ann 1951- WhoAmW 91, WhoEmL 91, WhoWor 91
Higgins, Paul Clifford 1945- WhoSSW 91
Higgins, Paula Elizabeth 1954- WhoWrEP 89
Higgins, Peter T. 1946- St&PR 91
Higgins, Pinky 1909-1969 Ballpl 90
Higgins, Prentiss C. 1939- St&PR 91
Higgins, R. Scott 1956- St&PR 91
Higgins, Richard B. 1937- St&PR 91
Higgins, Richard Carter 1938- WhoWrEP 89
Higgins, Richard Loren 1952- WhoE 91
Higgins, Robert Arthur 1924- WhoAm 90
Higgins, Robert Emmett 1932- St&PR 91
Higgins, Robert Francis 1947- WhoE 91
Higgins, Robert Gerard 1952- WhoEmL 91
Higgins, Robert J. 1945- St&PR 91
Higgins, Robert Louis 1919- WhoAm 90
Higgins, Ronald Clarence 1946- WhoEmL 91
Higgins, Shaun Brian 1950- St&PR 91
Higgins, Shaun O'Leary 1948- WhoEmL 91
Higgins, Stephen Boyd 1946- WhoEmL 91
Higgins, Stephen E. 1938- WhoAm 90
Higgins, Theresa Mary 1956- WhoE 91
Higgins, Therese 1925- WhoAm 90, WhoAmW 91
Higgins, Thomas James 1945- WhoEmL 91
Higgins, Thomas Joseph 1944- WhoWor 91
Higgins, Trumbull BioIn 16
Higgins, Trumbull NewYTBS 90
Higgins, Trumbull 1919-1990 ConAu 131
Higgins, Victor 1884-1949 WhoAmA 91N
Higgins, William Henry Clay, III 1908- WhoAm 90
Higgins, William R. BioIn 16
Higgins, William Waugh 1935- St&PR 91, WhoAm 90
Higgins-Stahulak, Elizabeth Jean 1950- WhoAmW 91
Higginsen, Vy DrBIPA 90
Higginson, Bernard E. 1932- St&PR 91
Higginson, Carla Jean 1955- WhoEmL 91
Higginson, Ella 1860?-1940 FemiCLE
Higginson, Francis 1586-1630 EncCRAm
Higginson, Gary Michael 1952- IntWWM 90
Higginson, James Jackson 1921- WhoAm 90
Higginson, Robert Lee 1949- WhoE 91
Higginson, Theodore N. 1935- WhoWor 91
Higginson, Thomas Lee 1920- WhoAm 90
Higginson, Thomas Lee 1920-1990 BioIn 16
Higginson, Thomas Wentworth 1823-1911 BioIn 16
Higginson, William J. 1938- WhoWrEP 89
Higgison, Peyton BioIn 16
Higgs, DeWitt A. 1907- WhoAm 90
Higgs, Elizabeth Jo 1960- WhoAmW 91
Higgs, Jeffrey B. 1948- St&PR 91
Higgs, John H. 1934- WhoAm 90, WhoE 91
Higgs, Lloyd Albert 1937- WhoAm 90
Higgs, Paul C BiDrAPA 89
Higgs, Peter John 1959- WhoWor 91
High Horn 1775?-1812 WhNaAH
High, Andy 1897-1981 Ballpl 90
High, Arrington BioIn 16
High, Calvin Glenn 1932- WhoAm 90
High, Dallas Milton 1931- WhoSSW 91
High, David Scherer 1940- St&PR 91
High, Dorothy Helen Frank 1935- WhoAmW 91
High, George Borman 1931- WhoAm 90
High, Hugh 1887-1962 Ballpl 90
High, James Russell 1943- BiDrAPA 89
High, Joshua 1950- St&PR 91
High, Lee E. 1951- St&PR 91
High, Michael B. 1948- St&PR 91
High, Monique Raphel 1949- WhoAmW 91, WhoWrEP 89
High, Ned W. ODwPR 91
High, S. Dale 1942- St&PR 91, WhoAm 90
High, Sharolyn Parker 1945- WhoAmW 91
High, Steve 1947- ODwPR 91
High, Steven Samuel 1956- WhoSSW 91
High, Thomas W. 1947- WhoAm 90
High, Timothy Griffin 1949- WhoAmA 91
High-Backed Wolf WhNaAH
Higham, Cynthia Mary 1938- IntWWM 90
Higham, David 1949- BioIn 16
Higham, Dick 1851-1905 Ballpl 90
Higham, John 1920- WhoAm 90
Higham, Jon Atlas 1960- BioIn 16
Higham, Robin 1925- ConAu 31NR, WhoAm 90, WhoWrEP 89
Highberg, Peter Alden 1941- WhoE 91
Highberger, Craig Bender 1953- WhoEmL 91, WhoWrEP 89
Highberger, William Foster 1950- WhoWor 91
Highbloom, Lloyd Henry 1939- WhoAm 90
Highet, Helen MajTwCW
Highfield, Jane Elizabeth 1956- IntWWM 90
Highfield, Robert Edward 1930- WhoAm 90
Highfield, Roger 1922- ConAu 130
Highfill, Philip Henry, Jr. 1918- WhoAm 90
Highhouse, Kent E. 1942- St&PR 91
Highland, Cecil Blaine, Jr. 1918- WhoAm 90
Highland, David C. 1954- WhoEmL 91
Highland, Dora TwCCr&M 91
Highland, Selby Arnett, Jr. 1945- WhoAm 90
Highland, Thomas C. WhoSSW 91
Highlands, Donald Bruce 1939- St&PR 91
Highley, Frank Shapley 1946- BiDrAPA 89
Highleyman, Leslie Ann 1957- WhoEmL 91
Highleyman, Samuel Locke, III 1928- WhoAm 90
Highman, Bruce James 1956- WhoEmL 91
Highsaw, James Leonard, Jr. 1914- WhoAm 90
Highsmith, Carol McKinney 1946- WhoAmW 91
Highsmith, Duncan 1948- St&PR 91
Highsmith, Hugh Purcell 1914- St&PR 91
Highsmith, Jasper Habersham 1940- WhoSSW 91
Highsmith, Jimmy D. 1933- St&PR 91
Highsmith, Linda Yvonne 1949- WhoAmW 91
Highsmith, Patricia 1921- BioIn 16, CurBio 90 [port], FemiCLE, MajTwCW, TwCCr&M 91, WorAlBi
Highsmith, Shelby 1929- WhoAm 90
Highsmith, Wanda Law 1928- WhoAmW 91
Highstein, Jene 1942- WhoAmA 91
Highstein, Max NewAgMG
Hight, B. Boyd 1939- St&PR 91
Hight, Donna Louise 1965- WhoEmL 91
Hight, Getrude E BiDrAPA 89
Hightower, Arlene Janice 1949- WhoAmW 91
Hightower, Carol Ann 1950- WhoEmL 91
Hightower, Caroline Warner 1935- WhoAm 90
Hightower, Denise Michelle 1958- WhoSSW 91
Hightower, Dennis F. BioIn 16
Hightower, Florence Cole 1916-1981 AuBYP 90
Hightower, Jack English 1926- WhoAm 90
Hightower, Jim BioIn 16
Hightower, Jim Allen 1943- WhoAm 90
Hightower, Joe Walter 1936- WhoAm 90
Hightower, John B 1933- WhoAmA 91
Hightower, John Brantley 1933- WhoAm 90
Hightower, Joyce M. 1925- St&PR 91
Hightower, Lloyd Arthur 1934- St&PR 91
Hightower, Marvin Alvert 1947- WhoE 91
Hightower, Mary Ann 1945- WhoAmW 91
Hightower, Michael 1957- WhoSSW 91
Hightower, Neil Hamilton 1940- St&PR 91, WhoAm 90, WhoSSW 91
Hightower, Nicholas Carr 1918- WhoSSW 91
Hightower, William Allen 1943- St&PR 91
Hightower, William Harrison, III 1936- St&PR 91
Highwater, Jamake 1942- WhoAm 90, WhoAmA 91, WhoWrEP 89, WorAu 1980 [port]
Highway 101 ConMus 4 [port], WhoNeCM [port]
Higi, William L. 1933- WhoAm 90
Higie, William F. 1926- St&PR 91
Higinbotham, Betty Louise Wilson 1910- WhoAmW 91
Higinbotham, Jacquelyn Joan 1951- WhoEmL 91
Higinbotham, William Alfred 1910- WhoAm 90
Higley, Albert M., Jr. 1928- St&PR 91
Higley, Bruce Wadsworth 1928- WhoAm 90
Higley, David L. 1952- St&PR 91
Higley, J. Douglas BioIn 16
Higley, Kathleen Ann 1948- WhoAm 90
Higley, Robert A. 1946- St&PR 91
Higley, Robert Allen 1946- WhoSSW 91
Higley, Thomas Carlton 1938- WhoSSW 91
Higman, Dennis J. 1940- ODwPR 91
Higman, Sally Lee 1945- WhoAmW 91
Higuchi, Ichiyo 1872-1896 BioIn 16
Higuchi, Takayoshi 1927- WhoWor 91
Higuera, Jesus 1950- WhoHisp 91
Higuera, Ted 1958- Ballpl 90, WhoHisp 91
Hijazi, Ihsan A. BioIn 16
Hijazi, Mohammed Saeed 1950- WhoWor 91
Hijikata, Takeshi 1915- St&PR 91
Hijikata, Tatsumi 1928-1986 BioIn 16
Hijuelos, Oscar BioIn 16
Hijuelos, Oscar 1951- HispWr 90
Hijuelos, Oscar 1952- WhoAm 90, WhoE 91
Hijuelos, Oscar J. 1951- WhoHisp 91
Hikawa, Christine 1951- St&PR 91
Hikel, Steven BioIn 16
Hiland, R. Bruce 1939- St&PR 91
Hilary, Sandra Marie 1938- WhoAmW 91
Hilb, Martin 1948- WhoWor 91
Hilber, Robin Shomo 1957- St&PR 91
Hilberdink, Fred Joannes 1942- WhoSSW 91
Hilberman, Elaine 1939- WhoE 91
Hilberry, Conrad Arthur 1928- WhoWrEP 89
Hilbert, Angelia H. 1949- WhoAmW 91
Hilbert, Bernard Charles 1921- WhoAm 90
Hilbert, Gregory J. 1950- WhoEmL 91
Hilbert, Jeffrey Lee 1953- WhoSSW 91
Hilbert, John Warren, II 1946- WhoEmL 91
Hilbert, Robert Backus 1929- WhoAm 90
Hilbert, Robert Saul 1941- WhoAm 90
Hilbert, Virginia Lois 1935- WhoAmW 91
Hilbish, Barbara Smith 1928- IntWWM 90
Hilborn, Michael G. 1943- WhoAm 90
Hilbrecht, Norman Ty 1933- WhoAm 90, WhoWor 91
Hilburn, John Charles 1946- WhoSSW 91
Hilburn, William Robert 1946- St&PR 91
Hilbush, Edward O. 1918- St&PR 91
Hilby, Bruce Titus 1944- WhoWor 91
Hild, Jack ConAu 130
Hild, Lawrence C. 1928- St&PR 91
Hild, Nancy 1942- WhoWrEP 89
Hildebolt, William Morton 1943- St&PR 91
Hildebrand, Carol Ilene 1943- WhoAmW 91
Hildebrand, Clive Perry 1937- WhoWor 91
Hildebrand, David Floyd 1955- WhoSSW 91

Hildebrand, Don Cecil 1943- *WhoWor 91*
Hildebrand, Donald Nelson 1954- *WhoSSW 91*
Hildebrand, Francis Begnaud 1915- *WhoAm 90*
Hildebrand, George 1878-1960 *Ballpl 90*
Hildebrand, John 1949- *ConAu 131*
Hildebrand, John Frederick 1940- *WhoAm 90*
Hildebrand, John Grant 1942- *WhoAm 90*
Hildebrand, John W. 1953- *St&PR 91*
Hildebrand, June Mary Ann 1930- *WhoAmA 91*
Hildebrand, Oral 1907-1977 *Ballpl 90*
Hildebrand, Peter Henry 1945- *WhoEmL 91*
Hildebrand, Richard Allen 1916- *WhoAm 90*
Hildebrand, Rodger Blake 1958- *WhoSSW 91*
Hildebrand, Roger Henry 1922- *WhoAm 90*
Hildebrand, Verna Lee 1924- *WhoAm 90*
Hildebrand, Willard Ray 1939- *WhoAm 90*
Hildebrandt, Bradford Walter 1940- *WhoAm 90*
Hildebrandt, Claudia Joan 1942- *WhoAmW 91*
Hildebrandt, Frederick Dean, Jr. 1933- *WhoE 91, WhoWor 91*
Hildebrandt, Greg 1939- *BioIn 16*
Hildebrandt, Johann Lucus Von 1668-1745 *WorAlBi*
Hildebrandt, Theodore Ware 1922- *WhoSSW 91*
Hildebrandt, Tim 1939- *BioIn 16*
Hildebrandt, William Albert 1917- *WhoAmA 91, WhoE 91*
Hildegard von Bingen 1098?-1179 *EncCoWW*
Hildegard, von Bingen, Saint 1098-1179 *BioIn 16*
Hildegarde 1906- *OxCPMus*
Hilden, Mikael Philip 1955- *WhoWor 91*
Hilden, Patricia Jane 1944- *WhoSSW 91*
Hilder, Philip Harlan 1955- *WhoEmL 91*
Hilderbrandt, Donald Franklin, II 1939- *WhoAm 90*
Hilderbrandt, Howard Logan 1874-1958 *WhoAmA 91N*
Hildermeier, Manfred 1948- *WhoWor 91*
Hildesheimer, Azriel 1820-1899 *BioIn 16*
Hildestad, Terry Dean 1949- *St&PR 91*
Hildick, E. W. 1925- *AuBYP 90*
Hilding, Jerel Lee 1949- *WhoAm 90*
Hilding, Ronald F 1938- *BiDrAPA 89*
Hildner, Ernest Gotthold, III 1940- *WhoAm 90*
Hildner, John F. 1940- *St&PR 91*
Hildner, Phillips Brooks, II 1944- *WhoWor 91*
Hildner, Thomas G. 1946- *WhoEmL 91*
Hildreth, Arthur M 1938- *BiDrAPA 89*
Hildreth, Clifford 1917- *WhoAm 90*
Hildreth, Eugene A. 1924- *WhoAm 90*
Hildreth, Horace Augustus 1902-1988 *BioIn 16*
Hildreth, James Robert 1927- *WhoAm 90*
Hildreth, Joseph Alan 1947- *WhoAmA 91, WhoE 91*
Hildreth, Richard 1807-1865 *BioIn 16, EncABHB 6 [port]*
Hildreth, Richard Mansfield 1948- *WhoSSW 91*
Hildreth, Rodger Paul 1946- *WhoSSW 91*
Hildreth, Roland James 1926- *WhoAm 90*
Hildreth, William Bartley 1949- *WhoEmL 91, WhoSSW 91*
Hileman, Ambrose F. 1851-1898 *AmLegL*
Hileman, Carl Ellsworth 1929- *WhoSSW 91*
Hiler, Dale Courtlan 1937- *St&PR 91*
Hiler, Edward Allan 1939- *WhoAm 90*
Hiler, Emerson G 1919- *BiDrAPA 89*
Hiler, Hilaire 1898-1966 *WhoAmA 91N*
Hiler, John Patrick 1953- *WhoAm 90*
Hiles, Kathryn Hass 1954- *WhoSSW 91*
Hiles, William Gayle, Jr. 1945- *WhoSSW 91*
Hiley, David 1947- *IntWWM 90*
Hiley, Muriel B. G. 1906- *BiDWomA*
Hilf, Franklin D *BiDrAPA 89*
Hilf, Russell 1931- *WhoAm 90*
Hilfer, Anthony Channell 1936- *WhoSSW 91*
Hilferding, Rudolf 1877-1941 *BioIn 16*
Hilferty, Robert D. 1952- *St&PR 91*
Hilfiger, Roger Henry 1945- *WhoAm 90*
Hilfiker, Mary Louise 1945- *WhoWor 91*
Hilfstein, Erna *WhoAmW 91, WhoE 91, WhoWor 91*
Hilgard, Ernest R 1904- *ConAu 32NR*
Hilgard, Ernest Ropiequet 1904- *WhoAm 90, WhoWor 91*
Hilgard, Heinrich 1835-1900 *BioIn 16*
Hilgard, Josephine R *BiDrAPA 89*
Hilgartner, Beth 1957- *BioIn 16*
Hilgartner, Margaret Wehr 1924- *WhoAm 90*
Hilgeman, Charles E. 1934- *St&PR 91*
Hilgeman, Frederick Raymond 1937- *WhoSSW 91*
Hilgenberg, Eve Brantly Handy 1942- *WhoAm 90, WhoAmW 91*
Hilgenberg, John Christian 1941- *WhoAm 90*
Hilgendorf, Robert Lee 1936- *St&PR 91*
Hilgendorf, Tom 1942- *Ballpl 90*
Hilger, Daniel 1940- *St&PR 91*
Hilger, David W 1915- *BiDrAPA 89*
Hilger, Elsa 1904- *IntWWM 90*
Hilger, Frederick Lee, Jr. 1946- *WhoWor 91*
Hilger, Urban Eugene 1939- *St&PR 91*
Hilger, William C *BiDrAPA 89*
Hilger, Wolfgang 1929- *WhoWor 91*
Hilgers, Hans *PenDiDA 89*
Hilgert, Raymond Lewis 1930- *WhoAm 90*
Hilinski, Chester C. 1917- *WhoAm 90*
Hilinski, Robert Harry 1957- *WhoEmL 91*
Hilke, John Coryell 1950- *WhoE 91*
Hilker, G. Daniel 1929- *WhoAm 90*
Hilker, Robert Richard 1927- *WhoAm 90*
Hilker, Walter Robert, Jr. 1921- *WhoAm 90*
Hilkert, Fred G 1929- *BiDrAPA 89*
Hilkert, Fred George 1929- *WhoE 91*
Hilkevitch, Aaron A *BiDrAPA 89*
Hilkevitch, Alex *BiDrAPA 89*
Hilkevitch, Joyce Turner 1921- *IntWWM 90*
Hill, Lord 1904-1989 *AnObit 1989*
Hill, Abram 1911-1986 *DrBIPA 90, EarBIAP*
Hill, Adrienne Nicole 1964- *WhoAmW 91*
Hill, Agnes LaVone Lyles 1953- *WhoAmW 91*
Hill, Alan Jackson 1944- *St&PR 91*
Hill, Alan R. 1942- *St&PR 91*
Hill, Albert Alan 1938- *WhoAm 90*
Hill, Albert Gordon 1910- *WhoAm 90*
Hill, Alden Eugene 1926- *St&PR 91*
Hill, Alex 1906-1936 *OxCPMus*
Hill, Alfred 1917- *WhoAm 90*
Hill, Alfred Daniel 1952- *WhoSSW 91*
Hill, Allen Frank 1952- *WhoE 91*
Hill, Allen M. 1945- *St&PR 91*
Hill, Alton David, Jr. 1933- *WhoAm 90*
Hill, Amelia Robertson 1820-1904 *BiDWomA*
Hill, Andrew William 1937- *WhoAm 90, WhoWor 91*
Hill, Anita Carraway 1928- *WhoAmW 91*
Hill, Anita Rae 1928- *WhoAmW 91*
Hill, Ann 1921- *BioIn 16*
Hill, Ann Geddes Stahlman 1921- *NotWoAT*
Hill, Ann Marie 1951- *WhoE 91*
Hill, Anna Marie 1938- *WhoAmW 91*
Hill, Anne *DcCanB 12*
Hill, Anne 1810-1890 *OxCCanT*
Hill, Anne Lynn 1944- *WhoE 91*
Hill, Archibald G. 1950- *WhoSSW 91*
Hill, Arthur 1922- *WorAlBi*
Hill, Arthur James 1948- *WhoEmL 91*
Hill, Arthur Johnston, Jr. 1942- *WhoE 91*
Hill, Austin Bradford 1897- *WhoWor 91*
Hill, Barbara Jean *BiDrAPA 89*
Hill, Barbara Mae 1924- *WhoAmW 91, WhoE 91*
Hill, Bennett David 1934- *WhoAm 90*
Hill, Bertha 1905-1950 *BioIn 16, OxCPMus*
Hill, Betty Jean 1937- *WhoAmW 91*
Hill, Bill *WhoWrEP 89*
Hill, Billy 1899-1940 *OxCPMus*
Hill, Boyd H., Jr. 1931- *WhoAm 90*
Hill, Brian Michael *WhoE 91*
Hill, Brian Rich 1934- *St&PR 91*
Hill, Bruce Marvin 1935- *WhoAm 90, WhoWor 91*
Hill, Bryce Dale 1930- *WhoWor 91*
Hill, Carl McClellan 1907- *WhoAm 90*
Hill, Carl Paul 1942- *WhoAm 90*
Hill, Carlene Bay 1957- *WhoWrEP 89*
Hill, Carmen 1895- *Ballpl 90*
Hill, Carmen 1895-1990 *BioIn 16*
Hill, Catherine *WhoWrEP 89*
Hill, Cecil 1936- *IntWWM 90*
Hill, Chad *ODwPR 91*
Hill, Charles 1805-1874 *OxCCanT*
Hill, Charles 1904-1989 *BioIn 16, ConAu 129*
Hill, Charles Bud 1929- *IntWWM 90*
Hill, Charles Christopher 1948- *WhoAmA 91*
Hill, Charles Edward 1932- *WhoSSW 91*
Hill, Charles Ireland 1926- *St&PR 91*
Hill, Charles K. 1928- *St&PR 91*
Hill, Charles Lee 1910- *IntWWM 90*
Hill, Charles Strunk 1919- *St&PR 91, WhoSSW 91*
Hill, Cherry Lynn 1947- *WhoWrEP 89*
Hill, Chippie 1905-1950 *BioIn 16*
Hill, Christopher 1912- *WhoWor 91*
Hill, Christopher John 1949- *WhoEmL 91*
Hill, Christopher Thomas 1942- *WhoE 91*
Hill, Clara Edith 1948- *WhoAmW 91*
Hill, Claudia Adams 1949- *WhoAmW 91*
Hill, Clifford Geoffrey 1935- *St&PR 91*
Hill, Clinton 1922- *WhoAm 90*
Hill, Clinton J 1922- *WhoAmA 91*
Hill, Clyde Cecil, Jr. 1914- *WhoAm 90*
Hill, Crag A. 1957- *WhoWrEP 89*
Hill, Curtis V. 1947- *St&PR 91*
Hill, Curtis Wayne 1954- *WhoSSW 91*
Hill, Cynthia Ann 1953- *WhoAmW 91*
Hill, Cynthia Leigh 1957- *WhoAmW 91*
Hill, Dan J. 1940- *St&PR 91*
Hill, Dave *ConAu 132*
Hill, David Allan 1942- *WhoAm 90*
Hill, David Denham 1925- *St&PR 91*
Hill, David Francis 1955- *St&PR 91*
Hill, David Jayne 1850-1932 *BioIn 16*
Hill, David Jerome 1948- *St&PR 91*
Hill, David John 1958- *ConAu 132*
Hill, David Neil 1957- *IntWWM 90*
Hill, David Owen 1950- *WhoSSW 91*
Hill, David Peter 1940- *BiDrAPA 89*
Hill, David Ronald *BiDrAPA 89*
Hill, David W. 1871- *AmLegL*
Hill, David Warren 1946- *WhoE 91*
Hill, David William 1949- *WhoEmL 91*
Hill, Dean Allen 1934- *WhoWor 91*
Hill, DeAnn Gail 1953- *WhoAmW 91, WhoEmL 91*
Hill, Debra Ann *BiDrAPA 89*
Hill, Delmas Carl 1906- *WhoAm 90*
Hill, Delores Jean 1937- *St&PR 91*
Hill, Denis 1913-1982 *DcNaB 1981*
Hill, Denise Ann 1954- *WhoEmL 91*
Hill, Dennis James 1943- *WhoSSW 91*
Hill, Dennis Patrick 1960- *WhoEmL 91, WhoWor 91*
Hill, Denny Eugene 1939- *WhoSSW 91*
Hill, Denson 1939- *WhoE 91*
Hill, Derek 1916- *BioIn 16*
Hill, Diana Joan 1936- *WhoAmW 91*
Hill, Diane Seldon 1943- *WhoAmW 91*
Hill, Don 1930- *ODwPR 91*
Hill, Donald Lee *WhoSSW 91*
Hill, Donald T. 1934- *St&PR 91*
Hill, Donna Marie 1957- *WhoAmW 91*
Hill, Donnie 1960- *Ballpl 90*
Hill, Dorothy Belle 1936- *WhoAmW 91*
Hill, Dorothy J. 1922- *WhoWrEP 89*
Hill, Dorothy Kent 1907- *WhoAmA 91N*
Hill, Dorothy S. 1926- *St&PR 91*
Hill, Douglas 1935- *BioIn 16*
Hill, Draper 1935- *WhoAm 90, WhoAmA 91*
Hill, Dumond Peck 1923- *WhoAm 90*
Hill, E. Burrow, III 1953- *WhoSSW 91*
Hill, Earl McColl 1926- *WhoAm 90, WhoWor 91*
Hill, Earlene Hooper *WhoAmW 91*
Hill, Ed 1937- *WhoAmA 91*
Hill, Eddie *BioIn 16*
Hill, Edward Burlingame 1872-1960 *BioIn 16*
Hill, Edwin Conger 1884-1957 *BioIn 16*
Hill, Elizabeth Starr 1925- *AuBYP 90, ConAu 31NR*
Hill, Elizabeth Trezise 1936- *WhoAmW 91*
Hill, Elizabeth Wolfe *BiDrAPA 89*
Hill, Ellen Brown 1944- *WhoAmW 91*
Hill, Emery F. 1943- *St&PR 91*
Hill, Emily Katharine 1921- *WhoWrEP 89*
Hill, Emita Brady 1936- *WhoAmW 91*
Hill, Emma Lee 1949- *WhoAmW 91*
Hill, Emma Willis 1952- *WhoAmW 91*
Hill, Eric *BioIn 16*
Hill, Ernestine 1899-1972 *FemiCLE*
Hill, Errol 1921- *DrBIPA 90*
Hill, Errol Gaston 1921- *WhoAm 90*
Hill, Eugene DuBose 1951- *WhoEmL 91*
Hill, Eula Vertner 1928- *WhoAmW 91*
Hill, Evelyn Ann 1942- *WhoAmW 91*
Hill, Evelyn K. *BioIn 16, NewYTBS 90*
Hill, Everett 1956- *BiDrAPA 89*
Hill, F. Trent, Jr. 1952- *St&PR 91*
Hill, Fontaine S 1922- *BiDrAPA 89*
Hill, Francis Frederick 1908- *WhoAm 90*
Hill, Frank Ernest 1888-1969 *AuBYP 90*
Hill, Frank Nelson 1958- *WhoSSW 91*
Hill, Frank Whitney, Jr. 1914- *WhoAm 90*
Hill, Fred Gene 1933- *WhoSSW 91*
Hill, Fred James 1945- *WhoSSW 91*
Hill, Gary C. 1948- *St&PR 91*
Hill, Geoffrey 1932- *MajTwCW*
Hill, George Gwynn 1952- *WhoE 91*
Hill, George H. 1936- *St&PR 91*
Hill, George Jackson, III 1932- *WhoAm 90*
Hill, George James 1932- *WhoAm 90*
Hill, George Morey 1908- *St&PR 91*
Hill, George R. 1943- *IntWWM 90*
Hill, George Richard 1921- *WhoAm 90*
Hill, George Ronald 1946- *WhoWrEP 89*
Hill, George Roy *WhoAm 90*
Hill, George Roy 1922- *BioIn 16, WorAlBi*
Hill, George S. 1926- *St&PR 91*
Hill, George Snow 1898-1969 *WhoAmA 91N*
Hill, George Watts 1901- *St&PR 91, WhoAm 90*
Hill, Gerald 1923- *BiDrAPA 89*
Hill, Gordon Charles, III 1948- *WhoE 91*
Hill, Grace L. 1865-1947 *BioAmW*
Hill, Grace Lucile 1930- *WhoSSW 91*
Hill, Graham 1929-1975 *WorAlBi*
Hill, Graham Lancelot 1939- *WhoWor 91*
Hill, Graham Roderick 1946- *WhoAm 90*
Hill, H. Jay 1939- *St&PR 91*
Hill, Hamlin Lewis, Jr. 1931- *WhoAm 90*
Hill, Harold Eugene 1918- *WhoAm 90*
Hill, Harold Nelson, Jr. 1930- *WhoAm 90*
Hill, Harold Wayne 1933- *WhoAmA 91*
Hill, Harry Edward, III 1948- *WhoE 91*
Hill, Harry G. 1900- *St&PR 91*
Hill, Helen Brooks- 1908- *BioIn 16*
Hill, Henry Allen 1933- *WhoAm 90*
Hill, Henry Forrest 1917- *WhoSSW 91*
Hill, Henry Parker 1918- *WhoAm 90*
Hill, Homer *WhoAmA 91N*
Hill, Howard Earl 1952- *WhoSSW 91*
Hill, Howard W. 1926- *St&PR 91*
Hill, Hulene Dian 1948- *WhoEmL 91, WhoSSW 91*
Hill, Hunter 1879-1959 *Ballpl 90*
Hill, Hyacinthe 1920- *WhoWrEP 89*
Hill, I. Kathryn 1950- *WhoAmW 91*
Hill, Isaac William 1908- *WhoAm 90, WhoWrEP 89*
Hill, Isabel 1800-1842 *FemiCLE*
Hill, J Arthur 1872-1951 *EncO&P 3*
Hill, J.B. 1927- *St&PR 91*
Hill, J. Kenneth 1928- *St&PR 91*
Hill, J. Leubrie *EarBIAP*
Hill, J. Newton *BioIn 16*
Hill, J. Stanley 1914- *St&PR 91*
Hill, J Tweed *WhoAmA 91*
Hill, Jack 1924- *WhoE 91*
Hill, Jack Erwin 1942- *St&PR 91*
Hill, Jack K. 1928- *WhoAm 90*
Hill, Jack Warren 1921- *BiDrAPA 89*
Hill, Jackson 1941- *IntWWM 90*
Hill, James Allen 1949- *WhoEmL 91*
Hill, James Bayer 1911- *St&PR 91*
Hill, James Benjamin, Jr. 1948- *WhoSSW 91, WhoWor 91*
Hill, James Berry 1945- *WhoAmA 91*
Hill, James Clinkscales 1924- *WhoAm 90, WhoSSW 91*
Hill, James F. 1935- *ODwPR 91*
Hill, James Grayson 1942- *BiDrAPA 89*
Hill, James H. 1947- *ODwPR 91*
Hill, James J. 1838-1916 *WorAlBi*
Hill, James Jerome 1838-1916 *BioIn 16*
Hill, James Lee 1941- *WhoSSW 91*
Hill, James Scott 1924- *WhoAm 90*
Hill, James Stanley 1914- *WhoAm 90*
Hill, James Thomas 1950- *WhoEmL 91*
Hill, James Tomilson 1948- *WhoE 91*
Hill, James Walter, IV 1951- *WhoEmL 91*
Hill, James Warren 1941- *St&PR 91*
Hill, Jan Christelman 1948- *WhoE 91*
Hill, Janet *AuBYP 90*
Hill, Jefferson Borden 1941- *WhoE 91*
Hill, Jeffrey Alan 1951- *WhoEmL 91*
Hill, Jennifer June 1944- *IntWWM 90*
Hill, Jenny 1848-1896 *OxCPMus*
Hill, Jeri Linda 1949- *WhoWor 91*
Hill, Jerome, II 1903- *WhoAmA 91N*
Hill, Jerrold Wayne 1952- *WhoE 91*
Hill, Jesse 1907- *Ballpl 90*
Hill, Jimmie Dale 1933- *WhoAm 90*
Hill, Joan *WhoAmA 91*
Hill, Joan Palmer 1957- *WhoE 91*
Hill, Joan R. 1931-1969 *BioAmW*
Hill, Joanne M. *BioIn 16*
Hill, Joe 1879-1915 *BioIn 16, EncAL [port]*
Hill, John *BioIn 16, MajTwCW*
Hill, John 1821-1884 *AmLegL*
Hill, John 1923- *St&PR 91*
Hill, John A. 1907- *St&PR 91*
Hill, John Alexander 1907- *WhoAm 90*
Hill, John Campbell 1938- *WhoAm 90*
Hill, John Conner 1945- *WhoAmA 91*
Hill, John David 1920- *St&PR 91*
Hill, John deKoven 1920- *WhoAm 90*
Hill, John Earl 1953- *WhoEmL 91*
Hill, John-Edward 1947- *WhoEmL 91*
Hill, John Henry 1839-1922 *WhoAmA 91N*
Hill, John Howard 1940- *WhoAm 90*
Hill, John Kevin *BioIn 16*
Hill, John McGregor 1921- *WhoWor 91*
Hill, John Rutledge, Jr. 1922- *WhoAm 90*
Hill, John Steven 1957- *WhoEmL 91*
Hill, John Walter 1942- *IntWWM 90*
Hill, John William 1812-1879 *WhoAmA 91N*
Hill, John William 1930- *WhoAm 90*
Hill, Johnson D., Jr. 1916- *St&PR 91*
Hill, Jonas Lee, Sr. 1947- *WhoEmL 91*
Hill, Jonel C. 1925- *St&PR 91, WhoAm 90*
Hill, Joseph Gray 1950- *St&PR 91*
Hill, Joyce 1929-1988 *BioIn 16*
Hill, Judith 1945- *WhoWrEP 89*
Hill, Judith Deegan 1940- *WhoAmW 91, WhoWor 91*
Hill, Judith Swigost 1942- *WhoAmW 91*

Hill, Karen Waterstrauss 1946- *WhoAmW 91*
Hill, Katharine Gay 1954- *WhoEmL 91*
Hill, Kathy Louise 1951- *WhoSSW 91*
Hill, Kathy Lynn 1955- *WhoAmW 91*
Hill, Keith Maurice 1954- *WhoE 91*
Hill, Keith Richard 1948- *IntWWM 90*
Hill, Ken 1965- *Ballpl 90*
Hill, Kenneth Douglas 1934- *WhoAm 90*
Hill, King J. *ODwPR 91*
Hill, Knox Calvin 1910- *WhoAm 90*
Hill, L. Gordon 1922-1990 *BioIn 16*
Hill, La Joyce Carmichael 1952- *WhoAmW 91*
Hill, Larkin Payne 1954- *WhoAmW 91, WhoEmL 91, WhoSSW 91*
Hill, Larry Michael 1948- *St&PR 91*
Hill, Laura Jo 1959- *WhoAmW 91*
Hill, Lawrence 1912-1988 *BioIn 16*
Hill, Lee *BioIn 16*
Hill, Lee H., Jr. 1924- *St&PR 91*
Hill, Lee Halsey, Jr. 1924- *WhoSSW 91*
Hill, Lee Wayne 1944- *WhoE 91*
Hill, Lenora Mae 1937- *WhoAmW 91*
Hill, Leona Bowman *BioIn 16*
Hill, Leonard Franklin 1947- *WhoEmL 91*
Hill, Leslie Clyde 1934- *WhoWor 91*
Hill, Leslie Pinckney 1880-1960 *EarBlAP*
Hill, Levi Walter 1928- *St&PR 91*
Hill, Linda Lee 1947- *WhoAmW 91*
Hill, Lois Jane 1949- *WhoEmL 91*
Hill, Lorna 1902- *AuBYP 90*
Hill, Louis Allen, Jr. 1927- *WhoAm 90*
Hill, Louise B. 1952- *WhoAmW 91*
Hill, Luther Lyons, Jr. 1922- *St&PR 91, WhoAm 90*
Hill, Lynix S. 1940- *St&PR 91*
Hill, Lynn *BioIn 16*
Hill, Lynn 1961?- *News 91-2*
Hill, Malcolm 1930- *BiDrAPA 89*
Hill, Malcolm R 1942- *ConAu 130*
Hill, Marc 1952- *Ballpl 90*
Hill, Marcella Elaine Washington 1927- *WhoAm 90*
Hill, Marcus Edward 1947- *WhoEmL 91*
Hill, Margaret 1915- *AuBYP 90*
Hill, Margaret F. *St&PR 91*
Hill, Marilyn J. 1929- *WhoAmW 91*
Hill, Marion Gundy 1933- *WhoSSW 91*
Hill, Marion Thelma 1937- *WhoAmW 91*
Hill, Martyn 1944- *IntWWM 90, PenDiMP*
Hill, Mary Ann *WhoAmW 91*
Hill, Mary Christina 1949- *WhoAmW 91*
Hill, Mary Lou 1936- *WhoAmW 91*
Hill, Mary Rae 1923- *WhoAmW 91*
Hill, Maureen Kelley 1951- *WhoAmW 91*
Hill, Maurice Neville 1919-1966 *DcScB S2*
Hill, Max E. 1940- *St&PR 91*
Hill, Max Lloyd, Jr. 1927- *WhoSSW 91*
Hill, Megan Lloyd *WhoAmA 91*
Hill, Melvin James 1919- *WhoAm 90*
Hill, Michael Alan 1954- *BiDrAPA 89*
Hill, Michael Evans 1947- *WhoSSW 91*
Hill, Michael John Anthony 1937- *IntWWM 90*
Hill, Michael Nelson, III 1945- *WhoEmL 91*
Hill, Millicent Elizabeth *WhoWrEP 89*
Hill, Milton Monroe 1919- *St&PR 91*
Hill, Milton Simpson 1942- *St&PR 91, WhoSSW 91*
Hill, Monte Scott 1950- *St&PR 91*
Hill, Morris *BioIn 16*
Hill, Neal 1952- *WhoE 91*
Hill, Nolanda Sue 1944- *WhoAmW 91*
Hill, Norman Ellison 1939- *St&PR 91*
Hill, Norman Julius 1925- *WhoAm 90, WhoWrEP 89*
Hill, Octavia 1838-1912 *BioIn 16*
Hill, Orion Alvah, Jr. 1920- *WhoAm 90*
Hill, Owen Leslie, Jr. 1938- *St&PR 91*
Hill, Pamela 1938- *WhoAmW 91*
Hill, Pati 1921- *LiHiK*
Hill, Patricia 1932- *WhoWrEP 89*
Hill, Patricia Arnold 1936- *WhoAmW 91*
Hill, Patricia Francine 1955- *WhoAmW 91*
Hill, Patricia Kaye *BiDrAPA 89*
Hill, Patricia Lispenard 1937- *WhoAmW 91*
Hill, Paul Bryan 1959- *BiDrAPA 89*
Hill, Paul Drennen 1941- *St&PR 91, WhoAm 90*
Hill, Paul Stevens *BiDrAPA 89*
Hill, Penny *ODwPR 91*
Hill, Pete 1880-1951 *Ballpl 90*
Hill, Peter 1933- *WhoAmA 91*
Hill, Peter 1948- *IntWWM 90*
Hill, Peter W. *BioIn 16*
Hill, Peter Waverly 1953- *WhoE 91, WhoEmL 91, WhoWor 91*
Hill, Philip Carteret 1821-1894 *DcCanB 12*
Hill, Phillippina *FemiCLE*
Hill, Polly Knipp 1900-1990 *WhoAmA 91N*
Hill, Prescott F. 1934- *St&PR 91*
Hill, Ralph H. 1914- *St&PR 91*
Hill, Ralph Harold 1914- *WhoAm 90*
Hill, Ralph Kelly 1952- *WhoSSW 91*
Hill, Ralph Nading 1917- *AuBYP 90*
Hill, Randall William 1933- *St&PR 91*
Hill, Regina Eileen 1962- *WhoAmW 91*
Hill, Reginald 1936- *ConAu 32NR, TwCCr&M 91*
Hill, Renee Yvette 1959- *BiDrAPA 89*
Hill, Reuben 1912-1985 *ConAu 131*
Hill, Richard 1951- *WhoEmL 91*
Hill, Richard Allen 1932- *WhoAm 90*
Hill, Richard D. 1919- *St&PR 91*
Hill, Richard Devereux 1919- *WhoAm 90*
Hill, Richard Earl 1929- *WhoAm 90*
Hill, Richard Edwin 1928- *WhoAm 90*
Hill, Richard Garland 1953- *WhoSSW 91*
Hill, Richard Keith 1928- *WhoAm 90*
Hill, Richard Lee 1931- *WhoWor 91*
Hill, Richard M. *WhoAm 90*
Hill, Richard Wayne 1950- *WhoAmA 91*
Hill, Richard Wm *BiDrAPA 89*
Hill, Richard Wright 1959- *WhoEmL 91*
Hill, Robert *BioIn 16*
Hill, Robert 1931- *WhoSSW 91*
Hill, Robert A. 1943- *ConAu 132*
Hill, Robert Anthony 1958- *WhoEmL 91*
Hill, Robert Arthur 1961- *WhoAm 90*
Hill, Robert B. 1933- *St&PR 91*
Hill, Robert Cameron, Jr. 1952- *WhoEmL 91*
Hill, Robert Charles 1952- *WhoE 91*
Hill, Robert F. 1936- *St&PR 91*
Hill, Robert Folwell, Jr. 1946- *WhoSSW 91*
Hill, Robert James 1951- *WhoEmL 91*
Hill, Robert Lee 1928- *WhoAm 90*
Hill, Robert Mason 1922- *WhoAm 90*
Hill, Robert Stephen 1953- *IntWWM 90*
Hill, Robert Thomas 1940- *WhoWor 91*
Hill, Robert W. 1927- *St&PR 91*
Hill, Robert Wayne 1927- *WhoAm 90*
Hill, Robert White 1919-1982 *AuBYP 90*
Hill, Robin 1955- *WhoAmA 91*
Hill, Robyn Lesley 1942- *WhoAmA 91, WhoAmW 91*
Hill, Roger *ConAu 31NR*
Hill, Roger Webb, Jr. 1932- *St&PR 91*
Hill, Rolla B. 1929- *WhoAm 90*
Hill, Ronald Charles 1948- *WhoSSW 91*
Hill, Ronald Guy 1934- *WhoSSW 91*
Hill, Ronald Roy 1952- *WhoEmL 91*
Hill, Rowland 1795-1879 *BioIn 16*
Hill, Roy D, Jr. 1933- *BiDrAPA 89*
Hill, Ruby 1922- *DrBlPA 90*
Hill, Rubye Robinson 1926- *WhoAmW 91*
Hill, Rufus Sadler, Jr. 1935- *WhoE 91*
Hill, Ruth Foell 1931- *WhoAmW 91*
Hill, Samuel 1857-1931 *BioIn 16*
Hill, Samuel P. 1823-1874 *AmLegL*
Hill, Samuel Richardson, Jr. 1923- *WhoAm 90*
Hill, Sandy *BioIn 16*
Hill, Sara Frances 1953- *WhoAmW 91*
Hill, Sara Lenox *BioIn 16*
Hill, Sarah Conover 1951- *WhoEmL 91*
Hill, Selima 1945- *FemiCLE*
Hill, Sheila Karen 1948- *WhoWrEP 89*
Hill, Shirley Aline 1956- *WhoAmW 91*
Hill, Shirley Ann 1927- *WhoAm 90, WhoAmW 91*
Hill, Stephen John 1809-1891 *DcCanB 12*
Hill, Stephen M. 1930- *St&PR 91, WhoAm 90*
Hill, Steven 1922- *ConTFT 8*
Hill, Steven Richard 1947- *WhoEmL 91*
Hill, Sue Annette 1964- *WhoAmW 91*
Hill, Susan 1942- *BioIn 16, FemiCLE, MajTwCW*
Hill, Susan Sloan 1952- *WhoAmW 91, WhoSSW 91, WhoWor 91*
Hill, Teddy 1909-1978 *OxCPMus*
Hill, Terrance Allan 1957- *WhoEmL 91*
Hill, Terrell Leslie 1917- *WhoAm 90*
Hill, Terrence 1944- *ODwPR 91*
Hill, Thomas A. 1924- *St&PR 91*
Hill, Thomas Allen 1958- *WhoEmL 91, WhoWor 91*
Hill, Thomas Bowen, III 1929- *WhoAm 90, WhoSSW 91*
Hill, Thomas Clark 1946- *WhoEmL 91*
Hill, Thomas Dana 1940- *WhoE 91*
Hill, Thomas Glenn, III 1942- *WhoAm 90*
Hill, Thomas M *BiDrAPA 89*
Hill, Thomas S. 1936- *St&PR 91*
Hill, Thomas Stewart 1936- *WhoAm 90*
Hill, Thomas William, Jr. 1924- *WhoE 91, WhoWor 91*
Hill, Tracey 1946- *WhoAmW 91*
Hill, Trafford, Jr. 1934- *BiDrAPA 89*
Hill, Ureli Corelli 1802?-1875 *PenDiMP*
Hill, Valerie Charlotte 1932- *WhoAmW 91, WhoE 91, WhoWor 91*
Hill, Van E. 1945- *WhoSSW 91*
Hill, Victor Ernst, IV 1939- *WhoAm 90*
Hill, Virgil Lusk, Jr. 1938- *WhoAm 90*
Hill, Virginia Lee 1955- *BiDrAPA 89*
Hill, W M *ConAu 31NR*
Hill, Walter 1942- *BioIn 16, WhoAm 90*
Hill, Walter James 1935- *BiDrAPA 89*
Hill, Warren Gardiner 1918- *WhoAm 90*
Hill, Wendell Talbot, Jr. 1924- *WhoAm 90*
Hill, Wendy Paulen 1952- *WhoAmW 91, WhoEmL 91*
Hill, Wesley S. 1930- *St&PR 91, WhoE 91*
Hill, William Edwin 1910-1988 *BioIn 16*
Hill, William Gilbert, Jr. 1941- *WhoE 91*
Hill, William Granville 1941- *WhoWor 91*
Hill, William H. 1925- *St&PR 91*
Hill, William Mansfield 1925- *WhoAmA 91*
Hill, William Plummer 1908- *WhoE 91, WhoWor 91*
Hill, William Thomas 1925- *WhoAm 90*
Hill, William Victor, II 1936- *WhoSSW 91*
Hill, Wilmer Bailey 1928- *WhoAm 90*
Hill, Winfred Farrington 1929- *WhoAm 90*
Hill, Winslow Smith 1925- *WhoE 91*
Hill-Beuf, Ann Harper 1938- *WhoWrEP 89*
Hill-Donisch, Karla 1959- *WhoAmW 91*
Hill of Luton, Charles Hill, Baron 1904-1989 *BioIn 16*
Hill Smith, Marilyn 1952- *IntWWM 90, WhoWor 91*
Hillage, Steve *NewAgMG*
Hillard, Claire Fox 1958- *IntWWM 90*
Hillard, Ida McCree 1942- *BiDrAPA 89*
Hillard, James Randolph 1951- *BiDrAPA 89*
Hillard, Lloyd C., Jr. 1946- *St&PR 91*
Hillard, Robert Ellsworth 1917- *WhoAm 90*
Hillard, William E 1925- *BiDrAPA 89*
Hillary, Edmund *BioIn 16*
Hillary, Edmund 1919- *WorAlBi*
Hillary, Edmund Percival 1919- *WhoWor 91*
Hillas, Roger S. 1927- *BioIn 16*
Hillback, Ella 1915-1979 *EncCoWW*
Hillberg, Marylou Elin 1950- *WhoEmL 91*
Hillberry, Benny Max 1937- *WhoAm 90*
Hillbom, Eero *BiDrAPA 89*
Hillborg, Anders Per 1954- *IntWWM 90*
Hillcourt, William 1900- *AuBYP 90, WhoAm 90*
Hilldrup, Mary Eileen 1946- *WhoAmW 91*
Hille, Bertil 1940- *WhoAm 90*
Hille, David Charles 1948- *WhoE 91*
Hille, Stanley James 1937- *WhoAm 90*
Hillebrand, Melanie 1952- *WhoWor 91*
Hillebrand, Nikolaus 1948- *IntWWM 90*
Hillebrand, Wendy Ann 1952- *BiDrAPA 89*
Hillebrandt, Friedrich *PenDiDA 89*
Hillebrecht, Hildegard 1927- *IntWWM 90, PenDiMP*
Hillegas, Michael 1729-1804 *EncCRAm*
Hillegas, Shawn 1964- *Ballpl 90*
Hillegass, Christine Ann 1952- *WhoAmW 91, WhoEmL 91*
Hillegass, Clifton Keith 1918- *WhoAm 90*
Hillegass, William Grimes, Sr. 1950- *WhoSSW 91*
Hillegeist, Willard McConkey 1940- *St&PR 91*
Hillel, David D'Bet *BioIn 16*
Hilleman, Jeryl Lynn 1957- *WhoAmW 91*
Hillen, James McLaren *BiDrAPA 89*
Hillen, Kees 1946- *IntWWM 90*
Hillenbrand, Charles J *BiDrAPA 89*
Hillenbrand, Charles R 1943- *BiDrAPA 89*
Hillenbrand, Daniel A. 1923- *WhoAm 90*
Hillenbrand, Martin Joseph 1915- *BioIn 16, WhoAm 90*
Hillenbrand, W. August 1940- *St&PR 91, WhoAm 90*
Hillengass, Eugen Georges 1930- *WhoWor 91*
Hillenmeyer, Ernest Bernard, Jr. 1922- *St&PR 91*
Hillenmeyer, Henry Reiling 1943- *St&PR 91*
Hillenmeyer, Henry Reiling, Jr. 1943- *WhoSSW 91*
Hillenmeyer, Jacques Henri 1946- *WhoWor 91*
Hiller, Arthur 1923- *ConTFT 8, WhoAm 90, WorAlBi*
Hiller, Betty R 1925- *WhoAmA 91*
Hiller, Bruce H 1934- *BiDrAPA 89*
Hiller, Carl E. *AuBYP 90*
Hiller, Chuck 1934- *Ballpl 90, BioIn 16*
Hiller, Dagmar C. 1962- *WhoAmW 91*
Hiller, Eli 1936- *WhoE 91*
Hiller, Ferdinand 1811-1885 *PenDiMP*
Hiller, Frank 1920-1987 *Ballpl 90*
Hiller, Ilo 1938- *BioIn 16*
Hiller, John 1943- *Ballpl 90*
Hiller, John Richard 1953- *WhoEmL 91*
Hiller, Karen Sue 1952- *WhoEmL 91*
Hiller, Lee 1941- *St&PR 91*
Hiller, Lejaran Arthur 1924- *IntWWM 90*
Hiller, Lejaren Arthur, Jr. 1924- *WhoAm 90*
Hiller, Melvin Jackson 1941- *St&PR 91*
Hiller, Phyllis Lillian *WhoAmW 91*
Hiller, Robert Stanford 1951- *WhoEmL 91*
Hiller, Stanley, Jr. *BioIn 16*
Hiller, Stanley, Jr. 1924- *St&PR 91, WhoAm 90*
Hiller, Susan 1942- *BiDWomA*
Hiller, Walter W, Jr. *BiDrAPA 89*
Hiller, Wendy *WhoAm 90*
Hiller, Wendy 1912- *WorAlBi*
Hiller, William Arlington 1928- *St&PR 91, WhoAm 90*
Hillerbrand, Hans Joachim 1931- *WhoAm 90*
Hillerich, John A. 1940- *St&PR 91*
Hillerman, John 1932- *ConTFT 8 [port], WorAlBi*
Hillerman, Tony *BioIn 16*
Hillerman, Tony 1925- *Au&Arts 6 [port], ConLC 62 [port], TwCCr&M 91, WhoWrEP 89, WorAlBi*
Hillers, Delbert Roy 1932- *WhoAm 90*
Hillers, John K. 1843-1925 *BioIn 16, WhNaAH*
Hillert, Gloria Bonnin 1930- *WhoAmW 91*
Hillert, Margaret 1920- *WhoWrEP 89*
Hillery, Julian Swoop 1937- *WhoSSW 91*
Hillery, Mary Jane Larato 1931- *WhoAmW 91, WhoE 91, WhoWor 91*
Hillery, Patrick John 1923- *WhoWor 91*
Hilles, Helen 1905- *AuBYP 90*
Hillestad, Charles Andrew 1945- *WhoEmL 91*
Hillesum, Esther 1914-1943 *EncCoWW*
Hillgard, Else M B 1925- *BiDrAPA 89*
Hillgren, James Stuart 1945- *St&PR 91*
Hillgren, Sonja Dorothy 1948- *WhoAmW 91*
Hillgrove, Sara Meyerdierks 1952- *WhoE 91*
Hillgruber, Andreas 1925-1989 *AnObit 1989, BioIn 16*
Hilliam, B. C. 1890-1968 *OxCPMus*
Hilliard, Bob 1918-1971 *OxCPMus*
Hilliard, Earl Frederick 1942- *WhoSSW 91*
Hilliard, Frederick 1935- *St&PR 91*
Hilliard, Garrison Lee 1960- *WhoWrEP 89*
Hilliard, Henning 1916- *St&PR 91*
Hilliard, James M. 1921- *St&PR 91*
Hilliard, James William 1958- *WhoEmL 91*
Hilliard, John 1945- *WhoWor 91*
Hilliard, John K. 1901-1989 *BioIn 16*
Hilliard, John Stanley 1947- *IntWWM 90*
Hilliard, Katharine A *BiDrAPA 89*
Hilliard, Landon 1939- *St&PR 91, WhoAm 90*
Hilliard, Lawrence L. *ODwPR 91*
Hilliard, Lester Earl 1945- *WhoEmL 91*
Hilliard, Nicholas 1547?-1619? *IntDcAA 90*
Hilliard, Quincy Charles 1954- *IntWWM 90*
Hilliard, Robert A. 1952- *ODwPR 91*
Hilliard, Robert Glenn 1943- *St&PR 91, WhoAm 90*
Hilliard, Royce M. 1922- *WhoSSW 91*
Hilliard, Sam Bowers 1930- *WhoAm 90*
Hilliard, Sharen Anne 1942- *WhoAmW 91*
Hilliard, Stephen Mark 1955- *St&PR 91*
Hilliard, Thomas Lee 1930- *IntWWM 90*
Hilliard, Wendy *BioIn 16*
Hilliard, William Raymond, Jr. 1953- *WhoEmL 91*
Hillier, Caroline *AuBYP 90*
Hillier, Harold George Knight 1905-1985 *DcNaB 1981*
Hillier, James 1915- *WorAlBi*
Hillier, James Robert 1937- *WhoAm 90*
Hillier, Jay D. 1949- *St&PR 91*
Hillier, Judith A. 1951- *WhoAmW 91*
Hillier, Paul Douglas 1949- *IntWWM 90*
Hillier, Stanley Kenneth 1918- *WhoSSW 91*
Hillier, Tristram Paul 1905-1983 *DcNaB 1981*
Hilligoss, Martha M 1928-1987 *WhoAmA 91N*
Hilliker, John Arthur Charles 1928- *St&PR 91*
Hillila, Bernhard Hugo Paul 1919- *WhoAm 90*
Hillin, Henderson, Jr. 1930- *WhoWrEP 89*
Hillings, E. Joseph *ODwPR 91*
Hillion, Pierre Theodore Marie 1926- *WhoWor 91*
Hillips, Gordon 1929- *St&PR 91*
Hillis Hayo *WhNaAH*
Hillis, Llewellya W. 1930- *WhoAmW 91*
Hillis, Margaret 1921- *IntWWM 90, PenDiMP, WhoAm 90, WhoAmW 91*
Hillis, Mark 1942- *St&PR 91*
Hillis, Richard K 1936- *WhoAmA 91*
Hillis, Shelby Ross 1940- *WhoSSW 91*
Hillis, William Daniel 1933- *WhoAm 90*
Hillman, Aaron Waddell 1926- *WhoWrEP 89*
Hillman, Alex L 1900-1968 *WhoAmA 91N*
Hillman, Arthur Burgess, III 1945- *WhoEmL 91*

Hillman, Arthur Stanley 1945- WhoAmA 91
Hillman, Bessie 1889-1970 WorAlBi
Hillman, Bill 1922- WhoAm 90
Hillman, Brenda 1951- ConAu 129
Hillman, Brenda Lynn 1951- WhoWrEP 89
Hillman, Bruce John 1938- St&PR 91
Hillman, Carol B. 1940- ODwPR 91
Hillman, Carol Barbara 1940- WhoAmW 91
Hillman, Charlene ODwPR 91
Hillman, Charles W. 1929- St&PR 91
Hillman, Chris WhoNeCM A
Hillman, Constance Pappas 1948- WhoEmL 91
Hillman, Dave 1927- Ballpl 90
Hillman, David W. 1956- St&PR 91
Hillman, Dean Elof 1936- WhoAm 90
Hillman, Deborah Jeanne 1962- WhoAmW 91
Hillman, Douglas Woodruff 1922- WhoAm 90
Hillman, Farrell A BiDrAPA 89
Hillman, Gary 1938- St&PR 91
Hillman, George 1906- DrBlPA 90
Hillman, Gordon F. 1923- St&PR 91
Hillman, Henry L. 1918- St&PR 91, WhoAm 90, WhoWor 91
Hillman, Howard Budrow 1934- WhoAm 90, WhoWrEP 89
Hillman, Jack Brittian 1934- BiDrAPA 89
Hillman, James 1926- EncO&P 3
Hillman, James Calvin 1944- St&PR 91
Hillman, Jennifer 1944- IntWWM 90
Hillman, Julie Renae 1962- WhoAmW 91
Hillman, May AuBYP 90
Hillman, Melville Ernest Douglas 1926- WhoAm 90
Hillman, Patrick WhoAm 90
Hillman, Priscilla 1940- BioIn 16
Hillman, Richard B. 1944- St&PR 91
Hillman, Richard Ephraim 1940- WhoAm 90
Hillman, Rita 1912- WhoAmW 91, WhoE 91
Hillman, Robert George 1937- BiDrAPA 89
Hillman, S.E.G. 1911- St&PR 91
Hillman, Sidney 1887-1946 WorAlBi
Hillman, Stanley Eric Gordon 1911- WhoAm 90
Hillman, William Chernick 1935- WhoE 91
Hillman-Jones, Gladys Cornelia 1938- WhoAmW 91, WhoE 91
Hillmann, Hans 1925- ConDes 90
Hillmer, Duane H. 1916- St&PR 91
Hillner, Kathleen Anhalt 1956- WhoAmW 91
Hillquit, Morris 1869-1933 EncAL
Hills, Alan Lee 1954- WhoEmL 91
Hills, Austin Edward 1934- St&PR 91, WhoAm 90
Hills, Carla 1934- News 90 [port], -90-3 [port], WorAlBi
Hills, Carla A. 1934- St&PR 91
Hills, Carla Anderson 1934- BiDrUSE 89, BioIn 16, WhoAm 90, WhoAmW 91
Hills, Christiana ODwPR 91
Hills, Christopher EncO&P 3
Hills, Claude Hibbard 1912- WhoE 91
Hills, Cornell Dexter 1953- WhoEmL 91
Hills, Edith BioIn 16
Hills, Frank Stanley 1935- WhoAm 90
Hills, Frederic Wheeler 1934- WhoAm 90
Hills, George 1816-1895 DcCanB 12
Hills, George Burkhart, Jr. 1925- WhoAm 90
Hills, Joan BioIn 16
Hills, John Merrill 1944- WhoAm 90
Hills, Laura Coombs 1859-1952 WhoAmA 91N
Hills, Lawrence Donegan 1911-1990 ConAu 132
Hills, Lee 1906- St&PR 91
Hills, Linda Launey 1947- WhoEmL 91, WhoWor 91
Hills, Marilla Turner Marks Hutchins 1807-1901 BioIn 16
Hills, P. J. ConAu 129
Hills, Patricia 1936- WhoAmA 91
Hills, Patricia Gorton Schulze 1936- WhoAm 90
Hills, Patti Lynn 1953- WhoAmW 91
Hills, Philip ConAu 129
Hills, Philip J 1933- ConAu 129
Hills, Regina J. 1953- WhoAm 90
Hills, Richard A., Jr. 1940- St&PR 91
Hills, Roderick M. 1931- WhoAm 90
Hillsborough, Will Hills, Earl of 1718-1793 EncCRAm
Hillsdon-Hutton, Valerie 1943- WhoWrEP 89
Hillsman, Philip Lee 1959- BiDrAPA 89
Hillsman, Walter Lee 1943- IntWWM 90
Hillsmith, Fannie 1911- WhoAmA 91
Hillson, Jan Leslie 1952- WhoAmW 91
Hillsten, Kenneth Leroy 1937- WhoSSW 91
Hillstrom, Paul John 1930- St&PR 91
Hillway, Tyrus 1912- WhoAm 90
Hillyard, Ira William 1924- WhoAm 90
Hillyer, Carter Sinclair 1948- WhoWrEP 89
Hillyer, Dolores Hocutt 1935- WhoSSW 91
Hillyer, Raphael PenDiMP
Hillyer, Virgil Mores 1875-1931 AuBYP 90
Hillyer, William Hudson 1928- St&PR 91
Hilman, Eric 1954- WhoEmL 91
Hilmers, David C. 1950- BioIn 16
Hilpert, Brunette Kathleen Powers 1909- WhoAmW 91
Hilpert, Dale W. WhoAm 90
Hilpert, Friedrich PenDiMP
Hilsabeck, Frank H. 1944- St&PR 91
Hilscher, Hubert 1924- ConDes 90
Hilsen, John C. 1931- St&PR 91
Hilsenrath, Lee Betty 1934- WhoE 91
Hilser, Richard J. 1940- St&PR 91
Hilsinger, Arthur R., Jr. 1927- St&PR 91
Hilsinger, Ellen Alice BiDrAPA 89
Hilsman, Gray BiDrAPA 89
Hilsman, Gray 1947- WhoSSW 91
Hilsman, Hoyt Roger 1948- WhoEmL 91
Hilsman, Roger 1919- BioIn 16, WhoAm 90
Hilson, Douglas 1941- WhoAmA 91
Hilson, M. Douglas 1941- WhoE 91
Hilstad, Paul Arnold 1942- St&PR 91
Hilt, Diane Elaine 1944- WhoAmW 91, WhoSSW 91
Hiltbrunner, Venita Katheleene 1944- WhoSSW 91
Hiltgen, Dale Edward 1946- BiDrAPA 89
Hiltner, William Albert 1914- WhoAm 90
Hilton, Alice Mary 1929- WhoAm 90
Hilton, Andrew C. 1928- St&PR 91
Hilton, Andrew Carson 1928- WhoAm 90
Hilton, Arleen Antoinette 1961- WhoAmW 91
Hilton, Barron 1927- WhoAm 90
Hilton, Claude Meredith 1940- WhoAm 90, WhoSSW 91
Hilton, Clifford Thomas 1934- WhoSSW 91
Hilton, Conrad N. 1887-1979 WorAlBi
Hilton, Dave 1950- Ballpl 90
Hilton, Emmett Walters 1926- BiDrAPA 89
Hilton, Eric Michael 1933- WhoAm 90
Hilton, Eva Mae 1950- WhoAmW 91
Hilton, Gary Michael 1941- St&PR 91
Hilton, George Q 1946- BiDrAPA 89
Hilton, Jack 1937- ODwPR 91
Hilton, James 1900-1954 WorAlBi
Hilton, James Gorton 1923- WhoAm 90
Hilton, James L. 1930- WhoAm 90
Hilton, James Monroe BiDrAPA 89
Hilton, Janet Lesley 1945- IntWWM 90
Hilton, John Buxton 1921-1986 TwCCr&M 91
Hilton, John David 1958- WhoE 91
Hilton, Joseph 1934- WhoE 91
Hilton, Linda Ann 1948- WhoWrEP 89
Hilton, Mark Howard 1951- WhoE 91
Hilton, Michael R. 1951- St&PR 91
Hilton, Ordway 1913- WhoAm 90
Hilton, Peter John 1923- WhoAm 90, WhoE 91
Hilton, Randall Craig 1949- WhoEmL 91
Hilton, Robert Leroy 1928- WhoSSW 91, WhoWor 91
Hilton, Robert Parker, Sr. 1927- WhoAm 90, WhoWor 91
Hilton, Ronald 1911- WhoAm 90
Hilton, Ronald James 1932- WhoWrEP 89
Hilton, Suzanne 1922- AuBYP 90, ConAu 30NR
Hilton, Thomas Scott 1952- WhoAm 90
Hilton, William Barron 1927- St&PR 91
Hilton, William D. 1929- St&PR 91
Hilton-Regan, Judith Ann 1938- WhoWrEP 89
Hilts, Alvin 1908- WhoAmA 91
Hilts, Margarete Louise 1912- WhoAm 90
Hilts, Philip James 1947- WhoE 91
Hiltunen, Eila 1922- BiDWomA
Hiltunen, Jon S. ODwPR 91
Hilty, Everett Jay 1910- IntWWM 90
Hilty, Louise BiDrAPA 89
Hilty, Thomas R 1943- WhoAmA 91
Hiltz, Dawn Papp 1959- WhoAmW 91, WhoE 91, WhoEmL 91, WhoWor 91
Hiltz, Paul Christopher 1959- WhoEmL 91
Hiltz, William Fowler 1952- BiDrAPA 89
Hiltz, William Otis 1951- St&PR 91
Hilzendeger, Connie Colleen 1950- WhoAmW 91
Him, George 1900-1982 ConDes 90
Himber, Victor Roy 1945- BiDrAPA 89
Himebauch, Steven Frederick 1951- St&PR 91
Himebaugh, Arthur Elliott 1925- St&PR 91
Himel, Edmond E., Jr. 1921- St&PR 91
Himel, Elizabeth Grace 1960- WhoAmW 91
Himelein, Larry M. 1949- WhoEmL 91
Himeles, Martin Stanley 1923- St&PR 91
Himeles, Martin Stanley, Jr. 1956- WhoEmL 91
Himelfarb, Richard Jay 1942- St&PR 91, WhoAm 90
Himelfarb, Stephen Roy 1954- WhoEmL 91
Himelstein, Peggy Donn 1932- WhoAmW 91
Himelstein, Philip Nathan 1923- WhoAm 90, WhoSSW 91
Himelstein, Theodore Karl 1906-1990 BioIn 16
Himes, Chester 1909-1984 BioIn 16, MajTwCW, TwCCr&M 91
Himes, Geoffrey 1952- WhoWrEP 89
Himes, Jane Ann 1923- WhoAmW 91
Himes, Jay Leslie 1948- WhoEmL 91
Himes, Jerry Bryant 1951- WhoEmL 91
Himes, Laurence Austin 1940- WhoAm 90
Himes, Norman S. 1943- St&PR 91
Himid, Lubaina 1954- BiDWomA
Himiko EncJap, WomWR
Himler, J. Renee BioIn 16
Himler, James B. 1944- St&PR 91
Himler, Peter B. ODwPR 91
Himler, Ronald BioIn 16
Himmel, Larry William 1953- St&PR 91
Himmel, Mitchell A. 1942- St&PR 91
Himmel, Patricia A. 1947- St&PR 91
Himmel, Richard C. 1920- WhoAm 90
Himmelbauer, Linda Dianne 1965- WhoAmW 91
Himmelberg, Charles John, III 1931- WhoAm 90
Himmelberg, Robert Franklin 1934- WhoAm 90
Himmelblau, David Mautner 1923- WhoAm 90
Himmelfarb, Gertrude 1922- WhoAm 90, WhoWrEP 89, WorAu 1980 [port]
Himmelfarb, John David 1946- WhoAm 90, WhoAmA 91
Himmelfarb, Milton 1918- WhoAm 90
Himmelhoch, Jonathan M BiDrAPA 89
Himmell, Samuel BioIn 16
Himmell, Samuel S. St&PR 91N
Himmelman, Gerald Leon 1934- St&PR 91
Himmelman, John 1959- AuBYP 90, BioIn 16
Himmelreich, David Baker 1954- WhoEmL 91
Himmelreich, Faith 1921- St&PR 91
Himmelright, Robert John, Jr. 1926- WhoAm 90
Himmelstein, Carole Shapiro WhoAmW 91
Himmer, Richard Edward 1945- St&PR 91
Himmler, Heinrich 1900-1945 BioIn 16, WorAlBi
Himms-Hagen, Jean Margaret 1933- WhoAm 90, WhoAmW 91
Himnechildis WomWR
Himot, Linda Jean BiDrAPA 89
Himoto, Teruo 1923- St&PR 91
Himsworth, Harold Percival 1905- WhoWor 91
Himsworth, Winston E. 1940- St&PR 91
Hinault, Bernard BioIn 16
Hinch, John De Courteille 1942- IntWWM 90
Hinchcliffe, Peter R. M. 1937- WhoWor 91
Hinchey, Keith 1933- St&PR 91
Hinchey, Patricia Ann 1952- WhoAmW 91
Hinchliffe, Gwendolyn Ann 1948- WhoAmW 91, WhoEmL 91
Hinchliffe, Joseph G BiDrAPA 89
Hinchliffe, Stephen F., Jr. 1933- St&PR 91
Hinchman, Bill 1883-1963 Ballpl 90
Hinchman, John Sanger 1931- St&PR 91
Hinchman, Kearn David BiDrAPA 89
Hinckle, Warren James, III 1938- WhoAm 90
Hinckley, Benjamin Barrett, Jr. 1913- St&PR 91
Hinckley, Charles Clarence 1933- St&PR 91
Hinckley, Clark Bryant 1947- WhoEmL 91
Hinckley, Dawn Margaret 1949- WhoAmW 91
Hinckley, Gordon B. 1910- WhoAm 90
Hinckley, Gregory K. 1946- St&PR 91
Hinckley, Gregory Keith 1946- WhoAm 90
Hinckley, Helen 1903- AuBYP 90
Hinckley, John, Jr. 1956- WorAlBi
Hinckley, Kenneth R. 1946- St&PR 91
Hinckley, Robert Craig 1947- St&PR 91
Hinckley, Robert H. 1891-1988 BioIn 16
Hincks, Elizabeth BiDEWW, FemiCLE
Hind al-Hirah WomWR
Hind, Dolores 1931- BioIn 16, ConAu 129
Hind, Harry William 1915- WhoAm 90
Hind, Joseph Edward, Jr. 1923- WhoAm 90
Hind, Robert James 1931- WhoWor 91
Hind O'Malley, Pamela 1923- IntWWM 90
Hindash, Osama Saad BiDrAPA 89
Hinde, Bobbie Torla 1946- WhoAmW 91
Hinde, Edward J., IV 1947- WhoEmL 91
Hinde, Robert A 1923- ConAu 30NR
Hinde, Robert Aubrey 1923- WhoWor 91
Hindelang, Robert Louis 1946- WhoEmL 91
Hindemith, Paul PenDiMP
Hindemith, Paul 1895-1963 BioIn 16, PenDiMP A, WorAlBi
Hinden, Stanley Jay 1927- WhoAm 90
Hindenburg, Paul von 1847-1934 BioIn 16, WorAlBi
Hinder, David 1950- St&PR 91
Hinderaker, Ivan 1916- WhoAm 90
Hinderas, Natalie 1937?-1987 DrBlPA 90
Hinderer, Walter Hermann 1934- WhoAm 90
Hinderhofer, Kathryn M. 1951- St&PR 91
Hinderliter, Marie A. 1952- St&PR 91
Hindermann, Mark John 1935- St&PR 91
Hindermann, Richard Lane 1923- St&PR 91
Hindert, Kristina Falk 1951- BiDrAPA 89
Hindery, Leo Joseph, Jr. 1947- WhoEmL 91
Hindes, Chuck 1942- WhoAmA 91
Hindin, Lee BiDrAPA 89
Hindin, Russell 1946- WhoEmL 91
Hinding, Andrea 1942- WhoAm 90
Hindle, Brooke 1918- WhoAm 90
Hindle, Elizabeth Christine 1952- WhoSSW 91
Hindle, Paula Alice 1952- WhoAmW 91
Hindle, Winston Russell, Jr. 1930- St&PR 91, WhoAm 90
Hindley, Edward Dal 1938- St&PR 91
Hindman, Don J. 1926- St&PR 91, WhoAm 90
Hindman, Earl ConTFT 8
Hindman, Harold 1917- St&PR 91
Hindman, Ira Eugene 1931- WhoE 91
Hindman, Joanne O'Rourke 1954- St&PR 91
Hindman, John William, III 1951- WhoE 91
Hindman, Lee H., IV 1949- St&PR 91
Hindman, Leslie Susan 1954- WhoAmW 91
Hindman, Mary Kathryn 1951- WhoEmL 91
Hindman, Randall Kevin 1952- WhoSSW 91
Hindman, Robert A. 1939- St&PR 91
Hindmarsh, Dale J BiDrAPA 89
Hindmarsh, F. Charles R. 1947- WhoEmL 91
Hindo, Walid Afram 1940- WhoAm 90, WhoWor 91
Hinds, Ann M. 1949- WhoAmW 91
Hinds, Barbara Marie 1949- WhoAmW 91
Hinds, Bo-Verner 1941- WhoWor 91
Hinds, Cathy BioIn 16
Hinds, Charles Franklin 1923- WhoAm 90
Hinds, Derald G. 1934- St&PR 91
Hinds, Douglas Wade 1954- WhoEmL 91
Hinds, Esther 1943- IntWWM 90
Hinds, Geoffrey William John 1950- IntWWM 90
Hinds, Jackson C. 1921- St&PR 91
Hinds, Jackson Ceivers, Jr. 1921- WhoAm 90
Hinds, Jean Phillips 1931- WhoSSW 91
Hinds, Joe M., Jr. 1937- St&PR 91
Hinds, John A. 1936- St&PR 91
Hinds, John G. 1941- St&PR 91
Hinds, Paula Anderson 1955- WhoEmL 91
Hinds, Randal Eugene 1951- WhoSSW 91
Hinds, Richard Clayton 1948- St&PR 91
Hinds, Sallie Ann 1930- WhoWrEP 89
Hinds, Thomas Sheldon 1943- WhoAm 90
Hinds, Warren Ted 1936- WhoE 91
Hindsley, Harold Eugene 1929- St&PR 91, WhoAm 90
Hindsley, Mark Hubert 1905- IntWWM 90
Hindus, Maurice Gerschon 1891-1969 BioIn 16
Hindus, Milton 1916- WhoAm 90, WhoWrEP 89
Hine, Alfred Blakelee 1915- AuBYP 90
Hine, Charles W. BioIn 16
Hine, Darlene Clark 1947- WhoAmW 91
Hine, Daryl BioIn 16
Hine, Daryl 1936- WhoAm 90, WorAu 1980 [port]
Hine, Donald F. BioIn 16
Hine, Edward, Jr. 1952- WhoSSW 91
Hine, Frederick R 1925- BiDrAPA 89
Hine, Gilbert Clarendon, Sr. 1917- WhoAm 90
Hine, John P. 1924- St&PR 91
Hine, Lewis Wickes 1874-1940 BioIn 16
Hine, Robert Van Norden, Jr. 1921- WhoAm 90
Hine, S. J. AuBYP 90

Hineman, Kalo Albert 1922- *WhoAm 90*
Hineman, Nancy Lee 1951- *WhoAmW 91, WhoWor 91*
Hinematioro *WomWR*
Hiner, Gladys Webber 1907- *WhoSSW 91*
Hiner, Leslie Davis 1957- *WhoAmW 91, WhoEmL 91*
Hiner, William Chase 1932- *WhoE 91*
Hinerfeld, Joshua Gordon 1961- *WhoE 91, WhoEmL 91*
Hinerfeld, Norman M. 1929- *St&PR 91*
Hinerfeld, Norman Martin 1929- *WhoAm 90*
Hinerfeld, Robert Elliot 1934- *WhoAm 90*
Hinerfeld, Ruth J. 1930- *WhoAm 90, WhoAmW 91*
Hines, Andrew Hampton, Jr. 1923- *St&PR 91, WhoAm 90*
Hines, Angus I., Jr. 1923- *St&PR 91*
Hines, Angus Irving, Jr. 1923- *WhoAm 90*
Hines, Anna Grossnickle 1946- *AuBYP 90, BioIn 16*
Hines, Anthony Loring 1941- *WhoAm 90*
Hines, Barbara Hohman *ODwPR 91*
Hines, Christa Louise 1957- *BiDrAPA 89*
Hines, Daisy Marie 1913- *WhoAmW 91*
Hines, Danny Ray 1947- *WhoSSW 91*
Hines, Donald William 1935- *St&PR 91*
Hines, Duncan 1880-1959 *WorAlBi*
Hines, Earl 1903-1983 *OxCPMus*
Hines, Earl 1905-1983 *BioIn 16, DrBlPA 90, WorAlBi*
Hines, Edward Francis, Jr. 1945- *WhoAm 90*
Hines, Glenn Morris 1950- *WhoE 91*
Hines, Gregory 1946- *DrBlPA 90, WorAlBi*
Hines, Gregory Oliver 1946- *WhoAm 90*
Hines, Hugh Francis 1932- *WhoAm 90*
Hines, Hugh Van 1958- *WhoSSW 91*
Hines, James Robert 1937- *IntWWM 90*
Hines, James Rodger 1923- *WhoAm 90*
Hines, James William 1950- *WhoEmL 91*
Hines, Jerome 1921- *ConAu 130, IntWWM 90, PenDiMP, WorAlBi*
Hines, Jesse Knock 1829-1889 *AmLegL*
Hines, Jessica 1958- *WhoAmA 91*
Hines, John H. 1925- *St&PR 91*
Hines, John M *WhoAmA 91N*
Hines, Jonathan Eugene 1952- *WhoEmL 91*
Hines, Judith Dunbar 1947- *WhoAmW 91*
Hines, Lawrence Gregory 1915- *WhoAm 90*
Hines, Linda Marie 1940- *WhoAmW 91*
Hines, Marion Ernest 1918- *WhoAm 90*
Hines, Marion Louise 1920- *WhoAmW 91*
Hines, Marshall 1923- *St&PR 91*
Hines, Mary Jane 1934- *WhoAmW 91*
Hines, Maurice *BioIn 16*
Hines, Maurice 1944- *DrBlPA 90*
Hines, Merrill Odom 1909- *WhoAm 90, WhoWor 91*
Hines, Michael Stephen 1946- *WhoEmL 91*
Hines, N. William 1936- *WhoAm 90*
Hines, Norris Lee 1929- *St&PR 91*
Hines, Patricia 1947- *WhoAmW 91, WhoE 91*
Hines, Paul 1852-1935 *Ballpl 90*
Hines, Paul Garry 1937- *WhoAm 90*
Hines, Robert Stephan 1926- *IntWWM 90*
Hines, Ruth Ann 1958- *WhoAmW 91*
Hines, Samuel G. *WhoAm 90*
Hines, Sherman Edwards, Jr. 1940- *St&PR 91*
Hines, Vincent J. 1912-1990 *BioIn 16*
Hines, Voncile 1945- *WhoAmW 91*
Hines, Walter J. 1947- *St&PR 91*
Hines, Wilbur Eugene 1948- *WhoAm 90*
Hines, William Eugene 1914- *WhoAm 90*
Hines, Yvonne Maria 1953- *WhoAmW 91*
Hines, Zoe Ann 1949- *St&PR 91*
Hinesley, R Kent 1936- *BiDrAPA 89*
Hiney, Eileen 1952- *St&PR 91*
Hinghofer-Szalkay, Helmut G. 1948- *WhoWor 91*
Hingle, Pat 1923- *ConTFT 8 [port], WorAlBi*
Hingle, Pat 1924- *WhoAm 90*
Hingoranee, Ramesh Ram 1960- *WhoEmL 91*
Hingsbergen, John Edward 1950- *WhoEmL 91*
Hingson, Ralph W. 1948- *WhoAm 90*
Hingson, Robert Andrew 1913- *WhoAm 90, WhoWor 91*
Hingst, Lawrence W. 1940- *St&PR 91*
Hingston, Ann Guthrie 1946- *WhoEmL 91*
Hingtgen, Joseph Nicholas 1936- *WhoAm 90*
Hinich, Melvin Jay 1939- *WhoAm 90*
Hinkaty, Charles J. 1950- *St&PR 91*
Hinkaty, Charles John 1950- *WhoAm 90, WhoE 91*
Hinke, Karl H. *NewYTBS 90*
Hinkel, Richard Robert 1935- *St&PR 91*
Hinkelman, Kenneth William 1940- *WhoAm 90*
Hinkelman, Ruth A. 1949- *St&PR 91*
Hinkelman, Ruth Amidon 1949- *WhoAmW 91*
Hinken, Johann Heyen 1946- *WhoWor 91*
Hinkens, Andrew George 1955- *BiDrAPA 89*
Hinkfuss, Rosemary 1931- *WhoAmW 91*
Hinkhouse, Forest Melick 1925- *WhoAmA 91*
Hinkins, Virginia *AuBYP 90*
Hinkle, Anthony Brooks 1950- *WhoEmL 91*
Hinkle, B. J. 1922- *WhoAm 90*
Hinkle, Barbara Carolina 1951- *WhoSSW 91*
Hinkle, Barton Leslie 1925- *WhoAm 90*
Hinkle, Betty Ruth 1930- *WhoAmW 91*
Hinkle, Charles Leonard 1960- *WhoEmL 91*
Hinkle, Clarence 1880-1960 *WhoAmA 91N*
Hinkle, Clarke *BioIn 16*
Hinkle, David Olin *BiDrAPA 89*
Hinkle, Donald Earl 1952- *St&PR 91, WhoEmL 91*
Hinkle, James Donald 1935- *BiDrAPA 89*
Hinkle, James Robert, II 1948- *WhoEmL 91*
Hinkle, John M. 1948- *St&PR 91*
Hinkle, Larry W. 1946- *St&PR 91*
Hinkle, Michael Glenn 1947- *St&PR 91*
Hinkle, Muriel Ruth Nelson 1929- *WhoAm 90, WhoAmW 91*
Hinkle, Philip E *BiDrAPA 89*
Hinkle, Richard Paul 1946- *WhoWrEP 89*
Hinkle, Robert Alan 1944- *St&PR 91*
Hinkle, Robert Lewis 1951- *WhoEmL 91*
Hinkle, Talmadge Gray 1924- *St&PR 91*
Hinkle, Thomas Clark 1876-1949 *AuBYP 90*
Hinkle, Vernon 1935- *ConAu 30NR*
Hinkley, Carol Edward 1929- *St&PR 91*
Hinkley, Everett David, Jr. 1936- *WhoAm 90*
Hinklin, Alan Dee 1937- *WhoAm 90*
Hinko, Edward N *BiDrAPA 89*
Hinkson, Katharine Tynan 1861-1931 *BioIn 16*
Hinlopen, Francina 1908- *IntWWM 90*
Hinman, Brian L. 1961- *St&PR 91*
Hinman, Charles B 1932- *WhoAm 90, WhoAmA 91*
Hinman, David N. 1950- *St&PR 91*
Hinman, Elaine Marie 1960- *WhoAmW 91, WhoWor 91*
Hinman, Frank, Jr. 1915- *WhoAm 90*
Hinman, George Lyon 1905- *WhoAm 90*
Hinman, Myra Mahlow 1926- *WhoAmW 91, WhoWor 91*
Hinman, Ralph Moe, III 1950- *WhoEmL 91*
Hinman, Richard Leslie 1927- *WhoAm 90*
Hinnah, Daniel Bryon 1946- *St&PR 91*
Hinnant, Charles Asbell 1950- *WhoE 91*
Hinnant, Clarence Henry, III 1938- *WhoSSW 91*
Hinnant, Hilari Anne 1953- *WhoAmW 91*
Hinnant, Kathryn *BioIn 16*
Hinnant, Skip 1940- *WhoE 91*
Hinnenkamp, Dirk Schleicher 1956- *WhoEmL 91*
Hinojos, Alfred 1941- *WhoHisp 91*
Hinojosa, Carlos M. 1944- *WhoHisp 91*
Hinojosa, David Andres 1959- *WhoHisp 91*
Hinojosa, Gilberto Miguel 1942- *WhoHisp 91*
Hinojosa, Hector Oscar 1950- *WhoHisp 91*
Hinojosa, Jesus Hector 1935- *WhoHisp 91*
Hinojosa, Juan 1946- *WhoHisp 91*
Hinojosa, Liborio *WhoHisp 91*
Hinojosa, R. Marie 1940- *WhoHisp 91*
Hinojosa, Raul 1928- *WhoAm 90*
Hinojosa, Ricardo H. 1950- *WhoHisp 91*
Hinojosa, Rolando 1929- *BioIn 16, ConAu 131, HispWr 90*
Hinojosa, Santiago Noel 1943- *WhoAm 90*
Hinojosa Antezana, Mario Raul 1930- *WhoWor 91*
Hinojosa-S., Rolando R. *ConAu 131, HispWr 90*
Hinojosa-Smith, R. Rolando 1929- *WhoHisp 91*
Hinojosa-Smith, Roland 1929- *WhoAm 90*
Hinojosa-Smith, Rolando *ConAu 131, HispWr 90*
Hinrichs, Gina Burns 1954- *WhoEmL 91*
Hinrichs, Horst 1933- *St&PR 91*
Hinrichsen, Georg 1941- *WhoWor 91*
Hinrichsen, Klaus Volquardt 1927- *WhoWor 91*
Hinsch, Gertrude Wilma 1932- *WhoAmW 91*
Hinsch, Kathryn *ODwPR 91*
Hinsch, Thomas Robert 1968- *WhoEmL 91*
Hinsch, Wilhelm Albert 1945- *WhoWor 91*
Hinsdill, Ronald Dwight 1933- *WhoAm 90*
Hinshaw, Carroll Elton 1936- *WhoSSW 91*
Hinshaw, Donald Gray 1934- *IntWWM 90, WhoSSW 91*
Hinshaw, Edward Banks 1940- *WhoAm 90*
Hinshaw, Ernest T., Jr. 1928- *St&PR 91*
Hinshaw, Ernest Theodore, Jr. 1928- *WhoAm 90*
Hinshaw, Gaylord Carlyle 1933- *St&PR 91*
Hinshaw, Horton Corwin 1902- *WhoAm 90, WhoWor 91*
Hinshaw, Juanita H. 1945- *St&PR 91*
Hinshaw, Lerner Brady 1921- *WhoAm 90*
Hinshaw, Mark Waldo 1938- *BiDrAPA 89*
Hinshaw, Randall 1915- *WhoAm 90*
Hinshaw, Virgil Goodman, Jr. 1919- *WhoAm 90*
Hinshaw, W. Eric 1949- *St&PR 91*
Hinshelwood, Cyril N. 1897-1967 *WorAlBi*
Hinske, Gerd 1932- *St&PR 91*
Hinske, Gerd Friedrich Heinrich 1932- *WhoWor 91*
Hinsley-Loeber, Charles Ernest 1962- *WhoWrEP 89*
Hinsman, David Carl 1943- *BiDrAPA 89*
Hinson, Catherine Brewer 1951- *WhoSSW 91*
Hinson, David *BioIn 16*
Hinson, David R. *WhoAm 90*
Hinson, David R. 1933- *St&PR 91*
Hinson, Everette C. 1929- *St&PR 91*
Hinson, H. Douglas 1960- *WhoEmL 91*
Hinson, Howard Houston 1913- *WhoAm 90, WhoWor 91*
Hinson, Jack Allsbrook 1944- *WhoSSW 91*
Hinson, James *WhoSSW 91*
Hinson, James 1924- *St&PR 91*
Hinson, James Lyle 1955- *BiDrAPA 89*
Hinson, Jerry Lee 1951- *WhoWrEP 89*
Hinson, John Morgan 1945- *St&PR 91*
Hinson, Laura K. 1961- *St&PR 91*
Hinson, Robert Wayne 1949- *WhoSSW 91*
Hinson, Robert William 1944- *WhoAm 90, WhoE 91*
Hinson, Robin Ledbetter 1931- *St&PR 91*
Hinson, Sharon Foster *BiDrAPA 89*
Hinson, Tom Everett 1944- *WhoAmA 91*
Hinson, Warren Anthony *BiDrAPA 89*
Hinson, William H. 1915- *St&PR 91*
Hinterhaeuser, Herman 1941- *St&PR 91*
Hinterhaeuser, Hermann 1941- *WhoE 91*
Hintermann, Eric G. 1936- *WhoWor 91*
Hintikka, Harri Juhani 1937- *WhoWor 91*
Hintikka, Jaakko 1929- *WhoAm 90*
Hintlian, James T. 1924- *St&PR 91*
Hinton, C. Bruce *St&PR 91*
Hinton, C. Bruce 1936- *WhoAm 90*
Hinton, Charles 1948- *WhoSSW 91*
Hinton, Charles Louis 1869-1950 *WhoAmA 91N*
Hinton, Christopher 1901-1983 *DcNaB 1981, WorAlBi*
Hinton, Christopher Jerrod 1961- *WhoAm 90*
Hinton, Chuck 1934- *Ballpl 90*
Hinton, Deane R. 1923- *BioIn 16*
Hinton, Deane Roesch 1923- *WhoAm 90, WhoWor 91*
Hinton, Howard W. 1946- *St&PR 91*
Hinton, Jennie Louise *BiDrAPA 89*
Hinton, Laura Geddes 1961- *WhoSSW 91*
Hinton, Leslie Frank 1944- *WhoAm 90*
Hinton, Michael R. 1954- *St&PR 91*
Hinton, Patrick *ODwPR 91*
Hinton, Rich 1947- *Ballpl 90*
Hinton, S. E. *BioIn 16*
Hinton, S. E. 1948- *ChlLR 23 [port]*
Hinton, S. E. 1950- *AuBYP 90*
Hinton, S E 1950- *ConAu 32NR, MajTwCW*
Hinton, S. E. 1950- *WorAlBi*
Hinton, Susan Eloise 1948- *WhoAmW 91*
Hinton, Troy *BioIn 16*
Hinton, W Ladson, III 1934- *BiDrAPA 89*
Hinton, Walter Ladson, IV 1958- *BiDrAPA 89*
Hinton, Warren S. 1921- *WhoAm 90*
Hinton, William Harwood 1921- *WhoAm 90*
Hintz, Bernd Jurgen 1942- *WhoAm 90*
Hintz, Charles Bradley 1949- *WhoE 91*
Hintz, D Charles *BiDrAPA 89*
Hintz, Gerald Ramon 1933- *St&PR 91*
Hintz, Luther Maron 1945- *WhoEmL 91*
Hintz, Martin 1945- *BioIn 16, ConAu 30NR*
Hintz, Mel 1932- *WhoE 91*
Hintz, Monica E. 1947- *WhoAmW 91*
Hintz, Peter Edward 1960- *WhoEmL 91*
Hintz, Robert L. 1930- *St&PR 91*
Hintz, Robert Louis 1930- *WhoAm 90, WhoSSW 91*
Hintz, Russell Berg 1944- *St&PR 91*
Hintz, Sonya Diane *BiDrAPA 89*
Hintz, Thomas F. 1945- *St&PR 91*
Hintz, Walter Gene 1945- *St&PR 91*
Hintz, Walter Richard 1937- *St&PR 91*
Hintze, Barry John 1956- *St&PR 91*
Hintze, Courtland T. 1945- *St&PR 91*
Hintze, Frank D. 1919- *St&PR 91*
Hinueber, Mark Arthur 1952- *WhoEmL 91*
Hinz, Carl Frederick, Jr. 1927- *WhoAm 90*
Hinz, James Thomas 1926- *St&PR 91*
Hinz, Mittie Dean 1941- *WhoAmW 91*
Hinz, Walter Fred 1946- *St&PR 91*
Hios, Theo 1908- *WhoAmA 91*
Hiott, Yvonne *ODwPR 91*
Hipchen, Donald E. 1932- *St&PR 91*
Hipkin, Leslie John 1935- *WhoWor 91*
Hipolito, Abel *BiDrAPA 89*
Hipp, Catherine *ConDes 90*
Hipp, Francis Moffett 1911- *St&PR 91, WhoAm 90, WhoSSW 91*
Hipp, Frederick R. 1950- *St&PR 91*
Hipp, James William 1934- *IntWWM 90*
Hipp, Urban 1913- *St&PR 91*
Hipp, W. Hayne 1940- *St&PR 91*
Hipp, William Hayne 1940- *WhoAm 90, WhoSSW 91*
Hipparchus 190?BC-120?BC *WorAlBi*
Hippe, Norman Douglas 1939- *St&PR 91*
Hippel, Theodor Gottlieb von 1741-1796 *DcLB 97 [port]*
Hippel, Ursula Von *AuBYP 90*
Hippert, Linda Buchek 1954- *WhoE 91*
Hippisley Coxe, Antony 1912-1988 *AnObit 1988*
Hippius, Hanns *BiDrAPA 89*
Hippius, Zinaida *EncCoWW*
Hipple, James Blackman 1934- *St&PR 91, WhoAm 90*
Hipple, Walter John 1921- *WhoAm 90*
Hippner, Richard 1938- *St&PR 91*
Hippocrates *BioIn 16*
Hippocrates 460BC-370?BC *WorAlBi*
Hippopotamus, Eugene H. *AuBYP 90*
Hipps, Alan Stanley 1952- *WhoEmL 91*
Hipps, J. Robert 1939- *St&PR 91*
Hipps, Larry Clay 1953- *WhoEmL 91*
Hipps, Michael Francis 1950- *WhoEmL 91*
Hipshman, Lawrence *BiDrAPA 89*
Hipshman, May 1919- *AuBYP 90*
Hipsley, Jane Frances 1926- *WhoAmW 91*
Hiraga, Masaharu 1939- *WhoWor 91*
Hirahara, Patti 1955- *WhoWor 91*
Hirai, Denitsu 1943- *WhoWor 91*
Hirai, Hajime *ODwPR 91*
Hirai, Kiyotaka 1955- *St&PR 91*
Hiraishi, Nagahisa 1925- *WhoWor 91*
Hiraizumi, Wataru 1929- *BioIn 16*
Hiraki, Schunichi 1941- *BioIn 16*
Hiraki, Tokato 1950- *WhoWor 91*
Hiramoto, Koichiro 1934- *St&PR 91*
Hiranand, Kishore 1967- *WhoWor 91*
Hiranandani, Hiro R. 1938- *St&PR 91*
Hiranandani, Hiro Rewachand 1938- *WhoAm 90*
Hirani, Bansilal M 1933- *BiDrAPA 89*
Hirano, Asao 1926- *WhoAm 90*
Hirano, June Yamada 1943- *WhoAmW 91*
Hirano, Ken-ichi 1927- *WhoWor 91*
Hirano, Masami 1936- *WhoWor 91*
Hirano, Steven S. 1946- *St&PR 91*
Hirano, Takakuni 1930- *WhoWor 91*
Hiranuma Kiichiro 1867-1952 *EncJap*
Hirao, Yasuo 1930- *WhoWor 91*
Hiraoka, Chiyuki 1930- *WhoWor 91*
Hiraoka, Kimitake 1925-1970 *MajTwCW*
Hirasawa, Shigeru 1920- *IntWWM 90*
Hirata, Hironori 1948- *WhoWor 91*
Hirata, Naohiko *BioIn 16*
Hiratsuka Raicho *EncJap*
Hiratsuka, Toshio 1936- *St&PR 91*
Hirayama, Chisato 1923- *WhoWor 91*
Hirbe, Richard Andrew, Jr. 1952- *WhoEmL 91*
Hird, Sydelle Druckman 1925- *WhoE 91*
Hire, R.C. 1928- *St&PR 91*
Hire, Richard O 1945- *BiDrAPA 89*
Hirejo zu Hortowey, Anovo *EncCoWW*
Hires, Peter Van Zanthier 1923- *WhoE 91*
Hires, Thomas Louis, Sr. 1930- *WhoAm 90*
Hires, William Leland 1918- *WhoAm 90, WhoE 91*
Hirigoyen, Hector 1947- *WhoEmL 91, WhoSSW 91*
Hirko, Joseph M. 1956- *St&PR 91*
Hirl, J. Roger 1931- *St&PR 91*
Hirman, Arland E. 1941- *St&PR 91*
Hirn, Doris Dreyer 1933- *WhoAmW 91*
Hiro, Crown Prince *EncJap*
Hiro, Dilip *ConAu 32NR*
Hirohito 1901-1989 *WorAlBi*
Hirohito, Emperor 1901-1989 *AnObit 1989, EncJap*
Hirohito, Emperor of Japan 1901-1989 *BioIn 16*
Hiromoto, Toshiro 1952- *WhoWor 91*
Hiron, Jean-Claude Jules 1943- *WhoWor 91*
Hirondelle, Anne E 1966- *WhoAmA 91*
Hironimus, Sharon Lynn 1936- *WhoAmW 91*
Hirono, Mazie Keiko 1947- *WhoAmW 91*
Hirose, Akira 1941- *WhoAm 90*

Hirose, Sadao 1918- *BiDrAPA 89*
Hirose, Teruo Terry 1926- *WhoAm 90*
Hiroshige 1797-1858 *EncJap*
Hiroshima *NewAgMG*
Hiroshima, Koji Edmund 1924- *WhoAm 90*
Hirota, Jitsuya 1924- *WhoWor 91*
Hirotani, Atsushi 1934- *WhoWor 91*
Hirsbrunner, Theo 1931- *IntWWM 90*
Hirsch, Alan 1937- *ODwPR 91*
Hirsch, Alan Richard *BiDrAPA 89*
Hirsch, Alex 1924- *St&PR 91*
Hirsch, Allen Vernon 1953- *St&PR 91, WhoAm 90*
Hirsch, Anita 1947- *BiDrAPA 89*
Hirsch, Arlene Sharon 1951- *WhoEmL 91*
Hirsch, Arthur S. 1908-1989 *BioIn 16*
Hirsch, Barry 1933- *St&PR 91, WhoAm 90*
Hirsch, Bernard D. 1957- *WhoEmL 91*
Hirsch, Bruce Wangman 1946- *WhoEmL 91*
Hirsch, Carl E. 1946- *WhoAm 90*
Hirsch, Carl Herbert 1934- *St&PR 91, WhoAm 90*
Hirsch, Charles Bronislaw 1919- *WhoAm 90*
Hirsch, Charles J 1937- *BiDrAPA 89*
Hirsch, Charlotte Teller *EarBlAP*
Hirsch, Daniel *BioIn 16*
Hirsch, Daniel 1940- *St&PR 91, WhoE 91*
Hirsch, David M. 1944- *St&PR 91*
Hirsch, Deborah A. *BioIn 16*
Hirsch, Donald Earl 1924- *WhoSSW 91*
Hirsch, Dorothy T. 1919- *St&PR 91*
Hirsch, E. D., Jr. 1928- *MajTwCW*
Hirsch, E. Franklin 1931- *St&PR 91*
Hirsch, Edward 1950- *WhoWrEP 89*
Hirsch, Edward Mark 1950- *WhoAm 90, WhoSSW 91*
Hirsch, Edwin Waixel 1904- *St&PR 91*
Hirsch, Elizabeth *BioIn 16*
Hirsch, Emil Gustav 1851-1923 *BioIn 16*
Hirsch, Eric Donald *BioIn 16*
Hirsch, Eric Donald, Jr. 1928- *WhoAm 90*
Hirsch, Gary D. *BioIn 16*
Hirsch, George Aaron 1934- *WhoAm 90, WhoWrEP 89*
Hirsch, Gerson T. *BioIn 16*
Hirsch, Gilah Yelin 1944- *WhoAmA 91*
Hirsch, Glenn David *BiDrAPA 89*
Hirsch, Glenn Stuart *BiDrAPA 89*
Hirsch, Glenn Stuart 1954- *WhoE 91*
Hirsch, Gregory Lee 1952- *WhoEmL 91*
Hirsch, H.E. 1933- *St&PR 91*
Hirsch, Hans Joachim 1929- *WhoWor 91*
Hirsch, Harold S. *NewYTBS 90*
Hirsch, Harold S. 1907- *St&PR 91*
Hirsch, Harold Seller 1907- *WhoAm 90*
Hirsch, Harvey S *BiDrAPA 89*
Hirsch, Harvey Stuart 1950- *WhoE 91*
Hirsch, Henry David 1943- *WhoSSW 91*
Hirsch, Horst Eberhard 1933- *WhoAm 90*
Hirsch, Hortense *NewYTBS 90 [port]*
Hirsch, Howard Davis *WhoAm 90*
Hirsch, Hyman *BioIn 16*
Hirsch, Irma Lou Kolterman 1934- *WhoAmW 91*
Hirsch, James L. 1952- *St&PR 91*
Hirsch, Jay G 1930- *BiDrAPA 89, WhoAm 90*
Hirsch, Jeffrey Allan 1950- *WhoEmL 91*
Hirsch, John *BioIn 16*
Hirsch, John 1930-1989 *AnObit 1989, OxCCanT*
Hirsch, Jon H. 1955- *St&PR 91*
Hirsch, Joseph 1910-1981 *WhoAmA 91N*
Hirsch, Judd 1935- *BioIn 16, WhoAm 90, WorAlBi*
Hirsch, Judith Ilberman *BiDrAPA 89*
Hirsch, June Schaut 1925- *WhoAmW 91*
Hirsch, Karen 1941- *SmATA 61 [port]*
Hirsch, Kenneth Harris 1945- *WhoEmL 91*
Hirsch, Larry Joseph 1938- *WhoE 91*
Hirsch, Laurence E. 1945- *St&PR 91, WhoAm 90, WhoSSW 91*
Hirsch, Lawrence Leonard 1922- *WhoAm 90*
Hirsch, Leon C. 1927- *St&PR 91*
Hirsch, Leon Charles 1927- *WhoAm 90*
Hirsch, Leonard 1902- *IntWWM 90*
Hirsch, Lore *BiDrAPA 89*
Hirsch, Loren Phillip 1958- *WhoEmL 91*
Hirsch, Louis A. 1887-1924 *OxCPMus*
Hirsch, Mark D. 1910-1989 *BioIn 16*
Hirsch, Mark Lee 1954- *WhoEmL 91*
Hirsch, Martin S 1944- *BiDrAPA 89*
Hirsch, Mary Tone 1944- *WhoWrEP 89*
Hirsch, Melinda S *BiDrAPA 89*
Hirsch, Melvin L. 1923- *St&PR 91, WhoE 91*
Hirsch, Michael *BioIn 16*
Hirsch, Michael Alan 1940- *BiDrAPA 89*
Hirsch, Michael D. 1945- *St&PR 91*
Hirsch, Michelle Linda 1947- *BiDrAPA 89*
Hirsch, Morris William 1933- *WhoAm 90*
Hirsch, Nathan *BiDrAPA 89*
Hirsch, Neil S. 1947- *St&PR 91, WhoAm 90*
Hirsch, Norman Isak 1948- *BiDrAPA 89*
Hirsch, Otto 1885-1941 *BioIn 16*
Hirsch, Paul J. 1937- *WhoE 91*
Hirsch, Paula Jean 1944- *WhoAmW 91*
Hirsch, Peter *ODwPR 91*
Hirsch, Peter B 1949- *BiDrAPA 89*
Hirsch, Philip Francis 1925- *WhoAm 90*
Hirsch, Raymond Robert 1936- *WhoAm 90*
Hirsch, Richard 1941- *St&PR 91*
Hirsch, Richard Arthur 1925- *WhoE 91*
Hirsch, Richard B. 1921- *St&PR 91*
Hirsch, Richard George 1926- *WhoAm 90*
Hirsch, Robert *BiDrAPA 89*
Hirsch, Robert Allen 1946- *WhoEmL 91*
Hirsch, Robert Bruce 1926- *WhoAm 90*
Hirsch, Robert F. 1933- *St&PR 91*
Hirsch, Robert Louis 1935- *WhoAm 90*
Hirsch, Robert W. 1939- *St&PR 91, WhoAm 90*
Hirsch, Robert W., Jr. 1947- *St&PR 91*
Hirsch, Robert William 1925- *WhoAm 90*
Hirsch, Roseann Conte 1941- *WhoAm 90*
Hirsch, S. Carl 1913- *AuBYP 90*
Hirsch, Samson Raphael 1808-1888 *BioIn 16*
Hirsch, Seev 1931- *WhoWor 91*
Hirsch, Sharon Louise *BiDrAPA 89*
Hirsch, Shelly *BioIn 16*
Hirsch, Sidney Mttron *BioIn 16*
Hirsch, Solomon 1926- *BiDrAPA 89*
Hirsch, Stefan 1899-1964 *WhoAmA 91N*
Hirsch, Stephen A 1930- *BiDrAPA 89*
Hirsch, Steven J 1936- *BiDrAPA 89*
Hirsch, Steven R 1937- *ConAu 32NR*
Hirsch, Steven Richard *BiDrAPA 89*
Hirsch, Stuart David 1938- *BiDrAPA 89*
Hirsch, Ully *BioIn 16*
Hirsch, Walter 1917- *WhoWor 91*
Hirsch, Werner Zvi 1920- *WhoAm 90*
Hirsch-Fikejs, Judith Ann 1939- *WhoAmW 91*
Hirschberg, Arthur A. 1927- *St&PR 91*
Hirschberg, Gary Edward 1939- *WhoWor 91*
Hirschberg, Gerald A. 1945- *St&PR 91*
Hirschberg, Gunter 1920-1989 *BioIn 16*
Hirschberg, J Cotter 1915- *BiDrAPA 89*
Hirschberg, John H 1925- *BiDrAPA 89*
Hirschberg, Joseph Gustav 1921- *WhoAm 90*
Hirschberg, Mark Gerald 1958- *St&PR 91*
Hirschberg, Stephen Edwin 1947- *WhoEmL 91*
Hirschberg, Thomas Vincent 1924- *St&PR 91*
Hirschberg, Vera Hilda 1929- *WhoAmW 91*
Hirschberg, Walter J. 1922- *St&PR 91*
Hirschburg, Peter Lofton 1922- *St&PR 91*
Hirschel, Lieselotte Anne 1926- *WhoWrEP 89*
Hirschenberger, Richard Henry 1950- *WhoEmL 91*
Hirschenfang, Gail 1954- *WhoAmW 91*
Hirschey, Laura Lynne 1965- *WhoE 91*
Hirschfeld, Abraham Jacob 1919- *WhoE 91*
Hirschfeld, Albert 1903- *WhoAm 90, WhoAmA 91, WhoE 91*
Hirschfeld, Alexander Herzog 1914-1988 *BioIn 16*
Hirschfeld, Arlene F. 1944- *WhoAmW 91*
Hirschfeld, Burt 1923- *AuBYP 90*
Hirschfeld, Eckhard Friedrich 1938- *WhoWor 91*
Hirschfeld, Gerald Joseph 1921- *WhoAm 90*
Hirschfeld, I. Alan *St&PR 91*
Hirschfeld, Linda Evelyn 1947- *WhoAmW 91*
Hirschfeld, Michael 1950- *WhoEmL 91*
Hirschfeld, Robert M A 1943- *BiDrAPA 89*
Hirschfeld, Ronald Colman 1930- *WhoAm 90*
Hirschfeld, Sue Ellen 1941- *WhoAmW 91*
Hirschfeld, Walter *BiDrAPA 89*
Hirschfelder, Joseph O 1911-1990 *CurBio 90N*
Hirschfelder, Joseph Oakland *NewYTBS 90*
Hirschfelder, Joseph Oakland 1911-1990 *BioIn 16, ConAu 131*
Hirschfield, Robert S. 1928- *WhoAm 90*
Hirschhausen, Christian Roland von 1964- *WhoWor 91*
Hirschhorn, Austin 1936- *WhoAm 90*
Hirschhorn, Eric Leonard 1946- *WhoE 91, WhoEmL 91*
Hirschhorn, Fred, Jr. 1919- *St&PR 91*
Hirschhorn, Joseph H 1899-1981 *WhoAmA 91N*
Hirschhorn, Joyce Donen 1926- *WhoAmW 91*
Hirschhorn, Kurt 1926- *WhoAm 90*
Hirschhorn, Laurence H. 1936- *St&PR 91*
Hirschhorn, Richard S. 1935- *St&PR 91*
Hirschhorn, Wendy *ODwPR 91*
Hirschi, Ron *BioIn 16*
Hirschkind, Roger Allen 1938- *St&PR 91*
Hirschklau, Morton 1932- *WhoE 91*
Hirschland, Paul M. *BioIn 16*
Hirschle, Ulrich Wolfgang 1952- *WhoWor 91*
Hirschler, Edward S. 1914- *St&PR 91*
Hirschler, Philip 1955- *WhoE 91*
Hirschler, Rene 1905-1944 *BioIn 16*
Hirschman, Bernardo 1932- *BiDrAPA 89*
Hirschman, Frank Frederick 1936- *St&PR 91*
Hirschman, Howard 1927- *St&PR 91*
Hirschman, Shalom Zarach 1936- *WhoAm 90*
Hirschmann, Franz Gottfried 1945- *WhoEmL 91, WhoWor 91*
Hirschmann, Ira Arthur 1901-1989 *BioIn 16*
Hirschmann, Ralph Franz 1922- *WhoAm 90*
Hirschorn, Martin 1921- *St&PR 91*
Hirschovits-Gerz, Fred 1952- *WhoEmL 91*
Hirschowitz, Basil Isaac 1925- *WhoAm 90*
Hirschowitz, Jack 1945- *BiDrAPA 89*
Hirschson, Niel 1934- *WhoWor 91*
Hirschvogel, Augustin 1503-1553 *PenDiDA 89*
Hirsekorn, Robert Dean 1949- *St&PR 91*
Hirsh, Albert 1915- *IntWWM 90*
Hirsh, Allan Thurman, Jr. 1920- *WhoAm 90*
Hirsh, Annette Marie 1921- *WhoAmA 91*
Hirsh, Connie Kessler *BiDrAPA 89*
Hirsh, Cynthia O'Connor 1943- *WhoAmW 91*
Hirsh, Ethan 1947- *ODwPR 91, WhoEmL 91*
Hirsh, Ira Jean 1922- *WhoAm 90*
Hirsh, Leonard Steven 1951- *WhoEmL 91*
Hirsh, Marilyn 1944- *AuBYP 90*
Hirsh, Marilyn 1944-1988 *BioIn 16*
Hirsh, Norman Barry 1935- *WhoAm 90, WhoWor 91*
Hirsh, Philip Reid 1938- *BiDrAPA 89*
Hirsh, Richard Allan 1953- *WhoE 91*
Hirsh, Stephanie Abraham 1954- *WhoSSW 91*
Hirsh, Sylvia *St&PR 91*
Hirsh-Pasek, Kathryn Ann 1953- *WhoAmW 91*
Hirshberg, Al 1910-1973 *Ballpl 90*
Hirshberg, Albert Simon 1909-1973 *AuBYP 90*
Hirshberg, Marcie Sue 1959- *WhoAmW 91*
Hirshen, Sanford 1935- *WhoAm 90*
Hirshfield, Daniel S. 1942- *ODwPR 91*
Hirshfield, Jane 1953- *WhoWrEP 89*
Hirshfield, Jay Leonard 1931- *WhoAm 90*
Hirshfield, Morris 1872-1946 *MusmAFA*
Hirshfield, Pearl *WhoAmA 91*
Hirshfield, Stuart 1941- *WhoE 91*
Hirshhorn, Joseph H. 1899-1981 *WorAlBi*
Hirshman, Harold Carl 1945- *WhoAm 90*
Hirshman, Karl Jonathan 1936- *St&PR 91*
Hirshman, Melvin 1931- *WhoE 91*
Hirshson, Stanley Philip 1928- *WhoAm 90*
Hirson, Estelle *WhoAmW 91*
Hirssig, James Earl 1926- *St&PR 91*
Hirst, Heston Stillings 1915- *WhoAm 90*
Hirst, John Malcolm 1921- *BioIn 16*
Hirst, Julian Fravel 1921- *WhoAm 90*
Hirst, Lawrence Martin 1949- *St&PR 91*
Hirst, Lee 1922- *ODwPR 91*
Hirst, Linda 1950- *IntWWM 90*
Hirst, Marie R. 1922- *ODwPR 91*
Hirst, Robert Lynn 1947- *WhoEmL 91*
Hirst, Ronald Keene 1952- *WhoEmL 91*
Hirst, Wilma Elizabeth *WhoAmW 91, WhoWor 91*
Hirt, Al 1922- *ConMus 5 [port], WorAlBi*
Hirt, Evelyn Helen 1952- *WhoEmL 91*
Hirt, Howard 1924-1987 *ConAu 131*
Hirt, Norman B *BiDrAPA 89*
Hirte, Klaus 1937- *IntWWM 90*
Hirth, John Price 1930- *WhoAm 90*
Hirtle, Robert David 1932- *St&PR 91*
Hirvela, Harold J. 1932- *St&PR 91*
Hirvonen, Leo Leopold 1924- *WhoWor 91*
Hiryok, Kathryn Ann 1942- *WhoAmW 91*
Hirzebruch, Friedrich 1927- *BioIn 16*
Hirzebruch, Friedrich Ernst Peter 1927- *WhoWor 91*
Hirzel, Nancy Jeanne 1948- *WhoEmL 91*
Hisamatsu Shin'ichi 1898-1976 *EncJap*
Hisashige, Tadao 1936- *WhoWor 91*
Hiscock, Bruce *AuBYP 90*
Hiscock, Bruce 1940- *BioIn 16*
Hiscock, Eric 1899-1989 *AnObit 1989*
Hise, Elijah 1801-1867 *BioIn 16*
Hise, Mark Allen 1950- *WhoEmL 91*
Hiser, Berniece T. *AuBYP 90*
Hiser, Harold R., Jr. 1931- *St&PR 91*
Hisey, Richard M. 1958- *St&PR 91*
Hishinuma, Kathleen K. 1954- *WhoAmW 91*
Hishmeh, Bassem L. 1941- *St&PR 91*
Hisiger, Kerri Ileen 1955- *WhoAmW 91*
Hisle, Dewitt T. 1934- *St&PR 91*
Hisle, Larry 1947- *Ballpl 90*
Hisle, Randall William 1962- *WhoEmL 91*
Hislop, Gordon Stuart 1939- *WhoE 91*
Hislop, Joseph 1884-1977 *PenDiMP*
Hislop, Mervyn Warren 1937- *WhoAm 90*
Hisrich, Robert Dale 1944- *WhoSSW 91*
Hiss, Alger *BioIn 16, EncAL*
Hiss, Alger 1904- *WorAlBi*
Hiss, Donald 1906-1989 *BioIn 16*
Hiss, Philip Hanson *BioIn 16*
Hiss, Roland Graham 1932- *WhoAm 90*
Hissey, Jane *AuBYP 90*
Hissey, Jane 1952- *BioIn 16*
Histed, Bradley John 1954- *WhoEmL 91*
Hit-Him-Home, Joan *BiDEWW*
Hitachi, Prince *EncJap*
Hitam, Musa bin 1934- *BioIn 16*
Hitch, Charles Johnston 1910- *WhoAm 90*
Hitch, Horace 1921- *WhoAm 90, WhoWor 91*
Hitch, Jean Leason 1918- *WhoAmA 91*
Hitch, Robert A 1920- *WhoAmA 91*
Hitch, Stewart 1940- *WhoAmA 91*
Hitchborn, James Brian 1938- *WhoSSW 91*
Hitchcock, Alfred 1899-1980 *BioIn 16, WorAlBi*
Hitchcock, Billy 1916- *Ballpl 90*
Hitchcock, Christopher Brian 1947- *WhoE 91, WhoEmL 91, WhoWor 91*
Hitchcock, Connie Ginevra 1954- *WhoAmW 91*
Hitchcock, David Gridley 1956- *St&PR 91*
Hitchcock, Donald Simon 1929- *St&PR 91, WhoAm 90*
Hitchcock, Ethan Allen 1798-1870 *WhNaAH*
Hitchcock, Ethan Allen 1835-1909 *BiDrUSE 89, BioIn 16*
Hitchcock, Ethan Allen 1909- *WhoAm 90*
Hitchcock, Frank Harris 1867-1935 *BiDrUSE 89*
Hitchcock, George 1914- *ConAu 12AS [port]*
Hitchcock, George Parks 1914- *WhoAm 90, WhoWrEP 89*
Hitchcock, Georgia Magdalene 1904- *WhoAmW 91*
Hitchcock, Gregory Todd 1947- *St&PR 91*
Hitchcock, Harry Addington 1945- *WhoE 91*
Hitchcock, Henry Perry 1921- *WhoAm 90*
Hitchcock, Henry Russell 1903-1986 *WhoAmA 91N*
Hitchcock, Henry Russell 1903-1987 *BioIn 16*
Hitchcock, Hugh Wiley 1923- *IntWWM 90*
Hitchcock, J. Gareth 1914- *WhoWor 91*
Hitchcock, John 1931- *BiDrAPA 89*
Hitchcock, Karen Ruth 1943- *WhoAm 90, WhoAmW 91*
Hitchcock, Lambert 1795-1852 *PenDiDA 89*
Hitchcock, Lillian Dorothy Staw 1922- *WhoAmW 91*
Hitchcock, Lloyd 1932- *St&PR 91*
Hitchcock, Patricia *AuBYP 90*
Hitchcock, Patti Ann 1945- *WhoEmL 91*
Hitchcock, Ray 1947- *WhoEmL 91*
Hitchcock, Raymond 1865-1929 *OxCPMus*
Hitchcock, Robert B. *St&PR 91*
Hitchcock, Timothy Randall 1941- *St&PR 91*
Hitchcock, Walter Anson 1918- *WhoAm 90*
Hitchens, Bert *TwCCr&M 91*
Hitchens, Dolores *TwCCr&M 91*
Hitching, Harry James 1909- *WhoAm 90*
Hitchings, George H. 1905- *BioIn 16, WorAlBi*
Hitchings, George Herbert 1905- *WhoAm 90, WhoSSW 91, WhoWor 91*
Hitchings, Herbert William 1930- *St&PR 91*
Hitchings, Owen Lyman 1937- *WhoSSW 91*
Hitchins, Ronald Joseph 1940- *St&PR 91*
Hitchman, Margaret E *BiDrAPA 89*
Hitchman, William 1830- *AmLegL*
Hitchner, Dell Gillette 1914- *WhoAm 90*
Hitchock, Thomas Strack 1939- *St&PR 91*
Hite, Arthur Joseph 1942- *St&PR 91*
Hite, Catharine Leavey 1924- *WhoAmW 91*
Hite, David Nelson 1938- *St&PR 91*
Hite, Gary Paul 1935- *WhoAm 90*
Hite, James Cleveland 1941- *WhoSSW 91*
Hite, James Tillman, III 1938- *WhoAm 90*
Hite, Joseph Patrick 1948- *St&PR 91*
Hite, Mark 1935- *WhoE 91*
Hite, R. Lee 1944- *St&PR 91*
Hite, Robert Edelen 1937- *St&PR 91*
Hite, Shere *BioIn 16*

Hite, Shere 1942- *ConAu 31NR, MajTwCW*
Hite, Shere D. *WhoWrEP 89*
Hite, Shere D. 1942- *WhoAm 90, WhoAmW 91, WorAlBi*
Hite, Shirley L. 1935- *WhoAmW 91*
Hites, Robert William, Jr. 1952- *WhoEmL 91*
Hites, Ronald Atlee 1942- *WhoAm 90*
Hitler, Adolf 1889-1945 *BioIn 16, WorAlBi*
Hitler, Adolph 1889-1945 *EncPaPR 91*
Hitlin, David George 1942- *WhoAm 90*
Hitner, Chuck 1943- *WhoAmA 91*
Hitpas, Robert E. 1938- *St&PR 91*
Hitt, David H. 1925- *WhoAm 90*
Hitt, Iola Haley 1919- *WhoAmW 91*
Hitt, Leo N. 1955- *WhoEmL 91*
Hitt, Mary Jane 1947- *WhoEmL 91*
Hitt, Michael A. 1946- *WhoAm 90*
Hitt, Robert M., III 1949- *WhoSSW 91*
Hitte, Ernie Lawrence 1941- *WhoSSW 91*
Hitte, Kathryn *AuBYP 90*
Hittinger, William Charles 1922- *St&PR 91, WhoAm 90*
Hittle, David William 1947- *WhoWor 91*
Hittle, James D. 1915- *WhoAm 90*
Hittle, James Q. 1915- *St&PR 91*
Hittle, Keith Richard 1944- *St&PR 91*
Hittle, Lloyd 1924- *Ballpl 90*
Hittle, Richard Howard 1923- *WhoAm 90*
Hittleman, Ben 1920- *St&PR 91*
Hittmair, Otto Heinrich 1924- *WhoWor 91*
Hittner, Carol Brenner 1942- *WhoAm 90*
Hittner, David 1939- *WhoSSW 91*
Hitz, Demi 1942- *BioIn 16*
Hitz, Frederick Porter 1939- *WhoAm 90*
Hitz, Kingman L. 1948- *WhoSSW 91*
Hitz, Michael Ellis *BiDrAPA 89*
Hitzig, Bernard Michael 1935- *WhoWor 91*
Hitzig, Walter Hermann 1922- *WhoWor 91*
Hively, Charles Edward 1947- *WhoEmL 91*
Hively, Neal Otto 1950- *WhoEmL 91*
Hivry, Arnold Herbert 1945- *St&PR 91*
Hix, James William 1947- *WhoEmL 91*
Hix, John 1908-1944 *EncACom*
Hix, Robert Ernest 1939- *BiDrAPA 89*
Hixenbaugh, Lyle H. 1931- *St&PR 91*
Hixon, Robert Charles 1922- *WhoAm 90*
Hixson, Jerome C. *BioIn 16*
Hixson, Nathan Hanks 1913- *WhoSSW 91*
Hixson, Sheila Ellis 1933 *WhoAmW 91*
Hiykel, James William, Jr. 1947- *St&PR 91*
Hizon, Josefina L *BiDrAPA 89*
HJ Zainal Abidin, Azasahibul 1955- *WhoWor 91*
Hjalmarsson, Johann 1939- *DcScanL*
Hjalmarsson, Lennart Anders 1944- *WhoWor 91*
Hjartarson, Snorri 1906-1986 *DcScanL*
Hjelde, Hans Jorgen 1936- *St&PR 91*
Hjelle, Mary Ann 1930- *WhoAmW 91*
Hjellum, John 1910- *WhoAm 90*
Hjelm, Peter Robert 1942- *St&PR 91*
Hjelm, Ralph Oscar 1923- *WhoAm 90*
Hjelmborg, Bjorn 1911- *IntWWM 90*
Hjelmqvist, Bengt A. 1949- *WhoWor 91*
Hjerpe, Edward Alfred, III 1959- *WhoE 91*
Hjerpsted, Erik 1947- *WhoWor 91*
Hjort, Howard Warren 1931- *WhoAm 90*
Hjorth, William Thomas 1937- *St&PR 91, WhoAm 90*
Hjorth-Andersen, Christian 1944- *WhoWor 91*
Hjortsberg, William Reinhold 1941- *WhoAm 90, WhoWrEP 89*
Hjortsvang, Kenneth W 1928- *BiDrAPA 89*
Hlad, Gregory Michael 1947- *WhoSSW 91*
Hladkyj, Stephan 1955- *WhoEmL 91*
Hlasek, Jakob *BioIn 16*
Hlass, I. Jerry *WhoAm 90*
Hlathein, Dennis 1935- *St&PR 91*
Hlava, Diane Elizabeth 1948- *WhoAmW 91*
Hlavac, Phyllis Joan Idle 1949- *WhoAmW 91*
Hlavacek, James J. 1946- *St&PR 91*
Hlavacek, Roy George 1937- *St&PR 91, WhoAm 90*
Hlavaty, Joel Robert 1955- *WhoEmL 91*
Hlavaty, Marie L. 1936- *St&PR 91*
Hlavay, Jay Alan 1956- *WhoE 91, WhoEmL 91*
Hlavin, Miles L. 1932- *St&PR 91*
Hlavina, Rasto R 1943- *WhoAmA 91*
Hlavinka, Paul Thomas 1950- *WhoSSW 91*
Hlavka, Edwin J. 1937- *St&PR 91*
Hlavka, Edwin John 1937- *WhoAm 90*
Hlawitschka, Eduard Gottfried 1928- *WhoWor 91*
Hlinka, Andreas 1864-1938 *BioIn 16*
Hlopoff, Rostislav *BioIn 16*
Hlousek, George J. 1931- *St&PR 91*
Hlousek, Timothy J. 1947- *St&PR 91*
Hlozek, Carole Diane Quast 1959- *WhoAmW 91, WhoEmL 91*
Hlubek, Jeffry J. 1946- *ODwPR 91*
Hmieleski, Carol Lydia 1950- *WhoAmW 91*
Hnatiuk, Miroslaw W 1917- *BiDrAPA 89*
Hnatyshyn, Ramon *BioIn 16*
Hnatyshyn, Ramon John 1934- *WhoAm 90, WhoWor 91*
Hnetila, Carol Ann 1950- *BiDrAPA 89*
Hnizdovsky, Jacques 1915-1985 *WhoAmA 91N*
Ho Chi Minh 1890-1969 *WorAlBi*
Ho Joong Choi 1930- *WhoWor 91*
Ho Quang Minh *BioIn 16*
Ho, Allan Benedict 1955- *IntWWM 90*
Ho, Chi Minh 1890-1969 *BioIn 16*
Ho, Chien 1934- *WhoAm 90*
Ho, Chong 1896-1988 *BioIn 16*
Ho, David K. 1948- *WhoEmL 91*
Ho, Donald Tai Loy 1930- *WhoAm 90*
Ho, Edward 1939- *IntWWM 90*
Ho, Francis T 1938- *WhoAmA 91*
Ho, Frank F. 1950- *St&PR 91*
Ho, Fung 1955- *IntWWM 90*
Ho, Iwan 1925- *WhoWor 91*
Ho, James K. 1952- *St&PR 91*
Ho, John Jen-Yeang 1955- *BiDrAPA 89*
Ho, Kenneth Kin-Leung 1954- *St&PR 91*
Ho, Leo Chi Chien 1940- *WhoWor 91*
Ho, Mary Hao Tze 1958- *WhoE 91*
Ho, Oi Lan *BiDrAPA 89*
Ho, Paul S. 1936- *WhoE 91*
Ho, Pauline 1954- *WhoEmL 91*
Ho, Ping-Ti 1917- *WhoAm 90*
Ho, Raymond Yap 1954- *WhoSSW 91*
Ho, Reggie *BioIn 16*
Ho, Samuel Pao-San 1936- *WhoAm 90*
Ho, Sau Nan 1931- *WhoWor 91*
Ho, Sylvia 1952- *IntWWM 90*
Ho, Sze-Key *BiDrAPA 89*
Ho, Tao 1936- *WhoWor 91*
Ho, Thomas Inn Min 1948- *WhoAm 90, WhoEmL 91*
Ho, Vincent Wing Kin 1951- *WhoWor 91*
Ho, Weifan L. 1951- *WhoAmW 91*
Ho, Yhi-Min 1934- *WhoAm 90*
Ho, Ying-Chin 1889-1987 *BioIn 16*
Ho, Yu-Chi 1934- *WhoAm 90*
Hoadley, David N. 1933- *St&PR 91*
Hoadley, Garrick Little 1936- *WhoE 91*
Hoadley, Irene Braden 1938- *WhoAm 90, WhoAmW 91*
Hoadley, Peter George 1934- *WhoAm 90*
Hoadley, Russell S. 1944- *ODwPR 91*
Hoadley, Walter E. 1916- *St&PR 91*
Hoadley, Walter Evans 1916- *WhoAm 90, WhoWor 91*
Hoag, David Garratt 1925- *WhoAm 90, WhoE 91*
Hoag, David H. *St&PR 91*
Hoag, David H. 1939- *WhoAm 90, WhoSSW 91*
Hoag, Edwin 1926- *AuBYP 90*
Hoag, Jack Carter 1952- *WhoEmL 91*
Hoag, Jean Marie 1916- *BiDrAPA 89*
Hoag, John Arthur 1932- *St&PR 91*
Hoag, Myril 1908-1971 *Ballpl 90*
Hoag, Paul Sterling 1913- *WhoAm 90*
Hoag, Robert C. *BioIn 16*
Hoag, Robert R. 1908-1987 *BioIn 16*
Hoag, Sharon Kay 1963- *WhoAmW 91*
Hoag, Thomas Robert 1947- *St&PR 91*
Hoag, William Gifford 1909- *WhoWor 91*
Hoag, William James 1939- *St&PR 91*
Hoagberg, Karen Anne *BiDrAPA 89*
Hoagland, Albert Joseph, Jr. 1939- *WhoWor 91*
Hoagland, Albert Smiley 1926- *WhoAm 90*
Hoagland, Alexander Campbell, Jr. 1927- *WhoAm 90*
Hoagland, C. Thomas, Jr. 1925- *St&PR 91*
Hoagland, Donald Romeyne 1928- *St&PR 91*
Hoagland, Donald Wright 1921- *WhoAm 90*
Hoagland, Edward *BioIn 16*
Hoagland, Edward 1932- *ConAu 31NR, WhoAm 90, WhoWrEP 89*
Hoagland, Guy Whitney 1920- *WhoWrEP 89*
Hoagland, Jack Charles 1918- *WhoAm 90*
Hoagland, James Lee 1922- *WhoAm 90*
Hoagland, Jimmie Lee 1940- *WhoAm 90*
Hoagland, John H., Jr. *St&PR 91*
Hoagland, Karl King, Jr. 1933- *St&PR 91, WhoAm 90*
Hoagland, Laurance Redington, Jr. 1936- *WhoAm 90*
Hoagland, Mahlon B. 1921- *BioIn 16*
Hoagland, Mahlon Bush 1921- *WhoAm 90*
Hoagland, Peter 1941- *BioIn 16*
Hoagland, Peter Jackson 1941- *WhoAm 90*
Hoagland, Porter, Jr. 1925- *WhoE 91*
Hoagland, Robert Earl 1951- *WhoE 91*
Hoagland, Samuel Albert 1953- *WhoEmL 91*
Hoagland, Steven William 1948- *WhoE 91*
Hoagland, Thomas V 1908- *BiDrAPA 89*
Hoagland, Thomas Walter 1941- *St&PR 91*
Hoagland, William Thomas 1955- *WhoSSW 91*
Hoaglund, Glenn Carl 1937- *WhoAm 90*
Hoak, Don 1928-1969 *Ballpl 90*
Hoak, J.M. 1918- *St&PR 91*
Hoak, James McClain, Jr. 1944- *St&PR 91*
Hoak, John Charles 1928- *WhoAm 90*
Hoaken, Paul C S 1930- *BiDrAPA 89*
Hoan, Dan *EncAL*
Hoang, Duc Van 1926- *WhoAm 90*
Hoang, Joy Gonzales 1949- *WhoAmW 91*
Hoang, Ke Guy 1933- *BiDrAPA 89*
Hoang, Ngoc-Tuan 1956- *IntWWM 90*
Hoang, Trung Quang 1950- *WhoEmL 91*
Hoar, Barbara Reddy *BiDrAPA 89*
Hoar, Ebenezer Rockwood 1816-1895 *BiDrUSE 89*
Hoar, Frederick M. *ODwPR 91*
Hoar, James J. 1918- *St&PR 91*
Hoar, John F. 1931- *St&PR 91*
Hoar, John Kenderdine 1954- *WhoSSW 91*
Hoar, Richard Nichols 1913- *St&PR 91*
Hoar, Samuel 1927- *WhoAm 90*
Hoar, Wayne Nichols 1950- *St&PR 91*
Hoar, William Patrick 1945- *WhoE 91*
Hoar, William Stewart 1913- *WhoAm 90*
Hoard, Linda Jane 1947- *WhoEmL 91*
Hoard, Philip H. *St&PR 91*
Hoare, Antony Michael 1943- *WhoWor 91*
Hoare, Diane *BioIn 16*
Hoare, Oliver *BioIn 16*
Hoare, Richard David 1927- *WhoAm 90*
Hoare, Tyler James 1940- *WhoAm 90, WhoAmA 91*
Hoarty, John Joseph 1950- *WhoAm 90*
Hoatson, Grant Cameron 1930- *WhoSSW 91*
Hoback, Florence K 1922- *BiDrAPA 89*
Hoback, Florence Kunst 1922- *WhoAmW 91*
Hoback, Ronald Dean 1935- *WhoSSW 91*
Hoban, Anne Kathryn *BiDrAPA 89*
Hoban, Bruce Randall 1954- *WhoEmL 91*
Hoban, George Savre 1914- *WhoAm 90*
Hoban, James 1762?-1831 *WorAlBi*
Hoban, Julia *AuBYP 90*
Hoban, Lillian *WhoAmW 91*
Hoban, Lillian 1925- *AuBYP 90*
Hoban, Michael *BioIn 16*
Hoban, Russell 1925- *AuBYP 90, MajTwCW*
Hoban, Russell Conwell 1925- *WhoAm 90*
Hoban, Tana *AuBYP 90, SmATA 12AS [port]*
Hoban, Walter *EncACom*
Hobart, Alice 1882-1967 *FemiCLE*
Hobart, David Edward 1949- *WhoEmL 91*
Hobart, Garret Augustus 1844-1899 *AmLegL, BiDrUSE 89*
Hobart, James L. 1933- *St&PR 91*
Hobart, Lawrence Scott 1931- *WhoAm 90*
Hobart, Lois Elaine *AuBYP 90*
Hobart, Marie Helen *BiDrAPA 89*
Hobart, Peter Cahill 1934- *St&PR 91, WhoWor 91*
Hobart, Richard B. 1944- *St&PR 91*
Hobart, Sharon L. 1946- *WhoEmL 91*
Hobart, William Harrison, Jr. 1924- *St&PR 91, WhoAm 90*
Hobaugh, Ed 1934- *Ballpl 90*
Hobbema, Meindert 1638?-1709 *IntDcAA 90, WorAlBi*
Hobbes, John Oliver 1867-1906 *BioIn 16, FemiCLE*
Hobbes, Thomas 1588-1679 *WorAlBi, WrPh P*
Hobbie, A. Clark, Jr. 1941- *St&PR 91*
Hobbie, Glen 1936- *Ballpl 90, BioIn 16*
Hobbie, Lucille 1915- *WhoAmA 91, WhoE 91*
Hobbie, Russell Klyver 1934- *WhoAm 90*
Hobbie, Susan Janet 1943- *WhoAmW 91, WhoE 91*
Hobbs, Allen 1937- *IntWWM 90*
Hobbs, Ann Todd 1926- *WhoAmW 91*
Hobbs, Becky *WhoNeCM [port]*
Hobbs, Bradley Keith 1956- *WhoSSW 91*
Hobbs, Carl Fredric 1931- *WhoAm 90*
Hobbs, Charles Alexander *St&PR 91N*
Hobbs, Christopher 1950- *IntWWM 90*
Hobbs, Claire Mary 1961- *IntWWM 90*
Hobbs, Estel Milton 1937- *WhoAm 90*
Hobbs, Franklin Dean, III 1952- *WhoEmL 91*
Hobbs, Franklin Warren 1924- *St&PR 91*
Hobbs, Franklin Warren, IV 1947- *WhoAm 90, WhoEmL 91*
Hobbs, Fredric 1931- *WhoAmA 91*
Hobbs, Gerald S 1941- *WhoAmA 91*
Hobbs, J. Edwin 1916- *WhoAm 90*
Hobbs, Jack Arthur 1930- *WhoAmA 91*
Hobbs, James Allen 1930- *St&PR 91, WhoAm 90*
Hobbs, James Beverly 1930- *WhoAm 90*
Hobbs, James D. 1943- *St&PR 91*
Hobbs, James Durham 1951- *IntWWM 90*
Hobbs, James Steven 1953- *WhoEmL 91*
Hobbs, Jerry Chilton 1939- *St&PR 91*
Hobbs, Jewell Elizabeth 1945- *WhoAmW 91*
Hobbs, Joan Pizzo 1957- *WhoAmW 91*
Hobbs, Joe Ferrell 1934- *WhoAmA 91*
Hobbs, John Henry 1938- *St&PR 91*
Hobbs, John Robert 1941- *WhoE 91*
Hobbs, Kenneth L. 1951- *WhoEmL 91*
Hobbs, Leonard S. 1896-1977 *WorAlBi*
Hobbs, Lewis Mankin 1937- *WhoAm 90*
Hobbs, Lewis Ray 1955- *St&PR 91, WhoAm 90*
Hobbs, Linder Charlie 1925- *WhoAm 90*
Hobbs, Lyndall *BioIn 16*
Hobbs, Marcus Edwin 1909- *WhoAm 90*
Hobbs, Matthew Hallock 1946- *WhoE 91*
Hobbs, Michael Edwin 1940- *WhoAm 90*
Hobbs, Nila Alene 1949- *WhoEmL 91*
Hobbs, Odell *BioIn 16*
Hobbs, Patricia Ann 1934- *WhoAmW 91*
Hobbs, Patricia Anne 1954- *WhoE 91*
Hobbs, Ranald Purcell 1907- *WhoAm 90*
Hobbs, Richard, Jr. *BioIn 16*
Hobbs, Richard Allen 1950- *WhoEmL 91*
Hobbs, Richard F. 1947- *St&PR 91*
Hobbs, Robert Carleton 1946- *WhoAmA 91*
Hobbs, Robert Dean 1928- *WhoAmA 91*
Hobbs, Robert E. 1930- *St&PR 91*
Hobbs, Robert Wesley 1938- *WhoAm 90*
Hobbs, Roland L. 1932- *St&PR 91*
Hobbs, Roland Lee 1932- *WhoAm 90*
Hobbs, Sharon Stanley 1953- *WhoSSW 91*
Hobbs, Thomas Alan 1944- *St&PR 91*
Hobbs, Thomas D. 1946- *St&PR 91*
Hobbs, Truman McGill 1921- *WhoAm 90, WhoSSW 91*
Hobbs, W. Keith 1940- *ODwPR 91*
Hobbs, William Barton Rogers 1949- *WhoE 91*
Hobbs, William P. 1924- *St&PR 91*
Hobbs, William Ralph 1945- *BiDrAPA 89*
Hobbs, William Robert, II 1944- *St&PR 91*
Hobby, Carolyn Patrice 1953- *WhoSSW 91*
Hobby, Charles 1665?-1715 *EncCRAm*
Hobby, Elaine 1956- *ConAu 130*
Hobby, Kenneth L. 1932- *St&PR 91*
Hobby, Kevin James 1970- *WhoSSW 91*
Hobby, Oveta Culp 1905- *BiDrUSE 89, St&PR 91, WhoAm 90, WorAlBi*
Hobby, Paul William 1960- *WhoEmL 91*
Hobby, William Matthews, III 1935- *WhoSSW 91*
Hobby, William Pettus 1878-1964 *BioIn 16*
Hobby, William Pettus 1932- *St&PR 91, WhoAm 90, WhoSSW 91*
Hobcroft, Rex Kelvin 1925- *IntWWM 90*
Hobday, Charles 1917- *ConAu 132*
Hobday, John Charles 1935- *WhoAm 90*
Hobe, Robert Donald 1958- *St&PR 91*
Hobe, Seiichi *St&PR 91*
Hobel, Phil *ConAu 32NR*
Hobelman, Carl Donald 1931- *WhoAm 90, WhoWor 91*
Hoben, Marian William *WhoAmW 91*
Hober, Rudolf Otto Anselm 1873-1953 *DcScB S2*
Hoberecht, Earnest 1918- *WhoAm 90*
Hoberman, Henry Don 1914- *WhoAm 90*
Hoberman, Mary Ann 1930- *AuBYP 90, BioIn 16, ChlLR 22 [port]*
Hoberman, Max 1924- *St&PR 91*
Hoberman, Sharlene 1942- *WhoE 91*
Hobgood, E Wade 1953- *WhoAmA 91*
Hobgood, George 1923- *ODwPR 91*
Hobgood-Brown, Lucy 1954- *ODwPR 91*
Hobhouse, Mary 1864-1901 *FemiCLE*
Hobin, Gary Russell 1946- *WhoSSW 91*
Hobler, Herbert Windsor 1922- *WhoAm 90*
Hobler, Ruth *ODwPR 91*
Hoblin, Philip J., Jr. 1929- *WhoAm 90*
Hoblitzell, Alan Penniman, Jr. 1931- *St&PR 91, WhoE 91*
Hoblitzell, Dick 1888-1962 *Ballpl 90*
Hoblitzell, Fetter Schrier 1838-1900 *AmLegL*
Hoblitzelle, George Knapp 1921- *WhoAm 90*
Hobomok *WhNaAH*
Hobomoko *WhNaAH*
Hobor, Nancy 1946- *ODwPR 91*
Hobor, Nancy Allen 1846- *WhoAmW 91*
Hobowsky, M Richard *BiDrAPA 89*
Hobratschk, Martin Glenn 1944- *St&PR 91*
Hobsbaum, Philip Dennis 1932- *WhoWor 91*
Hobson, Anne Glen 1925- *WhoWor 91*
Hobson, Bernard Edward 1953- *WhoEmL 91*

Hobson, Bruce *AuBYP 90*
Hobson, Bruce 1950- *SmATA 62*
Hobson, Burton H. 1933- *St&PR 91*
Hobson, Burton Harold 1933- *WhoAm 90*
Hobson, Butch 1951- *Ballpl 90*
Hobson, Carroll Dean 1928- *St&PR 91*
Hobson, Charles Blagrove 1936- *WhoE 91*
Hobson, Cynthia Regina 1940- *WhoAmW 91*
Hobson, Douglas Paul 1952- *BiDrAPA 89*
Hobson, Ervin A. 1956- *St&PR 91*
Hobson, Ervin J. *St&PR 91*
Hobson, Fred C. 1943- *BioIn 16*
Hobson, Ginger Kay 1959- *WhoAmW 91*
Hobson, Harry E., Jr. 1948- *WhoEmL 91, WhoWor 91*
Hobson, Harry Lee, Jr. 1929- *WhoAm 90*
Hobson, Howard L. 1938- *St&PR 91*
Hobson, Ian 1952- *PenDiMP*
Hobson, Ian 1953- *IntWWM 90*
Hobson, James Richmond 1937- *WhoAm 90, WhoE 91*
Hobson, John Allan 1933- *WhoAm 90*
Hobson, John Atkinson 1858-1940 *BioIn 16*
Hobson, John David 1941- *WhoAm 90*
Hobson, Julius W. 1922?-1977 *AuBYP 90*
Hobson, Karen Louise 1953- *WhoEmL 91*
Hobson, Katherine Thayer 1889-1982 *WhoAmA 91N*
Hobson, Laura 1900-1986 *FemiCLE*
Hobson, Laura Keane Zametkin 1900-1986 *BioIn 16*
Hobson, Leahanne *ODwPR 91*
Hobson, Lois Renee 1949- *WhoAmW 91*
Hobson, Mary Quinn 1857-1892? *BioAmW*
Hobson, Polly 1913- *AuBYP 90*
Hobson, Richard F., Jr. 1954- *IntWWM 90*
Hobson, Robert Wayne, II 1939- *WhoAm 90, WhoWor 91*
Hobson, Thomas R. 1944- *ODwPR 91*
Hoburg, James Frederick 1946- *WhoAm 90*
Hoby, Elizabeth 1528-1609 *BiDEWW*
Hoby, Margaret 1571-1633 *BiDEWW, FemiCLE*
Hocevar, Gregory Paul 1948- *WhoEmL 91*
Hoch, Andrew W. *St&PR 91*
Hoch, Edward D 1930- *TwCCr&M 91, WhoWrEP 89*
Hoch, Edward Dentinger 1930- *SpyFic, WhoAm 90*
Hoch, Frank W. 1921- *St&PR 91*
Hoch, Frank William 1921- *WhoAm 90*
Hoch, Frederic Louis 1920- *WhoAm 90*
Hoch, Hannah 1889-1978 *BiDWomA*
Hoch, Hans Peter 1924- *ConDes 90*
Hoch, John Joseph 1927- *St&PR 91*
Hoch, Mary Camp 1960- *WhoE 91*
Hoch, Orion Lindel 1928- *WhoAm 90*
Hoch, Rand 1955- *WhoEmL 91*
Hoch, Robert Charles 1948- *St&PR 91*
Hoch, Roland Franklin 1940- *WhoAm 90*
Hoch, Samuel *BiDrAPA 89*
Hoch, Scott *BioIn 16*
Hoch, Standley Howard *WhoAm 90*
Hoch, Standley Howard 1933- *St&PR 91*
Hoch, William O. 1948- *ODwPR 91*
Hochachka, Peter William 1937- *WhoAm 90*
Hochadel, Jack Birch *St&PR 91*
Hochbaum, Godfrey Martin 1916- *WhoAm 90*
Hochbaum, H. Albert 1911-1988 *BioIn 16*
Hochbaum, Hans Albert 1911-1988 *BioIn 16*
Hochberg, Bayard Zabdial 1932- *WhoAm 90*
Hochberg, Fred P. 1952- *St&PR 91*
Hochberg, Fred Philip 1952- *WhoAm 90*
Hochberg, Jerome A. 1933- *WhoAm 90*
Hochberg, Joel Morton 1939- *WhoAm 90*
Hochberg, Julian 1923- *WhoAm 90*
Hochberg, Kenneth J. 1950- *WhoWor 91*
Hochberg, Marilyn B. 1926- *St&PR 91*
Hochberg, Mark S. 1947- *WhoE 91*
Hochberg, Martin J. 1931- *St&PR 91*
Hochberg, Richard Alan *BiDrAPA 89*
Hochberg, Samuel Israel 1950- *WhoEmL 91*
Hochberger, John Richard 1960- *WhoEmL 91*
Hochberger, Simon 1912- *WhoAm 90*
Hochbrueckner, George J. 1938- *WhoAm 90, WhoE 91*
Hochderffer, Kris 1948- *St&PR 91*
Hoche, Philip Anthony 1906- *WhoAm 90*
Hochenegg, Leonhard 1942- *WhoWor 91*
Hochhalter, Gordon Ray 1946- *WhoEmL 91, WhoWor 91*
Hochhauser, Marilyn Helsenrott 1928- *WhoAmA 91*
Hochhauser, Richard Michael 1944- *St&PR 91*
Hochheimer, Laura 1933- *IntWWM 90*
Hochheiser, Joseph Herman *BiDrAPA 89*
Hochhuth, Rolf 1931- *ConAu 33NR, MajTwCW*
Hochi, Shozo *BioIn 16*
Hochman, Bert 1925- *ODwPR 91*
Hochman, Gloria *BioIn 16*
Hochman, Harold Marvin 1936- *WhoE 91*
Hochman, Jeffrey J. 1952- *WhoEmL 91*
Hochman, John Ira 1945- *BiDrAPA 89*
Hochman, Kitty *WhoAmA 91*
Hochman, Larry 1953- *WhoEmL 91*
Hochman, Marilyn Joy 1958- *WhoEmL 91*
Hochman, Neal Stuart 1934- *St&PR 91*
Hochman, Richard H. 1945- *St&PR 91*
Hochman, William Russell 1921- *WhoAm 90*
Hochmeister, Angela Beth 1958- *WhoAmW 91, WhoEmL 91*
Hochmuth, Robert Milo 1939- *WhoAm 90*
Hochreither, Karl 1933- *IntWWM 90*
Hochron, Beryl Judith 1947- *WhoAmW 91*
Hochschild, Adam 1942- *WhoAm 90*
Hochschild, Carroll Shepherd 1935- *WhoAmW 91*
Hochschwender, Herman Karl 1920- *WhoWor 91*
Hochschwender, Karl Albert 1927- *WhoWor 91*
Hochstadt, Doug *BioIn 16*
Hochstadt, Harry 1925- *WhoAm 90, WhoE 91*
Hochstadt, Joy 1939- *WhoAm 90, WhoAmW 91*
Hochstedler, Rowen M 1943- *BiDrAPA 89*
Hochstein, Anatoly Boris 1932- *WhoAm 90*
Hochstein, Eric Cameron 1956- *WhoE 91*
Hochstein, John 1941- *St&PR 91*
Hochster, Melvin 1943- *WhoAm 90*
Hochstetler, T Max 1941- *WhoAmA 91*
Hochstrasser, Barbara *BiDrAPA 89*
Hochstrasser, Donald Lee 1927- *WhoAm 90*
Hochwaelder, Fritz 1911-1986 *MajTwCW*
Hock, Bertold 1939- *WhoWor 91*
Hock, Delwin D. 1935- *St&PR 91*
Hock, Harlan H. *St&PR 91*
Hock, Morton 1929- *WhoAm 90, WhoWor 91*
Hock, Nicholas George 1917- *WhoAm 90*
Hock, Roy E. 1929- *St&PR 91*
Hock, Vincent Michael 1942- *St&PR 91*
Hock, W. Fletcher, Jr. 1931- *St&PR 91*
Hock, Winifred Lehman 1952- *WhoEmL 91*
Hockaday, Hugh 1892-1968 *WhoAmA 91N*
Hockaday, Irvine O., Jr. 1936- *St&PR 91, WhoAm 90*
Hockeborn, Margaret Lankford 1959- *WhoAmW 91*
Hockeimer, Henry Eric 1920- *WhoAm 90, WhoWor 91*
Hockemeier, J. Curt 1948- *WhoSSW 91*
Hockenberg, Harlan David 1927- *WhoAm 90*
Hockenberry, Debra Pearl 1961- *WhoWrEP 89*
Hockenbrocht, David William 1935- *St&PR 91*
Hockensmith, Hadley *NewAgMG*
Hocker, Douglas William 1945- *WhoE 91*
Hocker, Johann Michael *PenDiDA 89*
Hocker, John Kells 1949- *WhoSSW 91*
Hocker, Karla 1946- *WhoWrEP 89*
Hockersmith, Harold M. 1927- *St&PR 91*
Hockett, Charles Francis 1916- *WhoAm 90*
Hockett, Harry G 1903- *BiDrAPA 89*
Hockett, Oris 1909-1969 *Ballpl 90*
Hockett-Korman, Debra Jean *BiDrAPA 89*
Hockey, John Albert 1936- *St&PR 91*
Hockin, Alan Bond 1923- *St&PR 91*
Hockin, Thomas Alexander 1938- *WhoE 91*
Hocking, Anne 189-?- *TwCCr&M 91*
Hocking, James Robert 1929- *WhoAm 90*
Hocking, John Edwin 1926- *St&PR 91*
Hocking, John Gilbert 1920- *WhoAm 90*
Hocking, Leslie Beth 1957- *BiDrAPA 89*
Hocking, William E. 1873-1966 *WorAlBi*
Hocking-Fetter, Julie 1965- *St&PR 91*
Hockley, Frederick 1809-1885 *EncO&P 3*
Hockley, Nancy Evelyn 1936- *IntWWM 90*
Hockman, Bruce Richard 1948- *St&PR 91*
Hockman, Richard Elton 1945- *WhoAm 90*
Hockney, David *BioIn 16*
Hockney, David 1937- *IntDcAA 90, IntWWM 90, WhoAm 90, WhoWor 91, WorAlBi*
Hockridge, Robert George 1920- *St&PR 91*
Hocks, Paula Jeanne *WhoWrEP 89*
Hocott, Claude Richard 1909- *WhoAm 90*
Hocott, Joe Bill 1921- *WhoSSW 91, WhoWor 91*
Hocter, William J., Jr. *BiDrAPA 89*
Hocutt, Max Oliver 1936- *WhoAm 90*
Hoda, Bernice E. 1923- *St&PR 91*
Hoda, Mohammad Mansurul 1930- *WhoWor 91*
Hodapp, Don Joseph 1937- *St&PR 91, WhoAm 90*
Hodapp, Johnny 1905-1980 *Ballpl 90*
Hodapp, Larry Frank 1956- *WhoEmL 91*
Hodapp, Robert Louis 1910-1989 *BioIn 16*
Hodapp, Volker Artur 1944- *WhoWor 91*
Hodara, Henri 1926- *St&PR 91*
Hodas, Arnold J 1933- *BiDrAPA 89*
Hodas, Gordon R 1947- *BiDrAPA 89*
Hodas, Morton M 1931- *BiDrAPA 89*
Hodas, Sidney M 1911- *BiDrAPA 89*
Hodder, Kent Holmes 1956- *WhoEmL 91*
Hodder, Michael John 1946- *WhoE 91*
Hodder, William Alan 1931- *St&PR 91, WhoAm 90*
Hoddeson, Cynthia A. 1954- *WhoE 91*
Hoddinott, Alun 1929- *IntWWM 90, PenDiMP A*
Hoddy, Raymond Arthur 1921- *WhoAm 90*
Hodeir, Andre 1921- *OxCPMus*
Hodel, Christian M. 1936- *WhoWor 91*
Hodel, Donald Paul 1935- *BiDrUSE 89, BioIn 16*
Hodel, George H *BiDrAPA 89*
Hodes, Alan 1943- *St&PR 91*
Hodes, Barbara 1941- *WhoAmW 91*
Hodes, Barney 1943- *WhoAmA 91*
Hodes, Barton L. 1940- *WhoAm 90*
Hodes, Bernard S. 1931- *WhoAm 90*
Hodes, Horace L. 1907-1989 *BioIn 16*
Hodes, Joel L. 1947- *WhoEmL 91*
Hodes, Linda *WhoAm 90*
Hodes, Lisa Brett 1963- *WhoE 91*
Hodes, Marion Edward 1925- *WhoAm 90*
Hodes, Paul William 1951- *WhoEmL 91*
Hodes, Robert B. 1925- *St&PR 91*
Hodes, Robert Bernard 1925- *WhoAm 90*
Hodes, Robert Joseph 1926- *St&PR 91*
Hodes, Scott 1937- *St&PR 91, WhoAm 90*
Hodes, Stuart T. 1925- *St&PR 91*
Hodes, Thomas H. 1928- *St&PR 91*
Hodes, William Dierks 1934- *St&PR 91*
Hodgdon, Harry Edward 1946- *WhoAm 90, WhoE 91*
Hodgdon, Herbert James 1924- *WhoAm 90*
Hodge, Alan M. *St&PR 91*
Hodge, Angela Karen *BiDrAPA 89*
Hodge, Anne Harkness 1951- *WhoAmW 91*
Hodge, Bobby Lynn 1956- *WhoSSW 91*
Hodge, Carleton Taylor 1917- *WhoAm 90*
Hodge, Cathy M. *BioIn 16*
Hodge, Charles Joseph 1956- *WhoSSW 91*
Hodge, Charles Joseph, Jr. 1941- *WhoAm 90*
Hodge, Deborah Lou 1956- *WhoSSW 91*
Hodge, Decca Renee Carter 1956- *WhoSSW 91*
Hodge, Ernest Edward 1951- *WhoEmL 91*
Hodge, Frederick Webb 1864-1956 *WhNaAH*
Hodge, G. Lowrance 1934- *St&PR 91*
Hodge, Gameel Byron 1917- *WhoWor 91*
Hodge, Gary Vincent 1951- *WhoE 91*
Hodge, Gerald Britton 1934- *St&PR 91*
Hodge, Hester Wayne 1931- *St&PR 91*
Hodge, James Lee 1935- *WhoAm 90*
Hodge, James R 1927- *BiDrAPA 89*
Hodge, James Robert 1927- *WhoAm 90*
Hodge, Jane 1917- *FemiCLE*
Hodge, Jane Aiken 1917- *AuBYP 90*
Hodge, Karen *BioIn 16*
Hodge, Kerwyn Christopher 1964- *WhoE 91*
Hodge, Kimberley Sue 1957- *WhoAmW 91*
Hodge, Lynda Sobczyk 1951- *WhoEmL 91*
Hodge, Malcolm H. 1942- *St&PR 91*
Hodge, Mary Gretchen Farnam 1943- *WhoAmW 91*
Hodge, Mary Jo 1935- *WhoAmW 91*
Hodge, Merle 1944- *FemiCLE*
Hodge, Nicholas Sim 1954- *WhoEmL 91*
Hodge, Orlando J. 1828-1911 *AmLegL*
Hodge, Patricia 1946- *ConTFT 8*
Hodge, Paul William 1934- *WhoAm 90*
Hodge, Pearl Mcdonald 1950- *WhoAmW 91*
Hodge, Philip Gibson, Jr. 1920- *WhoAm 90*
Hodge, R Garey 1937- *WhoAmA 91*
Hodge, Raymond Joseph 1922- *WhoAm 90*
Hodge, Robert E. *St&PR 91*
Hodge, Robert H *BiDrAPA 89*
Hodge, Robert Joseph 1937- *WhoAm 90*
Hodge, Rusty Harvey 1962- *WhoEmL 91*
Hodge, Scottie 1940- *WhoAmA 91*
Hodge, Shovel 1893-1967 *Ballpl 90*
Hodge, Verne Antonio 1933- *WhoAm 90*
Hodge, William Vallance Douglas 1903-1975 *DcScB S2*
Hodgell, Murlin Ray 1924- *WhoAm 90*
Hodgell, Patricia Christine 1951- *WhoWrEP 89*
Hodgell, Robert Overman 1922- *WhoAm 90, WhoAmA 91*
Hodgen, Maurice Denzil 1929- *WhoAm 90*
Hodgens, Helen W 1897- *BiDrAPA 89*
Hodges, A Gerry 1942- *BiDrAPA 89*
Hodges, Allan Adolf 1938- *WhoE 91*
Hodges, Allen M. 1947- *St&PR 91*
Hodges, Ann E. 1931- *WhoAmW 91*
Hodges, Bessie Bell 1923- *St&PR 91*
Hodges, Bruce Allen 1954- *WhoEmL 91*
Hodges, C.A. 1924- *St&PR 91*
Hodges, Carl G. 1902-1964 *AuBYP 90*
Hodges, Carol Ann 1942- *WhoAmW 91*
Hodges, Cheryl D. 1952- *St&PR 91*
Hodges, Clarence Eugene 1939- *WhoAm 90*
Hodges, Courtney H. 1887-1966 *WorAlBi*
Hodges, Cyril Walter 1909- *AuBYP 90*
Hodges, Daniel M. 1949- *St&PR 91*
Hodges, David Albert 1937- *WhoAm 90*
Hodges, Dewey Harper 1948- *WhoEmL 91*
Hodges, Donald Wayne 1934- *St&PR 91*
Hodges, Eddie Valson 1932- *WhoSSW 91*
Hodges, Elbert Ray, Jr. *BiDrAPA 89*
Hodges, Elizabeth Jamison *AuBYP 90*
Hodges, Emory F, Jr. *BiDrAPA 89*
Hodges, Everett L. 1932- *St&PR 91*
Hodges, Frederick James 1939- *St&PR 91*
Hodges, Gayla Dianne 1950- *WhoAmW 91*
Hodges, George W. *EarBlAP*
Hodges, Gil 1924-1972 *Ballpl 90 [port], WorAlBi*
Hodges, H. Gaylord, Jr. 1941- *WhoAm 90*
Hodges, H. Raiford, Jr. 1932- *St&PR 91*
Hodges, Harland Edward 1950- *St&PR 91*
Hodges, J. Les *BioIn 16*
Hodges, Jack Douglas 1953- *WhoSSW 91*
Hodges, James Ronald 1952- *St&PR 91*
Hodges, James W. 1937- *St&PR 91*
Hodges, Janice Kay 1945- *WhoEmL 91, WhoSSW 91*
Hodges, John B. 1936- *St&PR 91*
Hodges, John Hendricks 1914- *WhoAm 90*
Hodges, John Raymond 1925- *WhoAm 90*
Hodges, Johnny 1906-1970 *BioIn 16, WorAlBi*
Hodges, Johnny 1907-1970 *DrBlPA 90, OxCPMus*
Hodges, Jolyne C. 1948- *WhoAmW 91*
Hodges, Jot Holiver, Jr. 1932- *WhoWor 91*
Hodges, Julia Elmira 1951- *WhoEmL 91*
Hodges, Kenneth Stuart 1955- *WhoE 91, WhoEmL 91*
Hodges, Lily Handal *BiDrAPA 89*
Hodges, Linda Susan 1961- *WhoAmW 91*
Hodges, Luther Hartwell 1898-1974 *BiDrUSE 89*
Hodges, Luther Hartwell, Jr. 1936- *St&PR 91, WhoAm 90*
Hodges, M. Ray 1931- *WhoAm 90*
Hodges, Margaret 1911- *AuBYP 90*
Hodges, Margaret Ann 1928- *WhoAmW 91*
Hodges, Margaret Moore 1911- *ConAu 30NR, WhoAm 90*
Hodges, Mitchell 1959- *WhoSSW 91*
Hodges, Nora *BioIn 16*
Hodges, Patricia *ConTFT 8*
Hodges, Patricia Ann 1954- *WhoEmL 91*
Hodges, Pauline Ruth 1944- *WhoAmW 91*
Hodges, Priscilla B. 1940- *WhoAmW 91*
Hodges, Ralph B. 1930- *WhoAm 90*
Hodges, Ralph G *BiDrAPA 89*
Hodges, Ralph Lee 1948- *WhoEmL 91*
Hodges, Richard E. 1928- *ODwPR 91, St&PR 91*
Hodges, Robert Edgar 1922- *WhoAm 90*
Hodges, Robert Leith 1941- *WhoSSW 91*
Hodges, Robert M 1921- *BiDrAPA 89*
Hodges, Ron 1949- *Ballpl 90*
Hodges, Russ 1910-1971 *Ballpl 90*
Hodges, Sheila Sue 1949- *WhoEmL 91*
Hodges, Terrell Scott 1940- *WhoSSW 91*
Hodges, Thomas Kent 1936- *WhoAm 90*
Hodges, Thomas Wayne 1945- *WhoEmL 91*
Hodges, Thompson Gene 1913- *WhoAm 90, WhoWor 91*
Hodges, William Terrell 1934- *WhoAm 90, WhoSSW 91*
Hodges, Zachary Ross 1947- *WhoSSW 91*
Hodgetts, John Edwin 1917- *WhoAm 90*
Hodgetts, William *PenDiDA 89*
Hodgin, John C. 1952- *WhoSSW 91*
Hodgin, Jon Darryl *BiDrAPA 89*
Hodgin, Ralph 1916- *Ballpl 90*
Hodgins, Agatha Cobourg 1877-1945 *BioIn 16*
Hodgins, Beatrice Davis 1932- *WhoE 91*
Hodgins, Debra Jean 1953- *WhoEmL 91*
Hodgins, Duncan Ross 1941- *St&PR 91*
Hodgins, Jack 1939- *BioIn 16*
Hodgins, Jack Stanley 1938- *WhoAm 90, WhoWrEP 89*
Hodgins, Theodore Sylvester, III 1966- *WhoEmL 91*
Hodgins, William *BioIn 16*
Hodgkin, Alan L. 1914- *WorAlBi*

Hodgkin, Alan Lloyd 1914- *WhoAm 90, WhoWor 91*
Hodgkin, Dorothy Crowfoot 1910- *BioIn 16, WhoAm 90, WhoWor 91*
Hodgkin, Howard 1932- *NewYTBS 90 [port]*
Hodgkin, John Pease 1909- *WhoAm 90*
Hodgkin, Thomas 1798-1866 *BioIn 16*
Hodgkins, Frances 1869-1947 *BiDWomA*
Hodgkins, H.F., Jr. 1928- *St&PR 91*
Hodgkins, Margaret H. 1939- *St&PR 91*
Hodgkins, Rosalind Selma 1942- *WhoAmA 91*
Hodgkinson, Charles Paul 1907- *WhoAm 90*
Hodgkinson, John 1767?-1805 *BioIn 16*
Hodgkinson, Virginia Humphreys 1941- *WhoE 91*
Hodgkinson, William James 1939- *WhoE 91, WhoWor 91*
Hodgman, Christopher H 1931- *BiDrAPA 89*
Hodgman, Christopher Hampton 1931- *WhoE 91*
Hodgman, Frank H., III 1944- *St&PR 91*
Hodgman, Helen 1945- *ConAu 131, FemiCLE*
Hodgman, Joan Elizabeth 1923- *WhoAm 90*
Hodgman, Thomas F. 1926- *St&PR 91*
Hodgman, Vicki Jean 1933- *WhoWor 91*
Hodgson, Alfreda 1940- *PenDiMP*
Hodgson, Alfreda Rose 1940- *IntWWM 90*
Hodgson, Allan Archibald 1937- *St&PR 91, WhoAm 90*
Hodgson, Arthur Clay 1907- *WhoWor 91*
Hodgson, Carole 1940?- *BiDWomA*
Hodgson, Charles Arthur 1920- *WhoAm 90*
Hodgson, Clague Pitman 1946- *WhoEmL 91*
Hodgson, Edward William, Jr. 1946- *WhoE 91*
Hodgson, Ernest 1932- *WhoAm 90, WhoWor 91*
Hodgson, Frederic 1907- *IntWWM 90*
Hodgson, Frederick Matthew 1930- *St&PR 91*
Hodgson, James D. 1915- *BiDrUSE 89*
Hodgson, James Stanley 1942- *WhoAm 90*
Hodgson, Jane *BioIn 16*
Hodgson, Judd Lawrence 1957- *WhoEmL 91*
Hodgson, Matthew Marshall Neil 1926- *WhoAm 90*
Hodgson, Maureen Laura *BiDrAPA 89*
Hodgson, Paul Edmund 1921- *WhoAm 90*
Hodgson, Peter John 1929- *IntWWM 90, WhoAm 90*
Hodgson, Reginald Hutchins, Jr. 1939- *WhoSSW 91*
Hodgson, Richard 1855-1905 *EncO&P 3, EncPaPR 91*
Hodgson, Richard 1917- *St&PR 91, WhoAm 90*
Hodgson, Robert James 1938- *St&PR 91*
Hodgson, Ryan Richard 1960- *WhoEmL 91*
Hodgson, Thomas Richard 1941- *St&PR 91, WhoAm 90*
Hodgson, Voigt Ralph 1923- *WhoAm 90*
Hodgson, Walter John Barry 1939- *WhoE 91*
Hodgson, William Hope 1877-1918 *TwCCr&M 91*
Hodgson, Winfred Hudson 1920- *WhoAmW 91*
Hodiak, John 1914-1955 *WorAlBi*
Hodierna of Jerusalem *WomWR*
Hodin, Joseph S. 1922- *St&PR 91*
Hodin, Michael W. *ODwPR 91*
Hodin, William 1920- *St&PR 91*
Hodinar, Michael 1954- *WhoE 91, WhoEmL 91*
Hodinko, Robert G. 1934- *St&PR 91*
Hodkinson, Sydney Phillip 1934- *WhoAm 90*
Hodler, Ferdinand 1853-1918 *IntDcAA 90*
Hodley, Jane *WhoAmA 91*
Hodne, Thomas Harold, Jr. 1927- *WhoAm 90*
Hodnett, Byron E. 1945- *St&PR 91*
Hodnett, Dianne Marie 1947- *WhoAmW 91*
Hodnett, Earnestine 1949- *WhoAmW 91, WhoWor 91*
Hodnik, David Francis 1947- *St&PR 91*
Hodo, David Ward 1943- *BiDrAPA 89*
Hodo, Edward Douglas *WhoAm 90*
Hodor, Jadwiga Wegrzyn 1946- *IntWWM 90*
Hodous, Robert Power 1945- *St&PR 91*
Hodowal, John Raymond 1945- *St&PR 91, WhoAm 90*
Hodsdon, Anne C. 1953- *St&PR 91*
Hodsdon, Kenneth Y. 1925- *St&PR 91*
Hodsoll, Christopher *BioIn 16*
Hodsoll, Francis Samuel Monaise 1938- *WhoAm 90*
Hodson, Charlton 1895-1984 *DcNaB 1981*
Hodson, Dale M. *St&PR 91*
Hodson, Janet Dawn 1947- *WhoAmW 91*
Hodson, Jimmy 1962- *WhoEmL 91*
Hodson, John Ralph 1948- *WhoSSW 91*
Hodson, Kenneth Joe 1913- *WhoAm 90*
Hodson, Loretta J. 1934- *St&PR 91*
Hodson, Martin Neil 1945- *IntWWM 90*
Hodson, Thane Raymond 1953- *WhoEmL 91*
Hodson, Thomas William 1946- *St&PR 91, WhoAm 90, WhoEmL 91*
Hodson, Tommy *BioIn 16*
Hodson, William Alan 1935- *WhoAm 90*
Hodulik, Charles James *BiDrAPA 89*
Hodus, Herbert J. 1930- *St&PR 91*
Hoe, Boon Long 1943- *St&PR 91*
Hoe, Richard March 1939- *WhoSSW 91*
Hoebel, Bartley Gore 1935- *WhoAm 90*
Hoebel, Edward Adamson 1906- *WhoAm 90*
Hoebens, Piet Hein 1948-1984 *EncO&P 3*
Hoeberichts, Joan B. 1942- *St&PR 91*
Hoechner, Carl Ludwig 1928- *WhoSSW 91*
Hoechstetter, Harvey 1941- *St&PR 91*
Hoecke, Valeria Konstantinovna 1904-1986 *EncCoWW*
Hoeckele, Stephan John 1947- *WhoE 91*
Hoeckele, Stephen John 1947- *St&PR 91*
Hoeckele, Walter J. 1921- *St&PR 91*
Hoecker, Burdet Wesley 1942- *St&PR 91*
Hoecker, David 1948- *WhoAm 90*
Hoecker, James John 1945- *WhoEmL 91*
Hoecker, Thomas Ralph 1950- *WhoEmL 91*
Hoedemaker, Frederick S 1933- *BiDrAPA 89*
Hoefel, H.T. 1927- *St&PR 91*
Hoefelmeyer, Albert Bernard 1928- *WhoWor 91*
Hoefer, Ann McCallum 1948- *BiDrAPA 89*
Hoefer, Margaret J. 1909- *WhoSSW 91*
Hoeffe, Dietmar 1942- *WhoWor 91*
Hoefflin, Richard Michael 1949- *WhoWor 91*
Hoeffner, Karol Ann 1952- *WhoEmL 91*
Hoeffner, Warren 1932- *St&PR 91*
Hoefle, Joel Matthew 1959- *WhoE 91*
Hoefler, William R. 1946- *St&PR 91*
Hoeflich, Charles Hitschler 1914- *WhoAm 90*
Hoeflin, Ruth Merle 1918- *WhoAm 90*
Hoefling, John Alan 1925- *WhoAm 90*
Hoefling, John Erwin 1927- *WhoWrEP 89*
Hoefling, Judy Elaine 1946- *WhoAmW 91*
Hoefling, Rudolf Joachim 1942- *WhoE 91*
Hoefling, Virginia Ann 1931- *WhoAmW 91, WhoE 91*
Hoeflinger, Norman Charles 1925- *WhoAm 90*
Hoeft, Billy 1932- *Ballpl 90*
Hoeft, Elizabeth Bayless 1942- *WhoAmW 91*
Hoeft, Julius Albert 1946- *WhoAm 90*
Hoeft, Pamela Ann 1946- *WhoEmL 91*
Hoeg, Donald Francis 1931- *WhoAm 90*
Hoegen Dijkhof, Hans Johannes 1947- *WhoWor 91*
Hoegle, Robert Louis 1952- *WhoEmL 91*
Hoehler, Fred Kenneth, Jr. 1918- *WhoAm 90*
Hoehling, Mary 1914- *AuBYP 90*
Hoehn, Elmer L. 1915- *WhoAm 90*
Hoehn, Harry 1918-1974 *WhoAmA 91N*
Hoehn, Robert A. 1941- *St&PR 91*
Hoehn, Robert David 1955- *WhoEmL 91*
Hoehn, William Edwin 1937- *WhoAm 90*
Hoehn-Saric, Rudolf 1929- *BiDrAPA 89*
Hoehne, William Hermann, Jr. 1948- *WhoEmL 91*
Hoei-shin *BioIn 16*
Hoek, Hans Wybrand 1955- *WhoWor 91*
Hoekelman, Thomas Pettie 1940- *St&PR 91*
Hoekema, David Andrew 1950- *WhoAm 90, WhoWor 91*
Hoekman, Guus 1913- *IntWWM 90*
Hoekman, Steven Kent 1953- *WhoEmL 91*
Hoeksema, Timothy E. *WhoSSW 91*
Hoekstra, Andrew Louis 1919- *BiDrAPA 89*
Hoekstra, Clarence S *BiDrAPA 89*
Hoekstra, Djoerd 1934- *St&PR 91*
Hoekwater, James Warren 1946- *St&PR 91, WhoAm 90*
Hoel, David Gerhard 1939- *WhoAm 90*
Hoel, Lester A. 1935- *WhoAm 90*
Hoel, Paul 1905- *WhoAm 90*
Hoel, Robert Fredrick, Jr. 1949- *WhoSSW 91*
Hoel, Roger Satrang 1938- *IntWWM 90*
Hoel, Sigurd 1890-1960 *DcScanL*
Hoel, Sonja Leslie 1966- *WhoAmW 91*
Hoelderle, Paul T. 1937- *St&PR 91*
Hoelker, Louise Catherine 1962- *WhoAmW 91*
Hoell, Noel Laramie 1939- *BiDrAPA 89*
Hoellering, Michael F. 1929- *St&PR 91*
Hoelmer, Karl Heinz 1941- *St&PR 91*
Hoelscher, John Henry 1932- *WhoAm 90*
Hoelscher, Ludwig 1907- *IntWWM 90*
Hoelscher, Robert James 1952- *WhoEmL 91*
Hoelter, Timothy K. 1946- *St&PR 91*
Hoelterhoff, Manuela Vali 1949- *WhoAm 90, WhoAmW 91*
Hoeltzel, David Albert 1954- *WhoE 91*
Hoelzli, Matthew Philip 1961- *WhoEmL 91*
Hoem, Edvard 1949- *DcScanL*
Hoeman, Shirley Pollock 1942- *WhoAmW 91*
Hoen, Hudson Philip, III 1945- *St&PR 91*
Hoenack, Peg Course 1916- *IntWWM 90*
Hoene, Mary Joan 1949- *St&PR 91*
Hoene-Wronski, Joseph Maria 1776-1853 *EncO&P 3*
Hoener, Arthur 1929- *WhoAm 90, WhoAmA 91*
Hoengen, Elisabeth *PenDiMP*
Hoenicke, Edward Henry 1930- *WhoAm 90*
Hoenig, Alan 1949- *WhoEmL 91*
Hoenig, Michael *NewAgMG*
Hoenig, Thomas Michael 1946- *St&PR 91*
Hoenig, William C. 1931- *St&PR 91*
Hoeniger, Berthold H. 1928- *WhoE 91*
Hoenigswald, Henry Max 1915- *WhoAm 90, WhoWor 91*
Hoenmans, Paul John 1932- *St&PR 91, WhoAm 90*
Hoenstine, Barbara Ann 1935- *WhoE 91*
Hoentschel, Georges 1855-1915 *PenDiDA 89*
Hoeper, Bonnie Mae 1940- *WhoE 91*
Hoeper, Edwin William *BiDrAPA 89*
Hoeper, Jeffrey David 1948- *WhoSSW 91*
Hoepfl, Harro 1943- *ConAu 129*
Hoepker, Wilhelm-Wolfgang 1942- *WhoWor 91*
Hoepner, Theodore J. 1941- *St&PR 91*
Hoepner, Theodore John 1941- *WhoAm 90, WhoSSW 91*
Hoeppner, Conrad Henry 1928- *WhoAm 90*
Hoeppner, Iona Ruth 1939- *WhoWrEP 89*
Hoeppner, Thomas Joseph 1941- *St&PR 91*
Hoeprich, Thomas Eric 1955- *IntWWM 90, WhoWor 91*
Hoerber, Mary Elizabeth 1960- *WhoAmW 91*
Hoerger, William E. *ODwPR 91*
Hoerig, Gerald Lee 1943- *WhoAm 90*
Hoermann, Helmut Heinz 1941- *St&PR 91, WhoAm 90*
Hoerner, Joe 1936- *Ballpl 90*
Hoerner, John Finch 1939- *WhoWor 91*
Hoerner, Robert Jack 1931- *WhoAm 90*
Hoerni, Jean Amedee 1924- *WhoAm 90*
Hoernig, Paul Ernst *BiDrAPA 89*
Hoeroldt, Dietrich 1927- *WhoWor 91*
Hoerr, Edward B. 1906- *St&PR 91*
Hoerr, Kenneth Edward 1937- *St&PR 91*
Hoerr, Mark Reeves 1954- *BiDrAPA 89*
Hoerschgen, Hans Eberhard 1936- *WhoWor 91*
Hoerst, Frank 1917- *Ballpl 90*
Hoerster, Samuel August, Jr. 1918- *BiDrAPA 89*
Hoes, Larry M. 1946- *St&PR 91*
Hoes, Tom L. 1953- *St&PR 91*
Hoesch, Edgar 1935- *WhoWor 91*
Hoesch, Henning *BioIn 16*
Hoeschler, Linda Lovas 1944- *WhoAm 90*
Hoess, Rudolf 1900-1947 *BioIn 16*
Hoessle, Charles Herman 1931- *WhoAm 90*
Hoest, Bill 1926-1988 *BioIn 16*
Hoest, William 1926-1988 *EncACom*
Hoesterey, Richard Kenneth 1942- *St&PR 91*
Hoetink, Harmannus 1931- *WhoWor 91*
Hoetink, Hendrik Richard 1929- *WhoWor 91*
Hoetker, William James 1932- *WhoAm 90*
Hoetzel, Richard 1943- *BiDrAPA 89*
Hoeve, Anthon Roelof 1953- *WhoWor 91*
Hoeveler, J. David, Jr. 1943- *ConAu 129*
Hoeveler, William M. *NewYTBS 90 [port]*
Hoexter, Corinne Rosenfelder Katz 1927- *WhoE 91*
Hoey, Allen S. 1952- *WhoWrEP 89*
Hoey, Clyde Roark, II 1939- *St&PR 91*
Hoey, Frances Sarah 1830-1908 *FemiCLE*
Hoey, Fred 1885-1932 *Ballpl 90*
Hoey, James Joseph 1936- *St&PR 91*
Hoey, Karen Elyse 1954- *WhoEmL 91, WhoSSW 91*
Hoey, Rita 1952- *ODwPR 91*
Hoey, Rita Marie 1950- *WhoAmW 91*
Hof, Liselotte Bertha 1937- *WhoAmW 91*
Hofacker, Charles Frederick 1953- *WhoSSW 91*
Hofacker, Ludwig Georg 1930- *WhoWor 91*
Hofacre, William M. 1933- *St&PR 91*
Hofacre, William Marion 1933- *WhoAm 90*
Hofbauer, Rita Anne 1936- *WhoAmW 91*
Hofe, G. Douglas *BioIn 16*
Hofeldt, John W. 1920- *WhoAm 90*
Hofeldt, Ronald Lloyd *BiDrAPA 89*
Hofer, Evelyn *WhoAmA 91*
Hofer, Ingrid *WhoAmA 91*
Hofer, Judith K. *WhoAmW 91*
Hofer, Milan Peter 1936- *WhoWor 91*
Hofer, Myron Arms 1931- *WhoE 91*
Hofert, Jack 1930- *WhoWor 91*
Hoff, B. J. 1940- *WhoWrEP 89*
Hoff, Charles Worthington, III 1934- *St&PR 91, WhoAm 90*
Hoff, David Jordan 1924- *St&PR 91*
Hoff, Donnafred Mary 1903- *WhoWrEP 89*
Hoff, Gary Ward 1962- *WhoSSW 91*
Hoff, Gerhardt Michael 1930- *St&PR 91, WhoAm 90*
Hoff, Jeanne *BiDrAPA 89*
Hoff, John F. 1939- *St&PR 91*
Hoff, Jonathan Morind 1955- *WhoEmL 91*
Hoff, Julian Theodore 1936- *WhoAm 90*
Hoff, Julienne Nora 1939- *WhoAmW 91*
Hoff, Kathleen Patricia 1927- *WhoAmW 91*
Hoff, Lawrence C. 1929- *St&PR 91*
Hoff, Margo *WhoAmA 91*
Hoff, Margo 1912- *WhoAm 90*
Hoff, Mary Kathryn 1953- *WhoAmW 91*
Hoff, Nicholas John 1906- *WhoAm 90*
Hoff, Randal Mark 1952- *St&PR 91*
Hoff, Randy A. 1949- *St&PR 91*
Hoff, Renae 1951- *WhoEmL 91*
Hoff, Samuel R. 1930- *St&PR 91*
Hoff, Shirley Arlene 1934- *WhoAmW 91*
Hoff, Syd 1912- *EncACom*
Hoff, Sydney 1912- *AuBYP 90, WhoAm 90*
Hoff, Timothy 1941- *WhoSSW 91*
Hoff-Jessen, Allan 1942- *WhoWor 91*
Hoffa, Harlan Edward 1925- *WhoAm 90*
Hoffa, James R. 1913-1975? *WorAlBi*
Hoffa, James Riddle *BioIn 16*
Hoffa, Jimmy *BioIn 16*
Hoffa, Portland *NewYTBS 90*
Hoffart, Louis Frank 1939- *St&PR 91*
Hoffbauer, Diane Kaye 1955- *WhoAmW 91*
Hoffberg, Judith A 1934- *WhoAmA 91, WhoWrEP 89*
Hoffberg, Norman Charles 1947- *St&PR 91*
Hoffberg, Theodore J. 1932- *St&PR 91*
Hoffberg, William E. 1923- *St&PR 91*
Hoffberger, Charles H. 1912- *St&PR 91*
Hoffberger, Jerold C. 1919- *St&PR 91*
Hoffberger, Jerold Charles 1919- *WhoAm 90*
Hoffberger, LeRoy E. 1925- *St&PR 91*
Hoffberger, LeRoy Edward 1925- *WhoAm 90*
Hoffberger, Stanley A. 1929- *St&PR 91*
Hoffe, Otfried 1943- *WhoWor 91*
Hoffecker, John Henry 1827-1900 *AmLegL*
Hoffecker, Pamela Hobbs 1942- *WhoWrEP 89*
Hoffecker, Savin 1908- *AuBYP 90*
Hoffee, Patricia Anne 1937- *WhoAmW 91*
Hoffeld, Jeffrey M 1945- *WhoAmA 91*
Hoffenberg, Harvey *BioIn 16*
Hoffenberg, Martin 1945- *St&PR 91, WhoAm 90*
Hoffenberg, Marvin 1914- *WhoAm 90*
Hoffenberg, Raymond 1923- *WhoWor 91*
Hoffer, Abram 1917- *EncO&P 3*
Hoffer, Alexander 1933- *BiDrAPA 89*
Hoffer, Alma Jeanne 1932- *WhoAmW 91*
Hoffer, Audrey S. *ODwPR 91*
Hoffer, Axel 1936- *BiDrAPA 89, WhoE 91*
Hoffer, Bill 1870-1959 *Ballpl 90*
Hoffer, Charles R. 1929- *WhoWrEP 89*
Hoffer, Eric 1902-1983 *WorAlBi*
Hoffer, John Louis 1931- *St&PR 91, WhoE 91*
Hoffer, Mary Jane 1947- *WhoAmW 91*
Hoffer, Michael G. 1939- *St&PR 91*
Hoffer, Mindy *BiDrAPA 89*
Hoffer, Paul B. 1939- *WhoAm 90*
Hoffer, Richard *BioIn 16*
Hoffer, Richard Scott 1950- *BiDrAPA 89*
Hoffer, Robert M. 1921- *St&PR 91*
Hoffer, Robert Morrison 1921- *WhoAm 90*
Hoffer, Sharon Kay Rife 1944- *WhoAmW 91*
Hoffer, Stuart H. 1937- *St&PR 91*
Hoffer, Thomas William 1938- *WhoSSW 91*
Hoffer, William A. 1949- *St&PR 91*
Hoffert, J. Stan 1947- *St&PR 91*
Hoffert, Martin Irving 1938- *WhoAm 90, WhoE 91*
Hoffert, Paul Washington 1923- *WhoE 91, WhoWor 91*
Hoffgen, Marga 1921- *PenDiMP*

Hoffgen, Marga 1926- IntWWM 90
Hoffheimer, Craig 1950- St&PR 91
Hoffheimer, Daniel Joseph 1950- WhoEmL 91
Hoffheimer, James M. 1955- St&PR 91
Hoffheimer, Michael Harry 1954- WhoEmL 91
Hoffland, Dorinda Ruth 1961- WhoEmL 91
Hoffleit, Ellen Dorrit 1907- WhoAm 90
Hoffler, Dietrich 1934- WhoWor 91
Hoffler, G. Wyckliffe 1934- WhoAm 90
Hoffman, Abbie BioIn 16
Hoffman, Abbie 1936-1989 AnObit 1989, EncAL, MajTwCW
Hoffman, Al 1902-1960 OxCPMus
Hoffman, Alan Jay 1948- WhoE 91
Hoffman, Alan Jerome 1924- WhoAm 90
Hoffman, Alan Michael 1946- WhoWor 91
Hoffman, Alfred John 1917- WhoAm 90
Hoffman, Alice BioIn 16
Hoffman, Alice 1952- MajTwCW, WorAu 1980 [port]
Hoffman, Allan Sachs 1932- WhoAm 90
Hoffman, Amy S BiDrAPA 89
Hoffman, Ann Fleisher 1942- WhoAmW 91
Hoffman, Arlene Faun 1941- WhoAmW 91
Hoffman, Arnold WhoAmA 91N
Hoffman, Arthur M 1941- BiDrAPA 89
Hoffman, Arthur Wolf 1921- WhoAm 90
Hoffman, Barbara A. 1940- WhoAmW 91
Hoffman, Barbara Allen 1943- WhoAmW 91
Hoffman, Ben G BiDrAPA 89
Hoffman, Bernadine M. 1947- WhoAmW 91
Hoffman, Bernard BiDrAPA 89
Hoffman, Bernard 1943- WhoE 91
Hoffman, Beth Lynn 1943- WhoAmW 91
Hoffman, Betty Jane 1933- WhoAmW 91
Hoffman, Bradley J. 1961- St&PR 91
Hoffman, Brian F 1942- BiDrAPA 89
Hoffman, C. Fenno, III 1958- WhoEmL 91
Hoffman, C.N., Jr. 1918- St&PR 91
Hoffman, Candy Lynn 1957- WhoAmW 91
Hoffman, Carl J BiDrAPA 89
Hoffman, Carol Knight 1943- WhoAmW 91, WhoE 91
Hoffman, Carol Maree 1944- WhoAmA 91
Hoffman, Catherine Mary 1946- WhoAmW 91
Hoffman, Charles A. BioIn 16
Hoffman, Charles Isaiah 1864-1945 BioIn 16
Hoffman, Charles J. 1929- St&PR 91
Hoffman, Christian Matthew 1944- WhoAm 90
Hoffman, Cindy Jane 1946- WhoWrEP 89
Hoffman, Claer-Marie 1960- WhoEmL 91
Hoffman, Clive 1937- ODwPR 91
Hoffman, D. 1932- St&PR 91
Hoffman, Dale Marland 1940- WhoSSW 91
Hoffman, Daniel 1923- WhoAm 90, WhoWrEP 89
Hoffman, Daniel Andrew 1948- BiDrAPA 89
Hoffman, Daniel Paul 1912- WhoWrEP 89
Hoffman, Daniel Steven 1931- WhoAm 90
Hoffman, Danny 1880-1922 Ballpl 90
Hoffman, Darleane Christian 1926- WhoAm 90, WhoAmW 91
Hoffman, Darnay Robert 1947- WhoE 91, WhoWor 91
Hoffman, Dave BioIn 16
Hoffman, David Alan 1947- WhoEmL 91
Hoffman, David Edward 1945- BiDrAPA 89
Hoffman, David Lloyd 1954- BiDrAPA 89
Hoffman, David N. 1910- St&PR 91
Hoffman, Dean Allen 1949- WhoWrEP 89
Hoffman, Dolores Garcia 1936- WhoHisp 91
Hoffman, Donald Howard 1933- St&PR 91, WhoAm 90, WhoE 91
Hoffman, Donald M. 1935- WhoAm 90
Hoffman, Donna Coy 1940- WhoAmW 91
Hoffman, Douglas Robert 1949- WhoEmL 91
Hoffman, Dustin 1937- BioIn 16, WorAlBi
Hoffman, Dustin Lee 1937- WhoAm 90, WhoE 91, WhoWor 91
Hoffman, E. T. A. 1776-1822 WorAlBi
Hoffman, Edward Fenno, III 1916- WhoAm 90, WhoAmA 91
Hoffman, Edward Richard, III 1928- WhoSSW 91
Hoffman, Edward Robert 1923- St&PR 91
Hoffman, Edwin D. BioIn 16
Hoffman, Edwin K. 1922- St&PR 91
Hoffman, Edwin Philip 1942- WhoAm 90
Hoffman, Elaine Janet WhoAmA 91
Hoffman, Elissa J. BiDrAPA 89
Hoffman, Ellen B. 1920- St&PR 91
Hoffman, Ercell H. 1941- WhoWrEP 89
Hoffman, Eric BioIn 16
Hoffman, Eric 1952- WhoAmA 91
Hoffman, Eric Jay 1942- WhoE 91
Hoffman, Ethan BioIn 16
Hoffman, Ethan NewYTBS 90
Hoffman, Eva BioIn 16
Hoffman, Eva 1945- ConAu 132
Hoffman, Floyd Gerry 1943- St&PR 91, WhoAm 90
Hoffman, Francis H BiDrAPA 89
Hoffman, Frank Lloyd 1956- WhoEmL 91
Hoffman, Frank V 1921- BiDrAPA 89
Hoffman, Franklin David, Jr. 1945- WhoAm 90
Hoffman, Fred S. 1922- WhoAm 90
Hoffman, Frederick 1903- St&PR 91
Hoffman, Frederick 1937- WhoSSW 91
Hoffman, Gene 1927- WhoAm 90
Hoffman, Gene D. 1927- St&PR 91
Hoffman, George BioIn 16
Hoffman, George A. 1959- WhoSSW 91
Hoffman, George Walter 1914- WhoAm 90
Hoffman, Gerald Allan 1931- BiDrAPA 89
Hoffman, Gerald K BiDrAPA 89
Hoffman, Gert 1931- WorAu 1980 [port]
Hoffman, Glenn 1958- Ballpl 90
Hoffman, Gloria AuBYP 90
Hoffman, Gloria L. 1933- WhoWrEP 89
Hoffman, Gloria Levy 1933- WhoWor 91
Hoffman, Grace 1925- PenDiMP
Hoffman, Grace 1926- IntWWM 90
Hoffman, Graham Walter, Jr. 1956- BiDrAPA 89
Hoffman, Gretel Bonneval Holcomb 1962- WhoAmW 91
Hoffman, Guy 1956- Ballpl 90
Hoffman, Harold Clifford BioIn 16
Hoffman, Harold Wayne 1930- WhoAm 90
Hoffman, Harry Theodore 1927- WhoAm 90
Hoffman, Harry Z 1908- WhoAmA 91
Hoffman, Helen Bacon 1930- WhoAmA 91
Hoffman, Henry William 1925- WhoWrEP 89
Hoffman, Herbert W. 1939- St&PR 91
Hoffman, Howard A 1936- BiDrAPA 89
Hoffman, Howard Carl 1942- WhoE 91
Hoffman, Howard Lee 1943- BiDrAPA 89
Hoffman, Howard Stanley 1925- WhoAm 90
Hoffman, Irwin 1924- IntWWM 90, WhoAm 90, WhoWor 91
Hoffman, Ivan Bruce 1949- BiDrAPA 89
Hoffman, Jack Leroy 1922- WhoAm 90
Hoffman, Jackie BioIn 16
Hoffman, James Paul 1943- WhoWor 91
Hoffman, Jane E. 1953- St&PR 91
Hoffman, Jane Ellen 1953- WhoEmL 91
Hoffman, Jeffrey Morse 1945- BiDrAPA 89
Hoffman, Jeffrey William 1952- St&PR 91
Hoffman, Jennifer Isobel 1948- WhoAmW 91
Hoffman, Jerry Carl 1943- St&PR 91
Hoffman, Joan Bentley 1946- WhoEmL 91
Hoffman, Joel Elihu 1937- WhoAm 90
Hoffman, Joel Harvey 1953- IntWWM 90, WhoEmL 91
Hoffman, Joel Jeffrey 1944- St&PR 91
Hoffman, Joel Stephen BiDrAPA 89
Hoffman, Johanna A 1936- BiDrAPA 89
Hoffman, John Ernest, Jr. 1934- WhoAm 90, WhoE 91
Hoffman, John Fletcher 1946- WhoE 91
Hoffman, John Raleigh 1926- WhoAm 90
Hoffman, John Raymond 1945- St&PR 91
Hoffman, Joseph Anthony 1956- WhoEmL 91
Hoffman, Joseph Frederick 1925- WhoAm 90
Hoffman, Joseph Henry, Jr. 1955- WhoEmL 91
Hoffman, Judith Louise BiDrAPA 89
Hoffman, Judy Greenblatt 1932- WhoAmW 91, WhoWor 91
Hoffman, Julien Ivor Ellis 1925- WhoAm 90
Hoffman, Julius 1921- BiDrAPA 89, WhoE 91
Hoffman, Karla Ann 1953- WhoE 91
Hoffman, Karla Leigh 1948- WhoSSW 91
Hoffman, Kenneth D. 1928- St&PR 91
Hoffman, Kenneth Jay BiDrAPA 89
Hoffman, Kenneth Myron 1930- WhoAm 90
Hoffman, Larry Gene 1933- WhoAmA 91
Hoffman, Lawrence Michael 1951- WhoEmL 91
Hoffman, Leon 1941- BiDrAPA 89
Hoffman, Linda R. 1940- WhoAmW 91
Hoffman, Lloyd O. 1927- St&PR 91
Hoffman, Lois Wladis 1929- WhoAm 90
Hoffman, Louis 1922- BiDrAPA 89
Hoffman, Lynne Francis 1953- BiDrAPA 89
Hoffman, Malvina 1887-1966 BioIn 16, WhoAmA 91N
Hoffman, Malvina Cornell 1885-1966 BiDWomA
Hoffman, Mandy Lippman 1956- WhoAmA 91
Hoffman, Margaret A. 1945- WhoEmL 91
Hoffman, Marilyn Friedman WhoAm 90, WhoAmA 91, WhoE 91
Hoffman, Marshall 1942- WhoWrEP 89
Hoffman, Martin 1933- St&PR 91
Hoffman, Martin 1935- WhoAmA 91
Hoffman, Martin Leon 1924- WhoAm 90
Hoffman, Marvin 1933- WhoWor 91
Hoffman, Mary 1945- BioIn 16, ConAu 131
Hoffman, Mary Catherine 1923- WhoAmW 91
Hoffman, Maryhelen H. Paulick 1943- WhoAm 90
Hoffman, Mathew 1954- WhoEmL 91
Hoffman, Melvin B. 1919- St&PR 91
Hoffman, Merle Holly 1946- WhoAmW 91, WhoE 91, WhoEmL 91, WhoWor 91
Hoffman, Michael Alan 1954- BiDrAPA 89
Hoffman, Michael Allen 1944-1990 ConAu 131
Hoffman, Michael B BiDrAPA 89
Hoffman, Michael Charles 1947- WhoEmL 91
Hoffman, Michael E 1942- WhoAmA 91
Hoffman, Michael Eugene 1942- WhoAm 90
Hoffman, Michael George 1947- St&PR 91
Hoffman, Michael Harris 1952- WhoEmL 91
Hoffman, Michael Jerome 1939- WhoAm 90
Hoffman, Michael Joseph 1954- WhoEmL 91
Hoffman, Michael Lindsay 1915- WhoE 91
Hoffman, Michael W. 1948- St&PR 91
Hoffman, Michael William 1955- WhoEmL 91
Hoffman, Nanci L. 1948- ODwPR 91
Hoffman, Nancy 1944- WhoAmA 91
Hoffman, Nathaniel A. 1949- WhoEmL 91
Hoffman, Neil James 1938- WhoAm 90, WhoAmA 91
Hoffman, Nito Joseph 1948- WhoWor 91
Hoffman, Oscar Allen 1920- WhoAm 90
Hoffman, Pat 1943-1988 BioIn 16
Hoffman, Pattie BioIn 16
Hoffman, Paul BioIn 16
Hoffman, Paul Felix 1941- WhoAm 90
Hoffman, Paul G. 1891-1974 BioIn 16
Hoffman, Paul Gray 1891-1974 EncABHB 5 [port]
Hoffman, Paul Roger 1934- WhoAm 90
Hoffman, Paul W. 1925- St&PR 91
Hoffman, Paul William 1956- WhoE 91
Hoffman, Pete 1919- EncACom
Hoffman, Peter Ivan 1954- WhoE 91
Hoffman, Peter Toll 1946- WhoAm 90, WhoEmL 91
Hoffman, Philip Andrew 1931- WhoAm 90
Hoffman, Philip D. 1932- ODwPR 91
Hoffman, Philip Guthrie 1915- WhoAm 90
Hoffman, R.J. 1932- St&PR 91
Hoffman, Ralph G. St&PR 91
Hoffman, Ramona Kay 1956- WhoAmW 91
Hoffman, Randy Michael 1965- WhoSSW 91, WhoWor 91
Hoffman, Richard 1831-1909 PenDiMP
Hoffman, Richard Allen BiDrAPA 89
Hoffman, Richard Bennett 1945- WhoEmL 91
Hoffman, Richard Bruce 1947- WhoAm 90, WhoEmL 91
Hoffman, Richard E. 1932- St&PR 91
Hoffman, Richard George 1949- WhoEmL 91
Hoffman, Richard James 1948- WhoSSW 91
Hoffman, Richard K. 1928- St&PR 91
Hoffman, Richard M. 1942- St&PR 91, WhoAm 90
Hoffman, Richard Peter 1911- WhoAmA 91
Hoffman, Richard Scott 1956- WhoEmL 91
Hoffman, Richard William 1918- WhoAm 90
Hoffman, Robert Alan 1946- St&PR 91
Hoffman, Robert David 1941- BiDrAPA 89
Hoffman, Robert Stanley 1944- BiDrAPA 89
Hoffman, Robin Rhoades Menge 1952- WhoAmW 91
Hoffman, Rodney James 1953- WhoEmL 91
Hoffman, Roger John 1949- WhoEmL 91
Hoffman, Roger P. 1944- St&PR 91
Hoffman, Roger Warren 1964- WhoE 91
Hoffman, Ronald 1945- WhoAm 90
Hoffman, Ronald Bruce 1939- WhoSSW 91
Hoffman, Ronald H. 1947- St&PR 91
Hoffman, Ronald Robert 1934- St&PR 91, WhoAm 90
Hoffman, Ronna BioIn 16
Hoffman, Roy A., Jr. 1940- WhoSSW 91
Hoffman, S. Joseph 1920- WhoAm 90
Hoffman, Sandra Bette 1943- WhoE 91
Hoffman, Sharon Accardo BiDrAPA 89
Hoffman, Sharon Ann 1958- WhoE 91
Hoffman, Stanley 1929- IntWWM 90
Hoffman, Stanley W. BioIn 16
Hoffman, Stephen M. 1945- St&PR 91
Hoffman, Steven Jacob 1954- WhoEmL 91
Hoffman, Sue Ellen 1945- WhoAmW 91, WhoEmL 91
Hoffman, Teresa Esther 1957- WhoAmW 91
Hoffman, Theodore E, Jr. BiDrAPA 89
Hoffman, Timothy Herman 1953- WhoE 91
Hoffman, Valerie Jane 1953- WhoAmW 91
Hoffman, Walter August 1926- St&PR 91
Hoffman, Walter Edward 1907- WhoAm 90
Hoffman, Warren Eugene, II 1954- WhoWor 91
Hoffman, Warren Mark 1926- St&PR 91
Hoffman, Wayne Melvin 1923- WhoAm 90
Hoffman, William A 1920- WhoAmA 91
Hoffman, William Franklin 1950- BiDrAPA 89
Hoffman, William Howard 1930- St&PR 91, WhoAm 90
Hoffman, William J. St&PR 91
Hoffman, William McKinley, Jr 1934- WhoAmA 91, WhoE 91
Hoffman, William P. BioIn 16
Hoffmann, Arnold, Jr 1915- WhoAmA 91
Hoffmann, Barry L. 1946- St&PR 91
Hoffmann, Bernhard 1932- St&PR 91
Hoffmann, Bruno 1913- IntWWM 90, PenDiMP
Hoffmann, Carol Tomb 1952- WhoAmW 91, WhoEmL 91
Hoffmann, Charles Wesley 1929- WhoAm 90
Hoffmann, Christoph L. 1944- St&PR 91
Hoffmann, Christoph Ludwig 1944- WhoAm 90
Hoffmann, Constance Wellings 1950- WhoAmW 91
Hoffmann, Donald 1933- WhoAm 90
Hoffmann, Gary David 1947- WhoAmA 91
Hoffmann, Gerhard BiDrAPA 89
Hoffmann, Gerhard Fedor Oskar 1917- WhoWor 91
Hoffmann, Guy 1916-1986 OxCCanT
Hoffmann, Hans Juergen 1943- WhoWor 91
Hoffmann, Horst 1935- IntWWM 90
Hoffmann, Joan Carol 1934- WhoAmW 91
Hoffmann, John Baldwin 1940- St&PR 91
Hoffmann, Josef 1870-1956 BioIn 16, PenDiDA 89
Hoffmann, Juan Miguel 1941- BiDrAPA 89
Hoffmann, Karel PenDiMP
Hoffmann, Klaus Hubert 1946- WhoWor 91
Hoffmann, Kurt George Joachim 1929- WhoWor 91
Hoffmann, Leesa L 1946- WhoAmA 91
Hoffmann, Leon Roger 1949- St&PR 91
Hoffmann, Louis Gerhard 1932- WhoAm 90
Hoffmann, Malcolm Arthur 1912- WhoAm 90
Hoffmann, Manfred Walter 1938- WhoSSW 91, WhoWor 91
Hoffmann, Margaret Jones AuBYP 90
Hoffmann, Mary Ann 1944- BiDrAPA 89
Hoffmann, Melane Kinney 1956- ODwPR 91
Hoffmann, Michael Richard 1947- WhoEmL 91
Hoffmann, Nancy Larraine WhoAmW 91
Hoffmann, Oswald Carl Julius 1913- WhoAm 90
Hoffmann, Peggy 1910- AuBYP 90, BioIn 16
Hoffmann, Peter Conrad Werner 1930- WhoAm 90, WhoWrEP 89
Hoffmann, Richard Arthur 1941- WhoSSW 91
Hoffmann, Roald 1937- BioIn 16, WhoAm 90, WhoE 91, WhoWor 91, WorAlBi
Hoffmann, Robert Shaw 1929- WhoAm 90, WhoWor 91
Hoffmann, Stanley 1928- WhoAm 90
Hoffmann, Thomas Russell 1933- WhoAm 90
Hoffmann, Timothy Jay 1958- WhoEmL 91
Hoffmann, Volker BiDrAPA 89
Hoffmann, W. PenDiDA 89

Hoffmann, William F. III 1940- *BiDrAPA 89*
Hoffmann, William Frederick 1933- *WhoAm 90*
Hoffmann, William Frederick, III 1940- *WhoE 91*
Hoffmann, Wolf-Dietrich 1945- *WhoWor 91*
Hoffmann-Erbrecht, Lothar 1925- *IntWWM 90*
Hoffmann-Ostenhof, Otto 1914- *WhoWor 91*
Hoffmann-Ostenhof, Peter 1955- *WhoWor 91*
Hoffmannsthal, Hugo Von 1874-1929 *WorAlBi*
Hoffmaster, Stephanie Joan 1953- *WhoAmW 91*
Hoffmeier, Kathy Ann 1956- *WhoAmW 91*
Hoffmeister, Bruce Francis 1961- *WhoEmL 91*
Hoffmeister, Donald Frederick 1916- *WhoAm 90*
Hoffmeister, Gerhart 1936- *ConAu 130*
Hoffmeister, Jana Marie *WhoAmW 91*
Hoffmeyer, Erik 1924- *WhoWor 91*
Hoffmeyer, Stanton David 1939- *WhoSSW 91*
Hoffmeyer, William Frederick 1936- *WhoWor 91*
Hoffner, Marilyn 1929- *WhoAmW 91, WhoE 91*
Hoffner, Pelagie Doane *AuBYP 90*
Hoffnung, Audrey Sonia 1928- *WhoAmW 91*
Hoffnung, Gerard 1925-1959 *PenDiMP*
Hofford, Suzanne 1957- *WhoAmW 91*
Hoffs, Joshua A 1933- *BiDrAPA 89*
Hoffs, Malcolm J *BiDrAPA 89*
Hoffs, Susanna *BioIn 16*
Hoffstein, Allen 1927- *BiDrAPA 89*
Hoffstein, Herbert 1928- *WhoE 91*
Hoffstetter, Armand A. 1910- *St&PR 91*
Hoffstot, Henry Phipps, Jr. 1917- *WhoAm 90*
Hofgesang, Paul Joseph 1957- *WhoEmL 91*
Hofinga, Tyler Hans 1957- *WhoEmL 91*
Hofland, Barbara 1770-1844 *FemiCLE*
Hofley, Carole S. *St&PR 91*
Hofley, Norman H. 1932- *St&PR 91*
Hofling, A. Alden 1929- *St&PR 91*
Hoflund, Charles J. 1834-1914 *BioIn 16*
Hofman, Bobby 1925- *Ballpl 90*
Hofman, Peter David 1946- *St&PR 91*
Hofman, Shlomo 1909- *IntWWM 90*
Hofman, Solly 1894-1956 *Ballpl 90*
Hofman, Steven Ira 1953- *WhoE 91*
Hofmann, Adele Dellenbaugh 1926- *WhoAmW 91*
Hofmann, Alan Frederick 1931- *WhoAm 90*
Hofmann, Armin 1920- *ConDes 90*
Hofmann, Bernard M. 1934- *St&PR 91*
Hofmann, Daniel 1930- *St&PR 91*
Hofmann, Douglas Allan 1950- *WhoEmL 91*
Hofmann, Douglas William 1945- *WhoAmA 91*
Hofmann, Franz 1942- *WhoWor 91*
Hofmann, Fred 1894-1964 *Ballpl 90*
Hofmann, Hans 1880-1961 *WhoAmA 91N*
Hofmann, Hans 1880-1966 *IntDcAA 90, WorAlBi*
Hofmann, Hans 1923- *WhoAm 90, WhoWrEP 89*
Hofmann, Harald 1932- *WhoWor 91*
Hofmann, Herbert Charles 1942- *St&PR 91*
Hofmann, Isabella *BioIn 16*
Hofmann, J. Michael 1943- *St&PR 91*
Hofmann, John Richard, Jr. 1922- *WhoAm 90*
Hofmann, Josef 1876-1957 *BioIn 16, PenDiMP*
Hofmann, Kay 1932- *WhoAmA 91*
Hofmann, Klaus 1911- *WhoAm 90*
Hofmann, Mark *BioIn 16*
Hofmann, Paul Bernard 1941- *WhoAm 90*
Hofmann, Peter *BioIn 16*
Hofmann, Peter 1944- *IntWWM 90, PenDiMP*
Hofmann, Robert D. 1960- *St&PR 91*
Hofmann, Theo 1924- *WhoAm 90*
Hofmann, Thomas J. 1942- *St&PR 91*
Hofmann, William F., III 1943- *WhoE 91*
Hofmans, Cornelis M. 1929- *St&PR 91*
Hofmeister, Adolf K. 1936- *St&PR 91*
Hofmeister, Burkhard 1931- *WhoWor 91*
Hofmeister, Franz 1850-1922 *DcScB S2*
Hofmeister, Giannina Lombardo 1942- *IntWWM 90*
Hofmo, Gunvor 1921- *DcScanL*
Hofmockel, Gerald 1926- *St&PR 91*
Hofrichter, David Alan 1948- *WhoWor 91*
Hofrichter, Lawrence S. 1947- *WhoEmL 91*
Hofsinde, Robert 1902-1973 *AuBYP 90*
Hofstadter, Albert 1910-1989 *BioIn 16*
Hofstadter, Douglas R 1945- *MajTwCW, WorAu 1980 [port]*
Hofstadter, Douglas Richard 1945- *WhoAm 90*
Hofstadter, Richard 1916-1970 *WorAlBi*
Hofstadter, Robert 1915- *WhoAm 90, WhoWor 91, WorAlBi*
Hofstadter, Robert 1915-1990 *NewYTBS 90 [port]*
Hofstaedter, Charles Andreas 1961- *WhoSSW 91*
Hofstaetter, Gabriele Anna 1953- *WhoWor 91*
Hofstatter, Leopold 1902- *BiDrAPA 89, WhoAm 90*
Hofstead, James Warner 1913- *WhoWor 91*
Hofsted, Jolyon Gene 1942- *WhoAmA 91, WhoE 91*
Hofstein, David Neal 1951- *WhoEmL 91*
Hofstetter, Georgene Louise Weigel 1954- *WhoAmW 91*
Hofstetter, Henry W 1914- *WhoAm 90*
Hofstetter, Igo 1926- *IntWWM 90*
Hofstetter, Kenneth John 1940- *WhoSSW 91*
Hofstra, John Lambert *BiDrAPA 89*
Hofstrand, Joanne Kalar *BiDrAPA 89*
Hoft, Lynne Ann 1945- *WhoAmW 91, WhoEmL 91*
Hoftiezer, Helen Louise 1950- *WhoAmW 91*
Hogan, Arthur Robert 1932- *St&PR 91*
Hogan, Barbara Jane 1939- *WhoAmW 91*
Hogan, Ben *NewYTBS 90 [port]*
Hogan, Ben 1912- *BioIn 16, WhoAm 90, WorAlBi*
Hogan, Brian Joseph 1943- *WhoE 91*
Hogan, Charlene Jo 1948- *WhoAmW 91*
Hogan, Charles C 1921- *BiDrAPA 89*
Hogan, Charles Carlton 1921- *WhoE 91*
Hogan, Clarence Lester 1920- *WhoAm 90, WhoWor 91*
Hogan, Claude Hollis 1920- *WhoAm 90*
Hogan, Curtis Jule 1926- *WhoAm 90, WhoWor 91*
Hogan, D.M. 1947- *St&PR 91*
Hogan, Daniel E., Jr. 1917- *St&PR 91*
Hogan, Daniel Michael 1950- *WhoE 91*
Hogan, David Earl 1949- *WhoAm 90, WhoEmL 91*
Hogan, Deborah Lynn *BiDrAPA 89*
Hogan, Deidre *ODwPR 91*
Hogan, Diarmuid M. 1944- *St&PR 91*
Hogan, Donald Jack 1945- *St&PR 91*
Hogan, Douglas William 1960- *WhoEmL 91*
Hogan, Edward J. *BioIn 16*
Hogan, Edward Joseph 1950- *WhoEmL 91*
Hogan, Edward Leo 1932- *WhoAm 90*
Hogan, Ellen Joan 1945- *St&PR 91*
Hogan, Eric E., Jr. 1950- *WhoSSW 91*
Hogan, Ernest *EarBlAP*
Hogan, Frances Alicia 1955- *BiDrAPA 89*
Hogan, Genie Merrell 1946- *WhoEmL 91*
Hogan, Gerald Francis *BioIn 16*
Hogan, Harlan Robert 1946- *WhoEmL 91*
Hogan, Henry Leon, III 1920- *WhoAm 90*
Hogan, Henry M., Jr. 1932- *St&PR 91*
Hogan, Hulk *BioIn 16*
Hogan, Ilona Modly 1947- *WhoAm 90*
Hogan, Inez 1895- *AuBYP 90*
Hogan, James Charles 1936- *WhoAm 90*
Hogan, James Donald 1927- *WhoAm 90*
Hogan, James Joseph 1829-1913 *AmLegL*
Hogan, James L. 1930- *St&PR 91*
Hogan, James P. 1941- *RGTwCSF*
Hogan, Jerry Harold 1937- *St&PR 91*
Hogan, Joanna Leigh 1951- *WhoEmL 91*
Hogan, John Donald 1927- *WhoAm 90*
Hogan, John H. 1946- *St&PR 91*
Hogan, John Henry *BioIn 16*
Hogan, John Paul 1919- *WhoAm 90*
Hogan, Joseph Burroughs 1942- *WhoSSW 91*
Hogan, Joseph Thomas 1943- *WhoE 91, WhoWor 91*
Hogan, Judy Fordham 1937- *WhoWrEP 89*
Hogan, Kenneth William 1944- *St&PR 91*
Hogan, Kristina A. 1948- *WhoAmW 91*
Hogan, Linda K. 1947- *WhoWrEP 89*
Hogan, Linda Rae 1948- *WhoEmL 91*
Hogan, Lois *ODwPR 91*
Hogan, Mark 1931- *WhoAm 90*
Hogan, Mark James 1956- *WhoEmL 91*
Hogan, Marshall D, Jr. 1919- *BiDrAPA 89*
Hogan, Mary Ann Egan *BioIn 16*
Hogan, Melody Ann 1958- *WhoSSW 91*
Hogan, Mervin Booth 1906- *WhoAm 90*
Hogan, Michael Ray 1953- *St&PR 91, WhoEmL 91*
Hogan, Molly 1945- *WhoEmL 91*
Hogan, Patricia Eileen 1953- *BiDrAPA 89*
Hogan, Patricia Susan 1944- *St&PR 91*
Hogan, Patrick 1947-1988 *BioIn 16*
Hogan, Paul *WhoWor 91*
Hogan, Paul 1941?- *BioIn 16, WorAlBi*
Hogan, Robert Ball 1947- *St&PR 91*
Hogan, Robert Francis, Jr. 1956- *WhoSSW 91*
Hogan, Robert Henry 1926- *WhoAm 90*
Hogan, Robert N.D. 1938- *St&PR 91*
Hogan, Ronald P. 1940- *WhoAm 90, WhoSSW 91*
Hogan, Shanty 1906-1967 *Ballpl 90, BioIn 16*
Hogan, Sheila Joan 1965- *WhoAmW 91*
Hogan, Terrence Patrick 1937- *WhoAm 90*
Hogan, Thomas Bernard *BioIn 16*
Hogan, Thomas Harlan 1944- *WhoAm 90*
Hogan, Thomas John 1946- *WhoE 91*
Hogan, Thomas Michael 1941- *St&PR 91*
Hogan, Timothy J. *ODwPR 91*
Hogan, Timothy J. 1951- *St&PR 91*
Hogan, William Joseph 1902- *WhoAm 90*
Hogan, William M 1945- *BiDrAPA 89*
Hogan, William Robert 1927- *St&PR 91*
Hogan, William T. 1933- *WhoAm 90*
Hogarth, Burne 1911- *EncACom, SmATA 63 [port], WhoAm 90, WhoAmA 91, WhoWor 91*
Hogarth, Charles *MajTwCW, TwCCr&M 91*
Hogarth, JoAnne Catherine 1963- *WhoSSW 91*
Hogarth, William 1697-1764 *IntDcAA 90, WorAlBi*
Hogben, George L *BiDrAPA 89*
Hogben, Lancelot 1895-1975 *BioIn 16*
Hogberg, Carl Gustav 1913- *WhoE 91, WhoWor 91*
Hogbin, Stephen James *WhoAmA 91*
Hoge, Douglas L. 1921- *St&PR 91*
Hoge, Franz Joseph 1944- *WhoAm 90*
Hoge, Geraldine Rajacich 1937- *WhoAmW 91*
Hoge, Hilary Whittle *BiDrAPA 89*
Hoge, James F., Jr. 1935- *St&PR 91*
Hoge, James Fulton, Jr. 1935- *WhoAm 90, WhoE 91*
Hoge, John Herman 1932- *St&PR 91*
Hoge, Marlin Boyd 1914- *WhoSSW 91*
Hoge, Phyllis *ConAu 30NR*
Hoge, Robert Clyde 1947- *St&PR 91*
Hoge, Robert Wilson 1947- *WhoAmA 91*
Hoge, Sharon King 1944- *WhoE 91*
Hoge, Steven *BioIn 16*
Hoge, Steven Kenny *BiDrAPA 89*
Hoge, Warren *BioIn 16*
Hoge, Warren M. 1941- *WhoAm 90*
Hoge, William Hamilton *BioIn 16, NewYTBS 90*
Hogeboom, Amy 1891- *AuBYP 90*
Hogeboom, G. W. *AmLegL*
Hogeboom, Jan C. 1944- *St&PR 91*
Hogeboom, Patricia Ann Schrack 1937- *WhoAmW 91*
Hogen, Glenn A. 1928- *St&PR 91*
Hogen, Philip Nere 1944- *WhoAm 90*
Hogenkamp, Thomas Allen 1958- *WhoEmL 91*
Hogensen, Margaret Hiner 1920- *WhoE 91*
Hogfors, Marie 1938- *WhoWor 91*
Hogg, Beth *AuBYP 90*
Hogg, Bill 1880-1909 *Ballpl 90*
Hogg, Brad 1888-1935 *Ballpl 90*
Hogg, Christopher Anthony 1936- *St&PR 91, WhoWor 91*
Hogg, David Clarence 1921- *WhoAm 90*
Hogg, Don 1924-1988 *BioIn 16*
Hogg, Elizabeth *AuBYP 90*
Hogg, Enderby *ConAu 130*
Hogg, Helen Battles Sawyer 1905- *WhoAm 90*
Hogg, James 1770?-1835 *DcLB 93 [port]*
Hogg, Mary Jean 1926- *WhoAmW 91*
Hogg, Michael John 1945- *St&PR 91*
Hogg, Rozalia Cruise 1931- *WhoAmW 91*
Hogg, Sara Marie 1949- *WhoWrEP 89*
Hogg, Thomas F. *St&PR 91*
Hoggard, James Martin 1941- *WhoSSW 91, WhoWrEP 89*
Hoggard, Lara Guldmar 1915- *WhoAm 90, WhoWor 91*
Hoggard, Michael 1953- *St&PR 91*
Hoggard, Thomas Gene 1940- *WhoSSW 91*
Hoggard, William Zack, Jr. 1951- *WhoSSW 91*
Hoggatt, Clela Allphin 1932- *WhoAmW 91*
Hoggatt-Lowman, William Earl 1937- *BiDrAPA 89*
Hogge, John William 1939- *St&PR 91*
Hogge, Paul Waverly 1943- *St&PR 91*
Hogh, Dawn Marie 1962- *WhoAmW 91*
Hogle, Ann Meilstrup 1927- *WhoAmA 91*
Hogle, Cheryl Mae 1945- *WhoAmW 91*
Hogle, George H 1915- *BiDrAPA 89*
Hoglund, Anders Hjalmer 1937- *WhoWor 91*
Hoglund, Erik 1932- *ConDes 90*
Hoglund, Forrest Eugene 1933- *WhoSSW 91*
Hoglund, John Andrew 1945- *WhoEmL 91, WhoWor 91*
Hoglund, John B. 1930- *St&PR 91*
Hoglund, Olof Anders 1923- *WhoWor 91*
Hoglund, Raymond C. *St&PR 91*
Hoglund, Richard Frank 1933- *WhoAm 90*
Hoglund, William Elis 1934- *WhoAm 90*
Hogner, Dorothy *AuBYP 90*
Hogner, Nils 1893-1970 *AuBYP 90*
Hogness, John Rusten 1922- *WhoAm 90*
Hognestad, Eivind 1921- *WhoAm 90*
Hogrebe, Wolfram 1945- *WhoWor 91*
Hogrogian, Nonny 1932- *AuBYP 90*
Hogseth, John M. 1939- *St&PR 91*
Hogsett, Chief 1903- *Ballpl 90*
Hogsett, Joseph *WhoAm 90*
Hogsette, Sarah Margaret 1948- *WhoAmW 91*
Hogsten, Paul Erick 1960- *BiDrAPA 89*
Hogue, Alexandre 1898- *WhoAm 90, WhoAmA 91*
Hogue, Bobby 1921- *Ballpl 90*
Hogue, Cal 1927- *Ballpl 90*
Hogue, Carol J. Rowland 1945- *WhoAmW 91*
Hogue, Don F. 1920- *St&PR 91*
Hogue, James Claude 1932- *St&PR 91*
Hogue, James Conlon *BiDrAPA 89*
Hogue, James Lawrence 1923- *WhoAm 90*
Hogue, John G. 1948- *St&PR 91*
Hogue, Michael E. 1942- *St&PR 91*
Hogue, Susan Carol 1949- *WhoEmL 91*
Hogue, Viola Maye 1948- *WhoAmW 91*
Hogue, William C. 1941- *St&PR 91*
Hoguet, David Dilworth 1951- *WhoEmL 91*
Hoguet, Robert Louis 1908- *WhoAm 90*
Hoguet, Susan Ramsay 1945- *AuBYP 90*
Hogwood, Christopher 1941- *PenDiMP, WorAlBi*
Hogwood, Christopher Jarvis Haley 1941- *IntWWM 90, WhoAm 90*
Hogya, Mary Golding 1946- *WhoAmW 91*
Hoh, Diane 1937- *BioIn 16*
Hohage, Frederick William 1938- *WhoAm 90*
Hohe, Kenneth William 1934- *WhoE 91*
Hoheb, Richard Winfield 1931- *BiDrAPA 89*
Hoheisel, Robert Arthur 1925- *St&PR 91*
Hohenberg, John 1906- *WhoAm 90, WhoWor 91*
Hohenberg, Pierre Claude 1934- *WhoAm 90*
Hohendahl, Peter Uwe 1936- *WhoAm 90*
Hohendorf, Paul *BioIn 16*
Hohenemser, Christoph 1937- *WhoAm 90*
Hohener, Conrad F., III 1952- *St&PR 91*
Hohener, Heidi Catherine *BiDrAPA 89*
Hohenheim, Franziska, Grafin von 1748-1811 *EncCoWW*
Hohenlohe, Prince 1794-1849 *EncO&P 3*
Hohenrath, William Edward 1922- *WhoAm 90*
Hohenschuh, Paul F. 1943- *St&PR 91*
Hohenwarter, Peter 1894- *EncO&P 3*
Hoher, Martin 1957- *WhoWor 91*
Hohl, Ludwig 1904-1980 *BioIn 16*
Hohler, G. Robert 1932- *WhoAm 90*
Hohly, Eve Katherine 1940- *BiDrAPA 89*
Hohm, Dale Jonathan 1958- *St&PR 91*
Hohman, Clifford C. 1909- *St&PR 91*
Hohman, William Frederick 1930- *St&PR 91*
Hohmann, Maria *BiDrAPA 89*
Hohn, Harry George 1932- *WhoAm 90*
Hohn, Harry George, Jr. 1932- *St&PR 91*
Hohn, Jayne Marie 1957- *WhoAmW 91*
Hohn, Michael 1948- *WhoEmL 91*
Hohnbaum, Carl 1936- *St&PR 91*
Hohne, Robert Joseph 1933- *WhoAm 90*
Hohner, Bill Bela 1948- *St&PR 91*
Hohner, Kenneth Dwayne 1934- *WhoWor 91*
Hohns, William Allin 1952- *St&PR 91*
Hohnstedt, Leo Frank 1924- *WhoAm 90*
Hohnstein, Robert P. 1930- *St&PR 91*
Hohnstein, William Conrad, Jr. 1952- *WhoEmL 91*
Hoialmen, Laura Lee 1950- *WhoEmL 91*
Hoiby, Lee 1926- *IntWWM 90, WhoAm 90*
Hoie, Claus 1911- *WhoAm 90, WhoAmA 91*
Hoie, Helen Hunt *WhoAmA 91*
Hoigaard, Conrad J. 1936- *St&PR 91*
Hoiland, Andrew Calvin 1926- *WhoAm 90*
Hoime, Bryan Lee 1958- *WhoEmL 91*
Hoinic, Bujor 1950- *IntWWM 90*
Hoinkes, Mary Elizabeth 1940- *WhoAmW 91*
Hoiseth, Kolbjorn 1932- *IntWWM 90*
Hoisington, Frederick Reed, III 1929- *WhoSSW 91*
Hoisington, John Thomas 1951- *WhoSSW 91*
Hoisington, Richard L. 1926- *St&PR 91*
Hoisington, Richard Reed 1948- *WhoE 91*
Hoit, Kenneth R. 1937- *St&PR 91*
Hoit-Thetford, Elizabeth 1948- *WhoAmW 91*

Hoitenga, Camilla 1954- *IntWWM 90*
Hoitt, Clifford *BioIn 16*
Hoitt, Kenneth 1947- *St&PR 91*
Hojo Clan *EncJap*
Hojsgaard, Erik 1954- *IntWWM 90*
Hokanson, Hans 1925- *WhoAmA 91*
Hokanson, Leonard Ray 1931- *IntWWM 90*
Hokanson, Lois Muriel *BiDrAPA 89*
Hoke, Alexander Peabody 1949- *WhoEmL 91*
Hoke, Bob *BiDrAPA 89*
Hoke, Charles Pawling 1942- *St&PR 91*
Hoke, Donald Edwin, Jr. 1948- *St&PR 91*
Hoke, Eugena Louise 1949- *WhoAmW 91*
Hoke, Frank *St&PR 91N*
Hoke, Helen *ConAu 131*
Hoke, Helen *NewYTBS 90*
Hoke, Helen 1903-1990 *BioIn 16*
Hoke, Helen L. 1903- *AuBYP 90*
Hoke, Jennifer Lynn 1958- *WhoEmL 91*
Hoke, Robert Alan 1954- *WhoEmL 91*
Hokenson, Frank E. 1931- *St&PR 91*
Hokenstad, Merl Clifford, Jr. 1936- *WhoAm 90, WhoWor 91*
Hokin, Lowell Edward 1924- *WhoAm 90*
Hoks, Barbara L. 1955- *WhoHisp 91*
Hoks, Barbara Louise 1955- *WhoEmL 91*
Hokusai 1760-1849 *BioIn 16, EncJap*
Holab, William Joshua 1958- *IntWWM 90*
Holabird, Jean 1946- *WhoAmA 91*
Holabird, John Augur, Jr. 1920- *WhoAm 90*
Holabird, Katharine *AuBYP 90*
Holabird, Katharine 1948- *SmATA 62 [port]*
Holaday, Allan Gibson 1916- *WhoAm 90*
Holaday, James Clifton 1935- *WhoWrEP 89*
Holaday, Susan Mirles 1938- *WhoAmW 91, WhoWrEP 89*
Holahan, Richard Vincent 1909- *WhoAm 90*
Holajter, David Michael 1952- *BiDrAPA 89*
Holamon, Gladys Marie Avery 1927- *WhoAmW 91*
Holan, Jerri-Ann 1959- *WhoAmW 91*
Holay, Sandeep Harishchandra 1963- *WhoEmL 91*
Holbach, Paul Henri Thiry, Baron d' 1723-1789 *LitC 14 [port]*
Holbein, Hans 1497?-1543 *IntDcAA 90, PenDiDA 89, WorAlBi*
Holbek, Karsten 1947- *WhoWor 91*
Holben, Ralph Erdman 1916- *WhoE 91*
Holberg, Ludvig 1684-1754 *DcScanL, WorAlBi*
Holberg, Ralph Gans, Jr. 1908- *WhoAm 90*
Holberg, Richard A. 1889-1942 *AuBYP 90*
Holberg, Ruth 1889- *AuBYP 90*
Holberg, Sven Ludvig 1927- *WhoSSW 91*
Holbert, Al *BioIn 16*
Holbert, Don Raymond 1928- *WhoSSW 91*
Holbert, Janice Hughes 1952- *WhoAmW 91*
Holbert, Sue E. *BioIn 16*
Holbert, Sue Elisabeth 1935- *WhoAmW 91*
Holbert, Theodore F. 1921- *St&PR 91*
Holbert, Theodore Frank 1921- *WhoAm 90*
Holberton, Philip Vaughan 1942- *WhoAm 90*
Holbik, Karel 1920- *WhoAm 90*
Holbik, Thomas 1960- *WhoE 91*
Holbrook, Alfred Samson, III 1957- *WhoSSW 91*
Holbrook, Anthony 1940- *WhoAm 90*
Holbrook, Barbara Carr San *WhoAmW 91*
Holbrook, Charles W. 1940- *St&PR 91*
Holbrook, Clyde A. *BioIn 16*
Holbrook, Clyde A 1911-1989 *ConAu 130*
Holbrook, Coit Conger 1936- *St&PR 91*
Holbrook, Dan Weddington 1948- *WhoEmL 91*
Holbrook, Donald Benson 1925- *WhoAm 90*
Holbrook, Douglas Cowan 1934- *WhoAm 90*
Holbrook, Elizabeth 1937- *IntWWM 90*
Holbrook, Elizabeth Bradford 1913- *WhoAm 90*
Holbrook, Eugene Edward, Jr. 1954- *WhoSSW 91*
Holbrook, Frank Malvin 1952- *WhoEmL 91*
Holbrook, Hal 1925- *WhoAm 90, WorAlBi*
Holbrook, Hollis Howard 1909-1984 *WhoAmA 91N*
Holbrook, James J. *WhoWrEP 89*
Holbrook, Jay Collins 1952-1988 *BioIn 16*
Holbrook, Joan 1934- *WhoAmW 91*
Holbrook, John *MajTwCW*
Holbrook, John Scott, Jr. 1939- *WhoAm 90*
Holbrook, Lawrence Alan 1956- *WhoE 91*
Holbrook, Lee Bruce 1950- *WhoSSW 91*
Holbrook, Margaret Kay 1958- *WhoEmL 91*
Holbrook, Nancy Lyn 1956- *WhoEmL 91*
Holbrook, Norma Jeannette 1939- *WhoAmW 91*
Holbrook, Peter Greene 1940- *WhoAmA 91*
Holbrook, R. James *St&PR 91*
Holbrook, Richard David *WhoE 91*
Holbrook, Richard E. *St&PR 91*
Holbrook, Robert Berryman 1941- *St&PR 91*
Holbrook, Robert Sumner 1932- *WhoAm 90*
Holbrook, Stewart Hall 1893-1964 *AuBYP 90*
Holbrook, Thomas L *BiDrAPA 89*
Holbrook, Vincent *ODwPR 91*
Holbrook, Vivian Nicholas 1913- *WhoAmA 91*
Holbrook, William D *BiDrAPA 89*
Holbrook, William Harold 1924- *St&PR 91*
Holbrooke, Richard Charles 1941- *St&PR 91*
Holbrow, Charles Howard 1935- *WhoAm 90*
Holby, Grethe Barrett 1948- *IntWWM 90*
Holc, Paul *BioIn 16*
Holcenberg, John Stanley 1935- *WhoAm 90*
Holch, Eric Sanford 1948- *WhoE 91*
Holch, Niels C. 1956- *ODwPR 91*
Holck, Frederick H. George 1927- *WhoAm 90*
Holcomb, Alice 1906-1977 *WhoAmA 91N*
Holcomb, Alice Willard Power 1922- *WhoAmW 91, WhoSSW 91*
Holcomb, Bruce D. 1947- *St&PR 91*
Holcomb, Caramine Kellam 1941- *WhoAmW 91*
Holcomb, Charles R. 1934- *ODwPR 91*
Holcomb, Constance L. 1942- *WhoAmW 91*
Holcomb, David Wallace, Jr. 1937- *WhoSSW 91*
Holcomb, Dennis Lamar 1946- *WhoSSW 91*
Holcomb, Donald Frank 1925- *WhoAm 90*
Holcomb, Edward Orr, Jr. 1941- *WhoSSW 91*
Holcomb, George Ruhle 1927- *WhoAm 90*
Holcomb, George U. *BioIn 16*
Holcomb, Grant 1944- *WhoAmA 91*
Holcomb, Grant, III 1944- *WhoAm 90, WhoE 91*
Holcomb, Henry H *BiDrAPA 89*
Holcomb, Horace Hale, III 1930- *St&PR 91*
Holcomb, Hubert D. 1930- *St&PR 91*
Holcomb, Jack 1951- *IntWWM 90*
Holcomb, James Robert 1937- *WhoSSW 91*
Holcomb, Jerry Kimble *WhoWrEP 89*
Holcomb, Karen S. *St&PR 91*
Holcomb, M. Staser 1932- *WhoAm 90*
Holcomb, Marcus Hensey 1844-1932 *AmLegL*
Holcomb, Norman C. 1944- *St&PR 91*
Holcomb, Raymond L. 1945- *St&PR 91*
Holcomb, Thomas 1843- *AmLegL*
Holcomb, Vicki L. Hanna 1953- *WhoEmL 91*
Holcomb, William A. 1926- *WhoAm 90*
Holcomb, William W. 1948- *WhoEmL 91*
Holcomb, Winford Honzel, Jr. 1948- *WhoEmL 91*
Holcombe, Anna Calluori 1952- *WhoAmA 91*
Holcombe, Blanche Keaton 1912- *WhoAmA 91N*
Holcombe, Chester 1844-1912 *BioIn 16*
Holcombe, George Roland 1933- *WhoSSW 91*
Holcombe, Henry Jameson, Jr. 1963- *WhoEmL 91*
Holcombe, James C. 1945- *St&PR 91*
Holcombe, Ken 1918- *Ballpl 90*
Holcombe, Milton Winford 1932- *St&PR 91*
Holcombe, R Gordon, Jr 1913- *WhoAmA 91*
Holcombe, Randall Gregory 1950- *WhoAm 90*
Holcombe, Robert Swaine 1942- *WhoAm 90*
Holcombe, Wesley Glenn 1924- *St&PR 91*
Holcombe, William Jones 1925- *St&PR 91*
Holcroft, Frances 1778?-1844 *FemiCLE*
Holczer, Geoffrey M. 1949- *St&PR 91*
Hold, John *ConTFT 8*
Hold, Trevor James 1939- *IntWWM 90*
Holda, Margaret *ODwPR 91*
Holdeman, Richard John, Jr. 1943- *St&PR 91*
Holden, Al 1931- *St&PR 91*
Holden, Alexander Stallings 1944- *WhoSSW 91*
Holden, Andrea Rose 1958- *WhoEmL 91, WhoWor 91*
Holden, Ann *BioIn 16*
Holden, Ann Marie 1954- *St&PR 91*
Holden, Arthur Cort 1890- *WhoAm 90*
Holden, Dalby *TwCCr&M 91*
Holden, David Johnston 1930- *St&PR 91*
Holden, David Morgan 1938- *WhoAm 90*
Holden, Donald 1931- *BioIn 16, WhoAm 90, WhoAmA 91, WhoE 91*
Holden, Donnie Joe *BiDrAPA 89*
Holden, Edith 1871-1920 *BioIn 16*
Holden, Eva Rachel 1924- *IntWWM 90*
Holden, Frank Eugene 1861-1938 *AmLegL*
Holden, Frederick Douglass, Jr. 1949- *WhoEmL 91*
Holden, George Fredric 1937- *WhoWor 91*
Holden, George T. 1945- *WhoEmL 91*
Holden, Glen A. 1927- *WhoWor 91*
Holden, Isidore *BiDrAPA 89*
Holden, James Phillip 1932- *WhoAm 90*
Holden, James Stuart 1914- *WhoAm 90*
Holden, Joan 1939- *BioIn 16*
Holden, Joan Allan 1939- *NotWoAT*
Holden, John Bernard 1910- *WhoAm 90*
Holden, John Porter *OxCCanT [port]*
Holden, John S. *BioIn 16*
Holden, Jonathan 1941- *DcLB 105 [port], WhoWrEP 89*
Holden, Joseph Charles, Jr. 1946- *WhoSSW 91*
Holden, Joseph M C *BiDrAPA 89*
Holden, Joseph William 1844-1875 *AmLegL*
Holden, Justin Samuel 1946- *WhoEmL 91*
Holden, Kenneth 1943- *WhoWor 91*
Holden, L Dwight *BiDrAPA 89*
Holden, Linda Anne 1939- *WhoAmW 91, WhoSSW 91*
Holden, Mary *BiDEWW*
Holden, Matthew, Jr. 1931- *WhoAm 90, WhoSSW 91*
Holden, Michael James 1951- *St&PR 91*
Holden, Molly 1927-1981 *BioIn 16*
Holden, Myretta *WhoSSW 91*
Holden, Norman Brooks, Jr. 1949- *BiDrAPA 89*
Holden, Patrick 1945- *BiDrAPA 89*
Holden, Patrick John 1949- *St&PR 91*
Holden, Peter Holt 1922- *BiDrAPA 89*
Holden, Randall LeConte 1943- *IntWWM 90*
Holden, Raymond 1894-1972 *AuBYP 90*
Holden, Raymond Henry 1924- *WhoE 91, WhoWor 91*
Holden, Raymond Thomas 1904- *WhoAm 90*
Holden, Reuben Andrus 1918- *WhoAm 90*
Holden, Rick Marshall 1952- *WhoE 91*
Holden, Robert Stuart 1929- *St&PR 91*
Holden, Ronnie Joe 1948- *WhoSSW 91*
Holden, Ruth Egri 1911- *WhoAmA 91*
Holden, Sandra Sue 1938- *WhoAmW 91*
Holden, Thomas B. 1948- *St&PR 91*
Holden, Thomas J. 1921- *St&PR 91*
Holden, W. W. 1818-1892 *BioIn 16*
Holden, William 1918-1981 *BioIn 16, WorAlBi*
Holden, William Hoyt, Jr. *WhoE 91*
Holden, William P. 1933- *WhoAm 90*
Holden, William Roger 1946- *WhoSSW 91*
Holden, William Vaughn 1949- *WhoEmL 91*
Holden, William Woods 1818-1892 *BioIn 16*
Holden-Brown, Derrick 1923- *WhoAm 90, WhoWor 91*
Holdenried, Frank Xavier 1932-1983 *BioIn 16*
Holdenried, John Richard 1950- *WhoEmL 91*
Holder, Angela Roddey 1938- *WhoAm 90, WhoAmW 91*
Holder, Barbara J. 1944- *WhoSSW 91*
Holder, Barry Keith 1933- *WhoWor 91*
Holder, Christopher Peirce 1947- *WhoEmL 91*
Holder, Elaine Edith 1926- *WhoAmW 91*
Holder, Gail Jillian 1953- *WhoAmW 91*
Holder, Geoffrey *BioIn 16*
Holder, Geoffrey 1930- *DrBIPA 90*
Holder, George H. 1936- *St&PR 91*
Holder, Glenn 1906- *AuBYP 90*
Holder, Harold Douglas, Sr. 1931- *WhoAm 90, WhoWor 91*
Holder, Holly Irene 1952- *WhoAmW 91*
Holder, Howard Randolph, Sr. 1916- *WhoSSW 91, WhoWor 91*
Holder, Janice Marie 1949- *WhoAmW 91*
Holder, Jim Ray 1961- *WhoSSW 91*
Holder, Joe Biles, Jr. 1936- *WhoSSW 91*
Holder, John Nathaniel 1868-1961 *AmLegL*
Holder, Joyce Fiorella 1926- *WhoAmW 91*
Holder, Kenneth Allen 1936- *WhoAmA 91*
Holder, Lee 1932- *WhoAm 90*
Holder, Patricia Wenzel 1925- *WhoAmW 91*
Holder, Ram John 1940?- *DrBIPA 90*
Holder, Richmond 1918- *BiDrAPA 89*
Holder, Robert James 1955- *WhoEmL 91*
Holder, Ruth Elsie 1953- *WhoAmW 91*
Holder, Sallie Lou 1939- *WhoAm 90, WhoE 91*
Holder, Sandra Sue 1938- *WhoAmW 91*
Holder, Susan McCaskill 1956- *WhoAmW 91*
Holder, Thomas Martin 1926- *WhoAm 90*
Holder, Tom 1940- *WhoAmA 91*
Holder, Virginia Mary 1942- *WhoAmW 91*
Holder, William G. 1937- *AuBYP 90*
Holderbaum, Linda Sue 1951- *WhoAmW 91*
Holderith, Erika *BioIn 16*
Holderlin, Friedrich 1770-1843 *WorAlBi, WrPh*
Holderman, James Bowker 1936- *WhoAm 90, WhoSSW 91*
Holderman, James F., Jr. 1946- *WhoAm 90*
Holderness, Algernon Sidney, Jr. 1938- *WhoAm 90*
Holderness, Cheryl Ann 1959- *WhoAmW 91*
Holderness, Susan Rutherford 1941- *WhoAmW 91*
Holdheim, William Wolfgang 1926- *WhoAm 90*
Holding, Elisabeth Sanxay 1889-1955 *TwCCr&M 91*
Holding, Harvey R. 1934- *St&PR 91*
Holding, James 1907- *AuBYP 90, TwCCr&M 91*
Holding, William Burton 1933- *WhoE 91*
Holditch, W. Kenneth 1933- *WhoWrEP 89*
Holditch, William Kenneth 1933- *WhoSSW 91*
Holdo, Nelson Andres 1959- *WhoEmL 91*
Holdowsky, Michael Martin 1953- *WhoE 91*
Holdread, Jon Wayne *BiDrAPA 89*
Holdredge, Robert Leslie 1946- *WhoE 91*
Holdren, Cynthia Wills 1948- *WhoSSW 91*
Holdren, John Paul 1944- *WhoAm 90*
Holdridge, Barbara 1929- *WhoAm 90, WhoWrEP 89*
Holdridge, Lee 1944- *ConTFT 8, IntWWM 90*
Holdridge, Thomas D. 1941- *St&PR 91*
Holdstein, Russell Simon 1946- *WhoEmL 91*
Holdstock, Robert *ConAu 131*
Holdstock, Robert P. 1948- *ConAu 131*
Holdsworth, Annie E. 1857?- *FemiCLE*
Holdsworth, Fred 1952- *Ballpl 90*
Holdsworth, Janet Nott 1941- *WhoAmW 91, WhoWor 91*
Holdt, Leland 1930- *St&PR 91*
Holdt, Leland LaMar Stark 1930- *WhoAm 90*
Holdway, Michael Leon 1952- *WhoSSW 91*
Hole, Donald E. 1951- *St&PR 91*
Hole, Richard W., Jr. 1948- *BiDrAPA 89*
Hole-in-the-Day *WhNaAH*
Hole-in-the-Day 1825-1868 *WhNaAH*
Holecek, Josef 1939- *IntWWM 90*
Holechek, James 1929- *St&PR 91*
Holeman, Marilyn Batey 1938- *WhoWrEP 89*
Holemon, Claude Hugh 1934- *St&PR 91*
Holemon, Dawn Michelle *BiDrAPA 89*
Holemon, Lance Douglas *BiDrAPA 89*
Holemon, R Eugene *BiDrAPA 89*
Holen, Eugene Dwayne 1928- *St&PR 91*
Holen, Harold Hampton 1935- *WhoAm 90*
Holen, Norman Dean 1937- *WhoAmA 91*
Holenbaugh, Robert Allan 1942- *St&PR 91*
Holender, Barbara D. 1927- *WhoWrEP 89*
Holey, Mercedes Garriga 1918- *WhoAmW 91*
Holey, Ronald Loren 1931- *St&PR 91*
Holfinger, Robert R. 1930- *St&PR 91*
Holford, Margaret 1761?-1834 *FemiCLE*
Holford, Margaret 1778-1852 *FemiCLE*
Holforty, Pearl Martha 1928- *WhoAmW 91*
Holgate, Edwin Headley 1892-1977 *WhoAmA 91N*
Holgate, George Jackson 1933- *WhoAm 90*
Holguin, Alfonso Hudson 1931- *WhoAm 90*
Holguin, Hector 1935- *WhoHisp 91*
Holian, Katherine Stover 1947- *WhoAmW 91*
Holickova, Elena *IntWWM 90*
Holiday, Billie 1915-1959 *BioAmW, BioIn 16, DrBIPA 90, OxCPMus, WorAlBi*
Holiday, Edith Elizabeth 1952- *WhoAm 90, WhoAmW 91*
Holiday, Gregory 1951- *WhoEmL 91*
Holiday, Patrick James 1947- *WhoEmL 91*

Holien, Kim Bernard 1948- *WhoE 91, WhoEmL 91, WhoSSW 91, WhoWor 91*
Holifield, Harold *EarBlAP*
Holifield, Patricia DiMiceli 1945- *WhoSSW 91*
Holiga, Ludomil Andrew 1920- *WhoAm 90*
Holik, William Veazey, Jr. 1925- *WhoAm 90*
Holiner, Joel Alan 1954- *BiDrAPA 89*
Holinger, Paul Campbell 1946- *BiDrAPA 89*
Holinger, Richard 1949- *WhoWrEP 89*
Holinger, William 1944- *WhoWrEP 89*
Holiver, Kimberly Lynn 1956- *WhoEmL 91*
Holke, Friedrich *PenDiDA 89*
Holke, Walter 1892-1954 *Ballpl 90*
Holkeri, Harri Hermanni 1937- *WhoWor 91*
Holko, Joseph Adams 1956- *WhoEmL 91*
Holl, Adelaide 1910- *AuBYP 90*
Holl, Donald Richard 1947- *WhoE 91*
Holl, Edwin G. *WhoE 91*
Holl, John William 1928- *WhoAm 90*
Holl, Kristi 1951- *BioIn 16*
Holl, Kristi Diane 1951- *AuBYP 90*
Holl, Richard Henry 1929- *St&PR 91*
Holl, Robert 1947- *IntWWM 90, PenDiMP*
Holl, Rose E. 1920- *St&PR 91*
Holl, Steven 1947- *BioIn 16*
Holl, Steven Myron 1947- *WhoAm 90*
Holla, Ronald J. 1958- *St&PR 91*
Hollabaugh, Mark 1949- *WhoWrEP 89*
Holladay, Charles Otis 1931- *St&PR 91*
Holladay, Harlan 1925- *WhoAm 90*
Holladay, Harlan H 1925- *WhoAmA 91*
Holladay, James Frank 1922- *WhoAm 90*
Holladay, John Henry 1923- *WhoSSW 91*
Holladay, K. David 1957- *BiDrAPA 89*
Holladay, Ronald Bell 1947- *WhoSSW 91*
Holladay, Wendell Gene 1925- *WhoAm 90*
Holladay, Wilhelmina Cole *WhoAmA 91*
Holladay, Wilhelmina Cole 1922- *WhoAmW 91, WhoE 91, WhoWor 91*
Hollan, Susan R. 1920- *WhoWor 91*
Holland, Dozier and Holland *OxCPMus*
Holland, Mrs. *EncPaPR 91*
Holland, Mrs. 1868-1948 *EncO&P 3*
Holland, Al 1952- *Ballpl 90*
Holland, Albert H. 1918-1988 *BioIn 16*
Holland, Andrew McDonald 1933- *St&PR 91*
Holland, Anthony *BioIn 16*
Holland, Arthur J. 1918-1989 *BioIn 16*
Holland, Barbara Lee 1948- *WhoEmL 91*
Holland, Bernard C 1916- *BiDrAPA 89*
Holland, Beth *WhoAm 90, WhoAmW 91*
Holland, Bill 1901- *Ballpl 90*
Holland, Bradford Wayne 1943- *WhoAm 90*
Holland, Brian 1941- *ConMus 5 [port], OxCPMus*
Holland, C. Gehrmann 1937- *St&PR 91*
Holland, Catherine 1635-1720 *BiDEWW*
Holland, Catherine 1637-1720 *FemiCLE*
Holland, Catherine Pauline 1951- *St&PR 91*
Holland, Charles 1908-1987 *DcAfAmP*
Holland, Charles Donald 1921- *WhoAm 90*
Holland, Charles F 1928- *BiDrAPA 89*
Holland, Charles Malcolm, Jr. 1932- *WhoAm 90*
Holland, Christie Anna 1950- *WhoAmW 91*
Holland, Claude M, Jr. 1925- *BiDrAPA 89*
Holland, Daniel E. 1918- *WhoAm 90*
Holland, Daniel Mark 1920- *WhoAm 90*
Holland, Dave *BioIn 16*
Holland, David Michael 1946- *St&PR 91*
Holland, David Scott 1931- *St&PR 91, WhoSSW 91*
Holland, David Thurston 1923- *WhoAm 90*
Holland, Denise Edgecombe 1948- *BiDrAPA 89*
Holland, Dianna Gwin 1948- *WhoAm 90*
Holland, Donald Joe 1959- *BiDrAPA 89*
Holland, Donald Ray 1943- *WhoSSW 91*
Holland, Donald Reginald 1940- *WhoAm 90*
Holland, Donna Sue 1954- *BiDrAPA 89*
Holland, Dorothy Winifred 1919- *WhoAm 90*
Holland, Dulcie Sybil 1913- *IntWWM 90*
Holland, Eddie 1939- *ConMus 5 [port], OxCPMus*
Holland, Elizabeth 1771-1845 *FemiCLE*
Holland, Eugene, Jr. 1922- *WhoAm 90*
Holland, Evan Marc 1955- *St&PR 91*
Holland, Gary Alexander 1933- *WhoAm 90*
Holland, Gary L. 1953- *WhoEmL 91*
Holland, Gary Richard 1942- *St&PR 91, WhoAm 90*
Holland, Gay Willman 1941- *WhoAmW 91*
Holland, Gene Grigsby 1928- *WhoAm 90, WhoAmW 91*
Holland, George H. *St&PR 91*
Holland, Gerald J. 1951- *St&PR 91*
Holland, Gerald M. 1935- *St&PR 91*
Holland, Harold Herbert 1932- *WhoAm 90*
Holland, Harold William 1956- *WhoSSW 91*
Holland, Harry Charles 1937- *WhoAmA 91*
Holland, Heinrich Dieter 1927- *WhoAm 90*
Holland, Henry 1745-1806 *PenDiDA 89*
Holland, Henry Davis 1939- *BiDrAPA 89*
Holland, Henry Preston 1948- *St&PR 91*
Holland, Hillman Randall 1950- *WhoAmA 91, WhoSSW 91*
Holland, Hubert Brian 1904- *WhoAm 90*
Holland, Iris Kaufman 1920- *WhoAmW 91*
Holland, Isabelle *BioIn 16*
Holland, Isabelle 1920- *AuBYP 90*
Holland, J.P. *St&PR 91*
Holland, James 1905- *ConDes 90*
Holland, James Michael 1945- *St&PR 91*
Holland, James Paul 1948- *WhoAm 90*
Holland, James R. 1929- *ODwPR 91*
Holland, James R. 1944- *WhoE 91, WhoWor 91*
Holland, James Richard, Jr. 1943- *WhoAm 90, WhoSSW 91*
Holland, James Ricks 1929- *WhoAm 90*
Holland, James T. 1940- *St&PR 91*
Holland, James Tulley 1940- *WhoAm 90*
Holland, Janice 1913-1962 *WhoAmA 91N*
Holland, Janice Arlene 1951- *WhoSSW 91*
Holland, Jari Lyn 1950- *WhoEmL 91*
Holland, Jeffrey 1946- *ConTFT 8*
Holland, Jeffrey R. 1940- *WhoAm 90*
Holland, Jerome V 1921- *BiDrAPA 89*
Holland, Jessica *BioIn 16*
Holland, Jimmie C. 1928- *WhoAm 90*
Holland, Jimmie C B 1928- *BiDrAPA 89*
Holland, John *AuBYP 90*
Holland, John Ben 1932- *WhoAm 90, WhoSSW 91, WhoWor 91*
Holland, John Madison 1927- *WhoAm 90*
Holland, Joy 1946- *WhoAmW 91, WhoEmL 91*
Holland, Joyce *WhoWrEP 89*
Holland, Kelly Gill 1934- *WhoAmW 91*
Holland, Kenneth John 1918- *WhoAm 90*
Holland, Kenneth M. 1923- *St&PR 91*
Holland, Kimberly Ann *BiDrAPA 89*
Holland, Lauren Susan 1952- *WhoEmL 91*
Holland, Leland J. *NewYTBS 90 [port]*
Holland, Lieselotte *BiDrAPA 89*
Holland, Lisa Ann 1959- *WhoAmW 91*
Holland, Lyman Faith, Jr. 1931- *WhoAm 90*
Holland, Malvern Carlyle 1926- *WhoSSW 91*
Holland, Marcella Amelia 1947- *WhoEmL 91*
Holland, Margaret McPheron 1906- *WhoAmW 91*
Holland, Marilyn Basye 1947- *WhoSSW 91*
Holland, Marion 1908- *AuBYP 90*
Holland, Marion 1908-1989 *SmATA 61*
Holland, Marjorie Miriam 1947- *WhoE 91*
Holland, Merle Susan 1945- *WhoAmW 91*
Holland, Michael Francis 1944- *WhoAm 90*
Holland, Michael Ward 1949- *BiDrAPA 89*
Holland, Nancy Hinkle 1921- *WhoAmW 91*
Holland, Nancy Marie 1948- *WhoAmW 91*
Holland, Noel Julian 1931- *WhoE 91*
Holland, Norman Norwood 1927- *BioIn 16*
Holland, Patricia Ann 1951- *WhoAmW 91*
Holland, Paul Deleval 1910- *WhoAm 90*
Holland, Peter Jay 1953- *BiDrAPA 89*
Holland, Peter John *BiDrAPA 89*
Holland, Peter John 1929- *WhoSSW 91*
Holland, Randy James 1947- *WhoAm 90, WhoE 91, WhoEmL 91*
Holland, Rebecca Lou 1949- *St&PR 91*
Holland, Richard 1944- *WhoWor 91*
Holland, Richard George, Jr. 1927- *St&PR 91*
Holland, Richard L. 1926- *St&PR 91*
Holland, Robert Campbell 1923- *WhoAm 90*
Holland, Robert Carl 1925- *WhoAm 90*
Holland, Robert E *BiDrAPA 89*
Holland, Robert Edward *BiDrAPA 89*
Holland, Robert L. 1939- *St&PR 91*
Holland, Robert Rolland, Jr. 1952- *WhoEmL 91*
Holland, Robert Stevens 1945- *WhoE 91*
Holland, Sandra Gunter 1952- *WhoAmW 91*
Holland, Stephen Murray 1950- *WhoEmL 91*
Holland, Stephen Thomas 1952- *WhoWrEP 89*
Holland, Steven William 1951- *WhoEmL 91*
Holland, Susan Palmieri 1956- *WhoWrEP 89*
Holland, Thomas Powell 1942- *WhoAm 90*
Holland, Tom 1936- *WhoAm 90, WhoAmA 91*
Holland, Viki *AuBYP 90*
Holland, Willard R. 1936- *St&PR 91*
Holland, Willard Raymond, Jr. 1936- *WhoAm 90*
Holland, William Jeremiah 1932- *WhoAm 90*
Holland, William Ray 1938- *St&PR 91, WhoAm 90, WhoSSW 91*
Holland, William T 1923- *BiDrAPA 89*
Holland, Zera Jane 1947- *WhoEmL 91*
Holland-Beachley, Jan Mary *BiDrAPA 89*
Holland-Dozier-Holland *ConMus 5 [port]*
Holland-Hull, N E *BiDrAPA 89*
Holland-Jones, Paula Elaine 1955- *WhoAmW 91*
Hollander, Anne 1930- *ConAu 131*
Hollander, Annette 1941- *BiDrAPA 89*
Hollander, Barbara S. 1938- *WhoE 91*
Hollander, Betty Ruth 1930- *WhoAm 90*
Hollander, Edwin Paul 1927- *WhoAm 90*
Hollander, Ella H. 1908- *WhoWrEP 89*
Hollander, Ellen Collins 1946- *WhoEmL 91, WhoWor 91*
Hollander, Ellen Lynne *BiDrAPA 89*
Hollander, Eric *BiDrAPA 89*
Hollander, Eric 1957- *WhoE 91*
Hollander, Frederick 1896-1976 *OxCPMus*
Hollander, Gerhard Ludwig 1922- *WhoAm 90*
Hollander, Gordon Dennis 1948- *WhoEmL 91*
Hollander, Herbert I. 1924- *St&PR 91, WhoE 91*
Hollander, Howard Robert 1952- *WhoE 91*
Hollander, Irwin Joel 1949- *WhoE 91*
Hollander, Jean *WhoWrEP 89*
Hollander, Jeffrey Michael 1961- *St&PR 91*
Hollander, John *BioIn 16*
Hollander, John 1929- *AuBYP 90, WhoAm 90, WhoWrEP 89*
Hollander, John Thorning 1941- *WhoSSW 91*
Hollander, Lawrence Jay 1940- *WhoE 91*
Hollander, Leonard *BiDrAPA 89*
Hollander, Lorin 1944- *WhoAm 90*
Hollander, Marshall J. 1919- *St&PR 91*
Hollander, Michael Frederic 1946- *WhoEmL 91*
Hollander, Milton Bernard 1928- *WhoAm 90*
Hollander, Morton Joseph 1913- *WhoAm 90*
Hollander, Paul *AuBYP 90, MajTwCW*
Hollander, Phyllis 1928- *AuBYP 90*
Hollander, Richard C. 1946- *St&PR 91*
Hollander, Richard Edward 1947- *WhoE 91*
Hollander, Robert B., Jr. 1933- *WhoAm 90*
Hollander, Samuel 1937- *WhoAm 90*
Hollander, Samuel 1939- *WhoE 91*
Hollander, Samuel Steven 1938- *St&PR 91*
Hollander, Sidney 1949- *WhoEmL 91*
Hollander, Toby Edward 1931- *WhoAm 90, WhoE 91*
Hollander, Zander 1923- *AuBYP 90, SmATA 63*
Hollands, John Henry 1929- *WhoAm 90*
Hollandsworth, Kenneth Peter 1934- *WhoWor 91*
Hollandsworth, Linda Padgett 1947- *WhoEmL 91*
Hollans, Irby Noah, Jr. 1930- *WhoAm 90*
Hollar, Constance 1880-1945 *FemiCLE*
Hollar, Jan H. 1955- *St&PR 91*
Hollar, Lloyd *DrBlPA 90*
Hollar, Milton C *BiDrAPA 89*
Hollas, Donna Marie 1962- *WhoSSW 91*
Hollaway, Raymond Lawson, Jr. 1924- *WhoAm 90*
Holldobler, Berthold Karl 1936- *WhoAm 90*
Holle, Brenda M. 1963- *St&PR 91*
Holle, Charles George 1898-1989 *BioIn 16*
Holle, Cheryl Lynn *BiDrAPA 89*
Holleb, Arthur Irving 1921- *WhoE 91*
Holleder, Don *BioIn 16*
Hollein, Hans 1934- *BioIn 16, ConDes 90, PenDiDA 89, WhoWor 91*
Hollein, Helen Conway 1943- *WhoAmW 91*
Holleman, Frank Sharp, III 1954- *WhoEmL 91*
Holleman, John Albert 1939- *St&PR 91, WhoAm 90, WhoSSW 91*
Holleman, Marian Isabel 1923- *WhoAm 90*
Holleman, Matthew Louis 1951- *St&PR 91*
Holleman, Sandy Lee 1940- *WhoAmW 91*
Hollen, Jane 1955- *WhoE 91*
Hollen, Patricia Jean 1945- *WhoAmW 91*
Hollen-Bolmgren, Donna 1935- *WhoAmA 91, WhoE 91*
Hollenbach, Barbara Louise 1953- *WhoEmL 91*
Hollenbach, Edwin A. 1918- *St&PR 91*
Hollenbach, Eleanor P. 1922- *St&PR 91*
Hollenbach, Mark A. 1954- *St&PR 91*
Hollenbach, Ruth F. *WhoAm 90, WhoAmW 91*
Hollenbaugh, Robert Allan 1942- *St&PR 91*
Hollenbeck, Burton G. 1927- *St&PR 91*
Hollenbeck, Donald Craig 1953- *St&PR 91*
Hollenbeck, Harold Capistran 1938- *WhoAm 90*
Hollenbeck, Jot Niclas 1954- *St&PR 91*
Hollenbeck, Marynell 1939- *WhoAmW 91*
Hollenbeck, Ralph Anthony 1925- *WhoAm 90*
Hollenberg, Harvard 1938- *WhoE 91*
Hollenberg, John Steven *BiDrAPA 89*
Hollender, Christoph Albert 1962- *WhoWor 91*
Hollender, John Edward 1941- *WhoWor 91*
Hollender, Marc H 1916- *BiDrAPA 89*
Hollenshead, David S. 1926- *St&PR 91*
Hollensteiner, James *BioIn 16*
Hollensworth, Mayme Stevens 1910- *WhoWrEP 89*
Holler, Adlai Cornwell, Jr. 1925- *WhoSSW 91*
Holler, Frank A. *ODwPR 91*
Holler, Grover M., Jr. 1921- *St&PR 91*
Holler, Kenny G. 1945- *St&PR 91*
Holler, York Georg 1944- *IntWWM 90*
Holleran, Eugene M. 1922- *EncO&P 3*
Holleran, Kevin Joseph 1951- *WhoEmL 91*
Holleran, Lawrence P. 1931- *St&PR 91*
Holleran, Paula Rizzo *WhoAmW 91*
Holleran, Sheila 1939- *WhoAmW 91*
Hollerbach, Louis V. 1930- *St&PR 91*
Hollerbach, Serge 1923- *WhoAmA 91*
Hollerith, Richard, Jr. 1926- *WhoAm 90*
Hollerman, Charles Edward 1929- *WhoAm 90*
Hollermann, Peter Wilhelm 1931- *WhoWor 91*
Hollesen, Hollie Marie 1959- *WhoAmW 91*
Hollett, Grant Thomas, Jr. 1942- *St&PR 91, WhoAm 90*
Holleweg dit Wegman, Willy 1934- *WhoWor 91*
Holley, Audrey Rodgers 1939- *WhoAmW 91*
Holley, Barbara Lee 1940- *WhoAmW 91*
Holley, C. Roy 1936- *St&PR 91*
Holley, Charlotte Marie 1950- *WhoWrEP 89*
Holley, Cyrus H. 1936- *St&PR 91*
Holley, Cyrus Helmer 1936- *WhoAm 90, WhoE 91*
Holley, Daniel Charles 1949- *WhoEmL 91*
Holley, David Russell 1950- *WhoWor 91*
Holley, Deborah Jon 1953- *St&PR 91*
Holley, Deborah Kathryn 1960- *WhoE 91*
Holley, Ed 1899-1986 *Ballpl 90*
Holley, Edward Gailon 1927- *WhoAm 90*
Holley, Frank Edward 1919- *WhoAm 90*
Holley, George M. 1878-1963 *EncABHB 4 [port], WorAlBi*
Holley, Gerald Neal 1938- *St&PR 91, WhoAm 90*
Holley, Howard George 1943- *St&PR 91*
Holley, Irving Brinton, Jr. 1919- *WhoAm 90*
Holley, Ishmael McKever, Jr. 1940- *WhoSSW 91*
Holley, James W., III *WhoAm 90*
Holley, John M. *St&PR 91N*
Holley, Joseph Cohron 1928- *St&PR 91*
Holley, Joseph Thomas 1946- *St&PR 91*
Holley, Larry Jay 1936- *St&PR 91*
Holley, Lauren Allana 1948- *WhoAmW 91*
Holley, Lawrence Alvin 1924- *WhoAm 90*
Holley, Lonnie 1950- *MusmAFA*
Holley, Major *NewYTBS 90 [port]*
Holley, Marietta 1836-1926 *BioAmW, FemiCLE*
Holley, Mary Austin 1784-1846 *BioAmW*
Holley, Monelle Boyett 1935- *WhoWrEP 89*
Holley, Robert B. 1944- *St&PR 91*
Holley, Robert W. 1922- *WorAlBi*
Holley, Robert William 1922- *WhoAm 90, WhoWor 91*
Holley, Russell G. 1919- *St&PR 91*
Holley, Sallie 1818-1893 *BioAmW*
Holley, Samuel Justin, Jr. 1947- *WhoE 91*
Holley, Sandra C. *BioIn 16*
Holley, Thomas R 1949- *BiDrAPA 89*

Holliday, Anne Elaine 1962- *WhoAmW 91*
Holliday, Bug 1867-1910 *Ballpl 90*
Holliday, Chanalarp P 1950- *BiDrAPA 89*
Holliday, Charles O., Jr. 1948- *WhoE 91*
Holliday, James 1936- *BioIn 16*
Holliday, Jennifer 1960- *DrBlPA 90*
Holliday, Jennifer Yvette 1960- *WhoAm 90, WhoAmW 91*
Holliday, John Moffitt 1935- *WhoAm 90*
Holliday, Judith 1938- *WhoAmA 91*
Holliday, Judy 1922-1965 *BioAmW, BioIn 16, OxCPMus, WorAlBi*
Holliday, Judy Tuvim 1922-1965 *NotWoAT*
Holliday, Karen Kahler 1959- *WhoAmW 91*
Holliday, Kene 1948?- *DrBlPA 90*
Holliday, Kent Alfred 1940- *IntWWM 90*
Holliday, Leslie Talbott 1948- *WhoEmL 91*
Holliday, Linda L. 1951- *WhoAmW 91*
Holliday, Mark Armiger 1956- *WhoSSW 91*
Holliday, Melanie 1951- *IntWWM 90*
Holliday, Polly Dean 1937- *WhoAm 90*
Holliday, Richard Carter 1938- *St&PR 91*
Holliday, Robert Kelvin 1933- *WhoSSW 91*
Holliday, Terry Lynn 1955- *WhoSSW 91*
Holliday, Tom E. 1929- *St&PR 91*
Holliday, William C 1947- *BiDrAPA 89*
Hollidge, Kenneth Blake, Jr. 1945- *St&PR 91*
Hollie, Joseph Alan 1961- *WhoSSW 91*
Hollien, Harry Francis 1926- *WhoAm 90, WhoSSW 91*
Hollien, Patricia Ann 1938- *WhoAmW 91*
Hollier, Donald Russell 1934- *IntWWM 90*
Hollier, Yves 1949- *WhoWor 91*
Hollies, The *EncPR&S 89, OxCPMus*
Hollies, Linda Hall 1943- *WhoAmW 91*
Holliger, Heinz 1939- *IntWWM 90, PenDiMP*
Holliger, Ursula 1937- *PenDiMP*
Holliman, Becky Sellers 1954- *WhoAmW 91*
Holliman, Dan Clark 1932- *WhoSSW 91*
Holliman, Joe M. 1921- *St&PR 91*
Holliman, Joe Milton 1921- *WhoAm 90*
Hollin, Betty A. 1956- *WhoAmW 91*
Hollin, Lawrence Bruce 1959- *WhoEmL 91*
Hollin, Shelby W. 1925- *WhoSSW 91*
Holling, Crawford Stanley 1930- *WhoAm 90*
Holling, Holling Clancy 1900-1973 *AuBYP 90*
Hollingdale, Richard Graham 1956- *IntWWM 90*
Hollinger, Arlene Utz 1916- *St&PR 91*
Hollinger, James Davidson 1955- *WhoSSW 91*
Hollinger, Martha Reese 1941- *WhoSSW 91*
Hollinger, Paula Colodny 1940- *WhoAmW 91, WhoE 91*
Hollinger, Peter Bracken 1948- *WhoSSW 91*
Hollings, Ernest F. 1922- *BioIn 16*
Hollings, Ernest Frederick 1922- *WhoAm 90, WhoSSW 91, WhoWor 91*
Hollings, Peter Fernhout 1945- *WhoE 91*
Hollingshead, August B. 1907- *BioIn 16*
Hollingshead, Joe Edger 1946- *WhoAmA 91*
Hollingshead, Melinda Gay 1953- *WhoEmL 91*
Hollingshead, Susan Lynn Pearson 1946- *WhoEmL 91*
Hollingsworth, Al 1908- *Ballpl 90*
Hollingsworth, Alvin Carl 1930- *WhoAmA 91*
Hollingsworth, Bobby J. 1927- *WhoSSW 91*
Hollingsworth, Brian 1923- *ConAu 130*
Hollingsworth, Carey Ferguson, Jr. 1929- *St&PR 91*
Hollingsworth, Clyde Dixon, Jr. 1920- *WhoSSW 91*
Hollingsworth, Cornelia Ann 1957- *WhoAmW 91*
Hollingsworth, D. Vertrees 1937- *WhoE 91*
Hollingsworth, David S. 1928- *St&PR 91*
Hollingsworth, David Southerland *WhoAm 90, WhoE 91*
Hollingsworth, Dennis L. 1934- *St&PR 91*
Hollingsworth, Donald Lee 1947- *WhoEmL 91*
Hollingsworth, Edward P. 1932- *St&PR 91*
Hollingsworth, Gary Mayes 1944- *WhoWor 91*
Hollingsworth, Harry D., Jr. 1945- *ODwPR 91*
Hollingsworth, J. J. 1956- *IntWWM 90*
Hollingsworth, Jack Waring 1924- *WhoAm 90*
Hollingsworth, James William 1943- *WhoSSW 91*
Hollingsworth, Jeffrey Alan 1951- *WhoEmL 91*
Hollingsworth, John Allen 1929- *St&PR 91, WhoAm 90*
Hollingsworth, John D. *BioIn 16*
Hollingsworth, Joseph Rogers 1932- *WhoAm 90, WhoWrEP 89*
Hollingsworth, Kent 1929- *WhoWrEP 89*
Hollingsworth, Margaret 1940- *BioIn 16*
Hollingsworth, Margaret 1942- *OxCCanT*
Hollingsworth, Margaret Camille 1929- *WhoAmW 91*
Hollingsworth, Martha Lynette 1951- *WhoAmW 91*
Hollingsworth, Mary Carolyn 1947- *WhoWrEP 89*
Hollingsworth, Meredith Beaton 1941- *WhoAmW 91*
Hollingsworth, Michael 1950- *OxCCanT*
Hollingsworth, Penelope Kay 1944- *WhoE 91*
Hollingsworth, Perlesta Arthur 1936- *WhoSSW 91*
Hollingsworth, Robert Edgar 1918- *WhoAm 90*
Hollingsworth, Samuel Hawkins, Jr. 1922- *WhoAm 90*
Hollingsworth, Stuart W 1927- *BiDrAPA 89*
Hollingsworth, Thomas L. 1937- *St&PR 91*
Hollingworth, Leta S. 1886-1939 *BioAmW*
Hollingworth, Leta Stetter 1886-1939 *BioIn 16*
Hollingworth, Pamela 1936- *ODwPR 91*
Hollins, Alfred 1865-1942 *PenDiMP*
Hollins, Arthur, III 1930- *St&PR 91*
Hollins, Michael 1949- *WhoEmL 91*
Hollins, Mitchell Leslie 1947- *WhoEmL 91*
Hollins, Samuel 1748-1820 *PenDiDA 89*
Hollinshead, Ariel Cahill 1929- *WhoAm 90*
Hollinshead, Byron S., Jr. 1929- *WhoAm 90*
Hollinshead, Earl Darnell, Jr. 1927- *WhoE 91, WhoWor 91*
Hollinshead, Mary Hanton 1940- *WhoAmW 91*
Hollinshead, May Block 1913- *WhoAmW 91*
Hollinshead, Phillip Anthony 1957- *WhoE 91*
Hollis, Charles Carroll 1911- *WhoAm 90*
Hollis, Charles Eugene, Jr. 1948- *St&PR 91, WhoAm 90*
Hollis, Dan, Jr. 1951- *WhoSSW 91*
Hollis, Donald Roger 1936- *St&PR 91, WhoAm 90*
Hollis, Eleanor Hannah 1931- *WhoAmW 91*
Hollis, Everett Loftus 1914- *WhoAm 90*
Hollis, Howell 1919- *St&PR 91*
Hollis, Jocelyn 1927- *WhoWrEP 89*
Hollis, Johnnie Olyn 1926- *St&PR 91*
Hollis, Julie Ellen 1952- *WhoEmL 91*
Hollis, Kathleen Sue 1955- *WhoAmW 91, WhoEmL 91*
Hollis, Linda Eardley 1948- *WhoE 91, WhoEmL 91*
Hollis, Mark C. *WhoAm 90, WhoSSW 91*
Hollis, Mark D. 1908- *WhoAm 90*
Hollis, Mary J. 1837- *EncO&P 3*
Hollis, Peter B. 1943- *WhoE 91*
Hollis, Reginald 1932- *WhoAm 90*
Hollis, Samuel Brinson 1929- *St&PR 91*
Hollis, Sheila Slocum 1948- *WhoAm 90, WhoWor 91*
Hollis, William S. 1930- *WhoAm 90*
Hollis-Allbritton, Cheryl Dawn 1959- *WhoAmW 91*
Hollis-Billing, Mrs. 1837- *EncO&P 3*
Hollister, A.D. *St&PR 91*
Hollister, Charles Davis 1936- *WhoAm 90*
Hollister, Charles Warren 1930- *WhoAm 90*
Hollister, Charlotte Ann 1940- *WhoAmW 91*
Hollister, David Manship 1929- *IntWWM 90*
Hollister, Jeffrey Lynn 1949- *St&PR 91*
Hollister, John Baker, Jr. 1925- *WhoAm 90*
Hollister, Leo Edward 1920- *BiDrAPA 89, WhoAm 90*
Hollister, Lynda Jeanne 1960- *WhoAmW 91*
Hollister, Paul *WhoAmA 91*
Hollister, Peter H. *ODwPR 91*
Hollister, Susan Pender 1934- *WhoSSW 91*
Hollister, Valerie 1939- *WhoAmA 91*
Hollister, Vincent Loy 1951- *WhoEmL 91*
Hollister, William Gray *BiDrAPA 89*
Hollister, William Gray 1915- *WhoAm 90*
Hollitt, Raye *BioIn 16*
Hollman, Arthur 1923- *WhoWor 91*
Hollman, Richard Martin 1932- *St&PR 91*
Hollmann, Werner G. 1908-1989 *BioIn 16*
Hollocher, Charlie 1896-1940 *Ballpl 90*
Hollom, Chuck *BioIn 16*
Holloman, Bobo 1925-1987 *Ballpl 90*
Holloman, Charles James 1926- *St&PR 91*
Holloman, Charlotte *BioIn 16*
Holloman, G. H., Jr. *BiDrAPA 89*
Holloman, Haskell Andrew 1907- *WhoSSW 91*
Holloman, Hugh Jerry 1947- *WhoWrEP 89*
Holloman, John Lawrence Sullivan, Jr. 1919- *WhoAm 90*
Holloman, Otis Jack 1926- *St&PR 91*
Holloman, Rochelle 1952- *WhoSSW 91*
Hollon, William Eugene 1913- *WhoAm 90, WhoWrEP 89*
Hollopeter, Vincent E. 1953- *WhoE 91*
Holloran, Thomas Edward 1929- *St&PR 91*
Hollos, Mate 1954- *IntWWM 90*
Hollow Horn Bear 1850-1913 *WhNaAH [port]*
Hollow, John Walter 1939- *WhoAm 90*
Holloway, Anthony Wynne 1954- *WhoSSW 91*
Holloway, Barbara Jean Chambers 1938- *WhoAmW 91*
Holloway, Barry Victor, Jr. 1949- *WhoSSW 91*
Holloway, Benjamin Duke 1925- *St&PR 91, WhoAm 90*
Holloway, Bruce Keener 1912- *WhoAm 90*
Holloway, Carol Lee 1948- *St&PR 91*
Holloway, Charles Arthur 1936- *WhoAm 90*
Holloway, Cindy 1960- *WhoAmW 91*
Holloway, Clyde Cecil 1943- *WhoAm 90, WhoSSW 91*
Holloway, David 1942- *IntWWM 90, WhoAm 90*
Holloway, David Edwin *BiDrAPA 89*
Holloway, Donald Lee 1943- *WhoSSW 91*
Holloway, Donald Phillip 1928- *WhoWor 91*
Holloway, Douglas P. 1938- *St&PR 91*
Holloway, Douglas Patrick 1938- *WhoAm 90*
Holloway, Edgar Austin 1925- *WhoAm 90*
Holloway, Edna LaRue 1942- *WhoAmW 91*
Holloway, Emory 1885-1977 *DcLB 103*
Holloway, Frank Burnley 1931- *St&PR 91*
Holloway, Glenna Preston 1938- *WhoWrEP 89*
Holloway, Gordon Arthur 1938- *WhoSSW 91*
Holloway, H Maxson *WhoAmA 91N*
Holloway, Harry C, Jr. *BiDrAPA 89*
Holloway, Hiliary Hamilton 1928- *St&PR 91, WhoAm 90*
Holloway, Hiliary Hamilton, Jr. 1953- *WhoE 91*
Holloway, Jacque E. 1947- *St&PR 91*
Holloway, James J. 1936- *St&PR 91*
Holloway, James Joseph 1951- *WhoEmL 91*
Holloway, James Lemuel, III 1922- *WhoAm 90, WhoE 91, WhoWor 91*
Holloway, James Young 1927- *WhoAm 90*
Holloway, Jean *ConAu 130*
Holloway, Jerome Knight 1923- *WhoAm 90*
Holloway, Jodie Susan 1961- *BiDrAPA 89*
Holloway, John George 1937- *WhoWor 91*
Holloway, John Laws, III 1937- *St&PR 91*
Holloway, John Thomas 1922- *WhoAm 90*
Holloway, Joseph Wesley 1930- *WhoAm 90*
Holloway, Julia Bolton 1937- *WhoAmW 91*
Holloway, Karen *BiDrAPA 89*
Holloway, Ken 1897-1968 *Ballpl 90*
Holloway, Laurence 1938- *IntWWM 90*
Holloway, Lawrence Milton, Sr. 1913- *WhoWor 91*
Holloway, Leonard Leveine 1923- *WhoAm 90*
Holloway, Lisabeth Marie 1926- *WhoAmW 91*
Holloway, Lucy Ariel Williams 1905-1973 *HarlReB*
Holloway, Marcella Marie 1913- *WhoWrEP 89*
Holloway, Markita Rachelle 1965- *IntWWM 90*
Holloway, Marvin Lawrence 1911- *WhoAm 90*
Holloway, Muriel D. *WhoAmW 91*
Holloway, Paul Fayette 1938- *WhoAm 90*
Holloway, Paul Howard 1943- *WhoSSW 91*
Holloway, Redmond Thomas 1929- *WhoWor 91*
Holloway, Renee Diane *BiDrAPA 89*
Holloway, Richard A. 1941- *St&PR 91*
Holloway, Richard Allen 1941- *WhoAm 90*
Holloway, Robert A. 1930- *St&PR 91*
Holloway, Robert John 1921- *WhoAm 90*
Holloway, Robert Ross 1934- *WhoAm 90*
Holloway, Robert Wester 1945- *WhoEmL 91*
Holloway, Robin 1943- *PenDiMP A*
Holloway, Robin Greville 1943- *IntWWM 90, WhoWor 91*
Holloway, Rubin L. 1948- *St&PR 91*
Holloway, Stanley 1890-1982 *OxCPMus*
Holloway, Stanley Augustus 1890-1982 *DcNaB 1981*
Holloway, Stephen Francis *BiDrAPA 89*
Holloway, Thomas F. 1947- *St&PR 91*
Holloway, William H 1924- *BiDrAPA 89*
Holloway, William J., Jr. 1923- *WhoAm 90, WhoSSW 91*
Holloway, William Jimmerson 1917- *WhoAm 90*
Holloway, Willis, Jr. *BiDrAPA 89*
Hollowell, William George 1931- *St&PR 91*
Hollowood, James Richard 1943- *WhoE 91*
Hollreiser, Heinrich 1913- *IntWWM 90, PenDiMP*
Holls, William M., Jr. 1923- *St&PR 91*
Hollstein, Brian R. *BioIn 16*
Hollweg, Ilse 1922- *IntWWM 90*
Hollweg, Werner 1936- *IntWWM 90, PenDiMP*
Hollworth, Raymond Joseph 1939- *St&PR 91*
Holly, Buddy 1936-1959 *EncPR&S 89, OxCPMus, WorAlBi*
Holly, Charles F. *AmLegL*
Holly, Ellen 1931- *DrBlPA 90*
Holly, Ellistine Perkins 1934- *WhoSSW 91*
Hollyday, Chris *BioIn 16*
Hollyfield, Judy Lynn 1956- *WhoSSW 91*
Hollywood Argyles, The *EncPR&S 89*
Hollywood Quartet *PenDiMP*
Hollywood, Edwin L. 1923- *St&PR 91*
Hollywood, John Matthew 1910- *WhoAm 90*
Holm, Bertil K. 1925- *WhoE 91*
Holm, Bill 1925- *WhoAmA 91*
Holm, Bill 1943- *BioIn 16*
Holm, Carl-Eric Ove 1946- *WhoWor 91*
Holm, Carol Elizabeth Sachs 1932- *WhoAmW 91*
Holm, Cassie 1957- *ODwPR 91*
Holm, Celeste 1919- *BioIn 16, NotWoAT, WhoAm 90, WorAlBi*
Holm, Floyd W. 1953- *WhoEmL 91*
Holm, Gary Lunde 1947- *WhoEmL 91*
Holm, Gerald Lange 1938- *St&PR 91*
Holm, Gro 1878-1949 *EncCoWW*
Holm, Hannebo *AuBYP 90*
Holm, Hans-Henrik 1951- *WhoWor 91*
Holm, Hanya *WhoAm 90, WhoAmW 91*
Holm, Hanya 1893- *BioIn 16, NotWoAT*
Holm, Ian 1931- *WhoAm 90*
Holm, Jeanne M 1921- *ConAu 130*
Holm, Jeanne Marjorie 1921- *WhoAm 90*
Holm, Jens T. *BioIn 16*
Holm, Kevin Eugene 1957- *WhoEmL 91*
Holm, Lillemor *DcScanL*
Holm, Milton W *WhoAmA 91*
Holm, Mogens Winkel 1936- *IntWWM 90*
Holm, Peder 1926- *IntWWM 90*
Holm, Peter Christian Achilles 1936- *WhoWor 91*
Holm, Phillip Howard 1931- *WhoAm 90*
Holm, Renate 1931- *IntWWM 90, PenDiMP*
Holm, Richard 1912-1988 *PenDiMP*
Holm, Richard Eugene 1946- *WhoEmL 91*
Holm, Richard Hadley 1933- *WhoAm 90*
Holm, Robert Arthur 1935- *WhoAm 90*
Holm, Ronald Herbert 1944- *St&PR 91*
Holm, Soren 1944- *WhoWor 91*
Holm, Sven 1940- *DcScanL*
Holm, Victor Martin 1929- *BiDrAPA 89*
Holm, Wattie 1901-1950 *Ballpl 90*
Holm-Moller, Oliva 1875-1970 *BiDWomA*
Holman, Alan B. 1944- *St&PR 91*
Holman, Anne Whitsett 1938- *BiDrAPA 89*
Holman, Arthur 1926- *WhoAmA 91*
Holman, Arthur Stearns 1926- *WhoAm 90*
Holman, Betty Ann 1937- *WhoAmW 91*
Holman, Bill 1903-1987 *EncACom*
Holman, Bob 1948- *WhoWrEP 89*
Holman, Brian 1965- *Ballpl 90*
Holman, Bud George 1929- *WhoAm 90*
Holman, Carl Reyburn 1942- *St&PR 91*
Holman, Charles Richardson 1915- *WhoAm 90*
Holman, Cranston William 1907- *WhoAm 90*
Holman, Currier J. 1911-1977 *ConAmBL*
Holman, D.V. 1914- *St&PR 91*
Holman, Daniel G. 1945- *St&PR 91*
Holman, David Wallace 1947- *WhoEmL 91*
Holman, Derek 1931- *IntWWM 90*
Holman, Donald Reid 1930- *St&PR 91, WhoAm 90*
Holman, Felice 1919- *AuBYP 90*
Holman, Francis Wade, Jr. 1939- *WhoE 91*
Holman, Granville W. 1929- *St&PR 91*

Holman, Halsted Reid 1925- *WhoAm 90*
Holman, Harland Eugene 1914- *St&PR 91, WhoAm 90*
Holman, James Bradley 1935- *St&PR 91*
Holman, James Henry 1824-1891 *DcCanB 12*
Holman, James Lewis 1926- *WhoWor 91*
Holman, John Foster 1946- *WhoEmL 91, WhoWor 91*
Holman, John Leonard 1929- *St&PR 91, WhoAm 90, WhoWor 91*
Holman, Jon Barstow *BiDrAPA 89*
Holman, Karen Marie 1962- *WhoAmW 91*
Holman, Kermit Layton 1935- *WhoAm 90*
Holman, Libby 1906-1971 *BioAmW, OxCPMus*
Holman, M. Carl *BioIn 16*
Holman, Margaret Mezoff 1951- *WhoE 91*
Holman, Ralph Theodore 1918- *WhoAm 90*
Holman, Robert Carpenter 1945- *WhoE 91*
Holman, Russell A. 1955- *St&PR 91*
Holman, Scott 1958- *Ballpl 90*
Holman, W Thomas 1925- *BiDrAPA 89*
Holman-Hunt, William 1827-1910 *BioIn 16*
Holmans, The *OxCCanT*
Holmay, Patrick James 1957- *WhoEmL 91*
Holmberg, A. William 1923- *St&PR 91*
Holmberg, Albert William, Jr. 1923- *WhoAm 90*
Holmberg, Branton Kieth 1936- *WhoWor 91*
Holmberg, C.W., Jr. 1928- *St&PR 91*
Holmberg, Erik 1908- *BioIn 16*
Holmberg, Georgia McKee 1946- *WhoAmW 91*
Holmberg, James J. 1928- *St&PR 91*
Holmberg, Joyce 1930- *WhoAmW 91*
Holmberg, Robert Alan 1935- *WhoE 91*
Holmberg, Ronald Keith 1932- *St&PR 91*
Holmberg, Ruth S. 1921- *St&PR 91*
Holmberg, Ruth Sulzberger 1921- *WhoAm 90*
Holmboe, Vagn 1909- *IntWWM 90*
Holme, Bryan *NewYTBS 90*
Holme, Bryan 1913- *AuBYP 90*
Holme, Bryan 1913-1990 *ConAu 132*
Holme, Constance 1880-1955 *BioIn 16, FemiCLE*
Holme, Richard Phillips 1941- *WhoAm 90*
Holme, Thomas Timings 1913- *WhoAm 90*
Holme, Timothy *TwCCr&M 91*
Holmen, Ardyce M *BiDrAPA 89*
Holmen, George Robert 1933- *St&PR 91*
Holmen, Orrie Jeffrey 1953- *WhoSSW 91*
Holmen, Robert 1933- *WhoAm 90, WhoE 91*
Holmer, Edwin C. *BioIn 16*
Holmer, Edwin C. 1921- *St&PR 91*
Holmer, Edwin Carl 1921- *WhoAm 90*
Holmer, Paul *BiDrAPA 89*
Holmer, Paul L. *BioIn 16*
Holmes, Abraham S 1821?-1908 *DcLB 99*
Holmes, Albert R. 1924- *St&PR 91*
Holmes, Albert William, Jr. 1932- *WhoAm 90*
Holmes, Allen Cornelius 1920- *WhoAm 90*
Holmes, Ann Hitchcock 1922- *WhoAm 90*
Holmes, Anna *WhoWrEP 89*
Holmes, Archie E., Jr. 1935- *St&PR 91*
Holmes, Barbara Ann Krajkoski 1946- *WhoAmW 91*
Holmes, Barbara Jean 1948- *WhoE 91*
Holmes, Barbara Ware 1945- *WhoWrEP 89*
Holmes, Bert Otis E., Jr. 1921- *WhoAm 90*
Holmes, Bonnie Tansill 1946- *WhoSSW 91*
Holmes, Brenda *BioIn 16*
Holmes, Broox Garrett 1932- *WhoAm 90*
Holmes, Bruce John 1948- *WhoSSW 91*
Holmes, Carl Dean 1940- *WhoWor 91*
Holmes, Carolyn Coggin 1939- *WhoAmW 91*
Holmes, Charles Harvey 1918- *WhoAm 90*
Holmes, Christopher Francis 1959- *WhoE 91*
Holmes, Clint *BioIn 16*
Holmes, Colgate Frederick 1935- *WhoAm 90*
Holmes, Cynthia Misao Bell 1949- *WhoAmW 91*
Holmes, D. Brainerd 1921- *St&PR 91*
Holmes, Daniel Henry 1851-1908 *LiHiK*
Holmes, Daniel W., Jr. 1938- *St&PR 91*
Holmes, Darrell 1921- *WhoAm 90*
Holmes, David *BioIn 16, ODwPR 91*
Holmes, David Bryan 1936- *WhoAmA 91, WhoE 91*
Holmes, David Gordon 1943- *WhoAm 90*
Holmes, David Grover 1938- *WhoSSW 91*
Holmes, David Larson 1948- *WhoEmL 91*
Holmes, David M *BiDrAPA 89*
Holmes, David Richard 1940- *St&PR 91*
Holmes, David S. *BioIn 16*
Holmes, David Valentine 1945- *WhoAmA 91*
Holmes, Deborah Lynn 1954- *WhoE 91*
Holmes, Denise Marianne 1937- *St&PR 91*
Holmes, Doloris Grant *BioIn 16*
Holmes, Donald J 1924- *BiDrAPA 89*
Holmes, Dorothy Ellen 1910- *WhoE 91*
Holmes, Ducky 1869-1932 *Ballpl 90*
Holmes, Dwight Ellis 1938- *WhoAm 90*
Holmes, Edgar Parsons 1936- *IntWWM 90*
Holmes, Edward Walker 1939- *WhoE 91*
Holmes, Eileen Martinez 1952- *WhoHisp 91*
Holmes, Elkanah 1744-1832 *BioIn 16*
Holmes, Eugene 1934- *IntWWM 90*
Holmes, Francis Simmons 1815-1882 *BioIn 16*
Holmes, Francis William 1929- *WhoAm 90*
Holmes, Frankie Ann 1950- *WhoAmW 91*
Holmes, Fred Gillespie 1913- *WhoAm 90*
Holmes, Frederic Lawrence 1932- *WhoAm 90*
Holmes, Geoffrey Kenneth Towndrow 1942- *WhoWor 91*
Holmes, Gerald E. 1940- *St&PR 91*
Holmes, Gladys Viola 1898- *BiDrAPA 89*
Holmes, Gordon *TwCCr&M 91*
Holmes, Grace Idalia 1932- *WhoE 91*
Holmes, Grant *TwCCr&M 91*
Holmes, Gregory Lawrence 1948- *WhoE 91*
Holmes, H. H. *TwCCr&M 91*
Holmes, Harry L. 1945- *St&PR 91*
Holmes, Helen *ODwPR 91*
Holmes, Helen Bequaert 1929- *WhoAmW 91*
Holmes, Helen Juanita *WhoWrEP 89*
Holmes, Henry Allen 1933- *WhoAm 90*
Holmes, Houston Eccleston, Jr. 1938- *St&PR 91*
Holmes, Howard S. 1913- *St&PR 91*
Holmes, Jack David Lazarus 1930- *WhoAm 90, WhoWor 91*
Holmes, Jack Edward 1934- *St&PR 91*
Holmes, Jack Oliver 1905- *WhoAm 90*
Holmes, Jacquelin Ann 1947- *WhoAmW 91*
Holmes, James 1919- *WhoAm 90*
Holmes, James Everett *BiDrAPA 89*
Holmes, James Hillman 1922- *BiDrAPA 89*
Holmes, James Parker 1940- *WhoWor 91*
Holmes, Jane *BiDEWW*
Holmes, Janet Alice 1956- *WhoWrEP 89*
Holmes, Jay Thorpe 1942- *St&PR 91, WhoAm 90*
Holmes, Jenanne Nelson *WhoSSW 91*
Holmes, Jeri 1910- *WhoAmW 91*
Holmes, Jerry Dell 1935- *WhoAm 90*
Holmes, John *WorAu 1980*
Holmes, John *BioIn 16*
Holmes, John 1921- *SmATA X [port]*
Holmes, John Alfred, Jr. 1944- *WhoE 91*
Holmes, John Clellon 1926-1988 *AnObit 1988, BioIn 16*
Holmes, John Leonard 1931- *WhoAm 90*
Holmes, John Michael 1946- *St&PR 91*
Holmes, John Richard 1917- *WhoAm 90*
Holmes, John Robert 1952- *WhoEmL 91*
Holmes, Joseph *DrBIPA 90*
Holmes, Kenneth Howard 1936- *WhoAm 90*
Holmes, Larry *BioIn 16*
Holmes, Larry 1949- *WhoAm 90, WorAlBi*
Holmes, Larry W 1942- *WhoAmA 91*
Holmes, Lisa Ramona 1963- *WhoE 91*
Holmes, Lucille Martin 1921- *WhoWor 91*
Holmes, Malcolm Herbert 1934- *St&PR 91, WhoAm 90*
Holmes, Marilyn Adams 1930- *WhoWrEP 89*
Holmes, Marilyn Chattin 1949- *WhoAm 90*
Holmes, Marjorie Rose *WhoAm 90, WhoWrEP 89*
Holmes, Marjorie Rose 1910- *AuBYP 90*
Holmes, Marjory Ann 1931- *St&PR 91*
Holmes, Martin M. 1939- *St&PR 91*
Holmes, Mary Jane *LiHiK*
Holmes, Mary Jane 1825-1907 *FemiCLE*
Holmes, Mary Jane 1828-1907 *LiHiK*
Holmes, Mary L. Grier 1961- *WhoEmL 91*
Holmes, Maurice F. *BioIn 16*
Holmes, Max Jacob 1926- *WhoAm 90*
Holmes, Melvin Almont 1919- *WhoAm 90*
Holmes, Michael Denison 1935- *St&PR 91, WhoAm 90*
Holmes, Michael Elwyn 1949- *WhoEmL 91*
Holmes, Miller P., Jr. 1943- *St&PR 91*
Holmes, Nancy Ruth 1948- *WhoEmL 91*
Holmes, Natalie *BioIn 16*
Holmes, Ned Sweeney 1944- *WhoSSW 91*
Holmes, Neil E. 1944- *St&PR 91*
Holmes, Neil Edward 1944- *WhoAm 90*
Holmes, Nelson *EncO&P 3, EncPaPR 91*
Holmes, Nelson, Mrs. *EncO&P 3, EncPaPR 91*
Holmes, Norman Leonard 1928- *WhoAm 90*
Holmes, Obadiah 1607-1682 *BioIn 16*
Holmes, Oliver Wendell 1809-1894 *BioIn 16, WorAlBi*
Holmes, Oliver Wendell 1809-1904 *EncPaPR 91*
Holmes, Oliver Wendell 1841-1935 *BioIn 16*
Holmes, Oliver Wendell, Jr. 1841-1935 *WorAlBi*
Holmes, P.H. 1943- *St&PR 91*
Holmes, Patricia Anne 1927- *WhoAmW 91*
Holmes, Patricia Brown 1960- *WhoEmL 91*
Holmes, Peggy 1898- *SmATA 60 [port]*
Holmes, Peter Allen 1949- *WhoE 91*
Holmes, Ralph 1937-1984 *PenDiMP*
Holmes, Ralph Harris 1948- *WhoE 91*
Holmes, Ralph W. 1930- *WhoAm 90*
Holmes, Randall Kent 1940- *WhoAm 90*
Holmes, Raymond *WorAu 1980*
Holmes, Raymond 1921- *SmATA X [port]*
Holmes, Raymond V. 1937- *St&PR 91*
Holmes, Reed M. 1917- *WhoAm 90*
Holmes, Richard Andrew 1946- *IntWWM 90*
Holmes, Richard Hugh Morris 1925- *WhoAm 90*
Holmes, Richard V. 1929- *St&PR 91*
Holmes, Richard Winn 1923- *WhoAm 90*
Holmes, Robert Allen 1947- *WhoWor 91*
Holmes, Robert Bigelow 1931- *WhoAm 90*
Holmes, Robert Edward 1922- *WhoAm 90*
Holmes, Robert Glasgow, Jr. 1930- *St&PR 91*
Holmes, Robert Lawrence 1935- *WhoAm 90*
Holmes, Robert Raymond 1937- *WhoSSW 91*
Holmes, Robert William, Jr. 1953- *WhoE 91*
Holmes, Samuel 1813-1868 *AmLegL*
Holmes, Samuel Frederick 1963- *WhoSSW 91*
Holmes, Sarah 1841-1908 *FemiCLE*
Holmes, Sheila Louise 1956- *WhoSSW 91*
Holmes, Sue Baird 1955- *WhoEmL 91*
Holmes, Susan G. 1955- *WhoAmW 91*
Holmes, Susan K. 1951- *St&PR 91*
Holmes, T Stephenson 1944- *BiDrAPA 89*
Holmes, Terry 1949- *BiDrAPA 89*
Holmes, Thomas A. 1923- *WhoAm 90*
Holmes, Thomas Ewen 1954- *WhoWor 91*
Holmes, Thomas H *BiDrAPA 89*
Holmes, Thomas H. 1918-1988 *BioIn 16*
Holmes, Thomas James, Jr. 1948- *WhoSSW 91*
Holmes, Tommy 1904-1975 *Ballpl 90*
Holmes, Tommy 1917- *Ballpl 90*
Holmes, Valerie Frances *BiDrAPA 89*
Holmes, Valerie Frances 1954- *WhoE 91*
Holmes, Vance Bradley 1960- *WhoEmL 91*
Holmes, Vern H. 1920- *St&PR 91*
Holmes, Vernon Harrison 1920- *WhoAm 90*
Holmes, Walter John 1906- *WhoE 91*
Holmes, Walter S., Jr. 1919- *St&PR 91*
Holmes, Walter Stephen, Jr. 1919- *WhoAm 90*
Holmes, Wendy 1946- *WhoAmA 91*
Holmes, Willard *WhoAm 90, WhoAmA 91*
Holmes, William Charles, Jr. 1917- *WhoAm 90*
Holmes, William D. 1929- *St&PR 91*
Holmes, William Dee 1929- *WhoAm 90*
Holmes, William Dewayne 1961- *BiDrAPA 89*
Holmes, William Henry 1846-1933 *WhNaAH*
Holmes, William James *WhoAm 90, WhoE 91*
Holmes, William Paul 1945- *St&PR 91*
Holmes a Court, Robert 1937-1990 *NewYTBS 90 [port], WhoAm 90, WhoWor 91*
Holmgaard, Jorgen Henning 1946- *WhoWor 91*
Holmgren, Edwin Surl 1934- *WhoAm 90, WhoE 91*
Holmgren, Jeffrey Paul 1949- *BiDrAPA 89*
Holmgren, Laton Earle 1915- *WhoAm 90, WhoWor 91*
Holmgren, Patricia Kern 1940- *WhoE 91*
Holmgren, Paul *WhoAm 90, WhoE 91*
Holmgren, R John 1897-1963 *WhoAmA 91N*
Holmgren, Robert B 1924- *BiDrAPA 89*
Holmgren, Robert Bruce 1920- *WhoAm 90*
Holmgren, Theodore Joseph 1927- *WhoAm 90*
Holmgren, Virginia Cunningham *AuBYP 90*
Holmin, Torsten 1935- *WhoWor 91*
Holmlund, James Adrian 1956- *BiDrAPA 89*
Holmlund, Lisa Lynne 1960- *WhoEmL 91*
Holmquest, Donald Lee 1939- *WhoAm 90*
Holmquist, Ake 1943- *IntWWM 90*
Holmquist, John Edward 1955- *IntWWM 90*
Holmquist, Walter Richard 1934- *WhoAm 90*
Holmquist, William Randall 1925- *St&PR 91*
Holms, A Campbell 1861-1954 *EncO&P 3*
Holmsten, Victoria Lynn 1953- *WhoWrEP 89*
Holmstrom, Gregory Leonard 1948- *WhoEmL 91*
Holmstrom, Michael Edward 1942- *St&PR 91*
Holmwood, James Morley 1937- *WhoE 91*
Holness, Gordon V.R. 1939- *St&PR 91*
Holnick, Catherine Sigmund 1959- *WhoWrEP 89*
Holo, Selma R 1943- *WhoAmA 91*
Holo, Selma Reuben 1943- *WhoAm 90, WhoAmW 91*
Holoch, Stephen Alan 1947- *WhoEmL 91*
Holofcener, Lawrence 1926- *WhoE 91*
Holograf, Michael R. 1946- *St&PR 91*
Holoman, D. Kern 1947- *IntWWM 90*
Holoman, Dallas Kern 1947- *WhoAm 90*
Holoman, Eric L. *BioIn 16*
Holonyak, Nick, Jr. 1928- *WhoAm 90*
Holoubek, Gustaw 1923- *WhoWor 91*
Holoubek, Ladislav 1913- *IntWWM 90*
Holoun, Harold Dean 1939- *WhoAmA 91*
Holoviak, Stephen Julian 1948- *WhoE 91*
Holowesko, Mark Gordon 1960- *WhoEmL 91*
Holoyda, Basil B. 1953- *WhoEmL 91*
Holp, Carolyn Elaine 1947- *WhoWrEP 89*
Holquist, James Michael 1935- *WhoAm 90*
Holroyd, Gregory E. 1955- *St&PR 91*
Holroyd, Joseph Armitage 1939- *WhoE 91*
Holroyd, Louis Vincent 1925- *WhoAm 90*
Holroyd, Michael *BioIn 16*
Holroyd, Michael 1935- *MajTwCW, WhoAm 90*
Holsaert, Eunice *AuBYP 90*
Holsaert, Faith S. 1943- *WhoWrEP 89*
Holsch, Robert Fred 1952- *WhoAmA 91*
Holscher, Edward C, Jr. *BiDrAPA 89*
Holscher, Franz Foster 1921- *St&PR 91*
Holscher, Knud 1930- *ConDes 90*
Holscher, Richard Harry 1928- *St&PR 91*
Holschuh, Fred 1902- *WhoAmA 91*
Holschuh, John David 1926- *WhoAm 90*
Holsclaw, Robert Graydon 1934- *St&PR 91, WhoAm 90*
Holsen, James Noble, Jr. 1924- *WhoAm 90*
Holsen, Robert Charles 1913- *WhoAm 90*
Holsenbeck, Linton S, III *BiDrAPA 89*
Holsendolph, Ernest 1935- *WhoSSW 91*
Holshey, Michael L. 1941- *St&PR 91*
Holshouser, Don Franklin 1920- *WhoAm 90*
Holshouser, Thomas Edward 1958- *WhoSSW 91*
Holsinger, Candice Doreen 1955- *WhoEmL 91*
Holsinger, Fran 1938- *WhoAmW 91*
Holsinger, George Robert, Jr. 1925- *WhoAm 90*
Holsinger, James Wilson, Jr. 1939- *WhoSSW 91, WhoWor 91*
Holsinger, Jane Lumley *AuBYP 90*
Holsinger, Kent Eugene 1956- *WhoE 91*
Holsinger, W. Preston 1942- *St&PR 91, WhoAm 90*
Holsinger, Wayne Townsend 1931- *WhoAm 90*
Holsman, Daniel *AmLegL*
Holsonback, James F. 1920- *St&PR 91*
Holst, Gull-May 1941- *WhoWor 91*
Holst, Gustav 1874-1934 *PenDiMP A, WorAlBi*
Holst, Henry 1899- *PenDiMP*
Holst, Imogen 1907-1984 *PenDiMP*
Holst, Imogen Clare 1907-1984 *DcNaB 1981*
Holst, Johan Jorgen 1937- *WhoWor 91*
Holst, Norman Dolcy 1943- *St&PR 91*
Holst, Willem 1911- *WhoE 91*
Holste, Thomas James 1943- *WhoAmA 91*
Holstead, John Burnham 1938- *WhoAm 90*
Holstein, Bruce Jay 1947- *BiDrAPA 89, WhoE 91*
Holstein, Charlotte Garelick 1925- *WhoAmW 91*
Holstein, David 1934- *WhoE 91*
Holstein, Henry Lincoln 1865-1942 *AmLegL*
Holstein, Jay Allen 1938- *WhoAm 90*
Holstein, Ludvig Ditlef 1864-1943 *DcScanL*
Holstein, Marilyn Anne 1958- *WhoAm 90*
Holstein, Peter Lawrence 1942- *WhoAm 90*
Holstein, William Kurt 1936- *WhoAm 90*
Holster, Robert Marc 1946- *WhoAm 90*
Holsti, Kalevi Jacque 1935- *WhoAm 90*

Holsti, Ole Rudolf 1933- *WhoAm 90*
Holston, James Benjamin, III 1958- *WhoE 91*
Holston, James Eugene 1951- *WhoWrEP 89*
Holston, Sharon Smith 1945- *WhoAmW 91*
Holstrom, Carleton Arthur 1935- *WhoAm 90*
Holstrom, Gustaf Werner 1923- *WhoWor 91*
Holswade, Larry Haig 1937- *St&PR 91*
Holsworth, William C. 1944- *WhoAm 90*
Holt, Amos E. 1940- *St&PR 91*
Holt, Arthur Roland, Jr. 1953- *BiDrAPA 89*
Holt, Barbara Bertany 1940- *WhoAmW 91*
Holt, Barry 1945- *ODwPR 91*
Holt, Ben *BioIn 16, NewYTBS 90*
Holt, Ben 1955- *DrBIPA 90*
Holt, Bertha Merrill 1916- *WhoAmW 91*
Holt, Beverly Elaine 1945- *WhoAmW 91*
Holt, Carol Rosemary Smedley 1939- *IntWWM 90*
Holt, Charles Carter 1921- *WhoAm 90*
Holt, Charlotte Sinclair 1914-1990 *WhoAmA 91N*
Holt, Cheryl Adams 1947- *WhoSSW 91*
Holt, Darrel M. 1915- *St&PR 91*
Holt, David Earl 1928- *WhoAm 90, WhoSSW 91*
Holt, Dennis F. *WhoAm 90*
Holt, Donald A. 1932- *WhoAm 90*
Holt, Donald Dale 1936- *WhoAm 90, WhoWrEP 89*
Holt, Donald Edward, Jr. 1945- *WhoAm 90*
Holt, Douglas Eugene 1924- *WhoAm 90*
Holt, Earl Kendall, III 1945- *WhoEmL 91*
Holt, Edward James 1942- *WhoSSW 91*
Holt, Edwin Joseph *WhoSSW 91*
Holt, Elizabeth Hunter 1727?-1788 *BioIn 16*
Holt, Eric Francis *BiDrAPA 89*
Holt, Felix 1898-1954 *LiHiK*
Holt, Georgia *BioIn 16*
Holt, Georgia 1927- *ConAu 129*
Holt, Georgina L. 1934- *WhoAmW 91*
Holt, Gerald F. 1923- *St&PR 91*
Holt, Gordon Arthur 1951- *WhoE 91, WhoWor 91*
Holt, Hamilton 1872-1951 *BioIn 16*
Holt, Helen *ConAu 31NR*
Holt, Helen Keil 1937- *WhoAmW 91*
Holt, Henry 1840-1926 *EncO&P 3*
Holt, Henry Vance 1951- *WhoSSW 91*
Holt, Herbert *BiDrAPA 89*
Holt, Herbert 1912- *WhoE 91*
Holt, Ivan Lee, Jr. 1913- *WhoAm 90*
Holt, Jack Wilson, Jr. 1929- *WhoAm 90, WhoSSW 91*
Holt, James 1955- *WhoSSW 91*
Holt, Jim 1944- *Ballpl 90*
Holt, John 1721-1784 *BioIn 16, EncCRAm*
Holt, John 1923-1985 *ConAu 32NR*
Holt, John B. 1915- *WhoAm 90*
Holt, John C. *St&PR 91*
Holt, John C. 1940- *WhoAm 90*
Holt, John Caldwell 1923-1985 *BioIn 16*
Holt, John I. 1861-1920 *AmLegL*
Holt, John William, Jr. 1948- *WhoEmL 91*
Holt, Jonathan H *BiDrAPA 89*
Holt, Joseph 1807-1894 *BiDrUSE 89*
Holt, Judith Ann 1940- *WhoAmW 91*
Holt, Kare 1917- *DcScanL*
Holt, Karen Anita Young 1949- *WhoSSW 91*
Holt, Kay Gurine 1943- *BiDrAPA 89*
Holt, Larry D. 1940- *St&PR 91*
Holt, Leon C., Jr. 1925- *St&PR 91*
Holt, Leon Conrad, Jr. 1925- *WhoAm 90*
Holt, Louise 1924- *WhoAmA 91*
Holt, Margaret 1937- *AuBYP 90*
Holt, Margaret Mary 1935- *WhoAmW 91*
Holt, Marjorie Sewell 1920- *WhoAm 90, WhoAmW 91*
Holt, Martha *BioIn 16*
Holt, Martha A 1945- *WhoAmA 91*
Holt, Michael Bartholomew 1956- *WhoEmL 91*
Holt, Nancy 1943- *BioIn 16*
Holt, Nancy Louise 1938- *WhoAm 90, WhoAmA 91*
Holt, Nora 1895?-1974 *DrBIPA 90*
Holt, Pamela Gail 1958- *WhoAmW 91*
Holt, Patricia Lester 1944- *WhoAm 90*
Holt, Peter Rolf 1930- *WhoAm 90*
Holt, Philetus Havens, III 1928- *WhoAm 90*
Holt, Ralph Manning, Jr. 1931- *St&PR 91, WhoAm 90*
Holt, Rex *BioIn 16*
Holt, Robert Emery 1945- *BiDrAPA 89*
Holt, Robert LeRoi 1920- *WhoAm 90*
Holt, Robert McKindly 1956- *WhoEmL 91*
Holt, Robert Theodore 1928- *WhoAm 90*
Holt, Robert W. 1949- *St&PR 91*
Holt, Rochelle Lynn 1946- *WhoWrEP 89*
Holt, Ronald Lee 1952- *WhoEmL 91*
Holt, Simon 1958- *IntWWM 90*
Holt, Smith Lewis, Jr. 1938- *WhoAm 90*
Holt, Stephen *AuBYP 90*
Holt, Stephen 1894-1987 *BioIn 16*
Holt, Stephen S. 1940- *WhoAm 90*
Holt, Steven Hamilton Humphrey 1957- *WhoEmL 91*
Holt, Thomas Michael 1831-1896 *AmLegL*
Holt, Timothy Arthur 1953- *St&PR 91*
Holt, Tonie *BioIn 16*
Holt, Valmai *BioIn 16*
Holt, Victoria *WhoAm 90, WhoWrEP 89*
Holt, Victoria 1906- *BestSel 90-4 [port], TwCCr&M 91, WorAlBi*
Holt, Wayne Gary 1937- *St&PR 91*
Holt, William E 1920- *BiDrAPA 89*
Holt, William H. 1929- *St&PR 91*
Holt, William Henry 1939- *WhoSSW 91*
Holt, William L 1906- *BiDrAPA 89*
Holt-Harris, John Evan, Jr. 1917- *WhoWor 91*
Holt-Jensen, Arild 1937- *WhoWor 91*
Holtan, Boyd DeVere 1928- *WhoSSW 91*
Holtan, Daniel A. 1945- *St&PR 91*
Holtan, Maurice O. 1901- *St&PR 91*
Holtby, Winifred 1898-1935 *BioIn 16, FemiCLE*
Holte, David B. 1944- *St&PR 91*
Holte, Debra Leah 1952- *WhoAmW 91*
Holtel, Bob *BioIn 16*
Holten, Bo 1948- *IntWWM 90*
Holten, Virginia Lois Zewe 1938- *WhoAmW 91*
Holter, Arlen Rolf 1946- *WhoEmL 91*
Holter, Don Wendell 1905- *WhoAm 90*
Holter, Gail L. 1937- *St&PR 91*
Holter, Gary S. 1954- *St&PR 91*
Holter, Marvin Rosenkrantz 1922- *WhoAm 90*
Holter, Wesley Keith 1937- *St&PR 91*
Holtfreter, Johannes Friedrich Karl 1901- *WhoAm 90*
Holthaus, Dennis B. 1949- *St&PR 91*
Holthaus, Gerard Gustav 1962- *St&PR 91*
Holthaus, Hollis Lee 1936- *WhoWor 91*
Holtkamp, Dorsey Emil 1919- *WhoAm 90*
Holtkamp, Richard T. 1934- *St&PR 91*
Holtmann, Antonius 1936- *WhoWor 91*
Holtmann, Heidrun 1961- *IntWWM 90*
Holton, A. Linwood, Jr. 1923- *WhoAm 90*
Holton, Anne Lysbeth 1950- *WhoAmW 91*
Holton, Brian 1959- *Ballpl 90*
Holton, Gerald 1922- *WhoAm 90*
Holton, Grace Holland 1957- *WhoE 91*
Holton, James Jerome 1963- *WhoSSW 91*
Holton, John J. 1933- *St&PR 91*
Holton, Leonard *AuBYP 90*
Holton, Leonard 1915-1983 *TwCCr&M 91*
Holton, Mary Pearce 1939- *WhoSSW 91*
Holton, Raymond William 1929- *WhoAm 90*
Holton, Richard Henry 1926- *WhoAm 90*
Holton, Robert Page 1938- *WhoAm 90*
Holton, Susan A. 1948- *WhoAmW 91, WhoE 91*
Holton, William Chester 1939- *WhoWor 91*
Holton, William Coffeen 1930- *WhoAm 90*
Holton, William Milne 1931- *WhoAm 90*
Holtrop, Marijke Elizabet 1932- *WhoE 91*
Holtsclaw, Gwendolyn Pheagin 1945- *WhoAmW 91*
Holtsinger, Christine L. 1899- *St&PR 91*
Holtsmark, Eric Birger 1937- *WhoWor 91*
Holttum, John Robert *BiDrAPA 89*
Holty, Carl Robert 1900-1973 *WhoAmA 91N*
Holty, Ludwig Christoph Heinrich 1748-1776 *DcLB 94 [port]*
Holtz, Abel *WhoHisp 91*
Holtz, Abel 1935- *St&PR 91*
Holtz, Anthony John 1945- *WhoEmL 91*
Holtz, Daniel M. 1959- *St&PR 91*
Holtz, Donald J. 1949- *St&PR 91*
Holtz, Edgar Wolfe 1922- *WhoAm 90*
Holtz, Gail Ramagnano Pinto 1947- *WhoAmW 91*
Holtz, Gilbert Joseph 1924- *WhoE 91, WhoWor 91*
Holtz, Glenn Edward 1938- *WhoAm 90*
Holtz, Harry Lawrence 1918- *St&PR 91*
Holtz, Herman 1919- *WhoWrEP 89*
Holtz, Itshak 1925- *WhoE 91*
Holtz, Itshak Jack 1925- *WhoAmA 91*
Holtz, Lou *BioIn 16*
Holtz, Lou 1937- *WorAlBi*
Holtz, Louis Leo 1937- *WhoAm 90*
Holtz, Mary Heston 1926- *WhoSSW 91*
Holtz, Richard L. *St&PR 91*
Holtz, Robert Joseph 1950- *WhoE 91*
Holtz, Sidney 1925- *WhoAm 90*
Holtz, W. Bradley 1955- *WhoEmL 91*
Holtzapfel, Patricia Kelly 1948- *WhoAmW 91, WhoWor 91*
Holtzclaw, Diane Smith 1936- *WhoAmW 91*
Holtze, Sally Holmes 1952- *SmATA 64*
Holtzendorff, Richard Lee 1926- *St&PR 91*
Holtzer, Alfred Melvin 1929- *WhoAm 90*
Holtzer, Marilyn Emerson 1938- *WhoAmW 91*
Holtzinger, Albert Harrison 1901- *WhoE 91, WhoWor 91*
Holtzman, Alan M *BiDrAPA 89*
Holtzman, Andrew Jay 1953- *ODwPR 91*
Holtzman, Arnold Harold 1932- *WhoE 91*
Holtzman, Edward 1924- *BiDrAPA 89*
Holtzman, Elizabeth 1941- *WhoAm 90, WhoAmW 91, WorAlBi*
Holtzman, Garry Lynn *BiDrAPA 89*
Holtzman, Gary Yale 1936- *WhoAm 90*
Holtzman, Gilbert E *BiDrAPA 89*
Holtzman, Jay H. 1942- *BiDrAPA 89*
Holtzman, Jerome 1926- *Ballpl 90, BioIn 16, WhoAm 90*
Holtzman, Jerome Joseph 1930- *WhoWor 91*
Holtzman, Joseph 1953- *WhoE 91*
Holtzman, Ken 1945- *Ballpl 90, BioIn 16*
Holtzman, Marc Lawrence 1960- *WhoE 91*
Holtzman, Richard Edward 1919- *WhoAm 90*
Holtzman, Sandra 1951- *WhoEmL 91*
Holtzman, Saul C *BiDrAPA 89*
Holtzman, Seymour 1935- *St&PR 91*
Holtzman, Wayne Harold 1923- *WhoAm 90*
Holtzman, William Scott 1951- *WhoE 91*
Holtzmann, Fanny E. 1903- *BioAmW*
Holtzmann, Howard Marshall 1921- *WhoAm 90, WhoWor 91*
Holtzschue, Karl Bressem 1938- *WhoE 91, WhoWor 91*
Holub, Martin 1938- *WhoAm 90*
Holub, Miroslav 1923- *WhoWor 91, WorAlBi*
Holum-Hardegen, Laura Lynn 1956- *WhoAmW 91*
Holverson, John 1946- *WhoAmA 91, WhoE 91*
Holvey, Samuel Boyer 1935- *WhoAmA 91, WhoE 91*
Holway, James Colin 1927- *WhoWor 91*
Holway, John 1929- *Ballpl 90*
Holway, Michael Paul 1955- *WhoEmL 91*
Holway, Richard A. 1937- *St&PR 91*
Holwerda, Robert Dale *BiDrAPA 89*
Holwick, Robert Keith 1932- *St&PR 91*
Holwill, Richard Newton 1945- *WhoAm 90, WhoWor 91*
Holwin, Mic *NewAgMG*
Holyer, Erna Maria 1925- *WhoWrEP 89*
Holyfield, Evander *BioIn 16*
Holyfield, James Robert 1940- *WhoSSW 91*
Holyoak, William Heber *BiDrAPA 89*
Holyoake, George Jacob 1817-1906 *BioIn 16*
Holz, George H. 1922- *St&PR 91*
Holz, Hans Heinz 1927- *WhoWor 91*
Holz, Harold A. 1925- *WhoAm 90*
Holz, Harry George 1934- *WhoAm 90*
Holz, K. Jacqueline 1942- *ODwPR 91*
Holz, Kenneth 1959- *St&PR 91*
Holz, Robert Kenneth 1930- *WhoSSW 91*
Holzach, Robert 1922- *WhoWor 91*
Holzapfel, Christina Marie 1942- *WhoAmW 91*
Holzbach, Raymond Thomas 1929- *WhoAm 90*
Holzberg, Ida R *BiDrAPA 89*
Holzberg, Robert 1927- *WhoSSW 91*
Holzberg, Stanley I 1929- *BiDrAPA 89*
Holzberger, Sheila Marie 1960- *WhoAmW 91*
Holzberger, William George 1932- *WhoWrEP 89*
Holzel, David Benjamin 1958- *WhoAm 90*
Holzel, Hans *BioIn 16*
Holzel, Thomas Martin 1940- *WhoE 91*
Holzendorf, Betty Smith 1939- *WhoAmW 91*
Holzenthal, Leo Leonhard, Jr. 1957- *WhoSSW 91*
Holzer, Adela *BioIn 16*
Holzer, Barry D 1958- *BiDrAPA 89*
Holzer, Edwin 1933- *WhoAm 90*
Holzer, Edwin H. 1933- *St&PR 91*
Holzer, Hans *WhoAm 90*
Holzer, Hans 1920- *EncPaPR 91*
Holzer, Hans W. 1920- *EncO&P 3*
Holzer, Harold *ODwPR 91*
Holzer, Hellfried Peter 1926- *WhoAm 90*
Holzer, Jacob Chaim *BiDrAPA 89*
Holzer, Jenny *BioIn 16*
Holzer, Jenny 1950- *CurBio 90 [port], WhoAmA 91*
Holzer, Joseph Alfred 1914- *WhoWor 91*
Holzer, Kenneth D. 1929- *St&PR 91*
Holzer, Marc 1945- *WhoE 91*
Holzer, Thomas Lequear 1944- *WhoAm 90*
Holzgang, Anthony James 1947- *BiDrAPA 89*
Holzheimer, Jorge 1945- *St&PR 91*
Holzherr, Katherine 1957- *WhoE 91*
Holzinger, James Jay 1935- *St&PR 91*
Holzmacher, Robert Gustav 1927- *WhoAm 90*
Holzman, Arthur David 1914- *WhoE 91*
Holzman, Beth Frances 1954- *WhoEmL 91*
Holzman, Bruce R 1940- *BiDrAPA 89*
Holzman, D. Keith 1936- *WhoAm 90*
Holzman, Eric 1949- *WhoAmA 91*
Holzman, Evan Mark 1954- *WhoSSW 91*
Holzman, Franklyn Dunn 1918- *WhoAm 90*
Holzman, Herbert S. 1934- *St&PR 91*
Holzman, Irwin Lloyd 1929- *St&PR 91*
Holzman, Malcolm *BioIn 16*
Holzman, Malcolm 1940- *WhoAm 90*
Holzman, Philip Seidman 1922- *WhoAm 90, WhoWor 91*
Holzman, Red 1920- *BioIn 16*
Holzman, Robert Stuart 1907- *AuBYP 90, WhoAm 90, WhoWor 91*
Holzman, Ronald R. 1931- *St&PR 91*
Holzman, Stephen R 1944- *BiDrAPA 89*
Holzman, Todd F 1942- *BiDrAPA 89*
Holzmann, Abe 1874-1939 *OxCPMus*
Holzmann, Hans 1929- *WhoWor 91*
Holzmeister, Alicia Lynn 1954- *WhoEmL 91*
Holzner, Burkart 1931- *WhoAm 90*
Holzsager, Mel 1921- *WhoE 91*
Holzwasser, Harry A. 1924- *St&PR 91*
Holzwasser, Robert A. 1954- *St&PR 91*
Hom, Doris Soo 1953- *WhoEmL 91*
Hom, Marlon Kau 1947- *ConAu 131*
Hom, Richard Yee 1950- *WhoEmL 91*
Hom, William Lim *BiDrAPA 89*
Homan, Benjamin Keith 1959- *WhoEmL 91*
Homan, Charles I. 1943- *St&PR 91*
Homan, Gerlof 1930- *St&PR 91*
Homan, John F. 1943- *St&PR 91*
Homan, Mary Carolyn 1958- *WhoAmW 91*
Homan, Ralph William 1951- *WhoEmL 91, WhoWor 91*
Homann, Juergen *BiDrAPA 89*
Homans, George Caspar 1910-1989 *BioIn 16*
Homans, Peter Chardon Brooks 1955- *IntWWM 90*
Homar, Lorenzo 1913- *WhoAmA 91*
Homayssi, Ruby Lee 1945- *WhoAmW 91*
Hombs, Margaret Mavourneen 1934- *WhoAmW 91*
Homburg, Al 1937- *IntWWM 90*
Homburger, Eve Alice 1955- *WhoSSW 91*
Homburger, Freddy 1916- *WhoAm 90, WhoWrEP 89*
Homburger, Thomas Charles 1941- *WhoAm 90*
Home, Charles Cospatrick Douglas- 1937-1985 *DcNaB 1981*
Home, Daniel Dunglas 1833-1886 *EncO&P 3, EncPaPR 91*
Home, Michael *TwCCr&M 91*
Home, William Douglas 1912- *BioIn 16*
Home of the Hirsel, Baron 1903- *BioIn 16*
Homeier, Lon Williams 1927- *St&PR 91*
Homeier, Skip 1930- *ConTFT 8*
Homer *WorAlBi*
Homer, Agnes Mabel Narney 1946- *WhoAmW 91*
Homer, Arthur B. 1896-1972 *WorAlBi*
Homer, Ben R. 1936- *St&PR 91*
Homer, Bruce A. 1931- *St&PR 91*
Homer, C. James 1936- *St&PR 91*
Homer, Charles Christopher 1847-1914 *EncABHB 6*
Homer, Charles T. 1938- *St&PR 91*
Homer, Edward John 1925- *St&PR 91*
Homer, F.G. 1937- *St&PR 91*
Homer, Irvin 1924- *WhoE 91*
Homer, John Thomas 1945- *St&PR 91*
Homer, Louise 1871-1947 *BioAmW, PenDiMP*
Homer, Marion 1948- *St&PR 91*
Homer, Paul Robert 1928- *IntWWM 90*
Homer, Tamara Kukrycka 1932- *WhoAmW 91*
Homer, William Innes 1929- *WhoAm 90, WhoAmA 91*
Homer, Winslow 1836-1910 *BioIn 16, IntDcAA 90, WorAlBi*
Homes, Geoffrey 1902-1978 *TwCCr&M 91*
Homesley, Horace Edward 1928- *WhoWrEP 89*
Homestead, Susan 1937- *WhoAmW 91, WhoWor 91*
Homewood, Charles H. 1914-1984 *SpyFic*
Homewood, Harry 1914-1984 *SpyFic*
Homeyer, Fred Carl 1920- *WhoWor 91*
Homeyer, Howard C. 1933- *St&PR 91, WhoAm 90*
Homick, Daniel John 1947- *WhoSSW 91*
Homisak, Theresa 1950- *WhoEmL 91*

Homitzky, Peter 1942- *WhoAmA 91*
Homma, Hitoshi 1948- *WhoEmL 91*
Homma, Kazufumi 1943- *WhoAmA 91*
Hommell, Adrienne Elizabeth 1934- *WhoAmW 91*
Hommen, Jan H.M. 1943- *St&PR 91*
Hommen, Jan H. M. 1943- *WhoAm 90*
Hommer, Daniel W 1948- *BiDrAPA 89*
Hommes, Frits Aukustinus 1934- *WhoAm 90*
Hommes, Robert Lee 1934- *St&PR 91*
Homo-Lechner, Catherine Anne Francoise 1958- *IntWWM 90*
Homola, Ivan E 1933- *BiDrAPA 89*
Homola, Joseph T. *ODwPR 91*
Homolka, Oscar 1898-1978 *WorAlBi*
Homolya, Istvan 1940- *ConAu 131*
Hompe, John Thomas 1961- *WhoEmL 91*
Hompson, Davi Det 1939- *WhoAmA 91*
Homrich-Henderson, Jean Marie 1964- *WhoAmW 91*
Homsey, Harvey Harold Harry 1960- *WhoEmL 91*
Homsey, Victorine duPont 1900- *WhoAm 90*
Homsky, Marie D. *St&PR 91*
Homsy, Paul Tamer *BiDrAPA 89*
Hon, David Nyok-Sai 1947- *WhoSSW 91*
Honack, Richard P. *ODwPR 91*
Honadle, Beth Walter 1954- *WhoAmW 91*
Honahan, Henry Robert 1937- *WhoSSW 91*
Honaman, David Gerald 1951- *St&PR 91*
Hon'ami Koetsu 1558-1637 *EncJap*
Honan, James Terry 1946- *WhoAm 90*
Honan, Thomas M. *AmLegL*
Honan, William Holmes 1930- *WhoAm 90*
Honanyawas 1725-1815 *WhNaAH*
Honasan, Gregorio *BioIn 16*
Honayawas 1725-1815 *WhNaAH*
Honberg, Lynda Ellen 1952- *WhoE 91*
Honda, Margaret 1961- *WhoAmA 91*
Honda, Natsuo 1930- *WhoWor 91*
Honda, Soichiro 1906- *BioIn 16, WorAlBi*
Honda, Yuzo 1947- *WhoWor 91*
Hondeghem, Luc M. 1944- *WhoAm 90*
Honderd, Gaele 1933- *WhoWor 91*
Honderich, Beland H. *BioIn 16*
Honderich, Beland Hugh 1918- *WhoAm 90*
Honderich, John Allen 1946- *WhoAm 90*
Hondius, Ewoud Herman 1942- *WhoWor 91*
Hondl, Edeltraud A 1939- *BiDrAPA 89*
Hondo, Med *DrBIPA 90*
Hondre, Anthony Rodney 1939- *St&PR 91*
Hondrich, Karl Otto 1937- *WhoWor 91*
Hone, Evie 1894-1955 *BiDWomA*
Hone, Francis James, Jr. 1958- *WhoEmL 91*
Hone, Frederick *BioIn 16*
Hone, Galyon *PenDiDA 89*
Hone, James A. 1944- *St&PR 91*
Hone, Joseph 1937- *SpyFic, TwCCr&M 91*
Hone, Kimberly *BioIn 16*
Hone, L. Michael 1949- *St&PR 91*
Hone, Louis Raymond 1950- *WhoEmL 91*
Hone, Michael Curran 1937- *St&PR 91*
Honea, James Michael 1959- *WhoE 91, WhoEmL 91, WhoWor 91*
Honecker, Erich *BioIn 16*
Honecker, Erich 1912- *WhoWor 91*
Honegger, Arthur 1892-1955 *PenDiMP A*
Honegger, Artur 1892-1955 *WorAlBi*
Honegger, Henri Charles 1904- *IntWWM 90*
Honegger-Moyse, Blanche *PenDiMP*
Honek, Andrew P. 1960- *St&PR 91*
Honek, J. Frank 1958- *St&PR 91*
Honemann, Daniel Henry 1929- *WhoAm 90*
Honemann, Volker Hans 1943- *WhoWor 91*
Honen 1133-1212 *EncJap*
Honer, Anne Stifel 1940- *WhoE 91*
Honer, Robert B. 1926- *St&PR 91*
Honer, William G *BiDrAPA 89*
Honer, William George 1957- *WhoE 91*
Honey, Martha S 1945- *ConAu 31NR*
Honey, Raymond J. 1938- *St&PR 91*
Honey, Richard Churchill 1924- *WhoAm 90*
Honey, Richard David 1927- *WhoAm 90*
Honeycheck, Linda Jean 1949- *WhoAmW 91*
Honeychurch, Denis Arthur 1946- *WhoEmL 91*
Honeychurch, Dorothy Anne 1925- *WhoAmW 91, WhoE 91*
Honeycutt, Ann *BioIn 16*
Honeycutt, Ann 1902?-1989 *ConAu 129*
Honeycutt, Earl Dwight, Jr. 1947- *WhoSSW 91*
Honeycutt, George Leonard 1936- *WhoAm 90*
Honeycutt, James Michael 1956- *WhoSSW 91*
Honeycutt, Natalie *AuBYP 90*
Honeycutt, Rick 1954- *Ballpl 90*
Honeyford, George John 1921- *St&PR 91*
Honeyman, David Lee *BiDrAPA 89*
Honeyman, Louise Mary 1933- *IntWWM 90*
Honeystein, Karl 1932- *WhoAm 90*
Honeywell, Larry G. 1935- *St&PR 91*
Honeywell, Larry Gene 1935- *WhoAm 90, WhoWor 91*
Hong, Doo Pyo 1943- *BiDrAPA 89*
Hong, Hei-Kyung 1957- *BioIn 16*
Hong, Howard Vincent 1912- *WhoAm 90*
Hong, Inpow David 1940- *BiDrAPA 89*
Hong, James M. 1940- *St&PR 91*
Hong, James Ming 1940- *WhoSSW 91*
Hong, John Joonpyo 1938- *WhoWor 91*
Hong, Ki Moon *BiDrAPA 89*
Hong, Mae Sien *BioIn 16*
Hong, Norman G. Y. 1947- *WhoWor 91*
Hong, Ock Lan *BiDrAPA 89*
Hong, Ok Ro *BiDrAPA 89*
Hong, Perry 1965- *WhoEmL 91*
Hong, Richard 1929- *WhoAm 90*
Hong, Se June 1944- *WhoAm 90*
Hong, Stanley W. 1936- *St&PR 91*
Hong, Sungdo David 1945- *BiDrAPA 89*
Hong, Yong Shik 1932- *WhoWor 91*
Hong Bailar, Theresa Yumee 1964- *WhoAmW 91*
Hongen, Elisabeth 1906- *IntWWM 90, PenDiMP*
Hongo, Garrett Kaoru 1951- *WhoWrEP 89*
Hongo, Kohei 1939- *WhoWor 91*
Hongo, Yoshihiro 1936- *St&PR 91*
Honick, Joseph J. *ODwPR 91*
Honick, Murray Glenn 1953- *BiDrAPA 89*
Honig, Arnold 1928- *WhoAm 90*
Honig, Barry Hirsh 1941- *WhoAm 90*
Honig, Bill 1937- *WhoAm 90*
Honig, Burton A. 1937- *St&PR 91*
Honig, Daniel Martin 1948- *WhoEmL 91*
Honig, Donald 1931- *Ballpl 90*
Honig, Edwin 1919- *WhoAm 90*
Honig, Edwin B. 1919- *WhoWrEP 89*
Honig, Emanuel M 1915- *BiDrAPA 89*
Honig, George Raymond 1936- *WhoAm 90*
Honig, John 1924- *St&PR 91*
Honig, Lawrence Edward 1948- *St&PR 91, WhoAm 90*
Honig, Mark I *BiDrAPA 89*
Honig, Mervin 1920- *WhoAm 90, WhoAmA 91*
Honig, Orie Charles 1918- *WhoAm 90*
Honig, Paul 1905- *St&PR 91*
Honig, Richard G 1945- *BiDrAPA 89*
Honig, Steven 1931- *St&PR 91*
Honigberg, Bronislaw Mark 1920- *WhoAm 90*
Honigman, Daniel M. 1933- *St&PR 91*
Honiss, Robin 1937- *St&PR 91, WhoE 91*
Honjo, Masako 1948- *WhoAmA 91*
Honkanen, William *BioIn 16*
Honley, Russell Loran 1948- *WhoEmL 91*
Honma, Hiroki 1936- *WhoWor 91*
Honnecourt, Villard de *BioIn 16*
Honnef, Klaus Bernhard Wilhelm 1939- *WhoWor 91*
Honner, B. Joan 1952- *WhoAmW 91*
Honness, Elizabeth 1904- *AuBYP 90*
Honnold, John Otis, Jr. 1915- *WhoAm 90*
Honnold, Kathryn S. 1936- *WhoAmW 91*
Honnold, W. Dean 1940- *St&PR 91*
Honochick, Jim 1917- *Ballpl 90*
Honohan, Robert Leo, Jr. 1960- *WhoE 91*
Honolulu *EncCoWW*
Honore, Anthony *St&PR 91*
Honore, Carla A. 1959- *WhoAmW 91*
Honorton, Charles 1946- *EncO&P 3, EncPaPR 91*
Honroth, Dale Kenneth 1945- *St&PR 91*
Honroth, Kenneth Arthur 1914- *St&PR 91*
Hons, Craig E. 1951- *St&PR 91*
Honsinger, Vernon Bertram 1917- *WhoAm 90*
Honstead, Loren Lee 1947- *WhoEmL 91*
Honthorst, Gerrit van 1590-1656 *IntDcAA 90*
Hontzas, Thomas Milton 1944- *St&PR 91*
Honzel, Andrew J. 1931- *St&PR 91*
Honzik, Marjorie Knickerbocker Pyles 1908- *WhoAmW 91*
Honzl, John Joseph 1942- *St&PR 91*
Hooberman, Daniel 1954- *BiDrAPA 89*
Hoobler, Icie Gertrude Macy 1892-1984 *BioIn 16*
Hoobler, James Ferguson 1938- *WhoE 91*
Hoobler, Raymond Taylor 1941- *WhoE 91*
Hoobler, Sibley Worth 1911- *WhoAm 90*
Hooch, Pieter de 1629-1684? *IntDcAA 90*
Hood, A. Thomas 1946- *St&PR 91*
Hood, Alexander 1930- *IntWWM 90*
Hood, Basil 1864-1917 *OxCPMus*
Hood, Bruce 1936- *ConAu 130*
Hood, Charles David, Jr. 1954- *WhoEmL 91*
Hood, Charles Harvey 1929- *St&PR 91, WhoAm 90*
Hood, Charles Hurlburt 1938- *WhoAm 90*
Hood, Charles R. 1948- *St&PR 91*
Hood, Clifford C. R. 1927- *WhoE 91*
Hood, David Davies 1942- *St&PR 91*
Hood, David Murl 1950- *St&PR 91*
Hood, Don 1949- *Ballpl 90*
Hood, Dorothy *WhoAmA 91*
Hood, Dorothy 1919- *WhoWor 91*
Hood, Douglas Crary 1932- *WhoWor 91*
Hood, Edward Exum, Jr. 1930- *St&PR 91, WhoAm 90, WhoE 91*
Hood, Eric L. 1951- *ODwPR 91*
Hood, Ernest Alva 1910- *WhoE 91*
Hood, Ethel Painter 1908-1982 *WhoAmA 91N*
Hood, Gary Allen 1943- *WhoAmA 91*
Hood, George W 1869-1949 *WhoAmA 91N*
Hood, Graham Stanley 1936- *WhoAmA 91*
Hood, Gwenyth Elise 1955- *WhoWrEP 89*
Hood, Henry Lyman 1921- *WhoE 91*
Hood, Hugh 1928- *ConAu 33NR, WorAu 1980 [port]*
Hood, James Byron 1951- *WhoWrEP 89*
Hood, James W. *ODwPR 91*
Hood, John Bell 1831-1879 *WorAlBi*
Hood, John Edward 1925- *WhoAm 90*
Hood, Lamartine Frain 1937- *WhoAm 90*
Hood, Leroy Edward 1938- *WhoAm 90*
Hood, Mary Bryan 1938- *WhoAm 90, WhoAmA 91, WhoSSW 91*
Hood, Mather Daniel 1946- *WhoEmL 91*
Hood, Melinda Brewer 1952- *WhoSSW 91*
Hood, Ollie Ruth 1947- *WhoAmW 91*
Hood, Paul Bernard 1927- *St&PR 91*
Hood, Philip Boyce 1951- *WhoWrEP 89*
Hood, Raymond 1881-1934 *WorAlBi*
Hood, Richard *WhoAmA 91*
Hood, Robert E. 1926- *AuBYP 90*
Hood, Robert Eric 1926- *WhoWrEP 89*
Hood, Robert H., Jr. *WhoAm 90*
Hood, Robert R. 1949- *St&PR 91*
Hood, Robin *BioIn 16*
Hood, Sarah *ConAu 32NR*
Hood, Sarah 1942- *SmATA X [port]*
Hood, Stuart 1915- *WorAu 1980 [port]*
Hood, Thomas 1799-1845 *BioIn 16, DcLB 96 [port]*
Hood, Thomas R.C. *BioIn 16*
Hood, Timothy Michael 1968- *WhoEmL 91*
Hood, Virginia Ford 1905- *WhoAmW 91*
Hood, Walter Kelly 1928- *WhoAmA 91*
Hood, William Boyd, Jr. 1932- *WhoAm 90*
Hood, William Clarence 1921- *WhoAm 90*
Hood, William Joseph 1920- *SpyFic*
Hoodenpyle, Richard Lee 1946- *WhoWor 91*
Hoods, David R. 1936- *ODwPR 91*
Hoodwin, Lou W. 1915- *St&PR 91*
Hoof, David Lorne 1945- *WhoWrEP 89*
Hoof, James Bruce 1948- *WhoEmL 91*
Hoofman, Cliff 1943- *WhoSSW 91*
Hoofman, Robert Sidney 1954- *WhoEmL 91*
Hoofnagle, Jay Houston 1943- *WhoAm 90*
Hoog, Marjorie 1947- *WhoWor 91*
Hoog, Michel 1932- *WhoWor 91*
Hoog, Patrick Edward 1954- *WhoEmL 91*
Hoogenakker, Virginia Ruth 1921- *IntWWM 90*
Hoogenboom, Ari Arthur 1927- *WhoAm 90*
Hoogeveen, Linda Lorraine 1958- *WhoEmL 91*
Hoogewind, William H. 1948- *St&PR 91*
Hoogland, Robert Frederics 1955- *WhoEmL 91*
Hoogmoed, Neil 1934- *St&PR 91*
Hoogmoed, Walter Leonard 1938- *St&PR 91*
Hoogsteden, Aloysius Franciscus 1936- *WhoWor 91*
Hoogstra, Eric John 1962- *WhoEmL 91*
Hoogstraten, Louise *BioIn 16*
Hook, Andrew Dunnet 1932- *WhoWor 91*
Hook, Clyde Edward 1948- *WhoEmL 91*
Hook, Cornelius Henry 1929- *WhoSSW 91*
Hook, Daryl Gayle 1928- *St&PR 91*
Hook, David John 1960- *WhoEmL 91*
Hook, Edward Watson, Jr. 1924- *WhoAm 90*
Hook, Frances A 1912-1981 *WhoAmA 91N*
Hook, George Matthew Verity 1917- *WhoWor 91*
Hook, Harold S. 1931- *St&PR 91*
Hook, Harold Swanson 1931- *WhoAm 90, WhoSSW 91, WhoWor 91*
Hook, Henry *BioIn 16*
Hook, Henry B. 1909- *St&PR 91*
Hook, Hilary *BioIn 16*
Hook, Hilary 1917-1990 *ConAu 132*
Hook, Jay 1936- *Ballpl 90*
Hook, Jeffrey Robbins 1954- *St&PR 91*
Hook, Jerry Bruce 1937- *WhoAm 90*
Hook, John Burney 1928- *WhoAm 90*
Hook, Julia Jane 1955- *WhoAmW 91, WhoEmL 91*
Hook, Lewis William 1924- *St&PR 91*
Hook, Martha Ann 1936- *WhoWrEP 89*
Hook, Philipps Joseph 1935- *WhoSSW 91*
Hook, Ralph Clifford, Jr. 1923- *WhoAm 90*
Hook, Robert 1935- *BiDrAPA 89*
Hook, Rodney N. 1946- *St&PR 91*
Hook, Sanders H.B. 1939- *St&PR 91*
Hook, Sidney 1902-1989 *AnObit 1989, BioIn 16, ConAu 129, EncAL*
Hook, Vicki Sue *BiDrAPA 89*
Hook, Virginia May 1932- *WhoAmW 91*
Hook, William George 1913- *IntWWM 90*
Hook-Haygood, Marsha *WhoAmW 91*
Hooke, Anne Morris 1939- *WhoAmW 91*
Hooke, Christopher 1949- *St&PR 91*
Hooke, Robert 1635-1703 *WorAlBi*
Hooke, Roger LeBaron 1939- *WhoAm 90*
Hooker Jim 1825?-1879 *WhNaAH*
Hooker, Alice Louise Ingram *WhoAmW 91, WhoSSW 91*
Hooker, Brian *BioIn 16*
Hooker, Charles Hollingswort, Jr. 1946- *WhoSSW 91*
Hooker, David Andrew 1954- *WhoE 91*
Hooker, Harry Edward 1950- *WhoEmL 91*
Hooker, Isabella Beecher 1822-1907 *BioIn 16*
Hooker, Ivan R. 1947- *St&PR 91*
Hooker, J. Clyde, Jr. 1920- *St&PR 91*
Hooker, James A. 1936- *St&PR 91*
Hooker, James Todd 1946- *WhoEmL 91*
Hooker, John Lee *BioIn 16*
Hooker, John Lee 1917- *DrBIPA 90, EncPR&S 89, OxCPMus, WhoAm 90*
Hooker, John Patrick 1926- *WhoSSW 91*
Hooker, Joseph 1814-1879 *WorAlBi*
Hooker, Karen Ann 1955- *WhoAmW 91*
Hooker, Michael Kenneth 1945- *WhoAm 90, WhoE 91*
Hooker, Roger Wolcott, Jr. 1941- *WhoAm 90*
Hooker, Ruth *AuBYP 90*
Hooker, Stanley George 1907-1984 *DcNaB 1981*
Hooker, Steven L. 1954- *St&PR 91*
Hooker, Thomas 1586-1647 *EncCRAm, WorAlBi*
Hooker, Van Dorn 1921- *WhoAm 90*
Hooker-Haring, Christopher Alan 1950- *WhoE 91*
Hookham, Eleanor King *WhoAmA 91*
Hooks, Benjamin L. 1924- *BioIn 16*
Hooks, Benjamin L. 1925- *WorAlBi*
Hooks, Benjamin Lawson 1925- *WhoAm 90*
Hooks, Charles Vernon 1930- *WhoAmA 91*
Hooks, Clifton F. 1935- *St&PR 91*
Hooks, Earl J 1927- *WhoAmA 91*
Hooks, Frances *BioIn 16*
Hooks, Geri 1935- *WhoAmA 91*
Hooks, Gregory Eugene 1949- *St&PR 91*
Hooks, Julia Ann 1852-1942 *BioAmW*
Hooks, Kevin 1958- *DrBIPA 90*
Hooks, Lornetta Boyer 1953- *IntWWM 90*
Hooks, Marla *BiDrAPA 89*
Hooks, Penelope Jo *BiDrAPA 89*
Hooks, Robert 1937- *DrBIPA 90*
Hooks, Vandalyn Lawrence 1935- *WhoAmW 91*
Hooks, Vendie Hudson, III 1948- *WhoSSW 91*
Hooks, William Gary 1927- *WhoAm 90*
Hooks, William H. *BioIn 16*
Hooks, William Harris 1921- *AuBYP 90*
Hookstratten, Edward Gregory 1932- *WhoAm 90, WhoWor 91*
Hookway, Warren Arthur 1936- *St&PR 91*
Hoolaart, G.H. 1716?-1772 *PenDiDA 89*
Hoole, James Edward 1947- *St&PR 91*
Hoole, William Stanley 1903- *WhoAm 90*
Hooley, James Robert 1932- *WhoAm 90*
Hooley, Robert C. 1927- *St&PR 91*
Hooley, Robert Childs 1927- *WhoAm 90*
Hoop, William C. *ODwPR 91*
Hooper, Adrian John 1953- *IntWWM 90*
Hooper, Anne Dodge 1926- *WhoAmW 91*
Hooper, Arthur G. 1942- *St&PR 91*
Hooper, Arthur William 1919- *WhoAm 90*
Hooper, Barbara Bush 1909- *St&PR 91*
Hooper, Billy Ernest 1931- *WhoAm 90*
Hooper, Blake Howard 1922- *WhoAm 90*
Hooper, Bruce Charles 1948- *WhoEmL 91*
Hooper, Carl Glenn 1936- *WhoSSW 91*
Hooper, David Charles 1963- *WhoEmL 91*
Hooper, Frederick Richard 1908- *WhoAm 90*
Hooper, Harry 1887-1974 *Ballpl 90 [port]*
Hooper, Henry Olcott 1935- *WhoAm 90*
Hooper, Ian 1941- *WhoAm 90*
Hooper, Ian Derek 1941- *St&PR 91*
Hooper, Jack Meredith 1928- *WhoAmA 91*
Hooper, James F, IV 1947- *BiDrAPA 89*
Hooper, James Fullerton, IV 1947- *WhoSSW 91*
Hooper, James William 1937- *WhoSSW 91*
Hooper, Jane Ann 1964- *WhoAmW 91*
Hooper, Jere Mann 1933- *St&PR 91*
Hooper, John Allen 1922- *WhoAm 90*

Hooper, Jon J. 1942- *ODwPR 91*
Hooper, Jon O. 1937- *St&PR 91*
Hooper, Lois 1947- *WhoAmW 91*
Hooper, Lucien Obed 1896-1988 *BioIn 16*
Hooper, Lucy 1816-1841 *FemiCLE*
Hooper, Lucy Hamilton 1835-1893 *FemiCLE*
Hooper, Michael Stone *BioIn 16*
Hooper, Patricia 1941- *WhoWrEP 89*
Hooper, Peter, III 1947- *WhoE 91*
Hooper, Robert Earle 1954- *WhoSSW 91*
Hooper, Sidney Francis 1941- *St&PR 91*
Hooper, Susan Jeanne 1950- *WhoEmL 91*
Hooper, T. d'Aute *EncO&P 3*
Hooper, William 1742-1790 *EncCRAm*
Hooper, William Douglas 1949- *WhoEmL 91*
Hooper, William John, Jr. 1935- *WhoSSW 91*
Hoopere, Bob 1922-1980 *Ballpl 90*
Hoopers, John Michael 1947- *St&PR 91*
Hoopes, Darlington 1896-1989 *BioIn 16*
Hoopes, Donelson 1932- *WhoE 91*
Hoopes, Janet Louise 1923- *WhoAm 90*
Hoopes, Joseph Coudon, Jr. 1943- *St&PR 91*
Hoopes, Lorenzo Neville 1913- *WhoAm 90*
Hoopes, Lyn Littlefield 1953- *BioIn 16*
Hoopes, Roy 1922- *AuBYP 90*
Hoopes, Spencer Wendell 1947- *St&PR 91, WhoEmL 91*
Hoopes, Townsend Walter 1922- *WhoAm 90*
Hoopes, Walter Ronald 1933- *WhoE 91*
Hoopingarner, John Martin 1954- *WhoEmL 91*
Hoople, Cheryl G. *AuBYP 90*
Hoople, Sally Crosby 1930- *WhoWrEP 89*
Hoops, Diane Kinuko 1961- *WhoAmW 91*
Hoops, Jeffrey Robert 1953- *WhoE 91*
Hoornstra, E.H. 1921- *St&PR 91*
Hoornstra, Edward H. 1921- *WhoAm 90*
Hoort, Steven Thomas 1949- *WhoEmL 91*
Hoorweg, Frits Peter Adriaan 1947- *WhoWor 91*
Hoose, Alfred 1918- *IntWWM 90*
Hoose, Quincey Shelley 1955- *WhoWrEP 89*
Hoosin, Janice Lautt 1942- *WhoAmW 91*
Hoot, Patricia Lynch 1921- *WhoWrEP 89*
Hoot, William John 1916- *St&PR 91*
Hooten, Mickey L. *BioIn 16*
Hootman, Harry Edward 1933- *WhoSSW 91, WhoWor 91*
Hootnick, Kenneth 1939- *St&PR 91*
Hooton, Archie B 1926- *BiDrAPA 89*
Hooton, Bruce Duff 1928- *WhoAmA 91, WhoE 91, WhoWor 91*
Hooton, Burt 1950- *Ballpl 90*
Hooton, Donald M. 1950- *St&PR 91*
Hooton, Donald Milton 1950- *WhoE 91*
Hooton, Elizabeth 1600?-1670 *FemiCLE*
Hooton, Elizabeth 1600?-1671? *BiDEWW*
Hooton, Michael Edward 1950- *WhoEmL 91*
Hoots, Helen Hardin *WhoWrEP 89*
Hooven, Wendy Lee 1963- *WhoEmL 91*
Hoover, Benjamin Andrew, II 1937- *WhoE 91*
Hoover, Betty-Bruce Howard 1939- *WhoAmW 91*
Hoover, Bob *BioIn 16*
Hoover, Carol Faith 1921- *WhoWrEP 89*
Hoover, Carolyn Bishop *BiDrAPA 89*
Hoover, Clarence Edward 1942- *St&PR 91*
Hoover, Claude W. 1953- *St&PR 91*
Hoover, Cove *BioIn 16, NewYTBS 90*
Hoover, Cynthia Jane 1953- *WhoAmW 91*
Hoover, David Carlson 1950- *WhoE 91, WhoEmL 91, WhoWor 91*
Hoover, Dean Robert 1935- *St&PR 91*
Hoover, Donald Leroy 1952- *WhoEmL 91*
Hoover, Dorothy R. 1907- *St&PR 91*
Hoover, Dwight Wesley 1926- *WhoAm 90*
Hoover, Eric John 1944- *IntWWM 90*
Hoover, Francis Louis 1913- *WhoAm 90, WhoAmA 91*
Hoover, George Nicholas, III 1927- *St&PR 91*
Hoover, George Schweke 1935- *WhoAm 90*
Hoover, H. M. 1935- *BioIn 16, WhoWrEP 89*
Hoover, Harold Lee 1953- *WhoE 91*
Hoover, Harry W., Jr. *ODwPR 91*
Hoover, Herbert 1874-1964 *BioIn 16*
Hoover, Herbert, III 1927- *St&PR 91*
Hoover, Herbert Arnold 1930- *St&PR 91*
Hoover, Herbert C. 1874-1964 *WorAlBi*
Hoover, Herbert Clark 1874-1964 *BiDrUSE 89*
Hoover, Herbert William, Jr. 1918- *WhoAm 90*
Hoover, Howard S., Jr. 1938- *St&PR 91*
Hoover, J. Edgar 1895-1972 *BioIn 16, WorAlBi*
Hoover, James Bentley 1955- *St&PR 91*
Hoover, James Lloyd 1945- *WhoAm 90*
Hoover, James Otis 1939- *BiDrAPA 89*
Hoover, Jesse Wilbert 1908- *WhoWrEP 89*
Hoover, Jimmie Hartman 1930- *WhoSSW 91*
Hoover, Joe 1915-1965 *Ballpl 90*
Hoover, John Edgar 1895-1972 *BioIn 16*
Hoover, John Elwood 1924- *WhoAm 90*
Hoover, John Jay 1919- *WhoAmA 91*
Hoover, Judith Ann 1941- *WhoAmW 91*
Hoover, Julie T. *St&PR 91*
Hoover, Julie Tarachow *WhoAmW 91*
Hoover, Katherine 1937- *BioIn 16, IntWWM 90*
Hoover, Ken 1938- *St&PR 91*
Hoover, Kenneth R 1940- *ConAu 132*
Hoover, Kim Gloria *BiDrAPA 89*
Hoover, Lawrence Richard 1935- *St&PR 91*
Hoover, Lewis Dean 1948- *BiDrAPA 89*
Hoover, Lola Mae 1947- *WhoAmW 91, WhoEmL 91*
Hoover, Lou Henry *BioIn 16*
Hoover, Lyle Leslie 1929- *St&PR 91*
Hoover, Mae Morgan 1940- *WhoWrEP 89*
Hoover, Marie Louise 1895-1976 *WhoAmA 91N*
Hoover, Mary Nell 1946- *WhoEmL 91*
Hoover, Mary Sue Millen 1929- *WhoAmW 91*
Hoover, Molly Ann 1948- *WhoAmW 91*
Hoover, Paul Russell 1941- *St&PR 91*
Hoover, Pearl Rollings 1924- *WhoWor 91*
Hoover, R.E. 1929- *St&PR 91*
Hoover, Rayallen 1932- *St&PR 91*
Hoover, Rena Virginia 1925- *WhoAmW 91*
Hoover, Rodger S. 1927- *St&PR 91*
Hoover, Roland Armitage 1929- *WhoAm 90*
Hoover, Susan Frantz 1939- *WhoWrEP 89*
Hoover, Walter B. 1898-1989 *BioIn 16*
Hoover, William Howard 1951- *WhoSSW 91*
Hoover, William Ray 1930- *St&PR 91, WhoAm 90*
Hoovler, Matthew Reed 1952- *WhoEmL 91*
Hoovler, Paul Vincent 1927- *St&PR 91*
Hopcke, Klaus 1933- *WhoWor 91*
Hopcroft, John Edward 1939- *WhoAm 90*
Hope, A.D. 1907- *ConAu 33NR, MajTwCW*
Hope, Akua Lezli 1957- *WhoWrEP 89*
Hope, Amanda *AuBYP 90*
Hope, Ammie Deloris 1946- *WhoAmW 91*
Hope, Arlene 1913-1989 *BioIn 16*
Hope, Barbara *BioIn 16*
Hope, Bob *ODwPR 91*
Hope, Bob 1903- *BestSel 90-4 [port], BioIn 16, OxCPMus, WhoAm 90, WhoWor 91, WorAlBi*
Hope, Brian *MajTwCW*
Hope, Charles *EncPaPR 91*
Hope, Christopher 1944- *SmATA 62 [port], WorAu 1980*
Hope, Clarence Caldwell, Jr. 1920- *WhoAm 90*
Hope, David Terence 1946- *WhoWor 91*
Hope, Garland Howard 1911- *WhoAm 90*
Hope, Gerri Danette 1956- *WhoAmW 91, WhoEmL 91*
Hope, Henry 1905-1989 *BioIn 16*
Hope, John Charles, Jr. 1948- *WhoEmL 91*
Hope, Judith Richards 1940- *WhoAm 90*
Hope, Kenneth Weaver 1947- *WhoEmL 91*
Hope, Laurence 1865-1904 *FemiCLE*
Hope, Lawrence Latimer 1939- *WhoAm 90*
Hope, Margaret *ConAu 33NR*
Hope, Margaret Lauten *WhoAmW 91, WhoSSW 91*
Hope, Mark Alan 1960- *WhoSSW 91*
Hope, Maury M. 1949- *St&PR 91*
Hope, Michael S. 1942- *St&PR 91*
Hope, Nicholas Martin 1944- *WhoWor 91*
Hope, Phelps Richard 1959- *WhoSSW 91*
Hope, Quentin Manning 1923- *WhoAm 90*
Hope, Robert John 1946- *St&PR 91*
Hope, Samuel Howard 1946- *IntWWM 90, WhoAm 90*
Hope, T. E. 1923-1987 *BioIn 16*
Hope, Theodore Sherwood, Jr. 1903- *WhoWor 91*
Hope, Thomas 1769-1831 *PenDiDA 89*
Hope, Thomas Edwin 1923-1987 *BioIn 16*
Hope, Thomas Walker 1920- *WhoAm 90*
Hope, William 1863-1933 *EncO&P 3, EncPaPR 91*
Hope, William Duane 1935- *WhoAm 90*
Hopekirk, Helen 1856-1945 *BioIn 16*
Hopelain, Rick 1954- *ODwPR 91*
Hopen, Herbert John 1934- *WhoAm 90*
Hopen, Stuart Neil 1953- *WhoEmL 91*
Hopenwasser, Karen 1953- *BiDrAPA 89*
Hopes, David Brendan 1953- *WhoWrEP 89*
Hopf, Alice 1904- *AuBYP 90*
Hopf, Alice Lightner 1904-1988 *BioIn 16*
Hopf, Frank Rudolph 1920- *WhoE 91, WhoWor 91*
Hopf, Hans 1916- *IntWWM 90, PenDiMP*
Hopfenbeck, George Martin, Jr. 1929- *WhoAm 90*
Hopfer, Samuel *WhoAm 90*
Hopferweiser, Josef 1938- *IntWWM 90*
Hopfield, John Joseph 1933- *WhoAm 90*
Hopgood, Debra Jo 1958- *WhoEmL 91, WhoWor 91*
Hopgood, James F. 1943- *WhoSSW 91, WhoWor 91*
Hopgood, Winthrop C 1920- *BiDrAPA 89*
Hopkin, Alfred W. *St&PR 91*
Hopkin, John Arden 1947- *IntWWM 90*
Hopkin, John Taggart *BiDrAPA 89*
Hopkins, A. T. *AuBYP 90*
Hopkins, Albert Lafayette, Jr. 1931- *WhoAm 90*
Hopkins, Alfred A. *WhoE 91*
Hopkins, Ann B. *BioIn 16*
Hopkins, Anne *FemiCLE*
Hopkins, Anne Dankmeyer 1929- *WhoE 91*
Hopkins, Anthony 1937- *ConTFT 8 [port], WorAlBi*
Hopkins, Anthony Philip 1937- *WhoAm 90, WhoWor 91*
Hopkins, Antony 1921- *IntWWM 90, PenDiMP A*
Hopkins, Arlene Marie 1945- *WhoEmL 91*
Hopkins, Benjamin 1936- *WhoAmA 91*
Hopkins, Beverly M. 1952- *WhoSSW 91*
Hopkins, Billy *BioIn 16*
Hopkins, Bridget Ann 1960- *WhoAmW 91*
Hopkins, Bruce Bond 1949- *WhoSSW 91*
Hopkins, Bruce Wallace 1945- *WhoEmL 91*
Hopkins, Budd 1931- *WhoAm 90, WhoAmA 91*
Hopkins, Calvin Sylvester, III 1949- *WhoSSW 91*
Hopkins, Carl Edward 1912- *WhoAm 90*
Hopkins, Cecilia Ann 1922- *WhoAmW 91*
Hopkins, Charlene Martha 1934- *WhoAmW 91*
Hopkins, Charles L., Jr. 1927- *St&PR 91*
Hopkins, Charles Peter, II 1953- *WhoE 91, WhoEmL 91, WhoWor 91*
Hopkins, Chester Arthur 1928- *St&PR 91*
Hopkins, Christopher James 1957- *WhoEmL 91*
Hopkins, Clark 1895-1976 *AuBYP 90, ConAu 129*
Hopkins, Claude *BioIn 16*
Hopkins, Claude 1903-1984 *DrBIPA 90, OxCPMus*
Hopkins, Clyde C. 1929- *WhoSSW 91*
Hopkins, Clyde L. 1937- *ODwPR 91*
Hopkins, Dan Walton 1937- *WhoAm 90*
Hopkins, David L., Jr. 1928- *WhoAm 90*
Hopkins, David Moody 1921- *BioIn 16*
Hopkins, Donald Roswell 1941- *WhoAm 90*
Hopkins, Douglas Edward 1902- *IntWWM 90*
Hopkins, Drusilla K. 1956- *St&PR 91*
Hopkins, Duane A. 1959- *WhoEmL 91*
Hopkins, Edith Cary 1959- *WhoEmL 91, WhoSSW 91*
Hopkins, Edward Donald 1937- *St&PR 91, WhoAm 90*
Hopkins, Edwina Weiskittel 1947- *WhoAmW 91, WhoWor 91*
Hopkins, Ernest Loyd 1930- *WhoAm 90*
Hopkins, Esek 1718-1802 *WorAlBi*
Hopkins, Esther Arvilla Harrison 1926- *WhoE 91*
Hopkins, Everett Harold 1912- *WhoAm 90*
Hopkins, Frederick G. 1861-1947 *WorAlBi*
Hopkins, Gail 1943- *Ballpl 90*
Hopkins, Gary B. 1949- *St&PR 91*
Hopkins, Gary L. 1955- *St&PR 91*
Hopkins, Gary Wayne 1942- *WhoWor 91*
Hopkins, George 1958- *WhoSSW 91*
Hopkins, George Mathews Marks 1923- *WhoAm 90, WhoSSW 91, WhoWor 91*
Hopkins, George Pearce, Jr. 1926- *WhoSSW 91*
Hopkins, George Washington 1804-1861 *AmLegL*
Hopkins, Gerard Manley 1844-1889 *BioIn 16, WorAlBi, WrPh*
Hopkins, Gerri Lynne 1945- *WhoEmL 91*
Hopkins, Grover Prevatte 1933- *WhoWor 91*
Hopkins, Harlow Eugene 1931- *IntWWM 90*
Hopkins, Harold Anthony, Jr. *WhoAm 90*
Hopkins, Harrison *WhoWrEP 89*
Hopkins, Harry L. 1890-1946 *WorAlBi*
Hopkins, Harry Lloyd 1890-1946 *BiDrUSE 89, BioIn 16*
Hopkins, Henry Tyler 1928- *WhoAm 90, WhoAmA 91*
Hopkins, J. Wallace *BioIn 16*
Hopkins, Jack Walker 1930- *WhoAm 90*
Hopkins, James 1928- *BioIn 16*
Hopkins, James D. 1961- *WhoWrEP 89*
Hopkins, James R. 1936- *St&PR 91*
Hopkins, James William 1946- *WhoWrEP 89*
Hopkins, Janice A. 1953- *WhoEmL 91*
Hopkins, Jasper 1936- *ConAu 31NR*
Hopkins, Jeanne Sulick 1952- *WhoAmW 91, WhoE 91*
Hopkins, Jeannette E. 1922- *WhoAm 90*
Hopkins, Jeffery Boyd 1955- *WhoEmL 91*
Hopkins, Jerome Kirklin 1934- *St&PR 91*
Hopkins, Jerry Berl 1945- *WhoSSW 91*
Hopkins, Jerry Wayne 1947- *St&PR 91*
Hopkins, Jim D. 1935- *St&PR 91*
Hopkins, Joan Munn 1954- *WhoEmL 91*
Hopkins, Joe Warren 1928- *St&PR 91*
Hopkins, Johanna M. *BioIn 16*
Hopkins, John 1927- *PenDiMP*
Hopkins, John David 1938- *WhoAm 90*
Hopkins, John J. 1933- *St&PR 91*
Hopkins, John Jay 1893-1957 *WorAlBi*
Hopkins, John Lee 1947- *WhoEmL 91*
Hopkins, John Raymond 1927- *IntWWM 90*
Hopkins, John Robert 1930- *St&PR 91*
Hopkins, John T. 1956- *St&PR 91*
Hopkins, John Thomas *BiDrAPA 89*
Hopkins, Judith Owen 1952- *WhoAmW 91*
Hopkins, Keith 1934- *ConAu 130*
Hopkins, Kendal Coles 1908- *WhoAmA 91*
Hopkins, Kenneth 1914-1988 *BioIn 16*
Hopkins, Kenneth R 1922- *WhoAmA 91*
Hopkins, L. Wallace 1925- *St&PR 91*
Hopkins, Larry J. 1933- *WhoAm 90, WhoSSW 91*
Hopkins, Larry Mark 1940- *WhoSSW 91*
Hopkins, Lee Bennett 1938- *AuBYP 90, BioIn 16, WhoE 91*
Hopkins, Lila *AuBYP 90*
Hopkins, Linda *BioIn 16*
Hopkins, Linda 1925- *DrBIPA 90*
Hopkins, Linda Ann 1937- *WhoAmW 91*
Hopkins, Lloyd Travers, Jr. 1943- *St&PR 91*
Hopkins, Lyman *AuBYP 90*
Hopkins, Malcolm John 1948- *St&PR 91*
Hopkins, Marjorie 1911- *AuBYP 90*
Hopkins, Mark 1802-1887 *WorAlBi*
Hopkins, Mark 1813-1878 *WorAlBi*
Hopkins, Mary Evelyn 1919- *WhoAmW 91*
Hopkins, Matthew *EncO&P 3*
Hopkins, Miriam 1902-1972 *WorAlBi*
Hopkins, Muriel-Beth Norbrey 1951- *WhoEmL 91*
Hopkins, Paul Jeffrey 1940- *WhoSSW 91*
Hopkins, Pauline 1859-1930 *FemiCLE*
Hopkins, Pauline Elizabeth 1859-1930 *EarBlAP, HarlReB*
Hopkins, Peter 1911- *WhoAmA 91*
Hopkins, Philip Joseph 1954- *WhoEmL 91*
Hopkins, Rachel Pomeroy 1944- *WhoE 91*
Hopkins, Raymond Frederick 1939- *WhoAm 90*
Hopkins, Rebecca Anne 1961- *WhoEmL 91*
Hopkins, Robert Elliott 1931- *IntWWM 90, WhoWor 91*
Hopkins, Robert Howard 1939- *WhoE 91*
Hopkins, Robert Parker 1939- *BiDrAPA 89*
Hopkins, Robert Sydney *SpyFic*
Hopkins, Sam 1912-1982 *OxCPMus, WorAlBi*
Hopkins, Samuel 1721-1803 *EncCRAm*
Hopkins, Samuel 1913- *WhoAm 90*
Hopkins, Sarah 1958- *IntWWM 90*
Hopkins, Sarah Winnemucca 1844?-1891 *BioIn 16, FemiCLE*
Hopkins, Shelley *BioIn 16*
Hopkins, Stephen 1707-1785 *WorAlBi*
Hopkins, Stephen H. 1955- *WhoEmL 91*
Hopkins, Suzanne 1964- *WhoAmW 91*
Hopkins, Telma *DrBIPA 90*
Hopkins, Telma 1948- *WorAlBi*
Hopkins, Thayer, Jr. 1951- *WhoEmL 91*
Hopkins, Thomas Arscott 1931- *WhoAm 90*
Hopkins, Thomas Duvall 1942- *WhoE 91*
Hopkins, Thomas Matthews 1927- *WhoAm 90*
Hopkins, W. Dean 1909- *St&PR 91*
Hopkins, Wanda Sue 1935- *St&PR 91*
Hopkins, Wayne W. *ODwPR 91*
Hopkins, Wayne W. 1947- *St&PR 91*
Hopkins, William Leatherbury 1938- *St&PR 91*
Hopkins, Woodrow Justin 1957- *WhoEmL 91*
Hopkinson, B. Todd 1946- *St&PR 91*
Hopkinson, Charles 1869-1962 *WhoAmA 91N*
Hopkinson, Charles C., Jr. 1931- *St&PR 91*
Hopkinson, Francis 1737-1791 *EncCRAm, WorAlBi*
Hopkinson, Harold I 1918- *WhoAmA 91*

Hopkinson, Henry Thomas 1905-1990 ConAu 132
Hopkinson, Joan E. 1934- WhoAmW 91
Hopkinson, Shirley Lois 1924- WhoAmW 91
Hopkinson, Tom ConAu 132
Hopkinson, Tom M. ODwPR 91
Hopley, David Philip 1932- St&PR 91
Hopley, George TwCCr&M 91
Hopley, George 1903-1968 BioIn 16
Hopley-Woolrich, Cornell George 1903-1968 BioIn 16
Hoplin, Herman Peter 1920- WhoE 91
Hopmann, Philip Terrence 1942- WhoE 91
Hopmeier, Arthur P. 1928- St&PR 91
Hopocan 1725?-1794 WhNaAH
Hopokan 1725?-1794 WhNaAH
Hopp, Anthony J. 1945- St&PR 91
Hopp, Daniel Frederick 1947- St&PR 91, WhoAm 90
Hopp, James Lee 1949- WhoWrEP 89
Hopp, Johnny 1916- Ballpl 90
Hopp, Kevin R. 1960- WhoEmL 91
Hopp, Manfred Ernst 1936- St&PR 91, WhoAm 90
Hopp, Richard Louis 1943- WhoE 91
Hopp, Roy Allen 1951- IntWWM 90
Hopp, William A. 1942- St&PR 91
Hoppa, Mary Ann 1959- WhoAmW 91
Hoppe, Arthur Watterson 1925- WhoAm 90
Hoppe, Charles William 1935- St&PR 91
Hoppe, Craig Allen 1950- WhoEmL 91
Hoppe, Edward Henry, III 1927- St&PR 91
Hoppe, Hal F. 1938- St&PR 91
Hoppe, Heinz 1924- IntWWM 90
Hoppe, Klaus D 1922- BiDrAPA 89
Hoppe, Manley Robert 1910- St&PR 91
Hoppe, Murl Vern 1941- St&PR 91
Hoppe, Paul Werner 1910-1974 BioIn 16
Hoppe, Peter Christian 1942- WhoAm 90
Hoppe, Robert Roderick 1951- WhoEmL 91
Hoppe, William L. 1947- ODwPR 91
Hoppe, Willie 1887-1959 WorAlBi
Hoppe, Wolfgang 1933- WhoAm 90
Hoppe-Seyler, Ernst Felix 1825-1895 WorAlBi
Hoppen, Stephanie BioIn 16
Hoppenhaupt, Johann Christian 1719-1786 PenDiDA 89
Hoppenhaupt, Johann Michael 1685-1751 PenDiDA 89
Hoppenhaupt, Johann Michael 1709-1769 PenDiDA 89
Hoppensteadt, Frank Charles 1938- WhoAm 90
Hoppenstein, Abraham Solomon 1931- WhoWor 91
Hopper Inc WhoAmA 91
Hopper, Anita Klein 1945- WhoAmW 91
Hopper, Bill BioIn 16
Hopper, Carl Jefferson 1944- St&PR 91
Hopper, Dave M. 1932- St&PR 91
Hopper, David A. 1941- St&PR 91
Hopper, David Henry 1927- WhoAm 90
Hopper, De Wolf 1858-1935 OxCPMus
Hopper, Dennis BioIn 16
Hopper, Dennis 1936- WhoAm 90, WorAlBi
Hopper, Edward 1882-1967 BioIn 16, IntDcAA 90, WhoAmA 91N, WorAlBi
Hopper, Elizabeth BiDEWW
Hopper, Frank J 1924- WhoAmA 91
Hopper, Gary C. 1945- IntWWM 90
Hopper, George Drew 1950- WhoE 91
Hopper, Grace BioIn 16
Hopper, Grace M. 1906- WhoAm 90, WhoAmW 91
Hopper, Hedda 1885-1966 BioAmW
Hopper, Hedda 1890-1966 WorAlBi
Hopper, James Edwin 1945- WhoEmL 91
Hopper, Jeannette M. 1959- WhoWrEP 89
Hopper, Jerry 1907-1988 BioIn 16
Hopper, John Elisha Peck 1841-1895 DcCanB 12
Hopper, Jon WhoAmA 91N
Hopper, Lloyd Wade 1956- WhoEmL 91
Hopper, Lyn Watson 1953- WhoSSW 91
Hopper, Margaret Sue 1937- WhoSSW 91
Hopper, Marianne Seward 1904- WhoAmA 91N
Hopper, Mary A. 1942- St&PR 91
Hopper, Max Dean 1934- St&PR 91
Hopper, Michel C. 1941- St&PR 91
Hopper, Nora 1871-1906 FemiCLE
Hopper, Sally WhoAmW 91
Hopper, Sheila Marie 1962- WhoAmW 91
Hopper, Sherry Leigh 1954- WhoAmW 91
Hopper, Stephen B 1956- BiDrAPA 89
Hopper, Victor D. 1918- St&PR 91
Hopper, Virginia Shearer 1940- WhoWrEP 89
Hopper, W. David 1927- WhoAm 90
Hopper, Walter Everett 1915- WhoAm 90, WhoWor 91
Hopper, Wilbert Hill 1933- WhoAm 90
Hoppert, Earl William 1939- WhoWor 91
Hopperton, Richard H. ODwPR 91
Hoppes, Lowell E 1913- WhoAmA 91
Hoppesteyn, Jacob Wemmertsz PenDiDA 89
Hoppesteyn, Rochus Jacobsz PenDiDA 89
Hoppin, Thomas E. 1941- ODwPR 91, St&PR 91
Hoppin, Thomas Edward 1941- WhoAm 90
Hopping, Michael Wayne BiDrAPA 89
Hopping, Richard Lee 1928- WhoAm 90
Hopple, Lynwood M BiDrAPA 89
Hoppmann, Barbara Elsie 1953- WhoAmW 91, WhoEmL 91
Hoppmann, Erich 1923- WhoWor 91
Hoppner, John 1758-1810 IntDcAA 90
Hopps, Howard Carl 1914- WhoAm 90
Hopps, Sidney Bryce 1934- WhoAm 90
Hoppus, Mary 1843-1916 FemiCLE
Hopson, George H 1925- BiDrAPA 89
Hopson, Howel H. 1924- St&PR 91
Hopson, James Ferrell 1946- WhoE 91
Hopson, James Warren 1946- St&PR 91
Hopson, Raymond Duane BiDrAPA 89
Hopson, Winthrop Howell, III 1951- WhoEmL 91
Hopta, Anna Marie 1961- WhoAmW 91
Hoptner, Richard 1921- WhoAmA 91
Hopton, Lester C. 1902-1989 BioIn 16
Hopton, Susanna 1627-1709 BiDEWW, BioIn 16, FemiCLE
Hopwood, Avery 1884-1928 BioIn 16
Hopwood, D. Caroline FemiCLE
Hopwood, Gillian 1927- WomArch [port]
Hopwood, Stafford Leopold, Jr. 1926- WhoE 91
Hoque, Asraul 1949- WhoWor 91
Hora, Heinrich 1931- WhoWor 91
Hora, Michael E. 1943- St&PR 91
Hora, Thomas BiDrAPA 89
Horace 65BC-8BC WorAlBi
Horace, Charles C. 1924- St&PR 91
Horacek, Frank J. 1945- St&PR 91
Horacek, Jaroslav 1924- IntWWM 90
Horack, Thomas Borland 1946- WhoAm 90
Horadam, Weyman Wilson 1916- WhoAm 90
Horahan, Edward Bernard, III 1951- WhoEmL 91
Horaitis, Angelica Polito 1952- WhoAmW 91
Horak, Josef 1931- IntWWM 90, PenDiMP
Horak, William Charles 1950- WhoE 91
Horakova, Zdenka Zahutova 1925- WhoAmW 91
Horan, Clark J., III 1950- WhoEmL 91, WhoWor 91
Horan, Donald Burke 1934- St&PR 91
Horan, Edward J. 1921- St&PR 91
Horan, Eugene Francis 1931- WhoE 91
Horan, Francis James 1927- St&PR 91
Horan, Harold Eugene 1927- WhoAm 90
Horan, Hume Alexander 1934- WhoAm 90
Horan, James Daniel 1925- St&PR 91
Horan, James Joseph 1936- St&PR 91
Horan, John J. 1920- WhoAm 90
Horan, John Joseph 1928- WhoE 91
Horan, Justin Thomas 1927- WhoAm 90
Horan, Leo Gallaspy 1925- WhoAm 90
Horan, Raymond Edward, Jr. 1917- St&PR 91
Horan, Roy Allison 1953- WhoSSW 91
Horan, Thomas 1938- St&PR 91
Horan, William Joseph 1947- WhoE 91
Horatio MajTwCW
Horbach, Stephen 1917- St&PR 91
Horbal, John St&PR 91
Horbatiuk, Kevin Gerard 1957- WhoE 91
Horberg, Samuel Bernard 1926- St&PR 91
Horbert, Janet L.H. WhoWrEP 89
Horbiger, Hans 1860-1931 EncO&P 3
Horch, Louis L 1889-1979 WhoAmA 91N
Horchhaimer, Nicholas PenDiDA 89
Horchow, S. Roger 1928- BioIn 16, St&PR 91
Horchow, Samuel Roger 1928- WhoAm 90, WhoSSW 91
Hord, Donal 1902-1966 WhoAmA 91N
Hordeman, Agnes Marie 1929- WhoAmW 91
Horden, John 1828-1893 DcCanB 12
Horder, Jacqueline Elizabeth 1953- IntWWM 90
Hordern, Anthony BiDrAPA 89
Hore, John Edward 1929- WhoE 91, WhoWor 91
Hore, Marlene Carole 1944- WhoAm 90, WhoAmW 91
Hore-Ruthven, Alexander Patric Greysteil 1939- BioIn 16
Hore y Ley, Maria Gertrudis 1742-1801 EncCoWW
Horecker, Bernard Leonard 1914- WhoAm 90
Horein, James R. 1937- St&PR 91
Horel, Lisa Stander 1955- WhoAmW 91
Horel, Tom 1947- St&PR 91
Horelova, Eliska 1925- EncCoWW
Horen, I. Richard 1946- St&PR 91
Horenci, John Paul, Jr. 1944- St&PR 91
Horenstein, Jascha 1887-1973 PenDiMP
Horenstein, Simon 1927- BiDrAPA 89
Horetzky, Charles George 1838-1900 DcCanB 12
Horevitz, Richard Paul 1945- WhoEmL 91
Horewitz, James S 1935- BiDrAPA 89
Horey, Edward C. 1937- St&PR 91
Horgan, Cornelius Oliver 1944- WhoSSW 91
Horgan, Dianne Daugherty 1948- WhoSSW 91
Horgan, Edward Daniel, III 1942- WhoWor 91
Horgan, John J. 1942- St&PR 91
Horgan, John Joseph, Jr. 1925- WhoAm 90
Horgan, John P. 1924- St&PR 91
Horgan, John Paul 1928- WhoSSW 91
Horgan, Maryellyn 1945- WhoSSW 91
Horgan, Paul 1903- AuBYP 90, DcLB 102 [port], MajTwCW, WhoAm 90
Horgan, Stephen Henry 1854-1941 BioIn 16
Horgan, Thaddeus D. BioIn 16
Horgan, William P. 1947- St&PR 91
Horger, Edgar Olin, III 1937- WhoAm 90
Horger, Robert V. 1911- St&PR 91
Hori, Keiko 1954- WhoWor 91
Hori, Saburo 1918- St&PR 91
Hori, Toshikazu 1924- WhoWor 91
Hori, Yukio 1927- WhoWor 91
Horianopoulos, Gus 1938- St&PR 91
Horide, Ichiro 1931- WhoWor 91
Horie, Akio 1931- WhoWor 91
Horie, Shigeo 1928- WhoWor 91
Horigome, Yuzuko 1960- IntWWM 90
Horiguchi, Mitsuo BioIn 16
Horiike, Hideto 1949- WhoWor 91
Horikawa, Akira 1922- WhoWor 91
Horin, Marc B. 1953- WhoEmL 91
Horine, Nelson Charles, II 1947- WhoE 91
Horioka, Charles Yuji 1956- WhoWor 91
Horisk, Anthony Bane 1947- St&PR 91
Horitz, Gill Anne 1947- WhoWor 91
Horiuchi, Atsushi 1929- WhoWor 91
Horiuchi, Katsuaki 1931- WhoWor 91
Horiuchi, Paul C 1906- WhoAmA 91
Horiuchi, Tsuneo 1948- Ballpl 90
Horkey, William R. 1925- St&PR 91
Horkey, William Richard 1925- WhoAm 90
Horkheimer, Jack BioIn 16
Horkovich, Robert Michael 1954- WhoEmL 91
Horky-Malloy, Laurel Meredith 1963- WhoAmW 91
Horland, Ephraim BiDrAPA 89
Horlander, Walter Franklin 1932- WhoSSW 91
Horlen, Joe 1937- Ballpl 90
Horler, Sydney 1888-1954 SpyFic, TwCCr&M 91
Horlick, Gary Norman 1947- WhoAm 90, WhoE 91
Horlick, Robert Allan 1956- WhoE 91
Horlick, William 1846-1936 WorAlBi
Horlock, John Harold 1928- WhoWor 91
Horman, Charles H. 1939- St&PR 91
Horman, Richard Eliot 1945- WhoE 91
Hormander, Lars 1931- BioIn 16
Hormats, Robert David 1943- WhoAm 90
Hormel, George A. 1860-1946 WorAlBi
Horn, Agneta 1629-1672 EncCoWW
Horn, Andrew 1952- WhoAmA 91
Horn, Andrew Warren 1946- WhoEmL 91, WhoWor 91
Horn, Bonnie Phyllis 1951- WhoEmL 91
Horn, Bruce 1946- WhoAmA 91
Horn, Carl, Jr. 1921- St&PR 91
Horn, Carol Ellen 1936- WhoAmW 91
Horn, Charles G. 1939- WhoAm 90, WhoE 91
Horn, Christian F. 1927- St&PR 91
Horn, Christian Friedrich 1927- WhoAm 90
Horn, Claire Helen 1934- WhoWor 91
Horn, Daisy Anderson 1929- WhoAmW 91
Horn, David Brecht 1946- WhoAm 90
Horn, David C. 1939- St&PR 91
Horn, David D. St&PR 91
Horn, David Dinsmore 1941- WhoAm 90
Horn, David Scott 1951- BiDrAPA 89, WhoE 91
Horn, Deborah Sue 1954- WhoAm 90
Horn, Donald Noel 1928- St&PR 91
Horn, Dwain R. 1930- St&PR 91
Horn, Everett Byron, Jr. 1927- St&PR 91
Horn, F. Christian ODwPR 91
Horn, Francis Henry 1908- WhoAm 90
Horn, Frederick William 1815-1893 AmLegL
Horn, Gary Allen 1949- WhoEmL 91
Horn, Gaye Burkholder WhoAmW 91
Horn, Gerald Anthony 1941- WhoAm 90
Horn, Guenther 1943- St&PR 91
Horn, Gyula 1932- WhoWor 91
Horn, Hartmut Gerhard 1930- WhoWor 91
Horn, Heiner 1920- IntWWM 90
Horn, Henry Stainken 1941- WhoE 91
Horn, James Kennith 1949- WhoEmL 91
Horn, Jerry Dean 1937- St&PR 91
Horn, Jim Nathan 1941- WhoSSW 91
Horn, Joan Kelly WhoAmW 91
Horn, John C. 1915- St&PR 91
Horn, John Chisolm 1915- WhoAm 90, WhoE 91, WhoWor 91
Horn, John F. 1941- WhoAm 90
Horn, Joseph Robert BiDrAPA 89
Horn, Karen BioIn 16
Horn, Karen Carol 1957- WhoEmL 91
Horn, Karen Nicholson 1943- WhoAm 90, WhoAmW 91
Horn, Kate M 1826?-1896 DcCanB 12
Horn, Keith Donald 1958- WhoEmL 91
Horn, Kim Marie 1964- WhoAmW 91
Horn, Lawrence Alan 1949- WhoEmL 91
Horn, Linda Anne 1943- WhoAmW 91
Horn, Lisa A. 1959- ODwPR 91
Horn, Lois Burley 1928- IntWWM 90
Horn, Ludwig Paul 1930- St&PR 91, WhoAm 90
Horn, Marian Blank 1943- WhoAm 90, WhoAmW 91
Horn, Martin I. 1951- WhoEmL 91
Horn, Martin Louis, Jr. 1927- WhoAm 90
Horn, Martin Robert 1928- WhoAm 90
Horn, Michiel Steven Daniel 1939- WhoE 91
Horn, Milton 1906- WhoAm 90, WhoAmA 91
Horn, Myron Kay 1930- WhoAm 90
Horn, Pamela 1936- ConAu 30NR
Horn, Patrice Daily 1927- WhoAm 90
Horn, Paul NewAgMG
Horn, Paul 1930- NewAgE 90
Horn, Paul Joseph 1930- WhoAm 90
Horn, Paul M. 1946- WhoAm 90
Horn, Paula Lois 1947- WhoAmW 91
Horn, Peter M. BioIn 16
Horn, Ralph E. 1937- St&PR 91
Horn, Rebecca 1944- BiDWomA
Horn, Richard 1930- St&PR 91
Horn, Richard 1954-1989 BioIn 16
Horn, Richard G. 1928- St&PR 91
Horn, Robert E 1935- BiDrAPA 89
Horn, Robert Ernest 1926- St&PR 91
Horn, Robert Nelson 1947- WhoAmA 91
Horn, Roberta Claire WhoAmW 91
Horn, Roger Alan 1942- WhoAm 90, WhoE 91
Horn, Roger Garland 1932- WhoE 91
Horn, Roni 1955- WhoAmA 91
Horn, Rose Mary 1921- WhoAmW 91
Horn, Russell Eugene 1912- St&PR 91
Horn, Russell Eugene, Jr. 1934- WhoE 91
Horn, Sheila Turner 1951- St&PR 91
Horn, Stephen 1931- WhoAm 90, WhoWor 91
Horn, Susan Andrews 1946- WhoAmW 91
Horn, Susan Dadakis 1943- WhoAmW 91
Horn, Ted 1910-1948 BioIn 16
Horn, Thomas Carl 1916- WhoAm 90
Horn, Thomas Darrough 1918- WhoAm 90
Horn, Thomas Landes 1946- BiDrAPA 89
Horn, Thomas Lefler, Jr. 1922- St&PR 91
Horn, Thomas Russell 1938- St&PR 91
Horn, Todd Richard Wendell 1955- WhoEmL 91
Horn, Tom 1860-1903 BioIn 16, WhNaAH
Horn, Volker 1945- IntWWM 90
Horn, Will Henry 1935- WhoE 91
Horn-Dalton, Kathy Ellen 1952- WhoAmW 91
Horna, Alan Roger 1949- St&PR 91
Hornaday, David Samuel 1959- St&PR 91
Hornaday, F.D. 1950- St&PR 91
Hornaday, Jon Russell 1935- WhoSSW 91
Hornaday, Richard Hoyt 1927- WhoAmA 91
Hornaday, Scott Dickson 1958- WhoEmL 91
Hornady, John R., III 1929- St&PR 91
Hornak, Anna Frances 1922- WhoAm 90
Hornak, Ian John 1944- WhoAmA 91
Hornak, Thomas 1924- WhoAm 90
Hornback, Joseph Hope 1910- WhoAm 90
Hornback, May Shiga 1924-1976 BioIn 16
Hornbaker, Alice Joy 1927- WhoAmW 91
Hornbeck, Stanley Kuhl 1883-1966 BioIn 16
Hornbein, Thomas Frederic 1930- WhoAm 90
Hornbein, Victor 1913- WhoAm 90
Hornberger, Deborah Ann 1957- WhoAmW 91
Hornberger, Frederick Charles, Jr. 1960- WhoEmL 91, WhoSSW 91
Hornberger, George Milton 1942- WhoAm 90

Hornberger, H.D. 1927- *St&PR 91*
Hornberger, Kevin Frederick *BiDrAPA 89*
Hornberger, Ronald 1943- *WhoSSW 91*
Hornblass, Bernice Miriam 1951- *WhoE 91*
Hornblow, Leonora 1920- *AuBYP 90*
Hornbogen, Erhard 1930- *WhoWor 91*
Hornbostel, Charles C. *BioIn 16*
Hornbostel, John F., Jr. 1940- *St&PR 91*
Hornbruch, Frederick William, Jr. 1913- *WhoWor 91*
Hornbuckle, Franklin L. 1941- *WhoE 91*
Hornbuckle, James Kenneth 1945- *St&PR 91*
Hornburg, Tanya V. 1960- *WhoAmW 91*
Hornby, David Brock 1944- *WhoE 91*
Hornby, Jack David 1948- *BiDrAPA 89*
Hornby, Lesley 1949- *WhoAm 90*
Hornby, Thomas Richard 1936- *WhoAm 90*
Horne, Carl A. 1929- *St&PR 91*
Horne, Charles E., III 1932- *St&PR 91*
Horne, Charlotte Ann Holcombe 1938- *WhoAmW 91*
Horne, Cleeve 1912- *WhoAmA 91*
Horne, Diana D *BiDrAPA 89*
Horne, Douglas Stuart 1934- *WhoE 91*
Horne, Eddie Belle 1938- *WhoSSW 91*
Horne, Elliott 1922-1989 *BioIn 16, ConAu 129*
Horne, Eugene Barron, Jr. 1942- *St&PR 91*
Horne, Frederick Herbert 1934- *WhoAm 90*
Horne, George *BioIn 16, NewYTBS 90 [port]*
Horne, George R. 1936- *St&PR 91*
Horne, Grant N. *ODwPR 91*
Horne, Grant N. 1931- *St&PR 91*
Horne, Grant Nelson 1931- *WhoAm 90*
Horne, Harold Field *BioIn 16*
Horne, Homa Judson 1921- *WhoAm 90*
Horne, Howard *ConAu 31NR*
Horne, James Barron 1926- *BiDrAPA 89*
Horne, Janis Mayo 1955- *WhoAmW 91*
Horne, John R. 1938- *St&PR 91*
Horne, L. Donald 1933- *St&PR 91, WhoAm 90*
Horne, Lena *BioIn 16*
Horne, Lena 1917- *BioAmW, DrBlPA 90, OxCPMus, WhoAm 90, WorAlBi*
Horne, Linda Sue *BiDrAPA 89*
Horne, Malcolm *BioIn 16*
Horne, Marcy Anne 1961- *WhoAmW 91*
Horne, Marilyn 1934- *IntWWM 90, PenDiMP, WhoAm 90, WhoWor 91, WorAlBi*
Horne, Michael John *BiDrAPA 89*
Horne, Michael Stewart 1938- *WhoAm 90*
Horne, Patricia Guest 1950- *WhoEmL 91*
Horne, Paul Adams, Jr. 1957- *WhoEmL 91*
Horne, Ralph Sheldon, Jr. 1935- *WhoSSW 91*
Horne, Richard Henry 1803-1884 *BioIn 16*
Horne, Robert Lynn 1949- *BiDrAPA 89*
Horne, Scott Jeffrey 1955- *WhoE 91, WhoEmL 91*
Horne, Thomas Charles 1945- *WhoEmL 91*
Horne, Timothy P. 1938- *St&PR 91*
Horne, Tom Lee, III 1950- *WhoEmL 91*
Horne, Vernon Alvin 1947- *St&PR 91*
Horne, William E. 1946- *St&PR 91*
Horne, William Parrish 1924- *St&PR 91*
Horne, William T *BiDrAPA 89*
Hornecker, Wendell E. 1941- *WhoAm 90*
Horner, Althea Jane 1926- *WhoAm 90, WhoWor 91*
Horner, Barbara Jeanne *BiDrAPA 89*
Horner, Bob *BioIn 16*
Horner, Bob 1957- *Ballpl 90*
Horner, Carl Matthew 1930- *WhoE 91*
Horner, Charles Albert 1936- *WhoAm 90*
Horner, Constance J. 1942- *WhoAm 90, WhoAmW 91*
Horner, David G. *WhoAm 90, WhoSSW 91*
Horner, David John 1953- *WhoWor 91*
Horner, Donald G. 1950- *St&PR 91*
Horner, Evan Wayne 1950- *WhoEmL 91*
Horner, H. R. *WhoE 91*
Horner, Harry 1910- *ConDes 90, WhoAm 90*
Horner, Jack *BioIn 16*
Horner, Jack B. 1927- *St&PR 91*
Horner, James *BioIn 16*
Horner, James A. 1931- *St&PR 91*
Horner, James M, Jr. 1922- *BiDrAPA 89*
Horner, John Githens 1872- *AmLegL*
Horner, John R. *AuBYP 90, BioIn 16*
Horner, Kenneth D. 1935- *St&PR 91*
Horner, Larry Dean 1934- *WhoAm 90*
Horner, Laura S. 1959- *ODwPR 91*
Horner, Leonard M. 1927- *St&PR 91*
Horner, Mary Kay 1940- *St&PR 91*
Horner, Mary Kay Hall 1940- *WhoAmW 91*
Horner, Matina Souretis 1939- *WhoAm 90, WhoAmW 91, WhoWor 91*
Horner, Maxine Edwyna Cissel 1933- *WhoAmW 91, WhoSSW 91*
Horner, Richard E. 1917- *St&PR 91*
Horner, Richard Elmer 1917- *WhoAm 90*
Horner, Robert D. *BioIn 16*
Horner, Robert David 1947- *WhoAm 90*
Horner, Russell W. 1925- *St&PR 91*
Horner, Sally McKay Melvin 1935- *WhoAmW 91*
Horner, Stephen R. *St&PR 91*
Horner, Susan *ODwPR 91*
Horner, Terry David 1955- *WhoEmL 91*
Horner, Thomas Harvey 1928- *WhoAm 90*
Horner, Timothy Matthew 1959- *WhoE 91*
Horner, William Edwin, III 1963- *St&PR 91*
Horner, William Frederick 1946- *WhoEmL 91*
Horner, William Harry 1923- *WhoAm 90*
Horner, Winifred Bryan 1922- *WhoAmW 91*
Horness, Cindy Kay 1959- *WhoEmL 91*
Horne'y, Christel Adele 1938- *WhoAmW 91*
Horney, Karen 1885-1952 *BioIn 16, WorAlBi*
Horney, Stephen Henry 1946- *WhoSSW 91*
Hornfeldt, Berndt Eric 1939- *WhoWor 91*
Horngren, Charles Thomas 1926- *WhoAm 90*
Hornick, Erasmus *PenDiDA 89*
Hornick, Gerald Charles 1932- *St&PR 91*
Hornick, John Francis 1956- *WhoEmL 91*
Hornick, Katherine Joyce Kay 1940- *WhoAmW 91*
Hornick, Leslee Goodman 1953- *WhoSSW 91*
Hornick, Richard Bernard 1929- *WhoAm 90*
Hornick, Samuel L. 1949- *WhoEmL 91*
Hornig, Donald F. 1920- *St&PR 91*
Hornig, Donald Frederick 1920- *WhoAm 90*
Hornig, Doug 1943- *TwCCr&M 91*
Hornig, Douglas 1943- *WhoWrEP 89*
Hornig, George R. 1954- *St&PR 91*
Hornig-Rohan, Mady *BiDrAPA 89*
Hornik, Gottfried 1940- *IntWWM 90*
Hornik, Henry 1927- *WhoAm 90*
Hornik, Irena Helena 1930- *BiDrAPA 89*
Hornik, Joseph William 1929- *WhoAm 90, WhoWor 91*
Horning, Gregory Mason 1950- *WhoEmL 91*
Horning, Jerome Kay 1935- *WhoAm 90*
Horning, Leonard Bernard 1928- *St&PR 91*
Horning, Martin Stuart 1942- *St&PR 91*
Horning, Michael F. 1957- *St&PR 91*
Horning, Ross Charles, Jr. 1920- *WhoAm 90, WhoWor 91*
Horning, Thomas L. 1931- *St&PR 91*
Horning-Norris, Lois Dale 1928- *St&PR 91*
Hornor, Frank Berkshire 1923- *WhoAm 90*
Horns, Howard Lowell 1912- *WhoAm 90*
Hornsby, Bruce *BioIn 16*
Hornsby, Clarence Hood 1926- *St&PR 91*
Hornsby, Cyrus Edward, III 1943- *WhoSSW 91*
Hornsby, Gerald 1934- *WhoAm 90*
Hornsby, Henry H. 1910- *LiHiK*
Hornsby, Lawrence G 1930- *BiDrAPA 89*
Hornsby, Richard L. 1936- *St&PR 91*
Hornsby, Roger Allen 1926- *WhoAm 90*
Hornsby, Rogers 1896-1963 *Ballpl 90 [port], BioIn 16, WorAlBi*
Hornsby, Sonny *WhoSSW 91*
Hornsby, Tenna Middleton 1961- *WhoSSW 91*
Hornschemeier, Patrick 1945- *WhoEmL 91*
Hornstein, Alvin S. 1926- *ODwPR 91*
Hornstein, Andrew 1947- *BiDrAPA 89*
Hornstein, Eugene 1940- *St&PR 91*
Hornstein, George D. 1904-1990 *BioIn 16*
Hornstein, Harold 1920- *WhoWrEP 89*
Hornstein, John Stanley 1941- *WhoE 91*
Hornstein, Nancy Louise *BiDrAPA 89*
Hornstein, Norbert Richard 1951- *WhoE 91*
Hornstein, Reuben Aaron 1912- *SmATA 64*
Hornsten, Lawrence A. *WhoSSW 91*
Hornstra, Robijn K 1926- *BiDrAPA 89*
Hornthal, Philipp Richard 1950- *WhoEmL 91*
Hornung, Clarence Pearson 1899- *WhoAmA 91*
Hornung, E W 1866-1921 *TwCCr&M 91*
Hornung, Franz E *BiDrAPA 89*
Hornung, Gertrude Seymour *WhoAmA 91*
Hornung, Gertrude Seymour 1939- *WhoWor 91*
Hornung, Hans Georg 1934- *WhoAm 90*
Hornung, Leonard Matthew 1934- *St&PR 91*
Hornung, Paul 1935- *BioIn 16, WorAlBi*
Hornung, Paul Andrew 1917- *WhoAm 90*
Hornung, Robert Paul 1923- *St&PR 91*
Hornyak, Eugene Augustine 1919- *WhoAm 90*
Hornyak, Ronald F. 1947- *St&PR 91*
Hornynsky, Nicholas 1896-1965 *WhoAmA 91N*
Horoldt, Johann Gregor 1696-1775 *PenDiDA 89*
Horos, Laura 1849-1906? *EncO&P 3*
Horos, Theodore 1866?- *EncO&P 3*
Horoshak, Richard J 1940- *WhoAmA 91*
Horoszewicz, Juliusz Stanislaw 1931- *WhoE 91*
Horovitz, Adam *BioIn 16*
Horovitz, Frances 1938-1983 *FemiCLE*
Horovitz, Israel Arthur 1939- *WhoAm 90*
Horovitz, Jacques Henri 1947- *WhoWor 91*
Horovitz, Jeffrey H *BiDrAPA 89*
Horovitz, Joseph 1926- *IntWWM 90, OxCPMus*
Horovitz, Stanley 1933- *St&PR 91*
Horovitz, Zola Philip 1934- *St&PR 91, WhoAm 90*
Horowitz, Barney Louis 1938- *WhoWor 91*
Horowitz, Barry Martin 1943- *WhoAm 90*
Horowitz, Ben 1914- *WhoWor 91*
Horowitz, Benjamin 1912- *WhoAmA 91*
Horowitz, Beverly Phyllis 1949- *WhoAmW 91*
Horowitz, Carl 1923- *St&PR 91*
Horowitz, Carol Rose *BiDrAPA 89*
Horowitz, Daniel L. 1916- *WhoAm 90, WhoE 91*
Horowitz, David 1939- *BioIn 16*
Horowitz, David 1943- *WhoE 91*
Horowitz, David Charles 1937- *WhoAm 90*
Horowitz, David H. 1928- *St&PR 91, WhoAm 90*
Horowitz, David Joel 1939- *WhoWrEP 89*
Horowitz, David Morris *BiDrAPA 89*
Horowitz, Don Roy 1930- *WhoAm 90*
Horowitz, Dona Weinstein 1948- *WhoE 91*
Horowitz, Donald B *BiDrAPA 89*
Horowitz, Donald Leonard 1939- *WhoAm 90*
Horowitz, Edwin 1931- *St&PR 91*
Horowitz, Elizabeth McGinnis 1955- *WhoEmL 91*
Horowitz, Esther 1920- *WhoAmW 91*
Horowitz, Frances Degen 1932- *WhoAm 90*
Horowitz, Fred L. 1954- *WhoWor 91*
Horowitz, Gedale B. 1932- *St&PR 91*
Horowitz, Gedale Bob 1932- *WhoAm 90*
Horowitz, George C. 1952- *WhoEmL 91*
Horowitz, George Gary 1938- *WhoE 91*
Horowitz, Harold 1927- *WhoAm 90*
Horowitz, Harold A. 1950- *WhoEmL 91*
Horowitz, Harry I. 1915- *WhoSSW 91*
Horowitz, Harvey Alan 1942- *BiDrAPA 89*
Horowitz, Helen Joyce *BiDrAPA 89*
Horowitz, Henry *BiDrAPA 89*
Horowitz, Herbert Eugene 1930- *WhoAm 90*
Horowitz, Irene 1923- *St&PR 91*
Horowitz, Irving Louis 1929- *WhoAm 90, WhoWrEP 89*
Horowitz, Jack 1931- *WhoAm 90*
Horowitz, Janice Elayne 1951- *BiDrAPA 89*
Horowitz, Jonathan Marc *BiDrAPA 89*
Horowitz, Lenore Wisney 1946- *WhoWrEP 89*
Horowitz, Leonard *BioIn 16*
Horowitz, Lewis J. 1935- *St&PR 91*
Horowitz, Lewis Jay 1935- *WhoAm 90*
Horowitz, Lynette Joy *BiDrAPA 89*
Horowitz, Marcia 1952- *ODwPR 91*
Horowitz, Mardi J 1934- *BiDrAPA 89*
Horowitz, Mark R. 1949- *ODwPR 91*
Horowitz, Mary Curtis 1946- *WhoAm 90*
Horowitz, Milton H *BiDrAPA 89*
Horowitz, Morris A. 1919- *WhoAm 90, WhoE 91*
Horowitz, Nadia *WhoAmA 91*
Horowitz, Norman *BioIn 16*
Horowitz, Norman Harold 1915- *WhoAm 90*
Horowitz, Raymond J *WhoAmA 91*
Horowitz, Raymond J. 1916- *St&PR 91, WhoAm 90*
Horowitz, Raymond J, Mrs *WhoAmA 91*
Horowitz, Richard Andrew 1950- *St&PR 91*
Horowitz, Roberta Sharon 1951- *WhoEmL 91*
Horowitz, Ryszard *BioIn 16*
Horowitz, Samuel Boris 1927- *WhoAm 90*
Horowitz, Shel Alan 1956- *WhoWrEP 89*
Horowitz, Sidney 1920- *St&PR 91, WhoAm 90*
Horowitz, Stephen Paul 1943- *WhoWor 91*
Horowitz, Steven *BioIn 16*
Horowitz, Steven Leslie 1950- *WhoEmL 91*
Horowitz, Sylvia Teich 1922- *WhoAmW 91*
Horowitz, Vladimir 1903?-1989 *CurBio 90N, News 90, PenDiMP*
Horowitz, Vladimir 1904-1989 *AnObit 1989, BioIn 16, WorAlBi*
Horowitz, Wanda *BioIn 16*
Horowitz, William 1907- *St&PR 91*
Horowitz, Zachary I. 1953- *WhoAm 90, WhoWor 91*
Horr, David A. 1938- *St&PR 91*
Horr, William Henry 1914- *WhoAm 90*
Horrall, Allyson Denise 1962- *WhoEmL 91*
Horrall, Bob G. 1932- *St&PR 91*
Horrall, Curtis L. 1930- *St&PR 91*
Horrell, Fred Thomas 1947- *WhoSSW 91*
Horrell, Jeffrey L 1952- *WhoAmA 91*
Horrell, Karen Holley 1952- *St&PR 91, WhoAm 90*
Horres, Charles Russell, Jr. 1945- *WhoEmL 91*
Horrey, C. Douglas 1937- *St&PR 91*
Horricks, Raymond 1933- *ConAu 129*
Horridge, George Adrian 1927- *WhoWor 91*
Horridge, Patricia Emily 1937- *WhoAmW 91*
Horrigan, Alfred Frederic 1914- *WhoAm 90*
Horrigan, Brian Richard 1951- *WhoE 91*
Horrigan, D. Gregory 1943- *St&PR 91*
Horrigan, Edward A., Jr. 1929- *WhoAm 90, WhoSSW 91*
Horrigan, Joseph Patrick 1962- *BiDrAPA 89*
Horrigan, Patricia Ann 1934- *WhoWrEP 89*
Horrigan, Thomas H. 1926- *WhoE 91*
Horrocks, Brian Gwynne 1895-1985 *DcNaB 1981*
Horrocks, Jay B. 1930- *St&PR 91*
Horrocks, John 1927- *WhoAm 90*
Horrocks, Norman 1927- *St&PR 91, WhoAm 90*
Horrox, Alberta W. 1938- *St&PR 91*
Horsbrugh, Patrick 1920- *WhoAm 90*
Horsch, Kathleen Joanne 1936- *WhoAm 90*
Horsch, Lawrence Leonard 1934- *St&PR 91, WhoAm 90*
Horsell, Mary Kay 1917- *WhoAm 90, WhoWor 91*
Horsely, Ramsbottom *MajTwCW*
Horseman, Elaine 1925- *AuBYP 90*
Horsey, Henry Ridgely 1924- *WhoAm 90, WhoE 91*
Horsey, James J. 1949- *St&PR 91*
Horsey, William Grant 1915- *WhoAm 90*
Horsfall, Bruce D. 1933- *St&PR 91*
Horsfield, Debbie 1955- *FemiCLE*
Horsford, Anna Maria *BioIn 16*
Horsford, Anna Maria 1947- *DrBlPA 90*
Horsford, Eben Norton 1818-1893 *BioIn 16*
Horsford, Howard Clarke 1921- *WhoAm 90*
Horska, Katarina 1951- *WhoWor 91*
Horsky, Charles Antone 1910- *WhoAm 90*
Horsley, Colin 1920- *IntWWM 90*
Horsley, David 1873-1933 *BioIn 16*
Horsley, Jack Everett 1915- *WhoAm 90, WhoWor 91*
Horsley, Lee 1955- *WorAlBi*
Horsley, Lee Herbert 1936- *WhoSSW 91*
Horsley, Paula Rosalie 1924- *WhoAmW 91, WhoWor 91*
Horsley, Richard D. 1942- *WhoAm 90*
Horsley, Richard David 1942- *St&PR 91*
Horsley, Waller Holladay 1931- *WhoAm 90*
Horsman, David A. Elliott 1932- *WhoAm 90, WhoE 91, WhoWor 91*
Horsman, James Deverell 1935- *WhoAm 90*
Horsman, John G., Jr. 1938- *St&PR 91*
Horsman, John Gordon, Jr 1938- *WhoAm 90*
Horsman, Lenore Lynde *IntWWM 90*
Horsman, Reginald 1931- *WhoAm 90*
Horsnell, Walter Cecil 1911- *WhoWor 91*
Horst, Bruce Everett 1921- *WhoAm 90*
Horst, David Lester 1939- *St&PR 91*
Horst, Donald John 1932- *St&PR 91*
Horst, Elmer Leaman 1912- *BiDrAPA 89*
Horst, Harriette Mathilda 1948- *WhoEmL 91*
Horst, Nancy Carroll 1933- *WhoAmW 91*
Horst, Neal A. 1941- *St&PR 91*
Horst, Pamela Jane 1957- *WhoAmW 91*
Horst, R.G. 1919- *St&PR 91*
Horst, Richard Harley 1958- *WhoEmL 91*
Horst, Robert Lee 1930- *WhoE 91*
Horst, Timothy Lee 1949- *WhoSSW 91*
Horst, Tom Emil 1951- *WhoSSW 91*
Horstman, Arden William 1930- *WhoSSW 91*
Horstman, Nancy Jean Crocker 1945- *WhoAmW 91*

Horstman, Neil Williard 1946- *WhoSSW 91*
Horstman, Randall L. *St&PR 91*
Horstman, Suzanne Rucker 1945- *WhoAmW 91*
Horstmann, Claus 1949- *WhoWor 91*
Horstmann, Dorothy Millicent 1911- *WhoAm 90, WhoAmW 91*
Horstmann, James Douglas 1933- *WhoAm 90*
Horstmann, Victoria *ODwPR 91*
Horstmyer, Kenneth LeRoy 1921- *WhoAm 90*
Horszowski, Mieczyslaw 1892- *IntWWM 90, PenDiMP*
Hort, Michael David 1941- *St&PR 91*
Horta, Maria Teresa 1937- *EncCoWW*
Horta, Victor 1861-1947 *PenDiDA 89*
Horten, Carl Frank 1914- *WhoAm 90*
Hortense de Beauharnais 1783-1837 *WomWR*
Horthy, Miklos 1868-1957 *BioIn 16, WorAlBi*
Hortman, Carolyn L. 1957- *WhoAmW 91*
Horton, Aaron Wesley 1919- *WhoAm 90*
Horton, Alonzo Erastus 1813-1909 *BioIn 16*
Horton, Anita A. 1952- *WhoSSW 91*
Horton, Ann Mitchell 1949- *WhoAmW 91*
Horton, Barbara Elizabeth 1953- *WhoAmW 91*
Horton, Barbara Marion Deady 1930- *WhoAmW 91*
Horton, Bernard Francis 1916- *WhoAm 90*
Horton, Brewer Tate, Jr. 1943- *WhoAm 90*
Horton, Byron W. 1909- *St&PR 91*
Horton, Claude Wendell 1915- *WhoAm 90*
Horton, Cleveland Bradford 1955- *WhoEmL 91*
Horton, David Alan 1957- *WhoSSW 91*
Horton, E. Dennis 1950- *WhoSSW 91*
Horton, Edward Everett 1886-1970 *WorAlBi*
Horton, Edward Everett, Jr. 1931- *WhoE 91*
Horton, Elliott Argue, Jr. 1926- *WhoAm 90*
Horton, Finis Gene 1953- *WhoEmL 91*
Horton, Frank 1919- *WhoAm 90, WhoE 91*
Horton, Frank Elba 1939- *WhoAm 90*
Horton, Frederick T, Jr. *BiDrAPA 89*
Horton, Gary Bruce 1943- *WhoAm 90*
Horton, George Vaughn 1911-1988 *BioIn 16*
Horton, Gerald Talmadge 1934- *WhoAm 90*
Horton, Gerald W. 1943- *St&PR 91*
Horton, Granville Eugene 1927- *WhoSSW 91*
Horton, Guy M. 1933- *ODwPR 91*
Horton, H. Hollis, III 1955- *WhoEmL 91*
Horton, Hamilton Cowles, Jr. 1931- *St&PR 91*
Horton, Horace Robert 1935- *WhoAm 90*
Horton, J.T. 1928- *St&PR 91*
Horton, Jack King 1916- *St&PR 91*
Horton, James Bawden 1930- *WhoAm 90*
Horton, James C. 1930- *St&PR 91*
Horton, James L. *ODwPR 91*
Horton, James Lee, Jr. 1944- *WhoE 91*
Horton, James Wright 1919- *WhoAm 90*
Horton, Jared C. 1924- *WhoAm 90*
Horton, Jeanette 1938- *WhoAmW 91, WhoSSW 91*
Horton, John Alden 1920- *WhoAm 90*
Horton, John Edward 1930- *WhoAm 90*
Horton, John Michael 1946- *BiDrAPA 89*
Horton, John Tod 1928- *WhoAm 90*
Horton, John Warner *DrBlPA 90*
Horton, John William 1905- *IntWWM 90*
Horton, Johnathan David 1941- *IntWWM 90*
Horton, Joseph Julian, Jr. 1936- *WhoE 91*
Horton, K.C. 1956- *St&PR 91*
Horton, Keith A 1933- *BiDrAPA 89*
Horton, Keith Willard *BioIn 16*
Horton, Larry Bruce 1942- *WhoSSW 91*
Horton, Leonard M. *BioIn 16*
Horton, Louis Charles 1918- *WhoE 91*
Horton, Madeline Mary 1939- *WhoAmW 91*
Horton, Marcia L. 1947- *St&PR 91*
Horton, Michael 1916- *ODwPR 91*
Horton, Michael 1918- *WhoE 91*
Horton, Michael Patrick 1942- *St&PR 91*
Horton, Mildred G. 1929- *WhoAmW 91*
Horton, Myles *BioIn 16*
Horton, Myles 1905- *EncAL*
Horton, Myles 1905-1990 *NewYTBS 90 [port]*
Horton, Odell 1929- *WhoAm 90, WhoSSW 91*
Horton, Paul Bradfield 1920- *WhoAm 90, WhoSSW 91, WhoWor 91*
Horton, Paul Chester 1942- *BiDrAPA 89, WhoE 91*
Horton, Peter *BioIn 16, ConTFT 8*
Horton, Philip C. *BioIn 16*
Horton, Philip C. 1911?-1989 *ConAu 129*
Horton, Philip Giles 1930- *St&PR 91*
Horton, Richard 1932- *WhoAm 90*
Horton, Richard L. 1943- *St&PR 91*
Horton, Richard Murphy 1921- *St&PR 91*
Horton, Rick 1959- *Ballpl 90*
Horton, Rick Ray *BiDrAPA 89*
Horton, Robert Baynes 1939- *St&PR 91, WhoAm 90, WhoWor 91*
Horton, Robert Carlton 1926- *WhoAm 90*
Horton, Robert Lawrence 1959- *WhoEmL 91*
Horton, Ronald Lee 1948- *IntWWM 90*
Horton, Susan Raye *WhoE 91*
Horton, Theodore Thompson, Jr. 1951- *St&PR 91*
Horton, Thomas Edward, Jr. 1935- *WhoAm 90*
Horton, Thomas Leon 1954- *WhoSSW 91*
Horton, Thomas Mark 1952- *WhoEmL 91, WhoSSW 91*
Horton, Thomas R. 1926- *WhoAm 90*
Horton, Tony 1944- *Ballpl 90*
Horton, William D 1917- *BiDrAPA 89*
Horton, William H. 1921- *St&PR 91*
Horton, William R. 1931- *St&PR 91*
Horton, Willie 1942- *Ballpl 90*
Horton, Yvonne *WhoE 91*
Horty, J.F. 1928- *St&PR 91*
Horvat, Edwina Marie 1953- *WhoAmW 91*
Horvat, Martin Michael 1946- *WhoWrEP 89*
Horvat, Milan 1919- *IntWWM 90, PenDiMP*
Horvat, Peter Daniel 1937- *St&PR 91*
Horvath, Betty 1927- *AuBYP 90*
Horvath, Csaba 1930- *WhoAm 90*
Horvath, Dennis Paul 1913- *BiDrAPA 89*
Horvath, Diane Ellen 1961- *WhoEmL 91*
Horvath, Elemer 1933- *WhoWrEP 89*
Horvath, Gary 1946- *St&PR 91*
Horvath, Ian *BioIn 16*
Horvath, Ian *NewYTBS 90*
Horvath, Imre E *BiDrAPA 89*
Horvath, James Julius 1945- *St&PR 91, WhoAm 90, WhoEmL 91*
Horvath, John 1948- *St&PR 91, WhoWrEP 89*
Horvath, John Michael 1924- *WhoE 91*
Horvath, Jordan A. 1961- *WhoEmL 91*
Horvath, Joseph John 1936- *St&PR 91, WhoAm 90*
Horvath, Juliana 1948- *WhoEmL 91*
Horvath, Laszlo 1945- *IntWWM 90*
Horvath, Michael R. 1951- *St&PR 91*
Horvath, Polly 1957- *ConAu 132*
Horvath, Ronald Frank 1950- *WhoEmL 91*
Horvath, Ronald Joseph 1939- *WhoAm 90*
Horvath, Stephen Anthony 1955- *WhoEmL 91*
Horvath, Steven M. 1932- *St&PR 91*
Horvath, Vincent V. 1942- *St&PR 91*
Horvay, Gabriel 1908- *WhoSSW 91*
Horve, Leslie A. 1938- *St&PR 91*
Horvick, Neil M. 1954- *St&PR 91*
Horvitz, Daniel Goodman 1921- *WhoAm 90*
Horvitz, Howard Robert 1947- *WhoAm 90*
Horvitz, Paul Michael 1935- *WhoAm 90*
Horvitz, Suzanne Joan *WhoAmA 91*
Horvitz, Wayne *BioIn 16*
Horwath, Ewald 1953- *BiDrAPA 89*
Horwedel, Lowell Charles 1932- *St&PR 91*
Horwich, Allan 1944- *WhoAm 90*
Horwich, Frances 1908- *AuBYP 90*
Horwich, George 1924- *WhoAm 90*
Horwin, Gary Steven 1951- *WhoEmL 91*
Horwith, Susan Kardos *WhoAmW 91*
Horwits, Al 1903- *Ballpl 90*
Horwitt, Max Kenneth 1908- *WhoAm 90*
Horwitt, Nathan George *NewYTBS 90*
Horwitt, Will 1934-1985 *WhoAmA 91N*
Horwitz, Alan Fredrick 1944- *WhoAm 90*
Horwitz, Alan Steven 1955- *St&PR 91*
Horwitz, Albert Abram 1935- *St&PR 91*
Horwitz, Alexander E 1958- *BiDrAPA 89*
Horwitz, Allan Barry 1947- *WhoEmL 91*
Horwitz, Carey *ODwPR 91*
Horwitz, Channa 1932- *WhoAmA 91*
Horwitz, David Larry 1942- *WhoWor 91*
Horwitz, David Michael 1953- *St&PR 91*
Horwitz, Donald P. 1936- *St&PR 91*
Horwitz, Donald Paul 1936- *WhoAm 90*
Horwitz, Eleanor Catherine 1941- *WhoE 91*
Horwitz, Elinor Lander *AuBYP 90*
Horwitz, Gary Joseph 1951- *BiDrAPA 89*
Horwitz, Harry 1927- *WhoAm 90*
Horwitz, Helen L. 1940- *ODwPR 91*
Horwitz, Irwin Daniel 1920- *WhoAm 90*
Horwitz, Jack *NewYTBS 90 [port]*
Horwitz, Judy *ODwPR 91*
Horwitz, Kathryn Bloch 1941- *WhoAmW 91*
Horwitz, Lawrence David 1939- *WhoAm 90*
Horwitz, Lawrence Paul 1930- *WhoWor 91*
Horwitz, Louis B. 1927- *St&PR 91*
Horwitz, Marc Jeffry *BiDrAPA 89*
Horwitz, Michael M. 1948- *St&PR 91*
Horwitz, Morton J. 1938- *WhoAm 90*
Horwitz, Orville 1909- *WhoAm 90*
Horwitz, Paul 1938- *WhoAm 90*
Horwitz, Ralph Irving 1947- *WhoAm 90*
Horwitz, Robert P. 1932- *St&PR 91*
Horwitz, Robin *BiDrAPA 89*
Horwitz, Ronald M. 1938- *WhoAm 90*
Horwitz, Saul 1925- *St&PR 91*
Horwitz, Steven Cary *BiDrAPA 89*
Horwood, Ellis George 1911- *WhoWor 91*
Horwood, Harold Andrew 1923- *BioIn 16*
Horwood, Michael Stephen 1947- *IntWWM 90*
Horyn, Gene 1927- *St&PR 91*
Horysa, Inghild 1944- *IntWWM 90*
Horzinek, Marian Christian 1936- *WhoWor 91*
Hosage, Daniel A. 1932- *St&PR 91*
Hosain, Attia 1913- *FemiCLE*
Hosaka, Sakae 1930- *St&PR 91*
Hosansky, Mel *BioIn 16*
Hosbach, Howard D. *NewYTBS 90*
Hosbach, Howard D. 1931-1990 *BioIn 16*
Hosbach, Howard Daniel 1931-1990 *WhoAm 90, WhoWor 91*
Hosch, Burton B. 1947- *St&PR 91*
Hoschna, Karl 1877-1911 *OxCPMus*
Hose, Anthony Paul 1944- *IntWWM 90*
Hosea, Julia Hiller 1952- *WhoAmW 91, WhoEmL 91*
Hosea, Linda Marx 1954- *WhoAmW 91*
Hosek, Ankica 1949- *WhoWor 91*
Hosek, Chaviva Milada 1946- *WhoAmW 91*
Hosek, Laverne R. 1933- *St&PR 91*
Hosek, Louis Otto, III 1952- *WhoSSW 91*
Hosenball, S. Neil *WhoAm 90*
Hosenbocus, Nazim *BiDrAPA 89*
Hosenfeller, Heinrich Christian F. *PenDiDA 89*
Hosfield, William B *BiDrAPA 89*
Hosford, Dorothy 1900-1952 *AuBYP 90*
Hosford, William R. 1935- *St&PR 91*
Hoshall, Paul Clifford 1943- *WhoAm 90*
Hoshaw, Robert Alan 1950- *WhoEmL 91*
Hoshino, Arthur *BiDrAPA 89*
Hosiasson, Jose 1931- *WhoWor 91*
Hosick, Howard Lawrence 1943- *WhoAm 90*
Hosie, John James 1940- *WhoE 91*
Hosie, William Carlton 1936- *WhoAm 90*
Hosier, John 1928- *IntWWM 90*
Hosken, Richard Bruce 1942- *WhoSSW 91*
Hoskens, Jane 1693-1770? *FemiCLE*
Hosker, Rayford Peter, Jr. 1943- *WhoAm 90*
Hoskin, Sandra Ruble 1935- *WhoAmW 91*
Hoskin, William Dickel 1920- *WhoE 91*
Hosking, Craig *BioIn 16*
Hosking, Eric John 1909- *BioIn 16*
Hosking, Robert L. *BioIn 16*
Hosking, Sharon B. 1942- *WhoE 91*
Hoskins, Allen Clayton 1920-1980 *DrBlPA 90*
Hoskins, B. Wayne 1949- *St&PR 91, WhoSSW 91*
Hoskins, Barbara Bruno 1948- *WhoEmL 91*
Hoskins, Bob 1942- *BioIn 16, CurBio 90 [port], WhoAm 90, WorAlBi*
Hoskins, Charles Ross 1941- *St&PR 91*
Hoskins, Curtis Lynn 1937- *St&PR 91*
Hoskins, David Springer 1959- *WhoEmL 91*
Hoskins, Deborah Lebo 1960- *WhoAmW 91*
Hoskins, Edwin Campbell 1928- *St&PR 91*
Hoskins, Frank L. 1919-1976 *BioIn 16*
Hoskins, George Gilbert 1824-1883 *AmLegL*
Hoskins, Geraldine 1940- *WhoAmW 91*
Hoskins, James Jay 1950- *WhoEmL 91*
Hoskins, Jane 1693-1770? *FemiCLE*
Hoskins, John 1595?-1665 *IntDcAA 90*
Hoskins, John H. 1934- *WhoAm 90*
Hoskins, Laetitia *ODwPR 91*
Hoskins, Lowell 1927- *St&PR 91*
Hoskins, Percy 1904-1989 *AnObit 1989*
Hoskins, Richard Jerold 1945- *WhoAm 90*
Hoskins, Robert Nathan 1917- *WhoAm 90, WhoSSW 91*
Hoskins, Ryland L. 1940- *ODwPR 91*
Hoskins, Trevor C. 1934- *ODwPR 91*
Hoskins, W. Lee 1941- *WhoAm 90*
Hoskins, William Darrell 1930- *WhoSSW 91*
Hoskins, William John 1940- *WhoAm 90, WhoWor 91*
Hoskins, William Keller 1935- *St&PR 91, WhoAm 90*
Hoskinson, Carol Rowe 1947- *WhoAmW 91*
Hoskinson, David Wilber 1935- *St&PR 91*
Hoskinson, Francis Bryan 1963- *WhoSSW 91*
Hoskinson, Jean H. *St&PR 91*
Hoskinson, William R. 1948- *St&PR 91*
Hosler, Charles Luther, Jr. 1924- *WhoAm 90*
Hosler, David Eugene 1950- *St&PR 91*
Hosler, Russell John 1906- *WhoAm 90*
Hosley, Edward Howard 1930- *WhoE 91*
Hosley, Richmond B. 1947- *St&PR 91*
Hosmanek, Jane *ODwPR 91*
Hosmer, Bradley Edwin 1940- *WhoE 91*
Hosmer, Bruce E. 1942- *WhoE 91*
Hosmer, Harriet 1830-1908 *BioIn 16*
Hosmer, Harriet Goodhue 1830-1908 *BiDWomA*
Hosmer, Katherine 1928- *WhoAmW 91*
Hosmer, Max Edmonds 1924- *St&PR 91*
Hosmer, Rachel *BioIn 16*
Hosmon, Robert Stahr 1943- *WhoSSW 91*
Hosner, James Robert 1944- *WhoWor 91*
Hosoe, Eikoh 1933- *WhoWor 91*
Hosokawa Clan *EncJap*
Hosokawa Gracia 1563-1600 *EncJap*
Hosokawa, Morihiro 1938- *WhoWor 91*
Hosokawa, Peter E. 1948- *St&PR 91*
Hosokawa, William K. 1915- *WhoAm 90*
Hospers, John 1918- *WhoAm 90*
Hospital, Janette 1942- *FemiCLE*
Hospital, Maria Carolina 1957- *WhoHisp 91*
Hospodar, R.S. 1929- *St&PR 91*
Hospodor, Andrew Thomas 1937- *WhoAm 90*
Hoss, Ann 1959- *ODwPR 91*
Hoss, Donald Adron 1940- *WhoWor 91*
Hoss, Janalee 1939- *WhoAmW 91*
Hossack, Charles H. 1935- *ODwPR 91*
Hossack, Charles Henry 1935- *St&PR 91*
Hossack, John Edward 1924- *St&PR 91*
Hossain, Anwar 1931- *WhoWor 91*
Hossain, Mosaddeq Khondker 1953- *WhoE 91*
Hossain, S M Moazzem *BiDrAPA 89*
Hossein Barkat Siraj *WhoWor 91*
Hossellman, Vernon Christopher, Jr. 1921- *St&PR 91*
Hossent, Harry 1916- *SpyFic*
Hossfeld, Walter Edward 1932- *St&PR 91*
Host, Stig 1926- *WhoAm 90*
Host, Thorkil *BioIn 16*
Hostage, John Brayne Arthur 1952- *WhoEmL 91*
Hosten, Edward Bernarr *BiDrAPA 89*
Hoster, David H. *St&PR 91*
Hoster, Fred William 1939- *WhoSSW 91*
Hoster, Geroge S., Jr. 1931- *St&PR 91*
Hoster, Richard Henry 1921- *St&PR 91*
Hoster, William Henry, Jr. 1912- *WhoSSW 91*
Hostetler, Dave 1956- *Ballpl 90*
Hostetler, Donna Fordyce 1950- *WhoEmL 91*
Hostetler, Joyce Detwiler 1939- *WhoAmW 91*
Hostetler, Richard Carl 1930- *St&PR 91*
Hostetler, Roger *BioIn 16*
Hostetler, Sheri Ann 1962- *WhoWrEP 89*
Hostetter, Abram M 1929- *BiDrAPA 89*
Hostetter, Abram Martin 1929- *WhoE 91*
Hostetter, Charles Heiges 1950- *WhoAm 90*
Hostetter, Jay Tabb 1949- *St&PR 91*
Hostetter, Madonna M. 1941- *St&PR 91*
Hostetter, Mary Elizabeth Nieha 1961- *WhoSSW 91*
Hostetter, Robin E *BiDrAPA 89*
Hostettler, Stephen John 1931- *WhoAm 90*
Hostler, Charles Warren 1919- *WhoAm 90*
Hostler, Sharon Lee 1939- *WhoAm 90*
Hostos, Adolfo de 1887- *ConAu 131, HispWr 90*
Hostos, E. M. de *ConAu 131, HispWr 90*
Hostos, Eugenio M. de *ConAu 131, HispWr 90*
Hostos, Eugenio Maria *ConAu 131, HispWr 90*
Hostos, Eugenio Maria de 1839-1903 *BioIn 16, ConAu 131, HispWr 90*
Hostos y Bonilla, Eugenio Maria de 1839-1903 *HispWr 90*
Hostrop, Richard Winfred 1925- *WhoWrEP 89*
Hot Tuna *EncPR&S 89*
Hotaling, Danal L. 1914- *St&PR 91*
Hotaling, Denise Lowery 1957- *WhoEmL 91*
Hotchkies, Barry 1945- *WhoE 91*
Hotchkis, John 1916- *IntWWM 90*
Hotchkiss, Bill 1936- *WhoWrEP 89*
Hotchkiss, Charles Albert 1927- *St&PR 91*
Hotchkiss, Clarence Francis, Jr. 1928- *St&PR 91*
Hotchkiss, David Robert 1936- *St&PR 91*
Hotchkiss, Eugene, III 1928- *WhoAm 90*
Hotchkiss, Linda S *BiDrAPA 89*
Hotchkiss, Robert Kenneth 1954- *BiDrAPA 89*

Hotchkiss, Robert S. 1903-1989 *BioIn 16*
Hotchkiss, Rollin Douglas 1911- *WhoAm 90*
Hotchkiss, Sally McMurdo 1929- *WhoAmW 91*
Hotchkiss, Wesley Akin 1919- *WhoAm 90*
Hotchkiss, Winchester Fitch 1928- *WhoAm 90*
Hotchner, Aaron Edward 1920- *WhoAm 90*
Hotchner, John Mc Clure 1943- *WhoWrEP 89*
Hotelling, Harold 1945- *WhoEmL 91*
Hotes, William Joseph 1931- *WhoE 91*
Hoth, Agustin Carlos 1939- *St&PR 91*
Hothem, Bobbie Carol 1948- *WhoEmL 91*
Hotoke, Shigeru 1927- *IntWWM 90*
Hotopp, Thomas Bruce 1941- *St&PR 91*
Hott, Katherine May 1948- *BiDrAPA 89*
Hotta, Yasushi 1931- *St&PR 91*
Hotte, A. Paul L. 1920- *St&PR 91*
Hottel, Hoyt Clarke 1903- *WhoAm 90*
Hottenstein, Evelyn Jeanette Kenny 1948- *WhoAmW 91*
Hotter, Hans 1909- *IntWWM 90, PenDiMP*
Hotteterre, Jacques 1674-1762 *PenDiMP*
Hottin, Paule *BiDrAPA 89*
Hottinger, John Creighton 1945- *WhoEmL 91*
Hottinger, Michael Richard 1951- *WhoAm 90*
Hottinger, Paul *St&PR 91*
Hottois, Lawrence Daniel 1933- *St&PR 91, WhoAm 90*
Hotvedt, Kris J 1943- *WhoAmA 91*
Hotz, Gunter 1931- *WhoWor 91*
Hotz, Henry Palmer 1925- *WhoAm 90*
Hotz, Jimmy Christian 1953- *WhoEmL 91*
Hotz, John A. 1943- *St&PR 91*
Hotz, Peter Rudolf 1942- *WhoWor 91*
Hotz, Rachelle *BiDrAPA 89*
Hotz, Robert H. 1944- *St&PR 91*
Hotz, Robert Henry 1944- *WhoAm 90*
Hotze, Charles Wayne 1919- *WhoAm 90*
Hotze, Henry 1834-1887 *BioIn 16*
Hou, Chi Ming 1924- *WhoAm 90*
Hou, Runyu 1945- *IntWWM 90*
Hou, Tien-Kuei *BiDrAPA 89*
Houben, Francine 1955- *WomArch*
Houbolt, John Cornelius 1919- *WhoAm 90*
Houbrick, Richard Stephen 1937- *WhoAm 90*
Houchard, Michael Harlow 1935- *WhoSSW 91*
Houchin, John Frederick 1945- *WhoE 91*
Houck, Arthur Dean 1938- *St&PR 91*
Houck, Byron 1891-1969 *Ballpl 90*
Houck, Carl Augustus 1955- *BiDrAPA 89*
Houck, Charles Weston 1933- *WhoAm 90*
Houck, Donald 1932- *St&PR 91*
Houck, Donald Lee 1935- *WhoE 91*
Houck, Edward Bernard, II 1948- *WhoSSW 91*
Houck, James I. 1941- *WhoAm 90, WhoE 91*
Houck, John Burton 1928- *WhoAm 90*
Houck, John Candee 1931- *WhoAm 90*
Houck, John H 1919- *BiDrAPA 89*
Houck, John M. 1946- *St&PR 91*
Houck, John Roland 1923- *WhoAm 90*
Houck, Lewis Daniel, Jr. 1932- *WhoE 91, WhoWor 91*
Houck, Oliver Austin 1939- *WhoAm 90*
Houck, Robert Edward 1950- *WhoSSW 91*
Houck, Sharon Lu Thomas 1952- *WhoAmW 91*
Houck, William 1953- *WhoSSW 91*
Houck, William Russell 1926- *WhoAm 90, WhoSSW 91*
Houde, James Armand 1945- *WhoSSW 91*
Houde, John Michael 1959- *WhoEmL 91*
Houdek, Robert G. 1940- *WhoAm 90*
Houdeshel, William R. 1928- *St&PR 91*
Houdin, Jean-Eugene Robert- 1805-1871 *BioIn 16*
Houdini *MajTwCW*
Houdini, Harry 1874-1926 *BioIn 16, EncO&P 3, EncPaPR 91, WorAlBi*
Houdon, Jean Antoine 1741-1828 *IntDcAA 90, WorAlBi*
Houdret, Jeffrey John 1945- *WhoEmL 91*
Houel, Patrick 1942- *WhoWor 91*
Houfek, Edward Emil 1925- *BiDrAPA 89*
Hougan, Carolyn Aileen 1943- *WhoAmW 91*
Hougan, Tom McKay 1935- *St&PR 91*
Hougen, H. Montgomery 1935- *St&PR 91*
Hougen, Jon Torger 1936- *WhoAm 90*
Hough, Aubrey Johnston, Jr. 1944- *WhoAm 90*
Hough, Bonnie Arline *BiDrAPA 89*
Hough, C. Royce 1937- *WhoAm 90, WhoSSW 91*
Hough, Cass Sheffield 1904- *St&PR 91*
Hough, Charles N., Jr. 1934- *St&PR 91*
Hough, Charles Royce, III 1937- *St&PR 91*
Hough, Charlie 1948- *Ballpl 90*
Hough, David Allen 1946- *WhoWor 91*
Hough, David W 1956- *BiDrAPA 89*
Hough, Eldred Wilson 1916- *WhoAm 90*
Hough, Frank *Ballpl 90*
Hough, George Anthony, III 1920- *WhoAm 90*
Hough, Graham 1908-1990 *ConAu 132*
Hough, Grant H. 1941- *St&PR 91*
Hough, Gregory Glenn 1960- *WhoEmL 91*
Hough, Jack Van Doren 1920- *WhoSSW 91*
Hough, Janet Gerda Campbell 1948- *WhoAmW 91, WhoEmL 91*
Hough, Jennine 1948- *WhoAmA 91*
Hough, John Gordon 1936- *St&PR 91*
Hough, Joseph H. 1953- *WhoEmL 91*
Hough, Judy Taylor 1932- *SmATA 63 [port]*
Hough, Lawrence Alan 1944- *St&PR 91*
Hough, Margaret Brooks 1939- *WhoSSW 91*
Hough, Mark Taylor 1949- *WhoE 91*
Hough, Patricia L *BiDrAPA 89*
Hough, R.T. 1923- *St&PR 91*
Hough, Richard Alexander 1922- *AuBYP 90*
Hough, Richard Ralston 1917- *WhoAm 90*
Hough, S B 1917- *TwCCr&M 91*
Hough, Stephen 1961- *IntWWM 90*
Hough, Thomas Henry Michael 1933- *WhoAm 90*
Hough-Dunnette, Leaetta Marie 1947- *WhoAmW 91*
Hough-Goldstein, Judith Anne 1950- *WhoAmW 91*
Houghtalen, Rory Philip 1959- *BiDrAPA 89*
Houghtaling, Colleen Joy 1957- *WhoWrEP 89*
Houghtaling, Pamela Ann 1949- *WhoEmL 91*
Houghtelin, Cheryl Ann 1957- *WhoAmW 91*
Houghteling, James Lawrence 1920-1990 *BioIn 16*
Houghton, A.E. 1931- *St&PR 91*
Houghton, Alan Nourse 1924- *WhoAm 90*
Houghton, Alanson Bigelow 1863-1941 *BioIn 16*
Houghton, Amory 1899-1981 *BioIn 16*
Houghton, Amory, Jr. *BioIn 16*
Houghton, Amory, Jr. 1926- *WhoAm 90, WhoE 91*
Houghton, Arthur A., Jr. 1906-1990 *NewYTBS 90, WhoAmA 91N*
Houghton, Arthur Amory 1906-1990 *BioIn 16*
Houghton, Arthur Amory, Jr. 1906- *WhoAm 90*
Houghton, Arthur Boyd 1836-1875 *WhNaAH*
Houghton, Barbara Jean 1947- *WhoAmA 91*
Houghton, Charles Frederick 1839-1898 *DcCanB 12*
Houghton, Charles Norris 1909- *WhoAm 90*
Houghton, David Drew 1938- *WhoAm 90*
Houghton, David L. 1953- *St&PR 91*
Houghton, Donald Cary 1946- *WhoAm 90*
Houghton, Donald Charles 1934- *St&PR 91*
Houghton, Eric 1930- *AuBYP 90*
Houghton, George Knight 1929- *St&PR 91*
Houghton, Georgiana 1814-1884 *BiDWomA*
Houghton, Georgina *EncO&P 3*
Houghton, James O. *BioIn 16*
Houghton, James R. 1936- *St&PR 91*
Houghton, James Richardson 1936- *WhoAm 90, WhoE 91, WhoWor 91*
Houghton, Judith Dean 1939- *WhoAmW 91*
Houghton, Katharine 1945- *ConAu 130, WhoAm 90*
Houghton, Kenneth L. 1960- *WhoE 91*
Houghton, Mary Alice 1940- *BiDrAPA 89*
Houghton, Michael *EncO&P 3*
Houghton, Proctor Willis 1916- *St&PR 91*
Houghton, R E C 1896-1990 *ConAu 132*
Houghton, Richard Monckton Milnes, Baron 1809-1885 *BioIn 16*
Houghton, Rodney Adam *BiDrAPA 89*
Houghton, Sidney Paul 1938- *St&PR 91*
Houghton, Stephen W. 1939- *WhoAm 90*
Houghton, Timothy Dane 1955- *WhoWrEP 89*
Houghton, William John, Jr. 1938- *BiDrAPA 89*
Houghton, Woodson Plyer 1893- *WhoAm 90, WhoWor 91*
Hougland, Curtis R. *St&PR 91*
Houk, Edwynn L 1952- *WhoAmA 91*
Houk, Lawrence Ernest 1924- *St&PR 91*
Houk, Marion D. 1933- *St&PR 91*
Houk, Nancy 1940- *WhoAmW 91*
Houk, Pamela P 1935- *WhoAmA 91*
Houk, Ralph 1919- *Ballpl 90*
Houk, Robert Louis 1937- *BiDrAPA 89*
Houk, Stephen Donald 1956- *St&PR 91, WhoEmL 91*
Houk, Vernon Neal 1929- *WhoAm 90*
Houlbrooke, Ralph 1944- *ConAu 132*
Houlding, John D. 1921- *St&PR 91*
Houle, Cyril Orvin 1913- *WhoAm 90*
Houle, Diane Elizabeth 1930- *WhoAmW 91*
Houle, Eugene S. 1936- *St&PR 91*
Houle, Frances Anne 1952- *WhoAmW 91*
Houle, Gerard 1953- *St&PR 91*
Houle, Guy 1935- *St&PR 91*
Houle, J. Barker 1920- *St&PR 91*
Houle, Joseph E. 1930- *WhoAm 90*
Houle, Leopold 1883-1953 *OxCCanT*
Houle, Rita C. 1947- *WhoAmW 91*
Houlgate, Deke 1930- *ODwPR 91*
Houlgate, Jack Leonard 1940- *WhoSSW 91*
Houlihan, Brian T. 1944- *WhoWrEP 89*
Houlihan, Christina Erin 1962- *WhoWrEP 89*
Houlihan, Hilda Imelio 1937- *WhoAm 90*
Houlihan, Joseph Patrick 1949- *WhoEmL 91*
Houlihan, Patrick T 1942- *WhoAmA 91*
Houlihan, Phillip 1956- *IntWWM 90*
Houlihan, Richard Patrick 1933- *St&PR 91*
Houlihan, Robert A. 1938- *St&PR 91*
Houlihan, Timothy De Quetteville 1954- *IntWWM 90*
Houliston, George Baillie 1834?-1891 *DcCanB 12*
Houlne, Paul Joseph 1931- *St&PR 91*
Hoult, Norah 1898-1984 *FemiCLE*
Hoult, Peter John 1943- *WhoAm 90*
Houlton, Loyce J. 1926- *WhoAm 90*
Houlton, Peggy Mann *NewYTBS 90*
Houminer, Ehud *St&PR 91, WhoAm 90*
Houndjahoue, Michel 1949- *WhoWor 91*
Hounsfield, Godfrey N. 1919- *WorAlBi*
Hounsfield, Godfrey Newbold 1919- *WhoWor 91*
Hounshell, Charles David 1920- *WhoAm 90*
Hounshell, David A. 1950- *ConAu 129*
Hountras, Peter Timothy 1927- *WhoAm 90*
Houphouet-Boigny, Felix 1905- *BiDFrPL, WhoWor 91*
Houpis, Constantine Harry 1922- *WhoAm 90*
Houpt, Charles Landon 1928- *St&PR 91*
Houpt, Gary Lynn 1936- *WhoE 91*
Houpt, Grover K. 1932- *St&PR 91*
Houpt, Jeffrey Lyle 1941- *BiDrAPA 89*
Houpt, Jeffrey Lyle 1942- *WhoAm 90*
Houpt, Waynbe Edison, Jr. 1951- *BiDrAPA 89*
Hourani, Cecil 1917- *ConAu 129*
Hourcade, Jack Joseph 1953- *WhoEmL 91*
Houren, Jay Randle 1958- *WhoEmL 91*
Hourican, Thomas P. 1954- *St&PR 91*
Hourigan, Diane Renae 1949- *WhoEmL 91*
Hourihan, Thomas J. 1934- *St&PR 91*
Housand, Jonathan W 1939- *St&PR 91*
House, Adrian *BioIn 16*
House, Amelia *FemiCLE*
House, Arthur H. 1942- *St&PR 91*
House, Arthur Kinnear 1932- *St&PR 91*
House, Arthur Stephen 1921- *WhoAm 90*
House, Carleen Faye 1950- *WhoAmW 91, WhoEmL 91, WhoWor 91*
House, Charles Albert 1916- *AuBYP 90*
House, Charles Brewer, Jr. 1927- *WhoAm 90*
House, Charles Robert 1930- *St&PR 91*
House, Charles Staver 1908- *WhoAm 90*
House, Delpha LeAnn 1953- *WhoEmL 91*
House, Donald Lee, Sr. 1941- *WhoAm 90, WhoSSW 91*
House, Edward Howard 1836-1901 *BioIn 16*
House, Edward M. 1858-1938 *WorAlBi*
House, Edward Mandell 1858-1938 *BioIn 16*
House, Edwin Wesley 1939- *WhoAm 90*
House, Eric 1923- *OxCCanT*
House, Floyd L *BiDrAPA 89*
House, Frank 1930- *Ballpl 90*
House, James Charles, Jr 1902- *WhoAmA 91N*
House, Jerry L. 1950- *WhoEmL 91*
House, John David *BioIn 16*
House, John W. 1941- *WhoAm 90*
House, Joseph Wayne 1931- *WhoSSW 91*
House, Karen Elliott 1947- *ConAu 130, WhoAm 90, WhoAmW 91, WhoWor 91*
House, Kenneth M *BiDrAPA 89*
House, Leland Ralph 1929- *WhoWor 91*
House, Mary Anne 1950- *WhoAmW 91*
House, Patricia Joyce 1962- *WhoSSW 91*
House, Richard Calvin 1927- *WhoWrEP 89*
House, Robert E. 1924- *St&PR 91*
House, Robert James 1932- *WhoAm 90*
House, Robert Martin, Jr. *BiDrAPA 89*
House, Robert Stanley 1944- *WhoE 91*
House, Robert William 1920- *IntWWM 90, WhoAm 90*
House, Robert William 1927- *WhoAm 90*
House, Roy C. 1917- *WhoAm 90*
House, Sherwood G. 1935- *St&PR 91*
House, Stanley Gartenhaus 1920- *WhoSSW 91*
House, Suda Kay 1951- *WhoAmA 91*
House, Susan Patricia 1959- *WhoAmW 91, WhoEmL 91*
House, Tom 1947- *Ballpl 90*
House, William A. *BioIn 16*
Houseal, John Irving, Jr. 1945- *WhoSSW 91*
Household, Geoffrey 1900-1988 *AnObit 1988, BioIn 16, TwCCr&M 91*
Household, Geoffrey Edward West 1900-1988 *SpyFic*
Householder, Paul 1958- *Ballpl 90*
Houseknecht, Thomas R 1928- *BiDrAPA 89*
Housel, Glenda Joy *BiDrAPA 89*
Housel, Jerry Winters 1912- *WhoAm 90*
Houselander, Caryll 1901-1954 *BioIn 16*
Houseman, Ann Elizabeth Lord 1936- *WhoAmW 91, WhoE 91*
Houseman, David E. 1941- *St&PR 91*
Houseman, Jack 1940- *ODwPR 91*
Houseman, John *BioIn 16*
Houseman, John 1902- *WorAlBi*
Houseman, John 1902-1988 *AnObit 1988*
Housen, Sevrin 1948- *WhoWrEP 89*
Houser, Allan C 1914- *WhoAmA 91*
Houser, Caroline Mae *WhoAmA 91*
Houser, Carrol D. 1929- *St&PR 91*
Houser, Christopher I.M. 1936- *St&PR 91*
Houser, Douglas Guy 1935- *WhoAm 90*
Houser, Dwane R. 1935- *St&PR 91*
Houser, Gregory John 1948- *St&PR 91*
Houser, Harold Byron 1921- *WhoAm 90*
Houser, James Cowing, Jr. 1928- *WhoSSW 91*
Houser, Jim 1928- *WhoAmA 91*
Houser, John Edward 1928- *WhoSSW 91, WhoWor 91*
Houser, John W. *BioIn 16*
Houser, Keith A. 1948- *WhoSSW 91*
Houser, Kris Dauene 1961- *BiDrAPA 89*
Houser, Louise Kelley 1919- *WhoAmW 91*
Houser, Michael Lawrence 1952- *WhoSSW 91*
Houser, Michael Robert 1951- *St&PR 91*
Houser, Norman W. *AuBYP 90*
Houser, Richard Allan *BiDrAPA 89*
Houser, Theodore V. 1892-1963 *WorAlBi*
Houser, William Douglas 1921- *WhoAm 90*
Houseworth, Richard Court 1928- *St&PR 91, WhoAm 90*
Housewright, Artemis Skevakis 1927- *WhoAmA 91*
Housewright, James Tipton 1956- *WhoEmL 91*
Housewright, Riley Dee 1913- *WhoAm 90*
Housewright, Wiley Lee 1913- *IntWWM 90, WhoAm 90*
Housey, John James 1917- *St&PR 91*
Housey, John James, Jr. 1942- *St&PR 91*
Housh, E. William 1932- *BioIn 16*
Houshiary, Shirazeh 1955- *BiDWomA*
Houska, Charles Robert 1927- *WhoAm 90*
Houskeeper, Barbara 1922- *WhoAmA 91*
Housley, John Howard 1953- *WhoE 91*
Housman, A. E. 1859-1936 *BioIn 16*
Housman, A E 1859-1936 *MajTwCW, PoeCrit 2 [port]*
Housman, A. E. 1859-1936 *WorAlBi*
Housman, Alfred Edward 1859-1936 *BioIn 16, EncPaPR 91*
Housman, Arthur Lloyd 1928- *WhoAm 90*
Housman, Charles J. 1927- *St&PR 91*
Housman, H *BiDEWW, FemiCLE*
Housman, Harry J. 1942- *St&PR 91*
Housman, Kenneth A. 1955- *St&PR 91*
Housman, Russell F 1928- *WhoAmA 91*
Houssa, Nicole 1930-1959 *EncCoWW*
Houssay, Bernardo A. 1887-1971 *WorAlBi*
Houston, Alfred Dearborn 1940- *St&PR 91, WhoAm 90*
Houston, Alma Faye 1944- *BiDrAPA 89*
Houston, B. Ord 1912- *St&PR 91*
Houston, Beverle Ann 1935-1988 *BioIn 16*
Houston, Bruce 1937- *WhoAmA 91*
Houston, Caroline Margaret 1964- *WhoAmW 91*
Houston, Cissy *BioIn 16, DrBIPA 90*
Houston, David Franklin 1866-1940 *BiDrUSE 89*
Houston, David Robert 1941- *St&PR 91*
Houston, Dorine Syme 1951- *WhoAmW 91*
Houston, Elisha Hilton 1940- *WhoSSW 91*
Houston, Elizabeth Reece Manasco 1935- *WhoAmW 91, WhoWor 91*
Houston, Frederick 1917- *BiDrAPA 89*
Houston, Gary William 1948- *St&PR 91*

Houston, Gloria 1940- *WhoAmW 91, WhoSSW 91*
Houston, Heather Ann 1955- *WhoEmL 91*
Houston, Howard Edwin 1910- *WhoAm 90*
Houston, Ian 1941- *ODwPR 91*
Houston, Ian Briercliffe 1932- *WhoWor 91*
Houston, Ivan J. 1925- *St&PR 91*
Houston, Ivan James 1925- *WhoAm 90*
Houston, J. Gorman, Jr. 1933- *WhoAm 90*
Houston, James A. 1921- *BioIn 16, WhoAmA 91*
Houston, James Archibald 1921- *WhoAm 90*
Houston, James D. 1933- *WhoWrEP 89*
Houston, Jean *EncO&P 3, EncPaPR 91, NewAgE 90*
Houston, Jeanna Beth 1951- *WhoSSW 91*
Houston, Joan 1928- *AuBYP 90*
Houston, Joe *BioIn 16*
Houston, John Albert 1914- *WhoAm 90*
Houston, John Albert 1940- *WhoSSW 91*
Houston, John Coates, Jr. 1909- *WhoAm 90*
Houston, John Phillip 1949- *BiDrAPA 89*
Houston, John Stewart *WhoAmA 91*
Houston, Johnny Lee 1941- *WhoSSW 91*
Houston, Joseph S *BiDrAPA 89*
Houston, Karl LaVon 1964- *WhoSSW 91*
Houston, Lee Hammond, Jr. 1944- *WhoSSW 91*
Houston, Libby 1941- *FemiCLE*
Houston, Lock E. 1820?- *AmLegL*
Houston, Margaret L. 1819-1867 *BioAmW*
Houston, Margaret Moffette Lea 1819-1867 *BioIn 16*
Houston, Mary Etta 1912- *WhoAmA 91*
Houston, Mora *ODwPR 91*
Houston, Nancy Marie 1948- *WhoEmL 91*
Houston, Neal Bryan 1928- *WhoSSW 91*
Houston, Peyton Hoge 1910- *WhoAm 90, WhoWor 91*
Houston, R. B. *TwCCr&M 91*
Houston, Ralph M. 1903-1988 *BioIn 16*
Houston, Robert Alan 1946- *St&PR 91*
Houston, Robert Ewing, Jr. 1943- *WhoSSW 91*
Houston, Robert Stroud 1923- *WhoAm 90*
Houston, Rodney Guy 1954- *WhoSSW 91*
Houston, Roy T. 1945- *St&PR 91*
Houston, Sam 1793-1863 *WorAlBi*
Houston, Sam 1932- *St&PR 91*
Houston, Samuel 1793-1863 *BioIn 16, WhNaAH*
Houston, Samuel Lee 1951- *WhoEmL 91*
Houston, Seawadon L. 1942- *St&PR 91*
Houston, Shepard P. *AmLegL*
Houston, Shirley Mae 1938- *WhoWor 91*
Houston, Temple Lea 1860-1905 *BioIn 16*
Houston, Thelma *DrBlPA 90*
Houston, Tom *BioIn 16*
Houston, Whitney *BioIn 16*
Houston, Whitney 1963- *DrBlPA 90, EncPR&S 89, OxCPMus, WhoAm 90, WhoAmW 91, WorAlBi*
Houston, Will *ConAu 31NR*
Houston, William 1755-1813 *BioIn 16*
Houston, William Churchill 1746?-1788 *BioIn 16*
Houston, William Robert Montgomery 1922- *WhoWor 91*
Houston, William Tennent 1950- *St&PR 91*
Houstoun, Lawrence Orson, Jr. 1929- *WhoAm 90*
Houstoun, Matilda Charlotte 1815?-1892 *FemiCLE*
Houstoun, William 1755-1813 *BioIn 16*
Hout, Lucien van *PenDiMP*
Houtchens, Barnard 1911- *WhoAm 90*
Houtchens, C. J. 1952- *WhoE 91*
Houtchens, Robert Austin, Jr. 1953- *WhoAm 90*
Houtepen, Anton Willem Joseph 1940- *WhoWor 91*
Houthakker, Hendrik S. 1924- *BioIn 16*
Houthakker, Hendrik Samuel 1924- *WhoAm 90*
Houts, Don Lewis 1950- *BiDrAPA 89*
Houts, Marshall Wilson 1919- *WhoAm 90, WhoWor 91*
Houtte, Melissa 1950- *WhoAm 90*
Houtteman, Art 1927- *Ballpl 90*
Houtz, Heywood Barron 1936- *St&PR 91*
Houtz, Jim H. 1936- *St&PR 91*
Houtz, K.H. 1927- *St&PR 91*
Houx, Shirley Ann 1931- *WhoAmW 91*
Houze De L'Aulnoit, Patrick Gaspard 1954- *WhoWor 91*
Houziaux, Leo Narcisse Omer 1932- *WhoWor 91*
Hovanec, Robert Michael 1954- *St&PR 91*
Hovanesian, Joseph Der 1930- *WhoAm 90*
Hovanessian, Shahen Alexander 1931- *WhoAm 90*
Hovannes, John 1904-1973 *WhoAmA 91N*
Hovannesian, Albert S. 1924- *St&PR 91*
Hovannesian, Rose A. 1920- *St&PR 91*
Hovannisian, Richard G. 1932- *WhoAm 90*
Hovany, Cherie 1955- *WhoEmL 91*
Hovda, Allen A *BiDrAPA 89*
Hovde, Carl Frederick 1926- *WhoAm 90*
Hovde, Howard *BioIn 16*
Hovdesven, Arne 1928- *WhoAm 90*
Hovdey, Suzanne Shirley 1953- *ODwPR 91*
Hove, Julian Phillops 1937- *St&PR 91*
Hoveland, Janet Rae *BiDrAPA 89*
Hovell, Lucille A. *AuBYP 90*
Hovell, Lucy A. 1916- *AuBYP 90*
Hovell, Susan M. 1961- *WhoAmW 91*
Hovell, Walter Lee 1928- *St&PR 91*
Hovelmann, Gerd 1956- *EncPaPR 91*
Hovelson, Doug 1950- *ODwPR 91*
Hoven, Deborah Camille 1955- *WhoAmW 91*
Hovenier, Joachim W. 1936- *WhoWor 91*
Hover, John Calvin, II 1943- *St&PR 91, WhoAm 90*
Hovermale, Lisa Simone *BiDrAPA 89*
Hovermale, Ronald L. 1939- *St&PR 91*
Hoverstad, Ronald Alan 1951- *WhoSSW 91*
Hoversten, Philip Everard 1947- *WhoAm 90*
Hovet, Mary R. 1917- *WhoAmW 91*
Hovey, Alan Edwin, Jr. 1933- *WhoE 91*
Hovey, Alvah 1820-1903 *BioIn 16*
Hovey, Charles F. 1909- *St&PR 91*
Hovey, George Melvin 1929- *St&PR 91*
Hovey, Justus Allan, Jr. 1922- *WhoAm 90, WhoWor 91*
Hovey, Louis Mealus 1930- *St&PR 91*
Hovey, Serge 1920-1989 *BioIn 16*
Hovey, Walter Read 1949-1982 *WhoAmA 91N*
Hovgard, Carl 1905- *WhoAm 90*
Hovgard, Carl 1905-1989 *BioIn 16*
Hovhaness, Alan *BioIn 16*
Hovhaness, Alan 1911- *IntWWM 90, PenDiMP A, WhoAm 90*
Hovin, Arne William 1922- *WhoAm 90*
Hoving, John Hannes Forester 1923- *WhoAm 90, WhoWor 91*
Hoving, Thomas 1931- *WhoAm 90, WhoAmA 91, WhoWrEP 89*
Hoving, Walter 1897-1989 *AnObit 1989, BioIn 16, CurBio 90N*
Hovis, Cherie Lynn 1952- *WhoAmW 91*
Hovis, Janet Fowler 1931- *WhoSSW 91*
Hovis, Lorraine Baugher 1942- *WhoAmW 91*
Hovis, Melanie *ODwPR 91*
Hovley, Steve 1944- *Ballpl 90*
Hovman, Klavs 1957- *IntWWM 90*
Hovnanian, Armen 1930- *St&PR 91*
Hovnanian, H. Philip 1920- *WhoAm 90, WhoWor 91*
Hovsepian, Abraham 1926- *St&PR 91*
Hovsepian, Leon 1915- *WhoAmA 91, WhoE 91*
Hovsepian, Vatche 1930- *WhoAm 90*
How, Julia Beatrice 1867-1932 *BiDWomA*
How, Martin John Richard 1931- *IntWWM 90*
How Joo, Tan 1955- *WhoWor 91*
Howald, Alan Bert 1945- *WhoEmL 91*
Howalt, F. Harvey, Jr. 1926- *St&PR 91*
Howalt, Frederick Harvey, Jr. 1926- *WhoAm 90*
Howar, Barbara 1934- *BioIn 16*
Howard, Dr. *DcCanB 12*
Howard, Alan Mackenzie 1937- *WhoWor 91*
Howard, Albert Jesse 1929- *St&PR 91*
Howard, Albert Warren 1913- *St&PR 91*
Howard, Allen Richmond, Jr. 1920- *WhoWor 91*
Howard, Alton Johnathan 1951- *WhoSSW 91*
Howard, Alvis *BioIn 16*
Howard, Andrew Blair 1960- *WhoEmL 91*
Howard, Ann 1936- *IntWWM 90, PenDiMP*
Howard, Ann Hubbard 1938- *WhoE 91*
Howard, Ann Johnson 1957- *BiDrAPA 89*
Howard, Anne *FemiCLE*
Howard, Anne 1558-1630 *BiDEWW*
Howard, Arabella 1655-1746 *BiDEWW*
Howard, Arlene Henley *WhoE 91*
Howard, Arthur Ellsworth Dick 1933- *WhoAm 90*
Howard, Aughtum Luciel Smith 1906- *WhoAmW 91*
Howard, August 1910-1988 *BioIn 16*
Howard, Barbara 1926- *WhoAmA 91*
Howard, Barbara June 1957- *WhoSSW 91*
Howard, Barbara Sue Mesner 1944- *WhoAm 90*
Howard, Barnaby John 1925- *WhoE 91*
Howard, Barry 1949- *WhoEmL 91*
Howard, Benjamin W. 1944- *WhoWrEP 89*
Howard, Bernard Eufinger 1920- *WhoSSW 91, WhoWor 91*
Howard, Betty Ruth 1946- *WhoWrEP 89*
Howard, Bion Bradbury 1912- *WhoAm 90*
Howard, Bion Dickerson 1950- *WhoE 91*
Howard, Bruce 1943- *Ballpl 90*
Howard, Bruce Frank 1924- *WhoSSW 91*
Howard, Bruce L. *St&PR 91*
Howard, Burton D. 1938- *St&PR 91*
Howard, Byron Laburt 1940- *BiDrAPA 89*
Howard, C Jeriel 1939- *ConAu 31NR*
Howard, C. Robert 1914- *St&PR 91*
Howard, Carl 1920- *WhoAm 90*
Howard, Carole M. *ODwPR 91*
Howard, Carole Margaret 1945- *St&PR 91*
Howard, Catherine Mary 1683-1753 *BiDEWW*
Howard, Cecil 1888-1956 *WhoAmA 91N*
Howard, Cecil Ray 1937- *WhoAmA 91*
Howard, Charles 1919- *WhoAm 90*
Howard, Charles T. *AmLegL*
Howard, Cheryl Lynn 1947- *WhoAmW 91*
Howard, Christina Schneider 1945- *St&PR 91*
Howard, Cindy Lee 1959- *WhoEmL 91*
Howard, Clark 1934- *TwCCr&M 91*
Howard, Clifford Norman 1926- *St&PR 91*
Howard, Clifton M 1922- *BiDrAPA 89*
Howard, Clifton Merton 1922- *WhoE 91*
Howard, Clinton H. 1928- *St&PR 91*
Howard, Cordelia 1848-1941 *BioIn 16, NotWoAT*
Howard, Daggett Horton 1917- *WhoAm 90, WhoE 91, WhoWor 91*
Howard, Dan F 1931- *WhoAmA 91*
Howard, David *WhoAmA 91*
Howard, David 1929- *WhoE 91, WhoWor 91*
Howard, David 1937- *WhoAm 90*
Howard, David E. 1952- *WhoAm 90*
Howard, David H. 1944- *WhoWrEP 89*
Howard, David John 1947- *WhoEmL 91*
Howard, Davis Jonathan 1954- *WhoE 91*
Howard, Dean Denton 1927- *WhoAm 90*
Howard, Deborah 1957- *WhoEmL 91*
Howard, Deborah Ann 1950- *WhoEmL 91*
Howard, Deborah Susanne 1956- *WhoAmW 91*
Howard, Del 1877-1956 *Ballpl 90*
Howard, Dennis Martin 1930- *WhoE 91*
Howard, Derek 1934- *St&PR 91*
Howard, Dewnzar Delia 1960- *BiDrAPA 89*
Howard, Don 1940- *WhoWrEP 89*
Howard, Donald F. 1928- *St&PR 91*
Howard, Donald Lee 1938- *St&PR 91*
Howard, Donald Roy 1927-1987 *BioIn 16*
Howard, Donald Searcy 1928- *St&PR 91, WhoAm 90*
Howard, Donna Marie 1953- *WhoSSW 91*
Howard, Donna Marie 1965- *WhoSSW 91*
Howard, Dorette Marie 1958- *WhoEmL 91*
Howard, Dudley Robin 1947- *WhoWor 91*
Howard, Duncan Lent 1940- *WhoAm 90*
Howard, Ebenezer 1850-1928 *BioIn 16*
Howard, Edward Lee *BioIn 16*
Howard, Elizabeth *ConAu 31NR*
Howard, Elizabeth 1907- *AuBYP 90*
Howard, Elizabeth 1950- *WhoAmW 91, WhoEmL 91*
Howard, Elizabeth Crawford 1939- *WhoWrEP 89*
Howard, Elizabeth Jane *BioIn 16*
Howard, Elizabeth Jane 1923- *FemiCLE*
Howard, Ellen 1943- *ConAu 130*
Howard, Elston 1929-1980 *Ballpl 90 [port]*
Howard, Ernest E., III 1943- *St&PR 91*
Howard, Esme 1863-1939 *BioIn 16*
Howard, Etchell 1942- *St&PR 91*
Howard, Eugene 1881-1965 *OxCPMus*
Howard, Eugene C. 1921- *St&PR 91*
Howard, Eugene W. 1923- *St&PR 91*
Howard, Frances N *BiDrAPA 89*
Howard, Frank 1936- *Ballpl 90 [port]*
Howard, Fred J. 1920-1989 *BioIn 16*
Howard, Frederick J. 1912- *St&PR 91*
Howard, Fredric Timothy 1939- *WhoSSW 91*
Howard, Gail Frances 1946- *WhoEmL 91*
Howard, Gary Scott 1951- *WhoEmL 91*
Howard, Gene Claude 1926- *WhoAm 90*
Howard, George 1944- *WhoSSW 91*
Howard, George, Jr. 1924- *WhoAm 90*
Howard, George Eulan 1935- *WhoAm 90*
Howard, George Marshall 1930- *WhoE 91*
Howard, George Sallade 1903- *IntWWM 90, WhoAm 90*
Howard, Gerald Kenneth 1934- *WhoAm 90*
Howard, Gerald Thomas 1938- *St&PR 91*
Howard, Gertrude 1892-1934 *DrBlPA 90*
Howard, Graeme Keith, Jr. 1932- *St&PR 91*
Howard, Gregory Charles 1947- *WhoE 91*
Howard, Harry Clay 1929- *WhoAm 90*
Howard, Hartley *TwCCr&M 91*
Howard, Helen Arlene 1927- *WhoAm 90*
Howard, Henrietta 1681-1767 *BioIn 16*
Howard, Herbert Hoover 1928- *WhoSSW 91*
Howard, Hildegarde 1901- *WhoAm 90*
Howard, Hillard *BioIn 16*
Howard, Howell H. 1927- *St&PR 91*
Howard, Howell James, Jr. *BiDrAPA 89*
Howard, Hubert Wendell 1927- *WhoAm 90*
Howard, Hugh C. 1929- *St&PR 91*
Howard, Humbert L 1915- *WhoAmA 91*
Howard, Irmgard Keeler 1941- *WhoAmW 91*
Howard, J. Daniel 1943- *WhoAm 90*
Howard, J. L. 1941- *WhoSSW 91*
Howard, J. Woodford, Jr. 1931- *WhoAm 90*
Howard, Jack 1924- *WhoAm 90*
Howard, Jack Monroe 1931- *WhoSSW 91, WhoWor 91*
Howard, Jack Rohe 1910- *WhoAm 90*
Howard, Jacqueline Sue 1954- *WhoAmW 91*
Howard, James, III 1935- *St&PR 91*
Howard, James Arthur *BiDrAPA 89*
Howard, James Dale *BiDrAPA 89*
Howard, James J. *BioIn 16*
Howard, James Joseph 1950- *WhoE 91*
Howard, James Joseph, III 1935- *WhoAm 90*
Howard, James Kenton 1943- *WhoSSW 91*
Howard, James Merriam, Jr. 1922- *WhoAm 90*
Howard, James Michael 1954- *WhoSSW 91*
Howard, James Thomas 1945- *BiDrAPA 89, WhoSSW 91*
Howard, James Webb 1925- *WhoAm 90, WhoWor 91*
Howard, Jane Temple 1935- *WhoWrEP 89*
Howard, Janet Anne 1946- *WhoAmW 91*
Howard, Janet Schlenker 1950- *WhoAmW 91*
Howard, Jay Lloyd 1951- *St&PR 91*
Howard, Jeffrey *BioIn 16*
Howard, Jeffrey Hjalmar 1944- *WhoAm 90*
Howard, Jerry A. 1942- *St&PR 91*
Howard, Jerry Wayne 1944- *St&PR 91*
Howard, Jesse 1885-1983 *MusmAFA*
Howard, Joan Alice 1929- *WhoAmW 91, WhoE 91, WhoWor 91*
Howard, Joe 1878-1961 *OxCPMus*
Howard, Joe L. 1941- *St&PR 91*
Howard, Joerena Young *WhoAmW 91*
Howard, John 1943- *SmATA X [port]*
Howard, John A. 1950- *WhoAm 90*
Howard, John Addison 1921- *WhoAm 90*
Howard, John Arnold 1915- *WhoAm 90*
Howard, John Brigham 1912- *WhoAm 90*
Howard, John Fitzallen 1930- *St&PR 91*
Howard, John Fred 1941- *St&PR 91*
Howard, John G, Jr. *BiDrAPA 89*
Howard, John Lindsay 1931- *WhoAm 90*
Howard, John Michael 1949- *St&PR 91*
Howard, John Raymond 1938- *WhoAm 90*
Howard, John Robert 1940- *St&PR 91*
Howard, John Stuart 1950- *IntWWM 90*
Howard, John Tasker 1911- *WhoAm 90*
Howard, John Vincent 1933- *St&PR 91*
Howard, John Wilfred 1924- *WhoSSW 91, WhoWor 91*
Howard, John Winston 1939- *BioIn 16, WhoWor 91*
Howard, Joseph Clemens 1922- *WhoAm 90*
Howard, Joseph Edgar 1867-1961 *BioIn 16*
Howard, Joseph Harvey 1931- *WhoAm 90*
Howard, Judith Lois 1936- *WhoAmW 91*
Howard, Karen A. *BioIn 16*
Howard, Kathleen 1947- *WhoAmW 91, WhoEmL 91*
Howard, Kathleen Janet 1949- *WhoEmL 91*
Howard, Ken 1944- *WorAlBi*
Howard, Kenneth Calvin, Jr. 1947- *WhoEmL 91*
Howard, Kenneth Joseph, Jr. 1944- *WhoAm 90*
Howard, Kid 1908-1966 *BioIn 16*
Howard, Kingston Lee 1929- *St&PR 91, WhoAm 90*
Howard, Kirk E. 1952- *St&PR 91*
Howard, L. Wayne 1947- *WhoEmL 91, WhoWor 91*
Howard, La Rue Cooke 1914- *WhoWrEP 89*
Howard, Laura Dianne Dobson 1951- *WhoE 91*
Howard, Laura K *BiDrAPA 89*
Howard, Lawrence A *BiDrAPA 89*
Howard, Lawrence Cabot 1925- *WhoAm 90*
Howard, Lee Milton 1922- *WhoAm 90*
Howard, Lee Scott 1959- *WhoE 91*
Howard, Leon *WhoAm 90*
Howard, Leslie 1893-1943 *WorAlBi*
Howard, Leslie James 1960- *WhoSSW 91*
Howard, Leslie John 1948- *IntWWM 90*
Howard, Linda 1934- *WhoAmA 91*
Howard, Linda Ann 1953- *WhoAmW 91*
Howard, Linda Kay *WhoSSW 91*
Howard, M. Francine 1939- *WhoAmW 91*

Howard, Marghanita Laski 1915-1988 *BioIn 16*
Howard, Marguerite Evangeline Barker 1921- *WhoAmW 91*
Howard, Marian Carmean 1926- *St&PR 91*
Howard, Mary Cynthia 1950- *WhoWrEP 89*
Howard, Mary Helen 1957- *WhoEmL 91*
Howard, Mary Matilda 1804-1893 *FemiCLE*
Howard, Mary Merle Prunty 1942- *WhoAmW 91*
Howard, Mary of the Holy Cross 1653-1735 *BiDEWW*
Howard, Maureen 1930- *BioIn 16, ConAu 31NR, MajTwCW*
Howard, Maurine Carroll 1945- *WhoEmL 91*
Howard, Melvin 1935- *St&PR 91, WhoAm 90*
Howard, Merrill J. 1930- *St&PR 91*
Howard, Michael *BioIn 16*
Howard, Michael D. 1954- *St&PR 91*
Howard, Michael Stockwin 1922- *IntWWM 90*
Howard, Michael Thomas 1950- *WhoE 91*
Howard, Mildred *BioIn 16*
Howard, Moses Leon 1928- *BioIn 16*
Howard, Moses William, Jr. 1946- *WhoAm 90*
Howard, Nathan Southard 1941- *WhoAm 90*
Howard, Nikki Speck 1953- *WhoEmL 91*
Howard, Noel S 1940- *BiDrAPA 89*
Howard, Noel Scott 1940- *WhoE 91*
Howard, Nora Oakes 1954- *WhoE 91*
Howard, Norman 1926- *WhoWor 91*
Howard, Norman E. 1947- *St&PR 91*
Howard, Norman Wrigley 1911- *WhoE 91*
Howard, Oliver Otis 1830-1909 *WhNaAH, WorAlBi*
Howard, Patricia 1937- *IntWWM 90*
Howard, Patricia Ann 1950- *WhoAmW 91*
Howard, Patrick Edward 1947- *St&PR 91*
Howard, Paul B. 1955- *St&PR 91*
Howard, Paul Leroy 1925- *St&PR 91*
Howard, Paul M *BiDrAPA 89*
Howard, Paul Noble, Jr. 1922- *WhoAm 90*
Howard, Paula Walton Ollick 1944- *WhoAmW 91*
Howard, Randy DeWayne 1934- *WhoWor 91*
Howard, Richard 1929- *BioIn 16, WhoAm 90, WhoWrEP 89*
Howard, Richard Alden 1917- *WhoE 91*
Howard, Richard James 1952- *WhoE 91*
Howard, Richard Ralston, II 1948- *WhoSSW 91*
Howard, Richard Turner 1935- *WhoAm 90*
Howard, Robert A 1922- *WhoAmA 91*
Howard, Robert Boardman 1896-1983 *WhoAmA 91N*
Howard, Robert C. 1931- *St&PR 91*
Howard, Robert Campbell, Jr. 1951- *WhoEmL 91*
Howard, Robert Clark 1931- *WhoAm 90*
Howard, Robert D. 1927- *St&PR 91*
Howard, Robert E. 1906-1936 *RGTwCSF*
Howard, Robert Ervin 1906-1936 *BioIn 16*
Howard, Robert Franklin 1932- *WhoAm 90*
Howard, Robert Frederick 1947- *WhoEmL 91*
Howard, Robert Miller 1919- *WhoAm 90*
Howard, Robert P. 1922- *St&PR 91*
Howard, Robert Pickrell 1905- *WhoE 91*
Howard, Robert Staples 1924- *WhoAm 90*
Howard, Robert W. 1954- *St&PR 91*
Howard, Robin 1924-1989 *AnObit 1989, BioIn 16*
Howard, Ron *BioIn 16*
Howard, Ron 1954- *WhoAm 90, WorAlBi*
Howard, Rosalind 1845-1921 *BioIn 16*
Howard, Roy B. 1929- *St&PR 91*
Howard, Roy W. 1883-1964 *WorAlBi*
Howard, Roy Wilson 1883-1964 *BioIn 16*
Howard, Royal M. 1922-1989 *BioIn 16*
Howard, Russell 1931- *IntWWM 90*
Howard, Ruth Colette 1958- *WhoAmW 91*
Howard, Sally *EarBlAP*
Howard, Sandria Gail 1969- *WhoEmL 91*
Howard, Sandy 1927- *WhoAm 90*
Howard, Sedgwick 1923- *St&PR 91*
Howard, Shirley Ann 1935- *WhoSSW 91*
Howard, Stanley Louis 1948- *WhoE 91, WhoEmL 91*
Howard, Stephen D 1937- *BiDrAPA 89*
Howard, Stephen Wrigley 1940- *WhoE 91*
Howard, Steven H. 1951- *St&PR 91*
Howard, Sumner 1835- *AmLegL*
Howard, Suzanne M. 1941- *St&PR 91*
Howard, Theodore Walter 1942- *St&PR 91, WhoAm 90*
Howard, Thomas Bailey, Jr. 1928- *WhoAm 90, WhoSSW 91*
Howard, Thomas Jackson 1942- *St&PR 91*
Howard, Thomas Smith 1950- *WhoEmL 91*
Howard, Timothy George 1946- *St&PR 91*
Howard, Timothy John 1950- *WhoEmL 91*
Howard, Trevor 1916-1988 *AnObit 1988, BioIn 16, WorAlBi*
Howard, Troy *ConAu 31NR*
Howard, Vance F. 1937- *St&PR 91*
Howard, Vernon Linwood 1918- *AuBYP 90*
Howard, W. Wayne 1949- *St&PR 91*
Howard, Walter Burke 1916- *WhoAm 90*
Howard, Warren F. *MajTwCW*
Howard, Wayne 1942- *IntWWM 90*
Howard, Wilbur 1947- *Ballpl 90*
Howard, William Allen 1912- *WhoE 91*
Howard, William Bradley 1957- *WhoEmL 91*
Howard, William C. 1933- *St&PR 91*
Howard, William F. 1916- *St&PR 91*
Howard, William Francis 1960- *WhoE 91*
Howard, William H. *St&PR 91*
Howard, William Herbert 1953- *WhoEmL 91*
Howard, William Jack 1922- *WhoAm 90*
Howard, William Peter *BioIn 16*
Howard, William Templeton, Jr. 1958- *WhoSSW 91*
Howard, Willie 1886-1949 *OxCPMus*
Howard-Carter, Theresa 1929- *WhoAm 90*
Howard-Hill, Trevor Howard 1933- *WhoSSW 91*
Howard-Howard, Margo Chanler 1935- *WhoWrEP 89*
Howard-Jones, Ray 1903- *BiDWomA*
Howard of Effingham, Baron 1643-1695 *BioIn 16*
Howard of Effingham, Francis 1643-1695 *EncCRAm*
Howarth, Anna 1854?-1943 *FemiCLE*
Howarth, Christopher Douglas 1948- *WhoWor 91*
Howarth, David H. 1936- *WhoAm 90*
Howarth, Elgar 1935- *IntWWM 90, PenDiMP, -A*
Howarth, Henry 1955- *WhoEmL 91*
Howarth, Judith 1960- *IntWWM 90*
Howarth, Richard Harper 1932- *WhoAm 90*
Howarth, Robert 1931- *St&PR 91*
Howarth, Shirley Reiff 1944- *WhoAmA 91*
Howarth, T. E. B. 1914-1988 *BioIn 16*
Howarth, Thomas 1921- *WhoAm 90*
Howarth, Thomas Edward Brodie 1914-1988 *BioIn 16*
Howat, Amy *BioIn 16*
Howat, Bruce Bradshaw, Jr. 1945- *St&PR 91*
Howat, John Keith 1937- *WhoAm 90, WhoAmA 91*
Howat, Robert Van Skiver 1933- *IntWWM 90*
Howatson, Marianne 1948- *WhoAm 90, WhoAmW 91*
Howatt, Cornelius 1810-1895 *DcCanB 12*
Howatt, Helen Clare 1927- *WhoAmW 91, WhoWor 91*
Howbert, Edgar Charles 1937- *WhoAm 90*
Howd, Janet 1940- *IntWWM 90*
Howdeshell, Angela I *BiDrAPA 89*
Howe, Art 1946- *Ballpl 90, WhoAm 90*
Howe, Brian Leslie 1936- *WhoWor 91*
Howe, Carroll Victor 1923- *WhoE 91*
Howe, Charles Chaffee 1945- *WhoE 91*
Howe, Charles H.S. 1933- *St&PR 91*
Howe, Daniel Walker 1937- *WhoAm 90*
Howe, Dean R. 1946- *St&PR 91*
Howe, Deborah 1946-1978 *BioIn 16*
Howe, Dianne Shelden 1949- *WhoEmL 91*
Howe, Don Duvall 1945- *BiDrAPA 89*
Howe, Donald Edward 1962- *WhoEmL 91*
Howe, Douglas James 1950- *WhoE 91*
Howe, E. W. 1853-1937 *BioIn 16*
Howe, Edmund Grant *BiDrAPA 89*
Howe, Edmund Grant, III 1944- *WhoE 91*
Howe, Elias 1819-1867 *WorAlBi*
Howe, Ellic 1910- *EncO&P 3*
Howe, Evelyn Freeman 1929- *WhoAmW 91*
Howe, Everett R. 1942- *St&PR 91*
Howe, F. L. 1926- *ODwPR 91*
Howe, Fanny *BioIn 16*
Howe, Fisher 1914- *WhoAm 90*
Howe, Florence 1929- *WhoAm 90*
Howe, Frank E. 1870-1956 *AmLegL*
Howe, Frederic Clemson 1867-1940 *BioIn 16*
Howe, Gary Lee *BiDrAPA 89*
Howe, Gary Woodson 1936- *WhoAm 90*
Howe, Geoffrey *BioIn 16*
Howe, Geoffrey 1926- *WhoWor 91, WorAlBi*
Howe, George Augustus 1724?-1758 *EncCRAm*
Howe, Gordie *BioIn 16*
Howe, Gordie 1928- *WorAlBi*
Howe, Gordon 1928- *WhoAm 90, WhoE 91*
Howe, Graham Lloyd 1950- *WhoAm 90*
Howe, Herbert Marshall 1912- *WhoAm 90*
Howe, Hugh Philip 1932- *WhoAm 90*
Howe, Irving *BioIn 16*
Howe, Irving 1920- *EncAL, MajTwCW, WhoAm 90, WhoWrEP 89, WorAlBi*
Howe, Irwin M. 1866-1934 *Ballpl 90*
Howe, James 1946- *AuBYP 90, BioIn 16*
Howe, James Everett 1930- *WhoE 91, WhoWor 91*
Howe, James Murray 1924- *WhoAm 90*
Howe, James Robert 1943- *WhoE 91*
Howe, James Tarsicius 1924- *St&PR 91, WhoAm 90*
Howe, Jas Murray 1924- *St&PR 91*
Howe, Jerald Shropshire, Jr. 1956- *WhoEmL 91*
Howe, John Kingman 1945- *WhoEmL 91, WhoWor 91*
Howe, John L. *BioIn 16*
Howe, John Perry 1910- *WhoAm 90*
Howe, John Prentice, III 1943- *WhoAm 90, WhoWor 91*
Howe, Jonathan Thomas 1940- *WhoAm 90*
Howe, Joseph 1804-1873 *DcLB 99 [port]*
Howe, Julia 1819-1910 *FemiCLE*
Howe, Julia Ward 1819-1910 *BioAmW, BioIn 16, WorAlBi*
Howe, Katherine L Mallet *WhoAmA 91N*
Howe, Kevin Paul 1934- *St&PR 91*
Howe, Lawrence 1921- *WhoAm 90*
Howe, Lenore Ann 1948- *WhoAmW 91*
Howe, Lyman Harold, III 1938- *WhoSSW 91*
Howe, Mark Steven 1955- *WhoAm 90*
Howe, Marolyn Louise 1957- *WhoAmW 91*
Howe, Martha Morgan 1945- *WhoAm 90*
Howe, Michael William 1948- *WhoAm 90*
Howe, Murray Joseph 1931- *St&PR 91*
Howe, Murrill Norton, Jr. 1937- *St&PR 91*
Howe, Neil 1951- *ConAu 132*
Howe, Nelson S 1935- *WhoAmA 91*
Howe, Oscar 1915- *WhoAmA 91*
Howe, Oscar 1915-1983 *WhoAmA 91N*
Howe, Quincy 1900-1977 *BioIn 16*
Howe, Richard 1726-1799 *EncCRAm [port], WorAlBi*
Howe, Richard Cuddy 1924- *WhoAm 90*
Howe, Richard Davis 1939- *WhoSSW 91*
Howe, Richard Esmond, Jr. 1927- *WhoAm 90*
Howe, Richard J. 1928- *WhoAm 90*
Howe, Richard J. 1937- *ODwPR 91*
Howe, Richard Karl 1943- *WhoAm 90*
Howe, Richard Marshall 1952- *WhoE 91*
Howe, Robert 1732-1786 *EncCRAm*
Howe, Robert C. 1831-1915 *AmLegL*
Howe, Robert M. 1939- *St&PR 91*
Howe, Robert Melvin 1939- *WhoAm 90*
Howe, Robert Wilson 1932- *WhoAm 90*
Howe, Roger Evans 1945- *WhoAm 90, WhoE 91*
Howe, Russell Warren 1925- *WhoE 91*
Howe, Sally Ann 1930- *WorAlBi*
Howe, Samuel G. 1801-1876 *WorAlBi*
Howe, Stanley M. 1924- *St&PR 91*
Howe, Stanley Merrill 1924- *WhoAm 90*
Howe, Steve *BioIn 16*
Howe, Steve 1958- *Ballpl 90*
Howe, Timothy Otis 1816-1883 *BiDrUSE 89*
Howe, Tina *BioIn 16*
Howe, Tina 1937- *CurBio 90 [port], FemiCLE, NotWoAT*
Howe, Victor H. 1928- *St&PR 91*
Howe, Wallace Brady 1926- *WhoAm 90*
Howe, Walter C. 1934- *St&PR 91*
Howe, Wayne H. *ODwPR 91*
Howe, Wesley Jackson 1921- *St&PR 91, WhoAm 90, WhoE 91*
Howe, William 1729-1814 *EncCRAm, WorAlBi*
Howe, William Hugh 1928- *WhoWor 91*
Howe-Ellison, Patricia Mary 1928- *WhoAmW 91*
Howell, Alfred Hunt 1912- *WhoAm 90*
Howell, Allen Windsor 1949- *WhoEmL 91*
Howell, Allie Rhea 1927- *WhoAmW 91*
Howell, Alvin Harold 1908- *WhoAm 90*
Howell, Ann *FemiCLE*
Howell, Archie Curtis 1928- *St&PR 91*
Howell, Arthur 1918- *WhoAm 90*
Howell, Barbara Fennema 1924- *WhoAmW 91*
Howell, Barbara Miles 1937- *WhoWrEP 89*
Howell, Benjamin Franklin, Jr. 1917- *WhoAm 90*
Howell, Beth Ann *BiDrAPA 89*
Howell, Bette 1920- *ConAu 130*
Howell, Bonnie Howard 1947- *WhoAmW 91, WhoEmL 91*
Howell, Brian L. 1929- *St&PR 91*
Howell, Bruce Inman 1942- *WhoSSW 91*
Howell, C. Thomas 1966- *ConTFT 8 [port], WorAlBi*
Howell, Catharine Ann 1949- *WhoAmW 91*
Howell, Charles Douglas 1939- *St&PR 91*
Howell, Charles L., Jr. 1946- *WhoSSW 91*
Howell, Charles Maitland 1914- *WhoAm 90, WhoWor 91*
Howell, Clark 1863-1936 *AmLegL, BioIn 16*
Howell, Claude Flynn 1915- *WhoAmA 91*
Howell, Columbus Leo, III 1950- *WhoEmL 91*
Howell, David Arthur Russell 1936- *WhoWor 91*
Howell, David S. 1944- *St&PR 91*
Howell, Dean Myral 1932- *WhoWrEP 89*
Howell, Dixie 1919- *Ballpl 90*
Howell, Dixie 1920-1960 *Ballpl 90*
Howell, Donald Herbert 1942- *St&PR 91*
Howell, Donald Lee 1935- *WhoAm 90, WhoSSW 91, WhoWor 91*
Howell, Donald Lewis, II 1951- *WhoEmL 91*
Howell, E Jane *BiDrAPA 89*
Howell, Elizabeth Ann 1932- *WhoAmA 91*
Howell, Elizabeth F *BiDrAPA 89*
Howell, Elizabeth Fulton 1955- *WhoEmL 91*
Howell, Elizabeth M. 1932- *St&PR 91*
Howell, Embry Martin 1945- *WhoAmW 91*
Howell, Everette Irl 1914- *WhoAm 90*
Howell, Francis Clark 1925- *WhoAm 90*
Howell, Gary Allen 1943- *St&PR 91*
Howell, George Bedell 1919- *WhoAm 90*
Howell, George Cook, III 1956- *WhoEmL 91*
Howell, George Washington 1927- *WhoAm 90*
Howell, Grover Elmer 1916- *St&PR 91*
Howell, Gwynne 1938- *PenDiMP*
Howell, Gwynne Richard 1938- *IntWWM 90*
Howell, H. Michael 1945- *ODwPR 91*
Howell, H. Scott 1929- *St&PR 91*
Howell, Hannah Johnson 1905-1988 *WhoAmA 91N*
Howell, Harley Thomas 1937- *WhoAm 90, WhoE 91, WhoWor 91*
Howell, Harry 1876-1956 *Ballpl 90*
Howell, Hugh Hawkins, Jr. 1920- *WhoSSW 91*
Howell, Jack 1961- *Ballpl 90*
Howell, James 1594?-1666 *LitC 13 [port]*
Howell, James Burt, III 1933- *WhoE 91*
Howell, James E. 1945- *ODwPR 91*
Howell, James Edwin 1928- *WhoAm 90*
Howell, James Melton 1933- *WhoAm 90, WhoE 91*
Howell, James Theodore 1919- *WhoAm 90*
Howell, James William 1946- *WhoEmL 91*
Howell, Jay 1955- *Ballpl 90*
Howell, Jimmy Frank 1932- *WhoAm 90*
Howell, John Alfred 1929- *WhoAm 90*
Howell, John Floyd 1932- *WhoAm 90*
Howell, John McDade 1922- *WhoAm 90*
Howell, John R. 1933- *WhoAm 90*
Howell, John Reid 1936- *WhoAm 90*
Howell, John Williams 1941- *St&PR 91*
Howell, Joseph Jarvis 1928- *WhoSSW 91*
Howell, Josh *ODwPR 91*
Howell, Joyce Ann 1955- *WhoAmW 91*
Howell, Julian Erwin, III 1954- *WhoSSW 91*
Howell, Ken 1960- *Ballpl 90*
Howell, Kristin K. 1951- *WhoSSW 91*
Howell, Laura Sue 1937- *WhoAmW 91*
Howell, Linda Kay 1946- *WhoAmW 91*
Howell, Louis Peyton 1932- *St&PR 91*
Howell, Lynda Edwina 1959- *WhoSSW 91*
Howell, Mary Elizabeth 1942- *WhoAmW 91*
Howell, Mary L. 1952- *WhoAm 90*
Howell, Mary Oakley 1955- *WhoE 91*
Howell, Michael Wayne 1945- *WhoEmL 91*
Howell, Michael William Davis 1947- *St&PR 91*
Howell, Nadia Diaa 1954- *WhoSSW 91*
Howell, Park Louis 1961- *WhoEmL 91*
Howell, Paul Neilson 1918- *St&PR 91, WhoAm 90*
Howell, Ralph Rodney 1931- *WhoAm 90, WhoSSW 91, WhoWor 91*
Howell, Rebecca Elizabeth 1952- *WhoAmW 91*
Howell, Richard Louis 1933- *St&PR 91*
Howell, Richard Paul, Sr. 1927- *WhoE 91, WhoWor 91*
Howell, Robert Barey 1948- *WhoE 91*
Howell, Robert James 1925- *WhoAm 90*
Howell, Robert Leslie 1931- *St&PR 91*
Howell, Robert Thomas, Jr. 1942- *St&PR 91, WhoAm 90*
Howell, Robert Wayne 1916- *WhoAm 90*
Howell, Robert Wayne 1961- *WhoSSW 91*
Howell, Roger 1936-1989 *BioIn 16*
Howell, Roy 1953- *Ballpl 90*
Howell, Sarah E *BiDrAPA 89*

Howell, Saundra Leah 1945- *WhoAmW 91*
Howell, Stephen Haviland 1932- *St&PR 91*
Howell, Steven Kendrick 1949- *WhoAm 90*
Howell, Stewart Leslie 1942- *St&PR 91*
Howell, Thomas 1944- *WhoAm 90*
Howell, Thomas Edwin 1918- *WhoAm 90*
Howell, Timothy 1947- *BiDrAPA 89*
Howell, Tom *ConTFT 8*
Howell, Vicki Thompson 1942- *WhoSSW 91*
Howell, Wilbur Samuel 1904- *WhoAm 90*
Howell, William Ashley, III 1949- *WhoEmL 91, WhoSSW 91*
Howell, William C. *WhoAm 90*
Howell, William James 1929- *WhoAm 90*
Howell, William Robert 1936- *St&PR 91, WhoAm 90, WhoSSW 91*
Howell, William Smiley 1914- *WhoAm 90*
Howell, Wilson Nathaniel 1939- *WhoAm 90, WhoWor 91*
Howell-Price, Owen 1926- *WhoWor 91*
Howells, Anne 1941- *IntWWM 90, PenDiMP*
Howells, Annie *BioAmW*
Howells, Edgar H. 1946- *St&PR 91*
Howells, Elinor Mead 1837-1910 *BioIn 16*
Howells, Henry C. *BioIn 16*
Howells, Herbert Norman 1892-1983 *DcNaB 1981*
Howells, John Gwilym 1918- *BiDrAPA 89*
Howells, Liz *ODwPR 91*
Howells, Martha Louise 1951- *WhoE 91*
Howells, Muriel Gurdon Seabury 1910- *WhoWor 91*
Howells, William Dean 1837-1920 *BioIn 16, EncAL, WorAlBi*
Howells, William White 1908- *WhoAm 90, WhoWor 91*
Hower, Debra Kay 1954- *WhoSSW 91*
Hower, Edward 1941- *WhoWrEP 89*
Hower, Frank Beard, Jr. 1928- *St&PR 91, WhoAm 90*
Howerton, Bill 1921- *Ballpl 90*
Howerton, George 1905- *WhoAm 90*
Howerton, Helen V. 1933- *WhoAm 90*
Howerton, James R *BiDrAPA 89*
Howery, Donald E. 1941- *St&PR 91, WhoSSW 91*
Howery, Sharon C. 1962- *WhoAmW 91*
Howes, Alfred Spencer 1917- *WhoWor 91*
Howes, Barbara 1914- *FemiCLE, WhoAm 90, WhoWrEP 89*
Howes, Benjamin Durward, III 1922- *WhoAm 90*
Howes, Bobby 1895-1972 *OxCPMus*
Howes, Carol Susan 1960- *WhoAmW 91*
Howes, Kei H 1925- *BiDrAPA 89*
Howes, Lorraine de Wet 1933- *WhoAm 90*
Howes, Michael Frank 1951- *WhoE 91*
Howes, Robert Alan 1928- *WhoAm 90*
Howes, Royce Bucknam 1950- *WhoAmA 91*
Howes, Sally Ann 1930- *OxCPMus*
Howes, Theodore Clark 1929- *WhoE 91*
Howes, Thomas P. 1934- *St&PR 91*
Howes, Wendy Elizabeth 1951- *WhoAmW 91*
Howes, William Browning 1937- *St&PR 91, WhoAm 90*
Howes, William Carter 1936- *St&PR 91*
Howeth, Robert W. 1948- *St&PR 91*
Howett, John 1926- *WhoAmA 91*
Howey, Gilbert Edward *BiDrAPA 89*
Howey, Gregory Blair 1942- *St&PR 91*
Howey, John Richard 1933- *WhoAm 90*
Howey, Robert Swanson, Sr. 1930- *WhoSSW 91*
Howgate, Bernard *BioIn 16*
Howgill, Dorothy *BiDEWW*
Howgill, Mary *FemiCLE*
Howgill, Mary 1623-1681? *BiDEWW*
Howie, Alan Crawford 1942- *IntWWM 90*
Howie, Archibald 1934- *WhoWor 91*
Howie, Bruce Griffith 1953- *WhoEmL 91*
Howie, John Robert 1946- *WhoSSW 91*
Howie, John S 1934- *BiDrAPA 89*
Howie, Laverne M 1904- *BiDrAPA 89*
Howie, Tomas Vincent 1957- *WhoEmL 91*
Howington, Pamela Kay 1958- *WhoAmW 91*
Howitt, Geoffrey 1926- *WhoWor 91*
Howitt, John Newton 1885-1958 *WhoAmA 91N*
Howitt, Loretta Y. 1956- *BiDrAPA 89*
Howitt, Mary 1799-1888 *FemiCLE*
Howitt, Mary Botham 1799-1888 *BioIn 16*
Howitt, William 1792-1879 *BioIn 16, EncO&P 3*
Howker, Janni *BioIn 16*
Howkins, John 1945- *ConAu 32NR*
Howkins, John H 1921- *BiDrAPA 89*
Howl, Joanne Healey 1957- *WhoAmW 91*
Howland, Allen H. 1921- *St&PR 91*
Howland, David G. 1929- *St&PR 91*
Howland, Edith *WhoAmA 91N*
Howland, Elihu S 1912- *BiDrAPA 89*
Howland, Garth 1887-1950 *WhoAmA 91N*
Howland, James Chase 1916- *St&PR 91*
Howland, Joan Sidney 1951- *WhoEmL 91*
Howland, Jobyna 1880-1936 *OxCPMus*
Howland, John Hathaway 1946- *St&PR 91*
Howland, John S 1942- *BiDrAPA 89*
Howland, John Seymour 1942- *WhoE 91*
Howland, June C Huston *BiDrAPA 89*
Howland, Lewis S. 1901- *St&PR 91*
Howland, Marie 1836-1921 *FemiCLE*
Howland, Murray Shipley, Jr. 1911- *WhoAm 90*
Howland, Peter A 1936- *BiDrAPA 89*
Howland, Rebekah Gwen *BiDrAPA 89*
Howland, Richard C. 1934- *WhoAm 90, WhoWor 91*
Howland, Richard Henry 1925- *WhoAm 90*
Howland, Richard Hubbard 1910- *WhoAm 90, WhoAmA 91*
Howland, Richard Moulton 1940- *WhoE 91*
Howland, Robert A. 1923- *St&PR 91*
Howland, Robert G. 1928- *St&PR 91*
Howland, Robert H *BiDrAPA 89*
Howland, Robert Herbert 1960- *WhoE 91*
Howland, Walter Warren 1933- *St&PR 91*
Howland, Willard J. 1927- *WhoAm 90*
Howland, William Goldwin Carrington 1915- *WhoAm 90*
Howland, William Holmes 1844-1893 *DcCanB 12*
Howland, William Stapleton 1919- *WhoAm 90*
Howle, C. Tycho 1949- *WhoSSW 91*
Howle, Jerry Albert 1945- *BiDrAPA 89*
Howlett, C.T. 1945- *St&PR 91*
Howlett, Carolyn Chance 1915- *WhoAm 90*
Howlett, Carolyn Svrluga 1914- *WhoAm 90, WhoAmA 91*
Howlett, Chris Richard 1952- *BiDrAPA 89*
Howlett, Clifford Theodore, Jr. 1945- *WhoAm 90*
Howlett, D Roger 1945- *WhoAmA 91*
Howlett, Joan Gail 1943- *WhoWrEP 89*
Howlett, Joe Richard 1928- *St&PR 91*
Howlett, John Reginald 1940- *SpyFic*
Howlett, Lisa Jo 1957- *St&PR 91*
Howlett, Neil Baillie 1934- *IntWWM 90*
Howlett, Phyllis Lou 1932- *WhoAmW 91, WhoWor 91*
Howlett-Gonzalez, Stephanie Ann 1957- *WhoAmW 91*
Howley, Dan 1885-1944 *Ballpl 90*
Howley, James Rogers 1942- *WhoE 91*
Howley, W.N., Jr. 1927- *St&PR 91*
Howlin' Wolf 1910-1976 *EncPR&S 89, OxCPMus*
Howling Wolf 1850?-1927 *WhNaAH*
Howman-Giles, Robert 1947- *WhoWor 91*
Howorth, Lucy Somerville 1895- *WhoAm 90, WhoAmW 91, WhoSSW 91, WhoWor 91*
Howorth, M. K. *ConAu 32NR*
Howren, Philip Bruce 1950- *WhoEmL 91*
Howrey, Edward F. 1903- *WhoAm 90*
Howrey, Eugene Philip 1937- *WhoAm 90*
Howsare, Leora Alic Nagel 1908- *WhoAmW 91*
Howse, Anita Louise 1955- *WhoEmL 91*
Howse, Ben T. 1952- *St&PR 91*
Howse, Ernest Marshall 1902- *WhoAm 90*
Howse, Harold D. 1928- *WhoWrEP 89*
Howse, Harold Darrow 1928- *WhoAm 90*
Howse, Robert Davis 1908- *WhoAm 90*
Howser, Dick 1936-1987 *BioIn 16*
Howser, Dick 1937-1987 *Ballpl 90*
Howsley, Richard Thornton 1948- *WhoEmL 91*
Howson, Bruce Kenneth 1942- *St&PR 91*
Howson, Robert E. 1932- *WhoSSW 91*
Howton, Ronald Jeffrey 1955- *WhoEmL 91*
Howze, James Dean 1930- *WhoAmA 91*
Howze, Joseph Lawson Edward 1923- *WhoAm 90, WhoSSW 91*
Howze, Karen Aileen 1950- *WhoAm 90*
Howze, Wendell Morgan 1947- *WhoSSW 91*
Hoxie, Henry Wayne 1947- *St&PR 91*
Hoxie, Ralph Gordon 1919- *WhoAm 90, WhoE 91, WhoWor 91*
Hoxie, Robert E. 1941- *ODwPR 91*
Hoxie, Russell Evan, Jr. 1960- *BiDrAPA 89*
Hoxie, Vinnie 1847-1914 *BiDWomA*
Hoxie, Vinnie R. *BioAmW*
Hoxit, Garland Kellogg 1946- *WhoEmL 91*
Hoxit-Smith, Linda Caroline 1953- *WhoAmW 91*
Hoxter, Curtis Joseph 1922- *WhoAm 90, WhoE 91, WhoWor 91*
Hoxworth, Dan Hardy 1960- *WhoEmL 91*
Hoy, Anne Tawes *WhoAm 90*
Hoy, Cyrus Henry 1926- *WhoAm 90*
Hoy, Dummy 1862-1961 *Ballpl 90 [port]*
Hoy, Harold H 1941- *WhoAmA 91*
Hoy, Harold Joseph 1934- *WhoE 91*
Hoy, Harry Eugene 1908- *WhoAm 90*
Hoy, John Craven 1933- *WhoAm 90*
Hoy, Linda 1946- *ConAu 130*
Hoy, Marjorie Ann 1941- *WhoAm 90*
Hoy, Michael John 1945- *WhoEmL 91*
Hoy, Robert Joseph 1929- *WhoE 91, WhoWor 91*
Hoy, Ronald Raymond 1939- *WhoAm 90*
Hoy, William Ivan 1915- *WhoAm 90*
Hoyal, Dorothy 1918- *WhoAmA 91*
Hoydal, Annika 1945- *IntWWM 90*
Hoye, Clara L *BiDrAPA 89*
Hoye, Daniel Francis 1946- *WhoAm 90*
Hoye, Walter Brisco 1930- *WhoWor 91*
Hoyem, Andrew Lewison 1935- *WhoAm 90*
Hoyem, David S. 1944- *St&PR 91*
Hoyer, Aviva S 1917- *BiDrAPA 89*
Hoyer, David J 1943- *BiDrAPA 89*
Hoyer, David Ralph 1931- *WhoAm 90*
Hoyer, Francis Joseph 1922- *St&PR 91*
Hoyer, Harvey Conrad 1907- *WhoAm 90*
Hoyer, Jesse Lee 1960- *WhoAmW 91*
Hoyer, Phyllis Scarborough 1938- *WhoAmW 91, WhoE 91*
Hoyer, Steny H. *BioIn 16*
Hoyer, Steny Hamilton 1939- *WhoAm 90, WhoE 91*
Hoyer, Thomas V *BiDrAPA 89*
Hoyer, Ulrich Oskar 1938- *WhoWor 91*
Hoyer, Vincent Edgar 1924- *St&PR 91, WhoAm 90*
Hoyer, Werner H. 1951- *WhoWor 91*
Hoyerman, William Richard 1958- *St&PR 91*
Hoyers, Anna Ovena 1584-1655 *EncCoWW*
Hoyland, Barbara 1764-1829 *FemiCLE*
Hoyland, Fred 1940- *WhoSSW 91*
Hoyland, Janet Louise 1940- *WhoAmW 91*
Hoyland, Vic 1945- *IntWWM 90*
Hoyle, Cynthia Lynn 1957- *WhoAmW 91*
Hoyle, Fred 1915- *MajTwCW, RGTwCSF*
Hoyle, Kenneth Samuel 1953- *BiDrAPA 89, WhoE 91*
Hoyle, Lawrence Truman, Jr. 1938- *WhoE 91*
Hoyle, Mark 1972-1986 *BioIn 16*
Hoyle, Randy Lowell 1953- *WhoEmL 91*
Hoyle, Ruth Pamela 1945- *WhoAmA 91, WhoEmL 91*
Hoyle, Ted 1942- *IntWWM 90*
Hoyler, Geraldine M. *BioIn 16*
Hoyme, Chad E. 1933- *St&PR 91*
Hoyme, Chad Earl 1933- *WhoAm 90*
Hoyme, James B 1935- *BiDrAPA 89*
Hoyne, Andrew Thomas 1947- *WhoEmL 91*
Hoyne, Scott William 1950- *WhoEmL 91*
Hoyne, Thomas Temple 1935- *WhoWor 91*
Hoynes, Louis L., Jr. 1935- *St&PR 91*
Hoynes, Louis LeNoir, Jr. 1935- *WhoAm 90*
Hoyo, Jose Azcona *BioIn 16*
Hoyos, Angela de 1940?- *ConAu 131, HispWr 90*
Hoyos, Arturo 1948- *WhoWor 91*
Hoyt, Arthur W *BiDrAPA 89*
Hoyt, Brooks Pettingill 1929- *WhoAm 90*
Hoyt, Caroline *DcCanB 12*
Hoyt, Charlee Ildora 1936- *WhoAmW 91*
Hoyt, Charles Lindsay 1925- *St&PR 91*
Hoyt, Charles Orcutt 1929- *WhoAm 90*
Hoyt, Christopher H. 1956- *ODwPR 91*
Hoyt, Clark Freeland 1942- *WhoAm 90*
Hoyt, Coleman Williams 1925- *WhoWor 91*
Hoyt, Craig Robert 1949- *St&PR 91*
Hoyt, David Lemire 1951- *WhoAm 90*
Hoyt, David P. 1959- *St&PR 91*
Hoyt, David Richard 1950- *WhoAm 90*
Hoyt, Dennis *BioIn 16*
Hoyt, Earl Edward, Jr. 1936- *WhoE 91*
Hoyt, Edmund *St&PR 91*
Hoyt, Edward Jonathan 1840-1918 *BioIn 16*
Hoyt, Edwin Palmer *BioIn 16*
Hoyt, Edwin Palmer, Jr. 1923- *AuBYP 90*
Hoyt, Elizabeth B *BiDrAPA 89*
Hoyt, Ellen 1933- *WhoAmA 91, WhoE 91*
Hoyt, Frances Weston 1908- *WhoAmA 91*
Hoyt, Frank Russell 1916- *WhoAm 90*
Hoyt, George Washington 1936- *WhoAm 90*
Hoyt, H. Gunther *St&PR 91*
Hoyt, Harry Edward 1931- *St&PR 91*
Hoyt, Helen 1887-1972 *FemiCLE*
Hoyt, Henry H. 1895- *St&PR 91*
Hoyt, Henry Hamilton, Jr. 1927- *WhoAm 90*
Hoyt, Herbert Austin Aikins 1937- *WhoAm 90*
Hoyt, Heusted W. R. 1842-1894 *AmLegL*
Hoyt, James Lawrence 1943- *WhoAm 90*
Hoyt, John Arthur 1932- *WhoAm 90*
Hoyt, John P. 1841- *AmLegL*
Hoyt, John Taylor, Jr. 1942- *St&PR 91*
Hoyt, Kathleen Elizabeth 1953- *WhoAmW 91*
Hoyt, Kenneth Boyd 1924- *WhoAm 90*
Hoyt, LaMarr 1955- *Ballpl 90*
Hoyt, Leon G., Jr. 1925- *St&PR 91*
Hoyt, Lupe Ann Gonzalez 1952- *WhoEmL 91*
Hoyt, Mary Finch *WhoAm 90*
Hoyt, Mary Finch 1924?- *AuBYP 90*
Hoyt, Matthew Buckingham 1957- *WhoSSW 91*
Hoyt, Millard L *BiDrAPA 89*
Hoyt, Mont Powell 1940- *WhoAm 90, WhoSSW 91*
Hoyt, Monty 1944- *WhoAm 90, WhoE 91*
Hoyt, Nelly Schargo 1920- *WhoAm 90*
Hoyt, Norris H. *BioIn 16*
Hoyt, Olga 1922- *AuBYP 90*
Hoyt, Richard 1941- *ConAu 129, SpyFic, TwCCr&M 91*
Hoyt, Roger Wilson 1937- *St&PR 91*
Hoyt, Susan 1944- *WhoAm 90*
Hoyt, Thomas L *BiDrAPA 89*
Hoyt, Wade Arthur 1943- *WhoAm 90*
Hoyt, Waite 1899-1984 *Ballpl 90 [port], BioIn 16*
Hoyt, Whitney F 1910-1980 *WhoAmA 91N*
Hoyt, William C. 1946- *WhoAm 90*
Hoyt, William Vernor 1937- *WhoAm 90*
Hoyt, Winthrop 1900-1989 *BioIn 16*
Hoyt-Hoch, Peggy Jane 1954- *WhoAmW 91*
Hoyte, David S. 1947- *St&PR 91*
Hoyte, Hugh Desmond 1929- *WhoWor 91*
Hrabak, William Henry, Jr. 1955- *WhoEmL 91*
Hrabal, Bohumil 1914- *ConAu 12AS [port]*
Hrabarchuk, Eugene 1920- *BiDrAPA 89*
Hrabosky, Al 1949- *Ballpl 90*
Hrabovsky, Joseph Emil 1942- *St&PR 91*
Hrachovina, Frederick Vincent 1926- *WhoAm 90*
Hradel, Elizabeth Hard 1908- *WhoAmW 91*
Hradesky, Christine L *BiDrAPA 89*
Hrascinski, Jo Anne Victoria 1967- *WhoWrEP 89*
Hrawi, Elias 1930- *WhoWor 91*
Hrayssi, Walid 1934- *WhoWor 91*
Hrbek, Kent 1960- *Ballpl 90*
Hrdlicka, Charles R. 1938- *St&PR 91*
Hrdlicka, Richard F. 1932- *St&PR 91*
Hreczny, Bohdan Nicholai *BiDrAPA 89*
Hreha, Donald William 1934- *St&PR 91*
Hreha, Karen Sue 1953- *WhoEmL 91*
Hreidarsson-Downey, Robert Arni 1946- *WhoWor 91*
Hresan, Sally L. 1946- *WhoSSW 91*
Hresko, Michael Basil 1935- *BiDrAPA 89*
Hrg, Franjo 1933- *IntWWM 90*
Hribar, Frank 1922- *St&PR 91*
Hribernik, Robert Martin 1945- *WhoEmL 91*
Hric, Patricia Ann 1944- *WhoAmW 91*
Hriljac, Michael James 1950- *WhoEmL 91*
Hrinko, Daniel Dean 1955- *WhoEmL 91*
Hrisak, Daniel Michael 1945- *WhoE 91, WhoEmL 91, WhoWor 91*
Hriskevich, Michael Edward 1926- *WhoAm 90*
Hriso, Emmanuel 1958- *BiDrAPA 89*
Hrisoscoleu, Sofia *EncCoWW*
Hristakis, Barbara 1951- *WhoAmW 91*
Hrivnak, David James 1959- *WhoSSW 91*
Hrivnak, Pavol 1931- *WhoWor 91*
Hrna, Daniel Joseph 1940- *WhoSSW 91, WhoWor 91*
Hromadka, Josef 1936- *WhoWor 91*
Hromadko, George 1920- *WhoAm 90*
Hromnak, George *BiDrAPA 89*
Hron, Richard W. 1940- *St&PR 91*
Hronas, Michael J. 1961- *St&PR 91*
Hroncich, Edward F. 1934- *St&PR 91*
Hrones, John Anthony 1912- *WhoAm 90*
Hroswitha *EncCoWW*
Hrotsvit *EncCoWW*
Hrotsvita *EncCoWW*
Hrotsvitha *EncCoWW*
Hruby, Blahoslav S. *NewYTBS 90*
Hruby, F. Michael 1946- *WhoEmL 91*
Hruby, Frank M. 1918- *WhoAm 90*
Hruby, Norbert Joseph 1918- *WhoAm 90*
Hruby, Roger Francis 1935- *St&PR 91*
Hrushevs'kyi, Mykhailo 1866-1934 *BioIn 16*
Hrushka, Myroslaw *BiDrAPA 89*
Hruska, Alan J. 1933- *WhoAm 90*
Hruska, Elias Nicolas 1943- *WhoWrEP 89*
Hruska, Francis John 1935- *WhoWor 91*
Hruska, Roman Lee 1904- *WhoAm 90*
Hruzek, S. Leonard 1954- *St&PR 91*
Hrycak, Peter 1923- *WhoAm 90, WhoE 91, WhoWor 91*
Hryhorczuk, Linda Louise 1944- *BiDrAPA 89*
Hrynyk, John Paul 1949- *St&PR 91*
Hryvniak, Michael R. *BiDrAPA 89*

Hsi, David Ching Heng 1928- *WhoAm 90*
Hsi, Edward Yang 1957- *WhoWor 91*
Hsia, James Ching 1946- *St&PR 91*
Hsiao, Alice 1964- *WhoEmL 91*
Hsiao, Chin 1935- *WhoAmA 91*
Hsiao, John Kao *BiDrAPA 89*
Hsiao, Ling 1940- *WhoWor 91*
Hsiao, Mu-Yue 1933- *WhoAm 90*
Hsiao, Peter 1960- *WhoEmL 91*
Hsiao, Roger Chenfang 1955- *WhoSSW 91*
Hsiao-shih *WomWR*
Hsie, Jen-Yah *BiDrAPA 89*
Hsieh, Dennis P. H. 1937- *WhoAm 90*
Hsieh, Henry Lien 1930- *WhoSSW 91*
Hsieh, Hudson H 1949- *BiDrAPA 89*
Hsieh, Jui Sheng 1921- *WhoAm 90, WhoWor 91*
Hsieh, Lamont 1946- *St&PR 91*
Hsieh, Michael Thomas 1958- *WhoEmL 91*
Hsieh, You-Lo 1953- *WhoEmL 91*
Hsin, Victor Jun-Kuan 1945- *WhoE 91*
Hsiung, Robert C. *BiDrAPA 89*
Hsiung, Robert Yuan Chun 1935- *WhoAm 90*
Hsu, Charles Jui-cheng 1930- *WhoE 91*
Hsu, Chen Chao 1940- *WhoAm 90*
Hsu, Chen-chin 1927- *WhoWor 91*
Hsu, Cheng 1951- *WhoE 91*
Hsu, Chieh Su 1922- *WhoAm 90*
Hsu, Chih Yun 1915- *WhoWor 91*
Hsu, Ching-Hsin 1956- *WhoAmW 91*
Hsu, Ching-yu 1898- *WhoAm 90, WhoWor 91*
Hsu, Cho-yun 1930- *WhoAm 90*
Hsu, Chung Yi 1944- *WhoSSW 91*
Hsu, Donald Kung-Hsing 1947- *WhoEmL 91*
Hsu, Francis Lang Kwang 1911- *WhoAm 90*
Hsu, Hsi Fan *NewYTBS 90*
Hsu, Hsi Fan 1906-1990 *BioIn 16*
Hsu, Hsiung 1920- *WhoAm 90*
Hsu, Immanuel Chung Yueh 1923- *WhoAm 90*
Hsu, Isaac Hou-An 1946- *WhoEmL 91*
Hsu, Jing *BiDrAPA 89*
Hsu, John J *BiDrAPA 89*
Hsu, John J. 1919- *WhoAm 90*
Hsu, John T. 1931- *IntWWM 90*
Hsu, John Tseng Hsin 1931- *WhoAm 90*
Hsu, Jong-Pyng 1951- *WhoSSW 91*
Hsu, Kenneth Jinghwa 1929- *WhoWor 91*
Hsu, Laura Hwei Nien Ling 1939- *WhoAmW 91*
Hsu, Lee-Keung G *BiDrAPA 89*
Hsu, Leslie Chia-Mei 1948- *BiDrAPA 89*
Hsu, Madeleine 1938- *IntWWM 90*
Hsu, Ming-Yu 1925- *WhoSSW 91*
Hsu, Paul Sho-Po 1939- *WhoWor 91*
Hsu, Richard Kingwei 1933- *WhoE 91*
Hsu, Roger Y.K. 1927- *St&PR 91*
Hsu, Samuel 1947- *IntWWM 90, WhoE 91*
Hsu, Simon Ta Kuang 1923- *WhoWor 91*
Hsu, Tao-Chang 1927- *WhoWor 91*
Hsu, Thomas Tseng-Chuang 1933- *WhoSSW 91*
Hsu, Timothy 1952- *BiDrAPA 89*
Hsu, Tony M. 1963- *WhoSSW 91*
Hsu, Yau Que 1953- *WhoWor 91*
Hsu, Yu-Chih *WhoAm 90*
Hsu, Zuey-Shin 1930- *WhoWor 91*
Hsueh, Chun-tu 1922- *WhoAm 90*
Hu *WomWR*
Hu Qili 1929- *WhoWor 91*
Hu Yaobang 1915-1989 *AnObit 1989, BioIn 16*
Hu, Can Beven 1949- *WhoWor 91*
Hu, Chenyi 1948- *WhoEmL 91*
Hu, Chi Chung 1927- *WhoAmA 91*
Hu, Chi Yu 1933- *WhoAm 90*
Hu, Chin-ch'uan 1931- *BioIn 16*
Hu, Da-Shih 1958- *BiDrAPA 89, WhoE 91*
Hu, John Chih-An 1922- *WhoWor 91*
Hu, Joseph Chi-Ping 1946- *WhoE 91*
Hu, King 1931- *BioIn 16*
Hu, Mary Lee 1943- *WhoAmA 91*
Hu, Richard Jun-Teh *BiDrAPA 89*
Hu, Scarlett Hsichia 1957- *WhoAmW 91*
Hu, Shau-chung 1941- *WhoWor 91*
Hu, Shiu-Lok 1949- *WhoEmL 91*
Hu, Steve Seng-Chiu 1922- *WhoAm 90, WhoWor 91*
Hu, Sze-Tsen 1914- *WhoAm 90*
Hu, Weibai 1922- *WhoWor 91*
Hu, Yao-pang 1915-1989 *BioIn 16*
Hu, Yao-Su 1946- *WhoWor 91*
Hua Guofeng *WhoWor 91*
Hua Kuo-Feng 1920?- *WorAlBi*
Huan Xiang 1910-1989 *AnObit 1989*
Huang Zhen 1910-1989 *BioIn 16*
Huang, Alice Shih-hou 1939- *WhoAmW 91*
Huang, Belle 1947- *BiDrAPA 89*
Huang, Chao-Ming 1938- *WhoSSW 91*
Huang, Chin Tang 1928-1988 *BioIn 16*
Huang, Choung Chun 1936- *BiDrAPA 89*
Huang, Ethan 1958- *WhoEmL 91*
Huang, Eugene Yuching 1917- *WhoAm 90*
Huang, Francis Fu-Tse 1922- *WhoAm 90*
Huang, Hua-Feng 1935- *WhoAm 90*
Huang, Hubert Hwa-chou 1939- *WhoAm 90*
Huang, Huey Wen 1940- *WhoSSW 91*
Huang, Jacob Chen-ya 1937- *WhoE 91, WhoWor 91*
Huang, Jenmming Stephen 1947- *WhoEmL 91*
Huang, Joseph Chen-Huan 1933- *WhoE 91, WhoWor 91*
Huang, Kee Chang 1917- *WhoAm 90*
Huang, Kerson 1928- *WhoAm 90*
Huang, Kuang-Jen 1946- *BiDrAPA 89*
Huang, Kun-Huang *BiDrAPA 89*
Huang, Lena Grace 1950- *BiDrAPA 89*
Huang, Ling *BiDrAPA 89*
Huang, Patrick Fuh-Shyong 1943- *WhoWor 91*
Huang, Peter C.R. 1935- *St&PR 91*
Huang, Pien Chien 1931- *WhoAm 90*
Huang, Shikang 1937- *WhoWor 91*
Huang, Sun-Yi 1940- *WhoWor 91*
Huang, Theresa C. *WhoAmW 91, WhoWor 91*
Huang, Thomas Shi-Tao 1936- *WhoAm 90*
Huang, Thomas Tao-shing 1939- *WhoSSW 91*
Huang, Thomas Weishing 1941- *WhoWor 91*
Huang, Victor Tsangmin 1951- *WhoEmL 91, WhoWor 91*
Huang, Xia 1965- *WhoE 91*
Huang, Yao-wen 1947- *WhoSSW 91*
Huang, Yijun 1915- *IntWWM 90*
Huapaya, Luis V M 1926- *BiDrAPA 89*
Huard, Bernadette L *BiDrAPA 89*
Huat, Tan Keng 1945- *WhoWor 91*
Huaud l'aine 1647-1700 *PenDiDA 89*
Huaud le puine 1655-1723 *PenDiDA 89*
Huaud, Ami 1657-1724 *PenDiDA 89*
Huaud, Jean-Pierre 1655-1723 *PenDiDA 89*
Huaud, Pierre 1612?-1680 *PenDiDA 89*
Huaud, Pierre, II 1647-1700 *PenDiDA 89*
Huband, A. Rolph 1929- *St&PR 91*
Huband, Earnest A. *BioIn 16*
Hubard, William S. 1923- *St&PR 91*
Hubatsch, Hermann Hugo *PenDiDA 89*
Hubay, Charles Alfred 1918- *WhoAm 90*
Hubay, Jeno 1858-1937 *PenDiMP*
Hubay, Karoly 1828-1885 *PenDiMP*
Hubay, Tibor Steven 1941- *WhoWor 91*
Hubback, Catherine *FemiCLE*
Hubball, James Miles *BioIn 16*
Hubbard, Amy Nix 1949- *WhoE 91*
Hubbard, Arthur Thornton 1941- *WhoAm 90*
Hubbard, Barbara Marx 1929- *NewAgE 90*
Hubbard, Cal 1900-1977 *Ballpl 90 [port], WorAlBi*
Hubbard, Carroll, Jr. 1937- *WhoAm 90, WhoSSW 91*
Hubbard, Charles Allen 1931- *WhoAm 90*
Hubbard, Charles D 1876-1951 *WhoAmA 91N*
Hubbard, David Allan 1928- *WhoAm 90*
Hubbard, David G 1920- *BiDrAPA 89*
Hubbard, Dean Leon 1939- *WhoAm 90*
Hubbard, Elaine Marjorie 1950- *WhoEmL 91*
Hubbard, Elbert 1856-1915 *BioIn 16, PenDiDA 89*
Hubbard, Elizabeth *WhoAm 90*
Hubbard, Elizabeth Louise 1949- *WhoAmW 91*
Hubbard, Eugene P. 1922- *St&PR 91*
Hubbard, Frank G. 1937- *St&PR 91*
Hubbard, Freddie 1938- *BioIn 16, DrBlPA 90*
Hubbard, Frederick Dewayne 1938- *WhoAm 90*
Hubbard, Glenn 1957- *Ballpl 90*
Hubbard, Glenn Richard 1934- *St&PR 91*
Hubbard, Gregory Scott 1948- *WhoEmL 91, WhoWor 91*
Hubbard, Harlan *BioIn 16*
Hubbard, Harold M. 1924- *St&PR 91*
Hubbard, Harold Mead 1924- *WhoAm 90*
Hubbard, Harvey Hart 1921- *WhoAm 90*
Hubbard, Henry W. 1933- *ODwPR 91*
Hubbard, Herbert Hendrix 1922- *WhoAm 90*
Hubbard, Howard James 1938- *WhoAm 90, WhoE 91*
Hubbard, Howard L. 1927- *St&PR 91*
Hubbard, Howard Leland 1931- *WhoAm 90*
Hubbard, Jasper 1938- *WhoSSW 91*
Hubbard, Jeanne Delaney 1948- *WhoSSW 91*
Hubbard, Jesse Donald 1920- *WhoAm 90*
Hubbard, John 1931- *WhoAmA 91*
Hubbard, John Barry 1917- *WhoAm 90*
Hubbard, John David 1955- *BiDrAPA 89*
Hubbard, John Henry 1934- *St&PR 91*
Hubbard, John Kimber 1953- *WhoSSW 91*
Hubbard, John L. 1935- *St&PR 91*
Hubbard, John Lewis 1947- *WhoSSW 91*
Hubbard, John O'Connor 1933- *St&PR 91*
Hubbard, John Perry *NewYTBS 90*
Hubbard, John Pertillo 1836-1904 *AmLegL*
Hubbard, John Randolph 1918- *WhoAm 90*
Hubbard, John Robert 1952- *WhoSSW 91*
Hubbard, John Thomas 1949- *WhoSSW 91*
Hubbard, Jonathan V. 1946- *ODwPR 91*
Hubbard, Julia Faye 1948- *WhoAmW 91, WhoEmL 91*
Hubbard, Kenneth Earl 1942- *WhoSSW 91*
Hubbard, L. Ron *NewAgE 90*
Hubbard, L. Ron 1911-1986 *BioIn 16*
Hubbard, L Ron 1911-1986 *EncO&P 3*
Hubbard, L. Ron 1911-1986 *RGTwCSF, WorAlBi*
Hubbard, La Fayette Ron 1911-1986 *BioIn 16*
Hubbard, Margaret Anna 1947- *WhoAmW 91*
Hubbard, Mark O. 1949- *St&PR 91*
Hubbard, Michal Ann 1943- *WhoSSW 91*
Hubbard, Orville L. 1903-1982 *BioIn 16*
Hubbard, Oscar E 1903- *BiDrAPA 89*
Hubbard, Oscar Edwin 1903- *WhoE 91*
Hubbard, P M 1910-1980 *TwCCr&M 91*
Hubbard, Paul Stancyl, Jr. 1931- *WhoAm 90*
Hubbard, Peter E. 1942- *WhoAm 90*
Hubbard, Philip Gamaliel, Jr. 1946- *WhoEmL 91*
Hubbard, Philip Hollister 1900-1988 *BioIn 16*
Hubbard, Phillip *WhoHisp 91*
Hubbard, Randall D. 1935- *St&PR 91*
Hubbard, Randall Dee 1935- *WhoAm 90, WhoSSW 91*
Hubbard, Reginald Hampton 1948- *St&PR 91*
Hubbard, Richard Bennett 1832-1901 *BioIn 16*
Hubbard, Richard Buell, III 1938- *WhoSSW 91*
Hubbard, Richmond C 1916- *BiDrAPA 89*
Hubbard, Robert 1928- *WhoAmA 91*
Hubbard, Robert Glenn 1958- *WhoE 91*
Hubbard, Robert Hamilton 1916- *WhoAm 90, WhoWrEP 89*
Hubbard, Robert Lynwood 1934- *St&PR 91*
Hubbard, Roger D. 1957- *St&PR 91*
Hubbard, Roy 1918- *St&PR 91*
Hubbard, Russell Bruce *BiDrAPA 89*
Hubbard, Ruth 1924- *BioIn 16, WhoAm 90*
Hubbard, Ruth 1942- *WhoAm 90*
Hubbard, S. Wayne 1949- *WhoSSW 91*
Hubbard, Samuel Dickinson 1799-1855 *BiDrUSE 89*
Hubbard, Samuel Walton, Jr. 1929- *WhoAm 90*
Hubbard, Sandra Beamer 1962- *WhoAmW 91*
Hubbard, Sandra Sue 1959- *WhoAmW 91*
Hubbard, Scott David 1957- *WhoEmL 91*
Hubbard, Sonja Y. 1961- *St&PR 91*
Hubbard, Stanley Eugene 1897- *WhoAm 90*
Hubbard, Stanley S. 1933- *St&PR 91*
Hubbard, Stanley Stub 1933- *WhoAm 90*
Hubbard, Susie Dee 1954- *WhoEmL 91*
Hubbard, Thomas Edwin 1944- *WhoSSW 91, WhoWor 91*
Hubbard, Vance Matthew 1940- *St&PR 91*
Hubbard, Vaughn 1922- *St&PR 91*
Hubbard, Veronica Lynne 1960- *WhoAmW 91*
Hubbard, William Bogel 1940- *WhoAm 90*
Hubbard, William Neill, Jr. 1919- *WhoAm 90*
Hubbard, William Peyton 1842-1935 *BioIn 16*
Hubbeling, Edwin L. 1933- *St&PR 91*
Hubbell, Bill 1897-1980 *Ballpl 90*
Hubbell, Billy James 1949- *WhoEmL 91*
Hubbell, Carl 1903-1988 *AnObit 1988, Ballpl 90 [port], BioIn 16, WorAlBi*
Hubbell, Ernest 1914- *WhoAm 90, WhoWor 91*
Hubbell, Frederick S. 1951- *St&PR 91*
Hubbell, George L., Jr. 1894- *St&PR 91*
Hubbell, Harriet Weed 1909- *AuBYP 90*
Hubbell, Henry Salem 1870-1949 *WhoAmA 91N*
Hubbell, James Randolph 1824-1890 *AmLegL*
Hubbell, James Windsor, Jr. 1922- *St&PR 91, WhoAm 90*
Hubbell, John Howard 1925- *WhoE 91*
Hubbell, Joseph G. 1933- *St&PR 91*
Hubbell, Lorenzo 1854-1930 *BioIn 16*
Hubbell, Patricia Ann 1928- *WhoWrEP 89*
Hubbell, Raymond 1879-1954 *OxCPMus*
Hubbell, Robert C. 1949- *ODwPR 91*
Hubbell, Thomas C. 1936- *St&PR 91*
Hubbell, William L. 1943- *St&PR 91*
Hubbert, James F. 1939- *St&PR 91*
Hubbert, Marion King 1903-1989 *BioIn 16*
Hubble, Beverly *WhoWrEP 89*
Hubble, Don W. 1939- *WhoAm 90*
Hubble, Edwin P. 1889-1953 *WorAlBi*
Hubble, Edwin Powell 1889-1953 *BioIn 16*
Hubble, Nicholas *PenDiDA 89*
Hubbs, Alyce Leah 1934- *WhoWrEP 89*
Hubbs, Carl Leavitt 1894-1979 *DcScB S2*
Hubbs, Clark 1921- *WhoAm 90*
Hubbs, Donald Harvey 1918- *WhoAm 90*
Hubbs, Flora Amelia *DcCanB 12*
Hubbs, Galen Jay 1941- *WhoWrEP 89*
Hubbs, Jack Rolland 1937- *WhoAm 90, WhoE 91*
Hubbs, Ken 1941-1964 *Ballpl 90*
Hubbs, Ronald M. 1908- *WhoWor 91*
Hubel, David H. 1926- *WorAlBi*
Hubel, David Hunter 1926- *WhoAm 90, WhoE 91, WhoWor 91*
Hubele, Donald Edwin 1954- *WhoSSW 91*
Huben, Dolores Quevedo 1951- *WhoHisp 91*
Hubener, Frank G. *BioIn 16*
Hubenthal, Karl Samuel 1917- *WhoAmA 91*
Huber, Albert Frank 1953- *St&PR 91*
Huber, Alberta 1917- *WhoAm 90*
Huber, Allan J. 1929- *WhoAm 90*
Huber, Bruce C. 1947- *St&PR 91*
Huber, Calvin R. 1925- *IntWWM 90*
Huber, Charles B *BiDrAPA 89*
Huber, Clarence 1897-1965 *Ballpl 90*
Huber, Clayton Lloyd 1955- *WhoSSW 91*
Huber, David *BioIn 16*
Huber, Deanna Lynn 1959- *WhoAmW 91*
Huber, Don Lawrence 1928- *WhoAm 90*
Huber, Franz 1925- *WhoWor 91*
Huber, Fred W. 1931- *St&PR 91*
Huber, G. Ben 1934- *St&PR 91*
Huber, George P. *WhoAm 90*
Huber, Gordon Floyd 1921- *St&PR 91*
Huber, James A. 1951- *St&PR 91*
Huber, Joan Althaus 1925- *WhoAm 90*
Huber, John David 1946- *WhoAm 90*
Huber, John Lawrence 1944- *St&PR 91*
Huber, Joseph Fowler 1946- *St&PR 91*
Huber, Katherine Jeanne 1958- *WhoEmL 91*
Huber, Klaus 1924- *IntWWM 90*
Huber, Laurence Edward 1961- *WhoSSW 91*
Huber, Louis Anthony, III 1952- *WhoEmL 91*
Huber, Ludwig Ferdinand *EncCoWW*
Huber, Margaret Ann 1949- *WhoAmW 91*
Huber, Marsha Anne 1953- *WhoAmW 91*
Huber, Max 1919- *ConDes 90*
Huber, Michael Henry 1953- *WhoE 91*
Huber, Miriam Elaine 1940- *WhoAmW 91*
Huber, Mortimer G. 1932- *St&PR 91*
Huber, Norman Joseph 1925- *St&PR 91*
Huber, Oskar Richard 1933- *WhoE 91*
Huber, Paul Edward 1939- *WhoAm 90*
Huber, Peter C. 1930- *WhoAm 90*
Huber, Richard Alan 1949- *WhoEmL 91*
Huber, Richard G. 1947- *St&PR 91*
Huber, Richard Glen 1937- *WhoWor 91*
Huber, Richard Gregory 1919- *WhoAm 90*
Huber, Richard Leslie 1936- *St&PR 91, WhoAm 90*
Huber, Richard Miller 1922- *WhoE 91*
Huber, Rita Norma 1931- *WhoAmW 91*
Huber, Robert 1937- *BioIn 16, WhoWor 91, WorAlBi*
Huber, Robert Edger 1931- *WhoWrEP 89*
Huber, Robert Josef 1950- *WhoWor 91*
Huber, Ronald Frank 1923- *St&PR 91*
Huber, Ronald R. 1947- *WhoSSW 91*
Huber, Terry Stewart 1957- *WhoSSW 91*
Huber, Therese 1764-1829 *EncCoWW*
Huber, Thomas 1937- *WhoE 91*
Huber, Thomas Martin 1919- *WhoAm 90*
Huber, Vandra Lee 1949- *WhoAmW 91, WhoEmL 91*
Huber, Vicki *BioIn 16*
Huber, Walter Leroy 1883-1960 *BioIn 16*
Huber, William H., Jr. 1922- *WhoAm 90*
Huber, Wolfgang K *BiDrAPA 89*
Huberman, B. A. 1943- *BioIn 16*
Huberman, Benjamin 1938- *WhoE 91*
Huberman, Bernardo A. 1943- *BioIn 16*
Huberman, Bronislav 1882-1947 *PenDiMP*
Huberman, Richard Lee 1953- *WhoEmL 91*
Huberman, Roberta 1941- *BiDrAPA 89*
Hubers, David R. 1943- *St&PR 91*
Hubert, Bishop of Angers 980?-1047 *BioIn 16*
Hubert, Andre Jules 1933- *WhoWor 91*
Hubert, Anne M *WhoAmA 91*
Hubert, Bernard 1929- *WhoAm 90*
Hubert, Edgar F *WhoAmA 91*
Hubert, Emile Herman 1915- *WhoWor 91*
Hubert, Frank William Rene 1915- *WhoAm 90*
Hubert, Gabrielle Mary 1922- *WhoAmW 91*

Hubert, Helen Betty 1950- *WhoAmW 91*
Hubert, Jean-Luc 1960- *WhoEmL 91, WhoWor 91*
Hubert, Thaddeus Joseph, III 1950- *WhoEmL 91*
Hubert, Veronique C *BiDrAPA 89*
Hubert-Grenier, Stephanie Rae 1959- *WhoAmW 91*
Hubertina, Cornelia *EncCoWW*
Huberty, Daniel John 1943- *St&PR 91*
Hubicki, Margaret Olive 1915- *IntWWM 90*
Hubl, Milan 1927-1989 *AnObit 1989*
Hubler, Bruce A. 1944- *St&PR 91*
Hubler, Bruce Albert 1944- *WhoAm 90*
Hubler, David Elliot 1941- *WhoWrEP 89*
Hubler, H. Clark 1910- *WhoWrEP 89*
Hubler, James T. 1943- *St&PR 91*
Hubler, James Terrence 1943- *WhoAm 90*
Hubler, Julius 1919- *WhoAm 90, WhoAmA 91, WhoWor 91*
Hubley, Faith Elliot 1924- *BioIn 16*
Hubley, Faith Elliott 1924- *WhoAm 90*
Hubley, John 1914-1977 *BioIn 16*
Hubley, Reginald Allen 1928- *WhoAm 90*
Hubley, Robert H. 1926- *St&PR 91*
Hubli, Heinz 1930- *St&PR 91*
Hublitz, Sue 1940- *WhoAmW 91*
Hubner, Donald Anthony 1926- *St&PR 91*
Hubner, Fritz 1933- *IntWWM 90*
Hubner, Jean Alice 1933- *St&PR 91*
Hubner, John 1840-1920 *AmLegL*
Hubner, John A. 1932- *St&PR 91*
Hubner, Peter 1944- *WhoWor 91*
Hubner, Robert Wilmore 1918- *WhoAm 90*
Hubner, Zygmunt *BioIn 16*
Hubscher, William Donald 1956- *WhoWrEP 89*
Hubschman, David Neil 1946- *St&PR 91*
Hubschmid, Johannes 1916- *WhoWor 91*
Hubsher, Merritt Seth *BiDrAPA 89*
Hubshman, Emanuel Edward 1916- *St&PR 91*
Huby, Pamela M Clark 1922- *EncO&P 3*
Huby, Pamela Margaret 1922- *EncPaPR 91*
Huc, Pierre Vincent Francois 1935- *WhoWor 91*
Huch, Friedrich 1873-1913 *BioIn 16*
Huch, Ricarda 1864-1947 *EncCoWW*
Huch, Ricarda Octavia 1864-1947 *BioIn 16*
Huchel, Frederick M 1947- *WhoAmA 91*
Huchital, David A. 1942- *St&PR 91*
Huchok, James Paul 1952- *St&PR 91*
Huchteman, Ralph Douglas 1946- *WhoSSW 91*
Huchthausen, David Richard 1951- *WhoAmA 91*
Huck, Charlotte S. *AuBYP 90*
Huck, Gabe 1941- *ConAu 30NR*
Huck, John Lloyd 1922- *St&PR 91, WhoAm 90*
Huck, Leonard William 1922- *WhoAm 90*
Huck, Lewis Francis 1912- *WhoSSW 91, WhoWor 91*
Huck, Mary Lippert 1951- *WhoEmL 91*
Huck, Robert E 1923-1961 *WhoAmA 91N*
Huckabee, Carol Brooks 1945- *WhoAmW 91*
Huckaby, Thomas Jerald 1941- *WhoAm 90, WhoSSW 91*
Hucke, Samuel Theodore, III 1949- *BiDrAPA 89*
Hucker, Charles Oscar 1919- *WhoAm 90*
Hucker, Charles William 1947- *St&PR 91, WhoEmL 91*
Hucker, George J. 1893-1988 *BioIn 16*
Huckins, Donald E. 1925- *St&PR 91*
Huckins, Robert Michael 1957- *WhoEmL 91*
Huckins, William Judd 1927- *WhoAm 90*
Huckman, Michael Saul 1936- *WhoAm 90*
Hucknall, Nanette Veda 1933- *WhoAmW 91*
Huckvale, John Frederick 1937- *St&PR 91, WhoAm 90*
Hudacek, Stephen J. *BioIn 16*
Hudak, Cheryl M. 1947- *ODwPR 91*
Hudak, Gary Russell 1951- *BiDrAPA 89*
Hudak, Kristen M. *WhoAmW 91*
Hudak, Thomas F. 1942- *St&PR 91*
Hudak, Thomas Francis 1942- *WhoAm 90*
Huddart, Elinor Louisa 1853-1902 *FemiCLE*
Huddilston, Robert P. 1934- *St&PR 91*
Huddle, David 1942- *WhoWrEP 89*
Huddleson, Edwin Emmet, Jr. 1914- *WhoAm 90*
Huddleson, Scott Alden 1952- *WhoEmL 91*
Huddleston, C. Lawrence 1950- *St&PR 91*
Huddleston, Christie Ann 1952- *BiDrAPA 89, WhoE 91*
Huddleston, David William 1930- *WhoAm 90*
Huddleston, Donna Ruth 1958- *WhoAmW 91*
Huddleston, Eugene Lee 1931- *WhoAm 90*
Huddleston, George *BioIn 16*
Huddleston, James E., Jr. 1934- *BiDrAPA 89*
Huddleston, Kathy Nash 1949- *WhoAmW 91*
Huddleston, Lauren B. 1933- *WhoAmW 91, WhoWor 91*
Huddleston, Lee W. 1919- *St&PR 91*
Huddleston, Marilyn Anne 1953- *WhoAmW 91*
Huddleston, Victor Glenn 1948- *WhoEmL 91*
Huddleston, Virginia Byrn 1959- *WhoAmW 91*
Huddleston, Wayne Allan 1937- *St&PR 91*
Hudec, Robert Emil 1934- *WhoAm 90*
Hudecek, Vaclav 1952- *IntWWM 90*
Hudepohl, James Joseph 1952- *St&PR 91*
Hudez, Karl 1904- *IntWWM 90*
Hudgens, Alletta Jervey 1930- *WhoAmW 91*
Hudgens, Janet Walden 1964- *WhoSSW 91*
Hudgens, Michael Thomas, Sr. 1938- *WhoWor 91*
Hudgens, Richard W 1931- *BiDrAPA 89*
Hudgens, Robert Pierce 1915- *St&PR 91*
Hudgens, William Thomas 1954- *St&PR 91*
Hudgin, Donald Edward 1917- *WhoAm 90, WhoWor 91*
Hudgins, Andrew 1951- *ConAu 132, WhoWrEP 89*
Hudgins, B. B. *AmLegL*
Hudgins, Barbara 1932- *WhoWrEP 89*
Hudgins, Carol Johnston 1952- *WhoEmL 91*
Hudgins, Catherine Harding 1913- *WhoAmW 91, WhoSSW 91, WhoWor 91*
Hudgins, Clay Erwin 1961- *WhoEmL 91*
Hudgins, David Drake 1955- *WhoSSW 91*
Hudgins, David Lee 1961- *WhoSSW 91*
Hudgins, J. Thomas 1940- *WhoAm 90*
Hudgins, Jack Sanders, Jr. 1959- *St&PR 91*
Hudgins, Mary K. 1938- *St&PR 91*
Hudgins, Patricia Montague 1938- *WhoAmW 91*
Hudgins, William Freeman, Jr. 1953- *WhoWrEP 89*
Hudgins, William Sheppard, Jr. 1944- *St&PR 91*
Hudgins-Bonafield, Christine Ann 1954- *WhoAmW 91*
Hudiak, David Michael 1953- *WhoE 91, WhoEmL 91, WhoWor 91*
Hudiburg, John Justus, Jr. 1928- *St&PR 91, WhoSSW 91*
Hudick, Andrew Michael, II 1958- *WhoSSW 91*
Hudik, Martin Francis 1949- *WhoEmL 91*
Hudkins, Daniel F. 1951- *St&PR 91*
Hudkins, James Allen 1953- *WhoEmL 91*
Hudler, Rex 1960- *Ballpl 90*
Hudlin, Reginald Alan 1961- *WhoEmL 91*
Hudlin, Willis 1906- *Ballpl 90*
Hudnall, David Harrison 1948- *St&PR 91*
Hudner, Philip 1931- *WhoAm 90*
Hudnut, David Beecher 1935- *WhoAm 90*
Hudnut, Robert Kilborne 1934- *WhoAm 90*
Hudnut, Stewart 1939- *St&PR 91*
Hudnut, William Herbert, III 1932- *WhoAm 90*
Hudock, George B *BiDrAPA 89*
Hudolin, Vladimir *BiDrAPA 89*
Hudon, Victor 1812-1897 *DcCanB 12*
Hudson 1950- *WhoAmA 91*
Hudson, Alice M. 1930- *St&PR 91*
Hudson, Anthony Webster 1937- *WhoAm 90*
Hudson, Arlene 1936- *WhoAmW 91*
Hudson, Arthur Lee, Jr. 1944- *St&PR 91*
Hudson, Barton 1936- *IntWWM 90*
Hudson, Bernard O'Grady *BiDrAPA 89*
Hudson, Betty *ODwPR 91*
Hudson, Betty Elizabeth Hamilton 1945- *WhoAmW 91*
Hudson, Bill *BioIn 16*
Hudson, Bill 1937- *ODwPR 91*
Hudson, Bill 1949- *ConTFT 8*
Hudson, Bonnor E., Jr. 1924- *St&PR 91*
Hudson, Brian Paige 1945- *WhoWor 91*
Hudson, C. B., Jr. 1947- *WhoSSW 91*
Hudson, Carolyn E. 1944- *St&PR 91*
Hudson, Cecil C 1935- *BiDrAPA 89*
Hudson, Charles 1959- *Ballpl 90*
Hudson, Charles Daugherty 1927- *WhoSSW 91, WhoWor 91*
Hudson, Charles J 1937- *BiDrAPA 89*
Hudson, Charles K. *ODwPR 91*
Hudson, Charles Melvin, Jr. 1932- *WhoSSW 91*
Hudson, Charles Ralph 1942- *WhoE 91*
Hudson, Claude Earl 1946- *WhoAm 90, WhoEmL 91*
Hudson, Clifford 1954- *St&PR 91*
Hudson, Courtney Morley 1955- *WhoSSW 91*
Hudson, Dale L. 1930- *IntWWM 90*
Hudson, Dale Monroe 1934- *St&PR 91*
Hudson, Dennis Lee 1936- *WhoWor 91*
Hudson, Dennis S., III 1955- *St&PR 91*
Hudson, Donald Ellis 1916- *WhoAm 90*
Hudson, Donald J. 1930- *WhoAm 90*
Hudson, Douglas Fillmore, Jr. 1945- *St&PR 91*
Hudson, Edward Voyle 1915- *WhoWor 91*
Hudson, Elizabeth 1949- *WhoAmW 91*
Hudson, Elizabeth Gault 1906- *WhoAmW 91*
Hudson, Ellen Matilda 1915- *WhoWrEP 89*
Hudson, Ernie *ConTFT 8, DrBlPA 90*
Hudson, Frank N. 1949- *WhoAm 90*
Hudson, Frank Parker 1918- *WhoSSW 91*
Hudson, Franklin Donald 1933- *WhoAm 90*
Hudson, Frederic 1819-1875 *BioIn 16*
Hudson, Frederick A. *EncO&P 3, EncPaPR 91*
Hudson, G. Kirk 1941- *St&PR 91*
Hudson, Gary Michael 1946- *WhoEmL 91*
Hudson, Gary Van Voorhees 1936- *WhoSSW 91*
Hudson, George Elbert 1916- *WhoAm 90*
Hudson, Gladys W. 1926- *St&PR 91*
Hudson, Grace Debrovner 1932- *WhoSSW 91*
Hudson, Gregory E. 1946- *St&PR 91*
Hudson, Hal D. 1931- *St&PR 91*
Hudson, Harold Jordon, Jr. 1924- *WhoAm 90*
Hudson, Harriet Dufresne 1912- *WhoAm 90*
Hudson, Harry Landrum 1936- *WhoSSW 91*
Hudson, Heber S 1924- *BiDrAPA 89*
Hudson, Henry *WorAlBi*
Hudson, Henry *EncCRAm*
Hudson, Henry *BioIn 16*
Hudson, Henry 1550?-1611? *WhNaAH*
Hudson, Henry Claude 1886-1989 *BioIn 16*
Hudson, Henry Norman 1814-1886 *BioIn 16*
Hudson, Hosea 1898- *EncAL*
Hudson, Howard V. 1945- *St&PR 91*
Hudson, Hubert R. 1928- *WhoWor 91*
Hudson, Hugh *BioIn 16*
Hudson, Hugh Thomas 1933- *WhoSSW 91*
Hudson, J. Clifford 1954- *St&PR 91*
Hudson, J.W. 1939- *St&PR 91*
Hudson, Jack William, Jr. 1926- *WhoAm 90*
Hudson, Jacqueline *WhoAmA 91, WhoAmW 91*
Hudson, James Irvin 1953- *BiDrAPA 89*
Hudson, James T. 1924- *WhoAm 90*
Hudson, Janet R. 1956- *St&PR 91*
Hudson, Jeffery *MajTwCW*
Hudson, Jeffrey *TwCCr&M 91*
Hudson, Jerry E. 1938- *WhoAm 90*
Hudson, Jesse Tucker, Jr. 1920- *WhoSSW 91*
Hudson, John Irvin 1932- *WhoAm 90*
Hudson, John Lester 1937- *WhoAm 90*
Hudson, John Robert 1947- *WhoWor 91*
Hudson, Johnny 1912-1970 *Ballpl 90*
Hudson, Jon Barlow 1945- *WhoAmA 91*
Hudson, Joseph L *EncABHB 4*
Hudson, Josie Ann 1952- *BiDrAPA 89*
Hudson, Joy Marlaine *BiDrAPA 89*
Hudson, Joyce Ann 1938- *WhoAmW 91*
Hudson, Karl Grier, Jr. 1919- *St&PR 91*
Hudson, Katherine M. *BioIn 16*
Hudson, Leonard Harlow 1915- *WhoAm 90*
Hudson, Leonard Lester 1910- *WhoWor 91*
Hudson, Lester A., Jr. 1939- *St&PR 91*
Hudson, Lincoln T. *BioIn 16*
Hudson, Linda 1950- *WhoAmW 91, WhoEmL 91*
Hudson, Linda Marie 1951- *WhoEmL 91*
Hudson, Lionel 1916- *BioIn 16*
Hudson, Louis Mark 1952- *WhoSSW 91*
Hudson, Manley O., Jr. 1932- *WhoAm 90*
Hudson, Marcus Allan 1947- *WhoWrEP 89*
Hudson, Margaret Stover 1947- *WhoAmW 91*
Hudson, Mark 1957- *ConAu 132*
Hudson, Martin Russell 1957- *WhoEmL 91*
Hudson, Mary 1912- *WhoAm 90*
Hudson, Mary Henderson 1937- *WhoSSW 91*
Hudson, Meg *ConAu 30NR*
Hudson, Michael Craig 1938- *WhoAm 90, WhoE 91*
Hudson, Michael H. *ODwPR 91*
Hudson, Michael T. 1947- *WhoAm 90*
Hudson, Miles 1925- *ConAu 132*
Hudson, Molly Ann 1941- *St&PR 91, WhoAmW 91*
Hudson, Myra Linden Frank 1950- *WhoAmW 91, WhoEmL 91, WhoSSW 91*
Hudson, Nan 1868-1957 *BiDWomA*
Hudson, Nat *BioIn 16*
Hudson, O.W. *St&PR 91N*
Hudson, Patti *BioIn 16*
Hudson, Ralph Magee 1907- *WhoAmA 91*
Hudson, Ralph P. 1924- *WhoAm 90*
Hudson, Richard Lloyd 1920- *WhoE 91*
Hudson, Robert Francis 1922- *WhoWor 91*
Hudson, Robert Franklin, Jr. 1946- *WhoSSW 91*
Hudson, Robert H 1938- *WhoAmA 91*
Hudson, Robert J 1913- *BiDrAPA 89*
Hudson, Rock 1925-1985 *BioIn 16, WorAlBi*
Hudson, Roy Davage 1930- *WhoAm 90*
Hudson, Samuel Eugene, Jr. 1946- *WhoEmL 91*
Hudson, Samuel T. 1927- *St&PR 91*
Hudson, Sid 1915- *Ballpl 90*
Hudson, Stanton H., Jr. 1951- *ODwPR 91*
Hudson, Suncerray Ann 1960- *WhoAmW 91*
Hudson, Tajquah Jaye 1959- *WhoAmW 91*
Hudson, Thomas 1791-1844 *OxCPMus*
Hudson, Thomas 1954- *WhoSSW 91*
Hudson, Thomas Jay 1834-1903 *EncPaPR 91*
Hudson, Thomas W. *BioIn 16*
Hudson, Thomson Jay 1834-1903 *EncO&P 3*
Hudson, Timothy B 1955- *BiDrAPA 89*
Hudson, Virginia Cary 1894-1954 *LiHiK*
Hudson, W H 1841-1922 *DcLB 98 [port]*
Hudson, Will 1908- *OxCPMus*
Hudson, William Mark 1932- *WhoSSW 91*
Hudson, William Ronald 1933- *WhoAm 90*
Hudson, William Stuart *BiDrAPA 89*
Hudson, William Thomas 1929- *WhoAm 90*
Hudson, Winthrop Still 1911- *WhoAm 90*
Hudson, Woodruff Lylle 1958- *St&PR 91*
Hudson, Yeager 1931- *WhoAm 90*
Hudson-White, Carmen *BioIn 16*
Hudson-Young, Jane Smither 1937- *WhoAmW 91*
Hudspeth, Albert James 1945- *WhoAm 90*
Hudspeth, Chalmers Mac 1919- *WhoAm 90*
Hudspeth, Emmett LeRoy 1916- *WhoAm 90*
Hudspeth, George Laverne, Jr. 1947- *WhoEmL 91, WhoSSW 91*
Hudspeth, Harry Lee 1935- *WhoAm 90, WhoSSW 91*
Hudspeth, Robert S. 1853-1929 *AmLegL*
Hudspeth, Robert Scott 1936- *St&PR 91*
Hudspeth, William Junia, Jr. 1939- *St&PR 91*
Hudspeth, William R. 1944- *St&PR 91*
Hudzik, Richard Francis 1952- *WhoEmL 91*
Hue, Joseph Alphonse 1932- *WhoWor 91*
Huebbers, Carl George, Jr. 1952- *WhoE 91*
Hueber, Kurt Anton 1928- *IntWWM 90*
Hueber, Wolf 1485?-1553 *IntDcAA 90*
Huebl, Lothar 1941- *WhoWor 91*
Huebl, Milan *BioIn 16*
Huebler, Douglas 1924- *WhoAmA 91*
Huebner, Donald Frank 1925- *St&PR 91*
Huebner, Gregory Karl 1953- *WhoEmL 91*
Huebner, Hans Frieder 1940- *BiDrAPA 89*
Huebner, Harlan Pierce 1927- *WhoAm 90*
Huebner, Jay Stanley 1939- *WhoSSW 91*
Huebner, John Stephen 1940- *WhoAm 90*
Huebner, Kurt 1921- *ConAu 132*
Huebner, Kurt Walter 1960- *WhoSSW 91*
Huebner, Lee William 1940- *WhoWor 91*
Huebner, Louise *EncO&P 3*
Huebner, Rosemarita 1932- *WhoAmA 91*
Huebner, Ted Raymond 1950- *WhoEmL 91*
Huebschman, Martin John 1947- *St&PR 91*
Hueffer, Catherine 1850-1927 *BiDWomA*
Hueffer, Ford Madox *ConAu 132, MajTwCW*
Huegele, Vinson Sebastian 1919- *WhoSSW 91*
Huegli, Albert G. *BioIn 16*
Huegy, Harvey W. *BioIn 16*
Hueholt, Richard L. 1929- *St&PR 91*
Hueholt, Therese Marie 1955- *BiDrAPA 89*
Huelbig, Larry Leggett 1944- *WhoAm 90*
Huelke, Donald Fred 1930- *WhoAm 90*
Huelke, Donna Jean 1956- *WhoEmL 91*
Huelskamp, Raymond L. 1927- *St&PR 91*
Huelsman, Albert John, Jr. 1936- *St&PR 91*
Huelsman, Frank 1874-1959 *Ballpl 90*
Huelsmann, Carl 1914- *ConAu 130*
Huelsmann, Thomas Cyril 1940- *St&PR 91*

Huemer, Christina Gertrude 1947- *WhoAmA 91*
Huemer, Joseph Wilson 1913- *WhoWrEP 89*
Huene, Friedrich Von 1875-1969 *DcScB S2*
Huenefeld, Robert C. 1936- *St&PR 91*
Huenefeld, Thomas Ernst 1937- *St&PR 91*
Hueneke, Terry A. 1942- *WhoAm 90*
Huenemann, Linda Christine 1954- *WhoEmL 91*
Huenemann, Ruben Henry 1909- *WhoAm 90*
Huening, Walter Carl, Jr. 1923- *WhoAm 90, WhoWor 91*
Huenink, Dirk William 1935- *St&PR 91*
Hueppi, Rolf 1943- *WhoWor 91*
Huergo, Eduardo Rodolfo 1939- *BiDrAPA 89*
Huerta, Albert 1943- *WhoHisp 91*
Huerta, Dolores 1930- *BioIn 16, WorAlBi*
Huerta, Dolores Fernandez 1930- *WhoHisp 91*
Huerta, Jorge *ConAu 131, HispWr 90*
Huerta, Jorge A 1942- *ConAu 131, HispWr 90*
Huerta, Lynn Ellen 1961- *WhoE 91*
Huerta, Ramon 1924- *WhoHisp 91*
Huerta, Victoriano 1854-1916 *BioIn 16, WorAlBi*
Huerta-Garcia, Enrique 1941- *BiDrAPA 89*
Huerter, Nancy Jane 1958- *BiDrAPA 89*
Huesca, Robert Thomas 1959- *WhoHisp 91*
Huesca Pacheco, Rosendo 1932- *WhoAm 90*
Hueser, Claudia *ODwPR 91*
Huesing, Elizabeth T. 1908- *St&PR 91*
Huesped, Estimado Huevos 1923- *WhoAm 90*
Huessy, Hans R 1921- *BiDrAPA 89*
Huestis, Charles Benjamin 1920- *WhoAm 90, WhoWor 91*
Huestis, Dorothy Louise 1911- *WhoAmW 91*
Huestis, Robert David 1945- *BiDrAPA 89*
Hueston, Allen Lee 1950- *BiDrAPA 89*
Hueston, Frederick Martin 1953- *WhoSSW 91*
Hueston, Robert Edward 1929- *St&PR 91*
Huet, Christophe *PenDiDA 89*
Huet, Jean-Baptiste 1745-1811 *PenDiDA 89*
Huet, Marie-Helene Jaqueline 1944- *WhoAm 90*
Huet, Pierre-Daniel 1620-1721 *EncO&P 3*
Huet, Raul *BiDrAPA 89*
Huet, Thomas Victor 1955- *WhoEmL 91*
Hueter, Ernest B. 1920- *St&PR 91*
Hueter, James Warren 1925- *WhoAmA 91*
Huether, Barbara Lee 1954- *WhoAmW 91*
Huether, Cynthia Ryan 1955- *WhoEmL 91*
Hueting, Juergen 1956- *WhoWor 91*
Huetsch, Larry C. 1947- *St&PR 91*
Huetteman, Raymond Theodore, Jr. 1929- *WhoAm 90*
Huetteman, Susan Ann Bice 1934- *WhoWrEP 89*
Huettner, Frederick A. *BioIn 16*
Huettner, Richard Alfred 1927- *WhoAm 90*
Huey, Bill 1947- *ODwPR 91*
Huey, Bruce Edward 1947- *WhoEmL 91*
Huey, E. G. *AuBYP 90*
Huey, Elizabeth A. 1953- *St&PR 91*
Huey, Florence Greene 1872-1961 *WhoAmA 91N*
Huey, John Wesley, Jr. 1948- *WhoSSW 91*
Huey, Leighton Y 1942- *BiDrAPA 89*
Huey, Richard *EarBlAP*
Huey, Sandra Agee 1948- *WhoEmL 91*
Huey, Wayne Cowan 1943- *WhoSSW 91*
Huf, Carol Elinor 1940- *WhoAmW 91*
Huf, Ernst Gustav Rudolf 1907- *WhoWor 91*
Hufbauer, Gary Clyde 1939- *WhoAm 90, WhoWor 91*
Huff, Al R. 1938- *St&PR 91*
Huff, Barbara A. *AuBYP 90*
Huff, Bruce N. 1950- *St&PR 91*
Huff, Caroline *BioIn 16*
Huff, Clarence Ronald 1945- *WhoWor 91*
Huff, Clayton 1914-1989 *BioIn 16*
Huff, David L. *WhoAm 90*
Huff, David Richard 1948- *WhoEmL 91*
Huff, Douglas *BioIn 16*
Huff, Edgar J. *St&PR 91*
Huff, Elizabeth *BioIn 16*
Huff, Elizabeth 1907- *BiDrAPA 89*
Huff, Gayle Compton 1956- *WhoAmW 91, WhoEmL 91, WhoWor 91*
Huff, George F. 1923- *St&PR 91*
Huff, Henry Blair 1924- *WhoSSW 91*
Huff, Howard Lee 1941- *WhoAmA 91*
Huff, Jimmy Laurence 1950- *WhoSSW 91*
Huff, John Craig, Jr. 1920- *St&PR 91*
Huff, John David 1952- *WhoEmL 91*
Huff, John Rossman 1946- *St&PR 91, WhoAm 90, WhoSSW 91, WhoWor 91*
Huff, Judith 1947- *BiDrAPA 89*
Huff, Kenneth Robert 1927- *WhoAm 90*
Huff, Laura Weaver 1930- *WhoAmA 91*
Huff, Margaret Joan Farris 1925- *WhoSSW 91*
Huff, Nancy Ruth *WhoAmW 91*
Huff, Norman Nelson 1933- *WhoWor 91*
Huff, Pamela Jean 1946- *WhoSSW 91*
Huff, Paul Emlyn 1916- *WhoAm 90*
Huff, Penny 1944- *St&PR 91*
Huff, Robert 1945- *WhoAmA 91*
Huff, Roderick Remmele 1920- *AuBYP 90*
Huff, Russell Joseph 1936- *WhoSSW 91*
Huff, Sam 1934- *BioIn 16*
Huff, Samuel B. 1943- *ODwPR 91*
Huff, Sheila Leverne Williams 1953- *WhoAmW 91*
Huff, Sita 1933- *BiDrAPA 89*
Huff, Stanley Eugene 1918- *WhoAm 90*
Huff, Talbot S., Jr. 1940- *St&PR 91*
Huff, Thomas A. 1939- *St&PR 91*
Huff, Vivian 1948- *BioIn 16*
Huff, William Braid 1950- *WhoAm 90*
Huff, William Henry, III 1937- *St&PR 91*
Huff, William Jennings 1919- *WhoSSW 91, WhoWor 91*
Huffaker, Carla Sue 1951- *WhoAmW 91*
Huffaker, Clair 1926?-1990 *ConAu 131*
Huffaker, John Boston 1925- *WhoAm 90*
Huffard, Elsie May 1927- *WhoSSW 91*
Huffard, Jay C. 1941- *St&PR 91*
Huffenus, Alan Michael 1947- *St&PR 91*
Huffer, Dan L. 1937- *St&PR 91, WhoAm 90*
Huffer, Virginia *BiDrAPA 89*
Huffine, Charles W, Jr. 1941- *BiDrAPA 89*
Huffine, Coy Lee 1924- *WhoAm 90*
Huffine, Gary Wayne 1948- *St&PR 91*
Huffines, Diane Souza 1964- *WhoSSW 91*
Huffington, Arianna Stassinopoulos *BioIn 16*
Huffington, Arianna Stassinopoulos 1950- *ConAu 129*
Huffington, Roy M. 1917- *St&PR 91*
Huffington, Roy Michael 1917- *WhoAm 90*
Huffman, Bernard Leslie, Jr. 1929- *WhoAm 90*
Huffman, Celia Ann 1953- *WhoAmW 91*
Huffman, Charles Lyndale 1937- *WhoSSW 91*
Huffman, Claudia Sue 1954- *WhoAmW 91*
Huffman, Delia Gonzalez 1953- *WhoHisp 91*
Huffman, Delton Cleon, Jr. 1943- *WhoAm 90*
Huffman, Dennis A. 1951- *St&PR 91*
Huffman, Edgar Joseph 1939- *St&PR 91, WhoAm 90*
Huffman, Eugene Henry *EarBlAP*
Huffman, Galen C *BiDrAPA 89*
Huffman, Gary Claud 1944- *St&PR 91*
Huffman, George Garrett 1916- *WhoAm 90*
Huffman, George L., Jr. 1938- *St&PR 91*
Huffman, Grady Lee *BioIn 16*
Huffman, Gregory *BioIn 16*
Huffman, Gregory Scott Combest 1946- *WhoEmL 91*
Huffman, H. Arlene 1933- *WhoAmW 91*
Huffman, Harold Melvin, Jr. 1926- *WhoE 91*
Huffman, James Thomas 1947- *St&PR 91*
Huffman, James Thomas William 1947- *WhoAm 90*
Huffman, Joan Brewer 1937- *WhoSSW 91*
Huffman, John William 1932- *WhoSSW 91*
Huffman, Karen *BioIn 16*
Huffman, Kenneth J. *ODwPR 91*
Huffman, Kenneth Jay 1953- *St&PR 91*
Huffman, Mary Frances 1911- *WhoAmW 91*
Huffman, Mona Lou 1956- *WhoAmW 91*
Huffman, Nona Gay 1942- *WhoAmW 91*
Huffman, Pamela Ione 1948- *WhoAmW 91*
Huffman, Percival Knox 1925- *St&PR 91*
Huffman, Phil 1958- *Ballpl 90*
Huffman, Richard Wesley 1957- *WhoSSW 91*
Huffman, Robert Allen, Jr. 1950- *WhoSSW 91, WhoWor 91*
Huffman, Robert Earl 1928- *St&PR 91*
Huffman, Robert Edward 1937- *BiDrAPA 89*
Huffman, Teela Louise Lewellen 1948- *WhoAmW 91*
Huffman, Thorn Clifton 1947- *WhoSSW 91*
Huffman, Wendell Alan 1952- *WhoEmL 91*
Huffman, William L. 1947- *St&PR 91*
Huffman-Hine, Ruth Carson 1925- *WhoAmW 91*
Huffman Sleeper, Kathryn Rae 1960- *IntWWM 90*
Hufford, David Clinton 1945- *WhoSSW 91*
Huffstetler, Noah Haywood, III 1951- *WhoEmL 91*
Huffstetler, Palmer Eugene 1937- *St&PR 91, WhoAm 90*
Huffstickler, James Edward 1942- *WhoSSW 91*
Huffstickler, Patrick Lee 1960- *WhoEmL 91*
Huffstodt, Karen *WhoAm 90*
Hufft, John Carlton 1925- *St&PR 91, WhoAm 90*
Hufham, Barbara Frances 1939- *St&PR 91*
Hufhines, Bobby Ray 1943- *St&PR 91*
Hufnagel, Charles A. 1916-1989 *AnObit 1989, BioIn 16*
Hufnagel, Ellen M. 1948- *WhoAmW 91*
Hufnagel, Linda Ann 1939- *WhoAmW 91*
Hufnagel, Robert Joseph 1953- *St&PR 91*
Hufnagle, Richard Angell 1950- *St&PR 91*
Hufschmidt, Maynard Michael 1912- *WhoAm 90*
Hufstedler, Seth Martin 1922- *WhoAm 90*
Hufstedler, Shirley Mount 1925- *BiDrUSE 89, WhoAm 90, WhoAmW 91*
Huftalen, Lisa Freeman 1953- *WhoE 91*
Hug, Adolf H 1926- *BiDrAPA 89*
Hug, Joan Tonning 1951- *WhoEmL 91, WhoSSW 91*
Hug, Procter Ralph, Jr. 1931- *WhoAm 90*
Hug, Richard E. 1935- *St&PR 91*
Hug, Richard Ernest 1935- *WhoAm 90, WhoE 91*
Hug, Robert Charles, Jr. 1940- *St&PR 91*
Hug, Stephen Louis 1956- *WhoE 91*
Hug, Theo 1906- *IntWWM 90*
Hugander, Anders 1946- *WhoWor 91*
Huge, Arthur W. 1945- *St&PR 91*
Huge, Arthur William 1945- *WhoAm 90*
Huge, Harry 1937- *WhoAm 90*
Huge, Thomas Arnold 1944- *WhoWor 91*
Hugeburc of Heidenheim *EncCoWW*
Hugel, Charles E. 1928- *St&PR 91, WhoAm 90*
Hugel, Philip Rudolph, IV 1940- *WhoSSW 91*
Hugel, Robert W 1931- *BiDrAPA 89*
Hugelin, Andre Henri 1923- *WhoWor 91*
Huger, Raymond A 1917- *BiDrAPA 89*
Hugessen, James K. 1933- *WhoE 91*
Huget, Eugene Floyd 1931- *WhoSSW 91*
Hugford, Don Enrico *PenDiDA 89*
Hugg, Terry Wayne *BiDrAPA 89*
Huggard, Eileen Elisabeth 1957- *WhoAmW 91*
Huggard, Ernest Douglas 1933- *St&PR 91, WhoAm 90*
Huggard, John Parker 1945- *WhoEmL 91*
Hugghins, Beverly Kennon 1927- *St&PR 91*
Hugghins, Ernest Jay 1920- *WhoAm 90*
Hugghins, Joseph Harris 1925- *St&PR 91*
Huggins, Allan Wesley 1949- *WhoEmL 91*
Huggins, Charles B. 1901- *WorAlBi*
Huggins, Charles Brenton 1901- *WhoAm 90, WhoWor 91*
Huggins, Charles Edward *NewYTBS 90*
Huggins, Charles Edward 1929- *WhoAm 90*
Huggins, Charles Edward 1929-1990 *BioIn 16*
Huggins, Frederick Anthony 1935- *St&PR 91*
Huggins, Laura Linn 1959- *WhoSSW 91*
Huggins, Marion D., Jr. 1941- *St&PR 91*
Huggins, Mary Louise White 1933- *WhoAmW 91*
Huggins, Miller 1879-1929 *Ballpl 90 [port], BioIn 16, WorAlBi*
Huggins, Nancy J. 1952- *St&PR 91*
Huggins, Nathan I 1927- *SmATA 63*
Huggins, Nathan Irvin 1927-1989 *BioIn 16, ConAu 130*
Huggins, Norman Dee 1947- *BiDrAPA 89*
Huggins, P Kenneth 1932- *BiDrAPA 89*
Huggins, R. Troy 1936- *St&PR 91*
Huggins, Randall D. 1959- *WhoEmL 91*
Huggins, Richard *BioIn 16*
Huggins, Rollin Charles, Jr. 1931- *WhoAm 90*
Huggins, Sara Espe 1913- *WhoAm 90*
Huggins, Tryon K., Jr. 1931- *St&PR 91*
Huggins, Victor, Jr 1936- *WhoAmA 91*
Huggins, William 1824-1910 *WorAlBi*
Huggins, William Herbert 1919- *WhoAm 90*
Huggins, William Hooper 1927- *St&PR 91*
Huggler, Max Melchior 1903- *WhoWor 91*
Hugh, Lori Evan 1959- *WhoAmW 91*
Hughan, Jessie Wallace 1875-1955 *EncAL*
Hughen, Lowell Harry 1937- *WhoAm 90*
Hughes, Aidan 1952- *St&PR 91*
Hughes, Alan 1952- *St&PR 91*
Hughes, Albert R., Jr. 1927- *St&PR 91*
Hughes, Alfred Clifton 1932- *WhoAm 90*
Hughes, Allan Bebout 1924- *WhoAm 90*
Hughes, Allen 1921- *WhoAm 90*
Hughes, Andy Karl 1958- *WhoEmL 91*
Hughes, Anita Hart 1960- *WhoAmW 91*
Hughes, Ann 1944- *WhoAmW 91*
Hughes, Ann H 1929- *BiDrAPA 89*
Hughes, Ann Hightower 1938- *WhoAm 90, WhoAmW 91*
Hughes, Ann Nolen 1933- *WhoAmW 91*
Hughes, Anne *FemiCLE*
Hughes, Anne Rosemarie 1955- *WhoAmW 91*
Hughes, Anthony D. 1934- *ODwPR 91*
Hughes, Arthur 1832-1915 *BioIn 16*
Hughes, Arthur Hyde 1952- *WhoEmL 91, WhoSSW 91*
Hughes, Arwel 1909-1988 *PenDiMP*
Hughes, Author E. 1929- *WhoAm 90*
Hughes, Barbara Ann 1938- *WhoAmW 91*
Hughes, Barbara Bradford 1941- *WhoAmW 91, WhoWor 91*
Hughes, Barbara Lynn 1961- *WhoEmL 91*
Hughes, Barbara Suzanne 1943- *WhoAmW 91*
Hughes, Barnard 1915- *WhoAm 90*
Hughes, Beldon Earl 1947- *WhoEmL 91*
Hughes, Bernard A. 1930- *St&PR 91*
Hughes, Betty *ODwPR 91*
Hughes, Beverly 1949- *WhoAmA 91*
Hughes, Bill *ODwPR 91*
Hughes, Bradley Richard 1954- *WhoEmL 91*
Hughes, Brian Gordon Richard 1954- *WhoEmL 91*
Hughes, Calvin Hoover *BiDrAPA 89*
Hughes, Carl Andrew 1948- *WhoSSW 91*
Hughes, Carl Wilson 1914- *WhoAm 90*
Hughes, Carolyn 1921- *WhoAmW 91*
Hughes, Carolyn Jeanne 1957- *WhoAmW 91, WhoEmL 91*
Hughes, Carolyn S. 1921- *WhoHisp 91*
Hughes, Carroll Thornton, Jr. 1931- *St&PR 91*
Hughes, Charles Campbell 1929- *WhoAm 90*
Hughes, Charles Evans 1862-1948 *BiDrUSE 89, BioIn 16, WorAlBi*
Hughes, Charles Evans 1938- *St&PR 91*
Hughes, Charles Jackson 1954- *WhoSSW 91*
Hughes, Charles William 1900- *IntWWM 90*
Hughes, Christine Georgette 1946- *WhoAmW 91, WhoSSW 91*
Hughes, Christopher 1786-1849 *BioIn 16*
Hughes, Claudette J 1959- *BiDrAPA 89*
Hughes, Colin *MajTwCW*
Hughes, Cynthia *BioIn 16*
Hughes, Dana T. 1922- *ODwPR 91*
Hughes, David 1930- *ConAu 129, WorAu 1980*
Hughes, David Emery 1947- *St&PR 91*
Hughes, David H. 1928- *WhoAm 90*
Hughes, David Henry 1943- *WhoSSW 91*
Hughes, David John 1942- *St&PR 91*
Hughes, David Joseph 1940- *WhoAm 90*
Hughes, David Michael 1939- *St&PR 91, WhoAm 90*
Hughes, David W. *St&PR 91*
Hughes, David Weirick 1945- *IntWWM 90*
Hughes, Dean 1943- *AuBYP 90, BioIn 16, WhoWrEP 89*
Hughes, Deborah Pifer 1963- *WhoSSW 91*
Hughes, Debra Lynn *BiDrAPA 89*
Hughes, Delbert E 1925- *BiDrAPA 89*
Hughes, Delia Ann 1947- *WhoAmW 91*
Hughes, Delos Dyson 1934- *WhoAm 90*
Hughes, Dennis Edward 1954- *WhoSSW 91*
Hughes, Dennis William 1951- *St&PR 91*
Hughes, Derek Dominic *BiDrAPA 89*
Hughes, Dick 1938- *Ballpl 90*
Hughes, Donald Duane *BiDrAPA 89*
Hughes, Donald J. 1941- *St&PR 91*
Hughes, Donald R. 1929- *WhoAm 90*
Hughes, Dorothy B. 1904- *FemiCLE, TwCCr&M 91*
Hughes, Dorothy Todd 1898- *WhoAmW 91*
Hughes, Douglas H 1954- *BiDrAPA 89*
Hughes, Douglas Histed 1954- *WhoE 91*
Hughes, Dusty *ConAu 131*
Hughes, Earl Mulford 1907- *WhoAm 90*
Hughes, Edgar Clayton 1939- *WhoSSW 91*
Hughes, Edward Cyril 1935- *WhoE 91*
Hughes, Edward D. 1942- *St&PR 91*
Hughes, Edward Hunter 1921- *WhoAm 90*
Hughes, Edward James 1930- *BioIn 16*
Hughes, Edward John 1913- *WhoAm 90, WhoAmA 91*
Hughes, Edward T. 1920- *WhoAm 90, WhoE 91*
Hughes, Edward W 1934- *BiDrAPA 89*
Hughes, Edwin Ross 1928- *WhoAm 90*
Hughes, Elinor Lambert 1906- *WhoAm 90*
Hughes, Eril Barnett 1953- *WhoSSW 91*
Hughes, Ethel Lena 1933- *WhoAmW 91*
Hughes, Eugene Morgan 1934- *WhoAm 90*
Hughes, Everett Clark 1904- *WhoAm 90*

Hughes, Faye Adele 1946- *WhoAmW 91, WhoE 91*
Hughes, Finola *BioIn 16*
Hughes, Fred *BioIn 16*
Hughes, Frieda *BioIn 16*
Hughes, Garry *NewAgMG*
Hughes, George Allen 1940- *St&PR 91*
Hughes, George David 1930- *WhoAm 90*
Hughes, George Edward 1950- *WhoSSW 91*
Hughes, George Edward Harcourt 1944- *WhoWor 91*
Hughes, George Farant, Jr. 1923- *WhoSSW 91*
Hughes, George Maxwell Knight 1928- *WhoE 91*
Hughes, George Michael 1939- *WhoAm 90*
Hughes, George S 1920- *BiDrAPA 89*
Hughes, George Vincent 1930- *St&PR 91*
Hughes, George Wendell 1929- *WhoAm 90*
Hughes, Gerald 1875-1956 *EncABHB 7*
Hughes, Gordon Elliot 1922- *St&PR 91*
Hughes, Grace-Flores 1946- *WhoAm 90*
Hughes, Grant B 1917- *BiDrAPA 89*
Hughes, Harold Hasbrouck, Jr. 1930- *WhoAm 90, WhoSSW 91*
Hughes, Harriet S. 1946- *WhoEmL 91*
Hughes, Heidi 1948- *WhoEmL 91*
Hughes, Helen Ruth 1914- *WhoWrEP 89*
Hughes, Henry Stuart 1916- *WhoAm 90*
Hughes, Herbert Leslie *St&PR 91N*
Hughes, Howard R., Jr. 1905-1976 *WorAlBi*
Hughes, Ian Frank 1940- *St&PR 91, WhoAm 90*
Hughes, Irene *EncO&P 3*
Hughes, J. Deborah 1948- *WhoAmW 91, WhoEmL 91*
Hughes, J. Lawrence *BioIn 16*
Hughes, James A. 1912- *St&PR 91*
Hughes, James Baker, Jr. 1938- *WhoSSW 91*
Hughes, James Donald 1951- *WhoEmL 91*
Hughes, James Eugene *BiDrAPA 89*
Hughes, James F. *ODwPR 91*
Hughes, James Francis 1943- *WhoE 91*
Hughes, James Joseph 1956- *St&PR 91*
Hughes, James M. 1950- *St&PR 91*
Hughes, James Paul 1920- *WhoAm 90*
Hughes, James Sinclair 1934- *WhoE 91*
Hughes, Jane Wolford 1920- *WhoAmW 91*
Hughes, Jeffry Scott 1954- *WhoEmL 91*
Hughes, Jim 1874-1924 *Ballpl 90*
Hughes, Jim 1951- *Ballpl 90*
Hughes, Jimmy H. 1921- *St&PR 91*
Hughes, Jo Blair *BioIn 16*
Hughes, Joan Linda 1947- *WhoEmL 91*
Hughes, Jodie C. *ODwPR 91*
Hughes, Joe *BioIn 16*
Hughes, Joe Don 1933- *WhoSSW 91*
Hughes, Joe Kenneth 1927- *WhoAm 90*
Hughes, John *BioIn 16*
Hughes, John 1926-1988 *AnObit 1988*
Hughes, John 1943- *WhoAm 90*
Hughes, John 1950?- *ConAu 129*
Hughes, John David 1935- *WhoE 91*
Hughes, John Edward 1922- *WhoAm 90*
Hughes, John Edwin 1927- *St&PR 91*
Hughes, John Farrell 1946- *St&PR 91, WhoAm 90*
Hughes, John L *BiDrAPA 89*
Hughes, John Lawrence 1925- *St&PR 91, WhoAm 90*
Hughes, John M. 1934- *St&PR 91*
Hughes, John Patrick 1947- *WhoE 91*
Hughes, John R. 1937- *St&PR 91*
Hughes, John Russell 1928- *WhoAm 90*
Hughes, John Russell 1949- *BiDrAPA 89, WhoE 91*
Hughes, John Vance 1946- *WhoEmL 91*
Hughes, John W. *WhoAm 90*
Hughes, Jon Christopher 1945- *WhoWrEP 89*
Hughes, Jonathan Roberts Tyson 1928- *WhoAm 90*
Hughes, Joseph D. 1910- *WhoAm 90*
Hughes, Josephine Blair *NewYTBS 90*
Hughes, Juanita Q. 1940- *St&PR 91*
Hughes, Judith Ann 1940- *BiDrAPA 89*
Hughes, Judith Lee 1940- *WhoAmW 91*
Hughes, Judy Lynne 1939- *WhoAmW 91*
Hughes, Judy Sanders 1957- *WhoAmW 91*
Hughes, Juliana Genine 1962- *WhoAmW 91*
Hughes, Karen Gray 1954- *WhoEmL 91*
Hughes, Karen Lu 1947- *WhoAmW 91*
Hughes, Karen S. 1954- *St&PR 91*
Hughes, Karen Woodbury 1940- *WhoAmW 91, WhoSSW 91*
Hughes, Katherine *ODwPR 91*
Hughes, Katherine Elaine 1950- *WhoWrEP 89*
Hughes, Kathleen Ann *BiDrAPA 89*
Hughes, Keith W. 1946- *St&PR 91*
Hughes, Keith William 1946- *WhoAm 90, WhoSSW 91*
Hughes, Kenneth Joseph 1943- *WhoAm 90*
Hughes, Kenneth Russell 1925- *WhoAm 90*
Hughes, Kennette Ann 1961- *WhoSSW 91*
Hughes, Kent Higgon 1941- *WhoE 91*
Hughes, Kerry C *BiDrAPA 89*
Hughes, Kevin Bernard *BiDrAPA 89*
Hughes, Kevin Bernard 1947- *WhoE 91*
Hughes, Kim Knox 1953- *WhoWrEP 89*
Hughes, Kristine Fugal 1938- *St&PR 91*
Hughes, L. Jane 1950- *WhoAmW 91*
Hughes, Langston 1902-1967 *BioIn 16, DrBlPA 90, EarBlAP, EncAL, MajTwCW, PoeCrit 1 [port], ShSCr 6 [port], WorAlBi*
Hughes, Langston 1902-1969 *AuBYP 90*
Hughes, Lark 1949- *BiDrAPA 89*
Hughes, Lenore Harris 1914- *WhoWrEP 89*
Hughes, Linda J. 1950- *WhoAmW 91*
Hughes, Linda Renate 1947- *WhoEmL 91*
Hughes, Linda Ruth *BiDrAPA 89*
Hughes, Long Tom 1878-1956 *Ballpl 90*
Hughes, Louis B. 1938- *St&PR 91*
Hughes, Lynn Feeney 1939- *St&PR 91*
Hughes, Lynn Nettleton 1941- *WhoAm 90, WhoSSW 91*
Hughes, Marcia Anne 1962- *WhoAmW 91*
Hughes, Margaret Eileen 1943- *WhoAm 90*
Hughes, Marie Sharon 1955- *WhoAmW 91*
Hughes, Marija Matich *WhoAm 90*
Hughes, Marjorie Kefover 1943- *WhoE 91*
Hughes, Mark Andrew *BiDrAPA 89*
Hughes, Mark Brian 1956- *WhoEmL 91*
Hughes, Martin Glyn 1950- *IntWWM 90*
Hughes, Mary Elizabeth 1940- *WhoAmW 91*
Hughes, Mary Elizabeth 1946- *WhoE 91*
Hughes, Max Madoc *BiDrAPA 89*
Hughes, Michael C 1937- *BiDrAPA 89*
Hughes, Michael Charles 1949- *St&PR 91*
Hughes, Michael E. *ODwPR 91*
Hughes, Michael Joseph 1951- *WhoSSW 91*
Hughes, Michael Murray 1937- *WhoAm 90*
Hughes, Michaela Kelly *WhoAm 90*
Hughes, Mike 1948- *WhoAm 90*
Hughes, Molly 1867-1956 *BioIn 16*
Hughes, Monica *BioIn 16*
Hughes, Monica 1925- *SmATA 11AS [port]*
Hughes, Nicholas David 1945- *St&PR 91*
Hughes, Owain Arwel 1942- *IntWWM 90, PenDiMP*
Hughes, Patricia Saddler 1931- *WhoWrEP 89*
Hughes, Patrick H 1934- *BiDrAPA 89*
Hughes, Patrick L 1955- *BiDrAPA 89*
Hughes, Patrick Paul 1952- *WhoEmL 91*
Hughes, Paul Cecil 1946- *WhoSSW 91*
Hughes, Paul Craig 1921- *St&PR 91*
Hughes, Paul Jones, III 1949- *WhoEmL 91*
Hughes, Paul Lucien 1938- *WhoAmA 91*
Hughes, Paula Guilfoyle 1955- *WhoAmW 91*
Hughes, Peter 1921- *AuBYP 90*
Hughes, Peter James 1933- *WhoAm 90*
Hughes, Peter William 1947- *WhoE 91*
Hughes, Philip C. 1940- *St&PR 91*
Hughes, Phillip Samuel 1917- *WhoAm 90*
Hughes, Ralph Lyle 1924- *St&PR 91*
Hughes, Randall James 1962- *WhoEmL 91*
Hughes, Ray Harrison 1924- *WhoAm 90*
Hughes, Raymond Hargett 1927- *WhoSSW 91*
Hughes, Revella E 1895-1987 *DcAfAmP*
Hughes, Rhetta *DrBlPA 90*
Hughes, Richard 1900-1976 *MajTwCW*
Hughes, Richard 1937- *St&PR 91*
Hughes, Richard Glynne 1955- *WhoWrEP 89*
Hughes, Richard Holland 1947- *ConAu 131*
Hughes, Richard William 1933- *St&PR 91*
Hughes, Robert *BioIn 16*
Hughes, Robert 1938?- *WorAu 1980 [port]*
Hughes, Robert Carey 1940- *WhoAm 90*
Hughes, Robert E. *BioIn 16*
Hughes, Robert Edward 1924- *WhoAm 90*
Hughes, Robert Edwin 1931- *St&PR 91, WhoAm 90*
Hughes, Robert F. 1932- *St&PR 91*
Hughes, Robert Harrison 1917- *WhoAm 90*
Hughes, Robert John 1946- *WhoAm 90, WhoE 91*
Hughes, Robert King 1936- *WhoSSW 91*
Hughes, Robert Michael 1955- *WhoEmL 91*
Hughes, Robert S F 1938- *WhoAmA 91*
Hughes, Robert Studley Forrest 1938- *WhoAm 90*
Hughes, Robert William 1935- *St&PR 91*
Hughes, Roger Louis 1945- *St&PR 91*
Hughes, Ronald F 1945- *BiDrAPA 89*
Hughes, Roy 1911- *Ballpl 90*
Hughes, Roy Elward 1924- *WhoAm 90*
Hughes, Russell Clair, III 1951- *WhoEmL 91*
Hughes, Russell Meriwether 1898-1988 *BioIn 16*
Hughes, Sammy 1910-1981 *Ballpl 90*
Hughes, Sandi *BioIn 16*
Hughes, Sara *ODwPR 91*
Hughes, Shirley 1929- *AuBYP 90*
Hughes, Simon Henry Ward 1951- *BioIn 16*
Hughes, Simon P. 1830-1906 *BioIn 16*
Hughes, Spike 1908-1987 *OxCPMus*
Hughes, Stacey 1927- *IntWWM 90*
Hughes, Stan *BioIn 16*
Hughes, Stanley John 1918- *WhoAm 90*
Hughes, Stanley Ray 1940- *WhoSSW 91*
Hughes, Stephen David 1955- *WhoSSW 91*
Hughes, Stephen Edward 1953- *WhoEmL 91*
Hughes, Steven Jay 1948- *WhoEmL 91, WhoSSW 91, WhoWor 91*
Hughes, Steven William 1952- *St&PR 91*
Hughes, Sue Margaret *WhoAm 90, WhoAmW 91, WhoSSW 91, WhoWor 91*
Hughes, Susan Curtis 1952- *WhoSSW 91*
Hughes, Ted 1930- *AuBYP 90, BioIn 16, ConAu 33NR, MajTwCW, WhoAm 90, WhoWor 91, WorAlBi*
Hughes, Ted Warrington 1934- *St&PR 91*
Hughes, Thomas 1822-1896 *BioIn 16, WorAlBi*
Hughes, Thomas H. 1929- *St&PR 91, WhoAm 90*
Hughes, Thomas Joseph 1926- *WhoAm 90*
Hughes, Thomas Joseph 1943- *WhoAm 90*
Hughes, Thomas Leland 1924- *WhoE 91*
Hughes, Thomas Lowe 1925- *WhoAm 90*
Hughes, Thomas Michael 1959- *WhoEmL 91*
Hughes, Thomas Parke 1923- *WhoAm 90*
Hughes, Tom *BioIn 16*
Hughes, Tom 1884-1961 *Ballpl 90*
Hughes, Tommy 1919- *Ballpl 90*
Hughes, Tracy *BiDrAPA 89, WhoWrEP 89*
Hughes, Vester Thomas, Jr. 1928- *WhoAm 90, WhoWor 91*
Hughes, Vincent George 1958- *St&PR 91*
Hughes, Walter *AuBYP 90*
Hughes, Walter Jay, Sr. 1942- *WhoWrEP 89*
Hughes, Walter T. 1930- *WhoAm 90*
Hughes, Waunell M 1928- *BiDrAPA 89*
Hughes, Waunell McDonald 1928- *WhoAmW 91*
Hughes, Wendy Lenore 1961- *WhoEmL 91*
Hughes, Wiley R. 1940- *St&PR 91*
Hughes, William Alan 1952- *St&PR 91*
Hughes, William Anthony 1921- *WhoAm 90, WhoSSW 91*
Hughes, William Cofer 1936- *St&PR 91*
Hughes, William Drennan 1928- *St&PR 91*
Hughes, William Fanning 1952- *WhoSSW 91*
Hughes, William Frank 1930- *WhoAm 90*
Hughes, William Franklin, Jr. 1913- *WhoAm 90*
Hughes, William John 1932- *WhoAm 90, WhoE 91*
Hughes, William Lesley 1924- *St&PR 91*
Hughes, William Lewis 1926- *WhoAm 90*
Hughes, William Nolin 1918- *WhoAm 90*
Hughes, William Taylor 1936- *WhoAm 90*
Hughes, Winston C *BiDrAPA 89*
Hughes, Woody 1956- *BioIn 16*
Hughes, Yvonne Lee 1940- *WhoAmW 91*
Hughes-Calero, Heather 1938- *WhoWrEP 89*
Hughett, Arthur, Jr. *BiDrAPA 89*
Hughett, Bryce G *BiDrAPA 89*
Hughett, John Paul 1946- *WhoSSW 91*
Hughey, Bill G. 1935- *St&PR 91*
Hughey, Don W. 1941- *St&PR 91*
Hughey, Eric Joseph 1950- *WhoSSW 91*
Hughey, Jane Bond 1935- *WhoSSW 91*
Hughey, Jim 1869-1945 *Ballpl 90*
Hughey, Jo A. 1966- *WhoWrEP 89*
Hughey, John Emory 1939- *St&PR 91*
Hughey, Kirk 1940- *WhoAmA 91*
Hughey, Lucinda Kay 1962- *WhoAm 90*
Hughey, Richard 1953- *IntWWM 90*
Hughey, Roberta 1942- *SmATA 61 [port]*
Hughitt, Jeremiah Keefe 1930- *WhoAm 90*
Hughlett, Robert Brooks 1918- *WhoAm 90*
Hughs, Mary Geraldine 1929- *WhoAmW 91*
Hughs, Richard Earl 1936- *WhoAm 90*
Hughs, Robert Nathaniel 1917- *WhoAm 90*
Hughson, Tex 1916- *Ballpl 90, BioIn 16*
Hughson, William J.C. 1926- *St&PR 91*
Hughston, Lane Palmer 1951- *WhoWor 91*
Hughto, Darryl Leo 1943- *WhoAmA 91*
Hughto, Margie A 1944- *WhoAmA 91*
Hugin, Adolph Charles Eugene 1907- *WhoSSW 91, WhoWor 91*
Hugo d'Oignies *PenDiDA 89*
Hugo, Grant *ConAu 33NR*
Hugo, Joan 1930- *WhoAmA 91*
Hugo, Matile 1940- *IntWWM 90*
Hugo, Michel *BioIn 16*
Hugo, Norman Eliot 1933- *WhoAm 90, WhoE 91*
Hugo, Richard *EncCoWW*
Hugo, Victor 1802-1885 *BioIn 16, EncO&P 3, WorAlBi*
Hugo, Victor Marie 1802-1885 *BiDFrPL, EncPaPR 91*
Hugstad, Paul Steven 1943- *WhoAm 90*
Huguenard, James Aaron 1954- *WhoEmL 91*
Huguenin, G. Richard 1937- *St&PR 91*
Hugues, Jeanne 1855-1914? *BiDWomA*
Huguet, Jaume 1414-1492 *IntDcAA 90*
Hugunin, James Richard 1947- *WhoAmA 91*
Hugus, Richard Denny 1949- *St&PR 91*
Hugus, Z Zimmerman, Jr. 1923- *WhoAm 90*
Huhmann, Paula M. 1934- *St&PR 91*
Huhmann, William Joseph 1938- *St&PR 91*
Huhn, David Raymond 1937- *WhoAm 90*
Huhn, Gary R. 1949- *St&PR 91*
Huhn, Jochen 1930- *WhoWor 91*
Huhndorf, Susan Koura 1954- *WhoEmL 91*
Huhta, Art *EncACom*
Huhta, James Kenneth 1937- *WhoSSW 91, WhoWor 91*
Huhta, Richard S. 1931- *WhoWrEP 89*
Huhtamo, Kari Kauko Johannes 1943- *WhoWor 91*
Huhtanen, Wayne H. 1954- *St&PR 91*
Huhtaniemi, Ilpo Tapani 1947- *WhoWor 91*
Hui, Jacques A. 1933- *WhoWor 91*
Hui, Pat 1943- *WhoAmA 91*
Hui, Sek Wen 1935- *WhoE 91*
Hui, Steve L.W. 1949- *St&PR 91*
Hui, Yin Fat 1936- *WhoWor 91*
Huiatt, Ronald Dean 1950- *WhoEmL 91*
Huidobro, Matias Montes 1931- *BioIn 16*
Huidobro, Vicente *ConAu 131, HispWr 90*
Huidobro, Vicente 1893-1948 *BioIn 16, WorAlBi*
Huidobro Fernandez, Vicente Garcia 1893-1948 *ConAu 131, HispWr 90*
Huie, Irving Raymond 1928- *WhoAm 90*
Huie, Robert Edwin 1929- *St&PR 91*
Huie, William Orr 1911- *WhoAm 90*
Huisgen, Rolf K.J. 1920- *WhoWor 91*
Huisman, Arvid Elton 1948- *WhoEmL 91*
Huismann, Mark 1958- *Ballpl 90*
Huitfeldt, Henrik Jorgen 1936- *WhoWor 91*
Huitt, Jimmie L. 1923- *WhoAm 90, WhoWor 91*
Huitt, Sigmon 1945- *ODwPR 91*
Huizenga, H. Wayne *BioIn 16*
Huizenga, John Robert 1921- *WhoAm 90*
Huizenga, Judith N 1938- *BiDrAPA 89*
Huizenga, Linda Ann 1962- *WhoEmL 91*
Huizenga, Philip Buryl *BiDrAPA 89*
Huizer, Gerrit Jan 1929- *WhoWor 91*
Huizingh, William 1919- *WhoAm 90*
Hujdich, Brian Michael 1963- *WhoE 91*
Huk, Stephen G. 1955- *BiDrAPA 89*
Huk, William J. 1943- *St&PR 91*
Hukill, Beth Ann 1962- *WhoAmW 91*
Hukkinen, Lars Johan 1928- *WhoWor 91*
Hulack, Lawrence B. *ODwPR 91*
Hulbert, Bruce Walker 1937- *WhoAm 90*
Hulbert, Jack 1892-1978 *OxCPMus*
Hulbert, Mark *BioIn 16*
Hulbert, Mary Frances 1942- *WhoAmW 91*
Hulbert, Randall Craig 1949- *BiDrAPA 89*
Hulbert, Richard Woodward 1929- *WhoAm 90*
Hulbert, Samuel Foster 1936- *WhoAm 90*
Hulbert, Sidney Z 1917- *BiDrAPA 89*
Hulbert, William 1832-1882 *Ballpl 90 [port]*
Hulbert, William Ambrose 1832-1882 *BioIn 16*
Hulce, Tom 1953- *WhoAm 90, WorAlBi*
Hulcher, Julia M 1956- *BiDrAPA 89*
Hulden, Lars 1926- *DcScanL*
Huldt, Bo Kristofer 1941- *WhoWor 91*
Huldt, Johan 1942- *ConDes 90*
Huldt, Lennart Sten 1918- *WhoWor 91*
Hulen, James Rozier 1933- *St&PR 91*
Hulet, Ervin Kenneth 1926- *WhoAm 90*
Hulett, Simonne R *WhoAmA 91*
Hulett, Tim 1960- *Ballpl 90*
Hulfachor, Lester Eugene 1937- *WhoSSW 91*
Hulford, Denise Lovona 1944- *IntWWM 90*

Hulick, Diana Emery WhoAmA 91
Hulick, Timothy P. 1942- St&PR 91
Hulin-Salkin, Belinda 1954- WhoAmW 91
Huling, Kendall Faye 1965- WhoAmW 91
Hulings, Henry B. 1937- St&PR 91
Hulings, Norman McDermott, Jr. 1923- WhoAm 90
Hulka, Barbara Sorenson 1931- WhoAm 90, WhoAmW 91
Hulka, Jaroslav Fabian 1930- WhoAm 90
Hulkower, Jonathan Lee BiDrAPA 89
Hulkower, Neal David 1949- WhoE 91
Hull, Ann Pekrul 1949- WhoEmL 91
Hull, Bobby BioIn 16
Hull, Bobby 1939- WhoAm 90, WorAlBi
Hull, Brenda Sue 1953- WhoEmL 91
Hull, Brett BioIn 16
Hull, Brett 1969- WorAlBi
Hull, Cathy 1946- WhoAm 90, WhoAmA 91
Hull, Charles Eugene 1944- St&PR 91
Hull, Charles William 1936- WhoWor 91
Hull, Cordell 1871-1955 BiDrUSE 89, BioIn 16, WorAlBi
Hull, Cordell William 1933- WhoAm 90, WhoWor 91
Hull, Dallas C. 1949- ODwPR 91
Hull, Daniel Louis 1956- WhoEmL 91
Hull, David Frank 1951- WhoEmL 91
Hull, David George 1937- WhoAm 90
Hull, David P. 1935- St&PR 91
Hull, David Stewart 1938- WhoE 91
Hull, Derek 1931- WhoWor 91
Hull, Donald R. St&PR 91
Hull, Douglas Michael 1952- WhoEmL 91
Hull, Doyle E. 1933- St&PR 91
Hull, Doyle Edwin 1933- WhoAm 90
Hull, Dwight Sigworth, II 1943- WhoSSW 91
Hull, E. M. FemiCLE
Hull, Earl J. 1933- St&PR 91
Hull, Elaine Mangelsdorf 1940- WhoAmW 91
Hull, Elizabeth Anne 1937- WhoAmW 91
Hull, Eugene R. 1933- St&PR 91
Hull, Fred T. 1937- St&PR 91
Hull, George H 1925- BiDrAPA 89
Hull, Gregory Stewart 1950- WhoAmA 91
Hull, Gretchen Gaebelein BioIn 16
Hull, Harry 1912- WhoAm 90
Hull, Helen Rose 1888-1971 FemiCLE
Hull, Henrietta Goodnough 1889-1967 BioIn 16
Hull, Herbert Mitchell 1919- WhoAm 90
Hull, Isaac 1773-1843 WorAlBi
Hull, J. Richard 1933- St&PR 91
Hull, James C. 1937- St&PR 91
Hull, James Charles 1937- WhoAm 90
Hull, James Donald 1946- WhoEmL 91
Hull, James Richard 1933- WhoAm 90
Hull, Jane Laurel Leek 1923- WhoAmW 91
Hull, Jesse Redding 1932- BioIn 16
Hull, John BioIn 16, WhoAmA 91
Hull, John 1624-1683 PenDiDA 89
Hull, John Laurence 1924- St&PR 91
Hull, John T., Jr. 1944- St&PR 91
Hull, John Thomas, Jr. 1944- WhoAm 90
Hull, Joseph Stephen 1933- WhoSSW 91
Hull, Josephine 1884-1957 BioAmW
Hull, Kathryn B. 1928- IntWWM 90
Hull, Kathryn Blomquist 1928- WhoAmW 91
Hull, Kenneth J. 1936- St&PR 91
Hull, Kenneth James 1936- WhoAm 90
Hull, Larry Wayne 1950- WhoEmL 91
Hull, Lewis Woodruff 1916- St&PR 91, WhoAm 90, WhoE 91, WhoWor 91
Hull, Louise Knox 1912- WhoAmW 91
Hull, Margaret Ruth 1921- WhoAmW 91, WhoSSW 91
Hull, Marie WhoAmA 91N
Hull, McAllister Hobart, Jr. 1923- WhoAm 90
Hull, Nicole Karol 1964- WhoAmW 91
Hull, Norman J., Jr. 1918- St&PR 91
Hull, Paul G. 1940- St&PR 91
Hull, Peggy 1889-1967 BioIn 16
Hull, Philip Glasgow 1925- WhoAm 90, WhoE 91
Hull, Piatt Harold 1914- St&PR 91
Hull, Ralph F BiDrAPA 89
Hull, Raymond Whitford 1946- WhoE 91, WhoEmL 91
Hull, Richard 1896-1973 TwCCr&M 91
Hull, Richard 1907-1989 AnObit 1989
Hull, Rita Prizler 1936- WhoAmW 91
Hull, Robert C 1921- BiDrAPA 89
Hull, Robert Fulton 1943- WhoSSW 91
Hull, Robert Glenn 1929- St&PR 91, WhoAm 90
Hull, Robert Kingsley 1951- WhoE 91
Hull, Roger Harold 1942- WhoAm 90
Hull, Ronald H 1925- BiDrAPA 89
Hull, Suzanne White 1921- WhoAm 90, WhoAmW 91
Hull, Thomas AmLegL
Hull, Thomas Gray 1926- WhoAm 90, WhoSSW 91
Hull, Treat Clark 1921- WhoAm 90, WhoE 91
Hull, Wesley Vannoy 1937- WhoAm 90
Hull, William 1753-1825 WorAlBi
Hull, William 1818?- AmLegL
Hull, William Edward 1930- WhoAm 90
Hull, William Floyd, Jr. 1920- WhoAm 90
Hull, William Henry 1918- WhoAm 90
Hull, William Martin, Jr. 1937- WhoSSW 91
Hullar, Theodore Lee 1935- WhoAm 90, WhoWor 91
Hullemann, Klaus-Diethart 1938- WhoWor 91
Hullen, Werner 1927- WhoWor 91
Hulley, Clair Montrose 1925- WhoAm 90
Hulley, Keith R. 1940- St&PR 91
Hulley-Liverman, Joan Frances BiDrAPA 89
Hullfish, William Rouse 1937- IntWWM 90
Hullin, Susan ODwPR 91
Hullin, Tod R. ODwPR 91
Hulme, Darlys Mae 1937- WhoAmW 91
Hulme, George 1913- WhoWor 91
Hulme, Keri 1947- FemiCLE, WorAu 1980 [port]
Hulme, Patrick James 1944- St&PR 91
Hulme, T. E. 1883-1917 WorAlBi
Hulmer, Eric Claus 1915-1988 WhoAmA 91N
Hulnick, Mary R. 1944- WhoAmW 91
Hulsbos, Cornie Leonard 1920- WhoAm 90
Hulse, Dexter Curtis 1952- WhoWor 91
Hulse, George Althouse 1934- WhoAm 90
Hulse, James William 1935- St&PR 91
Hulse, Jerry 1924- WhoAm 90, WhoWor 91
Hulse, Jesse Gifford 1955- WhoSSW 91
Hulse, John Edward 1933- WhoAm 90
Hulse, Paul Stephen St&PR 91
Hulse, Stewart Harding, Jr. 1931- WhoAm 90
Hulsebosch, Charles J. 1933- St&PR 91
Hulsebosch, Charles Joseph 1933- WhoAm 90
Hulsey, Michael David 1957- WhoEmL 91
Hulsey, Sam Byron 1932- WhoAm 90
Hulsey, Tammy Kaye 1961- WhoAmW 91
Hulsing, Darel John 1942- BiDrAPA 89
Hulsizer, Robert Inslee, Jr. 1919- WhoAm 90
Hulslander, Richard T. 1937- St&PR 91
Hulst, John B. WhoAm 90
Hulston, John K. 1915- St&PR 91
Hulston, John Kenton 1915- WhoAm 90
Hulstra, Johannes F W 1926- BiDrAPA 89
Hulswitt, Rudy 1877-1950 Ballpl 90
Hult, Karen Marie 1956- WhoAmW 91
Hultberg, John 1922- WhoAm 90, WhoAmA 91
Hultgren, Dennis N. 1946- St&PR 91
Hultgren, E. Anders 1952- WhoWor 91
Hultgren, Herbert Nils 1917- WhoAm 90
Hultine, Carl J. 1947- St&PR 91
Hulting, Wayne Allan 1951- St&PR 91
Hultkrantz, Aake G. B. 1920- ConAu 130
Hultkrantz, Ake G. B. ConAu 130
Hultkvist, Rudolf Nils 1926- WhoWor 91
Hultman, Charles William 1930- WhoAm 90
Hultmann, Barbara BioIn 16
Hultmark, Anders Nils 1954- WhoWor 91
Hultmark, Dete A. 1962- WhoEmL 91
Hultmark, Emil 1872-1943 BioIn 16
Hulton, Ann 1668-1697 BiDEWW
Hulton, Edward 1906-1988 AnObit 1988, BioIn 16
Hultquist, Joshua Keith 1932- St&PR 91
Hultquist, Paul Fredrick 1920- WhoAm 90
Hultquist, Steven John 1949- WhoEmL 91
Hultquist, Timothy Allen 1950- WhoAm 90, WhoEmL 91
Hultstrand, Donald Maynard 1927- WhoAm 90
Humaid ibn Rashid Al-Nuami, Sheikh 1930- WhoWor 91
Human League, The OxCPMus
Human, Jacob 1932- IntWWM 90
Human, Mel 1954- WhoE 91
Humann, Walter Johann 1937- WhoAm 90
Humaydan, Hasib Shaheen 1945- WhoEmL 91
Humbach, Helmut 1921- WhoWor 91
Humberd, Scott Wesley 1955- WhoEmL 91
Humberstone, Augustina BiDEWW
Humberstone, K.J. 1917- St&PR 91
Humbert, James Ronald 1938- WhoSSW 91
Humbert, John O. WhoAm 90
Humbert, Pamela 1941- WhoAmW 91
Humble Pie EncPR&S 89
Humble, Douglas Boaz, III 1958- WhoEmL 91
Humble, Jimmy Logan 1944- WhoWor 91
Humble, Joseph Elgin 1953- WhoSSW 91
Humble, Richard 1945- SmATA 60
Humble, Stephen Crenshaw BiDrAPA 89
Humboldt, Alexander von 1769-1859 ArtLatA
Humboldt, Friedrich, Freiherr Von 1769-1859 WorAlBi
Humboldt, Wilhelm, Freiherr von 1767-1835 BioIn 16
Humbracht, Loyal Charles 1925- St&PR 91
Hume, Alexander Britton 1943- WhoAm 90
Hume, Anna BiDEWW, FemiCLE
Hume, Basil 1923- WhoWor 91
Hume, Ben BioIn 16
Hume, Brit BioIn 16
Hume, David 1711-1776 BioIn 16, DcLB 104 [port], WorAlBi, WrPh P
Hume, David Cady 1919- St&PR 91
Hume, David DesJardins 1928- WhoAm 90
Hume, David Lang 1914- WhoAm 90
Hume, Ellen Hunsberger 1947- WhoAm 90
Hume, Ernest Harding 1924- WhoAm 90
Hume, Fergus 1859-1932 TwCCr&M 91
Hume, Frederick Raymond 1943- WhoAm 90
Hume, H.D. 1898- St&PR 91
Hume, Horace Delbert 1898- WhoWor 91
Hume, James Borden 1950- WhoAm 90
Hume, James Nairn Patterson 1923- WhoAm 90
Hume, James Ord 1864-1932 OxCPMus
Hume, John BioIn 16
Hume, John 1937- WhoWor 91
Hume, John L. 1939- St&PR 91
Hume, John Mitchell 1929- BiDrAPA 89
Hume, Leonard John 1926- WhoWor 91
Hume, Mary Catherine 1824-1885 FemiCLE
Hume, Michael H. 1955- St&PR 91
Hume, Paul Chandler 1915- WhoAm 90
Hume, Robert Alan 1936- WhoAm 90
Hume, Robert C BiDrAPA 89
Hume, Ruth 1922-1980 AuBYP 90
Hume, Sophia 1702-1774 FemiCLE
Hume, Sophia Wigington 1702-1774 EncCRAm
Hume, Stephen 1947- WhoAm 90
Hume, Susan Rachel 1952- WhoE 91
Hume, Tom 1953- Ballpl 90
Hume, Warren Charles 1916- WhoAm 90
Humelsine, Carlisle H. 1915-1989 BioIn 16
Humenansky, Diane Bay 1935- BiDrAPA 89
Humenesky, Gregory 1951- St&PR 91
Humeniuk, Orest 1935- St&PR 91
Humes, Alexander B BiDrAPA 89
Humes, David Walker 1954- WhoSSW 91
Humes, Edward WhoAm 90
Humes, Graham 1932- St&PR 91, WhoAm 90, WhoE 91
Humes, Helen 1913-1981 BioIn 16, DrBIPA 90, OxCPMus
Humes, James Calhoun 1934- WhoAm 90
Humes, Lawrence Thomas 1934- WhoE 91
Humes, Ralph H 1902-1981 WhoAmA 91N
Humes, Robert Ernest 1943- WhoAm 90, WhoE 91
Humes, Samuel, IV 1930- WhoWor 91
Humfleet, Harolyn J. 1946- WhoAmW 91
Humiston, Ronald S. 1944- ODwPR 91
Humiston, Ronald Squier 1944- St&PR 91
Humke, Ramon L. 1932- St&PR 91, WhoAm 90
Huml, Donald Scott 1946- St&PR 91, WhoAm 90
Humlicek, Evelyn Clarice 1923- WhoAmW 91
Hummel, Andries 1936- WhoWor 91
Hummel, Carl William 1929- St&PR 91
Hummel, Charles Frederick 1932- WhoAm 90, WhoAmA 91
Hummel, Charles Leroy 1947- WhoEmL 91
Hummel, Dana D. Mallett WhoAmW 91
Hummel, Daniel Lee 1951- WhoEmL 91
Hummel, Daryl G. 1948- St&PR 91
Hummel, Dean Loil 1923- WhoSSW 91
Hummel, Don W. 1933- St&PR 91
Hummel, Fred Ernest 1927- WhoAm 90
Hummel, Frederick Eugene 1935- WhoSSW 91
Hummel, Gene Maywood 1926- WhoAm 90
Hummel, James Arthur 1942- St&PR 91
Hummel, Johann Nepomuk 1778-1837 PenDiMP A
Hummel, John 1883-1959 Ballpl 90
Hummel, Kay Jean 1943- WhoSSW 91
Hummel, Kermit 1954- St&PR 91
Hummel, Marilyn Mae 1931- WhoAmW 91
Hummel, Michael John 1949- St&PR 91
Hummel, Ralph T BiDrAPA 89
Hummel, Robert Jensen 1935- St&PR 91
Hummel, Robert Paul 1928- WhoAm 90
Hummell, Burton Howard 1932- St&PR 91, WhoAm 90, WhoSSW 91
Hummell, Ross Bennett 1957- St&PR 91
Hummer, Charles Walter, Jr. 1937- WhoSSW 91, WhoWor 91
Hummer, David Graybill 1934- WhoAm 90
Hummer, Larry Jay 1937- St&PR 91
Hummer, Paul F. 1941- St&PR 91
Hummer, Paul F., II 1941- WhoAm 90
Hummer, Paul Jacob, Jr. 1932- WhoWrEP 89
Hummer, Thomas Michael 1942- St&PR 91
Hummer, William B. 1924- St&PR 91
Hummerhielm, Sharon J. 1949- WhoSSW 91
Hummingbird, Rita G. 1951- WhoEmL 91
Hummler, Richard J. NewYTBS 90
Hump WhNaAH
Humperdinck, Engelbert 1854-1921 BioIn 16, PenDiMP A, WorAlBi
Humperdinck, Engelbert 1936- EncPR&S 89, WhoAm 90, WorAlBi
Humperdinck, Englebert 1936- OxCPMus
Humpert, John E. 1962- WhoWrEP 89
Humpert, Samuel Jay 1947- WhoEmL 91
Humpf, Gregory Joseph 1939- St&PR 91
Humpfner, Winfried G 1889-1962 EncO&P 3
Humphery-Smith, Cecil Raymond Julian 1928- WhoWor 91
Humphreville, John David 1953- WhoEmL 91
Humphreville, Neil E. 1921- St&PR 91
Humphrey, Arthur Earl 1927- WhoAm 90
Humphrey, Arthur L. 1860?- AmLegL
Humphrey, Betty EncPaPR 91
Humphrey, Bingham Johnson 1906- WhoE 91, WhoWor 91
Humphrey, Bobbi 1950- DrBIPA 90
Humphrey, Carletta Sue 1954- WhoAmW 91
Humphrey, Carlos Andres Pasalagua 1937- WhoWor 91
Humphrey, Charles Durham 1943- WhoAm 90
Humphrey, Charles Edward, Jr. 1943- WhoAm 90
Humphrey, Cliff 1942- WhoE 91
Humphrey, David Aiken 1955- WhoAmA 91, WhoE 91
Humphrey, Dennis Dewayne 1958- WhoWrEP 89
Humphrey, Donald Gray 1920- WhoAmA 91
Humphrey, Donna Claire 1962- WhoAmW 91
Humphrey, Doris 1895-1958 BioAmW, WorAlBi
Humphrey, Edward William 1926- WhoAm 90
Humphrey, Edwin Lowell 1920- WhoWrEP 89
Humphrey, Edwin Murray 1917- WhoAm 90
Humphrey, Faye L. 1939- St&PR 91
Humphrey, Fred A. 1896- WhoAm 90
Humphrey, Frederick J, II 1940- BiDrAPA 89
Humphrey, George M. AmLegL
Humphrey, George Magoffin 1890-1970 BiDrUSE 89
Humphrey, George Magoffin, II 1942- St&PR 91, WhoAm 90
Humphrey, Gordon John 1940- WhoAm 90, WhoE 91, WhoWor 91
Humphrey, Graeme 1948- IntWWM 90
Humphrey, Gwen 1934- WhoSSW 91
Humphrey, Hubert Ben, Jr. 1928- WhoAm 90
Humphrey, Hubert H. 1911-1978 WorAlBi
Humphrey, Hubert Horatio, III 1942- WhoAm 90
Humphrey, Hubert Horatio, Jr. 1911-1978 BiDrUSE 89
Humphrey, Irving L, III 1941- BiDrAPA 89
Humphrey, J. Steven 1951- WhoE 91
Humphrey, Jack Weldon WhoAmA 91N
Humphrey, Jayne Hulbert 1947- WhoAmW 91
Humphrey, Jeffrey Hauger 1957- WhoEmL 91
Humphrey, John Edward, Jr. BiDrAPA 89
Humphrey, John William 1937- St&PR 91, WhoWor 91
Humphrey, Joseph Anthony Christie 1948- WhoEmL 91
Humphrey, Judy Lucille 1949- WhoAmA 91, WhoSSW 91
Humphrey, Karen 1945- WhoAmW 91
Humphrey, Kay Lynn 1960- WhoAmW 91
Humphrey, Lawrence Holden 1934- St&PR 91
Humphrey, Louise Ireland 1918- WhoAmW 91
Humphrey, Neil Darwin 1928- WhoAm 90
Humphrey, Nene 1947- WhoAmA 91
Humphrey, Paul 1915- WhoWrEP 89
Humphrey, Paul Elmo 1913- St&PR 91

Humphrey, Philip Strong 1926- *WhoAm 90*
Humphrey, Ralph 1932-1990 *NewYTBS 90*
Humphrey, Richard Sears *BioIn 16*
Humphrey, Robert C. 1918- *St&PR 91*
Humphrey, Robin Andrew 1955- *WhoEmL 91*
Humphrey, Roger Cleveland 1940- *St&PR 91*
Humphrey, Ronald D. 1938- *WhoSSW 91*
Humphrey, S L 1941- *WhoAmA 91*
Humphrey, Samuel Stockwell 1923- *WhoE 91*
Humphrey, Shirley Joy 1937- *WhoAmW 91*
Humphrey, Terry 1949- *Ballpl 90*
Humphrey, Thomas C. 1846- *AmLegL*
Humphrey, Thomas M. 1935- *St&PR 91*
Humphrey, Watts Sherman 1927- *WhoAm 90*
Humphrey, William *BioIn 16*
Humphrey, William Albert 1927- *St&PR 91, WhoAm 90*
Humphrey, William Edwin 1939- *WhoSSW 91*
Humphrey, William Roland 1917- *WhoE 91, WhoWor 91*
Humphrey, William Swift 1939- *WhoE 91*
Humphreys, Alwyn 1944- *IntWWM 90*
Humphreys, Bob 1935- *Ballpl 90*
Humphreys, Carey 1922- *IntWWM 90*
Humphreys, Carlos 1951- *WhoSSW 91*
Humphreys, Christmas 1901-1983 *DcNaB 1981, EncO&P 3*
Humphreys, David Carlysle 1951- *WhoSSW 91*
Humphreys, David John 1936- *WhoAm 90*
Humphreys, Donald Robert 1923- *WhoAm 90*
Humphreys, Edward J 1903- *BiDrAPA 89*
Humphreys, Edward Jackson 1903- *WhoE 91*
Humphreys, Eliza M. Y. *EncO&P 3*
Humphreys, Elizabeth Stockton 1955- *WhoE 91*
Humphreys, Fred C. 1923- *St&PR 91*
Humphreys, Garry Paul 1946- *IntWWM 90*
Humphreys, George Gary 1949- *WhoSSW 91*
Humphreys, Holly E. 1947- *WhoEmL 91*
Humphreys, Homer Alexander 1902- *WhoSSW 91*
Humphreys, James R. 1955- *WhoEmL 91*
Humphreys, James W. 1915- *WhoAm 90*
Humphreys, Joe *BioIn 16*
Humphreys, John Richard Adams 1918- *WhoWrEP 89*
Humphreys, Joshua 1751-1838 *EncCRAm*
Humphreys, Kenneth Jerome 1944- *St&PR 91*
Humphreys, Kenneth King 1938- *WhoAm 90*
Humphreys, Lloyd Girton 1913- *WhoAm 90*
Humphreys, Mabel Gweneth 1911- *WhoAm 90*
Humphreys, Michael Edward 1953- *WhoSSW 91*
Humphreys, R A 1907- *ConAu 129*
Humphreys, Robert Russell 1938- *WhoAm 90*
Humphreys, Robert T.C., Jr. 1932- *St&PR 91*
Humphreys, Roberta Marie 1944- *WhoAmW 91*
Humphreys, Robin A. *ConAu 129*
Humphreys, Thomas Hadden 1865-1951 *AmLegL*
Humphreys, Trevor L. 1937- *St&PR 91*
Humphries, Barry 1934- *ConAu 129*
Humphries, Bert 1880-1945 *Ballpl 90*
Humphries, Beverly Nell 1930- *WhoAm 90*
Humphries, D. Keith 1943- *St&PR 91*
Humphries, David M. *ODwPR 91*
Humphries, Deborah Ann 1955- *WhoAmW 91*
Humphries, Dempsey Marshall, Jr. 1919- *St&PR 91*
Humphries, Edward Francis 1957- *WhoEmL 91*
Humphries, Ellen Thom 1947- *WhoAmW 91, WhoWor 91*
Humphries, Frederick S. 1935- *WhoAm 90, WhoSSW 91*
Humphries, Harold Lee 1931- *St&PR 91*
Humphries, Jack Wood 1936- *WhoAm 90*
Humphries, Joan Ropes 1928- *WhoAmW 91, WhoSSW 91, WhoWor 91*
Humphries, John 1915-1965 *Ballpl 90*
Humphries, John Bertram 1918- *St&PR 91*
Humphries, John O'Neal 1931- *WhoAm 90*
Humphries, Judy Lynn 1946- *WhoWor 91*
Humphries, Kenneth B. 1928- *WhoAm 90*
Humphries, Laurie Lee *BiDrAPA 89*
Humphries, Michael William 1940- *St&PR 91*
Humphries, Robert H 1938- *BiDrAPA 89*
Humphries, Robert Lee, Jr. 1930- *WhoSSW 91*
Humphries, Weldon R. 1937- *St&PR 91, WhoAm 90*
Humphries, William Charles 1948- *WhoEmL 91*
Humphries, William Henry, III 1950- *WhoE 91*
Humphris, Susan *BioIn 16*
Humphry, Derek John 1930- *WhoWrEP 89*
Humphry, James, III 1916- *WhoAm 90*
Humphry, John A. 1916-1989 *BioIn 16*
Humphrys, C.M. 1921- *St&PR 91*
Humphrys, Richard 1917- *WhoAm 90*
Humway, Ronald Jimmie 1945- *WhoSSW 91*
Hun Sen 1950- *WhoWor 91*
Hun Sen 1951- *CurBio 90 [port]*
Hun, Sen *BioIn 16*
Hunan, James Terry *WhoSSW 91*
Huncke, Herbert 1915- *BioIn 16*
Huncke, Herbert E 1915- *ConAu 130*
Hund, Ferdinand 1704?-1758 *PenDiDA 89*
Hund, Friedrich H. 1896- *WhoWor 91*
Hund, Morris Alan 1958- *BiDrAPA 89*
Hund, Robert Arthur 1927- *WhoWrEP 89*
Hundal, Sarbjit Singh 1950- *WhoWor 91*
Hundere, Myriam Goldsmith 1933- *St&PR 91*
Hundert, Edward Mark *BiDrAPA 89*
Hundertmark, Thad R. 1929- *St&PR 91*
Hundertwasser, Friedensreich 1928- *WhoWor 91*
Hundley, Frank T. 1932- *St&PR 91*
Hundley, Garry Wayne 1951- *WhoE 91*
Hundley, Hot Rod *BioIn 16*
Hundley, James R 1949- *BiDrAPA 89*
Hundley, John W. *NewYTBS 90*
Hundley, John W. 1899-1990 *BioIn 16*
Hundley, Maritha Renee 1961- *WhoAmW 91*
Hundley, Norris Cecil, Jr. 1935- *WhoAm 90*
Hundley, Randy 1942- *Ballpl 90*
Hundman, Robert Louis 1935- *WhoWrEP 89*
Hundt, Ferdinand 1704?-1758 *PenDiDA 89*
Hundt, Paul Robert 1939- *St&PR 91*
Hundt, Reed Eric 1948- *WhoEmL 91*
Hundziak, Marcel *BiDrAPA 89*
Hune, Nancy Jean 1954- *WhoEmL 91*
Huneke, John George 1931- *WhoE 91*
Huneke, John Henry, III 1945- *WhoAm 90*
Huneker, James Gibbons 1860-1921 *BioIn 16*
Hunerberg, David W. 1943- *WhoAm 90*
Huneycutt, Alice Ruth 1951- *WhoAmW 91*
Huneycutt, Sarah E. 1933- *St&PR 91*
Hung, George Wen-Chi 1932- *WhoSSW 91*
Hung, James Chen 1929- *WhoAm 90*
Hung, Lien Ai *BiDrAPA 89*
Hung, Mimi Wong *WhoWor 91*
Hung, Nguyen Manh 1937- *WhoWor 91*
Hung, Pham 1911-1988 *AnObit 1988*
Hung, Ru J. 1934- *WhoSSW 91*
Hung, Tin-Kan 1936- *WhoAm 90*
Hung, William 1893- *BioIn 16*
Hung, Yen-Con 1954- *WhoSSW 91*
Hungarian Quartet *PenDiMP*
Hungate, Sue Carol 1957- *WhoAmW 91*
Hungate, William Leonard 1922- *WhoAm 90*
Hunger, Christoph Conrad *PenDiDA 89*
Hunger, Gunther Karl 1922- *WhoWor 91*
Hunger, Jack Edward 1934- *St&PR 91*
Hunger, John David 1941- *WhoWor 91*
Hunger, Kingsley W. 1945- *St&PR 91*
Hungerford, Brian Edward 1955- *WhoEmL 91*
Hungerford, Constance Cain 1948- *WhoAmA 91*
Hungerford, Dale 1936- *St&PR 91*
Hungerford, David S. 1938- *WhoAm 90*
Hungerford, Ed Vernon, III 1939- *WhoAm 90*
Hungerford, Edward Buell 1900- *AuBYP 90*
Hungerford, Gary A. 1948- *WhoE 91*
Hungerford, Hans Jorg *WhoAm 90*
Hungerford, Herbert Eugene 1918- *WhoAm 90*
Hungerford, Hesba Brinsmead 1922- *BioIn 16*
Hungerford, Margaret 1855?-1897 *FemiCLE*
Hungerford, Margaret Hamilton Wolfe 1855-1897 *BioIn 16*
Hungerford, Mark C. *St&PR 91*
Hungler, Charles E. 1936- *St&PR 91*
Hungsberg, Gottfried Heinrich 1944- *IntWWM 90*
Huning, Allan Arthur 1938- *St&PR 91*
Huning, Deborah Gray 1950- *WhoAmW 91*
Hunisak, John Michael 1944- *WhoAmA 91*
Hunjan, Bhajan 1956- *BiDWomA*
Hunkel, Cary Christiana 1945- *WhoEmL 91*
Hunker, T. Allen 1957- *WhoWrEP 89*
Hunkin, Mary Louise 1950- *WhoAmW 91*
Hunkin, Tim 1950- *BioIn 16*
Hunkins, Francis Peter 1938- *WhoAm 90*
Hunkler, Dennis 1943- *WhoAmA 91*
Hunley, Leann *BioIn 16*
Hunley, W. Helen 1920- *WhoAm 90, WhoAmW 91*
Hunn, Fredric A. 1938- *St&PR 91*
Hunnefield, Bill 1899-1976 *Ballpl 90*
Hunnewell, Ruthann Baffo 1954- *WhoAmW 91*
Hunnewell, Walter, Jr. 1956- *WhoEmL 91*
Hunnicutt, Benjamin Kline 1943- *ConAu 130*
Hunnicutt, Charles Alvin 1950- *WhoE 91*
Hunnicutt, H. Richard, Jr. 1938- *WhoSSW 91*
Hunnicutt, Mary Sharon 1942- *WhoWor 91*
Hunnicutt, Richard P. 1926- *St&PR 91*
Hunnicutt, Robert William 1954- *WhoEmL 91*
Hunnings, Wardie Giles 1929- *St&PR 91*
Huno, Lawrence Gerard 1956- *St&PR 91*
Hunsaker, Floyd B. 1915- *WhoWor 91*
Hunsaker, Harold Jeff 1927- *WhoAm 90*
Hunsaker, Richard E. 1948- *St&PR 91*
Hunsaker, Richard Kendall 1960- *WhoEmL 91, WhoWor 91*
Hunsberger, Robert Earl 1947- *WhoEmL 91*
Hunsinger, B. Frank 1943- *St&PR 91*
Hunsinger, Doyle J. 1947- *WhoE 91, WhoEmL 91, WhoWor 91*
Hunsinger, Edward Eugene 1945- *WhoSSW 91*
Hunsperger, Elizabeth Jane 1938- *WhoWor 91*
Hunstad, Robert Edward 1940- *St&PR 91, WhoAm 90*
Hunsucker, Elmore Glenn 1949- *WhoSSW 91*
Hunsucker, Philip Carl 1957- *WhoEmL 91*
Hunsucker, Robert Dean 1925- *St&PR 91, WhoAm 90, WhoSSW 91*
Hunsucker, Timothy Lyn 1955- *BiDrAPA 89*
Hunt, Albert Andrew 1923- *St&PR 91*
Hunt, Albert Barker 1910- *St&PR 91, WhoAm 90*
Hunt, Albert R. 1942- *WhoE 91*
Hunt, Alexandra *IntWWM 90*
Hunt, Andrew Donaldson, Jr. 1948- *WhoEmL 91*
Hunt, Annice Elizabeth 1934- *WhoWrEP 89*
Hunt, Arabella 1645?-1705 *PenDiMP*
Hunt, Avery 1943- *ODwPR 91*
Hunt, Barbara Evelyn 1958- *WhoEmL 91*
Hunt, Bernice 1920- *WhoWrEP 89*
Hunt, Bernice Kohn *AuBYP 90*
Hunt, Bob 1948- *St&PR 91*
Hunt, Bobby Ray 1941- *WhoAm 90*
Hunt, Brenda Leigh 1960- *WhoAmW 91*
Hunt, Brian William 1950- *IntWWM 90*
Hunt, Bryan 1947- *WhoAm 90, WhoAmA 91, WhoE 91*
Hunt, Carl C. *St&PR 91*
Hunt, Carl C. 1936- *WhoAm 90*
Hunt, Carl G. 1912- *St&PR 91*
Hunt, Carl V *BiDrAPA 89*
Hunt, Carol Ann 1955- *WhoEmL 91*
Hunt, Caroline Collins 1941- *WhoSSW 91*
Hunt, Charles Brownlow, Jr. 1916- *WhoAm 90*
Hunt, Charles Butler 1906- *WhoAm 90*
Hunt, Cheryl Ruth 1946- *WhoE 91*
Hunt, Christina Lee 1959- *WhoEmL 91*
Hunt, Christine Sapp 1927- *WhoSSW 91*
Hunt, Clifford Onufry 1917- *IntWWM 90*
Hunt, Courtenay 1917- *WhoAmA 91*
Hunt, Daniel S. 1938- *St&PR 91*
Hunt, David 1942- *WhoWor 91*
Hunt, David Claude 1957- *WhoEmL 91*
Hunt, David Curtis 1935- *WhoAmA 91*
Hunt, David Daniel 1947- *BiDrAPA 89*
Hunt, David Ford 1931- *WhoAm 90, WhoSSW 91*
Hunt, David Kenneth 1946- *St&PR 91*
Hunt, Deborah Lee 1960- *WhoWrEP 89*
Hunt, Diana Dilger 1953- *WhoE 91*
Hunt, Donald 1930- *IntWWM 90*
Hunt, Donald R. 1921- *WhoAm 90*
Hunt, Donald Samuel 1938- *St&PR 91, WhoAm 90*
Hunt, Donnell Ray 1926- *WhoAm 90*
Hunt, Douglass 1924- *WhoAm 90*
Hunt, E. Howard 1918- *TwCCr&M 91*
Hunt, E. Howard, Jr. 1918- *WorAlBi*
Hunt, Earl Busby 1933- *WhoAm 90*
Hunt, Edgar Hubert 1909- *IntWWM 90*
Hunt, Effie Neva 1922- *WhoAm 90*
Hunt, Enid Clara 1911- *IntWWM 90*
Hunt, Ethan Wayne, Jr. 1954- *WhoSSW 91*
Hunt, Everette Howard 1918- *SpyFic*
Hunt, F V *ConAu 132*
Hunt, Forrest L. 1947- *St&PR 91*
Hunt, Francis Howard 1919- *WhoE 91*
Hunt, Frank Bouldin 1915- *WhoAm 90*
Hunt, Frank M. 1928- *WhoAm 90*
Hunt, Franklin Griggs 1930- *WhoAm 90*
Hunt, Frederick Vinton 1905-1972 *DcScB S2*
Hunt, G. W. 1825-1904 *OxCPMus*
Hunt, George *BioIn 16*
Hunt, George 1854-1933 *WhNaAH*
Hunt, George Nelson 1931- *WhoAm 90*
Hunt, George Pinney 1918- *AuBYP 90*
Hunt, Gordon 1934- *WhoAm 90*
Hunt, Gregory Lynn 1947- *WhoAm 90, WhoEmL 91, WhoWor 91*
Hunt, H Ernest *EncO&P 3*
Hunt, H. Guy 1933- *WhoAm 90, WhoSSW 91, WhoWor 91*
Hunt, H. L. 1889-1974 *BioIn 16, WorAlBi*
Hunt, Harold E. 1931- *St&PR 91*
Hunt, Harold Keith 1938- *WhoAm 90*
Hunt, Harrison *TwCCr&M 91*
Hunt, Helen 1963- *ConTFT 8*
Hunt, Henry Carter 1952- *St&PR 91*
Hunt, Herman Turner, Jr. 1921- *WhoSSW 91*
Hunt, Hilton Adair 1955- *St&PR 91*
Hunt, Holman 1827-1910 *WorAlBi*
Hunt, Howard Francis 1918- *WhoAm 90*
Hunt, Irene 1907- *AuBYP 90*
Hunt, Isobel Violet 1866-1942 *BioIn 16*
Hunt, Jacob Tate 1916- *WhoAm 90*
Hunt, James Baxter, Jr. 1937- *WhoAm 90*
Hunt, James Calvin 1925- *WhoAm 90*
Hunt, James D. 1939- *St&PR 91*
Hunt, James Dennis 1931- *WhoSSW 91*
Hunt, James Frank 1858-1917 *AmLegL*
Hunt, James Gerald 1932- *ConAu 31NR, WhoAm 90*
Hunt, James Robert 1925- *WhoAm 90*
Hunt, James Simon Wallis 1947- *WhoWor 91*
Hunt, Jane Jewett 1945- *WhoWrEP 89*
Hunt, Jean 1932- *WhoAmW 91*
Hunt, Jeffrey Brian 1958- *WhoEmL 91*
Hunt, Jeffrey Ivan 1957- *BiDrAPA 89*
Hunt, Joe Harold 1925- *WhoAm 90*
Hunt, John *ConAu 31NR*
Hunt, John August 1929- *St&PR 91*
Hunt, John Clinton 1925- *WhoAm 90*
Hunt, John David 1925- *St&PR 91, WhoAm 90*
Hunt, John E. 1908-1989 *BioIn 16*
Hunt, John Edwin 1918- *WhoSSW 91*
Hunt, John Edwin, Sr. 1918- *St&PR 91*
Hunt, John Floyd 1946- *WhoEmL 91*
Hunt, John Miles 1932- *St&PR 91*
Hunt, John R. 1952- *St&PR 91*
Hunt, John Richard 1937- *St&PR 91*
Hunt, John Wesley 1927- *WhoAm 90*
Hunt, Johnnie B. 1924- *WhoSSW 91*
Hunt, Joseph *BioIn 16*
Hunt, Joseph Francis 1941- *WhoAm 90*
Hunt, Joseph McVicker 1906- *WhoAm 90*
Hunt, Judith Ann 1939- *WhoAmW 91*
Hunt, Julian Courtenay 1917- *WhoSSW 91*
Hunt, Kari 1920- *AuBYP 90*
Hunt, Ken 1934- *Ballpl 90*
Hunt, Kevan *BioIn 16*
Hunt, Kyle *MajTwCW, TwCCr&M 91*
Hunt, Lacy Harris, II 1942- *St&PR 91*
Hunt, Lamar 1932- *WhoAm 90*
Hunt, Lamar 1933- *BioIn 16*
Hunt, Leigh 1784-1859 *DcLB 96 [port]*
Hunt, Leigh S. J. 1855-1933 *BioIn 16*
Hunt, Leslie B. 1906-1987 *BioIn 16*
Hunt, Linda *BioIn 16, WhoAmA 91*
Hunt, Linda 1945- *WhoAm 90, WhoAmW 91, WorAlBi*
Hunt, Linda Johnson 1947- *WhoSSW 91*
Hunt, Linda K. *ODwPR 91*
Hunt, Linda Marie 1947- *WhoAmW 91*
Hunt, Lois A. 1947- *St&PR 91*
Hunt, Lora Lynn 1948- *WhoSSW 91*
Hunt, Lynda Joyce 1951- *WhoAmW 91*
Hunt, Lynn 1878-1960 *WhoAmA 91N*
Hunt, Lynn 1945- *ConAu 131*
Hunt, Mabel Leigh 1892-1971 *AuBYP 90*
Hunt, Margaret 1831-1912 *FemiCLE*
Hunt, Marion Paul 1926- *St&PR 91*
Hunt, Marjorie Kalteyer 1915- *St&PR 91*
Hunt, Mark Alan 1949- *WhoAm 90*
Hunt, Marsha 1917- *BioIn 16*
Hunt, Marshall James 1945- *WhoEmL 91*
Hunt, Martha 1924- *WhoAmW 91*
Hunt, Mary Lou 1932- *WhoAmW 91*
Hunt, Mary Reilly 1921- *WhoAmW 91*
Hunt, Maurice Arthur 1942- *WhoWrEP 89*
Hunt, Melissa *BiDrAPA 89*
Hunt, Michael Francis 1945- *IntWWM 90*
Hunt, Morton M. 1920- *WhoWrEP 89*
Hunt, Nelson Bunker 1926- *BioIn 16*

Hunt, Norman Crowther 1920-1987 *BioIn 16*
Hunt, Norman Edwin 1916- *WhoE 91*
Hunt, P.G. 1935- *St&PR 91*
Hunt, Patricia 1922?-1983 *AuBYP 90*
Hunt, Patrick Eugene 1946- *WhoE 91*
Hunt, Pee Wee 1907-1979 *OxCPMus*
Hunt, Peter 1916-1988 *AnObit 1988*
Hunt, Peter 1945- *ConAu 32NR*
Hunt, Peter Huls 1938- *WhoAm 90*
Hunt, Peter Kevin 1946- *St&PR 91*
Hunt, Peter Leonard 1945- *WhoWor 91*
Hunt, Polly Lybrook *BiDrAPA 89*
Hunt, Ray Lee 1943- *WhoAm 90*
Hunt, Raymon Earl 1947- *WhoEmL 91*
Hunt, Reid 1870-1948 *DcScB S2*
Hunt, Richard B. 1948- *St&PR 91*
Hunt, Richard Howard 1935- *WhoAmA 91*
Hunt, Richard M. 1827-1895 *WorAlBi*
Hunt, Richard Morris 1827-1895 *BioIn 16*
Hunt, Robert C *BiDrAPA 89*
Hunt, Robert Chester 1923- *St&PR 91*
Hunt, Robert Cushman 1905-1989 *BioIn 16*
Hunt, Robert J. *BioIn 16*
Hunt, Robert J. 1949- *St&PR 91*
Hunt, Robert James 1921- *WhoAmA 91*
Hunt, Robert Wayne 1940- *WhoWor 91*
Hunt, Robert William 1947- *WhoEmL 91*
Hunt, Robin Ray 1935- *St&PR 91*
Hunt, Roger Schermerhorn 1943- *WhoAm 90*
Hunt, Ron 1941- *Ballpl 90*
Hunt, Ronald Duncan 1935- *WhoAm 90*
Hunt, Ronald Forrest 1943- *St&PR 91, WhoAm 90*
Hunt, Samuel P *BiDrAPA 89*
Hunt, Samuel Pancoast, III 1943- *WhoAm 90*
Hunt, Stanley Eugene 1930- *St&PR 91*
Hunt, Stephen Christopher 1962- *WhoE 91*
Hunt, Stoker *ConAu 131*
Hunt, Stuart 1921- *St&PR 91*
Hunt, Sue Whittington 1952- *WhoAmW 91, WhoSSW 91, WhoWor 91*
Hunt, T.M. *St&PR 91*
Hunt, Thomas E. *ODwPR 91*
Hunt, Thomas Reed, Jr. 1948- *WhoE 91, WhoEmL 91*
Hunt, Thomas Sterry 1826-1892 *DcCanB 12*
Hunt, Timothy A. 1949- *WhoWrEP 89*
Hunt, V. Daniel 1939- *WhoSSW 91*
Hunt, V. William 1944- *St&PR 91*
Hunt, Violet 1866-1942 *BioIn 16, FemiCLE*
Hunt, W. Kenneth 1953- *St&PR 91*
Hunt, Walter Kenneth, III 1953- *WhoEmL 91*
Hunt, Walter L. 1941- *St&PR 91, WhoAm 90*
Hunt, Wanda Holder 1944- *WhoAmW 91*
Hunt, Wanda Sue 1950- *WhoAmW 91*
Hunt, Wayne Wolf Robe 1905-1977 *WhoAmA 91N*
Hunt, William 1934- *WhoWrEP 89*
Hunt, William Clay 1942- *St&PR 91*
Hunt, William Edward 1921- *WhoAm 90*
Hunt, William Henry 1823-1884 *BiDrUSE 89, BioIn 16*
Hunt, William Herbert *BioIn 16*
Hunt, William Holman 1827-1910 *BioIn 16, IntDcAA 90*
Hunt, William J. 1925- *St&PR 91*
Hunt, William Joseph, Jr. 1950- *WhoE 91*
Hunt, William Martin, III *BiDrAPA 89*
Hunt, William O. 1933- *St&PR 91*
Hunt, William Walter, III 1951- *WhoEmL 91*
Hunt, Wilson Price 1783-1842 *WhNaAH*
Hunt, Winslow Robert *BiDrAPA 89*
Hunt Piccirillo, Maureen 1942- *WhoSSW 91*
Hunt-Rivera, Marsha *BiDrAPA 89*
Hunte, Beryl Eleanor *WhoAmW 91*
Hunte, Christopher *BioIn 16*
Hunten, Donald Mount 1925- *WhoAm 90*
Hunter, Alan 1922- *TwCCr&M 91*
Hunter, Alan F. 1939- *St&PR 91*
Hunter, Alberta 1895?-1984 *BioAmW, BioIn 16, DrBIPA 90, OxCPMus*
Hunter, Alexis 1948- *BiDWomA*
Hunter, Allan B. 1916- *St&PR 91*
Hunter, Anita *ODwPR 91*
Hunter, Anne 1742-1821 *FemiCLE*
Hunter, Archibald Stewart 1936- *WhoWor 91*
Hunter, Aubrey *St&PR 91*
Hunter, Austin Brough 1949- *WhoWor 91*
Hunter, Barbara W. 1927- *ODwPR 91*
Hunter, Beatrice Trum 1918- *WhoWrEP 89*
Hunter, Betty Turner 1948- *WhoSSW 91*
Hunter, Bill R. 1932?-1990 *ConAu 131*
Hunter, Billy 1928- *Ballpl 90*
Hunter, Billy Ray 1947- *BiDrAPA 89*
Hunter, Brian 1953- *WhoEmL 91*
Hunter, Buddy D. 1930- *WhoAm 90*
Hunter, Bynum Merritt 1925- *WhoAm 90*
Hunter, Carol Ann 1918- *BiDrAPA 89*
Hunter, Carole A. 1941- *WhoAmW 91*
Hunter, Catfish 1946- *Ballpl 90 [port], BioIn 16*
Hunter, Charles A. *EarBIAP*
Hunter, Charles David 1929- *St&PR 91, WhoAm 90*
Hunter, Charles W. 1876-1906 *OxCPMus*
Hunter, Charlotte Rae 1942- *WhoAmW 91*
Hunter, Christopher Douglas *BiDrAPA 89*
Hunter, Clarence Cal 1927- *WhoSSW 91*
Hunter, Clarence H. 1925- *St&PR 91*
Hunter, Clementine 1886?-1988 *BioIn 16, MusmAFA*
Hunter, D. Michael 1942- *St&PR 91*
Hunter, Dard *PenDiDA 89*
Hunter, David D. 1940- *St&PR 91*
Hunter, David Motz 1950- *WhoEmL 91*
Hunter, David Wittmer 1928- *WhoAm 90*
Hunter, Debbie Ann 1952- *WhoAmW 91*
Hunter, Debora 1950- *WhoAmA 91*
Hunter, Don Michael 1942- *WhoAm 90*
Hunter, Donald 1934- *St&PR 91, WhoAm 90*
Hunter, Donna Vene 1958- *WhoAmW 91*
Hunter, Donnell Walker 1930- *WhoWrEP 89*
Hunter, Dorian 1932- *WhoAm 90*
Hunter, Doris M *BiDrAPA 89*
Hunter, Duncan Lee 1948- *WhoAm 90*
Hunter, E. Waldo *ConAu 32NR, MajTwCW*
Hunter, Earle Leslie, III 1929- *WhoAm 90*
Hunter, Eddie *EarBIAP*
Hunter, Eddie 1888-1980 *DrBIPA 90*
Hunter, Edgar Hayes 1914- *WhoAm 90*
Hunter, Edwin Ford, Jr. 1911- *WhoAm 90*
Hunter, Elizabeth Ives-Valsam 1945- *WhoAmW 91*
Hunter, Elmo Bolton 1915- *WhoAm 90, WhoWor 91*
Hunter, Ernest B., Jr. 1924- *St&PR 91*
Hunter, Evan *TwCCr&M 91*
Hunter, Evan 1926- *AuBYP 90, MajTwCW, WhoAm 90, WhoWrEP 89, WorAlBi*
Hunter, Forrest Walker 1950- *WhoEmL 91*
Hunter, Francis Tipton 1896- *WhoAmA 91N*
Hunter, Frank Herbert 1901- *WhoAm 90*
Hunter, Garrett B. 1937- *St&PR 91*
Hunter, Garrett Bell 1937- *WhoAm 90*
Hunter, George Richard 1917- *St&PR 91*
Hunter, Gerald R. 1948- *ODwPR 91*
Hunter, Gordon Waterman 1942- *WhoSSW 91*
Hunter, Harlen Charles 1940- *WhoAm 90*
Hunter, Harold Cooper, Jr. 1945- *St&PR 91*
Hunter, Harold Raymond 1956- *WhoSSW 91*
Hunter, Harriot *BiDrAPA 89*
Hunter, Henry H. 1922- *ODwPR 91*
Hunter, Henry Hamilton 1922- *WhoAm 90*
Hunter, Hilda 1921- *AuBYP 90*
Hunter, Holly *BioIn 16*
Hunter, Holly 1958- *WhoAm 90, WhoAmW 91*
Hunter, Holly 1959- *WorAlBi*
Hunter, Holly P. 1958- *St&PR 91*
Hunter, Ian Timothy 1942- *IntWWM 90*
Hunter, J.D. *St&PR 91*
Hunter, Jack Corbett 1930- *WhoAm 90*
Hunter, Jack Duval 1937- *St&PR 91, WhoAm 90*
Hunter, Jack Duval, II 1959- *WhoEmL 91, WhoSSW 91*
Hunter, Jack Laird 1927- *St&PR 91*
Hunter, Jairy C., Jr. 1942- *WhoAm 90, WhoSSW 91*
Hunter, James 1916-1989 *BioIn 16*
Hunter, James 1946- *WorAlBi*
Hunter, James Alexander 1928- *WhoAm 90*
Hunter, James Austen, Jr. 1941- *WhoAm 90*
Hunter, James Galbraith, Jr. 1942- *WhoAm 90, WhoWor 91*
Hunter, James Gregory 1949- *BiDrAPA 89*
Hunter, James H. 1935- *St&PR 91*
Hunter, James Paul 1934- *WhoAm 90*
Hunter, Jane Edna 1882-1971 *HarlReB*
Hunter, Jeffery A. 1954- *WhoEmL 91*
Hunter, Jesse Thomas, Jr. 1924- *St&PR 91*
Hunter, Jill B. 1962- *WhoAmW 91*
Hunter, Jim 1946- *BioIn 16*
Hunter, Joan Elizabeth *WhoAmW 91*
Hunter, John 1728-1793 *BioIn 16*
Hunter, John 1821-1899 *DcCanB 12*
Hunter, John, Jr. 1925- *St&PR 91*
Hunter, John Alfred 1921- *WhoSSW 91*
Hunter, John Barton 1921- *St&PR 91*
Hunter, John H 1934- *WhoAmA 91*
Hunter, John Harnden 1934- *WhoAm 90*
Hunter, John R. 1931- *St&PR 91*
Hunter, John Robert 1936- *WhoAm 90*
Hunter, John Stuart 1923- *WhoAm 90*
Hunter, Joseph Anthony 1952- *WhoE 91*
Hunter, Joseph Edward 1927- *IntWWM 90*
Hunter, Joseph Vincent 1925- *WhoAm 90*
Hunter, Karen A. *ODwPR 91*
Hunter, Karen Ann 1945- *WhoAmW 91*
Hunter, Karen Ann 1959- *WhoEmL 91*
Hunter, Karen Mary 1962- *WhoE 91*
Hunter, Kathy 1944- *WhoWrEP 89*
Hunter, Kay Frances Turner 1934- *WhoAmW 91*
Hunter, Kenneth James 1953- *WhoSSW 91*
Hunter, Kermit Houston 1910- *WhoAm 90*
Hunter, Kim 1922- *BioIn 16, NotWoAT, WhoAm 90, WhoAmW 91, WorAlBi*
Hunter, Kristin *WhoWrEP 89*
Hunter, Kristin 1931- *AuBYP 90, BioIn 16, FemiCLE*
Hunter, Larry Dean 1950- *WhoAm 90*
Hunter, Larry Lee 1938- *WhoSSW 91*
Hunter, Leland Clair 1925- *St&PR 91*
Hunter, Leonard Legrande, III 1940- *WhoAmA 91*
Hunter, Leslie Stannard 1890-1983 *DcNaB 1981*
Hunter, Madeline 1916?- *News 91-2 [port]*
Hunter, Malcolm Kenmore 1934- *WhoSSW 91*
Hunter, Margaret 1948- *BiDWomA*
Hunter, Margaret King 1919- *WhoAm 90*
Hunter, Martha Louise 1948- *WhoEmL 91*
Hunter, Mary Anderson 1949- *WhoAmW 91*
Hunter, Mathew 1934- *WhoAm 90*
Hunter, Matthew 1934- *St&PR 91*
Hunter, Mel 1927- *WhoAmA 91*
Hunter, Michael 1941- *WhoAm 90*
Hunter, Michael Bourne 1947- *WhoWrEP 89*
Hunter, Michael Thomas 1949- *St&PR 91*
Hunter, Mollie 1922- *AuBYP 90, BioIn 16*
Hunter, Morgan 1923- *WhoAm 90*
Hunter, Nadene Denison *BiDrAPA 89*
Hunter, Nadene Denison 1918- *WhoAmW 91, WhoE 91*
Hunter, Naomi Elizabeth 1916- *WhoAmW 91*
Hunter, Nell Pierce 1889- *DcAfAmP*
Hunter, Norman L. 1932- *WhoAm 90*
Hunter, O. 1938- *St&PR 91*
Hunter, Olivia *EarBIAP*
Hunter, Paul 1954- *WhoAmA 91*
Hunter, Peter William 1930- *WhoAm 90*
Hunter, Rachel 1754-1813 *FemiCLE*
Hunter, Richard A. 1930- *St&PR 91*
Hunter, Richard Edward 1919- *WhoAm 90*
Hunter, Richard Grant, Jr. 1938- *WhoSSW 91*
Hunter, Richard Samford, Jr. 1954- *WhoEmL 91*
Hunter, Rita 1933- *IntWWM 90, PenDiMP*
Hunter, Robert *EncCRAm*
Hunter, Robert B 1954- *BiDrAPA 89*
Hunter, Robert C. 1929- *St&PR 91*
Hunter, Robert Coleman 1941- *WhoAm 90*
Hunter, Robert Douglas 1928- *WhoAmA 91*
Hunter, Robert E. 1940- *ConAu 33NR*
Hunter, Robert Frank 1923- *WhoAm 90*
Hunter, Robert Grams 1927- *WhoAm 90*
Hunter, Robert Howard 1929- *WhoAmA 91*
Hunter, Robert J. 1943- *St&PR 91*
Hunter, Robert J., Jr. *ODwPR 91*
Hunter, Robert Mercer Taliaferro 1809-1887 *BioIn 16*
Hunter, Robert Nelson 1930- *St&PR 91, WhoAm 90*
Hunter, Robert P., Jr. 1935- *St&PR 91*
Hunter, Robert T., Jr. 1934- *St&PR 91*
Hunter, Robert Tweedy, Jr. 1934- *WhoAm 90*
Hunter, Robert W. 1937- *ODwPR 91*
Hunter, Rodney John 1940- *WhoSSW 91*
Hunter, Ronald L. 1936- *St&PR 91*
Hunter, Ronald V. 1944- *St&PR 91*
Hunter, Rosemary S *BiDrAPA 89*
Hunter, Ross 1921- *WorAlBi*
Hunter, Ross 1926- *WhoAm 90*
Hunter, Roy, Jr. 1930- *WhoSSW 91*
Hunter, Sally Irene 1936- *WhoAmW 91, WhoWor 91*
Hunter, Sam 1923- *WhoAm 90, WhoAmA 91*
Hunter, Samuel Paul 1944- *St&PR 91*
Hunter, Samuel Richard 1929- *St&PR 91*
Hunter, Sarah M 1949- *BiDrAPA 89*
Hunter, Sheryl Lynn 1958- *WhoWrEP 89*
Hunter, Sonia L. 1933- *WhoAmW 91*
Hunter, Stacy H. 1963- *WhoAmW 91*
Hunter, Steven Lawrence 1955- *WhoEmL 91*
Hunter, Sue Persons 1921- *WhoAmW 91*
Hunter, Susan Gail 1950- *St&PR 91, WhoAmW 91, WhoEmL 91*
Hunter, Tab 1931- *WorAlBi*
Hunter, Thom Hugh 1918- *WhoAm 90*
Hunter, Thomas 1831-1915 *WorAlBi*
Hunter, Thomas A. *BiDrAPA 89*
Hunter, Thomas C. 1933- *ODwPR 91*
Hunter, Thomas Harrison 1913- *WhoAm 90*
Hunter, Timothy Joseph 1955- *WhoE 91*
Hunter, Valerie Jean Dexter 1943- *WhoAmW 91*
Hunter, Wanda Mae 1937- *WhoWrEP 89*
Hunter, Warren Aiken, Jr. 1948- *WhoSSW 91*
Hunter, Willard 1934- *Ballpl 90*
Hunter, William B, III 1941- *BiDrAPA 89*
Hunter, William Jay, Jr 1944- *WhoAm 90*
Hunter, William Mill, II 1949- *St&PR 91*
Hunter, William Schmidt 1931- *St&PR 91*
Hunter Blair, Pauline Clarke 1921- *WhoAm 90*
Hunter-Blank, Lawrence D. 1952- *WhoEmL 91*
Hunter-Bone, Maureen Claire 1946- *WhoAmW 91*
Hunter-Duvar, John 1821-1899 *DcCanB 12, DcLB 99 [port], OxCCanT*
Hunter-Gault, Charlayne 1942- *WhoWrEP 89*
Hunter-Stiebel, Penelope *WhoAmA 91, WhoE 91*
Hunthausen, Raymond Gerhardt 1921- *WhoAm 90*
Hunting, Anne Ritchie 1944- *WhoWor 91*
Hunting, Constance Coulter 1925- *WhoAm 90*
Hunting, D.D., Jr. 1926- *St&PR 91*
Hunting, David D. 1892- *St&PR 91*
Hunting, David D., Jr. 1926- *WhoAm 90*
Hunting, David D., Sr. 1892- *WhoAm 90*
Huntington, A Montgomery *WhoAmA 91N*
Huntington, Ann V Hyatt 1876-1973 *WhoAmA 91N*
Huntington, Anna Vaughn 1876-1973 *BiDWomA*
Huntington, Charles Ellsworth 1919- *WhoAm 90*
Huntington, Curtis Edward 1942- *St&PR 91, WhoAm 90*
Huntington, Cynthia 1951- *WhoWrEP 89*
Huntington, David Carew 1922- *WhoAm 90*
Huntington, David Mack Goode 1926- *WhoAm 90*
Huntington, Earl L. 1929- *St&PR 91*
Huntington, Earl Lloyd 1929- *WhoAm 90*
Huntington, Harriet Elizabeth 1909- *AuBYP 90*
Huntington, Henry E. 1850-1927 *WorAlBi*
Huntington, Hillard Bell 1910- *WhoAm 90*
Huntington, James C., Jr. 1928- *St&PR 91*
Huntington, James Cantine, Jr. 1928- *WhoAm 90*
Huntington, Jim 1941- *WhoAmA 91*
Huntington, John W 1910-1976 *WhoAmA 91N*
Huntington, Karen Rae 1945- *WhoWrEP 89*
Huntington, Lawrence S. 1935- *St&PR 91*
Huntington, Lawrence Smith 1935- *WhoAm 90*
Huntington, Margaret Wendell 1867-1958 *WhoAmA 91N*
Huntington, Nathaniel 1830-1888 *AmLegL*
Huntington, Robert Graham, Jr. 1926- *St&PR 91*
Huntington, Robert Hubbard 1937- *St&PR 91, WhoAm 90*
Huntington, Samuel *BioIn 16*
Huntington, Samuel 1731-1796 *BiDrUSE 89, EncCRAm*
Huntington, Samuel Phillips 1927- *WhoAm 90*
Huntington, Stephen Patrick 1948- *WhoEmL 91*
Huntington, Susan 1791-1823 *FemiCLE*
Huntington, Thomas Foster 1920- *WhoAm 90*
Huntington, William Reed *BioIn 16, NewYTBS 90*
Huntley, Alice Mae 1917- *WhoAmW 91*
Huntley, Arthur C 1930- *BiDrAPA 89*
Huntley, Charles William 1913- *WhoAm 90*
Huntley, Chet 1911-1974 *BioIn 16*
Huntley, David Austin 1933- *St&PR 91*
Huntley, David C 1930- *WhoAmA 91*
Huntley, Elizabeth Maddox *EarBIAP*
Huntley, Harlan Harrison 1928- *St&PR 91*
Huntley, Harvey Lewis, Jr. 1945- *WhoSSW 91*
Huntley, James Robert 1923- *WhoAm 90*
Huntley, Marcia Lynn 1951- *St&PR 91*
Huntley, Raymond *NewYTBS 90*
Huntley, Robert Edward Royall 1929- *WhoAm 90*

Huntley, Robert Joseph 1924- *WhoWor 91*
Huntley, Robert Ross 1926- *WhoAm 90*
Huntley, Robin S. 1948- *St&PR 91*
Huntley, Victoria Hutson 1900-1971 *WhoAmA 91N*
Hunton, Addie D. Waites 1870-1943 *HarlReB*
Hunton, Augustus Pingry 1816-1911 *AmLegL*
Hunton, Donald Bothen 1927- *WhoAm 90*
Huntoon, Abby E 1951- *WhoAmA 91*
Huntoon, Barry *BioIn 16*
Huntoon, Robert Brian 1927- *WhoE 91, WhoWor 91*
Huntress, E. Charles 1938- *WhoSSW 91*
Huntress, Keith Gibson 1913- *WhoAm 90*
Hunts, Barney D. *St&PR 91*
Huntsbarger, Bruce Edward 1950- *WhoEmL 91*
Huntsinger, Fritz Roy 1935- *WhoAm 90*
Huntsinger, Martha Elaine 1944- *WhoSSW 91*
Huntsman, John Robert 1951- *WhoSSW 91*
Huntsman, Lawrence Darrow 1934- *WhoE 91*
Huntsman, Leslie D. 1948- *St&PR 91*
Huntsman, Stanley Houser 1932- *WhoAm 90*
Huntting, Cynthia Cox 1936- *WhoAmW 91*
Huntz, Steve 1945- *Ballpl 90*
Huntzicker, Jon Noble 1939- *St&PR 91*
Huntzinger, James Allyn 1927- *BiDrAPA 89*
Hunyadi, Steve 1937- *St&PR 91*
Hunzeker, Hubert La Von 1920- *WhoAm 90*
Hunzicker, Warren John 1920- *WhoAm 90*
Hunziker, Catherine *BioIn 16*
Hunziker, Don A. 1927- *WhoSSW 91*
Hunziker, Don Allen 1927- *St&PR 91*
Hunziker, Frederick John, Jr. 1928- *St&PR 91*
Hunziker, Robert McK 1932- *St&PR 91*
Hunziker, Robert McKee 1932- *WhoAm 90*
Hunziker, Rudy 1946- *BioIn 16*
Hunzinger, George 1835-1898 *PenDiDA 89*
Huon, Hubert John 1936- *WhoWor 91*
Huot, Alexandre 1897-1953 *OxCCanT*
Huot, Guy Eugene 1943- *WhoWor 91*
Huot, Jean J *BiDrAPA 89*
Huot, Rachel Irene 1950- *WhoAmW 91*
Huot, Robert 1935- *WhoAmA 91, WhoE 91*
Huot, William J. 1926- *St&PR 91*
Huovie, Curtis Oliver 1947- *St&PR 91*
Hupalo, Meredith Topliff 1917- *WhoAmW 91*
Hupf, Robert Edmund 1948- *St&PR 91*
Hupfeld, Herman 1894-1951 *OxCPMus*
Hupfeld, Stanley Francis 1944- *WhoSSW 91*
Hupfer, L. Lee *St&PR 91*
Hupp, Frederick Duis 1938- *WhoAmA 91*
Hupp, Harry L. 1929- *WhoAm 90*
Hupp, Jack Scott 1930- *St&PR 91, WhoAm 90*
Hupp, Patricia Ellen 1950- *WhoAmW 91*
Hupp, Robert Craig 1877-1931 *EncABHB 4*
Hupp, Robert Paul 1915- *WhoAm 90*
Hupp, Terry L. 1941- *St&PR 91*
Huppe, Alex 1947- *WhoE 91*
Huppe, Bernard Felix 1911-1989 *BioIn 16*
Huppe, Francis Frowin 1934- *WhoAm 90*
Hupper, John Roscoe 1925- *WhoAm 90*
Huppert, Ernest 1922- *WhoWor 91*
Huppert, Herbert Eric 1943- *WhoWor 91*
Huppert, Isabelle *BioIn 16*
Huppert, Jack George 1933- *WhoSSW 91*
Huppert, Victor F *BiDrAPA 89*
Hupy, Art 1924- *WhoAmA 91*
Hupy, Michael Frederick 1946- *WhoEmL 91*
Huque, Ahmed Shafiqul 1952- *WhoWor 91*
Huquier, Jacques-Gabriel 1695-1772 *PenDiDA 89*
Hurajt, Andrea Ruth 1948- *WhoAmW 91, WhoEmL 91*
Huras, William David 1932- *WhoAm 90*
Hurayt, Andrew Joseph *BiDrAPA 89*
Hurbanis, Brenda Louise 1949- *WhoAmW 91, WhoEmL 91*
Hurchalla, Maggy Reno 1940- *WhoAmW 91*
Hurches, Carlos E. *WhoHisp 91*
Hurcomb, Thomas J. 1937- *St&PR 91*
Hurd, Benjamin *PenDiDA 89*
Hurd, Bruce Edward 1954- *WhoEmL 91*
Hurd, Byron Thomas 1933- *WhoWor 91*
Hurd, Carl Bently 1919- *WhoAm 90*
Hurd, Charles Buell 1894-1979 *BioIn 16*
Hurd, Charles W. 1927- *St&PR 91*
Hurd, Clement 1908-1988 *AuBYP 90, BioIn 16, SmATA 64 [port]*
Hurd, Cuthbert C. 1911- *WhoAm 90*
Hurd, Douglas 1930- *BioIn 16, CurBio 90 [port]*
Hurd, Douglas Richard 1930- *SpyFic, WhoWor 91*
Hurd, Edith 1910- *AuBYP 90*
Hurd, Edith Thacher 1910- *SmATA 64 [port]*
Hurd, Eric Ray 1936- *WhoSSW 91, WhoWor 91*
Hurd, Frederick *BioIn 16*
Hurd, G. David 1929- *St&PR 91, WhoAm 90*
Hurd, Gale Anne *BioIn 16*
Hurd, Hazel Ruth 1934- *WhoSSW 91*
Hurd, J. Nicholas 1942- *St&PR 91, WhoAm 90*
Hurd, Jacob 1703-1758 *PenDiDA 89*
Hurd, Michael Edward William 1947- *WhoWrEP 89*
Hurd, Michael John 1928- *IntWWM 90*
Hurd, Nathaniel 1729-1777 *PenDiDA 89*
Hurd, Paul DeHart 1905- *BioIn 16*
Hurd, Paul Gemmill 1946- *WhoEmL 91*
Hurd, Peter 1904- *WhoAmA 91N*
Hurd, Richard M. 1924- *St&PR 91*
Hurd, Richard Nelson 1926- *WhoAm 90, WhoWor 91*
Hurd, Shirley Dyer 1940- *WhoAmW 91*
Hurd, Suzanne Sheldon 1939- *WhoAm 90*
Hurd, Thacher *BioIn 16*
Hurd, Thacher 1949- *AuBYP 90*
Hurd, Tom 1924-1982 *Ballpl 90*
Hurd, W. Russell 1946- *St&PR 91*
Hurdle, Clint 1957- *Ballpl 90*
Hurdle, Les *NewAgMG*
Hurdle, Thomas Gray 1919- *WhoSSW 91*
Huret, Barry S. 1938- *WhoE 91*
Hurewicz, Witold 1904-1956 *DcScB S2*
Hurewitz, Florence K *WhoAmA 91*
Hurewitz, Jacob Coleman 1914- *WhoE 91*
Hurewitz, Sharon Joy 1959- *WhoAmW 91*
Hurford, Gary T. 1936- *St&PR 91*
Hurford, John Boyce 1938- *WhoAm 90, WhoWor 91*
Hurford, Peter 1930- *PenDiMP*
Hurford, Peter John 1930- *IntWWM 90*
Huriaux, Richard Dana 1944- *WhoE 91*
Hurkos, Peter 1911-1988 *AnObit 1988, BioIn 16, EncO&P 3, EncPaPR 91*
Hurlbert, Clark D. 1941- *St&PR 91*
Hurlbert, Gordon C. 1924- *St&PR 91*
Hurlbert, Gordon Charles 1924- *WhoAm 90*
Hurlbert, John A. 1923- *St&PR 91*
Hurlburt, Allen 1910-1983 *ConDes 90*
Hurlburt, Frances Alice 1937- *WhoSSW 91*
Hurlburt, Harley Ernest 1943- *WhoWor 91*
Hurlburt, Jack 1925- *St&PR 91*
Hurlburt, Sidney Hollady 1940- *WhoE 91*
Hurlbut, Cornelius Searle, Jr. 1906- *WhoAm 90*
Hurlbut, Dan *BioIn 16*
Hurlbut, Edwin W. 1854- *AmLegL*
Hurlbut, Elvin Millard, Jr. 1921- *WhoWor 91*
Hurlbut, Robert H. 1935- *St&PR 91*
Hurlbut, Robert Harold 1935- *WhoE 91, WhoWor 91*
Hurlbut, Robert St. Clair 1924- *St&PR 91, WhoAm 90*
Hurlbut, Stephen Augustus 1815-1882 *BioIn 16*
Hurlbutt, Guy Gordon 1942- *WhoAm 90*
Hurley, Albert M *BiDrAPA 89*
Hurley, Albert Rowe 1939- *St&PR 91*
Hurley, Alfred Francis 1928- *WhoAm 90, WhoSSW 91*
Hurley, Allyson Kingsley 1949- *WhoAmW 91*
Hurley, Anne Irene 1958- *WhoE 91*
Hurley, Augustus H., Jr. 1928- *St&PR 91*
Hurley, Carol *ODwPR 91*
Hurley, Cheryl Joyce 1947- *WhoAm 90, WhoAmW 91*
Hurley, Dale W 1922- *BiDrAPA 89*
Hurley, Dean C. 1954- *WhoE 91*
Hurley, Denzil H 1949- *WhoAmA 91*
Hurley, Donald G. 1933- *St&PR 91*
Hurley, Dorothea *BioIn 16*
Hurley, Ed 1910-1969 *Ballpl 90*
Hurley, Edward Bradley 1965- *WhoE 91*
Hurley, Edward Timothy 1869-1950 *WhoAmA 91N*
Hurley, Elaine Margaret 1958- *WhoAmW 91*
Hurley, Eleanor Jane 1939- *WhoSSW 91*
Hurley, Elizabeth *BioIn 16*
Hurley, Francis T. 1927- *WhoAm 90*
Hurley, Frank Thomas, Jr. 1924- *WhoSSW 91*
Hurley, Giovanna Maria 1952- *WhoAmW 91*
Hurley, Harry James, Jr. 1926- *WhoAm 90*
Hurley, James F. *ODwPR 91*
Hurley, James F. 1937- *St&PR 91*
Hurley, James Frederick 1941- *WhoE 91*
Hurley, James R. 1932- *WhoE 91*
Hurley, James Raymond *BiDrAPA 89*
Hurley, John Kenneth 1931- *WhoSSW 91*
Hurley, John Neal 1951- *St&PR 91*
Hurley, John William 1929- *St&PR 91*
Hurley, Kay Weaver 1954- *WhoEmL 91*
Hurley, Laurel 1927- *IntWWM 90*
Hurley, Laurence Harold 1944- *WhoAm 90*
Hurley, Lawrence Joseph 1946- *WhoEmL 91*
Hurley, Leslie John 1911- *AuBYP 90*
Hurley, Linda Kay 1951- *WhoAmW 91*
Hurley, Lucille S. 1922-1988 *BioIn 16*
Hurley, Lucille Shapson 1922- *WhoWrEP 89*
Hurley, Marjorie Bryan 1941- *St&PR 91, WhoAmW 91*
Hurley, Mark Joseph 1919- *WhoAm 90*
Hurley, Marlene Emogene 1938- *WhoAmW 91, WhoWor 91*
Hurley, Mary Stupnik 1952- *WhoEmL 91*
Hurley, Maureen Viola 1952- *WhoWrEP 89*
Hurley, Michael J. 1938- *St&PR 91*
Hurley, Morris Elmer, Jr. 1920- *WhoAm 90*
Hurley, Pat *BioIn 16*
Hurley, Patrick J. 1883-1963 *BioIn 16*
Hurley, Patrick Jay 1883-1963 *BiDrUSE 89*
Hurley, Patrick Mason 1912- *WhoAm 90*
Hurley, Patrick T. 1954- *BiDrAPA 89*
Hurley, Peyton 1919- *St&PR 91*
Hurley, Priscilla R. 1940- *WhoAmW 91*
Hurley, Robert Joseph 1932- *WhoAm 90*
Hurley, Samuel Clay, III 1936- *WhoAm 90*
Hurley, Steven Ray 1947- *WhoE 91*
Hurley, Thomas J 1922- *BiDrAPA 89*
Hurley, Thomas O. 1951- *St&PR 91*
Hurley, Webster H. 1921- *St&PR 91*
Hurley, Willard Lee 1926- *WhoAm 90*
Hurley, William Joseph 1926- *WhoAm 90*
Hurley, William Joseph 1939- *WhoE 91*
Hurley, Wilson 1924- *WhoAmA 91*
Hurlock, James Bickford 1933- *WhoAm 90, WhoE 91, WhoWor 91*
Hurlock, Roger W. 1912- *St&PR 91*
Hurlow-Hannah, Elizabeth F. 1941- *WhoE 91*
Hurlstone, Robert William 1952- *WhoAmA 91*
Hurman, David Charles 1952- *WhoWor 91*
Hurmence, Belinda 1921- *BioIn 16*
Hurn, David 1934- *WhoWor 91*
Hurn, William Thomas 1933- *St&PR 91*
Hurney, Kate 1941- *IntWWM 90*
Hurni, Richard Jay 1934- *St&PR 91*
Hurnik, Ilja 1922- *IntWWM 90*
Hurnyak, Christina Kaiser 1949- *WhoEmL 91*
Hurok, Oscar Joseph 1906- *BiDrAPA 89*
Hurok, Sol 1888-1974 *WorAlBi*
Hurowitz, Gerald *BiDrAPA 89*
Hurrelmann, Klaus 1944- *WhoWor 91*
Hurry, Robert Otis 1938- *St&PR 91*
Hursch, James Alexander 1961- *WhoE 91*
Hursey, Ann *BioIn 16*
Hursey, B. Edward 1927- *St&PR 91*
Hursh, Yvonne Machelle 1959- *WhoEmL 91*
Hursky, Jacob P. 1923- *WhoAm 90*
Hurson, Brian John 1945- *WhoWor 91*
Hurson, Daniel L. 1920- *St&PR 91*
Hurson, Michael 1941- *WhoAmA 91*
Hurst, Allen Harvey 1960- *WhoEmL 91*
Hurst, Bruce 1958- *Ballpl 90*
Hurst, Carolyn Jean 1958- *WhoAmW 91*
Hurst, Catherine Beyer 1944- *WhoAmW 91*
Hurst, Charles Jackson 1941- *WhoAm 90*
Hurst, Christina Marie 1955- *WhoAmW 91*
Hurst, Clyde Oren *BiDrAPA 89*
Hurst, David Alan 1950- *WhoSSW 91*
Hurst, David Michael 1937- *BiDrAPA 89*
Hurst, Don 1905-1952 *Ballpl 90*
Hurst, Donald David 1928- *St&PR 91*
Hurst, Donald Geoffrey 1911- *WhoAm 90*
Hurst, Elizabeth C 1959- *BiDrAPA 89*
Hurst, Elton L 1952- *BiDrAPA 89*
Hurst, Ernest C. 1926- *St&PR 91*
Hurst, Fannie 1887?-1968 *FemiCLE*
Hurst, Fannie 1889-1968 *WorAlBi*
Hurst, Flora Mia Moley 1953- *WhoAmW 91*
Hurst, Frances Ethel Weekley 1919- *WhoAmW 91*
Hurst, George 1926- *IntWWM 90, PenDiMP*
Hurst, Gregory Squire 1947- *WhoEmL 91, WhoWor 91*
Hurst, Hal N. 1935- *St&PR 91*
Hurst, Harvey Edward 1924- *St&PR 91*
Hurst, Hollis Christopher 1924- *WhoSSW 91*
Hurst, Howard Cates 1957- *WhoSSW 91*
Hurst, James Paul, Jr. 1932- *BiDrAPA 89*
Hurst, James Willard 1910- *ConAu 130, WhoAm 90*
Hurst, Janet Leigh 1950- *WhoEmL 91*
Hurst, John Emory, Jr. 1928- *St&PR 91, WhoAm 90*
Hurst, Karen E. 1946- *St&PR 91, WhoE 91*
Hurst, Kenneth Thurston 1923- *WhoAm 90*
Hurst, Lawrence Page 1937- *IntWWM 90*
Hurst, Leland L. 1930- *St&PR 91*
Hurst, Leland Lyle 1930- *WhoAm 90*
Hurst, Lewis Alfred 1911- *BiDrAPA 89*
Hurst, Lionel Alexander 1950- *WhoWor 91*
Hurst, Margery 1913-1989 *AnObit 1989*
Hurst, Mark Andrew 1959- *BiDrAPA 89*
Hurst, Michael William 1947- *WhoE 91*
Hurst, Phillip Gordon 1951- *WhoEmL 91*
Hurst, Ralph N 1918- *WhoAmA 91*
Hurst, Robert J. 1945- *St&PR 91*
Hurst, Robert Jay 1945- *WhoAm 90*
Hurst, Susan Diane 1957- *WhoAmW 91*
Hurst, Thomas Lee 1924- *St&PR 91*
Hurst, Tim 1865-1915 *Ballpl 90*
Hurst, Vernon James 1923- *WhoAm 90*
Hurston, Ronald Orne 1938- *BiDrAPA 89*
Hurston, Zora Neale 1891-1960 *ConLC 61 [port], EarBlAP, FemiCLE, HarlReB [port]*
Hurston, Zora Neale 1901-1960 *BioAmW*
Hurston, Zora Neale 1903-1960 *DrBlPA 90, MajTwCW*
Hurston, Zora Neale 1907-1960 *BioIn 16*
Hurt, Bob *BioIn 16*
Hurt, Charlie Deuel, III 1950- *WhoAm 90, WhoEmL 91*
Hurt, Daniel I. 1951- *WhoEmL 91*
Hurt, Edward P. *BioIn 16*
Hurt, Frank Benjamin 1899- *WhoSSW 91, WhoWor 91*
Hurt, Hubert Olyn 1925- *WhoSSW 91*
Hurt, James Riggins 1934- *WhoAm 90*
Hurt, John *BioIn 16, NewYTBS 90 [port]*
Hurt, John 1940- *WorAlBi*
Hurt, John O *BiDrAPA 89*
Hurt, John O., Jr. *BiDrAPA 89*
Hurt, John Richard, II *BiDrAPA 89*
Hurt, John Vincent 1940- *WhoAm 90*
Hurt, Joseph Richard 1953- *WhoEmL 91*
Hurt, Katha Connor 1947- *WhoAmW 91*
Hurt, Mary Beth *WhoAm 90*
Hurt, Mary Beth 1948- *WorAlBi*
Hurt, Mississippi John 1892-1966 *DrBlPA 90*
Hurt, Pamela Denise 1964- *WhoAmW 91*
Hurt, Robert C. 1909- *St&PR 91*
Hurt, Robert Glenn 1919- *WhoWor 91*
Hurt, Robert Lee 1959- *WhoEmL 91*
Hurt, Stan Charles 1939- *St&PR 91*
Hurt, Susanne M *WhoAmA 91*
Hurt, Susanne Morris *WhoE 91*
Hurt, William 1950- *BioIn 16, WhoAm 90, WorAlBi*
Hurt, William Holman 1927- *WhoAm 90*
Hurta, Glenn R. 1942- *St&PR 91*
Hurtado, Albert L. 1946- *ConAu 130*
Hurtado, Angel 1927- *WhoE 91*
Hurtado, Ciro 1954- *WhoHisp 91*
Hurtado, I. Jay *WhoHisp 91*
Hurtado, Luis Victor 1954- *WhoE 91*
Hurtado, Miguel de la Madrid *BioIn 16*
Hurtado Miller, Carlos *WhoWor 91*
Hurtarte, Susana Penalosa 1946- *WhoHisp 91*
Hurteau, Gilles David 1928- *WhoAm 90*
Hurter, Arthur Patrick *WhoAm 90*
Hurter, Bruce P. 1948- *BiDrAPA 89*
Hurth, James Philip 1955- *BiDrAPA 89*
Hurtig, Martin Russell 1929- *WhoAmA 91*
Hurtig, Serge 1927- *WhoWor 91*
Hurtt, Caleb Brown 1931- *St&PR 91, WhoAm 90, WhoE 91*
Hurtt, Claude David 1947- *WhoEmL 91, WhoSSW 91*
Hurtubise, Jacques 1939- *WhoAmA 91*
Hurtubise, Jim *BioIn 16*
Hurvell, Bengt Olof 1935- *WhoWor 91*
Hurvich, Leo Maurice 1910- *WhoAm 90*
Hurvitz, Carole Hughes 1942- *WhoAm 90, WhoAmW 91*
Hurvitz, Martin 1918- *BiDrAPA 89*
Hurwich, Robert Allen 1941- *St&PR 91*
Hurwicz, Leonid 1917- *WhoAm 90*
Hurwit, Robert Harold 1935- *St&PR 91*
Hurwitch, John Edward 1942- *WhoE 91*
Hurwitz, Alan Joel 1951- *BiDrAPA 89*
Hurwitz, Charles E. 1940- *St&PR 91*
Hurwitz, Charles Edwin 1940- *WhoAm 90*
Hurwitz, David 1905- *WhoAm 90*
Hurwitz, David Louis 1967- *WhoEmL 91*
Hurwitz, Donald Lee 1952- *WhoEmL 91*
Hurwitz, Ellen Stiskin 1942- *WhoAm 90*
Hurwitz, Emanuel 1919- *IntWWM 90, PenDiMP*
Hurwitz, Henry, Jr. 1918- *WhoAm 90*
Hurwitz, Herbert Neal 1942- *BiDrAPA 89*
Hurwitz, Hy 1910-1966 *Ballpl 90*

Hurwitz, Isadore E 1931- *BiDrAPA 89*
Hurwitz, Johanna *BioIn 16*
Hurwitz, Johanna 1937- *AuBYP 90, WhoWrEP 89*
Hurwitz, Lawrence B *BiDrAPA 89*
Hurwitz, Lawrence Neal 1939- *WhoAm 90*
Hurwitz, Leo *BioIn 16*
Hurwitz, Mervin H *BiDrAPA 89*
Hurwitz, Michele Leslie Weber 1959- *WhoAmW 91*
Hurwitz, Mitchell Seth 1953- *WhoEmL 91*
Hurwitz, Myron R 1937- *BiDrAPA 89*
Hurwitz, Robert Irving 1939- *IntWWM 90*
Hurwitz, Sidney J 1932- *WhoAmA 91*
Hurwitz, Stanley M. 1949- *WhoEmL 91*
Hurwitz, Stephen Allen 1942- *St&PR 91*
Hurwitz, Thomas David 1945- *BiDrAPA 89*
Hurwiz, Melvin H. 1932- *St&PR 91*
Hurwood, Bernhardt J. *BioIn 16*
Hurzeler, Marc A *BiDrAPA 89*
Hus, Walter 1959- *IntWWM 90*
Husa, Karel 1921- *BioIn 16, IntWWM 90*
Husa, Karel Jaroslav 1921- *WhoAm 90, WhoWor 91*
Husain, Arif 1952- *BiDrAPA 89*
Husain, Asim *BiDrAPA 89*
Husain, Farzana *BiDrAPA 89*
Husain, Jaweed *BiDrAPA 89*
Husain, Maimoona Hakim *BiDrAPA 89*
Husain, Mazhar 1949- *WhoWor 91*
Husain, Mubarak 1939- *WhoWor 91*
Husain, Rafe Asim 1959- *WhoEmL 91*
Husain, S Arshad *BiDrAPA 89*
Husain, Taqdir 1929- *WhoAm 90*
Husak, Gustav 1913- *WhoWor 91, WorAlBi*
Husak, Susan M. V. 1961- *WhoAmW 91*
Husar, Emile 1915- *WhoE 91*
Husar, John Paul 1937- *WhoAm 90*
Husarik, Stephen 1944- *IntWWM 90*
Husayn, Saddam *BioIn 16*
Husayni, Amin al- *BioIn 16*
Husband, Charles 1908-1983 *DcNaB 1981*
Husband, Harold 1905- *St&PR 91*
Husband, James Francis, II 1946- *St&PR 91*
Husband, Lowell S 1942- *BiDrAPA 89*
Husband, Phillip Lyle 1962- *WhoEmL 91*
Husband, Richard Lorin, Sr. 1931- *WhoAm 90, WhoWor 91*
Husband, W. Wayne 1950- *St&PR 91*
Husby, Donald Evans 1927- *WhoAm 90*
Husby, John Richard 1950- *WhoEmL 91*
Husch, Gerhard 1901-1984 *PenDiMP*
Husch, Peter H. 1912- *St&PR 91*
Huschka, Martin F. 1949- *St&PR 91*
Huschka, Pius A. 1930- *St&PR 91*
Huse, Betty *BiDrAPA 89*
Huse, Frank Peter 1948- *St&PR 91*
Huse, Henry Howard 1839-1890 *AmLegL*
Huse, Robert J. *BioIn 16*
Huse, Stephen M. 1942- *St&PR 91*
Husebye, Terry L 1945- *WhoAmA 91*
Husemann, Robert William 1931- *WhoAm 90*
Husemoller, Roger Paul 1939- *St&PR 91*
Husen, Torsten 1916- *WhoWor 91*
Huser, Lawrence Roy 1945- *WhoEmL 91*
Husevaag, Marit 1932- *WhoWor 91*
Hushen, John W. 1935- *WhoAm 90*
Hushen, John Wallace 1935- *St&PR 91*
Hushing, William Collins 1918- *WhoAm 90*
Hushlak, Gerald 1945- *WhoAmA 91*
Husi, Donald Lester 1963- *WhoEmL 91*
Husing, Edward Britt 1901-1962 *BioIn 16*
Husing, Ted 1901-1961 *Ballpl 90*
Husing, Ted 1901-1962 *BioIn 16*
Husk, Cecil 1847-1920 *EncO&P 3*
Husk, G. Ronald 1937- *WhoAm 90, WhoSSW 91*
Husk, John Ramsden 1956- *WhoEmL 91*
Huskey, Harry Douglas 1916- *WhoAm 90*
Huskey, Tom 1954- *St&PR 91*
Huskins, Joseph Patterson 1908- *St&PR 91*
Huslap, James R. 1945- *St&PR 91*
Husman, Catherine Bigot 1943- *WhoAm 90*
Husman, Michael Rosche 1953- *WhoSSW 91*
Husmann, Don 1930- *St&PR 91*
Husovsky, Ivan 1927- *WhoAm 90*
Huss, Claudia Speroff 1959- *WhoEmL 91*
Huss, Edward Eugene 1932- *St&PR 91*
Huss, Hugo Jan 1934- *IntWWM 90*
Huss, Jack Lewis 1931- *WhoAm 90*
Huss, John 1372-1415 *WorAlBi*
Huss, John Anthony 1935- *St&PR 91*
Huss, John Jay 1936- *St&PR 91*
Huss, Joseph James 1957- *WhoEmL 91*
Huss, Salim Al- *WhoWor 91*
Huss, William Lee 1956- *WhoEmL 91*
Hussain, Akmal *WhoWor 91*
Hussain, Al 1949- *St&PR 91*
Hussain, Amjed 1930- *BiDrAPA 89*
Hussain, Hansa S *BiDrAPA 89*
Hussain, Kuhurani A *BiDrAPA 89*
Hussain, Mushtaq 1954- *WhoWor 91*
Hussain, Sajjad Fazal *BiDrAPA 89*
Hussainun, Salih Abu Bakr Bin *WhoWor 91*
Hussar, Daniel Alexander 1941- *WhoAm 90*
Hussar, Susan Rae 1951- *WhoAmW 91*
Hussar, Susan Vickery 1958- *WhoAmW 91*
Hussar, Sybil Anne 1929- *WhoAmW 91*
Hussein bin Onn 1922-1990 *BioIn 16*
Hussein Bin Talal 1935- *WhoWor 91*
Hussein Ibn Talal 1935- *PolLCME*
Hussein I, King *NewYTBS 90 [port]*
Hussein, King of Jordan 1935- *BioIn 16*
Hussein Onn 1922-1990 *NewYTBS 90 [port]*
Hussein Talal Ibn 1935- *WorAlBi*
Hussein, Ahmed Dia 1941- *WhoE 91*
Hussein, Pattie Yu 1956- *WhoAmW 91*
Hussein, Rafaat Mahmoud 1950- *WhoE 91*
Hussein, Saddam *BioIn 16*
Hussein, Saddam 1937- *NewYTBS 90 [port], News 91-1 [port], PolLCME, WhoWor 91*
Husseini, Haj Amin 1893-1974 *BioIn 16*
Husseini, Hussein *WhoWor 91*
Husseini, Ishak Mousa *NewYTBS 90*
Husselman, Grace 1923- *WhoAmW 91*
Husserl, Consuelo R. 1948- *WhoHisp 91*
Husserl, Edmund 1859-1938 *WrPh P*
Husserl, Fred E. 1946- *WhoHisp 91*
Hussey, Carol Ann 1955- *WhoAmW 91*
Hussey, John Dixon 1935- *WhoAm 90*
Hussey, John F. 1940- *ODwPR 91*
Hussey, John Fleming 1940- *St&PR 91*
Hussey, Jolee Childs 1948- *WhoAmW 91*
Hussey, Nan Marie 1957- *WhoAmW 91*
Hussey, Patricia *BioIn 16*
Hussey, Peter A. 1933- *St&PR 91*
Hussey, Philip W., Jr. 1931- *St&PR 91*
Hussey, Ward MacLean 1920- *WhoAm 90*
Hussey, William Bertrand 1915- *WhoAm 90*
Hussin, Vincent Gerard 1914- *St&PR 91*
Husson, Maurice *PenDiMP*
Husson, Philippe *BioIn 16*
Husson, Robert Farrin 1938- *IntWWM 90*
Husson, Suzanne 1943- *IntWWM 90*
Hussong, Wallace B 1919- *BiDrAPA 89*
Hust, Anne-Marie de Claviere d' *BioIn 16*
Hust, Bernard de Claviere d' *BioIn 16*
Hust, Bruce Kevin 1957- *WhoEmL 91, WhoWor 91*
Hustad, Marvin Allan 1928- *St&PR 91*
Hustad, Thomas Pegg 1945- *WhoEmL 91, WhoWor 91*
Husted, James William 1833-1892 *AmLegL*
Husted, John Edwin 1915- *WhoAm 90*
Husted, Marlin K. 1930- *St&PR 91*
Husted, Ralph Waldo 1911- *WhoAm 90, WhoWor 91*
Husted, Stewart Winthrop 1946- *WhoSSW 91*
Hustin, Jacques *PenDiDA 89*
Hustin, Jacques-Dennis-Ferdinand *PenDiDA 89*
Husting, Bert 1878-1948 *Ballpl 90*
Hustoles, Paul John 1952- *WhoEmL 91*
Huston, Allan Smith, Jr. 1944- *WhoAm 90*
Huston, Anjelica *BioIn 16, WhoAm 90, WhoAmW 91*
Huston, Anjelica 1951- *CurBio 90 [port]*
Huston, Anjelica 1952- *WorAlBi*
Huston, Annette Lynn 1963- *WhoAmW 91*
Huston, Beatrice Louise 1932- *WhoAm 90*
Huston, Bernard K. 1939- *St&PR 91*
Huston, Charles Lukens, III 1934- *St&PR 91*
Huston, Daniel Cliff 1955- *WhoEmL 91*
Huston, Danny *BioIn 16*
Huston, Dennis Robert 1952- *St&PR 91*
Huston, Edwin Allen 1938- *St&PR 91, WhoAm 90*
Huston, Harland Watson 1924- *St&PR 91*
Huston, Harris Hyde 1907- *WhoAm 90, WhoWor 91*
Huston, J. Dennis *BioIn 16*
Huston, James A. 1918- *ConAu 33NR*
Huston, James Alvin 1918- *WhoAm 90*
Huston, John 1906-1987 *BioIn 16, WorAlBi*
Huston, John Albert 1920- *WhoAm 90*
Huston, John Boyd 1813-187-? *AmLegL*
Huston, John Charles 1927- *WhoAm 90*
Huston, John Leo 1944- *WhoAm 90*
Huston, John Lewis 1919- *WhoAm 90*
Huston, John Oliver 1945- *St&PR 91*
Huston, John Wilson 1925- *WhoAm 90*
Huston, Jonathan Boyd 1964- *WhoEmL 91*
Huston, Joseph Hollingsworth, Jr. 1949- *WhoEmL 91*
Huston, Margo 1943- *WhoAm 90, WhoAmW 91*
Huston, Michael Everett 1959- *WhoSSW 91*
Huston, Nancy Elizabeth 1947- *WhoSSW 91*
Huston, Norman Earl 1919- *WhoAm 90*
Huston, Paul E *BiDrAPA 89*
Huston, Perry Clark 1933- *WhoAmA 91*
Huston, Preston D. 1925- *St&PR 91*
Huston, Richard Thomas 1946- *St&PR 91*
Huston, Ted Laird 1943- *WhoAm 90*
Huston, Thelma Diane 1956- *WhoHisp 91*
Huston, Tom Charles 1941- *WhoAm 90*
Huston, Walter 1884-1950 *OxCCanT, WorAlBi*
Huston, Wanda 1948- *BioIn 16*
Huszar, Arlene Celia 1952- *WhoEmL 91*
Huszar, Kenneth D. 1937- *ODwPR 91*
Huszar, Lajos 1948- *IntWWM 90*
Huszar, Marta Jean 1953- *WhoE 91*
Huszonek, John Joseph 1950- *BiDrAPA 89*
Huszti, Joseph Bela 1936- *IntWWM 90*
Huta, Henry Nicholaus 1947- *WhoWor 91*
Hutabarat, Binsar Hamonangan 1942- *WhoWor 91*
Hutaff, William Rhett, III 1956- *St&PR 91*
Hutchcraft, A. Stephen 1930- *St&PR 91*
Hutchcraft, A. Stephens, Jr. 1930- *WhoAm 90*
Hutchcroft, John C. 1941- *IntWWM 90*
Hutchcroft, John Carter 1941- *WhoSSW 91*
Hutchence, Michael *BioIn 16*
Hutchens, Gail Rakes 1938- *St&PR 91*
Hutchens, John Kennedy 1905- *WhoAm 90*
Hutchens, John Oliver 1914- *WhoAm 90*
Hutchens, Steve Randall 1957- *WhoSSW 91*
Hutchens, Teresa Andrews 1949- *WhoSSW 91*
Hutchens, Thomas D. *WhoSSW 91*
Hutchens, Tyra Thornton 1921- *WhoAm 90*
Hutcheon, Duncan Elliot 1922- *WhoAm 90*
Hutcheon, Linda 1947- *ConAu 131*
Hutcheon, Peter David 1943- *WhoE 91*
Hutcheon, Wallace Schoonmaker 1933- *WhoSSW 91*
Hutcherson, Bobby *BioIn 16*
Hutcherson, Bobby 1941- *WhoAm 90*
Hutcherson, Carolyn Ann 1944- *WhoAmW 91*
Hutcherson, Christopher Alfred 1950- *WhoEmL 91*
Hutcherson, Cyrus Booker, Jr. 1939- *WhoSSW 91*
Hutcherson, James Michael 1949- *WhoEmL 91*
Hutcherson, John Rogers 1943- *WhoSSW 91*
Hutcherson, Karen F. 1951- *WhoAmW 91*
Hutcherson, Reginald Kenneth 1929- *St&PR 91*
Hutcheson, Bellenden *BiDrAPA 89*
Hutcheson, Carolyn Pirtle 1930- *WhoWrEP 89*
Hutcheson, Donald Wade 1933- *WhoSSW 91*
Hutcheson, Ernest 1871-1951 *PenDiMP*
Hutcheson, Fritz 1915- *St&PR 91*
Hutcheson, Harold Leo 1916- *WhoAm 90*
Hutcheson, James Sterling 1919- *WhoAm 90, WhoWor 91*
Hutcheson, Janet Reid 1934- *WhoAmW 91, WhoE 91*
Hutcheson, Jere Trent 1938- *IntWWM 90*
Hutcheson, Jerry Dee 1932- *WhoWor 91*
Hutcheson, Joseph Chappell, III 1907- *WhoAm 90*
Hutcheson, Mark Andrew 1942- *WhoAm 90*
Hutcheson, Mary Lee 1954- *BiDrAPA 89*
Hutcheson, Philip Charles 1948- *WhoSSW 91*
Hutcheson, Thad T., Jr. 1941- *WhoSSW 91*
Hutcheson, Zenas *BioIn 16*
Hutcheson, Zenas Willard, III 1953- *WhoE 91*
Hutchey, Brenda Jean 1952- *WhoEmL 91*
Hutchings, Alan Arthur 1944- *St&PR 91*
Hutchings, Arthur James Bramwell 1906- *IntWWM 90*
Hutchings, Brian LaMar 1915- *WhoAm 90*
Hutchings, George Henry 1922- *WhoAm 90*
Hutchings, John Barrie 1941- *WhoAm 90*
Hutchings, Johnny 1916-1963 *Ballpl 90*
Hutchings, La Vere 1918- *WhoAmA 91*
Hutchings, LeAnne von Neumeyer *WhoAmW 91*
Hutchings, Leo George 1924- *St&PR 91*
Hutchings, Peter Lounsbery 1943- *WhoAm 90*
Hutchins, Constantine, Jr. 1928- *St&PR 91*
Hutchins, Cynthia Ann 1962- *WhoAmW 91*
Hutchins, Diane Marie 1960- *St&PR 91*
Hutchins, Dianne 1953- *WhoAmW 91*
Hutchins, Donald B. 1948- *St&PR 91*
Hutchins, Donald Bruce 1947- *WhoEmL 91*
Hutchins, Frank McAllister 1922- *WhoAm 90*
Hutchins, Gene Robert 1949- *WhoEmL 91*
Hutchins, Grace 1885-1969 *EncAL*
Hutchins, Guy Edward, Jr. 1948- *WhoSSW 91*
Hutchins, Guy Starr 1905- *IntWWM 90*
Hutchins, H. J. 1952- *BioIn 16*
Hutchins, Hazel J. 1952- *BioIn 16*
Hutchins, Henry Alexander 1944- *WhoSSW 91*
Hutchins, James Joseph 1950- *BiDrAPA 89*
Hutchins, Jeane M. 1947- *WhoWrEP 89*
Hutchins, John Osborne 1920- *WhoAm 90*
Hutchins, John Richard, III *WhoAm 90*
Hutchins, MaryGail Kinzer 1940- *WhoAmW 91*
Hutchins, Pamela Elizabeth 1947- *WhoAmW 91*
Hutchins, Pat 1942- *AuBYP 90, ConAu 32NR*
Hutchins, Ralph 1937- *St&PR 91*
Hutchins, Ralph E. 1944- *St&PR 91*
Hutchins, Ralph Edwin, Jr. 1944- *WhoAm 90*
Hutchins, Robert Gordon *BiDrAPA 89*
Hutchins, Robert Maynard 1899-1977 *BioIn 16*
Hutchins, Robert Senger 1907- *WhoAm 90*
Hutchins, Ross Elliott 1906- *AuBYP 90*
Hutchins, Shirley M. 1933- *WhoWrEP 89*
Hutchins, Stilson 1838-1912 *BioIn 16*
Hutchins, Thomas 1730-1789 *EncCRAm*
Hutchins, Thomas Williams 1948- *St&PR 91*
Hutchins, Waldo 1895-1989 *BioIn 16*
Hutchins, William Bruce, III 1943- *St&PR 91, WhoAm 90*
Hutchinson Family *OxCPMus*
Hutchinson, A.L., Jr. 1933- *St&PR 91*
Hutchinson, Alan Bradford 1927- *WhoE 91*
Hutchinson, Anne 1591-1643 *BioAmW, WorAlBi*
Hutchinson, Anne Marbury 1591-1643 *BioIn 16, EncCRAm*
Hutchinson, Bill 1859-1926 *Ballpl 90*
Hutchinson, Carroll Ray 1933- *St&PR 91*
Hutchinson, Cecil Clair 1934- *St&PR 91*
Hutchinson, Charles Edgar 1935- *WhoAm 90*
Hutchinson, Charles Kimball 1928- *St&PR 91*
Hutchinson, Charles Smith, Jr. 1930- *WhoAm 90*
Hutchinson, Deborah Gibson 1956- *WhoEmL 91*
Hutchinson, Douglas 1960- *St&PR 91*
Hutchinson, Edith Margaret Emily 1907- *WhoWor 91*
Hutchinson, Edward Prince 1906- *WhoAm 90*
Hutchinson, Everett 1915- *WhoAm 90, WhoE 91*
Hutchinson, F. James *WhoE 91*
Hutchinson, Frank David, III 1929- *St&PR 91*
Hutchinson, Fred 1919-1964 *Ballpl 90 [port]*
Hutchinson, Frederick Edward 1930- *WhoAm 90*
Hutchinson, George Evelyn 1903- *WhoAm 90*
Hutchinson, George J. 1937- *WhoAm 90*
Hutchinson, George Joseph 1937- *St&PR 91*
Hutchinson, Harold David 1931- *WhoAm 90*
Hutchinson, Henry Hamilton 1919- *St&PR 91*
Hutchinson, Ira 1910-1973 *Ballpl 90*
Hutchinson, James Emlen 1937- *BiDrAPA 89*
Hutchinson, James Henry *BiDrAPA 89*
Hutchinson, Janet L 1917- *WhoAmA 91*
Hutchinson, Janice Gertrude *BiDrAPA 89*
Hutchinson, Jean Leslie 1952- *IntWWM 90*
Hutchinson, John *BioIn 16*
Hutchinson, John Woodside 1939- *WhoAm 90*
Hutchinson, Joseph D. 1941- *WhoE 91*
Hutchinson, Joseph Wood, III 1953- *WhoEmL 91*
Hutchinson, Julien Reay 1930- *St&PR 91*
Hutchinson, Karen Andrea *BiDrAPA 89*
Hutchinson, Leslie 1900-1969 *OxCPMus*
Hutchinson, Liberty Haven 1844-1882 *AmLegL*
Hutchinson, Loren Kelley 1916- *St&PR 91*

Hutchinson, Lucie Mary 1919- *IntWWM 90*
Hutchinson, Lucy 1620-1675? *BiDEWW, FemiCLE*
Hutchinson, Lucy Apsley 1620- *BioIn 16*
Hutchinson, M. Curry 1939- *St&PR 91*
Hutchinson, Margaret Blakeslee 1942- *WhoAmW 91*
Hutchinson, Max 1925- *WhoAmA 91*
Hutchinson, Melvin J. 1918- *St&PR 91*
Hutchinson, Michael Peter 1947- *WhoSSW 91*
Hutchinson, Mindy Beth *BiDrAPA 89*
Hutchinson, Olin Fulmer, Jr. 1943- *WhoSSW 91*
Hutchinson, Patricia Ann *BioIn 16*
Hutchinson, Pemberton 1931- *St&PR 91, WhoAm 90, WhoE 91*
Hutchinson, Peter Arthur 1930- *WhoE 91*
Hutchinson, Peter Arthur 1932- *WhoAmA 91*
Hutchinson, Philip A., Jr. 1938- *St&PR 91*
Hutchinson, Raymond Alexander 1937- *St&PR 91*
Hutchinson, Richard Armstrong 1944- *St&PR 91*
Hutchinson, Richard C 1929- *BiDrAPA 89*
Hutchinson, Richard William 1928- *WhoAm 90*
Hutchinson, Robert *BioIn 16*
Hutchinson, Robert Joseph 1957- *WhoWrEP 89*
Hutchinson, Ronald Porter 1951- *WhoE 91*
Hutchinson, Stephanie 1957- *IntWWM 90*
Hutchinson, Stuart 1956- *IntWWM 90*
Hutchinson, Thomas 1711-1780 *EncCRAm, WorAlBi*
Hutchinson, Thomas Eugene 1936- *WhoAm 90*
Hutchinson, Travis George 1942- *St&PR 91*
Hutchinson, Virginia Nettles 1936- *WhoAmW 91*
Hutchinson, William Burke 1909- *WhoAm 90*
Hutchinson, William David 1932- *WhoAm 90*
Hutchinson-Arm, Lillian Jahns 1937- *St&PR 91*
Hutchison, Alexander C. 1934- *St&PR 91*
Hutchison, Bert 1926- *St&PR 91*
Hutchison, Bruce *BioIn 16*
Hutchison, Cathleen Smith 1949- *WhoWor 91*
Hutchison, Clyde Allen, III 1938- *WhoAm 90*
Hutchison, Clyde Allen, Jr. 1913- *WhoAm 90*
Hutchison, Coe 1953- *St&PR 91*
Hutchison, Craig Austin 1952- *St&PR 91, WhoAm 90*
Hutchison, D. Warner 1930- *IntWWM 90*
Hutchison, David A. 1946- *WhoWrEP 89*
Hutchison, Dorris Jeannette 1918- *WhoAm 90*
Hutchison, Douglas B. 1957- *WhoSSW 91*
Hutchison, Elizabeth May 1924- *WhoAmW 91*
Hutchison, Elizabeth S *WhoAmA 91*
Hutchison, James Arthur, Jr. 1917- *WhoE 91*
Hutchison, James Donald 1932- *WhoE 91*
Hutchison, Jane Campbell 1932- *WhoAmA 91*
Hutchison, Jeanne Slaninger 1942- *WhoAmW 91*
Hutchison, John Michael 1944- *WhoWor 91*
Hutchison, Joseph G., Jr. 1950- *WhoWrEP 89*
Hutchison, Karon Elaine 1951- *WhoAmW 91*
Hutchison, Kay Bailey 1943- *WhoAmW 91*
Hutchison, Linda Taylor 1952- *WhoAmW 91*
Hutchison, Mary Elizabeth 1904-1970 *WhoAmA 91N*
Hutchison, Michael S. *WhoWrEP 89*
Hutchison, Murray Hunter 1938- *St&PR 91*
Hutchison, Pat 1943- *WhoAmW 91*
Hutchison, Ralph Oswald 1923- *WhoSSW 91*
Hutchison, Ron 1954- *St&PR 91*
Hutchison, Stanley Philip 1923- *WhoAm 90*
Hutchison, T W 1912- *ConAu 129*
Hutchison, Theodore Murtagh 1932- *St&PR 91, WhoAm 90*
Hutchison, Victor Hobbs 1931- *WhoAm 90*
Hutchison, William Forrest 1925- *WhoAm 90*
Hutchison, William Leete 1932- *WhoAm 90*
Hutchison, William Robert 1930- *WhoAm 90*
Hutchison-Hall, William Ellsworth H., IV 1963- *WhoE 91, WhoEmL 91*
Hutchisson, James Marvin 1961- *WhoSSW 91*
Huth, Edward Janavel 1923- *WhoAm 90*
Huth, John A. 1941- *St&PR 91*
Huth, John H. 1930- *St&PR 91*
Huth, John Harvey 1922- *WhoE 91*
Huth, Robert D. 1946- *St&PR 91, WhoAm 90*
Huth, William Edward 1931- *WhoAm 90*
Huthnance, Robert Thompson 1942- *St&PR 91*
Huthsteiner, George *BiDrAPA 89*
Hutin, Magdeleine 1898-1989 *ConAu 130*
Hutin, Serge Roger Jean 1929- *EncO&P 3*
Hutka, Glenn 1939- *St&PR 91*
Hutlitz, Philip N. 1940- *WhoE 91*
Hutmacher, Rahel 1944- *EncCoWW*
Hutman, Burton S 1932- *BiDrAPA 89*
Hutner, Herbert L. *WhoAm 90*
Hutner, Isaac 1906-1980 *BioIn 16*
Hutner, Robert Wolf 1931- *St&PR 91*
Hutner, Seymour Herbert 1911- *WhoAm 90, WhoE 91*
Hutsaliuk, Lubo 1923- *WhoAmA 91, WhoE 91*
Hutschnecker, Arnold A 1898- *BiDrAPA 89*
Hutsell, Thomas Carlyle 1939- *St&PR 91*
Hutsenpiller, Charles William 1942- *WhoSSW 91*
Hutson, Alan R. 1945- *St&PR 91*
Hutson, Charles Randolph 1949- *St&PR 91*
Hutson, Dan C., II 1953- *St&PR 91*
Hutson, Danny James 1957- *WhoSSW 91*
Hutson, Don 1913- *BioIn 16, WorAlBi*
Hutson, Don 1931- *WhoAm 90*
Hutson, Don D. 1936- *St&PR 91, WhoAm 90*
Hutson, Jack Karl 1948- *WhoEmL 91*
Hutson, James Harold, Jr. 1957- *WhoSSW 91*
Hutson, Jean Blackwell 1914- *WhoAm 90*
Hutson, Jim W. 1948- *WhoEmL 91*
Hutson, Keith Eugene 1925- *St&PR 91*
Hutson, Lockhart W. 1898-1986 *BioIn 16*
Hutson, Peggy B 1935- *BiDrAPA 89*
Hutt, Eric John Villette 1915- *WhoWor 91*
Hutt, Joanna Cravey 1943- *WhoWrEP 89*
Hutt, Laurence Jeffrey 1950- *WhoEmL 91*
Hutt, Peter Barton 1934- *WhoAm 90*
Hutt, W. H. 1899-1988 *AnObit 1988*
Hutt, William 1920- *BioIn 16, OxCCanT [port]*
Hutt, William H. *BioIn 16*
Huttenbach, Dirk E 1938- *BiDrAPA 89*
Huttenback, Robert Arthur 1928- *WhoAm 90*
Huttenlocher, Philippe 1942- *IntWWM 90*
Huttenstine, Marian Louise 1940- *WhoSSW 91*
Hutter, Adolph Matthew, Jr. 1937- *WhoAm 90, WhoE 91*
Hutter, Albert David 1941- *ConAu 130*
Hutter, Donald S. *NewYTBS 90*
Hutter, Donald S. 1932-1990 *BioIn 16*
Hutter, Dunald Stephen 1932- *WhoWrEP 89*
Hutter, James Risque 1924- *WhoAm 90, WhoWor 91*
Hutter, Joseph Gerard 1953- *St&PR 91*
Hutter, Robert Victor Paul 1929- *WhoAm 90*
Hutter, Rudolf Gustav Emil 1910- *WhoAm 90*
Huttig, Hans 1894- *BioIn 16*
Huttinger, Richard C. 1924- *St&PR 91*
Huttner, Jonny *BioIn 16*
Huttner, Marian Alice 1920- *WhoAm 90*
Hutto, Burton Roy *BiDrAPA 89*
Hutto, Earl 1926- *WhoAm 90, WhoSSW 91*
Hutto, James Calhoun 1931- *WhoAm 90*
Hutto, John L. 1941- *St&PR 91*
Hutto, Mark Craton *BiDrAPA 89*
Hutto, Ruth Bishop 1927- *WhoWor 91*
Hutto, Tommye Whitt 1939- *WhoAm 90*
Hutton, Albert Edward 1925- *St&PR 91*
Hutton, Ann Hawkes 1909- *WhoAm 90*
Hutton, Barbara *BioIn 16*
Hutton, Barbara 1912-1979 *BioAmW, WorAlBi*
Hutton, Barbara 1920- *ConAu 132*
Hutton, Betty 1921- *OxCPMus, WorAlBi*
Hutton, Catherine 1756-1846 *FemiCLE*
Hutton, David Krar 1944- *St&PR 91*
Hutton, Dorothy Wackerman 1899- *WhoAmA 91*
Hutton, Edward L. 1919- *St&PR 91*
Hutton, Edward Luke 1919- *WhoAm 90, WhoWor 91*
Hutton, Eleanor Hall 1936- *WhoSSW 91*
Hutton, Ernest Watson, Jr. 1944- *WhoE 91*
Hutton, Geoffrey 1909- *ConAu 130*
Hutton, George Norman, Jr. 1929- *St&PR 91*
Hutton, George Thompson 1946- *WhoEmL 91*
Hutton, Graham 1904-1988 *BioIn 16*
Hutton, Hugh McMillen 1897-1976 *WhoAmA 91N*
Hutton, Ian 1942- *WhoWor 91*
Hutton, Jack Gossett, Jr. 1931- *WhoE 91, WhoWor 91*
Hutton, James 1726-1797 *WorAlBi*
Hutton, James M., III 1927- *St&PR 91*
Hutton, James Morgan, III 1927- *WhoAm 90*
Hutton, James Scott 1833-1891 *DcCanB 12*
Hutton, John *BioIn 16*
Hutton, John Patrick 1948- *BiDrAPA 89*
Hutton, Joseph 1928- *St&PR 91*
Hutton, Lauren *BioIn 16*
Hutton, Lauren 1943- *WorAlBi*
Hutton, Leonard *WhoAmA 91*
Hutton, Leonard *BioIn 16, NewYTBS 90*
Hutton, Linda Jo 1947- *WhoWrEP 89*
Hutton, Lucy *FemiCLE*
Hutton, May Arkwright 1860-1915 *BioIn 16*
Hutton, Paul Andrew 1949- *WhoWrEP 89*
Hutton, Richard Holt 1826-1897 *BioIn 16*
Hutton, Robert Wackerman 1932- *WhoE 91*
Hutton, Robert William 1921- *St&PR 91*
Hutton, Robin R. 1945- *St&PR 91*
Hutton, Ronald 1953- *ConAu 131*
Hutton, Samuel 1845-1894 *DcCanB 12*
Hutton, Shirley *BioIn 16*
Hutton, Thomas Hays 1921- *St&PR 91*
Hutton, Timothy 1961- *WhoAm 90, WorAlBi*
Hutton, Tom 1946- *Ballpl 90*
Hutton, Walter Pandrich, Jr. 1916- *WhoE 91*
Hutton, Warwick *BioIn 16*
Hutton, Will 1950- *ConAu 130*
Hutton, William 1926- *WhoAm 90, WhoAmA 91*
Huttrer, Gerald William 1939- *St&PR 91*
Hutts, Joseph Clair, Jr. 1941- *St&PR 91*
Huttunen, Harri Juhani 1957- *WhoWor 91*
Huttunen, Matti O *BiDrAPA 89*
Huttunen, Reino *BiDrAPA 89*
Hutz, James Alan 1949- *St&PR 91*
Hutzell, Jeffrey Scott 1949- *WhoSSW 91*
Hutzler, Jeffery C 1943- *BiDrAPA 89*
Hutzli, Martin 1958- *WhoWor 91*
Huusko, Gary Lawrence 1957- *WhoEmL 91*
Huvos, Andrew 1930- *WhoE 91*
Huvos, Christopher L. 1946- *WhoE 91*
Huvos, Kornel 1913- *WhoAm 90*
Hux, Eugene L. 1927- *St&PR 91*
Hux, Robert C. *St&PR 91*
Hux, Ronald Wayne 1957- *St&PR 91*
Huxley, Aldous 1894-1963 *BioIn 16, DcLB 100 [port], EncO&P 3, EncPaPR 91, MajTwCW, RGTwCSF, SmATA 63 [port], WorAlBi, WrPh*
Huxley, Andrew 1917- *WhoAm 90, WhoWor 91*
Huxley, Andrew F. 1917- *WorAlBi*
Huxley, Craig *NewAgMG*
Huxley, Elspeth 1907- *BioIn 16, FemiCLE, SmATA 62 [port], TwCCr&M 91*
Huxley, Hugh Esmor 1924- *WhoAm 90*
Huxley, Julian 1887-1975 *MajTwCW*
Huxley, Marcus Richard 1949- *IntWWM 90*
Huxley, Thomas H. 1825-1895 *WorAlBi*
Huxley, Thomas Henry 1825-1895 *BioIn 16*
Huxsahl, John Edward 1953- *BiDrAPA 89*
Huxster, Evelyn Rachel 1931- *BiDrAPA 89*
Huxster, Howard K 1924- *BiDrAPA 89*
Huxster, Howard Knight 1924- *WhoE 91*
Huxta, Richard Alan 1947- *WhoE 91*
Huxtable, Ada Louise *WhoAm 90, WhoAmA 91*
Huy *PenDiDA 89*
Huybrechs, Thomas Hubert 1955- *WhoWor 91*
Huybrechts, Francois 1946- *IntWWM 90*
Huyck, Willard *WhoAm 90*
Huyer, Adriana 1945- *WhoAmW 91*
Huyett, Daniel Henry, III 1921- *WhoAm 90*
Huyffer, Paul *St&PR 91*
Huygens, Christiaan 1629-1695 *BioIn 16, WorAlBi*
Huygens, Remmert William 1932- *WhoAm 90, WhoE 91*
Huygens, Robert Burchard Constantijn 1931- *WhoWor 91*
Huyghe, Rene Louis 1906- *WhoWor 91*
Huyghebaert, Jan 1945- *WhoWor 91*
Huyghue, Douglas Smith 1816-1891 *DcLB 99*
Huyghue, Samuel Douglass Smith 1816-1891 *DcCanB 12*
Huyler, Jean Wiley 1935- *WhoAm 90, WhoWrEP 89*
Huyler, John 1808-1870 *AmLegL*
Huyler, Martha Juanita 1941- *WhoAmW 91*
Huynh, Huon Van 1920- *BiDrAPA 89*
Huynh, Kiet Tuan 1952- *WhoEmL 91*
Huynh, Tan Phat 1913-1989 *BioIn 16*
HuYoung, Michael 1956- *WhoEmL 91*
Huyser, Robert Ernest 1924- *WhoAm 90*
Huysman, Arlene Weiss 1929- *WhoAm 90, WhoAmW 91, WhoSSW 91*
Huysmans, J.-K. 1848-1907 *BioIn 16*
Huysmans, Joris-Karl 1848-1907 *BioIn 16, WorAlBi*
Huyssen, Andreas 1942- *WhoAm 90*
Huzar, Eleanor Goltz 1922- *WhoAm 90*
Huze, Cyril Michel 1949- *WhoEmL 91, WhoWor 91*
Huzii, Mituaki 1936- *WhoWor 91*
Huzinec, Mary Suzanne 1956- *WhoE 91*
Huzvar, Barbara Jo 1950- *WhoWrEP 89*
Hvidt, Kristian 1929- *ConAu 130*
Hvidt, Peter 1916- *PenDiDA 89*
Hvistendahl, Joyce Kilmer 1918- *WhoAm 90*
Hvitadal, Stefan fra *DcScanL*
Hwa, Erh-Cheng 1945- *WhoE 91*
Hwa, Millie Hui *WhoAmW 91*
Hwa, Stephen Chi-Ping 1933- *St&PR 91*
Hwaletz, Otto Josef 1951- *WhoWor 91*
Hwang, Andrew Sutaeg *BiDrAPA 89*
Hwang, Bun Chin C. 1943- *WhoWor 91*
Hwang, Cordelia Jong 1942- *WhoWor 91*
Hwang, David Henry *BioIn 16*
Hwang, David Henry 1957- *ConAu 132, WhoAm 90*
Hwang, K. Philip 1936- *St&PR 91*
Hwang, K. Phillip 1936- *WhoAm 90*
Hwang, Kao 1916- *WhoE 91*
Hwang, Kyupin Philip *BioIn 16*
Hwang, Michael Yongyou 1956- *BiDrAPA 89*
Hwang, Robert Wansung 1929- *BiDrAPA 89*
Hwang, Roland 1949- *WhoEmL 91*
Hwang, Yao-Chung 1933- *BiDrAPA 89*
Hwass, Edward Robert, Jr. 1959- *WhoSSW 91*
Hwong, Lucia *BioIn 16, NewAgMG*
Hyams, Barry 1911-1989 *BioIn 16, ConAu 129*
Hyams, Harriet 1929- *WhoAmA 91*
Hyams, James William 1946- *WhoSSW 91*
Hyams, Joe 1923- *WhoWrEP 89*
Hyams, Joseph W. 1865- *AmLegL*
Hyatt, Anna Vaughn 1876-1973 *BiDWomA*
Hyatt, Dennis Michael 1940- *St&PR 91*
Hyatt, Donald Bishop 1924- *WhoAm 90*
Hyatt, Elaine Miller 1951- *WhoAmW 91*
Hyatt, Guy William 1909- *WhoWor 91*
Hyatt, Joel Z. 1950- *WhoAm 90*
Hyatt, John W. 1837-1920 *WorAlBi*
Hyatt, John Wesley 1837-1920 *EncABHB 4 [port]*
Hyatt, Kenneth Austin 1940- *WhoWor 91*
Hyatt, Kenneth Ernest 1940- *St&PR 91, WhoAm 90*
Hyatt, Lawrence Eliot 1954- *WhoEmL 91*
Hyatt, Margaret Elizabeth 1959- *WhoAmW 91*
Hyatt, Mark C. *BiDrAPA 89*
Hyatt, Phillip Steven 1935- *St&PR 91*
Hyatt, Robert *BioIn 16*
Hyatt, Stuart Q. *ODwPR 91*
Hyatt-Smith, Ann Rose 1953- *WhoE 91, WhoEmL 91*
Hybl, William J. 1942- *St&PR 91*
Hyckes, Richard *PenDiDA 89*
Hyde, Alan Litchfield 1928- *WhoAm 90*
Hyde, Anne *BiDEWW*
Hyde, Anne 1637-1671 *BioIn 16*
Hyde, Anthony 1946- *SpyFic*
Hyde, Arthur Mastick 1877-1947 *BiDrUSE 89*
Hyde, Charles H. 1914- *WhoAm 90*
Hyde, Charles Henry, III 1952- *St&PR 91*
Hyde, Clarence Brodie, II 1937- *WhoAm 90, WhoSSW 91*
Hyde, David Rowley 1929- *WhoAm 90*
Hyde, Dawn Stauffer 1954- *WhoAmW 91*
Hyde, Dayton O. 1925- *BioIn 16*
Hyde, Dayton Ogden *AuBYP 90*
Hyde, Dick 1928- *Ballpl 90*
Hyde, Douglas G. 1943- *St&PR 91*
Hyde, Douglas Gaylord 1943- *WhoAm 90, WhoE 91*
Hyde, Edward 1609-1674 *BioIn 16, WorAlBi*
Hyde, Edward 1661-1723 *EncCRAm*
Hyde, Elizabeth Howe 1920- *WhoAmW 91*
Hyde, Estella M. 1946- *WhoEmL 91*
Hyde, Frederick Bill 1908- *IntWWM 90*
Hyde, Geoffrey 1930- *WhoAm 90*
Hyde, Geoffrey N L 1940- *BiDrAPA 89*
Hyde, George Charles, Jr. 1947- *WhoE 91*
Hyde, George H. 1922- *St&PR 91*
Hyde, Geraldine Veola 1926- *WhoAmW 91*

Hyde, Gordon E. 1898-1989 *BioIn 16*
Hyde, H. Montgomery 1907-1989 *AnObit 1989*
Hyde, H Montgomery 1907-1989 *ConAu 129*
Hyde, Henry J. *BioIn 16*
Hyde, Henry John 1924- *WhoAm 90*
Hyde, Howard Laurence 1957- *WhoE 91, WhoEmL 91*
Hyde, Ida Henrietta 1857-1945 *BioIn 16*
Hyde, Jack 1916- *WhoAm 90, WhoE 91*
Hyde, John Michael 1930- *WhoAm 90*
Hyde, John Paul 1934- *WhoAm 90*
Hyde, Joseph R., III 1942- *St&PR 91, WhoSSW 91*
Hyde, Kenneth R. 1944- *St&PR 91*
Hyde, Kent Owen 1959- *WhoEmL 91*
Hyde, Kevin Oliver 1945- *WhoWor 91*
Hyde, Lawrence H. 1924- *St&PR 91*
Hyde, Lawrence Henry, Jr. 1924- *WhoAm 90, WhoE 91*
Hyde, Lewis 1899- *IntWWM 90*
Hyde, Lewis 1945- *WhoWrEP 89*
Hyde, Margaret O 1917- *ChlLR 23 [port]*
Hyde, Margaret Oldroyd 1917- *AuBYP 90*
Hyde, Mary Morley Crapo 1912- *WhoAm 90*
Hyde, Michael Arthur 1942- *WhoWor 91*
Hyde, Miriam Beatrice 1913- *IntWWM 90*
Hyde, Nina *BioIn 16, NewYTBS 90 [port]*
Hyde, Nina Solomon 1932-1990 *ConAu 131*
Hyde, Peter Dawson 1924- *WhoSSW 91*
Hyde, Ray 1928- *ODwPR 91*
Hyde, Richard C. 1935- *ODwPR 91*
Hyde, Richard Mark 1955- *WhoSSW 91*
Hyde, Robert Burke, Jr. 1928- *WhoAm 90*
Hyde, Robert P. *BioIn 16*
Hyde, Robin 1906-1939 *FemiCLE*
Hyde, Scott 1926- *WhoAmA 91*
Hyde, Stuart Wallace 1923- *WhoAm 90*
Hyde, Thomas D. 1948- *St&PR 91*
Hyde, Walter 1875-1951 *PenDiMP*
Hyde, Walter Lewis 1919- *WhoAm 90*
Hyde, William 1946- *WhoEmL 91*
Hyde, William Frederick 1942- *WhoE 91*
Hyde de Neuville, A-M Rouille de Marigny 1749?-1849 *BioIn 16*
Hyde de Neuville, Jean-Guillaume 1776-1857 *BioIn 16*
Hyde-Jackson, M. Deborah 1949- *WhoAmW 91*
Hyde-Smith, Christopher *PenDiMP*
Hyde-Smith, Christopher 1935- *IntWWM 90*
Hyde-White, Wilfred 1903- *WorAlBi*
Hyde-White, Wilfrid 1903- *WhoAm 90*
Hyden, Dorothy Louise 1948- *WhoAmW 91*
Hyden, Elaine 1949- *WhoAmW 91, WhoEmL 91*
Hyden, Holger Viktor 1917- *WhoWor 91*
Hyden, Joe Bailey 1939- *WhoSSW 91*
Hyder, Clyde Kenneth 1902- *WhoE 91*
Hyder, Jeanne McEachern 1962- *WhoAmW 91*
Hydman-Vallien, Ulrica 1938- *ConDes 90*
Hydok, Joseph Thomas 1928- *St&PR 91, WhoAm 90*
Hydrick, Bob Durrett 1939- *WhoSSW 91*
Hyduk, Dennis Michael 1951- *St&PR 91*
Hyer, Frank Sidney 1933- *St&PR 91*
Hyer, Frederick L., Jr. 1940- *St&PR 91*
Hyer, John L. 1937- *WhoAm 90, WhoE 91*
Hyer, Margaret Kay 1944- *WhoSSW 91*
Hyer, Martha *BioIn 16*
Hyer, Michael Edward 1945- *WhoE 91*
Hyer, Paul Jones, Jr. 1943- *WhoSSW 91*
Hyera, Asterius Magnus 1942- *WhoAm 90*
Hyers, Emma Louise *BioIn 16*
Hyers, Judith G. *St&PR 91*
Hyers, Judith Gegenheimer 1945- *St&PR 91, WhoAmW 91*
Hyers, Kemper Kent 1929- *St&PR 91*
Hyett, Doyle Gregory 1948- *WhoE 91, WhoEmL 91*
Hyett, Kathy M. 1953- *ODwPR 91*
Hyjek, Walter John 1937- *St&PR 91*
Hykel, Richard Daniel 1944- *St&PR 91*
Hykes, David, and the Harmonic Choir *NewAgMG*
Hyla, James Franklin 1945- *WhoE 91*
Hyland, Christopher Samuel 1947- *WhoE 91*
Hyland, Douglas K. S. 1949- *WhoAm 90*
Hyland, Douglas K S 1949- *WhoAmA 91*
Hyland, Douglas K. S. 1949- *WhoSSW 91*
Hyland, Edward B. 1942- *St&PR 91*
Hyland, Edward W. 1925- *St&PR 91*
Hyland, Edward William 1925- *WhoAm 90*
Hyland, Frances 1927- *OxCCanT [port]*
Hyland, Geoffrey F. *St&PR 91*
Hyland, John P. 1928- *St&PR 91*
Hyland, Joseph Michael 1945- *WhoAm 90*
Hyland, Lawrence A. 1897-1989 *BioIn 16*
Hyland, Mary Pat 1956- *WhoE 91*
Hyland, Oonagh Mary 1948- *WhoWor 91*
Hyland, Richard Francis 1937- *St&PR 91*
Hyland, Robert J., Jr. 1949- *St&PR 91*
Hyland, Thomas Robert 1932- *WhoSSW 91*
Hyland, Thomas Sheridan, Jr. 1943- *St&PR 91*
Hyland, Timothy Mylo 1957- *WhoWor 91*
Hyland, Virginia Ling 1947- *WhoEmL 91*
Hyland, William Francis 1923- *WhoAm 90*
Hyland, William George 1929- *WhoAm 90*
Hylander, Clarence John 1897-1964 *AuBYP 90*
Hylander, Walter Raymond, Jr. 1924- *WhoSSW 91*
Hylbert, K William 1953- *BiDrAPA 89*
Hyle, Charles Thomas 1961- *WhoSSW 91*
Hyle, Jack 1929- *WhoE 91, WhoWor 91*
Hyle, Tom 1933- *WhoAm 90*
Hyler, Irene G *BiDrAPA 89*
Hyler, Steven E *BiDrAPA 89*
Hylin, Birgitta Charlotta Kristina 1915- *IntWWM 90*
Hylton, Gale Lynette *BiDrAPA 89*
Hylton, Hannelore Menke 1936- *WhoAm 90*
Hylton, Jack 1892-1965 *OxCPMus*
Hylton, Jane W. 1929- *St&PR 91*
Hylton, Joseph Gordon 1952- *WhoEmL 91*
Hylton, Kevin Earl 1956- *St&PR 91*
Hylton, Richard Maurice 1954- *WhoSSW 91*
Hylton, Thomas James 1948- *WhoAm 90, WhoE 91*
Hyman, Albert Lewis 1923- *WhoAm 90, WhoWor 91*
Hyman, Anthony 1928- *ConAu 132*
Hyman, Barbara S. 1953- *ODwPR 91*
Hyman, Betty Harpole 1938- *WhoAmW 91*
Hyman, Bruce 1944- *St&PR 91*
Hyman, Bruce Malcolm 1943- *WhoAm 90, WhoE 91, WhoWor 91*
Hyman, Carl Samuel 1955- *WhoEmL 91*
Hyman, David Nell 1943- *WhoWrEP 89*
Hyman, Dick *BioIn 16*
Hyman, Dick 1927- *OxCPMus*
Hyman, Donald R. 1948- *ODwPR 91*
Hyman, Earle 1926- *BioIn 16, DrBIPA 90, WhoAm 90, WorAlBi*
Hyman, Edward Sidney 1925- *WhoWor 91*
Hyman, Eric Lee 1956- *WhoEmL 91*
Hyman, Florence Joy 1926- *WhoE 91*
Hyman, Harvey 1937- *St&PR 91*
Hyman, Herbert Hiram 1918-1985 *BioIn 16*
Hyman, Isabelle 1930- *WhoAmA 91*
Hyman, Jerome Elliot 1923- *WhoAm 90*
Hyman, Johanna Jessica 1955- *WhoEmL 91*
Hyman, John Adams 1840-1891 *BlkAmsC [port]*
Hyman, Joseph 1928- *St&PR 91*
Hyman, Joy 1926- *IntWWM 90*
Hyman, Laura 1927- *WhoE 91*
Hyman, Lawrence Robert *BiDrAPA 89*
Hyman, Lawrence Robert 1940- *WhoE 91*
Hyman, Lester Samuel 1931- *WhoAm 90*
Hyman, Libbie H. 1888-1969 *BioIn 16*
Hyman, Libbie Henrietta 1888-1969 *DcScB S2*
Hyman, Linda *AuBYP 90*
Hyman, Linda 1940- *WhoAmA 91*
Hyman, Lloyd George 1928- *WhoAm 90*
Hyman, M. David 1934- *St&PR 91*
Hyman, Marshall Leonard 1924- *St&PR 91*
Hyman, Mary Bloom *WhoAmW 91, WhoE 91, WhoWor 91*
Hyman, Michael Richard 1954- *WhoSSW 91*
Hyman, Milton 1905- *WhoAm 90*
Hyman, Milton Bernard 1941- *WhoAm 90*
Hyman, Milton David 1934- *WhoAm 90*
Hyman, Miranda *ConAu 132*
Hyman, Morton P. 1936- *St&PR 91*
Hyman, Morton Peter 1936- *WhoAm 90, WhoE 91*
Hyman, Paula Ellen *WhoAm 90*
Hyman, Phyllis *DrBIPA 90*
Hyman, Ralph Alan 1928- *WhoAm 90*
Hyman, Ray *EncPaPR 91*
Hyman, Robin Philip 1931- *WhoWor 91*
Hyman, Ronald Terry 1933- *WhoE 91*
Hyman, Seymour 1927- *WhoAm 90*
Hyman, Seymour Charles 1919- *WhoAm 90*
Hyman, Sonia W 1934- *BiDrAPA 89*
Hyman, Steven Edward 1952- *BiDrAPA 89*
Hyman, Trina Schart 1939- *BioIn 16, WhoAm 90, WhoAmW 91*
Hyman, W. Maier 1930- *St&PR 91*
Hymans, Frank Alexander 1947- *WhoWor 91*
Hymel, Gary 1933- *ODwPR 91*
Hymel, Gary Gerard 1933- *WhoAm 90*
Hymer, Robert Mike 1953- *WhoSSW 91*
Hymes, Dell Hathaway 1927- *WhoAm 90, WhoSSW 91*
Hymes, Norma 1949- *WhoAmW 91*
Hymoff, Edward 1924- *WhoAm 90*
Hymowitz, Abraham 1910- *BiDrAPA 89*
Hymowitz, Mitchell I. 1956- *St&PR 91*
Hyms, Kevin L. 1955- *WhoE 91, WhoEmL 91*
Hynd, Noel *SpyFic*
Hynde, Chrissie *BioIn 16*
Hynde, Chrissie 1951- *EncPR&S 89, News 91-1 [port]*
Hynde, Chrissie, and the Pretenders *EncPR&S 89*
Hyndman, H. M. 1842-1921 *BioIn 16*
Hyndman, Henry Mayers 1842-1921 *BioIn 16*
Hyndman, Jane Lee *AuBYP 90*
Hyndman, Lloyd G 1928- *BiDrAPA 89*
Hyndman, Thomas M., Jr. 1924- *St&PR 91*
Hyne, James Bissett 1929- *WhoAm 90*
Hynek, J Allen 1910-1986 *EncO&P 3*
Hynek, Josef Allen 1910-1986 *EncPaPR 91*
Hynes, Charles Joseph 1935- *BioIn 16*
Hynes, Hugh Bernard Noel 1917- *WhoAm 90*
Hynes, J. Peter 1933- *ODwPR 91*
Hynes, John F. 1935- *St&PR 91*
Hynes, John J. 1927- *St&PR 91*
Hynes, Mary Ann 1947- *St&PR 91, WhoAm 90, WhoAmW 91*
Hynes, Michael Kevin 1935- *WhoSSW 91*
Hynes, Neil John 1935- *St&PR 91*
Hynes, Samuel 1924- *ConAu 32NR, WhoAm 90*
Hynes, Samuel Lynn *BioIn 16*
Hynninen, Jorma 1941- *IntWWM 90, WhoWor 91*
Hynning, Clifford James 1913- *WhoAm 90*
Hynson, George Beswick 1932- *St&PR 91*
Hyora, Henry Curtis 1950- *WhoE 91*
Hyppolite, Hector 1894-1948 *ArtLatA*
Hyre, Frank F. 1934- *St&PR 91*
Hyre, James G. 1941- *WhoAm 90*
Hyre, Marcus A. 1928- *St&PR 91*
Hyre, Rexford C. 1940- *St&PR 91*
Hyrick, Marie Lynne 1954- *WhoE 91*
Hyry, Antti 1931- *DcScanL*
Hysell, Nial R. 1854-1921 *AmLegL*
Hyslop, George H. 1892-1965 *EncPaPR 91*
Hyslop, George Hall 1892-1965 *EncO&P 3*
Hyslop, James Hervey 1854-1920 *EncO&P 3, EncPaPR 91*
Hyslop, James Robert 1944- *St&PR 91*
Hyslop, William T 1913- *BiDrAPA 89*
Hysmith, Tony Wane 1958- *WhoEmL 91*
Hyson, Charles David 1915- *WhoAm 90*
Hyson, Jean 1933- *WhoAmA 91*
Hyson, Winifred Prince 1925- *IntWWM 90*
Hysong, James Wilson 1947- *St&PR 91*
Hytche, William Percy 1927- *WhoAm 90, WhoE 91*
Hytha, Robert J. 1928- *WhoAm 90*
Hytier, Adrienne Doris *WhoAm 90*
Hytken, Franklin Harris 1948- *WhoEmL 91*
Hytner, Nicholas 1955- *IntWWM 90*
Hyun, Min J 1944- *BiDrAPA 89*
Hyvonen, C.W. 1946- *St&PR 91*
Hyvonen, Veikko Olavi 1929- *WhoWor 91*

I

I.B.M. *EncCoWW*
I Schuster, Jose Martin *BiDrAPA 89*
Iacangelo, Peter August 1948- *WhoEmL 91*
Iaccheo, Armand R. 1923- *St&PR 91*
Iachelli, Carmelo L *BiDrAPA 89*
Iachetti, Rose Maria Anne 1931- *WhoAmW 91, WhoWor 91*
Iaco, Steven J. 1961- *ODwPR 91*
Iacobell, Frank Peter 1937- *WhoAm 90*
Iacobelli, John Louis 1931- *WhoWor 91*
Iacobelli, Mark Anthony 1957- *WhoEmL 91*
Iacobellis, Sam Frank 1929- *WhoAm 90*
Iacoboni, Thomas Camillo 1930- *WhoE 91*
Iacobucci, Frank 1937- *WhoAm 90, WhoE 91, WhoWor 91*
Iacobucci, Guillermo Arturo 1927- *WhoWor 91*
Iacocca, Lee 1924- *WhoAm 90, WhoWor 91, WorAlBi*
Iacocca, Lee A. *BioIn 16*
Iacocca, Lee A. 1924- *St&PR 91*
Iacocca, Lido 1924- *WhoAm 90*
Iacocca, Lido Anthony 1924- *EncABHB 5 [port], WhoWor 91*
Iacoi, Joseph James 1951- *WhoE 91*
Iacone, Marge 1943- *WhoAmW 91*
Iaconelli, William B. 1933- *St&PR 91*
Iacono, George *BioIn 16*
Iacono, William G. *BioIn 16*
Iacovelli, Guido David 1932- *St&PR 91*
Iacovetti, Benedict John 1956- *WhoE 91*
Iacovou, George 1938- *WhoWor 91*
Iacueo, Louis Frank *BiDrAPA 89*
Iacurto, Francesco 1908- *WhoAmA 91*
Iadanza, Eugene Anthony 1948- *WhoE 91*
Iadarola, Stephen J. 1958- *St&PR 91*
Iadavaia, Elizabeth Ann 1960- *WhoAmW 91*
Iaderosa, Gina Marie 1960- *WhoAmW 91*
Iadicicco, Robert George 1963- *WhoE 91*
Iafrate, John P 1937- *BiDrAPA 89*
Iakovidis, Spyros Eustace 1923- *WhoAm 90*
IAkovlev, A. S. 1906-1989 *BioIn 16*
IAkovlev, Aleksandr Sergeevich 1906-1989 *BioIn 16*
IAkovleva, Varvara Nikolaevna 1885-1944 *BioIn 16*
Iakovos, Bishop *WhoAm 90*
Iakovos, Demetrios A. Coucouzis 1911- *WhoAm 90*
Iammartino, Nicholas R. 1947- *ODwPR 91*
Iams, David Aveling 1938- *WhoAm 90*
Iams, Jack *ConAu 130*
Iams, Jack 1910-1990 *BioIn 16, NewYTBS 90*
Iams, Leslie Ann 1961- *WhoEmL 91*
Iams, Richard 1950- *BioIn 16*
Iams, Samuel H. 1910-1990 *BioIn 16*
Iams, Samuel Harvey, Jr. 1910-1990 *ConAu 130*
Ian 1933- *BioIn 16*
Ian, Janis 1950- *WorAlBi*
Ian, Janis 1951- *ConMus 5 [port], EncPR&S 89*
Iannaccone, Anthony 1943- *IntWWM 90*
Iannarelli, Janine Kathryn 1961- *WhoEmL 91*
Iannazzone, Ralph L. 1933- *St&PR 91*
Iannelli, Fons 1917-1988 *BioIn 16*
Iannetti, Pasquale Francesco Paolo 1940- *WhoAmA 91*
Ianni, Francis Alphonse 1931- *WhoAm 90*
Ianni, Jerry Girolamo 1970- *WhoEmL 91*
Ianni, Lawrence Albert 1930- *WhoAm 90*
Ianni, Ronald William 1935- *WhoAm 90*
Ianniello, Robert Michael 1954- *WhoE 91*
Iannone, Abel Pablo 1940- *WhoE 91*
Iannotti, Lawrence William 1929- *St&PR 91*
Iannotti, Robert Anthony, Jr. 1963- *WhoE 91*
Iannucci, Flavio 1955- *WhoWor 91*
Iannucci, Patricia J. *St&PR 91*
Iannucci, Salvatore Joseph, Jr. 1927- *St&PR 91*
Iannuzzi, Daniel Andrew 1934- *WhoE 91*
Iannuzzi, John Nicholas 1935- *WhoWor 91*
I'Anson, Lawrence Warren 1907- *WhoAm 90, WhoWor 91*
Iantosca, Maryann 1958- *WhoAmW 91*
Ianuzzi, Ralph J. 1931- *St&PR 91*
Ianziti, Adelbert John 1927- *WhoWor 91*
Ianzito, Benjamin M 1942- *BiDrAPA 89*
Iaquinto, James J. 1947- *St&PR 91*
IAroslavskii, Emel'ian 1878-1943 *BioIn 16*
Iarossi, Nancy Semler 1949- *WhoAmW 91*
Iasillo, Peter 1929- *WhoE 91, WhoWor 91*
Iason, Lawrence 1945- *WhoEmL 91*
Iasos *NewAgMG*
Iatesta, John Michael 1944- *WhoE 91, WhoWor 91*
Iati, Anthony P. 1933- *St&PR 91*
Iatropoulos, Michael John 1938- *WhoE 91*
Iavarone, Grace 1961- *WhoAmW 91*
Iavicoli, Mario Anthony 1939- *WhoAm 90*
Iba, Barbara Jean Young 1937- *WhoAmW 91, WhoE 91*
Iba, Hank 1904- *BioIn 16*
Iba, Henry Payne 1904- *BioIn 16*
Ibaceta, Herminia D. 1933- *WhoHisp 91*
Ibach, Douglas Theodore 1925- *WhoE 91, WhoWor 91*
Ibach, Robert W., Jr. *ODwPR 91*
Ibanez, Delfin George C. *BiDrAPA 89*
Ibanez, Manuel L. 1935- *WhoHisp 91*
Ibanez, Manuel Luis 1935- *WhoAm 90*
Ibanez, Maria Elena *WhoHisp 91*
Ibanez, Mario 1921- *BiDrAPA 89*
Ibanez, Roberto 1940- *WhoWor 91*
Ibanez, Vicente Blasco *ConAu 131, HispWr 90, MajTwCW*
Ibanez, Vicente Blasco 1867-1928 *BioIn 16*
Ibanez del Campo, Carlos 1877-1960 *BioIn 16*
Ibarbourou, Juana de 1895-1979 *BioIn 16, HispWr 90*
Ibarguen, Alberto 1944- *WhoHisp 91*
Ibarguen, Carlos 1951- *St&PR 91*
Ibarguengoitia, Jorge 1928-1983 *HispWr 90*
Ibarra, Hector H. 1946- *St&PR 91*
Ibarra, J Luis *BiDrAPA 89*
Ibarra, Josee Maria Velasco 1893-1979 *BioIn 16*
Ibarra, Oscar 1952- *WhoHisp 91*
Ibarra, Oscar Hererra 1941- *WhoAm 90*
Ibarra de Piedra, Rosano *BioIn 16*
Ibarreta, Nelson Yerro *BiDrAPA 89*
Ibarria, Antonio *WhoHisp 91*
Ibarruri, Delores 1895-1989 *WorAlBi*
Ibarruri, Dolores 1895- *EncCoWW*
Ibarruri, Dolores 1895-1989 *AnObit 1989, BioIn 16, CurBio 90N*
Ibay, Manuel S 1938- *BiDrAPA 89*
Ibay, Rosaline Hofilena *BiDrAPA 89*
Ibayashi, Tsuguio 1931- *WhoWor 91*
Ibbotson, Roger G. *BioIn 16*
Ibbott, Daphne 1918- *IntWWM 90*
Ibbs, Patricia Johnson 1938- *WhoAmW 91*
Ibe, Ibe Onuka 1945- *BiDrAPA 89*
Ibele, Warren Edward 1924- *WhoAm 90*
Iben, Icko, Jr. 1931- *WhoAm 90*
Iberall, Arthur Saul 1918- *WhoAm 90*
Ibers, James Arthur 1930- *WhoAm 90*
Ibert, Jacques 1890-1962 *PenDiMP A*
Iberville, Pierre Le Moyne, Sieur D' 1661-1706 *EncCRAm, WhNaAH, WorAlBi*
Ibieta, Gabriella 1953- *WhoHisp 91*
Iblacker, Reinhold A. 1930- *ConAu 130*
Ibn Battuta 1304-1377 *BioIn 16*
Ibn Saud 1880?-1953 *WorAlBi*
ibn Abdul-Aziz, Abdullah 1924- *WhoWor 91*
Ibragimov, Mirzaolim I. 1928- *WhoWor 91*
Ibrahim, Abdullah *BioIn 16*
Ibrahim, Fayez Fares 1941- *St&PR 91*
Ibrahim, Ibrahim N. 1940- *WhoAm 90*
Ibrahim, Ilyas 1945- *WhoWor 91*
Ibrahim, Izzat 1942- *WhoWor 91*
Ibrahim, Kashim 1910- *BioIn 16*
Ibrahim, Khaled 1960- *St&PR 91*
Ibrahim, Lucy Wadie 1957- *BiDrAPA 89*
Ibrahim, Michel Ayoub 1934- *WhoAm 90*
Ibrahim, Mohamed 1938- *St&PR 91*
Ibrahim, Mohamed Abdalla 1938- *WhoAm 90*
Ibrahim, Mounir Labib 1948- *BiDrAPA 89*
Ibrahimov, Galimjan 1887-1938 *BioIn 16*
Ibsen, Henrik 1828-1906 *TwCLC 37 [port], WorAlBi, WrPh*
Ibsen, Henrik Johan 1828-1906 *DcScanL*
Ibuka, Nobuo 1941- *WhoWor 91*
Ibur, Jane Ellen 1950- *WhoWrEP 89*
Iburg, Bill *BioIn 16*
Ibuse, Masuji 1898- *BioIn 16, WorAu 1980*
Icahn, Carl C. *BioIn 16*
Icahn, Carl C. 1936- *WhoAm 90, WhoE 91, WorAlBi*
Icahn, Carl Celian 1936- *ConAmBL*
Icaza, Carmen de 1899- *EncCoWW*
Icaza, Jorge 1906-1978 *BioIn 16*
Icaza, Jorge 1906-1979 *HispWr 90*
Ice, Billie Oberta 1962- *WhoAmW 91*
Ice, John David 1959- *WhoSSW 91*
Ice, John F 1927- *BiDrAPA 89*
Ice, Noel Carlysle 1951- *WhoEmL 91*
Ice, Rodney Dean 1937- *WhoSSW 91*
Ice, Ruth 1928- *WhoWrEP 89*
Ice, Susan M 1946- *BiDrAPA 89*
Icenhower, Joseph Bryan 1913- *AuBYP 90*
Icenogle, Ronald Dean 1951- *WhoE 91, WhoEmL 91*
Ichihara, Taro 1950- *BioIn 16*
Ichiishi, Tatsuro 1943- *WhoAm 90*
Ichikawa Fusae 1893-1981 *EncJap*
Ichikawa Kon 1915- *EncJap*
Ichikawa, Hidehiko 1919- *WhoWor 91*
Ichikawa, Kon *BioIn 16*
Ichikawa, Satomi 1949- *BioIn 16*
Ichikawa, Yoshio 1914- *WhoWor 91*
Ichimura, Shinichi 1925- *ConAu 129*
Ichino, Yoko *WhoAm 90, WhoAmW 91*
Ichinohe, Saeko *BioIn 16, IntWWM 90*
Ichinyu *PenDiDA 89*
Ichiyama, Dennis Yoshihide 1944- *WhoAm 90*
Ichord, Richard Howard 1926- *WhoAm 90*
Ickes, Arthur Dennis 1946- *WhoEmL 91*
Ickes, Harold Le Clair 1874-1953 *BiDrUSE 89*
Icks, Robert J. 1900- *AuBYP 90*
Icks, Robert Joseph 1899-1985 *BioIn 16*
Icone, Joe Al 1942- *St&PR 91*
Ida, Vera 1952- *WhoAmW 91*
Idaherma *WhoAmA 91*
Idarius, Eric Wiley 1946- *WhoEmL 91*
Idaszak, Jerome Joseph 1945- *WhoAm 90*
Iddings, Kathleen Ann *WhoWrEP 89*
Ide d'Alsace *WomWR*
Ide, Gary L. 1953- *St&PR 91*
Ide, Henry Clay 1844-1921 *BioIn 16*
Ide, Patricia Louise 1935- *WhoWrEP 89*
Idel, Harlan W. 1943- *St&PR 91*
Idelman, Steve *BioIn 16*
Idelson, Charles K. 1949- *St&PR 91, WhoSSW 91*
Ideman, James M. 1931- *WhoAm 90*
Iden, Sheldon 1933- *WhoAmA 91*
Idenburg, Philip Abraham 1934- *WhoWor 91*
Idinsaw *DcCanB 12*
Idle, Eric *BioIn 16*
Idleman, Holland B. *BioIn 16*
Idleman, Jerry Gene 1939- *St&PR 91*
Idleman, Larry Lynn 1938- *St&PR 91, WhoAm 90*
Idleman, Lee Hillis 1933- *WhoAm 90*
Idler, David Richard 1923- *WhoAm 90, WhoWor 91*
Idol, Billy 1955- *EncPR&S 89, WorAlBi*
Idol, James Daniel, Jr. 1928- *WhoAm 90*
Idol, Lance Harris 1953- *WhoSSW 91*
Idol, Lorna Jeanne 1947- *WhoSSW 91*
Idorn, Gunnar Morten 1920- *WhoWor 91*
Idota, Akira 1928- *WhoWor 91*
Idris I 1889-1983 *PolLCME*
Idriss, Farouk Salim 1928- *WhoAm 90*
Idriss, Izzat M. 1935- *WhoAm 90*
Idrissu, Alhadj *WhoWor 91*
Idupuganti, Sudharam 1952- *BiDrAPA 89*
Idzerda, Stanley John 1920- *WhoAm 90*
Idzik, Martin Francis 1942- *WhoAm 90*
Idzorek, Scott 1944- *BiDrAPA 89*
Ie, Masaji 1937- *WhoWor 91*
Iehl, Bruce Herbert 1949- *WhoEmL 91*
Ielmini, John Alfonso 1929- *St&PR 91*
Ienaga, Yasumitsu 1925- *WhoWor 91*
Iengo, Valerie 1955- *WhoAmW 91*
Ienni, Philip Camillo 1930- *IntWWM 90*
Ierardi, Eric Joseph 1950- *WhoE 91*
Ieuter, Fredric E. 1938- *St&PR 91*
Ieyasu *EncJap*
Ieyasu 1543-1616 *WorAlBi*
Ifarraguerri, Agustin *BiDrAPA 89*
Ifeagwu, Sam Chukwudi 1952- *WhoWor 91*
Iffland, August Wilhelm 1759-1814 *DcLB 94 [port]*
Iffrig, Greg Frank 1954- *WhoEmL 91*
Iffy, Leslie 1925- *WhoAm 90*
Ifield, Frank 1937- *OxCPMus*
Ifield, Henry *PenDiDA 89*
Ifill, Gordon G L 1931- *BiDrAPA 89*
Ifkovic, Edward 1943- *ConAu 33NR*

Igama, Juliet Ruiz *BiDrAPA 89*
Igarashi, Takenobu 1944- *BioIn 16, ConDes 90*
Igarashi, Takeshi 1946- *WhoWor 91*
Igasaki, Masao, Jr. 1925- *WhoAm 90*
Igasaki, Toshio 1925- *WhoWor 91*
Ige, Tom 1916- *BioIn 16*
Igel, George Daniel 1946- *BiDrAPA 89*
Igel, George Joseph, Jr. 1924- *St&PR 91*
Iger, Howard George 1936- *BiDrAPA 89*
Iger, Jerry 1910- *EncACom*
Iger, Martin *AuBYP 90*
Iger, Robert *BioIn 16*
Igersheimer, Walter W *BiDrAPA 89*
Igesz, Bodo 1935- *IntWWM 90, WhoAm 90*
Iggers, Georg G. 1926- *ConAu 33NR*
Iggers, Georg Gerson 1926- *WhoAm 90, WhoWor 91*
Igi, Keiji 1933- *WhoWor 91*
Igiel, Robert E. *BioIn 16*
Iglar, Albert Francis 1939- *WhoSSW 91*
Iglecia-Fernandez, Raymond *BiDrAPA 89*
Iglehart, Alison Rowe 1956- *WhoEmL 91*
Iglehart, James *DrBlPA 90*
Iglehart, John K. 1939- *WhoAm 90*
Iglehart, Robert L 1912- *WhoAmA 91*
Igleheart, Elizabeth Robbin 1957- *WhoAmW 91*
Igleheart, James B. 1922- *St&PR 91*
Iglesias, Carlos 1934- *St&PR 91*
Iglesias, Eduardo Hector 1936- *WhoWor 91*
Iglesias, Elizabeth Ivette 1951- *WhoHisp 91*
Iglesias, Enrique V. 1930- *WhoWor 91*
Iglesias, Julio *BioIn 16*
Iglesias, Julio 1943- *WhoAm 90, WhoHisp 91, WhoWor 91, WorAlBi*
Iglesias, Maria Adela 1950- *WhoAmW 91, WhoEmL 91*
Iglesias, Mario A. 1957- *WhoEmL 91*
Iglesias, Nieves *BiDrAPA 89*
Iglesias Castro, Rafael 1861-1924 *BioIn 16*
Iglesias Pantin, Santiago 1872-1939 *BioIn 16*
Igleski, Thomas Robert 1934- *St&PR 91, WhoAm 90*
Iglewicz, Boris 1939- *WhoAm 90*
Iglewicz, Raja 1945- *WhoAmW 91*
Iglhaut, Ludwig E. 1936- *St&PR 91*
Iglitzen, Marlene *BioIn 16*
Ignacio, Elmer Pedere 1946- *BiDrAPA 89*
Ignacio, Lourdes Ladrido 1939- *BiDrAPA 89*
Ignacio, Luis Faustino 1949- *BiDrAPA 89*
Ignacz, Rozsa 1910-1979 *EncCoWW*
Ignaczak, Carol Ann *WhoE 91*
Ignaczak, Jozef 1935- *WhoWor 91*
Ignath, Lujza Linczegh 1891- *EncO&P 3*
Ignatiadis, Varvara 1955- *WhoE 91*
Ignatius, of Loyola, Saint 1491-1556 *BioIn 16*
Ignatius of Loyola, Saint 1491-1556 *WorAlBi*
Ignatius, David Reynolds 1950- *SpyFic*
Ignatius, Paul Robert 1920- *WhoAm 90, WhoE 91*
Ignatow, David 1914- *BioIn 16, ConAu 31NR, WhoAm 90, WhoWrEP 89*
Ignoffo, Carlo Michael 1928- *WhoAm 90*
Ignoffo, Flori Frances 1928- *WhoWrEP 89*
Igo, John N., Jr. 1927- *ConAu 33NR*
Igo, Louis Daniel 1939- *WhoWor 91*
Igo, Peter Alexander 1956- *WhoAmA 91*
Igoa, Jose Esteban 1954- *BiDrAPA 89*
Igoe, Francis Daniel 1961- *WhoE 91*
Igoe, James Thomas 1911- *St&PR 91*
Igoe, Peter Michael 1942- *St&PR 91*
Igoe, William Joseph 1928- *St&PR 91*
Igram, Richard Eric 1954- *WhoEmL 91*
Iguchi, Kenji 1949- *WhoWor 91*
Iguina, Luis Alberto *BiDrAPA 89*
Igusa, Jun-Ichi 1924- *WhoAm 90*
Ihamuotila, Jaakko 1939- *WhoWor 91*
Ihara, Michio 1928- *WhoAm 90, WhoAmA 91*
Ihara, Yasuo *BioIn 16*
Ihara, Yasuo 1945- *WhoWor 91*
I'Haya, Yasumasa John 1928- *WhoWor 91*
Ihde, Aaron John 1909- *WhoAm 90*
Ihde, Don 1934- *WhoAm 90*
Ihgari, Joseph C. *St&PR 91*
Ihlanfeldt, William 1936- *WhoWor 91*
Ihle, Herbert Duane 1939- *WhoAm 90*
Ihle, John Livingston 1925- *WhoAm 90, WhoAmA 91*
Ihlenfeld, Charles L 1937- *BiDrAPA 89*
Ihling, Edward L. 1926- *St&PR 91*
Ihloff, Jutta-Renate 1944- *IntWWM 90*
Ihori, Toshihiro 1952- *WhoWor 91*
Ihrie, Robert 1925- *St&PR 91, WhoAm 90*
Ihrig, Judson La Moure 1925- *WhoAm 90*
Ihrke, Walter Rudolph 1908- *IntWWM 90*
Ihsanoglu, Ekmeleddin 1943- *WhoWor 91*
Ii Naosuke *EncJap*
Ii, Jack Morito 1926- *WhoWor 91*
Iida, Tatsuji *BiDrAPA 89*
Iimura, Takahiko 1937- *WhoAmA 91*
Iizuka, Tetsuya 1947- *WhoWor 91*
Ijiri, Yuji 1935- *WhoE 91*
Ik, Kim Yong *AuBYP 90*
Ikard, Frank Neville 1913- *WhoAm 90*
Ikard, Frank Neville, Jr. 1942- *WhoAm 90*
Ikard, James Asa 1947- *WhoEmL 91*
Ikard, Thomas Emmett 1935- *WhoSSW 91*
Ikasia *EncCoWW*
Ikawa-Smith, Fumiko 1930- *WhoAm 90*
Ike, Rev. 1935?- *EncO&P 3*
Ike, John Edward 1924- *St&PR 91*
Ike, Nobutaka 1916- *WhoAm 90*
Ikeda Clan *EncJap*
Ikeda Terumasa *EncJap*
Ikeda, Donna Rika 1939- *WhoAmW 91*
Ikeda, Hajime 1927- *WhoWor 91*
Ikeda, Kikuei *PenDiMP*
Ikeda, Makoto 1922- *WhoWor 91*
Ikeda, Moss Marcus Masanobu 1931- *WhoWor 91*
Ikeda, Yoshiko 1924- *BiDrAPA 89*
Ikeda, Yoshiro 1947- *WhoAmA 91*
Ikeda, Yutaka 1949- *WhoWor 91*
Ikeda-Gerling, Mariko M. 1935- *WhoWor 91*
Ikegami, Toshiroh 1948- *WhoWor 91*
Ikegami, Yusaku 1930- *WhoWor 91*
Ikegawa, Shiro 1933- *WhoAmA 91*
Ikegaya, Takashi 1930- *WhoWor 91*
Ikenberry, Henry Cephas, Jr. 1920- *WhoAm 90, WhoWor 91*
Ikenberry, Lynn David 1936- *BiDrAPA 89*
Ikenberry, Stanley Oliver 1935- *WhoAm 90, WhoWor 91*
Ikhnaton *BioIn 16, WorAlBi*
Ikkyu Sojun 1394-1481 *EncJap*
Ikle, Doris Margret 1928- *WhoAmW 91*
Ikle, Frank William 1921- *WhoAm 90*
Ikle, Fred Charles 1924- *WhoAm 90*
Ikonomidou, Fotini 1856-1883 *EncCoWW*
Ikramullah, Sultana *BiDrAPA 89*
Ikuta, Linda MacKenna 1952- *WhoAmW 91*
Ilano, Maria Daisy 1957- *BiDrAPA 89*
Ilaria, Robert Leslie *BiDrAPA 89*
Ilaskivi, Raimo 1928- *WhoWor 91*
Ilberman, Barry 1950- *St&PR 91*
Ilchman, Alice Stone 1935- *WhoAm 90, WhoAmW 91*
Ilchman, Warren Frederick 1933- *WhoAm 90*
Ilderton, Jane Wallace 1936- *WhoAmW 91, WhoSSW 91*
Ileana *EncCoWW*
Ileana-Fatma *EncCoWW*
Ilem, Priscilla G *BiDrAPA 89*
Iler, Russell Evans *BiDrAPA 89*
Ilerio, Pedro Julio 1920- *WhoHisp 91*
Iles, Bert *ConAu 130*
Iles, Edna *IntWWM 90*
Iles, Francis *TwCCr&M 91*
Iles, Ronald A. 1935- *St&PR 91*
Ilett, Frank, Jr. 1940- *WhoAm 90*
Iley, Janet Mathis 1959- *WhoAmW 91*
Ilfeld, Frederic W, Jr. 1940- *BiDrAPA 89*
Ilg, John Herold 1926- *St&PR 91*
Ilg, Ruth Merkle 1945- *WhoWrEP 89*
Ilgen, Daniel Richard 1943- *WhoAm 90*
Ilic, Mirko *BioIn 16*
Ilich, Daniel Frank 1931- *St&PR 91*
Ilich, Richard Joseph 1959- *St&PR 91*
Ilie, Paul 1932- *WhoAm 90*
Ilieff, Mois M *BiDrAPA 89*
Iliescu, Ion *BioIn 16*
Iliescu, Ion 1930- *CurBio 90 [port], WhoWor 91*
Iliff, Maria *FemiCLE*
Iliff, Warren Jolidon 1936- *WhoAm 90*
Iligan, Ralph W 1894-1960 *WhoAmA 91N*
Ilin, M. *AuBYP 90*
Il'ina, Nataliya Iosifovna 1914- *EncCoWW*
Iliprandi, Giancarlo 1925- *ConDes 90*
Ilitch, Michael *WhoAm 90*
Ilivitsky, Vadim B 1940- *BiDrAPA 89*
Ilku, Elyse Yockey 1928- *IntWWM 90*
Illakowiczowna, Kazimiera 1892-1970 *EncCoWW*
Illar, Louis S. 1946- *WhoSSW 91*
Ille, B.G. 1927- *St&PR 91*
Ille, Bernard Glenn 1927- *WhoAm 90*
Ille, Robert G. 1945- *St&PR 91*
Illes, Brian 1959- *WhoEmL 91*
Illia, Arturo Umberto 1900-1983 *BioIn 16*
Illian, C.R. 1941- *St&PR 91*
Illich, Ivan 1926- *MajTwCW, WhoAm 90*
Illig, Carl 1909- *WhoAm 90*
Illig, James Michael 1913- *WhoAm 90*
Illing, Vincent Charles 1890-1969 *DcScB S2*
Illingworth, Heidi Louise 1966- *WhoE 91*
Illingworth, Ronald Stanley 1909-1990? *ConAu 131*
Illion, Larry Steven 1949- *St&PR 91*
Illman, Deborah Louise 1955- *WhoEmL 91*
Illner, Pavel 1937- *WhoE 91*
Illnick, Sheryl Evanne 1955- *WhoAm 90*
Illouz, Gabriel 1920- *WhoWor 91*
Illsley, Rolf F. 1921- *St&PR 91*
Illson, Dorothy Spence *BioIn 16, NewYTBS 90*
Illuzzi, Michael D. 1926- *WhoE 91*
Illuzzi, Vincent 1953- *WhoE 91*
Illyes, Andrew Earl 1949- *St&PR 91*
Ilma, Viola 1910?-1989 *BioIn 16*
Ilma, Viola 1911?-1989 *ConAu 129*
Ilmark, John Erik 1946- *WhoWor 91*
Ilmonen, Eino Ossian 1908- *WhoWor 91*
Ilmonen, Urho Kustaa 1953- *WhoWor 91*
Ilmoniemi, Risto Juhani 1954- *WhoWor 91*
Ilnicky, Michaline Katherine 1948- *WhoEmL 91*
Ilosvalvy, Robert 1927- *IntWWM 90*
Ilosvay, Maria Von 1913- *IntWWM 90*
Ilowitz, Theodora 1921- *WhoE 91*
Ilson, Bernard *ODwPR 91*
Ilstad, Geir Are 1955- *WhoWor 91*
Ilstam, Anders B. 1941- *WhoWor 91*
Ilten, David Frederick 1938- *WhoWor 91*
Iltis, Hugh Hellmut 1925- *WhoAm 90*
Iltis, John Frederic 1940- *WhoAm 90*
Iltzsch, Henry H. 1929- *St&PR 91*
Iltzsch, Max Henry 1957- *WhoEmL 91*
Ilutovich, Leon *WhoAm 90*
Im, Chhoodeth 1929- *WhoWor 91*
Im, Won-Gi *BiDrAPA 89*
Im, Yung Kook 1928- *WhoSSW 91*
Im Hof, Ulrich Walter 1917- *WhoWor 91*
Imagawa, David Tadashi 1922- *WhoAm 90*
Imahara, John K 1939- *BiDrAPA 89*
Imai, Ken-ichi 1931- *WhoWor 91*
Imai, Kenji 1895-1987 *BioIn 16*
Imai, Masaaki 1930- *ConAu 129*
Imai, Nobuko 1943- *IntWWM 90, PenDiMP*
Imaizumi, Akitoshi 1949- *WhoWor 91*
Imam, Abd El Rahman 1920- *WhoWor 91*
Imamura, Shohei *BioIn 16*
Iman *BioIn 16*
Imana, Jorge Garron 1930- *WhoAmA 91*
Imani, Parviz 1932- *BiDrAPA 89*
Imani, Pouran A *BiDrAPA 89*
Imbault, James Joseph 1944- *WhoAm 90*
Imbeau, Stephen Alan 1947- *WhoSSW 91*
Imbeault, Raynald 1944- *WhoAm 90*
Imbembo, Anthony Louis 1942- *WhoWor 91*
Imber, Barry 1945- *St&PR 91*
Imber, Brian Lee 1959- *WhoEmL 91*
Imber, Jonathan 1950- *WhoAmA 91*
Imberman, Marcie *BioIn 16*
Imbert, Enrique Anderson *HispWr 90*
Imbert, Enrique Anderson 1910- *BioIn 16*
Imbert, Richard Conrad 1941- *WhoE 91*
Imbert, Segundo Antonio 1943- *BiDrAPA 89*
Imbler, Martin Ray 1948- *St&PR 91*
Imboden, John B *BiDrAPA 89*
Imboden, Patrica Altom 1961- *WhoAmW 91*
Imboden, Ronald Gordon 1931- *WhoAm 90*
Imbriani, Michael Rocco 1943- *St&PR 91*
Imbrie, Andrew 1921- *IntWWM 90*
Imbrie, Andrew Welsh 1921- *WhoAm 90*
Imbrie, John Zeller 1956- *WhoE 91*
Imbrigato-Fesson, Pauline-Maria 1946- *WhoAmW 91*
Imbrogno, Edward Nicola 1922- *St&PR 91*
Imburg, Irving Jerome 1924- *WhoSSW 91*
Imbus, Harold Roger 1928- *WhoSSW 91*
Imdahl, Heinz 1924- *IntWWM 90*
Imel, Priscilla Brown 1954- *WhoAmW 91*
Imelman, Jan Dirk 1939- *WhoWor 91*
Imershein, Betsy 1953- *SmATA 62 [port]*
Imershein, Charles J. 1923- *St&PR 91*
Imershein, Richard Edward 1927- *WhoE 91*
Imershein, Ruth Elizabeth 1950- *BiDrAPA 89*
Imershein, William Leonard 1922- *St&PR 91*
Imes, Birney 1951- *WhoAmA 91*
Imesch, Joseph Leopold 1931- *WhoAm 90*
Imgrund, Bernadine Wojtanowski 1936- *WhoAmW 91*
Imhauser, Gunter 1912- *WhoWor 91*
Imhof, Ralph Edward 1946- *WhoSSW 91*
Imhoff, Herbert F. 1926- *St&PR 91*
Imhoff, Herbert Franklin, Jr. 1950- *St&PR 91*
Imhoff, John Edward 1950- *St&PR 91*
Imhoff, John Leonard 1923- *WhoAm 90*
Imhoff, Joseph Martin 1934- *St&PR 91*
Imhoff, Peter H. 1956- *St&PR 91*
Imhoff, W. Joseph 1940- *St&PR 91*
Imhoff, Walter Francis 1931- *St&PR 91, WhoAm 90*
Imielowska, Dorota Maria 1966- *IntWWM 90*
Imig, David Gregg 1939- *WhoAm 90*
Imlay, Gilbert 1754?-1828? *LiHiK*
Imlay, John Prescott, Jr. 1936- *St&PR 91, WhoAm 90*
Imle, John Frederick, Jr. 1940- *St&PR 91*
Imler, Russell Eugene 1936- *St&PR 91*
Immel, Calvin Louis 1929- *St&PR 91*
Immel, Cynthia Luanne 1958- *WhoAmW 91*
Immel, Mary Blair 1930- *AuBYP 90, WhoWrEP 89*
Immel, Nancy Kay 1946- *WhoEmL 91*
Immel, Vincent Clare 1920- *WhoAm 90*
Immelman, Nettie 1917- *IntWWM 90*
Immelmann, Klaus 1935-1987 *BioIn 16*
Immelt, Mark W. 1945- *St&PR 91*
Immenga, Ulrich 1934- *WhoWor 91*
Immerman, Richard H. 1949- *ConAu 129*
Immerman, Ronald Stuart 1952- *BiDrAPA 89*
Immesberger, Helmut 1934- *WhoWor 91*
Imming, Marie Elizabeth 1966- *WhoEmL 91*
Immler, Michael Earl 1952- *WhoEmL 91*
Immler, Richard Edward *BiDrAPA 89*
Immonen, Gerald 1936- *WhoAmA 91*
Imoda, Enrico *EncO&P 3*
Imoh, Unwana Ben 1948- *WhoWor 91*
Imonen, Robb Edwin 1941- *BiDrAPA 89*
Imp, John F 1910- *BiDrAPA 89*
Impaglia, Charles *BioIn 16*
Imparato, Anthony Michael 1922- *WhoAm 90*
Imparator, Peter George 1930- *St&PR 91*
Impastato, Arthur 1930- *BiDrAPA 89*
Impellizzeri, Irene Helen *WhoAm 90*
Imperato, Donna A. 1960- *ODwPR 91*
Imperato, Pascal James 1937- *WhoAm 90, WhoWor 91, WhoWrEP 89*
Imperatore, Arthur E. 1925- *WhoAm 90*
Imperial, Boris Serrano 1928- *BiDrAPA 89*
Impiglia, Giancarlo 1940- *WhoAmA 91*
Impollonia, Michael Edward 1955- *WhoE 91*
Impressions, The *EncPR&S 89, OxCPMus*
Imray, Thomas John 1939- *WhoAm 90*
Imre, David M. 1957- *WhoE 91, WhoEmL 91*
Imre, Ereg M. 1933- *St&PR 91*
Imrhan, Sheik Nazir 1950- *WhoSSW 91*
Imrich, Wilfried 1941- *WhoWor 91*
Imura, Akiya *WhoAm 90*
Imura, Michael Ken *BiDrAPA 89*
Imus, A Austin 1913- *BiDrAPA 89*
Imus, Neil Winston 1953- *WhoEmL 91*
Imus, Richard Howard 1938- *WhoAm 90*
Imus, Russel Walter 1935- *St&PR 91*
Imwalle, Dennis Edward 1941- *St&PR 91*
Imwinkelried, Edward John 1946- *WhoAm 90*
Inabinet, George Walker, Jr. 1927- *WhoSSW 91*
Inabinet, Rhett E. 1955- *St&PR 91*
Inabinette, Norma Bartin 1942- *WhoAm 90*
Inacker, Charles John 1936- *WhoAm 90*
Inadomi, Robert John 1948- *St&PR 91, WhoEmL 91*
Inagami, Tadashi 1931- *WhoAm 90*
Inaganti, Prasad V. 1945- *St&PR 91*
Inaganti, Venkateswara R 1951- *BiDrAPA 89*
Inait, M. Yousaf 1935- *WhoWor 91*
Inalcik, Halil 1916- *WhoAm 90*
Inamdar, Subhash C 1942- *BiDrAPA 89*
Inamori, Kazuo 1932- *WhoWor 91*
Inamura, Kobo 1948- *WhoWor 91*
Inanaga, Kazutoyo 1922- *WhoWor 91*
Inao, Iron Man 1938- *Ballpl 90*
Inatome, Rick 1953- *WhoAm 90*
Inbal, Eliahu 1936- *IntWWM 90, PenDiMP, WhoWor 91*
Inbau, Fred Edward 1909- *WhoAm 90*
Inber, Vera 1890-1972 *EncCoWW*
Inbody, Donald R 1930- *BiDrAPA 89*
Incalicchio, Mario 1936- *St&PR 91*
Incandela, Gerald Jean-Marie 1952- *WhoAmA 91, WhoE 91*
Incaprera, Frank Philip 1928- *WhoSSW 91, WhoWor 91*
Incaudo, Claude J. 1936- *WhoAm 90*
Incaudo, Joseph A. 1940- *St&PR 91*
Incaviglia, Pete 1964- *Ballpl 90*
Ince, Elizabeth 1936- *IntWWM 90*
Ince, Eugene St. Clair, Jr. 1926- *WhoAm 90*
Ince, Ralph 1887-1937 *BioIn 16*
Ince, Richard W. 1938- *St&PR 91*
Ince, W. N. 1926-1988 *BioIn 16*
Ince, Walter Newcombe 1926-1988 *BioIn 16*
Ince, William 1752?-1804 *PenDiDA 89*
Inch, Morris Alton 1925- *WhoAm 90*
Inchbald, Mrs. 1753-1821 *BioIn 16*
Inchbald, Elizabeth 1753-1821 *FemiCLE*
Inchbald, Elizabeth Simpson 1753-1821 *BioIn 16*
Inchbald, Peter 1919- *ConAu 130*
Inchcape, Earl of 1917- *WhoWor 91*
Inchcape, James Lyle Mackay, Earl of 1852-1932 *BioIn 16*

Inclan, Ramon del Valle 1870-1936 BioIn 16
Incogniteau, Jean-Louis MajTwCW
Incredible String Band, The OxCPMus
Incropera, Frank Paul 1939- WhoAm 90
Inculet, Ion I. 1921- WhoAm 90
Inda, Kevin S. ODwPR 91
Indahl, Dennis Deltyne 1935- St&PR 91
Indart, Monica Jeanne-Marie 1958- WhoAmW 91
Indelicato, Albert D. 1950- St&PR 91
Indelicato, Dorothy L. 1933- St&PR 91
Indelicato, Venerando J. 1932- St&PR 91
Indelicato, Vincent 1933- St&PR 91
Inden, Gerhard 1938- WhoWor 91
Inderbitzin, Lawrence Ben 1939- BiDrAPA 89
Inderbitzin, Paul Herold 1948- WhoAm 90
Inderfurth, Karl Frederick 1946- WhoAm 90
Indest, George Felix, III 1951- WhoEmL 91
Indiana, Robert 1928- BioIn 16, WhoAm 90, WhoAmA 91
Indianer, Mickey W BiDrAPA 89
Indick, Janet 1932- WhoAmA 91, WhoAmW 91
Indik, Jonathan Howard BiDrAPA 89
Indin, Bert M BiDrAPA 89
Indiradevi, Ayyagari BiDrAPA 89
Indiviglia, Salvatore Joseph 1919- WhoAmA 91, WhoE 91
Indovina, Vincent A 1929- BiDrAPA 89
Indra Devi 1899- EncO&P 3
Indrasutanta, Waskita 1954- WhoWor 91
Indridason, Indridi 1883-1912 EncO&P 3, EncPaPR 91
Indridi G. Thorsteinsson DcScanL
Indukuri, Padmanabha R 1952- BiDrAPA 89
Indy, Vincent d' 1851-1931 PenDiMP A
Ineichen, Gustav 1929- WhoWor 91
Ines de la Cruz, Juana 1651-1695 BioIn 16
Inez, Colette 1931- WhoAm 90, WhoWrEP 89
Infante, Christine Marie 1952- WhoWrEP 89
Infante, Daisy Inocentes 1946- WhoAmW 91, WhoEmL 91
Infante, Ettore Ferrari 1938- WhoAm 90
Infante, G Cabrera HispWr 90, MajTwCW
Infante, G. Cabrera 1929- BioIn 16
Infante, Gabriel A. 1945- WhoHisp 91
Infante, Lindy 1940- WhoAm 90
Infante, Olga L BiDrAPA 89
Infanti, Nello Leo 1921- WhoE 91
Inferrera, Marie Antoinette 1958- WhoAmW 91
infield, Marthea Mae 1929- WhoAmW 91
Infiesta, Felix WhoHisp 91
Infiesta, Felix Orlando 1942- WhoSSW 91
Infusino, Jeffrey Scott 1950- WhoE 91
Infuso, Joseph 1927- WhoWor 91
Ing, Sheridan C.F. 1923- St&PR 91
Ingaglio, Diego Augustus 1922- WhoE 91, WhoWor 91
Ingal, Ann BiDEWW
Ingala, Rose A. 1955- BiDrAPA 89
Ingall, David 1930- WhoAm 90
Ingall, Francis BioIn 16
Ingall, Michael A 1940- BiDrAPA 89
Ingall, Michael Alexander 1940- WhoE 91
Ingalls, Anna May 1941- WhoAmW 91
Ingalls, Caroline Celestia 1870-1946 BioIn 16
Ingalls, Daniel H.H. 1916- St&PR 91
Ingalls, Daniel H.H., Jr. 1944- St&PR 91
Ingalls, Daniel Henry Holmes 1916- WhoAm 90
Ingalls, Eve 1936- WhoAmA 91
Ingalls, Everett Palmer, III 1947- WhoEmL 91
Ingalls, Grace Pearl 1877-1941 BioIn 16
Ingalls, Jeremy 1911- WhoAmW 91, WhoWor 91, WhoWrEP 89
Ingalls, John James 1833-1900 WorAlBi
Ingalls, Leonard AuBYP 90
Ingalls, Marie Cecelie 1936- WhoAmW 91
Ingalls, Mary Amelia 1865-1928 BioIn 16
Ingalls, Rachel 1940- WorAu 1980 [port]
Ingalls, Robert Lynn 1934- WhoAm 90
Ingalls, Roscoe C., Jr. 1920- St&PR 91
Ingalls, Stephen David 1954- WhoEmL 91
Ingalls, William G. 1930- St&PR 91
Ingalsbee, Charles Fenn 1950- St&PR 91
Ingamells, John 1934- WhoWor 91
Ingamells, Julia Irene 1945- WhoWrEP 89
Ingbar, Sidney H. BioIn 16
Ingber, Barbara 1932- WhoAmA 91
Ingber, Jeffrey Fred 1954- St&PR 91
Ingber, Pamela Sheryl 1952- BiDrAPA 89
Ingberg, Donald Dennis 1936- St&PR 91
Ingberg, Earl Eugene, Jr. 1947- St&PR 91
Inge, Milton Thomas 1936- WhoAm 90
Inge, Ronald Eugene 1956- St&PR 91
Inge, William 1860-1954 WorAlBi
Inge, William 1913-1973 BioIn 16, WorAlBi
Inge, William Bullock 1933- St&PR 91
Inge, William Motter 1913-1973 MajTwCW
Inge, William Murphy 182-?- AmLegL
Ingebrand, George B. 1927- St&PR 91
Ingebrigtsen, Catherine Williams 1955- WhoAmW 91
Ingel, Florence Courtney 1963- ConAu 130
Ingelow, Jean 1820-1897 BioIn 16, FemiCLE
Ingels, Graham 1915- EncACom
Ingels, Jack Edward 1942- WhoE 91
Ingels, Larry Tyson 1934- WhoE 91
Ingels, Marty 1936- WhoAm 90
Ingeman, Jerry Andrew 1950- WhoEmL 91, WhoWor 91
Ingemann, Bernhard Severin 1789-1862 DcScanL
Ingemi, Martha Catherine 1963- WhoAmW 91
Ingenhousz, Jan 1730-1799 WorAlBi
Ingenito, Gennaro Peter BiDrAPA 89
Ingenthron, Gerard D. 1941- ODwPR 91
Ingerman, Michael Leigh 1937- WhoWor 91
Ingerman, Peter Zilahy 1934- WhoE 91, WhoWor 91
Ingersol, Jared ConAu 31NR
Ingersoll, Alfred Cajori 1920- WhoAm 90
Ingersoll, C. Jared 1894-1988 BioIn 16
Ingersoll, Charles H. 1865-1948 WorAlBi
Ingersoll, Charles John 1951- WhoSSW 91
Ingersoll, Jared 1749-1822 BioIn 16
Ingersoll, John Gregory 1948- WhoEmL 91
Ingersoll, Joseph Reed 1786-1868 BioIn 16
Ingersoll, Paul Mills 1928- WhoAm 90
Ingersoll, Ralph, II BioIn 16
Ingersoll, Ralph McAllister, II 1946- WhoAm 90
Ingersoll, Robert Green 1833-1899 BioIn 16
Ingersoll, Robert H. 1859-1928 WorAlBi
Ingersoll, Robert Stephen 1914- BioIn 16
Ingersoll, Roy WhoWrEP 89
Ingersoll, Royal E. 1883-1976 WorAlBi
Ingersoll, William Boley 1938- WhoE 91, WhoSSW 91, WhoWor 91
Ingerson, Charles Richard 1925- St&PR 91
Ingevaldson, Paul Martin 1945- St&PR 91
Ingham, Albert Joseph, Jr. 1934- St&PR 91
Ingham, Denise Ann BiDrAPA 89
Ingham, George Alexander 1936- WhoWor 91
Ingham, Kenneth LeRoy 1962- WhoEmL 91
Ingham, Richard Reed 1954- IntWWM 90
Ingham, Robert Edwin 1944- WhoAm 90
Ingham, Samuel 1793-1881 AmLegL
Ingham, Samuel Delucenna 1779-1860 BiDrUSE 89
Ingham, Thomas Edgar 1942- WhoAmA 91
Inghelbrecht, Desire-Emile 1880-1965 PenDiMP
Inghram, Mark Gordon 1919- WhoAm 90
Ingis, Gail 1935- WhoE 91
Ingish, Karen S. 1947- WhoAmW 91
Ingish, Stephen J. ODwPR 91
Ingle, Alexander W. 1942- St&PR 91
Ingle, Don W. ODwPR 91
Ingle, Gary Luther 1954- IntWWM 90
Ingle, H. Larry 1936- WhoSSW 91
Ingle, Henry Thomas 1943- WhoAm 90
Ingle, James Chesney, Jr. 1935- WhoAm 90
Ingle, John David 1940- WhoWor 91
Ingle, John Ide 1919- WhoAm 90
Ingle, John S 1933- WhoAmA 91
Ingle, John Stuart BioIn 16
Ingle, Leo Ray, Jr. BiDrAPA 89
Ingle, Marcus David 1943- WhoE 91
Ingle, Marleen Bengel 1932- WhoSSW 91
Ingle, Morton Blakeman 1942- St&PR 91
Ingle, Richard Maurice 1946- WhoSSW 91
Ingle, Robert D. 1939- WhoAm 90
Ingle, Robert P. 1933- WhoAm 90, WhoSSW 91
Ingle, Tom 1920-1973 WhoAmA 91N
Ingle, William 1934- IntWWM 90
Inglehart, Marita Rosch 1951- WhoAmW 91
Ingleman, John A. 1946- St&PR 91
Ingles, Luis L., Jr. 1942- St&PR 91
Ingles, Thelma Marguerite 1909-1983 BioIn 16
Inglesby, Beverly Fisher 1954- WhoAmW 91
Inglett, Betty Lee 1930- WhoAmW 91
Inglis, Andrew Even BiDrAPA 89
Inglis, Andrew Franklin 1920- WhoAm 90
Inglis, Brian 1916- EncO&P 3, EncPaPR 91
Inglis, Charles 1734-1816 EncCRAm
Inglis, David Rittenhouse 1905- WhoAm 90
Inglis, Donald Scott 1935- St&PR 91
Inglis, Esther BiDEWW
Inglis, Frances Erskine 1804-1882 BioIn 16
Inglis, Ivan Leslie 1926- St&PR 91
Inglis, Robert Shepherd, Jr. 1929- WhoSSW 91
Inglot, Peter B. 1924- St&PR 91
Inglove, Herbert M BiDrAPA 89
Ingman, Elias Magnus PenDiDA 89
Ingman, Nicholas 1948- BioIn 16
Ingman, Richard Wilson 1944- St&PR 91
Ingmire, Gary Dean 1943- WhoSSW 91
Ingo, Luang Eng Lie- 1918-1989 BioIn 16
Ingold, Catherine White 1949- WhoAm 90, WhoWor 91
Ingold, Keith U. BioIn 16
Ingold, Keith Usherwood 1929- WhoAm 90
Ingold, Robert Glen 1950- WhoEmL 91
Ingoldsby, Arthur W. 1907- St&PR 91
Ingoldsby, Roderick 1944- St&PR 91
Ingraham, David W. St&PR 91
Ingraham, Deborah Rachel 1956- WhoSSW 91
Ingraham, Edward Clarke, Jr. 1922- WhoAm 90
Ingraham, Helen Madeline BioIn 16
Ingraham, Joe McDonald 1903-1990 BioIn 16
Ingraham, John Douglas 1955- WhoAmA 91
Ingraham, John Wright 1930- WhoAm 90, WhoE 91, WhoWor 91
Ingraham, Merle R 1924- BiDrAPA 89
Ingraham, Michael Lee 1930- St&PR 91
Ingraham, Sears Wilson 1927- WhoAm 90
Ingram, Albert L, Jr. 1916- BiDrAPA 89
Ingram, Alvin John 1914- WhoAm 90
Ingram, Alyce M. 1914- WhoWrEP 89
Ingram, B.N. 1927- St&PR 91
Ingram, Charles Clark, Jr. 1916- St&PR 91, WhoAm 90
Ingram, Conley 1930- WhoAm 90
Ingram, David 1944- WhoAm 90
Ingram, David Eric 1939- WhoWor 91
Ingram, David Vernon 1939- WhoWor 91
Ingram, Denny Ouzts, Jr. 1929- WhoAm 90
Ingram, Don V. 1935- St&PR 91
Ingram, Dorothy Stamps 1946- WhoAmW 91
Ingram, Douglas H 1943- BiDrAPA 89
Ingram, E. Michael 1952- St&PR 91
Ingram, Edgar W., Jr. 1910- St&PR 91
Ingram, Ernest M. 1926- St&PR 91
Ingram, Erskine Bronson 1931 St&PR 91
Ingram, George 1920- WhoAm 90
Ingram, George Conley 1930- WhoAm 90
Ingram, Helen Moyer 1937- WhoWrEP 89
Ingram, Jaime Ricardo Jaen 1928- IntWWM 90
Ingram, James WhoAm 90
Ingram, James 1952?- DrBIPA 90
Ingram, James Carlton 1922- WhoAm 90
Ingram, James Charles 1928- WhoWor 91
Ingram, James P. 1940- St&PR 91
Ingram, Joyce Elaine 1947- WhoAmW 91
Ingram, Judith 1926- WhoAmA 91
Ingram, Kenneth Lloyd 1948- WhoSSW 91
Ingram, Lawrence Warren 1921- WhoAm 90
Ingram, M. Lynda 1948- WhoSSW 91
Ingram, Michael Alexander 1958- WhoSSW 91
Ingram, Patricia Kay 1961- WhoSSW 91
Ingram, R W 1930-1989 ConAu 129
Ingram, Rex EarBlAP
Ingram, Rex 1895-1969 DrBIPA 90
Ingram, Robert M., Jr. 1922- St&PR 91
Ingram, Robert Palmer 1917- WhoAm 90
Ingram, Roland Harrison, Jr. 1935- WhoAm 90
Ingram, Roy Lee 1921- WhoAm 90
Ingram, Sam Harris 1928- WhoAm 90, WhoSSW 91
Ingram, Samuel William, Jr. 1933- WhoAm 90
Ingram, Susan Schaefer 1950- ODwPR 91
Ingram, Temple Byrn, Jr. 1949- WhoEmL 91
Ingram, William Austin 1924- WhoAm 90
Ingram, William Leon 1920- BiDrAPA 89
Ingram, William Truitt 1908- WhoAm 90
Ingrao, Deborah Ann 1950- WhoAmW 91
Ingrassia, Paul Joseph 1950- WhoAm 90
Ingres, Jean Auguste Dominique 1780-1867 BioIn 16, IntDcAA 90, WorAlBi
Ingrish, Elizabeth Beasley 1944- WhoSSW 91
Ingstrup, Ole Michaelsen 1941- WhoAm 90
Ingui, John 1952- BiDrAPA 89
Ingulfsen, Charlene 1964- WhoAmW 91
Ingvar, David Henschen 1924- WhoWor 91
Ingwell, Scott V. 1957- St&PR 91
Ingwersen, Martin Lewis 1919- St&PR 91, WhoAm 90
Ingwersen, Will 1905-1990 ConAu 132
Inhofe, James M. 1934- WhoAm 90, WhoSSW 91
Inhorn, Stanley Lee 1928- WhoAm 90
Iniguez, Calixto Garcia 1839-1898 BioIn 16
Iniguez, Diego Angulo 1901-1986 BioIn 16
Injerd, William George 1951- WhoEmL 91
Injeyan, Seta L 1946- WhoAmA 91
Ink Spots, The OxCPMus
Ink, Dwight A. 1922- WhoAm 90
Inkeles, Alex 1920- WhoAm 90
Inkellis, Barbara G. 1949- WhoEmL 91
Inkley, John James, Jr. 1945- WhoEmL 91
Inkley, Scott Russell 1921- WhoAm 90
Inkley, Scott Russell, Jr. 1952- WhoAm 90
Inkpaduta 1815?-1882? WhNaAH
Inkpen, Ross McKay 1936- WhoAm 90
Inks, Allen Walcott 1954- WhoEmL 91
Inkster, Norman David 1938- WhoAm 90
Inlow, Edgar Burke 1915- WhoAm 90
Inlow, Lawrence W. 1950- St&PR 91
Inlow, Linda Bishop 1948- WhoSSW 91
Inlow, Patti P. 1950- St&PR 91
Inman, Bobby R. St&PR 91
Inman, Bobby Ray BioIn 16
Inman, Bobby Ray 1931- WhoAm 90
Inman, Christal D. 1964- WhoAmW 91
Inman, Daniel 1921- IntWWM 90
Inman, Daniel John 1947- WhoE 91, WhoEmL 91
Inman, Della Bates 1930- WhoE 91
Inman, Grant Muir 1941- St&PR 91
Inman, Henry Joseph 1946- WhoEmL 91
Inman, James Carlton, Jr. 1945- WhoSSW 91
Inman, Lydia Lucille 1918- WhoWor 91
Inman, Margaret Anne 1929- St&PR 91
Inman, Mary 1894-1985 EncAL
Inman, Pauline Winchester 1904-1990 WhoAmA 91N
Inman, Peter T. 1948- WhoWrEP 89
Inman, Robert Frederick 1943- WhoSSW 91
Inman, Ross Banks 1931- WhoAm 90
Inman, Terry W. 1940- WhoAm 90
Inman, W.O., III St&PR 91
Inman, Will 1923- WhoWrEP 89
Inman, William Peter 1936- WhoAm 90
Inmon-Loeffler, Kathy Marie 1962- WhoEmL 91
Innace, Joseph J. ODwPR 91
Innamorato, Anthony John 1936- St&PR 91
Innanen, Larry John 1950- St&PR 91, WhoAm 90
Innaurato, Albert BioIn 16
Innaurato, Albert 1947- WorAu 1980 [port]
Innaurato, Albert 1948?- ConLC 60 [port]
Innaurato, Albert Francis 1947- WhoAm 90
Innelli, Hope 1960- WhoEmL 91
Innerst, Mark 1958?- BioIn 16
Innerst, Preston Eugene 1927- WhoAm 90
Innes, Audrey Muriel 1936- IntWWM 90
Innes, David Lyn 1941- WhoSSW 91
Innes, Donn 1927- St&PR 91
Innes, Georgette Meyer 1918- WhoAmW 91
Innes, Hammond AuBYP 90
Innes, Hammond 1913- BioIn 16, TwCCr&M 91
Innes, John Phythian, II 1934- St&PR 91, WhoAm 90
Innes, Kenneth Frederick, III 1950- WhoEmL 91, WhoSSW 91
Innes, Michael MajTwCW
Innes, Michael 1906- BioIn 16, TwCCr&M 91, WorAlBi
Innes, P. Kim Sturgess 1955- WhoAmW 91
Innes, Peter Bruce 1941- WhoAm 90
Innes, Ralph Hammond- 1913- BioIn 16
Innes, Ruth 1929- WhoWrEP 89
Innes, Zondra F. 1953- St&PR 91
Inness, George 1825-1894 WorAlBi
Inness-Brown, Elizabeth Ann 1954- WhoWrEP 89
Innis, Bertha June Bower 1940- WhoSSW 91
Innis, Gail Marie 1957- WhoEmL 91
Innis, Jeff 1962- Ballpl 90
Innis, Pauline WhoAmW 91
Innis, Robert Bryan BiDrAPA 89
Innis, Robert E 1941- ConAu 130
Innis, Roy Emile Alfredo 1934- WhoAm 90
Innis, Yvonne Phyllis-Jean 1948- WhoE 91
Innis-Jurko, Angela Renee 1961- WhoAmW 91
Inniss, Rosalyn E 1946- BiDrAPA 89
Inno, Karl 1908- WhoE 91, WhoWor 91
Innocent, Antoine J 1933- BiDrAPA 89
Innocente, Salvatore Steven 1954- WhoEmL 91
Innocenti, Antonio 1915- WhoWor 91
Innocenti, Ray D. 1935- St&PR 91

Innocenti, Robert Edward 1937- *St&PR 91*
Inns, Harry Douglas Ellis 1922- *WhoWor 91*
Inocalla, Marilou V. *BiDrAPA 89*
Inoguchi, Kuniko 1952- *WhoWor 91*
Inoguchi, Takashi 1944- *ConAu 131, WhoWor 91*
Inonu, Ismet 1884-1973 *PolLCME*
Inoue Yasushi 1907- *WorAu 1980 [port]*
Inoue, Enryo 1859-1919 *EncPaPR 91*
Inoue, Haruoki *BioIn 16*
Inoue, Hisashi 1947- *WhoE 91*
Inoue, Kazuko 1946- *WhoAmA 91*
Inoue, Kazuo 1935- *WhoWor 91*
Inoue, Osamu 1940- *WhoWor 91*
Inoue, Shinya 1921- *WhoAm 90*
Inoue, Shun 1938- *WhoWor 91*
Inoue, Takeshi 1932- *WhoWor 91*
Inoue, Yoshio 1929- *WhoWor 91*
Inoue, Yoshisuke 1932- *WhoWor 91*
Inouye, Barry Isamu 1954- *WhoEmL 91*
Inouye, Daniel K. *BioIn 16*
Inouye, Daniel K. 1924- *WorAlBi*
Inouye, Daniel Ken 1924- *WhoAm 90, WhoWor 91*
Inouye, Stanley K. *BioIn 16*
Inouye, Zuiken 1936- *WhoWor 91*
Inquart, Artur von Seyss- 1892-1946 *BioIn 16*
Insani, John Louis 1925- *St&PR 91*
Insco, Michael Andrew 1950- *WhoEmL 91*
Inscoe, Jennifer Lynn 1947- *WhoAmW 91*
Insel, Paul Anthony 1945- *WhoEmL 91*
Inselbuch, Harriet 1940- *ODwPR 91*
Inselman, Laura Sue 1944- *WhoAmW 91*
Inselman-Temkin, Barbara Ruth 1948- *WhoEmL 91*
Inserra, Donna Louise 1948- *WhoEmL 91*
Insingel, Mark 1935- *ConAu 131*
Insinna, Paul William 1958- *WhoEmL 91*
Inskeep, Gordon Charles 1922- *WhoAm 90*
Inskeep, Richard Darwin 1951- *WhoEmL 91*
Insler, Stanley 1937- *WhoAm 90*
Insley, Richard Langrall 1927- *WhoAm 90*
Insley, Will 1929- *WhoAm 90, WhoAmA 91*
Instone, John C. 1924- *St&PR 91*
Instone, John Clifford 1924- *WhoAm 90, WhoE 91, WhoWor 91*
Intan, Princess of Malaysia *BioIn 16*
Intemann, Robert Louis 1938- *WhoAm 90*
Interdonato, Anthony Paul 1949- *WhoEmL 91*
Inti-Illimani *NewAgMG*
Intihar, Stanley V. 1934- *St&PR 91*
Intile, Patricia Ann 1950- *WhoE 91*
Intilli, Sharon Marie 1950- *WhoAmW 91*
Intorre, Benjamin Joseph, Sr. 1929- *WhoE 91*
Intrator, Joanne Ruth *BiDrAPA 89*
Intrator, Richard L. 1952- *St&PR 91*
Intriligator, Marc Steven 1952- *WhoE 91, WhoEmL 91*
Intriligator, Michael David 1938- *WhoAm 90, WhoWor 91*
Introcaso, John Charles 1947- *WhoE 91*
IntVeld, Marjorie Lee 1936- *WhoAmW 91*
Inukai, Kyohei 1913- *WhoAmA 91*
Inveen, Laura Campbell 1955- *WhoEmL 91*
Inver, Marc Robert 1950- *BiDrAPA 89*
Inverarity, Robert Bruce 1909- *WhoAmA 91*
Invernizio, Carolina 1858-1916 *EncCoWW*
Inwood, David Gerald 1946- *BiDrAPA 89, WhoE 91*
Inwood, Mary Ruth Brink 1928- *IntWWM 90*
Iny, George S. 1933- *St&PR 91*
Inyart, Gene *AuBYP 90*
Inzano, Karen Lee 1946- *WhoEmL 91*
Inzitari, Frank 1935- *St&PR 91*
Ioachimescu, Calin 1949- *IntWWM 90*
Ioan, Magdalena 1948- *IntWWM 90*
Ioannides, Alkis 1929- *BiDrAPA 89*
Ioannou, Costas Demosthenous 1944- *WhoWor 91*
Ioannou, Paul 1942- *WhoWor 91*
Iodice, Elaine 1947- *WhoAmW 91*
Iodice, Emilio Francis 1946- *WhoEmL 91*
Iodice, Jody DiMeno 1953- *WhoAmW 91*
Iodice, Ruth Genevieve Work 1925- *WhoWrEP 89*
Ioffe, Adolf Abramovich 1883-1927 *BioIn 16*
Iokibe, Makoto 1943- *WhoWor 91*
Iommi, Enio 1926- *ArtLatA*
Iona, Mario 1917- *WhoAm 90*
Ionesco, Eugene 1912- *EuWr 13, MajTwCW, WhoAm 90, WhoWor 91, WorAlBi*
Ionesco-Vovu, Constantin 1932- *IntWWM 90*
Ionescu, George 1917- *IntWWM 90*
Ionescu Tulcea, Cassius 1923- *WhoAm 90, WhoWor 91*
Ionni, Ray *St&PR 91*
Ionno, Joseph A 1926- *BiDrAPA 89*
Ioppolo, Frank Sebastian 1942- *WhoAm 90*
Iordanides, Yiannes 1943- *WhoE 91*
Iordanidou, Maria 1897- *EncCoWW*
Iordanou, Constantine P. 1950- *St&PR 91*
Iorfida, Diane Mary 1954- *WhoAmW 91*
Iorg, Dane 1950- *Ballpl 90*
Iorg, Garth 1954- *Ballpl 90*
Iorillo, John R. 1935- *St&PR 91*
Iorillo, Mario Angelo 1939- *WhoAm 90*
Iorio, Adrian J 1879-1957 *WhoAmA 91N*
Iorio, Ralph A. 1925- *St&PR 91*
Iorio, Ralph Arthur 1925- *WhoAm 90*
Iorio, Rosemarie Ann 1966- *WhoE 91*
Iosa Ghini, Massimo *BioIn 16*
Iosilevich, Miron A *BiDrAPA 89*
Iosue, Michael Allen 1945- *WhoSSW 91*
Iosue, Robert V. *WhoAm 90*
Iott, Gregory Lawrence 1951- *WhoEmL 91*
Iott, Richard B. 1951- *St&PR 91*
Iott, Timothy Lee 1950- *St&PR 91*
Iott, Wallace D. 1915- *St&PR 91, WhoAm 90*
Iotti, Robert C. 1941- *St&PR 91*
Iovenko, Michael 1930- *WhoAm 90*
Ip, Matthew Wai-Fan 1951- *WhoSSW 91*
Ipach, Cynthia Ann 1963- *WhoAmW 91*
Ipaktchian, Sidney 1933- *WhoAm 90*
Ipar, Omar Joffre *BiDrAPA 89*
Ipatieff, Vladimir 1867-1952 *WorAlBi*
Ipcar, Dahlov 1917- *AuBYP 90, BioIn 16, WhoAm 90, WhoAmA 91*
Ipcar, Dhalov 1917- *BiDWomA*
Ipousteguy 1920- *WhoAmA 91*
Ipousteguy, Jean 1920- *WhoWor 91*
Ippel, Gerald L. 1927- *St&PR 91*
Ippen, Erich Peter 1940- *WhoAm 90*
Ippolito, Andrew V. 1932- *St&PR 91*
Ippolito, Angelo 1922- *WhoAm 90, WhoAmA 91*
Ippolito, Giuseppe 1954- *WhoWor 91*
Ipsen, Brad *St&PR 91*
Ipsen, Carol Anne 1951- *BiDrAPA 89, WhoE 91*
Ipsen, Detlev 1945- *WhoWor 91*
Ipsen, Ernest L 1869-1951 *WhoAmA 91N*
Ipsen, Joern 1944- *WhoWor 91*
Ipsen, Kent Forrest 1933- *WhoAmA 91*
Ipsen, Poul Janus 1936- *WhoAmA 91*
Iqbal, Azad 1946- *WhoWor 91*
Iqbal, M Javed 1941- *BiDrAPA 89*
Iqbal, Mohammad Zafar 1945- *WhoEmL 91*
Iqbal, Rafi Q *BiDrAPA 89*
Iqbal, Zafar 1946- *WhoAm 90*
Iradier, Eduardo Dato 1856-1921 *BioIn 16*
Iraha, Michael Masaichi 1948- *WhoEmL 91*
Irahola, Rene C. 1928- *WhoHisp 91*
Irani, Jamshed Jiji 1936- *WhoWor 91*
Irani, Joseph H. 1927- *St&PR 91*
Irani, Ray R. *BioIn 16*
Irani, Ray R. 1935- *St&PR 91, WhoAm 90*
Irani, Raymond Reza 1928- *WhoAm 90*
Iranyi, Gabriel 1946- *IntWWM 90*
Irateba 1814?-1878 *WhNaAH*
Irby, Benjamin Freeman 1938- *WhoSSW 91*
Irby, Charles Lyons 1954- *St&PR 91*
Irby, Jack Daniel 1953- *St&PR 91*
Irby, John Laurens Manning 1854-1900 *AmLegL*
Irby, Kenneth 1936- *WhoWrEP 89*
Irby, Richard Logan 1918- *WhoAm 90*
Irby, Stuart C., Jr. 1923- *St&PR 91*
Irby, Stuart Charles, Jr. 1923- *WhoAm 90*
Irby, Stuart M. 1953- *St&PR 91*
Irby, Stuart McIlwaine 1953- *WhoAm 90*
Irby, Yvette Renata 1963- *WhoEmL 91*
Iredell, Denise 1926- *EncPaPR 91*
Iredell, Robert, IV 1941- *St&PR 91*
Iredell, Russell 1889-1959 *WhoAmA 91N*
Irelan, John Ralph Smiley 1935- *WhoSSW 91*
Ireland, Andrew P. 1930- *WhoAm 90, WhoSSW 91*
Ireland, Carol E. 1956- *WhoAmW 91*
Ireland, Cindy Jean 1959- *WhoAmW 91*
Ireland, David *BioIn 16*
Ireland, Harry Bert 1938- *St&PR 91*
Ireland, Herbert Orin 1919- *WhoAm 90*
Ireland, Jacqueline Mayhew *BioIn 16*
Ireland, James Duane, III 1950- *St&PR 91, WhoAm 90, WhoEmL 91*
Ireland, Jill *BioIn 16, ConAu 131*
Ireland, Jill *NewYTBS 90 [port]*
Ireland, Jill 1936-1990 *News 90, WorAlBi*
Ireland, Joan E. 1949- *St&PR 91*
Ireland, John 1838-1918 *BioIn 16*
Ireland, John 1879-1962 *PenDiMP A*
Ireland, John 1914- *WorAlBi*
Ireland, John 1916- *ConTFT 8*
Ireland, Marvin Edwin 1947- *WhoSSW 91*
Ireland, Norman C. 1927- *St&PR 91*
Ireland, Norman Charles 1927- *WhoWor 91*
Ireland, Pamela Woodhull 1957- *WhoAmW 91*
Ireland, Patrick *PenDiMP*
Ireland, Patrick 1935- *WhoAm 90, WhoAmA 91*
Ireland, R.L., III 1920- *St&PR 91*
Ireland, Robert Livingtston, III 1920- *WhoAm 90*
Ireland, Robin *PenDiMP*
Ireland, William Patrick 1923- *IntWWM 90*
Irell, Lawrence Elliott 1912- *WhoAm 90*
Iremonger, Lucille *EncO&P 3*
Iremonger, Lucille 1919- *FemiCLE*
Irene 752?-803 *WomWR [port]*
Irene, Eugene Arthur 1941- *WhoSSW 91*
Ireson, Nathaniel *PenDiDA 89*
Ireton, John Francis, Jr. 1939- *WhoAm 90*
Ireton, Thomas Francis 1940- *St&PR 91, WhoE 91*
Ireton-Hewitt, John H. 1937- *St&PR 91*
Ireton-Hewitt, John Howard 1937- *WhoE 91*
Irey, Charlotte York 1918- *WhoAm 90*
Irey, Nelson Sumner 1911- *WhoAm 90*
Iri, Masao 1933- *WhoWor 91*
Iribar, Manuel R. 1953- *WhoSSW 91*
Iribarren, Norma Carmen 1938- *WhoHisp 91*
Iribe, Paul 1883-1935 *PenDiDA 89*
Irigaray, Luce *EncCoWW*
Irigaray, Luce 1939- *FemiCLE*
Irigaray, Pedro J 1932- *BiDrAPA 89*
Irigoyen, David E 1927- *BiDrAPA 89*
Irigoyen, Fructuoso Rascon 1949- *WhoHisp 91*
Irigoyen, Hipolito 1852-1933 *BioIn 16*
Irigoyen, Matilde M. 1949- *WhoHisp 91*
Irigoyen, Sal A. 1954- *WhoHisp 91*
Irigoyen-Rascon, Fructuoso 1949- *BiDrAPA 89, WhoSSW 91*
Irion, Arthur Lloyd 1918- *WhoAm 90*
Irion, James V. 1950- *St&PR 91*
Irion, Mary Jean 1922- *WhoWrEP 89*
Irions, Charles Carter 1929- *WhoAm 90*
Irish, Chas. A. 1929- *St&PR 91*
Irish, D.C. *St&PR 91*
Irish, Frank Sylvester 1932- *St&PR 91*
Irish, Jerry Arthur 1936- *WhoAm 90*
Irish, K. Michael *ODwPR 91*
Irish, Larry Gordon 1944- *St&PR 91*
Irish, Leon Eugene 1938- *WhoAm 90, WhoE 91*
Irish, Marilyn Eleanor 1943- *WhoE 91*
Irish, Patrick Leon 1925- *St&PR 91*
Irish, William *TwCCr&M 91*
Irish, William 1903-1968 *BioIn 16*
Iriuchijima, Juro 1931- *WhoWor 91*
Iriye, Akira 1934- *WhoAm 90*
Irizarry, Annabelle 1949- *WhoSSW 91*
Irizarry, Carmen P *BiDrAPA 89*
Irizarry, Rachel Socas *BioIn 16*
Irizarry-Graziani, Carmen 1948- *WhoHisp 91*
Irizarry-Yunque, Carlos Juan 1922- *WhoAm 90*
Irland, David *ConAu 33NR, MajTwCW*
Irland, Lorraine 1946- *WhoAmW 91*
Irlando, Richard Anthony *BiDrAPA 89*
Irmas, Sydney Milton 1925- *St&PR 91*
Irmiere-Marchitto, Amy Frances 1961- *WhoEmL 91*
Irminger, Eldon R. 1947- *St&PR 91*
Irminger, Eugene H. 1929- *St&PR 91*
Irminger, Eugene Herman 1929- *WhoAm 90*
Irmscher, Hans Dietrich 1929- *WhoWor 91*
Irmscher, Wallace G. 1923- *St&PR 91*
Iron Butterfly *EncPR&S 89*
Iron Maiden *EncPR&S 89*
Iron Tail 1850?-1916 *WhNaAH*
Iron, Ralph 1855-1920 *BioIn 16*
Irons, Barry Lynn *BiDrAPA 89*
Irons, Dennis Michael 1951- *WhoSSW 91*
Irons, Edi *BioIn 16*
Irons, George Vernon 1902- *WhoAm 90*
Irons, Jeremy 1948- *BioIn 16, WorAlBi*
Irons, Jeremy John 1948- *WhoAm 90, WhoWor 91*
Irons, Neil L. 1936- *WhoAm 90*
Irons, Richard R. 1948- *WhoEmL 91*
Irons, William George 1933- *WhoAm 90*
Irons, William Lee 1941- *WhoWor 91*
Ironside, Jetske 1940- *SmATA 60 [port]*
Ironside, Wallace 1917- *BiDrAPA 89*
Irosch, Mirjana 1939- *IntWWM 90*
Irrmann, Robert Henry 1916- *WhoAm 90*
Irrthum, Henri Emile 1947- *WhoWor 91*
Irsay, James Steven 1959- *WhoAm 90*
Irsay, Robert 1923- *WhoAm 90*
Irsfeld, John Henry 1937- *WhoWrEP 89*
Irsfeld, Lynn Irene 1960- *WhoEmL 91*
Irvan, Robert P. 1937- *St&PR 91*
Irvin, Charles Richard 1932- *St&PR 91*
Irvin, David Rand 1948- *WhoSSW 91*
Irvin, Eames 1928- *St&PR 91*
Irvin, Isaiah Tucker 1816-1860 *AmLegL*
Irvin, John 1940- *ConTFT 8*
Irvin, Kathryn Jeanette 1947- *WhoAmW 91*
Irvin, Lynda Elare 1950- *WhoAmW 91*
Irvin, Marjory Ruth 1925- *IntWWM 90*
Irvin, Michael Richard 1951- *St&PR 91*
Irvin, Monte 1919- *Ballpl 90 [port], BioIn 16*
Irvin, Rea 1881-1972 *WhoAmA 91N*
Irvin, Robert Andrew 1948- *WhoSSW 91*
Irvin, Robert H. 1952- *St&PR 91*
Irvin, Stephen Ross 1947- *WhoSSW 91*
Irvin, Tinsley Hoyt 1933- *St&PR 91, WhoAm 90, WhoE 91*
Irvin, W. Lynn 1935- *St&PR 91*
Irvin, William M *BiDrAPA 89*
Irvine, Betty Jo 1943- *WhoAmA 91*
Irvine, Douglas Ross 1960- *WhoEmL 91*
Irvine, Florence C *BiDrAPA 89*
Irvine, Frances Geraldene 1940- *WhoAmW 91*
Irvine, George 1826-1897 *DcCanB 12*
Irvine, George 1948- *WhoAm 90*
Irvine, George A. 1941- *St&PR 91*
Irvine, Gretchen Krantz 1946- *WhoAmW 91*
Irvine, Horace Hills, II 1937- *WhoAm 90, WhoE 91*
Irvine, James Bosworth 1914- *WhoSSW 91*
Irvine, Jeffrey K. 1953- *IntWWM 90*
Irvine, John Alexander 1947- *WhoAm 90, WhoSSW 91, WhoWor 91*
Irvine, John Michael 1954- *WhoE 91*
Irvine, Louise *BioIn 16*
Irvine, Louva Elizabeth 1939- *WhoAm 90*
Irvine, Marion *BioIn 16*
Irvine, Olive A *BiDrAPA 89*
Irvine, Peter Bennington 1951- *WhoE 91*
Irvine, Phyllis Eleanor Kuhnle 1940- *WhoAmW 91*
Irvine, Robert 1936- *TwCCr&M 91*
Irvine, Robert 1963- *IntWWM 90*
Irvine, Roger Kenneth 1933- *St&PR 91*
Irvine, Stewart Edward 1950- *St&PR 91*
Irvine, Thomas Francis, Jr. 1922- *WhoAm 90*
Irving, Adam, Jr. 1943- *St&PR 91*
Irving, Amy *BioIn 16*
Irving, Amy 1953- *WhoAm 90, WhoAmW 91, WorAlBi*
Irving, Anna Duer 1873-1957 *WhoAmA 91N*
Irving, Arthur *BioIn 16*
Irving, Carolyn Elizabeth 1969- *WhoEmL 91*
Irving, Clarence 1955- *BioIn 16*
Irving, David Gerow 1935- *IntWWM 90*
Irving, Donald J 1933- *WhoAmA 91*
Irving, Edward 1792-1834 *EncO&P 3*
Irving, Edward M. 1928- *St&PR 91*
Irving, Edward Muir 1928- *WhoAm 90*
Irving, Ernest 1877-1953 *OxCPMus*
Irving, Ernest 1878-1953 *PenDiMP*
Irving, George Steven 1922- *WhoAm 90*
Irving, George Washington, III 1940- *WhoAm 90*
Irving, Gitte Nielsen 1954- *WhoAmW 91, WhoE 91, WhoWor 91*
Irving, Glenn Alexander 1931- *St&PR 91*
Irving, Henry 1838-1905 *BioIn 16*
Irving, Sir Henry 1838-1905 *WorAlBi*
Irving, Herbert 1917- *WhoAm 90*
Irving, Howard Lee 1951- *IntWWM 90*
Irving, I.A.L. 1938- *St&PR 91*
Irving, Ian *BioIn 16*
Irving, J. Lawrence 1935- *WhoAm 90*
Irving, Jack Howard 1920- *WhoAm 90*
Irving, James *BioIn 16*
Irving, Joan 1916- *WhoAmA 91*
Irving, John *BioIn 16*
Irving, John 1942- *BioIn 16, MajTwCW, WorAlBi*
Irving, John Winslow 1942- *WhoE 91, WhoWrEP 89*
Irving, Joyce Arlene 1945- *WhoAmW 91*
Irving, Kenneth Colin *BioIn 16*
Irving, Larry 1955- *BioIn 16*
Irving, Laurence 1897-1988 *AnObit 1988*
Irving, Michael Henry 1923- *WhoAm 90*
Irving, Nancy *AuBYP 90*
Irving, Richard *NewYTBS 90*
Irving, Robert 1913- *PenDiMP*
Irving, Robert, III *BioIn 16*
Irving, Robert Augustine 1913- *IntWWM 90*
Irving, Robert Churchill 1928- *WhoE 91*
Irving, Ronald 1931- *St&PR 91*
Irving, Stephen Miller 1950- *WhoEmL 91*
Irving, Terry 1951- *WhoE 91*
Irving, Wanda Elaine 1953- *WhoAmW 91*
Irving, Washington 1783-1859 *BioIn 16, WorAlBi*
Irving, William *AuBYP 90*
Irwin, Agnes 1841-1914 *BioAmW*
Irwin, Alice W. 1943- *St&PR 91*
Irwin, Ann 1915- *BioIn 16*
Irwin, Anne 1696?-1764 *FemiCLE*
Irwin, Arthur Mead *BioIn 16*
Irwin, Arthur Samuel 1912- *WhoAm 90, WhoE 91*
Irwin, Bill *BioIn 16*
Irwin, Charlie 1869-1925 *Ballpl 90*

Irwin, Christopher Wayne 1948- *St&PR 91*
Irwin, David Herman, Jr. 1950- *WhoSSW 91*
Irwin, David S 1940- *BiDrAPA 89*
Irwin, David Samuel 1944- *BiDrAPA 89*
Irwin, Deborah Jo 1952- *WhoEmL 91, WhoWor 91*
Irwin, Don Dennis 1936- *WhoSSW 91*
Irwin, Douglas Alexander 1962- *WhoE 91*
Irwin, F Michael 1940- *BiDrAPA 89*
Irwin, Fay *WhoWrEP 89*
Irwin, G. Stormy 1929- *WhoAmW 91*
Irwin, George M 1921- *WhoAmA 91*
Irwin, George Rankin 1907- *WhoAm 90*
Irwin, Glenn Ward, Jr. 1920- *WhoAm 90*
Irwin, Grace *AuBYP 90*
Irwin, Grace Lillian 1907- *FemiCLE*
Irwin, Graham Wilkie 1920- *WhoAm 90*
Irwin, H J 1943- *EncO&P 3*
Irwin, H. Thomas 1943- *St&PR 91*
Irwin, Hale S. 1945- *WhoAm 90*
Irwin, Harvey Jon 1943- *EncPaPR 91*
Irwin, Helen Trathen 1939- *WhoAm 90*
Irwin, Inez 1873-1970 *FemiCLE*
Irwin, Ira 1932- *St&PR 91*
Irwin, James Benson 1930- *BioIn 16, WhoAm 90, WhoWor 91*
Irwin, James Burke, V 1947- *WhoEmL 91*
Irwin, James Carson 1932- *St&PR 91*
Irwin, Joe Robert 1936- *St&PR 91, WhoAm 90*
Irwin, John David 1939- *WhoAm 90*
Irwin, John Joseph 1949- *WhoSSW 91*
Irwin, John Nichol 1913- *BioIn 16*
Irwin, John Nichol, II 1913- *WhoAm 90*
Irwin, John Rice *BioIn 16*
Irwin, John Robert 1945- *St&PR 91, WhoEmL 91*
Irwin, John Thomas 1940- *WhoAm 90*
Irwin, John Wesley 1937- *WhoAm 90*
Irwin, Joseph A. 1936- *St&PR 91*
Irwin, Joseph Augustus 1936- *WhoAm 90*
Irwin, Joseph James 1908 *WhoAm 90*
Irwin, Lani Helena 1947- *WhoAmA 91*
Irwin, Leo Howard 1917- *WhoAm 90*
Irwin, Linda Belmore 1950- *WhoAmW 91, WhoWor 91*
Irwin, Lisa Dru 1953- *WhoAmA 91*
Irwin, Mark 1953- *WhoWrEP 89*
Irwin, Martin 1949- *WhoE 91*
Irwin, Martin Abraham *BiDrAPA 89*
Irwin, Mary Frances 1925- *WhoAmW 91*
Irwin, May 1862-1938 *BioIn 16, NotWoAT, OxCCanT, OxCPMus*
Irwin, Michael Henry Knox 1931- *WhoWor 91*
Irwin, Miriam Dianne Owen 1930- *WhoAmW 91*
Irwin, Miriam Owen 1930- *WhoWrEP 89*
Irwin, Myron Richard 1912- *St&PR 91, WhoAm 90*
Irwin, P. K. *MajTwCW*
Irwin, Pat 1921- *WhoAm 90*
Irwin, Patrick H. 1923- *St&PR 91*
Irwin, Peter John 1934- *St&PR 91*
Irwin, Philip Donnan 1933- *WhoAm 90*
Irwin, Phyllis Ann 1929- *IntWWM 90*
Irwin, Raymond Richard 1928- *St&PR 91*
Irwin, Richard Dorsey 1905- *WhoAm 90*
Irwin, Richard Dorsey 1905-1989 *BioIn 16*
Irwin, Richard Loren 1924- *WhoAm 90*
Irwin, Richard Warren 1951- *WhoAm 90*
Irwin, Robert 1928- *WhoAmA 91*
Irwin, Robert J.A. 1927- *St&PR 91*
Irwin, Robert James Armstrong, Jr. 1927- *WhoAm 90, WhoWor 91*
Irwin, S. Macdonald 1927- *St&PR 91*
Irwin, Samuel Macdonald 1927- *WhoAm 90*
Irwin, Scott *BioIn 16*
Irwin, Scott Arnold 1951- *St&PR 91*
Irwin, Susan 1946- *ODwPR 91*
Irwin, T.B. 1930- *St&PR 91*
Irwin, Theodore 1907- *WhoAm 90*
Irwin, William Henry 1873-1948 *BioIn 16*
Irwin, William Lyman 1942- *WhoE 91*
Irwin, William R. 1944- *WhoAm 90*
Irwin, William Richard 1944- *St&PR 91*
Irwinsky, Larry Don 1954- *WhoSSW 91*
Isa bin Salman Al-Khalifa, Sheikh 1933- *WhoWor 91*
Isa Bin Sulman Al-Khalifah 1933- *PolLCME*
Isa, Tomas Jorge 1928- *BiDrAPA 89*
Isaac of Holland *EncO&P 3*
Isaac, Adele 1854-1915 *PenDiMP*
Isaac, Bina Susan 1958- *WhoAmW 91, WhoEmL 91*
Isaac, Cecil 1930- *IntWWM 90*
Isaac, Charles D. 1932- *St&PR 91*
Isaac, George, Jr. 1923- *St&PR 91*
Isaac, George A., III 1953- *St&PR 91*
Isaac, Gerald Duane 1947- *WhoWor 91*
Isaac, John Rees 1945- *St&PR 91*
Isaac, Luis *WhoHisp 91*
Isaac, Merle John 1898- *BioIn 16*
Isaac, Paul Edward 1926- *WhoSSW 91*
Isaac, Rhys Llywelyn 1937- *WhoWor 91*
Isaac, Robert H *BiDrAPA 89*
Isaac, Robert Michael 1928- *WhoAm 90*
Isaac, Sol Morton 1911- *WhoAm 90*
Isaac, Steven Richard 1947- *WhoAm 90, WhoSSW 91*
Isaac, Walter Lon 1956- *WhoSSW 91*
Isaac, William Michael 1943- *WhoAm 90*
Isaac, Yvonne Renee 1948- *WhoAmW 91*
Isaac Nash, Eva Mae 1936- *WhoAmW 91, WhoWor 91*
Isaacman, Steven 1930- *WhoE 91*
Isaacoff, Dana Margolia 1960- *WhoAmW 91*
Isaacs, Andrea 1952- *WhoEmL 91*
Isaacs, Antony Rufus- *BioIn 16*
Isaacs, Avrom 1926- *WhoAmA 91*
Isaacs, Betty Lewis 1894-1971 *WhoAmA 91N*
Isaacs, Carole Schaffer 1931-1980 *WhoAmA 91N*
Isaacs, Claire Naomi 1933- *WhoAmA 91*
Isaacs, Dorothy Ann 1948- *WhoSSW 91*
Isaacs, Edith Juliet Rich 1878-1956 *BioIn 16, NotWoAT*
Isaacs, Edward 1881-1953 *PenDiMP*
Isaacs, Florence 1937- *WhoWrEP 89*
Isaacs, Gerald William 1927- *WhoAm 90*
Isaacs, Godfrey Leonard 1924- *WhoE 91*
Isaacs, Heide Rufus- *BioIn 16*
Isaacs, Helen Coolidge Adams 1917- *WhoAmW 91, WhoE 91, WhoWor 91*
Isaacs, Howard David 1940- *BiDrAPA 89*
Isaacs, Irving A. 1903-1990 *BioIn 16*
Isaacs, James Lawrence 1960- *WhoEmL 91*
Isaacs, John H. 1922- *WhoAm 90*
Isaacs, John Henry 1949- *WhoSSW 91*
Isaacs, Jon T. 1945- *St&PR 91*
Isaacs, Jorge 1837-1895 *BioIn 16*
Isaacs, Juanita Joyce *BiDrAPA 89*
Isaacs, Kendall George Lamon 1925- *BioIn 16*
Isaacs, Kenneth L. 1904- *WhoAm 90, WhoWor 91*
Isaacs, Kenneth Sidney 1920- *WhoAm 90, WhoWor 91*
Isaacs, Madelyn Lisa 1953- *WhoSSW 91*
Isaacs, Mark D. 1955- *WhoWrEP 89*
Isaacs, Maurice 1922- *IntWWM 90*
Isaacs, Michael Burton 1947- *WhoE 91*
Isaacs, Moses Legis 1899-1970 *BioIn 16*
Isaacs, Myron S. 1911-1988 *BioIn 16*
Isaacs, Nicholas Stephen 1945- *IntWWM 90*
Isaacs, Norman Ellis 1908- *WhoAm 90*
Isaacs, R.J. 1905- *St&PR 91*
Isaacs, Richard Hart 1949- *WhoAm 90*
Isaacs, Robert Wolfe 1931- *WhoWor 91*
Isaacs, Roger D. 1925- *ODwPR 91*
Isaacs, Roger David 1925- *WhoAm 90, WhoWor 91*
Isaacs, Ron 1941- *WhoAmA 91*
Isaacs, Russell L. 1932- *St&PR 91*
Isaacs, S.F. 1937- *St&PR 91*
Isaacs, S. Fred 1937- *WhoAm 90*
Isaacs, S. Ted 1914- *WhoWor 91*
Isaacs, Scott *BioIn 16*
Isaacs, Susan 1943- *MajTwCW, WhoE 91*
Isaacs, Thomas K. 1949- *St&PR 91*
Isaacs, Timothy F 1943- *BiDrAPA 89*
Isaacson, Arline Levine 1946- *WhoAmW 91*
Isaacson, Bernard 1936- *St&PR 91*
Isaacson, Edith Lipsig 1920- *WhoAmW 91*
Isaacson, Gene Lester 1936- *WhoAmA 91*
Isaacson, Gerald Neil 1943- *WhoE 91*
Isaacson, Gerald Sidney 1927- *WhoAm 90*
Isaacson, Henry C. 1927- *St&PR 91*
Isaacson, John Magyar 1946- *WhoE 91*
Isaacson, Lynn Judith 1948- *WhoAmA 91*
Isaacson, M.S. 1932- *St&PR 91*
Isaacson, Marcia Jean 1945- *WhoAmA 91*
Isaacson, Marvin G *BiDrAPA 89*
Isaacson, Marvin Gerald 1918- *WhoSSW 91, WhoWor 91*
Isaacson, Milton Stanley 1932- *WhoAm 90*
Isaacson, Philip Marshal 1924- *WhoAmA 91*
Isaacson, Robert Lee 1928- *WhoAm 90*
Isaacson, Robert Louis 1944- *WhoWor 91*
Isaacson, Ronald G 1948- *WhoAmA 91*
Isaacson, Ronald Glenn 1948- *WhoEmL 91*
Isaacson, Vivienne *BiDrAPA 89*
Isaacson, Walter Seff 1952- *WhoE 91*
Isaak, Nicholas, Jr 1944- *WhoAmA 91*
Isabel 1846-1921 *WomWR*
Isabell, Robert *BioIn 16*
Isabella *WomWR*
Isabella *WomWR*
Isabella *WomWR*
Isabella 1180?- *EncCoWW*
Isabella I 1451-1504 *WorAlBi*
Isabella II 1830-1904 *WomWR*
Isabella Clara Eugenia of Austria 1566-1633 *WomWR [port]*
Isabella d'Este *WomWR*
Isabella Farnese of Parma 1692-1766 *WomWR*
Isabella Leonarda 1620-1704 *BioIn 16*
Isabella of Bavaria 1371-1435 *WomWR [port]*
Isabella of Cyprus *WomWR*
Isabella I, Queen of Spain 1451-1504 *BioIn 16*
Isabella II, Queen of Spain 1830-1904 *BioIn 16*
Isabella I the Catholic 1451-1504 *WomWR [port]*
Isabella, Thomas A. 1938- *St&PR 91*
Isabelle, Didier Bernard 1934- *WhoWor 91*
Isackes, Richard Morgan 1945- *WhoEmL 91*
Isacoff, Mark 1953- *WhoWor 91*
Isadora, Rachel *BioIn 16*
Isadore *DcCanB 12*
Isaia, Nana 1934- *EncCoWW*
Isaiah *WorAlBi*
Isakoff, Sheldon Erwin 1925- *WhoAm 90*
Isakov, Viktor Fedorovich 1932- *WhoWor 91*
Isakovic, Smiljka 1953- *IntWWM 90*
Isakow, Selwyn 1952- *WhoAm 90*
Isakson, John Philip 1939- *WhoSSW 91*
Isaksson, Ulla 1916- *DcScanL*
Isaksson, Ulla Margareta 1916- *EncCoWW*
Isalski, Zbigniew *BiDrAPA 89*
Isaminger, James C. 1881-1946 *Ballpl 90*
Isanos, Magda 1916-1944 *EncCoWW*
Isard, Walter 1919- *WhoAm 90*
Isasi-Diaz, Ada Maria 1943- *WhoHisp 91*
Isatai *WhNaAH*
Isay, Jane Franzblau 1939- *WhoAm 90*
Isay, Richard A. *BiDrAPA 89*
Isay, Richard Alexander *WhoE 91*
Isbell, Charles Edwin 1931- *St&PR 91*
Isbell, David Bradford 1929- *WhoAm 90*
Isbell, Frank 1875-1941 *Ballpl 90*
Isbell, Garnett Knowlten 1946- *St&PR 91*
Isbell, Garnett Knowlten, II 1946- *WhoSSW 91*
Isbell, Gary K. 1946- *St&PR 91*
Isbell, George H. 1937- *St&PR 91*
Isbell, Horace Smith 1898- *WhoAm 90*
Isbell, Jack Robert 1946- *WhoSSW 91*
Isbell, John Rolfe 1930- *WhoE 91*
Isbell, Marion William 1905-1988 *BioIn 16*
Isbell, Patricia Gonzales 1958- *BiDrAPA 89*
Isbell, Robert 1923- *WhoAm 90*
Isbell, Virginia 1932- *WhoAmW 91*
Isberg, Roberta S *BiDrAPA 89*
Isbin, Herbert Stanford 1919- *WhoAm 90*
Isbin, Sharon 1956- *IntWWM 90*
Isbister, David Kent 1940- *WhoAm 90*
Isbister, James David 1937- *WhoAm 90*
Isbister, Jenefir Diane Wilkinson 1936- *WhoSSW 91*
Ischer, Robert 1950- *IntWWM 90*
Isdaner, Lawrence Arthur 1934- *WhoE 91*
Isdell, E. Neville 1943- *St&PR 91*
Isdell, Sarah *FemiCLE*
Ise, Carolyn E *BiDrAPA 89*
Isele, David Clark 1946- *IntWWM 90*
Isele, Elizabeth 1942- *WhoWrEP 89*
Iseley, R.F. 1939- *St&PR 91*
Iseli, Andre W. 1932- *St&PR 91*
Iselin, Barry Martin 1947- *WhoEmL 91*
Iselin, Donald Grote 1922- *WhoAm 90*
Iselin, John Jay 1933- *WhoAm 90*
Iselin, Lewis 1913- *WhoE 91*
Iselin, Madeline Mary 1955- *WhoEmL 91*
Iselin, Peter 1920- *St&PR 91*
Iselin, Sally Cary 1915- *WhoAmW 91, WhoE 91*
Isely, Duane 1918- *WhoAm 90*
Isely, Henry Philip 1915- *WhoWor 91*
Iseman, Joseph S. 1916- *St&PR 91*
Iseman, Joseph Seeman 1916- *WhoAm 90*
Iseman, Michael Dee 1939- *WhoAm 90*
Iseman, Murray 1943- *St&PR 91*
Iseman, Robert D. 1948- *St&PR 91*
Isen, Alice M. *WhoAm 90*
Isenberg, Abraham Charles 1914- *WhoAm 90*
Isenberg, Bruce Kenneth 1946- *WhoEmL 91*
Isenberg, Dave 1936- *St&PR 91*
Isenberg, Eugene M. 1929- *St&PR 91*
Isenberg, Henry David 1922- *WhoAm 90*
Isenberg, Howard 1936- *St&PR 91*
Isenberg, Howard Lee 1936- *WhoAm 90*
Isenberg, Jon Irwin 1937- *WhoAm 90*
Isenberg, Keith Eugene 1951- *BiDrAPA 89*
Isenberg, Morris 1906- *BiDrAPA 89*
Isenberg, Paul David 1949- *WhoEmL 91, WhoSSW 91*
Isenberg, Phillip L 1930- *BiDrAPA 89*
Isenberg, Phillip L. 1939- *WhoAm 90*
Isenberg, Phillip Louis 1930- *WhoE 91*
Isenberg, Sidney 1921- *BiDrAPA 89*
Isenberg, Steven Lawrence 1940- *WhoE 91*
Isenbergh, Max 1913- *WhoAm 90*
Isenburger, Eric 1902- *WhoAm 90, WhoAmA 91*
Isengard, Chris S. 1948- *WhoEmL 91*
Isenhower, Eleanor Anne 1946- *WhoEmL 91*
Isenman, David Morris *BiDrAPA 89*
Isennock, Mary Rose 1925- *WhoAmW 91*
Isenor, Linda Darlene 1955- *WhoAmW 91*
Isepp, Martin Johannes Sebastian 1930- *IntWWM 90*
Iserbyt, Georgina 1915- *BiDWomA*
Iseri, Hirofumi 1947- *WhoWor 91*
Iseri, Mike 1954- *St&PR 91*
Iserman, Jim 1955- *WhoAmA 91*
Isermann, Michael Ralph 1946- *St&PR 91*
Isern, Raul Dario, Jr. *BiDrAPA 89*
Isetani, Hiroshi 1926- *WhoWor 91*
Isgro, Joseph Anthone 1938- *St&PR 91*
Isgur, Nathan Gerald 1947- *WhoAm 90*
Ish, Daniel Russell 1946- *WhoAm 90*
Ish-Kishor, Sulamith 1896-1977 *AuBYP 90*
Ishac, Fathy F *BiDrAPA 89*
Ishak, Samira A *BiDrAPA 89*
Isham, A Chapman *BiDrAPA 89*
Isham, Alfred H. *BioIn 16*
Isham, Carolynn Clough 1947- *WhoAmW 91*
Isham, Chris *BioIn 16*
Isham, Dewey Edward, Jr. 1947- *WhoSSW 91*
Isham, Kathryn Lane 1955- *WhoAmW 91*
Isham, Mark *NewAgMG*
Isham, Sheila Eaton 1927- *WhoAm 90*
Ishaque, Saleem 1949- *BiDrAPA 89*
Ishaque, Sultana N 1953- *BiDrAPA 89*
Ishatai *WhNaAH*
Ishay, Ram Raymond 1931- *WhoWor 91*
Ishee, Dixie White 1955- *WhoSSW 91*
Ishee, Robert Raymond 1934- *St&PR 91*
Ishee, William Willis, Jr. *WhoSSW 91, WhoWor 91*
Isherwood, Charles S. 1933- *St&PR 91*
Isherwood, Christopher 1904-1986 *MajTwCW, WorAlBi, WrPh*
Isherwood, Diane Marie *BiDrAPA 89*
Isherwood, John S. 1940- *St&PR 91, WhoAm 90*
Isherwood, Robert P. *BioIn 16*
Isherwood, Robert Paul 1940- *St&PR 91*
Ishi 1862?-1916 *WhNaAH*
Ishi, Hiromitsu 1937- *WhoWor 91*
Ishibashi, Fusao 1922- *WhoWor 91*
Ishibashi, Yoshikazu 1957- *WhoWor 91*
Ishida, Koshiro 1930- *WhoWor 91*
Ishida, Yoichi 1935- *WhoWor 91*
Ishigaki, Emiko Hannah 1931- *WhoWor 91*
Ishiguro, Kazuo 1954- *BioIn 16, ConLC 59 [port], CurBio 90 [port], MajTwCW, NewYTBS 90 [port], WhoWor 91*
Ishiguro, Naobumi 1931- *WhoWor 91*
Ishihara, Hideo 1929- *WhoWor 91*
Ishihara, Minoru 1928- *WhoWor 91*
Ishihara, Ren 1928- *WhoWor 91*
Ishihara, Shintaro *BioIn 16*
Ishii Mitsujiro 1889-1981 *EncJap*
Ishii, Ben Twotom 1935- *WhoWor 91*
Ishii, Robert F. 1956- *St&PR 91*
Ishii, Takashi 1935- *WhoWor 91*
Ishii, Takemi 1941- *WhoWor 91*
Ishikawa Jun 1899- *EncJap*
Ishikawa, Brenda 1952- *IntWWM 90*
Ishikawa, Hiroshi 1930- *St&PR 91*
Ishikawa, Joseph 1919- *WhoAmA 91*
Ishikawa, Kazuo 1927- *WhoWor 91*
Ishikawa, Kozo 1947- *WhoWor 91*
Ishikawa, Minoru Keizo 1927- *WhoWor 91*
Ishikawa, Shigeru 1918- *WhoWor 91*
Ishikawa, Shizuka 1954- *IntWWM 90*
Ishikawa, Tadahisa 1932- *WhoWor 91*
Ishikawa, Tadao 1922- *WhoWor 91*
Ishikawa, Takuboku 1886-1912 *BioIn 16*
Ishikawa, Tetsuro 1945- *IntWWM 90*
Ishikawa, Yoshiyuki 1953- *IntWWM 90*
Ishikawa, Zenzaburo 1922- *St&PR 91*
Ishiki, Dean Mitsuo 1941- *BiDrAPA 89*
Ishimaru, Akira 1928- *WhoAm 90*
Ishimoto, Fujiwo 1941- *ConDes 90*
Ishizaka, Jiro 1927- *St&PR 91*
Ishizaki, Hatsuo 1921- *WhoWor 91*
Ishizaki, Tatsushi 1915- *WhoWor 91*
Ishizuka, Yukio 1938- *BiDrAPA 89*
Ishkanian, Mark A. *ODwPR 91*
Ishler, Norman H. 1914- *St&PR 91*
Ishmael, Darrell Lewis 1952- *WhoEmL 91*
Ishoy, Steen 1941- *WhoWor 91*
Isidoro, Edith Annette 1957- *WhoEmL 91*
Isidro, Romeo L. 1957- *BiDrAPA 89*
Isidro, Rose Marie 1940- *BiDrAPA 89*
Ising, E. James 1941- *St&PR 91*
Iskandar, Hani Lawendy *BiDrAPA 89*
Iskandar, Nanang Rachmatullah Ibnu 1945- *WhoWor 91*
Iskandarani, Nimer Mahmoud 1935- *BiDrAPA 89*
Iskander, Atef 1946- *St&PR 91*
Iskander, Felib Youssef 1949- *WhoSSW 91*

Iskander, Trevor Nagib 1930- *BiDrAPA 89*
Iskeliunas, Irena 1949- *ODwPR 91*
Isko, Irving David 1927- *WhoAm 90*
Isko, Norman S. 1930- *St&PR 91*
Iskowitz, Gershon 1921-1988 *WhoAmA 91N*
Islam, Kazi Azizul *BiDrAPA 89*
Islam, Manzurul 1943- *WhoWor 91*
Islam, Mohammed S 1946- *BiDrAPA 89*
Islam, Nurul 1929- *WhoE 91*
Islam, Saiful Kamal 1948- *WhoWor 91*
Islam, Sajan Saiful 1951- *WhoWor 91*
Islam, Shaheen Momtaz 1951- *WhoSSW 91*
Islam, Yusuf *BioIn 16*
Islan, Gregory deFontaine 1947- *WhoE 91, WhoEmL 91*
Islander, Steve 1946- *St&PR 91*
Islas, Arturo 1938- *ConAu 131, HispWr 90, WhoHisp 91*
Islas, Maya C. 1947- *WhoHisp 91*
Isle, John Stanley 1923- *WhoAm 90*
Isler, Ralph Charles 1933- *WhoSSW 91*
Isler, Vicki Jan 1955- *WhoAmW 91*
Isles, Marvin Lee 1946- *WhoAm 90*
Isles, Thomas Aquinas 1952- *WhoEmL 91*
Islew, Bert 1861- *BioIn 16*
Isley Brothers *EncPR&S 89, OxCPMus*
Isley, Ernie *BioIn 16*
Isley, John Charles 1950- *WhoAm 90*
Isley, O'Kelly 1937-1986 *EncPR&S 89, OxCPMus*
Isley, Robert Arnold 1947- *WhoSSW 91*
Isley, Ronald 1941- *EncPR&S 89, OxCPMus*
Isley, Rudolph 1939- *EncPR&S 89, OxCPMus*
Isley, Timothy Charles *BiDrAPA 89*
Islinger, Robert Scott 1956- *WhoEmL 91*
Ismach, Arnold Harvey 1930- *WhoAm 90*
Ismael, Hirosi Harold 1936- *WhoWor 91*
Ismail Petra Ibni Al-Marhum Tuanku *WhoWor 91*
Ismail, Abd Al-Fattah 1939-1986 *PolLCME*
Ismail, Amr A. 1940- *St&PR 91*
Ismail, Ismail Mahmoud Kamal 1945- *WhoEmL 91*
Ismail, Mohamed A. 1938- *WhoSSW 91*
Ismail, Mohammad 1952- *WhoE 91*
Ismail, Moosa 1945- *WhoWor 91*
Ismail, Raghib *BioIn 16*
Ismail, Yahia Hassan 1938- *WhoAm 90*
Isman, Lloyd Ellis 1946- *WhoEmL 91*
Isoda, Takuro 1936- *St&PR 91*
Isola, Aimaro Oreglia d' *PenDiDA 89*
Isola, Joseph Charles 1947- *St&PR 91*
Isole, Louise d' *EncCoWW*
Isom, Harriet Winsar 1936- *WhoAm 90, WhoAmW 91, WhoWor 91*
Isom, Lawrence E *BiDrAPA 89*
Isom, Lloyd Warren 1928- *St&PR 91*
Isomura, Kazuhide *PenDiMP*
Isomura, Theresa *BiDrAPA 89*
Ison, Christopher John 1957- *WhoAm 90*
Ison, J.D. 1928- *St&PR 91*
Ison, James Ratcliffe 1935- *WhoAm 90*
Ison, Robert Elwood 1955- *WhoEmL 91*
Isono, Kunio 1946- *WhoWor 91*
Isorni, Jacques Alfred Antoine Tibere 1911- *BiDFrPL*
Isozaki, Arata *BioIn 16*
Isozaki, Arata 1931- *News 90 [port], WhoWor 91*
Ispahani, Abbas *BiDrAPA 89*
Ispahecher 1829-1902 *WhNaAH*
Isparheche 1829-1902 *WhNaAH*
Ispass, Alan Benjamin 1953- *WhoAm 90, WhoSSW 91*
Isquith, Fred Taylor 1947- *WhoE 91, WhoEmL 91, WhoWor 91*
Israel, Adrian C. 1915- *St&PR 91*
Israel, Adrian Cremieux 1915- *WhoAm 90*
Israel, Betsy 1958- *BioIn 16*
Israel, David 1951- *WhoAm 90*
Israel, Dennis Robert 1942- *WhoAm 90*
Israel, Diana Kelleher 1947- *WhoEmL 91*
Israel, Edouard 1946- *WhoAm 90, WhoE 91*
Israel, Ellen *BioIn 16*
Israel, Franklin David 1945- *BioIn 16*
Israel, Fred Carl 1933- *WhoAm 90*
Israel, Harold *BioIn 16*
Israel, Ira M. *BiDrAPA 89*
Israel, Ira M. 1919- *WhoE 91*
Israel, James Ray 1936- *BiDrAPA 89*
Israel, Jerold Harvey 1934- *WhoAm 90*
Israel, Joseph S. 1928- *St&PR 91*
Israel, Kenneth *BiDrAPA 89*
Israel, Lawrence 1929- *St&PR 91*
Israel, Lesley Lowe 1938- *ODwPR 91, WhoE 91*
Israel, Lucien Isidore 1926- *WhoWor 91*
Israel, Lynne Charlene 1946- *WhoE 91*
Israel, Marcel Salvator 1945- *WhoWor 91*
Israel, Marcia 1930- *St&PR 91*
Israel, Margie Olanoff 1927- *WhoAmW 91, WhoE 91*
Israel, Maria Caunca *BiDrAPA 89*
Israel, Marvin 1924-1985 *WhoAmA 91N*
Israel, Michael 1933- *St&PR 91*
Israel, Mimi *BiDrAPA 89*
Israel, Nancy Diane 1955- *WhoWor 91*
Israel, Patrick 1922- *BiDrAPA 89*
Israel, Ricardo Zipper 1950- *WhoWor 91*
Israel, Richard Jerome 1930- *WhoAm 90*
Israel, Robert Allan 1933- *WhoAm 90, WhoE 91*
Israel, Robert H *BiDrAPA 89*
Israel, Saul 1910-1990 *BioIn 16, ConAu 131*
Israel, Steven Barry *BiDrAPA 89*
Israel, Steven Max 1953- *WhoEmL 91*
Israel, Vivianne Winters 1954- *WhoAmW 91, WhoEmL 91*
Israel, Werner 1931- *WhoAm 90*
Israelievitch, Jacques Herbert 1948- *WhoAm 90*
Israelowitz, Oscar 1949- *ConAu 32NR*
Israels, Lyonel Garry 1926- *WhoAm 90*
Israelsen, Loren David 1955- *St&PR 91*
Israelsen, Ned Alma 1954- *WhoEmL 91*
Israelsky, Roberta Schwartz 1954- *WhoAmW 91*
Israelson, Chase 1933- *St&PR 91*
Israelstam, David Michael 1939- *BiDrAPA 89*
Israely, Robert Alvin 1941- *BiDrAPA 89*
Israili, Zafar Hasan 1934- *WhoAm 90*
Israni, Kim 1935- *WhoWor 91*
Isroff, Lola K *WhoAmA 91*
Issa, Aswad Hashim Asim 1948- *WhoEmL 91, WhoWor 91*
Issa, Daniel J. 1952- *WhoE 91*
Issa, Fuad 1956- *BiDrAPA 89*
Issacharoff, Ammon 1927- *BiDrAPA 89*
Issaeva, Lyudmila 1926- *EncCoWW*
Issari, Mohammad Ali 1921- *WhoAm 90*
Issawi, Charles Philip 1916- *WhoAm 90*
Issei Miyake *EncJap*
Issel, Dan 1948- *WorAlBi*
Issel, Leila *BioIn 16*
Issel, Shahieda *BioIn 16*
Isselbacher, Kurt Julius 1925- *WhoAm 90*
Isser, Michael 1939- *ODwPR 91*
Isserlis, Steven 1958- *IntWWM 90*
Isserman, Joan Louise 1952- *WhoAmW 91*
Isseroff, Avraham Z *BiDrAPA 89*
Isserstedt, Dorothea Carus *WhoAmA 91*
Issigonis, Alec 1906-1988 *AnObit 1988, BioIn 16, ConDes 90*
Issing, Otmar 1936- *WhoWor 91*
Issleib, Lutz E. 1944- *St&PR 91*
Issleib, Lutz E. 1945- *WhoAm 90*
Issler, Harry 1935- *WhoAm 90, WhoE 91, WhoWor 91*
Issler, Robert F. 1951- *St&PR 91*
Issokson-Silver, Karen Lee 1965- *WhoAmW 91*
Istel, Jacques Andre 1929- *WhoAm 90*
Istel, Yves-Andre 1936- *St&PR 91*
Istock, Verne George 1940- *St&PR 91, WhoAm 90*
Istomin, Eugene 1925- *PenDiMP*
Istomin, Eugene George 1925- *IntWWM 90*
Istomin, Marta Casals 1936- *WhoAm 90, WhoAmW 91, WhoE 91, WhoHisp 91*
Istvan, Kristo Nagy 1921- *WhoWor 91*
Istvan, Miloslav 1928- *IntWWM 90*
Isvekov, Sergey Mikhailovich 1910-1990 *BioIn 16*
Iszard, Calvin Oscar, Jr. 1943- *WhoE 91*
Iszard, Robert French 1919- *St&PR 91*
Itabashi, Hideo Henry 1926- *WhoAm 90*
Itagaki Taisuke 1837-1919 *EncJap*
Italiaander, Rolf Bruno Maximilian 1913- *WhoWor 91*
Italiano, Joan *WhoAmA 91*
Italiano, Joseph John, III 1955- *WhoEmL 91*
Italiano, Quartetto *PenDiMP*
Itameri-Kinter, Terry 1953- *St&PR 91*
Itami Juzo *EncJap*
Itami, Juzo *BioIn 16*
Itami, Juzo 1933- *CurBio 90 [port]*
Itano, Harvey Akio 1920- *WhoAm 90*
Itano, Leslie Michiya 1954- *WhoEmL 91*
Itasse, Jeanne 1867- *BiDWomA*
Itatani, Michiko 1948- *WhoAmA 91*
Itchkawich, David Michael 1937- *WhoAmA 91*
Itchy Fingers *NewAgMG*
Iten, C. John 1955- *St&PR 91*
Iten, Joseph 1943- *WhoWor 91*
Ites, William Jay 1950- *St&PR 91*
Itil, Turan M *BiDrAPA 89*
Itim, Talang *ConAu 130*
Itin, James Richard 1933- *St&PR 91, WhoAm 90*
Itjen, Phyllis D. 1951- *WhoAmW 91*
Itkin, Robert Jeffrey 1956- *WhoEmL 91*
Itnyre, John Francis 1950- *WhoEmL 91*
Ito Hirobumi 1841-1909 *EncJap*
Ito, Atsuko 1933- *WhoWor 91*
Ito, Hirobumi 1841-1909 *WorAlBi*
Ito, Kentaro 1939- *WhoWor 91*
Ito, Midori 1969- *NewYTBS 90 [port]*
Ito, Rikuma 1931- *St&PR 91*
Ito, Shima 1937- *ConDes 90*
Ito, Takeo 1895- *BioIn 16*
Ito, Yoshitada Zen 1917- *WhoWor 91*
Ito, Zenichi 1924- *WhoWor 91*
Itoh, Akira *NewAgMG*
Itoh, Seishichi 1935- *St&PR 91*
Itoh, Tatsuo 1940- *WhoAm 90*
Itoigawa, Naosuke 1935- *WhoWor 91*
Itokawa, Yoshinori 1933- *WhoWor 91*
Itskovitz, Harold David 1929- *WhoAm 90*
Itskowitz, Harvey Z 1943- *BiDrAPA 89*
Itson, Sonja Patrica 1943- *WhoAmW 91*
Itteilag, Anthony L. 1942- *WhoAm 90*
Itter, Diane 1946-1989 *BioIn 16*
Ittiara, Theethaye L 1941- *BiDrAPA 89*
Ittleson, Henry, Jr 1900-1973 *WhoAmA 91N*
Ittleson, Henry Anthony 1937- *WhoAm 90, WhoE 91*
Ittleson, Nancy S. *BioIn 16*
Itts, Elizabeth Ann Dunham 1928- *WhoAmW 91*
Ittzes, Mihaly 1938- *IntWWM 90*
Iturbi, Amparo 1898-1969 *PenDiMP*
Iturbi, Jose 1895-1980 *PenDiMP, WorAlBi*
Iturbide, Agustin de 1783-1824 *BioIn 16*
Iturralde, George 1921- *BiDrAPA 89*
Iturralde, Therese 1963- *WhoAmA 91*
Iturralde Ballivian, Carlos 1941- *WhoWor 91*
Iturrino, Luis Felipe 1936- *BiDrAPA 89*
Itzcowitz, Eden Beth 1962- *WhoAmW 91*
Itzin, Charles Francis 1946- *WhoWrEP 89*
Itzkoff, Norman Jay 1940- *WhoE 91*
Itzkowitz, Norman 1931- *WhoAm 90*
Itzler, Ronald Stephen 1937- *St&PR 91*
Iudica, Ross C. 1941- *St&PR 91*
Iuliano, Ronald Anthony 1950- *WhoEmL 91*
Ivan III 1440-1505 *EncO&P 3*
Ivan IV 1530-1584 *WorAlBi*
Ivan, Gustave *AuBYP 90*
Ivan, Marian O'Loane 1956- *WhoAmW 91*
Ivan, Martha Miller Pfaff 1909- *AuBYP 90*
Ivan, Thomas Nathaniel 1911- *WhoAm 90*
Ivanauskaite, Sofija Psibiliauskiene- 1867-1926 *EncCoWW*
Ivancevic, Walter Charles 1920- *WhoAm 90*
Ivancie, Francis J. 1924- *WhoAm 90*
Ivancin, Maria 1955- *ODwPR 91*
Ivanhoe, Herman 1908- *WhoE 91*
Ivanhoe, Ruth 1931- *St&PR 91*
Ivanick, Carol W. Trencher 1939- *WhoAm 90*
Ivanick, Joseph 1922- *St&PR 91*
Ivanier, Isin 1906- *WhoAm 90, WhoWor 91*
Ivanier, Paul 1932- *WhoAm 90, WhoWor 91*
Ivanissevich, Guillermo O *BiDrAPA 89*
Ivanoff, Bernard Nicolas 1939- *WhoWor 91*
Ivanoff, Georges Michel 1911- *WhoWor 91*
Ivanoff, Grigori Kiril 1960- *WhoEmL 91*
Ivanoff, Iraida Gustavovna 1909- *EncCoWW*
Ivanoff, Vassili *PenDiDA 89*
Ivanov, Konstantin 1907- *PenDiMP*
Ivanov, Nikola 1861- *BioIn 16*
Ivanov, Sergey 1949- *WhoWor 91*
Ivanov, Vyacheslav 1866-1949 *WrPh*
Ivanova, Barbara *EncO&P 3*
Ivanova, Barbara Mikhailovna 1917- *EncPaPR 91*
Ivans, W.S. 1920- *St&PR 91*
Ivans, William Stanley 1920- *WhoAm 90*
Ivanson, Gary Stephen 1948- *WhoEmL 91*
Ivany, Robert Rudolph 1947- *WhoAm 90*
Ivanyi, Jozef *PenDiMP*
Ivashko, Vladimir *WhoWor 91*
Ivaska, Astride 1926- *EncCoWW*
Ive, M. *EncCoWW*
Ivens, Georg Henri Anton 1898?-1989 *ConAu 129*
Ivens, Joris *ConAu 129*
Ivens, Joris 1898-1989 *AnObit 1989, BioIn 16*
Ivens, Mary Sue 1929- *WhoAmW 91, WhoSSW 91*
Iveroth, Carl Axel 1914- *WhoWor 91*
Ivers, Donald Louis 1941- *WhoAm 90*
Ivers, Louise H 1964- *WhoAmA 91*
Iversen, Earl Harvey 1943- *WhoAmA 91*
Iversen, James Delano 1933- *WhoAm 90*
Iversen, Nancy M. 1928- *WhoAmW 91*
Iversen, Robert W. *BioIn 16*
Iverson, Ann Cummings 1941- *WhoAmW 91*
Iverson, Betty L. 1934- *WhoSSW 91*
Iverson, Carl John 1940- *St&PR 91*
Iverson, Carrold K *BiDrAPA 89*
Iverson, F. Kenneth *BioIn 16*
Iverson, F Kenneth 1925- *ConAmBL*
Iverson, F. Kenneth 1925- *St&PR 91*
Iverson, Francis Kenneth 1925- *WhoAm 90, WhoSSW 91*
Iverson, Genie *WhoAmW 91*
Iverson, Genie 1942- *AuBYP 90, BioIn 16*
Iverson, John B. 1946- *St&PR 91*
Iverson, Jon Kermit 1956- *WhoEmL 91*
Iverson, Lucille Karin 1925- *WhoWrEP 89*
Iverson, Meegan *BioIn 16*
Iverson, Peter James 1944- *WhoAm 90*
Iverson, Robert F 1924- *BiDrAPA 89*
Iverson, Wayne Dahl 1931- *WhoAm 90*
Ives, Adriene Diane 1951- *WhoAmW 91, WhoE 91, WhoEmL 91*
Ives, Burl 1909- *OxCPMus, WorAlBi*
Ives, Charles 1874-1954 *PenDiMP A, WorAlBi*
Ives, Charles C. 1935- *St&PR 91*
Ives, Charles Edward 1874-1954 *BioIn 16*
Ives, Charles L. 1815-1880 *AmLegL*
Ives, Colta Feller 1943- *WhoAm 90, WhoAmA 91, WhoAmW 91*
Ives, David Otis 1919- *WhoAm 90*
Ives, Dermod 1904- *WhoAm 90*
Ives, Donald G 1925- *BiDrAPA 89*
Ives, Edward Dawson 1925- *WhoAm 90*
Ives, Elinor Randolph 1906- *WhoAmW 91*
Ives, Elsa Mott *BioIn 16*
Ives, Fredrick Eugene 1856-1937 *BioIn 16*
Ives, George *BioIn 16*
Ives, George Skinner 1922- *WhoAm 90*
Ives, J. Atwood 1936- *St&PR 91, WhoAm 90*
Ives, James Merritt 1824-1895 *WorAlBi*
Ives, John David 1931- *WhoAm 90*
Ives, John Othniel 1939- *BiDrAPA 89*
Ives, Kenneth Holbrook 1916- *WhoWrEP 89*
Ives, Lister Cornelius, Jr. 1952- *WhoSSW 91*
Ives, Margaret 1903- *WhoAm 90*
Ives, Norman S 1924-1978 *WhoAmA 91N*
Ives, Rich Lee 1951- *WhoWrEP 89*
Ives, Ronn Brian 1950- *WhoAm 90*
Ives, Stephen Bradshaw, Jr. 1924- *WhoE 91*
Ives, Suzanne Lintz 1941- *WhoE 91*
Ives, Timothy R. 1928- *St&PR 91*
Ives, W. Byron 1928- *St&PR 91*
Ives, Washington 1843-1925 *BioIn 16*
Ives, William Bullock 1841-1899 *DcCanB 12*
Ivester, Hubert Clifford, Jr. 1931- *WhoAm 90*
Ivester, J. Harold 1940- *St&PR 91*
Ivester, Mark Allen 1947- *WhoSSW 91*
Ivester, Melvin Douglas 1947- *WhoAm 90*
Ivester, Robert Donald 1932- *WhoSSW 91*
Ivey, Anthony D. *St&PR 91*
Ivey, Charles McKinnon, Jr. 1922- *St&PR 91*
Ivey, David Malcolm 1952- *WhoSSW 91*
Ivey, Elizabeth S. 1935- *WhoAm 90*
Ivey, Harriet M. 1949- *St&PR 91*
Ivey, Helene Gores *WhoAmW 91*
Ivey, James Burnett 1925- *WhoAm 90, WhoAmA 91*
Ivey, Jean Eichelberger 1923- *WhoAm 90*
Ivey, John Allen 1963- *WhoE 91*
Ivey, John Courtney 1903-1989 *BioIn 16*
Ivey, John Smith, Sr. 1942- *WhoE 91*
Ivey, Judith 1951- *ConTFT 8 [port], WhoAm 90, WhoAmW 91*
Ivey, Kay Ellen 1944- *WhoAmW 91*
Ivey, Michael Wayne 1964- *WhoSSW 91*
Ivey, Reanee Nanette 1957- *WhoAmW 91*
Ivey, Reef Challance, II 1943- *WhoAm 90*
Ivey, Richard Macaulay 1925- *St&PR 91, WhoAm 90*
Ivey, Robert Carl 1939- *WhoAm 90, WhoSSW 91*
Ivey, Robert Gene 1940- *WhoSSW 91*
Ivey, William Hamilton 1951- *WhoEmL 91*
Ivey, William James 1944- *WhoAm 90, WhoSSW 91*
Ivey-Davis, Evelyn P 1914- *BiDrAPA 89*
Ivey-Davis, Evelyn Parker 1914- *WhoE 91*
Ivezaj, Frano Leka 1958- *WhoEmL 91*
Ivie, Leslie Todd 1960- *WhoE 91*
Ivie, Mike 1952- *Ballpl 90*
Ivie, Theodosia *BiDEWW*
Ivimey, John W. *AuBYP 90*
Ivins, J Leonard *BiDrAPA 89*
Ivins, Marsha S. 1951- *WhoAmW 91*
Ivins, Samuel P 1920- *BiDrAPA 89*
Ivins, Steven David 1937- *WhoE 91*
Ivins, William M, Jr 1881-1961 *WhoAmA 91N*
Ivkovich, Walter Michael, Jr. 1948- *WhoSSW 91*
Ivo, Ledo *BioIn 16*
Ivo, Ledo 1924- *ConAu 129*
Ivogun, Maria 1891-1987 *PenDiMP*
Ivory, Hugh Gordon 1929- *WhoWor 91*
Ivory, J. Angus 1932- *St&PR 91*
Ivory, James *BioIn 16*
Ivory, James Francis 1928- *WhoAm 90*
Ivory, Ming Marie 1949- *WhoAmW 91*

Ivory, Neil B. *St&PR 91N*
Ivory, Peter B C B 1927- *BiDrAPA 89*
Ivory, Peter B. C. B. 1927- *WhoAm 90*
Ivry, Alfred Lyon 1935- *WhoAm 90*
Ivry, Patricia Weisman 1950- *WhoEmL 91*
Ivsic, Mathieu Michel 1934- *WhoWor 91*
Ivy, Conway Gayle 1941- *WhoAm 90*
Ivy, David E. 1934- *St&PR 91*
Ivy, Edward Everett 1913- *WhoWor 91*
Ivy, Lesley *ODwPR 91*
Ivy, Robert Adams, Jr. 1947- *WhoEmL 91, WhoSSW 91*
Ivy, Robert E. 1933- *St&PR 91*
Ivy, Stephen Craig 1945- *WhoEmL 91*
Ivy, Woodland Howell 1925- *St&PR 91*
Iwai, Kazuo 1925- *WhoWor 91*
Iwaki, Hidehiro 1956- *WhoWor 91*
Iwaki, Hiroyuki 1932- *PenDiMP*
Iwakura *EncJap*
Iwamasa, Ken 1943- *WhoAmA 91*
Iwamatsu, Jun Altsushi 1908- *AuBYP 90*
Iwamoto, Jani 1960- *WhoEmL 91*
Iwamoto, Ralph Shigeto 1927- *WhoAmA 91*
Iwamoto, Roy 1928-1987 *BioIn 16*
Iwamura, Kazuo 1939- *ConAu 129*
Iwan, Wilfred Dean 1935- *WhoAm 90*
Iwanami, Yujiro 1919- *WhoWor 91*
Iwaniuk, Wactaw 1915- *ConAu 130*
Iwanski, Marie Ida 1948- *WhoAmW 91*
Iwasa, Shinichi 1947- *WhoEmL 91*
Iwasaka, Dennis K. 1944- *St&PR 91*
Iwasaki, Iwao 1929- *WhoAm 90*
Iwasaki, Ko 1944- *IntWWM 90*
Iwasaki, Kojiro Mike 1922- *St&PR 91*
Iwasaki, Tadaaki 1934- *WhoWor 91*
Iwasaki, Tetsuo *St&PR 91*
Iwasaki, Tetsuya 1935- *WhoWor 91*
Iwasaki, Tsutomu 1948- *WhoWor 91*
Iwasaki, Zensuke 1933- *WhoWor 91*
Iwashita, Takeki 1931- *WhoWor 91*
Iwashyna, Basil 1939- *WhoE 91*
Iwata, Jan Lei 1959- *WhoE 91*
Iwata, Yasuo 1932- *WhoWor 91*
Iwata, Yoshio 1925- *WhoWor 91*
Iway, Olivia Nunez *BiDrAPA 89*
Iwersen, Alfred, Jr. 1939- *St&PR 91*
Iwicki, Stanley D. 1946- *St&PR 91*
Iwinski, James Phillip 1960- *WhoEmL 91, WhoWor 91*
Iworsley, Arthur W. 1946- *WhoE 91*
Iwuc, John J. *BiDrAPA 89*
Ix, Robert Edward 1929- *WhoAm 90*
Iyannos *WhNaAH*
Iyanough *WhNaAH*
Iyengar, B. K. S. 1918- *BioIn 16*
Iyengar, Srinivasa 1934- *WhoAm 90*
Iyengar, Srinivasa T.K. 1933- *WhoWor 91*
Iyer, B. Rajam 1922- *WhoAm 90*
Iyer, Mala Sridhar *BiDrAPA 89*
Iyoda, Mitsuhiko 1943- *WhoWor 91*
Izaak, Martin 1945- *WhoEmL 91*
Izac, Ed V 1891-1990 *CurBio 90N*
Izac, Edouard V. M. *NewYTBS 90*
Izac, Edouard V. M. 1891-1990 *BioIn 16*
Izadi, Hossein J 1919- *BiDrAPA 89*
Izaguirre, Leandro 1867-1941 *ArtLatA*
Izant, Robert James, Jr. 1921- *WhoAm 90*
Izard, Anne R. 1916-1990 *BioIn 16*
Izard, Carroll Ellis 1923- *WhoAm 90*
Izard, John 1923- *WhoAm 90*
Izard, Ralph 1741-1804 *EncCRAm*
Izard, Ralph 1742-1804 *BioIn 16*
Izard, Ralph Sidney 1935- *WhoSSW 91*
Izatt, Jerald Ray 1928- *WhoSSW 91*
Izdebski, Christy Isabel 1946- *IntWWM 90*
Izen, Raymond Larry 1941- *WhoE 91*
Izenberg, Jerry *AuBYP 90*
Izenberg, Jerry 1930- *Ballpl 90*
Izenour, Christine 1949- *WhoAmW 91*
Izenour, George Charles 1912- *WhoAm 90*
Izenstark, Joseph Louis 1919- *WhoAm 90*
Izenstark, Robert C. *St&PR 91*
Izenzon, Pearl *BioIn 16*
Izlar, Robert Lee 1949- *WhoSSW 91*
Izlar, William Henry, Jr. 1931- *WhoAm 90*
Izmitli, Ara 1945- *WhoWor 91*
Izner, Sanford M 1920- *BiDrAPA 89*
Izon, Noel Maria 1946- *WhoAm 90*
Izquierdo, Maria 1902-1955 *ArtLatA*
Izquierdo, Maria 1906-1955 *BioIn 16*
Izquierdo, Maria B *BiDrAPA 89*
Izquierdo, Martin *BioIn 16*
Izuka, Kunio 1939- *WhoAmA 91, WhoE 91*
Izumi Shikibu *EncJap*
Izumi, Kiyoshi 1921- *WhoAmA 91*
Izumi, Masuko Inoue 1927- *WhoWor 91*
Izumi, Yoji 1942- *St&PR 91*
Izurieta, Fabian 1946- *WhoWor 91*
Izutsu, Satoru 1928- *WhoAm 90*
Izza, Michael *BioIn 16*
Izzi, Anthony J. 1947- *St&PR 91*
Izzi, John Donald 1931- *WhoE 91, WhoWor 91*
Izzi, Peter W., Jr. 1947- *St&PR 91*
Izzidien, Jousif 1922- *WhoWor 91*
Izzo, Francis Edmund 1950- *WhoEmL 91*
Izzo, George Martin 1949- *WhoSSW 91*
Izzo, Henry J. 1935- *St&PR 91*
Izzo, Louis Dominic 1925- *WhoE 91*
Izzo, Lucille Anne 1954- *WhoAmW 91*
Izzo, Ralph 1957- *WhoEmL 91*
Izzo, Richard S. 1951- *WhoE 91*
Izzo D'Amico, Fiamma 1964- *IntWWM 90*

J

J J 1932- *WhoAmA 91*
J L-M *ConAu 31NR*
Ja'afar Ibni Al-Marhum Abdul Rahman 1922- *WhoWor 91*
Jaafar, Mohamed Ali 1924- *WhoWor 91*
Jaakkola, Jouko Matti 1944- *WhoWor 91*
Jaar, Alfredo 1956- *WhoAmA 91*
Jabalpurwala, Kaizer Esufali 1932- *WhoWor 91*
Jabara, Francis Dwight 1924- *WhoAm 90*
Jabara, Michael Dean 1952- *WhoEmL 91*
Jabavu, Noni 1919?- *FemiCLE*
Jabbar, Kareem Abdul- 1947- *BioIn 16*
Jabbar-Malik, M.A. 1933- *St&PR 91*
Jaben, Edward 1926- *St&PR 91*
Jaben, Jan Elaine 1952- *WhoWrEP 89*
Jaber al-Ahmad al-Jaber al-Sabah 1926- *BioIn 16*
Jabir Al-Ahmad 1926- *PolLCME*
Jabir al-Ahmad al-Jabir Al-Sabah, Sheikh 1926- *WhoWor 91*
Jablecki, Donna Mae 1943- *WhoAmW 91*
Jablin, Laurie Clark 1921- *WhoAmW 91*
Jablon, Elaine 1950- *WhoSSW 91*
Jablon, Norman C *BiDrAPA 89*
Jablon, Scott William 1954- *WhoEmL 91*
Jablonowski, Adam Robert 1944- *WhoSSW 91*
Jablonski, David 1949- *St&PR 91*
Jablonski, Edward 1922- *AuBYP 90, WhoAm 90, WhoWrEP 89*
Jablonski, James Joseph 1944- *St&PR 91*
Jablonski, Louis John, Jr. 1950- *WhoEmL 91*
Jablonski, Michael J. 1941- *ODwPR 91*
Jablonski, Ray 1926-1985 *Ballpl 90*
Jablonski, Richard J. 1939- *St&PR 91*
Jablonski, Ronald E. 1954- *St&PR 91*
Jablonski, Wanda Mary *WhoWor 91*
Jablonsky, Harvey 1909-1989 *BioIn 16*
Jablow, Arnold 1942- *St&PR 91*
Jablow, Jeffrey *St&PR 91*
Jablow, Peter Anthony 1950- *WhoE 91*
Jabotinsky, Vladimir 1880-1940 *BioIn 16*
Jabs, Jacob 1930- *St&PR 91*
Jacangelo, Pia Maria 1954- *WhoAmW 91*
Jacaruso, Yvette C. 1938- *WhoE 91*
Jaccard, Walter B. 1953- *St&PR 91*
Jaccottet, Philippe 1925- *ConAu 129*
Jacenko, Brian G. 1952- *St&PR 91*
Jacey, Charles Frederick, Jr. 1936- *WhoE 91*
Jachacz, Bogdan Witold 1941- *WhoWor 91*
Jache, Albert William 1924- *WhoAm 90*
Jache, Heidi 1956- *BiDrAPA 89*
Jachera, J.T. 1930- *St&PR 91*
Jachmann, Christine 1949- *WomArch [port]*
Jachmann-Wagner, Johanna *PenDiMP*
Jachna, John Stanley *BiDrAPA 89*
Jachna, Joseph D. 1935- *WhoAm 90*
Jachna, Joseph David 1935- *WhoAmA 91*
Jachowski, Jan 1891- *EncO&P 3*
Jacinto, George Anthony 1949- *WhoEmL 91, WhoSSW 91, WhoWor 91*
Jacisin, John James 1942- *BiDrAPA 89*
Jack *WhNaAH*
Jack the Ripper *BioIn 16, EncO&P 3, EncPaPR 91, WorAlBi*
Jack, Charles R. 1935- *St&PR 91*
Jack, Elizabeth L *BiDrAPA 89*
Jack, Gary Adamson 1959- *WhoEmL 91*
Jack, George Washington 1855-1932 *PenDiDA 89*
Jack, Homer Alexander 1916- *WhoAm 90*
Jack, James Clyde, Jr. 1919- *St&PR 91*
Jack, James E. 1941- *St&PR 91, WhoAm 90*
Jack, Nancy Rayford 1939- *WhoAm 90, WhoAmW 91*
Jack, Phyllis Harris 1934- *WhoAmW 91, WhoSSW 91*
Jack, Richard *WhoAmA 91N*
Jack, Richard Wright 1949- *St&PR 91*
Jack, Timothy Charles 1958- *BiDrAPA 89*
Jack, Wayne Elmo 1943- *WhoAm 90*
Jack, William Irvine 1935- *WhoAm 90*
Jack, William S. 1888-1960 *WorAlBi*
Jackamets, Michael 1907- *BiDrAPA 89*
Jackamonis, Edward George 1939- *WhoAm 90*
Jackanin, Albina Veronica 1924- *WhoWrEP 89*
Jackard, Jerald Wayne *WhoAmA 91*
Jackee *BioIn 16, DrBlPA 90*
Jackee 19--?- *WorAlBi*
Jackel, Lawrence *WhoAm 90*
Jackel, Lawrence 1939- *St&PR 91*
Jackel, Merl M *BiDrAPA 89*
Jackel, Simon Samuel 1917- *WhoWor 91*
Jackels, Curt R. 1946- *St&PR 91*
Jackendoff, Nathaniel 1919- *WhoAm 90*
Jackendoff, Ray Saul 1945- *WhoAm 90*
Jackendoff, Ruth *BioIn 16*
Jacker, Corinne 1933- *AuBYP 90, FemiCLE*
Jacker, Corinne Litvin 1933- *WhoAm 90, WhoWrEP 89*
Jacker, Lauren Krent 1954- *BiDrAPA 89*
Jackier, Joseph Harold *St&PR 91N*
Jackins, Joseph A. 1947- *St&PR 91*
Jackle, Karen Dee 1945- *WhoAmW 91*
Jacklich, Joel 1948- *IntWWM 90*
Jacklin, Kathleen Bessie 1924- *WhoE 91*
Jacklin, Tony *BioIn 16*
Jacklin, Tony 1944- *WhoWor 91*
Jacklin, William Thomas 1940- *WhoWor 91*
Jacklitsch, Fred 1876-1937 *Ballpl 90*
Jackman, David G. 1947- *St&PR 91*
Jackman, David Gordon 1947- *WhoEmL 91*
Jackman, Francis Sweet 1921- *WhoSSW 91*
Jackman, Henry N.R. 1932- *St&PR 91*
Jackman, Jay M 1939- *BiDrAPA 89*
Jackman, Lloyd Miles 1926- *WhoAm 90*
Jackman, Michele 1944- *WhoWor 91*
Jackman, Robert Alan 1939- *WhoAm 90, WhoE 91, WhoWor 91*
Jackman, Roy P. 1924- *St&PR 91*
Jacko, Diane Newell *WhoWrEP 89*
Jackobs, Miriam Ann 1940- *WhoAmW 91*
Jackont, Amnon 1948- *ConAu 130*
Jackowiak, Patricia 1959- *WhoAmW 91, WhoEmL 91, WhoWor 91*
Jackowitz, Carol 1944- *St&PR 91*
Jackowitz, Edward C. *St&PR 91*
Jackowska, Nicki 1942- *FemiCLE*
Jackowski, Bill 1914- *Ballpl 90*
Jacks, Brian Paul 1943- *BiDrAPA 89*
Jacks, Bruce William 1947- *WhoEmL 91*
Jacks, Hugh H. 1932- *WhoSSW 91*
Jacks, L P 1860-1955 *EncO&P 3*
Jacks, Lawrence Pearsall 1860-1955 *EncPaPR 91*
Jacks, Oliver *TwCCr&M 91*
Jacks, Richard Kane 1941- *BiDrAPA 89*
Jackson 5 *EncPR&S 89*
Jackson family *BioIn 16*
Jackson Five, The *OxCPMus*
Jackson, A B 1925-1981 *WhoAmA 91N*
Jackson, Ada Jean Work *WhoSSW 91*
Jackson, Al 1935- *Ballpl 90*
Jackson, Alexander Young 1882-1974 *WhoAmA 91N*
Jackson, Alfred *BiDrAPA 89*
Jackson, Alfred, Jr. 1959- *WhoEmL 91*
Jackson, Allen Keith 1932- *WhoAm 90*
Jackson, Alvin 1935- *BioIn 16*
Jackson, Andrea Carroll 1945- *WhoAmW 91*
Jackson, Andrew 1767-1845 *BiDrUSE 89, BioIn 16, WhNaAH, WorAlBi*
Jackson, Andrew 1948- *WhoE 91*
Jackson, Andrew McBurney 1907-1989 *BioIn 16*
Jackson, Angela Ramona 1952- *WhoAmW 91*
Jackson, Ann *WhoAmA 91N*
Jackson, Anne *WhoAm 90, WhoAmW 91*
Jackson, Anne 1925- *WorAlBi*
Jackson, Annie Hurlburt 1877- *WhoAmA 91N*
Jackson, Anthony Haig *BiDrAPA 89*
Jackson, Arthur Howard 1956- *WhoE 91*
Jackson, Arthur Richard *BioIn 16*
Jackson, B.L., Jr. 1924- *St&PR 91*
Jackson, Barbara Ann Garvey 1929- *IntWWM 90*
Jackson, Barbara Bagley *BiDrAPA 89*
Jackson, Barbara Ward 1914- *BioIn 16*
Jackson, Bart 1941- *St&PR 91*
Jackson, Basil *BiDrAPA 89*
Jackson, Benita Marie 1956- *WhoAmW 91*
Jackson, Betty Eileen 1925- *WhoAmW 91, WhoWor 91*
Jackson, Betty Lou 1927- *WhoAmW 91, WhoWor 91*
Jackson, Bill D. 1937- *WhoAm 90*
Jackson, Billy Morrow 1926- *WhoAm 90, WhoAmA 91*
Jackson, Blaine Albert 1947- *WhoEmL 91*
Jackson, Blair *ODwPR 91*
Jackson, Blyden 1910- *WhoAm 90, WhoSSW 91*
Jackson, Bo *BioIn 16*
Jackson, Bo 1962- *Ballpl 90, WorAlBi*
Jackson, Bobby Rand 1931- *WhoAm 90*
Jackson, Bonnie L. *ODwPR 91*
Jackson, Brian 1926- *OxCCanT*
Jackson, Brian Anthony 1932-1983 *DcNaB 1981*
Jackson, Bruce 1933- *ODwPR 91*
Jackson, Bruce L. 1946- *St&PR 91*
Jackson, C. Robert 1939- *St&PR 91*
Jackson, Caary Paul 1902- *AuBYP 90*
Jackson, Carl Anthony 1958- *IntWWM 90*
Jackson, Carl Robert 1928- *WhoAm 90*
Jackson, Carl Sergei *BiDrAPA 89*
Jackson, Carlisle *St&PR 91N*
Jackson, Carmault Benjamin, Jr. 1924- *WhoAm 90*
Jackson, Carol Frances 1938- *WhoAmW 91, WhoSSW 91*
Jackson, Carolyn Laughlin 1938- *WhoSSW 91*
Jackson, Carolyn Wittorff 1953- *WhoAmW 91*
Jackson, Charles Ian 1935- *WhoAm 90*
Jackson, Charles Robert 1939- *WhoAm 90*
Jackson, Charles Wayne 1930- *WhoSSW 91*
Jackson, Charles Wilfrid 1933- *WhoE 91*
Jackson, Charlotte E 1903?-1989 *SmATA 62*
Jackson, Chris *BioIn 16*
Jackson, Claude *BioIn 16*
Jackson, Claude Gene 1925- *WhoSSW 91*
Jackson, Claudine Edith 1934- *WhoAmW 91*
Jackson, Clayton LeRoy 1917- *WhoAm 90*
Jackson, Constance Cordice *WhoAmW 91*
Jackson, Crawford Motley 1820-1860 *AmLegL*
Jackson, Curtis Maitland 1933- *WhoAm 90*
Jackson, D. Brooks 1941- *WhoAm 90*
Jackson, Dale Edward 1950- *WhoWor 91*
Jackson, Daniel *ODwPR 91*
Jackson, Daniel Francis 1925- *WhoAm 90*
Jackson, Daniel Kelvin 1950- *WhoEmL 91*
Jackson, Daniel Leslie *BiDrAPA 89*
Jackson, Danny *BioIn 16*
Jackson, Danny 1962- *Ballpl 90*
Jackson, Darrell 1956- *Ballpl 90*
Jackson, Darrin 1963- *Ballpl 90*
Jackson, Darryl Robert 1957- *St&PR 91*
Jackson, Daryl Sanders 1937- *WhoWor 91*
Jackson, David Allen 1955- *St&PR 91*
Jackson, David E. 1933- *WhoAm 90*
Jackson, David Gibson 1939- *St&PR 91*
Jackson, David Gordon 1947- *St&PR 91*
Jackson, David H. 1930- *St&PR 91*
Jackson, David Lee 1946- *WhoEmL 91*
Jackson, David Martin 1954- *WhoSSW 91*
Jackson, David Munro 1925- *WhoAm 90*
Jackson, David Pingree 1931- *WhoAm 90*
Jackson, David R. 1952- *WhoSSW 91*
Jackson, Della Rosetta Hayden 1905- *WhoAmW 91*
Jackson, Dempster McKee 1930- *WhoAm 90*
Jackson, Derek Ainslie 1906-1982 *DcNaB 1981*
Jackson, Dewey 1900- *BioIn 16*
Jackson, Diana Jean 1949- *WhoSSW 91*
Jackson, Diane Patricia 1947- *WhoEmL 91*
Jackson, Dolly Joyce 1932- *WhoAmW 91*
Jackson, Don J. 1934- *St&PR 91*
Jackson, Don Merrill 1913- *WhoAm 90*
Jackson, Donald Kenneth 1944- *WhoAm 90*
Jackson, Donald Raymond 1928- *St&PR 91*
Jackson, Donald Richard 1938- *WhoE 91*
Jackson, Donna Ann 1951- *WhoSSW 91*
Jackson, Donnie Leon 1956- *WhoE 91*
Jackson, Dudley Pennington 1924- *WhoAm 90*
Jackson, Earl B. 1936- *St&PR 91*
Jackson, Edison *WhoAm 90*
Jackson, Edwin Sydney 1922- *St&PR 91*
Jackson, Elaine Francis 1945- *WhoAmW 91*
Jackson, Eleanor Alexander *BioIn 16*

Jackson, Elizabeth Irene *BiDrAPA 89*
Jackson, Elmer C. 1909- *St&PR 91*
Jackson, Elmer J. 1920- *St&PR 91*
Jackson, Elmer Joseph 1920- *WhoAm 90*
Jackson, Elmer Martin, Jr. 1906- *WhoAm 90, WhoWor 91*
Jackson, Elmore 1910-1989 *BioIn 16*
Jackson, Ernestine *DrBlPA 90*
Jackson, Esther 1922- *NotWoAT*
Jackson, Esther Merle 1922- *BioIn 16*
Jackson, Eugene Bernard 1915- *WhoAm 90*
Jackson, Eugene Wesley 1928- *WhoAm 90*
Jackson, Everett Gee 1900- *WhoAm 90, WhoAmA 91*
Jackson, F.H. 1927- *St&PR 91*
Jackson, Fleda Brown 1944- *WhoWrEP 89*
Jackson, Flora Elizabeth 1940- *WhoSSW 91*
Jackson, Francis 1917- *PenDiMP*
Jackson, Francis Alan 1917- *IntWWM 90*
Jackson, Francis Charles 1917- *WhoAm 90*
Jackson, Francis Ivan 1932- *WhoE 91*
Jackson, Francis Joseph 1932- *St&PR 91, WhoAm 90*
Jackson, Freda Lucille 1928- *WhoAmW 91, WhoWrEP 89*
Jackson, Freddie *BioIn 16*
Jackson, Freddie 1959- *DrBlPA 90*
Jackson, Frederick Herbert 1919- *WhoAm 90*
Jackson, G. Mark 1952- *ConAu 132*
Jackson, Garfield *PenDiMP*
Jackson, Geoffrey H. S. 1915-1987 *BioIn 16*
Jackson, George A. 1931- *St&PR 91*
Jackson, George Lyman 1923- *WhoAm 90*
Jackson, George W *BiDrAPA 89*
Jackson, George Wallace 1948- *WhoSSW 91*
Jackson, George Woodrow 1914- *WhoAm 90*
Jackson, Geraldine 1934- *WhoAmW 91*
Jackson, Glenda *BioIn 16*
Jackson, Glenda 1936- *WhoAm 90, WhoWor 91*
Jackson, Glenda 1938- *WorAlBi*
Jackson, Gordon 1923-1990 *BioIn 16, NewYTBS 90 [port]*
Jackson, Gordon Alexander 1913- *WhoWor 91*
Jackson, Gordon Stuart 1949- *WhoEmL 91*
Jackson, Granbery, III 1945- *WhoAm 90*
Jackson, Grant 1942- *Ballpl 90*
Jackson, Gregory Wayne 1950- *WhoEmL 91, WhoWor 91*
Jackson, Hal 1922- *DrBlPA 90*
Jackson, Harold Milton 1953- *WhoSSW 91*
Jackson, Harper Scales, Jr. 1951- *WhoSSW 91*
Jackson, Harriet Marie 1957- *WhoEmL 91*
Jackson, Harry Andrew 1900-1989 *BioIn 16*
Jackson, Harry Andrew 1924- *WhoAm 90, WhoAmA 91*
Jackson, Harry D. 1926- *St&PR 91*
Jackson, Hazel 1963- *WhoAmW 91*
Jackson, Hazel Brill *WhoAmA 91*
Jackson, Helen Cassandra 1951- *WhoAmW 91*
Jackson, Helen Hunt 1830-1885 *BioAmW, BioIn 16, FemiCLE, WhNaAH, WorAlBi*
Jackson, Henry Alden *WhoAmA 91N*
Jackson, Henry Daniel 1964- *WhoE 91*
Jackson, Henry F. 1939- *ConAu 129*
Jackson, Henry M. 1912-1983 *WorAlBi*
Jackson, Herb 1945- *WhoAm 90, WhoAmA 91*
Jackson, Hermina *BioIn 16*
Jackson, Hermoine Prestine 1945- *WhoAmW 91*
Jackson, Holbrook 1874-1948 *DcLB 98 [port]*
Jackson, Horace Franklin 1934- *WhoSSW 91*
Jackson, Howard Francis, Jr. 1949- *WhoEmL 91*
Jackson, Howard Lee 1957- *WhoE 91*
Jackson, Ian Vaughan 1942- *BiDrAPA 89*
Jackson, Irving 1920- *BiDrAPA 89*
Jackson, Isaiah *BioIn 16*
Jackson, Isaiah 1945- *DrBlPA 90, IntWWM 90, PenDiMP*
Jackson, J. T. Ross 1938- *WhoWor 91*
Jackson, Jack 1907-1978 *OxCPMus*
Jackson, Jack 1946- *WhoEmL 91*
Jackson, Jack Eldon 1928- *St&PR 91*
Jackson, Jackie 1951- *OxCPMus*
Jackson, Jacqueline *BioIn 16*
Jackson, Jacqueline 1928- *AuBYP 90*
Jackson, Jacqueline Dougan 1928- *WhoAm 90*
Jackson, Jacquelyne Johnson 1932- *WhoAm 90*
Jackson, James 1757-1806 *BioIn 16*
Jackson, James Alan 1952- *WhoEmL 91*
Jackson, James J. 1944- *St&PR 91*
Jackson, James L. 1945- *St&PR 91*
Jackson, James Leonard 1932- *WhoSSW 91*
Jackson, James O *SpyFic*
Jackson, James Robert 1922- *WhoE 91*
Jackson, James Sidney 1944- *WhoAm 90*
Jackson, James Wesley 1952- *IntWWM 90*
Jackson, Jane Elizabeth *BiDrAPA 89*
Jackson, Jane W. 1944- *WhoAmW 91*
Jackson, Janet *BioIn 16*
Jackson, Janet 1965- *WorAlBi*
Jackson, Janet 1966?- *News 90 [port]*
Jackson, Janet Merrill 1956- *WhoE 91*
Jackson, Janice Theresa 1960- *WhoAmW 91*
Jackson, Jean Berryman *BiDrAPA 89*
Jackson, Jeffrey E. 1950- *St&PR 91*
Jackson, Jeffrey Lewis 1955- *WhoEmL 91*
Jackson, Jeffrey Pendleton 1949- *St&PR 91*
Jackson, Jennifer Clay 1960- *WhoAmW 91*
Jackson, Jenny Tench 1952- *WhoSSW 91*
Jackson, Jermaine 1954- *EncPR&S 89, OxCPMus, WorAlBi*
Jackson, Jerry Donald 1944- *St&PR 91*
Jackson, Jerry Francis 1938- *WhoSSW 91*
Jackson, Jerry Thomas 1941- *St&PR 91*
Jackson, Jesse *BioIn 16*
Jackson, Jesse 1908-1983 *AuBYP 90*
Jackson, Jesse 1941- *WorAlBi*
Jackson, Jesse B., Jr. 1923- *St&PR 91*
Jackson, Jesse Jefferson 1936- *WhoSSW 91*
Jackson, Jesse L. 1941- *BioIn 16*
Jackson, Jesse L., Jr. *BioIn 16*
Jackson, Jesse Louis 1941- *WhoAm 90*
Jackson, Jewel 1942- *WhoAmW 91, WhoWor 91*
Jackson, Jim 1877-1955 *Ballpl 90*
Jackson, Joan *BioIn 16*
Jackson, Joe *WhoAm 90*
Jackson, Joe 1887-1951 *Ballpl 90 [port], BioIn 16*
Jackson, Joe 1955- *ConMus 4 [port], EncPR&S 89*
Jackson, Joe Alan *BiDrAPA 89*
Jackson, Joe Clarence 1911- *WhoSSW 91*
Jackson, Joe S. *Ballpl 90*
Jackson, Joe William, Jr. 1955- *WhoSSW 91*
Jackson, John Alan 1952- *WhoSSW 91*
Jackson, John Arthur 1947- *WhoWrEP 89*
Jackson, John Baptist 1701?-1780? *PenDiDA 89*
Jackson, John Brinckerhoff 1862-1920 *BioIn 16*
Jackson, John Charles 1939- *WhoWor 91*
Jackson, John David 1937- *St&PR 91*
Jackson, John E. 1945- *St&PR 91*
Jackson, John Edgar 1942- *WhoAm 90*
Jackson, John Edwin 1875- *WhoAmA 91N*
Jackson, John Edwin 1945- *WhoWor 91*
Jackson, John H. *BioIn 16*
Jackson, John Howard 1932- *WhoAm 90*
Jackson, John Mathews 1908- *WhoAm 90*
Jackson, John N 1925- *ConAu 31NR*
Jackson, John R. *AmLegL*
Jackson, John T. 1921- *St&PR 91*
Jackson, John Tillson 1921- *WhoAm 90*
Jackson, John W. F. *AmLegL*
Jackson, John Wingfield 1905- *WhoSSW 91*
Jackson, John Wyant 1944- *WhoAm 90*
Jackson, Jonathan Steven 1961- *WhoSSW 91*
Jackson, Joseph *BioIn 16, WhoWrEP 89*
Jackson, Joseph 1944- *WhoE 91*
Jackson, Joseph H. *BioIn 16*
Jackson, Joy Juanita 1928- *WhoAmW 91*
Jackson, Julian Ellis 1913- *WhoAm 90*
Jackson, June Johnson 1943- *WhoE 91*
Jackson, Karl Francis 1935- *WhoAm 90*
Jackson, Karla Lynn 1956- *WhoAmW 91*
Jackson, Kate 1948- *WorAlBi*
Jackson, Kate 1949- *WhoAmW 91*
Jackson, Katherine *BioIn 16*
Jackson, Kay Lyn 1962- *WhoAmW 91*
Jackson, Keith MacKenzie 1928- *WhoAm 90*
Jackson, Kenneth Arthur 1930- *WhoAm 90*
Jackson, Kenneth Terry 1939- *WhoAm 90*
Jackson, Kingsbury Temple 1917- *WhoAm 90*
Jackson, L. Craig *St&PR 91N*
Jackson, Laird Gray 1930- *WhoAm 90*
Jackson, Larry 1931- *Ballpl 90*
Jackson, Larry Artope 1925- *WhoAm 90*
Jackson, Larry Todd 1964- *WhoSSW 91*
Jackson, LaToya *BioIn 16*
Jackson, Laura 1901- *BioIn 16, WhoAm 90*
Jackson, Lawrence 1937- *St&PR 91*
Jackson, Lawrence E *BiDrAPA 89*
Jackson, Lee *BiDrAPA 89, WhoAm 90*
Jackson, Lee 1909- *WhoAmA 91*
Jackson, Lela Evelyne 1941- *WhoAmW 91*
Jackson, Leland Brooks 1940- *WhoAm 90*
Jackson, Leon Karl 1934- *St&PR 91*
Jackson, Leonard 1928- *DrBlPA 90*
Jackson, LeRoy Eugene 1933- *WhoAm 90*
Jackson, Lesley 1866-1958 *WhoAmA 91N*
Jackson, Leslie Ann 1958- *WhoWrEP 89*
Jackson, Lewis Albert 1912- *WhoAm 90*
Jackson, Lewis Duane 1949- *WhoAm 90, WhoE 91*
Jackson, Linda 1950- *BioIn 16*
Jackson, Linda Hall 1942- *BiDrAPA 89*
Jackson, Lionel L *BiDrAPA 89*
Jackson, Lisa Amaya 1960- *BiDrAPA 89*
Jackson, Livia Bitton *ConAu 130*
Jackson, Lois Kathryn 1927- *WhoAmW 91*
Jackson, Lola Hirdler 1942- *WhoAmW 91*
Jackson, Lora Ruthe Thompson 1920- *WhoAmW 91*
Jackson, Loretta Young 1935- *WhoAmW 91*
Jackson, Loyd Appleby 1946- *WhoAmW 91*
Jackson, Lynda Kay 1949- *WhoAmW 91*
Jackson, Mack Willie 1960- *WhoEmL 91, WhoSSW 91*
Jackson, Maga Essie *BiDrAPA 89*
Jackson, Mahalia 1911-1972 *BioAmW, DrBlPA 90, OxCPMus, WorAlBi*
Jackson, Marette McCauley 1931- *WhoSSW 91*
Jackson, Maria Pilar 1949- *WhoHisp 91*
Jackson, Marilynn Bock 1937- *WhoSSW 91*
Jackson, Marion Elizabeth 1941- *WhoAmA 91*
Jackson, Marion Leroy 1914- *WhoAm 90*
Jackson, Mark *BioIn 16, WhoWrEP 89*
Jackson, Marlon *BioIn 16*
Jackson, Marlon 1957- *OxCPMus*
Jackson, Marlon David 1957- *EncPR&S 89*
Jackson, Martha *WhoAmA 91N*
Jackson, Mary 1910- *WhoAm 90*
Jackson, Mary A. *ODwPR 91*
Jackson, Mary Coleman *AuBYP 90*
Jackson, Mary L. 1938- *WhoAmW 91, WhoWor 91*
Jackson, Mary V *BiDrAPA 89*
Jackson, Maynard 1938- *WorAlBi*
Jackson, Melbourne Leslie 1915- *WhoAm 90*
Jackson, Michael 1958- *BioIn 16, DrBlPA 90, EncPR&S 89, OxCPMus, WorAlBi*
Jackson, Michael John 1938- *WhoAm 90*
Jackson, Michael Joseph 1958- *WhoAm 90*
Jackson, Michael Stewart 1954- *WhoEmL 91*
Jackson, Michele Chickerella 1954- *WhoEmL 91*
Jackson, Mike 1964- *Ballpl 90*
Jackson, Miles Merrill 1929- *WhoAm 90*
Jackson, Millie *DrBlPA 90*
Jackson, Milt *BioIn 16*
Jackson, Milt 1923- *DrBlPA 90, OxCPMus, WorAlBi*
Jackson, Mona Bethel 1947- *WhoAmW 91*
Jackson, Mona Maria 1944- *WhoAmW 91*
Jackson, Muriel Grace 1929- *WhoAmW 91*
Jackson, Myron Eaton 1927- *St&PR 91*
Jackson, Nancy Kay 1950- *WhoEmL 91*
Jackson, Nicholas Fane St George 1934- *IntWWM 90*
Jackson, Norman Eugene 1937- *St&PR 91*
Jackson, O. B. *AuBYP 90*
Jackson, Oliver Lee 1935- *WhoAmA 91*
Jackson, Orpha *AuBYP 90*
Jackson, Patricia Lee 1916- *WhoAmW 91, WhoE 91*
Jackson, Patricia Pike 1960- *WhoAmW 91*
Jackson, Patrick 1932- *ODwPR 91*
Jackson, Patrick John 1932- *WhoAm 90, WhoE 91*
Jackson, Paul Ernest 1956- *WhoEmL 91*
Jackson, Paul I. 1951- *St&PR 91*
Jackson, Paulette White 1949- *WhoAmW 91*
Jackson, Pauline M 1936- *BiDrAPA 89*
Jackson, Peter Vorious, III 1927- *WhoAm 90*
Jackson, Philip C. 1935- *St&PR 91*
Jackson, Philip Chappell, Jr. 1928- *St&PR 91*
Jackson, Philip Douglas *WhoAm 90*
Jackson, Phillip 1950- *St&PR 91*
Jackson, Phillis Kitchen 1948- *WhoEmL 91*
Jackson, Preston 1903-1983 *BioIn 16*
Jackson, Quintin T. 1947- *St&PR 91*
Jackson, R.A. 1946- *St&PR 91*
Jackson, R. Graham 1913- *WhoAm 90*
Jackson, Rachel D. 1767-1828 *BioAmW*
Jackson, Rachel Donelson Robards 1767-1828 *BioIn 16*
Jackson, Ralph 1928- *ODwPR 91*
Jackson, Ralph Neel 1952- *IntWWM 90*
Jackson, Randall Vaughan 1948- *IntWWM 90*
Jackson, Randy 1926- *Ballpl 90*
Jackson, Raymond T. 1933- *IntWWM 90*
Jackson, Rebecca 1795-1871 *FemiCLE*
Jackson, Rebecca A. 1955- *St&PR 91*
Jackson, Rebecca Ann 1955- *WhoAmW 91*
Jackson, Rebecca Cox 1795-1871 *BioAmW*
Jackson, Reggie *BioIn 16*
Jackson, Reggie 1946- *Ballpl 90 [port], WorAlBi*
Jackson, Reginald 1945- *IntWWM 90*
Jackson, Reginald Sherman 1910- *WhoAm 90*
Jackson, Richard *IntWWM 90*
Jackson, Richard 1936- *IntWWM 90*
Jackson, Richard Brooke 1947- *WhoEmL 91*
Jackson, Richard Delyn 1937- *WhoAm 90, WhoSSW 91*
Jackson, Richard Evan *BiDrAPA 89*
Jackson, Richard George 1940- *WhoAm 90*
Jackson, Richard Landrum *BiDrAPA 89*
Jackson, Richard Lee 1931- *St&PR 91*
Jackson, Richard Montgomery 1920- *WhoAm 90*
Jackson, Richard Paul 1946- *WhoWrEP 89*
Jackson, Richard Seymour 1915- *WhoE 91*
Jackson, Richard Steven 1960- *BiDrAPA 89*
Jackson, Richard Wayne 1926- *St&PR 91*
Jackson, Robert *BioIn 16*
Jackson, Robert B *BiDrAPA 89*
Jackson, Robert Blake 1926- *AuBYP 90*
Jackson, Robert Bruce, Jr. 1929- *WhoSSW 91*
Jackson, Robert Dale 1930- *St&PR 91*
Jackson, Robert Deverr, Jr. 1961- *WhoSSW 91*
Jackson, Robert Doster 1920- *BiDrAPA 89*
Jackson, Robert Everette 1930- *WhoSSW 91*
Jackson, Robert Frederick 1947- *WhoSSW 91*
Jackson, Robert H. 1892-1954 *WorAlBi*
Jackson, Robert Harold 1940- *WhoSSW 91*
Jackson, Robert Houghwout 1892-1954 *BiDrUSE 89*
Jackson, Robert Keith 1943- *WhoSSW 91*
Jackson, Robert Lawrence 1909- *WhoAm 90*
Jackson, Robert Ludovic 1927- *St&PR 91*
Jackson, Robert Raymond 1951- *WhoEmL 91*
Jackson, Robert Scott 1946- *WhoE 91*
Jackson, Robert Sherwood 1945- *WhoAm 90*
Jackson, Robert Street 1943- *WhoAm 90*
Jackson, Robert Thomas 1946- *St&PR 91*
Jackson, Robert W. 1930- *St&PR 91*
Jackson, Robert William 1930- *WhoAm 90*
Jackson, Roberta Plant *WhoAmW 91*
Jackson, Robins H. 1924- *St&PR 91*
Jackson, Rochelle P *BiDrAPA 89*
Jackson, Roger Keith *BiDrAPA 89*
Jackson, Rollin Ashby, Jr. 1934- *WhoSSW 91*
Jackson, Ron 1953- *Ballpl 90*
Jackson, Ronald Lee 1936- *St&PR 91*
Jackson, Rosa Catherine 1948- *WhoWrEP 89*
Jackson, Rose Valdez 1953- *WhoHisp 91*
Jackson, Roy A. 1950- *St&PR 91*
Jackson, Roy Lee 1954- *Ballpl 90*
Jackson, Royce Van 1928- *BiDrAPA 89*
Jackson, Rudolph Ellsworth 1935- *WhoAm 90*
Jackson, Ruth 1902- *WhoAm 90*
Jackson, Ruth Amelia *WhoAmA 91*
Jackson, Ruth Amelia 1912- *WhoAm 90*
Jackson, Ruth Robertson 1939- *WhoAmW 91*
Jackson, Ruthie Fay 1948- *WhoEmL 91*
Jackson, Sally *AuBYP 90*
Jackson, Sally D. 1946- *ODwPR 91*
Jackson, Sally Gavin 1954- *WhoEmL 91*
Jackson, Samuel E., Jr. 1928- *St&PR 91*
Jackson, Sarah 1924- *WhoAmA 91*
Jackson, Sarah Charlotte 1948- *WhoWor 91*
Jackson, Sarah Curry 1934- *WhoAmW 91*
Jackson, Sarah Jeanette 1924- *WhoAm 90*
Jackson, Schuyler Brinckerhoff 1849-1914 *AmLegL*
Jackson, Sharon Patrice 1958- *WhoAmW 91, WhoEmL 91*
Jackson, Shaun Bryan 1960- *WhoEmL 91*
Jackson, Sherry 1942- *ConTFT 8*

Jackson, Shirley 1919-1965 *BioAmW, BioIn 16, ConLC 60 [port], FemiCLE, WorAlBi*
Jackson, Shirley Crite 1940- *WhoAmW 91*
Jackson, Shirley Strother 1940- *WhoAmW 91*
Jackson, Sigmund Esco 1951- *EncPR&S 89*
Jackson, Sonny 1944- *Ballpl 90*
Jackson, Stacy H. 1958- *St&PR 91*
Jackson, Stanley W 1920- *BiDrAPA 89*
Jackson, Stanley Webber 1920- *WhoE 91*
Jackson, Stephanie Ann 1960- *WhoSSW 91*
Jackson, Stephen Eric 1946- *WhoSSW 91*
Jackson, Stephen Keith 1939- *St&PR 91*
Jackson, Steven Randall 1961- *EncPR&S 89*
Jackson, Stonewall *WhoNeCM C [port]*
Jackson, Stonewall 1824-1863 *BioIn 16*
Jackson, Stu *BioIn 16, WhoAm 90, WhoE 91*
Jackson, Susan Adams 1953- *WhoEmL 91*
Jackson, Susan Roberta 1949- *WhoAmW 91*
Jackson, Suzanne Fitzallen 1944- *WhoAmA 91*
Jackson, Sylvia *WhoAmW 91*
Jackson, Tammy Lolita 1969- *WhoEmL 91*
Jackson, Tarra 1964- *WhoAmW 91*
Jackson, Ted M. 1928- *St&PR 91*
Jackson, Terry Wayne 1955- *WhoSSW 91*
Jackson, Theodore Marshall 1928- *WhoAm 90*
Jackson, Theresa Ann 1959- *WhoAmW 91*
Jackson, Theresa Pittman 1945- *WhoSSW 91*
Jackson, Thomas 1824-1863 *WorAlBi*
Jackson, Thomas Cline 1930- *St&PR 91*
Jackson, Thomas Clyde 1949- *WhoE 91*
Jackson, Thomas Francis, III 1940- *WhoWor 91*
Jackson, Thomas H. 1930- *WhoWrEP 89*
Jackson, Thomas Humphrey 1950- *WhoAm 90*
Jackson, Thomas Jonathan 1824-1863 *BioIn 16*
Jackson, Thomas Penfield 1937- *WhoAm 90, WhoE 91*
Jackson, Thomas W *BiDrAPA 89*
Jackson, Thunderbolt *BioIn 16*
Jackson, Tito 1953- *OxCPMus*
Jackson, Tom 1957- *BioIn 16*
Jackson, Tony 1876-1921 *OxCPMus*
Jackson, Tonya Elishe 1965- *WhoAmW 91*
Jackson, Toriano Adaryl 1953- *EncPR&S 89*
Jackson, Travis 1903-1987 *Ballpl 90 [port]*
Jackson, Twyla Douglas 1957- *WhoEmL 91*
Jackson, Velma Louise 1945- *WhoAmW 91, WhoE 91, WhoEmL 91, WhoWor 91*
Jackson, Vernice Prewitt 1929- *WhoAmW 91*
Jackson, Victor Louis 1933- *WhoAm 90*
Jackson, Victoria *BioIn 16*
Jackson, Victoria 1959- *WorAlBi*
Jackson, Victoria Padgett 1949- *WhoSSW 91*
Jackson, W. Bruce 1943- *WhoAm 90*
Jackson, Walter Francis 1946- *WhoE 91*
Jackson, Ward 1928- *WhoAm 90, WhoAmA 91*
Jackson, Wes *BioIn 16*
Jackson, Wes 1936- *WhoWrEP 89*
Jackson, Willard *BioIn 16*
Jackson, William *EarBlAP*
Jackson, William C. 1932- *St&PR 91*
Jackson, William Clark, Jr. 1932- *WhoAm 90*
Jackson, William David 1927- *WhoAm 90*
Jackson, William E. 1956- *St&PR 91*
Jackson, William Edward, III 1953- *WhoE 91*
Jackson, William Eldred 1919- *WhoAm 90, WhoE 91*
Jackson, William Gene 1946- *WhoWor 91*
Jackson, William Henry 1843-1942 *BioIn 16, WhNaAH*
Jackson, William Lloyd 1927- *WhoAm 90*
Jackson, William Longstreth 1948- *WhoEmL 91*
Jackson, William MacLeod 1926- *WhoAm 90*
Jackson, William Paul, Jr. 1938- *WhoAm 90, WhoWor 91*
Jackson, William R. 1908- *St&PR 91*
Jackson, William Turrentine 1915- *WhoAm 90*
Jackson, William Vernon 1926- *WhoAm 90*
Jackson, William Ward 1913- *WhoAm 90*
Jackson, Wilma *WhoAmW 91*
Jackson, Woody *BioIn 16*
Jackson, Wynn K *BiDrAPA 89*
Jackson-Gillison, Helen Lucille 1944- *WhoAmW 91*
Jackson Of Lodsworth, Baroness 1914-1981 *DcNaB 1981*
Jackson-Randolph, Marie *BioIn 16*
Jacksons, The *EncPR&S 89, OxCPMus*
Jacky, Doris Victoria 1928- *WhoAmW 91*
Jaclot, Francois C. 1949- *St&PR 91*
Jaclot, Francois Charles 1949- *WhoAm 90*
Jaco, C. D. *BioIn 16*
Jaco, William Howard 1940- *St&PR 91*
Jacob, Mr. 1850?-1921 *EncO&P 3*
Jacob of Simla 1850?-1921 *EncO&P 3*
Jacob the Zouave 1828-1913 *EncO&P 3*
Jacob, Auguste Henri 1828-1913 *EncO&P 3*
Jacob, Benjamin 1778-1829 *PenDiMP*
Jacob, Bernard Michel 1930- *WhoAm 90*
Jacob, Bruce Robert 1935- *WhoAm 90*
Jacob, Carol G *BiDrAPA 89*
Jacob, Charles Elmer 1931- *WhoAm 90*
Jacob, Charles Waldemar 1943- *WhoAm 90*
Jacob, Daisy 1948- *BiDrAPA 89*
Jacob, Donald Gary 1942- *WhoE 91*
Jacob, Edwin J. 1927- *WhoAm 90*
Jacob, Ellis 1953- *St&PR 91*
Jacob, Emerson Donald 1914- *WhoAm 90*
Jacob, Francois 1920- *BioIn 16, WhoAm 90, WhoWor 91, WorAlBi*
Jacob, Francois-Honore-Georges 1770-1841 *PenDiDA 89*
Jacob, Gary Steven 1949- *WhoE 91*
Jacob, Georges 1739-1814 *PenDiDA 89*
Jacob, Georges, II 1768-1803 *PenDiDA 89*
Jacob, Gordon 1895-1984 *PenDiMP A*
Jacob, Gordon Percival Septimus 1895-1984 *DcNaB 1981*
Jacob, Gunther M *BiDrAPA 89*
Jacob, Harry Myles 1913- *WhoAm 90*
Jacob, Harry Samuel 1933- *WhoAm 90*
Jacob, Henri 1753-1824 *PenDiDA 89*
Jacob, Henri Maurice 1925- *St&PR 91*
Jacob, Herbert 1933- *WhoAm 90*
Jacob, J. R. *ConAu 132*
Jacob, James R. 1940- *ConAu 132*
Jacob, Jeremy D. *ODwPR 91*
Jacob, Jerry R. 1933- *St&PR 91*
Jacob, John C. 1950- *WhoWrEP 89*
Jacob, John Edward 1934- *WhoAm 90, WhoE 91*
Jacob, Joseph *PenDiMP*
Jacob, Joseph S 1915- *BiDrAPA 89*
Jacob, Judith Elizabeth 1940- *WhoE 91*
Jacob, Karen Hite 1947- *IntWWM 90*
Jacob, Lawrence 1945- *St&PR 91*
Jacob, Louise Helen 1924- *WhoAmW 91*
Jacob, M. Teresa C. 1948- *WhoAmW 91*
Jacob, Mark Craig 1951- *WhoEmL 91*
Jacob, Marvin Eugene 1935- *WhoAm 90*
Jacob, Mary Ellen L. 1939- *WhoWrEP 89*
Jacob, Mary Jane 1952- *WhoAmA 91, WhoAmW 91*
Jacob, Merle Lynn 1945- *WhoEmL 91*
Jacob, Nancy Louise 1943- *WhoAmW 91*
Jacob, Naomi 1884-1964 *BioIn 16, FemiCLE*
Jacob, Ned 1938- *WhoAmA 91*
Jacob, Paul Bernard, Jr. 1922- *WhoAm 90*
Jacob, Peyton, Jr. 1919- *BiDrAPA 89*
Jacob, Pius 1955- *BiDrAPA 89*
Jacob, Richard Carl 1936- *WhoE 91*
Jacob, Richard J. 1919- *St&PR 91*
Jacob, Robert *St&PR 91*
Jacob, Robert Edward 1954- *WhoEmL 91*
Jacob, Rolf G 1942- *BiDrAPA 89*
Jacob, Ruth Ann 1945- *WhoAmW 91*
Jacob, Said Isaac *BiDrAPA 89*
Jacob, Stanley Wallace 1924- *WhoAm 90*
Jacob, Thomas Bernard 1934- *WhoAm 90*
Jacob, Thomas N *BiDrAPA 89*
Jacob, Thresiamma 1939- *BiDrAPA 89*
Jacob, W Lindsay *BiDrAPA 89*
Jacob, William F. 1941- *St&PR 91*
Jacob-Desmalter, Francois-Honore-Georges 1770-1841 *PenDiDA 89*
Jacob-Desmalter, Georges-Alphonse 1799-1870 *PenDiDA 89*
Jacoba *WomWR*
Jacober, Dale Stuart 1962- *St&PR 91*
Jacober, Todd J. 1960- *St&PR 91*
Jacobey, John Arthur, III 1929- *WhoAm 90, WhoE 91*
Jacobi, Derek 1938- *WorAlBi*
Jacobi, Derek George 1938- *WhoAm 90, WhoWor 91*
Jacobi, Eileen M. 1918- *WhoAm 90*
Jacobi, Frederick A. *ODwPR 91*
Jacobi, Fredrick Thomas 1953- *WhoSSW 91*
Jacobi, Friedrich Heinrich 1743-1819 *DcLB 94 [port]*
Jacobi, Georg 1840-1906 *PenDiMP*
Jacobi, George T. 1922- *St&PR 91*
Jacobi, George Thomas 1922- *WhoAm 90*
Jacobi, Herbert J. 1907-1989 *BioIn 16*
Jacobi, Johann Georg 1740-1814 *DcLB 97 [port]*
Jacobi, John Albert 1947- *WhoEmL 91*
Jacobi, John Edward 1907- *WhoAm 90*
Jacobi, Jolande Szekacs 1890- *EncO&P 3*
Jacobi, Lotte *NewYTBS 90*
Jacobi, Lotte 1896-1990 *BioIn 16*
Jacobi, Mary Putnam 1842-1906 *BioAmW*
Jacobi, Neal Henry 1952- *BiDrAPA 89*
Jacobi, Peter *ODwPR 91*
Jacobi, Peter Paul 1930- *WhoAm 90, WhoWrEP 89*
Jacobi, Robert V., Jr. *WhoWrEP 89*
Jacobi, Roger Edgar 1924- *IntWWM 90*
Jacobo, John Rodriguez 1942- *WhoHisp 91*
Jacobovitz, Jeffrey Steven 1955- *WhoEmL 91*
Jacobowitz, Ellen Sue 1948- *WhoAmA 91*
Jacobowitz, John 1940- *St&PR 91*
Jacobowitz, Judah L. *WhoWrEP 89*
Jacobozzi, Vivian Marie 1933- *WhoAmW 91*
Jacobs *WhNaAH*
Jacobs, Abigail Conway 1942- *WhoAmW 91*
Jacobs, Adam *BioIn 16*
Jacobs, Alan Martin 1932- *WhoAm 90*
Jacobs, Alan Neil *BiDrAPA 89*
Jacobs, Alton Ramon 1936- *WhoSSW 91*
Jacobs, Andrew, Jr. 1932- *WhoAm 90*
Jacobs, Anna C. 1939- *WhoAmW 91*
Jacobs, Arnold Stephen 1940- *WhoAm 90*
Jacobs, Arthur A. *BioIn 16*
Jacobs, Arthur David 1922- *IntWWM 90*
Jacobs, Arthur Dietrich 1933- *WhoWor 91*
Jacobs, Arthur R 1947- *BiDrAPA 89*
Jacobs, Arthur Russell 1947- *WhoE 91*
Jacobs, Arthur Theodore 1912- *WhoAm 90*
Jacobs, Audrey Ardys 1927- *WhoAmW 91*
Jacobs, Augusta Adelle 1925- *WhoAmW 91*
Jacobs, Barbara Frank 1942- *WhoE 91*
Jacobs, Barbara J. 1949- *ODwPR 91*
Jacobs, Barry Alan Holland 1946- *WhoE 91*
Jacobs, Bella Hertzberg 1919- *WhoAmW 91*
Jacobs, Bernard B. 1916- *St&PR 91, WhoAm 90*
Jacobs, Bernard J *BiDrAPA 89*
Jacobs, Bertrand R 1927- *BiDrAPA 89*
Jacobs, Beth *AuBYP 90*
Jacobs, Bradford McElderry 1920- *WhoAm 90*
Jacobs, Bruce Edmund 1947- *St&PR 91*
Jacobs, Burleigh E. 1920- *St&PR 91*
Jacobs, Burleigh Edmund 1920- *WhoAm 90*
Jacobs, C. Bernard 1918- *WhoAm 90*
Jacobs, Charles Robinson 1918- *WhoSSW 91*
Jacobs, Chris *BioIn 16*
Jacobs, Christie Jean 1961- *WhoAmW 91*
Jacobs, Christie Stiegman 1946- *WhoE 91*
Jacobs, Cindy J. 1962- *WhoEmL 91*
Jacobs, Clyde Edward 1925- *WhoAm 90*
Jacobs, Conrad R 1935- *BiDrAPA 89*
Jacobs, Dale Maynard *BiDrAPA 89*
Jacobs, Daniel Howard 1937- *BiDrAPA 89*
Jacobs, David 1932- *WhoAm 90, WhoAmA 91*
Jacobs, David Calhoun 1949- *BiDrAPA 89*
Jacobs, Debra McQuaia 1950- *WhoAmW 91*
Jacobs, Dennis E. 1949- *St&PR 91*
Jacobs, Diana Pietrocarli 1950- *WhoEmL 91*
Jacobs, Donald G. 1930- *St&PR 91*
Jacobs, Donald P. 1927- *WhoAm 90*
Jacobs, Donald Paul 1942- *WhoAm 90*
Jacobs, Donald Richard *BiDrAPA 89*
Jacobs, Donald Warren 1932- *WhoE 91*
Jacobs, Douglas G 1945- *BiDrAPA 89*
Jacobs, E Gardner 1926- *BiDrAPA 89*
Jacobs, E. Gardner 1926- *WhoE 91*
Jacobs, Edwin Max 1925- *WhoAm 90*
Jacobs, Eleanor Alice 1923- *WhoAm 90, WhoAmW 91, WhoE 91, WhoWor 91*
Jacobs, Eli S. 1937- *St&PR 91*
Jacobs, Elmer 1892-1958 *Ballpl 90*
Jacobs, Eric *BiDrAPA 89*
Jacobs, Erwin M 1925- *BiDrAPA 89*
Jacobs, Eugene L 1933- *BiDrAPA 89*
Jacobs, Eugene William 1933- *St&PR 91*
Jacobs, Flora Gill 1918- *AuBYP 90*
Jacobs, Francis Albin 1918- *WhoAm 90*
Jacobs, Frank 1929- *AuBYP 90*
Jacobs, Franklin A. 1932- *St&PR 91*
Jacobs, Frederick Carl 1946- *St&PR 91*
Jacobs, George 1924- *WhoAm 90*
Jacobs, Gretchen Huntley 1941- *BiDrAPA 89*
Jacobs, Harold 1932- *WhoAmA 91*
Jacobs, Harold Robert 1936- *WhoAm 90, WhoWor 91*
Jacobs, Harriet 1818-1896 *FemiCLE*
Jacobs, Harry A., Jr. 1921- *St&PR 91*
Jacobs, Harry Milburn, Jr. 1928- *WhoAm 90, WhoSSW 91, WhoWor 91*
Jacobs, Harvey Collins 1915- *WhoAm 90*
Jacobs, Harvey S. 1958- *WhoE 91*
Jacobs, Helen Hull 1908- *AuBYP 90, WhoAm 90, WorAlBi*
Jacobs, Helen Nichols 1924- *WhoAmA 91, WhoE 91*
Jacobs, Horace 1911- *WhoWrEP 89*
Jacobs, Howard 1937- *WhoAm 90*
Jacobs, Ilene B. 1947- *WhoAm 90, WhoAmW 91*
Jacobs, Ira 1931- *WhoAm 90*
Jacobs, Irwin L. 1941- *St&PR 91*
Jacobs, Irwin Lawrence 1941- *WhoAm 90*
Jacobs, Irwin S 1923- *BiDrAPA 89*
Jacobs, Isaac *PenDiDA 89*
Jacobs, J. Ethan 1940- *St&PR 91*
Jacobs, James Nathan 1955- *WhoSSW 91*
Jacobs, James P. 1952- *St&PR 91*
Jacobs, James Paul 1930- *WhoSSW 91*
Jacobs, James S L 1916- *BiDrAPA 89*
Jacobs, James Walter 1962- *WhoEmL 91*
Jacobs, Jane 1916- *WhoAm 90, WhoAmW 91*
Jacobs, Jeff C. 1950- *EncPaPR 91*
Jacobs, Jeffrey Bruce 1943- *WhoWor 91*
Jacobs, Jeffrey Lee 1951- *WhoE 91*
Jacobs, Jerome L 1931- *BiDrAPA 89*
Jacobs, Jim 1930-1988 *BioIn 16*
Jacobs, Jim 1942- *WhoAm 90*
Jacobs, Jim 1945- *WhoAmA 91*
Jacobs, John *BioIn 16*
Jacobs, John D. 1943- *St&PR 91*
Jacobs, John Edward 1920- *WhoAm 90*
Jacobs, John Howard 1925- *WhoAm 90*
Jacobs, John P. 1943- *St&PR 91*
Jacobs, John William 1943- *BiDrAPA 89*
Jacobs, Jon Robert 1950- *WhoEmL 91*
Jacobs, Joseph 1854-1916 *BioIn 16*
Jacobs, Joseph Donovan 1908- *WhoAm 90*
Jacobs, Joseph J. 1916- *St&PR 91*
Jacobs, Joseph John 1916- *WhoAm 90*
Jacobs, Julian I. 1937- *WhoAm 90*
Jacobs, Karen J *BiDrAPA 89*
Jacobs, Karen Louise 1943- *WhoAmW 91, WhoWor 91*
Jacobs, Katherine M *BiDrAPA 89*
Jacobs, Kathleen Caldwell 1940- *WhoAmW 91*
Jacobs, Keith William 1944- *WhoWor 91*
Jacobs, Kenneth A. 1948- *WhoSSW 91*
Jacobs, Kent Frederick 1938- *WhoWor 91*
Jacobs, Lambert W. 1931- *St&PR 91*
Jacobs, Laurence P *BiDrAPA 89*
Jacobs, Laurence Stanton 1940- *WhoAm 90*
Jacobs, Lawrence H. 1955- *WhoEmL 91*
Jacobs, Lawrence-Hilton 1953- *DrBlPA 90*
Jacobs, Lazarus *PenDiDA 89*
Jacobs, Leland Blair 1907- *AuBYP 90*
Jacobs, Leo I *BiDrAPA 89*
Jacobs, Leon 1915- *WhoAm 90*
Jacobs, Leonard John 1940- *St&PR 91*
Jacobs, Leonard S 1939- *BiDrAPA 89*
Jacobs, Leonard S. 1946- *St&PR 91*
Jacobs, Leslie William 1944- *WhoAm 90*
Jacobs, Libby 1947- *WhoAmW 91*
Jacobs, Linda *ConAu 30NR*
Jacobs, Linda Joan 1941- *WhoE 91*
Jacobs, Linda Lee 1961- *WhoAmW 91*
Jacobs, Lou 1921- *AuBYP 90*
Jacobs, Louis 1910- *BiDrAPA 89*
Jacobs, Louis J 1933- *BiDrAPA 89*
Jacobs, Louis Sullivan *WhoWor 91*
Jacobs, Lynne Rose *BiDrAPA 89*
Jacobs, Marc 1963- *BioIn 16*
Jacobs, Marc Harris 1949- *BiDrAPA 89*
Jacobs, Marian Beckmann 1935- *WhoAmW 91, WhoE 91*
Jacobs, Marilyn Susan 1952- *WhoAmW 91*
Jacobs, Marion Kramer 1938- *WhoAmW 91*
Jacobs, Mark Neil 1946- *St&PR 91, WhoAm 90*
Jacobs, Mark Steven 1952- *BiDrAPA 89*
Jacobs, Mary Kathryn 1947- *WhoAmW 91*
Jacobs, Matthew Stephen 1943- *St&PR 91*
Jacobs, Melvin 1926- *St&PR 91, WhoE 91*
Jacobs, Michael L. 1942- *St&PR 91*
Jacobs, Michael Lee 1957- *WhoSSW 91*
Jacobs, Michael William 1943- *St&PR 91*
Jacobs, Michel 1877-1958 *WhoAmA 91N*
Jacobs, Michel Camille 1936- *WhoWor 91*
Jacobs, Milton 1920- *WhoAm 90*
Jacobs, Morton *BiDrAPA 89*
Jacobs, Natalie 1961- *WhoE 91*
Jacobs, Nathan L. 1905-1989 *BioIn 16*
Jacobs, Nicholas John Denham 1946- *WhoEmL 91*
Jacobs, Nora C. *ODwPR 91*
Jacobs, Norman A. 1937- *St&PR 91*
Jacobs, Norman Allan 1937- *St&PR 91*
Jacobs, Norman Gabriel 1924- *WhoAm 90*
Jacobs, Norman Joseph 1932- *WhoAm 90*

Jacobs, Otto Helmut 1939- *WhoWor 91*
Jacobs, Paul 1930-1983 *PenDiMP*
Jacobs, Paul Eugene 1932- *WhoSSW 91*
Jacobs, Peter 1950- *ODwPR 91*
Jacobs, Peter Alan 1939- *WhoAmA 91*
Jacobs, Peter Nelson 1955- *WhoEmL 91*
Jacobs, Rachel Isabelle 1945- *WhoAmW 91*
Jacobs, Ralph, Jr 1940- *WhoAmA 91*
Jacobs, Randall Brian 1951- *WhoEmL 91*
Jacobs, Randi S. 1955- *WhoAmW 91*
Jacobs, Rene 1946- *IntWWM 90, PenDiMP*
Jacobs, Richard *BioIn 16*
Jacobs, Richard Alan 1934- *WhoAm 90*
Jacobs, Richard Allen 1936- *St&PR 91, WhoAm 90*
Jacobs, Richard James 1941- *WhoAm 90, WhoE 91*
Jacobs, Richard Marc 1953- *WhoE 91*
Jacobs, Richard Matthew 1924- *WhoAm 90*
Jacobs, Richard Michael 1955- *WhoSSW 91*
Jacobs, Rita Goldman 1927- *WhoAmW 91*
Jacobs, Robert 1913- *WhoAm 90*
Jacobs, Robert J. 1929- *St&PR 91*
Jacobs, Robert Lee 1910- *St&PR 91*
Jacobs, Robert Louis 1904- *IntWWM 90*
Jacobs, Robert Louis 1939- *WhoAm 90*
Jacobs, Roger Bruce 1951- *WhoEmL 91*
Jacobs, Roland William *BiDrAPA 89*
Jacobs, Rosetta 1932- *WhoAmW 91*
Jacobs, Ruth Ann 1940- *WhoSSW 91*
Jacobs, Ruth Harriet 1924- *ConAu 33NR, WhoAm 90*
Jacobs, Sally 1932- *ConDes 90*
Jacobs, Salvador *BiDrAPA 89*
Jacobs, Selby C *BiDrAPA 89*
Jacobs, Sheila Gail McNeil 1953- *WhoAmW 91*
Jacobs, Sherry Raphael 1943- *St&PR 91, WhoAm 90*
Jacobs, Spook 1925- *Ballpl 90*
Jacobs, Stephen 1954- *WhoEmL 91*
Jacobs, Stephen Benjamin 1939- *WhoAm 90*
Jacobs, Susan Gail 1956- *WhoE 91*
Jacobs, Ted Seth 1927- *WhoAmA 91, WhoWor 91*
Jacobs, Teri Gould 1946- *WhoEmL 91*
Jacobs, Terry Stewart 1942- *St&PR 91*
Jacobs, Theodore J 1931- *BiDrAPA 89*
Jacobs, Thomas E. 1938- *St&PR 91*
Jacobs, Thomas Melvin 1943- *WhoE 91*
Jacobs, Travis Beal 1936- *WhoAm 90*
Jacobs, Vicki Ann 1951- *WhoE 91*
Jacobs, Victoria Lonigro 1947- *WhoEmL 91*
Jacobs, Warren David 1943- *BiDrAPA 89*
Jacobs, Wendell Early, Jr. 1945- *WhoEmL 91*
Jacobs, Wilfred Ebenezer 1919- *WhoWor 91*
Jacobs, Willard L. 1917- *St&PR 91*
Jacobs, William Harold 1933- *St&PR 91*
Jacobs, William M., Jr. 1939- *St&PR 91*
Jacobs, William Michael 1951- *WhoEmL 91*
Jacobs, William Paul 1919- *WhoAm 90*
Jacobs, William Thomas 1958- *WhoEmL 91*
Jacobs-Meadway, Roberta Lee 1950- *WhoEmL 91*
Jacobsberg, Lawrence Bruce 1949- *BiDrAPA 89*
Jacobsen, Adolf Marcelius Bergh 1926- *WhoAm 90*
Jacobsen, Arne 1902-1971 *ConDes 90, PenDiDA 89*
Jacobsen, Arnold 1898-1989 *BioIn 16*
Jacobsen, Arthur 1921- *St&PR 91, WhoAm 90*
Jacobsen, Arthur Francis 1942- *St&PR 91*
Jacobsen, Bruce Frederik 1946- *St&PR 91*
Jacobsen, Diane 1944- *St&PR 91*
Jacobsen, Donald Martin 1931- *St&PR 91*
Jacobsen, Eigil 1948- *WhoWor 91*
Jacobsen, Eric 1927- *St&PR 91*
Jacobsen, Frederick M 1954- *BiDrAPA 89*
Jacobsen, Frederick Marius 1954- *WhoE 91*
Jacobsen, Herbert B. 1919- *St&PR 91*
Jacobsen, James C. 1935- *St&PR 91*
Jacobsen, James Conrad 1935- *WhoAm 90*
Jacobsen, Jens Peter 1847-1885 *DcScanL*
Jacobsen, Johan Adrian 1853-1947 *WhNaAH*
Jacobsen, John A. 1944- *WhoE 91*
Jacobsen, John S. 1947- *St&PR 91*
Jacobsen, Jorgen-Frantz 1900-1938 *DcScanL*
Jacobsen, Joseph Theodore 1959- *St&PR 91*
Jacobsen, Josephine 1908- *FemiCLE*
Jacobsen, Josephine Winder Boylan 1908- *WhoAm 90*
Jacobsen, Keith M *BiDrAPA 89*
Jacobsen, Laura Beth 1951- *WhoWrEP 89*
Jacobsen, Michael A 1942- *WhoAmA 91*
Jacobsen, Michael A. 1957- *WhoWrEP 89*
Jacobsen, Norman Howard 1947- *WhoWrEP 89*
Jacobsen, Ole A. 1935- *St&PR 91*
Jacobsen, Pamela 1947- *WhoAmW 91*
Jacobsen, Paul Stephen 1958- *WhoEmL 91*
Jacobsen, Rebecca Hanson 1949- *WhoAmW 91*
Jacobsen, Richard T. 1941- *WhoAm 90*
Jacobsen, Robert Gail 1947- *WhoSSW 91*
Jacobsen, Rolf 1907- *DcScanL*
Jacobsen, Soren Lange 1951- *WhoWor 91*
Jacobsen, Susan Marie 1949- *WhoAmW 91*
Jacobsen, Theodore Harvey 1933- *WhoE 91*
Jacobsen, Thomas H. *St&PR 91*
Jacobsen, Thomas Herbert 1939- *WhoAm 90*
Jacobsen, Thomas Warren 1935- *WhoAm 90*
Jacobsen, William Ludwig, Jr. 1936- *WhoAm 90, WhoWor 91*
Jacobsen, William Peter 1932- *St&PR 91*
Jacobsen-McKeague, Mary Mae 1952- *WhoEmL 91*
Jacobshagen, N Keith, II 1941- *WhoAmA 91*
Jacobsohn, Howard G. 1916- *St&PR 91*
Jacobsohn, Richard H. 1944- *St&PR 91*
Jacobsohn, Ulrich B 1928- *BiDrAPA 89*
Jacobsohn-Lask, Berta *EncCoWW*
Jacobson, Lord 1908-1988 *AnObit 1988*
Jacobson, A. F. 1905-1990 *BioIn 16*
Jacobson, Abraham S. 1911-1988 *BioIn 16*
Jacobson, Alan Marc 1944- *BiDrAPA 89*
Jacobson, Albert Sigfried 1931- *WhoAm 90*
Jacobson, Alfred Thurl 1919- *St&PR 91, WhoAm 90*
Jacobson, Allen Frank 1926- *St&PR 91, WhoAm 90*
Jacobson, Alma Frank 1905-1990 *BioIn 16*
Jacobson, Andrea *BiDrAPA 89*
Jacobson, Ann Reisner 1926- *WhoAmW 91*
Jacobson, Anna Sue 1940- *WhoAmW 91*
Jacobson, Antone Gardner 1929- *WhoAm 90*
Jacobson, Arent John 1925- *WhoWor 91*
Jacobson, Arnold Palmer 1932- *WhoAm 90*
Jacobson, Arthur 1924- *WhoAmA 91*
Jacobson, Baby Doll 1890-1977 *Ballpl 90*
Jacobson, Barry Stephen 1955- *WhoE 91, WhoEmL 91, WhoWor 91*
Jacobson, Beany 1881-1933 *Ballpl 90*
Jacobson, Bernard 1930- *St&PR 91*
Jacobson, Bernard Isaac 1936- *IntWWM 90*
Jacobson, Bertil 1923- *WhoWor 91*
Jacobson, Beverly Greenberg 1927- *WhoE 91*
Jacobson, Bonnie Brown 1952 *WhoAmW 91, WhoE 91, WhoEmL 91*
Jacobson, Buddy 1930-1989 *BioIn 16*
Jacobson, Burton J. 1929-1989 *BioIn 16*
Jacobson, Carl E. 1930- *St&PR 91*
Jacobson, Charles Allen 1925- *WhoSSW 91*
Jacobson, Charles R 1927- *BiDrAPA 89*
Jacobson, Clifford R 1950- *BiDrAPA 89*
Jacobson, Cye Barry 1948- *WhoEmL 91*
Jacobson, D. Blaine 1955- *WhoEmL 91*
Jacobson, Dan 1929- *MajTwCW, WhoAm 90, WhoWor 91*
Jacobson, Daniel 1923- *AuBYP 90*
Jacobson, Daniel Raymond 1960- *WhoEmL 91*
Jacobson, David 1909- *WhoAm 90*
Jacobson, David J. *BioIn 16*
Jacobson, David Russell 1955- *BiDrAPA 89*
Jacobson, David Scott 1942- *St&PR 91*
Jacobson, Dennis John 1953- *WhoEmL 91*
Jacobson, Dennis L. 1945- *St&PR 91*
Jacobson, Donald Melvin 1955- *BiDrAPA 89*
Jacobson, Edward 1922- *WhoAm 90*
Jacobson, Edwin 1929- *St&PR 91*
Jacobson, Elaine Zeporah 1942- *WhoAmW 91*
Jacobson, Eli Asher 1947- *St&PR 91, WhoEmL 91, WhoWor 91*
Jacobson, Eric Michael 1947- *BiDrAPA 89*
Jacobson, Eugene Donald 1930- *WhoAm 90*
Jacobson, Eve Maxine 1961- *WhoAmW 91*
Jacobson, Florence Dorfman 1918- *WhoE 91*
Jacobson, Frank 1948- *WhoAmA 91*
Jacobson, Fred F.A. 1924- *St&PR 91*
Jacobson, Gary *BiDrAPA 89*
Jacobson, Gaynor I. 1912- *WhoAm 90*
Jacobson, George 1925- *BiDrAPA 89*
Jacobson, George D. *BioIn 16*
Jacobson, George Donald, Jr. 1947- *St&PR 91*
Jacobson, Gerald F *BiDrAPA 89*
Jacobson, Gerald M. 1938- *St&PR 91*
Jacobson, Glenn Erle 1935- *IntWWM 90*
Jacobson, Grant H. 1943- *WhoSSW 91*
Jacobson, Harold Gordon 1912- *WhoAm 90, WhoWor 91*
Jacobson, Harold Karan 1929- *WhoAm 90, WhoWor 91*
Jacobson, Harold LeLand 1926- *WhoAm 90*
Jacobson, Harvey *BiDrAPA 89*
Jacobson, Helen Gugenheim *WhoAmW 91, WhoSSW 91, WhoWor 91*
Jacobson, Henrietta *BioIn 16*
Jacobson, Herbert Laurence 1915- *WhoAm 90*
Jacobson, Herbert Leonard 1940- *WhoAm 90*
Jacobson, Howard 1928- *St&PR 91*
Jacobson, Howard 1940- *WhoAm 90*
Jacobson, Irving *BioIn 16*
Jacobson, Irving 1926- *WhoAm 90*
Jacobson, Ishier 1922- *St&PR 91, WhoAm 90*
Jacobson, Jacob G 1928- *BiDrAPA 89*
Jacobson, James Bassett *St&PR 91*
Jacobson, James Bassett 1922- *WhoAm 90*
Jacobson, James Edmund 1934- *WhoAm 90*
Jacobson, James L. 1951- *BiDrAPA 89*
Jacobson, James Lamma, Jr. 1946- *WhoSSW 91, WhoWor 91*
Jacobson, James Martin 1926- *St&PR 91*
Jacobson, James Nelson 1958- *BiDrAPA 89*
Jacobson, Jay Stanley 1934- *WhoE 91*
Jacobson, Jeffrey Eli 1956- *WhoEmL 91*
Jacobson, Jeffrey Lee 1948- *St&PR 91*
Jacobson, Jeffrey Steven 1944- *St&PR 91*
Jacobson, Jerome 1921- *St&PR 91*
Jacobson, Jerome E 1928- *BiDrAPA 89*
Jacobson, Joan 1924- *WhoAmW 91*
Jacobson, Joel *BioIn 16*
Jacobson, John D. 1929- *St&PR 91*
Jacobson, John Howard, Jr. 1933- *WhoAm 90*
Jacobson, Judith Helen 1939- *WhoAmW 91*
Jacobson, Lee 1927- *St&PR 91*
Jacobson, Leon Orris 1911- *WhoAm 90*
Jacobson, Leonard 1921- *WhoAm 90*
Jacobson, Leonard H. 1924- *St&PR 91*
Jacobson, Leonard I. 1940- *WhoAm 90, WhoWor 91*
Jacobson, Leslie Sari 1933- *WhoAm 90*
Jacobson, Louise 1927- *BiDrAPA 89*
Jacobson, Louise Groves 1938- *WhoAmW 91*
Jacobson, Lyle Gordon 1941- *St&PR 91*
Jacobson, Marc 1952- *WhoEmL 91*
Jacobson, Marcus 1930- *WhoAm 90*
Jacobson, Mark *BioIn 16*
Jacobson, Martin 1933- *St&PR 91*
Jacobson, Maura *BioIn 16*
Jacobson, Melvin Joseph 1928- *WhoAm 90*
Jacobson, Merlin Francis 1951- *WhoEmL 91*
Jacobson, Merwin 1894-1978 *Ballpl 90*
Jacobson, Michael Faraday 1943- *WhoAm 90*
Jacobson, Michael M. 1959- *WhoEmL 91*
Jacobson, Milton Murray 1952- *WhoEmL 91*
Jacobson, Mindy Sue 1954- *WhoAmW 91, WhoE 91*
Jacobson, Miriam Nachamah 1941- *WhoAmW 91*
Jacobson, Mitchell 1951- *St&PR 91*
Jacobson, Nancy Dee 1942- *St&PR 91*
Jacobson, Nancy Helen 1947- *WhoAmW 91*
Jacobson, Natalie *BioIn 16*
Jacobson, Nathan 1910- *WhoAm 90*
Jacobson, Neda *BiDrAPA 89*
Jacobson, Neil H. *BiDrAPA 89*
Jacobson, Nils O. 1937- *EncPaPR 91*
Jacobson, Norman L. 1918- *WhoAm 90*
Jacobson, Patricia Anne Fitts 1946- *WhoAmW 91*
Jacobson, Paul Allen *BiDrAPA 89*
Jacobson, Peter A. 1944- *St&PR 91*
Jacobson, Phillip Lee 1928- *WhoAm 90*
Jacobson, Ralph H. 1931- *WhoAm 90*
Jacobson, Raymond E. 1922- *St&PR 91*
Jacobson, Richard A. 1925- *St&PR 91*
Jacobson, Richard Arthur 1928- *St&PR 91*
Jacobson, Richard Harvey 1952- *BiDrAPA 89*
Jacobson, Richard Lee 1942- *WhoAm 90, WhoWor 91*
Jacobson, Richard N. 1942- *St&PR 91*
Jacobson, Richard William 1937- *St&PR 91*
Jacobson, Robert Andrew 1932- *WhoAm 90*
Jacobson, Robert Manfred 1930- *WhoAm 90*
Jacobson, Robert Neil 1957- *WhoAm 90*
Jacobson, Roger Edward 1951- *BiDrAPA 89*
Jacobson, Rut 1927- *IntWWM 90*
Jacobson, Ruth Krause 1925- *ODwPR 91*
Jacobson, Sandra Ann 1953- *BiDrAPA 89*
Jacobson, Sanford 1936- *BiDrAPA 89*
Jacobson, Saul P. 1916- *WhoAm 90*
Jacobson, Seymour B 1918- *BiDrAPA 89*
Jacobson, Sharon Diane 1942- *BiDrAPA 89*
Jacobson, Sharyn Renee 1946- *WhoAmW 91, WhoSSW 91*
Jacobson, Sheldon 1938- *WhoAm 90*
Jacobson, Sheldon Albert 1903- *WhoSSW 91*
Jacobson, Sid 1952- *WhoWrEP 89*
Jacobson, Sidney 1918- *St&PR 91*
Jacobson, Sidney 1929- *WhoAm 90*
Jacobson, Stuart E. *BioIn 16*
Jacobson, Sue Anne 1953- *WhoEmL 91*
Jacobson, Susan Dene 1949- *WhoAmW 91*
Jacobson, Sverre Theodore 1922- *WhoAm 90*
Jacobson, Victor *BioIn 16*
Jacobson, Walter Fredrick 1942- *St&PR 91*
Jacobson, Wayne E 1922- *BiDrAPA 89*
Jacobson, Wendy 1954- *BiDrAPA 89, WhoE 91*
Jacobson, William Henry 1948- *WhoSSW 91*
Jacobson, William T. 1946- *St&PR 91*
Jacobson, Yolande 1921- *WhoAmA 91*
Jacobsson, John-Eric 1931- *IntWWM 90*
Jacobsson, Sten Wilhelm John 1899-1983 *WhoAmA 91N*
Jacobstein, Joseph Myron 1920- *WhoAm 90*
Jacobus, Charles Joseph 1947- *WhoWor 91*
Jacobus, David Dinkel 1900-1988 *BioIn 16*
Jacobus, Fred D. 1926- *St&PR 91*
Jacobus, George Anthony Bodley 1938- *WhoWor 91*
Jacobus, John M 1927- *WhoAmA 91*
Jacobus, John M., Jr. 1927- *WhoAm 90*
Jacobus, Lee A 1935- *ConAu 30NR*
Jacobvitz, Robin Smith 1953- *WhoAmW 91*
Jacoby, A. James 1939- *St&PR 91, WhoAm 90, WhoE 91*
Jacoby, Brook 1959- *Ballpl 90*
Jacoby, Dolores P. 1951- *WhoSSW 91*
Jacoby, George Alonzo 1904- *WhoAm 90*
Jacoby, George V. 1918- *WhoAm 90*
Jacoby, Henry Donnan 1935- *WhoAm 90*
Jacoby, Jacob 1940- *WhoAm 90*
Jacoby, Jacob Herman 1943- *BiDrAPA 89*
Jacoby, John Primm 1941- *WhoAm 90*
Jacoby, Mary Jean 1955- *WhoAmW 91*
Jacoby, Monte Herrmann 1931- *WhoE 91, WhoWor 91*
Jacoby, Robert E. *BioIn 16*
Jacoby, Robert Eakin, Jr. 1928- *St&PR 91*
Jacoby, Robert Edward, II 1946- *WhoEmL 91*
Jacoby, Robert John 1940- *IntWWM 90*
Jacoby, Sidney B 1908-1990 *ConAu 130*
Jacoby, Stanley Arthur 1927- *WhoE 91*
Jacoby, Tamar 1954- *WhoAm 90, WhoE 91*
Jacoby, Teresa Michelle 1956- *WhoAmW 91, WhoEmL 91, WhoSSW 91*
Jacoby, William D *BiDrAPA 89*
Jacoby, William H. 1938- *St&PR 91*
Jacoby, William Jerome, Jr. 1925- *WhoAm 90*
Jacocks, Henry Miller 1953- *WhoSSW 91*
Jacoel, Anita 1956- *WhoWor 91*
Jacoff, Sydney 1915- *St&PR 91*
Jacolow, Melvin F. 1934- *WhoE 91*
Jacomb, Martin 1929- *BioIn 16, WhoWor 91*
Jacomo da Pesaro *PenDiDA 89*
Jaconetty, Thomas Anthony 1953- *WhoEmL 91*
Jacopo *PenDiDA 89*
Jacot, H. Dean 1941- *St&PR 91*
Jacovec, Joanne Mellow 1946- *WhoAmW 91*
Jacover, Jerold Alan 1945- *WhoEmL 91, WhoWor 91*
Jacovini, Joseph Henry 1940- *WhoAm 90*
Jacovitch, John 1930- *WhoWor 91*
Jacox, Ada Kathryn *WhoAm 90, WhoAmW 91*
Jacox, Ralph Franklin 1913- *WhoAm 90*
Jacqmin, Michael R. *St&PR 91*
Jacquard 1937- *WhoAmA 91*
Jacquard, Joseph-Marie 1752-1834 *PenDiDA 89*

Jacqueau, Olivier Marie 1961- *WhoEmL 91*
Jacqueline *HispWr 90*
Jacqueline *WomWR*
Jacquemart, Nelie Barbe Hyacinthe 1841-1912 *BiDWomA*
Jacquemart-Andre, Nelie Barbe Hyacinthe 1841-1912 *BiDWomA*
Jacquemin, Bob *BioIn 16*
Jacquemon, Pierre 1935- *WhoAmA 91*
Jacques, Andre Charles 1921- *WhoAm 90*
Jacques, Beau *WhoWrEP 89*
Jacques, Brian 1939- *ChlLR 21 [port], SmATA 62 [port]*
Jacques, Carole 1960- *WhoAmW 91*
Jacques, Charles-Symphorien *PenDiDA 89*
Jacques, Michael Louis 1945- *WhoAmA 91*
Jacques, Norman A. 1938- *St&PR 91*
Jacques, Robin 1920- *BioIn 16*
Jacques, Russell Kenneth 1943- *WhoAmA 91*
Jacques, Serge A. 1935- *St&PR 91*
Jacques, Wilfred James, Jr. 1932- *WhoSSW 91*
Jacquet d'Arras *PenDiDA 89*
Jacquet, Illinois *BioIn 16*
Jacquet, Illinois 1922- *DrBlPA 90, OxCPMus*
Jacquette, Yvonne Helene 1934- *WhoAm 90, WhoAmA 91*
Jacquez, Albert S. *WhoHisp 91*
Jacquier, Ivy 1890- *BioIn 16*
Jacquillat, Thierry 1938- *WhoWor 91*
Jacquinet, Damien Jean 1962- *WhoE 91*
Jacuzzi, Aldo Joseph 1921-1989 *BioIn 16*
Jacuzzi, Candido 1903-1986 *BioIn 16*
Jacuzzi, Dante Paul 1948- *St&PR 91*
Jadd, Robert Ira 1949- *WhoEmL 91*
Jade Warrior *NewAgMG*
Jaderborg, Jean Ann 1955- *WhoAmW 91*
Jadick, Harry J. 1956- *St&PR 91, WhoEmL 91*
Jadlowker, Hermann 1877-1953 *PenDiMP*
Jadot, Jean Lambert Octave 1909- *WhoAm 90*
Jadra, Ramon *WhoHisp 91*
Jadresic, Alfredo Arturo 1925- *WhoWor 91*
Jadro, William John, Jr. 1956- *WhoEmL 91*
Jadunath Sarkar 1870-1958 *BioIn 16*
Jadwiga 1373?-1399 *WomWR*
Jadwiga, Queen of Poland 1371?-1399 *BioIn 16*
Jae 1947- *WhoAmA 91, WhoAmW 91*
Jaeckel, James Carl 1944- *WhoE 91*
Jaeckel, Max *BiDrAPA 89*
Jaeckel, Richard 1926- *WorAlBi*
Jaeckels, Donald Davis 1947- *St&PR 91*
Jaeckle, Fred William 1943- *St&PR 91*
Jaeckle, Harvey 1917- *St&PR 91*
Jaeckle, Richard G 1936- *BiDrAPA 89*
Jaegel, Jeffrey James 1951- *St&PR 91*
Jaeger, Andrea *BioIn 16*
Jaeger, Andrei-Claudian 1953- *BiDrAPA 89*
Jaeger, Brenda Kay 1950- *WhoAmA 91, WhoWrEP 89*
Jaeger, Clara *BioIn 16*
Jaeger, David 1947- *IntWWM 90*
Jaeger, David A. 1938- *St&PR 91*
Jaeger, David Arnold 1938- *WhoAm 90*
Jaeger, Ed *BioIn 16*
Jaeger, Frank 1926-1977 *DcScanL*
Jaeger, George W. 1926- *WhoE 91*
Jaeger, Ina Claire Burlingham 1929- *IntWWM 90*
Jaeger, James L. 1948- *St&PR 91*
Jaeger, Judy Durrance 1950- *WhoAmW 91*
Jaeger, Leonard Henry 1905- *WhoAm 90, WhoWor 91*
Jaeger, Lowell Larry 1951- *WhoWrEP 89*
Jaeger, Muriel 1893?- *FemiCLE*
Jaeger, Richard Charles 1944- *WhoAm 90*
Jaeger, Robert J. 1948- *St&PR 91*
Jaeger, Roberta Alice *BiDrAPA 89*
Jaeger, Ruth 1900-1990 *BioIn 16*
Jaeger, Ruth E *BiDrAPA 89*
Jaeger, Sharon Ann 1945- *WhoWor 91, WhoWrEP 89*
Jaeger, Stephen Owen 1944- *St&PR 91*
Jaeger, Thomas *BiDrAPA 89*
Jaeger-Lee, Dorothy 1917- *BiDrAPA 89*
Jaegermann, Ephraim Josef 1949- *WhoWor 91*
Jaegers, Beverly Carol 1935- *WhoWrEP 89*
Jaeggi, Eva Maria 1934- *WhoWor 91*
Jaeggi, Kenneth Vincent 1945- *WhoAm 90*
Jaeggi, Urs 1937- *IntWWM 90*
Jaekels, Christopher John 1960- *WhoEmL 91*
Jaenicke, Lothar 1923- *WhoWor 91*
Jaenike, Richard C *BiDrAPA 89*
Jaenike, William F. 1937- *St&PR 91*
Jaenke, Edwin August 1930- *St&PR 91*
Jafek, Bruce William 1941- *WhoAm 90*
Jaff, Alvin Martin 1931- *St&PR 91*
Jaffa, David 1929- *St&PR 91*
Jaffa, Harry Victor 1918- *WhoAm 90*
Jaffa, Max 1911- *IntWWM 90*
Jaffan, Heather 1938- *St&PR 91*
Jaffar, Sayed *BioIn 16*
Jaffe, Abraham 1932- *St&PR 91*
Jaffe, Alan *BiDrAPA 89*
Jaffe, Alan Steven 1939- *WhoAm 90*
Jaffe, Andrew Mark 1938- *WhoWor 91*
Jaffe, Andrew Michael 1923- *WhoWor 91*
Jaffe, Aniela 1903- *EncO&P 3, EncPaPR 91*
Jaffe, Annette Gail 1954- *WhoE 91*
Jaffe, Arnold 1930- *St&PR 91*
Jaffe, Arthur Michael 1937- *WhoAm 90*
Jaffe, Austin Jay 1952- *WhoE 91, WhoEmL 91*
Jaffe, Bernard M. 1923- *St&PR 91*
Jaffe, Bernard Michael *WhoAm 90*
Jaffe, Brian Dimitrios *WhoE 91*
Jaffe, Bruce Morgan 1944- *St&PR 91*
Jaffe, Caroline Ruth 1961- *WhoAmW 91*
Jaffe, Charles M 1947- *BiDrAPA 89*
Jaffe, Daniel S 1914- *BiDrAPA 89*
Jaffe, David *BiDrAPA 89*
Jaffe, David 1911- *WhoWrEP 89*
Jaffe, David 1911-1990 *ConAu 131, WhoAm 90, WhoWor 91*
Jaffe, David Royce 1959- *WhoEmL 91*
Jaffe, Dennis T 1946- *ConAu 32NR*
Jaffe, Edward Ephraim 1928- *WhoAm 90*
Jaffe, Elliot S. 1926- *WhoAm 90*
Jaffe, Ernst Richard 1925- *WhoE 91*
Jaffe, Eugene Donald 1937- *WhoWor 91*
Jaffe, F. Filmore 1918- *WhoAm 90*
Jaffe, Harold 1940- *ConAu 30NR, WhoWrEP 89*
Jaffe, Harvey Jay 1960- *BiDrAPA 89*
Jaffe, Herbert J. 1934- *St&PR 91*
Jaffe, Herbert Leon 1928- *St&PR 91*
Jaffe, Herbert M. 1924- *St&PR 91*
Jaffe, Hilde 1927- *WhoAm 90*
Jaffe, Ira S 1943- *WhoAmA 91*
Jaffe, Irma B *WhoAmA 91*
Jaffe, Jan Paynter 1944- *WhoAm 90*
Jaffe, Jay M. *ODwPR 91*
Jaffe, Jay M. 1941- *St&PR 91*
Jaffe, Jeff Hugh 1920- *WhoSSW 91*
Jaffe, Jeffrey Martin 1954- *WhoAm 90*
Jaffe, Jerome H *BiDrAPA 89*
Jaffe, Joanne Wilson 1942- *WhoAmW 91*
Jaffe, Joseph *BiDrAPA 89*
Jaffe, Kenneth Eric 1951- *BiDrAPA 89*
Jaffe, Laurence Richard 1942- *WhoAm 90*
Jaffe, Lawrence Jay 1950- *BiDrAPA 89*
Jaffe, Leo 1909- *St&PR 91, WhoAm 90*
Jaffe, Leonard Sigmund 1916- *WhoAm 90*
Jaffe, Lewis 1956- *WhoE 91*
Jaffe, Lori Beth 1957- *St&PR 91*
Jaffe, Louise 1936- *WhoAmW 91*
Jaffe, Maggie 1948- *WhoWrEP 89*
Jaffe, Mark Lester 1958- *WhoEmL 91*
Jaffe, Marvin 1920- *BiDrAPA 89*
Jaffe, Marvin Eugene 1936- *St&PR 91*
Jaffe, Maurice H. 1912- *St&PR 91*
Jaffe, Melvin 1919- *WhoE 91*
Jaffe, Michael 1940- *St&PR 91, WhoAm 90*
Jaffe, Michael A *BiDrAPA 89*
Jaffe, Murray Sherwood 1926- *WhoAm 90*
Jaffe, Nora 1928- *WhoAm 90, WhoAmA 91*
Jaffe, Norman J. 1954- *WhoEmL 91*
Jaffe, Paul Lawrence 1928- *WhoAm 90, WhoE 91, WhoWor 91*
Jaffe, Phyllis Shelley 1925- *WhoAmW 91, WhoE 91*
Jaffe, Richard Louis *BiDrAPA 89*
Jaffe, Richard Louis 1952- *WhoE 91*
Jaffe, Robert 1923- *BiDrAPA 89*
Jaffe, Robert David 1952- *WhoEmL 91*
Jaffe, Rona 1932- *BestSel 90-3 [port], MajTwCW, WhoAm 90, WhoAmW 91, WhoWrEP 89, WorAlBi*
Jaffe, Sam 1891-1984 *WorAlBi*
Jaffe, Sanford I. 1926- *St&PR 91*
Jaffe, Seymour Sheppard 1930- *WhoE 91*
Jaffe, Shirley 1923- *BioIn 16*
Jaffe, Sigmund 1921- *WhoAm 90*
Jaffe, Stanley Richard 1940- *WhoAm 90*
Jaffe, Stephen 1954- *IntWWM 90*
Jaffe, Stephen Mark *BiDrAPA 89*
Jaffe, Steven L 1940- *BiDrAPA 89*
Jaffe, Susan *BioIn 16, WhoAmW 91*
Jaffe, Susan Lynn *WhoAmW 91*
Jaffe, Suzanne Denbo 1943- *WhoAmW 91, WhoE 91*
Jaffe, Sylvia 1926- *WhoWrEP 89*
Jaffe, Sylvia Sarah 1917- *WhoAmW 91, WhoSSW 91, WhoWor 91*
Jaffe, William B *WhoAmA 91N*
Jaffe-Barzach, Amy Eileen 1961- *WhoAmW 91*
Jaffe-Notier, Peter Andrew 1947- *WhoEmL 91*
Jaffee, Allan 1921- *EncACom*
Jaffee, Annette Williams 1945- *ConAu 131, WhoWrEP 89*
Jaffee, Dwight M. 1943- *WhoAm 90, WhoE 91*
Jaffee, Eileen Karen 1954- *WhoAmW 91*
Jaffee, Kay 1937- *IntWWM 90*
Jaffee, Keith W. 1960- *St&PR 91*
Jaffee, Mary L *ConAu 30NR*
Jaffee, Michael *IntWWM 90*
Jaffee, Michael 1938- *WhoAm 90*
Jaffee, Richard M. 1936- *St&PR 91*
Jaffee, Robert D. 1933- *St&PR 91*
Jaffee, Robert Isaac 1917- *WhoAm 90*
Jaffee, Sandra Schuyler 1943- *St&PR 91, WhoAm 90*
Jaffer, Azeezaly S. 1955- *ODwPR 91*
Jaffer, Frances E. 1921- *WhoWrEP 89*
Jaffer, Navin 1958- *WhoAmW 91*
Jaffeson, Richard Charles 1947- *WhoE 91*
Jaffin, Charles Leonard 1928- *WhoAm 90*
Jaffoni, Joseph *ODwPR 91*
Jaffrey, Saeed 1929- *ConTFT 8*
Jaffri, Syed Shams U 1941- *BiDrAPA 89*
Jaffurs, Lee Wardlaw 1955- *WhoEmL 91*
Jafri, Alima Bibi *BiDrAPA 89*
Jafri, Mokarram H 1935- *BiDrAPA 89*
Jagan, Cheddi 1918- *BioIn 16*
Jagan, Janet 1920- *BioIn 16, WhoWor 91*
Jagel, Abraham ben Hananiah dei Galicchi *BioIn 16*
Jagendorf, Andre Tridon 1926- *WhoAm 90*
Jagendorf, Moritz 1888-1981 *AuBYP 90*
Jager, Hendrik 1944- *WhoWor 91*
Jager, Karl 1888-1959 *BioIn 16*
Jager, Norbert 1925- *WhoWor 91*
Jager, Robert 1939- *BioIn 16*
Jager, Robert Edward 1939- *IntWWM 90*
Jager, Tom *BioIn 16*
Jaggard, Gary E. 1953- *WhoSSW 91*
Jaggears, Albert R. 1936- *St&PR 91*
Jagger, Bryony Phillips 1948- *IntWWM 90*
Jagger, C. Thomas 1937- *St&PR 91*
Jagger, David Michael 1941- *St&PR 91*
Jagger, Dean 1903- *WorAlBi*
Jagger, Gillian 1930- *WhoAmA 91, WhoE 91*
Jagger, Jade *BioIn 16*
Jagger, James Cloyd 1945- *WhoEmL 91*
Jagger, Kenneth 1925- *St&PR 91*
Jagger, Mick *BioIn 16*
Jagger, Mick 1943- *EncPR&S 89, WhoAm 90, WhoWor 91, WorAlBi*
Jaggers, Annielaura Mixon 1918- *WhoWrEP 89*
Jaggi, Rene C. 1948- *WhoWor 91*
Jaggin, Christoph 1956- *IntWWM 90*
Jagid, Bruce 1940- *St&PR 91*
Jagielski, Karen Irene 1962- *WhoAmW 91*
Jaglom, Andre Richard 1953- *WhoEmL 91*
Jaglom, Henry *BioIn 16*
Jaglom, Jacob 1927- *St&PR 91*
Jagman, Ed 1936- *WhoAmA 91*
Jagnow, Lawrence V. 1941- *ODwPR 91*
Jagoda, Andrew Lester 1959- *WhoEmL 91*
Jagoda, Barry Lionel 1944- *WhoAm 90*
Jagoda, Leonard Joseph 1947- *St&PR 91*
Jagodzinski, Heinz Ernst 1916- *WhoWor 91*
Jagow, Charles Herman 1910- *WhoWor 91*
Jagow, Elmer 1922- *WhoAm 90*
Jagric, Milan 1949- *WhoWor 91*
Jagt, Jack 1942- *St&PR 91*
Jagtiani, Ram Alimchand 1936- *WhoWor 91*
Jahagirdar, Keshav Tatacharya 1914- *EncO&P 3*
Jahan, Marine 1958- *WhoAmW 91*
Jahansetan, Seyed J *BiDrAPA 89*
Jahde, Judy A. 1949- *WhoAmW 91*
Jahiel, Rene Ino 1928- *WhoWor 91*
Jahkola, Kaarlo Antero 1931- *WhoWor 91*
Jahn, Billie Jane 1921- *WhoAmW 91, WhoWor 91*
Jahn, Earl W. 1918- *St&PR 91*
Jahn, Ellen Elizabeth 1951- *WhoEmL 91*
Jahn, Evelyn Eleanor 1909- *St&PR 91*
Jahn, Gertrude 1940- *IntWWM 90*
Jahn, Helmut *BioIn 16*
Jahn, Helmut 1940- *WhoAm 90*
Jahn, Jerome J. 1936- *St&PR 91*
Jahn, Laurence Roy 1926- *WhoAm 90*
Jahn, Norma Jean 1926- *WhoAmW 91*
Jahn, Patricia Lynn 1948- *St&PR 91*
Jahn, Paul Ronald 1942- *St&PR 91*
Jahn, Robert C. *St&PR 91*
Jahn, Robert G. 1930- *EncPaPR 91*
Jahn, Robert George 1930- *WhoAm 90*
Jahn, Robert William, II 1949- *WhoEmL 91*
Jahn, Virginia C. 1919- *St&PR 91*
Jahn, Wolfgang G. *St&PR 91*
Jahnke, Erich W. 1946- *St&PR 91*
Jahnke, Robert A. 1944- *St&PR 91*
Jahnn, Hans Henny 1894-1959 *BioIn 16*
Jahns, Jeffrey 1946- *WhoEmL 91*
Jahoda, Fritz 1909- *WhoAm 90*
Jahoda, Gustav 1920- *EncO&P 3*
Jahromi, Mahmood *BiDrAPA 89*
Jaicks, David P. 1925- *St&PR 91*
Jaicks, Frederick Gillies 1918- *WhoAm 90*
Jaicks, Wilson A., Jr. 1922- *St&PR 91*
Jaicomo, Ronald James 1932- *St&PR 91*
Jaidah, Ali Mohammed 1941- *WhoWor 91*
Jaidinger, Judith C 1941- *WhoAmA 91*
Jaime, Francisco 1960- *WhoHisp 91*
Jaime, Kalani 1961- *WhoHisp 91*
Jaimes Freyre, Ricardo 1866-1933 *BioIn 16*
Jaimes Freyre, Ricardo 1868-1933 *HispWr 90*
Jaimovich, David Gerard 1954- *WhoEmL 91*
Jain, Anil Kumar 1949- *BiDrAPA 89*
Jain, Ash *BioIn 16*
Jain, Brij Bhushan 1931- *St&PR 91*
Jain, Devinder K 1945- *BiDrAPA 89*
Jain, Mahavir Sohanlal 1952- *WhoWor 91*
Jain, Mohan H *BiDrAPA 89*
Jain, Padam Chand 1935- *BiDrAPA 89*
Jain, Padm Dant 1936- *WhoWor 91*
Jain, Piyare Lal 1921- *WhoAm 90*
Jain, Pushpa Rani 1935- *WhoAmW 91*
Jain, Sagar Chand 1930- *WhoAm 90*
Jain, Sanjeevani *BiDrAPA 89*
Jain, Shanti *BiDrAPA 89*
Jain, Subhash C 1941- *BiDrAPA 89*
Jain, Subhash Chandra 1950- *WhoWor 91*
Jain, Sudesh K. 1953- *WhoWor 91*
Jain, Sukhbir Prasad 1943- *WhoWor 91*
Jain, Sunita Duli 1938- *WhoAmW 91*
Jain, Surendra Kumar 1947- *WhoWor 91*
Jain, Surendra Mohan 1947- *St&PR 91, WhoEmL 91*
Jain, Sushil Kumar 1955- *WhoWor 91*
Jain, Umesh Ravi *BiDrAPA 89*
Jain, Vijay Prakash 1944- *WhoWor 91*
Jain, Vinary Kumar 1959- *WhoE 91*
Jain, Virendra K *BiDrAPA 89*
Jain, Yawantraj P *BiDrAPA 89*
Jaine, Hira C *BiDrAPA 89*
Jaini, Yolanda Marie Jimenez 1950- *WhoAmW 91*
Jair Lang, Roberto *WhoHisp 91*
Jairaj, Sudha 1949- *BiDrAPA 89*
Jais, Richard Benjamin 1930- *WhoWor 91*
Jaiven, Jack 1946- *St&PR 91*
Jajodia, Shyamalendu 1958- *WhoE 91*
Jajoor, Nagaraj Onkarappa *BiDrAPA 89*
Jakab, Irene *BiDrAPA 89, WhoAm 90, WhoAmW 91, WhoE 91, WhoWor 91*
Jakab, Veronica A *BiDrAPA 89*
Jakes, Jean Ann 1956- *WhoWrEP 89*
Jakes, John 1932- *AuBYP 90, BioIn 16, MajTwCW, SmATA 62 [port], WhoAm 90*
Jakes, John William 1932- *WhoWrEP 89*
Jakes, Karen Sorkin 1947- *WhoAmW 91*
Jakes, Milos *BioIn 16*
Jakes, Milos 1922- *WhoWor 91*
Jakes, Walter *BioIn 16*
Jakes, William Chester 1922- *WhoAm 90*
Jakhar, Bal Ram 1923- *BioIn 16, WhoWor 91*
Jaki, Stanley Ladislas 1924- *WhoAm 90*
Jakmas, Richard Gordon 1951- *St&PR 91*
Jakmauh, Edward 1942- *St&PR 91*
Jakob, Dennis H. 1948- *St&PR 91*
Jakob, Michel Alexandre 1962- *WhoWor 91*
Jakobe, Virginia Ellis 1922- *WhoE 91*
Jakobovits, Immanuel *BioIn 16*
Jakobowski, Thomas W. 1931- *St&PR 91*
Jakobs, Nancy Martha 1940- *St&PR 91*
Jakobsdottir, Svava 1930- *DcScanL*
Jakobsen, Jakob Knudsen 1912- *WhoAm 90*
Jakobsen, Katherine Ann 1952- *MusmAFA*
Jakobson, Irina *BioIn 16*
Jakobson, Mark John 1923- *WhoAm 90*
Jakobson, Roman 1896-1982 *ConAu 31NR*
Jakobsson, Claes 1924- *IntWWM 90*
Jakobsson, Jokull 1933-1978 *DcScanL*
Jakoby, Richard Matthias 1929- *IntWWM 90*
Jaksic, Djura 1924- *IntWWM 90*
Jakstas, Alfred John 1916- *WhoAm 90, WhoAmA 91*
Jakubanis, Paula Marie 1958- *WhoEmL 91*
Jakubauskas, Edward Benedict 1930- *WhoAm 90*
Jakubec, Paul John 1938- *WhoSSW 91*
Jakubowski, Donna Marie 1957- *WhoWrEP 89*
Jakubowski, Hieronim 1946- *WhoE 91*
Jakubowski, W. 1933- *St&PR 91*
Jakubowsky, Frank R. 1931- *WhoWrEP 89*
Jakucki, Sig 1909-1979 *Ballpl 90*
Jalal al-Din Muhammad 1542-1605 *BioIn 16*
Jalali, Behnaz *BiDrAPA 89*

Jalali, Mehrdad *BiDrAPA 89*
Jalan, Lalit 1956- *WhoWor 91*
Jalan, Suman Lata *BiDrAPA 89*
Jalas, Jussi 1908- *PenDiMP*
Jalayer, Behrooz 1938- *St&PR 91, WhoSSW 91*
Jalbert, Eugene Roland 1951- *WhoSSW 91*
Jalbert, Michael Eugene 1945- *St&PR 91*
Jalbert, Ronald Richard 1938- *St&PR 91*
Jalife, Jose 1947- *WhoAm 90*
Jalil, Abdul 1920- *St&PR 91*
Jalkut, Richard Alan 1944- *St&PR 91, WhoAm 90*
Jallais, Denise *EncCoWW*
Jallais, Denise D. *EncCoWW*
Jalonen, John William 1922- *St&PR 91*
Jalonick, George Washington, IV 1940- *WhoSSW 91, WhoWor 91*
Jalton, Frederic 1924- *BioIn 16*
Jam, The *OxCPMus*
Jam, Jimmy *BioIn 16*
Jamail, Joseph Dahr, Jr. 1925- *WhoSSW 91*
Jamal al-Din al-Afghani 1838-1897 *BioIn 16*
Jamal, Ahmad 1930- *BioIn 16, DrBIPA 90*
Jamal, Moez Ahamed 1955- *WhoWor 91*
Jamal, Parviz *BiDrAPA 89*
Jamali, Mohammed Fadhel al- 1903- *BioIn 16*
Jamaluddin, Jafri 1934- *WhoWor 91*
Jamandre, Vita Mallari 1932- *WhoSSW 91*
Jamar, Steven Dwight 1953- *WhoEmL 91*
Jambois, Beverly Ann 1954- *WhoEmL 91*
Jambois, Robert James 1952- *WhoEmL 91*
Jambor, Robert Vernon 1936- *WhoAm 90*
Jameel, Fathulla *WhoWor 91*
Jameikis, Brone Aleksandra *WhoAmA 91*
Jameison, Timothy C. 1930- *St&PR 91*
Jamell, Jeanne 1933- *St&PR 91*
Jamena, Jose Serrano 1951- *BiDrAPA 89*
James II, King of Great Britain 1633-1701 *BioIn 16*
James IV, King of Scotland 1473-1513 *BioIn 16*
James IV of Scotland 1473-1513 *EncO&P 3*
James Peter *DcCanB 12*
James, A Everette, Jr 1938- *WhoAmA 91*
James, Alice 1848-1892 *BioAmW, BioIn 16, FemiCLE*
James, Allen 1945- *St&PR 91*
James, Allix Bledsoe 1922- *WhoAm 90, WhoSSW 91*
James, Alton Everette, Jr. 1938- *WhoAm 90*
James, Amabel Boyce 1952- *WhoAmW 91*
James, Amalia *ConAu 30NR*
James, Anne 1956- *WhoAmW 91*
James, Arthur Giangiacomo 1912- *WhoAm 90*
James, Artis Edward, Jr. 1946- *St&PR 91*
James, Austin 1924- *St&PR 91*
James, Barbara Woodward 1936- *WhoAmW 91*
James, Barry Nelson 1933- *St&PR 91*
James, Benjamin David 1912 *WhoAm 90*
James, Bess *BioIn 16*
James, Bill *BioIn 16*
James, Bill 1887-1942 *Ballpl 90*
James, Bill 1892-1971 *Ballpl 90*
James, Bill 1943- *WhoAmA 91*
James, Bill 1949- *Ballpl 90*
James, Bob 1958- *Ballpl 90*
James, Brent Carl 1950- *WhoEmL 91*
James, Brian Robert 1936- *WhoAm 90*
James, Bruce M. 1935- *St&PR 91*
James, Byron S. 1932- *St&PR 91*
James, C. B. *WhoWrEP 89*
James, C. L. R. 1901-1989 *AnObit 1989, BioIn 16*
James, C.L.R. 1901-1989 *EncAL, MajTwCW*
James, Carl G. 1952- *St&PR 91*
James, Carolyne Faye 1945- *WhoAm 90*
James, Catherine French *WhoE 91*
James, Catti 1940- *WhoAmA 91*
James, Chappie *BioIn 16*
James, Charlene 1959- *WhoSSW 91*
James, Charles *BioIn 16*
James, Charles Franklin, Jr. 1931- *WhoAm 90*
James, Charles Griffin 1933- *WhoSSW 91*
James, Charles Leslie 1939- *St&PR 91*
James, Charles R. 1934- *St&PR 91*
James, Charlie 1937- *Ballpl 90*
James, Chris 1962- *Ballpl 90*
James, Christopher 1948- *WhoEmL 91*
James, Christopher P 1947- *WhoAmA 91*
James, Clarity 1945- *IntWWM 90*
James, Clive 1939- *MajTwCW*
James, Clive Vivian Leopold 1939- *WhoWor 91*
James, Colin *BioIn 16*
James, Craig 1941- *WhoAm 90, WhoSSW 91*
James, Craig T. 1941- *BioIn 16*
James, Cynthia Ann 1956- *WhoAmW 91*
James, Cyril Lionel Robert 1901-1989 *BioIn 16*
James, Dan 1951- *WhoEmL 91*
James, Daniel *BioIn 16*
James, Daniel, Jr. *BioIn 16*
James, Daniel, Jr. 1920-1978 *WorAlBi*
James, Daniel J. 1920- *WhoAm 90*
James, David Edward 1935- *WhoAm 90*
James, David Geraint 1922- *WhoWor 91*
James, David L. 1933- *St&PR 91*
James, David L. 1955- *WhoWrEP 89*
James, David Lee 1933- *WhoAm 90, WhoWor 91*
James, David Nicholas 1952- *WhoSSW 91*
James, David Randolph, Jr. 1924- *WhoSSW 91*
James, David Stever 1952- *WhoEmL 91*
James, David W. 1933- *St&PR 91*
James, Diana Marie 1955- *WhoAmW 91*
James, Diane Louise 1965- *WhoWrEP 89*
James, Dion 1962- *Ballpl 90*
James, Dorothy Buckton *WhoAm 90*
James, Dorris Clayton 1931- *WhoAm 90*
James, Dot 1938- *WhoAmW 91*
James, E. Pendleton *BioIn 16*
James, Earl Eugene, Jr. 1923- *WhoSSW 91, WhoWor 91*
James, Edith Joyce 1926- *WhoAmW 91*
James, Edward Foster 1927- *WhoWor 91*
James, Edwin *WhoWrEP 89*
James, Edwin Clark 1932- *WhoAm 90*
James, Edwin Hugh 1917- *St&PR 91*
James, Eirian 1952- *IntWWM 90*
James, Elinor *BiDEWW, FemiCLE*
James, Elizabeth *BioIn 16*
James, Elizabeth 1942- *AuBYP 90*
James, Elizabeth Wick 1950- *WhoAm 90*
James, Ellen Lawrence 1932- *WhoSSW 91*
James, Elmore 1918-1963 *OxCPMus*
James, Emlyn *WhoWrEP 89*
James, Emrys 1930-1989 *AnObit 1989*
James, Eric G. 1910-1988 *BioIn 16*
James, Estelle 1935- *WhoAm 90, WhoE 91*
James, Etta 193-?- *EncPR&S 89*
James, Francis Edward, Jr. 1931- *WhoAm 90, WhoWor 91*
James, Frank 1844-1915 *BioIn 16*
James, Frank M 1909- *BiDrAPA 89*
James, Frank Munger 1939- *WhoAm 90*
James, Frank Samuel, III 1945- *WhoEmL 91*
James, Frank William 1946- *WhoWrEP 89*
James, Frederick Calhoun 1922- *WhoAm 90*
James, G. Peter 1946- *St&PR 91*
James, Gene A. 1932- *St&PR 91*
James, Gene Albert 1932- *WhoSSW 91*
James, Geneva Behrens 1942- *WhoAmW 91*
James, George Barker 1937- *St&PR 91*
James, George Barker, II 1937- *WhoAm 90*
James, George C *BiDrAPA 89*
James, George William, Jr. 1932- *WhoAm 90*
James, Geraldine *BioIn 16*
James, Geraldine 1950- *ConTFT 8 [port]*
James, Gleda Jo *WhoAmW 91*
James, Hamilton Evans 1951- *WhoAm 90*
James, Harold Arthur 1903- *WhoAm 90*
James, Harry 1916-1983 *BioIn 16, OxCPMus, WorAlBi*
James, Heather 1914- *ConAu 31NR*
James, Helen Spencer 1936- *WhoAmW 91*
James, Henry 1811-1882 *BioIn 16, WorAlBi*
James, Henry 1843-1916 *BioIn 16, ConAu 132, MajTwCW, TwCLC 40 [port], WorAlBi, WrPh*
James, Henry 1940- *St&PR 91*
James, Henry Thomas 1915- *WhoAm 90*
James, Herman Delano 1943- *WhoAm 90, WhoE 91*
James, Howard Anthony, Jr. 1935- *WhoAm 90*
James, Howard P. 1923- *St&PR 91*
James, Hugh Neal 1952- *WhoSSW 91*
James, Hugh R. 1947- *St&PR 91*
James, I. M. 1928- *BioIn 16*
James, Ifor 1931- *IntWWM 90*
James, Ioan Mackenzie 1928- *BioIn 16*
James, Irving Arthur 1922- *WhoAm 90*
James, J. Douglas 1918- *St&PR 91*
James, J Frank 1937- *BiDrAPA 89*
James, Jack 1930- *St&PR 91*
James, James Rush, Jr. 1916- *St&PR 91*
James, James Younger *WhoWrEP 89*
James, Jeannie Henrietta 1921- *WhoAmW 91*
James, Jeff 1941- *Ballpl 90*
James, Jennifer Austin 1943- *WhoAmW 91, WhoWor 91*
James, Jesse 1847-1882 *BioIn 16, WorAlBi*
James, Jessica *BioIn 16, NewYTBS 90*
James, Jimmie, Jr. 1938- *IntWWM 90*
James, Joel Andrew 1953- *WhoSSW 91*
James, John 1956- *ConTFT 8 [port]*
James, John Delmar 1944- *WhoAm 90*
James, John Edward 1950- *WhoEmL 91*
James, John J. *BioIn 16*
James, John Randolph 1949- *WhoEmL 91*
James, John Robert *BioIn 16*
James, John Sullivan 1957- *WhoEmL 91*
James, John William, Jr. 1930- *WhoSSW 91*
James, Johnny 1933- *Ballpl 90*
James, Jonathan K. *ODwPR 91*
James, Joyce 1952- *St&PR 91*
James, Judith Vogel 1937- *WhoE 91*
James, Karl Chase 1949- *St&PR 91*
James, Kathryn Kanarek 1949- *WhoAmW 91*
James, Kay 1949- *WhoAm 90, WhoAmW 91*
James, Keith Alan 1957- *WhoEmL 91*
James, Keith William 1936- *WhoWor 91*
James, Ladonna Huntley *ODwPR 91*
James, Lance Fitzgerald 1954- *WhoE 91*
James, Lawrence D. 1914- *St&PR 91*
James, Linda Strong 1954- *WhoSSW 91*
James, Louis Meredith 1941- *WhoSSW 91*
James, Margaret Neal 1942- *WhoAmW 91*
James, Marge Elizabeth 1925- *WhoAmW 91*
James, Marian 1822?-1900 *FemiCLE*
James, Marie Moody 1928- *WhoAmW 91, WhoWor 91*
James, Marie Ruppert 1942- *WhoAmW 91*
James, Marion Ray 1940- *WhoAm 90, WhoWor 91*
James, Mark *WhoWrEP 89*
James, Mark Edward 1955- *BiDrAPA 89*
James, Maryellen 1960- *WhoAmW 91*
James, Michael A. 1943- *St&PR 91*
James, Michael Andrew 1953- *WhoE 91*
James, Michael Benjamin 1964- *WhoSSW 91*
James, Michael Lee 1955- *BiDrAPA 89*
James, Michael N. G. *WhoAm 90*
James, Michael Royston 1950- *WhoEmL 91*
James, Mona Hinkle 1935- *WhoAmW 91*
James, Norma Wood *AuBYP 90*
James, Norman M 1942- *BiDrAPA 89*
James, Olga *DrBIPA 90*
James, P. D. *BioIn 16*
James, P D *MajTwCW*
James, P. D. 1920- *FemiCLE*
James, P D 1920- *TwCCr&M 91, WhoWor 91*
James, P. D. 1920- *WorAlBi*
James, Patricia Ann 1933- *WhoAm 90*
James, Patricia Ann 1947- *WhoSSW 91*
James, Patrick J. 1910- *St&PR 91*
James, Paul Charles 1935- *WhoAm 90*
James, Peter Haydn 1940- *IntWWM 90*
James, Philip *MajTwCW*
James, Phyllis Dorothy 1920- *WhoAm 90*
James, Phyllis P. 1947- *St&PR 91*
James, Preston Everett 1899-1986 *BioIn 16*
James, Quinton C 1929- *BiDrAPA 89*
James, Raymond John 1937- *BiDrAPA 89*
James, Rhoda Ann Michaux 1953- *WhoEmL 91*
James, Richard Lowell *BiDrAPA 89*
James, Rick 1952- *EncPR&S 89*
James, Robert Brian 1950- *WhoEmL 91*
James, Robert Charles 1943- *St&PR 91, WhoAm 90*
James, Robert E *BiDrAPA 89*
James, Robert Gamble 1933- *St&PR 91*
James, Robert Leo *BioIn 16*
James, Robert Leo 1936- *WhoAm 90, WhoE 91*
James, Robert Logan 1945- *BiDrAPA 89*
James, Robert M. 1928- *WhoAm 90*
James, Robert S. 1939- *St&PR 91*
James, Robert Scott 1943- *WhoAm 90*
James, Robin 1953- *BioIn 16*
James, Roderick Vivian 1946- *WhoSSW 91*
James, Roger *BioIn 16*
James, Ronald *BioIn 16*
James, Ronald Bruce 1954- *St&PR 91*
James, Ronald Eugene 1954- *WhoEmL 91*
James, Roz H. *BioIn 16*
James, S. S. *WhoWrEP 89*
James, Sean Christopher 1940- *St&PR 91*
James, Sharpe 1936- *WhoAm 90, WhoE 91*
James, Sheila Ann 1937- *WhoAmW 91*
James, Sheila Feagley 1925- *WhoAmW 91*
James, Shelly, Jr. *BiDrAPA 89*
James, Sidney Lorraine 1906- *WhoAm 90*
James, Stan *BioIn 16*
James, Stanislaus Anthony 1919- *WhoWor 91*
James, Steven Parker 1952- *BiDrAPA 89, WhoE 91*
James, SuEllen Holliman 1931- *WhoAmW 91*
James, Sydney Vincent 1929- *WhoAm 90, WhoWrEP 89*
James, T. P. *EncO&P 3*
James, Theodore, Jr. 1934- *WhoWrEP 89*
James, Thomas 1593?-1635 *EncCRAm*
James, Thomas Alan 1942- *St&PR 91*
James, Thomas Lemuel 1831-1916 *BiDrUSE 89*
James, Thomas Naum 1925- *WhoAm 90, WhoSSW 91*
James, Timmy Joel 1963- *WhoSSW 91*
James, Tommy 1947- *EncPR&S 89*
James, Tommy, and the Shondells *EncPR&S 89*
James, Walter 1915- *WhoWor 91*
James, Wayne Lamar 1934- *St&PR 91*
James, Will 1892-1942 *AuBYP 90, BioIn 16*
James, William 1771-1832 *BioIn 16*
James, William 1842-1910 *BioIn 16, EncO&P 3, EncPaPR 91, WorAlBi, WrPh P*
James, William 1929- *BioIn 16, St&PR 91*
James, William Allen *BiDrAPA 89*
James, William Andrew 1838-1893 *AmLegL*
James, William Benjamin 1947- *WhoEmL 91*
James, William C. W. *BioIn 16*
James, William Fleming 1894- *St&PR 91, WhoAm 90*
James, William Hall 1910- *WhoE 91, WhoWor 91*
James, William Joseph 1922- *WhoAm 90*
James, William Joseph 1928- *BiDrAPA 89*
James, William M. 1931- *St&PR 91*
James, William N. *WhoWrEP 89*
James, William Ramsay 1933- *WhoAm 90*
James, William Scott *BiDrAPA 89*
James, William W. 1931- *WhoAm 90*
James, William Wesley, Jr. 1936- *WhoWor 91*
James Mayer, Susan Smyth 1955- *WhoAmW 91*
James-Price, Frances Antoinette 1961- *WhoE 91*
James-Roberts, Brenda 1957- *WhoAmW 91*
Jameson, Andrew *WhoAm 90*
Jameson, Anna 1794-1860 *DcLB 99 [port]*
Jameson, Anna Brownell 1794-1860 *BioIn 16, FemiCLE*
Jameson, Charles Scott Kennedy 1925- *WhoWor 91*
Jameson, Cynthia *AuBYP 90*
Jameson, Demetrios George 1919- *WhoAmA 91*
Jameson, Dorothea 1920- *WhoAm 90, WhoAmW 91*
Jameson, Fredric *BioIn 16*
Jameson, Grace K 1924- *BiDrAPA 89*
Jameson, Guilford Stanley 1897- *WhoE 91*
Jameson, J. Larry 1937- *St&PR 91*
Jameson, James Larry 1937- *WhoAm 90*
Jameson, Jay Marshall 1943- *WhoE 91*
Jameson, Johnette H. *AuBYP 90*
Jameson, Kenneth D. 1950- *St&PR 91*
Jameson, Larry Ernest 1949- *WhoSSW 91*
Jameson, Leander Starr 1853-1917 *BioIn 16*
Jameson, Malcolm 1891-1945 *AuBYP 90*
Jameson, Michael Hamilton 1924- *WhoAm 90*
Jameson, Patricia Marian 1945- *WhoAmW 91*
Jameson, Paula Ann 1945- *WhoAmW 91, WhoEmL 91*
Jameson, Philip Alexander 1952- *WhoAmA 91*
Jameson, R. Philip 1941- *IntWWM 90*
Jameson, Richard Willis 1851-1899 *DcCanB 12*
Jameson, Robert Benson Makeham 1933- *St&PR 91*
Jameson, Sanford Chandler 1932- *WhoE 91*
Jameson, Storm 1891-1986 *BioIn 16, FemiCLE*
Jameson, Victor Loyd 1924- *WhoAm 90*
Jameson, William James 1898- *WhoAm 90*
Jamieson, Brewster Howard 1960- *WhoEmL 91*
Jamieson, Charlie 1893-1969 *Ballpl 90*
Jamieson, Christopher W. 1954- *St&PR 91*
Jamieson, David Donald 1926- *WhoAm 90*
Jamieson, Graham A. 1929- *WhoAm 90*
Jamieson, H.L. 1911- *St&PR 91*
Jamieson, Henry Louis 1911- *WhoAm 90*
Jamieson, James Phillips 1953- *WhoEmL 91, WhoSSW 91*
Jamieson, John *BiDrAPA 89*
Jamieson, John B. 1940- *St&PR 91*
Jamieson, John Charles 1933- *WhoAm 90*
Jamieson, John Kenneth 1910- *WhoAm 90*
Jamieson, Margretta Elizabeth 1907- *WhoE 91*
Jamieson, Michael Lawrence 1940- *WhoAm 90*
Jamieson, Reginald Mac 1927- *St&PR 91*
Jamieson, Robert, Jr. 1936- *St&PR 91*

Jamieson, Robert C 1949- *BiDrAPA 89*
Jamieson, Russell Ladeau, Jr. 1958- *WhoSSW 91*
Jamieson, Stuart William 1947- *WhoAm 90*
Jamieson, Timm 1947- *St&PR 91*
Jamieson, W. Scott 1953- *St&PR 91*
Jamiesson, Max *BioIn 16*
Jamil, Ahmad Khan 1939- *WhoWor 91*
Jamin, G.A. 1941- *St&PR 91*
Jamin, Gerald Alan 1941- *WhoAm 90*
Jamison, Charles H. 1940- *St&PR 91*
Jamison, Harrison Clyde 1925- *WhoAm 90*
Jamison, Herbert L., Jr. 1924- *St&PR 91*
Jamison, Hubert Milton 1946- *WhoSSW 91*
Jamison, John Ambler 1916- *WhoAm 90, WhoSSW 91*
Jamison, John Callison 1934- *WhoAm 90*
Jamison, John Vincent, III 1911- *St&PR 91*
Jamison, Judith *BioIn 16*
Jamison, Judith 1934- *BioAmW*
Jamison, Judith 1943- *DrBlPA 90*
Jamison, Judith 1944- *News 90[port], -90-3[port], WhoAm 90, WhoE 91*
Jamison, Mark Peter 1955- *St&PR 91*
Jamison, Max Killian 1918- *WhoAm 90, WhoWor 91*
Jamison, Michael David 1955- *St&PR 91*
Jamison, Oliver Morton 1916- *WhoAm 90*
Jamison, Paul William *BiDrAPA 89*
Jamison, Philip 1925- *WhoAm 90, WhoAmA 91*
Jamison, Rex Lindsay 1933- *WhoAm 90*
Jamison, Richard Bryan 1932- *WhoAm 90*
Jamison, Richard Melvin 1938- *WhoAm 90*
Jamison, Robert Irwin 1939- *St&PR 91*
Jamison, Roger 1937- *IntWWM 90*
Jamison, Sheila Ann English 1950- *WhoAmW 91, WhoEmL 91, WhoWor 91*
Jamison, Sheila D. *ODwPR 91*
Jamison, Susan Clapp 1929- *WhoAmW 91, WhoE 91*
Jamison, Thomas Jefferson 1917- *St&PR 91*
Jamison, Virginia Patterson 1918- *WhoAmW 91*
Jamison, Wallace Glenn 1945- *BiDrAPA 89*
Jamison, Zean, Jr. 1932- *St&PR 91*
Jammal, Jamal Mohamad 1959- *WhoWor 91*
Jamme, Albert Joseph 1916- *WhoAm 90*
Jamme, Anna C. 1865-1939 *BioIn 16*
Jamnitzer, Albrecht *PenDiDA 89*
Jamnitzer, Bartel 1548?-1596 *PenDiDA 89*
Jamnitzer, Christoph 1563-1618 *PenDiDA 89*
Jamnitzer, Hans *PenDiDA 89*
Jamnitzer, Hans, II 1539-1603 *PenDiDA 89*
Jamnitzer, Wenzel 1508-1585 *PenDiDA 89*
Jamora, Augusto Magno 1941- *BiDrAPA 89*
Jamora, Mariflor S 1955- *BiDrAPA 89*
Jamora, Sylvia Jacinto 1939- *WhoWor 91*
Jampala, V Chowdary 1955- *BiDrAPA 89*
Jampala, Vijayababu *BiDrAPA 89*
Jampel, Robert Steven 1926- *WhoAm 90*
Jamplis, Robert Warren 1920- *WhoAm 90*
Jampol, Glenn D 1950- *WhoAmA 91*
Jampole, Diana Patricia 1958- *WhoAmW 91*
Jampolsky, Gerald Gersham 1925- *NewAgE 90*
Jamrich, John Xavier 1920- *WhoAm 90*
Jamsek-Tehlirian, Marieta 1947- *BiDrAPA 89, WhoEmL 91*
Jamshidi, Simin 1956- *WhoAmW 91*
Jan and Dean *EncPR&S 89, WorAlBi*
Jan, Chenhuan Jack 1961- *WhoEmL 91*
Janacek Quartet *PenDiMP*
Janacek, Bedrich 1920- *IntWWM 90*
Janacek, Jim W. 1942- *St&PR 91*
Janacek, Leos 1854-1928 *BioIn 16, PenDiMP A, WorAlBi*
Janakiramaiah, Nimmagadda 1941- *BiDrAPA 89*
Janas, Adam 1938- *St&PR 91*
Janauschek, Fanny 1830-1904 *BioIn 16, NotWoAT*
Janazzo, Donna Lynn 1948- *WhoAmW 91*
Jancauskas, Don 1946- *WhoEmL 91*
Jance, Judy 1944- *BioIn 16*
Jancewicz, Robert Stanley, Sr. 1951- *St&PR 91*
Jancso, Miklos 1921- *BioIn 16*
Jancuk, Wilma Ann 1944- *WhoAmW 91, WhoE 91*
Janda, Robert Louis 1936- *St&PR 91*
Jandeni *WhoWor 91*
Jander, Owen 1930- *IntWWM 90*
Jandial, Satish Rai 1938- *St&PR 91*
Jandl, Ernst 1925- *WorAu 1980[port]*
Jandl, Henry Anthony 1910- *WhoAm 90*
Jandl, James Harriman 1925- *WhoAm 90*
Jandura, Paula 1952- *WhoAmW 91*
Jane *WomWR*
Jane, John Anthony 1931- *WhoAm 90*
Jane, Mary Childs 1909- *AuBYP 90*
Janecek, James 1933- *BiDrAPA 89*
Janecek, Lenore Elaine 1944- *WhoAmW 91*
Janecke, Ronald Brian 1939- *WhoAm 90*
Janecky, David Richard 1953- *WhoEmL 91*
Janeczko, Paul B. 1945- *BioIn 16, WhoWrEP 89*
Janelsins, Veronica 1910- *WhoAmA 91*
Janenka, Stephen James 1960- *WhoE 91*
Janensch, Paul 1938- *WhoAm 90*
Janerus, Ingolf Valentin 1943- *St&PR 91*
Janes, Clara 1940- *EncCoWW*
Janes, Edward Clarence 1908- *AuBYP 90*
Janes, George Sargent 1927- *WhoAm 90*
Janes, J. Robert 1935- *BioIn 16*
Janes, Janina Z. P. 1955- *WhoEmL 91*
Janes, John Anthony 1943- *St&PR 91*
Janes, John Joseph, Jr. 1957- *St&PR 91*
Janes, Joseph Robert 1935- *BioIn 16*
Janes, Judy *WhoWrEP 89*
Janes, Maronee Fleming 1929- *WhoAmW 91*
Janes, Robert Grant *BiDrAPA 89*
Janes, Robert James 1925- *WhoE 91*
Janes, Steven M. 1954- *WhoWrEP 89*
Janes, William Sargent 1953- *WhoE 91*
Janesch, Mary Jean 1928- *WhoAmW 91*
Janeski, Gerry 1946- *Ballpl 90*
Janet, Pierre 1859-1947 *EncO&P 3, EncPaPR 91*
Janetos, Andrew E. 1936- *St&PR 91*
Janetos, Paul E., Sr. 1931- *St&PR 91*
Janevicius, Vincas *BiDrAPA 89*
Janevski, Blagoja Kame 1934- *WhoWor 91*
Janeway, Carol *BioIn 16*
Janeway, David Lee *BiDrAPA 89*
Janeway, Eliot 1913- *ConAu 130, WhoE 91, WorAlBi*
Janeway, Elizabeth 1913- *AuBYP 90, FemiCLE*
Janeway, Elizabeth Hall 1913- *WhoAm 90, WhoAmW 91, WhoWrEP 89*
Janeway, Michael Charles 1940- *WhoAm 90, WhoWrEP 89*
Janeway, Richard 1933- *WhoAm 90*
Jang, Song-Hyon 1939- *WhoWor 91*
Jangaard, Norman Olaf 1941- *St&PR 91, WhoAm 90*
Jani, Niranjan N *BiDrAPA 89*
Jani, Robert F. *BioIn 16*
Jani, Sushma Niranjan 1959- *BiDrAPA 89, WhoE 91*
Janiak, A. Richard 1946- *St&PR 91*
Janiak, Anthony Richard, Jr. 1946- *WhoAm 90*
Janiak, Jane Marie 1947- *WhoAmW 91*
Janicak, Philip G 1946- *BiDrAPA 89*
Janice *AuBYP 90*
Janich, Daniel Nicholas 1952- *WhoEmL 91*
Janich, George Peter 1929- *WhoAm 90*
Janicker, Lynn Ruth 1936- *WhoE 91*
Janicki, Anna Josepha *BiDrAPA 89*
Janicki, Hazel 1918-1976 *WhoAmA 91N*
Janicki, Natalia J *BiDrAPA 89*
Janicki, Peggy *BioIn 16*
Janicki, Robert Stephen 1934- *St&PR 91, WhoAm 90*
Janicki, Suzanne Lynn 1961- *WhoAmW 91*
Janics, John T *BiDrAPA 89*
Janiger, Oscar *BiDrAPA 89*
Janigro, Antonio 1918-1989 *PenDiMP*
Janik, Andrew Stephen *BiDrAPA 89*
Janik, Carolyn 1940- *ConAu 33NR*
Janikowski, Constance Janelle 1934- *St&PR 91*
Janin, Pierre Raymond 1941- *St&PR 91*
Janis, Allen Ira 1930- *WhoAm 90*
Janis, Byron 1924- *IntWWM 90*
Janis, Byron 1928- *PenDiMP*
Janis, Conrad *WhoAm 90*
Janis, Conrad 1928- *WhoAmA 91*
Janis, Donald E. 1942- *St&PR 91*
Janis, Donald Emil 1942- *WhoAm 90*
Janis, Donald Leon 1931- *WhoAm 90*
Janis, Elsie 1889-1956 *BioIn 16, NotWoAT, OxCPMus*
Janis, Eugenia Parry 1940- *WhoAmA 91*
Janis, Irving L. *NewYTBS 90*
Janis, Irving Lester 1918- *WhoAm 90*
Janis, Jay 1932- *St&PR 91*
Janis, Juliane *BiDrAPA 89*
Janis, Leon O 1926- *BiDrAPA 89*
Janis, N. Richard 1946- *WhoEmL 91*
Janis, Sidney 1896-1989 *AnObit 1989, BioIn 16, ConAu 130, CurBio 90N, WhoAmA 91N*
Janischewskyj, Wasyl 1925- *WhoAm 90*
Janiszewski, Edward J. 1928- *St&PR 91*
Janitschek, Maria 1859-1927 *EncCoWW*
Janjigian, Edward R 1908- *BiDrAPA 89*
Janjigian, Lucy Elizabeth 1932- *WhoAmA 91*
Janjigian, Vahan 1956- *WhoE 91*
Janjua, Pervez Zamurrad 1955- *WhoWor 91*
Jankauskas, Benedict S *BiDrAPA 89*
Janke, Igor Edward 1958- *BiDrAPA 89*
Janke, Paul Gordon 1955- *BiDrAPA 89*
Janke, Tom Michael 1943- *St&PR 91*
Janklow, Mort *BioIn 16*
Janklow, Morton Lloyd 1930- *WhoAm 90, WhoWor 91*
Janko, May 1926- *WhoAm 90, WhoAmA 91, WhoE 91*
Janko, Richard 1955- *ConAu 30NR*
Jankoff, John Henry 1943- *WhoE 91*
Jankovic, Joseph 1948- *WhoAm 90, WhoWor 91*
Jankowiak, Jeffrey R. 1960- *St&PR 91*
Jankowiak, Richard Alan *BiDrAPA 89*
Jankowitsch, Peter 1933- *WhoWor 91*
Jankowitz, Abraham 1935- *BiDrAPA 89*
Jankowski, Gene F. 1934- *St&PR 91, WhoAm 90, WhoE 91*
Jankowski, James Paul 1937- *WhoAm 90*
Jankowski, Joseph John 1936- *BiDrAPA 89*
Jankowski, Kazimierz W *BiDrAPA 89*
Jankowski, Loretta 1950- *IntWWM 90*
Jankowski, Stanislaw 1946- *WhoWor 91*
Jankowski, Theodore Andrew 1946- *WhoAmA 91*
Jankowski, Walter Joseph 1920- *St&PR 91*
Jankowsky, Joseph Simon 1934- *St&PR 91*
Janku, Hana 1940- *IntWWM 90*
Jankun, Robert Edward 1949- *WhoEmL 91*
Jankura, Donald Eugene 1929- *St&PR 91, WhoAm 90*
Janky, Gladyce O. 1953- *St&PR 91*
Janle, Elsa Marie 1941- *WhoAmW 91*
Jannarone, John Robert 1914- *WhoAm 90*
Janne, Henri G. 1908- *WhoWor 91*
Jannen, Robert L. 1927- *St&PR 91*
Janner, Barnett 1892-1982 *DcNaB 1981*
Jannett, Carl Paskie 1952- *WhoEmL 91*
Jannetta, Peter J. *BioIn 16*
Jannetta, Samuel Michael 1940- *WhoSSW 91*
Jannetti, Tony 1947- *WhoAmA 91*
Janney, Christopher Draper 1950- *WhoAmA 91*
Janney, Donald Wayne 1952- *WhoEmL 91*
Janney, Richard Neil 1941- *St&PR 91*
Janney, Samuel McPherson 1801-1880 *WhNaAH*
Janney, Stuart Symington 1907-1988 *BioIn 16*
Janney, Thomas Michael 1949- *St&PR 91*
Jannicelli, Matteo 1935- *WhoWrEP 89*
Janning, Mary Bernadette 1917- *WhoAm 90*
Jannings, Emil 1886-1950 *WorAlBi*
Jannini, Ralph H. 1932- *St&PR 91*
Jannini, Ralph Humbert, III 1932- *WhoAm 90*
Jannis, Dorothy *WhoWrEP 89*
Jannoni, Richard F. 1935- *St&PR 91*
Jannott, Frederick P. 1938- *St&PR 91*
Jannotta, Edgar D. 1931- *St&PR 91*
Jannuzi, Eugene F. 1915- *St&PR 91*
Jannuzzi, Janice Gertrude 1962- *WhoEmL 91*
Janock, Marcia Linda 1960- *WhoAmW 91*
Janoff, Aaron 1930-1988 *BioIn 16*
Janofsky, Bonnie Ruth 1953- *WhoEmL 91*
Janofsky, Jeffrey S *BiDrAPA 89*
Janofsky, Jeffrey Stuart 1957- *WhoE 91*
Janofsky, Leonard S. 1909- *WhoAm 90*
Janos, Greg 1947- *St&PR 91*
Janos, Joseph A. 1941- *St&PR 91*
Janosik, Edward Gabriel 1918- *WhoAm 90*
Janosik, Evelyn Joyce 1933- *WhoAmW 91*
Janoska, Judith 1931- *WhoWor 91*
Janoski, Henry Valentine 1933- *WhoAm 90, WhoE 91*
Janosko, Linda 1949- *WhoEmL 91*
Janosko, Rudolph E M 1930- *BiDrAPA 89*
Janosko, Rudolph E. M. 1930- *WhoE 91*
Janotha, Natalie 1856-1932 *BioIn 16, PenDiMP*
Janousek, Judith Ann 1940- *WhoAmW 91*
Janov, Lauren Lynn 1958- *WhoEmL 91*
Janovec, Madeline Meza 1935- *WhoAmW 91*
Janover, H.G. 1916- *St&PR 91*
Janover, Robert H. 1930- *WhoWor 91*
Janovich, Alvin C. 1946- *St&PR 91*
Janovicky, Karel 1930- *IntWWM 90*
Janovitz, William Paul 1942- *St&PR 91*
Janovy, David Lee 1934- *WhoAm 90*
Janow, Chris 1953- *WhoE 91*
Janowiak, Sandra Logan 1955- *WhoAmW 91*
Janowich, Ronald 1948- *WhoAmA 91*
Janowicz, Peter Francis 1940- *WhoWor 91*
Janowicz, Vic 1930- *Ballpl 90*
Janowitz, Gundula 1937- *IntWWM 90, PenDiMP, WhoWor 91*
Janowitz, Henry David 1915- *WhoAm 90*
Janowitz, Joel 1945- *WhoAmA 91*
Janowitz, Morris *BioIn 16*
Janowitz, Phyllis *WhoWrEP 89*
Janowitz, Tama *BioIn 16*
Janowitz, Tama 1957- *WhoWrEP 89*
Janowitz, Warren Robert 1947- *WhoEmL 91*
Janowski, Edward *St&PR 91*
Janowski, Marek 1939- *IntWWM 90, PenDiMP*
Janowski, Thaddeus Marian 1923- *WhoAm 90, WhoWor 91*
Janowsky, Carol 1939- *St&PR 91*
Janowsky, David Steffan 1939- *BiDrAPA 89*
Janowsky, Sy 1928- *St&PR 91*
Jans, Candace 1952- *WhoAmA 91, WhoE 91*
Jans, James Patrick 1927- *WhoAm 90*
Jans, Joan Marie 1962- *WhoE 91*
Jansa, Karlene Rae 1946- *WhoAmW 91*
Janschka, Fritz 1919- *WhoAmA 91*
Jansen, Angela Bing 1929- *WhoAm 90, WhoAmA 91, WhoE 91*
Jansen, August Harry 1883-1955 *BioIn 16*
Jansen, Barbara 1954- *WhoAmW 91*
Jansen, Catherine Sandra 1950- *WhoAmA 91*
Jansen, Dale L., III 1942- *St&PR 91*
Jansen, Dan *BioIn 16*
Jansen, Dirk Adriaan 1956- *WhoWor 91*
Jansen, Donald Orville 1939- *WhoAm 90*
Jansen, G. Thomas 1926- *WhoAm 90*
Jansen, Gert Peter 1936- *WhoWor 91*
Jansen, Gwendolyn Beth 1955- *WhoAmW 91*
Jansen, Henry 1918 *St&PR 91, WhoAm 90, WhoWor 91*
Jansen, Isabel 1906- *WhoWor 91*
Jansen, Jacques 1913- *IntWWM 90*
Jansen, Jared *ConAu 30NR*
Jansen, Johannes Felix Johanna Maria 1923- *IntWWM 90*
Jansen, Joseph A. *ODwPR 91*
Jansen, Larry 1920- *Ballpl 90*
Jansen, Marius B 1922- *ConAu 130*
Jansen, Marius Berthus 1922- *WhoAm 90*
Jansen, Martin Henry 1931- *BiDrAPA 89*
Jansen, Michael 1940- *ConAu 130*
Jansen, Patrick J. 1927- *St&PR 91*
Jansen, Ralph 1927- *St&PR 91*
Jansen, Raymond A., Jr. 1939- *St&PR 91*
Jansen, Richard *St&PR 91*
Jansen, Robert Bruce 1922- *WhoAm 90*
Jansen, Robert Paul Siebrand 1946- *WhoWor 91*
Jansen, Rudolf 1940- *IntWWM 90*
Jansen, Ruth K 1920- *BiDrAPA 89*
Jansen, Walter B. 1945- *St&PR 91*
Jansen/Barbieri *NewAgMG*
Janshekar, Hossein 1947- *WhoWor 91*
Jansing, John Curry 1925- *St&PR 91*
Jansky, Karl G. 1905-1950 *WorAlBi*
Jansma, John Dean 1933- *WhoE 91*
Janson, Agnes *WhoAmA 91*
Janson, Anthony Frederick 1943- *WhoAm 90*
Janson, Anthony Fredrick 1943- *WhoAmA 91*
Janson, Astrid 1947- *OxCCanT*
Janson, Barbara Jean 1942- *WhoAmW 91, WhoE 91*
Janson, Dora Jane 1916- *AuBYP 90*
Janson, Horst Woldemar 1913-1982 *AuBYP 90, WhoAmA 91N*
Janson, Joseph Bror, II 1928- *WhoAm 90*
Janson, Raymond Kenneth 1927- *St&PR 91*
Janson, Richard Wilford 1926- *St&PR 91*
Jansons, Andrejs 1938- *IntWWM 90*
Jansons, Mariss 1943- *IntWWM 90, PenDiMP*
Janss, Edwin *BioIn 16*
Janss, Glenn Cooper 1932- *WhoAmA 91*
Janssen, Alfred Guthrie 1949- *WhoWrEP 89*
Janssen, Cydney Dawn 1958- *WhoEmL 91*
Janssen, David 1930-1980 *BioIn 16, WorAlBi*
Janssen, Erwin T 1936- *BiDrAPA 89, WhoAm 90*
Janssen, Felix Gerard 1925- *WhoAm 90*
Janssen, Hans *WhoAmA 91N*
Janssen, Henri Jean 1940- *WhoWor 91*
Janssen, Herbert 1895-1963 *PenDiMP*
Janssen, Mark Anthony 1958- *WhoEmL 91*
Janssen, Martin Christopher 1948- *WhoWor 91*
Janssen, Paul Adriaan Jan 1926- *WhoWor 91*
Janssen, Peter Anton 1936- *WhoAm 90*

Janssen, Werner *NewYTBS 90 [port]*
Janssen, Werner 1899- *PenDiMP*
Janssens, Joseph William, Jr. 1935- *WhoAm 90*
Jansson, Henrik Daniel Johannes 1916- *IntWWM 90*
Jansson, Jan-Erik 1921- *WhoWor 91*
Jansson, Jan Helge 1941- *WhoWor 91*
Jansson, John Phillip 1918- *WhoWor 91*
Jansson, Kurt Gunnar 1915- *WhoWor 91*
Jansson, Tove Maria 1914- *DcScanL*
Jansson, Tove Marika 1914- *EncCoWW*
Janszen, Herbert H *BiDrAPA 89*
Janszen, Wilbur John, Jr. 1940- *St&PR 91*
Jantio, Roger Blanchard 1959- *WhoE 91*
Jantunen, Kauko Ilmari 1941- *WhoWor 91*
Jantz, Cynthia M. 1957- *WhoAmW 91*
Jantz, Harold 1907-1987 *BioIn 16*
Jantz, Kenneth M. 1942- *St&PR 91*
Jantzen, John Marc 1908- *WhoAm 90, WhoWor 91*
Jantzen, Ronald Edward 1946- *WhoSSW 91*
Jantzen, William J. 1909- *St&PR 91*
Januarius, Saint *EncPaPR 91*
January, Lewis Edward 1910- *WhoAm 90*
January, Mildred H *BiDrAPA 89*
January, Richard George 1947- *WhoEmL 91*
Janulaitis, M. Victor 1945- *WhoEmL 91*
Janulako, Vassilio 1933- *IntWWM 90*
Janulis, Peter T 1926- *BiDrAPA 89*
Janura, Jan Arol 1949- *WhoEmL 91, WhoWor 91*
Janus, Paul William 1939- *St&PR 91*
Janus, Thomas Gerald 1942- *WhoE 91*
Janutolo, Sarah Catherine 1935- *WhoAmW 91*
Januz, Lauren Robert 1930- *WhoWrEP 89*
Janvier, C. A. *BiDWomA*
Janvier, Rosemary Farley 1939- *WhoE 91*
Janville, duchess of Martel de 1849-1932 *EncCoWW*
Janvrin, Hal 1892-1962 *Ballpl 90*
Janzen, Calvin Lewis 1940- *BiDrAPA 89*
Janzen, Daniel H. *BioIn 16*
Janzen, Daniel Hunt 1939- *WhoAm 90*
Janzen, Eldon A. 1928- *IntWWM 90*
Janzen, Howard E. 1954- *St&PR 91*
Janzen, Norine Madelyn Quinlan 1943- *WhoAmW 91*
Janzer, Georges *PenDiMP*
Janzer, Jerome Mark 1957- *WhoEmL 91*
Janzer, Norman M *BiDrAPA 89*
Janzou, Steven Howard 1963- *WhoEmL 91*
Janzow, Walter Theophilus 1918- *WhoAm 90*
Japar, Susan Elizabeth 1949- *WhoAmW 91*
Jape, Mijndert 1932- *IntWWM 90*
Japelli, Giuseppe 1783-1852 *PenDiDA 89*
Japhet, Ernest Israel 1921- *St&PR 91*
Japhet, James Hagen 1953- *WhoSSW 91*
Jappelli, Tullio 1956- *WhoWor 91*
Japrisot, Sebastien 1931- *BioIn 16, TwCCr&M 91B*
Jaqua, Frederick W. 1921- *St&PR 91*
Jaqua, Richard Allen 1938- *WhoAm 90*
Jaque, Louis 1919- *WhoAmA 91*
Jaques, E. Vernon 1942- *St&PR 91*
Jaques, Louis Barker 1911- *WhoAm 90*
Jaques, Susan Hosterman 1953- *WhoEmL 91*
Jaques, Thomas Francis 1938- *WhoSSW 91*
Jaques, William Everett 1917- *WhoWor 91*
Jaquet, Brent Michael 1949- *WhoE 91*
Jaquet, James R. 1929- *St&PR 91*
Jaquette, John J. 1918- *St&PR 91*
Jaquette, John Joseph 1918- *WhoAm 90*
Jaquin, Noel 1894-1974 *EncO&P 3*
Jaquint, Robert W. 1925- *St&PR 91*
Jaquith, Donald S. 1925- *St&PR 91*
Jaquith, George Oakes 1916- *WhoWor 91*
Jaquith, Martha Ann 1962- *WhoAmW 91*
Jaquith, Priscilla 1908- *BioIn 16*
Jaquith, Richard Herbert 1919- *WhoAm 90*
Jaquith, William L *BiDrAPA 89*
Jaquith, William Walter 1944- *St&PR 91*
Jara, Jose Maria 1866-1939 *ArtLatA*
Jaramillo, Anthony B. 1959- *WhoHisp 91*
Jaramillo, Cleofas Martinez 1878-1956 *BioIn 16*
Jaramillo, Ernesto 1963- *WhoHisp 91*
Jaramillo, Florence *BioIn 16*
Jaramillo, George *WhoHisp 91*
Jaramillo, Henry, Jr. 1928- *WhoHisp 91*
Jaramillo, Jaime *BiDrAPA 89*
Jaramillo, James D C *BiDrAPA 89*
Jaramillo, Jeannine D. 1960- *WhoHisp 91*
Jaramillo, Mari-Luci 1928- *BioIn 16, WhoAm 90, WhoHisp 91*
Jaramillo, Pedro *BioIn 16*
Jaramillo, Rudy *WhoHisp 91*
Jaramillo, Virginia 1939- *WhoAmA 91*
Jaramillo, Yasmin M *BiDrAPA 89*
Jaranson, James Melvin *BiDrAPA 89*
Jarass, Hans Dieter 1945- *WhoWor 91*
Jarausch, Konrad H 1941- *ConAu 130*
Jarausch, Konrad Hugo 1941- *WhoAm 90*
Jaray, Tess 1937- *BiDWomA*
Jarblum, Marc 1887-1972 *BioIn 16*
Jarboe, Edward Joseph 1935- *WhoE 91*
Jarboe, Greg *ODwPR 91*
Jarboe, John Melvin 1930- *St&PR 91, WhoAm 90*
Jarboe, Mark Alan 1951- *WhoEmL 91*
Jarboro, Caterina 1903-1986 *BioIn 16, DrBIPA 90*
Jarc, Frank Robert 1942- *WhoAm 90*
Jarda, Jean Carl 1953- *BiDrAPA 89*
Jardetzky, Oleg 1929- *WhoAm 90*
Jardin, Alain D. 1937- *WhoWor 91*
Jardine, Andrew *BioIn 16*
Jardine, David Henry 1947- *St&PR 91*
Jardine, Don L. 1926- *St&PR 91*
Jardine, Donald Leroy 1926- *WhoAmA 91*
Jardine, James Quintus 1954- *WhoSSW 91*
Jardine, John *BioIn 16*
Jardine, John Wallace, Jr. 1927- *St&PR 91*
Jardine, Larry L. 1936- *St&PR 91*
Jardine, Thomas D. 1928- *ODwPR 91*
Jardine, William Marion 1879-1955 *BiDrUSE 89*
Jardiolin, Pearl C *BiDrAPA 89*
Jardon, Cesar Alberto 1932- *BiDrAPA 89*
Jardon, Claude Earl, Jr. 1941- *St&PR 91*
Jardon, John Raymond 1948- *WhoEmL 91*
Jarecki, Henry G 1933- *BiDrAPA 89*
Jarecki, Henry George 1933- *WhoE 91*
Jareckie, Stephen Barlow 1929- *WhoAm 90*
Jarema, Maria 1908-1958 *BiDWomA*
Jarema, Stephen J. 1905-1988 *BioIn 16*
Jaresko, Natalie Ann 1965- *WhoE 91*
Jaret, Julian 1924- *St&PR 91*
Jaret, Kathe A. 1952- *WhoAmW 91*
Jaret, Leroy R 1939- *BiDrAPA 89*
Jaret, Stanley 1929- *St&PR 91*
Jarett, Leonard 1936- *WhoAm 90*
Jarislowsky, Stephen Arnold 1925- *St&PR 91*
Jarkovsky, Isaac 1926- *St&PR 91, WhoWor 91*
Jarmain, Edwin Roper 1907- *St&PR 91*
Jarman, A O H 1911- *ConAu 130*
Jarman, Archibald Seymour 1909- *EncO&P 3*
Jarman, David L. 1949- *WhoEmL 91*
Jarman, Derek 1942- *BioIn 16*
Jarman, Douglas 1942- *IntWWM 90*
Jarman, Joseph 1937- *WhoAm 90*
Jarman, Mark Foster 1952- *WhoSSW 91*
Jarman, Maureen Casey 1949- *WhoEmL 91*
Jarman, Richard Sinclair 1947- *St&PR 91*
Jarman, Walton Maxey 1904-1980 *WhoAmA 91N*
Jarmick, Christopher James 1956- *WhoEmL 91*
Jarmie, Nelson 1928- *WhoAm 90*
Jarmine, Lori S. *ODwPR 91*
Jarmul, Ruth Barbara 1949- *WhoEmL 91*
Jarmus, Stephan Onysym 1925- *WhoAm 90*
Jarmusch, Jim *BioIn 16*
Jarmusch, Jim 1953?- *ConAu 132, CurBio 90 [port]*
Jarmusch, Robert Thomas 1922- *St&PR 91*
Jarmusch, Roland J. 1945- *St&PR 91*
Jarnagan, Harry William, Jr. 1953- *WhoEmL 91*
Jarnefelt, Arvid 1861-1932 *DcScanL*
Jarnot Billias, Andrea Marie 1960- *WhoE 91*
Jaroch, Raymond *St&PR 91*
Jaroff, Leon Morton 1927- *WhoAm 90, WhoWor 91*
Jaron, Dov 1935- *WhoAm 90*
Jaros, Arthur G. 1922- *St&PR 91*
Jaros, Dean 1938- *WhoAm 90*
Jaros, George A. *St&PR 91N*
Jaros, Robert James 1939- *WhoE 91*
Jaroski, Edward L. 1946- *St&PR 91*
Jaroski, Jill Ann 1956- *WhoAmW 91*
Jaross, Richard Harvey 1944- *WhoE 91*
Jarosz, Frederick John 1929- *St&PR 91*
Jaroszewski, Edward, II 1952- *BiDrAPA 89*
Jaroszewski, Leo Francis 1939- *WhoSSW 91*
Jarowski, Charles Ignatius 1946- *WhoE 91*
Jarrahi, Ali *BiDrAPA 89*
Jarrar, Hala Y. Jarrah 1947- *WhoE 91*
Jarrard, Jerald Osborne 1917- *WhoAm 90*
Jarrard, Leonard Everett 1930- *WhoAm 90*
Jarrard, Terry Sue 1945- *BiDWomA*
Jarrard-Dimond, Terry 1945- *WhoAmA 91*
Jarrard-Dimond, Terry Sue 1945- *BiDWomA*
Jarrat, Henri Aaron 1938- *WhoAm 90*
Jarratt, Devereux 1733-1801 *EncCRAm*
Jarratt, Mary Claiborne 1942- *WhoAm 90*
Jarratt, Robert Devereux 1941- *WhoSSW 91*
Jarre, Jean-Michel *NewAgMG*
Jarre, Maurice 1924- *OxCPMus*
Jarreau, Al *BioIn 16*
Jarreau, Al 1940- *DrBIPA 90, WhoAm 90, WorAlBi*
Jarrell, Donald Ray 1963- *WhoSSW 91*
Jarrell, Elaine Thurman 1943- *WhoSSW 91*
Jarrell, Iris Bonds 1942- *WhoAmW 91*
Jarrell, James Michael 1957- *St&PR 91*
Jarrell, Randall 1914-1965 *AuBYP 90, BioIn 16, MajTwCW, WhoAmA 91N, WorAlBi*
Jarrell, Richard Wayne 1951- *WhoEmL 91*
Jarrell, Sheree Gipson 1955- *WhoAmW 91*
Jarrell, Valerie Cantrelle 1962- *WhoAmW 91*
Jarrett, Alexis 1948- *WhoAmW 91*
Jarrett, Anthony 1930- *WhoAm 90*
Jarrett, Charles Edward 1924- *WhoAm 90*
Jarrett, David Bernard 1947- *BiDrAPA 89*
Jarrett, Dennis Eugene 1946- *WhoE 91*
Jarrett, Diana Louise *WhoAmW 91*
Jarrett, Elbert Loy 1940- *WhoSSW 91*
Jarrett, Graham Edmund 1935- *St&PR 91*
Jarrett, Guy 1881-1972 *BioIn 16*
Jarrett, Harry Berton 1933- *St&PR 91*
Jarrett, Hugh *BioIn 16*
Jarrett, James W. 1944- *ODwPR 91*
Jarrett, James Warren 1944- *St&PR 91*
Jarrett, Jerry Vernon 1931- *St&PR 91*
Jarrett, John Crow, II 1950- *WhoWor 91*
Jarrett, Keith *BioIn 16*
Jarrett, Keith 1945- *IntWWM 90*
Jarrett, Noel 1921- *WhoAm 90*
Jarrett, Paul S 1921- *BiDrAPA 89*
Jarrett, Randall F. 1943- *St&PR 91*
Jarrett, Richard Scott 1946- *St&PR 91*
Jarrett, Rosalind 1948- *WhoEmL 91*
Jarrett, Steven P. 1954- *St&PR 91*
Jarrett, Teresa Yvonne 1953- *WhoAmW 91*
Jarricot, Jean 1877-1962 *EncO&P 3*
Jarrin, Jaime 1935- *WhoHisp 91*
Jarris, Raymond F *BiDrAPA 89*
Jarrott, Charles 1927- *WhoAm 90*
Jarrow, Emil 1874-1959 *BioIn 16*
Jarrow, Myles Atlass 1922- *St&PR 91*
Jarrow, Robert Alan 1952- *WhoAm 90*
Jarrow, Stanley L. 1919- *St&PR 91*
Jarry, Alfred 1873-1907 *WorAlBi*
Jarry, Jacques *PenDiDA 89*
Jarry, Paul Rudger 1937- *WhoWrEP 89*
Jartman, Marc R. *St&PR 91*
Jaruzelski, Janina Anne 1958- *WhoAmW 91, WhoE 91*
Jaruzelski, Katharine Heywood 1929- *WhoAmW 91*
Jaruzelski, Wojciech 1923- *WhoWor 91*
Jarvefelt, Goran *BioIn 16*
Jarvefelt, Goran 1947-1989 *AnObit 1989*
Jarvenkyla, Jyri Jaakko 1947- *WhoWor 91*
Jarves, Deming *PenDiDA 89*
Jarvi, Neeme 1937- *IntWWM 90, PenDiMP, WhoAm 90, WhoWor 91*
Jarvik, Lissy F *BiDrAPA 89, WhoAm 90*
Jarvik, Murray Elias 1923- *WhoAm 90*
Jarvik, Robert *BioIn 16*
Jarvik, Robert 1946- *WhoAm 90, WhoE 91*
Jarvik, Robert K. 1946- *WorAlBi*
Jarvill-McCord, Judi Lynne 1944- *WhoAmW 91*
Jarvis, Adrian Andrew 1930- *WhoE 91*
Jarvis, Allan P., Jr. 1949- *St&PR 91*
Jarvis, Barbara Ann 1946- *WhoAmW 91*
Jarvis, Barbara Anne 1934- *WhoAmW 91*
Jarvis, Billy Britt 1943- *WhoSSW 91*
Jarvis, Christopher L. 1948- *St&PR 91*
Jarvis, Craig Holloway 1947- *WhoEmL 91*
Jarvis, Delvra I. *BioIn 16*
Jarvis, Donald 1923- *WhoAmA 91*
Jarvis, Douglas LaVern 1957- *BiDrAPA 89*
Jarvis, E. K. *MajTwCW*
Jarvis, Edward Curtis 1951- *WhoE 91, WhoWor 91*
Jarvis, Edward Keith 1939- *IntWWM 90*
Jarvis, Erich David 1965- *WhoE 91*
Jarvis, Fred *BioIn 16*
Jarvis, Frederick D., Jr. *BiDrAPA 89*
Jarvis, Frederick Gordon 1930- *WhoWrEP 89*
Jarvis, Frederick Henry 1928- *WhoAm 90*
Jarvis, Gary Lee 1955- *WhoE 91*
Jarvis, Gilbert Andrew 1941- *WhoAm 90*
Jarvis, Gregory B. 1944-1986 *BioIn 16*
Jarvis, Howard A. 1902-1986 *WorAlBi*
Jarvis, Jack R *BiDrAPA 89*
Jarvis, James Howard, II 1937- *WhoAm 90, WhoSSW 91*
Jarvis, James M. 1912- *St&PR 91*
Jarvis, John Brent 1946- *WhoAmA 91*
Jarvis, John Cecil 1949- *WhoEmL 91*
Jarvis, John E. 1943- *St&PR 91*
Jarvis, John Heber 1933- *BiDrAPA 89*
Jarvis, Joseph Boyer 1923- *WhoAm 90*
Jarvis, Juliet Alicia 1968- *WhoEmL 91*
Jarvis, Lucy 1927- *WhoAmA 91*
Jarvis, Michael Richard 1956- *BiDrAPA 89*
Jarvis, Morris O. 1940- *WhoAm 90*
Jarvis, Oscar T., Jr. 1930- *WhoAm 90*
Jarvis, Pat 1941- *Ballpl 90*
Jarvis, Ray 1946- *Ballpl 90*
Jarvis, Robert Mark 1959- *WhoEmL 91, WhoSSW 91, WhoWor 91*
Jarvis, Ronald Dean 1937- *WhoAm 90*
Jarvis, Scott *BioIn 16*
Jarvis, Scott Edward 1938- *WhoSSW 91*
Jarvis, Shirley Kaye 1942- *WhoAmW 91*
Jarvis, Stephen P. 1956- *BiDrAPA 89*
Jarvis, Terrance Carlyle 1943- *WhoAm 90*
Jarvis, Thomas Jordan 1836-1915 *AmLegL*
Jarvis, Thomas Lee 1948- *WhoEmL 91*
Jarvis, Walter M, Jr. *BiDrAPA 89*
Jarvis, Wilbur *BiDrAPA 89*
Jarvis, William 1770-1859 *BioIn 16*
Jarvis, William Esmond 1931- *WhoAm 90*
Jarvis, William Eugene 1925- *WhoAm 90*
Jarvis, William Hyde 1964- *WhoSSW 91*
Jarvis, William Robert 1948- *WhoEmL 91*
Jarvlepp, Jan Eric 1953- *IntWWM 90*
Jary, Mary Canales 1936- *WhoAmW 91*
Jarzombek, Susan Marlena 1956- *WhoEmL 91*
Jarzyk, Susan 1952- *WhoAm 90*
Jasani, Ramesh Narandas 1945- *WhoSSW 91*
Jaschke, Kurt-Ulrich 1938- *WhoWor 91*
Jaschke, Virginia Amanda 1954- *BiDrAPA 89*
Jasek, Caroline Mary 1962- *WhoE 91*
Jaselskis, Catherine Anne 1957- *BiDrAPA 89*
Jasen, Matthew Joseph 1915- *WhoAm 90*
Jasica, Andrea Lynn 1945- *WhoAmW 91*
Jasinowski, Jerry Joseph 1939- *WhoAm 90*
Jasinski, Arnold Robert 1933- *WhoE 91*
Jasinski, Roman 1900- *BioIn 16*
Jasinski-Caldwell, Mary L. 1959- *WhoAmW 91*
Jaskiewicz, Leonard Albert 1927- *WhoAm 90*
Jaskiewicz, Linda Sue 1955- *WhoEmL 91*
Jaskiw, George Eugene 1956- *BiDrAPA 89*
Jasko, Lillian Evelyn 1933- *St&PR 91, WhoAmW 91*
Jasko, Margaret *St&PR 91*
Jasko, Paul George 1947- *WhoEmL 91*
Jaskol, Earl 1943- *St&PR 91*
Jaskol, Leonard R. 1937- *St&PR 91*
Jaskol, Norman 1933- *St&PR 91*
Jaskot, John Joseph 1921- *WhoAm 90*
Jaskot, Marty J. 1937- *St&PR 91*
Jaslow, Albert C 1920- *BiDrAPA 89*
Jasmin, Claude 1930- *BioIn 16, OxCCanT, WhoWrEP 89*
Jasmin, Edwin Herard 1933- *St&PR 91*
Jasmin, Gaetan 1924- *WhoAm 90*
Jasnow, David Michael 1943- *WhoAm 90*
Jasny, George Roman 1924- *WhoAm 90*
Jasny, Vojtech *BioIn 16*
Jaso, Hector 1925- *BiDrAPA 89*
Jason *ConAu 129, -132*
Jason, Hilliard 1933- *BiDrAPA 89*
Jason, J. Julie 1949- *WhoEmL 91*
Jason, Judith Noodleman 1956- *WhoEmL 91*
Jason, Philip Kenneth 1941- *WhoWrEP 89*
Jason, Stuart *TwCCr&M 91*
Jason, Stuart 1937- *St&PR 91*
Jason, Veronica *TwCCr&M 91*
Jaspan, Jacqueline 1948- *BiDrAPA 89*
Jaspar, Francis E. 1953- *WhoWor 91*
Jaspen, Nathan 1917- *WhoAm 90, WhoWor 91*
Jasper, David 1951- *WhoWor 91*
Jasper, David Westwater 1916- *WhoAm 90*
Jasper, Donald Edward 1918- *WhoAm 90*
Jasper, Doris Jean Berry 1933- *WhoAmW 91, WhoWor 91*
Jasper, Herbert Henri 1906- *WhoAm 90*
Jasper, J. Alan 1920- *ODwPR 91*
Jasper, James Macdonald 1957- *WhoE 91*
Jasper, John 1812-1901 *BioIn 16*
Jasper, Norman Hans 1918- *WhoSSW 91*
Jasper, Ronald Claud Dudley 1917-1990 *ConAu 131*
Jaspers, Karl 1883-1969 *WorAlBi, WrPh P*
Jaspersen, Frederick Zarr 1938- *WhoAm 90*
Jasperson, Paul *BioIn 16*

Jasser, Ira L. *BiDrAPA 89*
Jasser, Ronald Maury 1948- *St&PR 91, WhoE 91*
Jasso, Gayle *ODwPR 91*
Jasso, Joseph B. 1936- *St&PR 91*
Jasso, Paula Inosencia 1951- *WhoHisp 91*
Jassy, Everett Lewis 1937- *WhoAm 90*
Jaster, Larry 1944- *Ballpl 90*
Jastrebski, Linda Marie 1958- *WhoEmL 91*
Jastrow, Joseph 1863- *EncPaPR 91*
Jastrow, Joseph 1863-1944 *EncO&P 3*
Jastrow, Robert 1925- *WhoAm 90*
Jastrow, Werner 1934- *WhoE 91*
Jastrzebski, Ronald Joseph 1959- *WhoEmL 91*
Jasukaityte, Vidmante 1948- *EncCoWW*
Jaszczak, John 1947- *St&PR 91*
Jaszczak, Ronald Jack 1942- *WhoAm 90, WhoWor 91*
Jaszi, Jean Yourd *AuBYP 90*
Jatala, Ijaz Ahmad *BiDrAPA 89*
Jatlow, Peter I. 1936- *WhoAm 90*
Jatras, Stephen James 1926- *St&PR 91, WhoSSW 91*
Jatusipitak, Som 1950- *WhoWor 91*
Jatzkewitz, Horst Waldemar 1912- *WhoWor 91*
Jaubert, Maurice 1900-1940 *OxCPMus*
Jaubert, Richard J. 1912- *St&PR 91*
Jauch, Ronald R. 1945- *St&PR 91*
Jauchem, Clarence Ralph 1916- *WhoAm 90*
Jauchem, Esquire 1947- *WhoEmL 91*
Jaudes, Robert Christian 1933- *St&PR 91*
Jaudes, William E. 1937- *St&PR 91*
Jaudon, Valerie 1945- *WhoAm 90, WhoAmA 91*
Jauhiainen, Jyrki Paavo 1955- *WhoWor 91*
Jaumot, Frank Edward, Jr. 1923- *WhoAm 90*
Jaumotte, Andre Louis 1919- *WhoWor 91*
Jaunaux, Yves 1944- *WhoWor 91*
Jaunich, Robert, II 1940- *St&PR 91*
Jauquet-Kalinoski, Barbara 1948- *WhoAmW 91*
Jauregui, Gabriel Ruben, Sr. 1941- *WhoHisp 91*
Jauregui, Gaston A. 1943- *WhoHisp 91*
Jauregui, Paul Luis 1941- *St&PR 91*
Jaures, Jean Leon 1859-1914 *BiDFrPL*
Jauss, Anne Marie 1907- *AuBYP 90*
Jauss, David Russell 1951- *WhoWrEP 89*
Javacheff, Christo Vladimirov 1935- *WhoAm 90, WhoE 91*
Javaid, Ghazala 1946- *BiDrAPA 89*
Javaid, Mohammed Hafeez *BiDrAPA 89*
Javal, Camille 1934- *WhoWor 91*
Javaras, Barbara Kariotis 1946- *WhoAmW 91*
Javel, Alan F 1948- *BiDrAPA 89*
Javellana, Cynthia Tarrosa *BiDrAPA 89*
Javers, Ron *WhoWrEP 89*
Javery, Al 1918-1977 *Ballpl 90*
Javid, Manucher J. 1922- *WhoAm 90*
Javier, Julian 1936- *Ballpl 90*
Javier, Stan 1965- *Ballpl 90, WhoHisp 91*
Javierre Ortas, Antonio Maria 1921- *WhoWor 91*
Javitch, Gary Richard 1947- *WhoAm 90*
Javitch, Jonathan Allen *BiDrAPA 89*
Javits, Eric *BioIn 16*
Javits, Eric M. 1931- *St&PR 91*
Javits, Jacob K. 1904-1986 *WorAlBi*
Javits, Joshua Moses 1950- *WhoEmL 91*
Javits, Michael D. 1937- *St&PR 91*
Javitt, Daniel 1958- *BiDrAPA 89*
Javna, John *BioIn 16*
Javorek, Judeth Newham 1950- *WhoAmW 91*
Jawaharlal Nehru 1889-1964 *BioIn 16*
Jawara, Dawda Kairaba 1924- *WhoWor 91*
Jawetz, Ernest 1916- *WhoAm 90*
Jawetz, Ilse K *BiDrAPA 89*
Jaworska, Tamara *WhoAmA 91*
Jaworski, Carole L. 1939- *WhoE 91*
Jaworski, Edward Joseph 1944- *WhoE 91*
Jaworski, Irene D. *AuBYP 90*
Jaworski, Janice Ann 1958- *WhoEmL 91*
Jaworski, Karen Arnold 1941- *WhoAmW 91*
Jaworski, Leon 1905-1982 *WorAlBi*
Jaworski, Mavis Webster *BiDrAPA 89*
Jaworski, Michael T *BiDrAPA 89*
Jaworski, Philip Joseph 1927- *St&PR 91*
Jaworsky, Janice Loveland 1947- *WhoWor 91*
Jaxkson, Vaughn L 1920- *WhoAmA 91*
Jay and the Americans *EncPR&S 89*
Jay, Bill 1940- *WhoAmA 91*
Jay, Burton Dean 1937- *St&PR 91, WhoAm 90*
Jay, Byron *BioIn 16*
Jay, Carol Ann 1950- *WhoEmL 91*
Jay, Charles Douglas 1925- *WhoAm 90*
Jay, Charlotte 1919- *TwCCr&M 91*
Jay, David Jakubowicz 1925- *WhoWor 91*
Jay, Frank Peter 1922- *WhoAm 90, WhoE 91*
Jay, G M *TwCCr&M 91*
Jay, Gregory S. 1952- *ConAu 130*
Jay, Harriett 1857-1932 *FemiCLE*
Jay, Herbert Lloyd 1924- *WhoAm 90*
Jay, Hilary *BioIn 16*
Jay, James Albert 1916- *WhoSSW 91, WhoWor 91*
Jay, Joey 1935- *Ballpl 90*
Jay, John *BioIn 16*
Jay, John 1745-1829 *BiDrUSE 89, BioIn 16, EncCRAm [port], WorAlBi*
Jay, Leslie *ODwPR 91*
Jay, Mel *ConAu 32NR*
Jay, Michael Eliot 1949- *WhoE 91, WhoEmL 91*
Jay, Nigel N. 1963- *St&PR 91*
Jay, Norma Joyce *WhoAmA 91*
Jay, Norma Joyce 1925- *WhoAmW 91*
Jay, Peter 1937- *WhoWor 91*
Jay, Ralph *WhoWrEP 89*
Jay, Stanley Bernard 1924- *St&PR 91*
Jay, Stephen Jordan 1941- *WhoAm 90*
Jay, Thelma Gertrude Allen 1923- *WhoWrEP 89*
Jay, Thomas G. 1915- *St&PR 91*
Jayabalan, Vemblaserry 1937- *WhoAm 90*
Jayachandran, Sanker *BiDrAPA 89*
Jayakar, Kushalata R 1939- *BiDrAPA 89*
Jayaprakash, Srinivasa K S 1950- *BiDrAPA 89*
Jayaram, Geetha *BiDrAPA 89*
Jayaram, Susan Ann 1930- *WhoWor 91*
Jayaratna, Mahinda A *BiDrAPA 89*
Jayasinghe, Asoka W 1945- *BiDrAPA 89*
Jayasinghe, Gamini S 1939- *BiDrAPA 89*
Jayasuriya, Dharmasoka Laksiri 1931- *WhoWor 91*
Jaycox, Ann G. 1962- *WhoSSW 91*
Jaycox, Elbert Ralph 1923- *WhoWrEP 89*
Jaye, David Robert, Jr. 1930- *WhoAm 90*
Jayewardene, Junius Richard *BioIn 16*
Jayewardene, Junius Richard 1906- *WhoWor 91*
Jayjock, Michael Anthony 1946- *WhoE 91*
Jayme, Bill *NewYTBS 90*
Jayme, Vincente *BioIn 16*
Jayne, Benjamin Anderson 1928- *WhoAm 90, WhoE 91*
Jayne, Cynthia Elizabeth 1953- *WhoAmW 91*
Jayne, Robyn Christina 1969- *WhoAmW 91*
Jayne, Theodore Douglas 1929- *WhoAm 90*
Jayne, Thomas Mitchell 1958- *BiDrAPA 89*
Jayne, Timothy Randal 1965- *WhoEmL 91*
Jaynes, Barry S. 1943- *St&PR 91*
Jaynes, Clara *AuBYP 90*
Jaynes, Robert Henry, Jr. 1948- *WhoE 91, WhoEmL 91*
Jaynes, Sharon Lynne 1947- *BiDrAPA 89*
Jayson, Diane Frankie 1948- *WhoE 91*
Jayson, Floyd H. 1936- *WhoE 91*
Jayson, Lester Samuel 1915- *WhoAm 90*
Jayson, Melinda Gayle 1956- *WhoEmL 91*
Jayson, Paul *BiDrAPA 89*
Jazayery, Mohammad Ali 1924- *WhoAm 90*
Jazrawi, Taha Yassin Rama dan al- 1939- *WhoWor 91*
Jeake, Samuel, Jr. *AuBYP 90, MajTwCW*
Jeamel, Joseph Francis 1939- *St&PR 91*
Jean 1921- *WhoWor 91*
Jean Baptiste *DcCanB 12*
Jean d'Arras *EncO&P 3*
Jean de Mehun 1250?-1305? *EncO&P 3*
Jean de Meung 1250?-1305? *EncO&P 3*
Jean, Bernard 1929- *BiDrAPA 89*
Jean, Fred *BiDrAPA 89*
Jean, Marcel 1900- *BioIn 16*
Jean, Sally Lucas 1878-1971 *BioIn 16*
Jean, Wilmer Francis 1915- *WhoSSW 91, WhoWor 91*
Jean-Louis *MajTwCW*
Jean-Louis, Don 1937- *WhoAmA 91*
Jean-Noel, Pierre A *BiDrAPA 89*
Jean-Pierre, Antoine 1938- *BiDrAPA 89*
Jeanblanc, Dean Baylor 1933- *WhoE 91*
Jeanblanc, William 1957- *BiDrAPA 89*
Jeane, Martin Keller 1955- *WhoEmL 91*
Jeanes, Joe W. 1927- *WhoAm 90*
Jeanes, Joe Wesley 1927- *St&PR 91*
Jeanes, Sherry Lynn 1959- *WhoEmL 91*
Jeanette, Gertrude 1918- *DrBlPA 90*
Jeanloz, Raymond *BioIn 16*
Jeanloz, Raymond 1952- *WhoAm 90*
Jeanloz, Roger William 1917- *WhoAm 90*
Jeanmart, Claude Rene Gustave 1933- *WhoWor 91*
Jeanmougin, David T. 1940- *St&PR 91*
Jeanmougin, Michel Marcel 1949- *WhoWor 91*
Jeanne I *WomWR*
Jeanne I *WomWR*
Jeanne II *WomWR*
Jeanne d'Albret 1528?-1572? *WomWR*
Jeanne d'Albret, Queen of Navarre 1528-1572 *BioIn 16*
Jeanne d'Arc, Saint 1412-1431 *BioIn 16*
Jeanne D'Arc, St. 1412-1431 *EncO&P 3*
Jeanne de Castile *WomWR*
Jeanne de Chatillon *WomWR*
Jeanne de Nemours *WomWR*
Jeanne II, Queen of Navarre 1311?-1349 *BioIn 16*
Jeanne, Robert Lawrence 1942- *WhoAm 90*
Jeanneney, Jean Marcel 1910- *BiDFrPL*
Jeanneney, Jules Emile 1864-1957 *BiDFrPL*
Jeanneret, Marsh *NewYTBS 90*
Jeanneret, Marsh 1917- *St&PR 91, WhoAm 90*
Jeanneret, Marsh 1917-1990 *ConAu 132*
Jeanneret, Paul Richard *WhoSSW 91*
Jeanneret-Gris, Charles Edouard 1887-1965 *BioIn 16*
Jeannero, Douglas M. 1926- *St&PR 91*
Jeannest, Pierre-Emile *PenDiDA 89*
Jeannette, Gertrude *EarBlAP*
Jeanniot, Pierre Jean 1933- *WhoAm 90*
Jeanrenaud, Joan *PenDiMP*
Jeans, Carl E. 1941- *St&PR 91*
Jeans, James H. 1877-1946 *WorAlBi*
Jeans, John Berger 1931- *St&PR 91*
Jeans, Susi 1911- *IntWWM 90*
Jeanselme Jeune 1818- *PenDiDA 89*
Jeanselme, Charles-Joseph-Henri 1856- *PenDiDA 89*
Jeanselme, Charles-Joseph-Marie 1827-1871? *PenDiDA 89*
Jeanselme, Godin *PenDiDA 89*
Jeanselme, Joseph-Pierre-Francois *PenDiDA 89*
Jeanselme, Pierre-Antoine 1818- *PenDiDA 89*
Jeansonne, Lawrence Bob 1938- *St&PR 91*
Jeansson, Bo Lars Gosta 1943- *WhoWor 91*
Jeantelot, Charles Marcel Jean 1925- *WhoWor 91*
Jeanty, Maxence 1940- *BiDrAPA 89*
Jeanty, Ninette Helene *ConAu 132*
Jeas, William C. 1938- *WhoE 91*
Jeatran, Stephen John 1951- *WhoSSW 91*
Jeavons, Norman Stone 1930- *WhoAm 90*
Jeavons, Robert W. 1925- *St&PR 91*
Jebb, Ann 1735-1812 *FemiCLE*
Jebb, Robert Dudley 1944- *WhoWrEP 89*
Jech, Thomas J. 1944- *WhoE 91*
Jeck, Lida Morawetz 1952- *BiDrAPA 89*
Jeckel, Lawrence Lee 1951- *BiDrAPA 89*
Jeckeln, Friedrich 1895-1946 *BioIn 16*
Jecklin, Arthur C., Jr. 1909- *St&PR 91*
Jecklin, G.D. 1935- *St&PR 91*
Jecklin, Lois U. 1934- *WhoAmW 91*
Jeckyll, Thomas 1827-1881 *PenDiDA 89*
Ject-Key, David *WhoAmA 91N*
Jedel, Peter Harold 1939- *WhoAm 90*
Jedenoff, George Alexander 1917- *WhoAm 90*
Jedinak, Audrey Grace 1930- *St&PR 91*
Jedinak, Thomas Joseph 1947- *WhoEmL 91*
Jedlicka, Dalibor 1929- *IntWWM 90*
Jedlicka, Rudolf 1920- *IntWWM 90*
Jedlinkski, Henryk 1924-1987 *BioIn 16*
Jedruch, Jacek 1927- *WhoE 91*
Jedwill, Judith Mary 1941- *WhoAmW 91*
Jedynak, Beverly L. 1952- *ODwPR 91*
Jedziniak, Lee Peter 1956- *WhoEmL 91*
Jee, Justin Soonho 1951- *WhoE 91, WhoEmL 91, WhoWor 91*
Jeeloff, Gerrit 1927- *WhoE 91*
Jeetun, Beeharrylall 1960- *WhoWor 91*
Jefcoat, James Robert 1943- *St&PR 91*
Jeffares, Robert Travis 1935- *St&PR 91*
Jeffay, Henry 1927- *WhoAm 90*
Jeffcoat, A. E. 1924- *ODwPR 91*
Jeffcoat, Gaines R. 1922- *St&PR 91*
Jeffcoat, Hal 1924- *Ballpl 90*
Jeffcoat, Mike 1959- *Ballpl 90*
Jeffcoat, Otis Allen, III 1948- *WhoEmL 91*
Jeffe, Barbara Elaine 1940- *WhoE 91*
Jeffe, Douglas I. 1943- *ODwPR 91*
Jeffe, Huldah C *WhoAmA 91*
Jeffe, Huldah Cherry *WhoAm 90*
Jeffe, Robert Allan 1950- *WhoAm 90*
Jeffe, Sidney D. 1927- *St&PR 91*
Jeffe, Sidney David 1927- *WhoAm 90*
Jeffer, Edward K 1940- *BiDrAPA 89*
Jeffer, Edward Kenneth 1940- *WhoSSW 91*
Jefferds, Joseph Crosby, III 1944- *St&PR 91*
Jefferds, Joseph Crosby, Jr. 1919- *St&PR 91*
Jefferds, Mary Lee 1921- *WhoAmW 91, WhoWor 91*
Jefferds, Vincent H. 1916- *BioIn 16*
Jefferies, Boyd L. *BioIn 16*
Jefferies, Gregg *BioIn 16*
Jefferies, Gregg 1967- *Ballpl 90*
Jefferies, Jack P. 1928- *WhoAm 90*
Jefferies, John Trevor 1925- *WhoAm 90*
Jefferies, Joyce *BiDEWW*
Jefferies, Michael John 1941- *WhoAm 90*
Jefferies, Michael Lewis *BiDrAPA 89*
Jefferies, Richard 1848-1887 *DcLB 98 [port]*
Jefferies, Richard Lynn 1956- *WhoEmL 91*
Jefferies, Robert Aaron 1941- *St&PR 91*
Jefferies, Robert Aaron, Jr. 1941- *WhoAm 90*
Jefferies, Walter M. *BioIn 16*
Jefferis, Barbara 1917- *FemiCLE*
Jefferis, Elle 1952- *WhoSSW 91*
Jeffers, Avanella Carmen 1922- *WhoWrEP 89*
Jeffers, Donald E. 1925- *WhoAm 90*
Jeffers, Gregory *BiDrAPA 89*
Jeffers, Harry Paul 1934- *AuBYP 90*
Jeffers, Harvey Parker 1931- *WhoSSW 91*
Jeffers, Ida Pearle 1935- *WhoAmW 91*
Jeffers, John James 1937- *St&PR 91*
Jeffers, John L. 1942-1989 *BioIn 16*
Jeffers, John Robinson 1887-1962 *BioIn 16*
Jeffers, Michael Bogue 1940- *St&PR 91, WhoAm 90*
Jeffers, Robert, Jr. 1948- *WhoE 91*
Jeffers, Robert K. 1926- *St&PR 91*
Jeffers, Robinson 1887-1962 *BioIn 16, MajTwCW, WorAlBi, WrPh*
Jeffers, Suzanne 1949- *WhoAmW 91*
Jeffers, Thomas Arthur 1938- *St&PR 91*
Jeffers, Walter Wilson 1915-1989 *BioIn 16*
Jeffers, Wellington 1814-1896 *DcCanB 12*
Jeffers, Wendy Jane 1948- *WhoAmA 91*
Jefferson Airplane *ConMus 5 [port], EncPR&S 89, OxCPMus*
Jefferson Starship *ConMus 5 [port], EncPR&S 89*
Jefferson, Alan Rigby 1921- *IntWWM 90*
Jefferson, Anne Morgan 1935- *WhoAmW 91*
Jefferson, Arthur 1938- *WhoAm 90*
Jefferson, Blind Lemon 1897-1930 *DrBlPA 90, WorAlBi*
Jefferson, Charmaine *BioIn 16*
Jefferson, Cheryl May 1954- *WhoAmW 91*
Jefferson, Clarence 1897-1929 *OxCPMus*
Jefferson, David Rowe 1931- *WhoE 91*
Jefferson, Eddie 1918-1979 *BioIn 16*
Jefferson, Edward Graham 1921- *St&PR 91*
Jefferson, Herbert, Jr. 1946- *DrBlPA 90*
Jefferson, James, Jr. 1951- *WhoEmL 91*
Jefferson, James Walter 1937- *BiDrAPA 89, WhoAm 90*
Jefferson, Janet *MajTwCW*
Jefferson, Jesse 1949- *Ballpl 90*
Jefferson, John H. 1947- *St&PR 91*
Jefferson, Kristin Marie 1947- *WhoAmW 91*
Jefferson, Lila Rae 1953- *WhoAmW 91*
Jefferson, Martha Wayles Skelton 1748-1782 *BioIn 16*
Jefferson, Owen Collin 1932- *WhoWor 91*
Jefferson, Roland A C 1901- *BiDrAPA 89*
Jefferson, Samuel *AmLegL*
Jefferson, Sandra Traylor 1942- *WhoAmW 91, WhoSSW 91, WhoWor 91*
Jefferson, Sherri Jean *WhoSSW 91*
Jefferson, Stan 1962- *Ballpl 90*
Jefferson, Thomas 1743-1826 *BiDrUSE 89, BioIn 16, EncCRAm [port], WhNaAH, WorAlBi*
Jefferson, Thomas 1923- *BioIn 16*
Jefferson, Thomas Bradley 1924- *WhoAm 90*
Jefferson, Thomas Richard 1945- *WhoSSW 91*
Jefferson, Tommy Payton 1943- *St&PR 91*
Jefferson, W. J. *EarBlAP*
Jefferson, William F. 1949- *St&PR 91*
Jefferson, William Harrison 1929- *St&PR 91*
Jefferson, William Jackson 1929- *St&PR 91*
Jeffery, Alan G. 1938- *St&PR 91*
Jeffery, Charles *EncABHB 4*
Jeffery, Geoffrey Marron 1919- *WhoAm 90*
Jeffery, Grant *ODwPR 91*
Jeffery, Joseph 1829-1894 *DcCanB 12*
Jeffery, Joseph 1907- *St&PR 91*
Jeffery, Lawrence 1953- *ConAu 130*
Jeffery, Lilian Hamilton 1915-1986 *BioIn 16*
Jeffery, Maria Aoling Chea 1962- *WhoSSW 91*
Jeffery, Maurice Stanley 1932- *St&PR 91*
Jeffery, Peter 1953- *IntWWM 90*
Jeffery, Richard P., Jr. 1932- *St&PR 91*
Jeffery, Stephen Robert 1938- *St&PR 91*
Jeffery, Thomas B *EncABHB 4*
Jeffery, William Richard 1944- *WhoAm 90*
Jefferys, Charles William 1869-1951 *WhoAmA 91N*

Jefferys, William Hamilton, III 1940- *WhoAm 90*
Jeffes, Peter 1948- *IntWWM 90*
Jeffett, Frank Asbury 1927- *WhoAm 90*
Jeffett, Nancy Pearce 1928- *WhoSSW 91*
Jefford, Charles William 1929- *WhoWor 91*
Jeffords, Edward Alan 1945- *WhoEmL 91, WhoSSW 91, WhoWor 91*
Jeffords, Gail *ODwPR 91*
Jeffords, James *BioIn 16*
Jeffords, James Merrill 1934- *WhoAm 90, WhoE 91, WhoWor 91*
Jeffords, Jean Garrett 1921- *WhoSSW 91*
Jeffords, Lynn Redding 1957- *WhoAmW 91*
Jeffords, Thomas J. 1832-1914 *WhNaAH*
Jeffords, Walter M. *BioIn 16*
Jeffords, Walter M., Jr. *NewYTBS 90*
Jeffredo, John Victor 1927- *WhoWor 91*
Jeffress, Lloyd A. *BioIn 16*
Jeffress, Robert J. 1955- *WhoEmL 91*
Jeffrey, Bob *BioIn 16*
Jeffrey, Dennis John 1947- *WhoEmL 91*
Jeffrey, Francis 1950- *WhoEmL 91*
Jeffrey, Graham Keith 1933- *WhoE 91*
Jeffrey, Howard *BioIn 16*
Jeffrey, James R. 1937- *St&PR 91*
Jeffrey, Lisa C. 1958- *St&PR 91*
Jeffrey, Louis Robert 1927- *St&PR 91*
Jeffrey, Maurine L. 1900- *HarlReB*
Jeffrey, Noela Mary 1941- *WhoAmW 91*
Jeffrey, R. Mitchell 1948- *WhoEmL 91*
Jeffrey, R. Mitchell, Jr. 1948- *ODwPR 91*
Jeffrey, Richard Carl 1926- *WhoAm 90*
Jeffrey, Robert Campbell 1927- *WhoAm 90*
Jeffrey, Robert George, Jr. 1933- *WhoAm 90*
Jeffrey, Robert Howard 1946- *WhoEmL 91*
Jeffrey, Sharon Lee 1944- *WhoAmW 91*
Jeffrey, Susan Winder 1951- *WhoAmW 91*
Jeffrey, Walter Leslie 1908- *WhoAm 90*
Jeffrey, William *ConAu 32NR, TwCCr&M 91*
Jeffrey, William Alan 1960- *WhoSSW 91*
Jeffrey, William David *BiDrAPA 89*
Jeffrey-Smith, Lilli Ann 1944- *WhoWor 91*
Jeffreys, Anne 1923- *WorAlBi*
Jeffreys, Elystan Geoffrey 1926- *WhoAm 90, WhoSSW 91*
Jeffreys, Garland 194-?- *EncPR&S 89*
Jeffreys, Harold 1891-1989 *BioIn 16*
Jeffreys, J. G. *TwCCr&M 91*
Jeffreys, Jane Kilgore 1934- *BiDrAPA 89*
Jeffreys, John Michael 1927- *IntWWM 90*
Jeffreys, Margaret Villar 1953- *WhoAmW 91, WhoSSW 91*
Jeffreys, Matthew David 1959- *BiDrAPA 89*
Jeffries, Betty *WhoWrEP 89*
Jeffries, Betty Sarah 1925- *WhoAmW 91*
Jeffries, Carson Dunning 1922- *WhoAm 90*
Jeffries, Charles Dean 1929- *WhoAm 90*
Jeffries, Donald George 1934- *St&PR 91*
Jeffries, Georgia Thomas 1951- *WhoEmL 91*
Jeffries, Herb 1916- *DrBlPA 90*
Jeffries, J. Joel 1939- *BiDrAPA 89*
Jeffries, Marsha Denell 1954- *WhoAmW 91*
Jeffries, McChesney Hill 1922- *WhoAm 90*
Jeffries, McChesney Hill, Jr. 1954- *WhoEmL 91*
Jeffries, R.J. 1923- *St&PR 91*
Jeffries, Robert Alan 1933- *WhoAm 90*
Jeffries, Robert Joseph 1923- *WhoAm 90*
Jeffries, Roderic 1926- *AuBYP 90, TwCCr&M 91*
Jeffries, Rosalyn Ann 1961- *WhoEmL 91*
Jeffries, Seymour Barnard 1916- *WhoE 91*
Jeffries, Thomas A. 1954- *St&PR 91*
Jeffries, William Spence 1925- *St&PR 91*
Jeffris, Ronald Duane 1937- *St&PR 91, WhoAm 90*
Jeffs, G.W. 1925- *St&PR 91*
Jeffs, Thomas H., II 1938- *WhoAm 90*
Jeffs, Thomas Hamilton, II 1938- *St&PR 91*
Jefroykin, Jules 1911-1987 *BioIn 16*
Jegasothy, Brian Vasanthakumar 1943- *WhoAm 90*
Jegede, R Olukayode *BiDrAPA 89*
Jegede, Victor Adebayo 1944- *St&PR 91*
Jegen, Carol Frances 1925- *WhoAmW 91*
Jegen, Lawrence A., III 1934- *WhoAm 90*
Jeggle, David Alan 1940- *St&PR 91*
Jeghers, Harold Joseph 1904- *WhoAm 90, WhoE 91, WhoWor 91*
Jeghers, Sanderson John 1945- *WhoEmL 91*
Jeglinski, Patricia Ann 1938- *WhoAmW 91*
Jegou, Carol Kulina 1949- *WhoEmL 91*
Jeha, Abdallah Henry 1962- *WhoWor 91*
Jehan, Sayed Shah *BiDrAPA 89*
Jehangir, Alam 1934- *WhoWor 91*
Jehin-Prume, Frantz 1839-1899 *DcCanB 12*
Jehl, Louis C. 1924- *St&PR 91*
Jehle, Michael Edward 1954- *St&PR 91, WhoAm 90*
Jeier, Thomas *BioIn 16*
Jekel, Benita D'Andrea 1934- *St&PR 91*
Jekel, James Franklin 1934- *WhoAm 90*
Jekel, Pamela L. 1948- *WhoWrEP 89*
Jeknavorian, Aram A. 1939- *St&PR 91*
Jekyll, Gertrude 1843-1932 *BioIn 16*
Jelalian, Albert V. 1933- *WhoE 91*
Jelasko, Michael Joseph 1949- *WhoE 91*
Jelavich, Barbara 1923- *WhoAm 90*
Jelensperger, Francis F. 1943- *St&PR 91*
Jelensperger, Francis J. 1943- *WhoAm 90*
Jelin, Martin *BioIn 16*
Jelin, Stephen Jacob 1934- *WhoE 91*
Jelinek, Elfriede 1946- *EncCoWW*
Jelinek, Frederick 1932- *WhoAm 90*
Jelinek, Hans *WhoAmA 91*
Jelinek, Hans 1910- *WhoAm 90*
Jelinek, John Joseph 1955- *WhoAm 90*
Jelinek, John Peter 1916- *WhoAm 90*
Jelinek, Josef Emil 1928- *WhoAm 90*
Jelinek, Otto John 1940- *WhoAm 90, WhoE 91*
Jelinek, Richard Carl 1937- *WhoAm 90*
Jelinek, Robert 1929- *WhoAm 90*
Jelks, Edward Baker 1922- *WhoAm 90*
Jellema, Rod Hartigh 1927- *WhoWrEP 89*
Jellett, Mainie 1897-1944 *BiDWomA*
Jellico, John Anthony 1914- *WhoAmA 91*
Jellico, Nancy R 1939- *WhoAmA 91*
Jellicoe, Ann *BioIn 16*
Jellicoe, Ann 1927- *FemiCLE*
Jellicoe, Hon Earl 1918- *WhoWor 91*
Jellicoe, Patricia Ruiz de Castilla 1950- *WhoWor 91*
Jellicorse, John Lee 1937- *WhoAm 90*
Jelliff, John 1813-1893 *PenDiDA 89*
Jelliffe, Charles Gordon 1914- *WhoAm 90*
Jelliffe, Roger Woodham 1929- *WhoAm 90*
Jelliffe, Rowena Woodham 1892- *BioIn 16, NotWoAT*
Jellinek, George 1919- *WhoAm 90*
Jellinek, Michael Steven 1948- *WhoEmL 91*
Jellinek, Roger 1938- *WhoAm 90, WhoWrEP 89*
Jellinek, Theodore M 1940- *BiDrAPA 89*
Jellinek, Tristram *BioIn 16*
Jellinger, Robert Martin *BiDrAPA 89*
Jellinghaus, Carl F. 1917-1989 *BioIn 16*
Jellinghaus, Fritz *ODwPR 91*
Jellison, Gretchen Gayhart 1908- *WhoAmW 91*
Jellovitz, John Charles 1942- *St&PR 91*
Jellows, Tracy Patrick 1951- *WhoE 91, WhoEmL 91*
Jelstrom, Evelyn Maja 1955- *WhoAmW 91*
Jeltsch, Rolf 1945- *WhoWor 91*
Jeltz, Steve 1959- *Ballpl 90*
Jembere, Berhanu *BioIn 16*
Jemelian, John Nazar 1933- *WhoAm 90*
Jemerin, John Michael 1953- *BiDrAPA 89*
Jemian, Wartan Armin 1925- *WhoAm 90*
Jemilo, Carol Cecile 1958- *WhoEmL 91*
Jemison, Cheryl Lynne 1959- *WhoAmW 91*
Jemison, Frank Zimmerman, Jr. 1948- *St&PR 91*
Jemison, John Snow, III 1949- *St&PR 91*
Jemison, Mae C. *BioIn 16*
Jemison, Marie Stokes *BioIn 16*
Jemison, Mary 1743-1833 *BioAmW, EncCRAm, WhNaAH*
Jemison, Shirley J. *ODwPR 91*
Jemison, Theodore Judson 1918- *WhoSSW 91*
Jemmat, Catherine 1714-1766 *FemiCLE*
Jemmott, Elizabeth Joy 1941- *WhoSSW 91*
Jen, Frank Chifeng 1931- *WhoAm 90*
Jen, Joanne Pauline 1967- *WhoAmW 91*
Jen, Joseph Jwu-Shan 1939- *WhoSSW 91*
Jen, Kai-Lin Catherine 1949- *WhoAmW 91*
Jen Kin, James Henry 1936- *BiDrAPA 89*
Jena, Ruth Michaelis- 1905- *BioIn 16*
Jenckes, Joseph 1632-1717 *EncCRAm*
Jenckes, Joseph S. 1935- *St&PR 91*
Jencks, Christopher Sandys 1936- *WhoAm 90*
Jencks, Stephen F 1940- *BiDrAPA 89*
Jencks, William Platt 1927- *WhoAm 90*
Jenden, Donald James 1926- *WhoAm 90*
Jenders, Thomas 1942- *St&PR 91*
Jendusa, David James *BiDrAPA 89*
Jenefsky, Jack 1919- *WhoWor 91*
Jenes, Theodore George, Jr. 1930- *WhoAm 90*
Jeng, Raymond Ing-Song 1940- *WhoAm 90*
Jenifer, Daniel of St. Thomas 1723-1790 *BioIn 16*
Jenifer, Franklyn Green *WhoAm 90*
Jenike, Michael Andrew 1945- *BiDrAPA 89, WhoE 91*
Jenison, Eric Lee 1950- *WhoEmL 91*
Jenk, Jorgen *BioIn 16*
Jenk, Lloyd F 1919- *BiDrAPA 89*
Jenke, Arthur 1945- *St&PR 91*
Jenkin, Douglas Alan 1932- *WhoSSW 91*
Jenkin, Henrietta Camilla 1807?-1885 *FemiCLE*
Jenkin, Margaret 1892-1912 *BiDWomA*
Jenkins, Adrienne Beth 1963- *WhoAmW 91*
Jenkins, Alan Bradford 1936- *St&PR 91*
Jenkins, Albert Felton, Jr. 1941- *WhoAm 90*
Jenkins, Albert Gallatin 1830-1864 *BioIn 16*
Jenkins, Alexander, III 1934- *St&PR 91, WhoAm 90*
Jenkins, Andrew *WhoE 91*
Jenkins, Anne Elizabeth Green 1944- *WhoAmW 91*
Jenkins, Anne MacGregor 1924- *WhoSSW 91*
Jenkins, Anthony Charles 1956- *WhoE 91*
Jenkins, B. Larry 1938- *St&PR 91*
Jenkins, Benjamin Larry 1938- *WhoAm 90*
Jenkins, Billie Beasley 1943- *WhoAmW 91*
Jenkins, Brenda Gwenetta 1949- *WhoAmW 91*
Jenkins, Britt 1943- *St&PR 91*
Jenkins, Bruce Armand 1933- *WhoWor 91*
Jenkins, Bunny Gloria 1953- *WhoEmL 91*
Jenkins, Burris 1897-1966 *WhoAmA 91N*
Jenkins, Carl Anthony 1958- *WhoSSW 91*
Jenkins, Carol 1944- *DrBlPA 90*
Jenkins, Carol Ann 1948- *WhoAmW 91*
Jenkins, Carol Anne 1945- *WhoAmW 91, WhoEmL 91*
Jenkins, Carrell Ray 1930- *WhoAm 90*
Jenkins, Charles B. 1941- *WhoE 91*
Jenkins, Chester W 1942- *BiDrAPA 89*
Jenkins, Clara Barnes 1943- *WhoAmW 91, WhoSSW 91, WhoWor 91*
Jenkins, Claude B. 1929- *St&PR 91*
Jenkins, Clifford Gordon, Jr. 1955- *WhoSSW 91*
Jenkins, Colleen Theresa 1961- *WhoEmL 91*
Jenkins, Connie Webster 1955- *WhoSSW 91*
Jenkins, Damita Jo 1963- *WhoAmW 91*
Jenkins, Daniel Edwards, Jr. 1916- *WhoAm 90*
Jenkins, David B. *WhoE 91*
Jenkins, David E. *BioIn 16*
Jenkins, Dennis Robert 1957- *WhoSSW 91*
Jenkins, Donald John 1931- *WhoAm 90, WhoAmA 91*
Jenkins, Donald M. 1928- *WhoAm 90*
Jenkins, E. Clark 1940- *St&PR 91*
Jenkins, Edgar Lanier *BioIn 16*
Jenkins, Edgar Lanier 1933- *WhoAm 90, WhoSSW 91*
Jenkins, Elizabeth *BioIn 16*
Jenkins, Elizabeth 1915- *FemiCLE*
Jenkins, Ernest B. 1934- *St&PR 91*
Jenkins, Fats 1898-1968 *Ballpl 90*
Jenkins, Ferguson 1943- *Ballpl 90 [port], WorAlBi*
Jenkins, Floyd T. 1942- *St&PR 91*
Jenkins, Frances Owens 1924- *WhoAmW 91*
Jenkins, Fred Arnold 1940- *St&PR 91*
Jenkins, George 1908- *WhoAm 90*
Jenkins, George 1911- *ConDes 90*
Jenkins, George Edward 1914- *BiDrAPA 89*
Jenkins, George Edward 1942- *BiDrAPA 89*
Jenkins, George Henry 1929- *WhoWor 91*
Jenkins, George P. 1915- *St&PR 91*
Jenkins, George W. 1907- *WhoAm 90, WhoSSW 91*
Jenkins, Glenna Glee 1918- *WhoWrEP 89*
Jenkins, Gloria Delores *WhoAmW 91*
Jenkins, Gordon 1910-1984 *OxCPMus*
Jenkins, Graeme James Ewers 1958- *IntWWM 90*
Jenkins, Harold Richard *BioIn 16*
Jenkins, Harold Thomas 1956- *St&PR 91*
Jenkins, Harvey Wayne 1956- *WhoEmL 91*
Jenkins, Helen Ann 1945- *WhoSSW 91*
Jenkins, Helen Heath 1952- *WhoAmW 91*
Jenkins, Helen Williams 1921- *WhoSSW 91*
Jenkins, Herbert T., Sr. *NewYTBS 90 [port]*
Jenkins, Hudson Augustus 1855-1902 *AmLegL*
Jenkins, Ian Ross 1942- *BiDrAPA 89*
Jenkins, Irene *WhoAmW 91*
Jenkins, J.M. 1942- *St&PR 91*
Jenkins, J.S.B. 1943- *St&PR 91*
Jenkins, James Allister 1923- *WhoAm 90*
Jenkins, James Edward *BiDrAPA 89*
Jenkins, James L. 1939- *St&PR 91*
Jenkins, James P. 1948- *St&PR 91*
Jenkins, James Pollock 1948- *WhoAm 90*
Jenkins, James Robert 1945- *WhoAm 90*
Jenkins, James Sherwood, Jr. 1941- *WhoSSW 91*
Jenkins, James Thomas 1951- *St&PR 91*
Jenkins, Jeanne Boutin 1948- *WhoEmL 91*
Jenkins, Jerry Bruce 1949- *WhoWrEP 89*
Jenkins, Jerry G. 1931- *St&PR 91*
Jenkins, Jesse Frank 1918- *St&PR 91*
Jenkins, John 1813-1898 *DcCanB 12*
Jenkins, John Anthony 1926- *WhoAm 90*
Jenkins, John Charles 1935- *BiDrAPA 89*
Jenkins, John Douglas 1939- *WhoSSW 91*
Jenkins, John Edgar 1925- *St&PR 91*
Jenkins, John Edward, Sr. 1914- *St&PR 91*
Jenkins, John Holmes 1940-1989 *BioIn 16*
Jenkins, John J. 1937- *ConAu 132*
Jenkins, John Logan 1950- *WhoEmL 91*
Jenkins, John Smith 1932- *WhoAm 90*
Jenkins, John Tierce 1920- *WhoWrEP 89*
Jenkins, Kathleen Kay 1952- *WhoEmL 91*
Jenkins, Kathy 1955- *WhoAmW 91*
Jenkins, Kempton Boyce 1926- *St&PR 91*
Jenkins, Kenneth Vincent *WhoAm 90, WhoE 91*
Jenkins, Laine Maureen *BiDrAPA 89*
Jenkins, Larry *ODwPR 91*
Jenkins, Larry E. 1941- *St&PR 91*
Jenkins, Lawrence Eugene 1933- *WhoAm 90*
Jenkins, Leroy *BioIn 16*
Jenkins, Leroy 1932- *WhoAm 90*
Jenkins, Linda Hudak *BiDrAPA 89*
Jenkins, Louis 1947- *WhoSSW 91*
Jenkins, Louise Sherman 1943- *WhoAmW 91*
Jenkins, M. T. 1917- *WhoAm 90*
Jenkins, Madge Marie 1938- *WhoAmW 91*
Jenkins, Margaret Aikens 1925- *WhoAmW 91*
Jenkins, Marie Hooper 1929- *WhoSSW 91*
Jenkins, Marie Magdalen 1909- *AuBYP 90*
Jenkins, Marilyn *BioIn 16*
Jenkins, Marjorie C. 1911- *WhoWrEP 89*
Jenkins, Marshall Whitfield 1952- *WhoSSW 91*
Jenkins, Martin Robert 1953- *WhoEmL 91*
Jenkins, Mary *BioIn 16*
Jenkins, Mary Anne Keel 1929- *WhoAmA 91*
Jenkins, Mary Ebener *BiDrAPA 89*
Jenkins, Mary Frances 1968- *WhoEmL 91*
Jenkins, Melody Stinson 1951- *WhoAmW 91, WhoSSW 91*
Jenkins, Michael Austin 1942- *WhoSSW 91*
Jenkins, Michael D *BiDrAPA 89*
Jenkins, Michael Romilly Heald 1936- *WhoWor 91*
Jenkins, Mildred N. 1928- *WhoAmW 91*
Jenkins, Myra Ellen 1916- *WhoAmW 91*
Jenkins, Neil 1945- *IntWWM 90*
Jenkins, Neil Edmund 1949- *St&PR 91*
Jenkins, Newell 1915- *IntWWM 90, WhoAm 90*
Jenkins, Orville Wesley 1913- *WhoAm 90, WhoWor 91*
Jenkins, Patricia Ann 1954- *WhoSSW 91*
Jenkins, Paul 1923- *WhoAm 90, WhoAmA 91*
Jenkins, Paul H *BiDrAPA 89*
Jenkins, Paul N. 1939- *St&PR 91*
Jenkins, Paul R. 1942- *WhoWrEP 89*
Jenkins, Paul Ripley 1904-1974 *WhoAmA 91N*
Jenkins, Peter Edwin 1940- *WhoAm 90*
Jenkins, Phillip L. 1923- *St&PR 91*
Jenkins, R. *St&PR 91*
Jenkins, R. Lee 1929- *St&PR 91*
Jenkins, Reese V. *BioIn 16*
Jenkins, Richard L 1903- *BiDrAPA 89*
Jenkins, Richard Lee 1931- *WhoAm 90*
Jenkins, Richard N. 1944- *St&PR 91*
Jenkins, Richard Walter 1925-1984 *DcNaB 1981*
Jenkins, Rick Lee 1958- *BiDrAPA 89*
Jenkins, Robert Ashley 1959- *WhoEmL 91*
Jenkins, Robert Berryman 1950- *WhoSSW 91*
Jenkins, Robert Harrington 1943- *St&PR 91*
Jenkins, Robert Jeffery 1959- *WhoSSW 91*
Jenkins, Robert Nesbit 1951- *WhoE 91*
Jenkins, Robert Spurgeon 1921- *WhoAm 90*
Jenkins, Rodger Kiley 1938- *St&PR 91*
Jenkins, Roy 1920- *ConAu 30NR*
Jenkins, Roy Harris 1920- *WhoWor 91*
Jenkins, Royal Gregory 1936- *WhoAm 90*
Jenkins, Ruben Lee 1929- *WhoAm 90*
Jenkins, Scott R. 1949- *St&PR 91*
Jenkins, Simon David 1943- *WhoWor 91*

Jenkins, Speight *BioIn 16*
Jenkins, Speight 1937- *WhoAm 90*
Jenkins, Susan Carol 1955- *BiDrAPA 89*
Jenkins, Sylvia *BioIn 16*
Jenkins, Terry 1941- *IntWWM 90*
Jenkins, Thomas A. 1942- *St&PR 91*
Jenkins, Thomas Canfield, IV 1949- *WhoSSW 91*
Jenkins, Thomas Llewellyn 1927- *WhoAm 90*
Jenkins, Thomas Michael 1951- *St&PR 91*
Jenkins, Travis Wayne 1941- *BiDrAPA 89*
Jenkins, Tudor Emlyn 1949- *WhoWor 91*
Jenkins, Warren C. 1925- *St&PR 91*
Jenkins, Wendell L. *St&PR 91*
Jenkins, William 1920- *St&PR 91, WhoAm 90*
Jenkins, William Atwell 1922- *WhoAm 90*
Jenkins, William C, Jr. *BiDrAPA 89*
Jenkins, William Kenneth 1947- *WhoAm 90*
Jenkins, William Lawrence 1943- *St&PR 91*
Jenkins, William M. 1919- *St&PR 91*
Jenkins, William Martyn Peter 1954- *WhoWor 91*
Jenkins, William Nelson 1928- *St&PR 91*
Jenkins, William R. *St&PR 91*
Jenkins, William R. 1940- *ODwPR 91*
Jenkins, William Robert 1927- *WhoAm 90*
Jenkins, William Russell 1938- *WhoSSW 91*
Jenkins, William Stanyarne 1955- *WhoSSW 91*
Jenkins-Turner, Judy 1948- *WhoAmW 91*
Jenkinson, David Michael 1929- *WhoWor 91*
Jenkinson, Judith Apsey 1943- *WhoAmW 91*
Jenkis, Helmut Walter 1927- *WhoWor 91*
Jenks, Carolyn Boyd 1935- *WhoWrEP 89*
Jenks, Clifford James, Jr. 1928- *WhoE 91*
Jenks, Downing Bland 1915- *WhoAm 90*
Jenks, Elisabeth R *BiDrAPA 89*
Jenks, George Merritt 1929- *WhoAm 90*
Jenks, George S. 1927- *St&PR 91*
Jenks, George Schuyler 1927- *WhoAm 90*
Jenks, Homer Simeon 1914- *WhoAm 90*
Jenks, John Bernard 1937- *St&PR 91*
Jenks, Lisa *BioIn 16*
Jenks, Sarah Isabel 1913- *WhoAmW 91*
Jenks, Schuyler T. 1956- *St&PR 91*
Jenks, Thomas Edward 1929- *WhoAm 90*
Jenks, Tom *BioIn 16*
Jenks, Vina Jane 1931- *WhoAmW 91*
Jenks, William Elliott 1946- *WhoEmL 91*
Jenks, William P. 1957- *St&PR 91*
Jenks-Davies, Kathryn Ryburn 1916- *WhoAmW 91*
Jenks-Jordal, Mary Ellen 1933- *St&PR 91*
Jenkusky, Steven *BiDrAPA 89*
Jenkyns, Chris 1924- *BioIn 16*
Jenne, Kenneth Clarence, II *WhoSSW 91*
Jenne, Kirk 1945- *WhoEmL 91*
Jenneke, L.E. 1923- *St&PR 91*
Jennens, Charles 1700-1773 *BioIn 16*
Jennens, Trevor R. 1944- *St&PR 91*
Jenner, Albert E. 1907-1988 *BioIn 16*
Jenner, Alexander 1929- *IntWWM 90*
Jenner, Bruce 1949- *WhoAm 90, WorAlBi*
Jenner, Edward 1749-1823 *WorAlBi*
Jenner, Heather *ConAu 31NR*
Jenner, Richard H. 1930- *St&PR 91*
Jenner, Robert Ernest 1952- *WhoE 91*
Jenner, Robert Keith 1960- *WhoEmL 91*
Jenner, William Alexander 1915- *WhoWor 91*
Jennerich, Edward John 1945- *WhoAm 90*
Jennerjahn, W P 1922- *WhoAmA 91*
Jenness, M. Ian 1943- *WhoSSW 91*
Jenness, Robert 1917- *WhoAm 90*
Jennett, J. Charles 1940- *WhoSSW 91*
Jennett, Shirley Marie Shimmick 1937- *WhoAmW 91*
Jennewein, C Paul 1890-1978 *WhoAmA 91N*
Jennewein, James Joseph 1929- *WhoAm 90*
Jenney, Neil 1945- *WhoAmA 91*
Jenney, Neil Franklin, Jr. 1945- *WhoAm 90*
Jenney, Peter B *BiDrAPA 89*
Jenney, Robert M. 1918- *St&PR 91*
Jenney, William Le Baron 1832-1907 *WorAlBi*
Jenney-West, Roxanne Elizabeth 1960- *WhoAmW 91*
Jenni, Donald Alison 1932- *WhoAm 90*
Jenni, Donald Martin 1937- *IntWWM 90*
Jennings, A. Drue *WhoAm 90*
Jennings, Albert L. 1934- *St&PR 91*
Jennings, Alston 1917- *WhoAm 90*
Jennings, Alvin R. *BioIn 16, NewYTBS 90*
Jennings, Amelia Clotilda *DcCanB 12*
Jennings, B. Joelle 1944- *WhoAmW 91*
Jennings, Bonnie K *BiDrAPA 89*
Jennings, Burgess Hill 1903- *WhoAm 90*
Jennings, Carl Anthony 1944- *St&PR 91*
Jennings, Clark Lindsay 1956- *BiDrAPA 89*
Jennings, Clifford R. 1911- *St&PR 91*
Jennings, Coleman A 1933- *SmATA 64*
Jennings, Cynthia Ann 1950- *WhoE 91*
Jennings, David Reese 1957- *WhoEmL 91*
Jennings, David S. 1942- *St&PR 91*
Jennings, Deborah Sue 1956- *BiDrAPA 89*
Jennings, Dennis Raymond 1942- *WhoSSW 91*
Jennings, Diane B. 1953- *St&PR 91*
Jennings, E.C., Jr. 1946- *St&PR 91*
Jennings, E. Paul, Jr. 1932- *St&PR 91*
Jennings, Edward Harrington 1937- *WhoAm 90, WhoWor 91*
Jennings, Edward Morton, Jr. 1906- *WhoAm 90*
Jennings, Eileen Marie O'Brien 1946- *WhoE 91*
Jennings, Eileen O *BiDrAPA 89*
Jennings, Elizabeth 1926- *BioIn 16, FemiCLE, MajTwCW, WhoWor 91*
Jennings, Francis 1910- *WhoAmA 91*
Jennings, Frank Gerard 1915- *WhoAm 90*
Jennings, Frank Louis *WhoE 91*
Jennings, Frederic Beach, Jr. 1945- *WhoE 91*
Jennings, Frederick G. 1950- *St&PR 91*
Jennings, Gary 1928- *AuBYP 90*
Jennings, Gerald Douglas 1945- *WhoSSW 91*
Jennings, Gerald M. *BioIn 16, St&PR 91N*
Jennings, Gertrude *FemiCLE*
Jennings, Glenn Earl 1953- *BiDrAPA 89*
Jennings, Glenn Ray 1949- *St&PR 91*
Jennings, Gordon *AuBYP 90*
Jennings, Guy McFarland 1947- *WhoSSW 91*
Jennings, Harold B. 1921- *BioIn 16*
Jennings, Herbert Erwin 1928- *St&PR 91*
Jennings, Hughie 1869-1928 *Ballpl 90 [port]*
Jennings, Irvin Ray *BiDrAPA 89*
Jennings, James 1949- *WhoHisp 91*
Jennings, James Burnett 1940- *St&PR 91*
Jennings, James Courtney 1945- *ODwPR 91, WhoAm 90*
Jennings, James Floyd 1933- *BiDrAPA 89*
Jennings, James Harold 1931- *MusmAFA*
Jennings, James K., Jr. 1941- *St&PR 91*
Jennings, James Kelly 1951- *WhoEmL 91*
Jennings, Jan 1943- *WhoAmA 91*
Jennings, Jay *BioIn 16*
Jennings, Jay Bradford 1957- *WhoEmL 91, WhoWor 91*
Jennings, Jeanne Elizabeth 1961- *WhoAmW 91*
Jennings, Jeffrey Howells 1919- *WhoWor 91*
Jennings, Jeffrey L 1958- *BiDrAPA 89*
Jennings, Jennifer Angelene 1968- *WhoWrEP 89*
Jennings, Jerry D. 1940- *WhoAm 90*
Jennings, Jesse David 1909- *WhoAm 90*
Jennings, John Edward, Jr. 1906-1973 *AuBYP 90*
Jennings, John Robert Rogers 1937- *WhoE 91*
Jennings, Joseph A. 1920- *St&PR 91*
Jennings, Joseph Ashby 1920- *WhoAm 90*
Jennings, Joseph H. 1945- *ODwPR 91*
Jennings, Joseph Leslie 1937- *St&PR 91*
Jennings, Joseph Leslie, Jr. 1937- *WhoAm 90, WhoSSW 91*
Jennings, Kenneth *BioIn 16*
Jennings, Kevin Patrick 1947- *WhoWor 91*
Jennings, Leander Warren 1928- *WhoAm 90*
Jennings, Lee Byron 1927- *WhoAm 90*
Jennings, Lynn *NewYTBS 90 [port]*
Jennings, Madelyn Pulver *BioIn 16*
Jennings, Madelyn Pulver 1934- *St&PR 91, WhoAm 90, WhoAmW 91*
Jennings, Marcella Grady 1920- *WhoAmW 91, WhoWor 91*
Jennings, Michael 1931- *AuBYP 90*
Jennings, Michael Dean 1946- *WhoSSW 91*
Jennings, Michael E. 1945- *St&PR 91*
Jennings, Myron Kent 1934- *WhoAm 90*
Jennings, Nancy Ann 1932- *WhoAmW 91*
Jennings, Paul 1918-1989 *AnObit 1989*
Jennings, Paul Christian 1936- *WhoAm 90*
Jennings, Peter 1938- *BioIn 16*
Jennings, Peter C. 1938- *WorAlBi*
Jennings, Peter Charles 1938- *WhoAm 90, WhoE 91*
Jennings, Ralph Edward, Jr. 1958- *WhoSSW 91*
Jennings, Ralph Merwin 1938- *WhoE 91*
Jennings, Richard K 1928- *BiDrAPA 89*
Jennings, Richard Louis 1933- *WhoAm 90*
Jennings, Richard Wormington 1907- *WhoAm 90*
Jennings, Robert Burgess 1926- *WhoAm 90, WhoSSW 91*
Jennings, Robert Edward 1939- *WhoSSW 91*
Jennings, Robert G. 1938- *St&PR 91*
Jennings, Robert Kevin *BiDrAPA 89*
Jennings, Robert Lee 1946- *WhoE 91*
Jennings, Robert Leroy 1928- *WhoAm 90*
Jennings, Robert William, Jr. 1956- *WhoEmL 91*
Jennings, Roger L. 1940- *St&PR 91*
Jennings, Roy, Jr. *St&PR 91*
Jennings, Royce Merlyn 1920- *St&PR 91*
Jennings, Sandra *BioIn 16*
Jennings, Stephen Grant 1946- *WhoAm 90, WhoEmL 91*
Jennings, Susan Jane 1952- *WhoEmL 91*
Jennings, Thomas P. 1947- *St&PR 91*
Jennings, Thomas Parks 1947- *WhoAm 90*
Jennings, Toni 1949- *WhoAmW 91, WhoSSW 91*
Jennings, Vance Shelby 1925- *IntWWM 90*
Jennings, Vivien Ann 1934- *WhoAmW 91*
Jennings, Walter H. 1961- *WhoE 91*
Jennings, Walter Stanley, Jr. 1952- *BiDrAPA 89*
Jennings, Wanda Beth 1947- *WhoAmW 91*
Jennings, Ward Allyn, Sr. 1939- *WhoSSW 91*
Jennings, Waylon *WhoNeCM A [port]*
Jennings, Waylon 1937- *ConMus 4 [port], OxCPMus, WorAlBi*
Jennings, William Bryan, Jr. 1939- *WhoSSW 91*
Jennings, William Christopher 1939- *St&PR 91*
Jennings, William Scott *BioIn 16*
Jennings, William Sherman 1863-1920 *AmLegL*
Jennings-Wainwright, A. Terea *WhoE 91*
Jennison, Beverly Petersen 1952- *WhoEmL 91*
Jennison, Brian L. 1950- *WhoEmL 91*
Jennison, C. S. *AuBYP 90*
Jennison, James S. 1934- *St&PR 91*
Jennison, Keith Warren 1911- *AuBYP 90*
Jennison, Peter Saxe 1922- *WhoWrEP 89*
Jennrich, John Harold 1941- *WhoE 91*
Jennrich, William Frank 1940- *St&PR 91*
Jenny, Albert 1918- *WhoE 91*
Jenny, Charlotte L *BiDrAPA 89*
Jenny, Frederick Franklin 1935- *WhoSSW 91*
Jenrette, Pamela Anne 1947- *WhoAmA 91*
Jenrette, Richard Hampton 1929- *St&PR 91, WhoAm 90, WhoE 91*
Jenrette, Rita Carpenter 1949- *WhoAmW 91*
Jenrette, Thomas Shepard, Jr. 1946- *WhoSSW 91*
Jenrich, Charles Lester 1947- *WhoWor 91*
Jens, Elizabeth Lee Shafer 1915- *WhoWor 91*
Jens, Kurtis David *BiDrAPA 89*
Jens, Patricia Ann 1955- *BiDrAPA 89*
Jens, Ruth 1911- *BiDrAPA 89*
Jens, Walter 1923- *WhoWor 91*
Jensen, A. Kris 1927- *St&PR 91*
Jensen, Adolph Robert 1915- *WhoAm 90*
Jensen, Alfred 1903-1981 *WhoAmA 91N*
Jensen, Alvin L. 1930- *St&PR 91*
Jensen, Andrea Fox 1956- *WhoEmL 91*
Jensen, Andrew Oden 1920- *WhoSSW 91*
Jensen, Anita Kristina 1955- *WhoEmL 91*
Jensen, Anne Turner 1926- *WhoAmW 91*
Jensen, Arthur Seigfried 1917- *WhoAm 90*
Jensen, Barbara Wood 1927- *WhoWor 91*
Jensen, Bernard 1908- *NewAgE 90*
Jensen, Bill 1945- *WhoAm 90, WhoAmA 91*
Jensen, Bill G. 1933- *St&PR 91*
Jensen, Birger Steen 1947- *WhoWor 91*
Jensen, Bo Green 1955- *WhoWor 91*
Jensen, Bruce Lamont 1937- *BiDrAPA 89*
Jensen, Carl Frank 1952- *BiDrAPA 89*
Jensen, Carol Ann 1951- *WhoEmL 91*
Jensen, Cecil 1902-1976 *EncACom*
Jensen, Cecil Leon 1902-1976 *WhoAmA 91N*
Jensen, Charles Patrick 1931- *WhoE 91*
Jensen, Christian Reid 1940- *WhoSSW 91*
Jensen, Clay Easton 1952- *WhoAmA 91*
Jensen, Clayne R. 1930- *WhoAm 90*
Jensen, Craig William 1951- *WhoSSW 91*
Jensen, D. Clifford *St&PR 91*
Jensen, D. Lowell 1928- *WhoAm 90*
Jensen, Dale Alan 1949- *WhoWrEP 89*
Jensen, Dale Martin 1949- *St&PR 91*
Jensen, Daniel Thomas 1966- *WhoEmL 91*
Jensen, Daryl D. 1939- *St&PR 91*
Jensen, David Chris 1958- *WhoE 91*
Jensen, David E. *AuBYP 90*
Jensen, David Elden 1921- *St&PR 91*
Jensen, David Lynn 1941- *WhoE 91*
Jensen, David R. 1942- *St&PR 91*
Jensen, Dean N 1938- *WhoAmA 91*
Jensen, Deborah MacLurg 1900-1962 *BioIn 16*
Jensen, Delores 1944- *WhoAmW 91*
Jensen, Dennis Mark 1946- *WhoEmL 91*
Jensen, Dick Leroy 1930- *WhoAm 90*
Jensen, Don Arlen 1935- *St&PR 91, WhoAm 90*
Jensen, Donald Reed 1934- *BiDrAPA 89*
Jensen, Doris Eileen 1949- *BiDrAPA 89*
Jensen, Doris J. 1939- *WhoAmW 91*
Jensen, Dwight William 1934- *WhoWrEP 89*
Jensen, Edmund Paul 1937- *St&PR 91, WhoAm 90*
Jensen, Elwood Vernon 1920- *WhoAm 90, WhoWor 91*
Jensen, Eric Finn 1927- *WhoAm 90*
Jensen, Eric Webb *BiDrAPA 89*
Jensen, Erik Henning 1933- *WhoWor 91*
Jensen, Ernest 1915- *WhoWor 91*
Jensen, Ethel Roxanne 1938- *WhoAmW 91*
Jensen, Gary A. 1941- *St&PR 91*
Jensen, Georg 1866-1935 *PenDiDA 89*
Jensen, George Aaron 1934- *St&PR 91*
Jensen, George Albert 1929-1990 *WhoAm 90*
Jensen, Gerald L. 1940- *St&PR 91*
Jensen, Gerald Randolph 1924- *WhoWrEP 89*
Jensen, Gerreit *PenDiDA 89*
Jensen, Gordon D 1926- *BiDrAPA 89*
Jensen, Grady Edmonds 1922- *WhoAm 90*
Jensen, Grete Stenbaek 1925- *EncCoWW*
Jensen, Gwendolyn Evans 1936- *WhoAm 90*
Jensen, Hanne Margrete 1935- *WhoAmW 91*
Jensen, Hans Jorgen 1929- *WhoWor 91*
Jensen, Harlan Ellsworth 1915- *WhoAm 90*
Jensen, Harold Leroy 1926- *WhoAm 90*
Jensen, Harold Sherwood 1930- *WhoAm 90*
Jensen, Helen 1919- *IntWWM 90, WhoAmW 91*
Jensen, Helene Wickstrom 1929- *WhoE 91*
Jensen, Henry 1933- *WhoAm 90*
Jensen, Herluf Matthias 1923- *WhoE 91*
Jensen, J. Christopher 1947- *WhoEmL 91*
Jensen, J. David 1948- *St&PR 91*
Jensen, J. Hans Daniel 1907-1973 *WorAlBi*
Jensen, Jackie 1927-1982 *Ballpl 90*
Jensen, Jakki Renee 1959- *WhoAmW 91, WhoEmL 91*
Jensen, James Herbert 1906- *WhoAm 90*
Jensen, James Robert 1922- *WhoAm 90*
Jensen, Jane Mary 1951- *WhoWor 91*
Jensen, Jane Thielke 1933- *WhoAmW 91*
Jensen, Jay R. *BioIn 16*
Jensen, Jeffrey Carl 1955- *WhoE 91*
Jensen, Jennifer Jo 1960- *WhoAmW 91, WhoEmL 91, WhoWor 91*
Jensen, Jim *BioIn 16*
Jensen, Jodeen Marie 1964- *WhoAmW 91*
Jensen, Joel E. 1935- *St&PR 91*
Jensen, Johan Laurentz 1800-1865 *BioIn 16*
Jensen, Johannes Vilhelm 1873-1950 *DcScanL*
Jensen, John E. 1928- *St&PR 91*
Jensen, John Edward 1921-1982 *WhoAmA 91N*
Jensen, John Lawrence 1942- *WhoAm 90*
Jensen, Jon 1960- *BioIn 16*
Jensen, Jonathan Alan *WhoE 91*
Jensen, Jorgen Fris 1927- *WhoWor 91*
Jensen, Joseph S 1926- *BiDrAPA 89*
Jensen, Judy Dianne 1948- *WhoEmL 91*
Jensen, Julie Mae 1943- *WhoAm 90*
Jensen, Julius, III 1933- *St&PR 91*
Jensen, Katherine Kemp 1955- *WhoAmW 91*
Jensen, Kathryn Patricia 1950- *WhoAmW 91*
Jensen, Kenneth R. 1914- *St&PR 91*
Jensen, Knud Werner Koch 1935- *WhoWor 91*
Jensen, Kristen A. *ODwPR 91*
Jensen, Laura Linnea 1948- *WhoWrEP 89*
Jensen, Lawrence Jeremy 1950- *WhoAm 90*
Jensen, Leo 1926- *WhoAmA 91*
Jensen, Loren Ann 1953- *WhoAmW 91*
Jensen, Loren D. 1937- *St&PR 91*
Jensen, Louis 1924- *BiDrAPA 89*
Jensen, Marilyn Moore 1935- *St&PR 91*
Jensen, Marit *WhoAmA 91N*
Jensen, Marlene F. 1947- *WhoAm 90, WhoAmW 91*
Jensen, Marvin Eli 1926- *WhoAm 90*
Jensen, Mary Brandt 1959- *WhoEmL 91*
Jensen, Mary-Jane 1924- *BiDrAPA 89*
Jensen, Maxine Elizabeth 1919- *WhoWrEP 89*
Jensen, Michael C. *BioIn 16*
Jensen, Michael C 1939- *ConAu 32NR*
Jensen, Michael Charles 1934- *WhoAm 90*
Jensen, Michael Cole 1939- *WhoAm 90, WhoE 91*
Jensen, Mikael 1953- *WhoWor 91*
Jensen, Millard 1922- *BiDrAPA 89*

Jensen, Muriel 1945- *WhoWrEP 89*
Jensen, Oliver B *BiDrAPA 89*
Jensen, Oliver Ormerod 1914- *WhoAm 90*
Jensen, Owen Franklin, III 1950- *St&PR 91*
Jensen, Owen Franklin, Jr. *St&PR 91*
Jensen, Peter J. 1939- *St&PR 91*
Jensen, Peter S. 1949- *BiDrAPA 89*
Jensen, Peter Scott 1949- *WhoE 91*
Jensen, Poul Erik 1956- *WhoWor 91*
Jensen, Poul Guldberg 1953- *WhoWor 91*
Jensen, Ralph D. 1950- *St&PR 91*
Jensen, Randy J. 1949- *WhoEmL 91*
Jensen, Regina Brunhild 1951- *WhoAmW 91, WhoWor 91*
Jensen, Reuben Rolland 1920- *WhoAm 90*
Jensen, Richard d'Arcambal 1955- *IntWWM 90*
Jensen, Richard Gerald 1951- *WhoSSW 91*
Jensen, Rita Ann 1955- *WhoEmL 91*
Jensen, Robert 1938-1990 *ConAu 132*
Jensen, Robert E. *ODwPR 91*
Jensen, Robert Granville 1935- *WhoAm 90*
Jensen, Robert L. 1928- *St&PR 91*
Jensen, Robert Trygve 1922- *WhoAm 90*
Jensen, Roger A. 1939- *St&PR 91*
Jensen, Roger Christian 1945- *WhoSSW 91*
Jensen, Roland J. 1929- *St&PR 91*
Jensen, Roland Jens 1929- *WhoAm 90*
Jensen, Ronald Eugene 1949- *WhoEmL 91*
Jensen, Ronnie Blaine 1950- *WhoSSW 91*
Jensen, Sam 1935- *WhoAm 90*
Jensen, Scott D. 1952- *St&PR 91*
Jensen, Sheryl Rufenacht 1956- *WhoAmW 91*
Jensen, Soren Georg 1917- *PenDiDA 89*
Jensen, Soren Stistrup 1956- *WhoE 91*
Jensen, Stanley A. 1924- *St&PR 91*
Jensen, Susan Ann 1946- *WhoE 91, WhoEmL 91*
Jensen, Sven Engell 1926- *BiDrAPA 89*
Jensen, Teresa Elaine 1948- *WhoEmL 91*
Jensen, Thomas *PenDiMP*
Jensen, Thomas H. 1932- *St&PR 91*
Jensen, Thomas Scott *BiDrAPA 89*
Jensen, Thomas W. *ODwPR 91*
Jensen, Viggo W 1923- *BiDrAPA 89*
Jensen, Wallace Quentin 1945- *WhoEmL 91*
Jensen, Walter Edward 1937- *WhoSSW 91*
Jensen, Welby Neal *BiDrAPA 89*
Jensen, Wiers 1866-1925 *EncO&P 3*
Jensen, Woody 1907- *Ballpl 90*
Jensen, Yvonne Marie 1946- *WhoEmL 91*
Jensh, Ronald Paul 1938- *WhoAm 90*
Jenson, Andrew 1850-1941 *BioIn 16*
Jenson, Charles David 1952- *WhoEmL 91*
Jenson, Dylana 1961- *IntWWM 90*
Jenson, James Joseph *BiDrAPA 89*
Jenson, Jan K. 1946- *WhoWrEP 89*
Jenson, Jennifer Ann 1959- *WhoEmL 91*
Jenson, Jon Eberdt 1934- *WhoAm 90*
Jenson, Paul Gerhard 1925- *WhoAm 90*
Jenson, Richard Leon 1952- *WhoEmL 91*
Jenson, Ronald Allen 1948- *WhoEmL 91*
Jenson, Taylor R. 1938- *St&PR 91*
Jenssen, Arthur H. 1923- *St&PR 91*
Jensvold, Margaret F 1956- *BiDrAPA 89*
Jent, William Riley *BioIn 16*
Jentes, William Robert 1932- *WhoAm 90*
Jentner, Bruce Alan 1954- *WhoEmL 91*
Jentoft, Arthur Philip 1927- *St&PR 91*
Jentz, Gaylord A 1931- *ConAu 31NR*
Jentz, Gaylord Adair 1931- *WhoAm 90, WhoSSW 91, WhoWor 91*
Jenzano, Anthony Francis 1919- *WhoAm 90*
Jeon, Bang Nam 1954- *WhoE 91*
Jeon, Kwang Wu 1934- *WhoSSW 91*
Jeorger, Leopold Henri 1933- *WhoWor 91*
Jephson, Ina *EncO&P 3*
Jephson, Ina 189-?-1961 *EncPaPR 91*
Jeppesen, Elrey Borge *BioIn 16*
Jeppesen, Myron Alton 1905- *WhoAm 90*
Jeppesen, Robert Eugene 1951- *WhoEmL 91*
Jeppesen, Susan Quandt 1954- *WhoAmW 91*
Jeppsen, Ernest Alan 1939- *BiDrAPA 89*
Jeppson, Calvin W. 1933- *St&PR 91*
Jeppson, J. O. 1926- *BioIn 16*
Jeppson, Janet 1926- *BiDrAPA 89*
Jeppson, Jay Herald 1926- *WhoAm 90*
Jeppson, John 1916- *WhoE 91*
Jeppsson, Kerstin Maria 1948- *IntWWM 90*
Jepsen, Glenn Lowell 1903-1974 *DcScB S2*
Jepsen, Henrik Bent 1957- *WhoWor 91*
Jepsen, John Robert 1955- *WhoEmL 91*
Jepsen, Jonathan M. 1945- *St&PR 91*
Jepsen-Lozano, Lisa 1952- *WhoE 91*
Jepson, Franklin T. *ODwPR 91*
Jepson, Hans Godfrey 1936- *WhoAm 90, WhoWor 91*
Jepson, Helen Anna 1947- *WhoAmW 91*
Jepson, John Willisford 1931- *St&PR 91*
Jepson, Robert Scott, Jr. 1942- *WhoAm 90*
Jepson, Selwyn 1899-1989 *TwCCr&M 91*
Jepson, Steven Baker 1960- *WhoAm 90*
Jepson, William W 1926- *BiDrAPA 89*
Jerabek, Karel 1943- *WhoWor 91*
Jerauld, Charlotte Ann 1820-1845 *FemiCLE*
Jerauld, Gordon Otis 1921- *St&PR 91*
Jerde, Jon Adams *WhoAm 90*
Jerde, Roxanne Garske 1953- *WhoEmL 91*
Jerdee, Thomas Harlan 1927- *WhoAm 90*
Jerding, Frederick Noel 1938- *WhoE 91*
Jereb, Marjan Josip 1930- *WhoWor 91*
Jeremiah 650?BC-585?BC *WorAlBi*
Jeremiah, David Elmer 1934- *WhoAm 90*
Jeremias, Gerald S. *BioIn 16*
Jeremy, David J. 1939- *ConAu 129*
Jerge, Dale Robert 1951- *WhoE 91*
Jerge, Marie Charlotte 1952- *WhoAmW 91*
Jergens, Robert Joseph 1938- *WhoAmA 91*
Jerger, Alfred 1889-1976 *PenDiMP*
Jerger, Edward William 1922- *WhoAm 90*
Jeri, Federico R *BiDrAPA 89*
Jeria, Jorge 1947- *WhoHisp 91*
Jerichau, Elizabeth Maria Anna 1819-1881 *BiDWomA*
Jerie, Marek Jan 1947- *IntWWM 90*
Jerin, Kay 1943- *ODwPR 91*
Jerina, Donald Michael 1940- *WhoE 91*
Jerins, Edgar 1958- *WhoAmA 91*
Jerison, Meyer 1922- *WhoAm 90*
Jeritza, Maria 1887-1982 *PenDiMP*
Jerkins, Catherine A. 1959- *St&PR 91*
Jerkins, Grace Mae 1904- *WhoAmW 91*
Jerkins, Ken M. 1944- *St&PR 91*
Jerkku, Jorma Severi 1938- *WhoWor 91*
Jerkofsky, MaryAnn 1943- *WhoAmW 91*
Jermany, Mertine Reece *BiDrAPA 89*
Jermyn, Helen Williams 1957- *WhoSSW 91*
Jermyn, Rebecca *BiDEWW*
Jerndal, Jens 1934- *WhoWor 91*
Jerne, Niels Kai 1911- *WorAlBi*
Jerne, Niels Kaj 1911- *WhoAm 90, WhoWor 91*
Jerner, R. Craig 1938- *WhoSSW 91*
Jernigan, Alicia 1944- *WhoHisp 91*
Jernigan, Eddie Dean 1956- *WhoSSW 91*
Jernigan, Finith Ewin, II 1952- *WhoE 91*
Jernigan, Gail Fiveash 1951- *WhoAmW 91*
Jernigan, Harry 1946- *WhoSSW 91*
Jernigan, James Earl 1925- *WhoSSW 91*
Jernigan, James Paul 1954- *WhoEmL 91*
Jernigan, Kenneth 1926- *WhoAm 90*
Jernigan, Marian Sue 1940- *WhoAmW 91*
Jernigan, Michael O'Neal 1953- *WhoSSW 91*
Jernigan, Nancy E *BiDrAPA 89*
Jernigan, Ralph W. 1946- *St&PR 91*
Jernigan, Robert Goode 1936- *WhoSSW 91*
Jernigan, Thomas Edward 1948- *WhoSSW 91*
Jernow, Jane Liu 1938- *WhoAmW 91*
Jernstedt, Rich 1947- *ODwPR 91*
Jernstedt, Richard Don 1947- *WhoAm 90*
Jerolimic, Nevio P. 1950- *St&PR 91*
Jerome, Saint *BioIn 16*
Jerome, Saint 342?-420 *WorAlBi*
Jerome, Albert *BioIn 16*
Jerome, Albert D. 1942- *St&PR 91*
Jerome, Fred Louis 1939- *WhoAm 90*
Jerome, James Alexander 1933- *WhoAm 90, WhoE 91*
Jerome, Jerrold V. 1929- *WhoAm 90*
Jerome, Jerrold Vincent 1929- *St&PR 91*
Jerome, Joseph Ben 1950- *WhoEmL 91*
Jerome, Joseph Walter 1939- *WhoAm 90*
Jerome, Judson 1927- *DcLB 105 [port], WhoWrEP 89*
Jerome, M. K. 1893- *OxCPMus*
Jerome, Maryanne Lee 1936- *BiDrAPA 89*
Jerome, Nancy Cawley 1930- *IntWWM 90*
Jerome, Norge Winifred 1930- *WhoAm 90*
Jerome, Norman A. 1925- *St&PR 91*
Jerome, Richard William 1922- *IntWWM 90*
Jeromson, James Robert, Jr. 1924- *St&PR 91*
Jeroski, Anthony Joseph, Jr. 1948- *WhoEmL 91, WhoWor 91*
Jerow, James Edward 1933- *WhoAm 90*
Jeroy, Frederick Daly 1937- *WhoSSW 91*
Jerr, William A. *AuBYP 90*
Jerrard, John Ralston 1930- *St&PR 91*
Jerrard, Richard Patterson 1925- *WhoAm 90*
Jerrett, Cathy Louise 1953- *WhoWrEP 89*
Jerrett, Robert, III 1943- *St&PR 91*
Jerris, Sidney David 1933- *St&PR 91*
Jerritts, Stephen G. 1925- *WhoAm 90, WhoWor 91*
Jerrold, Douglas William 1803-1857 *BioIn 16*
Jerry, Michael John 1937- *WhoAmA 91*
Jerry, Robert Howard 1923- *WhoAm 90*
Jersey, Deirdre Irene 1946- *WhoAmW 91*
Jersild, Arthur T. 1902- *WhoWrEP 89*
Jersild, Casper Anders 1939- *WhoWor 91*
Jersild, Jorgen 1913- *IntWWM 90*
Jersild, P. C. *ConAu 130*
Jersild, Per Christian 1935- *ConAu 130, DcScanL*
Jersild, Thomas Nielsen 1936- *WhoAm 90, WhoWor 91*
Jersky, Brian 1957- *WhoE 91*
Jerson, Carol Anne 1957- *WhoAmW 91*
Jerusalem, Siegfried *BioIn 16*
Jerusalem, Siegfried 1940- *IntWWM 90, PenDiMP*
Jervey, Harold Edward, Jr. 1920- *WhoAm 90*
Jerving, John Wesley 1950- *WhoEmL 91*
Jervis, Robert 1940- *WhoAm 90*
Jervis, Robert E. 1927- *WhoAm 90*
Jervis, Sally Ann 1937- *WhoAmW 91*
Jervis Read, Charles John Christian 1947- *WhoWor 91*
Jervis-Read, Diana Isabel 1945- *WhoWor 91*
Jerviss, Joy 1941- *WhoAmA 91*
Jerviss, Joy J. 1941- *WhoE 91*
Jervois, William Francis Drummond 1821-1897 *DcCanB 12*
Jerwood, John *BioIn 16*
Jesalva, Edmundo *BiDrAPA 89*
Jeschelnig, Richard John 1951- *St&PR 91*
Jeschke, Channing Renwick 1927- *WhoAm 90, WhoSSW 91*
Jeschke, Mark Walter 1956- *WhoEmL 91*
Jeschonnek, Hans 1899-1943 *BioIn 16*
Jeseseke, Ellen Frances 1954- *WhoAmW 91, WhoEmL 91*
Jeskalian, Barbara Jean 1936- *IntWWM 90*
Jeske, Debora Rae 1952- *WhoAmW 91*
Jeske, Howard Leigh 1917- *WhoAm 90*
Jeske, Kathlynn Jeanne 1950- *WhoSSW 91*
Jeske, Lucille 1931- *WhoAmW 91*
Jesko, Milan 1941- *IntWWM 90*
Jesky, T. J. 1947- *WhoWor 91*
Jespersen, Charles Zinck 1941- *St&PR 91*
Jespersen, Jesper Jorgen 1952- *WhoWor 91*
Jespersen, Knud Jesper Vinggaard 1942- *WhoWor 91*
Jespersen, Robert Carl *BiDrAPA 89*
Jespersen, Vagn 1918- *WhoWor 91*
Jesperson, Daryl Lee 1947- *WhoAm 90*
Jess 1923- *WhoAmA 91*
Jess, Frank B. 1870- *AmLegL*
Jesse, F. Tennyson 1888-1958 *FemiCLE*
Jesse, F Tennyson 1888-1958 *TwCCr&M 91*
Jesse, Fryniwyd Tennyson 1888-1958 *BioIn 16*
Jesse, Mary Jane 1918- *WhoAm 90*
Jessee, John Thomas 1955- *WhoEmL 91*
Jessee, Lance 1943- *St&PR 91*
Jessee, Salley Sue 1948- *BiDrAPA 89*
Jessel, George 1898-1981 *WorAlBi*
Jessel, Leon 1871-1942 *OxCPMus*
Jesselson, Robert 1949- *IntWWM 90*
Jesseman, Wendell William 1934- *St&PR 91*
Jessen, Albert V 1920- *BiDrAPA 89*
Jessen, David Wayne 1950- *WhoAm 90*
Jessen, John Henry, Sr. 1923- *St&PR 91*
Jessen, Shirley Agnes 1921- *WhoAmA 91*
Jesseph, Steven Austin 1951- *WhoSSW 91*
Jesser, Benn Wainwright 1915- *WhoAm 90*
Jesser, Edward A., Jr. 1916- *St&PR 91*
Jesser, Roger Franklyn 1926- *WhoAm 90*
Jesseramsing, Chitmansing *BioIn 16*
Jesseramsing, Chitmansing 1933- *WhoAm 90, WhoWor 91*
Jesserson, Susanna *BiDEWW, FemiCLE*
Jessey, John Joseph, Jr. 1953- *WhoEmL 91*
Jessiman, Alistair 1957- *WhoE 91*
Jesson, Casey *BioIn 16*
Jesson, Valerie *BioIn 16*
Jessop, Dorothy Emma 1929- *WhoWrEP 89*
Jessop, Douglas Wayne 1951- *WhoEmL 91*
Jessor, Herman J. 1896-1990 *BioIn 16*
Jessup, James Barry *St&PR 91N*
Jessup, Joe Lee 1913- *WhoAm 90, WhoSSW 91, WhoWor 91*
Jessup, John Baker 1921- *WhoAm 90*
Jessup, Lynne E. 1944- *IntWWM 90*
Jessup, Paul Frederick 1939- *WhoAm 90*
Jessup, Philip C. 1897-1986 *BioIn 16*
Jessup, Philip Caryl, Jr. 1926- *WhoAm 90*
Jessup, Rachel Lutz 1962- *WhoAmW 91*
Jessup, Richard 1925-1982 *TwCCr&M 91*
Jessup, Robert 1952- *WhoAmA 91*
Jessup, Robert Judd 1947- *WhoEmL 91*
Jessup, Steve R. 1952- *St&PR 91*
Jessup, Steven Lee 1954- *WhoSSW 91*
Jessup, Stewart E. 1924- *WhoSSW 91*
Jessup, W. Edgar, Jr. 1922- *St&PR 91*
Jessup, Warren T. 1916- *WhoAm 90, WhoWor 91*
Jessup, William McClellan, Jr. 1928- *WhoE 91*
Jessup, William Royall 1933- *WhoSSW 91*
Jessurun D'Oliveira, Hans Ulrich 1933- *WhoWor 91*
Jessye, Eva 1895- *DrBIPA 90*
Jessye, Eva Alberta 1895- *DcAfAmP*
Jessye, Eva Alberta 1897- *HarlReB*
Jeste, Dilip V *BiDrAPA 89*
Jeste, Dilip Vishwanath 1944- *WhoAm 90*
Jester, Dana Edward 1939- *St&PR 91*
Jester, Guy Earlscourt 1929- *St&PR 91*
Jester, Mary George 1946- *WhoSSW 91*
Jester, R. Charles, Jr. 1917- *St&PR 91*
Jester, Roberts Charles, Jr. 1917- *WhoAm 90, WhoE 91*
Jester, Tod Krueger 1942- *St&PR 91, WhoAm 90*
Jestice, Aaron Lowell 1930- *St&PR 91*
Jestin, Heimwarth B. 1918- *WhoAm 90*
Jesup, Thomas Sidney 1788-1860 *WhNaAH*
Jesurin, Arthur J. *ODwPR 91*
Jesurun, Harold Mendez 1915- *WhoAm 90*
Jesus Christ *BioIn 16*
Jesus Christ 6?BC-30AD *EncPaPR 91, WorAlBi*
Jesus, Magdeleine de 1898-1989 *BioIn 16*
Jeswald, Joseph 1927- *WhoAmA 91*
Jesweak, Clayton C. 1931- *St&PR 91*
Jeszeck, Charles Anthony 1953- *WhoE 91*
Jet, Jammo 1955- *WhoSSW 91*
Jet, Jimmy 1950- *WhoEmL 91*
Jetelova, Magdalena *BioIn 16*
Jetelova, Magdalena 1946- *BiDWomA*
Jeter, Allen Hunter 1927- *St&PR 91*
Jeter, Clifton B., Jr. 1944- *WhoE 91*
Jeter, Duane *St&PR 91*
Jeter, George W. 1935- *St&PR 91*
Jeter, James 1949- *IntWWM 90*
Jeter, Jeremiah Bell 1802-1880 *BioIn 16*
Jeter, John 1944- *Ballpl 90*
Jeter, Katherine Leslie Brash 1921- *WhoAmW 91, WhoSSW 91, WhoWor 91*
Jeter, Kelli Jo 1961- *WhoEmL 91*
Jeter, Randy Joe 1937-1987 *WhoAmA 91N*
Jeter, Wayburn Stewart 1926- *WhoAm 90*
Jethanandani, Vijay *BiDrAPA 89*
Jethro Tull *EncPR&S 89, OxCPMus*
Jethroe, Sam 1922- *Ballpl 90*
Jetmalani, Ajit Naraindas *BiDrAPA 89*
Jetmalani, Naraindas B 1916- *BiDrAPA 89*
Jett, Benjamin P. 1808-1865 *AmLegL*
Jett, Bill 1944- *St&PR 91*
Jett, Charles Cranston 1941- *WhoAm 90, WhoWor 91*
Jett, Edward Stephen 1945- *WhoEmL 91*
Jett, Jamie Denise 1963- *WhoE 91*
Jett, Joan 1960- *EncPR&S 89, WorAlBi*
Jett, Nancy Jensen 1956- *WhoSSW 91*
Jett, Stephen Clinton 1938- *WhoAm 90*
Jetton, Girard Reuel, Jr. 1924- *WhoAm 90*
Jetton, Michael T. *St&PR 91*
Jetzer, Alap *NewAgMG*
Jeub, Michael Leonard 1943- *St&PR 91, WhoAm 90*
Jeub, Robert P *BiDrAPA 89*
Jeuck, John Edward 1916- *WhoAm 90*
Jeun, Kong Ryeul 1942- *BiDrAPA 89*
Jeurissen, Herman G. A. 1952- *IntWWM 90*
Jevon, Rachel *FemiCLE*
Jevon, Rachel 1627?- *BiDEWW*
Jevons, Mary Ann 1795-1845 *FemiCLE*
Jevons, William Stanley 1835-1882 *BioIn 16*
Jew, Henry 1950- *WhoSSW 91*
Jewel, Ian *PenDiMP*
Jewell, Alice Karnes 1943- *WhoSSW 91*
Jewell, Byron Frank 1946- *WhoAm 90, WhoSSW 91*
Jewell, Charles Edwin 1945- *WhoEmL 91, WhoSSW 91*
Jewell, Diana Kay 1959- *WhoSSW 91*
Jewell, E. Harvey *IntWWM 90*
Jewell, Gayla Dawne 1951- *WhoEmL 91*
Jewell, George Hiram 1922- *WhoAm 90*
Jewell, Harvey 1820-1881 *AmLegL*
Jewell, James Wade 1954- *WhoEmL 91*
Jewell, Joyce 1945- *WhoAmA 91*
Jewell, Marshall 1825-1883 *BiDrUSE 89*
Jewell, Richard 1949- *WhoWrEP 89*
Jewell, Rob *ODwPR 91*
Jewell, Robert B. 1906- *St&PR 91*
Jewell, Robert Burnett 1906- *WhoAm 90, WhoSSW 91*
Jewell, Sally *BioIn 16*
Jewell, Sarah *BioIn 16*
Jewell, Steven Charles 1959- *WhoE 91*
Jewell, Steven William *BiDrAPA 89*
Jewell, Thomas Lawrence 1944- *St&PR 91*

Jewell, Timothy Powell 1939- *WhoSSW 91*
Jewell, William M 1904- *WhoAmA 91*
Jewell, William MacIntyre 1904- *WhoAm 90*
Jewell, William Sylvester 1932- *WhoAm 90*
Jewels, Mary 1886-1977 *BiDWomA*
Jewers, Kenneth 1931- *WhoWor 91*
Jewess, Kathleen *ConAu 130*
Jewett, Cathy Ann 1946- *WhoEmL 91*
Jewett, Charles Edgar 1952- *St&PR 91*
Jewett, Charles LaFayette 1848-1931 *AmLegL*
Jewett, David Stuart 1941- *WhoAm 90*
Jewett, Edgar Boardman, III 1928- *WhoAm 90*
Jewett, Edward T *BiDrAPA 89*
Jewett, Frank S 1932- *BiDrAPA 89*
Jewett, Frank Sniffen 1932- *WhoE 91*
Jewett, G.F., Jr. 1927- *St&PR 91*
Jewett, George Frederick, Jr. 1927- *WhoAm 90*
Jewett, Gerald Anson, Jr. 1925- *St&PR 91*
Jewett, Hugh Judge 1903-1990 *BioIn 16*
Jewett, John Persinger 1943- *WhoE 91*
Jewett, John Rhodes 1922- *WhoAm 90*
Jewett, Raymond L. 1924- *St&PR 91*
Jewett, Richard Kirk 1926- *St&PR 91*
Jewett, Robert William 1952- *St&PR 91*
Jewett, Sally Jean 1953- *WhoAmW 91*
Jewett, Sarah Orne 1849-1909 *AuBYP 90, BioAmW, BioIn 16, FemiCLE, ShSCr 6 [port], WorAlBi*
Jewett, Stephen Shannon 1858-1932 *AmLegL*
Jewison, Norman *BioIn 16*
Jewison, Norman 1926- *WorAlBi*
Jewison, Norman Frederick 1926- *WhoAm 90*
Jewitt, David Willard Pennock 1921- *WhoAm 90*
Jewitt, John Rodgers 1783-1821 *DcLB 99, WhNaAH*
Jewitt, Thomas Lee 1951- *BiDrAPA 89*
Jewkes, Gordon Wesley 1931- *WhoWor 91*
Jewkes, John 1902-1988 *AnObit 1988*
Jewsbury, Geraldine 1812-1880 *BioIn 16, FemiCLE*
Jewsbury, Maria Jane 1800-1833 *BioIn 16, FemiCLE*
Jex-Blake, Sophia Louisa 1840-1912 *BioIn 16*
Jeydel, Richard K. 1950- *St&PR 91, WhoAm 90, WhoEmL 91*
Jeye, Peter Austin 1959- *WhoSSW 91*
Jeynes, Paul 1927- *WhoAmA 91*
Jez, Jacob 1928- *IntWWM 90*
Jez, John B. 1935- *St&PR 91*
Jezard, Alison 1919- *BioIn 16*
Jezerinac, Joseph 1936- *St&PR 91*
Jezewski, James Edward 1948- *St&PR 91*
Jezina, Carol Susan 1946- *WhoEmL 91*
Jeziorkowski, John G. 1952- *St&PR 91*
Jezl, Barbara Ann 1947- *WhoE 91*
Jezuit, Leslie James 1945- *WhoAm 90*
Jha, Bal Krishna 1929- *BiDrAPA 89*
Jha, L. K. 1913-1988 *AnObit 1988*
Jhabvala, Ruth 1927- *FemiCLE*
Jhabvala, Ruth Prawer *BioIn 16*
Jhabvala, Ruth Prawer 1927- *MajTwCW, WhoAm 90, WhoWor 91, WhoWrEP 89*
Jhaveri, Mukesh J *BiDrAPA 89*
Jhawar, Shiv Ratan 1948- *WhoEmL 91*
Jhin, Michael Kontien 1950- *WhoAm 90*
Jhirad, David John 1939- *WhoE 91*
Ji Pengfei 1910- *WhoWor 91*
Ji Zhiguang *BioIn 16*
Ji, Shanyu 1955- *WhoSSW 91*
Jia Zuoguang *BioIn 16*
Jia, Pingwa 1952- *WhoWor 91*
Jia-Yuan, Charlotte 1958- *WhoAmW 91*
Jialanella, Gloria Jean 1942- *WhoAmW 91*
Jiang Jialiang *BioIn 16*
Jiang Kun *BioIn 16*
Jiang Qing 1910- *BioIn 16*
Jiang Wen *BioIn 16*
Jiang Zemin *BioIn 16*
Jiang Zemin 1926- *WhoWor 91*
Jiang, John Jianzhong 1960- *WhoEmL 91*
Jiang, Paul Yun-ming 1939- *WhoWor 91*
Jiang, Renfang 1952- *WhoEmL 91*
Jibben, Laura Ann 1949- *WhoAmW 91*
Jicha, Louis Ray 1951- *WhoEmL 91*
Jicha, Victoria Poullette 1944- *IntWWM 90*
Jickling, John Ward 1921- *WhoAm 90*
Jigyasu, Dharam Jit 1915- *WhoE 91*
Jilek, John P. 1952- *St&PR 91*
Jiler, William Laurence 1925- *WhoAm 90*
Jilg, Michael Florian 1947- *WhoAmA 91*
Jilhewar, Ashok 1947- *WhoWor 91*
Jillette, Penn *BioIn 16*
Jillian, Ann *BioIn 16*
Jillian, Ann 1950- *WorAlBi*
Jillson, Francello George 1841-1912 *AmLegL*
Jimenez, A. Jimmy *WhoHisp 91*
Jimenez, Alberto Vasquez *BioIn 16*
Jimenez, Andres L 1943- *BiDrAPA 89*
Jimenez, Angel F. *WhoHisp 91*
Jimenez, Arlene Marie 1959- *WhoAmW 91*
Jimenez, Bettie Eileen 1932- *WhoAmW 91*
Jimenez, Cristobal 1932- *WhoHisp 91*
Jimenez, Daniel 1936- *WhoHisp 91*
Jimenez, Donna 1961- *WhoHisp 91*
Jimenez, Emmanuel 1952- *WhoE 91*
Jimenez, Enrique Adolfo 1888-1970 *BioIn 16*
Jimenez, Felix J. 1944- *WhoHisp 91*
Jimenez, Francisco 1943- *BioIn 16, ConAu 131, HispWr 90, WhoHisp 91, WhoWrEP 89*
Jimenez, Houston 1957- *Ballpl 90*
Jimenez, Iris C. 1951- *WhoHisp 91*
Jimenez, Juan Carlos 1952- *WhoHisp 91*
Jimenez, Juan Ramon *BioIn 16*
Jimenez, Juan Ramon 1881-1958 *ConAu 131, HispWr 90, MajTwCW, WorAlBi*
Jimenez, Luis 1940- *BioIn 16*
Jimenez, Luis A. 1940- *WhoHisp 91*
Jimenez, Luis Alberto 1945- *WhoE 91*
Jimenez, Luis Alfonso, Jr. 1940- *WhoAm 90, WhoAmA 91*
Jimenez, Manny 1938- *Ballpl 90*
Jimenez, Marcos Perez 1914- *BioIn 16*
Jimenez, Maria C. *WhoHisp 91*
Jimenez, Maria J. 1964- *WhoHisp 91*
Jimenez, Marie John 1932- *WhoHisp 91*
Jimenez, Mario Echandi 1915- *BioIn 16*
Jimenez, Menardo R., Sr. 1932- *WhoWor 91*
Jimenez, Ramon *ConAu 131, HispWr 90, MajTwCW*
Jimenez, Raul, Jr. *WhoHisp 91*
Jimenez, Richard Gonzales 1956- *BiDrAPA 89*
Jimenez, Robert Leo *BiDrAPA 89*
Jimenez, Rolando Daniel 1938- *WhoSSW 91*
Jimenez, Sergio A. 1942- *WhoHisp 91*
Jimenez Casasnovas, Alberto 1949- *WhoWor 91*
Jimenez de Cisneros, Francisco 1436?-1517 *BioIn 16*
Jimenez-Faro, Luzmaria 1937- *EncCoWW*
Jimenez Hyre, Silvia 1950- *WhoHisp 91*
Jimenez Mantecon, Juan *ConAu 131, HispWr 90, MajTwCW*
Jimenez Oreamuno, Ricardo 1859-1945 *BioIn 16*
Jimenez P., Rodrigo *WhoHisp 91*
Jimenez-Penaloza, Rosa 1955- *WhoHisp 91*
Jimenez-Soto, Jesus Raul *BiDrAPA 89*
Jimenez-Velez, Jose L. 1927- *WhoHisp 91*
Jimenez-Wagenheim, Olga 1941- *WhoHisp 91*
Jimerson, David Cedric *BiDrAPA 89*
Jimerson, James Compere, Sr. 1936- *WhoAm 90*
Jimerson, Robert Charles *BiDrAPA 89*
Jimirro, James P. 1937- *WhoAm 90*
Jimma, Takashi 1932- *WhoWor 91*
Jimmu Tenno *EncJap*
Jimmy Jock *DcCanB 12*
Jimmy the Greek *BioIn 16*
Jin, Marvin Y J 1946- *BiDrAPA 89*
Jin, Marvin Young-Jong 1946- *WhoSSW 91*
Jin, Meiling 1956- *FemiCLE*
Jin, Sungho *BioIn 16*
Jinadu, Musa Kolawole 1940- *WhoWor 91*
Jinasena, Ranjit Tissaweera 1945- *WhoWor 91*
Jindal, Ramesh K *BiDrAPA 89*
Jindan *WomWR*
Jindrich, William Lee 1940- *St&PR 91*
Jinga 1582-1663 *BioIn 16*
Jingo-kogo 169?-269? *WomWR [port]*
Jingu, Empress *EncJap*
Jinkens, Rosalyn S. 1948- *St&PR 91*
Jinks, Jill Karen 1957- *WhoEmL 91*
Jinks, Robert Larry 1929- *WhoAm 90*
Jinks, Sharon Jean 1947- *WhoAmW 91*
Jinnah, Mohamed Ali 1876-1948 *BioIn 16*
Jinner, Sara *BiDEWW*
Jinner, Sarah *FemiCLE*
Jinnett, Robert Jefferson 1949- *WhoE 91, WhoEmL 91, WhoWor 91*
Jinno, Yoh 1951- *WhoE 91*
Jiral, Jeannine Carol 1955- *WhoSSW 91*
Jiranek, Leo *BioIn 16, NewYTBS 90*
Jiricna, Eva 1939- *WomArch*
Jirikovec, Leroy Edward 1925- *St&PR 91*
Jirka, Frank Joseph, Jr. 1922- *WhoAm 90*
Jiron, Arnoldo Jose *BiDrAPA 89*
Jiron, Herardo A. 1926- *WhoHisp 91*
Jirousek, Jaroslav Wenceslas 1931- *WhoWor 91*
Jirovec, Ronald Arthur 1948- *St&PR 91*
Jirran, Raymond Joseph 1934- *WhoSSW 91*
Jirsa, James Otis 1938- *WhoAm 90*
Jischke, Martin C. 1941- *WhoAm 90*
Jison, Asuncion G *BiDrAPA 89*
Jitkoff, Andrew *BioIn 16*
Jito, Empress 645-703 *EncJap*
Jito-tenno 625-701 *WomWR [port]*
Jiwkow, Wasil 1926- *IntWWM 90, WhoWor 91*
Jnanadeva *BioIn 16*
Joachim Quartet *PenDiMP*
Joachim, Brigitta Golden *WhoAmW 91, WhoE 91*
Joachim, Dana 1957- *ODwPR 91*
Joachim, Joseph 1831-1907 *PenDiMP*
Joachim, Miroslav Vaclav Jan 1919- *WhoWor 91*
Joachim, Otto 1910- *IntWWM 90*
Joan *WhoWrEP 89*
Joan I 1326-1382 *WomWR*
Joan II 1371-1435 *WomWR*
Joan of Arc 1412-1431 *WorAlBi*
Joan, of Arc, Saint 1412-1431 *BioIn 16*
Joan of Arc, Saint 1412-1431 *EncPaPR 91*
Joanna *WomWR*
Joanna I 1326-1382 *WomWR*
Joanna II 1371-1435 *WomWR*
Joanna of Austria *WomWR*
Joanna I, Queen of Naples 1327?-1382 *BioIn 16*
Joanna II, Queen of Naples 1371-1435 *BioIn 16*
Joannette, Vianney 1940- *St&PR 91*
Joanning, Harold Theodore 1927- *St&PR 91, WhoAm 90*
Joanou, Phillip 1933- *WhoAm 90*
Joaquim, Leandro 1738?-1798? *ArtLatA*
Joaquim, Richard Ralph 1936- *WhoWor 91*
Joaquin, Wilfredo Serrano 1949- *WhoE 91*
Job, Anne Marie 1956- *WhoAmW 91*
Job, Donald D. 1942- *WhoWrEP 89*
Job, Gilberto Souza Gomes 1932- *WhoWor 91*
Job, Reuben Philip 1928- *WhoAm 90*
Jobe, Alice 1935- *WhoAmW 91*
Jobe, Don Larry 1946- *WhoEmL 91*
Jobe, Frank Wilson 1925- *WhoAm 90*
Jobe, G. David 1943- *St&PR 91*
Jobe, George Henry, Jr. 1941- *WhoAm 90*
Jobe, Jared Bruce 1951- *WhoEmL 91*
Jobe, Larry Alton 1940- *WhoAm 90*
Jobe, Shirley A. 1946- *WhoAmW 91*
Jobe, Thomas Harmon *BiDrAPA 89*
Jobe, Warren Yancey 1940- *St&PR 91*
Jobert, Michel 1921- *BiDFrPL*
Jobes, Nancy *BioIn 16*
Jobim, Antonio Carlos *BioIn 16*
Jobim, Antonio Carlos 1927- *OxCPMus*
Jobin, Raoul 1906-1974 *PenDiMP*
Jobs, Stephen P. 1955- *WorAlBi*
Jobs, Steven *BioIn 16*
Jobs, Steven Paul 1955- *ConAmBL*
Jobson, Eddie *NewAgMG*
Jobson, Edward R. *BioIn 16*
Jobson, Kenneth Owens 1943- *BiDrAPA 89*
Jobson, Mareda Bell 1946- *WhoAmW 91, WhoEmL 91*
Jobson, Mary *EncO&P 3*
Jobson, Thomas Wootten 1925- *WhoAm 90*
Jocda 1926- *WhoAmA 91*
Jocelin, Elizabeth 1595?-1622 *FemiCLE*
Jocelin, Elizabeth 1596-1622 *BioIn 16*
Jocelyn, Ada Maria 1860-1931 *FemiCLE*
Jocelyn, Henry David 1933- *WhoWor 91*
Jochim, Michael Allan 1945- *WhoAm 90*
Jochim, Michael Eugene 1945- *WhoSSW 91*
Jochim, W. Steve 1942- *WhoSSW 91*
Jochimsen, Earl 1928- *BiDrAPA 89*
Jocho *EncJap*
Jochsberger, Tzipora H. 1920- *IntWWM 90*
Jochum, Eugen 1902-1987 *PenDiMP*
Jochum, Otto 1898-1969 *PenDiMP*
Jochum, Veronica *IntWWM 90, WhoAm 90*
Jochumsson, Matthias 1835-1920 *DcScanL*
Jockusch, Carl Groos, Jr. 1941- *WhoAm 90*
Jocobs, Herman 1936- *WhoWor 91*
Jocobsohn, James S *BiDrAPA 89*
Jodl, Alfred 1890-1946 *BioIn 16, WorAlBi*
Jodoin, Kenneth Francis 1941- *WhoE 91*
Jodoin, Maurice 1939- *St&PR 91*
Jodsaas, Larry Elvin 1935- *St&PR 91, WhoAm 90*
Jody, Darlene 1955- *BiDrAPA 89*
Joe, Oreland *BioIn 16*
Joel, Amos Edward, Jr. 1918- *WhoAm 90*
Joel, Billy 1949- *EncPR&S 89, OxCPMus, WhoAm 90, WorAlBi*
Joel, Irving 1928- *St&PR 91*
Joel, Samuel W 1913- *BiDrAPA 89*
Joel, William Lee, II 1933- *WhoAm 90*
Joels, Frederick David 1925- *St&PR 91*
Joelson, Edith Weisskopf- 1910-1983 *BioIn 16*
Joelson, Mark Rene 1934- *WhoAm 90*
Joelson, Suzanne *WhoAmA 91*
Joenpelto, Eeva 1921- *DcScanL, EncCoWW*
Joenson, Gunilla Gundel Tora 1943- *WhoWor 91*
Joeres, Manfred K 1937- *BiDrAPA 89*
Joergensen, Per Bay 1945- *WhoWor 91*
Joerger, Erica Ann 1965- *WhoAmW 91*
Joerling, Dale Raymond 1949- *WhoEmL 91*
Joern, Lester Carroll, Jr. 1950- *WhoEmL 91*
Joest, Douglas P. 1953- *St&PR 91*
Jofen, Jean *WhoAm 90*
Joffe, Bertha *WhoAmA 91*
Joffe, Bruce Howard 1949- *WhoEmL 91*
Joffe, Charles 1929- *WhoAm 90*
Joffe, Irwin *BioIn 16*
Joffe, Jeffrey Ephraim 1939- *WhoSSW 91*
Joffe, Joy Ruth *BiDrAPA 89*
Joffe, Robert David 1943- *WhoAm 90*
Joffe, Roland *BioIn 16*
Joffe, Russell Trevor 1954- *BiDrAPA 89*
Joffe, Wendy A. 1947- *WhoAmW 91*
Joffre, Joseph 1852-1931 *WorAlBi*
Joffre, Joseph Jacques Cesaire 1852-1931 *BiDFrPL*
Joffre, Stephen Paul 1913- *WhoAm 90*
Joffrey, Robert *BioIn 16*
Joffrey, Robert 1930-1988 *AnObit 1988, WorAlBi*
Jofre, Manuel Alcides 1947- *WhoWor 91*
Jogand-Pages, Gabriel 1854-1906? *EncO&P 3*
Jogezai, Naseema Schaikh 1948- *WhoWor 91*
Joglekar, Prafulla Narayan 1947- *WhoE 91*
Jogues, Isaac 1607-1646 *WhNaAH*
Joh, Harold Euiyol *BiDrAPA 89*
Johan, Morton *BiDrAPA 89*
Johanknecht, Lori Jo 1961- *WhoAmW 91*
Johann Hjalmarsson *DcScanL*
Johann Sigurjonsson *DcScanL*
Johanna *WomWR*
Johanna *WomWR*
Johanne, Inger *EncCoWW*
Johannes Bjarni Jonasson *DcScanL*
Johannes ur Kotlum 1899-1972 *DcScanL*
Johannes, Geoffry Sunny 1950- *WhoWor 91*
Johannes, George Robert 1938- *St&PR 91*
Johannes, John Roland 1943- *WhoAm 90*
Johannes, Virgil Ivancich 1930- *WhoAm 90*
Johannes, Wilfred Clemens 1924- *WhoAm 90*
Johannes-German, Kym *ODwPR 91*
Johannesen, Georg 1931- *DcScanL*
Johannesen, Grant 1921- *IntWWM 90, PenDiMP*
Johannesen, Thomas M. 1946- *St&PR 91*
Johanneson, Gerald B. 1940- *WhoAm 90*
Johanneson, Gerald Benedict 1940- *St&PR 91*
Johannessen, Dag O. 1932- *St&PR 91*
Johannessen, Donald Jon *BiDrAPA 89*
Johannessen, Matthias 1930- *DcScanL*
Johannet, Christopher M *BiDrAPA 89*
Johannet, Pierre *BiDrAPA 89*
Johanningmeier, Robert Alan 1946- *WhoAmA 91*
Johannisson, Elizabeth Ingrid 1934- *WhoWor 91*
Johanns, Charles F. *ODwPR 91*
Johannsen, Chris Jakob 1937- *WhoAm 90*
Johannsen, Gunnar 1940- *WhoWor 91*
Johannsen, Peter George 1942- *WhoAm 90*
Johannsen, Robert Walter 1925- *WhoAm 90*
Johannson, Joyce *ODwPR 91*
Johannsson, Victoria Ann 1964- *WhoAmW 91*
Johanos, Donald 1928- *IntWWM 90, WhoAm 90*
Johansen, Craig V. 1944- *St&PR 91*
Johansen, David *BioIn 16*
Johansen, David 1954?- *EncPR&S 89*
Johansen, Eivind Herbert 1927- *WhoAm 90, WhoWor 91*
Johansen, Eric Neil 1950- *WhoEmL 91*
Johansen, John C 1876-1964 *WhoAmA 91N*
Johansen, John MacLane 1916- *WhoAm 90*
Johansen, John W. 1943- *St&PR 91*
Johansen, John Wesley 1943- *WhoAm 90*
Johansen, Kathleen Marie 1961- *WhoAmW 91*
Johansen, Keith Hadley 1934- *BiDrAPA 89*
Johansen, Margaret 1896- *AuBYP 90*
Johansen, Norman Lee 1955- *IntWWM 90*
Johansen, Paul E. 1910- *St&PR 91*

Johansen, Peter Burnett 1947- BiDrAPA 89
Johansen, Phillip Mallory 1937- WhoSSW 91
Johansen, Richard W. 1951- St&PR 91
Johansen, Robert 1923- WhoAmA 91
Johansen, Robert W 1945- BiDrAPA 89
Johansen, Ulla Christine 1927- WhoWor 91
Johansky, Peter Paul 1950- WhoEmL 91
Johanson, Donald C. BioIn 16
Johanson, Donald Carl 1943- WhoAm 90
Johanson, Elise 1958- ODwPR 91
Johanson, George E 1928- WhoAmA 91
Johanson, Norman Eric 1940- St&PR 91
Johanson, Patricia 1940- BiDWomA, WhoAmA 91
Johanson, Patricia Maureen 1940- WhoAm 90
Johanson, W. F. Walker 1945- WhoEmL 91, WhoSSW 91
Johanson, Waldemar G., Jr. 1937- WhoAm 90
Johansson, Barbro Birgitta 1933- WhoWor 91
Johansson, Bjorn 1947- WhoWor 91
Johansson, Gunnar Alfred Helge 1918- IntWWM 90
Johansson, Ingemar BioIn 16
Johansson, Jerker Mats 1956- WhoE 91
Johansson, Lars DcScanL
Johansson, Nils A. 1948- St&PR 91
Johansson, Per Ole 1934- WhoWor 91
Johansson, Sven Vage Kenneth 1945- WhoWor 91
Johar, Surendar Nath 1944- WhoE 91
John WhNaAH
John 1167-1216 WorAlBi
John of Nottingham EncO&P 3
John of the Cross, Saint 1542-1591 WorAlBi
John Paul II, His Holiness Pope 1920- WhoWor 91
John Paul I, Pope 1912-1978 BioIn 16
John Paul II, Pope 1920- BioIn 16
John Paul I 1912-1978 WorAlBi
John Paul II 1920- WorAlBi
John XXII, Pope 1244?-1334 EncO&P 3
John XXIII, Pope 1881-1963 BioIn 16
John III Sobieski 1629-1696 WorAlBi
John, Prince 1944- WhoWor 91
John, Augustus 1878-1961 IntDcAA 90
John, Betty 1907- WhoWrEP 89
John, Brynmor 1934-1988 BioIn 16
John, Bubba Free EncO&P 3
John, Caspar 1903-1984 DcNaB 1981
John, Cheryl Annette 1957- St&PR 91
John, Da Free 1939- EncO&P 3
John, David W. BiDrAPA 89
John, Dewitt, Jr. 1942- WhoE 91
John, Donas WhoWrEP 89
John, Doreen Ann 1949- WhoAmW 91
John, Elizabeth Mani BiDrAPA 89
John, Elton BioIn 16
John, Elton 1947- EncPR&S 89, OxCPMus, WorAlBi
John, Elton Hercules 1947- WhoAm 90, WhoWor 91
John, Errol DrBlPA 90
John, Errol 1924-1988 AnObit 1988
John, Frederick Elias 1946- St&PR 91
John, Friederike Christiane Henriette EncCoWW
John, Grace Spaulding 1890-1972 BioIn 16, WhoAmA 91N
John, Gwen 1876-1939 BiDWomA
John, Hugo Herman 1929- WhoAm 90
John, James Edward Albert 1933- WhoAm 90
John, Jerome Francis 1940- St&PR 91
John, Joby 1957- WhoEmL 91
John, Joseph 1938- St&PR 91, WhoAm 90
John, Joyce BioIn 16
John, Leonard Keith 1949- WhoWor 91
John, Nicholas David BiDrAPA 89
John, Patricia Spaulding 1916- IntWWM 90
John, Patrick Roland 1937- BioIn 16
John, Puthenpurayil BiDrAPA 89
John, Ralph Candler 1919- WhoAm 90
John, Richard Rodda 1929- WhoAm 90
John, Robert WhoE 91
John, Robert 1921- BiDrAPA 89
John, Robert McClintock 1947- WhoEmL 91
John, Ronald David 1948- WhoEmL 91
John, Russell T. 1946- St&PR 91
John, Tommy BioIn 16
John, Tommy 1943- Ballpl 90 [port], WorAlBi
John, Yvonne Maree 1944- WhoAmW 91
John-Roger BioIn 16
Johncock, Gordon Walter 1936- WhoAm 90
Johnee WhoWrEP 89
Johnes, Geraint 1958- WhoWor 91
Johnes, Lawrence A. 1944- WhoAm 90
Johng, Hae Wohn 1925- BiDrAPA 89
Johngren, Peter Morgan BiDrAPA 89
Johnigan, Sandra Kay 1947- WhoAmW 91
Johnloz, Gregory Lee 1948- St&PR 91
Johnopolos, Stephen Gary 1950- WhoE 91
Johns, Albert Cameron 1914- WhoAm 90
Johns, Avery AuBYP 90
Johns, Avis Shetter 1935- WhoAmW 91
Johns, B. F. 1830- AmLegL
Johns, Beverley Anne Holden 1946- WhoAmW 91
Johns, Carol Johnson 1923- WhoAmW 91
Johns, Celeste Athena 1955- BiDrAPA 89
Johns, Charley Eugene 1905-1990 BioIn 16
Johns, Charley Jerome 1928- St&PR 91
Johns, Christopher George 1951- WhoAm 90
Johns, Christopher K 1952- WhoAmA 91
Johns, Claude Jackson, Jr. 1930- WhoAm 90
Johns, David Lee 1951- WhoSSW 91
Johns, Dianna Rose 1951- WhoAmW 91
Johns, Don Herbert 1925- WhoAm 90
Johns, Donald Charles 1926- IntWWM 90
Johns, Elizabeth Jane Hobbs 1941- WhoAmW 91, WhoSSW 91
Johns, Emerson Thomas 1947- WhoEmL 91
Johns, Emile 1798?-1860 PenDiMP
Johns, Gary BioIn 16
Johns, George John 1928- BiDrAPA 89
Johns, Glynis 1923- WorAlBi
Johns, Horace Edward 1945- WhoEmL 91
Johns, James Edward 1938- St&PR 91
Johns, James Haight 1926- St&PR 91
Johns, Janetta ConAu 33NR
Johns, Jasper BioIn 16
Johns, Jasper 1930- IntDcAA 90, WhoAmA 91, WhoWor 91, WorAlBi
Johns, Jerry Marvin 1946- St&PR 91
Johns, John Edward, Jr. 1946- WhoAm 90
Johns, John Edwin 1921- WhoAm 90
Johns, John Richards 1952- WhoE 91
Johns, Joni BioIn 16
Johns, Lee Rhea 1956- WhoAmW 91
Johns, Margaret K. 1952- St&PR 91
Johns, Margy Gover 1931- WhoAmW 91
Johns, Marston ConAu 32NR
Johns, Perry 1934- St&PR 91
Johns, R.W. 1948- St&PR 91
Johns, Richard James 1925- WhoAm 90
Johns, Robert Powell, Jr. 1937- WhoAm 90
Johns, Robert S. 1946- St&PR 91
Johns, Roy 1929- WhoWrEP 89
Johns, Stephanie Bernardo 1947- ConAu 30NR
Johns, Ted 1942- OxCCanT
Johns, Traci Lorraine 1964- WhoAmW 91, WhoE 91
Johns, Tracy Camila BioIn 16
Johns, Varner Jay, Jr. 1921- WhoAm 90
Johns, Veronica Parker 1907- TwCCr&M 91
Johns, W. E. 1893-1968 BioIn 16
Johns, W E 1893-1968 ConAu 30NR
Johns, Warren LeRoi 1929- WhoE 91
Johns, Wayne Groh 1951- WhoE 91
Johns, William Davis, Jr. 1925- WhoAm 90
Johns, William Earl 1893-1968 BioIn 16
Johns, William Howard 1941- BiDrAPA 89, WhoWor 91
Johns, William Patrick 1941- WhoAm 90
Johnsen, Clifford Andrew 1941- St&PR 91
Johnsen, Dan 1951- IntWWM 90
Johnsen, Debra Lee 1257- WhoAmW 91
Johnsen, Erik Frithjof 1925- WhoAm 90
Johnsen, Eugene Carlyle 1932- WhoAm 90
Johnsen, Gordon Norman 1926- WhoAm 90
Johnsen, Gretchen Lynne 1952- WhoWrEP 89
Johnsen, Howard H. St&PR 91
Johnsen, John Herbert 1923- WhoAm 90
Johnsen, John R. BioIn 16
Johnsen, Kjell BioIn 16
Johnsen, Kjell 1945- IntWWM 90
Johnsen, Leigh Dana 1952- WhoEmL 91
Johnsen, May Anne WhoAmA 91
Johnsen, Niels Winchester 1922- WhoAm 90
Johnsen, Richard A. 1946- St&PR 91
Johnsen, Richard Alan 1946- WhoAm 90
Johnsen, Ronald A. 1937- St&PR 91
Johnsen, Russell Harold 1922- WhoAm 90
Johnsen, Walter Craig 1950- WhoE 91
Johnsen, William A. 1955- St&PR 91
Johnsen, William Arthur 1955- WhoAm 90
Johnsey, Walter F. 1924- St&PR 91
Johnson WhNaAH
Johnson, A Findlay 1947- ConAu 132
Johnson, A. Paul 1955- WhoWrEP 89
Johnson, A. Ross 1939- WhoWor 91
Johnson, Adam 1888-1972 Ballpl 90
Johnson, Addie Collins WhoAmW 91, WhoE 91
Johnson, Adelaide 1859-1955 BiDWomA
Johnson, Adele Cunningham 1934- WhoE 91
Johnson, Aimee Shereen BiDrAPA 89
Johnson, Aimee Von Eichles 1966- WhoE 91
Johnson, Alan Arthur 1930- WhoAm 90, WhoWor 91
Johnson, Alan Clair 1946- WhoEmL 91
Johnson, Alan G 1931- BiDrAPA 89
Johnson, Alan G. 1934- St&PR 91
Johnson, Alan R. 1952- ODwPR 91
Johnson, Alan Ray 1952- WhoSSW 91
Johnson, Alan W. 1925- St&PR 91
Johnson, Alan Woodworth 1917-1982 DcNaB 1981
Johnson, Albert Madden 1943- St&PR 91
Johnson, Albert Wesley BioIn 16
Johnson, Albert Wesley 1923- WhoAm 90
Johnson, Albert Willard 1926- WhoAm 90
Johnson, Alex 1942- Ballpl 90
Johnson, Alexander Bryan 1786-1867 EncABHB 6 [port]
Johnson, Alice 186-?-1940 EncO&P 3
Johnson, Alice 1860-1940 EncPaPR 91
Johnson, Alice Moore 1952- WhoE 91
Johnson, Alison ConAu 132
Johnson, Allan Edward 1941- St&PR 91
Johnson, Allan R. 1947- St&PR 91
Johnson, Allan Ray 1947- WhoAm 90
Johnson, Allen Dress 1941- WhoAm 90
Johnson, Allen Halbert 1922- WhoAm 90
Johnson, Allen Huggins 1937- WhoAm 90
Johnson, Allen Leroy 1935- WhoAm 90
Johnson, Alonza Casson BiDrAPA 89
Johnson, Alton Cornelius 1924- WhoAm 90
Johnson, Alva 1858- BioIn 16
Johnson, Alvin Donnel 1940- WhoE 91
Johnson, Alvin Harold 1914- IntWWM 90, WhoAm 90
Johnson, Alvin Roscoe 1942- WhoAm 90
Johnson, Alyn William 1933- WhoAm 90
Johnson, Amryl FemiCLE
Johnson, Amy 1903-1941 BioIn 16
Johnson, Amy L. 1954- BiDrAPA 89
Johnson, Amy Leigh 1955- WhoAmW 91
Johnson, Andean 1929- WhoAmA 91
Johnson, Andre Tennell 1961- WhoSSW 91
Johnson, Andrea BioIn 16
Johnson, Andrew 1808-1875 BiDrUSE 89, BioIn 16, WorAlBi
Johnson, Andrew Emerson, III 1931- WhoAm 90
Johnson, Andrew Myron 1935- WhoSSW 91
Johnson, Anita 1926- WhoAm 90
Johnson, Anita Locy 1955- WhoAmW 91
Johnson, Ann BiDEWW
Johnson, Ann Lutes 1936- BiDrAPA 89
Johnson, Annabel 1921- AuBYP 90
Johnson, Anne Bradstreet 1927- WhoAmW 91
Johnson, Anne MarcoVecchio 1931- WhoAm 90, WhoAmW 91
Johnson, Anne-Marie DrBlPA 90
Johnson, Anthony Keith 1943- WhoWor 91
Johnson, Anthony Rolfe BioIn 16, PenDiMP
Johnson, Antoinette Spanos 1953- WhoAmA 91
Johnson, Arlene Lytle 1937- WhoAm 90
Johnson, Arnold DrBlPA 90
Johnson, Arnold BioIn 16
Johnson, Arnold Cale 1925- WhoAm 90
Johnson, Arnold Ivan 1919- WhoAm 90
Johnson, Arondle L. 1933- St&PR 91
Johnson, Arthur Edward 1922- St&PR 91
Johnson, Arthur Gilbert 1926- WhoAm 90
Johnson, Arthur Joseph 1953- WhoSSW 91
Johnson, Arthur Menzies 1921- WhoAm 90
Johnson, Arthur William, Jr. 1949- WhoAm 90
Johnson, Arvid Conrad, III 1964- WhoE 91
Johnson, Ashmore Clark, Jr. 1930- WhoAm 90, WhoSSW 91
Johnson, Avery Fischer 1906-1990 WhoAmA 91N
Johnson, Avis E. 1934- St&PR 91
Johnson, B.A. 1944- St&PR 91
Johnson, B. Richard 1945- ODwPR 91
Johnson, Badri Nahvi 1934- WhoAmW 91
Johnson, Ban 1864-1931 Ballpl 90 [port]
Johnson, Barbara BioIn 16
Johnson, Barbara Ann BiDrAPA 89
Johnson, Barbara Ann 1948- WhoWrEP 89
Johnson, Barbara Anne 1939- WhoSSW 91
Johnson, Barbara Converse 1955- WhoAmW 91
Johnson, Barbara J. ODwPR 91
Johnson, Barbara Jane 1946- WhoAmW 91
Johnson, Barbara Jean 1952- WhoAmW 91
Johnson, Barbara Sue 1952- WhoAmW 91
Johnson, Barry Lee 1938- WhoAm 90
Johnson, Bart 1950- Ballpl 90
Johnson, Basia BioIn 16
Johnson, Beatrice A. BiDrAPA 89
Johnson, Beatrice Brookshire 1957- WhoAmW 91
Johnson, Belton Kleberg 1929- WhoAm 90
Johnson, Ben BioIn 16
Johnson, Ben 1858-1950 AmLegL
Johnson, Ben 1902-1967 WhoAmA 91N
Johnson, Ben 1919- WorAlBi
Johnson, Ben Eugene 1928- St&PR 91
Johnson, Ben Sigel 1929- IntWWM 90
Johnson, Benjamin 1918- WhoAm 90
Johnson, Benjamin Edgar 1921- WhoAm 90
Johnson, Benjamin Ford 1959- WhoSSW 91
Johnson, Benjamin Franklin, III 1943- WhoAm 90
Johnson, Benjamin Leibold 1950- WhoEmL 91, WhoSSW 91
Johnson, Bernard G. 1915- St&PR 91
Johnson, Beth Exum 1952- WhoAmW 91, WhoEmL 91, WhoSSW 91, WhoWor 91
Johnson, Betsey BioIn 16
Johnson, Betsey Lee 1942- WhoAm 90, WhoAmW 91
Johnson, Betty Anne 1924- WhoAmW 91
Johnson, Betty Jean 1958- WhoAmW 91
Johnson, Betty Zschiegner 1933- WhoAmW 91
Johnson, Beverley Peck IntWWM 90
Johnson, Beverly BioIn 16
Johnson, Beverly 1951- DrBlPA 90
Johnson, Beverly Kay 1939- WhoAmW 91
Johnson, Beverly Phillips 1963- WhoAmW 91
Johnson, Bill BioIn 16
Johnson, Billy 1918- Ballpl 90
Johnson, Bix McPhail 1946- St&PR 91
Johnson, Bob 1906- Ballpl 90 [port]
Johnson, Bob 1931- WhoAm 90
Johnson, Bob 1936- Ballpl 90
Johnson, Bob 1943- Ballpl 90
Johnson, Bob 1950- ConAu 130
Johnson, Boine T., Jr. 1931- St&PR 91
Johnson, Boine Theodore 1931- WhoAm 90
Johnson, Boreham Boyd 1952- WhoSSW 91
Johnson, Brad Arnold 1954- WhoSSW 91
Johnson, Brad Hart 1951- WhoWor 91
Johnson, Bradley C. 1942- WhoAm 90
Johnson, Brandy BioIn 16
Johnson, Brenda Faye 1953- WhoEmL 91, WhoWor 91
Johnson, Brenda Jean 1965- WhoAmW 91
Johnson, Brenda Lee 1950- WhoAmW 91
Johnson, Brenda Lee 1960- WhoAmW 91
Johnson, Brent 1941- WhoAmA 91
Johnson, Brian BiDrAPA 89
Johnson, Brian 1952- WhoE 91
Johnson, Bruce 1932- WhoAm 90
Johnson, Bruce 1944- WhoAmA 91
Johnson, Bruce 1949-1976 WhoAmA 91N
Johnson, Bruce Allan 1958- WhoEmL 91
Johnson, Bruce C. BioIn 16
Johnson, Bruce Carl BiDrAPA 89
Johnson, Bruce Marvin 1933- WhoAm 90
Johnson, Bryce G. 1953- St&PR 91
Johnson, Buddy 1915-1977 OxCPMus
Johnson, Buffie 1912- WhoAmA 91
Johnson, Bunk 1879-1949 BioIn 16, WorAlBi
Johnson, Bunk 1889-1949 OxCPMus
Johnson, Burdetta Faye AuBYP 90
Johnson, Burdette A. 1905- St&PR 91
Johnson, Burt Powers BiDrAPA 89
Johnson, Byron 1915- St&PR 91
Johnson, Byron Eugene 1936- WhoWor 91
Johnson, C. Bosworth ODwPR 91
Johnson, C. H. 1925- WhoAm 90
Johnson, C. Paul BioIn 16
Johnson, C. Richard 1941- WhoAm 90
Johnson, C. Scott 1944- WhoAm 90
Johnson, C. Terry 1937- WhoAm 90
Johnson, Calvert 1949- IntWWM 90
Johnson, Calvert Berry 1949- WhoSSW 91
Johnson, Camille BioIn 16
Johnson, Carl Anderson 1943- WhoAm 90
Johnson, Carl J. 1929-1988 BioIn 16
Johnson, Carl N. 1961- St&PR 91
Johnson, Carl P. ODwPR 91
Johnson, Carla Rae 1947- WhoAmA 91
Johnson, Carol Ann 1958- WhoEmL 91
Johnson, Carole Elizabeth 1939- WhoE 91
Johnson, Carolyn Anne 1948- WhoAmW 91
Johnson, Carolyn Elizabeth 1921- WhoAmW 91
Johnson, Carroll Frye 1913- WhoAm 90
Johnson, Carroll O. 1929- St&PR 91
Johnson, Carter Samuel 1961- WhoEmL 91
Johnson, Catherine Augusta Lewis 1937- WhoAmW 91

Johnson, Catherine Common 1914- *WhoAmW 91*
Johnson, Catherine Grymes 1952- *WhoAmW 91*
Johnson, Cathleen *WhoAmW 91*
Johnson, Cathy 1951- *ODwPR 91*
Johnson, Cato 1947- *WhoSSW 91*
Johnson, Cave 1793-1866 *BiDrUSE 89*
Johnson, Cecil V *BiDrAPA 89*
Johnson, Cecile Ryden *WhoAmA 91, WhoWor 91*
Johnson, Cecilia Ann 1940- *WhoAmW 91*
Johnson, Celia *BioIn 16*
Johnson, Celia 1908-1982 *DcNaB 1981*
Johnson, Chappie 1875- *Ballpl 90*
Johnson, Charles 1679-1748 *BioIn 16*
Johnson, Charles Austin 1930- *WhoAm 90*
Johnson, Charles Bartlett 1933- *WhoAm 90*
Johnson, Charles Blake 1952- *WhoWrEP 89*
Johnson, Charles Christopher, Jr. 1921- *WhoAm 90*
Johnson, Charles Floyd *WhoWor 91*
Johnson, Charles Foreman 1929- *WhoWor 91*
Johnson, Charles Frederick *AuBYP 90*
Johnson, Charles George 1954- *WhoEmL 91*
Johnson, Charles Henry, Jr. 1946- *WhoEmL 91*
Johnson, Charles John, Jr. 1932- *WhoAm 90*
Johnson, Charles Knox 1913- *St&PR 91*
Johnson, Charles L 1876-1950 *OxCPMus*
Johnson, Charles Lenard 1942- *WhoWor 91*
Johnson, Charles Leslie 1876-1950 *BioIn 16*
Johnson, Charles Lewis *BiDrAPA 89*
Johnson, Charles M. 1941- *WhoAm 90*
Johnson, Charles Owen 1926- *WhoSSW 91*
Johnson, Charles P. 1927- *St&PR 91*
Johnson, Charles Raymond 1925- *WhoAm 90*
Johnson, Charles Richard 1912- *WhoWor 91*
Johnson, Charles Richard 1948- *BioIn 16*
Johnson, Charles Ross *BiDrAPA 89*
Johnson, Charles Sidney, Jr. 1936- *WhoAm 90*
Johnson, Charles Simons 1940- *St&PR 91, WhoWor 91*
Johnson, Charles W, Jr 1938- *WhoAmA 91*
Johnson, Charles Wayne 1921- *WhoWor 91*
Johnson, Charlie 1891-1959 *OxCPMus*
Johnson, Charlotte Verne 1944- *WhoAmW 91*
Johnson, Chas. Floyd *ConTFT 8*
Johnson, Chas. W. 1938- *St&PR 91*
Johnson, Chauncey Paul 1931- *St&PR 91, WhoAm 90*
Johnson, Cheri Jean 1959- *WhoAmW 91*
Johnson, Cheryl Elizabeth 1952- *WhoEmL 91, WhoSSW 91*
Johnson, Cheryl June 1938- *WhoWrEP 89*
Johnson, Chic 1891-1962 *BioIn 16*
Johnson, Chief 1886-1922 *Ballpl 90*
Johnson, Chloe Rene 1939- *WhoAmW 91*
Johnson, Christina Michele 1960- *WhoE 91*
Johnson, Christine Ann 1951- *WhoEmL 91*
Johnson, Christine D. 1951- *ODwPR 91*
Johnson, Christine M. 1948- *WhoAmW 91*
Johnson, Christine Marie 1952- *WhoAmW 91*
Johnson, Christopher Charles 1962- *IntWWM 90*
Johnson, Christopher Mason 1960- *WhoWor 91*
Johnson, Christopher Ralph 1947- *WhoWrEP 89*
Johnson, Chrysta Lea 1949- *WhoAmW 91*
Johnson, Ciri Diane 1956- *WhoE 91*
Johnson, Claire M. 1912- *St&PR 91*
Johnson, Clarence L. 1910-1990 *NewYTBS 90 [port]*
Johnson, Clarence M *BiDrAPA 89*
Johnson, Clark Allen 1931- *St&PR 91*
Johnson, Clark Eugene, Jr. 1930- *WhoE 91*
Johnson, Clark Hughes 1935- *WhoAm 90*
Johnson, Clarke Courtney 1936- *WhoAm 90*
Johnson, Claudia 1912- *BioAmW*
Johnson, Claudia Alta 1912- *WorAlBi*
Johnson, Claudia Alta Taylor 1912- *BioIn 16*
Johnson, Clayton Errold 1921- *WhoWor 91*
Johnson, Cliff 1947- *Ballpl 90*
Johnson, Clifford Andrew, III 1945- *WhoE 91*
Johnson, Clifford J. *BioIn 16*
Johnson, Clifford R. 1923- *WhoAm 90*
Johnson, Clifton Herman 1921- *WhoSSW 91, WhoWor 91*
Johnson, Clinton A 1916- *BiDrAPA 89*
Johnson, Clyde 1935- *St&PR 91*
Johnson, Clyde Benton 1946- *WhoSSW 91*
Johnson, Colin 1939- *ConAu 130*
Johnson, Connie 1922- *Ballpl 90*
Johnson, Conor Deane 1943- *WhoAm 90*
Johnson, Constance Ann Trillich 1949- *WhoAmW 91, WhoSSW 91, WhoWor 91*
Johnson, Content *WhoAmA 91N*
Johnson, Cora Lee *BioIn 16*
Johnson, Corinne B. *AuBYP 90*
Johnson, Corwin Waggoner 1917- *WhoAm 90*
Johnson, Craig 1947- *St&PR 91*
Johnson, Craig G. 1952- *BiDrAPA 89*
Johnson, Craig Merril 1947- *WhoEmL 91*
Johnson, Craig Norman 1942- *WhoAm 90*
Johnson, Craig Robert 1951- *WhoEmL 91*
Johnson, Crawford Toy, III 1925- *WhoAm 90*
Johnson, Crocket 1906-1976 *WhoAmA 91N*
Johnson, Crockett *AuBYP 90*
Johnson, Crockett 1906-1975 *EncACom*
Johnson, Crystal Duane 1954- *WhoAmW 91*
Johnson, Curtis 1946- *St&PR 91*
Johnson, Curtis Lee 1928- *WhoAm 90, WhoWrEP 89*
Johnson, Curtiss Sherman 1899- *WhoE 91*
Johnson, Cyrus Edwin 1929- *St&PR 91, WhoAm 90*
Johnson, Dale A. 1937- *St&PR 91, WhoAm 90*
Johnson, Dale Eliot 1946- *WhoEmL 91*
Johnson, Dale L 1934- *ConAu 130*
Johnson, Dana Lisa 1958- *WhoAmW 91*
Johnson, Daniel 1944- *WhoAm 90*
Johnson, Daniel McDonald 1953- *WhoSSW 91*
Johnson, Daniel Patrick 1956- *WhoEmL 91*
Johnson, Daniel Robert 1938- *WhoE 91*
Johnson, Dara *BiDrAPA 89*
Johnson, Darrell 1928- *Ballpl 90*
Johnson, Dave 1948- *Ballpl 90*
Johnson, Davey 1943- *Ballpl 90 [port], WorAlBi*
Johnson, David 1939- *BiDrAPA 89*
Johnson, David Allen 1943- *WhoE 91*
Johnson, David Allen 1949- *WhoWor 91*
Johnson, David Allen 1954- *WhoEmL 91, WhoWor 91*
Johnson, David Blackwell 1954- *WhoE 91*
Johnson, David Carl 1942- *St&PR 91*
Johnson, David Charles 1942- *IntWWM 90*
Johnson, David Earl 1937- *St&PR 91, WhoAm 90*
Johnson, David Elliot 1933- *WhoAm 90, WhoE 91*
Johnson, David Eric Francis 1946- *IntWWM 90*
Johnson, David George 1948- *WhoEmL 91*
Johnson, David Harrover 1946- *WhoEmL 91*
Johnson, David Jordan 1946- *St&PR 91*
Johnson, David K. 1934- *St&PR 91*
Johnson, David L. 1937- *St&PR 91*
Johnson, David Lee *BiDrAPA 89*
Johnson, David Lewis 1951- *BiDrAPA 89*
Johnson, David Lincoln 1929- *WhoAm 90*
Johnson, David Lynn 1934- *WhoAm 90*
Johnson, David M *BiDrAPA 89*
Johnson, David Mathis 1947- *WhoAm 90*
Johnson, David N. 1922- *IntWWM 90*
Johnson, David Owen 1918- *St&PR 91*
Johnson, David Paul 1963- *WhoSSW 91*
Johnson, David Peter 1945- *St&PR 91*
Johnson, David R. 1953- *St&PR 91*
Johnson, David Ralph 1933- *WhoAm 90*
Johnson, David Randall *BiDrAPA 89*
Johnson, David Raymond 1946- *WhoEmL 91*
Johnson, David Raymond 1952- *WhoEmL 91*
Johnson, David Simonds 1924- *WhoAm 90*
Johnson, David W. 1959- *St&PR 91*
Johnson, David Wesley 1955- *WhoEmL 91*
Johnson, David Willis 1932- *WhoAm 90*
Johnson, David Wolcott 1940- *WhoAm 90, WhoWor 91*
Johnson, Dean Conway 1934- *WhoAm 90*
Johnson, Dean Evan 1931- *St&PR 91*
Johnson, Dean T. *St&PR 91*
Johnson, Deane Frank 1918- *St&PR 91, WhoAm 90, WhoE 91*
Johnson, Deanna K. 1942- *WhoWor 91*
Johnson, Deborah Jean 1953- *WhoAmW 91*
Johnson, Deborah Sue 1948- *WhoAmW 91, WhoEmL 91*
Johnson, D'Elaine A Herard *WhoAmA 91*
Johnson, d'Elaine Ann Herard 1932- *WhoAmW 91*
Johnson, Delbert Calvin 1952- *WhoEmL 91*
Johnson, Delores Scott 1931- *WhoSSW 91*
Johnson, Delos R., Jr. 1924- *St&PR 91*
Johnson, Denis 1949- *WorAu 1980 [port]*
Johnson, Dennis 1954- *WorAlBi*
Johnson, Dennis Burl 1949- *WhoSSW 91*
Johnson, Dennis D. 1939- *St&PR 91*
Johnson, Dennis Duane 1938- *WhoAm 90*
Johnson, Dennis Lee 1948- *WhoEmL 91*
Johnson, Dennis Lester 1938- *WhoAm 90*
Johnson, Dennis Owen 1946- *WhoSSW 91*
Johnson, Dennis Ray 1946- *WhoSSW 91*
Johnson, Dennis W. 1945- *St&PR 91*
Johnson, Deron 1938- *Ballpl 90*
Johnson, Dewey Edward 1935- *WhoSSW 91*
Johnson, Diana Carol 1949- *WhoSSW 91*
Johnson, Diana Lepow 1940- *WhoE 91*
Johnson, Diana Lynn 1954- *WhoAmW 91*
Johnson, Diane 1934- *FemiCLE, MajTwCW, WhoWrEP 89*
Johnson, Diane Chalmers 1943- *WhoAmA 91*
Johnson, Diane Kay 1937- *WhoWor 91*
Johnson, Diane Lain 1934- *WhoAm 90*
Johnson, Diane Weinberg 1951- *WhoAmW 91*
Johnson, Dianne Ball 1959- *WhoAmW 91*
Johnson, Dink 1892-1954 *OxCPMus*
Johnson, Dolores DeBower 1932- *WhoSSW 91*
Johnson, Don *BioIn 16*
Johnson, Don 1911- *Ballpl 90*
Johnson, Don 1926- *Ballpl 90*
Johnson, Don 1949- *WorAlBi*
Johnson, Don E *BiDrAPA 89*
Johnson, Don Robert 1942- *WhoE 91*
Johnson, Donal Dabell 1922- *WhoAm 90*
Johnson, Donald Allen 1926- *St&PR 91*
Johnson, Donald Arthur 1952- *WhoE 91*
Johnson, Donald E. *St&PR 91*
Johnson, Donald E. 1928- *St&PR 91*
Johnson, Donald E., Jr. *WhoAm 90*
Johnson, Donald E. L. 1941- *WhoAm 90*
Johnson, Donald Glen 1931- *WhoE 91*
Johnson, Donald Harry 1944- *WhoSSW 91*
Johnson, Donald Howard 1930- *St&PR 91*
Johnson, Donald Lee 1935- *WhoAm 90*
Johnson, Donald Lee 1947- *St&PR 91*
Johnson, Donald Ray 1942- *WhoAmA 91*
Johnson, Donald Ray 1955- *WhoSSW 91*
Johnson, Donna M. 1939- *WhoWrEP 89*
Johnson, Donnamae Elaine 1951- *WhoAmW 91*
Johnson, Donny Ray 1951- *WhoEmL 91*
Johnson, Dora Myrtle Knudtson 1900- *WhoAmW 91*
Johnson, Doris 1922- *AuBYP 90*
Johnson, Doris Miller 1909- *WhoAmA 91*
Johnson, Dorothy *WhoAmW 91*
Johnson, Dorothy Phyllis 1925- *WhoAmW 91*
Johnson, Dorothy Strathman Gullen 1931- *WhoWrEP 89*
Johnson, Dorothy Vena 1898-1970 *HarlReB*
Johnson, Dotts 1913- *DrBlPA 90*
Johnson, Doug *BioIn 16*
Johnson, Doug 1919- *WhoAm 90*
Johnson, Douglas *EncPaPR 91*
Johnson, Douglas 1909?-1988 *EncO&P 3*
Johnson, Douglas F. 1956- *WhoEmL 91*
Johnson, Douglas James 1937- *WhoWor 91*
Johnson, Douglas N 1935- *BiDrAPA 89*
Johnson, Douglas Sherman 1925- *BiDrAPA 89*
Johnson, Douglas W. 1934- *WhoWrEP 89*
Johnson, Douglas Walter 1946- *WhoAmA 91*
Johnson, Douglass F. 1913- *St&PR 91*
Johnson, Duane Fadinand 1940- *WhoAm 90*
Johnson, Duane Gordon 1943- *St&PR 91*
Johnson, Duane Michael 1949- *WhoEmL 91*
Johnson, Dudley *BioIn 16*
Johnson, E. Eric 1927- *St&PR 91, WhoWor 91*
Johnson, E. Ned *AuBYP 90*
Johnson, E Richard 1937- *TwCCr&M 91*
Johnson, Earl 1919- *Ballpl 90*
Johnson, Earl 1958- *St&PR 91*
Johnson, Earl, Jr. 1933- *WhoAm 90, WhoWrEP 89*
Johnson, Earl D. *NewYTBS 90*
Johnson, Earl D. 1905-1990 *BioIn 16*
Johnson, Earl LeRoy 1932- *St&PR 91*
Johnson, Earle Bertrand 1914- *WhoAm 90*
Johnson, Earvin 1959- *BioIn 16, WhoAm 90*
Johnson, Eastman 1824-1906 *BioIn 16, WhNaAH*
Johnson, Ector R., III 1948- *St&PR 91*
Johnson, Eddie Bernice 1935- *WhoAmW 91, WhoSSW 91*
Johnson, Edgar 1901- *DcLB 103 [port]*
Johnson, Edgar 1912-1960 *AuBYP 90*
Johnson, Edgar B. 1923- *St&PR 91*
Johnson, Edgar Ernest 1933- *St&PR 91*
Johnson, Edgar Frederick 1899- *WhoAm 90*
Johnson, Edna Hafner 1942- *WhoAmW 91*
Johnson, Edvard Arthur 1911- *WhoAmA 91*
Johnson, Edward *BiDrAPA 89*
Johnson, Edward 1598-1672 *EncCRAm*
Johnson, Edward 1878-1959 *PenDiMP*
Johnson, Edward A. 1917- *WhoAm 90*
Johnson, Edward C., III 1930- *St&PR 91*
Johnson, Edward Charles 1922- *WhoAm 90*
Johnson, Edward Crosby, III 1930- *WhoAm 90*
Johnson, Edward Elemuel 1926- *WhoAm 90*
Johnson, Edward Eric 1944- *St&PR 91*
Johnson, Edward Fuller 1921- *WhoE 91*
Johnson, Edward Nayland 1948- *WhoSSW 91*
Johnson, Edward O. 1919-1989 *BioIn 16*
Johnson, Edward Roy 1940- *WhoAm 90*
Johnson, Edwin Carver *BiDrAPA 89*
Johnson, Edwin F. 1934- *St&PR 91*
Johnson, Eileen Morgan 1957- *WhoEmL 91*
Johnson, Einar William 1955- *WhoEmL 91*
Johnson, Elaine McDowell 1942- *WhoAm 90*
Johnson, Eleanor Murdoch 1892-1987 *BioIn 16*
Johnson, Eliza McCardle 1810-1876 *BioIn 16*
Johnson, Elizabeth *BiDEWW, FemiCLE*
Johnson, Elizabeth 1911-1984 *AuBYP 90*
Johnson, Elizabeth 1961- *WhoEmL 91*
Johnson, Elizabeth Anne 1960- *ODwPR 91*
Johnson, Elizabeth Boyd 1948- *WhoSSW 91*
Johnson, Elizabeth Diane Long 1945- *WhoAmW 91, WhoEmL 91*
Johnson, Elizabeth Hill 1913- *WhoAmW 91*
Johnson, Elizabeth Jackson 1925- *WhoAmW 91*
Johnson, Elizabeth Jolene 1957- *WhoSSW 91*
Johnson, Elizabeth Katharine 1951- *WhoEmL 91*
Johnson, Elizabeth L. 1953- *St&PR 91*
Johnson, Elizabeth Rose 1952- *WhoE 91*
Johnson, Elizabeth V. 1923- *St&PR 91*
Johnson, Ellen *BiDrAPA 89*
Johnson, Ellen C. *ODwPR 91*
Johnson, Ellen Christine 1948- *WhoAmW 91, WhoEmL 91*
Johnson, Ellen Hulda 1910- *WhoAmA 91*
Johnson, Ellen Irene *BiDrAPA 89*
Johnson, Ellen Randel 1916- *WhoAmW 91, WhoSSW 91*
Johnson, Ellen Schultz 1918- *IntWWM 90*
Johnson, Elliott Amos 1907- *WhoAm 90*
Johnson, Elliott M. 1929- *St&PR 91*
Johnson, Ellis D 1920- *BiDrAPA 89*
Johnson, Ellis Lane 1938- *WhoAm 90*
Johnson, Ellsworth Levine 1918- *WhoWor 91*
Johnson, Elmer Marshall 1930- *WhoAm 90*
Johnson, Elmer W. 1932- *BioIn 16*
Johnson, Elmer William 1932- *WhoAm 90*
Johnson, Elsa Linnea *BiDrAPA 89*
Johnson, Emery Allen 1929- *WhoAm 90*
Johnson, Emily Pauline 1862-1913 *WhNaAH*
Johnson, Emma 1966- *IntWWM 90, PenDiMP*
Johnson, Enid 1892- *AuBYP 90*
Johnson, Eric *NewAgMG*
Johnson, Eric Austin 1964- *BiDrAPA 89*
Johnson, Eric Carl 1951- *WhoEmL 91*
Johnson, Eric Folke 1916- *WhoAm 90*
Johnson, Eric Lynn 1949- *St&PR 91*
Johnson, Eric Norman *St&PR 91*
Johnson, Eric W. 1918- *AuBYP 90*
Johnson, Erik G. *ODwPR 91*
Johnson, Erik R. 1945- *St&PR 91*
Johnson, Ernest 1924- *WhoAmA 91*
Johnson, Ernest A. 1920- *St&PR 91*
Johnson, Ernest Frederick 1918- *WhoAm 90*
Johnson, Ernestine Hedgecock 1938- *WhoSSW 91*
Johnson, Ernie 1888-1952 *Ballpl 90*
Johnson, Ernie 1924- *Ballpl 90*
Johnson, Ervin Albert 1931- *St&PR 91*
Johnson, Esther 1681-1728 *BioIn 16*
Johnson, Eugene Clare 1940- *WhoE 91*
Johnson, Eugene Joseph 1937- *WhoAmA 91*

Johnson, Eugene Laurence 1936- *WhoAm 90*
Johnson, Eugene R., Jr. 1924- *St&PR 91*
Johnson, Eugene Walter 1939- *WhoAm 90*
Johnson, Eunice W. *BioIn 16*
Johnson, Evelyn Bryan 1909- *WhoAmW 91*
Johnson, Evelyne 1922- *WhoWrEP 89*
Johnson, Everett Clark 1955- *WhoEmL 91*
Johnson, Everett Ramon 1915- *WhoAm 90*
Johnson, Ewell Calvin 1926- *WhoAm 90*
Johnson, Eyvind 1900-1976 *EuWr 12, WorAlBi*
Johnson, Eyvind Olof Verner 1900- *DcScanL*
Johnson, F. Michael 1953- *WhoEmL 91*
Johnson, F. Ross *BioIn 16*
Johnson, F. Ross 1931- *St&PR 91*
Johnson, Falk Simmons 1913- *WhoAm 90*
Johnson, Fatima Nunes 1939- *WhoAmW 91*
Johnson, Felicia Bryan Farrar 1937- *WhoSSW 91*
Johnson, Fenton 1888-1958 *EarBlAP*
Johnson, Ferd 1905- *EncACom, WhoAm 90*
Johnson, Fern L. *WhoAm 90*
Johnson, Florence Merriam 1875-1954 *BioIn 16*
Johnson, Frances E. 1936- *WhoAmW 91*
Johnson, Frances Flaherty 1916- *WhoAmW 91, WhoSSW 91, WhoWor 91*
Johnson, Francis Godschall 1817-1894 *DcCanB 12*
Johnson, Francis S. 1925- *St&PR 91*
Johnson, Francis Severin 1918- *WhoAm 90*
Johnson, Frank A 1928- *BiDrAPA 89*
Johnson, Frank Corliss 1927- *WhoAm 90*
Johnson, Frank Edward 1920- *WhoAm 90*
Johnson, Frank K *BiDrAPA 89*
Johnson, Frank Minis, Jr. 1918- *WhoAm 90*
Johnson, Frank S. 1930- *ODwPR 91*
Johnson, Frank Scott 1956- *WhoEmL 91*
Johnson, Frank Stanley, Jr. 1930- *St&PR 91, WhoAm 90*
Johnson, Frank William 1948- *WhoEmL 91*
Johnson, Franklin C 1934- *BiDrAPA 89*
Johnson, Franklin Ridgway 1912- *WhoAm 90*
Johnson, Franklyn Arthur 1921- *WhoAm 90, WhoWor 91*
Johnson, Franz Reed 1946- *WhoE 91*
Johnson, Fred 19--?-1982 *SmATA 63*
Johnson, Freda S. 1947- *St&PR 91, WhoAm 90*
Johnson, Freddie *EarBlAP*
Johnson, Frederick Dean 1911- *WhoSSW 91, WhoWor 91*
Johnson, Frederick Ross 1931- *WhoSSW 91, WhoWor 91*
Johnson, Frederick William 1947- *WhoWrEP 89*
Johnson, Fridolf 1905-1988 *BioIn 16*
Johnson, Fridolf Lester 1905-1988 *WhoAmA 91N*
Johnson, Fridthjofur O. 1956- *WhoWor 91*
Johnson, Gabriel Ampah 1930- *WhoWor 91*
Johnson, Gail Delories 1957- *WhoAmW 91, WhoEmL 91*
Johnson, Gale A. *ODwPR 91*
Johnson, Garry Wayne 1955- *WhoEmL 91*
Johnson, Gary Allen 1954- *WhoEmL 91*
Johnson, Gary E. 1935- *St&PR 91*
Johnson, Gary Keith 1951- *WhoEmL 91*
Johnson, Gary Lee 1933- *St&PR 91*
Johnson, Gary Ray 1949- *WhoSSW 91*
Johnson, Gary Thomas 1950- *WhoEmL 91, WhoSSW 91*
Johnson, Geneva Bolton *WhoAm 90*
Johnson, George 1920- *WhoAm 90*
Johnson, George, Jr. 1926- *WhoAm 90*
Johnson, George Andrew 1949- *St&PR 91*
Johnson, George Carl 1947- *WhoSSW 91*
Johnson, George Clayton 1929- *BioIn 16*
Johnson, George Croom 1948- *BiDrAPA 89*
Johnson, George E. *BioIn 16*
Johnson, George H. 1941- *St&PR 91*
Johnson, George Lee 1945- *WhoEmL 91*
Johnson, George Leonard 1947- *St&PR 91, WhoAm 90*
Johnson, George P. 1887-19--? *EarBlAP*
Johnson, George P. 1948- *St&PR 91*
Johnson, George Perry 1887-1939 *DrBlPA 90*
Johnson, George R. 1933- *St&PR 91*
Johnson, George Robert 1917- *WhoAm 90*
Johnson, George Robert 1927- *WhoWor 91*
Johnson, George W. 1811-1862 *AmLegL*
Johnson, George William 1928- *WhoAm 90, WhoSSW 91*
Johnson, Georgia Douglas 1877-1966 *HarlReB*
Johnson, Georgia Douglas 1880-1966 *FemiCLE*
Johnson, Georgia Douglas 1886-1966 *EarBlAP, NotWoAT*
Johnson, Georgia Douglas Camp 1886-1966 *BioIn 16*
Johnson, Georgia Kay 1952- *WhoEmL 91*
Johnson, Gerald A. 1948- *St&PR 91*
Johnson, Gerald Donald 1931- *St&PR 91*
Johnson, Gerald Lee 1938- *St&PR 91*
Johnson, Gerald White 1890-1980 *AuBYP 90*
Johnson, Geraldine Esch 1921- *WhoAmW 91*
Johnson, Geralyn Anne 1962- *WhoE 91*
Johnson, Gerard G. 1941- *WhoAm 90*
Johnson, Gerard Griffin 1941- *St&PR 91*
Johnson, Gertrude M 1905?- *EncPaPR 91*
Johnson, Gilbert Eugene 1933- *St&PR 91*
Johnson, Gilbert Fred 1931- *St&PR 91*
Johnson, Glade 1946- *WhoEmL 91*
Johnson, Glen Eric *BiDrAPA 89*
Johnson, Glen Roger 1929- *WhoAm 90*
Johnson, Glendon E. 1924- *St&PR 91*
Johnson, Glenn Thompson 1917- *WhoAm 90*
Johnson, Gordon 1930- *WhoWor 91*
Johnson, Gordon Duane 1946- *WhoEmL 91*
Johnson, Gordon Edward 1934- *WhoAm 90*
Johnson, Gordon James 1949- *IntWWM 90*
Johnson, Gordon O. 1933- *St&PR 91*
Johnson, Gordon S 1919- *BiDrAPA 89*
Johnson, Gordon Selby 1918- *WhoAm 90, WhoSSW 91*
Johnson, Graham 1950- *PenDiMP*
Johnson, Graham Rhodes 1950- *IntWWM 90*
Johnson, Grant 1874- *Ballpl 90*
Johnson, Grant D. 1930- *St&PR 91*
Johnson, Grant Lester 1929- *St&PR 91, WhoAm 90*
Johnson, Greg *WhoWrEP 89*
Johnson, Gregory David 1949- *WhoEmL 91*
Johnson, Gregory L. *WhoAm 90*
Johnson, Gregory Lee *BioIn 16*
Johnson, Gregory W. 1937- *St&PR 91*
Johnson, Gus LaRoy 1947- *WhoAm 90, WhoSSW 91*
Johnson, Gustav E. 1927- *St&PR 91*
Johnson, Guy 1740-1788 *EncCRAm, WhNaAH*
Johnson, Guy 1927- *WhoAmA 91*
Johnson, Guy, Jr. 1922- *WhoE 91*
Johnson, Guy Charles 1933- *IntWWM 90*
Johnson, Gwenavere Anelisa 1909- *WhoAmW 91*
Johnson, H. Arvid 1936- *WhoAm 90*
Johnson, H. Fisk 1958- *St&PR 91*
Johnson, H. Lynn 1933- *St&PR 91*
Johnson, H. Richard 1926- *St&PR 91*
Johnson, Hal Harold Gustav 1915- *WhoAm 90*
Johnson, Hall 1888-1970 *DcAfAmP, DrBlPA 90, EarBlAP*
Johnson, Hank 1906-1982 *Ballpl 90*
Johnson, Hannibal Barker 1959- *WhoEmL 91*
Johnson, Hardwick Smith, Jr. 1958- *WhoSSW 91, WhoWor 91*
Johnson, Harold 1884- *Ballpl 90*
Johnson, Harold D. 1934- *St&PR 91*
Johnson, Harold Earl 1939- *WhoAm 90*
Johnson, Harold H., III 1952- *St&PR 91*
Johnson, Harold Leonard 1944- *WhoSSW 91*
Johnson, Harold R. 1923- *St&PR 91*
Johnson, Harold R. 1926- *WhoAm 90*
Johnson, Harold R 1934- *BiDrAPA 89*
Johnson, Harold Timothy 1958- *WhoSSW 91*
Johnson, Harriet McBryde 1957- *WhoEmL 91*
Johnson, Harriett 1908-1987 *BioIn 16*
Johnson, Harrison F. 1904- *St&PR 91*
Johnson, Harry Alleyn 1921- *ConAu 31NR*
Johnson, Harry C. 1932- *St&PR 91*
Johnson, Harry E. 1931- *St&PR 91*
Johnson, Harry L. 1901- *St&PR 91*
Johnson, Harry Sten 1931- *St&PR 91*
Johnson, Harvey William 1921- *WhoAmA 91*
Johnson, Haynes Bonner 1931- *WhoAm 90*
Johnson, Hazel Lynn 1955- *WhoEmL 91*
Johnson, Helen *BiDrAPA 89*
Johnson, Helen 1921-1989 *BioIn 16*
Johnson, Helen Elizabeth Welty 1957- *WhoEmL 91*
Johnson, Helen Lossing *AuBYP 90*
Johnson, Helene 1907- *HarlReB*
Johnson, Henry *BioIn 16*
Johnson, Henry 1905- *St&PR 91*
Johnson, Henry Arna 1919- *WhoAm 90*
Johnson, Henry C. 1826-1892 *AmLegL*
Johnson, Henry Clay 1910- *WhoAm 90*
Johnson, Henry Clyde 1914- *WhoWor 91*
Johnson, Henry Eugene, III 1951- *WhoSSW 91*
Johnson, Henry Franklin, Mrs. 1922- *St&PR 91*
Johnson, Henry Parker 1951- *St&PR 91*
Johnson, Henry Samuel, Jr. 1914- *St&PR 91*
Johnson, Henry T. 1937- *WhoAm 90*
Johnson, Herbert Alan 1934- *WhoAm 90*
Johnson, Herbert Fisk 1901-1980 *WhoAmA 91N*
Johnson, Herbert Frederick 1934- *WhoAm 90*
Johnson, Herbert M. 1936- *St&PR 91*
Johnson, Herbert Michael 1936- *WhoAm 90*
Johnson, Herbert O. 1918- *St&PR 91*
Johnson, Hiram 1866-1945 *BioIn 16*
Johnson, Hiram W. 1866-1945 *WorAlBi*
Johnson, Hollis Eugene, III 1935- *WhoAm 90*
Johnson, Hollis Ralph 1928- *WhoAm 90*
Johnson, Homer 1925- *WhoAmA 91*
Johnson, Horace Richard 1926- *WhoAm 90*
Johnson, Horton Anton 1926- *WhoAm 90*
Johnson, Howard 1960- *Ballpl 90*
Johnson, Howard E. 1888?-1941 *WorAlBi*
Johnson, Howard Nicholas 1924- *WhoSSW 91*
Johnson, Howard Russell 1944- *WhoSSW 91*
Johnson, Howard Wesley 1922- *WhoAm 90, WhoWor 91*
Johnson, Hubert C. 1930- *ConAu 130*
Johnson, Hugh Bailey 1904- *WhoAm 90*
Johnson, Hugh E. 1929- *St&PR 91*
Johnson, Hulette M. 1943- *St&PR 91*
Johnson, I. Dean 1942- *St&PR 91*
Johnson, Ian Derek 1955- *St&PR 91*
Johnson, Ingolf Birger 1913- *WhoAm 90*
Johnson, Irving Stanley 1925- *WhoAm 90*
Johnson, Ivan Earl 1911- *WhoAmA 91*
Johnson, J. Alan 1944- *WhoAm 90*
Johnson, J. D. 1949- *WhoSSW 91*
Johnson, J. J. *WhoAm 90*
Johnson, J. J. 1924- *BioIn 16*
Johnson, J J 1924- *DrBlPA 90, WorAlBi*
Johnson, J.M. Hamlin 1925- *St&PR 91*
Johnson, J. M. Hamlin 1925- *WhoAm 90*
Johnson, J. Mitchell 1951- *WhoEmL 91*
Johnson, J. R. *MajTwCW*
Johnson, J. Richard *ODwPR 91*
Johnson, J. Rosamond *EarBlAP*
Johnson, J Rosamond 1873-1954 *DcAfAmP, DrBlPA 90*
Johnson, J. Rudolf *WhoWor 91*
Johnson, J Seward, Jr 1930- *WhoAmA 91*
Johnson, J Stewart 1925- *WhoAmA 91*
Johnson, J William 1936- *BiDrAPA 89*
Johnson, J. William 1941- *St&PR 91*
Johnson, Jack 1878-1946 *BioIn 16, WorAlBi*
Johnson, Jack Leo 1933- *St&PR 91*
Johnson, Jack Thomas 1915- *WhoAm 90*
Johnson, Jacquelyn Elnor 1949- *WhoWrEP 89*
Johnson, James A *BiDrAPA 89*
Johnson, James Alan 1945- *WhoAmA 91*
Johnson, James Albert, Jr. 1950- *WhoEmL 91*
Johnson, James Arnold 1939- *WhoAm 90*
Johnson, James Blair 1944- *WhoWrEP 89*
Johnson, James C. 1820-1912 *AmLegL*
Johnson, James C. 1896-1981 *OxCPMus*
Johnson, James David 1948- *IntWWM 90*
Johnson, James Donald, Jr. 1935- *WhoAm 90*
Johnson, James Douglas 1924- *WhoAm 90*
Johnson, James Doyle 1938- *WhoAm 90*
Johnson, James E. 1930- *St&PR 91*
Johnson, James Edwin 1942- *WhoAmA 91*
Johnson, James Edwin 1959- *WhoSSW 91*
Johnson, James Gann, Jr. 1915- *WhoAm 90*
Johnson, James Gibb 1937- *WhoAm 90*
Johnson, James H., Jr. 1944- *St&PR 91*
Johnson, James Harold 1944- *WhoAm 90*
Johnson, James Holbrook 1955- *WhoWrEP 89*
Johnson, James L. 1924- *St&PR 91*
Johnson, James L. 1927- *St&PR 91*
Johnson, James Lawrence 1927- *WhoE 91*
Johnson, James Leonard 1927-1987 *BioIn 16*
Johnson, James Louis 1924- *BioIn 16, OxCPMus*
Johnson, James Myron 1927- *WhoAm 90, WhoE 91*
Johnson, James P. 1891-1955 *BioIn 16*
Johnson, James P 1894-1955 *OxCPMus*
Johnson, James Ralph 1922- *AuBYP 90, WhoAmA 91*
Johnson, James Randall 1951- *WhoEmL 91*
Johnson, James Richard 1952- *WhoEmL 91*
Johnson, James Robert 1923- *WhoAm 90*
Johnson, James Ronald 1940- *BiDrAPA 89*
Johnson, James Terence 1942- *WhoAm 90, WhoWor 91*
Johnson, James Vernor 1923- *St&PR 91*
Johnson, James Walker 1953- *WhoWor 91*
Johnson, James Walton 1916- *St&PR 91, WhoSSW 91*
Johnson, James Waring 1959- *WhoSSW 91*
Johnson, James Weldon 1871-1938 *BioIn 16, DcAfAmP, DrBlPA 90, MajTwCW, OxCPMus*
Johnson, James Wiley 1940- *St&PR 91*
Johnson, James William 1927- *WhoAm 90*
Johnson, James Winston 1930- *WhoAm 90*
Johnson, Jamie 1947- *WhoAmW 91*
Johnson, Jan *ODwPR 91*
Johnson, Jane *WhoWrEP 89*
Johnson, Jane 1951- *BioIn 16*
Johnson, Jane Penelope 1940- *WhoSSW 91*
Johnson, Jane Sellers 1949- *St&PR 91*
Johnson, Janet A. 1940- *WhoAm 90*
Johnson, Janet Helen 1944- *WhoAm 90, WhoAmW 91*
Johnson, Janet Lou 1939- *WhoAmW 91*
Johnson, Janice C. 1956- *WhoAmW 91*
Johnson, Janice Cornelius 1940- *WhoSSW 91*
Johnson, Janice Denice 1955- *WhoAmW 91*
Johnson, Janice Kay 1946- *WhoAmW 91*
Johnson, Janice Marie 1954- *WhoAmW 91*
Johnson, Janis 1956- *St&PR 91*
Johnson, Jay *BioIn 16*
Johnson, Jay 1951?-1990 *ConAu 131*
Johnson, Jay A. 1945- *St&PR 91*
Johnson, Jay Blair 1952- *WhoSSW 91*
Johnson, Jay Francis 1934- *WhoE 91*
Johnson, Jean *AuBYP 90*
Johnson, Jean Elaine 1925- *WhoAm 90, WhoAmW 91*
Johnson, Jeanne Payne 1887-1958 *WhoAmA 91N*
Johnson, Jed *BioIn 16*
Johnson, Jed Joseph, Jr. 1939- *WhoE 91*
Johnson, Jeff *NewAgMG*
Johnson, Jeffrey Michael 1962- *WhoEmL 91*
Johnson, Jeffrey Moore 1954- *WhoEmL 91*
Johnson, Jeffrey Robert 1948- *WhoEmL 91*
Johnson, Jeh Vincent 1931- *WhoAm 90*
Johnson, Jennifer J. 1962- *ODwPR 91*
Johnson, Jennifer Jean *BiDrAPA 89*
Johnson, Jennifer Rhae 1964- *WhoAmW 91*
Johnson, Jere Macy 1954- *St&PR 91, WhoE 91*
Johnson, Jerry 1943 *Ballpl 90*
Johnson, Jerry A. 1931- *WhoAm 90*
Johnson, Jerry L. *BioIn 16*
Johnson, Jerry Morgan 1942- *St&PR 91*
Johnson, Jetsie Louise 1944- *WhoAmW 91*
Johnson, Jim *BioIn 16*
Johnson, Jimmy *BioIn 16*
Johnson, Jimmy 1943- *WhoAm 90*
Johnson, Jing 1894-1950 *Ballpl 90*
Johnson, Jo Ann 1938- *WhoAmW 91*
Johnson, Joan *BioIn 16*
Johnson, Joan B. *BioIn 16*
Johnson, Joan B. 1929- *WhoAmW 91*
Johnson, Joan Bernice 1939- *WhoAmW 91*
Johnson, Joan Bray 1926- *WhoAmW 91*
Johnson, Joan E. Stout 1944- *WhoWrEP 89*
Johnson, Joanna Mabel 1891-1971 *BioIn 16*
Johnson, Joanne Mary 1947- *WhoAmW 91, WhoEmL 91*
Johnson, Joe 1961- *Ballpl 90*
Johnson, Joe C. 1926- *WhoHisp 91*
Johnson, Joe Lawrence 1950- *WhoSSW 91*
Johnson, Joe Pat 1939- *WhoSSW 91*
Johnson, Joe William 1908- *WhoAm 90*
Johnson, Joel David 1948- *WhoEmL 91*
Johnson, Joey *BioIn 16*
Johnson, John 1742-1830 *EncCRAm, WhNaAH*
Johnson, John 1938- *DrBlPA 90*
Johnson, John A. 1915- *WhoAm 90*
Johnson, John A. 1926- *St&PR 91*
Johnson, John Albert 1945- *WhoEmL 91*
Johnson, John Allen 1950- *WhoEmL 91, WhoSSW 91*
Johnson, John Andrew 1942- *WhoWor 91*
Johnson, John B. 1916- *St&PR 91*
Johnson, John Blossner 1842-1899 *AmLegL*
Johnson, John Brayton 1916- *WhoAm 90*

Johnson, John Clifford 1955- WhoEmL 91
Johnson, John E. 1942- St&PR 91
Johnson, John E., Jr. 1940- St&PR 91
Johnson, John Francis 1947- WhoAm 90
Johnson, John Frank 1942- WhoAm 90
Johnson, John Gary 1958- WhoEmL 91
Johnson, John Gray 1924- WhoAm 90
Johnson, John H. BioIn 16
Johnson, John H. 1918- WhoAm 90
Johnson, John Henry 1951- WhoEmL 91
Johnson, John Henry 1956- Ballpl 90
Johnson, John Irwin, Jr. 1931- WhoAm 90
Johnson, John J. 1912- WhoAm 90
Johnson, John James 1932- St&PR 91
Johnson, John K. 1953- WhoEmL 91
Johnson, John Michael BiDrAPA 89
Johnson, John Philip 1949- WhoEmL 91
Johnson, John Prescott 1921- WhoAm 90
Johnson, John Rosamond 1873-1954 BioIn 16, OxCPMus
Johnson, John Warren 1929- WhoAm 90
Johnson, John William 1947- St&PR 91
Johnson, John William, Jr. 1932- WhoAm 90
Johnson, Johnnie D. ODwPR 91
Johnson, Johnny Paul 1964- WhoSSW 91
Johnson, Johnny Ray 1929- WhoAm 90
Johnson, Joia Mishaaron 1960- WhoSSW 91
Johnson, Jonas Talmadge 1947- WhoE 91
Johnson, Jonathan Edwin, II 1936- WhoAm 90
Johnson, Joseph Benjamin 1934- WhoAm 90, WhoSSW 91
Johnson, Joseph Bernard 1919- WhoAm 90
Johnson, Joseph E. NewYTBS 90
Johnson, Joseph Edward 1923- WhoAm 90
Johnson, Joseph Edward 1932- WhoE 91
Johnson, Joseph Eggleston, III 1930- WhoAm 90
Johnson, Joseph Eversole 1930- St&PR 91
Johnson, Joseph H. 1943- St&PR 91
Johnson, Joseph M 1937- BiDrAPA 89
Johnson, Joseph P. St&PR 91
Johnson, Josephine NewYTBS 90
Johnson, Josephine Ann 1938- St&PR 91
Johnson, Josephine Powell 1941- WhoAmW 91
Johnson, Josephine W. BioIn 16
Johnson, Josephine W. 1910- BioAmW, FemiCLE
Johnson, Josephine W 1910-1990 ConAu 131
Johnson, Joy Duvall 1932- WhoAmW 91
Johnson, Joyce 1929- WhoAmA 91
Johnson, Joyce 1935- ConAu 129
Johnson, Joyce 1936- St&PR 91
Johnson, Joyce Ann 1950- WhoAmW 91
Johnson, Joyce Marie 1952- BiDrAPA 89, WhoWor 91
Johnson, Judith A. 1939- WhoE 91
Johnson, Judith Ann WhoAmW 91
Johnson, Judith Ekberg St&PR 91
Johnson, Judith Evelyn 1936- WhoWrEP 89
Johnson, Judith Johns 1942- WhoSSW 91
Johnson, Judith Kay 1939- WhoAmW 91, WhoSSW 91
Johnson, Judy 1899-1989 Ballpl 90 [port], BioIn 16
Johnson, Judy Sherrill 1944- WhoAmW 91
Johnson, Julian Ernest 1925- St&PR 91
Johnson, Julian Ernest, III 1949- St&PR 91
Johnson, Julie Elizabeth 1962- WhoAmW 91
Johnson, Julius T BiDrAPA 89
Johnson, K.O. 1920- St&PR 91
Johnson, Karen 1940- BioIn 16
Johnson, Karen 1948- BiDrAPA 89
Johnson, Karen Anne 1962- WhoAmW 91, WhoEmL 91
Johnson, Karen B. 1942- WhoAmW 91
Johnson, Karen Bremer 1950- WhoWor 91
Johnson, Karen Jane 1953- WhoAmW 91
Johnson, Karen Kay 1949- WhoAmW 91
Johnson, Karen L. 1940- WhoAmW 91
Johnson, Karen Lavone 1940- St&PR 91
Johnson, Karen M 1947- BiDrAPA 89
Johnson, Kate Chamness WhoAmA 91
Johnson, Katharyn Price 1897- WhoAmW 91, WhoE 91
Johnson, Katherine BiDEWW
Johnson, Katherine Anne 1947- WhoEmL 91
Johnson, Katherine Holthaus 1961- WhoAmW 91, WhoEmL 91
Johnson, Katherine King 1906- WhoAmA 91N
Johnson, Kathleen Hughes BiDrAPA 89
Johnson, Kathleen Keane 1940- St&PR 91
Johnson, Kathleen Linda 1951- WhoEmL 91
Johnson, Kathleen R BiDrAPA 89
Johnson, Kathryn Barrett 1941- WhoAmW 91
Johnson, Kathy BioIn 16
Johnson, Kathy Ann 1956- WhoAmW 91
Johnson, Keith 1921- WhoWor 91
Johnson, Keith Edwin 1948- WhoSSW 91
Johnson, Keith G. 1931- St&PR 91
Johnson, Keith Gilbert 1931- WhoAm 90
Johnson, Keith L. 1939- St&PR 91
Johnson, Keith Leonard 1952- WhoEmL 91
Johnson, Keith Northey 1936- St&PR 91
Johnson, Keith Windsor 1952- WhoEmL 91
Johnson, Kelley Smith 1959- WhoEmL 91
Johnson, Ken 1923- Ballpl 90
Johnson, Ken 1933- Ballpl 90
Johnson, Kenn H 1927- BiDrAPA 89
Johnson, Kenneth E. 1915- St&PR 91
Johnson, Kenneth Edward BiDrAPA 89
Johnson, Kenneth Grant BiDrAPA 89
Johnson, Kenneth Harvey 1936- WhoAm 90
Johnson, Kenneth James 1935- St&PR 91
Johnson, Kenneth Major, II 1957- WhoSSW 91
Johnson, Kenneth Odell 1922- WhoAm 90, WhoWor 91
Johnson, Kenneth Oscar 1920- WhoAm 90
Johnson, Kenneth Owen 1920- WhoAm 90
Johnson, Kenneth Peter 1932- WhoAm 90
Johnson, Kennett Conrad 1927- St&PR 91, WhoAm 90
Johnson, Kent Robert 1946- WhoEmL 91
Johnson, Kerry Kaminsky 1956- WhoEmL 91
Johnson, Kevin 1966- BioIn 16, News 91-1 [port], WorAlBi
Johnson, Kevin A. 1955- St&PR 91
Johnson, Kevin Donell 1961- WhoE 91
Johnson, Kevin Raymond 1958- WhoEmL 91, WhoHisp 91
Johnson, Kyle DrBIPA 90
Johnson, Lady Bird 1912- BioIn 16, WhoAmW 91, WhoSSW 91
Johnson, Lael Frederic 1938- St&PR 91, WhoAm 90
Johnson, Lamar 1950- Ballpl 90
Johnson, Lance Gordon 1959- WhoEmL 91
Johnson, Larry 1949- BioIn 16
Johnson, Larry C. St&PR 91
Johnson, Larry E. 1950- St&PR 91
Johnson, Larry Glenn 1948- St&PR 91
Johnson, Larry James 1949- WhoSSW 91
Johnson, Larry Russell 1945- WhoEmL 91
Johnson, Larry Walter 1934- WhoAm 90
Johnson, Larry Wayne 1961- WhoEmL 91
Johnson, Larry Wilson 1938- WhoAm 90
Johnson, Laura BioIn 16
Johnson, Laura Ann 1959- WhoAmW 91
Johnson, Laurance F 1942- BiDrAPA 89
Johnson, Laurie 1927- OxCPMus
Johnson, LaVerne St. Clair WhoAmW 91
Johnson, Lavonne Bebler 1946- WhoEmL 91
Johnson, Lawrence Allan, Sr. 1943- WhoWor 91
Johnson, Lawrence E BiDrAPA 89
Johnson, Lawrence H. ODwPR 91
Johnson, Lawrence Henry 1862-1947 AmLegL
Johnson, Lawrence M. BioIn 16
Johnson, Lawrence M. 1940- St&PR 91
Johnson, Lawrence Wilbur, Jr. 1955- WhoEmL 91
Johnson, Leander Floyd 1926- WhoAm 90
Johnson, Lee 1935- WhoAmA 91
Johnson, Lee Harnie 1909- WhoAm 90, WhoWor 91
Johnson, Lee Roy W BiDrAPA 89
Johnson, Leon Bernard WhoAmA 91
Johnson, Leone Nancy 1955- WhoEmL 91
Johnson, Leopoldo A. 1935- St&PR 91
Johnson, Leslie Jones 1958- WhoAmW 91
Johnson, Lester Deane 1932- WhoAm 90
Johnson, Lester F 1919- WhoAmA 91
Johnson, Lester Fredrick 1919- WhoAm 90
Johnson, Lester L 1937- WhoAmA 91
Johnson, Lester O. 1912- St&PR 91
Johnson, Lewis Brandon 1922- St&PR 91
Johnson, Lewis P. 1922- St&PR 91
Johnson, Lillian Beatrice 1922- WhoAmW 91
Johnson, Lincoln F., Jr. 1920- WhoAm 90
Johnson, Linda WhoAmW 91
Johnson, Linda Arlene 1946- WhoAmW 91
Johnson, Linda Diane 1947- WhoAmW 91
Johnson, Linda Joyce 1956- WhoAmW 91
Johnson, Linda Lee Davis 1947- WhoSSW 91
Johnson, Linda Ligon 1949- WhoAmW 91
Johnson, Linda Marie 1940- WhoAmW 91
Johnson, Lionel Pigot 1867-1902 BioIn 16
Johnson, Lisa Webbe 1957- St&PR 91
Johnson, Lizabeth Lettie 1957- WhoAmW 91
Johnson, Lloyd Peter 1930- St&PR 91, WhoAm 90
Johnson, Loering M. 1926- WhoAm 90
Johnson, Lois Marlene 1942- WhoAmA 91
Johnson, Lois Walfrid 1936- WhoWrEP 89
Johnson, Lola N. ODwPR 91
Johnson, Lori Anne 1963- WhoAmW 91
Johnson, Lorraine B. 1952- St&PR 91
Johnson, Lou 1934- Ballpl 90
Johnson, Louis 1933- DrBIPA 90
Johnson, Louis Arthur 1891-1956 BiDrUSE 89
Johnson, Lowell F. 1912- St&PR 91
Johnson, Lowell Ferris 1912- WhoAm 90
Johnson, Lowell W. 1944- WhoAm 90
Johnson, LuAn 1956- WhoAmW 91, WhoEmL 91
Johnson, Luanne Elizabeth 1949- WhoWor 91
Johnson, Luci 1947- BioAmW
Johnson, Luci Baines BioIn 16
Johnson, Lucille Lewis 1943- WhoE 91
Johnson, Lulu BioIn 16
Johnson, Lyle R. 1931- St&PR 91
Johnson, Lyman T. 1906- BioIn 16
Johnson, Lynda 1943- BioAmW
Johnson, Lynda Bird 1943- BioIn 16
Johnson, Lyndon B. 1908-1973 BioIn 16
Johnson, Lyndon Baines 1908-1973 BiDrUSE 89, WorAlBi
Johnson, Lynn EncACom
Johnson, Lynn Cravat 1953- WhoEmL 91
Johnson, Lynn Esther 1964- WhoE 91
Johnson, Lynn Kimmel 1958- WhoEmL 91
Johnson, Lynn Raymond 1952- WhoEmL 91
Johnson, Lynne Ardell 1951- WhoAmW 91
Johnson, M. Alanson, II 1933- St&PR 91
Johnson, M.E. 1922- St&PR 91
Johnson, M L J 1947- WhoAmA 91
Johnson, Magic 1959- BioIn 16, WhoAm 90, WorAlBi
Johnson, Malcolm Clinton, Jr. 1925- WhoAm 90
Johnson, Malvin Gray 1896-1934 WhoAmA 91N
Johnson, Manuel Holman, Jr. 1949- WhoAm 90
Johnson, Marc Kimball 1954- WhoEmL 91
Johnson, Marcelite Elaine 1949- WhoAmW 91
Johnson, Margaret Helen 1933- WhoAmW 91, WhoWor 91
Johnson, Margaret Hill 1923- WhoAmW 91
Johnson, Margaret Kathleen 1920- WhoAm 90, WhoAmW 91
Johnson, Margaret Mary Joyce 1948- WhoEmL 91
Johnson, Margaret Sweet 1893-1964 AuBYP 90
Johnson, Margery Ruth 1950- BiDrAPA 89
Johnson, Maria E. 1955- St&PR 91
Johnson, Marian Willard 1904- WhoAmA 91N
Johnson, Marie 1920- BiDWomA
Johnson, Marie Louise 1933- WhoAmW 91
Johnson, Marie-Louise Tully 1927- WhoAm 90
Johnson, Marijo Anne 1935- WhoE 91
Johnson, Marilyn Ann 1946- WhoAmW 91
Johnson, Marilyn June 1934- WhoAmW 91
Johnson, Marilyn Rae 1958- WhoAmW 91
Johnson, Marion 1914-1988 BioIn 16
Johnson, Marion Joyce Frye 1932- WhoAmW 91
Johnson, Marion Phillip 1931- WhoAm 90
Johnson, Marjean 1951- ODwPR 91
Johnson, Mark Alan 1960- WhoEmL 91
Johnson, Mark Cundiff BiDrAPA 89
Johnson, Mark Curtis 1948- WhoEmL 91
Johnson, Mark Edward 1953- WhoEmL 91
Johnson, Mark Leonard 1954- St&PR 91
Johnson, Mark M 1950- WhoAmA 91
Johnson, Mark Matthew 1950- WhoSSW 91
Johnson, Mark Musgrave 1946- St&PR 91, WhoAm 90
Johnson, Mark Oliver 1945- St&PR 91
Johnson, Mark Scott 1951- WhoEmL 91
Johnson, Mark Thomas 1930- WhoAm 90
Johnson, Mark Wayne 1959- WhoEmL 91
Johnson, Markham P., III 1953- WhoWrEP 89
Johnson, Marlene 1946- WhoAm 90, WhoAmW 91
Johnson, Marlin J.E. 1922- St&PR 91
Johnson, Marlys Dianne 1948- WhoAm 90
Johnson, Marques Kevin 1956- WhoAm 90
Johnson, Marson Harry 1941- WhoSSW 91
Johnson, Martha AuBYP 90
Johnson, Martha C. BioIn 16
Johnson, Martha Jo 1947- WhoAmW 91
Johnson, Martin EncPaPR 91
Johnson, Martin Allen 1931- WhoAm 90
Johnson, Martin Arthur BiDrAPA 89
Johnson, Martin Brian 1951- WhoAmA 91
Johnson, Martin Earl 1929- WhoAm 90
Johnson, Martin Elmer 1884-1937 BioIn 16
Johnson, Martin McDermid 1945- BiDrAPA 89
Johnson, Martin T. 1951- St&PR 91
Johnson, Marty Jo 1947- WhoWrEP 89
Johnson, Marvin Dave 1928- St&PR 91
Johnson, Marvin Donald 1928- WhoAm 90, WhoWor 91
Johnson, Marvin Melrose 1925- WhoAm 90
Johnson, Marvin Richard Alois 1916- WhoAm 90
Johnson, Mary Alice 1942- WhoAmW 91
Johnson, Mary Ann 1933- BiDrAPA 89
Johnson, Mary Ann 1945- WhoAmW 91
Johnson, Mary Ann 1950- WhoAmW 91
Johnson, Mary E. BioIn 16
Johnson, Mary Elizabeth 1905- WhoAmW 91
Johnson, Mary Ellen 1946- St&PR 91
Johnson, Mary Ignacia 1933- WhoHisp 91
Johnson, Mary Lou 1953- WhoWrEP 89
Johnson, Mary Louise 1932- WhoWrEP 89
Johnson, Mary Lynn 1938- WhoAmW 91
Johnson, Mary Murphy 1940- WhoAmW 91
Johnson, Mary Susan 1937- WhoAmW 91, WhoWor 91
Johnson, Mary Teel 1921- WhoAmW 91
Johnson, Mary Veronica 1945- WhoAmW 91
Johnson, Maryann Elaine 1943- WhoAmW 91
Johnson, Maryanna Morse 1936- WhoAmW 91
Johnson, Matthew Lee 1956- BiDrAPA 89
Johnson, Maurice Glen 1936- WhoAm 90
Johnson, Max E 1915- BiDrAPA 89
Johnson, Maxine Frahm 1939- WhoAmW 91
Johnson, Maynard B. 1921- St&PR 91
Johnson, Melinda 1936- WhoWor 91
Johnson, Melinda Ann 1962- IntWWM 90
Johnson, Melissa Bruce 1952- WhoAmW 91
Johnson, Melissa Ramirez 1953- WhoAmW 91
Johnson, Melvin Edward 1939- St&PR 91
Johnson, Melvin Herbert 1938- St&PR 91
Johnson, Melvyn BiDrAPA 89
Johnson, Merle L. 1923- St&PR 91
Johnson, Merlin H 1922- BiDrAPA 89
Johnson, Merlin J. 1906- WhoSSW 91
Johnson, Miani Guthrie 1948- WhoAmA 91
Johnson, Micah William 1963- WhoSSW 91
Johnson, Michael WhoNeCM [port]
Johnson, Michael Chee 1953- WhoEmL 91
Johnson, Michael Eure 1956- IntWWM 90
Johnson, Michael Ferguson 1932- St&PR 91
Johnson, Michael L. 1945- ODwPR 91
Johnson, Michael P 1941- ConAu 132
Johnson, Michael Reid 1957- BiDrAPA 89
Johnson, Michael William 1953- WhoEmL 91, WhoWor 91
Johnson, Mike BioIn 16
Johnson, Mildred D. ConAu 132
Johnson, Mildred Irene 1924- WhoAmW 91
Johnson, Millard Wallace, Jr. 1928- WhoAm 90
Johnson, Miller Alanson, II 1933- WhoAm 90
Johnson, Millicent Vivian 1910- WhoAmW 91
Johnson, Milton Jerrell 1941- WhoSSW 91
Johnson, Milton Raymond, Jr. 1919- WhoSSW 91
Johnson, Mitchell Allen 1942- St&PR 91
Johnson, Monte S. 1958- WhoEmL 91
Johnson, Murray H. 1956- WhoSSW 91
Johnson, Nancie Schalk 1949- WhoE 91
Johnson, Nancy ODwPR 91
Johnson, Nancy Ann 1955- WhoAmW 91
Johnson, Nancy C. Pickles 1950- WhoAmW 91
Johnson, Nancy Elizabeth 1953- WhoAmW 91
Johnson, Nancy Faye 1951- WhoAmW 91
Johnson, Nancy Lee 1935- WhoAm 90, WhoAmW 91
Johnson, Nancy Marie 1947- WhoEmL 91
Johnson, Nancy Plattner 1938- WhoSSW 91
Johnson, Naomi Marie 1910- WhoAmW 91
Johnson, Natalie ConAu 30NR
Johnson, Nathan 1795-1880 BioIn 16

Johnson, Ned 1926- WhoAm 90
Johnson, Neil Gordon 1927- St&PR 91
Johnson, Neil Richard 1945- BiDrAPA 89, WhoE 91
Johnson, Nelson Trusler 1887-1954 BioIn 16
Johnson, Nicholas 1934- WhoWrEP 89
Johnson, Noble M 1881-1978 DrBlPA 90
Johnson, Noel Lars 1957- WhoAm 90
Johnson, Noel McKinley 1936- BiDrAPA 89
Johnson, Nora Ann Toner 1952- WhoAmW 91
Johnson, Norbert Jeffrey 1961- WhoEmL 91
Johnson, Nordahl Kent 1942- WhoSSW 91
Johnson, Norine Goode 1935- WhoAmW 91
Johnson, Norma Alice 1932- WhoWrEP 89
Johnson, Norma Holloway WhoAmW 91
Johnson, Norma J. 1925- WhoAmW 91
Johnson, Norma Jean Wilson 1935- WhoWor 91
Johnson, Norman 1928- WhoAm 90
Johnson, Norman Gary 1942- IntWWM 90
Johnson, Norman James 1921- WhoSSW 91
Johnson, Norman Kenneth 1928- IntWWM 90
Johnson, Nota 1923- WhoAmA 91
Johnson, Olive M. 1871?-1952 EncAL
Johnson, Oliver 1821-1907 BioIn 16
Johnson, Oliver Thomas, Jr. 1946- WhoE 91, WhoEmL 91
Johnson, Opal Burton 1929- WhoAmW 91
Johnson, Ora Mae 1944- WhoWrEP 89
Johnson, Orlin E. 1948- St&PR 91
Johnson, Orrin Wendell 1920- WhoAm 90
Johnson, Osa Helen 1894-1953 AuBYP 90
Johnson, Osa Helen Leighty 1894-1953 BioIn 16
Johnson, Owen H. 1929- WhoE 91
Johnson, P. B. 1837- AmLegL
Johnson, Pam McAllister 1945- WhoAmW 91
Johnson, Pamela Beth 1946- WhoEmL 91
Johnson, Pamela Hansford 1912-1981 BioIn 16, DcNaB 1981, FemiCLE, MajTwCW
Johnson, Patrice Jeanine BiDrAPA 89
Johnson, Patricia 1934- IntWWM 90
Johnson, Patricia Anita 1944- WhoAmW 91
Johnson, Patricia Burke 1941- WhoAmW 91
Johnson, Patricia Duren 1943- WhoAmW 91
Johnson, Patricia Gayle 1947- WhoAmW 91
Johnson, Patricia Hardy 1933- WhoAmW 91
Johnson, Patricia Mary 1937- WhoAmW 91
Johnson, Patrick BioIn 16
Johnson, Patrick, Jr. 1955- WhoEmL 91, WhoSSW 91
Johnson, Patrick Eugene 1958- WhoSSW 91
Johnson, Patrick Michael 1954- WhoEmL 91
Johnson, Patrick Trench 1926- WhoAm 90
Johnson, Paul BioIn 16
Johnson, Paul 1928- BioIn 16
Johnson, Paul A. 1919- St&PR 91
Johnson, Paul A. 1955- IntWWM 90
Johnson, Paul Christian 1928- WhoAm 90
Johnson, Paul Edwin 1933- WhoSSW 91
Johnson, Paul Eugene 1959- WhoEmL 91
Johnson, Paul Franklin 1956- WhoE 91
Johnson, Paul Howard 1924- WhoAm 90
Johnson, Paul J. 1923- St&PR 91
Johnson, Paul Martin 1946- WhoEmL 91
Johnson, Paul Oren 1937- WhoAm 90
Johnson, Paul S 1924- BiDrAPA 89
Johnson, Paula Barnes WhoAmW 91
Johnson, Pauline 1861-1913 DcLB 92 [port], FemiCLE
Johnson, Pauline 1959- WhoAmW 91
Johnson, Payne ODwPR 91
Johnson, Peggy Joyce 1939- WhoSSW 91
Johnson, Perry H. 1946- St&PR 91
Johnson, Pete 1904-1967 BioIn 16, OxCPMus
Johnson, Peter 1956- WhoWor 91
Johnson, Peter Christopher 1954- WhoWrEP 89
Johnson, Peter Forbes 1934- WhoSSW 91
Johnson, Peter K. 1938- ODwPR 91
Johnson, Peter Lars 1953- WhoSSW 91
Johnson, Philip Biesinger 1949- WhoEmL 91
Johnson, Philip C. 1906- WorAlBi
Johnson, Philip C. 1946- St&PR 91
Johnson, Philip Cortelyou 1906- BioIn 16, WhoWor 91
Johnson, Philip Edward 1947- WhoEmL 91
Johnson, Philip Martin 1940- WhoE 91
Johnson, Philip McBride 1938- WhoAm 90
Johnson, Phillip Eugene 1937- WhoAm 90
Johnson, Phyllis Kay 1955- WhoAmW 91
Johnson, Phyllis Michelle 1954- WhoE 91
Johnson, Pierre Marc 1946- WhoAm 90
Johnson, Preston Lewis 1934- St&PR 91
Johnson, R.C., Jr. 1920- St&PR 91
Johnson, R. Horace 1944- WhoSSW 91
Johnson, Rachel Ramirez 1937- WhoHisp 91, WhoSSW 91
Johnson, Rady Alan 1936- WhoAm 90
Johnson, Rafer 1935- DrBlPA 90, WorAlBi
Johnson, Rafer Lewis 1935- BioIn 16
Johnson, Ralph N. 1901- St&PR 91
Johnson, Ralph P. BioIn 16
Johnson, Ralph Raymond 1943- WhoAm 90
Johnson, Ralph S. 1943- St&PR 91
Johnson, Randy BioIn 16
Johnson, Randy 1963- Ballpl 90
Johnson, Ray BioIn 16
Johnson, Ray 1927- WhoAmA 91
Johnson, Ray Clifford 1927- WhoAm 90
Johnson, Ray DeForest 1926-1989 ConAu 130
Johnson, Ray Loring 1933- BiDrAPA 89
Johnson, Raymond Alfred 1922- WhoE 91
Johnson, Raymond Ard BiDrAPA 89
Johnson, Raymond Ard 1942- WhoE 91
Johnson, Raymond Coles 1907- WhoAm 90
Johnson, Raymond Craig 1950- WhoEmL 91
Johnson, Raymond Edward 1904- WhoAm 90
Johnson, Raymond Harold 1939- St&PR 91
Johnson, Raymond L. 1931- St&PR 91
Johnson, Raymond Sherman 1948- IntWWM 90
Johnson, Raymond W. 1934- WhoWor 91
Johnson, Raymonda Theodora Greene 1939- WhoAmW 91
Johnson, Raynor C 1901- EncO&P 3
Johnson, Raynor C. 1901-1987 EncPaPR 91
Johnson, Rebecca Lynne BiDrAPA 89
Johnson, Rebecca McGeorge 1948- WhoAmW 91
Johnson, Reed Moery BiDrAPA 89
Johnson, Renee Grace 1962- WhoE 91
Johnson, Reverdy 1796-1876 BiDrUSE 89, BioIn 16
Johnson, Reverdy 1937- WhoAm 90
Johnson, Rheta Grimsley 1953- BioIn 16
Johnson, Rhoda Ann Brown 1938- WhoE 91
Johnson, Richard St&PR 91
Johnson, Richard 1930- WhoSSW 91
Johnson, Richard A. WhoAm 90
Johnson, Richard A. 1936- St&PR 91
Johnson, Richard A 1942- WhoAmA 91
Johnson, Richard Abraham 1910- WhoAm 90
Johnson, Richard Alan 1942- WhoAm 90
Johnson, Richard Arlo 1952- WhoWor 91
Johnson, Richard Arnold 1937- WhoAm 90
Johnson, Richard Arthur 1936- WhoAm 90
Johnson, Richard August 1937- WhoAm 90
Johnson, Richard Clark 1937- WhoAm 90
Johnson, Richard Clayton 1930- WhoAm 90
Johnson, Richard D. 1932- ODwPR 91, St&PR 91
Johnson, Richard Damerau 1934- WhoAm 90
Johnson, Richard David 1927- WhoAm 90, WhoE 91
Johnson, Richard Dean 1936- WhoWor 91
Johnson, Richard E. 1929- St&PR 91
Johnson, Richard E. 1946- St&PR 91
Johnson, Richard Edward 1954- WhoEmL 91
Johnson, Richard Fred 1944- WhoWor 91
Johnson, Richard G 1921- BiDrAPA 89
Johnson, Richard H BiDrAPA 89, St&PR 91
Johnson, Richard J.V. 1930- St&PR 91
Johnson, Richard James Vaughn 1930- WhoAm 90, WhoSSW 91
Johnson, Richard John 1947- WhoSSW 91
Johnson, Richard Karl 1947- WhoEmL 91
Johnson, Richard Kent 1952- WhoE 91
Johnson, Richard L 1929- BiDrAPA 89
Johnson, Richard Lewis BiDrAPA 89
Johnson, Richard Mentor 1781-1850 BiDrUSE 89
Johnson, Richard Merrill 1934- WhoAm 90
Johnson, Richard S. 1932- St&PR 91
Johnson, Richard T. 1931- WhoAm 90
Johnson, Richard Tenney 1930- WhoAm 90
Johnson, Richard Walter 1928- WhoAm 90, WhoWor 91
Johnson, Richard Warloe 1942- St&PR 91
Johnson, Richard Warren 1939- WhoAm 90
Johnson, Richard Wesley BioIn 16
Johnson, Richard William 1916- WhoAm 90
Johnson, Rick Paul 1951- St&PR 91
Johnson, Ricky Leon 1952- WhoSSW 91
Johnson, Robert BioIn 16
Johnson, Robert BioIn 16
Johnson, Robert 1911-1938 OxCPMus
Johnson, Robert Alan 1944- WhoAm 90
Johnson, Robert Allan 1919- WhoAm 90
Johnson, Robert Allen 1948- BiDrAPA 89
Johnson, Robert Allison 1928- St&PR 91, WhoAm 90
Johnson, Robert B. 1934- St&PR 91
Johnson, Robert Britten 1924- WhoAm 90
Johnson, Robert Bruce 1912- WhoAm 90
Johnson, Robert Clyde 1919- WhoAm 90
Johnson, Robert Dale 1965- WhoWor 91
Johnson, Robert Dudley 1945- WhoSSW 91
Johnson, Robert E. AuBYP 90
Johnson, Robert E. 1926- St&PR 91
Johnson, Robert E. 1936- WhoAm 90
Johnson, Robert Edward 1959- WhoEmL 91
Johnson, Robert Edward, Jr. 1952- WhoE 91
Johnson, Robert Eugene 1911- WhoAm 90
Johnson, Robert Everett 1956- WhoSSW 91
Johnson, Robert Flynn 1948- WhoAmA 91
Johnson, Robert Gerald 1928- WhoAm 90
Johnson, Robert Graham 1953- WhoE 91
Johnson, Robert Henry 1921- WhoAm 90
Johnson, Robert Hersel 1923- WhoAm 90
Johnson, Robert Ivar 1933- WhoAm 90
Johnson, Robert J. 1921- St&PR 91
Johnson, Robert Jay 1951-1990 WhoAmA 91N
Johnson, Robert Joseph 1938- WhoAm 90
Johnson, Robert Lawrence 1919- WhoAm 90
Johnson, Robert Lawrence 1950- WhoWor 91
Johnson, Robert Lawrence, Jr. 1945- WhoAm 90
Johnson, Robert Lewis, Jr. 1935- WhoAm 90
Johnson, Robert Louis 1946- WhoAm 90
Johnson, Robert Maurice 1945- WhoAm 90, WhoE 91
Johnson, Robert Merrill 1926- WhoAm 90
Johnson, Robert Raymond 1917- WhoAm 90
Johnson, Robert Richard 1932- St&PR 91
Johnson, Robert Royce BiDrAPA 89
Johnson, Robert Royce 1928- WhoAm 90
Johnson, Robert T. 1923- St&PR 91
Johnson, Robert T. 1948- BioIn 16
Johnson, Robert Thomas WhoWrEP 89
Johnson, Robert Willard 1921- WhoAm 90
Johnson, Robert William 1954- BiDrAPA 89
Johnson, Roberts, Mrs. EncO&P 3
Johnson, Rodell C 1913- WhoAmA 91
Johnson, Roderick Gerard 1949- WhoEmL 91
Johnson, Rodney C 1932- BiDrAPA 89
Johnson, Rodney Marcum 1947- WhoSSW 91
Johnson, Roger Alan 1940- BiDrAPA 89
Johnson, Roger N. 1939- WhoWrEP 89
Johnson, Roger W. 1934- St&PR 91
Johnson, Rogers Bruce 1928- WhoAm 90
Johnson, Roland Edward 1933- St&PR 91
Johnson, Rolla L. 1916- St&PR 91
Johnson, Rolland Clair 1944- WhoAm 90
Johnson, Ronald 1935- WhoAm 90, WhoWrEP 89
Johnson, Ronald B. 1928- St&PR 91
Johnson, Ronald Carl 1935- WhoAm 90
Johnson, Ronald Cleve 1941- St&PR 91
Johnson, Ronald D. 1945- St&PR 91
Johnson, Ronald Earl 1942- BiDrAPA 89
Johnson, Ronald Erik BiDrAPA 89
Johnson, Ronald Kay 1939- WhoWor 91
Johnson, Ronald La Var 1942- St&PR 91
Johnson, Ronald Lee 1954- WhoEmL 91
Johnson, Ronald Leroy 1943- WhoWrEP 89
Johnson, Ronald M. 1950- St&PR 91
Johnson, Ronald Roy 1928- WhoSSW 91
Johnson, Ronald W 1931- BiDrAPA 89
Johnson, Ronald W 1937- WhoAmA 91
Johnson, Ronald Wayne 1942- WhoAm 90
Johnson, Ronnie 1948- WhoSSW 91
Johnson, Rosa Townsend Johnson 1928- WhoSSW 91
Johnson, Rose-Marie 1931- IntWWM 90
Johnson, Rosemary Wrucke 1924- WhoAmW 91
Johnson, Rosi K. 1951- St&PR 91
Johnson, Ross W. St&PR 91
Johnson, Roy 1903-1973 Ballpl 90
Johnson, Roy Hamlin 1929- IntWWM 90
Johnson, Roy M. 1947- St&PR 91
Johnson, Roy Ragnar 1932- WhoAm 90
Johnson, Roy S. BioIn 16
Johnson, Roy W. 1945- St&PR 91
Johnson, Roy W. 1948- St&PR 91
Johnson, Roy William 1945- WhoSSW 91
Johnson, Rubidoux Early WhoAmA 91
Johnson, Rupert Harris BioIn 16
Johnson, Russell 1923- IntWWM 90
Johnson, Russell F. 1928- St&PR 91
Johnson, Russell W. BioIn 16
Johnson, Ruth 1937- WhoE 91
Johnson, Ruth Ann 1947- WhoAmW 91
Johnson, Ruth Brammer 1955- WhoEmL 91
Johnson, Ryerson 1901- AuBYP 90
Johnson, Sally C 1953- BiDrAPA 89
Johnson, Sam BioIn 16
Johnson, Sam D. 1920- WhoAm 90
Johnson, Sammye La Rue 1946- WhoWrEP 89
Johnson, Sammye LaRue 1946- WhoSSW 91
Johnson, Samuel 1696-1772 EncCRAm
Johnson, Samuel 1709-1784 BioIn 16, DcLB 104 [port], -95 [port], EncPaPR 91, LitC 15 [port], WorAlBi
Johnson, Samuel C. 1928- St&PR 91
Johnson, Samuel Curtis 1928- WhoAm 90
Johnson, Sandra H. BioIn 16
Johnson, Sandra Jean 1945- WhoAmW 91
Johnson, Sandra Joyce 1949- WhoAmW 91
Johnson, Sanford A. 1918- St&PR 91
Johnson, Sankey Anton 1940- WhoAm 90
Johnson, Sarah Carolyn 1947- WhoEmL 91
Johnson, Sarala Devi BiDrAPA 89
Johnson, Sargent 1888-1967 WhoAmA 91N
Johnson, Sarilyn Joan 1932- WhoAmW 91
Johnson, Scott William 1940- WhoAm 90
Johnson, Searcy Lee 1908- WhoAm 90, WhoWor 91
Johnson, Selina WhoAmA 91
Johnson, Selina Tetzlaff 1906- WhoAm 90
Johnson, Sharon Jean 1962- WhoAmW 91, WhoEmL 91
Johnson, Sharon Kay Haneroff WhoAmW 91, WhoWor 91
Johnson, Sharon Marie Blom 1937- WhoAmW 91
Johnson, Shawana P. 1957- WhoAmW 91
Johnson, Sheldon Wayne 1947- WhoSSW 91
Johnson, Shelia M 1948- BiDrAPA 89
Johnson, Shelley A. 1951- St&PR 91
Johnson, Shelli Wright 1953- WhoEmL 91
Johnson, Sheree Ann 1954- WhoEmL 91
Johnson, Sherri Dale 1948- WhoAmW 91
Johnson, Sherri Lynn 1956- WhoE 91
Johnson, Shirley Ann 1944- WhoAmW 91
Johnson, Shirley Elaine 1946- WhoAmW 91
Johnson, Shirley Jeanne 1928- WhoWrEP 89
Johnson, Si 1900-1985 Ballpl 90
Johnson, Sid 1939- St&PR 91
Johnson, Siddie Joe 1905-1977 AuBYP 90
Johnson, Sidney K. 1942- ODwPR 91
Johnson, Sidney Malcolm 1924- WhoAm 90
Johnson, Sondra Lea 1952- WhoAmW 91, WhoEmL 91
Johnson, Stancil E D BiDrAPA 89
Johnson, Stanford Leland 1924- WhoAm 90
Johnson, Stanley David 1943- St&PR 91
Johnson, Stanley R. 1938- BioIn 16
Johnson, Stanley Webster 1938- WhoSSW 91
Johnson, Steamboat Ballpl 90
Johnson, Stephanie Lynn 1962- WhoAmW 91
Johnson, Stephen Anthony 1947- St&PR 91
Johnson, Stephen C. 1942- St&PR 91
Johnson, Stephen I. St&PR 91
Johnson, Sterling Cornaby 1940- St&PR 91
Johnson, Steven J. 1936- St&PR 91
Johnson, Steven Lloyd 1954- WhoSSW 91
Johnson, Steven M. 1951- St&PR 91
Johnson, Steven Olof 1955- WhoEmL 91
Johnson, Stuart 1936- IntWWM 90
Johnson, Stuart 1942- WhoAm 90, WhoSSW 91
Johnson, Susan 1952- ODwPR 91
Johnson, Susan Burgess 1948- WhoAmW 91
Johnson, Susan E. WhoE 91
Johnson, Susan Marcia 1944- IntWWM 90
Johnson, Susan Rose 1956- BiDrAPA 89

Johnson, Susannah 1730-1810 FemiCLE
Johnson, Susanne Pearl 1946- WhoEmL 91
Johnson, Susie Ann 1950- WhoE 91
Johnson, Suzanne Bennett 1948- WhoEmL 91
Johnson, Syl 1900-1984 Ballpl 90
Johnson, Sylvia BiDrAPA 89
Johnson, Sylvia A. BioIn 16
Johnson, Teresa Greiner BiDrAPA 89
Johnson, Terrance G. 1938- St&PR 91
Johnson, Terri Lynn 1947- WhoEmL 91
Johnson, Terry L. 1953- St&PR 91
Johnson, Terry Max BiDrAPA 89
Johnson, Theodore M. 1947- St&PR 91
Johnson, Theodore Marvin, Jr. 1947- WhoAm 90, WhoEmL 91
Johnson, Theodore Oliver 1929- IntWWM 90
Johnson, Theodore Oliver, Jr. 1929- WhoAm 90
Johnson, Theresa Mary 1863-1899 DcCanB 12
Johnson, Thomas 1714-1778? PenDiDA 89
Johnson, Thomas, Jr. 1760?-1820? LiHiK
Johnson, Thomas Allibone Budd 1955- WhoEmL 91, WhoSSW 91, WhoWor 91
Johnson, Thomas Edward 1938- WhoWor 91
Johnson, Thomas Floyd 1943- WhoAm 90
Johnson, Thomas Folsom 1918- WhoE 91
Johnson, Thomas Francis 1942- WhoE 91
Johnson, Thomas G. 1951- WhoEmL 91
Johnson, Thomas L., Jr. 1914- St&PR 91
Johnson, Thomas LeRoy 1933- WhoSSW 91
Johnson, Thomas N.P., Jr. 1918- St&PR 91
Johnson, Thomas Paul 1950- St&PR 91
Johnson, Thomas Pershing 1940- St&PR 91
Johnson, Thomas Phillips 1914- St&PR 91
Johnson, Thomas Russell 1944- St&PR 91, WhoAm 90
Johnson, Thomas S. 1940- St&PR 91
Johnson, Thomas Stephen 1940- WhoAm 90, WhoE 91
Johnson, Thomas Stuart 1942- WhoWor 91
Johnson, Thomas Webber, Jr. 1941- WhoAm 90
Johnson, Thor S. 1953- WhoE 91
Johnson, Thruston Charles 1914- WhoE 91, WhoWor 91
Johnson, Tim 1949- Ballpl 90
Johnson, Timothy Allen 1948- WhoSSW 91
Johnson, Timothy Peter 1946- WhoAm 90
Johnson, Timothy S. ODwPR 91
Johnson, Tod Stuart 1944- WhoAm 90, WhoWor 91
Johnson, Todd Anthony 1957- WhoEmL 91
Johnson, Tom 1939- IntWWM 90
Johnson, Tom 1941- BioIn 16
Johnson, Tom 1951- Ballpl 90
Johnson, Tom L. 1854-1911 WorAlBi
Johnson, Tom Milroy 1935- WhoAm 90
Johnson, Torrence Vaino 1944- WhoAm 90
Johnson, Trebbe 1948- WhoWrEP 89
Johnson, U. Alexis 1908- BioIn 16, WhoE 91
Johnson, Una E WhoAmA 91
Johnson, Ural Alexis 1908- BioIn 16
Johnson, Uwe 1934-1984 MajTwCW
Johnson, Valerie Sharon 1950- WhoAmW 91, WhoEmL 91
Johnson, Van 1916- BioIn 16, WorAlBi
Johnson, Van 1954- BiDrAPA 89
Johnson, Verbon Rogers, Sr. 1942- WhoSSW 91
Johnson, Verdenal Hoag 1924- WhoAm 90
Johnson, Vernon Alfred 1928- St&PR 91
Johnson, Vernon Eugene 1930- WhoSSW 91
Johnson, Vernon Leroy 1929- St&PR 91
Johnson, Vicki Lynn 1961- WhoAmW 91
Johnson, Vicki R. 1952- WhoAmW 91
Johnson, Vicki Sue 1959- WhoEmL 91
Johnson, Vicky Lynn 1955- WhoAmW 91
Johnson, Victor L. 1923- St&PR 91
Johnson, Victor Lawrence 1928- WhoAm 90
Johnson, Victoria Kaprielian 1959- WhoAmW 91
Johnson, Vilia Jocelyn 1953- WhoAmW 91
Johnson, Vincent Robert 1953- WhoEmL 91
Johnson, Virgil Allen 1921- WhoAm 90
Johnson, Virgil James 1948- WhoEmL 91
Johnson, Virginia 1950- BioIn 16
Johnson, Virginia B BiDrAPA 89
Johnson, Virginia B. 1954- St&PR 91
Johnson, W.E. 1928- St&PR 91
Johnson, W. Jacqueline 1937- WhoE 91
Johnson, W. Loy 1929- WhoSSW 91
Johnson, W.S. 1938- St&PR 91
Johnson, W Stacy 1927-1990 ConAu 131
Johnson, W. W. 1931- EncABHB 7 [port]
Johnson, Wade Lane BiDrAPA 89
Johnson, Waine Cecil 1928- WhoAm 90
Johnson, Walker Reed 1931- WhoAm 90
Johnson, Wallace BioIn 16
Johnson, Wallace 1939- WhoWor 91
Johnson, Wallace 1956- Ballpl 90
Johnson, Wallace E. 1901-1988 BioIn 16
Johnson, Wallace Richard 1944- St&PR 91
Johnson, Wallace Stephen, Jr. 1932- WhoAm 90
Johnson, Walter 1887-1946 Ballpl 90 [port], BioIn 16, WorAlBi
Johnson, Walter 1939- WhoE 91
Johnson, Walter C BiDrAPA 89
Johnson, Walter Conrad 1925- WhoAm 90
Johnson, Walter Curtis 1913- WhoAm 90
Johnson, Walter Frank, Jr. 1945- WhoEmL 91
Johnson, Walter Heinrick, Jr. 1928- WhoAm 90
Johnson, Walter Henry 1911- WhoE 91
Johnson, Walter Henry, III 1948- WhoE 91
Johnson, Walter L. 1927- WhoAm 90
Johnson, Warren BioIn 16
Johnson, Warren Allan 1958- WhoEmL 91
Johnson, Warren C BiDrAPA 89
Johnson, Warren C 1923- BiDrAPA 89
Johnson, Warren Charles 1923- WhoE 91
Johnson, Warren Donald 1922- WhoAm 90
Johnson, Warren Harold 1949- WhoEmL 91
Johnson, Warren R. 1920- WhoWor 91
Johnson, Warren Richard 1928- WhoAm 90, WhoE 91, WhoWor 91
Johnson, Warren T 1925- ConAu 131
Johnson, Wayne D. 1932- WhoAm 90
Johnson, Wayne David 1932- St&PR 91
Johnson, Wayne Eaton 1930- WhoAm 90
Johnson, Wayne Harold 1942- WhoAm 90
Johnson, Wayne Leslie 1953- WhoEmL 91, WhoSSW 91
Johnson, Weldon Howard 1937- WhoAm 90
Johnson, Wesley Dean 1957- WhoEmL 91
Johnson, Weyman Thompson, Jr. 1951- WhoSSW 91
Johnson, Willard Raymond 1935- WhoAm 90
Johnson, William EarBIAP
Johnson, William 1715-1774 BioIn 16, EncCRAm, WhNaAH [port]
Johnson, William A., Jr. 1953- St&PR 91
Johnson, William Alexander 1934- WhoAm 90
Johnson, William Benjamin 1918- WhoAm 90
Johnson, William Bruce 1940- WhoWor 91
Johnson, William Bullein 1782-1862 BioIn 16
Johnson, William C. 1940- St&PR 91
Johnson, William Carl 1958- WhoEmL 91
Johnson, William Cumming, Jr. 1904- WhoWor 91
Johnson, William David 1924- WhoAm 90
Johnson, William E. 1862-1945 WorAlBi
Johnson, William E. 1933- St&PR 91
Johnson, William E. 1941- St&PR 91
Johnson, William Fell 1951- BiDrAPA 89
Johnson, William G. 1947- St&PR 91
Johnson, William Glenn 1943- ODwPR 91
Johnson, William Hall 1943- WhoAm 90
Johnson, William Howard 1922- WhoAm 90
Johnson, William Hugh, Jr. 1935- WhoAm 90
Johnson, William James 1950- WhoEmL 91
Johnson, William Joseph 1941- WhoE 91
Johnson, William Kelly 1943- WhoSSW 91
Johnson, William Kyle, Jr. 1940- St&PR 91
Johnson, William Larry 1943- WhoSSW 91
Johnson, William Lee 1929- WhoAm 90
Johnson, William Lewis 1948- WhoAm 90
Johnson, William McAllister 1939- WhoAm 90
Johnson, William Michael 1940- WhoWor 91
Johnson, William Parks 1942- WhoSSW 91
Johnson, William Patrick 1942- St&PR 91
Johnson, William Potter 1935- WhoAm 90
Johnson, William R. 1930- WhoE 91
Johnson, William Ray 1930- WhoSSW 91
Johnson, William Richard 1928- WhoAm 90
Johnson, William Richard, Jr. BioIn 16
Johnson, William Richard, Jr. 1942- St&PR 91
Johnson, William Rudolph 1933- WhoAm 90, WhoSSW 91
Johnson, William Samuel 1727-1819 BioIn 16
Johnson, William Summer 1913- WhoAm 90
Johnson, William Theodore 1953- WhoEmL 91
Johnson, William Treby 1815-1881 AmLegL
Johnson, William Weber 1909- AuBYP 90
Johnson, William Woodward 1931- WhoAm 90
Johnson, Willie J. 1956- WhoEmL 91
Johnson, Willis Fletcher 1857-1931 BioIn 16
Johnson, Winston Conrad 1943- WhoSSW 91
Johnson, Woodruff B. 1916- St&PR 91
Johnson, Wyatt Thomas 1941- BioIn 16, St&PR 91
Johnson, Wyatt Thomas, Jr. 1941- WhoAm 90
Johnson, Wylie Pierson 1919- WhoSSW 91
Johnson, Zane Quentin 1924- WhoAm 90
Johnson, Zoe Ann 1960- WhoAmW 91
Johnson Blankenship, Elizabeth Ann 1952- WhoAmW 91
Johnson-Champ, Debra Sue 1955- WhoAmW 91
Johnson-Grayum, Jane Robin 1957- WhoAmW 91
Johnson Hubbell, Helene 1907- HarlReB
Johnson-Laub, Martha M. St&PR 91
Johnson-Lesson, Charleen Ann 1949- WhoAmW 91, WhoEmL 91
Johnson-Marshall, Stirrat Andrew William 1912-1981 DcNaB 1981
Johnson-Morris, Ingeborg BiDrAPA 89
Johnson-Ross, Robyn WhoAmA 91
Johnson-Tanis, Pamela Sue 1946- WhoEmL 91
Johnson-Tatelbaum, Diane Elizabeth 1961- WhoEmL 91
Johnson-Warren, Marjorie E BiDrAPA 89
Johnsonbaugh, Richard DeWayne 1953- WhoSSW 91
Johnsrud, Russell Lloyd 1909- WhoAm 90
Johnsson, Bengt Gustaf 1921- IntWWM 90
Johnsson, Hans ODwPR 91
Johnsson, Hillary Anne 1959- WhoE 91
Johnston, Alan Rogers 1914- WhoAm 90
Johnston, Alastair John Carmichael 1928- WhoWor 91
Johnston, Albert C. 1900-1988 BioIn 16
Johnston, Alfred G. 1922- St&PR 91
Johnston, Alfred H BiDrAPA 89
Johnston, Alistair D. 1937- St&PR 91
Johnston, Ann Elizabeth 1954- WhoEmL 91
Johnston, Annie Fellows 1863-1931 LiHiK
Johnston, Ardena Crowson 1929- WhoAmW 91
Johnston, Arthur James 1898-1954 OxCPMus
Johnston, Barry Woods WhoAmA 91
Johnston, Barry Woods 1941- WhoE 91
Johnston, Basil 1929- BioIn 16
Johnston, Ben Burwell 1926- IntWWM 90
Johnston, Ben Earl 1938- WhoAm 90
Johnston, Brad L. 1940- St&PR 91
Johnston, Brian 1912- BioIn 16
Johnston, Bruce Foster 1919- WhoAm 90
Johnston, Bruce Gilbert 1905- WhoAm 90
Johnston, Bryan E. St&PR 91
Johnston, Burleigh Clay 1946- WhoEmL 91
Johnston, C Eric 1918- BiDrAPA 89
Johnston, Carole Anne 1944- WhoWrEP 89
Johnston, Cecile M. ODwPR 91
Johnston, Charles Bernie, Jr. 1931- WhoAm 90
Johnston, Charles Edgar BiDrAPA 89
Johnston, Charles Enue 1943- St&PR 91
Johnston, Charles Frederick 1933- St&PR 91
Johnston, Christina Jane 1952- WhoAmW 91, WhoEmL 91, WhoWor 91
Johnston, Cicely Anne 1912- WhoWrEP 89
Johnston, Claire 1940-1987 BioIn 16
Johnston, Curtis Arnold 1951- WhoE 91
Johnston, Cyrus Conrad, Jr. 1929- WhoAm 90
Johnston, D.W. 1903- St&PR 91
Johnston, Daniel Fulper 1931- BiDrAPA 89
Johnston, Daniel Joseph 1950- St&PR 91
Johnston, David 1789-1854 PenDiDA 89
Johnston, David 1948- ConAu 131
Johnston, David Alan BiDrAPA 89
Johnston, David C 1925- BiDrAPA 89
Johnston, David Cay Boyle 1948- WhoE 91
Johnston, David Hervey 1951- WhoSSW 91
Johnston, David Ian 1932- WhoAm 90
Johnston, David L. 1941- St&PR 91
Johnston, David Lloyd 1941- WhoE 91
Johnston, David Ritchey 1950- WhoE 91, WhoEmL 91
Johnston, David T. 1921- St&PR 91
Johnston, David White 1921- St&PR 91
Johnston, David White, Jr. 1921- WhoAm 90
Johnston, Dee Ann BioIn 16
Johnston, Dennis Roy 1937- WhoE 91, WhoWor 91
Johnston, Doc 1887-1961 Ballpl 90
Johnston, Dolores Mae Mascik 1927- WhoAmW 91
Johnston, Don 1927- St&PR 91
Johnston, Donald O. 1929- IntWWM 90
Johnston, Donald Walter 1936- St&PR 91
Johnston, Donna Faye 1941- WhoAmW 91
Johnston, Dorothy BiDrAPA 89
Johnston, Dorothy 1948- FemiCLE
Johnston, Dorothy Grunbock 1915-1979 BioIn 16
Johnston, Edward Allan 1921- WhoAm 90
Johnston, Edward Elliott 1918- WhoAm 90
Johnston, Elizabeth Bryant 1833-1907 LiHiK
Johnston, Elizabeth W 1920- BiDrAPA 89
Johnston, Erin Elam 1958- WhoAmW 91
Johnston, Ernest John 1926- St&PR 91
Johnston, Frank TwCCr&M 91
Johnston, Fred B., II 1938- St&PR 91
Johnston, Fred William, Jr. 1933- WhoAm 90
Johnston, Frederick Charles 1916- AuBYP 90
Johnston, Frederick Thomas 1918- St&PR 91
Johnston, Gary 1946- WhoWrEP 89
Johnston, Gary 1948- WhoEmL 91
Johnston, George Elmer 1927- WhoWor 91
Johnston, George G. 1932- St&PR 91, WhoAm 90
Johnston, George S. 1924- St&PR 91
Johnston, George Sim 1924- WhoAm 90
Johnston, Gerald Andrew 1931- WhoAm 90
Johnston, Gerald McArthur 1942- St&PR 91, WhoAm 90
Johnston, Ginny AuBYP 90
Johnston, Ginny 1946- SmATA 60 [port]
Johnston, Grace Eliette 1957- WhoAmW 91
Johnston, Gwinavere 1943- ODwPR 91
Johnston, Gwinavere Adams 1943- WhoAmW 91
Johnston, H. Frederick 1927- St&PR 91
Johnston, H. Robert 1956- WhoE 91
Johnston, Harold B BiDrAPA 89
Johnston, Harold Sledge 1920- WhoAm 90
Johnston, Harry A. 1931- BioIn 16
Johnston, Harry A., II 1931- WhoAm 90, WhoSSW 91
Johnston, Harry Melville, III 1945- WhoEmL 91
Johnston, Helen Head WhoAmA 91N
Johnston, Henrietta BioAmW
Johnston, Henrietta 1670?-1728? EncCRAm
Johnston, Hugh Buckner 1913- WhoWrEP 89
Johnston, Hugh Frederick 1952- BiDrAPA 89
Johnston, J. Bruce 1930- St&PR 91
Johnston, J. Phillips L. 1939- St&PR 91
Johnston, James 1738-1808 BioIn 16
Johnston, James 1903- PenDiMP
Johnston, James B 1932- BiDrAPA 89
Johnston, James Bruce 1930- WhoAm 90
Johnston, James D. 1930- St&PR 91, WhoAm 90
Johnston, James Franklin 1937- WhoSSW 91
Johnston, James Jordon 1931- WhoAm 90
Johnston, James Kenneth 1935- WhoSSW 91
Johnston, James Wesley 1946- WhoAm 90
Johnston, Janis Clark 1947- WhoAmW 91, WhoEmL 91
Johnston, Jeffrey D. 1950- St&PR 91
Johnston, Jeffrey Monroe 1952- WhoSSW 91
Johnston, Jeffrey Scott 1953- WhoEmL 91
Johnston, Jennifer 1930- BioIn 16, FemiCLE
Johnston, Jerry Wayne 1946- St&PR 91
Johnston, Jerry Wilson 1932- WhoAm 90
Johnston, Jill 1929- FemiCLE
Johnston, Jimmy 1889-1967 Ballpl 90
Johnston, Jocelyn Elaine 1954- WhoEmL 91
Johnston, Johanna 1914-1982 AuBYP 90
Johnston, John Andrew 1923- WhoAm 90
Johnston, John B. 1840?- AmLegL

Johnston, John Bennett, Jr. 1932- *WhoAm 90, WhoSSW 91, WhoWor 91*
Johnston, John Devereaux, Jr. 1932- *WhoAm 90*
Johnston, John Gerard, Jr. 1926- *St&PR 91*
Johnston, John J. 1950- *WhoE 91*
Johnston, John Martin 1923- *WhoAm 90*
Johnston, John Philip 1935- *WhoAm 90*
Johnston, Joni Elizabeth 1960- *WhoAmW 91*
Johnston, Joseph Eggleston 1807-1891 *BioIn 16, WorAlBi*
Johnston, Josephine Rose 1926- *WhoAmW 91, WhoE 91, WhoWor 91*
Johnston, Karen Cecile 1952- *BiDrAPA 89*
Johnston, Karen Queally 1952- *WhoAmW 91, WhoEmL 91*
Johnston, Katherine Fortino 1956- *St&PR 91*
Johnston, Kenneth Richard 1938- *WhoAm 90*
Johnston, Kurt M. 1954- *St&PR 91*
Johnston, Kurt Malcolm 1954- *WhoEmL 91*
Johnston, Lane *ODwPR 91*
Johnston, Laurance Scott 1950- *WhoAm 90*
Johnston, Laurie *AuBYP 90*
Johnston, Lloyd Douglas 1940- *WhoAm 90*
Johnston, Logan T., Jr. 1925- *WhoAm 90*
Johnston, Lois Ann 1949- *WhoE 91*
Johnston, Lorene Gayle 1952- *WhoEmL 91*
Johnston, Louisa Mae *AuBYP 90*
Johnston, Lynn *BioIn 16*
Johnston, Lynn Henry 1931- *St&PR 91*
Johnston, Lynne S. C. 1947- *WhoAmW 91*
Johnston, Malcolm Andrew 1945- *WhoEmL 91*
Johnston, Malcolm Carlyle 1934- *WhoAm 90*
Johnston, Margaret Williams 1953- *WhoEmL 91*
Johnston, Marguerite 1917- *WhoAm 90*
Johnston, Marie E. *WhoWrEP 89*
Johnston, Marion Elizabeth 1946- *WhoEmL 91*
Johnston, Marshall William 1919- *St&PR 91*
Johnston, Mary *BioIn 16*
Johnston, Mary 1870-1936 *BioAmW, FemiCLE*
Johnston, Mary Ellen 1951- *WhoAmW 91*
Johnston, Maxene *BioIn 16*
Johnston, McClain *BiDrAPA 89*
Johnston, Means 1916-1989 *BioIn 16*
Johnston, Michael Anthony 1947- *St&PR 91*
Johnston, Michael F. *St&PR 91*
Johnston, Michael Joseph 1938- *St&PR 91*
Johnston, Michael Richard 1946- *WhoAm 90*
Johnston, Michael T. 1949- *St&PR 91*
Johnston, Murray Lloyd, Jr. 1940- *St&PR 91*
Johnston, Nancy Dahl 1954- *WhoAmW 91*
Johnston, Norma *BioIn 16, ConAu 32NR*
Johnston, Norman John 1918- *WhoAm 90*
Johnston, Patricia Caryl 1954- *WhoAmW 91*
Johnston, Peter O. Lawson- 1927- *BioIn 16*
Johnston, Phillip M 1944- *WhoAmA 91*
Johnston, Phillip Michael 1944- *WhoAm 90, WhoE 91*
Johnston, Ralph E. 1902- *AuBYP 90*
Johnston, Randall B. 1958- *St&PR 91*
Johnston, Randolph Page 1935- *BiDrAPA 89*
Johnston, Rhodes 1917- *St&PR 91*
Johnston, Richard 1917- *IntWWM 90*
Johnston, Richard Elton 1952- *WhoSSW 91*
Johnston, Richard Fourness 1925- *WhoAm 90*
Johnston, Richard M. 1935- *St&PR 91*
Johnston, Richard M 1942- *WhoAmA 91*
Johnston, Richard Park 1930- *St&PR 91*
Johnston, Robert Addison 1936- *St&PR 91*
Johnston, Robert Alan 1924- *WhoWor 91*
Johnston, Robert Chapman 1930- *WhoAm 90*
Johnston, Robert Cossin 1913- *WhoAm 90*
Johnston, Robert Cully 1916- *WhoSSW 91*
Johnston, Robert D., Jr. 1950- *St&PR 91*
Johnston, Robert Donaghy 1929- *WhoAm 90*
Johnston, Robert Elliott 1921- *WhoAm 90*
Johnston, Robert G M *BiDrAPA 89*
Johnston, Robert H. 1923- *St&PR 91*
Johnston, Robert Harold 1928- *WhoAmA 91*
Johnston, Robert Hugh, Jr. 1930- *WhoSSW 91*
Johnston, Robert L. 1931- *St&PR 91*
Johnston, Robert Lloyd, Jr. 1931- *WhoAm 90*
Johnston, Robert Lynn 1940- *WhoSSW 91*
Johnston, Ronald Carlyle 1907-1990 *ConAu 131*
Johnston, Roy G. 1914- *WhoAm 90*
Johnston, Ruby Charlotte 1918- *WhoAmW 91*
Johnston, S. Parker, Jr. 1915- *St&PR 91*
Johnston, Samuel Thomas 1924- *WhoAm 90*
Johnston, Sarah Virginia 1950- *St&PR 91*
Johnston, Sean Francois 1956- *WhoWor 91*
Johnston, Shepherd D. 1947- *St&PR 91*
Johnston, Susan Taylor *AuBYP 90*
Johnston, Theodore Allan 1930- *WhoAm 90*
Johnston, Thomas *PenDiDA 89*
Johnston, Thomas 1945- *AuBYP 90*
Johnston, Thomas Alix 1941- *WhoAmA 91*
Johnston, Thomas David 1953- *WhoEmL 91*
Johnston, Thomas Gayle 1909- *WhoWor 91*
Johnston, Thomas J. 1922- *St&PR 91*
Johnston, Thomas John 1922- *WhoAm 90*
Johnston, Thomas Warren 1951- *WhoEmL 91*
Johnston, Tony *BioIn 16*
Johnston, Tony 1942- *AuBYP 90*
Johnston, Velda *TwCCr&M 91*
Johnston, Virginia Evelyn 1933- *WhoAmW 91*
Johnston, Wallace Robert 1902- *St&PR 91*
Johnston, Walter Eugene, III 1936- *St&PR 91*
Johnston, Warren Eugene 1933- *WhoAm 90*
Johnston, William Arnold 1942- *WhoWrEP 89*
Johnston, William C 1902- *BiDrAPA 89*
Johnston, William David 1944- *WhoAm 90*
Johnston, William David 1957- *WhoEmL 91*
Johnston, William E., Jr. 1940- *St&PR 91*
Johnston, William M. 1946- *St&PR 91*
Johnston, William Martin 1941- *WhoSSW 91*
Johnston, William Medford 1941- *WhoAmA 91*
Johnston, William N. 1922-1989 *BioIn 16*
Johnston, William Noel 1919- *WhoAm 90*
Johnston, William Ralph 1936- *WhoAmA 91, WhoE 91*
Johnston, William Randolph 1953- *WhoSSW 91*
Johnston, William Webb 1933- *WhoAm 90*
Johnston, Ynez 1920- *WhoAm 90, WhoAmA 91*
Johnston-O'Connor, Elizabeth J. 1952- *WhoE 91, WhoEmL 91*
Johnstone, Bruce Beal *BiDrAPA 89*
Johnstone, C. Bruce 1940- *WhoWor 91*
Johnstone, Campbell 1929- *St&PR 91*
Johnstone, Chauncey Olcott 1943- *WhoE 91*
Johnstone, Christian Isobel 1781-1857 *FemiCLE*
Johnstone, D. Bruce *BioIn 16*
Johnstone, D. Bruce 1941- *WhoAm 90*
Johnstone, David Moore 1926- *WhoWrEP 89*
Johnstone, Donald Frederick 1930- *WhoAm 90*
Johnstone, Edmund Frank 1909- *WhoAm 90*
Johnstone, Edward H. 1922- *WhoAm 90, WhoSSW 91*
Johnstone, Edward K., II 1936- *St&PR 91*
Johnstone, Edward Ransom *BioIn 16*
Johnstone, Edwin Enoch *BiDrAPA 89*
Johnstone, Gregg Martin 1947- *WhoEmL 91*
Johnstone, Harry Diack 1935- *IntWWM 90*
Johnstone, Harry Inge 1903- *WhoAm 90*
Johnstone, Henry Webb, Jr. 1920- *WhoAm 90*
Johnstone, Irvine Blakeley, III 1948- *WhoEmL 91*
Johnstone, James *Ballpl 90*
Johnstone, James George 1920- *WhoAm 90*
Johnstone, Jay 1945- *Ballpl 90*
Johnstone, Jeffrey Marwill 1945- *WhoEmL 91*
Johnstone, John Wallace Claire 1931- *WhoAm 90*
Johnstone, John William, Jr. 1932- *St&PR 91, WhoAm 90, WhoE 91*
Johnstone, Keith *ConAu 129*
Johnstone, L. Knox 1945- *WhoEmL 91*
Johnstone, Larry Craig 1942- *WhoAm 90*
Johnstone, Mark 1953- *WhoAmA 91, WhoEmL 91*
Johnstone, Mildred *BioIn 16*
Johnstone, Paula Sue 1947- *WhoAmW 91*
Johnstone, Philip MacLaren 1961- *WhoE 91*
Johnstone, Quintin 1915- *WhoAm 90*
Johnstone, Robert Philip 1943- *WhoAm 90*
Johnstone, Rose Mamelak 1928- *WhoAm 90*
Johnstone, Sally Mac 1949- *WhoAmW 91*
Johnstone, William Mervyn 1946- *WhoWrEP 89*
Joiner, Burt L. 1919- *St&PR 91*
Joiner, Charles W. 1942- *St&PR 91*
Joiner, Donald Lee 1935- *St&PR 91*
Joiner, James Monroe, II 1944- *BiDrAPA 89*
Joiner, Joseph H. 1926- *St&PR 91*
Joiner, Larry J. 1939- *WhoAm 90*
Joiner, Lorell Howard 1945- *St&PR 91, WhoSSW 91*
Joiner, Marilyn Segura 1947- *WhoEmL 91*
Joiner, Stephen T. 1945- *St&PR 91*
Joiner, Steven Craig 1958- *WhoEmL 91*
Joiner, Webb F. 1933- *St&PR 91*
Joinville, Patricia Kay 1955- *WhoAmW 91*
Joire, Paul 1856- *EncO&P 3*
Joist, Johann Heinrich 1935- *WhoAm 90*
Jokai, Anna 1932- *EncCoWW*
Jokay, Alex 1927- *St&PR 91*
Jokei *PenDiDA 89*
Jokela, Robert Wain 1950- *WhoEmL 91*
Jokerst, Carol Ann 1939- *WhoAmW 91*
Jokl, Ernst F. 1907- *WhoSSW 91*
Joklik, Gunther Franz 1928- *WhoAm 90*
Joklik, Wolfgang Karl 1926- *WhoAm 90*
Jokull Jakobsson *DcScanL*
Jolas, Betsy 1926- *IntWWM 90*
Jolas, Eugene 1894-1952 *BioIn 16*
Jolas, Maria 1893-1987 *FemiCLE*
Jolbitado, Deusdedit L *BiDrAPA 89*
Jolepalem, Neelakantam R *BiDrAPA 89*
Jolicoeur, Louise 1953- *St&PR 91*
Jolicoeur, Paul 1945- *WhoAm 90*
Joliet, Louis 1645-1700 *WhNaAH*
Joliet, Robert L. 1929- *St&PR 91*
Jolin, Edith May *BiDrAPA 89*
Jolin, Peggy 1952- *WhoAmW 91*
Jolinski, Jenny Ramirez 1947- *WhoAmW 91*
Joliot-Curie, Irene 1897-1956 *BiDFrPL, BioIn 16, WorAlBi*
Joliot-Curie, Jean-Frederic 1900-1958 *BiDFrPL, WorAlBi*
Jolissaint, Stephen Lacy 1951- *WhoSSW 91*
Jolivet, Andre 1905-1974 *PenDiMP A*
Jolivet, Vincent 1930- *St&PR 91*
Jolivette, Thayer E. 1936- *St&PR 91*
Joll, Philip 1954- *IntWWM 90*
Jolles, Ira Hervey 1938- *WhoAm 90*
Jolles, Paul Rodolphe 1919- *WhoWor 91*
Jolles, Scott Alan 1960- *WhoSSW 91*
Jolley, Bob Ray 1954- *BiDrAPA 89*
Jolley, David 1942- *WhoAm 90*
Jolley, Diane Louise 1944- *WhoSSW 91*
Jolley, Donal Clark 1933- *WhoAmA 91*
Jolley, Elizabeth 1923- *BioIn 16, ConAu 13AS [port], FemiCLE, WorAu 1980 [port]*
Jolley, Geraldine H 1911- *WhoAmA 91N*
Jolley, Jack J. 1925- *WhoAm 90*
Jolley, Joseph Steve 1951- *WhoEmL 91*
Jolley, Olin Bradford 1963- *BiDrAPA 89*
Jolley, Smead 1902- *Ballpl 90*
Jolley, Weldon B. 1926- *St&PR 91*
Jollie, Tom *ODwPR 91*
Jolliet, Louis 1645-1700 *EncCRAm, WhNaAH, WorAlBi*
Jolliff, Carl R. 1926- *WhoAm 90*
Jolliff, David Everett 1951- *WhoEmL 91*
Jolliff, Donald Eugene 1930- *St&PR 91*
Jolliff, James W *BiDrAPA 89*
Jolliff, Robert A. 1943- *St&PR 91*
Jolliff, Robert Allen 1943- *WhoAm 90, WhoSSW 91, WhoWor 91*
Jolliffe, David J. *ODwPR 91*
Jolliffe, Richard W. 1927- *St&PR 91*
Jollivette, Cyrus Martin 1946- *WhoEmL 91, WhoSSW 91*
Jolly, Bruce Dwight 1943- *St&PR 91, WhoAm 90*
Jolly, Bruce Overstreet 1912- *WhoSSW 91*
Jolly, Charles Nelson 1942- *St&PR 91*
Jolly, Clayton Leon, III 1959- *WhoEmL 91*
Jolly, Daniel Ehs 1952- *WhoEmL 91, WhoWor 91*
Jolly, Dave 1924-1963 *Ballpl 90*
Jolly, E. Grady 1937- *WhoAm 90, WhoSSW 91*
Jolly, J. Mel 1942- *St&PR 91*
Jolly, John *WhNaAH*
Jolly, Judith Eleanor Apple 1939- *WhoSSW 91*
Jolly, Lynda S. 1957- *WhoSSW 91*
Jolly, Richard Carman 1947- *WhoSSW 91*
Jolly, Roy H. 1923- *St&PR 91*
Jolly, Wayne Travis 1940- *WhoAm 90, WhoWor 91*
Jolly, William Lee 1927- *WhoAm 90*
Jolsen, Ragnhild 1875-1908 *DcScanL, EncCoWW*
Jolson, Al *BioIn 16*
Jolson, Al 1886-1950 *OxCPMus, WorAlBi*
Jolson, Marvin Arnold 1922- *WhoAm 90*
Joly, Andre 1951- *St&PR 91*
Joly, Jean-Gil 1940- *WhoAm 90*
Joly, Jean Robert 1950- *WhoAm 90*
Joly, Rene D. 1926- *St&PR 91*
Joly, Simon 1952- *IntWWM 90*
Jomarron, Emilio A 1924- *BiDrAPA 89*
Jommersbach, Kristine 1955- *St&PR 91*
Jon *EncCoWW*
Jon Trausti *DcScanL*
Jon ur Vor 1917- *DcScanL*
Jonah *BioIn 16*
Jonaitis, Aldona 1948- *WhoAmA 91*
Jonaitis, Aldona Claire 1948- *WhoE 91*
Jonap, Lane 1923- *St&PR 91*
Jonas Hallgrimsson *DcScanL*
Jonas, Adolphe D *BiDrAPA 89*
Jonas, Alan Mark *BiDrAPA 89*
Jonas, Alfred Gordon 1950- *BiDrAPA 89*
Jonas, Ann *BioIn 16*
Jonas, Ann 1919- *WhoWrEP 89*
Jonas, Carl H *BiDrAPA 89*
Jonas, Charles Raper 1904-1988 *BioIn 16*
Jonas, David Lewis *BiDrAPA 89*
Jonas, Edward M. 1938- *St&PR 91*
Jonas, Emile 1827-1905 *OxCPMus*
Jonas, Fred Morgan 1948- *WhoEmL 91*
Jonas, Gary Fred 1945- *WhoE 91*
Jonas, George 1935- *ConAu 32NR*
Jonas, Gilbert 1930- *WhoE 91*
Jonas, Gordon Mark 1959- *WhoEmL 91*
Jonas, Harry S. 1926- *WhoAm 90*
Jonas, Hilda Klestadt 1913- *IntWWM 90*
Jonas, Jeffrey Martin 1953- *BiDrAPA 89*
Jonas, Jiri 1932- *WhoAm 90*
Jonas, Joan 1936- *BiDWomA, WhoAmA 91*
Jonas, Kathy Woolf 1957- *WhoEmL 91*
Jonas, Manfred 1927- *WhoAm 90*
Jonas, Murray 1924- *BiDrAPA 89*
Jonas, Peter 1946- *IntWWM 90*
Jonas, Saran 1931- *WhoAm 90*
Jonas, Stanislaw P 1933- *BiDrAPA 89*
Jonas, Steven 1936- *WhoAm 90*
Jonas, Trent Christopher 1968- *WhoEmL 91*
Jonassen, Gaylord D. 1932- *WhoE 91, WhoWor 91*
Jonassen, Hans Boegh 1912- *WhoAm 90*
Jonassen, James O. 1940- *WhoAm 90*
Jonassohn, Kurt 1920- *WhoAm 90*
Jonasson, Johannes Bjarni *DcScanL*
Jonatansson, Halldor 1932- *WhoWor 91*
Jonathan, Stephen Aaron 1953- *WhoE 91, WhoEmL 91*
Joncaire, Louis Thomas Chabert De 1670?-1739 *WhNaAH*
Jonckheer, Efrain 1910- *BioIn 16*
Jonckheere, Alan Mathew 1947- *WhoAm 90*
Jonckowski, David Lawrence 1948- *WhoEmL 91*
Jondahl, James Owen 1951- *WhoEmL 91*
Jondahl, Terri Elise 1959- *WhoAmW 91*
Jonec, Viliam Stefan *BiDrAPA 89*
Jones & Ginzel *WhoAmA 91*
Jones, Lady 1889-1981 *DcNaB 1981*
Jones, Mother 1830-1930 *BioIn 16*
Jones, Abbott C. 1934- *WhoAm 90*
Jones, Alan C. 1942- *WhoAm 90*
Jones, Alan Clifford 1938- *WhoSSW 91*
Jones, Alan Hedrick 1937- *WhoWrEP 89*
Jones, Alan Porter, Jr. 1925- *St&PR 91*
Jones, Alan Pryce- 1908- *BioIn 16*
Jones, Alan Richard 1939- *WhoAm 90*
Jones, Alan Roderick- *BioIn 16*
Jones, Albert Pearson 1907- *WhoAm 90, WhoSSW 91, WhoWor 91*
Jones, Albertus Eugene 1882-1957 *WhoAmA 91N*
Jones, Aled 1970- *PenDiMP*
Jones, Alex, and Friends *NewAgMG*
Jones, Alex S. 1946- *WhoAm 90*
Jones, Alexander Elvin 1920- *WhoAm 90*
Jones, Alfred D. 1814-1902 *AmLegL*
Jones, Alfred William, Jr. 1930- *St&PR 91*
Jones, Alfred Winslow 1900-1989 *BioIn 16*
Jones, Alice 1853-1933 *FemiCLE*
Jones, Alice Adams 1949- *BiDrAPA 89*
Jones, Alice C 1853-1933 *DcLB 92 [port]*
Jones, Alice Palache 1907-1989 *BioIn 16*
Jones, Allan 1907- *WorAlBi*
Jones, Allan 1908- *OxCPMus*
Jones, Allan Gwynne- 1892-1982 *DcNaB 1981*
Jones, Allen 1937- *BioIn 16, WhoWor 91*
Jones, Allen H. 1927- *St&PR 91*
Jones, Allen K. 1947- *St&PR 91*
Jones, Allen Lee 1959- *WhoEmL 91*
Jones, Allen Pedarre 1956- *WhoSSW 91*
Jones, Alun Arthur Gwynne 1919- *BioIn 16*

Jones, Amanda Theodocia 1835-1914 *FemiCLE*
Jones, Andrew Berrien 1961- *WhoEmL 91*
Jones, Andrew N. 1943- *ODwPR 91*
Jones, Andrew Nolan 1943- *WhoE 91*
Jones, Andrew Richard Johan 1932- *WhoE 91*
Jones, Andrew T. 1939- *St&PR 91*
Jones, Angela 1959- *WhoAmW 91*
Jones, Anita Lucille 1961- *WhoSSW 91*
Jones, Ann *BioIn 16*
Jones, Ann 1937- *WhoWrEP 89*
Jones, Annabel 1907-1988 *SmATA X*
Jones, Annabel Marie 1953- *WhoAmW 91*
Jones, Anne 1935- *BioIn 16*
Jones, Anne Elizabeth 1945- *WhoAmW 91, WhoSSW 91*
Jones, Anne Markey 1953- *WhoAmW 91*
Jones, Anne Patricia 1935- *WhoAm 90*
Jones, Annie Walton 1952- *WhoAmW 91*
Jones, Anthony Edward 1944- *WhoAm 90, WhoWor 91*
Jones, Archer 1926- *WhoAm 90*
Jones, Ardith Brocka 1940- *WhoAmW 91*
Jones, Arthur Curtis, III 1947- *WhoEmL 91*
Jones, Arthur Edwin, Jr. 1918- *WhoAm 90*
Jones, Arthur Frank 1946- *BiDrAPA 89*
Jones, Arthur L. 1938- *WhoAm 90*
Jones, Arthur McDonald, Sr. 1947- *St&PR 91, WhoAm 90*
Jones, Audrey Howard 1928- *WhoAmW 91, WhoE 91*
Jones, B. Calvin 1925- *ODwPR 91*
Jones, B. Paul 1931- *WhoAm 90*
Jones, Bailey Armstrong 1961- *WhoWrEP 89*
Jones, Barbara A. P. 1943- *WhoSSW 91*
Jones, Barbara Ann 1957- *WhoSSW 91*
Jones, Barbara Archer 1945- *WhoSSW 91*
Jones, Barbara Christine 1942- *WhoAmW 91*
Jones, Barbara Clifford 1916- *St&PR 91*
Jones, Barclay Gibbs 1960- *St&PR 91*
Jones, Barclay Gibbs, III 1960- *WhoE 91, WhoEmL 91, WhoWor 91*
Jones, Barnie Philip, Jr. 1947- *WhoSSW 91*
Jones, Barry 1963- *Ballpl 90*
Jones, Barry Kent 1955- *WhoEmL 91*
Jones, Beatrice 1953- *WhoAmW 91*
Jones, Ben *BioIn 16*
Jones, Ben 1912- *St&PR 91, WhoAm 90*
Jones, Ben 1924- *WhoWor 91*
Jones, Ben 1941- *WhoAm 90, WhoSSW 91*
Jones, Ben 1942- *WhoAmA 91*
Jones, Benjamin F. 1922- *St&PR 91*
Jones, Benjamin Franklin 1870-1935? *AmLegL*
Jones, Bennet Spencer 1939- *WhoSSW 91*
Jones, Bernadette Robinson 1962- *WhoSSW 91*
Jones, Bernard 1957- *WhoEmL 91, WhoSSW 91*
Jones, Bernice 1941- *WhoAmW 91*
Jones, Betty *IntWWM 90*
Jones, Betty Kate 1952- *WhoAmW 91*
Jones, Betty Millsaps 1940- *BioIn 16*
Jones, Beverly Ann Miller 1927- *WhoAmW 91*
Jones, Bill T. *BioIn 16*
Jones, Billie McCleary 1913- *WhoAmW 91*
Jones, Billy Emanuel *BiDrAPA 89*
Jones, Billy Ernest 1933- *WhoAm 90*
Jones, Billy Mac 1925- *WhoAm 90*
Jones, Birgit K S *BiDrAPA 89*
Jones, Bob 1889-1964 *Ballpl 90*
Jones, Bob, III *WhoAm 90*
Jones, Bob, Jr. 1911- *WhoAm 90*
Jones, Bob Gordon 1932- *WhoAm 90*
Jones, Bobby 1902-1971 *WorAlBi*
Jones, Bobby 1949- *Ballpl 90*
Jones, Bobette 1928- *St&PR 91*
Jones, Boyd T. 1932- *St&PR 91*
Jones, Bradley 1944-1989 *BioIn 16*
Jones, Bradley Mitchell 1952- *WhoEmL 91*
Jones, Branson Coltrane 1927- *St&PR 91*
Jones, Brenda Anne 1943- *WhoWor 91*
Jones, Brenda Lee 1944- *WhoSSW 91*
Jones, Brent Michael 1946- *WhoEmL 91*
Jones, Brereton C. 1939- *WhoAm 90, WhoSSW 91*
Jones, Brian W. 1938- *St&PR 91*
Jones, Bruce Alan *BiDrAPA 89*
Jones, Bruce E. 1942- *BioIn 16*
Jones, Bruce Hardin 1922- *St&PR 91*
Jones, Bruce Wayne 1947- *St&PR 91*
Jones, Buffalo 1844?- *BioIn 16*
Jones, Bunny Paine 1946- *WhoEmL 91*
Jones, C. Edward 1908- *St&PR 91*
Jones, C. J. 1844?- *BioIn 16*
Jones, C. J. 1943- *WhoAm 90*
Jones, C. Kevin 1963- *WhoSSW 91*
Jones, C. Mark 1935- *St&PR 91*
Jones, C. Paul 1927- *WhoAm 90*
Jones, C Robert 1932- *ConAu 129*
Jones, C. W. 1921- *WhoWor 91*
Jones, Calvin B 1934- *WhoAmA 91*
Jones, Calvin K. 1946- *St&PR 91*
Jones, Candy *BioIn 16, NewYTBS 90 [port]*
Jones, Candy 1925-1990 *ConAu 130, CurBio 90N*
Jones, Carl A. 1912- *St&PR 91*
Jones, Carl E., Jr. *WhoSSW 91*
Jones, Carleton Shaw 1942- *WhoAm 90*
Jones, Carol Ann 1950- *WhoSSW 91*
Jones, Carol Dawn 1935- *St&PR 91*
Jones, Carol Leigh 1949- *WhoWor 91*
Jones, Carol M. E. 1949- *WhoAmW 91*
Jones, Carole Widmaier 1941- *BiDrAPA 89*
Jones, Caroline Robinson *WhoAmW 91*
Jones, Carolyn 1933- *WorAlBi*
Jones, Carolyn Elizabeth 1931- *WhoAmW 91*
Jones, Carolyn Ellis 1928- *WhoAmW 91*
Jones, Carter R, Jr 1945- *WhoAmA 91*
Jones, Casey 1863-1900 *BioIn 16*
Jones, Catesby B. 1925- *St&PR 91*
Jones, Catesby Baytop *BioIn 16*
Jones, Catesby Brooke 1925- *WhoAm 90*
Jones, Catherine Ann 1936- *WhoAm 90*
Jones, Catherine Quailes 1967- *WhoEmL 91*
Jones, Cecil B 1928- *EncPaPR 91*
Jones, Charles *WhoAm 90*
Jones, Charles Davis 1917- *WhoE 91, WhoWor 91*
Jones, Charles Edward 1918- *WhoAm 90*
Jones, Charles Edward 1920- *WhoAm 90*
Jones, Charles Eric, Jr. 1957- *WhoEmL 91, WhoSSW 91*
Jones, Charles Frank 1927- *St&PR 91*
Jones, Charles Franklin 1911- *WhoAm 90*
Jones, Charles Hill, Jr. 1933- *St&PR 91, WhoAm 90*
Jones, Charles Irving 1943- *WhoAm 90*
Jones, Charles J. 1940- *WhoWor 91*
Jones, Charles M 1912- *ConAu 129*
Jones, Charles Oscar 1931- *WhoAm 90*
Jones, Charles R. *BioIn 16*
Jones, Charles Stansfeld 1886-1950 *EncO&P 3*
Jones, Charles Thomas 1951- *WhoEmL 91*
Jones, Charley 1850- *Ballpl 90*
Jones, Charlie *WhoAm 90*
Jones, Charlie 1876-1947 *Ballpl 90*
Jones, Charlott Ann 1927- *WhoAm 90, WhoAmA 91*
Jones, Chris *BioIn 16*
Jones, Christine Elizabeth 1959- *WhoAmW 91*
Jones, Christine M. 1929- *St&PR 91*
Jones, Christine Massey 1929- *WhoAm 90*
Jones, Christopher Austin 1961- *WhoSSW 91*
Jones, Christopher K. 1951- *St&PR 91*
Jones, Christopher Shaw 1940- *WhoWor 91*
Jones, Chuck *ConAu 129*
Jones, Chuck 1912- *BioIn 16*
Jones, Claiborne Stribling 1914- *WhoAm 90*
Jones, Clare Lynelle *IntWWM 90*
Jones, Clarence Joseph 1937- *WhoE 91*
Jones, Clarice Carmody 1906- *WhoAmW 91*
Jones, Claris Eugene, Jr. 1942- *WhoAm 90*
Jones, Clark David 1935- *St&PR 91*
Jones, Clarke Chastain 1948- *St&PR 91*
Jones, Claudella Archambeault 1938- *WhoAmW 91*
Jones, Claudia 1915?-1952 *EncAL*
Jones, Cleon 1942- *Ballpl 90*
Jones, Cleve *BioIn 16*
Jones, Clifford A. 1912- *St&PR 91*
Jones, Clifford Aaron 1912- *WhoAm 90, WhoWor 91*
Jones, Clifton Clyde 1922- *WhoAm 90*
Jones, Clifton S., Jr. 1934- *St&PR 91*
Jones, Clive B. 1941- *St&PR 91*
Jones, Clyde Adam 1924- *WhoE 91, WhoWor 91*
Jones, Clyde Wayne 1962- *WhoEmL 91*
Jones, Connie R. 1959- *WhoEmL 91*
Jones, Courtney Frederick 1940- *WhoAm 90*
Jones, Courtney John 1933- *WhoWor 91*
Jones, Cowboy 1874-1958 *Ballpl 90*
Jones, Coy Aaron 1944- *WhoSSW 91*
Jones, Craig R. 1946- *St&PR 91*
Jones, Craig Ward 1947- *WhoEmL 91*
Jones, Cranston Edward 1918- *WhoAm 90*
Jones, Curtis Harvey 1929- *St&PR 91*
Jones, Cynthia Cavenaugh 1938- *WhoE 91*
Jones, Cyril David 1922- *BiDrAPA 89*
Jones, D. Michael 1942- *WhoAm 90*
Jones, D. Paul, Jr. 1942- *WhoAm 90*
Jones, Dale C. 1948- *St&PR 91*
Jones, Dale Edwin 1948- *WhoE 91*
Jones, Dale P. 1936- *St&PR 91, WhoAm 90, WhoSSW 91*
Jones, Dalton 1943- *Ballpl 90*
Jones, Dan Lewis 1951- *WhoSSW 91*
Jones, Daniel Elven 1943- *WhoSSW 91*
Jones, Daniel Hare 1949- *WhoAm 90*
Jones, Daniel Jenkyn 1912- *IntWWM 90*
Jones, Daniel Webster 1839-1918 *BioIn 16*
Jones, Darby *DrBlPA 90*
Jones, Darlene Frances 1959- *WhoAmW 91*
Jones, Dave Mickel 1948- *WhoSSW 91*
Jones, David 1880-1972 *Ballpl 90*
Jones, David 1895-1974 *DcLB 100 [port], MajTwCW*
Jones, David 1938- *WorAlBi*
Jones, David A. 1931- *St&PR 91*
Jones, David Allen 1931- *WhoAm 90, WhoSSW 91*
Jones, David B. 1943- *St&PR 91, WhoAm 90*
Jones, David C. 1944- *St&PR 91*
Jones, David C. 1946- *WhoAm 90*
Jones, David Charles 1921- *WhoAm 90*
Jones, David Charles 1935- *WhoSSW 91*
Jones, David Eugene 1942- *WhoAm 90*
Jones, David Evan 1946- *IntWWM 90*
Jones, David Henry 1937- *St&PR 91*
Jones, David Hugh 1934- *WhoAm 90*
Jones, David John 1933- *St&PR 91*
Jones, David John 1934- *WhoAm 90*
Jones, David LaRue 1945- *WhoEmL 91*
Jones, David Lawrence *BiDrAPA 89*
Jones, David Lee 1948- *WhoAmA 91, WhoSSW 91*
Jones, David Lynn *WhoNeCM*
Jones, David Milton 1938- *WhoAm 90*
Jones, David Norris 1948- *St&PR 91*
Jones, David R 1934- *BiDrAPA 89*
Jones, David R. 1937- *St&PR 91, WhoAm 90, WhoSSW 91*
Jones, David Ray *BiDrAPA 89*
Jones, David Rhodes 1932- *WhoAm 90*
Jones, David Robert 1941- *WhoAm 90*
Jones, David W 1950- *ConAu 131*
Jones, David Wayne 1948- *WhoEmL 91*
Jones, Dean 1935- *WorAlBi*
Jones, Deborah 1954- *WhoE 91*
Jones, Debra Renee *BiDrAPA 89*
Jones, Della *IntWWM 90*
Jones, Denise Ann 1963- *WhoEmL 91*
Jones, Dennis M. 1938- *St&PR 91*
Jones, Dennis T *BiDrAPA 89*
Jones, Derry Wynn 1928- *WhoWor 91*
Jones, Dewey Michael 1953- *WhoEmL 91*
Jones, Dexter 1926- *WhoAmA 91N*
Jones, Diana Wynne 1934- *ChlLR 23 [port]*
Jones, Diane Catherine 1938- *WhoWrEP 89*
Jones, Dianne Powell 1963- *WhoAmW 91*
Jones, Don 1938- *WhoWrEP 89*
Jones, Donald Esplin 1931- *St&PR 91*
Jones, Donald George 1930- *WhoWor 91*
Jones, Donald H. 1937- *St&PR 91*
Jones, Donald K 1930- *BiDrAPA 89*
Jones, Donald Ray 1932- *WhoSSW 91*
Jones, Donald Richard 1930- *WhoAm 90*
Jones, Donald Richard, III 1952- *WhoEmL 91*
Jones, Donna Marilyn 1939- *WhoAmW 91*
Jones, Doris Elaine 1955- *WhoAmW 91*
Jones, Doris Mae 1938- *WhoAmW 91, WhoWor 91*
Jones, Doug 1929- *WhoAmA 91*
Jones, Doug 1957- *Ballpl 90*
Jones, Douglas 1949- *WhoHisp 91*
Jones, Douglas C. 1924- *BioIn 16*
Jones, Douglas Clyde 1924- *WhoAm 90, WhoWrEP 89*
Jones, Douglas Samuel 1964- *WhoSSW 91*
Jones, Duane 1937?-1988 *DrBlPA 90*
Jones, Duane L. 1937-1988 *BioIn 16*
Jones, Dwain L. 1927- *St&PR 91*
Jones, Dwight W. 1931- *St&PR 91*
Jones, E. B. C. 1893-1966 *FemiCLE*
Jones, E. Bradley 1927- *St&PR 91*
Jones, E. Fay 1921- *BioIn 16*
Jones, E. Stewart, Jr. 1941- *WhoE 91, WhoWor 91*
Jones, Earl 1925- *WhoAm 90*
Jones, Earl 1934- *WhoWor 91*
Jones, Earl Irven 1928- *St&PR 91*
Jones, Ebon Richard 1944- *WhoAm 90*
Jones, Ed 1912- *WhoAm 90*
Jones, Ed 1951- *WorAlBi*
Jones, Edgar Albert 1951- *WhoE 91*
Jones, Edith Augusta *WhoAm 90*
Jones, Edith Hollan 1949- *WhoAm 90, WhoAmW 91*
Jones, Edith Irby 1927- *WhoAmW 91*
Jones, Edloe Pendleton, III 1939- *WhoSSW 91*
Jones, Edna Ruth 1932- *WhoSSW 91*
Jones, Ednah *WhoWrEP 89*
Jones, Edward 1935- *WhoAm 90*
Jones, Edward A. 1939- *St&PR 91*
Jones, Edward Ames 1952- *WhoE 91, WhoEmL 91*
Jones, Edward Burne- 1833-1898 *BioIn 16*
Jones, Edward C. 1936- *St&PR 91*
Jones, Edward Claude 1948- *BiDrAPA 89*
Jones, Edward David 1920- *WhoAm 90*
Jones, Edward Douglass, III 1945- *WhoE 91*
Jones, Edward George 1939- *WhoAm 90*
Jones, Edward Lambert, Jr. 1936- *St&PR 91*
Jones, Edward Louis 1922- *WhoWor 91*
Jones, Edward Magruder 1928- *WhoAm 90*
Jones, Edward Marshall 1926- *WhoAm 90, WhoSSW 91*
Jones, Edward Powis 1919- *WhoAm 90, WhoAmA 91*
Jones, Edward R. *BioIn 16*
Jones, Edward Witker 1929- *WhoAm 90*
Jones, Edwin C., Jr. 1934- *WhoAm 90*
Jones, Edwin Carroll 1946- *BiDrAPA 89*
Jones, Edwin Lee, Jr. 1921- *WhoAm 90*
Jones, Edwin Michael 1916- *WhoAm 90*
Jones, Eiddon Lloyd 1904- *WhoAm 90*
Jones, Eldred D 1925- *ConAu 30NR*
Jones, Eldred Durosimi 1925- *WhoWor 91*
Jones, Eleanor Illston 1924- *WhoAmW 91*
Jones, Elin Denise 1955- *WhoE 91*
Jones, Elizabeth A B 1935- *WhoAmA 91*
Jones, Elizabeth Bartholomew 1924- *WhoWrEP 89*
Jones, Elizabeth Kennedy *St&PR 91*
Jones, Elizabeth M. *WhoAmW 91*
Jones, Elizabeth Nordwall 1934- *WhoAm 90*
Jones, Elizabeth Orton 1910- *AuBYP 90*
Jones, Elizabeth Winifred 1939- *WhoAmW 91*
Jones, Elmer Leroy 1935- *St&PR 91*
Jones, Elvin 1927- *BioIn 16*
Jones, Elwood L *BiDrAPA 89*
Jones, Elwyn 1929- *IntWWM 90*
Jones, Emily Strange 1919- *WhoAm 90*
Jones, Eric 1948- *IntWWM 90*
Jones, Eric Phillip 1947- *WhoEmL 91*
Jones, Erika Ziebarth 1955- *WhoAmW 91*
Jones, Ernest 1879-1958 *BioIn 16*
Jones, Ernest Donald 1943- *WhoSSW 91*
Jones, Ernest Edward 1931- *WhoAm 90, WhoSSW 91*
Jones, Ernest L. 1950- *St&PR 91*
Jones, Ethelene Dyer 1930- *WhoWrEP 89*
Jones, Eugene D. 1925- *St&PR 91*
Jones, Euine Fay 1921- *WhoAm 90*
Jones, Eva 1913- *ConAu 131*
Jones, Eva Joyce 1934- *WhoSSW 91*
Jones, Evan 1788-1873 *BioIn 16*
Jones, Evelyn Clementine 1921- *WhoAmW 91*
Jones, Evelyn Kirby *BiDrAPA 89*
Jones, Everett L 1915-1990 *ConAu 131*
Jones, F. E. 1907-1988 *AnObit 1988*
Jones, F. H. 1853- *AmLegL*
Jones, Farrell 1926- *WhoE 91*
Jones, Fay 1921- *BioIn 16*
Jones, Ferdinand *BioIn 16*
Jones, Ferdinand Taylor, Jr. 1932- *WhoAm 90*
Jones, Fielder 1874-1934 *Ballpl 90 [port]*
Jones, Frances Follin 1913- *WhoAm 90*
Jones, Frances Oconnell 1950- *St&PR 91*
Jones, Francis Clark 1933- *WhoWor 91*
Jones, Frank Albert 1900-1969 *MusmAFA*
Jones, Frank Cater 1925- *WhoAm 90*
Jones, Frank D 1924- *BiDrAPA 89*
Jones, Frank Edward 1917- *WhoAm 90*
Jones, Frank Pierce, Jr. 1929- *St&PR 91*
Jones, Frank R. 1945- *St&PR 91*
Jones, Frank Ray 1945- *WhoAm 90*
Jones, Frank Sidney *WhoAm 90*
Jones, Frank William 1915- *WhoAm 90*
Jones, Frank Wyman 1940- *St&PR 91, WhoAm 90*
Jones, Franklin Albert 1939- *EncO&P 3*
Jones, Franklin D 1933- *BiDrAPA 89*
Jones, Franklin Del 1935- *BiDrAPA 89, WhoE 91*
Jones, Franklin Reed 1921- *WhoAmA 91, WhoE 91*
Jones, Franklin Ross 1921- *WhoAm 90, WhoWor 91*
Jones, Franklyn *ODwPR 91*
Jones, Fred 1940- *BioIn 16*
Jones, Fred Eugene 1926- *WhoAm 90*
Jones, Fred Richard 1947- *WhoAm 90, WhoE 91*
Jones, Frederick Elwyn- 1909-1989 *BioIn 16*
Jones, Frederick George 1940- *WhoAmA 91*
Jones, Frederick Martin 1954- *WhoEmL 91*
Jones, G. Wayman *TwCCr&M 91*
Jones, G. William 1927- *WhoAm 90, WhoSSW 91*
Jones, Gail *WhoAmW 91*
Jones, Galen Everts 1928- *WhoAm 90, WhoE 91*
Jones, Garth Nelson 1925- *WhoAm 90*
Jones, Gary D. 1937- *WhoAm 90*
Jones, Gary Ralph 1947- *WhoEmL 91*
Jones, Gayl 1949- *FemiCLE, LiHiK, MajTwCW*

Jones, Gaynor Elizabeth Grace 1945- *IntWWM 90*
Jones, Gene Paul 1951- *WhoSSW 91*
Jones, Gene Stanley 1951- *WhoE 91*
Jones, Genene *BioIn 16*
Jones, Genia K. 1954- *WhoAmW 91*
Jones, Geoffrey John Charles 1927- *St&PR 91*
Jones, Geoffrey Melvill 1923- *WhoAm 90*
Jones, George *BioIn 16*, *WhoNeCM C [port]*
Jones, George 1811-1891 *BioIn 16*
Jones, George 1931- *ConMus 4 [port]*, *WhoAm 90*
Jones, George Bobby 1946- *WhoAmA 91*, *WhoE 91*
Jones, George Edward 1916- *WhoAm 90*
Jones, George Edward, III 1961- *WhoEmL 91*
Jones, George Eugene 1922- *St&PR 91*
Jones, George Henry 1942- *WhoAm 90*
Jones, George J. 1942- *St&PR 91*
Jones, George W., Jr. 1953- *WhoEmL 91*
Jones, Geraint 1917- *PenDiMP*
Jones, Geraint Iwan 1917- *IntWWM 90*
Jones, Gladys Hurt 1920- *WhoSSW 91*
Jones, Glenn Earle 1946- *WhoEmL 91*
Jones, Glenn R. 1930- *St&PR 91*
Jones, Gloria Ellen 1948- *WhoAmW 91*
Jones, Glyn 1942- *EncPaPR 91*
Jones, Gordon 1930- *Ballpl 90*
Jones, Gordon Edwin 1921- *WhoE 91*, *WhoWor 91*
Jones, Gordon Kempton 1946- *WhoEmL 91*
Jones, Gordon Wayne 1930- *St&PR 91*
Jones, Grace 1952- *DrBIPA 90*
Jones, Grace 1953?- *EncPR&S 89*
Jones, Grant 1922- *WhoSSW 91*
Jones, Grant D 1941- *ConAu 129*
Jones, Gregory Clifton 1953- *WhoSSW 91*
Jones, Gregory Wynn, Sr. 1948- *WhoAm 90*
Jones, Grey Wilbur 1950- *WhoEmL 91*
Jones, Grier Patterson 1942- *WhoSSW 91*
Jones, Gwenyth *WhoE 91*
Jones, Gwenyth Ellen 1952- *WhoAm 90*
Jones, Gwyn Owain 1917- *WhoWor 91*
Jones, Gwyneth 1936- *IntWWM 90*, *PenDiMP*, *WhoAm 90*, *WhoWor 91*
Jones, H Ivor 1924- *BiDrAPA 89*
Jones, Harold 1936- *IntWWM 90*
Jones, Harold Antony 1943- *St&PR 91*, *WhoAm 90*
Jones, Harold Calvert, II 1949- *WhoEmL 91*
Jones, Harold Foy 1930- *St&PR 91*
Jones, Harold Gilbert, Jr. 1927- *WhoAm 90*
Jones, Harold Henry 1940- *WhoAmA 91*
Jones, Harold Hudson, Jr. 1927- *WhoSSW 91*
Jones, Harold W *BiDrAPA 89*
Jones, Harry Gordon 1950- *WhoEmL 91*, *WhoSSW 91*
Jones, Harry Willmer 1911- *WhoAm 90*
Jones, Harvey Davis 1939- *WhoSSW 91*
Jones, Harvie Paul 1930- *WhoAm 90*
Jones, Helen Hinckley *AuBYP 90*
Jones, Henry 1912- *WhoAm 90*
Jones, Henry Arthur 1851-1929 *BioIn 16*
Jones, Henry Earl 1940- *WhoAm 90*
Jones, Henry Glenn 1957- *WhoEmL 91*
Jones, Henry V. 1938- *St&PR 91*
Jones, Henry Wanton 1925- *WhoAmA 91*
Jones, Herb, Jr 1923- *WhoAmA 91*
Jones, Herbert C. *BioIn 16*
Jones, Herbert M. *St&PR 91*
Jones, Herman Otto, Jr. 1933- *WhoSSW 91*
Jones, Hettie 1934- *AuBYP 90*, *BioIn 16*
Jones, Hilary Pollard 1863-1938 *BioIn 16*
Jones, Hilton Pressley, III 1948- *WhoWrEP 89*
Jones, Homer Walter, Jr. 1925- *WhoWor 91*
Jones, Horace C., II 1916- *St&PR 91*
Jones, Horace Charles 1910- *WhoAm 90*
Jones, Houston Gwynne 1924- *WhoSSW 91*
Jones, Howard E. 1935- *St&PR 91*
Jones, Howard Langworthy 1917- *WhoAm 90*
Jones, Howard Lenhardt 1957- *WhoEmL 91*
Jones, Howard St. Claire, Jr. 1921- *WhoAm 90*
Jones, Howard Wilbur, Jr. 1910- *WhoAm 90*
Jones, Howard William 1922- *WhoAmA 91*
Jones, Hugh H., Jr. 1930- *St&PR 91*
Jones, Hugh Henry, Jr. 1930- *WhoSSW 91*
Jones, Hugh McKittrick 1919- *WhoAm 90*
Jones, Hugh Richard 1914- *WhoAm 90*
Jones, Hugh Richard, Jr. 1938- *WhoAm 90*
Jones, Huw Leonard 1957- *WhoWor 91*
Jones, Ian Frederick 1952- *WhoSSW 91*
Jones, Ieuan *IntWWM 90*
Jones, Ieuan 1942- *EncPaPR 91*
Jones, Inigo 1573?-1652 *WorAlBi*
Jones, Ira Boyd 1851-1927 *AmLegL*
Jones, Irene Margaret 1965- *WhoAmW 91*
Jones, Isaac, Jr. 1933- *WhoE 91*
Jones, Isham 1894-1956 *BioIn 16*, *OxCPMus*
Jones, Isola 1949- *IntWWM 90*
Jones, J. Barrie 1946- *ConAu 131*
Jones, J. Benton, Jr. 1930- *WhoAm 90*
Jones, J David *BiDrAPA 89*
Jones, J. Dulin 1957- *WhoAmW 91*
Jones, J Farragut *ConAu 31NR*
Jones, J. Gilbert 1922- *WhoWor 91*
Jones, J. Kenley 1935- *WhoAm 90*
Jones, J. Kenneth 1945- *WhoAm 90*
Jones, J. Knox, Jr. 1929- *WhoAm 90*
Jones, J. Larry 1941- *St&PR 91*
Jones, J. Nicholas 1944- *WhoWrEP 89*
Jones, J. R. 1873-1936 *BioIn 16*
Jones, J Sidney *BiDrAPA 89*
Jones, Jack 1938- *WhoAm 90*, *WorAlBi*
Jones, Jack Alan 1948- *WhoWor 91*
Jones, Jack Benjamin 1944- *WhoAm 90*
Jones, Jack Dellis 1925- *WhoAm 90*
Jones, Jack Edward 1930- *WhoSSW 91*
Jones, Jack Parker 1924- *WhoAm 90*
Jones, Jack Payne 1928- *WhoWrEP 89*
Jones, Jack Raymond 1950- *WhoEmL 91*
Jones, Jack W. 1940- *WhoSSW 91*
Jones, Jacobine *WhoAmA 91N*
Jones, Jacqueline 1948- *WhoAm 90*
Jones, Jacqueline Laurette 1959- *WhoWrEP 89*
Jones, Jake 1920- *Ballpl 90*
Jones, James 1921-1977 *BioIn 16*, *MajTwCW*, *WorAlBi*
Jones, James 1931-1978 *WorAlBi*
Jones, James Alfred 1958- *WhoE 91*
Jones, James Arnold 1948- *WhoSSW 91*
Jones, James Arthur 1917- *WhoAm 90*
Jones, James Blake *BiDrAPA 89*
Jones, James Earl 1931- *DrBIPA 90*, *WhoAm 90*, *WorAlBi*
Jones, James Edward 1937- *WhoAmA 91*, *WhoE 91*
Jones, James Edward, Jr. 1924- *WhoAm 90*
Jones, James Fleming, Jr. 1947- *WhoAm 90*
Jones, James Haskell 1934- *WhoSSW 91*
Jones, James Joseph 1932- *St&PR 91*
Jones, James Kenna 1919- *WhoE 91*
Jones, James Landon, Jr. 1950- *St&PR 91*
Jones, James Martin 1942- *WhoSSW 91*
Jones, James McKernon 1924- *WhoSSW 91*
Jones, James Ogden 1935- *WhoSSW 91*
Jones, James Parker 1940- *WhoSSW 91*
Jones, James R. 1935- *St&PR 91*
Jones, James R. 1939- *WhoAm 90*
Jones, James Rees 1916- *WhoAm 90*
Jones, James Richard 1940- *WhoAm 90*
Jones, James Richard 1947- *WhoSSW 91*
Jones, James Robert 1934- *WhoAm 90*
Jones, James Thomas 1942- *WhoAm 90*
Jones, James Thomas 1949- *WhoEmL 91*, *WhoSSW 91*
Jones, James Thomas, Jr. 1946- *WhoSSW 91*
Jones, James Tilford 1927- *WhoSSW 91*
Jones, James William 1946- *St&PR 91*
Jones, James William, Jr. 1947- *WhoSSW 91*
Jones, Jamie Denise 1955- *WhoAmW 91*
Jones, Jane Wright 1948- *BiDrAPA 89*
Jones, Janet *BioIn 16*
Jones, Janet Hall 1945- *BiDrAPA 89*
Jones, Janet Sue 1946- *St&PR 91*
Jones, Janice Annette *BiDrAPA 89*
Jones, Janice Joanne 1953- *WhoAmW 91*
Jones, Janice Louise 1956- *WhoAmW 91*
Jones, Jean Melody 1949- *WhoAmW 91*
Jones, Jean R. 1919- *WhoWrEP 89*
Jones, Jean Souther 1937- *WhoSSW 91*
Jones, Jeanne Elise Dumas 1949- *WhoAmW 91*
Jones, Jeannie Cromeans 1949- *WhoAmW 91*
Jones, Jeff *BiDrAPA 89*
Jones, Jeff 1956- *Ballpl 90*
Jones, Jeffery Richard 1956- *WhoSSW 91*
Jones, Jeffrey 1947- *ConTFT 8 [port]*
Jones, Jeffrey Todd 1961- *WhoEmL 91*
Jones, Jeffrey Warren 1949- *WhoEmL 91*
Jones, Jenk, Jr. 1936- *WhoAm 90*
Jones, Jenkin Lloyd 1911- *WhoAm 90*, *WhoSSW 91*
Jones, Jennifer 1919- *BioAmW*, *BioIn 16*, *WhoAm 90*, *WorAlBi*
Jones, Jennifer Lee 1949- *St&PR 91*
Jones, Jennings Hinch 1913- *WhoAm 90*
Jones, Jerome B. 1947- *WhoAm 90*
Jones, Jerome Payne, Jr. 1951- *WhoEmL 91*
Jones, Jerral *BioIn 16*
Jones, Jerry Lynn 1933- *WhoAm 90*
Jones, Jerry Perkinson *BiDrAPA 89*
Jones, Jerry Travis *BiDrAPA 89*
Jones, Jerry Wayne 1945- *WhoSSW 91*
Jones, Jerve Maldwyn 1918- *WhoAm 90*
Jones, Jesse H. 1874-1956 *EncABHB 7 [port]*
Jones, Jesse Holman 1874-1956 *BiDrUSE 89*
Jones, Jim 1931-1978 *EncO&P 3*
Jones, Jim Dean 1942- *St&PR 91*
Jones, Jimmie LeRoy 1947- *WhoEmL 91*
Jones, Jimmy 1964- *Ballpl 90*
Jones, Jo 1911-1985 *BioIn 16*, *OxCPMus*
Jones, Joan Megan 1933- *WhoAmW 91*
Jones, Joe A. 1938- *St&PR 91*
Jones, Joe Frank, III 1949- *WhoSSW 91*
Jones, Joel Mackey 1937- *WhoAm 90*
Jones, John A. 1946- *St&PR 91*
Jones, John Arthur 1921- *WhoAm 90*
Jones, John Barclay, Jr. 1928- *WhoAm 90*
Jones, John Buttrick 1824-1876 *BioIn 16*
Jones, John Charles 1921- *WhoAm 90*
Jones, John D. 1849-1914 *AmLegL*
Jones, John E. 1934- *St&PR 91*
Jones, John Earl 1934- *WhoAm 90*
Jones, John Edwin 1934- *WhoE 91*
Jones, John Ellis 1941- *WhoSSW 91*
Jones, John Eric *BiDrAPA 89*
Jones, John Evan 1930- *WhoAm 90*
Jones, John F 1929- *ConAu 130*
Jones, John H., Jr. 1944- *St&PR 91*
Jones, John Harris 1922- *WhoAm 90*, *WhoWor 91*
Jones, John Harvey- *BioIn 16*
Jones, John J. *MajTwCW*
Jones, John Kipling 1944- *BiDrAPA 89*
Jones, John Lou 1929- *St&PR 91*, *WhoAm 90*
Jones, John Martin, Jr. 1928- *WhoAm 90*
Jones, John Paul 1747-1792 *BioIn 16*, *EncCRAm [port]*, *WorAlBi*
Jones, John Paul 1924- *WhoAmA 91*
Jones, John Paul 1935- *WhoSSW 91*
Jones, John Philip 1930- *ConAu 130*
Jones, John Walker 1943- *WhoSSW 91*
Jones, Johnie H. 1929- *WhoSSW 91*
Jones, Joie Pierce 1941- *WhoAm 90*
Jones, Jon Rex 1935- *St&PR 91*
Jones, Jonah 1909- *BioIn 16*, *DrBIPA 90*
Jones, Joseph Edward 1935- *WhoE 91*
Jones, Joseph Hayward 1924- *WhoE 91*
Jones, Joseph John 1909-1963 *WhoAmA 91N*
Jones, Joseph Louis 1923- *St&PR 91*, *WhoAm 90*
Jones, Joseph M 1933- *BiDrAPA 89*
Jones, Joseph Marion *NewYTBS 90*
Jones, Joseph Marion, Jr. 1908-1990 *ConAu 132*
Jones, Joseph Rudolph 1923-1985 *BioIn 16*
Jones, Joseph S. 1913- *St&PR 91*
Jones, Joseph Wayne 1936- *WhoAm 90*, *WhoSSW 91*
Jones, Juanita Nuttall 1912- *AuBYP 90*
Jones, Judith Decherd 1943- *WhoSSW 91*
Jones, Judith Lennon 1940- *WhoSSW 91*
Jones, Julia Faye Griggs 1945- *WhoAmW 91*
Jones, Julie 1935- *WhoAm 90*
Jones, K. C. *BioIn 16*
Jones, K. C. 1932- *WhoAm 90*
Jones, Karen Annette 1941- *WhoAmW 91*
Jones, Karl David *BiDrAPA 89*
Jones, Kasey 1952- *WhoE 91*
Jones, Kate Verrier 1946- *WhoWor 91*
Jones, Kathleen Ann 1964- *WhoAmW 91*
Jones, Kathleen Naefeli 1947- *WhoAmW 91*
Jones, Kathryn Cherie 1955- *WhoAmW 91*
Jones, Kathryn Kristy 1958- *WhoAmW 91*
Jones, Kathy Elaine 1958- *WhoAmW 91*
Jones, Keith Alden 1941- *WhoAm 90*
Jones, Kelly *BioIn 16*
Jones, Ken D 1930- *ConAu 31NR*
Jones, Kenneth A. 1950- *St&PR 91*
Jones, Kenneth Bruce 1953- *WhoSSW 91*
Jones, Kenneth D *BiDrAPA 89*
Jones, Kenneth R *BiDrAPA 89*
Jones, Kenneth T. 1963- *St&PR 91*
Jones, Kenneth Victor 1924- *IntWWM 90*
Jones, Kensinger 1919- *WhoAm 90*
Jones, Kent Albert 1953- *WhoE 91*
Jones, Kermit E. 1928- *St&PR 91*
Jones, Keva 1948- *DrBIPA 90*
Jones, Kevin Lamar 1960- *WhoEmL 91*
Jones, Kevin Raymond 1953- *WhoE 91*
Jones, Kevin Scott 1958- *WhoSSW 91*
Jones, Kiki *BioIn 16*
Jones, Klebert 1945- *BiDrAPA 89*
Jones, Kristin *WhoAmA 91*
Jones, L Ralph 1942- *BiDrAPA 89*
Jones, Lamar S. *St&PR 91*
Jones, Lana J. 1951- *St&PR 91*
Jones, Landon Y., Jr. *WhoAm 90*, *WhoE 91*
Jones, Larry Deland 1946- *WhoSSW 91*
Jones, Larry Hudson 1948- *WhoSSW 91*
Jones, Larry L. 1936- *St&PR 91*
Jones, Larry William 1940- *WhoAm 90*
Jones, Laura Ann 1963- *WhoAmW 91*
Jones, Laura Ann 1968- *WhoAmW 91*
Jones, Lauren 1942- *DrBIPA 90*
Jones, Lauren Evans 1952- *WhoEmL 91*
Jones, Lauren S. 1948- *WhoSSW 91*
Jones, Lauretta Marie 1953- *WhoAm 90*, *WhoAmW 91*
Jones, Laurie Lynn 1947- *WhoAm 90*
Jones, Laurie Pitts 1921- *WhoAm 90*
Jones, Lawassa B. 1938- *WhoAmW 91*
Jones, Lawrence Campbell 1913- *St&PR 91*
Jones, Lawrence D. 1928- *St&PR 91*
Jones, Lawrence J. 1870?-1955 *EncPaPR 91*
Jones, Lawrence Marion 1931- *St&PR 91*, *WhoAm 90*
Jones, Lawrence McCeney, Jr. 1924- *WhoAm 90*
Jones, Lawrence Neale 1921- *WhoAm 90*
Jones, Lawrence T. 1940- *St&PR 91*
Jones, Lawrence Tunnicliffe 1950- *WhoE 91*, *WhoEmL 91*, *WhoWor 91*
Jones, Lawrence William 1925- *WhoAm 90*
Jones, Lee Bennett 1938- *WhoAm 90*
Jones, Lee O. 1940- *St&PR 91*
Jones, Leeland Anthony 1946- *BiDrAPA 89*
Jones, Leighton W *BiDrAPA 89*
Jones, Leland Carson 1946- *St&PR 91*, *WhoSSW 91*
Jones, Lenny Karl 1952- *WhoE 91*
Jones, Leon 1936- *WhoE 91*
Jones, Leon Herbert, Jr. 1923- *WhoAm 90*, *WhoSSW 91*, *WhoWor 91*
Jones, Leon Ralph 1930- *St&PR 91*
Jones, Leonade Diane 1947- *St&PR 91*, *WhoAm 90*, *WhoE 91*, *WhoEmL 91*
Jones, Leroi *DrBIPA 90*, *MajTwCW*
Jones, LeRoi 1934- *BioIn 16*, *DcLB DS8 [port]*, *WhoAm 90*
Jones, Lesley Mitchell 1948- *St&PR 91*
Jones, Leslie A. 1939- *St&PR 91*
Jones, Leslie Alan 1939- *WhoAm 90*, *WhoE 91*
Jones, Leslie Julian 1910- *OxCPMus*
Jones, Lewanna 1955- *WhoAmW 91*
Jones, Lewis Bevel, III 1926- *WhoAm 90*, *WhoSSW 91*
Jones, Lewis Howard 1942- *WhoSSW 91*
Jones, Lillie Agnes 1910- *WhoAmW 91*
Jones, Lillie Madison 1942- *WhoAmW 91*
Jones, Lincoln, III 1933- *WhoAm 90*
Jones, Linda Louise 1946- *WhoAmW 91*
Jones, Linda R. Wolf 1943- *WhoAmW 91*
Jones, Linnea J 1933- *BiDrAPA 89*
Jones, Lisa 1961- *ConAu 130*
Jones, Lisa Day *BiDrAPA 89*
Jones, Lisa Ellen 1959- *WhoAmW 91*
Jones, Lisa Gail 1960- *WhoAmW 91*
Jones, Lisa Marie 1963- *WhoEmL 91*
Jones, Lisa Stievater *BiDrAPA 89*
Jones, Lloid 1908- *AuBYP 90*
Jones, Lloyd T. *BioIn 16*
Jones, Lloyd W. 1938- *St&PR 91*
Jones, Lois Mailou 1905- *BiDWomA*, *BioIn 16*, *WhoAmA 91*
Jones, Lois Swan 1927- *WhoAmA 91*
Jones, Lora Lee 1962- *WhoAmW 91*
Jones, Lorella Margaret 1943- *WhoAmW 91*
Jones, Loren Farquhar 1905- *WhoE 91*
Jones, Lou *BioIn 16*, *WhoAmA 91*
Jones, Louie Johnson 1856-1912? *BiDWomA*
Jones, Louis Alvin 1945- *WhoEmL 91*
Jones, Louis C. *NewYTBS 90*
Jones, Louis C 1908- *WhoAmA 91*
Jones, Lowell Robert 1931- *WhoE 91*
Jones, Loy David 1924- *St&PR 91*
Jones, Lyle Vincent 1924- *WhoAm 90*
Jones, Lynn 1953- *Ballpl 90*
Jones, Lynn Louise 1949- *WhoEmL 91*
Jones, Lynne Christine Heilenman 1956- *WhoEmL 91*
Jones, M. Colleen 1950- *WhoAmW 91*
Jones, M. Hume 1950- *St&PR 91*
Jones, Mack 1938- *Ballpl 90*
Jones, Madison Ralph, III 1938- *WhoSSW 91*
Jones, Madonna Mary 1940- *WhoAmW 91*
Jones, Mair Wyn 1957- *IntWWM 90*
Jones, Maitland, Jr. 1937- *WhoAm 90*
Jones, Malcolm Anthony 1947- *WhoWor 91*
Jones, Malinda Thiessen 1947- *WhoAmW 91*, *WhoEmL 91*, *WhoSSW 91*, *WhoWor 91*
Jones, Mallory 1939- *WhoWor 91*
Jones, Marc Edmund 1888- *EncO&P 3*
Jones, Marcia White 1959- *WhoSSW 91*
Jones, Margaret Bridwell 1939- *WhoWrEP 89*
Jones, Margaret Doris 1942- *WhoAmW 91*
Jones, Margaret Eileen Zee 1936- *WhoAm 90*

Jones, Margaret L. 1954- St&PR 91
Jones, Margaret Mary 1963- WhoAmW 91
Jones, Margie Irene 1951- WhoAmW 91
Jones, Margo 1912?-1955 BioIn 16, NotWoAT
Jones, Marguerite Jackson 1949- WhoAmW 91, WhoSSW 91, WhoWor 91
Jones, Marian Ilene 1929- WhoAmW 91, WhoWor 91
Jones, Marion Kittle 1927- BiDrAPA 89
Jones, Marion Patrick 1934- FemiCLE
Jones, Marjorie Gillette 1924- WhoWrEP 89
Jones, Marjory Maffitt 1931- WhoSSW 91
Jones, Mark E. 1939- St&PR 91
Jones, Mark Elmer, Jr. 1920- WhoAm 90
Jones, Mark Logan 1950- WhoE 91
Jones, Marnie 1948- WhoAm 90
Jones, Marshall W 1934- BiDrAPA 89
Jones, Martha Nyvall 1933- St&PR 91
Jones, Martin A. 1956- St&PR 91
Jones, Marva Jane Batson 1938- WhoSSW 91
Jones, Marvin Harold 1940- WhoAmA 91
Jones, Marvin Leroy 1937- St&PR 91
Jones, Mary FemiCLE
Jones, Mary 1830-1930 WorAlBi
Jones, Mary Alice 1898?-1980 AuBYP 90
Jones, Mary Alice 1965- WhoAmW 91
Jones, Mary Cover 1896-1987 BioIn 16
Jones, Mary Dailey WhoWor 91
Jones, Mary Elizabeth BioIn 16, WhoSSW 91
Jones, Mary Ellen 1922- WhoAm 90, WhoAmW 91
Jones, Mary Harris 1830-1930 BioIn 16
Jones, Mary Harris 1836-1930 EncAL
Jones, Mary Holmes 1921- WhoWrEP 89
Jones, Mary Letitia 1865-1946 BioIn 16
Jones, Mary Louise Helfrich 1944- WhoAmW 91
Jones, Mary Louise Jordan 1916- WhoSSW 91
Jones, Mary Virginia 1931- St&PR 91
Jones, Mason 1919- WhoAm 90
Jones, Mattie Saunders 1942- WhoSSW 91
Jones, Melda Renee 1954- WhoSSW 91
Jones, Melvin R. 1934- ODwPR 91
Jones, Mervyn BioIn 16
Jones, Mervyn 1922- MajTwCW
Jones, Michael NewAgMG
Jones, Michael Butler 1946- WhoAmA 91
Jones, Michael Calhoun 1936- St&PR 91
Jones, Michael H. 1947- St&PR 91
Jones, Michael J. 1939- St&PR 91
Jones, Michael Joseph, Jr. 1963- WhoE 91
Jones, Michael Robert 1953- IntWWM 90
Jones, Mick 1944- BioIn 16
Jones, Mick 1956- BioIn 16
Jones, Mike 1959- Ballpl 90
Jones, Milnor 1925- WhoSSW 91, WhoWor 91
Jones, Milo Corey BiDrAPA 89
Jones, Milton Wakefield 1930- WhoAm 90
Jones, Monika 1949- WhoAmW 91
Jones, Murray WhoAmA 91N
Jones, Nancy C. 1942- WhoAmW 91
Jones, Nancy Gex 1952- WhoWor 91
Jones, Nancy Joy 1939- WhoWrEP 89
Jones, Nancy Langdon 1939- WhoAmW 91
Jones, Nancy Lynne 1938- WhoAmW 91
Jones, Nancy Scott 1951- WhoSSW 91
Jones, Nathaniel B., IV 1945- WhoEmL 91
Jones, Nathaniel Raphael 1926- WhoAm 90
Jones, Neil Ford 1948- WhoWor 91
Jones, Nell 1879-1981 BiDWomA
Jones, Nina Williams 1936- WhoSSW 91
Jones, Nippy 1925- Ballpl 90
Jones, Noel K. 1932- WhoSSW 91
Jones, Norma Henry 1929- WhoWrEP 89
Jones, Norma L WhoAmA 91
Jones, Norma Louise WhoAm 90
Jones, Norman M. 1930- St&PR 91, WhoAm 90
Jones, Norman T. 1936- St&PR 91
Jones, Norman Thomas 1936- WhoAm 90
Jones, O. K., III 1942- WhoAm 90
Jones, Odell 1953- Ballpl 90
Jones, Oliver 1821-1899 DcCanB 12
Jones, Oliver Hastings 1922- WhoAm 90
Jones, Olivet Benbow 1954- WhoAmW 91
Jones, Orlo D. 1938- St&PR 91
Jones, Orlo Dow 1938- WhoAm 90
Jones, Oscar 1879-1946 Ballpl 90
Jones, Otho Eli 1936- WhoE 91
Jones, Owen 1809-1874 BioIn 16, PenDiDA 89
Jones, Owen Craven, Jr. 1936- WhoAm 90
Jones, Owen John, III 1949- WhoE 91, WhoEmL 91
Jones, Pamela Lorraine 1956- WhoWrEP 89
Jones, Parry 1891-1963 PenDiMP
Jones, Patricia Ann 1953- WhoSSW 91
Jones, Patricia H. 1938- WhoSSW 91
Jones, Patricia Pearce 1947- WhoAmW 91
Jones, Patrick S. 1944- St&PR 91
Jones, Patsy D. 1926- WhoAmW 91
Jones, Patty Sue 1949- WhoAmA 91
Jones, Paul BioIn 16
Jones, Paul A 1906- BiDrAPA 89
Jones, Paul C. 1938- St&PR 91
Jones, Paul Davis 1940- WhoE 91
Jones, Paul H. 1928- St&PR 91
Jones, Paul M. 1950- WhoWrEP 89
Jones, Percy 1899-1979 Ballpl 90
Jones, Percy Coleman 1947- WhoSSW 91
Jones, Percy E. BioIn 16
Jones, Perry 1936- IntWWM 90
Jones, Peter 1802-1856 WhNaAH
Jones, Peter 1941- WhoWor 91
Jones, Peter A. 1955- St&PR 91
Jones, Peter d'Alroy 1931- WhoAm 90, WhoWrEP 89
Jones, Peter David 1948- WhoE 91
Jones, Peter Norman 1940- IntWWM 90
Jones, Peter T. BioIn 16
Jones, Philip 1928- PenDiMP
Jones, Philip Alan 1944- WhoAm 90
Jones, Philip Burnell Rees 1951- IntWWM 90
Jones, Philip Davis 1932- WhoAm 90
Jones, Philip Howard 1937- WhoAm 90
Jones, Philip Mark 1928- IntWWM 90
Jones, Philip Newton 1924- WhoAm 90
Jones, Philip S. 1943- St&PR 91
Jones, Phillip Clarence 1942- St&PR 91
Jones, Phillip Sanford 1912- WhoAm 90
Jones, Philly Joe 1923-1985 BioIn 16, OxCPMus
Jones, Phyllis Atkins 1949- WhoSSW 91
Jones, Phyllis Edith 1924- WhoAm 90
Jones, Pirkle 1914- WhoAm 90, WhoAmA 91
Jones, Pythias Damon 1951- BiDrAPA 89
Jones, Quincy BioIn 16, NewYTBS 90 [port]
Jones, Quincy 1933- ConTFT 8, DrBlPA 90, EncPR&S 89, News 90 [port], OxCPMus, WhoAm 90, WorAlBi
Jones, R J 1934- BiDrAPA 89
Jones, R Terry BiDrAPA 89
Jones, Rachel M. 1929- WhoAmW 91, WhoWor 91
Jones, Ralph ODwPR 91
Jones, Randall Sidney 1955- WhoWor 91
Jones, Randy 1950- Ballpl 90
Jones, Ray Glenn, Jr. 1929- WhoSSW 91
Jones, Ray Neill 1953- WhoSSW 91
Jones, Rayford Scott 1936- WhoAm 90
Jones, Raymond Edward, Jr. 1927- WhoAm 90
Jones, Raymond Harold 1926- St&PR 91
Jones, Raymond Moylan 1942- WhoE 91
Jones, Raymond Robert 1928- St&PR 91
Jones, Rebecca Alvina Patronis 1952- WhoEmL 91
Jones, Rebecca Ann 1946- WhoAmW 91
Jones, Rebecca C. 1947- WhoWrEP 89
Jones, Rebecca Kay 1963- WhoEmL 91
Jones, Rebecca M BiDrAPA 89
Jones, Reese T 1932- BiDrAPA 89
Jones, Regina Nickerson 1942- WhoAm 90, WhoAmW 91
Jones, Reginald Lorrin 1951- WhoEmL 91
Jones, Renae Spencer 1960- WhoAmW 91
Jones, Renee Kauerauf 1949- WhoAmW 91, WhoEmL 91, WhoSSW 91, WhoWor 91
Jones, Retha Simmons 1945- WhoE 91
Jones, Richard ODwPR 91
Jones, Richard 1790-1855 BioIn 16
Jones, Richard 1904-1989 BioIn 16
Jones, Richard A. 1947- St&PR 91
Jones, Richard Allen 1931- WhoE 91
Jones, Richard Andrew 1953- WhoWrEP 89
Jones, Richard Cyrus 1928- WhoAm 90, WhoWor 91
Jones, Richard Eugene 1937- St&PR 91
Jones, Richard Hutton 1914- WhoAm 90
Jones, Richard L. 1923- WhoAm 90
Jones, Richard Lee 1961- WhoEmL 91
Jones, Richard M. 1889-1945 OxCPMus
Jones, Richard M. 1926- St&PR 91, WhoAm 90, WhoSSW 91
Jones, Richard Michael 1952- WhoEmL 91
Jones, Richard Norman 1913- WhoAm 90
Jones, Richard P. 1942- WhoWrEP 89
Jones, Richard T. 1946- St&PR 91
Jones, Richard Theodore 1929- WhoAm 90
Jones, Richard Victor 1929- WhoAm 90
Jones, Richard Wallace 1929- WhoAm 90, WhoWor 91
Jones, Richmond Addison 1937- WhoWor 91
Jones, Rick 1955- Ballpl 90
Jones, Rickie Lee BioIn 16
Jones, Rickie Lee 1954- ConMus 4 [port], CurBio 90 [port], EncPR&S 89
Jones, Rita Ann 1947- WhoSSW 91
Jones, Robert Allen 1949- WhoSSW 91
Jones, Robert Allison 1935- St&PR 91
Jones, Robert Alonzo 1937- WhoWor 91
Jones, Robert Anthony 1957- WhoEmL 91
Jones, Robert Buckner BiDrAPA 89
Jones, Robert C. 1943- WhoAm 90
Jones, Robert Clinton, Jr. 1945- WhoSSW 91
Jones, Robert D. ODwPR 91
Jones, Robert D 1925- BiDrAPA 89
Jones, Robert Doyne 1933- WhoAm 90
Jones, Robert Earl 1900- DrBlPA 90
Jones, Robert Edward 1927- WhoAm 90
Jones, Robert Emmet 1928- WhoAm 90
Jones, Robert Fredrick 1930- WhoWrEP 89
Jones, Robert G 1936- DrBlPA 90
Jones, Robert Gean 1925- WhoAm 90
Jones, Robert H. 1925- St&PR 91
Jones, Robert Henry 1935- WhoAm 90
Jones, Robert Huhn 1927- WhoAm 90
Jones, Robert Keith 1949- WhoEmL 91
Jones, Robert Kemp 1924- BiDrAPA 89
Jones, Robert Lawton 1925- WhoAm 90
Jones, Robert Lee 1920- WhoAm 90
Jones, Robert Lyle 1959- WhoEmL 91
Jones, Robert Marion 1919- WhoAm 90
Jones, Robert McKittrick 1933- St&PR 91
Jones, Robert Mims 1937- WhoAm 90
Jones, Robert P. 1955- ODwPR 91
Jones, Robert Penfield 1917- St&PR 91
Jones, Robert Roland, Jr. 1942- WhoSSW 91, WhoWor 91
Jones, Robert Russell 1927- WhoAm 90
Jones, Robert S 1939- BiDrAPA 89
Jones, Robert Sinclair 1929- St&PR 91
Jones, Robert T. 1939- BioIn 16
Jones, Robert Thomas 1910- WhoAm 90
Jones, Robert Thomas 1947- WhoEmL 91
Jones, Robert Trent 1906- BioIn 16
Jones, Robert Trent, Jr. 1939- WhoAm 90
Jones, Robert Trent, Sr. 1906- WhoAm 90
Jones, Robert V. 1934- ODwPR 91
Jones, Roberts Titus 1940- WhoAm 90
Jones, Robin 1949- WhoEmL 91
Jones, Robin Allen 1954- WhoSSW 91
Jones, Robin Arbuckle 1962- WhoAmW 91
Jones, Rocky WhoWrEP 89
Jones, Roddis Stewart 1930- WhoWor 91
Jones, Roderick Cashman 1946- IntWWM 90
Jones, Rodney Anthony 1961- WhoSSW 91
Jones, Rodney W. 1943- ConAu 33NR
Jones, Roger Alan 1947- WhoE 91
Jones, Roger C. 1947- St&PR 91
Jones, Roger Clyde 1919- WhoAm 90, WhoWor 91
Jones, Roger W. 1920- St&PR 91
Jones, Roger Walton 1953- WhoWrEP 89
Jones, Roland Leo 1932- IntWWM 90
Jones, Ron 1964- Ballpl 90
Jones, Ronald Bamber 1952- WhoSSW 91
Jones, Ronald D. 1948- St&PR 91
Jones, Ronald David 1930- WhoAm 90
Jones, Ronald G. 1935- St&PR 91
Jones, Ronald Lee, Jr 1942- WhoAmA 91
Jones, Ronald Lloyd 1938- St&PR 91
Jones, Ronald Neu 1939- St&PR 91
Jones, Ronald Vance 1946- WhoEmL 91
Jones, Ronald Warren 1952- WhoAmA 91
Jones, Ronald Winthrop 1931- WhoE 91
Jones, Ronald Woodbridge 1932- St&PR 91
Jones, Roosevelt, Jr. 1959- St&PR 91
Jones, Rosie BioIn 16
Jones, Ross Tilghman BiDrAPA 89
Jones, Roxanne Harper 1928- WhoAmW 91, WhoE 91
Jones, Roy BioIn 16
Jones, Royal Maurice 1937- WhoSSW 91
Jones, Ruppert 1955- Ballpl 90
Jones, Russel C. 1935- BioIn 16
Jones, Russel Cameron 1935- WhoAm 90, WhoE 91, WhoWor 91
Jones, Russell Eugene 1928- WhoWrEP 89
Jones, Russell H. 1944- St&PR 91
Jones, Russell Lane 1962- WhoSSW 91
Jones, Ruthe Blalock 1939- WhoAmA 91
Jones, Sad Sam 1892-1966 Ballpl 90
Jones, Sally Daviess Pickrell 1923- WhoAmW 91, WhoE 91, WhoWor 91
Jones, Sam 1925-1971 Ballpl 90
Jones, Sam Willis, Jr. 1942- St&PR 91
Jones, Samuel 1935- IntWWM 90, WhoAm 90
Jones, Samuel M. 1936- St&PR 91
Jones, Sandra 1937- ConAu 132
Jones, Sandra LaVern 1948- WhoE 91
Jones, Sanford Logan, Jr. 1958- BiDrAPA 89
Jones, Sarah BiDEWW, FemiCLE
Jones, Sarah J. 1940- St&PR 91
Jones, Sarah Lynn 1952- BiDrAPA 89
Jones, Sarah Sheffield 1948- WhoEmL 91
Jones, Scott Dean BiDrAPA 89
Jones, Seaborn Gustavus, Jr. 1942- WhoWrEP 89
Jones, Shalley Ann Matthews 1954- WhoEmL 91
Jones, Shari L. BioIn 16
Jones, Sharon Gibson 1954- WhoEmL 91
Jones, Sharon Kay 1952- WhoSSW 91
Jones, Sharon Lester 1944- WhoAmW 91
Jones, Shelby L. 1936- St&PR 91
Jones, Sheldon 1922- Ballpl 90
Jones, Sheliah Jeffcoat 1953- WhoEmL 91
Jones, Sherman 1935- Ballpl 90
Jones, Sherman J. 1946- WhoAm 90
Jones, Sheryl Cassandra 1947- WhoAmW 91
Jones, Shields Landon 1901- MusmAFA
Jones, Shirley BioIn 16, WhoAm 90
Jones, Shirley 1934- WorAlBi
Jones, Sidney 1861-1946 OxCPMus
Jones, Sidney Eugene 1936- WhoE 91
Jones, Sidney Francis, Jr. 1937- St&PR 91
Jones, Sidney Lewis 1933- WhoAm 90
Jones, Sisseretta 1869-1933 DrBlPA 90
Jones, Sissieretta 1868-1933 PenDiMP
Jones, Sissieretta 1870-1933 BioIn 16
Jones, Slim 1913-1938 Ballpl 90
Jones, Sonia BioIn 16
Jones, Spike 1911-1965 ConMus 5, OxCPMus, WorAlBi
Jones, Stacy V. 1894-1989 BioIn 16
Jones, Stanley Boyd 1938- WhoAm 90
Jones, Stanley Ernest 1933- WhoE 91
Jones, Stanley Houston 1935- St&PR 91
Jones, Stephan Lowry 1935- St&PR 91
Jones, Stephen 1940- WhoSSW 91, WhoWor 91
Jones, Stephen Craig 1952- WhoEmL 91
Jones, Stephen Dunbar 1946- St&PR 91
Jones, Stephen Graf 1947- IntWWM 90
Jones, Stephen Lane 1945- WhoSSW 91
Jones, Stephen Maxwell 1944- WhoSSW 91
Jones, Stephen Powell 1941- WhoE 91
Jones, Steve 1948- St&PR 91
Jones, Steven E. BioIn 16
Jones, Steven G. 1949- St&PR 91
Jones, Steven Gibb 1949- WhoEmL 91, WhoSSW 91
Jones, Steven Marlin 1942- St&PR 91
Jones, Stormie BioIn 16
Jones, Stuart A. 1947- WhoE 91
Jones, Susan 1864?-1926 FemiCLE
Jones, Susan Ann 1959- WhoAmW 91
Jones, Susan Dorfman 1939- WhoAmW 91, WhoE 91, WhoWor 91
Jones, Susan Emily 1948- WhoAm 90
Jones, Suzanne Whitmore 1950- WhoSSW 91
Jones, Sydney Tucker, III 1944- St&PR 91
Jones, T. Gordon BioIn 16
Jones, Tad W. WhoAm 90
Jones, Terri 1962- BioIn 16
Jones, Terry 1942- BioIn 16, WhoAm 90
Jones, Terry Bruce 1944- WhoSSW 91
Jones, Terry L. 1933- St&PR 91
Jones, Thad BioIn 16
Jones, Thad 1923-1986 DrBlPA 90, OxCPMus
Jones, Thatcher C. BioIn 16
Jones, Theodore Joseph 1938- WhoAmA 91
Jones, Theodore Lawrence 1920- WhoAm 90, WhoWor 91
Jones, Theodore William 1924- St&PR 91, WhoAm 90
Jones, Thomas 1870-1955 BioIn 16
Jones, Thomas Carlyle 1912- WhoAm 90
Jones, Thomas Charles 1934- St&PR 91
Jones, Thomas Edward 1948- WhoEmL 91
Jones, Thomas Goode 1844-1914 AmLegL
Jones, Thomas H. 1916- St&PR 91
Jones, Thomas J. BioIn 16
Jones, Thomas Lee 1944- ODwPR 91
Jones, Thomas N. 1952- WhoSSW 91
Jones, Thomas Neal 1930- WhoAm 90
Jones, Thomas Neil 1945- St&PR 91
Jones, Thomas Robert 1949- BiDrAPA 89
Jones, Thomas Robert 1950- WhoEmL 91, WhoWor 91
Jones, Thomas S. 1845- BioIn 16
Jones, Thomas Victor 1920- BioIn 16, WhoAm 90
Jones, Thomas Walter 1945- WhoAm 90
Jones, Thomas William 1942- WhoAmA 91
Jones, Thornton Keith 1923- WhoWor 91
Jones, Tim Wynne- BioIn 16
Jones, Timothy Dale 1949- WhoWrEP 89
Jones, Tobin Jack 1959- BiDrAPA 89
Jones, Tom 1877-1923 Ballpl 90
Jones, Tom 1940- BioIn 16, EncPR&S 89, OxCPMus, WhoAm 90, WorAlBi
Jones, Tommy Lee 1946- WhoAm 90, WorAlBi
Jones, Tony Everett 1920- WhoAm 90
Jones, Tony Ray- 1941-1972 BioIn 16
Jones, Tonya Gale 1948- WhoAmW 91
Jones, Tracey Kirk, Jr. 1917- WhoAm 90
Jones, Tracy 1961- Ballpl 90

Jones, Trevor Alfred Charles 1949- IntWWM 90
Jones, Trevor Owen 1930- WhoAm 90, WhoWor 91
Jones, Tristan 1924- BioIn 16
Jones, Valerie Kaye 1956- WhoAmW 91, WhoEmL 91
Jones, Vaughn Paul 1947- WhoSSW 91
Jones, Veda Rae 1948- WhoWrEP 89
Jones, Vernon T. 1929- St&PR 91
Jones, Vernon Thomas 1929- WhoAm 90, WhoSSW 91
Jones, Vicki Sue 1957- WhoWrEP 89
Jones, Victoria Lynn 1955- WhoAmW 91
Jones, Vincent Starbuck 1906- WhoAm 90
Jones, Virgil Carrington 1906- WhoWrEP 89
Jones, Vivian Dianne BiDrAPA 89
Jones, Volney Hurt 1903-1982 BioIn 16
Jones, W J 1932- ConAu 129
Jones, W Mitchell, Jr. 1931- BiDrAPA 89
Jones, W. Rhys 1894-1990 BioIn 16
Jones, W.T. 1914- St&PR 91
Jones, W. Thomas 1937- WhoSSW 91
Jones, Waldo Clyde, Jr. 1943- WhoSSW 91
Jones, Walk Claridge, III 1933- WhoSSW 91
Jones, Walter Beaman 1913- WhoAm 90, WhoSSW 91
Jones, Walter Charles 1959- WhoSSW 91
Jones, Walter Edward 1951- WhoEmL 91, WhoSSW 91
Jones, Walter Harrison 1922- WhoAm 90, WhoWor 91
Jones, Walter Jennings 1865-1935 DcScB S2
Jones, Walter Leon 1955- WhoSSW 91, WhoWor 91
Jones, Walton Linton 1918- WhoAm 90
Jones, Wanda 1923- BioIn 16
Jones, Wanda Faye 1949- WhoAmW 91
Jones, Warren 1951- IntWWM 90
Jones, Warren Casey, Jr. 1942- WhoSSW 91
Jones, Warren David 1914- WhoAm 90
Jones, Warren L 1924- BiDrAPA 89
Jones, Warren LeRoy 1895- WhoAm 90
Jones, Warren Rentz 1957- St&PR 91
Jones, Warren Thomas 1942- WhoAm 90
Jones, Warren W. 1937- ODwPR 91
Jones, Wayne Charles 1942- BiDrAPA 89
Jones, Wendell Willis 1941- WhoSSW 91
Jones, Weyman 1928- AuBYP 90, SmATA 11AS [port]
Jones, Weyman B. 1928- ODwPR 91
Jones, Weyman Beckett 1928- St&PR 91
Jones, Wilbur Stone 1945- St&PR 91
Jones, Wiley N. St&PR 91
Jones, Willa Saunders 1901-1979 EarBlAP
Jones, William 1760-1831 BiDrUSE 89
Jones, William A 1940- BiDrAPA 89
Jones, William Alfred 1817-1900 BioIn 16
Jones, William Allen 1941- St&PR 91, WhoAm 90
Jones, William Arnold 1924- WhoAm 90
Jones, William Augustus, Jr. 1927- WhoAm 90
Jones, William Benjamin, Jr. 1924- WhoAm 90
Jones, William Bowdoin 1928- WhoAm 90
Jones, William Catron 1926- WhoAm 90
Jones, William Claude 1818?- AmLegL
Jones, William Ernest 1936- WhoAm 90
Jones, William Eugene St&PR 91
Jones, William Frank 1951- WhoEmL 91
Jones, William H. ODwPR 91
Jones, William Henry, Jr. 1919- St&PR 91
Jones, William James 1957- WhoEmL 91
Jones, William John 1926- IntWWM 90
Jones, William Kenefick 1916- WhoAm 90
Jones, William Kenneth 1930- WhoAm 90
Jones, William Kinzy 1946- WhoSSW 91
Jones, William Leicester 1906- St&PR 91
Jones, William Maurice 1930- WhoAm 90
Jones, William McKendrey 1927- WhoAm 90
Jones, William N. 1926- St&PR 91
Jones, William Orville 1910- WhoAm 90
Jones, William Randall 1955- WhoAm 90, WhoEmL 91
Jones, William Rex 1922- WhoAm 90
Jones, William Riley, Jr. 1947- WhoEmL 91, WhoSSW 91
Jones, William Wood, Jr. 1954- St&PR 91
Jones, Willie 1925-1983 Ballpl 90
Jones, Willis B., Jr. 1936- St&PR 91
Jones, Winona Nigels 1928- WhoAmW 91, WhoSSW 91
Jones, Winson 1925- St&PR 91
Jones, Wyman H. 1929- WhoAm 90
Jones, Wynford Lyn 1948- IntWWM 90
Jones, Yasmin Marie 1958- WhoEmL 91
Jones-Mixon, Robyn Ann 1944- St&PR 91
Jones-Smith, Jayne E. 1952- WhoAmW 91
Jones-Wilson, Faustine Clarisse 1927- WhoAm 90
Jones y Diez Arguelles, Gaston Roberto 1910- WhoWor 91
Joneson, Michael G. 1946- St&PR 91
Joneston, Micheal 1950- WhoWor 91
Jong, Allan Young 1934- BiDrAPA 89
Jong, Anthony 1938- WhoAm 90
Jong, Erica BioIn 16
Jong, Erica 1942- FemiCLE, MajTwCW, WorAlBi
Jong, Erica Mann 1942- WhoAm 90, WhoAmW 91, WhoWor 91, WhoWrEP 89
Jong, Patrick Edward de Josselin de 1922- BioIn 16
Jonge, Nicolaas Marinus de 1920- BioIn 16
Jongejans, George ConTFT 8
Jongkind, Johan Barthold 1819-1891 IntDcAA 90
Jonish, Arley Duane 1927- WhoAm 90
Jonish, James Edward 1941- WhoAm 90
Jonker, Mary BioIn 16
Jonker, Pieter 1937- WhoWor 91
Jonker, Pieter 1950- WhoWor 91
Jonker, Robert James 1960- WhoEmL 91
Jonkers, Martinus Karel Petrus 1924- WhoWor 91
Jonkheer Testa, Andreas Lodewyk F M 1942- WhoWor 91
Jonkman, Hans 1925- WhoWor 91
Jonkouski, Jill Ellen WhoAmW 91
Jonnalagadda, Rao 1941- BiDrAPA 89
Jonnard, Bubber 1897-1977 Ballpl 90
Jonnard, Claude 1897-1959 Ballpl 90
Jonquieres, T. BiDWomA
Jonsdottir, Thorgunnur 1948- WhoWor 91
Jonsen, Albert R. 1931- WhoAm 90
Jonsen, Helen 1957- WhoE 91
Jonsgarden, Kenneth Bo 1946- WhoWor 91
Jonson, Mr. 1854- EncO&P 3
Jonson, Ben 1572-1637 EncPaPR 91, WorAlBi
Jonson, Ben 1573?-1637 BioIn 16
Jonson, Guy IntWWM 90
Jonson, J. B., Mrs. EncO&P 3
Jonson, Jon M 1893-1947 WhoAmA 91N
Jonson, Kerstin 1945- WhoWor 91
Jonson, Raymond 1891-1982 WhoAmA 91N
Jonsson, Anders Karl 1930- WhoWor 91
Jonsson, Bjarni 1920- WhoAm 90
Jonsson, Carl R. 1935- St&PR 91
Jonsson, Gerd Margareta 1945- WhoWor 91
Jonsson, Gisli 1929- WhoWor 91
Jonsson, Jens Johannes 1922- WhoAm 90
Jonsson, Jon DcScanL
Jonsson, Kjartan A. 1940- WhoE 91
Jonsson, Lars Olov 1952- WhoWor 91
Jonsson, Olaf EncO&P 3
Jonsson, Olof 1918- EncPaPR 91
Jonsson, Richard Eugene Thomas 1935- WhoWrEP 89
Jonsson, Thorsteinn DcScanL
Jonsson, Tor 1916-1951 DcScanL
Jonte, John Haworth 1918- WhoAm 90
Jontry, Jerry 1911- WhoAm 90
Jontry, Richard 1942- WhoWor 91
Jontz, Dennis Eugene 1948- WhoEmL 91
Jontz, James Prather 1951- WhoAm 90
Jontz, Pauline 1928- WhoAmW 91
Jonzen, Karin 1914- BiDWomA
Joo, Christopher J 1923- BiDrAPA 89
Joos Van Ghent 1430?-1480? IntDcAA 90
Joos, Felipe Miguel 1952- WhoE 91, WhoEmL 91
Joos, Heidi Louise BiDrAPA 89
Jooss, Kurt 1901-1979 WorAlBi
Joosse, Barbara M. 1949- BioIn 16
Joosse, Barbara Monnot 1949- WhoWrEP 89
Joosse, Peter C 1947- BiDrAPA 89
Joost, Eddie 1916- Ballpl 90
Joost-Gaugier, Christiane L WhoAmA 91
Jooste, Stephanus Jacobus 1953- IntWWM 90
Jooste, Waldie 1947- St&PR 91
Joostema, Brenda Ann 1958- WhoAmW 91
Joosten, Ferdinand Louis 1928- WhoWrEP 89
Joosten, George C 1925- BiDrAPA 89
Joplin, Graham Frank 1927- WhoWor 91
Joplin, Janis 1943-1970 BioAmW, BioIn 16, EncPR&S 89, OxCPMus, WorAlBi
Joplin, John Francis 1924- St&PR 91
Joplin, Julian Mike 1936- WhoAm 90
Joplin, Scott 1868-1917 BioIn 16, DrBlPA 90, OxCPMus, WorAlBi
Jopling, Carol Farrington 1916- WhoE 91
Jopling, Louise 1843-1933 BiDWomA
Jopling-Rowe, Louise 1843-1933 BiDWomA
Joppa, Robert Glenn 1922- WhoAm 90
Joranko, Sara R. 1936- WhoAmW 91
Joravsky, David 1925- WhoAm 90
Jorda, Enrique 1911- IntWWM 90, PenDiMP
Jorda, Lou 1893-1964 Ballpl 90
Jordaens, Jacob 1593-1678 IntDcAA 90
Jordahl, Rodney C. 1956- St&PR 91
Jordan, Alexander Joseph, Jr. 1938- WhoAm 90
Jordan, Amos Azariah, Jr. 1922- WhoAm 90, WhoE 91
Jordan, Angel Goni 1930- WhoAm 90
Jordan, Anne Harrison 1959- WhoEmL 91
Jordan, Armin PenDiMP
Jordan, Armin Georg 1932- IntWWM 90
Jordan, Arno BioIn 16
Jordan, Barbara BioIn 16
Jordan, Barbara 1936- WorAlBi
Jordan, Barbara C. 1936- WhoAm 90, WhoAmW 91
Jordan, Barbara Charline 1936- BlkAmsC [port]
Jordan, Barbara Leslie 1915- WhoWrEP 89
Jordan, Barbara Moore BiDrAPA 89
Jordan, Barbara Schwinn WhoAmA 91, WhoAmW 91, WhoE 91, WhoWor 91
Jordan, Benjamin Everett, Jr. 1926- St&PR 91
Jordan, Beth McAninch 1918- WhoAmA 91
Jordan, Betty Sue 1920- WhoAmW 91
Jordan, Bonita Adele 1948- WhoAm 90
Jordan, Boyd E. 1937- St&PR 91
Jordan, Bryce 1924- WhoAm 90, WhoE 91, WhoWor 91
Jordan, Buck 1907- Ballpl 90
Jordan, C. Edward, Jr. 1943- St&PR 91
Jordan, Carl Frederick 1935- WhoAm 90
Jordan, Carol Lynn 1956- WhoAmW 91
Jordan, Charles Edward 1938- WhoE 91
Jordan, Charles Morrell 1927- WhoAm 90
Jordan, Charlyn Laskey 1948- WhoWor 91
Jordan, Chester Bradley 1839-1914 AmLegL
Jordan, Clifford 1919- St&PR 91
Jordan, Clifford Henry 1921- WhoAm 90
Jordan, Crystal Lee 1940- BioAmW
Jordan, Dale Charles 1950- WhoSSW 91
Jordan, Daniel P., Jr. 1938- ConAu 130
Jordan, Daniel Porter, Jr. 1938- WhoSSW 91
Jordan, Danny Clyde 1951- WhoSSW 91
Jordan, David K BiDrAPA 89
Jordan, David Lewis 1937- WhoAm 90
Jordan, Don AuBYP 90
Jordan, Don D. 1932- St&PR 91, WhoAm 90, WhoSSW 91
Jordan, Don Reece 1928- WhoSSW 91
Jordan, Dorothy BioIn 16
Jordan, Douglas Saunders 1942- St&PR 91
Jordan, DuPree, Jr. 1929- WhoAm 90
Jordan, Earl Clifford 1916- WhoWor 91
Jordan, Edward 1800-1869 BioIn 16
Jordan, Edward 1945- St&PR 91
Jordan, Edward Conrad 1910- WhoAm 90
Jordan, Edward Daniel 1931- WhoAm 90
Jordan, Edward George 1929- WhoAm 90
Jordan, Edward S 1882-1958 EncABHB 4
Jordan, Edwin Eugene, Jr. 1948- WhoEmL 91
Jordan, Eithne 1954- BiDWomA
Jordan, Elke 1937- WhoAm 90
Jordan, Ernst Pascual 1902-1980 DcScB S2
Jordan, F. Gene 1932- WhoSSW 91
Jordan, G. Gary 1940- St&PR 91
Jordan, Gary Lee 1953- WhoEmL 91
Jordan, Gene Morrison 1931- WhoWor 91
Jordan, George Edwin 1940- WhoAmA 91
Jordan, George Lyman, Jr. 1921- WhoAm 90
Jordan, George R., Jr. 1920- St&PR 91
Jordan, George Robert, Jr. 1945- WhoE 91
Jordan, George Washington, Jr. 1938- WhoSSW 91
Jordan, Gerda Petersen 1927- WhoSSW 91
Jordan, Glenn 1936- WhoAm 90
Jordan, Grace Ellen 1928- WhoAmW 91
Jordan, H. Glyn 1937- WhoSSW 91
Jordan, H. Mendall 1941- WhoSSW 91
Jordan, Hamilton 1944- WorAlBi
Jordan, Harold R BiDrAPA 89
Jordan, Harold W 1937- BiDrAPA 89
Jordan, Harriet Marie 1959- WhoAmW 91
Jordan, Henry Hellmut, Jr. 1921- WhoSSW 91, WhoWor 91
Jordan, Henry Kevin 1956- St&PR 91
Jordan, Henry Preston, Jr. 1926- WhoSSW 91
Jordan, Howard Emerson 1926- WhoAm 90
Jordan, I. King BioIn 16
Jordan, Irving King WhoAm 90
Jordan, J. Luther, Jr. 1921- St&PR 91
Jordan, Jack 1927- WhoAmA 91
Jordan, Jack 1929- DrBlPA 90
Jordan, Jack Gerald 1929- WhoSSW 91
Jordan, James BioIn 16
Jordan, James A 1933- BiDrAPA 89
Jordan, James Daniel, Jr. 1933- WhoAm 90
Jordan, James Dee 1956- WhoEmL 91
Jordan, James Joseph BiDrAPA 89
Jordan, James Peter 1948- WhoEmL 91
Jordan, James Pinson 1925- St&PR 91
Jordan, Jerry Dale 1934- WhoAm 90
Jordan, Jerry Lee 1941- WhoAm 90
Jordan, Jerry Neville 1928- WhoAm 90
Jordan, Jim 1896-1988 BioIn 16
Jordan, Jimmy 1908-1957 Ballpl 90
Jordan, Joan Kowalski 1941- WhoAmW 91
Jordan, Joe 1882-1971 OxCPMus
Jordan, John 1927- IntWWM 90
Jordan, John Allen, Jr. 1935- St&PR 91
Jordan, John Emory 1919- WhoAm 90
Jordan, John L 1944- WhoAmA 91
Jordan, John Patrick 1934- WhoAm 90, WhoE 91
Jordan, John R., Jr. 1939- WhoAm 90
Jordan, John Richard, Jr. 1921- WhoAm 90
Jordan, Joseph 1919- WhoAm 90
Jordan, Joseph 1927- St&PR 91
Jordan, Joseph Michael 1922- WhoE 91
Jordan, Joseph Rembert 1947- WhoAm 90
Jordan, Joseph William 1948- St&PR 91
Jordan, Judith Victoria 1943- WhoAmW 91, WhoE 91
Jordan, June 1936- AuBYP 90, BioIn 16, FemiCLE, MajTwCW
Jordan, June M. 1936- WhoAm 90
Jordan, Karen Gail 1950- WhoAmW 91
Jordan, Karen Schifelbein- BioIn 16
Jordan, Karl 1861-1959 DcScB S2
Jordan, Kate 1862-1926 FemiCLE
Jordan, King 1943?- News 90 [port]
Jordan, Lambert Whitfield 1940- WhoSSW 91
Jordan, Larry Clinton 1943- St&PR 91
Jordan, Lawrence E. 1958- St&PR 91
Jordan, Lena E WhoAmA 91N
Jordan, Lennon Douglas, Jr. 1953- WhoSSW 91
Jordan, Leo C. 1943- St&PR 91
Jordan, Leo Clayton 1943- WhoAm 90
Jordan, Leo F. 1932- St&PR 91
Jordan, Leonard ConAu 31NR
Jordan, Leonard E. 1930- St&PR 91
Jordan, Lewis H. WhoAm 90
Jordan, Lorna 1958- WhoAmW 91
Jordan, Louis 1908-1975 BioIn 16, DrBlPA 90, OxCPMus
Jordan, Louis Hampton 1922- WhoAm 90
Jordan, Lucille Galloway WhoAmW 91
Jordan, Marian 1898-1961 BioIn 16
Jordan, Mark Henry 1915- WhoAm 90
Jordan, Mary Ann 1940- WhoAmW 91
Jordan, Max 1895-1977 BioIn 16
Jordan, Michael BioIn 16
Jordan, Michael 1963- WorAlBi
Jordan, Michael Hugh 1936- WhoAm 90, WhoSSW 91, WhoWor 91
Jordan, Michael Jeffery 1963- WhoAm 90
Jordan, Michael Joseph 1948- BiDrAPA 89
Jordan, Michelle 1948- ODwPR 91
Jordan, Michelle Denise 1954- WhoEmL 91
Jordan, Michelle Henrietta 1948- WhoAm 90
Jordan, Morris Reginald, Jr. 1951- WhoSSW 91
Jordan, Nancy Ingram 1956- WhoEmL 91
Jordan, Neal Harvlin 1939- St&PR 91
Jordan, Neil 1950?- ConAu 130
Jordan, Nicholas Theodore 1940- St&PR 91
Jordan, Octavio Manuel 1912- WhoHisp 91
Jordan, Pacual 1902- EncO&P 3
Jordan, Pamela 1953- WhoSSW 91
Jordan, Pat BioIn 16
Jordan, Pat 1941- Ballpl 90
Jordan, Patrice Marie 1957- St&PR 91
Jordan, Paul 1939- IntWWM 90
Jordan, Paul Howard, Jr. 1919- WhoAm 90
Jordan, Paul Richard 1926- WhoWrEP 89
Jordan, Peter C. 1936- WhoAm 90
Jordan, Peter Wilson 1943- WhoWrEP 89
Jordan, Philip Dillon 1903- AuBYP 90
Jordan, Philip Harding, Jr. 1931- WhoAm 90
Jordan, Randall Clark 1950- BiDrAPA 89
Jordan, Ray BioIn 16
Jordan, Richard Charles 1909- WhoAm 90
Jordan, Richard D. WhoSSW 91
Jordan, Richard Thomas 1948- WhoEmL 91
Jordan, Ricky 1965- Ballpl 90
Jordan, Robert WhoWrEP 89
Jordan, Robert 1925- WhoAmA 91
Jordan, Robert 1940- IntWWM 90, WhoAm 90
Jordan, Robert Andrew 1944- IntWWM 90

Jordan, Robert Andrew 1955- *WhoSSW 91*
Jordan, Robert Byrd, III 1932- *WhoAm 90, WhoSSW 91*
Jordan, Robert Elijah, III 1936- *WhoAm 90*
Jordan, Robert Frederick 1950- *WhoEmL 91*
Jordan, Robert Furneaux *TwCCr&M 91*
Jordan, Robert L *BiDrAPA 89*
Jordan, Robert Leon 1928- *WhoAm 90*
Jordan, Robert Leslie 1947- *WhoEmL 91*
Jordan, Robert Maynard 1924- *WhoAm 90*
Jordan, Robert Oliver 1933- *St&PR 91*
Jordan, Robert Paul 1952- *WhoWor 91*
Jordan, Robert Smith 1929- *WhoAm 90*
Jordan, Robert T. 1937- *St&PR 91*
Jordan, Roger 1933- *St&PR 91*
Jordan, Roger Lynn 1953- *WhoEmL 91*
Jordan, Ronald E. 1943- *St&PR 91*
Jordan, Ronald Lee 1939- *St&PR 91*
Jordan, Roy Wilcox 1911- *WhoAm 90*
Jordan, Russell Leigh 1927- *WhoE 91*
Jordan, Sheila *BioIn 16*
Jordan, Stanley *BioIn 16*
Jordan, Stephen Christopher 1933- *WhoWor 91*
Jordan, Steven Jeffrey 1945- *St&PR 91*
Jordan, Susan *BioIn 16*
Jordan, Susan Foreman 1952- *WhoEmL 91*
Jordan, Terry Gilbert 1938- *WhoAm 90*
Jordan, Thomas Edison, Jr. *BiDrAPA 89*
Jordan, Thomas Edison, Jr. 1951- *WhoE 91*
Jordan, Thomas Eugene 1929- *WhoSSW 91*
Jordan, Thomas Fredrick 1936- *WhoAm 90*
Jordan, Thomas Hillman 1948- *WhoAm 90*
Jordan, Thomas R. 1928- *ODwPR 91*
Jordan, Thomas Richard 1928- *WhoAm 90*
Jordan, Tim 1879-1949 *Ballpl 90*
Jordan, Tommy Henry *BiDrAPA 89*
Jordan, V. Craig 1947- *WhoAm 90, WhoWor 91*
Jordan, Vance 1943- *WhoAmA 91*
Jordan, Vernon E., Jr. 1935- *St&PR 91*
Jordan, Vernon Eulion, Jr. 1935- *WhoAm 90, WhoWor 91*
Jordan, Wayne Clifford 1949- *St&PR 91*
Jordan, Wiley 1938- *BiDrAPA 89*
Jordan, William B 1940- *WhoAmA 91*
Jordan, William B., III 1920- *St&PR 91*
Jordan, William Bryan, Jr. 1940- *WhoAm 90*
Jordan, William Chester 1948- *WhoAm 90*
Jordan, William G 1933- *BiDrAPA 89*
Jordan, William H. 1849-1939 *AmLegL*
Jordan, William James 1942- *St&PR 91*
Jordan, William John 1919- *WhoAm 90*
Jordan, William McLendon 1944- *St&PR 91*
Jordan, William Reynier Van Evera, Sr. *WhoAm 90, WhoSSW 91, WhoWor 91*
Jordan, William Stone, III 1949- *WhoEmL 91*
Jordan, Winthrop Donaldson 1931- *WhoAm 90*
Jordan Pena, Jose Luis 1932- *EncPaPR 91*
Jordana, Ann M. 1935- *WhoAmW 91*
Jordania, Vakhtang 1942- *WhoAm 90, WhoSSW 91*
Jorden, Doris Marie 1943- *WhoWrEP 89*
Jorden, Eleanor Harz *WhoAm 90*
Jorden, James Roy 1934- *WhoAm 90*
Jorden, William John 1923- *WhoAm 90*
Jordon, David Lewis 1937- *St&PR 91*
Jordon, Deborah Elizabeth 1951- *WhoAmW 91, WhoE 91, WhoEmL 91*
Jordon, Robert Earl 1938- *WhoAm 90*
Jordy, William Henry 1917- *WhoAm 90*
Jorganxhi, Zhuljana G. 1946- *EncCoWW*
Jorge, Antonio *WhoHisp 91*
Jorge, Gerardo Luis *BiDrAPA 89*
Jorge, Nuno Maria Roque 1947- *WhoWor 91*
Jorge, Silvia 1945- *WhoHisp 91*
Jorgen, Ulm 1934- *WhoWor 91*
Jorgens, Arndt 1905-1980 *Ballpl 90*
Jorgens, Orville 1908- *Ballpl 90*
Jorgens, Thomas Phillip 1947- *WhoEmL 91*
Jorgensen, Alfred H. 1934- *WhoWor 91*
Jorgensen, Charles Everett 1932- *St&PR 91*
Jorgensen, Chester Neil 1925- *St&PR 91*
Jorgensen, Christine 1926-1989 *AnObit 1989*
Jorgensen, Dean Stafford 1956- *WhoE 91*
Jorgensen, Earle M. 1898- *St&PR 91*
Jorgensen, Edvard 1950- *WhoE 91*
Jorgensen, Erik 1921- *WhoAm 90*
Jorgensen, Erik 1934- *St&PR 91*
Jorgensen, Erik Holger 1916- *WhoWor 91*
Jorgensen, Estelle Ruth 1945- *IntWWM 90, WhoEmL 91*
Jorgensen, Evelyn 1910- *St&PR 91*
Jorgensen, Flemming 1934- *WhoAmA 91*
Jorgensen, Gordon David 1921- *WhoAm 90*
Jorgensen, Gordon Dean 1932- *St&PR 91*
Jorgensen, Gregory A. *ODwPR 91*
Jorgensen, Gregory A. 1956- *WhoEmL 91*
Jorgensen, Ivar *ConAu 130, MajTwCW*
Jorgensen, Jack J. 1914-1990 *BioIn 16*
Jorgensen, Janet L. 1957- *St&PR 91*
Jorgensen, Johannes 1866-1956 *DcScanL*
Jorgensen, John Daniel 1945- *WhoE 91*
Jorgensen, John W. *BioIn 16*
Jorgensen, Judith Ann *BiDrAPA 89, WhoAmW 91*
Jorgensen, Judith Strong *ODwPR 91*
Jorgensen, Judith Strong 1959- *WhoE 91*
Jorgensen, Lennart Andrew 1947- *WhoWor 91*
Jorgensen, Mary Venn *AuBYP 90*
Jorgensen, Michael William 1954- *WhoEmL 91*
Jorgensen, Mike 1948- *Ballpl 90*
Jorgensen, Mogens Hugo 1943- *WhoWor 91*
Jorgensen, Nora June 1927- *WhoAmW 91*
Jorgensen, Palle O. 1941- *WhoWor 91*
Jorgensen, Paul Alfred 1916- *WhoAm 90, WhoWor 91*
Jorgensen, Paul J. 1930- *St&PR 91, WhoAm 90*
Jorgensen, Paul Robert 1942- *St&PR 91*
Jorgensen, Poul 1934- *IntWWM 90*
Jorgensen, Richard Edward 1948- *WhoWrEP 89*
Jorgensen, Robert K. 1921- *St&PR 91*
Jorgensen, Robert Westengaard 1907- *WhoWor 91*
Jorgensen, Roger M 1919- *WhoAmA 91*
Jorgensen, Roger McKenzie 1919- *WhoE 91*
Jorgensen, Ron 1957- *St&PR 91*
Jorgensen, Sandra 1934- *WhoAmA 91*
Jorgensen, Spider 1919- *Ballpl 90*
Jorgensen, Virginia T 1923- *BiDrAPA 89*
Jorgensen, William Ernest 1913- *WhoAm 90*
Jorgenson, Christine 1926-1989 *BioIn 16*
Jorgenson, Dale Alfred 1926- *IntWWM 90, WhoAmA 91*
Jorgenson, Dale K. 1939- *St&PR 91*
Jorgenson, Dale Weldeau 1933- *WhoAm 90, WhoE 91*
Jorgenson, Everett Thomas 1952- *WhoEmL 91*
Jorgenson, George 1926-1989 *BioIn 16*
Jorgenson, Ivar *AuBYP 90, MajTwCW*
Jorgenson, James Richard 1926- *IntWWM 90*
Jorgenson, Wallace James 1923- *WhoAm 90*
Jorgenson, Wayne D. 1949- *St&PR 91*
Jorio, Maati 1928- *WhoAm 90*
Joris, Agnese 1850-1922 *BiDWomA*
Joris, Jean Louis 1948- *WhoWor 91*
Joris, Leopoldo O'Donnell y 1809-1867 *BioIn 16*
Jorjorian, Thomas 1957- *WhoSSW 91*
Jorkasky, Richard Joseph 1929- *St&PR 91*
Jorn, Asger 1914-1973 *IntDcAA 90, WhoAmA 91N*
Jorndt, L. Daniel 1941- *St&PR 91*
Jorndt, Louis Daniel 1941- *WhoAm 90*
Jorne, Jacob 1941- *WhoAm 90*
Jorns, Byron Charles 1898-1958 *WhoAmA 91N*
Jorns, David Lee 1944- *WhoAm 90*
Jornter, Joshua 1933- *WhoWor 91*
Jorstad, Erling 1930- *ConAu 30NR*
Jortberg, Robert Francis 1926- *WhoE 91*
Jortner, Alan Jeffery 1951- *St&PR 91*
Jortner, Joshua 1933- *WhoWor 91*
Jory, Marcia Lynn 1955- *WhoAmW 91*
Jorysz, Walter 1919- *IntWWM 90*
Jos, C J 1943- *BiDrAPA 89*
Josceline, Elizabeth 1592-1622 *BiDEWW*
Joscelyn, Kent Buckley 1936- *WhoAm 90*
Joscelyn, Robert G. 1923- *St&PR 91*
Jose, James Robert 1939- *WhoAm 90*
Josef, Norma Castro *BiDrAPA 89*
Joseff, Joan Castle 1922- *WhoWor 91*
Joseffy, Rafael 1852-1915 *BioIn 16, PenDiMP*
Josefowicz, Leila *BioIn 16*
Josefsen, Turi 1936- *WhoAm 90*
Josell, Jessica 1943- *WhoAmW 91*
Joseloff, Stanley S. 1907-1989 *BioIn 16*
Joselson, Tedd 1954- *IntWWM 90*
Joselyn, Jo Ann 1943- *WhoAm 90*
Josendale, James E. 1917- *St&PR 91*
Joseph *BioIn 16*
Joseph *PenDiDA 89*
Joseph 1790?-1871 *WhNaAH*
Joseph 1840-1904 *BioIn 16, WhNaAH [port], WorAlBi*
Joseph Baumhauer *PenDiDA 89*
Joseph Bonaparte, King of Spain 1768-1844 *BioIn 16*
Joseph Friedrich 1702-1787 *BioIn 16*
Joseph of Copertino, Saint 1603-1663 *EncPaPR 91*
Joseph, A. David 1932- *St&PR 91*
Joseph, Alexander 1907-1976 *AuBYP 90*
Joseph, Allan Jay 1938- *WhoAm 90*
Joseph, Anthony Barnett 1955- *BiDrAPA 89, WhoE 91*
Joseph, Antony *BiDrAPA 89*
Joseph, Brian Salit 1942- *BiDrAPA 89*
Joseph, Brian W 1938- *BiDrAPA 89*
Joseph, Burton M. 1921- *St&PR 91, WhoAm 90*
Joseph, Charles duPont 1943- *WhoE 91*
Joseph, Charles M. 1946- *IntWWM 90*
Joseph, Daniel Donald 1929- *WhoAm 90*
Joseph, David Alan *BiDrAPA 89*
Joseph, David I 1941- *BiDrAPA 89*
Joseph, David J., Jr. 1916- *St&PR 91, WhoAm 90*
Joseph, Denise Elaine *BiDrAPA 89*
Joseph, Edna Whitehead 1924- *WhoE 91*
Joseph, Edward D 1919- *BiDrAPA 89*
Joseph, Edward David 1919- *WhoAm 90*
Joseph, Eleanor Ann 1944- *WhoAmW 91*
Joseph, Frank E. 1904- *St&PR 91*
Joseph, Frank Samuel 1940- *WhoE 91, WhoWrEP 89*
Joseph, Fred, Jr. 1942- *WhoWrEP 89*
Joseph, Frederick Harold 1937- *WhoAm 90*
Joseph, George *BiDrAPA 89*
Joseph, George 1921- *St&PR 91*
Joseph, George 1935- *BiDrAPA 89*
Joseph, George M 1943- *BiDrAPA 89*
Joseph, Geri Mack 1923- *WhoAm 90*
Joseph, Gregory Paul 1951- *WhoE 91*
Joseph, Harriet 1919- *WhoAmW 91*
Joseph, Harry Sheridan 1866-1943 *AmLegL*
Joseph, Helen 1905- *BioIn 16*
Joseph, Holly J. 1956- *WhoAmW 91*
Joseph, J. Jonathan 1932- *WhoE 91*
Joseph, Jack *WhoWrEP 89*
Joseph, James *BioIn 16*
Joseph, Janice K *BiDrAPA 89*
Joseph, Jennifer 1961- *WhoWrEP 89*
Joseph, Jenny 1932- *FemiCLE*
Joseph, Jerome 1918- *St&PR 91*
Joseph, John 1923- *WhoAm 90*
Joseph, John James 1953- *WhoEmL 91*
Joseph, John Lawrence 1945- *WhoAm 90*
Joseph, Jon A. 1947- *St&PR 91*
Joseph, Joyce Marie 1947- *WhoAmW 91*
Joseph, Judith R. 1948- *WhoAmW 91*
Joseph, Jules K. 1927- *ODwPR 91, WhoAm 90*
Joseph, Kalappuracka1 C *BiDrAPA 89*
Joseph, Keith *BioIn 16*
Joseph, Leonard 1919- *WhoAm 90*
Joseph, Lily 1864-1940 *BiDWomA*
Joseph, Llewellyn W 1944- *BiDrAPA 89*
Joseph, Lura Ellen 1947- *WhoEmL 91, WhoSSW 91*
Joseph, Marjory L. *BioIn 16*
Joseph, Mary *BiDrAPA 89*
Joseph, Mary Sharon 1942- *ODwPR 91*
Joseph, Mary Thomas 1958- *WhoAmW 91*
Joseph, Maxwell 1910-1982 *DcNaB 1981*
Joseph, Michael, Jr. 1913- *St&PR 91*
Joseph, Michael Anthony 1944- *St&PR 91, WhoAm 90, WhoWor 91*
Joseph, Michael Sarkies 1950- *WhoAm 90*
Joseph, Michael Thomas 1927- *WhoAm 90, WhoE 91*
Joseph, Monica Anna Bilcheck 1926- *IntWWM 90*
Joseph, Monte L *BiDrAPA 89*
Joseph, Moolamannil A *BiDrAPA 89*
Joseph, Nebbie Peter 1929- *St&PR 91*
Joseph, P. A. 1944- *WhoWor 91*
Joseph, Paul R 1951- *WhoEmL 91*
Joseph, R. F. *ConAu 129*
Joseph, Ramon Rafael 1930- *WhoAm 90*
Joseph, Richard Isaac 1936- *WhoAm 90*
Joseph, Richard Michael 1937- *St&PR 91*
Joseph, Rick 1940-1979 *Ballpl 90*
Joseph, Robert C 1950- *BiDrAPA 89*
Joseph, Robert D. 1935- *St&PR 91*
Joseph, Robert Edward 1935- *WhoAm 90*
Joseph, Robert F. *ConAu 129*
Joseph, Robert Farras 1935- *ConAu 129*
Joseph, Robert J 1925- *BiDrAPA 89*
Joseph, Robert L. 1948- *St&PR 91*
Joseph, Roger David 1941- *St&PR 91*
Joseph, Ronald K. 1962- *WhoWrEP 89*
Joseph, Rosaline R. 1929- *WhoAmW 91*
Joseph, Ruth Rhodes 1916- *WhoWrEP 89*
Joseph, Samuel Kenneth 1949- *WhoEmL 91*
Joseph, Simon Philip 1940- *WhoWor 91*
Joseph, Sonny Valooran 1950- *BiDrAPA 89*
Joseph, Stephanie R. 1946- *WhoAm 90, WhoEmL 91*
Joseph, Stephen C. *BioIn 16*
Joseph, Susan *ODwPR 91*
Joseph, Susan 1957- *WhoEmL 91*
Joseph, Susan B. 1958- *WhoAmW 91, WhoE 91, WhoEmL 91*
Joseph, Thomas A. 1945- *WhoE 91*
Joseph, Thomas G. 1936- *St&PR 91*
Joseph, William Gerard 1954- *WhoE 91*
Josepho, C Adele *BiDrAPA 89*
Josephs, Anna Catherine *AuBYP 90*
Josephs, Babette 1940- *WhoAmW 91*
Josephs, Bonnie Priscilla 1938- *WhoAmW 91*
Josephs, Carolyn Brenda 1964- *WhoAmW 91*
Josephs, Jess J. 1917- *WhoAm 90*
Josephs, John P. 1936- *St&PR 91*
Josephs, Larry *BioIn 16*
Josephs, Lois B. 1956- *St&PR 91*
Josephs, Nathana Claire 1959- *WhoE 91*
Josephs, Norman Arthur 1943- *IntWWM 90*
Josephs, Ray 1912- *WhoAm 90, WhoE 91*
Josephs, Wilfred 1927- *ConTFT 8, IntWWM 90, PenDiMP A, WhoWor 91*
Josephs, William Vincent, Jr. 1945- *WhoSSW 91*
Josephs-Spencer, Herta *BiDrAPA 89*
Josephsen, Niels Brondum 1951- *WhoWor 91*
Josephson, Allan Mark 1951- *BiDrAPA 89*
Josephson, Barney 1902-1988 *BioIn 16*
Josephson, Brian D. 1940- *WorAlBi*
Josephson, Brian David 1940- *WhoWor 91*
Josephson, Diana Hayward 1936- *WhoAm 90*
Josephson, Duane 1942- *Ballpl 90*
Josephson, Erland *BioIn 16*
Josephson, Erland 1923- *ConTFT 8, WhoWor 91*
Josephson, Gloria Agrin 1923-1988 *BioIn 16*
Josephson, Jay Larry 1950- *WhoEmL 91*
Josephson, John E. 1947- *St&PR 91*
Josephson, John H. 1961- *WhoE 91*
Josephson, Joseph Paul 1933- *WhoAm 90*
Josephson, Kenneth Bradley 1932- *WhoAm 90, WhoAmA 91*
Josephson, Mark Eric 1943- *WhoAm 90*
Josephson, Martin M 1927- *BiDrAPA 89*
Josephson, Marvin 1927- *St&PR 91, WhoAm 90*
Josephson, Morton *BiDrAPA 89*
Josephson, Staffan 1930- *WhoWor 91*
Josephson, Stanley M. 1934- *St&PR 91*
Josephson, Susan Phyllis *BiDrAPA 89*
Josephson, Thomas Selmer *BiDrAPA 89*
Josephson, William Howard 1934- *WhoAm 90, WhoE 91*
Josephthal, Daniel H 1935- *BiDrAPA 89*
Josephy, Alvin M., Jr. 1915- *WhoAm 90*
Josetsu *EncJap*
Josey, Deborah K. 1949- *WhoAmW 91*
Josey, Elonnie Junius 1924- *WhoAm 90, WhoWor 91*
Josey, Victoria Sue Harley 1957- *WhoSSW 91*
Joshi, Arun Dattatraya 1937- *WhoSSW 91*
Joshi, Chandrashekhar Janardan 1953- *WhoWor 91*
Joshi, Kumudben *BioIn 16*
Joshi, Paramjit Kaur *BiDrAPA 89*
Joshi, Praful M 1945- *BiDrAPA 89*
Joshi, S T 1958- *ConAu 131*
Joshi, Sadanand Dattatray 1950- *WhoSSW 91*
Joshi, Suresh Meghashyam *WhoAm 90*
Joshi, Uma S 1942- *BiDrAPA 89*
Joshi, Usha Praful 1943- *BiDrAPA 89*
Joshi, Vasant L 1950- *BiDrAPA 89*
Joshi, Vijay S. 1939- *WhoSSW 91*
Joshua, Susan Caroline *BiDrAPA 89*
Josiah, Walter James 1933- *St&PR 91*
Josimovich, George 1894- *WhoAmA 91N*
Josipovic, Ivo 1957- *IntWWM 90*
Josipovici, Gabriel 1940- *WorAu 1980 [port]*
Joskow, Jules *WhoAm 90*
Joskow, Paul Lewis 1947- *WhoAm 90*
Joslin, Alfred Hahn 1914- *WhoAm 90*
Joslin, Charlotte *BioIn 16*
Joslin, Rodney D. 1944- *St&PR 91*
Joslin, Roger 1936- *St&PR 91*
Joslin, Scott Andrew 1963- *BiDrAPA 89*
Joslin, Sesyle 1929- *AuBYP 90*
Joslin, Stuart Lorin 1916- *BiDrAPA 89*
Joslyn, Betsy Ann 1954- *WhoAmW 91*
Joslyn, Lee W. 1955- *St&PR 91*
Joslyn, Robert Bruce 1945- *WhoWor 91*
Joslyn, Sandy Lynne 1958- *WhoEmL 91*
Joslyn, Veronica Joan 1920- *WhoWrEP 89*
Joslyn, William 1950- *WhoEmL 91*
Jospe, Jack D. 1920- *St&PR 91*
Jospe, Joseph Lewis 1951- *St&PR 91*
Jospin, Lionel Robert 1937- *BiDFrPL, WhoWor 91*
Jospitre, Jacques *BiDrAPA 89*
Joss, Addie 1880-1911 *Ballpl 90 [port]*
Joss, George Smith 1926- *WhoWor 91*

Joss, Judy Harue 1953- *WhoEmL 91*
Joss, Paul Christopher 1945- *WhoAm 90*
Josselin, Ralph 1617-1683 *BioIn 16*
Josselin de Jong, Patrick Edward de 1922- *BioIn 16*
Josselsohn, Phyllis Sandra 1955- *WhoEmL 91*
Josselson, Diana 1921- *WhoWor 91*
Josselson, Jack Bernard 1905- *WhoAm 90*
Josselyn, John *EncCRAm*
Josselyn, Sharon Holladay 1950- *WhoAmW 91*
Josset, Raoul 1900-1957 *WhoAmA 91N*
Jossey-Bass, Allen Quitman 1928- *St&PR 91, WhoAm 90*
Jost, Barbara Dinger 1947- *WhoAmW 91*
Jost, Harry P. 1945- *WhoWor 91*
Jost, Helen Christine 1944- *St&PR 91*
Jost, Lawrence John 1944- *WhoAm 90*
Jost, Mack 1918- *IntWWM 90*
Jost, Mary *ODwPR 91*
Jost, Robert Alan 1952- *WhoEmL 91*
Jost, Wesley William 1930- *WhoE 91, WhoWor 91*
Josue, Vic Ramayan *BiDrAPA 89*
Jotaki, Tomosada 1915- *WhoWor 91*
Jotcham, Thomas Denis 1918- *WhoE 91*
Jotuni, Maria 1880-1943 *EncCoWW*
Jotuni, Maria Gustava 1880-1943 *DcScanL*
Jotwani, Nandlal C 1944- *BiDrAPA 89*
Jou, Jeanette Bikling 1945- *WhoAmW 91*
Jouandet, Jean 1938- *WhoWor 91*
Jouanel, Frederic 1967- *WhoWor 91*
Joubert, Curtis *BioIn 16*
Joubert, Francois *PenDiDA 89*
Joubert, Gilles 1689-1775 *PenDiDA 89*
Joubert, John Pierre Herman 1927- *IntWWM 90*
Joubert, Molly 1925- *IntWWM 90*
Joudrie, Herbert Earl 1934- *St&PR 91*
Joudry, Patricia 1921- *FemiCLE, OxCCanT*
Jouffroy D'Abbans, Marquis De 1751-1832 *WorAlBi*
Jouhaux, Leon 1879-1954 *WorAlBi*
Jouhaux, Leon Henri 1879-1954 *BiDFrPL*
Joukhadar, Kristina 1952- *WhoAmA 91*
Joukhadar, Moumtaz 1940- *WhoAmA 91*
Joukowsky, Artemis A.W. 1930- *WhoE 91*
Joule, James P. 1818-1889 *WorAlBi*
Joulia, Elisabeth *PenDiDA 89*
Jouno, Randolph James *WhoAm 90*
Jourdain, Alice Marie 1923- *WhoAm 90*
Jourdain, Francis 1876-1958 *PenDiDA 89*
Jourdain, Frantz 1847-1935 *PenDiDA 89*
Jourdan, Louis 1919- *WorAlBi*
Jourdan, Louis 1921- *WhoAm 90*
Jourdan-Morhange, Helene 1888-1961 *PenDiMP*
Jourden, Lewis E. 1938- *St&PR 91*
Jourdian, George William 1929- *WhoAm 90*
Jourdren, Marc Henri 1960- *WhoWor 91*
Journeay, Glen Eugene 1925- *WhoSSW 91*
Journet, Marcel 1867-1933 *PenDiMP*
Journey *EncPR&S 89*
Journey, Drexel Dahlke 1926- *WhoAm 90, WhoE 91, WhoWor 91*
Journeycake, Charles 1817-1894 *BioIn 16, WhNaAH*
Jousset, Gerard Marie 1944- *WhoWor 91*
Joutel, Henri 1645?-1723 *EncCRAm*
Jouvenel, Bertrand de 1903-1987 *BioIn 16*
Jova, Henri Vatable 1919- *WhoAm 90*
Jova, Joseph John 1916- *BioIn 16, WhoAm 90, WhoHisp 91*
Jovan, John Dimitri 1940- *WhoE 91*
Jovanovic, Milan Miodrag 1952- *WhoSSW 91*
Jovanovic, Miodrag 1936- *WhoAm 90*
Jovanovic, Miroslav N. 1957- *WhoWor 91*
Jovanovic, Vladimir Zivojina 1937- *IntWWM 90*
Jovanovich, Peter William 1949- *WhoAm 90, WhoSSW 91*
Jovanovich, William 1920- *WhoAm 90, WhoSSW 91, WhoWrEP 89*
Jovanovitch, Milena 1951- *WhoAmW 91*
Jovellanos, Gaspar de 1744-1811 *BioIn 16*
Jovic, Borisav *WhoWor 91*
Jovine, Marcel 1921- *WhoAmA 91*
Jovovich, Milla *BioIn 16*
Jowaiszas, Susan G. *ODwPR 91*
Jowdy, Jeffrey William 1959- *WhoSSW 91*
Jowers, Jerry Earl 1949- *WhoSSW 91*
Jowers, Lawrence Victor 1921- *WhoWrEP 89*
Jowers, Ronnie Lee 1951- *WhoSSW 91*
Jowett, Benjamin 1817-1893 *BioIn 16*
Jowsey, Shiela G *BiDrAPA 89*
Joxe, Louis 1901- *BiDFrPL*
Joxe, Pierre 1934- *BiDFrPL*
Joy, Charles Rhind 1885- *AuBYP 90*
Joy, Charles Richard 1952- *BiDrAPA 89, WhoE 91*
Joy, Edward Bennett 1941- *WhoSSW 91*
Joy, Genevieve 1919- *PenDiMP*
Joy, George Andrew 1896-1974 *EncO&P 3*
Joy, Henry Bourne 1864-1936 *EncABHB 4 [port]*
Joy, James Everett 1941- *BiDrAPA 89*
Joy, Lucinda Jean 1952- *WhoSSW 91*
Joy, O. Maurice 1938- *WhoAm 90*
Joy, Paul W. 1924- *St&PR 91*
Joy, Perihan Dursun *WhoWrEP 89*
Joyaux, Alain Georges 1950- *WhoAm 90, WhoAmA 91*
Joyce, Alfred R 1920- *BiDrAPA 89*
Joyce, Anne Raine 1942- *WhoAmW 91*
Joyce, Archibald 1873-1963 *OxCPMus*
Joyce, Bernita Anne *WhoAmW 91, WhoWor 91*
Joyce, Beverly Joan 1945- *WhoAmW 91*
Joyce, Bill 1865-1941 *Ballpl 90*
Joyce, Burton M. 1942- *St&PR 91*
Joyce, Charles Herbert 1830-1916 *AmLegL*
Joyce, Christopher P. 1949- *St&PR 91*
Joyce, Claude Clinton 1931- *St&PR 91, WhoAm 90*
Joyce, David Edward 1951- *WhoE 91*
Joyce, Diane *BioIn 16*
Joyce, Dorothy Jill *BiDrAPA 89*
Joyce, Edward F. 1944- *St&PR 91*
Joyce, Eileen 1912- *IntWWM 90, PenDiMP*
Joyce, Florence V. Mienert 1923- *WhoAmW 91*
Joyce, Harry Richard, Jr. 1950- *WhoEmL 91*
Joyce, Helen Marie 1938- *St&PR 91*
Joyce, J David 1946- *WhoAmA 91*
Joyce, Jack R. 1942- *St&PR 91*
Joyce, James 1882-1941 *AuBYP 90, BioIn 16, MajTwCW, WorAlBi, WrPh*
Joyce, James Avery *BioIn 16*
Joyce, James Daniel 1921- *WhoAm 90*
Joyce, James E. 1926- *St&PR 91*
Joyce, James Joseph, Jr. 1947- *WhoE 91*
Joyce, Jerry Haines 1936- *WhoAm 90, WhoSSW 91*
Joyce, John J. 1943- *St&PR 91*
Joyce, John M. 1908-1989 *BioIn 16*
Joyce, John Mark *BiDrAPA 89*
Joyce, John T. 1935- *WhoAm 90*
Joyce, Joseph James 1943- *WhoAm 90*
Joyce, Joseph Michael 1951- *St&PR 91*
Joyce, Joseph Patrick 1951- *WhoE 91*
Joyce, Kenneth T. 1947- *St&PR 91*
Joyce, Linda *BioIn 16*
Joyce, Marilyn Schmidt 1942- *WhoAmW 91*
Joyce, Marion *ODwPR 91*
Joyce, Marshall Woodside 1912- *WhoAmA 91*
Joyce, Michael J. 1942- *WhoAm 90*
Joyce, Michael Ray 1950- *WhoE 91*
Joyce, Michael Stewart 1942- *WhoAm 90*
Joyce, Morton D. *BioIn 16*
Joyce, Neal Allan 1940- *St&PR 91*
Joyce, Nora Barnacle 1884-1951 *BioIn 16*
Joyce, Pamela-Ann Leong 1948- *WhoAmW 91*
Joyce, Paul Roberts 1947- *St&PR 91*
Joyce, Peggy Hopkins 1893-1957 *BioIn 16*
Joyce, Peter 1941- *IntWWM 90*
Joyce, Peter C. 1942- *WhoSSW 91*
Joyce, Philip Halton 1928- *WhoAm 90*
Joyce, Robert J. 1948- *St&PR 91*
Joyce, Sheila Mary 1953- *WhoEmL 91*
Joyce, Stephen F. 1941- *St&PR 91*
Joyce, Stephen Francis 1941- *WhoAm 90*
Joyce, Stephen Michael 1945- *WhoEmL 91*
Joyce, Thomas C. 1937- *St&PR 91*
Joyce, Timothy David 1957- *WhoE 91*
Joyce, W. Seavey 1913-1988 *BioIn 16*
Joyce, Walter Joseph 1930- *WhoSSW 91*
Joyce, William *AuBYP 90, BioIn 16*
Joyce, William 1906-1946 *BioIn 16*
Joyce, William Frank 1960- *WhoEmL 91*
Joyce, William Leonard 1942- *WhoAm 90*
Joye, Afrie Songco 1942- *WhoAmW 91*
Joye, Jennings Bryant, Jr. *BiDrAPA 89*
Joyner, Al *BioIn 16*
Joyner, Billy N. 1932- *St&PR 91*
Joyner, Claude Reuben, Jr. 1925- *WhoAm 90*
Joyner, Conrad Francis 1931- *WhoAm 90*
Joyner, Dee Ann 1947- *WhoEmL 91*
Joyner, Diane Bishop 1951- *WhoSSW 91*
Joyner, Earl Scarboro 1934- *St&PR 91*
Joyner, Edd Ray 1948- *WhoSSW 91*
Joyner, Florence Griffith *BioIn 16*
Joyner, Floyd T., Jr. 1927- *St&PR 91*
Joyner, Floyd Talmage, Jr. 1927- *WhoAm 90*
Joyner, Gary Kelton 1957- *WhoEmL 91*
Joyner, John Brooks 1944- *WhoAm 90, WhoAmA 91*
Joyner, John Erwin 1935- *WhoAm 90*
Joyner, Leon Felix 1924- *WhoAm 90*
Joyner, Michelle Denise 1961- *WhoEmL 91*
Joyner, Robert Carter 1947- *WhoEmL 91*
Joyner, Roy Elton 1922- *WhoAm 90*
Joyner, Suzanne DiMascio 1942- *WhoAmW 91, WhoE 91*
Joyner, Wally 1962- *Ballpl 90*
Joyner, Walton Kitchin 1933- *WhoAm 90*
Joyner, Weyland Thomas 1929- *WhoAm 90, WhoWor 91*
Joyner-Kersee, Jackie *BioIn 16*
Joyner-Kersee, Jackie 1962- *WorAlBi*
Joyner-Kersee, Jacqueline 1962- *WhoAm 90, WhoAmW 91*
Joynes, Ralph Carlisle 1928- *WhoAm 90*
Joynes, Thomas J 1927- *BiDrAPA 89*
Joynson-Hicks, William 1865-1932 *BioIn 16*
Joynt, Carey Bonthron 1924- *WhoAm 90*
Joynt, James E. *St&PR 91*
Joynt, Robert James 1925- *WhoAm 90*
Joynton, Stanley Forrest 1951- *WhoEmL 91*
Jozef, Sally Schley 1962- *WhoAmW 91*
Jozefiak, Richard Chester 1960- *WhoEmL 91*
Jozefiak, Stanley Walter 1957- *WhoEmL 91*
Jozoff, Malcolm 1939- *St&PR 91, WhoAm 90*
Jozsef, Stephen Michael 1954- *BiDrAPA 89*
Jozwiak, Ronald D. 1947- *St&PR 91*
Jozwik, Francis Xavier 1940- *WhoWor 91, WhoWrEP 89*
Jozzo, Alfonso 1942- *WhoWor 91*
Jraige, Wassim Gebran 1952- *WhoWor 91*
Jrmen, Hans-Josef 1938- *WhoWor 91*
Ju, Chester 1949- *St&PR 91*
Ju, Chow-Soon Chuang 1924- *WhoWrEP 89*
Ju, I-Hsiung 1923- *WhoAmA 91*
Ju, Semmy 1945- *WhoEmL 91*
Ju, Teresa Lin 1950- *WhoAmW 91*
Juan Carlos I 1938- *WhoWor 91, WorAlBi*
Juan Carlos I, King of Spain 1938- *BioIn 16*
Juan, Gerardo A 1941- *BiDrAPA 89*
Juan, Henry Walter, III 1953- *WhoE 91*
Juan, Ronaldo de 1931-1989 *BioIn 16*
Juana 1479- *WomWR [port]*
Juana I 1273-1305 *WomWR*
Juana II 1312-1349 *WomWR*
Juana Ines de la Cruz 1651-1695 *BioIn 16*
Juana, la Loca, Queen of Castile 1479-1555 *BioIn 16*
Juana II, Queen of Navarre 1311?-1349 *BioIn 16*
Juanarena, Douglas B. *WhoHisp 91*
Juarbe, Jose Arturo *BiDrAPA 89*
Juarez, Antonio 1952- *WhoEmL 91, WhoSSW 91, WhoWor 91*
Juarez, Benito 1806-1872 *BioIn 16, WorAlBi*
Juarez, Jacinto P. 1944- *WhoHisp 91*
Juarez, Jesus R *BiDrAPA 89*
Juarez, Jesus R. 1952- *WhoHisp 91*
Juarez, Jose 1955- *WhoHisp 91*
Juarez, Leo J. 1939- *WhoHisp 91*
Juarez, Maretta Liya Calimpong 1958- *WhoWor 91*
Juarez, Mario Hernandez 1962- *WhoSSW 91*
Juarez, Martin 1946- *WhoEmL 91, WhoHisp 91*
Juarez, Nicandro *WhoHisp 91*
Juarez, Robert Carrillo 1935- *WhoHisp 91*
Juarez, Roberto 1952- *WhoAmA 91*
Juarez-Nunez, Ciro Francisco *BiDrAPA 89*
Juarez Robles, Jennifer Jean 1957- *WhoHisp 91*
Juarez-West, Debra Ann 1958- *WhoHisp 91*
Juarroz, Roberto 1925- *ConAu 131, HispWr 90*
Juba, Dorothy Virginia Margaret *BioIn 16*
Juba, Robert David 1948- *WhoWrEP 89*
Jubany Arnau, Narcisco 1913- *WhoWor 91*
Jube, Edward H. 1929- *St&PR 91*
Jubeark, Sandraa Melvin 1948- *WhoAmW 91*
Jubelirer, Robert C. 1937- *WhoE 91*
Jubilee Singers *OxCPMus*
Jubinville, Alain Maurice Joseph 1928- *WhoAm 90*
Jubinville, Luc A. 1935- *St&PR 91*
Jubitz, Monroe A. 1916- *St&PR 91*
Jubitz, Monroe Albin, Jr. 1944- *St&PR 91*
Jubliee Singers *DcAfAmP*
Juboori, Michael A *BiDrAPA 89*
Juceam, Eleanor Pam 1936- *WhoE 91*
Juceam, Robert E. 1940- *WhoAm 90, WhoE 91, WhoWor 91*
Juchatz, Wayne Warren 1946- *WhoAm 90*
Juchems, Rudolf Hans 1929- *WhoWor 91*
Juckem, Wilfred Philip 1915- *WhoAm 90*
Juckett, Margaret Gregory *WhoAmW 91*
Jucovy, Milton Edward 1918- *BiDrAPA 89*
Jud, Rudolf 1923- *WhoWor 91*
Juda, Walter 1916- *St&PR 91*
Judah, Douglas Fraser 1942- *St&PR 91*
Judah, Janeen Sue 1959- *WhoAmW 91*
Judah, Jay Stillson 1911- *WhoAm 90*
Judas Maccabaeus *WorAlBi*
Judas Priest *EncPR&S 89*
Judas, Ilse 1924- *BiDrAPA 89*
Judas, Maccabaeus *BioIn 16*
Judd, A Bradford 1929- *BiDrAPA 89*
Judd, Alan 1947- *SpyFic*
Judd, Arnold Walter, Jr. 1942- *St&PR 91*
Judd, Barry Lewis *BiDrAPA 89*
Judd, Brian Raymond 1931- *WhoAm 90*
Judd, Cyril *MajTwCW*
Judd, De Forrest Hale 1916- *WhoAmA 91*
Judd, Dennis L. 1954- *WhoEmL 91*
Judd, Donald Clarence 1928- *WhoAmA 91*
Judd, Dorothy Heiple 1922- *WhoWor 91*
Judd, Frederick Lee 1957- *St&PR 91*
Judd, Garry 1962- *IntWWM 90*
Judd, Gary 1942- *WhoAm 90*
Judd, Harrison *TwCCr&M 91*
Judd, Jacqueline Vogel 1939- *WhoAmW 91*
Judd, James 1949- *IntWWM 90*
Judd, Jerome *St&PR 91*
Judd, Joel Stanton 1951- *WhoEmL 91*
Judd, John E. 1930- *St&PR 91*
Judd, John William 1930- *St&PR 91*
Judd, Karen Bumgarner 1948- *WhoEmL 91*
Judd, Leonard Robert 1939- *St&PR 91*
Judd, Lewis L 1930- *BiDrAPA 89*
Judd, Lewis Lund 1930- *WhoAm 90*
Judd, Mary Jo 1949- *WhoAmW 91*
Judd, Naomi *BioIn 16, WhoAm 90, WhoAmW 91*
Judd, Norman Buel 1815-1878 *BioIn 16*
Judd, Norman R. 1948- *St&PR 91*
Judd, O'Dean P. 1937- *WhoAm 90*
Judd, Oscar 1908- *Ballpl 90*
Judd, Patricia Hoffman 1946- *WhoEmL 91*
Judd, Pearl 1908- *EncO&P 3*
Judd, Ralph Waverly 1930- *WhoWrEP 89*
Judd, Richard Louis 1937- *WhoE 91*
Judd, Robert Carpenter 1921- *WhoAm 90, WhoWor 91*
Judd, Roger Langley 1944- *IntWWM 90*
Judd, Wilfred *IntWWM 90*
Judd, William Reid 1951- *WhoSSW 91*
Judd, William Robert 1917- *WhoAm 90*
Judd, Winnie Ruth 1905- *WorAlBi*
Judd, Wynonna *BioIn 16*
Judd, Wynonna 1964- *WhoAm 90, WhoAmW 91*
Judds, The *WhoNeCM [port]*
Jude, James Roderick 1928- *WhoAm 90*
Judell, Cynthia N. 1924- *WhoAmW 91*
Judell, Robert B. 1923- *St&PR 91*
Judelson, Robert A. 1939- *WhoAm 90*
Judenkunig, Hans 1450?-1526 *PenDiMP*
Judge, Bernard Martin 1940- *WhoAm 90*
Judge, Bruce *BioIn 16*
Judge, David Howard 1928- *St&PR 91*
Judge, Hugh Gordon 1939- *St&PR 91*
Judge, James Carl 1945- *WhoEmL 91*
Judge, James Eugene 1939- *St&PR 91*
Judge, Joanne Mary 1952- *WhoAmW 91, WhoEmL 91*
Judge, Joe 1894-1963 *Ballpl 90*
Judge, John Emmet 1912- *WhoAm 90, WhoWor 91*
Judge, Mary Frances 1935- *WhoAmA 91*
Judge, Michael Ronald 1952- *WhoEmL 91*
Judge, Rosemary Ann *WhoAm 90*
Judge, Sheila *BiDrAPA 89*
Judge, Stanley J. 1927- *St&PR 91*
Judge, Thomas J. 1927- *St&PR 91*
Judge, Thomas Joseph 1927- *WhoAm 90*
Judge, William Q 1851-1896 *EncO&P 3, EncPaPR 91*
Judge, William Quan *NewAgE 90*
Judihardianto, Alex *WhoWor 91*
Judith *WomWR*
Judkins, Donald Ward 1912- *WhoAm 90*
Judkins, Reba *BioIn 16*
Judkins, Sylvia *WhoAmA 91*
Judlin, James Walter, Sr. 1937- *WhoSSW 91*
Judnich, Walt 1917-1971 *Ballpl 90*
Judovitz, Dalia 1951- *ConAu 130*
Judson, Adoniram 1788-1850 *BioIn 16*
Judson, Alice *WhoAmA 91N*
Judson, Ann 1789-1826 *FemiCLE*
Judson, Ann H. 1789-1826 *BioAmW*
Judson, Ann Hasseltine 1789-1826 *BioIn 16*
Judson, Arnold Sidney 1927- *WhoE 91*
Judson, Arthur, II 1930- *St&PR 91*
Judson, Bruce David 1958- *WhoEmL 91*
Judson, Charles James 1944- *WhoAm 90*
Judson, Clara 1879-1960 *AuBYP 90*
Judson, Donald Rae 1948- *St&PR 91*
Judson, Edward 1844-1914 *BioIn 16*
Judson, Emily 1817-1854 *FemiCLE*
Judson, Emily C. 1817-1854 *BioAmW*
Judson, Emily Chubbuck 1817-1854 *BioIn 16*

Judson, Franklyn Sylvanus 1915- *WhoAm 90*
Judson, Horace Freeland 1931- *WhoAm 90*
Judson, Howie 1926- *Ballpl 90*
Judson, Jeannette Alexander 1912- *WhoAm 90, WhoAmA 91*
Judson, Lou *NewAgMG*
Judson, Lyman Spicer Vincent 1903- *WhoAm 90*
Judson, Ray W. 1926- *WhoAm 90*
Judson, Ray Warner 1926- *St&PR 91*
Judson, Sarah B. 1803-1845 *BioAmW*
Judson, Sheldon 1918- *WhoAm 90*
Judson, Sylvia Shaw 1897-1978 *WhoAmA 91N*
Judson, Thomas Fearey, Jr. 1945- *St&PR 91*
Judson, William D 1939- *WhoAmA 91*
Judson, William Lees 1842-1928 *BioIn 16*
Judy, Bernard Francis 1920- *WhoAm 90*
Judy, John Wayne, Jr. 1931- *WhoAm 90*
Judy, Paul R. 1931- *St&PR 91*
Judy, Robert Dale 1924- *WhoSSW 91*
Judy, William Jerome 1931- *St&PR 91*
Judywhite *WhoWrEP 89*
Jue, Susan Lynne 1956- *WhoAmW 91*
Juech, Stephen Paul 1952- *WhoEmL 91*
Juel, Twila Eileen 1948- *WhoAmW 91*
Juelich, Richard James 1950- *WhoEmL 91*
Juell, Bruce Charles 1934- *St&PR 91*
Juenemann, Jean 1936- *WhoAmW 91*
Juengel, Eugene Thomas 1932- *St&PR 91*
Juenger, Friedrich Klaus 1930- *WhoAm 90*
Juerchko, Jack 1938- *St&PR 91*
Juergens, George Ivar 1932- *WhoAm 90*
Juergens, Rainer 1941- *St&PR 91, WhoWor 91*
Juergens, Steven Manley 1953- *BiDrAPA 89*
Juergensen, Holger 1957- *WhoWor 91*
Juergensmeyer, Jane Stuart *ConAu 31NR*
Juergensmeyer, Mark 1940- *ConAu 129*
Jug, Karl 1939- *WhoWor 91*
Jugel, Richard Dennis 1942- *WhoWor 91*
Jugenheimer, Donald Wayne 1943- *WhoAm 90*
Juglar, Clement 1819-1905 *BioIn 16*
Jugnauth, Anerood 1930- *WhoWor 91*
Juh *WhNaAH*
Juhasz, Joseph *St&PR 91*
Juhasz, Stephen 1913- *WhoAm 90*
Juhasz, Stephen E. 1923- *BiDrAPA 89*
Juhl, Daniel Leo 1935- *WhoAm 90*
Juhl, Finn 1912- *PenDiDA 89*
Juhl, Finn 1912-1989 *ConDes 90*
Juhl, Harold Alexander 1950- *WhoEmL 91, WhoSSW 91*
Juhl, Loren Earl 1918- *WhoAm 90*
Juhlin, Sven-Eric 1940- *ConDes 90*
Juillet, Pierre Armand 1921- *BiDFrPL*
Jukes, Beth 1910- *BiDWomA*
Jukes, Mavis *BioIn 16*
Jukes, Mavis 1947- *SmATA 12AS [port]*
Jukes, Thomas Hughes 1906- *WhoAm 90*
Jukkola, George Duane 1945- *WhoEmL 91*
Julander, Paula Foil 1939- *WhoAmW 91*
Jule, Thomas 1959- *St&PR 91*
Julen, Donald L. 1943- *St&PR 91*
Jules, Mervin 1912- *WhoAm 90, WhoAmA 91*
Julesberg, Elizabeth Rider Montgomery *AuBYP 90*
Julesz, Bela 1928- *WhoAm 90*
Julia *EncCoWW*
Julia Avita Mammaea *WomWR*
Julia Berenice 28?- *WomWR*
Julia Domna *WomWR*
Julia Maesa *WomWR*
Julia, Gaston 1893-1978 *BioIn 16*
Julia, Maria C. *WhoHisp 91*
Julia, Raul 1940- *WhoHisp 91*
Julia, Raul 1944- *WorAlBi*
Julia, Raul Rafael Carlos 1944- *WhoAm 90*
Julian of Norwich 1343?-1413? *FemiCLE*
Julian, of Norwich 1343-1443 *BioIn 16*
Julian, Alexander, II 1948- *WhoAm 90*
Julian, Alfred *WhoWrEP 89*
Julian, Ellen Ruth 1957- *WhoAmW 91*
Julian, George M. 1931- *St&PR 91*
Julian, James Joseph 1945- *WhoSSW 91*
Julian, Jane *ConAu 30NR*
Julian, Jerry B. 1933- *WhoAm 90*
Julian, Jim Lee 1954- *WhoEmL 91*
Julian, Lazaro 1945- *WhoAmA 91*
Julian, Michael 1951- *WhoSSW 91*
Julian, Michele Denise 1954- *WhoAmW 91*
Julian, Nancy R. *AuBYP 90*
Julian, Percy Lavon 1899-1975 *DcScB S2*
Julian, Rachel Ann *BiDrAPA 89*
Julian, Thomas Anthony 1930- *WhoE 91*
Julian, Wayne Edmond 1951- *BiDrAPA 89*
Juliana 1909- *WomWR*
Juliana, Anchoret 1343-1443 *BioIn 16*
Juliana, Queen of the Netherlands 1909- *BioIn 16*
Juliana, James Nicholas 1922- *WhoAm 90*
Juliana, Vincent Alphonso 1959- *WhoE 91*
Juliani, John 1940- *OxCCanT*
Juliano, Albert Joseph 1929- *St&PR 91*
Juliber, Irving Gerard 1913- *WhoAm 90*
Julich, Marvin Milam 1941- *WhoSSW 91*
Julie, David Brian 1939- *St&PR 91*
Julie, Loebe 1920- *St&PR 91*
Julie, Ora McBride 1939- *WhoAmW 91*
Julien, Alfred S. 1910-1989 *BioIn 16*
Julien, Antoine F 1931- *BiDrAPA 89*
Julien, Denis Alan 1945- *WhoEmL 91*
Julien, Max *DrBIPA 90*
Juliff, Peter Laurence 1938- *WhoWor 91*
Julifs, Sandra Jean 1939- *WhoAmW 91*
Julin, Joseph Richard 1926- *WhoAm 90, WhoWor 91*
Julio, Pat T 1923- *WhoAmA 91*
Julius, Demetrios A 1945- *BiDrAPA 89*
Julius, Emanuel Haldeman- 1889-1951 *BioIn 16*
Julius, Stevo 1929- *WhoAm 90*
Juliussen, Karen 1948- *WhoEmL 91*
Juliusson, Marguerite 1956- *WhoAmW 91, WhoEmL 91*
Julivert, Manuel 1930- *WhoWor 91*
Jull, Peter Sherman 1942- *WhoWor 91*
Julliard Quartet *PenDiMP*
Jullien, Joseph *PenDiDA 89*
Jullien, Louis 1812-1860 *PenDiMP*
Jullien, Louis Antoine 1812-1860 *OxCPMus*
Julstrom, Clifford Arthur 1907- *IntWWM 90*
Julstrom, Rosa Drake 1925- *IntWWM 90*
Jumabhoy, Rafiq 1951- *WhoWor 91*
Jumayyil, Amin *BioIn 16*
Jumayyil, Bashir 1948-1982 *BioIn 16*
Jumblatt, Kamal *BioIn 16*
Jumblatt, Kamal 1917-1977 *PolLCME*
Jumblatt, Walid *BioIn 16*
Jumblatt, Walid 1949- *PolLCME*
Jumel, Eliza Bowen 1769-1865 *BioAmW*
Jumonville, Felix Joseph, Jr. 1920- *WhoAm 90*
Jumonville, George R. 1942- *St&PR 91*
Jump, Bernard, Jr. 1938- *WhoAm 90*
Jump, Chester Jackson, Jr. 1918- *WhoAm 90*
Jump, Linda Gail 1949- *WhoWor 91*
Jumper 1790?-1838 *WhNaAH*
Jumper, Betty Mae 1927?- *WomWR*
Jumper, Cindy Ann 1954- *WhoAmW 91*
Jumper, John 1820?-1896 *WhNaAH*
Jumsai, Sumet 1939- *ConAu 129*
Junaid, Raja Muhammad *BiDrAPA 89*
Junaluska *WhNaAH*
Junankar, Pramod Nagorao 1943- *WhoWor 91*
Juncal, Cynthia Ann 1961- *WhoEmL 91*
Junchen, David Lawrence 1946- *WhoEmL 91, WhoWor 91*
Juncker, Karen Post 1944- *WhoAmW 91*
Junco, Marie 1956- *WhoSSW 91*
Junco, Ricardo Jorge 1959- *BiDrAPA 89*
Juncos, Jorge Luis 1952- *WhoSSW 91*
Jund, Daniel Edward 1946- *St&PR 91*
June, Ava 1931- *IntWWM 90*
June, Franz E. 1934- *St&PR 91*
Juneau, John Bradley 1959- *St&PR 91*
Juneau, John Lawrence 1947- *WhoE 91*
Juneau, Joseph *WhNaAH*
Juneau, Pierre *BioIn 16*
Juneau, Pierre 1922- *WhoAm 90, WhoE 91, WhoWor 91*
Juneau, Richard James 1933- *St&PR 91*
Juneja, Diljit Singh 1922- *WhoAm 90*
Juneja, Satish K. 1946- *St&PR 91*
Junejo, Anwar Ahmed 1944- *WhoWor 91*
Junejo, Mohammad Khan 1932- *WhoWor 91*
Junek, Elisabeth *BioIn 16*
Junell, Robert Frank 1914- *St&PR 91*
Jung, Andre 1939- *WhoWor 91*
Jung, Buck Leong 1931- *WhoSSW 91*
Jung, C. G. 1875-1961 *BioIn 16*
Jung, C G 1875-1961 *MajTwCW*
Jung, Carl 1875-1961 *WrPh P*
Jung, Carl Gustav 1875-1961 *BioIn 16, EncO&P 3, EncPaPR 91, WorAlBi*
Jung, Charlotte Jeanne 1924- *St&PR 91*
Jung, Dora 1906-1980 *ConDes 90*
Jung, Doranne 1948- *WhoEmL 91*
Jung, Doris 1924- *IntWWM 90, WhoAm 90, WhoAmW 91, WhoE 91*
Jung, Franz 1888-1963 *BioIn 16*
Jung, George Henry 1938- *St&PR 91*
Jung, Greg Mark 1963- *WhoSSW 91*
Jung, Henry Hung 1957- *WhoEmL 91*
Jung, Hilda Ziifle *WhoAmW 91*
Jung, James Hoyoung 1946- *BiDrAPA 89*
Jung, Jerrold Mark 1953- *St&PR 91*
Jung, Johann Heinrich 1740-1817 *EncO&P 3*
Jung, John Bernard 1926- *St&PR 91*
Jung, Juergen Alfred 1951- *WhoEmL 91*
Jung, Koock Elan *BiDrAPA 89*
Jung, Kwan Yee 1932- *WhoAmA 91*
Jung, LaDonna 1960- *WhoAmW 91, WhoEmL 91*
Jung, Laramie Jane 1951- *WhoAmW 91*
Jung, Manfred 1940- *IntWWM 90*
Jung, Manfred 1945- *PenDiMP*
Jung, Peter Michael 1955- *WhoEmL 91*
Jung, Peter U. 1937- *St&PR 91*
Jung, Reinhard Paul 1946- *WhoWor 91*
Jung, Rodney C. 1920- *WhoAm 90, WhoSSW 91*
Jung, Samson Pang 1963- *WhoEmL 91, WhoWor 91*
Jung, Tom *BioIn 16*
Jung, Yee Wah 1936- *WhoAmA 91*
Jung, Yoosuck 1940- *BiDrAPA 89*
Jung-Stilling, Johann Heinrich 1740-1817 *DcLB 94 [port]*
Jungbauer, Mary Ann 1934- *WhoAmW 91*
Jungbluth, Connie Carlson 1955- *WhoAmW 91, WhoEmL 91, WhoWor 91*
Jungbluth, Georg 1928- *WhoWor 91*
Jungbluth, John A. 1920- *St&PR 91*
Jungbluth, Kirk E. 1949- *WhoWor 91*
Jungbluth, William Charles 1924- *St&PR 91*
Jungclaus, Gregory Alan 1947- *WhoSSW 91*
Jungel, Eberhard 1934- *WhoWor 91*
Junger, Ernst 1895- *BioIn 16*
Junger, Miguel Chapero 1923- *WhoAm 90*
Jungerman, John Albert 1921- *WhoAm 90*
Jungermann, Eric 1923- *St&PR 91*
Jungers, Blaine Carroll 1944- *WhoAm 90*
Jungers, Francis 1926- *WhoAm 90*
Junghaene, Joan L. 1924- *St&PR 91*
Jungholm, Sven Johan 1921- *WhoWor 91*
Jungjohann, Eugen E 1930- *BiDrAPA 89*
Jungkind, Walter 1923- *WhoAm 90*
Jungkuntz, Richard Paul 1918- *WhoAm 90, WhoWor 91*
Jungman, Jonathan Wayne 1948- *WhoEmL 91*
Jungman, Robert Peter 1937- *WhoSSW 91, WhoWor 91*
Jungman, Young Frank 1929- *WhoSSW 91*
Jungmann, Frederick Arthur 1936- *WhoE 91*
Jungmann, Horst 1921- *WhoWor 91*
Jungquist, Paul Jerome 1961- *WhoEmL 91*
Jungraithmayr, Herrmann 1931- *WhoWor 91*
Jungwirth, Leonard D 1903-1964 *WhoAmA 91N*
Jungwirth, Manfred 1919- *IntWWM 90, PenDiMP*
Junius, Daniel M. 1952- *St&PR 91*
Junius, Frans Marcel 1930- *WhoWor 91*
Junius, Manfred 1929- *IntWWM 90*
Junius, Ralph W. 1923- *St&PR 91*
Junker, Christine Rosetta 1953- *WhoAmW 91, WhoEmL 91*
Junker, Detlef 1939- *WhoWor 91*
Junker, Edward Philip, III 1937- *St&PR 91*
Junker, George E. *St&PR 91*
Junker, Hans Dieter 1936- *WhoWor 91*
Junker, Ralph Daniel 1923-1988 *BioIn 16*
Junker, Sandra Jean 1947- *WhoAmW 91, WhoEmL 91*
Junkin, Elizabeth Darby 1958- *WhoEmL 91*
Junkin, Joseph Swan 1939- *St&PR 91*
Junkin, Marion Montague 1905-1977 *WhoAmA 91N*
Junkin, Scott Anthony 1946- *St&PR 91*
Junkins, Anita Goll 1956- *WhoEmL 91*
Junkins, David Wallace 1949- *WhoAm 90*
Junkins, Jerry R. 1937- *St&PR 91*
Junkins, Jerry Ray 1937- *WhoAm 90, WhoSSW 91*
Junlius, Steven Mark 1958- *St&PR 91*
Junlowjiraya, Viroj 1955- *WhoEmL 91*
Junquera, Mercedes 1930- *WhoHisp 91*
Junya, Yano 1932- *WhoWor 91*
Junz, Helen B. *WhoAm 90*
Juon, Lester Allen 1938- *St&PR 91, WhoAm 90*
Juottonen, Arvo Olavi 1950- *WhoWor 91*
Jupalli, Raja S 1950- *BiDrAPA 89*
Jupiter, Lona 1933- *St&PR 91*
Jupo, Frank J. 1904- *AuBYP 90*
Jupp, Michael John *BioIn 16*
Jupp, Mo 1938- *BioIn 16*
Juppe, Alain Marie 1945- *BiDFrPL*
Juppeau, Jean-Pierre 1943- *WhoWor 91*
Juquin, Pierre Louis Michel 1930- *BiDFrPL*
Jur, Barbara A. 1945- *WhoEmL 91*
Jura, James J. 1942- *WhoAm 90*
Juracsek, Valeria R *BiDrAPA 89*
Jurak, Danuta Smith 1952- *WhoEmL 91*
Juran, Joseph Moses 1904- *WhoAm 90*
Jurand, Joseph A *BiDrAPA 89*
Jurand, Julian *BiDrAPA 89*
Jurascheck, Francois Jacques 1931- *WhoWor 91*
Jurasek, Kris Charles 1947- *St&PR 91*
Juraska, Janice Marie 1949- *WhoAmW 91*
Jurasky, Jack A *BiDrAPA 89*
Jurczak, Dennis M 1935- *BiDrAPA 89*
Jurczak, Patricia Jean 1962- *WhoAmW 91*
Jurczyk, Irene Donohue 1949- *WhoWrEP 89*
Jurdana, Ernest J. 1944- *WhoAm 90*
Jurecic, Robert Louis 1950- *WhoE 91*
Jurecka, Cyril 1884- *WhoAmA 91N*
Jurecki, Casimer John Joseph 1952- *WhoEmL 91*
Juredine, David G. 1937- *St&PR 91*
Jurek, Eileen Jean 1947- *WhoAmW 91*
Jurek, Kenneth Rudolph 1950- *WhoEmL 91*
Jurena, Leonard Adolph 1936- *WhoSSW 91*
Jurewicz, Thomas 1958- *WhoEmL 91*
Jurgens, Conrad Robert 1947- *St&PR 91*
Jurgens, E.L. 1905- *St&PR 91*
Jurgens, Grethe 1899- *BiDWomA*
Jurgens, John F.B., III 1945- *St&PR 91*
Jurgens, Jurgen 1925- *IntWWM 90, PenDiMP*
Jurgens, Rainer 1941- *St&PR 91*
Jurgensen, Christian Adolph, III 1934- *WhoAm 90*
Jurgensen, Delbert Frederick 1909- *St&PR 91*
Jurgensen, John H., III 1939- *WhoAm 90*
Jurgensen, Warren P 1921- *BiDrAPA 89*
Jurgensen, Warren Peter 1921- *WhoAm 90*
Jurgensen, William Gerald 1951- *St&PR 91*
Jurgenson, Friedrich 1903-1987 *EncO&P 3, EncPaPR 91*
Jurgenson, Sonny 1934- *WorAlBi*
Jurges, Billy 1908- *Ballpl 90*
Jurich, Julie Ann 1946- *WhoAmW 91*
Jurick, Robert H. 1926- *WhoE 91*
Jurick, Robert Rudolph 1942- *WhoSSW 91*
Jurilla, Eduardo L *BiDrAPA 89*
Jurin, Benjamin M *BiDrAPA 89*
Jurin, Eric William 1952- *WhoE 91*
Jurinac, Sena 1921- *IntWWM 90, PenDiMP*
Jurinko, Andy *WhoAmA 91*
Juris, Hervey Asher 1938- *WhoAm 90*
Jurisich, Al 1921-1981 *Ballpl 90*
Jurist, James Alfred *WhoAm 90*
Jurista, Alan Peter 1961- *WhoEmL 91*
Jurji, Edward J. 1907-1990 *ConAu 132*
Jurjus, George Jamil *BiDrAPA 89*
Jurka, Edith M 1915- *BiDrAPA 89*
Jurka, Edith Mila 1915- *WhoE 91*
Jurkat, Martin Peter 1935- *WhoAm 90*
Jurkiewicz, Maurice John 1923- *WhoAm 90*
Jurkovic, Milos *IntWWM 90*
Jurkovich, Mike 1954- *WhoEmL 91*
Jurkowich, George J. 1938- *ODwPR 91*
Jurkowicz, Abel Marcos *BiDrAPA 89*
Jurkowski, Mark Alan 1967- *WhoEmL 91*
Jurkowski, Paul Meredith *BiDrAPA 89*
Jurmain, Alan *BioIn 16*
Jurman, Claudia Lynne 1956- *WhoAmW 91*
Jurmu, Stephen Inghart 1951- *WhoEmL 91*
Jurney, Donald 1945- *WhoAmA 91*
Jurney, Donald Benson 1945- *WhoE 91*
Jurney, Dorothy Misener 1909- *WhoAm 90*
Jurock, Oswald Erich 1944- *WhoAm 90*
Jurras, Mark Ivan 1924- *St&PR 91*
Jurriens, Henny 1949-1989 *BioIn 16*
Jurschak, Jay Aloysius 1952- *WhoEmL 91*
Jurse, Milan 1952- *WhoWor 91*
Jursevskis, Zigfrids 1910- *WhoAmA 91*
Jurtshuk, Peter, Jr. 1929- *WhoAm 90*
Jury, Eliahu Ibraham 1923- *WhoAm 90*
Jury, John Robert 1930- *St&PR 91*
Jurzitza, Gerhard Roman Anton 1929- *WhoWor 91*
Jus, Andrzej *BiDrAPA 89*
Jusino-Berrios, Carlos Manuel *BiDrAPA 89*
Jusino-Berrios, Carlos Manuel 1955- *WhoE 91*
Juskey, Frank Joseph 1949- *WhoSSW 91*
Jussie, Jeanne de 1500?-1557? *EncCoWW*
Just, Gemma Rivoli 1921- *WhoAmW 91*
Just, Jennifer Ramsay 1958- *WhoE 91*
Just, Philip Ray 1955- *WhoSSW 91*
Just, Richard Eugene 1948- *WhoE 91*
Just, Victor 1913- *IntWWM 90*
Just, Ward 1935- *ConAu 32NR*
Just, Ward S. *BioIn 16*
Just, Ward Swift 1935- *WhoAm 90, WhoWrEP 89*
Justa, Francine C. *WhoE 91*
Juste, Michael *EncO&P 3*
Juster, Daniel Calvin 1947- *WhoEmL 91*
Juster, Kenneth Ian 1954- *WhoE 91*
Juster, Martin W. *BioIn 16*
Juster, Norton 1929- *AuBYP 90*

Juster, Ronald Samuel 1943- *St&PR 91*
Juster, Sara Ann 1964- *WhoEmL 91*
Justesen, Bryce Everett 1953- *WhoEmL 91*
Justesen, Don Robert 1930- *WhoAm 90*
Justesen, Wayne Quay, Jr. 1946- *St&PR 91*
Justice, Blair 1927- *WhoAm 90*
Justice, Brady R., Jr. 1930- *St&PR 91*
Justice, Brady Richmond, Jr. 1930- *WhoAm 90*
Justice, Charles Richard 1930- *St&PR 91*
Justice, Donald Rodney 1925- *WhoAm 90, WhoWrEP 89*
Justice, Dorothy Dobbs 1932- *WhoAmW 91*
Justice, Edward J. 1867-1917 *AmLegL*
Justice, Elizabeth 1703-1752 *FemiCLE*
Justice, Eric Henry 1960- *WhoE 91*
Justice, Eun Joo Lee 1948- *BiDrAPA 89*
Justice, Frank K. 1941- *St&PR 91*
Justice, Frank P. 1938- *ODwPR 91*
Justice, Franklin Pierce, Jr. 1938- *WhoAm 90*
Justice, Gary A. 1946- *St&PR 91*
Justice, Ingrid Cooper 1958- *WhoAmW 91*
Justice, Jack Burton 1931- *WhoAm 90*
Justice, Jack Ronald 1940- *WhoWrEP 89*
Justice, Kathleen Murphy *WhoAmW 91*
Justice, Ledro Rogers 1943- *BiDrAPA 89*
Justice, Ora Lynn 1942- *WhoWor 91*
Justice, Susanne Dorothy 1942- *WhoAmW 91*
Justice, Thomas Hardwick, III 1955- *WhoEmL 91*
Justice, Timothy David *BiDrAPA 89*
Justice, William Wayne 1920- *WhoAm 90, WhoSSW 91*
Justiciar *ConAu 30NR*
Justin, John S., Jr. 1917- *St&PR 91*
Justin, Joseph Eugene 1945- *WhoEmL 91*
Justinger, Maryann Elizabeth 1951- *WhoAmW 91*
Justinian I 483-565 *WorAlBi*
Justiniano, Robert 1928- *St&PR 91*
Justiniano-Toro, Luis 1932- *BiDrAPA 89*
Justis, Gary 1953- *WhoAmA 91*
Justis, Nancy Ann 1950- *WhoAmW 91*
Justis, Robert Young, Jr. 1943- *WhoE 91*
Justiz, Manuel Jon 1948- *WhoAm 90*
Justman, Robert H. *BioIn 16*
Justo, Agustin P. 1878-1943 *BioIn 16*
Justo, Juan Bautista 1865-1928 *BioIn 16*
Justus, Betty I. 1930- *WhoAmW 91*
Justus, E. J. 1917- *BioIn 16*
Justus, May 1898- *AuBYP 90*
Justus, Roy Braxton 1901-1983 *WhoAmA 91N*
Juszczyk, James Joseph 1943- *WhoAmA 91*
Juszkiewicz, Henry Edward 1953- *St&PR 91*
Jute, Andre 1945- *ConAu 131, SpyFic*
Juten, John Russell 1907- *WhoAm 90*
Juter, Selwyn Oscar *BiDrAPA 89*
Juthani, Nalini Virendra 1946- *BiDrAPA 89, WhoE 91*
Jutovsky, Jean 1959- *WhoSSW 91*
Jutra, Claude 1930-1987 *BioIn 16*
Jutze, George A. 1927- *St&PR 91*
Jutze, Skip 1946- *Ballpl 90*
Juul, Clement O 1911- *BiDrAPA 89*
Juvarra, Filippo 1678-1736 *PenDiDA 89*
Juve, Arthur James 1951- *WhoEmL 91, WhoSSW 91*
Juve, Richard Henry 1920- *St&PR 91*
Juvelis, Priscilla Catherine 1945- *WhoAmW 91*
Juvenal 60?-140? *WorAlBi*
Juvet, Richard Spalding, Jr. 1930- *WhoAm 90*
Juviler, Peter Henry 1926- *WhoAm 90*
Juvonen, Helvi 1919-1959 *DcScanL, EncCoWW*
Juzwik, Frank L. 1922- *St&PR 91*
Jyotir Maya Nanda, Swami 1931- *EncO&P 3*
Jyrkiainen, Reijo Einari 1934- *IntWWM 90*
Jywook, Sam M. 1947- *St&PR 91*

K

K, M *BiDEWW*
K.C. and the Sunshine Band *EncPR&S 89*
K-Turkel, Judi 1934- *WhoAmW 91, WhoWrEP 89*
Kaak, Hans Otto 1938- *BiDrAPA 89*
Kaake, Norman Bradford 1954- *WhoEmL 91*
Kaapcke, Wallace Letcher 1916- *WhoAm 90, WhoWor 91*
Kaariainen, Jarmo Tapio 1952- *WhoWor 91*
Kaas, Jon H. *WhoAm 90*
Kaas, William M. 1927- *St&PR 91*
Kaat, Jim 1938- *Ballpl 90 [port]*
Kaatz, Margo Jeanne 1960- *WhoAmW 91*
Kaatz, Ronald B. 1934- *WhoAm 90*
Kaback, Deborah 1951- *St&PR 91*
Kaback, Elaine 1939- *WhoAmW 91*
Kabaivanska, Raina 1934- *IntWWM 90, PenDiMP*
Kabak, Douglas Thomas 1957- *WhoE 91, WhoEmL 91, WhoWor 91*
Kabak, Wayne Stuart 1950- *WhoAm 90*
Kabaker, Ray 1934?-1990 *ConAu 132*
Kabala, Edward John 1942- *WhoE 91, WhoWor 91*
Kabala, Karen Lynn 1963- *WhoAmW 91*
Kabalevsky, Dmitry 1904- *PenDiMP A*
Kabalka, George Walter 1943- *WhoSSW 91*
Kabaphes, Konstantinos Petrou 1863-1933 *BioIn 16*
Kabara, Jon Joseph 1926- *WhoAm 90*
Kabat, Douglas Charles 1946- *WhoEmL 91*
Kabat, Elvin Abraham 1914- *WhoAm 90*
Kabat, Jules Max 1942- *St&PR 91*
Kabat, Julie Phyllis 1947- *IntWWM 90*
Kabat, Linda Georgette 1951- *WhoEmL 91*
Kabatay, Romulo Villegas 1948- *WhoEmL 91*
Kabateck, Gladys Irene 1930- *WhoAmW 91*
Kabay, John K. 1942- *St&PR 91*
Kabcenell, Martin Joseph 1926- *St&PR 91*
Kabel, Joanne Lisa 1963- *WhoAmW 91*
Kabel, Robert James 1946- *WhoAm 90*
Kabel, Robert Lynn 1932- *WhoAm 90*
Kabengele, Ntanda 1942- *WhoWor 91*
Kaberon, Daniel Adam 1955- *WhoEmL 91*
Kabibble, Ish *ConAu 131*
Kabibble, Ish 1908- *BioIn 16*
Kabins, Darryl *BiDrAPA 89*
Kabir 1440?-1518 *EncO&P 3*
Kabir, Mohammed A 1931- *BiDrAPA 89*
Kable, Edward Everett 1939- *St&PR 91*
Kable, Mark 1948- *St&PR 91*
Kabos, Ilona 1893-1973 *PenDiMP*
Kaboth, Kurt R. 1951- *WhoE 91*
Kabrick, Randolph Marion 1952- *WhoSSW 91*
Kabriel, Marcia Gail 1938- *WhoAmW 91*
Kabureck, George Richard 1939- *St&PR 91*
Kac, Victor G. 1943- *WhoE 91*
Kacalieff, Louis D *BiDrAPA 89*
Kace, Morris *BiDrAPA 89*
Kacek, Don J. 1936- *St&PR 91, WhoAm 90*
Kacere, John C 1920- *WhoAmA 91*
Kacewicz, Laura Ann 1945- *WhoAmW 91*
Kachadoorian, Zubel 1924- *WhoAm 90, WhoAmA 91*
Kachadurian, Kachig *St&PR 91*
Kachajian, George Simon 1927- *St&PR 91*
Kachalsky, Hyman D 1929- *BiDrAPA 89*
Kachan, Darrel *ODwPR 91*
Kachel, Harold Stanley 1928- *WhoAmA 91*
Kachenmeister, Lois Ann 1929- *BiDrAPA 89*
Kachergis, George Joseph 1917-1974 *WhoAmA 91N*
Kachigian, Mark George 1952- *WhoEmL 91*
Kachinsky, Alexander 1888-1958 *WhoAmA 91N*
Kachka, Larry 1950- *St&PR 91*
Kachlein, George F., III 1934- *St&PR 91*
Kachlein, Mark R. 1961- *St&PR 91*
Kachline, Clifford 1922- *Ballpl 90*
Kachline, Evelyn Jerene Bates 1922- *WhoE 91*
Kachmar, Jessie K. 1913- *WhoWrEP 89*
Kachmarik, George Steven, VI 1953- *WhoSSW 91*
Kachmer, Michael Paul 1947- *WhoSSW 91*
Kachoris, Paul John *BiDrAPA 89*
Kachru, Braj Behari 1932- *WhoAm 90*
Kachru, Yamuna 1933- *WhoAm 90*
Kacin, William L. 1932- *St&PR 91*
Kacinski, John Joseph 1957- *WhoSSW 91*
Kacir, Barbara Brattin 1941- *WhoAmW 91*
Kaclik, Debi Louise 1953- *WhoAmW 91*
Kacoha, Margie 1955- *WhoWrEP 89*
Kacor, Laura Mary 1958- *WhoAmW 91*
Kacoyanis, Joyce *ODwPR 91*
Kacvinsky, Raymond C. 1949- *St&PR 91*
Kaczanowska, Anna *BiDrAPA 89*
Kaczanowska, Wieslawa K *BiDrAPA 89*
Kaczanowski, Carl Henry 1948- *WhoE 91, WhoEmL 91*
Kaczerginski, Shmaryahu 1908-1954 *BioIn 16*
Kaczey, Charles J *BiDrAPA 89*
Kaczmarek, Jack Jay *BiDrAPA 89*
Kaczmarek, Kenneth Kasimer 1939- *St&PR 91*
Kaczmarek, Zdzislaw 1928- *WhoWor 91*
Kaczmarski, Michael J. 1953- *St&PR 91*
Kaczynski, Bernice *BioIn 16*
Kaczynski, Stephen John 1954- *WhoEmL 91*
Kad, Surinder Kumar 1950- *WhoEmL 91*
Kadaba, Pankaja Kooveli 1928- *WhoAmW 91*
Kadah, Dianne 1957- *WhoEmL 91*
Kadak, Andrew C. 1945- *St&PR 91*
Kadakia, Shailesh Chandrakant 1952- *WhoSSW 91*
Kadakkal, Sreeja *BiDrAPA 89*
Kadalie, Rhoda Bertelsmann- 1953- *BioIn 16*
Kadan, Ranjit Singh 1935- *WhoSSW 91*
Kadane, Joseph B. 1941- *WhoAm 90*
Kadaner, Debbie 1956- *WhoE 91*
Kadanoff, Leo Philip 1937- *WhoAm 90*
Kadar, Jan 1918-1979 *BioIn 16*
Kadar, Janos 1912-1989 *AnObit 1989, BioIn 16*
Kadar, Laszlo *BiDrAPA 89*
Kadare, Elena 1943- *EncCoWW*
Kadas, Zsuzsanna Margit 1953- *WhoE 91*
Kadash, Kenneth Warren 1945- *WhoSSW 91*
Kadavy, Paul Dean 1943- *St&PR 91*
Kadel, Merl A *BiDrAPA 89*
Kadel, Paula Ruth Ritchie 1946- *WhoE 91*
Kadela, David Anthony 1956- *WhoEmL 91*
Kaden, Allen R. 1943- *St&PR 91*
Kadenbach, Bernhard Adolf Anton 1933- *WhoWor 91*
Kader, Adel Abdel 1941- *WhoAm 90*
Kader, Nancy Stowe 1945- *WhoE 91*
Kaderi, Nazem al- *BioIn 16*
Kades, Charles Louis 1906- *WhoAm 90*
Kadesch, Robert R. 1922- *AuBYP 90*
Kadey, Frederic Lionel, Jr. 1918- *WhoWor 91*
Kadhafi, Muammar Muhammad *WhoWor 91*
Kadijevic, Veljko Dusan 1925- *WhoWor 91*
Kadile, Eleazar Demira *BiDrAPA 89*
Kadile, Hermanegildo 1930- *BiDrAPA 89*
Kadin, Fred Martin 1942- *WhoAm 90*
Kadin, Marshall Edward 1939- *WhoAm 90*
Kading, David Richard 1958- *WhoEmL 91*
Kadis, Betty *BioIn 16*
Kadis, Leslie B *BiDrAPA 89*
Kadish, Alon 1950- *ConAu 131*
Kadish, Gerald M. 1937- *St&PR 91*
Kadish, Mark J. 1943- *WhoSSW 91*
Kadish, Richard L. 1943- *St&PR 91*
Kadish, Sanford Harold 1921- *WhoAm 90*
Kadish, William A 1957- *BiDrAPA 89*
Kadison, Douglas Bennett 1947- *WhoEmL 91*
Kadison, Richard David 1949- *BiDrAPA 89*
Kadison, Richard Vincent 1925- *WhoAm 90*
Kadison, Stuart L. 1923- *WhoAm 90*
Kadkhodaian, Hooshmand 1938- *BiDrAPA 89*
Kadlec, Rudolph Joseph 1932- *St&PR 91, WhoE 91*
Kadleck, Joseph J. 1936- *St&PR 91*
Kado, Clarence Isao 1936- *WhoAm 90*
Kadohata, Cynthia *ConLC 59 [port]*
Kadon, Karl Paul, III 1958- *WhoEmL 91*
Kadonada, George 1942- *St&PR 91*
Kadonsky, William James 1954- *WhoEmL 91*
Kadota, Takashi Theodore 1930- *WhoAm 90*
Kadoya, Tetsuo 1949- *St&PR 91*
Kadri, Tariq Rashid 1949- *WhoEmL 91*
Kadrmas, Arnold Edmund *BiDrAPA 89*
Kadrovach, Dan George 1920- *WhoSSW 91*
Kadry, Ahmed *NewYTBS 90*
Kadtke, James Bernard 1957- *WhoEmL 91*
Kadushin, Max 1895-1980 *BioIn 16*
Kady, Michael S. 1949- *St&PR 91*
Kady, Michael Stanley 1949- *WhoE 91*
Kaechele, David Paul 1940- *St&PR 91*
Kaefer, Gene John 1928- *St&PR 91, WhoAm 90*
Kaegel, Ray Martin 1925- *WhoWor 91*
Kaegel, Richard James 1939- *WhoAm 90*
Kaegi, Charles Edward, Jr. *BiDrAPA 89*
Kaegi, Richard John 1948- *St&PR 91*
Kaehler, Susan Lee *BiDrAPA 89*
Kaehr, Mitchael Raymond 1942- *WhoSSW 91*
Kael, Pauline *BioIn 16*
Kael, Pauline 1919- *FemiCLE, WhoAm 90, WhoAmW 91, WhoE 91, WhoWrEP 89, WorAlBi*
Kaelber, Charles Theodore 1938- *BiDrAPA 89, WhoE 91*
Kaelber, Don Edward 1933- *St&PR 91*
Kaelin, Elmer B. 1925- *WhoAm 90*
Kaelin, Eugene Francis 1926- *WhoAm 90*
Kaelin, Pamela Marie 1965- *WhoWrEP 89*
Kaemmerlen, Cathy June 1949- *WhoEmL 91, WhoSSW 91*
Kaempfert, Bert 1923-1980 *OxCPMus*
Kaempfert, Wade *MajTwCW*
Kaempffert, Waldemar B 1877-1956 *EncO&P 3*
Kaempffert, Waldemar Bernhard 1877-1956 *EncPaPR 91*
Kaendler, Johann Joachim *PenDiDA 89*
Kaenel, Reg Alfred 1929- *WhoAm 90*
Kaenzig, Joseph G., Jr. 1945- *St&PR 91*
Kaep, Louis Joseph 1903- *WhoAmA 91*
Kaercher, Robert Lloyd 1924- *St&PR 91*
Kaericher, C.W. 1921- *St&PR 91*
Kaericher, John Conrad 1936- *WhoAmA 91*
Kaesberg, Paul Joseph 1923- *WhoAm 90*
Kaese, Harold 1909-1975 *Ballpl 90*
Kaeser, Clifford Richard 1936- *St&PR 91, WhoAm 90*
Kaeser, Ernst Heini 1924- *WhoWor 91*
Kaeser, Hans Eugen 1924- *WhoWor 91*
Kaeslin, Laura M. 1917- *St&PR 91*
Kaessner, Michael L. 1950- *St&PR 91*
Kaeter, Margaret 1957- *WhoWrEP 89*
Kafadar, Ahmed D. 1915- *St&PR 91*
Kafadar, Charles Bell 1945- *St&PR 91*
Kafantaris, George Nicholas 1953- *WhoEmL 91*
Kafarova, Elmira Mikail Kyzy 1934- *WhoWor 91*
Kafarski, Mitchell I. 1917- *WhoAm 90*
Kafe, Said Madi 1937- *WhoWor 91*
Kafes, William O. 1935- *St&PR 91*
Kafes, William Owen 1935- *WhoAm 90*
Kaff, Albert Ernest 1920- *WhoAm 90*
Kaffen, A. Steven 1947- *St&PR 91*
Kaffenberger, Ernst Wilhelm 1931- *WhoWor 91*
Kaffenberger, Wilfried Ernst 1944- *St&PR 91*
Kaffer, Roger Louis 1927- *WhoAm 90*
Kaffer, William John 1929- *St&PR 91*
Kafferlin, William H. 1923- *St&PR 91*
Kaffka, Margit 1880-1918 *EncCoWW*
Kafi, Ahmad *BiDrAPA 89*
Kafin, William Joel *BiDrAPA 89*
Kafka, Alexandre 1917- *WhoE 91, WhoWor 91*
Kafka, Anne G. 1920- *WhoAmW 91, WhoWor 91*
Kafka, Ernest 1932- *BiDrAPA 89*
Kafka, Franz 1883-1924 *BioIn 16, MajTwCW, WorAlBi, WrPh*
Kafka, Gerald Andrew 1951- *WhoEmL 91*
Kafka, John S 1921- *BiDrAPA 89*
Kafka, Leon 1926- *ODwPR 91*
Kafka, Martin Paul 1947- *BiDrAPA 89*
Kafrissen, Steven R *BiDrAPA 89*
Kaftal, George 1897-1987 *BioIn 16*
Kagan, Alan Robert 1944- *BiDrAPA 89*

Kagan, Andrew Aaron 1947- WhoAmA 91
Kagan, Anna S BiDrAPA 89
Kagan, Arthur Myron 1919- St&PR 91
Kagan, Bruce L BiDrAPA 89
Kagan, Donald 1932- WhoAm 90
Kagan, Drew T. 1948- St&PR 91
Kagan, George Irwin 1939- WhoWor 91
Kagan, Henya 1946- WhoAmW 91
Kagan, Irving 1928- St&PR 91
Kagan, Irving 1936- WhoAm 90
Kagan, James Melvin 1943- BiDrAPA 89
Kagan, Jeremy Paul 1945- WhoAm 90
Kagan, Jerome BioIn 16
Kagan, Jerome 1929- WhoAm 90
Kagan, Julia Lee 1948- WhoAm 90
Kagan, Martin I. 1946- WhoEmL 91
Kagan, Michael 1939- St&PR 91
Kagan, Oleg PenDiMP
Kagan, Robert BiDrAPA 89
Kagan, Sioma 1907- WhoAm 90, WhoWor 91
Kagan, Stephen Bruce 1944- St&PR 91, WhoAm 90
Kagawa, Kathleen Hatsuyo 1952- WhoAmW 91, WhoEmL 91, WhoWor 91
Kagawa, Toyohiko 1888-1960 BioIn 16
Kagawa, Yukio 1935- WhoWor 91
Kagaya, Hiroshi Kan 1930- WhoWor 91
Kagda, Sakina Yusuf 1939- WhoWor 91
Kage, Wilhelm PenDiDA 89
Kagel, Mauricio 1931- BioIn 16, IntWWM 90, PenDiMP A, WhoAm 90
Kagemoto, Haro 1951- WhoAmA 91
Kagen, Irving N 1922- BiDrAPA 89
Kagen, James Gordon 1943- WhoAm 90
Kagey, Florence Eileen 1925- WhoAmW 91
Kageyama, Kiichi 1936- WhoWor 91
Kagiwada, Harriet Hatsune 1937- WhoAmW 91
Kagle, Joseph L, Jr 1932- WhoAmA 91
Kagle, Joseph Louis, Jr. 1932- WhoAm 90
Kagler, Kris ODwPR 91
Kagler, William George 1932- St&PR 91
Kagy, Sheffield Harold 1907-1989 WhoAmA 91N
Kahalas, Harvey 1941- WhoE 91
Kahan, Al E. 1922- St&PR 91
Kahan, Alexander WhoAmA 91
Kahan, Barry Donald 1939- WhoAm 90
Kahan, Bernard B BiDrAPA 89
Kahan, Eileen B 1945- BiDrAPA 89
Kahan, Herman L. 1954- WhoE 91
Kahan, James Paul 1942- WhoAm 90
Kahan, Joel BiDrAPA 89
Kahan, Joel 1953- WhoSSW 91
Kahan, Leonard 1935- WhoAmA 91
Kahan, Leonard H. 1924- St&PR 91
Kahan, Michael 1953- BiDrAPA 89
Kahan, Mitchell Douglas 1951- WhoAm 90, WhoAmA 91, WhoEmL 91
Kahan, Oscar 1910-1981 Ballpl 90
Kahan, Richard Lee 1940- BiDrAPA 89
Kahan, Sheldon Jeremiah 1948- WhoEmL 91
Kahana, Aron 1921- WhoAm 90
Kahana, Eva Frost 1941- WhoAm 90
Kahana, Ralph J 1924- BiDrAPA 89
Kahana, Ralph Jonah 1924- WhoE 91
Kahanamoku, Duke Paoa 1890-1968 WorAlBi
Kahane, Henry 1902- WhoAm 90
Kahane, Jack 1888-1939 BioIn 16
Kahane, Jeffrey Alan 1956- IntWWM 90
Kahane, Meir BioIn 16
Kahane, Meir 1932- WorAlBi
Kahane, Meir 1932-1990 News 91-2
Kahane, Melanie 1910-1988 BioIn 16
Kahaner, Kenneth Paul BiDrAPA 89
Kahanovitz, Neil 1949- WhoAm 90
Kahanpaa, Kari Veikko 1939- WhoWor 91
Kahen, Harold I. 1918- St&PR 91, WhoAm 90
Kahgan, Marc Paul 1948- BiDrAPA 89
Kahill, Joseph B 1882-1957 WhoAmA 91N
Kahin, George McTurnan 1918- WhoAm 90
Kahina WomWR
Kahl, Alfred Louis, Jr. 1932- WhoE 91
Kahl, Dan Robert 1924- St&PR 91
Kahl, Jeffrey Brian 1950- St&PR 91
Kahl, L Bruce BiDrAPA 89
Kahl, M. P. 1934- BioIn 16
Kahl, M.W. 1930- St&PR 91
Kahl, Marvin Philip 1934- BioIn 16
Kahl, Virginia 1919- AuBYP 90, BioIn 16
Kahl, William Frederick 1922- WhoAm 90
Kahle, Douglas St&PR 91
Kahle, Jack E. 1929- St&PR 91
Kahle, Lynn Richard 1950- WhoEmL 91
Kahle, Maria 1891-1975 EncCoWW
Kahle, Roger David 1940- St&PR 91
Kahle, Roger Raymond 1943- WhoWor 91
Kahlenbeck, Howard 1929- St&PR 91
Kahlenbeck, Paul R. St&PR 91
Kahlenberg, Jeannette Dawson 1931- WhoE 91
Kahlenberg, John B. 1915- St&PR 91
Kahlenberg, Karl W. 1933- St&PR 91
Kahler, Elizabeth Sartor 1911- WhoAm 90
Kahler, George 1889-1924 Ballpl 90
Kahler, Harlan P BiDrAPA 89
Kahler, Herbert Frederick 1936- St&PR 91, WhoAm 90
Kahler, Hermann August 1846-1917 PenDiDA 89
Kahler, Jeffrey Richard 1949- WhoEmL 91
Kahler, Julia Pemberton 1947- BiDrAPA 89
Kahler, Lee Daniel 1959- WhoEmL 91
Kahler, Nancee NewAgMG
Kahler, Tom 1943- WhoWor 91
Kahles, Charles William 1878-1931 EncACom
Kahles, John F. 1914- St&PR 91
Kahles, John Frank 1914- WhoAm 90
Kahlil, Khazem el- NewYTBS 90
Kahlo, Frida 1907-1954 ArtLatA, BioIn 16
Kahlon, Neenoo BiDrAPA 89
Kahlon, Ravinder BiDrAPA 89
Kahlon, Vasdev S. BiDrAPA 89
Kahlor, Robert A. WhoAm 90
Kahlow, Barbara Fenvessy 1946- WhoAmW 91
Kahn, Lord 1905-1989 AnObit 1989
Kahn, A Michael 1917- WhoAmA 91
Kahn, Alan Edwin 1929- WhoE 91
Kahn, Albert 1869-1942 BioIn 16, EncABHB 4 [port], WorAlBi
Kahn, Albert Michael 1917- WhoAm 90, WhoSSW 91, WhoWor 91
Kahn, Alex 1931- St&PR 91
Kahn, Alfred Edward 1917- BioIn 16, WhoAm 90
Kahn, Alfred J. 1919- ConAu 32NR
Kahn, Alfred Joseph 1919- WhoAm 90
Kahn, Alice 1943- BioIn 16
Kahn, Alice Joyce 1943- WhoAm 90
Kahn, Allen 1921- BiDrAPA 89
Kahn, Alvin 1928- BiDrAPA 89
Kahn, Andre Santamaria 1949- WhoWor 91
Kahn, Ann Jean 1950- IntWWM 90
Kahn, Anna L. 1923- St&PR 91
Kahn, Annelies Ruth 1927- WhoAmA 91
Kahn, Anthony 1961- BioIn 16
Kahn, Arnold N. 1941- St&PR 91
Kahn, Arthur H. 1931- WhoAm 90
Kahn, B. Franklin 1925- St&PR 91
Kahn, Bernd 1928- WhoAm 90
Kahn, Blossom 1936- WhoAmW 91
Kahn, Brian Aleck 1954- WhoSSW 91
Kahn, Bruce Alan 1953- BiDrAPA 89
Kahn, Carl Ronald 1944- WhoAm 90
Kahn, Charles 1903- St&PR 91
Kahn, Charles H 1928- ConAu 132
Kahn, Charles Howard 1926- WhoAm 90
Kahn, Coppelia 1939- ConAu 129
Kahn, Corinne Beth 1953- WhoEmL 91
Kahn, Dan BioIn 16
Kahn, Dan 1933?-1989 ConAu 129
Kahn, Daniel 1927- WhoE 91
Kahn, Daniel Gerald 1955- WhoE 91
Kahn, David 1912- WhoAm 90
Kahn, David A BiDrAPA 89
Kahn, David Alan 1953- BiDrAPA 89
Kahn, Debra Johnson 1950- St&PR 91
Kahn, Donald Paul 1925- WhoSSW 91
Kahn, Doris Chilton 1928- WhoE 91
Kahn, Douglas Allen 1934- WhoAm 90
Kahn, Douglas G 1946- BiDrAPA 89
Kahn, Douglas Gerard 1946- WhoAm 90
Kahn, E. J. 1916- BioIn 16
Kahn, Edgar Michael 1954- BiDrAPA 89
Kahn, Edward D. 1941- WhoAm 90
Kahn, Edward Stanton 1947- WhoEmL 91
Kahn, Edwin Leonard 1918- WhoAm 90
Kahn, Elliot 1920- St&PR 91
Kahn, Ellis Irvin 1936- WhoSSW 91
Kahn, Ely Jacques 1916- BioIn 16
Kahn, Ely Jacques, Jr. 1916- WhoAm 90
Kahn, Erich J. 1913-1990 BioIn 16
Kahn, Ernest 1919- BiDrAPA 89
Kahn, Faith-Hope 1921- WhoAmW 91, WhoE 91, WhoWor 91
Kahn, Florence Abraham BioIn 16
Kahn, Frank J. 1921- St&PR 91
Kahn, Franz 1896-1944 BioIn 16
Kahn, Fred A. 1932- WhoE 91
Kahn, Gary 1947-1974 WhoAmA 91N
Kahn, Gerald J. 1926- St&PR 91
Kahn, Gordon Barry 1931- WhoAm 90
Kahn, Gus 1886-1941 OxCPMus
Kahn, H. Bernard 1923- St&PR 91
Kahn, Hannah 1911- WhoWrEP 89
Kahn, Harry 1916- WhoAm 90
Kahn, Harry H. 1943- St&PR 91
Kahn, Herbert 1922- St&PR 91
Kahn, Herman Bernard 1923- WhoAm 90
Kahn, Herta Hess 1919- WhoAm 90
Kahn, Hugo 1932- St&PR 91
Kahn, I.B. 1917- St&PR 91
Kahn, Irving 1905- St&PR 91
Kahn, Irving B. 1917- WhoAm 90
Kahn, Irving I. 1916- St&PR 91
Kahn, Irwin 1912- St&PR 91
Kahn, Irwin William 1923- WhoWor 91
Kahn, Isadore J. 1914- St&PR 91
Kahn, James BioIn 16
Kahn, James Leslie 1942- BiDrAPA 89
Kahn, James Robert 1953- WhoEmL 91
Kahn, James Stanley 1947- WhoE 91, WhoEmL 91
Kahn, James Steven 1931- WhoAm 90
Kahn, Jeffrey H. 1939- St&PR 91
Kahn, Jeffrey Hay 1939- WhoAm 90
Kahn, Jeffrey Paul 1953- BiDrAPA 89
Kahn, Joan BioIn 16
Kahn, Joan 1914- AuBYP 90
Kahn, Joseph Gabriel 1913- WhoAm 90
Kahn, Joshua BiDrAPA 89
Kahn, Judith G. ODwPR 91
Kahn, Karen Lynn 1956- WhoE 91
Kahn, Kathy 1945- WhoAmW 91, WhoEmL 91
Kahn, Lawrence Alan 1953- WhoE 91
Kahn, Leonard 1929- BiDrAPA 89
Kahn, Leonard Richard 1926- WhoAm 90
Kahn, Leslie Ruth 1947- WhoAmW 91, WhoE 91, WhoEmL 91
Kahn, Linda Anne 1949- WhoAmW 91
Kahn, Linda McClure WhoAmW 91
Kahn, Lisa 1927- EncCoWW
Kahn, Lois Jean 1939- WhoSSW 91
Kahn, Lothar 1922-1990 BioIn 16
Kahn, Ludwig EncO&P 3
Kahn, Ludwig Werner 1910- WhoAm 90
Kahn, Madeline BioIn 16
Kahn, Madeline 1942- ConTFT 8 [port], WorAlBi
Kahn, Madeline Gail WhoAm 90
Kahn, Mark Leo 1921- WhoWor 91
Kahn, Melissa Jan 1956- WhoAmW 91
Kahn, Michael BioIn 16, WhoAm 90
Kahn, Michael William 1921- BiDrAPA 89
Kahn, Michele 1940- ConAu 130
Kahn, Mitchell Charles 1953- WhoEmL 91
Kahn, Mohammad Anwar 1953- WhoWor 91
Kahn, Myron 1930- St&PR 91
Kahn, Nancy Valerie 1952- WhoAmW 91
Kahn, Nathan Samuel 1954- St&PR 91
Kahn, Neil 1957- St&PR 91
Kahn, Neil Andrew BiDrAPA 89
Kahn, Norman 1932- WhoAm 90
Kahn, Otto H. 1867-1934 EncABHB 6 [port], WorAlBi
Kahn, Otto Hermann 1867-1934 BioIn 16
Kahn, Paul 1949- WhoWrEP 89
Kahn, Paul Frederick 1935- WhoAm 90
Kahn, Paul H. 1947- St&PR 91
Kahn, Paul Markham 1935- WhoWor 91
Kahn, Peter 1921- WhoAmA 91
Kahn, Peter Andrew BiDrAPA 89
Kahn, Peter B. 1935- WhoAm 90
Kahn, Philippe BioIn 16
Kahn, Ralph 1920-1987 WhoAmA 91N
Kahn, Raymond Lee 1917- WhoAm 90
Kahn, Reuben 1935- St&PR 91
Kahn, Richard Dreyfus 1931- WhoAm 90
Kahn, Richard J BiDrAPA 89
Kahn, Richard Paul 1926- WhoE 91
Kahn, Robert E. 1938- WhoAm 90
Kahn, Robert Irving 1918- WhoAm 90, WhoWor 91
Kahn, Robert L BiDrAPA 89
Kahn, Robert Louis 1918- BioIn 16
Kahn, Robert Phillip 1924- WhoE 91
Kahn, Robert Theodore 1933- WhoAm 90
Kahn, Robin WhoAmA 91
Kahn, Roger BioIn 16
Kahn, Roger 1927- AuBYP 90, Ballpl 90, WhoAm 90, WhoWrEP 89
Kahn, Roy J. 1932- St&PR 91
Kahn, S. Carroll, Jr. 1924- St&PR 91
Kahn, S David 1929- BiDrAPA 89
Kahn, S. David 1929- EncO&P 3, EncPaPR 91
Kahn, Sigmund Benham 1933- WhoE 91
Kahn, Stephen 1943- BiDrAPA 89
Kahn, Stephen Louis 1955- WhoEmL 91
Kahn, Steve BioIn 16
Kahn, Steven BiDrAPA 89
Kahn, Susan B 1924- WhoAmA 91
Kahn, Susan Beth 1924- WhoAm 90, WhoAmW 91
Kahn, Sy Myron 1924- WhoWrEP 89
Kahn, Tobi Aaron 1952- WhoAmA 91
Kahn, Tom 1938- WhoAm 90
Kahn, Tracy Lynn 1955- WhoAmW 91
Kahn, Walter 1917- St&PR 91, WhoAm 90
Kahn, Walter Kurt 1929- WhoAm 90
Kahn, Wolf 1927- WhoAm 90, WhoAmA 91, WhoE 91
Kahn-Goldfarb, Anna Lee 1923- St&PR 91
Kahne, Merton J 1924- BiDrAPA 89
Kahne, Stephen James 1937- WhoAm 90
Kahng, Dawon 1931- WhoAm 90, WhoWor 91
Kahoe, Mike 1873-1949 Ballpl 90
Kahoun, John Robert BiDrAPA 89
Kahr, Frank Millner 1947- BiDrAPA 89
Kahr, Toby Yale 1932- WhoSSW 91
Kahrs, Cynthia Anne 1948- WhoAmW 91
Kahrs, Daniel Henry 1933- St&PR 91
Kahrs, Steven Arthur 1959- WhoEmL 91
Kahrs, Susan Kimberley 1963- WhoAmW 91
Kai, Mutsuoki 1936- BiDrAPA 89
Kaia, Marilyn JoLoyce 1933- WhoAmW 91
Kaida, Ikuo 1931- WhoWor 91
Kaida, Tamarra 1946- WhoAmA 91
Kaiden, Shirley ODwPR 91
Kaiden, Thomas F. 1959- WhoE 91
Kaido, Bonnell Dolores 1951- WhoAmW 91
Kaifa, Stephen Simonovitch 1952- WhoE 91
Kaifu Toshiki 1931- EncJap
Kaifu, Toshiki BioIn 16
Kaifu, Toshiki 1931- CurBio 90 [port], WhoWor 91
Kaige, Alice Tubb 1922- WhoAmW 91
Kaikkonen, Gus 1951- ConAu 129
Kail, Daniel R. 1935- St&PR 91
Kail, Robert Lee WhoWrEP 89
Kaila, Martti Mikael 1933- WhoWor 91
Kailas, Indira Mohan 1949- BiDrAPA 89
Kailas, Uuno 1901-1933 DcScanL
Kailasanath, Kazhikathra 1953- WhoE 91
Kailath, Thomas 1935- WhoAm 90
Kailian, Aram Harry 1949- WhoE 91
Kailo, Meyer Mitchell BioIn 16
Kaim, Samuel C 1911- BiDrAPA 89
Kaiman, Charles 1947- WhoAmA 91
Kaiman, David S. 1955- St&PR 91
Kaiman, Jerome J. 1932- WhoAm 90
Kaiman, Marvin 1930- St&PR 91
Kaiman, Stan C. 1938- St&PR 91
Kain, Clayton A. 1946- St&PR 91
Kain, Edward Robert 1922- St&PR 91
Kain, Jack Allan 1929- St&PR 91
Kain, John Forrest 1935- WhoE 91
Kain, Karen BioIn 16
Kain, Karen Alexandria 1951- WhoAm 90
Kain, Philip J 1943- ConAu 132
Kain, Richard M. NewYTBS 90
Kain, Richard M. 1908-1990 BioIn 16, ConAu 131
Kain, Richard Yerkes 1936- WhoAm 90
Kain, Ronald Stuart 1899- WhoAm 90
Kain, Saul MajTwCW
Kain, Susan Lane 1946- St&PR 91
Kain, Virginia Rose WhoWrEP 89
Kain, William H. 1912- St&PR 91
Kaindl, Gunter 1940- WhoWor 91
Kaine, Robert Leonard 1941- BiDrAPA 89
Kainen, Jacob 1909- WhoAm 90, WhoAmA 91
Kainen, Paul Chester 1943- WhoE 91
Kainlauri, Eino Olavi 1922- WhoAm 90
Kainulainen, Hannu Lauri Olavi 1941- WhoWor 91
Kaipainen, Anu 1933- EncCoWW
Kaipainen, Jouni Ilari 1956- IntWWM 90
Kairaluoma, Matti Ilmari 1936- WhoWor 91
Kairey, Mindy Sue 1963- WhoAmW 91
Kairis, Paul J. 1957- St&PR 91
Kairys, Anatolijus 1914- ConAu 32NR
Kaiser, A. W. 1876- EncO&P 3
Kaiser, Adrian E., Jr. 1928 St&PR 91
Kaiser, Alan H. 1957- ODwPR 91
Kaiser, Albert Farr 1933- WhoAm 90
Kaiser, Ann Philomena 1948- WhoAmW 91
Kaiser, Antoinette Perrone 1935- WhoAmW 91
Kaiser, Armin Dale 1927- WhoAm 90
Kaiser, Barbara 1947- IntWWM 90
Kaiser, Benjamin 1943- WhoAmA 91
Kaiser, Bo Paul 1917- WhoWor 91
Kaiser, Charles BioIn 16
Kaiser, Charles James 1939- WhoAmA 91
Kaiser, Constance K. BioIn 16
Kaiser, Diane 1946- WhoAmA 91
Kaiser, Don 1935- Ballpl 90
Kaiser, Edgar, Jr. BioIn 16
Kaiser, Edgar Fosburgh, Jr. 1942- WhoAm 90, WhoWor 91
Kaiser, Emil Thomas 1938-1988 BioIn 16
Kaiser, Ernest Daniel 1915- WhoAm 90, WhoWrEP 89
Kaiser, F.E. St&PR 91
Kaiser, Franz Nicholas BiDrAPA 89
Kaiser, Fred 1906- WhoAm 90
Kaiser, Georg 1878-1945 WorAlBi
Kaiser, Gunther Willy Heinz 1928- WhoWor 91
Kaiser, Henry BioIn 16
Kaiser, Henry 1911-1989 BioIn 16
Kaiser, Henry Gerard 1956- WhoE 91
Kaiser, Henry J. 1882-1967 WorAlBi
Kaiser, Henry John 1882-1967 BioIn 16, EncABHB 5 [port]
Kaiser, I Howard 1925- BiDrAPA 89
Kaiser, Irwin Herbert 1918- WhoAm 90
Kaiser, Isabelle 1866-1925 EncCoWW
Kaiser, James G. 1943- St&PR 91
Kaiser, James W. 1946- St&PR 91
Kaiser, Jean Morgan 1932- WhoSSW 91
Kaiser, Jeffrey Anthony BiDrAPA 89
Kaiser, John Michael 1956- WhoEmL 91
Kaiser, Joseph P., Jr. 1948- St&PR 91

Kaiser, Joyce Ann 1939- *WhoAmW 91*
Kaiser, Karen 1945- *WhoAmA 91*
Kaiser, Karen Elizabeth 1957- *WhoAmW 91*
Kaiser, Karen June 1951- *WhoE 91, WhoEmL 91*
Kaiser, Ken 1945- *Ballpl 90*
Kaiser, Kenneth Joseph 1931- *St&PR 91*
Kaiser, Lloyd Eugene 1927- *WhoAm 90, WhoE 91*
Kaiser, Mark Alexander 1957- *WhoSSW 91*
Kaiser, Marvin Kent 1941- *St&PR 91*
Kaiser, Mary Agnes 1948- *WhoAmW 91, WhoEmL 91*
Kaiser, Mary Kister 1956- *WhoAmW 91, WhoEmL 91*
Kaiser, Michael J. 1946- *St&PR 91*
Kaiser, Nicholas Thomas 1933- *St&PR 91*
Kaiser, Norman Stanley 1949- *St&PR 91*
Kaiser, Philip Mayer 1913- *WhoAm 90, WhoSSW 91*
Kaiser, Richard *BiDrAPA 89*
Kaiser, Robert G 1943- *ConAu 31NR*
Kaiser, Robert Greeley 1943- *BioIn 16, WhoAm 90*
Kaiser, Robert Lee 1935- *WhoSSW 91, WhoWor 91*
Kaiser, Theodore H *BiDrAPA 89*
Kaiser, Thomas Griffeth 1947- *St&PR 91*
Kaiser, Valerie B *BiDrAPA 89*
Kaiser, Vitus J 1929- *WhoAmA 91*
Kaiser, Walter Ronald 1933- *St&PR 91*
Kaiser, Wolfgang Albert 1923- *WhoWor 91*
Kaiserlian, Penelope Jane 1943- *WhoAm 90*
Kaiserling, George 1893-1918 *Ballpl 90*
Kaiserman, David Norman 1937- *IntWWM 90*
Kaiserman, Terrance Zale 1950- *WhoSSW 91*
Kaish, Luise *WhoAmA 91*
Kaish, Luise Clayborn 1925- *WhoAm 90*
Kaish, Morton 1927- *WhoAm 90, WhoAmA 91*
Kaish, Olga M. 1927- *WhoAmW 91*
Kaisin, Johann Jacob *PenDiDA 89*
Kaising, Elmer A. 1933- *St&PR 91*
Kaistha, Krishan Kumar 1926- *WhoAm 90*
Kaitner, Bruce Edmund 1927- *St&PR 91*
Kaitschuk, Robert Charles 1934- *WhoWor 91*
Kaitz, Ronald Irwin 1952- *BiDrAPA 89*
Kaiya, Hisanobu *BiDrAPA 89*
Kaiyalethe, John Kuruvilla 1936- *WhoWor 91*
Kaizuka, Keimei 1934- *WhoWor 91*
Kajanto, Iiro Ilkka 1925- *WhoWor 91*
Kajanus, Robert 1856-1933 *PenDiMP*
Kajfez, Darko 1928- *WhoSSW 91*
Kaji, Hideko Katayama 1932- *WhoAmW 91*
Kajiwara, Takuma 1877-1960 *WhoAmA 91N*
Kajiwara, Yoshio 1933- *WhoWor 91*
Kajor, Michael Steven 1950- *WhoE 91*
Kakac, Kim Annette 1962- *WhoAmW 91*
Kakacek, Gen *AuBYP 90*
Kakalec, Joseph Michael 1930- *WhoE 91*
Kakanias, Konstantin *BioIn 16*
Kakari, Sophia Anastasiou *WhoWor 91*
Kakas, Christopher A 1941- *WhoAmA 91*
Kakas, George J. 1910- *St&PR 91*
Kakascik, Joan 1941- *WhoAmW 91*
Kakati, Nabajyoti 1948- *BiDrAPA 89*
Kakaty, Kenneth Joseph 1944- *St&PR 91*
Kakee-Manitou-Waya *DcCanB 12*
Kakiemon, II *PenDiDA 89*
Kakiemon, III *PenDiDA 89*
Kakiemon, Ensai 1574-1651 *PenDiDA 89*
Kakiemon, Sakaida 1596-1666 *PenDiDA 89*
Kakish, Stephen 1922- *St&PR 91*
Kakkad, Pradeep B *BiDrAPA 89*
Kakkar, S. 1938- *St&PR 91*
Kakogeorgiou, Charalampos *BiDrAPA 89*
Kakoyiannis, Michael 1942- *WhoAm 90*
Kaku, Michio 1947- *WhoE 91*
Kakusa, Cathy Jean 1949- *St&PR 91*
Kakuschka, Thomas *PenDiMP*
Kakusha, Daniel Wade *BiDrAPA 89*
KAL *BioIn 16*
Kal, Edmund F 1925- *BiDrAPA 89*
Kalaba, Robert Edwin 1926- *WhoAm 90*
Kalabis, Viktor 1923- *IntWWM 90*
Kaladish, Robert 1958- *BiDrAPA 89*
Kalaf, Walter Nadeem 1925- *WhoSSW 91*
Kalafut, George Wendell 1934- *St&PR 91, WhoAm 90, WhoSSW 91*
Kalahar, Patricia Ann 1956- *WhoAmW 91*
Kalahar, William L. 1941- *St&PR 91*
Kalaher, Richard Alan 1940- *St&PR 91, WhoAm 90*
Kalai, Ehud 1942- *WhoAm 90*
Kalaidjian, Berj Boghos 1936- *WhoWor 91*
Kalainov, Sam Charles 1930- *St&PR 91, WhoAm 90*
Kalal, Robert James 1946- *WhoEmL 91*
Kalamaros, Edward Nicholas 1934- *WhoAm 90*
Kalamotousakis, George John 1936- *WhoAm 90, WhoWor 91*
Kalamuniak, Helen Maria 1951- *IntWWM 90*
Kalan, George Richard 1944- *WhoE 91*
Kalanges, James George 1939- *WhoSSW 91*
Kalani, Bob 1953- *BiDrAPA 89*
Kalant, Harold 1923- *WhoAm 90*
Kalanta, James John 1953- *St&PR 91*
Kalapatapu, Sitha Gita *BiDrAPA 89*
Kalapatapu, Umamaheswara *BiDrAPA 89*
Kalas, Frank Joseph, Jr. 1943- *WhoE 91*
Kalas, Melvyn R. 1934- *St&PR 91*
Kalashian, Susan Welling 1933- *WhoSSW 91*
Kalaski, Robert John 1941- *WhoWrEP 89*
Kalat, Peter Anthony 1939- *WhoAm 90*
Kalata, John Joseph 1947- *St&PR 91*
Kalathas, John 1946- *WhoWor 91*
Kalayam, Balkrishna 1949- *BiDrAPA 89*
Kalayjian, Anie Sanentz *WhoAmW 91*
Kalb, Johann *PenDiDA 89*
Kalb, Johann 1721-1780 *EncCRAm*
Kalb, Jonah 1926- *AuBYP 90*
Kalb, Marty Joel 1941- *WhoAmA 91*
Kalb, Marvin *WhoAm 90*
Kalb, Mary Ann 1926- *WhoAmW 91*
Kalb, Nathan *BiDrAPA 89*
Kalb, Robert Joseph 1951- *WhoEmL 91*
Kalb, Ronald G. 1944- *ODwPR 91*
Kalba, Kas 1945- *WhoEmL 91*
Kalbach, Paul Douglas 1947- *WhoEmL 91*
Kalbag, Gayatri Sadanand *BiDrAPA 89*
Kalbaugh, Elmore Porter, Jr. 1921- *BiDrAPA 89*
Kalberer, Dolletta Ann 1951- *WhoE 91*
Kalberkamp, Carl H. 1930- *St&PR 91*
Kalbfeld, Brad Marshall 1954- *WhoEmL 91*
Kalbfleisch, George Randolph 1931- *WhoSSW 91*
Kalbfleisch, John McDowell 1930- *WhoAm 90, WhoSSW 91, WhoWor 91*
Kalcevic, Timothy Francis 1950- *WhoEmL 91, WhoWor 91*
Kalchbrenner, Thelsen Marjorie 1936- *WhoAmW 91*
Kaldahl, Wesley Glen 1924- *WhoAm 90*
Kalderen, Erik Erland 1931- *WhoWor 91*
Kaldewaay, Paul 1938- *WhoWor 91*
Kaldis, Guy Constantine 1937- *WhoE 91*
Kaldis, Panayiotis Efstratios 1960- *WhoWor 91*
Kaldor, Bruce T *BiDrAPA 89*
Kaldor, Nicholas 1908-1986 *BioIn 16*
Kale, Barbara Alice *WhoAmW 91*
Kale, Prabhaker B 1937- *BiDrAPA 89*
Kale, Shrikrishna Vasudeo 1924- *EncO&P 3*
Kalec, Robert Michael 1954- *WhoEmL 91*
Kalechofsky, Roberta 1931- *WhoWrEP 89*
Kaledin, Aleksei Maksimovich 1861-1918 *BioIn 16*
Kaledo, Grace Lucille 1928- *WhoAmW 91*
Kaleel, Mohamed Nawaz *BiDrAPA 89*
Kalekin-Fishman, Devorah 1929- *WhoWor 91*
Kaleko, Mascha 1907-1975 *EncCoWW*
Kalelkar, Ashok Satish 1943- *St&PR 91, WhoAm 90*
Kalellis, William 1917- *St&PR 91*
Kalen, Ragnar Helge Olov 1934- *WhoWor 91*
Kaler, Emile T., Jr. 1935- *St&PR 91*
Kaler, Eric William 1956- *WhoEmL 91*
Kaler, James Llewellyn, Jr. 1951- *WhoEmL 91*
Kaler, Robert Joseph 1956- *WhoEmL 91*
Kales, Anthony 1934- *BiDrAPA 89*
Kales, Joyce D 1934- *BiDrAPA 89*
Kales, Robert Gray 1904- *WhoAm 90*
Kaleta, Mary Ellen A *BiDrAPA 89*
Kalette, Stephen Richard 1950- *St&PR 91*
Kaley, Arthur Warren 1921- *St&PR 91, WhoAm 90*
Kaley, Gabor 1926- *WhoAm 90*
Kalf, Willem 1619-1693 *IntDcAA 90*
Kalfus, Alfred *BioIn 16*
Kalhorn, Gene Edward 1944- *St&PR 91*
Kali *WhoAmA 91*
Kalia, Madhu P. 1940- *WhoAm 90*
Kalia, Narendra Nath 1942- *ConAu 30NR*
Kalian, Robert P. 1939- *WhoWrEP 89*
Kalibat, Francis P 1941- *BiDrAPA 89*
Kalichman, Nathan 1922- *BiDrAPA 89*
Kalichstein, Joseph 1946- *IntWWM 90, PenDiMP*
Kalicki, Patricia Ann 1954- *WhoAmW 91*
Kalidasa *WorAlBi*
Kaliff, Joseph Alfred 1922- *WhoAm 90*
Kaliher, Larkin Lewis 1947- *WhoEmL 91*
Kaliher, Michael Dennis 1947- *WhoWor 91*
Kaliher, Paul L. 1946- *St&PR 91*
Kalik, Barbara Faith 1936- *WhoAmW 91*
Kalikow, Kevin Todd 1953- *BiDrAPA 89*
Kalikow, Peter *BioIn 16*
Kalikow, Peter Steven 1942- *WhoAm 90*
Kalikow, Sidney *BioIn 16*
Kalikow, Theodora J. 1941- *WhoAm 90*
Kalikstein, Kalman 1929-1987 *BioIn 16*
Kalil, Farris G. 1938- *St&PR 91*
Kalil, Farris George 1938- *WhoAm 90*
Kalimo, Esko Antero 1937- *WhoWor 91*
Kalin, David Arthur 1952- *WhoSSW 91*
Kalin, Dieter 1949- *WhoWor 91*
Kalin, Ivan Petrovich 1935- *WhoWor 91*
Kalin, Karin Bea 1943- *WhoAmW 91*
Kalin, Leslie Rae 1948- *WhoEmL 91*
Kalin, Nancy Jagger 1935- *WhoAmW 91*
Kalin, Robert 1921- *WhoAm 90, WhoSSW 91, WhoWor 91*
Kalin, Sharon J. *BioIn 16*
Kalin, Stanley Roy 1927- *WhoE 91*
Kalina, Bernard F 1923- *BiDrAPA 89*
Kalina, Eduardo 1937- *BiDrAPA 89*
Kalina, Joseph F. 1922- *ODwPR 91*
Kalina, Kent Michael 1953- *BiDrAPA 89*
Kalina, Lawrence Andrew 1951- *WhoEmL 91*
Kalina, Richard 1946- *WhoAm 90, WhoAmA 91*
Kalina, Robert Edward 1936- *WhoAm 90*
Kalina, Sigmund 1911-1977 *AuBYP 90*
Kalinauskas, Nancy McRae 1948- *WhoAmW 91*
Kaline, Al 1934- *Ballpl 90 [port], WorAlBi*
Kaliner, Michael Aron 1941- *WhoAm 90*
Kalinger, Daniel J. 1952- *ODwPR 91*
Kaliniak, Catherine Mary 1958- *WhoAmW 91*
Kalinich, Lila Joyce *BiDrAPA 89*
Kalinin, Mikhail Ivanovich 1875-1946 *BioIn 16*
Kalinina, Masha *BioIn 16*
Kalinka, Susan Carol 1949- *WhoEmL 91*
Kalinoski, Henry Thomas 1957- *WhoEmL 91*
Kalinowski, Katherine Mae 1952- *WhoE 91*
Kalinowski, Michael Francis 1947- *WhoWor 91*
Kalinowsky, Lothar B *BiDrAPA 89*
Kalinowsky, Lothar B. 1899- *WhoAm 90*
Kalins, Dorothy 1942- *WhoAm 90, WhoAmW 91, WhoWrEP 89*
Kalipolites, June Turner 1932- *WhoAmW 91, WhoE 91*
Kalir, Henry H *BiDrAPA 89*
Kalis, David B. *ODwPR 91*
Kalisch, Beatrice Jean 1943- *WhoAm 90, WhoAmW 91*
Kalisch, Paul *PenDiMP*
Kalisch, Philip A. 1942- *WhoAm 90*
Kalischer, Zebi Hirsch 1795-1874 *BioIn 16*
Kalish, Alexander Edward 1953- *WhoSSW 91*
Kalish, Arthur 1930- *WhoAm 90*
Kalish, Carl M. *St&PR 91*
Kalish, Donald 1919- *WhoAm 90*
Kalish, Gilbert 1935- *IntWWM 90*
Kalish, Herbert S. 1922- *St&PR 91*
Kalish, Mark A 1951- *BiDrAPA 89*
Kalish, Myron 1919- *St&PR 91, WhoAm 90*
Kalish, Paul E. 1930- *WhoE 91*
Kalish, Richard A. *BioIn 16*
Kalish, Ronald G. 1940- *St&PR 91*
Kalish, Steven Joseph 1946- *WhoEmL 91*
Kalish, William B. *St&PR 91*
Kalisher, Sheila Lynn 1944- *WhoAmW 91, WhoE 91*
Kalisher, Simpson 1926- *WhoAmA 91*
Kalishman, Reesa Joan 1959- *WhoAmW 91, WhoSSW 91*
Kaliski, Stephan Felix 1928- *WhoAm 90*
Kalisman, Michael 1945- *WhoEmL 91*
Kalista, James Alexander 1947- *WhoEmL 91*
Kalita, Arthur *BioIn 16*
Kalivas, Linda Lee *BiDrAPA 89*
Kalka, Robert Alois, Jr. 1966- *WhoE 91*
Kalkbrenner, Frederic 1785-1849 *PenDiMP*
Kalkbrenner, Friedrich Wilhelm Michael 1788-1849 *BioIn 16*
Kalker, Joost Jacques 1933- *WhoWor 91*
Kalkhof, Thomas Corrigan 1919- *WhoE 91, WhoWor 91*
Kalkhoff, Ronald Kenneth 1933- *WhoAm 90*
Kalkman, Donald Alfred 1927- *St&PR 91*
Kalkman, Vernon D. 1945- *St&PR 91*
Kalkreuth, Maria 1857-1897 *BiDWomA*
Kalkstein, David *BiDrAPA 89*
Kalkus, Stanley 1931- *WhoAm 90*
Kalkwarf, Leonard V. 1928- *WhoAm 90*
Kall, Janice Elena 1960- *WhoAmW 91*
Kallaher, Michael Joseph 1940- *WhoAm 90*
Kallai, Janos 1922- *BioIn 16*
Kalland, Lloyd Austin 1914- *WhoAm 90*
Kallas, Aino 1878-1956 *EncCoWW*
Kallas, Aino Julia Maria 1878-1956 *DcScanL*
Kallas, James Edward 1935- *WhoSSW 91*
Kallas, Phillip G. 1946- *WhoWrEP 89*
Kallaugher, Kevin *BioIn 16*
Kallay, Dusan 1948- *BioIn 16*
Kallay, Michael Frank, II 1944- *WhoWor 91*
Kallay, Nicholas 1887-1967 *BioIn 16*
Kallel, Abdallah 1943- *WhoWor 91*
Kallem, Henry 1912- *WhoAmA 91N*
Kallembach, Larry J. 1958- *St&PR 91*
Kallen, Arnold M *BiDrAPA 89*
Kallen, Horace Meyer 1882-1974 *WorAlBi*
Kallen, Lowell Hart 1943- *BiDrAPA 89, WhoE 91*
Kallen, Lucille 1926- *TwCCr&M 91*
Kallen, Thomas E. 1928- *St&PR 91*
Kallenberg, John Kenneth 1942- *WhoAm 90*
Kallenberg, Olav Herbert *WhoSSW 91*
Kallendorf, Craig William 1954- *WhoSSW 91*
Kaller, Robert Jameson *WhoAmA 91N*
Kallfelz, Francis A. 1938- *WhoAm 90*
Kallfelz, Hans Carlo 1933- *WhoWor 91*
Kallgren, Edward Eugene 1928- *WhoAm 90*
Kallgren, Joyce Kislitzin 1930- *WhoAm 90*
Kallgren-Miller, Janine Ann 1962- *WhoAmW 91*
Kallhovd, Roger Thomas 1941- *BiDrAPA 89, WhoE 91*
Kallianpur, Gopinath 1925- *WhoAm 90*
Kallick, Charles J 1933- *BiDrAPA 89*
Kallick, David A. 1945- *WhoEmL 91*
Kallick, Terry *BiDrAPA 89*
Kallio, Rudy 1892-1979 *Ballpl 90*
Kallir, Jane Katherine 1954- *WhoAmA 91, WhoE 91*
Kallir, John 1923- *WhoAm 90, WhoE 91, WhoWor 91*
Kallir, Lilian 1931- *IntWWM 90*
Kallir, Otto 1894-1978 *WhoAmA 91N*
Kallis, Jack A. 1919- *St&PR 91*
Kallis, John Hunt 1941- *St&PR 91*
Kallison, Perry M. 1934- *St&PR 91*
Kallison, Steven Gene 1944- *BiDrAPA 89*
Kallman, Donald Harry 1930- *St&PR 91, WhoAm 90*
Kallman, Ernest A. 1936- *St&PR 91*
Kallman, James Steven 1960- *WhoWor 91*
Kallman, Kathleen Barbara 1952- *WhoAmW 91, WhoEmL 91*
Kallman, Mary Jeanne 1948- *WhoAmW 91*
Kallman, Theodore William 1952- *WhoEmL 91*
Kallmann, Edward O. *BioIn 16*
Kallmann, Hans Jurgen 1908- *BioIn 16*
Kallmann, Helmut 1922- *IntWWM 90*
Kallmann, Helmut Max 1922- *WhoAm 90, WhoWrEP 89*
Kallmyer, C. Gregory 1950- *St&PR 91*
Kallmyer, Jerry Doane 1955- *WhoE 91*
Kallner, Nina Cory 1921- *WhoAmW 91*
Kallok, Michael John 1948- *WhoAm 90*
Kallon, Kelfala Morana 1954- *WhoE 91*
Kallop, William M. 1943- *St&PR 91*
Kallos, Bruce Oliver 1935- *WhoE 91*
Kallsen, Pamela Kay 1951- *WhoAmW 91, WhoEmL 91*
Kallsen, Theodore John 1915- *WhoAm 90, WhoSSW 91*
Kallstrand, Bo Gosta 1949- *WhoWor 91*
Kallstrom, James David 1950- *WhoEmL 91*
Kallstrom, Robert Elvir 1938- *St&PR 91*
Kallum, Bengt Olof 1938- *WhoWor 91*
Kallus, Richard *BiDrAPA 89*
Kalm, Arne 1936- *St&PR 91*
Kalm, Mart 1961- *WhoWor 91*
Kalm, Michael Alan 1946- *BiDrAPA 89*
Kalma, Ariel *NewAgMG*
Kalman, Andrew 1919- *WhoAm 90*
Kalman, Arlene Diane *BiDrAPA 89*
Kalman, Bobbie 1947- *SmATA 63 [port]*
Kalman, C. Arnold 1919- *St&PR 91*
Kalman, Emmerich 1882-1953 *OxCPMus*
Kalman, George J 1930- *BiDrAPA 89*
Kalman, Jerry L. 1941- *ODwPR 91*
Kalman, Rudolf Emil 1930- *WhoAm 90, WhoWor 91*
Kalman, Thomas Peter 1949- *BiDrAPA 89*
Kalman, Tibor *BioIn 16*
Kalmanoff, Herbert 1911- *BiDrAPA 89*
Kalmanoff, Martin 1920- *WhoAm 90*
Kalmanowicz, Max 1948- *WhoEmL 91*
Kalmanowitz, Abraham 1891-1964 *BioIn 16*
Kalmar, Bert 1884-1947 *OxCPMus*
Kalmar, Janice 1961- *ODwPR 91*
Kalmar, Laszlo 1905-1976 *DcScB S2*
Kalmar, Magda 1944- *IntWWM 90*
Kalmbach, Charles Frederic 1920- *St&PR 91*
Kalmbach, L.D. 1951- *St&PR 91*
Kalmus, Allan H. 1917- *ODwPR 91*
Kalmus, Allan Henry 1917- *WhoAm 90*

Kalmus, Ellin *WhoE 91*
Kalmus, Geoffrey M. 1934- *WhoAm 90*
Kalmus, Gerhard Wolfgang 1942- *WhoSSW 91*
Kalmus, Henry J., Jr. 1946- *St&PR 91*
Kalmus, Herbert T. 1881-1963 *WorAlBi*
Kalmutz, Sheldon E *BiDrAPA 89*
Kalnay, Eugenia 1942- *WhoHisp 91*
Kalnay, Francis 1899- *AuBYP 90*
Kalogerakis, Alexander D 1961- *BiDrAPA 89*
Kalogerakis, Michael G *BiDrAPA 89*
Kalogjera, Ikar Jaksa 1945- *BiDrAPA 89*
Kalomeris, Lucille 1949- *WhoE 91*
Kalomirakis, Theodore 1948- *St&PR 91*
Kalonaros, George Constanti 1954- *BiDrAPA 89*
Kalousek, George Edward *BiDrAPA 89*
Kaloustian, Shnork 1913-1990 *BioIn 16*
Kalov, Jerry 1936- *St&PR 91*
Kalow, Werner 1917- *WhoAm 90*
Kalpakian, Laura Anne 1945- *WhoWrEP 89*
Kalpokas, Donald *WhoWor 91*
Kalra, Anil 1951- *WhoWor 91*
Kalra, Beraldine Leli *WhoAmW 91*
Kalra, Gurjeet Singh 1955- *BiDrAPA 89*
Kalsner, Stanley 1936- *WhoAm 90*
Kalson, Albert E 1932- *ConAu 132*
Kalstad, Kristen Andrea 1948- *WhoAmW 91*
Kalt, Glenda Gail 1946- *WhoSSW 91*
Kalt, Howard *ODwPR 91*
Kaltenbach, Hubert Leonard 1922- *WhoAm 90*
Kaltenbach, Shirley Jean 1948- *WhoAmW 91*
Kaltenbach-Townsend, Jane Couffer 1922- *WhoE 91*
Kaltenbacher, Philip David 1937- *St&PR 91, WhoAm 90*
Kaltenborn, H. V. 1878-1965 *BioIn 16*
Kaltenborn, Hans Von 1878-1965 *BioIn 16*
Kaltenborn, Rolf 1915- *WhoSSW 91*
Kaltenbronn, Jon Arthur 1959- *WhoEmL 91*
Kaltenbrunner, Ernst *BioIn 16*
Kaltenthaler, Klaus 1938- *WhoWor 91*
Kalter, Doreen Barbara 1950- *BiDrAPA 89*
Kalter, Edmond Morey 1950- *WhoE 91*
Kalter, Robert L 1950- *BiDrAPA 89*
Kalter, Sabine 1889-1957 *PenDiMP*
Kalter, Seymour Sanford 1918- *WhoAm 90*
Kalthoff, Klaus Otto 1941- *WhoAm 90*
Kaltinick, Paul R. 1932- *WhoAm 90*
Kaltman, Eric 1942- *St&PR 91*
Kaltman, Florence D. *St&PR 91*
Kaltman, Jack 1925- *St&PR 91*
Kaltofen, Marco *BioIn 16*
Kalton, Graham 1936- *WhoAm 90*
Kalton, Robert Rankin 1920- *WhoAm 90*
Kaltreider, Nancy Bowen 1938- *BiDrAPA 89*
Kaltsos, Angelo John 1930- *WhoE 91, WhoWor 91*
Kaltsounis, Theodore 1930- *WhoAm 90*
Kaltwasser, Gustavo 1954- *WhoWor 91*
Kaludis, George 1938- *WhoAm 90*
Kalugin, Oleg D. *NewYTBS 90 [port]*
Kalunian, Douglas Alan 1957- *BiDrAPA 89*
Kalus, Oren 1954- *BiDrAPA 89*
Kalusin, Marilyn 1956- *WhoHisp 91*
Kalusky, Rebecca *AuBYP 90*
Kaluza, William J. 1954- *St&PR 91*
Kaluzniacki, Sophia Barbara 1942- *WhoAmW 91*
Kaluzny, Zigy 1947- *WhoSSW 91*
Kalver, Gail Ellen 1948- *WhoAm 90*
Kalvert, Sol E. *BioIn 16*
Kalwajtys, Ronald R. 1938- *St&PR 91*
Kalweit, Juliette Anne *BiDrAPA 89*
Kalweit, Werner 1926- *WhoWor 91*
Kalwinsky, Charles Knowlton 1946- *WhoAm 90*
Kalyanaraman, Palaiyur Sundarappie 1945- *WhoE 91*
Kalyanavati *WomWR*
Kam, Denis C.H. 1935- *St&PR 91*
Kam, Mei K 1938- *WhoAmA 91*
Kamada, Rodney Thomas 1957- *WhoEmL 91*
Kamaiakin 1800?-1877 *WhNaAH*
Kamal, Mafa Ribhi 1957- *BiDrAPA 89*
Kamal, Mohammed Anwar *WhoSSW 91*
Kamali, Norma *BioIn 16*
Kamali, Norma 1944- *ConDes 90*
Kamali, Norma 1945- *WhoAm 90, WhoAmW 91*
Kamalidenov, Zakash 1938- *WhoWor 91*
Kamalnath, Prakash Jayaraj *BiDrAPA 89*
Kaman, Charles Huron 1919- *St&PR 91, WhoAm 90*
Kaman, Robert Lawrence 1941- *WhoSSW 91*
Kamanitz, Joyce Rose 1949- *BiDrAPA 89*
Kamaraju, Lakshmi S 1952- *BiDrAPA 89*
Kamarck, Andrew Martin 1914- *WhoAm 90*
Kamarck, Lawrence 1927- *ConAu 32NR*
Kamarei, Ahmad Reza 1947- *WhoWor 91*
Kamath, Anil Vasudev 1950- *WhoWor 91*
Kamath, Gopalakrishna A 1931- *BiDrAPA 89*
Kamath, Prabhakar S 1945- *BiDrAPA 89*
Kamath, Prem Janardan 1949- *WhoWor 91*
Kamath, Vishwanath Narasinha 1936- *WhoWor 91*
Kamatoy, Lourdes Aguas 1945- *WhoAmW 91, WhoWor 91*
Kamb, Walter Barclay 1931- *WhoAm 90*
Kamba, Walter Joseph 1931- *WhoWor 91*
Kamban, Gudmundur 1888-1945 *DcScanL*
Kambara, George Kiyoshi 1916- *WhoAm 90*
Kamber, Victor 1944- *ODwPR 91*
Kamber, Victor Samuel 1944- *WhoAm 90*
Kamberg, Kenneth Edward 1915- *St&PR 91, WhoAm 90*
Kambhampati, Radha Krishna 1956- *BiDrAPA 89*
Kambic, Randy 1954- *ODwPR 91*
Kambli, Johann Melchior 1718-1783 *PenDiDA 89*
Kambour, Frances Provencher 1947- *ODwPR 91*
Kambour, Roger Peabody 1932- *WhoAm 90*
Kambourian, James Stewart 1944- *WhoSSW 91*
Kambun Master *EncJap*
Kamdar, Mukesh Nautam *BiDrAPA 89*
Kamdar, Raj N. 1946- *St&PR 91*
Kameen, John Paul 1941- *WhoE 91*
Kameese, Suzanne C. 1952- *St&PR 91*
Kamekura, Yusaku 1915- *ConDes 90*
Kamel, Kamel Louis *BiDrAPA 89*
Kamelhair, Nora Brantley 1948- *WhoEmL 91*
Kamemoto, Fred Isamu 1928- *WhoAm 90*
Kamemoto, Haruyuki 1922- *WhoAm 90*
Kamen, D. Jonathan 1953- *WhoE 91*
Kamen, Harry P. 1933- *St&PR 91*
Kamen, Harry Paul 1933- *WhoAm 90*
Kamen, Martin D. 1913- *WorAlBi*
Kamen, Martin David 1913- *WhoAm 90*
Kamen, Rebecca 1950- *WhoAmA 91*
Kamenar, Elizabeth *WhoE 91*
Kamenetz, Leo *BiDrAPA 89*
Kamenetz, Rodger 1950- *ConAu 30NR*
Kamenetz, Rodger Lee 1950- *WhoWrEP 89*
Kamenev, Lev Borisovich 1883-1936 *BioIn 16*
Kamenikova, Valentina Jurijevna 1930- *IntWWM 90*
Kamenka, Hippolyte *NewYTBS 90*
Kamenka, Hippolyte 1897-1990 *BioIn 16*
Kamenko, Vera 1947- *EncCoWW*
Kamenske, Bernard Harold 1927- *WhoAm 90*
Kamentsky, Louis Aaron 1930- *WhoAm 90*
Kameny, Nat 1923- *WhoAm 90*
Kamer, Joel Victor 1942- *St&PR 91, WhoAm 90*
Kamer, Martin *BioIn 16*
Kamerlinghonnes, Heike 1853-1926 *WorAlBi*
Kamerman, Jon 1960- *WhoEmL 91*
Kamerman, Sheila Brody 1928- *WhoAm 90, WhoAmW 91*
Kamerow, Martin Laurence 1931- *WhoAm 90*
Kamerschen, David Roy 1937- *WhoAm 90*
Kamerschen, Robert Jerome 1936- *WhoAm 90*
Kames, Lord 1696-1782 *DcLB 104 [port]*
Kames, Kenneth F. 1935- *St&PR 91*
Kametches, Chris L. 1935- *St&PR 91*
Kamhi, Samuel Vitali 1922- *WhoWor 91*
Kamholz, Barbara Addison 1949- *BiDrAPA 89*
Kamholz, Stephan L. 1947- *WhoE 91*
Kami, Michael John 1922- *St&PR 91*
Kamiak, Sandra Nancy 1952- *BiDrAPA 89*
Kamiakan 1800?-1877 *WhNaAH*
Kamiakin 1800?-1877 *WhNaAH*
Kamien, Marcia 1940- *WhoWrEP 89*
Kamienska, Anna 1920- *EncCoWW*
Kamihira, Ben 1925- *WhoAmA 91*
Kamikawa, Alden Tanemitsu 1940- *WhoE 91, WhoWor 91*
Kamil, Harvey 1944- *St&PR 91*
Kamimori, Satoru 1927- *WhoWor 91*
Kamin, Benjamin Alon 1953- *WhoAm 90*
Kamin, Chester Thomas 1940- *WhoAm 90*
Kamin, Isadore 1917- *BiDrAPA 89*
Kamin, Robert Jay 1933- *St&PR 91*
Kamin, Sherwin 1927- *WhoAm 90*
Kaminek, Miroslav 1933- *WhoWor 91*
Kaminer, Benjamin 1924- *WhoAm 90*
Kaminer, Gerald A. *St&PR 91N*
Kaminer, Henry 1934- *BiDrAPA 89*
Kaminer, Peter H. 1915- *WhoAm 90*
Kaminetzky, Harold Alexander 1923- *WhoAm 90*
Kaminkowitz, Grace 1935- *WhoAmW 91*
Kaminow, Ira Paul 1940- *St&PR 91*
Kaminow, Ivan Paul 1930- *WhoAm 90*
Kamins, Barry Michael 1943- *WhoE 91*
Kamins, Lloyd Philip *BiDrAPA 89*
Kamins, Michael Abraham 1952- *WhoEmL 91*
Kaminski, Donald Leon 1940- *WhoAm 90*
Kaminski, Janelle Kay 1962- *WhoAmW 91*
Kaminski, Joanne 1961- *WhoE 91*
Kaminski, John *WhoAm 90*
Kaminski, Joseph C. 1943- *St&PR 91*
Kaminski, Karen Sue 1955- *WhoAmW 91*
Kaminski, Leslie Kay *BiDrAPA 89*
Kaminski, Madolyn Andrea DeSilva 1952- *WhoAmW 91*
Kaminski, Robert Stanley 1936- *St&PR 91, WhoAm 90*
Kaminski, Stanley Ronald 1955- *WhoEmL 91*
Kaminski, Susan Denise 1955- *WhoEmL 91*
Kaminsky, Alice R. *WhoWrEP 89*
Kaminsky, Alice Richkin *WhoAm 90*
Kaminsky, Allan L. *St&PR 91*
Kaminsky, Arthur Charles 1946- *WhoAm 90*
Kaminsky, David Michael 1948- *BiDrAPA 89*
Kaminsky, Elisabeth M 1928- *BiDrAPA 89*
Kaminsky, Howard *BioIn 16*
Kaminsky, Howard 1940- *WhoAm 90*
Kaminsky, Jack 1922- *WhoE 91*
Kaminsky, Jack 1949- *WhoE 91*
Kaminsky, Jack Allan 1949- *WhoAmA 91*
Kaminsky, Judith Gerson 1942- *WhoAmW 91, WhoSSW 91*
Kaminsky, Larry E. 1938- *St&PR 91*
Kaminsky, Laura 1956- *WhoAmW 91*
Kaminsky, Manfred Stephan 1929- *WhoAm 90*
Kaminsky, Marc 1943- *WhoWrEP 89*
Kaminsky, Max 1908- *BioIn 16, OxCPMus*
Kaminsky, Phyllis *ODwPR 91*
Kaminsky, Ray 1950- *St&PR 91*
Kaminsky, Richard Alan 1951- *WhoEmL 91*
Kaminsky, Seth 1940- *St&PR 91*
Kaminsky, Stuart M. *BioIn 16*
Kaminsky, Stuart M 1934- *ConLC 59 [port], TwCCr&M 91*
Kaminstein, Philip 1928- *BiDrAPA 89*
Kamisar, Gordon Aaron 1960- *WhoEmL 91*
Kamisar, Sandra Lee 1937- *WhoAmW 91*
Kamisar, Yale 1929- *WhoAm 90, WhoWor 91*
Kamiya, Kyoji 1951- *WhoSSW 91*
Kamiya, Noburo 1913- *BioIn 16*
Kamlet, Barbara Lynn 1949- *WhoEmL 91*
Kamlet, Lee Gordon 1952- *WhoEmL 91*
Kamlot, Robert 1926- *WhoAm 90*
Kamm, Dorothy Lila 1957- *WhoAmA 91*
Kamm, Ervin *St&PR 91*
Kamm, Henry 1925- *WhoAm 90*
Kamm, Herbert 1917- *WhoAm 90*
Kamm, Ilse *BiDrAPA 89*
Kamm, Jacob Oswald 1918- *WhoAm 90, WhoWor 91*
Kamm, Laurence Richard 1939- *WhoAm 90*
Kamm, Linda Heller 1939- *WhoAm 90*
Kamm, Patrick W *BiDrAPA 89*
Kamm, Robert B. 1919- *WhoAm 90*
Kamm, Robert L 1919- *BiDrAPA 89*
Kamm, Ronald Lee 1943- *BiDrAPA 89*
Kamm, Thomas Allen 1925- *WhoAm 90*
Kamm, Willie 1900-1988 *Ballpl 90, BioIn 16*
Kamman, Alan Bertram 1931- *WhoAm 90, WhoWor 91*
Kamman, Curtis Warren 1939- *WhoAm 90*
Kamman, William 1930- *WhoAm 90*
Kammen, Michael 1936- *WhoAm 90*
Kammen, Michael G 1936- *MajTwCW*
Kammer, Harry Samuel 1954- *St&PR 91*
Kammer, Raymond Gerard, Jr. 1947- *WhoAm 90*
Kammer, Robert Arthur, Jr. 1945- *WhoEmL 91*
Kammer, Roselyn 1921- *St&PR 91*
Kammerdeiner, Nancy Alyce 1946- *WhoAmW 91*
Kammerdiener, Franklin Leslie, Jr. 1932- *EncO&P 3*
Kammerer, John A. 1942- *St&PR 91*
Kammerer, Kelly Christian 1941- *WhoWor 91*
Kammerer, Mike *BioIn 16*
Kammerer, Warren Louis, III *BiDrAPA 89*
Kammerer, William Henry 1912- *WhoAm 90*
Kammerer, William R 1940- *BiDrAPA 89*
Kammerman, Arthur C. 1915- *St&PR 91*
Kammerman, Arthur Charles Cyril 1915- *WhoE 91*
Kammeyer, Sonia Margaretha 1942- *WhoAmW 91*
Kammholz, Theophil Carl 1909- *WhoAm 90, WhoWor 91*
Kammhuber, Josef 1896-1986? *BioIn 16*
Kammiel, Rita R 1952- *BiDrAPA 89*
Kammu, Emperor *EncJap*
Kamnik, Ronald Shawn *BiDrAPA 89*
Kamnikar, Michael A. 1951- *St&PR 91*
Kamnitzer, Peter *PenDiMP*
Kamnitzer, Sophie Neorah *BiDrAPA 89*
Kamo no Chomei 1156?-1216 *EncJap*
Kamogawa, Hiroshi 1913- *WhoWor 91*
Kamon, Effie H. 1925- *St&PR 91*
Kamon, Pauline McDougal 1925- *WhoAmW 91*
Kamon, Robert B. 1927- *St&PR 91*
Kamp, Harry Van der 1947- *IntWWM 90*
Kamp, Peter Stephen *BiDrAPA 89*
Kamp, Thomas G. 1925- *St&PR 91*
Kamp, Thomas George 1925- *WhoAm 90*
Kampe, Lawrence 1935- *St&PR 91*
Kampelman, Max M. 1920- *BioIn 16, WhoAm 90, WhoWor 91*
Kampen, Bernhardt Anthony Van 1943- *IntWWM 90*
Kampen, Emerson 1928- *St&PR 91*
Kampf, Avram S 1920- *WhoAmA 91*
Kampf, Cindy 1961- *ODwPR 91*
Kampf, Cindy Alise 1961- *WhoAmW 91, WhoE 91*
Kampf, Joel *St&PR 91*
Kampf, Joel 1937- *WhoAm 90*
Kampf, Philip L. 1931- *St&PR 91*
Kamph, Patricia Ann 1956- *WhoAmW 91*
Kamphaus, John Nichalos *BiDrAPA 89*
Kamphoevener, Elsa Sophia von 1878-1963 *EncCoWW*
Kamphuisen, Hilbert Arie Cornelis 1931- *WhoWor 91*
Kampmeier, Donald G. 1944- *St&PR 91*
Kampmeier, Donald George 1944- *WhoAm 90*
Kampmeier, Jack August 1935- *WhoAm 90*
Kampmeier, Rudolph H. 1898- *BioIn 16*
Kampouris, Alex 1912- *Ballpl 90*
Kampouris, Emmanuel Andrew 1934- *WhoAm 90*
Kampschror, Leslie Dean 1932- *WhoAm 90*
Kamrowski, Gerome 1914- *WhoAm 90, WhoAmA 91*
Kamsky, Gata *BioIn 16, NewYTBS 90 [port]*
Kamsky, Leonard 1918- *WhoAm 90*
Kamsky, Rustam *BioIn 16, NewYTBS 90 [port]*
Kamsky, Virginia *BioIn 16*
Kamsler, Victoria Alexandra Ashcroft 1960- *WhoAmW 91*
Kamstra, Egbert 1930- *BiDrAPA 89*
Kamstra, Garrett Allen 1954- *St&PR 91*
Kamu, Okko 1946- *IntWWM 90, PenDiMP*
Kamuri, Rose T. *St&PR 91*
Kamys, Walter 1917- *WhoAmA 91*
Kamzan, Stephen 1949- *St&PR 91*
Kan, Diana 1926- *WhoAmA 91*
Kan, Diana Artemis Mann Shu 1926- *WhoAm 90, WhoWor 91*
Kan, Kit-Keung 1943- *WhoAmA 91, WhoSSW 91*
Kan, Lai-Bing *WhoWor 91*
Kan, Lydia A. 1962- *WhoE 91*
Kan, Michael 1933- *WhoAmA 91*
Kan, Paul Man-Lok 1947- *WhoEmL 91, WhoWor 91*
Kan, Yue-Sai *BioIn 16*
Kan, Yuet Wai 1936- *WhoAm 90*
Kana, Anthony T. 1935- *St&PR 91*
Kana, Jan S. 1952- *WhoWor 91*
Kana, Said Mohidine 1936- *WhoWor 91*
Kanabus, Henry 1949- *WhoWrEP 89*
Kanada, Margaret Miller 1953- *WhoWor 91*
Kanaday, Joseph, Jr. 1926- *St&PR 91*
Kanaga, Conseulo 1894-1978 *WhoAmA 91N*
Kanaga, William S. *BioIn 16*
Kanagawa, Diane Wiltshire 1955- *WhoWor 91*
Kanai, Hiroshi 1930- *WhoWor 91*
Kanai, Kazuhiko 1933- *WhoWor 91*
Kanakaraj, Annamaria Belle 1951- *WhoE 91*
Kanal, Laveen N. 1931- *WhoAm 90*
Kanaley, James Edward 1941- *WhoAm 90*
Kanaly, Steven Francis 1946- *WhoAm 90*
Kanami Kiyotsugu *EncJap*
Kanamori, Hitoshi 1932- *WhoWor 91*
Kanan, Sean *BioIn 16*
Kananowitz, Anna Gilson 1924- *WhoWrEP 89*
Kanapa, Jean 1924-1978 *BiDFrPL*
Kanapima 1813- *WhNaAH*
Kanarek, Anna Clare Victoria *BiDrAPA 89*
Kanarek, Carol Mock 1953- *WhoEmL 91*

Kanarek, Robert 1920- *St&PR 91*
Kanari, Norimichi 1946- *St&PR 91*
Kanarkowski, Edward J. 1947- *ODwPR 91*
Kanarkowski, Edward Joseph 1947- *WhoE 91*
Kanarowski, Stanley Martin 1912- *WhoE 91*
Kanary, Richard Lincoln 1934- *St&PR 91*
Kanas, John Adam 1946- *St&PR 91, WhoAm 90*
Kanas, Nick Andrew 1945- *BiDrAPA 89*
Kanashige, Toyo 1896-1967 *PenDiDA 89*
Kanawa, Kiri Te *PenDiMP*
Kanazawa, Takafumi 1926- *WhoWor 91*
Kanazawa, Yoshiki Paul 1929- *WhoWor 91*
Kanazir, Dusan 1921- *WhoWor 91*
Kanba, Shigenobu *BiDrAPA 89*
Kanbara, Bertram Teruo 1926- *WhoAm 90*
Kanbe, Keishiro 1928- *WhoWor 91*
Kancamagus *WhNaAH*
Kancelbaum, Joshua Jacob 1936- *WhoAm 90*
Kanchier, Carole *ConAu 132*
Kanda, Motohisa 1943- *WhoAm 90*
Kandaras, Homer Michael 1929- *WhoAm 90*
Kandathil, Valsamma T *BiDrAPA 89*
Kandel, Christopher Nelson 1960- *WhoWor 91*
Kandel, Emanuel 1938- *WhoE 91*
Kandel, Eric Richard 1929- *WhoAm 90*
Kandel, Nelson Robert 1929- *WhoE 91, WhoWor 91*
Kandel, Stephen *BioIn 16*
Kandelin, Albert *BiDrAPA 89*
Kandell, Marshall Jay 1937- *ODwPR 91*
Kander, John 1927- *OxCPMus*
Kander, John Harold 1927- *WhoAm 90*
Kandera, John *BiDrAPA 89*
Kandhal, Prithvi Singh 1935- *WhoSSW 91*
Kandil, Hassan Samy 1933- *WhoWor 91*
Kandil, Osama Abd El Mohsin 1944- *WhoWor 91*
Kandinsky, Vasily 1866-1944 *WorAlBi*
Kandinsky, Wassily 1866-1944 *BioIn 16, IntDcAA 90*
Kandler, Charles *PenDiDA 89*
Kandler, Henry O *BiDrAPA 89*
Kandler, Johann Friedrich *PenDiDA 89*
Kandler, Johann Joachim 1706-1775 *PenDiDA 89*
Kandoian, Ellen *AuBYP 90*
Kandravy, John 1935- *WhoE 91*
Kane, Agnes Brezak 1946- *WhoAmW 91*
Kane, Alice Theresa 1948- *St&PR 91, WhoAm 90, WhoEmL 91*
Kane, Andy 1936- *WhoE 91*
Kane, Andy 1956- *MusmAFA*
Kane, Annette P. 1933- *WhoAm 90*
Kane, Art 1925- *WhoAm 90*
Kane, Barbara Jeanne 1955- *BiDrAPA 89*
Kane, Barry Francis 1940- *St&PR 91*
Kane, Bartholomew Aloysius 1945- *WhoAm 90*
Kane, Bill 1951- *WhoAmA 91*
Kane, Bob *BioIn 16*
Kane, Bob 1916- *EncACom*
Kane, Bob Paul 1937- *WhoAmA 91*
Kane, Carol 1952- *BioIn 16, WhoAm 90, WhoAmW 91, WorAlBi*
Kane, Charles Fairweather, Jr. 1950- *WhoE 91*
Kane, Charles J. 1920- *St&PR 91*
Kane, Charles Joseph 1920- *WhoAm 90*
Kane, Daniel 1915- *St&PR 91, WhoAm 90*
Kane, Daniel Hipwell 1908- *WhoAm 90*
Kane, David C. 1949- *St&PR 91*
Kane, David Edward 1952- *St&PR 91*
Kane, Deborah Lange 1956- *WhoEmL 91*
Kane, Donald Barrett 1932- *St&PR 91*
Kane, E. Leonard 1929- *St&PR 91*
Kane, Edward J. 1930- *St&PR 91*
Kane, Edward James 1935- *WhoAm 90*
Kane, Edward Joseph 1951- *WhoE 91*
Kane, Edward K. 1929- *St&PR 91*
Kane, Edward L. 1938- *WhoAm 90*
Kane, Edward Leonard 1929- *WhoAm 90*
Kane, Edward Rynex 1918- *St&PR 91, WhoAm 90*
Kane, Elisha Kent 1820-1857 *EncO&P 3*
Kane, Francis J. Jr. 1929- *BiDrAPA 89*
Kane, Frank 1912-1968 *TwCCr&M 91*
Kane, Frank L. 1951- *WhoE 91*
Kane, Fred J *BiDrAPA 89*
Kane, Gary Allen 1936- *St&PR 91*
Kane, George 1943- *St&PR 91*
Kane, George Joseph 1916- *WhoAm 90*
Kane, Gerard *BioIn 16*
Kane, Gil 1926- *EncACom*
Kane, Henry 1918- *TwCCr&M 91*
Kane, Henry Bugbee 1902-1971 *AuBYP 90*
Kane, Herman William 1939- *WhoE 91*
Kane, Howard Edward 1927- *WhoAm 90*
Kane, Howard Jay 1947- *WhoE 91*
Kane, Jack Allison 1921- *WhoWor 91*
Kane, Jacqueline Jones 1917- *WhoE 91*
Kane, James G. 1926- *St&PR 91*
Kane, James Golden 1926- *WhoAm 90*
Kane, James Robert 1959- *WhoEmL 91*
Kane, Jay Brassler 1931- *WhoE 91*
Kane, Jerry Robert 1941- *St&PR 91*
Kane, Joe *BioIn 16*
Kane, John 1860-1934 *MusmAFA*
Kane, John C. 1939- *WhoAm 90*
Kane, John Dandridge Henley, Jr. 1921- *WhoAm 90*
Kane, John Lawrence, Jr. 1937- *WhoAm 90*
Kane, John Michael 1945- *BiDrAPA 89*
Kane, Jonathan A. 1945- *WhoEmL 91*
Kane, Joseph Charles 1935- *WhoE 91, WhoWor 91*
Kane, Joseph James, Jr. 1948- *WhoEmL 91*
Kane, Joseph T. 1924- *ODwPR 91*
Kane, Joseph Thomas 1933- *St&PR 91*
Kane, Joseph Thomas 1934- *WhoAm 90*
Kane, Julie Ellen 1952- *WhoEmL 91*
Kane, Kathleen Elizabeth 1961- *WhoAmW 91*
Kane, Kathleen M. *BioIn 16*
Kane, Leonard *BiDrAPA 89*
Kane, Louis Isaac 1931- *WhoAm 90*
Kane, Lucile Marie 1920- *WhoAm 90*
Kane, Manuel Edward 1920- *St&PR 91*
Kane, Margaret Brassler 1909- *WhoAm 90, WhoAmA 91, WhoAmW 91, WhoE 91, WhoWor 91*
Kane, Marilyn Elizabeth 1941- *WhoAmW 91*
Kane, Martin 1955- *WhoEmL 91*
Kane, Martin Stanley 1953- *BiDrAPA 89*
Kane, Michael Will *BiDrAPA 89*
Kane, Neil David 1963- *WhoEmL 91*
Kane, Patricia 1955- *WhoWrEP 89*
Kane, Patricia Lanegran 1926- *WhoAm 90*
Kane, Patrick J. 1924- *St&PR 91*
Kane, Paul 1810-1871 *BioIn 16, WhNaAH*
Kane, Penelope Susan 1945- *ConAu 131*
Kane, Penny *ConAu 131*
Kane, Peter E 1932- *ConAu 31NR*
Kane, Racquel E. 1929- *St&PR 91*
Kane, Richard 1928- *WhoE 91*
Kane, Richard Stephen 1937- *St&PR 91*
Kane, Robert B. 1940- *St&PR 91*
Kane, Robert Francis 1916- *ODwPR 91*
Kane, Robert Francis 1926- *WhoAm 90*
Kane, Robert John 1958- *WhoEmL 91*
Kane, Robert Louis 1940- *WhoAm 90*
Kane, Robert Marvin 1923- *WhoE 91*
Kane, Robert Peter 1937- *St&PR 91*
Kane, Rod *BioIn 16*
Kane, Ronald 1944- *WhoAm 90*
Kane, Ronald Charles 1933- *WhoE 91*
Kane, Rosamond 1926-1989 *BioIn 16*
Kane, Sam 1919- *WhoWor 91*
Kane, Stanley B. 1920- *St&PR 91*
Kane, Stanley Bruce 1920- *WhoAm 90, WhoE 91*
Kane, Stanley Phillip 1930- *WhoAm 90*
Kane, Steven Edward 1949- *WhoEmL 91*
Kane, Stratton J. 1938- *St&PR 91*
Kane, Terence Peter 1961- *WhoSSW 91*
Kane, Terry Richard 1947- *WhoEmL 91*
Kane, Thomas J. 1938- *St&PR 91*
Kane, Thomas Joseph 1934- *WhoE 91*
Kane, Thomas Patrick 1942- *WhoAm 90*
Kane, Thomas Patrick 1945- *WhoEmL 91*
Kane, Thomas Reif 1924- *WhoAm 90*
Kane, Timothy Patrick 1962- *WhoWor 91*
Kane, Trudy 1950- *IntWWM 90*
Kane, Warren F. 1923- *St&PR 91*
Kane, William James 1933- *WhoAm 90*
Kane, William L. 1938- *WhoWrEP 89*
Kane-Vanni, Patricia Ruth 1954- *WhoAmW 91, WhoEmL 91*
Kaneb, Elizabeth M. 1958- *WhoAmW 91*
Kaneda, Masanichi 1930- *Ballpl 90*
Kanee, Sol 1909- *St&PR 91*
Kaneff, Stephen 1926- *WhoWor 91*
Kanefield, Marvin 1935- *BiDrAPA 89*
Kanefsky, Joel 1947- *St&PR 91*
Kanegis, Sidney S 1922- *WhoAmA 91*
Kanehisa, Minoru 1948- *WhoWor 91*
Kanehl, Rod 1934- *Ballpl 90*
Kaneko Kentaro 1853-1942 *EncJap*
Kaneko, Eisaku 1947- *WhoWor 91*
Kaneko, Fumiko 1903-1926 *BioIn 16*
Kaneko, Haruo 1929- *WhoWor 91*
Kaneko, Hisashi 1933- *WhoAm 90*
Kaneko, Junichi 1936- *WhoWor 91*
Kaneko, Ziro 1915- *BiDrAPA 89*
Kanellakis, Nicholas Alexander 1963- *WhoEmL 91*
Kanellakis, Theodore *BioIn 16*
Kanellos, Helen 1943- *WhoAm 90*
Kanellos, Nicolas 1945- *ConAu 131, HispWr 90, WhoHisp 91*
Kanelos, Frank Theodore 1948- *BioIn 16*
Kanely, James R. 1941- *St&PR 91*
Kanemitsu, Matsumi 1922- *WhoAm 90, WhoAmA 91*
Kanenaka, Rebecca Yae 1958- *WhoEmL 91*
Kaner, Harvey Sheldon 1930- *St&PR 91, WhoAm 90*
Kaner, Walter 1920- *ODwPR 91*
Kaneria, Sumanlal J *BiDrAPA 89*
Kanes, William Henry 1934- *WhoAm 90*
Kaneshiro, Edna Sayomi 1937- *WhoWor 91*
Kanet, Roger Edward 1936- *WhoAm 90, WhoWor 91*
Kanfer, Frederick H. *WhoAm 90*
Kanfer, Frederick H. 1925- *ConAu 32NR*
Kanfer, Julian Norman 1930- *WhoAm 90*
Kanfer, Ruth 1955- *WhoAmW 91*
Kang Shien 1913- *WhoWor 91*
Kang Young Hoon 1922- *WhoWor 91*
Kang, Balvinder S 1947- *BiDrAPA 89*
Kang, Bann C. 1939- *WhoAmW 91*
Kang, Benjamin Toyeong 1931- *WhoE 91*
Kang, Chang Kyoo *BiDrAPA 89*
Kang, Chang-Wuk 1937- *BiDrAPA 89*
Kang, Chung-Wuk 1937- *WhoE 91*
Kang, Dong-Suk 1954- *IntWWM 90*
Kang, Edward Paotai 1942- *WhoE 91, WhoWor 91*
Kang, Gobindsharan *BiDrAPA 89*
Kang, Ho Ryun *BioIn 16, NewYTBS 90*
Kang, Hong Sik 1934- *BiDrAPA 89*
Kang, Hwa Ing 1936- *BiDrAPA 89*
Kang, Jae Ryong 1932- *BiDrAPA 89*
Kang, Jasbir Singh 1953- *BiDrAPA 89*
Kang, Jung Il 1942- *WhoWor 91*
Kang, Karen *ODwPR 91*
Kang, Kunn *BiDrAPA 89*
Kang, Kyoung Sook 1942- *WhoAmW 91*
Kang, Kyungsik 1936- *WhoAm 90*
Kang, Tai K *BiDrAPA 89*
K'ang, Versa Clarice 1939- *WhoAmW 91*
Kang, William 1955- *WhoSSW 91*
Kang, Young Ho 1937- *BiDrAPA 89*
K'ang-hsi, Emperor of China 1654-1722 *BioIn 16*
Kanga, Homi 1922- *IntWWM 90*
Kangas, Clare Michele 1956- *WhoEmL 91*
Kangas, Edward A. *WhoAm 90*
Kangas, Gene 1944- *WhoAmA 91*
Kangas, James Richard 1944- *WhoWrEP 89*
Kangas, Julie Elizabeth 1956- *WhoAmW 91*
Kangas, Robert Jacob 1951- *WhoEmL 91*
Kangas, Ronald Clinton 1941- *St&PR 91*
Kangun, Norman 1937- *WhoSSW 91*
Kangxi, Emperor 1662-1722 *PenDiDA 89*
Kani, Takeo 1932- *St&PR 91, WhoAm 90*
Kania, Alan James 1949- *WhoWor 91*
Kania, Edwin M. 1927- *St&PR 91*
Kania, Jay A. 1960- *WhoEmL 91*
Kania, John Robert 1944- *BiDrAPA 89*
Kania, Karin *BioIn 16*
Kania, Richard Roman Edward 1947- *WhoEmL 91*
Kanianthra, Joseph Ninan 1933- *WhoE 91*
Kanick, Robert W. 1962- *St&PR 91*
Kanick, Virginia 1925- *WhoAmW 91*
Kanidinc, Salahattin 1927- *WhoAm 90, WhoAmA 91*
Kaniecki, Michael Joseph 1935- *WhoAm 90*
Kanigan, William S. 1944- *St&PR 91*
Kanigel, Robert 1946- *ConAu 132, WhoWrEP 89*
Kanigel, Robert Joseph 1946- *WhoE 91*
Kanik, Beth Wendy 1961- *WhoEmL 91*
Kanin, Dennis Roy 1946- *WhoEmL 91*
Kanin, Fay *BioIn 16, WhoAm 90*
Kanin, Fay Mitchell 1916?- *NotWoAT*
Kanin, Garson 1912- *WhoAm 90, WorAlBi*
Kanis, Frank H. 1911- *St&PR 91*
Kanitz, Terry Wayne 1941- *St&PR 91*
Kaniuk, Yoram *BioIn 16*
Kanjani, Mulchand Assandas 1937- *WhoWor 91*
Kanjeng Gusti Mangkunegoro, King of Java *BioIn 16*
Kanji, Juliana *BiDrAPA 89*
Kanjorski, Paul Edmund 1937- *WhoAm 90, WhoE 91*
Kankel, Keith Victor 1942- *St&PR 91*
Kanmanthreddy, Vijaya K 1955- *BiDrAPA 89*
Kann, Hans 1927- *IntWWM 90*
Kann, Mark E. 1947- *ConAu 130*
Kann, Peter R. *BioIn 16, St&PR 91*
Kann, Peter Robert 1942- *WhoAm 90, WhoE 91*
Kann, Robert A 1906-1981 *ConAu 129*
Kannan, Dhandapani 1941- *WhoSSW 91*
Kannan, Hari Dasan *BiDrAPA 89*
Kannangara, Don Walter 1942- *WhoE 91*
Kannapell, John Trouy 1957- *WhoEmL 91*
Kannard, Janice Alisa 1952- *WhoAmW 91*
Kanne, Gerald M. 1930- *St&PR 91*
Kanne, Gerald Merle 1930- *WhoAm 90*
Kanne, Marvin George 1937- *St&PR 91*
Kanne, Michael Stephen 1938- *WhoAm 90*
Kannel, Alan Howard 1960- *WhoEmL 91*
Kannel, William Bernard 1923- *WhoAm 90*
Kannen, Gunter Von 1940- *IntWWM 90*
Kannenberg, Mark E. 1947- *St&PR 91*
Kanner, Abraham Pascal 1911- *St&PR 91*
Kanner, Andres Miguel *BiDrAPA 89*
Kanner, Bruce Mitchell 1956- *WhoEmL 91*
Kanner, Edwin B. 1922- *St&PR 91*
Kanner, Ellen 1961- *WhoAmW 91*
Kanner, Ellen Barbara 1950- *WhoAmW 91*
Kanner, Robert Howard 1947- *St&PR 91*
Kanner, Suzanne Rodin 1928- *WhoE 91*
Kanninen, Melvin Fred 1935- *WhoAm 90*
Kanno, Suga 1881-1911 *BioIn 16*
Kannry, Sybil 1931- *WhoAmW 91, WhoE 91*
Kano *NewAgMG*
Kano 1434-1530 *EncJap*
Kano, Susan Leslie 1959- *WhoWrEP 89*
Kanof, Naomi M. 1911-1988 *BioIn 16*
Kanofsky, Alvin Sheldon 1939- *WhoE 91*
Kanofsky, Jacob Daniel *BiDrAPA 89*
Kanofsky, Jacob Daniel 1948- *WhoE 91*
Kanoh, Minami 1927- *WhoWor 91*
Kanoh, Tokio 1935- *BioIn 16*
Kanokogi, Rusty *BioIn 16*
Kanon, Joseph A. 1946- *St&PR 91*
Kanopoulos, Nick 1956- *WhoEmL 91*
Kanouse, Thomas John 1936- *St&PR 91*
Kanov, Lubomir Mladenov 1944- *BiDrAPA 89*
Kanovitz, Bob Solomon *BiDrAPA 89*
Kanovitz, Howard 1929- *WhoAmA 91*
Kanovitz, Howard Earl 1929- *WhoAm 90*
Kanpak, Saffet Ali 1947- *WhoWor 91*
Kansagra, Chunilal H *BiDrAPA 89*
Kansal, Prem Kumar 1945- *BiDrAPA 89*
Kansara, Suryakant Ratilal *WhoWor 91*
Kansas *EncPR&S 89*
Kansbod, Lena *BioIn 16*
Kanski, Jozef Celestyn 1928- *IntWWM 90*
Kansky, Eugene W 1927- *BiDrAPA 89*
Kansky, Stanislav 1940- *WhoWor 91*
Kant, Chander 1948- *WhoE 91*
Kant, Harold Sanford 1931- *WhoAm 90*
Kant, Immanuel 1724-1804 *DcLB 94 [port], EncO&P 3, EncPaPR 91, NinCLC 27 [port], WorAlBi, WrPh P*
Kant, Ravi *BiDrAPA 89*
Kant, Steven Michael *BiDrAPA 89*
Kantabutra, Bundhit 1916- *WhoWor 91*
Kantack, Paul Wayne *BiDrAPA 89*
Kantack, Walter W 1889-1953 *WhoAmA 91N*
Kantamneni, Satyanarayana *BiDrAPA 89*
Kantar, William G 1936- *BiDrAPA 89*
Kantarelis, Demetrius 1951- *WhoE 91*
Kantaris, Sylvia 1936- *ConAu 129, FemiCLE*
Kantarizis, Sylvia *ConAu 129*
Kantarizis, Sylvia 1936- *FemiCLE*
Kantarjian, Artin D 1920- *BiDrAPA 89*
Kanter, Alan Michael 1954- *WhoEmL 91*
Kanter, Carl Irwin 1932- *St&PR 91, WhoAm 90*
Kanter, Donald Richard 1951- *WhoWor 91*
Kanter, Ellen V *BiDrAPA 89*
Kanter, Frederick S *BiDrAPA 89*
Kanter, Gary Lawrence *BiDrAPA 89*
Kanter, Gerald Alan 1931- *St&PR 91*
Kanter, Hal 1918- *WhoAm 90*
Kanter, Isaac 1908- *BiDrAPA 89*
Kanter, James I. 1920- *St&PR 91*
Kanter, Jay 1926- *WhoAm 90*
Kanter, Joel Stephen 1956- *WhoEmL 91*
Kanter, Joseph Hyman 1923- *WhoAm 90*
Kanter, Leonard *St&PR 91*
Kanter, Morton 1923- *St&PR 91*
Kanter, Rosabeth Moss *BioIn 16*
Kanter, Rosabeth Moss 1943- *WhoAm 90, WhoAmW 91*
Kanter, Shamai 1930- *WhoE 91*
Kanter, Stanley S 1917- *BiDrAPA 89*
Kantesaria, Atul Nandlal 1957- *BiDrAPA 89*
Kantharaj, Adisayam Joseph 1931- *WhoE 91*
Kanther, Manfred 1925- *BiDrAPA 89*
Kantlehner, Erv 1892- *Ballpl 90*
Kantner, John F. 1920- *WhoAm 90*
Kantner, Paul 1941- *WhoAm 90*
Kantor, Bernard 1930- *WhoE 91*
Kantor, Edwin 1932- *WhoAm 90*
Kantor, Eva Ida *IntWWM 90*
Kantor, Fred Stuart 1931- *WhoAm 90*
Kantor, Gideon 1925- *WhoAm 90, WhoE 91*
Kantor, Henry 1954- *WhoEmL 91*
Kantor, Jerry Steven 1951- *BiDrAPA 89*
Kantor, MacKinlay 1904-1977 *AuBYP 90, BioIn 16, DcLB 102 [port]*
Kantor, Maksim 1957- *BioIn 16*
Kantor, Mark Neil 1956- *St&PR 91*
Kantor, Martin 1933- *BiDrAPA 89*
Kantor, Marvin 1934- *WhoAm 90*
Kantor, McKinlay 1904-1977 *WorAlBi*
Kantor, Morris 1896-1974 *WhoAmA 91N*
Kantor, Nathan 1942- *St&PR 91, WhoAm 90*
Kantor, Russell S. 1951- *St&PR 91*
Kantor, Ruth Brenda 1943- *BiDrAPA 89*

Kantor, Seth 1926- *WhoAm 90*
Kantor, Shepard J 1944- *BiDrAPA 89*
Kantor, Simon William 1925- *WhoAm 90*
Kantor, Stanley Estrin 1933- *St&PR 91*
Kantor, Tadeusz 1915- *ConDes 90, WhoWor 91*
Kantor, Tadeusz 1915-1990 *NewYTBS 90*
Kantorek, Sandra Schwahl 1952- *WhoAmW 91*
Kantorksi, Alan Lloyd 1947- *St&PR 91*
Kantounis, Lizabeth Ann 1959- *WhoE 91*
Kantowitz, Robert Isaac 1956- *WhoEmL 91*
Kantrovitch, Vera Evelyn *IntWWM 90*
Kantrowitz, Adrian 1918- *WhoAm 90*
Kantrowitz, Arthur 1913- *WhoAm 90*
Kantrowitz, Betty 1942- *WhoE 91*
Kantrowitz, Jonathan Daniel 1945- *WhoE 91*
Kantrowitz, Mildred *AuBYP 90*
Kantz, Phil *BioIn 16*
Kantzer, Klaus Peter 1935- *St&PR 91*
Kantzler, George W 1924- *BiDrAPA 89*
Kanu-Oji, Nsa 1942- *WhoWor 91*
Kanuit, Robert B. 1944- *St&PR 91*
Kanuk, Leslie Lazar *WhoAm 90*
Kanwal, Gurmeet Singh *BiDrAPA 89*
Kanwit, Glen Harris 1943- *WhoAm 90*
Kany, Donald J. 1944- *St&PR 91*
Kany, Judy Casperson 1937- *WhoAmW 91, WhoE 91*
Kany, Steven C. 1943- *St&PR 91*
Kanya, Alberta 1942- *WhoE 91*
Kanyusik, James 1953- *WhoEmL 91*
Kanz, Heinrich Georg 1927- *WhoWor 91*
Kanzer, Mark 1908- *BiDrAPA 89, WhoE 91*
Kanzinger, Russell Christian 1940- *St&PR 91*
Kanzler, Ford *ODwPR 91*
Kao, Charles Kuen 1933- *WhoAm 90*
Kao, Cheng Chi 1941- *WhoWor 91*
Kao, George 1912- *ConAu 132*
Kao, Karen Patricia *WhoAmW 91*
Kao, Kuo Nan 1934- *WhoAm 90*
Kao, Pai Chih 1934- *WhoAm 90*
Kao, Ruth Lee *WhoAmA 91N*
Kao, Shou Carl 1924- *WhoSSW 91*
Kao, Teh-Hong 1925- *WhoWor 91*
Kao, Wen-Hong 1954- *WhoEmL 91*
Kaonis, Donna Christine 1949- *WhoWrEP 89*
Kapadia, Haresh K. 1950- *St&PR 91*
Kapahi, Naresh Chander 1950- *St&PR 91*
Kapalin, Jerman *WhoAm 90*
Kapanci, Yusuf 1929- *WhoWor 91*
Kapandji, Adalbert Ibrahim 1928- *WhoWor 91*
Kapania, Rakesh Kumar 1956- *WhoSSW 91*
Kapatkin, Fred 1927- *WhoE 91*
Kapchan, Jack 1922- *EncPaPR 91*
Kapche, Ronald Anthony 1941- *WhoSSW 91, WhoWor 91*
Kapcsandy, Louis Endre 1936- *WhoAm 90*
Kapecki, Walter Joseph 1933- *St&PR 91*
Kapek, Antonin 1922-1990 *BioIn 16*
Kapel, David Edward 1932- *WhoE 91*
Kapel, Kirk Frederick 1956- *St&PR 91*
Kapel, Saul E 1928- *BiDrAPA 89*
Kapell, Bernard L. 1926- *St&PR 91*
Kapell, Lydia Ann *BiDrAPA 89*
Kapell, William 1922-1953 *PenDiMP*
Kapelovitz, Leonard H 1939- *BiDrAPA 89*
Kaper, Bronislaw 1902-1983 *OxCPMus*
Kapfer, Kathleen Ann 1951- *WhoEmL 91*
Kaphan, Robert C. 1944- *St&PR 91*
Kapik, Armand B 1925- *BiDrAPA 89*
Kapikian, Albert Zaven 1930- *WhoE 91, WhoWor 91*
Kapila *EncO&P 3*
Kapila, Abi *BiDrAPA 89*
Kapila, Sneh 1950- *BiDrAPA 89*
Kapila, Soneet Ravi 1952- *WhoEmL 91*
Kapioltas, John 1927- *St&PR 91, WhoAm 90, WhoE 91, WhoWor 91*
Kapitsa, Pyotr 1894-1984 *WorAlBi*
Kapitza, Piotr Leonidovich 1894-1984 *DcNaB 1981*
Kapitzki, Herbert W 1925- *ConDes 90*
Kapkin, Ihsan A 1924- *BiDrAPA 89*
Kaplan, Abraham 1918- *St&PR 91*
Kaplan, Abraham I 1914- *BiDrAPA 89*
Kaplan, Abraham Irving 1914- *WhoE 91*
Kaplan, Alan 1941- *St&PR 91*
Kaplan, Albert A. *AuBYP 90*
Kaplan, Albert A 1940- *BiDrAPA 89*
Kaplan, Alex H 1912- *BiDrAPA 89*
Kaplan, Alexander 1920- *St&PR 91*
Kaplan, Allan Saul *BiDrAPA 89*
Kaplan, Allen Jack 1925- *WhoSSW 91*
Kaplan, Allen Stanford 1939- *WhoE 91*
Kaplan, Alvin 1941- *St&PR 91*
Kaplan, Alvin I. 1930- *WhoE 91*
Kaplan, Alvin Irving 1925- *WhoAm 90*
Kaplan, Amy Louise 1950- *WhoAmW 91, WhoEmL 91*
Kaplan, Andrea *ODwPR 91*
Kaplan, Ann Ruth 1938- *WhoAmW 91*
Kaplan, Anne Karp 1938- *WhoE 91*
Kaplan, Arnold H. 1939- *St&PR 91*
Kaplan, Barbara *WhoAm 90*
Kaplan, Barnett Morris 1947- *BiDrAPA 89*
Kaplan, Barry S 1938- *BiDrAPA 89*
Kaplan, Benjamin 1911- *WhoAm 90*
Kaplan, Bernard *BioIn 16*
Kaplan, Bernard Joseph 1918- *WhoE 91, WhoWor 91*
Kaplan, Bernice Antoville 1923- *WhoAm 90*
Kaplan, Carey 1943- *WhoAmW 91*
Kaplan, Carl E. 1939- *St&PR 91*
Kaplan, Carl Eliot 1939- *WhoAm 90*
Kaplan, Carline 1963- *ODwPR 91*
Kaplan, Carol 1949- *BioIn 16*
Kaplan, Carol Blakely 1945- *WhoAmW 91, WhoEmL 91*
Kaplan, Carole Jane 1959- *WhoE 91*
Kaplan, Chaim Aron 1880-1942? *BioIn 16*
Kaplan, Daniel I. 1943- *St&PR 91, WhoAm 90*
Kaplan, David Andrew 1956- *WhoE 91*
Kaplan, David E 1948- *BiDrAPA 89*
Kaplan, David Michael 1946- *WhoWrEP 89*
Kaplan, Diane Susan 1957- *WhoAmW 91*
Kaplan, Donald David 1930- *St&PR 91, WhoAm 90*
Kaplan, Eliot Fredric 1954- *BiDrAPA 89*
Kaplan, Ellen Wendy 1952- *WhoEmL 91*
Kaplan, Elliot S. 1936- *WhoAm 90*
Kaplan, Eric M 1960- *BiDrAPA 89*
Kaplan, Eric William 1957- *BiDrAPA 89*
Kaplan, Erica Lynn 1955- *WhoAmW 91, WhoEmL 91*
Kaplan, Eugene A 1933- *BiDrAPA 89*
Kaplan, Eugene H 1925- *BiDrAPA 89*
Kaplan, Fania 1887-1918 *BioIn 16*
Kaplan, Frank E 1911- *BiDrAPA 89*
Kaplan, Fred M. 1954- *St&PR 91*
Kaplan, Fred Martin 1948- *WhoEmL 91*
Kaplan, Frederic Clark 1948- *WhoAmA 91*
Kaplan, Gabe 1945- *WorAlBi*
Kaplan, Gabriel *BiDrAPA 89*
Kaplan, Gabriel 1956- *WhoE 91*
Kaplan, Gary 1939- *WhoAm 90*
Kaplan, Gary B. *BiDrAPA 89*
Kaplan, George C 1934- *BiDrAPA 89*
Kaplan, George R. 1919- *St&PR 91*
Kaplan, Georges *NewYTBS 90*
Kaplan, Gerson H *BiDrAPA 89*
Kaplan, Gilbert B. 1951- *WhoAm 90*
Kaplan, Gustave 1920- *St&PR 91*
Kaplan, Harley B. 1954- *St&PR 91*
Kaplan, Harley Lance 1961- *WhoE 91*
Kaplan, Harold 1916- *WhoAm 90*
Kaplan, Harold 1918- *WhoAm 90*
Kaplan, Harold I 1927- *BiDrAPA 89*
Kaplan, Harold Irving 1921- *WhoAm 90*
Kaplan, Harold Irwin 1927- *WhoAm 90*
Kaplan, Harold Morris 1908- *WhoAm 90*
Kaplan, Harold Paul 1939- *WhoE 91*
Kaplan, Harriet Smith 1929- *BiDrAPA 89*
Kaplan, Harry Allan 1954- *WhoE 91*
Kaplan, Harry Paul 1940- *WhoWor 91*
Kaplan, Hayyim Aaron 1880-1942? *BioIn 16*
Kaplan, Helen S *BiDrAPA 89*
Kaplan, Helene Lois 1933- *WhoAm 90, WhoAmW 91*
Kaplan, Henry Jerrold 1942- *WhoAm 90*
Kaplan, Herbert A 1939- *BiDrAPA 89*
Kaplan, Herman 1928- *BiDrAPA 89*
Kaplan, Howard Elliott 1956- *WhoE 91*
Kaplan, Howard Fred 1941- *St&PR 91*
Kaplan, Huette Myra 1933- *WhoAmW 91*
Kaplan, Ilee *WhoAmA 91*
Kaplan, Isaac Raymond 1929- *WhoAm 90*
Kaplan, Jacques 1924- *WhoAmA 91*
Kaplan, James *ConLC 59 [port]*
Kaplan, James Lee 1939- *WhoE 91*
Kaplan, Janet A 1945- *ConAu 130*
Kaplan, Janet Gordon 1938- *WhoAmW 91*
Kaplan, Jared 1938- *WhoWor 91*
Kaplan, Jean Caryl Korn *AuBYP 90*
Kaplan, Jean Gaither 1927- *WhoAmW 91*
Kaplan, Jeffrey Ira 1951- *WhoEmL 91*
Kaplan, Jeremiah 1926- *St&PR 91, WhoAm 90, WhoE 91*
Kaplan, Jerome Eugene 1920- *WhoAmA 91*
Kaplan, Jocelyn Rae 1952- *WhoAmW 91*
Kaplan, Joel Howard 1936- *BiDrAPA 89*
Kaplan, John *BioIn 16*
Kaplan, John 1929-1989 *ConAu 130*
Kaplan, John 1959- *WhoAm 90*
Kaplan, Jonathan *BiDrAPA 89*
Kaplan, Jonathan Harris 1957- *WhoE 91, WhoEmL 91, WhoWor 91*
Kaplan, Jonathan Stewart 1947- *WhoAm 90*
Kaplan, Josef 1913-1942 *BioIn 16*
Kaplan, Joseph 1900-1980 *WhoAmA 91N*
Kaplan, Judith E *BiDrAPA 89*
Kaplan, Judith Helene 1938- *St&PR 91, WhoAmW 91*
Kaplan, Julius David 1941- *WhoAmA 91*
Kaplan, Justin *BioIn 16*
Kaplan, Justin 1925- *WhoAm 90, WhoWrEP 89*
Kaplan, Kenneth F. 1945- *St&PR 91*
Kaplan, Kenneth H 1940- *BiDrAPA 89*
Kaplan, Kenneth L *BiDrAPA 89*
Kaplan, Kenneth Neil 1947- *WhoE 91*
Kaplan, Laura Beth 1965- *WhoSSW 91*
Kaplan, Laura Garcia 1957- *WhoAmW 91*
Kaplan, Laura Kay 1958- *WhoEmL 91*
Kaplan, Lawrence 1926- *WhoE 91*
Kaplan, Lawrence I *BiDrAPA 89*
Kaplan, Lawrence Irving 1917- *WhoAm 90*
Kaplan, Lawrence R. 1950- *St&PR 91*
Kaplan, Lee Landa 1952- *WhoEmL 91*
Kaplan, Lenora *ODwPR 91*
Kaplan, Leo 1912- *WhoAmA 91*
Kaplan, Leo Sylvan 1924- *WhoAm 90*
Kaplan, Leon 1908- *St&PR 91*
Kaplan, Leonard Eugene 1940- *WhoAm 90, WhoSSW 91*
Kaplan, Leonard M 1935- *BiDrAPA 89*
Kaplan, Lester 1941- *WhoE 91*
Kaplan, Lewis 1933- *IntWWM 90*
Kaplan, Lewis A. 1944- *WhoAm 90*
Kaplan, Linda F. 1951- *WhoAmW 91*
Kaplan, Lloyd Arthur 1934- *WhoAm 90*
Kaplan, Lois Jay 1932- *WhoAmW 91*
Kaplan, Madeline 1944- *WhoAmW 91, WhoE 91*
Kaplan, Manfred Harold 1928- *WhoWor 91*
Kaplan, Manuel E. 1928- *WhoAm 90*
Kaplan, Marcia Joan 1954- *BiDrAPA 89*
Kaplan, Margaret *AuBYP 90*
Kaplan, Marilyn Flashenberg *WhoAm 90, WhoAmA 91*
Kaplan, Mark 1953- *IntWWM 90*
Kaplan, Mark N. 1930- *St&PR 91*
Kaplan, Mark Norman 1930- *WhoE 91*
Kaplan, Mark Steven 1947- *WhoE 91*
Kaplan, Marshall Van 1959- *WhoEmL 91*
Kaplan, Martin Mark 1915- *WhoWor 91*
Kaplan, Marvin Alan 1948- *BiDrAPA 89*
Kaplan, Maurice 1907- *BiDrAPA 89*
Kaplan, Melvin Hyman 1920- *WhoAm 90*
Kaplan, Michael Irving 1941- *WhoAm 90*
Kaplan, Michael Jay 1951- *St&PR 91*
Kaplan, Michael Miller 1954- *BiDrAPA 89*
Kaplan, Michael Sebastian 1959- *WhoE 91*
Kaplan, Milton 1910- *WhoWrEP 89*
Kaplan, Mitchel A *BiDrAPA 89*
Kaplan, Mitchel Alan 1949- *WhoE 91*
Kaplan, Mordecai Menahem 1881-1983 *BioIn 16*
Kaplan, Morris *BiDrAPA 89*
Kaplan, Morris *BioIn 16*
Kaplan, Morton A. 1921- *WhoAm 90*
Kaplan, Morton H. 1931- *ODwPR 91*
Kaplan, Muriel 1924- *WhoAmA 91*
Kaplan, Muriel Sheerr 1924- *WhoAm 90, WhoSSW 91*
Kaplan, Murray S. *BioIn 16*
Kaplan, Myron Jay *BiDrAPA 89*
Kaplan, Nancy Wilma *BiDrAPA 89*
Kaplan, Norman Mayer 1931- *WhoAm 90*
Kaplan, Oscar Joel 1915- *WhoAm 90*
Kaplan, Patricia Ann 1952- *WhoAmW 91*
Kaplan, Penny *WhoAmA 91*
Kaplan, Perrin *ODwPR 91*
Kaplan, Peter 1943- *WhoAm 90*
Kaplan, Peter Benjamin 1939- *WhoAm 90*
Kaplan, Peter James 1943- *WhoAm 90*
Kaplan, Peter Jay 1954- *St&PR 91*
Kaplan, Philip Thomas 1928- *WhoAm 90*
Kaplan, Phillip S. *WhoAm 90*
Kaplan, Phyllis *BiDrAPA 89*
Kaplan, R.W. 1924- *St&PR 91*
Kaplan, Rachel 1937- *WhoAm 90*
Kaplan, Raymon T 1935- *BiDrAPA 89*
Kaplan, Reed Jay *BiDrAPA 89*
Kaplan, Reuben William 1924- *WhoAm 90*
Kaplan, Richard *BioIn 16*
Kaplan, Richard D 1951- *BiDrAPA 89*
Kaplan, Richard David 1951- *WhoE 91*
Kaplan, Robert Arthur 1927- *WhoAm 90*
Kaplan, Robert B. 1929- *WhoAm 90*
Kaplan, Robert Barnett 1924- *IntWWM 90*
Kaplan, Robert D. *BioIn 16*
Kaplan, Robert David 1955- *WhoEmL 91*
Kaplan, Robert Lee 1933- *WhoE 91*
Kaplan, Robert Malcolm 1947- *WhoAm 90, WhoEmL 91*
Kaplan, Robert Malcolm 1950- *WhoWor 91*
Kaplan, Robert Marshall 1936- *WhoWor 91*
Kaplan, Robert Phillip 1936- *WhoAm 90*
Kaplan, Ronald Alan 1943- *St&PR 91*
Kaplan, Ronald Martin 1948- *WhoE 91*
Kaplan, Ronald V. 1930- *St&PR 91, WhoAm 90*
Kaplan, Rose Glasser *BioIn 16*
Kaplan, Samuel 1916- *BiDrAPA 89*
Kaplan, Samuel 1922- *WhoAm 90, WhoWor 91*
Kaplan, Sandra 1943- *WhoAmA 91*
Kaplan, Sandra Janet *BiDrAPA 89*
Kaplan, Sandra Lee 1956- *WhoAmW 91*
Kaplan, Sanford 1916- *St&PR 91*
Kaplan, Sanford Sandy 1950- *WhoEmL 91, WhoWor 91*
Kaplan, Seymour R. *BioIn 16*
Kaplan, Shari Ann *WhoAmW 91*
Kaplan, Sheila *WhoAm 90, WhoAmW 91*
Kaplan, Sheldon 1915- *WhoAm 90*
Kaplan, Sheldon Zachary 1911- *WhoAm 90*
Kaplan, Sidney Joseph 1924- *WhoAm 90*
Kaplan, Slyvia Allison 1917- *WhoAmW 91*
Kaplan, Sol *NewYTBS 90*
Kaplan, Sollie 1917- *WhoSSW 91*
Kaplan, Stanley 1925- *WhoAmA 91*
Kaplan, Stanley Albert 1938- *WhoAm 90*
Kaplan, Stanley M 1922- *BiDrAPA 89*
Kaplan, Stanley Meisel 1922- *WhoAm 90*
Kaplan, Stephen 1940- *WhoSSW 91, WhoWor 91*
Kaplan, Stephen H. 1940- *St&PR 91*
Kaplan, Stephen P. 1939- *St&PR 91*
Kaplan, Stephen Robert 1937- *WhoAm 90*
Kaplan, Steven F. 1956- *WhoAm 90, WhoEmL 91*
Kaplan, Steven Leslie *BiDrAPA 89*
Kaplan, Steven Marc 1953- *WhoEmL 91*
Kaplan, Steven Zane 1946- *WhoEmL 91*
Kaplan, Stuart Lee 1939- *BiDrAPA 89*
Kaplan, Stuart R. 1932- *WhoWrEP 89*
Kaplan, Susan *WhoE 91*
Kaplan, Susan Robin 1954- *WhoE 91*
Kaplan, Sylvia Yalowitz Kaplan 1921- *WhoAmW 91*
Kaplan, Theodore Norman 1935- *WhoE 91*
Kaplan, Thomas R. *ODwPR 91*
Kaplan, V. Jerome 1926- *St&PR 91*
Kaplan, Warren 1937- *St&PR 91*
Kaplan, Warren J. 1942- *St&PR 91*
Kaplan, William 1934- *St&PR 91*
Kaplan, William Howard *BiDrAPA 89*
Kaplan, Yale Joseph 1928- *St&PR 91*
Kaplan-Sagal, Lauren Ellen 1962- *WhoEmL 91*
Kapland, Mitchell A. 1906- *St&PR 91*
Kapland, Mitchell Arthur 1906- *WhoAm 90*
Kaplansky, Irving 1917- *WhoAm 90*
Kaplansky-Gold, Cathy S *BiDrAPA 89*
Kaplen, Alexander *BioIn 16*
Kaplenk, Joseph Edward 1947- *WhoEmL 91*
Kapler, A. William, III 1951- *WhoE 91*
Kapley, David Joseph *BiDrAPA 89*
Kaplin, Arnold Jay 1934- *BiDrAPA 89*
Kaplin, Bernard Douglas 1950- *WhoSSW 91*
Kaplin, Julian M., Jr. 1953- *WhoEmL 91*
Kaplin, Randy Wayne 1949- *St&PR 91*
Kaplin, William Albert 1942- *WhoE 91*
Kaplinski, Buffalo 1943- *WhoAmA 91*
Kaplinski, Hirsch 1910-1942 *BioIn 16*
Kaplinski, Richard S. 1943- *St&PR 91*
Kaplitz, Renee Lynn 1963- *WhoEmL 91*
Kaplow, Herbert Elias 1927- *WhoAm 90*
Kaplow, Jonathan 1957- *WhoEmL 91*
Kaplow, Jonathan W. 1957- *St&PR 91*
Kaplow, Leonard Samuel 1920- *WhoAm 90*
Kaplow, Louis 1956- *WhoE 91*
Kaplowitz, Daniel 1917- *BiDrAPA 89*
Kaplowitz, Jane *BioIn 16*
Kaplowitz, Jeffrey Jay 1943- *St&PR 91*
Kaplowitz, Kenneth 1941- *WhoE 91*
Kaplun, Serge 1939- *WhoWor 91*
Kapnek, Wendy N. 1960- *WhoAmW 91*
Kapner, Jerry A. 1952- *WhoE 91*
Kapner, Stanley H. 1918- *ODwPR 91*
Kapnick, Harvey 1925- *St&PR 91*
Kapnick, Harvey Edward, Jr. 1925- *WhoAm 90, WhoWor 91*
Kapnick, Laura Beth 1951- *WhoEmL 91*
Kapnick, Richard Allan 1941- *WhoWor 91*
Kapnick, Richard Bradshaw 1955- *WhoEmL 91, WhoWor 91*
Kapnick, Stewart 1956- *WhoEmL 91*
Kapnoudhis, Paul Christos *BiDrAPA 89*
Kapochunas, Andrew 1947- *WhoEmL 91*
Kapoor, Ashok Kumar 1952- *WhoEmL 91*
Kapoor, Deepak *BiDrAPA 89*
Kapoor, Raj 1924-1988 *AnObit 1988, BioIn 16*
Kapoor, Shashi *BioIn 16*
Kapoor, Veena 1942- *BiDrAPA 89*
Kapoor, Vinod 1943- *St&PR 91*
Kapor, Mitch 1950- *News 90 [port], -90-3 [port]*
Kapor, Mitchell *BioIn 16*
Kapor, Mitchell David 1950- *WhoAm 90*
Kapoulas, George James 1953- *WhoEmL 91*
Kapp, Colin 1928?- *ConAu 132*
Kapp, John Paul 1938- *WhoAm 90, WhoSSW 91*
Kapp, M. Keith 1953- *WhoEmL 91*
Kapp, Marshall Barry 1949- *WhoEmL 91*
Kapp, Nancy Gladys 1945- *WhoAmW 91*
Kapp, Paul *AuBYP 90*

Kapp, Richard 1936- IntWWM 90
Kapp, Robert Harris 1934- WhoAm 90
Kapp, Roger W. 1936- St&PR 91, WhoAm 90
Kappa, Margaret McCaffrey 1921- WhoAmW 91
Kappagantula, Savithri WhoSSW 91
Kappas, Attallah 1926- WhoAm 90
Kappel, Gertrude 1884-1971 PenDiMP
Kappel, Joseph 1918- St&PR 91
Kappel, Philip 1901-1981 WhoAmA 91N
Kappeler, Beat Anton Gabriel 1946- WhoWor 91
Kappelmann, Douglas James 1949- WhoSSW 91
Kappenberg, Richard Paul 1944- WhoWor 91
Kappers, Jan 1914- EncO&P 3, EncPaPR 91
Kappes, Christopher A. 1958- St&PR 91
Kappes, Philip Spangler 1925- WhoAm 90
Kappesser, Robert Roy 1943- WhoE 91
Kapphahn, Ernest L. 1946- WhoEmL 91
Kappler, Edward James 1946- WhoEmL 91
Kappler, Frank K., II ODwPR 91
Kappler, Herbert 1907-1978 BioIn 16
Kappler, John Edward 1944- St&PR 91
Kappler, Lydia Patricia 1958- WhoAmW 91, WhoEmL 91
Kappler, Robert Paul 1938- WhoE 91
Kappmeyer, Keith Karl 1934- St&PR 91
Kappock, Thomas Joseph, III 1944- St&PR 91
Kappus, Harold C BiDrAPA 89
Kapr, Albert 1918- ConDes 90
Kapr, John Robert 1954- WhoE 91
Kapral, Frank Albert 1928- WhoAm 90
Kapral, Hilarion 1948- WhoAm 90
Kaprelian, Edward K. 1913- WhoAm 90
Kaprielian, Michael 1931- BiDrAPA 89
Kaprielian, Walter 1934- WhoAm 90
Kaprov, Susan 1946- WhoAmA 91
Kaps, Fred 1926-1980 BioIn 16
Kapsalis, Thomas Harry 1925- WhoAmA 91
Kapsen, Terrance John 1951- St&PR 91
Kapshandy, Timothy Edward 1956- WhoEmL 91
Kapsten, Seymour C. 1922- St&PR 91
Kapteyn, Paul Joan G. 1928- WhoWor 91
Kaptsan, Helen 1960- WhoAmW 91
Kaptur, Marcia Carolyn 1946- WhoAm 90, WhoAmW 91
Kapuchinski, Stanley 1944- BiDrAPA 89
Kapuler, William P 1911- BiDrAPA 89
Kapur, Brahm 1949- BiDrAPA 89
Kapur, Harish Chandra 1929- WhoWor 91
Kapur, Kailash Chander 1941- WhoAm 90
Kapur, Krishan Kishore 1930- WhoAm 90
Kapur, Shitij BiDrAPA 89
Kapus, Josephine DiStefano 1928- WhoE 91
Kapuscinski, Richard PenDiMP
Kapuscinski, Ryszard 1932- WhoWor 91
Kapwepwe, Simon Mwansa BioIn 16
Kara-Dodhia, Munira N BiDrAPA 89
Karaba, Frank Andrew 1927- WhoAm 90
Karabanow, Oscar BiDrAPA 89
Karabatsos, Elizabeth Ann 1932- WhoAmW 91
Karabel, Jerome Bernard 1950- WhoEmL 91
Karabey, Turgut 1926- BiDrAPA 89
Karabots, Nick George 1933- St&PR 91
Karacan, Ismet BiDrAPA 89
Karadja, Mary EncO&P 3
Karady, George Gyorgy 1930- WhoAm 90
Karafel, Lorraine 1956- WhoAmA 91
Karafolas, Simeon 1958- WhoWor 91
Karagannis, Ted 1958- WhoE 91
Karageorge, Michael AuBYP 90, MajTwCW
Karageorghis, Vassos 1929- ConAu 33NR, WhoWor 91
Karagianis, James Andrew 1947- St&PR 91
Karagianis, Maria Elizabeth 1948- WhoWrEP 89
Karagiorga, Olympia 1934- EncCoWW
Karagozian, Serge Varenack 1948- WhoWor 91
Karagulla, Shafica EncO&P 3
Karagulla, Shafica 1914-198-? EncPaPR 91
Karai, Jozsef 1927- IntWWM 90
Karajan, Herbert von BioIn 16
Karajan, Herbert von 1908-1989 AnObit 1989, PenDiMP, WorAlBi
Karakas, Rita S. WhoAm 90
Karakash, John J. 1914- WhoAm 90
Karakashian, Marlene Lenore 1933- WhoE 91
Karakey, Sherry Joanne 1942- St&PR 91
Karaki, Yukihiko 1943- WhoWor 91
Karakitsos, Elias 1948- WhoWor 91
Karalekas, Anne 1946- WhoE 91
Karalekas, George Steven 1939- WhoAm 90
Karales, James Harry 1930- WhoAm 90
Karalis, John Peter 1938- WhoAm 90
Karam, Elie George 1950- BiDrAPA 89
Karam, Victor Abraham 1934- St&PR 91
Karamanlis, Constantine G. 1907- WhoWor 91
Karamanlis, Konstantine 1907- WorAlBi
Karamatsu, Yoshikazu 1937- WhoWor 91
Karambelas, John 1923- St&PR 91
Karambelkar, Jagannath P BiDrAPA 89
Karami, Rashid 1921-1987 PolLCME
Karamigios, George John 1950- BiDrAPA 89
Karan, Donna BioIn 16
Karan, Donna 1948- ConDes 90, CurBio 90 [port], WhoAm 90, WhoAmW 91, WorAlBi
Karan, Donna/Dell'Olio, Louis ConDes 90
Karan, Toni Shostak St&PR 91
Karanfilova, Ganka Slavova 1934- EncCoWW
Karanian, Ralph Edward 1955- WhoEmL 91
Karanik, John A. 1944- St&PR 91
Karanikas, Alexander 1916- WhoAm 90
Karanja, Josphat Njuguna 1931- WhoWor 91
Karanjia, Russy K. 1912- WhoWor 91
Karantokis, Nicolas Georgiou 1917- WhoWor 91
Karaosmanoglu, Attila 1932- WhoAm 90
Karapanou, Margarita 1946- EncCoWW
Karapashev, Ljubka Nicerska BiDrAPA 89
Karapetian, David 1947- St&PR 91
Karapostoles, Demetrios Aristides 1936- WhoWor 91
Karas, Anton 1906-1985 OxCPMus, PenDiMP
Karas, Donald A. 1931- St&PR 91, WhoAm 90
Karas, Howard Robert 1927- St&PR 91
Karas, James 1950- St&PR 91
Karas, Michael Victor, III 1958- WhoE 91
Karas, Richard Andrew 1942- St&PR 91
Karas, Scott A. 1948- St&PR 91
Karasaki, Shuichi 1931- WhoWor 91
Karase, Chakanyuka 1952- WhoWor 91
Karasek, Victoria Jane 1955- WhoSSW 91
Karasic, Jerome BiDrAPA 89
Karasick, Carol 1941- St&PR 91, WhoAm 90, WhoAmW 91
Karasik, Brenda-Lee 1947- WhoAmW 91
Karasik, Gita 1949- IntWWM 90
Karasik, Myron Solomon 1950- WhoEmL 91
Karasu, Sylvia Rabson 1949- BiDrAPA 89
Karasu, Toksoz Byram 1935- BiDrAPA 89, WhoAm 90
Karasz, Frank Erwin 1933- WhoAm 90
Karasz, Ilonka 1896-1981 PenDiDA 89
Karasz, Mariska 1898-1960 PenDiDA 89, WhoAmA 91N
Karatela, Mohammed I BiDrAPA 89
Karatjas, Nicholas 1949- WhoE 91
Karatsu, Hajime 1919- WhoWor 91
Karatsu, Osamu 1947- WhoEmL 91, WhoWor 91
Karatz, Bruce E. 1945- St&PR 91, WhoAm 90
Karatz, William Warren 1926- WhoAm 90
Karatzoglou, John 1946- WhoWor 91
Karau, Jon Olin 1918- WhoSSW 91
Karavaeva, Anna Aleksandrovna 1893- EncCoWW
Karavites, Peter 1932- WhoE 91
Karavolas, Harry John 1936- WhoAm 90
Karawina, Erica WhoAmA 91
Karawina, Erica 1904- WhoAm 90
Karayannis, Nicholas Marios 1931- WhoAm 90
Karayn, James, Jr. 1933- WhoAm 90
Karayusuf, Alford Sami BiDrAPA 89
Karaz, Samy Sobhy 1952- BiDrAPA 89
Karban, Robert, Jr. 1945- WhoEmL 91
Karben, Shelley Valerie 1944- WhoE 91
Karbowiak, Carol Jean 1966- WhoWrEP 89
Karch, George Frederick, Jr. 1933- WhoAm 90
Karch, Hans-Dieter 1942- WhoWor 91
Karch, Robert E. 1933- WhoSSW 91
Karcher, Charles William 1920- WhoAm 90
Karcher, Nicholaus PenDiDA 89
Karchin, Louis S. 1951- IntWWM 90
Karchmer, David Kary 1941- St&PR 91
Karchon, James 1949- St&PR 91
Karczykowski, Ryszard 1942- IntWWM 90
Kardas, Barbara Jean 1931- WhoAm 90
Kardashian, Frank 1934- St&PR 91
Kardec, Allan 1804-1869 EncO&P 3, EncPaPR 91
Kardener, Sheldon H 1933- BiDrAPA 89
Kardish, Laurence 1945- ConAu 30NR
Kardon, Janet WhoAm 90, WhoAmA 91, WhoAmW 91
Kardon, Leroy 1951- St&PR 91
Kardon, Robert St&PR 91
Kardon, Robert 1922- WhoAm 90
Kardong, Don BioIn 16
Kardong, Gloria Marie 1956- BiDrAPA 89
Kardos, Dezider 1914- IntWWM 90
Kardos, Marianne BiDrAPA 89
Kardos, Mel D. 1947- WhoE 91, WhoWor 91
Kardys, Joseph Anthony 1925- WhoE 91
Kardys, Richard 1946- St&PR 91
Kare P. EncCoWW
Kare, Graciela Salinas 1957- WhoHisp 91
Kare, Morley R. NewYTBS 90
Kare, Morley Richard 1922- WhoAm 90
Kareda, Urjo 1944- OxCCanT
Kareff, Jack Fredrick 1955- WhoSSW 91
Karega, Deborah Annette 1953- WhoAmW 91
Kareken, Francis A. 1930- WhoAm 90
Kareklas, Petros Michael 1949- WhoWor 91
Karel, Frank, III 1935- ODwPR 91
Karel, Marcus 1928- WhoAm 90
Karel, Martin Lewis 1944- WhoE 91
Karelis, Charles Howard 1945- WhoAm 90
Karelitz, Robert Nelson 1948- St&PR 91, WhoEmL 91
Karelitz-LeShay, Maxine Hoffman 1942- WhoAmW 91
Karell, Patricia Payne 1955- WhoAmW 91
Karelli, Zoe 1901- EncCoWW
Karen, James 1923- ConTFT 8 [port]
Karen, Ruth 1922- AuBYP 90
Karen, Ruth 1922-1987 BioIn 16
Karet, Jack A. 1934- St&PR 91
Karfiol, Bernard 1886-1952 WhoAmA 91N
Kargacos, Charles Edwin 1954- WhoE 91
Kargados, Panagiotis 1942- WhoWor 91
Kargas, Aristomenis K BiDrAPA 89
Karger, Ed 1883-1957 Ballpl 90
Karger, Thomas Jakob 1930- WhoWor 91
Karges, Edwin Ferdinand, Jr. 1922- St&PR 91
Kargin, Valentin Alekseevich 1907-1969 DcScB S2
Kargman, Jeffrey Mark 1954- BiDrAPA 89
Kargus, Jeffrey R. 1954- St&PR 91
Karhama, Pertti Aarre 1930- WhoWor 91
Kari, Paul BioIn 16
Kari, Shelley Lynn 1957- WhoAmW 91
Karigan, James Andrew 1927- WhoAm 90
Karim, Alia BiDrAPA 89
Karim, Ashir 1958- WhoE 91
Karimi, Farid BiDrAPA 89
Karin, Steven Norman 1941- WhoE 91
Karina, Anna 1940- ConTFT 8
Kariotis, George Stephen 1923- St&PR 91
Karis, Joseph John BiDrAPA 89
Karish, David Alan 1946- St&PR 91
Kariya, Hiroshi 1948- WhoAmA 91
Kariya, Tetsuro 1957- WhoWor 91
Karja, Juhani Aukusti 1934- WhoWor 91
Kark, David S. 1951- St&PR 91
Kark, Joanne Barbara 1953- WhoAmW 91
Kark, Nina Mary AuBYP 90
Kark, Robert M. 1911- WhoAm 90
Karka, Ilona 1959- BiDrAPA 89
Karkalas, John 1921- BiDrAPA 89
Karkalits, Olin Carroll, Jr. 1916- WhoSSW 91
Karkas, John D. 1926- WhoE 91
Karkhanis, Sharad 1935- WhoE 91
Karkheck, John Peter 1945- WhoEmL 91
Karklins, Vija L. 1929- WhoAm 90
Karkoff, Maurice Ingvar 1927- IntWWM 90
Karkoschka, Erhard 1923- IntWWM 90
Karkovice, Ron 1963- Ballpl 90
Karkus, Harvey D 1928- BiDrAPA 89
Karkut, Bonnie Lee 1934- WhoAmW 91
Karkut, Emil Joseph 1916- WhoAm 90
Karl, Archduke of Austria 1771-1847 BioIn 16
Karl, Andy 1914- Ballpl 90
Karl, Anita Katherine 1941- WhoWor 91
Karl, Barry Dean 1927- WhoAm 90
Karl, Conrad Paul, Sr. 1933- St&PR 91
Karl, Eric Alan 1956- WhoE 91
Karl, Frederick Brennan 1924- WhoAm 90
Karl, Frederick Robert 1927- WhoWor 91
Karl, Gabriel 1937- WhoAm 90
Karl, Helen Weist 1948- WhoAmW 91
Karl, Jean 1927- AuBYP 90, BioIn 16
Karl, Jean Edna 1927- WhoAm 90, WhoWrEP 89
Karl, Leo Emil, Jr. 1929- WhoE 91
Karl, Michael WhoWrEP 89
Karl, Robert Harry 1947- WhoSSW 91
Karl, Robert John 1949- WhoEmL 91
Karl, Ronald Joseph 1956- WhoEmL 91
Karl, Thomas John 1956- WhoEmL 91
Karlan, Luann Florio 1954- WhoAmW 91
Karlan, Samuel C BiDrAPA 89
Karlander, Lars Stig 1955- WhoWor 91
Karlberg, John R. 1941- St&PR 91
Karle, Isabella 1921- WhoAm 90, WhoAmW 91
Karle, Isabella L. 1921- BioIn 16
Karle, Jerome 1918- WhoAm 90, WhoE 91, WhoWor 91, WorAlBi
Karlen, Delmar 1912-1988 BioIn 16
Karlen, Janice Marie 1953- WhoAmW 91
Karlen, John Adam 1933- WhoAm 90
Karlen, Peter H WhoAmA 91
Karlen, Saul H 1909- BiDrAPA 89
Karleskint, George Anthony, Jr. 1950- WhoEmL 91
Karlfeldt, Erik Axel 1864-1931 DcScanL
Karlin, Calvin Joseph 1952- WhoEmL 91
Karlin, Elyse Zorn 1950- WhoAmW 91, WhoEmL 91
Karlin, Muriel Schlosberg 1940- WhoAmW 91
Karlin, Nurit SmATA 63
Karlin, Robert Lowell 1929- St&PR 91
Karlin, Samuel 1924- WhoAm 90
Karlin, Steven F BiDrAPA 89
Karlin, Teri Lea 1963- WhoEmL 91
Karliner, William 1910- BiDrAPA 89
Karling, Sten Ingvar 1906-1987 BioIn 16
Karlins, M. William 1932- IntWWM 90
Karlins, Martin William 1932- WhoAm 90
Karlinsky, Elizabeth 1904- BiDWomA
Karlinsky, Harry BiDrAPA 89
Karlinsky, Simon 1924- WhoAm 90
Karlinsky-Scherfig, Elizabeth 1904- BiDWomA
Karlitz, Herb S. ODwPR 91
Karloff, Boris 1887-1969 BioIn 16, WorAlBi
Karlos, Anthony Christ 1912- WhoWor 91
Karlovec, Lucien B., Jr. 1936- St&PR 91
Karlovec, Robert V. 1922- St&PR 91
Karlovich, Stephen P. 1963- WhoE 91
Karlowska, Stanislawa de 1876-1952 BiDWomA
Karls, John Spencer 1942- WhoE 91
Karls, William Joel 1956- BiDrAPA 89
Karlsberg, Robert Charles 1940- BiDrAPA 89
Karlsdottir, Sigurlaug M. 1952- BiDrAPA 89
Karlson, David J. St&PR 91
Karlson, Dixie D. 1941- WhoAmW 91
Karlson, Karen Louise 1950- WhoAmW 91
Karlson, Karl Eugene 1920- WhoAm 90, WhoWor 91
Karlson, Lawrence Carl 1942- WhoAm 90, WhoE 91, WhoWor 91
Karlson, P. 1918- BioIn 16
Karlson, Peter 1918- BioIn 16
Karlsoon, Lars Olof 1953- IntWWM 90
Karlsson, Christer B. 1944- WhoWor 91
Karlsson, Fred Goran 1946- WhoWor 91
Karlsson, Hans Ragnar 1925- St&PR 91
Karlsson, Linda Marie 1949- WhoE 91
Karlsson, Ragnar K 1924- BiDrAPA 89
Karlstrand, James Edward 1946- WhoEmL 91
Karlstrom, Paul Johnson 1941- WhoAm 90, WhoAmA 91
Karma NewAgMG
Karmal, Babrak BioIn 16
Karmal, Babrak 1929- WhoWor 91
Karman, James A. 1937- St&PR 91
Karman, James Anthony 1937- WhoAm 90
Karmason, Marilyn G 1928- BiDrAPA 89
Karmazin, J. Donald 1941- St&PR 91
Karmazin, John, Jr. 1924- St&PR 91
Karmazin, Nelly 1930- WhoAmW 91
Karme, Alan B 1934- BiDrAPA 89
Karmeier, Delbert Fred 1935- WhoAm 90
Karmel, Leslie 1923- St&PR 91
Karmel, Roberta S. 1937- WhoAm 90
Karmelin, Michael Allen 1947- WhoE 91
Karmen, Arthur 1930- WhoAm 90
Karmin, Monroe William 1929- WhoAm 90, WhoE 91
Karmol, David Laurence 1953- WhoE 91, WhoEmL 91
Karn, Gloria Stoll 1923- WhoAmA 91
Karn, Richard Wendall 1927- WhoAm 90
Karn, Robert Burns, III 1942- WhoAm 90
Karn, William N., Jr. 1923- BiDrAPA 89
Karnafel, Eugene T 1933- BiDrAPA 89
Karnath, Joan Edna 1947- WhoAmW 91
Karnatz, William E. 1937- St&PR 91
Karnaugh, Maurice 1924- WhoAm 90
Karnavas, C.A. 1929- St&PR 91
Karnbach, William Francis Marmion 1938- St&PR 91
Karner, Theodor PenDiDA 89
Karnes, Bettejane 1926- WhoAmW 91
Karnes, David 1948- WhoAm 90
Karnes, Evan Burton, II WhoWor 91
Karnes, Karen 1925- WhoAmA 91
Karnes, Lucia Rooney 1921- WhoAmW 91
Karney, Dea Ilene 1965- WhoAmW 91
Karney, Joe D. 1933- St&PR 91
Karney, Joe Dan 1933- WhoAm 90
Karney, Mark Steven 1948- WhoEmL 91
Karni, Edi 1944- WhoAm 90, WhoE 91
Karni, Michaela Jordan 1941- WhoWrEP 89
Karni, Shlomo 1932- WhoAm 90
Karnicki, Alfred Michael, Jr. BiDrAPA 89
Karnig, Albert WhoAm 90
Karnig, Veronica Anne 1961- WhoEmL 91

Karniol, Hilda 1910- WhoAmA 91
Karniol, Hilda Hutterer 1910- WhoAmW 91
Karnitz, Jane Connie 1958- St&PR 91
Karno, Marvin 1933- BiDrAPA 89
Karnofsky, Brian Lee 1954- WhoSSW 91
Karnoouh-Vertalier, Martine 1947- WhoWor 91
Karnovsky, Manfred L. 1918- WhoAm 90
Karnovsky, Morris John 1926- WhoAm 90
Karnow, Stanley 1925- ConAu 31NR, MajTwCW, WhoAm 90, WhoE 91
Karnowsky, Deborah WhoAmW 91
Karns, B. Lee 1930- St&PR 91
Karns, Barry Wayne 1946- WhoSSW 91
Karns, William George 1920- St&PR 91
Karo, Douglas Paul 1947- WhoE 91
Karodia, Farida 1942- FemiCLE
Karol, Bernard John 1953- WhoE 91
Karol, Cecilia K BiDrAPA 89
Karol, Frederick J. BioIn 16
Karol, Frederick John 1933- WhoAm 90
Karol, K. S. BioIn 16
Karol, Meryl H. 1940- WhoAmW 91
Karol, Nathaniel H. 1929- WhoAm 90
Karol, Pamala Marie 1950- WhoAmW 91
Karol, Reuben Hirsh 1922- WhoAm 90, WhoE 91, WhoWor 91
Karolak, Dale Walter 1959- WhoEmL 91
Karolevitz, Robert Francis 1922- WhoWrEP 89
Karolin, Stella H BiDrAPA 89
Karoll, Craig Alan BiDrAPA 89
Karolyi, Bela BioIn 16
Karolyi, Bela 1942- WorAlBi
Karolyi, Mihaly 1875-1955 BioIn 16
Karolyi, Otto Jozsef 1934- IntWWM 90
Karos, Gus 1923- St&PR 91
Karoui, Hamed 1927- WhoWor 91
Karousou, Marianna EncCoWW
Karow, Alann F. 1939- St&PR 91
Karow, Charles Stanley 1954- WhoE 91
Karow, Thomas R. ODwPR 91
Karowe, Harris E 1921- BiDrAPA 89
Karp, Aaron S 1947- WhoAmA 91
Karp, Abraham J. 1921- BioIn 16
Karp, Abraham Joseph 1921- WhoAm 90
Karp, Daniel S. 1918- St&PR 91
Karp, Donald Mathew 1937- WhoAm 90
Karp, Harry R. BioIn 16, NewYTBS 90
Karp, Harvey Lawrence 1927- WhoAm 90
Karp, Herbert Rubin 1921- WhoAm 90
Karp, Jack Lee 1936- WhoAm 90
Karp, Jane F BiDrAPA 89
Karp, Judith Esther 1946- WhoAmW 91
Karp, Leon WhoAmA 91N
Karp, Leopold 1900- BiDrAPA 89
Karp, Mark Edward 1946- St&PR 91
Karp, Martin Everett 1922- WhoAm 90
Karp, Naomi 1926- AuBYP 90
Karp, Nathan 1915- WhoAm 90
Karp, Norman 1935- WhoE 91
Karp, Peter Simon 1935- WhoE 91
Karp, Richard Gordon 1933- WhoAmA 91, WhoE 91
Karp, Richard M. 1929- St&PR 91, WhoAm 90
Karp, Rick Alvin 1954- WhoE 91
Karp, Robert 1934- WhoAm 90
Karp, Robert Alan 1947- BiDrAPA 89
Karp, Robert L 1944- BiDrAPA 89
Karp, Ronald Alvin 1945- WhoEmL 91
Karp, Steven Jay 1955- BiDrAPA 89
Karp, Walter AuBYP 90, BioIn 16
Karp, Walter 1934?-1989 ConAu 129
Karpacs, Joanne Mary 1945- WhoWrEP 89
Karpan, Kathleen Marie 1942- WhoAm 90, WhoAmW 91
Karpas, Alan K. 1940- St&PR 91
Karpati, Ferenc 1926- WhoWor 91
Karpati, Janos 1932- IntWWM 90, WhoWor 91
Karpatkin, Margaret 1932- WhoAm 90
Karpatkin, Rhoda Hendrick 1930- WhoAm 90
Karpe, Keith H. 1950- ODwPR 91
Karpechenko, Georgii Dmitrievich 1899-1942 DcScB S2
Karpel, Eli 1916- WhoAmA 91
Karpeles, Michael Dean 1958- WhoEmL 91
Karpen, Marian Joan 1944- WhoAmW 91, WhoE 91, WhoWor 91
Karpen, Richard L. 1926- St&PR 91
Karpf, Gary Allan 1953- BiDrAPA 89
Karpf, H. Scott 1954- St&PR 91
Karpf, Juanita 1951- WhoAmW 91
Karpf, Richard James BiDrAPA 89
Karpf, Robin Rigell 1953- BiDrAPA 89
Karpf, Ronald Jay 1948- WhoE 91
Karpick, John 1884-1960 WhoAmA 91N
Karpiel, Doris Catherine 1935- WhoAmW 91
Karpienia, Joseph Francis 1949- WhoEmL 91
Karpinski, Jacek 1927- WhoWor 91
Karpinski, Patricia Anne 1948- WhoAmW 91
Karpinsky, Len Vyacheslavovich 1929- BioIn 16
Karpiscak, John, III 1957- WhoEmL 91
Karplus, Esteban J. 1937- St&PR 91
Karplus, Martin 1930- WhoAm 90
Karplus, Robert NewYTBS 90
Karplus, Robert 1927-1990 BioIn 16
Karplus, Walter J. 1927- WhoAm 90
Karpman, Harold Lew 1927- WhoAm 90
Karpman, Stephen Benjamin BiDrAPA 89
Karpoff-Mandell, Gina D. 1964- WhoAmW 91
Karpov, Anatoly 1951- WhoWor 91
Karpowicz, Ray Anthony 1925- WhoAm 90
Karpowicz, Terrence Edward 1948- WhoAmA 91
Karppinen, Pertti BioIn 16
Karr, Alan Francis 1947- WhoE 91
Karr, Benn 1893-1968 Ballpl 90
Karr, Cheryl Lofgreen 1954- WhoEmL 91
Karr, Daniel John 1946- WhoEmL 91
Karr, Daryl Kelly Paul James 1954- WhoEmL 91
Karr, David Maurice 1932- St&PR 91
Karr, Elizabeth McRae 1953- WhoAmW 91
Karr, Gary 1941- IntWWM 90, PenDiMP
Karr, Herbert W. 1925-1990 BioIn 16
Karr, Howard Henry 1943- St&PR 91
Karr, Inez ODwPR 91
Karr, James BioIn 16
Karr, James Richard 1943- WhoSSW 91
Karr, Jay Miles 1926- WhoWrEP 89
Karr, Joseph Peter 1925- WhoWor 91
Karr, Kari Bethany Ward 1951- WhoAmW 91
Karr, Lloyd 1912-1990 WhoAm 90
Karr, Norman 1927- WhoAm 90
Karr, Norman W 1916- BiDrAPA 89
Karr, Paul Michael James 1950- WhoEmL 91
Karr, Robert Irving 1924- St&PR 91
Karr, William Lee 1951- WhoWor 91
Karr-Bertoli, Julius 1920- IntWWM 90
Karr i Alfonsetti, Carme 1865-1943 EncCoWW
Karr-Kidwell, P. J. 1952- WhoEmL 91
Karras, Alex 1935- WhoAm 90, WorAlBi
Karrell, Roy BioIn 16
Karrels, Edward W. WhoAm 90
Karrer, Otto 1888-1976 BioIn 16
Karrh, Bruce Wakefield 1936- WhoAm 90
Karron, Betty BiDrAPA 89
Karrys, William G. 1923- St&PR 91
Kars, Jean-Rodolphe 1947- PenDiMP
Karsan, Nooruddin 1957- WhoE 91
Karsch, Anna Louisa 1722-1791 DcLB 97 [port]
Karsch, Anna Luise 1722-1791 EncCoWW
Karsch, Christian 1940- WhoWor 91
Karsch, Daniel Selwyn 1923- WhoAm 90
Karschin, Anna Luise 1722-1791 EncCoWW
Karsen, Sonja Petra 1919- WhoAm 90, WhoAmW 91, WhoE 91, WhoWor 91
Karsenti, Rene M. 1950- WhoE 91
Karsh, Richard Bruce 1944- WhoSSW 91
Karsh, Robert Charles 1942- BiDrAPA 89
Karsh, Yousuf 1908- BioIn 16, WhoAm 90, WhoAmA 91, WhoWor 91
Karshner, Roger Kay 1928- WhoWrEP 89
Karsk, Bruce 1952- St&PR 91
Karski, Jan 1914- BioIn 16
Karson, Allen Ronald 1947- WhoEmL 91, WhoWor 91
Karson, Burton Lewis 1934- WhoAm 90
Karson, Craig Neal 1949- BiDrAPA 89
Karson, Stanley WhoHisp 91
Karst, Judy Ward-Steinman 1941- WhoAmW 91
Karst, Kenneth L 1929- ConAu 132
Karst, Kenneth Leslie 1929- WhoAm 90
Karsten, John Alan 1932- St&PR 91
Karsten, Philip 1920- WhoE 91
Karsten, Robert Edgar 1930- WhoAm 90, WhoE 91
Karsten, Thomas Loren 1915- WhoAm 90
Karstien, Diana C. 1946- WhoAmW 91
Karszes, Arthur J. 1936- St&PR 91
Kart, Barry Harold 1943- WhoE 91
Kart, Richard M. 1953- St&PR 91
Kartalia, Mitchell P. 1913- St&PR 91
Kartan, Usha Kumari BiDrAPA 89
Kartanowicz, John Joseph 1939- St&PR 91
Karten, Terry 1947- WhoAm 90
Karter, Elias M. 1940- WhoAm 90
Karthauser, Brad C. 1957- St&PR 91
Karthauser, Patricia Farley 1952- WhoAmW 91
Kartheiser, Josiane 1950- EncCoWW
Kartiganer, Joseph 1935- WhoAm 90
Kartje, Jean Van Landuyt 1953- WhoEmL 91
Kartoz, Deborah Ellen 1954- WhoEmL 91
Kartsev, Vladimir Petrovich 1938- WhoWor 91
Kartun, Derek 1919- SpyFic
Kartus, Irving 1913- BiDrAPA 89
Kartzinel, Ronald 1945- WhoE 91
Kartzke, Klaus Wilhelm 1922- WhoWor 91
Karu, Gilda M. 1951- WhoAmW 91, WhoEmL 91
Karukstis, Kerry Kathleen 1955- WhoAmW 91
Karumanchi, Veeraiah Choudary 1946- BiDrAPA 89
Karunatilake, Halwalage Neville Sepala 1930- WhoWor 91
Karush, Aaron 1912- BiDrAPA 89
Karush, Larry 1946- IntWWM 90
Karush, Nathaniel P 1941- BiDrAPA 89
Karush, Ruth K 1941- BiDrAPA 89
Karvas, Jozef 1950- WhoWor 91
Karvonen, Jaakko Mikko 1945- WhoWor 91
Karwelis, Donald Charles 1934- WhoAmA 91
Karwoski, Glenn ODwPR 91
Karwoski, Glenn John 1955- WhoEmL 91
Karwoski, Richard Charles 1938- WhoAmA 91, WhoE 91
Kary, Jodi Heflin St&PR 91
Kary, Susan E. 1950- WhoEmL 91
Karydas, Pamela Roseman 1961- ODwPR 91
Karzel, Karlfried Heinz Erich 1929- WhoWor 91
Kasa, Pamela D. 1943- WhoAmW 91
Kasa, Pamela Dorothy 1943- St&PR 91
Kasack, Wolfgang 1927- WhoWor 91
Kasahara, Hiroshi 1937- WhoWor 91
Kasahara, Susumu 1940- WhoWor 91
Kasahara, Tosio 1947- EncPaPR 91
Kasahara, Yasushi 1941- WhoWor 91
Kasai, Kazuhiko BioIn 16
Kasak, Donna Beth 1967- WhoSSW 91
Kasak, Nikolai WhoAmA 91
Kasakove, Susan 1938- WhoAmW 91, WhoE 91
Kasanin, Mark Owen 1929- WhoAm 90
Kasarda, John Dale 1945- WhoAm 90
Kasarjian, Levon, Jr. 1937- St&PR 91
Kasatkina, Natalya Dmitriyevna 1934- WhoWor 91
Kasavana, Toby Stuart 1946- WhoEmL 91
Kasbeer, Stephen Frederick 1925- WhoAm 90
Kasbergen, Hendrik P. 1944- WhoWor 91
Kasch, James Alan 1946- St&PR 91
Kasch, Jeffrey Clark 1942- St&PR 91
Kaschak, Lillian Anne WhoWor 91
Kaschnitz, Marie Luise 1901-1974 EncCoWW
Kaschub, William John 1942- St&PR 91
Kasckow, John William 1958- BiDrAPA 89
Kasdagle, Lina 1921- EncCoWW
Kasdagli, Lina EncCoWW
Kasdan, Lawrence BioIn 16
Kasdan, Lawrence Edward 1949- WhoAm 90
Kasden, Allen J. 1949- St&PR 91
Kasdin, Mark Benjamin 1944- St&PR 91
Kase, Kingdon 1957- WhoEmL 91
Kase, Max 1898-1974 Ballpl 90
Kase, Nathan Ginden 1930- WhoAm 90
Kase, Paul St&PR 91
Kase, Robert Warren 1951- WhoEmL 91
Kase, Shigeo 1922- WhoWor 91
Kase, William A BiDrAPA 89
Kase-Polisini, Judith Baker 1932- WhoAmW 91
Kasebier, Gertrude 1852-1934 BioIn 16
Kaseff, Fred 1957- St&PR 91
Kasel, Francis X., Jr. 1931- St&PR 91
Kasem, Casey NewYTBS 90 [port]
Kasem, Casey 1932- BioIn 16
Kaseman, James 1964- WhoEmL 91
Kasen, Donald Michael 1946- St&PR 91
Kasen, Martin 1934- St&PR 91
Kasen, Stewart Michael 1939- WhoAm 90
Kasenetz, Harriet ODwPR 91
Kasenter, Robert Albert 1946- St&PR 91
Kaser, David 1924- WhoAm 90
Kaser, Peter G. 1945- St&PR 91
Kaser, Richard Todd 1952- WhoEmL 91
Kaser, Wayne M. 1938- St&PR 91
Kasevich, Lawrence Stanley 1952- WhoE 91, WhoEmL 91
Kasey, Arthur R, Jr. BiDrAPA 89
Kash, Don Eldon 1934- WhoAm 90
Kash, Francys Kaygey 1921- WhoAmW 91
Kash, Graham Stephens 1937- WhoSSW 91
Kash, Kathleen 1953- WhoEmL 91
Kash, Wyatt Keith 1955- WhoEmL 91, WhoWrEP 89
Kasha, Lawrence NewYTBS 90
Kasha, Lawrence N. 1934- WhoAm 90
Kasha, Lawrence N 1934?-1990 ConAu 132
Kashani, Javad H 1937- BiDrAPA 89
Kashdin, Gladys Shafran 1921- WhoAmA 91, WhoAmW 91
Kashdin, Laurence M. 1947- St&PR 91
Kasher, Menahem 1895-1983 BioIn 16
Kashfi, Mansour Seid 1939- WhoWor 91
Kashfi-Lari, Ali Asghar BiDrAPA 89
Kashgarian, Michael 1933- WhoAm 90
Kashima, Tomoyoshi 1937- WhoWor 91
Kashin, Jeffrey D BiDrAPA 89
Kashiwa, Akifumi 1944- WhoWor 91
Kashiwagi, Yusuke 1917- St&PR 91, WhoWor 91
Kashiwahara, Ken WhoAm 90
Kashka, Maisie Schmidt 1938- WhoAmW 91
Kashkashian, Kim 1952- IntWWM 90
Kashkin, Kenneth Blair 1950- BiDrAPA 89
Kashmeri, Sarwar Aghajani 1942- WhoWor 91
Kashner, Albert Edward 1955- WhoE 91
Kashou, Jean Lee 1945- WhoAmW 91
Kashtan, Judith F 1951- BiDrAPA 89
Kashyap, Kripa Shanker 1942- BiDrAPA 89
Kashyap, Rangasami Lakshmi Narayan 1938- WhoAm 90
Kasi, Leela Peshkar 1939- WhoAmW 91
Kasia EncCoWW
Kasich, John R. 1952- WhoAm 90
Kasim, Husayn Sudki 1924- WhoWor 91
Kasimer, Eli 1926- St&PR 91
Kasin, Edwin 1914- BiDrAPA 89
Kasindorf, Blanche Robins 1925- WhoAmW 91, WhoE 91, WhoWor 91
Kasinec, Edward 1945- WhoAm 90
Kasinoff, Bernard H 1920- BiDrAPA 89
Kasinoff, Bernard Herman 1920- WhoAm 90
Kaskan, Lisa Joy 1953- BiDrAPA 89
Kaske, Carol Margaret Vonckx 1933- WhoAmW 91
Kaske, Robert Earl 1921-1989 BioIn 16, ConAu 129
Kaskel, Edward 1910- St&PR 91
Kaskel, Murry 1915- St&PR 91
Kaskell, Joseph 1892-1989 BioIn 16
Kaskell, Peter Howard 1924- WhoAm 90
Kaskey, Dale Edward 1944- St&PR 91
Kaskey, Gary Brent 1951- BiDrAPA 89
Kaskey, Raymond J. BioIn 16
Kaskey, Raymond John 1943- WhoAmA 91, WhoE 91
Kaskey, Richard A. 1921- St&PR 91
Kaskie, Stephen John 1950- WhoSSW 91
Kaskinen Riesberg, Barbara Kay 1952- WhoAmW 91
Kaskiw, Pamela Irene 1948- WhoAmW 91
Kasko, Eddie 1932- Ballpl 90
Kasko, William Paul 1942- St&PR 91
Kaskowitz, Edwin 1936- WhoAm 90
Kasky, Rita 1940- WhoE 91
Kasle, Anita L. 1929- WhoAmW 91
Kasle, Gertrude 1917- WhoAmA 91
Kasle, Irwin G BiDrAPA 89
Kasle, Myron J. WhoAm 90
Kasle, Richard L. 1927- St&PR 91
Kasle, Thomas Ross 1953- St&PR 91
Kasler, Richard Eugene 1925- St&PR 91
Kasler, Richard Eugene Jeff 1925- WhoAm 90
Kasley, Helen Mary 1951- St&PR 91
Kaslick, Ralph Sidney 1935- WhoAm 90
Kaslik, Vaclav 1917- IntWWM 90
Kaslik, Zdenek 1948- WhoWor 91
Kasloff, Philip 1918- St&PR 91
Kaslow, Arthur Louis 1913- WhoAm 90
Kaslow, Audrey A. Rojas BioIn 16
Kaslow, John Francis 1932- St&PR 91, WhoAm 90
Kaslusky, Anne 1948- WhoE 91
Kasm, Abdel Rauf al- WhoWor 91
Kasman, Barbara F. 1946- ODwPR 91
Kasmeier, Julia Crystine 1899-1979 BioIn 16
Kasmir, Gail Alice 1958- WhoAmW 91, WhoEmL 91
Kasmire, Robert D. 1926- ODwPR 91
Kasnowski, Chester N 1944- WhoAmA 91
Kasoff, Lawrence Elliot 1949- WhoEmL 91
Kaspar, Dan A. 1955- St&PR 91
Kaspar, David C. 1953- St&PR 91
Kaspar, Don G. 1928- St&PR 91
Kaspar, Douglas D. 1958- St&PR 91
Kaspar, James E. 1935- St&PR 91
Kaspar, Jean 1941- BiDFrPL
Kaspar, Robert Stephen 1958- St&PR 91
Kaspar, Valfrids R. 1939- St&PR 91
Kasparek, Christopher BiDrAPA 89
Kasparian, Kaspar 1940- St&PR 91
Kasparov, Garri Kimovich 1963- WhoWor 91
Kasparov, Gary BioIn 16
Kasparov, Gary 1963- NewYTBS 90 [port]
Kasper, Bruce M. 1948- WhoEmL 91
Kasper, Casimir W. 1919- St&PR 91
Kasper, Connie Jo Irvin 1955- St&PR 91
Kasper, Frank W. 1921- St&PR 91
Kasper, George Martin 1951- WhoSSW 91
Kasper, Herbert 1926- WhoAm 90
Kasper, Horst Manfred 1939- WhoE 91, WhoWor 91
Kasper, James Michael 1945- WhoEmL 91

Kasper, John Andrew, Jr. 1961- *BiDrAPA 89*
Kasper, M. 1947- *WhoWrEP 89*
Kasper, Michael Anthony 1946- *WhoEmL 91*
Kasper, Ronald Wayne 1944- *WhoSSW 91*
Kasper, Russell Richard 1932- *WhoAm 90*
Kasper, Stanley Frank 1920- *WhoWrEP 89*
Kasper, Susan Kathryn 1944- *WhoAmW 91*
Kasper, Timothy C. 1956- *St&PR 91*
Kasper, Walter 1933- *ConAu 130*
Kasper, Wolfgang Ernst 1939- *WhoWor 91*
Kasperczyk, Jurgen 1941- *WhoWor 91*
Kasperko, Jean Margaret 1949- *WhoEmL 91*
Kasperson, Richard Willet 1927- *St&PR 91, WhoAm 90*
Kasprick, Lyle Clinton 1932- *St&PR 91, WhoAm 90, WhoWor 91*
Kasprzak, Joyce Ann 1946- *WhoAmW 91*
Kasprzak, Lucian Alexander 1943- *WhoAm 90*
Kasprzik, Waldemar 1941- *WhoWor 91*
Kasprzyk, Jacek *IntWWM 90*
Kasputys, Joseph E. 1936- *St&PR 91*
Kasputys, Joseph Edward 1936- *WhoAm 90, WhoSSW 91*
Kasraie, Bijan 1947- *WhoSSW 91*
Kasrashvili, Makvala 1942- *IntWWM 90*
Kasriel, Bernard L. 1946- *WhoAm 90, WhoSSW 91*
Kass, Benny Lee 1936- *WhoAm 90*
Kass, Bernard *St&PR 91*
Kass, David *BioIn 16*
Kass, David Joseph *BiDrAPA 89*
Kass, Deborah 1952- *WhoAmA 91*
Kass, Dennis Miles 1950- *WhoAm 90*
Kass, Douglas *BioIn 16*
Kass, Edward H. *NewYTBS 90*
Kass, Edward H 1917- *ConAu 129*
Kass, Edward H. 1917-1990 *BioIn 16*
Kass, Edward J. 1928- *St&PR 91*
Kass, Ethan Ben 1958- *BiDrAPA 89*
Kass, Frederic I 1944- *BiDrAPA 89*
Kass, Fredrik J. 1929- *St&PR 91*
Kass, Jacob James 1910- *WhoAmA 91*
Kass, Jeffrey F. 1943- *St&PR 91*
Kass, Julius 1905-1989 *BioIn 16*
Kass, Leon Richard 1939- *WhoAm 90*
Kass, Marshall I. 1929- *St&PR 91*
Kass, Martin David 1952- *BiDrAPA 89*
Kass, Matthew Anthony 1937- *St&PR 91*
Kass, Myron 1921- *BiDrAPA 89*
Kass, Ray 1944- *WhoAmA 91*
Kass, Steven R. *St&PR 91*
Kass, Wayne E. *St&PR 91*
Kass, William *BiDrAPA 89*
Kassab, Charles Shaw 1928- *WhoWor 91*
Kassabian, David, Jr. *ODwPR 91*
Kassak, Lajos 1887-1967 *BioIn 16*
Kassal, Randy Elliot 1952- *WhoSSW 91*
Kassam, Amirali Hassanali 1943- *WhoWor 91*
Kassander, Arno Richard, Jr. 1920- *WhoAm 90*
Kassapoglou, Christos 1959- *WhoE 91*
Kassebaum, Donald Gene 1931- *WhoAm 90*
Kassebaum, John Philip *BioIn 16*
Kassebaum, John Philip 1932- *WhoWor 91*
Kassebaum, Kenneth G *BiDrAPA 89*
Kassebaum, Nancy 1932- *News 91-1 [port]*
Kassebaum, Nancy Landon *BioIn 16*
Kassebaum, Nancy Landon 1932- *WhoAm 90, WhoAmW 91, WhoWor 91*
Kassekent, Craig Robert 1950- *WhoEmL 91*
Kassel, Barbara 1952- *WhoAmA 91, WhoE 91*
Kassel, Kenneth 1955- *St&PR 91*
Kassel, Miriam 1930- *St&PR 91*
Kassel, Richard 1953- *IntWWM 90*
Kassel, Theodore 1925- *St&PR 91*
Kassel, Tichi Wilkerson 1932- *St&PR 91*
Kassel, Virginia Weltmer *WhoAm 90*
Kassell, Martin B 1918- *BiDrAPA 89*
Kassell, Neal Frederic 1946- *WhoAm 90*
Kassem, Lou *BioIn 16*
Kassem, Lou 1931- *SmATA 62 [port]*
Kassenaar, John D.C. 1929- *St&PR 91*
Kasses, Kenneth George 1945- *WhoAm 90*
Kassewitz, Ruth Eileen Blower 1928- *WhoAmW 91*
Kassi *WomWR*
Kassia 805?-865? *EncCoWW*
Kassiane *EncCoWW*
Kassin, Michael Barry 1947- *WhoE 91*
Kassinger, Theodore William 1953- *WhoE 91*
Kassirer, Norma *AuBYP 90*
Kassler, Haskell A. 1936- *WhoWor 91*
Kassler, Jamie Croy *IntWWM 90*
Kassman, Andrew Lance 1950- *WhoEmL 91*
Kassman, Edward Irving *BiDrAPA 89*
Kassman, Herbert Seymour 1924- *WhoAm 90*
Kassman, Shirley 1929- *WhoAmA 91*
Kassner, Michael Ernest 1950- *WhoEmL 91*
Kassner, Pam *ODwPR 91*
Kassoff, David Barry 1947- *BiDrAPA 89*
Kassoff, Edwin 1924- *WhoAm 90*
Kasson, James Matthews 1943- *WhoAm 90*
Kasson, John Adam 1822-1910 *BioIn 16*
Kassor, Gerd S.J. 1935- *St&PR 91*
Kassos, T. George 1935- *St&PR 91*
Kassoy, Bernard 1914- *WhoAmA 91*
Kassoy, Hortense 1917- *WhoAmA 91*
Kassur, Michael Maciej *BiDrAPA 89*
Kast, Fremont Ellsworth 1926- *WhoAm 90*
Kast, George F. 1946- *St&PR 91*
Kast, Karin Annette *BiDrAPA 89*
Kastantin, Joseph Thomas 1947- *WhoEmL 91*
Kastel, August Paul 1936- *St&PR 91*
Kastel, Warren *MajTwCW*
Kastelen, Lillian 1937- *St&PR 91*
Kastelic, Robert Frank 1934- *St&PR 91, WhoAm 90*
Kasten, Diane Lynn 1947- *WhoAmW 91*
Kasten, Jack 1927- *St&PR 91*
Kasten, Karl Albert 1916- *WhoAm 90, WhoAmA 91*
Kasten, Katherine Elaine Clark 1958- *WhoSSW 91*
Kasten, Paul Rudolph 1923- *WhoAm 90*
Kasten, Richard John 1938- *WhoAm 90*
Kasten, Robert W. *BioIn 16*
Kasten, Robert W., Jr. 1942- *WhoAm 90, WhoWor 91*
Kasten, Stanley Harvey 1952- *WhoAm 90, WhoSSW 91*
Kasten, Stephen A 1938- *BiDrAPA 89*
Kasten, Walter, II 1936- *St&PR 91*
Kastenmeier, Robert William 1924- *WhoAm 90*
Kastens, Kipp Verling *BiDrAPA 89*
Kastiel, Ray William 1926- *St&PR 91*
Kastigar, Susan Marie 1959- *WhoEmL 91*
Kastin, Abba Jeremiah 1934- *WhoAm 90, WhoSSW 91*
Kastl, Curtis Alan 1952- *WhoEmL 91*
Kastl, Dian Evans 1953- *WhoAmW 91, WhoEmL 91*
Kastle, Leonard Gregory 1929- *IntWWM 90*
Kastler, B.Z. 1920- *St&PR 91*
Kastler, Bonnie Lou 1956- *WhoAmW 91*
Kastler, Nancy Jane Meade 1959- *WhoAmW 91*
Kastner, Christine Kriha 1951- *WhoWrEP 89*
Kastner, Erich 1899- *AuBYP 90*
Kastner, Erich 1899-1974 *BioIn 16*
Kastner, Richard H 1923- *BiDrAPA 89*
Kastner, Robert George 1939- *St&PR 91*
Kastner, Shay Davidson 1944- *WhoAmW 91*
Kastner, Thomas Mortimer 1926- *WhoSSW 91*
Kastner, William Joseph 1928- *WhoE 91*
Kastor, Frank Sullivan 1933- *WhoAm 90*
Kastor, Hugo *WhoAmA 91N*
Kastor, John Alfred 1931- *WhoAm 90*
Kastu, Matti 1945- *IntWWM 90*
Kasturi, Gopalan 1924- *WhoWor 91*
Kasturirangan, Usha *BiDrAPA 89*
Kastury, Uma R. 1948- *St&PR 91*
Kasuba, Aleksandra 1923- *WhoAmA 91*
Kasuboski, David Allen 1942- *BiDrAPA 89*
Kasuga, Ikko 1910-1989 *BioIn 16*
Kasuya, Masahiro 1937- *BioIn 16*
Kaswell, Ernest Ralph 1917- *WhoAm 90*
Kaswell, Stuart Joel 1954- *WhoEmL 91*
Kasyjanski, Richard J. 1950- *WhoE 91*
Kasza, Elizabeth A. 1958- *WhoAmW 91*
Kasza, Katalin 1940- *IntWWM 90*
Kasza, Keiko *AuBYP 90*
Kaszniak, Alfred Wayne 1949- *WhoAm 90*
Kasztner, Rezso 1906-1957 *BioIn 16*
Kaszubski, Elizabeth D. 1950- *WhoEmL 91*
Kat, Willem 1902- *EncO&P 3*
Kata, Edward John 1941- *St&PR 91*
Katai, Andrew A. 1937- *St&PR 91*
Katai, Andrew Andras 1937- *WhoAm 90*
Kataja, Eero Ilmari 1927- *WhoWor 91*
Katakia, Manjula Nagin *BiDrAPA 89*
Katalinas, Ed *Ballpl 90*
Katano, Marc 1952- *WhoAmA 91*
Kataoka, Katsutaro 1915- *WhoWor 91*
Kataphusin *ConAu 129*
Kataria, Purshotam B *BiDrAPA 89*
Katarincic, Joseph Anthony 1931- *WhoAm 90*
Katase, Takafumi 1930- *WhoWor 91*
Katayama, Alyce Coyne 1950- *WhoEmL 91*
Katayama, Arthur Shoji 1927- *WhoAm 90*
Katayama, Atsushi 1931- *WhoWor 91*
Katayama, Nihachiro *WhoWor 91*
Katayama, Robert Nobuichi 1924- *WhoAm 90*
Katayama, Takashi 1930- *WhoWor 91*
Katayama, Toshihiro 1928- *ConDes 90, WhoAm 90*
Katayama, Tsuneo 1939- *WhoWor 91*
Katayama, Yutaka *BioIn 16*
Katayev, Valentin 1897-1986 *ConAu 131*
Katchen, Julius 1926-1969 *PenDiMP*
Katcher, Alan Barry 1943- *WhoE 91, WhoWor 91*
Katcher, Andrew Charles 1956- *WhoEmL 91*
Katcher, Avrum Labe 1925- *WhoE 91*
Katcher, Jerome Fred 1933- *St&PR 91*
Katcher, Lewis H. 1942- *St&PR 91*
Katcher, Monroe I. 1908-1989 *BioIn 16*
Katcher, Philip M. 1944- *WhoE 91*
Katcher, Richard 1918- *WhoAm 90*
Katchur, Edward George 1951- *WhoE 91*
Katchur, Marlene Martha 1946- *WhoAmW 91*
Kateb, George Anthony 1931- *WhoAm 90*
Kateley, Richard 1944- *St&PR 91*
Katell, Sidney 1915- *WhoAm 90*
Kater, Kathryn *WhoAmW 91*
Kater, Louis 1938- *WhoWor 91*
Kater, Mitchell Jay 1956- *WhoE 91*
Kater, Peter *NewAgMG*
Katerli, Nina 194-?- *EncCoWW*
Kates, Gerald Saul 1932- *WhoE 91*
Kates, Harold H *BiDrAPA 89*
Kates, Henry *BioIn 16*
Kates, Henry E. 1939- *St&PR 91, WhoAm 90, WhoE 91, WhoWor 91*
Kates, Josef 1921- *St&PR 91, WhoAm 90*
Kates, Morris 1923- *WhoAm 90*
Kates, Nick Simon 1952- *BiDrAPA 89*
Kates, Phillip Brown 1919- *St&PR 91*
Kates, Robert William 1929- *WhoAm 90*
Kates, Stephen 1943- *IntWWM 90*
Kates, William Wolfe 1939- *BiDrAPA 89*
Katf, Nicola Y 1932- *BiDrAPA 89*
Kath, Camelia *BioIn 16*
Kathan, Elizabeth *ODwPR 91*
Katheder, Thomas 1959- *WhoEmL 91*
Katherine, of Sutton *BioIn 16*
Katherine, Robert Andrew 1941- *WhoAm 90*
Kathka, David Arlin *WhoAm 90*
Kathol, Anthony Louis 1964- *WhoEmL 91*
Kathol, Robert F. 1941- *St&PR 91*
Kathol, Roger Gerald 1948- *BiDrAPA 89*
Kathpalia, Salil 1955- *BiDrAPA 89*
Kathrein, Michael Lee 1953- *WhoEmL 91*
Kathuria, Nirmal B *BiDrAPA 89*
Kathuria, Nirmal Bhatia 1948- *WhoEmL 91*
Kathwari, M. Farooq 1944- *St&PR 91, WhoE 91*
Katims, Milton 1909- *IntWWM 90, PenDiMP*
Katin, Peter 1930- *PenDiMP*
Katin, Peter Roy 1930- *IntWWM 90, WhoWor 91*
Katis, James G 1933- *BiDrAPA 89*
Katis, Lauma Upelnieks *BiDrAPA 89*
Katkar, Kirti Keshav 1945- *WhoEmL 91*
Katke, Mary Lou 1959- *WhoAmW 91*
Katkin, Daniel 1945- *WhoAm 90*
Katkin, Edward Samuel 1937- *WhoAm 90*
Katlein, Glen Jeffrey 1956- *WhoEmL 91*
Katleman, Harris L. *WhoAm 90*
Katlian *WhNaAH*
Katlic, John E. *BioIn 16*
Katlic, John E. 1928- *St&PR 91*
Katlic, John Edward 1928- *WhoAm 90*
Katlin, Burt 1930- *WhoWor 91*
Kato Takaaki 1860-1926 *EncJap*
Kato, Hajime 1900-1968 *PenDiDA 89*
Kato, Hidetoshi 1930- *WhoWor 91*
Kato, Kay *WhoAmA 91*
Kato, Koichi *BioIn 16*
Kato, Koichi 1939- *WhoWor 91*
Kato, Masaaki 1913- *BiDrAPA 89*
Kato, Masanobu 1946- *WhoWor 91*
Kato, Minobu 1953- *St&PR 91*
Kato, Nobuo 1930- *WhoWor 91*
Kato, Peter Eiichi 1934- *WhoWor 91*
Kato, Shunsaku 1923- *WhoWor 91*
Kato, Tokuro 1898- *PenDiDA 89*
Kato, Walter Yoneo 1924- *WhoAm 90*
Kato, Yuriko 1927- *WhoWor 91*
Katoll, John 1872-1955 *Ballpl 90*
Katon, John Edward 1929- *WhoAm 90*
Katon, Wayne Jay *BiDrAPA 89*
Katona, Joseph William 1929- *St&PR 91*
Katona, Peter Geza 1937- *WhoAm 90*
Katope, Christopher George 1918- *WhoAm 90*
Katopes, Peter James 1947- *WhoWrEP 89*
Katopodes, Nikolaos Demetrios 1949- *WhoEmL 91*
Kator, Steven W. 1948- *St&PR 91*
Katovic, Zvonimir 1933- *WhoWor 91*
Katovich, John C. 1953- *St&PR 91*
Katrina and the Waves *EncPR&S 89*
Katritzky, Alan Roy 1928- *WhoAm 90*
Kats, Gregory Hollins 1959- *WhoWor 91*
Katsahnias, Thomas George 1928- *St&PR 91, WhoAm 90*
Katsakiores, Phyllis 1934- *WhoAmW 91*
Katsampes, Theodore Peter 1949- *St&PR 91*
Katsaros, Constantine 1926- *WhoE 91*
Katsh, Abraham Isaac 1908- *WhoAm 90*
Katsiaficas, Mary Diane 1947- *WhoEmL 91*
Katsianis, Estelle Jo-Ann 1969- *WhoEmL 91*
Katsianis, John Nick 1960- *WhoWor 91*
Katsiff, Bruce 1945- *WhoAmA 91, WhoE 91*
Katsimbris, George Michael 1942- *WhoE 91*
Katskee, Melvin Robert 1945- *WhoEmL 91*
Katson, Roberta Marina 1947- *WhoAmW 91*
Katsonov, Florence Jean *WhoWrEP 89*
Katsoulis, Larry N. 1945- *St&PR 91*
Katsu Kaishu 1823-1899 *EncJap*
Katsuki, Hirohiko 1921- *WhoWor 91*
Katsuki, Yoshito 1915- *WhoWor 91*
Katsura, Fumiko 1944- *WhoWor 91*
Katsushika, Hokusai 1760-1849 *BioIn 16*
Katt, Bonita Kay 1941- *WhoAmW 91*
Katt, Elmer A. 1917- *St&PR 91*
Katt, Ray 1927- *Ballpl 90*
Katt, William 1951- *WorAlBi*
Katta, Sreenivasulu *BiDrAPA 89*
Kattan, Naim 1928- *WhoWor 91*
Kattawar, George Williford 1937- *WhoAm 90*
Kattrup, Per Elmann 1939- *WhoWor 91*
Kattwinkel, John 1941- *WhoAm 90*
Katus, Eli Margrethe *BiDrAPA 89*
Katz, Abraham *BioIn 16*
Katz, Abraham 1926- *WhoAm 90, WhoWor 91*
Katz, Abraham Jacobo *BiDrAPA 89*
Katz, Adrian Izhack 1932- *WhoAm 90*
Katz, Alan Ira 1951- *WhoEmL 91*
Katz, Alan S *BiDrAPA 89*
Katz, Alex 1927- *ModArCr 1 [port], News 90, -90-3, WhoAm 90, WhoAmA 91*
Katz, Alix Martha 1948- *WhoE 91*
Katz, Allan Jack 1947- *WhoSSW 91*
Katz, Allan Robert 1942- *WhoSSW 91*
Katz, Amnon 1935- *WhoWrEP 89*
Katz, Anthony R. *ODwPR 91*
Katz, Arni 1954- *WhoSSW 91*
Katz, Arnold 1930- *WhoE 91*
Katz, Arnold M. 1954- *St&PR 91*
Katz, Arthur Shaye 1955- *WhoEmL 91*
Katz, Austin Morton 1934- *BiDrAPA 89*
Katz, Avrum Sidney 1939- *WhoWor 91*
Katz, Barbara 1952- *WhoE 91*
Katz, Bernard 1911- *WhoAm 90, WhoWor 91, WorAlBi*
Katz, Bernard 1936- *WhoE 91*
Katz, Bernard A 1936- *BiDrAPA 89*
Katz, Bertha 1908- *BioIn 16*
Katz, Brenda Rochelle 1946- *WhoE 91*
Katz, Carlos 1934- *WhoAm 90*
Katz, Charles J *BiDrAPA 89*
Katz, Colleen 1936- *WhoAm 90*
Katz, Colleen Burke 1936- *WhoWrEP 89*
Katz, Dan 1955- *WhoEmL 91*
Katz, Daniel Barry 1948- *WhoSSW 91*
Katz, Daniel S. 1960- *IntWWM 90*
Katz, David 1955- *IntWWM 90*
Katz, David Allan 1933- *St&PR 91*
Katz, David Allen 1945- *WhoE 91*
Katz, David Carey 1940- *St&PR 91*
Katz, David Lawrence 1956- *BiDrAPA 89*
Katz, David Robert 1947- *WhoEmL 91*
Katz, Debra Miriam 1958- *BiDrAPA 89*
Katz, Donald 1948- *WhoEmL 91*
Katz, Donald L. 1907-1989 *BioIn 16*
Katz, Donald Paul 1947- *St&PR 91*
Katz, Earl L. 1918- *St&PR 91*
Katz, Edward K 1948- *BiDrAPA 89*
Katz, Edward M. 1921- *St&PR 91*
Katz, Edward Morris 1921- *WhoAm 90*
Katz, Edward Petroff 1933- *St&PR 91*
Katz, Elaine Marcia 1942- *WhoAmW 91*
Katz, Eli 1954- *BiDrAPA 89*
Katz, Eliot 1957- *WhoWrEP 89*
Katz, Elizabeth A. 1959- *St&PR 91*
Katz, Ellen *BiDrAPA 89*
Katz, Elsa S 1927- *BiDrAPA 89*
Katz, Emanuel *BioIn 16*
Katz, Eric Stephen 1946- *WhoSSW 91*
Katz, Erwin I. *St&PR 91*
Katz, Eugene *BioIn 16*
Katz, Eunice *WhoAmA 91*
Katz, Evan 1931- *BiDrAPA 89*
Katz, Eve G. 1938- *WhoE 91*
Katz, Fred N. 1941- *WhoSSW 91*
Katz, Frederick 1898-1989 *BioIn 16*
Katz, Gary Michael 1959- *ODwPR 91*
Katz, George 1931-1989 *BioIn 16*
Katz, George L. 1933- *IntWWM 90*
Katz, George R. *BioIn 16*
Katz, Gerald 1938- *St&PR 91*
Katz, Gerald 1939- *WhoAm 90*

Katz, Gloria WhoAm 90
Katz, Glory Weisberger 1928- WhoAmW 91
Katz, Gregory 1950- St&PR 91
Katz, Hannah L 1904- BiDrAPA 89
Katz, Harold 1937- WhoAm 90, WhoE 91
Katz, Harold 1944- WhoAm 90
Katz, Harold Ambrose 1921- WhoAm 90
Katz, Harold W. BioIn 16
Katz, Harry 1907- BiDrAPA 89
Katz, Harvey A. 1927- St&PR 91
Katz, Harvey L. 1925- ODwPR 91
Katz, Henry 1937- WhoAm 90
Katz, Herbert 1930- AuBYP 90
Katz, Herman BioIn 16, NewYTBS 90 [port]
Katz, Hilda 1909- WhoAm 90, WhoAmA 91, WhoAmW 91, WhoE 91
Katz, Hilliard Joel 1918- WhoAm 90
Katz, Howard M 1948- BiDrAPA 89
Katz, Ira Ralph BiDrAPA 89
Katz, Irwin Howard 1927- St&PR 91
Katz, Jack 1934- WhoAm 90
Katz, Jack L 1936- BiDrAPA 89
Katz, Jacqueline Hunt AuBYP 90
Katz, James Martin 1942- St&PR 91
Katz, Jane 1943- WhoAmW 91
Katz, Jason Herbert 1930- St&PR 91
Katz, Jason L. 1947- St&PR 91
Katz, Jason Lawrence 1947- WhoAm 90
Katz, Jay BiDrAPA 89
Katz, Jeffrey Harvey 1947- WhoE 91, WhoEmL 91, WhoWor 91
Katz, Jerome BioIn 16
Katz, Jerome Abraham 1952- WhoEmL 91
Katz, Jerome B BiDrAPA 89
Katz, Jerome I 1925- BiDrAPA 89
Katz, Jerrold Pinya 1939- WhoE 91
Katz, Joel BiDrAPA 89
Katz, John 1938- WhoAm 90
Katz, John Bruce 1951- WhoSSW 91
Katz, Jonathan Garber 1950- WhoAm 90
Katz, Joseph 1920-1988 BioIn 16
Katz, Joseph Jacob 1912- WhoAm 90
Katz, Joseph Louis 1938- WhoAm 90
Katz, Joseph M 1913- WhoAmA 91
Katz, Joseph Morris 1913- WhoAm 90
Katz, Judith T. 1946- St&PR 91
Katz, Judy ODwPR 91
Katz, Julian 1937- WhoAm 90, WhoE 91, WhoWor 91
Katz, Kathy Silver 1947- WhoAmW 91
Katz, Lawrence Andrew 1948- St&PR 91
Katz, Lawrence Edward 1947- WhoE 91
Katz, Leandro 1938- WhoAmA 91, WhoE 91
Katz, Leon 1919- WhoAm 90
Katz, Leon 1921- WhoAm 90
Katz, Leslie George 1918- WhoAm 90
Katz, Lewis 1923- WhoAm 90
Katz, Lewis Robert 1938- WhoAm 90
Katz, Lillian Menasche 1927- ConAmBL
Katz, Lillian Vernon BioIn 16
Katz, Lillian Vernon 1927- St&PR 91
Katz, Louis Howard 1950- WhoSSW 91
Katz, Lynn Frances WhoAmW 91
Katz, Marc 1949- WhoE 91
Katz, Marc Paul 1953- St&PR 91
Katz, Marcia ODwPR 91
Katz, Mariann 1948- St&PR 91
Katz, Marilyn Faye 1945- WhoAmW 91
Katz, Marjorie P. 1934- AuBYP 90
Katz, Mark Roy BiDrAPA 89
Katz, Marshall Paul 1939- St&PR 91
Katz, Martha Lessman 1952- WhoAmW 91
Katz, Martin 1945- IntWWM 90
Katz, Martin Howard 1931- WhoAm 90
Katz, Martin Jay 1943- St&PR 91
Katz, Marty 1947- WhoEmL 91
Katz, Marvin 1930- WhoAm 90
Katz, Marvin G. 1935- ODwPR 91
Katz, Marvin Gerald 1935- WhoE 91
Katz, Maurice Harry 1937- WhoAm 90
Katz, Maurice Joseph 1937- WhoAm 90
Katz, Max 1919- BiDrAPA 89, WhoE 91
Katz, Menke 1906- WhoWrEP 89
Katz, Michael 1928- WhoAm 90
Katz, Michael 1939- WhoAm 90
Katz, Michael Howard 1956- BiDrAPA 89
Katz, Michael Jeffery 1950- WhoEmL 91, WhoWor 91
Katz, Michael Ray 1944- WhoAm 90
Katz, Michele Wynne 1962- WhoAmW 91
Katz, Mickey 1909-1985 BioIn 16
Katz, Milton 1907- WhoAm 90
Katz, Mindru 1925-1978 PenDiMP
Katz, Miriam Lesser 1942- WhoAmW 91
Katz, Morris WhoAmA 91
Katz, Morris 1915- St&PR 91
Katz, Morton H. 1934- St&PR 91
Katz, Morton Howard 1945- WhoEmL 91
Katz, Nachum M BiDrAPA 89
Katz, Nancy Sue 1954- WhoAmW 91
Katz, Natasha BioIn 16
Katz, Norman 1925- WhoAm 90, WhoE 91
Katz, Norman 1942- St&PR 91
Katz, Paul PenDiMP
Katz, Paul 1907- WhoAm 90
Katz, Paul William 1944- BiDrAPA 89
Katz, Pete Christopher 1953- St&PR 91
Katz, Peter 1947- WhoAm 90
Katz, Philip 1923- BiDrAPA 89
Katz, Philip 1930- BiDrAPA 89
Katz, Philip Arthur 1942- WhoE 91
Katz, Phyllis Alberts WhoAmW 91
Katz, Phyllis Pollak 1939- WhoAm 90
Katz, Raananah Swirsky 1951- WhoSSW 91
Katz, Raymond 1895-1974 WhoAmA 91N
Katz, Richard 1948- WhoEmL 91, WhoWor 91
Katz, Richard Jon 1932- WhoE 91
Katz, Richard William 1954- WhoEmL 91
Katz, Robert A 1955- BiDrAPA 89
Katz, Robert Arvin 1927- WhoAm 90
Katz, Robert H. 1925- St&PR 91
Katz, Robert Langdon 1917- WhoAm 90
Katz, Robert Lee 1926- WhoAm 90
Katz, Robert Nathan 1939- WhoE 91
Katz, Robin Nancy 1963- WhoAmW 91
Katz, Roger Martin 1945- WhoE 91, WhoWor 91
Katz, Ronald Alan 1949- St&PR 91
Katz, Ronald Lewis 1932- WhoAm 90
Katz, Ronald S. 1946- WhoEmL 91
Katz, S. Stanley 1928- WhoAm 90
Katz, Samuel 1914- St&PR 91
Katz, Samuel 1923- WhoAm 90
Katz, Samuel E BiDrAPA 89
Katz, Samuel Irving 1916- WhoE 91
Katz, Samuel Lawrence 1927- WhoAm 90, WhoSSW 91
Katz, Sanford Noah 1933- WhoAm 90
Katz, Saul Milton 1915- WhoAm 90
Katz, Sharon F. 1955- WhoE 91
Katz, Sidney BiDrAPA 89
Katz, Sidney L 1915-1978 WhoAmA 91N
Katz, Sol 1913- WhoAm 90
Katz, Solomon 1909- WhoAm 90
Katz, Solomon Stuart 1947- WhoEmL 91
Katz, Stanley Bernard 1949- WhoWor 91
Katz, Stanley H. 1923- WhoAm 90
Katz, Stanley Nider 1934- WhoAm 90, WhoWor 91
Katz, Stephen Eric 1948- WhoAm 90
Katz, Steve Robert 1935- WhoWrEP 89
Katz, Steven E. 1937- BiDrAPA 89
Katz, Steven Edward 1937- WhoAm 90, WhoE 91
Katz, Steven Martin 1941- WhoWor 91
Katz, Steven T 1944- ConAu 132
Katz, Steven Theodore 1944- WhoAm 90
Katz, Stuart 1964- WhoE 91
Katz, Stuart Charles 1937- WhoAm 90
Katz, Susan A. 1939- WhoWrEP 89
Katz, Susan Audrey 1956- WhoAmW 91
Katz, Susan Campbell 1952- BiDrAPA 89
Katz, Susan J. 1935- St&PR 91
Katz, Susan Kohl 1938- WhoE 91
Katz, Susie BioIn 16
Katz, Sydney L. 1941- St&PR 91
Katz, Ted 1937- WhoAmA 91
Katz, Tobi Cheryl BiDrAPA 89
Katz, Warren Allen 1936- WhoAm 90
Katz, Welwyn Wilton 1948- SmATA 62 [port]
Katz, William Armstrong 1926- WhoAm 90
Katz, William David 1915- WhoAm 90
Katz, William E. 1924- St&PR 91
Katz, William Emanuel 1924- WhoAm 90
Katz, William Loren 1927- AuBYP 90, WhoAm 90, WhoWrEP 89
Katz, William Michael 1940- WhoE 91, WhoWor 91
Katz-Bearnot, Sherry Pearl BiDrAPA 89
Katzberg, Jane Michaels 1940- WhoE 91
Katze, Jennifer Anne 1948- BiDrAPA 89
Katzel, Jeanine Alma 1948- WhoAmW 91
Katzel, Joseph Samuel 1926- St&PR 91
Katzell, Raymond A. 1919- WhoAm 90
Katzelnick, David Joel BiDrAPA 89
Katzen, Barry Jay 1954- WhoEmL 91
Katzen, Hal Zachery 1954- WhoAmA 91
Katzen, Jack 1921- WhoAm 90
Katzen, Jay Kenneth 1936- WhoAm 90
Katzen, Lila WhoAmA 91
Katzen, Lila 1932- BiDWomA
Katzen, Lila Pell 1932- WhoAm 90
Katzen, Raphael 1915- WhoAm 90
Katzen, Sally 1942- WhoAm 90, WhoAmW 91
Katzenbach, Nicholas de Belleville 1922- BiDrUSE 89
Katzenbach, Nicholas DeB 1922- St&PR 91
Katzenbach, Nicholas deBelleville 1922- WhoAm 90
Katzenbach, William E 1904-1975 WhoAmA 91N
Katzenberg, Dena S WhoAmA 91
Katzenberg, Jeffrey 1950- WhoAm 90
Katzenellenbogen, Adolf E M 1901-1964 WhoAmA 91N
Katzenelson, Itzhak 1886-1944 BioIn 16
Katzenstein, Benjamin Bailis 1958- WhoE 91
Katzenstein, Gary Jay 1956- WhoE 91
Katzenstein, Irving 1902- WhoAmA 91N
Katzenstein, Robert John 1951- WhoEmL 91
Katzenstein, Thea 1927- WhoAmW 91, WhoSSW 91
Katzer, Georg 1935- IntWWM 90
Katzfey, Patricia Ann 1956- WhoAmW 91
Katzin, Alfred G. 1906-1989 BioIn 16
Katzin, Dick 1934- WhoE 91
Katzin, Jerome S. 1918- St&PR 91
Katzin, Michael Lee 1956- WhoEmL 91
Katzir, Ephraim 1916- WhoWor 91
Katzir, Levy 1932- St&PR 91
Katzir, Pamela 1938- WhoAmW 91
Katzive, David H 1942- WhoAmA 91
Katzka, Gabriel BioIn 16, NewYTBS 90
Katzman, Anita 1920- WhoAmW 91
Katzman, Debbie ODwPR 91
Katzman, Diane Krivit 1960- ODwPR 91
Katzman, Donna Jeanne 1945- WhoAmW 91
Katzman, Elliot M. 1956- St&PR 91
Katzman, Elliot Mark 1956- WhoEmL 91
Katzman, Gerald Harvey 1947- WhoEmL 91
Katzman, Herbert 1923- WhoAmA 91
Katzman, Herbert Henry 1923- WhoAm 90
Katzman, Lawrence 1922- St&PR 91
Katzman, Leonard BioIn 16
Katzman, Lori Ann BiDrAPA 89
Katzman, Marshall B 1936- BiDrAPA 89
Katzman, Patricia Diane 1964- WhoAmW 91
Katzman, Robert 1925- WhoAm 90
Katzmann, Fred Leonard 1929- BioIn 16
Katzmann, Fritz 1906-1957 BioIn 16
Katzmann, Gary Stephen 1953- WhoE 91, WhoEmL 91
Katzmann, Herbert WhoAmA 91N
Katzmann, Robert Allen 1953- WhoE 91
Katzner, Donald Wahl 1938- WhoE 91
Katzner, Fred E. BioIn 16
Katzoff, Arnold Neal 1936- BiDrAPA 89
Katzoff, Michael M. BioIn 16
Katzow, Jacob J 1936- BiDrAPA 89
Katzowitz, Lauren WhoAmW 91
Kau, Lawrie Elizabeth 1942- WhoWrEP 89
Kauachi, Jose 1939- St&PR 91
Kauahikaua, James Puupai 1951- WhoEmL 91
Kaub, Peter St&PR 91
Kaucheck, Larry J. 1943- St&PR 91
Kauderer, Bernard Marvin 1931- WhoAm 90
Kauf, David Karl 1933- St&PR 91
Kauf, Gary D. 1943- St&PR 91
Kaufelt, David A. WhoWrEP 89
Kaufelt, Roy M. 1942- St&PR 91
Kaufelt, Stanley Philip 1920- St&PR 91, WhoAm 90
Kaufer, Daniel Ian 1959- BiDrAPA 89
Kauff, Benny 1890-1961 Ballpl 90
Kauffman, Audrey Jean WhoSSW 91
Kauffman, Barbara Ellen 1955- WhoE 91
Kauffman, Bruce William 1934- WhoAm 90, WhoE 91, WhoWor 91
Kauffman, Camille Andrene 1905- WhoAmA 91
Kauffman, Daun Howard 1957- WhoEmL 91
Kauffman, Dean Ronald 1921- St&PR 91
Kauffman, Ellwood 1928- St&PR 91
Kauffman, Erle Galen 1933- WhoAm 90
Kauffman, Ewing Marion 1916- WhoAm 90
Kauffman, George Bernard 1930- WhoAm 90
Kauffman, Gerald Galen 1943- BiDrAPA 89
Kauffman, James Harold 1944- St&PR 91
Kauffman, James Milton 1940- WhoAm 90
Kauffman, Janet 1945- WhoWrEP 89
Kauffman, John George 1923- St&PR 91
Kauffman, John Thomas 1926- St&PR 91
Kauffman, Juanita Eileen 1946- St&PR 91
Kauffman, Kenneth Mark 1930- WhoAm 90
Kauffman, Laura Tavel 1956- WhoAmW 91
Kauffman, Leon A. 1934- WhoE 91
Kauffman, Luke Edward 1941- WhoE 91
Kauffman, M. Jane 1935- WhoAmW 91
Kauffman, Margaret Anne 1945- WhoAmW 91
Kauffman, Mark 1922- WhoAm 90
Kauffman, Marvin E. 1933- WhoAm 90
Kauffman, Pamela Lynn 1963- WhoEmL 91
Kauffman, Patricia Litke 1949- BiDrAPA 89
Kauffman, Peg 1944- WhoAmW 91
Kauffman, Ralph Ira 1931- WhoE 91
Kauffman, Richard N. 1916- St&PR 91
Kauffman, Robert Craig 1932- WhoAm 90, WhoAmA 91
Kauffman, Robert Louis 1926- St&PR 91
Kauffman, Sandra D. 1933- WhoAmW 91
Kauffman, Scott Lawrence 1956- WhoEmL 91
Kauffman, Stanley C. 1924- St&PR 91
Kauffman, Stanley Chester 1924- WhoAm 90
Kauffman, Timothy Jay 1949- St&PR 91
Kauffmann, Angelica 1741-1807 BioIn 16, IntDcAA 90
Kauffmann, Franklin Lane 1921-1988 BioIn 16
Kauffmann, Howard C. 1923- St&PR 91, WhoAm 90
Kauffmann, Jean-Paul BioIn 16
Kauffmann, Lane 1921- WhoWrEP 89
Kauffmann, Stanley Jules 1916- WhoAm 90, WhoWrEP 89
Kauffmann, Thekla BioIn 16
Kauffmann, Thomas 1924- WhoWor 91
Kaufinger, George 1934- St&PR 91
Kaufman, Alan Joel 1943- St&PR 91
Kaufman, Albert Nick 1924- WhoWor 91
Kaufman, Alex 1924- WhoAm 90
Kaufman, Allan M. 1948- WhoAm 90
Kaufman, Amy Rebecca 1951- WhoWrEP 89
Kaufman, Andrea Vita BiDrAPA 89
Kaufman, Andrew Lee 1931- WhoAm 90
Kaufman, Andy 1949-1984 BioIn 16
Kaufman, Ann 1954- WhoAmW 91
Kaufman, Antoinette D. 1939- WhoAm 90
Kaufman, Armin 1925- St&PR 91
Kaufman, Arnold M. 1935- St&PR 91
Kaufman, Arnold Marvin 1935- WhoE 91
Kaufman, Barbara H BiDrAPA 89
Kaufman, Bel BioIn 16, WhoAm 90, WhoWrEP 89
Kaufman, Benjamin BiDrAPA 89
Kaufman, Charles Rudolph 1908- WhoAm 90
Kaufman, Charlotte Gordon 1959- WhoE 91
Kaufman, Charlotte King 1920- WhoAmW 91
Kaufman, Colin Kelly 1946- WhoEmL 91
Kaufman, Daniel Andrew 1945- BiDrAPA 89
Kaufman, David BiDrAPA 89
Kaufman, David A. 1915- St&PR 91
Kaufman, David Harold BiDrAPA 89
Kaufman, Deborah A ODwPR 91
Kaufman, Debra Jane 1951- WhoWrEP 89
Kaufman, Diane Beatrice 1944- WhoSSW 91
Kaufman, Diane Leslie BiDrAPA 89
Kaufman, Donald Leroy 1931- WhoAm 90
Kaufman, Donald Saul 1945- WhoE 91
Kaufman, Edward 1936- BiDrAPA 89
Kaufman, Elaine BioIn 16
Kaufman, Elaine Sue Sommers 1933- WhoAmW 91
Kaufman, Elliot Martin BiDrAPA 89
Kaufman, Enit 1898-1961 WhoAmA 91N
Kaufman, Enrique N 1933- BiDrAPA 89
Kaufman, Erwin R. St&PR 91
Kaufman, Frank Albert 1916- WhoAm 90
Kaufman, Frank J. 1944- St&PR 91
Kaufman, George S. 1889-1961 OxCPMus, WorAlBi
Kaufman, Gordon Dester 1925- WhoAm 90
Kaufman, Harold Richard 1926- WhoAm 90
Kaufman, Harry 1937- WhoE 91
Kaufman, Harvey !931- WhoSSW 91, WhoWor 91
Kaufman, Harvey Isidore 1937- WhoWor 91
Kaufman, Henry 1927- WhoAm 90
Kaufman, Herbert 1922- WhoAm 90
Kaufman, Herbert 1928- St&PR 91
Kaufman, Herbert Edward 1931- WhoAm 90
Kaufman, Herbert Mark 1946- WhoWor 91
Kaufman, Hugh BioIn 16
Kaufman, I Charles BiDrAPA 89
Kaufman, Ira Gladstone 1909- WhoWor 91
Kaufman, Ira Jeffrey 1928- WhoAm 90
Kaufman, Irving BiDrAPA 89
Kaufman, Irving 1920- WhoAmA 91
Kaufman, Irving 1925- WhoAm 90
Kaufman, Irving N. 1924- WhoE 91
Kaufman, Irving Robert 1910- WhoAm 90
Kaufman, Isaac 1947- St&PR 91
Kaufman, James E. 1950- St&PR 91
Kaufman, James Harry 1937- St&PR 91
Kaufman, James Mark 1951- WhoSSW 91
Kaufman, Jane 1938- WhoAm 90, WhoAmA 91
Kaufman, Jane 1947- WhoAmW 91
Kaufman, Janice Horner 1949- WhoAmW 91
Kaufman, Jeffrey Allen 1952- WhoWor 91
Kaufman, Jerome Edward 1949- BiDrAPA 89
Kaufman, Jerome J. 1917- WhoAm 90
Kaufman, Jerome L. 1933- WhoAm 90

Kaufman, Jess 1920- WhoE 91, WhoWor 91
Kaufman, Joanne BioIn 16
Kaufman, Joe 1911- WhoAmA 91, WhoE 91
Kaufman, John E. 1927- WhoAm 90
Kaufman, John Gilbert, Jr. 1931- WhoAm 90
Kaufman, Jonathan 1943- ODwPR 91
Kaufman, Jonathan Reed 1956- WhoAm 90
Kaufman, Judith Lasker 1942- WhoAmW 91
Kaufman, Julian Mortimer 1918- WhoAm 90
Kaufman, Karl Lincoln 1911- WhoAm 90
Kaufman, Laurence 1930- ODwPR 91
Kaufman, Lawrence H. 1936- ODwPR 91
Kaufman, Leon I. 1927- St&PR 91
Kaufman, Lester Robert 1946- WhoEmL 91
Kaufman, Loretta Ana 1946- WhoAmA 91
Kaufman, Lori Hokin 1951- WhoAmA 91
Kaufman, Louis 1905- PenDiMP
Kaufman, Malvin 1929- St&PR 91
Kaufman, Marcus Maurice 1929- WhoAm 90
Kaufman, Margo BioIn 16
Kaufman, Mark 1950- St&PR 91
Kaufman, Mark Stuart 1947- WhoEmL 91
Kaufman, Martin 1940- WhoWrEP 89
Kaufman, Martin M. 1921- St&PR 91
Kaufman, Martin Theodore 1945- St&PR 91
Kaufman, Melvin 1939- St&PR 91
Kaufman, Mervyn BioIn 16
Kaufman, Mervyn Douglas 1932- WhoAm 90
Kaufman, Michael David 1941- WhoAm 90
Kaufman, Mico 1924- WhoAmA 91
Kaufman, Monte Irvin BiDrAPA 89
Kaufman, Morris Enouch BioIn 16
Kaufman, Nancy WhoAmA 91
Kaufman, Nathan 1915- WhoAm 90
Kaufman, Paul 1923- WhoAm 90
Kaufman, Paul 1931- BiDrAPA 89
Kaufman, Paul Albert 1915- St&PR 91
Kaufman, Paula T. 1946- WhoAm 90, WhoSSW 91
Kaufman, Peter Bishop 1928- WhoAm 90
Kaufman, Philip BioIn 16
Kaufman, Philip 1936- WhoAm 90
Kaufman, Phyllis Cynthia 1945- WhoAmW 91
Kaufman, Ralph Mark BiDrAPA 89
Kaufman, Ray G. 1944- St&PR 91
Kaufman, Raymond 1917- St&PR 91
Kaufman, Raymond Henry 1925- WhoAm 90
Kaufman, Richard BioIn 16
Kaufman, Richard 1936- WhoAm 90
Kaufman, Richard 1937- BiDrAPA 89
Kaufman, Richard 1959- St&PR 91
Kaufman, Richard A. 1951- St&PR 91
Kaufman, Richard Louis 1955- St&PR 91
Kaufman, Robert David 1947- WhoEmL 91
Kaufman, Robert Edward 1934- St&PR 91
Kaufman, Robert Jules 1921- WhoAm 90
Kaufman, Robert L. BioIn 16
Kaufman, Robert Max 1929- WhoAm 90
Kaufman, Robert Perry 1949- St&PR 91
Kaufman, Rolf 1930- St&PR 91
Kaufman, Ronald Paul 1929- WhoAm 90
Kaufman, Russell Eugene 1946- WhoSSW 91
Kaufman, S Harvard 1913- BiDrAPA 89
Kaufman, Samuel S 1913- BiDrAPA 89
Kaufman, Samuel William BiDrAPA 89
Kaufman, Sanford Paul 1928- WhoAm 90
Kaufman, Seymour 1924- WhoAm 90
Kaufman, Shelley S. 1953- WhoAmW 91
Kaufman, Shirley 1923- FemiCLE
Kaufman, Sidney 1908- WhoE 91
Kaufman, Sol 1916- St&PR 91
Kaufman, Stephen E. 1932- WhoE 91, WhoWor 91
Kaufman, Stephen Lawrence 1942- WhoSSW 91
Kaufman, Stephen P. 1941- St&PR 91, WhoAm 90, WhoE 91
Kaufman, Stuart J. 1950- WhoWrEP 89
Kaufman, Stuart Martin 1926- WhoAmA 91
Kaufman, Susan Jane 1942- WhoAmW 91
Kaufman, Thomas Frederick 1949- WhoE 91
Kaufman, Victor BioIn 16
Kaufman, Victor A. St&PR 91
Kaufman, Victor A. 1943- ConTFT 8
Kaufman, Walter J. 1917- St&PR 91
Kaufman, William B. 1936- St&PR 91
Kaufman, William Morris 1931- WhoAm 90
Kaufman-Diamond, Sharon BiDrAPA 89
Kaufman-Jacobs, Louise Jackson 1932- WhoE 91
Kaufman-Levy, Barbara 1954- WhoAmW 91
Kaufmann, Charles Arthur 1951- BiDrAPA 89
Kaufmann, D.B. 1934- St&PR 91
Kaufmann, Edgar 1910-1989 BioIn 16
Kaufmann, Edgar, Jr. 1910-1989 ConAu 129
Kaufmann, Helen 1887- AuBYP 90
Kaufmann, Henry Mark 1929- WhoE 91
Kaufmann, James A. 1923- WhoAm 90, WhoSSW 91, WhoWor 91
Kaufmann, Joseph Gregory, Jr. 1953- WhoWrEP 89
Kaufmann, Julie 1954- IntWWM 90
Kaufmann, Kenneth K. 1930- St&PR 91
Kaufmann, Margaret C 1952- BiDrAPA 89
Kaufmann, Mark S. 1932- St&PR 91
Kaufmann, Mark Steiner 1932- WhoAm 90, WhoE 91, WhoWor 91
Kaufmann, Michael William BiDrAPA 89
Kaufmann, Paul D 1928- BiDrAPA 89
Kaufmann, Paul T. 1936- St&PR 91
Kaufmann, Paul Theodor 1936- WhoAm 90
Kaufmann, Paulette Clark 1944- WhoAm 90
Kaufmann, Peter J. 1935- WhoSSW 91
Kaufmann, Ralph 1936- St&PR 91
Kaufmann, Ralph James 1924- WhoAm 90
Kaufmann, Richard K. BioIn 16
Kaufmann, Rick 1947- WhoAmA 91
Kaufmann, Robert 1914-1959 WhoAmA 91N
Kaufmann, Robert Carl 1937- WhoAmA 91
Kaufmann, Robert John BiDrAPA 89
Kaufmann, Robert W. 1949- St&PR 91
Kaufmann, Roy Leslie 1953- WhoEmL 91
Kaufmann, Sally Havner 1935- BiDrAPA 89
Kaufmann, Stephan 1926- St&PR 91
Kaufmann, Sylvia Nadeau 1940- WhoAmW 91
Kaufmann, Thomas DaCosta 1948- ConAu 129
Kaufmann, Thomas David 1922- WhoAm 90
Kaufmann, Tony 1900-1982 Ballpl 90
Kaufmann, Vicki Marie M. 1946- WhoEmL 91
Kaufmann, Werner Karl Hermann 1924- WhoWor 91
Kaufmann, Yadin Bernard 1959- WhoWor 91
Kaufold, Leroy 1924- WhoAm 90
Kaufthal, Ilan 1947- St&PR 91
Kaugars, George Edward 1949- WhoSSW 91
Kauger, Yvonne 1937- WhoAm 90, WhoAmW 91, WhoSSW 91
Kaul, Ashok K BiDrAPA 89
Kaul, Hari Krishen 1941- WhoWor 91
Kaul, Karan 1945- WhoSSW 91
Kaul, Kenneth Lee 1945- WhoEmL 91
Kaul, Mani 1942- BioIn 16
Kaul, Om Prakash 1943- WhoWor 91
Kaul, Udo 1939- St&PR 91
Kaula, Edna Mason 1906- AuBYP 90
Kaula, William Mason 1926- WhoAm 90
Kaulakis, Arnold Francis 1916- WhoAm 90
Kaulitz, Garry Charles 1942- WhoAmA 91
Kaulkin, Donna Brookman 1943- WhoAm 90
Kaull, George H. 1931- St&PR 91
Kaulukou, John Lot 1841-1917 AmLegL
Kaunas, Roman R 1944- BiDrAPA 89
Kaunda, Kenneth 1924- WorAlBi
Kaunda, Kenneth David 1924- WhoWor 91
Kaung, Thomas T.S. 1937- St&PR 91
Kaung, Thomas T. S. 1937- WhoAm 90
Kaung, William Hsueh Ping 1945- WhoAm 90
Kaunitz, Paul E 1914- BiDrAPA 89
Kaunitz, Paul Ehrlich 1914- WhoE 91
Kaup, Bruce Allen 1952- BiDrAPA 89
Kaup, David Earle 1952- WhoSSW 91
Kaupe, Walter BiDrAPA 89
Kaupelis, Robert John 1928- WhoAmA 91, WhoE 91
Kauper, Thomas Eugene 1935- WhoAm 90
Kauppila, Veikko Aulis 1937- WhoWor 91
Kaur, Bibi Bhani NewAgMG
Kaur, Jasjit BiDrAPA 89
Kaur, Prabhjot 1927- WhoWor 91
Kaur, Sat Kartar NewAgMG
Kaur, Singh NewAgMG
Kaur Khalsa, Dayal 1943?-1989 ConAu 129
Kaurala, Wesley 1940- St&PR 91
Kauranen, Gail 1957- ODwPR 91
Kaus, Otto Michael 1920- WhoAm 90
Kausch, Otto BiDrAPA 89
Kausch, Otto 1950- WhoEmL 91
Kausel, Cecilia Lewis 1945- WhoEmL 91
Kauser, Janson Allen 1949- WhoEmL 91
Kausler, Donald Harvey 1927- WhoAm 90
Kautsky, Karl 1854-1938 BioIn 16
Kautt, Glenn Gregory 1948- WhoEmL 91, WhoWor 91
Kautter, David John 1948- WhoE 91
Kautz, John Terry 1945- St&PR 91
Kautz, Richard C. 1916- St&PR 91
Kautz, Richard Carl 1916- WhoAm 90
Kautz, Walter Cordes 1924- St&PR 91
Kautz, Wayne Paul 1940- St&PR 91
Kautzman, Edward J. 1935- St&PR 91
Kauvar, Abraham J. 1915- WhoAm 90
Kauvar, Charles Eliezer Hillel 1879-1971 BioIn 16
Kauwell, Gail P. Abbott 1952- WhoEmL 91
Kauzlarich, James Joseph 1927- WhoAm 90
Kauzlarich, Richard Dale 1944- WhoAm 90
Kauzmann, Walter Joseph 1916- WhoAm 90
Kavadas-Pappas, Iphigenia Katherine 1958- WhoAmW 91
Kavafian, Ani 1948- IntWWM 90
Kavafian, Ida 1952- IntWWM 90
Kavage, William 1940- St&PR 91
Kavalek, Lubomir 1943- WhoAm 90
Kavaler, Lucy 1930- AuBYP 90
Kavaler, Lucy E. St&PR 91
Kavaler, Rebecca WhoWrEP 89
Kavaler, Susan Adler 1950- WhoAmW 91
Kavaler, Thomas J. 1948- WhoEmL 91
Kavalerist-devitsa EncCoWW
Kavan, Anna 1901-1968 BioIn 16, FemiCLE, MajTwCW
Kavanagh, Dan 1946- TwCCr&M 91
Kavanagh, J E Terence BiDrAPA 89
Kavanagh, Jane Lavonne 1961- WhoEmL 91
Kavanagh, Julia 1824-1877 BioIn 16, FemiCLE
Kavanagh, Kevin Patrick 1932- St&PR 91, WhoAm 90
Kavanagh, Marty 1891-1960 Ballpl 90
Kavanagh, Patrick 1904-1967 MajTwCW
Kavanagh, Paul TwCCr&M 91
Kavanagh, Paul M. 1928- St&PR 91
Kavanagh, Peter 1916- ConAu 132
Kavanagh, Preston Breckenridge 1932- WhoAm 90
Kavanaugh, Everett Edward, Jr. 1941- WhoAm 90
Kavanaugh, James G BiDrAPA 89
Kavanaugh, John BioIn 16
Kavanaugh, John Michael 1952- WhoEmL 91
Kavanaugh, Kelly H. 1960- ODwPR 91
Kavanaugh, Patrick T. 1954- WhoEmL 91
Kavanaugh, Paul Fred 1959- WhoEmL 91
Kavanaugh, Richard BioIn 16
Kavandi, Janet Lynn 1959- WhoEmL 91
Kavasch, Deborah Helene 1945- IntWWM 90
Kavass, Igor Ivar 1932- WhoAm 90
Kavaya, Michael Joseph 1951- WhoEmL 91
Kavee, Robert Charles 1934- WhoE 91
Kavehrad, Mohsen 1951- WhoE 91
Kavelin, Howard Borrah BioIn 16
Kavensky, Jodie Shagrin 1957- WhoEmL 91
Kaverman, Donald Lee 1952- WhoWrEP 89
Kavesh, Robert A. 1927- WhoAm 90
Kavett, Henry C. ODwPR 91
Kavey, Neil Barton BiDrAPA 89
Kavey, Richard Plaut 1947- BiDrAPA 89, WhoE 91
Kavin, Rebecca Jean 1946- WhoAmW 91, WhoEmL 91
Kavka, Audrey Beth 1951- BiDrAPA 89
Kavka, Georgine A 1922- BiDrAPA 89
Kavka, Jerome 1921- BiDrAPA 89
Kavli, Fred 1927- St&PR 91
Kavlie, Gaylord Jerome 1953- WhoEmL 91
Kavner, Julie 1951- WorAlBi
Kavner, Robert M. BioIn 16
Kavner, Robert M. 1943- WhoAm 90, WhoE 91
Kavounas, Anita Marie 1956- WhoAmW 91
Kavouras, Freida 1962- WhoE 91
Kavouras, Patricia 1955- WhoE 91
Kavoussi, Richard J. BiDrAPA 89
Kavrakos, Dimitri 1946- IntWWM 90
Kavtschitsch, Joseph 1926- BiDrAPA 89
Kavulic, Richard A. 1950- St&PR 91
Kavy, Susan 1955- WhoEmL 91
Kavzanjian, John Daniel 1951- St&PR 91
Kaw, Autar Krishen 1960- WhoSSW 91
Kawa, Florence Kathryn 1912- WhoAmA 91
Kawa, Marcia Lynne 1957- WhoAmW 91
Kawabata Yasunari 1899-1972 EncJap, WorAlBi
Kawabata, Minoru 1911- WhoAmA 91
Kawabuchi, Hiroshi St&PR 91
Kawade, Yoshimi 1924- WhoWor 91
Kawaguchi, Harry Harumitsu 1928- WhoSSW 91, WhoWor 91
Kawaguchi, Meredith Ferguson 1940- WhoAmW 91, WhoSSW 91, WhoWor 91
Kawaguchi, Minoru 1928- WhoWor 91
Kawaguchi, Yoriko 1941- BioIn 16
Kawahara, Hisashi 1930- WhoWor 91
Kawahara, Yoko 1939- IntWWM 90
Kawahito, Makiko 1956- IntWWM 90
Kawai, Kanjiro 1890-1966 PenDiDA 89
Kawai, Ryoichi 1917- WhoWor 91
Kawai, Ryoichi 1950- WhoWor 91
Kawakami, Takaya 1936- St&PR 91
Kawakami, Tetsuharu Ballpl 90
Kawakita, Takashi 1948- WhoWor 91
Kawakubo Rei EncJap
Kawalerowicz, Jerzy 1922- BioIn 16
Kawamitsu, Isao 1944- WhoWor 91
Kawamura, Shigekuni BioIn 16
Kawamura, Takeo 1934- BiDrAPA 89
Kawana, Koichi 1930- WhoAm 90, WhoWor 91
Kawano, Ietoshi 1941- WhoWor 91
Kawano, James Conrad WhoE 91
Kawano, Kenji 1916- WhoWor 91
Kawano, Randall Toshio 1959- WhoEmL 91
Kawano, Tadasu 1917- WhoWor 91
Kawano, Yosh BioIn 16
Kawasaki, Kyoji 1957- WhoWor 91
Kawasaki, Masaru 1924- IntWWM 90
Kawasaki, Seiichi 1922- WhoWor 91
Kawashima, Kiko BioIn 16
Kawashima, Masao 1929- WhoWor 91
Kawashima, Takeshi 1930- WhoAmA 91, WhoE 91
Kawata, Hiroshi 1933- IntWWM 90
Kawecki, Annette R. BiDrAPA 89
Kawecki, Jean Mary 1926- WhoAmA 91
Kawecki, John Anthony Boleslaw 1959- WhoEmL 91
Kawecki, Leon Stanley 1921- WhoWor 91
Kawecki, Witold 1929- BiDrAPA 89
Kawi, Ali A BiDrAPA 89
Kawin, Bruce Frederick 1945- WhoEmL 91
Kawitzky, Ronald David 1953- St&PR 91
Kawmy, Susan Yost 1950- WhoAmW 91
Kawuki, Joseph Nsanusi 1934- WhoWor 91
Kawula, John Michael 1947- WhoE 91, WhoEmL 91
Kay, Alan BioIn 16
Kay, Alan 1940- WhoAm 90
Kay, Alan Francis 1925- WhoAm 90
Kay, Albert 1914- WhoAm 90
Kay, Andrew F. 1919- St&PR 91
Kay, Andrew John 1954- WhoSSW 91
Kay, Arnold Melvin 1933- St&PR 91
Kay, Barry S. St&PR 91
Kay, Bernard Melvin 1932- WhoAm 90
Kay, Carl 1938- ODwPR 91
Kay, Carol McGinnis 1941- WhoAm 90
Kay, Charles D. 1950- WhoSSW 91
Kay, Cyril Max 1931- WhoAm 90
Kay, David C BiDrAPA 89
Kay, Dickie 1953- BiDrAPA 89
Kay, Douglas Casey 1932- WhoAm 90
Kay, Douglass Allan 1947- BiDrAPA 89
Kay, Elizabeth Alison 1928- WhoAmW 91
Kay, Elizabeth Ann 1956- WhoAmW 91
Kay, Ernest 1915- WhoWor 91
Kay, Gersil Newmark St&PR 91
Kay, Helen AuBYP 90
Kay, Helen 1912- WhoAmW 91, WhoE 91, WhoWor 91
Kay, Herbert 1924- St&PR 91, WhoAm 90
Kay, Herma Hill 1934- WhoAm 90
Kay, Hershy 1919-1981 OxCPMus
Kay, Jack Garvin 1930- WhoAm 90
Kay, Jane Holtz 1938- WhoWrEP 89
Kay, Jeffrey Robert 1952- St&PR 91
Kay, Jerald 1945- BiDrAPA 89, WhoEmL 91
Kay, Jerome 1920- BiDrAPA 89, WhoE 91
Kay, Jerome Harold 1921- WhoAm 90
Kay, Joel Phillip 1936- WhoAm 90
Kay, Judith 1952- WhoEmL 91
Kay, Kenneth J. 1955- St&PR 91
Kay, Kenneth Jeffrey 1955- WhoAm 90
Kay, Kenneth Robert 1951- WhoEmL 91
Kay, Larry Alan 1947- St&PR 91
Kay, Larry David 1954- St&PR 91
Kay, M. Jane 1925- St&PR 91, WhoAmW 91
Kay, Margaret J. 1951- WhoAmW 91
Kay, Marshall 1904-1975 DcScB S2
Kay, Mary Ellen 1947- WhoAmW 91
Kay, Mary Patricia 1947- WhoAmW 91
Kay, Monte BioIn 16
Kay, Norman Forber 1929- IntWWM 90
Kay, Patricia A J BiDrAPA 89
Kay, Patrick 1904-1983 DcNaB 1981
Kay, Paul 1920- BiDrAPA 89
Kay, Paul A. 1951- St&PR 91
Kay, Paul de Young 1934- WhoAm 90
Kay, Peter Patrick 1949- WhoEmL 91
Kay, Reed 1925- WhoAmA 91, WhoE 91

Kay, Rena Lynn 1943- *BiDrAPA 89*
Kay, Richard Frederick 1947- *WhoAm 90*
Kay, Robert Leo 1924- *WhoAm 90*
Kay, Ronald James 1947- *WhoAm 90*
Kay, Saul 1914- *WhoAm 90*
Kay, Stanley L. 1942- *St&PR 91*
Kay, Stanley R. *NewYTBS 90*
Kay, Stephen B. 1934- *St&PR 91*
Kay, Stephen William 1953- *WhoEmL 91*
Kay, Susan Barcus 1948- *WhoAmW 91*
Kay, Suzanne *BioIn 16*
Kay, Suzanne Mahlburg 1947- *WhoAmW 91*
Kay, Thomas Oliver 1929- *WhoAm 90*
Kay, Thomas Richard 1945- *WhoE 91*
Kay, Thomas Robert 1960- *WhoSSW 91*
Kay, Tom 1946- *WhoEmL 91*
Kay, Tracy Ralph 1953- *WhoEmL 91*
Kay, Ulysses 1917- *WhoAm 90*
Kay, Ulysses Simpson 1917- *DrBlPA 90, IntWWM 90*
Kay, Vicki M. 1937- *St&PR 91*
Kay, Walter Anthony 1945- *St&PR 91*
Kay, William Gemmill, Jr. 1930- *WhoAm 90*
Kay, William Richard, Jr. 1948- *WhoEmL 91*
Kay-Shuttleworth, James 1804-1877 *BioIn 16*
Kaya, Robert Masayoshi 1914- *WhoWor 91*
Kayan, Sabih 1939- *BiDrAPA 89*
Kayastha, Veena *BiDrAPA 89*
Kayatenna *WhNaAH*
Kayatennae *WhNaAH*
Kayden, Mimi R. 1933- *St&PR 91*
Kaye, A Stanley 1909- *BiDrAPA 89*
Kaye, Abraham 1918- *BiDrAPA 89*
Kaye, Alan 1934- *BiDrAPA 89*
Kaye, Bernard 1930- *St&PR 91*
Kaye, Buddy 1918- *IntWWM 90*
Kaye, D Michael *BiDrAPA 89*
Kaye, Danny *BioIn 16*
Kaye, Danny 1913-1987 *OxCPMus, WorAlBi*
Kaye, David 1942- *ODwPR 91*
Kaye, David Haigh 1947- *WhoAmA 91*
Kaye, David Laurence 1951- *BiDrAPA 89*
Kaye, Donald 1931- *WhoAm 90*
Kaye, Elizabeth *BioIn 16*
Kaye, Elizabeth Ann 1951- *WhoAmW 91*
Kaye, Evelyn 1937- *WhoWrEP 89*
Kaye, Evelyn Patricia 1937- *WhoAm 90*
Kaye, Gene Warren 1950- *WhoSSW 91*
Kaye, George 1911- *WhoAmA 91*
Kaye, George M. 1931- *St&PR 91*
Kaye, Geraldine 1925- *WhoWor 91*
Kaye, Gordon Israel 1935- *WhoAm 90*
Kaye, Harvey E 1927- *BiDrAPA 89*
Kaye, Harvey N. 1940- *St&PR 91*
Kaye, Jack Alan 1954- *WhoE 91*
Kaye, Jerome 1923- *WhoSSW 91*
Kaye, Jerome R. 1928- *St&PR 91, WhoAm 90*
Kaye, Jesse J *BiDrAPA 89*
Kaye, Judith Smith 1938- *WhoAm 90, WhoAmW 91, WhoE 91*
Kaye, Judy 1948- *WhoAmW 91*
Kaye, Laurence H. *BioIn 16*
Kaye, Lenard Wayne 1950- *WhoE 91*
Kaye, M M 1908- *SmATA 62 [port]*
Kaye, M M 1909- *MajTwCW*
Kaye, Marc Mendell 1959- *WhoEmL 91*
Kaye, Marilyn *BioIn 16*
Kaye, Marilyn 1949- *AuBYP 90*
Kaye, Melanie Fern 1960- *WhoAmW 91*
Kaye, Mildred Elaine 1929- *WhoAmA 91*
Kaye, Miriam 1932- *BiDrAPA 89*
Kaye, Mollie *MajTwCW*
Kaye, Mollie 1908- *SmATA X [port]*
Kaye, Neil S. 1958- *BiDrAPA 89*
Kaye, Neil Scott 1958- *WhoE 91*
Kaye, Nora *BioIn 16*
Kaye, Norman Edwin 1941- *WhoSSW 91*
Kaye, Rasa *WhoWrEP 89*
Kaye, Richard Leon 1925- *WhoE 91*
Kaye, Richard Paul 1953- *WhoEmL 91*
Kaye, Sammy 1910-1987 *BioIn 16, WorAlBi*
Kaye, Simon 1899- *BiDrAPA 89*
Kaye, Stephen Frederick 1946- *St&PR 91*
Kaye, Stephen J. 1943- *ODwPR 91, St&PR 91*
Kaye, Stephen Rackow 1931- *WhoAm 90*
Kaye, Tony *BioIn 16*
Kaye, Victoria Ann 1941- *WhoE 91*
Kaye, Walter 1927- *WhoAm 90, WhoE 91*
Kaye, Walter H *BiDrAPA 89*
Kaye, Wilbur Irving 1922- *WhoAm 90*
Kaye, William Herbert 1947- *WhoEmL 91*
Kaye, William R. 1952- *St&PR 91*
Kaye, William S. 1953- *St&PR 91*
Kaye, William Samuel 1953- *WhoAm 90, WhoWor 91*
Kaye-Smith, Sheila 1887-1956 *BioIn 16, FemiCLE*
Kayes, Evan R. 1949- *St&PR 91*
Kayko, Meg *ODwPR 91*
Kaylan, Howard Lawrence 1947- *WhoEmL 91, WhoWor 91*
Kayll, Joseph Robert 1914- *WhoWor 91*
Kaylor, Andrea Lynn 1946- *WhoEmL 91*
Kaylor, Barbara Brotman 1959- *St&PR 91, WhoAmW 91*
Kaylor, David Owen 1944- *WhoSSW 91, WhoWor 91*
Kaylor, Ronald Dean 1938- *St&PR 91*
Kaymor, Patrice Maguilene *MajTwCW*
Kayn, Hilde B 1903-1950 *WhoAmA 91N*
Kayne, Ernst M 1937- *BiDrAPA 89*
Kayne, Nancy D. 1954- *BiDrAPA 89*
Kaynes, Robert J., Jr. 1956- *St&PR 91*
Kaynes, Robert Jacob 1927- *St&PR 91*
Kaynor, Sanford Bull 1926- *WhoAm 90*
Kays, B. Thomas 1944- *WhoSSW 91, WhoWor 91*
Kays, James William 1924- *St&PR 91*
Kays, Nancy E. 1948- *ODwPR 91*
Kays, Nancy Elizabeth 1948- *WhoEmL 91*
Kays, Robert M. *ODwPR 91*
Kays, William Morrow 1920- *WhoAm 90*
Kaysen, Carl 1920- *St&PR 91, WhoAm 90, WhoWor 91*
Kaysen, David Brookes 1949- *St&PR 91*
Kayser, Allen 1949- *BiDrAPA 89*
Kayser, Donald R. 1930- *St&PR 91*
Kayser, Donald Robert 1930- *WhoAm 90*
Kayser, Engelbert 1840-1911 *PenDiDA 89*
Kayser, Kenneth Wayne 1947- *WhoEmL 91*
Kayser, Leif 1919- *IntWWM 90*
Kayser, Paul W. 1918-1990 *BioIn 16*
Kayser, Robert Justin 1946- *WhoE 91*
Kayser, Terry M. 1957- *St&PR 91*
Kayser, Thomas Arthur 1935- *WhoAm 90, WhoAmA 91*
Kayson, Mary Beth 1955- *WhoEmL 91*
Kaysone Phomvihan 1920- *WhoWor 91*
Kaytennae *WhNaAH*
Kayton, Lawrence 1938- *BiDrAPA 89*
Kayton, Myron 1934- *WhoAm 90*
Kaywin, Louis *BiDrAPA 89*
Kaywood, George *BioIn 16*
Kayye, Paul Thomas 1937- *BiDrAPA 89*
Kaz 1922- *WhoAmA 91*
Kaz, Joyce Zickerman 1936-1979 *WhoAmA 91N*
Kaz, Nathaniel 1917- *WhoAm 90, WhoAmA 91*
Kaz, William Jacob 1932- *BiDrAPA 89*
Kaza, Basavapunna R *BiDrAPA 89*
Kaza, Paul 1951- *WhoEmL 91*
Kazak, Eddie 1920- *Ballpl 90*
Kazak, Joseph 1905- *BiDrAPA 89*
Kazakoff, Michael 1923- *St&PR 91*
Kazakov, Sergey *BiDrAPA 89*
Kazakov, Yuri Pavlovich 1927- *MajTwCW*
Kazala, Michael J. 1952- *St&PR 91*
Kazamatsuri, Hajime 1934- *WhoWor 91*
Kazan, Avraam T *BiDrAPA 89*
Kazan, Basil Gibran 1914- *WhoE 91*
Kazan, Benjamin 1917- *WhoAm 90*
Kazan, Elia *BioIn 16*
Kazan, Elia 1909- *ConAu 32NR, ConLC 63 [port], WhoAm 90, WorAlBi*
Kazan, Kathryn Lukins 1957- *WhoAmW 91*
Kazan, Lainie 1942- *WhoAm 90*
Kazan, Lanie 1942- *WorAlBi*
Kazan, Richard 1945- *St&PR 91*
Kazan, Robert Peter 1947- *WhoEmL 91*
Kazaniwskyj, Lubomyra Maria 1957- *WhoAmW 91*
Kazanjian, Robert Kapriel 1951- *WhoSSW 91*
Kazankina, Tatyana 1951- *BioIn 16*
Kazanowski, Albin Daniel 1926- *WhoAm 90*
Kazanski, Ted 1934- *Ballpl 90*
Kazantzaki, Galatea 1886-1962 *EncCoWW*
Kazantzakis, Nikos 1883?-1957 *ConAu 132, MajTwCW, WorAlBi*
Kazantzis, Judith 1940- *FemiCLE*
Kazarian, Ann Huston 1932- *BiDrAPA 89*
Kazarian, Richard Steven 1954- *WhoEmL 91*
Kazarinoff, Nicholas D. 1929- *WhoAm 90*
Kazazis, Kostas 1934- *WhoAm 90*
Kazda, Louis Frank 1916- *WhoAm 90*
Kazdan, Aralee 1935- *WhoE 91*
Kaze, James Michael 1948- *WhoEmL 91*
Kazel, Dorothy 1939-1980 *BioIn 16*
Kazem, Ismail 1931- *WhoE 91*
Kazem, Taheya *BioIn 16*
Kazemi, Abbas Ashtiani 1956- *WhoE 91*
Kazemi, Farhad 1943- *WhoAm 90*
Kazemi, Homayoun 1934- *WhoAm 90*
Kazemzadeh, Firuz 1924- *WhoAm 90*
Kazen, George Philip 1940- *WhoAm 90*
Kazezski, Stanley G. 1934- *St&PR 91*
Kazik, John S. 1942- *St&PR 91*
Kazik, John Stanley 1942- *WhoAm 90*
Kazim, Victor 1942- *WhoWor 91*
Kazimierczuk, Marian Kazimierz 1948- *WhoWor 91*
Kazimir, Edward Oliver 1943- *St&PR 91*
Kazimir, Gina Ann 1964- *WhoAmW 91*
Kazin, Alfred 1915- *BioIn 16, WhoAm 90, WhoWor 91, WhoWrEP 89, WorAlBi*
Kazlauskas, Romas Joseph 1956- *WhoEmL 91*
Kazle, Elynmarie 1958- *WhoAmW 91, WhoEmL 91*
Kazmark, Karen *ODwPR 91*
Kazmayer, Robert Henderson 1908- *WhoAm 90*
Kazmerski, Lawrence Lee 1945- *WhoAm 90*
Kazmi Syed, Irshad Ali 1938- *WhoWor 91*
Kazmierczak, Kenneth J. 1948- *St&PR 91*
Kazmierczak, Steven Craig 1959- *WhoSSW 91*
Kazmierski, Paul Regis 1936- *WhoE 91*
Kazon, Bernard 1924- *St&PR 91*
Kazor, Virginia Ernst 1940- *WhoAmA 91*
Kazor, Walter Robert 1922- *WhoSSW 91, WhoWor 91*
Kazovsky, Leonid Gregory 1947- *WhoE 91*
Kazovszkij, El 1948- *BiDWomA*
Kazragys, Linda Kayan Bublis 1946- *WhoEmL 91*
Kazuo, Omata 1925- *WhoWor 91*
Kazuyoshi, Kamachi 1925- *WhoWor 91*
Kazzaz, David *BiDrAPA 89*
Kczlowski, Jerzy Marek 1931- *WhoWor 91*
Ke, Paul Jenn 1934- *WhoE 91*
Keach, Benjamin 1640-1704 *BioIn 16*
Keach, Kenneth Lowell 1946- *WhoEmL 91*
Keach, Stacy 1941- *WorAlBi*
Keach, Stacy, Jr. 1941- *WhoAm 90*
Keach, Stacy, Sr. 1914- *WhoAm 90*
Keadle, Homer Lee 1924- *WhoSSW 91*
Keadle, W. Glenn 1950- *St&PR 91*
Keady, George Cregan, Jr. 1924- *WhoAm 90*
Keady, Michael J. 1926- *St&PR 91*
Keady, William C. 1913-1989 *BioIn 16*
Keady, William P. 1850-1917 *AmLegL*
Keala, Francis Ahloy 1930- *WhoAm 90*
Kealey, Steve 1947- *Ballpl 90*
Kealey, Thomas F. 1951- *St&PR 91*
Keally, Francis 1889-1978 *WhoAmA 91N*
Kealy, Arthur Philip 1945- *St&PR 91*
Kealy, William James 1940- *WhoAm 90*
Keam, Thomas V. 1846-1904 *BioIn 16*
Keams, Geraldine *BioIn 16*
Kean, Benjamin Harrison 1912- *WhoAm 90*
Kean, Charles John 1811?-1868 *BioIn 16*
Kean, Charles Thomas 1941- *WhoE 91, WhoWor 91*
Kean, Hamilton Fish 1925- *WhoAm 90, WhoWor 91*
Kean, John *BioIn 16*
Kean, John 1929- *St&PR 91, WhoAm 90*
Kean, John Vaughan 1917- *WhoE 91, WhoWor 91*
Kean, Michael *PenDiDA 89*
Kean, Robert W., Jr. 1922- *St&PR 91*
Kean, Thomas H. *BioIn 16*
Kean, Thomas H. 1935- *WhoAm 90, WhoE 91, WhoWor 91*
Kean, Thomas Joseph 1933- *St&PR 91*
Kean, Vivian Elaine 1945- *WhoE 91*
Kean, Warren Paul 1959- *WhoEmL 91*
Keanan, Staci *BioIn 16*
Keane, Anthony John 1961- *WhoSSW 91*
Keane, Bil *EncACom*
Keane, Bil 1922- *BioIn 16, WhoAm 90, WhoAmA 91*
Keane, Brian *NewAgMG*
Keane, Brian Teagan 1961- *WhoE 91*
Keane, Daniel J. 1939- *St&PR 91, WhoAm 90*
Keane, David *IntWWM 90*
Keane, David L. 1952- *St&PR 91*
Keane, Doris 1881-1945 *BioIn 16, NotWoAT*
Keane, Edmund J., Jr. 1933- *WhoAm 90*
Keane, Edward Webb 1930- *WhoAm 90*
Keane, Frederick William 1958- *WhoEmL 91*
Keane, Glen 1954- *BioIn 16*
Keane, Gregory George 1947- *WhoEmL 91*
Keane, Gustave Robert 1914- *WhoAm 90*
Keane, Helen *BioIn 16*
Keane, James Michael 1938- *St&PR 91*
Keane, John F. 1931- *St&PR 91*
Keane, John G. 1930- *WhoAm 90*
Keane, Johnny 1911-1967 *Ballpl 90*
Keane, Keith M 1920- *BiDrAPA 89*
Keane, Kevin G. 1951- *WhoEmL 91*
Keane, Kevin P. 1954- *St&PR 91*
Keane, Kevin Thomas 1933- *St&PR 91*
Keane, Laura Meacham 1962- *WhoAmW 91*
Keane, Mark Edward 1919- *WhoAm 90*
Keane, Mary Elizabeth 1953- *WhoE 91*
Keane, Michael *BioIn 16*
Keane, Michael 1960- *WhoEmL 91*
Keane, Molly *BioIn 16*
Keane, Molly 1904- *FemiCLE, WorAu 1980 [port]*
Keane, Paul Edward 1938- *St&PR 91*
Keane, Peter Leo 1917- *WhoAm 90*
Keane, Stephen Edward 1943- *St&PR 91*
Keane, Tina 1948?- *BiDWomA*
Keane, Tom *BioIn 16*
Keaney, John Joseph 1932- *WhoAm 90*
Keaney, William Regis 1937- *WhoAm 90, WhoWor 91*
Keany, Sutton 1943- *WhoAm 90*
Kear, Arthur Thomas 1934- *St&PR 91*
Kear, Bernard Henry 1931- *WhoAm 90*
Kear, Carl I. 1904- *St&PR 91*
Kear, Maria Martha Ruscitella 1954- *WhoEmL 91*
Kearfott, Kelly S *BiDrAPA 89*
Kearins, Michael J. 1946- *St&PR 91*
Kearl, Bryant Eastham 1921- *WhoAm 90*
Kearl, Stanley Brandon 1913- *WhoAmA 91, WhoE 91*
Kearney, Annette Gaines 1939- *WhoE 91*
Kearney, Austin E., Jr. 1952- *St&PR 91*
Kearney, Austin Eugene, Jr. 1952- *WhoEmL 91*
Kearney, Bob 1956- *Ballpl 90*
Kearney, Connie W. 1938- *WhoWrEP 89*
Kearney, Edward R. *ODwPR 91*
Kearney, Edward Rutledge 1931- *St&PR 91*
Kearney, Elizabeth Irene 1934- *WhoAmW 91*
Kearney, Gretchen Warner 1955- *WhoAmW 91*
Kearney, Hugh Francis 1924- *WhoAm 90*
Kearney, James T. *BioIn 16*
Kearney, Jennifer Rego 1956- *BiDrAPA 89*
Kearney, John *BioIn 16*
Kearney, John 1924- *WhoAmA 91*
Kearney, John F. 1951- *St&PR 91*
Kearney, John Joseph, Jr. 1924- *St&PR 91, WhoAm 90*
Kearney, John Walter 1924- *WhoAm 90*
Kearney, Joseph Laurence 1927- *WhoAm 90*
Kearney, Judy Miller 1940- *WhoAmW 91*
Kearney, Kevin Joseph Patrick 1935- *WhoWor 91*
Kearney, Lawrence 1789-1868 *BioIn 16*
Kearney, Lawrence Michael 1948- *WhoWrEP 89*
Kearney, Lynn Haigh 1927- *WhoAmA 91*
Kearney, Marietta *BioIn 16*
Kearney, Matthew Bernard 1940- *St&PR 91*
Kearney, Patricia Ann 1943- *WhoAmW 91*
Kearney, Richard Craig 1946- *WhoEmL 91*
Kearney, Richard David 1914- *WhoAm 90*
Kearney, Richard James 1927- *WhoSSW 91, WhoWor 91*
Kearney, Rose Theresa 1951- *WhoAmW 91*
Kearney, Sheila Jane 1961- *WhoEmL 91*
Kearney, Sheila Patricia 1933- *WhoAmW 91*
Kearney, Stephen M. 1956- *St&PR 91*
Kearney, Steve 1958- *WhoSSW 91*
Kearney, William Edward, Jr. 1964- *WhoEmL 91*
Kearney, William J *BiDrAPA 89*
Kearns, Allen 1893-1956 *OxCPMus*
Kearns, Amos R., Jr. 1935- *St&PR 91*
Kearns, David Todd 1930- *St&PR 91, WhoAm 90, WhoE 91, WhoWor 91*
Kearns, Donn Kenyon 1949- *WhoEmL 91*
Kearns, Francis Emner 1905- *WhoAm 90*
Kearns, James Frances 1928- *St&PR 91*
Kearns, James Francis 1928- *WhoAm 90*
Kearns, James Joseph 1924- *WhoAm 90, WhoAmA 91*
Kearns, James Thomas 1938- *St&PR 91*
Kearns, Janet Catherine 1940- *WhoAm 90*
Kearns, Jerome Barton 1939- *WhoAm 90*
Kearns, John Francis, III 1957- *WhoEmL 91*
Kearns, John J., III 1951- *WhoEmL 91*
Kearns, John Joseph 1929- *St&PR 91*
Kearns, John W. 1933- *WhoSSW 91*
Kearns, John William 1935- *WhoSSW 91*
Kearns, Josephine Anna 1954- *WhoWrEP 89*
Kearns, Kenneth D. 1942- *ODwPR 91*
Kearns, Lauri Jones *BiDrAPA 89*
Kearns, Norbert W, Jr. *BiDrAPA 89*
Kearns, Patricia Louise 1944- *WhoAmW 91*
Kearns, Robert Francis 1945- *St&PR 91*
Kearns, Ruth Mary Schiller 1946- *WhoEmL 91, WhoSSW 91*
Kearns, Terrance Brophy 1946- *WhoSSW 91*
Kearns, Thomas Richard 1948- *WhoEmL 91*
Kearns, Vincent E. 1939- *St&PR 91*
Kearns, Warren Kenneth 1929- *St&PR 91, WhoAm 90*
Kearns, William John, Jr. 1940- *WhoE 91*
Kearns, William Michael, Jr. 1935- *WhoAm 90*
Kearns, William Stanley 1941- *WhoE 91*
Kearny, Philip 1815-1862 *BioIn 16*

Kearny, Stephen 1794-1848 *WorAlBi*
Kearny, Stephen Watts 1794-1848 *BioIn 16, WhNaAH*
Kearse, Amalya Lyle 1937- *WhoAm 90, WhoAmW 91*
Kearsley, Barry Andrew *BioIn 16*
Kearsley, Steven N. 1941- *St&PR 91*
Kearton, Reginald R. 1910- *St&PR 91*
Keary, Annie 1825-1879 *FemiCLE*
Keasbey, Aertsen P. *BioIn 16*
Keasing, Dale A. 1943- *St&PR 91*
Keasling, John F. 1931- *St&PR 91*
Keast, Colleen D. *ODwPR 91*
Keat, Diana Pauline 1955- *WhoE 91*
Keat, James Sussman 1929- *WhoE 91*
Keate, Kenneth Earl 1951- *WhoEmL 91*
Keaten, Dennis Earl 1947- *St&PR 91*
Keath, Mary Lee *BioIn 16*
Keathley, Frank Maben, Jr. 1947- *WhoSSW 91*
Keathley, Michael N. 1957- *St&PR 91*
Keathley, Naymond Haskins 1940- *WhoSSW 91*
Keathly, David Mark 1962- *WhoEmL 91*
Keating, Anne Elizabeth 1946- *WhoEmL 91*
Keating, Anne Fraser 1955- *WhoAmW 91*
Keating, Charles H., Jr. *BioIn 16*
Keating, Charles H., Jr. 1923- *News 90 [port]*
Keating, Cornelius F. 1925- *St&PR 91*
Keating, Cornelius Francis 1925- *WhoAm 90*
Keating, Daniel Gerard 1956- *WhoEmL 91*
Keating, Donald Francis 1931- *St&PR 91*
Keating, Edward Thomas 1961- *WhoEmL 91*
Keating, Eugene Kneeland 1928- *WhoAm 90*
Keating, Francis Anthony, II 1944- *WhoAm 90*
Keating, Frank J. 1928- *WhoWor 91*
Keating, Gordon W 1940- *BiDrAPA 89*
Keating, H R F 1926- *MajTwCW, TwCCr&M 91*
Keating, James Bernard 1935- *WhoE 91*
Keating, Janis Lynne 1952- *WhoEmL 91*
Keating, John Richard 1934- *WhoAm 90, WhoSSW 91*
Keating, John Roderick 1941- *WhoWrEP 89*
Keating, John U *BiDrAPA 89*
Keating, Joseph T. 1952- *St&PR 91*
Keating, Joseph William 1939- *St&PR 91*
Keating, K. Murray 1952- *St&PR 91*
Keating, Kenneth Barnard 1900-1975 *BioIn 16*
Keating, Kerry W. 1935- *St&PR 91*
Keating, Larry Grant 1944- *WhoWor 91*
Keating, Laura Anne 1969- *WhoE 91*
Keating, Laurel 1924- *WhoAmW 91*
Keating, Lawrence Alfred 1903-1966 *AuBYP 90*
Keating, Louis Clark 1907- *WhoAm 90*
Keating, Marian *BioIn 16*
Keating, Mary Jo 1952- *ODwPR 91*
Keating, Michael 1943- *ConAu 129*
Keating, Michael Burns 1940- *WhoAm 90*
Keating, Michael Francis 1947- *WhoEmL 91*
Keating, Micheline *BioIn 16*
Keating, Norma *AuBYP 90*
Keating, Patrick 1937- *St&PR 91*
Keating, Paul 1944- *WhoWor 91*
Keating, Ray 1891-1963 *Ballpl 90*
Keating, Raymond John 1931- *St&PR 91*
Keating, Richard P. 1935- *ODwPR 91, St&PR 91*
Keating, Richard W. *WhoAm 90*
Keating, Robert B. 1924- *WhoAm 90*
Keating, Robert E. 1937- *ODwPR 91*
Keating, Robert J. 1918- *St&PR 91*
Keating, Roderic Maurice 1941- *IntWWM 90*
Keating, Salvatrice Farinella 1941- *WhoE 91*
Keating, Thomas E. 1933- *St&PR 91*
Keating, Thomas Edward 1933- *WhoAm 90*
Keating, Thomas J., Jr. 1940- *ODwPR 91*
Keating, Thomas James, Jr. 1940- *WhoE 91*
Keating, Thomas Michael 1949- *WhoEmL 91*
Keating, Thomas Patrick 1917-1984 *DcNaB 1981*
Keating, Thomas Patrick 1949- *WhoEmL 91, WhoSSW 91*
Keating, William *BioIn 16*
Keating, William John 1927- *St&PR 91, WhoAm 90*
Keatinge, Richard *ODwPR 91*
Keatinge, Richard Harte 1919- *WhoAm 90, WhoWor 91*
Keatinge, Robert Reed 1948- *WhoEmL 91*
Keaton, Buster 1895-1966 *BioIn 16, WorAlBi*
Keaton, David L. 1939- *St&PR 91*
Keaton, Diane *BioIn 16*
Keaton, Diane 1946- *WhoAm 90, WorAlBi*
Keaton, Frances Marlene 1944- *WhoAmW 91*
Keaton, Joseph Francis 1895-1966 *BioIn 16*
Keaton, Kenneth Dillard 1953- *WhoEmL 91*
Keaton, Mary Elizabeth 1955- *WhoEmL 91*
Keaton, Michael *BioIn 16*
Keaton, Michael 1951- *WhoAm 90, WorAlBi*
Keaton, Reggie Edward 1959- *WhoEmL 91*
Keaton, Russell 1910-1945 *EncACom*
Keaton, William Capelle, Jr. 1935- *St&PR 91*
Keaton, William Richard 1955- *WhoEmL 91*
Keats, An *BioIn 16*
Keats, Christopher J 1943- *BiDrAPA 89*
Keats, Christopher John 1943- *WhoE 91*
Keats, Donald 1929- *IntWWM 90*
Keats, Donald Howard 1929- *WhoAm 90*
Keats, Douglas Edward 1950- *St&PR 91*
Keats, Ezra 1916-1983 *AuBYP 90*
Keats, Ezra Jack 1916-1983 *BioIn 16, WhoAmA 91N*
Keats, Frank Joseph 1950- *WhoEmL 91, WhoWor 91*
Keats, Harold Alan 1913- *WhoAm 90*
Keats, Joe *WhoWrEP 89*
Keats, John 1795-1821 *BioIn 16, DcLB 96 [port], PoeCrit 1 [port], WorAlBi, WrPh*
Keats, Matthew Mason 1952- *BiDrAPA 89*
Keats, Sheila 1929- *WhoAmW 91*
Keats, Theodore Eliot 1924- *WhoAm 90*
Keaty, Robert Burke 1949- *WhoSSW 91*
Keaty, Thomas St. Paul, II 1943- *WhoSSW 91*
Keaty, William Armshaw 1944- *WhoSSW 91*
Keaveney, David Michael 1935- *St&PR 91*
Keaveney, Sydney Starr 1939- *WhoAmA 91, WhoE 91*
Keaveney, Thomas William 1945- *WhoAm 90*
Keaveny, Denis James 1946- *St&PR 91, WhoAm 90*
Keay, Nigel David 1955- *IntWWM 90*
Keays, Wayne Chesley 1940- *St&PR 91*
Kebabian, Paul Blakeslee 1917- *WhoAm 90*
Kebblish, John Basil 1925- *WhoAm 90, WhoWor 91*
Keber, Kenneth James 1954- *WhoEmL 91*
Keberle, David Scott 1952- *IntWWM 90*
Keble, John 1792-1866 *BioIn 16*
Kecala, Sophia M *BiDrAPA 89*
Kececioglu, Dimitri Basil 1922- *WhoAm 90*
Kechley, David Stevenson 1947- *IntWWM 90*
Kecik, Omer Avni 1926- *BiDrAPA 89*
Keck, Albert Philip 1934- *WhoE 91*
Keck, Barbara Anne 1946- *WhoAmW 91, WhoEmL 91*
Keck, Cactus 1899-1981 *Ballpl 90*
Keck, Charles 1875-1951 *WhoAmA 91N*
Keck, David Randal 1950- *St&PR 91*
Keck, Hardu 1940- *WhoAmA 91, WhoE 91*
Keck, Harry 1897- *Ballpl 90*
Keck, James Collyer 1924- *WhoAm 90*
Keck, James Moulton 1921- *WhoAm 90*
Keck, Jeanne Gentry 1938- *WhoAmA 91*
Keck, John Stanley 1947- *WhoSSW 91*
Keck, Judith Marie Burke 1938- *WhoAmW 91, WhoWor 91*
Keck, Leander Earl 1928- *WhoAm 90*
Keck, Merel Fogg 1928- *WhoAm 90*
Keck, Michael 1946- *ConTFT 8 [port]*
Keck, Otto 1944- *WhoWor 91*
Keck, Paul E, Jr. 1957- *BiDrAPA 89*
Keck, Philip Walter 1947- *WhoEmL 91*
Keck, Richard Paul 1960- *WhoEmL 91*
Keck, Robert Clifton 1914- *WhoAm 90, WhoWor 91*
Keck, Sheldon Waugh 1910- *WhoAmA 91*
Keck, William 1908- *WhoAm 90*
Keckel, Peter J. 1942- *WhoSSW 91*
Keckich, Walter A 1945- *BiDrAPA 89*
Keckley, Elizabeth 1818?-1907 *FemiCLE*
Keckley, James D. 1924- *St&PR 91*
Kecskemeti, Istvan 1920- *IntWWM 90*
Kedderis, Pamela Jean 1956- *WhoAmW 91*
Keddie, Roland Thomas 1928- *WhoAm 90, WhoE 91*
Keddis, Evelyn Nagib *BiDrAPA 89*
Keddy, Wayne Richard 1945- *WhoAm 90*
Keding, Ann Clyrene 1944- *WhoAmW 91*
Kedney, Skip *BioIn 16*
Kedo, Paul Nicholas 1949- *WhoEmL 91*
Kedourie, Elie 1926- *ConAu 31NR*
Kee, Chandra A *BiDrAPA 89*
Kee, Cornelis 1900- *IntWWM 90*
Kee, Gregory Michael 1957- *WhoEmL 91*
Kee, Howard Clark 1920- *WhoAm 90*
Kee, James 1917-1989 *BioIn 16*
Kee, Piet 1927- *IntWWM 90*
Kee, Robert 1919- *ConAu 130*
Kee, Walter Andrew 1914- *WhoAm 90*
Kee Borges, Saundra A. 1959- *WhoEmL 91*
Keeble, Edwin Augustus 1807-1868 *AmLegL*
Keeble, John Robert 1944- *WhoWrEP 89*
Keeble, Kezia *NewYTBS 90 [port]*
Keeble, Sydney Frazer, Jr. 1928- *St&PR 91*
Keebler, Barbara A. *ODwPR 91*
Keebler, Lois Marie 1955- *WhoAmW 91*
Keech, Diana 1945- *IntWWM 90*
Keech, John H 1943- *WhoAmA 91*
Keedwell, Douglas Robert 1920- *St&PR 91*
Keedy, David M 1910- *BiDrAPA 89*
Keedy, Mervin L. 1920- *WhoAm 90*
Keefe, Bob 1882-1964 *Ballpl 90*
Keefe, Dave 1897-1978 *Ballpl 90*
Keefe, George Evans 1909- *WhoWor 91*
Keefe, Harry V. *BioIn 16*
Keefe, Harry Victor, Jr. 1922- *St&PR 91, WhoAm 90, WhoE 91*
Keefe, James Michael 1951- *WhoEmL 91*
Keefe, James Vincent 1936- *St&PR 91*
Keefe, Janet Cathryn 1947- *WhoAmW 91*
Keefe, John Webster 1941- *WhoAm 90*
Keefe, Peter Huntley 1952- *BiDrAPA 89*
Keefe, Roger Manton 1919- *WhoAm 90*
Keefe, Stanley A. 1933- *St&PR 91*
Keefe, Tim 1856-1933 *BioIn 16*
Keefe, Tim 1857-1933 *Ballpl 90 [port]*
Keefe, William Joseph 1925- *WhoAm 90*
Keefer, Brenda Lynn 1948- *BiDrAPA 89*
Keefer, Christine Ann 1962- *WhoWrEP 89*
Keefer, David A. 1948- *St&PR 91*
Keefer, Dwight Edwin 1948- *WhoEmL 91*
Keefer, Ivan Earl 1944- *St&PR 91*
Keefer, R. Scott 1947- *St&PR 91*
Keefer, Rhonda Jean 1959- *WhoAmW 91, WhoEmL 91*
Keefer, Robert Edward 1925- *St&PR 91*
Keefer, Yvonne June Kelsoe 1935- *WhoAmW 91*
Keeffe, Arthur J. *BioIn 16*
Keeffe, Bernard 1925- *IntWWM 90*
Keefover, Marvin Dale 1944- *St&PR 91*
Keefover, Robert Ward *BiDrAPA 89*
Keegan, Bob 1920- *Ballpl 90*
Keegan, Bridget Ann 1951- *WhoAmW 91*
Keegan, David Lloyd 1939- *BiDrAPA 89, WhoAm 90*
Keegan, Dennis F. 1939- *ODwPR 91*
Keegan, Harry E. 1922- *St&PR 91*
Keegan, James B. 1941- *St&PR 91*
Keegan, James Joseph 1947- *WhoEmL 91*
Keegan, Jane Ann 1950- *WhoAmW 91, WhoEmL 91, WhoWor 91*
Keegan, John 1934- *BestSel 90-3 [port], BioIn 16, ConAu 130, WorAu 1980 [port]*
Keegan, K. Brian 1959- *WhoE 91*
Keegan, Marcia 1943- *ConAu 32NR*
Keegan, Peter William 1944- *St&PR 91, WhoAm 90*
Keegan, Richard John 1924- *WhoAm 90*
Keegan, Rita 1949- *BiDWomA*
Keegan, William R. 1955- *ODwPR 91*
Keehn, Neil Francis 1948- *WhoEmL 91*
Keehn, Silas 1930- *St&PR 91, WhoAm 90*
Keehner, Michael Arthur Miller 1943- *St&PR 91, WhoAm 90*
Keel, Alton Gold, Jr. 1943- *WhoAm 90*
Keel, Cheryl Ann 1946- *WhoAmW 91*
Keel, Howard 1917- *OxCPMus, WorAlBi*
Keel, John A 1930- *EncO&P 3*
Keel, Jolene Mar-Jen 1951- *WhoEmL 91*
Keel, Michael C. *St&PR 91*
Keel, Michael Clarence 1940- *WhoAm 90*
Keel, Page Clark, Jr. 1946- *St&PR 91*
Keel, William Clifford 1957- *WhoSSW 91*
Keel-Williams, Mildred Yvonne 1954- *WhoWrEP 89*
Keelan, Kevin Robert 1921- *WhoAm 90*
Keeland, Delpha Florine 1925- *WhoAmW 91*
Keele, Lyndon A. 1928- *St&PR 91*
Keelean, John S. 1939- *St&PR 91*
Keeler, Barbara Allen 1946- *WhoE 91*
Keeler, Christine 1941?- *BioIn 16*
Keeler, Clifford E *BiDrAPA 89*
Keeler, David Boughton 1931- *WhoAmA 91*
Keeler, Fred Ashmead 1925- *St&PR 91*
Keeler, Harry Stephen 1890-1967 *TwCCr&M 91*
Keeler, James L. 1935- *St&PR 91*
Keeler, James Leonard 1935- *WhoAm 90*
Keeler, Janet Bradford 1947- *WhoAmW 91*
Keeler, John F. 1956- *St&PR 91*
Keeler, Kathleen Marie 1957- *WhoAmW 91*
Keeler, Linda Lorene *BiDrAPA 89*
Keeler, Marian Rita 1930- *WhoAmW 91*
Keeler, Martin H 1927- *BiDrAPA 89*
Keeler, Pierre L.O.A. *EncO&P 3*
Keeler, Ronald F. 1913-1983 *BioIn 16*
Keeler, Ruby 1909- *OxCPMus, WorAlBi*
Keeler, Steven Robert 1954- *WhoEmL 91*
Keeler, Theodore Edwin 1945- *WhoAm 90*
Keeler, W Raymond *BiDrAPA 89*
Keeler, Wally *PenDiDA 89*
Keeler, Walter 1942?- *BioIn 16*
Keeler, William Henry 1931- *WhoAm 90, WhoE 91*
Keeler, William M. *EncO&P 3*
Keeler, Willie 1872-1923 *Ballpl 90, WorAlBi*
Keeley, A. H. *WhoWrEP 89*
Keeley, Alvin William 1937- *St&PR 91*
Keeley, Craig Thomas 1952- *WhoE 91*
Keeley, Edmund 1928- *WhoWrEP 89*
Keeley, Edmund LeRoy 1928- *WhoAm 90*
Keeley, John Lemuel 1904- *WhoAm 90*
Keeley, Kim A 1938- *BiDrAPA 89*
Keeley, Michael Clark 1947- *WhoEmL 91*
Keeley, Pamela Ann 1950- *WhoAmW 91*
Keeley, Philip Max 1941- *St&PR 91*
Keeley, Robert Vossler 1929- *WhoAm 90, WhoWor 91*
Keeley, Wayne Joseph 1956- *WhoE 91*
Keeling, Charles David 1928- *WhoAm 90*
Keeling, Faris Eldon 1952- *BiDrAPA 89*
Keeling, Geraldine Ann 1946- *IntWWM 90, WhoEmL 91*
Keeling, Henry Cornelious 1923- *WhoAmA 91*
Keeling, Joe Keith 1936- *WhoAm 90*
Keeling, Marita Jane 1952- *BiDrAPA 89*
Keeling, Terry Lee 1950- *WhoSSW 91*
Keelser, James Martin 1935- *WhoSSW 91*
Keely, Eugene Joseph 1935- *St&PR 91*
Keely, George Clayton 1926- *WhoAm 90*
Keely, John Worrell 1837-1898 *EncO&P 3*
Keem, Michael Dennis 1950- *WhoE 91, WhoEmL 91*
Keen, Brenda Denniston 1949- *WhoAmW 91, WhoEmL 91, WhoSSW 91*
Keen, Charlotte Elizabeth 1943- *WhoAm 90, WhoAmW 91*
Keen, Constantine 1925- *WhoAm 90*
Keen, Constantine 1926- *St&PR 91*
Keen, Cynthia Elaine 1948- *WhoEmL 91*
Keen, Fred J. 1935- *St&PR 91*
Keen, Fred Jacob 1935- *St&PR 91*
Keen, Helen Boyd *WhoAmA 91*
Keen, Howard 1948- *WhoEmL 91*
Keen, Lamont J. 1952- *St&PR 91*
Keen, Leonard 1957- *WhoEmL 91*
Keen, Maria Elizabeth 1918- *WhoAmW 91*
Keen, Martin L. 1913- *AuBYP 90*
Keen, Michael John 1935- *WhoAm 90*
Keen, Vic 1899-1976 *Ballpl 90*
Keena, Janet Laybourn 1928- *WhoAmA 91*
Keenan, Anthony Lee 1949- *WhoEmL 91, WhoWor 91*
Keenan, Beverly Owen 1948- *WhoAmW 91*
Keenan, Boyd Raymond 1928- *WhoAm 90*
Keenan, C. Robert, III 1954- *WhoEmL 91*
Keenan, Clarke Meredith 1946- *St&PR 91*
Keenan, Deborah 1950- *ConAu 30NR*
Keenan, Edmund Terrence 1965- *WhoE 91*
Keenan, Edward Louis 1935- *WhoAm 90*
Keenan, F.D. 1922- *St&PR 91*
Keenan, Gerard Patrick 1945- *WhoWrEP 89*
Keenan, Hugh Thomas 1936- *WhoSSW 91*
Keenan, Jack A. 1915- *St&PR 91*
Keenan, James George 1944- *WhoAm 90*
Keenan, James Ignatius, Jr. 1932- *St&PR 91*
Keenan, James L. 1937- *St&PR 91*
Keenan, James Lee 1937- *WhoAm 90, WhoWor 91*
Keenan, James Robert 1950- *St&PR 91*
Keenan, Joan Marie 1949- *WhoAmW 91*
Keenan, John Fontaine 1929- *WhoAm 90*
Keenan, John H. 1938- *St&PR 91*
Keenan, Joseph T. 1944- *St&PR 91*
Keenan, Kathleen Gloria 1955- *WhoE 91*
Keenan, Kathleen Margaret 1934- *WhoAmW 91*
Keenan, Mary Ann 1950- *WhoAm 90*
Keenan, Michael Edgar 1934- *WhoAm 90, WhoWor 91*
Keenan, Mike *WhoAm 90*
Keenan, P.J. 1932- *St&PR 91*
Keenan, Retha Ellen Vornholt 1934- *WhoAmW 91*
Keenan, Richard Lawrence 1923- *St&PR 91*
Keenan, Robert 1950- *WhoEmL 91*
Keenan, Robert Anthony 1930- *WhoAm 90*
Keenan, Stephen Patrick 1955- *WhoEmL 91*
Keenan, T.J. *St&PR 91*
Keenan, Terence W. 1946- *St&PR 91*
Keenan, Terrance 1924- *WhoAm 90*
Keenan, Willis J. 1918- *St&PR 91*
Keenan-Abilay, Georgia Ann 1936- *WhoAmW 91*
Keene, Bess Ritchey 1926- *WhoSSW 91*

Keene, Charles T. 1945- *ODwPR 91*
Keene, Charles Thornton 1945- *WhoE 91*
Keene, Christopher 1946- *BioIn 16, CurBio 90 [port], IntWWM 90, PenDiMP, WhoAm 90, WhoE 91*
Keene, Clifford Henry 1910- *WhoAm 90, WhoWor 91*
Keene, Darlene Jacqueline *BiDrAPA 89*
Keene, Day *TwCCr&M 91*
Keene, Donald 1922- *BioIn 16*
Keene, Donald L. *St&PR 91*
Keene, Donald Lane 1933- *WhoAm 90*
Keene, Edward F. 1928- *St&PR 91*
Keene, Elizabeth M *BiDrAPA 89*
Keene, Evelyn 1922- *WhoAmW 91*
Keene, Floyd Stanley 1949- *St&PR 91, WhoAm 90*
Keene, Howard B. 1942- *St&PR 91*
Keene, Irene 1953- *WhoWrEP 89*
Keene, James L. 1945- *St&PR 91*
Keene, John Clark 1931- *WhoE 91*
Keene, John Gilbert 1948- *WhoE 91*
Keene, Laura 1826?-1873 *BioIn 16, NotWoAT*
Keene, Margaret Girthel 1915- *WhoAmW 91*
Keene, Mildred T 1928- *BiDrAPA 89*
Keene, Pamela A. 1952- *WhoEmL 91, WhoSSW 91*
Keene, Paul 1920- *WhoAmA 91*
Keene, Robert Gilmore 1917- *WhoE 91*
Keene, Stephen Winslow 1938- *St&PR 91*
Keene, Thomas Joel 1936- *WhoE 91*
Keene, William Blair 1933- *WhoAm 90, WhoE 91*
Keene, William Patrick 1938- *St&PR 91*
Keene-Burgess, Ruth Frances 1948- *WhoAmW 91*
Keenen, Bruce G. 1949- *St&PR 91*
Keenen, George *AuBYP 90*
Keener, Bruce, III 1924- *WhoAm 90*
Keener, Carl L *BiDrAPA 89*
Keener, Charles Richard 1939- *WhoAm 90*
Keener, Jefferson W., Jr. 1932- *St&PR 91*
Keener, Larkelyn 1945- *WhoAmW 91*
Keener, Linda Marie 1953- *WhoAmW 91*
Keener, Marvin Stanford 1943- *WhoSSW 91*
Keener, Polly Leonard 1946- *WhoAmA 91*
Keener, Richard N. 1928- *St&PR 91*
Keener, Robert *ODwPR 91*
Keener, Robert P. 1958- *WhoSSW 91*
Keener, Robert W. 1931- *St&PR 91, WhoAm 90*
Keener, Sid C. 1888- *Ballpl 90*
Keeney, Allen Lloyd 1933- *WhoAmA 91*
Keeney, Arthur Hail 1920- *WhoAm 90, WhoSSW 91*
Keeney, Cecil Madison 1927- *St&PR 91*
Keeney, Dan F 1920- *BiDrAPA 89*
Keeney, Debra Ann 1954- *WhoAmW 91*
Keeney, Dennis Raymond 1937- *WhoAm 90*
Keeney, Edmund Ludlow 1908- *WhoAm 90, WhoWor 91*
Keeney, John Christopher 1922- *WhoAm 90*
Keeney, John Christopher, Jr. 1951- *WhoEmL 91*
Keeney, Kristopher K. 1952- *WhoEmL 91*
Keeney, L. Douglas 1951- *WhoSSW 91*
Keeney, Lafayette 1926- *St&PR 91*
Keeney, Norwood Henry, Jr. 1924- *WhoAm 90*
Keeney, Robert Lee 1955- *WhoE 91*
Keeney, Virginia T *BiDrAPA 89*
Keenlyside, Raymond *PenDiMP*
Keenlyside, Raymond 1928- *IntWWM 90*
Keenon, Una H. R. 1933- *WhoAmW 91*
Keeny, Spurgeon Milton 1893-1988 *BioIn 16*
Keeny, Spurgeon Milton, Jr. 1924- *WhoAm 90*
Keep, Judith N. 1944- *WhoAm 90, WhoAmW 91*
Keeper, Gary *BioIn 16*
Keepers, George Alan 1950- *BiDrAPA 89*
Keepin, George Robert, Jr. 1923- *WhoAm 90*
Keeping, Cecil E. 1948- *St&PR 91*
Keeping, Charles 1924- *BioIn 16*
Keeping, Charles 1924-1988 *AnObit 1988*
Keeping, Sharon Marie 1954- *WhoAmW 91*
Keepper, Lester Haywood, III 1957- *WhoEmL 91*
Keer, Kathleen *WhoWrEP 89*
Keer, Leon Morris 1934- *WhoAm 90*
Keerl, Bayat 1948- *WhoAmA 91*
Keersmaeker, Anne Teresa de *BioIn 16*
Kees, Weldon *BioIn 16*
Keesari, Manohar 1940- *BiDrAPA 89*
Keesee, Allen Randolph Key 1919- *St&PR 91*
Keesee, Christian Kirkpatrick 1961- *WhoSSW 91*
Keesee, Roger N. 1937- *WhoAm 90*
Keesee, Thomas Woodfin, Jr. 1915- *WhoAm 90*
Keesey, Richard L. 1948- *St&PR 91*
Keesey, Ulker Tulunay 1932- *WhoAm 90*
Keeshan, Bob *BioIn 16*
Keeshan, Bob 1927- *WhoAm 90, WorAlBi*
Keeshan, Michael *WhoAm 90*
Keeshan, William Francis, Jr. 1934- *WhoE 91*
Keeshen, Kathleen Kearney 1937- *WhoAmW 91*
Keeshin, Scott Avery 1952- *St&PR 91*
Keesing, Nancy 1923- *FemiCLE*
Keesler, Allen J., Jr. 1938- *St&PR 91*
Keesler, Allen John, Jr. 1938- *WhoAm 90, WhoSSW 91*
Keesler, Lenoir Chambers 1927- *St&PR 91*
Keesling, Francis Valentine, Jr. 1908- *WhoAm 90, WhoWor 91*
Keesling, James Edgar 1942- *WhoSSW 91*
Keesling, Karen Ruth 1946- *WhoAm 90, WhoAmW 91*
Keet, Ernest E. 1941- *St&PR 91*
Keeton, Darra Rathbun 1947- *WhoE 91*
Keeton, David Paul 1944- *WhoE 91*
Keeton, J E *BiDrAPA 89*
Keeton, James Hamilton 1910- *St&PR 91*
Keeton, John Toliver, Jr. 1923- *WhoSSW 91*
Keeton, Kathy Merle 1939- *WhoAmW 91, WhoE 91*
Keeton, Morris Teuton 1917- *WhoAm 90*
Keeton, Robert Ernest 1919- *WhoAm 90*
Keeven, Judy L. *BiDrAPA 89*
Keever, Herbert Weller 1927- *St&PR 91*
Keever, Kim 1950- *WhoAmA 91, WhoE 91*
Keever, Melville Marie 1941- *St&PR 91*
Keevil, N.B., Jr. 1938- *St&PR 91*
Keevil, Norman Bell 1910- *St&PR 91*
Keevil, Norman Bell, Jr. 1938- *WhoAm 90*
Keevil, Philip C. 1946- *St&PR 91*
Keevil, Philip Clement 1946- *WhoAm 90*
Keezer, Ronald N. W. 1940- *IntWWM 90*
Kefala, Antigone 1934- *FemiCLE*
Kefalanitis, Andrew 1949- *St&PR 91*
Kefauver, Alan Pierce 1947- *WhoEmL 91*
Kefauver, Estes 1903-1963 *WorAlBi*
Kefauver, Nancy *WhoAmA 91N*
Kefauver, Weldon Addison 1927- *WhoAm 90*
Keffer, Charles Joseph 1941- *WhoAm 90*
Kegel, Gerhard 1912- *WhoWor 91*
Kegel, Herbert 1920- *IntWWM 90, PenDiMP*
Kegel, Scott R. 1956- *St&PR 91*
Kegel, William George 1922- *WhoAm 90*
Kegeles, Gerson 1917- *WhoAm 90*
Kegerreis, Robert James 1921- *WhoAm 90*
Kegg, James Franklin 1927- *St&PR 91*
Kegler, Brenda Jean 1949- *WhoAmW 91*
Kegler, James Francis 1949- *St&PR 91*
Kegley, Jacquelyn Ann 1938- *WhoAmW 91*
Kegley, James Henry 1912- *St&PR 91*
Kegley, Terry *BioIn 16*
Keh, Milagros S *BiDrAPA 89*
Kehaya, Ery W. 1923- *WhoAm 90, WhoSSW 91*
Kehl, Randall Herman 1954- *WhoEmL 91*
Kehl, Sigrid 1932- *IntWWM 90*
Kehlbeck, Kenneth Alfred 1928- *St&PR 91*
Kehle, Anthony George, III 1938- *WhoAm 90*
Kehle, Mary Jane 1937- *WhoAmW 91*
Kehle, Ralph O. 1934- *St&PR 91*
Kehle, Robert Gordon 1951- *WhoEmL 91*
Kehler, James S 1937- *BiDrAPA 89*
Kehler, Thomas P. 1947- *St&PR 91*
Kehley, Deborah Anne 1966- *WhoAmW 91*
Kehlibareva, Nadya 1933- *EncCoWW*
Kehlmann, Robert 1942- *WhoAmA 91*
Kehm, Walter Carl 1926-1990 *BioIn 16*
Kehm, Walter H. 1937- *WhoAm 90*
Kehne, Christine W 1920- *BiDrAPA 89*
Kehne, W Deaver 1920- *BiDrAPA 89*
Kehnle, Jeffrey Bill 1941- *St&PR 91*
Kehoe, Dennis M. 1949- *St&PR 91*
Kehoe, James W. 1925- *WhoAm 90*
Kehoe, John C. 1953- *St&PR 91*
Kehoe, John E 1933- *BiDrAPA 89*
Kehoe, John Edward 1947- *WhoE 91*
Kehoe, John P. 1938- *ODwPR 91, WhoAm 90*
Kehoe, L. Paul 1938- *WhoE 91*
Kehoe, Michael J *BiDrAPA 89*
Kehoe, Patrice 1952- *WhoAmA 91*
Kehoe, Patricia D. 1951- *ConAu 132*
Kehoe, Steven C. 1955- *WhoEmL 91*
Kehoe, Susan 1947- *WhoAmW 91*
Kehoe, Veronica McAuley *WhoAmW 91*
Kehoe, William Anthony, III 1950- *WhoE 91*
Kehoe, William Francis 1933- *WhoAm 90*
Kehr, Bruce Alan 1949- *BiDrAPA 89*
Kehr, Gunther 1920- *IntWWM 90*
Kehr, Pierre Henri 1937- *WhoWor 91*
Kehrer, Daniel M. 1953- *WhoAm 90, WhoWrEP 89*
Kehrl, Howard Harmon 1923- *WhoAm 90*
Kehrli, Ronald Louis 1932- *WhoAm 90*
Kehs, Michael *ODwPR 91*
Keible, Edward A. 1943- *St&PR 91*
Keicher, Werner Alex 1944- *WhoWor 91*
Keider, Norman B. 1931- *St&PR 91*
Keider, Stephen Philip 1935- *St&PR 91*
Keifer, Mary Carter 1946- *WhoAmW 91*
Keifetz, Corey J. 1951- *St&PR 91*
Keiffer, E. Gene 1929- *St&PR 91*
Keiffer, Edwin Gene 1929- *WhoAm 90, WhoSSW 91*
Keigher, Sharon 1965- *ODwPR 91*
Keighley, Sydney Augustus 1900- *BioIn 16*
Keigler, John E. 1929- *WhoAm 90*
Keil, Alfred Adolf Heinrich 1913- *WhoAm 90*
Keil, Beverly 1946- *WhoAmW 91*
Keil, Charles Emanuel 1936- *WhoAm 90*
Keil, Ernest W *BiDrAPA 89*
Keil, Gordon Bruce 1960- *WhoE 91*
Keil, H H J 1930- *EncO&P 3*
Keil, Jeffrey C. 1943- *WhoAm 90, WhoE 91*
Keil, Jeffrey Craig 1943- *St&PR 91*
Keil, John M. *BioIn 16*
Keil, John Mullan 1922- *WhoAm 90*
Keil, Jurgen 1930- *EncPaPR 91*
Keil, Klaus 1934- *WhoAm 90*
Keil, M. David 1931- *WhoAm 90*
Keil, Robert Matthes 1926- *St&PR 91, WhoAm 90*
Keilberth, Joseph 1908-1968 *PenDiMP*
Keilholtz, Otis 1838?- *AmLegL*
Keilholtz, Patricia Diane 1950- *WhoE 91*
Keilholtz, Scott R. 1936- *St&PR 91*
Keilin, Eugene Jacob 1942- *WhoAm 90*
Keill, Stuart L 1927- *BiDrAPA 89*
Keill, Stuart Langdon 1927- *WhoAm 90*
Keiller, James Bruce 1938- *WhoSSW 91, WhoWor 91*
Keillor, Elaine 1939- *IntWWM 90*
Keillor, Garrison *BioIn 16, MajTwCW*
Keillor, Garrison 1942- *WorAlBi*
Keillor, Garrison Edward 1942- *WhoAm 90*
Keillor, Gary 1942- *MajTwCW*
Keillor, Sharon Ann 1945- *WhoAm 90, WhoE 91*
Keilman, Louis, II 1960- *WhoSSW 91*
Keilman, Robert E. 1945- *St&PR 91*
Keilson, Julian 1924- *WhoAm 90*
Keim, John D. 1945- *St&PR 91*
Keim, Lewis P. 1930- *ODwPR 91*
Keim, Robert Phillip 1920- *WhoAm 90*
Keim, Robert R, Jr. *BiDrAPA 89*
Keim, S.G. 1924- *St&PR 91*
Keim, Wayne Franklin 1923- *WhoAm 90*
Keimach, Brad 1953- *IntWWM 90*
Keimach, Brad M. 1953- *WhoEmL 91*
Keimel, Klaus Heinz 1939- *WhoWor 91*
Keinath, Steven Ernest 1954- *WhoEmL 91*
Keiner, Robert Bruce, Jr. 1942- *WhoAm 90*
Keinlen, Helen Horsley 1927- *WhoAmW 91*
Keino, Kip *BioIn 16*
Keinonen, Mirja Ilona 1949- *WhoWor 91*
Keins, Judith Anne 1956- *BiDrAPA 89*
Keipi, Kari Juhani 1946- *WhoEmL 91*
Keir, Douglas Charles 1949- *WhoSSW 91*
Keir, Duncan Wray 1946- *WhoEmL 91*
Keir, Elizabeth *FemiCLE*
Keir, Rick *ODwPR 91*
Keirnan, Ellen Louise 1949- *WhoAmW 91*
Keirns, Harry D. 1938- *St&PR 91*
Keirstead, Allan Guy 1944- *St&PR 91*
Keirstead, Phillip Owen 1938- *WhoSSW 91*
Keiser, Aelbregt Cornelisz de *PenDiDA 89*
Keiser, Bernhard Edward 1928- *WhoAm 90*
Keiser, Charles Arthur 1943- *St&PR 91*
Keiser, Cornelis *PenDiDA 89*
Keiser, Donald Matson 1939- *St&PR 91*
Keiser, Edmund Davis, Jr. 1934- *WhoAm 90, WhoSSW 91*
Keiser, Harry Robert 1933- *WhoAm 90*
Keiser, Henry Bruce 1927- *WhoE 91, WhoWor 91*
Keiser, John Howard 1936- *WhoAm 90*
Keiser, Karen Lynne 1960- *WhoAmW 91*
Keiser, Kris *DrBIPA 90*
Keiser, Morton 1918- *St&PR 91*
Keiser, Nancy Eyman 1947- *WhoAmW 91*
Keiser, Norman Michael 1919- *St&PR 91, WhoAm 90*
Keiser, Paul David 1955- *WhoEmL 91*
Keiser, Paul Harold 1927- *WhoAm 90*
Keiser, Reinhard 1674-1739 *PenDiMP A*
Keiser, Robert L. 1942- *St&PR 91*
Keiser, Ross Edward 1951- *WhoEmL 91, WhoSSW 91*
Keiser, Stanley Thomas 1950- *WhoEmL 91*
Keiser, Stephen Charles 1955- *St&PR 91*
Keiser, Sylvan *BiDrAPA 89*
Keiser, Sylvan 1907-1990 *BioIn 16*
Keisler, Howard Jerome 1936- *WhoAm 90*
Keisler, Peter Douglas 1960- *WhoEmL 91*
Keisling, Gary M. 1951- *St&PR 91*
Keisling, Robert West 1947- *BiDrAPA 89*
Keisling, William *ODwPR 91*
Keister, Bill 1874-1924 *Ballpl 90*
Keister, David C. 1940- *WhoAm 90*
Keister, Lawrence D. 1950- *St&PR 91*
Keister, Steve 1949- *WhoAmA 91*
Keistler, Betty Lou 1935- *WhoAmW 91*
Keita, Salif *BioIn 16*
Keitel, Harvey 1947- *WhoAm 90, WorAlBi*
Keitel, Wilhelm 1882-1946 *BioIn 16, WorAlBi*
Keiter, Robert Harvey 1941- *BiDrAPA 89*
Keiter, Timothy Stuart 1960- *WhoEmL 91*
Keith, Barry Harold 1954- *WhoE 91*
Keith, Brian 1921- *WorAlBi*
Keith, Brian Michael 1921- *WhoAm 90*
Keith, Carl Walter 1927- *WhoAm 90*
Keith, Carlton *AuBYP 90*
Keith, Charles R 1932- *BiDrAPA 89*
Keith, Clyde H. 1912- *St&PR 91*
Keith, Damon Jerome 1922- *WhoAm 90*
Keith, Dave 1934- *ODwPR 91*
Keith, David *BioIn 16*
Keith, David 1930- *IntWWM 90*
Keith, David 1954- *WorAlBi*
Keith, David Vernon *BiDrAPA 89*
Keith, Debra L. 1956- *WhoEmL 91*
Keith, Donald Raymond 1927- *WhoAm 90*
Keith, Edward Oliver 1951- *WhoSSW 91*
Keith, Elizabeth Miller 1911- *WhoE 91*
Keith, Eros 1942- *BioIn 16, WhoAmA 91*
Keith, Garnett Lee, Jr. 1935- *St&PR 91, WhoAm 90*
Keith, Gordon 1913- *WhoWor 91*
Keith, Hamish *ConAu 33NR*
Keith, Harold Verne 1903- *AuBYP 90*
Keith, Hastings 1915- *WhoAm 90*
Keith, Hosmer H. 1846-1910 *AmLegL*
Keith, Hugh 1950- *St&PR 91*
Keith, J. Kilmeny *TwCCr&M 91*
Keith, James E. 1924- *St&PR 91*
Keith, James French, Jr. 1935- *WhoSSW 91*
Keith, Jennie 1942- *WhoAm 90*
Keith, Juanita Orton 1917- *WhoAmW 91*
Keith, Kenneth James 1937- *WhoWor 91*
Keith, Kent Marsteller 1948- *WhoAm 90, WhoEmL 91, WhoWor 91*
Keith, Lawrence Edward 1945- *WhoSSW 91*
Keith, Leroy, Jr. 1939- *WhoAm 90*
Keith, Marian 1874?-1961 *DcLB 92 [port]*
Keith, Mary Ellen 1938- *WhoAmW 91*
Keith, Michael C 1945- *ConAu 132*
Keith, Minor C. 1848-1929 *WorAlBi*
Keith, Minor Cooper 1848-1929 *BioIn 16*
Keith, Nancy *BioIn 16*
Keith, Nancy 1916-1990 *NewYTBS 90 [port]*
Keith, Paul Richard 1943- *BiDrAPA 89*
Keith, Pauline Mary 1924- *WhoAmW 91*
Keith, Penny Sue 1949- *WhoAmW 91, WhoSSW 91*
Keith, Quentin Gangewere 1919- *WhoE 91*
Keith, Robert Drake 1935- *St&PR 91*
Keith, Robert E. 1941- *St&PR 91*
Keith, Robert M *BiDrAPA 89*
Keith, Robert Ralph 1941- *St&PR 91*
Keith, Robert Taylor Scott *BioIn 16*
Keith, Robert William 1926- *WhoAm 90*
Keith, Samuel John *BiDrAPA 89*
Keith, Slim *BioIn 16*
Keith, Stephen S. 1948- *St&PR 91*
Keith, Susan Beth Knobbs 1951- *WhoAmW 91*
Keith, Theresa Day 1962- *WhoAmW 91*
Keith, Timothy Jones 1948- *St&PR 91*
Keith, Timothy Zook 1952- *WhoEmL 91*
Keith, Warren Gray 1908- *WhoAm 90*
Keith, William John 1934- *WhoWrEP 89*
Keith-Muselin, Brenda Kay 1947- *WhoAmW 91*
Keith-Spiegel, Patricia Cosette *WhoAm 90*
Keithley, Bradford Gene 1951- *St&PR 91, WhoAm 90, WhoSSW 91*
Keithley, George 1935- *WhoWrEP 89*
Keithley, George Frederick 1935- *WhoAm 90*
Keithley, Joseph Faber 1915- *St&PR 91, WhoAm 90*
Keithly, Levi J. 1810?- *AmLegL*
Keitlen, Seymour *BiDrAPA 89*
Keitner, Gabor Istvan 1947- *BiDrAPA 89*
Keizer, Aelbregt Cornelisz de *PenDiDA 89*
Keizer, Cornelis *PenDiDA 89*
Keizer, Garret *BioIn 16*
Keizer, Joel Edward 1942- *WhoAm 90*
Kekes, John 1936- *WhoAm 90*
Kekich, Mike 1945- *Ballpl 90*
Kekst, Gershon 1934- *WhoAm 90, WhoWor 91*
Kekule, Friedrich August 1829-1896 *BioIn 16*
Kekule Von Stradonitz, Friedrich August 1829-1896 *WorAlBi*
Kelada, Nadine Helmy *BiDrAPA 89*

Kelahan, John Anthony, Jr. 1952- *WhoE 91, WhoEmL 91*
Kelaiditis, Anestis 1948- *WhoWor 91*
Kelalis, Barbara Anna Lisa 1940- *WhoSSW 91, WhoWor 91*
Kelalis, Panayotis 1932- *WhoAm 90*
Kelbaugh, Douglas Stewart 1945- *WhoAm 90*
Kelbley, Stephen Paul 1942- *WhoAm 90*
Kelby, David E. 1937- *St&PR 91*
Kelch, Ray Alden 1923- *WhoAm 90*
Kelch, Robert Paul 1942- *WhoAm 90*
Kelchner, Charles *Ballpl 90*
Kelchner, Diane Lynn 1956- *WhoAmW 91, WhoE 91*
Kelchner, Rod C. *WhoAm 90*
Kelder, Diane M 1934- *WhoAmA 91*
Kelder, Maarten Albert 1963- *WhoE 91*
Kelder, William Richard 1948- *St&PR 91*
Kele, Judit *BioIn 16*
Kelehan, James Lawrence 1914- *WhoAm 90*
Kelehear, Carole Marchbanks Spann 1945- *WhoAmW 91*
Keleher, James P. 1931- *WhoAm 90*
Keleher, Michael Cassat 1955- *WhoSSW 91*
Kelejian, Harry Herand 1937- *WhoE 91*
Kelemen, Charles F. 1943- *WhoAm 90*
Kelemen, Eugene 1899- *BiDrAPA 89*
Kelemen, Milko 1924- *PenDiMP A*
Kelemen, Pal 1894- *WhoAm 90, WhoAmA 91*
Kelemen, Zoltan 1926-1979 *PenDiMP*
Kelen, Emery 1896-1978 *AuBYP 90*
Kelen, Erwin Anton 1935- *St&PR 91*
Keler, Marianne Martha 1954- *WhoEmL 91*
Keleti, Georg 1925- *WhoE 91*
Keligian, David Leo 1956- *WhoEmL 91*
Kelk, Constantin 1943- *WhoWor 91*
Kell, Adolf Heinrich Karl 1934- *WhoWor 91*
Kell, Carla Sue 1952- *WhoAmW 91*
Kell, Ernest Eugene, Jr. 1928- *WhoAm 90*
Kell, George 1922- *Ballpl 90 [port]*
Kell, James Herbert 1930- *WhoAm 90, WhoWor 91*
Kell, Jean Bruyere 1909- *WhoWrEP 89*
Kell, John F., Jr. 1937- *St&PR 91*
Kell, John McIntosh 1823-1900 *BioIn 16*
Kell, Joseph *MajTwCW*
Kell, Reginald 1906-1981 *PenDiMP*
Kella, John J. 1948- *WhoE 91*
Kella, John Jake 1948- *IntWWM 90*
Kellaigh, Kathleen 1955- *WhoAmW 91*
Kellam, Diane Celine Fidi 1950- *WhoAmW 91*
Kellam, Lucius James 1911- *St&PR 91*
Kellam, Lucius James, Jr. 1911- *WhoWor 91*
Kellam, Sheppard G *BiDrAPA 89*
Kellams, Daniel R. *ODwPR 91*
Kellams, Jeffrey J 1944- *BiDrAPA 89*
Kelland, Michael B. 1943- *St&PR 91*
Kelland, Michael Buckner 1943- *WhoAm 90, WhoWor 91*
Kellar, Elizabeth Kaenzig 1948- *WhoEmL 91*
Kellar, Gerald Dean 1916- *WhoSSW 91*
Kellar, Jeff 1949- *WhoAmA 91*
Kellar, Lorrence T. 1937- *St&PR 91*
Kellar, Lorrence Theodore 1937- *WhoAm 90*
Kellar, Marshal M. 1932- *St&PR 91*
Kellar, Mary L. 1920- *WhoSSW 91*
Kellar, Paul Timothy 1950- *WhoEmL 91*
Kellar, Steven Marshal 1956- *St&PR 91*
Kellaway, Cecil 1894-1973 *WorAlBi*
Kellbach, Harley H. 1922- *St&PR 91*
Kelleher, Debra Lee 1958- *WhoAmW 91, WhoEmL 91*
Kelleher, Edward J *BiDrAPA 89*
Kelleher, Frank 1937- *IntWWM 90*
Kelleher, Hal 1913- *Ballpl 90*
Kelleher, Herbert David 1931- *St&PR 91, WhoAm 90, WhoSSW 91*
Kelleher, James Joseph 1958- *WhoEmL 91*
Kelleher, James P. 1914- *WhoWrEP 89*
Kelleher, John 1949- *WhoEmL 91*
Kelleher, John Edward, Jr. *BiDrAPA 89*
Kelleher, Judith Charlene 1923- *WhoAmW 91*
Kelleher, Karen A. 1948- *St&PR 91*
Kelleher, Kathleen 1951- *WhoEmL 91, WhoWor 91*
Kelleher, Kevin John 1953- *WhoE 91*
Kelleher, Kevin John 1954- *WhoE 91*
Kelleher, Lisa Ann 1960- *WhoAmW 91, WhoEmL 91*
Kelleher, Michael Joseph 1933- *WhoSSW 91*
Kelleher, Mick 1947- *Ballpl 90*
Kelleher, Patrick Joseph 1917-1985 *WhoAmA 91N*
Kelleher, Richard Cornelius 1949- *WhoEmL 91, WhoWor 91*
Kelleher, Robert J. *BioIn 16*
Kelleher, Robert Joseph 1913- *WhoAm 90*
Kelleher, Thomas F. 1923- *WhoAm 90, WhoE 91*
Kelleher, Thomas M. 1953- *St&PR 91*
Kelleher, Thomas Patrick 1964- *WhoE 91*
Kelleher, Timothy John 1940- *St&PR 91, WhoAm 90*
Kelleher, Timothy Joseph 1954- *WhoEmL 91*
Kelleher, Victor 1939- *BioIn 16*
Kellen, Michael Leo 1948- *St&PR 91*
Kellen, Stephen Max 1914- *St&PR 91, WhoAm 90*
Kellens, Georges 1941- *WhoWor 91*
Keller, Alan Seth 1950- *BiDrAPA 89*
Keller, Alex Stephen 1928- *WhoAm 90*
Keller, Alfred 1882- *BioIn 16*
Keller, Alfred S. 1911-1989 *BioIn 16*
Keller, Alfred Samuel 1911- *WhoAm 90*
Keller, Alvin G. 1909- *St&PR 91*
Keller, Arthur Michael 1957- *WhoEmL 91, WhoWor 91*
Keller, Barbara Alexander 1931- *St&PR 91*
Keller, Ben Robert, Jr. 1936- *WhoSSW 91*
Keller, Beverly L. *AuBYP 90*
Keller, Bill *WhoAm 90, WhoE 91, WhoWor 91*
Keller, Bradly Jay 1953- *BiDrAPA 89*
Keller, Bruce Alan 1950- *St&PR 91*
Keller, Bryan J. 1950- *WhoAm 90*
Keller, C. Graden, Jr. 1949- *WhoSSW 91*
Keller, Carl Albert 1920- *WhoWor 91*
Keller, Carl H 1931- *BiDrAPA 89*
Keller, Charles 1942- *AuBYP 90*
Keller, Charles Henry 1947- *WhoWrEP 89*
Keller, Charles Walter 1925- *WhoAm 90*
Keller, Charlie *NewYTBS 90 [port]*
Keller, Charlie 1916- *Ballpl 90*
Keller, Charlie 1916-1990 *BioIn 16*
Keller, Christoph, Jr. 1915- *WhoAm 90*
Keller, Clarence Cornelius 1930- *St&PR 91*
Keller, Dale *BioIn 16*
Keller, Daniel R. 1949- *St&PR 91*
Keller, Darla Lynn 1956- *WhoAmW 91*
Keller, David M. 1941- *WhoWrEP 89*
Keller, David Wayne 1960- *WhoEmL 91*
Keller, Deane 1901- *WhoAmA 91*
Keller, Deane Galloway *BioIn 16*
Keller, Dennis James 1941- *WhoWor 91*
Keller, Donald H. 1933- *St&PR 91*
Keller, Donald John 1932- *WhoAm 90*
Keller, Donald R. 1943- *St&PR 91*
Keller, Donald S. 1939- *St&PR 91*
Keller, Edward Clarence, Jr. 1932- *WhoAm 90*
Keller, Edward Lowell 1939- *WhoAm 90*
Keller, Eliot Aaron 1947- *WhoAm 90*
Keller, Elizabeth Ann 1949- *WhoEmL 91*
Keller, F. Merrill 1937- *WhoSSW 91*
Keller, Frances Ruth 1911- *AuBYP 90*
Keller, Frank S 1951- *WhoAmA 91*
Keller, Frank Steven 1948- *WhoEmL 91*
Keller, Gary 1941- *St&PR 91*
Keller, Gary Aron *BiDrAPA 89*
Keller, Gary Charles 1942- *WhoSSW 91*
Keller, Gary D. 1943- *ConAu 131, HispWr 90, WhoHisp 91*
Keller, Gary William 1948- *WhoSSW 91*
Keller, George *DcScanL*
Keller, George Charles 1928- *WhoE 91*
Keller, George Henrik 1931- *WhoAm 90*
Keller, George M. 1923- *St&PR 91*
Keller, George Matthew 1923- *WhoAm 90*
Keller, Glen Elven, Jr. 1938- *WhoAm 90*
Keller, Glenn Walter 1944- *St&PR 91*
Keller, Greta 1913-1977 *OxCPMus*
Keller, H. Dietz 1908- *St&PR 91*
Keller, Heinrich 1940- *IntWWM 90*
Keller, Helen 1880-1967 *EncAL*
Keller, Helen 1880-1968 *BioIn 16, MajTwCW, WorAlBi*
Keller, Helen Adams 1880-1968 *BioAmW*
Keller, Henry A. *BioIn 16*
Keller, Henry Frederick 1933- *St&PR 91*
Keller, Henry Fredrick 1933- *St&PR 91*
Keller, Henry G 1870-1949 *WhoAmA 91N*
Keller, Holly *AuBYP 90, BioIn 16*
Keller, Ignacio Javier 1702-1759 *EncCRAm*
Keller, J Michael 1944- *BiDrAPA 89*
Keller, Jack 1928- *WhoAm 90*
Keller, Jackie 1940- *St&PR 91*
Keller, Jaime Roberto 1936- *WhoWor 91*
Keller, James B. 1944- *St&PR 91*
Keller, James J. 1948- *St&PR 91*
Keller, James T. *St&PR 91*
Keller, James Wesley 1958- *WhoEmL 91, WhoWor 91*
Keller, Jay Arthur 1939- *WhoAm 90*
Keller, Jimmy Ray 1952- *WhoEmL 91*
Keller, John Caldwell 1965- *WhoSSW 91*
Keller, John Francis 1925- *WhoAm 90*
Keller, John Greenway, Jr. 1958- *WhoAm 90*
Keller, John J. 1918- *St&PR 91*
Keller, John Mahlon 1939- *WhoAm 90*
Keller, John Paul 1939- *St&PR 91*
Keller, John Richard 1924- *WhoE 91*
Keller, Jorgen Rothe Keith 1924- *WhoWor 91*
Keller, Joseph A. 1926- *St&PR 91*
Keller, Joseph Bishop 1923- *WhoAm 90*
Keller, Joseph Steve 1935- *St&PR 91*
Keller, Joyce Garver 1947- *WhoAmW 91*
Keller, Kaufman Thuma 1885-1966 *EncABHB 5 [port]*
Keller, Kenneth Harrison 1934- *WhoAm 90*
Keller, Kenneth John 1950- *WhoEmL 91*
Keller, Kent Earl 1936- *BiDrAPA 89*
Keller, Kjell 1942- *IntWWM 90*
Keller, Kurt Joseph 1925- *St&PR 91*
Keller, Larry Jay 1941- *St&PR 91*
Keller, Lawrence G. 1934- *ODwPR 91*
Keller, LeRoy 1905- *WhoAm 90, WhoWor 91*
Keller, Lora *ODwPR 91*
Keller, Loretta Schertz 1928- *WhoAmW 91*
Keller, Louis William 1931- *St&PR 91*
Keller, Lynn Robin 1952- *WhoEmL 91*
Keller, Margaret Gilmer 1911- *WhoAmW 91, WhoE 91, WhoWor 91*
Keller, Margaret Marie 1944- *WhoAmW 91*
Keller, Marian Jean 1953- *WhoEmL 91*
Keller, Marisa *ODwPR 91*
Keller, Mark 1907- *WhoE 91*
Keller, Martha *WhoAmA 91*
Keller, Martin Barry *BiDrAPA 89*
Keller, Mary Lynn 1958- *WhoAmW 91*
Keller, Michael 1934- *ODwPR 91*
Keller, Michael A. 1945- *IntWWM 90*
Keller, Michael Alan 1945- *WhoE 91*
Keller, Michael Goldwyn 1947- *St&PR 91*
Keller, Michael John 1966- *WhoSSW 91*
Keller, Michael Roger 1952- *WhoSSW 91*
Keller, Mollie *BioIn 16*
Keller, Myla 1932- *BioIn 16*
Keller, Neil Richard 1954- *St&PR 91*
Keller, Niklaus J A 1923- *BiDrAPA 89*
Keller, Pamela Diane 1958- *WhoAmW 91*
Keller, Patricia *BioIn 16*
Keller, Paul 1921- *WhoAm 90*
Keller, Reed T. 1938- *WhoAm 90*
Keller, Rene 1926- *WhoWor 91*
Keller, Renee Susan 1960- *WhoAmW 91*
Keller, Richard B. 1929- *St&PR 91*
Keller, Richard Charles 1937- *WhoAm 90*
Keller, Richard W. 1950- *ODwPR 91*
Keller, Robert 1942- *WhoE 91*
Keller, Robert A 1940- *BiDrAPA 89*
Keller, Robert Alexander 1930- *St&PR 91*
Keller, Robert John 1913- *WhoAm 90*
Keller, Robert Joseph 1930- *St&PR 91*
Keller, Robert L. 1946- *St&PR 91*
Keller, Robert R. 1913- *St&PR 91*
Keller, Robert Scott 1945- *WhoEmL 91, WhoWor 91*
Keller, Robert Thomas 1950- *BiDrAPA 89*
Keller, Robert Wayne *BiDrAPA 89*
Keller, Ronald 1958- *WhoWor 91*
Keller, Ronald L. 1943- *St&PR 91*
Keller, Ross W. 1940- *St&PR 91*
Keller, Roy Alan 1928- *WhoAm 90*
Keller, Sebastian *PenDiDA 89*
Keller, Shelly B. 1948- *WhoEmL 91*
Keller, Stanley 1938- *WhoAm 90*
Keller, Stephen Francis 1938- *WhoAm 90*
Keller, Stephen P. 1942- *St&PR 91*
Keller, Steven Leigh 1947- *BiDrAPA 89*
Keller, Steven Ray 1947- *WhoSSW 91*
Keller, Susan Agnes 1952- *WhoAmW 91*
Keller, Teresa Gale 1958- *WhoAmW 91*
Keller, Thomas *BioIn 16*
Keller, Thomas 1924-1989 *AnObit 1989*
Keller, Thomas Clements 1938- *St&PR 91, WhoAm 90*
Keller, Thomas Franklin 1931- *WhoAm 90, WhoSSW 91*
Keller, Thomas J. 1940- *ODwPR 91*
Keller, Thomas Walter, II 1952- *WhoE 91*
Keller, Tillman J., III 1941- *St&PR 91*
Keller, Tim A. 1942- *St&PR 91*
Keller, Timothy W 1939- *BiDrAPA 89*
Keller, Wanda Kate 1961- *WhoAmW 91*
Keller, Wayne F 1937- *BiDrAPA 89*
Keller, William D. 1934- *WhoAm 90*
Keller, William Francis 1922- *WhoAm 90*
Keller, William G. 1915- *St&PR 91*
Keller, William K *BiDrAPA 89*
Keller, William Martin 1916- *WhoAm 90*
Keller, William Martin, Jr. 1940- *St&PR 91*
Keller-Cohen, Deborah 1948- *WhoEmL 91*
Keller-Harris, Karen Louise 1958- *WhoEmL 91*
Keller Sarmiento, Carlos Oscar 1934- *WhoE 91*
Kellerhals, Bernhard Emanuel 1933- *WhoWor 91*
Kellerman, Christopher Allan 1942- *St&PR 91*
Kellerman, David 1918- *St&PR 91*
Kellerman, Edgar A *BiDrAPA 89*
Kellerman, Faye 1952- *TwCCr&M 91*
Kellerman, Hillel 1956- *St&PR 91*
Kellerman, Joan M. 1953- *WhoAmW 91*
Kellerman, Jonathan 1949- *TwCCr&M 91*
Kellerman, Jonathan Seth 1949- *WhoAm 90*
Kellerman, Sally 1937- *WorAlBi*
Kellerman, Sally Claire 1937- *WhoAm 90, WhoAmW 91*
Kellerman, Sylvia 1920- *St&PR 91*
Kellermann, Donald S. *ODwPR 91*
Kellermann, Kenneth Irwin 1937- *WhoAm 90*
Kellermann, Robert F. 1948- *St&PR 91*
Kellermeyer, Robert William 1929- *WhoAm 90*
Kellers, Kathleen Marie 1956- *WhoAmW 91*
Kellerthaler, Daniel 1575?-1651? *PenDiDA 89*
Kellerthaler, Hans 1562?-1611 *PenDiDA 89*
Kellett, David Lee 1961- *WhoSSW 91*
Kellett, Edgar A. 1951- *St&PR 91*
Kellett, Edgar W. 1912- *St&PR 91*
Kellett, Morris C. 1935- *WhoAm 90*
Kellett, William Hiram, Jr. 1930- *WhoAm 90, WhoWor 91*
Kelley, Albert Benjamin 1936- *WhoAm 90*
Kelley, Albert D. 1858-1925 *AmLegL*
Kelley, Albert Joseph 1924- *St&PR 91, WhoAm 90*
Kelley, Alfred 1789-1859 *EncABHB 6 [port]*
Kelley, Alice Mary 1920- *WhoAmW 91*
Kelley, Allen Charles 1937- *WhoAm 90*
Kelley, Aloysius Paul 1929- *WhoAm 90, WhoE 91*
Kelley, Amy Rickly 1962- *BiDrAPA 89*
Kelley, Arleon Leigh 1935- *WhoE 91*
Kelley, Arthur Evans 1949- *BiDrAPA 89*
Kelley, B. G. *WhoWrEP 89*
Kelley, Bernard Inui 1935- *WhoSSW 91*
Kelley, Betty Marie 1955- *WhoAmW 91*
Kelley, Bobbe Jone 1952- *BiDrAPA 89*
Kelley, Brenda Carole 1945- *WhoAmW 91*
Kelley, Bridget Ann 1955- *WhoEmL 91*
Kelley, Brooks Mather 1929- *WhoE 91*
Kelley, Bruce Gunn 1954- *St&PR 91, WhoEmL 91*
Kelley, Christine Ruth 1951- *WhoAmW 91, WhoEmL 91*
Kelley, Christopher Donald 1957- *WhoE 91, WhoEmL 91*
Kelley, Clarence M. *BioIn 16*
Kelley, Colin Thomas *BiDrAPA 89*
Kelley, Dale Russell 1939- *WhoSSW 91*
Kelley, Dan B. 1938- *St&PR 91*
Kelley, Daniel James 1949- *WhoEmL 91*
Kelley, Daniel M. 1925- *St&PR 91*
Kelley, Daniel McCann 1925- *WhoAm 90*
Kelley, David *BioIn 16*
Kelley, David Lee 1936- *St&PR 91, WhoAm 90*
Kelley, Dean Maurice 1926- *WhoAm 90*
Kelley, Deborah Maverick 1953- *WhoAmA 91*
Kelley, DeForest 1920- *BioIn 16, ConTFT 8, WorAlBi*
Kelley, Dick 1940- *Ballpl 90*
Kelley, Donald Castell *WhoAmA 91*
Kelley, Donald Eugene 1937- *WhoSSW 91*
Kelley, Donald Hayden 1929- *WhoAm 90*
Kelley, Donald Reed 1931- *WhoAm 90*
Kelley, Donald William 1939- *WhoAmA 91*
Kelley, Edith 1884-1956 *FemiCLE*
Kelley, Edith Summers 1884-1956 *LiHiK*
Kelley, Edward Watson, Jr. 1932- *WhoAm 90, WhoWor 91*
Kelley, Emma Dunham *FemiCLE*
Kelley, Estel W. 1917- *St&PR 91*
Kelley, Eugene John 1922- *WhoAm 90, WhoSSW 91*
Kelley, Everette Eugene 1938- *WhoAm 90*
Kelley, Florence 1859-1932 *BioAmW, EncAL*
Kelley, Frank *BioIn 16*
Kelley, Frank Joseph 1924- *WhoAm 90*
Kelley, G. Daniel, Jr. 1940- *WhoAm 90*
Kelley, G. Larry 1916- *St&PR 91*
Kelley, G. Richard 1932- *St&PR 91*
Kelley, Gaynor N. 1931- *St&PR 91*
Kelley, Gaynor Nathaniel 1931- *WhoAm 90, WhoE 91*
Kelley, Georgia 1947- *WhoAmW 91*
Kelley, Glen P. 1948- *St&PR 91*
Kelley, Harold Harding 1921- *WhoAm 90*
Kelley, Harry 1906-1958 *Ballpl 90*
Kelley, J Whitney 1909- *BiDrAPA 89*
Kelley, Jackson DeForest 1920- *WhoAm 90*
Kelley, Jacquelyn Larson 1945- *WhoEmL 91*
Kelley, Jacquie *WhoAmW 91*
Kelley, James Charles, III 1940- *WhoAm 90*
Kelley, James Edward 1951- *WhoSSW 91*
Kelley, James Francis 1941- *St&PR 91, WhoAm 90*
Kelley, James G. 1948- *St&PR 91*

Kelley, James H. 1939- St&PR 91
Kelley, James J., Jr. 1949- WhoWrEP 89
Kelley, James Michael 1950- WhoEmL 91
Kelley, James R. AmLegL
Kelley, James William 1922- WhoSSW 91
Kelley, Jay Hilary 1920- WhoAm 90
Kelley, Jean Ann Jacobs 1930- WhoSSW 91
Kelley, Jerry Francis 1933- St&PR 91
Kelley, Joe 1871-1943 Ballpl 90 [port]
Kelley, John A. 1949- St&PR 91
Kelley, John Byron 1961- WhoEmL 91
Kelley, John Dearing, Jr. 1932- WhoAm 90
Kelley, John Dennis 1900- WhoAm 90
Kelley, John F 1931- BiDrAPA 89
Kelley, John H. 1941- St&PR 91
Kelley, John Joseph, Jr. 1936- WhoAm 90
Kelley, John L. 1918- St&PR 91
Kelley, John Paul 1919- WhoAm 90
Kelley, John R., Jr. 1949- St&PR 91
Kelley, Joseph Cosgrove 1949- St&PR 91
Kelley, Joseph George, Jr. 1924- St&PR 91
Kelley, Joseph Patrick 1929- WhoE 91
Kelley, Joseph V. 1922- St&PR 91
Kelley, Kate 1955- WhoWrEP 89
Kelley, Kathleen BioIn 16
Kelley, Kathleen Ann ODwPR 91
Kelley, Kathleen Marie BiDrAPA 89
Kelley, Kevin Patrick 1954- WhoEmL 91
Kelley, Kitty BioIn 16
Kelley, Lavern 1928- MusmAFA
Kelley, Leigh Barton 1950- WhoSSW 91
Kelley, Leldon Stratton 1955- WhoEmL 91
Kelley, Linda Eileen 1950- WhoAmW 91, WhoEmL 91
Kelley, Lyn Schraff 1956- WhoAmW 91
Kelley, Marian Herbst 1959- WhoAmW 91
Kelley, Mariceleste 1948- WhoEmL 91
Kelley, Mark A 1940- BiDrAPA 89
Kelley, Marsha Christine 1965- WhoAmW 91
Kelley, Martha Maywood 1947- St&PR 91
Kelley, Maurice Leslie, Jr. 1924- WhoAm 90, WhoWor 91
Kelley, Melissa ODwPR 91
Kelley, Michael Curtis 1947- WhoWor 91
Kelley, Michael Dwaine 1945- St&PR 91
Kelley, Michael J. 1951- St&PR 91
Kelley, Michael James 1955- WhoEmL 91
Kelley, Michael John 1942- WhoAm 90
Kelley, Michael L. Stephen 1952- St&PR 91
Kelley, Michael T. 1952- St&PR 91
Kelley, Michael Vincent 1951- WhoEmL 91
Kelley, Mike 1954- WhoAmA 91
Kelley, Nanette Noland 1958- WhoSSW 91
Kelley, Noble Henry 1901- WhoAm 90
Kelley, Norman 1917- IntWWM 90
Kelley, Patricia Hagelin 1953- WhoAmW 91
Kelley, Paul Joseph 1941- St&PR 91
Kelley, Paul Reed 1945- BiDrAPA 89
Kelley, Paul Xavier 1928- WhoAm 90
Kelley, Peggy Elaine 1960- WhoEmL 91
Kelley, Phil O. 1950- St&PR 91
Kelley, Phillip Gregory 1948- WhoEmL 91
Kelley, R. Leslie BioIn 16
Kelley, Ramon 1939- WhoAmA 91
Kelley, Ray ConAu 31NR
Kelley, Richard Allen, Jr. 1954- WhoEmL 91
Kelley, Richard Gilbert 1931- St&PR 91, WhoAm 90
Kelley, Richard M. 1932- ODwPR 91
Kelley, Richard Roy 1933- WhoAm 90
Kelley, Robb Beardsley 1917- St&PR 91, WhoAm 90
Kelley, Robert E. 1938- WhoAm 90
Kelley, Robert Edward, Jr. 1947- WhoEmL 91
Kelley, Robert L BiDrAPA 89
Kelley, Robert Lloyd 1925- WhoAm 90
Kelley, Robert Otis 1944- WhoAm 90
Kelley, Ronald Lee 1939- BiDrAPA 89
Kelley, Samuel Keith 1957- BiDrAPA 89
Kelley, Sandra Dee 1937- WhoAmW 91
Kelley, Sean Patrick 1957- St&PR 91
Kelley, Severance B 1934- BiDrAPA 89
Kelley, Sheila S. ODwPR 91
Kelley, Sheila Seymour St&PR 91, WhoAmW 91, WhoE 91
Kelley, Stafford K. 1932- St&PR 91
Kelley, Steve BioIn 16
Kelley, Terry G. 1940- ODwPR 91
Kelley, Timothy A. 1954- WhoE 91
Kelley, Timothy Edward 1954- WhoEmL 91
Kelley, Timothy Joseph 1950- St&PR 91
Kelley, Tom 1944- Ballpl 90
Kelley, Vincent Charles 1916- WhoAm 90
Kelley, W. Michael 1947- St&PR 91
Kelley, Wallace Ryan 1950- WhoEmL 91
Kelley, Wayne Plumbley, Jr. 1933- WhoAm 90
Kelley, Wendell J. 1926- St&PR 91, WhoAm 90
Kelley, Wilbur E. BioIn 16
Kelley, William Frederick 1914- WhoAm 90
Kelley, William Lewis 1932- WhoWor 91
Kelley, William Nimmons 1939- WhoAm 90
Kelley, William Rufus, Jr. 1950- WhoEmL 91
Kelley, William Thomas 1917- WhoAm 90
Kellgren, George Lars 1943- WhoSSW 91, WhoWor 91
Kellgren, Johan Henric 1751-1795 DcScanL
Kelliher, Daniel Joseph, Jr. 1944- St&PR 91
Kelliher, Donald J. 1943- St&PR 91
Kelliher, John M. 1951- St&PR 91
Kelliher, Lyle F. 1945- St&PR 91
Kelliher, Peter Maurice 1912- WhoAm 90
Kelling, David Henry 1953- WhoEmL 91, WhoSSW 91
Kelling, Douglas G BiDrAPA 89
Kellison, Donna Louise George 1950- WhoAmW 91, WhoEmL 91
Kellison, James Bruce 1922- WhoAm 90
Kellison, Stephen George 1942- WhoAm 90
Kellman, Barnet BioIn 16
Kellman, Barnet Kramer 1947- WhoAm 90
Kellman, Brian 1945- WhoEmL 91
Kellman, Cheryl Anne 1962- WhoAmW 91
Kellman, H David BiDrAPA 89
Kellman, Ira Stuart 1940- WhoE 91
Kellman, Jerold L. 1945- WhoWrEP 89
Kellman, Joseph 1920- WhoAm 90
Kellman, Mark Alec 1953- WhoEmL 91
Kellman, Steven G. 1947- WhoSSW 91
Kelln, Albert Lee 1929- WhoAm 90
Kellner, Aaron 1914- WhoAm 90
Kellner, Alex 1924- Ballpl 90
Kellner, Alison Bender ODwPR 91
Kellner, Allen 1915- St&PR 91
Kellner, Charles Horn BiDrAPA 89
Kellner, Douglas Ernest 1956- WhoE 91
Kellner, Eileen Wynne 1929- WhoAmW 91
Kellner, George Andrew 1942- St&PR 91
Kellner, Henry L. 1905- St&PR 91
Kellner, Irwin L. 1938- St&PR 91, WhoAm 90
Kellner, Jack 1957- WhoEmL 91
Kellner, Richard George 1943- WhoWor 91
Kellner, Robert BiDrAPA 89
Kellner, Robert Dean 1956- WhoSSW 91
Kellner, Robert Douglas 1940- WhoSSW 91
Kellner, Robert G. 1953- St&PR 91
Kellner, Robert Scott 1941- WhoAm 90
Kello, Esther 1571-1624 BiDEWW
Kellock, Alan Converse 1942- WhoAm 90
Kellock, Judith Graham 1952- IntWWM 90
Kellog, Chester Elijah 1888-1948 EncPaPR 91
Kellogg, Ansel Nash 1832-1886 BioIn 16
Kellogg, Bruce Michael 1947- WhoEmL 91, WhoWor 91
Kellogg, C. Burton, II 1934- St&PR 91
Kellogg, C.T. 1931- St&PR 91
Kellogg, Cal Stewart 1947- IntWWM 90
Kellogg, Carol Kay 1941- WhoAm 90
Kellogg, Clara 1842-1916 PenDiMP
Kellogg, Claude Carroll 1935- St&PR 91
Kellogg, Dorothy M. 1920- WhoAmW 91
Kellogg, Douglas Elliott 1919- St&PR 91
Kellogg, Dwight Alva 1940- St&PR 91
Kellogg, Ensign Hosmer 1812-1881 AmLegL
Kellogg, Fernanda Wanamaker Munn BioIn 16
Kellogg, Frank B. 1856-1937 WorAlBi
Kellogg, Frank Billings 1856-1937 BiDrUSE 89, BioIn 16
Kellogg, Frederic Hartwell 1904- WhoAm 90
Kellogg, Frederic Rogers 1942- WhoAm 90
Kellogg, Gene AuBYP 90
Kellogg, George A. BioIn 16
Kellogg, George W BiDrAPA 89
Kellogg, Harold Field BioIn 16
Kellogg, Harry E. 1923- St&PR 91
Kellogg, Herbert Humphrey 1920- WhoAm 90
Kellogg, Jean 1916-1978 AuBYP 90
Kellogg, Jimmie Dale 1949- WhoSSW 91
Kellogg, John Harvey 1852-1943 NewAgE 90, WorAlBi
Kellogg, John Mahon, Jr. 1929- St&PR 91
Kellogg, Josiah 1831-1890 AmLegL
Kellogg, Marjorie Bradley BioIn 16
Kellogg, Marjorie Bradley 1946- NotWoAT
Kellogg, Mark BioIn 16
Kellogg, Mark Wentworth 1942- St&PR 91
Kellogg, Martin Nykes 1930- St&PR 91
Kellogg, Maurice Dale 1919-1984 WhoAmA 91N
Kellogg, Nancy Jean 1957- WhoAmW 91
Kellogg, Oliver P. 1830- AmLegL
Kellogg, Pamela P 1952- BiDrAPA 89
Kellogg, Peter Newman 1956- WhoE 91
Kellogg, Peter R. 1942- WhoAm 90
Kellogg, Ralph Henderson 1920- WhoAm 90
Kellogg, Robert Leland 1928- WhoAm 90
Kellogg, Robert LeRoy 1952- WhoEmL 91
Kellogg, Robert Towne BiDrAPA 89
Kellogg, Steven 1941- AuBYP 90, BioIn 16
Kellogg, Tommy Nason 1936- St&PR 91, WhoAm 90
Kellogg, Will Keith BioIn 16
Kellogg, Will Keith 1860-1951 NewAgE 90, WorAlBi
Kellogg, William K., III 1930- St&PR 91
Kellogg, William Welch 1917- WhoAm 90
Kellogg-Smith, Peter 1920- WhoE 91, WhoWor 91
Kellor, Frances Alice 1873-1952 BioIn 16
Kellow, James Harry 1939- WhoAm 90, WhoWor 91
Kellow, Martha Shaffer 1954- WhoE 91
Kells, Doris M BiDrAPA 89
Kells, Peter Charles 1938- St&PR 91
Kells, Phyllis Elaine 1932- WhoAmW 91
Kellum, C. Richard 1926- St&PR 91
Kellum, Carmen Kaye 1952- WhoAmW 91, WhoEmL 91
Kellum, Norman Bryant, Jr. 1937- WhoSSW 91
Kellum, Ron McFarlin 1952- WhoEmL 91
Kellum, Win 1876-1951 Ballpl 90
Kelly, Alan D. 1957- ODwPR 91
Kelly, Alan W. 1948- WhoE 91
Kelly, Alex R 1917- BiDrAPA 89
Kelly, Alison Mary 1955- WhoAmW 91
Kelly, Alonzo Hyatt, Jr. 1922- WhoAm 90
Kelly, Anastasia Donovan 1949- WhoAmW 91
Kelly, Andrew Dighton 1926- St&PR 91
Kelly, Anne C. 1916- WhoAmW 91
Kelly, Anthony Odrian 1935- WhoAm 90
Kelly, Arleen P WhoAmA 91
Kelly, Armandine Frances 1947- WhoWrEP 89
Kelly, Arthur Lloyd 1937- WhoAm 90, WhoWor 91
Kelly, Arthur Paul 1938- WhoAm 90
Kelly, Aurel Maxey 1923- WhoAm 90
Kelly, Austin Patrick, Jr. 1935- St&PR 91
Kelly, Barbara Reynolds 1953- WhoAmW 91
Kelly, Belinda Sue 1949- WhoSSW 91
Kelly, Bernard J. 1936- St&PR 91
Kelly, Bob 1927- Ballpl 90
Kelly, Bonnie Davis 1959- WhoSSW 91
Kelly, Brenda Joyce 1950- WhoAmW 91
Kelly, Brian Christopher 1951- St&PR 91
Kelly, Brian Daniel 1956- WhoE 91
Kelly, Brian J. 1934- St&PR 91
Kelly, Bruce 1949- BioIn 16
Kelly, Bryan 1934- IntWWM 90
Kelly, Buena V. EarBlAP
Kelly, Burton Vincent 1932- WhoAm 90
Kelly, Carl Neal 1937- St&PR 91
Kelly, Carol White 1946- WhoAmW 91
Kelly, Carolyn BiDrAPA 89
Kelly, Catherine M. BioIn 16
Kelly, Catherine Makem 1948- WhoAmW 91
Kelly, Charles ODwPR 91
Kelly, Charles 1937- ODwPR 91
Kelly, Charles Arthur 1932- WhoAm 90, WhoWor 91
Kelly, Chester John 1952- WhoEmL 91
Kelly, Christine Ann 1952- WhoAmW 91
Kelly, Colleen BioIn 16
Kelly, Colleen Phyllis 1955- WhoEmL 91
Kelly, Coriene 1926- St&PR 91
Kelly, Cynthia Ference WhoAmA 91
Kelly, Dan BioIn 16
Kelly, Dan Michael 1946- St&PR 91
Kelly, Daniel Grady, Jr. 1951- WhoAm 90, WhoEmL 91
Kelly, Daniel Joseph WhoAm 90
Kelly, David Austin 1938- St&PR 91, WhoAm 90
Kelly, David Marsh 1841- AmLegL
Kelly, David Michael 1938- WhoWrEP 89
Kelly, Deborah E. 1946- ODwPR 91
Kelly, Deborah Elise 1946- St&PR 91
Kelly, Declan Patrick 1943- WhoWor 91
Kelly, Dee J. 1929- WhoAm 90, WhoSSW 91
Kelly, Dennis John 1947- WhoE 91
Kelly, Dennis P. 1946- St&PR 91
Kelly, Dennis Patricia 1945- WhoEmL 91
Kelly, Dennis Ray 1948- WhoEmL 91, WhoWor 91
Kelly, Donald P. BioIn 16
Kelly, Donald Philip 1922- St&PR 91, WhoAm 90
Kelly, Doris L. 1921- WhoE 91, WhoWor 91
Kelly, Dorothy Ann 1929- WhoAm 90, WhoAmW 91
Kelly, Dorothy Helen 1944- WhoAmW 91
Kelly, Douglas Laird 1949- WhoEmL 91
Kelly, Dwight Franklin 1945- WhoSSW 91
Kelly, Eamon Michael 1936- WhoAm 90, WhoSSW 91, WhoWor 91
Kelly, Edgar B. 1942- St&PR 91
Kelly, Edmund Joseph 1937- WhoAm 90, WhoWor 91
Kelly, Edward F. 1940- EncPaPR 91
Kelly, Edward Francis 1932- WhoE 91
Kelly, Edward John, V 1936- WhoSSW 91
Kelly, Edward Thomas 1957- St&PR 91
Kelly, Edwin Frost 1946- WhoEmL 91
Kelly, Eileen Patricia 1955- WhoAmW 91, WhoSSW 91, WhoWor 91
Kelly, Eleanor Mercein 1880-1968 LiHiK
Kelly, Ellen Veronica 1937- WhoE 91
Kelly, Ellsworth 1923- WhoAm 90, WhoAmA 91, WorAlBi
Kelly, Emmett 1898-1979 WorAlBi
Kelly, Eric Damian 1947- WhoEmL 91, WhoWor 91
Kelly, Eric Philbrook 1884-1960 AuBYP 90
Kelly, Eugene Walter, Jr. 1936- WhoAm 90
Kelly, Eula Mae Currie 1906- WhoAmW 91
Kelly, Florence Finch 1858-1939 BioIn 16
Kelly, Francis Daniel 1909- WhoAm 90
Kelly, Francis J., Jr. 1929- St&PR 91, WhoE 91
Kelly, Francis Thomas 1947- WhoEmL 91
Kelly, Francis W 1913- BiDrAPA 89
Kelly, Frank Bryan 1957- WhoSSW 91
Kelly, Frank J. 1948- WhoAm 90, WhoEmL 91
Kelly, Frank Joseph, Jr. 1944- WhoSSW 91
Kelly, Franklin Wood 1953- WhoAm 90, WhoAmA 91, WhoE 91
Kelly, Frederick W. 1937- St&PR 91
Kelly, Gary Clayton 1955- St&PR 91
Kelly, Gary M. 1934- St&PR 91
Kelly, Gene 1912- BioIn 16, OxCPMus, WorAlBi
Kelly, Gene Curran 1912- WhoAm 90
Kelly, George 1895-1984 Ballpl 90 [port]
Kelly, George 1897-1954 WorAlBi
Kelly, George Anthony 1916- AuBYP 90, WhoAm 90, WhoWrEP 89
Kelly, George Armstrong 1932-1987 BioIn 16
Kelly, George E. 1908- St&PR 91
Kelly, George Philip 1944- BiDrAPA 89
Kelly, Georgia NewAgMG
Kelly, Gerald James 1947- St&PR 91
Kelly, Gerald Wayne 1944- WhoSSW 91, WhoWor 91
Kelly, Grace 1929-1982 BioAmW, BioIn 16, WorAlBi
Kelly, Gwen 1922- FemiCLE
Kelly, H A 1934- ConAu 30NR
Kelly, H Vincent 1933- BiDrAPA 89
Kelly, Hamilton M 1936- BiDrAPA 89
Kelly, Harley Lawrence 1937- WhoSSW 91
Kelly, Harold Vernon 1931- WhoAm 90
Kelly, Helen I. 1947- WhoAm 90
Kelly, Henry Aloysius 1921- WhoSSW 91
Kelly, Henry Ansgar 1934- WhoAm 90
Kelly, Herman 1951- WhoEmL 91
Kelly, Hugh Padraic 1931- WhoAm 90
Kelly, Hugh Rice 1942- WhoAm 90
Kelly, Irene M. 1949- WhoSSW 91
Kelly, Isaac Perry 1925- WhoAmA 91
Kelly, Isabella BioIn 16
Kelly, Isabella 1758?-1857 FemiCLE
Kelly, J. Fredrick, Jr. 1950- St&PR 91
Kelly, J.J., III 1945- St&PR 91
Kelly, J. Ronald ODwPR 91
Kelly, Jack Edward 1946- WhoEmL 91
Kelly, James 1913- WhoAm 90, WhoAmA 91
Kelly, James A. 1932- St&PR 91
Kelly, James Andrew 1936- WhoAm 90
Kelly, James Arthur, Jr. 1934- WhoAm 90
Kelly, James Barton 1927- St&PR 91, WhoAm 90
Kelly, James Christopher 1939- St&PR 91
Kelly, James Curry 1956- IntWWM 90
Kelly, James Dewitt 1918- St&PR 91
Kelly, James Edward BiDrAPA 89
Kelly, James Edward 1944- St&PR 91
Kelly, James F. 1922- St&PR 91
Kelly, James Joseph, Jr. 1951- WhoAm 90
Kelly, James McGirr WhoAm 90
Kelly, James Michael 1947- WhoEmL 91
Kelly, James Patrick 1946- WhoEmL 91
Kelly, James Patrick, Jr. 1933- WhoAm 90
Kelly, Jean McCormick 1938- WhoAmW 91, WhoSSW 91
Kelly, Jeffrey AuBYP 90
Kelly, Jeffrey Stephen 1947- St&PR 91
Kelly, Jerome Joseph BiDrAPA 89
Kelly, Jerrold J. 1930- St&PR 91
Kelly, Jim DrBlPA 90
Kelly, Joan Larson 1927- WhoE 91
Kelly, Joe 1886-1977 Ballpl 90
Kelly, Joel 1944- St&PR 91
Kelly, John 1856-1926 Ballpl 90
Kelly, John Alexander, Jr. 1953- WhoE 91
Kelly, John C., Jr. 1936- St&PR 91

Kelly, John Charles 1928- *WhoWor 91*
Kelly, John David, Jr. 1941- *St&PR 91*
Kelly, John F 1931- *BiDrAPA 89*
Kelly, John F. 1939- *ODwPR 91*
Kelly, John Fleming 1926- *WhoAm 90*
Kelly, John Fredrick 1933- *St&PR 91*
Kelly, John G. *ODwPR 91*
Kelly, John G. 1927- *St&PR 91*
Kelly, John Hubert 1939- *WhoAm 90, WhoWor 91*
Kelly, John Keene 1938- *ODwPR 91*
Kelly, John P. 1935- *St&PR 91*
Kelly, John Patrick 1924- *WhoAm 90*
Kelly, John Patrick 1933- *WhoAm 90*
Kelly, John Thomas *BiDrAPA 89*
Kelly, John Thomas 1925- *St&PR 91*
Kelly, Jonathan R *BiDrAPA 89*
Kelly, Jonathan Richard 1949- *WhoEmL 91*
Kelly, Joseph Edward 1937- *WhoAm 90*
Kelly, Joseph Elton, III 1927- *St&PR 91*
Kelly, Joseph Francis, Jr. 1938- *WhoAm 90*
Kelly, Joseph John 1948- *WhoWrEP 89*
Kelly, Josephine Kaye 1944- *WhoAmW 91*
Kelly, Junea Wangeman 1886-1969 *BioIn 16*
Kelly, Kate 1950- *WhoEmL 91*
Kelly, Kathleen *BioIn 16*
Kelly, Kathleen Anne 1955- *WhoWor 91*
Kelly, Kathleen C. 1947- *St&PR 91*
Kelly, Kathleen Margaret 1921- *WhoE 91*
Kelly, Kathleen Sue 1943- *WhoAmW 91, WhoE 91*
Kelly, Kathryn 1953- *WhoEmL 91*
Kelly, Kathryn Elizabeth 1958- *WhoEmL 91*
Kelly, Keith John 1954- *WhoE 91*
Kelly, Kenneth Constantine 1928- *WhoAm 90*
Kelly, Kenneth James 1932- *St&PR 91*
Kelly, Kevin 1934- *ConAu 130, WhoAm 90*
Kelly, Kevin Blake 1959- *WhoSSW 91*
Kelly, Kevin Richard 1949- *WhoAm 90*
Kelly, Kevin Thomas 1960- *WhoE 91, WhoEmL 91*
Kelly, Kevin Vincent 1951- *BiDrAPA 89*
Kelly, King 1857-1894 *Ballpl 90 [port]*
Kelly, L. Thomas 1945- *WhoAm 90, WhoE 91*
Kelly, Lawrence B *BiDrAPA 89*
Kelly, Lawrence Joseph 1933- *St&PR 91*
Kelly, Lee F. 1942- *St&PR 91*
Kelly, Leontine T. C. *WhoAm 90, WhoAmW 91*
Kelly, Leslie Ray 1941- *St&PR 91*
Kelly, Lewis Andrew 1943- *WhoSSW 91*
Kelly, Lucie Stirm Young 1925- *WhoAm 90*
Kelly, Luther Wrentmore, Jr. 1925- *WhoAm 90*
Kelly, Margaret 1898-1990 *BioIn 16, NewYTBS 90*
Kelly, Margaret D *BiDrAPA 89*
Kelly, Marguerite Stehli 1931- *WhoAmW 91*
Kelly, Marilyn Veronica 1947- *WhoAmW 91*
Kelly, Mark E. 1947- *St&PR 91*
Kelly, Mark Hamilton 1953- *WhoSSW 91*
Kelly, Martin J, Jr. *BiDrAPA 89*
Kelly, Mary 1927- *TwCCr&M 91*
Kelly, Mary 1941- *BiDWomA*
Kelly, Mary 1955- *WhoE 91*
Kelly, Mary Jo 1947- *WhoWrEP 89*
Kelly, Mary Lee 1949- *WhoWrEP 89*
Kelly, Mary Louise 1952- *WhoAmW 91*
Kelly, Matthew Edward 1928- *WhoAm 90*
Kelly, Mattie Caroline May 1912- *WhoAmW 91*
Kelly, Maureen Ann 1965- *WhoAmW 91*
Kelly, Maureen C. 1944- *St&PR 91*
Kelly, Maxine Ann 1931- *WhoAmW 91*
Kelly, Mercedes *BioIn 16*
Kelly, Michael *ODwPR 91*
Kelly, Michael 1762-1826 *PenDiMP*
Kelly, Michael Garcin 1946- *WhoSSW 91*
Kelly, Michael John 1928- *St&PR 91*
Kelly, Mike 1857-1894 *BioIn 16*
Kelly, Moira 1951- *WhoAmA 91*
Kelly, Neil Joseph 1940- *St&PR 91*
Kelly, Pamela Sue 1953- *WhoAmW 91*
Kelly, Patricia *WhoWrEP 89*
Kelly, Patricia 1935- *ODwPR 91*
Kelly, Patricia Ann 1953- *WhoEmL 91*
Kelly, Patricia Marguerite Mary 1930- *WhoAmW 91*
Kelly, Patrick *BioIn 16, TwCCr&M 91*
Kelly, Patrick *NewYTBS 90 [port]*
Kelly, Patrick 1954?-1990 *CurBio 90N, News 90*
Kelly, Patrick Chastain 1947- *WhoSSW 91*
Kelly, Patrick J. 1926- *WhoAm 90*
Kelly, Patrick Richard 1959- *WhoWor 91*
Kelly, Patrick T. 1935- *St&PR 91*
Kelly, Paul E. 1912- *St&PR 91*
Kelly, Paul Edward 1912- *WhoAm 90, WhoWor 91*
Kelly, Paul Howard 1947- *IntWWM 90*
Kelly, Paul Knox 1940- *WhoAm 90, WhoE 91, WhoWor 91*
Kelly, Paul L. 1956- *St&PR 91*
Kelly, Paul Lance 1939- *St&PR 91*
Kelly, Paul Thomas 1936- *St&PR 91*
Kelly, Paul Timothy 1958- *WhoEmL 91*
Kelly, Paula 1943- *DrBIPA 90*
Kelly, Prescott Vail 1943- *WhoE 91*
Kelly, Preston W. 1936- *St&PR 91*
Kelly, Quentin Patrick 1959- *WhoEmL 91*
Kelly, Ray *ConAu 31NR*
Kelly, Ray 1914-1988 *Ballpl 90*
Kelly, Raymond Boone, III 1947- *WhoSSW 91*
Kelly, Raymond Francis 1939- *St&PR 91*
Kelly, Raymond John, III 1943- *WhoAm 90*
Kelly, Richard 1937- *WhoWrEP 89*
Kelly, Richard 1957- *WhoE 91*
Kelly, Richard Baskott 1946- *WhoAm 90*
Kelly, Richard Evans 1943- *St&PR 91*
Kelly, Richard S. 1951- *St&PR 91*
Kelly, Richard Smith 1925- *WhoAm 90*
Kelly, Robert 1916- *IntWWM 90*
Kelly, Robert 1934- *WhoWrEP 89*
Kelly, Robert 1935- *WhoAm 90, WorAu 1980 [port]*
Kelly, Robert A. 1931- *ODwPR 91*
Kelly, Robert B. *BioIn 16*
Kelly, Robert Dale, Sr. 1949- *WhoEmL 91*
Kelly, Robert Donald 1929- *WhoAm 90*
Kelly, Robert E. 1926- *WhoWrEP 89*
Kelly, Robert Emmett 1929- *WhoAm 90*
Kelly, Robert F. 1930- *St&PR 91*
Kelly, Robert Francis 1958- *WhoEmL 91*
Kelly, Robert H. 1929- *St&PR 91*
Kelly, Robert J. *WhoAm 90, WhoE 91*
Kelly, Robert Joseph 1957- *WhoEmL 91*
Kelly, Robert Kevin 1946- *WhoSSW 91*
Kelly, Robert Lynn 1939- *WhoAm 90, WhoE 91*
Kelly, Robert Thomas 1924- *WhoAm 90*
Kelly, Robert Timothy 1953- *St&PR 91*
Kelly, Robert Vincent, Jr. 1938- *St&PR 91, WhoAm 90, WhoWor 91*
Kelly, Robert Weber 1916- *St&PR 91, WhoSSW 91*
Kelly, Roberto 1964- *Ballpl 90*
Kelly, Roberto Conrado 1964- *WhoHisp 91*
Kelly, Rochelle-Louise 1961- *WhoAmW 91*
Kelly, Ronald Vincent 1936- *St&PR 91*
Kelly, Ruth Eileen 1921- *St&PR 91*
Kelly, Sally Marie *WhoAmW 91*
Kelly, Sandra L. 1957- *St&PR 91*
Kelly, Sean *BioIn 16*
Kelly, Shannon Lynn 1956- *WhoAmW 91*
Kelly, Sharon Lee 1965- *WhoAmW 91*
Kelly, Sharon Marie 1950- *WhoEmL 91*
Kelly, Stephen John 1940- *WhoE 91*
Kelly, Stewart Ragan 1957- *WhoSSW 91*
Kelly, Susan Croce 1947- *ConAu 129, ODwPR 91, WhoAmW 91*
Kelly, Susan Kathleen 1961- *WhoSSW 91*
Kelly, Suzanne Woodward 1946- *WhoAmW 91*
Kelly, Sylvia Hayden Neahr 1938- *WhoWrEP 89*
Kelly, Tammas *BiDrAPA 89*
Kelly, Teresa Sparks 1963- *WhoAmW 91*
Kelly, Thomas A. 1951- *St&PR 91*
Kelly, Thomas Brooke 1943- *WhoAm 90*
Kelly, Thomas Cajetan 1931- *WhoAm 90, WhoSSW 91*
Kelly, Thomas Charles 1952- *WhoEmL 91*
Kelly, Thomas Francis 1942- *St&PR 91*
Kelly, Thomas J. *BioIn 16*
Kelly, Thomas J. 1927- *St&PR 91*
Kelly, Thomas Jervey 1938- *BiDrAPA 89*
Kelly, Thomas Jesse, Jr. 1941- *WhoAm 90*
Kelly, Thomas Joseph, III 1947- *WhoAm 90*
Kelly, Thomas Mortimer 1953- *WhoE 91*
Kelly, Thomas Paine, Jr. 1912- *WhoAm 90*
Kelly, Timothy Michael 1947- *WhoAm 90, WhoEmL 91*
Kelly, Tom 1950- *Ballpl 90*
Kelly, Vernon C, Jr. 1944- *BiDrAPA 89*
Kelly, Viana Eileen 1953- *WhoAmW 91, WhoEmL 91*
Kelly, Victor Clayton, Jr. 1943- *St&PR 91*
Kelly, Vincent Michael, Jr. 1933- *WhoSSW 91*
Kelly, W. Richard, Jr. 1929- *St&PR 91*
Kelly, Wallace McElroy 1910- *LiHiK*
Kelly, Walt 1913-1973 *EncACom [port]*
Kelly, Walter R. 1926- *St&PR 91*
Kelly, Wanda Sue 1948- *WhoEmL 91*
Kelly, William 1914- *WhoAm 90, WhoSSW 91, WhoWor 91*
Kelly, William A 1935- *BiDrAPA 89*
Kelly, William Charles, Jr. 1946- *WhoEmL 91*
Kelly, William Clark 1922- *WhoAm 90*
Kelly, William Crowley 1929- *WhoAm 90*
Kelly, William E 1914- *BiDrAPA 89*
Kelly, William F., III 1951- *St&PR 91*
Kelly, William Harold 1926- *WhoAm 90*
Kelly, William Joseph 1943- *WhoAmA 91*
Kelly, William L *BiDrAPA 89*
Kelly, William M., Jr. 1929- *WhoAm 90*
Kelly, William P. *BioIn 16*
Kelly, William R. 1905- *WhoAm 90*
Kelly, William Russell 1906- *ConAmBL*
Kelly, William S. 1948- *ODwPR 91*
Kelly, William Watkins 1928- *WhoAm 90*
Kelly, Winfield M. 1935- *WhoE 91*
Kelm, Bonnie G 1947- *WhoAmA 91*
Kelm, George 1928- *St&PR 91*
Kelm, Jack *BioIn 16*
Kelm, Linda 1944- *WhoAm 90*
Kelman, Arthur 1918- *WhoAm 90*
Kelman, David 1934- *St&PR 91*
Kelman, Gary Allen 1951- *WhoE 91*
Kelman, Harvey *BiDrAPA 89*
Kelman, Herbert Chanoch 1927- *WhoAm 90*
Kelman, John Brian 1957- *WhoE 91*
Kelman, John Matheson 1938- *St&PR 91*
Kelman, Norman 1914- *BiDrAPA 89*
Kelman, Wolfe 1923-1990 *BioIn 16, NewYTBS 90*
Kelmenson, Leo-Arthur 1927- *WhoAm 90, WhoE 91*
Kelmenson, Lita 1932- *WhoAmA 91*
Kelms, Betty Jo 1945- *St&PR 91*
Kelne, Nathan 1918- *WhoAm 90*
Kelnhofer, Maria Ibanez *BiDrAPA 89*
Kelpe, Paul 1902-1985 *WhoAmA 91N*
Kelpe, Paul Robert 1948- *WhoEmL 91*
Kels, Hans *PenDiDA 89*
Kelsall, Tabitha *BiDEWW*
Kelsay, Royal Edward 1930- *St&PR 91*
Kelsen, Peter Foster 1956- *WhoEmL 91*
Kelsey, Alice 1896- *AuBYP 90*
Kelsey, Barbara Helen 1926- *St&PR 91*
Kelsey, Clyde Eastman, Jr. 1924- *WhoAm 90*
Kelsey, F. A. D. 1928- *ODwPR 91*
Kelsey, Floyd Lamar, Jr. 1925- *WhoAm 90*
Kelsey, Frances Oldham 1914- *WhoAmW 91*
Kelsey, Henry 1667?-1724 *EncCRAm*
Kelsey, Henry 1667?-1729 *WhNaAH*
Kelsey, Jarel Robert 1937- *St&PR 91*
Kelsey, John *EncABHB 4*
Kelsey, John L. 1925- *St&PR 91*
Kelsey, Julie Ann 1961- *WhoAmW 91*
Kelsey, Linda Miller 1938- *WhoE 91*
Kelsey, Mary F. 1925- *St&PR 91*
Kelsey, Maynard James 1939- *St&PR 91*
Kelsey, Robert Louis 1930- *St&PR 91*
Kelsh, Karen Teresa 1963- *WhoAmW 91, WhoEmL 91*
Kelshaw, Terence *WhoAm 90*
Kelsky, Richard Brian 1955- *WhoEmL 91*
Kelso, Alec John 1930- *WhoAm 90*
Kelso, Ann Breeding 1945- *WhoSSW 91*
Kelso, Bill 1940- *Ballpl 90*
Kelso, David William 1948- *WhoAmA 91*
Kelso, Eveline Maria 1951- *WhoEmL 91*
Kelso, Frank Benton, II 1933- *WhoAm 90, WhoWor 91*
Kelso, Gwendolyn Lee 1935- *WhoAmW 91*
Kelso, Harold Glen 1929- *WhoAm 90*
Kelso, J. Richard *WhoAm 90*
Kelso, James Richard 1949- *St&PR 91*
Kelso, John Hodgson 1925- *WhoAm 90*
Kelso, John Morris 1922- *WhoAm 90*
Kelso, Louis Orth 1913- *WhoAm 90, WhoWor 91*
Kelso, Terry A. 1948- *St&PR 91*
Kelsoe, John Rice, Jr. *BiDrAPA 89*
Kelson, Allen Howard 1940- *WhoAm 90, WhoWrEP 89*
Kelt, Sidney Arthur 1957- *BiDrAPA 89*
Kelter, Jolie *BioIn 16*
Kelterborn, Rudolf 1931- *IntWWM 90*
Keltner, David E. 1950- *WhoEmL 91*
Keltner, J. Robert 1921- *St&PR 91*
Keltner, Judith *ODwPR 91*
Keltner, Ken 1916- *Ballpl 90*
Keltner, Raymond Marion, Jr. 1929- *WhoAm 90*
Keltner, Richard *WhoAm 90*
Keltner, Thomas Nethery, Jr. 1946- *WhoEmL 91*
Kelton, Arthur Marvin, Jr. 1939- *WhoWor 91*
Kelton, Beulah Mai Hogan 1929- *IntWWM 90*
Kelton, David J. 1925- *St&PR 91*
Kelton, Elmer 1926- *BioIn 16*
Kelts, Susan Margaret 1949- *WhoAmW 91*
Keltsch, Donald Robert 1924- *St&PR 91*
Keltsch, Maurice Carl 1927- *St&PR 91*
Kelty, Karen Ann 1946- *St&PR 91*
Kelty, Mary Ann 1789-1873 *FemiCLE*
Kelty, Michael P. 1950- *St&PR 91*
Kelty, Paul David 1947- *WhoEmL 91*
Keltz, Martin J. 1944- *St&PR 91*
Keltz, Michael J. *St&PR 91*
Kelvin, William Thomson 1824-1907 *WorAlBi*
Kelvin, William Thomson, Baron 1824-1907 *BioIn 16*
Kelwala, Surendra 1951- *BiDrAPA 89*
Kelz, Arnold 1933- *BiDrAPA 89*
Kem, Richard Samuel 1934- *WhoAm 90*
Kemal, Yasar 1923- *WhoWor 91*
Kemball, Christopher 1946- *WhoAm 90*
Kemball, Christopher Ross 1946- *St&PR 91*
Kemble, Adelaide 1814?-1879 *BioIn 16, PenDiMP*
Kemble, Adelaide 1816-1879 *FemiCLE*
Kemble, Ernest Dell 1935- *WhoAm 90*
Kemble, Fanny 1809-1893 *BioIn 16*
Kemble, Fanny 1809-1903 *FemiCLE*
Kemble, John Hasking *NewYTBS 90*
Kemble, John Hasking 1912-1990 *BioIn 16*
Kemble, Maria Theresa 1775-1838 *FemiCLE*
Kemble, Richard 1932- *WhoAmA 91*
Kemble, Robert D *BiDrAPA 89*
Kemble, Stephen Brooks 1947- *BiDrAPA 89, WhoEmL 91*
Kemble-Heisinger, Anne 1956- *WhoAmW 91*
Kemelhor, Robert Elias 1919- *WhoE 91*
Kemelman, Harry 1908- *TwCCr&M 91, WhoAm 90, WhoWrEP 89, WorAlBi*
Kemenczky, Judit 1948- *EncCoWW*
Kemeny, Alexander 1943- *IntWWM 90*
Kemeny, Gyorgy 1936- *ConDes 90*
Kemeny, John George 1926- *WhoAm 90*
Kemenyffy, Steven 1943- *WhoAmA 91, WhoE 91*
Kemenyffy, Susan B Hale 1941- *WhoAmA 91*
Kemerling, James Lee 1939- *St&PR 91*
Kemler, Katherine Penelope 1951- *WhoSSW 91*
Kemler, Raphael Leonard 1918- *WhoE 91, WhoWor 91*
Kemmel, William Anthony, Jr. 1930- *St&PR 91*
Kemmer, Nicholas 1911- *WhoWor 91*
Kemmer, Richard Julius 1945- *WhoE 91*
Kemmerer, Donald Lorenzo 1905- *WhoAm 90*
Kemmerer, John L., Jr. 1911- *St&PR 91*
Kemmerer, Peter Ream 1942- *WhoE 91*
Kemmerer, Russ 1931- *Ballpl 90*
Kemmerer, Sharon Jean 1956- *WhoAmW 91*
Kemmerer, Terry *St&PR 91*
Kemmerly, Jack Dale 1936- *WhoAm 90*
Kemmet, Gerald William 1939- *St&PR 91*
Kemmett, William J. *WhoWrEP 89*
Kemmis, Daniel Orra 1945- *WhoAm 90*
Kemner, Mark H. 1945- *St&PR 91*
Kemnitz, Louis A. *BioIn 16*
Kemnitz, Thomas Milton *WhoAm 90*
Kemp, Anna *BiDEWW*
Kemp, Anthony Eric 1934- *IntWWM 90*
Kemp, Arthur 1916- *WhoAm 90*
Kemp, Aubrey L. 1939- *St&PR 91*
Kemp, Barbara 1881-1959 *PenDiMP*
Kemp, Bernard 1955- *WhoWor 91*
Kemp, Betty Ruth 1930- *WhoAm 90, WhoAmW 91, WhoSSW 91*
Kemp, Brian George 1940- *IntWWM 90*
Kemp, Danial Schaeffer 1936- *WhoAm 90*
Kemp, David 1947- *ODwPR 91*
Kemp, David Westley 1958- *WhoEmL 91*
Kemp, Edgar Ray, Jr. 1924- *St&PR 91*
Kemp, Elizabeth 1957- *ConTFT 8 [port]*
Kemp, Emory Leland 1931- *WhoAm 90*
Kemp, Evan Jennings, Jr. 1937- *WhoAm 90*
Kemp, Ferrell T., Jr. 1954- *St&PR 91*
Kemp, Francis Bolling, III 1940- *WhoSSW 91*
Kemp, Frank 1927- *St&PR 91*
Kemp, Frank Willes, Jr. 1929- *BiDrAPA 89*
Kemp, Geoffrey Thomas Howard 1939- *WhoAm 90*
Kemp, Harris Atteridge 1912- *WhoAm 90*
Kemp, J. Robert 1920- *WhoAm 90*
Kemp, Jack *BioIn 16*
Kemp, Jack 1935- *BiDrUSE 89, News 90 [port], WorAlBi*
Kemp, Jack French 1935- *WhoAm 90, WhoE 91, WhoWor 91*
Kemp, James C. *BioIn 16*
Kemp, Jan *BioIn 16*
Kemp, Jeremy 1935- *ConTFT 8 [port]*
Kemp, Jim *BioIn 16*
Kemp, John Dan 1951- *WhoEmL 91*
Kemp, John W. *St&PR 91*
Kemp, June 1933- *WhoWor 91*
Kemp, Katharine V *BiDrAPA 89*
Kemp, Kenneth Duane *BiDrAPA 89*
Kemp, Kenneth Lawrence 1949- *WhoEmL 91*
Kemp, Maury Page 1929- *WhoAm 90*
Kemp, Michael Allan 1943- *WhoE 91*
Kemp, Nettie Emmerine 1908- *WhoWrEP 89*
Kemp, Patrick Samuel 1932- *WhoAm 90*
Kemp, Paul Zane 1928- *WhoAmA 91*

Kemp, Penny 1944- *ConAu 130*
Kemp, Ralph Gene, Jr. 1944- *WhoAm 90, WhoE 91*
Kemp, Robert Bowers, Jr. 1941- *St&PR 91*
Kemp, Robert William 1943- *St&PR 91*
Kemp, Roger L. *BioIn 16*
Kemp, Samuel Leon 1945- *WhoSSW 91*
Kemp, Shawn *BioIn 16*
Kemp, Steve 1954- *Ballpl 90*
Kemp, Suzanne Leppart 1929- *WhoAmW 91*
Kemp, Theresa Anne 1956- *WhoE 91*
Kemp, Thomas H., Jr. 1834?- *AmLegL*
Kemp, Walter Herbert 1938- *IntWWM 90*
Kemp, Walter W *BiDrAPA 89*
Kemp, Wesley Barton 1946- *St&PR 91*
Kemp-Welch, Lucy Elizabeth 1869-1958 *BiDWomA*
Kempa, Gerald 1934- *WhoE 91*
Kempe, Lloyd Lute 1911- *WhoAm 90*
Kempe, Ludwig George 1915- *WhoSSW 91*
Kempe, Margery 1373?- *BioIn 16*
Kempe, Marjery 1373?-1439? *FemiCLE*
Kempe, Mirdza 1907-1974 *EncCoWW*
Kempe, Richard Joseph 1922- *WhoAmA 91*
Kempe, Robert A. 1922- *St&PR 91*
Kempe, Robert Aron 1922- *WhoWor 91*
Kempe, Rudolf 1910-1976 *PenDiMP*
Kempe, Ruth Irene S 1921- *BiDrAPA 89*
Kempe, Samuel *PenDiDA 89*
Kempema, James L. 1931- *St&PR 91*
Kempen, Gerard A.M. 1943- *WhoWor 91*
Kempen, Paul van 1893-1955 *PenDiMP*
Kemper, Casey Randolph 1947- *WhoAm 90*
Kemper, David W. 1950- *St&PR 91*
Kemper, David Woods, II 1950- *WhoAm 90*
Kemper, Dorla Dean 1929- *WhoAmW 91*
Kemper, Hans-Georg 1941- *WhoWor 91*
Kemper, Jackson, Jr. 1935- *St&PR 91*
Kemper, James Lawson 1823-1895 *AmLegL*
Kemper, James M., Jr. 1921- *St&PR 91*
Kemper, James Madison, Jr. 1921- *WhoAm 90*
Kemper, James W. 1927- *WhoSSW 91*
Kemper, John Dustin 1924- *WhoAm 90*
Kemper, John Garner 1909- *WhoAmA 91*
Kemper, Jonathan McBride 1953- *St&PR 91, WhoAm 90*
Kemper, Kathi Jill 1957- *WhoAmW 91*
Kemper, Klaus Gunter 1947- *WhoWor 91*
Kemper, Kurt C. 1946- *St&PR 91*
Kemper, Lee Howard 1921- *St&PR 91*
Kemper, Marlyn J. 1943- *WhoAm 90, WhoAmW 91, WhoWor 91*
Kemper, Marlyn Janofsky 1943- *WhoSSW 91*
Kemper, Patricia Louise 1948- *WhoEmL 91*
Kemper, Philip Ray 1964- *WhoSSW 91*
Kemper, Rufus Crosby 1927- *BioIn 16*
Kemper, Rufus Crosby, Jr. 1927- *St&PR 91*
Kemper, Steven E. 1951- *WhoE 91*
Kemper, Steven Edward 1951- *WhoWrEP 89*
Kemper, Troxey 1915- *WhoWrEP 89*
Kemper, Walker Warder, Jr. 1924- *WhoWor 91*
Kemper, William Thornton 1903- *St&PR 91*
Kempers, Roger Dyke 1928- *WhoAm 90*
Kempf, Cecil Joseph 1927- *WhoAm 90*
Kempf, Davorin 1947- *IntWWM 90*
Kempf, Donald G., Jr. 1937- *WhoAm 90*
Kempf, Douglas Paul 1954- *WhoEmL 91*
Kempf, Eugen Karl 1932- *WhoWor 91*
Kempf, Martine 1958- *WhoAmW 91, WhoEmL 91, WhoWor 91*
Kempf, Paul Stuart 1918- *WhoAm 90*
Kempf, Reva Ann 1947- *WhoSSW 91*
Kempfer, Homer 1911- *WhoAm 90*
Kempff, Diana 1945- *EncCoWW*
Kempff, Wilhelm 1895- *PenDiMP*
Kempff, Wilhelm Walter Friedrich 1895- *IntWWM 90*
Kemph, John P 1919- *BiDrAPA 89*
Kempin, Frederick Gustav, Jr. 1922- *WhoAm 90*
Kempin, Linda Jeanne 1951- *WhoE 91, WhoEmL 91*
Kempinger, Herwig *BioIn 16*
Kempinski, Chester F. 1942- *St&PR 91*
Kempis, Thomas a 1380-1471 *BioIn 16*
Kempker, Adele C *BiDrAPA 89*
Kemple, Joseph Nephi 1921- *WhoAm 90*
Kempler, Irwin *BiDrAPA 89*
Kempley, Rita Jane 1945- *WhoAm 90*
Kemplin, Richard D. *ODwPR 91*
Kemplin, Richard D. 1929- *St&PR 91*
Kempner, Friederike 1836-1904 *EncCoWW*
Kempner, Harris L. 1903- *St&PR 91*
Kempner, Helen Hill 1938- *WhoAmA 91*
Kempner, Isaac Herbert, III 1932- *WhoAm 90*
Kempner, Jack Julian 1917- *WhoAm 90*
Kempner, James Carroll 1939- *WhoAm 90*
Kempner, Jonathan 1951- *WhoE 91*
Kempner, Joseph 1923- *WhoAm 90*
Kempner, Kenneth Marc 1947- *WhoEmL 91*
Kempner, Maximilian Walter 1929- *WhoAm 90*
Kempner, Michael W. 1958- *ODwPR 91*
Kempner, Robert Max Wasilii 1899- *WhoAm 90, WhoE 91*
Kempner, Thomas Lenox 1927- *St&PR 91*
Kempner, Walter 1903- *WhoAm 90*
Kempowski, Walter 1929- *WorAu 1980*
Kempski, Ralph Aloisius 1934- *WhoAm 90*
Kempson, Rachel 1910- *ConAu 130*
Kempster, Norman Roy 1936- *WhoAm 90*
Kempster, Stephen W *BiDrAPA 89*
Kempter, John Daniel 1930- *St&PR 91*
Kempthorne, Dirk Arthur 1951- *WhoAm 90*
Kempthorne, Oscar 1919- *WhoAm 90*
Kempton, Alan George 1932- *WhoAm 90, WhoWor 91*
Kempton, George Roger 1934- *St&PR 91*
Kempton, Greta 1903- *WhoAmA 91*
Kempton, Greta M. *WhoWor 91*
Kempton, James Murray 1918- *WhoAm 90*
Kempton, Karl 1943- *WhoWrEP 89*
Kempton, Leo V 1921- *BiDrAPA 89*
Kemske, Floyd Steven 1947- *WhoWrEP 89*
Kemsley, William George, Jr. 1928- *WhoAm 90*
Kenady, James S. 1946- *St&PR 91*
Kenaga, Eugene Ellis 1917- *WhoWor 91*
Kenagy, Donald Allan 1941- *WhoSSW 91*
Kenagy, John Warner 1945- *WhoAm 90*
Kenagy, Robert C. 1931- *St&PR 91*
Kenakuk 1785?-1852 *WhNaAH*
Kenan, Frank H. 1912- *St&PR 91*
Kenan, Owen Graham 1943- *St&PR 91*
Kenan, Randall *BioIn 16*
Kenan, Richard Pearson 1931- *WhoSSW 91*
Kenan, Wilfred Mills 1930- *St&PR 91*
Kenary, Daniel Charles 1960- *WhoE 91*
Kenawell, William Wooding 1920- *EncO&P 3*
Kenczewicz, Timothy 1953- *St&PR 91*
Kenda, Juanita Echeverria 1922- *WhoAmW 91*
Kenda, Juanita Echeverria 1923- *WhoAmA 91*
Kendal, Felicity 1946- *WhoWor 91*
Kendall, Alan 1939- *ConAu 131*
Kendall, Amos 1789-1869 *BiDrUSE 89, BioIn 16, EncABHB 6 [port]*
Kendall, Arnold L *BiDrAPA 89*
Kendall, Carol Seeger 1917- *AuBYP 90*
Kendall, Christopher 1949- *WhoAm 90*
Kendall, Christopher Wolff 1949- *IntWWM 90*
Kendall, Clifford M. 1931- *St&PR 91*
Kendall, Curtis Allen 1933- *St&PR 91*
Kendall, David Benjamin 1959- *WhoEmL 91*
Kendall, David Nelson 1916- *WhoSSW 91*
Kendall, David R. 1958- *St&PR 91*
Kendall, Dolores Diane Pisapia 1946- *WhoAmW 91*
Kendall, Donald M. 1921- *St&PR 91*
Kendall, Donald McIntosh 1921- *ConAmBL*
Kendall, Donald Sargent 1948- *St&PR 91*
Kendall, Edward C. 1886-1972 *WorAlBi*
Kendall, Edward McDonnell *BiDrAPA 89*
Kendall, Frank, III 1949- *WhoAm 90*
Kendall, Fred 1949- *Ballpl 90*
Kendall, G. Preston, Sr. 1909- *St&PR 91*
Kendall, Gary K. 1943- *IntWWM 90*
Kendall, George Jason 1937- *WhoE 91*
Kendall, George P., Jr. 1934- *St&PR 91*
Kendall, George P., Jr. 1935- *WhoAm 90*
Kendall, George Preston, Sr. 1909- *WhoAm 90*
Kendall, George Wilkins 1809-1867 *BioIn 16*
Kendall, Henry W. *WhoAm 90*
Kendall, James William 1932- *St&PR 91*
Kendall, John Seedoff 1928- *WhoAm 90*
Kendall, John Walker, Jr. 1929- *WhoAm 90*
Kendall, Julie Ellen 1952- *WhoE 91, WhoWor 91*
Kendall, Julius 1919- *St&PR 91, WhoE 91*
Kendall, Katharine Kerr 1921- *WhoAmW 91*
Kendall, Katherine Anne 1910- *WhoAm 90*
Kendall, Kay Lynn 1950- *WhoAmW 91*
Kendall, Kenneth C. 1928- *St&PR 91*
Kendall, Kenneth Edward 1948- *WhoE 91, WhoWor 91*
Kendall, Kim Elizabeth 1952- *WhoAmW 91*
Kendall, Laurel Ann 1956- *WhoAmW 91*
Kendall, Leigh Wakefield 1937- *WhoE 91*
Kendall, Leon Thomas 1928- *WhoAm 90*
Kendall, Lloyd David 1936- *WhoWor 91*
Kendall, Marie *BioIn 16*
Kendall, Maurice George 1907-1983 *DcNaB 1981*
Kendall, May 1861-1931? *FemiCLE*
Kendall, Michael *WhoAmA 91*
Kendall, Nancy Melching 1951- *WhoE 91*
Kendall, Nathan Edward 1868-1936 *AmLegL*
Kendall, Patricia L. 1921-1990 *BioIn 16*
Kendall, Patricia Louise 1921-1990 *ConAu 131*
Kendall, Peter Landis 1936- *WhoAm 90*
Kendall, Richard H. 1930- *St&PR 91*
Kendall, Robert E. 1923- *St&PR 91*
Kendall, Robert Louis, Jr. 1930- *WhoAm 90*
Kendall, Robert McCutcheon 1931- *St&PR 91, WhoAm 90*
Kendall, Ronald Edward 1942- *St&PR 91*
Kendall, Sarah Lucille 1930- *WhoSSW 91*
Kendall, Scipiaruth 1955- *WhoAmW 91*
Kendall, Sharon Jean 1956- *WhoEmL 91*
Kendall, Steven Walter 1947- *St&PR 91, WhoEmL 91, WhoSSW 91*
Kendall, Thomas Lyle 1949- *WhoAmA 91*
Kendall, Walter C. 1924- *St&PR 91*
Kendall, Walter J. *BioIn 16*
Kendall, William Denis 1903- *WhoAm 90, WhoWor 91*
Kendall, William E. 1914- *St&PR 91*
Kendall, William Franklin 1948- *WhoEmL 91*
Kendall, William James 1947- *St&PR 91*
Kende, Andrew Steven 1932- *WhoAm 90*
Kende, Hans Janos 1937- *WhoAm 90*
Kendell, Iain Philip 1931- *IntWWM 90*
Kendell, Ross Ezra 1934- *St&PR 91, WhoAm 90*
Kender, James Larry 1946- *St&PR 91*
Kender, Laura Logan 1959- *WhoEmL 91*
Kender, Walter John 1935- *WhoAm 90*
Kenderdine, Augustus Frederick *WhoAmA 91N*
Kenderdine, John Marshall 1912- *WhoAm 90, WhoSSW 91*
Kendig, Diane Lyn 1950- *WhoWrEP 89*
Kendig, Edwin Lawrence, Jr. 1911- *WhoAm 90, WhoWor 91*
Kendig, Ellsworth Harold, Jr. 1922- *WhoAm 90*
Kendig, Martin William 1945- *WhoEmL 91*
Kendig, Patricia Hale 1934- *WhoAmW 91*
Kendig, William L. 1938- *WhoE 91*
Kendler, Bernhard 1934- *WhoAm 90, WhoWrEP 89*
Kendler, Hayden Brian 1947- *WhoWor 91*
Kendler, Howard Harvard 1919- *WhoAm 90*
Kendler, Kenneth Seedman 1950- *BiDrAPA 89*
Kendrake, Carleton *MajTwCW, TwCCr&M 91*
Kendrew, John Cowdery 1917- *WhoAm 90, WhoWor 91*
Kendrick, Baynard H 1894-1977 *TwCCr&M 91*
Kendrick, Budd Leroy 1944- *WhoAm 90*
Kendrick, Caldwell C. 1910- *St&PR 91*
Kendrick, Cheryl Donofrio 1948- *WhoAmW 91*
Kendrick, Curtis 1921- *BiDrAPA 89*
Kendrick, David Andrew 1937- *WhoAm 90*
Kendrick, Dennis 1944- *WhoE 91*
Kendrick, Eddie 1939- *EncPR&S 89*
Kendrick, Edmund H. 1921- *St&PR 91*
Kendrick, Ernest A *BiDrAPA 89*
Kendrick, George P. *PenDiDA 89*
Kendrick, Greene 1798-1873 *AmLegL*
Kendrick, Harold F 1922- *BiDrAPA 89*
Kendrick, James Earl 1940- *WhoAm 90, WhoE 91, WhoWor 91*
Kendrick, James M. *ODwPR 91*
Kendrick, James Richard 1929- *St&PR 91*
Kendrick, James William 1953- *WhoSSW 91*
Kendrick, Jody Weiss 1964- *ODwPR 91*
Kendrick, John W. 1943- *St&PR 91*
Kendrick, John Whitefield 1917- *WhoAm 90*
Kendrick, Joseph Trotwood 1920- *WhoAm 90*
Kendrick, Mel 1949- *WhoAmA 91*
Kendrick, Nathaniel 1777-1848 *BioIn 16*
Kendrick, Nona Caroline 1932- *WhoWrEP 89*
Kendrick, Pamela Ann 1943- *WhoAmW 91, WhoSSW 91*
Kendrick, Peter Murray 1936- *WhoAm 90*
Kendrick, Richard Lofton 1944- *WhoSSW 91, WhoWor 91*
Kendrick, Ronald Edward 1935- *WhoAm 90*
Kendrick, Ronald H. 1941- *WhoAm 90*
Kendrick, Stephanie Bird 1953- *WhoAmW 91*
Kendrick, Thomas Rudolph 1933- *WhoAm 90*
Kendrick, William J. 1932- *ODwPR 91, St&PR 91*
Kendricks, Eddie 1939- *EncPR&S 89*
Kendricks, Eddie 1940- *DrBIPA 90*
Kendy, Joseph Stephen, Jr. 1942- *St&PR 91*
Kendzierski, Lottie Henryka 1917- *WhoAm 90*
Keneally, Maryann Paglia 1942- *WhoAmW 91*
Keneally, Thomas *BioIn 16*
Keneally, Thomas 1935- *MajTwCW*
Keneally, Thomas Michael 1935- *WhoWor 91*
Kenealy, Annesley 1861- *FemiCLE*
Kenealy, Arabella 1864-1938 *FemiCLE*
Kenealy, Jim 1927- *BioIn 16*
Kenealy, Matthew H., III 1956- *WhoE 91*
Kenealy, Michael 1854-1916 *AmLegL*
Kenealy, Patrick 1959- *WhoWrEP 89*
Kenedi, Robert 1931- *St&PR 91*
Kenedy, Reid 1938- *St&PR 91*
Kenefick, John Henry, Jr. 1921- *WhoAm 90*
Kenefick, Thomas Aquinas, III 1946- *WhoEmL 91*
Kenekuk *BioIn 16*
Kenelly, John Willis, Jr. 1935- *WhoAm 90*
Kenemer, Kerry Durant 1953- *WhoSSW 91*
Kenen, I. L. 1905-1988 *BioIn 16*
Kenen, Isaiah Leo 1905-1988 *BioIn 16*
Kenen, Peter Bain 1932- *WhoAm 90, WhoE 91*
Kenerleber, A.J. 1923- *St&PR 91*
Kenerson, Robert Foster *BiDrAPA 89*
Kenesi, Claude 1930- *WhoWor 91*
Kenfield, Laurie Ann *BiDrAPA 89*
Kenfield, William John 1921- *BiDrAPA 89*
Kengen, Kund-Erik 1947- *IntWWM 90*
Kengo Wa Dondo 1935- *WhoWor 91*
Kenig, Noe 1923- *WhoWor 91*
Kenigsberg, Marvin Donald 1935- *St&PR 91*
Kenilorea, Peter 1943- *WhoWor 91*
Kenin, Michael 1936- *BiDrAPA 89*
Kenins, Talivaldis 1919- *IntWWM 90*
Kenison, Raymond Robert 1932- *WhoWor 91*
Kenitzer, Richard Edward 1958- *WhoEmL 91*
Kenkel, Robert August 1934- *WhoAm 90*
Kenley, Elizabeth Sue 1945- *WhoAmW 91, WhoEmL 91, WhoSSW 91, WhoWor 91*
Kenly, F. Corning, Jr. 1915- *WhoAm 90*
Kenly, Granger Farwell 1919- *WhoAm 90*
Kenly, Jacqueline Sueann 1945- *WhoAmW 91*
Kenna, E. Douglas 1924- *St&PR 91*
Kenna, Edgar Douglas 1924- *WhoAm 90*
Kenna, Edward F. 1945- *St&PR 91*
Kenna, Frank 1923- *St&PR 91*
Kenna, Gary Franklin 1954- *St&PR 91*
Kenna, James Joseph 1932- *St&PR 91*
Kenna, Marita D *BiDrAPA 89*
Kenna, Michael 1953- *WhoAmA 91*
Kennamer, Elton Leon, Jr. 1930- *WhoSSW 91*
Kennamer, Lorrin Garfield, Jr. 1924- *WhoAm 90*
Kennan, Christopher James 1949- *WhoEmL 91*
Kennan, Elizabeth Topham 1938- *WhoAm 90, WhoAmW 91, WhoE 91*
Kennan, George F. 1904- *WorAlBi*
Kennan, George Frost 1904- *BioIn 16, WhoAm 90*
Kennan, James Harley 1946- *WhoWor 91*
Kennan, Kent Wheeler 1913- *IntWWM 90, WhoAm 90*
Kennard, David William 1923- *BiDrAPA 89*
Kennard, Francis M. 1929- *St&PR 91*
Kennard, Joyce *WhoAmW 91*
Kennard, Kenneth Clifton 1923- *WhoAm 90*
Kennard, Mary Eliza *FemiCLE*
Kennard, Nina 1844-1926 *FemiCLE*
Kennard, Robert Morrison, Jr. 1951- *WhoEmL 91*
Kennard Race, Daphne Jean 1927- *IntWWM 90*
Kennaugh, Ralph Christopher 1947- *WhoEmL 91*
Kennaway, Adrienne 1945- *SmATA 60 [port]*
Kenne, David C. 1947- *St&PR 91*
Kenneally, Dennis Michael 1946- *WhoAm 90*
Kennedy family *BioIn 16*
Kennedy, Adele Pattin 1936- *WhoWrEP 89*
Kennedy, Adrienne *BioIn 16*
Kennedy, Adrienne 1931- *DrBIPA 90, FemiCLE, NotWoAT*
Kennedy, Adrienne Lita 1931- *WhoAm 90*
Kennedy, Aida Marie 1954- *WhoEmL 91*

Kennedy, Alexander J. 1931- *St&PR 91*
Kennedy, Anthony M. *BioIn 16*
Kennedy, Anthony McLeod 1936- *WhoAm 90, WhoE 91*
Kennedy, Arthur 1914-1990 *BioIn 16, NewYTBS 90 [port], WorAlBi*
Kennedy, Austin Milton 1867- *AmLegL*
Kennedy, Barbara L *BiDrAPA 89*
Kennedy, Barbara L. 1938- *WhoE 91*
Kennedy, Barbara Lucille 1938- *WhoSSW 91*
Kennedy, Barton *WhoWrEP 89*
Kennedy, Berenice Connor *WhoAm 90*
Kennedy, Bernard D. 1925- *WhoAm 90*
Kennedy, Bernard J. 1931- *St&PR 91*
Kennedy, Bernard Joseph 1931- *WhoAm 90, WhoE 91*
Kennedy, Beth Blumenreich 1950- *WhoAmW 91*
Kennedy, Beverly Burris 1943- *WhoSSW 91*
Kennedy, Bill 1921-1983 *Ballpl 90*
Kennedy, Bob 1920- *Ballpl 90*
Kennedy, Brenda Elizabeth 1962- *WhoEmL 91*
Kennedy, Brendan 1970- *BioIn 16*
Kennedy, Brian Charles 1952- *WhoWor 91*
Kennedy, Brian James 1941- *St&PR 91*
Kennedy, Brickyard 1867-1915 *Ballpl 90*
Kennedy, Bruce A. 1950- *St&PR 91*
Kennedy, Burt 1923- *BioIn 16*
Kennedy, Burt Raphael 1922- *WhoAm 90*
Kennedy, Byrl James 1921- *WhoAm 90*
Kennedy, Caroline *BioIn 16*
Kennedy, Catherine *BiDrAPA 89*
Kennedy, Charlotte Irene 1947- *WhoAmW 91*
Kennedy, Cheryl Ann *BiDrAPA 89*
Kennedy, Cheryl Lynn 1946- *WhoAmW 91*
Kennedy, Chester Ralph, Jr. 1926- *WhoAm 90, WhoE 91, WhoWor 91*
Kennedy, Christie Ann 1950- *WhoAmW 91*
Kennedy, Christopher Robin 1948- *WhoAm 90*
Kennedy, Colleen Geralyn 1955- *WhoAmW 91*
Kennedy, Cornelia Groefsema 1923- *WhoAm 90, WhoAmW 91*
Kennedy, Cornelius Bryant 1921- *WhoAm 90, WhoE 91, WhoWor 91*
Kennedy, Craig Allen 1951- *WhoEmL 91*
Kennedy, D. James 1930- *BioIn 16*
Kennedy, Daisy *PenDiMP*
Kennedy, Dan W., III 1945- *St&PR 91*
Kennedy, Daniel Floyd 1945- *WhoSSW 91*
Kennedy, Danielle Rae 1945- *WhoEmL 91*
Kennedy, David *NewYTBS 90 [port]*
Kennedy, David 1825-1886 *PenDiMP*
Kennedy, David Boyd 1933- *WhoAm 90*
Kennedy, David Burl *BiDrAPA 89*
Kennedy, David Burl 1950- *WhoWor 91*
Kennedy, David F *BiDrAPA 89*
Kennedy, David M. 1905- *BiDrUSE 89*
Kennedy, David Michael 1941- *WhoAm 90*
Kennedy, David Tinsley 1919- *WhoWor 91*
Kennedy, David Woodford 1941- *WhoE 91*
Kennedy, Davis Lee 1938- *WhoE 91*
Kennedy, Debra Joyce 1955- *WhoAmW 91*
Kennedy, Denis Thomas 1940- *BiDrAPA 89*
Kennedy, Dennis James 1930- *BioIn 16*
Kennedy, Diana *BioIn 16*
Kennedy, Donald 1931- *WhoAm 90, WhoWor 91*
Kennedy, Donald A. 1927- *St&PR 91*
Kennedy, Donald Davidson, Jr. 1931- *St&PR 91*
Kennedy, Donald Parker 1918- *St&PR 91, WhoAm 90*
Kennedy, Donna Virginia 1948- *WhoAmW 91*
Kennedy, Dora Funari 1921- *WhoAmW 91*
Kennedy, Dorothy M. 1931- *BioIn 16*
Kennedy, Douglas 1893-1988 *BioIn 16*
Kennedy, Edward M. 1932- *WorAlBi*
Kennedy, Edward Moore 1932- *BioIn 16, WhoAm 90, WhoE 91, WhoWor 91*
Kennedy, Edwin L. 1904- *St&PR 91*
Kennedy, Elaine Therese 1937- *WhoAmW 91*
ennedy, Elizabeth Mae 1949- *WhoAmW 91*
Kennedy, Emmet 1941- *ConAu 132*
Kennedy, Ethel S. 1928- *BioAmW*
Kennedy, Eugene Cullen 1928- *WhoAm 90*
Kennedy, Eugene Patrick 1919- *WhoAm 90*
ennedy, Eugene Richard 1919- *WhoAm 90*
ennedy, Evelyn Siefert 1927- *WhoAmW 91, WhoWor 91*
ennedy, F. Frederick, Jr. 1943- *WhoSSW 91, WhoWor 91*
ennedy, Frances Midlam *BioIn 16*
Kennedy, Frank Robert 1914- *WhoAm 90*
Kennedy, Franklin, Jr. 1915- *St&PR 91*
Kennedy, Gary J 1948- *BiDrAPA 89*
Kennedy, Gene 1946- *WhoAmA 91*
Kennedy, George 1926- *WorAlBi*
Kennedy, George Alexander 1928- *WhoAm 90*
Kennedy, George D. 1926- *St&PR 91, WhoAm 90*
Kennedy, George Hunt 1936- *WhoAm 90*
Kennedy, Gerald Owen 1942- *St&PR 91*
Kennedy, Gerald Studdert *ConAu 131*
Kennedy, H. Philip *St&PR 91*
Kennedy, Hal 1933- *ODwPR 91*
Kennedy, Harold David 1945- *St&PR 91*
Kennedy, Harold Edward 1927- *St&PR 91, WhoAm 90, WhoWor 91*
Kennedy, Harriet Forte *WhoAmA 91*
Kennedy, Harry E. *BioIn 16*
Kennedy, Harvey Edward 1928- *WhoAm 90*
Kennedy, Helene A. 1956- *ODwPR 91*
Kennedy, Ian Glen 1945- *WhoAm 90*
Kennedy, J. Jack, Jr. 1956- *WhoEmL 91, WhoSSW 91, WhoWor 91*
Kennedy, J William 1903- *WhoAmA 91*
Kennedy, Jack Edward 1945- *WhoEmL 91*
Kennedy, Jack Leland 1924- *WhoAm 90*
Kennedy, Jack W. 1924- *St&PR 91*
Kennedy, Jacob M. 1864- *AmLegL*
Kennedy, Jacqueline Ann 1947- *WhoAmW 91*
Kennedy, Jacqueline B. 1929- *BioAmW*
Kennedy, James 1902-1984 *DcNaB 1981*
Kennedy, James A *BiDrAPA 89*
Kennedy, James Andrew 1937- *St&PR 91*
Kennedy, James Anthony 1958- *WhoEmL 91*
Kennedy, James Cox 1947- *WhoSSW 91*
Kennedy, James Drake, Jr. 1924- *St&PR 91*
Kennedy, James Edward 1933- *WhoAmA 91*
Kennedy, James Harrington 1924- *WhoWrEP 89*
Kennedy, James J. *WhoSSW 91*
Kennedy, James J. 1933- *St&PR 91*
Kennedy, James Joseph *BiDrAPA 89*
Kennedy, James L. 1937- *WhoAm 90*
Kennedy, James Lowery *BiDrAPA 89*
Kennedy, James Russell 1935- *BiDrAPA 89*
Kennedy, James Waite 1937- *WhoAm 90*
Kennedy, Jane Allen *BiDrAPA 89*
Kennedy, Janet A. 1913- *BiDrAPA 89*
Kennedy, Janet Lee 1951- *WhoEmL 91*
Kennedy, Janet Robson 1902-1974 *WhoAmA 91N*
Kennedy, Jay *BioIn 16*
Kennedy, Jay Richard 1911- *WhoWor 91*
Kennedy, Jayne *BioIn 16*
Kennedy, Jayne 1951- *DrBlPA 90*
Kennedy, Jean Marie 1957- *WhoAm 90*
Kennedy, Jelane Anne 1961- *WhoSSW 91*
Kennedy, Jerry Wayne 1947- *WhoEmL 91*
Kennedy, Jimmy 1902-1984 *OxCPMus*
Kennedy, Joan *BioIn 16*
Kennedy, Joan B. 1936- *BioAmW*
Kennedy, Joan Canfield 1931- *WhoAmW 91*
Kennedy, JoAnne 1957- *WhoE 91*
Kennedy, John *BioIn 16*
Kennedy, John 1941- *Ballpl 90*
Kennedy, John A. 1921- *St&PR 91*
Kennedy, John B. 1951- *WhoEmL 91*
Kennedy, John F. 1917-1963 *BioIn 16, WorAlBi*
Kennedy, John F. 1960- *BioIn 16*
Kennedy, John F., Jr. 1960- *News 90 [port]*
Kennedy, John Fisher 1933- *WhoAm 90*
Kennedy, John Fitzgerald 1917-1963 *BiDrUSE 89, EncPaPR 91, MajTwCW*
Kennedy, John Harley 1956- *WhoEmL 91*
Kennedy, John Joseph 1914- *WhoAm 90*
Kennedy, John Joseph 1948- *WhoEmL 91*
Kennedy, John L *EncPaPR 91*
Kennedy, John L. 1913-1984 *BioIn 16*
Kennedy, John Leonard 1956- *WhoE 91*
Kennedy, John M. 1921- *WhoWrEP 89*
Kennedy, John Maxwell 1934- *WhoWor 91*
Kennedy, John Patrick 1943- *WhoAm 90*
Kennedy, John Pendleton 1795-1870 *BiDrUSE 89*
Kennedy, John Raymond 1930- *St&PR 91, WhoAm 90*
Kennedy, John Robert 1927- *WhoSSW 91*
Kennedy, John S *BiDrAPA 89*
Kennedy, John Stewart 1830-1909 *EncABHB 6 [port]*
Kennedy, John Wesley 1920- *WhoAm 90*
Kennedy, John William 1956- *WhoE 91*
Kennedy, John William, Jr. 1944- *WhoE 91*
Kennedy, Jon Reid 1942- *WhoWrEP 89*
Kennedy, Joseph Charles 1929- *ConAu 30NR*
Kennedy, Joseph Everett 1930- *WhoSSW 91*
Kennedy, Joseph P. 1888-1969 *BioIn 16, WorAlBi*
Kennedy, Joseph Patrick, II *BioIn 16*
Kennedy, Joseph Patrick, II 1952- *WhoAm 90, WhoE 91*
Kennedy, Joseph Paul 1928- *WhoAm 90*
Kennedy, Josepha Marie 1928- *WhoWrEP 89*
Kennedy, Josephine 1914- *WhoAmW 91*
Kennedy, Joyce Lain *BioIn 16*
Kennedy, Junior 1950- *Ballpl 90*
Kennedy, Kael Behan 1941- *WhoWor 91*
Kennedy, Karen Syence 1943- *ODwPR 91, WhoSSW 91*
Kennedy, Katharine E. 1947- *ODwPR 91*
Kennedy, Kathleen *BioIn 16*
Kennedy, Kathleen 1920-1948 *BioAmW*
Kennedy, Kathy Irene 1956- *WhoAmW 91*
Kennedy, Kay *BioIn 16*
Kennedy, Kay J. *WhoAmW 91*
Kennedy, Keith Furnival 1925- *St&PR 91, WhoAm 90*
Kennedy, Keith Sanford 1945- *WhoEmL 91*
Kennedy, Kenneth Adrian Raine 1930- *WhoAm 90*
Kennedy, Kieran Anthony 1935- *WhoWor 91*
Kennedy, L. James 1927- *St&PR 91*
Kennedy, Larry Alan 1954- *WhoSSW 91*
Kennedy, Lawrence Allan 1937- *WhoAm 90*
Kennedy, Lawrence L *BiDrAPA 89*
Kennedy, Lawrence Robert *St&PR 91N*
Kennedy, Leon Isaac 1949- *DrBlPA 90*
Kennedy, LeRoy Errett 1924- *WhoAm 90*
Kennedy, Linda Eve 1953- *WhoEmL 91*
Kennedy, Louise St John 1950- *WomArch*
Kennedy, Lucille A. 1923- *St&PR 91*
Kennedy, Lyle H. 1933- *WhoE 91*
Kennedy, Marc J. 1945- *WhoAm 90, WhoSSW 91, WhoWor 91*
Kennedy, Margaret 1896-1967 *BioIn 16, FemiCLE*
Kennedy, Margaret Swierz 1941- *WhoWrEP 89*
Kennedy, Marilyn Moats 1943- *ConAu 32NR, WhoAmW 91*
Kennedy, Marilyn Ruth 1958- *BiDrAPA 89*
Kennedy, Mark 1952- *WhoAm 90*
Kennedy, Mary *St&PR 91*
Kennedy, Mary Morrison *BioIn 16*
Kennedy, Matthew Washington 1921- *IntWWM 90, WhoAm 90*
Kennedy, Melanie Sproul 1942- *WhoAmW 91*
Kennedy, Melvin H. 1922- *St&PR 91*
Kennedy, Michael *BioIn 16*
Kennedy, Michael 1926- *IntWWM 90*
Kennedy, Michael Craufurd 1932- *WhoWor 91*
Kennedy, Michael James 1958- *WhoEmL 91*
Kennedy, Michael Reed 1940- *WhoSSW 91*
Kennedy, Milward 1894-1968 *TwCCr&M 91*
Kennedy, Mimi 1948- *ConTFT 8*
Kennedy, Monica Margaret 1957- *BiDrAPA 89*
Kennedy, Monte 1922- *Ballpl 90*
Kennedy, Moorhead 1930- *WhoAm 90*
Kennedy, Nancy Mohr *WhoAm 90*
Kennedy, Nigel 1956- *PenDiMP*
Kennedy, Nigel Paul 1956- *IntWWM 90*
Kennedy, Patricia Ann Sullivan 1936- *WhoSSW 91*
Kennedy, Patricia Michele 1966- *WhoEmL 91*
Kennedy, Patrick J. *BioIn 16*
Kennedy, Patrick Kenyon 1933- *St&PR 91*
Kennedy, Patrick W. 1956- *St&PR 91*
Kennedy, Paul 1945- *ConAu 30NR*
Kennedy, Paul M *ConAu 30NR*
Kennedy, Paul M. 1945- *BioIn 16*
Kennedy, Paul Michael 1945- *WhoAm 90*
Kennedy, Paul Vincent 1946- *BiDrAPA 89*
Kennedy, Philip L. 1932- *St&PR 91*
Kennedy, Quentin J., Sr. 1933- *WhoAm 90*
Kennedy, Quentin James 1933- *St&PR 91*
Kennedy, R. Michael, Jr. 1943- *St&PR 91*
Kennedy, Raoul Dion 1944- *WhoAm 90, WhoWor 91*
Kennedy, Ray *BioIn 16*
Kennedy, Richard 1910-1989 *AnObit 1989, SmATA 60*
Kennedy, Richard A. 1938- *WhoE 91*
Kennedy, Richard Carl 1945- *WhoEmL 91*
Kennedy, Richard D. 1940- *St&PR 91*
Kennedy, Richard Frederick 1933- *WhoAm 90*
Kennedy, Richard Jerome 1932- *WhoAm 90, WhoWrEP 89*
Kennedy, Richard Thomas 1919- *WhoAm 90*
Kennedy, Rita M. 1948- *WhoHisp 91*
Kennedy, Robert 1938- *SmATA 63 [port]*
Kennedy, Robert A. 1948- *St&PR 91*
Kennedy, Robert Alan 1958- *WhoSSW 91*
Kennedy, Robert Charles 1943- *WhoE 91*
Kennedy, Robert Cobb 1835-1865 *BioIn 16*
Kennedy, Robert D. 1945- *St&PR 91*
Kennedy, Robert Delmont 1932- *WhoAm 90, WhoE 91*
Kennedy, Robert Emmet 1910- *WhoAm 90, WhoWor 91*
Kennedy, Robert Emmet, Jr. 1941- *WhoAm 90*
Kennedy, Robert Eugene 1942- *WhoAm 90*
Kennedy, Robert F. 1925-1968 *BioIn 16, WorAlBi*
Kennedy, Robert Francis 1925-1968 *BiDrUSE 89*
Kennedy, Robert J. 1913- *St&PR 91*
Kennedy, Robert Joseph, Jr. 1952- *WhoE 91*
Kennedy, Robert Meyer 1933- *St&PR 91*
Kennedy, Robert Norman 1932- *WhoAm 90*
Kennedy, Robert Spayde 1933- *WhoAm 90*
Kennedy, Robert William 1931- *WhoAm 90*
Kennedy, Robinn Rodgers 1955- *WhoEmL 91*
Kennedy, Roger G. 1940- *St&PR 91*
Kennedy, Roger George 1926- *WhoAm 90, WhoE 91*
Kennedy, Rosario 1945- *WhoHisp 91*
Kennedy, Rose F. 1890- *BioAmW*
Kennedy, Rose Fitzgerald 1890- *WhoAm 90, WorAlBi*
Kennedy, Ruth Lee 1895-1988 *BioIn 16*
Kennedy, Sam Delk 1926- *WhoSSW 91*
Kennedy, Sandra Hays 1945- *WhoWrEP 89*
Kennedy, Sara L *BiDrAPA 89*
Kennedy, Scott 1927- *DrBlPA 90*
Kennedy, Seward Jones 1925- *WhoWor 91*
Kennedy, Shirley Duglin 1951- *WhoSSW 91*
Kennedy, Shirley Lou 1958- *WhoEmL 91*
Kennedy, Sidney 1951- *BiDrAPA 89*
Kennedy, Stephen Dandridge 1942- *St&PR 91, WhoE 91*
Kennedy, Susan Fichter 1941- *ODwPR 91*
Kennedy, Suzanne *BioIn 16*
Kennedy, Tamyra Machele 1958- *WhoAmW 91*
Kennedy, Ted 1932- *BioIn 16*
Kennedy, Terry 1941- *WhoWrEP 89*
Kennedy, Terry 1956- *Ballpl 90*
Kennedy, Theodore Clifford 1930 *WhoAm 90*
Kennedy, Thomas 1887-1963 *WorAlBi*
Kennedy, Thomas B. *St&PR 91*
Kennedy, Thomas Chester 1940- *St&PR 91*
Kennedy, Thomas Edgar 1958- *WhoEmL 91*
Kennedy, Thomas Eugene 1944- *WhoWor 91, WhoWrEP 89*
Kennedy, Thomas J. 1948- *WhoE 91*
Kennedy, Thomas James, Jr. 1920- *WhoAm 90*
Kennedy, Thomas Leo 1936- *WhoAm 90*
Kennedy, Thomas M *BiDrAPA 89*
Kennedy, Thomas Marcellus 1951- *WhoE 91*
Kennedy, Thomas Patrick 1932- *WhoE 91, WhoSSW 91, WhoWor 91*
Kennedy, Thomas Riley 1934- *St&PR 91*
Kennedy, Traver Hall 1952- *WhoE 91*
Kennedy, Tyrone George 1944- *WhoSSW 91*
Kennedy, Varina 1940- *WhoAmW 91*
Kennedy, Vern 1907- *Ballpl 90*
Kennedy, W. Keith 1943- *St&PR 91*
Kennedy, W. M. 1924- *WhoAm 90*
Kennedy, Wallace 1895- *WhoSSW 91*
Kennedy, Walter Jeff, Jr. 1928- *WhoWor 91*
Kennedy, Wilbert Keith, Jr. 1943- *WhoAm 90*
Kennedy, Wilbert Keith, Sr. 1919- *WhoAm 90*
Kennedy, William 1928- *BioIn 16, ConAu 31NR, MajTwCW, WhoWrEP 89, WorAlBi*
Kennedy, William Bean 1926- *WhoAm 90*
Kennedy, William Brittain 1961- *WhoEmL 91*
Kennedy, William E., Jr. 1919- *St&PR 91*
Kennedy, William Edward 1955- *St&PR 91*
Kennedy, William Francis 1918- *WhoAm 90*
Kennedy, William H., Jr. 1917- *St&PR 91*
Kennedy, William Jesse, III 1922- *St&PR 91, WhoAm 90*
Kennedy, William Joseph 1928- *WhoAm 90*
Kennedy, William Petersen 1950- *WhoEmL 91*
Kennedy, William S. 1926- *WhoWrEP 89*
Kennedy, William Thomas 1947- *WhoWor 91*

Kennedy, X. J. *BioIn 16*
Kennedy, X J *ConAu 30NR*
Kennedy, X. J. 1929- *WhoAm 90, WhoWrEP 89*
Kennedy, Yvonne Kennington 1919- *WhoAmW 91*
Kennedy-Fraser, Marjorie 1857-1930 *OxCPMus*
Kennedy-Fraser, Marjory 1857-1930 *PenDiMP*
Kennedy-Heath, Jill 1954- *BiDrAPA 89*
Kennedy-Minott, Rodney *WhoAm 90, WhoWor 91*
Kennedy-Shields, Kathleen Ann 1951- *WhoAmW 91*
Kennedy-Takahashi, Charlotte Aline 1946- *WhoWor 91*
Kennedy-Verbel, Jeanne Marie 1965- *WhoWrEP 89*
Kennekuk 1785?-1852 *WhNaAH*
Kennel, Charles Frederick 1939- *WhoAm 90*
Kennel, Raymund Justin 1944- *WhoWor 91*
Kennel, Robert Philip 1936- *St&PR 91*
Kennell, Arthur C. 1931- *St&PR 91*
Kennell, Kevin J. 1961- *St&PR 91*
Kennell, Richard Wayne 1952- *WhoEmL 91*
Kennelly, Arthur E. 1861-1939 *WorAlBi*
Kennelly, Barbara B. 1936- *WhoAm 90, WhoAmW 91, WhoE 91*
Kennelly, Daniel J *BiDrAPA 89*
Kennelly, John Jerome 1918- *WhoWor 91*
Kennelly, Karen Margaret 1933- *WhoAm 90, WhoAmW 91*
Kennelly, Robert Andrew 1919- *WhoAm 90*
Kennelly, Stacy Ann 1958- *WhoEmL 91*
Kenner, Bruce Bell 1940- *St&PR 91*
Kenner, Carole Ann 1953- *WhoAmW 91*
Kenner, David Vaupel 1958- *WhoEmL 91*
Kenner, Fred A. 1952- *St&PR 91*
Kenner, Hugh *BioIn 16*
Kenner, Mary Ellen 1941- *WhoSSW 91*
Kenner, R Robertson 1937- *BiDrAPA 89*
Kenner, Rhonda Shultz 1960- *WhoEmL 91*
Kenner, William Davis, III 1943- *BiDrAPA 89*
Kenner, William Hugh 1923- *WhoWrEP 89*
Kennerley, John Randall 1939- *WhoWor 91*
Kennerly, David Hume 1947- *WhoEmL 91, WhoWor 91*
Kennerly, James Edward 1924- *St&PR 91*
Kennet, Kathleen Young 1878-1947 *BiDWomA*
Kenneth *BioIn 16*
Kennett, Colette Ann 1951- *WhoEmL 91*
Kennett, Jiyu 1924- *WhoWrEP 89*
Kennett, Robert L. 1939- *St&PR 91*
Kennett, William Alexander 1932- *WhoAm 90*
Kennevan, Walter James 1912- *WhoE 91*
Kenneweg, Hartmut 1940- *WhoWor 91*
Kenney, Annie 1879-1953 *FemiCLE*
Kenney, Donald J. 1947- *St&PR 91*
Kenney, Douglas 1962- *WhoAmA 91*
Kenney, Emelie Agnes 1950- *WhoE 91*
Kenney, Emmet M 1931- *BiDrAPA 89*
Kenney, Emmet Michael, Jr. *BiDrAPA 89*
Kenney, Estelle Koval 1928- *WhoAmA 91*
Kenney, F. Donald 1918- *WhoWor 91*
Kenney, Francis Joseph 1925- *St&PR 91*
Kenney, Frank Deming 1921- *WhoAm 90*
Kenney, George C. 1889-1977 *BioIn 16, WorAlBi*
Kenney, Gerald Raymond 1956- *WhoEmL 91*
Kenney, Harry Wesley, Jr. 1926- *WhoAm 90, WhoWor 91*
Kenney, Howard Washington 1917- *WhoAm 90*
Kenney, James Donald 1927- *St&PR 91*
Kenney, James Francis 1921- *WhoAm 90*
Kenney, Jerry 1945- *Ballpl 90*
Kenney, John Arthur 1948- *WhoEmL 91*
Kenney, John Michel 1938- *WhoE 91, WhoWor 91*
Kenney, John Patrick 1946- *WhoEmL 91*
Kenney, Lawrence James 1930- *WhoAm 90*
Kenney, Leonard Allen 1945- *St&PR 91*
Kenney, Lisa Michelle 1962- *WhoAmW 91*
Kenney, Louis Augustine 1917- *WhoAm 90*
Kenney, Neil Patrick 1932- *WhoAm 90*
Kenney, Raymond Joseph, Jr. 1932- *WhoAm 90*
Kenney, Richard Alec 1924- *WhoAm 90*
Kenney, Robert 1947- *ODwPR 91*
Kenney, Robert Timothy 1942- *St&PR 91*
Kenney, Rosemary 1945- *WhoAmW 91*
Kenney, Thomas F. 1941- *St&PR 91*
Kenney, Thomas Frederick 1941- *WhoAm 90*
Kenney, Thomas Michael 1947- *WhoAm 90*
Kenney, Tricia *ODwPR 91*
Kenney, Vincent Paul 1927- *WhoAm 90*
Kenney-Wallace, Geraldine 1943- *WhoAm 90, WhoAmW 91*
Kennick, William Elmer 1923- *WhoAm 90*
Kennicott, James W. 1945- *WhoEmL 91, WhoWor 91*
Kennicott, Thomas C. 1940- *St&PR 91*
Kenniff, James A. 1951- *St&PR 91*
Kenniff, James M. *St&PR 91*
Kennington, Robert E., II 1932- *St&PR 91*
Kennish, Katharine *WhoWrEP 89*
Kennison, James Dudley 1920- *St&PR 91*
Kennison, Warren Samuel *BiDrAPA 89*
Kennon, Alfred W. 1941- *St&PR 91*
Kennon, Arthur Bruce 1933- *WhoAmA 91*
Kennon, Paul 1934-1990 *BioIn 16*
Kennon, Paul A. *NewYTBS 90*
Kennon, Robert Floyd 1902-1988 *BioIn 16*
Kenny G *BioIn 16*
Kenny, Adele M. 1948- *WhoWrEP 89*
Kenny, Alexander Donovan 1925- *WhoAm 90*
Kenny, Bill *DrBlPA 90*
Kenny, Charles D. 1945- *St&PR 91*
Kenny, Charles J. *MajTwCW*
Kenny, Courtney Arthur Lloyd 1933- *IntWWM 90*
Kenny, Dennis James 1935- *St&PR 91*
Kenny, Douglas Timothy 1923- *WhoAm 90*
Kenny, Edmund Joyce 1920- *WhoAm 90*
Kenny, Edward 1800-1891 *DcCanB 12*
Kenny, Elizabeth 1886-1952 *BioIn 16*
Kenny, Elizabeth A. 1961- *ODwPR 91*
Kenny, Ellsworth Newcomb 1909-1971 *AuBYP 90*
Kenny, Herbert A. 1912- *WhoWrEP 89*
Kenny, Herbert Andrew 1912- *WhoAm 90*
Kenny, Hugh 1909-1971 *AuBYP 90*
Kenny, James C. 1926- *St&PR 91*
Kenny, Jane A. 1945- *WhoAm 90, WhoAmW 91*
Kenny, John B. *BioIn 16*
Kenny, John Kevin 1936- *St&PR 91*
Kenny, John Thomas 1938- *St&PR 91*
Kenny, Kathryn *WhoWrEP 89*
Kenny, Kevin J. *BiDrAPA 89*
Kenny, Lawrence P 1942- *BiDrAPA 89*
Kenny, Luis Federico 1955- *WhoWor 91*
Kenny, Maurice F. 1929- *WhoWrEP 89*
Kenny, Michael 1923-1986 *BioIn 16*
Kenny, Raymond James 1927- *St&PR 91*
Kenny, Robert R. 1927- *St&PR 91*
Kenny, Robert Wayne 1932- *WhoAm 90*
Kenny, Roger Michael 1938- *WhoAm 90*
Kenny, Shirley Strum 1934- *ConAu 31NR, WhoAm 90, WhoAmW 91*
Kenny, Vernon B. 1922- *St&PR 91*
Kenny, William Crecca 1959- *WhoEmL 91*
Kenny, William F 1935- *BiDrAPA 89*
Kenny, William Francis, Jr. 1935- *WhoE 91*
Kenny, William J 1934- *BiDrAPA 89*
Kenny, William James 1950- *WhoSSW 91*
Kenny, William M *BiDrAPA 89*
Kenny, Yvonne 1950- *IntWWM 90*
Kenny-Welch, Susan Marie 1955- *WhoAmW 91*
Keno, Robert Peter 1924- *St&PR 91*
Kenoeigh, Donald Charles 1939- *St&PR 91*
Kenojuak 1933- *WhoAmA 91*
Kenrich, John L. 1929- *St&PR 91*
Kenrich, John Lewis 1929- *WhoAm 90*
Kenrick, Tony 1935- *TwCCr&M 91*
Kenschaft, Patricia Clark 1940- *WhoE 91*
Kensel, Neven Michael 1940- *WhoSSW 91*
Kenshalo, Daniel Ralph 1922- *WhoAm 90*
Kensick, Helen Lorraine 1948- *WhoAmW 91*
Kensicki, Paul Ray 1952- *BiDrAPA 89*
Kensil, James Lewis 1930- *WhoE 91*
Kensing, Henry V. 1933- *St&PR 91*
Kensinger, Jack William *BiDrAPA 89*
Kensinger, Richard Gerald 1947- *WhoE 91*
Kensinger, Tina R. 1961- *WhoAmW 91*
Kensit, Patsy *BioIn 16*
Kensky, James Francis 1946- *St&PR 91*
Kent, Alexander 1924- *SmATA X [port]*
Kent, Allen 1921- *WhoAm 90*
Kent, Andrew Adam 1959- *BiDrAPA 89*
Kent, Bartis Milton 1925- *WhoSSW 91, WhoWor 91*
Kent, Brad C. 1949- *St&PR 91*
Kent, Calvin Albert 1941- *WhoAm 90*
Kent, Carol 1944- *WhoWrEP 89*
Kent, Christopher 1940- *ConAu 129*
Kent, Christopher John 1949- *IntWWM 90*
Kent, Conrad *BioIn 16*
Kent, Corita *BioIn 16*
Kent, David Arthur 1957- *BiDrAPA 89*
Kent, David Charles 1953- *WhoEmL 91*
Kent, Deborah 1948- *BioIn 16*
Kent, Donald Alan 1949- *WhoEmL 91*
Kent, Donald Charles 1923- *WhoAm 90*
Kent, Earl B. 1921- *St&PR 91*
Kent, Edgar Robert, Jr. 1941- *WhoAm 90*
Kent, Edward A 1909- *BiDrAPA 89*
Kent, Eileen Caroline 1956- *WhoE 91*
Kent, Elizabeth Grey, Countess of *BiDEWW*
Kent, Emma M 1910- *BiDrAPA 89*
Kent, Frank Ward 1912-1977 *WhoAmA 91N*
Kent, Frederick Heber 1905- *WhoAm 90, WhoWor 91*
Kent, Frederick James 1928- *IntWWM 90*
Kent, Gary Warner 1933- *WhoSSW 91*
Kent, Gayle Steverson 1938- *WhoSSW 91*
Kent, Geoffrey 1914- *WhoAm 90*
Kent, George Cantine, Jr. 1914- *WhoAm 90*
Kent, George Virgil *BiDrAPA 89*
Kent, Greg B. 1947- *St&PR 91*
Kent, H Latham 1930- *WhoAmA 91*
Kent, Harry Christison 1930- *WhoAm 90*
Kent, Helen *ConAu 129*
Kent, Ian 1915- *BiDrAPA 89*
Kent, Jack 1920-1985 *EncACom, WhoAmA 91N*
Kent, James A. 1922- *WhoAm 90*
Kent, James Daniel 1941- *St&PR 91*
Kent, James Everett 1936- *WhoSSW 91*
Kent, James Howard 1923- *St&PR 91*
Kent, James Simpson, Jr. 1954- *WhoSSW 91*
Kent, Jesse Gaston, Jr. 1946- *St&PR 91*
Kent, Jill Elspeth 1948- *WhoAm 90, WhoAmW 91*
Kent, Joan Swafford 1927- *WhoAmW 91*
Kent, John Francis 1950- *WhoSSW 91*
Kent, Karen Irene 1944- *WhoAmW 91*
Kent, Kate Peck 1914-1987 *BioIn 16*
Kent, Kaye Robinson 1957- *WhoEmL 91*
Kent, Kenneth Mitchell 1938- *WhoE 91*
Kent, Leslie Ann 1955- *WhoAmW 91*
Kent, Linda *BioIn 16*
Kent, Linda Gail 1946- *WhoAm 90*
Kent, Lori Marian 1957- *WhoEmL 91*
Kent, Louise 1886-1969 *AuBYP 90*
Kent, Michael Louis 1946- *WhoE 91*
Kent, Mollie 1933- *WhoWrEP 89*
Kent, Nancy Lee 1956- *WhoAmW 91*
Kent, Neil 1951- *ConAu 129*
Kent, Norman 1903-1972 *WhoAmA 91N*
Kent, Patricia *BiDrAPA 89*
Kent, Paula *WhoAm 90*
Kent, Perry *BioIn 16*
Kent, Peter Blodget 1948- *St&PR 91*
Kent, Peter J. 1946- *St&PR 91*
Kent, Raymond Knezevich 1929- *WhoAm 90*
Kent, Richard Vincent 1949- *WhoWrEP 89*
Kent, Robert Brydon 1921- *WhoAm 90*
Kent, Robert Joel *BiDrAPA 89*
Kent, Robert John 1835-1893 *DcCanB 12*
Kent, Robert John 1947- *WhoEmL 91*
Kent, Robert John 1948- *WhoE 91*
Kent, Robert Warren 1935- *St&PR 91, WhoAm 90*
Kent, Roberta B. 1945- *WhoAmW 91*
Kent, Rockwell 1882-1971 *WhoAmA 91N, WorAlBi*
Kent, Roderick Sidney 1946- *WhoEmL 91*
Kent, Rolly 1946- *WhoWrEP 89*
Kent, Roy Norman 1944- *St&PR 91, WhoE 91*
Kent, Sally Litherland 1937- *WhoAmW 91*
Kent, Samuel Louis 1951- *BiDrAPA 89*
Kent, Sandra Lee 1946- *WhoWrEP 89*
Kent, Sherman 1903-1986 *BioIn 16*
Kent, Sherman B. 1927- *St&PR 91*
Kent, Steven Peter 1950- *St&PR 91*
Kent, Steven Robert 1943- *St&PR 91*
Kent, Theodore Charles *WhoWor 91*
Kent, Thomas Andrew *BiDrAPA 89*
Kent, Thomas Frederick 1940- *St&PR 91*
Kent, Walter 1911- *OxCPMus*
Kent, Warren T. 1925- *St&PR 91*
Kent, William 1685-1748 *PenDiDA 89*
Kent, William A. 1942- *WhoSSW 91*
Kent, William B. 1955- *St&PR 91*
Kent, Zachary *AuBYP 90*
Kentish, John William 1938- *St&PR 91*
Kentner, Louis 1905-1987 *PenDiMP*
Kenton, Frank Joseph 1950- *WhoEmL 91*
Kenton, James Alan 1955- *WhoAm 90*
Kenton, Ken 1942- *WhoSSW 91*
Kenton, Mary Jean 1946- *WhoAmA 91*
Kenton, Simon 1755-1836 *WhNaAH*
Kenton, Stan 1912-1979 *BioIn 16, OxCPMus, WorAlBi*
Kenton Smith, Wanda Gayle 1957- *WhoAmW 91*
Kentsmith, David K 1940- *BiDrAPA 89*
Kentucky Headhunters *ConMus 5 [port]*
Kenvin, Helene Enid 1941- *WhoAmW 91*
Kenward, John F 1913- *BiDrAPA 89*
Kenward, John Franklin 1913-1989 *BioIn 16*
Kenway, Reginald G. 1912- *St&PR 91*
Kenworthey, Charles Warner 1925- *WhoSSW 91, WhoWor 91*
Kenworthy, Bud *BioIn 16*
Kenworthy, James Lawrence 1937- *WhoE 91*
Kenworthy, Jean Marie 1960- *WhoAmW 91*
Kenworthy, Ken L. 1935- *St&PR 91*
Kenworthy, Lucretia Mina 1962- *WhoAmW 91*
Kenworthy, N. Paul 1925- *BioIn 16*
Kenworthy, Nelson A. *BioIn 16*
Kenyatta, Jomo 1891?-1978 *MajTwCW*
Kenyatta, Jomo 1894?-1978 *WorAlBi*
Kenyhercz, Thomas Michael 1950- *WhoE 91, WhoWor 91*
Kenyon, Bruce Davis 1943- *St&PR 91, WhoE 91*
Kenyon, Bruce Guy 1929- *WhoWrEP 89*
Kenyon, Cecelia M. *BioIn 16*
Kenyon, Charles Moir 1916- *WhoAm 90*
Kenyon, Colleen Frances 1951- *WhoAmA 91*
Kenyon, Daphne Anne 1952- *WhoAmW 91*
Kenyon, Edward Tipton 1929- *WhoAm 90*
Kenyon, Gary Michael 1949- *WhoAm 90*
Kenyon, Hewitt 1920- *WhoAm 90*
Kenyon, Jack Munro 1915- *BiDrAPA 89*
Kenyon, James A. 1938- *St&PR 91*
Kenyon, John Michael 1949- *St&PR 91*
Kenyon, Josephine 1944- *WhoAmW 91*
Kenyon, Judith Eleanor 1948- *WhoAmW 91*
Kenyon, Julia Caroline 1919- *WhoAmW 91*
Kenyon, Karen Beth 1938- *WhoWrEP 89*
Kenyon, Kate *ConAu 31NR*
Kenyon, Laurin McAlister 1963- *WhoEmL 91*
Kenyon, Michael *BioIn 16*
Kenyon, Michael 1931- *TwCCr&M 91*
Kenyon, Michael Lee 1943- *WhoE 91*
Kenyon, Nicholas Roger 1951- *IntWWM 90*
Kenyon, Raymond G. 1922- *AuBYP 90*
Kenyon, Richard Albert 1933- *WhoAm 90*
Kenyon, Richard John 1943- *St&PR 91*
Kenyon, Robert Edwin, Jr. 1908- *WhoAm 90, WhoE 91*
Kenyon, Roger Alan 1953- *WhoE 91, WhoEmL 91*
Kenyon, Sidney Eugene 1959- *WhoSSW 91*
Kenyon, Thomas Leo 1938- *WhoE 91*
Kenyon, Victor Gerard 1926- *WhoAm 90*
Kenyon, William Riley 1833-1914 *AmLegL*
Kenzan 1663-1743 *EncJap*
Kenzan VI *PenDiDA 89*
Kenzan VII *PenDiDA 89*
Kenzan, Korin *PenDiDA 89*
Kenzan, Ogata Shinsei 1663-1743 *PenDiDA 89*
Kenzer, Gary Edward 1957- *WhoEmL 91*
Kenzie, Ross Bruce 1931- *WhoAm 90*
Kenzingen, Magdalena von *EncCoWW*
Kenzo *WhoWor 91*
Kenzo 1939- *ConDes 90*
Kenzo Takada *EncJap*
Keogh, Edward 1835-1898 *AmLegL*
Keogh, Eugene James 1907-1989 *BioIn 16*
Keogh, Heidi Helen Dake 1950- *WhoAmW 91*
Keogh, James 1916- *WhoAm 90*
Keogh, Jeanne Marie 1924- *WhoWor 91*
Keogh, Monica Leverone 1954- *WhoAmW 91*
Keohane, Nannerl Overholser 1940- *WhoAm 90, WhoAmW 91, WhoE 91*
Keohane, Philip M *ODwPR 91*
Keohane, Robert O. 1941- *ConAu 33NR*
Keohane, Robert Owen 1941- *WhoAm 90*
Keokuk 1783?-1848 *WhNaAH [port]*
Keon, Linda Elizabeth 1950- *WhoAmW 91*
Keosseian, Charles Jospeh 1929- *St&PR 91*
Keough, Daniel *BioIn 16*
Keough, Danielle Riley *BioIn 16*
Keough, Donald L. 1941- *St&PR 91*
Keough, Donald Raymond 1926- *St&PR 91, WhoAm 90, WhoSSW 91*
Keough, Francis Paul 1917- *WhoAm 90*
Keough, James Gillman, Jr. 1947- *WhoWor 91*
Keough, James Gordon 1946- *WhoAm 90, WhoE 91*
Keough, Jeffrey 1953- *WhoAmA 91*
Keough, Joe 1946- *Ballpl 90*
Keough, Marty 1935- *Ballpl 90*
Keough, Matt 1955- *Ballpl 90*
Keough, William D. *ODwPR 91*
Keough, William H. 1937- *St&PR 91*
Keough-Lewis, Patricia Ann 1957- *WhoE 91*
Keoun, L. Craig 1939- *St&PR 91*
Keowen, Sheralee June 1939- *St&PR 91*
Keown, Richard C 1946- *BiDrAPA 89*
Kepalas *WhoAmA 91*
Kepecs, Joseph G 1912- *BiDrAPA 89*
Kepecs, Joseph Goodman 1912- *WhoAm 90*
Kepes, Gyorgy 1906- *ConDes 90, WhoAmA 91, WhoWor 91*
Kepes, Juliet Appleby 1919- *AuBYP 90*

Kepets, Hugh Michael 1946- *WhoAm 90, WhoAmA 91*
Kephart, A. Evans 1905- *WhoAm 90*
Kephart, H. Harrison, Jr. 1940- *St&PR 91*
Kephart, James William 1955- *WhoEmL 91*
Kephart, Larry Robert 1949- *WhoEmL 91*
Kephart, Lori Maureen Du'Mont 1968- *WhoAmW 91*
Kephart, Mirrel, Jr. 1946- *ODwPR 91*
Kephart, William Milton 1919- *WhoAm 90*
Kepler, Elise Anne 1964- *WhoAmW 91, WhoE 91*
Kepler, Jimmie Aaron 1953- *WhoSSW 91*
Kepler, Johann 1571-1630 *EncO&P 3*
Kepler, Johannes 1571-1630 *BioIn 16, WorAlBi*
Kepler, Patricia Anne 1942- *WhoAmW 91*
Kepler, Raymond Glen 1928- *WhoAm 90*
Kepley, James Spencer 1942- *WhoAm 90*
Kepley, Thomas Alvin 1928- *WhoAm 90*
Kepley, Thomas Howard 1933- *WhoWor 91*
Keplinger, Bruce 1952- *WhoEmL 91*
Keplinger, Duane 1926- *WhoSSW 91*
Keplinger, Robert B., Jr. 1932- *St&PR 91*
Kepner, Janet Sumner 1936- *WhoAmW 91*
Kepner, Rita 1944- *WhoAmA 91*
Kepner, Rita Marie 1944- *WhoAmW 91, WhoWor 91*
Kepner, Woody 1920- *ODwPR 91, WhoAm 90, WhoWor 91*
Kepp, John Ward, Jr. 1945- *WhoEmL 91*
Keppard, Freddie 1890-1933 *OxCPMus*
Keppel, Alice 1869-1947 *BioIn 16*
Keppel, Charlotte *TwCCr&M 91*
Keppel, Christina C 1951- *BiDrAPA 89*
Keppel, Francis *NewYTBS 90 [port]*
Keppel, Francis 1916-1990 *CurBio 90N*
Keppel, Francis C. *BioIn 16*
Keppel, James D. 1944- *St&PR 91*
Keppel, John 1917- *WhoAm 90*
Keppel, Robert F. 1918- *St&PR 91*
Keppel, William Henry *BiDrAPA 89*
Kepple, Ronald Lee 1934- *St&PR 91*
Kepple, Thomas Ray, Jr. 1948- *WhoAm 90*
Keppler, Billie Jo 1949- *WhoAmW 91*
Keppler, Herbert 1925- *WhoAm 90*
Keppler, Jodell Anne 1959- *St&PR 91*
Keppler, Johannes 1571-1630 *BioIn 16*
Keppler, William Edmund 1922- *WhoAm 90*
Kepshire, Kurt 1959- *Ballpl 90*
Kepuraitis, Peggy Mary 1961- *WhoAmW 91*
Ker, Ann Steele 1937- *IntWWM 90*
Ker, Anne 1766?-1820? *FemiCLE*
Ker, Jill *ConAu 130*
Ker, Louisa Theresa Bellenden *FemiCLE*
Ker, Neil Ripley 1908-1982 *DcNaB 1981*
Keracher, John 1880-1958 *EncAL*
Keraga, Gloria Theresa *BiDrAPA 89*
Keram, Stevan *BiDrAPA 89*
Keran, Jerry E. 1941- *St&PR 91*
Keran, Michael William 1931- *St&PR 91*
Keranen, Gary John 1948- *St&PR 91*
Kerbawy, Nick *BioIn 16*
Kerbel, John J. 1944- *St&PR 91*
Kerbel, Marcos Alan 1946- *WhoEmL 91*
Kerber, John L. 1926- *St&PR 91*
Kerber, Kevin Brian 1953- *BiDrAPA 89*
Kerber, Linda Kaufman 1940- *WhoAm 90*
Kerber, Ronald L. 1943- *St&PR 91*
Kerber, Ronald Lee 1943- *WhoAm 90*
Kerber, Walter Josef 1926- *WhoWor 91*
Kerbeshian, Jacob 1944- *BiDrAPA 89*
Kerbiriou, Yves Raymond 1950- *WhoWor 91*
Kerbis, Gertrude Lempp *WhoAm 90*
Kerbow, Odis Doyce 1932- *St&PR 91*
Kerby, Philip Pearce 1911- *WhoAm 90*
Kerby, Robert Browning 1938- *WhoSSW 91, WhoWor 91*
Kerby, Stewart L. 1936- *St&PR 91*
Kerby, Stewart Lawrence 1936- *WhoAm 90*
Kerby, William 1908-1989 *AnObit 1989*
Kerby, William F. 1908-1989 *BioIn 16*
Kerch, John G., Jr. 1931- *St&PR 91*
Kercher, Arthur J. *BioIn 16*
Kercher, Edwin C. 1946- *St&PR 91*
Kercher, Eugene Edward 1939- *BiDrAPA 89*
Kercher, Robert A. *BioIn 16*
Kercheval, Ken 1935- *WhoAm 90*
Kercheville, R. James 1939- *ODwPR 91*
Kerchner, Charles F., Jr. 1945- *St&PR 91*
Kerchner, Charles Frederick, Jr. 1945- *WhoE 91*
Kercho, Randy S. 1956- *St&PR 91*
Kerckhoff, Alan C 1924- *ConAu 32NR*
Kerckhoff, Richard Daniel 1905- *St&PR 91*
Kerdasha, Robert J. *BioIn 16*
Kerekou, Mathieu 1933- *WhoWor 91*
Keremes, Constance Andrea 1958- *WhoWrEP 89*
Keren, Ron 1954- *BiDrAPA 89*
Kerensky, Aleksandr Fyodorovich 1881-1970 *BioIn 16*
Kerensky, Alexander 1881-1970 *WorAlBi*
Kerensky, Oleg Alexander 1905-1984 *DcNaB 1981*
Kerenyi, Gyorgy 1902- *IntWWM 90*
Kerenyi, Kristine K. 1955- *ODwPR 91*
Keres, Karen Lynne 1945- *WhoAmW 91, WhoEmL 91*
Keresey, Thomas M. 1931- *St&PR 91*
Kerester, Charles John 1927- *WhoAm 90*
Kerestes, Michael C. 1946- *St&PR 91*
Keresztesi, Koloman 1916- *WhoWor 91*
Kerezy, John D. 1957- *ODwPR 91*
Kerfeld, Charlie 1963- *Ballpl 90*
Kerferd, G B 1915- *ConAu 132*
Kerfoot, Glenn Warren 1921- *WhoWrEP 89*
Kerfoot, Henry Bartlett 1952- *WhoEmL 91*
Kergosien, Harold A. 1947- *St&PR 91*
Kerich, J. Patrick 1938- *St&PR 91*
Kerillis, Henri Adrien Calloc'h de 1889-1958 *BiDFrPL*
Kerina, Mburumba 1932- *ConAu 129*
Kerins, Francis Joseph 1927- *WhoAm 90*
Kerins, Paul T. 1943- *St&PR 91*
Kerins, Thomas Edward 1945- *St&PR 91*
Keriotis, Constantinos Gus 1917- *WhoSSW 91*
Kerivan, William Robert 1945- *WhoSSW 91*
Kerkam, Earl 1890-1965 *WhoAmA 91N*
Kerkel, Lynn 1942- *WhoAmW 91*
Kerker, Gustav 1857-1923 *OxCPMus*
Kerker, Milton 1920- *WhoAm 90*
Kerkhoff, Susanne 1918-1950 *EncCoWW*
Kerkorian, Kirk 1917- *WhoAm 90*
Kerkovius, Ida 1879-1970 *BiDWomA*
Kerler, William R. 1929- *St&PR 91*
Kerley, F. Michael 1945- *WhoEmL 91*
Kerley, Gary Lee 1949- *WhoWrEP 89*
Kerley, James Homer, Jr. 1925- *St&PR 91*
Kerley, Janice Johnson 1938- *WhoAmW 91*
Kerley, Thomas O. 1941- *St&PR 91*
Kerlikowsky, Horst 1939- *WhoWor 91*
Kerlin, Donald James 1942- *WhoE 91*
Kerlin, Gilbert 1909- *St&PR 91*
Kerlin, Richard M. *ODwPR 91*
Kerman, Edward F *BiDrAPA 89*
Kerman, Edward R. 1943- *St&PR 91*
Kerman, Gertrude *ConAu 31NR*
Kerman, Joseph 1924- *WorAu 1980 [port]*
Kerman, Joseph Wilfred 1924- *IntWWM 90, WhoAm 90*
Kerman, Judith Berna 1945- *WhoWrEP 89*
Kerman, Jules 1944- *BiDrAPA 89*
Kerman, Susan H 1946- *BiDrAPA 89*
Kermani, Peter Rustam 1940- *WhoAm 90*
Kermath, Nancy Ann 1950- *BiDrAPA 89*
Kermeen, J.S. 1930- *St&PR 91*
Kermeen, Sharon Kay 1938- *WhoAmW 91*
Kermes, Constantine John 1923- *WhoAmA 91, WhoE 91*
Kermode, Frank 1919- *WhoAm 90*
Kermon, Margaret Anne 1956- *WhoEmL 91*
Kermott, Cameron Hayes *BiDrAPA 89*
Kern, Adele 1901-1980 *PenDiMP*
Kern, Angeline Frazier 1939- *WhoAmW 91*
Kern, Arthur 1931- *WhoAmA 91*
Kern, Barbara Patricia 1935- *WhoAmW 91*
Kern, Benjamin Jordan 1818-1849 *WhNaAH*
Kern, Bernard Donald 1919- *WhoAm 90*
Kern, Canyon *WhoWrEP 89*
Kern, Charles William 1935- *WhoAm 90, WhoWor 91*
Kern, Constance Elizabeth 1937- *WhoAmW 91*
Kern, Daniel Edmund 1965- *WhoE 91*
Kern, David Jeffrey 1950- *WhoEmL 91*
Kern, Dennis Matthew 1948- *WhoSSW 91*
Kern, Edith 1912- *WhoAm 90, WhoWrEP 89*
Kern, Edna Ruth 1945- *WhoEmL 91*
Kern, Edward Evans *BiDrAPA 89*
Kern, Edward Meyer 1834-1863 *WhNaAH*
Kern, Ellyn R. 1938- *WhoWrEP 89*
Kern, Eugene Francis 1919- *WhoWor 91*
Kern, Frank Norton 1920- *WhoE 91, WhoWor 91*
Kern, Franklin Lorenz 1932- *WhoAm 90*
Kern, Fred, Jr. 1918- *WhoAm 90*
Kern, Fred Robert, Jr. 1943- *WhoE 91*
Kern, Geof *BioIn 16*
Kern, George C. 1926- *St&PR 91*
Kern, George Calvin, Jr. 1926- *WhoAm 90*
Kern, Gerald N. 1938- *St&PR 91*
Kern, Harry Frederick 1911- *BioIn 16, WhoAm 90*
Kern, Herbert *BiDrAPA 89*
Kern, Howard M 1925- *BiDrAPA 89*
Kern, Irving John 1914- *WhoAm 90*
Kern, Jerome 1885-1945 *BioIn 16, OxCPMus, PenDiMP A, WorAlBi*
Kern, Jerome H. 1937- *WhoAm 90*
Kern, Jill Phelps 1956- *WhoAmW 91*
Kern, Jim 1949- *Ballpl 90*
Kern, John Sheldon 1960- *BiDrAPA 89*
Kern, John Worth, III 1928- *WhoE 91*
Kern, Joseph F. *BioIn 16*
Kern, Judy *BiDrAPA 89*
Kern, Mark Sherwood 1959- *WhoSSW 91*
Kern, Martin H. 1941- *St&PR 91*
Kern, Martin Harold 1941- *WhoAm 90*
Kern, Patricia 1927- *IntWWM 90, PenDiMP*
Kern, Patricia Joan 1933- *WhoAmW 91*
Kern, Paul Alfred 1958- *WhoEmL 91, WhoWor 91*
Kern, Paul R. 1926- *St&PR 91*
Kern, Portia *BioIn 16*
Kern, Regina Flora 1948- *WhoAmW 91*
Kern, Richard Hovendon 1821-1853 *WhNaAH*
Kern, Stanley R 1928- *BiDrAPA 89*
Kern, Stanley Robert 1928- *WhoE 91*
Kern, Thomas G *BiDrAPA 89*
Kern, Vincent James 1951- *WhoEmL 91*
Kern, W. Michael 1946- *ODwPR 91*
Kern, William Ira 1938- *St&PR 91*
Kern-Foxworth, Marilyn Louise 1954- *WhoAmW 91, WhoEmL 91, WhoSSW 91, WhoWor 91*
Kern John, McDougall 1946- *WhoEmL 91*
Kernahan, Dennis Arthur 1948- *St&PR 91*
Kernan, Alvin B. 1923- *ConAu 33NR*
Kernan, Alvin Bernard 1923- *WhoAm 90*
Kernan, Barbara Desind 1939- *WhoAm 90, WhoAmW 91, WhoE 91, WhoWor 91*
Kernan, Mary Catherine 1957- *WhoAmW 91*
Kernberg, Otto F 1928- *BiDrAPA 89*
Kernberg, Paulina F *BiDrAPA 89*
Kerne, Barbara Davis 1938- *WhoAmA 91*
Kernell, John *ODwPR 91*
Kernen, Jules Alfred 1929- *WhoAm 90*
Kerner, Barry Ira *BiDrAPA 89*
Kerner, Ben *AuBYP 90*
Kerner, Carol A. 1939- *ODwPR 91*
Kerner, Carol Ann 1939- *St&PR 91*
Kerner, Deborah Ann 1961- *WhoWrEP 89*
Kerner, Fred 1921- *WhoAm 90, WhoE 91, WhoWor 91, WhoWrEP 89*
Kerner, Justinus 1786-1862 *EncO&P 3*
Kerner, Martin 1947- *WhoEmL 91, WhoSSW 91*
Kerney, Evelyn Loretta 1945- *WhoAmW 91*
Kerney, Suzanne Elizabeth 1953- *BiDrAPA 89*
Kerney, Thomas Lincoln, II 1950- *WhoE 91, WhoWor 91*
Kernfeld, Barry Dean 1950- *IntWWM 90*
Kernig, Claus Dieter 1927- *WhoWor 91*
Kernisan, Junie Marie *BiDrAPA 89*
Kernn-Larsen, Rita 1904- *BiDWomA*
Kernochan, John Marshall 1919- *WhoAm 90*
Kernodle, Rigdon Wayne 1919- *WhoAm 90*
Kernodle, Una Mae 1947- *WhoAmW 91*
Kerns, Christianne Finch 1958- *WhoAmW 91, WhoEmL 91*
Kerns, Ed, Jr 1945- *WhoAmA 91*
Kerns, Gertrude Yvonne 1931- *WhoAmW 91, WhoWor 91*
Kerns, Ginger 1948- *WhoAmA 91*
Kerns, Joanna *BioIn 16*
Kerns, Joanna 1953- *ConTFT 8*
Kerns, Joanna 1955- *WorAlBi*
Kerns, Kim Ann 1960- *WhoAmW 91*
Kerns, Lawrence L. *BiDrAPA 89*
Kerns, Rhonda Lynn 1959- *WhoEmL 91*
Kerns, Robert 1933-1989 *AnObit 1989*
Kerns, Robert Louis 1929- *WhoAm 90*
Kerns, Robert Owen 1933- *St&PR 91*
Kerouac, Jack *MajTwCW*
Kerouac, Jack 1922-1969 *BioIn 16, ConLC 61 [port], WorAlBi*
Kerouac, Jean-Louis Lebrid de 1922-1969 *MajTwCW*
Kerouac, John *MajTwCW*
Kerpchar, Michael 1924- *WhoE 91*
Kerpelman, Larry C. 1939- *St&PR 91*
Kerpelman, Larry Cyril 1939- *WhoE 91*
Kerper, Duane J. 1939- *St&PR 91*
Kerper, Meike 1929- *WhoAmW 91*
Kerr, Alva Rae 1926- *WhoSSW 91*
Kerr, Andy *BioIn 16*
Kerr, Anthony Robert 1941- *WhoAm 90*
Kerr, Arthur 1926-1979 *WhoAmA 91N*
Kerr, Baine Perkins 1919- *St&PR 91*
Kerr, Banks D. 1922- *St&PR 91*
Kerr, Ben *TwCCr&M 91*
Kerr, Blair M. 1930- *St&PR 91*
Kerr, Bonnie Lynn 1943- *WhoAmW 91*
Kerr, Breene Mitchell, Jr. 1952- *WhoEmL 91*
Kerr, Buddy 1922- *Ballpl 90, BioIn 16*
Kerr, Carol Mary 1958- *WhoSSW 91*
Kerr, Charles Giese 1956- *WhoEmL 91*
Kerr, Charles H. 1860- *EncAL*
Kerr, Charles M 1935- *BiDrAPA 89*
Kerr, Charles Randall 1933- *WhoSSW 91*
Kerr, Charlotte Herman 1920- *WhoAmW 91*
Kerr, Chester Brooks 1913- *WhoAm 90, WhoWor 91*
Kerr, Christen McCullough *BiDrAPA 89*
Kerr, Christopher Richard 1947- *WhoAm 90*
Kerr, Clarence William 1923- *WhoAm 90*
Kerr, Clark 1911- *WhoAm 90*
Kerr, Cynthia Joan 1947- *WhoEmL 91*
Kerr, Darlene Buckley 1947- *WhoE 91*
Kerr, David Wylie 1943- *WhoAm 90*
Kerr, Deborah 1921- *WorAlBi*
Kerr, Deborah Jane 1921- *WhoAm 90, WhoWor 91*
Kerr, Deborah Lee 1950- *WhoEmL 91*
Kerr, Deborah MacPhail 1951- *WhoAmW 91*
Kerr, Dickey 1893-1963 *Ballpl 90*
Kerr, Donald Jon 1938- *St&PR 91*
Kerr, Donald MacLean, Jr. 1939- *WhoAm 90*
Kerr, Dorothy Marie Burmeister 1935- *WhoAm 90*
Kerr, E Coe 1914-1973 *WhoAmA 91N*
Kerr, Edmund H. 1924- *St&PR 91*
Kerr, Edmund Hugh 1924- *WhoAm 90*
Kerr, Edward Lawrence 1934- *St&PR 91*
Kerr, Elizabeth Margaret 1905- *WhoAmW 91*
Kerr, Ewing Thomas 1900- *WhoAm 90*
Kerr, Frank John 1918- *WhoAm 90, WhoE 91, WhoWor 91*
Kerr, Fred 1947- *St&PR 91*
Kerr, Gordon J. 1953- *St&PR 91*
Kerr, Harris Eastham 1951- *WhoSSW 91*
Kerr, Hugh Thomson 1909- *WhoAm 90*
Kerr, Ian 1925- *ODwPR 91*
Kerr, J. S. *AmLegL*
Kerr, James Joseph 1926- *St&PR 91, WhoE 91*
Kerr, James Roderick 1948- *WhoAm 90*
Kerr, James W. 1914- *St&PR 91, WhoAm 90*
Kerr, James Wilfrid 1897- *WhoAmA 91*
Kerr, James Wilson 1921- *WhoWor 91*
Kerr, Janice Allen 1949- *WhoEmL 91*
Kerr, Jean *BioIn 16*
Kerr, Jean 1923- *FemiCLE, NotWoAT, WhoAm 90, WhoWrEP 89, WorAlBi*
Kerr, Jessica 1901- *AuBYP 90*
Kerr, Jim Forrest, Jr. *BiDrAPA 89*
Kerr, Joan Ziegler 1949- *WhoAmW 91*
Kerr, John 1898-1980 *Ballpl 90*
Kerr, John, Jr. 1925- *St&PR 91*
Kerr, John E. 1940- *St&PR 91*
Kerr, John G. 1953- *St&PR 91*
Kerr, John R. *ODwPR 91*
Kerr, Johnny *BioIn 16*
Kerr, Judith 1923- *AuBYP 90*
Kerr, Kathryn Ann 1946- *WhoWrEP 89*
Kerr, Kleon Harding 1911- *WhoWor 91*
Kerr, Laura 1904- *AuBYP 90*
Kerr, Leslie Ann 1949- *WhoEmL 91, WhoWrEP 89*
Kerr, Lisa Bruening 1962- *WhoAmW 91*
Kerr, Lois Reynolds 1908- *OxCCanT*
Kerr, Louise A. 1938- *WhoHisp 91*
Kerr, M Dorthea *BiDrAPA 89*
Kerr, M. E. *BioIn 16*
Kerr, M E *MajTwCW*
Kerr, M. E. 1927- *AuBYP 90*
Kerr, M E 1927- *SmATA X [port]*
Kerr, Mabel Dorothea *WhoAmW 91*
Kerr, Merle Duane 1947- *St&PR 91, WhoEmL 91*
Kerr, Michael Alan 1956- *St&PR 91*
Kerr, Michael E 1940- *BiDrAPA 89*
Kerr, Myron Thomas, Jr. 1932- *St&PR 91*
Kerr, Nancy Helen 1947- *WhoAmW 91, WhoSSW 91*
Kerr, Norman Charles, Jr. 1930- *WhoWor 91*
Kerr, Pat *BioIn 16*
Kerr, Paul William 1930- *St&PR 91*
Kerr, Robert S. *BioIn 16*
Kerr, Robert S. 1896-1963 *WorAlBi*
Kerr, Robert Samuel 1896-1963 *ConAmBL*
Kerr, Robert Samuel, III 1950- *WhoSSW 91*
Kerr, Robert Shaw 1917- *WhoE 91*
Kerr, Robert Willis, Jr. 1947- *WhoEmL 91*
Kerr, Ron 1947- *WhoSSW 91*
Kerr, Sandria Neidus 1940- *WhoSSW 91*
Kerr, Stanley B. 1928- *St&PR 91, WhoAm 90*
Kerr, Stephen Denton 1939- *WhoSSW 91*
Kerr, Stephen Robert *WhoE 91*
Kerr, Steve *BioIn 16*
Kerr, Sylvia Joann 1941- *WhoAmW 91*
Kerr, Thomas Adolphus 1923- *WhoAm 90*
Kerr, Thomas J. 1945- *St&PR 91*
Kerr, Thomas Jefferson, IV 1933- *WhoAm 90*
Kerr, Thomas Robert 1950- *WhoEmL 91*
Kerr, Tim 1930- *WorAlBi*
Kerr, Tim 1960- *WhoAm 90*

Kerr, Tom 1929- OxCCanT
Kerr, Virginia May 1928- St&PR 91
Kerr, W.H. PenDiDA 89
Kerr, Walter 1913- WorAlBi
Kerr, Walter F. 1913- WhoAm 90, WhoWrEP 89
Kerr, Walter H. 1914- WhoWrEP 89
Kerr, Walter Hughes 1927- St&PR 91
Kerr, Warwick Estevam 1922- WhoWor 91
Kerr, William 1919- WhoAm 90
Kerr, William Andrew 1934- WhoAm 90, WhoWor 91
Kerr, William Donald 1948- St&PR 91
Kerr, William T. 1941- WhoAm 90
Kerr, William Turnbull 1941- St&PR 91
Kerrebrock, Jack Leo 1928- WhoAm 90
Kerremans, Andre E.M.C. 1935- WhoWor 91
Kerrey, Bob 1943- WhoAm 90, WhoWor 91
Kerrey, Joseph Robert 1943- WorAlBi
Kerrey, Robert BioIn 16
Kerrick, David Ellsworth 1951- WhoEmL 91
Kerrick, Gray 1943- WhoAm 90
Kerrick, Jill Maureen 1964- WhoAmW 91
Kerrick, Jon Paul 1939- St&PR 91
Kerridge, Isaac C., Jr. 1924- St&PR 91
Kerridge, Isaac Curtis, Jr. 1924- WhoAm 90
Kerrigan, Amelia Burnham BiDrAPA 89
Kerrigan, Anthony 1918- WhoAm 90, WhoWrEP 89
Kerrigan, James Leo 1929- WhoSSW 91
Kerrigan, James W. 1936- St&PR 91
Kerrigan, Joe 1954- Ballpl 90
Kerrigan, Juanita Irene 1946- St&PR 91
Kerrigan, Mauric 1951- WhoAmA 91
Kerrigan, Patrick J. 1952- St&PR 91
Kerrigan, Walter W., II 1953- WhoEmL 91
Kerrigan, William Paul 1953- WhoEmL 91
Kerry, John 1825-1896 DcCanB 12
Kerry, John Forbes 1943- BioIn 16, WhoAm 90, WhoE 91, WhoWor 91
Kerry, Lois AuBYP 90
Kersavage, Carol Joan 1934- WhoWrEP 89
Kersch, Robert Stanley 1928- St&PR 91
Kerschbaum, Wesley Edward BiDrAPA 89
Kerschbaumer, Luisa BiDrAPA 89
Kerschbaumer, Marie-Therese 1936- EncCoWW
Kerschner, Joan Gentry 1945- WhoAmW 91
Kerschner, Lee Ronald 1931- WhoAm 90
Kersee, Jackie Joyner- BioIn 16
Kersey, Dallas M. ODwPR 91
Kersey, Dallas Manyette 1942- WhoE 91
Kersey, David Leonard BiDrAPA 89
Kersey, Eda 1904-1944 PenDiMP
Kersey, John TwCCr&M 91
Kersey, Terry Lee 1947- WhoEmL 91, WhoWor 91
Kersey, Timothy Lee 1962- WhoSSW 91
Kersh, Bert Yarbrough 1927- WhoAm 90
Kersh, Gerald 1911-1968 TwCCr&M 91
Kersh, John Danzey, Jr. 1950- WhoEmL 91
Kershaw, Carol Jean 1947- WhoAmW 91
Kershaw, James Robert 1946- WhoWrEP 89
Kershaw, John J. 1944- St&PR 91
Kershaw, Joseph 1927- WhoAm 90
Kershaw, Joseph A. 1913-1989 BioIn 16
Kershaw, R.A. St&PR 91
Kershaw, Thomas Abbott 1938- WhoE 91
Kershaw, Thomas Martin 1933- WhoE 91
Kershbaumer, Louis August 1931- St&PR 91
Kershner, Howard E. NewYTBS 90
Kershner, Howard E. 1891-1990 BioIn 16
Kershner, Irvin BioIn 16
Kershner, Lori Evangelos 1960- WhoE 91
Kershner, Raymond D. 1925- ODwPR 91
Kershner, Thomas Gordon 1941- St&PR 91
Kershul, Victor W 1923- BiDrAPA 89
Kersjes, Anton Frans Jan 1923- IntWWM 90, WhoWor 91
Kerski, David Lawrence BiDrAPA 89
Kerski, Karen Lee 1955- WhoE 91, WhoEmL 91
Kerslake, Kenneth Alvin 1930- WhoAm 90, WhoAmA 91
Kerson, Don 1954- BiDrAPA 89
Kerson, Paul Eugene 1951- WhoEmL 91
Kerst, Donald William 1911- WhoAm 90
Kerste, Donald L BiDrAPA 89
Kerstein, David Louis 1944- St&PR 91
Kerstein, Lawrence 1922- St&PR 91
Kersten, Albert Emmanuel 1943- WhoWor 91
Kersten, Horst PenDiDA 89
Kersten, Jan Martinus Lambertus M. 1931- WhoWor 91
Kersten, Paul M 1919- BiDrAPA 89
Kersten, Walter Heinrich 1926- WhoWor 91
Kerstetter, Michael James 1936- WhoAm 90
Kerstetter, Raymond John, Jr. 1936- St&PR 91
Kerstetter-Hull, Joanne Rita 1952- WhoAmW 91
Kerstiens, Ludwig 1924- WhoWor 91
Kersting, Edwin Joseph 1919- WhoAm 90
Kersting, John William 1940- BiDrAPA 89
Kersting-Kraus, Simone 1955- WhoEmL 91
Kerstner, Ralph Melvin 1932- St&PR 91
Kerswill, J W Roy 1925- WhoAmA 91
Kerswill, Randy Michael BiDrAPA 89
Kertess, Hans William 1939- St&PR 91
Kertesz, Attila 1942- IntWWM 90
Kertesz, George Joseph 1928- St&PR 91
Kertesz, Istvan 1929-1973 PenDiMP
Kertesz, Ivan 1930- IntWWM 90
Kertesz, Louis R. 1947- St&PR 91
Kerth, Alfred H., III ODwPR 91
Kerth, Leroy T. 1928- WhoAm 90
Kertz, Hubert Leonard 1910- WhoAm 90
Kertzner, Robert Michael 1952- BiDrAPA 89
Kerwin, Brian 1949- ConTFT 8
Kerwin, John Michael 1920- St&PR 91
Kerwin, Joseph Peter 1932- WhoAm 90
Kerwin, Larkin 1924- WhoAm 90, WhoWor 91
Kerwin, Lawrence J., Jr. 1927- St&PR 91
Kerwin, Patrick Joseph 1947- St&PR 91
Kerwin, Thomas Hugh 1930- St&PR 91, WhoAm 90
Kerwin, William James 1922- WhoAm 90
Kerwood, Lewis O. 1917- WhoE 91
Kerxton, Alan Smith 1938- WhoAm 90
Kery, Patricia Ann 1960- WhoE 91
Keryan, James Louis 1951- WhoEmL 91
Keryczynskyj, Leo Ihor 1948- WhoEmL 91
Keryk, Wendy Margaret 1951- St&PR 91
Kerz, Leo 1912-1976 ConDes 90
Kerze, Allan Richard 1946- WhoAm 90
Kerzie, Ted L 1943- WhoAmA 91
Kerzman, Norberto Luis-Maria 1943- WhoSSW 91
Kerzner, Stephen Douglas 1948- BiDrAPA 89
Kes, Willem 1856-1934 PenDiMP
Kesala, Raimo Olavi 1950- WhoWor 91
Keschl, Constance Frances 1949- WhoAmW 91
Kesegi, Pamela Lynne 1951- WhoAmW 91
Keser, Paul David 1927- WhoWor 91
Kesert, Benjamin H BiDrAPA 89
Keseru, Ilona 1933- BiDWomA
Kesey, Ken 1935- ConLC 64 [port], MajTwCW, WhoAm 90, WorAlBi
Kesey, Ken Elton 1935- WhoWrEP 89
Keshavadas, Satguru Sant NewAgE 90
Keshavan, Matcheri 1953- WhoE 91
Keshavan, Matcheri S BiDrAPA 89
Keshavarzi, Susan Ross 1947- WhoAmW 91
Keshtmand, Soltan Ali WhoWor 91
Kesisoglu, Garbis 1936- WhoWor 91
Keskiner, Ali 1929- BiDrAPA 89
Kesler, Clyde Ervin 1922- WhoAm 90
Kesler, Darrel J. 1949- WhoEmL 91
Kesler, Jay Lewis 1935- WhoAm 90
Kesler, Larry Badger 1938- WhoAm 90
Kesler, Olivia 1939- St&PR 91
Kesler, Stephen Edward 1940- WhoAm 90
Kesler-Corneil, Dian St&PR 91
Kesling, Annette Elizabeth 1931- WhoAmW 91
Kesling, Keith Kenton 1923- WhoWor 91
Kesper, Jeffrey Alan 1947- WhoE 91
Kessel, Alice Magaw 1860-1928 BioIn 16
Kessel, Barney 1923- BioIn 16
Kessel, Barry Lee 1949- WhoEmL 91
Kessel, Brina 1925- WhoAm 90
Kessel, Charles Ervin 1950- WhoSSW 91
Kessel, Dagobert Guntram 1935- WhoWor 91
Kessel, Frank 1948- St&PR 91
Kessel, Jeffrey Brian 1960- WhoWrEP 89
Kessel, Jerome Harvey 1943- BiDrAPA 89
Kessel, John Howard 1928- WhoAm 90, WhoWrEP 89
Kessel, Julie Beth BiDrAPA 89
Kessel, Martin 1901- BioIn 16
Kessel, Richard Glen 1931- WhoAm 90
Kessel, Shirley Kerner 1926- WhoE 91
Kesselbrenner, Israel BiDrAPA 89
Kesseler, Roger L. 1936- St&PR 91
Kesseler, Roger Louis 1936- WhoAm 90
Kesselhaut, Arthur 1935- St&PR 91
Kesselhaut, Arthur Melvyn 1935- WhoAm 90
Kessell, Mary 1914- BiDWomA
Kesselman, Bruce Alan 1951- WhoE 91, WhoEmL 91
Kesselman, Edward Charles 1952- WhoEmL 91
Kesselman, Frederic B. 1942- St&PR 91
Kesselman, Gayle BiDrAPA 89
Kesselman, Jonathan Rhys 1946- WhoAm 90
Kesselman, Madeline Elizabeth 1958- WhoEmL 91
Kesselman, Martin S 1936- BiDrAPA 89
Kesselman, Theodore Leonard 1932- WhoAm 90
Kesselman, Wendy 1940- NotWoAT
Kesselman, Wendy Ann BioIn 16
Kesselring, Albert 1885-1960 BioIn 16, WorAlBi
Kessen, William 1925- WhoAm 90
Kessiakoff, Robert Boris Alexander 1949- WhoWor 91
Kessinger, Don 1942- Ballpl 90
Kessinger, John Roy 1940- St&PR 91
Kessinger, Margaret Anne 1941- WhoAmW 91
Kessinger, Tom George 1941- WhoAm 90
Kesslen, Sheldon Robert 1936- St&PR 91
Kessler, A. D. 1923- WhoAm 90, WhoWor 91
Kessler, Alan 1945- WhoAmA 91
Kessler, Alan Craig 1950- WhoEmL 91, WhoWor 91
Kessler, Alan Lee 1950- WhoE 91
Kessler, Allen John, Jr. 1938- St&PR 91
Kessler, Andjela Loncaric 1952- WhoSSW 91
Kessler, Andrew Jay BiDrAPA 89
Kessler, Avraham Albert 1924- WhoWor 91
Kessler, Bryan K D 1948- BiDrAPA 89
Kessler, Christoph 1955- WhoWor 91
Kessler, Christopher C 1951- BiDrAPA 89
Kessler, David BioIn 16
Kessler, David R 1930- BiDrAPA 89
Kessler, Dietrich 1936- WhoAm 90
Kessler, Donald McWilliams 1952- WhoAm 90
Kessler, Doris Henrietta 1935- WhoAmW 91
Kessler, Edwin 1928- WhoAm 90
Kessler, Edwin S 1917- BiDrAPA 89
Kessler, Ethel 1922- AuBYP 90
Kessler, Gerald 1922- St&PR 91
Kessler, Harold David 1945- WhoE 91
Kessler, Herbert Leon 1941- WhoAm 90, WhoAmA 91, WhoE 91
Kessler, Irving Isar 1931- WhoAm 90
Kessler, Jacques Isaac 1929- WhoAm 90
Kessler, Jane Q 1946- WhoAmA 91
Kessler, Jascha Frederick 1929- WhoWrEP 89
Kessler, Jean S. 1954- WhoAmW 91, WhoE 91
Kessler, Jeffrey L. 1954- WhoEmL 91
Kessler, Joachim 1930- WhoWor 91
Kessler, John Edward 1941- St&PR 91
Kessler, John Henry 1945- St&PR 91
Kessler, John Otto 1928- WhoAm 90
Kessler, John W. 1919- WhoAm 90
Kessler, John Whitaker 1936- WhoAm 90
Kessler, Julie Lealoha 1960- WhoEmL 91
Kessler, Karen 1956- ODwPR 91
Kessler, Karl 1954- BiDrAPA 89
Kessler, Karl Gunther 1919- WhoAm 90
Kessler, Kenneth A BiDrAPA 89
Kessler, Kenneth Jay BiDrAPA 89
Kessler, Lawrence Bert 1946- WhoAm 90, WhoWor 91
Kessler, Lawrence Devlin 1936- WhoSSW 91
Kessler, Lawrence W. 1942- WhoWor 91
Kessler, Leizer R. 1939- St&PR 91
Kessler, Len 1927- ODwPR 91
Kessler, Leona Hanover 1925- WhoAmW 91
Kessler, Leonard 1937- BiDrAPA 89
Kessler, Leonard H 1921- WhoAmA 91
Kessler, Leonard P. 1921- AuBYP 90
Kessler, Linda Rudich 1949- BiDrAPA 89
Kessler, Luba BiDrAPA 89
Kessler, Marcia Sue 1947- WhoEmL 91
Kessler, Margaret Jennings 1944- WhoAmA 91
Kessler, Margaret Marie 1944- WhoAmW 91
Kessler, Mark Keil 1936- WhoAm 90
Kessler, Martin WhoAm 90
Kessler, Mary Elizabeth 1957- WhoEmL 91
Kessler, Maxine 1935- WhoAmW 91
Kessler, Milton 1917- St&PR 91, WhoWor 91
Kessler, Milton 1930- WhoAm 90, WhoWrEP 89
Kessler, Minuetta 1914- BioIn 16, IntWWM 90
Kessler, Minuetta Shumiatcher 1914- WhoAmW 91
Kessler, Morris H. 1920- St&PR 91
Kessler, Nathan 1923- WhoAm 90
Kessler, Otto H. 1910- St&PR 91
Kessler, Ralph Kenneth 1943- WhoAm 90
Kessler, Richard Jan 1948- BiDrAPA 89
Kessler, Robert Jack 1933- WhoAm 90
Kessler, Robert Richard 1935- St&PR 91
Kessler, Rod 1949- WhoWrEP 89
Kessler, Ronald Borek 1943- WhoAm 90
Kessler, Samuel BiDrAPA 89
Kessler, Shirley WhoAmA 91
Kessler, Stephen Lee 1943- St&PR 91
Kessler, Steven Gary BiDrAPA 89
Kessler, Theodore 1955- BiDrAPA 89
Kessler, Thomas Stuart 1951- WhoEmL 91
Kessler, Wallace Frank 1938- WhoE 91
Kessler, William Eugene 1944- WhoAm 90
Kessler, William Henry 1924- WhoAm 90
Kessler, Wirt Duane 1911- WhoWrEP 89
Kessler-Harris, Alice 1941- ConAu 32NR
Kessler-Hodgson, Lee Gwendolyn 1947- WhoAmW 91, WhoEmL 91
Kessman, Alan Stuart 1946- WhoAm 90
Kessmann, Roy William 1941- WhoSSW 91
Kessner, Daniel Aaron 1946- IntWWM 90, WhoEmL 91
Kessner, David NewAgMG
Kessner, David M 1932- BiDrAPA 89
Kesson, Jessie 1916- BioIn 16
Kesten, Hermann 1900- BioIn 16
Kesten, Mark M BiDrAPA 89
Kestenbaum, Clarice BiDrAPA 89
Kestenbaum, Harold L. 1949- St&PR 91
Kestenbaum, Harold Lee 1949- WhoEmL 91
Kestenbaum, Mel 1937- St&PR 91
Kestenberg, Judith S BiDrAPA 89
Kester, Eugene F BiDrAPA 89
Kester, Howard 1904-1977 EncAL
Kester, John Gordon 1938- WhoAm 90
Kester, Lenard 1917- WhoAm 90, WhoAmA 91
Kester, Randall Blair 1916- WhoAm 90
Kester, Stewart Randolph 1927- WhoAm 90
Kesteren, John Van 1921- IntWWM 90
Kesterke, Donald J. 1910- St&PR 91
Kesterke, Norman W. 1934- St&PR 91
Kesterman, Frank Raymond 1937- WhoE 91
Kesterson, David Bert 1938- WhoAm 90
Kesterson, Jeffery Doyle 1955- WhoSSW 91
Kesterson, Michael Denis 1932- St&PR 91
Kestin, Howard H. 1937- WhoAm 90
Kestin, Joan B. 1944- WhoAmW 91
Kestin, Joseph 1913- WhoAm 90
Kesting, Theodore 1918- WhoAm 90
Kestler, Francis J. 1944- St&PR 91
Kestler, Jeffrey Lewis 1947- WhoAm 90
Kestler, Joseph Allen 1945- WhoEmL 91
Kestnbaum, Albert S. 1939- WhoAm 90
Kestnbaum, Gertrude Dana WhoAmA 91N
Kestnbaum, Robert Dana 1932- WhoAm 90
Kestner, Arlene Katherine 1939- WhoAmW 91
Kestner, Neil Richard 1937- WhoAm 90
Keston, Joan Balboul 1937- WhoAmW 91
Kestrel, Steve BioIn 16
Keswani, Doulat L BiDrAPA 89
Keswani, Shanti BiDrAPA 89
Keswick, John Henry 1906-1982 DcNaB 1981
Keswick, William BioIn 16
Ketai, Richard Mark 1942- BiDrAPA 89
Ketcham, Alfred Schutt 1924- WhoAm 90
Ketcham, Geoffrey C. 1951- St&PR 91
Ketcham, Hank 1920- EncACom
Ketcham, Henry King 1920- WhoAm 90, WhoAmA 91
Ketcham, Jeffrey H. 1942- St&PR 91
Ketcham, John Burns BioIn 16
Ketcham, Julia Ann 1943- WhoAmW 91
Ketcham, Max 1953- WhoSSW 91
Ketcham, Orman Weston 1918- WhoAm 90
Ketcham, Ralph 1927- WhoE 91
Ketcham, Ralph Louis 1927- BioIn 16
Ketcham, Ray Newton BiDrAPA 89
Ketcham, Ray Winfred, Jr 1922- WhoAmA 91
Ketcham, Robert Edward 1949- BiDrAPA 89
Ketcham, Robert Thomas 1889-1978 BioIn 16
Ketcherside, James Lee 1935- St&PR 91
Ketchman, Jeffrey 1942- WhoE 91
Ketchum, Alton Harrington 1904- WhoAm 90, WhoWor 91
Ketchum, Chandler Griswold 1922- WhoWor 91
Ketchum, Cliff ConAu 31NR
Ketchum, David Storey 1920- WhoAm 90
Ketchum, Douglas Edward 1951- WhoEmL 91
Ketchum, Ezekiel Sargent 1935- St&PR 91, WhoAm 90
Ketchum, Frank ConAu 31NR
Ketchum, Harold A. 1912- St&PR 91
Ketchum, Henry George Clopper 1839-1896 DcCanB 12
Ketchum, Jack ConAu 31NR
Ketchum, Jack B. 1907- St&PR 91
Ketchum, James Roe 1939- WhoAm 90, WhoE 91
Ketchum, James S BiDrAPA 89
Ketchum, John Bunten 1955- WhoSSW 91

Ketchum, Kevin Lee *BiDrAPA 89*
Ketchum, Marshall D. 1905-1989 *BioIn 16*
Ketchum, Michael Jeremy 1932- *St&PR 91*
Ketchum, Perry D. 1946- *ODwPR 91*
Ketchum, Richard Malcolm 1922- *WhoAm 90*
Ketchum, Robert Glenn 1947- *WhoAm 90, WhoAmA 91*
Ketchum, Robert Scott 1937- *WhoAm 90*
Ketchum, Robert V A 1942- *BiDrAPA 89*
Ketchum, William Clarence, Jr. 1931- *WhoE 91*
Ketel, Bernard Jerome 1959- *WhoEmL 91*
Ketelbey, Albert 1875-1959 *OxCPMus*
Ketelhohn, Erika Frances 1950- *WhoE 91*
Ketelsen, James Lee 1930- *WhoAm 90, WhoSSW 91, WhoWor 91*
Ketkar, Suhas Laxman 1943- *WhoE 91*
Ketley, Jeanne Nelson 1938- *WhoAmW 91*
Ketlogetswe, Serara T. *BioIn 16*
Ketner, Kenneth Laine 1939- *WhoAm 90*
Ketner, Ralph W. 1920- *St&PR 91*
Ketner, Ralph Wright 1920- *WhoAm 90, WhoSSW 91*
Keto, Clement Tsehloane 1937- *WhoE 91*
Keto, John Edwin 1909- *WhoAm 90*
Ketola, Seppo Juhani 1939- *WhoWor 91*
Ketonen, Arvo Keijo Kalevi 1942- *WhoWor 91*
Ketonen, Arvo Mikko Olavi 1945- *WhoWor 91*
Ketover, Richard 1935- *St&PR 91*
Ketover, Steve Mitchel 1951- *WhoSSW 91*
Ketsoglou, Sophia *BiDrAPA 89*
Kett, Herbert Joseph 1933- *St&PR 91, WhoAm 90*
Kett, Joseph Francis 1938- *WhoAm 90*
Kettaneh, Tarek Michael 1947- *WhoE 91, WhoEmL 91*
Kettel, Louis John 1929- *WhoAm 90*
Kettelkamp, Donald Benjamin 1930- *WhoAm 90*
Kettelkamp, Larry 1933- *AuBYP 90*
Kettell, Leedom 1939- *St&PR 91*
Ketten, Darlene R. 1947- *WhoAm 90, WhoE 91*
Kettenhofen, Gretchen Maria 1935- *WhoAmW 91*
Ketter, David Lee 1929- *WhoAm 90*
Ketter, James Patrick 1956- *WhoEmL 91*
Ketter, Pam *WhoWrEP 89*
Ketter, Robert L. 1928-1989 *BioIn 16*
Ketter, Terence Arthur 1950- *BiDrAPA 89*
Ketterer, David 1942- *WhoWrEP 89*
Ketterer, Kenneth C. 1939- *St&PR 91*
Kettering, Charles Franklin *BioIn 16*
Kettering, Charles Franklin 1876-1958 *EncABHB 5 [port]*
Kettering, Eugene Williams 1908-1969 *BioIn 16*
Kettering, G.L. 1954- *St&PR 91*
Kettering, Jon Harris 1965- *WhoEmL 91*
Ketteringham, John M. *BioIn 16*
Ketteringham, John Malcolm *St&PR 91N*
Ketterman, Grace H. 1926- *WhoWrEP 89*
Ketterman, Grace Horst 1926- *BiDrAPA 89*
Kettinger, David John 1954- *WhoE 91, WhoEmL 91*
Kettis, Par Axel 1933- *WhoWor 91*
Kettl, Paul Andrew 1954- *BiDrAPA 89, WhoE 91*
Kettle, John Robert, III 1951- *WhoEmL 91*
Kettle, Peter *ConAu 30NR*
Kettle, Sally Anne 1938- *WhoAmW 91*
Kettler, Richard E 1941- *BiDrAPA 89*
Kettlewell, Henry Bernard Davis 1907-1979 *DcScB S2*
Kettlewell, Jeanne Kay 1955- *WhoEmL 91*
Kettlewood, Bea Card 1929- *WhoAmW 91*
Kettner, David Allen 1943- *WhoAmA 91*
Kettner, Frederick *EncO&P 3*
Kettunen, Kaarina Maire 1937- *BiDrAPA 89*
Kettyle, Cynthia N 1945- *BiDrAPA 89*
Kety, Seymour S 1915- *BiDrAPA 89*
Kety, Seymour Solomon 1915- *WhoAm 90*
Ketz, Louise Bilebof 1945- *WhoAmW 91*
Ketzler, Adolph C. *St&PR 91N*
Ketzner, J.A. 1951- *St&PR 91*
Keuchen, Toister Elaine 1930- *WhoAmW 91*
Keuchenius, T. Paul E. 1929- *St&PR 91*
Keuhnelian, John G. 1927-1988 *BioIn 16*
Keulegan, Emma Pauline 1930- *WhoAmW 91, WhoSSW 91, WhoWor 91*
Keulen, Mensje van 1946- *EncCoWW*
Keuler, Roland Leo 1933- *St&PR 91, WhoAm 90*
Keulks, George William 1938- *WhoAm 90*
Keun, Irmgard 1905-1982 *EncCoWW*
Keung, Chi Man 1944- *St&PR 91*
Keuning, Patricia Dubrava 1944- *WhoWrEP 89*
Keup, Arthur J. 1927- *St&PR 91*
Keuper, Philip J. 1933- *ODwPR 91*
Keupper, Lillian Marie 1920- *WhoAmW 91*
Keur, Dorothy Louise 1904-1989 *BioIn 16*
Keuris, Tristan 1946- *IntWWM 90*
Kevan, Douglas Keith McEwan 1920- *WhoAm 90*
Kevan, Larry 1938- *WhoAm 90*
Keve, Florence *WhoAmA 91N*
Kevenides, Herve Arnaud 1938- *WhoE 91*
Kevern, John F. 1942- *St&PR 91*
Kevern, Niles Russell 1931- *WhoAm 90*
Keves, Gyorgy 1935- *WhoWor 91*
Keveson, Florence *WhoAmA 91*
Keveson, Florence 1926- *WhoE 91*
Keviczky, Laszlo 1945- *WhoWor 91*
Kevill, Dennis Neil 1935- *WhoAm 90*
Kevins, David Vincent 1954- *WhoEmL 91*
Kevles, Daniel Jerome 1939- *WhoAm 90*
Kevlin, Mary Louise 1948- *WhoEmL 91*
Kevonian, Arlene V *BiDrAPA 89*
Kevorkian, Aram Trevor *St&PR 91*
Kevorkian, Jack *BioIn 16*
Kevorkian, Jirair 1933- *WhoAm 90*
Kevorkian, Richard 1937- *WhoAm 90, WhoAmA 91*
Kew, Robert James 1938- *St&PR 91*
Kewish, Alan E *BiDrAPA 89*
Kewitz, Helmut Paul 1920- *WhoWor 91*
Kewley, Sharon Lynn 1958- *WhoAmW 91*
Key, Alexander 1904-1979 *AuBYP 90*
Key, Bettye Ann 1945- *WhoSSW 91*
Key, Chapin 1922- *WhoAm 90*
Key, Charlie Earnest 1944- *WhoSSW 91*
Key, David McKendree 1824-1900 *BiDrUSE 89*
Key, David McKendree 1900-1988 *BioIn 16*
Key, Derrick N. 1947- *St&PR 91*
Key, Donald 1923- *WhoAm 90, WhoWrEP 89*
Key, Dorothy Lausberg 1947- *WhoAmW 91*
Key, Francis Scott 1779-1843 *WorAlBi*
Key, Jack D 1934- *ConAu 30NR*
Key, Jack Dayton 1934- *WhoAm 90*
Key, Jimmy 1961- *Ballpl 90*
Key, Kenneth James 1962- *WhoSSW 91*
Key, Marcella Ann 1947- *WhoEmL 91*
Key, Mary Ritchie 1924- *WhoAm 90, WhoAmW 91*
Key, Ramona Thornton 1939- *WhoAmW 91*
Key, Robert Edward Lee 1917- *WhoAm 90*
Key, Ted *WhoAmA 91*
Key, Ted 1912- *WhoAm 90*
Key, Thomas H. 1937- *St&PR 91*
Key-Oberg, Ellen Burke 1905- *WhoAmA 91N*
Key-Oberg, Rolf 1900-1959 *WhoAmA 91N*
Keydel, Frederick Reid 1928- *WhoAm 90*
Keye, Paul Failor 1929- *WhoAm 90*
Keyes, Albert Vincent 1932- *St&PR 91*
Keyes, Arthur Hawkins, Jr. 1917- *WhoAm 90*
Keyes, Baldwin L *BiDrAPA 89*
Keyes, Bernard M 1898-1973 *WhoAmA 91N*
Keyes, Charles Fenton 1937- *WhoAm 90*
Keyes, Cheryl Lynette 1957- *IntWWM 90*
Keyes, Daniel 1927- *RGTwCSF, WhoAm 90, WhoWrEP 89*
Keyes, Darlynn Ladd 1948- *WhoAmW 91*
Keyes, Edward Lawrence, Jr. 1929- *St&PR 91, WhoAm 90*
Keyes, Emmalou 1931- *WhoAmW 91*
Keyes, Fenton 1915- *WhoAm 90*
Keyes, Fenton George 1916- *St&PR 91*
Keyes, Gordon Lincoln 1920- *WhoAm 90*
Keyes, James C. 1926- *St&PR 91*
Keyes, James H. 1940- *St&PR 91*
Keyes, James Henry 1940- *WhoAm 90*
Keyes, James L., Jr. 1928- *St&PR 91*
Keyes, James Lyman, Jr. 1928- *WhoWor 91*
Keyes, Jo Anne *BioIn 16*
Keyes, Joan Ross Rafter 1924- *WhoAmW 91*
Keyes, John J. *St&PR 91N*
Keyes, Johnny *DrBlPA 90*
Keyes, Judith Droz 1946- *WhoAmW 91, WhoEmL 91*
Keyes, Ken 1921- *BioIn 16, NewAgE 90*
Keyes, Margaret Naumann 1918- *WhoAm 90*
Keyes, Marion Alvah, IV 1938- *WhoWor 91*
Keyes, Nelson 1886-1939 *OxCPMus*
Keyes, Nelson Beecher 1894- *AuBYP 90*
Keyes, R.A., Jr. 1952- *St&PR 91*
Keyes, Ralph Jeffry 1945- *WhoWrEP 89*
Keyes, Robert James 1952- *WhoEmL 91*
Keyes, Robert William 1921- *WhoAm 90*
Keyes, Saundra Elise 1945- *WhoAm 90*
Keyfitz, Nathan 1913- *WhoAm 90*
Keyhoe, Donald Edward 1897-1988 *BioIn 16*
Keyhoe, Donald Edwards 1897- *EncO&P 3*
Keyishian, M. Deiter *WhoWrEP 89*
Keyko, David Andrew 1946- *WhoE 91, WhoEmL 91*
Keylon, Charles David 1947- *WhoSSW 91*
Keynes, Lady 1892-1981 *DcNaB 1981*
Keynes, Geoffrey Langdon 1887-1982 *DcNaB 1981*
Keynes, John Maynard 1883-1946 *BioIn 16, EncABHB 7 [port], WorAlBi*
Keynes, John Neville 1852-1949 *BioIn 16*
Keys, Alice deSaavedra *BiDrAPA 89*
Keys, Brady, Jr. *BioIn 16*
Keys, Christopher Bennett 1946- *WhoEmL 91*
Keys, Desley Kay 1951- *St&PR 91*
Keys, Elizabeth Jaffer 1946- *WhoEmL 91*
Keys, Ivor 1919- *IntWWM 90, PenDiMP*
Keys, Kerry Shawn 1946- *WhoWrEP 89*
Keys, Lloyd Kenneth 1939- *WhoSSW 91*
Keys, Martha *ODwPR 91*
Keys, Michael *BioIn 16*
Keys, Michael Arnold 1956- *BiDrAPA 89*
Keys, Robert 1914- *IntWWM 90*
Keys, Samuel Robert 1922- *WhoAm 90*
Keys, Steven Franklin 1958- *WhoEmL 91*
Keys, Thomas Edward 1908- *WhoAm 90*
Keys, Walter Anthony 1948- *WhoSSW 91*
Keys, William G. 1947- *St&PR 91*
Keyser, Ernest Wise 1876-1959 *WhoAmA 91N*
Keyser, F. Ray, Jr. 1927- *St&PR 91*
Keyser, Frank Ray, Jr. 1927- *WhoAm 90*
Keyser, Gloria Jean 1939- *WhoAmW 91*
Keyser, John Alden, Jr. 1943- *St&PR 91*
Keyser, John J. *St&PR 91*
Keyser, Joseph W 1945- *BiDrAPA 89*
Keyser, Les 1943- *WhoE 91*
Keyser, Martha F. *ODwPR 91*
Keyser, Nancy Leola 1943- *WhoAmW 91*
Keyser, Richard Lee 1941- *WhoAm 90*
Keyser, Richard Lee 1942- *WhoAm 90*
Keyser, Robert G 1924- *WhoAmA 91*
Keyser, Robert L. 1945- *ODwPR 91*
Keyser, Robert N. 1934- *St&PR 91*
Keyser, Samuel Jay 1935- *WhoAm 90*
Keyser, Stephen Allen 1948 *St&PR 91*
Keyser, William Alphonse, Jr 1936- *WhoAmA 91*
Keyserling, Eduard von 1855-1918 *BioIn 16*
Keyserling, Harriet H. 1922- *WhoAmW 91*
Keyserling, Mary Dublin 1910- *WhoAm 90, WhoE 91, WhoWor 91*
Keyserlingk, Robert H. 1933- *ConAu 131*
Keyston, Stephani Ann 1955- *WhoAmW 91, WhoEmL 91*
Keyt, David 1930- *WhoAm 90*
Keyt, George 1901- *BioIn 16*
Keyte, Christopher Charles 1935- *IntWWM 90*
Keyte, June Margaret Rowland 1938- *IntWWM 90*
Keyton, Michael 1944- *IntWWM 90*
Keyworth, George Albert, II 1939- *WhoAm 90*
Keyworth, R. Allen 1910- *St&PR 91*
Kezele, Duane 1953- *St&PR 91*
Kezer, Claude Dean 1933- *WhoSSW 91*
Kezlarian, Jeffrey A *BiDrAPA 89*
Kezlarian, Nancy Kay 1948- *WhoAmW 91*
Kezur, Edward 1915- *BiDrAPA 89*
Kezys, Algimantas 1928- *ConAu 31NR*
Khabbaz, Abdallah Morris 1941- *WhoWor 91*
Khabibulayev, Pulat 1936- *WhoWor 91*
Khachadurian, Avedis 1926- *WhoAm 90*
Khachaturian, Aram 1903-1978 *PenDiMP A, WorAlBi*
Khachaturian, Henry 1951- *WhoE 91, WhoWor 91*
Khachigian, Kenneth Larry 1944- *WhoAm 90*
Khachigian, Meredith J. 1944- *WhoAmW 91*
Khadafy, Moammar *WhoWor 91*
Khaddam, Abdulhalim 1932- *WhoWor 91*
Khadduri, Farid Majid 1945- *WhoEmL 91, WhoSSW 91*
Khadduri, Majid 1909- *WhoAm 90*
Khadem-Missagh, Bijan 1948- *IntWWM 90*
Khader, Hanna *BioIn 16*
Khadouri, Hakham Sasson *BioIn 16*
Khadri, Syed Yousuf *BiDrAPA 89*
Khaghani, Hedayat *BiDrAPA 89*
Khaikin, Boris 1904-1978 *PenDiMP*
Khailo, Vladimir *BioIn 16*
Khair-el-Din, Abd-el-Hamid Mahmoud 1928- *WhoWor 91*
Khairallah, Adnan *BioIn 16*
Khairallah, Edward Amin 1936- *WhoE 91*
Khairullah, Zahid Yahya 1945- *WhoAm 90, WhoE 91, WhoWor 91*
Khaitov, Rakhim Musaevich 1944- *WhoWor 91*
Khaja, Yousufuddin 1961- *WhoWor 91*
Khajavi, Soheila Sedigeh *BiDrAPA 89*
Khajavi-Noori, Farrokh 1940- *BiDrAPA 89*
Khakee, Abdul 1938- *WhoWor 91*
Khakee, Abdulaziz G 1929- *BiDrAPA 89*
Khakee, Lois Lynette 1939- *WhoSSW 91*
Khalatov, Leonid Z *BiDrAPA 89*
Khaled, Hassan 1921-1989 *BioIn 16*
Khaled, Sheikh Abu Masum 1948- *WhoE 91*
Khaleel, Richard E. 1950- *St&PR 91*
Khalef, Bachir 1937- *WhoWor 91*
Khalid Bin Abdul Aziz 1913-1982 *WorAlBi*
Khalid, Sheba *BiDrAPA 89*
Khalid, Uzma 1946- *BiDrAPA 89*
Khalidi, Rashid Ismail 1948- *WhoEmL 91*
Khalifa bin Salman Al-Khalifa, Sheikh 1935- *WhoWor 91*
Khalifah Ibn Hamad Al Thani 1932- *PolLCME*
Khalife, Ilham Moussa 1949- *WhoWor 91*
Khalil, Amer *BioIn 16*
Khalil, Claire Anne 1944- *WhoAmA 91*
Khalil, Khazem el- *BioIn 16*
Khalil, Michael O. 1954- *WhoAm 90*
Khalil, Mohammad Omer *BioIn 16*
Khalil, Tarek Mohamed 1941- *WhoAm 90*
Khalily, Cyma *BiDrAPA 89*
Khalilzadeh-Shirazi, Javad 1944- *WhoE 91*
Khalimsky, Efim 1938- *WhoE 91*
Khaliq-Kareemi, Mian Abdul 1923- *BiDrAPA 89*
Khalique, Abdul 1949- *St&PR 91*
Khalique, Mujeeb A *BiDrAPA 89*
Khaliqyar, Fazil Haq *WhoWor 91*
Khalsa, Dayal Kaur *BioIn 16*
Khalsa, Dayal Kaur 1943-1989 *SmATA 62 [port]*
Khalsa, Liv Singh *NewAgMG*
Khalsa, Sat Want Kaur *NewAgMG*
Khambatta, Hoshang Jal 1931- *WhoWor 91*
Khamenei, Hojatoleslam Ali 1940- *BioIn 16*
Khamenei, Hojatoleslam Ali Hoseini 1940- *WhoWor 91*
Khamerernebti II *WomWR*
Khamis, Edward Albert 1952- *WhoEmL 91*
Khamisa, Azim Noordin 1949- *WhoEmL 91, WhoSSW 91, WhoWor 91*
Khamsi, Mohamed Amine 1959- *WhoSSW 91*
Khamtai Siphandon *WhoWor 91*
Khan, Abdul Ghaffar *BioIn 16*
Khan, Abdul Hafeez *BiDrAPA 89*
Khan, Abdul Qavi 1943- *WhoSSW 91*
Khan, Al Gromer *NewAgMG*
Khan, Amanullah 1940- *WhoAm 90, WhoWor 91*
Khan, Amir U. 1927- *WhoAm 90*
Khan, Aurangzeb 1954- *BiDrAPA 89*
Khan, Barkat U *BiDrAPA 89*
Khan, Chaka 1953- *DrBlPA 90, EncPR&S 89, WhoAm 90, WhoAmW 91, WorAlBi*
Khan, Edna M. *BiDrAPA 89*
Khan, Farzana Aquil *BiDrAPA 89*
Khan, Ghulam Ishaq 1915- *WhoWor 91*
Khan, Gordon Simeon 1943- *WhoAm 90*
Khan, Hazrat Inayat *NewAgE 90*
Khan, Hussain Ahmad 1936- *St&PR 91*
Khan, Iftikhar Ahmad 1930- *WhoWor 91*
Khan, Ikram-Ullah 1962- *WhoWor 91*
Khan, Imam Basheer *BiDrAPA 89*
Khan, Ishrat Husain 1938- *St&PR 91*
Khan, Ishrat Mahmood 1956- *WhoSSW 91*
Khan, Jamil Akber 1952- *WhoE 91*
Khan, Jehangir Alam 1958- *WhoE 91*
Khan, Kabir-Ur-Rahman 1925- *WhoWor 91*
Khan, Khawla 1935- *BiDrAPA 89*
Khan, M. Mir Nawab Mir Nawaz Jung 1904- *WhoWor 91*
Khan, Mazhar Iqbal 1947- *WhoEmL 91, WhoSSW 91*
Khan, Mohammad Asad 1940- *WhoAm 90, WhoWor 91*
Khan, Mohammad Farrukh Ali 1952- *WhoEmL 91*
Khan, Mohammad Khalid 1956- *BiDrAPA 89, WhoE 91*
Khan, Mohammed Masud R. 1927?-1989 *ConAu 129*
Khan, Muhammad Alamgir *BiDrAPA 89*
Khan, Muhammad I 1943- *BiDrAPA 89*
Khan, Muhammad Zahir 1951- *WhoWor 91*
Khan, Mujeeb Hasan *BiDrAPA 89*
Khan, Munir Ahmad 1926- *WhoWor 91*
Khan, Muzaffar Ali 1938- *WhoWor 91*
Khan, Muzaffar M 1947- *BiDrAPA 89*
Khan, Naeem Ahmad 1928- *WhoWor 91*
Khan, Nasim F *BiDrAPA 89*
Khan, Nasir Ali 1939- *BiDrAPA 89*
Khan, Pir Vilayat Inayat *NewAgE 90*
Khan, Raees Ahmed 1949- *WhoWor 91*
Khan, Sagheer Ahmad *BiDrAPA 89*
Khan, Shaukat Ali 1950- *BiDrAPA 89*
Khan, Steve *BioIn 16*
Khan, Steve Harris 1947- *WhoEmL 91*
Khan, Tamizuddin *BioIn 16*

Khan, Tariq 1940- *WhoWor 91*
Khan, Wakil *BiDrAPA 89*
Khan, Yasmin *BioIn 16*
Khan, Zohra Rashid *BiDrAPA 89*
Khanamirian, Soren Leon 1924- *WhoWor 91*
Khandelwal, Sudhir K 1951- *BiDrAPA 89*
Khandheria, Priyamvada 1950- *BiDrAPA 89*
Khandwala, Atul S. 1942- *St&PR 91*
Khandwalla, Pradip Navin 1940- *WhoWor 91*
Khaner, Jeffrey 1958- *WhoAm 90*
Khang, Chulsoon 1935- *WhoAm 90*
Khanga, Yelena *BioIn 16*
Khanh, Emmanuelle 1937- *ConDes 90*
Khankhanian, Moiez 1949- *BiDrAPA 89*
Khanna, Pragna Suresh 1961- *BiDrAPA 89*
Khanna, Purushottam 1942- *WhoWor 91*
Khanna, Pyare Lal 1945- *WhoEmL 91*
Khanna, Ravi 1954- *WhoWor 91*
Khansary, Phyllis June 1960- *WhoAmW 91*
Khantzian, Edward J 1935- *BiDrAPA 89*
Khanzadian, Vahan 1939- *WhoAm 90*
Khanzadian, Vahan Avedis 1939- *IntWWM 90*
Kharafi, Mohammed Al- *BioIn 16*
Kharasch, Virginia Sison 1956- *WhoAmW 91*
Khare, Mohan 1942- *WhoE 91, WhoWor 91*
Kharitonova, V Pormeister & N Zakharina *WomArch*
Kharitonova, Zoe *WomArch*
Kharod, Upendrakumar J 1938- *BiDrAPA 89*
Khasat, Namita 1960- *WhoEmL 91*
Khasawneh, Ali Mahmoud 1929- *WhoWor 91*
Khashoggi, Adnan *BioIn 16*
Khashu, Santosh K 1942- *BiDrAPA 89*
Khatain, Kenneth George 1953- *BiDrAPA 89*
Khatami, Mahin 1943- *WhoAmW 91*
Khatami, Manoochehr *BiDrAPA 89*
Khatau, Dhanvir *BioIn 16*
Khatena, Joe 1925- *WhoAm 90*
Khatib, Ghassan Khatib 1962- *WhoE 91*
Khaton, Sabrina Roslyn 1955- *WhoSSW 91*
Khayat, A Victor *BiDrAPA 89*
Khayat, Azeez Victor 1933- *WhoE 91*
Khayata, AbdulWahab Ismail 1924- *WhoWor 91*
Khayatt, Shaker Albert 1935- *WhoAm 90*
Khazan, Lorraine 1947- *WhoE 91*
Khazan, Tanya S. *BiDrAPA 89*
Khazeh, Khashayar 1948- *WhoE 91*
Kheel, Constance 1945- *WhoAmA 91*
Kheel, Theodore Woodrow 1914- *WhoAm 90*
Khelil, Ismail *WhoWor 91*
Khelil, Najat Arafat 1942- *WhoAmW 91*
Khentkaues *WomWR*
Kher, Harish *BiDrAPA 89*
Khera, Gurbir Singh *BiDrAPA 89*
Kherdian, David 1931- *WhoAm 90, WhoWrEP 89*
Kherumian, Raphael 1903- *EncO&P 3*
Khianey, Deepa *BiDrAPA 89*
Khidir, Mohammed Osman 1937- *WhoWor 91*
Khieu Samphan 1932- *WhoWor 91*
Khilnani, Mansho T. 1919-1990 *BioIn 16*
Khim, Jay Wook 1940- *WhoAm 90, WhoWor 91*
Khindaria, Brijesh Kumar 1945- *WhoWor 91*
Khinoo, Evelyn Mildred 1945- *WhoEmL 91*
Khireiwish, Laurie Owen 1957- *WhoAmW 91*
Khlebnikov, Velemir 1885-1922 *WorAlBi*
Khlebnikov, Velimir 1885-1922 *BioIn 16*
Khlentzos, Michael T *BiDrAPA 89*
Kho, Eusebio 1933- *WhoWor 91*
Khoe, Giok-djan 1946- *WhoWor 91*
Khokhlov, Pavel 1854-1919 *PenDiMP*
Khokhlov, Rem Victorovich 1926-1977 *DcScB S2*
Kholoussy, A. Mohsen 1947- *WhoAm 90*
Khomeini, Ayatollah 1902-1989 *AnObit 1989*
Khomeini, Ahmad *BioIn 16*
Khomeini, Ruhollah *BioIn 16*
Khomeini, Ruhollah 1901?-1989 *WorAlBi*
Khomeini, Ruhollah 1902-1989 *PolLCME*
Khoraiche, Antoine Pierre 1907- *WhoWor 91*
Khorana, Anand Bhushan 1938- *BiDrAPA 89*
Khorana, H. Gobind 1922- *WorAlBi*
Khorana, Har Gobind 1922- *WhoAm 90, WhoE 91, WhoWor 91*
Khorasanee, A Modarres *BiDrAPA 89*
Khorramzadeh, Enayat *BiDrAPA 89*
Khosho, Francis Kalo 1950- *WhoEmL 91*
Khosla, Nandini *BiDrAPA 89*
Khosla, Rajinder Paul 1933- *WhoAm 90*
Khosla, Ved Mitter 1926- *WhoAm 90*
Khosrovi, Behzad 1944- *St&PR 91*
Khot, Vikram S *BiDrAPA 89*
Khouberman, Jean Claude 1941- *WhoWor 91*
Khouri, Alfred *WhoAmA 91N*
Khouri, Fred John 1916- *WhoAm 90, WhoWor 91*
Khouri, George A. 1947- *WhoAm 90*
Khouri, Greta Matson *WhoAmA 91*
Khouri, Philippe John 1947- *BiDrAPA 89, WhoE 91*
Khouri-Haddad, S Eker 1929- *BiDrAPA 89*
Khoury, Ada Celeste 1964- *BiDrAPA 89*
Khoury, Christopher P 1949- *BiDrAPA 89*
Khoury, Gregory Charles 1954- *BiDrAPA 89*
Khoury, Henry B. 1947- *WhoE 91*
Khoury, Kenneth Alan 1944- *BiDrAPA 89*
Khoury, Said *BioIn 16*
Khoury, Virginia 1955- *BiDrAPA 89*
Khouw, Boen Tie 1934- *WhoWor 91*
Khouzam, Hani Raoul 1950- *BiDrAPA 89, WhoSSW 91*
Khrennikov, Tikhon Nikolayevich 1913- *IntWWM 90, WhoWor 91*
Khristoradnov, Yuriy Nikolayevich 1929- *WhoWor 91*
Khruschev, Nikita 1894-1971 *BioIn 16*
Khrushchev, Nikita 1894-1971 *WorAlBi*
Khrushchev, Nikita Sergeevich 1894-1971 *BioIn 16*
Khubchandani, Indru Tekchand *WhoWor 91*
Khufu *BioIn 16*
Khun Sa *BioIn 16*
Khuner, Felix *PenDiMP*
Khunrath, Heinrich 1560-1605 *EncO&P 3*
Khurana, Baljeet *BiDrAPA 89*
Khurana, Rajiv *BiDrAPA 89*
Khurana, Ramesh K. *BiDrAPA 89*
Khurana, Sat Pal 1942- *St&PR 91*
Khurana, Sudershan Kumar 1944- *WhoSSW 91*
Khuri, Nicola Najib 1933- *WhoAm 90*
Khuri, Radwan Rafik *BiDrAPA 89*
Khush, Gurdev Singh 1935- *WhoWor 91*
Khushalani, Ashok Issardas 1951- *BiDrAPA 89*
Khvoshchinskaia, Nadezhda 1824-1889 *EncCoWW*
Khvoshchinskaia, Sofia 1828-1865 *EncCoWW*
Kiah, Virginia Jackson 1911- *WhoAmA 91*
Kiam, Victor K., II *BioIn 16*
Kiam, Victor K., II 1926- *St&PR 91*
Kiam, Victor Kermit, II 1926- *WhoAm 90, WhoE 91*
Kianes, Reinaldo E 1946- *BiDrAPA 89*
Kiang, Assumpta 1939- *WhoWor 91*
Kiang, Nelson Yuan-Sheng 1929- *WhoAm 90*
Kianto, Ilmari 1874-1970 *DcScanL*
Kiashuta *WhNaAH*
Kibaki, Mwai 1931- *WhoWor 91*
Kibbe, James William 1926- *WhoE 91*
Kibbe, Milton H 1911- *BiDrAPA 89*
Kibbe, Pat *SmATA 60*
Kibbey, Ilah Marian 1883-1958 *WhoAmA 91N*
Kibel, Howard David 1937- *BiDrAPA 89, WhoE 91*
Kibira, Josiah *BioIn 16*
Kibkalo, Yevgeny 1932- *PenDiMP*
Kibler, Gary Albin 1943- *St&PR 91*
Kibler, James Everett, Jr. 1944- *WhoWrEP 89*
Kibler, John 1929- *Ballpl 90*
Kibler, Larry Warren 1947- *St&PR 91*
Kibler, Thomas Bryant 1950- *WhoSSW 91*
Kibler, Virginia Elaine 1951- *WhoAmW 91*
Kibler, Wallace Edward 1936- *WhoWrEP 89*
Kibler, William Westcott 1942- *WhoAm 90*
Kibrick, Anne 1919- *WhoAm 90*
Kibrick, Anne K. 1919- *WhoAmW 91*
Kice, James V. 1925- *St&PR 91*
Kice, John Edward 1949- *St&PR 91*
Kicher, Thomas Patrick 1937- *WhoAm 90*
Kichline, Diane Donchez 1957- *WhoE 91*
Kickham, Michael Francis 1929- *St&PR 91*
Kicking Bear *WhNaAH*
Kicking Bird 1835-1875 *WhNaAH*
Kickler, James Arnold 1927- *St&PR 91*
Kicklighter, Claude Milton 1933- *WhoAm 90*
Kicklighter, Clois Earl 1939- *WhoAm 90*
Kicknosway, Faye 1936- *WhoWrEP 89*
Kiczales, Adolphe C *BiDrAPA 89*
Kid Antrim *BioIn 16*
Kid Chocolate 1910-1988 *BioIn 16*
Kid 'n Play *ConMus 5*
Kid, Senorita *BioIn 16*
Kid, Thomas 1558-1594 *BioIn 16*
Kida, Eugene 1944- *St&PR 91*
Kidd, A. Paul 1939- *WhoAm 90*
Kidd, Adam 1802?-1831 *DcLB 99 [port]*
Kidd, Agnes Juanita 1918- *WhoAmW 91*
Kidd, Andre Charles *BiDrAPA 89*
Kidd, Billy *BioIn 16*
Kidd, Charles Vincent 1914- *WhoAm 90*
Kidd, Darlene Joyce 1935- *WhoSSW 91*
Kidd, Debra Jean 1956- *WhoAmW 91, WhoWor 91*
Kidd, Gerald Steele, II 1945- *WhoAm 90*
Kidd, I G 1922- *ConAu 132*
Kidd, James 1879-1949? *EncO&P 3, EncPaPR 91*
Kidd, James F. 1939- *St&PR 91*
Kidd, James M., Jr. *St&PR 91*
Kidd, Janet 1908-1988 *AnObit 1988*
Kidd, Janet Aitken 1908-1988 *BioIn 16*
Kidd, John Edward 1936- *WhoAm 90*
Kidd, John F. 1931- *St&PR 91*
Kidd, Karen Kay 1949- *WhoEmL 91*
Kidd, Langford 1931- *WhoAm 90*
Kidd, Lawrie K. 1931- *St&PR 91*
Kidd, Margaret 1900-1989 *AnObit 1989*
Kidd, Mark 1953- *WhoSSW 91*
Kidd, Michael *WhoAm 90*
Kidd, Michael 1919- *WorAlBi*
Kidd, Patricia Eileen 1952- *WhoAmW 91*
Kidd, Rebecca Montgomery 1942- *WhoAm 90, WhoAmA 91, WhoAmW 91, WhoSSW 91, WhoWor 91*
Kidd, Robert H. 1944- *St&PR 91*
Kidd, Robert Hugh 1944- *WhoAm 90*
Kidd, Vallee Melvina 1918- *WhoSSW 91*
Kidd, William 1645?-1701 *WorAlBi*
Kidd, Wilmot Higgins, III 1941- *St&PR 91*
Kidde, Harald 1878-1918 *DcScanL*
Kidde, John Lyon 1934- *St&PR 91, WhoAm 90, WhoWor 91*
Kiddell-Monroe, Joan 1908-1972 *BioIn 16*
Kidder, Alfred 1911-1984 *BioIn 16*
Kidder, Alice Eltha 1941- *WhoE 91*
Kidder, C. Robert 1944- *St&PR 91*
Kidder, Fred Dockstater 1922- *WhoAm 90*
Kidder, Jerome 1909-1988 *BioIn 16*
Kidder, John Newell 1932- *WhoAm 90*
Kidder, Margot *BioIn 16*
Kidder, Margot 1948- *WhoAm 90, WhoAmW 91, WorAlBi*
Kidder, Michael G. 1941- *ODwPR 91*
Kidder, Norman Kent 1951- *St&PR 91*
Kidder, Priscilla *St&PR 91*
Kidder, Tracy *BioIn 16*
Kidder, Tracy 1945- *MajTwCW*
Kiddoo, Richard Clyde 1927- *WhoSSW 91*
Kiddoo, Robert James 1936- *St&PR 91*
Kidera, George Jerome 1913- *WhoAm 90*
Kidman, Fiona 1940- *FemiCLE*
Kidney, Michael James 1959- *St&PR 91*
Kido Koichi 1889-1977 *EncJap*
Kido Takayoshi 1833-1877 *EncJap*
Kidrick, Valerie Anne 1961- *WhoAmA 91*
Kidson, Frank 1855-1926 *OxCPMus*
Kidston, Alan R. 1928- *St&PR 91*
Kidwell, David William 1956- *BiDrAPA 89*
Kidwell, Eugene R, Jr. 1942- *BiDrAPA 89*
Kidwell, Richard Patrick 1954- *WhoEmL 91*
Kiebala, Susan Marie 1952- *WhoAmW 91, WhoEmL 91*
Kiechlin, Robert Jerome 1919- *WhoAm 90*
Kieckhafer, Thomas William 1938- *St&PR 91*
Kieckhefer, Guy Norton 1926- *St&PR 91*
Kiecolt-Glaser, Janice Kay 1951- *WhoEmL 91*
Kiedaisch, Howard G. 1945- *St&PR 91*
Kiedrowski, Dale Michael 1950- *St&PR 91*
Kiedrowski, Michael Joseph 1955- *WhoEmL 91*
Kief, Paul Allan 1934- *WhoAm 90*
Kiefaber, John McReynolds 1950- *St&PR 91*
Kiefaber, Warner H., III 1942- *St&PR 91*
Kiefaber, Warner H., Jr. 1917- *St&PR 91*
Kiefer, Alfred W. 1912- *St&PR 91*
Kiefer, Alfred William 1912- *WhoE 91*
Kiefer, Anselm 1945- *BioIn 16, ModArCr 1, News 90*
Kiefer, Anselm Karl Albert 1945- *WhoWor 91*
Kiefer, Bruno 1923- *IntWWM 90*
Kiefer, C Raymond 1919- *BiDrAPA 89*
Kiefer, Carl Omer 1942- *St&PR 91*
Kiefer, Charles F. 1950- *St&PR 91*
Kiefer, Henry E. *BioIn 16*
Kiefer, J. Richard, Jr. 1928- *WhoE 91*
Kiefer, Kali Ann 1961- *WhoEmL 91*
Kiefer, Karen Hope 1947- *BiDrAPA 89*
Kiefer, Karen LaVerne 1952- *WhoEmL 91*
Kiefer, Kit Annette 1958- *WhoAmW 91*
Kiefer, Louis, Sr. 1936- *ConAu 131*
Kiefer, Nicholas Maximilian 1951- *WhoEmL 91*
Kiefer, Raymond H. 1927- *WhoAm 90*
Kiefer, Richard Otto 1937- *St&PR 91*
Kiefer, Stanley Clarence 1941- *St&PR 91*
Kiefer, Walter G. *St&PR 91*
Kiefer, William Lee 1946- *WhoWor 91*
Kieferndorf, Frederick George 1921- *WhoAmA 91*
Kiefert, Alice Stockwell 1929- *WhoAmW 91*
Kieff, Elliott Dan 1943- *WhoAm 90*
Kieffer, Barbara 1952- *St&PR 91*
Kieffer, Bernard L. 1933- *St&PR 91*
Kieffer, Burton L. 1919- *St&PR 91*
Kieffer, James Milton 1921- *WhoAm 90*
Kieffer, Jarold Alan 1923- *WhoAm 90*
Kieffer, John E 1959- *BiDrAPA 89*
Kieffer, Joyce Loretta 1940- *WhoAm 90*
Kieffer, Mary Jane *WhoAmA 91*
Kieffer, Richard William 1937- *St&PR 91*
Kieffer, Rosemarie 1932- *EncCoWW*
Kieffer, Sherman N 1919- *BiDrAPA 89*
Kieffer, Stephen Aaron 1935- *WhoAm 90*
Kieffer, Susan Faye 1962- *WhoAmW 91*
Kieffer, Susan Werner 1942- *WhoAm 90, WhoAmW 91*
Kieffer, William Franklinn 1915- *WhoAm 90*
Kieffer-Andrews, Marilyn Joanne 1947- *WhoAmW 91*
Kiefner, John Robert, Jr. 1946- *WhoEmL 91*
Kieft, Gerald Nelson 1946- *WhoEmL 91*
Kieft, Lester 1912- *WhoAm 90*
Kieft, Willem 1597-1647 *EncCRAm, WhNaAH*
Kiehl, David William 1948- *WhoE 91*
Kiehl, Royal Pearson 1943- *BiDrAPA 89*
Kiehne, Frank Charles, Jr. 1925- *WhoWor 91*
Kiehne, Thomas Merill 1947- *WhoSSW 91*
Kiekel, William Edward 1939- *St&PR 91*
Kiekhaefer, Carl *BioIn 16*
Kiel, Catherine 1961- *ODwPR 91*
Kiel, Edward J. 1938- *St&PR 91*
Kiel, Frederick Orin 1942- *WhoAm 90*
Kiel, Steve John 1956- *BiDrAPA 89*
Kielar, Loretta 1960- *BioIn 16*
Kielar, Richard M. *ODwPR 91*
Kiele, Jan Eric *BiDrAPA 89*
Kielenniva, Jorma Reijo 1945- *WhoWor 91*
Kielholz, Paul *BiDrAPA 89*
Kielkopf, James Robert 1939- *WhoAmA 91*
Kiell, Paul J *BiDrAPA 89*
Kielland, Alexander L. 1840-1906 *DcScanL*
Kielland, Alexander Lange 1849-1906 *WorAlBi*
Kielland, Else Christie 1903- *BiDWomA*
Kielland, Kitty 1843-1914 *BiDWomA*
Kielley, James Edward 1931- *St&PR 91*
Kielpikowski, Gary L *BiDrAPA 89*
Kielsmeier, Catherine Jane *WhoAmW 91*
Kielty, Bernardine *AuBYP 90*
Kielty, John L., III 1943- *WhoAm 90*
Kielty, Robert J. 1945- *St&PR 91*
Kielty, William R. 1937- *St&PR 91*
Kiely, Dan R. 1944- *St&PR 91*
Kiely, Dan Ray 1944- *WhoE 91, WhoWor 91*
Kiely, Edmond R. *BioIn 16*
Kiely, Laurie *ODwPR 91*
Kiely, Leo 1929-1984 *Ballpl 90*
Kiely, Michael Hughes 1944- *WhoE 91*
Kiely, Michael Sean 1948- *WhoEmL 91*
Kiely, Patrick J. 1951- *St&PR 91*
Kiely, Robert 1931- *ConAu 131*
Kiely, William L. 1942- *St&PR 91*
Kiemle, Fred William, Jr. 1934- *WhoSSW 91*
Kienast, Hansjuergen W *BiDrAPA 89*
Kienast, Wallace Frank Elliott 1923- *St&PR 91*
Kienbaum, Karen Smith 1943- *WhoAmW 91*
Kienbaum, Thomas Gerd 1942- *WhoAm 90*
Kienbusch, William Austin 1914-1979 *WhoAmA 91N*
Kiene, Julia *AuBYP 90*
Kiener, Franz Xaver 1910- *WhoWor 91*
Kiener, Jerome M. 1944- *WhoWor 91*
Kiener, Mary Elaine 1950- *WhoAmW 91*
Kiener, Ronald Charles 1954- *WhoE 91*
Kienholz, Edward 1927- *BioIn 16, IntDcAA 90*
Kienholz, Lyn *WhoAmA 91*
Kieninger, Richard George 1927- *WhoWrEP 89*
Kienker, Karen Ann 1951- *WhoAmW 91*
Kientz, Roland Charles 1956- *WhoWor 91*
Kientzy, Daniel 1951- *IntWWM 90*
Kieny, Albert Joseph, Jr. 1924- *St&PR 91*
Kienz, Glenn Charles 1953- *WhoE 91, WhoEmL 91*
Kienzl, Heinz 1922- *WhoWor 91*
Kienzle, William X 1928- *ConAu 31NR, MajTwCW, TwCCr&M 91*
Kienzler, Klaus 1944- *WhoWor 91*
Kiepert, Donniece Ann 1957- *WhoSSW 91*
Kiepper, Alan Frederick 1928- *WhoE 91*
Kiepper, James Julius 1933- *WhoE 91*

Kiepura, Jan 1902-1966 *PenDiMP*
Kier, Ann B. 1949- *WhoAmW 91*
Kier, Kearney Kay 1936- *St&PR 91*
Kier, Porter Martin 1927- *WhoAm 90*
Kier, Porter Sawyer 1935- *WhoE 91*
Kieran, James 1920- *WhoAm 90*
Kieran, John 1882-1981 *Ballpl 90*
Kieran, John 1892-1981 *AuBYP 90*
Kieren, Thomas Henry 1941- *St&PR 91, WhoAm 90, WhoE 91*
Kierkegaard, Soren 1813-1855 *BioIn 16, DcScanL, WorAlBi, WrPh P*
Kierman, Steven Wayne 1950- *St&PR 91*
Kiernan, Benedict Francis 1953- *WhoWor 91*
Kiernan, Edwin A., Jr. 1926- *WhoAm 90*
Kiernan, Jerald Robert 1945- *St&PR 91*
Kiernan, John Burke 1931- *St&PR 91*
Kiernan, John J. 1926- *St&PR 91*
Kiernan, Kevin Wight *BiDrAPA 89*
Kiernan, M. C. 1956- *WhoAmW 91*
Kiernan, Marianne C. *ODwPR 91*
Kiernan, Owen Burns 1914- *WhoAm 90*
Kiernan, Peter D. 1923-1988 *BioIn 16*
Kiernan, Peter Joseph 1939- *St&PR 91*
Kiernan, Richard Francis 1935- *WhoAm 90*
Kiernan, V. G. 1913- *BioIn 16*
Kiernan, Victor Gordon 1913- *BioIn 16*
Kiernan, William Joseph, Jr. 1932- *WhoAm 90, WhoSSW 91*
Kiernon, John Francis, Jr. 1938- *WhoSSW 91*
Kiersch, George Alfred 1918- *WhoAm 90*
Kiersch, Theodore A 1916- *BiDrAPA 89*
Kiersch, Theodore Alan 1943- *WhoAm 90*
Kierscht, Charles Mason 1939- *St&PR 91*
Kierski, Jozef 1935- *WhoWor 91*
Kierszenbaum, Hugo S 1940- *BiDrAPA 89*
Kierulff, Charles Taylor 1919- *WhoWrEP 89*
Kierulff, Stephen 1942- *WhoWrEP 89*
Kierzkowski, John Philip 1939- *St&PR 91*
Kies, Constance Virginia 1934- *WhoAmW 91*
Kies, Cosette Nell 1936- *WhoAm 90*
Kieschnick, John Henry 1942- *WhoSSW 91*
Kiesel, Bernard 1953- *WhoEmL 91*
Kiesel, Marjorie Jean 1960- *WhoAmW 91*
Kieselstein-Cord, Barry *BioIn 16*
Kieselstein-Cord, Cece *BioIn 16*
Kieser, Gunther 1930- *ConDes 90*
Kieser, Nita Irene 1960- *St&PR 91*
Kiesewetter, William Van Santen 1937- *WhoSSW 91*
Kiesinger, Kurt 1904-1988 *AnObit 1988*
Kiesinger, Kurt Georg 1904-1988 *BioIn 16*
Kiesler, Charles Adolphus 1934- *WhoAm 90*
Kiesler, Frank 1917- *BiDrAPA 89*
Kiesler, Frederick J 1892-1966 *WhoAmA 91N*
Kiesler, Frederick John 1890-1965 *PenDiDA 89*
Kiesling, Ernst Willie 1934- *WhoAm 90*
Kiesling, Gerald K. 1933- *St&PR 91*
Kiesling, Juanita Haseloff 1935- *WhoAmW 91*
Kiesow, Paul Frederick, Jr. 1928- *WhoSSW 91*
Kiesow-Webb, Nancy Anne *BiDrAPA 89*
Kiessel, Ruth Ann 1945- *WhoAmW 91*
Kiessling, Alice H 1903- *BiDrAPA 89*
Kiest, Alan Scott 1949- *WhoWor 91*
Kiest, Lauren J. 1932- *St&PR 91*
Kiev, Ari 1933- *BiDrAPA 89*
Kiev, Isaac Edward 1905-1975 *BioIn 16*
Kievari, Seppo Kalevi 1943- *WhoWor 91*
Kieve, Carola Anne 1954- *BiDrAPA 89*
Kiever, Paul K. 1946- *St&PR 91*
Kievman, Carson 1949- *IntWWM 90*
Kiewiet, Paul Alan 1953- *WhoEmL 91*
Kiffe, Mitchell Walter 1953- *WhoEmL 91*
Kiffin, William 1616-1701 *BioIn 16*
Kifner, John William 1941- *WhoAm 90*
Kiger, Joseph Charles 1920- *WhoAm 90*
Kiggen, James D. 1932- *St&PR 91*
Kiggins, Gilbert M. 1931- *WhoAm 90*
Kiggins, Gilbert Macgillivray 1931- *St&PR 91*
Kiggins, Mildred L. 1927- *WhoAmW 91*
Kight, Charles Walter, III 1938- *St&PR 91*
Kight, Edward H. 1935- *St&PR 91*
Kight, Edward Hill 1935- *WhoAm 90*
Kight, James Alan 1950- *St&PR 91*
Kightlinger, Ray Milton 1931- *St&PR 91*
Kigin, Thomas Edward 1928- *St&PR 91*
Kigin, Thomas John 1948- *WhoEmL 91*
Kigoshi, Kunihiko 1919- *WhoWor 91*
Kihara, Yasushi 1932- *WhoWor 91*
Kihle, Donald Arthur 1934- *WhoSSW 91, WhoWor 91*
Kihlken, Henry Bernhard 1939- *IntWWM 90*
Kihlman, Christer 1930- *DcScanL*
Kihlstrom, Kenneth Edward 1954- *WhoEmL 91*
Kihn, Greg 195-?- *EncPR&S 89*
Kihn, Harry 1912- *WhoAm 90*
Kihn, William Langdon 1898-1957 *WhoAmA 91N*
Kiihr, Elizabeth Marie 1963- *WhoAmW 91*
Kiil, Leevi 1940- *St&PR 91*
Kiilerich, Jens Ole 1946- *IntWWM 90*
Kijac, Peter 1932- *St&PR 91*
Kijanka, Stanley Joseph 1937-1981 *WhoAmA 91N*
Kijanka, Theodore H. 1942- *St&PR 91*
Kijima, Kanetaka 1943- *WhoWor 91*
Kikel, Rudy John 1942- *WhoWrEP 89*
Kiken, Norman Paul 1942- *St&PR 91*
Kiker, Billy Frazier 1936- *WhoAm 90*
Kiker, Edward Bruce 1947- *WhoEmL 91, WhoWor 91*
Kiker, Evelyn Coalson 1932- *WhoAmA 91*
Kiker, John D. *ODwPR 91*
Kiki De Montparnasse 1901- *BiDWomA*
Kiki, de Montparnasse 1901-1953? *BioIn 16*
Kikkawa, Akikazu 1937- *St&PR 91*
Kikol, John Charles 1944- *St&PR 91*
Kikuchi, Eiichi 1942- *WhoWor 91*
Kikuchi, Kazuhiro 1934- *WhoWor 91*
Kikuchi, Kazumasa 1935- *WhoWor 91*
Kikuchi, Kokichi 1932- *WhoWor 91*
Kikuchi, Masahiro 1934- *WhoWor 91*
Kikuchi-Yngojo, Alan 1949- *WhoAmA 91*
Kikugawa, Kiyomi 1940- *WhoWor 91*
Kikut, Aksi 1940- *St&PR 91*
Kikutake, Kiyonori 1928- *WhoWor 91*
Kilalea, Donal Francis 1956- *WhoWor 91*
Kilambi, Raj V. 1933- *WhoSSW 91*
Kiland, Lance Edward 1947- *WhoAmA 91*
Kilander, Anders Fredrik 1945- *WhoWor 91*
Kilanowski, Michael Charles, Jr. 1948- *WhoAm 90, WhoEmL 91*
Kilaru, Raghavendra Rao *BiDrAPA 89*
Kilbane, Adrienne F. 1933- *WhoAmW 91*
Kilbane, Thomas Stanton 1941- *WhoAm 90*
Kilberg, Bobbie Greene 1944- *WhoAm 90*
Kilberg, Richard Lloyd 1948- *WhoEmL 91*
Kilberg, William Jeffrey 1946- *WhoAm 90*
Kilborne, George Briggs 1930- *WhoWor 91*
Kilborne, Robert Stewart 1905- *WhoSSW 91, WhoWor 91*
Kilborne, William Skinner 1912- *WhoAm 90*
Kilbourn, Elbridge Gerry 1816?-1873 *AmLegL*
Kilbourn, Joan Priscilla 1936- *WhoAmW 91*
Kilbourne, Barbara Jean 1941- *WhoAmW 91*
Kilbourne, Clara Anne 1939- *WhoWrEP 89*
Kilbourne, Douglas M. 1948- *St&PR 91*
Kilbourne, Edwin Dennis 1920- *WhoAm 90*
Kilbourne, William Truman 1934- *St&PR 91, WhoAm 90*
Kilbride, John *BioIn 16*
Kilbridge, James X. 1926- *WhoAm 90*
Kilbridge, Maurice D. 1920- *WhoAm 90*
Kilbuck, John H. 1920- *St&PR 91*
Kilburn, Bettina Baechtold *BiDrAPA 89*
Kilburn, Edwin A. 1933- *St&PR 91*
Kilburn, Edwin Allen 1933- *WhoAm 90*
Kilburn, H. Thomas, Jr. 1931- *St&PR 91*
Kilburn, Henry Thomas, Jr. 1931- *WhoAm 90*
Kilburn, Lionel Clarence 1930- *St&PR 91*
Kilbury, Robert Hugh 1945- *St&PR 91*
Kilby, Jack St. Clair 1923- *WhoAm 90*
Kilby, Peter 1935- *WhoAm 90*
Kilby, Ronn Leonard 1951- *WhoEmL 91*
Kilchenstein, Michael W 1936- *BiDrAPA 89*
Kilcline, Thomas John 1925- *WhoAm 90*
Kilcollin, Thomas Eric *WhoAm 90*
Kilcoyne, John Francis 1922- *St&PR 91*
Kilcup, Clara Griego 1960- *WhoAmW 91*
Kilcur, James Francis 1951- *WhoEmL 91*
Kildare, H. Bernard 1919- *St&PR 91*
Kildee, Dale E. 1929- *WhoAm 90*
Kilduff, Brian L. 1945- *WhoAm 90*
Kilduff, Brian Lawrence 1945- *St&PR 91*
Kilduff, Pete 1893-1930 *Ballpl 90*
Kile, Jane Tucker Spindler 1949- *WhoEmL 91*
Kile, Thomas Charles 1946- *St&PR 91*
Kileen, Charles Michel 1942- *St&PR 91*
Kilenyi, Edward A. 1911- *IntWWM 90*
Kilenyi, Julio 1886-1959 *WhoAmA 91N*
Kiley, Bernard John, Jr. 1958- *WhoEmL 91*
Kiley, Bruce Edward 1955- *WhoEmL 91*
Kiley, Constance Schrader 1939- *St&PR 91*
Kiley, Dan 1942- *ConAu 132*
Kiley, Daniel Urban 1912- *WhoAm 90*
Kiley, Gregory Thomas 1966- *WhoE 91*
Kiley, James William 1944- *WhoAm 90*
Kiley, Jim *BioIn 16*
Kiley, John Lawrence 1936- *BiDrAPA 89*
Kiley, Richard 1922- *WorAlBi*
Kiley, Richard Paul 1922- *WhoAm 90*
Kiley, Susan Joan 1946- *WhoEmL 91*
Kiley, Wesley J. 1923- *St&PR 91*
Kilfedder, James Alexander 1928- *WhoWor 91*
Kilgallen, Dorothy 1913-1965 *BioAmW, BioIn 16*
Kilgannon, Rena Klein 1955- *WhoSSW 91*
Kilgariff, Sonja Jean 1940- *WhoE 91*
Kilgo, Robert Lawton, Jr. 1949- *WhoEmL 91*
Kilgore, Al 1927- *WhoAmA 91*
Kilgore, Bernard 1908-1967 *BioIn 16*
Kilgore, Bernice Jewelene 1918- *WhoAmW 91*
Kilgore, Byron *BiDrAPA 89*
Kilgore, Byron William *BiDrAPA 89*
Kilgore, Catherine C. 1956- *WhoAmW 91*
Kilgore, David 1804-1879 *AmLegL*
Kilgore, Dawson L. 1823-189-? *AmLegL*
Kilgore, Donald Gibson, Jr. 1927- *WhoAm 90, WhoSSW 91, WhoWor 91*
Kilgore, Edwin Carroll 1923- *WhoAm 90*
Kilgore, Eugene Sterling, Jr. 1920- *WhoAm 90*
Kilgore, Gary Allen 1945- *WhoEmL 91*
Kilgore, James Bernard 1948- *WhoE 91*
Kilgore, James M, Jr. 1928- *BiDrAPA 89*
Kilgore, Jerry G. 1945- *St&PR 91*
Kilgore, Joe Madison 1918- *WhoAm 90*
Kilgore, John *ConAu 31NR*
Kilgore, John Edward, Jr. 1921- *WhoAm 90*
Kilgore, Jon W. 1943- *St&PR 91*
Kilgore, Judith Shamille 1955- *WhoEmL 91*
Kilgore, Katherine Gayle 1945- *WhoAmW 91*
Kilgore, Kevin Patrick 1951- *WhoEmL 91*
Kilgore, Morris W 1916- *BiDrAPA 89*
Kilgore, Phillip Arthur 1957- *WhoEmL 91*
Kilgore, Rupert 1910-1971 *WhoAmA 91N*
Kilgore, Samuel R 1918- *BiDrAPA 89*
Kilgore, Scott *BioIn 16*
Kilgore, Terry Lee 1948- *WhoEmL 91*
Kilgore, William Jackson 1917- *WhoAm 90, WhoWor 91*
Kilgore, Wilson Roy 1949- *WhoEmL 91*
Kilgour, Frederick Gridley 1914- *WhoAm 90, WhoWor 91*
Kilgrow, Julie Maynes 1940- *WhoAmW 91*
Kilgus, Edward Louis 1920- *St&PR 91*
Kilgus, Lowell Keith 1945- *St&PR 91*
Kilgus, Paul 1962- *Ballpl 90*
Kilguss, Fred C. 1910- *St&PR 91*
Kilgust, Mary Lynn 1955- *WhoAm 90*
Kilham, Hannah 1774-1832 *FemiCLE*
Kilham, Lawrence 1910- *BioIn 16*
Kilham, Peter 1943-1989 *BioIn 16*
Kilham, Susan Soltau 1943- *WhoAmW 91*
Kilham, Walter H 1868-1948 *WhoAmA 91N*
Kilham, Walter H., Jr. 1904- *WhoAm 90*
Kilian, Austin Farland 1920- *WhoAmA 91*
Kilian, Brian Quentin 1954- *WhoSSW 91*
Kilian, Crawford 1941- *WhoWrEP 89*
Kilian, John James, II 1952- *WhoEmL 91*
Kilian, Mark Kenneth 1961- *WhoEmL 91*
Kilicozlu, Meral Can 1931- *BiDrAPA 89*
Kilitis, Aris 1926- *WhoWor 91*
Kiljunen, Kimmo 1951- *ConAu 132*
Kiljunen, Kimmo Roobert 1951- *WhoWor 91*
Kilkeary, Nan 1943- *ODwPR 91, WhoWrEP 89*
Kilkeary, Nan M. 1943- *WhoAmW 91, WhoWor 91*
Kilkelly, Marjorie Lee 1954- *WhoAmW 91*
Kilkenny, John F. 1901- *WhoAm 90*
Kilkenny, Mike 1945- *Ballpl 90*
Kilker, William Robert 1954- *WhoEmL 91*
Kill, Lawrence 1935- *WhoAm 90*
Kill, Robert H. 1947- *St&PR 91*
Killackey, Dorothy Helen 1927- *WhoAmW 91*
Killam, Eva King 1921- *WhoAm 90*
Killam, Joan *BiDEWW*
Killam, Margaret *BiDEWW, FemiCLE*
Killam, Terri *BioIn 16*
Killam, Walt 1907-1979 *WhoAmA 91N*
Killanin, Lord 1914- *WhoWor 91*
Kille, Mary Jean 1937- *WhoAmW 91*
Kille, Willard Bronson, III 1946- *WhoSSW 91*
Killea, Lucy 1922- *WhoHisp 91*
Killea, Lucy Lytle 1922- *WhoAmW 91*
Killebrew, Betty Rackley 1931- *WhoSSW 91*
Killebrew, Eleanor *BioIn 16*
Killebrew, Ellen Jane 1937- *WhoAmW 91*
Killebrew, George Buckley 1939- *St&PR 91*
Killebrew, Gwendolyn 1939- *IntWWM 90*
Killebrew, Harmon 1936- *Ballpl 90 [port], BioIn 16, WorAlBi*
Killebrew, James Robert 1918- *WhoAm 90*
Killeen, Edward F. 1930- *St&PR 91*
Killeen, Henry Walter 1946- *WhoEmL 91*
Killeen, Joann E. *ODwPR 91*
Killeen, Luann G. 1938- *St&PR 91*
Killeen, Melissa Helen 1955- *WhoAmA 91*
Killefer, Bill 1887-1960 *Ballpl 90*
Killefer, Red 1884-1958 *Ballpl 90*
Killefer, Tom 1917- *WhoAm 90*
Killeffer, Louis MacMillan 1954- *WhoEmL 91*
Killen, Carroll Gorden 1919- *St&PR 91, WhoAm 90*
Killen, Frank 1870-1939 *Ballpl 90*
Killen, James S. 1908- *BioIn 16*
Killen, Joel Davis 1950- *WhoEmL 91*
Killen, Melanie Ann 1957- *WhoAmW 91*
Killen, William D. 1932- *WhoAm 90*
Killen-Wolf, Anne 1959- *WhoAmW 91*
Killenberg, George Andrew 1917- *WhoAm 90*
Killens, John Oliver 1916-1987 *BioIn 16, DrBlPA 90*
Killgallon, William C. 1939- *St&PR 91*
Killgore, Andrew Ivy 1919- *WhoAm 90*
Killgore, Kenneth Wayne 1948- *WhoEmL 91*
Killhour, William Gherky 1925- *WhoE 91, WhoWor 91*
Killian, Donald Joseph 1934- *WhoAm 90*
Killian, Ed 1876-1928 *Ballpl 90*
Killian, George Ernest 1924- *WhoAm 90*
Killian, Grant Aram 1949- *WhoSSW 91*
Killian, Iris Louise 1962- *WhoAmW 91*
Killian, James Rhyne 1904-1988 *BioIn 16*
Killian, Joe *BioIn 16*
Killian, Jonathan D. 1960- *WhoE 91*
Killian, Lewis Martin 1919- *WhoAm 90, WhoSSW 91*
Killian, Nathan Rayne 1935- *WhoSSW 91*
Killian, Richard M. 1942- *WhoAm 90*
Killian, Robert Kenneth 1919- *WhoAm 90*
Killian, Robert Kenneth, Jr. 1947- *WhoEmL 91*
Killian, Terry Michael 1954- *BiDrAPA 89*
Killian, William Paul 1935- *St&PR 91, WhoAm 90*
Killiany, Catherine Ann 1957- *WhoAmW 91*
Killigrew, Anne 1660-1685 *BiDEWW, BioIn 16, FemiCLE*
Killigrew, Thomas 1612-1683 *BioIn 16*
Killin, Charles Clark 1923- *WhoAm 90*
Killin, Joan *BiDEWW*
Killin, Margaret *BiDEWW, FemiCLE*
Killingback, Julia 1944- *SmATA 63 [port]*
Killingbeck, Linda Ann 1961- *WhoAmW 91*
Killinger, Friedrich C. 1938- *St&PR 91*
Killinger, Georg Friedrich *PenDiDA 89*
Killinger, George Glenn 1908- *WhoAm 90*
Killinger, Manfred Von 1886-1944 *BioIn 16*
Killingsworth, Charles Clinton 1917- *WhoAm 90*
Killion, Kenneth Howard 1950- *WhoAm 90*
Killion, Paul Sheehan *BiDrAPA 89*
Killion, Wayne Worden 1925- *St&PR 91*
Killip, Chris 1946- *BioIn 16*
Killips, Danforth 1918- *WhoAm 90*
Killman, Sam *WhoSSW 91*
Killmaster, John H 1934- *WhoAmA 91*
Killoran, Sean M 1940- *BiDrAPA 89*
Killoren, Glenn Arthur 1935- *St&PR 91*
Killoren, Jack K. 1952- *St&PR 91*
Killoren, Robert 1950- *WhoWrEP 89*
Killorin, Edward Wylly 1928- *WhoWor 91*
Killorin, Mary Katherine 1951- *WhoEmL 91*
Killory, Diane Silberstein 1954- *WhoAm 90, WhoAmW 91*
Killough, Jack Christopher 1948- *WhoEmL 91*
Killough, James Stuart 1940- *St&PR 91*
Killough, John Edwin 1947- *WhoAm 90*
Killough, Kevin Charles 1958- *WhoEmL 91*
Killough, Larry Neil 1932- *WhoAm 90*
Killough, Lee 1942- *ConAu 32NR, SmATA 64 [port]*
Killough, Stephen Pinckney 1935- *St&PR 91*
Killough, Walter J. 1931- *St&PR 91*
Killpack, J. Robert 1922- *St&PR 91*
Killpack, James Hewett 1950- *BiDrAPA 89*
Killpack, James Robert 1922- *WhoAm 90*
Killpatrick, James Carl 1931- *WhoAm 90*
Killy, Jean Claude 1943- *BioIn 16, WorAlBi*
Kilman, James William 1931- *WhoAm 90, WhoWor 91*
Kilmann, Ralph Herman 1946- *WhoAm 90, WhoE 91, WhoEmL 91, WhoWor 91*
Kilmartin, Edward John 1923- *WhoAm 90, WhoWor 91*
Kilmartin, Joseph Francis, Jr. 1924- *WhoE 91*
Kilmartin, Suzanne 1945- *WhoAmW 91*
Kilmer, Douglas Aaron 1952- *WhoEmL 91*
Kilmer, Joanne Whalley- *BioIn 16*
Kilmer, John Henry 1917- *St&PR 91*

Kilmer, Joyce 1886-1918 *WorAlBi*
Kilmer, Kenton 1909- *WhoWrEP 89*
Kilmer, Nicholas 1941- *ConAu 129*
Kilmer, Sheila Agnes 1942- *WhoAmW 91*
Kilmurry, David Wallace 1931- *WhoWor 91*
Kilnapp, George L., Sr. 1931- *St&PR 91*
Kilner, Walter J 1847-1920 *EncO&P 3*
Kilner, Walter John 1847-1920 *EncPaPR 91*
Kilonzo, Gad Paul 1940- *WhoWor 91*
Kilov, Haim Israel 1946- *WhoE 91*
Kilpatric, Michael N. *ODwPR 91*
Kilpatrick, Ada Arilla *WhoAmA 91N*
Kilpatrick, Anita 1947- *WhoAmW 91*
Kilpatrick, Bill J. 1928- *St&PR 91*
Kilpatrick, Carole Camp 1959- *WhoEmL 91*
Kilpatrick, Carolyn Cheeks 1945- *WhoAmW 91*
Kilpatrick, Charles Otis 1922- *WhoAm 90, WhoSSW 91*
Kilpatrick, David *BioIn 16*
Kilpatrick, Ellen Perkins 1877-1951 *WhoAmA 91N*
Kilpatrick, Frank Stanton 1950- *WhoEmL 91*
Kilpatrick, George 1910-1989 *AnObit 1989*
Kilpatrick, George H. 1936- *St&PR 91, WhoAm 90*
Kilpatrick, Hugh Judson 1836-1881 *BioIn 16*
Kilpatrick, James Jackson, Jr. 1920- *WhoAm 90*
Kilpatrick, Lester L. 1923- *St&PR 91*
Kilpatrick, Lincoln 1936- *DrBlPA 90*
Kilpatrick, Melissa Ross 1960- *WhoEmL 91*
Kilpatrick, Mike 1952- *WhoEmL 91*
Kilpatrick, Richard Joseph 1961- *WhoE 91*
Kilpatrick, Richardo I. 1952- *WhoEmL 91*
Kilpatrick, Robert D. 1924- *St&PR 91*
Kilpatrick, Robert Donald 1924- *WhoAm 90, WhoSSW 91*
Kilpatrick, Ronald Wade 1945- *St&PR 91*
Kilpatrick, Ruby Nappier 1925- *WhoAmW 91*
Kilpatrick, Stephen Paul 1959- *WhoEmL 91*
Kilpatrick, William Heard *BioIn 16*
Kilpi, Eeva 1928- *DcScanL*
Kilpi, Volter Adalbert 1874-1939 *DcScanL*
Kilpinen, Yrjo 1892-1959 *PenDiMP A*
Kilquist, Helen Leonard 1912- *WhoAmW 91*
Kilquss, Fred C. 1910- *St&PR 91*
Kilroe, Frank E. 1912- *St&PR 91*
Kilroy, James Francis 1935- *WhoAm 90*
Kilroy, John Muir 1918- *WhoAm 90*
Kilroy, Linda Marie 1950- *WhoE 91*
Kilroy, Mark *BioIn 16*
Kilroy, Mary A *WhoAmA 91*
Kilroy, Matt 1866-1940 *Ballpl 90*
Kilroy, R.J. 1942- *St&PR 91*
Kilsby, Nicholas E. 1944- *ODwPR 91*
Kilsdonk, John A. 1954- *St&PR 91*
Kilsdonk-Biggs, Rachel Constance 1915- *WhoWrEP 89*
Kilson, Martin Luther, Jr. 1931- *WhoAm 90*
Kilton, Donald E. 1942- *St&PR 91*
Kilts, Albert F. 1945- *St&PR 91*
Kilts, Douglas Walter 1946- *WhoE 91*
Kilty, Jerome Timothy 1922- *WhoAm 90*
Kilty, Leaola Angelleana 1936- *WhoAmW 91*
Kilvert, Francis 1840-1879 *BioIn 16*
Kilwien-Meck, Sherri Rae 1960- *WhoAmW 91*
Kilwin, Cheryl Anne 1962- *WhoEmL 91*
Kilzieh, Nael 1961- *BiDrAPA 89*
Kim *ConAu 129, MajTwCW*
Kim Il-Sung 1912- *WhoWor 91, WorAlBi*
Kim Mahn Je 1934- *WhoWor 91*
Kim Yong-nam *WhoWor 91*
Kim, Andrew Byong-Soo 1936- *WhoE 91*
Kim, Andrew Byongsoo 1936- *St&PR 91*
Kim, Anthony H *BiDrAPA 89*
Kim, Bouh Hur *BiDrAPA 89*
Kim, Byung Ock *BiDrAPA 89*
Kim, C. I. Eugene 1930-1988 *BioIn 16*
Kim, Charles Wesley 1926- *WhoE 91*
Kim, Charles Y 1938- *BiDrAPA 89*
Kim, Chin-Woo 1936- *WhoAm 90*
Kim, Chong Ik Eugene 1930-1988 *BioIn 16*
Kim, Chong Il *BioIn 16*
Kim, Chong Soo *BiDrAPA 89*
Kim, Chong Soong 1945- *WhoSSW 91*
Kim, Choong-Ki 1942- *WhoWor 91*
Kim, Chung Hee 1937- *WhoAmW 91*
Kim, Chung-Lim *BiDrAPA 89*
Kim, Chung Wook 1934- *WhoAm 90*
Kim, Cyril K 1935- *BiDrAPA 89*
Kim, Dae-Jung 1925- *WhoWor 91*
Kim, Damian Byungsuk *BiDrAPA 89*
Kim, Daniel Dongsun 1933- *BiDrAPA 89*
Kim, David Y 1945- *BiDrAPA 89*
Kim, Dewey Hongwoo 1928- *WhoWor 91*
Kim, Dongmin 1941- *BiDrAPA 89*
Kim, Donna Marie 1957- *WhoEmL 91*
Kim, E. Han 1946- *WhoAm 90, WhoWor 91*
Kim, Earl 1920- *IntWWM 90, WhoAm 90*
Kim, Edward 1962- *BiDrAPA 89*
Kim, Edward William 1949- *WhoAm 90, WhoEmL 91*
Kim, Elaine *BioIn 16*
Kim, Elaine H 1942- *ConAu 130*
Kim, Emily Eurme *BiDrAPA 89*
Kim, Gew-rae 1954- *WhoE 91*
Kim, Gill-Ryoung 1926- *WhoWor 91*
Kim, Gunil G 1941- *BiDrAPA 89*
Kim, Hae Ahm 1933- *BiDrAPA 89*
Kim, Haeja Grace *BiDrAPA 89*
Kim, Heaza 1944- *BiDrAPA 89*
Kim, Heemong 1957- *WhoE 91*
Kim, Hei-Jung C. 1957- *BiDrAPA 89*
Kim, Hong Sik 1964- *WhoE 91*
Kim, Hoyon 1926- *BiDrAPA 89*
Kim, Hyojong Theresa 1962- *WhoE 91*
Kim, Hyun Joon 1955- *WhoWor 91*
Kim, Ih Chin 1925- *WhoE 91, WhoWor 91*
Kim, Il-Chung 1951- *WhoWor 91*
Kim, Il Sung 1912- *BioIn 16*
Kim, Ilpyong John 1931- *WhoAm 90*
Kim, Jae Chul *BiDrAPA 89*
Kim, Jaegwon 1934- *WhoAm 90*
Kim, Jai Soo 1925- *WhoAm 90*
Kim, James J. 1936- *St&PR 91*
Kim, James Joo-Jin 1936- *WhoAm 90*
Kim, Jin Kyung 1939- *WhoAmW 91*
Kim, Jin-Tek 1934- *BiDrAPA 89*
Kim, Jong Il *BioIn 16*
Kim, Jun Young 1951- *WhoWor 91*
Kim, Jung Hyeon *BiDrAPA 89*
Kim, Jung Il 1936- *BiDrAPA 89*
Kim, Jung Kwoun 1937- *BiDrAPA 89*
Kim, Kathleen Mekyung 1958- *BiDrAPA 89*
Kim, Ke Chung 1934- *WhoE 91*
Kim, Ki Tae 1953- *WhoWor 91*
Kim, Kisik 1930- *BiDrAPA 89*
Kim, Kong-Keun 1925- *BiDrAPA 89*
Kim, Kuke Ik C 1930- *BiDrAPA 89*
Kim, Kum Ock 1941- *BiDrAPA 89*
Kim, Kwang Chin 1943- *BiDrAPA 89*
Kim, Kwang Joon *BiDrAPA 89*
Kim, Kye Young 1949- *BiDrAPA 89*
Kim, Kyo Sool 1942- *WhoSSW 91*
Kim, Kyong-Hae 1946- *WhoWor 91*
Kim, Kyung Sun 1932- *IntWWM 90*
Kim, Kyung Young 1948- *WhoWor 91*
Kim, Laura Kyung-Hwa 1961- *WhoAmW 91*
Kim, Lawrence *BiDrAPA 89*
Kim, MaeJa 1944- *WhoWor 91*
Kim, Mi Ja 1940- *WhoAmW 91*
Kim, Michelle Anne *BiDrAPA 89*
Kim, Millie 1960- *WhoEmL 91*
Kim, Moon Hyun 1934- *WhoAm 90*
Kim, Myong Won *BiDrAPA 89*
Kim, Myun-Ki *BiDrAPA 89*
Kim, Myunghee 1932- *BiDrAPA 89*
Kim, Oksuk Mary 1939- *BiDrAPA 89*
Kim, Po *WhoAmA 91*
Kim, Rhyn Hyun 1936- *WhoSSW 91*
Kim, Richard E. 1932- *WhoAm 90, WhoWrEP 89*
Kim, S. John 1943- *BiDrAPA 89*
Kim, S Peter 1939- *BiDrAPA 89*
Kim, Sang-Hoon 1940- *WhoE 91*
Kim, Sang-Min 1931- *WhoWor 91*
Kim, Sangduk 1930- *WhoAmW 91*
Kim, Sanghee *BiDrAPA 89*
Kim, Se Jung 1931- *WhoWor 91*
Kim, Seung Jin 1948- *WhoWor 91*
Kim, Si-Wook 1950- *WhoWor 91*
Kim, Soo-Ryong 1951- *WhoE 91, WhoEmL 91, WhoWor 91*
Kim, Soon Kuyn *BiDrAPA 89*
Kim, Soon-Kyu 1932- *WhoE 91*
Kim, Stephan Sou-Hwan 1922- *WhoWor 91*
Kim, Suck Won 1940- *BiDrAPA 89*
Kim, Suk Hi 1937- *WhoAm 90*
Kim, Suk Sik 1937- *BiDrAPA 89, WhoE 91*
Kim, Sun-Joo 1929- *IntWWM 90*
Kim, Sun Yong 1960- *BiDrAPA 89*
Kim, Sung-Hou 1937- *WhoAm 90*
Kim, Synja P. *WhoAmW 91*
Kim, Tae Mook 1938- *BiDrAPA 89*
Kim, Thomas Kunhyuk 1929- *WhoAm 90*
Kim, Tong-Su 1927- *BiDrAPA 89*
Kim, Ung Soo 1949- *WhoE 91*
Kim, Wan Hee 1926- *WhoAm 90*
Kim, Wayne Y 1939- *BiDrAPA 89*
Kim, Willa *BioIn 16*
Kim, Willa 1930?- *NotWoAT*
Kim, Wonshik 1956- *WhoWor 91*
Kim, Woo-Ki 1942- *WhoWor 91*
Kim, Woo Tack 1943- *WhoWor 91*
Kim, Wun Jung *BiDrAPA 89*
Kim, Y William 1942- *BiDrAPA 89*
Kim, Yon Soo 1895-1979 *BioIn 16*
Kim, Yong Choon 1935- *WhoAm 90*
Kim, Yong-Kook A 1939- *BiDrAPA 89*
Kim, Yongmin 1953- *WhoWor 91*
Kim, Yoon Berm 1929- *WhoAm 90*
Kim, Yoon Hoon 1946- *BiDrAPA 89*
Kim, Young *BioIn 16*
Kim, Young H 1942- *BiDrAPA 89*
Kim, Young Ho 1927- *WhoE 91*
Kim, Young Kil *BiDrAPA 89*
Kim, Young Uck 1947- *IntWWM 90, PenDiMP*
Kim, Yuhn-Bok 1942- *WhoWor 91*
Kimak, George 1921-1972 *WhoAmA 91N*
Kimata, Glenn Tetsuo 1951- *BiDrAPA 89*
Kimatian, Stephen H. 1941- *WhoAm 90, WhoE 91*
Kimball, Allyn Winthrop 1921- *WhoAm 90*
Kimball, Bradford Miles 1961- *WhoE 91*
Kimball, Bruce *BioIn 16*
Kimball, Bruce Arnold 1941- *WhoAm 90*
Kimball, Charles Arthur 1939- *WhoWrEP 89*
Kimball, Charles Henry Gallwey 1909- *St&PR 91*
Kimball, Charles Newton 1911- *WhoAm 90*
Kimball, Charles Thomas 1945- *WhoWor 91*
Kimball, Chase Patterson *BiDrAPA 89*
Kimball, Clyde William 1928- *WhoAm 90*
Kimball, Connie E. *WhoWrEP 89*
Kimball, Dan Anderson 1951- *WhoEmL 91*
Kimball, Daniel Webster 1946- *WhoSSW 91*
Kimball, David T. 1927- *St&PR 91*
Kimball, Dean 1912- *AuBYP 90*
Kimball, Donald Victor 1948- *WhoE 91*
Kimball, Edward Lawrence 1930- *WhoAm 90*
Kimball, Frances Adrienne 1939- *WhoAmW 91*
Kimball, Frank *ConAu 31NR*
Kimball, Frank *BioIn 16*
Kimball, Irving S. 1918- *St&PR 91*
Kimball, J. Wayland *PenDiDA 89*
Kimball, James L. 1919- *St&PR 91*
Kimball, Joan Harwood 1956- *WhoAmW 91*
Kimball, Judith Ann 1928- *WhoE 91*
Kimball, Karen Lynn 1966- *WhoE 91*
Kimball, Kevin E. 1952- *ODwPR 91*
Kimball, Kim 1917- *SmATA X [port]*
Kimball, Kurt Frederick 1950- *WhoEmL 91*
Kimball, Leo Robert 1923- *St&PR 91*
Kimball, Lindsley Fiske 1894- *WhoAm 90*
Kimball, Louis Charles 1962- *WhoSSW 91*
Kimball, Mary Holt 1934- *WhoAmW 91*
Kimball, Natalie D. 1951- *St&PR 91*
Kimball, Newt 1915- *Ballpl 90*
Kimball, Paul C. 1903- *St&PR 91*
Kimball, Penn Townsend, II 1915- *WhoAm 90*
Kimball, Ralph *ConAu 31NR*
Kimball, Raymond Alonzo 1918- *WhoAm 90*
Kimball, Raymond Michael 1957- *BiDrAPA 89*
Kimball, Reid R 1926- *BiDrAPA 89*
Kimball, Reid Roberts 1926- *WhoAm 90*
Kimball, Richard A., Jr. *St&PR 91*
Kimball, Richard Arthur, Jr. 1930- *WhoAm 90*
Kimball, Richard Wilson 1938- *WhoWrEP 89*
Kimball, Robert Davern 1956- *WhoEmL 91*
Kimball, Robert Eric 1939- *WhoAm 90, WhoWrEP 89*
Kimball, Roland Baldwin 1921- *WhoAm 90*
Kimball, Sarah Wright 1942- *ODwPR 91*
Kimball, Sue Laslie *WhoWrEP 89*
Kimball, Sue Laslie 1921- *WhoSSW 91*
Kimball, Walter Henry 1953- *WhoE 91*
Kimball, Warren Forbes 1935- *WhoAm 90*
Kimball, Wilford Wayne, Jr 1943- *WhoAmA 91*
Kimball, Yeffe 1914-1978 *WhoAmA 91N*
Kimball-Brooke, Helen Chase 1947- *WhoWor 91*
Kimbell, Anthony *PenDiDA 89*
Kimbell, David Alan 1929- *St&PR 91*
Kimbell, Marion Joel 1923- *WhoWor 91*
Kimbell, Steven W 1940- *BiDrAPA 89*
Kimbell, Wilhelm 1766-1875 *PenDiDA 89*
Kimbell, William H *BiDrAPA 89*
Kimberlin, John H. 1943- *St&PR 91*
Kimberlin, Sam Owen, Jr. 1928- *St&PR 91, WhoSSW 91*
Kimberlin-Harris, Cecilia Louise 1947- *WhoEmL 91*
Kimberling, C. Ronald 1950- *St&PR 91*
Kimberly, John Robert 1942- *WhoAm 90*
Kimberly, William Essick 1933- *WhoE 91, WhoWor 91*
Kimble, Barry William 1961- *WhoSSW 91*
Kimble, Gladys Augusta Lee 1906- *WhoAmW 91, WhoWor 91*
Kimble, Gregory Adams 1917- *WhoAm 90*
Kimble, Raymond V 1944- *BiDrAPA 89*
Kimble, Robert P. 1946- *St&PR 91*
Kimble, William Earl 1926- *WhoAm 90*
Kimbleton, Dennis Paul 1948- *WhoEmL 91*
Kimbrel, Monroe 1916- *St&PR 91, WhoAm 90*
Kimbrell, Anna Margaret 1927- *WhoAmW 91*
Kimbrell, Grady Ned 1933- *WhoWrEP 89*
Kimbrell, Horace Warren 1916- *WhoAm 90*
Kimbrell, John Everett 1933- *WhoSSW 91*
Kimbrell, Leonard Buell 1922- *WhoAmA 91*
Kimbrell, Murvin Jackson 1930- *WhoSSW 91*
Kimbrell, Odell C., Jr. 1927- *St&PR 91*
Kimbrell, Odell Culp, Jr. 1927- *WhoAm 90*
Kimbrell, W. Duke 1924- *St&PR 91*
Kimbrell, Willard Duke 1924- *WhoAm 90*
Kimbro, Exall L, Jr. *BiDrAPA 89*
Kimbro, Harriet *ConAu 30NR*
Kimbro, Henry 1912- *Ballpl 90*
Kimbrough, Allen Wayne 1953- *WhoAm 90*
Kimbrough, Charles *BioIn 16*
Kimbrough, Emily 1899-1989 *BioIn 16*
Kimbrough, James Edward *BiDrAPA 89*
Kimbrough, James H. *WhoSSW 91*
Kimbrough, Kevin Edward 1962- *WhoEmL 91*
Kimbrough, Mary Alice 1932- *WhoSSW 91*
Kimbrough, Ralph Bradley, Sr. 1922- *WhoAm 90*
Kimbrough, Sara Dodge *WhoAmA 91N*
Kimbrough, Steven 1936- *IntWWM 90*
Kimbrough, William Adams, Jr. 1935- *WhoAm 90*
Kimbrough, William W 1928- *BiDrAPA 89*
Kimbrough, William Walter, III 1928- *WhoAm 90, WhoWor 91*
Kimchi, Dan *St&PR 91*
Kime, Bradley J. 1960- *St&PR 91*
Kime, Harold Howard 1924- *WhoSSW 91*
Kime, Wayne Raymond 1941- *WhoSSW 91*
Kimelman, Donald Bruce 1947- *WhoAm 90*
Kimelman, Henry L. 1921- *WhoAm 90*
Kimenye, Barbara 1940?- *FemiCLE*
Kimerer, John Vastine 1930- *St&PR 91*
Kimerer, Neil B 1918- *BiDrAPA 89*
Kimerer, Neil Banard, Sr. 1918- *WhoAm 90, WhoWor 91*
Kimes, Beverly Rae 1939- *WhoAmW 91, WhoWor 91*
Kimes, Don 1950- *WhoAmA 91*
Kimes, Don Mark 1950- *WhoE 91*
Kimes, J.D. 1936- *St&PR 91*
Kimes, Sheryl Elaine 1954- *WhoAmW 91*
Kimker, Klaholt P. 1945- *St&PR 91*
Kimlioka, Stefan 1943- *WhoWor 91*
Kimm, Barbara Chandler 1936- *WhoAmW 91*
Kimm, Fiona *IntWWM 90*
Kimm, Fiona 1952- *PenDiMP*
Kimm, Sue Young Sook 1938- *WhoE 91*
Kimmel, Carole Anne 1944- *WhoAmW 91*
Kimmel, Charles R. *St&PR 91*
Kimmel, Gary Dean 1937- *St&PR 91*
Kimmel, George Stuart 1934- *St&PR 91, WhoAm 90, WhoE 91*
Kimmel, H. Steven 1946- *WhoAm 90*
Kimmel, Husband Edward 1882-1968 *WorAlBi*
Kimmel, Irvine 1918- *St&PR 91*
Kimmel, Jerold 1946- *St&PR 91*
Kimmel, Jesse A. 1916- *St&PR 91*
Kimmel, Joyce Frances 1948- *WhoAmW 91*
Kimmel, Mark 1940- *WhoWor 91*
Kimmel, Mark J. 1959- *St&PR 91*
Kimmel, Patricia Temple 1930- *St&PR 91*
Kimmel, Peter Robin *BiDrAPA 89*
Kimmel, Peter Scott 1947- *WhoSSW 91*
Kimmel, Robert Irving 1922- *WhoAm 90, WhoE 91*
Kimmel, Robert L. 1933- *ODwPR 91*
Kimmel, Susan Elizabeth 1959- *BiDrAPA 89*
Kimmel, Troy Max, Jr. 1957- *WhoEmL 91, WhoSSW 91*
Kimmel, Victor 1921- *St&PR 91*
Kimmel-Cohn, Roberta 1937- *WhoAmA 91*
Kimmell, Garman Oscar 1913- *St&PR 91*
Kimmell, Lee *BioIn 16*
Kimmell, Lee H. 1950- *WhoAm 90*
Kimmell, Paul Michael *BiDrAPA 89*
Kimmell, Susan C 1894- *EncO&P 3*
Kimmelman, Burt Joseph 1947- *WhoWrEP 89*
Kimmelman, David H. 1955- *WhoEmL 91*
Kimmelman, Harold 1923- *WhoAmA 91*
Kimmelman, Leslie 1958- *ConAu 132*
Kimmelman, Peter 1944- *St&PR 91*
Kimmerle, Gerald W. 1928- *St&PR 91*
Kimmerle, Gerald William 1928- *WhoAm 90*

Kimmett, Robert M. *BioIn 16*
Kimmey, James Richard, Jr. 1935- *WhoAm 90*
Kimmich, Rainer Helmut 1941- *WhoWor 91*
Kimmich, Robert A 1920- *BiDrAPA 89*
Kimmich, Sara Jane 1963- *WhoAmW 91*
Kimmitt, Robert Michael 1947- *WhoAm 90*
Kimmle, Manfred 1942- *St&PR 91*, *WhoAm 90*
Kimn, Ha-Jine 1939- *WhoWor 91*
Kimnach, Myron William 1922- *WhoAm 90*
Kimpel, Benjamin Franklin 1905- *WhoAm 90*
Kimple, Scott Carlisle 1966- *WhoSSW 91*
Kimsey, Alice Darlene 1948- *WhoEmL 91*
Kimsey, Chad 1905-1942 *Ballpl 90*
Kimsey, Karl Keith 1953- *WhoSSW 91*
Kimsey, Larry Mark 1958- *BiDrAPA 89*
Kimsey, Rustin Ray 1935- *WhoAm 90*
Kimura, Akira 1936- *WhoWor 91*
Kimura, Doreen *WhoAm 90*
Kimura, Harlan Yoshito 1955- *WhoEmL 91*
Kimura, Joan Alexandra 1934- *WhoAmA 91*
Kimura, Kazuo 1934- *ConDes 90*
Kimura, Kimi Takeuchi 1914- *WhoE 91*
Kimura, Kiyoshi 1931- *BiDrAPA 89*
Kimura, Lillian Chiyeko 1929- *WhoAmW 91*
Kimura, Mary S. 1928- *St&PR 91*
Kimura, Riisaburo 1924- *WhoAmA 91*
Kimura, Sueko M *WhoAmA 91*
Kimura, William Yusaburo 1920- *WhoAmA 91*
Kimura, Yoshimasa Frank 1936- *WhoWor 91*
Kimzey, Jackie R. 1952- *St&PR 91*
Kimzey, Louis Lee 1928- *WhoAm 90*
Kimzey, Robin Lynn 1965- *WhoSSW 91*
Kin, Frederick Robert 1934- *St&PR 91*
Kinache *WhNaAH*
Kinaci, Ilhan 1932- *St&PR 91*
Kinal, Murl E. *BioIn 16*
Kinard, Agnes Dodds *WhoAmW 91*, *WhoE 91*
Kinard, Clifford James 1962- *WhoSSW 91*
Kinard, Fredrick William 1906- *WhoSSW 91*
Kinard, Glenn E. 1947- *St&PR 91*
Kinard, Hargett Yingling 1912- *WhoAm 90*
Kinard, John R. *BioIn 16*
Kinard, Mike 1939- *St&PR 91*
Kinard, William Carlton 1919- *St&PR 91*
Kinariwala, Bharat 1926- *WhoAm 90*
Kinasz, Thomas John 1957- *WhoEmL 91*
Kinberg, Judy 1948- *WhoAm 90*
Kincade, A.W. *St&PR 91N*
Kincade, H. Patricia 1930- *St&PR 91*
Kincade, William Hadley 1939- *WhoE 91*
Kincaid, Allen Wayne 1946- *WhoSSW 91*
Kincaid, Charles Vernon 1930- *WhoE 91*
Kincaid, Elsie Elizabeth 1929- *WhoSSW 91*
Kincaid, Hugh Reid 1934- *WhoAm 90*
Kincaid, Jamaica 1949- *FemiCLE*, *NewYTBS 90 [port]*, *WorAu 1980 [port]*
Kincaid, James, Jr. 1954- *WhoEmL 91*
Kincaid, James Alan 1930- *St&PR 91*
Kincaid, Kelly 1958- *WhoEmL 91*
Kincaid, Owings Wilson 1921- *WhoAm 90*
Kincaid, Ray L. 1935- *St&PR 91*
Kincaid, Rodney Lyle 1933- *WhoWor 91*
Kincaid, Steven Randall 1953- *WhoE 91*
Kincannon, Felice *BioIn 16*, *WhoAmW 91*
Kincannon, Karen Courtney 1945- *WhoSSW 91*
Kincare, Patricia Marie *BiDrAPA 89*
Kincart, Robert Owen 1949- *WhoSSW 91*
Kinch, Martin 1943- *OxCCanT*
Kincheloe, R.L. 1930- *St&PR 91*
Kinchen, James Benjamin 1952- *IntWWM 90*
Kinchen, Robert Preston 1933- *WhoAm 90*, *WhoE 91*
Kinck, Hans Ernst 1865-1926 *DcScanL*
Kincses, Veronica 1949- *IntWWM 90*
Kincszes, Veronika 1948- *PenDiMP*
Kind, Joshua B 1933- *WhoAmA 91*
Kind, Kenneth Wayne 1948- *WhoWor 91*
Kind, Margaret Ruth 1945- *BiDrAPA 89*
Kind, Phyllis *WhoAmA 91*
Kind, Phyllis Dawn 1933- *WhoAmW 91*
Kind, Richard John 1941- *WhoAm 90*
Kind, Stephen Joseph 1936- *St&PR 91*, *WhoAm 90*
Kindahl, Connie *WhoAmA 91*
Kindall, Charlotte Eloise 1944- *WhoAmW 91*
Kindall, Jerry 1935- *Ballpl 90*
Kindel, James Horace, Jr. 1913- *WhoAm 90*
Kindel, Robert James 1947- *WhoWrEP 89*
Kinder, Dolores *ODwPR 91*
Kinder, Ellis 1914-1968 *Ballpl 90*, *BioIn 16*
Kinder, Eugene J 1926- *BiDrAPA 89*
Kinder, Harold M. 1911- *WhoAm 90*, *WhoWor 91*
Kinder, James S. 1895- *WhoAm 90*
Kinderfather, Kathleen McShane *BioIn 16*
Kinderman, A. Sandford 1943- *WhoE 91*
Kindermann, Helmmo 1947- *WhoAmA 91*
Kindermann, Udo 1941- *WhoWor 91*
Kindermann, Wilfried 1940- *WhoWor 91*
Kindersley, Jemima 1741?-1809 *FemiCLE*
Kinderwater, Joseph C. 1922- *WhoAm 90*
Kindig, Cepha Pasek *BioIn 16*
Kindig, Everett William 1936- *WhoSSW 91*
Kindig, Fred Eugene 1920- *WhoAm 90*
Kindl, Fred Henry 1920- *WhoAm 90*
Kindleberger, Charles P., II 1910- *WhoAm 90*
Kindler, Alan Ronald *BiDrAPA 89*
Kindler, Albert *BioIn 16*
Kindler, Andrew Eugene 1956- *WhoEmL 91*
Kindler, Bob *NewAgMG*
Kindler, Hans 1892-1949 *PenDiMP*
Kindler, Steve *NewAgMG*
Kindley, Jeffrey 1945- *ConAu 130*
Kindlund, Joanne M. 1949- *St&PR 91*
Kindlund, Newton C. 1940- *St&PR 91*
Kindness, Thomas Norman 1929- *WhoAm 90*
Kindred, George Charles 1898- *WhoE 91*
Kindred, Guy Ben *BiDrAPA 89*
Kindred, Joan Hover 1930- *WhoAmW 91*
Kindrick, Charles Henry 1951- *St&PR 91*
Kindrick, Robert LeRoy 1942- *WhoAm 90*
Kinds, Herbert Eugene 1933- *WhoWor 91*
Kindschuh, Mark William *BiDrAPA 89*
Kindschy, Carroll Phillip 1939- *St&PR 91*
Kindsvater, Carl Edward 1913- *WhoAm 90*
Kindt, John Warren 1950- *WhoAm 90*
Kindt, Thomas James 1939- *WhoE 91*
Kindwald, Donald James 1961- *WhoEmL 91*
Kindwall, Josef A *BiDrAPA 89*
Kiner, Ralph 1922- *Ballpl 90 [port]*, *BioIn 16*, *WorAlBi*
Kinert, Reed Charles 1912?- *AuBYP 90*
Kines, Barbara *BioIn 16*
Kines, Joan Elaine 1949- *WhoEmL 91*, *WhoWor 91*
King Crimson *EncPR&S 89*
King, Mrs. *EncPaPR 91*
King Payne *WhNaAH*
King Philip *WhNaAH*
King, A. Thomas 1944- *WhoE 91*
King, Alan 1927- *WorAlBi*
King, Alan C. 1951- *St&PR 91*
King, Alan Jonathan 1954- *WhoE 91*
King, Albert 1924?- *EncPR&S 89*
King, Aldine *DrBlPA 90*
King, Alexander Hyatt 1911- *IntWWM 90*
King, Algin Braddy 1926- *WhoAm 90*, *WhoSSW 91*, *WhoWor 91*
King, Alice 1839-1894 *FemiCLE*
King, Alvin Thomas 1944- *WhoWrEP 89*
King, Ambrose Yeo-chi 1935- *WhoWor 91*
King, Amy Cathryne Patterson 1928- *WhoSSW 91*
King, Amy Jane 1961- *WhoE 91*
King, Andre Richardson 1931- *WhoAm 90*
King, Andrea *ODwPR 91*
King, Ann Beatrice 1957- *WhoAmW 91*
King, Ann Clare 1958- *WhoEmL 91*
King, Ann Stockman 1931- *WhoAmW 91*
King, Anne 1621-1684? *BiDEWW*
King, Anthony Gabriel 1953- *WhoAm 90*, *WhoE 91*
King, Arnold Kimsey 1901- *WhoAm 90*
King, Arnold Kimsey, Jr. 1931- *WhoWor 91*
King, Arthur *AuBYP 90*
King, Arthur Hood 1927- *St&PR 91*, *WhoAm 90*
King, Augusta Ada Byron 1815-1852 *BioIn 16*
King, B. B. *BioIn 16*
King, B B 1925- *DrBlPA 90*, *EncPR&S 89*
King, B. B. 1925- *OxCPMus*
King, B.B. 1925- *WorAlBi*
King, Barbara *ODwPR 91*
King, Barbara Jean 1941- *WhoAmW 91*
King, Barrett Taylor 1947- *WhoSSW 91*
King, Ben E 1938- *DrBlPA 90*, *EncPR&S 89*
King, Ben Tavera *NewAgMG*
King, Bernard *BioIn 16*
King, Bernard David 1949- *WhoE 91*, *WhoEmL 91*
King, Bernice *BioIn 16*
King, Bertrand E. 1930- *St&PR 91*
King, Betty Blake 1957- *WhoSSW 91*
King, Billie Jean *BioIn 16*
King, Billie Jean 1943- *WorAlBi*
King, Billie Jean Moffitt 1943- *WhoAm 90*, *WhoAmW 91*
King, Blondie Cherry 1933- *WhoAmW 91*
King, Bob *BioIn 16*
King, Brian Maxwell 1933- *WhoAm 90*
King, Brian Pierce 1948- *St&PR 91*
King, Bruce 1897-1976 *EncO&P 3*
King, Bruce 1925- *IntWWM 90*
King, Bruce Donald 1947- *St&PR 91*
King, Bryan Harry 1957- *BiDrAPA 89*
King, Bud *BioIn 16*
King, C. B. 1923-1988 *BioIn 16*
King, Candice Meriwether 1950- *WhoAmW 91*
King, Carl B. 1942- *WhoAm 90*
King, Carol Louise 1948- *WhoAmW 91*
King, Carol Soucek 1943- *WhoWrEP 89*
King, Carol Weiss 1895-1952 *EncAL*
King, Carole 1942- *EncPR&S 89*, *OxCPMus*, *WorAlBi*
King, Carolyn *BioIn 16*
King, Carolyn Dineen 1938- *WhoAm 90*, *WhoAmW 91*, *WhoSSW 91*
King, Carolyn Mae 1946- *WhoAmW 91*
King, Cary Judson, III 1934- *WhoAm 90*
King, Cecil 1901-1987 *EncO&P 3*
King, Charles 1844-1933 *WhNaAH*
King, Charles Bird 1785-1862 *WhNaAH*
King, Charles Brady 1868-1957 *EncABHB 4 [port]*
King, Charles C. *BioIn 16*
King, Charles C. 1929- *WhoSSW 91*
King, Charles Conaway 1929- *St&PR 91*
King, Charles D. 1953- *St&PR 91*
King, Charles E. 1874-1950 *OxCPMus*
King, Charles Glen 1896-1988 *BioIn 16*
King, Charles Glyn 1956- *WhoEmL 91*
King, Charles Henry, IV 1951- *St&PR 91*
King, Charles L. 1926- *St&PR 91*
King, Charles Mark 1952- *WhoEmL 91*, *WhoSSW 91*
King, Charles McDonald, Jr. 1934- *WhoAm 90*
King, Charles Ross 1925- *WhoAm 90*, *WhoWor 91*
King, Charles Thomas 1911- *WhoE 91*, *WhoWor 91*
King, Charmion 1925- *OxCCanT*
King, Charolette Elaine 1945- *WhoEmL 91*
King, Cheryl Waller 1957- *WhoAmW 91*
King, Chester Harding, Jr. 1913- *WhoAm 90*
King, Chevene Bowers 1923-1988 *BioIn 16*
King, Christine Ledesma 1945- *WhoAmW 91*, *WhoEmL 91*
King, Christine Paran 1949- *WhoAmW 91*
King, Christopher Burnette 1956- *WhoEmL 91*
King, Christopher Kevin 1959- *WhoE 91*
King, Clarence 1842-1901 *BioIn 16*, *WhNaAH*
King, Clarence Carleton, II 1956- *WhoEmL 91*
King, Clark E. 1934- *St&PR 91*
King, Claudia Louan 1940- *WhoAmW 91*
King, Clinton Blair 1901-1979 *WhoAmA 91N*
King, Clyde 1925- *Ballpl 90*
King, Clyde Richard 1924- *WhoAm 90*
King, Colbert Isaiah 1939- *WhoAm 90*
King, Coretta Scott 1927- *BioAmW*, *WhoAm 90*, *WhoAmW 91*, *WorAlBi*
King, Cynthia Bregman 1925- *WhoWrEP 89*
King, Cynthia Remington 1956- *WhoE 91*
King, Cyril E. 1921-1978 *BioIn 16*
King, Damon D. 1934- *WhoAm 90*
King, Dan E. 1952- *St&PR 91*
King, Dana Leland 1955- *WhoEmL 91*
King, Daniel J. 1952- *St&PR 91*
King, David Alderson 1936- *St&PR 91*
King, David Edgar 1936- *WhoAm 90*
King, David Leroy 1927- *St&PR 91*
King, David P. 1949- *St&PR 91*
King, David Randall 1953- *WhoEmL 91*
King, David Roy 1950- *WhoEmL 91*
King, David Scott 1957- *WhoEmL 91*
King, David Stephen *BiDrAPA 89*
King, Deborah 1950- *ConAu 31NR*
King, Deborah S. 1964- *ODwPR 91*
King, Debra Rowlett 1954- *WhoEmL 91*
King, Delores Luvina 1937- *WhoAmW 91*
King, Dennis 1897-1971 *OxCPMus*
King, Dennis 1941- *ConAu 130*
King, Dennis Eugene 1936- *St&PR 91*
King, Dennis L. 1946- *WhoEmL 91*
King, Dennis Maurice *BiDrAPA 89*
King, Dennis Michael 1946- *St&PR 91*
King, Diane R. 1950- *St&PR 91*
King, Dominic Benson 1928- *St&PR 91*, *WhoAm 90*
King, Don *ODwPR 91*
King, Don 1929- *BioIn 16*
King, Don 1932- *DrBlPA 90*
King, Donald C. 1930- *WhoAm 90*
King, Donald G. 1925- *St&PR 91*
King, Donald West, Jr. 1927- *WhoAm 90*
King, Douglas Lohr 1941- *St&PR 91*, *WhoAm 90*, *WhoWor 91*
King, Doyle D. 1936- *St&PR 91*
King, Dwight Lyman 1917- *St&PR 91*
King, E. *BiDWomA*
King, E. W. *AmLegL*
King, Edith Lawrence 1883?-1975 *BioIn 16*
King, Edith Lawrence 1884-1975 *NotWoAT*
King, Edward, Jr. 1951- *WhoSSW 91*
King, Edward Louis 1920- *WhoAm 90*
King, Edward William 1923- *WhoAm 90*
King, Edwin Henry 1828-1896 *DcCanB 12*
King, Edwina L. 1952- *WhoAmW 91*
King, Elaine A 1947- *WhoAmA 91*
King, Elaine Slatton 1947- *WhoAmW 91*
King, Eleanor 1906- *BioAmW*, *BioIn 16*
King, Eleanor 1909- *WhoAmA 91*
King, Elizabeth *BiDrAPA 89*
King, Elizabeth Chiu 1935- *WhoWrEP 89*
King, Elizabeth Maureen 1957- *WhoAmW 91*
King, Elizabeth Raymond 1923- *WhoAmW 91*
King, Elmer Richard 1916- *WhoAm 90*
King, Elton, Jr. 1934- *St&PR 91*
King, Emmett Alonzo, III 1942- *WhoE 91*, *WhoWor 91*
King, Eric 1964- *Ballpl 90*
King, Erika *BioIn 16*
King, Erika Irene 1942- *WhoWor 91*
King, Ernest J. 1878-1956 *WorAlBi*
King, Errol Gladstone 1942- *WhoE 91*
King, Evelyn 1960- *EncPR&S 89*
King, Florence *BioIn 16*
King, Francine Ellen 1946- *St&PR 91*
King, Francis 1904- *EncO&P 3*
King, Francis 1923- *ConAu 33NR*, *MajTwCW*
King, Francis Henry 1923- *WhoWor 91*
King, Frank *BioIn 16*
King, Frank 1883-1969 *EncACom*
King, Frank O 1883-1969 *WhoAmA 91N*
King, Frank Theodore 1923- *St&PR 91*
King, Frederick Alexander 1925- *WhoAm 90*
King, George 1919?- *EncO&P 3*
King, George, III 1947- *WhoE 91*
King, George Edward 1931- *WhoAm 90*
King, George F. 1938- *St&PR 91*
King, George Gerard 1940- *WhoAm 90*
King, George Raleigh 1931- *WhoWor 91*
King, George S. 1938- *St&PR 91*
King, George Smith, Jr. 1928- *WhoAm 90*
King, George W. 1932- *St&PR 91*
King, Gerard Francis 1935- *St&PR 91*
King, Glenn Richard 1928- *St&PR 91*
King, Gloria Reed 1946- *WhoAmW 91*
King, Godfre Ray 1878-1939 *EncO&P 3*
King, Gordon C. 1933- *St&PR 91*
King, Grace E. 1851-1932 *BioAmW*
King, Grace Elizabeth 1851?-1932 *FemiCLE*
King, Graham 1930- *ConAu 132*
King, Gundar Julian 1926- *WhoAm 90*, *WhoWor 91*
King, Guy David, Jr. 1931- *WhoSSW 91*, *WhoWor 91*
King, Gwendolyn Bair 1915- *WhoAmW 91*
King, Gwendolyn S. *BioIn 16*, *WhoAm 90*
King, H. Joe, Jr. 1932- *St&PR 91*
King, Hal 1944- *Ballpl 90*
King, Hamilton 1871-1952 *WhoAmA 91N*
King, Harold 1887-1956 *DcScB S2*
King, Harold 1898-1990 *ConAu 132*
King, Harold 1945- *SpyFic*
King, Harold D. 1932- *St&PR 91*
King, Harold Raymond 1945- *WhoSSW 91*
King, Harold Thomas, Jr. 1949- *WhoE 91*
King, Harriet 1840-1920 *FemiCLE*
King, Harry R. *St&PR 91*
King, Harry Robert *WhoAm 90*
King, Harry Warnock 1942- *St&PR 91*
King, Harvey Bills 1929- *St&PR 91*
King, Hazel Caudle 1947- *WhoWrEP 89*
King, Helen Dean 1869-1955 *DcScB S2*
King, Helen Jelks 1958- *WhoAmW 91*
King, Henrietta 1832-1925 *WorAlBi*
King, Henry Hayes, Jr. 1932- *WhoAm 90*
King, Henry Lawrence 1928- *WhoAm 90*
King, Hiram Bronson 1931- *WhoE 91*
King, Horatio 1811-1897 *BiDrUSE 89*
King, Howard J. 1933- *St&PR 91*
King, Hugh Aly, Jr. 1936- *BiDrAPA 89*
King, Imogene Martina 1923- *WhoAm 90*, *WhoAmW 91*
King, Indle Gifford 1934- *WhoAm 90*
King, Irving Henry 1935- *WhoE 91*
King, Ivan Robert 1927- *WhoAm 90*
King, Jack 1930-1987 *OxCCanT*
King, Jack Howell 1952- *WhoSSW 91*
King, James 1848-1900 *DcCanB 12*
King, James 1925- *BioIn 16*, *IntWWM 90*, *PenDiMP*
King, James A. 1948- *St&PR 91*
King, James Arthur 1920- *St&PR 91*
King, James B. 1935- *WhoAm 90*
King, James Cecil 1924- *WhoAm 90*
King, James Claude 1924- *WhoAm 90*
King, James Edward 1940- *WhoAm 90*
King, James Edward 1954- *WhoEmL 91*
King, James Elmer 1949- *WhoSSW 91*
King, James Forrest, Jr. 1949- *WhoEmL 91*

King, James Howard 1952- WhoEmL 91
King, James Lawrence 1927- WhoSSW 91
King, James Lawrence, Jr. 1935- WhoWor 91
King, James Manford 1951- WhoSSW 91
King, James Nedwed 1947- St&PR 91, WhoAm 90
King, James P BiDrAPA 89
King, James P 1938- ODwPR 91
King, James Pearson 1938- WhoE 91
King, James Richard 1943- WhoSSW 91
King, James Robert, III 1957- WhoSSW 91
King, James Russell 1954- WhoE 91
King, Jean Doster 1937- ODwPR 91
King, Jeannette Wertz 1937- WhoAmW 91
King, Jeffrey Charles 1949- WhoE 91
King, Jeffrey Norman 1953- WhoEmL 91
King, Jennifer Carolyn 1960- WhoAmW 91
King, Jesse Herman 1947- WhoSSW 91
King, Jessie M. 1875-1949 BiDWomA
King, Jim 1932- Ballpl 90
King, Joe BioIn 16
King, Joe 1909-1979 Ballpl 90
King, Joel Harris BiDrAPA 89
King, John Allison 1935- WhoE 91
King, John Barre BiDrAPA 89
King, John C. ODwPR 91
King, John Charles Peter 1949- WhoAm 90
King, John D. 1913- St&PR 91
King, John Edouard 1820- AmLegL
King, John Ethelbert, Jr. 1913- WhoAm 90
King, John Francis 1925- WhoAm 90
King, John Gordon 1925- WhoAm 90
King, John Herbert BiDrAPA 89
King, John Joseph 1938- St&PR 91
King, John Lane 1924- WhoAm 90
King, John Mark 1829-1899 DcCanB 12
King, John N. 1945- ConAu 32NR
King, John P. 1951- St&PR 91
King, John Quill Taylor 1921- WhoAm 90
King, John R. 1938- St&PR 91
King, John Reymes 1910- IntWWM 90
King, John Talbott, Jr. 1945- WhoE 91
King, Jon C. 1946- St&PR 91
King, Jon J. 1940- St&PR 91
King, Jonathan 1925- WhoAm 90
King, Joni D. St&PR 91
King, Joseph Bertram 1924- WhoAm 90
King, Joseph Clement 1922- WhoWor 91
King, Joseph Edward 1941- St&PR 91
King, Joseph P 1927- BiDrAPA 89
King, Joseph Paul 1941- St&PR 91, WhoAm 90
King, Joseph Willet 1934- BiDrAPA 89
King, Joseph Willett 1934- WhoSSW 91
King, Joyce Calistri 1927- WhoAmW 91
King, Judi Brown BioIn 16
King, Judith Ann 1950- WhoAmW 91
King, Judith Helene 1946- BiDrAPA 89
King, Julia Marion 1939- WhoWor 91
King, Julian Rex 1944- WhoWor 91
King, Karen Jeanne 1953- WhoWrEP 89
King, Karl L. 1891-1971 OxCPMus
King, Katherine Chungho 1937- WhoAmW 91
King, Kathleen Murphy 1944- WhoAmW 91
King, Kathryn Elizabeth 1926- WhoWrEP 89
King, Kelly S. WhoAm 90
King, Kelly Stuart 1948- St&PR 91
King, Kendall Willard 1926- WhoAm 90
King, Kenneth BioIn 16
King, Kenneth Ray BiDrAPA 89
King, Kernan Francis 1944- St&PR 91, WhoAm 90
King, Kimball 1934- ConAu 31NR
King, L. Ellis 1939- WhoSSW 91
King, Larry 1933- BioIn 16, WhoAm 90, WorAlBi
King, Larry Dale 1949- St&PR 91
King, Larry L 1929- MajTwCW, WhoAm 90, WhoE 91
King, Larry Peyton BioIn 16, NewYTBS 90
King, Larry R. 1939- St&PR 91
King, Laura Jane 1947- WhoAmW 91
King, Lauren Elizabeth 1963- WhoEmL 91
King, Lauren Juanita 1951- WhoAmW 91
King, Lawrence, III 1952- WhoSSW 91
King, Lawrence Edward 1948- WhoEmL 91
King, Lawrence Philip 1929- WhoAm 90, WhoE 91
King, Lee 1892-1967 Ballpl 90
King, Lee A. 1924- St&PR 91
King, Leland W. 1907- WhoAm 90
King, Leon 1921- WhoAm 90
King, LeRoy Francis 1928- St&PR 91
King, Leslie John 1934- WhoAm 90
King, Linda Orr 1948- WhoAmW 91
King, Lis ODwPR 91
King, Lis Sonder 1932- WhoAmW 91
King, Llewellyn Willings 1939- WhoE 91
King, Lloyd Joseph BiDrAPA 89
King, Louis Douglass BiDrAPA 89
King, Louise Howland 1865-1945 BioIn 16
King, Lowell Restell 1932- WhoAm 90
King, Lucy Jane BiDrAPA 89
King, Lucy Jane 1932- WhoSSW 91
King, Lyndel Irene Saunders 1943- WhoAm 90, WhoAmA 91
King, Lynne Mohrmann 1945- WhoEmL 91
King, Lynnette Lee 1946- WhoEmL 91
King, Mabel DrBlPA 90
King, Mabel Debra 1895-1950 WhoAmA 91N
King, Marcia 1940- WhoAm 90, WhoAmW 91
King, Marcia Gygli 1931- WhoAmW 91
King, Marcia Jones 1934- WhoAmW 91, WhoE 91
King, Marcia Louise 1950- WhoWrEP 89
King, Margaret Ann 1936- WhoAmW 91
King, Margaret Leah 1947- WhoAm 90
King, Margaret Mary 1953- St&PR 91
King, Marian BioIn 16
King, Marianne E. 1953- ODwPR 91
King, Marie Mincher 1956- WhoEmL 91
King, Mark A. 1951- St&PR 91
King, Mark Charles 1961- St&PR 91
King, Martha 1645-1740 BiDEWW
King, Martha Bennett AuBYP 90
King, Martin Luther 1929-1968 BioIn 16
King, Martin Luther 1958?- BioIn 16
King, Martin Luther, Jr. 1929-1968 MajTwCW, WorAlBi
King, Mary BioIn 16
King, Mary Alsop 1769-1819 BioIn 16
King, Mary Ann 1963- WhoE 91
King, Mary-Claire 1946- WhoAmW 91
King, Mary Jane 1950- WhoAmW 91
King, Mary Lois 1936- WhoSSW 91
King, Mary Smothers 1937- WhoAmW 91
King, Marylee Hansen 1946- WhoAmW 91
King, Maurice Athelstan 1936- WhoWor 91
King, Michael C. 1940- St&PR 91
King, Michael Dumont 1949- WhoE 91
King, Michael Gordon BioIn 16
King, Michael John 1938- St&PR 91
King, Michael Lewis 1949- WhoSSW 91
King, Monica Kayla 1962- WhoAmW 91
King, Monique V BiDrAPA 89
King, Morris Kenton 1924- WhoAm 90
King, Myron Lyzon 1921- WhoAmA 91
King, Ned P. 1919- St&PR 91
King, Nellie 1928- Ballpl 90
King, Nina Davis 1941- WhoAm 90
King, Norman Wyatt 1954- WhoSSW 91
King, Olin B. 1934- St&PR 91, WhoAm 90, WhoSSW 91
King, Ordie Herbert, Jr. 1933- WhoAm 90
King, Oswald M. 1909- St&PR 91
King, Pamela Ann 1951- WhoE 91
King, Patricia 1941- WhoAm 90
King, Patricia Miller 1937- WhoAm 90, WhoAmW 91
King, Patrick J 1951- WhoAmA 91
King, Patrick Joseph 1951- WhoEmL 91
King, Paul 1867-1947 WhoAmA 91N
King, Paul 1945- BiDrAPA 89
King, Paul Clinton 1928- BiDrAPA 89
King, Paul Hamilton 1936- WhoAm 90
King, Paul L. 1934- St&PR 91
King, Paul Lewis WhoE 91
King, Perry 1948- WhoAm 90
King, Perry M. 1931- St&PR 91
King, Peter 1957- BioIn 16
King, Peter Cotterill 1930- WhoAm 90
King, Peter D 1927- BiDrAPA 89
King, Peter J., Jr. 1921- St&PR 91
King, Peter Joseph, Jr. 1921- WhoAm 90
King, Phil John 1940- WhoWrEP 89
King, Philip Gordon 1922- WhoE 91, WhoWor 91
King, Preston 1923- St&PR 91
King, Preston Cloud, Jr. 1904- WhoAm 90
King, R Taylor 1925- BiDrAPA 89
King, Rachel Hadley 1904- WhoAmW 91, WhoWor 91
King, Ray 1950- WhoAmA 91
King, Ray John 1933- WhoAm 90
King, Ray Wallace 1916- St&PR 91
King, Raymond Stanley 1946- WhoEmL 91
King, Rey Reginald 1954- WhoWrEP 89
King, Richard 1825-1885 WorAlBi
King, Richard Allen 1944- WhoAm 90
King, Richard Allen, Sr. 1939- WhoWrEP 89
King, Richard Arthur 1940- St&PR 91
King, Richard Auld 1947- WhoEmL 91
King, Richard D 1946- BiDrAPA 89
King, Richard Eugene 1948- WhoE 91, WhoEmL 91, WhoWor 91
King, Richard Gordon BioIn 16
King, Richard H. St&PR 91
King, Richard Harding 1925- WhoAm 90
King, Richard Hood 1934- St&PR 91, WhoAm 90
King, Richard Lloyd BiDrAPA 89
King, Richard S 1915- BiDrAPA 89
King, Robert 1869- EncO&P 3
King, Robert A. 1862-1932 OxCPMus
King, Robert A 1943- BiDrAPA 89
King, Robert Ansel 1933- WhoSSW 91
King, Robert Augustin 1910- WhoAm 90, WhoWor 91
King, Robert Bainton 1922- WhoAm 90
King, Robert Bennett 1928- WhoSSW 91
King, Robert Bruce 1938- WhoAm 90
King, Robert Charles 1928- WhoAm 90
King, Robert Charles 1944- WhoSSW 91
King, Robert Cotton 1931- WhoAm 90
King, Robert D. 1936- WhoAm 90
King, Robert E. 1935- St&PR 91
King, Robert Elwin 1923- WhoAm 90
King, Robert Gardner 1906- WhoE 91
King, Robert Howard 1941- St&PR 91
King, Robert J. 1946- St&PR 91
King, Robert James 1937- WhoE 91
King, Robert John 1935- WhoAm 90
King, Robert John Stephen 1960- IntWWM 90
King, Robert L. 1938- St&PR 91
King, Robert Leonard 1904- WhoAm 90
King, Robert Leroy 1931- WhoAm 90
King, Robert Lewis 1950- WhoEmL 91
King, Robert Lucien 1936- WhoAm 90, WhoWor 91
King, Robert M. 1945- St&PR 91
King, Robert Thomas 1930- WhoAm 90
King, Robert W., Jr. 1946- WhoSSW 91
King, Roger Leo 1945- St&PR 91
King, Roger Monroe BioIn 16
King, Roland H. 1940- ODwPR 91
King, Roland Hemsley, Jr. 1940- WhoE 91
King, Rollin White 1931- St&PR 91
King, Ronald Baker 1953- WhoEmL 91
King, Ronold Wyeth Percival 1905- WhoAm 90
King, Rosalyn Mercita 1948- WhoAmW 91
King, Roy Lee 1935- St&PR 91, WhoAm 90
King, Ruby Thompson WhoAmW 91, WhoWor 91
King, Rufus 1755-1827 BioIn 16, WorAlBi
King, Rufus 1893-1966 TwCCr&M 91
King, Rufus 1917- WhoAm 90
King, Ruth Allen 1910- WhoAmW 91
King, Sam Cline 1936- WhoE 91
King, Sam S. 1924- St&PR 91
King, Sandra 1944- WhoAmW 91
King, Sandra Jane BiDrAPA 89
King, Seth S. AuBYP 90
King, Sharon Ann 1944- WhoAmW 91
King, Sharon Elizabeth 1938- WhoSSW 91
King, Sheldon Selig 1931- WhoAm 90, WhoWor 91
King, Sherry Anne BiDrAPA 89
King, Sheryl Jayne 1945- WhoAmW 91, WhoWor 91
King, Silver 1868-1938 Ballpl 90 [port]
King, Sophia 1781?- BioIn 16
King, Sophia 1782?- FemiCLE
King, Stacey BioIn 16
King, Stanley 1930- IntWWM 90
King, Stephen 1944- WhoSSW 91
King, Stephen 1947- BioIn 16, ConAu 30NR, ConLC 61 [port], ConTFT 8, MajTwCW, WorAlBi, WorAu 1980 [port]
King, Stephen Edwin 1947- WhoAm 90, WhoE 91, WhoWrEP 89
King, Stephen M. 1957- St&PR 91
King, Stephen P. BioIn 16
King, Stephen Scott 1937- WhoAm 90
King, Steve ConAu 30NR, MajTwCW
King, Steve Mason 1951- WhoSSW 91
King, Steven 1960- WhoE 91
King, Steven A BiDrAPA 89
King, Steven Alan 1951- BiDrAPA 89, WhoE 91
King, Susan Bennett 1940- WhoAm 90, WhoAmW 91
King, Susan Elizabeth 1947- WhoAmW 91
King, Susanne Lucille BiDrAPA 89
King, Suzanne M. BiDrAPA 89
King, Sylvia Lynn 1938- WhoAmW 91
King, Tabitha 1949- ConAu 30NR
King, Teresa Lynne 1953- WhoAmW 91
King, Teresita Lim 1952- WhoAmW 91
King, Terry B. 1947- IntWWM 90
King, Terry Bower 1947- WhoEmL 91
King, Thad Denton 1951- WhoEmL 91
King, Thea 1925- IntWWM 90, PenDiMP
King, Thomas Allen 1942- WhoAm 90
King, Thomas Bittle 1946- BiDrAPA 89
King, Thomas Creighton 1928- WhoAm 90
King, Thomas H. 1934- WhoAm 90
King, Thomas Howard 1955- St&PR 91
King, Thomas Jeremy 1933- WhoWor 91
King, Thomas L BiDrAPA 89
King, Thomas L. 1930- St&PR 91
King, Thomas Syme 1946- St&PR 91
King, Thomas Wade 1938- ODwPR 91
King, Thomas Wesley 1954- WhoEmL 91
King, Todd Richard 1959- WhoEmL 91
King, Tom 1957- BioIn 16
King, Tony DrBlPA 90
King, Valerie Ann 1965- WhoEmL 91
King, Vinetta Ellen 1949- WhoAmW 91
King, W L Mackenzie 1936- BiDrAPA 89
King, W. Russell 1949- WhoAm 90
King, Wallace Albert 1921- St&PR 91
King, Walter Clair 1927- St&PR 91
King, Warren Colvin 1925- St&PR 91
King, Warren L 1926- BiDrAPA 89
King, Warren Thomas 1916-1978 WhoAmA 91N
King, Wayne 1901-1985 OxCPMus
King, Weldon 1911- WhoWor 91
King, Willard Fahrenkamp 1924- WhoAm 90
King, William 1812-1895 DcCanB 12
King, William A 1937- BiDrAPA 89
King, William Beresford 1929- WhoE 91
King, William Bernard Robinson 1889-1963 DcScB S2
King, William Bruce 1932- WhoAm 90
King, William Carl 1944- WhoAm 90
King, William Collins 1921- WhoAm 90
King, William Dickey 1925- WhoAmA 91
King, William Douglas 1941- WhoAm 90
King, William Emery 1912- WhoAm 90
King, William Gary 1940- St&PR 91
King, William Henry 1907-1987 BioIn 16
King, William J. 1929- WhoAm 90
King, William James 1924- BiDrAPA 89
King, William John 1947- WhoEmL 91
King, William Joseph 1929- St&PR 91
King, William Kimble, Jr. 1946- WhoEmL 91
King, William Lyon Mackenzie 1874-1950 EncPaPR 91, WorAlBi
King, William M. 1800-1869 AmLegL
King, William N. BioIn 16
King, William Patrick 1947- St&PR 91
King, William Richard 1938- WhoAm 90
King, William Rufus de Vane 1786-1853 BiDrUSE 89
King, William Rufus Devane 1786-1853 BioIn 16
King, William Warren 1944- WhoWrEP 89
King, Woodie, Jr. 1937- ConTFT 8 [port], DrBlPA 90, WhoAm 90
King, Woods, Jr. 1928- St&PR 91, WhoAm 90
King, Yolanda BioIn 16
King-Atallah, Helen Louise 1958- WhoAmW 91
King Calkins, Carol Coleman 1949- WhoAmW 91
King-Ettema, Elizabeth Dorothy 1953- WhoAmW 91
King-Griswold, Kathy Ann 1957- WhoAmW 91
King-Haden, Kelly Louise 1959- WhoAmW 91
King-Hamilton, Alan 1904- ConAu 130
King-Hammond, Leslie 1944- WhoE 91
King-Hele, Desmond 1927- ConAu 32NR
King-Johnson, Marcia 1958- WhoAmW 91
King-Smith, Dick 1922- AuBYP 90, BioIn 16, WhoAm 90
Kingdom, Roger BioIn 16
Kingdon, Henry Shannon 1934- WhoAm 90
Kingdon, John Wells 1940- WhoAm 90
Kingdon, Robert McCune 1927- WhoAm 90
Kingery, Lionel Bruce 1921- WhoWrEP 89
Kingery, Lou Gene 1942- BiDrAPA 89
Kingery, Mike 1961- Ballpl 90
Kingery, Thomas Lloyd 1939- WhoSSW 91
Kingery, William David 1926- WhoAm 90
Kinget, G. Marian 1910- WhoAm 90
Kingett, Kathie Lee 1946- WhoEmL 91
Kingham, Richard Frank 1946- WhoE 91, WhoWor 91
Kinghan, Charles Ross 1895-1984 WhoAmA 91N
Kinghorn, Kenneth Cain 1930- ConAu 31NR
Kingma, Paul Edward 1958- WhoEmL 91
Kingma, Stanley George 1937- IntWWM 90
Kingman, Brian 1954- Ballpl 90
Kingman, Dave 1948- Ballpl 90
Kingman, Dong 1911- BioIn 16, WhoAm 90
Kingman, Dong, Jr. 1936- ODwPR 91, WhoE 91
Kingman, Dong M 1911- WhoAmA 91
Kingman, Eugene 1909-1975 WhoAmA 91N
Kingman, John Delano 1937- St&PR 91
Kingman, Mary Lee 1919- AuBYP 90
Kingman, William Lockwood 1930- WhoAm 90
Kingman-Brundage, Jane 1941- WhoE 91
Kingo, Thomas 1634-1703 DcScanL
Kingren, John Fred 1960- WhoEmL 91
Kingrey, Burnell Wayne 1921- WhoAm 90
Kingsberg, Harold J. 1927- St&PR 91
Kingsberg, Harold Joseph 1927- WhoAm 90
Kingsbery, Walton Waits, Jr. 1928- WhoAm 90

Kingsbury, Arthur F. 1948- *St&PR 91*
Kingsbury, Arthur French, III 1948- *WhoAm 90*
Kingsbury, Carolyn Ann 1938- *WhoAmW 91*
Kingsbury, Cyrus 1786-1870 *WhNaAH*
Kingsbury, David T. 1940- *WhoAm 90*
Kingsbury, Dorothy Louise 1946- *WhoWrEP 89*
Kingsbury, Frederick H., Jr. *St&PR 91N*
Kingsbury, Frederick Hutchinson 1907-1989 *BioIn 16*
Kingsbury, John Merriam 1928- *WhoAm 90*
Kingsbury, Read Austin 1925- *WhoAm 90*
Kingsbury, Robert Richmond 1936- *St&PR 91*
Kingsbury, Steven J. 1948- *BiDrAPA 89*
Kingsbury-Smith, Joseph 1908- *St&PR 91*
Kingsford, Anna 1846-1888 *FemiCLE*
Kingsford, Anna Bonus 1846-1888 *EncO&P 3*
Kingsford, William 1819-1898 *DcCanB 12*
Kingsford, William C. 1946- *St&PR 91*
Kingsland, James Arthur 1924- *WhoAm 90*
Kingsland, John Michael *BioIn 16*
Kingsley, Alvin B. 1936- *St&PR 91*
Kingsley, April 1941- *WhoAmA 91*
Kingsley, Ben *BioIn 16*
Kingsley, Ben 1943- *WhoAm 90, WhoWor 91, WorAlBi*
Kingsley, Charles 1819-1875 *AuBYP 90, BioIn 16*
Kingsley, Colin 1925- *IntWWM 90*
Kingsley, Daniel Francis 1953- *St&PR 91*
Kingsley, David Irwin 1935- *WhoE 91*
Kingsley, Frederick William 1932- *St&PR 91*
Kingsley, Gordon F. 1928- *St&PR 91*
Kingsley, James Gordon 1933- *WhoAm 90*
Kingsley, John M., Jr. 1931- *St&PR 91*
Kingsley, John McCall, Jr. 1931- *WhoAm 90*
Kingsley, Lee Goode *BioIn 16*
Kingsley, Margaret 1939- *IntWWM 90*
Kingsley, Mary 1862-1900 *FemiCLE*
Kingsley, Mary Henrietta 1862-1900 *BioIn 16*
Kingsley, Oliver Dowling, Jr. 1942- *St&PR 91*
Kingsley, Pat 1932- *News 90*
Kingsley, Paul L *BiDrAPA 89*
Kingsley, Richard Sewall *BiDrAPA 89*
Kingsley, Richard Thomas 1942- *WhoSSW 91*
Kingsley, Robert 1903-1988 *BioIn 16*
Kingsley, Sarah Du Bois 1958- *WhoE 91*
Kingsley, Scott Anton 1953- *WhoE 91*
Kingsley, Sidney 1906- *WhoAm 90*
Kingsley, Thomas Drowne 1916- *WhoAm 90*
Kingsley, Thomas Edward, Jr. 1947- *WhoSSW 91*
Kingsley, Walter Ingalls 1923- *WhoAm 90*
Kingsley, William Earl 1944- *St&PR 91*
Kingsmill, A.S. 1927- *St&PR 91*
Kingsmill, Suzanne Foster 1952- *WhoWrEP 89*
Kingsolver, Barbara 1955- *ConAu 129*
Kingson, Charles I. 1938- *WhoAm 90*
Kingson, Eric Roger 1946- *WhoE 91*
Kingston, Cecelia M. *WhoWrEP 89*
Kingston, Frederick Temple 1925- *WhoAm 90*
Kingston, James Burke 1953- *WhoSSW 91*
Kingston, John Russell, Earl 1792-1878 *BioIn 16*
Kingston, Maxine Hong *BioIn 16*
Kingston, Maxine Hong 1940- *CurBio 90 [port], FemiCLE, MajTwCW, WhoAm 90, WhoAmW 91*
Kingston, Robert Charles 1928- *WhoAm 90*
Kingston, Robert Hildreth 1928- *WhoAm 90*
Kingstone, Edward 1931- *BiDrAPA 89*
Kington, Barry Clark 1942- *WhoWor 91*
Kington, L Brent 1934- *WhoAmA 91*
Kington, Miles 1941- *ConAu 130*
Kingwill, David G. 1940- *St&PR 91*
Kini, Ranjan Bailur 1954- *WhoSSW 91*
Kinigakis, Panagiotis 1949- *WhoE 91, WhoEmL 91, WhoWor 91*
Kinigstein, Jonah 1923- *WhoAmA 91*
Kinion, Darrell G. 1954- *St&PR 91*
Kinison, Sam *BioIn 16*
Kinkade, Edgar D. 1950- *St&PR 91*
Kinkade, Kate 1951- *WhoAmW 91*
Kinkade, Maurice Edward 1942- *St&PR 91*
Kinkade, Richard P 1939- *ConAu 31NR*
Kinkade, Thomas 1958- *BioIn 16*
Kinkaid, Thomas Cassin 1888-1972 *BioIn 16*
Kinkead, Cleves 1882-1955 *LiHiK*
Kinkead, Eleanor Talbot *LiHiK*
Kinkead, Ellen Jane 1915- *WhoAmW 91*
Kinkead, Joseph C. 1933- *St&PR 91*
Kinkead, Robin *BioIn 16*
Kinkead, Verda Christine 1931- *WhoAmW 91*
Kinkel, Johanna 1810-1858 *EncCoWW*
Kinkle, George Phillip, Jr. 1925- *WhoAm 90*
Kinks, The *EncPR&S 89, OxCPMus*
Kinlan, Joan Evelyn *BiDrAPA 89*
Kinlan, Joan Evelyn 1943- *WhoE 91*
Kinlaw, Dennis Franklin 1922- *WhoAm 90*
Kinlein, Mary Lucille 1921- *WhoAmW 91*
Kinley, John A. 1924- *ODwPR 91*
Kinloch, Johnny 1936- *St&PR 91*
Kinlow, Eugene 1940- *WhoAm 90*
Kinman, James Walter 1930- *St&PR 91*
Kinman, Joseph Franklin, Jr 1956- *WhoEmL 91*
Kinmartin, Paul D., Sr. 1946- *St&PR 91*
Kinmartin, Paul David, Sr. 1946- *WhoE 91*
Kinn, John Matthias 1925- *WhoE 91, WhoWor 91*
Kinnaird, Charles Roemler 1932- *WhoAm 90*
Kinnaird, Margaret Mary 1949- *WhoAmW 91*
Kinnaird, Nancy Webster *WhoAmW 91*
Kinnaird, Richard William 1931- *WhoAmA 91*
Kinnaird, W.H. 1923- *St&PR 91*
Kinnaman, David L. 1938- *St&PR 91*
Kinnamon, David Lucas 1941- *WhoAm 90*
Kinnamon, Keneth 1932- *WhoAm 90*
Kinnamon, Noel James 1943- *WhoSSW 91*
Kinnane, Harry Earl *BiDrAPA 89*
Kinnard, William James, Jr. 1932- *WhoAm 90*
Kinne, David Weir 1936- *WhoAm 90, WhoWor 91*
Kinne, Frances Bartlett *WhoAm 90, WhoSSW 91*
Kinne, Jack Robert 1948- *St&PR 91*
Kinne, Morris Y., Jr. 1928- *WhoAm 90*
Kinnear, David W. 1942- *St&PR 91*
Kinnear, George 1923- *IntWWM 90*
Kinnear, George E.R., II 1928- *St&PR 91*
Kinnear, George E. R., II 1928- *WhoAm 90, WhoE 91*
Kinnear, James W. 1928- *BioIn 16, St&PR 91*
Kinnear, James Wesley, III 1928- *WhoAm 90, WhoE 91*
Kinnear, Roy 1934-1988 *AnObit 1988, BioIn 16*
Kinneberg, Arthur Hempton 1921- *WhoAm 90*
Kinnebrew, Jackson Metcalfe 1941- *WhoAm 90*
Kinnee, Sandy 1947- *WhoAmA 91*
Kinneir, Jock 1917- *ConDes 90*
Kinnel, Mary L. 1945- *WhoAmW 91*
Kinnell, Galway 1927- *MajTwCW, WhoWrEP 89*
Kinneman, Robert Eugene, Jr. *BiDrAPA 89*
Kinnen, Edwin 1925- *WhoAm 90*
Kinner, Albert Vernon 1927- *St&PR 91*
Kinner, Clara Webb *ODwPR 91*
Kinner, Donald Evan 1957- *WhoEmL 91*
Kinner, Peter Cummings 1947- *WhoE 91*
Kinney, Abbott Ford 1909- *WhoSSW 91, WhoWor 91*
Kinney, Aldon M., Jr. 1921- *St&PR 91*
Kinney, Aldon Monroe, Jr. 1921- *WhoAm 90*
Kinney, Allan G. 1951- *St&PR 91*
Kinney, Bernard E. 1929- *St&PR 91*
Kinney, Charles 1906- *MusmAFA*
Kinney, Cle 1915- *AuBYP 90*
Kinney, Dale Francis 1930- *St&PR 91*
Kinney, Daniel William 1950- *IntWWM 90*
Kinney, Dennis 1952- *Ballpl 90*
Kinney, Dita Hopkins 1854-1921 *BioIn 16*
Kinney, Douglas Merrill 1917- *WhoAm 90*
Kinney, E. Robert 1917- *St&PR 91*
Kinney, Earl Robert 1917- *WhoAm 90*
Kinney, Eleanor De Arman 1947- *WhoEmL 91*
Kinney, Elizabeth 1810-1889 *FemiCLE*
Kinney, Francis L. 1932- *ODwPR 91, St&PR 91*
Kinney, Gilbert Ford 1907- *WhoAm 90*
Kinney, Gilbert Hart 1931- *WhoAmA 91*
Kinney, Gordon Crawford *BioIn 16*
Kinney, Harry Edwin 1924- *WhoAm 90*
Kinney, Jean 1912- *AuBYP 90*
Kinney, Kathleen O'Leary 1942- *WhoAmW 91*
Kinney, Kenneth Parrish 1921- *WhoAm 90*
Kinney, Lisa Frances 1951- *WhoAmW 91*
Kinney, Louis D. 1936- *St&PR 91*
Kinney, Lowell D. 1936- *ODwPR 91*
Kinney, Marjorie Sharon 1940- *WhoAmW 91*
Kinney, Michael James 1937- *WhoSSW 91*
Kinney, Noah 1912- *MusmAFA*
Kinney, Ormond B. 1932- *St&PR 91*
Kinney, Richard J. *ODwPR 91*
Kinney, Richard R. 1933- *St&PR 91*
Kinney, Robert Bruce 1937- *WhoAm 90*
Kinney, Taz William *BiDrAPA 89*
Kinney, Walt 1893-1971 *Ballpl 90*
Kinney, William Burnet 1799-1880 *BioIn 16*
Kinney, William James Apolo 1948- *WhoEmL 91*
Kinney, William Light, Jr. 1933- *WhoAm 90*
Kinney, William Rudolph, Jr. 1942- *WhoAm 90*
Kinney Hanson, Sharon D. 1942- *WhoWrEP 89*
Kinniburgh, John Alan 1929- *WhoSSW 91*
Kinnicutt, Philip Heywood 1941- *St&PR 91*
Kinning, Ronald Lee 1939- *St&PR 91*
Kinnison, William Andrew 1932- *WhoAm 90*
Kinnock, Glenys Elizabeth 1944- *WhoWor 91*
Kinnock, Neil *BioIn 16, NewYTBS 90 [port]*
Kinnock, Neil 1942- *WorAlBi*
Kinnock, Neil Gordon 1942- *WhoWor 91*
Kinnune, William P. 1939- *WhoAm 90*
Kino, Eusebio Francisco 1644-1711 *BioIn 16*
Kino, Eusebio Francisco 1645?-1711 *EncCRAm, WhNaAH*
Kino, Gordon Stanley 1928- *WhoAm 90*
Kinoshita, Gene 1935- *WhoAmA 91*
Kinoshita, Hiroo 1932- *WhoWor 91*
Kinoshita, Isaac Shinichi 1933- *St&PR 91*
Kinoshita, Kay 1954- *WhoAmW 91*
Kinoshita, Shinji 1931- *WhoWor 91*
Kinoshita, Tomio 1944- *WhoWor 91*
Kinosian, Janet Marie 1957- *WhoAmW 91*
Kinross-Wright, John 1922- *BiDrAPA 89*
Kinsala, Scott Douglas 1955- *WhoEmL 91*
Kinsbury, Arthur F. 1948- *St&PR 91*
Kinsel, Michael Leslie 1947- *WhoAmA 91*
Kinsela, David Pentreath 1941- *IntWWM 90*
Kinsell, Jeffrey C. 1951- *St&PR 91*
Kinsella, Helen Louise *BiDrAPA 89*
Kinsella, John Edward 1938- *WhoAm 90*
Kinsella, Katherine M. *ODwPR 91*
Kinsella, Ralph Aloysius, Jr. 1919- *WhoAm 90*
Kinsella, Richard 1862-1939 *Ballpl 90*
Kinsella, Thomas 1928- *MajTwCW, WhoWor 91*
Kinsella, W. P. *Ballpl 90*
Kinsella, W P 1935- *MajTwCW*
Kinsella, W. P. 1935- *WhoWrEP 89*
Kinser, Carolynn Hipps *WhoAmW 91*
Kinser, Charleen *AuBYP 90, BioIn 16*
Kinser, Dennis 1944- *St&PR 91*
Kinser, Kirte Matheu 1957- *WhoEmL 91*
Kinser, Michael Dean 1951- *WhoEmL 91*
Kinser, Richard Edward 1936- *WhoWor 91*
Kinser, Steve *BioIn 16*
Kinsey, Alfred Charles 1894-1956 *WorAlBi*
Kinsey, Daniel L *BiDrAPA 89*
Kinsey, David North 1947- *WhoEmL 91*
Kinsey, Elizabeth *AuBYP 90*
Kinsey, Jack L 1905- *BiDrAPA 89*
Kinsey, James Lloyd 1934- *WhoAm 90*
Kinsey, Norman Victor 1921- *St&PR 91*
Kinsey, Raymond Alexander 1929- *St&PR 91*
Kinsey, Robert A *BiDrAPA 89*
Kinsey, Tony 1930- *IntWWM 90*
Kinsey, William Charles 1935- *St&PR 91, WhoAm 90*
Kinshofer, Christa *BioIn 16*
Kinsinger, Jack Burl 1925- *WhoAm 90*
Kinsinger, Robert Earl 1923- *WhoAm 90*
Kinski, Klaus 1926- *BioIn 16, WorAlBi*
Kinski, Nastassia 1959- *WorAlBi*
Kinski, Nastassja *WhoAm 90*
Kinsler, Bruce Whitney 1947- *WhoEmL 91*
Kinsler, Richard Gary 1929- *St&PR 91*
Kinsley, Michael *BioIn 16*
Kinsley, Michael E. 1951- *WhoAm 90*
Kinsley, Terrence D. 1952- *St&PR 91*
Kinsley, William Benton 1934- *WhoAm 90, WhoWrEP 89*
Kinslow, Marta Benavides 1941- *WhoAmW 91*
Kinslow, William Edward 1938- *St&PR 91*
Kinsman, Frank William 1925- *WhoE 91*
Kinsman, Lawrence Charles 1953- *WhoWrEP 89*
Kinsman, Robert Donald 1929- *WhoAm 90, WhoAmA 91*
Kinsman, Robert G 1925- *BiDrAPA 89*
Kinsman, Robert Preston 1949- *WhoEmL 91, WhoWor 91*
Kinsman, Rodney *PenDiDA 89*
Kinsolving, Augustus Blagden 1940- *St&PR 91*
Kinsolving, Charles McIlvaine, Jr. 1927- *WhoE 91*
Kinsolving, Laurence Edwin 1941- *WhoAm 90, WhoSSW 91*
Kinsolving, Sylvia Crockett 1931- *WhoSSW 91*
Kinst, Thomas A. 1941- *St&PR 91*
Kinstler, Everett Raymond 1926- *WhoAm 90, WhoAmA 91*
Kinstlinger, Jack 1931- *St&PR 91, WhoE 91*
Kinstrey, Robert Bruce 1944- *WhoSSW 91*
Kintaro *EncJap*
Kinter, Bruce Timothy 1949- *WhoE 91*
Kintigh, Allen E. 1924- *WhoAm 90*
Kintigh, Allen Ellis 1924- *St&PR 91*
Kintigh, William Thomas 1946- *St&PR 91*
Kintner, Earl Wilson 1912- *WhoAm 90*
Kintner, Jerome Worthy 1915- *St&PR 91*
Kintner, Judith Ann 1938- *WhoAmW 91*
Kintner, Treva Carpenter 1920- *WhoAmW 91*
Kintner, William Roscoe 1915- *WhoAm 90, WhoWor 91*
Kintpuash *WhNaAH*
Kinturi, Marja Liisa 1943- *WhoWor 91*
Kintz, George Jerome 1931- *St&PR 91*
Kintz, Virginia J. 1917- *St&PR 91*
Kintzele, John A. 1936- *WhoAm 90*
Kinugasa, Sachio 1947- *Ballpl 90*
Kinyatti, Maina Wa *BioIn 16, ConAu 132*
Kinyomi, Babatunde Olayide 1927- *WhoWor 91*
Kinyon, Duane Wallace 1911- *St&PR 91*
Kinyon, Jamie Michele 1954- *WhoAmW 91*
Kinzel, Dotti 1950- *BioIn 16*
Kinzel, Richard L. 1940- *St&PR 91*
Kinzelberg, Harvey 1945- *WhoAm 90*
Kinzer, Donald Louis 1914- *WhoAm 90*
Kinzer, Donald Marshall 1943- *St&PR 91, WhoAm 90*
Kinzer, James Raymond 1928- *WhoAm 90*
Kinzer, William Luther 1929- *WhoAm 90*
Kinzey, Hilliard Allen 1935- *WhoSSW 91*
Kinzey, Ouida Blackerby 1922- *WhoAmW 91*
Kinzey, Warren Glenford 1935- *WhoAm 90*
Kinzie, John David 1937- *BiDrAPA 89*
Kinzie, Juliette 1806-1870 *FemiCLE*
Kinzie, Mary 1944- *WhoWrEP 89*
Kinzie, Miriam Annette 1953- *WhoAmW 91*
Kinzie, Raymond Wyant 1930- *St&PR 91, WhoAm 90*
Kinzie, Robert William 1933- *St&PR 91*
Kinzler, Alexander C. 1958- *St&PR 91*
Kinzler, Kennard A. 1943- *St&PR 91*
Kinzler, Morton H. 1925- *St&PR 91*
Kinzly, Robert Edward 1939- *WhoAm 90*
Kiolbasa, Charles G., Jr. 1951- *St&PR 91*
Kionka, Edward James 1939- *WhoAm 90*
Kioulafas, Kyriacos 1940- *WhoWor 91*
Kioulpapas, Tassos 1943- *WhoWor 91*
Kiousis, Linda Weber *WhoAmA 91*
Kiousis, Martin John 1930- *St&PR 91*
Kiper, Ali Muhlis 1924- *WhoE 91*
Kipling, Rudyard 1865-1936 *AuBYP 90, BioIn 16, ConAu 33NR, EncPaPR 91, MajTwCW, WorAlBi*
Kiplinger, Austin Huntington 1918- *St&PR 91, WhoAm 90, WhoWrEP 89*
Kiplinger, Christina Louise 1957- *WhoWrEP 89*
Kiplinger, Glenn Francis 1930- *WhoAm 90*
Kiplinger, Knight Austin 1948- *St&PR 91*
Kiplinger, Willard 1891- *WorAlBi*
Kipnis, Alexander 1891-1978 *PenDiMP*
Kipnis, Barry Evan 1949- *WhoE 91*
Kipnis, David Morris 1927- *WhoAm 90*
Kipnis, Igor 1930- *IntWWM 90, PenDiMP, WhoAm 90*
Kipnis, Kenneth 1943- *ConAu 129*
Kipniss, Robert 1931- *WhoAm 90, WhoAmA 91, WhoE 91*
Kipp, Daniel Wayne 1959- *WhoEmL 91*
Kipp, Dean Carl 1918- *WhoAm 90*
Kipp, Fred 1931- *Ballpl 90*
Kipp, Jerry Steven 1952- *WhoEmL 91*
Kipp, John H. 1943- *St&PR 91*
Kipp, Karl *PenDiDA 89*
Kipp, Lyman 1929- *WhoAmA 91, WhoSSW 91*
Kipp, Martin-Heinrich 1945- *WhoWor 91*
Kipp, Orval 1904- *WhoAmA 91*
Kipp, Robert Almy 1932- *WhoAm 90*
Kipp, William Hugh 1941- *WhoE 91*
Kippel, Gary M. *WhoAm 90*
Kippen, Richard Marlin 1932- *WhoAm 90*
Kippenberger, Martin 1953- *BioIn 16, WhoAmA 91*
Kippenhahn, Rudolf 1926- *ConAu 130*
Kippenhan, Charles Jacob 1919- *WhoAm 90*
Kipper, Barbara Levy 1942- *St&PR 91, WhoAm 90*
Kipper, Bob 1964- *Ballpl 90*
Kipperman, Allan L 1947- *BiDrAPA 89*
Kipperman, Richard W. 1934- *WhoE 91*

Kippert, Robert John, Jr. 1952- *WhoEmL 91*
Kipping, Hans F. 1924- *WhoE 91*
Kipping, Vernon Louis 1921- *WhoWor 91*
Kipple, C. Wayne 1942- *St&PR 91*
Kipple, Helen M *BiDrAPA 89*
Kiprov, Dobri Dobrev 1949- *WhoEmL 91*
Kiralfy, Bolossy *BioIn 16*
Kiraly, James Francis 1933- *St&PR 91*
Kiraly, Karch 1961?- *BioIn 16*
Kiraly, Leslie Tamas 1948- *BiDrAPA 89*
Kiraly, Thomas E. 1960- *St&PR 91*
Kiratli, Cemile *ConAu 132*
Kirban, Lloyd 1931- *WhoAm 90*
Kirbo, Bruce, Sr. *St&PR 91*
Kirbo, Charles Hughes 1917- *WhoAm 90*
Kirby, Allan Price, Jr. 1931- *St&PR 91, WhoAm 90*
Kirby, Anthony John 1935- *WhoWor 91*
Kirby, Bernard C 1907- *EncO&P 3*
Kirby, Brenda Ruth 1948- *WhoEmL 91*
Kirby, Bruce Robert William 1929- *WhoE 91*
Kirby, Bruno *BioIn 16*
Kirby, Charles William, Jr. 1926- *WhoAm 90*
Kirby, Charlotte Ives Cobb Godbe *BioIn 16*
Kirby, Clay 1948- *Ballpl 90*
Kirby, Colleen 1948- *WhoAmW 91*
Kirby, Dan L. 1946- *St&PR 91*
Kirby, Daniel B. 1950- *St&PR 91*
Kirby, David R. 1939- *ODwPR 91*
Kirby, Deborah MacDonald 1948- *WhoAmW 91*
Kirby, Donald N. 1928- *St&PR 91*
Kirby, Dorothy Manville 1917- *WhoWor 91*
Kirby, Edward C, Jr. 1928- *BiDrAPA 89*
Kirby, Emily Baruch 1929- *WhoAm 90*
Kirby, Francis L. 1944- *St&PR 91*
Kirby, Frank Eugene 1928- *IntWWM 90*
Kirby, Fred M. 1861-1940 *WorAlBi*
Kirby, Fred M., II 1919- *St&PR 91*
Kirby, Fred Morgan, II 1919- *WhoAm 90, WhoE 91*
Kirby, George 1924- *DrBIPA 90*
Kirby, Georgiana Bruce 1818-1887 *BioIn 16*
Kirby, Henry L. 1953- *WhoEmL 91*
Kirby, Herbert Weldon 1933- *St&PR 91*
Kirby, Ian John 1934- *WhoWor 91*
Kirby, Jack 1917- *EncACom*
Kirby, James *ConAu 130*
Kirby, James 1928-1989 *BioIn 16*
Kirby, James A. 1945- *St&PR 91*
Kirby, James C., Jr. 1928-1989 *ConAu 130*
Kirby, James Edmund, Jr. 1933- *WhoAm 90*
Kirby, James Wallace 1947- *WhoSSW 91*
Kirby, Jean *AuBYP 90*
Kirby, Jeri Patricia Hall 1947- *WhoAmW 91*
Kirby, John *BioIn 16*
Kirby, John 1908-1952 *OxCPMus*
Kirby, John Delbert 1932- *St&PR 91*
Kirby, John Joseph, Jr. 1939- *WhoE 91*
Kirby, John Pendy 1905- *WhoSSW 91*
Kirby, Juanita F 1927- *BiDrAPA 89*
Kirby, Kasey 1940- *WhoSSW 91*
Kirby, Kate Page 1945- *WhoAmW 91*
Kirby, Kathryn 1923- *BiDrAPA 89*
Kirby, Kenneth William 1923- *St&PR 91*
Kirby, Kent Bruce 1934- *WhoAm 90, WhoAmA 91*
Kirby, Kristie Lynn 1953- *WhoAmW 91*
Kirby, Laurie Butler 1958- *WhoEmL 91*
Kirby, Mary Weeks 1947- *WhoAmW 91*
Kirby, Maurice Helm, Jr. 1926- *St&PR 91, WhoAm 90*
Kirby, Michael Donald 1939- *WhoWor 91*
Kirby, Paula Marie 1952- *WhoE 91*
Kirby, Philip Dorsey 1931- *St&PR 91*
Kirby, Rex Windell 1945- *WhoSSW 91*
Kirby, Rita Maye Knowles 1941- *WhoWor 91*
Kirby, Robert Lanham 1930- *WhoAm 90, WhoSSW 91*
Kirby, Robert Stephen 1925- *St&PR 91*
Kirby, Ronald Eugene 1947- *WhoEmL 91*
Kirby, Russell Stephen 1954- *WhoEmL 91*
Kirby, Stephen C. 1951- *St&PR 91*
Kirby, Steve Thomas 1952- *St&PR 91*
Kirby, Susan Alice *AuBYP 90*
Kirby, Susan E 1949- *SmATA 62 [port]*
Kirby, Tom *WhoWrEP 89*
Kirby, Turner E. 1931- *St&PR 91*
Kirby, Ward Nelson 1939- *St&PR 91, WhoAm 90*
Kirby, William 1817-1906 *DcLB 99 [port]*
Kirby, William Joseph 1937- *St&PR 91, WhoAm 90*
Kirby, William Murray Maurice 1914- *WhoAm 90*
Kirby, William T. *NewYTBS 90*
Kirby-Smith, Edmund 1824-1893 *WorAlBi*
Kirch, Darrell Gene *BiDrAPA 89*
Kirch, Eugene 1933- *St&PR 91*
Kirch, Margaret T. *ODwPR 91*
Kirch, Max Samuel 1915- *WhoAm 90*
Kirch, Patrick Vinton 1950- *WhoAm 90, WhoEmL 91*
Kirch, Paul *BiDrAPA 89*
Kirchberg, Elisabeth von 13--?- *EncCoWW*
Kirchen, Elaine D. 1942- *St&PR 91*
Kirchen, Richard Henry 1945- *St&PR 91*
Kirchenbauer, Bill 1953- *ConTFT 8 [port]*
Kircher, Carl Converse 1956- *WhoEmL 91*
Kircher, Dudley P. 1934- *St&PR 91*
Kircher, Girard Franklyn 1933- *WhoSSW 91*
Kircher, John Joseph 1938- *WhoWor 91*
Kircher, Joyce Megginson 1928- *WhoWrEP 89*
Kircher, Robert E. 1933- *WhoAm 90*
Kirchgassner, Marianne 1769-1808 *PenDiMP*
Kirchgraber, Frederick W. 1947- *St&PR 91*
Kirchheimer, Arthur Edward 1931- *WhoAm 90*
Kirchhof, Paul 1943- *WhoWor 91*
Kirchhofer, John A. 1937- *St&PR 91*
Kirchhoff, Charles L. *St&PR 91*
Kirchhoff, Gustav Robert 1824-1887 *WorAlBi*
Kirchhoff, Helga 1930- *WhoWor 91*
Kirchhoff, Keith Erwin 1954- *St&PR 91*
Kirchhoff, Michael Kent 1963- *WhoEmL 91*
Kirchhoff, Susan Ida 1949- *WhoEmL 91*
Kirchman, Charles Vincent 1935- *WhoE 91, WhoWor 91*
Kirchmann, Gerhardt Paul 1927- *St&PR 91*
Kirchmayer, Leon Kenneth 1924- *WhoAm 90*
Kirchner, Alfred F., Jr. 1930- *WhoAm 90*
Kirchner, Bruce M. 1948- *St&PR 91*
Kirchner, Bruce McHarg 1948- *WhoE 91*
Kirchner, Edwin James 1924- *WhoAm 90*
Kirchner, Elizabeth Parsons 1928- *WhoAmW 91*
Kirchner, Emil J. 1942- *ConAu 130*
Kirchner, Ernst Ludwig 1880-1938 *IntDcAA 90*
Kirchner, Frank H *BiDrAPA 89*
Kirchner, James William 1920- *WhoAm 90, WhoWor 91*
Kirchner, Jane Backstrom 1945- *IntWWM 90*
Kirchner, Johann Gottlob 1706?- *PenDiDA 89*
Kirchner, John Albert 1915- *WhoAm 90*
Kirchner, Katherine Ann 1948- *WhoAmW 91*
Kirchner, King P. 1927- *St&PR 91*
Kirchner, Leon 1919- *IntWWM 90, WhoAm 90, WorAlBi*
Kirchner, Louis John 1942- *St&PR 91*
Kirchner, Lynn Marie 1956- *WhoAmW 91*
Kirchner, Noel 1931- *St&PR 91*
Kirchner, Richard Martin 1941- *WhoE 91*
Kirchner, Robert Paul 1933- *St&PR 91*
Kirchner, Suzanne Cornelia 1955- *WhoAmW 91*
Kirchner, William Louis, Jr. 1926- *St&PR 91*
Kirchoff, Michael Joseph 1945- *St&PR 91*
Kirchoff, Shaila Rae 1962- *WhoAmW 91*
Kirchstein, Leonore 1933- *IntWWM 90*
Kirchwey, Freda 1911-1976 *BioAmW*
Kirdar, Nemir Amin 1936- *WhoWor 91*
Kiremitci, Nafi *BiDrAPA 89*
Kirgis, Frederic L. 1907- *WhoAm 90*
Kirgis, Frederic Lee, Jr. 1934- *WhoAm 90*
Kirhofer, Walter Joseph 1925- *St&PR 91*
Kiriakos, Ramzi Zaki *BiDrAPA 89*
Kirichenko, Yuri Alekseyevich *WhoWor 91*
Kirila, Carol Elizabeth 1952- *WhoEmL 91, WhoWor 91*
Kirilenko, Andrei P. 1906-1990 *NewYTBS 90 [port]*
Kirilenko, Andrei Pavlovich 1906-1990 *BioIn 16*
Kiripolsky, Ronald George 1940- *St&PR 91*
Kirjassoff, Gordon Louis 1922- *WhoAm 90*
Kirk, Alan Goodrich 1888-1963 *BioIn 16*
Kirk, Andy 1898- *BioIn 16, DrBIPA 90*
Kirk, Arthur F. 1946- *WhoEmL 91*
Kirk, Colleen Jean 1918- *IntWWM 90, WhoAm 90*
Kirk, Constance Ione 1951- *WhoAmW 91*
Kirk, Cynthia Ann 1957- *WhoE 91*
Kirk, Dana *BioIn 16*
Kirk, Daniel Lee 1919- *WhoAm 90*
Kirk, David 1952- *WhoEmL 91*
Kirk, David Guertin 1941- *St&PR 91*
Kirk, Dennis Dean 1950- *WhoE 91, WhoEmL 91*
Kirk, Diane Loraine 1957- *St&PR 91*
Kirk, Donald 1938- *WhoAm 90, WhoWor 91*
Kirk, Donald James 1932- *WhoAm 90*
Kirk, Dudley 1913- *WhoAm 90*
Kirk, Earl, Jr. 1927- *WhoAm 90*
Kirk, Edgar Lee 1923- *IntWWM 90, WhoAm 90*
Kirk, Elise Kuhl 1932- *IntWWM 90*
Kirk, Frank C 1889-1963 *WhoAmA 91N*
Kirk, Frank Harold, Jr. 1955- *BiDrAPA 89*
Kirk, Gerald Arthur 1940- *WhoAm 90*
Kirk, Gerald E. 1941- *St&PR 91*
Kirk, Grayson Louis 1903- *WhoAm 90*
Kirk, Hans Rudolf 1898-1962 *DcScanL*
Kirk, Helene Lisa 1959- *WhoAmW 91*
Kirk, Jack Lewis 1947- *WhoSSW 91*
Kirk, Jackson A. 1941- *St&PR 91*
Kirk, James Eric 1942- *St&PR 91*
Kirk, James Gerald 1939- *St&PR 91*
Kirk, James Lawrence, II 1926- *WhoAm 90*
Kirk, James Robert 1941- *WhoAm 90*
Kirk, Jerome 1923- *WhoAmA 91*
Kirk, Jerry Worth 1946- *St&PR 91*
Kirk, John 1832-1922 *BioIn 16*
Kirk, John Mark 1951- *BiDrAPA 89*
Kirk, John W. 1932- *ConAu 129*
Kirk, Kenneth Alan 1953- *WhoSSW 91*
Kirk, Kevin Lee 1950- *WhoSSW 91*
Kirk, Larry G. 1940- *St&PR 91*
Kirk, Larry Wayne 1957- *St&PR 91*
Kirk, Lisa *NewYTBS 90 [port]*
Kirk, Lynda Pounds 1946- *WhoAm 90, WhoAmW 91, WhoEmL 91, WhoSSW 91, WhoWor 91*
Kirk, Mark A. 1957- *St&PR 91*
Kirk, Mark-Lee *ConDes 90*
Kirk, Mary Powell 1954- *WhoAmW 91*
Kirk, Maurice Blake 1921- *WhoAm 90*
Kirk, Meldon Clark 1932- *St&PR 91*
Kirk, Michael *TwCCr&M 91*
Kirk, Michael 1947- *WhoAm 90, WhoAmA 91*
Kirk, Michael Thomas 1946- *WhoEmL 91, WhoSSW 91*
Kirk, Norman Andrew 1937- *WhoWrEP 89*
Kirk, Patrick Laine 1948- *WhoEmL 91*
Kirk, Paul Grattan, Jr. 1938- *WhoAm 90*
Kirk, Paul John 1962- *WhoE 91*
Kirk, Pearl Louise 1930- *WhoWrEP 89*
Kirk, Peter Francis 1953- *WhoE 91*
Kirk, Philip *ConAu 31NR*
Kirk, Preston F. 1945- *ODwPR 91*
Kirk, Preston Floyd 1945- *WhoEmL 91*
Kirk, Rahsaan Roland *BioIn 16*
Kirk, Rahsaan Roland 1936-1977 *OxCPMus*
Kirk, Rahsaan Roland 1937-1977 *DrBIPA 90*
Kirk, Randolph William 1948- *WhoEmL 91*
Kirk, Rhina *AuBYP 90*
Kirk, Richard A. 1930- *St&PR 91*
Kirk, Richard Augustus 1930- *WhoAm 90*
Kirk, Robert Allen 1958- *BiDrAPA 89*
Kirk, Robert H. 1931- *WhoAm 90*
Kirk, Robert L. 1929- *St&PR 91*
Kirk, Robert Leonard 1929- *WhoAm 90, WhoSSW 91*
Kirk, Robley Gordon 1944- *WhoSSW 91*
Kirk, Roger 1930- *WhoAm 90, WhoWor 91*
Kirk, Rudolf 1898-1989 *BioIn 16, ConAu 130*
Kirk, Russell 1918- *MajTwCW*
Kirk, Russell Amos 1918- *WhoAm 90, WhoWor 91, WhoWrEP 89*
Kirk, Ruth 1925- *AuBYP 90*
Kirk, Samuel 1793- *PenDiDA 89*
Kirk, Samuel Alexander 1904- *WhoAm 90*
Kirk, Sherwood 1924- *WhoAm 90, WhoWor 91*
Kirk, Stanley Butcher 1891-1989 *BioIn 16*
Kirk, Susan Lautz 1945- *WhoWor 91*
Kirk, Susan Murray 1953- *WhoAmW 91*
Kirk, Terence Sumner *BioIn 16*
Kirk, Theresa Lee 1961- *WhoEmL 91*
Kirk, Thomas Garrett, Jr. 1943- *WhoAm 90*
Kirk, Thomas Kent 1940- *WhoAm 90*
Kirk, Thomas L. *St&PR 91*
Kirk, Virginia 1895- *WhoWor 91*
Kirk, William Arthur, Jr. 1954- *WhoSSW 91*
Kirk, William E 1933- *BiDrAPA 89*
Kirk, William Smith 1928- *WhoSSW 91*
Kirk-Duggan, Michael Allan 1931- *WhoSSW 91*
Kirkaldy, John F 1908-1990 *ConAu 132*
Kirkbride, Chalmer Gatlin 1906- *WhoAm 90, WhoWor 91*
Kirkbride, Earle R 1891-1968 *WhoAmA 91N*
Kirkby, Emma 1949- *IntWWM 90, PenDiMP*
Kirkby, Maurice Anthony 1929- *WhoAm 90, WhoWor 91*
Kirkby-Lunn, Louise 1873-1930 *PenDiMP*
Kirke, Jay 1888-1968 *Ballpl 90*
Kirkeby, Edwin O. 1903- *St&PR 91*
Kirkeby, Gary John 1944- *IntWWM 90*
Kirkegaard, Mogens 1939- *WhoWor 91*
Kirkegaard, Raymond Lawrence, Jr. 1937- *WhoAm 90*
Kirkeide, John M. 1955- *St&PR 91*
Kirkemo, Elizabeth Ellen 1962- *WhoAmW 91*
Kirkendale, Ursula 1932- *IntWWM 90*
Kirkendale, Warren 1932- *IntWWM 90*
Kirkendall, Dean Alan 1957- *BiDrAPA 89*
Kirkendall, Donald Eugene 1939- *WhoAm 90*
Kirkendall, Richard Stewart 1928- *WhoAm 90*
Kirkenmeier, Thomas Edward 1955- *WhoEmL 91*
Kirkeride, Walter Terry 1946- *St&PR 91*
Kirkham, Don 1908- *WhoAm 90, WhoWor 91*
Kirkham, Francis Robison 1904- *WhoAm 90*
Kirkham, James Alvin 1935- *St&PR 91*
Kirkham, James E, Jr. *BiDrAPA 89*
Kirkham, John Anthony 1943- *St&PR 91*
Kirkham, M. B. *WhoAm 90, WhoAmW 91, WhoWor 91*
Kirkham, Shirley A. 1935- *St&PR 91*
Kirkhart, Barbara Jean 1960- *WhoEmL 91*
Kirkhoff, James Bruce 1921- *St&PR 91*
Kirkien-Rzeszotarski, Alicia Maria *WhoAmW 91*
Kirkland, Alfred Younges 1917- *WhoAm 90*
Kirkland, Bertha Theresa 1916- *WhoAmW 91*
Kirkland, Bryant Mays 1914- *WhoAm 90*
Kirkland, Caroline Matilda 1801-1864 *FemiCLE*
Kirkland, Charles 1947- *WhoEmL 91*
Kirkland, Gelsey 1952- *WorAlBi*
Kirkland, George Robert 1944- *WhoSSW 91*
Kirkland, Gerry P. 1943- *St&PR 91*
Kirkland, Gordon Laidlaw, Jr. 1943- *WhoE 91*
Kirkland, Hunter Moss Fry 1956- *St&PR 91*
Kirkland, John Cyril *St&PR 91*
Kirkland, John David 1933- *WhoAm 90*
Kirkland, Joseph J. 1925- *WhoAm 90*
Kirkland, Joseph Lane 1922- *WhoAm 90, WhoE 91*
Kirkland, Lane 1922- *WorAlBi*
Kirkland, Lawrence 1950- *BioIn 16*
Kirkland, Luther Joseph Sam 1927- *WhoSSW 91*
Kirkland, Malcolm 1943- *St&PR 91*
Kirkland, Mary Jane 1937- *WhoAmW 91*
Kirkland, N. L. 1946- *WhoWrEP 89*
Kirkland, Peggy Ann 1947- *WhoAmW 91*
Kirkland, Robert G 1929- *BiDrAPA 89*
Kirkland, Robert Taft 1935- *WhoSSW 91*
Kirkland, Russell Kermit 1942- *WhoSSW 91*
Kirkland, Sally *BioIn 16*
Kirkland, Sally 1912-1989 *BioIn 16, ConAu 129*
Kirkland, Samuel 1741-1808 *EncCRAm, WhNaAH*
Kirkland, Thomas Ray 1959- *WhoEmL 91*
Kirkland, Vance Hall 1904-1981 *WhoAmA 91N*
Kirkland, Virgil Wayne 1939- *WhoWor 91*
Kirkland, William George 1922- *St&PR 91*
Kirkland, Willie 1934- *Ballpl 90*
Kirkley, Leslie 1911-1989 *AnObit 1989*
Kirkley, T. A. *WhoAm 90*
Kirkman, Ada Darleen *BiDrAPA 89*
Kirkman, Elwood F. 1904- *St&PR 91*
Kirkman, Gilbert W. 1930- *St&PR 91*
Kirkman, James A. 1942- *St&PR 91*
Kirkman, Kay 1935- *WhoAmW 91*
Kirkman, Melinda Lee 1958- *WhoEmL 91*
Kirkman, Raymon Lee 1941- *St&PR 91*
Kirkman, Roger Norman 1949- *St&PR 91*
Kirkman, Sidney Chevalier 1895-1982 *DcNaB 1981*
Kirkman, Stacy Norman 1924- *St&PR 91*
Kirkop, Oreste 1923- *IntWWM 90*
Kirkorian, Roy 1945- *WhoAm 90*
Kirkpatrick, Andrew Booth, Jr. 1929- *WhoAm 90*
Kirkpatrick, Anne Saunders 1938- *WhoAmW 91, WhoWor 91*
Kirkpatrick, Charles C. 1907-1988 *BioIn 16*
Kirkpatrick, Charles Harvey 1931- *WhoAm 90*
Kirkpatrick, Clayton 1915- *WhoAm 90*
Kirkpatrick, David Cowan *BiDrAPA 89*
Kirkpatrick, Debbie Ann 1952- *WhoSSW 91*
Kirkpatrick, Diane 1933- *WhoAmA 91*
Kirkpatrick, Ed 1944- *Ballpl 90*
Kirkpatrick, Edward Thomson 1925- *WhoAm 90*
Kirkpatrick, Eleanor Blake 1909- *WhoAmW 91*
Kirkpatrick, Elwood *WhoAm 90*

Kirkpatrick, Evron Maurice 1911- *WhoAm 90*
Kirkpatrick, Floyd Robert 1925- *St&PR 91*
Kirkpatrick, Forrest H. 1905- *St&PR 91*
Kirkpatrick, Forrest Hunter 1905- *WhoAm 90, WhoWor 91*
Kirkpatrick, Francis Hubbard, Jr. 1943- *WhoAm 90*
Kirkpatrick, George Airey 1841-1899 *DcCanB 12*
Kirkpatrick, Helen 1909- *BioIn 16*
Kirkpatrick, James Daniel 1944- *WhoSSW 91*
Kirkpatrick, Jeane Duane Jordan 1926- *WhoAm 90, WhoAmW 91, WhoE 91, WhoWor 91, WhoWrEP 89*
Kirkpatrick, Jeane J. 1926- *BioIn 16*
Kirkpatrick, Joey *BioIn 16*
Kirkpatrick, John 1905- *IntWWM 90, PenDiMP*
Kirkpatrick, John Alton 1933- *WhoAm 90*
Kirkpatrick, John Blake 1944- *WhoE 91*
Kirkpatrick, John E. 1929- *St&PR 91*
Kirkpatrick, John Elson 1908- *WhoAm 90, WhoSSW 91*
Kirkpatrick, John Everett 1929- *WhoAm 90*
Kirkpatrick, John Gildersleeve 1917- *WhoAm 90*
Kirkpatrick, Joycelyn 1947- *WhoAmW 91*
Kirkpatrick, L.F. 1916- *St&PR 91*
Kirkpatrick, Martha J *BiDrAPA 89*
Kirkpatrick, Mary Beth 1951- *WhoAmW 91*
Kirkpatrick, Oliver 1911-1987 *BioIn 16*
Kirkpatrick, Philip R. 1947- *WhoE 91*
Kirkpatrick, Ralph 1911-1984 *PenDiMP*
Kirkpatrick, Robert Hugh 1954- *WhoEmL 91, WhoWor 91*
Kirkpatrick, Robert James 1946- *WhoAm 90*
Kirkpatrick, Samuel M. 1815-1892 *AmLegL*
Kirkpatrick, Sheila *BioIn 16*
Kirkpatrick, Thomas Herbert 1932- *WhoSSW 91*
Kirkpatrick, Tricia Thomson 1946- *WhoAmW 91*
Kirkpatrick, Vicki Karen 1952- *WhoAmW 91*
Kirkpatrick, William B. 1924- *St&PR 91*
Kirkpatrick, William Edward 1940- *St&PR 91*
Kirkpatrick-Ghene, Jeanne L *BiDrAPA 89*
Kirkpatrik, Samuel A. *WhoAm 90*
Kirks, Nicholas Brian *BioIn 16*
Kirksey, Avanelle 1926- *WhoAm 90*
Kirksey, Dianne *DrBlPA 90*
Kirksey, John Edward 1957- *St&PR 91*
Kirksey, Kirk 1943-1986 *DrBlPA 90*
Kirksey, Robert Edward 1930- *WhoAm 90*
Kirksey, Terrie Lynn 1958- *WhoAmW 91, WhoEmL 91*
Kirksey, William Boyd 1951- *WhoEmL 91*
Kirkup, James 1918- *BioIn 16*
Kirkwood, Byron D. 1949- *St&PR 91*
Kirkwood, Byron Ray 1946- *WhoSSW 91*
Kirkwood, Catherine 1949- *WhoAmW 91*
Kirkwood, Charles W. *BioIn 16*
Kirkwood, David Herbert Waddington 1924- *WhoAm 90*
Kirkwood, Dennis Michael 1948- *WhoEmL 91*
Kirkwood, Don 1950- *Ballpl 90*
Kirkwood, G.W. 1937- *St&PR 91*
Kirkwood, Gene 1945- *WhoAm 90*
Kirkwood, George Joseph 1939- *WhoE 91*
Kirkwood, James 1924?-1989 *AnObit 1989*
Kirkwood, James 1930-1989 *BioIn 16*
Kirkwood, Mary Burnette 1904- *WhoAmA 91*
Kirkwood, Maurice Richard 1920- *WhoAm 90*
Kirkwood, Michele Lea 1963- *WhoSSW 91*
Kirkwood, Robert 1923- *WhoAm 90*
Kirkwood, Samuel Jordon 1813-1894 *BiDrUSE 89*
Kirley, Marion Rachel 1934- *WhoAmW 91, WhoWor 91*
Kirley, Paul O. 1947- *St&PR 91*
Kirlian *EncPaPR 91*
Kirlin, John A. 1918- *St&PR 91*
Kirman, Alan Peter 1939- *WhoWor 91*
Kirman, Charles Gary 1949- *WhoAm 90*
Kirmayer, Laurence Jay *BiDrAPA 89*
Kirmse, Anne-Marie Rose 1941- *WhoAmW 91, WhoE 91*
Kirmse, Werner K. 1921- *St&PR 91*
Kirmser, Philip George 1919- *WhoAm 90*
Kirn, Ann Minette 1910- *AuBYP 90*
Kirn, Bob Joseph 1947- *St&PR 91*
Kirnan, Matthew James 1960- *WhoEmL 91*
Kirner, Paul Timothy 1947- *WhoEmL 91*
Kirner, Thomas Charles 1948- *St&PR 91*
Kironde-Kigozi, Sams Sendawula 1943- *WhoWor 91*
Kirov, Sergei Mironovich 1886-1934 *BioIn 16*
Kirpalaney, Ramon *WhoWor 91*
Kirpalani, Naresh Kishu 1950- *WhoWor 91*
Kirsch, Anthony Thomas 1930- *WhoAm 90*
Kirsch, Arthur S. 1952- *WhoAm 90*
Kirsch, Arthur W. 1941- *St&PR 91*
Kirsch, Arthur William 1941- *WhoAm 90*
Kirsch, Carl Michael 1938- *BiDrAPA 89*
Kirsch, Christine Jo 1950- *WhoAmW 91*
Kirsch, Daniel Jonathan 1950- *BiDrAPA 89*
Kirsch, Debra Frances *BiDrAPA 89*
Kirsch, Donald 1931- *St&PR 91*
Kirsch, Edwin Joseph 1924- *WhoAm 90*
Kirsch, Jack Frederick 1934- *WhoAm 90*
Kirsch, Jeffrey Scott 1947- *WhoEmL 91*
Kirsch, Joachim 1907- *WhoWor 91*
Kirsch, Kenneth C. 1943- *St&PR 91*
Kirsch, Laurence Stephen 1957- *WhoE 91, WhoEmL 91, WhoWor 91*
Kirsch, Michael Alan *BiDrAPA 89*
Kirsch, Miera Roybal 1949- *WhoEmL 91*
Kirsch, Ralph M. 1928- *St&PR 91, WhoAm 90*
Kirsch, Robert Dean 1953- *WhoSSW 91*
Kirsch, Sarah 1935- *EncCoWW*
Kirsch, Stephen William 1962- *WhoEmL 91*
Kirsch, William Joseph 1956- *WhoE 91*
Kirschbaum, Alan Ira 1948- *WhoSSW 91*
Kirschbaum, Charlotte von 1899-1975 *BioIn 16*
Kirschbaum, James Louis 1940- *WhoAm 90*
Kirschbaum, Myron 1949- *WhoEmL 91*
Kirschberg, Nancy Jeanne Miller 1948- *WhoSSW 91*
Kirschbrown, Lita Bryna 1952- *WhoAmW 91, WhoSSW 91*
Kirschen, Borell L. 1937- *St&PR 91*
Kirschen, Herman Leonard 1927- *WhoE 91*
Kirschen, Howard 1952- *BiDrAPA 89*
Kirschenbaum, Bernard Edwin 1924- *WhoAmA 91*
Kirschenbaum, Jules 1930- *WhoAmA 91*
Kirschenbaum, Richard H. 1939- *St&PR 91*
Kirschenbaum, Robert 1928- *St&PR 91*
Kirschenbaum, William 1944- *St&PR 91, WhoAm 90, WhoE 91, WhoWor 91*
Kirschenmann, Henry George, Jr. 1930- *WhoAm 90*
Kirscher, John C. 1934- *St&PR 91*
Kirschner, Barbara Starrels 1941- *WhoAm 90*
Kirschner, James Edward 1945- *St&PR 91*
Kirschner, Jay Larry 1955- *WhoEmL 91*
Kirschner, Kenneth M. *St&PR 91*
Kirschner, L Gordon *BiDrAPA 89*
Kirschner, Leon C. 1940- *St&PR 91*
Kirschner, Paul David 1955- *WhoEmL 91*
Kirschner, Richard Michael 1949- *WhoEmL 91, WhoWor 91*
Kirschner, Ronald Allen 1942- *WhoE 91, WhoWor 91*
Kirschner, Ruth Brin 1924- *WhoAmW 91*
Kirschner, Sidney 1934- *St&PR 91, WhoAm 90, WhoSSW 91*
Kirschner, Stanley 1927- *WhoAm 90*
Kirschner-Bromley, Victoria Ann 1960- *WhoEmL 91*
Kirschstein, Ruth Lillian 1926- *WhoAm 90, WhoAmW 91*
Kirscht, Judith Mary 1933- *WhoWrEP 89*
Kirschten, Barbara Louise 1950- *WhoAmW 91*
Kirsebom, Michael Fredrik 1964- *WhoE 91*
Kirsebom, Vendela *BioIn 16*
Kirsh, Andrea 1951- *WhoAmA 91*
Kirsh, James T., Jr. 1953- *St&PR 91*
Kirsh, James Theodore 1925- *St&PR 91*
Kirshbaum, Bernard 1910- *IntWWM 90*
Kirshbaum, Howard M. 1938- *WhoAm 90*
Kirshbaum, Kenneth David *BiDrAPA 89*
Kirshbaum, Ralph 1946- *PenDiMP*
Kirshbaum, Ronald Michael 1938- *St&PR 91*
Kirshenbaum, Isidor 1917- *WhoE 91*
Kirshenbaum, William Albert 1936- *St&PR 91*
Kirshner, Caroline Dok *BiDrAPA 89*
Kirshner, Judith Russi 1942- *WhoAmA 91*
Kirshner, Lewis A 1940- *BiDrAPA 89*
Kirshner, Norman 1923- *WhoAm 90*
Kirshner, Robert Paul 1949- *WhoAm 90*
Kirsner, Joseph Barnett 1909- *WhoAm 90*
Kirsner, Laura T. 1945- *St&PR 91*
Kirsner, Robert 1921- *WhoAm 90*
Kirst, Hans Hellmut 1914-1989 *AnObit 1989, BioIn 16, TwCCr&M 91B*
Kirstein, Gregory William 1954- *WhoEmL 91*
Kirstein, Isabella Johanna *WhoWor 91*
Kirstein, Jack *PenDiMP*
Kirstein, Kenneth *BiDrAPA 89*
Kirstein, Larry S 1946- *BiDrAPA 89*
Kirstein, Lincoln 1907- *CurBio 90 [port], WhoAm 90, WhoE 91, WorAlBi*
Kirstein, Naomi Wagman 1937- *WhoAmW 91*
Kirsten, Dorothy 1917- *IntWWM 90, PenDiMP*
Kirsten, Dorothy 1919- *WhoAm 90*
Kirsten, Markham 1949- *BiDrAPA 89*
Kirsten, Nicholas 1947- *WhoAmA 91*
Kirsten-Daiensai, Richard Charles 1920- *WhoAmA 91*
Kirsteuer, Ernst Karl Eberhart 1933- *WhoAm 90*
Kirtland, G. B. *AuBYP 90*
Kirtley, Donald R. 1938- *St&PR 91*
Kirtley, Jane Elizabeth 1953- *WhoEmL 91*
Kirtley, Mary Elizabeth 1935- *WhoAmW 91, WhoE 91*
Kirtley, Olivia Faulkner 1950- *St&PR 91*
Kirtley, Phyllis *WhoWrEP 89*
Kirtley, Samuel Coleman 1936- *WhoSSW 91*
Kirts, Thomas Edmund 1940- *BiDrAPA 89*
Kirubakaran, Vellore R 1944- *BiDrAPA 89*
Kirven, Gerald 1922- *WhoSSW 91*
Kirven, J.D., Jr. 1917- *St&PR 91*
Kirven, Leo E, Jr. 1923- *BiDrAPA 89*
Kirven, Peyton Edward 1924- *WhoAm 90*
Kirvesniemi, Harri *BioIn 16*
Kirwan, John Phillip, Jr. 1948- *WhoSSW 91*
Kirwan, Katharyn Grace 1913- *WhoAmW 91*
Kirwan, Peter James 1947- *WhoWor 91*
Kirwan, Thomas M. 1940- *St&PR 91, WhoAm 90, WhoE 91*
Kirwan, William English, II 1938- *WhoAm 90, WhoE 91, WhoWor 91*
Kirwin, Kenneth F. 1941- *WhoAm 90*
Kirya, Barnabas George 1939- *WhoWor 91*
Kiryu, Keiji 1935- *WhoWor 91*
Kirzner, Bernard M 1945- *BiDrAPA 89*
Kis, Danilo *BioIn 16*
Kis, Danilo 1935- *MajTwCW*
Kis, Danilo 1935-1989 *AnObit 1989, ConAu 129*
Kis, John *St&PR 91*
Kis, Miklos Totfalusi 1650-1702 *BioIn 16*
Kisak, Paul Francis 1956- *WhoEmL 91, WhoSSW 91, WhoWor 91*
Kiscaden, Laura Linnea 1950- *WhoAmW 91*
Kisch, Ethan Hillary 1951- *BiDrAPA 89*
Kisch, Gloria 1941- *WhoAmA 91, WhoE 91*
Kisch, Louis U.C. 1935- *St&PR 91*
Kisch, Royalton 1919- *IntWWM 90*
Kischuk, Richard Karl 1949- *WhoAm 90, WhoEmL 91*
Kise, James Nelson 1937- *WhoE 91*
Kisekka, Samson 1913- *WhoWor 91*
Kiselewski, Joseph 1901-1986 *WhoAmA 91N*
Kiselik, Paul Howard 1937- *WhoE 91*
Kiser, Arthur George 1943- *St&PR 91*
Kiser, Clyde Vernon 1904- *WhoAm 90*
Kiser, Donald L. 1933- *St&PR 91*
Kiser, Dorothy Mae Houston 1944- *WhoAmW 91*
Kiser, Ellen F *BiDrAPA 89*
Kiser, Glenn, Jr. 1951- *WhoSSW 91*
Kiser, Glenn Augustus 1917- *WhoSSW 91*
Kiser, Jackson L. 1929- *WhoAm 90, WhoSSW 91*
Kiser, James W. 1934- *St&PR 91*
Kiser, James Webb 1934- *WhoAm 90*
Kiser, Kimberly Anne 1958- *WhoAmW 91*
Kiser, Martha Gwinn *AuBYP 90*
Kiser, Mose, III 1956- *WhoSSW 91*
Kiser, Nagiko Sato 1923- *WhoAmW 91, WhoWor 91*
Kiser, Omer Lee 1943- *WhoSSW 91*
Kiser, Roy Sanford, Jr. *BiDrAPA 89*
Kiser, Sharon Ann 1945- *WhoAmW 91*
Kiser, Wieslaw Maria 1937- *IntWWM 90*
Kiser, William Francis 1935- *St&PR 91*
Kiser, William R. 1925- *St&PR 91*
Kiser, William Sites 1928- *WhoAm 90*
Kish, Joseph Laurence, Jr. 1933- *WhoAm 90*
Kish, Leslie 1910- *WhoAm 90*
Kish, Michael Stephen 1961- *WhoE 91*
Kish, Zaven Avedis 1911- *WhoSSW 91*
Kishi Nobusuke *EncJap*
Kishi, Takeo 1937- *WhoWor 91*
Kishi, Yoshito 1937- *WhoAm 90*
Kishibe, Shigeo 1912- *IntWWM 90*
Kishimori, Phillip T. 1936- *St&PR 91*
Kishimoto, Hiroko 1943- *IntWWM 90*
Kishimoto, Kenji 1947- *WhoWor 91*
Kishimoto, Yasuo 1925- *WhoAm 90*
Kishimoto, Yuji 1938- *WhoSSW 91, WhoWor 91*
Kishner, Ira Alexander 1933- *BiDrAPA 89*
Kishore, Nand *BiDrAPA 89*
Kishpaugh, Allan Richard 1937- *WhoWor 91*
Kisielewski, Stefan 1911- *IntWWM 90*
Kisinger, Grace Gelvin 1913-1965 *AuBYP 90*
Kiska, Timothy Olin 1952- *WhoAm 90*
Kiskadden, Robert Morgan 1918- *WhoAmA 91*
Kisken, Freda Voorhees 1938- *WhoE 91*
Kisla, Judy Bernadette 1954- *BiDrAPA 89*
Kislak, Jean Hart 1931- *WhoAmW 91*
Kislevitz, Joshua Luther 1957- *St&PR 91*
Kisley, Anthony J 1933- *BiDrAPA 89*
Kislik, Louis A. 1931- *WhoAm 90*
Kislik, Richard William 1927- *WhoAm 90*
Kisling, Norbert Erwin 1959- *WhoWor 91*
Kislowski, Richard John 1942- *St&PR 91*
Kismaric, Carole Lee 1942- *WhoAm 90*
Kisnadwala, Hiten Vithal 1958- *BiDrAPA 89, WhoE 91*
Kisner, Jacob 1926- *WhoAm 90, WhoE 91, WhoWor 91*
Kisner, Ronald Harris 1948- *St&PR 91*
Kison, Bruce 1950- *Ballpl 90*
Kisor, Henry 1940- *BioIn 16*
Kisor, Henry Du Bois 1940- *WhoAm 90*
Kiss *ConMus 5 [port], EncPR&S 89*
Kiss, Agnes Ildiko 1955- *WhoE 91*
Kiss, Anna 1939- *EncCoWW*
Kiss, John B. 1948- *St&PR 91*
Kiss, John Michael 1948- *WhoEmL 91*
Kiss, Laszlo 1950- *WhoWor 91*
Kiss, Stephen Paul 1924- *WhoWor 91*
Kissa, Erik 1923- *WhoE 91*
Kissane, James Donald 1930- *WhoAm 90*
Kissane, Jean Charlotte 1946- *WhoAmW 91, WhoE 91*
Kissane, Leedice McAnelly 1905- *WhoAmW 91*
Kissane, Richard F. 1951- *St&PR 91*
Kissane, Thomas 1927- *WhoE 91*
Kissane, William F. 1933- *St&PR 91*
Kissaun, Maryann 1930- *IntWWM 90*
Kisseberth, Paul Barto 1932- *WhoAm 90*
Kissel, David Eric 1953- *BiDrAPA 89*
Kissel, Edward William 1942- *WhoE 91*
Kissel, Elizabeth McCombs 1958- *WhoAmW 91*
Kissel, Frank Nolan 1952- *WhoE 91*
Kissel, Howard William 1942- *WhoAm 90*
Kissel, John Andrew 1959- *WhoEmL 91*
Kissel, Joseph F. 1947- *St&PR 91*
Kissel, Lester 1903- *St&PR 91*
Kissel, Louis *EncABHB 4*
Kissel, Michael Case *WhoE 91, WhoWor 91*
Kissel, Phillip 1954- *WhoEmL 91*
Kissel, Walter J. 1933- *St&PR 91*
Kissel, Wesley A *BiDrAPA 89*
Kissel, William Thorn, Jr 1920- *WhoAmA 91, WhoE 91, WhoWor 91*
Kissell, George *BioIn 16*
Kissell, Robin Leslie *BiDrAPA 89*
Kissick, Gary Richard 1946- *WhoWrEP 89*
Kissick, Luther Cleveland, Jr. 1919- *WhoWor 91*
Kissick, W. Norman *St&PR 91*
Kissick, W. Norman 1930- *WhoAm 90*
Kissick, William Lee 1932- *WhoAm 90*
Kissiloff, William 1929- *WhoAm 90*
Kissinger, Charles C. *BioIn 16*
Kissinger, Harold Arthur 1922- *WhoAm 90*
Kissinger, Henry 1923- *BioIn 16, WorAlBi*
Kissinger, Henry A. 1923- *ConAu 33NR, MajTwCW*
Kissinger, Henry Alfred 1923- *BiDrUSE 89, WhoAm 90, WhoE 91, WhoWor 91*
Kissinger, Marilyn Ruth 1947- *WhoAmW 91*
Kissinger, Stephen Neil 1955- *BiDrAPA 89*
Kissinger, Walter Bernhard 1924- *St&PR 91, WhoAm 90*
Kissko, John Martin 1945- *WhoE 91*
Kissling, John R., Jr. 1945- *St&PR 91*
Kissling, Walter 1931- *St&PR 91*
Kisslinger, Carl 1926- *WhoAm 90*
Kisslinger, Leonard Sol 1930- *WhoAm 90*
Kissmann, Edna *ODwPR 91*
Kissmeyer-Nielsen, Perla M.S. *BiDrAPA 89*
Kissner, Mary Jean 1957- *St&PR 91*
Kissner, Michael Stuart 1948- *St&PR 91*
Kist, Ewald 1944- *St&PR 91*
Kistenmacher, Patricia Lee 1934- *WhoSSW 91*
Kister, Benjamin Joseph 1951- *WhoEmL 91, WhoWor 91*
Kister, James Milton 1930- *WhoAm 90*
Kistiakowsky, Vera 1928- *WhoAm 90, WhoAmW 91*
Kistler, Alan Lee 1928- *WhoAm 90*
Kistler, Darci *BioIn 16*
Kistler, Darci Anna 1964- *WhoAm 90, WhoE 91*
Kistler, George Clifford 1934- *St&PR 91*
Kistler, Herbert Donald 1908- *WhoE 91*
Kistler, Irene Brady 1943- *BioIn 16*

Kistler, John Joseph, Jr. 1926- *WhoSSW 91*
Kistler, Thomas Carl 1947- *WhoEmL 91*
Kistler, Thomas King 1957- *WhoEmL 91*
Kistner, David Harold 1931- *WhoAm 90, WhoWor 91*
Kistner, Jennifer Ruth 1957- *WhoAmW 91*
Kistner, Jerry Lee 1950- *WhoE 91, WhoEmL 91*
Kistner, Klaus-Peter 1940- *WhoWor 91*
Kistner, Richard Allen 1948- *WhoE 91*
Kistner, Robert W. 1917-1990 *BioIn 16*
Kiszczak, Czeslaw 1925- *BioIn 16, WhoWor 91*
Kiszko, Martin Edmund 1958- *IntWWM 90*
Kit Carson *WhNaAH*
Kit, Saul 1920- *WhoAm 90*
Kita, Bernice *BioIn 16*
Kita, Hiroshi 1933- *WhoWor 91*
Kitada, Shinichi 1948- *WhoEmL 91, WhoWor 91*
Kitadai, Reiichiro 1926- *WhoWor 91*
Kitagami, Yasuharu 1939- *St&PR 91*
Kitagawa Utamaro *EncJap*
Kitagawa, Audrey Emiko 1951- *WhoAmW 91*
Kitagawa, Masanobu 1933- *WhoWor 91*
Kitahara, Shizuo 1922- *WhoWor 91*
Kitaj, R. B. *BioIn 16*
Kitaj, R. B. 1932- *WhoAm 90*
Kitaj, R B 1932- *WhoAmA 91*
Kitaj, Ronald B. *BioIn 16*
Kitajima, Heiichiro 1925- *WhoWor 91*
Kitajima, Osamu *NewAgMG*
Kitajima, Yoshitoshi 1933- *St&PR 91*
Kitamura, Kazuo 1925- *WhoWor 91*
Kitamura, Ryuji 1937- *St&PR 91*
Kitamura, Satoshi 1956- *SmATA 62*
Kitamura, Toshinori 1947- *WhoWor 91*
Kitani, Osamu 1935- *WhoWor 91*
Kitano, Hirohisa 1931- *WhoWor 91*
Kitano, Masanori 1935- *WhoWor 91*
Kitao, T Kaori 1933- *WhoAmA 91*
Kitaro *BioIn 16, NewAgMG*
Kitasato, Shibasaburo 1852-1931 *WorAlBi*
Kitay, Harvey Robert 1931- *WhoE 91*
Kitayama, Katsuhiko 1937- *WhoWor 91*
Kitayenko, Dimitri Georgievitch 1940- *WhoWor 91*
Kitazaki, Jeanne Durnford 1940- *WhoAmW 91*
Kitbunchu, Michael Michai 1929- *WhoWor 91*
Kitch, Edmund Wells 1939- *WhoAm 90*
Kitch, Frederick David 1928- *St&PR 91, WhoAm 90*
Kitchel, Denison 1908- *WhoAm 90*
Kitchell, James Wallace 1927- *St&PR 91*
Kitchell, Kenneth Francis, Jr. 1947- *WhoSSW 91*
Kitchell, Margaret Anne 1948- *BiDrAPA 89*
Kitchen, Alice Dean 1927- *BiDrAPA 89*
Kitchen, Anna Louise 1930- *WhoAmW 91*
Kitchen, Carol Anne 1941- *WhoAmW 91*
Kitchen, Charles B *BiDrAPA 89*
Kitchen, James Edward 1931- *St&PR 91*
Kitchen, John Howard 1957- *WhoE 91*
Kitchen, John Martin 1936- *WhoAm 90, WhoWrEP 89*
Kitchen, John Milton 1912- *WhoAm 90, WhoWor 91*
Kitchen, Lawrence O. 1923- *St&PR 91*
Kitchen, Lawrence Oscar 1923- *WhoAm 90*
Kitchen, Linda 1960- *IntWWM 90*
Kitchen, Michael 1948- *ConTFT 8*
Kitchen, Paul Howard 1937- *WhoAm 90*
Kitchen, Robert R 1926- *BiDrAPA 89*
Kitchen, Sidney Chuck 1954- *WhoEmL 91*
Kitchen, Steven L. 1945- *St&PR 91*
Kitchen, Tella 1902-1988 *MusmAFA*
Kitchener, Horatio Herbert 1850-1916 *WorAlBi*
Kitchener, Horatio Herbert, Earl 1850-1916 *BioIn 16*
Kitchener, Murray 1920- *BiDrAPA 89*
Kitchener, S. Alan 1932- *St&PR 91*
Kitchens, Clarence Wesley, Jr. 1943- *WhoE 91*
Kitchens, Debra Dianne 1958- *WhoSSW 91*
Kitchens, Frederick Lynton, Jr. 1940- *WhoSSW 91, WhoWor 91*
Kitchens, Larry Edwin 1940- *WhoSSW 91*
Kitchens, Leonard H. 1943- *St&PR 91*
Kitchens, O. W. 1901-1986 *MusmAFA*
Kitchens, Steven Bradley 1960- *WhoE 91*
Kitchens, William Rodgers 1944- *WhoSSW 91*
Kitcher, Philip Stuart 1947- *WhoAm 90*
Kitchi-Manito-Waya 1875?-1897 *DcCanB 12*
Kitchin, C H B 1895-1967 *TwCCr&M 91*
Kitchin, Carolyn T 1931- *BiDrAPA 89*
Kitchin, James D., III 1931- *WhoAm 90*
Kitchin, Kate Parks 1911- *WhoAmW 91*
Kitchin, Laurence Tyson 1913- *WhoAm 90*
Kitchin, Rosemarie A. 1939- *WhoWrEP 89*
Kitchin, Rosemarie Atkin 1939- *WhoAmW 91*
Kitchin, Winston Henry 1955- *BiDrAPA 89*
Kitchiner, John 1933- *IntWWM 90*
Kitchner, Irving 1939- *BiDrAPA 89*
Kite, Alvin E., Jr. 1933- *St&PR 91*
Kite, Christopher James 1947- *IntWWM 90*
Kite, J. Sellers 1928- *St&PR 91*
Kite, Jerry Marie 1934- *WhoSSW 91*
Kite, Tom 1949- *News 90 [port], -90-3 [port], WorAlBi*
Kite-Powell, Jeffery T. 1941- *IntWWM 90*
Kiteley, Brian 1956- *ConAu 132*
Kitingan, Jeffrey Gapari 1947- *WhoWor 91*
Kitlas, Ronald Allan 1953- *WhoEmL 91*
Kitner, Harold 1921- *WhoAmA 91*
Kito, Shiro 1934- *WhoWor 91*
Kito, Shozo 1927- *WhoWor 91*
Kitscha, Hector 1930- *St&PR 91*
Kitsko, William T 1922- *BiDrAPA 89*
Kitson, Alfred 1855-1934 *EncO&P 3*
Kitson, David *BioIn 16*
Kitson, Frank 1872-1930 *Ballpl 90*
Kitson, Stephan James *BiDrAPA 89*
Kitson, Theo Alice 1871-1932 *BiDWomA*
Kitsos, Petros 1965- *WhoWor 91*
Kitt, Eartha 1928- *DrBIPA 90, OxCPMus, WorAlBi*
Kitt, Eartha Mae 1928- *WhoAm 90*
Kitt, Walter 1925- *BiDrAPA 89*
Kitta, George Edward 1953- *WhoAmA 91*
Kittappa, Rethinasamy Kit *WhoE 91*
Kittas, Joel Richard 1936- *St&PR 91*
Kittel, Charles 1916- *WhoAm 90*
Kittel, Ernst Wolfram 1940- *WhoWor 91*
Kittel, Peter 1945- *WhoEmL 91*
Kittell, Donald D. 1937- *WhoAm 90*
Kittelson, David Burnelle 1942- *WhoAm 90*
Kittides, Christopher P. 1940- *St&PR 91*
Kittle, Bernard Wayne 1931- *WhoAm 90*
Kittle, Cecil W. 1945- *St&PR 91*
Kittle, Charles Frederick 1921- *WhoAm 90*
Kittle, Hub *BioIn 16*
Kittle, Ron 1958- *Ballpl 90*
Kittleson, Henry Marshall 1929- *WhoAm 90*
Kittlitz, Linda Gale 1949- *WhoAmW 91*
Kittlitz, Rudolf Gottlieb, Jr. 1935- *WhoAm 90*
Kitto, Armand E. 1927- *St&PR 91*
Kitto, Franklin Curtis 1954- *WhoEmL 91*
Kitto, John Buck, Jr. 1952- *WhoEmL 91*
Kitto, Thomas C. 1955- *St&PR 91*
Kittock, Claudia Jean 1952- *WhoEmL 91*
Kittredge, Chessman 1918- *St&PR 91*
Kittredge, George Washington 1805-1880 *AmLegL*
Kittredge, John Kendall 1927- *WhoAm 90*
Kittredge, Malachi 1869-1928 *Ballpl 90*
Kittredge, Nancy 1938- *WhoAmA 91*
Kittredge, Robert P. 1925- *St&PR 91*
Kittredge, Sidney 1932- *St&PR 91*
Kittredge, William *BioIn 16*
Kittrell, Steven Dan 1953- *WhoEmL 91*
Kittrie, Nicholas Norbert Nehemiah 1930- *WhoAm 90, WhoE 91, WhoWor 91*
Kittross, John Michael 1929- *WhoAm 90*
Kitts, Carson Dean 1934- *St&PR 91*
Kitts, Christopher Martin 1943- *IntWWM 90*
Kitts, Dean Carson 1934- *WhoAm 90*
Kitts, Jeffrey Brad 1956- *WhoEmL 91*
Kittson, Augustan Daniel 1955- *St&PR 91*
Kittson, Myrna Ann 1925- *St&PR 91*
Kitz, Richard John 1929- *WhoAm 90*
Kitzes, William Fredric 1950- *WhoEmL 91*
Kitzhaber, John Albert 1947- *WhoAm 90*
Kitzie, John, Jr. 1954- *St&PR 91, WhoAm 90*
Kitzing, Llona S. *St&PR 91*
Kitzinger, Ernst 1912- *WhoAmA 91*
Kitzinger, Sheila 1929- *BioIn 16*
Kitzinger, Stanley Albert 1916- *St&PR 91*
Kitzinger, Uwe 1928- *WhoWor 91*
Kitzke, Eugene David 1923- *WhoAm 90*
Kitzler, Elroy B. 1926- *St&PR 91*
Kitzman, Irene Roda 1950- *BiDrAPA 89*
Kitzmiller, Howard Lawrence 1930- *St&PR 91*
Kitzmiller, John 1913-1965 *DrBIPA 90*
Kitzmiller, Karen Maureen 1943- *St&PR 91*
Kitzmiller, William Michael 1931- *WhoAm 90*
Kivel, Maxine Nancy 1934- *WhoAmW 91, WhoE 91*
Kivelson, Margaret Galland 1928- *WhoAm 90, WhoAmW 91*
Kivelson, Robert D. *ODwPR 91*
Kivengere, Festo *BioIn 16*
Kivenko, Kenneth *WhoAm 90*
Kives, Philip *BioIn 16*
Kivett, Clarence 1905- *St&PR 91*
Kivett, Marvin Franklin 1917- *WhoAm 90*
Kivette, Ruth Montgomery 1926- *WhoAm 90*
Kivi, Aleksis 1834-1872 *DcScanL, NinCLC 30 [port]*
Kivi-Koskinen, Timo Ilari 1942- *WhoWor 91*
Kiviat, Philip Jay 1937- *WhoE 91*
Kiviat, Stephen Howard 1941- *WhoE 91*
Kiviet, Jan Frederik 1948- *WhoWor 91*
Kivikkaho, Eila 1921- *EncCoWW*
Kivowitz, Julian *BiDrAPA 89*
Kiwitt, Sidney 1928- *St&PR 91, WhoAm 90*
Kiwus, Karin 1942- *EncCoWW*
Kiyak, Yahya *BiDrAPA 89*
Kiyohara, Michiya 1919- *WhoWor 91*
Kiyota, Masuaki 1962- *EncO&P 3, EncPaPR 91*
Kiyota, Minoru 1923- *ConAu 32NR*
Kizer, Carolyn *BioIn 16*
Kizer, Carolyn 1925- *FemiCLE*
Kizer, Carolyn Ashley 1925- *WhoAm 90, WhoAmW 91, WhoWrEP 89*
Kizer, Jack D. 1925- *St&PR 91*
Kizer, John Tom 1910- *St&PR 91*
Kizer, Roy Arron 1948- *WhoSSW 91*
Kizzee, Margaret Leigh *WhoAmW 91*
Kizzia, Don Bradley 1954- *WhoEmL 91*
Kizziar, Janet Wright *WhoAm 90*
Kjaer, George C D 1932- *BiDrAPA 89*
Kjaer, Nils 1870-1924 *DcScanL*
Kjaerholm, Poul 1929-1980 *ConDes 90, PenDiDA 89*
Kjartansson, Kristjan Georg 1934- *WhoWor 91*
Kjeldaas, Terje, Jr. 1924- *WhoAm 90*
Kjeldsen-Kragh, Soren 1938- *WhoWor 91*
Kjelgaard, James Arthur 1910-1959 *AuBYP 90*
Kjelland, James Martin 1948- *IntWWM 90*
Kjellmark, Eric William, Jr. 1928- *WhoE 91*
Kjellstrom, Elving Joel 1922- *St&PR 91*
Kjenaas, Ervin A 1923- *BiDrAPA 89*
Kjer, Henning 1939- *WhoWor 91*
Kjerulff, Georgiana Ludlow Greene 1917- *WhoAmW 91*
Kjos, Victoria Ann 1953- *WhoAmW 91, WhoEmL 91*
Kjosa, David Leroy 1941- *WhoE 91*
Klaas, Nicholas Paul 1925- *WhoAm 90*
Klaas, Rainer Maria 1950- *IntWWM 90*
Klaas, Richard Lee 1945- *WhoSSW 91*
Klaassen, Carol S. 1951- *WhoWrEP 89*
Klaassen, Katherine L *BiDrAPA 89*
Klaaste, Aggrey *BioIn 16*
Klaatsch, Heinz H *BiDrAPA 89*
Klabbatz, Chester George 1933- *St&PR 91*
Klaben, Arthur S. 1937- *St&PR 91*
Klabin, Laura Jill 1948- *WhoE 91*
Klabo, Lincoln C. 1937- *St&PR 91*
Klabosh, Charles Joseph 1920- *WhoSSW 91*
Klabund 1890-1928 *BioIn 16*
Klabunde, Charles Spencer 1935- *WhoAmA 91*
Klabunde, Florence Alice 1938- *WhoWrEP 89*
Klacsmann, John Anthony 1921- *St&PR 91, WhoAm 90*
Klaczynski, Joseph Charles 1930- *St&PR 91*
Klad, Jeffrey Sanford 1949- *WhoEmL 91*
Kladias, Nikolaos Antonios 1964- *WhoWor 91*
Klaehn, Robert Lindsay 1955- *BiDrAPA 89*
Klaerner, C.M. 1920- *St&PR 91*
Klaerner, Curtis Maurice 1920- *WhoAm 90*
Klafter, Cary Ira 1948- *WhoEmL 91*
Klages, William A., Jr. 1952- *WhoEmL 91*
Klagsbrun, Samuel C 1932- *BiDrAPA 89, St&PR 91, WhoE 91*
Klagsbrunn, Hans Alexander 1909- *WhoAm 90*
Klagstad, Robert Edgar 1923- *WhoAm 90*
Klah, Hasteen 1867-1937 *BioIn 16*
Klaholz, Larry Robert 1946- *St&PR 91*
Klahr, Aryeh Leslie 1952- *BiDrAPA 89*
Klahr, David 1939- *WhoAm 90*
Klahr, David 1963- *BiDrAPA 89*
Klahr, Myra Blossom 1933- *WhoWrEP 89*
Klahr, Saulo 1935- *WhoAm 90*
Klaiber, Bernd Michael 1948- *WhoWor 91*
Klaiber, Teresa Lynn Martin 1949- *WhoWrEP 89*
Klaif, Charles H 1932- *BiDrAPA 89*
Klaits, Barrie 1944- *BioIn 16*
Klajbor, Dorothea M. 1915- *WhoAmW 91*
Klakowich, Robert John 1947- *IntWWM 90*
Klamann, Dieter Paul Max 1924- *WhoWor 91*
Klamen, Debra Lee *BiDrAPA 89*
Klamerus, Karen Jean 1957- *WhoAmW 91, WhoE 91*
Klamon, Lawrence P. 1937- *St&PR 91*
Klamon, Lawrence Paine 1937- *WhoAm 90, WhoSSW 91*
Klampert, Arthur Ronald 1941- *WhoE 91*
Klamt, Robert R 1920- *BiDrAPA 89*
Klancer, Richard 1937- *St&PR 91*
Klancher, Faye Romelle 1941- *WhoAmW 91*
Klanderman, Joel Dean 1947- *WhoEmL 91*
Klaniczay, Tibor 1923- *ConAu 132, WhoWor 91*
Klann, Julie Ann 1945- *WhoAmW 91*
Klansky, Ivan 1948- *IntWWM 90*
Klaperman, Gilbert 1921- *St&PR 91, WhoAm 90*
Klapes, Nancy Arlene 1955- *WhoAmW 91*
Klaphaak, Peter John, Jr. *BiDrAPA 89*
Klapheke, Martin Moyer 1953- *BiDrAPA 89*
Klapholz, Sue 1953- *BiDrAPA 89*
Klapinsky, Raymond Joseph 1938- *St&PR 91*
Klapman, Howard J *BiDrAPA 89*
Klapp, Enrique H. *WhoHisp 91*
Klapp, Irving *BiDrAPA 89*
Klapp, William Riddell, Jr. 1951- *WhoSSW 91*
Klapper, Carol L. 1923- *WhoE 91*
Klapper, Gail Heitler 1943- *WhoAmW 91*
Klapperich, Frank Lawrence, Jr. 1934- *St&PR 91, WhoAm 90*
Klappert, Peter 1942- *WhoAm 90, WhoE 91, WhoWrEP 89*
Klar, Howard M *BiDrAPA 89*
Klare, George Roger 1922- *WhoAm 90*
Klare, Michael T 1942- *ConAu 130*
Klare, Michael Thomas 1942- *WhoAm 90*
Klarfeld, Jonathan Michael 1937- *WhoE 91*
Klarfeld, Nathan 1950- *WhoEmL 91*
Klarich, Nina Marie *WhoAm 90*
Klarin, Winifred Erlick 1912- *WhoAmA 91*
Klarman, Edward L 1936- *BiDrAPA 89*
Klarman, Herbert Elias 1916- *WhoAm 90*
Klarwein, Franz 1914- *IntWWM 90*
Klas, Robert C. 1928- *St&PR 91*
Klase, William Roy 1925- *St&PR 91*
Klasko, Herbert Ronald 1949- *WhoEmL 91*
Klasky, Charles Maurice 1949- *WhoWor 91*
Klasnic, John Charles 1939- *WhoWor 91*
Klass, David Brian 1942- *BiDrAPA 89*
Klass, Donald Leroy 1926- *St&PR 91*
Klass, Irene 1916- *St&PR 91*
Klass, Jacob 1945- *St&PR 91*
Klass, Joel Victor 1942- *BiDrAPA 89*
Klass, Kathie 1951- *WhoAmW 91*
Klass, Lisa Ann 1962- *WhoAmW 91*
Klass, Morton 1927- *AuBYP 90, WhoAm 90*
Klass, Paul Mitchell 1959- *WhoE 91*
Klass, Perri Elizabeth 1958- *WhoAmW 91*
Klass, Philip Julian 1919- *WhoAm 90*
Klass, Phyllis Constance 1927- *WhoAmW 91*
Klass, Rosanne Traxler *WhoE 91*
Klass, Sheila Solomon 1927- *WhoWrEP 89*
Klass, Sidney 1916- *St&PR 91*
Klassen, David Morris 1939- *WhoSSW 91*
Klassen, Doreen Helen 1944- *IntWWM 90*
Klassen, Elmer T. *NewYTBS 90 [port]*
Klassen, Elmer T 1908-1990 *CurBio 90N*
Klassen, Elmer Theodore 1908-1990 *BioIn 16*
Klassen, Margreta 1928- *WhoAmW 91*
Klassen, Otto D 1927- *BiDrAPA 89*
Klassen, Peter James 1930- *WhoAm 90*
Klasson, Charles R., Jr. 1958- *St&PR 91*
Klatell, Jack 1918- *WhoAm 90*
Klatell, Robert Edward 1945- *St&PR 91, WhoAm 90*
Klatman, Michael F. 1950- *ODwPR 91*
Klatskin, Bertram 1916- *WhoAm 90*
Klatsky, Bruce J. 1948- *WhoAm 90*
Klatsky, Robert H. 1949- *St&PR 91*
Klatt, Albert Arthur 1920- *WhoAm 90*
Klatt, Gordon Roy 1942- *WhoAm 90*
Klatt, James A. *ODwPR 91*
Klatte, Ernest W 1926- *BiDrAPA 89*
Klatte, Eugene Carl 1928- *WhoAm 90*
Klatzkin Bochner, Robin Jane 1960- *WhoAmW 91*
Klatzky, Sheila R. *WhoAmW 91*
Klaube, Joerg Herbert 1941- *St&PR 91*
Klauber, Edward 1887-1954 *BioIn 16*
Klauber, Rick 1950- *WhoAmA 91*
Klauber, Steven 1947- *St&PR 91*
Klauberg, W.J. 1926- *St&PR 91*
Klauburg, Kurt 1957- *BiDrAPA 89*
Klaucke, Volkert 1944- *WhoAm 90, WhoE 91*
Klauder, Gerard John 1946- *WhoEmL 91, WhoSSW 91*
Klauder, John Rider 1932- *WhoSSW 91*
Klauer, Robert E. 1943- *St&PR 91*
Klauer, William R. 1942- *St&PR 91*
Klaui, Wolfgang 1945- *WhoWor 91*

Klaum, Arthur Damian 1961- WhoEmL 91
Klaus, Billy 1928- Ballpl 90
Klaus, Bobby 1937- Ballpl 90
Klaus, Carl Hanna 1932- WhoAm 90
Klaus, Charles 1935- WhoAm 90
Klaus, David Armin 1945- WhoEmL 91
Klaus, Elmer Erwin 1921- WhoAm 90
Klaus, Francois WhoWor 91
Klaus, Kenneth Sheldon 1952- IntWWM 90
Klaus, Kim Matthews 1955- WhoSSW 91
Klaus, Philip W. 1915- St&PR 91
Klaus, Robert Francis 1932- St&PR 91
Klaus, Roger Dean 1945- WhoEmL 91
Klausen, Raymond 1939- WhoAm 90
Klausing, Lavern H. 1928- St&PR 91
Klausler, Alfred Paul 1910- WhoAm 90
Klausman, Michael St&PR 91
Klausmann, Walter J. 1937- St&PR 91
Klausmeier, Herbert John 1915- WhoAm 90
Klausmeyer, David Michael 1934- St&PR 91
Klausner, Betty 1928- WhoAmA 91
Klausner, Edmond S 1939- BiDrAPA 89
Klausner, Michael David 1954- WhoEmL 91
Klausner, Morley 1948- WhoEmL 91
Klausner, Samuel Zundel 1923- WhoAm 90
Klausner, Tiberius 1931- IntWWM 90
Klavans, Minnie 1915- WhoAmA 91
Klaven, Marvin L 1931- WhoAmA 91
Klavens, George S 1938- BiDrAPA 89
Klavens, Kent Joel 1949- WhoEmL 91
Klaver, Kenneth John 1932- St&PR 91
Klavins, Janis Viliberts 1921- IntWWM 90
Klaviter, Helen Lothrop 1944- WhoAm 90
Klavun, Betty 1916- BiDWomA
Klaw, Barbara Van Doren 1920- WhoAm 90
Klaw, Spencer 1920- WhoAm 90
Klayf, Bernard S. 1921- St&PR 91
Klayman, Avi 1959- WhoWor 91
Klayman, Barry Martin 1952- WhoEmL 91
Klayman, Daniel L. 1929- WhoE 91
Klayman, Norman S. 1936- St&PR 91
Klayman, Raphael 1952- WhoEmL 91
Klayohn, Irvin Louis 1927- St&PR 91
Kleb, Elmer BioIn 16
Kleb, Kathryn 1945- St&PR 91
Kleb, Mary Jane 1917- St&PR 91
Kleb, Melvin E. 1917- St&PR 91
Kleb, William E. 1939- St&PR 91
Kleback, James John 1950- WhoEmL 91
Kleban, Carl H 1945- BiDrAPA 89
Klebanoff, David Michael 1956- BiDrAPA 89
Klebanoff, Philip Samuel 1918- WhoAm 90, WhoE 91
Klebanoff, Seymour Joseph 1927- WhoAm 90
Klebanoff, Stanley Milton 1926- WhoE 91
Klebanov, Roman B BiDrAPA 89
Klebanov, Sofya A BiDrAPA 89
Klebanov, Vladimir BiDrAPA 89
Klebanow, Barbara Elaine 1936- WhoAmW 91
Klebanow, Sheila 1932- BiDrAPA 89
Klebansky, Victor 1930- St&PR 91
Klebba, John Arthur 1956- WhoEmL 91
Klebba, Robert H. 1928- St&PR 91
Klebe, Gene 1918- WhoAmA 91N
Klebe, Giselher 1925- IntWWM 90, WhoWor 91
Kleber, Herbert David 1934- BiDrAPA 89
Kleber, John E. 1941- BioIn 16
Kleberg, Jack Carl 1930- WhoAm 90
Klecan, Eugene Edward 1943- BiDrAPA 89
Kleck, Robert Eldon 1937- WhoAm 90
Kleckner, Ann Cashan 1954- BiDrAPA 89
Kleckner, Dean Ralph 1932- WhoAm 90
Kleckner, Susan 1941- WhoAmA 91
Kleckner, Willard Richards 1937- WhoE 91
Klecko, Joe 1953- BioIn 16
Kleczka, Gerald D. 1943- WhoAm 90
Kleczka, John Casimir, III 1943- St&PR 91
Kledzik, Ronald Bruce 1932- BiDrAPA 89
Klee, Bernhard 1936- IntWWM 90, PenDiMP
Klee, Gerald D 1927- BiDrAPA 89
Klee, Gerald D'Arcy 1927- WhoE 91
Klee, Karl Heinz WhoWor 91
Klee, Kenneth Nathan 1949- WhoEmL 91
Klee, Marc Howard 1955- St&PR 91
Klee, Paul 1879-1940 BioIn 16, IntDcAA 90, WorAlBi
Klee, Robert Erhart 1930- WhoAm 90
Klee, Victor La Rue 1925- WhoAm 90
Kleeberg, Irene Cumming 1932- AuBYP 90
Kleefield, Richard 1936- WhoE 91
Kleeger, Andrew Stanley 1947- WhoSSW 91
Kleeman, James A 1922- BiDrAPA 89
Kleeman, Karen Eve BiDrAPA 89
Kleeman, Michael Jeffrey 1949- WhoAm 90
Kleeman, Neil BioIn 16
Kleeman, Rosslyn Aneta Shore 1922- WhoAmW 91
Kleeman, Susan T 1934- BiDrAPA 89
Kleeman, Walter Benton, Jr. 1918- WhoAm 90
Kleemann, Ron 1937- WhoAmA 91
Kleemann, Ronald Allen 1937- WhoE 91
Kleen, Juergen F BiDrAPA 89
Kleen, Reiner 1951- WhoWor 91
Kleerekoper, Michael 1944- WhoAm 90
Klees, Edward Harris 1959- WhoEmL 91
Kleffman, Carolee Schafer 1937- St&PR 91
Kleger, Barbara S. 1945- WhoE 91
Klegman, Barry H BiDrAPA 89
Klegon, Kenneth Louis 1951- WhoEmL 91
Klehm, Karen Isabel 1957- WhoE 91
Klehm, Michael Early 1955- WhoEmL 91
Klehn, Henry, Jr. 1936- St&PR 91
Kleiber, Carlos BioIn 16
Kleiber, Carlos 1930- PenDiMP, WhoWor 91
Kleiber, Erich 1890-1956 PenDiMP
Kleiber, James William 1934- St&PR 91
Kleid, Wallace 1946- WhoWor 91
Kleidon, Dennis Arthur 1942- WhoAmA 91
Kleihues, Josef Paul 1933- BioIn 16, WhoAm 90
Kleiman, Alan 1938- WhoAmA 91
Kleiman, Alan Boyd 1930- WhoAm 90
Kleiman, Ansel 1925- St&PR 91, WhoAm 90
Kleiman, Bernard 1928- WhoAm 90
Kleiman, David Harold 1934- WhoAm 90
Kleiman, Edwin Jordan 1926- St&PR 91
Kleiman, Gary Howard 1952- WhoAm 90, WhoE 91, WhoWor 91
Kleiman, Ida 1914- St&PR 91
Kleiman, Joseph 1919- WhoAm 90
Kleiman, Macklen 1913- St&PR 91
Kleiman, Stanley 1938- St&PR 91
Kleiman, Steven Lawrence 1942- WhoAm 90
Klein, Aaron E. 1930- AuBYP 90
Klein, Abraham 1927- WhoAm 90
Klein, Albert William 1956- WhoEmL 91
Klein, Alexandria M BiDrAPA 89
Klein, Allen 1938- ConAu 131
Klein, Andreas 1949- IntWWM 90
Klein, Andrew Manning 1941- WhoAm 90
Klein, Anne 1923?-1974 ConAmBL, ConDes 90
Klein, Anne Carolyn 1947- WhoSSW 91
Klein, Anne Sceia 1942- ODwPR 91, WhoAmW 91, WhoE 91, WhoWor 91
Klein, Arnold William 1945- WhoEmL 91, WhoWor 91
Klein, Arthur BioIn 16
Klein, Arthur 1934- WhoE 91
Klein, Arthur Deo WhoSSW 91
Klein, Arthur Luce 1916- WhoAm 90, WhoE 91
Klein, Barbara Pincus 1936- WhoAmW 91
Klein, Barry 1936- St&PR 91
Klein, Barry Todd 1949- WhoE 91
Klein, Beatrice Mary BiDrAPA 89
Klein, Benjamin 1943- WhoAm 90
Klein, Bernard BiDrAPA 89
Klein, Bernard 1921- WhoAm 90, WhoSSW 91, WhoWor 91
Klein, Bernard Elliot 1947- St&PR 91
Klein, Bertram W. 1930- St&PR 91
Klein, Beth Laurie 1953- WhoE 91
Klein, Bradley S. BioIn 16
Klein, Bradley Scott BiDrAPA 89
Klein, Bruce Peter 1933- St&PR 91
Klein, C. Robert 1923- St&PR 91
Klein, Calvin BioIn 16
Klein, Calvin 1942- ConDes 90, WorAlBi
Klein, Calvin Richard 1942- ConAmBL, WhoAm 90, WhoE 91
Klein, Cecelia F 1938- WhoAmA 91
Klein, Cerry Martin 1955- WhoEmL 91
Klein, Charles 1900- WhoAm 90
Klein, Charles H. 1908- St&PR 91
Klein, Charlotte Conrad 1923- WhoAmW 91
Klein, Cheryl Goodrich 1963- WhoEmL 91
Klein, Chuck 1904-1958 Ballpl 90 [port]
Klein, Clifford BioIn 16
Klein, Daniel 1913- St&PR 91
Klein, Daniel Ethan BiDrAPA 89
Klein, Daniel W. 1942- St&PR 91
Klein, David 1919- AuBYP 90, BioIn 16, WhoAm 90, WhoWor 91
Klein, David 1943- WhoAm 90
Klein, David J. AuBYP 90
Klein, David Mark 1946- St&PR 91
Klein, Deborah Cheryl 1953- WhoAmW 91, WhoSSW 91
Klein, Deborah Rae 1951- WhoEmL 91
Klein, Deena R. BiDrAPA 89
Klein, Dona Vellek 1955- WhoAmW 91
Klein, Donald C. BioIn 16
Klein, Donald F 1928- BiDrAPA 89
Klein, Donald Franklin 1928- WhoAm 90, WhoE 91
Klein, Doris 1918- WhoAmA 91
Klein, Doris Elaine 1929- WhoAmW 91
Klein, Dyann Leslie 1951- WhoAmW 91, WhoEmL 91
Klein, E. Gary 1931- St&PR 91
Klein, Edward BiDrAPA 89
Klein, Edward Joel 1936- WhoAm 90
Klein, Edward Peter 1930- St&PR 91
Klein, Elaine 1929- WhoAmW 91
Klein, Elizabeth Archer 1963- WhoAmW 91
Klein, Ellen Lee WhoAmA 91, WhoE 91
Klein, Emery I. 1928- St&PR 91
Klein, Erica BioIn 16
Klein, Ernest Victor 1933- WhoAm 90
Klein, Esther M 1907- WhoAmA 91
Klein, Esther Moyerman 1907- WhoAmW 91
Klein, Eugene V. St&PR 91N
Klein, Eva 1925- WhoWor 91
Klein, Farrel Ivan 1955- BiDrAPA 89
Klein, Fay Magid 1929- WhoAmW 91
Klein, Francis Charles 1949- WhoEmL 91
Klein, Frank J. 1942- St&PR 91
Klein, Frederic William 1922- St&PR 91, WhoE 91
Klein, Frederick William 1950- St&PR 91
Klein, Gary Arnold 1946- BiDrAPA 89
Klein, Gene BioIn 16
Klein, Gene NewYTBS 90 [port]
Klein, George 1925- WhoWor 91
Klein, George deVries 1933- WhoAm 90, WhoWor 91
Klein, George Robert 1909- WhoWor 91
Klein, Gerald W. 1948- St&PR 91
Klein, Gerda Doris 1934- WhoAmW 91
Klein, Gerhart L. 1948- ODwPR 91
Klein, Gregory Alan 1950- St&PR 91
Klein, Gwenda J 1949- WhoAmA 91
Klein, H. Joseph 1942- St&PR 91
Klein, Harold BiDrAPA 89
Klein, Harold Charles 1937- St&PR 91
Klein, Harold Paul 1921- WhoAm 90
Klein, Harriet Farber 1948- WhoAmW 91
Klein, Harry 1909- BiDrAPA 89
Klein, Harvey Allen 1947- WhoSSW 91
Klein, Harvey Jay BiDrAPA 89
Klein, Helen BioIn 16
Klein, Helmut Hermann 1940- St&PR 91
Klein, Henrietta BioIn 16
Klein, Henriette R BiDrAPA 89
Klein, Henry 1920- WhoAm 90
Klein, Henry 1949- WhoEmL 91
Klein, Herbert Arthur AuBYP 90
Klein, Herbert George 1918- St&PR 91, WhoAm 90
Klein, Herbert Sanford 1936- WhoAm 90
Klein, Howard Bruce 1950- WhoE 91
Klein, Ira Steven BiDrAPA 89
Klein, Irma Frances 1936- WhoAmW 91
Klein, Irving 1954- St&PR 91
Klein, Isaac 1905-1979 BioIn 16
Klein, Israel BiDrAPA 89
Klein, James B. St&PR 91
Klein, James Edwin 1951- WhoEmL 91
Klein, James Mikel 1953- WhoEmL 91
Klein, James Ronald 1936- WhoWor 91
Klein, Jan 1936- WhoWor 91
Klein, Jean-Marc Yves 1941- WhoWor 91
Klein, Jeffrey Bernard 1956- BiDrAPA 89
Klein, Jeffrey Mark 1954- WhoEmL 91
Klein, Jeffrey S. 1953- WhoAm 90, WhoEmL 91
Klein, Jerry Louis 1939- WhoSSW 91
Klein, Jill BioIn 16
Klein, Jo Ann Martucci 1947- WhoAmW 91, WhoEmL 91
Klein, Joan Dempsey 1924- WhoAm 90
Klein, John E. 1945- WhoAm 90
Klein, John Francis 1947- WhoSSW 91
Klein, John H. 1946- St&PR 91
Klein, Jonas B. 1922- St&PR 91
Klein, Joseph M. 1931- St&PR 91
Klein, Joseph Mark 1921- St&PR 91, WhoAm 90, WhoWor 91
Klein, Joseph Michelman 1936- WhoAm 90
Klein, Judah Harold 1935- WhoE 91
Klein, Judy Lynn 1945- WhoEmL 91
Klein, Julia Meredith 1955- WhoAm 90
Klein, June Robbins 1948- WhoEmL 91
Klein, Jurgen 1945- WhoWor 91
Klein, Karen 1955- St&PR 91
Klein, Karen Helene 1960- WhoAmW 91
Klein, Kathleen Gregory 1946- ConAu 130
Klein, Kay Janis 1942- WhoAmW 91, WhoSSW 91
Klein, Kenneth 1939- IntWWM 90
Klein, Laura B. BiDrAPA 89
Klein, Laura Jean 1952- BiDrAPA 89
Klein, Lauren Marsha 1957- WhoAmW 91
Klein, Lawrence R. 1920- WorAlBi
Klein, Lawrence Robert 1920- WhoAm 90, WhoE 91, WhoWor 91
Klein, Leonore 1916- AuBYP 90
Klein, Lewis 1927- BioIn 16
Klein, Linda Ann 1959- WhoEmL 91
Klein, Linda Diana 1955- BiDrAPA 89
Klein, Lothar 1932- IntWWM 90
Klein, Lou 1918-1976 Ballpl 90
Klein, Louis David 1951- BiDrAPA 89
Klein, Luella 1924- WhoAm 90
Klein, Lynn 1950- WhoAmA 91
Klein, M. Rosalie WhoAm 90
Klein, Madeline Iris 1947- WhoE 91
Klein, Manuel 1876-1919 OxCPMus
Klein, Marcie ODwPR 91
Klein, Marilyn Weiland 1928- WhoAm 90
Klein, Marina Shank 1950- WhoEmL 91
Klein, Marion Ann 1926- St&PR 91
Klein, Mark Bennett 1949- St&PR 91
Klein, Mark Joel 1943- BiDrAPA 89
Klein, Martin 1927- St&PR 91
Klein, Martin I. 1947- WhoE 91, WhoEmL 91, WhoWor 91
Klein, Martin Jesse 1924- WhoAm 90
Klein, Marvin 1936-1989 BioIn 16
Klein, Matthew J 1952- BiDrAPA 89
Klein, Maurice J. 1908- WhoAm 90
Klein, Max David 1885-1973 BioIn 16
Klein, Melvyn N. BioIn 16
Klein, Melvyn Norman 1941- WhoAm 90
Klein, Michael Bernard 1941- BiDrAPA 89
Klein, Michael D. 1949- St&PR 91
Klein, Michael Elihu 1946- WhoE 91
Klein, Michael Eugene 1940- WhoAmA 91
Klein, Michael Lawrence 1940- WhoAm 90
Klein, Michael Roger 1942- WhoAm 90, WhoWor 91
Klein, Michael Sherman 1951- WhoAm 90, WhoEmL 91
Klein, Michael William 1931- WhoAm 90
Klein, Michele Schutte WhoAmW 91
Klein, Miles M. 1927- St&PR 91
Klein, Milton Martin 1917- WhoAm 90
Klein, Mitchell Sardou 1947- IntWWM 90
Klein, Monika 1953- St&PR 91
Klein, Morton 1925- WhoAm 90
Klein, Morton Joseph 1928- WhoAm 90
Klein, Nancy ODwPR 91
Klein, Nancy Hopkins 1931- WhoAmW 91
Klein, Nancy Kirkland 1954- WhoSSW 91
Klein, Norma 1938- WhoWrEP 89
Klein, Norma 1938-1989 AnObit 1989, AuBYP 90, BioIn 16
Klein, Norman J. 1935- St&PR 91
Klein, Oscar Roy, Jr. 1927- St&PR 91, WhoAm 90
Klein, Oskar Benjamin 1894-1977 DcScB S2
Klein, Patricia Windrow WhoAmA 91
Klein, Paul E. 1934- WhoE 91
Klein, Peter 1907- IntWWM 90, PenDiMP
Klein, Peter 1940- WhoWor 91
Klein, Peter 1946- WhoEmL 91
Klein, Peter L BiDrAPA 89
Klein, Peter Martin 1934- St&PR 91, WhoAm 90
Klein, Peter William 1955- St&PR 91, WhoEmL 91
Klein, Philip Alexander 1927- WhoAm 90
Klein, Philipp 1849-1926 BioIn 16
Klein, Phyllis Katz St&PR 91
Klein, Ralph BiDrAPA 89, BioIn 16
Klein, Raymond Martin 1947- WhoEmL 91
Klein, Raymond S. 1934- WhoE 91
Klein, Raymond W. 1927- St&PR 91
Klein, Richard B. 1938- St&PR 91
Klein, Richard D. 1932- St&PR 91
Klein, Richard Dean 1932- WhoAm 90
Klein, Richard Grant 1942- St&PR 91
Klein, Richard Louis 1936- WhoSSW 91
Klein, Richard Rudolf 1921- IntWWM 90
Klein, Richard Stephen 1938- WhoAm 90, WhoWor 91
Klein, Richard Temple, Jr. 1956- St&PR 91
Klein, Robert 1924- WhoAm 90
Klein, Robert 1942- WhoAm 90, WorAlBi
Klein, Robert Allan 1944- WhoAm 90
Klein, Robert Edward 1926- WhoWor 91
Klein, Robert Leo 1946- WhoEmL 91
Klein, Robert Michael 1939- WhoAm 90
Klein, Robert Milgram BiDrAPA 89
Klein, Robert S. 1926- St&PR 91
Klein, Roberta Phyllis 1934- WhoSSW 91, WhoWor 91
Klein, Robin 1936- BioIn 16, ChlLR 21 [port]
Klein, Rona Elaine B BiDrAPA 89
Klein, Ronald Lloyd 1939- WhoAm 90
Klein, Ruth B. St&PR 91
Klein, Ruth B. 1908- WhoAmW 91
Klein, Sami Weiner 1939- WhoAm 90
Klein, Sandor C 1912- WhoAmA 91
Klein, Seymour M. 1909-1988 BioIn 16
Klein, Sheila Margaret 1943- WhoAmW 91
Klein, Sheldon 1935- WhoAm 90
Klein, Sheldon 1951- St&PR 91
Klein, Sherry Hope 1952- WhoEmL 91
Klein, Shlomo Wolf 1808-1867 BioIn 16
Klein, Snira Lubovsky WhoWor 91
Klein, Solomon A. 1906-1988 BioIn 16
Klein, Stanley Joseph 1916- WhoE 91

Klein, Stephen Thomas 1947- *WhoE 91*
Klein, Steve *BioIn 16*
Klein, Susan E. 1942- *St&PR 91*
Klein, Susan Marsha 1953- *WhoAmW 91, WhoE 91, WhoEmL 91*
Klein, Ted 1926- *ODwPR 91, St&PR 91*
Klein, Theodore Eibon Donald 1947- *WhoAm 90*
Klein, Thomas Ferdinand 1928- *WhoSSW 91*
Klein, Thomas James 1947- *WhoWrEP 89*
Klein, Thomas Martin 1928- *WhoE 91*
Klein, Thomas P. 1953- *St&PR 91*
Klein, Verle Wesley 1933- *WhoAm 90*
Klein, Virginia S. 1936- *WhoWrEP 89*
Klein, Virginia Sue 1936- *WhoAmW 91*
Klein, Walter Charles 1918- *WhoAm 90*
Klein, William David 1954- *WhoEmL 91*
Klein, William Harry 1951- *WhoWrEP 89*
Klein, William J *BiDrAPA 89*
Klein, William Julius, Jr. 1936- *WhoE 91*
Klein, William Kenneth 1916- *WhoAm 90*
Klein, William Wesley 1938- *WhoSSW 91*
Klein, Wolfgang Weissberger 1924- *WhoWor 91*
Klein-Rauner, Harro 1942- *WhoWor 91*
Kleinau, Karl Jurgen 1959- *WhoE 91*
Kleinbardt, Ernest 1875-1962 *WhoAmA 91N*
Kleinbart, David Alan 1947- *WhoEmL 91*
Kleinbauer, W Eugene 1937- *WhoAmA 91*
Kleinberg, David Lewis 1943- *WhoAm 90*
Kleinberg, Fredric Laufer 1949- *WhoWrEP 89*
Kleinberg, Howard J. 1932- *WhoAm 90*
Kleinberg, Israel 1930- *WhoAm 90*
Kleinberg, Jacob 1914- *WhoAm 90*
Kleinberg, Lawrence 1943- *WhoAm 90*
Kleinberg, Marvin H. 1927- *WhoAm 90*
Kleinberg, Susan *WhoAmA 91*
Kleinberger, Elizabeth *BiDrAPA 89*
Kleindienst, Richard Gordon 1923- *BiDrUSE 89, WhoAm 90*
Kleine, Herman 1920- *WhoAm 90*
Kleinelp, William Charles, III 1948- *WhoE 91*
Kleiner, Aaron 1947- *St&PR 91*
Kleiner, Brian 1959- *WhoEmL 91*
Kleiner, Charlotte A 1922- *BiDrAPA 89*
Kleiner, Dick *ConAu 129*
Kleiner, Fred Scott 1948- *WhoAm 90*
Kleiner, Henry T 1922- *BiDrAPA 89*
Kleiner, Henry Thomas 1922- *WhoE 91*
Kleiner, Jillian Anne *BiDrAPA 89*
Kleiner, Joel Howard 1949- *St&PR 91*
Kleiner, Kathleen Allen 1958- *WhoAmW 91*
Kleiner, Mark 1946- *WhoE 91*
Kleiner, Richard Arthur 1921- *ConAu 129, WhoAm 90, WhoWrEP 89*
Kleinerman, Gerald *BiDrAPA 89*
Kleinert, Harold Earl 1922- *WhoAm 90*
Kleinert, Robert William 1923- *St&PR 91*
Kleinfeld, Erwin 1927- *WhoAm 90*
Kleinfeld, Stefanie Lynn 1962- *WhoAmW 91*
Kleinfeldt, Richard C. 1941- *St&PR 91*
Kleinfelter, Mary Ann 1949- *WhoAmW 91*
Kleinhans, Ted 1899-1985 *Ballpl 90*
Kleinhans, Theodore John 1924- *WhoWrEP 89*
Kleinhans-Kelleher, Joan Mary 1954- *WhoAmW 91*
Kleinhanz, Frank J. 1932- *St&PR 91*
Kleinhenz, Christopher 1941- *WhoAm 90*
Kleinhenz, Karen R. 1954- *St&PR 91*
Kleinhenz, Michael J. 1955- *St&PR 91*
Kleinholz, Lewis Hermann 1910- *WhoAm 90*
Kleinke, Joan Ann 1945- *WhoEmL 91*
Kleinknecht, Christian Frederick 1924- *WhoAm 90*
Kleinknecht, Kenneth Samuel 1919- *WhoAm 90*
Kleinlein, Kathy Lynn 1950- *WhoAmW 91, WhoE 91, WhoEmL 91, WhoWor 91*
Kleinlogel, Alexander Ludwig Wilhelm 1929- *WhoWor 91*
Kleinmaier, D.N. *St&PR 91*
Kleinman, Arthur M 1941- *BiDrAPA 89*
Kleinman, Arthur Michael 1941- *WhoAm 90*
Kleinman, Carol Cole 1945- *BiDrAPA 89*
Kleinman, Chester Joseph 1948- *WhoEmL 91*
Kleinman, Edwin 1925- *BiDrAPA 89*
Kleinman, Elissa Corey 1956- *BiDrAPA 89*
Kleinman, Frederick F. 1947- *St&PR 91*
Kleinman, Gary E. 1951- *WhoSSW 91*
Kleinman, George 1951- *WhoWor 91*
Kleinman, Hynda Karen 1947- *WhoAmW 91*
Kleinman, Jerome J 1940- *BiDrAPA 89*
Kleinman, Joel Edward 1945- *BiDrAPA 89*
Kleinman, Judith Martin *BiDrAPA 89*
Kleinman, Kathryn *BioIn 16*
Kleinman, L. Frank 1945- *St&PR 91*
Kleinman, Laurence V. 1942- *ODwPR 91, St&PR 91*
Kleinman, Martin 1952- *WhoE 91*
Kleinman, Martin Ira 1945- *WhoEmL 91*
Kleinman, Marvin E. 1925- *St&PR 91*
Kleinman, Paul Bruce 1953- *BiDrAPA 89*
Kleinman, Peter Donald 1942- *BiDrAPA 89*
Kleinman, Philip 1925- *St&PR 91*
Kleinman, Philip 1932- *ConAu 131*
Kleinman, Philip Julian 1932- *WhoWor 91*
Kleinman, Robert E 1949- *BiDrAPA 89*
Kleinman, Stephen C *BiDrAPA 89*
Kleinman, Steven Charles 1943- *WhoE 91*
Kleinman, Stuart Bruce *BiDrAPA 89*
Kleinman, Stuart Bruce 1959- *WhoE 91*
Kleinman, Sue *WhoAmA 91*
Kleinmann, Leanne *BioIn 16*
Kleinmann, Mortimer V *BiDrAPA 89*
Kleinmanns, Robert Harry 1928- *St&PR 91*
Kleinn, Volker 1939- *St&PR 91*
Kleinow, Red 1879-1929 *Ballpl 90*
Kleinpeter, Edie Wagner 1931- *WhoSSW 91*
Kleinpeter, Sidney Harrison 1942- *WhoWor 91*
Kleinrock, Leonard 1934- *WhoAm 90*
Kleinrock, Lewis James 1932- *WhoAm 90*
Kleinschmidt, Donn Craig *BiDrAPA 89*
Kleinschmidt, Edward Joseph 1951- *WhoWrEP 89*
Kleinschmidt, Hans Joachim *BiDrAPA 89*
Kleinschmidt, Julia J. *WhoAmW 91*
Kleinschmidt, Robert *BioIn 16*
Kleinschmidt, Trude 1956- *BiDrAPA 89*
Kleinschnitz, Barbara Joy 1944- *WhoAmW 91*
Kleinschrod, Walter Andrew 1928- *WhoAm 90, WhoWrEP 89*
Kleinschuster, Stephen John 1939- *WhoAm 90, WhoWor 91*
Kleinsinger, George 1914-1982 *OxCPMus*
Kleinsmith, Bruce John *WhoAmA 91*
Kleinsmith, Bruce John 1942- *ConAu 132*
Kleinsmith, Gene 1942- *WhoAmA 91*
Kleinsmith, Lewis Joel 1942- *WhoAm 90*
Kleinsorge, William Peter 1941- *WhoSSW 91*
Kleinzeller, Arnost 1914- *WhoAm 90*
Kleis, Brian Neal 1958- *BiDrAPA 89*
Kleis, Margaret Anne 1950- *WhoAmW 91*
Kleiser, John Randal 1946- *WhoAm 90*
Kleisner, George Harry 1909-1987 *WhoAm 90*
Kleist, Ewald von 1715-1759 *DcLB 97 [port]*
Kleist, Frank W 1929- *BiDrAPA 89*
Kleist, Heinrich Von 1777-1811 *WorAlBi, WrPh*
Kleist, Peter D. 1918- *St&PR 91*
Kleist, Robert A. *St&PR 91*
Kleister, Tami Rae 1963- *WhoAmW 91*
Klejka, James Patrick *BiDrAPA 89*
Klejment, Anne 1950- *WhoEmL 91*
Klejmont, Rick Joseph 1954- *WhoEmL 91*
Klekoda-Baker, Antonia Marie 1939- *WhoAmW 91*
Klem, Bill 1874-1951 *Ballpl 90 [port], BioIn 16*
Klem, Peter Anton *BiDrAPA 89*
Klem, Robert Bruce 1953- *WhoEmL 91*
Klem, Robert Emmett 1943- *St&PR 91*
Klema, Ernest Donald 1920- *WhoAm 90*
Klembeth, John P. 1926- *St&PR 91*
Klemens, Eberhard Rudolf 1950- *WhoWor 91*
Klemens, Paul Gustav 1925- *WhoAm 90*
Klemens, Roney W. 1938- *St&PR 91*
Klement, Jerry Charles 1940- *St&PR 91*
Klement, Jonathan Joseph 1939- *St&PR 91*
Klement, Maria *BiDrAPA 89*
Klement, Timothy J. 1946- *St&PR 91*
Klement, Vera 1929- *WhoAm 90, WhoAmA 91*
Klemes, Marvin A 1921- *BiDrAPA 89*
Klemin, Diana *AuBYP 90*
Klemke, Elmer Daniel 1926- *WhoAm 90*
Klemke, Werner 1917- *ConDes 90*
Klemm, J Martin 1953- *BiDrAPA 89*
Klemm, Richard Henry 1931- *WhoE 91*
Klemm, William Robert 1934- *WhoSSW 91*
Klemme, Carl William 1928- *St&PR 91, WhoAm 90*
Klemme, Darrell Arthur 1934- *WhoE 91*
Klemme, Donald D. 1945- *St&PR 91*
Klemme, Herbert Lee 1922- *BiDrAPA 89*
Klemme, Howard Charles 1930- *WhoAm 90*
Klemmer, Herbert 1911- *BiDrAPA 89*
Klemons, Barry Allen 1951- *WhoSSW 91*
Klemow, Kenneth Mark 1953- *WhoE 91*
Klemperer, Otto 1885-1973 *PenDiMP, WorAlBi*
Klemperer, Werner 1919- *WorAlBi*
Klemperer, William 1927- *WhoAm 90*
Klemstine, Evelyn Renee 1958- *WhoAmW 91, WhoSSW 91*
Klenda, L.D. 1937- *St&PR 91*
Klengel, August Alexander 1783-1852 *PenDiMP*
Klengel, Julius 1859-1933 *PenDiMP*
Klenicki, Leon 1930- *WhoE 91*
Klenk, Ann Shirley 1951- *WhoSSW 91*
Klenk, Ernst 1896-1971 *DcScB S2*
Klenner, Wolfgang 1942- *WhoWor 91*
Klenoshek, William James 1943- *St&PR 91*
Klenotich, Joseph M. 1946- *St&PR 91*
Klenov, Aleksandr Vladimirovich 1896-1971 *BioIn 16*
Klens, Rick 1952- *WhoE 91*
Klensch, Elsa *BioIn 16*
Klenze, Leo von 1784-1864 *PenDiDA 89*
Klepac, Robert Karl 1943- *WhoSSW 91*
Klepcyk, Ronald Andrew 1946- *WhoSSW 91*
Kleper, Michael Laurence 1947- *WhoE 91*
Klepetar, Wendy Spanglet 1951- *WhoEmL 91*
Klepfer, Ed 1888-1950 *Ballpl 90*
Klepfer, Walter Frank 1952- *WhoSSW 91*
Klepfisz, Irene 1941- *FemiCLE*
Klepinger, John William 1945- *WhoEmL 91*
Klepitsch, Frank John 1957- *WhoEmL 91*
Kleppe, John Arthur 1939- *St&PR 91, WhoAm 90*
Kleppe, Martin I. *WhoAm 90*
Kleppe, Thomas Savig 1919- *BiDrUSE 89*
Klepper, Lawrence R. 1928- *St&PR 91*
Klepper, Lesa Kay 1961- *WhoAmW 91*
Klepper, Michael *ODwPR 91*
Klepper, Robert Fred 1917- *IntWWM 90*
Klepper, Sidney Lester 1914- *St&PR 91*
Kleppner, Daniel 1932- *WhoAm 90*
Klepzig, James K. 1943- *St&PR 91*
Klerekoper, Lise Chamblee 1964- *WhoAmW 91*
Klerk, Albert 1917- *IntWWM 90*
Klerman, Gerald L 1928- *BiDrAPA 89*
Klerman, Gerald Lawrence 1928- *WhoAm 90, WhoE 91*
Klesch, Gary *BioIn 16*
Klesius, Phillip Harry 1938- *WhoAm 90*
Klesmer, Jordan *BiDrAPA 89*
Klesper, Ernst Friedrich Gunter 1927- *WhoWor 91*
Klespies, Linda Sue 1952- *WhoAmW 91*
Klesse, William R. 1946- *St&PR 91*
Kletschka, Harold Dale 1924- *WhoAm 90, WhoWor 91*
Klett, Edwin Lee 1935- *WhoAm 90, WhoE 91*
Klett, Gordon A. 1925- *WhoAm 90*
Klett, Walter Charles 1897-1966 *WhoAmA 91N*
Kletti, Nicholas Burke *BiDrAPA 89*
Klettke, William August 1952- *St&PR 91*
Kletzien, James William 1962- *WhoEmL 91*
Kletzki, Paul 1900-1973 *PenDiMP*
Kleucker, Malinda Finch 1949- *IntWWM 90*
Kleucker, Wallace Harry 1947- *IntWWM 90*
Klevana, Leighton Quentin Joseph 1934- *WhoE 91, WhoWor 91*
Klevans, Edward Harris 1935- *WhoAm 90*
Kleve, Stella *EncCoWW*
Kleven, Clifford Ingemar 1930- *St&PR 91*
Kleven, Stanley Herbert 1940- *WhoAm 90*
Klevens, Stephen S *BiDrAPA 89*
Klever, Anita *AuBYP 90*
Klevins, Richard A. 1946- *St&PR 91*
Kley, Alfred Julius 1895-1957 *WhoAmA 91N*
Kley, John Arthur 1921- *WhoAm 90*
Kley, Juergen 1944- *St&PR 91*
Kleyman, Felix *BiDrAPA 89*
Kleyman, Felix Leo 1948- *WhoE 91*
Kleyn, Edward Gerald 1947- *St&PR 91*
Kleywegt, Adrianus Jan 1932- *WhoWor 91*
Kliban, B 1935-1990 *ConAu 132, NewYTBS 90*
Kliban, Bernard 1935- *WhoAm 90*
Klibaner, Richard B. 1951- *WhoE 91*
Klibanov, Alexander Maxim 1949- *WhoAm 90*
Klibanski, Aron S *BiDrAPA 89*
Klich, William Russell 1944- *St&PR 91*
Klick, Jean E. 1943- *WhoAmW 91*
Klick, Ronald C. *St&PR 91*
Klickmann, Flora 1867-1958 *FemiCLE*
Kliebhan, Jerome L. 1932- *WhoWrEP 89*
Kliebhan, Mary Camille 1923- *WhoAm 90, WhoAmW 91*
Kliefoth, Arthur Bernhard, III 1942- *WhoAm 90, WhoSSW 91*
Kliegl, Eugene F. 1926- *St&PR 91*
Kliegl, John H. *St&PR 91*
Kliegman, Paula Golden 1937- *WhoAmW 91*
Kliem, Peter O. 1938- *St&PR 91*
Kliem, Peter Otto 1938- *WhoAm 90*
Kliem, Ralph Leonard 1951- *WhoEmL 91*
Klieman, Eddie 1918-1979 *Ballpl 90*
Kliemann, Joao Lauro 1918- *WhoWor 91*
Klien, Erika Giovanna 1900-1957 *BiDWomA*
Klien, Walter 1928- *IntWWM 90, PenDiMP*
Kliese, Kenneth Alan 1939- *BiDrAPA 89*
Kliethermes, Mary Alice 1960- *WhoEmL 91*
Kliewer, Kenneth Lee 1935- *WhoAm 90*
Kliewer, Mary Helen Bigham 1952- *WhoEmL 91*
Kliewer, Vernon L 1931- *BiDrAPA 89*
Kliewer, Warren 1931- *WhoWrEP 89*
Kliger, David Michael 1960- *BiDrAPA 89*
Kliger, Milton Richard 1922- *WhoAm 90*
Kligerman, Charles 1916- *BiDrAPA 89*
Kligerman, Morton M. 1917- *WhoAm 90*
Kligerman, Sidney 1915- *BiDrAPA 89*
Kligfeld, Michael 1941- *BiDrAPA 89, WhoE 91*
Kligge, Joseph C. 1947- *St&PR 91*
Kligman, Albert Montgomery *BioIn 16*
Kligman, Ruth *BioIn 16*
Klijn, Anton 1937- *St&PR 91*
Klima, Dennis P. *St&PR 91*
Klima, Ivan 1931- *WorAu 1980 [port]*
Klima, Karen Ann 1960- *WhoAmW 91*
Klima, Martha Scanlan 1938- *WhoAmW 91*
Klima, Petr 1964- *BioIn 16*
Kliman, Gilbert W 1929- *BiDrAPA 89*
Kliman, Merwin 1932- *St&PR 91*
Kliman, Susan Schaefer 1963- *WhoAmW 91*
Klimas, Antanas 1924- *WhoAm 90*
Klimchock, Lou 1939- *Ballpl 90*
Klimczak, Janice Beverly 1944- *WhoE 91*
Kliment, Robert Michael 1933- *WhoAm 90, WhoWor 91*
Kliment, Stephen Alexander 1930- *WhoAm 90*
Klimes, Cyril Stefan 1935- *St&PR 91*
Klimesz, Henry Roman 1926- *WhoE 91*
Klimisch, Richard Leo 1938- *WhoAm 90*
Klimko, Ronald James 1936- *IntWWM 90*
Klimkowski, M. Ann Francis 1931- *WhoAmW 91*
Klimkowski, Ron 1945- *Ballpl 90*
Klimley, April Withington 1944- *ODwPR 91*
Klimov, Elem *BioIn 16*
Klimov, Valery Alexandrovich 1931- *IntWWM 90, PenDiMP*
Klimova, Rita *BioIn 16, NewYTBS 90 [port]*
Klimowicz, Barbara 1927- *AuBYP 90*
Klimowicz, Donna W 1958- *BiDrAPA 89*
Klimowski, Andrzej 1949- *ConDes 90*
Klimstra, Willard David 1919- *WhoAm 90*
Klimt, Gustav 1862-1918 *BioIn 16, IntDcAA 90*
Klimusko, Allan Jon 1961- *St&PR 91*
Klinck, Harold Rutherford 1922- *WhoAm 90*
Klinck, Patricia Ewasco 1940- *WhoAm 90, WhoAmW 91*
Klinckowstroem, Carl von 1884-1969 *EncO&P 3, EncPaPR 91*
Klinda, Ferdinand 1929- *IntWWM 90*
Klindt, Steven 1947- *WhoAm 90, WhoAmA 91*
Klindt, William C 1958- *BiDrAPA 89*
Klindtworth, Kenneth Francis 1934- *WhoAm 90*
Klindworth, Karl 1830-1916 *PenDiMP*
Kline, Alan David 1949- *St&PR 91*
Kline, Alan H. 1934- *St&PR 91*
Kline, Allen Haber, Jr. 1954- *WhoEmL 91*
Kline, Allene *BioIn 16*
Kline, Alma *WhoAmA 91N*
Kline, Amy Jo 1960- *WhoAmW 91*
Kline, Arnold Wolfe 1932- *St&PR 91*
Kline, Barry L. 1946- *St&PR 91*
Kline, Beebe *ODwPR 91*
Kline, Bernard Herman 1916- *St&PR 91*
Kline, Bernard Melvin 1925- *St&PR 91*
Kline, Billy Dan 1935- *St&PR 91*
Kline, Bob 1909- *Ballpl 90*
Kline, Bruce L. 1926- *St&PR 91*
Kline, Claire Benton, Jr. 1925- *WhoAm 90*
Kline, Claire Ellen 1955- *WhoAmW 91*
Kline, David Adam 1923- *WhoSSW 91, WhoWor 91*
Kline, David Gellinger 1934- *WhoAm 90, WhoWor 91*
Kline, David Lamar 1947- *St&PR 91, WhoE 91*
Kline, Donald 1933- *St&PR 91*
Kline, Donald 1948- *WhoAm 90, WhoEmL 91*
Kline, Edmund 1935- *St&PR 91*
Kline, Edward Charles, Jr. 1925- *WhoSSW 91*
Kline, Edward William 1947- *WhoE 91*
Kline, Elliot Howard 1940- *WhoAm 90*
Kline, Eric Hart 1951- *WhoEmL 91*
Kline, Eugene R. 1931- *ODwPR 91*
Kline, Franz 1910-1962 *IntDcAA 90, WhoAmA 91N*

Kline, Franz 1919-1962 *WorAlBi*
Kline, Gary Dean 1949- *St&PR 91*
Kline, George L. Jr. *BiDrAPA 89*
Kline, George Louis 1921- *WhoAm 90, WhoWor 91*
Kline, George T 1874-1956 *WhoAmA 91N*
Kline, George William, II 1949- *WhoEmL 91, WhoSSW 91*
Kline, Gerald Ray 1945- *WhoEmL 91*
Kline, Gloria Jean 1946- *WhoAmW 91*
Kline, Gordon Mabey 1903- *WhoAm 90*
Kline, Gregory Chisholm 1945- *St&PR 91*
Kline, H. Charles 1929- *WhoE 91*
Kline, Harriet 1916- *WhoAmA 91*
Kline, Harry Byrd *WhoAm 90, WhoSSW 91*
Kline, Harvey Franklin 1943- *WhoAm 90*
Kline, Jacob 1917- *WhoAm 90*
Kline, Jacques Howard 1940- *St&PR 91*
Kline, James Edward 1941- *WhoAm 90*
Kline, James Freeman 1939- *WhoSSW 91*
Kline, James L. 1933- *St&PR 91*
Kline, John Alvin 1939- *WhoAm 90*
Kline, John Anthony 1938- *WhoAm 90*
Kline, John William 1919- *WhoAm 90*
Kline, Joseph, Jr. 1947- *BiDrAPA 89*
Kline, Joyce Sheryl 1965- *WhoAmW 91*
Kline, Karen L. 1940- *WhoAmW 91*
Kline, Keith Lawrence 1925- *St&PR 91*
Kline, Kelly Ann 1962- *WhoEmL 91*
Kline, Kenneth Alan 1939- *WhoAm 90*
Kline, Kevin 1947- *WorAlBi*
Kline, Kevin Delaney 1947- *WhoAm 90, WhoE 91*
Kline, Kevin Fredric 1954- *WhoSSW 91*
Kline, Kristine Jo 1957- *WhoAmW 91*
Kline, L. Patton 1928- *St&PR 91*
Kline, Lawrence Y 1940- *BiDrAPA 89*
Kline, Lee B. 1914- *WhoAm 90*
Kline, Linda 1940- *WhoAmW 91*
Kline, Linda Rose 1961- *WhoEmL 91*
Kline, Lloyd Wartel 1931- *WhoWrEP 89*
Kline, Lois Darlene 1926- *St&PR 91*
Kline, Lois Twombley 1949- *WhoEmL 91*
Kline, Louise Letha 1944- *WhoAmW 91*
Kline, Mable Cornelia Page 1928- *WhoAmW 91, WhoWor 91*
Kline, Marc Aaron 1960- *WhoSSW 91*
Kline, Mark Douglas 1952- *BiDrAPA 89*
Kline, Martin Scott 1948- *WhoSSW 91*
Kline, Marvin I. 1952- *WhoEmL 91*
Kline, Mary Frances 1961- *WhoEmL 91*
Kline, Milton Vance 1923- *WhoAm 90, WhoE 91*
Kline, Miriam Marie 1934- *WhoAmW 91*
Kline, Morton *BioIn 16*
Kline, Nancy Mattoon 1937- *WhoE 91*
Kline, Neal Alan 1944- *BiDrAPA 89*
Kline, Pamela Boyce 1946- *WhoE 91*
Kline, Pamela Iris 1958- *WhoEmL 91*
Kline, Patricia Lee 1941- *WhoAmW 91*
Kline, Paul W.M. 1928- *St&PR 91*
Kline, Raymond Adam 1926- *WhoAm 90*
Kline, Richard H. 1927- *St&PR 91*
Kline, Richard R *WhoAmA 91*
Kline, Richard S. *ODwPR 91*
Kline, Richard Stephen 1948- *WhoAm 90*
Kline, Robert Allan 1932- *St&PR 91*
Kline, Robert Lorenzo, III 1960- *WhoEmL 91*
Kline, Robert Reeves 1918- *WhoAm 90*
Kline, Robert Samuel 1938- *WhoSSW 91*
Kline, Robert Vincent 1958- *WhoEmL 91*
Kline, Roberta Lane 1939- *WhoSSW 91*
Kline, Ron 1932- *Ballpl 90*
Kline, Ronald Alan 1952- *WhoSSW 91*
Kline, Ronald Steven 1947- *WhoSSW 91*
Kline, Ronald Wayne 1949- *WhoAmA 91*
Kline, S. Allan *BioIn 16*
Kline, Sanford E. 1928- *St&PR 91*
Kline, Stephen Alan *BiDrAPA 89*
Kline, Stephen Edward 1945- *ConAu 132*
Kline, Stephen Jay 1922- *WhoAm 90*
Kline, Stephen Parks 1954- *WhoEmL 91*
Kline, Steve *ConAu 132*
Kline, Steve 1947- *Ballpl 90*
Kline, Suzy 1943- *AuBYP 90, BioIn 16*
Kline, Timothy Deal 1949- *WhoEmL 91*
Klineberg, John Michael 1938- *WhoAm 90*
Klinedinst, Clare Alane 1947- *WhoE 91*
Klinedinst, John David 1950- *WhoEmL 91*
Klinedinst, Pamela Liane 1948- *WhoAmW 91*
Klinefelter, Hylda Catharine 1929- *WhoAmW 91*
Klinefelter, James Louis 1925- *WhoAm 90*
Klinefelter, Sarah Stephens 1938- *WhoAmW 91*
Klinestiver, Donald Gerould, Jr. *BiDrAPA 89*
Klinetob, Darwin Dana, Jr. *WhoSSW 91*
Kling, Arthur 1929- *BiDrAPA 89*
Kling, David G. 1949- *St&PR 91*
Kling, Gloria S. 1923- *St&PR 91*
Kling, Ian Andrew 1950- *BiDrAPA 89*
Kling, Jean Louise 1939- *WhoAmA 91*
Kling, John J. 1912- *St&PR 91*
Kling, Johnny 1875-1947 *Ballpl 90 [port]*
Kling, Kenneth Raymond 1947- *St&PR 91*
Kling, Merle 1919- *WhoAm 90*
Kling, Mitchel Allan 1956- *BiDrAPA 89*
Kling, Phradie 1933- *WhoAmW 91*
Kling, Richard Stephen 1945- *WhoEmL 91*
Kling, Richard William 1940- *St&PR 91, WhoAm 90*
Kling, S. Lee 1928- *St&PR 91*
Kling, Seena Fran 1949- *WhoE 91*
Kling, Suzanne K *BiDrAPA 89*
Kling, Vincent G 1916- *ConDes 90*
Kling, Wiley B., Jr. 1947- *St&PR 91*
Kling, William 1915- *WhoAm 90, WhoWor 91*
Kling, William Hugh 1942- *WhoAm 90*
Kling, Woody *BioIn 16*
Klingaman, Robert LeRoy 1914- *WhoE 91, WhoWor 91*
Klingberg, Alice Lillian 1914- *WhoAmW 91*
Klingbiel, Paul Herman 1919- *WhoSSW 91*
Klingel, Martin Allen 1941- *WhoSSW 91*
Klingeman, Ellis Dudley 1932- *St&PR 91*
Klingenberg, Peter 1953- *WhoSSW 91*
Klingenberg, William Henry, Jr. 1934- *St&PR 91*
Klingensmith, Arthur Paul 1949- *WhoEmL 91, WhoWor 91*
Klingensmith, Thelma Hyde 1904- *WhoAmW 91*
Klingenstein, Alan Lee 1954- *WhoEmL 91*
Klingenstein, Frederick Adler 1931- *WhoAm 90*
Klingenstein, R. James 1948- *WhoEmL 91*
Klinger, Alan Mark 1956- *WhoEmL 91*
Klinger, Allen 1937- *WhoAm 90*
Klinger, Bob 1908-1977 *Ballpl 90*
Klinger, David Jonathan 1954- *WhoE 91*
Klinger, Ernest T. 1935- *St&PR 91*
Klinger, Friedrich Maximilian 1752-1831 *DcLB 94 [port]*
Klinger, Harry Ernest *WhoWrEP 89*
Klinger, Johann Gottfried 1711-1781 *PenDiDA 89*
Klinger, Joseph R. 1942- *St&PR 91*
Klinger, Judith Ann 1943- *WhoAmW 91*
Klinger, Linda Anne 1949- *WhoAmW 91*
Klinger, Max 1857-1920 *IntDcAA 90*
Klinger, Michael 1921-1989 *AnObit 1989*
Klinger, Oliver Cecil 1910- *WhoAm 90*
Klinger, Philip W. 1935- *St&PR 91*
Klinger, Rochelle Lynn 1958- *BiDrAPA 89*
Klinger, Sherry Nadine 1953- *WhoEmL 91*
Klinger, Stephen *BiDrAPA 89*
Klinger, Walter Theodor 1934- *WhoWor 91*
Klingerman, Robert Harvey 1939- *St&PR 91*
Klinges, David Henry 1928- *St&PR 91, WhoAm 90*
Klinghoffer, Clara 1900-1970 *BiDWomA*
Klinghoffer, June Florence 1921- *WhoAmW 91*
Klinghoffer, Steven Harold 1950- *WhoEmL 91*
Klingle, Philip Anthony 1950- *WhoEmL 91*
Klingler, Eugene Herman 1932- *WhoAm 90*
Klingler, Raymond P. 1947- *St&PR 91*
Klingman, Alicia Lynn 1954- *WhoEmL 91*
Klingman, Darwin 1944-1989 *BioIn 16*
Klingsberg, David 1934- *WhoAm 90*
Klink, Arlene Marie *BiDrAPA 89*
Klink, Bruce C. 1950- *St&PR 91*
Klink, Fredric J. 1933- *WhoAm 90*
Klink, Hans-Jurgen Theodor 1933- *WhoWor 91*
Klink, Harold Anthony 1942- *St&PR 91*
Klink, J. Donald 1936- *St&PR 91*
Klink, Karin Elizabeth 1937- *WhoWor 91*
Klink, Patricia de Blank 1945- *WhoAmW 91*
Klinker, Orpha *WhoAmA 91N*
Klinkert, Kenneth F. *BioIn 16*
Klinkhamer, Frans Richard 1956- *WhoEmL 91*
Klinkowitz, Jerome 1943- *WhoWrEP 89*
Klinman, Jerome J 1934- *BiDrAPA 89*
Klinman, Jerome Joseph 1934- *WhoE 91*
Klinman, Judith Pollock 1941- *WhoAm 90*
Klinman, Norman Ralph 1937- *WhoAm 90*
Klinsky, Arnold 1944- *WhoE 91*
Klinsky, Steven Bruce 1956- *WhoE 91*
Klint, Douglas Earl 1950- *St&PR 91*
Klint, Hilma af 1862-1944 *BiDWomA, BioIn 16*
Klint, Kaare 1888-1954 *PenDiDA 89*
Klint, P.V. Jensen *PenDiDA 89*
Klinzman, Frank Watkins 1928- *St&PR 91*
Klion, Stanley Ring 1923- *WhoAm 90*
Klip, Eduard Cornelis 1939- *WhoWor 91*
Klipfel, Karl Jacob Christian *PenDiDA 89*
Klipfell, John Martin 1949- *St&PR 91*
Klipfell, John Martin, III 1949- *WhoAm 90, WhoEmL 91*
Kliphardt, Raymond A. 1917- *WhoAm 90*
Kliphouse, Everett A. 1941- *St&PR 91*
Klippel, Terry J. 1952- *St&PR 91*
Klipper, Daniel Stephen 1953- *WhoEmL 91*
Klipper, Harold 1932- *St&PR 91*
Klipper, Stuart David 1941- *WhoAm 90, WhoAmA 91*
Klippert, Richard Hobdell, Jr. 1940- *WhoWor 91*
Klippstatter, Kurt 1934- *IntWWM 90*
Klippstatter, Kurt L. 1934- *WhoAm 90*
Klippstein, Johnny 1927- *Ballpl 90*
Klipsch, M. David 1941- *St&PR 91*
Klipstein, Charlotte von 1837-1898 *EncCoWW*
Klipstein, Editha 1880-1953 *EncCoWW*
Klipstein, Kenneth H. 1900- *St&PR 91*
Klipstine, Geo. L. 1925- *St&PR 91*
Klipstine, John L. 1947- *St&PR 91*
Klir, George Jiri 1932- *WhoAm 90, WhoE 91*
Kliris, Angeliki 1956- *WhoE 91*
Klisart, Luke H. 1930- *St&PR 91*
Klitgaard, Robert J. 1916- *St&PR 91*
Klitzing, Klaus von 1943- *WhoWor 91, WorAlBi*
Klitzke, Theodore Elmer 1915- *WhoAm 90, WhoAmA 91, WhoWor 91*
Klitzman, Robert *BioIn 16*
Klitzman, Robert Lloyd 1958- *BiDrAPA 89, WhoE 91*
Klitzsch, Hans Eberhard 1933- *WhoWor 91*
Kliuchevskii, V. O. 1841-1911 *BioIn 16*
Kliuchevskii, Vasilii Osipovich 1841-1911 *BioIn 16*
Kliuev, Nikolai Alekseevich 1887-1937 *BioIn 16*
Klivans, Norman R. 1918- *St&PR 91*
Klobasa, John Anthony 1951- *WhoEmL 91*
Klobe, Tom 1940- *WhoAmA 91*
Klobedanz, Fred 1871-1940 *Ballpl 90*
Klobucar, Berislav 1924- *IntWWM 90, PenDiMP*
Klobusicky, Tibor Bela 1911- *St&PR 91*
Kloc, Clifford John 1946- *St&PR 91*
Klocek, Gary R. 1950- *St&PR 91*
Klocek, Kathleen Anne 1948- *WhoAmW 91*
Klock, Benny Leroy 1934- *WhoSSW 91*
Klock, Joseph Peter, Jr. 1949- *WhoAm 90, WhoWor 91*
Klock, Lawrence 1947- *WhoEmL 91*
Klocke, Mary Margaret 1961- *WhoAmW 91*
Klockenga, Michael Edwin 1950- *WhoEmL 91*
Klockhaus, Ruth Irmgard 1923- *WhoWor 91*
Klodnicki, Z. George 1923- *St&PR 91*
Klodowski, Amy Martha Auslander 1952- *WhoAmW 91*
Klodt, Gerald Joseph 1949- *WhoEmL 91*
Klodzinski, Beatrice Davis 1950- *WhoAmW 91*
Klodzinski, Joseph Anthony 1942- *WhoWor 91*
Kloeber, Ken Wade 1953- *WhoEmL 91*
Kloecker, John F. 1923- *St&PR 91*
Kloepfer, Marguerite Fonnesbeck 1916- *WhoAmW 91, WhoWor 91*
Kloesel, George W. 1950- *St&PR 91*
Kloesel, Mark Anthony 1953- *St&PR 91*
Kloesmeyer, Iliana Marisa 1958- *WhoAmW 91, WhoE 91*
Kloft, Werner Jakob 1925- *WhoWor 91*
Klohn, Earle Jardin 1927- *WhoAm 90*
Klohn, Franklin James, Jr. 1951- *WhoWor 91*
Klohr, James Walter 1924- *St&PR 91*
Kloiber, Lawrence A. *St&PR 91*
Kloker, Rebecca Jean *BiDrAPA 89*
Klombers, Norman 1923- *WhoAm 90*
Klomburg, Albert Henry 1933- *St&PR 91*
Klonarides, Carole Ann 1951- *WhoAmA 91*
Klonaris, Mary 1928- *WhoAmW 91*
Klong, Lawrence Alan 1938- *St&PR 91*
Klonglan, Gerald Edward 1936- *WhoAm 90*
Klonis, Bernard 1906-1957 *WhoAmA 91N*
Klonis, Stewart 1902-1989 *BioIn 16*
Klonoff, Harry 1924- *WhoAm 90, WhoWor 91*
Klonoff, Robert Howard 1955- *WhoEmL 91*
Klonowski, Joan Theresa *BiDrAPA 89*
Klontz, Virgil J. 1916- *WhoWor 91*
Klontz, William J 1951- *BiDrAPA 89*
Kloor, Morris John, Jr. 1936- *BiDrAPA 89*
Kloos, Jeanette Doris Burns 1950- *WhoAmW 91*
Klooster, Frederique Fako 1935- *WhoE 91*
Klooster, Judson 1925- *WhoAm 90*
Klooster, Willem Gerrit 1935- *WhoWor 91*
Kloosterman, Simke 1876-1938 *EncCoWW*
Klopf, Gordon John 1917- *WhoAm 90*
Klopf, John Lance 1945- *WhoEmL 91*
Klopfenstein, Edward Lee 1941- *St&PR 91*
Klopfenstein, Melinda Lee 1944- *WhoAmW 91*
Klopfenstein, Philip Arthur 1937- *WhoAm 90, WhoAmA 91*
Klopfer, Joanne 1954- *WhoAmW 91*
Klopfleisch, Stephanie Squance 1940- *WhoAmW 91*
Klopman, Gilles 1933- *WhoAm 90*
Klopman, William Allen 1921- *WhoSSW 91*
Klopott, Zvi Simcha *BiDrAPA 89*
Klopott, Zvi Simcha 1948- *WhoE 91*
Kloppel, Thomas Mathew 1950- *WhoEmL 91*
Kloppenburg, Aloka *BioIn 16*
Kloppenburg, Bonaventura 1919- *EncO&P 3*
Klopper, Jeffrey Howard *BiDrAPA 89*
Klopper, Ralph M 1935- *BiDrAPA 89*
Kloppers, Jacobus Joubert Krige 1937- *IntWWM 90*
Klopping, Martin Louis 1953- *St&PR 91*
Klopstock, Friedrich Gottlieb 1724-1803 *DcLB 97 [port]*
Klopstock, Margareta Moller 1728-1758 *EncCoWW*
Klopstock, Meta 1728-1758 *DcLB 97 [port]*
Klopstock, William J 1928- *BiDrAPA 89*
Klos, Elmar 1910- *BioIn 16*
Klos, Elmer 1910- *WhoWor 91*
Klos, Jerome John 1927- *WhoAm 90*
Klos, Wolfgang 1953- *IntWWM 90*
Klose, Christopher 1945- *ODwPR 91*
Klose, Hyacinthe Eleonore 1808-1880 *PenDiMP*
Klose, Karl W. 1924- *St&PR 91*
Klose, Margarete 1902-1968 *PenDiMP*
Klose, Patsy Mae Ellen 1941- *WhoAmW 91*
Klosk, Steven Mark 1957- *WhoE 91*
Kloska, Ronald Frank 1933- *St&PR 91, WhoAm 90*
Kloske, Dennis Edward 1954- *WhoAm 90*
Kloskowska, Antonina 1919- *WhoWor 91*
Kloskowski, Vincent John, Jr. 1934- *WhoE 91, WhoWor 91*
Klosner, Jerome Martin 1928- *WhoAm 90*
Kloss, Gene 1903- *WhoAm 90, WhoAmA 91, WhoWor 91*
Kloss, Henry E. *St&PR 91*
Kloss, Jethro 1863-1946 *NewAgE 90*
Kloss, John J. 1949- *St&PR 91*
Kloss, Raymond John *BiDrAPA 89*
Kloss, Richard C. 1954- *St&PR 91*
Kloss, Robert William 1949- *WhoAm 90, WhoWor 91*
Kloss, William 1937- *WhoAmA 91*
Klosson, Boris Hansen *NewYTBS 90*
Klosson, Michael 1949- *WhoAm 90*
Klossowski, Michel Balthazar 1908- *BioIn 16*
Kloster, Burton J., Jr. 1931- *St&PR 91*
Kloster, Burton John, Jr. 1931- *WhoAm 90*
Kloster, Doris *BioIn 16*
Kloster, Einar 1937- *WhoAm 90, WhoE 91*
Kloster, Frank Ellis 1929- *WhoAm 90*
Klosterhoff, Bruce Eugene 1945- *BiDrAPA 89*
Klostermaier, Klaus Konrad 1933- *WhoAm 90*
Klosterman, Albert L. 1942- *St&PR 91*
Klosterman, Albert Leonard 1942- *WhoAm 90*
Klosterman, Patricia Ann 1959- *WhoAmW 91*
Klosterman, Robert John 1951- *WhoEmL 91*
Kloth, Edward W 1918- *BiDrAPA 89*
Kloth, Rachell Darden 1939- *WhoAmW 91*
Kloth, Timothy Tom 1954- *IntWWM 90, WhoSSW 91*
Klotman, Robert Howard 1918- *IntWWM 90, WhoAm 90*
Klots, Alexander Barrett 1903-1989 *BioIn 16, SmATA 62*
Klotter, John Charles 1918- *WhoAm 90*
Klotter, Ronald Lawrence 1960- *WhoEmL 91*
Klotz, Arthur Paul 1913- *WhoAm 90*
Klotz, Charles Rodger 1942- *WhoAm 90*
Klotz, Criston Eugene 1954- *WhoEmL 91*
Klotz, David Wayne 1952- *WhoSSW 91*
Klotz, Dorothea Gloria 1945- *WhoAmW 91*
Klotz, Florence *WhoAm 90, WhoAmW 91*
Klotz, Florence 1920- *ConDes 90*
Klotz, Gary Willard 1951- *WhoEmL 91*
Klotz, Harold Andrew, Jr. 1956- *WhoEmL 91*
Klotz, Henrietta Stein 1901-1988 *BioIn 16*
Klotz, Howard S. 1939- *St&PR 91*
Klotz, Irving Myron 1916- *WhoAm 90*
Klotz, John Wesley 1919- *WhoAm 90*
Klotz, Richard G. 1954- *St&PR 91*
Klotz, Suzanne 1944- *WhoAmA 91*
Klotz, Thomas Albert *BiDrAPA 89*

Klotz, William Henry 1919- *St&PR 91*
Klotz-Chamberlin, Peter *BioIn 16*
Klotzbach, Robert James 1922- *WhoAm 90*
Klotzback, Walter E. *BioIn 16*
Klotzer, Charles Lothar 1925- *WhoWrEP 89*
Klouda, Naomi Gladys 1960- *WhoWrEP 89*
Klove, Carole Ann 1958- *WhoEmL 91*
Klozotsky, John K. 1937- *St&PR 91*
Kluber, Eugene Clare 1941- *St&PR 91*
Klubnikin, Kheryn 1951- *WhoAmW 91*
Kluck, Alexander Von 1846-1934 *WorAlBi*
Kluck, Clarence Joseph 1929- *WhoWor 91*
Kluck, John James, Jr. 1944- *BiDrAPA 89*
Kluckko, Thomas M. 1940- *St&PR 91*
Kluckowski, Stanley A., Jr. 1933- *St&PR 91*
Kludt, James B *BiDrAPA 89*
Klue, Harold Ellis *BioIn 16*
Klueh, Kenneth Cyril 1937- *St&PR 91, WhoAm 90*
Klueting, Harm 1949- *WhoWor 91*
Kluff, Barry *WhoWrEP 89*
Kluft, Gerald McElroy 1947- *WhoSSW 91*
Kluft, Richard P *BiDrAPA 89*
Kluft, Richard P. 1943- *WhoE 91*
Klug, Aaron 1926- *WhoAm 90, WhoWor 91, WorAlBi*
Klug, Mark William 1926- *St&PR 91*
Klug, Richard Paul 1934- *St&PR 91*
Klug, Ronald Allan 1939- *WhoWrEP 89*
Klug, William Frederick, IV 1939- *St&PR 91*
Kluge, Alexander 1932- *BioIn 16*
Kluge, J. Hans 1928- *WhoE 91*
Kluge, John 1914- *News 91-1 [port]*
Kluge, John Werner *BioIn 16*
Kluge, John Werner 1914- *ConAmBL, St&PR 91, WhoAm 90, WhoWor 91*
Kluge, Juergen 1953- *WhoWor 91*
Kluge, Len H. 1945- *WhoWor 91*
Kluge, Patricia *BioIn 16*
Kluge, Randy Scott 1962- *WhoSSW 91*
Kluger, Barry D. *ODwPR 91*
Kluger, Joseph Harris 1955- *WhoAm 90, WhoE 91*
Kluger, Richard 1934- *WhoAm 90*
Kluger, Ruth 1931- *WhoAm 90*
Klugh, James Richard 1931- *WhoAm 90, WhoWor 91*
Klugheit, Marianne Nebel *BiDrAPA 89*
Klugman, Edgar 1925- *ConAu 132*
Klugman, Jack 1922- *WhoAm 90, WorAlBi*
Klugman, Jeffry 1947- *BiDrAPA 89*
Klugman, Peter Jay 1942- *WhoE 91*
Klugman, Robert 1944- *BiDrAPA 89*
Klugman, Robert 1947- *St&PR 91*
Klugman, Yale Lee 1931- *BiDrAPA 89*
Kluk, Nada 1946- *WhoAmW 91*
Klukiewicz, Avis Margaret 1953- *WhoE 91*
Klumb, Richard A. 1931- *St&PR 91*
Klumb, Ted *ODwPR 91*
Klumpke, Anna Elizabeth 1856-1942 *BiDWomA*
Klumpner, George H 1924- *BiDrAPA 89*
Klumpner, Inger Olson 1925- *WhoAmW 91*
Klumpp, Anna Marie *BiDrAPA 89*
Klumpp, Donald K. 1943- *St&PR 91*
Klumpp, Gustav 1902-1980 *MusmAFA*
Klumpp, Larry Carl 1944- *St&PR 91*
Klumpp, Michael John 1941- *St&PR 91*
Klumpp, Theodore G. 1903- *St&PR 91*
Klundt, Irwin L. 1936- *St&PR 91*
Kluner, Kerry Joel *BiDrAPA 89*
Klunk, Walter Edward 1924- *St&PR 91*
Klunk, William E. 1956- *BiDrAPA 89*
Klunzinger, Dwight L. 1954- *St&PR 91*
Klurfeld, James Michael 1945- *WhoAm 90*
Klus, William Joseph 1943- *WhoSSW 91*
Klusak, Jan-Filip 1934- *IntWWM 90*
Kluski, Franek 1874- *EncO&P 3, EncPaPR 91*
Klussendorf, Michael John 1950- *WhoEmL 91*
Klussmann, Rudolf 1937- *WhoWor 91*
Kluszewski, Ted 1924-1988 *Ballpl 90 [port], BioIn 16*
Klutchko, Bruce Stewart 1951- *BiDrAPA 89*
Klute, Peter P. 1941- *ODwPR 91*
Klutts, Mickey 1954- *Ballpl 90*
Kluttz, Clyde 1917-1979 *Ballpl 90*
Kluttz, Joseph Branch Craige 1951- *WhoEmL 91*
Klutz, Anthony Aloysius, Jr. 1954- *WhoSSW 91*
Klutznick, Philip M. 1907- *BiDrUSE 89, WhoAm 90, WhoWor 91*
Klutznick, Thomas Joseph 1939- *WhoAm 90*
Kluver, Billy 1927- *WhoAmA 91*
Kluwin, John Andrew 1907- *WhoAm 90*
Kluxen, Herman Anthony, III 1950- *St&PR 91*
Kluxen, Wolfgang 1922- *WhoWor 91*
Kluznik, John Cooke *BiDrAPA 89*
Klyashtorny, Boris N. 1940- *BiDrAPA 89*
Klyce, Dorothy Jean Walleck 1942- *WhoAmW 91*
Klykylo, William M *BiDrAPA 89*
Klykylo, William Michael 1948- *WhoEmL 91*
Klyman, Anne Griffiths 1936- *WhoWrEP 89*
Klyman, Cassandra M 1938- *BiDrAPA 89*
Kmentt, Waldemar 1929- *IntWWM 90*
Kmiec, Douglas William 1951- *WhoAm 90*
Kmiecik, Tadeusz 1920- *BiDrAPA 89*
Kmiecik, Thomas T. 1959- *St&PR 91*
Kmietowicz, Zbigniew Wawrzyniec 1935- *WhoWor 91*
Knaack, Howard 1924- *St&PR 91*
Knaack, Keith Otto 1928- *WhoAm 90*
Knab, Donald Ralph 1922- *WhoAm 90*
Knab, Doris Elisabeth 1928- *WhoWor 91*
Knabb, Albert Stanley 1937- *St&PR 91*
Knabe, George William, Jr. 1924- *WhoAm 90*
Knabe, Otto 1884-1961 *Ballpl 90*
Knabenbauer, Alan Lee 1952- *WhoEmL 91*
Knable, Michael Boyd *BiDrAPA 89*
Knabusch, Charles Thair 1939- *WhoAm 90*
Knachel, Philip Atherton 1926- *WhoAm 90*
Knack, Thomas Michael 1950- *WhoEmL 91*
Knackert, Julian Martin 1933- *WhoSSW 91*
Knackstedt, Mary V. 1940- *WhoE 91*
Knadle, Richard D. *WhoAm 90*
Knafo, Danielle Sylvia 1953- *WhoAmW 91*
Knafo, Jerry Robert 1957- *WhoEmL 91*
Knag, Howard A. *BioIn 16*
Knag, Paul Everett 1948- *WhoEmL 91*
Knaggs, Nelson Stuart 1907- *WhoAm 90*
Knak, Roger Dale 1958- *WhoEmL 91*
Knake, Barry Edward 1946- *WhoEmL 91, WhoWor 91*
Knake, Ellery Louis 1927- *WhoAm 90*
Knape, Raymond E. 1931- *St&PR 91*
Knapen, Hugo 1950- *WhoWor 91*
Knapheide, Harold W., III 1945- *St&PR 91*
Knapp, Alexander Victor 1945- *IntWWM 90*
Knapp, Ann Hall 1947- *WhoSSW 91*
Knapp, Barbara Curtis 1933- *WhoAmW 91*
Knapp, Bernard Louis 1952- *WhoEmL 91*
Knapp, Bettina Liebowitz 1926- *WhoAm 90, WhoWrEP 89*
Knapp, Carolyn Marie 1956- *WhoEmL 91*
Knapp, Charles B. 1946- *WhoAm 90, WhoSSW 91*
Knapp, Chris 1953- *Ballpl 90*
Knapp, Clement B., Jr. 1942- *St&PR 91*
Knapp, Cleon Talboys 1937- *WhoAm 90, WhoWor 91*
Knapp, Constance Anne 1948- *WhoAmW 91, WhoE 91, WhoEmL 91*
Knapp, David Arthur 1960- *WhoSSW 91*
Knapp, David Curtis 1927- *WhoAm 90, WhoE 91*
Knapp, David Hebard 1938- *WhoAm 90*
Knapp, David L. 1939- *St&PR 91*
Knapp, David W. 1936- *St&PR 91*
Knapp, Dennis Raymond 1912- *WhoAm 90*
Knapp, Edward Alan 1932- *WhoAm 90*
Knapp, Edward D. 1934- *St&PR 91*
Knapp, Elizabeth-Ann Campbell *BioIn 16*
Knapp, Frederick J. 1944- *WhoAm 90*
Knapp, Gary Alan 1951- *WhoSSW 91*
Knapp, Gary W. 1956- *St&PR 91*
Knapp, Gene Lewis 1934- *St&PR 91*
Knapp, George Griff Prather 1923- *WhoAm 90*
Knapp, George Owen 1940- *St&PR 91*
Knapp, George Robert 1947- *WhoEmL 91*
Knapp, Gregory Peter 1942- *St&PR 91*
Knapp, Harold A. *BioIn 16*
Knapp, Horst Herbert 1925- *WhoWor 91*
Knapp, Ilana A. 1952- *St&PR 91*
Knapp, Jacob 1799-1874 *BioIn 16*
Knapp, James Ian Keith 1943- *WhoAm 90*
Knapp, Jean Carmen 1921- *WhoAmW 91*
Knapp, John C. *ODwPR 91*
Knapp, John F. 1848-1912 *AmLegL*
Knapp, John Merrill 1914- *WhoAm 90*
Knapp, John Williams 1932- *WhoAm 90*
Knapp, Joseph A. 1943- *WhoE 91*
Knapp, Jules F. 1928- *St&PR 91*
Knapp, K. Brad 1955- *WhoEmL 91*
Knapp, Kevin Douglas 1960- *WhoEmL 91*
Knapp, Lee A. 1958- *St&PR 91*
Knapp, Lillian *BioIn 16*
Knapp, Lloyd W. 1931- *St&PR 91*
Knapp, Louis H. 1942- *St&PR 91*
Knapp, Marc Steven 1944- *WhoE 91*
Knapp, Margo *BiDrAPA 89*
Knapp, Marilee Tiberio 1942- *WhoAmW 91*
Knapp, Michael 1946- *St&PR 91*
Knapp, Mildred Florence 1932- *WhoAmW 91*
Knapp, Nancy Hay 1922- *WhoAmW 91*
Knapp, Patrick William 1951- *WhoE 91*
Knapp, Paul Raymond 1945- *St&PR 91*
Knapp, Peter 1947- *IntWWM 90*
Knapp, Peter Hobart 1916- *BiDrAPA 89, WhoE 91*
Knapp, Peter O. 1930- *St&PR 91*
Knapp, Peter Osborn 1930- *WhoAm 90*
Knapp, Philip Bernard 1923- *WhoE 91, WhoWor 91*
Knapp, Richard Bruce 1933- *WhoAm 90*
Knapp, Richard D *BiDrAPA 89*
Knapp, Richard David 1946- *BiDrAPA 89*
Knapp, Richard Elwood 1928- *St&PR 91*
Knapp, Richard Maitland 1941- *WhoAm 90*
Knapp, Robert Charles 1927- *WhoAm 90*
Knapp, Robert S. 1931- *ODwPR 91*
Knapp, Robert Sinclair *BiDrAPA 89*
Knapp, Ronald Gary 1940- *ConAu 30NR, WhoE 91*
Knapp, Roselyn M. 1930- *WhoE 91*
Knapp, Sadie Magnet 1909- *WhoAmA 91*
Knapp, Samuel L. 1783-1838 *BioIn 16*
Knapp, Susan E. 1947- *WhoE 91*
Knapp, Theresa Daniel 1926- *WhoAmW 91*
Knapp, Thomas Edwin 1925- *WhoAm 90*
Knapp, Tillmann Wilhelm 1941- *WhoWor 91*
Knapp, Tom 1925- *WhoAmA 91*
Knapp, Vaughn Robert 1933- *WhoAm 90*
Knapp, Victor Richard 1955- *BiDrAPA 89*
Knapp, Virginia Estella 1919- *WhoAmW 91*
Knapp, Whitman 1909- *WhoAm 90*
Knapp, William Arnold, Jr. 1925- *WhoSSW 91*
Knapp, William Bernard 1921- *WhoWor 91*
Knapp, William R. *NewYTBS 90*
Knapp, William R. 1920?-1990 *ConAu 132*
Knappe, Eckhard Dietrich 1943- *WhoWor 91*
Knappenberger, Dorothy Lavina 1906- *WhoAmW 91*
Knappenberger, Jonathan Charles 1966- *WhoEmL 91*
Knappenberger, Paul Henry, Jr. 1942- *WhoAm 90*
Knappertsbusch, Gerda *BioIn 16*
Knappertsbusch, Hans 1888-1965 *PenDiMP*
Knappman, Edward William 1943- *WhoAm 90*
Knappman, Elizabeth Frost 1943- *WhoWrEP 89*
Knarr, Willard A. 1947- *St&PR 91*
Knatchbull, Lucy 1584-1629 *BiDEWW, FemiCLE*
Knatchbull, Mary *BiDEWW*
Knatchbull, Mary *BiDEWW*
Knaths, Karl 1891-1971 *BioIn 16, WhoAmA 91N*
Knaub, Charlotte Juanita 1933 *WhoAmW 91*
Knaub, Donald E 1936- *WhoAmA 91*
Knaub, Donald Edward 1936- *WhoAm 90*
Knaub, Ray *BioIn 16*
Knaub, Raymond L 1940- *WhoAmA 91*
Knauer, Carl 1940- *St&PR 91*
Knauer, Edward 1934- *St&PR 91*
Knauer, Georg Nicolaus 1926- *WhoAm 90*
Knauer, James A. 1946- *WhoEmL 91*
Knauer, Joseph D. 1918- *St&PR 91*
Knauer, Karen Lee 1960- *WhoEmL 91*
Knauer, Nancy J. 1961- *WhoAmW 91*
Knauer, Velma Stanford 1918- *WhoAmW 91*
Knauer, Virginia Harrington 1915- *WhoAm 90, WhoE 91*
Knauert, Arthur Paul 1944- *BiDrAPA 89*
Knauf, Alan Jon 1956- *WhoEmL 91*
Knauf, Albert E. 1943- *St&PR 91*
Knaur, John Sherman, Jr. 1924- *St&PR 91*
Knaus, Robert A. 1936- *ODwPR 91*
Knaus, Ronald L 1937- *BiDrAPA 89*
Knauss, Earl L. 1933- *WhoAm 90*
Knauss, Jeffery Paul 1953- *St&PR 91*
Knauss, John Atkinson 1925- *BioIn 16, WhoAm 90*
Knauss, Keith David 1945- *WhoEmL 91*
Knauss, Peter R. *BioIn 16*
Knauss, Peter R 1937-1990 *ConAu 131*
Knauss, Robert Lynn 1931- *WhoAm 90*
Knauss, Thomas Russell 1953- *WhoEmL 91*
Knauss, Walter W., Jr. 1921- *St&PR 91*
Knauth, Stephen Craig 1950- *WhoWrEP 89*
Knautz, Robert Francis 1942- *WhoE 91*
Kneale, Martha Hurst 1909- *EncO&P 3*
Kneale, Nigel 1922- *ConAu 132*
Kneavel, Thomas Charles, Jr. 1941- *WhoE 91*
Knebel, Donald Earl 1946- *WhoEmL 91*
Knebel, Fletcher 1911- *WhoAm 90*
Knebel, Jack Gillen 1939- *WhoAm 90*
Knebel, John Albert 1936- *BiDrUSE 89, WhoAm 90*
Knebel, Spear *BioIn 16*
Knecht, Charles Daniel 1932- *WhoAm 90*
Knecht, Dennis Fred 1943- *St&PR 91*
Knecht, George Bruce 1958- *WhoE 91, WhoEmL 91*
Knecht, James Herbert 1925- *WhoAm 90*
Knecht, John 1947- *WhoAmA 91*
Knecht, Julia Ann 1959- *WhoAmW 91*
Knecht, Mathilda *BioIn 16*
Knecht, Raymond L. 1948- *St&PR 91*
Knecht, Robert Douglas 1947- *WhoEmL 91*
Knecht, Robert Jean 1926- *WhoWor 91*
Knecht, Roland Edward 1929- *St&PR 91, WhoAm 90*
Knecht, Ronald Lee 1949- *WhoEmL 91*
Knechtel, Baird 1937- *IntWWM 90*
Knechtges, David Richard 1942- *WhoAm 90*
Knee, Ruth Irelan 1920- *WhoAmW 91*
Knee, Steven Thomas *BiDrAPA 89*
Kneebone, Peter 1923-1990 *ConDes 90*
Kneece, Daniel Rufus, III 1956- *WhoEmL 91*
Kneedler, Alvin Richard 1943- *WhoAm 90*
Kneeland, Bryan E. 1952- *St&PR 91*
Kneeland, Douglas Eugene 1929- *WhoAm 90*
Kneeland, Roland Joseph 1932- *WhoAm 90*
Kneen, James Russell 1955- *WhoWor 91*
Kneen, Russell Packard 1923- *WhoAm 90*
Kneer, Joseph 1949- *WhoWor 91*
Kneer, Thomas T. 1921- *St&PR 91*
Knego, Frank Michael 1929- *St&PR 91*
Knehans, Douglas 1957- *IntWWM 90*
Kneib, Joseph A. 1948- *St&PR 91*
Kneip, Frederick Evoy *BioIn 16*
Kneip, Robert Charles 1948- *St&PR 91*
Kneip, Robert Charles, III 1948- *WhoAm 90*
Kneipp, John A 1914- *BiDrAPA 89*
Kneipp, Sebastian *NewAgE 90*
Kneisel, Ann H. 1926- *St&PR 91*
Kneisel, Franz 1865-1926 *PenDiMP*
Kneiser, Richard John 1938- *WhoAm 90*
Kneissl, Ala von Auersperg *BioIn 16*
Kneissl, William Lee 1936- *St&PR 91, WhoE 91*
Kneitel, Thomas Stephen 1933- *WhoAm 90, WhoWrEP 89*
Knell, Gary Evan 1954- *WhoAm 90, WhoE 91*
Knell, Harvey G. *BioIn 16*
Knell, Walter Lee 1953- *St&PR 91*
Kneller, Eckart Friedrich 1928- *WhoWor 91*
Kneller, Godfrey 1646-1723 *IntDcAA 90, OxCPMus*
Kneller, John William 1916- *WhoAm 90*
Kneller, William Arthur 1929- *WhoAm 90*
Knelson, Nelda Lorain Rife 1915- *WhoWor 91*
Knemeyer, Franz-Ludwig 1937- *WhoWor 91*
Knepell, Rosalyn Israel 1947- *BiDrAPA 89*
Knepler, Henry 1922- *WhoAm 90*
Knepp, Wallace R., Jr. 1924- *St&PR 91*
Kneppar, Stanley Robert 1930- *St&PR 91*
Knepper, Barry Michael 1950- *St&PR 91*
Knepper, Bob *BioIn 16*
Knepper, Bob 1954- *Ballpl 90*
Knepper, George W. 1926- *WhoAm 90*
Knepper, Jimmy 1927- *BioIn 16*
Knepper, Orcena F *BiDrAPA 89*
Knepper, Susan Baggerly 1949- *WhoEmL 91*
Knepper, William Edward 1909- *WhoAm 90*
Kneppers, Leonardus Cornelis M. 1943- *WhoWor 91*
Knerly, Mary Johnson 1925- *WhoAmW 91, WhoWor 91*
Knerly, Vicky W. 1961- *WhoAmW 91*
Knerr, Elizabeth Lorraine 1949- *WhoAmW 91*
Knerr, Harold H. 1882-1949 *EncACom*
Knerr, Lou 1921-1980 *Ballpl 90*
Knerr, Reinhard H. 1939- *WhoAm 90*
Knerr, Thomas T. 1921- *St&PR 91*
Knesel, Ernest Arthur, Jr. 1945- *WhoAm 90, WhoSSW 91*
Knesel, John Arthur 1949- *WhoEmL 91*
Knesevich, John William 1948- *BiDrAPA 89*
Knesper, David James 1943- *BiDrAPA 89*
Kness, Richard Maynard 1937- *IntWWM 90, WhoAm 90, WhoE 91, WhoWor 91*
Kness, Russell Austin 1953- *WhoEmL 91*
Knetzer, Elmer 1885-1975 *Ballpl 90*
Knetzer, Thelma T. 1927- *St&PR 91*
Knevel, Adelbert Michael 1922- *WhoAm 90*
Knevitt, Charles 1952- *ConAu 132*
Knezevich, Alan David 1953- *WhoEmL 91*

Knezinskis, Jekabs *BiDrAPA 89*
Knezo, Genevieve Johanna 1942- *WhoAmW 91*
Knezovic, Donald C. 1942- *St&PR 91*
Kniaz, Albert *BiDrAPA 89*
Kniaz, Harry 1936- *BiDrAPA 89*
Knibb, Grace B. 1931- *St&PR 91*
Knicely, H.V. 1936- *St&PR 91*
Knicely, Howard V. *BioIn 16*
Knickerbocker, Bill 1911-1963 *Ballpl 90*
Knickerbocker, Cholly *ConAu 129*
Knickerbocker, Daniel Candee, Jr. 1919- *WhoAm 90*
Knickerbocker, Hubert Renfro 1898-1949 *BioIn 16*
Knickerbocker, Kenneth Leslie 1905- *WhoAm 90*
Knickerbocker, Robert Henry 1920- *St&PR 91*
Knickerbocker, Robert Platt, Jr. 1944- *WhoAm 90*
Knickerbocker, Suzy *BioIn 16*
Knickerbocker, William L. 1904-1988 *BioIn 16*
Knie, Roberta 1938- *IntWWM 90*
Knie-Andersen, Bent 1942- *WhoWor 91*
Knief, Helen Jeanette 1907- *WhoAmA 91*
Knieps, Franz 1956- *WhoWor 91*
Knier, Frederick Wallis 1943- *St&PR 91*
Knierim, Kim Phillip 1945- *WhoAm 90, WhoEmL 91*
Knies, Paul Henry 1918- *WhoAm 90*
Kniesler, Frederick Cornelius, Jr. 1954- *WhoE 91*
Kniess, Terry Lon 1950- *WhoSSW 91*
Kniest, Thomas William 1956- *WhoSSW 91*
Knievel, Arthur William 1920- *St&PR 91*
Knievel, Evel *BioIn 16*
Knievel, Robbie *BioIn 16*
Knievel, Robbie 1963- *News 90 [port]*
Kniewasser, Andrew Graham 1926- *WhoAm 90*
Kniffen, Jan R. 1948- *St&PR 91*
Kniffen, Jan Rogers 1948- *WhoAm 90, WhoEmL 91*
Kniffin, F. Robert 1934- *ODwPR 91*
Kniffin, Hazen G 1930- *BiDrAPA 89*
Kniffin, Judith Eileen *BiDrAPA 89*
Kniffin, Ralph Gus 1946- *WhoAmA 91*
Kniffin, Renate M 1930- *BiDrAPA 89*
Knigge, Adolph Franz F L, Freiherr von 1752-1796 *DcLB 94 [port]*
Knigge, Robert *BioIn 16*
Knight, Alanna *ConAu 33NR*
Knight, Alexa Davey 1949- *WhoEmL 91*
Knight, Alfred Bishop 1920- *WhoAm 90*
Knight, Alice Dorothy Tirrell 1903- *WhoAmW 91*
Knight, Allen M. 1949- *St&PR 91*
Knight, Anne Haskell 1937- *WhoAmW 91*
Knight, Arthur 1916- *WhoAm 90*
Knight, Arthur Lee, Jr. 1937- *St&PR 91*
Knight, Arthur Robert 1938- *WhoAm 90*
Knight, Arthur Winfield 1937- *WhoWrEP 89*
Knight, Athelia Wilhelmenia 1950- *WhoAm 90*
Knight, Becky 1941- *WhoWrEP 89*
Knight, Bobby *BioIn 16*
Knight, Carolyn Williams 1943- *WhoSSW 91*
Knight, Catherine Anne 263- *WhoAmW 91*
Knight, Charles F. 1936- *St&PR 91*
Knight, Charles Field 1936- *WhoAm 90*
Knight, Charles Frasuer 1932- *WhoSSW 91*
Knight, Charles Landon 1867-1933 *BioIn 16*
Knight, Chet 1939- *St&PR 91*
Knight, Christopher Allen 1950- *WhoAmA 91*
Knight, Chuck *BioIn 16*
Knight, Clayton *EncACom*
Knight, Clayton 1891-1969 *AuBYP 90*
Knight, Clifford 1886- *TwCCr&M 91*
Knight, Damon 1922- *RGTwCSF*
Knight, Dan P. 1941- *WhoSSW 91*
Knight, David *TwCCr&M 91*
Knight, David Bates 1939- *WhoSSW 91*
Knight, David Carpenter 1925- *AuBYP 90*
Knight, Dean Burson, Jr. 1946- *WhoSSW 91*
Knight, Dean L. *St&PR 91N*
Knight, Delos L. 1931- *ODwPR 91*
Knight, Donald W. 1940- *St&PR 91*
Knight, Douglas Maitland 1921- *St&PR 91, WhoAm 90, WhoE 91, WhoWor 91*
Knight, Douglas Walker 1952- *St&PR 91*
Knight, Edward 1936- *WhoSSW 91*
Knight, Edward H 1922- *BiDrAPA 89*
Knight, Edward Howden 1933- *WhoAm 90*
Knight, Edward R. 1917- *WhoE 91*
Knight, Elizabeth Ann 1957- *WhoSSW 91*
Knight, Ellis Cornelia 1758-1837 *FemiCLE*
Knight, Eric Mowbray 1897-1943 *AuBYP 90*
Knight, Ernest Lee 1933- *WhoE 91*
Knight, Frank Bardsley 1933- *WhoAm 90*
Knight, Fred Barrows 1925- *WhoAm 90*
Knight, Frederic Charles 1898-1979 *WhoAmA 91N*
Knight, Gary 1939- *WhoAm 90*
Knight, George Blanchard 1923- *St&PR 91*
Knight, George Fredrick 1943- *St&PR 91*
Knight, Gerald 1948- *St&PR 91*
Knight, Gillian 1934- *PenDiMP*
Knight, Gillian 1939- *IntWWM 90*
Knight, Gladys *BioIn 16*
Knight, Gladys 1944- *DrBlPA 90, EncPR&S 89, OxCPMus, WhoAm 90, WhoAmW 91, WorAlBi*
Knight, Gladys, & the Pips *EncPR&S 89*
Knight, H. Stuart 1921- *WhoAm 90*
Knight, Harold Edwin Holm, Jr. 1930- *St&PR 91, WhoAm 90*
Knight, Harry W. 1909- *WhoAm 90, WhoWor 91*
Knight, Haven A. 1929- *St&PR 91*
Knight, Helen King *ODwPR 91*
Knight, Herbert B. 1928- *St&PR 91*
Knight, Herbert Borwell 1928- *WhoAm 90*
Knight, Hilary *BioIn 16*
Knight, Hilary 1926- *AuBYP 90*
Knight, Howard Atwood 1942- *WhoE 91*
Knight, Howard Audway, Jr. 1943- *WhoSSW 91*
Knight, Ida Brown 1918- *WhoAmW 91*
Knight, J.A. 1927- *St&PR 91*
Knight, J. Z. *BioIn 16*
Knight, J.Z. *EncO&P 3*
Knight, J. Z. *EncPaPR 91*
Knight, J. Z. 1946- *NewAgE 90*
Knight, Jack 1895-1976 *Ballpl 90*
Knight, Jacob Jaskoviak 1938- *WhoAmA 91*
Knight, James A 1918- *BiDrAPA 89*
Knight, James A. 1927- *WhoAm 90*
Knight, James Allen 1918- *WhoAm 90*
Knight, James Arthur 1934- *WhoAm 90*
Knight, James H. 1939- *St&PR 91*
Knight, James P. 1929- *St&PR 91*
Knight, Janet Susan 1950- *WhoWrEP 89*
Knight, Janie S. 1936- *WhoSSW 91*
Knight, Jeffrey Lin 1959- *WhoEmL 91*
Knight, Jeffrey Richard 1962- *WhoWor 91*
Knight, Jeffrey Russell 1936- *WhoWor 91*
Knight, Jeffrey William 1949- *WhoAm 90*
Knight, Jerry Glenn 1938- *WhoAm 90, WhoSSW 91*
Knight, Jesse F. 1946- *ConAu 129*
Knight, John 1606- *EncCRAm*
Knight, John 1885-1965 *Ballpl 90*
Knight, John 1945- *WhoAmA 91*
Knight, John Allan 1931- *WhoAm 90*
Knight, John F. 1919- *St&PR 91*
Knight, John Francis 1919- *WhoAm 90*
Knight, John Lord 1936- *WhoAm 90*
Knight, John Phillips, Jr. 1944- *St&PR 91*
Knight, John Shively 1894-1981 *BioIn 16*
Knight, Joseph Adams 1930- *WhoAm 90*
Knight, Joyce Evelyn 1942- *WhoSSW 91*
Knight, Judy Zebra *BioIn 16*
Knight, June Elizabeth 1920- *WhoWrEP 89*
Knight, June J. 1935- *WhoAmW 91*
Knight, June Juanita 1935- *St&PR 91*
Knight, Karen A. 1939- *WhoAmW 91*
Knight, Kathleen Moore *TwCCr&M 91*
Knight, Kathryn Ross 1927- *WhoAmW 91*
Knight, Kathy 1950- *WhoAmW 91*
Knight, Keith Desmond St. Aubyn *WhoWor 91*
Knight, Kenneth George 1956- *WhoEmL 91*
Knight, Laura 1877-1970 *BiDWomA*
Knight, Laurie Jean 1963- *WhoAmW 91*
Knight, Lester B. *St&PR 91N*
Knight, Lester B. 1907-1989 *BioIn 16*
Knight, Margarett Lee 1923- *WhoAmW 91, WhoWor 91*
Knight, Margo Hauck 1954- *WhoAmW 91*
Knight, Martha Vestal 1949- *WhoSSW 91*
Knight, Mary *BiDEWW*
Knight, Mary Ann *BiDrAPA 89*
Knight, Mary Ann 1944- *WhoAmW 91*
Knight, Max *AuBYP 90*
Knight, Merrill Donnaldson, III 1930- *St&PR 91*
Knight, Michael Comer 1939- *St&PR 91*
Knight, Michael Joseph *BiDrAPA 89*
Knight, Nancy Carol 1947- *WhoWrEP 89*
Knight, Norman 1924- *WhoAm 90, WhoE 91, WhoWor 91*
Knight, Paul Ford 1947- *St&PR 91*
Knight, Peter *AuBYP 90*
Knight, Philip *St&PR 91*
Knight, Philip H. *BioIn 16*
Knight, Philip H. 1938- *ConAmBL, St&PR 91*
Knight, Philip Hampson 1938- *WhoAm 90*
Knight, Ray 1952- *Ballpl 90*
Knight, Rebecca R. 1941- *WhoWrEP 89*
Knight, Reo Lindsay 1931- *WhoWor 91*
Knight, Rey N. 1928- *St&PR 91*
Knight, Rick Jay 1956- *St&PR 91*
Knight, Robert Allen, Jr. 1956- *WhoEmL 91*
Knight, Robert Edward 1941- *WhoWor 91*
Knight, Robert G. 1941- *WhoAm 90*
Knight, Robert Huntington 1919- *WhoAm 90, WhoWor 91*
Knight, Robert Jackson, Jr. 1926- *WhoAm 90*
Knight, Robert Montgomery 1940- *WhoAm 90*
Knight, Robert P *BiDrAPA 89*
Knight, Robert Patrick 1935- *WhoAm 90*
Knight, Robert Vernon 1928- *St&PR 91*
Knight, Robert Vernon, Jr. 1928- *WhoAm 90*
Knight, Ruth Adams 1898-1974 *AuBYP 90*
Knight, Sam L. 1936- *St&PR 91*
Knight, Samuel Howell 1892-1975 *DcScB S2*
Knight, Sandra *ODwPR 91*
Knight, Sarah 1666-1727 *FemiCLE*
Knight, Sarah Kemble 1666-1727 *EncCRAm*
Knight, Shirlann D *BiDrAPA 89*
Knight, Shirley 1936- *WhoAm 90, WhoAmW 91*
Knight, Shirley M. 1908- *St&PR 91*
Knight, Stephen 1938- *WhoAm 90*
Knight, Stephen James, III 1947- *St&PR 91*
Knight, Stillman Depauw, Jr. 1947- *WhoSSW 91*
Knight, T.E. 1939- *St&PR 91*
Knight, Tack 1895-1976 *EncACom, WhoAmA 91N*
Knight, Ted 1923-1986 *WorAlBi*
Knight, Thomas Peter 1946- *WhoEmL 91*
Knight, Tom, Jr 1925- *WhoAmA 91*
Knight, Toni Cecille Frye 1949- *WhoSSW 91*
Knight, V. C. 1904- *WhoAm 90*
Knight, Verne C. 1904- *St&PR 91*
Knight, Virginia Cork 1952- *WhoEmL 91*
Knight, Walker Leigh 1924- *WhoAm 90*
Knight, Wallace E. 1926- *ODwPR 91*
Knight, Wallace Edward 1926- *LiHiK*
Knight, Walter David 1919- *WhoAm 90*
Knight, Walter Early 1911- *WhoAm 90*
Knight, Wendell Morgan 1936- *WhoSSW 91*
Knight, William E *BiDrAPA 89*
Knight, William Edwards 1922- *WhoAm 90*
Knight, William J. 1929- *WhoAm 90*
Knight, William Thomas 1937- *St&PR 91, WhoAm 90*
Knight, William Wilton, Jr. 1922- *WhoWor 91*
Knight, Wilson 1897-1985 *DcNaB 1981*
Knight-Richardson, Norwood *BiDrAPA 89*
Knight-Weiler, Rene Margaret 1953- *WhoWrEP 89*
Knighton, David Reed 1949- *WhoAm 90*
Knighton, George William 1926- *WhoWor 91*
Knighton, Robert Syron 1914- *WhoAm 90*
Knights, Edwin Munroe 1924- *WhoAm 90*
Knights, Jo *WhoNeCM B*
Knights, Winifred Margaret 1899-1947 *BiDWomA*
Knigin, Michael Jay 1942- *WhoAmA 91*
Knijff, Henri W. de 1931- *WhoWor 91*
Knilans, Kyleen 1953- *St&PR 91*
Knilans, Michael Jerome 1927- *WhoAm 90*
Knill, Bruce T.H. 1933- *St&PR 91*
Knill, James Reginald 1933- *St&PR 91*
Knill, Keefer Leslie 1949- *WhoEmL 91*
Knill, Ronald John 1935- *WhoSSW 91*
Knill, William Scott 1950- *WhoWor 91*
Knipe, Clarice Lynn *BiDrAPA 89*
Knipe, Robert W. 1939- *St&PR 91*
Kniplova, Nadezda 1932- *IntWWM 90, PenDiMP*
Knipp, Fred M. 1931- *St&PR 91*
Knipp, Helmut 1943- *WhoAm 90, WhoSSW 91*
Knipp, Stephen S. 1933- *St&PR 91*
Knippenburg, Tracy 1962- *WhoAmW 91*
Knippers, Edward 1946- *WhoAmA 91*
Knipple, Wendy Lyn 1958- *WhoAmW 91*
Knipscher, Gerard Allen 1935- *WhoAmA 91*
Knipschild, Robert 1927- *WhoAm 90, WhoAmA 91*
Knipstein, Robert C 1943- *BiDrAPA 89*
Knisel, Russell H. 1933- *WhoAm 90*
Knisel, Russell Henry 1933- *St&PR 91*
Knisely, Anne M. *ODwPR 91*
Knisely, Anne Marie 1955- *WhoAmW 91*
Knisely, Gary Theodore 1948- *St&PR 91*
Knisely, Jo Ann 1958- *St&PR 91*
Knisely, Marjorie L. 1924- *St&PR 91*
Knisely, Robert August 1940- *WhoAm 90*
Knisely, Robert D. 1922- *St&PR 91*
Knisely, Sally 1917- *WhoAmW 91*
Kniskern, Gary Dale 1945- *St&PR 91*
Kniskern, Joseph Warren 1951- *WhoSSW 91*
Kniskern, Maynard 1912- *WhoAm 90, WhoWor 91*
Knisley, Larry Ray 1942- *St&PR 91*
Knispel, Barry 1944- *St&PR 91*
Knister, James Alan 1937- *St&PR 91*
Knittel, Robert *BioIn 16*
Knitter, Paul F 1939- *ConAu 129*
Knittle, Frank Edward 1942- *St&PR 91*
Knizeski-Hollander, Justine Estelle 1954- *WhoAmW 91*
Knobel, Dale Thomas 1949- *WhoSSW 91*
Knobel, Mauricio 1922- *BiDrAPA 89*
Knobil, Ernst 1926- *WhoAm 90*
Knoblauch, Arlene Nock 1950- *BiDrAPA 89*
Knoblauch, Frank White *BiDrAPA 89*
Knoblauch, Joel Philip 1955- *WhoE 91*
Knoblauch, Leo Charles 1909- *St&PR 91*
Knoblauch, Marilyn Deatrick 1945- *WhoSSW 91*
Knoblauch, Mark George 1947- *WhoAm 90*
Knobler, Alfred Everett 1915- *WhoAm 90*
Knobler, Carolyn Berk 1934- *WhoAmW 91*
Knobler, Joanna Gabin 1951- *BiDrAPA 89*
Knobler, Lois Jean 1929- *WhoAmA 91*
Knobler, Nathan 1926- *WhoAmA 91*
Knobler, Peter Stephen 1946- *WhoAm 90, WhoWrEP 89*
Knobloch, Carl W., Jr. 1930- *St&PR 91*
Knobloch, Carl William, Jr. 1930- *WhoAm 90, WhoSSW 91*
Knobloch, Ferdinand J 1916- *BiDrAPA 89, WhoAm 90*
Knobloch, Hilda 1915- *WhoAmW 91*
Knobloch, Johann 1919- *WhoWor 91*
Knobloch, Thomas Georg 1966- *WhoE 91*
Knoblowitz, Martin 1949- *St&PR 91*
Knoch, Robert H. 1932- *St&PR 91*
Knoche, Donald Irving 1931- *St&PR 91*
Knoche, Everett, Jr. 1930- *St&PR 91*
Knochen, Helmut 1910- *BioIn 16*
Knock, Corky John 1933- *St&PR 91*
Knock, Peter Benjamin 1948- *WhoE 91*
Knodel, Elinor Livingston *WhoAmW 91*
Knodel, John Edwin 1940- *WhoAm 90*
Knodell, Clayton William 1927- *St&PR 91*
Knodt, Gerrit Janus 1938- *WhoSSW 91*
Knodt, William Charles 1936- *EncO&P 3*
Knoebel, Betty Lou Margaret 1931- *St&PR 91*
Knoebel, Cynthia 1960- *ODwPR 91*
Knoebel, David Jon 1949- *WhoAmA 91, WhoE 91*
Knoebel, Richard Henry 1927- *St&PR 91*
Knoebel, Suzanne Buckner 1926- *WhoAm 90*
Knoedler, Daniel William 1955- *BiDrAPA 89*
Knoedler, Elmer L. 1912- *WhoAm 90*
Knoedler, Gunther H. 1929- *St&PR 91*
Knoelke, Michael W *BiDrAPA 89*
Knoell, William H. 1924- *St&PR 91*
Knoeller, Christian T. 1926- *St&PR 91*
Knoepfle, John 1923- *AuBYP 90, WhoWrEP 89*
Knoepfler, Peter T 1929- *BiDrAPA 89*
Knoepfler, Peter Tamas 1929- *WhoAm 90*
Knoepflmacher, Ulrich Camillus 1931- *WhoAm 90*
Knoernschild, Katherine Mary 1948- *WhoAmW 91*
Knoff, William F 1921- *BiDrAPA 89*
Knoke, David Harmon 1947- *WhoAm 90*
Knoles, George Harmon 1907- *WhoAm 90*
Knoll, Andrew Herbert 1951- *WhoAm 90*
Knoll, Bruce Evans 1953- *WhoAm 90*
Knoll, David E. 1944- *St&PR 91*
Knoll, Denys W. 1907-1989 *BioIn 16*
Knoll, Erwin 1931- *WhoAm 90, WhoWrEP 89*
Knoll, Florence 1917- *ConDes 90*
Knoll, Florence Schust 1917- *PenDiDA 89, WhoAm 90*
Knoll, Frank J. 1948- *St&PR 91*
Knoll, Glenn Frederick 1935- *WhoAm 90*
Knoll, Hans 1914-1955 *PenDiDA 89*
Knoll, Isabel A Giampietro *WhoAmA 91*
Knoll, James B. *St&PR 91*
Knoll, James Lyle, III 1944- *BiDrAPA 89*
Knoll, Jerry 1924- *WhoAm 90*
Knoll, Joseph Carl 1948- *WhoEmL 91*
Knoll, Robert D *BiDrAPA 89*
Knoll, Rose Ann 1954- *WhoAmW 91*
Knoll, Samuel H. 1940- *St&PR 91*
Knolle, Mary Anne Ericson 1941- *WhoAmW 91, WhoSSW 91*
Knollenberg, Walter Thomas 1945- *St&PR 91*
Knoller, Guy David 1946- *WhoEmL 91*
Knoller, Johann Georg *PenDiDA 89*
Knoller, Karen A. 1959- *St&PR 91*
Knollys, Hanserd 1599?-1691 *BioIn 16*
Knoop, Bobby 1938- *Ballpl 90*

Knoor, Raymond R. 1918- *St&PR 91*
Knop, Joachim 1943- *BiDrAPA 89*
Knopf, Adolph 1882-1966 *DcScB S2*
Knopf, Alfred, Jr. 1918- *WhoAm 90*
Knopf, Alfred A. 1892-1984 *WorAlBi*
Knopf, Donna Braverman *WhoAmA 91*
Knopf, Edwin Ronald 1938- *BiDrAPA 89*
Knopf, Irwin Jay 1924- *WhoAm 90*
Knopf, Kenyon Alfred 1921- *WhoAm 90*
Knopf, Michael Irwin 1943- *WhoE 91*
Knopf, Paul Mark 1936- *WhoAm 90*
Knopf, Susan Lewis 1956- *WhoAmW 91*
Knopfelmacher, Frank 1923- *WhoWor 91*
Knopfler, Mark 1949- *ConTFT 8*
Knopman, David S. 1950- *WhoAm 90*
Knopoff, Leon 1925- *WhoAm 90*
Knopp, Marvin Isadore 1933- *WhoAm 90, WhoE 91*
Knoppel, Terri Boyd 1956- *WhoE 91*
Knopper, Dorothy *BioIn 16*
Knoppers, Antonie Theodoor 1915- *WhoAm 90*
Knopsnyder, Donald Dwayne 1953- *WhoEmL 91*
Knor, Zlatko 1933- *WhoWor 91*
Knorr, Betty Jewel Benkert 1928- *WhoWor 91*
Knorr, Gerard K. 1939- *St&PR 91*
Knorr, Jeanne Boardman *WhoAmA 91*
Knorr, Judith R. 1941- *WhoWrEP 89*
Knorr, Klaus *ConAu 131*
Knorr, Klaus E 1911-1990 *ConAu 131, NewYTBS 90*
Knorr, Klaus Eugen 1911-1990 *BioIn 16*
Knorr, Ludwig 1859-1921 *DcScB S2*
Knorr, Martin J. 1906-1989 *BioIn 16*
Knorr, Norman John *BiDrAPA 89*
Knorr, Norman John 1930- *WhoAm 90*
Knorr, Steven Joseph *BiDrAPA 89*
Knorr von Rosenroth, Christian 1636-1689 *EncO&P 3*
Knorring, Sophie von 1797-1848 *EncCoWW*
Knortz, Herbert Charles 1921- *WhoAm 90*
Knortz, Walter Robert 1919- *WhoAm 90*
Knospe, William Herbert 1929- *WhoAm 90*
Knost, Tony Alan 1961- *WhoSSW 91*
Knoth, Marge June 1944- *WhoAmW 91*
Knott, David Howard *BiDrAPA 89*
Knott, Dee D 1943- *WhoAmA 91*
Knott, Douglas Ronald 1927- *WhoAm 90*
Knott, Elizabeth B. 1927- *WhoAmW 91*
Knott, Henry J. 1906- *St&PR 91*
Knott, Henry Joseph 1906- *WhoAm 90*
Knott, Jack 1907-1981 *Ballpl 90*
Knott, James *BioIn 16*
Knott, James Robert 1910- *WhoAm 90*
Knott, John Ray, Jr. 1937- *WhoAm 90*
Knott, Mark D. 1948- *St&PR 91*
Knott, Martin E. 1926- *St&PR 91*
Knott, Mary 1653?-1718 *BiDEWW*
Knott, Robert H. 1939- *St&PR 91*
Knott, Stuart Blanoing 1925- *St&PR 91*
Knott, Tara Davis 1943- *WhoAmW 91*
Knott, Theodore Kenneth 1935- *WhoWor 91*
Knott, Wiley Eugene 1938- *WhoWor 91*
Knott, William C. 1927- *WhoWrEP 89*
Knott, William Cecil 1927- *AuBYP 90*
Knottnerus, John David 1946- *WhoEmL 91*
Knotts, Don 1924- *WhoAm 90, WorAlBi*
Knotts, Glenn Richard 1934- *WhoAm 90, WhoSSW 91, WhoWor 91*
Knotts, Louis Howard 1951- *WhoE 91*
Knotts, Max Leon 1922- *St&PR 91*
Knotts, Robert Lee 1942- *WhoSSW 91*
Knotts, Sarah April 1952- *WhoAmW 91*
Knotts, William Norman 1940- *St&PR 91*
Knouse, Charles Allison 1921- *WhoAm 90, WhoWor 91*
Knowlan, Michael Norman 1951- *BiDrAPA 89*
Knowland, Raymond Reginald 1930- *WhoWor 91*
Knowland, William F. 1908-1974 *WorAlBi*
Knowler, Faith Marion 1911- *WhoAmW 91*
Knowler, Lloyd A. 1908- *WhoWor 91*
Knowler, William C. 1946- *WhoWor 91*
Knowles, Alison 1933- *WhoAm 90, WhoAmA 91*
Knowles, Asa S. *NewYTBS 90 [port]*
Knowles, Asa S 1909-1990 *ConAu 132*
Knowles, Bvodley Nordmark 1936- *St&PR 91*
Knowles, Caroline Hoffberg 1926- *WhoAmW 91*
Knowles, Christopher Allan 1949- *WhoE 91*
Knowles, Christopher G. 1943- *St&PR 91*
Knowles, Clifford C. 1944- *St&PR 91*
Knowles, Colin George 1939- *WhoWor 91*
Knowles, Darold 1941- *Ballpl 90*
Knowles, Edward Frank 1929- *WhoAm 90*
Knowles, Edward L. *BioIn 16*
Knowles, Elizabeth 1958- *WhoAmA 91*
Knowles, Elizabeth Pringle 1943- *WhoE 91*
Knowles, Elsie A G 1908- *EncO&P 3*
Knowles, Emmitt Clifton 1951- *WhoEmL 91*
Knowles, Frederick E, III *BiDrAPA 89*
Knowles, Frederick W 1911- *EncO&P 3*
Knowles, Gary Gene 1946- *WhoEmL 91*
Knowles, George Ernest 1921- *WhoSSW 91*
Knowles, Gregory Adams 1947- *WhoSSW 91*
Knowles, Hugh S. *BioIn 16*
Knowles, Jack Oliver 1916- *WhoAm 90*
Knowles, Jack W. 1945- *St&PR 91*
Knowles, James H., Jr. 1940- *WhoAm 90*
Knowles, James Kenyon 1931- *WhoAm 90*
Knowles, Jeremy Randall 1935- *WhoAm 90*
Knowles, Jocelyn Wagner 1918- *WhoAmW 91, WhoE 91*
Knowles, John 1926- *MajTwCW, WhoWrEP 89, WorAlBi*
Knowles, Leo A. 1930- *St&PR 91*
Knowles, Malcolm Shepherd *BioIn 16*
Knowles, Malcolm Shepherd 1913- *WhoAm 90*
Knowles, Marjorie Fine 1939- *WhoAm 90*
Knowles, Mary 1733-1807 *FemiCLE*
Knowles, Nancy Welch 1930- *St&PR 91*
Knowles, Phyllis Bradfute 1927- *WhoAmW 91, WhoSSW 91*
Knowles, R. G. 1858-1919 *OxCPMus*
Knowles, Richard H 1934- *WhoAmA 91*
Knowles, Richard James Robert 1943- *WhoE 91, WhoWor 91*
Knowles, Richard Norris 1935- *WhoWor 91*
Knowles, Robert E. 1950- *St&PR 91*
Knowles, Robert Gordon, Jr. 1943- *WhoSSW 91*
Knowles, Robert R *BiDrAPA 89*
Knowles, Roy C 1913- *BiDrAPA 89*
Knowles, Stephen G. 1946- *St&PR 91*
Knowles, Susan Williams 1952- *WhoAmA 91*
Knowles, Thomas George 1928- *WhoSSW 91, WhoWor 91*
Knowles, Velma Merlee 1963- *WhoWor 91*
Knowles, Warren P. 1908- *St&PR 91*
Knowles, William James 1940- *WhoAm 90*
Knowles, William Leroy 1935- *WhoAm 90*
Knowles, William Townsend 1935- *St&PR 91, WhoAm 90*
Knowlton, Austin E. *WhoAm 90*
Knowlton, Charles Wilson 1923- *WhoAm 90*
Knowlton, Daniel Gibson 1922- *WhoAmA 91*
Knowlton, David Conde 1910- *St&PR 91*
Knowlton, Edgar Colby, Jr. 1921- *WhoAm 90, WhoWrEP 89*
Knowlton, Elizabeth *BioIn 16*
Knowlton, Grace Farrar 1932- *WhoAmA 91*
Knowlton, Helen Mary 1832-1918 *BiDWomA*
Knowlton, Jack W. 1926- *St&PR 91*
Knowlton, Jonathan 1937- *WhoAmA 91*
Knowlton, Joseph Smith 1931- *St&PR 91*
Knowlton, Kevin Charles 1957- *WhoEmL 91*
Knowlton, Maude Briggs 1876-1956 *WhoAmA 91N*
Knowlton, Peter 1916- *BiDrAPA 89*
Knowlton, Richard L. 1932- *St&PR 91, WhoAm 90*
Knowlton, Robert Charles 1929- *WhoSSW 91*
Knowlton, Thomas 1740-1776 *EncCRAm*
Knowlton, Thomas A. 1946- *WhoAm 90*
Knowlton, William Allen 1920- *St&PR 91, WhoAm 90, WhoSSW 91, WhoWor 91*
Knowlton, Winthrop 1930- *St&PR 91, WhoAm 90*
Knox, Agnes Ruth 1911- *WhoAmW 91*
Knox, Ann Brewer 1926- *WhoWrEP 89*
Knox, Archibald *PenDiDA 89*
Knox, Arthur Lloyd 1932- *St&PR 91*
Knox, Bernard MacGregor Walker 1914- *WhoAm 90*
Knox, Bernie *St&PR 91*
Knox, Betty Agee 1936- *WhoAmW 91, WhoE 91, WhoWor 91*
Knox, Bill 1928- *TwCCr&M 91*
Knox, C Frank, Jr. 1926- *BiDrAPA 89*
Knox, C. Neal 1935- *WhoAm 90*
Knox, Calvin M. *AuBYP 90, MajTwCW*
Knox, Carolyn Mullikin 1950- *IntWWM 90*
Knox, Charles 1929- *IntWWM 90*
Knox, Charles Henry 1950- *WhoSSW 91*
Knox, Charles Robert 1932- *WhoAm 90*
Knox, Chuck *BioIn 16*
Knox, Daryl Keith *BiDrAPA 89*
Knox, David Glen 1950- *WhoEmL 91*
Knox, Deborah Carolyn 1962- *WhoAmW 91*
Knox, Douglas Richard 1951- *St&PR 91*
Knox, Edward Chapman 1939- *WhoAm 90*
Knox, Elizabeth 1944- *WhoAmA 91*
Knox, Ellen Porter *BiDrAPA 89*
Knox, Ernest Rudder 1916- *WhoAm 90*
Knox, Franklin 1874-1944 *BioIn 16*
Knox, Frederick J. 1930- *St&PR 91*
Knox, George 1922- *WhoAmA 91*
Knox, George Edward, Jr. 1948- *WhoEmL 91*
Knox, George L. 1943- *St&PR 91*
Knox, George L., III 1943- *ODwPR 91*
Knox, George Levi, III 1943- *WhoAm 90*
Knox, Gerald Malm 1935- *WhoAm 90*
Knox, Harold L. 1918- *St&PR 91*
Knox, Havolyn Crocker 1937- *WhoAmW 91*
Knox, Henry 1750-1806 *BiDrUSE 89, EncCRAm [port], WhNaAH*
Knox, Jack Dill 1937- *St&PR 91, WhoSSW 91*
Knox, Jacqueline Mae 1932- *WhoAmW 91*
Knox, James *ConAu 30NR, TwCCr&M 91*
Knox, James E. 1937- *St&PR 91*
Knox, James Edwin 1937- *WhoAm 90*
Knox, James Lester 1919- *WhoAm 90*
Knox, James Lloyd 1929- *WhoAm 90*
Knox, James W. 1919- *WhoE 91*
Knox, John 1514-1572 *EncPaPR 91, WorAlBi*
Knox, John 1900-1990 *ConAu 132*
Knox, John, Jr. 1932- *WhoAm 90*
Knox, John Jay 1828-1892 *EncABHB 6 [port]*
Knox, Julie Johnson 1955- *BiDrAPA 89*
Knox, Lance Lethbridge 1944- *WhoWor 91*
Knox, Lucy 1845- *FemiCLE*
Knox, Michael Ross 1947- *St&PR 91*
Knox, Northrup R. 1928- *St&PR 91*
Knox, Northrup Rand 1928- *WhoAm 90*
Knox, Peter Seymour, III 1935- *St&PR 91*
Knox, Philander Chase 1853-1921 *BiDrUSE 89, BioIn 16, WorAlBi*
Knox, Rebecca Howland 1943- *WhoAmW 91*
Knox, Rhonda Lee 1960- *WhoAmW 91*
Knox, Richard Irol 1953- *WhoEmL 91*
Knox, Richard M. 1923- *St&PR 91*
Knox, Robert Burns 1917- *WhoSSW 91*
Knox, Robert Seiple 1931- *WhoAm 90, WhoE 91*
Knox, Ronald A 1888-1957 *TwCCr&M 91*
Knox, Sarah Margaret *BiDrAPA 89*
Knox, Seymour H. 1898- *BioIn 16*
Knox, Seymour H. 1898-1990 *NewYTBS 90*
Knox, Seymour Horace, III 1926- *WhoAm 90, WhoE 91*
Knox, Stanley Cramner 1928- *WhoAm 90*
Knox, Stephen Reid 1947- *WhoEmL 91*
Knox, Thomas Edward 1957- *BiDrAPA 89*
Knox, Thomas J. 1941- *WhoE 91*
Knox, Wallace John, II 1941- *WhoE 91*
Knox, Warren Barr 1925- *WhoAm 90*
Knox, Wendell Joseph 1948- *St&PR 91*
Knox, William David 1920- *WhoAm 90*
Knox, William Franklin 1874-1944 *BiDrUSE 89, BioIn 16*
Knox, Wilma Jones 1930- *WhoAmW 91*
Knox-Malewicki, Debra Suzanne 1954- *WhoAmW 91*
Knuckey, Michael 1936- *St&PR 91*
Knudsen, C. Calvert 1923- *St&PR 91*
Knudsen, Christian 1945- *WhoAmA 91*
Knudsen, Conrad Calvert 1923- *WhoAm 90*
Knudsen, David L. 1951- *St&PR 91*
Knudsen, Denis E. 1918- *St&PR 91*
Knudsen, Eric Ingvald 1949- *WhoAm 90*
Knudsen, Erik 1922- *DcScanL*
Knudsen, Erik Alfred 1872-1957 *AmLegL*
Knudsen, Gene Arthur 1948- *WhoE 91*
Knudsen, Gunnar 1918- *WhoWor 91*
Knudsen, Jakob 1858-1917 *DcScanL*
Knudsen, James George 1920- *WhoAm 90*
Knudsen, John Cyrill 1948- *WhoWor 91*
Knudsen, Kenneth Martin 1940- *St&PR 91*
Knudsen, Lauritz K. 1938- *St&PR 91*
Knudsen, Morten Vagner 1926- *WhoWor 91*
Knudsen, Raymond Barnett 1919- *WhoAm 90, WhoE 91*
Knudsen, Raymond Barnett, II 1941- *WhoE 91*
Knudsen, Robert LeRoy *BioIn 16*
Knudsen, Rudolph Edgar 1939- *St&PR 91*
Knudsen, Rudolph Edgar, Jr. 1939- *WhoAm 90*
Knudsen, Semon E. 1912- *St&PR 91*
Knudsen, Semon Emil 1912- *EncABHB 5 [port], WhoAm 90*
Knudsen, Vern Oliver 1893-1974 *DcScB S2*
Knudsen, William Claire 1925- *WhoAm 90*
Knudsen, William Signius 1879-1948 *EncABHB 5 [port]*
Knudslien, Dewey Victor 1929- *WhoWrEP 89*
Knudson, Alfred George, Jr. 1922- *WhoAm 90*
Knudson, Alvin B C *BiDrAPA 89*
Knudson, Ann Rankin 1933- *WhoAmW 91*
Knudson, Dean Kevin 1958- *BiDrAPA 89*
Knudson, George *BioIn 16*
Knudson, Harry Edward, Jr. 1921- *WhoAm 90*
Knudson, James Walter 1947- *BiDrAPA 89*
Knudson, John E., Jr. 1946- *St&PR 91*
Knudson, Knute S. 1943- *St&PR 91*
Knudson, Mark 1960- *Ballpl 90*
Knudson, Mark Bradley 1948- *WhoWor 91*
Knudson, R. Rozanne 1932- *BioIn 16*
Knudson-Fitzpatrick, Anne Howland 1952- *WhoWor 91*
Knudtson, Peter M 1947- *ConAu 129*
Knudtzon, Halvor, Jr. 1926- *WhoAm 90*
Knue, James Leroy 1953- *WhoEmL 91*
Knue, Paul Frederick 1947- *WhoAm 90*
Knuepfer, Jack Tarrant 1920- *St&PR 91*
Knuepfer, Robert Claude 1923- *St&PR 91*
Knup, Stephen Charles 1942- *WhoAm 90*
Knupfer, Genevieve 1914- *BiDrAPA 89*
Knupfer, Paul 1865-1920 *PenDiMP*
Knupp, Douglas Scott 1959- *WhoE 91*
Knuppel, Robert A. 1947- *WhoAm 90*
Knurek, Thomas Adam 1933- *St&PR 91*
Knushevitsky, Svyatoslav 1908-1963 *PenDiMP*
Knussen, Oliver 1952- *IntWWM 90*
Knutel, Kenneth Edward 1940- *St&PR 91*
Knuteson, Knut Jeffery 1949- *WhoEmL 91, WhoWor 91*
Knutgen, Anno *PenDiDA 89*
Knutgen, Bertram *PenDiDA 89*
Knutgen, Christian *PenDiDA 89*
Knutgen, Peter *PenDiDA 89*
Knutgen, Rutger *PenDiDA 89*
Knuth, Constance J. 1950- *St&PR 91*
Knuth, Cynthia Strout *WhoE 91*
Knuth, Eldon Luverne 1925- *WhoAm 90*
Knuth, Robert 1933- *St&PR 91*
Knuth, Stephen B. 1946- *St&PR 91*
Knuth, Terry Lynne 1952- *WhoEmL 91*
Knuths, Leroy R. 1932- *St&PR 91*
Knuths, Shalmerdean A. 1938- *St&PR 91*
Knuths, William Ronald 1955- *WhoEmL 91*
Knutsen, Alan Paul 1948- *WhoEmL 91*
Knutsen, Carl C.M. 1944- *St&PR 91*
Knutsen, Elaine J 1928- *BiDrAPA 89*
Knutson, David 1946- *IntWWM 90*
Knutson, David Harry 1934- *WhoAm 90*
Knutson, David Lee 1959- *WhoEmL 91*
Knutson, Donald C. 1930-1990 *BioIn 16*
Knutson, Donald C. 1931?-1990 *ConAu 131*
Knutson, Elliot Knut 1924- *St&PR 91, WhoAm 90*
Knutson, Greta 1899-1983 *BiDWomA*
Knutson, Janell Marie 1961- *WhoEmL 91*
Knutson, John Alfred 1940- *St&PR 91*
Knutson, John Franklin 1942- *WhoAm 90*
Knutson, Katherine Mellby 1910- *WhoAmW 91*
Knutson, Lee Thomas 1938- *St&PR 91*
Knutson, Lyle *St&PR 91*
Knutson, Ronald Dale 1940- *WhoAm 90*
Knutson, Steven John 1951 *WhoEmL 91*
Knutson, Timothy Russell 1956- *WhoEmL 91*
Knutson, Wayne Shafer 1926- *WhoAm 90*
Knutsson, Katherine H *BiDrAPA 89*
Knutti, Elizabeth Blanche 1945- *WhoAmW 91*
Knutzen, Raymond Edward 1941- *WhoWor 91*
Knye, Cassandra *MajTwCW*
Knyvett, Charles 1752-1822 *PenDiMP*
Ko, Allen Hiu-Ching 1953- *WhoWor 91*
Ko, Anthony 1934- *WhoAmA 91N*
Ko, Ensei 1927- *WhoWor 91*
Ko, Grant Norman *BiDrAPA 89*
Ko, Haeng S *BiDrAPA 89*
Ko, Hak Jin *BiDrAPA 89*
Ko, Pao Chung 1930- *BiDrAPA 89*
Ko, Sung-Won 1925- *WhoWrEP 89*
Ko, Wen-Hsiung 1923- *WhoAm 90*
Koach, Stephen Francis 1950- *WhoSSW 91*
Koart, Nellie Hart 1930- *WhoAmW 91*
Kobacker, Arthur J. 1924- *St&PR 91*
Kobak, Hope McEldowney 1922- *WhoE 91*
Kobak, James B. 1921- *St&PR 91*
Kobak, James Benedict 1921- *WhoAm 90, WhoWor 91*
Kobak, James Benedict, Jr. 1944- *WhoE 91*
Kobak, Sharon Torreano 1943- *BiDrAPA 89*
Kobasa, John David 1940- *St&PR 91*
Kobayashi, Albert Satoshi 1924- *WhoAm 90*
Kobayashi, Ann H. 1937- *WhoAmW 91*
Kobayashi, Atsumoto 1934- *WhoWor 91*
Kobayashi, Eiji 1947- *WhoWor 91*
Kobayashi, Fumito 1931- *WhoWor 91*
Kobayashi, Hideaki 1950- *WhoEmL 91*
Kobayashi, Hiroshi 1951- *WhoWor 91*
Kobayashi, Hisako 1946- *WhoAmA 91*
Kobayashi, Hisashi 1938- *WhoAm 90*
Kobayashi, Isao 1945- *WhoWor 91*
Kobayashi, Joyce Seiko *BiDrAPA 89*

Kobayashi, Kaetsu 1934- *St&PR 91*
Kobayashi, Koji 1907- *St&PR 91, WhoWor 91*
Kobayashi, Manji 1931- *WhoWor 91*
Kobayashi, Masaki *BioIn 16*
Kobayashi, Masako Matsuno *AuBYP 90*
Kobayashi, Masako Matsuno 1935- *ConAu 31NR*
Kobayashi, Masamichi 1933- *WhoWor 91*
Kobayashi, Noritake 1932- *WhoWor 91*
Kobayashi, Riki 1924- *WhoAm 90*
Kobayashi, Roger Hideo 1947- *WhoEmL 91*
Kobayashi, Shigeo 1927- *WhoWor 91*
Kobayashi, Shiro 1924- *WhoAm 90*
Kobayashi, Susumu 1939- *WhoWor 91*
Kobayashi, Tatsuya 1929- *WhoWor 91*
Kobayashi, Toshiji 1933- *WhoWor 91*
Kobayashi, Tsunehiro 1932- *WhoWor 91*
Kobayashi, Yashuhiro 1931- *WhoWor 91*
Kobayashi, Yotaro *BioIn 16*
Kobayashi, Yumi 1951- *WhoAmW 91*
Kobe Daishi *EncJap*
Kobe, Karen Louise 1962- *WhoAmW 91*
Kobe, Lan *WhoAmW 91*
Kobel, Kevin 1953- *Ballpl 90*
Kobelinski, Mitchell Peter 1928- *WhoAm 90*
Kobelski, Irene Catherine 1960- *WhoWrEP 89*
Kober, Alfred John 1937- *WhoAmA 91*
Kober, Arletta Refshauge 1919- *WhoAmW 91, WhoWor 91*
Kober, Carl Leopold 1913- *WhoAm 90*
Kober, Charles M. 1923- *St&PR 91*
Kober, Philip Mason 1952- *WhoEmL 91*
Kober, Theodore Earnest 1930- *St&PR 91*
Kobernusz, E. William 1940- *St&PR 91*
Kobert, Norman 1929- *St&PR 91*
Kobes, Rodger Dale 1941- *BiDrAPA 89*
Kobetz, Richard William 1933- *WhoSSW 91*
Kobialka, Daniel *NewAgMG*
Kobiashvili, Zurab S. 1942- *St&PR 91*
Kobie, Franklin L. 1933- *St&PR 91*
Kobilza, Siegfried 1954- *IntWWM 90*
Kobin, Herbert 1929- *St&PR 91*
Kobinia, Georg Stephan 1949- *WhoWor 91*
Kobke, Christen Schjellerup 1810-1848 *BioIn 16*
Koblentz, Aaron E *BiDrAPA 89*
Koblentz, Daniel Elliot 1946- *BiDrAPA 89*
Koblenz, Lawrence William 1948- *WhoEmL 91*
Koblenz, Michael Robert 1948- *WhoEmL 91*
Koblenzer, Habiba A *BiDrAPA 89*
Koblenzer, Jonathan 1953- *BiDrAPA 89*
Kobler, Fritz *BiDrAPA 89*
Kobler, John 1910- *WhoAm 90*
Kobler, Linda 1955- *IntWWM 90*
Kobler, Raymond 1945- *WhoAm 90*
Koblick, Andrew W. 1957- *St&PR 91*
Koblick, Jeffrey Mark 1947- *St&PR 91*
Koblitz, Karen *BioIn 16*
Koblitz, Michael Jay 1949- *WhoEmL 91*
Kobriger, Richard Roman, Jr. 1954- *WhoEmL 91*
Kobrin, Irving *BioIn 16*
Kobrin, Lawrence Alan 1933- *WhoAm 90, WhoE 91*
Kobrine, Arthur 1943- *WhoAm 90*
Kobro, Katarzyna 1898-1951 *BiDWomA*
Kobryns'ka, Natalija 1855-1920 *EncCoWW*
Kobs, Ann Elizabeth Jane 1944- *WhoAmW 91, WhoWor 91*
Kobs, James Fred 1938- *WhoAm 90*
Kobus, Mona Wright 1932- *WhoAmW 91*
Kobus, Thomas Andrew 1952- *St&PR 91*
Koby, Constance Kirkland 1944- *WhoSSW 91*
Koby, Elizabeth *BiDrAPA 89*
Koby, Jay S *BiDrAPA 89*
Kobylaret, Thomas L. 1939- *St&PR 91*
Kobylarz, Brian Fred 1956- *WhoEmL 91*
Kobyljans'ka, Ol'ha 1863-1942 *EncCoWW*
Kobylski, Thomas Paul 1961- *BiDrAPA 89*
Koc, Teoman 1930- *BiDrAPA 89*
Koc, Vehbi 1901- *WhoWor 91*
Kocache, Riad Mouhamed Adel 1942- *WhoWor 91*
Kocaoglu, Dundar F. 1939- *WhoAm 90, WhoWor 91*
Kocar, George Frederick 1948- *WhoAmA 91*
Kocbek, Marijan 1957- *WhoWor 91*
Kocen, Joel Evan 1936- *WhoAm 90*
Kocen, Steven Ellis 1949- *St&PR 91*
Koch, Alan 1938- *Ballpl 90*
Koch, Albert Acheson 1942- *WhoAm 90*
Koch, Albin Cooper 1933- *WhoAm 90*
Koch, Alexander 1932- *WhoWor 91*
Koch, Arne G. M. 1930- *WhoWor 91*
Koch, Arno Olaf Andreas 1955- *WhoWor 91*
Koch, Arnold T., Jr. 1930- *ODwPR 91*
Koch, Arthur Louis 1925- *WhoAm 90*
Koch, Arthur Robert 1934- *WhoAmA 91*
Koch, Bertha Couch 1899-1975 *WhoAmA 91N*
Koch, Bradley Christ 1935- *St&PR 91*
Koch, Brian David 1961- *WhoEmL 91*
Koch, Bruce K. 1947- *St&PR 91*
Koch, Bruno Alfons 1929- *WhoSSW 91*
Koch, Carl 1912- *WhoAm 90*
Koch, Carl G. 1931- *WhoAm 90*
Koch, Carol Higgins 1953- *WhoAmW 91*
Koch, Charles de Ganahl 1935- *WhoAm 90, WhoWor 91*
Koch, Charles G. 1935- *St&PR 91*
Koch, Charles Joseph 1919- *WhoAm 90*
Koch, Charles R *BiDrAPA 89*
Koch, Craig R. 1946- *WhoAm 90*
Koch, Daniel S. 1951- *WhoEmL 91*
Koch, David 1913- *St&PR 91*
Koch, David A. 1930- *St&PR 91*
Koch, David Alan 1961- *WhoEmL 91*
Koch, David Allan 1946- *BiDrAPA 89*
Koch, Diane Ruth 1956- *WhoAmW 91*
Koch, Diane Witman 1947- *WhoEmL 91*
Koch, Dietrich-Alex Gerhard 1942- *WhoWor 91*
Koch, Dorothy 1924- *AuBYP 90*
Koch, Eberhard Georg Johann 1951- *WhoWor 91*
Koch, Ed 1924- *BioIn 16*
Koch, Edna Mae 1951- *WhoAmW 91, WhoEmL 91, WhoWor 91*
Koch, Edward, Sr. 1907- *St&PR 91*
Koch, Edward I. 1924- *WhoAm 90, WhoE 91, WorAlBi*
Koch, Edward Richard 1953- *WhoE 91, WhoEmL 91, WhoWor 91*
Koch, Edwin B. 1937- *BioIn 16*
Koch, Edwin E 1915- *WhoAmA 91*
Koch, Edwin Ernest 1915- *WhoE 91*
Koch, Erich 1896-1986 *BioIn 16*
Koch, Fenton C. 1930- *St&PR 91*
Koch, Friedrich 1936- *WhoWor 91*
Koch, Gary Paul 1954- *St&PR 91*
Koch, Gerd 1929- *WhoAmA 91*
Koch, Guntram 1941- *WhoWor 91*
Koch, H. Thomas, Jr. 1926- *St&PR 91*
Koch, Harald Erich 1943- *WhoWor 91*
Koch, Harold V. 1921- *St&PR 91*
Koch, Helen Alice 1916- *WhoAmW 91*
Koch, Howard W. 1916- *BioIn 16*
Koch, Howard W., Jr. 1945- *WhoAm 90*
Koch, Howard Winchel 1916- *WhoAm 90*
Koch, Ilse 1906-1967 *BioIn 16*
Koch, Jacob, II *PenDiDA 89*
Koch, James Verch 1942- *WhoAm 90, WhoWrEP 89*
Koch, Jeffrey B. 1947- *St&PR 91*
Koch, Jerome A. *BioIn 16*
Koch, Jim *BioIn 16*
Koch, Joanne 1929- *WhoAmW 91*
Koch, Joanne 1940- *ConAu 32NR*
Koch, John 1909-1978 *WhoAmA 91N*
Koch, John Frederick W. 1925- *St&PR 91*
Koch, John Jacob, Jr. *BiDrAPA 89*
Koch, John Liveright 1944- *WhoAm 90*
Koch, Joseph M. 1934- *St&PR 91*
Koch, June Quint 1933- *WhoAmW 91*
Koch, Karen Jean 1945- *WhoWrEP 89*
Koch, Karl *BioIn 16*
Koch, Kathleen Jane 1953- *WhoEmL 91*
Koch, Kenneth 1925- *WhoAm 90, WhoWrEP 89*
Koch, Kenneth Hobson 1955- *St&PR 91*
Koch, Kenneth Joseph 1944- *St&PR 91*
Koch, Kenneth Richard 1955- *WhoEmL 91*
Koch, Kimberly Ann 1964- *WhoAmW 91*
Koch, Ky Marshall 1952- *WhoEmL 91*
Koch, Lawrence 1917- *St&PR 91*
Koch, Lisa C. 1961- *WhoEmL 91*
Koch, Marita *BioIn 16*
Koch, Martin 1882-1940 *DcScanL*
Koch, Martin Robert 1952- *St&PR 91*
Koch, Michael 1938- *St&PR 91*
Koch, Michael F *BiDrAPA 89*
Koch, Myron Harris 1936- *BiDrAPA 89*
Koch, Norman L. 1935- *St&PR 91*
Koch, Peter 1920- *WhoAm 90*
Koch, Peter F. 1933- *WhoAm 90*
Koch, Philip 1948- *WhoAmA 91*
Koch, Philip Frederick 1948- *WhoE 91*
Koch, R James *BiDrAPA 89*
Koch, Ralph Richard 1928- *WhoAm 90*
Koch, Richard 1921- *WhoAm 90*
Koch, Richard Edward 1928- *St&PR 91*
Koch, Richard F. 1945- *St&PR 91*
Koch, Richard G. 1925- *WhoSSW 91*
Koch, Richard Henry 1918- *WhoAm 90*
Koch, Richard Joseph 1947- *St&PR 91, WhoEmL 91*
Koch, Rita Elizabeth 1948- *WhoAmW 91*
Koch, Robert 1843-1910 *BioIn 16, WorAlBi*
Koch, Robert 1918- *WhoAmA 91*
Koch, Robert Alan 1919- *WhoAm 90*
Koch, Robert Louis *St&PR 91N*
Koch, Robert Louis, II 1939- *St&PR 91, WhoAm 90*
Koch, Robert M. 1930- *St&PR 91*
Koch, Robert Warren 1927- *St&PR 91*
Koch, Ronald Ray 1938- *St&PR 91*
Koch, Rosanna M *BiDrAPA 89*
Koch, Russell Gordon 1954- *WhoWor 91*
Koch, Sharon Lynne 1940- *WhoSSW 91*
Koch, Sidney 1935- *WhoAm 90*
Koch, Steven 1956- *WhoEmL 91*
Koch, Steven Alan 1952- *St&PR 91*
Koch, Susan Elsa 1944- *WhoAmW 91*
Koch, Tad Harbison 1943- *WhoAm 90*
Koch, Virginia *WhoAmA 91*
Koch, Virginia Greenleaf 1925- *WhoE 91*
Koch, Walter A 1895- *EncO&P 3*
Koch, William Albert 1915- *St&PR 91*
Koch, William Albert, Jr. 1961- *WhoEmL 91*
Koch, William Emery 1922-1987 *WhoAmA 91N*
Koch, William Franklin 1931- *St&PR 91*
Koch, William H *BiDrAPA 89*
Koch, William Henry 1941- *WhoSSW 91*
Koch, William I. *BioIn 16*
Koch, Wolfgang *BioIn 16*
Koch Lipman, Carel Evelynn 1960- *WhoAmW 91*
Kochakian, Charles Daniel 1908- *WhoAm 90*
Kochamp, Katherine Ellen 1946- *WhoAmW 91*
Kochan, Christopher Michael 1963- *WhoSSW 91*
Kochan, James Leo 1941- *WhoE 91*
Kochannek, Juergen 1946- *St&PR 91*
Kochanowski, Jan 1530-1584 *BioIn 16*
Kochanowski, Robert 1936- *WhoAm 90*
Kochanowsky, Boris Julius 1905- *WhoAm 90, WhoWor 91*
Kochanski, Adrian Joseph 1918- *WhoAm 90*
Kochanski, Paul 1887-1934 *PenDiMP*
Kochanski, Wladimir Jan 1936- *IntWWM 90*
Kochar, Hira 1942- *St&PR 91*
Kochar, Mahendr Singh 1943- *WhoAm 90*
Kochen, Ilana *BiDrAPA 89*
Kochen, Manfred 1928- *WhoAm 90*
Kochen, Manfred 1928-1989 *BioIn 16*
Kocher, Charles 1952- *St&PR 91*
Kocher, Donald Wallace 1963- *WhoWrEP 89*
Kocher, Emil T. 1841-1917 *WorAlBi*
Kocher, Frederick Lee 1943- *St&PR 91*
Kocher, Gary N. 1947- *St&PR 91*
Kocher, Gary Nielsen 1947- *WhoAm 90*
Kocher, Jo Ann Catherine 1946- *WhoEmL 91*
Kocher, Paul Harold 1907- *WhoAm 90*
Kocher, Robert Lee 1929- *WhoAmA 91*
Kocher, Walter W. 1934- *St&PR 91*
Kocherthaler, Mina *WhoAmA 91, WhoE 91*
Kochevar, John A. *ODwPR 91*
Kochheiser, George William 1925- *St&PR 91*
Kochheiser, Thomas H 1956- *WhoAmA 91*
Kochi, Jay Kazuo 1927- *WhoAm 90*
Kochinke, Clemens Joachim Maria 1952- *WhoEmL 91*
Kochis, George P 1925- *BiDrAPA 89*
Kochis, Paul Martin 1947- *St&PR 91*
Kochka, Al 1928- *WhoAm 90, WhoAmA 91*
Kochman, Alexandra D 1936- *WhoAmA 91*
Kochman, Edward 1948- *St&PR 91*
Kochman, Rosalind Axelrod 1937- *WhoAmW 91*
Kochno, Boris 1904-1990 *NewYTBS 90*
Kochs, Herbert William 1903- *WhoAm 90*
Kochta, Ruth Martha 1924- *WhoAmA 91*
Koci, Ludvik F. 1936- *St&PR 91*
Koci, Ludvik Frank 1936- *WhoAm 90*
Kocian, James J. 1935- *St&PR 91*
Kocian, Joseph Vince 1949- *WhoEmL 91*
Kocic, Vlajko 1953- *WhoWor 91*
Kocik, Dennis Edward 1955- *WhoEmL 91*
Kocikowski, Stefan 1924- *WhoWor 91*
Kocin, Sidney 1914- *WhoWrEP 89*
Kocinski, James Allen 1941- *St&PR 91*
Kocinski, John *BioIn 16*
Kocisko, Stephen John 1915- *WhoAm 90, WhoE 91*
Kock, Arlene Dorothy 1951- *WhoEmL 91*
Kock, Carl *AuBYP 90*
Kock, Lars Anders Wolfram 1913- *WhoWor 91*
Kock, Roland 1947- *St&PR 91*
Kockberg, Mats Borje 1950- *WhoWor 91*
Kockelmans, Joseph J. 1923- *WhoAm 90*
Kocks, Adriaen *PenDiDA 89*
Kocmieroski, Matthew 1953- *IntWWM 90*
Koco, Linda Gale 1945- *WhoWrEP 89*
Kocoras, Charles Petros 1938- *WhoAm 90*
Kocourek, Paul F. 1950- *St&PR 91*
Kocourek, Wayne C. 1937- *St&PR 91*
Kocsis, James H 1942- *BiDrAPA 89*
Kocsis, James Howard 1942- *WhoE 91*
Kocsis, James Paul 1936- *WhoAm 90, WhoAmA 91*
Kocsis, Zoltan 1952- *IntWWM 90, PenDiMP, WhoWor 91*
Kocur, John A. 1927- *St&PR 91*
Kocur, Shirley J *BiDrAPA 89*
Kocurek, Mary Jane 1939- *WhoAmW 91, WhoSSW 91*
Kocurek, Patricia Terrazas 1935- *WhoAmW 91*
Kocx, Adriaen *PenDiDA 89*
Koczur, Paula Marchewka 1949- *St&PR 91*
Kodah, Clara Mack 1945- *WhoE 91*
Kodaka, Kunio 1932- *St&PR 91*
Kodali, Swatantra B 1944- *BiDrAPA 89*
Kodaly, Zoltan 1882-1967 *PenDiMP A, WorAlBi*
Kode, Shubhada Kalidas *BiDrAPA 89*
Kodera, Takeshiro 1912- *WhoWor 91*
Kodesch, Fred 1956- *WhoSSW 91*
Kodet, Albert Charles 1958- *WhoE 91*
Kodis, Mary Caroline 1927- *WhoAmW 91*
Koditek, Robert Alan 1955- *WhoEmL 91*
Kodner, Martin 1934- *WhoAmA 91*
Kodosky, Jeffrey Leo 1949- *WhoSSW 91*
Kodousek, Joseph *PenDiMP*
Kodukula, Amruta Rao 1941- *BiDrAPA 89*
Koduri, Ramesh Babu *BiDrAPA 89*
Koduru, Banerje *BiDrAPA 89*
Koe, Bruce G. *St&PR 91*
Koe, Robert Edwards 1945- *St&PR 91, WhoAm 90*
Koebe, Paul 1882-1945 *DcScB S2*
Koebel, Wayne Robert 1947- *St&PR 91*
Koeburgge, H. Paul 1940- *WhoSSW 91*
Koechlein, Lois Jane Ellis 1951- *WhoEmL 91*
Koechler, Hans 1948- *WhoWor 91*
Koeckert Quartet *PenDiMP*
Koeckert, Robert A. 1947- *St&PR 91*
Koeckert, Rudolf 1913- *PenDiMP*
Koeckert, Rudolf Joachim *PenDiMP*
Koedel, John G., Jr. 1937- *St&PR 91*
Koedel, John Gilbert, Jr. 1937- *WhoAm 90*
Koedel, Robert Craig 1927- *WhoAm 90*
Koeder, Tamera Kathleen 1961- *WhoEmL 91*
Koegel, Albert J. 1926- *St&PR 91*
Koegel, William Fisher 1923- *WhoAm 90*
Koegler, Albert Charles 1952- *BiDrAPA 89*
Koegler, Ronald R 1927- *BiDrAPA 89*
Koegler, Shahin B *BiDrAPA 89*
Koehl, Camille Joan 1943- *WhoAmW 91, WhoWor 91*
Koehl, Stuart Laurence 1956- *WhoEmL 91*
Koehle, Siegfried Eugen 1931- *WhoAm 90*
Koehle, William Joseph 1950- *WhoEmL 91*
Koehler, Albert Max 1935- *St&PR 91*
Koehler, Corinne Anderson 1949- *WhoAmW 91*
Koehler, Daniel Walter 1950- *St&PR 91*
Koehler, David Gerard 1958- *WhoSSW 91*
Koehler, Donna *BioIn 16*
Koehler, Frank *ConAu 31NR*
Koehler, George Applegate 1921- *WhoAm 90*
Koehler, George F. *St&PR 91*
Koehler, Henry 1927- *WhoAmA 91, WhoE 91*
Koehler, Jane Ellen 1944- *WhoAmW 91*
Koehler, Jo Ann M. 1951- *WhoWrEP 89*
Koehler, John T. 1904-1989 *BioIn 16*
Koehler, Kurt Charles 1957- *WhoEmL 91*
Koehler, Margaret *ConAu 30NR*
Koehler, Mary Frances 1956- *BiDrAPA 89*
Koehler, Paul H. 1957- *WhoE 91*
Koehler, Philip Gene 1947- *WhoEmL 91*
Koehler, Phoebe 1955- *ConAu 132*
Koehler, Reginald Stafford, III 1932- *WhoAm 90*
Koehler, Ronald E. 1953- *WhoWrEP 89*
Koehler, Ronald Gene 1950- *WhoAmA 91*
Koehler, Rudolph August 1934- *St&PR 91, WhoAm 90*
Koehler, T. James 1935- *St&PR 91*
Koehler, T. Richard 1933- *St&PR 91*
Koehler, Ted 1894-1973 *OxCPMus*
Koehler, Truman Lester 1931- *WhoSSW 91*
Koehn, Charles William *WhoAm 90*
Koehn, George Waldemar 1943- *St&PR 91, WhoAm 90, WhoSSW 91*
Koehn, Hank E. *BioIn 16*
Koehn, John Edward 1932- *St&PR 91*
Koehn, Thomas K. 1949- *St&PR 91*
Koehn, William James 1936- *WhoWor 91*
Koehne, Graeme John 1956- *IntWWM 90*
Koehneke, Martin L. *BioIn 16*
Koehring, Klaus Heinrich 1941- *WhoWor 91*
Koehrsen, Lawrence G. 1937- *St&PR 91*
Koek, Ralph Jan 1958- *BiDrAPA 89*
Koekkoek, Kuindert Adriaan 1949- *WhoWor 91*
Koelb, Clayton T. 1920- *St&PR 91*
Koelb, Clayton T. 1942- *ConAu 132*
Koelb, Clayton Talmadge 1920- *WhoAm 90*
Koella, Carl Ohm, Jr. 1933- *WhoSSW 91*

Koelle, George Brampton 1918- *WhoAm 90*
Koelle, Mary L. 1948- *WhoE 91*
Koelle, Peter Otto 1945- *WhoEmL 91*
Koeller, Kirby F. 1936- *St&PR 91*
Koelling, Herbert Lee 1932- *WhoAm 90*
Koelmel, Lorna Lee 1936- *WhoAmW 91, WhoWor 91*
Koelsch, John M. *BioIn 16*
Koelsch, M. Oliver 1912- *WhoAm 90*
Koelsch, William Alvin 1933- *WhoWrEP 89*
Koelzer, Victor Alvin 1914- *WhoAm 90*
Koen, Benjamin Lawrence 1942- *St&PR 91*
Koen, Billy Vaughn 1938- *WhoAm 90*
Koen, Clifford Mock, Jr. 1949- *WhoSSW 91*
Koen, Fanny Blankers- 1918- *BioIn 16*
Koen, Joseph William 1942- *WhoSSW 91*
Koen, Philip Joseph 1952- *St&PR 91*
Koenecke, Carol Yvonne 1959- *WhoAmW 91*
Koenecke, Fred H 1924- *BiDrAPA 89*
Koenecke, Len 1904-1935 *Ballpl 90*
Koeneke, Karl Herbert 1929- *St&PR 91*
Koeneke, Michael S. 1947- *St&PR 91*
Koeneman, James P. 1948- *St&PR 91, WhoAm 90*
Koenhen, Dirk Marinus 1949- *WhoWor 91*
Koenig, A. Bertram 1910- *St&PR 91*
Koenig, A.W. 1928- *St&PR 91*
Koenig, Allen Edward 1939- *WhoAm 90*
Koenig, Alma Johanna 1887-1942? *EncCoWW*
Koenig, Angela C. *St&PR 91*
Koenig, Catherine Catanzaro 1921- *WhoAmA 91*
Koenig, Charles Louis 1911- *WhoAm 90*
Koenig, Eckard 1944- *WhoWor 91*
Koenig, Elizabeth 1937- *WhoAmA 91*
Koenig, Elizabeth Barbara 1937- *WhoAmW 91*
Koenig, Elliott Joseph 1928- *St&PR 91*
Koenig, Eric Stuart 1958- *WhoE 91*
Koenig, Franz 1905- *WhoWor 91*
Koenig, Gay Pennington 1956- *WhoAmW 91*
Koenig, George W. 1929- *St&PR 91*
Koenig, Ghisha 1921- *BiDWomA*
Koenig, H. Steve 1946- *WhoAm 90*
Koenig, Harold P. 1926- *St&PR 91*
Koenig, Hedwig 1895-1989 *BioIn 16*
Koenig, Herman Edward 1924- *WhoAm 90*
Koenig, James E. 1947- *St&PR 91*
Koenig, James Norman, Jr. 1961- *WhoEmL 91*
Koenig, John Franklin 1924- *WhoAmA 91*
Koenig, John Morris 1950- *WhoEmL 91*
Koenig, John Richard 1946- *WhoSSW 91*
Koenig, Karl Eric 1947- *WhoEmL 91*
Koenig, Karl Joseph 1955- *WhoSSW 91*
Koenig, Kenneth L 1938- *BiDrAPA 89*
Koenig, Kent Robert 1935- *St&PR 91*
Koenig, Kim Diane 1956- *WhoAmW 91*
Koenig, Laird *ConAu 32NR*
Koenig, Marie Harriet King 1919- *WhoAmW 91*
Koenig, Mark 1902- *Ballpl 90*
Koenig, Mark Edward 1955- *WhoSSW 91*
Koenig, Mary Gonzalez 1936- *WhoHisp 91*
Koenig, Michele Lorraine *BiDrAPA 89*
Koenig, Peter Edward 1956- *WhoEmL 91*
Koenig, Peter L 1933- *WhoAmA 91*
Koenig, Peter Laszlo 1933- *WhoE 91*
Koenig, Richard C 1923- *BiDrAPA 89*
Koenig, Richard Michael 1942- *WhoAm 90*
Koenig, Robert August 1933- *WhoWor 91*
Koenig, Robert J 1935- *WhoAmA 91*
Koenig, Robert John 1935- *WhoE 91*
Koenig, Robert W. 1932- *St&PR 91*
Koenig, Rodney Curtis 1940- *WhoAm 90*
Koenig, Ruth *BiDrAPA 89*
Koenig, Sharon Ann 1947- *WhoAmW 91*
Koenig, Sierra Sue 1954- *WhoAmW 91*
Koenig, Thomas L. 1940- *St&PR 91*
Koenig, Virgil 1913-1989 *WhoAm 90*
Koenig, Walter *BioIn 16*
Koenig, Werner T 1925- *BiDrAPA 89*
Koenig, William C. 1947- *St&PR 91*
Koenig, Wolfgang W. 1936- *St&PR 91, WhoAm 90*
Koenigs, Rita Scales 1952- *WhoAmW 91, WhoEmL 91*
Koenigsaecker, George Joseph, III 1945- *WhoEmL 91*
Koenigsberg, Alan 1954- *BiDrAPA 89*
Koenigsberg, Daniel M 1941- *BiDrAPA 89*
Koenigsberg, Harold Warren 1946- *BiDrAPA 89*
Koenigsberg, Martin 1912- *St&PR 91*
Koenigsberg, Marvin Lee 1918- *WhoAm 90*
Koenigsberg, Moses 1879-1945 *BioIn 16*
Koenigsberger, Helmut Georg 1918- *WhoWor 91*
Koenigsknecht, Roy A. 1942- *WhoAm 90*
Koenigswarter, Pannonica de 1913-1988 *BioIn 16*
Koenigswarter, Pannonica De 1914-1988 *AnObit 1988*
Koeninger, Edward Calvin 1930- *WhoAm 90*
Koeninger, Jimmy G. 1942- *WhoSSW 91*
Koeninger, Kay 1951- *WhoWrEP 89*
Koep, Richard Michael 1949- *WhoEmL 91*
Koepcke, F. Kristen 1935- *St&PR 91*
Koepeczi-Deak, Bajan 1945- *St&PR 91*
Koepf, Michael 1940- *WhoWrEP 89*
Koepfinger, Joseph Leo 1925- *WhoAm 90*
Koepke, Allen C. 1945- *St&PR 91*
Koepke, Frederick William 1926- *St&PR 91*
Koepke, Hans Heinrich *BiDrAPA 89*
Koepke, John Arthur 1929- *WhoAm 90*
Koepke, John D. 1935- *St&PR 91*
Koepke, Tom Allan *BiDrAPA 89*
Koepke, Wallace John 1949- *WhoEmL 91*
Koepnick, Donald Joseph 1945- *St&PR 91, WhoSSW 91*
Koepnick, Robert Charles 1907- *WhoAmA 91*
Koepp, Donald William 1929- *WhoAm 90*
Koeppe, Paul F. 1949- *St&PR 91*
Koeppel, Andrew E. 1943- *St&PR 91*
Koeppel, Gary Merle 1938- *WhoWor 91*
Koeppel, John Paul 1956- *BiDrAPA 89*
Koeppen, Albert W. 1930- *St&PR 91*
Koeppen, Raymond Bradley 1954- *WhoEmL 91*
Koepsel, Wellington Wesley 1921- *WhoAm 90*
Koepsell, Gilmore John 1925- *St&PR 91*
Koerber, Dirk 1940- *ODwPR 91, St&PR 91*
Koerber, Janet Pearl 1933- *WhoAmW 91*
Koerber, Joan Patricia 1929- *WhoAmW 91, WhoE 91*
Koerber, Marilynn Eleanor 1942- *WhoAmW 91*
Koerfer, Patrick C. *St&PR 91*
Koering, Marilyn Jean 1938- *WhoAm 90*
Koering, Ursula 1921-1976 *SmATA 64 [port]*
Koerner, Ernest Lee 1931- *St&PR 91*
Koerner, Frank 1955- *WhoEmL 91*
Koerner, Henry 1915- *WhoAmA 91*
Koerner, James David 1923- *WhoAm 90*
Koerner, Jerry Lynn 1950- *WhoAmW 91*
Koerner, Michael Milan 1928- *WhoAm 90*
Koerner, Philip Donald 1946- *St&PR 91*
Koerner, Victor Frederick 1911- *WhoAm 90*
Koertge, Noretta 1935- *WhoWrEP 89*
Koertge, Ronald *BioIn 16*
Koertge, Ronald 1940- *DcLB 105 [port]*
Koertge, Ronald Boyd 1940- *WhoWrEP 89*
Koerth, Leon Vincent 1947- *WhoSSW 91*
Koerting, Richard J. 1937- *St&PR 91*
Koessel, Donald Ray 1929- *WhoAm 90*
Koessler, Paul J. 1937- *St&PR 91*
Koesten, Gary Gilbert 1944- *WhoSSW 91*
Koestenblatt, Marlene Phylis 1945- *WhoEmL 91*
Koester, Berthold Karl 1931- *WhoWor 91*
Koester, Charles R. 1915- *WhoAm 90*
Koester, Charles William, Jr. 1945- *WhoAm 90, WhoEmL 91*
Koester, Fred William 1936- *St&PR 91*
Koester, Helmut Heinrich 1926- *WhoAm 90*
Koester, Robert Gregg 1932- *WhoAm 90*
Koester, Robert Joseph, Jr. 1948- *WhoWor 91*
Koester, Ronald 1956- *St&PR 91*
Koester, Ronald Dean 1935- *St&PR 91*
Koesterer, Martin George 1933- *WhoE 91*
Koesterer, Ralph J. 1926- *St&PR 91*
Koestler, Arthur 1905-1983 *BioIn 16, ConAu 33NR, DcNaB 1981, EncO&P 3, EncPaPR 91, MajTwCW, WorAlBi*
Koestler, Fred 1934- *WhoSSW 91*
Koestner, Adalbert 1920- *WhoAm 90*
Koestner, Don 1923- *WhoAmA 91*
Koeth, Leonard Alfred 1937- *WhoSSW 91*
Koether, Bernard Gustave, II 1937- *St&PR 91*
Koether, Paul Otto 1936- *St&PR 91*
Koether, Philip 1956- *WhoE 91*
Koetsch, Philip 1935- *St&PR 91*
Koetsier, Jan 1911- *IntWWM 90*
Koetsier, Johan Carel 1936- *WhoWor 91*
Koetsu *EncJap*
Koetsu, Hon'ami 1558-1637 *PenDiDA 89*
Koetter, Ludwig 1926- *WhoWor 91*
Koetters, Michael C. 1943- *St&PR 91*
Koetters, Michael Charles 1943- *WhoAm 90*
Koetters, Thomas Joseph 1943- *St&PR 91*
Koevenig, Brian Paul 1956- *WhoEmL 91*
Kofalk, Harriet 1937- *ConAu 30NR*
Koff, Marvin Saul 1938- *BiDrAPA 89*
Koff, Richard M 1926- *SmATA 62*
Koff, Richard Myram 1926- *St&PR 91, WhoAm 90*
Koff, Robert *PenDiMP*
Koff, Robert Hess 1938- *WhoAm 90*
Koff, William Edward 1954- *BiDrAPA 89*
Koffel, Martin M. 1939- *St&PR 91*
Koffler, Camilla *AuBYP 90*
Koffler, Henry 1922- *WhoAm 90*
Koffler, Irving 1932- *St&PR 91*
Koffler, Jeffrey Michael *BiDrAPA 89*
Koffman, Burton I. 1925- *St&PR 91*
Koffman, Earldene Johns 1927- *WhoSSW 91*
Koffman, Milton Aaron 1923- *St&PR 91, WhoAm 90*
Koffman, Mitchell J. 1931- *St&PR 91*
Koffman, Morley 1930- *St&PR 91*
Kofford, Cree-L 1933- *WhoWor 91*
Kofford, Kay G. 1948- *WhoEmL 91*
Koffskey, George Chester, Jr. 1921- *WhoSSW 91*
Koffsky, Peter Langer 1946- *WhoEmL 91*
Kofkin, Murray 1927- *BiDrAPA 89*
Kofler, Mark Bruno 1949- *BiDrAPA 89*
Kofler, Valentine Mathew 1927- *St&PR 91*
Kofman, Mary Anita 1942- *WhoAmW 91*
Kofoed, Jack 1894- *Ballpl 90*
Kofoed, Lial L *BiDrAPA 89*
Kofoed, William Carl 1934- *WhoSSW 91*
Koford, James Shingle 1938- *St&PR 91*
Koford, Kenneth John 1948- *WhoE 91, WhoEmL 91*
Koford, Stuart Keith 1953- *WhoEmL 91, WhoWor 91*
Kofranek, Anton Miles 1921- *WhoAm 90*
Kofsky, Maria P. 1963- *WhoAmW 91*
Koga, Elaine 1942- *WhoAmW 91*
Koga, Mary 1920- *WhoAm 90, WhoAmA 91*
Koga, Masayuki *NewAgMG*
Koga, Yoshiaki 1936- *WhoWor 91*
Kogan, Alan Otto 1941- *BiDrAPA 89*
Kogan, Bernard Robert 1920- *WhoAm 90*
Kogan, Deborah 1940- *BioIn 16, WhoAmA 91*
Kogan, Enrique A. *WhoHisp 91*
Kogan, Gerald 1933- *WhoAm 90*
Kogan, Herman 1914- *AuBYP 90*
Kogan, Herman 1914-1989 *BioIn 16*
Kogan, Inna 1940- *BiDrAPA 89*
Kogan, Leonid 1924-1982 *PenDiMP*
Kogan, Mario 1944- *BiDrAPA 89*
Kogan, Nina Osipovna 1887-1942? *BiDWomA*
Kogan, Ray *WhoWrEP 89*
Kogan, Richard 1955- *BiDrAPA 89*
Kogan, Richard Jay 1941- *St&PR 91, WhoAm 90, WhoE 91*
Kogawa, Joy 1935- *FemiCLE*
Kogel, Marcus David 1903-1989 *BioIn 16*
Kogel, Max 1895-1946 *BioIn 16*
Kogelnik, Herwig Werner 1932- *WhoAm 90*
Kogen, David Chaim 1919- *BioIn 16*
Kogen, Linda Sue 1961- *WhoAmW 91*
Koger, Ira M. 1912- *St&PR 91, WhoSSW 91*
Koger, Ira McKissick 1912- *WhoAmA 91*
Koger, Thomas Harlan 1951- *WhoEmL 91*
Kogi, Hiroko 1955- *WhoAmW 91*
Kogitz, Jeffrey Michael 1947- *St&PR 91*
Kogl, Richard C 1928- *BiDrAPA 89*
Kogod, Judith C 1949- *WhoAmA 91*
Kogon, Eugen 1903-1987 *BioIn 16*
Kogon, Irving Charles 1923- *WhoE 91*
Kogovsek, Conrad J. 1951- *St&PR 91*
Kogovsek, Daniel Charles 1951- *WhoEmL 91*
Kogucki, Jerry R. 1935- *St&PR 91*
Kogut, David H. *ODwPR 91*
Kogut, John Anthony 1942- *St&PR 91, WhoAm 90*
Kogut, Maurice David 1930- *WhoAm 90*
Kogyku-tenno 594- *WomWR*
Koh, Boon Piang Laurence 1927- *WhoWor 91*
Koh, Celedonia V *BiDrAPA 89*
Koh, Hesung Chun 1929- *WhoAm 90, WhoE 91*
Koh, Katsuo 1940- *St&PR 91*
Koh, Kenneth Siak Khee 1963- *WhoWor 91*
Koh, Kian Tee 1944- *WhoWor 91*
Koh, Kwang Lim 1920-1989 *BioIn 16*
Koh, Severino Legarda 1927- *WhoAm 90*
Koh, Tai Ann 1943- *WhoWor 91*
Koh, Tommy Thong Bee 1937- *WhoAm 90, WhoWor 91*
Kohak, Erazim V 1933- *ConAu 31NR*
Kohan, Dennis Lynn 1945- *WhoWor 91*
Kohan, Mario Alberto 1945- *BiDrAPA 89*
Kohan, Mark Anthony 1960- *WhoE 91*
Kohan, Theodore S. 1940- *St&PR 91*
Kohana, Sidney 1928- *St&PR 91*
Kohankie, Carol Langdon 1940- *WhoAmW 91, WhoSSW 91*
Kohanyi, Mioara A *BiDrAPA 89*
Kohl, Atlee Mitchell 1945- *St&PR 91*
Kohl, Barbara 1940- *WhoAmA 91*
Kohl, Benedict M. 1931- *WhoAm 90*
Kohl, Dora Dierks 1922- *WhoWor 91*
Kohl, Ernst 1935- *WhoWor 91*
Kohl, Harold 1923- *WhoWor 91*
Kohl, Helmut 1930- *BioIn 16, NewYTBS 90 [port], WhoWor 91, WorAlBi*
Kohl, Herbert *BioIn 16*
Kohl, Herbert 1935- *WhoAm 90*
Kohl, Herbert R. *BioIn 16*
Kohl, Jan *BiDrAPA 89*
Kohl, John Clayton 1908- *WhoAm 90, WhoWor 91*
Kohl, Judith Cleek 1939- *WhoE 91*
Kohl, Marguerite *AuBYP 90*
Kohl, Marvin 1932- *WhoE 91*
Kohl, Mary Ann 1947- *WhoEmL 91*
Kohl, Mary E 1922- *BiDrAPA 89*
Kohl, Peter 1925- *St&PR 91*
Kohl, Roy *BioIn 16*
Kohl, Stewart Allen 1955- *WhoAm 90, WhoEmL 91*
Kohlberg, Irving Joel *BiDrAPA 89*
Kohlberg, Jerome, Jr. 1925- *WhoAm 90*
Kohlberg, Lawrence 1927-1987 *BioIn 16*
Kohlbry, S.T. 1928- *St&PR 91*
Kohlenberg, Eldon August 1936- *St&PR 91*
Kohlenberg, Stanley *BioIn 16*
Kohlenberg, Stanley 1932- *WhoE 91*
Kohler, Alison Daryl 1956- *WhoEmL 91*
Kohler, Barry Lee 1947- *WhoEmL 91*
Kohler, Carrie Ann 1963- *WhoAmW 91*
Kohler, Charlotte 1908- *WhoAm 90*
Kohler, Donald H. *WhoAm 90*
Kohler, Foy 1908- *WhoAm 90*
Kohler, Foy D. 1908-1990 *NewYTBS 90 [port]*
Kohler, Foy David 1908- *BioIn 16*
Kohler, Georges J. F. 1946- *WhoWor 91, WorAlBi*
Kohler, Heinz 1934- *WhoAm 90*
Kohler, Herbert Vollrath, Jr. 1939- *St&PR 91, WhoAm 90*
Kohler, Irene 1912- *PenDiMP*
Kohler, Irene 1914- *IntWWM 90*
Kohler, Ivo *BioIn 16*
Kohler, Jerry L. 1944- *St&PR 91*
Kohler, John Dennis 1947- *WhoE 91*
Kohler, John Michael, Jr. 1934- *St&PR 91*
Kohler, Kaufmann 1843-1926 *BioIn 16, WorAlBi*
Kohler, Linda June *BiDrAPA 89*
Kohler, Max Adam 1915- *WhoAm 90*
Kohler, Michael X. 1937- *St&PR 91*
Kohler, Pat Jean 1951- *WhoEmL 91*
Kohler, Patricia Ann 1951- *WhoSSW 91*
Kohler, Peter G. 1934- *St&PR 91*
Kohler, Peter Ogden 1938- *WhoAm 90*
Kohler, Robert Eugene *St&PR 91N*
Kohler, Rose 1873-1947 *WhoAmA 91N*
Kohler, Ruth DeYoung 1941- *WhoAm 90, WhoAmA 91*
Kohler, Ted Raney 1950- *WhoEmL 91*
Kohler, Terry Jodok 1934- *St&PR 91*
Kohler, William R. 1940- *St&PR 91*
Kohler, Wolfgang 1887-1967 *BioIn 16, DcScB S2*
Kohlhepp, Dorothy Irene *WhoAmA 91N*
Kohlhepp, Norman *WhoAmA 91N*
Kohlhof, Lavern Louis 1929- *St&PR 91*
Kohlhorst, Gail Lewis 1946- *WhoAm 90*
Kohli, Manmohan Singh 1931- *WhoWor 91*
Kohli, Rajiv 1947- *WhoEmL 91*
Kohli, Vijay Kumar 1949- *WhoSSW 91*
Kohlman, David Leslie 1937- *WhoAm 90*
Kohlmann, Henry George 1939- *WhoAm 90*
Kohlmeier, Daniel Kimbrell 1960- *WhoE 91*
Kohlmeier, Louis Martin, Jr. 1926- *WhoAm 90*
Kohlmeyer, Albert C 1924- *BiDrAPA 89*
Kohlmeyer, Ida 1912- *BioIn 16, WhoAmA 91*
Kohlmeyer, Ida Renee 1912- *BiDWomA*
Kohlmeyer, Ida Rittenberg 1912- *WhoAm 90*
Kohlmeyer, Werner A. 1921- *BiDrAPA 89*
Kohloss, Frederick Henry 1922- *WhoAm 90*
Kohlross, Walter 1941- *St&PR 91*
Kohls, Carl William 1931- *WhoE 91*
Kohls, William Richard 1957- *St&PR 91*
Kohls-Stehman, Betty 1952- *WhoAmW 91*
Kohn, A. Eugene 1930- *WhoE 91*
Kohn, Barbara 1950- *ODwPR 91*
Kohn, Ben 1933- *BiDrAPA 89*
Kohn, Bernice Herstein 1920- *AuBYP 90*
Kohn, Clyde Frederick 1911-1989 *BioIn 16, ConAu 130*
Kohn, Daniel Reuben 1952- *St&PR 91*
Kohn, David 1940- *St&PR 91*
Kohn, Dennis Fredrich 1940- *WhoAm 90*
Kohn, Edward Ira *BiDrAPA 89*
Kohn, Eugene 1887-1977 *BioIn 16*
Kohn, Frederick *BioIn 16*
Kohn, Gabriel 1910-1975 *WhoAmA 91N*
Kohn, Harold Elias 1914- *WhoWor 91*
Kohn, Harry Jeremy 1943- *St&PR 91*

Kohn, Henry 1917- St&PR 91, WhoAm 90
Kohn, Henry Irving 1909- WhoAm 90
Kohn, Herbert N BiDrAPA 89
Kohn, Howard BioIn 16
Kohn, Immanuel 1926- WhoAm 90
Kohn, Jacob 1881-1968 BioIn 16
Kohn, James Paul 1924- WhoAm 90
Kohn, Jeffrey K BiDrAPA 89
Kohn, John Peter, Jr. 1902- WhoAm 90
Kohn, Joseph John 1932- WhoAm 90
Kohn, Julieanne 1946- WhoAmW 91
Kohn, Julius 1906- St&PR 91
Kohn, Karen Josephine 1951- WhoAmW 91
Kohn, Karl 1926- IntWWM 90
Kohn, Karl-Christian 1928- IntWWM 90
Kohn, Karl George 1926- WhoAm 90
Kohn, Lisa 1963- WhoAmW 91
Kohn, Lisa Salkovitz 1951- WhoEmL 91
Kohn, Mary Louise Beatrice 1920- WhoAmW 91
Kohn, Meir Gregory 1946- WhoAm 90
Kohn, Melvin L. 1928- WhoE 91
Kohn, Michael Bundy 1958- WhoAmA 91
Kohn, Misch 1916- WhoAmA 91
Kohn, Richard H. 1940- WhoAm 90
Kohn, Ricki BioIn 16
Kohn, Rik 1948- St&PR 91
Kohn, Robert 1959- BiDrAPA 89
Kohn, Robert David 1950- St&PR 91
Kohn, Robert G BiDrAPA 89
Kohn, Robert Samuel, Jr. 1949- WhoEmL 91, WhoWor 91
Kohn, Sidney Irving 1912-1989 BioIn 16
Kohn, Walter 1923- WhoAm 90
Kohn, William Henry 1915- WhoAm 90
Kohn, William Irwin 1951- WhoEmL 91, WhoWor 91
Kohn, William Roth 1931- WhoAmA 91
Kohne, Richard Edward 1924- WhoAm 90
Kohnen, Robert Eugene 1933- St&PR 91
Kohnen, Robert Lee 1952- WhoEmL 91
Kohnen, Robert Stefan 1932- IntWWM 90
Kohner, Frederick 1905-1986 BioIn 16
Kohner, Paul BioIn 16
Kohner, Peter 1948- St&PR 91
Kohnhorst, Earl Eugene 1947- St&PR 91, WhoAm 90
Kohnke, Mary Florence 1932- WhoSSW 91
Kohon, Gregorio 1943- WhoWor 91
Kohonen, Kaarlo Pentti 1931- WhoWor 91
Kohout, Antonin PenDiMP
Kohout, David Blair 1952- WhoEmL 91
Kohout, Ladislav 1941- WhoWor 91
Kohout, Pavel BioIn 16
Kohoutek, Ctirad 1929- IntWWM 90
Kohr, Glenn Earl 1928- St&PR 91
Kohring, Dagmar Luzia 1951- WhoE 91
Kohrman, Arthur Fisher 1934- WhoAm 90
Kohrt, Carl Fredrick 1943- WhoAm 90
Kohs, Ellis Bonoff 1916- IntWWM 90
Kohtes, Paul J. 1945- WhoWor 91
Kohtz, Richard Lee 1952- WhoEmL 91
Kohut, Alexander 1842-1894 BioIn 16
Kohut, Heinz 1913-1981 BioIn 16
Kohut, John Joel 1939- BiDrAPA 89
Kohut, John Walter 1946- WhoE 91, WhoEmL 91, WhoWor 91
Kohut, Karl Ernst Georg 1936- WhoWor 91
Kohut, Lorene 1929- WhoAmA 91
Kohut, Stephen 1939- St&PR 91
Koi, Andrew Z. 1931- St&PR 91
Koide, Frank Takayuki 1935- WhoAm 90
Koide, Tan 1938-1986 BioIn 16, ConAu 132
Koike, Hisao 1921- WhoWor 91
Koike, Iwataro 1913- ConDes 90
Koike, Yoshiko BioIn 16
Koile, Earl 1917- WhoAm 90
Koilpillai, Isaac George BiDrAPA 89
Koinis, Steven W. 1956- WhoE 91
Koirala, Bharat Dutta 1942- WhoWor 91
Koirtyohann, Samuel Roy 1930- WhoAm 90
Koiso Kuniaki EncJap
Koita, Saida Yahya 1945- BiDrAPA 89
Koithan, Mary Susan 1956- WhoAmW 91
Koivisto, Erkki Lauri Matias 1927- WhoWor 91
Koivisto, Jussi Veikko 1964- WhoWor 91
Koivisto, Mauno BioIn 16
Koivisto, Mauno Henrik 1923- WhoWor 91
Koivo, Heikki Niilo 1943- WhoWor 91
Koivula, Steven John 1949- WhoEmL 91
Koivusalo, Martti Johannes 1930- WhoWor 91
Koizumi, Hisako Makino BiDrAPA 89
Koizumi, Kazuhiro 1949- IntWWM 90
Koizumi, Shunzo 1946- WhoWor 91
Koizumi, Yakumo 1850-1904 BioIn 16
Koj, Aleksander 1935- WhoWor 91
Kojak, George, Jr. 1940- BiDrAPA 89
Kojanec, Giovanni 1932- WhoWor 91
Kojian, Varujan 1935- IntWWM 90
Kojian, Varujan Haig 1935- WhoAm 90
Kojima, Kiyohide 1928- WhoWor 91
Kok, J. Juriaan PenDiDA 89
Kok, Karen Roselle 1963- WhoE 91
Kok, Willem 1938- WhoWor 91
Kok Kheng, Oliver Tan 1946- WhoWor 91
Kokalari, Musine 1920- EncCoWW
Kokaska, Charles James 1937- WhoAm 90
Koke, Jeffrey David 1957- WhoSSW 91
Koke, Richard Joseph 1916- WhoAm 90
Koken 716- WomWR
Koken, Bernd Krafft 1926- WhoAm 90
Koken, Richard E 1949- BiDrAPA 89
Kokenda, Robert Earl 1932- St&PR 91
Kokenzie, Henry Fayette 1918- WhoAm 90
Koker, Bernhard Chomse-B. 1949- WhoWor 91
Kokernot, Herbert, Jr. BioIn 16
Kokhanovskaia EncCoWW
Kokich, Vincent George 1944- WhoAm 90
Kokjer, Serena Strazzulla 1939- St&PR 91
Kokko, Juha Pekka 1937- WhoAm 90, WhoSSW 91
Kokkonen, Joonas 1921- IntWWM 90, WhoWor 91
Kokmeyer, Edward W. 1937- St&PR 91
Kokolakis-Kastrenakes, Maria 1963- WhoAmW 91
Kokoris, Jim ODwPR 91
Kokos, Dick 1928-1986 Ballpl 90
Kokoschka, Oskar 1886-1980 BioIn 16, IntDcAA 90, ModArCr 1 [port]
Kokoszka, John Gregory 1942- WhoWor 91
Kokoszka, Richard Jerome 1928-1986 Ballpl 90
Kokot, David Frank 1959- WhoEmL 91
Kokotovich, Nick M. 1948- St&PR 91
Kokt, Gerard Johannes 1953- WhoWor 91
Kokus, John, Jr. 1933- WhoE 91
Kol, Gustav BiDrAPA 89
Kolacz, Michael David 1963- WhoSSW 91
Koladich, Stephen 1931- BiDrAPA 89
Kolafa, Jiri 1930- IntWWM 90
Kolahifar, Jafar 1940- BiDrAPA 89
Kolakofsky, Daniel 1943- WhoWor 91
Kolansky, Harold BiDrAPA 89
Kolansky, Harold 1924- WhoAm 90, WhoE 91, WhoWor 91
Kolansky, S. Kalman 1937- BiDrAPA 89
Kolappa, Kalavathi BiDrAPA 89
Kolar, Anne Frances 1957- BiDrAPA 89
Kolar, Donald Joseph 1929- St&PR 91
Kolar, John Joseph 1927- WhoWrEP 89
Kolar, Madeleine C BiDrAPA 89
Kolar, Mary Jane 1941- WhoAm 90
Kolar, Milton Anton 1916- WhoAm 90
Kolarova, Jaromira 1919- EncCoWW
Kolars, John F. 1929- WhoAm 90
Kolarsick, Leroy D. 1921- St&PR 91
Kolasa, Kathryn Kelly 1949- WhoAmW 91
Kolasinski, Dominic Hippolytus 1838-1898 BioIn 16
Kolasinski, Leonard Thomas 1924- St&PR 91
Kolaskar, Ashok Sadanand 1950- WhoWor 91
Kolaski, Cynthia Bertha 1959- WhoAmW 91
Kolata, Gina 1948- WhoAmW 91
Kolatch, Alfred Jacob 1916- WhoAm 90
Kolatch, Myron 1929- WhoAm 90
Kolb, Annette 1870-1967 BioIn 16, EncCoWW
Kolb, Barbara 1939- BioIn 16
Kolb, Bertha Mae 1925- WhoAmW 91
Kolb, Charles E. M. 1950- WhoAm 90
Kolb, Charles Eugene 1945- WhoAm 90
Kolb, David Allen 1939- WhoAm 90
Kolb, David Allen 1946- WhoSSW 91
Kolb, David L. 1939- St&PR 91, WhoAm 90
Kolb, Doris 1927- WhoAmW 91
Kolb, Gisela Eva 1922- BiDrAPA 89
Kolb, Gwin Jackson 1919- WhoAm 90, WhoWrEP 89
Kolb, Henry Karl 1936- St&PR 91
Kolb, James Herman 1939- St&PR 91
Kolb, Jerry Wilbert 1935- WhoAm 90
Kolb, Jonathan E 1943- BiDrAPA 89
Kolb, Keith Robert 1922- WhoAm 90
Kolb, Ken Lloyd 1926- WhoAm 90
Kolb, Kenneth James 1956- WhoEmL 91
Kolb, Kenneth Lloyd 1926- WhoWrEP 89
Kolb, Lawrence C 1911- BiDrAPA 89
Kolb, Lawrence Coleman 1911- WhoAm 90
Kolb, Mary Lorraine 1947- WhoAmW 91
Kolb, Melvin M. 1945- BiDrAPA 89
Kolb, Mignon G. 1934- St&PR 91
Kolb, Nathaniel Key, Jr. 1933- WhoAm 90
Kolb, Thomas A. 1951- St&PR 91
Kolb, Vera M. 1948- WhoAmW 91
Kolb, W Payton BiDrAPA 89
Kolb, William Lester 1916- WhoAm 90
Kolbe, Adolph W. H. 1818-1884 WorAlBi
Kolbe, James Frank 1932- St&PR 91
Kolbe, James Thomas 1942- WhoAm 90
Kolbe, Jane Boegler 1944- WhoAm 90
Kolbe, Karl William, Jr. 1926- WhoAm 90
Kolbe, Margaret Ann 1948- WhoAmW 91
Kolbe, Maximilian 1894-1941 BioIn 16
Kolbe, Peter-Michael BioIn 16
Kolbel, Herbert Paul Alfred 1908- WhoWor 91
Kolbenheyer, Erwin Guido 1878-1962 BioIn 16
Kolber, Daniel Hackner 1953- WhoSSW 91
Kolbert, Jack 1927- WhoE 91
Kolbeson, Marilyn Hopf 1930- WhoAmW 91
Kolboom, Ingo 1947- WhoWor 91
Kolbowski, Silvia 1953- WhoAmA 91
Kolbrener, Jonathan 1957- WhoEmL 91
Kolbye, Albert Christian, Jr. 1935- WhoAm 90
Kolchak, Aleksandr 1873-1920 WorAlBi
Kolchak, Aleksandr Vasiliyevich 1873-1920 BioIn 16
Kolchin, Mark Andrew 1958- WhoE 91
Kolczynski, Charlotte Ann 1952- IntWWM 90
Kolde, Frederick William 1870- WhoAmA 91N
Kolden, Rolf Julius 1942- BiDrAPA 89
Kolditz, Daniel Paul 1959- WhoEmL 91
Koldorf, Irene Janet 1925- WhoAmA 91
Kole, Bernard Elliott 1959- BiDrAPA 89
Kole, Christian 1921- BiDrAPA 89
Kole, Delbert M BiDrAPA 89
Kole, Janet Stephanie 1946- WhoAmW 91, WhoEmL 91
Kole, Jeffrey Holitser 1960- WhoE 91
Kole, John William 1934- WhoAm 90
Kole-Harf, Patricia Jean 1937- WhoAmW 91, WhoWor 91
Koledo, Thomas John 1935- St&PR 91
Kolehmainen, Jan Waldroy 1940- WhoAm 90
Kolehmainen, John Ilmari 1910- WhoAm 90
Kolehouse, Bobbie Lee Susan 1954- WhoWrEP 89
Kolehouse, Donald Michael 1957- WhoEmL 91
Kolenbrander, Harold Mark 1938- WhoAm 90
Kolenc, Koleen M. 1951- WhoAmW 91
Kolenda, Frank Donald 1945- WhoEmL 91
Kolenda, Konstantin 1923- WhoAm 90
Kolender, William Barnett 1935- WhoAm 90
Kolenski, Josef BiDrAPA 89
Kolenut, Elisa S. 1958- WhoAmW 91
Koler, Robert Donald 1924- WhoAm 90
Kolesar, Edward Steven, Jr. 1950- WhoEmL 91
Kolesar, Peter John 1936- WhoAm 90
Koleszar, Alexander Sandor 1955- BiDrAPA 89
Kolevzon, Peter Stephen 1942- WhoAm 90
Koley, James Lawrence 1930- St&PR 91
Kolff, Willem J. BioIn 16
Kolff, Willem Johan 1911- WhoAm 90
Koli, Malathi Vijay BiDrAPA 89
Koli, Vijay Narayanrao Koh 1943- WhoSSW 91
Kolias, Lisa 1962- ODwPR 91
Kolick, David 1948- WhoEmL 91
Kolin, Irving S 1940- BiDrAPA 89
Kolin, Michael David 1950- BiDrAPA 89
Kolin, Sacha 1911-1975 WhoAmA 91N
Koling, Barry R. ODwPR 91
Kolingba, Andre-Dieudonne 1936- WhoWor 91
Kolinski, Anthony T. 1934- St&PR 91
Kolis, Annette 1948- WhoE 91
Kolisch Quartet PenDiMP
Kolisch, Rudolf 1896-1978 PenDiMP
Kolisnyk, Peter 1934- WhoAmA 91
Kolizeras, Kostas 1943- St&PR 91
Kolk, Joseph Michael 1960- WhoEmL 91
Kolker, Allan Erwin 1933- WhoAm 90
Kolker, Bonnie Lynne 1953- WhoE 91
Kolker, James David 1947- St&PR 91
Kolker, Jonas C BiDrAPA 89
Kolker, Joseph BiDrAPA 89
Kolker, Karel Ann 1952- WhoEmL 91
Kolker, Raymond F. 1942- St&PR 91
Kolker, Roger Russell 1929- WhoAm 90
Kolker, Sondra G. 1938- WhoAmW 91, WhoE 91
Kolkey, Daniel Miles 1952- WhoEmL 91, WhoWor 91
Kolkhorst, Kathryn Mackay 1949- WhoAmW 91
Kolko, Gabriel 1932- WhoAm 90, WhoWrEP 89
Kolko, Joyce 1933- ConAu 130
Koll, Richard Leroy 1925- WhoAm 90
Koll-Nesher, Uri 1949- St&PR 91
Kollaer, Jim C. 1943- WhoWor 91
Kollaritsch, Felix Paul 1925- WhoAm 90
Kollat, David Truman 1938- WhoAm 90
Kolle, Bernard Gerard 1962- IntWWM 90
Kolle, Tom E. 1936- St&PR 91
Kollegger, James G. 1942- WhoAm 90, WhoWor 91
Kollek, Teddy BioIn 16
Kollentz, Anton Dan 1929- St&PR 91
Koller, Alexander Joseph 1957- WhoE 91
Koller, Alois J. 1910- St&PR 91
Koller, Arnold Alois 1933- WhoWor 91
Koller, Brian Richard BiDrAPA 89
Koller, Frances E BiDrAPA 89
Koller, James 1936- BioIn 16
Koller, James Anthony 1936- WhoWrEP 89
Koller, Karen Kathryn 1949- WhoEmL 91
Koller, Karl 1898-1952 BioIn 16
Koller, Kay Pak BiDrAPA 89
Koller, Loren D. 1940- WhoAm 90
Koller, Marita A. 1955- WhoAmW 91
Koller, Mark Robert BiDrAPA 89
Koller, Marvin Robert 1919- WhoAm 90
Koller, Miriam M BiDrAPA 89
Koller, Timothy Michael 1958- WhoEmL 91
Koller-Davies, Eva 1925- WhoAmA 91
Kolli, Eino 1925- WhoWor 91
Kollias, Georgia Nicoletta 1961- WhoAmW 91
Kolliker, William Augustin 1905- WhoAmA 91
Kolliner-Kelly, Nonnie Kris 1946- WhoAmW 91
Kollman, Franz Gustav 1934- WhoWor 91
Kollmann, Hilda Hanna 1913- WhoAm 90
Kollmorgen, Leland Stanford 1927- WhoAm 90
Kollmorgen, Rodger C 1937- BiDrAPA 89
Kollner, Herbert 1926-1988 BioIn 16
Kollo, Rene 1937- BioIn 16, IntWWM 90, PenDiMP
Kollock, David Hall 1916- WhoE 91
Kollock, James Paul 1951- WhoSSW 91
Kollodziewski, Rene 1937- PenDiMP
Kolloff, Margaret Penelope Britton 1942- WhoAmW 91
Kollontai, A. 1872-1952 BioIn 16
Kollontai, Aleksandra 1872-1952 BioIn 16
Kollontai, Alexandra 1872-1952 EncCoWW
Kolloway, Don 1918- Ballpl 90
Kollros, Jerry John 1917- WhoAm 90
Kolls, John Randal 1951- WhoSSW 91
Kollu, Tahir 1959- WhoWor 91
Kollwitz, Kathe 1867-1945 BiDWomA, BioIn 16, EncCoWW, IntDcAA 90 [port]
Kolm, Harvard Brown 1929- St&PR 91
Kolm, Henry Herbert 1924- St&PR 91, WhoE 91
Kolman, David A. 1951- WhoEmL 91
Kolmar, Gertrud 1894-1943 TwCLC 40 [port]
Kolmer, John H. 1945- St&PR 91
Kolmer, Michael Gene 1952- WhoEmL 91
Kolmogorov, Andrei N. 1903-1987 BioIn 16
Kolodey, Fred James 1936- WhoAm 90
Kolodin, Irving 1908-1988 BioIn 16
Kolodner, Berko B BiDrAPA 89
Kolodner, George F BiDrAPA 89
Kolodner, Ignace Izaak 1920- WhoAm 90
Kolodner, Nathan K. BioIn 16
Kolodner, Nathan K 1950- WhoAmA 91N
Kolodner, Paul Robert 1953- WhoE 91
Kolodner, Richard David 1951- WhoE 91
Kolodner, Robert Mark 1948- BiDrAPA 89
Kolodney, Nathan Rothaus 1939- WhoE 91
Kolodny, Annette 1941- BioIn 16
Kolodny, Edwin Hillel 1936- WhoAm 90
Kolodny, Nancy Joan 1946- WhoAmW 91
Kolodny, Richard 1943- WhoAm 90
Kolodny, Robert Alan 1943- WhoSSW 91
Kolodny, Stanley Charles 1923- WhoAm 90
Kolodziej, Edward Albert 1935- WhoAm 90
Kolodziej, Krysia 1948- WhoWrEP 89
Koloff, Gary Fredric 1954- BiDrAPA 89
Kolok, Kenneth George 1938- St&PR 91
Kolokowsky, Henry S. 1939- St&PR 91
Kololgi, Vijayalakshmi A BiDrAPA 89
Kolombatovic, Vadja Vadim 1924- WhoE 91
Kolon, Aleksandar 1947- ConAu 30NR
Kolonel, Laurence Norman 1942- WhoAm 90
Kolooziej, D.G. 1936- St&PR 91
Kolopsky, Jerry 1926- St&PR 91
Kolor, Michael Garrett 1934- WhoE 91
Kolovakos, Gregory BioIn 16
Kolovat, David Victor 1945- St&PR 91
Kolowsky, Donald E. BioIn 16
Kolp, Ray 1894-1967 Ballpl 90
Kolpakchi, Ilya M BiDrAPA 89
Kolpin, Marc A. 1932- St&PR 91
Kolrud, Lisa ODwPR 91
Kolski, Stephen J. 1941- WhoAm 90
Kolsky, Allan 1932- St&PR 91, WhoSSW 91
Kolsky, Herbert 1916- WhoAm 90

Kolson, Harry 1915- *WhoAm 90*
Kolson, Richard Jay 1948- *St&PR 91*
Kolsrud, Gretchen Schabtach 1939- *WhoAmW 91*
Kolsrud, Henry Gerald 1923- *WhoWor 91*
Kolstad, Allen C. 1931- *WhoAm 90*
Kolstad, Chester James 1926- *St&PR 91*
Kolste, Debra Ann 1953- *WhoAmW 91*
Kolster, Frederick August 1883-1950 *BioIn 16*
Kolsti, Paul Arthur 1953- *WhoSSW 91*
Koltai, Ralph 1924- *ConDes 90*
Koltai, Stephen Miklos 1922- *WhoWor 91*
Koltenuk, Adrienne Ruth 1947- *WhoAmW 91*
Kolter, Joseph Paul 1926- *WhoAm 90, WhoE 91*
Kolterjahn, Paul Henry 1924- *St&PR 91, WhoAm 90*
Koltes, John A 1922- *BiDrAPA 89*
Koltes, Thomas G. 1928- *St&PR 91*
Kolthoff, Izaak Maurits *BioIn 16*
Koltnow, Emily *BioIn 16*
Koltnow, Peter Gregory 1929- *WhoAm 90*
Kolton, Marilyn Sylvia 1944- *WhoAmW 91*
Kolton, Paul 1923- *St&PR 91, WhoAm 90*
Koltonow, Lawrence *BiDrAPA 89*
Koltov, Nadine H. 1962- *WhoAmW 91*
Koltun, Frances Lang *WhoAmA 91, WhoE 91*
Koltun, Karyn Lynn 1965- *WhoEmL 91*
Koltz, Anise 1928- *EncCoWW*
Koltzow, Liv 1945- *DcScanL, EncCoWW*
Kolumban, Nicholas 1940- *WhoWrEP 89*
Kolve, V. A. 1934- *WhoAm 90*
Kolvenbach, Donald M. 1934- *St&PR 91*
Kolvenbach, Peter Hans 1928- *WhoWor 91*
Kolz, Beverly Anne 1946- *WhoEmL 91*
Kolz, Ernst 1929- *IntWWM 90*
Kom, Ambroise 1946- *WhoWor 91*
Komacek, Stanley Albert 1956- *WhoE 91*
Komaiko, Leah *AuBYP 90*
Komando, Kimberly Ann 1964- *WhoAmW 91*
Komanduri, Ramanujam V *BiDrAPA 89*
Komar And Melamid *WhoAmA 91*
Komar, Arthur B. 1931- *WhoAm 90*
Komar, Chris *BioIn 16*
Komar, Kathleen Lenore 1949- *WhoEmL 91*
Komar, M. Hikmet 1929- *WhoWor 91*
Komar, Mathias 1909- *WhoAmA 91N*
Komar, Vitaly *WhoAmA 91*
Komarek, Paul Anthony 1954- *WhoEmL 91*
Komarek, Thomas Charles *WhoAm 90*
Komarek, Valtr *WhoWor 91*
Komareth, Vijayakumar 1944- *BiDrAPA 89*
Komarin, Gary 1951- *WhoAmA 91, WhoE 91*
Komaroff, Stanley 1935- *WhoAm 90*
Komarovsky, Mirra *WhoAm 90*
Komatsu, Chikahiro 1933- *WhoWor 91*
Komatsu, Ralph Yoshio 1915- *St&PR 91*
Komatsu, Shigego Richard 1916- *WhoAm 90*
Komatsu, Teruo 1933- *WhoWor 91*
Komatz, George T. 1938- *St&PR 91*
Komei, Emperor *EncJap*
Komen, John Denis 1936- *St&PR 91*
Komenda, Pamela 1953- *St&PR 91*
Komenich, Kim 1956- *WhoAm 90*
Komer, Harry S. 1918- *St&PR 91*
Komer, Joseph *BiDrAPA 89*
Komer, Robert Allan *BiDrAPA 89*
Komer, Robert William 1922- *WhoAm 90*
Komer, Stuart 1926- *St&PR 91, WhoE 91*
Komericki, Josip 1944- *WhoWor 91*
Komidar, Joseph Stanley 1916- *WhoAm 90*
Komie, Stephen Mark 1949- *WhoEmL 91*
Komins, Burton L. 1930- *St&PR 91*
Komins, Roger A. 1964- *St&PR 91*
Komisar, Arnold 1947- *WhoAm 90, WhoE 91, WhoEmL 91, WhoWor 91*
Komisar, David Daniel 1917- *WhoAm 90*
Komisar, Jerome Bertram 1937- *WhoAm 90*
Komisar, Lucy 1942- *AuBYP 90*
Komisarczyk, Shirley Theresa 1930- *WhoAmW 91*
Komisarjevsky, Christopher P. A. 1945- *ODwPR 91*
Komisarof, Jerome Herman *BiDrAPA 89*
Komito, Edward 1958- *St&PR 91*
Komito, Sanford 1931- *St&PR 91*
Komkov, Vadim 1919- *WhoAm 90*
Komleva, Gabriela Trofimovna 1938- *WhoWor 91*
Komline, Elizabeth Marlow 1917- *St&PR 91*
Komline, Russell Marlow 1948- *St&PR 91*
Komline, Thomas Raymond 1944- *St&PR 91*
Komlos, Katalin 1945- *IntWWM 90*
Komlos, Peter *PenDiMP*
Komlos, Peter 1935- *IntWWM 90, WhoWor 91*
Komlossy, Erzsebet 1933- *IntWWM 90, PenDiMP*
Kommareddi, Nageswara Rao 1938- *BiDrAPA 89*
Kommedahl, Thor 1920- *WhoAm 90*
Kommerell, Victor Maurice 1964- *WhoWor 91*
Komminsk, Brad 1961- *Ballpl 90*
Kommor, Martin Jay *BiDrAPA 89*
Komodore, Bill 1932- *WhoAmA 91*
Komodore, Bill G. 1932- *WhoAm 90*
Komoly, Otto 1892-1945 *BioIn 16*
Komora, Edward J *BiDrAPA 89*
Komori, Hiroo 1925- *WhoWor 91*
Komornicka, Maria 1876-1949 *EncCoWW*
Komorous, Rudolf 1931- *IntWWM 90*
Komorowski, Cheryl Ann 1956- *WhoAmW 91*
Komorowski, Tadeusz 1895-1966 *BioIn 16*
Komosa, Adam Anthony 1913- *WhoSSW 91, WhoWor 91*
Komp, Barbara Ann 1954- *WhoAmW 91*
Komp, Diane Marilyn 1940- *WhoAm 90*
Kompas, John George 1946- *WhoEmL 91*
Kompass, Edward John 1926- *WhoAm 90*
Kompe, Lydia 1935- *BioIn 16*
Komrad, Mark Stephen 1957- *BiDrAPA 89*
Komroff, Manuel 1890-1974 *AuBYP 90*
Komry, Victor Hanna 1952- *BiDrAPA 89*
Komurek, Charles Francis 1947- *WhoEmL 91*
Komyo, Emperor *EncJap*
Kon, Mark Andrew 1952- *WhoE 91*
Kon, Oi-Lian 1947- *WhoWor 91*
Kon, Richard 1952- *St&PR 91*
Konan-Bedie, Henri 1934- *WhoWor 91*
Konandreas, Panos Athanasios 1946- *WhoWor 91*
Konarski, Feliks 1907- *WhoWor 91*
Koncak, Jon *BioIn 16*
Koncel, James E. 1929- *St&PR 91*
Koncelik, Joseph Arthur 1940- *WhoAm 90*
Konchalovsky, Andrei 1937- *ConTFT 8*
Konchanin, Lynn Marie 1957- *WhoAmW 91*
Konchegul, Leon *BiDrAPA 89*
Konczal, Dennis R. 1950- *St&PR 91*
Konczalski, Ronald Louis 1935- *St&PR 91*
Konczol, Csaba 1947- *WhoWor 91*
Kondakov, Ivan Petrovich 1905-1969 *BioIn 16*
Kondapaneni, Sarat B 1943- *BiDrAPA 89*
Kondas, Nicholas Frank 1929- *St&PR 91, WhoE 91, WhoWor 91*
Kondelik, John P. 1942- *WhoAm 90*
Kondelin, George John, Jr. 1949- *WhoSSW 91*
Kondert, Reinhart Ditmar 1943- *WhoSSW 91*
Kondic, Mirjana *BiDrAPA 89*
Kondo, Kenneth S. 1950- *St&PR 91*
Kondo, Masatoshi Stephan 1940- *WhoE 91, WhoWor 91*
Kondoh, Kazumi 1936- *WhoWor 91*
Kondonassis, Alexander John 1928- *WhoAm 90*
Kondonassis, Yolanda 1963- *IntWWM 90*
Kondos, George Michael 1948- *St&PR 91*
Kondra, Douglass Emil 1946- *St&PR 91*
Kondra, Emil Paul 1917- *St&PR 91*
Kondracke, Morton Matt 1939- *WhoAm 90*
Kondrashin, Kirill 1914-1981 *PenDiMP*
Kondratas, Anna *BioIn 16*
Kondratas, Skirma Anna 1944- *WhoAm 90*
Kondratieff, Nikolai Dmitrievich *BioIn 16*
Kondratowicz, Frank John 1927- *St&PR 91*
Kondy, Stephanie Mary 1949- *WhoAmW 91*
Kondziela, Henryk 1931- *WhoWor 91*
Kondziela, Joseph Richard *BiDrAPA 89*
Kondziela, Joseph Richard 1954- *WhoE 91*
Kone, Elliott H. 1920- *WhoAm 90*
Kone, James S. 1912- *St&PR 91*
Kone, James S., Jr. 1949- *St&PR 91*
Kone, Russell Joseph 1929- *WhoE 91*
Konecky, Gary 1957- *WhoE 91*
Konecky, Nathan 1943- *St&PR 91*
Konegen, Norbert Rheinhard 1939- *WhoWor 91*
Koner, Pauline *BioIn 16*
Koner, Pauline 1912- *ConAu 132, WhoAm 90*
Konerczny, Anny 1902-1968 *PenDiMP*
Konerczny, Hilde 1905-1980 *PenDiMP*
Kones, Ramona Katherine 1955- *WhoEmL 91*
Kones, Richard 1948- *WhoAm 90, WhoE 91, WhoSSW 91, WhoWor 91*
Konetchy, Ed 1885-1947 *Ballpl 90 [port]*
Konetzni, Anny 1902-1968 *PenDiMP*
Konetzni, Hilde 1905-1980 *PenDiMP*
Koneval, William Paul 1934- *St&PR 91*
Konezny, Lorette M. Sobol 1948- *WhoAmW 91, WhoEmL 91*
Kong, Eric Siu-Wai 1953- *WhoEmL 91*
Kong, Jin Au 1942- *WhoAm 90*
Kong, Julie Chan 1958- *WhoEmL 91*
Kong, Ling-Ren 1924- *WhoWor 91*
Kong, Luis John 1956- *WhoHisp 91*
Kong, Young Sun *BiDrAPA 89*
Kongabel, H. Fred 1929- *WhoAm 90*
Kongara, Rama Krishna R *BiDrAPA 89*
Kongsted, Ole Dan 1943- *IntWWM 90*
Konhauser, Joseph Daniel Edward 1924- *WhoAm 90*
Konheim, Carolyn *BioIn 16*
Koni, Nicolaus 1911- *WhoAmA 91*
Konia, Charles *BiDrAPA 89*
Konicek, Michael Richard 1952- *St&PR 91*
Konicki, P Eric 1950- *BiDrAPA 89*
Koniecko, Edward Stanley 1913- *WhoAm 90*
Konieczka, Cas Harry 1964- *WhoE 91*
Konieczny, Doug 1951- *Ballpl 90*
Konieczny, Glenn Francis 1951- *WhoEmL 91*
Konieczny, Sharon Louise 1952- *WhoAmW 91, WhoWor 91*
Konieczny, Zygmunt 1937- *IntWWM 90*
Konig, Alfred Otto *PenDiDA 89*
Konig, Dieter 1935- *WhoWor 91*
Konig, Heinz Johannes Erdmann 1929- *WhoWor 91*
Konig, Klaus 1934- *IntWWM 90*
Konigsberg, Neil George 1946- *WhoE 91*
Konigsberg, Richard Lee 1953- *WhoE 91*
Konigsberg, William Henry 1930- *WhoAm 90*
Konigsburg, E. L. *BioIn 16*
Konigsburg, E L 1930- *MajTwCW*
Konigsburg, Elaine L 1930- *AuBYP 90*
Konigsburg, Elaine Lobl 1930- *WhoAm 90*
Konigsdorf, Helga 1938- *EncCoWW*
Konigsmark, Gary Loyd 1959- *WhoEmL 91*
Konikiewicz, Leonard Wieslaw 1928- *WhoSSW 91*
Konikow, Antoinette Bucholz 1869-1946 *EncAL*
Koning, Hans 1924- *WhoAm 90, WhoWrEP 89*
Koningsberger, Hans 1924- *WhoAm 90*
Konior, Lynne Bartlett 1953- *WhoAmW 91*
Konishi, Masakazu 1933- *WhoAm 90*
Konishiki, Yasokichi *BioIn 16*
Konisky, Jordan 1941- *WhoAm 90*
Konitsky, Erma Rose 1967- *WhoE 91*
Konitz, Lee *BioIn 16*
Konkapot 1700?-1775? *WhNaAH*
Konkel, Kurt Frederick 1945- *WhoEmL 91*
Konkel, Richard Steven 1950- *WhoEmL 91*
Konkle, Amy Delores *BiDrAPA 89*
Konkle, B.L. 1931- *St&PR 91*
Konkle, Henry R. 1929- *St&PR 91*
Konkle, Janet Marie Everest 1917- *WhoWrEP 89*
Konkol, George 1923- *St&PR 91*
Konkol, Robert Anthony 1951- *BiDrAPA 89, WhoE 91*
Konn McCormick, Susan 1953- *St&PR 91*
Konner, Joan *BioIn 16*
Konner, Joan Weiner 1931- *WhoAm 90*
Konney, Paul E. 1944- *St&PR 91*
Konney, Paul Edward 1944- *WhoAm 90*
Konnick, Dianne Cheryl 1961- *WhoAmW 91*
Konnyu, Ernest Leslie 1937- *WhoAm 90*
Kono, Kenichiro 1932- *WhoWor 91*
Kono, Tetsuro 1925- *WhoAm 90*
Kono, Toshihiko 1930- *IntWWM 90, WhoWrEP 89*
Konoe Fumimaro 1891-1945 *EncJap*
Konold, George Edward 1956- *WhoEmL 91*
Konoma, Kazuhisa 1942- *St&PR 91, WhoSSW 91*
Konon, Neena Nicholai 1951- *WhoAmW 91*
Kononiuk, Stephen John 1946- *St&PR 91*
Konopinski, Emil J. *NewYTBS 90*
Konopinski, Emil J. 1911-1990 *BioIn 16*
Konopka, Frank Joseph 1946- *WhoEmL 91*
Konopka, Gisela Peiper 1910- *WhoAm 90*
Konopka, Joseph 1932- *WhoAmA 91*
Konopka, Joseph Stanley 1932- *WhoE 91*
Konopnicka, Maria 1842-1910 *EncCoWW*
Konowitz, Herbert Henry 1937- *WhoWor 91*
Konowitz, Sheldon H. 1923- *St&PR 91*
Konrad, Adolf Ferdinand *WhoAmA 91*
Konrad, Adolf Ferdinand 1915- *WhoAm 90*
Konrad, Alan Karl 1950- *WhoEmL 91*
Konrad, Bernd 1948- *IntWWM 90*
Konrad, Dusan 1935- *WhoAm 90*
Konrad, G. Gregory 1951- *WhoWrEP 89*
Konrad, Michael T. 1960- *St&PR 91*
Konrad, Thomas Edmund 1928- *WhoWor 91*
Konselman, Douglas Derek 1958- *WhoEmL 91*
Konski, James Louis 1917- *WhoAm 90*
Konstan, David 1940- *ConAu 32NR*
Konstantin Pavlovich 1779-1831 *BioIn 16*
Konstanty, Jim 1917-1976 *Ballpl 90 [port]*
Konsulov, Ivan 1946- *IntWWM 90*
Kont, Paul 1920- *IntWWM 90*
Kontarsky, Alfons 1932- *IntWWM 90, PenDiMP*
Kontarsky, Alois 1931- *IntWWM 90*
Kontarsky, Aloys 1931- *PenDiMP*
Kontnier, Robert D. 1941- *St&PR 91*
Kontny, Vincent L. 1937- *St&PR 91*
Kontny, Vincent Lawrence 1937- *WhoAm 90*
Kontorovich, Vladimir 1951- *WhoE 91*
Kontos, Peter Gus 1949- *BiDrAPA 89*
Kontostathis, Kyriakos 1959- *WhoE 91*
Kontras, Stella Bicouvaris 1928- *BiDrAPA 89*
Konvalinka, Marianne 1959- *WhoAmW 91*
Konvicka, Frank Thomas 1958- *WhoEmL 91*
Konvitz, Josef Wolf 1946- *WhoAm 90*
Konvitz, Joseph 1878-1944 *BioIn 16*
Konvitz, Milton Ridbaz 1908- *WhoAm 90, WhoWor 91*
Konwal, Roger Alan 1944- *BiDrAPA 89*
Konwicki, Tadeusz 1926- *MajTwCW, WhoWor 91, WorAu 1980 [port]*
Konwin, Thor Warner 1943- *WhoWor 91*
Konwitschny, Franz 1901-1962 *PenDiMP*
Konya, Sandor 1923- *BioIn 16, IntWWM 90, PenDiMP*
Konyha, Larry Dean 1956- *WhoEmL 91*
Konyha, Stephen Michael 1940- *WhoE 91*
Konz, Gerald Keith 1932- *St&PR 91, WhoAm 90*
Konz, Helen Katherine 1910- *WhoAmW 91*
Konz, L.A. *St&PR 91*
Konzal, Joseph 1905- *WhoAmA 91*
Konzal, Joseph Charles 1905- *WhoAm 90*
Konzertverein Quartet *PenDiMP*
Koo, Antonio Yin Lun 1961- *WhoWor 91*
Koo, Bon Chul *BiDrAPA 89*
Koo, Daniel Shing-Cheong 1923- *WhoWor 91*
Koo, George Ping Shan 1938- *WhoAm 90*
Koo, John Ying Ming 1955- *BiDrAPA 89*
Koo, Reginald Chewyat 1949- *WhoSSW 91*
Koob, Ernie 1893-1941 *Ballpl 90*
Koob, James Stephen 1957- *WhoSSW 91*
Koob, Raymond Joseph 1947- *WhoWrEP 89*
Koob, Robert Duane 1941- *WhoAm 90*
Koob, Theodora 1918- *AuBYP 90*
Koocher, Gerald Paul 1947- *WhoE 91*
Koock, Victor I. 1940- *St&PR 91*
Koogler, Robert Foster 1933- *St&PR 91*
Koogler, Robert Luin 1952- *WhoEmL 91*
Kooiker, John E 1920- *BiDrAPA 89*
Kooiker, Leonie 1927- *BioIn 16*
Kooiman, Petronella 1945- *IntWWM 90*
Kook, Abraham Isaac 1865-1935 *BioIn 16*
Kook, Edward F. 1903-1990 *NewYTBS 90 [port]*
Kooken, John F. *BioIn 16*
Kooken, John F. 1931- *St&PR 91*
Kooken, John Frederick 1931- *WhoAm 90*
Kool & the Gang *EncPR&S 89*
Kool, Lawrence Bernard 1952- *WhoE 91*
Kool, Timothy Jay 1959- *St&PR 91*
Koolhaas, Rem 1944- *BioIn 16*
Koomen, Cornelis Jan 1947- *WhoWor 91*
Koomen, Jacob, Jr. 1917- *WhoAm 90*
Koomen, John Chapin 1945- *BiDrAPA 89*
Koomey, Paul Clifton 1927- *St&PR 91*
Koon, George William 1942- *WhoSSW 91*
Koon, Norman Carroll 1938- *WhoAm 90*
Koon, Ray Harold 1934- *WhoWor 91*
Koon, Vivian Jenkins 1947- *WhoAmW 91*
Koonce, Alexander Eben 1958- *WhoE 91*
Koonce, Cal 1940- *Ballpl 90*
Koonce, Eileen Mary 1955- *WhoEmL 91*
Koonce, Frank William 1952- *IntWWM 90*
Koonce, Gene C. 1932- *St&PR 91*
Koonce, Joel L., Jr. 1937- *St&PR 91*
Koonce, John Peter 1932- *WhoWor 91*
Koonce, Kenneth Terry 1938- *WhoAm 90*
Koonce, Phillip Anderson, Jr. 1922- *WhoSSW 91*
Koonce, Rodney Llewellyn 1947- *WhoE 91*
Kooning, Elaine de 1920-1989 *AnObit 1989, BiDWomA*
Koons, Ann Veronica 1945- *IntWWM 90*
Koons, Charles A. 1943- *St&PR 91*
Koons, Darell J 1924- *WhoAmA 91*
Koons, Donaldson 1917- *WhoAm 90*
Koons, Irvin Louis 1922- *WhoAm 90, WhoWor 91*
Koons, Jeff 1955- *BioIn 16, CurBio 90 [port]*
Koons, Jonathan *EncO&P 3*
Koons, Michael Jon 1939- *St&PR 91*
Koons, Robert Charles 1957- *WhoSSW 91*
Koonts, Jones Calvin 1924- *WhoAm 90*
Koonts, Robert Henry 1927- *St&PR 91*
Koontz, Alfred Joseph, Jr. 1942- *St&PR 91, WhoAm 90*
Koontz, Charles Leonard 1931- *St&PR 91*

Koontz, Cherry Lynn 1951- *WhoE 91*
Koontz, Dean R 1945- *MajTwCW, TwCCr&M 91*
Koontz, Dean Ray 1945- *WhoAm 90*
Koontz, Edward Larry 1946- *St&PR 91, WhoSSW 91*
Koontz, Elizabeth Duncan 1919-1989 *BioIn 16*
Koontz, Eva Isabelle 1935- *WhoAmW 91, WhoWor 91*
Koontz, James Arthur 1942- *BiDrAPA 89*
Koontz, Judith Ann *BiDrAPA 89*
Koontz, Katy 1959- *WhoEmL 91*
Koontz, Norma Carolyn 1938- *WhoAmW 91*
Koontz, Norma Jean 1930- *WhoAmW 91*
Koontz, Raymond 1912- *St&PR 91, WhoAm 90*
Koontz, Richard H. 1940- *St&PR 91*
Koontz, Richard Harvey 1940- *WhoAm 90*
Koontz, Robin Michael *AuBYP 90*
Koontz, Ronald David 1943- *St&PR 91*
Koontz, Thomas Wayne 1939- *WhoWrEP 89*
Koontz, Warren Woodson, Jr. 1932- *WhoAm 90*
Koonz, Claudia *ConAu 131, WhoAmW 91*
Koonz, Claudia Ann *ConAu 131*
Koop, C. Everett *BioIn 16*
Koop, C. Everett 1916- *WorAlBi*
Koop, Carolyn Pascucci 1953- *WhoEmL 91*
Koop, Charles Everett 1916- *WhoAm 90, WhoE 91*
Koop, Chris R. 1960- *St&PR 91*
Koop, Dale Wayne 1939- *St&PR 91*
Koop, Tamara Terri 1950- *WhoEmL 91*
Koop, Theodore Frederick 1907-1988 *BioIn 16*
Koopalethes, Olivia *WhoAmA 91*
Kooper, Al 1944- *EncPR&S 89, WorAlBi*
Koopman, Barbara G *BiDrAPA 89*
Koopman, Cheryl 1950- *WhoAmW 91*
Koopman, George A. *BioIn 16*
Koopman, John R 1881-1949 *WhoAmA 91N*
Koopman, Richard Nelson 1945- *WhoEmL 91*
Koopman, Ton 1944- *IntWWM 90, PenDiMP*
Koopman, William James 1945- *WhoAm 90*
Koopmann, Menno G. 1925- *WhoWor 91*
Koopmann, Robert John 1946- *IntWWM 90*
Koopmann Parrish, Reta Collene 1944- *WhoAmW 91, WhoSSW 91, WhoWor 91*
Koopmans, Cheryl Bette 1950- *WhoAmW 91, WhoEmL 91*
Koornhof, Piet *BioIn 16*
Koornhof, Pieter Gerhardus Jacobus 1925- *WhoWor 91*
Koors, Thomas John 1935- *St&PR 91*
Koos, Brian John 1949- *WhoEmL 91*
Koos, Patricia Kay 1940- *WhoAmW 91*
Koos, Russell B. 1942- *St&PR 91*
Kooser, Ted 1939- *DcLB 105[port]*
Koosman, Jerry 1943- *Ballpl 90[port]*
Koot, Sheila Cassily 1944- *WhoAmW 91*
Kooy, Gerrit Andries 1926- *WhoWor 91*
Kooy, J M J 1902- *EncO&P 3*
Kooyker-Romijn, Johanna Maria 1927- *BioIn 16*
Kooyman, Richard E *WhoAmA 91*
Kooymans, Pieter Hendrik 1933- *WhoWor 91*
Kopac, Andrew Joseph 1947- *WhoEmL 91*
Kopac, Jordan Jack 1938- *St&PR 91*
Kopack, Pamela Lee 1951- *WhoAmW 91*
Kopacz, Stanley William, Jr. 1951- *WhoEmL 91*
Kopal, Zdenek 1914- *BioIn 16*
Kopala, E. Wayne 1947- *St&PR 91*
Kopala, Lili C *BiDrAPA 89*
Kopanycia, Teresa Maria 1961- *WhoE 91*
Kopar, Mark W. 1947- *St&PR 91*
opay, David *BioIn 16*
opcha, Stephen Christopher 1941- *St&PR 91*
opchik, Jeffrey M. 1954- *St&PR 91*
opcke, Richard William 1947- *St&PR 91*
opczyk, Raymond Anthony 1933- *WhoSSW 91*
opec, Frank John 1943- *WhoAm 90*
opec, Joseph A 1946- *ODwPR 91*
opec, Michael Joseph 1939- *St&PR 91*
opech, Joseph I. 1923- *St&PR 91*
opech, Robert Irving 1951- *WhoE 91*
opechne, Gwen *BioIn 16*
pechne, Joseph *BioIn 16*
pechne, Mary Jo 1941-1969 *BioIn 16*
opecky, Charles Rayner *BiDrAPA 89*
pecky, Ferdinand F. E. *BioIn 16*
pecky, Kenneth John 1943- *WhoE 91*
pecky, Pilar Rosario *WhoAmW 91*
pel, David 1910- *WhoAm 90, WhoWor 91*
pell, Bernard Morton 1933- *WhoAm 90*
Kopell, Bert Stanley *BiDrAPA 89*
Kopelman, Arie L. 1938- *St&PR 91, WhoAm 90*
Kopelman, Jerome N. 1952- *WhoEmL 91*
Kopelman, Larry Gordon 1949- *WhoEmL 91*
Kopelman, Leonard 1940- *WhoAm 90*
Kopelman, Mikhail *PenDiMP*
Kopelman, Paul 1929- *St&PR 91*
Kopelman, Richard Eric 1943- *WhoAm 90, WhoE 91*
Kopelove, Alan Brian 1954- *WhoEmL 91*
Kopen, Dan Francis 1948- *WhoE 91*
Kopen, Jack R. 1953- *St&PR 91*
Kopen, Oscar J. 1911- *St&PR 91*
Kopenhaver, Josephine Young 1908- *WhoAmW 91*
Kopenhaver, Patricia Ellsworth *WhoAm 90, WhoAmW 91, WhoE 91, WhoWor 91*
Kopensky, Jerome Harry 1927- *St&PR 91*
Koperwas, Sam Earl 1948- *WhoWrEP 89*
Kopf, Alfred Walter 1926- *WhoAm 90*
Kopf, Eugene Herbert 1937- *WhoAm 90*
Kopf, Hubert Josef 1942- *WhoWor 91*
Kopf, Larry 1890-1986 *Ballpl 90*
Kopf, R.E. 1940- *St&PR 91*
Kopf, Silas 1949- *WhoAmA 91*
Kopff, Richard G, Jr. 1935- *BiDrAPA 89*
Kopidlansky, Victor Raymond 1931- *St&PR 91*
Kopiloff, George *BiDrAPA 89*
Kopiloff, George 1939- *WhoAm 90*
Kopins, John Louis 1934- *St&PR 91*
Kopinski, Dale M. *St&PR 91*
Kopit, Alan Stuart 1952- *WhoEmL 91*
Kopit, Arthur 1937- *MajTwCW, WhoAm 90*
Kopits, Imre *BiDrAPA 89*
Kopits, Steven *BioIn 16*
Kopke, Russell W. 1947- *St&PR 91*
Kopkin, Theodore Jonathon 1924- *WhoSSW 91*
Kopko, Edward M. 1954- *St&PR 91*
Kopko, Edward Mark 1954- *WhoAm 90*
Koplan, Carol Roberta *BiDrAPA 89*
Koplan, Jeffrey Powell 1945- *WhoAm 90*
Koplar, Edward J. *BioIn 16*
Koplewicz, Harold Samuel 1953- *BiDrAPA 89, WhoE 91*
Koplewitz, Laura Ann 1956- *IntWWM 90*
Koplewski, Andrzej *St&PR 91*
Koplin, Donald Leroy 1932- *WhoWor 91*
Koplin, John Lee 1933- *St&PR 91, WhoAm 90*
Koplitz, Howie 1938- *Ballpl 90*
Koplitz, Richard A. 1937- *St&PR 91*
Koplovitz, Kay *BioIn 16*
Koplovitz, Kay 1945- *WhoAm 90, WhoAmW 91*
Koplowitz, Benjamin 1893- *WhoAmA 91N*
Kopman, Benjamin 1887-1965 *WhoAmA 91N*
Kopman, Elizabeth Suzanne 1950- *WhoAmW 91*
Kopnisky, James Richard 1938- *St&PR 91*
Kopolow, Albert 1906- *St&PR 91*
Kopolow, Louis Edward 1944- *BiDrAPA 89*
Koponen, Matti Eemeli 1940- *WhoWor 91*
Kopp, Albert A 1932- *BiDrAPA 89*
Kopp, Charles Gilbert 1933- *WhoAm 90*
Kopp, David Charles 1945- *St&PR 91, WhoAm 90*
Kopp, Eugene Howard 1929- *WhoAm 90*
Kopp, Eugene Paul 1934- *WhoAm 90*
Kopp, Harriet Green 1917- *WhoAm 90*
Kopp, Jennifer Lee 1949- *WhoAmW 91*
Kopp, Jim *ODwPR 91*
Kopp, John Louis 1940- *St&PR 91*
Kopp, Kristin Jean Svanoe *WhoAmW 91*
Kopp, Laurie 1964- *WhoAmW 91*
Kopp, Marlene L. 1936- *St&PR 91*
Kopp, Melisande 1943- *WhoAmW 91*
Kopp, Melvin 1930- *St&PR 91*
Kopp, Nancy Kornblith 1943- *WhoAmW 91*
Kopp, Richard 1934- *WhoE 91*
Kopp, Richard Edgar 1931- *WhoAm 90, WhoE 91*
Kopp, Ronald Sinclair 1954- *WhoEmL 91*
Kopp, Virginia Ann 1959- *WhoAmW 91*
Kopp, W. Brewster *WhoAm 90*
Kopp, W. Brewster 1925- *St&PR 91*
Koppe, Bruce A. 1931- *St&PR 91*
Koppe, Joe 1930- *Ballpl 90*
Koppe, Richard 1916- *WhoAmA 91N*
Koppe, Wilhelm 1896-1975 *BioIn 16*
Koppel, Audrey Feiler 1944- *WhoAmW 91*
Koppel, Elliott Louis 1944- *St&PR 91*
Koppel, Henning *PenDiDA 89*
Koppel, Henning 1918-1981 *ConDes 90*
Koppel, Herman D. 1908- *IntWWM 90*
Koppel, Lewis Michael 1943- *WhoE 91*
Koppel, Sheree Powers 1951- *WhoWrEP 89*
Koppel, Ted *BioIn 16*
Koppel, Ted 1940- *WhoAm 90, WhoE 91, WorAlBi*
Koppel, Thomas Paul 1943- *WhoWrEP 89*
Koppelman, Arthur Mitchell 1951- *WhoE 91*
Koppelman, Chaim 1920- *WhoAm 90, WhoAmA 91, WhoE 91*
Koppelman, David V. 1940- *St&PR 91*
Koppelman, Dorothy 1920- *WhoAmA 91*
Koppelman, Jeffrey Roy 1953- *St&PR 91*
Koppelman, Julius 1916- *St&PR 91*
Koppelman, Stephen *St&PR 91*
Koppelmann, David V. 1940- *St&PR 91*
Koppelmann, Udo 1939- *WhoWor 91*
Koppen, Jerry L. 1945- *St&PR 91*
Koppen, See Foon *WhoWor 91*
Koppenaal, Richard John 1930- *WhoAm 90*
Kopper, Edward A., Jr. 1937- *ConAu 33NR*
Kopper, Hilmar 1935- *WhoWor 91*
Kopper, James L. 1932- *St&PR 91*
Kopper, Lisa 1950- *BioIn 16*
Koppersmith, Daniel Leonce 1952- *BiDrAPA 89*
Koppes, Amy *BiDrAPA 89*
Koppes, Sarah Catherine 1962- *WhoAmW 91*
Koppes, Wayne Farland 1902- *WhoAm 90*
Koppett, Leonard 1923- *Ballpl 90, WhoAm 90*
Koppien, Kim Lee 1951- *St&PR 91*
Kopping, Karl 1848-1914 *PenDiDA 89*
Kopple, Kenneth D. 1930- *WhoAm 90*
Koppula, Moreen *WhoAmW 91, WhoWor 91*
Kopriva, Sharon 1948- *WhoAmA 91*
Koproski, Alexander Robert 1934- *WhoE 91*
Koprowicz, Eugene John 1943- *BiDrAPA 89*
Koprowska, Irena 1917- *WhoAmW 91*
Koprowski, Hilary *WhoAm 90*
Koprowski, Kenneth M. 1949- *ODwPR 91*
Koprowski, Kenneth Mitchell 1949- *WhoEmL 91*
Koprulu, Murat Nafiz 1957- *WhoE 91*
Kops, Paul F. 1937- *St&PR 91*
Kopsa, Louis Dickson 1942- *St&PR 91*
Koptiaeva, Antonina 1904- *EncCoWW*
Koptuck, Anthony Edward 1926- *St&PR 91*
Kopuri, Aparna *BiDrAPA 89*
Kopytman, Mark 1929- *IntWWM 90*
Kopytoff, Igor 1930- *WhoE 91*
Korab, William H. 1942- *St&PR 91*
Korach, Jeffrey L. 1941- *St&PR 91*
Korach, Lawrence I. 1915- *St&PR 91*
Korach, William Mark 1945- *WhoE 91*
Koran, Connie Jean 1953- *WhoWrEP 89*
Koran, Lorrin M 1940- *BiDrAPA 89*
Koranda, David Edward 1947- *WhoEmL 91*
Koranda, J. Timothy 1950- *WhoWor 91*
Koranyi, Adam 1932- *WhoAm 90, WhoE 91*
Koranyi, Erwin K 1924- *BiDrAPA 89*
Koras, George *WhoAmA 91*
Koras, William 1932- *WhoAm 90*
Korayem, Essam Ali 1941- *WhoWor 91*
Korb, Allan R *BiDrAPA 89*
Korb, Daniel Allen 1953- *BiDrAPA 89*
Korb, Donald Baird 1923- *St&PR 91*
Korb, Donald C. 1930- *St&PR 91*
Korb, Donald Lee 1948- *WhoEmL 91*
Korb, Jack Lionel 1927- *St&PR 91*
Korb, Kenneth Allan 1932- *WhoE 91*
Korb, Lawrence J. 1939- *BioIn 16*
Korb, William Brown, Jr. 1940- *WhoAm 90, WhoWor 91*
Korbar, Marcia Marie 1955- *WhoWrEP 89*
Korbecki, Gregory Alan 1955- *WhoEmL 91*
Korbecki, Thomas Anthony 1928- *St&PR 91*
Korbel, Edward 1929- *St&PR 91*
Korbel, Elaine Elizabeth 1941- *WhoAmW 91*
Korbel, John Joseph 1918- *WhoAm 90*
Korben, Donald Lee 1948- *WhoE 91, WhoEmL 91, WhoWor 91*
Korbitz, Bernard Carl 1935- *WhoWor 91*
Korbman, Szalom-Lew 1947- *WhoWor 91*
Korbonski, Stefan 1903-1989 *BioIn 16*
Korbut, Olga *BioIn 16*
Korbut, Olga 1955- *WorAlBi*
Korchagin, Alexander *PenDiMP*
Korchmar, Don 1922- *St&PR 91*
Korchynsky, Michael 1918- *WhoAm 90*
Korczak, Janusz 1878-1942 *BioIn 16*
Korczak-Marla, Rozka 1921-1988 *BioIn 16*
Kord, Kazimierz 1930- *IntWWM 90, PenDiMP, WhoWor 91*
Kord, Victor George 1935- *WhoAmA 91*
Korda, Alexander 1893-1956 *WorAlBi*
Korda, Michael 1933- *WorAlBi*
Korda, Michael Vincent 1933- *WhoWrEP 89*
Korda, Reva 1926- *WhoAm 90, WhoAmW 91*
Korda, Vincent *WhoAmA 91N*
Korda, Vincent 1897-1979 *ConDes 90*
Kordalski, Anthony Tadausz 1926- *WhoAm 90*
Korde, Shirish 1945- *IntWWM 90*
Kordek, John Florian 1938- *WhoAm 90, WhoWor 91*
Kordek, Kathleen Ann 1947- *WhoEmL 91*
Korden, Mary Ethel 1950- *WhoAmW 91*
Kordenbusch, Georg Friedrich *PenDiDA 89*
Korder, Howard *BioIn 16*
Kordes, Hagen 1942- *WhoWor 91*
Kordick, Joseph *BioIn 16*
Kordisch, Larry Wesley 1947- *St&PR 91, WhoAm 90*
Kordons, Uldis 1941- *St&PR 91, WhoAm 90, WhoWor 91*
Korducki, Barbara Joan 1956- *WhoAmW 91*
Kordylewska, Margaret D 1945- *BiDrAPA 89*
Koreen, Amy Rappaport *BiDrAPA 89*
Koreishi, Aziza F *BiDrAPA 89*
Korek, Joan Susan 1957- *WhoAmW 91*
Korelitz, Jean Hanff 1961- *ConAu 132*
Koren, Edward B 1935- *WhoAmA 91*
Koren, Edward Benjamin 1935- *WhoAm 90*
Koren, Edward Franz 1946- *WhoEmL 91*
Koren, Louis *BiDrAPA 89*
Koren, Mary Elaine 1950- *WhoAmW 91*
Koren, R. 1945- *St&PR 91*
Koren, Robert 1945- *WhoE 91*
Koren, Samuel M. 1941- *St&PR 91*
Korenblat, Ashley Lane 1961- *WhoE 91*
Korenic, Lynette Marie 1950- *WhoAmA 91*
Korenman, Philip David 1956- *BiDrAPA 89*
Korenman, Stanley George *WhoAm 90*
Koresh 1839-1908 *EncO&P 3*
Koret, Arthur Solomon 1916- *IntWWM 90*
Koretz, Donald Sidney 1942- *BiDrAPA 89*
Koretz, Jane Faith 1947- *WhoAmW 91*
Koretz, Zvi *BioIn 16*
Koretzki, Paul Richard 1940- *WhoE 91*
Korey, Lois Balk 1933- *WhoAm 90*
Korey, Stanley M. 1930- *St&PR 91*
Korey-Krzeczowski, George J. M. Kniaz 1921- *WhoAm 90*
Korf, Anthony 1951- *IntWWM 90*
Korf, Jakob 1942- *WhoWor 91*
Korfel, Jerzy T. 1942- *St&PR 91*
Korff, Donald Henry 1925- *St&PR 91*
Korff, Ira A. 1949- *WhoAm 90*
Korff, Serge A. 1906-1989 *BioIn 16*
Korfhage, Joyce 1948- *WhoAmW 91, WhoSSW 91*
Korfhage, Robert Roy 1930- *WhoE 91*
Korg, Jacob 1922- *WhoAm 90*
Korgen, Benjamin Jeffry 1931- *WhoWor 91*
Korgen, Judith Kay 1939- *WhoAmW 91*
Korger, John Norbert *BiDrAPA 89*
Korherr, Edgar Josef 1928- *WhoWor 91*
Korherr, Richard 1903- *BioIn 16*
Korhumel, Lee A. 1941- *St&PR 91*
Korin 1658-1716 *EncJap*
Korin, Bernard 1915- *BiDrAPA 89*
Korin, Joel Benjamin 1945- *WhoEmL 91*
Korinek, Karl 1940- *WhoWor 91*
Koritan, Van Lee 1948- *WhoEmL 91*
Koriyama, Naoshi 1926- *WhoWor 91*
Korjeff, Michael Gregory 1932- *St&PR 91*
Korjus, Miliza 1907-1980 *PenDiMP*
Korkolonis, Robert Stephen 1960- *St&PR 91*
Korkosz, Tanya Joanna 1946- *BiDrAPA 89*
Korkowski, Robert Joseph 1941- *St&PR 91*
Korkuczanska, Svetlana *BiDrAPA 89*
Korle, Hans-Heinrich 1934- *WhoWor 91*
Korman, Barbara 1938- *WhoAm 90, WhoAmA 91*
Korman, Bernard J. 1931- *St&PR 91*
Korman, Bernie *BioIn 16*
Korman, David Joel *BiDrAPA 89*
Korman, Edward R. 1942- *WhoAm 90*
Korman, Gerd 1928- *WhoAm 90*
Korman, Gordon 1963- *BioIn 16*
Korman, Harriet R 1947- *WhoAmA 91*
Korman, Harvey 1927- *WorAlBi*
Korman, Harvey Herschel 1927- *WhoAm 90*
Korman, Ira Bruce 1944- *WhoAm 90, WhoSSW 91*
Korman, James William 1943- *WhoAm 90, WhoSSW 91*
Korman, Jess J. 1933- *WhoAm 90*
Korman, Lewis J. 1945- *WhoAm 90*
Korman, Lisa Joy 1960- *BiDrAPA 89*
Korman, Nathaniel I. 1916- *St&PR 91*
Korman, Nathaniel Irving 1916- *WhoAm 90*
Korman, Robert 1947- *St&PR 91*
Korman, Ruth K. 1920- *St&PR 91*
Korman, Samuel J. 1909- *St&PR 91*

Kormanik, Carmela Javellana 1957- *BiDrAPA 89*
Kormano, Martti Johannes 1941- *WhoWor 91*
Kormendi, Eugene 1889-1959 *WhoAmA 91N*
Kormes, John Winston 1935- *WhoE 91, WhoWor 91*
Kormondy, Edward John 1926- *WhoAm 90*
Kormos, Harry R 1933- *BiDrAPA 89*
Kormos, Kathleen Misichko 1952- *WhoAmW 91*
Kormos, Keith J. 1947- *St&PR 91*
Korn, Alan Martin 1944- *St&PR 91*
Korn, Allan L. 1922- *WhoE 91*
Korn, Artur 1937- *IntWWM 90*
Korn, Barry Paul 1944- *WhoE 91*
Korn, Bennet *BioIn 16*
Korn, Bernard 1925- *St&PR 91, WhoAm 90*
Korn, Carl 1921- *St&PR 91*
Korn, Carole Ruth 1941- *WhoSSW 91*
Korn, David 1933- *WhoAm 90*
Korn, David 1934- *WhoAm 90*
Korn, David Gerard 1943- *WhoE 91*
Korn, Donald Louis 1933- *St&PR 91*
Korn, Edward David 1928- *WhoAm 90*
Korn, Elizabeth P 1900- *WhoAmA 91N*
Korn, Franklin A. *BioIn 16*
Korn, Henry 1945- *WhoWrEP 89*
Korn, Howard L. 1932- *St&PR 91, WhoSSW 91*
Korn, Joel 1946- *St&PR 91*
Korn, Judith Ann 1947- *WhoAmW 91*
Korn, Leonard 1943- *BiDrAPA 89*
Korn, Lester B. 1936- *St&PR 91*
Korn, Lester Bernard 1936- *WhoAm 90, WhoWor 91*
Korn, Martin Leonard 1951- *BiDrAPA 89*
Korn, Mel R. 1929- *St&PR 91*
Korn, Peter 1944- *St&PR 91*
Korn, Peter A. 1939- *WhoAm 90*
Korn, Robin 1961- *ODwPR 91*
Korn, Roy Joseph, Sr. 1920- *WhoAm 90*
Korn, Stephen 1945- *St&PR 91, WhoEmL 91*
Korn, Steven Arthur 1955- *BiDrAPA 89*
Korn, Walter 1908- *WhoWor 91*
Korn, William David 1957- *WhoEmL 91*
Kornacki, Richard Alfred 1952- *WhoSSW 91*
Kornadt, Hans-Joachim Kurt 1927- *WhoWor 91*
Kornahrens, Herman 1927- *St&PR 91*
Kornai, Janos 1928- *WhoWor 91*
Kornasiewicz, Pamela Louise 1959- *WhoAmW 91*
Kornberg, Alan William 1952- *WhoEmL 91*
Kornberg, Arthur 1918- *BioIn 16, WhoAm 90, WhoWor 91*
Kornberg, Fred 1936- *St&PR 91*
Kornberg, Hans Leo 1928- *WhoWor 91*
Kornberg, Warren Stanley 1927- *WhoAm 90*
Kornblatt, Barbara Rodbell 1931- *WhoAmA 91*
Kornblatt, David W. 1927- *St&PR 91*
Kornblatt, Stephen David 1943- *WhoE 91*
Kornblau, Gerald 1928- *WhoAmA 91*
Kornbleet, Lynda Mae 1951- *WhoAmW 91*
Kornblet, Donald Ross 1943- *WhoAm 90*
Kornblith, John Howard 1924- *WhoAm 90*
Kornblith, Sara-Jane *BiDrAPA 89*
Kornbluh, Walter 1931- *St&PR 91*
Kornblum, Carl B. 1938- *St&PR 91*
Kornblum, Myrtle 1909- *WhoAmA 91*
Kornbluth, C. M. 1923-1958 *RGTwCSF, WorAlBi*
Kornbluth, Frances 1920- *WhoAmA 91*
Kornbluth, Ralph R 1938- *BiDrAPA 89*
Kornbluth, Ralph Ross 1938- *WhoE 91*
Kornbluth, Sandra Joan 1951- *WhoAmW 91*
Kornbrekke, H.N. 1944- *St&PR 91*
Korndoerfer, Claus Wolfgang 1925- *St&PR 91*
Korndorffer, William Earl 1930- *WhoSSW 91*
Kornecki, Andrew Jan 1946- *WhoSSW 91*
Kornecki, Robert A. 1950- *ODwPR 91*
Kornegay, Horace Robinson 1924- *WhoAm 90*
Kornegay, Lynette 1954- *St&PR 91*
Kornegay, Merry Lynn 1951- *WhoAmW 91*
Kornegay, Robert Madrid 1952- *WhoWrEP 89*
Kornegay, Roy Aubry, Jr. 1937- *WhoSSW 91*
Kornel, Ludwig 1923- *WhoAm 90*
Korner, Alexis 1928-1984 *OxCPMus*
Korner, Alexis 1928-1985 *EncPR&S 89*
Korner, Ann Margaret 1947- *WhoEmL 91*
Korner, Carol Ann 1960- *WhoAmW 91, WhoEmL 91*
Korner, Harold 1923- *BiDrAPA 89*
Korner, Hilda 1931- *WhoAmW 91*
Korner, Jules Gilmer, III 1922- *WhoAm 90*
Korner, Russell Benjamin, Jr. 1957- *WhoEmL 91*
Kornetchuk, Elena 1948- *WhoAmA 91*
Korney, Arthur Francis, Jr. 1933- *St&PR 91*
Kornfeld, Allan 1937- *St&PR 91*
Kornfeld, Allan A. 1937- *WhoAm 90, WhoE 91*
Kornfeld, Daniel 1960- *WhoEmL 91*
Kornfeld, Donald S 1929- *BiDrAPA 89*
Kornfeld, Elise Joy 1957- *WhoEmL 91*
Kornfeld, Emily Davie 1915-1989 *BioIn 16*
Kornfeld, Itzchak Ehud 1953- *WhoEmL 91, WhoSSW 91, WhoWor 91*
Kornfeld, Julian Potash 1934- *WhoAm 90*
Kornfeld, Marvin William 1928- *St&PR 91*
Kornfeld, Peter 1925- *WhoE 91*
Kornfeld, Rosalind Hauk 1935- *WhoAmW 91*
Kornfeld, William 1929- *BiDrAPA 89*
Kornfield, Alfred Theodore 1918- *WhoAm 90*
Korngold, Alvin Leonard 1924- *WhoAm 90, WhoWor 91*
Korngold, Erich Wolfgang 1897-1957 *OxCPMus, PenDiMP A*
Kornhaber, Arthur *BiDrAPA 89*
Kornhaber, Eugene Martin 1941- *BiDrAPA 89*
Kornhaus, John Patrick 1952- *WhoEmL 91*
Kornheiser, Anthony I. 1948- *WhoAm 90*
Kornhiser, Harry Paul 1935- *BiDrAPA 89*
Kornhuber, Hans Helmut 1928- *WhoWor 91*
Korniewicz, Helen Marie 1952- *WhoEmL 91*
Kornilov, Lavrenti 1870-1918 *WorAlBi*
Kornmayer, J Gary 1934- *WhoAmA 91*
Kornmeyer, Robin A. 1948- *St&PR 91*
Kornreich, Carole Sue 1948- *BiDrAPA 89*
Kornreich, Donald Bruce 1937- *St&PR 91*
Kornreich, Joel Craig 1948- *St&PR 91*
Kornsey, Robert J. *St&PR 91*
Kornstein, Don Robert 1952- *St&PR 91, WhoAm 90*
Kornstein, Edward 1929- *St&PR 91*
Kornstein, Michael Allen 1951- *WhoEmL 91*
Kornstein, Susan Gaye *BiDrAPA 89*
Korntheuer, Elmar 1942- *WhoWor 91*
Kornwachs, Klaus 1947- *EncPaPR 91*
Kornylak, Thomas Andrew 1945- *St&PR 91*
Korodi, Andras *PenDiMP*
Korodi, Andras 1922- *IntWWM 90*
Korody, Anthony Vincent 1951- *WhoEmL 91*
Koroljow, Maria G *BiDrAPA 89*
Koroljow, Surgis A 1910- *BiDrAPA 89*
Korologos, Tom Chris 1933- *WhoAm 90*
Koroma, Abdul Karim *WhoWor 91*
Koromzay, Denes *PenDiMP*
Koropatkin, Nicholas 1946- *St&PR 91*
Koros, William John 1947- *WhoAm 90*
Korot, Beryl 1945- *WhoAmA 91, WhoE 91*
Korotich, Vitaly *BioIn 16*
Korotkin, Audrey Rhona 1957- *WhoAmW 91, WhoEmL 91*
Korotkin, Fred 1917- *WhoAm 90, WhoWor 91*
Korow, Elinore M *WhoAmA 91*
Korp, Patricia Anne 1942- *WhoAmW 91, WhoE 91*
Korpal, Eugene Stanley 1931- *WhoAm 90*
Korpel, Adrian 1932- *WhoAm 90*
Korpela, Jon E. 1953- *St&PR 91*
Korpela, Richard Allan 1943- *St&PR 91*
Korpell, Herbert S 1942- *BiDrAPA 89*
Korphage, George J. 1947- *St&PR 91*
Korpi, Veli 1930- *WhoWor 91*
Korpinen, Gunnar John 1947- *WhoAm 90*
Korreng, Suzanne K. Ternes 1966- *WhoSSW 91*
Korrol, Charles R 1934- *BiDrAPA 89*
Korrol, Charles Reuben 1934- *WhoE 91*
Kors, Michael *BioIn 16*
Kors, Pieter C 1921- *BiDrAPA 89*
Kors, R. Paul 1935- *WhoAm 90*
Kors, Terry L. 1946- *St&PR 91*
Korsakov, Nikolay Rimsky- 1844-1908 *BioIn 16*
Korsant, Philip Bowman *WhoAm 90*
Korschinska, Maria 1895-1979 *PenDiMP*
Korschot, Benjamin Calvin 1921- *WhoAm 90, WhoWor 91*
Korschot, John C. 1951- *St&PR 91*
Korsgaard, Sherry *BioIn 16*
Korshak, Shelley J. 1949- *BiDrAPA 89*
Korshak, Yvonne *WhoAmA 91*
Korshak, Yvonne 1936- *WhoAmW 91, WhoE 91*
Korshunov, Oleg Pavlovich 1926- *BioIn 16*
Korsmo, Gordon Marvin 1917- *St&PR 91*
Korsnack, J.J. 1954- *St&PR 91*
Korson, Selig M 1910- *BiDrAPA 89*
Korst, Mogens Flemming 1926- *WhoWor 91*
Korsu, Kenneth W. 1943- *St&PR 91*
Korsyn, Irene Hahne 1927- *WhoAm 90*
Kort, Gregorio 1931- *BiDrAPA 89*
Kort, Shirley *BioIn 16*
Kortbaek, Arne Frederik 1956- *WhoWor 91*
Korte, Bernard Michael 1953- *WhoEmL 91*
Korte, Bernhard Hermann 1938- *WhoWor 91*
Korte, Guenter Wilhelm 1932- *WhoWor 91*
Korte, Karl Richard 1928- *WhoSSW 91*
Korte, Loren A. *WhoAm 90*
Korte, Loren A. 1933- *St&PR 91*
Korte, Martin Roland 1947- *St&PR 91*
Korte, Quentin William 1928- *WhoSSW 91*
Kortekangas, Olli 1955- *IntWWM 90*
Korten, Gunther *BioIn 16*
Korten, Patrick 1948- *ODwPR 91*
Korten, Thomas C. 1947- *St&PR 91*
Kortenhaus, Lynne M 1951- *WhoAmA 91*
Kortenhaus, William James 1934- *St&PR 91*
Kortepeter, Carl Max 1928- *WhoWrEP 89*
Korteweg, Simon Maarten 1938- *WhoWor 91*
Korth, Charlotte Williams *St&PR 91, WhoAmW 91*
Korth, Eugene H. 1917-1987 *BioIn 16*
Korth, Fred 1909- *St&PR 91, WhoAm 90, WhoWor 91*
Korth, Fritz-Alan 1938- *St&PR 91, WhoAm 90*
Korth, Penne Percy 1942- *WhoAmW 91, WhoWor 91*
Korthals, Robert Willem 1933- *WhoAm 90*
Kortheuer, Dayrell 1906- *WhoAmA 91*
Korthoff, Herbert William 1944- *St&PR 91*
Kortlander, Myrna 1934- *WhoAmW 91*
Kortlander, William 1925- *WhoAmA 91*
Kortlandt, Adriaan 1918- *WhoWor 91*
Kortman, Joyce Elaine 1935- *WhoAmW 91*
Kortright, Fanny Aikin 1821-1900 *FemiCLE*
Kortright, Peter Funnell 1954- *WhoEmL 91*
Kortright, Suzanne Alaine 1954- *WhoAmW 91*
Kortsch, William Joseph 1954- *WhoEmL 91*
Kortschak, Sepp August 1933- *St&PR 91, WhoSSW 91*
Kortz, Edwin Wunderly 1910- *WhoAm 90*
Korvatch, Lynn *BioIn 16*
Korver, Gerry Rozeboom 1952- *WhoEmL 91*
Korvick, Maria Marinello 1946- *WhoHisp 91*
Korwek, Alexander D. 1932- *St&PR 91*
Korwek, Alexander Donald 1932- *WhoAm 90, WhoWor 91*
Kory, Robert Bruce 1950- *WhoEmL 91*
Kory, Roger 1939- *WhoSSW 91*
Kory, Steven Michael *BiDrAPA 89*
Koryagin, Anatoly *BioIn 16*
Koryagin, Anatoly I 1938- *BiDrAPA 89*
Korylak, John Raymond 1953- *St&PR 91*
Korzekwa, Marilyn I *BiDrAPA 89*
Korzenik, Armand Alexander 1927- *WhoAm 90*
Korzenik, Diana 1941- *WhoAmA 91, WhoE 91*
Korzenny, Felipe 1947- *WhoHisp 91*
Kos, Paul Joseph 1942- *WhoAmA 91*
Kosa, Emil J, Jr 1903-1968 *WhoAmA 91N*
Kosac, Ljarissa 1871-1913 *EncCoWW*
Kosaceva, Ol'ha Petrivna 1849-1930 *EncCoWW*
Kosacoff-Karp, Phyllis Joyce 1944- *WhoAmW 91*
Kosak, Raymond Joseph 1936- *WhoAm 90*
Kosaki, Masamitsu 1939- *WhoWor 91*
Kosakow, James Matthew 1954- *WhoE 91*
Kosakowski, Cynthia Mallett 1957- *WhoAmW 91*
Kosar, Bernie *BioIn 16*
Kosar, Robert W. 1929- *St&PR 91*
Kosaraju, S. Rao 1943- *WhoAm 90*
Kosarin, Jonathan Henry 1951- *WhoE 91, WhoEmL 91*
Kosasky, Harold Jack 1927- *WhoE 91, WhoWor 91*
Kosbab, F Paul 1922- *BiDrAPA 89*
Kosbab, F. Paul 1922- *WhoWrEP 89*
Kosc, Jean Rochelle 1936- *WhoE 91*
Kosch, Richard Patrick 1947- *St&PR 91*
Koscianski, Leonard J 1952- *WhoAmA 91*
Koscielniak, Thomas Peter 1944- *WhoE 91*
Koscielny, Margaret 1940- *WhoAmA 91*
Koscierzynski, Ronald John 1947- *WhoWor 91*
Kosciuczyk, Lisa Anne 1959- *WhoAmW 91*
Kosciuk, Lisa Marie 1965- *WhoAmW 91*
Kosciuszko, Patricia L. *ODwPR 91*
Kosciuszko, Tadeusz 1746-1817 *BioIn 16, WorAlBi*
Kosciuszko, Tadeusz Andrzej Bonaventura 1746-1817 *EncCRAm*
Kosco, Andy 1941- *Ballpl 90*
Kosecoff, Jacqueline Barbara 1949- *WhoEmL 91*
Kosel, Howard E. 1931- *St&PR 91*
Koselka, Rita *BioIn 16*
Kosewick, Sigmund A 1915- *BiDrAPA 89*
Kosh, Zelda Horner 1913- *WhoWrEP 89*
Koshalek, Richard 1941- *WhoAmA 91*
Koshar, Herbert Bernard 1917- *St&PR 91*
Koshar, Louis David 1928- *WhoAm 90*
Koshes, Ronald John *BiDrAPA 89*
Koshetar, Paul, Jr. 1945- *WhoE 91, WhoEmL 91*
Koshetz, Nina 1894-1965 *PenDiMP*
Koshi, Masaki 1934- *WhoWor 91*
Koshiro, Kazutoshi 1932- *WhoWor 91*
Koshitz, Nina Ivanova 1894-1965 *PenDiMP*
Koshkarian, Haig Aram 1938- *BiDrAPA 89*
Koshland, Daniel Edward 1892-1979 *ConAmBL*
Koshland, Daniel Edward, Jr. 1920- *WhoAm 90*
Koshland, Marian Elliott 1921- *WhoAm 90, WhoAmW 91*
Koshland, William A. 1906- *St&PR 91*
Koshollek, Mary Jane 1955- *WhoEmL 91*
Koshy, Koshy Vydhian 1943- *WhoWor 91*
Kosiancic, Terrence Joseph 1961- *WhoSSW 91*
Kosiba, Bradley Everett 1953- *WhoSSW 91*
Kosice, Gyula 1924- *ArtLatA*
Kosick, William David *ODwPR 91*
Kosidlo, Stanley P. *St&PR 91*
Kosiek, Lawrence J. 1947- *St&PR 91*
Kosier, Christine Marie 1956- *WhoAmW 91*
Kosieradzki, Danuta A S *BiDrAPA 89*
Kosieradzki, Henry 1918- *BiDrAPA 89*
Kosieradzki, Paul H. *BiDrAPA 89*
Kosikowski, Frank Vincent 1916- *WhoAm 90*
Kosinar, William James 1944- *St&PR 91*
Kosins, Mark Steven 1946- *BiDrAPA 89*
Kosinski, Dennis Steven 1946- *WhoWrEP 89*
Kosinski, Jerzy 1933- *MajTwCW, WorAlBi*
Kosinski, Jerzy Nikodem 1933- *WhoAm 90, WhoE 91, WhoWor 91, WhoWrEP 89*
Kosinsky, Barbara Timm 1942- *WhoAmW 91, WhoWrEP 89*
Kosiver, Jeffrey M. 1943- *St&PR 91*
Koskas, Yvan David 1934- *WhoWor 91*
Koske, William Craig 1953- *WhoEmL 91*
Koskenmaki, Rosalie *ConAu 130*
Koskenniemi, Veikko Antero 1885-1962 *DcScanL*
Koski, Ann Louise 1951- *WhoAm 90*
Koski, Conrad W. 1945- *St&PR 91*
Koski, Linda Mae 1947- *St&PR 91, WhoAm 90, WhoE 91*
Koski, Raymond Allen 1951- *WhoEmL 91*
Koski, Walter D. 1933- *St&PR 91*
Koski, Walter David 1933- *WhoAm 90*
Koski, Walter William 1939- *WhoSSW 91*
Koski-Ponton, Ellen Irene 1947- *WhoAmW 91*
Koskie, R. Edward 1930- *St&PR 91*
Koskikallio, Jouko Uolevi 1927- *WhoWor 91*
Koskinas, Silas 1919- *WhoAm 90*
Koskinas, Stephan Aristotle 1946- *WhoAm 90*
Koskinen, Donald Steward 1928- *St&PR 91*
Koskinen, Esko Hugo 1938- *WhoWor 91*
Koskinen, John Andrew 1939- *WhoE 91*
Koskinen, Jouko Tapani 1936- *WhoWor 91*
Koskinen, Kalevi 1929- *WhoWor 91*
Koskoff, Theodore I. 1913-1989 *BioIn 16*
Koskotas, George *BioIn 16*
Koslen, Joel M. 1957- *St&PR 91*
Kosler, Miroslav 1931- *IntWWM 90*
Kosler, Zdenek 1928- *IntWWM 90, PenDiMP, WhoWor 91*
Koslo, Dave 1920-1975 *Ballpl 90*
Kosloff, Mike 1912- *St&PR 91*
Koslosky, Adam Martin 1956- *St&PR 91*
Koslosky, Michael Paul 1951- *St&PR 91*
Koslosky, Pierce A. 1920- *St&PR 91*
Koslosky, Pierce Andrew, Jr. 1950- *St&PR 91*
Koslow, Harold 1926- *St&PR 91*
Koslowski, Dennis *BioIn 16*
Koslowski, Duane *BioIn 16*

Koslowski, George Bernard 1920-1975 *Ballpl 90*
Koslowski, Peter Franziskus Theodor 1952- *WhoWor 91*
Kosma, Joseph 1905-1969 *OxCPMus*
Kosmahl, Henry G. 1919- *WhoAm 90*
Kosmala, Witold Aleksander Jan 1953- *WhoSSW 91*
Kosman, John G. 1930- *St&PR 91*
Kosman, Josh Paul 1966- *WhoE 91*
Kosman, William D. *ODwPR 91*
Kosmes, Kara Marie 1958- *WhoAmW 91*
Kosmicke, Sterling Ralph 1941- *St&PR 91*
Kosmicki, Richard J. *ODwPR 91*
Kosmides, Pericles Theo 1950- *WhoWor 91*
Kosminsky, Jane *BioIn 16*
Kosmo, Jeffrey D. 1942- *St&PR 91*
Kosner, Edward A. 1937- *St&PR 91*
Kosner, Edward Alan 1937- *WhoAm 90, WhoE 91*
Kosnett, Jeffrey Russell 1955- *WhoE 91*
Kosnik, Edward F. 1944- *WhoAm 90*
Kosnik, Edward Francis 1944- *St&PR 91*
Kosof, Anna Clara *WhoE 91*
Kosoff, Flora May 1926- *WhoWrEP 89*
Kosoff, Richard *St&PR 91*
Kosolosky, Roland 1948- *WhoWor 91*
Koson, Dennis F *BiDrAPA 89*
Kosonen, Markku 1945- *ConDes 90*
Kosovich, Dushan Radovan 1926- *WhoAm 90*
Kosovsky, Harry *BiDrAPA 89*
Kosovsky, Karen Ann *BiDrAPA 89*
Kosow, Alan L. 1949- *St&PR 91*
Kosow, Irving Lionel 1919- *WhoSSW 91*
Kosower, Edward Malcolm 1929- *WhoWor 91*
Kosowicz, Francis John 1946- *IntWWM 90, WhoEmL 91*
Kosowsky, David I. 1930- *WhoAm 90*
Kosowsky, Nina 1946- *WhoE 91*
Kosrof, Wosene *BioIn 16*
Koss, Daniel 1914- *St&PR 91*
Koss, Gene H 1947- *WhoAmA 91*
Koss, Joel E. 1954- *St&PR 91*
Koss, John C. 1930- *St&PR 91*
Koss, John Charles 1930- *WhoAm 90*
Koss, Leopold G. 1920- *WhoAm 90, WhoWor 91*
Koss, Marvin 1949- *BiDrAPA 89*
Koss, Mary Lyndon Pease 1948- *WhoEmL 91*
Koss, Mayburn *ODwPR 91*
Koss, Michael Leonard 1948- *St&PR 91*
Koss, Peter 1932- *WhoWor 91*
Koss, Raoul M. 1930- *St&PR 91*
Koss, Rosabel Steinhauer 1913- *WhoAmW 91*
Kossack, Carl Frederick 1915- *WhoAm 90*
Kossack, Georg Wilhelm 1923- *WhoWor 91*
Kossack, Robert James 1954- *WhoEmL 91*
Kossak-Szatkowska, Zofia 1890-1968 *EncCoWW*
Kossak-Szczucka, Zofia 1890-1968 *BioIn 16*
Kossamak *WomWR*
Kossanyi, Maria 1926- *WhoAmW 91*
Kossel, Albrecht 1853-1927 *WorAlBi*
Kossel, Clifford George 1916- *WhoAm 90*
Kossens, Richard Schulze- *BioIn 16*
Kossiakoff, Alexander 1914- *WhoAm 90*
Kossick, Robert M. 1940- *St&PR 91*
Kossman, Jacob 1909-1989 *BioIn 16*
Kossman, Jay Alan 1946- *WhoEmL 91*
Kossoff, Burton 1923- *St&PR 91*
Kossoff, Leon 1926- *BioIn 16*
Kossoff, Phyllis L. 1936- *St&PR 91*
Kossoff, Stanley M. 1925- *St&PR 91*
Kosson, Harlan 1954- *BiDrAPA 89*
Kossow, Sophia 1910- *WhoAm 90*
Kossup, Stanley Joseph 1933- *WhoE 91*
Kossuth, Lajos 1802-1894 *WorAlBi*
Kossuth, Selwyn Barnett 1937- *WhoAm 90*
Kost, Arnulf 1941- *WhoWor 91*
Kost, Gerald Joseph 1945- *WhoEmL 91*
Kost, Glen Edmond 1936- *WhoSSW 91*
Kost, Paul F 1911- *BiDrAPA 89*
Kost, Richard Stephen, Sr. 1947- *WhoEmL 91*
Kost, Wayne L. 1951- *WhoAm 90*
Kosta, Angela *WhoAmA 91*
Kostabi, Mark *BioIn 16*
Kostabi, Mark 1960- *WhoAmA 91*
Kostaki, Georgii Dionisevich 1912-1990 *BioIn 16*
Kostakopoulos, Haralambos Sergios 1950- *WhoAm 90*
Kostal, John Alexander 1960- *WhoE 91*
Kostal, Katherine M 1950- *BiDrAPA 89*
Kostant, Bertram 1928- *WhoAm 90*
Kostant, Ralph Bennett 1951- *WhoEmL 91*
Kostar, Ronald Edward 1950- *WhoWrEP 89*
Kostas, Evans 1935- *St&PR 91*
Kostash, Myrna 1944- *FemiCLE*
Kostava, Merab 1939-1989 *BioIn 16*
Kostecka, Gloria *WhoAmA 91*
Kostecke, B. William 1925- *WhoAm 90*
Kostecky, Lubomir *PenDiMP*
Kostek, James R. 1947- *St&PR 91*
Kostek, Paul John 1957- *WhoEmL 91*
Kostek, Theodore Patrick 1947- *St&PR 91*
Kostel, Laura Everitt 1934- *WhoSSW 91*
Kostelanetz, Andre 1901-1980 *BioIn 16, OxCPMus, PenDiMP, WorAlBi*
Kostelanetz, Boris 1911- *WhoAm 90*
Kostelanetz, Richard 1940- *WhoAm 90, WhoAmA 91, WhoWrEP 89*
Kostelic, Thomas Patrick 1954- *WhoEmL 91*
Kostellow, Rowena Reed 1900-1988 *BioIn 16*
Kostelni, James C. 1935- *St&PR 91*
Kostelnik, Thomas M. 1943- *St&PR 91*
Kosten, Harold W. 1937- *St&PR 91*
Kosten, Richard M. 1945- *St&PR 91*
Kosten, Thomas Richard 1951- *BiDrAPA 89*
Kostenbader, Kimberly Rae *WhoSSW 91*
Koster, Carolee *BioIn 16*
Koster, Charlie *BioIn 16*
Koster, Elaine Landis *St&PR 91*
Koster, Eugene Stanley 1942- *St&PR 91*
Koster, Henry 1905-1988 *AnObit 1988, BioIn 16*
Koster, James 1948- *St&PR 91, WhoE 91*
Koster, James Walter 1945- *BiDrAPA 89*
Koster, Jean Nicolas 1948- *WhoEmL 91*
Koster, John Peter, Jr. 1945- *WhoAm 90*
Koster, Kevin Neil 1958- *WhoEmL 91*
Koster, Marjory Jean 1926- *WhoAmA 91*
Koster, Michael Jay 1954- *St&PR 91*
Koster, Noreen Catherine 1953- *WhoAmW 91*
Koster, William P. 1929- *St&PR 91*
Koster, William Pfeiffer 1929- *WhoAm 90*
Kostere, Kim Martin 1954- *WhoEmL 91*
Kostianovsky, Jorge Edgardo *BiDrAPA 89*
Kostich, Dragos D. 1921- *AuBYP 90*
Kostich, Shirley Ann 1944- *WhoAmW 91*
Kostick, Neil Seth 1946- *BiDrAPA 89*
Kostielney, Janet Leah 1951- *WhoAmW 91*
Kostiha, Kenneth James 1930- *St&PR 91*
Kostiner, Eileen T. 1938- *WhoWrEP 89*
Kosting, Gertrude Simon *BioIn 16*
Kostinko, Gail Ann 1951- *WhoEmL 91*
Kostinsky, Harvey 1949- *WhoAm 90*
Kostiuk, Eugene Steven 1936- *BiDrAPA 89*
Kostiuk, Michael Marion, Jr 1944- *WhoAmA 91*
Kostka, Gloria *BioIn 16*
Kostka, Jean *EncO&P 3*
Kostka, Peter 1933- *WhoWor 91*
Kostler, Hermann 1943- *WhoWor 91*
Kostmayer, Peter Houston 1946- *WhoAm 90, WhoE 91*
Kostohryz, Milan 1911- *IntWWM 90*
Kostolansky, Joseph P. 1933- *St&PR 91*
Kostov, Doncho *BioIn 16*
Kostov, Ivan 1913- *WhoWor 91*
Kostreva, Adrienne Lee Gaal 1945- *WhoAmW 91*
Kostrubala, Thaddeus L *BiDrAPA 89*
Kostrzewa, Joseph Gerald 1941- *St&PR 91*
Kostrzewski, David Andrew 1951- *WhoEmL 91*
Kostrzewski, Jan Karol 1915- *WhoWor 91*
Kostuch, Mitchell John 1931- *WhoE 91*
Kostuik, John 1911- *St&PR 91*
Kosty, Michael Paul 1950- *WhoEmL 91*
Kostyniuk, Ronald P 1941- *WhoAmA 91*
Kostyo, Jack Lawrence 1931- *WhoAm 90*
Kostyo, John Francis 1955- *WhoEmL 91*
Kostyuk, Platon Grigorevich 1924- *WhoWor 91*
Kosuge, Tsune 1925-1988 *BioIn 16*
Kosut, Kenneth Paul 1949- *WhoSSW 91*
Kosuth, Joseph 1945- *WhoAmA 91*
Kosygin, Alexei 1904-1980 *WorAlBi*
Koszarski, Richard Joseph 1947- *WhoAm 90*
Koszewski, Andrzej 1922- *IntWWM 90*
Koszewski, Bohdan Julius 1918- *WhoWor 91*
Koszka, Joseph Edward 1923- *St&PR 91*
Kosztolnyik, Zoltan Joseph 1930- *WhoSSW 91*
Koszulinski, Georg W. 1948- *St&PR 91*
Koszut, Urszula 1940- *IntWWM 90*
Kot, Sarina Ying-Lai 1962- *WhoEmL 91*
Kotait, Joanne 1949- *St&PR 91*
Kotala, Stanislaw Waclaw 1909- *WhoAmA 91*
Kotalac, Russell T. 1964- *St&PR 91*
Kotan, Willie *BioIn 16*
Kotani, Masao 1906- *WhoWor 91*
Kotas, John Peter 1955- *St&PR 91*
Kotas, Robert Vincent 1938- *WhoAm 90*
Kotay, Miles 1949- *ODwPR 91*
Kotch, Alex 1926- *WhoAm 90*
Kotch, John E. 1927- *St&PR 91*
Kotcheff, Ted 1931- *BioIn 16*
Kotcheff, William Theodore 1931- *WhoAm 90*
Kotcher, Peter Giles 1946- *BiDrAPA 89*
Kotcher, Raymond Lowell 1951- *ODwPR 91*
Kotcher, Shirley J. W. 1924- *WhoAmW 91*
Kotchian, A. Carl 1914- *St&PR 91*
Kotek, Freddie Mark 1956- *St&PR 91*
Koteles, William John 1953- *St&PR 91*
Kotelly, George Vincent 1931- *WhoAm 90, WhoWrEP 89*
Kotelnikov, Vitaly A. *WhoWor 91*
Koten, John A. 1929- *St&PR 91*
Koten, John Alfred 1929- *WhoAm 90*
Kotenberg, Kenneth Clark 1949- *WhoEmL 91*
Kotermanski, Mitchell L. 1941- *St&PR 91*
Koth, Erika 1925- *IntWWM 90*
Koth, Erika 1927-1989 *PenDiMP*
Kotha, Aranjyothi *BiDrAPA 89*
Kothari, Ajay Prasannajit 1954- *WhoE 91*
Kothari, Ashok Sanatkumar 1947- *WhoWor 91*
Kothari, Bijay Singh 1928- *WhoWor 91*
Kothari, Kinnari Ashok *BiDrAPA 89*
Kothari, Madhubala Atul *BiDrAPA 89*
Kothari, Nauttam J *BiDrAPA 89*
Kothari, Nauttam J. 1923- *WhoE 91*
Kothari, Renu Omprakash *BiDrAPA 89*
Kothari, Samir Prabodhchandra 1954- *WhoEmL 91*
Kothari, Sriprakash 1957- *WhoE 91*
Kothe, Charles Aloysius 1912- *WhoAm 90*
Kothe, Charles Donald 1922- *St&PR 91*
Kothe, Patrick Donald 1958- *WhoSSW 91*
Kotheeranurak, Charnvit 1954- *WhoWor 91*
Kotheimer, William Conrad 1925- *WhoAm 90*
Kothera, Lynne M. 1938- *WhoAmW 91*
Kothgasser, Anton 1769-1851 *PenDiDA 89*
Kothmann, Jamie R. 1928- *St&PR 91*
Koths, Kirston Edward 1948- *WhoEmL 91*
Kotick, John Alexander 1947- *WhoEmL 91*
Kotik, Charlotta 1940- *WhoAmA 91*
Kotik, Petr 1942- *IntWWM 90*
Kotilainen, Markku Kustaa 1953- *WhoWor 91*
Kotin, Albert 1907-1980 *WhoAmA 91N*
Kotin, Gabriel Gary 1933- *St&PR 91*
Kotin, Joel Tepper *BiDrAPA 89*
Kotin, Paul 1916- *WhoAm 90*
Kotiuga, Peter Robert 1958 *WhoE 91*
Kotker, Norman Richard 1931- *WhoAm 90, WhoWrEP 89*
Kotker, Zane 1934- *WhoWrEP 89*
Kotkin, Leonid *BiDrAPA 89*
Kotkins, Henry Louis, Jr. 1948- *St&PR 91, WhoEmL 91*
Kotler, Aaron 1892-1962 *BioIn 16*
Kotler, Donald Philip 1947- *WhoEmL 91*
Kotler, Louise Lichtman 1921- *WhoAmW 91*
Kotler, Milton 1935- *WhoAm 90*
Kotler, Philip 1931- *WhoAm 90*
Kotler, Scott Franklin 1962- *WhoEmL 91*
Kotler, Steven 1947- *St&PR 91, WhoAm 90*
Kotlier, Susan Ann *BiDrAPA 89*
Kotlowitz, Robert 1924- *WhoAm 90*
Kotlum, Johannes ur *DcScanL*
Kotnour, Richard J. 1932- *ODwPR 91*
Kotonias-Payne, Gregory T *BiDrAPA 89*
Kotonski, Wlodzimierz 1925- *IntWWM 90, WhoWor 91*
Kotoske, Roger Allen 1933- *WhoAm 90, WhoAmA 91*
Kotoski, Debra Ann *BiDrAPA 89*
Kotouc, John F. 1946- *St&PR 91*
Kotovnikov, Felix 1948- *St&PR 91*
Kotowski, Christine Anne 1947- *WhoAmW 91*
Kotowski, John Stanley 1953- *WhoE 91*
Kotra, Rama Krishna 1952- *WhoE 91*
Kotrla, Kathryn Jo *BiDrAPA 89*
Kotsher, Paul Scott 1952- *WhoEmL 91*
Kotsis, Eugenia *BiDrAPA 89*
Kott, Alan 1948- *WhoE 91*
Kott, David Russell 1952- *WhoEmL 91*
Kott, Gary Lynn 1942- *St&PR 91*
Kott, Jan K. 1914- *WhoAm 90*
Kott, Stanley Paul, II 1957- *WhoEmL 91*
Kottanner, Helene 1400?-1470? *EncCoWW*
Kottapalli, Sesi Bhushan Rao 1951- *WhoE 91*
Kottaram, Sibi Joseph *BiDrAPA 89*
Kottas, John Frederick 1940- *WhoAm 90*
Kottemann, George 1931- *WhoAmA 91*
Kottemann, Norma 1932- *WhoAmA 91*
Kotter, John Paul 1947- *WhoAm 90*
Kottick, Edward Leon 1930- *WhoAm 90*
Kottick, Gloria 1930- *WhoWrEP 89*
Kottje, Raymund *WhoWor 91*
Kottkamp, John Harlan 1930- *WhoAm 90*
Kottke, Daniel Gordon, Jr. 1954- *WhoEmL 91*
Kottke, Frederick Edward 1926- *WhoWor 91*
Kottke, Paul K. 1925- *St&PR 91*
Kottler, Dennis Bruce 1949- *BiDrAPA 89*
Kottler, Howard 1930-1989 *BioIn 16*
Kottler, Howard William 1930- *WhoAmA 91*
Kottler, Sylvia Bravman 1922- *WhoAmW 91*
Kottlowski, Frank Edward 1921- *WhoAm 90, WhoWor 91*
Kottman, Roy Milton 1916- *WhoAm 90*
Kottmeyer, John David 1950- *St&PR 91, WhoAm 90*
Kottmeyer, William 1910-1989 *BioIn 16*
Kotto, Yaphet 1937- *DrBlPA 90*
Kotto, Yaphet 1944- *WorAlBi*
Kottom, Paul Wayne 1954- *WhoSSW 91*
Kottraba, Robert Paul 1947- *WhoE 91, WhoEmL 91*
Kotts, John *St&PR 91*
Kottwitz, Tillie *BioIn 16*
Kotty, Robert B *BiDrAPA 89*
Kotuk, Andrea Mikotajuk 1948- *ODwPR 91, WhoAmW 91, WhoE 91*
Kotula, Gloria Anne 1946- *WhoEmL 91*
Kotula, Jeanne 1957- *WhoAmW 91*
Kotula, Karl Robert 1955- *WhoEmL 91*
Kotulak, Ronald 1935- *WhoAm 90*
Kotulka, Frank S. 1943- *St&PR 91*
Kotun, Henry Paul 1931- *WhoAm 90, WhoAmA 91*
Kotun, Joan *BiDrAPA 89*
Kotwal, Deepak Atmaram 1948- *St&PR 91*
Kotwal, Jehangir Keki 1932- *BiDrAPA 89*
Kotwal, Zarine Homi 1964- *WhoEmL 91*
Kotyk, Arnost 1930- *WhoWor 91*
Kotz, David Michael 1943- *WhoAm 90*
Kotz, Margaret Mary *BiDrAPA 89*
Kotz, Nathan Kallison 1932- *WhoAm 90*
Kotz, Nick 1932- *ConAu 32NR*
Kotz, Robert Alan 1951- *BiDrAPA 89*
Kotz, S.W. 1950- *St&PR 91*
Kotz, Samuel 1930- *WhoAm 90*
Kotzebue, August von 1761-1819 *DcLB 94 [port]*
Kotzebue, Kenneth Lee 1933- *WhoAm 90*
Kotzia, Eleftheria 1957- *IntWWM 90*
Kotzky, Alex 1923- *EncACom*
Kotzky, Alex Sylvester 1923- *WhoAmA 91*
Kotzsch, August 1836-1910 *BioIn 16*
Kotzwinkle, William *BioIn 16*
Kotzwinkle, William 1938- *WhoAm 90*
Kou, Jane *BiDrAPA 89*
Kouabenan, Dongo Remi 1957- *WhoWor 91*
Kouame, Bernadette Mappa 1959- *WhoE 91*
Kouba, Maria 1924- *IntWWM 90*
Kouba, Sandra Louise 1941- *WhoWrEP 89*
Koubourlis, Demetrius John 1938- *WhoAm 90*
Kouchoukos, Nicholas Thomas 1936- *WhoAm 90*
Koucky, John Richard 1934- *St&PR 91, WhoAm 90*
Koudelik, Helen *WhoE 91*
Koudelka, Josef 1938- *WhoWor 91*
Kouf, M. James, Jr. 1951- *WhoEmL 91*
Koufax, Sandy 1935- *Ballpl 90 [port], BioIn 16, WorAlBi*
Koughan, Francis Michael 1943- *St&PR 91*
Kouhi, Elizabeth 1917- *BioIn 16*
Koukl, George 1953- *IntWWM 90*
Kouklis, Norma Votaw *BiDrAPA 89*
Koukol-McGuire, Susan Marie 1953- *WhoEmL 91*
Koul, M.K. 1941- *St&PR 91*
Koulamas, Christos Panagiotis 1959- *WhoSSW 91*
Koumans, Alfred J R 1929- *BiDrAPA 89*
Koumatos, Gerry Dionysos 1958- *WhoE 91*
Koumoulides, John Anastasios 1938- *WhoAm 90*
Kounkel, Teryle Lee 1946- *WhoEmL 91*
Kountz, John R. 1927- *WhoAm 90*
Kountze, Augustus 1826-1892 *EncABHB 6*
Kountze, Charles B. 1845-1911 *EncABHB 6*
Kountze, Herman 1833-1906 *EncABHB 6*
Kountze, Luther 1841-1918 *EncABHB 6 [port]*
Koupal, Joyce Ann 1932- *WhoAmW 91, WhoWor 91*
Koupal, Lou 1898-1961 *Ballpl 90*
Kourajian, Steven Charles 1957- *WhoEmL 91*
Kourakos, William 1929- *St&PR 91*
Kourany, Ronald F C *BiDrAPA 89*
Kouretas, Nicholas D 1943- *BiDrAPA 89*
Kouri, Donald Jack 1938- *WhoAm 90, WhoSSW 91*
Kouri-Pelleya, Josephine *BiDrAPA 89*
Kourides, Peter Theologos 1910- *WhoAm 90*
Koursaros, Harry G 1928-1986 *WhoAmA 91N*

Kourteli, Emily Aenou 1887-1941 *EncCoWW*
Kourtoglou, Prodromos John 1952- *WhoWor 91*
Koury, Aleah George 1925- *WhoAm 90*
Koury, George John 1930- *St&PR 91*
Koury, Joanne Marie 1957- *WhoAmW 91*
Kousoulas, Dimitrios George 1923- *WhoAm 90*
Koussa, Harold Alan 1947- *WhoE 91, WhoWor 91*
Kousser, J Morgan 1943- *ConAu 32NR*
Kousser, Joseph Morgan 1943- *WhoAm 90*
Koussevitzky, Serge 1874-1951 *PenDiMP*
Koussevitzky, Serge Alexandrovitch 1874-1951 *WorAlBi*
Koutouzi, Marianna 1922?- *EncCoWW*
Koutras, Phoebus 1932- *WhoAm 90*
Koutros, Stephen Anthony 1955- *WhoEmL 91*
Koutroulis, Aris George 1938- *WhoE 91*
Koutsis, James *St&PR 91*
Koutsky, Carl D 1923- *BiDrAPA 89*
Koutsky, Dean Roger 1935- *St&PR 91, WhoAm 90*
Koutsogiannopoulos, Panagiotis S *BiDrAPA 89*
Koutsos, Martha A *BiDrAPA 89*
Kouvel, James Spyros 1926- *WhoAm 90*
Kouwenhoven, John A 1909- *WhoAmA 91*
Kouwenhoven, John A 1909-1990 *ConAu 132*
Kouwenhoven, John Atlee *NewYTBS 90*
Kouwenhoven, John Atlee 1909- *WhoAm 90*
Kouymjian, Dickran 1934- *WhoAm 90*
Kouyoumjian, Charles H. 1940- *WhoAm 90, WhoE 91, WhoWor 91*
Kouzel, Alfred *NewYTBS 90*
Kouzmanoff, Alan *BiDrAPA 89*
Kovac, Frederick James 1930- *St&PR 91, WhoAm 90*
Kovacevic, Dejan 1940- *WhoWor 91*
Kovacevic, Zivorad 1930- *WhoWor 91*
Kovacevich, Christopher 1928- *WhoAm 90*
Kovacevich, Miroslav M *BiDrAPA 89*
Kovach, Andrew Louis 1948- *WhoEmL 91*
Kovach, Barbara Ellen 1941- *WhoAm 90, WhoAmW 91*
Kovach, Bernard C. *BioIn 16*
Kovach, Bill *BioIn 16*
Kovach, Bill 1932- *WhoAm 90, WhoE 91*
Kovach, Deanna Kay 1946- *St&PR 91*
Kovach, Edward T. 1941- *St&PR 91*
Kovach, Elizabeth Anne 1953- *WhoE 91*
Kovach, Eugene George 1922- *WhoAm 90*
Kovach, George Daniel 1951- *WhoE 91*
Kovach, James P. 1936- *St&PR 91*
Kovach, John Richard 1943- *St&PR 91*
Kovach, John Stephen 1936- *WhoAm 90*
Kovach, Mary Jo 1959- *WhoAmW 91*
Kovach, Stephen R. 1949- *St&PR 91*
Kovach, Thomas A 1949- *ConAu 129*
Kovacheva, Kalina 1943- *EncCoWW*
Kovachevich, Elizabeth Anne 1936- *WhoAm 90, WhoAmW 91, WhoSSW 91*
Kovachy, Edward Miklos 1946- *BiDrAPA 89*
Kovacic, Ernst 1943- *IntWWM 90*
Kovacic, Karen Jean *BiDrAPA 89*
Kovacic, William Evan 1952- *WhoEmL 91, WhoWor 91*
Kovacik, Neal Stephen 1952- *WhoWor 91*
Kovack, Roger F. 1948- *St&PR 91*
Kovacs, Andras 1925- *BioIn 16*
Kovacs, Charles Joseph Leslie Thomas 1945- *WhoEmL 91*
Kovacs, Denes 1930- *IntWWM 90, PenDiMP, WhoWor 91*
Kovacs, Elizabeth Ann 1944- *WhoAm 90*
Kovacs, Endre 1936- *IntWWM 90*
Kovacs, Ernest *BiDrAPA 89*
Kovacs, Ernie 1919-1962 *BioIn 16, WorAlBi*
Kovacs, Gabor 1939- *WhoWor 91*
Kovacs, Janos 1951- *IntWWM 90*
Kovacs, Joseph Curtis 1941- *WhoSSW 91*
Kovacs, Louis Edward 1915- *St&PR 91*
Kovacs, R.A. 1927- *St&PR 91*
Kovacs, Steven 1946- *ConAu 130*
Kovacs, William F. 1955- *St&PR 91*
Kovacs, William Lawrence 1947- *WhoEmL 91*
Koval, Bernard C. 1935- *St&PR 91*
Koval, Charles Francis 1938- *WhoAm 90*
Kovalcik, Kenneth John 1946- *WhoE 91*
Kovalefsky, Edward W. 1953- *St&PR 91*
Kovaleski, John David 1962- *WhoE 91*
Kovalev, Mikhail Vasil'evich *WhoWor 91*
Kovalevskaia, Sofia 1850-1891 *EncCoWW*
Kovalik, Nada 1926- *AuBYP 90*
Kovalski, Maryann *AuBYP 90*
Kovalski, Maryann 1951- *BioIn 16*
Kovalsky, Barbara Jean 1951- *WhoEmL 91*
Kovaly, Heda *BioIn 16*
Kovaly, John Joseph 1928- *WhoAm 90*
Kovaly, Marlene Joan 1943- *WhoSSW 91*
Kovar, Milo 1926- *WhoWrEP 89*
Kovaricek, Frantisek 1924- *IntWWM 90*
Kovarik, Bert E. 1943- *St&PR 91*
Kovarik, Colleen Ann 1958- *WhoEmL 91*
Kovarik, Daniel Charles 1958- *WhoE 91, WhoEmL 91*
Kovarik, Eugene J. 1931- *St&PR 91*
Kovarovic, Karel 1862-1920 *PenDiMP*
Kovarskaya-Levit, Galina *BiDrAPA 89*
Kovasznay, Beatrice M 1950- *BiDrAPA 89*
Kovatch, Jak 1929- *WhoAmA 91*
Kovatch, Jak Gene 1929- *WhoAm 90*
Kovats, Barna 1920- *IntWWM 90*
Kovats, Kolos 1948- *IntWWM 90*
Kove, Irwin 1928- *WhoE 91*
Kove, Simon 1914- *BiDrAPA 89*
Koved, Lance J. 1949- *St&PR 91*
Kovel, Joel S. 1936- *ConAu 32NR*
Kovel, Ralph M. *WhoAm 90, WhoWrEP 89*
Kovel, Terry Horvitz 1928- *WhoAm 90, WhoWrEP 89*
Koveleski, Kathryn Delane 1925- *WhoAmW 91*
Koven, Gustav H. *BioIn 16*
Koven, Howard Richard 1921- *WhoAm 90*
Kovener, Ronald Richard 1932- *WhoE 91*
Kovens, Ed *BioIn 16*
Kovens, Irvin *BioIn 16*
Kovens, Michael Lee 1942- *St&PR 91*
Kovera, Robert Richard 1940- *WhoSSW 91*
Koves, Gabor 1926- *WhoSSW 91*
Kovi, Ati 1960- *WhoE 91*
Kovic, Ron 1946- *CurBio 90[port]*
Kovich, Ann E. 1952- *St&PR 91*
Kovich, Nicholas Joseph 1956- *WhoE 91*
Kovich, William Michael 1948- *WhoEmL 91*
Kovin, Joel Bruce 1944- *St&PR 91*
Kovinick, Philip Peter 1924- *WhoAmA 91*
Kovitz, Benjamin 1913- *BiDrAPA 89*
Kovitz, Nancy R. *WhoAmW 91*
Kovner, Abba 1918-1987 *BioIn 16*
Kovner, Joel Wyatt 1941- *St&PR 91*
Kovner, Matthew Robert 1955- *WhoE 91*
Kovpak, Sidor Artemevich 1887-1967 *BioIn 16*
Kovrig, Bennett 1940- *WhoAm 90*
Kovtynovich, Dan 1952- *WhoEmL 91, WhoWor 91*
Kowacic, Joseph Peter 1919- *WhoWrEP 89*
Kowal, Cal 1944- *WhoAmA 91*
Kowal, Charles Thomas 1940- *WhoAm 90*
Kowal, David Martin 1950- *WhoSSW 91*
Kowal, Dennis J 1937- *WhoAmA 91*
Kowal, Dennis Joseph, Jr. 1937- *WhoE 91*
Kowal, Peter M. 1957- *St&PR 91*
Kowalchik, Walter 1937- *St&PR 91*
Kowalchyk, Gayle 1955- *IntWWM 90*
Kowalczewski, Doreen Mary Thurlow 1926- *WhoAmW 91*
Kowalczyk, Deborah A. 1951- *WhoAmW 91*
Kowalczyk, Jeanne Stuart 1942- *WhoAmW 91*
Kowalczyk, Maciej Stanislaw 1956- *WhoWor 91*
Kowalczyk, Maryann Mercedes 1947- *WhoAmW 91*
Kowalczyk, Richard Leon 1935- *WhoAm 90*
Kowalek, Jon W 1934- *WhoAmA 91N*
Kowaleski, Jane Elizabeth 1948- *WhoEmL 91*
Kowaleski, Thomas J. *ODwPR 91*
Kowalewski, Jan 1892-1965 *BioIn 16*
Kowaliw, Steven Joseph 1952- *St&PR 91*
Kowalke, Kathy Joy *BiDrAPA 89*
Kowalke, Kim H. 1948- *ConAu 132, IntWWM 90, WhoAm 90*
Kowalke, Ronald Leroy 1936- *WhoAmA 91*
Kowalkowski, Martha Jean 1939- *St&PR 91*
Kowallis, George H *BiDrAPA 89*
Kowallis, George Hancock 1942- *WhoE 91*
Kowalska, Anka 1932- *EncCoWW*
Kowalska, Anna 1903-1969 *EncCoWW*
Kowalski, Anthony M *BiDrAPA 89*
Kowalski, Bernard L. 1931- *BioIn 16*
Kowalski, Bob *BioIn 16*
Kowalski, Charmaine Rose *BiDrAPA 89*
Kowalski, David Leon 1956- *IntWWM 90*
Kowalski, Dennis Allen 1938- *WhoAmA 91*
Kowalski, Donald Walter *BiDrAPA 89*
Kowalski, George R *BiDrAPA 89*
Kowalski, James Andrew 1938- *St&PR 91*
Kowalski, Jane Mae 1951- *WhoAmW 91*
Kowalski, Jerry Alvin 1942- *WhoSSW 91*
Kowalski, John 1928- *WhoWrEP 89*
Kowalski, Joseph John 1942- *BiDrAPA 89*
Kowalski, Karla 1941- *WomArch [port]*
Kowalski, Kenneth Lawrence 1932- *WhoAm 90*
Kowalski, Libby R 1940- *WhoAmA 91*
Kowalski, Louis J *BiDrAPA 89*
Kowalski, Michael L. 1953- *St&PR 91*
Kowalski, Miroslaw 1956- *WhoWor 91*
Kowalski, Neal Anthony 1945- *WhoEmL 91, WhoWor 91*
Kowalski, Raymond Alois 1933- *WhoAmA 91*
Kowalski, Richard J *BiDrAPA 89*
Kowalski, Robert E. *BioIn 16*
Kowalski, Ronald J. *St&PR 91N*
Kowalski, Sharon *BioIn 16*
Kowalski, Stephen Frank 1955- *BiDrAPA 89*
Kowalski, Stephen Wesley 1931- *WhoAm 90*
Kowalski, Sylvester Joseph 1929- *St&PR 91*
Kowalski, Timothy Joseph 1956- *BiDrAPA 89*
Kowalski, Wayne W. 1948- *St&PR 91*
Kowalski, Wladyslaw 1895-1975 *BioIn 16*
Kowalsky, Adrian Dion 1947- *WhoSSW 91*
Kowalsky, Jerold D. 1933- *St&PR 91*
Kowalsky, Mark Lee 1958- *WhoEmL 91*
Kowalsky, Stanley Raymond 1935- *WhoSSW 91*
Kowalsky, William Allen 1946- *WhoEmL 91*
Kowaluk, Ralph S. 1941- *St&PR 91*
Kowalyshyn, Theodore Jacob 1935- *WhoE 91*
Kowarski, Allen Avinoam 1927- *WhoAm 90, WhoWor 91*
Kowarski, Lew 1907-1979 *DcScB S2*
Kowatch, Robert Anthony 1954- *BiDrAPA 89*
Koweity, Steven 1914-1989 *BioIn 16*
Kowel, Stephen Thomas 1942- *WhoAm 90*
Kower, H Susan 1953- *BiDrAPA 89*
Kowert, Edward H 1918- *BiDrAPA 89*
Kowert, Gregory Clarence 1946- *St&PR 91*
Kowet, Don 1937- *AuBYP 90*
Kowieski, Thomas Edward 1949- *St&PR 91*
Kowit, Steve Mark 1938- *WhoWrEP 89*
Kowitz, Gerald Thomas 1928- *WhoAm 90*
Kowler, Daniel Edward 1944- *BiDrAPA 89*
Kowsky, John J. *BioIn 16*
Kowtna, Christopher Charles 1946- *WhoE 91*
Kowzan, Tadeusz 1922- *WhoWor 91*
Koy, Albert P 1931- *BiDrAPA 89*
Koy, Ernie 1909- *Ballpl 90*
Koyama, Hachiro 1922- *WhoAm 90*
Koyama, Hiromi Maria 1937- *WhoWor 91*
Koyama, Kosuke 1929- *WhoAm 90*
Koyama, Masayaki *Ballpl 90*
Koyano, Keiichirou 1953- *WhoWor 91*
Koz, Gabriel 1933- *BiDrAPA 89*
Koza, Joan Lorraine 1941- *WhoAmW 91*
Koza, Julia Eklund 1952- *WhoEmL 91*
Kozacko, Richard Leonard *BioIn 16*
Kozai, Yoshihide 1928- *WhoWor 91*
Kozak, Ellen M. 1944- *WhoWrEP 89*
Kozak, Marilyn S. 1943- *WhoAmW 91*
Kozak, Marlene Galante 1952- *WhoAmW 91*
Kozak, Roman *BioIn 16*
Kozakis, Ernest 1927- *St&PR 91*
Kozar, Al 1922- *Ballpl 90*
Kozar, Bradley Kenneth 1958- *WhoEmL 91*
Kozar, Jennifer Lea 1948- *WhoEmL 91*
Kozar, John 1946- *IntWWM 90*
Kozar, William C. 1941- *St&PR 91*
Kozarich, John W. *BioIn 16*
Kozarovich, Donna Lee 1961- *WhoAmW 91*
Kozbelt, Laurie 1963- *WhoWrEP 89*
Kozberg, Donna Walters 1952- *WhoAmW 91, WhoE 91, WhoWor 91*
Kozberg, Oscar *BiDrAPA 89*
Kozberg, Steven Freed 1953- *WhoEmL 91*
Kozdemba, Dorothy Ann 1949- *WhoAmW 91*
Kozdemba, Kathleen Mary 1954- *WhoAmW 91, WhoSSW 91*
Kozel, Dennis Dean 1956- *BiDrAPA 89*
Kozel, Frank Joseph, Jr. 1945- *St&PR 91*
Kozel, Robert W. 1921- *St&PR 91*
Kozel, Thomas Randall 1946- *WhoAm 90*
Kozeliski, Anthony 1912- *St&PR 91*
Kozeliski, Frank Anthony 1944- *St&PR 91*
Kozeluh, Robin Irene 1962- *WhoAmW 91*
Kozer, Jose 1940- *WhoHisp 91, WhoWrEP 89*
Kozerski, Cazmis 1936- *WhoE 91*
Kozhevnikova, Nadezhda *EncCoWW*
Kozhuharov, Christophor 1946- *WhoEmL 91, WhoWor 91*
Koziar, Stephen Francis, Jr. 1944- *WhoAm 90*
Kozicki, Daniel Raymond 1951- *WhoEmL 91*
Kozicki, Zvi Elazar 1950- *St&PR 91*
Kozik, Jerome Matthew 1949- *St&PR 91*
Kozik, Margaret Mary 1966- *WhoAmW 91*
Kozik, Robert Lawrence 1953- *WhoWor 91*
Kozikowski, Mitchell 1935- *ODwPR 91, St&PR 91, WhoAm 90*
Kozin, F. 1930-1990 *BioIn 16*
Kozin, Frank 1930-1990 *BioIn 16*
Kozin, Kenneth Stanley 1950- *WhoEmL 91*
Kozina, Thomas Joseph 1930- *WhoWor 91*
Kozinski, Alex 1950- *WhoAm 90*
Kozinski, Andrzej Wladyslaw 1925- *WhoAm 90*
Koziol, Donald John *BiDrAPA 89*
Koziol, Joseph S. *WhoSSW 91*
Koziol, Urszula 1931- *EncCoWW*
Kozitka, Richard Eugene 1934- *St&PR 91, WhoAm 90*
Koziupa, Diana Maria 1950- *BiDrAPA 89*
Kozlak, Michael Joseph 1953- *St&PR 91*
Kozloff, Joyce 1942- *BiDWomA, WhoAmA 91*
Kozloff, Lloyd M. 1923- *WhoAm 90*
Kozloff, Max 1933- *WhoAmA 91*
Kozlov, Leonid 1947- *WhoAm 90*
Kozlova, Valentina 1957- *WhoAm 90*
Kozlovsky, Yevgeniy Aleksandrovich 1929- *WhoWor 91*
Kozlow, Jeffrey Scott 1961- *WhoEmL 91*
Kozlow, Richard 1926- *WhoAmA 91*
Kozlowski, Alex J. 1949- *St&PR 91*
Kozlowski, Edward C 1927- *WhoAmA 91*
Kozlowski, Edward W. 1925- *St&PR 91*
Kozlowski, Janiece Rae 1959- *WhoEmL 91*
Kozlowski, Karol 1885-1969 *MusmAFA*
Kozlowski, L. Dennis 1946- *WhoAm 90, WhoE 91*
Kozlowski, Linda *BioIn 16*
Kozlowski, Mark J. 1953- *WhoEmL 91*
Kozlowski, Paul G. 1938- *St&PR 91*
Kozlowski, Peter David 1957- *WhoE 91, WhoEmL 91*
Kozlowski, Richard Walter 1931- *St&PR 91*
Kozlowski, Susan 1952- *St&PR 91*
Kozlowski, Tadeusz 1926- *St&PR 91*
Kozlowski, Theodore Thomas 1917- *WhoAm 90*
Kozlowski, Thomas Joseph, Jr. 1950- *WhoAm 90, WhoEmL 91*
Kozlowski, Walter George 1934- *St&PR 91*
Kozma, Adam 1928- *WhoAm 90*
Kozma, Lajos 1938- *IntWWM 90*
Kozman, Maher Shawky *BiDrAPA 89*
Kozmetsky, George 1917- *WhoAm 90*
Kozmetsky, George 1918- *St&PR 91*
Kozmon, George 1960- *WhoAmA 91*
Kozodoy, Neal 1942- *WhoAm 90*
Kozoil, Micah Eugene 1943- *WhoE 91*
Kozol, Harry L *BiDrAPA 89*
Kozol, Jonathan 1936- *WhoAm 90, WhoWrEP 89*
Kozol, Stephen Michael 1961- *WhoEmL 91*
Kozolchyk, Boris 1934- *WhoHisp 91*
Kozub, Michael Victor 1943- *St&PR 91*
Kozubek, Lidia 1927- *IntWWM 90*
Kozyra, Barry Alan 1953- *WhoEmL 91*
Kozyreff, Vladimir Nikolaevitch 1943- *WhoWor 91*
Kozyris, Phaedon John 1932- *WhoAm 90*
Kra, Ethan Emanuel 1948- *WhoE 91, WhoEmL 91, WhoWor 91*
Kra, Irwin 1937- *WhoAm 90, WhoE 91*
Kra, Pauline Skornicki 1934- *WhoAmW 91, WhoE 91, WhoWor 91*
Kra, Siegfried J. 1930- *ConAu 129*
Kraabel, Stephen Edward 1941- *St&PR 91*
Kraai, Melody *BioIn 16*
Kraak, Myron L. 1933- *St&PR 91*
Kraar, Louis 1934- *WhoE 91*
Krabbe, Jeroen *BioIn 16*
Krabbenhoft, Kenneth Lester 1923- *WhoAm 90*
Krach, Mitchell Peter 1924- *WhoE 91, WhoWor 91*
Kracke, Gerald Bruce, Sr. 1935- *St&PR 91*
Kracke, William Irvin 1940- *BiDrAPA 89*
Kraczkowski, Phil 1916- *WhoAmA 91*
Krader, Barbara Lattimer 1922- *IntWWM 90*
Kraegel, Frederick G. 1948- *St&PR 91*
Kraeger-Rovey, Catherine Eileen 1948- *WhoEmL 91*
Kraehe, Birgit Saquina 1948- *WhoWor 91*
Kraehe, Enno Edward 1921- *WhoAm 90*
Kraemer, David R. 1941- *St&PR 91*
Kraemer, J.G. 1942- *St&PR 91*
Kraemer, Nicholas *IntWWM 90, PenDiMP*
Kraemer, Philipp 1931- *WhoE 91*
Kraemer, Richard A. *St&PR 91*
Kraemer, Sandy Frederick 1937- *WhoAm 90, WhoWor 91*
Kraepelin, Emil 1856-1926 *BioIn 16*
Kraessel, Alfred *WhoE 91*
Kraeszig-Mulcahy, Karla Maria 1951- *WhoEmL 91*
Kraetzer, Mary C. 1943- *WhoAmW 91*
Kraeuter, John Norman 1942- *WhoE 91*
Kraf, Harry *BioIn 16*
Krafchick, Dana *BiDrAPA 89*

Kraff, Barton Lewis 1939- *BiDrAPA 89*
Krafft, Julia Steven *WhoAm 90*
Krafft, Karl Ernest 1900-1945 *EncO&P 3*
Krafft, Marie Elizabeth 1956- *WhoAmW 91*
Krafft, Olaf Winfried 1939- *WhoWor 91*
Krafft, William Andrew 1960- *WhoSSW 91*
Krafft-Ebbing, Richard 1840-1902 *WorAlBi*
Krafka, Karel *PenDiMP*
Krafsur, Howard *BioIn 16*
Kraft, Alan Jay 1927- *WhoE 91*
Kraft, Alan M 1925- *BiDrAPA 89*
Kraft, Alan Myron 1925- *WhoAm 90*
Kraft, Anton 1749-1820 *PenDiMP*
Kraft, Arthur 1944- *WhoAm 90, WhoE 91*
Kraft, Audrey Rona 1949- *WhoWor 91*
Kraft, Burnell D. 1931- *St&PR 91, WhoAm 90*
Kraft, C. William, Jr. 1903- *WhoAm 90*
Kraft, Charles H. 1880-1952 *WorAlBi*
Kraft, Christopher Columbus 1924- *WorAlBi*
Kraft, David Christian 1937- *WhoAm 90*
Kraft, David Marvin, Jr. 1937- *WhoWrEP 89*
Kraft, David P 1942- *BiDrAPA 89*
Kraft, Diana Marie 1948- *BiDrAPA 89*
Kraft, Donald B. 1927- *St&PR 91*
Kraft, Donald Bowman 1927- *WhoAm 90*
Kraft, Elaine Joy 1951- *WhoAmW 91, WhoWor 91*
Kraft, Elisabeth Allen 1937- *WhoAmW 91*
Kraft, Gerald 1935- *WhoAm 90, WhoE 91*
Kraft, Gerald G. *St&PR 91*
Kraft, Henry R. 1946- *WhoEmL 91*
Kraft, Herbert 1938- *WhoWor 91*
Kraft, Herbert Arnold 1923- *St&PR 91*
Kraft, Irvin A 1921- *BiDrAPA 89*
Kraft, Jean 1940- *IntWWM 90*
Kraft, John C. *WhoAm 90*
Kraft, John Christian 1929- *WhoAm 90*
Kraft, John F. 1941- *St&PR 91*
Kraft, Joseph 1924-1986 *BioIn 16*
Kraft, Kathleen M. *ODwPR 91*
Kraft, Kenneth Houston, Jr. 1934- *WhoWor 91*
Kraft, Klaus Herbert 1934- *St&PR 91*
Kraft, Leo 1922- *IntWWM 90*
Kraft, Leo Abraham 1922- *WhoAm 90*
Kraft, Linda Carol 1954- *WhoAmW 91*
Kraft, Paula Jeanne *BiDrAPA 89*
Kraft, Peter George 1960- *WhoE 91, WhoEmL 91*
Kraft, Philip B *BiDrAPA 89*
Kraft, Ralph Wayne 1925- *WhoAm 90*
Kraft, Richard A. *BioIn 16*
Kraft, Robert Alan 1934- *WhoAm 90*
Kraft, Robert Paul 1927- *WhoAm 90*
Kraft, Sumner Charles 1928- *WhoAm 90*
Kraft, William 1923- *IntWWM 90*
Kraft, Wolfgang S. 1939- *St&PR 91*
Kraft-Hodges, Judith Ann 1954- *WhoAmW 91*
Kraftman, Michael Benjamin 1957- *WhoWor 91*
Kraftner, Hertha 1928-1951 *EncCoWW*
Kraftson, Raymond H. 1940- *St&PR 91, WhoE 91*
Kraftwerk *EncPR&S 89*
Krafve, Allen Horton 1937- *WhoWor 91*
Krag, Bjarne 1952- *WhoWor 91*
Krag, Donald Richards 1927- *WhoAm 90*
Krag, James Lund *BiDrAPA 89*
Krag, Jean Anita *BiDrAPA 89*
Krag, Olga 1937- *WhoAmW 91, WhoWor 91*
Krage, Patricia Ann Sheridan 1952- *WhoAmW 91*
Kragh, John *BioIn 16*
Kragh, Ulf Wilhelm 1920- *WhoWor 91*
Kraham, Gene Stanley 1953- *WhoEmL 91*
Krahel, Thomas Stephen 1947- *WhoEmL 91, WhoWor 91*
Krahl, Enzo 1924- *WhoAm 90*
Krahn, Dean Dennis *BiDrAPA 89*
Krahn, Fernando 1935- *AuBYP 90, BioIn 16*
Krahn, Lois Elaine 1963- *BiDrAPA 89*
Kraig, Bruce *BioIn 16*
Kraig, Ellen 1953- *WhoAmW 91*
Kraines, Gerald Allen 1944- *BiDrAPA 89*
Kraines, Maurice H. 1920- *St&PR 91*
Kraines, Samuel H *BiDrAPA 89*
Krainev, Vladimir 1944- *PenDiMP*
Krainev, Vladimir Vsevolodovich 1944- *IntWWM 90*
Krainik, Ardis 1929- *IntWWM 90, WhoAm 90, WhoAmW 91*
Krainin, James Mark 1940- *BiDrAPA 89, WhoE 91*
Krainin, Julian Arthur 1941- *WhoAm 90*
Krainski, Joanna Donna 1947- *WhoE 91*
Kraipipadh, Pruthigrai 1930- *WhoWor 91*
Kraiss, Glenn Stephen 1933- *St&PR 91*
Kraiss, Wayne E. *WhoAm 90*
Kraiza, Edward Anthony 1947- *St&PR 91*
Krajcik, Jackie Lynn 1959- *WhoAmW 91*
Krajec, Richard A. 1929- *St&PR 91*
Krajeski, James Paul *BiDrAPA 89*
Krajewski, Kenneth J 1950- *BiDrAPA 89*
Krajewski, Thomas Frank 1948- *BiDrAPA 89*
Krajina, Vladimir Joseph 1905- *BioIn 16*
Krajnovich, Ronald E. 1941- *ODwPR 91*
Krajny, Boris 1945- *IntWWM 90*
Krajovic, Patricia Louise 1949- *WhoAmW 91*
Krakauer, Albert Alexander 1937- *St&PR 91, WhoAm 90*
Krakauer, Bennett 1918- *St&PR 91*
Krakauer, Charles S. *BioIn 16*
Krakauer, John L. 1941- *St&PR 91*
Krakauer, Lawrence Jay 1942- *St&PR 91*
Krakauer, Merrill 1927- *St&PR 91, WhoAm 90*
Krakauer, Randall Sheldon 1949- *WhoE 91*
Krakauer, Sidney *BioIn 16*
Krakauer, Sidney 1919- *St&PR 91*
Krakauer, Thomas Henry 1942- *WhoAm 90, WhoSSW 91*
Krakauer, William *BiDrAPA 89*
Krakauskas, Joe 1915-1960 *Ballpl 90*
Kraker, Alan John 1955- *WhoEmL 91*
Kraker, David Nelson 1961- *WhoEmL 91*
Krakoff, Irwin Harold 1923- *WhoAm 90*
Krakoff, Robert L. 1935- *St&PR 91*
Krakora, Joseph G. 1926- *St&PR 91*
Krakora-Looby, Janice Marie 1951- *WhoAmW 91*
Krakover, Bramby Ann 1962- *WhoAmW 91*
Krakow, Amy Ginzig 1950- *WhoAmW 91, WhoE 91, WhoWor 91*
Krakow, Barbara L 1936- *WhoAmA 91*
Krakow, Barbara Levy 1936- *WhoE 91*
Krakower, Bernard Hyman 1935- *WhoWor 91*
Krakower, Bernard Marvin 1932- *St&PR 91*
Krakower, Leon A 1927- *BiDrAPA 89*
Krakowiak, Edward Thomas 1928- *St&PR 91*
Krakowski, Adam J 1914- *BiDrAPA 89*
Krakowski, Frank M. 1946- *St&PR 91*
Krakowski, Menaham *BiDrAPA 89*
Krakowski, Michael 1952- *WhoWor 91*
Krakowski, Richard John 1946- *WhoEmL 91*
Krakowsky, Minnie *WhoE 91*
Kral, Anthony Howard 1957- *WhoSSW 91*
Kral, Elin 1944- *WhoAmW 91*
Kral, Frank 1940- *WhoAm 90*
Kral, Josef 1887- *EncO&P 3*
Kralick, Charles 1953- *St&PR 91, WhoEmL 91*
Kralick, Jack 1935- *Ballpl 90*
Krall, Anders Albert Walter 1925- *WhoAm 90*
Krall, Cathy Ann 1954- *WhoAmW 91*
Krall, George F. 1936- *St&PR 91*
Krall, Harry Levern 1907- *WhoE 91*
Krall, Patricia Mary 1953- *WhoE 91*
Krall, Vita 1923- *WhoAmW 91*
Krallinger, Joseph Charles 1931- *WhoAm 90*
Kram, David Ian 1948- *IntWWM 90*
Kram, Guenther Reinhard 1957- *WhoEmL 91*
Kram, Leonard W 1945- *BiDrAPA 89*
Kram, Michael Arnold 1950- *WhoSSW 91*
Kram, Shirley Wohl 1922- *WhoAmW 91*
Kraman, Cynthia 1950- *WhoWrEP 89*
Kraman, Lillian V 1948- *BiDrAPA 89*
Krambeck, Robert Harold 1943- *WhoE 91*
Kramer, Aaron 1921- *WhoAm 90, WhoWrEP 89*
Kramer, Alan D 1932- *BiDrAPA 89*
Kramer, Alan Sharfsin 1934- *WhoAm 90*
Kramer, Albert Hartman 1955- *St&PR 91*
Kramer, Alex-Ann 1957- *WhoAmW 91*
Kramer, Alfred Neil 1941- *WhoE 91*
Kramer, Alice Poulsen 1937- *WhoAmW 91*
Kramer, Allan Franklin, II 1950- *WhoE 91*
Kramer, Andrew *BioIn 16*
Kramer, Andrew Alan 1955- *WhoE 91*
Kramer, Anne Pearce 1926- *WhoAmW 91, WhoWor 91*
Kramer, Barry Alan 1948- *BiDrAPA 89, WhoEmL 91, WhoWor 91*
Kramer, Bernard 1922- *WhoAm 90*
Kramer, Billy J. 1943- *EncPR&S 89*
Kramer, Billy J, & The Dakotas *EncPR&S 89*
Kramer, Binnie Henrietta 1914- *WhoAm 90*
Kramer, Burton 1932- *WhoAm 90, WhoAmA 91*
Kramer, Carol Gertrude 1939- *WhoAmW 91*
Kramer, Cecile E. 1927- *WhoAm 90*
Kramer, Charlene Kahlor 1951- *St&PR 91*
Kramer, Charles 1915- *WhoAm 90*
Kramer, Charles H 1922- *BiDrAPA 89*
Kramer, Charles Henry 1922- *WhoAm 90*
Kramer, Charles Shy 1929- *WhoE 91*
Kramer, Charles Warren 1946- *WhoEmL 91*
Kramer, Charles William 1942- *St&PR 91*
Kramer, Corrinnie A. 1937- *St&PR 91*
Kramer, Dale Vernon 1936- *WhoAm 90*
Kramer, Danny *BioIn 16*
Kramer, Debora Dammann 1938- *WhoE 91*
Kramer, Deirdre Anne 1954- *WhoAmW 91*
Kramer, Diana 1928- *WhoAmW 91*
Kramer, Diana R. 1949- *WhoAmW 91, WhoEmL 91*
Kramer, Donald 1937- *St&PR 91*
Kramer, Donovan Mershon 1925- *St&PR 91*
Kramer, Douglas Alan 1945- *BiDrAPA 89*
Kramer, Douglas C. 1942- *St&PR 91*
Kramer, Earl 1933- *St&PR 91*
Kramer, Edith *BioIn 16*
Kramer, Edward *BioIn 16*
Kramer, Edward George 1950- *WhoWor 91*
Kramer, Edward John 1939- *WhoAm 90*
Kramer, Eleanor 1939- *WhoAmW 91, WhoWor 91*
Kramer, Emmanuel Martin 1928- *WhoE 91*
Kramer, Eugene L. 1939- *WhoAm 90*
Kramer, Ferdinand 1901- *WhoAm 90*
Kramer, Frank Raymond 1908- *WhoAm 90, WhoWor 91*
Kramer, Fred M 1923- *BiDrAPA 89*
Kramer, Fred Russell 1942- *WhoE 91*
Kramer, Gary H *BiDrAPA 89*
Kramer, George *AuBYP 90*
Kramer, George P. 1927- *WhoAm 90*
Kramer, George Paul 1941- *St&PR 91*
Kramer, Gerhardt Theodore 1909- *WhoAm 90*
Kramer, Gertrude M *WhoAmA 91*
Kramer, Gilda Lea 1954- *WhoEmL 91*
Kramer, Gunter 1931- *WhoE 91*
Kramer, Harry 1914- *St&PR 91*
Kramer, Harry John 1925- *WhoWrEP 89*
Kramer, Harry-Karl 1925- *WhoWor 91*
Kramer, Heinrich 1430?-1505 *EncO&P 3*
Kramer, Helmut G *BiDrAPA 89*
Kramer, Henry Herman 1930- *St&PR 91*
Kramer, Hilton 1928- *WhoAmA 91*
Kramer, Horace Z. 1918-1988 *BioIn 16*
Kramer, Irvin Raymond 1912- *WhoAm 90*
Kramer, Irving *St&PR 91*
Kramer, Irwin *BioIn 16*
Kramer, Jack 1918- *Ballpl 90, BioIn 16*
Kramer, Jack 1921- *BioIn 16, WorAlBi*
Kramer, Jack A. 1950- *WhoEmL 91*
Kramer, Jack N 1923-1984 *WhoAmA 91N*
Kramer, Jackson C. *St&PR 91*
Kramer, James 1927- *WhoAmA 91*
Kramer, James Joseph 1929- *WhoAm 90*
Kramer, James Matthew 1942- *St&PR 91*
Kramer, Jane 1938- *WhoAm 90, WhoWrEP 89*
Kramer, Janice Kay 1944- *WhoAmW 91*
Kramer, Janice Lynn 1962- *WhoEmL 91*
Kramer, Jeffrey 1936- *BiDrAPA 89*
Kramer, Joan Lynn 1952- *WhoEmL 91*
Kramer, Joan Whitney *NewYTBS 90*
Kramer, Joel 1937- *St&PR 91*
Kramer, Joel Roy 1948- *WhoAm 90*
Kramer, Johannes 1946- *WhoWor 91*
Kramer, John F *BiDrAPA 89*
Kramer, John Paul 1928- *WhoAm 90*
Kramer, John S. 1931- *St&PR 91*
Kramer, Jonathan *NewAgMG*
Kramer, Jonathan D. 1942- *ConAu 130, IntWWM 90*
Kramer, Josef 1906-1945 *BioIn 16*
Kramer, Joseph H., III 1949- *ODwPR 91*
Kramer, June Elizabeth 1947- *BiDrAPA 89*
Kramer, Karen Sue 1942- *WhoAmW 91*
Kramer, Keith 1959- *WhoWrEP 89*
Kramer, Ken 1940- *OxCCanT [port]*
Kramer, Kenneth B. 1946- *WhoE 91*
Kramer, Kenneth Bentley 1942- *WhoAm 90*
Kramer, Kenneth Robert 1945- *St&PR 91*
Kramer, Lance 1941- *St&PR 91*
Kramer, Larry *BioIn 16*
Kramer, Larry 1935- *News 91-2 [port]*
Kramer, Larry A. *St&PR 91*
Kramer, Laura Kean *BiDrAPA 89*
Kramer, Lawrence Stephen *BioIn 16*
Kramer, Lawrence Stephen 1950- *WhoAm 90*
Kramer, Lee Roy 1819?-1894 *AmLegL*
Kramer, Lila Seldin *BiDrAPA 89*
Kramer, Linda Lewis 1937- *WhoAmA 91*
Kramer, Loren 1929- *St&PR 91*
Kramer, Louise *WhoAmA 91*
Kramer, Louise 1942?- *BiDWomA*
Kramer, Luther E. 1942- *WhoSSW 91*
Kramer, Lynne Adair 1952- *WhoAmW 91*
Kramer, Marc B. 1944- *WhoE 91*
Kramer, Marcia Gail 1948- *WhoAm 90*
Kramer, Margia *WhoAmA 91*
Kramer, Mary Jo 1947- *WhoE 91*
Kramer, Mary Vincent 1957- *WhoAmW 91*
Kramer, Melany Beth 1954- *WhoAmW 91*
Kramer, Meyer 1919- *WhoAm 90*
Kramer, Michael Evan 1954- *WhoEmL 91*
Kramer, Michael Paul 1945- *St&PR 91*
Kramer, Milton 1929- *BiDrAPA 89*
Kramer, Morton 1914- *BiDrAPA 89, WhoAm 90*
Kramer, Nora 1896?-1984 *AuBYP 90*
Kramer, Paul C. 1931- *St&PR 91*
Kramer, Paul Jackson 1904- *WhoAm 90*
Kramer, Paul L. 1944- *St&PR 91*
Kramer, Paul R. 1936- *WhoE 91*
Kramer, Paula Lee 1952- *WhoE 91*
Kramer, Peter David 1948- *BiDrAPA 89, WhoE 91*
Kramer, Peter Joseph 1953- *St&PR 91*
Kramer, Peter Robin 1951- *WhoE 91*
Kramer, Philip 1921- *St&PR 91, WhoAm 90*
Kramer, Philip Earl 1940- *WhoWrEP 89*
Kramer, Phyllis R. 1946- *St&PR 91*
Kramer, Ralph Geren 1921- *WhoSSW 91*
Kramer, Ralph J. *ODwPR 91*
Kramer, Randy 1960- *Ballpl 90*
Kramer, Reuben 1909- *WhoAmA 91*
Kramer, Reuben Robert 1909- *WhoAm 90, WhoWor 91*
Kramer, Richard A. 1938- *WhoAm 90*
Kramer, Richard Elwin 1934- *St&PR 91*
Kramer, Richard Eugene 1946- *WhoEmL 91*
Kramer, Richard L. 1945- *St&PR 91*
Kramer, Richard Lawrence 1945- *WhoE 91*
Kramer, Richard T 1930- *BiDrAPA 89*
Kramer, Rita 1929- *ConAu 31NR*
Kramer, Robert 1913- *WhoAm 90*
Kramer, Robert Ivan 1933- *WhoAm 90*
Kramer, Roy Howard 1960- *WhoEmL 91*
Kramer, Ruth 1925- *WhoAmW 91, WhoE 91*
Kramer, Samuel 1931- *BiDrAPA 89*
Kramer, Samuel Noah 1897-1990 *NewYTBS 90*
Kramer, Sandra 1943- *WhoAmW 91*
Kramer, Selma 1920- *BiDrAPA 89*
Kramer, Sheldon I. *BioIn 16*
Kramer, Sherri Marcelle 1954- *WhoAmW 91*
Kramer, Sidney B. 1915- *WhoAm 90*
Kramer, Simon 1808-1887 *BioIn 16*
Kramer, Simon 1919- *WhoAm 90*
Kramer, Stanley 1913- *BioIn 16, WorAlBi*
Kramer, Stanley E. 1913- *WhoAm 90*
Kramer, Stepfanie 1956- *WorAlBi*
Kramer, Stephen I 1950- *BiDrAPA 89*
Kramer, Stephen James *BiDrAPA 89*
Kramer, Sue 1939-1978 *OxCCanT [port]*
Kramer, Susan Wendy 1954- *WhoEmL 91*
Kramer, Sylvia Malcmacher 1952- *WhoEmL 91*
Kramer, Terry Allen *BioIn 16*
Kramer, Thomas A M 1957- *BiDrAPA 89*
Kramer, Thomas E. 1921- *St&PR 91*
Kramer, Toni *BioIn 16*
Kramer, Toni 1943- *IntWWM 90*
Kramer, Vicki Lee 1949- *WhoAmW 91*
Kramer, Walter 1948- *WhoWor 91*
Kramer, Warren 1923- *St&PR 91*
Kramer, William 1924- *St&PR 91*
Kramer, William J., Jr. 1940- *St&PR 91*
Kramer, William Joseph 1939- *WhoAm 90*
Kramer, Winifred Anita 1946- *WhoAmW 91*
Kramer, Worth Alan 1941- *WhoWor 91*
Kramer, Yale 1929- *BiDrAPA 89*
Kramers, Hendrik Anthony 1894-1952 *BioIn 16*
Kramish, Arnold 1923- *WhoAm 90*
Kramish, Marc Eric 1958- *WhoSSW 91*
Kramlinger, Keith Gregory 1955- *BiDrAPA 89*
Kramm, Deborah Lucille *WhoAmW 91, WhoE 91, WhoWor 91*
Kramm, Gunnar 1939- *St&PR 91*
Kramme, Paul Edgar, Jr. 1923- *St&PR 91*
Kramme, Richard Grover 1933- *St&PR 91*
Kramnick, Isaac 1938- *WhoAm 90*
Kramp, Richard William 1945- *WhoAm 90, WhoEmL 91*
Kramp, Ronald Arthur 1938- *WhoWor 91*
Krampitz, Lester Orville 1909- *WhoAm 90*
Kramrisch, Stella *WhoAmA 91, WhoE 91*
Kranda, Michael L. 1953- *St&PR 91*
Krane, Robert A. 1933- *St&PR 91*
Krane, Robert Alan 1933- *WhoAm 90*
Krane, Stephen Martin 1927- *WhoAm 90*
Krane, Steven Charles 1957- *WhoEmL 91*
Krane, Susan 1954- *WhoAmA 91, WhoSSW 91*
Kranenburg, Hendrik J. 1955- *St&PR 91*
Kranendonk, Jan 1930- *WhoWor 91*
Kranepool, Ed 1944- *Ballpl 90*
Kraner, Florian G 1908- *WhoAmA 91N*
Kraner, Madeline R. *WhoWrEP 89*
Kranhold, Lester Charles 1925- *St&PR 91*
Kranich, Wilmer LeRoy 1919- *WhoAm 90*

Kranick, Lewis Girard 1914- *St&PR 91*
Kranig, Carol A 1947- *BiDrAPA 89*
Kranig, K.J. 1946- *St&PR 91*
Kranitz, Theodore Mitchell 1922- *WhoAm 90*
Kranitz, Wesley Chester 1948- *WhoEmL 91*
Kranitzky, Mary Lisa 1955- *WhoAmW 91*
Kranjac, Thomas 1949- *BiDrAPA 89*
Krank, Daniel F 1932- *BiDrAPA 89*
Kranking, Margaret Graham *BioIn 16*
Kranking, Margaret Graham 1930- *WhoAmA 91, WhoAmW 91, WhoE 91*
Krannich, Beverley Turner 1951- *St&PR 91*
Krans, Olof 1838-1916 *MusmAFA*
Kransdorf, Ronald Joseph 1935- *St&PR 91*
Kranseler, Arthur Sheldon 1934- *St&PR 91*
Kranser, Leonard Samuel 1932- *St&PR 91*
Kransnansky, Marvin L. 1930- *ODwPR 91*
Krantz, Douglas Stanley 1952- *WhoEmL 91*
Krantz, Gary Andrew 1959- *WhoE 91*
Krantz, Jeffrey Albert 1954- *WhoEmL 91*
Krantz, Jeffry Ostler 1952- *St&PR 91*
Krantz, Judith 1927- *ConAu 33NR, MajTwCW*
Krantz, Judith 1928- *WorAlBi*
Krantz, Judith Tarcher 1928- *WhoAm 90*
Krantz, Kermit Edward 1923- *WhoAm 90, WhoWor 91*
Krantz, Les 1945- *WhoAmA 91*
Krantz, Lucretia *AuBYP 90*
Krantz, Melissa Marianne 1954- *WhoAm 90*
Krantz, Palmer Eric 1950- *WhoAm 90*
Krantz, Robert E. 1946- *St&PR 91*
Krantz, Sanford Burton 1934- *WhoAm 90*
Krantz, Stephen Falk 1923- *WhoAm 90*
Krantzler, Leah *ODwPR 91*
Krantzman, Irving Emanuel 1917- *St&PR 91*
Kranyik, Elizabeth Ann 1957- *WhoAmW 91, WhoE 91*
Kranz, Arthur John 1959- *BiDrAPA 89*
Kranz, Audie M. 1954- *St&PR 91*
Kranz, Frederick *PenDiDA 89*
Kranz, Janet Lee 1947- *WhoAmW 91*
Kranz, Kenneth Louis, Jr. 1946- *WhoWor 91*
Kranz, Norman 1924- *WhoAm 90*
Kranz, Przemo Tadeusz 1945- *WhoSSW 91*
Kranz, Sally *ODwPR 91*
Kranz, Victoria Yasamin *BiDrAPA 89*
Kranz, Wilbur Joseph 1927- *St&PR 91*
Kranz-Johnson, Maureen Ann 1956- *St&PR 91*
Kranzberg, Kenneth 1937- *St&PR 91*
Kranzberg, Maurice Bernard 1911- *St&PR 91*
Kranzberg, Melvin 1917- *WhoAm 90, WhoSSW 91*
Kranzdorf, Jeffrey Paul 1955- *WhoEmL 91*
Kranzdorf, Norman M. 1930- *St&PR 91*
Kranzdorf, Norman Melvin 1930- *WhoE 91*
Kranzler, Elliot Mark 1951- *BiDrAPA 89*
Kranzler, Harvey Nathan 1946- *BiDrAPA 89*
Kranzler, Henry Richard 1950- *BiDrAPA 89*
Kranzler, Myles Mitchell 1928- *St&PR 91*
Kranzley, Arthur S. 1927- *St&PR 91*
Kranzow, Ronald Roy 1931- *St&PR 91*
Krapf, Gerhard W. 1924- *IntWWM 90*
Krapf, Norbert 1943- *WhoWrEP 89*
Krapf, Richard Clarence 1930- *St&PR 91*
Krapohl, James Roy 1945- *St&PR 91*
Krapp, Edgar 1947- *IntWWM 90*
Krapp, Gene 1887-1923 *Ballpl 90*
Krappinger, Herbert Ernst 1950- *WhoWor 91*
Kraras, Gust Christ 1921- *WhoE 91*
Krarup, Anthony Charles 1928- *WhoWor 91*
Krarup, Thorleif 1952- *WhoWor 91*
Krasavage, Kenneth William 1942- *St&PR 91*
Krase, Jerome 1943- *WhoE 91*
Krash, Abe 1927- *WhoAm 90*
Krashen, Stephen D. 1941- *ConAu 132*
Krashes, Barbara *WhoAmA 91, WhoE 91*
Krasilovsky, Alexis Rafael 1950- *WhoEmL 91*
Krasilovsky, Phyllis 1926- *AuBYP 90, BioIn 16*
Krasin, Leonid Borisovich 1870-1926 *BioIn 16*
Krasinski, Jerzy Slawomir 1940- *WhoE 91*
Kraske, Karl V. 1935- *St&PR 91*
Kraske, Karl Vincent 1935- *WhoAm 90*
Krasker, Elaine S. 1927- *WhoAmW 91*
Krasko, Michael John 1943- *WhoAm 90*
Kraslow, David 1926- *WhoAm 90, WhoSSW 91, WhoWor 91*
Krasna, Alvin Isaac 1929- *WhoAm 90*
Krasna, Gary Marc 1960- *WhoEmL 91*
Krasnansky, Marvin L. 1930- *St&PR 91, WhoAm 90*
Krasner, Herbert *St&PR 91*
Krasner, Lee 1908-1984 *BioIn 16, WhoAmA 91N*
Krasner, Lee 1908-1985 *BiDWomA*
Krasner, Lenore 1908-1984 *BioIn 16*
Krasner, Louis 1903- *IntWWM 90, PenDiMP, WhoAm 90*
Krasner, Milton 1904-1988 *BioIn 16*
Krasner, Oscar Jay 1922- *WhoWor 91*
Krasner, Ronald F 1944- *BiDrAPA 89*
Krasner, Sidney D. 1932- *St&PR 91*
Krasney, Josephine *St&PR 91*
Krasney, Samuel 1924- *ODwPR 91*
Krasney, Samuel A. 1924- *St&PR 91*
Krasney, Samuel Joseph 1925- *St&PR 91, WhoAm 90*
Krasniewski, Witold Stanislaw 1955- *BiDrAPA 89*
Krasnoff, Abraham *WhoAm 90*
Krasnoff, Jeffrey Paul 1955- *St&PR 91*
Krasnohorska, Eliska 1847-1926 *EncCoWW*
Krasnopolsky, Michael *BioIn 16*
Krasnoshchekhov, Aleksandr Mikhailovich 1880-1937 *BioIn 16*
Krasnov, Vladislav Georgievich 1937- *ConAu 132*
Krasnow, Charles Gale 1949- *BiDrAPA 89*
Krasnow, Jeffrey Harry 1946- *WhoEmL 91*
Krasnow, Marvin L. 1938- *St&PR 91*
Krasnow, Michael S *BiDrAPA 89*
Krasnow, Robert W 1942- *BiDrAPA 89*
Krasny, Charlotte Althea 1935- *WhoAmW 91*
Krasnyansky, Anatole Lvovich 1930- *WhoAm 90*
Krasovskaya, Vera 1915- *ConAu 130*
Krass, Marc Stern 1949- *WhoEmL 91*
Krass, Robert Peter 1936- *St&PR 91, WhoAm 90*
Krassner, Lenore 1908-1985 *BiDWomA*
Krassner, Michael B 1935- *BiDrAPA 89*
Krasts, Aivars 1938- *St&PR 91, WhoAm 90*
Krasucki, Henri 1924- *BiDFrPL*
Kraszewski, Muriel *BioIn 16*
Krat, Gary Walden 1947- *St&PR 91, WhoAm 90, WhoEmL 91*
Kratena, Kurt Heinz 1961- *WhoWor 91*
Krathen, David Howard 1946- *WhoEmL 91*
Krathwohl, David Reading 1921- *WhoAm 90*
Kratina, Fredric K 1926- *BiDrAPA 89*
Kratina, K George 1910- *WhoAmA 91*
Kratky, Jiri 1926- *WhoWor 91*
Kratochvil, Byron George 1932- *WhoAm 90*
Kratochvil, Jiri *PenDiMP*
Kratochvil, Louis Glen 1922- *WhoAm 90*
Kratochvil, Susan Marie 1958- *WhoAmW 91*
Kratoville, Harry J. 1930- *St&PR 91*
Kratt, Peter George 1940- *St&PR 91, WhoAm 90*
Kratter, Leslie Michael 1945- *St&PR 91*
Kratz, E. Lyn 1948- *WhoE 91, WhoEmL 91*
Kratz, George Frank 1930- *St&PR 91*
Kratz, Hans Lewis 1938- *St&PR 91*
Kratz, Marilyn June 1938- *WhoWrEP 89*
Kratz, Mildred Sands *WhoAmA 91*
Kratz, Paul James 1941- *WhoSSW 91*
Kratz, Vernon H *BiDrAPA 89*
Kratzer, Guy Livingston 1911- *WhoAm 90, WhoE 91, WhoWor 91*
Kratzer, Russell Elmer, III 1950- *WhoEmL 91*
Krauch, Carl Heinrich 1931- *WhoWor 91*
Krauch, Velma Ann 1916- *WhoAmW 91*
Krauchick, Dale Zobal 1955- *WhoAmW 91*
Kraujiete, Aina 1923- *EncCoWW*
Krauk, Elsie Alexandria 1919- *WhoAmW 91*
Kraul, Edward Garcia 1930- *WhoHisp 91*
Kraulis, Olaf Ernest 1943- *St&PR 91*
Kraus, Adalbert 1937- *IntWWM 90*
Kraus, Albert Andrew, Jr. 1948- *WhoEmL 91*
Kraus, Alfredo *BioIn 16*
Kraus, Alfredo 1924- *WhoAm 90*
Kraus, Alfredo 1927- *IntWWM 90, PenDiMP*
Kraus, Andreas 1922- *WhoWor 91*
Kraus, Anna Josephine 1927- *WhoE 91*
Kraus, C. Norman 1924- *ConAu 33NR*
Kraus, Carl E. 1947- *St&PR 91*
Kraus, Constantine Raymond *BioIn 16*
Kraus, Constantine Raymond 1900- *ConAu 129, WhoAm 90*
Kraus, David 1930- *WhoSSW 91*
Kraus, David Robert 1960- *WhoEmL 91*
Kraus, Eileen S. *WhoAmW 91*
Kraus, Ernst 1863-1941 *PenDiMP*
Kraus, Frederick O 1919- *BiDrAPA 89*
Kraus, Gary Paul 1953- *WhoSSW 91*
Kraus, George 1912- *IntWWM 90*
Kraus, Gerry James 1951- *WhoEmL 91*
Kraus, Hans-Joachim 1918- *WhoWor 91*
Kraus, Hans Peter 1907-1988 *BioIn 16*
Kraus, Helen Antoinette 1909- *WhoWrEP 89*
Kraus, Helmut 1930- *WhoWor 91*
Kraus, Henry 1905- *WhoWor 91*
Kraus, Herbert M. 1921- *ODwPR 91, St&PR 91*
Kraus, Herbert Myron 1921- *WhoAm 90*
Kraus, Irvin Martin *BiDrAPA 89*
Kraus, James Calvin *BiDrAPA 89*
Kraus, James Robert 1926- *St&PR 91*
Kraus, Jean Elizabeth Grau 1932- *WhoSSW 91, WhoWor 91*
Kraus, Jeanne Smith *BiDrAPA 89*
Kraus, Jerome Hilbert 1957- *WhoEmL 91*
Kraus, Joan Davida 1933- *WhoAmW 91*
Kraus, Joanna Halpert 1937- *WhoE 91, WhoWrEP 89*
Kraus, Joseph 1892- *EncO&P 3*
Kraus, Karl 1874-1936 *WrPh*
Kraus, Lawrence B. 1950- *St&PR 91*
Kraus, Lili 1903-1986 *PenDiMP*
Kraus, Marilyn Frances *BiDrAPA 89*
Kraus, Max Hochschild 1927- *WhoE 91*
Kraus, Max William 1920- *WhoE 91*
Kraus, Michael 1901-1990 *ConAu 132*
Kraus, Mozelle DeWitte Bigelow 1929- *WhoAmW 91, WhoE 91*
Kraus, N.J., Sr. 1928- *St&PR 91*
Kraus, Nancy Penne 1962- *WhoAmW 91*
Kraus, Norma Jean 1931- *WhoAmW 91, WhoE 91, WhoWor 91*
Kraus, Otakar 1909-1980 *PenDiMP*
Kraus, Pansy Daegling 1916- *WhoAmW 91, WhoWor 91*
Kraus, Philip A. 1950- *IntWWM 90*
Kraus, Richard 1902-1978 *PenDiMP*
Kraus, Richard Carl 1946- *St&PR 91*
Kraus, Richard Charles 1953- *WhoEmL 91*
Kraus, Richard T *BiDrAPA 89*
Kraus, Robert 1925- *AuBYP 90, SmATA 11AS [port]*
Kraus, Robert F 1930- *BiDrAPA 89, WhoAm 90*
Kraus, Rozann Baghdad 1952- *IntWWM 90*
Kraus, Stephen Victor 1929- *WhoE 91*
Kraus, Thayne L. 1933- *St&PR 91*
Kraus, Zili *WhoAmA 91*
Kraus-Friedmann, Naomi 1933- *WhoAmW 91*
Krause, Alan M. 1929- *St&PR 91*
Krause, Alvina 1893-1981 *BioIn 16*
Krause, Alvina E 1893-1981 *NotWoAT*
Krause, Benjamin D. 1936- *St&PR 91*
Krause, Bernard Leo 1938- *WhoAm 90*
Krause, Bernie *BioIn 16*
Krause, C.J. 1924- *St&PR 91*
Krause, Charles W. 1929- *St&PR 91*
Krause, Chester Lee 1923- *WhoAm 90, WhoWor 91*
Krause, Daphne Hylda 1927- *WhoAmW 91*
Krause, David James 1953- *WhoAm 90, WhoEmL 91*
Krause, David John 1941- *St&PR 91*
Krause, Donald L. 1939- *St&PR 91*
Krause, Ernst Henry 1913- *WhoAm 90*
Krause, Ernst Henry 1913-1989 *BioIn 16*
Krause, Eugene Franklin 1937- *WhoAm 90*
Krause, Friedhilde 1928- *WhoWor 91*
Krause, George 1937- *WhoAm 90, WhoAmA 91*
Krause, H. Werner 1934- *St&PR 91*
Krause, Harry 1887-1940 *Ballpl 90*
Krause, Harry Dieter 1932- *WhoAm 90*
Krause, Heather Dawn 1956- *WhoAmW 91*
Krause, Heinz Werner 1934- *WhoAm 90*
Krause, Jerry 1939- *WhoAm 90*
Krause, Joan Merry 1935- *WhoAmW 91*
Krause, John F. 1945- *St&PR 91*
Krause, John L. 1917- *WhoWor 91*
Krause, John Robert *NewAgMG*
Krause, Jurgen 1944- *WhoWor 91*
Krause, Karl Christian Friedrich 1781-1832 *BioIn 16*
Krause, Kenneth David 1949- *BiDrAPA 89*
Krause, Kenneth Keith 1956- *WhoEmL 91*
Krause, L. William 1942- *WhoAm 90*
Krause, Laverne Erickson 1924- *WhoAmA 91*
Krause, Lawrence Allen 1939- *WhoAm 90*
Krause, Manfred Otto 1931- *WhoAm 90*
Krause, Mary Alice 1950- *WhoSSW 91*
Krause, Michael S. 1940- *St&PR 91*
Krause, Nina 1932- *WhoWrEP 89*
Krause, Norman L. 1917- *St&PR 91*
Krause, Paul Edward 1956- *WhoE 91*
Krause, Philip C. 1920- *St&PR 91*
Krause, Raymond R. 1951- *St&PR 91*
Krause, Richard Arthur 1939- *St&PR 91*
Krause, Richard D. 1930- *St&PR 91*
Krause, Richard J. 1932- *St&PR 91*
Krause, Richard James 1942- *WhoE 91*
Krause, Richard Michael 1925- *WhoAm 90*
Krause, Richard William 1936- *WhoE 91*
Krause, Robert Frederick 1926- *St&PR 91*
Krause, Robert M. 1950- *St&PR 91*
Krause, Robert Stanley 1942- *WhoAm 90*
Krause, Ronald J. 1927- *WhoSSW 91*
Krause, Sonja 1933- *WhoAm 90*
Krause, Stephen M 1938- *BiDrAPA 89*
Krause, Steven Michael 1953- *WhoEmL 91*
Krause, Susan D. 1953- *St&PR 91*
Krause, Theodore Joseph 1935- *St&PR 91*
Krause, Tom 1934- *IntWWM 90, PenDiMP*
Krause, Walter 1919- *WhoAm 90*
Krause, Werner William 1937- *St&PR 91*
Krause, William Austin 1930- *St&PR 91, WhoAm 90*
Krause-Bodoky, Annamaria 1941- *IntWWM 90*
Krausen, Anthony Sharnik 1944- *WhoWor 91*
Kraushaar, Antoinette M *WhoAmA 91*
Kraushaar, John Florence 1932- *WhoAm 90*
Kraushaar, Otto F. 1901-1989 *BioIn 16*
Kraushaar, Philip F. 1923- *St&PR 91*
Kraushaar, William Lester 1920- *WhoAm 90*
Krauskopf, Konrad Bates 1910- *WhoAm 90*
Krauskopf, Kurt Jeffrey 1954- *St&PR 91*
Krauss, Alan Robert 1943- *WhoAm 90, WhoWor 91*
Krauss, Beatrice J. 1943- *WhoAmW 91*
Krauss, Charles A., Jr. 1931- *St&PR 91*
Krauss, Clemens 1893-1954 *PenDiMP*
Krauss, Clifford Hans 1954- *St&PR 91*
Krauss, David Arthur 1947- *WhoEmL 91*
Krauss, Fern 1944- *ODwPR 91*
Krauss, Gary Lee 1945- *WhoEmL 91*
Krauss, George 1933- *WhoAm 90*
Krauss, Henry Frederick, Jr. 1952- *WhoWor 91*
Krauss, Herbert Harris 1940- *WhoAm 90*
Krauss, Herbert N. 1932- *St&PR 91*
Krauss, Jack 1920- *BiDrAPA 89*
Krauss, Jamie Gail 1952- *WhoAmW 91*
Krauss, Janet 1935- *WhoWrEP 89*
Krauss, Jeffrey David 1946- *WhoAm 90*
Krauss, Jeffrey M. 1953- *St&PR 91*
Krauss, John B. 1935- *St&PR 91*
Krauss, John Edward 1949- *WhoEmL 91*
Krauss, Judith Belliveau 1947- *WhoAm 90*
Krauss, Marlene 1945- *WhoAm 90, WhoAmW 91*
Krauss, Michael Edward 1934- *WhoAm 90*
Krauss, Michael Ian 1951- *WhoE 91*
Krauss, Michael J. 1943- *St&PR 91*
Krauss, Nathan Harry 1908- *St&PR 91*
Krauss, Ray Herbert 1949- *WhoE 91*
Krauss, Robert Aron 1946- *St&PR 91*
Krauss, Robert Wallfar 1921- *WhoAm 90*
Krauss, Rosalind E 1940- *WhoAmA 91*
Krauss, Ruth 1911- *AuBYP 90*
Krauss, Steven James 1942- *WhoE 91, WhoWor 91*
Krauss, Sue Elizabeth 1951- *WhoAmW 91*
Krauss, Willy 1938- *BiDrAPA 89*
Krausse, Lew 1943- *Ballpl 90*
Krausz, Laszlo 1903-1979 *WhoAmA 91N*
Krausz, Michael 1942- *WhoAm 90*
Krausz, Susan *IntWWM 90*
Kraut, Arthur Paul *BiDrAPA 89*
Kraut, Beverly Ruth 1952- *WhoAmW 91*
Kraut, Evelyn Schlossman 1921- *WhoAmW 91*
Kraut, Gary A. 1944- *ODwPR 91*
Kraut, Gerald Anthony 1951- *WhoAm 90*
Kraut, Joanne Lenora 1949- *WhoAmW 91*
Kraut, Joel Arthur 1937- *WhoE 91, WhoWor 91*
Kraut, Richard 1944- *ConAu 130*
Krautblatt, Charles John 1950- *WhoWor 91*
Krauter, Thomas Francis 1927- *St&PR 91*
Krauth, Harald 1923- *WhoAmA 91*
Krauth, Norman Lee 1929- *St&PR 91*
Krauthammer, Charles 1950- *WhoAm 90*
Krautman, Harvey *St&PR 91*
Krautman, Jeff *St&PR 91*
Krautter, Elisa *AuBYP 90*
Krautter, Elisa 1912?-1990 *ConAu 131*
Krautter, Elisa Bialk *NewYTBS 90*
Krautter, Elisa Bialk 1912-1990 *BioIn 16*
Krautz, Erich August Paul 1906- *WhoWor 91*
Krauze, Zygmunt 1938- *IntWWM 90*
Kravchuk, Robert Sacha 1955- *WhoEmL 91*
Kravec, Barbara Baldwin 1940- *St&PR 91*
Kravec, Ken 1951- *Ballpl 90*
Kraver, Deborah 1949- *WhoEmL 91*
Kravet, Donald Jay 1957- *WhoEmL 91*
Kravets, Robert W *BiDrAPA 89*
Kravets, Torichan Pavlovich 1876-1955 *DcScB S2*

Kravetz, Beth 1949- *WhoAmW 91*
Kravetz, Carolyn F. 1966- *WhoAmW 91*
Kravetz, Ellen Michele 1960- *WhoEmL 91*
Kravetz, Russell S 1930- *BiDrAPA 89*
Kravinsky, Hilary Beth *BiDrAPA 89*
Kravis, Hedi *BioIn 16*
Kravis, Henry R. *BioIn 16, WhoAm 90*
Kravis, Henry R. 1944?- *ConAmBL*
Kravis, Irving Bernard 1916- *WhoAm 90, WhoE 91*
Kravis, Janis 1935- *WhoAmA 91*
Kravis, Nathan M. 1957- *BiDrAPA 89*
Kravis, Nathan Mark 1957- *WhoE 91*
Kravitch, Phyllis A. 1920- *WhoAm 90, WhoAmW 91*
Kravitt, Gregory Ian 1950- *St&PR 91*
Kravitz, Arthur Richard 1928- *BiDrAPA 89*
Kravitz, Bernard L. 1933- *St&PR 91*
Kravitz, Daniel Bruce *BiDrAPA 89*
Kravitz, Danny 1930- *Ballpl 90*
Kravitz, Ellen King 1929- *IntWWM 90, WhoAm 90*
Kravitz, Henry 1918- *BiDrAPA 89*
Kravitz, Howard Michael 1950- *BiDrAPA 89*
Kravitz, Jeffery Howard 1948- *WhoEmL 91*
Kravitz, Kerry D 1952- *BiDrAPA 89*
Kravitz, Lawrence Bruce *BiDrAPA 89*
Kravitz, Lawrence Charles 1932- *WhoAm 90*
Kravitz, Lenny *BioIn 16*
Kravitz, Lenny 1964?- *ConMus 5 [port], News 91-1 [port]*
Kravitz, Linda Delanne 1947- *WhoAmW 91*
Kravitz, Morris A. *BioIn 16*
Kravitz, Richard 1949- *St&PR 91*
Kravitz, Richard Elliot *BiDrAPA 89*
Kravitz, Rubin 1928- *WhoAm 90, WhoWor 91*
Kravitz, Walter 1938- *WhoAmA 91*
Kravjansky, Mikulas 1928- *WhoAmA 91*
Kravs, Thomas Peter 1945- *WhoE 91*
Kraw, George Martin 1949- *WhoEmL 91, WhoWor 91*
Kraw, Sarah Kenyon 1949- *WhoEmL 91*
Krawciw, Natalia 1955- *WhoE 91, WhoEmL 91*
Krawczyk, Frank *BioIn 16*
Krawczyk, John Gary *BiDrAPA 89*
Krawczynski, Johanna Wilhelmina 1937- *WhoWor 91*
Krawitz, Arnold S. 1937- *St&PR 91*
Krawitz, Herman Everett 1925- *WhoAm 90*
Kray, Elizabeth 1916-1987 *BioIn 16*
Kraybill, Harold Erb 1939- *BiDrAPA 89*
Kraybill, Paul Nissley 1925- *WhoAm 90*
Kraynak, Michael, Jr. 1930- *St&PR 91*
Kreader, Barbara Barlow 1946- *WhoWrEP 89*
Kreager, Eileen Davis 1924- *WhoAmW 91, WhoWor 91*
Kreager, H. Dewayne 1912- *St&PR 91*
Kreager, Henry Dewayne 1912- *WhoAm 90*
Kreamer, Barbara Osborn *WhoAmW 91*
Kreamer, John Harrison 1922- *WhoAm 90*
Kreamer, Karen Sue 1956- *WhoEmL 91*
Krebbers, Herman 1923- *IntWWM 90*
Krebs, Annette *BioIn 16*
Krebs, Arno William, Jr. 1942- *WhoAm 90*
Krebs, Bernt 1938- *WhoWor 91*
Krebs, Christopher Paul 1954- *WhoE 91*
Krebs, David Alan 1958- *WhoEmL 91*
Krebs, Edwin Gerhard 1918- *WhoAm 90*
Krebs, Gary Lynn 1943- *WhoSSW 91*
Krebs, George Henry, Jr. 1954- *BiDrAPA 89*
Krebs, Hans 1900-1981 *ConAu 129*
Krebs, Hans A. 1900-1981 *WorAlBi*
Krebs, Hans Adolf 1900-1981 *DcNaB 1981, DcScB S2*
Krebs, Helmut 1913- *IntWWM 90*
Krebs, James Arthur, Jr. 1948- *WhoE 91*
Krebs, John H. 1926- *WhoAm 90*
Krebs, Joseph Jackson, Jr. 1930- *St&PR 91*
Krebs, Julia Elizabeth 1943- *WhoAmW 91*
Krebs, Margaret Eloise 1927- *WhoAmW 91, WhoE 91*
Krebs, Max Vance 1916- *WhoAm 90*
Krebs, Robert Allen 1950- *St&PR 91*
Krebs, Robert D. 1942- *St&PR 91*
Krebs, Robert Duncan 1942- *WhoAm 90*
Krebs, Robert Preston 1948- *WhoEmL 91*
Krebs, Rockne 1938- *WhoAmA 91*
Krebs, Roger Donavon 1949- *WhoEmL 91*
Krebs, Ronald Edward 1938- *St&PR 91*
Krebs, William A. Wallace, Jr. 1916- *WhoE 91*
Krebsbach, Karen K. *WhoAmW 91*
Krechel, Ursula 1947- *EncCoWW*
Krecke, Charles Francis 1926- *WhoAm 90*
Krecko, Valentins *BiDrAPA 89*
Kredenser, Gail 1936- *AuBYP 90*
Kredi, Olga Amary 1960- *WhoAmW 91, WhoHisp 91*
Kreeft, Peter 1937- *ConAu 31NR*
Kreeger, David Lloyd *NewYTBS 90 [port]*
Kreeger, David Lloyd 1909- *St&PR 91, WhoAm 90*
Kreeger, Jean Ann 1950- *WhoAmW 91*
Kreek, Robert *BioIn 16*
Kreer, Irene Overman 1926- *WhoAmW 91, WhoWor 91*
Kreer, John Belshaw 1927- *WhoAm 90*
Kreevich, Mike 1908- *Ballpl 90*
Kreevoy, Maurice Mordecai 1928- *WhoAm 90*
Krefetz, David Gary 1958- *BiDrAPA 89*
Kreft, Donald Frank 1941- *WhoSSW 91*
Krefting, Carol Lee 1948- *WhoAmW 91*
Krefting, Mark Bruce 1954- *WhoEmL 91*
Krefting, Paul Anthony 1946- *St&PR 91*
Krefting, Robert John 1944- *WhoAm 90, WhoE 91*
Kregel, Jan Allen 1944- *WhoWor 91*
Kregel, Robert Louis 1919- *WhoAm 90*
Kreger, Brian Frederick 1947- *WhoEmL 91*
Kreger, Elwyn L. 1924- *St&PR 91*
Kreger, Melvin Joseph 1937- *WhoWor 91*
Kreger, Ronald Eugene 1952- *St&PR 91*
Kreger, Spencer 1945- *BiDrAPA 89*
Kreh, Kent Q. 1935- *St&PR 91*
Krehbiel, Clarice Weekley 1929- *St&PR 91*
Krehbiel, Floyd Harold 1923- *St&PR 91*
Krehbiel, Frederick August 1941- *WhoAm 90*
Krehbiel, Peter W. 1929- *St&PR 91*
Krehbiel, Robert C. 1921- *St&PR 91*
Krehbiel, Susannah *BiDrAPA 89*
Krehbiel, William R. 1932- *St&PR 91*
Krehel, Roberta Mae 1927- *WhoAmW 91*
Kreick, John R. 1944- *St&PR 91*
Kreider, Carl 1914- *WhoAm 90*
Kreider, Carole Compton 1939- *WhoAmW 91*
Kreider, Cynthia Louise 1963- *WhoAmW 91*
Kreider, Leonard Emil 1938- *WhoWor 91*
Kreider, Stanley J *BiDrAPA 89*
Kreider, Thomas Edmund 1957- *BiDrAPA 89*
Kreider, Thomas McRoberts 1922- *WhoAm 90*
Kreideweis, John Laurence 1942- *WhoSSW 91*
Kreidler, Robert Neil 1929- *WhoAm 90*
Kreifeldt, Howard A. 1916- *St&PR 91*
Kreig, James J. 1950- *St&PR 91*
Kreig, Raymond R. 1922- *St&PR 91*
Kreiger, Kathy Renee 1959- *WhoEmL 91*
Kreighbaum, John Scott 1946- *WhoAm 90*
Kreil, Curtis Lee 1955- *WhoEmL 91*
Kreil, Walter Nelson, Jr. 1947- *St&PR 91*
Kreilein, Robert Lee 1943- *St&PR 91*
Kreilick, Marjorie E 1925- *WhoAmA 91*
Kreilick, Robert W. 1938- *WhoAm 90*
Kreiman, Naum 1919- *EncPaPR 91*
Kreiman, Robert Theodore 1924- *St&PR 91*
Kreimer, Herbert Frederick 1936- *WhoSSW 91*
Krein, A. Z. 1920- *WhoWor 91*
Krein, William A. 1940- *WhoE 91*
Kreinbrook, Suzanne Boyer 1939- *BiDrAPA 89*
Kreindel, Mark Stephen 1952- *WhoEmL 91*
Kreindler, Doris Barsky 1901-1974 *WhoAmA 91N*
Kreindler, Simon 1940- *BiDrAPA 89*
Kreiniker, Thomas J. 1952- *St&PR 91*
Kreinin, Mordechai Eliahu 1930- *WhoAm 90*
Kreipe, Werner 1904- *BioIn 16*
Kreipke, Sven Axel 1926- *WhoAm 90*
Kreis, Gene S. 1939- *St&PR 91*
Kreis, Ingrid Bernice 1960- *WhoSSW 91*
Kreis, Robert R. 1926- *St&PR 91*
Kreis, Ronald W. 1942- *St&PR 91*
Kreis, Ursula Gerda 1928- *WhoE 91*
Kreisberg, Neil Ivan 1945- *St&PR 91, WhoAm 90*
Kreisel, Henry 1922- *WhoAm 90*
Kreiser, Cheryl Ann 1966- *WhoE 91*
Kreisky, Bruno 1911- *WorAlBi*
Kreisky, Bruno 1911-1990 *CurBio 90N, NewYTBS 90 [port]*
Kreisl, Gary M. 1954- *St&PR 91*
Kreisle, James Edwin, Jr. 1949- *BiDrAPA 89*
Kreisler, Barry Benjamin 1945- *WhoEmL 91*
Kreisler, Fritz 1875-1962 *OxCPMus, PenDiMP, WorAlBi*
Kreisler, Kathi *St&PR 91*
Kreisler, Larry *St&PR 91*
Kreisman, Arthur 1918- *WhoAm 90*
Kreisman, Herbert 1912- *St&PR 91*
Kreisman, Jane Schexnayder 1948- *WhoAmW 91*
Kreisman, Jerold Jay 1947- *BiDrAPA 89*
Kreiss, Kathleen 1947- *WhoAm 90*
Kreissl, J. Scott 1946- *St&PR 91*
Kreiter, Harry 1917- *St&PR 91*
Kreiter, Herbert M. 1928- *St&PR 91*
Kreitler, Thomas S. 1957- *St&PR 91*
Kreitman, Benjamin Zvi 1920- *BioIn 16, WhoAm 90, WhoE 91*
Kreitman, Lenore Roberts 1947- *WhoE 91, WhoEmL 91*
Kreitzberg, Fred Charles 1934- *WhoAm 90, WhoWor 91*
Kreitzberg, Richard Anthony 1934- *St&PR 91*
Kreitzer, David Martin 1942- *WhoAmA 91*
Kreitzer, Gary A. 1955- *St&PR 91*
Kreitzer, J. Karl 1942- *St&PR 91*
Kreitzer, Jack 1949- *WhoWrEP 89*
Kreitzer, Lois Helen 1933- *WhoAmW 91*
Kreitzman, Ralph J. 1945- *WhoEmL 91*
Kreizel, William J. 1921- *St&PR 91*
Krejci, Jaroslav 1916- *ConAu 31NR*
Krejcsi, Cynthia Ann 1948- *WhoAmW 91*
Krek, Uros 1922- *IntWWM 90*
Kreker, Jeannine H. 1940- *WhoAmW 91*
Krelina, Michael 1953- *BiDrAPA 89*
Krelitz, Philip James 1911- *St&PR 91*
Krell, Helen Aicher 1944- *BiDrAPA 89*
Krell, Keith Vincent 1948- *WhoEmL 91*
Krell, Robert 1940- *BiDrAPA 89*
Krell, Ted William 1943- *BiDrAPA 89*
Krell, William H. *OxCPMus*
Krelle, Wilhelm Ernst 1916- *WhoWor 91*
Kreloff, Michael Allen 1946- *WhoEmL 91*
Kremberg, Marvin Roy 1951- *BiDrAPA 89, WhoE 91*
Krembs, F Greg 1943- *BiDrAPA 89*
Kremen, Howard M 1934- *BiDrAPA 89*
Kremen, Mark E 1948- *BiDrAPA 89*
Kremenick, Kenneth John 1939- *WhoE 91*
Kremenitzer, Janet Pickard 1949- *WhoAmW 91*
Kremenliev, Boris 1911- *IntWWM 90*
Kremenliev, Boris 1911-1988 *BioIn 16*
Kremens, Jack B *BiDrAPA 89*
Krementz, Edward Thomas 1917- *WhoAm 90*
Krementz, Jill 1940- *AuBYP 90, WhoAm 90, WhoAmW 91, WhoWrEP 89*
Kremer, Dirk Jozef Louis 1959- *WhoWor 91*
Kremer, Erhard Karl 1953- *WhoWor 91*
Kremer, Eugene R. 1938- *WhoAm 90*
Kremer, Fred, Jr. 1926- *WhoAm 90*
Kremer, Gidon 1947- *BioIn 16, IntWWM 90, PenDiMP, WhoWor 91*
Kremer, Honor Frances 1939- *WhoAmW 91*
Kremer, John Frederick 1949- *WhoEmL 91, WhoWrEP 89*
Kremer, Jonny Simon 1942- *WhoWor 91*
Kremer, Laura Evelyn 1921- *WhoE 91*
Kremer, Mervin Carl 1930- *St&PR 91*
Kremer, Ray 1893-1965 *Ballpl 90*
Kremers, Al Henry 1934- *St&PR 91*
Kreml, Franklin Martin 1907- *WhoAm 90*
Kremp, Herbert 1928- *WhoWor 91*
Krempa, Frank Stanley 1935- *St&PR 91*
Krempel, Ralf 1935- *WhoAmA 91*
Krempl, Erhard 1934- *WhoAm 90*
Krems, Susan Alexander 1940- *WhoAmW 91*
Kremsdorf, Julian 1920- *St&PR 91*
Kren, Margo 1939- *WhoAmA 91*
Kren, Thomas John 1950- *WhoAm 90*
Krenchicki, Wayne 1954- *Ballpl 90*
Krendel, Ezra Simon 1925- *WhoAm 90*
Kreneck, Lynwood 1936- *WhoAmA 91*
Krenek, Ernst 1900- *BioIn 16, IntWWM 90, PenDiMP A, WhoAm 90*
Krenek, Wilfred M. 1953- *St&PR 91*
Krener, Penelope K 1943- *BiDrAPA 89*
Krenitsky, Michael V. 1915- *WhoAm 90*
Krenitsyn, Pyotr Kuzmich *EncCRAm*
Krenke, Kristine Renee 1948- *WhoAmW 91*
Krenkel, Peter Ashton 1930- *WhoAm 90*
Krenmayr, Peter 1932- *WhoWor 91*
Krenn, Martha Nelle *BiDrAPA 89*
Krenn, Werner 1942- *PenDiMP*
Krens, Thomas *BioIn 16, WhoAmA 91*
Krens, Thomas 1946- *WhoAm 90, WhoE 91*
Krensky, Harold 1912- *WhoAm 90*
Krensky, Stephen 1953- *BioIn 16*
Krent, Justin *BiDrAPA 89*
Krents, Milton Ellis 1911- *WhoAm 90*
Krentz, Eugene Leo 1932- *WhoAm 90*
Krentz, Richard D. 1942- *St&PR 91*
Krentzel, Elise 1957- *WhoE 91, WhoEmL 91*
Krentzin, Earl 1929- *WhoAmA 91*
Krenz, Dean A. 1930- *St&PR 91*
Krenz, Dean Albert 1930- *WhoAm 90*
Krenz, Egon *BioIn 16*
Krenz, Egon 1937- *CurBio 90 [port], WhoWor 91*
Krenz, Jan 1926- *IntWWM 90, PenDiMP, WhoWor 91*
Krenzel, Archibald R *BiDrAPA 89*
Krenzer, Gail Claire 1944- *WhoAmW 91*
Krenzler, Alvin Irving 1921- *WhoAm 90*
Krepinevich, Kevin W. 1954- *WhoAm 90*
Kreppel, Walter 1923- *IntWWM 90*
Kreps, Charles W. 1924- *St&PR 91*
Kreps, David Marc 1950- *WhoAm 90*
Kreps, Juanita M 1921- *ConAu 130*
Kreps, Juanita Morris 1921- *BiDrUSE 89, WhoAm 90, WhoAmW 91*
Kreps, Robert Wilson 1946- *WhoAm 90, WhoE 91*
Kreps, S Alexanndra *BiDrAPA 89*
Kresa, Kent 1938- *St&PR 91, WhoAm 90*
Kresch, Richard Allen 1945- *BiDrAPA 89*
Kresel, Mary Ann *BioIn 16*
Kresge, Alexander Jerry 1926- *WhoAm 90*
Kresge, Bruce Anderson 1931- *WhoAm 90*
Kresge, Clyde L 1929- *BiDrAPA 89*
Kresh, Norman N *BiDrAPA 89*
Kresh, Paul 1919- *SmATA 61 [port], WhoAm 90*
Kresh, Yasha Yasha 1948- *WhoAm 90*
Kreshwansingh, Raveen 1950- *WhoWor 91*
Kreski, Edward J. 1912- *St&PR 91*
Kreskin 1935- *EncO&P 3, EncPaPR 91, WhoWor 91*
Kresko, Daniel Andrew 1929- *St&PR 91*
Kresky, Michael 1954- *St&PR 91*
Kresl, Miles L., Jr. 1939- *St&PR 91*
Kress, Agnes Irene 1947- *WhoWrEP 89*
Kress, Edward C. 1944- *St&PR 91*
Kress, Edward Marshall 1949- *St&PR 91*
Kress, George 1903- *St&PR 91*
Kress, George F. 1903- *WhoAm 90*
Kress, Mary Elizabeth 1951- *WhoSSW 91*
Kress, Paul Frederick 1935- *WhoAm 90*
Kress, Ralph Herman 1904- *WhoAm 90*
Kress, Red 1907-1962 *Ballpl 90*
Kress, Robert Frederick 1941- *St&PR 91*
Kress, Roy Alfred 1916- *WhoAm 90*
Kress, Samuel H. 1863-1955 *WorAlBi*
Kress, Thomas George 1931- *WhoAm 90*
Kresse, William Joseph 1958- *WhoEmL 91*
Kressel, Henry 1934- *WhoAm 90*
Kressin, Lori Lee 1959- *WhoAmW 91*
Kressler, Amelia Julia Braun 1944- *WhoAmW 91*
Kressler, James Phillip 1931- *WhoAm 90*
Krestal, Goncer Morton 1931- *WhoAm 90*
Krestensen, Ann M 1939- *WhoAmA 91*
Kreston, Martin Howard 1931- *WhoAm 90*
Krestovsky, V. *EncCoWW*
Kretchmer, Norman 1923- *WhoAm 90*
Kreter, Charles R. 1956- *ODwPR 91*
Kreth, Wolfgang 1946- *IntWWM 90*
Kretlow, Lou 1923- *Ballpl 90*
Kretsch, Hans Walter 1913- *WhoAm 90*
Kretschmar, Helmut 1928- *IntWWM 90*
Kretschmer, Diane Elise 1946- *WhoAmW 91*
Kretschmer, Frank F., Jr. 1930- *WhoAm 90*
Kretschmer, Hildegard T *BiDrAPA 89*
Kretschmer, Keith Hughes 1934- *WhoAm 90*
Kretschmer, Paul Robert 1929- *WhoE 91*
Kretsinger, Mary Amelia 1915- *WhoAmA 91*
Krettek, Otmar Klaus 1934- *WhoWor 91*
Kretzmann, John Albert 1951- *WhoEmL 91*
Kretzmann, Justus Paul 1913- *WhoAm 90*
Kretzmann, Walter John 1943- *St&PR 91*
Kretzschmar, Jan Georges Valentyn 1942- *WhoWor 91*
Kretzschmar, John R. 1933- *St&PR 91*
Kretzschmar, William Addison, Jr. 1953- *WhoSSW 91*
Kreuch, Paul C., Jr. 1938- *St&PR 91*
Kreuger, Ivar 1880-1932 *WorAlBi*
Kreuger, Ralph Walter 1942- *St&PR 91*
Kreuscher, Ronald H. 1935- *St&PR 91*
Kreuter, Charles R. 1950- *St&PR 91*
Kreuter, Gretchen V. 1934- *WhoAm 90, WhoAmW 91*
Kreuter, Jorg Wilhelm Rudolf 1948- *WhoWor 91*
Kreutler, Patricia Ann 1945- *WhoAmW 91*
Kreutz, Robert Edward 1922- *IntWWM 90*
Kreutzberg, Georg W. 1932- *WhoWor 91*
Kreutzberger, Mario *BioIn 16*
Kreutzer, Allan C. 1943- *St&PR 91*
Kreutzer, Frank 1939- *Ballpl 90*
Kreutzer, Franklin David 1940- *WhoAm 90, WhoSSW 91, WhoWor 91*
Kreutzer, Louis G. 1929- *St&PR 91*
Kreutzer, Louis G., Jr. 1929- *WhoAm 90*
Kreutzer, Rodolphe 1766-1831 *PenDiMP*
Kreutzer, Ronald Leon 1960- *WhoEmL 91*
Kreutzer, S. Stanley 1907- *WhoWor 91*
Kreutzig, LeRoy Tinker 1913- *WhoSSW 91*
Kreutzjans, Rudy 1951- *WhoSSW 91*
Kreutzkampf, June Elizabeth 1940- *WhoAmW 91*
Kreuz, Leo Edward 1937- *BiDrAPA 89*

Kreuzer, Helmut 1927- WhoWor 91
Kreuzer, Theodore Robert 1947- WhoAm 90
Krevans, Julius Richard 1924- WhoAm 90, WhoWor 91
Krevsky, Benjamin 1952- WhoE 91
Krey, Mary Ann Reynolds 1947- WhoAm 90
Krey, Robert Dean 1929- WhoAm 90
Kreyche, Gerald Francis 1927- WhoAm 90
Kreyche, Laurence Eugene 1951- BiDrAPA 89
Kreykes, Kathleen Kay 1952- WhoAmW 91, WhoEmL 91
Kreyling, Edward George, Jr. 1923- WhoAm 90
Krez, Paul Agustin 1950- WhoEmL 91
Krezdorn, Alfred H. 1920-1989 BioIn 16
Kreznar, Richard J 1940- WhoAmA 91
Krga, Joan S. 1943- ODwPR 91
Kriak, John Michael 1947- St&PR 91, WhoAm 90
Kribben, Christian 1821-1865 AmLegL
Kribbs, D. Lee 1941- St&PR 91
Kribel, Robert Edward 1937- WhoAm 90
Kribs, Louis P 1857-1898 DcCanB 12
Krichell, Paul 1882-1957 Ballpl 90
Kricher, John Charles 1944- WhoE 91
Krick, Frederick Marlowe 1960- WhoEmL 91
Krick, Irving Parkhurst 1906- WhoAm 90, WhoWor 91
Krick, John 1947- St&PR 91
Krick, Kenneth A. 1934- St&PR 91
Krick, Marilyn A. 1952- WhoAmW 91
Kridel, Craig 1951- WhoSSW 91
Kridel, James S. 1940- WhoAm 90
Krider, Harold H. 1940- St&PR 91
Kridler, J.W. 1927- St&PR 91
Kriebel, Charles H. 1933- St&PR 91
Kriebel, Charles Hosey 1933- WhoAm 90
Kriebel, George W, Jr. BiDrAPA 89
Kriebel, Robert I. St&PR 91
Krieble, Robert H. 1916- WhoAm 90, WhoWor 91
Kriechman, Avron Mark BiDrAPA 89
Kriedman, Warren Steven 1948- BiDrAPA 89
Krieg, Adrian H. 1938- St&PR 91
Krieg, Arthur Frederick 1930- WhoAm 90
Krieg, Audrey 1942- St&PR 91
Krieg, Brian Franklin 1960- WhoEmL 91
Krieg, Dorothy Linden 1919- WhoAmW 91
Krieg, Harry J. 1924- St&PR 91
Krieg, Phyllis Cheek 1960- WhoAmW 91
Krieg, Rebecca Jane 1953- WhoAmW 91
Krieg, Robert R. 1939- St&PR 91
Kriegel, Beth Ann 1961- WhoAmW 91
Kriegel, Jay L. 1940- WhoAm 90
Kriegel, Leonard 1933- BioIn 16, WhoWrEP 89
Krieger, Abbott Joel 1939- WhoAm 90
Krieger, Benjamin William 1937- St&PR 91, WhoAm 90
Krieger, C.R. 1951- WhoEmL 91
Krieger, Carl 1928- St&PR 91
Krieger, Dolores EncPaPR 91
Krieger, Florence WhoAmA 91
Krieger, Geoffrey W. 1950- St&PR 91
Krieger, George BiDrAPA 89
Krieger, Harvey 1933- St&PR 91
Krieger, Irvin Mitchell 1923- WhoAm 90
Krieger, Jane Helen 1946- WhoAmW 91
Krieger, John Newton 1948- WhoEmL 91
Krieger, Leonard NewYTBS 90
Krieger, Leonard 1918-1990 ConAu 132
Krieger, Leonard P. 1936- St&PR 91
Krieger, Michael Thomas 1950- WhoEmL 91
Krieger, Murray 1923- BioIn 16, WhoAm 90, WhoWrEP 89
Krieger, Paul Edward 1942- WhoSSW 91, WhoWor 91
Krieger, Philip Sheridan 1947- St&PR 91
Krieger, Robert Edward 1925- WhoAm 90
Krieger, Robert Lee, Jr. 1946- WhoSSW 91, WhoWor 91
Krieger, Ruth M 1922- WhoAmA 91
Krieger, Stanley L. 1942- St&PR 91
Krieger, Stuart A. 1918- St&PR 91
Krieger, Suzanne Baruc 1924- WhoAmA 91
Krieger, Theodore Kent 1950- WhoWrEP 89
Kriegman, Janice Lee 1956- WhoEmL 91
Kriegsman, Martin I. 1942- St&PR 91
Kriegsman, William Edwin 1932- WhoE 91
Kriendler, Jeffrey F. 1946- ODwPR 91
Kriendler, Jeffrey Feller 1946- St&PR 91
Krienke, Carol Belle Manikowske 1917- WhoAmW 91, WhoWor 91
Krienke, Douglas Elliot 1947- WhoAmA 91
Krienke, Kendra-Jean Cliver WhoAmA 91
Kriensky 1917- WhoAmA 91
Kriensky, Morris E WhoAmA 91
Krieps, Martha J. 1963- WhoAmW 91
Krier, Cynthia Taylor 1950- WhoAmW 91, WhoSSW 91
Krier, James Edward 1939- WhoAm 90
Kries, Henry WhoAmA 91N
Kriesberg, Irving 1919- WhoAmA 91
Kriesberg, Simeon M. 1951- WhoE 91
Krietemeyer, George O. 1936- St&PR 91
Kriewall, Willet W. 1934- St&PR 91
Krigbaum, William Richard 1922- WhoAm 90
Kriger, Brian Elliott 1954- WhoEmL 91
Krigman, Steven Slava 1967- WhoEmL 91
Krigsman, Gary 1956- WhoEmL 91
Krigstein, Bernard 1919- WhoAmA 91, WhoE 91
Krigstein, Bernard 1919-1990 EncACom
Kriken, John Lund 1938- WhoAm 90
Krikorian, Thomas Michael 1951- WhoEmL 91
Krikos, George Alexander 1922- WhoAm 90, WhoWor 91
Krill, Arthur Melvin 1921- WhoAm 90
Krilov, Jill 1959- BiDrAPA 89
Krim, Arthur B. 1910- WhoAm 90
Krim, Mathilde 1926- BioIn 16
Krim, Seymour 1922- WhoAm 90, WhoWrEP 89
Krim, Seymour 1922-1989 BioIn 16, ConAu 129
Krimendahl, H. Frederick 1928- St&PR 91
Krimendahl, Herbert Frederick, II 1928- WhoAm 90
Krimerman, Eleanor E 1940- BiDrAPA 89
Krimigis, Stamatios Mike 1938- WhoAm 90
Krimm, Fred 1933- St&PR 91
Krimm, Samuel 1925- WhoAm 90
Krims, Les 1942- WhoAmA 91
Krims, Marvin B 1928- BiDrAPA 89
Krims, Marvin Bennett 1928- WhoE 91
Krims, Milton BioIn 16
Krimsky, L.C. 1940- St&PR 91
Krimsky, Sheldon 1941- ConAu 33NR
Krin, Sylvie ConAu 129
Kriner, Sally Gladys Pearl 1911- WhoAmW 91
Kring, C.I. St&PR 91
Kring, Maurice W. 1936- St&PR 91
Kring, Maurice William 1936- WhoAm 90
Kring, Walter Donald 1916- WhoAm 90
Kringel, John G. 1939- St&PR 91, WhoAm 90
Krings, David BioIn 16
Krings, Hermann 1913- WhoWor 91
Krinsky, Albert 1925- BiDrAPA 89
Krinsky, Carol Herselle 1937- WhoAm 90, WhoAmA 91, WhoAmW 91, WhoE 91
Krinsky, Charles M 1908- BiDrAPA 89
Krinsky, Mary McInerney 1946- WhoE 91
Krinsky, Norman Irving 1928- WhoAm 90
Krinsky, Paul Lewis 1928- WhoAm 90
Krinsky, Robert D. 1937- St&PR 91
Krinsky, Robert Daniel 1937- WhoAm 90
Krinsley, David Henry 1927- WhoAm 90
Krinsly, Stuart Z. 1917- St&PR 91, WhoAm 90
Krintzman, B. J. 1946- WhoAmW 91
Krinzman, Richard Neil 1947- WhoEmL 91
Kripke, Daniel F 1941- BiDrAPA 89
Kripke, Donald Louis 1941- BiDrAPA 89
Kripke, Kenneth Norman 1920- WhoAm 90
Kripke, Saul A 1940- ConAu 130
Krippendorff, Ekkehart Richard Arthur 1934- WhoWor 91
Krippner, Stanley 1932- ConAu 32NR, EncPaPR 91
Krippner, Stanley Curtis 1932- EncO&P 3, WhoAm 90
Krips, Henry 1912-1987 PenDiMP
Krips, Josef 1902-1974 PenDiMP
Kris, Anton Oscar 1934- BiDrAPA 89
Kris, Kathryn Beck 1933- BiDrAPA 89
Krisano, Maria Susana WhoHisp 91
Krisch, Adolph O. 1916- St&PR 91
Krisch, Adolph Oscar 1916-1990 BioIn 16
Krisch, Alan David 1939- WhoAm 90
Krisch, Jean Peck 1939- WhoAmW 91
Krisch, Joel 1924- St&PR 91, WhoAm 90, WhoSSW 91
Krisch, Ronald Avery 1952- BiDrAPA 89
Krischer, Barry BioIn 16
Krisciokaitis, Raymond John 1937- WhoAm 90
Krise, Patricia Love 1959- WhoAmW 91, WhoEmL 91, WhoWor 91
Kriser, Anka Angelowa 1931- WhoE 91
Krishen, Kumar 1939- WhoAm 90, WhoSSW 91, WhoWor 91
Krisher, Bernard 1931- WhoAm 90
Krisher, Patterson Howard 1933- WhoAm 90
Krisher, William K. 1931- WhoAm 90
Krishna Venta EncO&P 3
Krishna, Gollapudi Gopal 1952- WhoEmL 91
Krishna, R Murali 1949- BiDrAPA 89
Krishna, R Vasantha 1937- BiDrAPA 89
Krishnakumar, Vasu BiDrAPA 89
Krishnamoorthy, C V 1943- BiDrAPA 89
Krishnamoorthy, Manjeri Subramanian 1946- WhoWor 91
Krishnamoorti, Singa R 1931- BiDrAPA 89
Krishnamurthy, Bhanumathy BiDrAPA 89
Krishnamurthy, Gerbail Thimmegowda 1937- WhoAm 90
Krishnamurti, Jiddu NewAgE 90
Krishnamurti, Jiddu 1895-1986 EncO&P 3
Krishnan, Devika R 1946- BiDrAPA 89
Krishnan, K Ranga Rama BiDrAPA 89
Krishnan, Palaniappa 1953- WhoE 91
Krishnan, Parukutty M 1951- BiDrAPA 89
Krishnappa, Kachigere S 1951- BiDrAPA 89
Krishnaraj, Muthaiya P BiDrAPA 89
Krishnaraj, Rajabather 1946- WhoEmL 91
Krishnaswami, Sriringam Kuppuswami 1933- WhoE 91
Krishnaswamy, Subbanaicker 1954- WhoWor 91
Krishnaswamy, Sudha 1944- BiDrAPA 89
Krishnayya, Chandra Pasupulati 1932- WhoAm 90
Krislov, Samuel 1929- WhoAm 90
Kriss, Dorothy Jean 1947- WhoE 91
Krissel, Susan Hinkle 1947- WhoSSW 91
Krisst, Raymond John 1937- WhoAm 90
Krist, Betty Jane 1946- WhoE 91
Krist, Gary 1957- ConAu 132
Krist, Howie 1916- Ballpl 90
Kristal, Martin Charles 1953- WhoEmL 91
Kristek, Jiri 1942- WhoWor 91
Kristel, Ira B. 1927- St&PR 91
Kristel, Sylvia 1952- ConTFT 8
Kristeller, Paul Oskar WhoAm 90
Kristensen, Gail Marie 1924- WhoAmA 91
Kristensen, H Kromann 1903- EncO&P 3
Kristensen, Karl Johan Norvang 1946- WhoWor 91
Kristensen, Thorkil 1899-1989 ConAu 130
Kristensen, Tom 1893-1974 DcScanL
Kristeva, Julia 1941- FemiCLE, WorAu 1980 [port]
Kristiansen, Ingrid BioIn 16
Kristiansen, Magne 1932- WhoAm 90
Kristick, K. Randolph 1957- WhoEmL 91
Kristina, Queen of Sweden 1626-1689 BioIn 16
Kristinsson, Sigursveinn D. 1911- IntWWM 90
Kristmann Gudmundsson DcScanL
Kristmundsson, Adalsteinn DcScanL
Kristof, Ariane 1963- WhoWor 91
Kristof, Dennis Robert 1943- WhoSSW 91
Kristof, Ladis Kris Donabed 1918- WhoAm 90
Kristof, Nicholas D. 1959- WhoAm 90, WhoWor 91
Kristofco, Thomas John 1960- St&PR 91
Kristoff, Frank R. 1929- St&PR 91
Kristoff, James Christopher 1957- WhoE 91
Kristoffersen, Eva M. 1901- AuBYP 90
Kristofferson, Karl Eric 1929- WhoAm 90
Kristofferson, Kris WhoNeCM A [port]
Kristofferson, Kris 1936- ConMus 4 [port], EncPR&S 89, OxCPMus, WhoAm 90, WorAlBi
Kristol, Irving 1920- WhoAm 90
Kristol, William BioIn 16
Kriston, Michael E. 1940- St&PR 91
Kristopeit, Donald Julius 1926- St&PR 91
Kristwald-Kallefelz, Elfriede Hildegarde 1938- WhoWrEP 89
Kristy, James Eugene 1929- WhoWor 91
Krit, Robert Lee 1920- WhoWor 91
Kritchevsky, David 1920- WhoAm 90
Krites, Vance Richard 1942- WhoE 91
Kritsick, Stephen BioIn 16
Kritsick, Stephen Mark 1951- WhoAm 90, WhoEmL 91
Kritz, Morris 1913- St&PR 91
Kritzer, Donald L. 1934- St&PR 91
Kritzer, Margaret Rose 1959- WhoAmW 91
Kritzer, Paul Eric 1942- WhoAm 90
Kritzler, Zoe A BiDrAPA 89
Kritzman, Jeffrey D. 1954- St&PR 91
Krivacska, James Joseph 1957- WhoEmL 91
Krivetsky, Alexander 1914- WhoE 91
Krivine, Alain 1941- BiDFrPL
Krivisky, Stephen Jerold 1945- St&PR 91
Krivkovich, Peter BioIn 16
Krivkovich, Peter George 1946- WhoAm 90
Krivo, David Alan 1950- WhoEmL 91
Krivosha, Norman Marvin 1934- St&PR 91
Krivoy, Kathy Lynn 1956- WhoAmW 91
Krivsky, William A. 1929- St&PR 91
Kriyananda ConAu 132
Kriyananda, Sri ConAu 132
Kriyananda, Swami ConAu 132
Kriyananda, S ConAu 132
Kriz, Marjorie Minsk 1920- WhoAmW 91
Kriz, Vilem Francis 1921- WhoAm 90
Krizanc, John 1956- OxCCanT
Krizanosky, Mary Suzanna 1958- WhoAmW 91
Krizek, George Otakar 1932- BiDrAPA 89
Krizek, John L. 1933- ODwPR 91
Krizek, Randall E. 1951- St&PR 91
Krizek, Raymond John 1932- WhoAm 90
Krizek, Thomas Joseph 1932- WhoAm 90
Krmpotic, Vesna 1932- EncCoWW
Krnjevic, Kresimir Ivan 1927- WhoAm 90
Kroboth-Weber, Janet Marie 1956- WhoE 91
Kroc, Joan BioIn 16
Kroc, Ray BioIn 16
Kroc, Ray A. 1902-1984 WorAlBi
Kroch, Carl A. 1914- St&PR 91
Kroch, Carl Adolph 1914- WhoAm 90
Krochmal, Arnold 1919- WhoSSW 91
Krochmalny, Michael William 1949- WhoEmL 91
Krock, Arthur 1886?-1974 BioIn 16
Krock, Arthur 1887-1974 WorAlBi
Krodel, William Joseph 1928- St&PR 91
Krodman, Steven Barry 1952- WhoE 91
Kroeber, A L 1876-1960 ConAu 129
Kroeber, C. Kent 1939- St&PR 91, WhoAm 90
Kroeber, Clifton B 1921- ConAu 32NR
Kroeber, Clifton Brown 1921- WhoAm 90
Kroeber, Karl 1926- ConAu 32NR, WhoAm 90
Kroeber, Theodora 1897-1979 ConAu 32NR
Kroeger, Albert R. 1931- ODwPR 91
Kroeger, Arthur 1932- WhoAm 90
Kroeger, Arthur F. 1912- St&PR 91
Kroeger, Ingo Wilhelm 1936- St&PR 91
Kroeger, Karl 1932- IntWWM 90
Kroeger, Lin J. 1952- WhoEmL 91
Kroeger, Marie 1935- IntWWM 90
Kroeger, Ryta 1927- WhoE 91
Kroeger, Sandra P. 1941- ODwPR 91
Kroehl, Susan Ann 1945- WhoAmW 91
Kroehling, John H. 1923- St&PR 91
Kroekel, Juliette Ann 1947- WhoWrEP 89
Kroeker, Charlotte Y. 1948- IntWWM 90
Kroener, Peter H. 1942- St&PR 91
Kroenig, Wolfgang 1904- WhoWor 91
Kroening, Robert St&PR 91
Kroepelin, Hans Wolfram Dietrich 1901- WhoWor 91
Kroeplin, Karla Joan 1961- WhoAmW 91
Kroes, Gunter 1940- WhoWor 91
Kroese, Chris Coyle 1959- St&PR 91
Kroesen, Frederick James 1923- WhoAm 90
Kroesen, Jill Anne 1949- WhoWrEP 89
Kroessler, David E 1953- BiDrAPA 89
Kroetch, Patricia Ann Robinson 1935- WhoWor 91
Kroetsch, Peter Frank 1949- BiDrAPA 89
Kroetsch, Robert 1927- MajTwCW
Kroetsch, Robert Paul 1927- WhoAm 90
Kroetz, Franz ConAu 130
Kroetz, Franz Xaver 1946- ConAu 130
Kroez, Harold 1937- St&PR 91
Krofcheck, Joseph L 1932- BiDrAPA 89
Kroft, Steve BioIn 16
Krog, Arnold PenDiDA 89
Krog, Helge 1889-1962 DcScanL
Krog, Joel Thomas 1935- St&PR 91
Krogager, Eilif 1910- WhoWor 91
Kroger, Bernard H. 1860-1938 WorAlBi
Kroger, Dawn Virginia 1941- WhoSSW 91
Kroger, Ferdinand Anne 1915- WhoAm 90
Kroger, Fred 1945- WhoWor 91
Kroger, Joseph J. 1934- St&PR 91
Kroger, William Saul BiDrAPA 89
Kroger, William Saul 1906- WhoAm 90
Krogh, Grethe 1928- IntWWM 90
Krogh, Harry M. 1929- WhoAm 90
Krogh, Lester Christensen 1925- WhoAm 90
Krogh, Peter Frederic 1937- WhoAm 90
Krogh, Sarah Elizabeth 1956- WhoAmW 91
Krogius, Tristan Ernst Gunnar 1933- WhoAm 90
Krogman, Wilton M. 1903-1987 BioIn 16
Krogstad, Jack Lynn 1944- WhoAm 90
Krogstad, Robert Wellington 1919- WhoSSW 91
Krogulski, John Leo 1927- WhoE 91
Kroha, Bradford King 1926- WhoAm 90
Krohg, Oda 1860-1935 BiDWomA
Krohley, Thomas Michael 1944- WhoE 91
Krohn, Claus D. 1923- St&PR 91
Krohn, Claus Dankertsen 1923- WhoAm 90, WhoWor 91
Krohn, David D BiDrAPA 89
Krohn, Duane Ronald 1946- WhoAm 90
Krohn, Edward John 1942- WhoSSW 91
Krohn, Hans-Joachim 1943- St&PR 91
Krohn, John D. 1927- St&PR 91
Krohn, Kenneth Albert 1945- WhoEmL 91
Krohn, Kenneth Robert 1946- WhoE 91
Krohn, Pietro PenDiDA 89
Krohn, Robert Finley 1933- St&PR 91

Krohn, Sven I 1903- EncO&P 3
Krohn, William Eugene 1932- St&PR 91
Krojanker, David Niels 1958- BiDrAPA 89
Krojanker, Rolf 1922- BiDrAPA 89
Krok, Arlene BioIn 16
Krok, Loren BioIn 16
Krok, Sharon BioIn 16
Krok-Paszkowski, Jan 1925- ConAu 130
Krokenberger, Linda Rose 1954- WhoAmW 91, WhoEmL 91
Krokfors, Christer Filip Jakob 1941- WhoWor 91
Krol, Henryk Emanuel 1952- WhoWor 91
Krol, John 1910- WhoAm 90, WhoE 91, WhoWor 91
Krol, John Casimir 1949- WhoE 91
Krol, Joseph 1911- WhoSSW 91, WhoWor 91
Krol, Victor Joseph 1953- WhoEmL 91
Krolick, Edward John 1923- IntWWM 90
Krolikowski, Werner 1928- WhoWor 91
Kroll, Alexander BioIn 16
Kroll, Alexander S. 1937- WhoAm 90, WhoE 91
Kroll, Arnold Howard 1935- WhoAm 90
Kroll, Arthur Herbert 1939- WhoAm 90
Kroll, Barry Lewis 1934- WhoAm 90
Kroll, Beverley Jane 1929- WhoWor 91
Kroll, Boris 1913- ConDes 90
Kroll, Carolyn K. 1945- WhoAmW 91
Kroll, Charles Henry 1958- WhoSSW 91
Kroll, Elliott Mark 1953- WhoEmL 91
Kroll, Ernest 1914- WhoAm 90
Kroll, Gary 1941- Ballpl 90
Kroll, Jerome Lewis 1935- BiDrAPA 89
Kroll, Ken BioIn 16
Kroll, Leon 1884-1974 WhoAmA 91N
Kroll, Mark 1946- IntWWM 90
Kroll, Mark William 1952- St&PR 91
Kroll, Michael Joseph 1948- St&PR 91
Kroll, Milton Paul 1914- WhoE 91
Kroll, Norman Myles 1922- WhoAm 90
Kroll, Phillip D BiDrAPA 89
Kroll, Richard 1952- WhoE 91
Kroll, Robert James 1928- WhoAm 90
Kroll, Steven 1941- AuBYP 90
Kroll, Steven Alexander 1947- WhoWor 91
Kroll, Steven Lawrence 1941- WhoE 91
Kroll, Thomas Robert 1947- St&PR 91
Kroll, William 1901-1980 PenDiMP
Kroloff, George 1935- ODwPR 91
Kroloff, George Michael 1935- WhoAm 90
Krolopp, Rudolph William 1930- WhoAm 90
Krolopp, Wojciech Aleksander 1945- IntWWM 90
Krom, George Charles 1930- St&PR 91
Krom, Ruud Arne Finco 1941- WhoAm 90
Krombach, Juergen 1933- WhoWor 91
Krombein, Karl vonVorse 1912- WhoAm 90
Kromberg, William A. 1945- St&PR 91, WhoEmL 91
Krombholc, Jaroslav 1918-1983 PenDiMP
Kromenhoek, J.P. 1942- St&PR 91
Kromer, Mary Lou 1953- WhoEmL 91
Kromhout, Robert Andrew 1923- WhoAm 90
Kromka, James Thomas Michael 1954- WhoEmL 91, WhoWor 91
Kromm, David Valentine 1947- WhoEmL 91
Krompier, Andrew BiDrAPA 89
Kron, Frederick Andrew 1950- WhoEmL 91
Kron, Kenneth Avrom 1953- BiDrAPA 89
Kron, Kenneth M BiDrAPA 89
Kron, Lawrence F 1946- BiDrAPA 89
Kron, Reuben E 1930- BiDrAPA 89
Kron, Violet Selma BiDrAPA 89
Kronberg, Louis 1872-1965 WhoAmA 91N
Kronberger, Fritz Paul 1940- WhoSSW 91
Krone, Andrew Joseph 1952- WhoSSW 91
Krone, Debra Jean 1955- WhoAmW 91
Krone, Frank 1928- St&PR 91
Krone, Gerald Sidney 1933- WhoAm 90
Krone, Helmut 1925- WhoAm 90
Krone, Irene 1940- WhoE 91
Krone, Julie BioIn 16
Krone, Julie 1963- WhoAmW 91
Krone, Norman Bernard 1938- St&PR 91
Krone, Philip Sano 1948- St&PR 91
Krone, Roger A. 1956- WhoSSW 91
Kronegger, Maria Elisabeth 1932- WhoAm 90
Kronen, Larry B. 1955- WhoEmL 91
Kronen, Peter Heinrich 1921- WhoWor 91
Kronenberg, Inez V. 1937- WhoAmW 91
Kronenberg, Mindy H. 1954- WhoWrEP 89
Kronenberg, Mindy Hollis 1954- WhoEmL 91
Kronenberg, Nathan Walter 1924- BiDrAPA 89
Kronenberg, Norman 1936- St&PR 91
Kronenberg, Rose T BiDrAPA 89
Kronenberg, Susan L. 1948- WhoWrEP 89
Kronenberg, Warren D BiDrAPA 89
Kronenfeld, David Brian 1941- WhoAm 90
Kronengold, Eric A 1935- WhoAmA 91
Kronenwetter, Michael 1943- SmATA 62 [port]
Kroner, Lawrence R 1921- BiDrAPA 89
Kroner, Sally Ann BiDrAPA 89
Kronewitter, Joseph Ray 1949- St&PR 91
Kronfeld, Alan C. 1930- St&PR 91
Kronfeld, Fred N. 1929- St&PR 91
Kronfeld, Gary H. 1955- St&PR 91
Kronfeld, Lydia B 1929- BiDrAPA 89
Kronfol, Ziad BiDrAPA 89
Krongard, Alvin B. 1936- St&PR 91
Kronheim, Roberta S. WhoE 91
Kronholm, Louise Bailey 1934- WhoAmW 91
Kronick, David A. 1917- WhoAm 90
Kronick, Steven David BiDrAPA 89
Kronig, Michael Howard 1952- BiDrAPA 89
Kronik, John William 1931- WhoAm 90
Kronikar, P. EncCoWW
Kroninger, Luther H., Jr. 1930- St&PR 91
Kronman, Anthony Townsend 1945- WhoAm 90
Kronman, Carol Jane 1944- WhoE 91
Kronman, Joseph Henry 1931- WhoAm 90
Kronner, Joan Marie 1960- WhoAmW 91
Kronos Quartet PenDiMP
Kronos Quartet, The ConMus 5 [port]
Kronrad, Robert B. 1951- St&PR 91
Kronschnabel, George J. 1925- St&PR 91
Kronschnabel, Robert James 1935- St&PR 91
Kronsnoble, Jeffrey Michael 1939- WhoAmA 91
Kronstad-Judge, Elizabeth 1948- WhoAmW 91
Kronstadt, Arnold Mayo 1919- WhoAm 90
Kronstadt, Herbert S 1934- BiDrAPA 89
Kronstadt, Nat 1923- St&PR 91
Kronstat, Bradley David 1951- St&PR 91, WhoE 91
Kronstein, Werner J 1930- WhoAm 90
Kroo, Gyorgy 1926- IntWWM 90
Krook, Bertil Olof 1932- WhoWor 91
Kroon, Ciro de BioIn 16
Kroon, Edwin H 1930- BiDrAPA 89
Kroon, John C. 1939- St&PR 91
Kroop, Merle Sondra BiDrAPA 89
Kroop, Merle Sondra 1939- WhoE 91
Kroouze, Thomas Joseph 1942- WhoE 91
Kropack, John August 1930- WhoWor 91
Kropas, Claudia Victoria 1957- WhoAmW 91
Kropat, Loren Michael 1952- WhoE 91
Kropf, Joan R 1949- WhoAmA 91
Kropf, Richard Thomas 1909- St&PR 91
Kropiewnicki, Mark Edward 1952- WhoEmL 91
Kroplick, Lois Ellen BiDrAPA 89
Kropotkin, Peter Alekseevich 1842-1921 BioIn 16
Kropp, August Donald 1938- BiDrAPA 89
Kropp, Charles August 1937- St&PR 91
Kropp, David Arthur 1933- WhoAm 90
Kropp, David Edward 1941- St&PR 91
Kropp, William Allen 1928- WhoAm 90
Kropschot, Richard H. 1927- WhoAm 90
Kropsky, Michael Lee 1946- BiDrAPA 89
Krosche, Eric Rudolf 1957- WhoEmL 91
Krosnick, Aaron Burton 1937- IntWWM 90
Krosnick, Annette Susan 1948- WhoE 91
Krosnick, Joel PenDiMP
Krosnick, Joel 1941- IntWWM 90, WhoAm 90
Krosnick, Mary Lou Wesley 1934- IntWWM 90
Krosoczka, Joseph D. 1928- St&PR 91
Kross, Siegfried 1930- IntWWM 90
Krostich, Henry J. 1950- WhoE 91
Kroszner, Randall Scott 1962- WhoE 91
Kroth, Jeannie Mae 1944- WhoAmW 91
Krothapalli, Radha Krishna 1951- WhoSSW 91
Krotiuk, William John 1948- WhoE 91
Krotki, Karol Jozef 1922- WhoAm 90, WhoWor 91
Krotter, John R. 1910- St&PR 91
Krotter, Robert J. 1930- St&PR 91
Krouk, Marianne G. BiDrAPA 89
Kroulek, Jack James 1931- St&PR 91
Krouse, Ann Wolk 1945- WhoAmW 91, WhoWor 91
Krouse, Diane Murray 1954- WhoAmW 91
Krouse, Gwin M. 1952- WhoEmL 91
Krouse, Howard BiDrAPA 89
Krouskop, Janice Louise 1953- WhoAmW 91
Krout, Boyd M 1931- BiDrAPA 89
Krout, John Edward 1920- WhoAm 90
Krout, W. Vincent 1924- St&PR 91
Krovetz, L. Jerome 1929- WhoSSW 91
Krowe, Allen Julian 1932- WhoAm 90, WhoE 91
Krown, Susan Ellen 1946- WhoAmW 91
Krowzow, Alexander 1952- WhoE 91
Kroyer, Robert W. WhoAm 90
Kroyt, Boris PenDiMP
Krpan, Daniel R. 1938- St&PR 91
Krpan, Vladimir 1938- IntWWM 90
Krpata, Anne Marie 1933- WhoAmW 91, WhoEmL 91
KRS-ONE BioIn 16
Krsek, George 1920- St&PR 91
Krsul, John Aloysius, Jr. 1938- WhoAm 90
Krubeck, Richard 1945- St&PR 91
Kruchek, Joseph William 1954- WhoEmL 91
Kruchek, Thomas F 1922- BiDrAPA 89
Kruchkow, Diane 1947- WhoWrEP 89
Kruchten, Marcia Helen 1932- WhoWrEP 89
Kruck, Werner H. 1933- St&PR 91
Kruckeberg, Arthur Rice 1920- WhoAm 90
Krucks, William 1918- St&PR 91, WhoAm 90
Krueckeberg, Karin Emily 1942- BiDrAPA 89
Krueger, Alan Douglas 1937- WhoWor 91
Krueger, Alan Lee 1941- BiDrAPA 89
Krueger, Anne O. 1934- ConAu 32NR
Krueger, Betty Jane 1923- WhoAmW 91, WhoWor 91
Krueger, Betty L. 1929- St&PR 91
Krueger, Bill 1958- Ballpl 90
Krueger, Bonnie Lee 1950- WhoAm 90, WhoAmW 91, WhoEmL 91, WhoWor 91
Krueger, Caryl Waller 1929- WhoAmW 91, WhoWrEP 89
Krueger, Catherine Anne 1961- WhoAmW 91
Krueger, Charlie BioIn 16
Krueger, Cheryl Ann 1956- WhoEmL 91
Krueger, Darrell William 1943- WhoAm 90
Krueger, David W 1947- BiDrAPA 89
Krueger, David Wayne 1947- WhoWrEP 89
Krueger, Donald Marc 1952- WhoEmL 91
Krueger, Douglas Herbert 1944- St&PR 91
Krueger, Ernie 1890-1976 Ballpl 90
Krueger, Eugene Rex 1935- WhoAm 90
Krueger, Everett Heath 1950- WhoEmL 91
Krueger, Gretchen Marie Dewailly 1952- WhoSSW 91
Krueger, Harald S BiDrAPA 89
Krueger, Harvey M. 1929- St&PR 91
Krueger, Henrik S. 1938- ConAu 130
Krueger, James 1938- WhoAm 90, WhoWor 91
Krueger, James Wayne 1957- WhoEmL 91
Krueger, John Charles 1951- WhoEmL 91
Krueger, John E. 1942- St&PR 91
Krueger, John R. 1927- ConAu 33NR
Krueger, Katherine Kamp 1944- WhoAmW 91
Krueger, Kenneth John 1946- WhoAm 90, WhoWor 91
Krueger, Kurt Donn 1952- WhoEmL 91, WhoWor 91
Krueger, Lothar David 1919- WhoAmA 91
Krueger, Marty L. 1957- WhoEmL 91
Krueger, Maynard August, Jr. 1931- St&PR 91
Krueger, Maynard C. 1906- WhoAm 90
Krueger, Michael Paul 1950- WhoEmL 91
Krueger, Michelle Mary 1963- WhoAmW 91
Krueger, Nancy Asta 1947- WhoAmW 91
Krueger, Otto 1876-1961 Ballpl 90
Krueger, Pamela Ann Hicks 1952- WhoEmL 91
Krueger, Paul Eric 1948- WhoEmL 91
Krueger, Paul H. 1940- ODwPR 91
Krueger, Peter J. 1934- WhoAm 90
Krueger, Ralph Arthur 1952- WhoE 91
Krueger, Ralph Ray 1927- WhoAm 90
Krueger, Randy Ray 1955- WhoEmL 91
Krueger, Richard Bohn 1945- BiDrAPA 89
Krueger, Robert A. 1935- St&PR 91
Krueger, Robert Blair 1928- WhoAm 90
Krueger, Robert Charles 1935- WhoAm 90
Krueger, Robert James 1930- WhoAm 90
Krueger, Robert John 1948- WhoEmL 91
Krueger, Robert Kenneth 1941- WhoSSW 91
Krueger, Robert W. 1916- St&PR 91
Krueger, Robert William 1916- WhoAm 90
Krueger, Rolf 1937- WhoSSW 91
Krueger, Van NewAgMG
Krueger, Walter 1881-1967 BioIn 16, WorAlBi
Kruegler, Nancy Alice 1946- WhoAmW 91
Kruell, Marianne 1936- ConAu 132
Kruener, Harry Howard 1915- WhoAm 90
Kruesi, John, Jr. 1913- WhoSSW 91
Kruesi, Markus John Potter 1949- BiDrAPA 89
Kruesi, Paul R. 1928- St&PR 91
Kruess, James AuBYP 90
Kruesselberg, Hans-Guenter 1929- WhoWor 91
Kruft, Hanno-Walter 1938- WhoWor 91
Krug, Anthony Earle 1938- St&PR 91
Krug, David John 1949- St&PR 91
Krug, Harry Elno 1930- WhoAmA 91
Krug, Harry Everistus Peter, Jr. 1932- WhoWor 91
Krug, Hartman H. 1937- St&PR 91
Krug, John Carleton 1951- WhoSSW 91
Krug, Judith Fingeret 1940- WhoAmW 91
Krug, Julius Albert 1907-1970 BiDrUSE 89
Krug, Karen-Ann 1951- WhoAmW 91
Krug, Ludwig 1488?-1532 PenDiDA 89
Krug, Maurice F. 1929- St&PR 91
Krug, Othilda M 1913- BiDrAPA 89
Krug, Philip L. 1929- WhoAm 90
Krug, Rob Alan 1951- WhoEmL 91
Krug, Robert Edward 1925- WhoAm 90
Krugel, Marius Andre 1938- WhoWor 91
Kruger, Albert Aaron 1952- WhoEmL 91
Kruger, Allan Ira 1945- WhoSSW 91
Kruger, Art 1881-1949 Ballpl 90
Kruger, Arthur Martin 1932- WhoAm 90
Kruger, Arthur Newman 1916- WhoAm 90
Kruger, Barbara BioIn 16
Kruger, Barbara 1945- BiDWomA, WhoAmA 91
Kruger, Charles Herman, Jr. 1934- WhoAm 90
Kruger, Curtis Frank 1930- St&PR 91
Kruger, David Benson 1926- BiDrAPA 89
Kruger, David Wesley 1944- WhoE 91
Kruger, Dennis George 1946- WhoSSW 91
Kruger, Eric 1954- St&PR 91
Kruger, Fred Walter 1921- WhoAm 90
Kruger, Fredrick Christian 1912- WhoAm 90
Kruger, Friedrich Wilhelm 1894-1945 BioIn 16
Kruger, Gustav Otto, Jr. 1916- WhoAm 90
Kruger, Harris Norman 1938- St&PR 91
Kruger, Harry 1929- IntWWM 90
Kruger, Jerome 1927- WhoAm 90
Kruger, JoAnn 1930- WhoAmW 91
Kruger, Kenneth Charles 1930- WhoAm 90
Kruger, Lawrence 1929- WhoAm 90
Kruger, Melvin I. 1929- St&PR 91
Kruger, Mollee 1929- WhoWrEP 89
Kruger, Paul 1825-1904 BioIn 16, WorAlBi
Kruger, Reto 1953- WhoE 91
Kruger, Rudolf IntWWM 90
Kruger, Rudolf 1916- WhoAm 90
Kruger, Simcha Stanley 1937- WhoE 91
Kruger, Stephanus Johannes Paulus 1825-1904 BioIn 16
Kruger, Steven L. 1956- St&PR 91
Kruger, Tristram Coffin 1951- WhoE 91
Kruger, Weldon Dale 1931- WhoAm 90
Krugley, Richard Alan 1951- BiDrAPA 89
Krugliak, Samuel 1917- St&PR 91
Kruglik, Meyer 1914- BiDrAPA 89
Krugman, Craig Burton 1957- WhoEmL 91
Krugman, Jeff St&PR 91
Krugman, Paul R. BioIn 16
Krugman, Paul Robin 1953- WhoAm 90, WhoE 91
Krugman, Saul 1911- WhoAm 90
Krugman, Stanley L. 1925- St&PR 91
Krugman, Stanley Lee 1925- WhoAm 90
Kruguer, Ignacio 1939- WhoWor 91
Kruh, Alain Edwin BiDrAPA 89
Kruh, Robert F. 1925- WhoAm 90
Kruidenier, David 1921- St&PR 91, WhoAm 90
Kruijtbosch, Egbert Diederik 1925- WhoWor 91
Kruizenga, Richard John 1930- St&PR 91, WhoAm 90
Kruk, Herman 1897-1944 BioIn 16
Kruk, J.W. 1940- St&PR 91
Kruk, John BioIn 16
Kruk, John 1961- Ballpl 90
Kruk, Steven James St&PR 91
Kruklitis, A. 1941- St&PR 91
Krukow, Mike 1952- Ballpl 90
Krukowski, Lucian 1929- WhoAm 90, WhoAmA 91
Krukowski, Nancy Harrow WhoAm 90
Krul, Michael Henry 1948- WhoSSW 91
Krulak, Victor Harold 1913- WhoAm 90
Krulee, David Arnold 1957- BiDrAPA 89
Krulfeld, Ruth Marilyn 1931- WhoAm 90
Krulik, Barbara S 1955- WhoAmA 91
Krulik, Stephanie Miriam 1943- WhoWrEP 89
Krulin, Gregory S 1944- BiDrAPA 89
Krulisky, Thomas V 1945- BiDrAPA 89
Krulitz, Leo M. 1938- St&PR 91
Krulitz, Leo Morrion 1938- WhoAm 90
Krull, Charles Fred 1933- WhoAm 90
Krull, Edward Alexander 1929- WhoWor 91
Krull, Jeffrey Robert 1948- WhoEmL 91
Krull, Kathleen 1952- BioIn 16
Krull, Kevin Charles 1952- WhoAm 90
Krull, Marianne ConAu 132
Krull, Wolfgang 1899-1971 DcScB S2
Krulwich, Robert BioIn 16
Krulwich, Terry Ann 1943- WhoAmW 91

Krum, Charlotte 1886- *AuBYP 90*
Krum, Joseph C. 1937- *St&PR 91*
Krum, Paul R. 1912- *St&PR 91*
Krum, Robert 1935- *WhoE 91*
Kruman, Mark Steven 1953- *WhoWor 91*
Krumb, P.P. 1942- *St&PR 91*
Krumbein, Charles Harvey 1944- *St&PR 91, WhoAm 90*
Krumbiegel, Stanley E *BiDrAPA 89*
Krumboltz, John Dwight 1928- *WhoAm 90*
Krumey, Hermann 1905- *BioIn 16*
Krumgold, Joseph 1908-1980 *AuBYP 90, BioIn 16*
Krumhansl, Bernice Rosemary 1922- *WhoWrEP 89*
Krumhansl, James Arthur 1919- *WhoAm 90*
Krumhar, Kim Carleton 1952- *WhoSSW 91*
Krumhauer, Peter 1941- *WhoWor 91*
Krumholt, Ann 1933- *WhoAmA 91*
Krumholtz, Cheryl Lynn 1966- *WhoAmW 91*
Krumholz, Alfred F., Jr. 1921- *St&PR 91*
Krumholz, David Rand 1949- *WhoE 91*
Krumholz, Walter *BiDrAPA 89*
Krumholz, Wilhelm V *BiDrAPA 89*
Krumholz, Wilhelm Vilem 1915- *WhoE 91*
Krumins, Girts 1932- *St&PR 91, WhoAm 90*
Krumm, Daniel John 1926- *St&PR 91, WhoAm 90*
Krumm, James R. 1947- *St&PR 91*
Krumm, John McGill 1913- *WhoAm 90*
Krumm, Philip Edwin 1941- *IntWWM 90*
Krumm, Philip O. 1906-1988 *BioIn 16*
Krumm, William Frederick 1923- *WhoAm 90*
Krummacher, Hans-Henrik 1931- *WhoWor 91*
Krumme, Donald P. 1931- *St&PR 91*
Krumme, George W. 1922- *St&PR 91*
Krummel, Donald William 1929- *WhoAm 90*
Krummel, Stephen John 1955- *BiDrAPA 89*
Krump, Gary Joseph 1946- *WhoEmL 91*
Krump, John M. 1929?-1990 *ConAu 132*
Krumper, Barry Lester *BiDrAPA 89*
Krumpholtz, Jean-Baptiste 1742-1790 *PenDiMP*
Krumpholtz, Wenzel 1750?-1817 *PenDiMP*
Krumrie, Tim *BioIn 16*
Krupa, Gene 1909-1973 *BioIn 16, OxCPMus, WorAlBi*
Krupa, Jeffrey Allen 1960- *WhoE 91*
Krupa, Lori Davis 1960- *WhoE 91*
Krupansky, Blanche 1925- *WhoAm 90*
Krupansky, Robert Bazil 1921- *WhoAm 90*
Krupat, Arnold 1941- *WhoAm 90*
Krupczak, Ambrose M *BiDrAPA 89*
Kruper, John Gerald 1949- *WhoEmL 91, WhoWor 91*
Krupinsky, Jacquelyn Stowell 1932- *WhoWrEP 89*
Krupka, Eric Lawrence 1963- *WhoEmL 91*
Krupka, Robert George 1949- *WhoEmL 91*
Krupka, Tina Marie 1961- *WhoAmW 91*
Krupnick, Elizabeth R. 1949- *ODwPR 91*
Krupnick, Janice Lee 1950- *WhoE 91*
Krupnick, Jerold Barry 1943- *St&PR 91*
Krupnick, Mark L. 1939- *ConAu 130*
Krupnick, Michael Ira 1947- *WhoEmL 91*
Krupnick, Steven Barry 1949- *St&PR 91*
Krupnick, Wendy Susan 1965- *WhoAmW 91*
Krupnik, Vee M. *WhoAm 90, WhoAmW 91*
Krupp, Alfred 1812-1887 *WorAlBi*
Krupp, Brandon Harris *BiDrAPA 89*
Krupp, Clarence William 1929- *WhoAm 90*
Krupp, E. C. *BioIn 16*
Krupp, Edwin C. *BioIn 16*
Krupp, Edwin Charles 1944- *WhoAm 90, WhoWrEP 89*
Krupp, Frederic David 1954- *WhoAm 90*
Krupp, George *BiDrAPA 89*
Krupp, Iris Marie 1928- *WhoAmW 91*
Krupp, Jonathan Maurice 1948- *WhoEmL 91*
Krupp, Marcus Abraham 1913- *WhoAm 90*
Krupp, Margaret Ann 1956- *WhoAmW 91*
Krupp, Neal E 1930- *BiDrAPA 89*
Krupp, Robin Rector 1946- *BioIn 16*
Krupp, Sherman R. 1926-1988 *BioIn 16*
Krupp von Bohlen Und Halbach, Gustav 1870-1950 *BioIn 16*
Krupska, Dania 1923- *BioIn 16, NotWoAT*
Krupska, Danya 1921- *WhoAm 90*
Krupskaia, Nadezhda Konstantinovna 1869-1939 *BioIn 16*
Krupskaya, Nadezhda 1869-1939 *WorAlBi*
Krus, David James 1940- *WhoAm 90*
Krus, John F. 1949- *St&PR 91*
Krusch, Werner E. 1927- *AuBYP 90*
Krusche, Dietrich 1935- *WhoWor 91*
Kruschke, Earl Roger 1934- *WhoAm 90*
Kruse, Ann Gray 1941- *WhoAmW 91*
Kruse, Cathy Callahan 1960- *St&PR 91*
Kruse, David L. 1944- *St&PR 91*
Kruse, David Louis, II 1944- *WhoAm 90*
Kruse, Donna Hynes 1956- *WhoAmW 91*
Kruse, Douglas Lynn 1959- *WhoE 91*
Kruse, Earl H. 1906- *ODwPR 91*
Kruse, Edgar Christ 1912- *WhoAm 90*
Kruse, Edward H. 1918- *St&PR 91*
Kruse, Hans-Jorgen Lutz Kalodent 1938- *WhoWor 91*
Kruse, James Joseph 1932- *WhoAm 90*
Kruse, Jan Cecile 1959- *WhoAmW 91*
Kruse, Jennie C. 1927- *St&PR 91*
Kruse, John Alphonse 1926- *WhoAm 90*
Kruse, Kathryn Warren 1940- *WhoE 91*
Kruse, Lise Fiaux 1947- *WhoWor 91*
Kruse, Marlin L. 1936- *St&PR 91*
Kruse, Pamela Jean 1950- *WhoAmW 91, WhoEmL 91*
Kruse, Paul Robert 1912- *WhoAm 90*
Kruse, Paul Walters, Jr. 1927- *WhoAm 90*
Kruse, Richard Kareth, Jr. 1938- *WhoAm 90*
Kruse, Rudolf 1952- *WhoWor 91*
Kruse, Stephanie Sheryl 1956- *WhoAmW 91*
Kruse, Virginia Gilda 1921- *WhoAmW 91*
Kruse-Susser, Lawrence A 1932- *BiDrAPA 89*
Krusell, Charles Robert 1924- *WhoAm 90*
Kruseman, Mina 1839-1922 *EncCoWW*
Krusen, Donna Ingle *BiDrAPA 89*
Krusen, Edward Montgomery 1920- *WhoAm 90*
Krusen, Henry Stanley 1907- *WhoAm 90*
Krusenstjerna, Agnes Julie Frederika von 1894-1940 *EncCoWW*
Krusenstjerna, Agnes Julie Fredrika von 1894-1940 *DcScanL*
Krushchev, Nikita 1894-1971 *BioIn 16*
Krushenick, Frances Harriet 1930- *WhoAmW 91*
Krushenick, John 1927- *WhoAmA 91*
Krushenick, Nicholas 1929- *WhoAm 90, WhoAmA 91*
Krusie, Kathleen Rose 1960- *WhoAmW 91*
Kruska, Jay Lynn 1951- *WhoEmL 91*
Kruska, Kenneth John 1936- *St&PR 91*
Kruskal, Clyde Philip 1954- *WhoE 91*
Kruskal, Martin David 1925- *WhoAm 90, WhoE 91*
Kruskal, William Henry 1919- *WhoAm 90*
Kruskamp, Janet 1934- *WhoAmA 91*
Krusky, J. Roger 1941- *St&PR 91*
Krusos, Denis Angelo 1927- *WhoE 91*
Kruss, James 1926- *AuBYP 90*
Kruszewski, Krzysztof 1939- *WhoWor 91*
Krutan, George 1924- *St&PR 91*
Krutch, Joseph Wood 1893-1970 *BioIn 16*
Krutchkoff, Richard Gerald 1953- *WhoSSW 91*
Krutcck, Laurence R. 1941- *WhoE 91, WhoWor 91*
Krutein, Eva *BioIn 16*
Krutenat, Richard Carroll 1934- *WhoWrEP 89*
Krutilek, D.R. 1942- *St&PR 91*
Krutkov, Iurii Aleksandrovich 1890-1952 *DcScB S2*
Krutsick, Robert Stanley 1942- *WhoE 91*
Krutzch, Gus *MajTwCW*
Kruus, Harri Kullervo 1950- *WhoWor 91*
Kruvant, M. Charito *BioIn 16*
Kruvant, M. Charito 1945- *WhoHisp 91*
Kruy, Joseph F. 1931- *St&PR 91*
Kruzich, Thomas R 1937- *BiDrAPA 89*
Kry, Rebecca Ridley 1939- *WhoAmW 91*
Kry, Stig Adolf 1929- *St&PR 91*
Kryczko, Thaddeus Walter 1954- *WhoEmL 91*
Kryder, Mark Howard 1943- *WhoAm 90*
Kryder, Phillip Verne 1962- *WhoEmL 91*
Krygel, Barbara A. 1947- *WhoAmW 91*
Kryger, Rudolph J. 1937- *St&PR 91*
Krygowska, Zofia 1904-1988 *BioIn 16*
Kryhoski, Dick 1925- *Ballpl 90*
Krylenko, Nikolai Vasilievich 1885-1938 *BioIn 16*
Krymkowski, Eugene R. 1931- *ODwPR 91*
Krymskii, Victor 1883-1927 *BioIn 16*
Krynicki, Margaret 1953- *WhoAmW 91*
Krynski, Magnus Jan 1922-1989 *BioIn 16*
Krys, Sheldon Jack 1934- *WhoAm 90*
Krysakowski, John M. 1943- *St&PR 91*
Kryshak, Thaddeus Francis 1930- *WhoAm 90*
Krysiak, Joseph Francis 1915- *St&PR 91*
Krysiak, Julian A., Mrs. 1920- *St&PR 91*
Krysinska, Maria 1857-1908 *EncCoWW*
Krysinski, Linda Ann 1957- *WhoAmW 91*
Krysinski, Thomas Frank 1945- *WhoSSW 91*
Krysl, Marilyn 1942- *WhoWrEP 89*
Krystal, Andrew Darrell 1960- *BiDrAPA 89*
Krystal, Henry 1925- *BiDrAPA 89*
Krystal, John Harrison *BiDrAPA 89*
Krystal, John Harrison 1958- *WhoE 91*
Kryston, Rosalie B 1938- *BiDrAPA 89*
Krystosek, Paul Nelson 1951- *WhoEmL 91*
Kryszak, Alan John 1961- *IntWWM 90*
Kryter, Karl David 1914- *WhoAm 90*
Kryuchkov, Vladimir Aleksandrovich 1924- *BioIn 16, WhoWor 91*
Kryvicky, Robert Charles 1948- *WhoE 91*
Kryza, Elmer Gregory 1922- *WhoAm 90*
Kryzanowski, Leslie J *BiDrAPA 89*
Krzanowski, Andrzej 1951- *IntWWM 90*
Krzanowski, Joseph John, Jr. 1940- *WhoSSW 91*
Krzeminski, James Allan 1944- *St&PR 91*
Krzesinski, Thomas Steven 1947- *St&PR 91, WhoSSW 91*
Krzycki, Leo *EncAL*
Krzysztofiak, Miroslaw 1927- *WhoWor 91*
Krzysztofowicz, Roman 1947- *WhoAm 90*
Krzyzan, Judy Lynn 1951- *WhoAmW 91*
Krzyzanowski, Eve 1951- *WhoE 91*
Krzyzanowski, Richard L. 1932- *St&PR 91*
Krzyzanowski, Richard Lucien 1932- *WhoAm 90*
Ksansnak, James E. 1940- *St&PR 91, WhoAm 90*
Kseniak, Beth 1957- *ODwPR 91*
Kshetarpal, Amit Kumar *BiDrAPA 89*
Ksienski, Aharon Arthur 1924- *WhoAm 90*
Ksoll, Christina Maria 1964- *WhoAmW 91*
Kszepka, Joseph Anthony 1931- *WhoE 91*
Kszystyniak, William Robert 1952- *WhoE 91*
Ktorides, Stanley 1949- *WhoEmL 91*
Ku, Annette E. 1945- *St&PR 91*
Ku, Cecilia Chou Yuan 1942- *WhoAmW 91*
Ku, Chia-Soon 1946- *WhoEmL 91*
Ku, Jentung *WhoE 91*
Ku, Jerry Chih 1953- *WhoEmL 91*
Ku, R. Fashun 1949- *WhoE 91*
Ku, Thomas Hsiu-Heng 1948- *WhoWor 91*
Ku, Y. H. 1902- *WhoAm 90, WhoE 91, WhoWor 91*
Kuan, Nai-Chung 1939- *IntWWM 90*
Kuan, Shia Shiong 1933- *WhoSSW 91*
Kuba, Deborah Irene 1955- *WhoEmL 91*
Kuba, Jacqueline Renee 1954- *IntWWM 90*
Kuba, James F. 1948- *St&PR 91*
Kubach, Charles Howard 1950- *WhoSSW 91*
Kubal, Geeta Gopal *BiDrAPA 89*
Kubala, Thomas Edward 1948- *WhoEmL 91*
Kubale, Bernard Stephen 1928- *St&PR 91, WhoAm 90*
Kubas, Gregory Joseph 1945- *WhoEmL 91*
Kubasch, Marja 1890-1976 *EncCoWW*
Kubasec, Marja 1890-1976 *EncCoWW*
Kube, Barbara Lou 1939- *WhoAmW 91*
Kube, Harold Deming 1910- *WhoSSW 91, WhoWor 91*
Kube, Wilhelm 1887-1943 *BioIn 16*
Kube-McDowell, Michael Paul 1954- *WhoEmL 91*
Kubek, Anthony Christopher 1935- *WhoAm 90*
Kubek, Tony 1936- *Ballpl 90, WorAlBi*
Kubela, Jeannine Veryl 1929- *WhoAmW 91*
Kubelik, Jan 1880-1940 *PenDiMP*
Kubelik, Rafael 1914- *PenDiMP, WorAlBi*
Kubelik, Rafael Jeronym 1914- *IntWWM 90*
Kubena, Frank Albert 1955- *WhoSSW 91*
Kuberski, Frank J. 1941- *St&PR 91*
Kubersky, Zave 1936- *St&PR 91, WhoAm 90*
Kubert, Joe 1926- *EncACom*
Kubiak, John Michael 1935- *WhoE 91*
Kubiak, Jon S. 1935- *St&PR 91*
Kubiak, Ted 1942- *Ballpl 90*
Kubiak, Teresa 1937- *IntWWM 90, PenDiMP*
Kubicek, Dwayne Joseph 1963- *WhoSSW 91*
Kubicek, Peter John 1930- *St&PR 91*
Kubicek, R.T. 1942- *St&PR 91*
Kubicek, Robert Vincent 1935- *WhoAm 90, WhoWrEP 89*
Kubicka, Margarethe 1891- *BiDWomA*
Kubicka, Vitazoslav 1953- *IntWWM 90*
Kubicke, George John 1944- *St&PR 91*
Kubida, William Joseph 1949- *WhoEmL 91, WhoWor 91*
Kubie, Nora Benjamin 1899-1988 *BioIn 16*
Kubie, Nora Gottheil Benjamin 1899- *AuBYP 90*
Kubiet, Leo L. 1924- *St&PR 91*
Kubiet, Leo Lawrence 1924- *WhoAm 90*
Kubik, Adam Joseph 1931- *WhoE 91*
Kubik, Gerhard 1934- *IntWWM 90*
Kubik, Jack Roy 1929- *St&PR 91*
Kubik, Ladislav 1946- *IntWWM 90*
Kubik, Reinhold 1942- *IntWWM 90*
Kubik, Richard J. 1953- *St&PR 91*
Kubiliun, Helena 1936- *BiDrAPA 89*
Kubilus, Norbert John 1948- *WhoAm 90, WhoE 91, WhoEmL 91, WhoWor 91*
Kubin, Charles Calvin 1932- *St&PR 91*
Kubin, Michael Ernest 1951- *WhoAm 90*
Kubini, Zofia 16--?- *EncCoWW*
Kubiniova, Zofia *EncCoWW*
Kubinski, Henry Anthony 1933- *WhoAm 90*
Kubinyi, Zsofia *EncCoWW*
Kubis, Donna M. 1963- *ODwPR 91*
Kubisen, Steven Joseph, Jr. 1952- *WhoEmL 91*
Kubistal, Patricia Bernice 1938- *WhoAmW 91, WhoWor 91*
Kubitschek, Juscelino 1902-1976 *BioIn 16*
Kubitz, Jody Allen 1963- *WhoEmL 91*
Kubitzki, Klaus 1933- *WhoWor 91*
Kubizek, Augustin 1918- *IntWWM 90*
Kublai Khan 1216-1294 *BioIn 16, WorAlBi*
Kubler, Fred C., Jr. 1929- *St&PR 91*
Kubler, Friedrich Karl 1932- *WhoWor 91*
Kubler, George Alexander 1912- *WhoAmA 91, WhoE 91*
Kubler-Ross, Elisabeth *BioIn 16, EncO&P 3*
Kubler-Ross, Elisabeth 1926- *EncPaPR 91, WhoAm 90, WhoAmW 91, WhoWrEP 89, WorAlBi*
Kublin, Hyman 1919- *AuBYP 90*
Kubly, Herbert 1915- *WhoAm 90*
Kubly, Herbert Oswald 1915- *WhoWrEP 89*
Kubo, Keizaburo 1922- *WhoWor 91*
Kubo, Yoko 1956- *IntWWM 90*
Kubota, Joe *WhoAm 90*
Kubota, Koichi 1930- *WhoWor 91*
Kubota, Scott Edward Yukio 1958- *WhoEmL 91*
Kubota, Shigeko 1937- *WhoAmA 91*
Kubr, Milan 1930- *WhoWor 91*
Kubricht, Dottie Mae Weidemeyer 1942- *WhoAmW 91, WhoSSW 91*
Kubrick, Stanley *BioIn 16*
Kubrick, Stanley 1928- *ConAu 33NR, WhoAm 90, WhoWor 91, WorAlBi*
Kubrin, Gail M. *BiDrAPA 89*
Kubsch, Kim Karen 1956- *WhoAmW 91*
Kubski, George Marian *BiDrAPA 89*
Kubski, Nayda Lavinia *BiDrAPA 89*
Kuby, Barbara Eleanor 1944- *WhoAmW 91*
Kuby, Edward Raymond 1938- *St&PR 91, WhoAm 90*
Kuby, Jane *ODwPR 91*
Kuby, Lolette Beth 1943- *WhoWrEP 89*
Kuby, Stephen Allen 1925- *WhoAm 90*
Kuby, Stu *BioIn 16*
Kubzansky, Philip Eugene 1928- *WhoAm 90*
Kuc, Joseph A. 1929- *WhoSSW 91*
Kucab, Johnny 1919-1977 *Ballpl 90*
Kucek, Jack 1953- *Ballpl 90*
Kucera, Daniel Jerome 1939- *WhoAm 90*
Kucera, Daniel William 1923- *WhoAm 90*
Kucera, Ellen Carll 1947- *WhoE 91*
Kucera, Henry 1925- *WhoAm 90*
Kuch, Klaus 1941- *BiDrAPA 89*
Kuchak, Joann M. 1949- *St&PR 91*
Kuchak, JoAnn Marie 1949- *WhoAmW 91*
Kuchar, Kathleen Ann 1942- *WhoAmA 91*
Kucharavy, Robert M. 1946- *WhoE 91*
Kucharski, Anastasia *BiDrAPA 89*
Kucharski, John Michael 1936- *St&PR 91, WhoAm 90, WhoE 91*
Kucharski, Kathy Jo 1948- *St&PR 91*
Kucharski, Robert Joseph 1932- *St&PR 91, WhoAm 90*
Kucharsky, David Eugene 1931- *WhoAm 90*
Kuchel, Konrad G 1937- *WhoAmA 91*
Kucheman, Clark Arthur 1931- *WhoAm 90*
Kuchen, Wilhelm Peter 1926- *WhoWor 91*
Kuchenbecker, Robert O. 1934- *WhoAm 90*
Kuchera, Michael Louis 1955- *WhoEmL 91, WhoWor 91*
Kuchler, Kenneth Grant 1922- *IntWWM 90*
Kuchmak, Carol Ann 1953- *BiDrAPA 89*
Kuchner, Eugene Frederick 1945- *WhoE 91, WhoEmL 91, WhoWor 91*
Kuchta, Bernard Joseph 1936- *WhoAm 90*
Kuchta, Gladys 1923- *IntWWM 90*
Kuchta, John Andrew 1943- *WhoE 91*
Kuchta, Ronald A 1935- *WhoAmA 91*
Kuchta, Ronald Andrew 1935- *WhoAm 90, WhoE 91*
Kuchta, Thomas Walter 1942- *WhoAm 90*
Kucic, Joseph 1964- *WhoE 91*
Kucij, Timothy Michael 1954- *WhoEmL 91, WhoWor 91*
Kuck, David Jerome 1937- *WhoAm 90*
Kuck, John Howland 1932- *St&PR 91*
Kuck, Kurt Charles 1957- *WhoEmL 91*

Kuck, Marie Elizabeth Bukovsky 1910- *WhoAmW 91*
Kuckartz, Wilfried 1937- *WhoWor 91*
Kuckhoff, Carl, Jr. 1930- *St&PR 91*
Kucklaender, Uwe 1942- *WhoWor 91*
Kuckro, Lee Gerard 1941- *St&PR 91*
Kucks, Johnny 1933- *Ballpl 90*
Kucler, Edward Alan 1942- *St&PR 91*
Kucler, Jack J. 1948- *St&PR 91*
Kuczak, Sophie Marie 1952- *WhoAmW 91*
Kuczek, Richard Edward 1945- *WhoEmL 91*
Kuczinski, Anthony Joseph 1959- *St&PR 91*
Kuczkowski, Richard Joseph 1944- *WhoE 91*
Kuczmarski, Susan Smith 1951- *WhoWor 91*
Kuczun, Ann-Marie *WhoAmA 91*
Kuczwanski, John S. 1945- *St&PR 91*
Kuczwanski, John Sigmund 1945- *WhoSSW 91*
Kuczynski, John Raymond 1953- *St&PR 91*
Kuczynski, Pedro-Pablo 1938- *WhoAm 90*
Kuda Bux 1905- *EncO&P 3*
Kudarauskas, Edmund N *BiDrAPA 89*
Kuddous, Ihsan Abdel *BioIn 16*
Kudelka, James *WhoAm 90*
Kudenholdt, Sharon Sue 1942- *WhoAmW 91*
Kudesh, Stephen B. 1944- *St&PR 91*
Kudisch, Leonard 1912-1989 *BioIn 16*
Kudish, David J. 1943- *WhoAm 90*
Kudlack, Constance Dale 1942- *WhoE 91*
Kudler, Harold Stephen 1953- *BiDrAPA 89*
Kudler, Peter Howard 1949- *BiDrAPA 89*
Kudlow, Lawrence Alan 1947- *WhoAm 90*
Kudner, Richard Don 1927- *St&PR 91*
Kudo, Emiko Iwashita 1923- *WhoWor 91*
Kudo, Kaz 1933- *WhoAm 90*
Kudo, Kenneth Masaaki 1943- *WhoWor 91*
Kudrle, William Alan 1954- *WhoSSW 91*
Kudrna, Christopher R. 1954- *St&PR 91*
Kudrna, Perry Francis 1962- *WhoEmL 91*
Kudrnac, I.K. 1926- *St&PR 91*
Kudrnac, Kristian Ivoj 1949- *WhoE 91*, *WhoEmL 91*
Kudryavtsev, Vladimir 1923- *WhoWor 91*
Kudryk, Oleg 1912- *WhoAm 90*, *WhoWor 91*
Kudzma, J.C. *St&PR 91*
Kueber, Roland W. 1933- *WhoAm 90*
Kuebler, David 1947- *IntWWM 90*
Kuebler, David Wayne 1947- *WhoEmL 91*, *WhoSSW 91*, *WhoWor 91*
Kuebler, Patricia Irene 1942- *WhoAmW 91*
Kuechenmeister, Karl Thomas 1946- *WhoE 91*
Kuechler, James R *BiDrAPA 89*
Kueh, Yak Yeow 1937- *WhoWor 91*
Kuehl, Frederick A. *St&PR 91*
Kuehl, Hal C. 1923- *WhoAm 90*
Kuehl, Hal Charles 1923- *St&PR 91*
Kuehl, Hans Henry 1933- *WhoAm 90*
Kuehl, John Richard 1928- *WhoWrEP 89*
Kuehl, Nancy Louise 1947- *WhoAmW 91*, *WhoEmL 91*
Kuehler, Jack Dwyer 1932- *WhoAm 90*
Kuehn, Albert John 1925- *St&PR 91*
Kuehn, Carol Ann 1954- *St&PR 91*
Kuehn, David Laurance 1940- *WhoAm 90*
Kuehn, Edmund Karl 1916- *WhoAm 90*, *WhoAmA 91*
Kuehn, Frances 1943- *WhoAmA 91*
Kuehn, Gary 1939- *WhoAmA 91*
Kuehn, George E. 1946- *St&PR 91*, *WhoAm 90*
Kuehn, Heinz R. 1919- *ConAu 130*
Kuehn, Hermann Walter 1933- *WhoWor 91*
Kuehn, James H. 1918- *St&PR 91*
Kuehn, James Marshall 1926- *WhoAm 90*
Kuehn, John L 1930- *BiDrAPA 89*
Kuehn, Luise F *BiDrAPA 89*
Kuehn, Raymond Kenneth 1929- *St&PR 91*
Kuehn, Ronald L., Jr. 1935- *St&PR 91*, *WhoAm 90*, *WhoSSW 91*
Kuehn, Steven E. *ODwPR 91*
Kuehne, Donald James 1930- *St&PR 91*
Kuehne, Margaret Ann 1939- *WhoAmW 91*
Kuehne, Martin Eric 1931- *WhoAm 90*
Kuehner, Horst Karl 1937- *St&PR 91*
Kuehner, Louis C. *AuBYP 90*
Kuehnert, Deborah Anne 1949- *WhoAmW 91*
Kuehnert, Robert G *BiDrAPA 89*
Kuehnl, Claudia Ann 1948- *WhoAmA 91*
Kuehnle, Emery Charles, Jr. 1928- *St&PR 91*
Kuehnle, John C 1940- *BiDrAPA 89*
Kuehnle, Norman Bruce 1940- *WhoE 91*
Kuekes, Edward D 1901-1987 *WhoAmA 91N*
Kuekes, George Cleve 1928- *St&PR 91*
Kuemmel, Reiner 1939- *WhoWor 91*
Kuemmerle, John F. 1925- *St&PR 91*
Kuemmerlein, Janet 1932- *WhoAmA 91*
Kuen, Paul 1910- *IntWWM 90*
Kuendig, John *BioIn 16*
Kuenen, Philip Henry 1902-1976 *DcScB S2*
Kueng, Hans 1928- *MajTwCW*
Kuenn, Harvey 1930-1988 *Ballpl 90 [port]*, *BioIn 16*
Kuenne, Robert Eugene 1924- *WhoAm 90*
Kuenneth, John Robert 1932- *WhoSSW 91*
Kuenster, John Joseph 1924- *WhoAm 90*, *WhoWrEP 89*
Kuentz, Bruce J. 1953- *St&PR 91*
Kuentz, John Charles 1925- *St&PR 91*
Kuentzel, William Paul 1947- *BiDrAPA 89*
Kueny, Mary Ellen 1955- *WhoAmW 91*
Kuenzel, Steven Paul 1952- *WhoEmL 91*
Kuenzi, Curt William 1956- *WhoEmL 91*
Kuenzler, Edward Julian 1929- *WhoAm 90*
Kueper, Clement John 1928- *St&PR 91*
Kuerti, Anton Emil 1938- *IntWWM 90*, *WhoAm 90*
Kues, Mary Carolyn 1936- *WhoAmW 91*
Kuesel, Thomas Robert 1926- *St&PR 91*, *WhoAm 90*
Kuester, Dennis J. *WhoAm 90*
Kuethe, Peggy Sue 1958- *WhoWrEP 89*
Kuether, Ronald Clarence 1934- *St&PR 91*, *WhoAm 90*
Kuever, Nancy Jeanne 1947- *WhoAmW 91*, *WhoEmL 91*
Kufeld, William Manuel 1922- *WhoAm 90*
Kufeldt, James 1938- *WhoAm 90*, *WhoSSW 91*
Kuffel, Edmund 1924- *WhoAm 90*
Kuffner-Hirt, Mary Jane 1951- *WhoAmW 91*
Kuftinec, Dubravko M 1935- *BiDrAPA 89*
Kuftinec, Jasna *BiDrAPA 89*
Kuftinec, Zlatko M *BiDrAPA 89*
Kugel, James Lewis 1945- *WhoAm 90*
Kugel, Robert Benjamin 1923- *WhoAm 90*
Kugelberg, Donald Charles 1954- *WhoE 91*
Kugell, Robert Herbert 1935- *St&PR 91*
Kugelmass, Joseph Alvin 1910-1972 *AuBYP 90*
Kugelmass, Michael Ian 1944- *BiDrAPA 89*
Kughn, Dick *BioIn 16*
Kuglar, Everett C *BiDrAPA 89*
Kugle, J. Alan 1937- *WhoAm 90*
Kuglen, Francesca Bernadette 1961- *WhoAmW 91*
Kugler, Frank J., Jr. 1934- *St&PR 91*
Kugler, Lawrence Dean 1941- *WhoAm 90*
Kugler, Margaret M 1924- *BiDrAPA 89*
Kugler, Robert J. 1930- *St&PR 91*
Kugler, Seymour 1936- *St&PR 91*
Kugler, William Charles 1935- *St&PR 91*
Kugler-Poni, Matilda *EncCoWW*
Kuh, Elizabeth N *BiDrAPA 89*
Kuh, Ernest Shiu-Jen 1928- *WhoAm 90*
Kuh, Howard 1899- *WhoAmA 91*
Kuh, Katharine 1904- *BioIn 16*, *WhoAmA 91*
Kuh, Richard Henry 1921- *WhoAm 90*
Kuhagen, Lawrence K. 1954- *St&PR 91*
Kuhajek, Eugene James 1934- *WhoAm 90*
Kuhaneck, David 1949- *BiDrAPA 89*
Kuhar, Fred 1946- *St&PR 91*
Kuhar, June Carolynn 1935- *WhoAmW 91*
Kuhar, Timothy 1955- *St&PR 91*
Kuharic, Franjo 1919- *WhoWor 91*
Kuharski, James Paul 1935- *St&PR 91*
Kuharsky, Andrew Sergius 1957- *WhoSSW 91*
Kuhel, Joe 1906-1984 *Ballpl 90*
Kuhi, Leonard Vello 1936- *WhoAm 90*
Kuhl, David Edmund 1929- *WhoAm 90*
Kuhl, Dorothy L 1920- *BiDrAPA 89*
Kuhl, Josephine 1951- *BiDrAPA 89*
Kuhl, Kathy 1956- *WhoEmL 91*
Kuhl, Margaret Helen Clayton *WhoAmW 91*
Kuhl, Norman Ernest 1940- *St&PR 91*
Kuhl, Richard Allen 1949- *WhoEmL 91*
Kuhl, Thomas J. 1936- *St&PR 91*
Kuhlen, Rainer 1944- *WhoWor 91*
Kuhlengel, Barbara Greif 1954- *BiDrAPA 89*
Kuhlenschmidt, Richard Edward 1951- *WhoAmA 91*
Kuhler, Deborah G. 1952- *WhoAmW 91*
Kuhler, Otto August 1894-1977 *WhoAmA 91N*
Kuhler, Renaldo Gillet 1931- *WhoSSW 91*, *WhoWor 91*
Kuhlke, Kim Lee 1946- *WhoEmL 91*
Kuhlman, Donald Ray 1962- *WhoEmL 91*
Kuhlman, John Michael 1948- *WhoEmL 91*
Kuhlman, Kathryn 1907-1976 *EncO&P 3*, *EncPaPR 91*
Kuhlman, Kathryn 1910-1976 *BioAmW*, *WorAlBi*
Kuhlman, Lisa *BiDrAPA 89*
Kuhlman, Walter Egel 1918- *WhoAm 90*, *WhoAmA 91*
Kuhlmann, Arkadi 1946- *St&PR 91*
Kuhlmann, Fred L. 1916- *St&PR 91*, *WhoAm 90*
Kuhlmann, Fred Mark 1948- *St&PR 91*, *WhoAm 90*, *WhoEmL 91*
Kuhlmann, Kathleen 1950- *IntWWM 90*, *PenDiMP*
Kuhlmann, Kyloe Somae 1964- *WhoEmL 91*
Kuhlmann, Ralf 1948- *WhoWor 91*
Kuhlmann, Rolf F.W. 1937- *St&PR 91*
Kuhlmann, William Carl 1950- *St&PR 91*, *WhoEmL 91*
Kuhlmann-Wilsdorf, Doris 1922- *WhoAm 90*, *WhoSSW 91*
Kuhlmey, Walter Trowbridge 1918- *WhoAm 90*
Kuhlthau, Conrad William, III 1933- *WhoAm 90*
Kuhlthau, John Suydam 1937- *WhoE 91*
Kuhn, Albert Joseph 1926- *WhoAm 90*
Kuhn, Anne Naomi Wicker *WhoAmW 91*
Kuhn, Annette Frieda 1945- *WhoWor 91*
Kuhn, Arthur Richard 1931- *St&PR 91*
Kuhn, Barbara 1924-1988 *BioIn 16*
Kuhn, Beate *PenDiDA 89*
Kuhn, Bob 1920- *WhoAmA 91*
Kuhn, Bowie 1926- *Ballpl 90 [port]*, *WhoAm 90*
Kuhn, Brenda 1911- *WhoE 91*
Kuhn, Charles 1892-1989 *EncACom*
Kuhn, Charles W 1926- *BiDrAPA 89*
Kuhn, Clifford C 1941- *BiDrAPA 89*
Kuhn, Colleen Mae 1962- *WhoSSW 91*
Kuhn, Daniel 1943- *BiDrAPA 89*
Kuhn, David *ODwPR 91*
Kuhn, David A. 1929- *St&PR 91*
Kuhn, David Alan 1929- *WhoAm 90*
Kuhn, Delia 1903-1989 *ConAu 130*
Kuhn, Delia W. *BioIn 16*
Kuhn, Donald Marshall 1922- *WhoE 91*
Kuhn, Doris *AuBYP 90*
Kuhn, Eleanor G. 1922- *St&PR 91*
Kuhn, Ernesto 1929- *WhoWor 91*
Kuhn, Fred M. 1928- *WhoWor 91*
Kuhn, Gabriele 1950- *IntWWM 90*
Kuhn, Gustav 1947- *PenDiMP*
Kuhn, Hans Peter *BioIn 16*
Kuhn, Heinz R *ConAu 130*
Kuhn, Howard Arthur 1940- *WhoAm 90*
Kuhn, Howard Frederick 1938- *WhoSSW 91*
Kuhn, Irene Corbally 1900- *BioIn 16*
Kuhn, Irvin Nelson 1928- *WhoAm 90*
Kuhn, James E. 1946- *WhoSSW 91*
Kuhn, James Paul 1937- *St&PR 91*, *WhoAm 90*
Kuhn, James Peter, Jr. 1939- *WhoAm 90*
Kuhn, Joachim *BioIn 16*
Kuhn, John Mark 1955- *WhoEmL 91*, *WhoSSW 91*
Kuhn, Josef Leonz 1926- *St&PR 91*, *WhoAm 90*
Kuhn, Judy *BioIn 16*
Kuhn, Kathleen Jo 1947- *WhoAmW 91*
Kuhn, Kenneth Allen 1945- *WhoE 91*
Kuhn, Lawrence Fred 1946- *BiDrAPA 89*
Kuhn, Linda Marie 1953- *WhoAmW 91*
Kuhn, Lucille Ross 1927- *WhoAmW 91*
Kuhn, Maggie *BioIn 16*
Kuhn, Margaret 1905- *WhoAm 90*, *WhoAmW 91*, *WorAlBi*
Kuhn, Mary Croughan 1914- *WhoAmW 91*
Kuhn, Marylou 1923- *WhoAmA 91*
Kuhn, Michael Heinrich 1943- *WhoWor 91*
Kuhn, Nancy Jane 1946- *WhoEmL 91*
Kuhn, Nancy Lee 1950- *WhoE 91*
Kuhn, Nancy Zeleny 1931- *WhoAmW 91*
Kuhn, Nicholas G. *BioIn 16*
Kuhn, Othmar 1892-1969 *DcScB S2*
Kuhn, Otto 1955- *St&PR 91*
Kuhn, Paul Hubert, Jr. 1943- *WhoSSW 91*
Kuhn, Peter Mouat 1920- *WhoAm 90*
Kuhn, Raymond E. 1942- *St&PR 91*
Kuhn, Robert C. 1930- *WhoAm 90*
Kuhn, Robert Mitchell 1942- *St&PR 91*
Kuhn, Robert P. 1926- *St&PR 91*
Kuhn, Roland J. 1912- *St&PR 91*
Kuhn, Ronald Joseph 1944- *St&PR 91*
Kuhn, Ryan Anthony 1947- *WhoEmL 91*
Kuhn, Sarah 1952- *WhoEmL 91*
Kuhn, Sherman McAllister 1907- *WhoAm 90*
Kuhn, Stephen L. 1947- *St&PR 91*
Kuhn, Terry Lee 1941- *IntWWM 90*
Kuhn, Thomas 1922- *EncPaPR 91*
Kuhn, Thomas 1958- *WhoWor 91*
Kuhn, Thomas Samuel 1922- *WhoAm 90*
Kuhn, Thomas William 1960- *BiDrAPA 89*
Kuhn, Timothy Edward 1951- *WhoEmL 91*
Kuhn, Walt 1877-1949 *BioIn 16*
Kuhn, Walt 1880-1949 *WhoAmA 91N*
Kuhn, Warren Boehm 1924- *WhoAm 90*
Kuhn, William Frederick 1924- *WhoAm 90*
Kuhn, Wolfgang F 1945- *BiDrAPA 89*
Kuhne, Sharon Anglin 1951- *WhoWrEP 89*
Kuhner, Ben Richard 1937- *BiDrAPA 89*
Kuhner, Heiner 1943- *IntWWM 90*
Kuhnert, Robert Richard 1925- *St&PR 91*
Kuhnke, Thomas J. 1943- *St&PR 91*
Kuhnley, Edward John 1951- *BiDrAPA 89*, *WhoE 91*
Kuhnmuench, John R. 1944- *St&PR 91*
Kuhns, Barbara Anne 1948- *WhoSSW 91*
Kuhns, F.L. 1946- *St&PR 91*
Kuhns, Ralph Walter 1938- *St&PR 91*
Kuhns, Roberrt C. 1926- *St&PR 91*
Kuhns, Roger James 1922- *St&PR 91*
Kuhns, William G. 1922- *St&PR 91*
Kuhr, Bernard M 1926- *BiDrAPA 89*
Kuhr, Michael S. 1949- *St&PR 91*
Kuhrmeyer, Carl Albert 1928- *St&PR 91*, *WhoAm 90*
Kuhrt, Richard Lee 1959- *WhoEmL 91*
Kuhrt, Sharon Lee 1957- *WhoAmW 91*
Kuhs, Milton L *BiDrAPA 89*
Kuhse, Hanne-Lore 1925- *IntWWM 90*
Kuich, Thomas Edward *BiDrAPA 89*
Kuijken, Barthold 1949- *IntWWM 90*, *PenDiMP*
Kuijken, Sigiswald 1944- *IntWWM 90*, *PenDiMP*
Kuijken, Wieland 1938- *IntWWM 90*, *PenDiMP*
Kuik, Maarten 1954- *WhoSSW 91*
Kuiken, Bunny 1929- *WhoE 91*
Kuiper, Duane 1950- *Ballpl 90*
Kuiper, Erika Lura Schmidt 1946- *WhoEmL 91*
Kuiper, Franciscus Bernardus Jacobus 1907- *WhoWor 91*
Kuiper, Gerard P. 1905-1973 *WorAlBi*
Kuitert, Harminus Martinus 1924- *WhoWor 91*
Kuivila, Henry Gabriel 1917- *WhoAm 90*
Kuizon, Servando Ragas *BiDrAPA 89*
Kujala, Steve *NewAgMG*
Kujala, Walfrid Eugene 1925- *WhoAm 90*
Kujawski, Mary H. 1949- *WhoAm 90*
Kujoth, Jean 1935-1975 *AuBYP 90*
Kujundzic, Zeljko D 1920- *WhoAmA 91*
Kuk Lee, Won *Ballpl 90*
Kukai 774-835 *EncJap*
Kukanskis, Peter E. 1946- *St&PR 91*
Kukec, Anna Marie 1958- *WhoAmW 91*
Kukin, Ira 1924- *St&PR 91*
Kukkapuro, Yrjo 1933- *ConDes 90*
Kukkasjarvi, Irma 1941- *ConDes 90*
Kukla, Anne 1922- *St&PR 91*
Kukla, Helena Jasna *BiDrAPA 89*
Kukla, Judi Ann 1945- *St&PR 91*
Kukla, Robert John 1932- *WhoAm 90*
Kukla, T.J. 1918- *St&PR 91*
Kuklin, Anthony Bennett 1929- *WhoAm 90*
Kuklin, Jeffrey Peter 1935- *WhoWor 91*
Kuklin, Susan *AuBYP 90*
Kuklin, Susan 1941- *ConAu 130*, *SmATA 63 [port]*
Kuklinski, T.F. 1932- *St&PR 91*
Kukuk, Karen Eloise 1938- *WhoAmW 91*
Kukura, Rita Anne 1947- *WhoAmW 91*
Kula, Elsa *AuBYP 90*
Kula, Gary Paul 1951- *BiDrAPA 89*
Kulagina, Nina S *EncO&P 3*
Kulagina, Nina Sergeyevna 1925?- *EncPaPR 91*
Kulahcioglu, Muzaffer 1927- *BiDrAPA 89*
Kulason, Robert Alexander 1928- *St&PR 91*
Kulbaba, Terry John 1957- *WhoEmL 91*
Kulbertus, Henri Emile 1938- *WhoWor 91*
Kulcsar, Francis E *BiDrAPA 89*
Kulczycki, Michael Terry 1952- *WhoEmL 91*
Kulczynski, Edwina Mary 1935- *WhoAmW 91*
Kuldau, John M 1933- *BiDrAPA 89*
Kule, Sheldon 1936- *BiDrAPA 89*
Kule, Stephen Jay 1945- *WhoE 91*
Kulenkampff, Georg 1898-1948 *PenDiMP*
Kulesh, William Adam 1929- *WhoWor 91*
Kulesha, Gary Alan 1954- *IntWWM 90*
Kulesha, Kevin John 1956- *WhoE 91*
Kuleshova, Rosa *EncO&P 3*
Kuleshova, Rosa A. 1955-1978 *EncPaPR 91*
Kulesza, Frank W. 1920- *St&PR 91*
Kulewicz, John Joseph 1954- *WhoEmL 91*
Kulewicz, Stanley Francis 1928- *WhoE 91*
Kulharya, Himmat Singh 1945- *St&PR 91*
Kulick, Eric Michael *BiDrAPA 89*
Kulick, Florence Olivia Post 1923- *WhoAmW 91*
Kulick, Gary F. 1944- *WhoAm 90*
Kulicke, Charles Scott 1949- *St&PR 91*, *WhoAm 90*
Kulicke, Robert M 1924- *WhoAmA 91*

Kulik, Alcides V 1937- *BiDrAPA 89*
Kulik, Boles *WhoWrEP 89*
Kulik, Frank Albert 1938- *BiDrAPA 89*
Kulikov, Viktor Georgiyevich 1921- *WhoWor 91*
Kulild, James Clinton 1947- *WhoSSW 91*
Kulin, Keith David 1948- *WhoE 91*
Kulinski, Stephen Edward 1955- *WhoSSW 91*
Kulinsky, Bohumil 1959- *IntWWM 90*
Kuliseva, Oleksandra Myxajlivna 1828-1911 *EncCoWW*
Kuljian, Arthur H. 1923- *St&PR 91*
Kulka, Anna M *BiDrAPA 89*
Kulka, Ernest W. 1897-1990 *BioIn 16*
Kulka, Konstanty Andrzej 1947- *IntWWM 90*
Kulka, Kurt 1904- *WhoAm 90*
Kulka, Richard A. 1945- *ConAu 130*
Kulkarni, Arun *BiDrAPA 89*
Kulkarni, Arun Digambar 1947- *WhoSSW 91*
Kulkarni, Jagdish D *BiDrAPA 89*
Kulkarni, Jayant Vithal 1947- *WhoE 91*
Kulkarni, Satish *BiDrAPA 89*
Kulkarni, Subhash V *BiDrAPA 89*
Kulkarni, Vineet P 1950- *BiDrAPA 89*
Kulke, Christine *WhoWor 91*
Kulkosky, Paul Joseph 1949- *WhoEmL 91*
Kull, Barbara Anne 1946- *WhoAmW 91*
Kull, Bryan Paul 1960- *WhoSSW 91*
Kull, Lorenz Anthony 1937- *St&PR 91*
Kull, Richard Kevin 1951- *BiDrAPA 89*, *WhoE 91*
Kull, Robert Alan 1952- *WhoE 91*, *WhoEmL 91*
Kull, Ulrich Otto 1938- *WhoWor 91*
Kull, William Franklin 1956- *WhoEmL 91*
Kullak, Theodor 1818-1882 *PenDiMP*
Kullas, Albert John 1917- *WhoAm 90*
Kullberg, Duane Reuben 1932- *WhoAm 90*, *WhoWor 91*
Kullberg, John Francis 1939- *WhoAm 90*
Kullberg, Rolf Evert 1930- *WhoWor 91*
Kullenberg, Roger Dale 1930- *WhoAm 90*
Kuller, Jonathan Mark 1951- *WhoEmL 91*
Kuller, Lewis Henry 1934- *WhoAm 90*
Kuller, Mark David 1959- *WhoEmL 91*
Kullgren, Elwood M. 1911- *St&PR 91*
Kullick, Ronald H. 1942- *St&PR 91*
Kullman, Charles 1903-1983 *PenDiMP*
Kullman, Wilfred M. 1936- *St&PR 91*
Kullmann, Wolfgang Walter 1927- *WhoWor 91*
Kulman, Linda 1960- *ODwPR 91*
Kulmer, Morris H. 1945- *St&PR 91*
Kulok, William Allan 1940- *WhoE 91*, *WhoWor 91*
Kulomzin, Anatolii Nikolaevich 1838-1921 *BioIn 16*
Kulp, David W *BiDrAPA 89*
Kulp, Eileen Bodnar 1941- *WhoAmW 91*
Kulp, J. Robert 1935- *WhoE 91*
Kulp, Jonathan B. 1937- *WhoE 91*
Kulp, Nancy Jane 1921- *WhoAm 90*, *WhoAmW 91*
Kulp, Philip Masterton 1929- *WhoAm 90*
Kulp, Richard Wayne 1943- *WhoSSW 91*
Kulpa, John Edward 1929- *WhoAm 90*
Kulpa, Karen Joan 1965- *WhoAmW 91*
Kulper, Perry Dean 1953- *WhoAm 90*
Kulshreshtha, Anand Kumar 1947- *WhoWor 91*
Kulshrestha, Shashi Mohan 1934- *WhoWor 91*
Kulski, Julian Eugeniusz 1929- *WhoAm 90*
Kulstad, Guy Charles 1930- *WhoWor 91*
Kult, Robert Phillip 1940- *St&PR 91*
Kultermann, Udo 1927- *WhoAm 90*, *WhoAmA 91*
Kulukundis, Manuel *BioIn 16*
Kuluva, Will *NewYTBS 90*
Kulvi, Paul Michael 1954- *WhoSSW 91*
Kulvik, Hannes Gustav 1948- *WhoWor 91*
Kulvinskas, Victor P. 1950- *WhoWrEP 89*
Kulwin, Herbert 1930- *St&PR 91*
Kulyk, Mark C. 1956- *St&PR 91*
Kulynych, Petro 1921- *St&PR 91*
Kulzer-Hollen, Regina Dyanne 1951- *WhoAmW 91*
Kulzick, Kenneth Edmund 1927- *WhoAm 90*
Kumagai, Takashi 1931- *WhoWor 91*
Kumagai, Takenobu 1937- *WhoWor 91*
Kumagi, Yoshitaro 1947- *WhoWor 91*
Kumamaru, Takahiro 1936- *WhoWor 91*
Kumamoto, Chukei 1925- *WhoWor 91*
Kumar, Adarsh 1940- *WhoSSW 91*
Kumar, Anand *BiDrAPA 89*
Kumar, Anand 1950- *WhoEmL 91*
Kumar, Anil *BiDrAPA 89*
Kumar, Arun 1948- *WhoEmL 91*
Kumar, Arvind 1950- *BiDrAPA 89*
Kumar, Ashok *BiDrAPA 89*
Kumar, Devendra 1944- *WhoSSW 91*
Kumar, Dhananjaya 1949- *WhoE 91*
Kumar, Geetha *BiDrAPA 89*
Kumar, K Krishna *BiDrAPA 89*
Kumar, K M Druva 1942- *BiDrAPA 89*
Kumar, Kala Prithvi *BiDrAPA 89*
Kumar, Kaplesh 1947- *WhoWor 91*
Kumar, Krishan 1942- *ConAu 130*
Kumar, Krishna 1936- *WhoWor 91*
Kumar, Krishna 1944- *BiDrAPA 89*
Kumar, Kumud Vijay *BiDrAPA 89*
Kumar, Manjari *BiDrAPA 89*
Kumar, Nandan Puthezhath 1949- *BiDrAPA 89*
Kumar, Pamela Eileen 1944- *WhoAmW 91*
Kumar, Panganamala Ramana 1952- *WhoAm 90*
Kumar, Parmanand 1943- *WhoWor 91*
Kumar, Prem 1945- *WhoWrEP 89*
Kumar, Puskoor Manmadh *BiDrAPA 89*
Kumar, Rajendra 1947- *St&PR 91*
Kumar, Rajendra 1948- *WhoWor 91*
Kumar, Rajiv *BiDrAPA 89*
Kumar, Ram N. *St&PR 91*
Kumar, Ramesh Pal 1948- *WhoWor 91*
Kumar, Rashmi Goyle 1953- *BiDrAPA 89*
Kumar, Ravinder *BiDrAPA 89*
Kumar, Romesh 1944- *WhoAm 90*
Kumar, Seema 1957- *BiDrAPA 89*
Kumar, Shailendra 1934- *BiDrAPA 89*
Kumar, Smita Rajeev 1959- *WhoAmW 91*
Kumar, Sreedharan Kishore 1955- *WhoWor 91*
Kumar, Subodh 1948- *WhoE 91*
Kumar, Subodh 1953- *WhoWor 91*
Kumar, Sudhir 1942- *WhoWor 91*
Kumar, Surendra 1935- *St&PR 91*
Kumar, Surinder 1944- *WhoAm 90*
Kumar, Vasant 1949- *WhoWor 91*
Kumar, Vinod *BiDrAPA 89*
Kumar, Virinder *BiDrAPA 89*
Kumara Padmanabha Sivasankara Menon 1898-1982 *BioIn 16*
Kumari, Durga 1951- *WhoE 91*
Kumazawa, Shunji 1927- *WhoWor 91*
Kumble, Steven Jay 1933- *WhoAm 90*
Kumcu, Ahmet Erdogan 1950- *WhoEmL 91*
Kume, Tadashi *WhoWor 91*
Kume, Yutaka *BioIn 16*
Kumela, Olli Kaarlo Juhani 1942- *WhoWor 91*
Kumer, Roy L. 1908- *St&PR 91*
Kumetat, Bernard Bruno 1943- *BiDrAPA 89*
Kumin, Albert *BioIn 16*
Kumin, Ivri 1946- *BiDrAPA 89*
Kumin, Laura Ann 1956- *WhoWor 91*
Kumin, Laura Anne 1952- *WhoEmL 91*
Kumin, Libby Barbara 1945- *WhoAmW 91*, *WhoE 91*
Kumin, Maxine 1925- *AuBYP 90*, *FemiCLE*, *MajTwCW*, *WhoWrEP 89*, *WorAlBi*
Kumin, Maxine Winokur 1925- *WhoAm 90*, *WhoAmW 91*
Kumler, Kipton 1940- *WhoAmA 91*
Kumler, Kipton Cornelius 1940- *WhoAm 90*
Kumlin, Krister Ralf 1938- *WhoWor 91*
Kumm, Marguerite Elizabeth *WhoAmA 91*
Kummel, Eugene *BioIn 16*
Kummel, Eugene H. 1923- *WhoAm 90*
Kummer, Clare *BioIn 16*
Kummer, Clare 1873?-1958 *NotWoAT*
Kummer, Frederic Arnold 1873- *AuBYP 90*
Kummer, Glenn F. 1933- *WhoAm 90*
Kummer, Robert W., Jr. 1936- *St&PR 91*
Kummerfeld, Donald David 1934- *WhoAm 90*
Kummert, Richard Osborne 1932- *WhoAm 90*
Kummins, Joel Stephen 1942- *WhoSSW 91*
Kummler, Ralph H. 1940- *WhoAm 90*
Kump, Ernest Joseph 1911- *WhoAm 90*
Kump, Kary Ronald 1952- *WhoEmL 91*
Kump, Peter 1937- *BioIn 16*
Kump, Scott Anthony 1956- *St&PR 91*
Kump, Thomas George 1962- *WhoE 91*
Kumpa 1920- *SmATA X*
Kumpf, John E. 1929- *ODwPR 91*
Kumura, James Yutaka 1962- *WhoEmL 91*
Kun, Bela 1886-1939 *BioIn 16*
Kun, Joyce Anne 1946- *WhoEmL 91*
Kun, Michael 1962- *ConAu 132*
Kun, Neila *WhoE 91*
Kun, Neila 1951- *WhoAmA 91*
Kuna, Michael Allan 1953- *BiDrAPA 89*
Kuna, Thomas Alan 1947- *St&PR 91*
Kunam, Syam Prasad B *BiDrAPA 89*
Kunc, Karen 1952- *WhoAmA 91*
Kunckel, Johann F. 1630-1703 *PenDiDA 89*
Kuncl, Lawrence G. 1938- *St&PR 91*
Kundahl, George Gustavus 1940- *WhoAm 90*
Kundakci, Vace 1952- *WhoE 91*
Kunde, Robert William 1928- *St&PR 91*
Kundel, Harold Louis 1933- *WhoAm 90*
Kundell, Linda *ODwPR 91*
Kundera, Milan *BioIn 16*
Kundera, Milan 1929- *EuWr 13*, *MajTwCW*, *WhoWor 91*
Kundert, Alice E. 1920- *WhoAm 90*
Kundert, David Jon 1942- *St&PR 91*
Kundsin, Ruth Blumfeld 1916- *WhoAmW 91*
Kundtz, Ewald Edmund, III 1953- *BiDrAPA 89*
Kundtz, John Andrew 1933- *WhoAm 90*
Kundtz, Lee R. 1932- *St&PR 91*
Kundu, Ambares 1945- *WhoWor 91*
Kundu, Anjana 1946- *BiDrAPA 89*
Kundur, Prabha Shankar 1939- *WhoAm 90*
Kunel, Larry Gene 1938- *St&PR 91*
Kunemund, Stephen George 1950- *WhoEmL 91*
Kunen, James Simon 1948- *WhoE 91*
Kuner, Jakob 1692-1764 *PenDiDA 89*
Kunert, Gunter 1929- *BioIn 16*
Kunes, Daniel Joseph 1937- *St&PR 91*
Kunev, Nicola V *BiDrAPA 89*
Kung, Chao Yu *BiDrAPA 89*
Kung, Edward Y. 1934- *St&PR 91*
Kung, Hans *MajTwCW*
Kung, Hans 1928- *WhoWor 91*
Kung, Jeffrey 1939- *WhoE 91*
Kung, Patrick C. 1947- *St&PR 91*
Kung, Patrick Chung-Shu 1947- *WhoE 91*, *WhoEmL 91*
Kung, Philip Yue-Fei 1947- *WhoWor 91*
Kung, Shain-dow 1935- *WhoWor 91*
Kung, Sun-Yuan 1950- *WhoAm 90*
Kungel, Kerry L. 1948- *WhoSSW 91*
Kunhardt, Dorothy Meserve 1901-1979 *BioIn 16*
Kunhardt, Edith *AuBYP 90*, *BioIn 16*
Kunhart, Dorathy 1901-1979 *AuBYP 90*
Kunhart, Philip B. 1928- *AuBYP 90*
Kunik, Mark Edwin *BiDrAPA 89*
Kunin, Arthur *BioIn 16*
Kunin, Calvin Murray 1929- *WhoAm 90*
Kunin, Jay S. 1949- *WhoEmL 91*
Kunin, Jean E 1954- *BiDrAPA 89*
Kunin, Madeleine May 1933- *WhoAm 90*, *WhoAmW 91*, *WhoE 91*, *WhoWor 91*
Kunin, Myron *WhoAm 90*
Kunin, Richard A *BiDrAPA 89*
Kuninska-Opacka, Maria Felicyta 1918- *IntWWM 90*
Kunis, Solomon R. 1916- *ODwPR 91*
Kunisch, Robert Dietrich 1941- *St&PR 91*, *WhoAm 90*, *WhoE 91*
Kunishi, Tadao 1936- *St&PR 91*
Kunitz, Moses 1887-1978 *DcScB S2*
Kunitz, Stanley 1905- *MajTwCW*, *WorAlBi*
Kunitz, Stanley Jasspon 1905- *WhoAm 90*
Kunitzsch, Paul 1930- *WhoWor 91*
Kuniyoshi, Yasuo 1893-1953 *WhoAmA 91N*
Kunjukrishnan, Reghuvaran *BiDrAPA 89*
Kunkel, Bill 1936-1985 *Ballpl 90*
Kunkel, David Nelson 1943- *WhoAm 90*, *WhoE 91*
Kunkel, Edward T. *WhoAm 90*
Kunkel, Georgie Myrtia *WhoAmW 91*
Kunkel, Jeff 1962- *Ballpl 90*
Kunkel, Lauri *BioIn 16*
Kunkel, Louis Martens 1949- *WhoAm 90*
Kunkel, Monique P 1942- *BiDrAPA 89*
Kunkel, Robert L 1930- *BiDrAPA 89*
Kunkel, Russell J. 1942- *St&PR 91*
Kunkel, Russell Jeffrey 1942- *WhoAm 90*
Kunkel, Thomas G. 1935- *St&PR 91*
Kunkemueller, A. Henry 1935- *St&PR 91*
Kunkle, David *WhoSSW 91*
Kunkle, George M. 1953- *St&PR 91*
Kunkle, John H., Jr. 1927- *St&PR 91*
Kunkle, Mark Alan 1954- *WhoE 91*
Kunkle, Richard Laine 1930- *St&PR 91*
Kunkle, Sandra Lee 1960- *WhoAmW 91*
Kunkler, Arnold William 1921- *WhoAm 90*
Kunko, Richard F. 1954- *St&PR 91*
Kunnas, Mauri *AuBYP 90*
Kunneke, Eduard 1885-1953 *OxCPMus*
Kunnes, Richard *BiDrAPA 89*
Kuno, Hisashi 1910-1969 *DcScB S2*
Kunoff, Sharon 1932- *WhoE 91*
Kuns, Nancy Lee 1960- *WhoAmW 91*
Kunsch, Louis 1937- *WhoAmA 91*
Kunsman, David Marvin 1949- *WhoEmL 91*
Kunst, Linda F *BiDrAPA 89*
Kunst, Otto John Nicholas 1946- *WhoEmL 91*
Kunst, Robert Lance 1946- *WhoSSW 91*
Kunstadt, George H. 1922- *St&PR 91*
Kunstadter, Geraldine S. 1928- *WhoAmW 91*, *WhoE 91*, *WhoWor 91*
Kunstadter, John W. 1927- *St&PR 91*
Kunstler, David B. 1934- *WhoAm 90*
Kunstler, David Bruce 1934- *St&PR 91*
Kunstler, James Howard *BioIn 16*
Kunstler, Karl 1901-1945 *BioIn 16*
Kunstler, Morton 1931- *WhoAmA 91*, *WhoE 91*
Kunstler, William 1919- *WorAlBi*
Kunstler, William Moses 1919- *WhoAm 90*
Kunstman, Steven William 1950- *WhoEmL 91*
Kuntsch, Margarethe Susanna von 1651-1717 *EncCoWW*
Kuntz, Eric Warren 1952- *BiDrAPA 89*
Kuntz, Federico de Madrazo y 1815-1894 *BioIn 16*
Kuntz, Hal Goggan 1937- *WhoSSW 91*, *WhoWor 91*
Kuntz, James Thomas 1938- *St&PR 91*
Kuntz, Joel Dubois 1946- *WhoEmL 91*
Kuntz, L.G. 1950- *St&PR 91*
Kuntz, Marion Lucile Leathers 1924- *WhoAm 90*
Kuntz, Mary M. Kohls 1928- *WhoAmW 91*, *WhoWor 91*
Kuntz, Noella Mae 1950- *WhoAmW 91*, *WhoEmL 91*
Kuntz, Paul Grimley 1915- *WhoAm 90*
Kuntz, Richard Peter 1957- *WhoEmL 91*
Kuntz, Roger Edward 1926-1975 *WhoAmA 91N*
Kuntzelman, Michael Stephen 1950- *BiDrAPA 89*
Kuntzleman, Charles Thomas 1940- *WhoWrEP 89*
Kuntzman, Ronald 1933- *WhoAm 90*
Kunz, Charlie 1896-1958 *OxCPMus*
Kunz, David G. 1926- *St&PR 91*
Kunz, Eric Gibson 1940- *St&PR 91*
Kunz, Erich 1909- *IntWWM 90*, *PenDiMP*
Kunz, Janet Alice 1956- *WhoAmW 91*
Kunz, John P. 1934- *WhoE 91*
Kunz, Karl Ludwig 1947- *WhoWor 91*
Kunz, Larry P. *WhoAm 90*
Kunz, Lawrence Joseph *St&PR 91*
Kunz, Leonard George, Jr. 1954- *WhoE 91*
Kunz, Ludvik 1914- *IntWWM 90*
Kunz, Lyle B 1927- *BiDrAPA 89*
Kunz, Michelle Beth 1955- *WhoSSW 91*
Kunz, Phillip Ray 1936- *WhoAm 90*
Kunz, Robert Anthony 1949- *WhoSSW 91*
Kunz, Roxane Brown 1932- *BioIn 16*
Kunz, Sharon Kay 1951- *St&PR 91*
Kunz, Thomas Henry 1938- *WhoE 91*
Kunz, Willi *BioIn 16*
Kunz, William Edward 1939- *St&PR 91*
Kunze, George William 1922- *WhoAm 90*
Kunze, Hans-Joachim Dieter 1935- *WhoWor 91*
Kunze, Klaus 1933- *WhoWor 91*
Kunze, Ralph Carl 1925- *WhoAm 90*
Kunze, Reiner 1933- *WorAu 1980 [port]*
Kunze, Richard Spencer 1948- *WhoE 91*
Kunzel, Erich 1935- *PenDiMP*
Kunzel, Erich, Jr. 1935- *WhoAm 90*
Kunzig, Richard Jerome 1941- *WhoE 91*
Kunzler, John Eugene 1923- *WhoAm 90*
Kunzman, E Eugene 1937- *BiDrAPA 89*
Kuo, Anna 1951- *WhoE 91*
Kuo, Benjamin C. 1930- *WhoAm 90*
Kuo, Chang-Yang 1934- *IntWWM 90*
Kuo, Franklin F. 1934- *WhoAm 90*
Kuo, Gloria Liang-Hui 1926- *WhoWor 91*
Kuo, Kenneth K. *WhoAm 90*
Kuo, Kuan C *BiDrAPA 89*
Kuo, Ling-Cheng *BiDrAPA 89*
Kuo, Louise Ramona 1963- *WhoAmW 91*, *WhoE 91*, *WhoEmL 91*
Kuo, Nan-hung 1936- *WhoWor 91*
Kuo, Ping-chia 1908- *WhoAm 90*, *WhoWor 91*
Kuo, Shirley W. Y. 1930- *WhoWor 91*
Kuo, Wei Hua 1955- *BiDrAPA 89*
Kuo, Yue 1953- *WhoEmL 91*
Kuony, Liane *BioIn 16*
Kuopus, Clinton 1942- *WhoAmA 91*
Kupchick, Alan Charles 1942- *WhoAm 90*
Kupchik, George 1914-1989 *BioIn 16*
Kupcik, Peter F. 1923- *St&PR 91*
Kupcinet, Essee Solomon *WhoAmW 91*
Kupcinet, Irv 1912- *WhoAm 90*
Kupel, Frederick John 1929- *WhoAm 90*
Kuper, Adam Jonathan 1941- *WhoAm 90*, *WhoWor 91*
Kuper, Dennis L. 1947- *St&PR 91*
Kuper, Dennis Lee 1947- *WhoAm 90*
Kuper, Maurice R. 1924- *WhoAm 90*
Kuper, Yuri 1940- *WhoAmA 91*
Kuperman, Samuel 1953- *BiDrAPA 89*
Kuperman, Yuri *WhoAmA 91*
Kupers, Martinus Petrus 1946- *WhoWor 91*
Kupers, Terry Allen 1943- *BiDrAPA 89*
Kupersmith, A. Harry 1925- *WhoAm 90*
Kupersmith, Aaron H. 1925- *St&PR 91*
Kupersmith, Joel 1939- *WhoSSW 91*, *WhoWor 91*
Kupersmith, Judith R *BiDrAPA 89*
Kuperus, John Henry 1949- *WhoEmL 91*
Kupfer, Benneth James 1952- *WhoEmL 91*
Kupfer, Carl 1928- *WhoAm 90*
Kupfer, David J 1941- *BiDrAPA 89*
Kupfer, Harry *BioIn 16*
Kupfer, Harry 1935- *IntWWM 90*
Kupfer, Robert D. 1928- *St&PR 91*
Kupfer, Sherman 1926- *WhoAm 90*
Kupferman, Harvey S. 1935- *St&PR 91*

Kupferman, Lawrence 1909-1982 *WhoAmA 91N*
Kupferman, Meyer 1926- *IntWWM 90, WhoAm 90*
Kupferman, Murray *WhoAmA 91*
Kupferman, Theodore R. 1920- *WhoAm 90*
Kupferstein, Leon 1944- *BiDrAPA 89*
Kuphal, John Edward 1945- *St&PR 91*
Kupiec, Raymond David 1962- *WhoEmL 91*
Kupietz, Roberta 1953- *WhoAmW 91*
Kuplan, Louis 1906- *WhoAm 90*
Kupor, Robert 1946- *WhoEmL 91*
Kupper, Annelies 1906-1987 *PenDiMP*
Kupper, Annelies 1906-1988 *AnObit 1988*
Kupper, Bruce David 1952- *WhoEmL 91*
Kupper, Herbert I *BiDrAPA 89*
Kupperman, Helen Slotnick *WhoAmW 91*
Kupperman, Henry John 1957- *WhoEmL 91*
Kupperman, Jonathan M. 1958- *WhoEmL 91*
Kupperman, Louis Brandeis 1946- *WhoAm 90, WhoEmL 91*
Kupperman, Melvin 1935- *WhoAm 90*
Kupperman, Robert Harris 1935- *WhoAm 90*
Kuppers, Horst 1933- *WhoWor 91*
Kuppin, Lawrence L. 1948- *WhoAm 90*
Kuppler, Karl Brian 1956- *WhoEmL 91*
Kuppuswami, B 1907- *EncO&P 3*
Kupris, Eleanor Marie 1941- *St&PR 91*
Kupsch, Walter Oscar 1919- *WhoAm 90*
Kupst, Mary Jo 1945- *WhoAmW 91, WhoEmL 91*
Kur, Sally *ODwPR 91*
Kurabayashi, Ikushiro 1913- *WhoWor 91*
Kurachi, Tadashi 1936- *WhoWor 91*
Kurahara, Masaaki 1927- *St&PR 91*
Kurahara, Ted N 1925- *WhoAmA 91*
Kurahara, Ted Naomi 1925- *WhoE 91*
Kuralt, Charles 1934- *BioIn 16*
Kuralt, Charles Bishop 1934- *WhoAm 90, WhoE 91*
Kuralt, Thomas *St&PR 91*
Kuramata, Shiro 1934- *BioIn 16, PenDiDA 89*
Kuramoto, Roy 1927- *St&PR 91*
Kurani, Devendra 1952- *BiDrAPA 89*
Kurant, Martin J. *St&PR 91*
Kuras, Jean Mary 1944- *WhoAmW 91*
Kurasch, Teri J. 1956- *St&PR 91*
Kurasch, Teri Joyce 1956- *WhoEmL 91*
Kurat, Gero 1938- *WhoWor 91*
Kurata, Kunio 1931- *WhoWor 91*
Kurata, Yasushi 1946- *St&PR 91*
Kuratowski, Kazimierz 1896-1980 *DcScB S2*
Kurau, Robert James 1918- *St&PR 91*
Kurchatov, Igor 1903-1960 *WorAlBi*
Kurdwanowski, Jan M *BiDrAPA 89*
Kurdziel, Joseph 1938- *St&PR 91*
Kureishi, Hanif 1954- *ConLC 64 [port]*
Kurek, Dolores Bodnar 1935- *WhoAmW 91*
Kurelek, William 1927-1977 *AuBYP 90, WhoAmA 91N*
Kurella, Thomas Kevin 1946- *WhoSSW 91*
Kurens, Hope Laurie *BiDrAPA 89*
Kures, Ken M. 1948- *St&PR 91*
Kuretsky, Susan Donahue 1941- *WhoAm 90*
Kurey, Robert J *BiDrAPA 89*
Kurfees, Donald Bryson 1933- *St&PR 91*
Kurfehs, Harold Charles 1939- *WhoWor 91*
Kurhajec, Joseph A 1938- *WhoAmA 91*
Kuri, Angel Fernando 1950- *WhoWor 91*
Kurian, Leslie David 1941- *BiDrAPA 89*
Kurian, Milton *BiDrAPA 89*
Kurian, Verghese 1934- *WhoWor 91*
Kuriansky, Judith 1947- *ConAu 132*
Kuriansky, Judy 1947- *WhoAmW 91*
Kuric, Joan M *BiDrAPA 89*
Kurie, Andrew Edmunds 1932- *WhoSSW 91*
Kurien, Biji Kurien 1940- *WhoWor 91*
Kurien, Santha T. 1945- *WhoE 91*
Kurien, Santha Thomas *BiDrAPA 89*
Kurihara, Tat 1952- *WhoSSW 91*
Kurilecz, Michael, Jr. 1953- *WhoSSW 91*
Kurimoto, Soji 1930- *WhoWor 91*
Kurinsky, Emil Matthew 1948- *St&PR 91*
Kurisky, George A. 1937- *St&PR 91*
Kurit, Neil 1940- *WhoAm 90*
Kurita, Chushiro 1910- *WhoWor 91*
Kurita, Jin 1949- *WhoWor 91*
Kurita, Osamu 1930- *WhoWor 91*
Kuritsky, M.M. 1920- *St&PR 91*
Kurka, Donald Frank 1930- *WhoAmA 91*
Kurka, George Joseph, Jr. 1940- *WhoSSW 91*
Kurke, David Samuel 1955- *WhoE 91*
Kurke, Kathleen Tighe 1958- *WhoAmW 91*
Kurke, Lewis 1929- *BiDrAPA 89*
Kurkela, Kauko Oiva Antero 1941- *WhoWor 91*
Kurki, Lauri J., Jr. 1931- *St&PR 91*
Kurki, Marja Leena 1939- *WhoWor 91*
Kurkjian, Gregory Arthur, Jr. 1936- *St&PR 91*
Kurkjian, Stephen A 1943- *ConAu 129*
Kurkjian, Stephen Anoosh 1943- *WhoAm 90*
Kurko, Michael C. 1942- *St&PR 91*
Kurkul, Edward W. 1928- *St&PR 91*
Kurkul, Stephan H. 1946- *St&PR 91*
Kurlan, Marvin Zeft 1934- *WhoE 91, WhoWor 91*
Kurland, Albert A 1914- *BiDrAPA 89*
Kurland, Elissa Ruth 1961- *WhoEmL 91*
Kurland, Emmanuel 1906- *St&PR 91*
Kurland, Howard D 1934- *BiDrAPA 89*
Kurland, Leon Irwin 1941- *WhoE 91, WhoWor 91*
Kurland, Leonard J. 1925- *St&PR 91*
Kurland, Michael 1938- *BioIn 16, SpyFic*
Kurland, Morton D 1934- *BiDrAPA 89*
Kurland, Morton L 1932- *BiDrAPA 89*
Kurland, Philip B. 1921- *WhoAm 90*
Kurland, Rayfield B. 1929- *St&PR 91*
Kurland, Richard M. 1953- *St&PR 91*
Kurland, Stacey Blair 1955- *BiDrAPA 89*
Kurlander, Carl Litman 1959- *WhoEmL 91*
Kurlander, Honey W *WhoAmA 91*
Kurlander, Leroy F *BiDrAPA 89*
Kurlander, Richard Alan *BioIn 16*
Kurlansky, Louis Sandy *BiDrAPA 89*
Kurlansky, Mervyn 1936- *ConDes 90*
Kurlowicz, Theodore Thomas 1953- *WhoEmL 91*
Kurmann, Robert C. 1947- *St&PR 91*
Kurnit, Paul David 1948- *WhoAm 90*
Kurnit, Richard Alan 1951- *WhoEmL 91*
Kurnit, Shepard 1924- *WhoAm 90, WhoE 91*
Kurnitz, Harry *TwCCr&M 91*
Kurnow, Ernest 1912- *WhoAm 90*
Kuroda, Makoto 1932- *WhoWor 91*
Kuroda, Sige-Yuki 1934- *WhoAm 90*
Kuroda, Tatsuaki 1955- *WhoWor 91*
Kuroiwa, Yutaka 1910- *WhoWor 91*
Kurokawa, Kisho 1934- *WhoWor 91*
Kurokawa, Yoshiteru 1933- *WhoWor 91*
Kuromatsu, Tomokiyo 1948- *WhoE 91*
Kuropat, Rosemary Louise 1958- *WhoAmW 91*
Kurosawa Akira 1910- *EncJap*
Kurosawa, Akira 1910- *BioIn 16, News 91-1 [port], WhoWor 91*
Kurosawa, Kazukiyo 1926- *WhoWor 91*
Kurosky, Alexander 1938- *WhoAm 90*
Kurowski, B. *St&PR 91*
Kurowski, Theodore G. 1929- *St&PR 91*
Kurowski, Whitey 1918- *Ballpl 90*
Kuroyanagi, Tetsuko 1934- *WhoWor 91*
Kurra, Sureshbabu *BiDrAPA 89*
Kurras, Herbert L. 1932- *St&PR 91*
Kurre, James Anthony 1951- *WhoE 91*
Kurreck, Harry 1932- *WhoWor 91*
Kurrelmeyer, Louis Hayner 1928- *WhoE 91, WhoWor 91*
Kurri, Jari 1960- *WhoAm 90, WorAlBi*
Kurrus, Thomas William 1947- *WhoEmL 91*
Kurschner, Robert Rudolph 1935- *St&PR 91*
Kursel, Marcy Ann 1953- *WhoWrEP 89*
Kursh, H. David *St&PR 91*
Kursh, Raymond J. *St&PR 91*
Kursman, Jerome 1921- *St&PR 91*
Kursman, Peter Jed 1952- *St&PR 91*
Kursunoglu, Behram N. 1922- *WhoAm 90, WhoWor 91*
Kurt, Joanne Leslie *BiDrAPA 89*
Kurtag, Gyorgy 1926- *IntWWM 90, PenDiMP A*
Kurten, Bjoern 1924-1988 *SmATA 64*
Kurth, Carl Ferdinand 1928- *WhoAm 90*
Kurth, Carol Lynn 1948- *WhoAmW 91*
Kurth, Clarence J *BiDrAPA 89*
Kurth, Dick *BioIn 16*
Kurth, Frederick W 1928- *BiDrAPA 89*
Kurth, John Herman, Jr. 1958- *WhoEmL 91*
Kurth, Juliette Elizabeth 1960- *WhoAmW 91*
Kurth, Lieselotte 1923- *WhoAm 90*
Kurth, Sidney Charles 1955- *WhoWor 91*
Kurth, Tammie Elaine 1960- *WhoAmW 91*
Kurth, Walter Richard 1932- *WhoAm 90*
Kurth-Voigt, Lieselotte E. 1923- *BioIn 16*
Kurtin, Stephen L. 1944- *St&PR 91*
Kurtis, Leslie 1916- *BiDrAPA 89*
Kurtis, William Horton 1940- *WhoAm 90*
Kurtts, Mary Alta 1936- *WhoWor 91*
Kurtz, Anthony D. 1929- *St&PR 91*
Kurtz, Barbara Brandon 1941- *WhoAmW 91*
Kurtz, Bruce D 1943- *WhoAmA 91*
Kurtz, Bruce Edward 1936- *WhoAm 90*
Kurtz, Carmen *EncCoWW*
Kurtz, Carol Deanne 1956- *WhoAmW 91*
Kurtz, Charles Jewett, III 1940- *WhoWor 91*
Kurtz, David Corey 1938- *WhoSSW 91*
Kurtz, Dolores May 1933- *WhoAmW 91*
Kurtz, Donald R. 1930- *St&PR 91*
Kurtz, Edwin Bernard 1926- *WhoSSW 91*
Kurtz, Efrem 1900- *IntWWM 90, PenDiMP*
Kurtz, Elaine 1928- *WhoAmA 91*
Kurtz, Eugene Allen 1923- *IntWWM 90*
Kurtz, F. Anthony 1941- *St&PR 91*
Kurtz, Gary Douglas 1940- *WhoAm 90*
Kurtz, Gladys Fish *BiDrAPA 89*
Kurtz, Grant Wilson 1942- *St&PR 91*
Kurtz, Hyman 1929- *BiDrAPA 89*
Kurtz, James Eugene 1928- *WhoE 91*
Kurtz, Jerome 1931- *WhoAm 90*
Kurtz, Joel Barry 1944- *WhoE 91, WhoWor 91*
Kurtz, John Charles 1951- *WhoSSW 91*
Kurtz, John R. 1930- *St&PR 91*
Kurtz, Joseph H 1940- *BiDrAPA 89*
Kurtz, Jules 1914- *St&PR 91*
Kurtz, Karen Barbara 1948- *WhoAmW 91, WhoEmL 91, WhoWor 91*
Kurtz, Kenneth R. 1946- *St&PR 91*
Kurtz, Kevin John *BiDrAPA 89*
Kurtz, Larry 1950- *ODwPR 91*
Kurtz, Lloyd Sherer, Jr. 1934- *WhoAm 90*
Kurtz, Marcia Lynn 1956- *WhoEmL 91*
Kurtz, Mary Jo Sabik 1963- *WhoE 91*
Kurtz, Max 1920- *WhoE 91*
Kurtz, Maxine 1921- *WhoAmW 91*
Kurtz, Michael Earl 1940- *WhoSSW 91*
Kurtz, Michael L. 1941- *WhoSSW 91*
Kurtz, Myers Richard 1924- *WhoAm 90, WhoSSW 91*
Kurtz, Myra Berman 1945- *WhoAmW 91*
Kurtz, Neil Michael 1950- *BiDrAPA 89*
Kurtz, Olga Bechkowiak 1929- *WhoAmW 91*
Kurtz, Patti Joan 1957- *WhoWrEP 89*
Kurtz, Paul 1925- *EncPaPR 91, WhoAm 90, WhoE 91, WhoWor 91*
Kurtz, Robert Arthur 1943- *WhoSSW 91*
Kurtz, Robert Irwin 1939- *BiDrAPA 89*
Kurtz, Samuel Mordecai 1904- *WhoAm 90*
Kurtz, Sheldon Francis 1943- *WhoAm 90*
Kurtz, Stephen J. 1936- *St&PR 91*
Kurtz, Steven Peter 1954- *St&PR 91*
Kurtz, Swoosie *WhoAm 90, WhoAmW 91*
Kurtz, Theresa Ann 1951- *BiDrAPA 89*
Kurtz, Thomas Eugene 1928- *WhoAm 90*
Kurtz, Thomas Gordon 1941- *WhoAm 90*
Kurtzberg, Richard L. 1938- *WhoE 91*
Kurtze, Crystal Catherine 1949- *WhoAmW 91, WhoEmL 91*
Kurtze, Crystal Catherine Gard 1949- *WhoWrEP 89*
Kurtzig, Sandra L. *BioIn 16*
Kurtzig, Sandra L. 1946- *WhoAm 90, WhoAmW 91*
Kurtzke, John Francis, Sr. 1926- *WhoAm 90*
Kurtzman, Alan *WhoAm 90*
Kurtzman, Allan Roger 1933- *WhoAm 90*
Kurtzman, Clifford Roger 1959- *WhoSSW 91*
Kurtzman, Harvey 1924- *BioIn 16, EncACom*
Kurtzman, Howard Marc 1951- *BiDrAPA 89*
Kurtzman, Joel 1947- *ConAu 30NR*
Kurtzman, Neil A. 1936- *WhoAm 90, WhoWor 91*
Kurtzman, Zvi 1947- *St&PR 91*
Kurucz, Anna Maria 1926- *BiDrAPA 89*
Kurucz, Donald Michael 1939- *St&PR 91*
Kurucz, Janos 1924- *BiDrAPA 89*
Kurucz, John 1930- *WhoAm 90*
Kurumado, Minoru 1919- *WhoWor 91*
Kurup, Siva Prasad 1937- *BiDrAPA 89*
Kurusu, Munetaka 1920- *WhoWor 91*
Kurutz, Andrew Stephen 1952- *WhoEmL 91*
Kuruvilla, Kurien *BiDrAPA 89*
Kury, Franklin Leo 1936- *WhoAm 90*
Kuryk, David Neal 1947- *WhoEmL 91*
Kurylko, Bohdan I. 1928- *St&PR 91*
Kurylo, Carolyn Kreiter 1946- *WhoWrEP 89*
Kuryluk, Ewa 1946- *WhoAmA 91*
Kuryokhin, Sergey *BioIn 16*
Kurys, Diane 1949- *ConTFT 8*
Kurz, Carolyn Jane Heppler 1946- *WhoSSW 91*
Kurz, Clarence John 1918- *WhoSSW 91*
Kurz, Diana *WhoAmA 91, WhoE 91*
Kurz, Edward A. 1926- *St&PR 91*
Kurz, Edward Philip 1921- *WhoWor 91*
Kurz, George Edward 1948- *WhoSSW 91*
Kurz, Gertrude Alice *WhoAmA 91N*
Kurz, Herbert 1920- *St&PR 91*
Kurz, Herbert 1940- *WhoAm 90*
Kurz, Isolde 1853-1944 *BioIn 16, EncCoWW*
Kurz, Ivan 1947- *IntWWM 90*
Kurz, Jean-Francois *BioIn 16*
Kurz, Jerry Bruce 1949- *WhoWor 91*
Kurz, Joseph Louis 1933- *WhoAm 90*
Kurz, Kenneth William 1955- *St&PR 91*
Kurz, Mitchell Howard 1951- *WhoAm 90*
Kurz, Mordecai 1934- *WhoAm 90*
Kurz, Ron 1940- *WhoWrEP 89*
Kurz, Rudolph Friedrich 1818-1871 *WhNaAH*
Kurz, Selma 1874-1933 *PenDiMP*
Kurz, William Charles Frederick 1942- *WhoAm 90*
Kurz, William W. *St&PR 91*
Kurzban, Ira 1949- *BioIn 16*
Kurzban, Stanley A. *BioIn 16*
Kurzbard, Gary 1944- *WhoE 91*
Kurzeja, Ronald 1949- *St&PR 91*
Kurzman, Dan 1927- *ConAu 32NR*
Kurzman, Robert Graham 1932- *WhoAm 90, WhoE 91*
Kurzman, Stephen Alan 1945- *WhoE 91*
Kurzrock, Razelle 1954- *WhoAmW 91*
Kurzweg, Ulrich Hermann 1936- *WhoAm 90*
Kurzweil, Edith *WhoAm 90, WhoAmW 91*
Kurzweil, Harvey 1945- *WhoEmL 91*
Kurzweil, Raymond *BioIn 16*
Kurzweil, Raymond C. 1948- *WhoAm 90, WhoEmL 91*
Kusalic, Maria *BiDrAPA 89*
Kusama, Haruo *BiDrAPA 89*
Kusama, Yayoi 1929- *WhoAm 90, WhoAmA 91*
Kusan, Ivan 1933- *AuBYP 90*
Kusar, Daniel D. 1928- *St&PR 91*
Kusch, Polykarp 1911- *WhoAm 90, WhoSSW 91, WhoWor 91*
Kusche, Benno 1916- *IntWWM 90, PenDiMP*
Kusche, Herbert R. 1921- *St&PR 91*
Kusche, Lawrence David 1940- *EncO&P 3*
Kuschinsky, Klaus U. 1939- *WhoWor 91*
Kuse, James Russell 1930- *WhoAm 90, WhoSSW 91*
Kusek, Carol Joan 1955- *WhoAmW 91*
Kusek, John Martin 1952- *WhoEmL 91*
Kuser, Daniel M. 1944- *St&PR 91*
Kuser, James Kerney, II 1960- *WhoEmL 91*
Kuserk, Frank Thomas 1951- *WhoE 91*
Kush, Charles Andrew, III 1964- *WhoE 91*
Kush, Emil 1916-1969 *Ballpl 90*
Kushel, Glenn Elliot 1945- *WhoEmL 91*
Kusheloff, David Leon 1917- *WhoAm 90*
Kushen, Allan Stanford 1929- *St&PR 91, WhoAm 90*
Kushen, Betty Sandra 1933- *WhoE 91*
Kushi, Francis Xavier 1938- *WhoE 91*
Kushi, Michio 1926- *NewAgE 90*
Kushlan, Isabel Jane 1954- *WhoE 91*
Kushlan, Samuel Daniel 1912- *WhoAm 90*
Kushmeider, Rose Marie 1956- *WhoE 91*
Kushnar, Denise Margaret 1957- *WhoAmW 91*
Kushner, Adam Mark 1959- *WhoEmL 91*
Kushner, Allen M. 1931- *St&PR 91*
Kushner, Barry 1941- *St&PR 91*
Kushner, Barry 1946- *WhoE 91*
Kushner, David Zakeri 1935- *IntWWM 90, WhoAm 90*
Kushner, Donald *St&PR 91*
Kushner, Donn 1927- *BioIn 16*
Kushner, Donna Marie *BiDrAPA 89*
Kushner, Dorothy Browdy *WhoAmA 91*
Kushner, Edward I 1925- *BiDrAPA 89*
Kushner, Eva 1929- *WhoAm 90, WhoAmW 91*
Kushner, Gail Lori 1953- *WhoEmL 91*
Kushner, Gary Gerald *BiDrAPA 89*
Kushner, Geri Lynn 1959- *WhoEmL 91*
Kushner, Harold Joseph 1933- *WhoAm 90*
Kushner, Harold S. 1935- *BioIn 16*
Kushner, Harvey D. 1930- *St&PR 91*
Kushner, Harvey David 1930- *WhoAm 90*
Kushner, James A 1945- *ConAu 132*
Kushner, James Alan 1945- *WhoEmL 91*
Kushner, Jeffrey L. 1948- *St&PR 91, WhoAm 90*
Kushner, Jill Menkes 1951- *SmATA 62*
Kushner, Lawrence Maurice 1924- *WhoAm 90*
Kushner, Michael James 1951- *WhoE 91*
Kushner, Robert Arnold 1935- *St&PR 91, WhoAm 90*
Kushner, Robert Ellis 1949- *WhoAm 90, WhoAmA 91, WhoE 91*
Kushner, Rose *BioIn 16*
Kushner, Rose *NewYTBS 90*
Kushner, Rose 1929-1990 *ConAu 130, WhoE 91*
Kushner, Stephanie Kenyon 1955- *St&PR 91*
Kushner, Stuart F. *BiDrAPA 89*
Kushnir, Frederick Theodore 1933- *St&PR 91*
Kushon, Donald John, Jr. *BiDrAPA 89*
Kushtiwala, Nasir Usman *WhoWor 91*
Kusick, Craig 1948- *Ballpl 90*
Kusiewicz, Piotr 1953- *IntWWM 90*

Kusisto, Kathryn Haas 1958- *WhoAmW 91*
Kusisto, Oscar Perry 1915- *WhoWor 91*
Kuska, Edward Arthur 1937- *WhoWor 91*
Kuske, Edward Alan 1940- *WhoE 91*
Kuskie, Patricia Lynn 1953- *WhoAmW 91*
Kuskin, Gary S. 1950- *St&PR 91*
Kuskin, Karla 1932- *WhoAm 90, WhoWrEP 89*
Kuskin, Karla Seidman 1932- *AuBYP 90*
Kusler, Duane Allan 1963- *WhoEmL 91*
Kusler, James O'Dell 1947- *WhoAm 90*
Kusler, Janet L. *BiDrAPA 89*
Kusler, Rex Ernest 1952- *WhoWrEP 89*
Kusnerz, Peggy Ann F 1947- *WhoAmA 91*
Kusnetzov, Howard 1942- *WhoE 91*
Kuspit, Donald Burton 1935- *WhoAm 90, WhoAmA 91*
Kuss, Henry J., Jr. 1922-1990 *NewYTBS 90 [port]*
Kuss, Kathy *BioIn 16*
Kuss, Mark Davis 1956- *WhoEmL 91*
Kuss, Richard L. 1923- *WhoAm 90*
Kuss, Steve *BioIn 16*
Kussel, William Ferdinand, Jr. 1957- *WhoWor 91*
Kusserow, Richard Phillip 1940- *WhoAm 90*
Kussin, Dennis Joseph *BiDrAPA 89*
Kussman, Ardys Ann 1948- *St&PR 91, WhoAmW 91*
Kust, Leonard E. 1917-1989 *BioIn 16*
Kuster, Antonio Carlos 1955- *WhoWor 91*
Kuster, Friedrich Otto 1938- *WhoWor 91*
Kuster, Gordon I 1941- *BiDrAPA 89*
Kuster, William Walter, Jr. 1955- *WhoE 91, WhoEmL 91*
Kustes, John Thomas 1950- *St&PR 91*
Kustin, Kenneth 1934- *WhoAm 90*
Kustron, Konnie Gerlyn 1954- *WhoAmW 91*
Kusuda, Misao *BiDrAPA 89*
Kusui, Toshiroh 1932- *WhoWor 91*
Kusulas, Elias P. 1940- *St&PR 91*
Kusumi, Yoshitaro *BiDrAPA 89*
Kusunoki Masahige *EncJap*
Kusuoka, Hideo 1950- *WhoWor 91*
Kusy, Robert Peter 1947- *WhoSSW 91*
Kuta, Jeffrey Theodore 1947- *WhoEmL 91*
Kutasi, Katalin Erzsebet 1956- *WhoAmW 91, WhoE 91*
Kutch, John Thomas 1954- *WhoEmL 91*
Kutcher, Mark *BiDrAPA 89*
Kutcher, Randy 1960- *Ballpl 90*
Kutcher, Robert A. 1950- *WhoEmL 91*
Kutchin, Edward David 1953- *WhoEmL 91*
Kutchin, Jill 1952- *St&PR 91*
Kutchin, Joseph W. 1928- *ODwPR 91*
Kutchin, Joseph William 1928- *St&PR 91*
Kutchins, Michael Joseph 1941- *WhoAm 90*
Kuten, Jay *BiDrAPA 89*
Kuthen, Hans-Werner 1938- *IntWWM 90*
Kuthy, Arnold Robert 1932- *WhoE 91*
Kutka, Anne *WhoAmA 91*
Kutko, Rostyslaw Josaphat 1944- *St&PR 91*
Kutler, Stanley Ira 1934- *WhoAm 90*
Kutler, Stephanie Lynn *BiDrAPA 89*
Kutman, Mehmet 1960- *WhoSSW 91*
Kutner, Dorothy G. *St&PR 91*
Kutner, Janet 1937- *WhoAmA 91*
Kutney, James Peter 1932- *WhoAm 90*
Kutnick, Joel 1941- *BiDrAPA 89*
Kutorgiene-Buivydaite, Elena 1888-1963 *BioIn 16*
Kutrieb, Ronald E. 1942- *St&PR 91*
Kutrzeba, Joseph Stanislaw 1927- *WhoAm 90*
Kuts, Vladimir *BioIn 16*
Kutsch, Clifford Dale 1930- *St&PR 91*
Kutschbach, James William, Sr. 1923- *St&PR 91*
Kutscher, Eugene Bernard 1947- *WhoE 91*
Kutshamakin *WhNaAH*
Kutsumi, Fusako 1890-1980 *BioIn 16*
Kutta, Phyllis 1927- *St&PR 91*
Kutten, Lawrence Joseph 1953- *WhoE 91*
Kutter, Peter 1930- *WhoWor 91*
Kuttler, Carl Martin, Jr. 1940- *WhoAm 90*
Kuttler, James Robert 1941- *WhoE 91*
Kuttler, Wolfgang 1936- *WhoWor 91*
Kuttner, Bernard A. 1934- *WhoWor 91*
Kuttner, Charles H 1947- *BiDrAPA 89*
Kuttner, Fritz A. 1903- *IntWWM 90*
Kuttner, Henry 1915-1958 *RGTwCSF*
Kuttner, Ludwig G. 1946- *WhoSSW 91*
Kuttner, Michael *PenDiMP*
Kuttner, Michael 1953- *WhoWor 91*
Kuttner, Paul 1931- *ConAu 30NR, WhoWrEP 89*
Kutty, Ittamveetil N 1944- *BiDrAPA 89*
Kutty, Kesavan 1949- *WhoEmL 91*
Kutuzov, Mikhail 1745-1813 *WorAlBi*
Kutyna, Marty 1932- *Ballpl 90*
Kutz, Elizabeth Ann Grady 1954- *IntWWM 90*
Kutz, Joseph Edward 1928- *WhoAm 90*
Kutz, Kenneth John 1926- *WhoAm 90*
Kutz, Myer Paul 1939- *WhoAm 90, WhoWrEP 89*
Kutz, Robert H. 1943- *WhoWor 91*
Kutzen, Jerome Jefferies 1923- *St&PR 91*
Kutzen, Peggy Duke 1951- *St&PR 91*
Kutzer, Dennis Jan 1949- *BiDrAPA 89*
Kutzer, Jane Degenhardt 1958- *WhoAmA 91*
Kutzin, Lawrence M. 1952- *St&PR 91*
Kutzin, Milton 1917- *St&PR 91*
Kutzler, John D. 1948- *St&PR 91*
Kutzmark, George F. 1928- *St&PR 91*
Kutzscher, Bernd Michael 1950- *WhoEmL 91*
Kuulling, Ruedi 1935- *WhoWor 91*
Kuusinen, Otto Vil'gel'movich 1881-1964 *BioIn 16*
Kuusisto, Karla Ann *BiDrAPA 89*
Kuvalayananda, Swami 1883-1966 *EncO&P 3*
Kuvin, Seymour F 1924- *BiDrAPA 89, WhoE 91*
Kuvshinoff, Bertha Horne *WhoAmA 91*
Kuvshinoff, Nicolai *WhoAmA 91*
Kuwabara, Dennis Matsuichi 1945- *WhoWor 91*
Kuwahara, Mitsunori 1936- *WhoWor 91*
Kuwaski, Rex S. 1928- *St&PR 91*
Kuwayama, George 1925- *WhoAm 90, WhoAmA 91*
Kuwayama, Tadaaki 1932- *WhoAmA 91, WhoE 91*
Kuwik, Robert Alfred 1946- *BiDrAPA 89*
Kux, Dennis Henry 1931- *WhoAm 90, WhoWor 91*
Kuyatt, Chris Ernie Earl 1930- *WhoAm 90*
Kuyers, David J. 1949- *St&PR 91*
Kuyers, David Jon 1949- *WhoAm 90, WhoEmL 91*
Kuykendal, Robert Lee 1945- *BiDrAPA 89*
Kuykendall, Crystal Arlene 1949- *WhoAmW 91*
Kuykendall, John Wells 1938- *WhoAm 90*
Kuykendall, Ronald Edward 1952- *WhoEmL 91*
Kuykendall, Theodore Cramor 1947- *St&PR 91*
Kuyler, Pauline Lorvan 1937- *BiDrAPA 89*
Kuyper, Joan Carolyn 1941- *WhoAmW 91, WhoE 91*
Kuyper, Vicki Jean 1956- *WhoWrEP 89*
Kuzava, Bob 1923- *Ballpl 90*
Kuzbari, Nabil Rafik 1936- *WhoWor 91*
Kuzbyt, Robert *ODwPR 91*
Kuzell, William Charles 1914- *WhoAm 90*
Kuzina, Jan Celeste 1956- *WhoAmW 91*
Kuzma, David Richard 1945- *St&PR 91*
Kuzma, Gregory Paul 1950- *St&PR 91*
Kuzmak, Lubomyr Ihor 1931- *WhoWor 91*
Kuzmin, Mikhail 1872?-1936 *TwCLC 40 [port]*
Kuzminski, Lawrence N. 1941- *St&PR 91*
Kuzmych, Christina 1954- *IntWWM 90*
Kuznecoff, Irene Cecilia 1937- *WhoAmW 91*
Kuznesof, Paul Martin 1941- *WhoE 91*
Kuznets, Simon *BioIn 16*
Kuznetsoff family *PenDiDA 89*
Kuznetsov, Pavel Varfolomeevich 1878-1968 *BioIn 16*
Kuznetsov, Vasilii Vasil'evich 1901-1990 *BioIn 16*
Kuznetsov, Vasily V. 1901-1990 *NewYTBS 90 [port]*
Kuznetsova, Maria 1880-1966 *PenDiMP*
Kuznetzov, Vassili V 1901-1990 *CurBio 90N*
Kuznik, Mary Elizabeth 1955- *WhoEmL 91*
Kuznik, Robert William 1947- *WhoEmL 91*
Kuzwayo, Ellen 1914- *FemiCLE*
Kvalseth, Tarald Oddvar 1938- *WhoAm 90*
Kvamme, Peder 1918- *St&PR 91*
Kvapil, Radoslav 1934- *IntWWM 90, PenDiMP*
Kvasnicka, Joseph G. *St&PR 91N*
Kvasnicka, Joseph G. *BioIn 16*
Kvasnicka, Lad 1944- *St&PR 91* .
Kvech, Otomar 1950- *IntWWM 90*
Kvederis, Kathryn Anne *BiDrAPA 89*
Kvederis, Paul M. *ODwPR 91*
Kvenvold, Tony Mark 1956- *WhoE 91, WhoEmL 91, WhoWor 91*
Kveton, Charles J. 1928- *St&PR 91*
Kvitsinsky, Yuli A. 1936- *WhoWor 91*
Kwa, Chunglin 1953- *WhoWor 91*
Kwa, Raymond Pain-Boon 1944- *WhoE 91, WhoWor 91*
Kwait, Andrew 1949- *BiDrAPA 89*
Kwak, Byong-sun 1942- *WhoWor 91*
Kwak, Hoon 1941- *WhoAmA 91*
Kwak, Myung Sook *BiDrAPA 89*
Kwak, Syng Yong 1945- *BiDrAPA 89*
Kwall, Jeffrey Louis 1955- *WhoEmL 91*
Kwalwasser, Amy 1956- *WhoEmL 91*
Kwalwasser, Amy Sue 1956- *WhoWrEP 89*
Kwalwasser, Helen 1927- *IntWWM 90*
Kwamena-Poh, M 1932- *ConAu 132*
Kwamie, Yosef Kwaku 1951- *BiDrAPA 89*
Kwan, Hoi Shan 1952- *WhoWor 91*
Kwan, Kian Moon 1929- *WhoAm 90*
Kwan, Nancy 1938- *BioIn 16*
Kwan-Kisaichi, Shirley 1958- *WhoAmW 91, WhoEmL 91*
Kwandt, Joanne 1944- *WhoAmW 91*
Kwapien, Frederic J *BiDrAPA 89*
Kwapil, William Joseph, Jr. 1943- *St&PR 91*
Kwarara, Galeva 1942- *WhoWor 91*
Kwasha, H. Charles 1906- *St&PR 91, WhoWor 91*
Kwasizur, John Michael 1939- *St&PR 91*
Kwasnick, Paul Jack 1925- *WhoAm 90*
Kwasnick, Raymond Mark 1949- *WhoEmL 91*
Kwasnicki, Stanley F. 1936- *St&PR 91*
Kwasnik, Joseph Robert 1951- *St&PR 91*
Kwasnofski, Michele E. 1967- *WhoEmL 91*
Kwass, Sidney J. 1908- *WhoSSW 91*
Kwass, Stephen K *BiDrAPA 89*
Kwei, Gloria Yung Ching 1943- *WhoAmW 91*
Kwek, Kelvin Kusnardy 1953- *WhoWor 91*
Kwella, Patrizia 1953- *IntWWM 90*
Kwentus, Joseph Allen 1946- *BiDrAPA 89*
Kwestel, Sidney *WhoAm 90*
Kwiat, Arthur 1941- *St&PR 91*
Kwiat, Joseph J. *WhoAm 90*
Kwiat, Kenneth Bernard 1939- *St&PR 91*
Kwiatkowska, Barbara Jolanta *IntWWM 90*
Kwiatkowski, Alan Paul 1940- *St&PR 91*
Kwiatkowski, Anne Susan 1955- *WhoAmW 91*
Kwiatkowski, Deborah Ann 1965- *WhoAmW 91*
Kwiatkowski, Diana J. 1958- *WhoWrEP 89*
Kwiatkowski, Edward Louis 1950- *St&PR 91*
Kwiatkowski, Fernando D. 1955- *BiDrAPA 89*
Kwiatkowski, Stanley John 1930- *St&PR 91*
Kwiatkowski, Thomas David 1941- *St&PR 91*
Kwiecinski, Chester Martin 1924- *WhoAmA 91*
Kwiedorowicz, Laurie Ann 1957- *WhoEmL 91*
Kwiker, Louis A. 1935- *WhoAm 90*
Kwinn, David 1945- *WhoEmL 91*
Kwiram, Alvin L. 1937- *WhoAm 90*
Kwit, Robert Baxter *BiDrAPA 89*
Kwock, Laureen C. 1951- *WhoWrEP 89*
Kwoh, Theodore Jesse 1951- *WhoEmL 91*
Kwok, Ka Cheong Alex 1950- *WhoWor 91*
Kwok, Yen Mee 1947- *WhoEmL 91*
Kwon, Chul Soo 1948- *BiDrAPA 89*
Kwon, In-Won 1933- *BiDrAPA 89*
Kwon, Kang 1943- *BiDrAPA 89*
Kwon, Young Jo *BiDrAPA 89*
Kwong, Bengie Man-Hang 1948- *WhoWor 91*
Kwong, Eva 1954- *WhoAmA 91*
Kwong, Peter Kong Kit 1936- *WhoWor 91*
Kwong, Stephen T. *St&PR 91*
Kwong, Yui-Hoi Harris 1957- *WhoE 91*
Kwun, Kyung Whan 1929- *WhoAm 90*
Ky-Yo-Kosi *DcCanB 12*
Kya-Hill, Robert 1930- *DrBIPA 90*
Kyburg, Henry Guy Ely, Jr. 1928- *WhoAm 90*
Kyd, Charles William 1948- *WhoEmL 91, WhoWrEP 89*
Kyd, Marilyn Gratton 1948- *WhoEmL 91, WhoWrEP 89*
Kyd, Thomas 1558-1594 *BioIn 16, WorAlBi*
Kyd, Thomas 1901-1976 *TwCCr&M 91*
Kydan, Manfred 1911- *BiDrAPA 89*
Kydd, Frances Shand *BioIn 16*
Kyger, Jack Adolphus 1915- *WhoAm 90*
Kyger, Kent 1931- *BiDrAPA 89*
Kyhl, Curtis Daniel 1937- *St&PR 91*
Kyhl, Robert Louis 1917- *WhoAm 90*
Kyhn, K.C.T. *PenDiDA 89*
Kyhos, Thomas Flynn 1947- *WhoE 91*
Kyi, Khin May *BiDrAPA 89*
Kyker, Christine White 1925- *WhoSSW 91*
Kyl, John Henry 1919- *WhoAm 90*
Kyl, Jon Llewellyn 1942- *WhoAm 90*
Kyle, Andrew Crockett, III 1945- *WhoSSW 91*
Kyle, Donald Gordon 1950- *WhoSSW 91*
Kyle, Duncan *ConAu 31NR*
Kyle, Duncan 1930- *SpyFic, TwCCr&M 91*
Kyle, Elisabeth *AuBYP 90*
Kyle, Frank Ray 1947- *WhoSSW 91*
Kyle, Frederick W. 1932- *WhoAm 90*
Kyle, Jerry L. 1941- *St&PR 91*
Kyle, John Hamilton 1925- *WhoAm 90*
Kyle, Karen Margaret 1960- *BiDrAPA 89*
Kyle, Mary J. *WhoWrEP 89*
Kyle, Noeline June 1940- *WhoWor 91*
Kyle, Penelope Ward 1947- *WhoEmL 91*
Kyle, Richard Erwin 1905- *WhoAm 90*
Kyle, Robert Arthur 1928- *WhoAm 90*
Kyle, Robert Campbell, II 1935- *WhoAm 90, WhoWor 91*
Kyle, Ron 1941- *WhoE 91*
Kyle, Sefton *TwCCr&M 91*
Kyle, Terrence Wayne 1950- *WhoAm 90*
Kyle, Wallace 1910-1988 *AnObit 1988*
Kyle, William Davidson, Jr. 1915- *St&PR 91*
Kyle, William L., Jr. 1927- *St&PR 91*
Kyle, William Walsh 1946- *St&PR 91*
Kyle, Willis B. 1914- *St&PR 91*
Kyle-Vega, Annette E *BiDrAPA 89*
Kyle-White, Barbara Louise 1945- *WhoAmW 91*
Kyles, N Bruce *BiDrAPA 89*
Kylian, Jiri 1947- *WhoWor 91*
Kylin, Anders Olof 1925- *WhoWor 91*
Kyllonen, Ronald R 1931- *BiDrAPA 89*
Kyllonen, Timo-Juhani 1955- *IntWWM 90*
Kylstra, Johannes Arnold 1925- *WhoAm 90*
Kyman, Alexander L. 1929- *St&PR 91*
Kyman, Alexander Leon 1929- *WhoAm 90*
Kyman, Wendy 1947- *WhoAmW 91*
Kymissis, Pavlos I 1944- *BiDrAPA 89*
Kymlicka, Milan 1936- *IntWWM 90*
Kynaston, Nicolas 1941- *IntWWM 90, PenDiMP*
Kyne, Peter Thomas *BiDrAPA 89*
Kynes, James W. 1928-1988 *BioIn 16*
Kynhoff, Louanda McClure 1952- *BiDrAPA 89*
Kynoch, James Brent 1959- *WhoAm 90, WhoE 91*
Kyo Machiko 1924- *EncJap*
Kyogoku, Tamekane 1254-1332 *BioIn 16*
Kyomen, Helen Hisae *BiDrAPA 89*
Kyotani, Yoshihiro 1926- *WhoWor 91*
Kyprianou, Spyros 1932- *WhoWor 91*
Kyr, Robert Harry 1952- *IntWWM 90*
Kyra *WhoAmA 91*
Kyriacou, Chris 1950- *WhoWor 91*
Kyriakou, Linda G. *St&PR 91*
Kyriakou, Linda Grace 1943- *WhoAmW 91*
Kyriazis, Arthur John 1958- *WhoE 91, WhoEmL 91, WhoWor 91*
Kyrklund, Borje Ragnar Eugen 1932- *WhoWor 91*
Kyrklund, Christina Lynn 1950- *St&PR 91*
Kyrklund, Paul Wilhelm 1921- *DcScanL*
Kyrklund, Willy *DcScanL*
Kyropoulos, Constantine D 1938- *BiDrAPA 89*
Kysar, John E 1926- *BiDrAPA 89*
Kysela, William J. 1942- *St&PR 91*
Kyser, James Gregory 1956- *BiDrAPA 89*
Kyser, Kay 1906-1985 *OxCPMus*
Kyst, Kaare 1944- *WhoWor 91*
Kyster, Theodore Mathis 1928- *St&PR 91*
Kyte, Dennis 1947- *BioIn 16*
Kyte, Kathleen Sharar 1946- *BioIn 16*
Kyteler, Alice *EncO&P 3*
Kyuno, Shoji 1929- *WhoWor 91*
Kyzar, Kent Como 1953- *WhoSSW 91*
Kyzar, Ollie Jeanette 1933- *WhoAmW 91*

L

L., Elizabeth *BiDEWW*
L.A.V.G. *EncCoWW*
L. E. L. 1802-1838 *DcLB 96 [port], FemiCLE*
L. L. Cool J *BioIn 16*
L.L. Cool J. 1969?- *ConMus 5 [port]*
La Latina *EncCoWW*
Laabs, Chet 1912-1983 *Ballpl 90*
Laabs, Peter 1948- *St&PR 91*
Laade, Wolfgang 1925- *IntWWM 90*
Laaff, Ann Karelitz 1951- *WhoEmL 91*
Laage, Gerhart 1925- *WhoWor 91*
Laage, Thomas Allen 1951- *BiDrAPA 89*
Laage, Ulla 1949- *IntWWM 90*
Laajava, Jaakko Tapani 1947- *WhoE 91, WhoWor 91*
Laajoki, Kauko Veikko 1940- *WhoWor 91*
Laake, Heinz Te 1925- *BioIn 16*
Laakso, Seppo Sakari 1944- *WhoWor 91*
Laaksonen, Donna J. 1949- *WhoWrEP 89*
Laaly, Heshmat Ollah 1927- *WhoWor 91*
Laamanen, Kai Juhani 1955- *WhoWor 91*
Laan, Diyi 1927- *ArtLatA*
Laan, Remmert 1942- *WhoWor 91*
Laano, Archie Bienvenido Maano 1939- *WhoAm 90, WhoE 91, WhoWor 91*
Laarhoven, Wim Ohendrik 1924- *WhoWor 91*
Laartz, Esther Elizabeth 1913- *WhoAm 90*
Laasonen, Pentti 1928- *WhoWor 91*
Laatsch, Gary 1956- *WhoAmA 91N*
Labadie, Barbara Lee 1943- *WhoAmW 91*
Labadie, Jean 1610-1674 *EncO&P 3*
Labaeye, Pierrette 1932- *WhoWor 91*
Labaguis, Rose-Marie Quibilan 1942- *WhoAmW 91*
Labalme, Patricia Hochschild 1927- *WhoAm 90*
LaBan, Myron Miles 1936- *WhoAm 90*
Laban, Robert Y. 1935- *St&PR 91*
Labanick, George Michael 1950- *WhoSSW 91*
Labant, Cynthia Jean 1963- *WhoAmW 91*
LaBar, Flora M. 1931- *St&PR 91*
La Barbara, Joan Lotz 1947- *IntWWM 90*
LaBarbera, Jane Marie 1951- *WhoEmL 91*
LaBarbera, Jerome V. *WhoAm 90*
LaBarbera, Philip Theodore 1945- *WhoSSW 91*
LaBarbera, Richard N. 1948- *St&PR 91*
Labarca, Angela 1942- *WhoHisp 91*
Labardi, Jillian Gay 1945- *WhoSSW 91*
Labarge, Margaret Wade 1916- *WhoAmW 91*
LaBarge, Pierre L., Jr. 1925- *St&PR 91*
Labarowski, John Victor 1941- *St&PR 91*
LaBarre, Carl Anthony 1918- *WhoAm 90*
La Barre, Weston 1911- *WhoWrEP 89*
Labash, Elizabeth Baker 1944- *St&PR 91*
Labastida Ochoa, Francisco 1942- *WhoWor 91*
Labat, Gary Joseph, Jr. 1961- *WhoSSW 91*
Labat, Tony 1951- *WhoAmA 91*
Labath, Octave 1941- *St&PR 91*
Labato, Joseph R. 1946- *St&PR 91*
Labb, James *St&PR 91*
Labbadia, Lewis Reynold 1953- *WhoE 91*
Labbadia, Pasquale, III 1956- *WhoEmL 91*
Labbate, Lawrence A *BiDrAPA 89*
Labbe, Donald 1930- *St&PR 91*
L'abbe, Gerrit Karel 1940- *WhoWor 91*
Labbe, Romeo J. 1935- *St&PR 91*
Labbett, John Edgar 1950- *WhoAm 90, WhoE 91*
Labbette, Dora 1898-1984 *PenDiMP*
Labby, Daniel Harvey 1914- *BiDrAPA 89*
Labdon, Kenneth Charles 1949- *WhoEmL 91*
Labe, Louise 1522?-1566 *EncCoWW*
Labedz, Bernice R. 1919- *WhoAmW 91*
Labella, Gary M. *ODwPR 91*
LaBella, Guy Francis 1948- *WhoE 91*
Labella, John Sebastian 1953- *WhoE 91*
Labelle, Alain *BiDrAPA 89*
La Belle, Antoinette Eloise 1949- *WhoEmL 91*
Labelle, Ellen J *BiDrAPA 89*
Labelle, Elzear 1843-1875 *OxCCanT*
Labelle, Eugene Jean-Marc 1941- *WhoAm 90*
Labelle, Francois-Xavier-Antoine 1833-1891 *DcCanB 12*
LaBelle, Gary Lee 1944- *St&PR 91*
Labelle, Jean-Baptiste 1825-1898 *DcCanB 12*
LaBelle, Patti *BioIn 16*
LaBelle, Patti 1944- *DrBlPA 90, EncPR&S 89, WhoAm 90, WorAlBi*
LaBelle, Stephen F. 1948- *St&PR 91*
LaBelle, Thomas Jeffrey 1941- *WhoAm 90*
Labenskyj, Ihor Nicholas 1946- *WhoEmL 91*
Labeque, Katia 1950- *IntWWM 90, PenDiMP*
Labeque, Marielle 1952- *IntWWM 90, PenDiMP*
LaBerge, Ellen Therese 1958- *St&PR 91*
Laberge, Louis *BioIn 16*
Laberge, Marie 1950- *BioIn 16, OxCCanT*
Labes, Mortimer Milton 1929- *WhoE 91*
Labhardt, Christoph 1641?-1695 *PenDiDA 89*
Labhardt, Johann Christoph 1695-1742 *PenDiDA 89*
Labhardt, Johann Christoph, II 1741-1814 *PenDiDA 89*
La Bianca, Cory Jane 1948- *WhoAmW 91*
Labib, Nefertiti A *BiDrAPA 89*
Labiche, Walter Anthony 1924-1979 *WhoAmA 91N*
Labille-Guiard, Adelaide 1749-1803 *BioIn 16*
Labin, Bert *BiDrAPA 89*
Labin, Suzanne 1913- *ConAu 32NR*
Labine, Clem 1926- *Ballpl 90, BioIn 16*
Labino, Dominick 1910- *PenDiDA 89*
Labins, Zev W.E. *BiDrAPA 89*
Labinsky, Andrey 1871-1941 *PenDiMP*
Labisky, Ronald Frank 1934- *WhoSSW 91*
Lablache, Luigi 1794-1858 *PenDiMP*
La Blanc, Charles Wesley, Jr. 1925- *WhoAm 90*
LaBlanc, Robert Edmund 1934- *St&PR 91*
La Blanc, Robert Edmund 1934- *WhoAm 90*
Lablanche, Jean-Marc Andre 1946- *WhoWor 91*
Lable, Eliot *WhoAmA 91, WhoE 91*
Lable, Ira *BiDrAPA 89*
LaBlonde, Charles John 1940- *WhoE 91*
Labo, Flaviano 1927- *IntWWM 90*
La Bobgah, Robert Gordon 1936- *WhoAmA 91*
Laboe, Norman J. 1940- *WhoAm 90*
LaBonia, Michael J. 1936- *St&PR 91*
La Bonte, Anne *BiDrAPA 89*
La Bonte, Clarence Joseph 1939- *WhoE 91*
Labonte, Edith *BiDrAPA 89*
Labonte, John Joseph 1939- *WhoWrEP 89*
La Bonte, Joseph 1939- *WhoAm 90*
LaBonte, Jovite 1933- *St&PR 91, WhoAm 90, WhoWor 91*
Labonte, Michel 1945- *St&PR 91*
LaBoon, Lawrence Joseph 1938- *WhoE 91, WhoWor 91*
LaBoon, Robert Bruce 1941- *WhoAm 90*
Laborati, Juan Carlos 1928- *BiDrAPA 89*
Laborda Medir, Clemencia 1908-1980 *EncCoWW*
Laborde, Alden James 1915- *WhoAm 90*
Laborde, Ana Maria 1956- *WhoHisp 91*
LaBorde, Charles B. 1949- *WhoSSW 91*
Laborde, John P. 1923- *St&PR 91*
Laborde, John Peter 1923- *WhoAm 90*
Laborde, Kevin Ashton 1957- *WhoSSW 91*
Laborde, Ronald Anthony 1956- *St&PR 91*
Laborne, George P. 1908- *St&PR 91*
Labosky, John Joseph 1948- *WhoWor 91*
Labota, Dolores Bernadette 1954- *WhoAmW 91*
Labott, Susan Marie 1956- *WhoAmW 91*
Labouchere, Ronald Edward 1946- *WhoE 91*
LaBounty, David Edward 1937- *St&PR 91*
La Bounty, Hugh Orvice 1927- *WhoAm 90*
Labounty, James Philip 1943- *St&PR 91*
LaBounty, John Thomas *WhoE 91*
Labourdette, Irene 1930- *BiDrAPA 89*
Labovitz, Harry 1950- *St&PR 91*
Labowitz, Leslie 1946- *BiDWomA*
Labowsky, Dorothy 1920- *St&PR 91*
Laboy, Coco 1939- *Ballpl 90*
Labra, George P. 1928- *St&PR 91*
La Branche, George M. L. *BioIn 16*
LaBreche, George Joseph, Jr. 1945- *St&PR 91*
Labreche, Jean-Pierre *NewAgMG*
Labreck, Gerald R. 1944- *St&PR 91*
Labrecque, Raymond Roger 1932- *St&PR 91*
LaBrecque, Richard Joseph 1938- *St&PR 91, WhoAm 90*
Labrecque, Theodore Joseph 1903- *WhoAm 90, WhoE 91, WhoWor 91*
Labrecque, Thomas G. 1938- *BioIn 16, St&PR 91, WhoAm 90, WhoE 91*
Labrenz, Shari K. 1950- *St&PR 91*
Labrie, Fernand 1937- *WhoAm 90*
LaBrie, J. Roland 1948- *WhoE 91*
Labrie, Robert John 1927- *WhoAm 90*
Labrie, Rose 1916- *WhoAmA 91*
Labrie, Rose 1916-1986 *WhoAmA 91N*
LaBriola, Peter 1947- *St&PR 91*
Labro, Pierre 1920- *WhoWor 91*
Labrosse, Leo E. 1925- *St&PR 91*
Labrousse, Carl Fredrick 1960- *WhoE 91*
La Brue, Terry J. 1949- *WhoEmL 91*
LaBrun, Henry Anthony 1937- *St&PR 91*
La Bruyere, Jean De 1645-1696 *WorAlBi*
LaBruzza, Anthony Louis 1945- *BiDrAPA 89*
Labry, Robbie Shirley 1957- *WhoAmW 91*
Labs, Richnard J. 1956- *St&PR 91*
La Budde, Kenneth James 1920- *WhoAm 90*
LaBudde, Roy Christian 1921- *WhoWor 91*
Labunski, Stephen Bronislaw 1924- *WhoAm 90*
La Burt, Harry A *BiDrAPA 89*
LaBurt, Harry A. 1898-1989 *BioIn 16*
Labuta, Joseph Anthony 1931- *IntWWM 90*
Labuz, Ronald Matthew 1953- *WhoE 91, WhoEmL 91, WhoWor 91*
Lac, Ming Q. 1948- *St&PR 91*
Lacaci, Maria Elvira 1934- *EncCoWW*
Lacagnina, Michael Anthony 1932- *WhoAm 90*
Lacaillade, Raymond H. 1944- *St&PR 91*
Lacaille, Michel Xavier 1944- *WhoWor 91*
Lacalle Herrera, Luis Alberto 1941- *WhoWor 91*
LaCapra, Dominick Charles 1939- *WhoAm 90*
Lacas, Marie-Lise Charlotte 1933- *WhoWor 91*
Lacasa, Cristina 1929- *EncCoWW*
Lacasse, Gilbert 1940- *St&PR 91*
LaCasse, James Phillip 1948- *WhoWor 91*
LaCavera, Frank J. *BioIn 16*
Lacayo, Carmela Gloria 1943- *WhoAm 90*
Lacefield, David W. 1954- *St&PR 91*
Lacell, James Leroy 1953- *WhoEmL 91*
La Celle, Charles Foster 1949- *WhoSSW 91*
Lacer, Kathryn Lorene 1930- *WhoAmW 91, WhoSSW 91*
Lacerda, Carlos 1914-1977 *BioIn 16*
Lacey, Beatrice Cates 1919- *WhoAm 90, WhoAmW 91*
Lacey, Bob 1953- *Ballpl 90*
Lacey, Christina K. 1879-1972 *BioIn 16*
Lacey, Cloyd Eugene 1918- *WhoAm 90*
Lacey, Daniel Alfred 1939- *St&PR 91*
Lacey, Daniel Damian 1950- *WhoEmL 91*
Lacey, David Lee 1951- *WhoEmL 91*
Lacey, E. Ralph *NewYTBS 90*
Lacey, Elizabeth A. *AuBYP 90*
Lacey, Elizabeth A. 1954- *ConAu 132*
Lacey, Frederick Milburn, Jr. 1934- *WhoSSW 91*
Lacey, Ginger 1917-1989 *AnObit 1989*
Lacey, Howard Elton 1937- *WhoSSW 91*
Lacey, Howard Raymond 1919- *WhoWor 91*
Lacey, Hugh Matthew 1939- *WhoAm 90*
Lacey, J. Michael 1945- *St&PR 91*
Lacey, Janet *BioIn 16*
Lacey, Janet 1903-1988 *AnObit 1988*
Lacey, Joan Mary 1920- *WhoWrEP 89*
Lacey, John Irving 1915- *WhoAm 90*
Lacey, John Robert 1932- *St&PR 91*
Lacey, John S. *St&PR 91*
Lacey, John William Charles 1930- *WhoAm 90*
Lacey, Nicola 1958- *ConAu 130*
Lacey, Pamela Anne 1955- *WhoE 91*
Lacey, Pamela Sue 1953- *WhoEmL 91*
Lacey, Peeler Grayson 1954- *WhoEmL 91, WhoSSW 91*
Lacey, Richard Dale 1957- *WhoSSW 91*
Lacey, Robert 1944- *WhoSSW 91*
Lacey, Ronda Hubbard 1954- *WhoEmL 91*
Lacey, Sally C. 1949- *St&PR 91*
Lacey, Stanley Lenwood 1958- *St&PR 91*
Lacey, Tim Joseph 1947- *St&PR 91*
Lach, Alma *WhoWrEP 89*

Lach, Alma Elizabeth WhoAm 90, WhoAmW 91, WhoWor 91
Lach, Christine Marie 1956- WhoEmL 91
Lach, Donald F. 1917- WhoAm 90
Lach, Donna M. 1954- WhoEmL 91
Lach, Edward J. 1922- St&PR 91
Lach, Eileen Marie 1950- WhoAm 90, WhoAmW 91
Lach, Joseph Theodore 1934- WhoAm 90
LaChance, Candy 1870-1932 Ballpl 90
Lachance, Janice Rachel 1953- WhoAm 90, WhoAmW 91
LaChance, Leon Joseph 1939- WhoE 91
Lachance, Paul Albert 1933- WhoAm 90
Lachapelle, Andre 1931- WhoAm 90
Lachapelle, Joseph Robert 1943- WhoAmA 91
La Chapelle, Mary 1955- ConAu 132
LaChat, Michael Ray 1948- WhoEmL 91
Lachemann, Marcel 1941- Ballpl 90
Lachenal, Edmond 1855-1930 PenDiDA 89
Lachenal, Raoul 1885-1956 PenDiDA 89
Lachenauer, Eckhard Walter 1949- WhoWor 91
Lachenbruch, Arthur Herold 1925- WhoAm 90
Lachenbruch, David 1921- WhoAm 90, WhoWrEP 89
Lachenicht, Angela Marie 1955- WhoAmW 91
Lachenmann, Helmut 1935- IntWWM 90
Lacher, Carolyn Harper 1959- WhoAmW 91
Lacher, Egon Leonhardt 1950- WhoWor 91
Lacher, Gunther Wilhelm 1929- WhoWor 91
Lacher, Joseph P. 1945- WhoAm 90
Lacher, Miriam Rise 1942- WhoAmW 91
Lachman, Jordan H BiDrAPA 89
Lachman, Lawrence 1916- St&PR 91, WhoAm 90
Lachman, Marguerite Leanne 1943- WhoAm 90
Lachman, Morton 1918- WhoAm 90
Lachman, Norman Joel BiDrAPA 89
Lachman, Seymour P. 1933- WhoAm 90
Lachmon, Jagernath 1916- BioIn 16
Lachner, Bernard Joseph 1927- WhoAm 90
Lachout, Karel 1929- IntWWM 90
Lachover, Leonard W BiDrAPA 89
Lachs, John 1934- WhoAm 90, WhoSSW 91
Lachs, Manfred 1914- WhoWor 91
Lacitis, Erik 1949- WhoAm 90
Lack, David Lambert 1910-1973 DcScB S2
Lack, Francesca ODwPR 91
Lack, Frederick R. BioIn 16
Lack, James J. 1944- WhoE 91
Lack, Larry Henry 1952- WhoWor 91
Lack, Leon 1922- WhoAm 90
Lack, Richard Frederick 1928- WhoAmA 91
Lack, Robert Joel 1955- WhoEmL 91
Lack, Stanley A. 1942- St&PR 91
Lack, Stephen 1946- WhoAmA 91
Lackamp, Gregory E. 1949- St&PR 91
Lackas, John Christopher 1904- WhoAm 90
Lackemann, George Walter 1946- BiDrAPA 89
Lackenbauer, G.S. St&PR 91
Lackenmier, James Richard 1938- WhoAm 90
Lackens, John Wendell, Jr. 1934- WhoAm 90
Lackey, James Edward 1953- WhoE 91
Lackey, Jane W 1948- WhoAmA 91
Lackey, Larry Alton, Sr. 1940- WhoWor 91
Lackey, Lawrence Bailis, Jr. 1914- WhoAm 90
Lackey, Leon Agee, Jr. 1945- St&PR 91
Lackey, Paul K. 1943- St&PR 91
Lackey, Robert Shields 1936- WhoAm 90
Lackey, S. Allen 1942- St&PR 91
Lackey, Sharon Theresa 1953- WhoSSW 91
Lackey, Walter Jackson 1940- WhoSSW 91
Lacki, Melanie BioIn 16
Lacki, Ralph Stephen 1949- WhoEmL 91
Lacklan, Carli 1907- AuBYP 90
Lackland, John 1939- WhoAm 90
Lackland, Theodore Howard 1943- WhoAm 90
Lackman, Jack Gene 1939- St&PR 91
Lackman, James Stephen 1949- WhoEmL 91
Lackner, James Robert 1940- WhoAm 90
Lacko, Andras Gyorgy WhoSSW 91
Lackritz, Barbara Bank 1938- WhoAmW 91
Lackritz, Marc E. 1947- ODwPR 91
Lacks, Gayle BiDrAPA 89
Lacks, John P. 1904- St&PR 91
Lacktman, Michael 1938- WhoAmA 91
LaClair, Thomas 1938- WhoE 91
LaClaire, Phillip Marshall 1952- WhoE 91
La Clave, Alan J 1944- BiDrAPA 89
Laclede, Pierre 1724?-1778 EncCRAm
Laclette, Fernando Javier 1942- WhoHisp 91
Laclos, Pierre Choderlos De 1741-1803 WorAlBi
LaCluyse, Linda Marie 1959- WhoAmW 91
LaCock, Pete 1952- Ballpl 90
LaCocque, Andre 1927- ConAu 31NR
Lacoe, Bruce E. 1950- St&PR 91
La Colere, Francois MajTwCW
Lacom, Wayne Carl 1922- WhoAmA 91
Lacomba, Justo WhoHisp 91
Lacomba, Rafael R 1928- BiDrAPA 89
Lacombe, Albert 1827-1916 WhNaAH
Lacombe, Claire 1765- EncCoWW
Lacombe, Rita Jeanne 1947- WhoAmW 91, WhoEmL 91
Lacome, Paul 1838-1920 OxCPMus
Laconte, Robert James 1950- St&PR 91
Lacore, Ivan A BiDrAPA 89
Lacore, Marie Suzanne 1875-1975 BiDFrPL
LaCorte, Frank 1951- Ballpl 90
La Corte, John N. BioIn 16
LaCoss, Mike 1956- Ballpl 90
Lacoste, Paul 1923- WhoAm 90
Lacoste, Robert BiDrAPA 89
Lacoste, Robert 1898-1989 BiDFrPL
LaCounte, Cheryl DeWerff 1961- WhoAmW 91
La Counte, Max E. 1941- St&PR 91
LaCour, Caron Ann 1963- WhoAmW 91
La Cour, Niels 1944- IntWWM 90
La Cour, Paul 1902-1956 DcScanL
Lacour-Gayet, Philippe 1947- WhoAm 90
Lacoursiere, Roy B 1937- BiDrAPA 89
Lacouture, Felipe Ernesto 1928- WhoAm 90
Lacouture, Jean 1921- WorAu 1980 [port]
Lacouture, Leonard D. 1949- St&PR 91
Lacovara, Dominick J 1917- BiDrAPA 89
Lacovara, Philip A. 1943- St&PR 91
Lacovara, Philip Allen 1943- WhoAm 90
Lacraru, Ioan-Marius 1953- IntWWM 90
Lacret-Subirat, Fabian 1922- WhoE 91
La Creta, John Joseph 1932- St&PR 91
Lacretelle, Jacques de 1888-1985 BioIn 16
LaCroce, Joseph Rodney 1964- WhoEmL 91
Lacroix 1728-1799 PenDiDA 89
Lacroix, Christian BioIn 16
Lacroix, Christian Marie Marc 1951- WhoAm 90, WhoWor 91
Lacroix, Jean-Pierre 1929- WhoWor 91
La Croix, Joseph George 1936- WhoAm 90
Lacroix, Judith Lucy 1942- WhoSSW 91
Lacroix, M. Steven 1948- St&PR 91
LaCroix, Marcel 1930- St&PR 91
Lacroix, Mary 1937- WhoWrEP 89
LaCroix, Michael John 1948- WhoEmL 91
Lacroix, Muriel Claire 1939- WhoAmW 91
Lacroix, Pierre 1947- St&PR 91
Lacroix, Robert WhoAm 90
Lacruz Gutierrez, Jose Luis 1958- WhoWor 91
Lacter, Barry 1945- St&PR 91
Lactilla 1752-1806 BioIn 16
Lacy, Alan Jasper 1953- WhoAm 90
Lacy, Alexander Shelton 1921- WhoAm 90
Lacy, Andre B. 1939- St&PR 91
Lacy, Andre Balz 1939- WhoAm 90
Lacy, Benjamin Watkins 1839-1895 AmLegL
Lacy, Bill 1933- WhoAm 90, WhoE 91
Lacy, Burritt S, Jr. 1919- BiDrAPA 89
Lacy, Carol Angela 1943- WhoAmW 91
Lacy, Dan ODwPR 91
Lacy, Dan Mabry 1914- WhoAm 90
Lacy, Ed 1911-1968 TwCCr&M 91
Lacy, Edna B. 1906- St&PR 91
Lacy, Edna Balz 1906- WhoAm 90
Lacy, Elizabeth Bermingham 1945- WhoAmW 91
Lacy, Glyn L. 1957- St&PR 91
Lacy, Gordon R. 1940- St&PR 91
Lacy, Herman Edgar 1935- WhoAm 90
Lacy, James Daniel 1947- St&PR 91, WhoAm 90
Lacy, James Harris 1940- St&PR 91
Lacy, James Vincent 1952- WhoAm 90
Lacy, Jerry 1936- WhoAm 90
Lacy, Joseph Newton 1905- WhoAm 90
Lacy, Lawrence Roger 1956- BiDrAPA 89
Lacy, Lee 1948- Ballpl 90
Lacy, Lucy Goode G 1924- BiDrAPA 89
Lacy, Norris Joiner 1940- WhoAm 90
Lacy, Paul Eston 1924- WhoAm 90
Lacy, Peter Dempsey 1920- St&PR 91, WhoAm 90
Lacy, Rose Ann 1945- St&PR 91
Lacy, Steve BioIn 16
Lacy, Susan ODwPR 91
Lacy, Suzanne 1945- BiDWomA, BioIn 16, WhoAmA 91
Lacy, Terry Goodwin 1926- WhoWor 91
Lacy, William Frank 1945- WhoEmL 91
Lacy, William Howard 1945- St&PR 91
Ladage, Ellen Joy 1956- WhoEmL 91
Ladany, L. ConAu 132
Ladany, Laszlo 1914-1990 ConAu 132
Ladanyi, Branka Maria 1947- WhoAmW 91, WhoEmL 91
Ladanyi, Branko 1922- WhoAm 90
Ladar, Jerrold Morton 1933- WhoAm 90
Ladar, Samuel Abraham 1903- WhoAm 90
Ladas, Alice Kahn ConAu 129
Ladas, Harold S. BioIn 16
Ladatte, Francesco 1706-1787 PenDiDA 89
Ladau, Robert Francis 1940- WhoE 91
Ladd, A. Earl 1935- St&PR 91
Ladd, Alan 1913-1964 WorAlBi
Ladd, Alan Walbridge, Jr. 1937- WhoAm 90
Ladd, Barton Dyer 1936- St&PR 91
Ladd, Charles Cushing, III 1932- WhoAm 90
Ladd, Cheryl 1951- WorAlBi
Ladd, David L. 1931- St&PR 91
Ladd, David Niven 1938- St&PR 91
Ladd, Delano Wood, Jr. 1925- St&PR 91, WhoAm 90
Ladd, Diane BioIn 16
Ladd, Everett Carll 1937- WhoE 91
Ladd, Everett Carll, Jr. 1937- WhoWrEP 89
Ladd, George W. 1925- BioIn 16
Ladd, J.B. 1923- St&PR 91
Ladd, James Roger 1943- WhoAm 90
Ladd, Joseph C. 1927- St&PR 91
Ladd, Joseph Carroll 1927- WhoAm 90
Ladd, Marcia Lee 1950- St&PR 91
Ladd, P. Jeffrey 1943- WhoSSW 91
Ladd, Pete 1956- Ballpl 90
Ladd, Richard F. 1926- St&PR 91
Ladd, Robert Dwinell 1918- St&PR 91
Ladd, Roberta Kay 1953- WhoAmW 91
Ladd, William 1778-1841 BioIn 16
Ladd, William D. 1934- ODwPR 91
Ladd, William S. 1826-1893 EncABHB 6 [port]
Laddaga, Lawrence Alexander 1957- WhoEmL 91
Laddis, Andreas 1938- BiDrAPA 89
Laddon, Warren Milton 1933- WhoAm 90
Ladds, Brian J BiDrAPA 89
Ladds, Herbert Preston, Jr. 1933- WhoAm 90
Ladds, Philip Dawson 1945- WhoWor 91
Laddusaw-Lane, Lisa Ann-Michael 1954- WhoAmW 91
Lade, David Alan 1955- WhoEmL 91
Lade, Doyle 1921- Ballpl 90
Lade, John 1916- IntWWM 90
La De Route, Robert Wayne 1945- St&PR 91
Ladefoged, Paul Nielsen 1931- WhoSSW 91
Ladefoged, Peter Nielsen 1925- WhoAm 90
Ladehoff, Leo William 1932- St&PR 91, WhoAm 90
Ladehoff, Robert Louis 1932- WhoAm 90
La Demoiselle WhNaAH
La Demoiselle EncCRAm
Laden, Ben Ellis 1942- WhoAm 90
Laden, Karl 1932- WhoAm 90
Ladenheim, Kala Evelyn 1950- WhoWrEP 89
Lader, Lawrence 1919- WhoAm 90, WhoWrEP 89
Lader, Melvin Paul 1947- WhoAmA 91, WhoE 91
Lader, Philip 1946- WhoAm 90, WhoEmL 91
Lader, Wendy Friedman 1952- WhoAmW 91
Laderman, Ezra 1924- IntWWM 90, WhoAm 90
Laderman, Gabriel 1929- WhoAm 90, WhoAmA 91
Laderman, Peter 1920- BiDrAPA 89
Laderoute, Charles David 1948- WhoE 91
Laderoute, Laurin L., Jr. 1941- St&PR 91
Laderoute, Linda Dodd 1948- WhoAmW 91
La Deshabilleuse ConAu 129
Ladetti, Francesco 1706-1787 PenDiDA 89
Ladetto, Francesco 1706-1787 PenDiDA 89
Ladien, Kimball Henry 1951- BiDrAPA 89
Ladin, Eugene 1927- WhoAm 90, WhoWor 91
Ladinsky, Judith Louise 1938- WhoAmW 91
Ladish, John H. 1924- St&PR 91
Ladizesky, Kathleen Ann 1940- WhoWor 91
Ladjevardi, Hamid 1948- WhoE 91, WhoEmL 91, WhoWor 91
Ladky, Frank Jack 1921- St&PR 91
Ladly, Frederick B. 1930- St&PR 91
Ladly, Frederick Bernard 1930- WhoAm 90
Ladman, Aaron Julius 1925- WhoAm 90
Ladman, Jerry R. 1935- WhoAm 90
Ladner, Charles L. 1938- St&PR 91
Ladner, Charles Leon 1938- WhoAm 90
Ladner, George Dale 1936- BiDrAPA 89
Ladner, Heber 1902-1989 BioIn 16
Ladner, James Franz 1939- WhoWor 91
Ladner, Jennifer Ann 1957- WhoEmL 91
Ladner, John A. 1928- St&PR 91
Ladner, Karl Julius 1920- WhoAm 90
Ladner, Lee Russell 1934- St&PR 91
Ladner, Thomas E. 1916- WhoAm 90
Ladner, Thomas Ellis 1916- St&PR 91
Ladnier, Tommy 1900-1939 OxCPMus, WorAlBi
Ladov, Norman 1945- WhoE 91
Ladov, Norman Howard 1945- BiDrAPA 89
LaDow, C. Stuart 1925- WhoAm 90
La Du, Bert Nichols, Jr. 1920- WhoAm 90
La Duca, Nicholas 1951- WhoSSW 91
Ladue, Peter Whiting 1950- WhoEmL 91
LaDue, Wade William 1935- WhoAm 90
La Duke, Violet Marina Roy 1935- WhoE 91
Ladwig, Alan Michael 1948- WhoAm 90
Lady of Honour, A BiDEWW
Lady of Lawers EncO&P 3
Lady Wonder EncPaPR 91
Lady, Larry G. 1940- St&PR 91
Lady, Larry Gene 1940- WhoAm 90
Ladyman, Phyllis AuBYP 90
Ladzinski, Gerard Robert 1962- WhoE 91
Laederach, Monique 1938- EncCoWW
Laemmel, Klaus 1931- BiDrAPA 89
Laemmle, Cheryl 1947- WhoAmA 91
Laengrich, Arthur Richard 1933- St&PR 91
Laennec, Rene 1781-1826 WorAlBi
Laennec, Rene Theophile Hyacinthe 1781-1826 BioIn 16
Laens, Jean 1946- WhoWor 91
Laeri, John Howard, Jr. 1935- WhoAm 90
Laermann, Klaus 1939- WhoWor 91
Laessig, Robert 1920- WhoAmA 91
Laessig, Robert H. 1913- WhoAm 90
Laessig, Ronald Harold 1940- WhoAm 90
Laessig, Walter Bruce 1941- WhoAm 90
Laeuger, Max 1864-1952 PenDiDA 89
La Falaise, Lucie de BioIn 16
La Falaise, Maxime de BioIn 16
La Falce, John Joseph 1939- WhoAm 90, WhoE 91
La Falce, Joseph A. St&PR 91
Lafarge, Catherine 1935- WhoAm 90
La Farge, John 1835-1910 BioIn 16, PenDiDA 89, WorAlBi
La Farge, Louis Bancel 1900-1989 BioIn 16
LaFarge, Lucy Bergson 1948- BiDrAPA 89
La Farge, Oliver 1901-1963 AuBYP 90, ConAu 30NR, WorAlBi
La Farge, Phyllis AuBYP 90
LaFargue, Craig Joseph 1950- WhoEmL 91
Lafargue, Paul 1842-1911 BiDFrPL
LaFaro, Scott 1936-1961 BioIn 16
LaFauci, Horatio Michael 1917- WhoAm 90
LaFave, Bonnie Lynne 1945- WhoE 91
Lafave, Hugh G BiDrAPA 89
Lafave, Hugh Gordon John 1929- WhoAm 90
LaFave, LeAnn Larson 1953- WhoAmW 91
Lafaye, Cary DuPre 1945- WhoAmW 91
Lafaye, Claudine Yvonne Louise 1942- WhoWor 91
Lafaye, Nell Murray 1937- WhoAmA 91
Lafayette, Marie J du Motier, Marquis de 1757-1834 BioIn 16, WhNaAH [port]
Lafayette, Marie-Joseph, Marquis de 1757-1834 EncCRAm [port]
Lafayette, Marie Joseph Paul, Marquis De 1757-1834 WorAlBi
La Fayette, Marie Madeleine, Comtesse de 1634-1693 FemiCLE, WorAlBi
LaFeber, Walter Frederick 1933- WhoAm 90
Lafer, Fred S. 1929- St&PR 91
Lafer, Fred Seymour 1929- WhoAm 90
LaFerriere, Therese WhoAm 90
Lafertte Gavino, Elias 1886-1981 BioIn 16
Lafetra, Anthony W. 1940- St&PR 91
Lafever, Howard Nelson 1938- WhoAm 90
Lafever, Minard 1798-1854 BioIn 16
Laffal, Florence 1921- WhoWrEP 89
Laffan, May FemiCLE
Laffer, Paul Selby 1951- BiDrAPA 89
Lafferman, Jeffrey Allen 1956- BiDrAPA 89
Lafferty, Charles Douglas Joseph 1930- WhoE 91
Lafferty, James Martin 1916- WhoAm 90
Lafferty, John David 1960- WhoE 91
Lafferty, John Jacob 1933- St&PR 91
Lafferty, John Yeoman 1938- WhoE 91

Lafferty, Kenneth J. 1932- *St&PR 91*
Lafferty, Lawrence Elliott 1957- *WhoEmL 91*
Lafferty, R A 1914- *ConAu 32NR*
Lafferty, R. A. 1914- *RGTwCSF*
Lafferty, R. James 1946- *St&PR 91*
Lafferty, Richard Thomas 1932- *WhoAm 90*
Lafferty, Susan Lee 1948- *WhoWrEP 89*
Laffey, James Kevin 1952- *WhoEmL 91*
Laffin, John 1922- *AuBYP 90*
Laffin, John C. *ODwPR 91*
Laffite, Jean 1780?-1825 *WorAlBi*
Laffitte, Hector M. 1934- *WhoSSW 91*
Laffitte-Reguera, Mary E. *WhoAmW 91*
Laffoley, Paul George, Jr. 1935- *WhoE 91*
Laffond, Laura Jean 1956- *WhoEmL 91*
Laffont, Ingrid Caridad 1958- *WhoEmL 91*
Laffoon, Carthrae Merrette 1920- *St&PR 91, WhoAm 90*
Lafitau, Joseph Francois 1681-1746 *WhNaAH*
Lafitte, Ed 1886-1971 *Ballpl 90*
Lafitte y Perez del Pulgar, Maria 1902- *EncCoWW*
LaFlam, Jack Allen 1955- *WhoSSW 91*
LaFlame, Gregory F. 1949- *St&PR 91*
La Flame, Gregory Frank 1949- *WhoAm 90*
Laflamme, Toussaint-Antoine-Rodolphe 1827-1893 *DcCanB 12*
Lafleche, George Albert 1925- *St&PR 91*
Lafleche, Louis-Francois 1818-1898 *DcCanB 12*
Lafleche, Pierre 1892- *EncO&P 3*
Laflen, Jerry Mark 1947- *St&PR 91*
Lafler, John A. 1939- *St&PR 91*
Lafler-Botelho, Kendra Lois 1961- *WhoEmL 91*
La Flesche, Francis 1857-1932 *WhNaAH*
La Flesche, Joseph 1818?-1888 *WhNaAH*
La Flesche, Susan 1865-1915 *WhNaAH*
La Flesche, Susette *BioAmW*
La Flesche, Susette 1854-1903 *WhNaAH*
La Flesche Picotte, Susan 1865-1915 *WhNaAH*
La Flesche Tibbles, Yosette 1854-1903 *WhNaAH*
LaFleur, Grant Riley 1937- *WhoSSW 91*
Lafleur, Guy 1951- *BioIn 16, WhoAm 90, WorAlBi*
La Fleur, James Kemble 1930- *St&PR 91*
LaFleur, James Matthew 1939- *St&PR 91*
Lafley, Alan Frederick 1922- *WhoAm 90*
La Follette, Belle Case 1859-1931 *BioAmW*
LaFollette, Charles Sanborn 1929- *WhoAm 90*
La Follette, Douglas J. 1940- *WhoAm 90*
LaFollette, Larry Maurice 1943- *St&PR 91*
La Follette, Philip F. 1897-1965 *WorAlBi*
La Follette, Robert M. 1855-1925 *BioIn 16, WorAlBi*
La Follette, Robert Marion, Jr. 1895-1953 *WorAlBi*
Lafon, Dee J 1929- *WhoAmA 91*
La Fon, Dorothy N 1910- *BiDrAPA 89*
La Fon, Julia Anna 1919- *WhoAmA 91*
LaFond, Stephen Dennis 1947- *WhoEmL 91*
Lafond Piccolomini, Bernadette 1953- *WhoAmW 91*
Lafont, Gerardo 1930- *BiDrAPA 89*
Lafont, Jean 1918- *IntWWM 90*
Lafont, Jean-Philippe 1951- *IntWWM 90*
La Fontaine, Hernan 1934- *WhoE 91*
Lafontaine, Hernan 1934- *WhoHisp 91*
La Fontaine, Jean De 1621-1695 *WorAlBi*
Lafontaine, John B. 1935- *St&PR 91*
Lafontaine, Oskar *BioIn 16*
Lafontaine, Oskar 1943- *CurBio 90 [port]*
LaFontaine, Pat *BioIn 16*
Lafontaine, Sylvain *BiDrAPA 89*
Lafontant, Jewel Stradford 1922- *WhoAm 90, WhoAmW 91*
Lafora, Nicholas De 1730?-1789? *EncCRAm*
La Force, James Clayburn, Jr. 1928- *WhoAm 90*
La Force, Pierre Joseph 1936- *WhoE 91*
Laforce, Tina Horton 1961- *WhoAmW 91*
LaForce, William Leonard, Jr. 1940- *WhoAm 90, WhoWor 91*
LaFore, E. T. *WhoHisp 91*
La Forest, Gerard Vincent 1926- *WhoAm 90, WhoE 91*
LaForest, James John 1927- *WhoAm 90*
La Forest, Rachel Jamison 1954- *WhoAmW 91*
Laforet, Carmen 1921- *EncCoWW, IntvSpW [port]*
Laforge, Francis Kress 1933- *St&PR 91*
LaForge, Mary Cecile 1945- *WhoAmW 91*
La Forge, Raymond Bernard, Jr. 1933- *WhoSSW 91*
LaForrest, Barbara J. 1951- *BiDrAPA 89*
Lafortune, David T. *St&PR 91*
La Fosse, Robert *BioIn 16, WhoAm 90*
LaFourest, Judith Ellen *WhoAmW 91*
La Framboise, Josette *WhNaAH*
La France, Michael L. 1959- *WhoSSW 91*
Lafrance, P.D. *St&PR 91*
Lafrance, Paul E. 1931- *St&PR 91*
La Frange, Joseph William, III 1940- *WhoSSW 91*
LaFrankie, James V. 1927- *WhoAm 90, WhoE 91*
La Frankie, James Vincent 1927- *St&PR 91*
La Fratta, Charles A. 1925- *St&PR 91*
LaFrence, Alison Denise *BiDrAPA 89*
La Frenier, R Kenneth, Jr. 1948- *BiDrAPA 89*
La Freniere, Celine 1950- *ConAu 132*
La Freniere, Francois 1951- *St&PR 91*
La Fresnaye, Roger de 1885-1925 *BioIn 16*
La Fressange, Ines de *BioIn 16*
La Froscia, Elizabeth Jeanne 1942- *WhoAmW 91*
LaFurn, Gerry *BioIn 16*
LaFuze, Elizabeth Perry 1950- *WhoSSW 91*
Lagakos, William George 1911- *WhoE 91*
Lagally, Max Gunter 1942- *WhoAm 90*
La Gamma, Edmund Francis 1952- *WhoEmL 91*
Lagan, Constance Hallinan 1947- *WhoEmL 91, WhoWrEP 89*
LaGanga, Donna Brandeis 1950- *WhoAmW 91*
Lagardere, Jean-Luc *BioIn 16*
Lagarias, Jeffrey Clark 1949- *WhoE 91*
LaGasse, Alfred Bazil, III 1954- *WhoAm 90*
Lagasse, Jacques 1916- *St&PR 91*
Lagassey, Elizabeth W. 1955- *WhoAmW 91*
Lagatol, Nancy Lynn 1948- *WhoE 91, WhoEmL 91*
Lagatta, John 1894-1976 *WhoAmA 91N*
LaGattuta, Steve *BioIn 16*
Lagdon, James Robert, II 1947- *St&PR 91*
Lage, Gustavo A *BiDrAPA 89*
Lage, Jacy Martins 1954- *WhoWor 91*
Lage, Wally 1943- *St&PR 91*
Lager, Eric 1932- *BiDrAPA 89, WhoE 91*
Lager, Fannie 1911- *WhoAmA 91*
Lager, John A. 1934- *St&PR 91*
Lager, Kerstin Cecilia 1955- *WhoWor 91*
Lager, Linda Kaye 1951- *WhoEmL 91*
Lager, Marilyn 1939- *BioIn 16*
Lager, Robert John 1934- *WhoAm 90, WhoSSW 91, WhoWor 91*
Lagerfeld, Karl *BioIn 16*
Lagerfeld, Karl 1938- *ConDes 90*
Lagerfeld, Karl Otto 1938- *WhoAm 90, WhoWor 91*
Lagerkvist, Magnus Fredrik Hjalmar 1947- *WhoWor 91*
Lagerkvist, Paer 1891-1974 *MajTwCW*
Lagerkvist, Par 1891-1974 *DcScanL, WorAlBi*
Lagerlof, Selma 1858-1940 *WorAlBi*
Lagerlof, Selma Ottilia Lovisa 1858-1940 *DcScanL*
Lagerman, Susan Borden 1952- *WhoEmL 91*
Lagerqvist, Albin Gustav 1915- *WhoWor 91*
Lagerwei, Nijs Antoon Johan 1938- *WhoWor 91*
Lageschulte, Jack 1936- *St&PR 91*
Laggett, William J. 1930- *St&PR 91*
Laggner, Peter Heinrich 1944- *WhoWor 91*
Laghari, Javaid Rasoolbux 1950- *WhoWor 91*
Laghi, Franco 1943- *WhoSSW 91*
Lagier, Rene Joseph 1925- *WhoWor 91*
Lagin, Neil 1942- *WhoSSW 91*
Lagman, Bogard Abuton 1950- *St&PR 91*
Lagnevik, Magnus 1949- *WhoWor 91*
Lago, Jesus Angel 1961- *WhoEmL 91*
Lago, Mary McClelland 1919- *WhoAm 90, WhoWrEP 89*
Lago, Robert Joseph 1956- *WhoE 91*
Lagomarsino, Robert John 1926- *WhoAm 90*
Lagonegro, Edward Francis 1936- *St&PR 91*
Lagonegro, William A. 1933- *St&PR 91*
Lagoni, Patricia Ann 1933- *St&PR 91*
LaGonterie, Yvette Marie 1956- *WhoEmL 91*
LaGore, Carol Elaine 1950- *WhoAmW 91*
Lagoria, Georgianna Marie 1953- *WhoAm 90, WhoAmA 91*
Lagorio, Gina 1930- *EncCoWW*
Lagorio, Irene R 1921- *WhoAmA 91*
Lagos, Concha 1909- *EncCoWW*
Lagos, George Peter 1954- *St&PR 91, WhoAm 90*
Lagos, James Harry 1951- *WhoEmL 91, WhoWor 91*
La Gourgue, John Richard *BiDrAPA 89*
Lagoutaris, Demetrios E *BiDrAPA 89*
Lagow, Pat Couch 1950- *ODwPR 91*
Lagowski, Barbara Jean 1955- *WhoAm 90, WhoWrEP 89*
Lagowski, Joseph John 1930- *WhoAm 90*
Lagoya, Alexandre *PenDiMP*
LaGrand, Kenneth Lewis 1941- *St&PR 91*
Lagrange, Francois Leo 1900-1940 *BiDFrPL*
Lagrange, Guiseppe Ludovico 1736-1813 *BioIn 16*
Lagrange, Joseph Louis, Comte De 1736-1813 *WorAlBi*
LaGrange, William F. 1913-1988 *BioIn 16*
La Grant, Laurence John 1947- *WhoEmL 91*
La Grenade, Janet *BiDrAPA 89*
La Grenade, Keith Michael *BiDrAPA 89*
Lagrene, Bireli *BioIn 16*
LaGrone, Alfred Hall 1912- *WhoAm 90*
LaGrone, Bobby D. 1933- *St&PR 91*
LaGrone, Cynthia Althuser 1949- *WhoSSW 91*
LaGrone, Dawn Sheree *BiDrAPA 89*
La Grone, Don Michael *BiDrAPA 89*
LaGrone, Harold Everett 1931- *St&PR 91*
LaGrone, Lavenia Whiddon 1940- *WhoAmW 91*
LaGrone, William Taylor 1914- *WhoWor 91*
LaGrow, Lerrin 1948- *Ballpl 90*
La Grutta, Diane Babuin 1959- *WhoE 91*
LaGuardia, Diana 1945- *WhoE 91*
Laguardia, Fiorello H. 1882-1947 *WorAlBi*
La Guardia, Fiorello Henry 1882-1947 *BioIn 16*
Laguardia, Louis Manuel 1948- *WhoHisp 91*
La Guerre, Elisabeth Claude Jacquet de 1659-1729 *BioIn 16*
Laguerre, Enrique A. 1906- *BioIn 16, ConAu 131, HispWr 90*
La Guerre, Irma-Estel *WhoHisp 91*
Laguerre, Julius Jenner *BiDrAPA 89*
La Guette, Catherine Meurdrac de 1613-1680? *EncCoWW*
Lagueux, Paul B. *BioIn 16*
Lagueux, Ronald Rene 1931- *WhoAm 90*
Laguiller, Arlette 1940- *BiDFrPL*
La Guma, Alex 1925-1985 *MajTwCW, WorAu 1980 [port]*
Laguna, Mariella *WhoAmA 91*
Lagunoff, David 1932- *WhoAm 90*
Lagzdina, Vineta 1945- *IntWWM 90*
Laha, Radha Govinda 1930- *WhoAm 90*
Laha, Sarojini *BiDrAPA 89*
Laham, Sandra Lee 1950- *WhoEmL 91*
Lahanas, Constantine J. 1928- *WhoAm 90*
Lahanas, Constantine James 1928- *St&PR 91*
Lahart, F. Vern 1928- *WhoSSW 91*
LaHay, David George Michael 1949- *WhoAm 90*
La Haye, Jocelyn Joan *BiDrAPA 89*
LaHaye, Pam Matera 1955- *WhoAmW 91*
Lahaye, Thomas Gerard 1936- *St&PR 91*
Lahde, Seppo Tapani 1940- *WhoWor 91*
Lahera, Angel 1961- *WhoEmL 91*
Lahey, Edward Vincent 1939- *St&PR 91*
Lahey, Edward Vincent, Jr. 1939- *WhoAm 90*
Lahey, John L. *WhoAm 90*
Lahey, Joseph Patrick 1947- *WhoAm 90*
Lahey, Marguerite Duprez 1880-1958 *WhoAmA 91N*
Lahey, Marion Eugene 1917- *WhoAm 90*
Lahey, Regis Henry 1948- *WhoE 91*
Lahey, Richard 1893-1979 *WhoAmA 91N*
Lahey, Robert C. 1936- *St&PR 91*
Lahham, Ghassan 1938- *WhoWor 91*
Lahiri, Murali N *BiDrAPA 89*
Lahiri, Sajal 1950- *WhoWor 91*
Lahiri, Satyajeet 1951- *BiDrAPA 89*
Lahiri, Supriya 1948- *WhoE 91*
Lahl, Lynda Lea 1961- *WhoEmL 91*
Lahm, Diane Chesley 1942- *WhoAmW 91*
Lahmann, Walter A. 1941- *St&PR 91*
Lahmers, David Earl, Sr. 1950- *St&PR 91, WhoEmL 91*
Lahmers, Nancy Kay 1954- *WhoEmL 91*
Lahmeyer, Henry Walter *BiDrAPA 89*
Lahn, M.L. 1933- *St&PR 91*
Lahn, Mervyn Lloyd 1933- *WhoAm 90*
Lahontan, Baron de 1666-1715? *DcLB 99*
Lahontan, Louis Armand D'Arce, Baron De 1666?-1715 *WhNaAH*
Lahontan, Louis-Armand de Lom D'Arce 1666-1716? *EncCRAm*
LaHood, Mary Anne 1947- *WhoAmW 91*
Lahoski, James Andrew 1952- *WhoEmL 91*
La Hotan, Robert L 1927- *WhoAmA 91*
Lahoud, Joe 1947- *Ballpl 90*
Lahourcade, John B. 1924- *St&PR 91*
Lahourcade, John Brosius 1924- *WhoAm 90*
Lahr, Bert 1895-1967 *OxCPMus, WorAlBi*
Lahr, C. Dwight 1945- *WhoAm 90*
Lahr, Frank Frederick 1921- *St&PR 91*
Lahr, J Stephen 1943- *WhoAmA 91*
Lahr, Jack Leroy 1934- *WhoAm 90*
Lahr, John 1941- *WhoAm 90, WhoWrEP 89*
Lahr, Lawrence 1938- *St&PR 91*
Lahr, Michael Lincoln 1955- *WhoE 91*
Lahr, Robert A. 1925- *St&PR 91*
Lahrmann, William August, Jr. 1932- *WhoAm 90*
Lahti, Christine *BioIn 16*
Lahti, Christine 1950- *WhoAmW 91, WorAlBi*
Lahti, Jeff 1956- *Ballpl 90*
Lai, Andrew 1956- *WhoWor 91*
Lai, David Kwong-Wah 1948- *WhoEmL 91*
Lai, Francis 1932- *OxCPMus*
Lai, Harry *BiDrAPA 89*
Lai, Hsin-Yi 1953- *WhoSSW 91*
Lai, Joseph *St&PR 91*
Lai, Paul 1951- *St&PR 91*
Lai, Samuel 1949- *WhoWor 91*
Lai, Shin-Tse Jason 1951- *WhoWor 91*
Lai, Tsung-Hui 1953- *WhoSSW 91*
Lai, Waihang 1939- *WhoAmA 91*
Lai, Wei Michael 1930- *WhoAm 90*
Laib, Helen Wiedemer 1948- *WhoEmL 91*
Laible, Jon Morse 1937- *WhoAm 90*
Laibow, Rima Ellen *BiDrAPA 89*
Laibson, Peter Robert 1933- *WhoAm 90*
Laico, Colette *WhoAmA 91*
Laidig, M.R. 1938- *St&PR 91*
Laidig, William Rupert 1927- *St&PR 91, WhoAm 90, WhoE 91*
Laidlaw, A.K. *ConAu 33NR*
Laidlaw, A. K. *MajTwCW*
Laidlaw, Anna Robena 1819-1901 *PenDiMP*
Laidlaw, Harry Hyde, Jr. 1907- *WhoAm 90*
Laidlaw, Henry Bell *BioIn 16*
Laidlaw, Melinda Katherine 1955- *WhoAmW 91*
Laidlaw, R. G. 1927- *WhoE 91*
Laidlaw, Robert Richard 1923- *WhoAm 90, WhoSSW 91*
Laidlaw, Robert W 1901- *EncO&P 3*
Laidlaw, William Franklin 1933- *WhoAm 90*
Laidlaw, William Samuel Hugh 1956- *WhoAm 90*
Laidler, David Ernest William 1938- *WhoAm 90*
Laidler, Harry W. 1884-1970 *EncAL*
Laier, Peter Von Halling 1956- *WhoWor 91*
Laiken, Deidre S. *BioIn 16*
Laiken, Nora Dawn 1946- *WhoAmW 91*
Laikin, George J. 1910- *St&PR 91*
Laikin, George Joseph 1910- *WhoAm 90*
Laikin, Michael Frank 1955- *BiDrAPA 89*
Lail, Charlie Joel, Sr. 1939- *WhoSSW 91*
Lail, John Wilburn 1945- *WhoSSW 91*
Laiman, Leah 1946- *WhoEmL 91*
Laimbeer, Bill *BioIn 16*
Laimbeer, Bill 1957- *WhoAm 90*
Laimbeer, Francis Effingham, III 1929- *WhoSSW 91*
Laina, Maria 1947- *EncCoWW*
Laine, Cleo 1927- *DrBIPA 90, IntWWM 90, PenDiMP, WhoAm 90, WhoAmW 91, WhoE 91, WorAlBi*
Laine, Cleo 1928- *OxCPMus*
Laine, Erick J. 1933- *St&PR 91*
Laine, Frankie 1913- *OxCPMus, WorAlBi*
Laine, Katie Myers 1947- *WhoAmW 91*
Laine, Olli-Pekka 1948- *WhoWor 91*
Lainez, Manuel Mujica *ConAu 32NR, HispWr 90*
Laing, Alan 1944- *IntWWM 90*
Laing, Alan Kemp 1902- *WhoAm 90*
Laing, Dilys 1906-1960 *FemiCLE*
Laing, Earl John *BiDrAPA 89*
Laing, Gertrude Mary 1905- *WhoAm 90*
Laing, Hugh 1911-1988 *AnObit 1988, BioIn 16*
Laing, Joan Rae 1938- *WhoAmW 91*
Laing, Karel Ann 1939- *WhoAm 90, WhoAmW 91*
Laing, Malcolm Brian 1955- *WhoEmL 91, WhoSSW 91*
Laing, Neil Fullerton 1932- *WhoWor 91*
Laing, Patrick Gowans 1923- *WhoAm 90*
Laing, R. D. 1927-1989 *AnObit 1989, BioIn 16*
Laing, R D 1927-1989 *ConAu 129, MajTwCW, News 90*
Laing, Richard Harlow 1932- *WhoAmA 91*
Laing, Robert S. 1948- *St&PR 91*
Laing, Robert Scott 1952- *WhoEmL 91*
Laing, Ronald David 1927-1989 *BioIn 16*
Laing, Thomas Dallas, Jr. 1943- *WhoSSW 91*
Laingen, Lowell Bruce 1922- *WhoAm 90*
Laino, Lee 1940- *ODwPR 91*
Laino, Robert T. 1947- *St&PR 91*
Lainson, Gretchen Hollman 1916- *St&PR 91*
Lainson, Hal 1912- *St&PR 91*
Lainson, John Jennings 1920- *St&PR 91*

Laiou, Angeliki E. 1941- WhoAm 90
Lair, Helen May 1918- WhoWor 91
Lair, Jesse K. 1926- WhoWrEP 89
Lair, Robert Ed, Jr. 1939- WhoE 91
Lair, Robert Louis 1921- WhoAm 90
Lair, Thomas E. 1931- St&PR 91
Laird, Alan Douglas Kenneth 1914- WhoAm 90
Laird, Alexander 1830-1896 DcCanB 12
Laird, Betty A. 1925- ConAu 33NR
Laird, Charles David 1939- WhoAm 90
Laird, David 1927- WhoAm 90
Laird, Dewayne E. 1947- St&PR 91
Laird, Doris Anne Marley 1931- WhoAmW 91, WhoWor 91
Laird, E. Ruth 1921- WhoAm 90
Laird, E Ruth 1921- WhoAmA 91
Laird, Elizabeth W. 1936- WhoWrEP 89
Laird, Evalyn Walsh 1902- WhoAmW 91
Laird, James Craig 1923- St&PR 91
Laird, Jean Elouise Rydeski 1930- WhoAmW 91
Laird, Joe S. 1918- St&PR 91
Laird, John Evans, III 1947- St&PR 91
Laird, John Robert 1942- St&PR 91, WhoAm 90
Laird, Joseph Weldon 1934- WhoSSW 91
Laird, Larrie W. 1940- St&PR 91
Laird, Margaret 1954- WhoAmW 91
Laird, Mary WhoAm 90, WhoAmW 91, WhoWor 91
Laird, Melvin R 1922- BiDrUSE 89, WorAlBi
Laird, Melvin Robert 1922- WhoAm 90
Laird, Morris E. 1908- St&PR 91
Laird, Pamela Sue 1955- WhoEmL 91
Laird, Peter Alan 1954- WhoE 91
Laird, Peter D. 1944- St&PR 91
Laird, Robert Winslow 1936- WhoAm 90
Laird, Roy D. 1925- ConAu 33NR, WhoAm 90
Laird, Shirley ODwPR 91
Laird, Stanley Wesley 1919- St&PR 91
Laird, W.F. 1919- St&PR 91
Laird, Wilbur David, Jr. 1937- WhoAm 90
Laird, William Everette, Jr. 1934- WhoAm 90
Laird, William Winder BioIn 16
Laires, Fernando 1925- WhoE 91
Laite, Gina Elisa BiDrAPA 89
Laithwaite, Eric 1921- BioIn 16
Laiti, Dominic Aldo 1931- St&PR 91
Laitin, David Dennis 1945- WhoAm 90
Laitin, Joseph 1914- WhoAm 90
Laitinen, Kai Leo Kaarlo 1924- WhoWor 91
Laitinen, Linda Jean 1955- WhoAmW 91
Laitman, Leila Bender 1955- BiDrAPA 89
Laitner, Linda DeMarest 1947- WhoAmW 91
Laity, David George 1948- WhoEmL 91
Laiuppa, Mark Anthony 1957- WhoEmL 91
Lajara, Cecilio Nicolas 1942- WhoSSW 91
Lajeunesse, Charles Henri R 1954- BiDrAPA 89
Lajeunesse, Claude 1941- WhoAm 90
Lajeunesse, Marcel 1942- WhoAm 90
Lajewski, Kenneth W BiDrAPA 89
Lajoie, Brian Alan 1946- St&PR 91
La Joie, James Francis 1945- St&PR 91
Lajoie, Nap 1874-1959 Ballpl 90 [port]
Lajoie, Napoleon 1875-1959 WorAlBi
Lajoie, Peter Anthony 1938- St&PR 91
Lajoie, William Richard 1934- WhoAm 90
Lajoie, Yves BiDrAPA 89
Lajoinie, Andre Francois 1929- BiDFrPL
Lajonchere, Maria Cristina BiDrAPA 89
Lajonchere, Rinaldo BiDrAPA 89
Lajoue, Jacques de 1686-1761 PenDiDA 89
Lajous, Roberta 1954- WhoWor 91
Lakachman, Robert BioIn 16
Lakatos, Stefan Istvan 1895- IntWWM 90
Lakatos, Susan Carol 1960- WhoE 91
Lakatta, Patricia Louise 1946- WhoEmL 91
Lakdawala, Sharad R BiDrAPA 89
Lake, Alice 1916-1990 BioIn 16, ConAu 131
Lake, Ann Hillery BiDrAPA 89
Lake, Ann Winslow 1919- WhoAm 90
Lake, Barbara Lee 1934- WhoAmW 91
Lake, Blair Moody 1932- WhoAmW 91
Lake, Candace Loomis 1946- WhoEmL 91
Lake, Carnell BioIn 16
Lake, Carol Lee 1944- WhoAmW 91
Lake, Charles R 1943- BiDrAPA 89
Lake, Charles William, Jr. 1918- St&PR 91, WhoAm 90
Lake, Christopher Robert 1952- WhoE 91
Lake, Dale Fletcher 1936- St&PR 91
Lake, David J. 1929- RGTwCSF
Lake, David S. 1938- WhoAm 90
Lake, David Sanders 1938- St&PR 91
Lake, Eddie 1916- Ballpl 90
Lake, Edward 1641-1704 BioIn 16
Lake, Edward 1934- WhoAm 90
Lake, F. Edward 1934- St&PR 91
Lake, Frederic WhoAmA 91N
Lake, George Baker 1827-1910 AmLegL
Lake, George H. 1933- St&PR 91
Lake, Gerald Eugene BiDrAPA 89
Lake, Greg EncPR&S 89
Lake, Harriette ConTFT 8
Lake, Hobart 1934- St&PR 91
Lake, Hubert, Jr. 1948- WhoEmL 91, WhoSSW 91
Lake, James H. WhoAm 90
Lake, Jerome Glen 1932- WhoE 91, WhoWor 91
Lake, Jerry Lee 1941- WhoAmA 91
Lake, Joe 1881-1950 Ballpl 90
Lake, John Leo 1960- WhoSSW 91
Lake, Joseph Frank 1933- St&PR 91
Lake, Kevin Bruce 1937- WhoAm 90
Lake, Larry Wayne 1946- WhoAm 90, WhoSSW 91
Lake, Marla Dawn BiDrAPA 89
Lake, Michael Smith 1941- St&PR 91
Lake, Oliver BioIn 16
Lake, Peter Matthew 1960- BiDrAPA 89
Lake, R. Elaine 1954- WhoAmW 91
Lake, Randall 1947- WhoAmA 91
Lake, Richard Arthur 1946- St&PR 91
Lake, Ricki BioIn 16
Lake, Robert Charles 1941- WhoSSW 91
Lake, Robert R. 1944- St&PR 91
Lake, Ross Duane 1937- St&PR 91
Lake, Simon 1866-1945 BioIn 16
Lake, Steve 1957- Ballpl 90
Lake, Suzanne Philena 1929- WhoAmW 91
Lake, Veronica 1919-1973 BioAmW, WorAlBi
Lake, Victor Hugo 1919- WhoWor 91
Lake, William Augustus 1808-1861 AmLegL
Lake, William Thomas 1910- WhoAm 90
Lake, William Truman 1943- WhoAm 90
Lake, Willis Wayne 1927- St&PR 91
Lakebrink, Cynthia 1963- WhoAmW 91
Lakeman, Al 1918-1976 Ballpl 90
Laken, Keith J. 1945- WhoEmL 91
Lakenbach, Cary 1946- St&PR 91
Laker, Irving 1928- St&PR 91
Laker, Kenneth Robert 1946- WhoAm 90
Laker, Rosalind ConAu 130
Lakes, Gary 1950- IntWWM 90
Lakey, Arnold Neil 1937- St&PR 91
Lakhani, Ameer Ali 1950- WhoSSW 91
Lakhani, Hanif 1943- WhoWor 91
Lakhanpal, Sharad 1951- WhoSSW 91
Laki, Krisztina 1954- IntWWM 90
Laki, Peter 1954- IntWWM 90
Lakin, Deborah Anne 1947- WhoAmW 91
Lakin, Judith Louise 1956- WhoEmL 91
Lakin, Judy Shelton 1958- WhoAmW 91
Lakin, Robert M. ODwPR 91
Lakin, Sandra Fisher 1953- WhoAmW 91
Lakin, Thomas J. 1942- St&PR 91
Lakner, George Stephen 1940- BiDrAPA 89
Lakner, Yehoshua 1924- IntWWM 90
Lako, Charles Michael, Jr. 1947- WhoEmL 91
Lako, Natasha 1948- EncCoWW
Lakos, Marcille Harris 1917- WhoAmW 91
Lakoski, Roland Arthur 1931- WhoAm 90, WhoSSW 91
La Kosky, Randall A 1936- BiDrAPA 89
Lakovics, Magnus BiDrAPA 89
Lakritz, Isaac 1952- WhoAm 90
Lakritz, Kenneth B. BiDrAPA 89
Lakshmanan, Muthusamy 1946- WhoWor 91
Lakshmanan, Ramaswamy 1954- BiDrAPA 89
Lakshmi Bai 1833?-1858 WomWR
Lakshmi Bai, Rani of Jhansi BioIn 16
Lakshmikantham, Vangipuram 1926- WhoAm 90
Lakshminarayana, Budugur 1935- WhoAm 90
Lakshminarayana, Natarajan 1937- BiDrAPA 89
Lakshminarayanan, V. R. 1928- BioIn 16
Laky, Joseph E. 1941- St&PR 91
Lal, Archana 1963- BiDrAPA 89
Lal, Chandra Prabha BiDrAPA 89
Lal, Devendra 1929- WhoAm 90
Lal, Lalit 1938- WhoWor 91
Lal, Neeru 1966- WhoE 91
Lal, Samarthji 1938- BiDrAPA 89
Lal, Sunder 1933- WhoWor 91
Lala, Dominick J. 1928- St&PR 91, WhoAm 90
Lala, Jaynarayan Hotchand 1951- WhoE 91
Lala, Kanayo Hotchand 1949- WhoE 91
Lala, Peeyush Kanti 1934- WhoAm 90
Lalak, Irene Christine BiDrAPA 89
Lalak, John Anthony, III 1942- St&PR 91
Laland, Paul H. ODwPR 91
Lalandi, Lina Madeleine IntWWM 90
Lalanne, Claude BioIn 16, ConDes 90
Lalanne, Francois-Xavier 1924- BioIn 16
Lalanne, Francois-Xavier 1927- ConDes 90
Lalanne, Jean-Louis Georges 1938- WhoWor 91
Lalanne, Jimmy BioIn 16
Lalemant, Jerome 1593-1673 EncCRAm, WhNaAH
LaLena, John Charles 1931- WhoE 91
La Liberte, Ann Gillis 1942- WhoAmW 91
La Liberte, Clarence Emory 1917- St&PR 91
Laliberte, Guy BioIn 16
Laliberte, Marc-Andre BiDrAPA 89
Laliberte, Normand Julien, Jr. 1951- WhoE 91
Laliberte, Richard BiDrAPA 89
LaLiberte, Thomas Charles 1949- WhoE 91
Lalicki, Barbara SmATA 61
Lalik, Sharron BioIn 16
Lalime, Ruth E BiDrAPA 89
Lalique, Marie-Claude BioIn 16
Lalique, Rene 1860-1945 PenDiDA 89
Lalka, Judith Candelor 1947- St&PR 91, WhoAm 90
Lall, Arthur Samuel 1911- WhoAm 90
Lalla, Thomas Rocco, Jr. 1950- WhoEmL 91
Lallatin, Gerald J. 1940- St&PR 91
Lalley, Frank Edward 1944- WhoAm 90
Lalli, Cele Goldsmith 1933- WhoAm 90
Lalli, John M. 1942- St&PR 91
Lalli, Louis J. 1936- WhoAm 90
Lalli, Stephen Francis Michael 1951- WhoEmL 91
Lallier, Erna L. 1946- WhoAmW 91
L'Allier, Jean-Paul WhoE 91
Lallinger, E. Michael 1915- WhoAm 90
Lallinger, Manuela von Chielanski- BioIn 16
Lally, Ann Marie 1914- WhoAmW 91, WhoWor 91
Lally, Elizabeth H. 1936- St&PR 91
Lally, James Joseph 1945- WhoAm 90, WhoAmA 91
Lally, Margaret M. WhoWrEP 89
Lally, Michael 1942- ConAu 32NR
Lally, Michael David 1942- WhoAm 90, WhoWrEP 89
Lally, Norma Ross 1932- WhoAmW 91
Lally, Richard Francis 1925- WhoAm 90
Lally, Shirley Constance 1938- WhoE 91
Lally, Thomas Michael 1936- St&PR 91
Lally, William Joseph 1937- WhoE 91, WhoWor 91
Lally-Green, Maureen Ellen 1949- WhoEmL 91
Lalo, Edouard 1823-1892 WorAlBi
Lalo, Edouard 1829-1892 PenDiMP A
La Loca 1950- WhoWrEP 89
LaLonde, Bernard Joseph 1933- WhoAm 90
Lalonde, Brice 1946- BiDFrPL
Lalonde, Donny BioIn 16
Lalonde, Jeffrey A. 1947- St&PR 91
Lalonde, John Stephen, Sr. 1948- WhoEmL 91
Lalonde, Joseph Gerard BiDrAPA 89
Lalonde, Marc 1929- WhoAm 90
Lalonde, Michele 1937- BioIn 16
Lalonde, Pierre 1941- BiDrAPA 89
Lalonde, Richard de PenDiDA 89
Lalonde, Thomas J. 1951- St&PR 91
La Londe, William Salem, III 1932- WhoAm 90
Lalor, Gerald Cecil 1930- WhoWor 91
Lalor, Juvenal BioIn 16
Lalor, Owen Patrick 1952- WhoEmL 91
Lalor, R. Peter 1950- St&PR 91
Lalumandier, Ronald Wayne 1941- St&PR 91
Lalumia, Carl Risley 1928- St&PR 91
La Lumia, Frank 1948- BioIn 16, WhoAmA 91
Lalumiere, Catherine 1935- WhoWor 91
Laluque, Pierre Georges 1921- WhoWor 91
La Luz, Jose A. 1950- WhoHisp 91
LaLuzerne, Richard Lawrence 1931- WhoSSW 91
Lalvani, Taru Jethmal 1918- WhoWor 91
Lalwani, Deena S BiDrAPA 89
Lalwani, Narendra Dhanraj 1952- WhoSSW 91
Lam, Alec St&PR 91
Lam, Annie Siu-Hing 1950- WhoEmL 91
Lam, Annie Young Ying Yee WhoWor 91
Lam, Billy 1960- WhoWor 91
Lam, Charles C K BiDrAPA 89
Lam, David BioIn 16, WhoAm 90
Lam, Jennette 1911-1985 WhoAmA 91N
Lam, Judy Kuan-Ieng 1946- WhoEmL 91
Lam, Julia Kit L BiDrAPA 89
Lam, Nguyen 1921-1990 BioIn 16
Lam, Nora 1932- WhoWor 91
Lam, Raymond Wayne 1956- BiDrAPA 89
Lam, Robert Marcus 1925- WhoE 91
Lam, Samuel ODwPR 91
Lam, Sau-Hai 1930- WhoAm 90
Lam, Sau-Wing 1952- St&PR 91
Lam, Simon Shin-Sing 1947- WhoAm 90
Lam, Wendy Wing Chuen 1964- WhoWor 91
Lam, Wifredo 1902-1982 ArtLatA, BioIn 16
Lama, Alberto De WhoAmA 91
Lama, Lina 1932- IntWWM 90
Lama, Patrick J. 1939- St&PR 91
Lamabe, Jack 1936- Ballpl 90
LaMacchia, Al 1921- Ballpl 90
LaMacchia, John Thomas 1941- WhoAm 90
Lamagra, Anthony James 1935- WhoAm 90
Lamaina, Francis C. 1939- St&PR 91
LaMaina, Lawrence J., Jr. 1935- St&PR 91
Lamaison, Peter Laurens 1941- St&PR 91
La Malfa, James Thomas 1937- WhoAmA 91
Lamalie, Robert Eugene 1931- WhoAm 90
Laman, Jene Terry 1932- WhoSSW 91
Laman, Jerry T. 1947- St&PR 91
LaMancuso, John Lory 1954- WhoEmL 91
Lamando, Ruth B. 1920- WhoE 91
Lamanec, Tracy 1941- WhoAm 90
Lamanna, Carmen 1927- WhoAmA 91
Lamanna, Dominick BioIn 16
LaManna, Ross James 1955- WhoEmL 91
Lamanna, Vincenzo BioIn 16
Lamanno, Ray 1919- Ballpl 90
Lamanno, Richard Carl 1960- WhoE 91
LaManque, Susan Lynn 1952- WhoAmW 91
Lamantia, Angelo 1960- St&PR 91
LaMantia, Charles Robert 1939- St&PR 91, WhoAm 90
Lamantia, James 1923- WhoAmA 91
Lamantia, Paul Zombek 1938- WhoAmA 91
Lamantia, Philip 1927- BioIn 16
LaMar, Bert BioIn 16
Lamar, Bill 1897-1970 Ballpl 90
Lamar, Bonnie Jo Hock BiDrAPA 89
Lamar, Howard Roberts 1923- WhoAm 90
La Mar, John Joseph 1936- WhoE 91
Lamar, Lucius Quintus Cincinnatus 1825-1893 BiDrUSE 89
Lamar, Mario Anselmo 1946- WhoHisp 91
Lamar, Richard E. 1931- St&PR 91
Lamar, Steven Richard 1944- WhoE 91
Lamar, Thomas Allen, Jr. 1936- WhoAm 90
Lamarca, Howard J 1934- WhoAmA 91
LaMarca, Howard James 1934- WhoE 91
Lamarche, Alan Ray 1945- WhoSSW 91
Lamarche, F. Morgan 1938- St&PR 91
LaMarche, Geraldine Venora 1942- WhoAmW 91
Lamarche, Gustave 1895-1987 OxCCanT
La Marche, Judith Ann 1947- WhoAmW 91
LaMarche, Raymond B. 1923- St&PR 91
Lamarchina, Robert 1928- IntWWM 90
Lamarck, Jean Baptiste P, Chevalier De 1744-1829 WorAlBi
Lamarck, Jean Baptiste Pierre Antoine de 1744-1829 BioIn 16
Lamare, Nappy 1907-1988 AnObit 1988
Lamarque, Maurice P. St&PR 91
Lamarr, Hedy 1913- WorAlBi
Lamarre, Bernard C. 1931- WhoAm 90, WhoE 91, WhoWor 91
Lamarre, Charles Jules BiDrAPA 89
La Marre, Mildred Holtz 1917- WhoAmW 91
Lamarre, Monique BiDrAPA 89
Lamarre, Paul WhoAmA 91
Lamarre, Suzanne 1942- BiDrAPA 89
Lamartine, Alphonse De 1790-1869 WorAlBi
Lamas, Jose Francisco 1940- WhoHisp 91
Lamas, Lorenzo BioIn 16
Lamas, Lorenzo 1958- WhoAm 90, WhoHisp 91, WorAlBi
LaMaster, Coleman A. 1929- St&PR 91
LaMaster, Wayne 1907- Ballpl 90
LaMay, Joseph Charles 1947- WhoE 91
Lamb, Adrian S WhoAmA 91N
Lamb, Adrian S. 1901-1988 BioIn 16
Lamb, Alan F. 1941- St&PR 91
Lamb, Alberta Carmella WhoAmA 91
Lamb, Anthony Stuart 1947- IntWWM 90
Lamb, Arthur C, Jr. 1939- BiDrAPA 89
Lamb, Arthur Clifton 1909- EarBlAP
Lamb, Arthur J. 1870-1928 OxCPMus
Lamb, Barbara BiDEWW
Lamb, Bob G. 1931- St&PR 91
Lamb, Caroline 1785-1828 BioIn 16, FemiCLE
Lamb, Catherine BiDEWW
Lamb, Charles 1775-1834 BioIn 16, DcLB 93 [port], WorAlBi
Lamb, Charles Edward 1947- WhoSSW 91
Lamb, Darlis BioIn 16
Lamb, Darlis Carol WhoAmA 91
Lamb, David Layton 1960- WhoEmL 91
Lamb, Doris 1925- BiDrAPA 89
Lamb, Dorrance Winfield 1947- St&PR 91
Lamb, Douglas Booth 1918- St&PR 91

Lamb, Edward Buckton 1806-1869 *BioIn 16*
Lamb, Elizabeth Searle 1917- *WhoWrEP 89*
Lamb, Evelyn Lee 1947- *IntWWM 90*
Lamb, Felix *EncCoWW*
Lamb, Frederic Davis 1931- *St&PR 91, WhoAm 90*
Lamb, Frederick Keithley 1945- *WhoAm 90*
Lamb, Geoffrey *AuBYP 90*
Lamb, George A. 1906- *WhoAm 90, WhoWor 91*
Lamb, George Richard 1928- *WhoAm 90*
Lamb, Girard E. 1923- *St&PR 91*
Lamb, Gordon Howard 1934- *WhoAm 90*
Lamb, H Richard 1929- *BiDrAPA 89*
Lamb, Harold 1892-1962 *AuBYP 90, BioIn 16*
Lamb, Henry D *BiDrAPA 89*
Lamb, Henry Grodon 1906- *WhoE 91*
Lamb, Isabelle Smith *St&PR 91*
Lamb, James Allen 1941- *WhoAm 90*
Lamb, James Christian, IV 1951- *WhoE 91*
Lamb, James R., Jr. 1934- *ODwPR 91*
Lamb, James Warner 1945- *WhoEmL 91*
Lamb, Jamie Parker, Jr. 1933- *WhoAm 90*
Lamb, Jerry Coleman 1938- *WhoAm 90*
Lamb, John *EncO&P 3*
Lamb, Joseph 1887-1960 *OxCPMus*
Lamb, Joseph Peter 1927- *St&PR 91*
Lamb, Joseph Stephen 1934- *St&PR 91, WhoAm 90*
Lamb, Lawrence Edward 1926- *WhoAm 90*
Lamb, Marilyn Freeman 1933- *WhoAmW 91*
Lamb, Mary 1764-1847 *BioIn 16, FemiCLE*
Lamb, Michael Ernest 1953- *WhoE 91*
Lamb, Michael R. 1944- *St&PR 91*
Lamb, Milton T. *TwCCr&M 91*
Lamb, Myrna 1930- *FemiCLE*
Lamb, Myrna 1935- *BioIn 16, NotWoAT*
Lamb, Norman Arthur 1936- *St&PR 91*
Lamb, Patricia *ODwPR 91*
Lamb, Patrick George *BiDrAPA 89*
Lamb, Ray 1944- *Ballpl 90*
Lamb, Rex McNaughton, III 1949- *WhoSSW 91*
Lamb, Robert A. 1938- *WhoAm 90*
Lamb, Robert E. 1940- *St&PR 91*
Lamb, Robert Edward 1936- *WhoAm 90*
Lamb, Robert Lewis 1932- *WhoAm 90*
Lamb, Scott *BioIn 16*
Lamb, Sydney MacDonald 1929- *WhoAm 90*
Lamb, Thomas Howard 1929- *St&PR 91*
Lamb, Ursula Schaefer 1914- *WhoAm 90*
Lamb, Wanda M *BiDrAPA 89*
Lamb, Warren G. 1943- *ODwPR 91, St&PR 91*
Lamb, William 1779-1848 *BioIn 16*
Lamb, William R *BiDrAPA 89*
Lamb, Willis Eugene, Jr. 1913- *WhoAm 90, WhoWor 91*
Lamb, Yanick Rice 1957- *WhoAmW 91*
Lamba, Ameet *BiDrAPA 89*
Lamba, Jacqueline 1910- *BiDWomA*
Lambarth, David Arnold 1940- *WhoE 91*
Lambe, Michael 1950- *WhoE 91*
Lambeau, Curly 1898-1965 *WorAlBi*
Lambeck, Debra T. 1958- *St&PR 91*
Lamber, Juliette *EncCoWW*
Lamberg, Arnold 1934- *St&PR 91*
Lamberg, Joan Bernice 1935- *WhoAmW 91*
Lamberg, Stanley Lawrence 1933- *WhoE 91*
Lamberg, Walter Jerome 1942- *WhoWrEP 89*
Lamberg-Karlovsky, Clifford Charles 1937- *WhoAm 90, WhoE 91, WhoWor 91*
Lambers, Johannes Thieo 1950- *WhoWor 91*
Lamberson, John Roger 1933- *St&PR 91, WhoAm 90, WhoWor 91*
Lambert & Rawlings *PenDiDA 89*
Lambert, Lady *BiDEWW*
Lambert, Marquise de 1647-1733 *EncCoWW*
Lambert, Allen Thomas 1911- *St&PR 91*
Lambert, Anne Therese 1647-1733 *FemiCLE*
Lambert, Arthur G. 1934- *St&PR 91*
Lambert, Arthur Gorman 1899- *WhoE 91, WhoWor 91*
Lambert, Benjamin Joseph, III 1937- *WhoSSW 91*
Lambert, Betty *BioIn 16*
Lambert, Betty 1933-1983 *FemiCLE, OxCCanT*
Lambert, Bill *BioIn 16*
Lambert, Byron Cecil 1923- *WhoAm 90*
Lambert, Carol Ann 1947- *WhoAmW 91, WhoSSW 91, WhoWor 91*
Lambert, Charles F., Jr. 1931- *St&PR 91*
Lambert, Chris Bradley 1958- *WhoSSW 91*
Lambert, Constant 1905-1951 *PenDiMP, -A*
Lambert, Craig Arthur 1947- *WhoEmL 91*
Lambert, Dale John 1946- *WhoEmL 91*
Lambert, Daniel Michael 1941- *WhoAm 90*
Lambert, Dave 1917-1966 *OxCPMus*
Lambert, David 1932- *BioIn 16*
Lambert, David Armstrong 1959- *WhoEmL 91*
Lambert, David L. *WhoAm 90*
Lambert, Deborah Ketchum 1942- *WhoAmW 91*
Lambert, Deborah Sue 1952- *WhoAmW 91*
Lambert, Debra DePrato *BiDrAPA 89*
Lambert, Denis Clair 1932- *WhoWor 91*
Lambert, Dennis M 1943- *BiDrAPA 89*
Lambert, Derek 1929- *TwCCr&M 91*
Lambert, Derek William 1929- *SpyFic*
Lambert, Douglas Harold 1949- *WhoSSW 91*
Lambert, Ed 1949- *WhoAmA 91*
Lambert, Edythe Rutherford 1921- *WhoSSW 91*
Lambert, Eleanor *BioIn 16, ODwPR 91, WhoAm 90*
Lambert, Eugene Louis 1948- *St&PR 91, WhoE 91*
Lambert, Eva Fleg 1935- *WhoWor 91*
Lambert, Francis *PenDiDA 89*
Lambert, Frederick William 1943- *WhoAm 90*
Lambert, G W 1889-1983 *EncO&P 3*
Lambert, Gene *BioIn 16*
Lambert, George Robert 1933- *St&PR 91, WhoAm 90*
Lambert, Georgia Lynn 1948- *WhoWrEP 89*
Lambert, Gerald Maurice 1951- *WhoE 91*
Lambert, Guy William 1889-1983 *EncPaPR 91*
Lambert, Harold Carlton 1956- *WhoEmL 91*
Lambert, Harry W. 1933- *WhoAm 90*
Lambert, Henry A. 1935- *St&PR 91*
Lambert, Henry L *BiDrAPA 89*
Lambert, Henry Raymond 1951- *WhoEmL 91*
Lambert, Ian 1946- *St&PR 91, WhoAm 90*
Lambert, James A. 1956- *St&PR 91*
Lambert, James B. 1924- *St&PR 91*
Lambert, James Richard 1949- *WhoSSW 91*
Lambert, James William 1951- *IntWWM 90*
Lambert, Jane K. 1924- *WhoWrEP 89*
Lambert, Janet 1895?-1973 *AuBYP 90*
Lambert, Jean Marjorie 1943- *WhoAmW 91*
Lambert, Jeff Lee 1953- *WhoEmL 91*
Lambert, Jeffrey Ross 1963- *WhoEmL 91*
Lambert, Jeremiah Daniel 1934- *WhoAm 90*
Lambert, Jerline 1938- *WhoAmW 91*
Lambert, Johann Heinrich 1728-1777 *WorAlBi*
Lambert, John *St&PR 91*
Lambert, John Bernard 1948- *WhoE 91*
Lambert, John Boyd 1929- *St&PR 91, WhoAm 90*
Lambert, John Phillip 1944- *WhoAm 90*
Lambert, John W., Jr. 1945- *ODwPR 91*
Lambert, Joseph Buckley 1940- *WhoAm 90*
Lambert, Joseph Earl 1948- *WhoAm 90, WhoSSW 91*
Lambert, Jules *BiDrAPA 89*
Lambert, Julia Lauver 1946- *WhoEmL 91*
Lambert, Julie Louise 1953- *WhoAmW 91*
Lambert, Ken Ray 1950- *WhoSSW 91*
Lambert, LaDoyce 1935- *St&PR 91*
Lambert, Lee R. 1942- *St&PR 91*
Lambert, Leonard M. 1951- *WhoE 91*
Lambert, Lionel *BioIn 16, NewYTBS 90*
Lambert, Lisa Gaye 1955- *WhoAmW 91*
Lambert, Lorene Cook 1950- *WhoEmL 91*
Lambert, Marjorie Ferguson 1910- *BioIn 16*
Lambert, Martha Lowery 1937- *WhoAmW 91*
Lambert, Mary Ann 1946- *WhoEmL 91*
Lambert, Mary Clark 1931- *WhoE 91*
Lambert, Michael 1947- *WhoSSW 91*
Lambert, Michael Gerard 1952- *WhoE 91*
Lambert, Michael John *BioIn 16*
Lambert, Michael Malet 1930- *WhoAm 90*
Lambert, Nadine Murphy *WhoAm 90*
Lambert, Nancy S 1932- *WhoAmA 91*
Lambert, Paul Christopher 1928- *WhoAm 90*
Lambert, Philip 1925- *WhoAm 90*
Lambert, Phyllis 1927- *BioIn 16, WhoAmA 91*
Lambert, R S 1894- *EncO&P 3*
Lambert, Raymond *BiDrAPA 89*
Lambert, Raymond E. 1925- *St&PR 91*
Lambert, Raymond-Raoul 1894-1943 *BioIn 16*
Lambert, Rebecca Fotouhi 1947- *WhoAm 90, WhoE 91*
Lambert, Rene Joseph 1933- *BiDrAPA 89*
Lambert, Richard G. 1936- *St&PR 91*
Lambert, Richard H 1913- *BiDrAPA 89*
Lambert, Richard Kent *BiDrAPA 89*
Lambert, Robert Bradley 1953- *WhoEmL 91*
Lambert, Robert F. 1959- *St&PR 91*
Lambert, Robert Frank 1924- *WhoAm 90*
Lambert, Robert Gilbert 1930- *WhoAm 90, WhoSSW 91*
Lambert, Robert Joe 1921- *WhoAm 90*
Lambert, Robert Lowell 1923- *WhoAm 90*
Lambert, Robert Stansbury 1920- *WhoAm 90*
Lambert, Sanders R., Jr. 1931- *St&PR 91*
Lambert, Sheldon Marvin 1930- *St&PR 91*
Lambert, Stanley Lyle 1952- *WhoSSW 91*
Lambert, Thomas Wayne 1942- *St&PR 91*
Lambert, Tony *BioIn 16*
Lambert, Vincent 1929- *BiDrAPA 89*
Lambert, W.B. 1923- *St&PR 91*
Lambert, Walter N. 1935- *BioIn 16*
Lambert, William Darby, III 1947- *WhoEmL 91*
Lambert, William G. 1920- *WhoAm 90*
Lambert, William H. 1936- *St&PR 91*
Lambert, William Martin 1929- *St&PR 91*
Lambert, William Wilson 1919- *WhoAm 90*
Lambert, Yves *St&PR 91*
Lamberth, Edwin Eugene 1931- *WhoSSW 91*
Lamberth, Ella Ruth Wheeler 1927- *WhoAmW 91*
Lamberth, J. Michael 1948- *WhoEmL 91*
Lamberti, Armand J 1919- *BiDrAPA 89*
Lamberti, J Steven 1958- *BiDrAPA 89*
Lamberti, Joseph W 1929- *BiDrAPA 89*
Lamberti, Judith Ann 1951- *WhoAmW 91*
Lamberti, Marilyn 1935- *WhoAmW 91*
Lamberti, Marjorie 1937- *WhoAm 90*
Lamberts, Heath 1941- *OxCCanT*
Lambertsen, Christian James 1917- *WhoAm 90*
Lambertsen, Mary Ann 1939- *St&PR 91, WhoAmW 91*
Lambertson, David Floyd 1940- *WhoAm 90*
Lambertson, Wingate Augustus, Jr. 1920- *WhoSSW 91*
Lambertz, Richard H. 1940- *St&PR 91*
Lambesis, Gregory 1955- *WhoE 91*
Lambeth, Thomas Willis 1935- *WhoSSW 91*
Lambeth, Victor Neal 1920- *WhoAm 90*
Lambi, Ivo Nikolai 1931- *ConAu 132*
Lambie, James K. 1928- *St&PR 91*
Lambie, James T. 1942- *St&PR 91*
Lambing, Malcolm E. 1934- *St&PR 91*
Lambing, Steven Jay 1957- *WhoEmL 91, WhoSSW 91*
Lambiotte, Charles Joseph 1955- *WhoEmL 91*
Lambird, Mona Salyer 1938- *WhoAm 90, WhoAmW 91*
Lambly, Sharon A. 1940- *St&PR 91*
Lambo, Jerry Dean 1935- *WhoE 91*
Lambo, Thomas A *BiDrAPA 89*
Lambo, Thomas Adeoye 1923- *WhoWor 91*
Lamboley, Paul Henri 1940- *WhoAm 90*
Lambooy, John Peter 1914- *WhoAm 90*
Lamborn, Earle 1934- *St&PR 91*
Lamborn, LeRoy Leslie 1937- *WhoAm 90*
Lambrakis, Christos 1934- *WhoWor 91*
Lambrecht, Sally Borcher 1960- *WhoAmW 91*
Lambrecht, Sara M. 1930- *ODwPR 91*
Lambrecht, Sara Murray 1930- *St&PR 91*
Lambrechts, Herbert William 1923- *St&PR 91*
Lambremont, Edward Nelson, Jr. 1928- *WhoAm 90*
Lambright, Robert L 1926- *BiDrAPA 89*
Lambright, Stephen Kirk 1942- *St&PR 91, WhoAm 90*
Lambrix, Robert John 1939- *St&PR 91*
Lambro, Donald Joseph 1940- *WhoAm 90*
Lambro, Phillip 1935- *IntWWM 90, WhoAm 90*
Lambros, Lambros John 1935- *WhoAm 90*
Lambros, Thomas Demetrios 1930- *WhoAm 90*
Lambton, John George 1792-1840 *BioIn 16*
Lamburn, Richmal Crompton 1890-1969 *BioIn 16*
Lamdan, Ruth M 1949- *BiDrAPA 89*
Lamden, Evelyn Olson 1950- *WhoAmW 91*
Lamden, Jean Sallie 1927- *WhoAmW 91*
Lame Deer *WhNaAH*
Lameiro, Gerard Francis 1949- *WhoEmL 91, WhoWor 91*
Lamel, Linda H. *BioIn 16*
Lamel, Linda Helen 1943- *WhoAmW 91*
Lamell, Robert 1913- *WhoAmA 91*
Lamendola, Frank Philip 1949- *WhoEmL 91*
Lamendola, Jennifer Joyce 1962- *WhoAmW 91*
Lamendola, Ronald N. 1947- *St&PR 91*
Lamennais, Felicite Robert de 1782-1854 *BioIn 16*
Lamer, Antonio 1933- *WhoAm 90*
Lamere, Robert Kent 1926- *WhoAm 90*
La Meri 1898-1988 *BioIn 16*
Lamerie, Paul de 1688-1751 *PenDiDA 89*
Lamers, John Peter 1933- *WhoAm 90*
Lamers, Willem Jozef Maria 1942- *WhoWor 91*
Lamers, William Francis 1951- *St&PR 91*
Lamesch, Fernand L. 1934- *St&PR 91*
La Messine, Juliette *EncCoWW*
Lamey, Florian Kenneth 1951- *WhoSSW 91*
Lamey, William Daniel Alexander 1953- *WhoAm 90, WhoWor 91*
Lamey, William Lawrence, Jr. 1938- *St&PR 91, WhoAm 90*
Lami, Charles Nicholas 1954- *WhoE 91*
Lamia, Thomas Roger 1938- *WhoWor 91*
Lamigeon, Louise 1915- *IntWWM 90*
Lamiman, Phyllis *BioIn 16*
Lamirande, Emilien 1926- *WhoAm 90*
Lamis, Leroy 1925- *WhoAm 90, WhoAmA 91*
Lamison, Donald R. 1940- *St&PR 91*
Lamison-White, Leatha Mae 1953- *WhoAmW 91*
Lamit, Louis Gary 1949- *WhoEmL 91*
Lamkin, Bill Dan 1929- *WhoAm 90*
Lamkin, Billy M. 1945- *St&PR 91*
Lamkin, Frank J. 1930- *St&PR 91*
Lamkin, Leslie L. 1940- *ODwPR 91*
Lamkin, Linda Landeros 1960- *IntWWM 90*
Lamkin, Martha D. 1942- *St&PR 91*
Lamkin, Selma Hoffman 1925- *WhoE 91*
Lamkin, William Pierce 1919- *WhoAm 90*
Lamm, Carolyn Beth 1948- *WhoAmW 91, WhoE 91, WhoEmL 91, WhoWor 91*
Lamm, Charles P. 1923- *St&PR 91*
Lamm, Donald Stephen 1931- *St&PR 91, WhoAm 90*
Lamm, Edwin R. 1934- *WhoSSW 91*
Lamm, Franklin Charles 1945- *WhoWor 91*
Lamm, Harvey H. *BioIn 16*
Lamm, Harvey H. 1935- *WhoAm 90, WhoE 91*
Lamm, Jeffrey A. *St&PR 91*
Lamm, Joshua Baumol *BiDrAPA 89*
Lamm, LeRoy B 1921- *BiDrAPA 89*
Lamm, Lester Paul 1934- *WhoAm 90*
Lamm, Michael 1936- *WhoWrEP 89*
Lamm, Michael Emanuel 1934- *WhoAm 90*
Lamm, Norman 1927- *WhoAm 90*
Lamm, Renee Ruth *BiDrAPA 89*
Lamm, Richard Douglas 1935- *WhoAm 90*
Lamm, Roderick William 1929- *St&PR 91*
Lamm, Zvi 1921- *WhoWor 91*
Lamme, Bertha 1869-1954 *BioIn 16*
Lammel, Inge 1924- *IntWWM 90*
Lammel, Jeanette Osborn *WhoAm 90*
Lammers, Ann H *BiDrAPA 89*
Lammers, Edward August 1923- *St&PR 91*
Lammers, Gerda 1915- *IntWWM 90*
Lammers, Hans Heinrich 1879-1962 *BioIn 16*
Lammers, Lennis Larry 1937- *WhoE 91*
Lammers, Mark Edward 1931- *IntWWM 90*
Lammers, Steven Paul 1960- *BiDrAPA 89*
Lammert, Richard Alan 1949- *WhoAm 90*
Lammert, Thomas Edward 1947- *WhoEmL 91, WhoWor 91*
Lammertsma, Koop 1949- *WhoSSW 91*
Lammie, James Michael 1949- *WhoSSW 91*
Lamming, George 1927- *BioIn 16, MajTwCW*
Lammons, J. Howard 1929- *St&PR 91*
Lammot, Brooke W. 1931- *St&PR 91*
Lamneck, William C. 1937- *ODwPR 91*
Lamon, Gayle Morse 1953- *WhoEmL 91*
Lamon, Harry Vincent, Jr. 1932- *WhoAm 90*
Lamon, Lillian McInnis 1950- *WhoEmL 91*
Lamonaca, Inga Jennifer 1952- *St&PR 91*
Lamond, Frederic 1868-1948 *PenDiMP*
Lamond, John Patrick 1937- *St&PR 91*
Lamonds, Harold A. 1924- *St&PR 91*
Lamone, Rudolph Philip 1931- *WhoAm 90*
Lamonica, Filippo 1928- *St&PR 91*
Lamonica, John 1954- *WhoEmL 91*
LaMonica, Michael Joseph 1927- *WhoAm 90*
LaMonica, Michael Samuel 1941- *St&PR 91*
Lamons, Robert G. 1932- *St&PR 91*
Lamons, Robert P. 1923- *St&PR 91*
Lamonsoff, Norman C 1936- *BiDrAPA 89*
Lamont, Alastair M 1914- *BiDrAPA 89*

Lamont, Alice *WhoAmW 91, WhoSSW 91, WhoWor 91*
Lamont, Alton W. 1930- *WhoE 91*
LaMont, Andre 1957- *WhoSSW 91*
Lamont, Barbara 1939- *DrBlPA 90, WhoAmW 91*
LaMont, Barbara Gibson 1925- *WhoAm 90*
Lamont, Bridget Later 1948- *WhoAm 90*
Lamont, Corliss 1902- *WhoAm 90, WhoWor 91, WhoWrEP 89*
Lamont, Daniel Scott 1851-1905 *BiDrUSE 89*
Lamont, Donald B. 1919- *St&PR 91*
Lamont, Frances K *WhoAmA 91N*
Lamont, John Hopkins 1923- *BiDrAPA 89*
Lamont, Lansing 1930- *WhoAm 90*
Lamont, Lee *BioIn 16, WhoAm 90*
Lamont, Robert Patterson 1867-1948 *BiDrUSE 89*
Lamont, Rosette Clementine *WhoAm 90*
Lamont, Sam Celeste Catherine 1952- *WhoEmL 91*
Lamont, Thomas W. 1870-1948 *EncABHB 7 [port]*
Lamont, Thomas William 1870-1948 *BioIn 16*
Lamont-Brown, Raymond 1939- *ConAu 32NR*
Lamont-Havers, Ronald William 1920- *WhoAm 90*
Lamontagne, Armand M 1938- *WhoAmA 91*
Lamontagne, David Edward 1948- *St&PR 91*
Lamontagne, J. Gilles 1919- *WhoAm 90, WhoE 91*
Lamontagne, Myrna Lynne 1950- *WhoWrEP 89*
LaMontagne, Normand Edward 1925- *WhoE 91*
Lamontagne, Yves 1941- *BiDrAPA 89*
La Monte, Angela Mae 1944- *WhoAmA 91*
LaMore, Chet Harmon 1908-1980 *WhoAmA 91N*
LaMore, George Edward, Jr. 1930- *WhoAm 90*
LaMore, George L. 1926- *St&PR 91, WhoAm 90*
LaMore, Kenneth W. 1948- *WhoSSW 91*
LaMoreaux, James Wood 1946- *WhoEmL 91*
LaMoreaux, Philip Elmer 1920- *WhoAm 90*
Lamoreaux, William Morris 1946- *WhoEmL 91*
LaMoreux, Frederick Holmes 1941- *St&PR 91, WhoAm 90*
Lamorie, Clarence Carl 1928- *St&PR 91*
Lamoriello, Louis Anthony 1942- *WhoAm 90, WhoE 91*
Lamorisse, Albert 1922-1970 *BioIn 16*
Lamothe, Donat Romeo 1935- *IntWWM 90*
La Mothe, Esther Elizabeth 1946- *WhoEmL 91*
LaMothe, William Edward 1926- *St&PR 91, WhoAm 90*
Lamothe, Yvan 1952- *WhoE 91*
La Motta, Jake *BioIn 16*
Lamotte, Bernard *BioIn 16*
LaMotte, Ellen Newbold 1873-1961 *BioIn 16*
LaMotte, John Vincent, Jr. 1954- *WhoEmL 91*
LaMotte, William Mitchell 1938- *WhoAm 90*
Lamour, Dorothy 1914- *OxCPMus, WorAlBi*
Lamour, Jean 1698-1771 *PenDiDA 89*
L'Amour, Louis 1908-1988 *AnObit 1988, BioIn 16, MajTwCW, WorAlBi, WorAu 1980 [port]*
Lamoureux, Charles 1834-1899 *PenDiMP*
Lamoureux, Gloria Kathleen 1947- *WhoAmW 91, WhoEmL 91, WhoWor 91*
Lamoureux, Paul A. 1947- *St&PR 91*
Lamoureux, William A. 1938- *WhoSSW 91, WhoWor 91*
Lamp, Dennis 1952- *Ballpl 90*
Lamp, John Ernest 1943- *WhoAm 90*
Lamp, Robert Alexander 1951- *St&PR 91*
Lamp, Robert Harry 1936- *St&PR 91*
Lampa, Lita Regala *BiDrAPA 89*
Lampard, Catherine Ann 1951- *WhoAmW 91*
Lamparski, Richard *WhoAm 90, WhoWrEP 89*
Lamparter, Ellen 1957- *WhoEmL 91*
Lamparter, William C. 1929- *WhoAm 90*
Lamparter, William S.L. 1926- *St&PR 91*
Lampe, Annacarol 1951- *WhoAmW 91, WhoEmL 91*
Lampe, Carol Karnell 1945- *WhoAmW 91*
Lampe, Fred George 1925- *WhoSSW 91*
Lampe, Frederick Walter 1927- *WhoAm 90*
Lampe, Guy Lee 1956- *St&PR 91*
Lampe, Henry Oscar 1927- *WhoSSW 91*
Lampe, J. Bodewalt 1869-1929 *OxCPMus*
Lampe, Seth R. 1938- *ODwPR 91*
Lampe, Stefan Martin *BiDrAPA 89*
Lampe, Thomas Heyl 1950- *BiDrAPA 89*
Lampedusa, Giuseppe Di 1896-1957 *WorAlBi*
Lampedusa, Giuseppe Di Tomasi 1896-1957 *BioIn 16*
Lampel, Anita Kay 1946- *WhoAmW 91*
Lampen, Jorma Johannes 1928- *WhoWor 91*
Lampert, Anne B. *ODwPR 91*
Lampert, Barbara Joyce *BiDrAPA 89*
Lampert, Carl Matthew 1952- *WhoEmL 91*
Lampert, Eleanor Verna *WhoWor 91*
Lampert, Emily 1951- *BioIn 16*
Lampert, Fritz 1933- *WhoWor 91*
Lampert, John R. 1923- *St&PR 91*
Lampert, Jonathan Lowell *BiDrAPA 89*
Lampert, Joseph A. 1941- *St&PR 91*
Lampert, Murray A. 1921-1988 *BioIn 16*
Lampert, Richard H. 1947- *St&PR 91*
Lampert, S. Henry 1929- *WhoWor 91*
Lampert, Sidney 1931- *St&PR 91*
Lampert, Wayne M. 1941- *WhoSSW 91*
Lamperti, John Williams 1932- *WhoAm 90*
Lampeter, Kathleen Mary 1961- *WhoAmW 91*
Lamphear, Vivian Shaw 1954- *WhoAmW 91*
Lamphere, James Joseph 1935- *St&PR 91*
Lamphere, Robert Leo 1944- *WhoSSW 91*
Lampi, Kari 1946- *WhoWor 91*
Lamping, Mathild Helen Krueger 1869-1948 *BioIn 16*
Lampiris, Ann Renee 1951- *WhoEmL 91*
Lampitoc, Rol Ponce *WhoAmA 91*
Lampitt, Dinah 1937- *ConAu 132*
Lampke, Robert Stephen 1945- *BiDrAPA 89*
Lampkin, Barbara Jo 1947- *WhoAmW 91*
Lampkin, Charles *DrBlPA 90*
Lampkin, Charles 1913-1989 *ConTFT 8*
Lampkin, Emmett Michael *BiDrAPA 89*
Lampl, Jack W., Jr. 1921- *St&PR 91*
Lampl, Jack Willard, Jr. 1921- *WhoAm 90*
Lampl, John W. *ODwPR 91*
Lampl, Michael Scott 1962- *WhoEmL 91, WhoSSW 91*
Lampl, Peggy Ann 1930- *WhoAm 90*
Lampley, Bianca Schmidt 1964- *WhoAmW 91*
Lamplugh, Mary Beth 1948- *WhoAmW 91, WhoE 91*
Lampman, Archibald 1861-1899 *DcCanB 12, DcLB 92 [port]*
Lampman, Evelyn 1907-1980 *AuBYP 90*
Lamport, Allan Howard 1942- *St&PR 91*
Lamport, Anthony Matthew 1935- *WhoAm 90*
Lamport, Felicia 1916- *WhoAm 90*
Lamprecht, Friedhelm *BiDrAPA 89*
Lamprecht, Karl 1856-1915 *BioIn 16*
Lampredi, Aurelio 1917-1989 *BioIn 16*
Lampron, John Joseph 1944- *St&PR 91*
Lampros-Klein, Francine Demetra 1948- *WhoAmW 91*
Lampsa, Diana *BiDrAPA 89*
Lampson, Butler Wright 1943- *WhoAm 90*
Lampson, Elbert Leroy 1852-1930 *AmLegL*
Lampson, John E. 1936- *St&PR 91*
Lamptey, Jonathan Charles 1950- *WhoEmL 91, WhoWor 91*
Lampton, Christopher *BioIn 16*
Lampton, Dinwiddie, Jr. 1914- *St&PR 91*
Lampton, Mason Houghland 1947- *WhoAm 90*
Lams, Louis *BiDrAPA 89*
Lams, Monica Mary 1947- *WhoAmW 91*
Lamsa, Turo Simo 1941- *WhoWor 91*
Lamsen, Edward Aquino *BiDrAPA 89*
Lamson, David Frank 1924- *St&PR 91*
Lamson, George Herbert 1940- *WhoAm 90*
Lamson, Joan E. 1937- *St&PR 91*
Lamson, Newton W. *ODwPR 91*
Lamson, Ronald K. 1936- *St&PR 91*
Lamy, John Baptist 1814-1888 *WorAlBi*
Lamy, Mary Rebecca 1929- *WhoSSW 91*
Lamy, Maurice Lucien 1942- *WhoWor 91*
Lamy, Michele *BioIn 16*
Lamy, Peter Paul 1925- *WhoAm 90*
Lan, Donald Paul, Jr. 1952- *WhoEmL 91*
Lana, Robert Edward 1932- *WhoAm 90*
Lanahan, John A. 1935- *St&PR 91*
Lanahan, John Stevenson 1922- *WhoAm 90*
Lanahan, William Wallace, III 1943- *St&PR 91*
La Nasa, Katherine *BioIn 16*
Lancashire, Ben John 1928- *St&PR 91*
Lancaster, Albertine Thomas *WhoE 91*
Lancaster, Anthony 1938- *WhoE 91*
Lancaster, Bruce Morgan 1923- *WhoAm 90*
Lancaster, Burt 1913- *BioIn 16, WorAlBi*
Lancaster, Burton 1913- *WhoAm 90*
Lancaster, Carroll Townes, Jr. 1929- *WhoSSW 91*
Lancaster, David *ConAu 30NR*
Lancaster, Deborah Hammond 1959- *WhoSSW 91*
Lancaster, Diane Racine 1954- *WhoSSW 91*
Lancaster, Edmund Clifton 1912- *WhoSSW 91*
Lancaster, Edwin Beattie 1916- *WhoAm 90*
Lancaster, Elaine L. 1935- *WhoAmW 91*
Lancaster, Emanuel Leo 1948- *IntWWM 90, WhoEmL 91*
Lancaster, Frederick Wilfrid 1933- *WhoAm 90*
Lancaster, G. B. 1874-1925 *FemiCLE*
Lancaster, Harold Martin 1943- *WhoAm 90, WhoSSW 91*
Lancaster, Henry Carrington 1923- *St&PR 91*
Lancaster, Howard Erwin, Jr. *BiDrAPA 89*
Lancaster, John B 1891- *EncO&P 3*
Lancaster, Joseph 1778-1838 *WorAlBi*
Lancaster, Joseph Lawrence, Jr. 1925- *WhoAm 90*
Lancaster, Kelvin John 1924- *WhoAm 90*
Lancaster, Les 1962- *Ballpl 90*
Lancaster, Linda Lee 1947- *WhoEmL 91*
Lancaster, Lucy Lee 1905-1989 *BioIn 16*
Lancaster, Lydia 1682?-1761 *BiDEWW*
Lancaster, Lydia 1683-1761 *FemiCLE*
Lancaster, Mark *BioIn 16*
Lancaster, Mark 1938- *WhoAmA 91*
Lancaster, Michael Stewart 1949- *BiDrAPA 89*
Lancaster, Miriam Diemmer 1957- *WhoEmL 91*
Lancaster, Osbert 1908-1986 *BioIn 16*
Lancaster, Peggy *WhoAmW 91*
Lancaster, Peter 1929- *WhoAm 90*
Lancaster, Ralph Ivan, Jr. 1930- *WhoAm 90*
Lancaster, Robert C *BiDrAPA 89*
Lancaster, Robert Charles 1946- *St&PR 91*
Lancaster, Robert Samuel 1909- *WhoAm 90*
Lancaster, Roy G. 1923- *St&PR 91*
Lancaster, Suzanne Corbin 1947- *WhoAmW 91*
Lancaster, Thomas D. 1953- *WhoSSW 91*
Lancaster, Thomas J *BiDrAPA 89*
Lancaster, Whitney C. *ODwPR 91*
Lance, Albert 1925- *IntWWM 90*
Lance, Bert 1931- *WorAlBi*
Lance, George Milward 1928- *WhoAm 90*
Lance, James Alan 1948- *St&PR 91, WhoEmL 91*
Lance, James Waldo 1926- *WhoWor 91*
Lance, Jeanne Louise 1945- *WhoWrEP 89*
Lance, Jerome Ronald *BiDrAPA 89*
Lance, Jill Ann 1945- *St&PR 91*
Lance, Larry K. 1941- *St&PR 91*
Lance, Thomas Bertram 1931- *WhoAm 90*
Lance, Walter C. 1934- *St&PR 91*
Lance, William Campbell 1944- *St&PR 91*
Lancefield, Rebecca Craighill 1895-1981 *DcScB S2*
Lancel McElhinney, James 1952- *WhoAmA 91*
Lancelin, Charles *EncO&P 3*
Lancelot, James Bennett 1952- *IntWWM 90*
Lancetti, Federico *PenDiDA 89*
Lancetti, Pino 1932- *ConDes 90*
Lanchbery, John 1923- *IntWWM 90, PenDiMP*
Lanchester, Elsa 1902-1987 *WorAlBi*
Lanchner, Bertrand Martin 1929- *St&PR 91, WhoAm 90*
Lancia, Frederick Nicholas 1938- *St&PR 91*
Lancie, John de *PenDiMP*
Lancie, John De 1921- *IntWWM 90*
Lancione, Gregory 1928- *St&PR 91*
Lanciotti, Don 1956- *St&PR 91*
Lanciotti, Michael A. 1956- *St&PR 91*
Lancour, Karen Louise 1946- *WhoAmW 91, WhoEmL 91*
Lanctot, Thomas Edward 1954- *WhoEmL 91*
Land, Allan H. 1922- *St&PR 91*
Land, Arthur Julian 1933- *WhoSSW 91*
Land, Betty Lou Jackson 1947- *WhoSSW 91*
Land, Charles Edwards 1952- *WhoEmL 91*
Land, Dorothy Nadine *WhoAmW 91*
Land, Edwin H. *BioIn 16*
Land, Edwin H. 1909- *WorAlBi*
Land, Edwin Herbert 1909- *WhoAm 90*
Land, Ernest Albert 1918- *WhoAmA 91, WhoE 91*
Land, Frank G. 1936- *ODwPR 91*
Land, George Ainsworth 1933- *WhoAm 90, WhoWor 91*
Land, Judith Ann 1938- *WhoWrEP 89*
Land, Judy M. 1945- *WhoAmW 91, WhoWor 91*
Land, Julie Kay 1967- *WhoAmW 91*
Land, Kenneth Carl 1942- *WhoAm 90*
Land, Lynton S. 1940- *WhoAm 90*
Land, Milton *TwCCr&M 91*
Land, Ming Huey 1940- *WhoSSW 91*
Land, Rebekah Ruth 1946- *WhoSSW 91*
Land, Reginald Brian 1927- *WhoAm 90*
Land, Rhonda Mae 1956- *WhoAmW 91*
Land, Richard E 1933- *BiDrAPA 89*
Land, Richard Robert 1949- *WhoWor 91*
Land, Sarah Agnes Riley *WhoAmA 91*
Land, William Bernard *BiDrAPA 89*
Land-Weber, Ellen 1943- *WhoAm 90*
Land-Weber, Ellen E 1943- *WhoAmA 91*
Landa, Alfonso Beaumont, II 1961- *WhoEmL 91, WhoWor 91*
Landa, Howard M. 1943- *St&PR 91*
Landa, Howard Martin 1943- *WhoAm 90*
Landa, Louis A. 1901-1989 *BioIn 16*
Landa, Maria Costabile 1935- *WhoAmW 91*
Landa, Michelle Annette 1955- *WhoAmW 91*
Landa, William Robert 1919- *WhoAm 90*
Landaal, Thomas Green 1954- *St&PR 91*
Landacre, Paul 1893-1963 *WhoAmA 91N*
Landahl, Herbert D. 1913- *WhoAm 90*
Landais, Hubert 1921- *WhoWor 91*
Landale, Thomas David 1927- *St&PR 91*
Landaluze, Victor Patricio de 1828-1889 *ArtLatA*
Landau, Anneliese 1903- *IntWWM 90*
Landau, Annette Henkin 1921- *WhoWrEP 89*
Landau, Barry J *BiDrAPA 89*
Landau, Bernard Robert 1926- *WhoAm 90*
Landau, David *BiDrAPA 89*
Landau, Elaine 1948- *AuBYP 90*
Landau, Ellis 1944- *St&PR 91, WhoAm 90*
Landau, Ely 1920- *WhoAm 90*
Landau, Emmanuel M *BiDrAPA 89*
Landau, Felicia L *BiDrAPA 89*
Landau, Felix 1947- *WhoEmL 91*
Landau, George L. 1928- *St&PR 91*
Landau, George Walter 1920- *WhoAm 90*
Landau, Georges Daniel 1934- *WhoWor 91*
Landau, Herbert Bernard 1940- *WhoAm 90*
Landau, Howard C. 1945- *ODwPR 91*
Landau, Irwin *WhoAm 90*
Landau, Jacob 1917- *WhoAm 90, WhoAmA 91*
Landau, Kurt Heinz 1947- *WhoWor 91*
Landau, Lauri Beth 1952- *WhoAmW 91, WhoEmL 91*
Landau, Lev 1908-1968 *WorAlBi*
Landau, Lev Davidovich 1908-1968 *BioIn 16*
Landau, Lucian 1912- *EncO&P 3*
Landau, Mark M. 1952- *St&PR 91*
Landau, Martin *BioIn 16*
Landau, Martin 1921- *WhoAm 90*
Landau, Martin 1934- *WhoAm 90*
Landau, Michael R. 1946- *St&PR 91*
Landau, Michael Roy 1946- *WhoE 91*
Landau, Mitzi 1925- *WhoAmA 91*
Landau, Myra *WhoAmA 91*
Landau, Nathaniel I. 1935- *St&PR 91*
Landau, Paul Howard 1934- *St&PR 91*
Landau, Peter Edward 1933- *WhoAm 90, WhoWrEP 89*
Landau, Ralph 1916- *WhoAm 90*
Landau, Richard Edwin 1943- *WhoAm 90*
Landau, Richard L. 1916- *WhoAm 90*
Landau, Robert I. 1933- *St&PR 91*
Landau, Robert Irwin 1933- *WhoAm 90*
Landau, Roy Neil 1931- *St&PR 91*
Landau, Samuel 1906- *St&PR 91*
Landau, Samuel J. 1907-1989 *BioIn 16*
Landau, Saul 1936- *ConAu 130, WhoAm 90*
Landau, Shelly 1956- *WhoAmW 91, WhoEmL 91*
Landau, Siegfried 1921- *IntWWM 90, WhoAm 90*
Landau, Sol 1920- *ConAu 31NR*
Landau, Sonia 1937- *WhoAm 90*
Landau, Stephen G 1943- *BiDrAPA 89*
Landau, Sybil Harriet 1937- *WhoAm 90*
Landau, Walter Loeber 1931- *WhoAm 90*
Landau, William 1946- *BiDrAPA 89*
Landau, William Milton 1924- *WhoAm 90*
Landau-Crawford, Dorothy Ruth 1957- *WhoAmW 91, WhoEmL 91*
Landauer, Gustav 1870-1919 *BioIn 16*
Landauer, Jay Paul 1935- *WhoAm 90*
Landauer, Rolf William 1927- *WhoAm 90*
Landauer, Walter E. 1923- *St&PR 91*
Landaw, Stephen Arthur 1936- *WhoAm 90*
Landazuri Ricketts, Juan 1913- *WhoWor 91*
Landberg, Ann Laurel 1926- *WhoAmW 91*
Landberg, George E 1931- *BiDrAPA 89*
Landberg, George Gustaf 1939- *St&PR 91*
Landberg, Nils *PenDiDA 89*
Landbloom, Ronald Peter *BiDrAPA 89*

Lande, Gail Ruth 1962- WhoAmW 91
Lande, Gary Marc 1946- BiDrAPA 89
Lande, James Avra 1930- WhoAm 90
Lande, Lawrence Montague 1906- WhoE 91
Lande, Melinda ODwPR 91
Lande, Ruth Harriet 1929- WhoE 91
Lande, Sarah Dunkerton 1938- WhoAmW 91
Landeau, Ralph 1916- WhoAm 90
Landeck, Armin 1905- WhoAmA 91N
Landeck, Beatrice 1904- AuBYP 90
Landecker, Werner Siegmund 1911- WhoAm 90
Landeen, Robert Harold BiDrAPA 89
Landefeld, E. Kent 1933- St&PR 91
Landegger, Carl Clement 1930- WhoAm 90, WhoE 91
Landegger, Carl M. 1953- St&PR 91
Landel, Robert Davis 1940- WhoAm 90
Landel, Robert Franklin 1925- WhoAm 90
Landen, James E BiDrAPA 89
Landen, Robert Geran 1930- WhoAm 90, WhoWor 91
Landendorf, Virginia B BiDrAPA 89
Lander, Alan Anthony 1946- WhoE 91
Lander, Alfred O. 1908- St&PR 91
Lander, Bernard 1915- WhoAm 90
Lander, Charles Allen 1937- St&PR 91
Lander, Donald BioIn 16
Lander, Donald H. 1925- WhoAm 90
Lander, Guy Philip 1952- WhoEmL 91
Lander, Howard 1950- WhoEmL 91
Lander, James Rollin, Jr. 1943- WhoSSW 91
Lander, Jay 1945- WhoE 91
Lander, Raymond A., Jr. 1920- St&PR 91
Lander, Richard Leon 1928- WhoAm 90
Landerdahl, Brenda Huschka 1161- WhoAmW 91
Landers, Ann BioIn 16
Landers, Ann 1918- BioAmW, WhoAm 90, WhoAmW 91, WorAlBi
Landers, Bertha WhoAmA 91
Landers, Blaine Howard 1957- WhoEmL 91
Landers, Donald F. 1933- WhoAm 90
Landers, Gary Clinton 1951- WhoEmL 91
Landers, James A. 1940- St&PR 91
Landers, James Rayburn 1942- WhoSSW 91
Landers, Milton Harold 1950- WhoEmL 91
Landers, Ronald Wayne 1946- St&PR 91
Landers, Susan Mae WhoAmW 91
Landers, Thomas J. 1929- WhoAm 90
Landers, Vernette Trosper 1912- WhoAmW 91, WhoWor 91
Landerson, Louis BioIn 16, NewYTBS 90
Landes, Bertha Knight 1868-1943 BioIn 16
Landes, David S. 1924- WhoWrEP 89
Landes, George Miller 1928- WhoAm 90
Landes, John Brougher 1948- WhoEmL 91
Landes, John David 1942- WhoSSW 91
Landes, Julie ODwPR 91
Landes, Marie Gisele ConAu 129
Landes, Marjorie BiDrAPA 89
Landes, Robert Nathan 1930- St&PR 91, WhoAm 90
Landes, Sonia 1925- WhoWrEP 89
Landes, Stan 1923- Ballpl 90
Landes, Stephen 1938- St&PR 91
Landes, William-Alan 1945- WhoWrEP 89
Landes, William M. 1939- WhoAm 90
Landes-Fuss, Marie-Gisele 1936- ConAu 129
Landesberg, Lee Jay 1948- WhoE 91
Landesberg, Steve WhoAm 90
Landesman, Alter 1895-1980? BioIn 16
Landesman, Earl Stanley 1952- WhoEmL 91
Landesman, Erica ODwPR 91
Landesman, Jay BioIn 16
Landess, Fred S. 1933- WhoAm 90
Landestoy, Rafael 1953- Ballpl 90
Landeta, Matilde 1913- BioIn 16
andfair, Billy Lou 1933- St&PR 91
andfield, Ronnie 1947- WhoAmA 91
andgarten, Nathan 1918- St&PR 91
andgraf, Charles W., Jr. 1925- BiDrAPA 89
andgraf, Susan Manning 1961- WhoAmW 91
andgraver, Kenneth R., Jr. 1940- St&PR 91
andgrebe, Bernhard Hans BiDrAPA 89
andgrebe, David Allen 1934- WhoAm 90
andgrebe, John Allan 1937- WhoAm 90
andgren, Craig Randall 1947- WhoAm 90
andgren, George Lawrence 1919- WhoAm 90
andherr, Robert F. 1938- St&PR 91
andi, Beroccio de' 1447-1500 BioIn 16
andi, Dale Michael 1938- WhoAm 90
andi, Richard 1948- St&PR 91
andi, Stefano 1586?-1639 PenDiMP A
andin, Felix, Jr. 1941- WhoHisp 91
andin, Myron W. 1948- St&PR 91
andin, Thomas Milton 1937- WhoE 91

Landini, Richard George 1929- WhoAm 90
Landino, Richard Earl 1959- WhoE 91
Landis, Bill 1942- Ballpl 90
Landis, Brenda Reinhart 1960- WhoWrEP 89
Landis, Brent William 1947- WhoEmL 91
Landis, Donald Howard 1929- St&PR 91
Landis, Edgar David 1932- St&PR 91, WhoAm 90
Landis, Edward E 1907- BiDrAPA 89
Landis, Elizabeth Storey 1921- WhoE 91
Landis, Ellen Jamie 1941- WhoAmA 91
Landis, Elwood Winton 1928- WhoAm 90, WhoWrEP 89
Landis, Fred 1923- WhoAm 90
Landis, Frederick NewYTBS 90
Landis, Frederick 1912-1990 BioIn 16
Landis, J D 1942- SmATA 60
Landis, James David BioIn 16
Landis, James David 1942- St&PR 91, WhoAm 90
Landis, James M. 1899-1964 EncABHB 7 [port]
Landis, James McCauley 1899-1964 BioIn 16
Landis, James Richard, Jr. 1930- WhoWrEP 89
Landis, Jay L. 1930- St&PR 91
Landis, Jim 1934- Ballpl 90
Landis, John BioIn 16
Landis, John 1950- WorAlBi
Landis, John David 1950- WhoAm 90
Landis, John William 1917- WhoAm 90, WhoWor 91
Landis, Kenesaw Mountain 1866-1944 Ballpl 90 [port], WorAlBi
Landis, Larry Seabrook 1945- WhoEmL 91
Landis, Lewis Rex 1917- WhoAm 90
Landis, Lynn Lamberton 1949- WhoSSW 91
Landis, Mark Glenn 1942- St&PR 91
Landis, Pamela Ann Youngman 1941- WhoE 91
Landis, Richard G. 1920- St&PR 91
Landis, Robert Kumler, III 1953- WhoE 91
Landis, Robert M. 1920- WhoAm 90
Landis, Thomas Shepler 1927- St&PR 91
Landis, Tom Jay 1946- WhoEmL 91
Landis, Virginia H. 1953- St&PR 91
Landisman, Mark 1928- WhoSSW 91
Landman, Bette Emeline 1937- WhoAm 90, WhoAmW 91
Landman, David 1948- WhoEmL 91
Landman, Hubrecht Anton 1945- WhoWor 91
Landman, Lou 1927- St&PR 91
Landman, Louis 1910- BiDrAPA 89, WhoE 91
Landman, Max V. 1946- St&PR 91
Landman, Richard Marc 1952- WhoEmL 91
Landman, Uzi WhoAm 90
Landmann, Frederic Harrison 1933- WhoAm 90, WhoE 91
Lando, Dario 1933- WhoWor 91
Lando, Howard Milton 1949- WhoEmL 91
Lando, Jerome Burton 1932- WhoAm 90
Lando, Maxine Cohen 1950- WhoEmL 91
Lando, Robert 1915- St&PR 91
Lando, Robert N. 1915- WhoAm 90
Landolfi, Jennie L. 1955- WhoAmW 91
Landolph, Joseph Richard, Jr. 1948- WhoEmL 91
Landolt, Allison Booth BiDrAPA 89
Landolt, Allison Booth 1919- WhoE 91
Landolt, Arlo Udell 1935- WhoAm 90
Landolt, Robert George 1939- WhoSSW 91
Landolt-Bohus, Eleanor Ruth 1954- WhoE 91
Landon, Alf 1887-1987 WorAlBi
Landon, Barry R. 1947- ODwPR 91
Landon, Carl Everett 1947- St&PR 91
Landon, Deborah Dodge 1943- WhoE 91
Landon, Donald R. 1945- WhoEmL 91
Landon, Edward August 1911-1984 WhoAmA 91N
Landon, Forrest M. 1933- WhoAm 90
Landon, Forrest Malcolm 1933- St&PR 91
Landon, Fred Barry 1951- WhoE 91
Landon, H. Ray 1935- St&PR 91
Landon, Harry Raymond 1935- WhoAm 90
Landon, Howard Chandler Robbins 1926- IntWWM 90
Landon, Jack Nicholas, III 1951- WhoEmL 91
Landon, John Campbell 1937- St&PR 91
Landon, John William 1937- WhoSSW 91, WhoWor 91
Landon, Letitia Elizabeth 1802-1838 BioIn 16, DcLB 96 [port]
Landon, Lucinda 1950- BioIn 16
Landon, Margaret 1903- BioIn 16
Landon, Mark Bond 1962- WhoEmL 91
Landon, Michael BioIn 16

Landon, Michael 1936- WhoAm 90
Landon, Michael 1937- WorAlBi
Landon, Michael de L 1935- ConAu 30NR
Landon, Morris F. 1919- St&PR 91
Landon, R. Kirk 1929- St&PR 91
Landon, Robert Gray 1928- WhoAm 90
Landon, Robert Kirkwood 1929- WhoAm 90
Landon, Timothy Riley 1958- WhoEmL 91
Landor, Walter 1913- ConDes 90
Landor, Walter Savage 1775-1864 BioIn 16, DcLB 93 [port]
Landou, Bernard 1931- ODwPR 91
Landovitz, Leon Fred 1932- St&PR 91, WhoAm 90
Landovsky, Rosemary Reid 1933- WhoAmW 91, WhoWor 91
Landow, George Paul 1940- WhoAm 90
Landow, Stanley 1918- WhoAm 90
Landowne, Ann Elizabeth 1955- BiDrAPA 89
Landowska, Wanda 1877-1959 BioIn 16, PenDiMP
Landowska, Wanda 1879-1959 WorAlBi
Landowski, Marcel 1915- PenDiMP A
Landowski, Marcel Francois Paul 1915- IntWWM 90
Landphair, Douglas Alan 1952- WhoEmL 91
Landram, Christina Louella 1922- WhoAmW 91
Landrau, Marge 1939- WhoHisp 91
Landreau, Anthony Norman 1930- WhoAmA 91
Landreaux, Ken 1954- Ballpl 90
Landree, Hubert Henry 1919- St&PR 91
Landreneau, Janis Suchand 1948- WhoSSW 91
Landreneau, Rodney Edmund, Jr. 1929- WhoSSW 91
Landres, Peter David BiDrAPA 89
Landreth, Beverly Charlene 1963- IntWWM 90
Landreth, Charles Burnet 1947- St&PR 91
Landrian, Mario P BiDrAPA 89
Landriault, Jacques 1921- WhoAm 90
Landrieu, Mary 1955- WhoAmW 91, WhoSSW 91
Landrieu, Moon 1930- WorAlBi
Landrieu, Moon Edwin 1930- BiDrUSE 89
Landrieu, Pierre Raoul Henri 1941- St&PR 91
Landrigan, Penelope Savage 1939- WhoAmW 91
Landrigan, Philip John 1942- WhoAm 90
Landriscina, Ben 1944- St&PR 91
Landrith, Hobie 1930- Ballpl 90
Landron, Michel John 1946- WhoE 91
Landrum, Bill 1957- Ballpl 90
Landrum, Diedra Gansloser 1952- WhoSSW 91
Landrum, Dom 1936- Ballpl 90
Landrum, Larry James 1943- WhoWor 91
Landrum, Phil M. NewYTBS 90
Landrum, Tito 1954- Ballpl 90
Landrum-Brummund, Frances Ann 1918- WhoAmW 91, WhoSSW 91
Landry, Albert 1919- WhoAmA 91
Landry, Alfred Ronald 1936- WhoE 91
Landry, Barry T. 1958- St&PR 91
Landry, Donald G. 1945- WhoSSW 91
Landry, Elaine G. 1943- WhoAmW 91
Landry, G.Y. 1938- St&PR 91
Landry, Gary Keith 1957- WhoEmL 91
Landry, James Michael 1956- WhoEmL 91
Landry, Jane Lorenz 1936- WhoAm 90
Landry, Joan Adele 1933- St&PR 91
Landry, Karen Eremin 1959- WhoAmW 91
Landry, Larry David 1948- WhoEmL 91
Landry, Lawrence S. 1956- St&PR 91
Landry, Lynn Louis 1931- WhoSSW 91
Landry, Mark Edward 1950- WhoEmL 91
Landry, Michael Gerard 1946- WhoEmL 91
Landry, Monique 1937- WhoAm 90, WhoAmW 91, WhoE 91
Landry, Napoleon-P 1884-1956 DcLB 92 [port]
Landry, Philip A BiDrAPA 89
Landry, Raymond BioIn 16
Landry, Rejean 1952- St&PR 91
Landry, Richard Miles 1938- WhoAmA 91
Landry, Robert Edward 1929- WhoAm 90
Landry, Robert J. 1946- St&PR 91
Landry, Robert James 1950- WhoSSW 91
Landry, Robert Raymond 1947- WhoSSW 91
Landry, Roger D. 1934- WhoAm 90
Landry, Ronald Jude 1943- WhoSSW 91
Landry, Stephen Anthony 1960- WhoEmL 91
Landry, Thomas Henry 1946- St&PR 91, WhoAm 90
Landry, Tom BioIn 16
Landry, Tom 1924- WhoAm 90, WhoSSW 91, WorAlBi

Landsberg, Dennis Robert 1948- WhoAm 90, WhoWor 91
Landsberg, Hans Herman 1913- WhoE 91
Landsberg, Jerry 1933- WhoE 91, WhoWor 91
Landsberg, Steven Allen 1957- WhoEmL 91
Landsberger, David 1948- St&PR 91
Landsberger, Henry A. 1926- WhoAm 90
Landsberger, Kurt 1920- St&PR 91
Landsbergis, Vytautas BioIn 16, WhoWor 91
Landsbergis, Vytautas 1932- CurBio 90 [port], WorAlBi
Landsborough, Ron James 1955- WhoEmL 91
Landsburg, Alan William 1933- WhoAm 90
Landseer, Edwin Henry 1802-1873 BioIn 16
Landseer, Jessica 1807-1880 BiDWomA
Landshoff, Fritz BioIn 16
Landske, Dorothy Suzanne 1937- WhoAmW 91
Landskroner, Ray 1940- St&PR 91
Landsman, Dale Earl 1934- WhoAm 90
Landsman, Eliot BiDrAPA 89
Landsman, Jerome Leonard 1923- IntWWM 90
Landsman, Joseph K. 1934- WhoWrEP 89
Landsman, Samuel N.B. 1950- WhoWrEP 89
Landsman, Stanley 1930- WhoAmA 91N
Landsman, Stephen A. 1942- WhoAm 90
Landsmann, Leanna 1946- WhoAm 90, WhoWrEP 89
Landsteiner, Karl 1868-1943 WorAlBi
Landsverk, Wayne Douglas 1946- WhoEmL 91
Landureth, Lewis James 1943- WhoSSW 91
Landuyt, Bernard Francis 1907- WhoAm 90, WhoWor 91
Landwehr, Arthur John 1934- WhoWor 91
Landwehr, Judy Ann 1952- WhoEmL 91
Landwehr, William Charles 1941- WhoAm 90, WhoAmA 91
Landy, Burton Aaron 1929- WhoAm 90, WhoWor 91
Landy, Douglas Alan 1955- BiDrAPA 89
Landy, Eugene BioIn 16
Landy, Eugene W. 1933- St&PR 91
Landy, Joseph P. 1932- WhoAm 90
Landy, Mary Joesphine BiDrAPA 89
Landy, Maurice 1913- WhoAm 90
Landy, Ralph Lewis 1957- WhoEmL 91
Landy, Richard Allen 1931- WhoAm 90
Landzaat, John Adriaan 1947- WhoWor 91
Landzettel, Robert W. 1935- St&PR 91
Lane, Alfred Church 1863-1948 DcScB S2
Lane, Allen 1902-1970 WorAlBi
Lane, Alvin Huey, Jr. 1942- WhoAm 90
Lane, Alvin S 1918- WhoAmA 91
Lane, Alvin Seymour 1918- WhoAm 90
Lane, Andrea Neal 1957- WhoAmW 91
Lane, Angela Gail 1955- St&PR 91
Lane, Ann Judith 1931- WhoAmW 91
Lane, Arthur Alan 1945- WhoAm 90
Lane, Arthur Bliss 1894-1956 BioIn 16
Lane, Barbara Miller 1934- WhoAm 90
Lane, Benjamin Thomas 1957- IntWWM 90
Lane, Brian David 1962- WhoSSW 91
Lane, Brian M. 1951- St&PR 91
Lane, Brogan BioIn 16
Lane, Bruce Stuart 1932- WhoAm 90
Lane, Burton 1912- OxCPMus, WhoAm 90
Lane, Carl Daniel 1899- AuBYP 90
Lane, Carolyn 1926- AuBYP 90
Lane, Carolyn Blocker 1926- WhoWrEP 89
Lane, Charles BioIn 16
Lane, Charles S, III 1951- BiDrAPA 89
Lane, Charles Stuart 1924- WhoE 91, WhoWor 91
Lane, Constance Carmichael Renick 1921- WhoAmW 91
Lane, Dana Ellis 1946- St&PR 91
Lane, Daniel McNeel 1936- WhoSSW 91, WhoWor 91
Lane, David 1956- EncO&P 3
Lane, David Christopher 1956- WhoEmL 91
Lane, David Oliver 1931- WhoAm 90
Lane, Diane BioIn 16
Lane, Don Velension 1953- WhoEmL 91
Lane, Donald Scott 1958- WhoEmL 91
Lane, DonnaLee Ann Mucciarone 1945- WhoEmL 91
Lane, Edward Wood, Jr. 1911- WhoAm 90
Lane, Eli W 1922- BiDrAPA 89
Lane, Elinor 1864-1909 FemiCLE
Lane, Elisabeth Ann 1942- WhoE 91
Lane, Elizabeth 1905-1988 AnObit 1988
Lane, Elizabeth Ann 1959- WhoE 91
Lane, Ernest Edward, III 1948- WhoE 91
Lane, Eugene Numa 1936- WhoAm 90

Lane, F. C. 1885- *Ballpl 90*
Lane, Fielding H. 1926- *WhoAm 90*
Lane, Fitz Hugh 1804-1865 *WorAlBi*
Lane, Frank 1896- *Ballpl 90*
Lane, Frank Childress *BiDrAPA 89*
Lane, Frank Elmer 1955- *BiDrAPA 89*
Lane, Franklin K. 1864-1921 *BiDrUSE 89*
Lane, Frederic C. 1900-1984 *BioIn 16*
Lane, Frederick Carpenter 1949- *WhoAm 90*
Lane, Frederick M 1928- *BiDrAPA 89*
Lane, Frederick Stanley 1915- *WhoAm 90*
Lane, G. William 1921- *St&PR 91*
Lane, Gary 1946- *WhoEmL 91, WhoWor 91*
Lane, Gloria 1930- *IntWWM 90*
Lane, Gloria Julian 1932- *WhoAmW 91, WhoWor 91*
Lane, Grant *TwCCr&M 91*
Lane, Gregory Jay 1952- *WhoSSW 91*
Lane, Hana Umlauf 1946- *WhoAm 90*
Lane, Harold Edwin 1913- *WhoAm 90*
Lane, Harold J 1927- *BiDrAPA 89*
Lane, Harriet 1830-1903 *BioIn 16*
Lane, Hugh C. 1914- *EncABHB 7 [port]*
Lane, Iris Mary 1934- *WhoAmW 91*
Lane, James F. *ODwPR 91*
Lane, James F. 1953- *WhoEmL 91*
Lane, James Franklin 1931- *WhoAm 90*
Lane, James G. 1934- *St&PR 91*
Lane, James Garland, Jr. 1934- *WhoAm 90*
Lane, James Hamilton 1945- *WhoSSW 91*
Lane, James M. 1929- *St&PR 91*
Lane, James McConkey 1929- *WhoAm 90*
Lane, Jane *ConAu 30NR*
Lane, Janet Ann 1959- *WhoAmW 91*
Lane, Jeannie Mae 1959- *WhoAmW 91*
Lane, Jeffrey Bruce 1942- *St&PR 91, WhoAm 90*
Lane, Jerald Paul *BiDrAPA 89*
Lane, John Christian 1953- *WhoSSW 91*
Lane, John Dennis 1921- *WhoAm 90*
Lane, John Gary 1942- *WhoAm 90*
Lane, John M. 1941- *St&PR 91*
Lane, John Rodger 1944- *WhoAm 90, WhoAmA 91*
Lane, John Thomas 1942- *WhoE 91*
Lane, Joseph C. 1953- *St&PR 91, WhoAm 90*
Lane, Julia A. 1927- *WhoAmW 91*
Lane, K. *BiDWomA*
Lane, Kathleen Margaret 1946- *WhoAmW 91*
Lane, Kelly *ODwPR 91*
Lane, Kenneth Edwin 1928- *WhoAm 90*
Lane, Kenneth Jay 1932- *WhoAm 90*
Lane, Kenneth Robert 1942- *WhoE 91, WhoWor 91*
Lane, Laurence William, Jr. 1919- *WhoWor 91*
Lane, Lawrence Jubin 1927- *WhoAm 90, WhoWor 91*
Lane, Leonard C. 1919- *St&PR 91*
Lane, Lois 1948- *WhoAmA 91*
Lane, Lois M. White 1914- *WhoWrEP 89*
Lane, Lois N. 1948- *WhoAm 90*
Lane, Louis 1923- *IntWWM 90, WhoAm 90*
Lane, Loyd Carlton 1944- *St&PR 91*
Lane, Lupino 1892-1959 *OxCPMus*
Lane, M. 1934- *FemiCLE*
Lane, M. Travis 1934- *BioIn 16*
Lane, Malcolm Daniel 1930- *WhoAm 90*
Lane, Malia *WhoWrEP 89*
Lane, Marc J. 1946- *WhoWrEP 89*
Lane, Margaret Beynon Taylor 1919- *WhoAmW 91*
Lane, Marie Irene 1944- *WhoAmW 91*
Lane, Marilyn E. 1931- *St&PR 91*
Lane, Marilyn Edith 1931- *WhoAm 90*
Lane, Marion Jean Arrons *WhoAmA 91*
Lane, Marion Sue 1944- *WhoAmW 91*
Lane, Mark 1927- *WhoAm 90, WhoWrEP 89, WorAlBi*
Lane, Marvin Maskall, Jr. 1934- *WhoAm 90*
Lane, Marvin Maskell, Jr. 1934- *St&PR 91*
Lane, Mary C. 1939- *St&PR 91*
Lane, Mary Frances 1955- *WhoAmW 91*
Lane, Mary Hill 1943- *WhoAmW 91*
Lane, Maryl A. 1958- *WhoEmL 91*
Lane, Matthew Jay 1955- *WhoEmL 91*
Lane, Melvin B. 1922- *St&PR 91*
Lane, Melvin Bell 1922- *WhoAm 90*
Lane, Michael G. 1945- *St&PR 91*
Lane, Michael H. 1943- *St&PR 91*
Lane, Millicent Travis 1934- *BioIn 16*
Lane, Mills 1912-1989 *BioIn 16*
Lane, Mills Bee, Jr. 1912- *ConAmBL*
Lane, Montague 1929- *WhoAm 90*
Lane, Morton Noel 1944- *St&PR 91*
Lane, Nancy *BioIn 16*
Lane, Nancy 1938- *WhoAm 90, WhoWrEP 89*
Lane, Nancy Lee 1938- *WhoAmW 91*
Lane, Neal Francis 1938- *WhoAm 90*
Lane, Neola Tracy *AuBYP 90*
Lane, Newton A. 1915- *St&PR 91*
Lane, Newton Alexander 1915- *WhoAm 90*
Lane, Norman Edward, Jr. 1950- *WhoEmL 91*
Lane, Patricia Louise 1950- *WhoAmW 91*
Lane, Patricia Nadine 1939- *St&PR 91*
Lane, Patricia S. 1932- *WhoSSW 91*
Lane, Patrick 1939- *WhoAm 90, WhoWrEP 89*
Lane, Pinkie Gordon *WhoWrEP 89*
Lane, Ralph 1530?-1603 *EncCRAm*
Lane, Ralph, Jr. 1923- *WhoAm 90*
Lane, Randall Brent *BiDrAPA 89*
Lane, Rebecca Massie *WhoSSW 91*
Lane, Richard David 1952- *BiDrAPA 89*
Lane, Robert Alan 1955- *WhoSSW 91*
Lane, Robert Dale 1929- *St&PR 91*
Lane, Robert Gerald 1926- *St&PR 91*
Lane, Robert Gerhart 1931- *WhoAm 90, WhoWor 91*
Lane, Robert Myers 1939- *St&PR 91*
Lane, Robert Pitt 1954- *WhoEmL 91*
Lane, Robert Raymond 1948- *WhoSSW 91*
Lane, Rose 1887?-1968 *FemiCLE*
Lane, Rose Wilder 1887-1968 *AuBYP 90*
Lane, Rosemary Louise 1944- *WhoAmA 91*
Lane, Sarah Marie 1946- *WhoAmW 91, WhoEmL 91*
Lane, Shari Lea 1950- *WhoAmW 91*
Lane, Sharon Suzanne 1950- *WhoEmL 91*
Lane, Sherry 1942- *WhoE 91*
Lane, Stephen John 1949- *WhoEmL 91*
Lane, Stephen L. 1935- *WhoAm 90*
Lane, Steve Allen 1935- *WhoSSW 91*
Lane, Steven Jay 1955- *WhoEmL 91*
Lane, Suzanne 1947- *ODwPR 91*
Lane, Suzanne Kathryn 1947- *WhoE 91*
Lane, Sylvia *WhoAm 90*
Lane, Thomas Darles 1949- *WhoEmL 91*
Lane, W. C. 1847- *AmLegL*
Lane, Warren C., Jr. 1923- *WhoAm 90*
Lane, William 1936- *WhoAmA 91*
Lane, William 1951- *OxCCanT*
Lane, William Arthur 1958- *WhoEmL 91, WhoSSW 91, WhoWor 91*
Lane, William Caswell 1925- *WhoSSW 91*
Lane, William Robert 1948- *St&PR 91*
Lane, William W. 1934- *St&PR 91, WhoAm 90, WhoE 91, WhoWor 91*
Lane, Winston Earl, III *BiDrAPA 89*
Lane-Arrons, Marion J. 1928- *WhoE 91*
Lane Fox, Robin *BioIn 16*
Lane-Reticker, Edward 1926- *St&PR 91, WhoAm 90*
Laner, Richard Warren 1933- *WhoAm 90*
Lanergan, James West 1828-1886 *OxCCanT*
Lanes, Douglas M 1944- *BiDrAPA 89*
Lanes, Lawrence M 1948- *BiDrAPA 89*
Lanes, Samuel 1908- *BiDrAPA 89*
Lanes, Selma 1929- *AuBYP 90*
Lanes, Selma Gordon 1929- *WhoAm 90*
Lanese, Anthony L., Jr. 1928- *St&PR 91*
Lanese, Herbert Joseph 1945- *St&PR 91*
Lanese, Jill Renee 1952- *WhoE 91*
Laneuville, Eric 1952- *DrBIPA 90*
Laney, Benjamin Travis 1896-1977 *BioIn 16*
Laney, D. Randy 1954- *St&PR 91*
Laney, David Hart 1959- *WhoSSW 91*
Laney, David Randy 1954- *WhoAm 90, WhoSSW 91*
Laney, Gary R. *St&PR 91*
Laney, James B. 1935- *St&PR 91*
Laney, James Thomas 1927- *WhoAm 90, WhoSSW 91*
Laney, Landy B. 1932- *WhoSSW 91*
Laney, Michael L. 1945- *WhoAm 90*
Laney, Shareen *BioIn 16*
Lanez, Carmencita T 1952- *BiDrAPA 89*
Lanfeld, Alvin Jerome 1927- *St&PR 91*
Lanford, Herbert Alvin, Jr. 1948- *WhoSSW 91, WhoWor 91*
Lanford, John C. 1930- *St&PR 91*
Lanford, Luke Dean 1922- *WhoAm 90*
Lanford, Oscar Erasmus, III 1940- *WhoAm 90*
Lanford, Oscar Erasmus, Jr. 1914- *WhoAm 90*
Lanfranco, Giovanni 1582-1647 *IntDcAA 90*
Lanfrey, Claude-Francois *PenDiDA 89*
Lang, Al *Ballpl 90*
Lang, Alan E. 1933- *St&PR 91*
Lang, Albert W *BiDrAPA 89*
Lang, Andrew 1844-1912 *AuBYP 90, BioIn 16, DcLB 98 [port], EncO&P 3, EncPaPR 91*
Lang, Avis 1944- *WhoAmA 91*
Lang, Barbara Ann 1950- *WhoAmW 91*
Lang, Belinda 1953- *ConTFT 8 [port]*
Lang, Bernard Albert 1936- *St&PR 91*
Lang, Bernhard 1946- *WhoWor 91*
Lang, Bertha F. 1917- *IntWWM 90*
Lang, Bruce T. 1944- *St&PR 91*
Lang, C. Max 1937- *WhoAm 90*
Lang, Carol Elizabeth 1937- *WhoSSW 91*
Lang, Cay 1948- *WhoAmA 91*
Lang, Cecil Yelverton 1920- *WhoAm 90, WhoWrEP 89*
Lang, Charles B. 1940- *St&PR 91*
Lang, Christopher M. 1951- *BiDrAPA 89*
Lang, Clyde Everett 1943- *St&PR 91*
Lang, Daniel S. 1935- *WhoAm 90, WhoAmA 91*
Lang, David Wayne 1954- *WhoE 91*
Lang, Debbie Davis 1956- *WhoAmW 91*
Lang, Deborah Odom 1953- *WhoAmW 91*
Lang, Eddie 1902-1933 *BioIn 16, OxCPMus*
Lang, Edith 1927- *IntWWM 90*
Lang, Edward W. *BioIn 16*
Lang, Enid Asher 1944- *BiDrAPA 89*
Lang, Erich Karl 1929- *WhoAm 90*
Lang, Eugene M 1919- *News 90 [port], -90-3 [port], WhoAm 90*
Lang, Eugene Michael 1919- *St&PR 91*
Lang, Francis Harover 1907- *WhoAm 90, WhoWor 91*
Lang, Frank Alexander 1934- *St&PR 91*
Lang, Frederick Webber 1924- *St&PR 91*
Lang, Fritz 1890-1976 *ConAu 30NR, WorAlBi*
Lang, Gabriel 1931- *WhoWor 91*
Lang, George 1924- *WhoAm 90*
Lang, George A., Jr. 1925- *St&PR 91*
Lang, George Russell, Jr. 1952- *WhoEmL 91*
Lang, Gloria Helen 1932- *WhoAmW 91*
Lang, H. Jack 1904- *WhoAm 90*
Lang, H. Warren, Jr. 1928- *St&PR 91*
Lang, Hans Joachim 1912- *WhoAm 90*
Lang, Henry Spencer 1947- *St&PR 91*
Lang, I. Ward 1929- *St&PR 91*
Lang, Istvan 1933- *IntWWM 90*
Lang, J T 1931- *WhoAmA 91*
Lang, Jack 1921- *Ballpl 90*
Lang, Jack Mathieu Emile 1939- *BiDFrPL*
Lang, Jackie J. *ODwPR 91*
Lang, James F. 1934- *St&PR 91*
Lang, James Robert 1943- *St&PR 91, WhoAm 90*
Lang, Jean McKinney 1921- *WhoAmW 91*
Lang, Jeffrey 1941- *WhoSSW 91*
Lang, Jeffrey Francis 1942- *St&PR 91*
Lang, Joan A *BiDrAPA 89*
Lang, John Cleveland 1940- *WhoE 91*
Lang, John Gerald 1896-1984 *DcNaB 1981*
Lang, Josephine 1815-1880 *BioIn 16*
Lang, K. D. *BioIn 16*
Lang, k.d. *WhoNeCM [port]*
Lang, K D 1961- *ConMus 4 [port]*
Lang, K. D. 1961- *WhoAmW 91*
Lang, K.D. 1962- *WorAlBi*
Lang, Katherine Anne 1947- *WhoAmW 91*
Lang, Kevin 1955- *WhoE 91*
Lang, Lanny R. 1958- *St&PR 91*
Lang, Leon S. 1898-1956 *BioIn 16*
Lang, Leonard C *BiDrAPA 89*
Lang, Leonard W. 1932- *St&PR 91*
Lang, Leslie John Alden *BioIn 16*
Lang, Lillian Owen 1915- *WhoSSW 91*
Lang, Mabel Louise 1917- *WhoAm 90*
Lang, Margo Terzian *WhoAm 90, WhoAmA 91*
Lang, Martin 1915- *WhoAm 90*
Lang, Matheson 1879-1948 *OxCCanT*
Lang, Michael Josef Maximilian 1950- *WhoWor 91*
Lang, Michel 1939- *ConAu 129*
Lang, Miriam 1915- *WhoWrEP 89*
Lang, Nancy 1929- *WhoAmW 91*
Lang, Neil Stephan 1942- *St&PR 91*
Lang, Norton David 1940- *WhoAm 90*
Lang, Otto E. 1932- *WhoAm 90*
Lang, Patricia K. 1947- *St&PR 91*
Lang, Paul Andrew 1923- *WhoE 91*
Lang, Paul Henry 1901- *IntWWM 90*
Lang, Paul Louis 1940- *St&PR 91, WhoAm 90*
Lang, Pearl 1922- *WhoAm 90*
Lang, Philip David 1929- *WhoAm 90*
Lang, Phyllis Jean 1938- *WhoAmW 91*
Lang, Richard W., Jr. 1950- *St&PR 91*
Lang, Richard Warren 1949- *WhoAm 90, WhoE 91*
Lang, Richard Wenzel 1943- *WhoAm 90*
Lang, Robert 1942- *St&PR 91*
Lang, Robert E. *St&PR 91*
Lang, Robert Howard, Jr. 1935- *St&PR 91*
Lang, Robert Todd 1924- *St&PR 91, WhoE 91*
Lang, Rodger Alan 1942- *WhoAmA 91*
Lang, Ronald Anthony 1936- *WhoAm 90*
Lang, Ronald J. 1943- *St&PR 91*
Lang, Ronald William 1955- *St&PR 91*
Lang, Scott H. 1946- *St&PR 91*
Lang, Scott Howard 1946- *WhoAm 90*
Lang, Scott Wesley 1950- *WhoEmL 91*
Lang, Scott William 1959- *WhoE 91*
Lang, Serge 1927- *WhoAm 90*
Lang, Sidney Bertram 1934- *WhoWor 91*
Lang, Siegfried 1919- *IntWWM 90*
Lang, Stephen *BioIn 16*
Lang, Stephen R. 1934- *WhoAm 90*
Lang, Stuart A. 1955- *WhoAm 90*
Lang, Susan Rebecca 1955- *WhoEmL 91*
Lang, Terence Henry 1937- *St&PR 91*
Lang, Thierry Jean Luc 1952- *WhoWor 91*
Lang, Thompson Hughes 1946- *WhoAm 90*
Lang, Victor John, Jr. 1936- *St&PR 91*
Lang, Victoria Winifred 1955- *WhoAmW 91*
Lang, Vivian Luevenier 1927- *WhoAmW 91*
Lang, Wendy F 1938- *WhoAmA 91*
Lang, William Charles 1944- *WhoAm 90*
Lang, William H. 1911-1990 *BioIn 16*
Lang, William Joseph 1932- *St&PR 91*
Lang, William Steve 1954- *WhoEmL 91*
Lang, William Warner 1926- *WhoAm 90*
Lang-Grundler, Mary Jane 1919- *WhoAmW 91*
Lang-Miers, Elizabeth Ann 1950- *WhoEmL 91*
Langaas, Arild Odd 1936- *WhoWor 91*
Langacker, Ronald Wayne 1942- *WhoAm 90*
Langager, Craig T 1946- *WhoAmA 91*
Langaker, Arthur Stephen 1937- *WhoWor 91*
Langan, John Patrick 1940- *WhoE 91*
Langan, Keith Edward 1955- *WhoEmL 91*
Langan, Kevin J. 1955- *IntWWM 90*
Langan, Margaret Ann 1963- *WhoAmW 91*
Langan, Marie A. 1943- *WhoAmW 91*
Langan, Peter *BioIn 16*
Langan, Peter 1941-1988 *AnObit 1988*
Langart, Darrell T. *ConAu 130*
Langbacka, Ralf Runar 1932- *WhoWor 91*
Langbaum, Gary *BioIn 16*
Langbaum, Robert Woodrow 1924- *WhoAm 90, WhoWrEP 89*
Langbein, John Harriss 1941- *WhoAm 90*
Langbein, Leland Henry 1915- *WhoE 91*
Langberg, Peter 1945- *IntWWM 90*
Langbo, Arnold Gordon 1937- *St&PR 91, WhoAm 90*
Langbort, Polly 1938- *WhoAmW 91*
Langdale, Harley, Jr. 1914- *St&PR 91*
Langdale, John J. 1927- *St&PR 91*
Langdale, John W. 1917- *St&PR 91*
Langdale, Noah Noel, Jr. 1920- *WhoAm 90*
Langdale, Robert Harley 1948- *St&PR 91*
Langdale, W.P. 1921- *St&PR 91*
Langdana, Farrokh Keki 1958- *WhoE 91*
Langdell, John I 1922- *BiDrAPA 89*
Langdell, Robert Dana 1924- *WhoAm 90*
Langdon, Barbara Jane 1947- *St&PR 91*
Langdon, David 1914- *WhoWor 91*
Langdon, Diane Stone 1957- *WhoAmW 91*
Langdon, Edward A. 1951- *St&PR 91*
Langdon, Frank Corriston 1919- *WhoAm 90*
Langdon, George, Jr. *BioIn 16*
Langdon, George Dorland, Jr. 1933- *WhoAm 90, WhoE 91*
Langdon, Glen George, Jr. 1936- *WhoAm 90*
Langdon, Herschel Garrett 1905- *WhoAm 90*
Langdon, Ina M. 1920- *St&PR 91*
Langdon, James Lloyd 1918- *St&PR 91, WhoAm 90*
Langdon, James Robert 1919- *St&PR 91*
Langdon, John 1741-1819 *BioIn 16, EncCRAm*
Langdon, John David 1943- *IntWWM 90*
Langdon, Larry 1940- *WhoWrEP 89*
Langdon, Marilyn Jamison 1962- *WhoAmW 91*
Langdon, Mary G. *BiDrAPA 89*
Langdon, Michael 1920- *IntWWM 90, PenDiMP*
Langdon, Philip 1947- *ConAu 129*
Langdon, Philip Alan 1947- *WhoEmL 91*
Langdon, Sue Ane 1940- *BioIn 16*
Langdon, William Chauncey 1831-1895 *WorAlBi*
Lange, Alan B. 1932- *St&PR 91*
Lange, Arthur Ernest 1920- *St&PR 91*
Lange, Augusta Ann 1934- *WhoWrEP 89*
Lange, Bertram Jeremy 1912- *WhoAm 90, WhoE 91, WhoWor 91*
Lange, Bill 1871-1950 *Ballpl 90 [port]*
Lange, C. William 1946- *WhoEmL 91*
Lange, Carl James 1925- *WhoAm 90*
Lange, Chadwick Stephens 1938- *St&PR 91*
Lange, Clifford E. 1935- *WhoAm 90*
Lange, David *BioIn 16, NewAgMG*
Lange, David 1938- *WhoAm 90*
Lange, David O. 1939- *St&PR 91*
Lange, David Russell 1942- *WhoWor 91*
Lange, Dick 1948- *Ballpl 90*
Lange, Dieter Ernst 1933- *WhoWor 91*
Lange, Dietz Christian 1933- *WhoWor 91*
Lange, Dorothea 1895-1965 *BioIn 16, ModArCr 1 [port], WhoAmA 91N, WorAlBi*
Lange, Dorothea N. 1895-1965 *BioAmW*

Lange, Douglas Keith 1953- *WhoEmL 91*
Lange, Edward Niles 1935- *WhoAm 90*
Lange, Frank 1883-1945 *Ballpl 90*
Lange, Fred Joseph, Jr. 1950- *St&PR 91*
Lange, Frederick Edward, Jr. 1946- *WhoEmL 91*
Lange, George Willard, Jr. 1949- *WhoSSW 91*
Lange, Gerald William 1946- *WhoWrEP 89*
Lange, Hanna S *BiDrAPA 89*
Lange, Harald 1937- *WhoWor 91*
Lange, Helmut 1940- *WhoWor 91*
Lange, Hope 1931- *WorAlBi*
Lange, Hope 1938- *WhoAm 90*
Lange, Jack Damgaard 1906- *WhoWor 91*
Lange, James Braxton 1937- *WhoAm 90*
Lange, Jane Louise 1947- *WhoAmW 91*
Lange, Jessica *BioIn 16*
Lange, Jessica 1949- *WhoAm 90, WhoAmW 91, WorAlBi*
Lange, John *MajTwCW, TwCCr&M 91*
Lange, John A *BiDrAPA 89*
Lange, Karen Ellen 1938- *St&PR 91*
Lange, Katherine JoAnn 1957- *WhoAmW 91, WhoEmL 91, WhoWor 91*
Lange, Klaus Robert 1930- *St&PR 91*
Lange, Kurt 1906-1989 *BioIn 16*
Lange, Lawrence Robert 1955- *WhoSSW 91*
Lange, Lester Henry 1924- *WhoAm 90*
Lange, Linda S. 1949- *WhoEmL 91*
Lange, Lois Jean 1931- *WhoSSW 91*
Lange, Martin 1955- *ConAu 130*
Lange, Michael 1943- *WhoE 91*
Lange, Monique 1926- *EncCoWW*
Lange, Norman 1951- *St&PR 91*
Lange, Oscar Richard 1904-1965 *BioIn 16*
Lange, Otto L. 1927- *WhoWor 91*
Lange, Paul Allan 1941- *BiDrAPA 89*
Lange, Per 1901- *DcScanL*
Lange, Phil C. 1914- *WhoAm 90*
Lange, Phillip F. 1947- *St&PR 91*
Lange, Phyllis Louise 1942- *WhoAmW 91*
Lange, Reinhardt J. 1949- *St&PR 91*
Lange, Robert Dale 1920- *WhoAm 90, WhoSSW 91*
Lange, Robert William 1943- *WhoE 91*
Lange, Scott Elliot 1950- *WhoE 91*
Lange, Scott Leslie 1946- *WhoEmL 91*
Lange, Stephen Mark 1957- *WhoE 91*
Lange, Stephen Thomas 1950- *WhoSSW 91*
Lange, Steven Donald 1955- *WhoE 91*
Lange, Ted *WhoAm 90*
Lange, Ted 1947?- *DrBIPA 90*
Lange, Victor 1908- *WhoAm 90*
Lange, William Dennis 1953- *WhoSSW 91*
Lange, William F. 1942- *St&PR 91*
Lange-Muller, Katja 1951- *EncCoWW*
Lange-Seidl, Annemarie 1918- *WhoWor 91*
Langee, Harvey R 1925- *BiDrAPA 89*
Langel, Robert Allan, III 1937- *WhoAm 90*
Langel, Vernon Peter 1931- *St&PR 91*
Langella, Frank 1940- *WhoAm 90, WorAlBi*
Langemo, Diane Kay 1947- *WhoEmL 91*
Langenau, Edward E. *BioIn 16*
Langenauer, Bernard J *BiDrAPA 89*
Langenberg, Christopher Melvin 1946- *St&PR 91*
Langenberg, Donald Newton 1932- *WhoAm 90, WhoWor 91*
Langenberg, Douglas Patton 1945- *St&PR 91*
Langenberg, Frederick Charles 1927- *St&PR 91, WhoAm 90*
Langenberg, Patricia Warrington 1931- *WhoAmW 91*
Langenderfer, Harold Quentin 1925- *WhoAm 90*
Langendoen, Donald Terence 1939- *WhoAm 90*
Langenfass, Rolf *BioIn 16*
Langenfeld, Douglas Eugene 1952- *WhoAm 90*
Langenheim, Edward Priest 1940- *St&PR 91*
Langenheim, Jean Harmon 1925- *WhoAmW 91*
Langenheim, Ralph Louis, Jr. 1922- *WhoAm 90*
Langenkamp, Heather *BioIn 16*
Langenscheidt, Florian 1955- *WhoWor 91*
Langenthal, Stephen R. 1934- *WhoE 91*
Langenwalter, Robert George 1924- *St&PR 91*
Langer, Andrew *BioIn 16*
Langer, Andrew J. *WhoAm 90*
Langer, Bernhard *BioIn 16*
Langer, Carlton Earl 1954- *St&PR 91, WhoEmL 91*
Langer, David 1935- *St&PR 91*
Langer, Dennis H 1951- *BiDrAPA 89*
Langer, Dennis Henry 1951- *WhoWor 91*
Langer, Edward L. 1936- *WhoAm 90*
Langer, Edward Leo 1936- *St&PR 91*
Langer, Ellen J. 1947- *BioIn 16, ConAu 30NR*
Langer, Ellen Jane 1947- *WhoAmW 91, WhoEmL 91*
Langer, Eva Marie 1958- *WhoEmL 91*
Langer, Felicia *BioIn 16*
Langer, Fritz H. 1932- *St&PR 91*
Langer, George Edward 1936- *WhoAm 90*
Langer, Horst *WhoE 91*
Langer, James Stephen 1934- *WhoAm 90*
Langer, Klaus Ernst Oskar Ewald 1936- *WhoWor 91*
Langer, Lawrence Marvin 1913- *WhoAm 90*
Langer, Marian Martha 1936- *WhoAmW 91*
Langer, Marie 1910-1987 *BioIn 16*
Langer, Milan 1955- *IntWWM 90*
Langer, Morton 1941- *St&PR 91*
Langer, Nicholas M *BiDrAPA 89*
Langer, Pamela Joyce 1951- *WhoEmL 91*
Langer, Peter H. 1931- *St&PR 91*
Langer, Ralph Ernest 1937- *WhoAm 90, WhoSSW 91*
Langer, Robert Adolph 1942- *WhoAm 90*
Langer, Robert Samuel 1948- *WhoAm 90*
Langer, S.W. 1909- *St&PR 91*
Langer, Samuel Joseph 1945- *BiDrAPA 89*
Langer, Sandra Lois 1941- *WhoAmA 91*
Langer, Sheldon 1924- *St&PR 91*
Langer, Steve Hall 1941- *St&PR 91*
Langer, Susan Follett 1946- *BiDrAPA 89*
Langer, Susanne 1895-1985 *FemiCLE, WrPh P*
Langer, Susanne K 1895-1985 *MajTwCW*
Langer, Susanne M. 1955- *WhoAmW 91, WhoEmL 91*
Langer, Sydney E 1914- *BiDrAPA 89*
Langerak, Esley Oren 1920- *WhoAm 90*
Langerman, Harold Albert 1923- *WhoAm 90*
Langerman, Peter A. 1955- *St&PR 91*
Langerman, Wayne Richard 1952- *WhoEmL 91*
Langetieg, Terence C. *BioIn 16*
Langeveld, Dirk 1951- *St&PR 91*
Langevin, Andre 1927- *BioIn 16*
Langevin, Jean 1821-1892 *DcCanB 12*
Langevin, Louis *PenDiDA 89*
Langevin, Louis-de-Gonzague 1921- *WhoAm 90*
Langevin, Thomas Harvey 1922- *WhoAm 90*
Langewiesche, Dieter 1943- *WhoWor 91*
Langewiesche, Marianne 1908-1979 *EncCoWW*
Langfeld, Marilyn Irene 1951- *WhoAmW 91*
Langfeldt, Bent 1923- *WhoWor 91*
Langfitt, D. Richard 1933- *St&PR 91*
Langfitt, Thomas William 1927- *WhoAm 90*
Langford, Anthony 1942- *IntWWM 90*
Langford, Audrey 1912- *IntWWM 90*
Langford, Charles Douglass 1922- *WhoSSW 91*
Langford, Dan C. 1945- *St&PR 91*
Langford, Dean T. 1939- *St&PR 91*
Langford, Dean Ted 1939- *WhoAm 90*
Langford, Edward Edwards 1809-1895 *DcCanB 12*
Langford, Ella Hunt 1944- *WhoAmW 91*
Langford, Eugene Craig 1949- *WhoSSW 91*
Langford, Frances 1913- *OxCPMus*
Langford, George 1939- *WhoAm 90*
Langford, Gerald 1911- *ConAu 32NR*
Langford, Gerald Talmadge 1935- *WhoSSW 91*
Langford, Gordon 1930- *OxCPMus*
Langford, Irvin James 1927- *WhoAm 90*
Langford, James Rouleau 1937- *WhoAm 90*
Langford, Jeffrey Lynn 1964- *WhoEmL 91*
Langford, John S. *BioIn 16*
Langford, John William 1932- *WhoSSW 91, WhoWor 91*
Langford, Lorraine *WhoAmW 91*
Langford, Martin *ODwPR 91*
Langford, Rick 1952- *Ballpl 90*
Langford, Rick C. 1953- *WhoWrEP 89*
Langford, Robert D. 1936- *St&PR 91*
Langford, Robert E. 1912- *St&PR 91*
Langford, Robert L. 1950- *St&PR 91*
Langford, Roland Everett 1945- *WhoEmL 91, WhoWor 91*
Langford, Sherry K 1944- *WhoAmA 91*
Langford, Ted Lee 1931- *WhoSSW 91*
Langford, Thomas Anderson 1929- *WhoAm 90*
Langford, Thomas L. 1941- *St&PR 91*
Langford, Walter Martin 1931- *St&PR 91*
Langford, William Paul 1935- *St&PR 91*
Langgasser, Elisabeth 1899-1950 *EncCoWW*
Langguth, A J 1933- *ConAu 30NR, WhoWrEP 89*
Langham, Barbara Dee 1938- *WhoWrEP 89*
Langham, C. Scott, Jr. 1936- *WhoSSW 91*
Langham, Joan *WhoWrEP 89*
Langham, Max Raymond, Jr. 1955- *WhoSSW 91*
Langham, Michael 1919- *OxCCanT, WhoAm 90*
Langham, Norma *WhoAmW 91, WhoE 91, WhoWor 91*
Langham-Coe, Joan *WhoWrEP 89*
Langhans, Edward Allen 1923- *WhoAm 90*
Langhans, Lester Frank, III 1948- *WhoE 91*
Langhans, Richard A. 1945- *St&PR 91*
Langhart, Janet 1942?- *DrBIPA 90*
Langhenry, John Godfred, Jr. 1933- *WhoAm 90*
Langhetee, Edmond Joseph, Jr. 1928- *WhoAm 90*
Langhinrichs, Richard Alan 1921- *WhoWor 91*
Langholz, Robert Wayne 1930- *WhoAm 90*
Langhorne, Chiswell Dabney, Jr. 1940- *St&PR 91*
Langhorne, Diane *ODwPR 91*
Langhorne, Kathryn Payne 1905- *WhoAmW 91*
Langhorne, Rossiter W. 1938- *St&PR 91*
Langhorne, Samuel W. 1836- *AmLegL*
Langhorst, Gary Arlen 1928- *WhoWor 91*
Langie, Louis A., Jr. 1928- *St&PR 91*
Langille, Harold James 1943- *St&PR 91*
Langille-Mattei, Suzanne Yvonne 1954- *WhoWrEP 89*
Langin, John Mauger Barnes 1934- *WhoWor 91*
Langkraehr, Randall David 1961- *WhoEmL 91*
Langlade, Charles 1729-1800? *WhNaAH*
Langlais, Bernard 1921-1977 *WhoAmA 91N*
Langlais, Jacques Claude 1936- *WhoWor 91*
Langlais, Jean 1907- *BioIn 16, PenDiMP*
Langlais, Jean Francois Hyacinthe 1907- *IntWWM 90*
Langlais, Patricia Ann 1949- *WhoWrEP 89*
Langland, Harold 1939- *WhoAmA 91*
Langland, Joseph Thomas 1917- *WhoAm 90, WhoWrEP 89*
Langland, Sara Nell 1949- *WhoEmL 91*
Langland, William 1330?-1400? *WorAlBi*
Langlands, Bryan Wooleston 1928-1989 *BioIn 16*
Langlands, Ian Holmes 1926- *St&PR 91*
Langlands, Robert Phelan 1936- *WhoAm 90, WhoE 91*
Langleben, Manuel Phillip 1924- *WhoAm 90*
Langley, Ann 1942- *WhoAmW 91*
Langley, Anthony H. 1947- *St&PR 91*
Langley, Batty 1696-1751 *PenDiDA 89*
Langley, Beryl W 1941- *BiDrAPA 89*
Langley, Cynthia Murray 1954- *WhoAmW 91, WhoEmL 91, WhoWor 91*
Langley, David Leigh 1949- *WhoSSW 91*
Langley, Desmond 1930- *WhoWor 91*
Langley, Ellis Bradford 1923- *WhoAm 90*
Langley, Eugene Loyle 1924- *St&PR 91, WhoAm 90, WhoSSW 91*
Langley, Eve 1908-1974 *FemiCLE*
Langley, Gary Alfred 1946- *WhoEmL 91*
Langley, George Ross 1931- *WhoAm 90*
Langley, Hugh F. 1954- *St&PR 91*
Langley, James 1927- *IntWWM 90*
Langley, James Oran 1934- *WhoAm 90*
Langley, Jimmy Don 1952- *WhoEmL 91*
Langley, John H. *BioIn 16*
Langley, John J. 1932- *St&PR 91*
Langley, M. Beth *BioIn 16*
Langley, Margaret Carol 1965- *WhoAmW 91*
Langley, Mary Elizabeth *BiDrAPA 89*
Langley, Noel 1911-1980 *ConAu 30NR*
Langley, Patricia Ann 1938- *WhoAmW 91, WhoE 91*
Langley, Patricia Coffroth 1924- *WhoE 91*
Langley, Roger Richard 1930- *WhoE 91*
Langley, Roland L *BiDrAPA 89*
Langley, Samuel Pierpont 1834-1906 *WorAlBi*
Langley, Thomas 1702- *PenDiDA 89*
Langley, Tim *BioIn 16*
Langley, Todd Hyatt 1934- *WhoWor 91*
Langley, William Robert 1940- *St&PR 91*
Langlinais, Joseph Willis 1922- *WhoAm 90*
Langlitz, David Carl 1953- *IntWWM 90*
Langlois, Marie Jean 1942- *St&PR 91*
Langlois, Michael Arthur 1956- *WhoEmL 91*
Langlois, Philippe *PenDiMP*
Langlois, Pierre *PenDiDA 89*
Langlois, Robert J. 1929- *St&PR 91*
Langlois, Steve *BioIn 16*
Langlois, Walter Gordon 1925- *WhoAm 90*
Langlow, John Robins, III 1960- *BiDrAPA 89*
Langmaid, Bruce R. 1950- *St&PR 91*
Langman, Krzysztof Maria 1948- *IntWWM 90*
Langman, Marc Jay *BiDrAPA 89*
Langman, Ransom Harry 1927- *St&PR 91*
Langman, Richard Theodore 1937- *WhoAmA 91*
Langmann, Adelheid *EncCoWW*
Langmesser, James Emilien 1947- *WhoSSW 91*
Langmuir, Alexander Duncan 1910- *WhoAm 90*
Langmuir, Irving 1881-1957 *WorAlBi*
Langner, Fred W 1914- *BiDrAPA 89*
Langner, Guenther Otto 1926- *WhoE 91*
Langner, Helen P 1892- *BiDrAPA 89*
Langner, Herman Paul 1936- *BiDrAPA 89*
Langner, Ilse 1899-1987 *EncCoWW*
Langone, Richard A. *BiDrAPA 89*
Langren, Daniel David 1938- *St&PR 91*
Langridge, Philip 1939- *PenDiMP*
Langridge, Philip Gordon 1939- *IntWWM 90*
Langrock, Karl Frederick 1927- *WhoAm 90*
Langs, Robert J 1928- *BiDrAPA 89*
Langs, Robert Joseph 1928- *WhoE 91*
Langsam, Norbert 1925- *WhoE 91*
Langsdorf, Alexander, Jr. 1912- *WhoAm 90*
Langsdorf, Martyl Schweig *WhoAmA 91*
Langsdorf, Thomas Kline 1947- *St&PR 91*
Langseth, Muriel Avonne 1939- *WhoWrEP 89*
Langseth-Christensen, Lillian *BioIn 16*
Langsley, Donald G 1925- *BiDrAPA 89*
Langsley, Donald Gene 1925- *WhoAm 90*
Langsley, Pauline *BiDrAPA 89*
Langsner, Jules *WhoAmA 91N*
Langstaff, E. Kennedy 1923- *St&PR 91*
Langstaff, Eleanor Marguerite 1934- *WhoAmW 91, WhoE 91*
Langstaff, Elliot Kennedy 1923- *WhoAm 90*
Langstaff, Gary L. *BioIn 16*
Langstaff, Gary L. 1948- *St&PR 91*
Langstaff, George Quigley, Jr. 1925- *WhoAm 90*
Langstaff, John 1920- *AuBYP 90*
Langstaff, John Meredith 1920- *WhoAm 90*
Langston, Charles C., Jr. 1937- *St&PR 91*
Langston, Douglas F. 1956- *WhoSSW 91*
Langston, George C. 1930- *St&PR 91*
Langston, George Calhoun 1930- *WhoAm 90*
Langston, Hiram Thomas 1912- *WhoAm 90, WhoWor 91*
Langston, John Mercer 1829-1897 *BioIn 16, BlkAmsC [port]*
Langston, Linda Cubbedge 1950- *WhoSSW 91*
Langston, Mark *BioIn 16*
Langston, Mark 1960- *Ballpl 90, WorAlBi*
Langston, Michael Densmore 1945- *St&PR 91*
Langston, Mildred J 1902-1976 *WhoAmA 91N*
Langston, Paul T. 1928- *WhoAm 90*
Langston, Roy A. 1912- *WhoAm 90*
Langston, Sally J. 1947- *WhoEmL 91*
Langston, Wann, Jr. 1921- *WhoAm 90*
Langston, William B 1925- *BiDrAPA 89*
Langston-Harrison, Lee Ann 1957- *WhoEmL 91*
Langton, Anne 1804-1893 *DcCanB 12, DcLB 99 [port]*
Langton, Anne 1805-1893 *FemiCLE*
Langton, Berenice 1878-1959 *WhoAmA 91N*
Langton, Daniel J. 1927- *WhoWrEP 89*
Langton, David Austin 1961- *WhoEmL 91*
Langton, Dawn 1955- *WhoE 91*
Langton, Jane *BioIn 16*
Langton, Jane 1922- *AuBYP 90, FemiCLE, TwCCr&M 91*
Langton, John 1808-1894 *DcCanB 12*
Langton, Kenneth Patrick 1933- *WhoAm 90*
Langtry, Ian 1939- *BioIn 16*
Langtry, Lillie 1853-1929 *BioIn 16, WorAlBi*
Langtry, Lois Catherine 1937- *WhoE 91*
Langtry, Philip S. 1934- *St&PR 91*
Languido, Eriberto Umbay 1934- *WhoWor 91*
Languirand, Jacques 1931- *OxCCanT*
Langum, John Kenneth 1913- *St&PR 91, WhoAm 90*
Langum, W. Sue 1934- *WhoAmW 91*
Languth, Helen W 1920- *BiDrAPA 89*
Langwasser, George August 1938- *St&PR 91*
Langway, Richard Merritt 1939- *WhoAm 90*

Langway, Rod 1957- *WorAlBi*
Langwig, John Edward 1924- *WhoAm 90*
Langworthy, Audrey Hansen 1938- *WhoAmW 91*
Langworthy, Everett Walter 1918- *WhoAm 90*
Langworthy, Orthello R *BiDrAPA 89*
Langworthy, Robert Burton 1918- *WhoAm 90*
Langworthy, William Clayton 1936- *WhoAm 90*
Lanham, Arthur Abrel 1953- *WhoEmL 91*
Lanham, Ben T., III 1945- *St&PR 91*
Lanham, Betty Bailey 1922- *WhoAm 90*
Lanham, David A 1927- *BiDrAPA 89*
Lanham, Elizabeth 1912- *WhoAm 90*
Lanham, Kenneth E. 1952- *St&PR 91*
Lanham, Logan Everett 1926- *WhoAm 90*
Lanham, Mark Rogers 1954- *WhoAm 90*
Lanham, Richard Alan 1936- *WhoAm 90*
Lanham, Scott Ayres 1958- *WhoE 91*
Lanham, Urless Norton 1918- *WhoAm 90*
Laniak, David Konstantyn 1935- *St&PR 91, WhoAm 90*
Laniel, Joseph Rene 1889-1975 *BiDFrPL*
Lanier, Anita Suzanne 1946- *WhoAmW 91, WhoSSW 91*
Lanier, Bob 1948- *WorAlBi*
Lanier, Cathy Gibson 1957- *WhoAmW 91*
Lanier, Charles Bedingfield, Jr. 1948- *WhoEmL 91*
Lanier, Emilia 1569-1645 *BioIn 16*
Lanier, Gerald N. *NewYTBS 90*
Lanier, Gerald N. 1937-1990 *BioIn 16*
Lanier, Geraldine Fe 1951- *WhoWrEP 89*
Lanier, Hal 1942- *Ballpl 90*
Lanier, James Lester, Jr. 1946- *WhoSSW 91*
Lanier, James Olanda 1931- *WhoSSW 91*
Lanier, John Hicks 1940- *St&PR 91, WhoAm 90, WhoSSW 91*
Lanier, Joseph Lamar, Jr. 1932- *WhoAm 90, WhoSSW 91*
Lanier, Joseph Vaughan 1928- *St&PR 91*
Lanier, Julian E. 1931- *St&PR 91*
Lanier, Max 1915- *Ballpl 90*
Lanier, Richard Blackburn 1958- *WhoE 91*
Lanier, Sidney 1842-1881 *BioIn 16, WorAlBi*
Lanier, Sterling E 1927- *AuBYP 90*
Lanier, Thomas 1923- *WhoE 91, WhoWor 91*
Lanier, Thomas F. 1942- *St&PR 91*
Lanier, Viola Wilson 1927- *WhoAmW 91, WhoWor 91*
Lanier, William Todd 1964- *WhoEmL 91*
Laniewski, Laura Ann 1961- *WhoAmW 91*
Lanigan, Charles Frederic 1940- *St&PR 91*
Lanigan, Denis George 1926- *WhoAm 90*
Lanigan, Edward J. 1931- *St&PR 91*
Lanigan, Ernest J. 1873-1962 *Ballpl 90*
Lanigan, James J. *ODwPR 91*
Lanigan, Jeramy Elise 1939- *WhoAm 90*
Lanigan, John 1921- *IntWWM 90*
Lanigan, John Timothy 1941- *WhoE 91*
Lanigan, Kevin John 1946- *St&PR 91, WhoEmL 91*
Lanigan, Robert Arnold 1912- *St&PR 91*
Lanigan, Robert J. 1928- *St&PR 91, WhoAm 90*
Lanin, Lester *BioIn 16*
Lanin, Matthew 1950- *WhoEmL 91*
Lanin, Thomas Kenneth 1943- *St&PR 91*
Laning, J. Halcombe 1920- *WhoAm 90*
Laning, Robert Comegys 1922- *WhoAm 90*
Lanis, Violet Ann 1948- *WhoAmW 91, WhoEmL 91*
Lanitis, Nicholas Constantine 1917- *WhoWor 91*
Lanitis, Tony Andrew 1926- *WhoAm 90*
Lanius, Carl E. 1944- *St&PR 91*
Lanius, Gloria Helene 1917- *WhoWrEP 89*
Lank, Edith Handleman *WhoE 91*
Lank, Herbert 1925- *WhoWor 91*
Lanka, Alan S. 1939- *St&PR 91*
Lankenau, Helen M 1949- *BiDrAPA 89*
Lankes, Julius J 1884-1960 *WhoAmA 91N*
Lankester, Michael 1944- *IntWWM 90*
Lankester, Michael John 1944- *WhoAm 90*
Lankford, Alana Frances 1948- *WhoWrEP 89*
Lankford, Charles A. *St&PR 91*
Lankford, Francis Greenfield, Jr. 1906- *WhoAm 90*
Lankford, Fred, III 1951- *WhoSSW 91*
Lankford, Jefferson Lewis 1951- *WhoEmL 91*
Lankford, Linda Marie 1947- *WhoAmW 91*
Lankford, Ronald Sovey 1952- *St&PR 91*
Lankton, Barbara Ballow 1945- *BiDrAPA 89*
Lankton, Gordon B. 1931- *St&PR 91*
Lankton, Stephen Ryan 1947- *WhoAm 90, WhoEmL 91*
Lanman, Richard Burnham *BiDrAPA 89*
Lanmon, Dwight P 1938- *WhoAmA 91*
Lanmon, Dwight Pierson 1938- *WhoAm 90, WhoE 91*
Lann, Helen Deborah 1955- *BiDrAPA 89*
Lanna, Robert A. 1934- *St&PR 91*
Lannamann, Richard Stuart 1947- *WhoE 91, WhoWor 91*
Lanner, Josef 1801-1843 *OxCPMus*
Lannert, Robert C. 1940- *St&PR 91*
Lannert, Robert Cornelius 1940- *WhoAm 90*
Lannert, Stephen Charles 1951- *WhoSSW 91*
Lanni, Joseph Terrence 1943- *St&PR 91, WhoAm 90*
Lanni, Richard A. *St&PR 91*
Lannigan, Julie Beth 1953- *WhoWrEP 89*
Lannin, Thomas Forrest, Jr. 1958- *WhoWor 91*
Lanning, James J. 1928- *St&PR 91*
Lanning, Johnny 1910- *Ballpl 90*
Lanning, Joseph R 1938- *BiDrAPA 89*
Lanning, Judith Ann 1936- *WhoAmW 91*
Lanning, Michael Lee 1946- *WhoWrEP 89*
Lanning, Shirley *ODwPR 91*
Lannom, Edward Hicks, Jr. 1924- *St&PR 91*
Lannom, G. S. 1885-1953 *BioIn 16*
Lannom, George Sharp 1885-1953 *BioIn 16*
Lannom, Jim H. 1942- *St&PR 91*
Lannon, Carrie A. *ODwPR 91*
Lannon, Edwin Raymond 1922- *WhoE 91*
Lannon, John Joseph 1937- *St&PR 91, WhoAm 90*
Lannon, Kathleen Maria 1949- *WhoE 91*
Lannon, Richard A *BiDrAPA 89*
Lannuier, Charles-Honore 1779-1819 *PenDiDA 89*
Lannuier, Nicolas-Louis-Cyrille *PenDiDA 89*
L'Annunziata, Michael Frank 1943- *WhoWor 91*
Lano, Charles Jack 1922- *WhoAm 90*
Lanocha, Karl Ignatius *BiDrAPA 89*
Lanoff, Ian David 1942- *WhoAm 90*
Lanoff, Samuel M. 1907- *St&PR 91*
Lanois, Daniel *BioIn 16*
Lanois, Daniel 1951- *News 91-1 [port]*
Lanotte, Anthony Thomas 1952- *BiDrAPA 89*
LaNoue, Alcide Moodie 1934- *WhoAm 90*
Lanoue, Blaze Allen 1960- *WhoSSW 91*
La Noue, Terence 1941- *WhoAmA 91*
La Noue, Terence David 1941- *WhoAm 90*
Lanouette, William John 1940- *WhoAm 90*
Lanphear, Charles Edward 1947- *St&PR 91*
Lanphear, Shawna Rae 1957- *WhoAmW 91*
Lanphear, Thomas Merrill 1954- *WhoEmL 91*
Lanphere, Charles Allen 1930- *WhoSSW 91*
Lanphier, Robert Carr, III 1932- *St&PR 91*
Lans, Allan M *BiDrAPA 89*
Lansaw, Judy W. 1951- *St&PR 91*
Lansbury, Angela *BioIn 16*
Lansbury, Angela 1925- *OxCPMus, WorAlBi*
Lansbury, Angela Brigid 1925- *NotWoAT, WhoAm 90, WhoAmW 91*
Lansbury, Coral *WhoAm 90*
Lansbury, Edgar George 1930- *WhoAm 90*
Lansdale, Daryl L. 1940- *St&PR 91*
Lansdale, Edward G. 1908-1987 *BioIn 16*
Lansdale, Herbert *BioIn 16*
Lansdale, Joe R 1951- *ConAu 32NR, TwCCr&M 91*
Lansdell, Sarah 1778?-1816? *FemiCLE*
Lansdon, Gay Brandt 1931- *WhoAmA 91*
Lansdown, Brenda *NewYTBS 90*
Lansdowne, J F 1937- *ConAu 30NR*
Lansdowne, James Fenwick 1937- *WhoAm 90, WhoAmA 91*
Lansdowne, Karen Myrtle 1926- *WhoAmW 91*
Lanselle, Lee Penn 1954- *WhoWor 91*
Lansford, Carney 1957- *Ballpl 90 [port], BioIn 16, WorAlBi*
Lansford, L.R. 1946- *St&PR 91*
Lansing, Allan Meredith 1929- *WhoAm 90*
Lansing, Cornelius 1923- *BiDrAPA 89*
Lansing, Don *BioIn 16*
Lansing, Elizabeth Carleton 1911- *AuBYP 90*
Lansing, Jean Ann 1949- *IntWWM 90*
Lansing, John 1754-1829? *BioIn 16*
Lansing, Mark Daniel 1961- *WhoEmL 91*
Lansing, Mary Rose *BiDrAPA 89*
Lansing, Robert 1864-1928 *BiDrUSE 89, BioIn 16*
Lansing, Robert C. 1915- *IntWWM 90*
Lansing, Robert Howell 1928- *WhoAm 90*
Lansing, Sherry *BioIn 16*
Lansing, Sherry Lee 1944- *WhoAm 90, WhoAmW 91*
Lansipuro, Yrjo Juhani 1940- *WhoWor 91*
Lanska, Mary Jo 1958- *WhoAmW 91*
Lansky, Melvin Robert 1941- *BiDrAPA 89*
Lansky, Shirley Bean *BiDrAPA 89*
Lansky, Vicki Lee 1942- *WhoWrEP 89*
Lansky, Zdenek J. 1922- *WhoSSW 91*
Lansner, Fay *WhoAmA 91*
Lansner, Kermit Irvin 1922- *WhoAm 90*
Lanson, Snooky *NewYTBS 90*
Lansun, A. La *WhoWrEP 89*
Lant, Carol Jane 1943- *St&PR 91*
Lant, Jeffrey Ladd 1947- *ConAu 30NR, WhoWrEP 89*
Lant, Nancy Jane 1930- *WhoAmW 91*
Lantay, George Charles 1942- *WhoAm 90, WhoE 91, WhoWor 91*
Lanter, Kenneth E *BiDrAPA 89*
Lanter, Sean Keith 1953- *WhoEmL 91*
Lanterman, Joseph Barney 1914- *WhoAm 90*
Lanthier, Ronald Ross 1926- *WhoAm 90*
Lanthorn, William Richard 1926- *St&PR 91*
Lantieri, Brenda Jean 1944- *WhoAmW 91*
Lanting, William Harold 1961- *WhoSSW 91*
Lantner, Henry J 1918- *BiDrAPA 89*
Lanton, Thomas Robert 1955- *WhoE 91*
Lantos, Geoffrey Paul 1952- *WhoEmL 91*
Lantos, George J 1913- *BiDrAPA 89*
Lantos, Istvan 1949- *IntWWM 90*
Lantos, Robert *BioIn 16*
Lantos, Thomas Jay 1957- *BiDrAPA 89*
Lantos, Thomas Peter 1928- *WhoAm 90*
Lantrip, Kay Lynn 1953- *WhoAmW 91*
Lantry, Marilyn Martha 1932- *WhoAmW 91*
Lantto, Marcia Mabel 1944- *WhoAmW 91*
Lantwicki, Eugene John 1944- *BiDrAPA 89*
Lantz, Billie Joanne 1956- *WhoAmW 91*
Lantz, David B. 1946- *St&PR 91*
Lantz, Fran 1952- *SmATA X [port]*
Lantz, Francess L 1952- *SmATA 63 [port]*
Lantz, George Benjamin, Jr. 1936- *WhoAm 90*
Lantz, J.R. 1911- *St&PR 91*
Lantz, Joanne Baldwin 1932- *WhoAm 90, WhoAmW 91*
Lantz, Karen Marie 1946- *WhoAmW 91*
Lantz, Kenneth Eugene 1934- *WhoAm 90*
Lantz, Louise Kalaman 1930- *WhoAmW 91*
Lantz, Melinda S 1960- *BiDrAPA 89*
Lantz, Michael 1908-1988 *BioIn 16*
Lantz, Peggy Sias 1933- *WhoAmW 91*
Lantz, Phillip Edward 1938- *WhoAm 90, WhoE 91, WhoWor 91*
Lantz, Robert Lynn 1939- *St&PR 91*
Lantz, Stephen Hamilton 1950- *WhoEmL 91*
Lantz, W. Franklin 1930- *WhoE 91*
Lantz, Walter 1900- *WhoAm 90*
Lantz, William Charles 1946- *WhoEmL 91*
Lantzsch, Guenther Christian 1925- *WhoAm 90*
Lantzsch, Thomas Paul 1960- *WhoEmL 91*
Lantzy, Donald Michael 1942 *WhoAmA 91*
Lantzy, John Paul 1955- *WhoSSW 91*
Lanusse, Alejandro A. 1918- *BioIn 16*
Lanvin, Jeanne 1867?-1946 *BioIn 16, WorAlBi*
Lanvin, Maryll *BioIn 16*
Lanwehr, Helen 1918- *WhoAmW 91, WhoE 91*
Lanxton, Rodney Alan 1965- *WhoSSW 91*
Lanyer, Aemilia 1569-1645 *FemiCLE*
Lanyer, Aemilia 1570?-1645 *BiDEWW*
Lanyi, Janos Karoly 1937- *WhoAm 90*
Lanyon, Carla Lanyon 1906-1971 *FemiCLE*
Lanyon, Ellen 1926- *WhoAm 90, WhoAmA 91*
Lanyon, J. Ken 1940- *St&PR 91*
Lanyon, Wesley Edwin 1926- *WhoAm 90*
Lanz, David *NewAgMG*
Lanz, Johann Wilhelm *PenDiDA 89*
Lanz, John R. 1927- *St&PR 91*
Lanz, John Robert 1927- *WhoAm 90*
Lanz, Robert Francis 1942- *St&PR 91, WhoAm 90*
Lanz, Robert H. 1922- *St&PR 91*
Lanz, Robert James *BiDrAPA 89*
Lanz Von Liebenfels, Jorg 1874-1954 *EncO&P 3*
Lanza, Alcides Emigdio 1929- *IntWWM 90*
Lanza, Frank C. 1931- *WhoAm 90*
Lanza, Gwendolyn F Yvonne 1942- *BiDrAPA 89*
Lanza, Mario 1921-1959 *BioIn 16, OxCPMus, PenDiMP, WorAlBi*
Lanza, Tomasi Gioacchino 1934- *WhoWor 91*
Lanzalone, Charles James 1952- *WhoE 91, WhoEmL 91*
Lanzano, Ralph Eugene 1926- *WhoAm 90, WhoE 91, WhoWor 91*
Lanzara, Gary Michael 1950- *St&PR 91*
Lanzarotta, Santo Anthony 1928- *St&PR 91*
Lanze, Johann Wilhelm *PenDiDA 89*
Lanzel, Jerome E., Jr. 1931- *St&PR 91*
Lanzerotti, Louis John 1938- *WhoAm 90, WhoE 91*
Lanzetta, Teresa Ann 1958- *WhoEmL 91*
Lanzi, Ray J. 1938- *St&PR 91*
Lanzieri, Charles Frederick 1952- *WhoEmL 91, WhoWor 91*
Lanzillotta, A. Paul 1931- *St&PR 91, WhoAm 90*
Lanzillotti, Robert Franklin 1921- *WhoAm 90*
Lanzit, Stephen Ray 1931- *WhoE 91*
Lanzkowsky, Philip 1932- *WhoAm 90*
Lanzkron, Carolyn Kahn 1964- *WhoAmW 91*
Lanzkron, Rolf Wolfgang 1929- *WhoE 91*
Lanzl, Lawrence Herman 1921- *WhoAm 90*
Lanzoni, Vincent 1928- *WhoAm 90*
Lanzotti, Bill Andrew 1950- *St&PR 91*
Lao, Mary Ann 1959- *WhoAmW 91*
Lao-Tzu 600?BC- *WorAlBi*
Laor, Klara R *BiDrAPA 89*
Lapadot, Sonee Spinner 1936- *WhoAmW 91*
La Paglia, Joseph Thomas 1943- *St&PR 91*
Lapaglia, Louis T. 1939- *WhoAm 90*
La Palma, Marina De Bellagente 1949- *WhoWrEP 89*
LaPalme, Paul 1923- *Ballpl 90*
La Palombara, Joseph 1925- *ConAu 31NR*
LaPalombara, Joseph 1925- *WhoAm 90*
La Pasionaria 1895-1989 *BioIn 16*
Lapatin, Philip Stuart 1949- *WhoAm 90*
Lapautre, Rene 1930- *WhoWor 91*
Lapayowker, Andrew 1954- *WhoEmL 91*
Lapayowker, Marc Spencer 1927- *WhoE 91*
Lapchick, Richard Edward *BioIn 16*
Lapczynski, Susan Agnes 1960- *WhoAmW 91*
Lapedes, Clarence 1909- *St&PR 91*
Lapelle, Diane McDonnell 1952- *WhoAmW 91*
La Pelle, Rodger 1936- *WhoAmA 91*
Lapena, Frank Raymond 1937- *WhoAmA 91*
Lapena-Bonifacio, Amelia 1930- *ConAu 130*
Lapenieks, Vilis 1931-1987 *BioIn 16*
La Perriere, Renee Julienne 1958- *IntWWM 90*
Lapes, George A 1940- *BiDrAPA 89*
LaPeters, Norman 1926- *St&PR 91*
Lapeyra, Joseph J 1936- *BiDrAPA 89*
Lapham, Constance Sumner 1921- *WhoWrEP 89*
Lapham, Joan *BioIn 16*
Lapham, John Edward 1936- *St&PR 91*
Lapham, Lewis A. 1909- *St&PR 91*
Lapham, Lewis Abbot 1909- *WhoAm 90*
Lapham, Lewis H. *BioIn 16*
Lapham, Lewis H. 1935- *ConAu 33NR*
Lapham, Lewis Henry 1935- *WhoAm 90, WhoE 91, WhoWrEP 89*
Lapham, Lewis Jay 1920- *WhoAm 90*
Lapham, Sandra Lee 1957- *WhoEmL 91*
Lapicola, John J. 1946- *St&PR 91*
Lapicque, Charles 1898-1988 *AnObit 1988*
Lapid, Gary George 1945- *BiDrAPA 89*
Lapid-Bogda, Ginger Snapp 1946- *WhoAmW 91*
Lapides, Harvey Grant 1939- *BiDrAPA 89*
Lapides, Jack 1914- *WhoAm 90*
Lapides, Jeffrey Rolf 1954- *St&PR 91, WhoAm 90, WhoE 91*
Lapides, Julian Lee 1931- *WhoE 91*
Lapides, Morton M. 1929- *St&PR 91, WhoAm 90*
Lapides, Robert E. 1918- *St&PR 91*
Lapidus, Arnold 1933- *WhoE 91, WhoWor 91*
Lapidus, Herbert 1931- *St&PR 91*
Lapidus, Jacqueline 1941- *WhoWrEP 89*
LaPidus, Jules Benjamin 1931- *WhoAm 90*
Lapidus, Lawrence Searle 1945- *WhoEmL 91*
Lapidus, Leonard 1929- *St&PR 91, WhoE 91*
Lapidus, Michael S 1942- *BiDrAPA 89*
Lapidus, Morris 1902- *WhoAm 90*
Lapidus, Norman Israel 1930- *WhoE 91*
Lapidus, Richard 1935-1988 *BioIn 16*
Lapidus, Sidney *WhoE 91*
Lapidus, Ted 1929- *ConDes 90*
Lapierre, Arnaud *PenDiDA 89*
Lapierre, Dominique 1931- *WhoAm 90*
La Pierre, Douglas Bruce 1947- *WhoAm 90*
La Pierre, Thomas 1930- *WhoAmA 91*
LaPierre, William Charles 1957- *WhoEmL 91*
Lapierre, Yvon Denis 1936- *BiDrAPA 89*
La Pietra, Ugo 1938- *ConDes 90*

Lapin, Byron Richard 1941- *St&PR 91*
Lapin, Harvey I. 1937- *WhoAm 90*
Lapin, Jay Forman 1945- *WhoAm 90*
Lapin, Jeffry Mark 1953- *WhoAm 90*
Lapin, Michelle 1961- *WhoE 91*
Lapin, Robert 1930- *St&PR 91*
Lapin, Sergei G. *NewYTBS 90*
Lapin, Sharon Joyce Vaughn 1938- *WhoAmW 91, WhoWor 91*
Lapine, James 1949- *ConAu 130*
Lapine, James 1950?- *BioIn 16*
Lapine, James Elliot 1949- *WhoAm 90*
Lapins, Scott Michael 1955- *WhoEmL 91*
Lapinskas, Darius 1934- *IntWWM 90*
Lapinski, Frances Constance 1950- *WhoE 91*
Lapinski, Joan Carolyn Butler 1952- *WhoEmL 91*
Lapinski, Tadeusz 1928- *WhoAmA 91*
Lapinski, Tadeusz Andrew 1928- *WhoAm 90, WhoE 91*
Lapke, John Harrison 1960- *WhoEmL 91*
Lapkin, Milton 1929- *WhoAm 90*
LaPlaca, Alison *BioIn 16*
Laplaca, Chris 1957- *ODwPR 91*
LaPlaca, David S. 1929- *St&PR 91*
La Placa, Gerald R 1940- *BiDrAPA 89*
La Placa, Robert W 1945- *BiDrAPA 89*
Laplace, Pierre Simon, Marquis De 1749-1827 *WorAlBi*
La Plant, Mimi 1943- *WhoAmA 91*
Laplante, Bruno 1938- *IntWWM 90*
Laplante, Bruno T *BiDrAPA 89*
Laplante, Eduardo 1818?- *ArtLatA*
La Plante, J. Duncan 1956- *WhoWrEP 89*
La Plante, Laura 1904- *BioIn 16*
Laplante, Paul Allen 1924- *St&PR 91*
LaPlante, William A. 1930- *St&PR 91*
Laplantz, David 1944- *WhoAmA 91*
Laplantz, Shereen 1947- *WhoAmA 91*
La Plata, George 1924- *WhoAm 90, WhoHisp 91*
Lapman, Mark Charles 1950- *WhoEmL 91*
LaPoe, Wayne Gilpin 1924- *WhoAm 90*
Lapof, Ray Charles 1932- *St&PR 91*
LaPoint, Dave *BioIn 16*
LaPoint, Dave 1959- *Ballpl 90*
Lapointe, Carole *BiDrAPA 89*
LaPointe, Cynthia Ruth 1962- *WhoAmW 91*
Lapointe, Dawn Dunaway 1955- *WhoAmW 91*
Lapointe, Edward Joseph 1942- *St&PR 91*
Lapointe, Frank 1942- *WhoAmA 91*
Lapointe, J.R. 1946- *St&PR 91*
Lapointe, Jean L 1926- *BiDrAPA 89*
LaPointe-Shaw, Lucie 1954- *WhoWor 91*
Laponce, Jean Antoine 1925- *WhoAm 90*
LaPorta, Danielle Marie 1956- *WhoE 91*
La Porta, Elayne B *WhoAmA 91*
LaPorta, Lauren Deidra *BiDrAPA 89*
Laporta, Marc *BiDrAPA 89*
LaPorta, Ralph *St&PR 91*
La Porta, Robert Louis 1941- *St&PR 91*
Laporte, Andre 1931- *IntWWM 90*
Laporte, Cloyd, III 1959- *WhoE 91*
Laporte, Cloyd, Jr. 1925- *St&PR 91, WhoAm 90*
Laporte, Craig Aiston 1953- *WhoWor 91*
LaPorte, Frank 1880-1939 *Ballpl 90*
Laporte, Gerald Joseph Sylvestre 1946- *WhoEmL 91*
La Porte, James 1931- *St&PR 91*
LaPorte, Joseph James 1931- *St&PR 91*
Laporte, Leo Frederic 1933- *WhoAm 90*
La Porte, Michael J. 1937- *St&PR 91*
Laporte, Thomas B. 1940- *St&PR 91*
LaPorte, William F. 1913- *St&PR 91*
Laposky, Ben Francis 1914- *WhoAmA 91, WhoWor 91*
Lapotaire, Robert Louis 1959- *WhoSSW 91*
Lapovsky, Arthur J *BiDrAPA 89*
Lapp, Alice Weber 1931- *WhoAmW 91*
Lapp, Eleanor J. 1936- *AuBYP 90, SmATA 61*
Lapp, J. Parker 1953- *St&PR 91*
Lapp, Jack 1884-1920 *Ballpl 90*
Lapp, Mary Klemm *WhoAmW 91*
Lapp, Philip Alexander 1928- *WhoAm 90*
Lapp, Roger James 1933- *WhoSSW 91, WhoWor 91*
Lapp, Susan Bolster 1945- *WhoAmW 91*
Lappalainen, Kimmo 1944- *IntWWM 90*
Lappat, Hans-Juergen Vinzenz 1953- *WhoWor 91*
Lappawinze 1700?- *WhNaAH*
Lappe, Frances Moore *BioIn 16*
Lappe, Frances Moore 1944- *WhoAm 90, WhoAmW 91, WhoWrEP 89*
Lappen, Chester I. 1919- *WhoAm 90*
Lappen, Timothy 1947- *WhoEmL 91*
Lappin, Gerald David 1910- *St&PR 91*
Lappin, Richard C. 1944- *WhoAm 90*
Lappin, Robert I. 1922- *St&PR 91*
Lappin, Robert Sidney 1928- *WhoWor 91*
Laprade, Barbara 1925- *St&PR 91*
LaPrade, James Nicholas 1956- *WhoE 91*
La Prade, Robert Timothy 1952- *St&PR 91*
Lapsley, James Norvell, Jr. 1930- *WhoAm 90*
Lapsley, Susan *AuBYP 90*
Lapsley, William Winston 1910- *WhoAm 90*
Lapsys, Michael Thomas 1948- *WhoSSW 91*
Laptad, Maria Nita Rameriez 1947- *WhoAmW 91*
Laput, Amador J *BiDrAPA 89*
LaQua, John Francis, Jr. 1958- *WhoEmL 91*
Laquatra, Lisa Ann 1962- *WhoAmW 91*
Laqueur, Klaus Christian 1945- *WhoWor 91*
Laqueur, Peter 1941- *St&PR 91, WhoAm 90*
Laqueur, Walter 1921- *WhoAm 90*
Laquinta, Fred John 1949- *WhoEmL 91*
La Quintinie, Jean de 1626-1688 *BioIn 16*
Lara, Contessa *EncCoWW*
Lara, C M *BiDrAPA 89*
Lara, Guillermo Rodriguez 1923- *BioIn 16*
Lara, Ione V 1949- *BiDrAPA 89*
Lara, Joe *BioIn 16*
Lara, Patricio P 1939- *BiDrAPA 89*
Lara, Rodrigo 1958- *WhoSSW 91*
Lara, Tirso Gallard *BiDrAPA 89*
Lara Castro, Carmen de *BioIn 16*
Laraaji *NewAgMG*
Larabie, Eugene 1936- *St&PR 91*
Larabie, Theresa Jeanine 1932- *St&PR 91*
Larach, Marilyn Green 1952- *WhoAmW 91*
Larach, Randa Isell 1960- *WhoAmW 91*
Larade, Bernice D. *St&PR 91*
Laragh, John Henry 1924- *WhoAm 90*
Laraine, Barbara *IntWWM 90*
La Raja, Diane Louise 1951- *WhoEmL 91*
Laraki, Azedine 1929- *WhoWor 91*
Laramey, Mark S. 1950- *St&PR 91*
Laramore, Rosemary *BiDrAPA 89*
Larangeira, Crispin 1940- *ConAu 129*
Larar, Jeanette G. 1934- *WhoAmW 91*
Larash, William Wallace 1927- *St&PR 91*
Laraya-Cuasay, Lourdes Redublo 1941- *WhoAmW 91*
Larbalestrier, Deborah Elizabeth 1934- *WhoAmW 91*
Larberg, John Frederick 1930- *WhoE 91, WhoWor 91*
Larcada, Luis Ignacio *BioIn 16*
Larcada, Richard Kenneth 1935- *WhoAmA 91N*
Larcade, Lee Alan *BiDrAPA 89*
Larche, James Clifford, II 1946- *WhoSSW 91*
Larcher, Hubert 1921- *EncO&P 3*
Larcher, Jean 1947- *ConDes 90*
L'Archeveque, Andre Robert 1923- *WhoAmA 91*
Larco Cox, Guillermo *WhoWor 91*
Larcom, Lucy 1824-1893 *BioAmW, FemiCLE*
Larcum, Mary *BiDEWW*
Lard, Charles Walter 1946- *St&PR 91*
Lardas, Konstantinos N. 1927- *WhoWrEP 89*
Larde-Arthes, Enrique Rafael 1899- *WhoE 91, WhoWor 91*
Lardner, Breck Surbrug 1937- *St&PR 91*
Lardner, Henry Petersen 1932- *WhoAm 90*
Lardner, James F. 1924- *St&PR 91*
Lardner, James Francis 1924- *WhoAm 90*
Lardner, John 1912-1960 *Ballpl 90*
Lardner, Peter 1932- *St&PR 91*
Lardner, Rex *AuBYP 90*
Lardner, Ring *ConAu 131, MajTwCW*
Lardner, Ring 1885-1933 *Ballpl 90, BioIn 16, WorAlBi*
Lardner, Ring 1915- *BioIn 16*
Lardner, Ring, Jr. 1915- *EncAL*
Lardner, Ring W 1885-1933 *ConAu 131, MajTwCW*
Lardner, Ring W., Jr. *ConAu 131, MajTwCW*
Lardner, Ring Wilmer, Jr. 1915- *WhoAm 90, WhoWrEP 89*
Lardner, Thomas Joseph 1938- *WhoAm 90*
Lardy, Henry Arnold 1917- *WhoAm 90*
Lareau, Marybeth Bass 1941- *WhoAmW 91, WhoE 91*
Lareau, Richard G. 1928- *St&PR 91*
Lareau, Richard George 1928- *WhoAm 90*
Laredo, Jaime 1941- *IntWWM 90, PenDiMP*
Laredo, Julio Richard 1952- *WhoHisp 91*
Laredo, Ruth 1937- *IntWWM 90*
Laredo, Teresa 1939- *IntWWM 90*
Laredo Bru, Federico 1875-1946 *BioIn 16*
Laren, Kuno 1924- *St&PR 91, WhoAm 90, WhoWor 91*
Lares, Linda *WhoHisp 91*
Larese, Edward John 1935- *WhoAm 90*
Laret, Robert L. 1946- *St&PR 91*
Larew, William Theodore, Jr. 1947- *St&PR 91*
Largay, George H. 1944- *St&PR 91*
Largay, Vincent B. 1930- *St&PR 91*
Large, Bonnie Arlene 1947- *WhoEmL 91*
Large, Brian 1937- *IntWWM 90*
Large, Darlene Dintino 1935- *WhoAmW 91*
Large, Edward W. 1930- *WhoAm 90*
Large, Edward Wilson 1930- *St&PR 91*
Large, James M. *St&PR 91*
Large, James M. 1932- *BioIn 16*
Large, John Andrew 1947- *WhoAm 90*
Large, Robert Harris 1935- *St&PR 91*
Largen, Cheryl Renee 1957- *WhoAmW 91*
Largen, Joseph 1940- *WhoAm 90*
Largen, Robert Glenn 1947- *St&PR 91*
Largent, Roy 1879-1943 *Ballpl 90*
Largent, Steve *BioIn 16*
Largent, Steve 1954- *WhoAm 90*
Largey, Arthur M., Jr. 1932- *St&PR 91*
Largey, Gale Peter 1944- *WhoE 91*
Largey, Joseph Charles 1952- *WhoE 91*
Largier, Arnaud 1946- *WhoWor 91*
Largman, Kenneth 1949- *WhoWor 91*
Largo Caballero, Francisco 1869-1946 *BioIn 16*
Lari, Steven Jud *BiDrAPA 89*
Laria, Maria 1959- *WhoHisp 91*
La Riba, Enric Prat de 1870-1917 *BioIn 16*
Laric, Michael Victor 1945- *WhoE 91*
La Rico, David M. 1955- *St&PR 91*
Larigan, Jane *BioIn 16*
Larimer, Thomas Raymond 1930- *WhoWor 91*
Larios, Juan 1636-1675? *EncCRAm*
Larios, Rafael Humberto *WhoWor 91*
Lariosa, Marietta L *BiDrAPA 89*
Lariscy, Craig Stephen 1960- *WhoEmL 91*
Larish, Kenneth 1957- *WhoEmL 91*
Larivee, David 1958- *WhoSSW 91*
Lariviere, Lawrence Lewis 1945- *St&PR 91*
Lariviere, Marian *AuBYP 90*
Lariviere, Susan Marie 1967- *WhoE 91*
Larizadeh, Mohammed Reza 1947- *WhoEmL 91, WhoWor 91*
Lark, Raymond 1939- *WhoAm 90, WhoAmA 91, WhoWor 91*
Lark, Sylvia 1947- *WhoAmA 91*
Lark-Horovitz, Karl 1892-1958 *DcScB S2*
Larkam, Beverley McCosham 1928- *WhoSSW 91*
Larker, Norm 1930- *Ballpl 90*
Larkin, Alfred Sinnott, Jr. 1947- *WhoAm 90*
Larkin, Amy *ConAu 132*
Larkin, Anthony C. 1942- *St&PR 91*
Larkin, Anya 1945- *ConDes 90*
Larkin, Barry 1964- *Ballpl 90*
Larkin, Betty Ann 1951- *WhoE 91*
Larkin, Charles B 1924- *BiDrAPA 89*
Larkin, David *NewAgMG*
Larkin, Donald James 1933- *WhoAm 90*
Larkin, Emmet 1927- *WhoAm 90, WhoWrEP 89*
Larkin, Eugene 1921- *WhoAmA 91*
Larkin, Eugene David 1921- *WhoAm 90*
Larkin, Francis Xavier 1926- *St&PR 91, WhoAm 90*
Larkin, Gene 1962- *Ballpl 90*
Larkin, Jacqueline Lee 1948- *WhoAmW 91*
Larkin, James Thomas 1931- *WhoE 91*
Larkin, Jeffrey H. 1950- *St&PR 91*
Larkin, Joan 1939- *WhoAm 90*
Larkin, John 1874-1936 *DrBlPA 90*
Larkin, John E, Jr 1930- *WhoAmA 91*
Larkin, John Griffith 1955- *WhoEmL 91*
Larkin, John Montague 1936- *WhoSSW 91*
Larkin, June Noble 1922- *WhoAm 90*
Larkin, Karen Lynn 1943- *WhoAmW 91*
Larkin, Lee Roy 1928- *WhoAm 90*
Larkin, Leo Paul, Jr. 1925- *WhoAm 90*
Larkin, Martha Jane 1952- *WhoEmL 91*
Larkin, Mary Ann *WhoWrEP 89*
Larkin, Mary Sue 1948- *WhoAmW 91*
Larkin, Michael J. 1941- *St&PR 91, WhoAm 90*
Larkin, Michael John 1950- *WhoAm 90*
Larkin, Moscelyne *BioIn 16*
Larkin, Nelle Jean 1925- *WhoAmW 91, WhoWor 91*
Larkin, Oliver 1896-1970 *WhoAmA 91N*
Larkin, Patrick Joseph 1829-1900 *DcCanB 12*
Larkin, Paul L. 1947- *St&PR 91*
Larkin, Peter *BioIn 16*
Larkin, Peter Anthony 1924- *WhoAm 90*
Larkin, Philip *BioIn 16*
Larkin, Philip 1922- *WorAlBi*
Larkin, Philip 1922-1985 *ConLC 64 [port], MajTwCW*
Larkin, Philip Arthur 1922-1985 *DcNaB 1981*
Larkin, Richard Peter 1951- *St&PR 91*
Larkin, Robert 1963- *WhoEmL 91*
Larkin, Robert Leon 1931- *WhoE 91*
Larkin, Rufus 1958- *WhoSSW 91*
Larkin, Sharon 1955- *ODwPR 91*
Larkin, Thomas Oliver 1802-1858 *BioIn 16*
Larkin, William 1902-1969 *WhoAmA 91N*
Larkin, William Thomas 1923- *WhoAm 90, WhoSSW 91*
Larkins, Brian Allen 1946- *WhoAm 90*
Larkins, Ellis 1923- *DrBlPA 90*
Larkins, Ernest Radford 1955- *WhoSSW 91*
Larkins, Gary L. 1943- *St&PR 91*
Larkins, Geoffrey David 1921- *WhoWor 91*
Larkins, Grover Lamar 1926- *WhoSSW 91*
Larkins, John Davis, Jr. 1909- *WhoAm 90*
Larkins, Richard Gregory 1960- *WhoEmL 91*
Larko, Valeri 1959- *BioIn 16*
Larlee, William M. 1912- *St&PR 91*
Larmande, John Claude 1943- *WhoWor 91*
Larmer, Oscar Vance 1924- *WhoAm 90, WhoAmA 91*
Larmon, Robert Edwards 1927- *St&PR 91*
Larmor, Frederick J R *BiDrAPA 89*
Larmore, Charles Everett 1950- *WhoE 91*
Larmore, Kim Scott 1946- *BiDrAPA 89*
Larmour-Goldin, Gigi 1958- *WhoAmW 91*
Larnaud, Yves Robert 1933- *WhoWor 91*
Larned, Catherine C. *BiDrAPA 89*
Larned, Michael Chouteau 1945- *St&PR 91*
Larned, William Edmund, Jr. 1919- *WhoAm 90*
Larner, Gerald 1936- *IntWWM 90*
Larney, Dennis P. 1935- *St&PR 91*
Laro, David 1942- *St&PR 91*
La Rocca, Aldo Vittorio 1926- *WhoWor 91*
LaRocca, Charlotte Ann *BiDrAPA 89*
La Rocca, Dario Vittorio *BiDrAPA 89*
Larocca, Felix E F 1936- *BiDrAPA 89*
Larocca, James Lawrence 1943- *WhoAm 90*
LaRocca, Nick 1889-1961 *BioIn 16*
La Rocca, Nick 1889-1961 *OxCPMus*
LaRocca, Robert Kenneth 1943- *St&PR 91*
LaRocco, John Bernard 1951- *WhoEmL 91*
La Roche, Catherine *BiDrAPA 89*
LaRoche, Dave 1948- *Ballpl 90*
Laroche, Gilles 1937- *St&PR 91*
LaRoche, Gloria Rosemarie 1946- *WhoAmW 91*
Laroche, Guy 1921-1989 *AnObit 1989, BioIn 16*
Laroche, Lynda L 1947- *WhoAmA 91*
La Roche, Marie-Elaine 1949- *WhoAm 90*
LaRoche, Richard Frederick, Jr. 1945- *St&PR 91*
Laroche, Roland 1927- *OxCCanT*
La Roche, Sophie von 1730-1807 *DcLB 94 [port]*
La Rochefoucauld, Bernard 1922- *WhoWor 91*
La Rochefoucauld, Francois, Duc De 1613-1680 *WorAlBi*
LaRochelle, Diane Racine 1945- *WhoEmL 91, WhoSSW 91*
Larochelle, Donald Raymond 1930- *WhoAm 90*
Larochelle, Pauline Joan 1958- *WhoAmW 91*
La Rochelle, Pierre-Louis 1928- *WhoAm 90*
Larochelle, Richard C. 1945- *St&PR 91*
Larochelle, Richard Clement 1945- *WhoEmL 91*
La Rocque, Eugene Philippe 1927- *WhoAm 90*
La Rocque, Francois de 1885-1946 *BiDFrPL*
La Rocque, Gene Robert *BioIn 16*
La Rocque, Gene Robert 1918- *WhoAm 90*
La Rocque, Gilbert 1943-1984 *BioIn 16*
La Rocque, Marilyn Ross Onderdonk 1934- *WhoAmW 91, WhoWor 91*
Larocque De Rochbrune, Alphonse-Barnabe 1823-1893 *DcCanB 12*
LaRoe, Charles E., Jr. 1944- *ODwPR 91*
LaRoe, Edward Terhune, III 1943- *WhoE 91*
Larom, Henry V. 1903?-1975 *AuBYP 90*
Laron, Eve 1931- *WomArch [port]*
Larosa, A.D. 1928- *St&PR 91*
LaRosa, Christopher 1958- *St&PR 91*
La Rosa, Dominic Joseph 1942- *St&PR 91*
LaRosa, John S. 1954- *WhoE 91*
La Rosa, Julius *BioIn 16*
LaRosa, Julius 1956- *WhoE 91*
La Rosa, Paul S. 1942- *St&PR 91*
Larose, Arthur P. 1932- *St&PR 91*
Larose, Juanita M. 1931- *St&PR 91*
Larose, Lawrence Alfred 1958- *WhoE 91, WhoEmL 91, WhoWor 91*
Larose, Michael John 1952- *WhoSSW 91*
LaRose, Michele *BiDrAPA 89*
Larose, Roger 1910- *WhoAm 90*
LaRose, Sharon Therese 1958- *BiDrAPA 89*

LaRose, Susan Trummel 1954- *WhoEmL 91*
La Rose, Thomas Joseph 1930- *St&PR 91*
Larosiere de Champfeu, Jacques 1929- *WhoWor 91*
La Rossa, James Michael 1931- *WhoAm 90*
Larouche, Leon-Maurice *BiDrAPA 89*
LaRouche, Lyndon H. *BioIn 16*
Larouche, Lyndon H., Jr. 1922- *WhoAm 90, WorAlBi*
Larounis, George Philip 1928- *WhoAm 90, WhoWor 91*
Larounis, Mary George 1934- *WhoAmW 91*
Larousse, Pierre 1817-1875 *WorAlBi*
Larovere, Ralph W. 1935- *St&PR 91*
Larpent, Anna Margaretta *FemiCLE*
Larpenteur, James Albert, Jr. 1935- *WhoAm 90*
Larr, Peter 1939- *St&PR 91, WhoAm 90*
Larra, Mariano Jose de 1809-1837 *BioIn 16*
Larrabee, C. X. 1922- *ODwPR 91*
Larrabee, Donald Richard 1923- *WhoAm 90*
Larrabee, Eric 1922- *WhoAm 90, WhoWrEP 89*
Larrabee, Eric 1922-1990 *NewYTBS 90 [port]*
Larrabee, James Frank, Jr. *BiDrAPA 89*
Larrabee, June Hansen 1946- *WhoSSW 91*
Larrabee, Martin Glover 1910- *WhoAm 90*
Larrabee, Robert 1907- *St&PR 91*
Larrabee, Seth L. 1855-1910 *AmLegL*
Larragoite, Patricio C. 1950- *WhoHisp 91*
Larragoiti, Rafael J *BiDrAPA 89*
Larrain, Emiliano Figueroa 1866-1931 *BioIn 16*
Larralde, Elsa *AuBYP 90*
Larranaga, Antonio Jose *BiDrAPA 89*
Larrauri, Manuel S *BiDrAPA 89*
Larraz, Julio 1944- *BioIn 16*
Larraz, Julio F 1944- *WhoAmA 91*
Larrazolo, Octaviano Ambrosio 1859-1930 *BioIn 16*
Larreche, Jean-Claude 1947- *WhoWor 91*
Larrecq, Anthony James 1908- *St&PR 91*
Larrenaga, Alfred V. *St&PR 91*
Larreta, Enrique Rodriguez 1875-1961 *BioIn 16*
Larrick, James William 1950- *WhoEmL 91*
Larrick, Nancy *BioIn 16*
Larrick, Nancy G. 1910- *AuBYP 90*
Larrick, Warren Edward 1933- *St&PR 91*
Larriere, Claire 1929- *WhoWor 91*
Larrieu, Roger Claude 1932- *WhoWor 91*
Larrieu-Smith, Francie 1953?- *BioIn 16*
Larrimer, Jo Rossier 1951- *WhoEmL 91*
Larrimore, Gloria Dean 1949- *WhoWrEP 89*
Larrimore, Patsy Gadd 1933- *WhoAmW 91, WhoWor 91*
Larrimore, Randall Walter 1947- *WhoAm 90, WhoEmL 91*
Larris, Ann *AuBYP 90*
Larris, Donald M. *St&PR 91*
Larroca, Raymond G. 1930- *WhoAm 90*
Larrocha, Alicia de *BioIn 16*
Larrocha, Alicia De 1923- *IntWWM 90, PenDiMP*
Larrocha y de la Calle, Alicia de 1923- *PenDiMP*
Larroque, Roberto Eduardo *BiDrAPA 89*
Larroquette, John *BioIn 16*
Larroquette, John 1947- *WorAlBi*
Larroquette, John Bernard 1947- *WhoAm 90*
Larrouilh, Michel 1935- *St&PR 91, WhoAm 90*
Larrow, Robert William 1916- *WhoAm 90*
Larrowe, Charles Patrick 1916- *WhoAm 90*
Larry, R. Heath 1914- *WhoAm 90*
Larsen, Alf 1885-1967 *DcScanL*
Larsen, Andrew J. 1947- *St&PR 91*
Larsen, Anne 1941- *WhoAm 90*
Larsen, Annette 1951- *WhoE 91*
Larsen, Arthur Hoff 1907- *WhoAm 90*
Larsen, Asger Norgaard 1931- *WhoWor 91*
Larsen, Bjarne 1922- *IntWWM 90*
Larsen, Bjarne 1956- *WhoWor 91*
Larsen, Bob *BioIn 16*
Larsen, Carl B. 1953- *WhoSSW 91*
Larsen, Carl Christian Skat 1946- *WhoWor 91*
Larsen, Carl Erik 1911- *WhoAmA 91*
Larsen, Christian Steen *BiDrAPA 89*
Larsen, D Dane 1950- *WhoAmA 91*
Larsen, Don 1929- *Ballpl 90 [port], WorAlBi*
Larsen, Donald *BioIn 16*
Larsen, Donna Kay *WhoAmW 91*
Larsen, Douglas Arthur 1961- *WhoEmL 91*
Larsen, Edward G. 1951- *St&PR 91*
Larsen, Edwin Merritt 1915- *WhoAm 90*
Larsen, Elizabeth B. 1950- *IntWWM 90, WhoAmW 91*
Larsen, Eric 1941- *ConAu 132*
Larsen, Eric Lyle 1954- *WhoEmL 91, WhoSSW 91*
Larsen, Erik 1911- *WhoAm 90*
Larsen, Ethel Paulson 1918- *WhoAmW 91*
Larsen, Gary Loy 1945- *WhoAm 90*
Larsen, Gaye Gibson 1955- *WhoEmL 91*
Larsen, Gaylord 1932- *ConAu 30NR*
Larsen, Gordon Frank 1941- *WhoE 91*
Larsen, Grey *NewAgMG*
Larsen, Howard R. 1929- *St&PR 91*
Larsen, Jack Lenor 1927- *ConDes 90, PenDiDA 89, WhoAmA 91*
Larsen, Janet Julia 1913- *WhoAmW 91*
Larsen, Jeanette Lenore 1955- *WhoAmW 91, WhoEmL 91*
Larsen, Jeanne Louise 1950- *WhoWrEP 89*
Larsen, Jens Peter 1902-1988 *BioIn 16*
Larsen, John Christian *WhoAmA 91*
Larsen, John S. 1939- *St&PR 91*
Larsen, John W. *NewYTBS 90 [port]*
Larsen, John W. 1914-1990 *BioIn 16*
Larsen, Jonathan Zerbe 1940- *WhoAm 90*
Larsen, Kai 1926- *WhoWor 91*
Larsen, Karen Astri 1948- *BiDrAPA 89*
Larsen, Karen Marie 1954- *WhoEmL 91*
Larsen, Kenneth David 1947- *WhoE 91*
Larsen, Kent W. 1938- *St&PR 91*
Larsen, Lawrence E. 1930- *St&PR 91*
Larsen, Leo Bruno 1946- *WhoWor 91*
Larsen, Lloyd Ashley 1936- *WhoSSW 91*
Larsen, Louis Royter 1916- *WhoAm 90, WhoWor 91*
Larsen, Lynn Beck 1945- *WhoEmL 91*
Larsen, Lynne *BiDrAPA 89*
Larsen, Marget *BioIn 16*
Larsen, Marguerite G 1932- *BiDrAPA 89*
Larsen, Marguerite Goetke 1932- *WhoE 91*
Larsen, Marianne 1951- *DcScanL*
Larsen, Mark Arvid 1948- *WhoE 91*
Larsen, Mernet Ruth 1940- *WhoAmA 91*
Larsen, Mollie Fitzgerald 1963- *WhoAmW 91*
Larsen, Neil *BioIn 16*
Larsen, Nella 1891?-1964 *FemiCLE, HarlReB [port]*
Larsen, Nels C. 1929- *St&PR 91*
Larsen, Niels Erik 1954- *WhoWor 91*
Larsen, Niels Ove 1938- *WhoAm 90, WhoWor 91*
Larsen, Ole *WhoAmA 91N*
Larsen, Patrick Heffner 1945- *WhoAmA 91*
Larsen, Paul A. 1949- *St&PR 91*
Larsen, Paul Emanuel 1933- *WhoAm 90*
Larsen, Per Arne 1944- *St&PR 91*
Larsen, Peter Harry 1927- *IntWWM 90*
Larsen, Phillip Nelson 1929- *WhoAm 90*
Larsen, Ralph Irving 1928- *WhoSSW 91, WhoWor 91*
Larsen, Ralph S. 1938- *BioIn 16, St&PR 91*
Larsen, Ralph Stanley 1938- *WhoAm 90, WhoE 91*
Larsen, Rebecca 1944- *BioIn 16*
Larsen, Richard Gary 1948- *WhoAm 90*
Larsen, Richard Lee 1934- *WhoAm 90*
Larsen, Robert Charles 1952- *BiDrAPA 89*
Larsen, Robert Dhu 1922- *WhoAm 90*
Larsen, Robert Wesley 1923- *WhoAmA 91*
Larsen, Rolf 1934- *WhoAm 90, WhoE 91*
Larsen, Ronald Melvin *BiDrAPA 89*
Larsen, Roy *BioIn 16*
Larsen, Susan C 1946- *WhoAmA 91*
Larsen, Susan Carol 1946- *WhoAm 90*
Larsen, Terrance A. *WhoAm 90*
Larsen, Wayne E. 1954- *St&PR 91*
Larsen, Wendell W. 1929- *ODwPR 91*
Larsen, Wendy Wilder 1940- *WhoWrEP 89*
Larsen, William Lawrence 1926- *WhoAm 90*
Larsen-Basse, Jorn 1934- *WhoE 91*
Larsen Imes, Nella 1891-1964 *HarlReB [port]*
Larsh, Howard William 1914- *WhoAm 90*
Larson, Alan Andrew 1955- *WhoAm 90*
Larson, Alan Philip 1949- *WhoAm 90*
Larson, Alan W. 1938- *St&PR 91*
Larson, Alfred Leonard *BiDrAPA 89*
Larson, Allan Louis 1932- *WhoAm 90*
Larson, Andre Pierre 1942- *IntWWM 90*
Larson, Arleigh Gerald 1922- *St&PR 91*
Larson, Arthur Stanley 1925- *WhoWor 91*
Larson, Arvid Gunnar 1937- *WhoAm 90*
Larson, Bennett Charles 1941- *WhoAm 90*
Larson, Betty Joan 1931- *WhoAmW 91*
Larson, Blaine 1937- *WhoAmA 91*
Larson, Bradley E. 1954- *St&PR 91*
Larson, Brent T. 1942- *WhoAm 90*
Larson, Brett Allen 1955- *WhoEmL 91*
Larson, Brian Keith 1958- *St&PR 91*
Larson, Bruce 1925- *ConAu 30NR*
Larson, Bruce Alan 1951- *WhoEmL 91*
Larson, Bruce David 1954- *BiDrAPA 89*
Larson, Calvin J 1933- *ConAu 31NR*
Larson, Carl Everett 1939- *WhoAm 90*
Larson, Carol Ann *BiDrAPA 89*
Larson, Ceri *ODwPR 91*
Larson, Charles 1968- *WhoWrEP 89*
Larson, Charles Fred 1936- *WhoAm 90*
Larson, Charles Lester 1922- *WhoAm 90*
Larson, Charles Wesley, II 1935- *WhoSSW 91*
Larson, Chris Norman 1953- *BiDrAPA 89*
Larson, Clarence Edward 1909- *WhoAm 90*
Larson, Cynthia M. 1957- *St&PR 91*
Larson, Dale Irving 1937- *WhoAm 90*
Larson, Dan 1954- *Ballpl 90*
Larson, Daniel Edward 1945- *BiDrAPA 89*
Larson, Daniel M. *ODwPR 91*
Larson, Daniel William 1954- *WhoWrEP 89*
Larson, David Bruce *BiDrAPA 89*
Larson, David Bruce 1947- *WhoAm 90, WhoEmL 91*
Larson, David Lynn 1941- *BiDrAPA 89*
Larson, Diane LaVerne Kusler 1942- *WhoAmW 91*
Larson, Donald Harold 1959- *WhoEmL 91*
Larson, Donald Vernon 1934- *St&PR 91*
Larson, Donna Halling 1931- *BiDrAPA 89*
Larson, Doyle Eugene 1930- *WhoAm 90*
Larson, Earl Richard 1911- *WhoAm 90*
Larson, Edwin Arthur 1932- *BiDrAPA 89*
Larson, Edwin Robert 1947- *BiDrAPA 89*
Larson, Elaine Lucille 1943- *WhoAm 90*
Larson, Elwin S. 1926- *St&PR 91, WhoAm 90, WhoE 91*
Larson, Emilie Gustava 1919- *WhoAmW 91*
Larson, Eric *BioIn 16*
Larson, Eric Dennis 1959- *WhoSSW 91*
Larson, Eric Victor 1957- *WhoEmL 91*
Larson, Eric W 1957- *BiDrAPA 89*
Larson, Francine *BiDrAPA 89*
Larson, Frank Clark 1920- *WhoAm 90*
Larson, Fred A. 1940- *St&PR 91*
Larson, Frederick Albin 1951- *WhoEmL 91*
Larson, G. Bennett *BioIn 16*
Larson, Gary *BioIn 16*
Larson, Gary 1950- *EncACom, WhoAm 90, WorAlBi*
Larson, Gaylen Nevoy 1940- *St&PR 91, WhoAm 90*
Larson, Gene M. 1935- *IntWWM 90*
Larson, George Charles 1942- *WhoAm 90*
Larson, Gunnar Lawrence *BiDrAPA 89*
Larson, Harry Thomas 1921- *WhoAm 90*
Larson, Howard Bruce 1953- *WhoEmL 91, WhoWor 91*
Larson, Howard James 1931- *WhoE 91*
Larson, Jack *BioIn 16*
Larson, James Lionel 1943- *BiDrAPA 89*
Larson, James Robert 1950- *St&PR 91*
Larson, James Roger 1947- *St&PR 91*
Larson, James W 1932- *BiDrAPA 89*
Larson, Jane 1922- *WhoAmA 91*
Larson, Jean Russell 1930- *AuBYP 90*
Larson, Jeffrey Thomas 1958- *WhoSSW 91*
Larson, Jerry L. 1936- *WhoAm 90*
Larson, John A *BiDrAPA 89*
Larson, John A. 1892- *WorAlBi*
Larson, John August 1945- *St&PR 91*
Larson, John David 1941- *St&PR 91, WhoAm 90*
Larson, John Hyde 1930- *WhoAm 90*
Larson, John Keith *BiDrAPA 89*
Larson, John Walter *BiDrAPA 89*
Larson, John William 1935- *WhoAm 90*
Larson, Joseph A. 1920- *St&PR 91*
Larson, Joseph Stanley 1933- *WhoAm 90*
Larson, Judy L 1952- *WhoAmA 91*
Larson, Julia Louise Fink 1950- *WhoAmW 91, WhoEmL 91, WhoWor 91*
Larson, Karen Elaine 1947- *WhoAmW 91, WhoEmL 91, WhoWor 91*
Larson, Kari Michelle 1966- *WhoAmW 91*
Larson, Karin Louise 1938- *St&PR 91*
Larson, Katherine Andra *BiDrAPA 89*
Larson, Kay L 1946- *WhoAmA 91, WhoE 91*
Larson, Kaylene Marie 1945- *WhoWrEP 89*
Larson, Keith Robert 1958- *WhoEmL 91*
Larson, Keith Willis 1942- *St&PR 91*
Larson, Kenneth Duane 1940- *St&PR 91*
Larson, Kermit Dean 1939- *WhoAm 90*
Larson, L.G. 1931- *St&PR 91*
Larson, Larry 1940- *WhoAm 90*
Larson, Larry G. 1931- *WhoAm 90*
Larson, Lars-Yngve 1932- *WhoWor 91*
Larson, Lawrence J. 1904- *St&PR 91*
Larson, Lawrence John 1904- *WhoAm 90*
Larson, Lawrence Keville *BioIn 16*
Larson, Lawrence Milton 1903- *St&PR 91*
Larson, Leon Joseph 1940- *WhoSSW 91*
Larson, Linda K. 1942- *WhoE 91*
Larson, Lloyd Jack 1931- *St&PR 91*
Larson, Lois Ione 1922- *WhoAmW 91*
Larson, Lorell Vincent 1918- *WhoSSW 91*
Larson, Lynn Diane 1960- *WhoAmW 91*
Larson, Margaret *ODwPR 91*
Larson, Marjorie Marie 1922- *WhoWrEP 89*
Larson, Mark Allan 1948- *WhoAm 90*
Larson, Marlene Louise 1952- *WhoAmW 91*
Larson, Martin Alfred 1897- *WhoAm 90*
Larson, Mary C. 1953- *St&PR 91*
Larson, Maureen Inez 1955- *WhoWor 91*
Larson, Maurice Allen 1927- *WhoAm 90*
Larson, Melvin Leon 1929- *St&PR 91*
Larson, Meria Ellena 1942- *WhoAmW 91*
Larson, Merlin L. 1937- *St&PR 91*
Larson, Michael J. 1941- *St&PR 91*
Larson, Michael S 1947- *BiDrAPA 89*
Larson, Milton B. 1927- *WhoAm 90*
Larson, Miriam T. *BioIn 16*
Larson, Nancy Celeste 1951- *WhoAmW 91, WhoEmL 91, WhoWor 91*
Larson, Nancy Kay 1949- *WhoEmL 91*
Larson, Nancy Lorene 1954- *WhoEmL 91*
Larson, Neal *BioIn 16*
Larson, Ola Anders Oscar 1941- *WhoWor 91*
Larson, Orland 1931- *WhoAmA 91*
Larson, Paul E. 1952- *St&PR 91*
Larson, Paul Edward 1952- *WhoAm 90*
Larson, Pete *BioIn 16*
Larson, Philip Allen 1926- *St&PR 91*
Larson, Philip Seely 1944- *WhoAmA 91*
Larson, Phyllis Jean 1947- *WhoAmW 91*
Larson, Phyllis Shepherd 1933- *WhoAmW 91*
Larson, Randall D. 1954- *WhoWrEP 89*
Larson, Randy *WhoWrEP 89*
Larson, Ray B. 1923- *St&PR 91*
Larson, Reed Eugene 1922- *WhoAm 90*
Larson, Richard Albert 1930- *St&PR 91*
Larson, Richard Bondo 1941- *WhoAm 90*
Larson, Richard Charles 1943- *WhoAm 90*
Larson, Richard E. 1924- *St&PR 91*
Larson, Richard James 1954- *WhoEmL 91*
Larson, Richard Kenneth 1940- *WhoSSW 91*
Larson, Richard William 1948- *St&PR 91*
Larson, Robert B. *ODwPR 91*
Larson, Robert Craig 1934- *WhoAm 90*
Larson, Robert Karyl 1931- *St&PR 91*
Larson, Robert Roland 1931- *St&PR 91*
Larson, Roland Elmer 1939- *WhoE 91*
Larson, Rolf J. 1934- *St&PR 91*
Larson, Ronald Alan 1948- *St&PR 91*
Larson, Ronald Charles 1936- *St&PR 91*
Larson, Ronald Dale 1935- *St&PR 91*
Larson, Ronald G. 1930- *St&PR 91*
Larson, Ronald L. 1953- *St&PR 91*
Larson, Roy 1929- *WhoAm 90*
Larson, Russell Edward 1917- *WhoAm 90*
Larson, Russell George 1942- *WhoAm 90*
Larson, Ryan R. 1950- *St&PR 91*
Larson, Sally Joan 1948- *WhoEmL 91*
Larson, Sidney 1923- *WhoAmA 91*
Larson, Sophia 1954- *IntWWM 90*
Larson, Stanley E. 1925- *St&PR 91*
Larson, Steve 1944- *St&PR 91*
Larson, Taft Alfred 1910- *WhoAm 90*
Larson, Teresa Jeanne 1959- *WhoAmW 91*
Larson, Theodore G 1928- *BiDrAPA 89*
Larson, Theresa Gail *WhoAmA 91*
Larson, Thomas D. 1928- *WhoAm 90*
Larson, Tim Vernon *BiDrAPA 89*
Larson, Todd L. 1961- *St&PR 91*
Larson, Walter F. *St&PR 91*
Larson, Ward Jerome 1924- *WhoAm 90*
Larson, Wayne K. *ODwPR 91*
Larson, Wilfred Joseph 1927- *St&PR 91, WhoAm 90*
Larson, Willard A E *BiDrAPA 89*
Larson, William Beckwith 1937- *St&PR 91*
Larson, William G 1942- *WhoAmA 91*
Larson-Kulcsar, Agnes Judith 1948- *BiDrAPA 89*
Larsson, Donald Eric 1941- *WhoSSW 91*
Larsson, Evert A 1902- *BiDrAPA 89*
Larsson, Ingemar Teodor 1936- *WhoWor 91*
Larsson, Lars Karl 1929- *WhoWor 91*
Larsson, Lars Uno 1942- *WhoWor 91*
Larsson, William Dean 1945- *St&PR 91, WhoAm 90*
Larter, Jane Marie 1954- *WhoAmW 91*
Lartigue, Christopher W 1953- *BiDrAPA 89*
Lartigue, Susana 1942- *WhoAmW 91*
La Rue, Arlene Catherine 1912- *WhoWrEP 89*
Larue, Auguste 1814-1900 *DcCanB 12*
La Rue, Carl Forman 1929- *WhoAm 90*
LaRue, Ethel *BioIn 16*
LaRue, Gentry Carnelius, Jr. *BiDrAPA 89*
La Rue, Grace 1882-1956 *OxCPMus*
La Rue, Henry Aldred 1927- *WhoAm 90*
Larue, Hugh McElroy 1830-1906 *AmLegL*
La Rue, Jan 1918- *WhoAm 90*
La Rue, Jan Pieters 1918- *IntWWM 90*
LaRue, Janice NaDine 1936- *WhoAmW 91*

LaRue, Lash BioIn 16
La Rue, Marianna M 1933- BiDrAPA 89
LaRue, Ray 1945- St&PR 91
LaRue, Rita Renea 1957- WhoEmL 91
Larumbe, Dick Cuadra 1938- BiDrAPA 89
LaRussa, Anthony, Jr. 1944- WhoAm 90
LaRussa, Joseph Anthony 1925- WhoAm 90
La Russa, Paul Gerard 1958- BiDrAPA 89
LaRussa, Tony 1944- Ballpl 90
LaRusso, Anthony Carl 1949- WhoEmL 91
La Russo, Marianne Elizabeth 1949- WhoAmW 91
Larwood, Laurie 1941- WhoAm 90, WhoAmW 91
Lary, Buford Derald 1933- WhoAm 90
Lary, Frank 1930- Ballpl 90
Lary, Lyn 1906-1973 Ballpl 90
Larzalere, Alfred AmLegL
Larzelere, Judith Ann 1944- WhoAmA 91
Larzelere, William E., Jr. 1949- St&PR 91
Lasa, Madelaine Ivette 1954- WhoAmW 91, WhoEmL 91, WhoSSW 91
Lasaga, Antonio C. 1949- WhoAm 90
Lasaga, Manuel 1952- WhoHisp 91
Lasagna, Louis Cesare 1923- WhoAm 90
Lasagni, Alberto 1951- WhoWor 91
Lasak, John Joseph 1944- WhoE 91
La Sala, John 1946- St&PR 91
LaSala, Joseph Anthony 1923- St&PR 91
LaSalle Quartet PenDiMP
La Salle, Arthur Edward 1930- WhoAm 90, WhoSSW 91, WhoWor 91
La Salle, J. Frank WhoHisp 91
La Salle, Jean Baptiste De 1651-1719 WorAlBi
LaSalle, Patricia S. 1955- WhoAmW 91
La Salle, Peter 1947- WhoWrEP 89
Lasalle, Philippe de 1723-1805 PenDiDA 89
La Salle, Rene Robert Cavelier 1643-1687 BioIn 16
La Salle, Rene Robert Cavelier, Sieur De 1643-1687 WhNaAH
La Salle, Robert Cavelier, Sieur de 1643-1687 BioIn 16, EncCRAm, WorAlBi
La Salle, Roch 1929- WhoAm 90
La Salle, Victor ConAu 32NR
LaSalvia, Deborah Louise 1955- WhoEmL 91
Lasansky, Leonardo 1946- WhoAmA 91
Lasansky, Mauricio L 1914- WhoAmA 91
Lasarow, William Julius 1922- WhoAm 90
LaSarre, William Jolly 1931- St&PR 91
Lasater, Charles W. 1936- St&PR 91
Lasater, Donald E. 1925- WhoAm 90
Lasater, Donald Eugene 1925- St&PR 91
Lasater, Eric Martin 1953- WhoEmL 91
Lasater, Garland M., Jr. 1938- St&PR 91
Lasater, Thomas John 1957- WhoEmL 91
LaScala, Anthony Charles 1924- St&PR 91
Lascara, Vincent Alfred 1919- WhoAm 90
Lascaris EncO&P 3
Las Casas, Bartolome 1474-1566 BioIn 16
Las Casas, Bartolome De 1474-1566 EncCRAm, WhNaAH [port]
Lascelles, Alan Frederick 1887-1981 DcNaB 1981
Lasch, Christopher 1932- MajTwCW, WhoAm 90, WhoWrEP 89
Lasch, Pat 1944- WhoAmA 91
Lasch, Robert 1907- WhoAm 90
Laschenski, John Patrick 1937- WhoE 91
Laschenski, Mathilda Jane 1942- WhoAmW 91
Laschever, Barnett D. 1924- AuBYP 90
Laschuk, Roy Bogdan 1932- WhoAm 90
Lasdun, Denys Louis 1914- WhoWor 91
Lasecke, Margaret ODwPR 91
Lasek, Robert BioIn 16
Lasell, Chester K. 1936- ODwPR 91
Lasell, Chester Krum 1936- St&PR 91
Lasell, Eldridge L BiDrAPA 89
Lasell, Elinor H. AuBYP 90
Lasell, Fen 1929- AuBYP 90
Lasell, Raymond E. 1935- St&PR 91
Lasell, Ruth Lyon 1946- BiDrAPA 89
La Selva, Vincent 1929- WhoE 91
Lasenby, Jack 1931- ConAu 130
Laser, Kevin L BiDrAPA 89
Laserna, Amelia De Leon BiDrAPA 89
Laserstein, Lotte 1898- BiDWomA, BioIn 16
Lash, Fred 1945- St&PR 91
Lash, Fred C. ODwPR 91
Lash, Joseph P. 1909-1987 BioIn 16
Lash, Kenneth 1918-1985 WhoAmA 91N
Lash, Linda Marie 1948- WhoWor 91
Lash, Myles Perry 1946- WhoAm 90
Lash, Richard Anthony 1961- WhoEmL 91, WhoSSW 91, WhoWor 91
Lash, Stephen Sycle 1940- WhoAm 90
Lash, William Henry 1934- St&PR 91, WhoAm 90
Lashai, Kourosh 1938- BiDrAPA 89
Lashar, Walter Benjamin 1929- St&PR 91
Lashbrooke, Elvin Carroll, Jr. 1939- WhoAm 90
Lashelle, Charles S. 1947- St&PR 91
LaShelle, Charles Stanton 1947- WhoAm 90
LaShelle, Joe 1900-1989 BioIn 16
La Shelle, Joseph W. BioIn 16
Lasher, Donald Rex 1929- WhoAm 90
Lasher, Donna Maria 1948- WhoAmW 91
Lasher, Duncan M. 1926- St&PR 91
Lasher, Fred 1941- Ballpl 90
Lasher, Jordan BioIn 16
Lasher, Michael WhoWrEP 89
Lasher, Russell J. 1918- St&PR 91
Lasher, William John 1943- BiDrAPA 89
Lashlee, JoLynne Van Marsdon 1948- WhoAmW 91
Lashley, Curtis Dale 1956- WhoEmL 91, WhoWor 91
Lashley, J Richard 1939- BiDrAPA 89
Lashley, Mark Alan 1959- WhoE 91
Lashner, Howard Bruce 1962- WhoE 91
Lashner, Michael Allan 1960- WhoEmL 91
Lashnits, Thomas Peter 1948- WhoWrEP 89
LaShomb, Sherri Lee 1964- WhoEmL 91
Lashwood, George 1863-1942 OxCPMus
Lasiecka, Irena M. 1948- WhoAmW 91, WhoSSW 91
Lasiter, Eleanor Janet 1934- WhoAmW 91
Lask, Berta 1878-1967 EncCoWW
Laska, David 1920- WhoAmA 91
Laska, John L. 1941- St&PR 91
Laska, Richard Matthew 1946- WhoSSW 91
Laska, Vera 1928- WhoE 91
Laska-Kulba, Judith Kate 1949- WhoE 91
Laskaris, Aristotle Theodore 1933- WhoE 91
Laske, Lyle F 1937- WhoAmA 91
Laske, Otto E. 1936- IntWWM 90
Lasker, Albert D. 1880-1952 WorAlBi
Lasker, Burton H BiDrAPA 89
Lasker, Edward 1912- WhoAm 90
Lasker, Fredrick 1937- BiDrAPA 89
Lasker, Gabriel Ward 1912- WhoAm 90
Lasker, Harold BiDrAPA 89
Lasker, Jay BioIn 16
Lasker, Joe 1919- WhoAmA 91
Lasker, Joel Marc 1946- St&PR 91
Lasker, Jonathan 1948- WhoAmA 91
Lasker, Jonathan Lewis 1948- WhoAm 90
Lasker, Joseph L. 1919- WhoAm 90
Lasker, Judith N. 1947- ConAu 130
Lasker, Martin 1932- St&PR 91
Lasker, Mary WhoAm 90
Lasker, Norman 1926- WhoAm 90
Lasker-Schuler, Else 1869-1945 BioIn 16, EncCoWW
Laskey, Amelia 1885-1973 WomFie [port]
Laskey, Bill 1957- Ballpl 90
Laskey, Richard Anthony 1936- WhoAm 90
Laski, Frank Joseph 1929- St&PR 91, WhoAm 90
Laski, Harold 1893-1950 WorAlBi
Laski, Harold Joseph 1893-1950 BioIn 16
Laski, James Emil 1950- WhoEmL 91
Laski, Karen Elaine 1944- WhoAmW 91
Laski, Marghanita 1915-1988 AnObit 1988, BioIn 16, FemiCLE
Laskin, Arthur James 1927- St&PR 91
Laskin, Daniel M. 1924- WhoAm 90
Laskin, Lee B. 1936- WhoE 91
Laskin, Muriel 1929- BiDrAPA 89
Laskin, Myron, Jr. 1930- WhoAm 90, WhoAmA 91
Laskin, Richard Sheldon 1940- WhoWor 91
Laskine, Lily 1893-1988 AnObit 1988, PenDiMP
Lasko, John C. St&PR 91
Lasko, Warren Anthony 1940- WhoAm 90
Laskow, Lynda Therese 1947- WhoAmW 91
Laskowski, Irma Williams 1943- WhoAmW 91
Laskowski, Janusz Stanislaw 1936- WhoAm 90
Laskowski, Leonard Francis, Jr. 1919- WhoAm 90
Laskowski, Michael, Jr. 1930- WhoAm 90
Laskowski, Robert A. 1951- St&PR 91
Lasky, Barry St&PR 91
Lasky, David 1932- St&PR 91, WhoAm 90
Lasky, David 1946- BiDrAPA 89
Lasky, Frank Michael 1940- WhoE 91
Lasky, Jack Samuel 1930- St&PR 91
Lasky, Janet Louise 1955- WhoWrEP 89
Lasky, Jesse BioIn 16
Lasky, Jesse L., Jr. 1910-1988 AnObit 1988
Lasky, Kathryn BioIn 16
Lasky, Marc Evan 1945- St&PR 91
Lasky, Morris BioIn 16
Lasky, Moses 1907- WhoAm 90
Lasky, Victor NewYTBS 90 [port]
Lasky, Victor 1918-1990 BioIn 16, ConAu 131
Lasky-Langford, Margaret Roleen 1936- WhoAmW 91
Lasley, John 1927- St&PR 91
Lasnick, Julius 1929- WhoSSW 91
Lasnier, Rina 1910- WhoAmW 91
Laso, Francisco 1823-1869 ArtLatA
Lasocki, David 1947- IntWWM 90
Lasoen, Patricia 1948- EncCoWW
Lason, Sandra Woolman 1934- WhoAmW 91
Lasonde, Marilynn Joy 1956- WhoWrEP 89
La Sor, William Sanford 1911- WhoAm 90
Lasorda, Tom BioIn 16
Lasorda, Tom Charles 1927- WhoAm 90
Lasorda, Tommy 1927- Ballpl 90 [port]
Lasorda Sivieri, Helen Marie WhoE 91
Lasorsa, Joseph Francis 1947- WhoEmL 91
La Sorsa, William George 1945- WhoEmL 91
Lasota, George L 1936- BiDrAPA 89
LaSpagnoletta, Benjamin Joseph 1946- WhoE 91
Laspina, Peter Joseph 1951- WhoE 91
Lass, E. Donald 1938- St&PR 91
Lass, Ernest Donald 1938- WhoAm 90
Lass, Katherine Ann 1951- WhoAmW 91
Lass, Roger 1937- ConAu 132
Lassabe, Alessandra Crain 1954- WhoAmW 91
Lassaigne, Jacques 1910?-1982 ConAu 129
Lassalle, Ferdinand 1825-1864 WorAlBi
Lassaw, Ibram 1913- WhoAm 90, WhoAmA 91
Lassen, Anna Margrethe 1659-1738 EncCoWW
Lassen, Arne Christian 1938- St&PR 91
Lassen, Ben WhoAmA 91N
Lassen, John Kai 1942- WhoE 91, WhoWor 91
Lassen, John R. 1922- WhoAm 90
Lassen, John Richard 1922- St&PR 91
Lassen, Kate 1880-1956 BiDWomA
Lassen, Nancy Beth Giannelli 1956- WhoEmL 91
Lassen, Stuart Allan 1932- St&PR 91
Lassen, Thorbjorn J 1916- BiDrAPA 89
Lasser, Gail Maria 1952- WhoE 91
Lasser, Joseph R. 1923- St&PR 91
Lasser, Joseph Robert 1923- WhoAm 90
Lasser, Louise WhoAm 90
Lasser, Louise 1939- WorAlBi
Lassers, Elisabeth BiDrAPA 89
Lassers, Willard J. 1919- WhoAm 90
Lasseter, Charles Erwin 1932- St&PR 91, WhoAm 90
Lasseter, Kenneth Carlyle 1942- WhoSSW 91
Lassetter, Leslie 1955- IntWWM 90
Lassettre, Edwin Nichols 1911-1990 WhoAm 90, WhoWor 91
Lassick, Sydney 1922- WhoAm 90
Lassila, Maiju 1868-1918 DcScanL
Lassiter, Barbara Ann 1960- WhoAmW 91
Lassiter, Barry Wayn 1961- WhoSSW 91
Lassiter, Byron Anthony 1957- WhoEmL 91
Lassiter, Isaac Steele 1941- WhoWrEP 89
Lassiter, James Harrison 1940- St&PR 91
Lassiter, James Morris, Jr. 1941- WhoSSW 91
Lassiter, Joseph Baker, III 1947- St&PR 91
Lassiter, Kenneth T. 1935- WhoAm 90
Lassiter, Luther BioIn 16
Lassiter, Mary ConAu 131
Lassiter, Reynolds B. H. 1963- WhoSSW 91
Lassiter, Ronald Corbett 1932- St&PR 91, WhoAm 90
Lassiter, Stephen Howard 1950- WhoEmL 91
Lassiter, Wimpy BioIn 16
Lasslo, Andrew 1922- WhoAm 90, WhoWor 91
Lassner, Franz George 1926- WhoAm 90
Lassner, Jacob 1935- WhoAm 90
Lasso, Galo Plaza 1906-1987 BioIn 16
Lasson, Anna Margrethe 1659-1738 EncCoWW
Lasson, Robert 1922- AuBYP 90
Lassus, Orlande De 1532?-1594 WorAlBi
Lasswell, Fred EncACom
Lasswell, Fred 1916- WhoAm 90
Lasswell, Marcia Lee 1927- WhoAm 90
Lasswell, Mary 1905- WhoAm 90
Lasswell, Thomas Ely 1919- WhoAm 90
Last, Alvin I. 1932- St&PR 91
Last, James 1929- OxCPMus
Last, Joan Mary 1908- IntWWM 90
Last, Joel Irwin BiDrAPA 89
Last, Marian Helen 1953- WhoAmW 91, WhoEmL 91
Last, Norman H. 1962- St&PR 91
Last, Sondra Carole 1932- WhoAmW 91
Laster, Atlas, Jr. 1948- WhoEmL 91, WhoWor 91
Laster, Connie McDaniel 1960- WhoEmL 91
Laster, Elizabeth 1928- St&PR 91
Laster, Howard 1930-1986 BioIn 16
Laster, Israel BioIn 16
Laster, LaMar Frederick 1951- St&PR 91
Laster, Leonard 1928- WhoAm 90, WhoE 91
Laster, Oliver 1921- St&PR 91
Laster, Paul 1951- WhoAmA 91
Laster, Ralph W. 1951- St&PR 91
Laster, Richard 1923- St&PR 91, WhoAm 90, WhoE 91, WhoWor 91
Lastfogel, Abe 1898-1984 BioIn 16
Lastic, Georges de 1927-1988 BioIn 16
Lastick, Marjorie Alice 1948- WhoAmW 91
Lastinger, Allen L. 1942- St&PR 91
Lastinger, Allen Lane, Jr. 1942- WhoAm 90
Lastman, Melvin D. 1933- WhoAm 90
Lastofka, Arthur Daniel 1930- St&PR 91
Lastowka, James Anthony 1951- WhoAm 90
Lastra, Eduardo 1938- WhoWor 91
Lastra, Manuel Postrero 1940- WhoSSW 91
Lasuchin, Michael 1923- WhoAmA 91
Lasure, Linda Lee 1946- WhoEmL 91
La Susa, Lawrence R. 1960- WhoEmL 91
Laswell, Lucien Kroll 1939- St&PR 91
Laswell, Troy James 1920- WhoAm 90
Laszewski, Ronald Thomas 1949- WhoE 91
Laszlo, Anna 1926-1981 EncCoWW
Laszlo, Ferenc 1937- IntWWM 90
Laszlo, Ivan J 1924- BiDrAPA 89
Laszlo, Ivan Jozsef 1924- WhoE 91
Laszlo, Laszlo 1898-1936 EncO&P 3
Laszlo, Magda 1919- IntWWM 90
Laszlo, Pierre 1938- WhoWor 91
Laszynski, Robert Steven 1953- WhoEmL 91
Lataif, Louis Edward 1939- St&PR 91
Latane, Bibb 1937- WhoAm 90
Latane, John Holladay 1869-1932 BioIn 16
Latanich, Terry S. 1950- St&PR 91
Latanision, Ronald Michael 1942- WhoAm 90
Latarche, Vanessa Jayne 1959- IntWWM 90
Latcham, Franklin Chester 1922- WhoAm 90
Latchem, Malcolm Stephen 1931- IntWWM 90
Latchford, James J. 1944- St&PR 91
Latchum, James Levin 1918- WhoAm 90, WhoE 91
Lateef, Noel V. 1956- St&PR 91
Lateef, Yusef BioIn 16, NewAgMG
Lateef, Yusef 1920- DrBIPA 90, WhoAm 90
Latef, Javed Anver 1943- WhoE 91
Lateiner, Jacob 1928- IntWWM 90
Latella, Robert N. 1942- St&PR 91
Latella, Robert Natale 1942- WhoAm 90
Latella, Salvatore Philip 1919- WhoE 91
Lately Gone DcCanB 12
La Tendresse, John D BiDrAPA 89
Latendresse, Lanelle St&PR 91
Laterza, Vito 1926- WhoWor 91
Latey, Mary 1650-1713 BiDEWW
Latham, Aaron 1943- SpyFic
Latham, Alfred William 1937- St&PR 91
Latham, Alice Frances Patterson 1916- WhoAmW 91, WhoSSW 91, WhoWor 91
Latham, Allen, Jr. 1908- St&PR 91, WhoAm 90
Latham, Arlie 1859-1952 Ballpl 90
Latham, Christopher Daniel 1951- WhoE 91
Latham, Daniel Henry 1952- WhoEmL 91
Latham, Donald Crawford 1932- AuBYP 90
Latham, Eleanor Ruth Earthrowl 1924- WhoAmW 91
Latham, Eunice Stunkard 1923- WhoE 91, WhoWor 91
Latham, Frank B. 1910- AuBYP 90
Latham, Hollis Colleen 1954- WhoEmL 91
Latham, James D. 1942- St&PR 91
Latham, James Parker 1918- WhoSSW 91
Latham, James William 1930- WhoE 91
Latham, Jean Lee 1902- AuBYP 90, WhoAm 90
Latham, John Michael 1954- WhoSSW 91
Latham, Larry Lee 1945- WhoSSW 91
Latham, Lyndon Clint 1943- WhoSSW 91
Latham, Mary Elizabeth WhoAmW 91
Latham, Patricia Horan 1941- WhoE 91
Latham, Philip AuBYP 90
Latham, Raymond R., Jr. 1945- WhoEmL 91

Latham, Richard Carlton 1941- *WhoSSW 91*
Latham, Robert Allen 1922- *WhoWor 91*
Latham, Robert Jesse 1942- *St&PR 91*
Latham, Robin Lynne 1964- *WhoAmW 91*
Latham, Tommye Paul 1945- *WhoEmL 91, WhoSSW 91*
Latham, William B. 1925- *St&PR 91*
Latham, William Peters 1917- *IntWWM 90, WhoAm 90*
Latham-Koenig, Jan 1953- *IntWWM 90, PenDiMP*
Lathan, Bobbi Jo 1951- *ConTFT 8 [port]*
Lathan, Roamey A. 1943- *St&PR 91*
Lathan, Samuel Robert, Jr. 1938- *WhoSSW 91*
Lathan, Stan 1944?- *DrBlPA 90*
Lathan, Tiffany LaVerne 1964- *WhoSSW 91*
Lathbury, Roger 1945- *WhoSSW 91, WhoWrEP 89*
Lathem, Edward Connery 1926- *WhoAm 90*
Lathen, Emma *TwCCr&M 91, WorAlBi*
Lathen, Emma 1927- *FemiCLE*
Lathen, John William *BiDrAPA 89*
Lathlaen, Robert Frank 1925- *St&PR 91, WhoAm 90*
Lathram, Marvin Walter, Jr. 1917- *BiDrAPA 89*
Lathrop, Arthur Lester 1938- *St&PR 91*
Lathrop, Churchill Pierce 1900- *WhoAmA 91*
Lathrop, Dean Allen 1937- *St&PR 91*
Lathrop, Donald D 1928- *BiDrAPA 89*
Lathrop, Dorothy Pulis 1891-1980 *AuBYP 90*
Lathrop, Francis *MajTwCW*
Lathrop, Gertrude Adams 1921- *WhoAm 90, WhoAmW 91*
Lathrop, Gertrude K 1896-1986 *WhoAmA 91N*
Lathrop, Irvin T. 1927- *WhoWrEP 89*
Lathrop, Irvin Tunis 1927- *WhoAm 90*
Lathrop, Jaime D. 1931- *St&PR 91*
Lathrop, John M. 1949- *St&PR 91*
Lathrop, Joyce Keen 1939- *WhoAmW 91*
Lathrop, Julia 1858-1932 *BioAmW, WorAlBi*
Lathrop, Katherine Austin 1915- *WhoAm 90*
Lathrop, Kaye Don 1932- *WhoAm 90*
Lathrop, Mitchell Lee 1937- *WhoAm 90, WhoWor 91*
Lathrop, Nancy-Coalter *BiDrAPA 89*
Lathrop, Roger Alan 1951- *WhoEmL 91*
Lathrop, Rose 1851-1926 *FemiCLE*
Lathrop, Rose Hawthorne 1851-1926 *BioAmW, BioIn 16*
Lathrop, Thomas Albert 1941- *WhoWor 91*
Lathrop, Walter William, Jr. 1933- *St&PR 91*
Lathrop, Wendy Pam 1952- *WhoEmL 91*
Lathrop, William Hamilton 1939- *WhoAm 90*
Latiak, Dennis Joseph 1946- *WhoSSW 91*
Latics, Victor Gregory 1926- *WhoAm 90*
Latif, Sami Mohammad 1953- *WhoEmL 91*
Latimer, Cynthia Lesette 1958- *WhoEmL 91*
Latimer, Dean 1945- *ConAu 129*
Latimer, Donovan Gail 1933- *WhoSSW 91*
Latimer, Douglas Hamilton 1937- *WhoAm 90*
Latimer, George 1935- *WhoAm 90*
Latimer, George W. *NewYTBS 90 [port]*
Latimer, George W. 1900-1990 *BioIn 16*
Latimer, Hugh 1485?-1555 *WorAlBi*
Latimer, James Dunlap 1938- *St&PR 91*
Latimer, James Hearn 1941- *WhoE 91*
Latimer, James Wellington 1826-1859 *BioIn 16*
Latimer, John A., III 1950- *St&PR 91*
Latimer, John Francis 1903- *WhoAm 90*
Latimer, Jonathan 1906-1983 *TwCCr&M 91*
Latimer, Margaret Petta 1932- *WhoAmW 91*
Latimer, Mark J. *BioIn 16*
Latimer, Peyton Randolph 1938- *St&PR 91*
Latimer, Robert T 1930- *BiDrAPA 89*
Latimer, Roy Truett 1928- *WhoAm 90*
Latimer, Thomas E. 1935- *ODwPR 91*
Latimer, Thomas Emmett 1935- *WhoSSW 91*
Latimer, Walter George 1958- *WhoEmL 91*
Latimer, Wilbur Scott 1938- *WhoAm 90*
Latimer, William Perot 1935- *St&PR 91*
Latinazo, Guillermo Antiado 1933- *WhoWor 91*
Latini, Anthony A. 1942- *WhoAm 90*
Latini, Carlo 1959- *WhoWor 91*
Latiolais, Ken Dale 1946- *St&PR 91*
Latiolais, Rene Louis 1942- *St&PR 91, WhoAm 90*
Latkovic, Goran 1959- *WhoWor 91*
Latkovich, Sharon Ann 1957- *WhoEmL 91*
Latman, Barry 1936- *Ballpl 90*
Latno, Arthur Clement 1929- *St&PR 91*
Latno, Arthur Clement, Jr. 1929- *WhoAm 90*
Laton, Thomas Michael 1959- *BiDrAPA 89*
Latona, Raymond W. 1936- *St&PR 91*
Latoni, Alfonso Rafael 1958- *WhoEmL 91, WhoSSW 91, WhoWor 91*
Latore, Daniel Joseph 1939- *St&PR 91*
LaTorre, L. Donald 1937- *St&PR 91, WhoAm 90*
LaTorre, Marion Joseph 1933- *WhoE 91*
Latorre, Robert George 1949- *WhoSSW 91*
LaTorre, Ruben *WhoHisp 91*
La Torre, Victor Raul Haya de 1895-1979 *BioIn 16*
Latos-Valier, Paula 1946- *WhoWor 91*
La Touche, John 1917-1956 *OxCPMus*
La Touf, Larry 1939- *St&PR 91, WhoAm 90*
La Tour, George De 1593-1652 *WorAlBi*
La Tour, Georges de 1593-1652 *IntDcAA 90*
Latour, Malcolm L 1933- *BiDrAPA 89*
Latour, Thomas George 1936- *BiDrAPA 89*
Latour, Wallace Charles 1924- *WhoAm 90*
La Tour du Pin, Marquis de 1834-1924 *BiDFrPL*
Latourell, Harry E. 1903- *St&PR 91*
Latourelle, Rene 1918- *ConAu 130*
La Tourette, Aileen 1946- *FemiCLE*
Latourette, Harry Hewes 1915- *St&PR 91*
La Tourette, John Ernest 1932- *WhoAm 90*
LaTourrette, James Thomas 1931- *WhoAm 90*
Latovick, Paula Rae 1954- *WhoEmL 91*
Latrobe, Benjamin H. 1764-1820 *WorAlBi*
Latrobe, Benjamin Henry 1764-1820 *BioIn 16*
Latrobe, Ferdinand Claiborne 1833-1911 *AmLegL*
Latronica, Anthony Francis, Jr. 1948- *WhoE 91*
Latshaw, John 1921- *St&PR 91, WhoAm 90*
Latshaw, Patricia Joan Herget 1930- *WhoAmW 91*
Latshaw, Steve Thomas 1959- *WhoEmL 91*
Latsios, Barbara Lynn 1954- *WhoAmW 91*
Latt, Khin M 1930- *BiDrAPA 89*
Latt, Samuel Arch 1938-1988 *BioIn 16*
Latta, Diana Lennox 1936- *WhoWor 91*
Latta, Jean Carolyn 1943- *WhoAmW 91, WhoWor 91*
Latta, Jennie Davidson 1961- *WhoAmW 91*
Latta, John Alex 1954- *WhoWrEP 89*
Latta, Jonathan Kane 1955- *WhoWrEP 89*
Latta, William Braden, Jr. 1949- *WhoEmL 91*
Latta, William Charlton 1902- *WhoAm 90*
Lattal, Alice Darnell 1943- *WhoAmW 91, WhoSSW 91*
Lattany, Kristin Eggleston 1931- *WhoWrEP 89*
Lattanzi, Robert Marc 1958- *WhoSSW 91*
Lattanzio, David Albert 1942- *St&PR 91*
Lattanzio, Frances 1949- *WhoAmA 91*
Lattanzio, Stephen Paul 1949- *WhoEmL 91*
Lattanzio Sastre, Sergio Raul 1948- *WhoWor 91*
Lattavo, Philip Errol 1941- *St&PR 91*
Latter, Eugene *St&PR 91*
Latter, Mary 1722-1777 *FemiCLE*
Latterell, Mari Jean 1965- *WhoAmW 91*
Latteri, Joseph A *BiDrAPA 89*
Latte's, Jean-Claude 1941- *St&PR 91*
Lattes, Jean-Claude J. 1941- *WhoAm 90*
Lattes, Raffaele 1910- *WhoAm 90*
Lattie, Betty S. 1934- *ODwPR 91*
Lattimer, Gary Lee 1939- *WhoAm 90*
Lattimer, James Michael 1950- *WhoAm 90*
Lattimer, John Kingsley 1914- *WhoAm 90, WhoWor 91*
Lattimore, Eleanor Frances 1904- *AuBYP 90*
Lattimore, Eleanor Frances 1904-1986 *BioIn 16*
Lattimore, Jessie *ConAu 132*
Lattimore, Kenneth Robert *BiDrAPA 89*
Lattimore, Owen 1900-1989 *AnObit 1989, BioIn 16*
Lattin, Albert Floyd 1950- *WhoE 91*
Lattin, Clark P. 1916-1989 *BioIn 16*
Lattin, Harriet 1898- *AuBYP 90*
Lattin, Vernon E. 1938- *WhoHisp 91*
Lattin, Vernon Eugene 1938- *WhoAm 90*
Lattman, Laurence Harold 1923- *WhoAm 90*
Lattman, Norman S. 1936- *St&PR 91*
Lattner, Forrest Comer *BioIn 16*
Latto, Lawrence Jay 1920- *WhoAm 90*
Latto, Lewis M., Jr. 1940- *WhoAm 90*
Latture, James Paul, Jr. 1946- *WhoSSW 91*
La Tules 1800-1852 *BioIn 16*
Laturno, Dean Marilyn 1937- *WhoAmW 91*
Latus, Timothy Dexter 1946- *WhoSSW 91, WhoWor 91*
Latwin, Joseph Louis 1952- *WhoEmL 91*
Latz, Gary W. 1949- *St&PR 91*
Latz, Jean-Pierre 1691?-1754 *PenDiDA 89*
Latzer, Richard Neal 1937- *St&PR 91*
Lau, Adolfo 1939- *WhoWor 91*
Lau, Annie Yin Har 1944- *WhoWor 91*
Lau, Bobby Wai-Man 1944- *WhoWor 91*
Lau, Charlie 1933-1984 *Ballpl 90*
Lau, Cheryl *WhoAmW 91*
Lau, Constance H. 1952- *St&PR 91*
Lau, Danny Din 1956- *WhoEmL 91*
Lau, Elizabeth Martinez 1951- *WhoAmW 91, WhoEmL 91, WhoWor 91*
Lau, Eugene Wing Iu 1931- *WhoWor 91*
Lau, Girard Douglas 1959- *WhoEmL 91*
Lau, Herbert G 1936- *BiDrAPA 89*
Lau, Ian Van 1950- *WhoAm 90*
Lau, Jeffrey Daniel 1948- *WhoEmL 91*
Lau, Kei-Chuen John 1952- *BiDrAPA 89*
Lau, Lawrence H.W. 1946- *St&PR 91*
Lau, Lawrence Juen-Yee 1944- *WhoAm 90*
Lau, Luis F 1928- *BiDrAPA 89*
Lau, Man Pang *BiDrAPA 89*
Lau, Maureen Treacy 1946- *WhoWor 91*
Lau, Michele Denise 1960- *WhoAmW 91*
Lau, Pearl 1952- *WhoEmL 91*
Lau, Phillip M. 1946- *St&PR 91*
Lau, Richard John 1939- *St&PR 91*
Lau, Robert Keith 1958- *WhoE 91, WhoEmL 91, WhoWor 91*
Laub, Dori *BiDrAPA 89*
Laub, George Cooley 1912- *WhoE 91*
Laub, Jakob Johann 1882-1962 *DcScB S2*
Laub, Ronald J. 1943- *St&PR 91*
Laub, Stephen 1945- *WhoAmA 91*
Laub, William Murray 1924- *WhoAm 90*
Laub-Novak, Karen 1937- *WhoAmA 91*
Laubach, Gerald David 1926- *St&PR 91, WhoAm 90, WhoE 91*
Laubach, L.R. 1930- *St&PR 91*
Laubach, Larry Preston 1955- *WhoEmL 91*
Laubach, Mark Edward 1961- *IntWWM 90*
Laubach, Rene 1948- *WhoE 91*
Laubach, Roger Alvin 1922- *WhoAm 90*
Laubach, Susan Ann 1940- *WhoAmW 91*
Laubaugh, Frederick 1926- *WhoWor 91*
Laube, David R. 1948- *St&PR 91*
Laube, Heinrich 1938- *WhoWor 91*
Laube, Lois Ruth 1946- *WhoAmW 91*
Laube, Roger Gustav 1921- *WhoAm 90*
Laube, William Tell 1940- *St&PR 91*
Laubenthal, Horst 1938- *PenDiMP*
Laubenthal, Horst 1939- *IntWWM 90*
Laubenthal, Rudolf 1886-1971 *PenDiMP*
Lauber, Christopher Joseph 1958- *WhoE 91*
Lauber, Daniel M. 1949- *WhoEmL 91*
Lauber, Mignon Diane *WhoAmW 91, WhoWor 91*
Lauber, Patricia 1924- *AuBYP 90*
Lauber, Patricia F. *ODwPR 91*
Lauber, Patricia Grace 1924- *WhoAmW 91*
Lauber, Peg Carlson 1938- *WhoWrEP 89*
Lauber, Volkmar 1944- *ConAu 132*
L'Aubespine, Madeleine de 1546-1596 *EncCoWW*
Laubich, Arnold *St&PR 91*
Laubscher, John Michael Steyn 1943- *WhoWor 91*
Laubscher, Louis E. 1944- *St&PR 91*
Laubscher, William Roy 1943- *St&PR 91*
Lauchert, John Joseph, Jr. 1956- *St&PR 91*
Lauchland, Jane Stuart *BiDrAPA 89*
Lauchli, Linda Diane 1954- *WhoEmL 91*
Lauchu, Carlos Manuel 1932- *BiDrAPA 89*
Laucirica, Louis Frank *St&PR 91*
Laucius, Stephanie Eve 1915- *WhoAmW 91*
Lauck, Anthony Joseph 1908- *WhoAm 90, WhoAmA 91*
Lauck, Kevin Dale 1950- *St&PR 91*
Lauck, W. Lawrence 1954- *ODwPR 91*
Laucks, Stanley P 1922- *BiDrAPA 89*
Laud, William 1573-1645 *BioIn 16*
Lauda, Donald Paul 1937- *WhoAm 90*
Lauda, Niki 1949- *WorAlBi*
Laudan, Larry L. 1941- *ConAu 129*
Laudano, Peter James 1956- *WhoEmL 91*
Laudato, Gaetano Joseph, Jr. 1917- *WhoE 91*
Laude, Richard Horton *BiDrAPA 89*
Lauder, Billy 1874-1933 *Ballpl 90*
Lauder, Estee *BioIn 16, WhoAm 90, WhoAmW 91, WhoE 91, WorAlBi*
Lauder, Estee 1908- *BioAmW, ConAmBL*
Lauder, Evelyn *BioIn 16*
Lauder, Harry 1870-1950 *BioIn 16, OxCPMus, WorAlBi*
Lauder, Leonard *BioIn 16*
Lauder, Leonard Alan 1933- *WhoAm 90, WhoE 91*
Lauder, Norma J. 1949- *WhoAm 90*
Lauder, Ronald S. 1944- *BioIn 16*
Lauder, Ronald Stephen 1944- *WhoAm 90, WhoE 91*
Lauder, Valarie Anne 1926- *WhoAmW 91, WhoWor 91*
Lauderdale, Clint Arlen 1932- *WhoAm 90*
Lauderdale, Gary D. 1945- *St&PR 91*
Lauderdale, James Maitland, Earl of 1759-1839 *BioIn 16*
Lauderdale, James Sidney 1911- *St&PR 91*
Lauderdale, Robert Martine 1940- *WhoSSW 91*
Laudicina, Eleanor V. 1942- *WhoAmW 91*
Laudick, Lawrence A. 1947- *St&PR 91*
Laudise, Robert Alfred 1930- *WhoAm 90*
Laudner, Tim 1958- *Ballpl 90*
Laudone, Anita Helene 1948- *WhoAm 90*
Laudonniere, Rene Goulaine De *EncCRAm, WhNaAH*
Laue, Brant Mitchell 1961- *WhoEmL 91*
Laue, Cathy Shaffia *BiDrAPA 89*
Laue, Max Von 1879-1960 *WorAlBi*
Laue, Robert C. 1925- *St&PR 91*
Lauenstein, Ann Gail 1949- *WhoAmW 91, WhoEmL 91, WhoWor 91*
Lauenstein, Milton Charles 1926- *St&PR 91, WhoAm 90*
Lauenstein, Raymond James 1937- *WhoE 91*
Lauer, Bruce A. 1952- *St&PR 91*
Lauer, Clinton D. 1926- *St&PR 91*
Lauer, Clinton Dillman 1926- *WhoAm 90*
Lauer, Eleanor L. 1931- *ODwPR 91*
Lauer, Elizabeth 1932- *WhoAmW 91*
Lauer, George 1936- *WhoWor 91*
Lauer, Gerald Joseph 1934- *St&PR 91*
Lauer, Gordon A. 1940- *St&PR 91*
Lauer, James Lothar 1920- *WhoAm 90*
Lauer, James Ward 1935- *BiDrAPA 89*
Lauer, Jeanette Carol 1935- *WhoAmW 91*
Lauer, John Charles *BiDrAPA 89*
Lauer, John W *BiDrAPA 89*
Lauer, Jonathan David 1952- *WhoE 91*
Lauer, Keith G. 1953- *St&PR 91*
Lauer, Mark Wayne 1951- *WhoSSW 91*
Lauer, Robert L. 1933- *ODwPR 91*
Lauer, Robert Lee 1933- *St&PR 91, WhoAm 90*
Lauer, Roger Myles 1940- *BiDrAPA 89*
Lauer, Thomas Eugene *BiDrAPA 89*
Lauerman, Henry Joseph, Jr. 1936- *St&PR 91*
Lauerman, James L. 1933- *St&PR 91*
Lauersen, Niels H. 1939- *ConAu 33NR*
Lauersen, Niels Helth 1939- *WhoAm 90*
Lauf, Cornelia *WhoAmA 91*
Lauf, Paul Winthrop 1942- *WhoE 91*
Laufe, Martin B 1929- *BiDrAPA 89*
Laufenberg, Terre Lynn 1951- *WhoAmW 91*
Laufer, Beatrice *WhoAm 90, WhoAmW 91, WhoWor 91*
Laufer, Hans 1929- *WhoAm 90*
Laufer, Igor 1944- *WhoAm 90*
Laufer, Jacob 1949- *WhoEmL 91*
Laufer, Joel 1933- *St&PR 91*
Laufer, Leonard Justin 1965- *WhoE 91*
Laufer, Ludwig G 1923- *BiDrAPA 89*
Laufer, Murray 1929- *OxCCanT*
Laufer, Robert S. *BioIn 16*
Laufer, Robert S. 1942?-1989 *ConAu 129*
Lauff, George Howard 1927- *WhoAm 90*
Lauffenburger, David Lind 1945- *WhoEmL 91*
Lauffenburger, Douglas Alan 1953- *WhoAm 90*
Lauffenburger, Sandra Kay 1951- *WhoAmW 91*
Lauffer, Alice A. 1919- *WhoAm 90, WhoAmA 91*
Laufman, Harold 1912- *WhoAm 90, WhoWor 91*
Laufman, Leslie Rodgers 1946- *WhoEmL 91*
Laufman, Sidney 1891-1985 *WhoAmA 91N*
Laughead, George Ross 1953- *St&PR 91*
Laughery, Jack Arnold 1935- *St&PR 91, WhoAm 90, WhoSSW 91*
Laughery, Kenneth R. 1935- *WhoAm 90*
Laughlin, Alice D 1895-1952 *WhoAmA 91N*
Laughlin, Bob 1932- *St&PR 91*
Laughlin, C.B. 1953- *St&PR 91*
Laughlin, Clarence John 1905-1985 *BioIn 16*
Laughlin, David Eugene 1947- *WhoAm 90*
Laughlin, Don *BioIn 16*
Laughlin, Greg 1942- *WhoAm 90, WhoSSW 91*
Laughlin, Greg H. 1942- *BioIn 16*
Laughlin, Harry Williamson, III 1950- *WhoEmL 91*

Laughlin, Henry Prather 1916- *BiDrAPA 89, WhoE 91*
Laughlin, James 1914- *BioIn 16, WhoAm 90*
Laughlin, James Ernest 1953- *WhoSSW 91*
Laughlin, James Rodney 1946- *St&PR 91, WhoAm 90*
Laughlin, Jean Willoughby 1935- *WhoAmW 91*
Laughlin, John Daniel 1956- *WhoSSW 91*
Laughlin, John Seth 1918- *WhoAm 90*
Laughlin, Louis Gene 1937- *WhoSSW 91*
Laughlin, Lyle Hoyt 1924- *St&PR 91*
Laughlin, Mortimer 1918- *WhoAmA 91*
Laughlin, Naomi Myers 1913- *WhoAmW 91*
Laughlin, P. S. *ConAu 130*
Laughlin, Pamela J. *ODwPR 91*
Laughlin, Philip Daniel 1907- *St&PR 91*
Laughlin, Philip Melville 1947- *WhoWor 91*
Laughlin, R. Newton 1905-1989 *BioIn 16*
Laughlin, Robert Arthur 1939- *WhoE 91*
Laughlin, Robert Scott 1945- *St&PR 91*
Laughlin, Ruth *AuBYP 90*
Laughlin, Terry Xavier 1936- *WhoWor 91*
Laughlin, Thomas *WhoAmA 91N*
Laughlin, Thomas Edward 1947- *WhoEmL 91*
Laughlin, Tom *BioIn 16*
Laughlin, William Bedford 1955- *WhoEmL 91*
Laughlin, William Eugene 1936- *WhoSSW 91, WhoWor 91*
Laughlin, William G. 1944- *St&PR 91*
Laughon, F.E. 1937- *St&PR 91*
Laughren, Terry 1940- *WhoE 91*
Laughter, Ron D. 1948- *WhoEmL 91*
Laughton, Charles 1899-1962 *BioIn 16, WorAlBi*
Laughton, Gail *NewAgMG*
Laughton, John Charles 1946- *IntWWM 90*
Lauher, O. Don 1942- *St&PR 91*
Lauinger, Frank Thomas 1940- *St&PR 91*
Lauinger, George Peter 1920- *St&PR 91*
Lauinger, P. C. 1900-1988 *BioIn 16*
Lauinger, Philip C., Jr. 1935- *St&PR 91*
Laukkanen, Julie L. *ODwPR 91*
Laulhere, Bernard M. 1914- *St&PR 91*
Laulicht, Murray Jack 1940- *WhoE 91*
Lauman, Robert Milton 1925- *St&PR 91*
Lauman, Vona Weger 1929- *St&PR 91*
Laumann, Dennis James 1941- *St&PR 91*
Laumann, Edward Otto 1938- *WhoAm 90*
Laumas, Kesho R *BiDrAPA 89*
Laumer, Keith 1925- *RGTwCSF*
Laun, Arthur Henry, Jr. 1930- *WhoAm 90*
Laun, Harold George 1905- *WhoAm 90*
Laun, Louis Frederick 1920- *WhoAm 90*
Laun, Max Walter 1961- *WhoE 91*
Launch, Robert Michael, Jr. 1955- *WhoEmL 91*
Launder, Arthur William 1939- *St&PR 91*
Launder, William H. 1954- *St&PR 91*
Laundon, Averill 1938- *St&PR 91*
Launey, Richard Barry 1954- *WhoEmL 91*
Launhardt, Carl Friedrich Wilhelm 1832-1918 *BioIn 16*
Launois, John Rene *WhoAmA 91N*
Launstein, Howard Cleveland 1922- *WhoAm 90*
Lauper, Cyndi *BioIn 16*
Lauper, Cyndi 1953- *EncPR&S 89, WhoAm 90, WhoAmW 91, WorAlBi*
Lauppi, Urs Victor 1943- *WhoWor 91*
Laupus, William Edward 1921- *WhoAm 90*
Laura, Charles Philip 1919- *St&PR 91*
Laurance, Dale R. 1945- *WhoAm 90*
Laurance, John 1750-1810 *BioIn 16*
Laurance, Matthew *ConTFT 8*
Laurans, Patricia Webster 1939- *WhoE 91*
Laure, Esther L. 1912- *St&PR 91*
Laure, Ettagale 1940- *BioIn 16*
Laure, George R. 1912- *St&PR 91*
Laure, Jason 1940- *BioIn 16*
Laure, Maurice Fernand 1917- *St&PR 91*
Laureano-Vega, Manuel 1956- *WhoHisp 91*
Laurel, Deborah Spring 1948- *WhoEmL 91*
Laurel, Doy *BioIn 16*
Laurel, Salvador *BioIn 16*
Laurel, Salvador Hidalgo 1928- *WhoWor 91*
Laurel, Stan 1890-1965 *BioIn 16, WorAlBi*
Laurelle, Raymond Louis 1948- *WhoWor 91*
Lauren, Linda 1952- *WhoWrEP 89*
Lauren, Ralph *BioIn 16*
Lauren, Ralph 1939- *ConAmBL, ConDes 90, News 90 [port], WhoAm 90, WorAlBi*
Laurence Vitrearius *PenDiDA 89*
Laurence, Alfred Edward 1910- *WhoWor 91*
Laurence, Dan H. 1920- *ConAu 32NR, WhoAm 90*
Laurence, Elizabeth *IntWWM 90*
Laurence, Gerald 1948- *ConAu 131*
Laurence, Jeffrey Conrad 1952- *WhoEmL 91*
Laurence, John *WhoAm 90*
Laurence, Margaret 1926-1987 *BioIn 16, ConAu 33NR, ConLC 62 [port], FemiCLE, MajTwCW, ShSCr 7 [port]*
Laurence, Marilyn Ligon 1933- *St&PR 91*
Laurence, Michael M. 1940- *St&PR 91*
Laurence, Robert Lionel 1936- *WhoAm 90, WhoE 91*
Laurence, Ronald B. 1938- *St&PR 91*
Laurence, Timothy *BioIn 16*
Laurence, William Leonard 1888-1977 *BioIn 16*
Laurencin, Marie 1885-1956 *BiDWomA, BioIn 16, EncCoWW*
Laurens, Guillemette 1950- *IntWWM 90*
Laurens, Henry 1724-1792 *BiDrUSE 89, BioIn 16, EncCRAm*
Laurens, Jean-Paul Gian 1946- *WhoWor 91*
Laurens, Nicholas Joseph 1924- *St&PR 91*
Laurenson, Charles Philip 1927- *St&PR 91*
Laurenson, Robert Mark 1938- *WhoAm 90*
Laurent, Clement C. Jr. *BiDrAPA 89*
Laurent, Hector Francis 1947- *WhoSSW 91*
Laurent, John Louis 1921- *WhoAmA 91, WhoE 91*
Laurent, Lawrence Bell 1925- *WhoAm 90, WhoE 91*
Laurent, Pierre-Henri 1933- *WhoAm 90*
Laurent, Richard Crawford 1947- *WhoEmL 91*
Laurent, Robert 1890-1970 *WhoAmA 91N*
Laurent, Robert Louis, Jr. 1955- *St&PR 91*
Laurent, Susan Elizabeth 1962- *WhoAmW 91*
Laurent-Catrice, Nicole 1937- *EncCoWW*
Laurenti, Joseph L 1931- *ConAu 31NR*
Laurents, Arthur 1918- *WhoAm 90*
Laurenzano, Robert Salvatore 1946- *WhoEmL 91*
Laurenzi, Margarethe P. 1961- *ODwPR 91*
Laurenzo, Frederick C. *WhoHisp 91*
Laurenzo, Ninfa Maria *BioIn 16*
Laurenzo, Roland *WhoHisp 91*
Laurenzo, Vince D. 1939- *St&PR 91*
Laurenzo, Vincent Dennis 1939- *WhoAm 90*
Lauret, Curtis Bernard, Jr. 1945- *WhoE 91*
Lauret, Ronald Wayne 1941- *St&PR 91*
Lauri-Volpi, Giacomo 1892-1979 *PenDiMP*
Lauricella, Janet May 1944- *WhoAmW 91*
Lauricella, Mary Ann *ODwPR 91*
Lauricella, Remo 1918- *IntWWM 90*
Lauricella, Richard Charles 1936- *WhoE 91*
Laurich, Ivan William 1940- *BiDrAPA 89*
Lauridsen, Hanne *WhoAmA 91*
Lauridsen, Jan 1948- *WhoWor 91*
Lauridsen, Laurids Sandager 1951- *WhoWor 91*
Laurie, Alison Margaret 1935- *IntWWM 90*
Laurie, Annie *ConAu 131*
Laurie, Annie 1863-1936 *BioIn 16*
Laurie, Clayton David 1954- *WhoE 91*
Laurie, Cynthia 1924- *IntWWM 90*
Laurie, James Andrew 1947- *WhoAm 90*
Laurie, John Veldon 1952- *St&PR 91, WhoAm 90*
Laurie, Margaret Sanders 1926- *WhoWrEP 89*
Laurie, Marilyn *ODwPR 91, St&PR 91, WhoAm 90, WhoAmW 91*
Laurie, Piper 1932- *WhoAmW 91, WorAlBi*
Laurie, Rona *ConAu 33NR*
Laurie, Rona 1916- *BioIn 16*
Lauriello, John *BiDrAPA 89*
Laurier, Francisco Herminio 1942- *WhoSSW 91*
Laurier, Johan George 1942- *WhoWor 91*
Laurier, Jose Julien 1943- *WhoWor 91*
Laurimore, Ann 1943- *WhoAmW 91, WhoWor 91*
Laurin, David J. 1925- *St&PR 91*
Laurin, Pierre 1939- *WhoAm 90*
Laurino, John Alan 1949- *WhoE 91*
Laurisden, Morten Johannes 1943- *IntWWM 90*
Lauritsen, Jill Ann 1959- *WhoAmW 91*
Lauritsen, John P. *WhoWrEP 89*
Lauritsen, Kenneth Bruce 1942- *St&PR 91*
Lauritz, Paul 1889-1975 *WhoAmA 91N*
Lauritzen, Bruce Ronnow 1943- *St&PR 91, WhoAm 90*
Lauritzen, John R. 1917- *St&PR 91*
Lauritzen, John Ronnow 1917- *WhoAm 90, WhoWor 91*
Lauritzen, Ole 1933- *WhoWor 91*
Lauritzen, Peter Owen 1935- *WhoAm 90*
Lauro, Sylvia D S *BiDrAPA 89*
Laursen, Axel Norskov 1951- *WhoWor 91*
Laursen, Finn 1944- *WhoWor 91*
Laursen, Harry Leon 1924- *WhoSSW 91*
Laursen, Paul Herbert 1929- *WhoAm 90*
Laursen, Soren N.S. 1935- *St&PR 91*
Laurus, Archbishop 1928- *WhoAm 90*
Laury, Gabriel Vernet 1928- *BiDrAPA 89*
Laury, Gabriel Vernet 1932- *WhoE 91*
Laury, Thomas David 1944- *St&PR 91*
Laus, Eduardo C *BiDrAPA 89*
Lausche, Frank J 1895-1990 *CurBio 90N, NewYTBS 90 [port]*
Lausche, Frank John 1895-1990 *BioIn 16*
Lauscher, Hermann *MajTwCW*
Lausier, Ernest Alexander 1945- *St&PR 91*
Lausten, Esther Carleton- 1912- *BioIn 16*
Laut, Agnes 1871-1936 *FemiCLE*
Laut, Agnes Christina 1871-1936 *DcLB 92 [port]*
Lautamatti, Liisa Inkeri 1937- *WhoWor 91*
Lautenbach, Terry R. *BioIn 16*
Lautenbach, Terry Robert 1938- *WhoAm 90*
Lautenberg, Alexis Peter 1945- *WhoWor 91*
Lautenberg, Frank *BioIn 16*
Lautenberg, Frank R. 1924- *WhoAm 90, WhoE 91, WhoWor 91*
Lautenschlager, Eugene Louis 1926- *St&PR 91*
Lautenschlager, Gary Joseph 1949- *WhoSSW 91*
Lauter, Jonathan B 1956- *BiDrAPA 89*
Lauter, Josef Martin 1936- *WhoWor 91*
Lauter, Steven Abba 1946- *WhoEmL 91*
Lauterbach, Edward Charles 1955- *BiDrAPA 89*
Lauterbach, Henry S. 1915- *St&PR 91*
Lauterbach, Nancy Lee 1945- *WhoEmL 91*
Lauterbach, Sandra Mayzel *BiDrAPA 89*
Lauterbach, Shirley Susan Pfeiffer 1955- *WhoAmW 91, WhoSSW 91*
Lauterback, Thomas K. 1944- *ODwPR 91*
Lauterborn, Robert F. 1936- *WhoAm 90*
Lauterbur, Paul Christian 1929- *WhoAm 90*
Lauterer, Arch 1904- *WhoAmA 91N*
Lauterstein, Ingeborg 1935- *ConAu 130*
Lautezenheiser, Karen Read 1946- *WhoEmL 91*
Lauth, Harold V. 1933- *ODwPR 91*
Lauth, Richard Joseph 1935- *St&PR 91*
Lautier, Yves Laurent 1941- *BiDrAPA 89*
Lautin, Andrew Leonard 1949- *BiDrAPA 89, WhoE 91*
Lautman, Joan Harris 1932- *WhoE 91*
Lautrec, Henri de Toulouse- 1864-1901 *BioIn 16*
Lautz, Henry Williams 1941- *St&PR 91*
Lautz, Lindsay Allan 1947- *WhoAm 90*
Lautzenheiser, Barbara J. 1938- *St&PR 91*
Lautzenheiser, Barbara Jean 1938- *WhoAm 90, WhoAmW 91*
Lautzenheiser, Dennis K. 1951- *St&PR 91*
Lautzenheiser, Karen R. *ODwPR 91*
Lautzenheiser, Karen Read 1946- *St&PR 91*
Lauven, Peter Michael 1948- *WhoWor 91*
Lauver, David H. 1949- *ODwPR 91*
Lauver, E. Eugene 1947- *St&PR 91*
Lauver, Robert Howard 1946- *WhoE 91*
Lauver, S Huffstutter *BiDrAPA 89*
Lauvergne, Madame de *EncCoWW*
Lauweryns, Joseph Marie 1933- *WhoWor 91*
Lauwerys, Joseph Albert 1902-1981 *DcNaB 1981*
Laux, Bernard M. 1948- *IntWWM 90*
Laux, Dorothy 1920- *BioIn 16*
Laux, France *Ballpl 90*
Laux, Richard F. 1927- *St&PR 91*
Laux, Russell Frederick 1918- *WhoE 91, WhoWor 91*
Lauzerique, George 1947- *Ballpl 90*
Lauzon, Shelley Marie 1952- *WhoE 91*
Lauzon, Theophile A. 1929- *St&PR 91*
Lauzzana, Gail Anne 1945- *St&PR 91*
Lava, Leslie Michele 1957- *WhoAmW 91*
LaVacca, John Thomas 1958- *WhoEmL 91*
Lavagetto, Cookie 1912- *Ballpl 90*
Lavagetto, Harry *NewYTBS 90 [port]*
LaVail, Jennifer Hart 1943- *WhoAm 90, WhoAmW 91*
Laval, Pierre 1883-1945 *BiDFrPL, BioIn 16, WorAlBi*
Lavalee, Leo P. 1933- *St&PR 91*
LaValle, Edith 1919- *WhoAmW 91*
LaValle, Irving Howard 1939- *WhoAm 90, WhoSSW 91*
Lavalle, Manuel Pardo y 1834-1878 *BioIn 16*
Lavalle, Peter Lawrence *BiDrAPA 89*
LaValle, William Joseph, Jr. 1947- *WhoSSW 91*
Lavallee, Calixa 1842-1891 *DcCanB 12*
Lavallee, Charles Phillip 1928- *WhoWor 91*
Lavallee, Deirdre Justine 1962- *WhoAmW 91*
Lavallee, Jean Charles 1939- *BiDrAPA 89*
Lavallee, John N 1925- *BiDrAPA 89*
Lavallee, Joseph Andre 1956- *St&PR 91*
Lavallee, Leo Pierre 1959- *WhoEmL 91*
Lavallee, Lorraine Doris 1931- *WhoAmW 91, WhoE 91*
Lavallee, Roderick Leo 1936- *St&PR 91, WhoWor 91*
Lavallee, Yvon-Jacques J 1945- *BiDrAPA 89*
Lavalleja, Juan Antonio 1784-1853 *BioIn 16*
LaValliere, Mike *BioIn 16*
LaValliere, Mike 1960- *Ballpl 90*
Lavalou, Michel Jean 1930- *WhoWor 91*
Lavan, Doc 1890-1952 *Ballpl 90*
Lavan, Peter I. B. 1898-1988 *BioIn 16*
Lavan, Timothy Francis 1966- *WhoEmL 91*
Lavanoux, Maurice *WhoAmA 91N*
Lavant, Christine 1915- *EncCoWW*
Lavarnway, Gerard Thomas 1956- *WhoE 91*
Lavash, William Thomas 1958- *WhoEmL 91*
Lavatelli, Carla 1928- *WhoAmA 91, WhoE 91*
Lavater, Johann Kaspar 1741-1801 *DcLB 97 [port]*
Lavdiotis, Chris P. 1952- *WhoEmL 91*
Lave, Charles Arthur 1938- *WhoAm 90*
Lave, Judith Rice *WhoE 91*
Lave, Lester B. 1939- *ConAu 33NR*
Lave, Lester Bernard 1939- *WhoAm 90, WhoE 91*
Laveccia, Benjamin L. 1935- *St&PR 91*
LaVeck, Gerald DeLoss 1927- *WhoAm 90*
La Vee, Katie *WhoWrEP 89*
La Veglia, Geri 1943- *WhoWrEP 89*
Lavell, Alan Joseph 1946- *WhoEmL 91*
Lavell, Thomas Eugene 1928- *WhoE 91*
LaVelle, Arthur 1921- *WhoAm 90*
LaVelle, Betty Sullivan Dougherty 1941- *WhoAmW 91*
Lavelle, Brian Francis David 1941- *WhoSSW 91, WhoWor 91*
LaVelle, Faith Wilson 1921- *WhoAmW 91*
Lavelle, Francis William 1949- *St&PR 91*
Lavelle, Gary 1949- *Ballpl 90*
Lavelle, John D. 1930- *St&PR 91*
Lavelle, John Philip 1956- *WhoEmL 91*
Lavelle, June *BioIn 16*
Lavelle, Michael Joseph 1934- *WhoAm 90*
Lavelle, Paul M. 1949- *St&PR 91*
Lavelle, Paul Michael 1956- *WhoEmL 91*
Lavelle, Robert E. 1922- *St&PR 91*
LaVelle, Robin Ann 1959- *WhoEmL 91*
Lavelle, Thomas 1946- *St&PR 91*
Laven, Monette 1928- *St&PR 91*
Lavenas, Suzanne 1942- *WhoAmW 91*
Lavendel, Giuliana Avanzini *WhoAm 90*
Lavender, A. Knight 1911- *BiDrAPA 89*
Lavender, Adele 1924- *St&PR 91*
Lavender, David 1910- *AuBYP 90, SmATA 64*
Lavender, Douglas Wayne 1947- *St&PR 91*
Lavender, Fred Charles 1934- *St&PR 91*
Lavender, Jimmy 1884-1960 *Ballpl 90*
Lavender, Robert Eugene 1926- *WhoAm 90*
Lavengood, Lawrence Gene 1924- *WhoAm 90*
Lavenson, James H. 1919- *WhoAm 90*
Lavenson, Susan Barker 1936- *WhoAmW 91*
Laventhol, David A. 1933- *St&PR 91*
Laventhol, David Abram 1933- *WhoAm 90*
Laventhol, Hank 1927- *WhoAmA 91*
Laventhol, Henry Lee 1927- *WhoAm 90*
Laver, Augustus 1834-1898 *DcCanB 12*
Laver, Rod *BioIn 16*
Laver, Rod 1938- *WorAlBi*
Laver, Rodney George 1938- *WhoAm 90*
Laver, William Graeme 1929- *WhoWor 91*
Laverge, Hendrik Johannes 1941- *St&PR 91*
Laverge, Jan 1909- *WhoAm 90*
Lavergne, Bernard M 1928- *BiDrAPA 89*
Laverne, Andy *BioIn 16*
Laverne, Michel Marie-Jacques 1928- *WhoAm 90*
Lavernia, Milton 1935- *WhoHisp 91*
Laverov, Nikolai Pavlovitch 1930- *WhoWor 91*
Laverriere, Lorraine Moreau 1938- *WhoWrEP 89*
Lavers, Annette 1932- *ConAu 130*
Lavers, Norman 1935- *WhoWrEP 89*
Lavers, Richard Marshall 1947- *WhoEmL 91*
Laverty, Donald *MajTwCW*
Laverty, Maura 1907-1966 *FemiCLE*
Laverty, Roger Montgomery, III 1947- *WhoAm 90*
Laverty, William E. 1951- *St&PR 91*
Lavery, Bryony *FemiCLE*
Lavery, Michael Joseph 1946- *WhoEmL 91*

Lavery, Richard Joseph 1953- *St&PR 91*
Lavery, Sean 1956- *WhoAm 90*
Lavery, Thomas Francis 1945- *St&PR 91*
Laves, Fritz H 1906-1978 *DcScB S2*
Laves, Hans Juergen 1924- *WhoE 91*
Lavett, Diane K. 1944- *WhoAmW 91*
La Vey, Anton Szandor 1930- *EncO&P 3*
Lavey, Gilbert L. 1934- *St&PR 91*
Lavey, Kenneth Henry 1923- *WhoAm 90*
Lavey, Stewart Evan 1945- *WhoAm 90*
Lavey, Thomas James 1949- *WhoEmL 91*
Lavezzoli, Charles E. 1942- *WhoE 91*
Lavi, Aviva *ODwPR 91*
La Via, Mariano Francis 1926- *WhoSSW 91*
Lavian, Manouchehr 1940- *BiDrAPA 89*
Lavid, Jean Stern 1943- *WhoAmW 91, WhoWor 91*
Lavidge, Robert James 1921- *WhoAm 90*
Lavidge, William Robert 1955- *WhoEmL 91*
Lavier, Annabelle Theresa 1947- *WhoAmW 91, WhoEmL 91*
Laviera, Tato 1950- *BioIn 16*
Laviera, Tato 1951- *WhoHisp 91*
Lavieri, Annamarie 1945- *WhoEmL 91*
La Vietes, Ruth L 1923- *BiDrAPA 89*
LaVietes, Ruth Lucille 1923- *WhoE 91*
Lavigerie, Charles Martial Allemand- 1825-1892 *BiDFrPL*
LaVigna, Michael Paul 1940- *St&PR 91, WhoAm 90*
Lavigne, Gary David 1953- *St&PR 91*
La Vigne, Gregory Lloyd 1948- *BiDrAPA 89*
LaVigne, Gregory Paul 1943- *St&PR 91*
La Vigne, Harland K. 1940- *St&PR 91*
Lavigne, Laurent J. 1938- *St&PR 91*
Lavigne, Louis J., Jr. 1948- *St&PR 91*
LaVigne, Mark Kino 1961- *BiDrAPA 89*
Lavigueur, Guy A. 1937- *WhoAm 90*
Lavilla, Felix *PenDiMP*
LaVilla, Ronaldo Alberto 1935- *St&PR 91*
La Villette, Elodie 1843- *BiDWomA*
Lavin, Andrew R. *ODwPR 91*
Lavin, Bernice E. 1925- *WhoAm 90, WhoAmW 91*
Lavin, Bernice Elizabeth 1925- *St&PR 91*
Lavin, Charles Blaise, Jr. 1940- *WhoAm 90*
Lavin, David J. 1923- *WhoAm 90*
Lavin, Gerard M. 1942- *St&PR 91*
Lavin, Gordon Kyle 1950- *BiDrAPA 89*
Lavin, Irving 1927- *WhoAmA 91*
Lavin, Jenna Rae 1968- *WhoEmL 91*
Lavin, John Halley 1932- *WhoAm 90, WhoWrEP 89*
Lavin, Lawrence W. *BioIn 16*
Lavin, Leeann P. 1955- *ODwPR 91*
Lavin, Leeann Popik 1955- *WhoE 91, WhoEmL 91*
Lavin, Leonard H. 1919- *St&PR 91, WhoAm 90*
Lavin, Linda 1937- *WhoAm 90, WhoAmW 91, WorAlBi*
Lavin, Louise Miller 1947- *WhoEmL 91*
Lavin, Marilyn Aronberg 1925- *WhoAmA 91*
Lavin, Marjorie Helen 1954- *BiDrAPA 89*
Lavin, Mary 1912- *AuBYP 90, BioIn 16, ConAu 33NR, FemiCLE, MajTwCW*
Lavin, Nancy Jean 1952- *WhoAmW 91*
Lavin, Priscilla *ODwPR 91*
Lavin, Thomas J.A. 1949- *St&PR 91*
Lavin, William Kane 1944- *St&PR 91, WhoAm 90, WhoE 91*
Lavine, David 1928- *AuBYP 90*
Lavine, David Arthur 1925- *St&PR 91*
La Vine, Glen Edward 1932- *St&PR 91*
Lavine, Henry Wolfe 1936- *WhoAm 90*
Lavine, John M. 1941- *WhoAm 90*
La Vine, Kenneth N., Jr. 1945- *St&PR 91*
Lavine, Philip H 1951- *BiDrAPA 89*
Lavine, Sigmund Arnold 1908- *AuBYP 90*
Lavine, Steven David 1947- *WhoAm 90*
Lavine, Steven Richard *BiDrAPA 89*
Lavine, Thelma Zeno *WhoAm 90*
Lavington, Joi Bauer 1952- *WhoAmW 91, WhoEmL 91*
Lavington, Michael Richard 1943- *WhoAm 90, WhoSSW 91*
Lavinsky, Larry Monroe 1929- *WhoAm 90*
Lavinson, Paula Jane 1942- *BiDrAPA 89*
Laviola, Franklin N 1944- *BiDrAPA 89*
Laviolette, Bruce Edward 1949- *WhoSSW 91*
Laviolette, Emily A. *BioIn 16*
Laviolette, Godefroy 1826-1895 *DcCanB 12*
Lavista, Mario 1943- *IntWWM 90*
La Vita, Roberto 1950- *WhoE 91*
Lavitt, Mel S. 1937- *WhoAm 90*
Lavoie, Charles J. 1945- *St&PR 91*
Lavoie, Mario 1945- *WhoEmL 91*
Lavoie, Roger 1928- *WhoAm 90, WhoE 91*
Lavoie, Serge 1963- *WhoAm 90*
Lavoie, Serge P. 1951- *WhoAm 90*
Lavoie, Suzanne B. 1953- *St&PR 91*
Lavoisier, Antoine Laurent 1743-1794 *BioIn 16, WorAlBi*
Lavoisier, Marie Anne Pierrette Paulze 1758-1836 *BioIn 16*
Lavoll, Gunnbjorg B *BiDrAPA 89*
Lavond, Paul Dennis *MajTwCW*
Lavonen, Maija 1931- *ConDes 90*
Lavorato, Louis A. *WhoAm 90*
Lavoy, Peter R. 1941- *St&PR 91*
Lavrence, Thomas I 1932- *BiDrAPA 89*
Lavrich, Carol Celeste 1955- *WhoEmL 91*
Lavrich, Philip Lewis 1959- *WhoE 91*
Lavritch, Sophie Bentkowski 1905- *EncO&P 3*
Lavrov, Sergei Borisovich 1928- *BioIn 16*
Lavy, Lorenzo 1729-1789 *PenDiDA 89*
Law, Andrew Bonar 1858-1923 *WorAlBi*
Law, Arthur G 1922- *BiDrAPA 89*
Law, Benjamin 1947- *St&PR 91*
Law, Bernard Francis 1931- *WhoAm 90, WhoE 91, WhoWor 91*
Law, Betty Jo 1930- *WhoSSW 91*
Law, Brett *BioIn 16*
Law, C Anthony 1916- *WhoAmA 91*
Law, Carol Judith 1940- *WhoAmW 91*
Law, Carol Russell *IntWWM 90*
Law, Cursey Shelby 1933- *WhoAm 90*
Law, Dan Udall 1948- *WhoEmL 91*
Law, David Holbrook 1946- *WhoE 91*
Law, Diane A. 1949- *St&PR 91*
Law, E. Christopher *BioIn 16*
Law, Ellen Marie 1960- *WhoSSW 91*
Law, Francis Jerome 1930- *WhoWor 91*
Law, Frederick Masom 1934- *WhoAm 90*
Law, Gale 1945- *St&PR 91*
Law, Gordon *ODwPR 91*
Law, Holly Jayne 1955- *WhoE 91*
Law, Hugh Toner 1922- *WhoWrEP 89*
Law, Ina Floriene 1924- *WhoAmW 91*
Law, James G. *BioIn 16*
Law, Jane Hinton 1928- *WhoAmW 91*
Law, Janice *WhoWrEP 89*
Law, John 1671-1729 *BioIn 16*
Law, John 1861-1923 *BioIn 16*
Law, John Manning 1927- *WhoAm 90*
Law, Kevin M. 1952- *St&PR 91*
Law, L. William 1945- *St&PR 91*
Law, Lloyd William 1910- *WhoAm 90*
Law, Margaret *WhoAmA 91N*
Law, Margaret Irene 1954- *WhoAmW 91*
Law, Margaret Yuen-Ming 1945- *WhoEmL 91*
Law, Marvin A. 1938- *St&PR 91*
Law, Maureen Margaret 1940- *WhoAm 90*
Law, Patricia Anne 1958- *WhoSSW 91*
Law, Phillip Garth 1912- *WhoWor 91*
Law, R.D. 1933- *St&PR 91*
Law, Richard H. 1953- *WhoSSW 91*
Law, Rudy 1956- *Ballpl 90*
Law, Teresa Marie 1954- *WhoAmW 91*
Law, Thomas *PenDiDA 89*
Law, Thomas Hart 1918- *WhoAm 90*
Law, Vance 1956- *Ballpl 90*
Law, Vern 1930- *Ballpl 90 [port]*
Law, Wallace Vincent 1906- *WhoSSW 91*
Law, William 1686-1761 *EncO&P 3*
Law, William, III *BiDrAPA 89*
Law-Smith, David John 1940- *St&PR 91*
Law-Yone, Byron 1941- *BiDrAPA 89*
Lawal, Oluwole Aina 1947- *WhoWor 91*
Lawall, David Barnard 1935- *WhoAmA 91*
Lawanson, Ruth *BioIn 16*
La Ware, John Kevin 1956- *St&PR 91*
LaWare, John P. *BioIn 16*
LaWare, John Patrick 1928- *WhoAm 90*
LaWarre, William Michael 1941- *St&PR 91*
Lawatsch, Frank E., Jr. 1944- *St&PR 91*
Lawatsch, Frank Emil, Jr. 1944- *WhoAm 90*
Lawbaugh, Penelope 1945- *WhoWrEP 89*
Lawch, Michael Jay 1950- *WhoEmL 91*
Lawder, Douglas Ward, Jr. 1934- *WhoWrEP 89*
Lawe, John 1919-1989 *BioIn 16*
Lawe, John E. 1922-1989 *AnObit 1989*
Lawellin, Duane Donald 1931- *St&PR 91*
Lawergren, Bo 1937- *IntWWM 90*
Lawford, Paula 1960- *BioIn 16*
Lawford, Peter 1923-1984 *BioIn 16, WorAlBi*
Lawhead, Stephen R. 1950- *BioIn 16*
Lawhead, Steve 1950- *BioIn 16*
Lawhon, Charles Watson 1922- *St&PR 91*
Lawhon, John E., III 1934- *WhoAm 90*
Lawhon, William Griffith 1942- *WhoAm 90*
Lawhorn, Donald Samuel 1925- *WhoAm 90*
Lawhorn, Jess S. 1933- *St&PR 91*
Lawhorn, Jess Sherman 1933- *WhoSSW 91*
Lawhorn, Thomas William 1936- *St&PR 91*
Lawhun, Steven F. 1948- *St&PR 91*
Lawhun, Steven Francis 1948- *WhoAm 90*
Lawi, David S. 1935- *St&PR 91*
Lawi, David Steven 1935- *WhoAm 90*
Lawin, Bruce A. 1934- *St&PR 91*
Lawing, Alvin L., Jr. 1933- *St&PR 91*
Lawing, Jack Lee 1938- *St&PR 91*
Lawler, Alice Bonzi 1914- *WhoAmW 91, WhoWor 91*
Lawler, Bruce Gibbs 1927- *St&PR 91, WhoAm 90*
Lawler, Charles W. 1949- *St&PR 91*
Lawler, Jack 1930- *WhoSSW 91*
Lawler, James P. 1934- *St&PR 91*
Lawler, James Ronald 1929- *WhoAm 90*
Lawler, Joy Michele 1953- *WhoEmL 91*
Lawler, Karen Strand 1939- *WhoAmW 91*
Lawler, Lawrence Thomas, Jr. 1949- *St&PR 91*
Lawler, Lilia Elianne 1959- *WhoEmL 91*
Lawler, Michael Gerard 1933- *WhoAm 90*
Lawler, Paul Edmund, Jr. 1928- *BiDrAPA 89*
Lawler, Philip W *BiDrAPA 89*
Lawler, Robert Eugene 1939- *WhoWor 91*
Lawler, Theresa Anne 1950- *WhoEmL 91*
Lawler, Thomas Albert 1946- *WhoEmL 91*
Lawler, Thomas Aquin 1953- *St&PR 91*
Lawless, Anthony *TwCCr&M 91*
Lawless, Billie 1950- *WhoEmL 91*
Lawless, Emily 1845-1913 *FemiCLE*
Lawless, Gary Cameron 1951- *WhoWrEP 89*
Lawless, Gregory B. 1940- *St&PR 91*
Lawless, Isaac Jesse 1936- *BiDrAPA 89*
Lawless, John C. 1958- *St&PR 91*
Lawless, John Craig 1958- *WhoE 91*
Lawless, John Langie, Jr. 1955- *WhoEmL 91*
Lawless, Joseph Henry, Sr. 1941- *WhoSSW 91*
Lawless, K. Gordon 1924- *St&PR 91*
Lawless, Mark Joseph 1946- *St&PR 91*
Lawless, Regina *BiDrAPA 89*
Lawless, Robert 1937- *WhoSSW 91*
Lawless, Robert William 1937- *St&PR 91, WhoAm 90, WhoSSW 91*
Lawless, Ronald 1960- *WhoEmL 91*
Lawless, Ronald Edward 1924- *WhoAm 90*
Lawless, Tom 1956- *Ballpl 90*
Lawless, William D. 1933- *St&PR 91*
Lawless, William Josselyn, Jr. 1919- *St&PR 91, WhoAm 90*
Lawley, Alan 1933- *WhoAm 90*
Lawley, Esther Gminder Smith 1960- *WhoSSW 91*
Lawley, Karen R. 1947- *WhoAmW 91*
Lawley, Kenneth Larry 1932- *WhoSSW 91*
Lawley, Robert W. 1954- *St&PR 91*
Lawley, Susan Marc 1951- *WhoAmW 91, WhoE 91, WhoEmL 91, WhoWor 91*
Lawlis, Grover Milton 1949- *BiDrAPA 89*
Lawlis, Marjorie G 1926- *BiDrAPA 89*
Lawlis, Patricia Kite 1945- *WhoAmW 91, WhoEmL 91, WhoWor 91*
Lawlor, Brian J. 1951- *St&PR 91*
Lawlor, Charles B. 1852-1925 *OxCPMus*
Lawlor, Eugene *BiDrAPA 89*
Lawlor, Helen Anne 1944- *St&PR 91, WhoAmW 91*
Lawlor, John *AuBYP 90*
Lawlor, John Arthur 1945- *WhoEmL 91*
Lawlor, Pat *BioIn 16*
Lawlor, Rob 1936- *WhoAm 90*
Lawlor, Robert James 1936- *St&PR 91*
Lawlor, Teresa *NewAgMG*
Lawlor, Thomas Edward *BiDrAPA 89*
Lawmann, Dennis James 1941- *St&PR 91*
Lawn, Beryl B *BiDrAPA 89*
Lawn, Gregory T. 1950- *WhoE 91*
Lawn, Harold J *BiDrAPA 89*
Lawn, John C. 1935- *WhoAm 90*
Lawn, Richard John 1949- *WhoSSW 91*
Lawner, Lynne 1935- *WhoWrEP 89*
Lawnicki, Mary 1940- *St&PR 91*
Lawrance, Charles Holway 1920- *WhoAm 90*
Lawrason, F. Douglas 1919- *WhoAm 90*
Lawrence of Arabia 1888-1935 *EncPaPR 91*
Lawrence, Abbott 1792-1855 *BioIn 16, WorAlBi*
Lawrence, Albert A. *BioIn 16*
Lawrence, Albert James 1947- *WhoAm 90*
Lawrence, Albert W. 1928- *St&PR 91*
Lawrence, Albert Weaver 1928- *WhoAm 90, WhoE 91, WhoWor 91*
Lawrence, Amos A. 1814-1886 *WorAlBi*
Lawrence, Amy L. 1941- *WhoAmW 91*
Lawrence, Andrea Mead 1932- *WhoAm 90*
Lawrence, Ann 1942-1987 *BioIn 16*
Lawrence, Arlene Hart White 1916- *WhoE 91*
Lawrence, Arnie *BioIn 16*
Lawrence, Arthur Peter 1937- *IntWWM 90, WhoWrEP 89*
Lawrence, Ashley 1934-1990 *BioIn 16, NewYTBS 90*
Lawrence, Barbara 1944- *WhoAmW 91, WhoE 91*
Lawrence, Barbara Ann 1951- *WhoAmW 91*
Lawrence, Barbara C. 1927- *St&PR 91*
Lawrence, Barbara Lu 1943- *WhoSSW 91*
Lawrence, Barry Ross 1955- *WhoEmL 91*
Lawrence, Benjamin *BioIn 16*
Lawrence, Betsy Ellen 1947- *WhoE 91*
Lawrence, Brian Michael 1961- *WhoSSW 91*
Lawrence, Brooks 1925- *Ballpl 90*
Lawrence, Bryan H. 1942- *St&PR 91*
Lawrence, C H 1921- *ConAu 132*
Lawrence, C. Jennifer *ODwPR 91*
Lawrence, Caleb James 1941- *WhoAm 90*
Lawrence, Carol 1932- *BioIn 16*
Lawrence, Charles Edmund 1927- *WhoAm 90*
Lawrence, Christopher Rueckert 1953- *WhoE 91*
Lawrence, Cristenna Louissa 1953- *WhoAmW 91*
Lawrence, D. Baloti 1950- *ConAu 32NR*
Lawrence, D.H. 1885-1930 *BioIn 16, DcLB 98 [port], MajTwCW*
Lawrence, D. H. 1885-1930 *WorAlBi*
Lawrence, D H 1885-1930 *WrPh*
Lawrence, Daniel Joseph 1953- *WhoEmL 91*
Lawrence, David *BiDrAPA 89*
Lawrence, David 1888-1973 *BioIn 16, WorAlBi*
Lawrence, David, Jr. 1942- *WhoAm 90*
Lawrence, David Herbert 1885-1930 *BioIn 16*
Lawrence, David John 1955- *IntWWM 90*
Lawrence, David Michael 1943- *WhoAm 90*
Lawrence, David Paul 1961- *WhoSSW 91*
Lawrence, Dean Grayson 1901- *WhoAmW 91*
Lawrence, Denise Elaine *BiDrAPA 89*
Lawrence, Donald Walter 1936- *St&PR 91*
Lawrence, Donna Marie 1953- *WhoAmW 91*
Lawrence, E. A. *WhoWrEP 89*
Lawrence, Eleanor Baker 1936- *IntWWM 90*
Lawrence, Elizabeth Chapman 1829-1905 *BioIn 16*
Lawrence, Elliot 1925- *OxCPMus*
Lawrence, Ernest O. 1901-1958 *WorAlBi*
Lawrence, Ernest Orlando 1901-1958 *BioIn 16*
Lawrence, Estelene Yvonne 1933- *WhoAmW 91*
Lawrence, Eugenia Jewell 1965- *WhoAmW 91*
Lawrence, Everett Dean 1934- *St&PR 91*
Lawrence, Francis Leo 1937- *WhoAm 90*
Lawrence, Francis McQuaid 1946- *WhoEmL 91*
Lawrence, Frederic C. 1899-1989 *BioIn 16*
Lawrence, Frieda von Richthofen 1879-1956 *BioIn 16*
Lawrence, Garland R. 1933- *St&PR 91*
Lawrence, Gary Dale 1947- *WhoWor 91*
Lawrence, George D. 1950- *St&PR 91*
Lawrence, George Durwood, Jr. 1950- *WhoAm 90*
Lawrence, George H *BiDrAPA 89*
Lawrence, George H.C. 1937- *St&PR 91*
Lawrence, George Howard 1925- *WhoAm 90*
Lawrence, Gerald 1939- *St&PR 91, WhoAm 90*
Lawrence, Gerald Graham 1947- *WhoE 91, WhoEmL 91*
Lawrence, Gertrude 1898-1952 *OxCPMus, WorAlBi*
Lawrence, Glenn Robert 1930- *WhoAm 90*
Lawrence, Gordon Grant 1931- *WhoE 91*
Lawrence, Helen Humphreys 1878- *WhoAmA 91N*
Lawrence, Helen Ruth 1942- *IntWWM 90*
Lawrence, Henry R. 1873- *AmLegL*
Lawrence, Henry Sherwood 1916- *WhoAm 90*
Lawrence, Herbert Gordon 1939- *St&PR 91*
Lawrence, Hilda 1906?- *TwCCr&M 91*
Lawrence, Howard Ray 1936- *WhoAmA 91*
Lawrence, Isabelle *AuBYP 90*
Lawrence, Jack 1912- *OxCPMus*
Lawrence, Jacob *BioIn 16*
Lawrence, Jacob 1917- *WhoAm 90, WhoAmA 91*
Lawrence, James 1781-1813 *WorAlBi*
Lawrence, James A 1910- *WhoAmA 91*
Lawrence, James B *BiDrAPA 89*
Lawrence, James D. 1918- *AuBYP 90*
Lawrence, James Francis 1932- *St&PR 91*
Lawrence, James Gordon 1943- *WhoAm 90*
Lawrence, James Harold, Jr. 1932- *WhoAm 90*
Lawrence, James Kaufman Lebensburger 1940- *WhoAm 90*
Lawrence, James Michael 1941- *St&PR 91*
Lawrence, Janet Marion *BiDrAPA 89*
Lawrence, Janice Annette Merrill 1938- *WhoAmW 91*
Lawrence, Jaye A 1939- *WhoAmA 91*

Lawrence, Jean Hope 1944- *WhoAmW 91, WhoWrEP 89*
Lawrence, Jerome 1915- *WhoAm 90*
Lawrence, Jesse Alvah 1934- *WhoSSW 91*
Lawrence, Joanne Lee 1953- *WhoEmL 91*
Lawrence, Joe A. 1934- *St&PR 91*
Lawrence, John Charles 1943- *WhoWor 91*
Lawrence, John Edward 1941- *WhoSSW 91*
Lawrence, John Frederick 1934- *BioIn 16*
Lawrence, John Kidder 1949- *WhoEmL 91, WhoWor 91*
Lawrence, John Malcolm, Jr. 1934- *St&PR 91*
Lawrence, John Warren 1928- *St&PR 91*
Lawrence, Joseph Wilson 1818-1892 *DcCanB 12*
Lawrence, Joy Elizabeth 1926- *IntWWM 90*
Lawrence, Kevin John 1957- *IntWWM 90*
Lawrence, Larry Charles *BiDrAPA 89*
Lawrence, Larry James 1944- *WhoE 91*
Lawrence, Lee McManaway 1957- *WhoEmL 91*
Lawrence, Leonard E 1937- *BiDrAPA 89*
Lawrence, Les 1940- *WhoAm 90, WhoAmA 91*
Lawrence, Leslie Gail 1961- *WhoE 91*
Lawrence, Lois Vana 1947- *WhoAmW 91*
Lawrence, Louis F *BiDrAPA 89*
Lawrence, Louise 1943- *BioIn 16*
Lawrence, Louise 1952- *WhoAmW 91*
Lawrence, M. Larry 1926- *WhoAm 90*
Lawrence, Marc A. 1946- *St&PR 91*
Lawrence, Margaret 1914- *BioAmW*
Lawrence, Margaret Morgan 1914- *BiDrAPA 89, BioIn 16*
Lawrence, Margery 1896-1969 *FemiCLE*
Lawrence, Margot *ConAu 132*
Lawrence, Marjorie 1907-1979 *PenDiMP*
Lawrence, Mark *BioIn 16*
Lawrence, Mark Allen 1939- *BiDrAPA 89*
Lawrence, Mary Georgene Wells 1928- *WhoAm 90, WhoAmW 91*
Lawrence, Mary Jo B. 1931- *WhoAmW 91*
Lawrence, Mary Wells *BioIn 16*
Lawrence, Mary Wells 1928- *WorAlBi*
Lawrence, Merle 1915- *WhoAm 90*
Lawrence, Merloyd Ludington 1932- *WhoAm 90*
Lawrence, Michael *WhoAmA 91*
Lawrence, Mildred Elwood 1907- *AuBYP 90*
Lawrence, Nancy Ann 1959- *WhoAmW 91*
Lawrence, Patricia Ann 1926- *WhoAmW 91*
Lawrence, Paul Roger 1922- *WhoAm 90*
Lawrence, Paula Denise 1959- *WhoAmW 91*
Lawrence, Pelham Bissell 1945- *WhoAm 90*
Lawrence, Peter 1921-1987 *BioIn 16*
Lawrence, Peter Gordon 1944- *WhoE 91*
Lawrence, Peter J. 1956- *St&PR 91*
Lawrence, Phenis Joseph 1926- *WhoSSW 91*
Lawrence, Philip James 1919- *St&PR 91*
Lawrence, R. D. 1921- *BioIn 16*
Lawrence, Ralph Waldo 1941- *WhoWor 91*
Lawrence, Randolph Thomas 1949- *WhoE 91, WhoEmL 91*
Lawrence, Ray Vance 1910- *WhoSSW 91*
Lawrence, Richard 1946- *IntWWM 90*
Lawrence, Richard E. 1939- *St&PR 91*
Lawrence, Richard M. 1926- *St&PR 91*
Lawrence, Richard Sellers 1934- *WhoE 91*
Lawrence, Richard W., Jr. 1909- *St&PR 91*
Lawrence, Richard Wesley, Jr. 1909- *WhoAm 90*
Lawrence, Rick Lee 1954- *WhoEmL 91*
Lawrence, Robert Ashton 1926- *St&PR 91*
Lawrence, Robert Cutting, III 1938- *WhoAm 90*
Lawrence, Robert Swan 1938- *WhoAm 90*
Lawrence, Robert W *BiDrAPA 89*
Lawrence, Robert W. 1924- *St&PR 91*
Lawrence, Roderick John 1949- *WhoWor 91*
Lawrence, Rodney Steven 1951- *WhoAmA 91, WhoEmL 91*
Lawrence, Ronald M. *NewAgE 90*
Lawrence, Rose *FemiCLE*
Lawrence, Ruddick C. 1912- *ODwPR 91, St&PR 91*
Lawrence, Ruddick Carpenter 1912- *WhoAm 90, WhoWor 91*
Lawrence, S. T. E. 1900-1987 *BioIn 16*
Lawrence, Sally Clark 1930- *WhoAmW 91*
Lawrence, Sanford Hull 1919- *WhoWor 91*
Lawrence, Sarah *BiDEWW*
Lawrence, Scott 1952- *BiDrAPA 89*
Lawrence, Seymour 1926- *BioIn 16, WhoAm 90*
Lawrence, Sherman S. 1918- *St&PR 91*
Lawrence, Sidney 1948- *WhoAmA 91*
Lawrence, Sidney Smith 1948- *WhoE 91*
Lawrence, Spencer 1949- *WhoAmA 91*
Lawrence, Stanley 1900-1987 *BioIn 16*
Lawrence, Stephanie 1958- *WhoAmW 91*
Lawrence, Stephen R. 1921- *ODwPR 91*
Lawrence, Steve 1935- *OxCPMus, WhoAm 90, WorAlBi*
Lawrence, Steven B. 1960- *WhoEmL 91*
Lawrence, Steven Denis 1951- *WhoSSW 91*
Lawrence, Steven Porter 1950- *WhoEmL 91*
Lawrence, Stewart D. 1948- *St&PR 91*
Lawrence, Susan 1939- *WhoAmA 91*
Lawrence, Syd 1923- *OxCPMus*
Lawrence, Sylvia Yvonne 1937- *WhoAmW 91*
Lawrence, T. E. 1888-1935 *BioIn 16*
Lawrence, Telete Zorayda 1910- *WhoAm 90, WhoAmW 91, WhoWor 91*
Lawrence, Theresa Annette *BiDrAPA 89*
Lawrence, Thomas 1769-1830 *IntDcAA 90*
Lawrence, Thomas E. 1888-1935 *WorAlBi*
Lawrence, Thomas Edward 1888-1935 *BioIn 16, EncPaPR 91*
Lawrence, Thomas P. 1946- *ODwPR 91*
Lawrence, Thomas Patterson 1946- *WhoAm 90*
Lawrence, Vicki 1949- *WorAlBi*
Lawrence, Vicki Schultz 1949- *WhoAm 90*
Lawrence, Vinnedge Moore 1940- *WhoE 91*
Lawrence, Vint *BioIn 16*
Lawrence, Virgil Edward, Jr. 1933- *WhoSSW 91*
Lawrence, W. N. Murray *BioIn 16*
Lawrence, Walter, Jr. 1925- *WhoAm 90*
Lawrence, Walter Thomas 1950- *WhoSSW 91*
Lawrence, Wayne Allen 1938- *St&PR 91, WhoAm 90*
Lawrence, Willard Earl 1917- *WhoAm 90*
Lawrence, William Calder Anderson 1832-1860 *AmLegL*
Lawrence, William Charles 1922- *WhoSSW 91*
Lawrence, William Charles 1950- *WhoE 91*
Lawrence, William David *BiDrAPA 89*
Lawrence, William Dwight 1931- *St&PR 91*
Lawrence, William F. 1934- *St&PR 91*
Lawrence, William J., Jr. 1918- *St&PR 91*
Lawrence, William Joseph, Jr. 1918- *WhoAm 90*
Lawrence, William Louis, Jr. 1951- *St&PR 91*
Lawrence, William M. *ODwPR 91*
Lawrence, William Porter 1930- *WhoAm 90*
Lawrence, William S 1895-1981 *DcAfAmP*
Lawrence, William S. 1943- *St&PR 91*
Lawrence, William Walter 1929- *WhoE 91*
Lawrence, William Wilberforce 1956- *WhoWor 91*
Lawrence-Berrey, Robert Edmond 1934- *WhoSSW 91*
Lawrie, Caroline S. 1932- *St&PR 91*
Lawrie, Gerald Murray 1945- *WhoAm 90*
Lawrie, Lee 1877-1963 *WhoAmA 91N*
Lawrimore, Earl W. *ODwPR 91*
Lawroski, Harry 1928- *WhoAm 90*
Lawry, Sylvia *WhoAm 90, WhoE 91*
Lawryniuk, Viktor 1953- *WhoWrEP 89*
Laws, Curtis Lee 1868-1946 *BioIn 16*
Laws, David Garrard 1930- *St&PR 91, WhoAm 90*
Laws, Donald M. 1935- *St&PR 91*
Laws, Edward Raymond 1938- *WhoAm 90*
Laws, Hubert, Jr. 1939- *DrBlPA 90*
Laws, John Kohlsaat, Jr. 1947- *WhoEmL 91, WhoSSW 91*
Laws, John T. 1938- *St&PR 91*
Laws, Judith A. 1937- *WhoAmW 91*
Laws, Marjorie E. 1940- *St&PR 91*
Laws, Priscilla Watson 1940- *WhoAmW 91*
Laws, Richard Maitland 1926- *WhoWor 91*
Laws, Robert Franklin 1914- *WhoAm 90*
Laws, Robert Julian 1922- *WhoAm 90*
Laws, Sam *DrBlPA 90*
Laws-Coats, Laurie Ann 1954- *WhoEmL 91*
Laws-Moseley, Barbara Lee 1946- *WhoE 91*
Lawson, Abram Venable 1922- *WhoAm 90*
Lawson, Albert R 1924- *BiDrAPA 89*
Lawson, Alec William 1947- *WhoSSW 91*
Lawson, Alexander 1815-1895 *DcCanB 12*
Lawson, Alexander E., Jr. 1922- *St&PR 91*
Lawson, Andrew Lowell, Jr. 1938- *St&PR 91, WhoAm 90*
Lawson, Ann Marie McDonald *WhoAmW 91*
Lawson, Annette 1936- *ConAu 129*
Lawson, Barbara *BioIn 16*
Lawson, Barbara Ellen 1963- *WhoAmW 91*
Lawson, Benjamin Samuel, Jr. 1949- *St&PR 91*
Lawson, Betty Noyes 1928- *WhoAmW 91*
Lawson, Bruce Gilbert 1945- *WhoEmL 91*
Lawson, Carolyn Ruth 1948- *WhoEmL 91*
Lawson, Carroll D. 1956- *St&PR 91*
Lawson, Charlene Ann 1948- *WhoAmW 91*
Lawson, Charles Edmond 1935- *St&PR 91*
Lawson, Charles J., Jr. 1921- *St&PR 91*
Lawson, Clarence *BioIn 16*
Lawson, Colin James 1949- *IntWWM 90*
Lawson, David E. 1937- *WhoAm 90*
Lawson, David Jerald 1930- *WhoAm 90*
Lawson, David R. 1947- *WhoSSW 91*
Lawson, Don *BioIn 16*
Lawson, Don 1917-1990 *ConAu 130*
Lawson, Donald Elmer 1917- *AuBYP 90*
Lawson, Donald Stuart 1935- *WhoAm 90*
Lawson, Earl *Ballpl 90*
Lawson, Earl 1923- *BioIn 16*
Lawson, Eddie *BioIn 16*
Lawson, Edward Pitt 1927- *WhoAmA 91*
Lawson, Eric W., Jr. 1941- *WhoE 91*
Lawson, Eugene K. 1939- *St&PR 91*
Lawson, Frederick Hebel 1927- *St&PR 91, WhoAm 90*
Lawson, Frederick Henry 1897-1983 *DcNaB 1981*
Lawson, Gayla Hughes 1940- *WhoSSW 91*
Lawson, George 1827-1895 *DcCanB 12*
Lawson, George B 1928- *BiDrAPA 89*
Lawson, Harold D. 1947- *WhoSSW 91*
Lawson, Henry 1867-1922 *BioIn 16*
Lawson, Herbert Blaine 1942- *WhoE 91*
Lawson, J.C. 1923- *St&PR 91*
Lawson, James A. 1936- *St&PR 91*
Lawson, James Earl 1945- *WhoEmL 91*
Lawson, James Lee 1949- *WhoEmL 91, WhoWor 91*
Lawson, James Marshall 1863- *AmLegL*
Lawson, James Raymond 1919- *WhoAm 90*
Lawson, James Thomas, Jr. 1935- *St&PR 91*
Lawson, Jane E. *St&PR 91*
Lawson, Jane Elizabeth *WhoAm 90*
Lawson, Jean Kerr 1941- *WhoAmW 91*
Lawson, Jerry Edward 1936- *St&PR 91*
Lawson, Jessie 1838?-1917 *FemiCLE*
Lawson, Joan 1906- *BioIn 16*
Lawson, Joel Smith, III 1947- *WhoAm 90, WhoE 91*
Lawson, John *AuBYP 90*
Lawson, John *EncCRAm, WhNaAH*
Lawson, John H. *WhoAm 90*
Lawson, John Howard 1894-1977 *BioIn 16, EncAL*
Lawson, John K. 1940- *St&PR 91*
Lawson, John Quinn 1940- *WhoAm 90*
Lawson, John Robert 1947- *St&PR 91*
Lawson, John W. 1944- *ODwPR 91*
Lawson, Jonathan Nevin 1941- *WhoE 91*
Lawson, Joyce Marie Moses 1955- *WhoAmW 91*
Lawson, Kate 1894-1977 *BioIn 16*
Lawson, Kate Drain 1894-1977 *NotWoAT*
Lawson, Louisa 1848-1920 *FemiCLE*
Lawson, Margaret Avril 1957- *WhoEmL 91*
Lawson, Marie 1894-1956 *AuBYP 90*
Lawson, Mary Elizabeth W. 1940- *WhoSSW 91*
Lawson, Mary Jane 1828-1890 *FemiCLE*
Lawson, Mary Viv *WhoAmW 91*
Lawson, Michael Deyo 1953- *WhoSSW 91*
Lawson, Nancy Helen 1925- *WhoAmW 91*
Lawson, Nancy P. 1926- *St&PR 91*
Lawson, Neils Vinton 1922- *WhoAm 90*
Lawson, Nigel 1932- *WhoWor 91, WorAlBi*
Lawson, Patricia Ann 1945- *WhoAmW 91*
Lawson, Patrick *AuBYP 90*
Lawson, Pauline Price 1923- *St&PR 91*
Lawson, Peter 1950- *IntWWM 90*
Lawson, Randall Clayton, II 1948- *WhoAm 90*
Lawson, Richard *BioIn 16, DrBlPA 90*
Lawson, Rik Michael 1962- *WhoSSW 91*
Lawson, Robert 1892-1957 *AuBYP 90, WhoAmA 91N*
Lawson, Robert Bernard 1940- *WhoAm 90, WhoE 91*
Lawson, Robert Davis 1926- *WhoAm 90*
Lawson, Robert Eugene 1944- *St&PR 91, WhoAm 90*
Lawson, Robert William, Jr. 1908- *WhoAm 90*
Lawson, Robley H. *BioIn 16*
Lawson, Rosanne Tauber 1946- *WhoEmL 91*
Lawson, Roxie 1906-1977 *Ballpl 90*
Lawson, Sarah Anne 1943- *WhoWor 91*
Lawson, Susan Barksdale 1956- *WhoEmL 91*
Lawson, Thomas 1951- *WhoAmA 91*
Lawson, Thomas Cheney 1955- *WhoEmL 91, WhoWor 91*
Lawson, Thomas Elsworth 1937- *WhoAm 90*
Lawson, Thomas Richard 1940- *WhoSSW 91*
Lawson, Thomas Seay, Jr. 1935- *WhoSSW 91, WhoWor 91*
Lawson, Thomas W. 1857-1925 *WorAlBi*
Lawson, Thomas Walker 1940- *WhoSSW 91*
Lawson, Tim 1963- *BioIn 16*
Lawson, Tom F. 1915- *WhoAm 90*
Lawson, T'sari E *BiDrAPA 89*
Lawson, Verona Delores 1943- *BiDrAPA 89*
Lawson, Victor F. 1850-1925 *BioIn 16*
Lawson, Willard Francis, Jr. 1947- *WhoSSW 91*
Lawson, William Bradford 1945- *BiDrAPA 89*
Lawson, William Burton 1930- *WhoE 91*
Lawson, William David, III 1924- *WhoAm 90, WhoSSW 91*
Lawson, William Hogan 1937- *St&PR 91*
Lawson, William Hogan, III 1937- *WhoAm 90*
Lawson, William Jesse 1939- *WhoAm 90*
Lawson, Wilma Jean 1940- *WhoAmW 91*
Lawson, Winifred 1894-1961 *OxCPMus*
Lawson-Johnston, Peter O. 1927- *BioIn 16, St&PR 91*
Lawson-Johnston, Peter Orman 1927- *WhoE 91*
Lawther, John Wheeler 1931- *WhoE 91*
Lawton, Alexander Robert, III 1938- *WhoAm 90*
Lawton, Alfred Henry 1916- *WhoAm 90*
Lawton, Andrew Swaby 1951- *WhoEmL 91*
Lawton, Barbara Perry 1930- *ODwPR 91*
Lawton, Brigitta 1948- *St&PR 91*
Lawton, Charles *ConAu 30NR, WhoWrEP 89*
Lawton, Charles 1913- *WhoAm 90*
Lawton, Charles B. 1920- *St&PR 91*
Lawton, Edgar Herbert, Jr. 1929- *St&PR 91, WhoAm 90*
Lawton, Eric 1947- *WhoEmL 91, WhoWor 91*
Lawton, Eugene A. 1936- *St&PR 91*
Lawton, Eugene Alfred 1936- *WhoAm 90*
Lawton, Florian Kenneth 1921- *WhoAmA 91*
Lawton, Frank J. 1943- *St&PR 91*
Lawton, George 1900-1957 *EncO&P 3*
Lawton, George Albert 1914- *WhoAm 90*
Lawton, Gregory Moss 1958- *WhoEmL 91, WhoWor 91*
Lawton, H. Cranston 1921- *ODwPR 91*
Lawton, Henry Ware 1843-1899 *WhNaAH*
Lawton, Jacqueline Agnes 1933- *WhoAmW 91*
Lawton, James J, Jr. 1915- *BiDrAPA 89*
Lawton, James L 1944- *WhoAmA 91*
Lawton, James Patrick 1948- *WhoEmL 91*
Lawton, Jeffrey *IntWWM 90*
Lawton, Kenneth Alan 1940- *St&PR 91*
Lawton, LaJoyce Chatwell 1947- *WhoAmW 91*
Lawton, Lorilee Ann 1947- *WhoAmW 91, WhoE 91*
Lawton, Manny 1918-1986 *BioIn 16*
Lawton, Marcia Jean 1937- *WhoAmW 91, WhoSSW 91*
Lawton, Michael James 1953- *WhoWor 91*
Lawton, Nancy 1950- *WhoAmA 91*
Lawton, Peter 1932- *ODwPR 91*
Lawton, Randall W. 1945- *St&PR 91*
Lawton, Richard Graham 1934- *WhoAm 90*
Lawton, Richard Stanley 1931- *St&PR 91*
Lawton, Robert Clark 1957- *WhoE 91*
Lawton, Robert L 1948- *BiDrAPA 89*
Lawton, Sidney Maurice 1924- *IntWWM 90*
Lawton, Thomas 1931- *WhoAm 90, WhoAmA 91*
Lawton, Thomas Gerard Samuel 1962- *WhoWrEP 89*
Lawton, Thomas Oregon, III 1957- *WhoE 91*
Lawton, Thomas Patrick, Jr. 1928- *WhoAm 90*
Lawton, William Burton 1927- *St&PR 91*
Lawwill, Theodore 1937- *WhoAm 90*
Lawyer 1796-1876 *WhNaAH*
Lawyer, Verne 1923- *WhoAm 90*
Lawyer, Vivian Jury 1932- *WhoAmW 91*
Lax, David 1910-1990 *WhoAmA 91N*
Lax, David 1939- *St&PR 91*
Lax, Eugene H. 1949- *St&PR 91*
Lax, Harold *BioIn 16*
Lax, James David 1954- *WhoE 91*
Lax, Jonathan Reiner 1949- *WhoE 91, WhoEmL 91*
Lax, Melvin 1922- *WhoAm 90*
Lax, Michael 1929- *ConDes 90*
Lax, Michael H. 1949- *WhoWor 91*
Lax, Peter David 1926- *WhoAm 90, WhoWor 91*

Lax, Philip 1920- WhoAm 90, WhoWor 91
Laxalt, Dominique BioIn 16
Laxalt, Paul 1922- WhoAm 90, WhoWor 91, WorAlBi
Laxeiro 1908- BioIn 16
Laxer, Marc Alan 1947- WhoE 91
Laxman, R. K. BioIn 16
Laxness, Halldor 1902- EuWr 12, WhoWor 91, WorAlBi
Laxness, Halldor Kiljan 1902- DcScanL
Laxson, Ruth WhoAmA 91
Laxson, Susan Jensen Ourand 1949- WhoAmW 91
Laxton, Bill 1948- Ballpl 90
Lay, Chris Andrew 1927- St&PR 91
Lay, Christopher David 1946- WhoE 91
Lay, Donald Pomeroy 1926- WhoAm 90
Lay, Fernando BioIn 16
Lay, Joseph Lafayette 1952- St&PR 91
Lay, Kenneth Edward 1932- WhoSSW 91
Lay, Kenneth Lee 1942- St&PR 91, WhoAm 90, WhoSSW 91
Lay, Nancy Duke S. 1938- WhoWrEP 89
Lay, Norvie Lee 1940- WhoAm 90
Lay, Patricia Anne 1941- WhoAmA 91, WhoE 91
Lay, Patti Jane 1955- WhoEmL 91
Lay, Philipp Friedrich PenDiDA 89
Lay, Russell Alan 1956- WhoSSW 91
Lay, Skipper 1940- WhoSSW 91
Lay, Stephen A 1943- BiDrAPA 89
Lay, Thorne 1956- WhoEmL 91
Lay, William R., III BiDrAPA 89
Lay, William Sherman 1939- St&PR 91
Layard, Peter Richard Grenville 1934- WhoWor 91
Laybe, Suzanne Cramton 1956- WhoAmW 91
Laybourn, Jan Lind 1947- WhoWor 91
Laybourne, Everett Broadstone 1911- WhoAm 90
Laybourne, Paul Curtis, Jr. BiDrAPA 89
Laybourne, Roxie BioIn 16
Laycob, Lawrence Dale 1941- BiDrAPA 89
Laycock, Fred 1926- St&PR 91
Laycock, George Edwin 1921- AuBYP 90
Laycock, Harold Douglas 1948- WhoAm 90, WhoEmL 91
Laycock, Mark 1957- IntWWM 90
Laycock, Michael 1954- St&PR 91
Laycock, Ralph George 1920- IntWWM 90
Laycraft, George H. 1924- St&PR 91
Laycraft, James Herbert 1924- WhoAm 90
Layde, Durward Charles 1912- WhoAm 90
Layde, Joseph Bernard 1954- BiDrAPA 89
Layden, Donald William, Jr. 1957- WhoEmL 91
Layden, Francis Patrick 1932- WhoAm 90
Layden, Frank BioIn 16
Layden, John J. 1924- St&PR 91
Laye, Camara 1928-1980 MajTwCW, WorAlBi
Laye, Evelyn 1900- OxCPMus
Laye, Letchford B., Jr. 1948- WhoSSW 91
Layendecker, John P. 1945- St&PR 91
Layer, Meredith Mitchum 1946- WhoAm 90, WhoAmW 91, WhoE 91
Layfield, Arthur Wayne 1960- WhoE 91, WhoEmL 91
Laylin, Lewis Cass AmLegL
Layman, Caleb Maynard 1943- St&PR 91
Layman, David J. 1945- St&PR 91
Layman, David Michael 1955- WhoEmL 91, WhoSSW 91
Layman, Emma McCloy 1910- WhoAm 90
Layman, Lawrence 1930- WhoAm 90
Layman, Linda Anne 1936- WhoAmW 91
Layman, Margo Elaine 1952- WhoEmL 91
Layman, Robert Eugene 1921- St&PR 91
Layman, William A 1929- BiDrAPA 89
Layman, William Arthur 1929- WhoAm 90, WhoE 91
Laymon, Cynthia J 1948- WhoAmA 91
Laymon, Harold James 1951- WhoWrEP 89
Laymon, John L. 1917- St&PR 91
Layne, Barbara J 1952- WhoAmA 91
Layne, Donald Sainteval 1931- WhoAm 90
Layne, Donna WhoWrEP 89
Layne, Edward Noel 1947- St&PR 91
Layne, George Stark BiDrAPA 89
Layne, James Nathaniel 1926- WhoAm 90
Layne, John Francis 1928- WhoSSW 91
Layne, Kay Ellen 1941- WhoE 91
Layne, Mark Jay 1961- WhoEmL 91
Layng, Judith Clave 1933- IntWWM 90
Laynor, Harold Arthur 1922- WhoAmA 91
Layson, Ruby Lee 1927- WhoSSW 91
Layson, William McIntyre 1934- St&PR 91, WhoAm 90
Layson, Zed Clark, Jr. 1937- St&PR 91
Laystrom, Robert Arnold 1952- St&PR 91
Layton, Allan Patrick 1954- WhoWor 91
Layton, Billy C. 1946- St&PR 91
Layton, Billy Jim 1924- WhoAm 90
Layton, Deborah Sutton 1937- WhoAmW 91, WhoE 91
Layton, Donald Harvey 1950- St&PR 91
Layton, Eddie BioIn 16
Layton, Edwin Thomas, Jr. 1928- WhoAm 90
Layton, Elizabeth BioIn 16
Layton, Elizabeth 1909- MusmAFA [port]
Layton, Frederick BioIn 16
Layton, Garland Mason 1925- WhoWor 91
Layton, Gloria 1914- WhoAmA 91N
Layton, Harry Christopher 1938- WhoWor 91
Layton, Irving 1912- ConAu 33NR, MajTwCW
Layton, Joe 1931- WhoAm 90
Layton, John B. BioIn 16
Layton, John C. 1944- WhoAm 90
Layton, Laura ODwPR 91
Layton, Leon H. 1930- St&PR 91
Layton, M.R. 1947- St&PR 91
Layton, Richard 1929- WhoAmA 91
Layton, Richard E., Jr. 1960- WhoSSW 91
Layton, Robert 1930- IntWWM 90
Layton, Robert Edward John 1925- WhoAm 90
Layton, Robert Glenn 1946- WhoEmL 91
Layton, Susan Broyles 1949- WhoEmL 91
Layton, Thomas Ralph 1947- WhoWrEP 89
Layton, Turner 1894-1978 OxCPMus
Layton, Wilbur Leslie 1922- WhoAm 90
Layton, William George 1931- St&PR 91, WhoAm 90
Layton, William Isaac 1913- WhoSSW 91
Layton-Bowlby, Linda Sue BiDrAPA 89
Layzer, Arthur James 1927- WhoE 91
Layzer, David 1925- WhoAm 90
Lazar, Abraham 1924- St&PR 91
Lazar, Cathy BioIn 16
Lazar, Donald A. St&PR 91
Lazar, Elysa BioIn 16
Lazar, Gary Alan BiDrAPA 89
Lazar, Gerald K 1942- BiDrAPA 89
Lazar, Gerald Martin 1942- BiDrAPA 89
Lazar, Gerson 1911- St&PR 91
Lazar, Gyorgy 1924- WhoWor 91
Lazar, Harold P. 1928-1989 BioIn 16
Lazar, Howard 1945- WhoAm 90
Lazar, Ira 1947- BiDrAPA 89
Lazar, Irving Paul 1907- WhoAm 90
Lazar, Jack BioIn 16, NewYTBS 90
Lazar, Kenneth Stuart 1948- WhoE 91, WhoEmL 91
Lazar, Linda Sharon 1943- WhoE 91
Lazar, Marda Goldfine 1956- WhoEmL 91
Lazar, Mark Howard 1952- WhoE 91
Lazar, Susan Gaber BiDrAPA 89
Lazar, Susan Gaber 1944- WhoAmW 91
Lazar, Theodore Aaron 1920- WhoAm 90
Lazar, Virginia M. 1951- St&PR 91
Lazar, Zoe L. 1948- WhoAmW 91
Lazar-Meyn, Heidi Ann 1955- WhoEmL 91
Lazarchick, Susan BioIn 16
Lazarcik, Gregor 1923- WhoWor 91
Lazard, Jacques C. 1951- St&PR 91
Lazare, Aaron 1936- BiDrAPA 89, WhoAm 90
Lazare, Denys EncO&P 3
La Zare, Howard Ted 1936- St&PR 91
Lazarescu, Michael BiDrAPA 89
Lazareth, Karen Beth 1956- WhoAmW 91, WhoE 91
Lazarevich, Emil Robert 1910- WhoAm 90
Lazarini, Gary Leo 1941- St&PR 91
Lazarini, Gustavo 1918- ArtLatA
Lazaris, Nick George 1950- St&PR 91
Lazaris, Pamela Adriane 1956- WhoAmW 91, WhoEmL 91
Lazaro, Francisco 1932- IntWWM 90
Lazaro, Jaime E BiDrAPA 89
Lazaro, Maribel 1948- EncCoWW
Lazaro, Pedro 1956- BiDrAPA 89
Lazarof, Henri 1932- IntWWM 90
Lazaroff, Beatrice J. Stein 1951- WhoAmW 91
Lazaroff, Elizabeth Cohn BiDrAPA 89
Lazarovic, Karen 1947- WhoAm 90
Lazarre, Justin Joseph, Jr. 1939- St&PR 91
Lazarte, Jorge Alfredo BiDrAPA 89
Lazarus, A. L. 1914- WhoWrEP 89
Lazarus, Allan Matthew 1927- WhoAm 90, WhoSSW 91
Lazarus, Andrew J. 1924- ODwPR 91
Lazarus, Arlie Gary 1938- WhoAm 90, WhoE 91
Lazarus, Arnold Allan 1932- WhoAm 90, WhoWor 91
Lazarus, Arnold Leslie 1914- WhoAm 90, WhoWor 91
Lazarus, Arthur, Jr. 1926- WhoAm 90
Lazarus, Arthur Louis 1954- BiDrAPA 89, WhoE 91
Lazarus, Barbara Beth 1946- WhoAmW 91
Lazarus, Bruce 1956- IntWWM 90
Lazarus, Bruce I. 1954- WhoEmL 91
Lazarus, Charles 1923- ConAmBL, WhoAm 90, WhoE 91
Lazarus, Charles Y. 1914- St&PR 91
Lazarus, Darrell Harry 1924- WhoE 91
Lazarus, David 1921- WhoAm 90
Lazarus, Edward Hal 1959- WhoE 91
Lazarus, Emma 1849-1887 BioAmW, BioIn 16, FemiCLE, WorAlBi
Lazarus, Fred, IV 1942- WhoAm 90, WhoAmA 91
Lazarus, Fred R., Jr. 1884-1973 ConAmBL
Lazarus, George Milton 1932- WhoAm 90
Lazarus, Gerald Sylvan 1939- WhoAm 90
Lazarus, Harold 1927- WhoAm 90, WhoWor 91
Lazarus, Henry 1815-1895 PenDiMP
Lazarus, James J. 1937- St&PR 91
Lazarus, Jeremy Allan 1943- BiDrAPA 89
Lazarus, Jerome B. 1922- St&PR 91
Lazarus, Jerrold St&PR 91
Lazarus, John 1947- ConAu 132
Lazarus, Jonathan Doniel 1951- WhoEmL 91
Lazarus, Julian 1924- St&PR 91
Lazarus, Kenneth Anthony 1942- WhoAm 90
Lazarus, Keo Felker 1913- AuBYP 90, WhoWrEP 89
Lazarus, Lawrence W 1941- BiDrAPA 89
Lazarus, Marvin P 1918-1982 WhoAmA 91N
Lazarus, Maurice 1915- WhoAm 90
Lazarus, Mel 1927- EncACom
Lazarus, Mell WhoAm 90
Lazarus, Pat 1935- ConAu 130
Lazarus, Ralph 1914-1988 BioIn 16
Lazarus, Richard Stanley 1922- WhoAm 90
Lazarus, Rochelle Braff 1947- WhoAm 90
Lazarus, Rochelle J. ODwPR 91
Lazarus, Sara Louise 1948- WhoAmW 91
Lazay, Paul D. 1939- St&PR 91
Lazda, Zinaida 1902-1957 EncCoWW
Lazear, Edward P. 1948- ConAu 129
Lazear, Edward Paul 1948- WhoAm 90
Lazelle, Harold Keith 1932- St&PR 91
Lazenby, Dexter 1955- WhoAmA 91
Lazenby, Fred Wiehl 1932- St&PR 91, WhoAm 90
Lazenby, James O. 1925- St&PR 91
Lazenby, Pender Jordan 1950- St&PR 91
Lazenby, Robert E. 1940- St&PR 91
Lazenski, David Paul 1952- WhoEmL 91
Lazeroff, Jessie Marvin 1947- WhoE 91
Lazerson, Alan Martin BiDrAPA 89
Lazerson, Earl Edwin 1930- WhoAm 90
Lazerson, Jack 1936- WhoAm 90
Lazich, Daniel 1941- WhoSSW 91
Lazinsky, Jo Anne Marie WhoE 91
Lazo, Agustin 1898-1971 ArtLatA
Lazo, John, Jr. 1946- WhoEmL 91
Lazo, Josefina BiDrAPA 89
Lazo, Nelson 1957- WhoHisp 91
Lazo-Wasem, Edgar A. 1929- St&PR 91
Lazor, Johnny 1912- Ballpl 90
Lazor, Patricia Ann 1936- WhoAmW 91
Lazor, Theodosius 1933- WhoAm 90
Lazorchak, Joseph Michael 1957- WhoE 91
Lazorik, Michael Raymond 1945- St&PR 91
Lazoritz, Martin BiDrAPA 89
Lazorko, Jack 1956- Ballpl 90
Lazorski, Paul 1926- St&PR 91
Lazorwitz, Elaine Sherri 1954- WhoAmW 91
Lazovick, Paul B. ODwPR 91
Lazovick, Paul B. 1935- St&PR 91
Lazroff, J.J. 1946- St&PR 91
Lazrus, Julian 1919- St&PR 91
Lazy Young Man DcCanB 12
Lazzara, Bernadette 1948- WhoAm 90, WhoAmW 91
Lazzara, Dennis Joseph 1948- WhoWor 91
Lazzara, Joseph John 1951- St&PR 91
Lazzari, Bice 1900-1981 BiDWomA
Lazzari, Craig Clinton 1920- WhoSSW 91
Lazzari, Pietro 1898-1979 WhoAmA 91N
Lazzarino, Evie ODwPR 91
Lazzaro, Anthony Derek 1921- WhoAm 90, WhoWor 91
Lazzaro, Emanuel BioIn 16
Lazzaro, Robert Wayne 1952- WhoEmL 91
Lazzell, Blanche 1878-1956 BiDWomA, WhoAmA 91N
Lazzeri, Tony 1903-1946 Ballpl 90 [port]
Le Duc Anh WhoWor 91
Le Duc Tho 1911-1990 NewYTBS 90 [port], News 91-1
Le Quang Dao 1921- WhoWor 91
Le, Dao Mau 1939- WhoSSW 91
Le, Diep Ngoc 1928- BiDrAPA 89
Le, Thanh Nghi BioIn 16
Le, Truc Huy 1952- WhoEmL 91
Lea, Charlie 1956- Ballpl 90
Lea, Eleanor Lucille 1916- WhoAmW 91, WhoWor 91
Lea, F. Kay Amend 1941- WhoAmW 91
Lea, George A., Jr. 1950- St&PR 91
Lea, Homer 1876-1912 BioIn 16
Lea, James F 1945- ConAu 130
Lea, Laurie Jane 1948- WhoAmA 91
Lea, Lola Stendig 1934- WhoAm 90
Lea, Lorenzo Bates 1925- WhoAm 90
Lea, Pauline S. 1942- WhoAmW 91
Lea, Scott Carter 1931- St&PR 91, WhoAm 90
Lea, Stanley E. 1930- WhoAm 90, WhoAmA 91
Lea, Suzanne Moore 1944- WhoSSW 91
Lea, Sydney 1942- WhoWrEP 89
Lea, Thomas Nalle 1948- WhoE 91
Lea, Tom 1907- BioIn 16, WhoAm 90, WhoAmA 91
Lea, Warren E. 1941- St&PR 91
Lea-Cox, Graham Russell 1957- IntWWM 90
Lea-Stokes, Michele J BiDrAPA 89
Leab, Daniel Josef 1936- WhoE 91
Leacacos, Peter John 1943- WhoWor 91
Leach, Anthony Raymond 1939- St&PR 91
Leach, Barney H. 1944- St&PR 91
Leach, Bernard 1887-1979 ConDes 90
Leach, Bernard Howell 1887-1979 BioIn 16, EncJap, PenDiDA 89
Leach, Catherine Frances 1956- WhoSSW 91
Leach, Daylin Barry 1961- WhoEmL 91
Leach, Deborah M BiDrAPA 89
Leach, Duane Marshall 1935- WhoAm 90
Leach, Edmund 1910-1989 AnObit 1989
Leach, Edwin F. 1947- St&PR 91
Leach, Elizabeth A. Bieryla 1949- WhoAmW 91
Leach, Elizabeth Anne 1957- WhoAmA 9[1]
Leach, Franklin Rollin 1933- WhoSSW 91
Leach, Freddy 1897-1981 Ballpl 90
Leach, Harold Hunter 1926- St&PR 91, WhoAm 90
Leach, Harrison Langford 1923- WhoE 91
Leach, J. Frank 1921- St&PR 91
Leach, James Albert Smith 1942- WhoAm 90
Leach, James Edward 1944- WhoE 91
Leach, James Francis 1953- WhoSSW 91
Leach, James G. 1948- St&PR 91
Leach, James Hess 1959- WhoEmL 91
Leach, James Lindsay 1918- WhoAm 90
Leach, Janet 1918- BioIn 16
Leach, Jeffrey Edward 1956- St&PR 91
Leach, Jeffrey Kent 1959- WhoEmL 91
Leach, Joan Genevieve 1941- WhoE 91
Leach, John 1931- IntWWM 90
Leach, John Frank 1921- WhoAm 90
Leach, John Malcolm 1937- IntWWM 90
Leach, John Sanders 1937- St&PR 91
Leach, Joseph Lee 1921- WhoAm 90, WhoWrEP 89
Leach, Julian Gilbert 1894-1972 BioIn 16
Leach, Louis Lawrence 1885-1957 WhoAmA 91N
Leach, Lysle D. 1900-1987 BioIn 16
Leach, Mada 1939- WhoAmA 91
Leach, Madelyn Manning BiDrAPA 89
Leach, Maria 1892-1977 AuBYP 90
Leach, Mary Jane 1949- IntWWM 90
Leach, Maurice Derby, Jr. 1923- WhoAm 90
Leach, Max Russell 1935- St&PR 91
Leach, Penelope BioIn 16
Leach, Ralph F. 1917- St&PR 91, WhoAm 90
Leach, Richard Heald 1922- WhoAm 90
Leach, Richard Maxwell, Jr. 1934- WhoWor 91
Leach, Rick BioIn 16
Leach, Rick 1957- Ballpl 90
Leach, Robert Barry 1937- WhoWor 91
Leach, Robert Ellis 1931- WhoAm 90
Leach, Robin BioIn 16
Leach, Robin 1941- CurBio 90 [port]
Leach, Rodney Edward 1928- St&PR 91
Leach, Roger Humphrey 1942- WhoSSW 91
Leach, Ronald George 1938- WhoAm 90
Leach, Ronald Lee 1934- St&PR 91, WhoAm 90
Leach, Rosemary 1935- ConTFT 8 [port]
Leach, Russell 1922- WhoAm 90, WhoWor 91
Leach, Sandra Sinsel 1946- WhoSSW 91
Leach, Sheila Norma 1945- WhoAmW 91
Leach, Steve Alan 1943- WhoSSW 91
Leach, Steven Craig 1959- WhoSSW 91
Leach, Sydney Minturn 1951- WhoEmL 91
Leach, Terry 1954- Ballpl 90
Leach, Terry Lynn 1948- WhoEmL 91
Leach, Terry Ray 1949- WhoEmL 91
Leach, Tommy 1877-1969 Ballpl 90 [port]
Leach, Wilford BioIn 16
Leachman, Cloris BioIn 16
Leachman, Cloris 1926- WorAlBi
Leachman, Cloris 1930- WhoAm 90, WhoAmW 91
Leachman, Connie Jean Kennedy 1957- WhoEmL 91
Leachman, Karen L. 1942- WhoSSW 91
Leachman, Robert Briggs 1921- WhoAm 90
Leachman, Roger Mack 1942- WhoAm 90

Leacock, Eleanor Burke 1922-1987 EncAL
Leacock, Philip NewYTBS 90
Leacock, Richard 1921- BioIn 16
Leacock, Stephen 1869-1944 DcLB 92 [port], OxCCanT
Lead, Jane 1623-1704? BiDEWW
Lead, Jane 1624-1704 BioIn 16, FemiCLE
Leadbeater, C W 1847-1934 EncO&P 3
Leadbeater, Charles Webster 1854-1934 EncPaPR 91
Leadbeater, Mary 1758-1826 FemiCLE
Leadbelly 1885-1949 BioIn 16, DrBlPA 90
Leadbelly 1889-1949 OxCPMus
Leadbetter, Martin John 1945- IntWWM 90
Leadbetter, Robert A 1957- BiDrAPA 89
Leader, Alan H. 1938- St&PR 91
Leader, Alan Howard 1927- WhoE 91
Leader, Anton Morris BioIn 16
Leader, Carl WhoWrEP 89
Leader, David Scott BiDrAPA 89
Leader, Edward 1934- BiDrAPA 89
Leader, Francie Debra 1955- WhoAmW 91
Leader, Garnet Rosamonde WhoAmA 91
Leader, Morton 1928- WhoAm 90
Leader, Robert Wardell 1919- WhoAm 90
Leaderman, David M. 1944- St&PR 91
Leadholm, Janet Kittelson 1945- WhoEmL 91
Leaf, Alexander 1920- WhoAm 90
Leaf, Boris 1919- WhoAm 90
Leaf, Gregory D. ODwPR 91
Leaf, Horace 1886?-1971 EncO&P 3
Leaf, Howard Westley 1923- WhoAm 90
Leaf, June 1929- WhoAmA 91
Leaf, Margaret BioIn 16
Leaf, Mindy Glass 1952- WhoWrEP 89
Leaf, Munro 1905-1976 AuBYP 90
Leaf, Munro 1906-1977 WhoAmA 91N
Leaf, Paul 1929- ConAu 132, WhoAm 90, WhoWrEP 89
Leaf, Robert S. 1931- ODwPR 91
Leaf, Robert Stephen 1931- WhoAm 90
Leaf, Roger W. 1946- St&PR 91
Leaf, Roger Warren 1946- WhoE 91
Leaf, Ruth WhoAmA 91, WhoE 91
Leaf, Walter 1852-1927 EncO&P 3, EncPaPR 91
Leafe, Joseph A. WhoSSW 91
Leaff, Louis A BiDrAPA 89
Leaffer, Harry BiDrAPA 89
League, Alice Fay 1945- WhoAmW 91
League, Daniel Noel, Jr. 1936- St&PR 91
League, Ellamae Ellis 1899- WhoAm 90
League, Janet DrBlPA 90
Leahey, Miles Cary 1952- WhoE 91
Leahey, Raymond 1939- WhoSSW 91
Leahey, T. Burke 1943- St&PR 91
Leahigh, Alan K. 1944- ODwPR 91
Leahy, Arthur Stephen 1951- WhoE 91
Leahy, Arthur T. 1949- St&PR 91
Leahy, David M. 1958- WhoEmL 91
Leahy, Denis J. 1925- St&PR 91
Leahy, Donald J. 1923-1990 BioIn 16
Leahy, Edward Prior 1923- WhoSSW 91
Leahy, Harold Robert 1953- WhoE 91
Leahy, James Joseph 1942- WhoE 91
Leahy, James Michael 1927- St&PR 91
Leahy, John J. 1931- St&PR 91
Leahy, John Jacob 1921- WhoAm 90
Leahy, Lourdes C. 1962- WhoHisp 91
Leahy, Margo M BiDrAPA 89
Leahy, Maurice Lewis 1920- WhoWor 91
Leahy, Michael Dennis 1951- WhoEmL 91
Leahy, Michael Joseph 1939- WhoAm 90
Leahy, Osmund A. BioIn 16
Leahy, Patrick J 1940- CurBio 90 [port]
Leahy, Patrick Joseph 1940- WhoAm 90, WhoE 91, WhoWor 91
Leahy, Paulette E. R. 1951- WhoEmL 91
Leahy, Robert D. 1952- ODwPR 91
Leahy, Sidney M., Jr. 1930- WhoAm 90
Leahy, Thomas Francis 1937- St&PR 91, WhoAm 90, WhoE 91
Leahy, Vincent P.J. 1943- St&PR 91
Leahy, Virginia Klein 1910- St&PR 91
Leahy, William D. 1875-1959 BioIn 16, WorAlBi
Leahy, William F. 1913- St&PR 91, WhoAm 90
Leahy, William Joseph 1933- WhoWrEP 89
Leak, Allison G. 1938- WhoAm 90
Leak, David Keith 1932- St&PR 91
Leak, Margaret Elizabeth 1946- St&PR 91, WhoAmW 91, WhoE 91
Leak, Robert E. 1934- WhoAm 90
Leak, Sarah Elizabeth 1936- WhoSSW 91
Leake, Brenda Gail 1950- WhoAmW 91
Leake, Damien DrBlPA 90
Leake, Donald Lewis 1931- WhoAm 90
Leake, Eugene W 1911- WhoAmA 91
Leake, Gerald 1885-1975 WhoAmA 91N
Leake, Jim 1916- BioIn 16
Leake, Larry Bruce 1950- WhoSSW 91
Leake, Lucille Perkins 1913- WhoSSW 91
Leake, Preston Hildebrand 1929- WhoSSW 91
Leake, Vernell 1955- WhoEmL 91
Leake, William D. 1929- St&PR 91, WhoAm 90
Leakey, Caroline 1827-1881 FemiCLE
Leakey, Louis 1903-1972 WorAlBi
Leakey, Louis S B 1903-1972 MajTwCW
Leakey, Mary 1913- WorAlBi
Leakey, Mary Douglas 1913- WhoAm 90, WhoWor 91
Leakey, Richard E. NewYTBS 90 [port]
Leakey, Richard E. 1944- BioIn 16, WorAlBi
Leakey, Richard Erskine 1944- WhoWor 91
Leaks, Sylvester 1927- DrBlPA 90
Leal, Antonio, Jr. 1946- WhoHisp 91
Leal, Carol Ann BiDrAPA 89
Leal, Carolina Gonzales 1939- WhoSSW 91
Leal, Fernando 1900-1964 ArtLatA, BioIn 16
Leal, Herbert Allan Borden 1917- WhoAm 90
Leal, Joseph Rogers 1918- WhoE 91
Leal, Leslie Gary 1943- WhoAm 90
Leal, Luis 1907- ConAu 131, HispWr 90, WhoHisp 91
Leal, Luis 1957- Ballpl 90
Leal, Robert Barry 1935- WhoWor 91
Leal, Robert L. 1945- WhoHisp 91
Leale, B C 1930- ConAu 132
Lealtad, Catharine Deaver BioIn 16
Leaman, David Martin 1935- WhoAm 90
Leaman, J. Richard, Jr. 1934- St&PR 91, WhoAm 90, WhoE 91
Leaman, Jack Ervin 1932- WhoAm 90
Leaman, Samuel Ray 1947- WhoE 91
Leamer, Laurence Allen 1941- WhoAm 90
Leaming, Deryl Ray 1932- WhoSSW 91
Leamon, Martin H 1956- BiDrAPA 89
Lean Bear WhNaAH
Lean Elk WhNaAH
Lean, David BioIn 16
Lean, David 1908- WhoAm 90, WorAlBi
Lean, Eric Gung-Hwa 1938- WhoAm 90
Lean, Ralph E. 1945- St&PR 91
Leana EncCoWW
Leana, Carrie Renee 1953- WhoAmW 91
Leand, Andrea BioIn 16
Leander, Georg A. 1948-1988 BioIn 16
Leander, Henry Alan 1930- St&PR 91
Leandro, Jair Jorge 1950- WhoWor 91
Leaness, Charles Gabriel 1950- St&PR 91
Leaney, John Andrew 1948- WhoEmL 91
Leaning, Jennifer 1945- ConAu 132
Leaper, Elizabeth BiDEWW
Leaper, Eric John 1953- WhoWrEP 89
Leaper, Norman G. 1931- ODwPR 91
Leapley, Patricia Murray WhoSSW 91
Leapman, Edwina 1934- BiDWomA
Leapor, Mary 1722-1746 BioIn 16, FemiCLE
Lear, Charles Emil 1941- BiDrAPA 89
Lear, Edward 1812-1888 AuBYP 90, BioIn 16
Lear, Erwin 1924- WhoAm 90, WhoWor 91
Lear, Evelyn 1926- IntWWM 90, PenDiMP
Lear, Evelyn 1930- WhoAm 90
Lear, Frances BioIn 16
Lear, Frances Loeb 1923- WhoAm 90, WhoAmW 91
Lear, George 1879-1956 WhoAmA 91N
Lear, John 1909- WhoAm 90
Lear, Norman 1922- ConTFT 8, WorAlBi
Lear, Norman Milton 1922- WhoAm 90
Lear, Peter MajTwCW
Lear, Phillip Ephrian 1905- WhoE 91
Lear, Rex Verne BiDrAPA 89
Lear, Robert D. 1946- St&PR 91
Lear, Robert William 1917- St&PR 91, WhoAm 90
Lear, Tobias 1762-1816 BioIn 16
Lear, William Dennis 1960- WhoSSW 91
Lear, William Edward 1918- WhoAm 90
Lear, William Henry 1939- St&PR 91
Lear, William Powell 1902-1978 BioIn 16
Learch, Thomas J BiDrAPA 89
Leard, Norman Wright, III 1933- WhoE 91
Learey, Fred Don 1906- WhoAm 90
Learmonth, George J BiDrAPA 89
Learn, Doris Lynn 1949- WhoEmL 91
Learn, Elmer Warner 1929- WhoAm 90
Learn, Richard Lisle 1935- WhoE 91
Learnard, William Ewing 1935- WhoAm 90
Learned, Michael 1939- WhoAm 90, WorAlBi
Learner, Roberta BiDrAPA 89
Learning, Walter 1938- OxCCanT
Learning, Walter J. 1938- ConAu 130
Leary, Clifford Clarence 1930- St&PR 91
Leary, Daniel WhoAmA 91
Leary, Daniel J. 1957- ODwPR 91
Leary, Dennis William St&PR 91N
Leary, Edward Andrew 1913- WhoWrEP 89
Leary, Edward J. 1947- St&PR 91
Leary, Fairfax, Jr. BioIn 16
Leary, James Francis 1930- St&PR 91, WhoAm 90
Leary, James Henry 1950- WhoE 91
Leary, Jay Francis 1938- WhoAm 90
Leary, Kathryn D. BioIn 16
Leary, Kevin Michael 1955- WhoE 91
Leary, Leo William 1919- WhoAm 90
Leary, Lewis NewYTBS 90 [port]
Leary, Lewis 1906-1990 ConAu 131
Leary, Lewis Gaston 1906-1990 BioIn 16
Leary, Linda BioIn 16
Leary, Mark BiDrAPA 89
Leary, Mark Richard 1954- WhoEmL 91
Leary, Michael Joseph 1939- St&PR 91
Leary, Michael Warren 1949- WhoAm 90
Leary, Nancy Jane 1952- WhoAmW 91, WhoSSW 91
Leary, Nancy May 1955- WhoEmL 91
Leary, Thomas Barrett 1931- WhoAm 90
Leary, Tim 1958- Ballpl 90
Leary, Timothy 1920- EncO&P 3, MajTwCW, WhoAm 90, WorAlBi
Leary, Timothy Francis 1920- BioIn 16
Leary, William G 1915- ConAu 31NR
Leary, William James 1931- WhoAm 90, WhoE 91
Leary Jones, Barbara Jean 1955- WhoSSW 91
Leas, Philip Joseph 1949- WhoEmL 91
Leas, Speed 1937- ConAu 30NR
Leasburg, Ronald Henry 1933- WhoAm 90
Lease, Daniel H. 1926- St&PR 91
Lease, Daniel W. 1948- St&PR 91
Lease, Jack Michael 1943- St&PR 91
Lease, Jane Etta 1924- WhoAmW 91, WhoWor 91
Lease, Martin Harry, Jr. 1927- WhoAm 90
Lease, Richard Jay 1914- WhoWor 91
Lease, Ronald Charles 1940- WhoAm 90
Leason, Jack Walter 1921- WhoE 91
Leason, Robert Wales 1930- St&PR 91
Leasor, James 1923- BioIn 16, TwCCr&M 91
Leasor, Jane 1922- WhoAmW 91
Leasor, Thomas James 1923- BioIn 16, SpyFic
Leasure, Janet Lynn 1949- WhoWrEP 89
Leasure, June N. Ruff 1951- WhoEmL 91
Leasure, Mary Louise 1956- WhoAmW 91
Leasure, Vickey Ann 1949- WhoAmW 91
Leath, Charles Alexander, Jr. 1944- WhoSSW 91
Leath, James Marvin 1931- WhoAm 90, WhoSSW 91
Leath, Jerry L. 1941- St&PR 91
Leath, Paul Larry 1941- WhoAm 90, WhoE 91, WhoWor 91
Leatham, John Tonkin 1936- WhoAm 90
Leatham, Kate 1951- St&PR 91
Leatham, Louis Salisbury 1902- St&PR 91
Leather, Ela Miloszewski Rigby- BioIn 16
Leather, Geoffrey Rigby- BioIn 16
Leather, Richard Brenk 1932- St&PR 91, WhoAm 90
Leatherberry, Anne Knox Clark 1953- WhoAmW 91
Leatherby, Carol Ann IntWWM 90
Leatherby, Joann 1955- WhoAmW 91, WhoEmL 91
Leatherby, Ralph William 1925- St&PR 91
Leatherby, Russell E. 1953- St&PR 91
Leatherdale, Douglas West 1936- St&PR 91, WhoAm 90
Leatherdale, Marcus Andrew 1952- WhoAmA 91
Leatherlips 1732?-1810 WhNaAH
Leatherman, Edward H 1938- BiDrAPA 89
Leatherman, Hugh Kenneth, Sr. 1931- WhoSSW 91
Leatherman, John B. 1939- St&PR 91
Leatherman, Merrilee Streun 1942- WhoAmW 91
Leatherman, Steven Edward 1947- WhoEmL 91
Leathers, Burge Roberts 1959- WhoAmW 91
Leathers, James C. 1934- St&PR 91
Leathers, L. Hudson 1906- St&PR 91
Leathers, Margaret Weil 1949- WhoAmW 91, WhoEmL 91
Leathers, Robert BioIn 16
Leathers, Winston Lyle 1932- WhoAmA 91
Leatherwood, Richard L. WhoAm 90
Leatherwood, Thomas Lee, Jr. 1929- WhoSSW 91
Leatherwood, Wilfred McKittrick, Jr. 1936- WhoE 91
Leathley, Gil L. St&PR 91
Leaton, Anne 1932- ConAu 130, FemiCLE
Leaton, Edward K. 1928- St&PR 91, WhoE 91
Leaton, Marcella Kay 1952- WhoAmW 91, WhoEmL 91
Leautaud, Paul 1872-1956 BioIn 16
Leavell, Jeffrey 1958- WhoEmL 91
Leavell, Landrum Pinson, II 1926- WhoSSW 91
Leavell, Walter F. 1934- WhoAm 90
Leavell, William A. 1923- WhoSSW 91
Leavell, Winston J. 1950- ODwPR 91
Leavengood, Victor Price 1924- St&PR 91, WhoAm 90
Leavens, William Barry 1904-1988 BioIn 16
Leaventon, Barry Howard 1947- St&PR 91
Leaventon, Marc 1955- St&PR 91
Leavenworth, Donald H. 1930- St&PR 91
Leavenworth, Henry 1783-1834 WhNaAH
Leaver, Bernard BioIn 16
Leaver, Gabriel 1757-1795 PenDiDA 89
Leaver, Gardener NewYTBS 90
Leaverton, David R 1936- BiDrAPA 89
Leavey, Thomas E. 1934- St&PR 91
Leavins, Arthur 1917- IntWWM 90
Leavis, F R 1895-1978 MajTwCW
Leavis, Q. D. 1906-1981 BioIn 16, FemiCLE
Leavis, Queenie Dorothy 1906-1981 BioIn 16
Leavitt, A. Leroy 1943- St&PR 91
Leavitt, Aaron M BiDrAPA 89
Leavitt, Arnold Keith 1932- St&PR 91
Leavitt, Audrey Faye Cox 1932- WhoAm 90
Leavitt, Caroline Susan 1952- WhoWrEP 89
Leavitt, Charles Loyal 1921- WhoAm 90, WhoE 91, WhoWor 91
Leavitt, Chase L. 1944- St&PR 91
Leavitt, Dana G. 1925- St&PR 91
Leavitt, Dana Gibson 1925- WhoAm 90
Leavitt, David 1961- BioIn 16
Leavitt, Debbie 1954- WhoAmW 91
Leavitt, Donna Marzee 1958- WhoAmW 91, WhoWrEP 89
Leavitt, Gordon Hodsdon 1931- St&PR 91
Leavitt, Greg A. BioIn 16
Leavitt, H. Huntington 1947- St&PR 91
Leavitt, Harold Jack 1922- WhoAm 90
Leavitt, Henrietta Swan 1868-1921 BioIn 16
Leavitt, Horace M. 1929- St&PR 91
Leavitt, J. IntWWM 90
Leavitt, Jeffrey Stuart 1946- WhoEmL 91
Leavitt, Jerome Edward 1916- AuBYP 90, WhoAm 90
Leavitt, Joan Kazanjian 1926- WhoAmW 91
Leavitt, Joseph WhoAm 90
Leavitt, Joseph NewYTBS 90
Leavitt, Judith Ann 1947- WhoEmL 91
Leavitt, Lawrence Ronald 1943- St&PR 91
Leavitt, Maimon 1921- BiDrAPA 89
Leavitt, Martin Jack 1940- WhoWor 91
Leavitt, Mary Janice Deimel 1924- WhoAmW 91, WhoSSW 91, WhoWor 91
Leavitt, Neal 1955- ODwPR 91
Leavitt, Paul B. 1942- St&PR 91
Leavitt, Richard M 1946- BiDrAPA 89
Leavitt, Ronald 1934- St&PR 91
Leavitt, Stephen S 1936- BiDrAPA 89
Leavitt, Thomas Whittlesey 1930- WhoAm 90, WhoAmA 91, WhoE 91
Leavitt, Thomas William 1935- WhoE 91
Leavitt, Todd Page 1951- WhoEmL 91
Leavitt, Virginia Crawford 1948- WhoAmW 91, WhoEmL 91
Leavitt, William D. 1941- WhoWrEP 89
Leavy, Edward 1929- WhoAm 90
Leavy, Herbert Theodore 1927- WhoAm 90, WhoWor 91
Leavy, Roger S. 1957- St&PR 91
Leavy, Stanley A BiDrAPA 89
Leazar, Augustus 1843-1905 AmLegL
Leazer, Richard H. 1941- St&PR 91
Lebamoff, Ivan Argire 1932- WhoAm 90
Leban, Michael Eugene 1932- WhoAm 90
Lebar, Alvin B. 1922-1988 BioIn 16
Le Bar, Michael Lewis 1945- St&PR 91
Lebaron, Alice Anne 1953- IntWWM 90
LeBaron, Francis Newton 1922- WhoAm 90
Le Bas, Albert BioIn 16
Lebas, Jean-Baptiste 1878-1944 BiDFrPL
Lebas, Joseph Carswell 1944- St&PR 91
Le Batard, Paul 1886-1986 MusmAFA
Lebbin, Carole Sue 1948- WhoE 91
Lebby, Andrew Miller 1946- WhoE 91
Lebduska, Lawrence 1894-1966 MusmAFA
Lebe, Doryann M 1940- BiDrAPA 89
Lebeau, Bernard G. 1921- St&PR 91
LeBeau, Charles Paul 1944- WhoAm 90, WhoWor 91
LeBeau, Edward Charles 1929- WhoAm 90
LeBeau, Hector Alton, Jr. 1931- WhoAm 90
Lebeau, William E 1922- BiDrAPA 89
Le Beauf, Sabrina DrBlPA 90
Lebeaux, Lincoln BiDrAPA 89
Lebeck, Carol E 1931- WhoAmA 91
Lebeck, Robert 1929- WhoWor 91
Lebeck, Warren Wells 1921- WhoAm 90

Lebed, Hartzel Zangwill 1928- *WhoAm 90, WhoE 91, WhoWor 91*
Lebedeff, Sergej A. *NewYTBS 90*
Lebedev, Aleksandr Nikolaevich 1881-1938 *DcScB S2*
Lebedev, Boris *BiDrAPA 89*
Lebedev, Valentin 1942- *BioIn 16*
Lebedev, Vladimir 1910- *WhoAmA 91*
Lebedeva, Sarah Dmitrievna 1881-1968 *BiDWomA*
Lebedow, Aaron Louis 1935- *WhoAm 90*
Lebegue, Breck Jon 1951- *BiDrAPA 89*
Lebeiko, Carol Hyslop *BiDrAPA 89*
Lebeis, Kerwin, Jr. 1950- *BiDrAPA 89*
Lebel, Alain *BiDrAPA 89*
Lebel, Gregory Galen 1950- *WhoE 91*
Lebel, Robert 1924- *WhoAm 90*
LeBell, June 1944- *WhoAmW 91*
LeBell, Robert 1948- *WhoEmL 91*
Lebens, Jeffrey K. 1944- *WhoAm 90*
Lebens, Jeffrey Kent 1944- *St&PR 91*
Lebensfeld, Harry 1904- *St&PR 91, WhoAm 90, WhoE 91*
Lebensohn, Zigmond Meyer 1910- *BiDrAPA 89, WhoAm 90, WhoE 91*
Lebenzon, Joseph Edmond 1944- *BiDrAPA 89*
Leber, Lester 1913- *WhoAm 90*
Leberman, Joseph *BioIn 16*
Lebey, Barbara 1939- *WhoAmA 91*
LeBey, Barbara Sydell 1939- *WhoAmW 91*
Lebi-Akintan, Stella Folake 1959- *WhoWor 91*
Lebic, Lojze 1934- *IntWWM 90*
LeBien, Robert Frank 1934- *WhoAm 90*
Lebinger, Martin B 1952- *BiDrAPA 89*
Lebischak, J. Doris *BiDrAPA 89*
LeBlanc, Alvin Louis 1931- *WhoSSW 91*
Leblanc, Barry D. 1954- *St&PR 91*
Leblanc, Bryan 1946- *St&PR 91*
Leblanc, Doris E *BiDrAPA 89*
Le Blanc, Douglas R. *St&PR 91*
LeBlanc, Edward Oliver 1923- *BioIn 16*
Leblanc, Etienne 1839-1897 *DcCanB 12*
Leblanc, George T. 1930- *St&PR 91*
Leblanc, Gerard 1959- *BiDrAPA 89*
Le Blanc, Gilbert Gerard 1955- *WhoEmL 91*
LeBlanc, Hugh Linus 1927- *WhoAm 90*
Leblanc, Hugues 1924- *WhoAm 90*
Le Blanc, J Alfred 1933- *BiDrAPA 89*
Leblanc, Jean 1936- *BiDrAPA 89*
LeBlanc, John Keith 1945- *WhoEmL 91*
Le Blanc, Joy Comeaux 1937- *WhoWrEP 89*
Le Blanc, Lee 1913- *BioIn 16*
Leblanc, Leonard J. 1941- *St&PR 91*
LeBlanc, Leonard Joseph 1941- *WhoAm 90, WhoWor 91*
LeBlanc, Lillian Mary 1959- *WhoAmW 91*
Leblanc, Maurice 1864-1941 *TwCCr&M 91B*
LeBlanc, Michael Stephen 1952- *WhoEmL 91*
Leblanc, Raymond Paul 1945- *St&PR 91*
Leblanc, Roger Maurice 1942- *WhoAm 90*
Le Blanc, Romeo Adrien 1927- *WhoAm 90*
LeBlanc, Tina *BioIn 16*
Leblanc de Marconnay, Hyacinthe-Poirier 1794-1864 *OxCCanT*
LeBlanc-LeBlanc, Geraldine Nowlin B. 1932- *WhoSSW 91*
Leblang, Myles H. 1932- *St&PR 91*
LeBlang, Skip Alan 1953- *WhoEmL 91*
LeBlang, Theodore Raymond 1949- *WhoEmL 91*
LeBleu, David *BioIn 16*
Leblique, Leopold Benjamin 1926- *WhoSSW 91*
LeBlond, Billy *BioIn 16*
Leblond, Charles Philippe 1910- *WhoAm 90*
LeBlond, Dorothy Bush *BioIn 16*
LeBlond, Francis Celeste 1821-1902 *AmLegL*
Leblond, Richard K., II 1920- *St&PR 91*
LeBlond, Richard Knight, II 1920- *WhoAm 90*
Lebman, Robert Richard 1945- *WhoE 91*
Lebo, Arland 1909- *WhoE 91*
Lebo, Marie 1941- *WhoAmW 91*
Lebo, S. Sue 1928- *St&PR 91*
Lebo, William C. 1944- *St&PR 91*
Leboeuf, R.W. 1946- *St&PR 91*
Leboeuf, Steven J. 1948- *St&PR 91*
Leboff, Gail F 1950- *WhoAmA 91*
Lebor, John Francis 1906- *WhoAm 90*
LeBorg, Reginald 1902-1989 *BioIn 16*
Leboss, Bruce 1945- *ODwPR 91*
Lebouitz, Martin F. 1946- *WhoE 91, WhoWor 91*
LeBourveau, Bevo 1894-1947 *Ballpl 90*
LeBoutillier, John *WhoAm 90*
Lebovic, Dezider *BiDrAPA 89*
Lebovidge, Richard Nathaniel 1937- *St&PR 91*
Lebovitz, Donna Rudnick 1943- *WhoWrEP 89*
Lebovitz, Marcy 1955- *WhoAmW 91*
Lebovitz, Phil Stanley 1940- *BiDrAPA 89*
Lebovitz, Richard Paul 1953- *St&PR 91*
LeBow, Bennett S. *BioIn 16*
LeBow, Bennett S. 1938- *WhoE 91*
Lebow, Edward Michael 1948- *WhoEmL 91*
Lebow, Eileen F. 1925- *ConAu 132*
Lebow, Gerald M. *St&PR 91*
Lebow, Irwin Leon 1926- *WhoAm 90*
Lebow, Jeanne *WhoWrEP 89*
Lebow, Jeanne Gregory 1951- *WhoEmL 91*
Lebow, Laurel Mary Lavin 1956- *WhoSSW 91*
Lebow, Leonard S 1940- *BiDrAPA 89*
Lebow, Marcia Wilson 1919- *IntWWM 90*
Lebow, Michael Jeffrey 1956- *WhoEmL 91*
Lebow, Richard Ned 1942- *ConAu 129*
Lebow-Shepard, Jeanne Swift Gregory 1951- *WhoWrEP 89*
Lebowitz, Albert 1922- *WhoAm 90, WhoWrEP 89*
Lebowitz, Catharine Koch 1915- *WhoAmW 91*
Lebowitz, Donald Warren 1928- *St&PR 91, WhoE 91*
Lebowitz, Fran 1951?- *MajTwCW*
Lebowitz, Joel Louis 1930- *WhoAm 90*
Lebowitz, Marshall 1923- *WhoAm 90, WhoE 91*
Lebowitz, Michael 1953- *WhoE 91*
Lebowitz, Michael David 1939- *WhoAm 90*
Lebowitz, Michael S 1941- *BiDrAPA 89*
Lebrecht, Norman 1948- *IntWWM 90*
LeBreton, Jean Marie Rene 1927- *WhoWor 91*
LeBreton, Walter Joseph, Jr. 1961- *WhoSSW 91*
Lebright, Ronald Phillip 1934- *St&PR 91, WhoAm 90, WhoWor 91*
Le Bris, Michel 1944- *ConAu 131*
Lebro, Theodore Peter 1910- *WhoWor 91*
Le Brock, Kelly *BioIn 16*
Lebron, Edgardo R *BiDrAPA 89*
Lebron, Michael A 1954- *WhoAmA 91*
Lebron, Michael A., III 1954- *WhoHisp 91*
LeBron, Victor 1950- *WhoHisp 91*
Lebron-Esteras, Francisco A *BiDrAPA 89*
Le Broquy, Melanie 1919- *BiDWomA*
Lebrun, Albert Francois 1871-1950 *BiDFrPL*
Le Brun, Charles 1619- *IntDcAA 90*
Le Brun, Charles 1619-1690 *EncO&P 3, PenDiDA 89*
Lebrun, Louise-Elisabeth Vigee- 1755-1842 *BioIn 16*
Le Brun, Michael David 1956- *WhoEmL 91*
Lebrun, Pierre 1661-1729 *EncO&P 3*
Lebrun, Rico 1900-1964 *WhoAmA 91N*
Lebrun Moratinos, Jose Ali 1919- *WhoWor 91*
Le Brunn, George 1862-1905 *OxCPMus*
Lebsack, Phyllis Jean 1921- *WhoAmW 91*
Lebson, Evan Michael 1943- *St&PR 91*
Le Buffe, Francis Peter 1946- *BiDrAPA 89*
Le Buhn, Robert 1932- *WhoAm 90*
Lebwohl, Harold Benjamin 1954- *St&PR 91*
Le Cain, Errol 1941-1989 *AnObit 1989, BioIn 16, SmATA 60*
Le Cam, Lucien Marie 1924- *WhoAm 90*
Lecanuet, Jean Adrien Francois 1920- *BiDFrPL*
Le Caron, Henri *DcCanB 12*
le Carre, John *ConAu 33NR, MajTwCW*
Le Carre, John 1931- *BioIn 16, TwCCr&M 91, WhoAm 90, WhoWor 91, WorAlBi*
Lecash, Leon Paul 1951- *WhoE 91*
Lecavele, Roland 1886-1973 *BioIn 16*
Lecca, Pedro J. *WhoHisp 91*
Lecca, Radu *BioIn 16*
Lecce, Frank Anthony 1947- *WhoE 91*
Leccese, Kenneth E. 1943- *St&PR 91*
Lecerf, Olivier Maurice Marie 1929- *WhoWor 91*
Lechay, James 1907- *WhoAm 90, WhoAmA 91, WhoE 91*
Lecheler, Helmut 1941- *WhoWor 91*
Lechelt, Eugene Carl 1942- *WhoAm 90*
Lechevalier, Hubert Arthur 1926- *WhoAm 90*
Lechin Oquendo, Juan 1915- *BioIn 16*
Lechman, Wolodymr Bohdan 1932- *St&PR 91*
Lechner, Bernard Joseph 1932- *WhoAm 90*
Lechner, Dean *BioIn 16*
Lechner, Enrique S *BiDrAPA 89*
Lechner, George William 1931- *WhoWor 91*
Lechner, Herbert Dean 1932- *St&PR 91*
Lechner, Thomas Paul 1924- *St&PR 91*
Lecht, Leonard A. 1920- *WhoAm 90*
Lechtenberg, Michael F. 1938- *St&PR 91*
Lechter, George Steve 1954- *WhoE 91*
Lechter, Seymour C. *BioIn 16*
Lechtzin, Edwards S. *ODwPR 91*
Lechtzin, Stanley 1936- *WhoAmA 91, WhoE 91*
Lecinski, Alice R. 1956- *WhoEmL 91*
Leckenby, Nancy L. 1936- *WhoWrEP 89*
Lecker, Abraham 1916- *WhoAm 90*
Lecker, Lisa Joy 1958- *WhoAmW 91, WhoE 91*
Leckey, Andrew A. 1949- *WhoAm 90*
Lecki, Earle Edward 1953- *WhoEmL 91*
Leckie, Carol Mavis 1929- *WhoAmW 91*
Leckie, Frederick Alexander 1929- *WhoAm 90*
Leckie, James Edward 1953- *St&PR 91*
Leckie, Keith 1952- *ConAu 130*
Leckie, Robert 1920- *AuBYP 90*
Leckie, Robert B. 1947- *St&PR 91*
Leckie, Shirley Anne 1937- *WhoAmW 91*
Lecklider, Jerry A. 1952- *St&PR 91*
Lecklitner, Myron Lynn 1942- *WhoSSW 91, WhoWor 91*
Leckman, Arnold Lane *BiDrAPA 89*
Leckman, James F 1947- *BiDrAPA 89*
Leckner, Carole Hannah 1946- *WhoWrEP 89*
Leckrone, Charles Ronald 1945- *WhoE 91*
Leckrone, Michael 1937- *IntWWM 90*
Lecky, Renee Jeanne 1927- *WhoAmW 91, WhoWor 91*
Lecky, Robert Parke, Jr. 1949- *WhoE 91*
Lecky, Susan 1940- *WhoAmA 91*
Lecky, William Ralston, III 1940- *WhoSSW 91*
LeClair, Brian W. 1948- *WhoEmL 91*
Le Clair, Charles 1914- *WhoAmA 91*
Le Clair, Charles George 1914- *WhoAm 90*
Le Clair, Douglas Marvin 1955- *WhoEmL 91*
Le Clair, J.G. 1928- *St&PR 91*
Le Clair, Richard Alfred, Jr. 1943- *WhoE 91*
Leclaire, Harry W. 1914- *St&PR 91*
Le Claire, Harry Walter 1914- *WhoAm 90*
Leclant, Jean 1920- *ConAu 132*
Leclerc, Felix 1914-1988 *BioIn 16, OxCCanT*
Leclerc, Michel *BiDrAPA 89*
LeClerc, Paul 1941- *WhoAm 90, WhoE 91*
Leclercq, Raoul Felix 1939- *WhoWor 91*
Leclere, Jacques Francois 1935- *WhoWor 91*
Le Clere, Joseph Earl 1950- *WhoEmL 91*
Le Clezio, Sylvie *BioIn 16*
Lecno, John Ronald 1938- *St&PR 91*
Lecocq, Charles 1832-1918 *OxCPMus*
Lecoin, Louis 1888-1971 *BiDFrPL*
LeCompte, Elizabeth *BioIn 16*
LeCompte, Elizabeth Alice 1944- *NotWoAT*
LeCompte, Malcolm Aaron 1946- *WhoE 91*
Lecompte, Richard J.E. 1947- *St&PR 91*
Lecomte, Didier 1943- *WhoWor 91*
Le Comte, Edward 1916- *BioIn 16*
Le Comte, Edward Semple 1916- *WhoAm 90, WhoWrEP 89*
LeConey, Ann *BioIn 16*
Leconey, Douglas E. 1956- *St&PR 91*
Leconte, Henri *BioIn 16*
Leconte de Lisle, Charles-Marie-Rene 1818-1894 *NinCLC 29 [port]*
Le Coq, Monsieur *ConAu 129*
Lecoque 1891-1981 *WhoAmA 91N*
Lecoque, Ervin J. 1930- *St&PR 91*
Le Corbusier 1887-1965 *BioIn 16*
Le Corbusier, Charles-Edouard Jeanneret 1887-1965 *PenDiDA 89*
Lecount, Robert Ames 1925- *St&PR 91*
Le Count, Virginia G. 1917- *WhoAmW 91*
Lecour, Paul 1871-1954 *EncO&P 3*
Lecours, Harry Joseph 1932- *St&PR 91*
Lecours, Magda M. 1935- *WhoHisp 91*
Lecours, Philip Ruben 1935- *WhoHisp 91*
Lecouvreur, Adrienne 1692-1730 *EncCoWW*
Lecreux, Nicolas *PenDiDA 89*
Lecron, Leslie M. 1892- *EncO&P 3*
Lecroy, Hoyt Franklin 1941- *WhoSSW 91*
Le Croy, Thomas Gail 1946- *BiDrAPA 89*
Lecuona, Ernesto 1896-1963 *OxCPMus*
Lecuyer, Ellen Delphine 1956- *WhoAmW 91*
L'Ecuyer, Guy 1931-1985 *OxCCanT [port]*
L'Ecuyer, Richard 1940- *WhoAm 90*
Lecuyer-Coons, Georgeida Celene 1926- *WhoAmW 91*
Leczynski, Barbara Ann 1954- *WhoAmW 91*
Led Zeppelin *EncPR&S 89, OxCPMus, WorAlBi*
Le Dain, Gerald Eric 1924- *WhoAm 90*
Ledang, Ola Kai 1940- *IntWWM 90*
Le Dantec, Denise 1937- *EncCoWW*
Ledbetter, Barbara *St&PR 91*
Ledbetter, Calvin Reville, Jr. *WhoAm 90*
Ledbetter, Charles Edward, III 1946- *WhoSSW 91*
Ledbetter, Donald L. 1926- *St&PR 91*
Ledbetter, Huddie 1885-1949 *BioIn 16*
Ledbetter, Huddie 1888?-1949 *WorAlBi*
Ledbetter, J. Lee 1935- *St&PR 91*
Ledbetter, Marcialee 1957- *BiDrAPA 89*
Ledbetter, Patricia Lou 1931- *St&PR 91*
Ledbetter, Paul Mark 1947- *WhoEmL 91*
Ledbetter, Sharon Faye Welch 1941- *WhoAmW 91, WhoSSW 91*
Ledbetter, Sherry L. 1958- *St&PR 91*
Ledbetter, Steven John 1942- *IntWWM 90*
Ledbetter, William J. 1927- *St&PR 91*
Ledbetter-Straight, Nora Kathleen 1934- *WhoAmW 91, WhoSSW 91, WhoWor 91*
Ledbury, Diana Gretchen 1931- *WhoAmW 91*
Leddicotte, George Comer 1947- *WhoE 91, WhoEmL 91, WhoWor 91*
Leddon, Charles David 1932- *St&PR 91*
Leddy, John Henry 1929- *WhoAm 90*
Leddy, Susan 1939- *WhoAmW 91*
Ledea, Jacqueline M. 1961- *WhoSSW 91*
Ledebur, Linas Vockroth, Jr. 1925- *WhoAm 90*
Ledec, Jan 1922- *IntWWM 90*
Ledecky, Jonathan Joseph 1958- *WhoEmL 91*
Ledeen, Lydia 1938- *IntWWM 90*
Ledeen, Robert Wagner 1928- *WhoAm 90*
Leder, Jane M 1945- *SmATA 61*
Leder, Jane Mersky *BioIn 16*
Leder, Philip 1934- *WhoAm 90*
Lederberg, Edith Schaffer 1929- *WhoAmW 91*
Lederberg, Joshua 1925- *WhoAm 90, WhoE 91, WhoWor 91, WorAlBi*
Lederberg, Marguerite S *BiDrAPA 89*
Lederberg, Victoria 1937- *WhoAmW 91, WhoE 91*
Lederer, Clara *EarBlAP*
Lederer, D. Veola *BioIn 16*
Lederer, David B. 1939- *St&PR 91*
Lederer, Edith Madelon 1943- *WhoAm 90*
Lederer, Esther Pauline *BioIn 16*
Lederer, Eugene Anthony 1955- *WhoSSW 91*
Lederer, Fredric Ira 1946- *WhoEmL 91*
Lederer, Henry D 1914- *BiDrAPA 89*
Lederer, Jerome 1902- *WhoAm 90*
Lederer, Joan A. *BiDrAPA 89*
Lederer, John *EncCRAm*
Lederer, Katherine Gay 1932- *WhoWrEP 89*
Lederer, Leslie Theodore 1948- *St&PR 91*
Lederer, Louis Franklin 1935- *St&PR 91*
Lederer, Lucy Kemmerer 1892- *WhoAmW 91*
Lederer, Margaret Ellen 1952- *WhoEmL 91*
Lederer, Marion Irvine 1920- *WhoAm 90*
Lederer, Muriel 1929- *BioIn 16*
Lederer, Norman Henry 1938- *WhoE 91*
Lederer, Paul Edward 1942- *WhoSSW 91*
Lederer, Paul R. 1939- *St&PR 91*
Lederer, Peter David 1930- *WhoAm 90*
Lederer, Richard 1938- *BioIn 16, ConAu 132*
Lederer, Rolf August 1934- *BiDrAPA 89*
Lederer, William J 1912- *SmATA 62 [port]*
Lederer, William Julius 1912- *SpyFic, WhoAm 90, WhoWrEP 89*
Lederer, Wolfgang 1919- *BiDrAPA 89*
Lederer-Antonucci, Yvonne 1958- *WhoE 91*
Lederman, Alan Gerald 1943- *WhoE 91*
Lederman, Allen 1952- *St&PR 91*
Lederman, Cindy Shellenberger 1954- *WhoAmW 91*
Lederman, Florence 1932- *WhoAmW 91*
Lederman, Frank L. 1949- *WhoAm 90*
Lederman, Fred Bernard 1947- *WhoEmL 91*
Lederman, Ivan Irwin 1932- *BiDrAPA 89*
Lederman, JoAnn Volk 1942- *WhoWor 91*
Lederman, Laurence N 1942- *BiDrAPA 89, WhoE 91*
Lederman, Leon M. *BioIn 16*
Lederman, Leon M. 1922- *WorAlBi*
Lederman, Leon Max 1922- *WhoAm 90, WhoWor 91*
Lederman, Leonard Lawrence 1931- *WhoAm 90*
Lederman, Marie Jean 1935- *WhoAm 90*
Lederman, Michael Wainwright 1948- *WhoWor 91*
Lederman, Peter 1931- *WhoAm 90, WhoE 91*
Lederman, Peter B. 1931- *St&PR 91*
Lederman, Philippe 1961- *WhoWor 91*
Lederman, Raymond Karl 1950- *BiDrAPA 89*
Lederman, Sheya Newman *WhoAmA 91*
Lederman, Stephanie Brody *WhoAmA 91, WhoE 91*
Lederman, Zelda Hurwitz *BiDrAPA 89*
Ledermann, Volker Detlef 1932- *WhoWor 91*
Ledermann, Walter 1911- *ConAu 30NR*

Ledesma, Gabriel Fernandez 1900-1983 *BioIn 16*
Le Desma, Hector Escobar 1924- *WhoHisp 91*
Ledesma, Jane Leal 1946- *WhoHisp 91*
Ledesma, Mariano 1935- *WhoWor 91*
Ledesma, Victor Cervantes 1930- *WhoHisp 91*
Ledesma-Jimeno, Alfonso 1923- *BiDrAPA 89*
Ledet, Grace Dominque 1943- *WhoAmW 91*
Ledford, Frank Finley, Jr. 1934- *WhoAm 90*
Ledford, Jack Clarence 1920- *WhoAm 90*
Ledford, Karen Darlene 1950- *WhoEmL 91*
Ledford, Marie Smalley 1951- *WhoSSW 91*
Ledford, Richard Allison 1931- *WhoAm 90*
Ledford, Robert E. *WhoSSW 91*
Ledford, Toni Dandridge 1942- *WhoAmW 91, WhoSSW 91*
Ledford, William Lester 1935- *WhoSSW 91*
Ledger, Charles 1818-1905 *BioIn 16*
Ledger, Philip 1937- *PenDiMP*
Ledger, Philip Stevens 1937- *IntWWM 90, WhoWor 91*
Ledger, William Joe *WhoAm 90*
Ledgerwood, Claude Newell, Jr. 1926- *WhoSSW 91*
Ledgerwood, Ella Ray *WhoAmA 91N*
Ledgerwood, Helen Diane 1946- *WhoEmL 91*
Ledgerwood, Joe Allen 1954- *St&PR 91*
Ledgerwood, Washington Lafayette 1843-1911 *AmLegL*
Ledien, Ulrich F 1895- *BiDrAPA 89*
Ledin, George, Jr. 1946- *WhoEmL 91*
Ledin, Matthew Cameron 1961- *WhoEmL 91*
Ledingham, John 1846-1897 *DcCanB 12*
Ledingham, John Gerard Garvin 1929- *WhoWor 91*
Le-Dinh-Phuoc 1941- *WhoWor 91*
Le Dizes, Maryvonne 1940- *IntWWM 90*
Ledley, Fred David 1954- *WhoSSW 91*
Ledley, Gary Stewart 1957- *WhoE 91*
Ledlie, Douglas Edward 1954- *WhoEmL 91*
Ledlie, Joseph M. A. *ODwPR 91*
Ledlie, Joseph Maurice Antony 1943- *WhoSSW 91*
Ledlow, Verla *St&PR 91*
Ledman, Robert Earl 1949- *WhoSSW 91*
Ledner, David Michael *BiDrAPA 89*
Lednicer, Oliver 1934- *St&PR 91*
Ledogar, Raymond Anthony 1926- *WhoAm 90*
Ledon, Ann M. 1957- *WhoHisp 91*
Ledon, Henry Jean 1945- *WhoWor 91*
LeDonne, Robert J. 1929- *WhoE 91*
LeDoux, Harold Anthony 1926- *WhoAm 90*
Ledoux, Jacques 1921-1988 *AnObit 1988, BioIn 16*
LeDoux, John Clarence 1944- *WhoSSW 91*
Ledoux, Juan Ramon 1928- *WhoE 91*
Ledoux, Paul 1949- *ConAu 131*
Ledoux, Paul Joseph 1914- *WhoWor 91*
Ledoyen, Charles Eric 1943- *St&PR 91*
Ledsinger, Charles Albert, Jr. 1950- *St&PR 91*
Ledsky, Nelson Charles 1929- *WhoE 91*
Ledsome, John Russell 1932- *WhoAm 90*
Ledson, Richard L. 1947- *WhoEmL 91*
LeDuBois, Jacques-Laurent 1943- *WhoSSW 91*
Le Duc, Albert Louis, Jr. 1937- *WhoSSW 91*
Leduc, Bernard Maurice 1935- *St&PR 91*
Le Duc, Don R 1933- *ConAu 31NR*
Le Duc, Don Raymond 1933- *WhoAm 90*
Le Duc, Elizabeth Ann 1963- *WhoAmW 91, WhoSSW 91*
LeDuc, J. Adrien M. 1924- *WhoE 91*
Leduc, Jacques 1932- *IntWWM 90*
Leduc, Philippe M. 1940- *WhoWor 91*
Leduc, Violette 1907-1972 *EncCoWW*
Ledvora, Beth *BiDrAPA 89*
Ledwidge, Patrick Joseph 1928- *WhoAm 90*
Ledwig, Donald E. *BioIn 16*
Ledwig, Donald Eugene 1937- *WhoAm 90*
Ledwin, William Francis 1937- *St&PR 91*
Ledwith, Douglas Thomas 1949- *St&PR 91*
Ledy, David Martin 1949- *WhoE 91*
Ledyard, John 1751-1789 *EncCRAm, WhNaAH*
Ledyard, John Odell 1940- *WhoAm 90*
Ledyard, Robins Heard 1939- *WhoAm 90*
Ledzinski, Stanley Paul 1959- *WhoE 91*
Lee Huan 1917- *WhoWor 91*
Lee Kuan Yew 1923- *WhoWor 91*
Lee Sang Hoon 1933- *WhoWor 91*
Lee Teng-Hui 1923- *WhoWor 91*
Lee, A Robert 1941- *ConAu 130*
Lee, A Russell 1929- *BiDrAPA 89*
Lee, Addison Earl 1914- *WhoAm 90*
Lee, Adrian Iselin, Jr. 1920- *WhoAm 90*
Lee, Albert *WhoNeCM B [port]*
Lee, Alexis Anne 1956- *WhoAmW 91*
Lee, Alfred *OxCPMus*
Lee, Alice Saunders *BiDrAPA 89*
Lee, Alison Ann 1950- *WhoAmW 91*
Lee, Allan Wren 1924- *WhoAm 90, WhoSSW 91*
Lee, Alvin 1944- *EncPR&S 89*
Lee, Alvin A. 1930- *WhoAm 90*
Lee, Amalia F 1950- *BiDrAPA 89*
Lee, Amy 1945- *WhoEmL 91*
Lee, Amy Elaine 1960- *WhoAmW 91*
Lee, Amy Freeman 1914- *WhoAmA 91*
Lee, Amy Shiu 1947- *WhoAmW 91*
Lee, An-Shih *BiDrAPA 89*
Lee, Ana Rubi 1960- *WhoHisp 91*
Lee, Andrew *MajTwCW*
Lee, Andrew P. *BioIn 16*
Lee, Ann 1736-1784 *EncCRAm, WorAlBi*
Lee, Anne Natalie *WhoAmW 91, WhoSSW 91*
Lee, Anne S. *AuBYP 90*
Lee, Anthony Asa 1947- *WhoWrEP 89*
Lee, Arthur 1740-1792 *BioIn 16, EncCRAm*
Lee, Arthur 1881-1961 *WhoAmA 91N*
Lee, Arthur Virgil, III 1920- *WhoE 91*
Lee, Audrey *WhoWrEP 89*
Lee, Austin Paul *BiDrAPA 89*
Lee, B. Kyun 1952- *WhoSSW 91*
Lee, Barbara Marie 1955- *WhoEmL 91*
Lee, Benjamin 1933- *BiDrAPA 89*
Lee, Benny 1944- *St&PR 91*
Lee, Bernard J 1936- *BiDrAPA 89*
Lee, Bernard S. 1934- *St&PR 91*
Lee, Bernard Tunghao 1944- *WhoWor 91*
Lee, Bert 1881-1946 *OxCPMus*
Lee, Bertram M. *BioIn 16*
Lee, Bette Galloway 1927- *WhoSSW 91*
Lee, Betty Redding 1919- *WhoAm 90, WhoAmW 91, WhoSSW 91*
Lee, Beverly Ing 1932- *WhoAmW 91*
Lee, Bill 1909-1977 *Ballpl 90*
Lee, Bill 1946- *Ballpl 90*
Lee, Bob 1937- *Ballpl 90*
Lee, Bok Sin 1936- *WhoAmW 91, WhoSSW 91, WhoWor 91*
Lee, Bom Sang 1937- *BiDrAPA 89, WhoE 91*
Lee, Brenda 1944- *ConMus 5 [port], OxCPMus, WhoAmW 91*
Lee, Brenda 1945- *BioIn 16*
Lee, Brian Eugene 1943- *WhoWor 91*
Lee, Briant Hamor 1938- *WhoAmA 91*
Lee, Bruce 1940-1973 *BioIn 16*
Lee, Bum Yong 1944- *BiDrAPA 89*
Lee, Burns Wells 1913- *WhoAm 90*
Lee, Burton James, III 1930- *WhoAm 90*
Lee, Burtrand Insung 1952- *WhoSSW 91*
Lee, Byron, Jr. 1929- *St&PR 91, WhoAm 90*
Lee, Byung Hyun 1937- *WhoE 91*
Lee, Byung Kuk 1948- *WhoE 91*
Lee, Canada 1907-1952 *DrBlPA 90*
Lee, Candie Ching Wah 1950- *WhoWor 91*
Lee, Carl 1933-1986 *DrBlPA 90*
Lee, Carol Frances 1955- *WhoEmL 91*
Lee, Carol Mon 1947- *St&PR 91*
Lee, Caroline 1932- *BiDWomA*
Lee, Caroline D 1934- *WhoAmA 91*
Lee, Carolyn Beth 1949- *WhoE 91*
Lee, Carroll Russell 1949- *St&PR 91*
Lee, Catherine 1950- *WhoAmA 91*
Lee, Chang Rae 1946- *WhoSSW 91*
Lee, Charleme Esma 1949- *WhoAmW 91*
Lee, Charles 1731-1782 *WorAlBi*
Lee, Charles 1758-1815 *BiDrUSE 89*
Lee, Charles 1913- *WhoAm 90*
Lee, Charles H. 1927-1989 *BioIn 16*
Lee, Charles James 1925- *St&PR 91*
Lee, Charles Ray 1934- *WhoSSW 91*
Lee, Charles Robert 1939- *WhoAm 90, WhoE 91*
Lee, Chester Maurice 1919- *WhoAm 90*
Lee, Chester T. 1951- *St&PR 91*
Lee, Chi-Hung 1955- *WhoWor 91*
Lee, Chol John 1935- *BiDrAPA 89*
Lee, Chong-Sik 1931- *WhoAm 90*
Lee, Chong Suk 1935- *BiDrAPA 89*
Lee, Chong Taek 1940- *BiDrAPA 89*
Lee, Choong Hun 1943- *BiDrAPA 89*
Lee, Christopher 1922- *WorAlBi*
Lee, Christopher Choo Long 1948- *WhoWor 91*
Lee, Christopher Frank Carandini 1922- *WhoAm 90*
Lee, Chui-chun *WhoAmW 91*
Lee, Chun-Kyu *BiDrAPA 89*
Lee, Chung Ha 1939- *WhoWor 91*
Lee, Chung Kyoon 1929- *BiDrAPA 89, WhoWor 91*
Lee, Chungmin 1939- *WhoWor 91*
Lee, Clarence William 1931- *WhoE 91*
Lee, Clay F. *WhoAm 90*
Lee, Clement William Khan 1938- *WhoE 91, WhoWor 91*
Lee, Cliff 1896-1980 *Ballpl 90*
Lee, Clifford Leon, II 1957- *WhoSSW 91*
Lee, Clifton Edward 1944- *WhoSSW 91*
Lee, Connie Smith 1930- *WhoAmW 91*
Lee, Corinne Adams 1910- *WhoAmW 91*
Lee, Curtis Howard 1928- *WhoWor 91*
Lee, Cynthia Louise 1954- *WhoEmL 91*
Lee, D. William 1927- *St&PR 91*
Lee, Dai-Keong 1915- *WhoAm 90*
Lee, Dan M. 1926- *WhoAm 90*
Lee, Daniel Andrew 1951- *WhoEmL 91, WhoWor 91*
Lee, Daniel David 1941- *WhoWor 91*
Lee, Daniel Richard 1956- *WhoEmL 91*
Lee, Daniel Yong-geun 1954- *WhoE 91*
Lee, David Bailey 1944- *WhoE 91*
Lee, David Bierly 1937- *St&PR 91*
Lee, David C. 1930- *St&PR 91*
Lee, David D. 1934- *St&PR 91*
Lee, David G. 1948- *ODwPR 91*
Lee, David George 1947- *WhoEmL 91*
Lee, David Michael 1955- *WhoSSW 91*
Lee, David Raymond 1937- *WhoSSW 91*
Lee, David S. *BioIn 16*
Lee, David Sen-Lin 1937- *St&PR 91*
Lee, David Stoddart 1934- *St&PR 91, WhoAm 90*
Lee, David Wa K 1942- *BiDrAPA 89*
Lee, Denis *BioIn 16*
Lee, Dennis 1939- *ConAu 31NR*
Lee, Dennis Don *BiDrAPA 89*
Lee, Dennis Ean Hooi 1946- *IntWWM 90*
Lee, Diana *St&PR 91*
Lee, Diana Belinda 1953- *WhoAmW 91*
Lee, Diane B. 1954- *WhoEmL 91*
Lee, Dominic 1942- *WhoAm 90*
Lee, Don 1934- *Ballpl 90*
Lee, Don L. 1942- *DcLB DS8 [port]*
Lee, Dong-Mock *BiDrAPA 89*
Lee, Donna Anne *BiDrAPA 89*
Lee, Dora Fugh 1930- *WhoAmA 91*
Lee, Douglas *BiDrAPA 89*
Lee, Douglas Allen 1932- *IntWWM 90*
Lee, Douglas J *BiDrAPA 89*
Lee, Douglas K. *St&PR 91*
Lee, Drun-sun John 1944- *WhoE 91*
Lee, Duane Edward 1955- *WhoEmL 91*
Lee, Earl Victory 1929- *St&PR 91*
Lee, Edna Pritchard 1923- *WhoAmW 91*
Lee, Edward Brooke, Jr. 1917- *WhoWor 91*
Lee, Edward Chai 1935-1986 *BioIn 16*
Lee, Edward Yangung 1941- *BiDrAPA 89*
Lee, Eleanor 1896-1967 *BioIn 16*
Lee, Eleanor Gay *WhoAmA 91*
Lee, Eleanor M. 1931- *WhoAmW 91*
Lee, Eliza 1788?-1864 *FemiCLE*
Lee, Elizabeth Bobbitt 1928- *WhoAm 90, WhoAmW 91*
Lee, Elizabeth P 1957- *BiDrAPA 89*
Lee, Elizabeth Sosenheimer 1941- *WhoE 91*
Lee, Ellen Wardwell 1949- *WhoAmA 91*
Lee, Elmo S *BiDrAPA 89*
Lee, Eric M. 1949- *WhoEmL 91*
Lee, Eugene 1939- *ConDes 90*
Lee, Eugene Canfield 1924- *WhoAm 90*
Lee, Eugene Stanley 1930- *WhoAm 90*
Lee, Eui Yong 1943- *WhoE 91*
Lee, Eunie Shim 1948- *WhoEmL 91*
Lee, Evelyn Marie 1931- *WhoAmW 91*
Lee, Everett *DrBlPA 90*
Lee, Fitzhugh 1835-1905 *BioIn 16*
Lee, Frances Helen 1936- *WhoAmW 91, WhoE 91*
Lee, Francis Lightfoot 1734-1797 *EncCRAm, WorAlBi*
Lee, Francis Wilson 1927- *WhoE 91*
Lee, Franne 1941- *BioIn 16, NotWoAT*
Lee, Frederick Yuk Leong 1937- *WhoAm 90, WhoSSW 91, WhoWor 91*
Lee, Gabriel *NewAgMG*
Lee, Gary A. 1933- *WhoAm 90*
Lee, Gary Albert 1941- *WhoAm 90*
Lee, Gary Alcide 1933- *St&PR 91*
Lee, Gary Edward 1951- *St&PR 91*
Lee, Gary M 1927- *BiDrAPA 89*
Lee, Gene F. 1960- *WhoE 91*
Lee, Genevieve Bruggeman 1928- *WhoE 91*
Lee, George C. 1933- *WhoAm 90*
Lee, George J 1919-1976 *WhoAmA 91N*
Lee, George L., III 1956- *St&PR 91*
Lee, George Ludlow, Jr. 1926- *St&PR 91*
Lee, George Oscar 1930- *St&PR 91*
Lee, Georgia Mason 1923- *BiDrAPA 89*
Lee, Geraldine *WhoAmA 91*
Lee, Gil Sik 1953- *WhoSSW 91*
Lee, Gilbert Brooks 1913- *WhoWor 91*
Lee, Gilbert Lamont, Jr. 1919- *WhoAm 90*
Lee, Glen K. 1950- *WhoWor 91*
Lee, Glenn Richard 1932- *WhoAm 90*
Lee, Graves Simcoe 1828-1912 *OxCCanT*
Lee, Griff Calicutt 1926- *WhoAm 90*
Lee, Gypsy Rose *BioIn 16*
Lee, Gypsy Rose 1914-1970 *BioAmW, FemiCLE, NotWoAT, WorAlBi*
Lee, Hal 1905- *Ballpl 90*
Lee, Hamilton Hangtao 1921- *WhoE 91, WhoWor 91, WhoWrEP 89*
Lee, Han Jun 1946- *BiDrAPA 89*
Lee, Han Soo *BiDrAPA 89*
Lee, Hanheugn *BiDrAPA 89*
Lee, Hannah Farnham 1780-1865 *FemiCLE*
Lee, Harley Clyde 1901- *WhoAm 90*
Lee, Harold Philip 1944- *St&PR 91*
Lee, Harper 1926- *ConLC 60 [port], MajTwCW, WorAlBi*
Lee, Harriet 1757-1851 *BioIn 16, FemiCLE*
Lee, Helen Shores *BioIn 16*
Lee, Henry 1756-1818 *EncCRAm, WorAlBi*
Lee, Henry Lawrence, Jr. 1926- *St&PR 91*
Lee, Heo-Peh 1931- *WhoE 91*
Lee, Hi Bahl 1942- *WhoWor 91*
Lee, Ho Young 1932- *BiDrAPA 89*
Lee, Holme 1828-1900 *FemiCLE*
Lee, Hong Koo *BioIn 16*
Lee, Honkon 1920- *WhoWor 91*
Lee, Hope K. W. 1953- *IntWWM 90*
Lee, Howard 1925- *St&PR 91*
Lee, Howard Douglas 1943- *WhoAm 90*
Lee, Hwa-Wei 1933- *WhoAm 90*
Lee, Hye-ku 1909- *IntWWM 90*
Lee, Hyun-Chae 1929- *WhoWor 91*
Lee, Hyung Kon 1939- *BiDrAPA 89*
Lee, Hyung Mo 1926- *WhoAm 90*
Lee, I-Min 1960- *WhoEmL 91*
Lee, Ik-Hwan 1943- *WhoWor 91*
Lee, In Woo 1931- *BiDrAPA 89*
Lee, Isaiah Chong-Pie 1934- *WhoAm 90*
Lee, Ivy *BioIn 16*
Lee, J. Daniel, Jr. 1938- *WhoAm 90*
Lee, J. Terrence 1942- *St&PR 91*
Lee, Jack 1936- *WhoAm 90*
Lee, Jae Seung 1947- *BiDrAPA 89*
Lee, Jaedu 1936- *BiDrAPA 89*
Lee, James A. 1939- *St&PR 91*
Lee, James Arthur 1940- *BiDrAPA 89*
Lee, James Bernard 1927- *St&PR 91*
Lee, James Douglas *BiDrAPA 89*
Lee, James E. 1932- *St&PR 91*
Lee, James Forrest 1951- *WhoEmL 91*
Lee, James Gillis 1927- *WhoAm 90*
Lee, James H., Jr. 1920- *WhoE 91*
Lee, James Harvey, III 1947- *St&PR 91*
Lee, James Matthew 1937- *WhoAm 90*
Lee, James Michael 1931- *ConAu 30NR, WhoAm 90*
Lee, James Monroe 1941- *BiDrAPA 89*
Lee, James Robert 1938- *St&PR 91*
Lee, James Roger 1947- *WhoEmL 91*
Lee, Jane Tennyson 1954- *St&PR 91*
Lee, Janet Hyosoon *BiDrAPA 89*
Lee, Janet Washburn 1955- *WhoAmW 91*
Lee, Janie C 1937- *WhoAmA 91*
Lee, Janis 1945- *WhoAmW 91*
Lee, Jarena 1783-1837? *FemiCLE*
Lee, Jason 1803-1845 *WhNaAH*
Lee, Jason Davis 1949- *WhoEmL 91, WhoWor 91*
Lee, Jay Wook 1944- *BiDrAPA 89*
Lee, Jean Childress *BioIn 16*
Lee, Jeanne Kit Yew 1959- *WhoAmW 91*
Lee, Jennie 1904-1988 *AnObit 1988, BioIn 16*
Lee, Jerome G. 1924- *WhoAm 90*
Lee, Jimmy Che-Yung 1946- *WhoSSW 91*
Lee, Jimmy Ray 1957- *WhoSSW 91*
Lee, Jisoon 1949- *WhoWor 91*
Lee, Joan Winifred 1933- *WhoE 91*
Lee, Joe R. 1940- *WhoAm 90*
Lee, Joel Marvin 1949- *WhoEmL 91*
Lee, Joel Michael 1946- *WhoEmL 91*
Lee, John 1949- *ODwPR 91*
Lee, John Busteed 1951- *WhoWrEP 89*
Lee, John Chonghoon 1928- *WhoE 91*
Lee, John D. 1943- *St&PR 91*
Lee, John Doyle 1812-1877 *BioIn 16*
Lee, John Edward, Jr. 1933- *WhoE 91*
Lee, John Francis 1918- *WhoAm 90*
Lee, John Franklin 1927- *WhoAm 90, WhoWor 91*
Lee, John Glessner 1898-1988 *BioIn 16*
Lee, John Jin 1948- *WhoAm 90*
Lee, John Jongjin 1933- *WhoE 91*
Lee, John Joseph *BiDrAPA 89*
Lee, John Michael 1932- *WhoWor 91*
Lee, Johnie Clifton 1923- *WhoSSW 91*
Lee, Johnson Y. 1955- *WhoWor 91*
Lee, Jonas Phillip 1966- *WhoE 91*
Lee, Jonathan O. 1951- *St&PR 91*
Lee, Jonathan Owen 1951- *WhoE 91*
Lee, Jonathon *NewAgMG*
Lee, Jong Hyuk 1941- *WhoWor 91*
Lee, Jong Sung 1939- *BiDrAPA 89*
Lee, Jordan Tzeng-Horng 1956- *WhoEmL 91, WhoWor 91*
Lee, Joseph Chuen Kwun 1938- *WhoWor 91*
Lee, Joseph David 1938- *St&PR 91*
Lee, Joseph Finley, Jr. *WhoAm 90*
Lee, Joseph Henry *BiDrAPA 89*
Lee, Joseph Smith *OxCCanT*
Lee, Joseph Taylor 1925- *St&PR 91*

Lee, Joseph William 1943- St&PR 91, WhoE 91
Lee, Joyce Everson BiDrAPA 89
Lee, Joyce Marie 1954- WhoSSW 91
Lee, Judith C. 1936- WhoAmW 91
Lee, Julian AuBYP 90
Lee, Julie ODwPR 91
Lee, June Warren 1952- WhoAmW 91
Lee, Jung Ja WhoAmW 91
Lee, Jung-Koo 1939- WhoWor 91
Lee, Jungsoon Kim 1956- WhoEmL 91
Lee, Kam Shing 1947- WhoWor 91
Lee, Karl Olsen St&PR 91
Lee, Katherine Ann 1947- WhoAmW 91
Lee, Kathleen Mary 1948- WhoSSW 91
Lee, Kathryn Adele Bunding 1949- WhoAmW 91
Lee, Kathy 1949- St&PR 91
Lee, Keith Alan 1957- WhoEmL 91
Lee, Kenneth Amos 1948- BiDrAPA 89
Lee, Kenneth Duane 1949- St&PR 91
Lee, Kenneth Stuart 1955- WhoSSW 91
Lee, Kermit James, Jr. 1934- WhoAm 90
Lee, Keun Sok 1954- WhoE 91
Lee, Kimun 1946- WhoEmL 91
Lee, Kinson 1935- BiDrAPA 89
Lee, Kiwhang K BiDrAPA 89
Lee, Kok Wai 1945- BiDrAPA 89
Lee, Kristine Snyder 1952- WhoEmL 91
Lee, Kwang 1941- St&PR 91
Lee, Kwang Soo 1941- BiDrAPA 89
Lee, Kyung Hui 1948- BiDrAPA 89
Lee, Kyung-Wook 1929- WhoWor 91
Lee, L. Edgar BiDrAPA 89
Lee, Lance 1942- WhoWrEP 89
Lee, Larry ConAu 131
Lee, Larry 1942-1990 BioIn 16
Lee, Laurence Raymond 1928- WhoAm 90
Lee, Laurie 1914- ConAu 33NR, MajTwCW
Lee, Lawrence 1941-1990 ConAu 131
Lee, Lawrence Michael 1949- WhoE 91
Lee, Lawrence W. BioIn 16
Lee, Lawrence W. 1938- St&PR 91
Lee, Lawrence Winston 1938- WhoAm 90
Lee, Leo Ou-fan 1939- WhoAm 90
Lee, Leron 1948- Ballpl 90
Lee, Leslie 1935?- DrBlPA 90
Lee, Lester L. 1933- St&PR 91
Lee, Lester Wade 1951- WhoSSW 91
Lee, Li-Young 1957- BioIn 16
Lee, Lillian Vanessa 1951- WhoE 91
Lee, Lily Kiang 1946- WhoAmW 91, WhoEmL 91
Lee, Linda Diane 1956- WhoSSW 91
Lee, Linda Hope WhoWrEP 89
Lee, Linda M. ODwPR 91
Lee, Linda Mae 1948- WhoE 91
Lee, Low Kee 1916- WhoAm 90
Lee, Lucille 1942- WhoAmW 91
Lee, Lydia 1944- WhoWrEP 89
Lee, Lynda Mills 1944- WhoAmW 91
Lee, Maggie Virginia 1941- WhoAmW 91
Lee, Manfred B. TwCCr&M 91
Lee, Manfred B 1905-1971 AuBYP 90
Lee, Manny 1965- Ballpl 90, WhoHisp 91
Lee, Margaret Anne 1930- WhoAmW 91, WhoWor 91
Lee, Margaret F 1922- WhoAmA 91
Lee, Margaret Norma 1928- WhoAmW 91
Lee, Margaret Z. BioIn 16
Lee, Marianne Hollingsworth 1930- WhoAmW 91
Lee, Marietta Y.W.T. 1943- WhoAmW 91
Lee, Marjorie Hembree 1946- IntWWM 90
Lee, Mark 1953- Ballpl 90
Lee, Mark Richard 1949- WhoEmL 91
Lee, Martin 1923- St&PR 91
Lee, Marva Jean 1938- WhoAmW 91
Lee, Marvin William 1925- WhoSSW 91
Lee, Mary 1934- AuBYP 90
Lee, Mary Elizabeth 1813-1849 FemiCLE
Lee, Mary Wyant BioIn 16
Lee, Maryat BioIn 16
Lee, Maryat 1923-1989 ConAu 129
Lee, Matt ConAu 131
Lee, Maurice, Jr. 1925- WhoWrEP 89
Lee, May Dean-Ming Lu 1949- WhoAmW 91
Lee, Michael BioIn 16
Lee, Michael Brooks 1946- WhoSSW 91
Lee, Michael Charles 1948- WhoEmL 91
Lee, Michel Carla 1958- WhoEmL 91
Lee, Michele BioIn 16
Lee, Michele 1942- WhoAm 90, WhoAmW 91, WorAlBi
Lee, Michelle 1952- IntWWM 90
Lee, Mildred 1908- AuBYP 90, SmATA 12AS [port]
Lee, Milton 1931- BiDrAPA 89
Lee, Ming Cho BioIn 16
Lee, Ming Cho 1930- ConDes 90, IntWWM 90, WhoAm 90, WhoWor 91
Lee, Miranda 1952- WhoAmW 91
Lee, Moon Chin BiDrAPA 89
Lee, Murlin E. 1957- WhoEmL 91, WhoWor 91
Lee, Myoung S Moon 1929- BiDrAPA 89
Lee, Myoung Sun Moon 1929- WhoE 91
Lee, Myung Ae BiDrAPA 89
Lee, Myung Bak 1941- WhoWor 91
Lee, Nancy Ellen 1944- WhoAmW 91
Lee, Naomi Pearl 1948- WhoAmW 91
Lee, Nelda S. 1941- WhoAm 90, WhoAmA 91, WhoAmW 91
Lee, Noel 1924- IntWWM 90
Lee, Norma E. 1924- AuBYP 90
Lee, Norman Hubbard 1929- St&PR 91
Lee, Norman W. BioIn 16
Lee, Ock-Bum 1934- BiDrAPA 89
Lee, Ok-Rhyun BiDrAPA 89
Lee, Oscar 1953- WhoEmL 91
Lee, Pali Jae 1929- ConAu 31NR
Lee, Pamela Anne 1960- WhoAmW 91
Lee, Patricia Ann 1939- WhoAmW 91
Lee, Patricia Hureston 1957- WhoEmL 91
Lee, Patricia Taylor 1936- IntWWM 90
Lee, Patrick P. 1938- St&PR 91
Lee, Patrick Paul 1938- WhoE 91
Lee, Paul D. 1942- St&PR 91
Lee, Paul King-lung 1942- WhoE 91
Lee, Paul M. ODwPR 91
Lee, Paul P. 1960- WhoEmL 91
Lee, Peggy BioIn 16
Lee, Peggy 1920- OxCPMus, WorAlBi
Lee, Peter Bernard 1959- WhoE 91, WhoEmL 91
Lee, Peter James 1938- WhoAm 90, WhoSSW 91
Lee, Phillip WhoE 91
Lee, Phillip Dukeal Kwaiyuen 1956- WhoEmL 91
Lee, Polly Jae ConAu 31NR
Lee, R. Marilyn WhoAmW 91
Lee, R. William, Jr. 1930- St&PR 91
Lee, Ramona Carmen 1959- WhoAmW 91
Lee, Raymond William, III 1960- WhoEmL 91
Lee, Raymond William, Jr. 1930- WhoAm 90
Lee, Renee McEntire 1949- WhoAmW 91
Lee, Rensselaer Wright 1898-1984 WhoAmA 91N
Lee, Rex E. 1935- BioIn 16, WhoAm 90
Lee, Richard Bland 1761-1827 BioIn 16
Lee, Richard Cavett 1951- WhoEmL 91
Lee, Richard D. 1940- St&PR 91
Lee, Richard H BiDrAPA 89
Lee, Richard Harlo 1947- WhoEmL 91, WhoWor 91
Lee, Richard Henry 1732-1794 BiDrUSE 89, BioIn 16, WorAlBi
Lee, Richard Henry 1734-1794 EncCRAm
Lee, Richard Joseph 1954- WhoE 91
Lee, Richard Laurence 1946- St&PR 91
Lee, Richard Vaille 1937- WhoAm 90
Lee, Richard Vincent 1924- WhoSSW 91
Lee, Riley NewAgMG
Lee, Robert BiDrAPA 89
Lee, Robert 1929- WhoAm 90
Lee, Robert 1933- St&PR 91
Lee, Robert 1948- WhoAm 90
Lee, Robert Alan 1951- WhoEmL 91
Lee, Robert Bumjung 1937- WhoAm 90
Lee, Robert C. 1931- AuBYP 90
Lee, Robert Charles, Sr. 1936- WhoSSW 91
Lee, Robert E. 1807-1870 BioIn 16, WorAlBi
Lee, Robert E. 1912- WhoAm 90
Lee, Robert E.A. 1921- WhoWrEP 89
Lee, Robert Earl 1928- WhoAm 90
Lee, Robert Edward, Jr. 1941- WhoE 91
Lee, Robert Edwin 1918- WhoAm 90
Lee, Robert Emil 1926- WhoSSW 91
Lee, Robert Erich 1955- WhoEmL 91
Lee, Robert Erwin, Jr. 1940- St&PR 91
Lee, Robert Greene 1886-1978 BioIn 16
Lee, Robert J 1921- WhoAmA 91
Lee, Robert J.E. 1933- St&PR 91
Lee, Robert John 1929- WhoAm 90
Lee, Robert Justin 1945- WhoSSW 91
Lee, Robert M 1933- WhoAmA 91
Lee, Robert Sanford 1924- WhoAm 90
Lee, Robert Wesley 1928- St&PR 91
Lee, Roger 1942- WhoAmA 91
Lee, Roger Bing 1941- WhoAm 90
Lee, Roland V. St&PR 91
Lee, Ronald Barry 1932- WhoAm 90
Lee, Ronald Bruce 1952- WhoEmL 91
Lee, Ronald D. 1948- St&PR 91
Lee, Ronald George 1952- St&PR 91
Lee, Rosalyn Shen 1927- WhoE 91
Lee, Rosann Teller BioIn 16
Lee, Roy AuBYP 90, ConAu 129
Lee, Roy Noble 1915- WhoAm 90, WhoSSW 91
Lee, Ruben 1955- WhoHisp 91
Lee, Russell BioIn 16
Lee, Russell W 1903-1986 WhoAmA 91N
Lee, Ruth Mikkelson 1936- WhoAmW 91
Lee, Sally AuBYP 90
Lee, Sam Min 1938- BiDrAPA 89
Lee, Sammie French 1928- WhoAm 90
Lee, Sammy 1920- BioIn 16
Lee, Sammy, I 1920- WhoAm 90
Lee, Samuel C. 1909- St&PR 91
Lee, Samuel Dennis 1958- WhoE 91
Lee, Samuel J. AmLegL
Lee, Sandra Margaret 1957- WhoEmL 91, WhoSSW 91
Lee, Sang Moon 1939- WhoAm 90
Lee, Sang Oug BiDrAPA 89
Lee, Sara Ward 1941- WhoSSW 91
Lee, Sarah Tomerlin WhoAm 90
Lee, Sean F. 1940- St&PR 91
Lee, Seok Yoon 1938- BiDrAPA 89
Lee, Shayna Patrice 1958- BiDrAPA 89
Lee, Shepard 1926- St&PR 91
Lee, Sherman Emery 1918- WhoAm 90, WhoAmA 91
Lee, Shew Kuhn 1923- WhoWor 91
Lee, Shih-Ying 1918- WhoAm 90
Lee, Shin Jae BiDrAPA 89
Lee, Shin Young 1945- BiDrAPA 89
Lee, Shou-Dong 1946- WhoWor 91
Lee, Si Hyung 1934- BiDrAPA 89
Lee, Sidney 1859-1926 BioIn 16
Lee, Sidney P. 1920- St&PR 91
Lee, Sidney Phillip 1920- WhoAm 90
Lee, Sidney Reaves 1941- BiDrAPA 89
Lee, Sidney Seymour 1921- WhoAm 90
Lee, Silas, III 1954- WhoSSW 91
Lee, So Hee 1942- BiDrAPA 89
Lee, Song-Ho 1926- WhoWor 91
Lee, Soong Hyun 1938- BiDrAPA 89
Lee, Sophia 1750-1824 BioIn 16, FemiCLE
Lee, Spike BioIn 16
Lee, Spike 1957- DrBlPA 90, WhoAm 90
Lee, St. George Tucker 1946- WhoSSW 91
Lee, Stan BioIn 16
Lee, Stan 1922- Au&Arts 5 [port], EncACom
Lee, Stanley 1919- WhoAm 90
Lee, Stephen Erwin 1953- BiDrAPA 89
Lee, Stephen F. ODwPR 91
Lee, Stephen Sheng-hao 1945- WhoEmL 91
Lee, Steven 1950- WhoE 91
Lee, Steven Franklin 1948- WhoSSW 91
Lee, Steven Richard 1952- BiDrAPA 89
Lee, Sul Hi 1936- WhoAm 90
Lee, Sun-Ock 1943- WhoE 91
Lee, Sung Ho 1934- BiDrAPA 89
Lee, Sung-Sook 1948- IntWWM 90
Lee, Susan 1943- WhoAmW 91
Lee, Susan Previant 1948- WhoAmW 91
Lee, Suzanne Bosen BiDrAPA 89
Lee, Tae-Ahn 1943- BiDrAPA 89
Lee, Tanya Hayes 1947- WhoEmL 91
Lee, Teng-hui BioIn 16
Lee, Terrance H.M. 1940- St&PR 91
Lee, Terry Git BiDrAPA 89
Lee, Thai T. 1958- St&PR 91
Lee, Thomas B. 1925- St&PR 91
Lee, Thomas Donovan 1955- BiDrAPA 89
Lee, Thomas F. 1947- WhoE 91
Lee, Thomas Henry 1923- WhoAm 90
Lee, Thomas Joseph, Jr. 1921- WhoAm 90
Lee, Thomas Oboe 1945- IntWWM 90
Lee, Thomas Patrick 1938- St&PR 91
Lee, Thomas Roy 1955- WhoWrEP 89
Lee, Thomas Way 1943- WhoWor 91
Lee, Thornton 1906- Ballpl 90
Lee, Tien Pei 1933- WhoAm 90
Lee, Timothy Earl 1947- WhoWor 91
Lee, Timothy Guy 1939- WhoAm 90
Lee, Tom Stewart 1941- WhoSSW 91
Lee, Tong Hun 1931- WhoAm 90
Lee, Tonia Renee 1963- WhoAmW 91, WhoSSW 91, WhoWor 91
Lee, Tony Chung 1963- WhoEmL 91
Lee, Tsung-Dao 1926- WhoAm 90, WhoE 91, WhoWor 91, WorAlBi
Lee, Tsyr-Hsioung 1956- WhoWor 91
Lee, Tunney F. 1931- WhoAm 90
Lee, Vernon 1856-1935 BioIn 16, FemiCLE
Lee, Vicki 1944- WhoAmW 91
Lee, Victoria BiDrAPA 89
Lee, W. Douglass BioIn 16
Lee, W.S. 1929- St&PR 91
Lee, Wallace Williams, Jr. 1915- WhoAm 90
Lee, Walter Hisung 1932- BiDrAPA 89
Lee, Walter John BioIn 16
Lee, Warner ConAu 30NR
Lee, Watty 1879-1936 Ballpl 90
Lee, Wayne 1945- St&PR 91
Lee, Wayne Floyd 1952- St&PR 91
Lee, Wesley D. St&PR 91
Lee, William MajTwCW
Lee, William 1739-1795 EncCRAm
Lee, William Anthony 1946- St&PR 91
Lee, William Charles 1938- WhoAm 90
Lee, William Chien-Yeh 1932- WhoAm 90
Lee, William David 1944- WhoWrEP 89
Lee, William David 1947- WhoSSW 91
Lee, William Edwin 1852-1920 AmLegL
Lee, William Franklin 1929- IntWWM 90
Lee, William Franklin, III 1929- WhoAm 90
Lee, William Henry 1946- WhoEmL 91
Lee, William I. 1952- St&PR 91
Lee, William James 1922- WhoAm 90
Lee, William Marshall 1922- WhoAm 90, WhoWor 91
Lee, William S. BioIn 16
Lee, William States 1929- WhoAm 90, WhoSSW 91
Lee, William T. 1934- WhoWor 91
Lee, Willy MajTwCW
Lee, Wing-Ki BiDrAPA 89
Lee, Won Jay 1938- WhoE 91
Lee, Woon Soon 1934- BiDrAPA 89
Lee, Yasyn BiDrAPA 89
Lee, Yien-Hwei 1937- WhoE 91, WhoWor 91
Lee, Yong-Kak 1924- WhoWor 91
Lee, Young Kil 1937- BiDrAPA 89
Lee, Young W. 1941- St&PR 91
Lee, Young Yong 1939- BiDrAPA 89
Lee, Yuan T. 1936- WorAlBi
Lee, Yuan Tseh 1936- WhoAm 90, WhoWor 91
Lee, Yuan-Yuan 1950- IntWWM 90
Lee, Yung-Keun 1929- WhoAm 90
Lee, Yvonne A. 1933- St&PR 91
Lee, Yvonne Alberta 1933- WhoAm 90
Lee, Zuk-Nae 1940- WhoWor 91
Lee Chuy, Ismael Chan 1953- BiDrAPA 89
Lee-Dukes, Gwendolyn 1945- BiDrAPA 89
Lee-Hostetler, Jeri 1940- SmATA 63
Lee-Mann, Allison Ann 1957- WhoAmW 91
Lee-McDonald, Cynthia Ann 1954- WhoAmW 91
Lee-Miller, Stephanie 1950- WhoAm 90
Lee-Sissom, E 1934- WhoAmA 91
Lee Six, Abigail 1960- ConAu 132
Lee-Smith, Diana 1940- WomArch [port]
Lee-Smith, Hughie 1915- WhoAm 90, WhoAmA 91
Lee-Sweeney, Judy ODwPR 91
Leeb, Burton O. 1935-1989 BioIn 16
Leeb, Charles Samuel 1945- WhoWor 91
Leeb, Franz 1950- WhoWor 91
Leebens, Patricia Kay 1951- BiDrAPA 89
Leeber, Sharon Corgan 1940- WhoAmA 91
Leeby, L.R. St&PR 91
Leece, William Joseph WhoWrEP 89
Leech, Alan Bruce 1944- IntWWM 90
Leech, Bertram G. 1926- St&PR 91
Leech, Charles Russell, Jr. 1930- WhoAm 90
Leech, Hilton 1906-1969 WhoAmA 91N
Leech, James William 1947- St&PR 91, WhoAm 90
Leech, Margaret 1893-1974 BioIn 16
Leech, Noyes Elwood 1921- WhoAm 90
Leech, Peter John 1828?-1899 DcCanB 12
Leech, Richard BioIn 16
Leech, Robert Milton 1921- WhoAm 90
Leech, Robin BioIn 16
Leecing, Walden Albert 1932- WhoWor 91
Leed, Carol Ann 1949- WhoE 91
Leeder, Ellen Lismore 1931- WhoAmW 91
Leedom, E. Paul 1925- St&PR 91
Leedom, John Nesbett 1921- St&PR 91, WhoSSW 91
Leedom-Ackerman, Joanne 1947- WhoWrEP 89
Leeds, Annette WhoAmA 91
Leeds, Candace ODwPR 91
Leeds, Douglas B. 1947- St&PR 91
Leeds, Elizabeth Louise 1925- WhoAmW 91
Leeds, Harold Eliot 1919- ConDes 90
Leeds, Kenneth Warren 1940- St&PR 91
Leeds, Laurence Carroll, Jr. 1929- St&PR 91
Leeds, M Frederick 1916- BiDrAPA 89
Leeds, Mark ODwPR 91
Leeds, Michael Eric 1959- WhoEmL 91
Leeds, Nancy Brecker 1924- WhoAmW 91, WhoWor 91
Leeds, Oliver BioIn 16
Leeds, Paul BiDrAPA 89
Leeds, Robert 1930- WhoSSW 91
Leeds, Robert Lewis, Jr. 1930- WhoAm 90, WhoSSW 91
Leeds, Robert X. 1927- WhoWrEP 89
Leeds, Ronald P.E. 1939- St&PR 91
Leeds, Steven David 1950- WhoE 91
Leedskalnin, Edward 1887-1951 MusmAFA
Leedy, Daniel Loney 1912- WhoAm 90
Leedy, Douglas 1938- IntWWM 90
Leedy, Emily L. Foster 1921- WhoAmW 91
Leedy, Harold Walter 1947- St&PR 91
Leedy, Jack J BiDrAPA 89
Leedy, Loreen 1959- BioIn 16
Leedy, R. Allan, Jr. 1942- St&PR 91
Leedy, Robert Allan 1909- WhoAm 90
Leef, Audrey V. 1922- WhoAmW 91
Leef, Yinam Arie 1953- IntWWM 90
Leefe, James Morrison 1921- WhoAm 90
Leegant, Jo Anne 1946- WhoEmL 91
Leege, David Calhoun 1937- WhoAm 90
Leehey, Kevin John 1953- BiDrAPA 89
Leehey, Patrick 1921- WhoAm 90
Leek, Jay Wilbur 1928- WhoSSW 91, WhoWor 91
Leek, Margaret TwCCr&M 91
Leek, Sybil 1923-1982 EncPaPR 91

Leek, Sybil 1923-1983 *EncO&P 3*
Leeke, David 1957- *IntWWM 90*
Leekley, John Robert 1943- *WhoAm 90*
Leekley, Thomas Briggs 1910- *AuBYP 90*
Leeks, Raymond C.F. 1941- *St&PR 91*
Leeks, Raymond Charles Frank 1941- *WhoAm 90*
Leeman, Cavin P 1932- *BiDrAPA 89*
Leeman, Cavin Philip 1932- *WhoE 91*
Leeman, Eve *BiDrAPA 89*
Leeman, Galan E. 1937- *St&PR 91*
Leeman, Sharon Lynn 1956- *WhoAmW 91*
Leemhuis, John P. 1930- *St&PR 91*
Leeming, David John 1939- *WhoWor 91*
Leeming, E. Janice 1941- *WhoAmW 91*
Leeming, Joseph 1897-1968 *AuBYP 90*
Leen, Jerry *BioIn 16*
Leen, Steven 1956- *St&PR 91*
Leen, Todd Kevin 1955- *WhoEmL 91*
Leenders, Antoon G. 1939- *WhoWor 91*
Leener, Jack Joseph 1926- *WhoAm 90*
Leeney, Robert Joseph 1916- *WhoAm 90*
Leenhouts, Lillian Scott 1911- *WhoAm 90*
Leep, J. Roger 1943- *St&PR 91*
Leepa, Allen 1919- *WhoAm 90*, *WhoAmA 91*
Leeper, Charles Kendal 1923- *WhoAm 90*
Leeper, David R. 1939- *ODwPR 91*
Leeper, Doris Marie 1929- *WhoAmA 91*
Leeper, James Malone 1935- *St&PR 91*
Leeper, John Palmer 1921- *WhoAmA 91*
Leeper, John Richard 1948- *St&PR 91*
Leeper, Michael Edward 1917- *WhoAm 90*
Leeper, Patti *WhoWrEP 89*
Leeper, Ramon Joe 1948- *WhoEmL 91*, *WhoWor 91*
Leeper, Zane H. 1922- *WhoSSW 91*
Leer, Mary Kelley 1950- *WhoEmL 91*
Lees, Alan Barnhart 1926- *St&PR 91*
Lees, Benjamin 1924- *PenDiMP A*, *WhoAm 90*
Lees, Brian Paul 1953- *WhoE 91*
Lees, Carlton B. *BioIn 16*
Lees, Christine Brown 1943- *IntWWM 90*
Lees, David Bryan 1936- *WhoWor 91*
Lees, Francis Anthony 1931- *WhoAm 90*
Lees, George R. 1926- *St&PR 91*
Lees, Harry Hanson *WhoAmA 91N*
Lees, James Edward 1939- *WhoAm 90*
Lees, James Morgan 1943- *BiDrAPA 89*
Lees, Joseph Edward 1953- *WhoEmL 91*
Lees, Martin Henry 1929- *WhoAm 90*
Lees, Robert 1849-1931 *EncPaPR 91*
Lees, Robert H. 1952- *St&PR 91*
Lees, Robert James *EncO&P 3*
Lees, Sidney 1917- *WhoAm 90*
Lees, William A., Jr. 1931- *St&PR 91*, *WhoAm 90*
Lees-Milne, James *BioIn 16*
Lees-Milne, James 1908- *ConAu 31NR*
Leese, Laverne L. 1946- *St&PR 91*
Leese, Marianne Brod 1945- *WhoE 91*
Leese, Oliver 1894-1978 *BioIn 16*
Leeseberg, Hugh Scott 1929- *St&PR 91*
Leeseberg, Norbert H. 1930- *WhoE 91*
Leeser, Isaac 1806-1868 *BioIn 16*
Leeser, Mario Rafael 1953- *WhoWor 91*
Leeson, Cecil 1902-1989 *BioIn 16*
Leeson, Charles Roland 1926- *WhoAm 90*
Leeson, David B. 1937- *St&PR 91*
Leeson, Derrick Raymond 1918- *WhoWor 91*
Leeson, Janet Caroline Tollefson 1933- *WhoAmW 91*
Leeson, Lorraine 1951- *BiDWomA*
Leeson, Muriel 1920- *BioIn 16*
Leeson, Robert, Jr. 1932- *St&PR 91*, *WhoE 91*
Leeson, Tom 1945- *WhoAmA 91*
Leestma, Robert 1927- *WhoAm 90*
Leet, Marcelle D 1948- *BiDrAPA 89*
Leet, Mildred Robbins 1922- *WhoAm 90*, *WhoAmW 91*, *WhoWor 91*
Leet, Richard Eugene 1936- *WhoAmA 91*
Leet, Richard Hale 1926- *St&PR 91*, *WhoAm 90*
Leetaru, Ilse 1915- *WhoAmA 91*, *WhoWor 91*
Leetch, Brian *BioIn 16*
Leete, David Douglas 1958- *WhoWor 91*
Leete, Edward 1928- *WhoAm 90*
Leete, William White 1929- *WhoAm 90*, *WhoAmA 91*
Leeth, Dan Steven 1949- *WhoEmL 91*
Leetham, Michelle Munz 1957- *WhoEmL 91*
Leeti, John Alfred 1926- *St&PR 91*
Leets, Peter John 1946- *WhoAm 90*, *WhoWor 91*
Leetz, Kenneth L 1955- *BiDrAPA 89*
Leetzow, Leonard E. 1938- *WhoSSW 91*
Leeuw, Johanna Engelberta vanLohuizen-De 1919-1983 *BioIn 16*
Leeuwenhoek, Anton Van 1632-1723 *WorAlBi*
Leever, Harold 1914- *St&PR 91*, *WhoAm 90*
Leever, Sam 1871-1953 *Ballpl 90*
Leeves, Jane Ann *BiDrAPA 89*
Leevy, Carroll Moton 1920- *WhoAm 90*
Lefald, Sidney Clark 1947- *BiDrAPA 89*
Le Fan, Jack M. 1927- *St&PR 91*
Lefanu, Alicia 1795?-1826? *FemiCLE*
Le Fanu, Joseph Sheridan 1814-1873 *BioIn 16*
LeFanu, Joseph Sheridan 1814-1873 *BioIn 16*
Le Fanu, Joseph Sheridan 1814-1873 *WorAlBi*
Lefanu, Nicola Frances 1947- *IntWWM 90*
Le Fanu, Sheridan 1814-1873 *TwCCr&M 91A*
Lefcourt, Irwin 1910- *WhoAmA 91*
Lefcowitz, Barbara F. 1935- *WhoWrEP 89*
Lefeber, Edward James 1911- *WhoSSW 91*
Lefebre, John 1905-1986 *WhoAmA 91N*
Lefebure, Francis 1916- *EncO&P 3*
Le Febure, Francois *PenDiDA 89*
Lefebure, Molly *AuBYP 90*
Lefebvre, Arthur Henry 1923- *WhoAm 90*
Lefebvre, Camille 1831-1895 *DcCanB 12*
Lefebvre, Claude 1931- *IntWWM 90*
Lefebvre, Diane Louise 1961- *WhoEmL 91*
Le Febvre, Francois *PenDiDA 89*
Lefebvre, Gabriel Felicien 1932- *WhoAm 90*
Lefebvre, James Kenneth 1943- *WhoAm 90*
Lefebvre, Jean Pierre *BioIn 16*
Lefebvre, Jim 1943- *Ballpl 90*
Lefebvre, Joe 1956- *Ballpl 90*
Lefebvre, Marcel *BioIn 16*
Lefebvre, Marcel 1905- *WorAlBi*
Lefebvre, Paul 1925- *BiDrAPA 89*
Lefebvre, Thomas Henri 1927- *WhoAm 90*
Lefebvre, William Joseph 1949- *WhoE 91*
Lefebvre D'Argence, Rene-Yvon 1928- *WhoAmA 91*
Lefeld, Al 1959- *St&PR 91*
Lefer, Allan Mark 1936- *WhoAm 90*
Lefer, Gary Lee *BiDrAPA 89*
Lefer, Jay *BiDrAPA 89*
Lefer, Jay 1930- *WhoE 91*
Lefer, Leon 1921- *BiDrAPA 89*
Lefer, Lewis Gary 1943- *WhoE 91*
Lefever, Ernest W. 1919- *WhoAm 90*
LeFever, M. Denyse 1954- *WhoE 91*
Lefever, Maxine Lane 1931- *IntWWM 90*
LeFever, Michael Grant 1947- *WhoAm 90*
Lefever, Michael Martin 1948- *WhoEmL 91*
Lefever, Richard R. 1936- *WhoE 91*
Lefevere, Patricia Ann 1943- *WhoWrEP 89*
LeFevour, May Kay Catherine 1955- *WhoE 91*
LeFevre, Carol Baumann 1924- *WhoAmW 91*
Le Fevre, Clinton A 1939- *BiDrAPA 89*
LeFevre, David E. 1944- *WhoAm 90*, *WhoWor 91*
Lefevre, Eckard Traugott Richard 1935- *WhoWor 91*
LeFevre, Elbert Walter, Jr. 1932- *WhoAm 90*
LeFevre, Eugene de Daugherty 1926- *St&PR 91*
Lefevre, George, Jr. 1917- *WhoAm 90*
Lefevre, Greg 1947- *WhoEmL 91*
Lefevre, Harvard S. 1920- *St&PR 91*
Lefevre, Howard Edgar 1907- *St&PR 91*
Lefevre, Lawrence E 1904-1960 *WhoAmA 91N*
Lefevre, Marcel Robert 1932- *St&PR 91*
Lefevre, Paul H. 1942- *St&PR 91*
LeFevre, Perry Deyo 1921- *WhoAm 90*
Le Fevre, Philip J 1935- *BiDrAPA 89*
Le Fevre, Richard John 1931- *WhoAmA 91*
Lefevre, Robert Michael 1944- *St&PR 91*
LeFevre, Roger Stanley 1960- *WhoEmL 91*
Lefevre, Stephen Scott 1954- *St&PR 91*
Lefevre, Thomas Vernon 1918- *WhoAm 90*, *WhoE 91*
Le Fevre, William Mathias, Jr. 1927- *WhoAm 90*
Lefevre de Wirz, Elvia Emilia Ramona 1931- *WhoWor 91*
Le Few, Harris W. *ODwPR 91*
Leff, Abraham *BiDrAPA 89*
Leff, Alan Richard 1945- *WhoAm 90*
Leff, Arthur 1908- *WhoAm 90*
Leff, Barbara 1939- *ODwPR 91*
Leff, Barry Joseph 1955- *WhoEmL 91*
Leff, Carl 1897- *St&PR 91*, *WhoAm 90*
Leff, David 1933- *St&PR 91*
Leff, Gloria Carole 1940- *WhoE 91*
Leff, Joel Basil 1935- *WhoAm 90*
Leff, Joel Richard 1946- *BiDrAPA 89*
Leff, Joseph Norman 1923- *St&PR 91*, *WhoAm 90*
Leff, Lisa Amy 1958- *WhoAmW 91*
Leff, Mark Abraham 1932- *St&PR 91*
Leff, Nancy Lea 1946- *WhoEmL 91*
Leff, Naomi *BioIn 16*
Leff, Robert *BiDrAPA 89*
Leff, Ronnie H. 1954- *St&PR 91*
Leff, Samuel *BioIn 16*
Leff, Sandra H. 1939- *WhoAm 90*
Leff, Sanford Leonard 1918- *St&PR 91*
Leffall, LaSalle D., Jr. *BioIn 16*
Leffall, LaSalle Doheny, Jr. 1930- *WhoAm 90*
Leffek, Kenneth Thomas 1934- *WhoAm 90*
Leffel, Russell Calvin 1948- *WhoEmL 91*
Leffell, Mary Sue 1946- *WhoAmW 91*
Leffert, Mark 1944- *BiDrAPA 89*
Leffert, Robert H. 1930- *St&PR 91*
Lefferts, Craig 1957- *Ballpl 90*
Lefferts, George *WhoAm 90*, *WhoWor 91*
Lefferts, Gillet, Jr. 1923- *WhoAm 90*
Lefferts, Jacob R. Van Mater *BioIn 16*
Lefferts, Melissa Briggs 1962- *WhoAmW 91*
Lefferts, William Geoffrey 1943- *WhoAm 90*
Leffingwell, Russell Cornell 1878-1960 *BioIn 16*, *EncABHB 7 [port]*
Leffland, Ella *BioIn 16*
Leffler, Anne Charlotte 1842-1892 *DcScanL*
Leffler, Anne Charlotte 1849-1892 *EncCoWW*
Leffler, Carey 1929- *St&PR 91*
Leffler, David L. 1938- *St&PR 91*
Leffler, Diane L R 1952- *BiDrAPA 89*
Leffler, f. *EncCoWW*
Leffler, John Sutton 1949- *WhoWor 91*
Leffler, Kenneth 1928- *St&PR 91*
Leffler, Marvin 1922- *St&PR 91*
Lefko, Jeffrey Jay 1945- *WhoSSW 91*, *WhoWor 91*
Lefkovitz, Sidney 1917- *St&PR 91*
Lefkovitz, Tom 1944- *St&PR 91*
Lefkowits, Henry J 1928- *BiDrAPA 89*
Lefkowitz, Abraham 1949- *St&PR 91*
Lefkowitz, Barbara Melville 1945- *WhoAmW 91*
Lefkowitz, Bernard 1937- *ConAu 30NR*
Lefkowitz, David 1957- *St&PR 91*
Lefkowitz, David Neil 1964- *WhoEmL 91*
Lefkowitz, Howard N. 1936- *WhoAm 90*
Lefkowitz, Irving 1921- *WhoAm 90*
Lefkowitz, Jerry 1945- *WhoEmL 91*
Lefkowitz, Lawrence 1938- *St&PR 91*, *WhoAm 90*
Lefkowitz, Louis Hirsch 1937- *WhoE 91*
Lefkowitz, Mischa 1954- *IntWWM 90*
Lefkowitz, Richard Howard 1944- *St&PR 91*
Lefkowitz, Robert Arnold 1958- *WhoEmL 91*
Lefkowitz, Robert Joseph 1943- *WhoAm 90*
Lefkowitz, Rose Frances 1954- *WhoE 91*, *WhoEmL 91*
Lefkowitz, William 1937- *WhoSSW 91*
Le Flanchec, Roger 1915-1986 *BioIn 16*
Lefler, Irene Whitney 1917- *WhoWrEP 89*
Lefler, Jack Heatherly 1921- *St&PR 91*
Lefler, Lester L. *St&PR 91*
Lefler, Maurice Lloyd, Jr. 1914- *St&PR 91*
Lefler, Sally Gene 1936- *WhoAmW 91*
LeFlore, Byron Louis 1936- *St&PR 91*
Le Flore, Greenwood *WhNaAH*
Le Flore, John Frederick 1943- *St&PR 91*
LeFlore, John Frederick 1943- *WhoSSW 91*
LeFlore, Ron *BioIn 16*
LeFlore, Ron 1948- *Ballpl 90*
Leflot, Marc Karel Julia 1950- *WhoWor 91*
Lefond, Michele M. 1955- *WhoAmW 91*
Lefor, Michael William 1943- *WhoE 91*
Le Forestier, Jean-Paul 1953- *WhoWor 91*
Lefort, Denis 1953- *St&PR 91*
Le Fort, Gertrud, Freiin von 1876-1971 *BioIn 16*
le Fort, Gertrud von 1876-1971 *ConAu 31NR*
Lefort, P.W. 1941- *St&PR 91*
Lefrak, Joseph Saul 1930- *WhoAm 90*
LeFrak, Samuel J. *BioIn 16*
LeFrak, Samuel J. 1918- *WhoAm 90*, *WorAlBi*
Lefranc, Margaret *WhoAmA 91*
Lefschetz, Solomon 1884-1972 *DcScB S2*
Lefsrud, John B 1929- *BiDrAPA 89*
Lefstein, Norman 1937- *WhoAm 90*
Lefstin, Allen H *BiDrAPA 89*
Left Hand 1820?-1864? *BioIn 16*
Left Hand 1840?- *WhNaAH*
Lefterescu, Petre 1936- *IntWWM 90*
Leftin, Howard Irwin 1951- *BiDrAPA 89*
Lefton, Al Paul, Jr. 1928- *St&PR 91*, *WhoAm 90*
Lefton, Andrea 1961- *BiDrAPA 89*
Lefton, David Edward 1960- *WhoEmL 91*
Lefton, Lester Alan 1946- *WhoAm 90*
Lefton, Norman Barry 1934- *St&PR 91*
Lefton, Robert Eugene 1931- *ConAu 31NR*
Leftwich, Hal West 1955- *WhoEmL 91*
Leftwich, Richard Henry 1920- *WhoAm 90*
Leftwich, Samuel Gilmer 1926- *WhoAm 90*
Lega, Silvestro 1826-1895 *BioIn 16*
Legace, Josette 1809?-1896 *DcCanB 12*
Legaic, Paul *DcCanB 12*
Le Gaigneur, Louis Constantin *PenDiDA 89*
Legaik, Paul *DcCanB 12*
Legallet, Mary Marguerite 1962- *WhoAmW 91*
Le Gallic, Yves 1932- *WhoWor 91*
Le Gallienne, Eva 1899- *AuBYP 90*, *BioIn 16*, *FemiCLE*, *NotWoAT*, *WhoAm 90*
Legallienne, Eva 1899- *WorAlBi*
Legalos, Charles Norman 1943- *WhoWor 91*
Legan, Richard N. 1937- *St&PR 91*
Legan, Thomas Lee 1933- *St&PR 91*
Legany, Dezso 1916- *IntWWM 90*
LeGardeur, Armand 1929- *St&PR 91*
Legare, Gedeon 1615?-1676 *PenDiDA 89*
Legare, Henri Francis 1918- *WhoAm 90*
Legare, Hugh Swinton 1797-1843 *BiDrUSE 89*, *BioIn 16*
Legasov, Valery *BioIn 16*
Legaspi, Abbelane S *BiDrAPA 89*
Legaspi, Rufino Encarnacion 1921- *WhoE 91*
Legasse, David Stephen 1949- *WhoE 91*
Legat, William E *BiDrAPA 89*
LeGates, John Crews 1940- *WhoAm 90*, *WhoE 91*, *WhoWor 91*
Legatti, Raymond 1932- *St&PR 91*
Legault, Emile 1906- *OxCCanT*
Legault, Louis *BiDrAPA 89*
Legault, Oscar 1914- *BiDrAPA 89*
Legault, Pauline Rose 1940- *St&PR 91*
Legault, Suzanne E *BiDrAPA 89*
Legazpi, Luisa Castro 1966- *EncCoWW*
Legel, Michael Lee 1957- *WhoEmL 91*
Le Gendre, Charles William 1830-1899 *BioIn 16*
Legendre, Gertrude Sanford 1902- *BioIn 16*
LeGendre, Laurette Michele 1954- *WhoAmW 91*
Legendre, Sally Treis 1946- *WhoEmL 91*
Legener, John B. 1929- *St&PR 91*
Leger, Alexis Leger Saint- 1887-1975 *BiDFrPL*
Leger, Alexis Saint-Leger 1887-1975 *MajTwCW*
Leger, Fernand 1881-1955 *BioIn 16*, *IntDcAA 90*, *WorAlBi*
Leger, Paul-Emile 1904- *WhoAm 90*, *WhoWor 91*
Leger, Saintleger *MajTwCW*
Legeř, Walter John, Jr. 1951- *WhoSSW 91*
Legere, Laurence Joseph 1919- *WhoAm 90*
Legerton, Clarence William, Jr. 1922- *WhoAm 90*, *WhoSSW 91*
Legex, Paul *DcCanB 12*
Legeza, Laszlo 1934- *ConAu 32NR*
Legg, John Wallis 1936- *WhoSSW 91*
Legg, Larry Barnard 1941- *WhoSSW 91*
Legg, Louis E., Jr. 1928- *St&PR 91*
Legg, Robert H. 1917- *St&PR 91*
Legg, Robert Henry 1917- *WhoAm 90*
Legg, Ronald Otis 1945- *WhoEmL 91*
Legg, Stuart 1910-1988 *AnObit 1988*
Legg, Thomas Charles 1956- *St&PR 91*
Legg, William Jefferson 1925- *WhoAm 90*
Leggat, Janet Cochrane 1954- *WhoE 91*
Leggat, John William, III 1942- *St&PR 91*
Leggat, Richard Durning 1927- *WhoAm 90*
Leggat, Thomas E. 1926- *St&PR 91*
Leggate, Robin 1946- *IntWWM 90*
Leggatt, Alison *NewYTBS 90*
Legge, Charles Alexander 1930- *WhoAm 90*
Legge, Diane *WomArch*
Legge, H. Allan 1928- *St&PR 91*
Legge, Jacqueline Crosby 1961- *WhoAm 90*
Legge, Margaret *FemiCLE*
Legge, Walter *BioIn 16*
Leggeri, Maurizio 1932- *WhoWor 91*
Legget, Robert Ferguson 1904- *WhoAm 90*
Leggett, Gerald D *BiDrAPA 89*
Leggett, Glenn 1918- *WhoAm 90*
Leggett, Joe Edward *BiDrAPA 89*
Leggett, John Carl 1930- *WhoE 91*
Leggett, John Ward 1917- *WhoWrEP 89*
Leggett, Richard Preston *BiDrAPA 89*
Leggett, Robert D *BiDrAPA 89*
Leggett, Roberta Jean 1926- *WhoAm 90*
Leggett, Sonyia Elizabeth 1936- *WhoAmW 91*
Leggett, Stephen Charles 1949- *WhoWrEP 89*
Leggett, William *BioIn 16*
Leggett, William C. 1939- *WhoAm 90*
Leggette, Earl Charles 1940- *WhoSSW 91*
Leggio, Beverly Chambers 1953- *WhoAmW 91*
Leggitt, Don C. 1938- *St&PR 91*
Leggitt, Mildred E. 1911- *St&PR 91*
Leggon, Cheryl Bernadette 1948- *WhoE 91*
Leginska, Ethel 1886-1970 *PenDiMP*
Leginski, Janet 1949- *WhoEmL 91*
Legitimus, Hegepappe *BioIn 16*

Legler, Donald Wayne 1931- *WhoAm 90*
Legler, Glenn D *BiDrAPA 89*
Legler, Kenneth Charles 1936- *St&PR 91*
Legler, Philip 1928- *WhoWrEP 89*
Lego, P. E. 1930- *BioIn 16*
Lego, P.E. 1930- *St&PR 91*
Lego, Paul E. 1930- *BioIn 16*
Lego, Paul Edward 1930- *WhoAm 90, WhoE 91*
Le Goff, Jacques 1926- *WorAu 1980 [port]*
Le Goff, Jean Yves 1948- *WhoWor 91*
Le Goff, Rene Jean 1944- *WhoWor 91*
LeGore, Gayle Patricia 1947- *WhoEmL 91*
Legorreta, Eduardo Antonio 1943- *St&PR 91*
Legorreta, Ricardo 1931- *WhoAm 90, WhoWor 91*
Legow, Deborah 1958- *ODwPR 91*
Legrady, Thomas Theodore 1920- *IntWWM 90*
Legrain, Gerard 1937- *WhoWor 91*
Legrain, Pierre 1889-1929 *PenDiDA 89*
Le Grand *AuBYP 90*
LeGrand, Brendan Camp Gardner 1948- *WhoEmL 91*
Le Grand, Charles Heyward 1949- *WhoEmL 91*
Le Grand, Clay 1911- *WhoAm 90*
Le Grand, David D 1916- *BiDrAPA 89*
Legrand, Michel 1932- *OxCPMus, WorAlBi*
Legrand, Raymond 1908-1974 *OxCPMus*
Legrand, Shawn Pierre 1960- *WhoEmL 91*
LeGrand, Teresa M. *BioIn 16*
LeGrande, Margaret Estella 1931- *WhoAmW 91*
LeGrange, Jane Deborah 1953- *WhoEmL 91*
Le Grange, Louis 1928- *WhoWor 91*
LeGrange, Ulyesse John 1931- *St&PR 91*
Le Gros, John Edward 1923- *St&PR 91*
LeGros, John Edward 1923- *WhoAm 90*
Legros, Joseph 1739-1793 *PenDiMP*
Legros, L.J. 1937- *St&PR 91*
LeGros, Peter Arthur 1939- *St&PR 91*
Legros, Susan LeBlanc 1952- *WhoAmW 91, WhoSSW 91*
Legters, Lyman Howard 1928- *WhoAm 90*
Leguay, Jean *BioIn 16*
LeGuerrier, Jules 1915- *WhoAm 90*
Leguey-Feilleux, Jean-Robert 1928- *WhoWor 91*
Leguia y Salcedo, Augusto Bernardino 1863-1932 *BioIn 16*
Le Guin, Ursula 1929- *AuBYP 90*
LeGuin, Ursula 1929- *BioIn 16*
Le Guin, Ursula 1929- *FemiCLE, WorAlBi*
LeGuin, Ursula K. 1929- *BioAmW*
Le Guin, Ursula K. 1929- *BioIn 16, ConAu 32NR, MajTwCW, RGTwCSF*
Le Guin, Ursula Kroeber 1929- *WhoAm 90, WhoAmW 91, WhoWrEP 89*
Legum, Jeffrey A. 1941- *St&PR 91*
Legum, Jeffrey Alfred 1941- *WhoAm 90, WhoE 91, WhoWor 91*
Legum, Leslie 1911- *St&PR 91*
Legwaila, Legwaila Joseph 1937- *WhoWor 91*
Lehan, Richard D'Aubin 1930- *WhoAm 90, WhoWrEP 89*
Lehane, Maureen *IntWWM 90*
Lehar, Franz 1870-1948 *OxCPMus, PenDiMPA, WorAlBi*
Lehberger, Lois Marie 1956- *WhoEmL 91*
Lehe, James Eugene *WhoSSW 91*
Lehel, Gyorgy 1926- *IntWWM 90*
Lehel, Gyorgy 1926-1989 *PenDiMP*
Lehew, Elton Wilmot, Jr. 1941- *BiDrAPA 89*
Lehew, Willette Lewis 1935- *WhoSSW 91*
Lehey, Gregory Francis 1948- *WhoWor 91*
Lehfeldt, Martin Christopher 1940- *WhoSSW 91*
Lehigh, Earl F. 1930- *St&PR 91*
Lehigh, George Edward 1927- *WhoSSW 91*
Lehine, David E 1911- *BiDrAPA 89*
Lehiste, Ilse 1922- *WhoAm 90*
Lehman, Albert E. 1915- *St&PR 91*
Lehman, Alfred *EncO&P 3*
Lehman, Anthony F 1948- *BiDrAPA 89*
Lehman, Arnold L 1944- *WhoAmA 91*
Lehman, Arnold Lester 1944- *WhoAm 90*
Lehman, Barry Alan 1948- *WhoEmL 91*
Lehman, Benjamin *PenDiDA 89*
Lehman, Christopher M. 1948- *WhoAm 90*
Lehman, Christopher MacFarlane 1941- *WhoAm 90*
Lehman, Clara May Hileman 1901- *WhoAmW 91*
Lehman, David 1948- *BioIn 16, WhoWrEP 89*
Lehman, David A. 1955- *WhoEmL 91*
Lehman, David Walter 1956- *WhoEmL 91*
Lehman, Donald Ray 1947- *WhoSSW 91*
Lehman, Edward *BiDrAPA 89*
Lehman, Edward 1925- *St&PR 91*
Lehman, Edward William 1936- *WhoAm 90*
Lehman, Harold L. 1935- *St&PR 91*
Lehman, Harry Jac 1935- *WhoAm 90*
Lehman, Howard M. 1927- *St&PR 91*
Lehman, Irving 1900-1983 *WhoAmA 91N*
Lehman, Jack Henry, Jr. 1918- *St&PR 91*
Lehman, Jackson R. 1931- *St&PR 91*
Lehman, James Richard 1943- *BiDrAPA 89*
Lehman, Jane Bagley *BioIn 16*
Lehman, Jean-Pierre 1914-1981 *DcScB S2*
Lehman, Jeffrey H. 1960- *WhoEmL 91*
Lehman, Jeffrey Sean 1956- *WhoEmL 91*
Lehman, Jennifer C. 1962- *St&PR 91*
Lehman, Jesse J. 1915- *St&PR 91*
Lehman, Joani Stevens 1953- *St&PR 91*
Lehman, John F. *BioIn 16*
Lehman, John F., Jr. 1942- *WhoAm 90*
Lehman, Ken 1928- *Ballpl 90*
Lehman, Lawrence Herbert 1929- *WhoAm 90*
Lehman, Lillian *DrBIPA 90*
Lehman, Linda Lee 1945- *WhoEmL 91*
Lehman, Lois Joan 1932- *WhoAm 90*
Lehman, Mark Ammon 1930- *WhoAmA 91*
Lehman, Michael *BioIn 16*
Lehman, Orin 1922- *WhoAm 90*
Lehman, Pamela Kay 1963- *WhoAmW 91*
Lehman, Paul Robert 1931- *IntWWM 90*
Lehman, Richard Henry 1948- *WhoAm 90*
Lehman, Richard Leroy 1930- *WhoAm 90, WhoWor 91*
Lehman, Robert *WhoAmA 91N*
Lehman, Robert 1924- *WhoAm 90*
Lehman, Robert Byron 1947- *BiDrAPA 89*
Lehman, Robert Frank 1942- *WhoAm 90*
Lehman, Robert G. 1933- *St&PR 91*
Lehman, Robert J *BiDrAPA 89*
Lehman, Robert L. 1942- *St&PR 91*
Lehman, Robert Nathan 1911- *WhoAm 90*
Lehman, Ronald Frank, II 1946- *WhoAm 90*
Lehman, Ruth Gillespie 1924- *St&PR 91*
Lehman, Sara Rose 1965- *WhoE 91*
Lehman, Sherelynn 1941- *WhoAmW 91*
Lehman, Shirley Yvonne 1936- *WhoWrEP 89*
Lehman, Terry A 1939- *BiDrAPA 89*
Lehman, Wayne 1949- *St&PR 91*
Lehman, Wendy *BioIn 16*
Lehman, William 1913- *WhoAm 90, WhoSSW 91*
Lehmann, Alexander R. 1935- *St&PR 91*
Lehmann, Arnold O. 1914- *IntWWM 90*
Lehmann, August Herman *St&PR 91N*
Lehmann, Barbara Lowis 1934- *WhoAmW 91*
Lehmann, Behrend 1661-1730 *BioIn 16*
Lehmann, Bruce Neal 1955- *WhoE 91*
Lehmann, Charles Henry 1924- *St&PR 91*
Lehmann, Christine H. 1946- *WhoEmL 91*
Lehmann, Eric Stanley 1956- *WhoSSW 91*
Lehmann, Erich Leo 1917- *WhoAm 90*
Lehmann, Esther Strauss 1944- *WhoAmW 91*
Lehmann, Ewald *St&PR 91*
Lehmann, Frederick Gliessmann 1930- *WhoE 91*
Lehmann, Gary Lawrence 1957- *WhoE 91*
Lehmann, Hans Ulrich 1937- *IntWWM 90*
Lehmann, Heinz E 1911- *BiDrAPA 89*
Lehmann, Heinz Edgar 1911- *WhoAm 90*
Lehmann, Heinz R. 1929- *St&PR 91*
Lehmann, Helmuth August 1956- *WhoEmL 91*
Lehmann, Herbert *BiDrAPA 89*
Lehmann, Herman 1859-1932 *WhNaAH*
Lehmann, Johannes Theodor 1920- *WhoWor 91*
Lehmann, John 1907-1987 *DcLB 100 [port]*
Lehmann, Kaspar 1565?-1622 *PenDiDA 89*
Lehmann, Laurent S 1945- *BiDrAPA 89*
Lehmann, Lilli 1848-1929 *PenDiMP, WorAlBi*
Lehmann, Liza 1862-1918 *OxCPMus*
Lehmann, Lotte 1888-1976 *BioIn 16, PenDiMP*
Lehmann, Manfred Roderich 1942- *St&PR 91*
Lehmann, Nolan 1944- *St&PR 91*
Lehmann, Phyllis Williams 1912- *WhoAm 90*
Lehmann, Richard J. 1944- *St&PR 91*
Lehmann, Rosamond *NewYTBS 90*
Lehmann, Rosamond 1901-1990 *BioIn 16, ConAu 131, FemiCLE*
Lehmann, Ruth Preston Miller 1912- *WhoAm 90, WhoWrEP 89*
Lehmann, Siegfried B. 1930- *WhoWor 91*
Lehmann, Susan W *BiDrAPA 89*
Lehmann, Wilhelm 1882-1968 *BioIn 16*
Lehmann, William Leonardo 1924- *WhoAm 90*
Lehmann, Winfred Philipp 1916- *WhoAm 90*
Lehmann-Carssow, Nancy Beth 1949- *WhoAmW 91*
Lehmann-Grube, Fritz Gustav Bernhard 1927- *WhoWor 91*
Lehmann-Haupt, Christopher Charles H. 1934- *WhoAm 90, WhoWrEP 89*
Lehmberg, Stanford Eugene 1931- *WhoAm 90*
Lehmer, David Lawrence 1942- *St&PR 91*
Lehmkuhl, David *BioIn 16*
Lehmstedt, Sigrid 1929- *IntWWM 90*
Lehn, Clifford A. 1930- *St&PR 91*
Lehn, Jean-Marie 1939- *WorAlBi*
Lehn, Jean-Marie Pierre 1939- *WhoAm 90, WhoWor 91*
Lehn, Joseph *BioIn 16*
Lehne, John *BioIn 16*
Lehner, Christine Reine 1952- *WhoWrEP 89*
Lehner, George Alexander, Jr. 1948- *WhoEmL 91*
Lehner, Gerhard Hans 1924- *WhoWor 91*
Lehner, Jeno *PenDiMP*
Lehner, Paul 1920-1967 *Ballpl 90*
Lehner, Paul Michael 1941- *WhoSSW 91*
Lehner, Urban Charles 1947- *WhoAm 90*
Lehnerd, Alvin P. 1928- *St&PR 91*
Lehnert, Herbert Hermann 1925- *WhoAm 90*
Lehnert, Lawrence A., Jr. 1957- *St&PR 91*
Lehnert, Rick 1957- *St&PR 91*
Lehnerts, Frances *IntWWM 90*
Lehnhoff, Nikolaus *BioIn 16*
Lehnhoff, Nikolaus 1939- *IntWWM 90*
Lehnus, Gary Lee 1945- *St&PR 91*
Lehoczky, John Paul 1943- *WhoAm 90*
Lehotka, Gabor 1938- *IntWWM 90*
Lehr, Barbara Augusta 1924- *WhoE 91*
Lehr, Dwight Arden 1935- *St&PR 91*
Lehr, Ellen Delores 1920- *WhoWrEP 89*
Lehr, Erwin W. 1928- *St&PR 91*
Lehr, George *BioIn 16*
Lehr, Harry 1869-1929 *BioIn 16*
Lehr, Harvey Glenn 1937- *St&PR 91*
Lehr, James Jerome 1931- *WhoWor 91*
Lehr, James Philip 1948- *WhoSSW 91*
Lehr, Janet 1937- *WhoAm 90, WhoAmA 91*
Lehr, Laurence Jon 1943- *WhoSSW 91*
Lehr, Lewis Wylie 1921- *St&PR 91*
Lehr, Meredith Lee 1956- *WhoEmL 91*
Lehr, Mira 1938- *WhoAmA 91*
Lehr, Rhonda 1946- *BiDrAPA 89*
Lehr, Roland 1912- *St&PR 91*
Lehr, Seth Jonathan 1956- *WhoEmL 91*
Lehr, William, Jr. 1940- *St&PR 91, WhoAm 90*
Lehrer, Douglas Sidney 1959- *BiDrAPA 89*
Lehrer, James 1934- *WorAlBi*
Lehrer, James Charles 1934- *WhoAm 90, WhoWrEP 89*
Lehrer, Joel Fredric 1941- *WhoE 91*
Lehrer, Keith Edward 1936- *WhoAm 90*
Lehrer, Kenneth Eugene 1946- *WhoAm 90, WhoSSW 91*
Lehrer, Leonard 1935- *WhoAm 90, WhoAmA 91*
Lehrer, Merrill Clark 1955- *WhoSSW 91*
Lehrer, Phyllis Claire Alpert 1940- *IntWWM 90*
Lehrer, Robert Elliott 1945- *WhoEmL 91*
Lehrer, Stanley 1929- *WhoAm 90, WhoWor 91, WhoWrEP 89*
Lehrer, Thomas Andrew 1928- *IntWWM 90, WhoAm 90*
Lehrer, Tom 1928- *OxCPMus*
Lehrer, Warren I. 1955- *WhoWrEP 89*
Lehrfeld, Andrew David 1958- *WhoE 91*
Lehrling, Terry James 1950- *WhoEmL 91*
Lehrman, Ela-Joy 1949- *WhoAmW 91*
Lehrman, Emily Rosenstein 1923- *WhoAmW 91*
Lehrman, Hal 1911-1988 *BioIn 16*
Lehrman, Harold B 1918- *BiDrAPA 89*
Lehrman, Joseph 1924- *St&PR 91*
Lehrman, Leonard Jordan 1949- *IntWWM 90, WhoEmL 91*
Lehrman, Lewis Edward 1938- *WhoAm 90*
Lehrman, Margaret McBride 1944- *WhoE 91*
Lehrman, Maurice Allen 1925- *St&PR 91*
Lehrman, Michael L. 1932- *St&PR 91*
Lehrman, Nat 1929- *WhoAm 90*
Lehrman, Nathaniel S 1923- *BiDrAPA 89*
Lehrman, Nathaniel Saul 1923- *WhoE 91*
Lehrman, Paul D. 1952- *IntWWM 90*
Lehrman, Paul David 1952- *WhoEmL 91*
Lehrman, Robert O. 1934- *ODwPR 91*
Lehrman, Roy Edward 1953- *WhoSSW 91*
Lehrman, Samuel R 1912- *BiDrAPA 89*
Lehti, John 1912- *EncACom*
Lehtinen, Dexter *BioIn 16*
Lehtinen, Ileana Ros- *BioIn 16*
Lehtinen, Seppo Ilmari 1937- *WhoWor 91*
Lehto, Arto Juhani 1941- *WhoWor 91*
Lehto, Sakari Tapani 1923- *WhoWor 91*
Lehtonen, Joel 1881-1934 *DcScanL*
Lehtonen, Reijo Paivio 1930- *WhoWor 91*
Lei, Kuan-Shaur 1955- *WhoSSW 91*
Leib, Joseph M. 1909- *St&PR 91*
Leib, Pamela Louise 1957- *BiDrAPA 89*
Leib, Prudence T 1951- *BiDrAPA 89*
Leibel, Richard J. 1949- *St&PR 91*
Leibel, Shelley Joy 1957- *WhoAmW 91*
Leibenguth, Kathleen Curran 1954- *WhoE 91*
Leibenluft, Ellen 1953- *BiDrAPA 89*
Leiber, Fritz 1910- *MajTwCW, WhoWrEP 89*
Leiber, Fritz, Jr. 1910- *RGTwCSF, WhoAm 90*
Leiber, Gerson August 1921- *WhoAm 90, WhoAmA 91*
Leiber, Jerry 1933- *BioIn 16, OxCPMus*
Leiber, Judith Maria 1921- *WhoAm 90*
Leibert, Peter R 1941- *WhoAmA 91*
Leibert, Richard Martin 1951- *WhoEmL 91*
Leibfried, Erwin H. 1942- *WhoWor 91*
Leibholz, Stephen W. 1932- *St&PR 91*
Leibholz, Stephen Wolfgang 1932- *WhoAm 90*
Leibl, Wilhelm 1844-1900 *IntDcAA 90*
Leibler, Kenneth R. 1949- *St&PR 91*
Leibler, Kenneth Robert 1949- *WhoAm 90*
Leibman, Morris Irwin 1911- *WhoAm 90*
Leibman, Ron 1937- *WhoAm 90*
Leibmann, Susan *BiDrAPA 89*
Leibner, Richard *BioIn 16*
Leibniz, Gottfried 1646-1716 *WorAlBi, WrPh P*
Leibniz, Gottfried Wilhelm 1646-1716 *EncPaPR 91*
Leibniz, Gottfried Wilhelm, Freiherr von 1646-1716 *BioIn 16*
Leibo, Mark *BiDrAPA 89*
Leibold, Arthur William, Jr. 1931- *WhoAm 90*
Leibold, Charles Howard 1954- *St&PR 91*
Leibold, Gunter Joseph 1950- *WhoWor 91*
Leibold, Jay 1957- *BioIn 16*
Leibold, Nemo 1892-1977 *Ballpl 90*
Leibov, Ernest B *BiDrAPA 89*
Leibovich, Miguel A 1933- *BiDrAPA 89*
Leibovici, Adrian 1954- *BiDrAPA 89*
Leibovici, Jacques Adolphe 1943- *WhoE 91*
Leibovitz, Annie *BioIn 16*
Leibovitz, Annie 1949- *WhoAm 90, WhoAmW 91*
Leibovitz, Jehoshwa 1931- *St&PR 91*
Leibovitz, Mitchell G. 1945- *St&PR 91, WhoAm 90*
Leibovitz, Morris Phillip 1917- *St&PR 91*
Leibow, David B 1950- *BiDrAPA 89*
Leibow, Lois May 1937- *WhoAmW 91*
Leibowitz, Anita Zoe 1934- *WhoAmW 91*
Leibowitz, Bernard 1930- *St&PR 91*
Leibowitz, Bernice 1929- *WhoAmA 91*
Leibowitz, George 1937- *St&PR 91*
Leibowitz, Herbert Akiba 1935- *WhoAm 90, WhoWrEP 89*
Leibowitz, Howard Allan 1941- *St&PR 91*
Leibowitz, Howard Richard 1952- *WhoE 91*
Leibowitz, Jack Richard *WhoAm 90*
Leibowitz, Michael David 1948- *BiDrAPA 89*
Leibowitz, Norman 1947- *WhoE 91*
Leibowitz, Rene 1913-1972 *PenDiMP*
Leibowitz, Sam *St&PR 91*
Leibrandt, Charlie 1956- *Ballpl 90*
Leibrecht, John Joseph 1930- *WhoAm 90*
Leibson, Charles M. 1929- *WhoAm 90, WhoSSW 91*
Leibson, Irving 1926- *St&PR 91, WhoAm 90*
Leibson, Mitchell H. 1952- *St&PR 91*
Leibundguth, Suzanne Jean 1953- *WhoEmL 91*
Leiby, Bruce Richard 1947- *WhoE 91*
Leiby, George Martin, Jr. 1935- *BiDrAPA 89*
Leiby, Jack Leroy 1942- *St&PR 91*
Leicach, Jorge 1932- *BiDrAPA 89*
Leicach, Mario 1930- *BiDrAPA 89*
Leicester, Andrew John 1948- *WhoAmA 91*
Leicester, Edith *NewAgMG*
Leicester, Robert Dudley, Earl of 1532?-1588 *BioIn 16*
Leich, Mildred C. 1912- *St&PR 91*
Leich, Robert M., Jr. 1943- *St&PR 91*
Leichner, Pierre Paul 1947- *BiDrAPA 89*
Leicht, Theodore M. 1927- *St&PR 91*
Leichter, Harry *BioIn 16*
Leichtman, Harry MacGregor 1949- *WhoE 91*
Leichty, David Herman 1946- *IntWWM 90*
Leick, Frederick William 1943- *St&PR 91, WhoAm 90*
Leidel, David John 1945- *WhoSSW 91*
Leidel, Frederick Otto 1916- *WhoAm 90*
Leiden, Carl 1922- *WhoAm 90*
Leiden, Lucas Van 1489?-1533 *WorAlBi*
Leiden, Terry Patrick 1940- *WhoSSW 91*

Leiden, Warren Robert 1949- *WhoEmL 91*
Leider, Allan R 1921- *BiDrAPA 89*
Leider, Deborah J. 1954- *ODwPR 91*
Leider, Frida 1888-1975 *PenDiMP*
Leider, Gary 1954- *WhoEmL 91*
Leider, Gerald J. 1931- *WhoAm 90*
Leider, Robert J 1932- *BiDrAPA 89*
Leider, Thomas R *BiDrAPA 89*
Leiderman, Leonardo 1951- *WhoWor 91*
Leidesdorf, Arthur David 1918- *WhoAm 90, WhoWor 91*
Leidheiser, Henry, Jr. 1920- *WhoAm 90*
Leidich, Robert John 1946- *WhoAm 90*
Leidich-Ross, Lois Jean 1952- *WhoAmW 91*
Leidig-Reed, Cheryl Sue 1947- *WhoAmW 91*
Leidner, Harold Edward 1937- *WhoAm 90*
Leidner, Suzanne Carolyn 1942- *WhoAmW 91*
Leidy, Lu Ann 1956- *BiDrAPA 89*
Leidy, William Austin 1948- *St&PR 91*
Leies, John Alex 1926- *WhoAm 90*
Leifer, Andrew Erik *BiDrAPA 89*
Leifer, Calvin 1929- *WhoAm 90*
Leifer, Carol *BioIn 16*
Leifer, Herb Charles 1950- *WhoEmL 91*
Leifer, Marvin W 1945- *BiDrAPA 89*
Leifer, Marvin William 1945- *WhoE 91*
Leiferkus, Sergei 1946- *IntWWM 90*
Leiferman, Harold W. 1926- *St&PR 91*
Leiferman, Silvia Weiner *WhoAmW 91*
Leifeste, Mark 1952- *BiDrAPA 89*
Leifield, Lefty 1883-1970 *Ballpl 90*
Leifsson, Asgeir 1941- *WhoWor 91*
Leigh, Adele 1924- *IntWWM 90*
Leigh, Archibald D 1915- *BiDrAPA 89*
Leigh, Beverly E. 1924- *St&PR 91*
Leigh, Beverly Eugene 1924- *WhoAm 90*
Leigh, Carolyn 1926- *OxCPMus*
Leigh, Carrie *BioIn 16*
Leigh, Christian *BioIn 16*
Leigh, David Anthony 1953- *IntWWM 90*
Leigh, Donald Charles 1929- *WhoAm 90*
Leigh, Dorothy *FemiCLE*
Leigh, Dorothy *BiDEWW*
Leigh, Dorothy Kempe 1616?- *BioIn 16*
Leigh, Douglas 1907- *WorAlBi*
Leigh, Elbert H 1932- *BiDrAPA 89*
Leigh, Fiona Jean *BiDrAPA 89*
Leigh, Franes *AuBYP 90*
Leigh, Harry E 1931- *WhoAmA 91*
Leigh, Harry Edward 1931- *WhoE 91*
Leigh, Helen *FemiCLE*
Leigh, Hoyle 1942- *BiDrAPA 89*
Leigh, Irene Wolff 1944- *WhoAmW 91*
Leigh, Jack David 1948- *WhoAmA 91*
Leigh, James Henry 1952- *WhoEmL 91*
Leigh, Jane Ellen 1958- *WhoAmW 91*
Leigh, Janet 1927- *WhoAm 90, WorAlBi*
Leigh, Jennifer Jason 1958- *ConTFT 8 [port]*
Leigh, Leon B. 1940- *St&PR 91*
Leigh, Lynn Laverne 1925- *St&PR 91*
Leigh, Marlisa Kay MacLeod 1965- *WhoAmW 91*
Leigh, Matthew Andrew *ConAu 129*
Leigh, Michael I. 1952- *St&PR 91*
Leigh, Mike 1943- *ConAu 31NR*
Leigh, Mitch 1928- *OxCPMus*
Leigh, Monroe 1919- *WhoAm 90*
Leigh, Shari Greer 1959- *WhoAmW 91, WhoWor 91*
Leigh, Stephen 1931- *WhoAm 90, WhoE 91*
Leigh, Susan Jane 1951- *WhoAmW 91*
Leigh, Vivien 1913-1967 *BioIn 16, WorAlBi*
Leigh, Walter 1905-1942 *OxCPMus*
Leigh Fermor, Patrick 1915- *MajTwCW*
Leigh-Manuell, Robert Allen 1942- *WhoSSW 91*
Leigh-Pemberton, Robert 1927- *WhoWor 91*
Leigh-Smith, B. *BiDWomA*
Leighly, John 1895-1986 *BioIn 16*
Leight, Walter Gilbert 1922- *WhoE 91*
Leighten, Edward Henry 1914- *WhoAm 90*
Leighten, Patricia 1946- *WhoE 91*
Leighton, A C *WhoAmA 91N*
Leighton, Alexander H 1908- *BiDrAPA 89*
Leighton, Betty 1923- *OxCCanT*
Leighton, Charles M. 1935- *St&PR 91*
Leighton, Charles Milton 1935- *WhoAm 90*
Leighton, Claire Veronica Hope 1900?- *BiDWomA*
Leighton, Clare 1898-1989 *AnObit 1989*
Leighton, David S R 1928- *WhoAmA 91*
Leighton, David Struan Robertson 1928- *WhoAm 90*
Leighton, Dorothea C *BiDrAPA 89*
Leighton, Frances Spatz *ConAu 30NR, WhoAm 90, WhoWor 91, WhoWrEP 89*
Leighton, Frederic 1830-1896 *IntDcAA 90*
Leighton, George Neves 1912- *WhoAm 90*
Leighton, Gregory Timothy 1959- *WhoEmL 91*
Leighton, Jan *BioIn 16*
Leighton, John Crichton 1925- *St&PR 91*
Leighton, John Elliott 1959- *WhoEmL 91*
Leighton, Joseph 1921- *WhoAm 90*
Leighton, Kim Gregory 1952- *WhoSSW 91*
Leighton, Lawrence Ward 1934- *WhoE 91, WhoWor 91*
Leighton, Leslie Steven 1952- *WhoSSW 91*
Leighton, Liane *WhoE 91*
Leighton, Margaret 1896- *AuBYP 90*
Leighton, Margaret 1922-1976 *WorAlBi*
Leighton, Margaret Carver 1896-1987 *BioIn 16*
Leighton, Marie 1876?-1941 *FemiCLE*
Leighton, Miriam *WhoAmW 91, WhoE 91*
Leighton, Paul Joe 1953- *WhoEmL 91*
Leighton, Robert Benjamin 1919- *WhoAm 90*
Leighton, Thomas Charles 1913-1976 *WhoAmA 91N*
Leighton-Lundberg, Jeanne *BioIn 16*
Leighton of Stretton, Baron 1830-1896 *BioIn 16*
Leightty, David 1951- *WhoEmL 91*
Leigner, Joseph William, III 1946- *WhoSSW 91*
Leih, Grace Janet 1936- *WhoWrEP 89*
Leihamer, Abraham 1745-1774 *PenDiDA 89*
Leijonhufvud, Axel Stig Bengt 1933- *WhoAm 90*
Leiken, Stanley J 1934- *BiDrAPA 89*
Leikin, Marcia Elise *BiDrAPA 89*
Leile, George 1750?-1800? *BioIn 16*
Leiman, David Charles *BiDrAPA 89*
Leiman, Joan Maisel 1934- *WhoE 91*
Leiman, Sid Zalman 1941- *WhoAm 90*
Leimbach, Martha 1963- *ConAu 130*
Leimbach, Marti *BioIn 16, ConAu 130*
Leimenstoll, J.R. 1899- *St&PR 91*
Leimer, Phyllis Hancock 1936- *WhoAmW 91*
Leimert, Joseph William 1916- *St&PR 91*
Leimgruber, Annette 1947- *WhoWor 91*
Leimkuhler, Ferdinand Francis 1928- *WhoAm 90*
Leimkuhler, Gerard Joseph 1948- *St&PR 91*
Leimkuhler, Gerard Joseph, Jr. 1948- *WhoAm 90, WhoE 91*
Lein, Allen 1913- *WhoAm 90*
Lein, Charles D. 1941- *WhoAm 90*
Lein, Don Curtis 1934- *St&PR 91, WhoAm 90*
Lein, Hebe Beatriz 1945- *WhoAmW 91*
Lein, Malcolm Emil 1913- *WhoAm 90, WhoAmA 91*
Leinbach, Frederick S. 1910-1990 *BioIn 16*
Leinbach, Joseph K. 1934- *St&PR 91*
Leinbach, Peter T. 1951- *St&PR 91*
Leinbach, Philip Eaton 1935- *WhoAm 90*
Leinbach, Wilmer Daniel 1940- *WhoAm 90*
Leinberger, Christopher Brown 1951- *WhoWor 91*
Leinberger, Joan Schmidt 1942- *WhoAmW 91*
Leinberger, Paul Daniel 1947- *WhoEmL 91*
Leinenkugel, James M. 1925- *St&PR 91*
Leinenweber, Harry Daniel 1937- *WhoAm 90*
Leiner, Carl Elton 1952- *WhoEmL 91*
Leiner, Katherine *AuBYP 90*
Leiner, Katherine 1949- *ConAu 132*
Leiner, Murray J. 1929- *WhoE 91*
Leiner, Roseann Hartke 1960- *WhoEmL 91*
Leiner, Wolfgang 1925- *WhoWor 91*
Leingang, Henry J. 1949- *St&PR 91*
Leingang, Terrence A 1948- *BiDrAPA 89*
Leinieks, Valdis 1932- *WhoAm 90, WhoWor 91*
Leininger, Alan R. 1955- *St&PR 91*
Leininger, James V. 1920- *St&PR 91*
Leininger, Kenneth Alan 1924- *St&PR 91*
Leininger, Madeleine Monica 1925- *WhoAm 90*
Leininger, Wayne Carl 1949- *WhoEmL 91*
Leininger, William Joseph 1947- *WhoEmL 91*
Leininger, Wilmer J. 1942- *St&PR 91*
Leino, Deanna Rose 1937- *WhoAmW 91*
Leino, Eino 1878-1926 *DcScanL*
Leinsdorf, Erich 1912- *BioIn 16, IntWWM 90, PenDiMP, WhoAm 90, WorAlBi*
Leinss, Edward Albert 1941- *St&PR 91*
Leinster, Colin Ronald 1939- *WhoWrEP 89*
Leinster, Murray 1896-1975 *RGTwCSF*
Leinweber, Daniel S. 1949- *ODwPR 91*
Leiper, Dave 1962- *Ballpl 90*
Leiper, Esther M. 1946- *WhoWrEP 89*
Leiper, W.C. *St&PR 91*
Leiphart, Clarence Daron 1915- *WhoE 91*
Leipold, Jon David 1938- *BiDrAPA 89*
Leipper, Dale Frederick 1914- *WhoAm 90*
Leipunskii, Aleksandr Il'ich 1903-1972 *DcScB S2*
Leipzig, Arthur 1918- *WhoAm 90, WhoAmA 91, WhoE 91*
Leipzig, Libby Black 1925- *WhoAmW 91*
Leipzig, Nate 1873-1939 *BioIn 16*
Leiris, Louise 1902-1988 *BioIn 16*
Leiris, Michel 1901- *BioIn 16, ConLC 61 [port]*
Leiris, Michel 1901-1990 *ConAu 132, NewYTBS 90*
Leis, Henry Patrick, Jr. 1914- *WhoAm 90, WhoE 91, WhoWor 91*
Leis, Philip Edward 1931- *WhoAm 90*
Leis, Winogene B. 1919- *WhoAmW 91, WhoE 91, WhoSSW 91, WhoWor 91*
Leiseca, Sergio Alfredo, Jr. 1946- *WhoHisp 91*
Leisenring, Edward B., Jr. 1926- *St&PR 91*
Leiser, Burton Myron 1930- *WhoAm 90, WhoE 91*
Leiser, Ernest Stern 1921- *WhoAm 90*
Leiser, Thomas Edward 1938- *St&PR 91*
Leisewitz, Johann Anton 1752-1806 *DcLB 94 [port]*
Leish, Kenneth William 1936- *WhoAm 90*
Leisher, George Loy, Jr. 1945- *WhoAm 90, WhoWor 91*
Leisher, William Rodger 1941- *WhoAm 90*
Leishman, David John *BiDrAPA 89*
Leishman, John G. A. 1857-1924 *BioIn 16*
Leising, Jean *WhoAmW 91*
Leisk, David Johnson 1906-1975 *AuBYP 90*
Leisner, Anthony Baker 1941- *WhoWor 91*
Leisner, David 1953- *WhoEmL 91*
Leiss, Peter 1939- *St&PR 91*
Leissa, Arthur William 1931- *WhoAm 90*
Leist, Elisabeth Pasek 1927- *WhoAmW 91*
Leist, John W 1919- *BiDrAPA 89*
Leist, Ronald Robert 1937- *St&PR 91*
Leisten, Arthur Gaynor 1941- *St&PR 91, WhoAm 90*
Leister, Kenneth W. 1921- *St&PR 91*
Leister, Mary McFarland 1917- *WhoWrEP 89*
Leister, Roy A., Jr. 1950- *St&PR 91*
Leister, Thomas A. 1959- *St&PR 91*
Leistler, Carl *PenDiDA 89*
Leistner, Eckhard Walter 1941- *WhoWor 91*
Leistritz, John P. *ODwPR 91*
Leisure, George Stanley, Jr. 1924- *WhoAm 90*
Leisure, Peter Keeton 1929- *WhoAm 90, WhoE 91*
Leisy, James F. 1927-1989 *BioIn 16*
Leisy, James Franklin *St&PR 91N*
Leisy, Jerald Waldo *BiDrAPA 89*
Leisz, George W. 1923- *WhoAm 90*
Leisz, George Webster 1923- *St&PR 91*
Leisz, Stuart Joseph 1931- *St&PR 91*
Leita, Tony Scott 1958- *WhoEmL 91*
Leitao Da Cunha, Pedro Horacio J.M. 1933- *St&PR 91*
Leitch, Alma May 1924- *WhoAm 90, WhoSSW 91*
Leitch, Brian P. 1958- *WhoEmL 91*
Leitch, Donovan 1967- *BioIn 16*
Leitch, Gordon James 1937- *WhoAm 90*
Leitch, Jay Andrew 1948- *WhoEmL 91*
Leitch, Jennifer Louise *BiDrAPA 89*
Leitch, Joel Steven 1952- *WhoSSW 91*
Leitch, John A. 1951- *St&PR 91*
Leitch, John D. 1921- *St&PR 91*
Leitch, John Daniel 1921- *WhoAm 90*
Leitch, Robert E. 1918- *St&PR 91*
Leite, Eduardo Cerqueira 1950- *WhoSSW 91*
Leite, Rui Pereira 1957- *WhoWor 91*
Leite, Silvio Carlos 1952- *WhoWor 91*
Leiter, Al 1965- *Ballpl 90*
Leiter, Daniel Norman 1940- *St&PR 91*
Leiter, Donald Eugene 1932- *WhoSSW 91*
Leiter, Elliot 1933- *WhoE 91*
Leiter, John M. 1951- *WhoEmL 91*
Leiter, Michael *St&PR 91*
Leiter, Naomi 1935- *BiDrAPA 89*
Leiter, Robert Allen 1949- *WhoAm 90*
Leiter, Samuel L 1940- *ConAu 31NR*
Leiter, William C. 1939- *St&PR 91, WhoAm 90*
Leiterstein, Steven Jay 1947- *WhoE 91*
Leith, Cecil Eldon, Jr. 1923- *WhoAm 90*
Leith, Emmett Norman 1927- *WhoAm 90*
Leith, James Clark 1937- *WhoAm 90*
Leith, John Douglas *BioIn 16*
Leith, John Haddon 1919- *WhoAm 90*
Leith, Linda 1949- *ConAu 131*
Leith, Linda Joan 1959- *WhoAmW 91*
Leith, Roderick Gordon 1928- *WhoAm 90*
Leith, Ronald 1946- *IntWWM 90*
Leith, Ronnie Sue *BiDrAPA 89*
Leith-Ross, Harry 1886- *WhoAmA 91N*
Leith-Ross, Prudence 1922- *ConAu 132*
Leithauser, Brad 1953- *WorAu 1980 [port]*
Leithauser, Mark Alan 1950- *WhoAmA 91*
Leithner, Joseph *PenDiDA 89*
Leithwood, Doreen Marjory 1930- *WhoAmW 91*
Leitich, Ann Tizia 1896-1976 *EncCoWW*
Leitman, Samuel 1908-1981 *WhoAmA 91N*
Leitmann, George 1925- *WhoAm 90*
Leitner, Alfred 1921- *WhoAm 90*
Leitner, Cynthia Madden 1951- *WhoAmW 91*
Leitner, David Larry 1956- *WhoEmL 91*
Leitner, Elliot 1930- *St&PR 91*
Leitner, Ferdinand 1912- *IntWWM 90, PenDiMP*
Leitner, Gottfried Ludwig 1922- *WhoWor 91*
Leitner, Gregory Marc 1957- *WhoEmL 91*
Leitner, Jeannette C. 1943- *WhoSSW 91*
Leitner, Mark Matthew 1958- *WhoEmL 91*
Leitner, Mary Hathaway 1914- *St&PR 91*
Leitner, Paul R. 1928- *WhoAm 90*
Leitner, R. Elaine 1953- *WhoAmW 91*
Leitner, Rose Marie P. 1959- *WhoEmL 91*
Leitner, Yoram Benjamin 1953- *WhoEmL 91*
Leito, James Vincent, III 1956- *WhoEmL 91*
Leitschuh, Cheryl Ann 1955- *WhoAmW 91*
Leitschuh, Thomas Henry *BiDrAPA 89*
Leitstein, Robert 1937- *WhoAm 90*
Leitten, Brian Joseph 1949- *WhoEmL 91*
Leitz, Jerry 1957- *St&PR 91*
Leitz, Paul David 1933- *WhoSSW 91*
Leitzell, Terry Lee 1942- *WhoAm 90*
Leitzer, Joan Schaap *BiDrAPA 89*
Leitzinger, Sandra Mayes 1936- *WhoAmW 91, WhoE 91*
Leitzke, Jacque Herbert 1929- *WhoWor 91*
Leivant, Daniel Maurice 1947- *WhoEmL 91*
Leivesley, Thomas Leonard, Jr. 1923- *St&PR 91*
Leizaola, Jesus Maria de 1896-1989 *BioIn 16*
Leizear, Charles William 1922- *WhoAm 90*
Leja, Joseph R., Jr. 1953- *St&PR 91*
Lejet, Edith 1941- *IntWWM 90*
Lejeune *DcCanB 12*
Lejeune, Anthony 1928- *TwCCr&M 91*
LeJeune, Dennis Edward 1942- *WhoAm 90*
Le Jeune, Francis Ernest, Jr. 1929- *WhoAm 90*
Le Jeune, Harriet Peacock 1917- *IntWWM 90*
LeJeune, Joseph Bobby 1954- *WhoEmL 91*
LeJeune, Joseph Guillaume 1914- *WhoWor 91*
LeJeune, Larry 1885-1952 *Ballpl 90*
Lejeune, Michael Leonard 1918- *WhoAm 90*
Lejeune, Rita Marguerite Josephine 1906- *WhoWor 91*
Lejeune, Simon M W *BiDrAPA 89*
Lejins, Peter Pierre 1909- *WhoAm 90*
Lejnieks, L. Arno 1928- *St&PR 91*
Leka, George T. *St&PR 91*
Leka, Lavdie 1935- *EncCoWW*
Lekan, Briana Marker 1955- *WhoEmL 91*
Lekas, Joyce *ODwPR 91*
Lekas, Mary Despina 1930- *WhoAmW 91*
Lekas, Mitchell Achilles 1922- *St&PR 91*
Lekberg, Barbara Hult 1925- *WhoAmA 91*
Lekberg, Robert David 1920- *WhoWor 91*
Lekhanya, Justin 1938- *WhoWor 91*
Lekisch, Karl Peter 1912- *St&PR 91*
Lekki, Walter J. 1938- *St&PR 91*
Lekstutis, John Paul 1943- *St&PR 91*
Lekus, Diana Rose 1948- *WhoAmW 91*
Lekwauwa, Ureh N 1955- *BiDrAPA 89*
LeLaidier-James, Paula Claire 1947- *WhoAmW 91*
Lelak, John Michael 1934- *St&PR 91*
Leland, Alison Walton 1958- *WhoEmL 91*
Leland, Charles Godfrey 1824-1903 *EncO&P 3*
Leland, Christopher Towne 1951- *WhoWrEP 89*
Leland, David Arthur 1959- *WhoSSW 91*
Leland, David D. 1935- *WhoAm 90*
Leland, David Dale 1935- *St&PR 91*
Leland, George Thomas 1944-1989 *BlkAmsC [port]*
Leland, Harold Robert 1931- *St&PR 91*
Leland, Henry M. 1843-1932 *WorAlBi*
Leland, Henry Martyn 1843-1932 *EncABHB 4 [port]*
Leland, John 1754-1841 *BioIn 16, EncCRAm*
Leland, Joy Hanson 1927- *WhoAm 90*
Leland, Lawrence 1915- *St&PR 91, WhoAm 90*
Leland, Leslie *St&PR 91*
Leland, Marc Ernest 1938- *WhoAm 90, WhoE 91*
Leland, Mickey *BioIn 16*
Leland, Mickey 1944-1989 *AnObit 1989*

Leland, Paula Susan 1953- *WhoAmW 91*
Leland, Pound 1945- *St&PR 91*
Leland, Sara *WhoAm 90*
Leland, Timothy 1937- *WhoAm 90*
Leland, Tom W 1929- *BiDrAPA 89*
Leland, Warren Hanan 1915- *WhoAm 90*
Leland, Whitney Edward 1945- *WhoAmA 91*
Lelarge, Jean Baptiste 1743-1802 *PenDiDA 89*
Lelas, Srdan 1939- *WhoWor 91*
Lelaurin, Jacqueline Francoise 1947- *WhoWor 91*
Lelchuk, Alan *BioIn 16*
Lelchuk, Alan 1938- *WhoAm 90, WhoWrEP 89*
Lele, Eknath V. 1938- *WhoSSW 91*
Lele, Padmakar Pratap 1927- *WhoAm 90*
Leleszi, Jimmie Paul 1944- *BiDrAPA 89*
Leleu, Jean-Francois 1729-1807 *PenDiDA 89*
Lelewer, David Kann 1940- *WhoAm 90*
le Lievre, Audrey 1923- *ConAu 132*
Le Lievre, Robert E 1929- *BiDrAPA 89*
Lelivelt, Jack 1885-1941 *Ballpl 90*
Lella, Joseph William 1936- *WhoAm 90*
Leloir, Luis Federico 1906-1987 *BioIn 16*
Lelouch, Claude 1937- *BioIn 16, ConTFT 8*
Leloudis, James Linwood, II 1955- *WhoEmL 91*
Le Loyer, Pierre 1550-1634 *EncO&P 3*
Lely, Johannes van der *PenDiDA 89*
Lely, Peter 1618-1680 *IntDcAA 90*
Lelyveld, Arthur Joseph 1913- *WhoAm 90*
Lelyveld, Gail Annick 1948- *WhoAmW 91, WhoE 91, WhoEmL 91, WhoWor 91*
Lelyveld, Joseph *BioIn 16*
Lelyveld, Joseph Salem 1937- *WhoAm 90*
Lem, Richard Douglas 1933- *WhoAmA 91, WhoWor 91*
Lem, Stanislaw 1921- *ConAu 32NR, MajTwCW, RGTwCSF, WorAlBi*
Lema, Arnold H. 1938- *St&PR 91*
Lema, George R. 1924- *St&PR 91*
LeMahieu, James Joseph 1936- *WhoE 91*
Lemaigre Dubreuil, Bertrand 1929- *WhoWor 91*
LeMaire, Cathy Louise 1951- *WhoAmW 91*
Lemaire, Guy Francois 1938- *WhoWor 91*
Lemaire, Jean Henri 1947- *WhoE 91*
Lemaire, Joseph J. 1928- *St&PR 91*
Lemaire, Madeleine Jeanne 1845?-1928 *BiDWomA*
Le Maire, William Jan 1933- *WhoAm 90*
Le Maistre, Charles Aubrey 1924- *WhoAm 90, WhoSSW 91*
Le Maistre, David Joseph 1946- *St&PR 91*
Lemaitre, Georges 1894-1966 *DcScB S2*
Leman, Eugene D. 1942- *St&PR 91, WhoAm 90*
Leman, James 1688?-1745 *PenDiDA 89*
Lemanczyk, Dave 1950- *Ballpl 90*
Lemanek, Kathleen Lynn 1958- *WhoAmW 91*
Lemann, Bernard 1905- *WhoWrEP 89*
Lemann, Juan 1928- *IntWWM 90*
Lemann, Nancy *BioIn 16*
Lemann, Thomas B. 1926- *St&PR 91*
Lemann, Thomas Berthelot 1926- *WhoAm 90*
Lemanski, David Alan 1951- *WhoEmL 91*
Lemanski, Larry Fredrick 1943- *WhoAm 90*
LeMar, Bruce Richard 1946- *St&PR 91*
LeMarbe, Edward Stanley 1952- *WhoE 91*
Lemarbe, Edward Stanly 1952- *St&PR 91*
Lemarchand, Charles-Joseph 1759-1826 *PenDiDA 89*
Lemarchand, Elizabeth 1906- *TwCCr&M 91*
Lemarchand, Louis-Edouard 1795-1872 *PenDiDA 89*
Lemare, Iris Margaret Elsie *IntWWM 90*
Lemaster, Denny 1939- *Ballpl 90*
LeMaster, Edwin William 1940- *WhoSSW 91*
LeMaster, J R 1934- *ConAu 30NR*
LeMaster, Jimmie Ray 1934- *WhoSSW 91, WhoWrEP 89*
LeMaster, Johnnie 1954- *Ballpl 90*
Lemaster, Leslie Jean *AuBYP 90*
Lemaster, Marvin Dale *BiDrAPA 89*
Lemaster, Richard L. 1925- *St&PR 91*
LeMaster, Sherry Renee 1953- *WhoAmW 91, WhoEmL 91*
LeMaster, Susan M. 1953- *WhoAmW 91*
Lemasters, John N. *WhoAm 90, WhoSSW 91*
Lemasters, John N. 1933- *St&PR 91*
Lemasters, John Nelson, III 1933- *WhoAm 90*
Lemay, Curtis E. 1906- *WorAlBi*
Lemay, Curtis E 1906-1990 *CurBio 90N, NewYTBS 90 [port]*
LeMay, Dick 1938- *Ballpl 90*
Lemay, Harding 1922- *WhoWrEP 89*
Lemay, Helen Lillian Schneider 1947- *WhoAmW 91, WhoEmL 91*
LeMay, Jacques 1940- *WhoAm 90*
LeMay, James Tandy *BiDrAPA 89*
Lemay, Pamphile 1837-1918 *DcLB 99 [port]*
Lemay, Robert C. 1950- *St&PR 91*
Lemayev, Nikolay Vasil'yevich 1929- *WhoWor 91*
Lembeck, Robert James 1954- *WhoEmL 91*
Lembede, Anton 1914-1947 *BioIn 16*
Lemberg, Steven Floyd 1953- *WhoEmL 91*
Lemberg, Thomas Michael 1946- *WhoE 91*
Lemberger, August Paul 1926- *WhoAm 90*
Lemberger, Coleen F. 1952- *WhoAmW 91*
Lemberger, Louis 1937- *WhoAm 90*
Lemberger, Nancy Lee 1947- *WhoAmW 91*
Lemberger, Norma 1944- *WhoAmW 91, WhoE 91*
Lembersky, Mark Raphael 1945- *WhoEmL 91*
Lembi-Detert, Yvonne *BioIn 16*
Lembitz, Edward Lawrence 1926- *WhoAm 90*
Lembke, Christel E 1939- *BiDrAPA 89*
Lembke, Janet 1933- *WhoWrEP 89*
Lembo, Gloria Ann 1949- *St&PR 91*
Lembo, Stephen Ignatius 1945- *WhoSSW 91*
Lembo, Stephen J *BiDrAPA 89*
Lembong, Johannes Tarcicius 1930- *WhoWor 91*
Lemcoe, M. Marshall 1921- *WhoAm 90*
Lemeche, Ellen Gyrithe 1866-1945 *EncCoWW*
Lemelin, Roger 1919- *WhoWor 91*
LeMelle, Tilden John 1929- *WhoAm 90*
Lemelle, Wilbert John 1931- *WhoE 91*
Lemen, Richard Alan 1943- *WhoAm 90*
Le Mener, Georges Philippe 1948- *WhoAm 90*
LeMenestrel, Alain Paul 1930- *St&PR 91*
Lemens, William Vernon, Jr. 1935- *WhoSSW 91, WhoWor 91*
LeMense, Rodney Anthony 1937- *St&PR 91*
Lementowski, Michal 1943- *WhoE 91*
Lemer, Albert 1926- *St&PR 91*
Lemer, Ellen Terry 1943- *WhoAmA 91*
Lemere, Frederick *BiDrAPA 89*
Lemerle, Paul 1903-1989 *ConAu 129*
Lemert, Charles Clay 1937- *WhoAm 90*
Lemert, James Bolton 1935- *WhoAm 90*
Lemery, Francis Patton 1939- *St&PR 91*
Lemery, J.L. 1941- *St&PR 91*
Lemesh, Nicholas Thomas 1946- *WhoAm 90*
Lemeshev, Sergey 1902-1977 *PenDiMP*
Lemessurier, William James 1926- *St&PR 91, WhoAm 90*
Le Mesurier, John 1912-1983 *DcNaB 1981*
Lemeur, Henry E. 1931- *St&PR 91*
Lemeur, Patricia McGrath 1932- *St&PR 91*
Lemeur, William T. 1956- *St&PR 91*
Lemieux, Annette Rose 1957- *WhoAmA 91, WhoAmW 91*
Lemieux, Bonne A 1921- *WhoAmA 91*
Lemieux, Claude 1965- *BioIn 16*
LeMieux, Guy Frederic 1929- *St&PR 91*
Lemieux, Henry F. 1926- *St&PR 91*
Lemieux, Irenee 1931- *WhoAmA 91*
Lemieux, James P. 1935- *St&PR 91*
Lemieux, Jean Paul 1904- *WhoAmA 91*
Lemieux, Joseph H. 1931- *St&PR 91*
Lemieux, Joseph Henry 1931- *WhoAm 90*
Lemieux, Mario *BioIn 16*
Lemieux, Mario 1965- *WhoAm 90, WorAlBi*
Lemieux, Marjorie Dix 1921- *WhoAmW 91*
Lemieux, Raymond Urgel 1920- *WhoAm 90*
Lemieux, Suzanne 1946- *WhoAmA 91*
Leming, Donna Faye 1957- *WhoSSW 91*
Leming, Marcia Lou 1934- *St&PR 91*
Leming, William Vaughn 1945- *WhoSSW 91*
Lemire, Charles-Gabriel Sauvage 1741-1827 *PenDiDA 89*
Lemire, David H. 1947- *St&PR 91*
Lemire, David Stephen 1949- *WhoEmL 91*
Lemire, Isabelle *BiDrAPA 89*
Lemire, Laurent Pierre Alfred 1961- *WhoWor 91*
Lemkau, Curt William 1943- *WhoE 91*
Lemkau, Paul V 1909- *BiDrAPA 89*
Lemkau, Paul Victor 1909- *WhoE 91*
Lemke, Carlton Edward 1920- *WhoWrEP 89*
Lemke, Clark Elliott 1946- *St&PR 91*
Lemke, Corrine LaRue 1934- *WhoAmW 91*
Lemke, Donald Ervin 1948- *St&PR 91*
Lemke, Heinz Ulrich 1941- *WhoWor 91*
Lemke, James Underwood 1929- *WhoAm 90*
Lemke, John Raymond 1941- *St&PR 91*
Lemke, Judith A. 1952- *WhoAmW 91*
Lemke, Paul Arenz 1937- *WhoAm 90*
Lemke, Peter William 1941- *St&PR 91*
Lemke, Richard Warren 1953- *WhoSSW 91*
Lemkin, Raphael 1900-1959 *BioIn 16*
Lemle, Louis G. *St&PR 91N*
Lemle, Robert Spencer 1953- *WhoAm 90, WhoE 91, WhoEmL 91, WhoWor 91*
Lemlech, Johanna Kasin *WhoAm 90*
Lemler, Jerry Berl 1949- *BiDrAPA 89*
Lemley, Barbara Wink 1930- *WhoE 91*
Lemley, Jack Kenneth 1935- *St&PR 91*
Lemley, Steven S. 1945- *WhoAm 90*
Lemley, Thomas Blair 1945- *St&PR 91*
Lemlich, Robert 1926- *WhoAm 90*
Lemma, Annmarie 1962- *WhoAmW 91*
Lemma, Mangestu 1928-1988 *AnObit 1988*
Lemmel, Steven Allen 1953- *WhoEmL 91*
Lemmen, Craig Allen *BiDrAPA 89*
Lemmens, Alois Antoon 1948- *WhoWor 91*
Lemmens, Jaak Nikolaas 1823-1881 *PenDiMP*
Lemmens-Sherrington, Helen 1834-1906 *PenDiMP*
Lemmer, Bjorn 1942- *WhoWor 91*
Lemmermen, Jay Charles 1948- *WhoSSW 91*
Lemmey, Tara Lynn 1964- *WhoAmW 91*
Lemmon, Alfred E. 1949- *IntWWM 90*
Lemmon, Charles Wesley 1949- *WhoEmL 91*
Lemmon, David 1931- *ConAu 131*
Lemmon, Harry Thomas 1930- *WhoAm 90*
Lemmon, Jack *BioIn 16*
Lemmon, Jack 1925- *WhoAm 90, WorAlBi*
Lemmon, Marcia Hilary 1958- *WhoE 91*
Lemmon, Marilyn Sue 1939- *WhoAmW 91, WhoWor 91*
Lemmon, Philip Douglas 1943- *IntWWM 90*
Lemmon, Robert Stell 1885- *AuBYP 90*
Lemmon, Willard Lincoln 1924- *WhoSSW 91*
Lemmond, Charles D., Jr. *WhoE 91*
Lemmond, Mary Sheldon 1945- *WhoSSW 91*
Lemmons, Barry Joe 1958- *WhoSSW 91*
Lemmons, James Curtis 1948- *St&PR 91*
Lemmons, Jerry A. 1937- *St&PR 91*
Lemmons, Miriam Elise 1932- *WhoAmW 91*
Lemnios, Andrew Zachery 1931- *WhoAm 90, WhoE 91*
Lemnitz, Tiana 1897- *IntWWM 90, PenDiMP*
Lemnitzer, Lyman 1899-1988 *AnObit 1988*
Lemnitzer, Lyman 1899-1989 *WorAlBi*
Lemnitzer, Lyman Louis 1899-1988 *BioIn 16*
Le Moine, James MacPherson 1825-1912 *DcLB 99 [port]*
Lemole, Gerald Michael 1936- *WhoAm 90*
Lemon, Bob 1920- *Ballpl 90 [port], WorAlBi*
Lemon, Charles Richard 1925- *St&PR 91*
Lemon, Chet 1955- *Ballpl 90*
Lemon, David W. 1945- *St&PR 91*
Lemon, David William 1945- *WhoAm 90*
Lemon, George Edward 1907- *WhoWrEP 89*
Lemon, Henry Martyn 1915- *WhoAm 90*
Lemon, J.R. 1942- *St&PR 91*
Lemon, Jerry Wayne 1935- *WhoSSW 91*
Lemon, Jim 1928- *Ballpl 90*
Lemon, Leslie Gene 1940- *St&PR 91*
Lemon, Mark 1809-1870 *BioIn 16*
Lemon, Meadowlark *BioIn 16*
Lemon, Robert A., Jr. 1961- *St&PR 91*
Lemon, Robert S, Jr 1938- *WhoAmA 91*
Lemon, Verna M. 1950- *WhoAmW 91*
Lemon, William J. 1922- *St&PR 91*
LeMond, Greg 1961?- *BioIn 16*
LeMond, Gregory James 1961- *WhoAm 90, WhoWor 91*
Lemongello, Mark 1955- *Ballpl 90*
Lemonias, Peter J. 1952- *St&PR 91*
Lemonick, Aaron 1923- *WhoAm 90*
Lemonnier, Jean-Charles-Henri *PenDiDA 89*
Lemonnier, Louis-Francois *PenDiDA 89*
Lemons, Brian John 1959- *WhoEmL 91*
Lemons, James Lenford 1948- *WhoSSW 91*
Lemons, Keith David 1954- *WhoSSW 91*
Lemont, Paul Edwin 1940- *St&PR 91*
Lemor, Isaac 1951- *St&PR 91*
Lemos, Antonio V *BiDrAPA 89*
Lemos, Gloria Elliott 1946- *St&PR 91, WhoAmW 91*
Lemos, Ramon Marcelino 1927- *WhoAm 90*
Lemos, Robert Anthony 1941- *St&PR 91*
Le Moyne, Charles 1626-1685 *WhNaAH, WorAlBi*
Le Moyne, Jacques *EncCRAm*
Le Moyne, Jacques De Morgues *WhNaAH*
Lemper, Ute *BioIn 16*
Lempereur, Douglas Roddis 1949- *St&PR 91*
Lemperle, Virginia Maxine 1921- *WhoWrEP 89*
Lempert, Philip 1953- *WhoE 91*
Lempert, Richard A. 1932- *St&PR 91*
Lempert, Richard Owen 1942- *WhoAm 90*
Lempicka, Tamara de 1898?-1980 *BiDWomA*
Lempicki, Chester P.J. 1947- *St&PR 91*
Lempres, Michael Timothy 1960- *WhoEmL 91*
Lemus, Carmen Z 1955- *BiDrAPA 89*
Lemus, Fraterno 1948- *WhoEmL 91, WhoHisp 91*
Lemus, Luis C. 1949- *BiDrAPA 89*
Lena, Adolph J. 1925- *St&PR 91*
Lena, Adolph John 1925- *WhoAm 90, WhoE 91*
Lenaburg, David S. 1942- *St&PR 91*
Lenahan, Edward Patrick 1925-1988 *BioIn 16*
Lenahan, Mea Lorraine 1932- *WhoWrEP 89*
Lenahan, Walter Clair 1934- *WhoAm 90*
Le Nain, Antoine 1588-1648 *WorAlBi*
Le Nain, Louis 1593?-1648 *WorAlBi*
Le Nain, Louis 1600?-1648 *IntDcAA 90*
Le Nain, Mathieu 1607-1677 *WorAlBi*
Lenander, Melbert A. 1932- *St&PR 91*
Lenard, Andrew 1927- *WhoAm 90*
Lenard, Julia 1935- *St&PR 91*
Lenard, Philipp Eduard Anton 1862-1947 *BioIn 16*
Lenardon, Robert Joseph 1928- *WhoAm 90*
Lenarz, Larry Rudolph 1924- *St&PR 91*
Lenas, Paris Procopiou 1936- *WhoWor 91*
LeNay, Tom W. 1927- *St&PR 91*
Lenaz, Gerald Carl 1942- *WhoE 91*
Lencastre, Filipa de 1437-1497 *EncCoWW*
Lence, Julio G. *WhoHisp 91*
Lencek, Rado L. 1921- *WhoAm 90, WhoWor 91*
Lenchin, Julianne Marie 1956- *WhoAmW 91*
Lencicki, John *BioIn 16*
Lencker, Christoph *PenDiDA 89*
Lencker, Hans 1523-1585 *PenDiDA 89*
Lencker, Johannes 1570-1637 *PenDiDA 89*
Lencker, Zacharias *PenDiDA 89*
Lenclos, Anne de 1623?-1706 *EncCoWW*
Lenczycki, Joseph Aloysius, Jr. 1948- *WhoEmL 91*
Lendacki, Sandra Elaine 1955- *WhoAmW 91*
Lender, Adam 1921- *WhoAm 90*
Lender, Herman Joseph 1923- *WhoAm 90*
Lenderking, William Raymond, Jr. 1934- *WhoE 91*
Lenders, Jozef Gerard 1957- *WhoEmL 91*
Lendi, Martin 1933- *WhoWor 91*
Lending, Kenn 1955- *IntWWM 90*
Lendl, Ivan *BioIn 16*
Lendl, Ivan 1960- *WhoAm 90, WhoWor 91*
Lendl, Ivan 1970- *WorAlBi*
Lendman, Ernest Martin 1938- *St&PR 91*
Lendrum, James Thoburn 1907- *WhoAm 90*
Lendrum, John T. 1927- *St&PR 91*
Lendvai, Paul 1929- *ConAu 33NR*
Lendvay, Kamillo 1928- *IntWWM 90*
LeNeau, Peter Willard 1954- *WhoEmL 91*
Lenehan, Pamela F. 1952- *St&PR 91*
Lenehan, William Thurman 1930- *WhoAm 90*
Lener Quartet *PenDiMP*
Lener, Jeno *PenDiMP*
Leness, George Crawford 1936- *WhoAm 90*
Lenfant, Claude Jean-Marie 1928- *WhoAm 90*
L'Enfant, Pierre 1754-1825 *WorAlBi*
L'Enfant, Pierre Charles 1754-1825 *BioIn 16*
Leng, Shao Chuan 1921- *WhoAm 90*
Lengefeld, William Chris 1939- *IntWWM 90*
Lengel, Clifford John 1945- *St&PR 91*
Lengel, Elizabeth Hilscher 1953- *WhoEmL 91*
Lengel, Jerome Kenneth 1933- *WhoE 91*
Lengel, John *ODwPR 91*
Lengel, John Robert 1929- *St&PR 91*
Lengemann, Frederick William 1925- *WhoAm 90*
Lengemann, Robert Allen 1934- *St&PR 91*
Lenger, Charlene Jean 1957- *WhoSSW 91*
Lenger, Mark Duane *BiDrAPA 89*
L'Engle, Madeleine 1918- *AuBYP 90, BioIn 16, MajTwCW, RGTwCSF, WhoAm 90, WhoAmW 91, WhoWrEP 89, WorAlBi*

L'Engle, William Johnson 1884-1957 *WhoAmA 91N*
Lenglen, Suzanne 1899-1938 *BioIn 16, WorAlBi*
Lengyel, Alfonz 1921- *WhoAm 90, WhoAmA 91*
Lengyel, Andras 1952- *WhoWor 91*
Lengyel, Cornel Adam 1915- *WhoAm 90, WhoWrEP 89*
Lengyel, Erwin 1900- *BiDrAPA 89*
Lengyel, Laura La Foret 1946- *WhoAmW 91*
Lengyel, Peter Emery 1940- *St&PR 91*
Lengyel, Sandra Susan 1959- *BiDrAPA 89*
Lenhardt, Benjamin F., Jr. 1940- *St&PR 91*
Lenhardt, Don 1922- *Ballpl 90*
Lenhardt, Shirley M 1934- *WhoAmA 91*
Lenhart, Harold Blondin *BiDrAPA 89*
Lenhart, Julie Brown 1950- *WhoAmW 91*
Lenhart, Karen Camp *BiDrAPA 89*
Lenhart, Kermit Raymond 1922- *St&PR 91*
Lenhart, Pauline June House 1929- *WhoAmW 91*
Lenhart, Ralph Leroy 1910- *WhoSSW 91*
Lenhart, Sharyn Ann 1948- *BiDrAPA 89*
Lenher, Samuel 1905- *WhoAm 90*
Lenherr, Frederick Keith 1943- *WhoAm 90*
Lenhoff, Howard Maer 1929- *WhoAm 90*
Leniado-Chira, Joseph 1934- *IntWWM 90*
Lenica, Jan 1928- *ConDes 90*
Lenich, Martin J. 1959- *St&PR 91*
Lenig, Larry E., Jr. 1948- *St&PR 91*
Lenihan, Brian Joseph 1930- *WhoWor 91*
Lenihan, Judith Ann 1939- *St&PR 91*
Lenihan, Rita 1914-1989 *BioIn 16*
Lenihan, Ronald Raymond 1963- *WhoE 91*
Lenin, Vladimir Il'ich 1870-1924 *BioIn 16*
Lenin, Vladimir Ilyich 1870-1924 *WorAlBi*
Lenington, Kenneth Taber 1949- *BiDrAPA 89*
Lenja, Lotte 1898-1981 *PenDiMP*
Lenk, Hans Albert Paul 1935- *WhoWor 91*
Lenk, Krzysztof 1936- *ConDes 90*
Lenk, Kurt Heinz 1929- *WhoWor 91*
Lenk, Robert E. 1917- *St&PR 91*
Lenk, Thomas 1933- *WhoWor 91*
Lenkaitis, Lewis F. 1943- *St&PR 91*
Lenkay, Mary Anne *BiDrAPA 89*
Lenke, George H., Jr. 1924- *St&PR 91*
Lenker, Jay Alan 1949- *WhoEmL 91*
Lenker, Marlene N 1932- *WhoAmA 91*
Lenker, Robert E. 1928- *St&PR 91*
Lenkiewicz, R. O. *BioIn 16*
Lenkoski, L Douglas 1925- *BiDrAPA 89*
Lenkoski, Leo Douglas 1925- *WhoAm 90*
Lenkowsky, Leslie 1946- *WhoE 91*
Lenman, Bruce Philip 1938- *WhoAm 90*
Lenn, Stephen Andrew 1946- *WhoEmL 91*
Lennard-Jones, John Edward 1927- *WhoWor 91*
Lennartson, Leo Sherwood 1928- *WhoE 91*
Lennartsson, Karl Magnus 1961- *WhoWor 91*
Lennartz, Michelle R. 1956- *WhoEmL 91*
Lennarz, William Joseph 1934- *WhoAm 90*
Lenneberg, Hans H. 1924- *IntWWM 90*
Lennes, Gregory 1947- *St&PR 91, WhoAm 90*
Lenney, Annie 1910- *WhoAmA 91N*
Lenngren, Anna Maria 1754-1817 *DcScanL, EncCoWW*
Lennhoff, David Charles 1946- *WhoEmL 91*
Lenning, Diane Adele Benge 1946- *WhoAmW 91*
Lennon, Amelia Oles 1949- *WhoAmW 91*
Lennon, Brooke Daniel 1939- *St&PR 91*
Lennon, Dennis 1918- *ConDes 90*
Lennon, Dianne 1939?- *BioIn 16*
Lennon, Edward Joseph 1927- *WhoAm 90*
Lennon, Frank M. 1938- *WhoAm 90*
Lennon, Frank T. 1942- *St&PR 91*
Lennon, Frank Thomas *WhoAm 90*
Lennon, Harry K. *NewYTBS 90*
Lennon, Janet 1946?- *BioIn 16*
Lennon, John 1940-1980 *BioIn 16, EncPR&S 89, OxCPMus, WorAlBi*
Lennon, John, and Ono, Yoko *EncPR&S 89*
Lennon, John Anthony 1950- *IntWWM 90*
Lennon, Joseph Luke 1919- *WhoAm 90*
Lennon, Julian *BioIn 16*
Lennon, Julian 1963- *EncPR&S 89*
Lennon, Kathy 1943?- *BioIn 16*
Lennon, Marilyn 1954- *WhoAm 90, WhoE 91*
Lennon, Marilyn Ellen 1954- *WhoEmL 91*
Lennon, Max 1940- *WhoAm 90, WhoSSW 91*
Lennon, Peggy 1941?- *BioIn 16*
Lennon, Robert Lawrence 1933- *WhoE 91*
Lennon, Thomas Michael 1942- *WhoAm 90*
Lennon, Timothy 1938- *WhoAmA 91*
Lennox, Annie *BioIn 16*
Lennox, Charlotte 1729?-1804 *FemiCLE*
Lennox, Charlotte R. 1729?-1804 *BioAmW*
Lennox, Charlotte Ramsay 1720-1804 *BioIn 16*
Lennox, Charlotte Ramsey 1720-1804 *EncCRAm*
Lennox, Donald D. 1918- *St&PR 91*
Lennox, Donald Duane 1918- *WhoAm 90, WhoE 91*
Lennox, Ed 1885-1939 *Ballpl 90*
Lennox, Edward Newman 1925- *WhoSSW 91*
Lennox, Gloria 1931- *WhoAmW 91*
Lennox, Gregory P. 1955- *St&PR 91*
Lennox, Shirley Ann 1931- *WhoAmW 91*
Lennox, Vincent Joseph, Jr. 1947- *WhoEmL 91*
Lennox-Boyd, Alan Tindal 1904-1983 *DcNaB 1981*
Lennox Fisch, Carol Jeanine 1952- *WhoAmW 91*
Leno, Dan 1860-1904 *OxCPMus*
Leno, Jay *BioIn 16, NewYTBS 90 [port]*
Leno, Jay 1950- *WhoAm 90, WorAlBi*
Lenoard, Donald G. 1941- *St&PR 91*
Lenobel, Abraham M. 1931- *WhoE 91*
Le Noir, Elizabeth Anne 1754-1841 *FemiCLE*
Lenoir, Gloria Cisneros 1951- *WhoAmW 91, WhoEmL 91*
Lenoir, Jean 1891-1976 *OxCPMus*
Lenoir, Jean Joseph Etienne 1822-1900 *WorAlBi*
Lenoir, Maria Annette 1950- *WhoEmL 91*
LeNoire, Rosetta *BioIn 16*
Le Noire, Rosetta 1911- *BioIn 16, DrBlPA 90*
Lenoire, Rosetta 1911- *IntWWM 90*
Le Noire, Rosetta Burton 1911- *NotWoAT*
Lenon, Richard A. 1920- *St&PR 91*
Lenon, Richard Allen 1920- *WhoAm 90*
Le Normand, Marie-Anne Adelaide 1772-1843 *EncO&P 3*
Lenowitz, Arthur I. 1928- *St&PR 91*
Lenox, Cora Clinkscales 1908- *WhoAmW 91*
Lenox, Kimberly 1965- *WhoWrEP 89*
Lenox, Mary Frances 1944- *WhoAm 90*
Lenox, Robert Howard *BiDrAPA 89*
Lenox, Walter Scott *PenDiDA 89*
Lenroot, Irvine Luther 1869-1949 *AmLegL*
Lens, Sidney *BioIn 16*
Lens, Sidney 1912-1986 *AuBYP 90, EncAL*
Lensch, George Edward 1925- *St&PR 91*
Lenschow, Rolf Johan 1928- *WhoWor 91*
Lense, Edward Louis 1945- *WhoWrEP 89*
Lense, Frederick Thomas 1917- *St&PR 91*
Lensgraf, Samuel Jay *BiDrAPA 89*
Lensing, Charles Edmond 1930- *St&PR 91*
Lenski, Gerhard Emmanuel 1924- *WhoAm 90*
Lenski, Lois 1893- *WhoAmA 91N*
Lenski, Lois 1893-1974 *AuBYP 90*
Lenskold, Richard K. 1937- *St&PR 91*
Lenson, David 1945- *WhoWrEP 89*
Lenson, Michael 1903-1971 *WhoAmA 91N*
Lenssen, Heidi *WhoAmA 91*
Lent, Berkeley 1921- *WhoAm 90*
Lent, Blair 1930- *WhoAmA 91*
Lent, Diane Margaret 1955- *WhoE 91*
Lent, Henry Bolles 1901-1973 *AuBYP 90*
Lent, John A 1936- *ConAu 30NR*
Lent, John Anthony 1936- *WhoAm 90, WhoE 91, WhoWrEP 89*
Lent, Mary E. 1869-1946 *BioIn 16*
Lent, Norman Frederick, Jr. 1931- *WhoAm 90, WhoE 91*
Lent, Richard Martin 1952- *WhoEmL 91*
Lentczner, Bennett 1938- *IntWWM 90, WhoSSW 91*
Lentelli, Leo 1882-1962 *WhoAmA 91N*
Lentes, David Eugene 1951- *WhoWor 91*
Lenthall, Franklyn 1919- *WhoAm 90*
Lentine, John *WhoAmA 91N*
Lentine, John Anthony 1960- *WhoSSW 91, WhoWor 91*
Lentini, Tony *ODwPR 91*
Lentini, Vincent 1903- *BiDrAPA 89*
Lents, Ann 1949- *WhoAmW 91*
Lents, Don Glaude 1949- *St&PR 91, WhoEmL 91*
Lents, Peggy Iglauer 1950- *WhoEmL 91*
Lentsch, Eugene J. 1924- *St&PR 91*
Lentz, Bernard Frederic 1948- *WhoE 91*
Lentz, Christine Marie Anderson 1958- *WhoAmW 91*
Lentz, Daniel *NewAgMG*
Lentz, Daniel Kirkland 1942- *IntWWM 90*
Lentz, David Lee 1946- *WhoEmL 91*
Lentz, Frank *NewAgMG*
Lentz, John Max 1896-1989 *BioIn 16*
Lentz, Kathleen Elaine *BiDrAPA 89*
Lentz, L. Charles 1945- *St&PR 91*
Lentz, Malcolm Louis 1921- *St&PR 91*
Lentz, Richard D 1942- *BiDrAPA 89*
Lentz, Robert Allen 1950- *WhoE 91*
Lentz, Robert Henry 1924- *WhoAm 90*
Lentz, Robert J 1908- *BiDrAPA 89*
Lentz, Robert Raines 1943- *St&PR 91*
Lentz, Thomas Edward 1958- *WhoEmL 91*
Lentz, Vernon E., Jr. *St&PR 91*
Leny, Jean-Claude 1928- *BioIn 16*
Lenya, Lotte 1898-1981 *BioIn 16, OxCPMus, PenDiMP, WorAlBi*
Lenz, Bruce C. 1943- *St&PR 91*
Lenz, Charles Wangelin 1942- *St&PR 91*
Lenz, Cynthia Lowe 1951- *WhoAmW 91*
Lenz, Edward Arnold 1942- *WhoAm 90, WhoSSW 91*
Lenz, Fred William 1947- *St&PR 91*
Lenz, Frederick *NewAgE 90*
Lenz, Hanfried Wilhelm 1916- *WhoWor 91*
Lenz, Henry Paul 1925- *WhoAm 90*
Lenz, J M R 1751-1792 *DcLB 94 [port]*
Lenz, John Joseph 1934- *St&PR 91*
Lenz, Kay *BioIn 16*
Lenz, Kay 1953- *WhoAm 90*
Lenz, Lawrence Richard 1946- *WhoEmL 91*
Lenz, Linda Lee 1938- *WhoE 91*
Lenz, Randolph W. *BioIn 16*
Lenz, Richard Joseph 1928- *WhoSSW 91*
Lenz, Robert H. *WhoAm 90*
Lenz, Robert H. 1939- *St&PR 91*
Lenz, Rosa *BiDrAPA 89*
Lenz, Siegfried 1926- *WhoWor 91*
Lenz, William Harding 1953- *WhoE 91*
Lenz, William J, Jr. 1945- *BiDrAPA 89*
Lenza, Linda Kay 1957- *WhoE 91, WhoEmL 91*
Lenzi, Andrea 1953- *WhoWor 91*
Lenzie, Charles A. 1937- *St&PR 91*
Lenzie, Charles Albert 1937- *WhoAm 90*
Lenzini, Arthur Lee 1927- *WhoAm 90*
Lenzini, Rebecca T. 1952- *St&PR 91*
Lenzmeier, Allen 1943- *St&PR 91*
Lenzner, Abraham S 1915- *BiDrAPA 89*
Lenzner, Joseph B. 1903-1989 *BioIn 16*
Lenzy, Delores F. 1961- *WhoEmL 91*
Leo, Alan 1860-1917 *EncO&P 3*
Leo, Andre 1832-1900 *EncCoWW*
Leo, Christy Lynn 1960- *WhoAmW 91, WhoEmL 91*
Leo, Karen Joan 1951- *BiDrAPA 89*
Leo, Karl William 1957- *WhoEmL 91*
Leo, Robert Joseph 1939- *WhoAm 90*
Leo, Salvatore Saverio 1926- *St&PR 91*
Leobgyda 732?-780 *EncCoWW*
Leodas, Costa G. 1933- *St&PR 91*
Leof, David B 1938- *BiDrAPA 89*
LeoGrande, William Mark 1949- *WhoAm 90*
Leon, Abilio *WhoHisp 91*
Leon, Ana Eugenia 1964- *WhoSSW 91*
Leon, Angel Acosta 1930-1964 *ArtLatA*
Leon, Arthur Sol 1931- *WhoAm 90*
Leon, Benjamin Joseph 1932- *WhoAm 90, WhoE 91*
Leon, Bruce Frederick 1952- *WhoSSW 91*
Leon, Bruno 1924- *WhoAm 90*
Leon, Carlos A 1926- *BiDrAPA 89*
Leon, Carmen I 1951- *BiDrAPA 89*
Leon, Dennis 1933- *WhoAm 90, WhoAmA 91*
Leon, Donald Francis 1932- *WhoAm 90*
Leon, Eddie 1946- *Ballpl 90*
Leon, Heriberto 1956- *WhoHisp 91*
Leon, Jack Paul 1930- *WhoEmL 91, WhoSSW 91*
Leon, James Howard 1951- *WhoEmL 91*
Leon, James Robert 1922- *St&PR 91*
Leon, Jeffrey J. 1947- *St&PR 91*
Leon, Juana Aurora 1940- *WhoAmW 91*
Leon, Judene Marie 1931- *WhoWrEP 89*
Leon, Luis E. 1952- *St&PR 91, WhoAm 90*
Leon, Luis Manuel, Jr. 1955- *WhoHisp 91*
Leon, Margaret Adele 1948- *WhoAmW 91*
Leon, Maria Teresa 1904- *EncCoWW*
Leon, Marjorie Roth 1952- *WhoAmW 91*
Leon, Max 1950- *Ballpl 90*
Leon, Michael Ponce de 1922- *BioIn 16*
Leon, Pedro J, Jr. *BiDrAPA 89*
Leon, Ralph Bernard 1932- *WhoAmA 91*
Leon, Robert L 1925- *BiDrAPA 89*
Leon, Robert Leonard 1925- *WhoAm 90*
Leon, Robert S. 1947- *WhoHisp 91*
Leon, Ronald Lawrence 1954- *BiDrAPA 89*
Leon, Steve 1948- *WhoWrEP 89*
Leon, Tania *BioIn 16*
Leon, Tania J. 1943- *WhoHisp 91*
Leon, Tania Justina 1943- *WhoAm 90*
Leon, Vicki 1942- *ConAu 132*
Leon, Ynes 1950- *WhoE 91*
Leon-Andrade, Carlos 1953- *BiDrAPA 89*
Leon de Vivero, Fernando 1906- *BioIn 16*
Leon Dub, Marcelo 1946- *WhoWor 91*
Leon Guerrero, Juan Duenas 1935- *WhoHisp 91*
Leon Guerrero, Wilfred Pacelle 1942- *WhoAm 90*
Leon-Portilla, Miguel 1926- *ConAu 32NR, HispWr 90, WhoWor 91*
Leonard, A. Byron 1904- *AuBYP 90*
Leonard, Arthur Sherman 1952- *WhoE 91*
Leonard, Bill 1916- *BioIn 16*
Leonard, Bobby Frank 1932- *St&PR 91*
Leonard, Brian Francis 1948- *WhoEmL 91*
Leonard, Brian Kelly 1958- *WhoEmL 91*
Leonard, Bruce D *BiDrAPA 89*
Leonard, Buck 1907- *Ballpl 90 [port]*
Leonard, Cecil Ervin 1941- *WhoE 91*
Leonard, Charles E 1907- *BiDrAPA 89*
Leonard, Charles F 1943- *BiDrAPA 89*
Leonard, Cheryl Martschink 1952- *WhoAmW 91*
Leonard, Cicero *BioIn 16*
Leonard, Daniel 1740-1829 *EncCRAm*
Leonard, David Arthur 1928- *WhoAm 90*
Leonard, David Henry 1933- *WhoAm 90*
Leonard, Debi Lynn 1955- *WhoAmW 91*
Leonard, Dennis 1951- *Ballpl 90*
Leonard, Donald L. 1946- *St&PR 91*
Leonard, Dorothy Louise 1932- *WhoAmW 91*
Leonard, Douglas Mark 1953- *BiDrAPA 89*
Leonard, Dutch 1909-1983 *Ballpl 90*
Leonard, Earl Rex 1939- *St&PR 91*
Leonard, Eason Harris 1920- *WhoAm 90*
Leonard, Eddie 1875-1941 *OxCPMus*
Leonard, Edward C, Jr. 1938- *BiDrAPA 89*
Leonard, Edward Charles 1927- *St&PR 91*
Leonard, Edward F. 1932- *WhoAm 90*
Leonard, Edward Paul 1935- *WhoSSW 91*
Leonard, Edwin Deane 1929- *WhoAm 90, WhoE 91*
Leonard, Eileen Ann 1941- *WhoAmW 91*
Leonard, Elijah 1814-1891 *DcCanB 12*
Leonard, Ellen Marie 1944- *WhoAmW 91*
Leonard, Elmore *BestSel 90-4 [port]*
Leonard, Elmore 1925- *BioIn 16, MajTwCW, TwCCr&M 91, WorAlBi, WorAu 1980 [port]*
Leonard, Elmore John 1925- *WhoAm 90, WhoWrEP 89*
Leonard, Emilio Manuel, Jr. 1945- *WhoHisp 91*
Leonard, Emily 1928- *WhoE 91*
Leonard, Eugene Albert 1935- *WhoAm 90*
Leonard, George Burr 1923- *BioIn 16*
Leonard, George Edmund 1940- *WhoAm 90, WhoWor 91*
Leonard, George Edmund, Jr. 1940- *St&PR 91*
Leonard, George Jay 1946- *WhoAm 90, WhoWor 91*
Leonard, Gerald Dennis 1937- *St&PR 91*
Leonard, Gilbert Stanley 1941- *WhoSSW 91*
Leonard, Gladys Osborne 1882-1968 *EncO&P 3, EncPaPR 91*
Leonard, Graham *BioIn 16*
Leonard, Graham Douglas 1921- *WhoWor 91*
Leonard, Harry E. 1922- *St&PR 91*
Leonard, Henrietta L *BiDrAPA 89*
Leonard, Henry Siggins, Jr. 1930- *WhoAm 90*
Leonard, Henry V. *BioIn 16*
Leonard, Herman Beukema 1952- *WhoAm 90*
Leonard, Hub 1892-1952 *Ballpl 90*
Leonard, Irvin 1921- *St&PR 91*
Leonard, Jack *BioIn 16*
Leonard, Jack D'Artagnan 1937- *St&PR 91*
Leonard, James Barry 1953- *WhoE 91*
Leonard, James Frederick 1949- *WhoEmL 91*
Leonard, James Joseph 1924- *WhoAm 90*
Leonard, James O. 1942- *St&PR 91*
Leonard, Janet Tonka 1952- *WhoAmW 91, WhoEmL 91*
Leonard, Janice Eloise 1934- *WhoSSW 91*
Leonard, Jeffrey 1955- *Ballpl 90*
Leonard, Jeffrey S. 1945- *WhoEmL 91*
Leonard, Jennifer Clare 1952- *WhoAmW 91*
Leonard, Jim Thomas 1955- *BiDrAPA 89*
Leonard, Joan *BioIn 16*
Leonard, Joanne 1940- *WhoAm 90, WhoAmA 91*
Leonard, Joe 1894-1920 *Ballpl 90*
Leonard, John Dunbar 1933- *St&PR 91*
Leonard, John Edward 1947- *WhoEmL 91*
Leonard, John F 1931- *BiDrAPA 89*
Leonard, John Francis 1935- *WhoAm 90*
Leonard, John Harry 1922- *WhoAm 90*
Leonard, John Martin 1957- *WhoE 91*
Leonard, John-Paul 1948- *WhoWor 91*
Leonard, Joseph B. 1943- *WhoAm 90*
Leonard, Joseph Howard 1952- *WhoE 91*
Leonard, Juanita Louise Evans 1939- *WhoAmW 91*
Leonard, Lank 1896-1960 *EncACom*
Leonard, Laurence B., Jr. 1930- *St&PR 91*
Leonard, Laurence Barberie, Jr. 1930- *WhoAm 90*
Leonard, Lawrence 1928- *IntWWM 90*
Leonard, Lawrence Edwards 1934- *WhoAm 90*
Leonard, Leo Donald 1938- *WhoE 91*

Leonard, Lorraine 1954- WhoAmW 91
Leonard, Lucinda Elaine WhoAmW 91
Leonard, Marc St&PR 91
Leonard, Marie Therese Pierrette 1949- WhoEmL 91
Leonard, Martha Frances 1916- WhoAmW 91
Leonard, Martha Reed 1938- WhoAmW 91
Leonard, Mary Finley 1862- LiHiK
Leonard, Michael Steven 1947- WhoAm 90
Leonard, Nelson Jordan 1916- WhoAm 90
Leonard, Noble D BiDrAPA 89
Leonard, Norman J. 1941- St&PR 91
Leonard, Paul Haralson 1925- WhoAm 90
Leonard, Paul R. 1943- WhoAm 90
Leonard, Penny Sue Evans 1945- WhoSSW 91
Leonard, Phyllis G. 1924- WhoWrEP 89
Leonard, Rachel Rauh 1957- WhoE 91
Leonard, Randall NewAgMG
Leonard, Ray 1956- WorAlBi
Leonard, Ray Charles BioIn 16
Leonard, Raymond Wesley 1909- WhoSSW 91
Leonard, Richard Hart 1921- WhoAm 90
Leonard, Richard Manning 1908- WhoAm 90
Leonard, Robert Beau 1951- WhoEmL 91
Leonard, Robert Charles 1947- WhoWor 91
Leonard, Robert Warren 1926- WhoAm 90
Leonard, Roy Junior 1929- WhoAm 90
Leonard, Ruth Ann 1946- WhoAmW 91
Leonard, Sarah Jane 1953- IntWWM 90
Leonard, Selina Phyllis 1963- WhoAmW 91
Leonard, Sharen Crumrine 1953- WhoAmW 91
Leonard, Sheldon 1907- WhoAm 90, WorAlBi
Leonard, Sheron Rena 1959- WhoAmW 91
Leonard, Spring Bixby 1953- WhoEmL 91
Leonard, Sugar Ray BioIn 16
Leonard, Sugar Ray 1956- WhoAm 90, WhoE 91
Leonard, Susan Ruth 1955- WhoAmW 91
Leonard, Susan Scheinman 1946- WhoE 91
Leonard, Thomas A. 1946- WhoE 91
Leonard, Timothy Dwight 1940- WhoSSW 91
Leonard, Tom 1944- ConAu 31NR
Leonard, Virginia Kathryn 1944- WhoAmW 91
Leonard, Walter Raymond 1923- WhoAm 90
Leonard, Wilford A. 1927- St&PR 91
Leonard, Will Ernest, Jr. 1935- WhoAm 90
Leonard, William F. 1926- WhoSSW 91
Leonard, William Michael 1939- WhoAm 90
Leonard, William Norris 1912- WhoAm 90
Leonard, William Samuel 1929- St&PR 91
Leonard-Barton, Dorothy 1942- WhoAmW 91
Leonardi, Hector 1930- WhoAmA 91
Leonardi, Lewis John 1947- St&PR 91
Leonardi, Samuel Joseph 1940- St&PR 91
Leonardi, Susan J. 1946- ConAu 131
Leonardo, da Vinci 1452-1519 BioIn 16
Leonardo da Vinci 1452-1519 IntDcAA 90, WorAlBi
Leonardo di Ser Giovanni PenDiDA 89
Leonardo, Ann Adamson 1944- WhoAmW 91
Leonardo, Joseph Francis 1948- St&PR 91
Leonardo, Lawrence J. 1948- St&PR 91
Leonardo, Louis Charles 1953- WhoEmL 91
Leonardo, Susan Ann 1953- WhoEmL 91
Leonardos, Urylee DrBIPA 90
Leonberger, Frederick John 1947- WhoAm 90
Leoncavallo, Ruggero 1857-1919 PenDiMP A
Leoncavallo, Ruggiero 1858-1919 WorAlBi
Leondar, Barbara 1928- WhoAmW 91, WhoE 91
Leondias, Sapho 1832-1900 EncCoWW
Leone, da Modena 1571-1648 BioIn 16
Leone, Carole Anne 1946- WhoAmW 91
Leone, Dennis 1955- BiDrAPA 89
Leone, Esterino B. 1907- St&PR 91
Leone, George Frank 1926- St&PR 91, WhoAm 90
Leone, Ida A. 1922- WhoAmW 91
Leone, John A. 1934- St&PR 91
Leone, Joseph Michael 1953- St&PR 91
Leone, Judith Gibson 1945- WhoAmW 91, WhoEmL 91
Leone, Nelson F BiDrAPA 89
Leone, Norma Leonardi 1935- WhoWrEP 89
Leone, Paul Michael 1955- WhoEmL 91
Leone, Richard Carl 1941- WhoAm 90, WhoE 91
Leone, Sergio 1921-1989 BioIn 16
Leone, Sergio 1929-1989 AnObit 1989
Leone, Stephan Robert 1939- St&PR 91
Leone, Stephen Robert 1948- WhoAm 90
Leone, Vincent John 1937- St&PR 91
Leone, William A 1922- BiDrAPA 89
Leone, William C. 1924- St&PR 91
Leone, William Charles 1924- WhoAm 90
Leonesio-Mons, Claudia Carruth 1952- WhoEmL 91
Leonett, Anthony Arthur 1929- St&PR 91, WhoAm 90
Leonetti, B.V. 1944- St&PR 91
Leonetti, Matthew F. WhoAm 90
Leonetti, Michael Edward 1955- WhoEmL 91, WhoWor 91
Leong Chee Kheong 1954- WhoWor 91
Leong, Adeline Shuk Ken Pung 1949- WhoWor 91
Leong, Carol Jean 1942- WhoAmW 91
Leong, Che Kan BioIn 16
Leong, George Kuotung 1929- WhoWor 91
Leong, Gregory Bruce 1951- BiDrAPA 89
Leong, J.Y.H. 1925- St&PR 91
Leong, James Chan 1929- WhoAmA 91
Leong, Janet Mee 1961- WhoAmW 91
Leong, Jo-Ann Ching 1942- WhoAmW 91
Leong, Judith Muriel BiDrAPA 89
Leong, Samuel 1956- WhoWor 91
Leonhard, D.F. 1924- St&PR 91
Leonhard, Dave 1942- Ballpl 90
Leonhard, Gregory Forrest 1951- WhoEmL 91
Leonhard, William E. 1914- St&PR 91
Leonhardt, Gary Gene 1957- BiDrAPA 89
Leonhardt, Gustav 1928- IntWWM 90, PenDiMP
Leonhardt, Jerald Lee 1948- St&PR 91
Leonhardt, Merrilee Gay BiDrAPA 89
Leonhardt, Ronald David 1947- WhoEmL 91
Leonhardt, Rudolf Walter 1921- WhoWor 91
Leonhardt, William S. 1916- St&PR 91
Leoni, Angelo Vincent 1929- St&PR 91
Leoni, Michael PenDiMP
Leoni, Raul 1905?-1972 BioIn 16
Leonian, Phillip BioIn 16
Leonid 1896-1976 WhoAmA 91N
Leonidas I WorAlBi
Leonidoff, Leon 1895-1989 BioIn 16
Leonidow, Natasha Matrina 1958- WhoAmW 91
Leonoff, L.E. 1943- St&PR 91
Leonor, Queen of Navarre 1426-1479 BioIn 16
Leonora Christina 1621-1698 DcScanL
Leonora Telles WomWR
Leonora, John 1928- WhoAm 90
Leonov, Aleksei 1934- WorAlBi
Leonov, Leonid 1899- ConAu 129, MajTwCW
Leonova, Darya Mikhailovna 1829-1896 PenDiMP
Leonowens, Anna 1831-1914 FemiCLE
Leonowens, Anna 1834-1914 DcLB 99 [port]
Leontief, Wassily 1906- WhoAm 90, WhoE 91, WhoWor 91
Leontief, Wassily W. 1906- WorAlBi
Leontovich, Eugenie 1894- WorAlBi
Leopardi, Giacomo 1798-1837 WorAlBi
Leopold II, King of the Belgians 1835-1909 BioIn 16
Leopold, Aldo 1886-1948 BioIn 16
Leopold, Allison Kyle 1955- WhoE 91
Leopold, Anna Marie 1925- WhoAmW 91
Leopold, Carl Gustaf 1756-1829 DcScanL
Leopold, Estella Bergere 1927- WhoAm 90
Leopold, Gary 1955- ODwPR 91
Leopold, George William, Jr. 1947- St&PR 91
Leopold, Gretta 1940- BiDrAPA 89
Leopold, Harold S BiDrAPA 89
Leopold, Harold S. 1900-1989 BioIn 16
Leopold, Irving Henry 1915- WhoAm 90
Leopold, Jay V 1928- BiDrAPA 89
Leopold, Johann Gottlieb PenDiDA 89
Leopold, Jonathan P.A. 1926- BiDrAPA 89
Leopold, Luna B 1915- ConAu 31NR
Leopold, Luna Bergere 1915- WhoAm 90
Leopold, M. Edwin 1934- St&PR 91
Leopold, Michael Alan 1948- BiDrAPA 89
Leopold, Nathan, Jr. 1904-1971 WorAlBi
Leopold, Richard William 1912- WhoAm 90
Leopold, Robert L 1922- BiDrAPA 89
Leopold, Robert Livingston 1922- WhoAm 90
Leopold, Robert M. 1926- St&PR 91
Leopold, Susan 1960- WhoAmA 91
Leopoldt, Gerd Charles 1945- BiDrAPA 89
Leotard, Francois Gerard Marie 1942- BiDFrPL, WhoWor 91
Lepage, Antoine J 1925- BiDrAPA 89
Lepage, Denis Jean B 1947- BiDrAPA 89
Lepage, Frank Albright 1927- St&PR 91
Lepage, George Edward 1938- St&PR 91
Lepage, Henri BioIn 16
Lepage, Jane Weiner 1931- IntWWM 90
LePage, John Roy 1957- WhoEmL 91
Lepage, Monique 1930- OxCCanT
Lepage, Robert BioIn 16
Lepage, Robert J. 1932- St&PR 91
Lepage, Roland 1928- OxCCanT
LePage, Sue 1951- OxCCanT [port]
LePage, Wilbur Reed 1911- WhoAm 90
Le Pan, Douglas 1914- ConAu 129
Le Pan de Ligny, Yves 1942- WhoWor 91
Lepape, Harry L. 1930- St&PR 91
Lepard, Olin Keith 1936- BiDrAPA 89
Leparulo, Angelo 1928- St&PR 91
Le Pautre, Jean 1618-1682 PenDiDA 89
Le Pautre, Pierre PenDiDA 89
Le Pautre, Pierre 1648?-1716 PenDiDA 89
Lepawsky, Albert 1908- WhoAm 90, WhoWor 91
Lepcio, Ted 1930- Ballpl 90, BioIn 16
Le Pen, Jean-Marie BioIn 16
Le Pen, Jean-Marie 1928- BiDFrPL
Lepenies, Wolf Dietrich 1941- WhoWor 91
Le Pensec, Louis 1937- WhoWor 91
Lepercq, Xavier Beraro 1950- St&PR 91
Lepes, Jeffrey S. 1947- St&PR 91
Lepet, Sara Isabel 1951- WhoEmL 91
Lepetit, Jean-Francois Eugene 1942- WhoWor 91
Le Pichon, Xavier Thaddee 1937- WhoWor 91
Lepick, Fred C. 1925- St&PR 91
Lepine, Ambroise WhNaAH [port]
Lepine, Marc BioIn 16
Lepine, Maxime 1837?-1897 DcCanB 12
Lepiner, Michael BioIn 16
Lepke, Charma Davies 1919- IntWWM 90
Lepkowski, Cynthia Ann 1950- WhoEmL 91
Lepley, Russell L. 1917- St&PR 91
Le Plongeon, Alice BioIn 16
Le Plongeon, Augustus 1826-1908 BioIn 16
Lepofsky, Robert Jerry 1944- St&PR 91
LePome, Penelope Marie 1945- WhoAmW 91
Lepore, Domenick V 1930- BiDrAPA 89
Lepore, Dominick James 1911- WhoWrEP 89
Lepore, Gerardo J. 1923- St&PR 91
Lepore, Michael Joseph 1910- WhoAm 90, WhoE 91
Lepore, Ralph Thomas, III 1954- WhoEmL 91
Leporin, Dorothea 1715-1762 EncCoWW
Le Pors, Anicet 1931- BiDFrPL
Leporte, James L. 1954- St&PR 91
Le Poulain, Jean 1924-1988 AnObit 1988, BioIn 16
Lepow, Gloria Kantor 1955- WhoAmW 91
Lepowsky, James 1944- WhoE 91
Lepp, Henry 1922- WhoAm 90
Lepp, Keith Allan BiDrAPA 89
Leppanen, Peter Walter 1956- WhoEmL 91
Leppard, Dale LeRoy 1937- WhoE 91
Leppard, Raymond 1927- PenDiMP
Leppard, Raymond John 1927- IntWWM 90, WhoAm 90
Lepper, Robert Lewis 1906- WhoAmA 91, WhoE 91
Leppert, Don 1931- Ballpl 90
Leppert, Phyllis Carolyn 1938- WhoAmW 91, WhoE 91
Leppert, Richard David 1943- WhoAm 90
Leppiks, Anita ODwPR 91
Lepping, George WhoWor 91
Leppla, Bruce W 1922- BiDrAPA 89
Leppla, Bruce W. 1949- St&PR 91
Leppo, Sheldon Sydney 1934- St&PR 91
Lepre, Robert Nicholas 1942- WhoAm 90
Le Prevost, Stephen Raymond 1955- IntWWM 90
Lepri, Daniel B. 1953- St&PR 91
Lepri, John Joseph 1957- WhoSSW 91
Le Prince, Gabriella WhoAmA 91N
Le Prince de Beaumont, Jeanne-Marie 1711-1780 EncCoWW
Leprohon, Jean-Lukin 1822-1900 DcCanB 12
Leprohon, Rosanna 1829-1879 FemiCLE
Leprohon, Rosanna Eleanor 1829-1879 DcLB 99
Leps, Thomas MacMaster 1914- WhoAm 90
Leptich, Ronny Joseph 1943- St&PR 91
Le Quernec, Alain 1944- ConDes 90
Le Quesne, Philip William 1939- WhoAm 90
Le Queux, William 1864-1927 TwCCr&M 91
Le Queux, William Tufnell 1864-1927 SpyFic
Leraaen, Allen Keith 1951- WhoEmL 91
Lerat, Jacqueline PenDiDA 89
Lerat, Jean PenDiDA 89
Lerch, Carol 1938- St&PR 91
Lerch, John Albert 1950- St&PR 91
Lerch, Justine Fredericks 1948- WhoEmL 91, WhoSSW 91
Lerch, Randy 1954- Ballpl 90
Lerch, Richard Heaphy 1924- WhoAm 90
Lerch, Sharon 1940- WhoWrEP 89
Lerche, Preben 1948- WhoWor 91
Lerdahl, Fred 1943- IntWWM 90
Lerdo de Tejada, Sebastian 1823-1889 BioIn 16
Lere, John Covey 1945- WhoEmL 91
Lere, Mark Allen 1950- WhoAmA 91
Lerebour, Florent 1947- WhoWor 91
Le Renard, Jean-Louis 1940- BiDrAPA 89
LeResche, Stephen D. ODwPR 91
Lerian, Walt 1903-1929 Ballpl 90
Le Rider, Jacques Charles 1954- WhoWor 91
Leritz, Arthur F 1944- BiDrAPA 89
Leritz, Daniel Raymond 1945- WhoEmL 91
Leritz, Lawrence R. 1958- IntWWM 90
Leritz, Lawrence Robert 1952- WhoAm 90
Le Riverend, Pablo 1907- WhoHisp 91
Lerma, Francisco Gomez y Rojas, Duque de 1552-1625 BioIn 16
Lerma, Joe Lius 1953- WhoAm 90
Lerma, Rosanna 1963- WhoAmW 91
Lerma, Vicki Gayle White 1953- WhoAmW 91, WhoEmL 91
Lerman, Albert 1936- WhoWrEP 89
Lerman, Alexander C.L. BiDrAPA 89
Lerman, Allen H. 1943- WhoE 91
Lerman, David Louis 1940- St&PR 91
Lerman, Doris WhoAmA 91
Lerman, Eileen R. 1947- WhoAmW 91
Lerman, Gerald Frederick 1941- St&PR 91
Lerman, Hannah 1936- WhoAmW 91
Lerman, Jeanette Paula 1948- St&PR 91
Lerman, Jerry 1921- St&PR 91
Lerman, Leo 1914- WhoAmA 91, WhoE 91
Lerman, Leonard Solomon 1925- WhoAm 90
Lerman, Manuel 1943- WhoE 91
Lerman, Mark N 1950- BiDrAPA 89
Lerman, Ora WhoE 91
Lerman, Ora 1938- WhoAmA 91
Lerman, Rhoda 1936- WhoWrEP 89
Lerman, Sidney 1927- WhoE 91
Lerman, Terry Allen 1946- WhoE 91, WhoEmL 91
Lermand, Barbara Patricia WhoAmW 91
Lermen, Birgit Johanna WhoWor 91
Lermo, Margarita BiDrAPA 89
Lermontov, Mikhail 1814-1841 WorAlBi
Lerner, Abe 1908- WhoAmA 91
Lerner, Abram 1913- WhoAm 90, WhoAmA 91
Lerner, Alan Burton 1930- St&PR 91, WhoAm 90, WhoSSW 91
Lerner, Alan Charles 1944- St&PR 91
Lerner, Alan Jay 1918-1986 BioIn 16, ConAu 31NR, OxCPMus, WorAlBi
Lerner, Alexandria Sandra WhoAmA 91
Lerner, Alfred 1933- St&PR 91, WhoAm 90
Lerner, Arnold Stanley 1930- WhoAm 90
Lerner, Barbara 1935- WhoAmW 91, WhoE 91, WhoWor 91
Lerner, Brad Scott 1958- WhoEmL 91
Lerner, Burton A 1932- BiDrAPA 89
Lerner, Carol 1927- BioIn 16, SmATA 12AS [port]
Lerner, Carole Jean 1938- WhoAmW 91
Lerner, Deborah Mae 1952- WhoEmL 91
Lerner, Dennis Bruce 1947- WhoEmL 91
Lerner, Edward Michael 1942- WhoSSW 91
Lerner, Eric John 1947- WhoE 91
Lerner, Frederick Andrew 1945- WhoE 91
Lerner, Gerda 1920- WhoAm 90, WhoWrEP 89
Lerner, Harry 1939- WhoAm 90
Lerner, Harry Jonas 1932- WhoAm 90
Lerner, Harvey Robert 1927- BiDrAPA 89
Lerner, Herbert J. 1938- WhoAm 90
Lerner, Hershey 1920- St&PR 91
Lerner, Howard 1927- St&PR 91
Lerner, Ina Roslyn 1938- WhoAmW 91
Lerner, Joel Samuel 1953- St&PR 91
Lerner, Joey Adam 1951- BiDrAPA 89
Lerner, Joseph 1921- WhoWor 91
Lerner, Laurence 1925- WorAu 1980 [port]
Lerner, Linda WhoWrEP 89
Lerner, Linda Joyce 1944- St&PR 91
Lerner, Liza Ann 1951- WhoE 91, WhoWor 91
Lerner, Loren Ruth 1948- WhoAmA 91
Lerner, Lori A BiDrAPA 89
Lerner, M. Michael 1942- WhoWor 91
Lerner, Marguerite Rush 1924- AuBYP 90
Lerner, Marguerite Rush 1924-1987 BioIn 16
Lerner, Marilyn 1942- WhoAmA 91
Lerner, Martin 1936- WhoAm 90, WhoAmA 91, WhoE 91
Lerner, Max 1902- WhoAm 90, WorAlBi
Lerner, Michael BioIn 16

Lerner, Nathan Bernard 1913- *WhoAm 90, WhoAmA 91*
Lerner, Ralph 1949- *WhoAm 90*
Lerner, Richard Alan 1938- *WhoAm 90*
Lerner, Richard J 1929-1982 *WhoAmA 91N*
Lerner, Robert David *BiDrAPA 89*
Lerner, Robert Earl 1940- *WhoAm 90*
Lerner, Robert George 1936- *BiDrAPA 89*
Lerner, Sammy 1903-1989 *BioIn 16*
Lerner, Samuel Harold 1917- *BiDrAPA 89*
Lerner, Sandra *WhoAmA 91*
Lerner, Sandy R 1918- *WhoAmA 91*
Lerner, Sheldon 1939- *WhoWor 91*
Lerner, Stefan *BiDrAPA 89*
Lerner, Stuart Alan *BiDrAPA 89*
Lerner, Stuart L. 1930- *St&PR 91*
Lerner, Warren 1929- *WhoAm 90*
Lerner, William 1933- *St&PR 91*
Lerner-Lam, Eva I-Hwa 1954- *WhoAmW 91*
Lernoux, Penny 1940-1989 *BioIn 16, ConAu 129*
Leroe, Ellen 1949- *BioIn 16*
Leroe, Ellen W 1949- *SmATA 61 [port]*
Le Rossignol, James 1866-1969 *DcLB 92*
LeRoux, Frank *BioIn 16*
Leroux, Gaston 1868-1927 *TwCCr&M 91B, WorAlBi*
Leroux, Pierre 1958- *IntWWM 90*
Le Roy, Andre F. 1933- *WhoAm 90*
LeRoy, Anne Marie *BiDrAPA 89*
Le Roy, Bruce Murdock 1920- *WhoAm 90*
Leroy, Catherine *BioIn 16*
LeRoy, David Charles 1946- *WhoEmL 91*
Leroy, David Henry 1947- *WhoAm 90*
LeRoy, Edward Carwile 1933- *WhoAm 90*
LeRoy, G. Palmer 1929- *WhoAm 90*
LeRoy, Gen *BioIn 16*
Leroy, Guy *BioIn 16*
LeRoy, Harold M. 1905- *WhoAm 90*
Le Roy, Harold M 1905- *WhoAmA 91*
Leroy, Hugh Alexander 1939- *WhoAmA 91*
LeRoy, Isabel Hernandez 1951- *WhoAmW 91*
Le Roy, Jean Henri Servais 1865-1953 *BioIn 16*
Le Roy, Joseph Beene 1947- *BiDrAPA 89*
Leroy, Jules Gerard 1934- *WhoWor 91*
Le Roy, L. David 1920- *WhoAm 90*
Leroy, Louis *PenDiDA 89*
Leroy, Louis 1941- *WhoAmA 91*
Leroy, Marie-Claire *BiDrAPA 89*
Le Roy, Mervyn 1900-1987 *WorAlBi*
Leroy, Olivier-Gilbert 1884- *EncO&P 3*
Leroy, Paul 1955- *St&PR 91*
Leroy, Pierre Elie 1948- *St&PR 91*
Leroy-Beaulieu, Philippine *BioIn 16*
Le Royer, Eric 1963- *WhoEmL 91*
Lerpae, Paul Karl 1900-1989 *BioIn 16*
Lerrigo, Edith 1910-1989 *BioIn 16*
Lerro, Furey Anthony 1943- *BiDrAPA 89*
Lerroux, Alejandro 1864-1949 *BioIn 16*
Lersch, Barry 1944- *Ballpl 90*
Lerteth, Oban *ConAu 32NR*
Lertratanangkoon, Khingkan 1948- *WhoSSW 91*
Lesaca, Timothy Gordon 1958- *BiDrAPA 89*
Lesage, Alain Rene 1668-1747 *WorAlBi*
Lesage, Francois *BioIn 16*
Le Sage, Sally *IntWWM 90*
Le Sage, William A. 1949- *St&PR 91*
Lesar, Hiram Henry 1912- *WhoAm 90*
LeSatz, Stephen, Jr. 1937- *WhoWor 91*
Lesauvage, J.R. *St&PR 91*
Lescaille, Katherijne 1649-1711 *EncCoWW*
Lescano, Javier A. 1935- *WhoHisp 91*
Lescarbot, Marc 1570?-1642 *DcLB 99, OxCCanT*
Lesch, Alma Wallace 1917- *WhoAmA 91*
Lesch, George Henry 1909- *WhoAm 90*
Lesch, Harry *BiDrAPA 89*
Lesch, James R. 1921- *St&PR 91*
Lesch, John E 1945- *ConAu 132*
Lesch, Michael 1939- *WhoAm 90*
Lesch, Michael Oscar 1938- *WhoAm 90*
Leschak, Peter Max 1951- *WhoWrEP 89*
Leschetizky, Theodor 1830-1915 *BioIn 16, PenDiMP*
Leschi *WhNaAH*
Leschinski, Susan Virginia 1954- *WhoAmW 91*
Lescoriere, Marie *EncO&P 3*
Lescot, Elie 1883-1974 *BioIn 16*
Lescroart, Emmett James 1951- *St&PR 91*
Lese, Alan E. 1943- *St&PR 91*
Lese, William M. 1925- *St&PR 91*
Lesem, Michael David 1955- *BiDrAPA 89*
Leseman, Robert G. 1940- *St&PR 91*
Leser, Hans Georg 1928- *WhoWor 91*
Leser, Lawrence A. 1935- *WhoAm 90*
Leser, Lawrence Arthur 1935- *St&PR 91*
Lesesne, Joab Mauldin, Jr. 1937- *WhoAm 90*
Lesh, Angela Dawn 1947- *WhoE 91*
Lesh, Charles J 1944- *BiDrAPA 89*
Lesh, Norman 1930- *St&PR 91*
Lesh, Richard D 1927- *WhoAmA 91*
Le Shan, Eda J. 1922- *AuBYP 90, WhoWrEP 89*
LeShan, Lawrence 1920- *EncO&P 3, EncPaPR 91*
Le Shan, Lawrence L. 1920- *WhoWrEP 89*
Le Shana, David Charles 1932- *WhoAm 90*
LeShane, Patricia Roland 1954- *WhoAmW 91, WhoEmL 91*
Leshaw, Jay 1925- *St&PR 91*
Lesher, Dean Stanley 1902- *WhoAm 90*
Lesher, Donald M. 1915- *St&PR 91*
Lesher, Donald Miles 1915- *WhoAm 90*
Lesher, George Y. 1926-1990 *BioIn 16*
Lesher, George Yohe *NewYTBS 90*
Lesher, Jack Leiter, Jr. 1948- *WhoSSW 91*
Lesher, John Lee 1934- *St&PR 91*
Lesher, John Lee, Jr. 1934- *WhoAm 90*
Lesher, Marie Palmisano 1919- *WhoAmA 91*
Lesher, Richard Lee 1933- *WhoAm 90, WhoE 91*
Lesher, William Richard 1924- *WhoAm 90*
Leshin, Seymour 1916- *BiDrAPA 89*
Leshinski, Linda 1952- *WhoWrEP 89*
Leshner, Alan Irvin 1944- *WhoAm 90*
Leshnower, Alan Lee 1938- *WhoE 91*
Leshyk, Tonie 1950- *WhoAmA 91*
Lesiak, Lucille Ann 1946- *WhoAmW 91*
Lesiak, S. Dean 1952- *St&PR 91*
Le Sieg, Theo *AuBYP 90, BioIn 16*
LeSieg, Theo *ConAu 32NR, MajTwCW*
Lesieur-Desaulniers, Louis-Leon 1823-1896 *DcCanB 12*
Lesiger, Ilene Gloria 1943- *WhoAmW 91*
Lesikar, Raymond Vincent 1922- *WhoAm 90*
Lesinski, Roger John 1949- *St&PR 91, WhoEmL 91*
Lesjak, Lisa Mary 1963- *WhoAmW 91*
Lesjak, V. James 1934- *WhoE 91*
Lesk, Alan 1941- *St&PR 91*
Lesk, Steven 1950- *BiDrAPA 89*
Leske, Michael E. 1948- *St&PR 91*
Leski, Anton R. 1913- *St&PR 91*
Leskin, Louis W 1913- *BiDrAPA 89*
Leskis, Loren James 1945- *St&PR 91*
Lesko, Diane *WhoAmA 91*
Lesko, Harry Joseph 1920- *WhoAm 90*
Lesko, James Joseph 1939- *WhoE 91*
Lesko, James M. 1932- *WhoSSW 91*
Lesko, Leonard Henry 1938- *WhoAm 90*
Lesko, Lynna Mary *BiDrAPA 89*
Leskova, Tatiana *BioIn 16*
Leskowitz, Eric David 1951- *BiDrAPA 89*
Lesley, Susan 1823-1904 *BioAmW*
Leslie, Allan Roy 1948- *St&PR 91, WhoEmL 91*
Leslie, Amy 1855-1939 *NotWoAT*
Leslie, Amy 1860?-1939 *BioIn 16*
Leslie, Anita 1914-1985 *ConAu 32NR*
Leslie, Anne *ConAu 32NR*
Leslie, Austin *BioIn 16*
Leslie, Catherine Alexandra *BiDrAPA 89*
Leslie, Charles Miller 1923- *WhoAm 90*
Leslie, Charles Robert 1794-1859 *BioIn 16*
Leslie, Cheryl Lees 1947- *WhoAmW 91*
Leslie, David Stephen 1930- *St&PR 91*
Leslie, Desmond 1921- *EncO&P 3*
Leslie, Edgar 1885- *OxCPMus*
Leslie, Edward L 1935- *BiDrAPA 89*
Leslie, Ernest Garry 1940- *St&PR 91*
Leslie, Frank 1821-1880 *BioIn 16*
Leslie, Frank, Mrs. 1836-1914 *BioIn 16*
Leslie, Fred 1855-1892 *OxCPMus*
Leslie, Henry 1822-1896 *PenDiMP*
Leslie, Henry Arthur 1921- *WhoAm 90, WhoSSW 91*
Leslie, Jacques Robert, Jr. 1947- *WhoAm 90, WhoEmL 91*
Leslie, James H. 1930- *St&PR 91*
Leslie, James Hill 1930- *WhoAm 90*
Leslie, James K. 1944- *St&PR 91*
Leslie, Joan 1925- *OxCPMus, WorAlBi*
Leslie, John *WhoAmA 91*
Leslie, John 1923- *WhoE 91*
Leslie, John Andrew 1940- *ConAu 30NR*
Leslie, John Edward 1954- *WhoEmL 91*
Leslie, John Ethelbert 1910- *WhoAm 90, WhoWor 91*
Leslie, John W. 1923- *ODwPR 91*
Leslie, John Walter 1929- *WhoAm 90*
Leslie, John Webster, Jr. 1954- *WhoE 91*
Leslie, John William 1923- *WhoAm 90*
Leslie, Lew 1886-1963 *OxCPMus*
Leslie, Lottie Lyle 1930- *WhoWrEP 89*
Leslie, Michael Ross 1957- *WhoEmL 91*
Leslie, Miriam F. 1836-1914 *BioAmW*
Leslie, Miriam Florence Folline 1836-1914 *BioIn 16*
Leslie, Peter Evelyn 1931- *WhoWor 91*
Leslie, Phil *BioIn 16*
Leslie, Reo Napoleon, Jr. 1953- *WhoEmL 91*
Leslie, Richard Newton 1945- *WhoE 91*
Leslie, Robert D. 1945- *St&PR 91*
Leslie, Robert Lincoln 1885-1987 *BioIn 16*
Leslie, Robert Lorne 1947- *WhoEmL 91, WhoWor 91*
Leslie, Royal Conrad 1923- *WhoAm 90*
Leslie, Sam 1905-1979 *Ballpl 90*
Leslie, Seaver 1946- *WhoAmA 91*
Leslie, Seymour 1922- *St&PR 91*
Leslie, Seymour Marvin 1922- *WhoAm 90, WhoE 91*
Leslie, Thomas Edward Cliffe 1827-1882 *BioIn 16*
Leslie, Victoria Hall 1954- *WhoAmW 91*
Leslie, W. Grant 1925- *St&PR 91*
Leslie, William, Jr. 1918- *WhoAm 90*
Leslie, William Cairns 1920- *WhoAm 90*
Leslie-Melville, Betty *AuBYP 90*
Leslien, John Hampton 1914- *WhoAm 90*
Lesly, Philip 1918- *ODwPR 91, St&PR 91, WhoAm 90, WhoWor 91*
Lesman, Michael Steven 1953- *WhoE 91, WhoEmL 91, WhoWor 91*
Lesmez, Arthur Gerard 1959- *WhoEmL 91*
Lesnau, Marilyn Michele 1953- *St&PR 91*
Lesner, William Jay *BiDrAPA 89*
Lesnett, Thomas Jay 1948- *St&PR 91*
Lesniak, John Peter 1935- *BiDrAPA 89*
Lesniak, Rose 1955- *WhoWrEP 89*
Lesnick, Michael Thomas 1952- *WhoEmL 91*
Lesnick, Stephen William 1931- *WhoAmA 91*
Lesnik, Max 1930- *WhoWor 91*
Lesnik, Steven H. 1940- *ODwPR 91*
Lesnik, Steven Harris 1940- *St&PR 91*
Lesnikowski, Wojciech *WhoAm 90*
Lesok, Eddie Monroe 1948- *St&PR 91, WhoAm 90, WhoSSW 91*
LeSourd, Nancy Susan Oliver 1953- *WhoEmL 91*
Lesowitz, Robert Irwin 1939- *BiDrAPA 89*
L'Esperance, Alexandria 1988- *BioIn 16*
L'Esperance, Danielle 1988- *BioIn 16*
L'Esperance, Erica 1988- *BioIn 16*
Lesperance, Francois 1961- *BiDrAPA 89*
Lesperance, Jean *BiDrAPA 89*
Lesperance, John 1835-1891 *DcCanB 12, DcLB 99*
L'Esperance, Michele *BioIn 16*
L'Esperance, Raymond *BioIn 16*
L'Esperance, Raymond 1988- *BioIn 16*
L'Esperance, Veronica 1988- *BioIn 16*
Less, David Arnold 1952- *WhoEmL 91*
Less, Theodore D. 1930- *St&PR 91*
Lessac, Frane 1954- *SmATA 61*
Lessack, Ronald D. 1947- *St&PR 91*
Lessard, Donald Roy 1943- *WhoAm 90*
Lessard, Edward Thomas 1951- *WhoE 91*
Lessard, John Ayres 1920- *IntWWM 90*
Lessard, Lynn Marie 1953- *WhoAmW 91*
Lessard, Michel M. 1939- *WhoAm 90*
Lessard, Pierre H. 1942- *St&PR 91*
Lessard, Pierre Henri 1942- *WhoAm 90*
Lessard, Raymond W. 1930- *WhoAm 90, WhoSSW 91*
Lessard, Rupert *BiDrAPA 89*
Lesse, Etta Gordon *WhoAmW 91, WhoE 91*
Lesse, S Michael 1910- *BiDrAPA 89*
Lesse, Stanley 1922- *BiDrAPA 89*
Lessel, Arthur C 1840?-1895 *DcCanB 12*
Lessells, Gerald Alan 1926- *WhoAm 90*
Lessem, Paul Robert 1945- *BiDrAPA 89*
Lessen, Martin 1920- *WhoAm 90*
Lessenco, Gilbert Barry 1929- *WhoWor 91*
Lessenden, Edith Ann Fleming 1922- *WhoAmW 91*
Lesseps, Ferdinand, Vicomte De 1805-1894 *WorAlBi*
Lesser, Alexander 1902-1982 *BioIn 16*
Lesser, Allen 1907- *WhoE 91*
Lesser, Arthur Leonard 1932- *BiDrAPA 89*
Lesser, David 1955- *St&PR 91*
Lesser, Edward Arnold 1934- *St&PR 91*
Lesser, Felice A. 1953- *WhoEmL 91*
Lesser, George Hulett 1944- *WhoE 91*
Lesser, Gilbert *NewYTBS 90 [port]*
Lesser, Ira Marc 1949- *BiDrAPA 89*
Lesser, Jary M *BiDrAPA 89*
Lesser, Joseph M. 1928- *WhoAm 90*
Lesser, Joseph S. 1928- *St&PR 91*
Lesser, Laurence 1938- *IntWWM 90, WhoAm 90, WhoE 91, WhoWor 91*
Lesser, Lawrence J. 1939- *WhoE 91*
Lesser, Leonard I 1916- *BiDrAPA 89*
Lesser, Marshall W. 1931- *St&PR 91*
Lesser, Michael *BioIn 16*
Lesser, Michael Scott *BiDrAPA 89*
Lesser, Milton *TwCCr&M 91*
Lesser, Milton 1928- *AuBYP 90*
Lesser, Rika *BioIn 16*
Lesser, Rika Ellen 1953- *WhoWrEP 89*
Lesser, Stanley R *BiDrAPA 89*
Lesser, Walter Hunter 1957- *WhoSSW 91*
Lesser, Wendy Celia 1952- *WhoWrEP 89*
Lesser, William Craig 1956- *WhoEmL 91*
Lesses, Maurice F. 1932- *St&PR 91*
Lesses, Maurice Falcon 1932- *WhoAm 90*
Lessey, Robert Allen 1944- *BiDrAPA 89*
Lessey, Samuel K., Jr. 1923- *WhoAm 90*
Lessick, Mira L. 1949- *WhoAmW 91*
Lessien, Bruce T 1932- *BiDrAPA 89*
Lessig, V. Parker *WhoAm 90*
Lessin, Andrew *AuBYP 90*
Lessin, Andrew R. 1942- *St&PR 91*
Lessin, Andrew Richard 1942- *WhoE 91*
Lessin, Debra Jean 1954- *WhoEmL 91*
Lessin, Lawrence Stephen 1937- *WhoAm 90, WhoE 91*
Lessin, Robert Leonard 1930- *St&PR 91*
Lessing, Charlotte *WhoWor 91*
Lessing, Doris 1919- *ConAu 33NR, FemiCLE, MajTwCW, RGTwCSF, ShSCr 6 [port], WhoAm 90, WhoWor 91, WorAlBi, WrPh*
Lessing, Doris May 1919- *BioIn 16*
Lessing, Fred W. 1915- *St&PR 91*
Lessing, Fred W. 1915-1990 *BioIn 16*
Lessing, Gotthold Ephraim 1729-1781 *DcLB 97 [port], WorAlBi, WrPh*
Lessing, Kolja 1961- *IntWWM 90*
Lessing, Peter 1938- *WhoSSW 91*
Lessinger, Murray Richard 1954- *WhoEmL 91*
Lessiter, Frank Donald 1939- *WhoAm 90, WhoWrEP 89*
Lessler, Peter Rodney 1947-1989 *BioIn 16*
Lessler, Richard Sigmund 1924- *WhoAm 90*
Lessman, Jac *NewYTBS 90*
Lessmann, Marlin M. 1944- *St&PR 91*
Lessner, Harold J. 1943- *St&PR 91*
Lessner, Sidney F. 1926- *St&PR 91*
Lessoff, Howard 1930- *WhoE 91*
Lessor, Edith Schroeder 1930- *WhoAmW 91*
Lessore, Emile-Aubert 1805-1876 *PenDiDA 89*
Lessore, Therese 1884-1945 *BiDWomA*
Lessow, Herbert 1929- *BiDrAPA 89*
Lessy, Roy Paul, Jr. 1944- *WhoE 91, WhoWor 91*
Lestage, Donald, III 1939- *St&PR 91*
Lester, Alison 1952- *BioIn 16*
Lester, Andrew William 1956- *WhoEmL 91*
Lester, Barnett Benjamin 1912- *WhoAm 90*
Lester, Boyd K 1926- *BiDrAPA 89*
Lester, Charles William *BiDrAPA 89*
Lester, David *NewYTBS 90*
Lester, David 1942- *ConAu 31NR, WhoE 91*
Lester, David W 1911- *BiDrAPA 89*
Lester, Edgel Celsus 1950- *WhoEmL 91*
Lester, Edwin *NewYTBS 90*
Lester, Elenore *NewYTBS 90*
Lester, George S. 1905- *St&PR 91*
Lester, George Washington 1939- *St&PR 91*
Lester, Hazen Russell, Jr. 1929- *St&PR 91*
Lester, John *BioIn 16*
Lester, John Buckles 1945- *BiDrAPA 89*
Lester, John James Nathaniel, II 1952- *WhoEmL 91, WhoWor 91*
Lester, John Seerey- 1945- *BioIn 16*
Lester, Julius *BioIn 16*
Lester, Julius B. 1939- *AuBYP 90, WhoAm 90, WhoWrEP 89*
Lester, Kathiann 1957- *WhoEmL 91*
Lester, Ketty 1938- *DrBlPA 90*
Lester, Lois Butterworth 1934- *WhoE 91*
Lester, Lorraine *BioIn 16*
Lester, Malcolm 1924- *WhoAm 90*
Lester, Mark *TwCCr&M 91*
Lester, Melvin 1933- *St&PR 91*
Lester, Michelle 1942- *WhoAmA 91*
Lester, Paul Arthur 1950- *WhoEmL 91*
Lester, Richard 1932- *BioIn 16, WhoAm 90, WhoWor 91, WorAlBi*
Lester, Richard Allan 1947- *St&PR 91*
Lester, Richard Allen 1908- *WhoE 91*
Lester, Richard Garrison 1925- *WhoAm 90*
Lester, Robert A., III 1949- *WhoEmL 91*
Lester, Robert Carlton 1933- *WhoAm 90*
Lester, Roy David 1949- *WhoWor 91*
Lester, Susan E. 1956- *St&PR 91*
Lester, Tilden Jackson 1933- *St&PR 91*
Lester, Virginia Laudano 1931- *WhoAm 90*
Lester, William 1924- *St&PR 91*
Lester, William Alexander, Jr. 1937- *WhoAm 90*
Lester, William Bernard 1939- *WhoSSW 91*
Lesti, Mary Lynn *WhoWrEP 89*
Lestienne, Francis Gervais 1941- *WhoWor 91*
Lestina, Thomas L. *BioIn 16*
Lestor, Joan *BioIn 16*
Lestrade, David *PenDiDA 89*
L'Estrange, Alice *BiDEWW*
Lestrange, Kenneth J. 1957- *St&PR 91*
Lestz, Gerald Samuel 1914- *WhoE 91*
Lestz, Jeffrey Scott 1956- *WhoEmL 91*
LeSuer, Jeanne Anne 1956- *WhoE 91*

Lesueur, Alexander Armand 1923- *IntWWM 90*
LeSueur, Elizabeth Fontaine 1947- *St&PR 91*
Le Sueur, Hubert 1580?-1628? *BioIn 16*
Lesueur, Joan Kavanaugh 1929- *WhoAmW 91, WhoSSW 91, WhoWor 91*
Le Sueur, Meridel 1900- *ConAu 30NR, EncAL, FemiCLE, WorAu 1980 [port]*
LeSueur, William Dawson 1840-1917 *DcLB 92 [port]*
Lesure, Francois 1923- *IntWWM 90*
Lesure, John B. 1933- *St&PR 91*
Leszek, Jerzy Waldemar 1949- *BiDrAPA 89*
Letaconnoux, Calleen King 1948- *St&PR 91*
Le Tang, Henry 1915?- *DrBIPA 90*
Le Tart, Laurin Harold 1942- *St&PR 91*
Letaw, Harry, Jr. 1926- *St&PR 91*
Letcher, John Seymour, Jr. 1941- *WhoE 91*
Letcher, Tina H. 1938- *WhoWrEP 89*
Letchinger, Robert Samuel 1955- *WhoEmL 91*
Le Tellier, Carroll Nance 1928- *St&PR 91*
Letellier, Phyllis Mortensen 1931- *WhoWrEP 89*
Letendre, Rita 1928- *WhoAmA 91*
LeTerneau, Susan Marie 1945- *WhoAmW 91*
Leth, James R. 1940- *St&PR 91*
Leth, Steven Arthur 1948- *WhoSSW 91*
Lethaby, William Richard 1857-1931 *PenDiDA 89*
Lethbridge, Edgard E. 1866-1924 *AmLegL*
Lethbridge, Francis Donald 1920- *WhoAm 90*
Lethbridge, George Tempest 1919- *WhoWor 91*
Letherwood, Kenneth C. 1957- *WhoEmL 91*
Le Thous, Robert 1937- *WhoWor 91*
Letiche, John Marion 1918- *WhoAm 90*
Letizia, B. 1936- *St&PR 91*
Letko, Stephen G. 1939- *St&PR 91*
Letko, Stephen George 1939- *WhoSSW 91*
Letley, Emma 1949- *ConAu 131*
Leto, Francis Joseph 1959- *WhoE 91*
Leto, Sam S., Jr. *WhoHisp 91*
Letofsky, Alan R. 1941- *St&PR 91*
Le Tord, Bijou 1945- *BioIn 16, ConAu 31NR*
Letourneau, Andre Guy 1929- *BiDrAPA 89*
LeTourneau, Duane John 1926- *WhoAm 90*
Letourneau, Jean-Paul 1930- *WhoWor 91*
LeTourneau, Richard Howard 1925- *WhoAm 90*
Letourneau, Robert G. 1888-1969 *WorAlBi*
Le Tourneau, Robert Gilmore 1888-1969 *BioIn 16*
Letourneau, Thomas Gerard 1950- *BiDrAPA 89*
LeTrent-Jones, Tony Gupton 1950- *WhoEmL 91*
Letro, Stephen George 1939- *St&PR 91*
Le Troquer, Andre Lucien Alexandre 1884-1963 *BiDFrPL*
Le Trung, Q. 1943- *St&PR 91*
Letsinger, Robert Lewis 1921- *WhoAm 90*
Lett, Austin Sherwood, Jr. 1941- *St&PR 91*
Lett, Charles Leonard 1949- *WhoSSW 91*
Lett, Denny L. 1932- *St&PR 91*
Lett, James William 1955- *WhoSSW 91*
Lett, Philip Wood, Jr. 1922- *WhoAm 90*
Lett, Sherri J. 1949- *WhoAmW 91*
Lettau, Reinhard 1929- *WorAu 1980 [port]*
Letteleir, John Andrew 1948- *WhoSSW 91*
Lettenstrom, Dean Roger 1941- *WhoAmA 91*
Letterman, David *BioIn 16*
Letterman, David 1947- *WhoAm 90, WhoE 91, WorAlBi*
Lettermen, The *EncPR&S 89*
Letters, Kathleen Mary 1910- *IntWWM 90*
Lettes, Ann Burgess *BiDrAPA 89*
Lettich, Louise Marie *BiDrAPA 89*
Lettieri, Ronald John 1950- *WhoE 91, WhoEmL 91*
Lettmann, John William 1942- *St&PR 91*
Letton, Alva Hamblin 1916- *WhoAm 90*
Lettow, Charles Frederick 1941- *WhoE 91*
Letts, Christine Webb 1948- *WhoAmW 91*
Letts, Nancy *BioIn 16*
Letts, Thomas Clinton 1911- *WhoSSW 91, WhoWor 91*
Lettvin, Daniel Stuart *BiDrAPA 89*
Lettvin, Theodore 1926- *IntWWM 90, WhoAm 90, WhoWor 91*
Letven, Ronelle *BiDrAPA 89*
Letwin, Jeffrey William 1953- *WhoEmL 91*
Letwin, Leon 1929- *WhoAm 90*
Letwin, Oliver 1956- *WhoWor 91*
Letwin, Stephen J. 1955- *St&PR 91*
Letzig, Frank William, Jr. 1925- *St&PR 91*
Leu, Olaf 1936- *ConDes 90*
Leu, Olaf 1937- *BioIn 16*
Leuba, Christopher 1929- *IntWWM 90*
Leuba, Clarence J. *BioIn 16*
Leubert, Alfred O.P. 1922- *St&PR 91*
Leubert, Alfred Otto Paul 1922- *WhoAm 90, WhoE 91*
Leubsdorf, Carl Philipp 1938- *WhoE 91*
Leuchter, Andrew Francis *BiDrAPA 89*
Leuchter, Heinrich J 1920- *BiDrAPA 89*
Leuchtman, Stephen Nathan 1945- *WhoEmL 91*
Leuchtmann, Horst 1927- *IntWWM 90*
Leuenberger, Martin Jakob 1949- *WhoEmL 91*
Leugers, William J., Jr. 1942- *St&PR 91*
Leugoud, Robert John 1953- *WhoEmL 91*
Leukefeld, Carl George 1943- *WhoE 91, WhoWor 91*
Leuliette, Connie Jane 1941- *WhoAmW 91*
Leung, Betty Brigid 1949- *WhoEmL 91*
Leung, George W. 1952- *St&PR 91*
Leung, Ida Marie 1951- *WhoEmL 91*
Leung, Jack Koon Keung 1954- *WhoWor 91*
Leung, Jacqueline M. 1958- *WhoAmW 91*
Leung, Lina Lee 1932- *WhoAmW 91*
Leung, Pak Tong 1945- *WhoEmL 91*
Leung, Paul Kahing 1955- *BiDrAPA 89*
Leung, Raymond Chung-chun 1952- *WhoSSW 91*
Leung, Roderick Chi-tak 1949- *WhoEmL 91, WhoWor 91*
Leung, Ted Tit-Hung 1941- *WhoE 91*
Leuos, Bob 1943- *St&PR 91*
Leupena, Tupua *WhoWor 91*
Leupin, Herbert 1916- *ConDes 90*
Leupold, Carol Jean Gilbert 1944- *WhoE 91*
Leupp, Alex Max 1939- *St&PR 91*
Leurpandeur, Max W. 1921- *St&PR 91*
Leus McFarlen, Patricia Cheryl 1954- *WhoEmL 91*
Leuschen, Donald Matthew 1925- *St&PR 91*
Leuschen, Mary Patricia 1943- *WhoAmW 91*
Leute, W.R. 1945- *St&PR 91*
Leutgeb, Ignaz 1745?-1811 *PenDiMP*
Leuthard, Joy Lynne 1952- *WhoAmW 91*
Leuther, Michael Doyle 1948- *WhoWor 91*
Leuthold, David 1932- *WhoAm 90*
Leuthold, Raymond Martin 1940- *WhoAm 90*
Leutwiler, Fritz 1924- *WhoWor 91*
Leutze, James Richard 1935- *WhoAm 90*
Leuzinger, George *ArtLatA*
Leuzinger, Rudolf 1911- *IntWWM 90*
Leuzzi, Anthony Peter 1916- *BiDrAPA 89*
Lev, Baruch Itamar 1938- *WhoAm 90*
Lev, Daniel Saul 1933- *WhoAm 90*
Lev, Eliat *St&PR 91*
Lev, Iza 1928- *BiDrAPA 89*
Lev, Judith Wilkens 1944- *WhoAmW 91*
Lev, L. Jay 1944- *WhoE 91*
Lev-Landau 1895-1979 *WhoAmA 91N*
Le Va, Barry 1941- *WhoAmA 91*
Leva, Charles R. 1914- *St&PR 91*
Leva, James Robert 1932- *St&PR 91, WhoAm 90*
Leva, Marx 1915- *WhoAm 90*
Leva, Michael *BioIn 16*
Leva, Neil Irwin 1929- *WhoE 91*
Levack, Arthur Paul 1909- *WhoAm 90*
Levada, William Joseph 1936- *WhoAm 90*
Levadi, David I 1932- *BiDrAPA 89*
Levai, Marian A *BiDrAPA 89*
Levai, Pierre Alexandre 1937- *WhoAm 90*
Leval, Pierre Nelson 1936- *WhoAm 90*
LeValley, Guy Glenn 1942- *WhoE 91*
LeValley, Joan Catherine 1931- *WhoAmW 91*
Le Valley, John *BiDrAPA 89*
Levan, B.W. 1941- *St&PR 91*
Le Van, Daniel Hayden 1924- *WhoE 91, WhoSSW 91, WhoWor 91*
Levan, David M. 1945- *St&PR 91*
Levan, Jack Alan 1954- *St&PR 91*
LeVan, Nolan Gerald 1934- *WhoAm 90*
LeVan, Suzanne Adell 1952- *WhoEmL 91*
Levandowski, Barbara Sue 1948- *WhoAmW 91*
Levandowski, Donald William 1927- *WhoAm 90*
Levandowsky, Michael 1935- *WhoE 91*
Levant, Oscar 1906-1972 *OxCPMus, WorAlBi*
Levanti, Salvatore Joseph 1928- *WhoE 91*
Levari, Henry K. 1948- *St&PR 91*
Levarie, Siegmund 1914- *IntWWM 90, WhoAm 90*
Levasseur jeune *PenDiDA 89*
Levasseur, Etienne 1721-1798 *PenDiDA 89*
LeVasseur, Paula Ann 1961- *WhoAmW 91*
Levasseur, Pierre-Etienne *PenDiDA 89*
LeVasseur, Richard Arthur 1942- *St&PR 91*
Levasseur, William Ryan 1935- *WhoAm 90, WhoE 91*
Levati, Giuseppe *PenDiDA 89*
Levatich, Julius *BiDrAPA 89*
Levatino, Anthony Samuel 1940- *St&PR 91*
Levato, Joseph Anthony 1941- *St&PR 91*
Levav, Itzak *BiDrAPA 89*
Levavasseur, Jacques-Nicolas *PenDiDA 89*
Levavasseur, Marie-Thomas-Philemon *PenDiDA 89*
Levay, Alexander N 1932- *BiDrAPA 89*
LeVay, Hal 1934- *ODwPR 91*
LeVay, John Paul 1941- *St&PR 91*
Levbarg, Diane 1950- *WhoAmW 91*
Levchenko, Anatoly *BioIn 16*
Levchenko, Stanislav Aleksandrovich *BioIn 16*
Leve, Alan Donald 1927- *WhoAm 90*
Leve, Howard B 1915- *BiDrAPA 89*
Leve, Jay Howard 1956- *WhoEmL 91*
Leveaux, Mark Frederick 1951- *BiDrAPA 89*
Levee, Didier Alain 1954- *WhoWor 91*
Levee, John H 1924- *WhoAmA 91*
Levee, John Harrison 1924- *WhoAm 90*
Levee, Marijane *ODwPR 91*
Levee, Mary Carol Reynolds 1947- *WhoEmL 91*
LeVeen, Robert Frederick 1946- *WhoE 91*
Leveille, Ernest-Baptiste *PenDiDA 89*
Leveille, Guy *BiDrAPA 89*
Leveille, Jean 1931- *WhoAm 90*
Leveille, Walter Henry, Jr. 1945- *WhoSSW 91*
Leveillee, Louis Roger 1934- *WhoE 91*
Levein, Ulf Ingvar 1950- *WhoWor 91*
Level, Leon Jules 1940- *St&PR 91, WhoAm 90*
Levelius, William H. 1927- *St&PR 91*
Levels, Calvin 1954- *DrBIPA 90*
Levelt, Willem Johannes 1938- *WhoWor 91*
Leven, Ann R 1940- *WhoAmA 91*
Leven, Ann Ruth 1940- *WhoAm 90*
Leven, Boris 1912- *ConDes 90*
Leven, Charles Louis 1928- *WhoAm 90*
Leven, Leonard I 1951- *BiDrAPA 89*
Leven, Michael Alan 1937- *WhoAm 90*
Leven, Richard Michael 1940- *St&PR 91, WhoE 91*
Levenberg, Alvin 1944- *St&PR 91*
Levenberg, David *BiDrAPA 89*
Levenberg, Lee H. 1951- *WhoEmL 91*
Levenberg, Nathan 1919- *St&PR 91*
Levendosky, Charles Leonard 1936- *WhoWrEP 89*
Levendula, Dezso *BiDrAPA 89*
Levendusky, Philip George 1946- *WhoAm 90*
Levene, Doreen 1947- *WhoSSW 91*
Levenfeld, Milton Arthur 1927- *WhoAm 90*
Levengood, Robert Andrew 1942- *BiDrAPA 89*
Levengood, William Camburn 1925- *WhoAm 90*
Levens, Marcia Civin 1926- *WhoSSW 91*
Levensaler, Walter Louis 1934- *WhoE 91*
Levenson, Alan Bradley 1935- *WhoAm 90, WhoE 91, WhoWor 91*
Levenson, Alan I 1935- *BiDrAPA 89*
Levenson, Alan Ira 1935- *WhoAm 90*
Levenson, Albert Murray 1931- *WhoAm 90*
Levenson, Alvin Jerome *BiDrAPA 89*
Levenson, Amy Beth *BiDrAPA 89*
Levenson, Carl 1905- *WhoE 91, WhoWor 91*
Levenson, Edgar A 1924- *BiDrAPA 89*
Levenson, Harvey S. 1940- *St&PR 91*
Levenson, Harvey Stuart 1940- *WhoAm 90*
Levenson, Hubert S 1938- *BiDrAPA 89*
Levenson, Jacob Clavner 1922- *WhoAm 90*
Levenson, James Lloyd 1951- *BiDrAPA 89*
Levenson, Jon Alan *BiDrAPA 89*
Levenson, Jordan *WhoWrEP 89*
Levenson, Judy Ann 1951- *WhoAmW 91, WhoE 91*
Levenson, Kathe Tanous *AuBYP 90*
Levenson, Lawrence Neil *BiDrAPA 89*
Levenson, Lewis 1934- *St&PR 91*
Levenson, Mark R. 1947- *St&PR 91*
Levenson, Mark Steven 1957- *WhoEmL 91*
Levenson, Marya Randall 1942- *WhoE 91*
Levenson, Milton 1923- *WhoAm 90*
Levenson, Nathan S. 1916- *WhoE 91*
Levenson, Paul Joshua 1959- *WhoEmL 91*
Levenson, Robert *BioIn 16*
Levenson, Robert Harold 1929- *WhoAm 90*
Levenson, Robert J. 1941- *St&PR 91, WhoAm 90*
Levenson, Rustin S 1947- *WhoAmA 91*
Levenson, Rustin Steele 1947- *WhoE 91*
Levenson, Stanley R. 1933- *ODwPR 91*
Levenson, Stanley Richard 1933- *WhoAm 90*
Levenson, Steven G. 1940- *St&PR 91*
Levenstein, Alan Peter 1936- *WhoAm 90*
Levenstein, Arnold 1930- *St&PR 91*
Levenstein, Robert 1926- *WhoAm 90*
Leventakis, Nicholas 1956- *WhoWor 91*
Levental, Harry E. 1916- *St&PR 91*
Leventer, Richard J. 1930- *St&PR 91*
Leventhal, A. Linda 1943- *WhoWor 91*
Leventhal, Alice Walker 1944- *BioIn 16*
Leventhal, Ann Z. 1936- *WhoWrEP 89*
Leventhal, Bennett L *BiDrAPA 89*
Leventhal, Carl M. 1933- *WhoAm 90*
Leventhal, Cyndi 1963- *WhoAmW 91*
Leventhal, David 1958- *St&PR 91*
Leventhal, Edwin H. 1930- *St&PR 91*
Leventhal, George *BiDrAPA 89*
Leventhal, Herbert 1941- *EncO&P 3*
Leventhal, Jeanne Louise 1956- *BiDrAPA 89*
Leventhal, Markham Richard 1959- *WhoEmL 91*
Leventhal, Mary E *BiDrAPA 89*
Leventhal, Ray L. 1920- *St&PR 91*
Leventhal, Ruth 1940- *WhoAmW 91*
Leventhal, Ruth Lee 1923- *WhoAmA 91*
Leventhal, Sheila Smith 1941- *WhoAmW 91*
Leventhal, Stuart Gary 1947- *WhoE 91*
Leventhal, Teri V. 1932- *WhoAmW 91*
Leventon, Rosie 1949- *BiDWomA*
LeVeque, Eddie *BioIn 16*
Leveque, Jean-Maxime 1923- *WhoWor 91*
Lever, Fat *BioIn 16*
Lever, James Jefferson, III 1947- *WhoSSW 91*
Lever, Lafayette *BioIn 16*
Lever, Peter Gordon *BiDrAPA 89*
Lever, R Hayley 1876-1968 *WhoAmA 91N*
Lever, Walter Frederick 1909- *WhoAm 90, WhoWor 91*
Lever, William Hesketh 1851-1925 *BioIn 16*
Levere, Jane Lois 1950- *WhoAmW 91, WhoEmL 91*
Levere, Richard David 1931- *WhoAm 90, WhoWor 91*
Leverenz, Walt 1887-1973 *Ballpl 90*
Leverett, Dixie 1894-1957 *Ballpl 90*
Leverett, Frank 1859-1943 *DcScB S2*
Leverett, John 1662-1724 *EncCRAm*
Leverett, Miles Corrington 1910- *WhoAm 90*
Leverett, Thomas DeWitt 1956- *WhoSSW 91*
Leverette, Robert S. 1946- *St&PR 91*
Levergood, John H. 1934- *WhoAm 90, WhoSSW 91*
Leverhulme, William H Lever, Viscount 1851-1925 *BioIn 16*
Leverhulme, William H. Lever, Viscount 1851-1925 *WorAlBi*
Leveridge, Richard 1670?-1758 *PenDiMP*
Levering, Donald Warren 1949- *WhoWrEP 89*
Levering, Eugene Henry 1932- *WhoAm 90*
Levering, Robert K 1919- *WhoAmA 91*
Leverkus, C. Erich 1926- *WhoWor 91*
Levermann, Thomas Werner 1943- *WhoE 91*
Levermore, Charles Herbert 1856-1927 *BioIn 16*
Levernier, Thomas John 1930- *St&PR 91*
Le Verrier, Regina Y *BiDrAPA 89*
LeVerrier, Regina Yvonne 1962- *WhoEmL 91*
Leversee, Gordon Jepson 1944- *WhoE 91*
Leverson, Ada 1862-1933 *BioIn 16, FemiCLE*
LeVert, John 1946- *BioIn 16*
Levert, John Bertels, Jr. 1931- *WhoSSW 91*
Levert, Joseph Albert 1959- *WhoEmL 91*
Levertin, Oscar Ivar 1862-1906 *DcScanL*
Levertov, Denise 1923- *BioAmW, BioIn 16, FemiCLE, MajTwCW, WhoWrEP 89, WorAlBi*
Leveson, Irving Frederick 1939- *WhoAm 90*
Levesque, Georges-Henri 1903- *WhoAm 90*
Levesque, Louis 1908- *WhoAm 90*
Levesque, Lucien C. 1930- *St&PR 91*
Levesque, Pascal 1923- *St&PR 91*
Levesque, Rene 1922-1987 *BioIn 16*
Levesque, Rene Jules Albert 1926- *WhoAm 90*
Levetin Avery, Estelle 1945- *WhoAmW 91*
Leveton, Alan F *BiDrAPA 89*
Levetown, Robert Alexander 1935- *WhoAm 90*
Levett, Mark A. 1949- *St&PR 91*
Levett, Michael John 1939- *St&PR 91*
Levey, Barry 1930- *WhoAm 90*
Levey, Bernard *BiDrAPA 89*
Levey, Brigid Brophy 1929- *BioIn 16*
Levey, Burton Robert 1931- *St&PR 91*
Levey, Ethel 1881-1955 *OxCPMus*
Levey, Gerald Saul 1937- *WhoAm 90*

Levey, J. Gerald St&PR 91
Levey, J. Gerald 1933- WhoAm 90
Levey, Jim 1906-1970 Ballpl 90
Levey, Lewis Jay 1960- WhoEmL 91
Levey, Mark 1944- BiDrAPA 89
Levey, Merton David 1925- St&PR 91
Levey, Michael 1927- WhoWor 91
Levey, Robert Frank 1945- WhoAm 90
Levey, Samuel 1932- WhoAm 90
Levi, Albert William 1911-1988 BioIn 16
Levi, Arlo Dane 1933- St&PR 91, WhoAm 90
Levi, Barbara Goss 1943- WhoAmW 91
Levi, Carlo 1902-1975 BioIn 16, WhoAmA 91N
Levi, Darrell E 1940- ConAu 131
Levi, David M. 1942- St&PR 91
Levi, David Ries 1960- WhoEmL 91
Levi, Dorothy Hoffman 1942- WhoE 91
Levi, Edward Hirsch 1911- BiDrUSE 89, WhoAm 90
Levi, Eliphas 1810-1875 EncO&P 3
Levi, Francis Albert 1949- WhoWor 91
Levi, Gary Kenneth 1951- WhoE 91, WhoEmL 91
Levi, Gershon ConAu 131
Levi, Harold Leslie 1947- WhoEmL 91
Levi, Herbert Walter 1921- WhoAm 90, WhoE 91
Levi, Hermann 1839-1900 PenDiMP
Levi, Ilan M. 1943- WhoAm 90
Levi, Isaac 1930- WhoAm 90
Levi, James Harry 1939- WhoAm 90, WhoE 91
Levi, Jan Heller 1954- WhoWrEP 89
Levi, Josef 1938- WhoAmA 91
Levi, Josef Alan 1938- WhoAm 90, WhoE 91
Levi, Julian 1900-1982 WhoAmA 91N
Levi, Julian Hirsch 1909- WhoAm 90
Levi, Kurt 1910- WhoAm 90
Levi, L David 1938- BiDrAPA 89
Levi, Lennart 1930- WhoWor 91
Levi, Linda S. 1957- ODwPR 91
Levi, Luigi 1859-1939 BioIn 16
Levi, Malcolm A. 1916- St&PR 91
Levi, Maurice David 1945- WhoAm 90
Levi, Patrizia A BiDrAPA 89
Levi, Peter Chad Tigar 1931- SpyFic
Levi, Primo 1919-1987 BioIn 16, ConAu 33NR, MajTwCW, WorAu 1980 [port]
Levi, Rafael N. BiDrAPA 89
Levi, Robert Henry 1915- WhoAm 90
Levi, Romano BioIn 16
Levi, S. Gershon NewYTBS 90
Levi, S Gershon 1908-1990 ConAu 131
Levi, Samuel Gershon 1908-1990 BioIn 16
Levi, Steven C. 1948- WhoWrEP 89
Levi, Suzanne Evans 1938- WhoAmW 91
Levi, Tamara 1947- WhoAmW 91
Levi, Theodore 1924- St&PR 91
Levi, Toni Mergentime 1941- WhoWrEP 89
Levi, Vicki Gold 1941- WhoE 91
Levi, Yoel 1950- IntWWM 90, WhoSSW 91
Levi Minzi, Carlo 1954- IntWWM 90
Levi-Minzi, Sergio 1938- BiDrAPA 89
Levi-Montalcini, Paola 1909- BioIn 16
Levi-Montalcini, Rita 1909- BioIn 16, WhoAm 90, WhoWor 91, WorAlBi
Levi-Strauss, Claude 1908- ConAu 32NR, MajTwCW, WhoWor 91, WorAlBi
LeVias, Jerry 1946- BioIn 16
Leviatin, David 1961- ConAu 130
Levich, Cecilia Cortes 1947- BiDrAPA 89
Levick, Bruce W. 1954- St&PR 91
Levick, Douglas Guinness Gwynne, III 1935- WhoAm 90
Levick, George Michael 1953- WhoEmL 91
Levick, Irving WhoAmA 91
Levick, Irving, Mrs WhoAmA 91
Levick, Ruby Winifred BiDWomA
Levick, Stephen E 1951- BiDrAPA 89
Levick, Stephen Eric 1951- WhoE 91
Levick, William Russell 1931- WhoWor 91
Levicki, John S. St&PR 91
Levicki, John Sullivan 1940- WhoAm 90
Levicky, Allen Paul 1948- St&PR 91
Levie, Charles A 1941- BiDrAPA 89
Levie, Howard Sidney 1907- WhoAm 90
Levie, Joseph Henry WhoAm 90
Le Vielleuze, Francisco Silvela y de 1845-1905 BioIn 16
Le Vien, John Douglas 1918- WhoAm 90
Levien, Roger E. 1935- St&PR 91
Levin, A. Leo 1919- WhoAm 90
Levin, Aaron Reuben 1929- WhoE 91
Levin, Abraham 1880-1957 MusmAFA
Levin, Alan Edward 1953- WhoSSW 91
Levin, Alan M. 1926- WhoAm 90
Levin, Alan Michael 1948- St&PR 91
Levin, Amy Beth 1942- WhoWrEP 89
Levin, Amy Beth 1945- WhoAm 90
Levin, Amy Elizabeth 1943- WhoE 91
Levin, Andrew Paul 1953- BiDrAPA 89
Levin, Arnold 1939- WhoE 91
Levin, Barton John 1944- WhoAm 90
Levin, Benjamin 1899- St&PR 91, WhoAm 90
Levin, Bernard 1942- WhoAm 90
Levin, Bertram 1920- WhoAm 90
Levin, Betsy 1935- WhoAm 90
Levin, Betty 1927- BioIn 16, SmATA 11AS [port]
Levin, Betty Bergman 1941- WhoAmW 91
Levin, Bruce Alan 1939- St&PR 91, WhoAm 90
Levin, Bruce Jay 1956- BiDrAPA 89
Levin, Burton 1930- WhoAm 90, WhoWor 91
Levin, Carl WhoAm 90
Levin, Carl 1934- WhoAm 90, WhoWor 91
Levin, Carol Arlene 1945- WhoAmW 91
Levin, Carol B 1945- BiDrAPA 89
Levin, Carol Simon 1959- WhoE 91
Levin, Charles Leonard 1926- WhoAm 90
Levin, Charles Robert 1945- WhoE 91, WhoEmL 91
Levin, Dan 1914- WhoWrEP 89
Levin, Daniel Neal 1954- WhoEmL 91
Levin, David 1924- WhoAm 90, WhoWrEP 89
Levin, David Harold 1928- WhoSSW 91
Levin, David Richard 1913- WhoE 91
Levin, David Saul 1934- St&PR 91
Levin, Debbe Ann 1954- WhoAmW 91, WhoEmL 91
Levin, Diana Phyllis Karasik 1938- WhoAmW 91
Levin, Diane ODwPR 91
Levin, Donald Barry 1942- BiDrAPA 89
Levin, Donald M. ODwPR 91
Levin, Donald Matthew 1939- WhoE 91
Levin, Doron P. 1950- ConAu 130
Levin, Edith Wegner 1939- WhoAmW 91
Levin, Edmund C 1931- BiDrAPA 89
Levin, Edward Jesse 1951- WhoEmL 91
Levin, Edward M. 1934- WhoE 91
Levin, Elena 1942- BiDrAPA 89
Levin, Elizabeth H 1950- BiDrAPA 89
Levin, Ellen Kodish BiDrAPA 89
Levin, Elliot M. St&PR 91
Levin, Eric Marc BiDrAPA 89
Levin, Ezra Gurion 1934- WhoAm 90
Levin, Frances Rudnick BiDrAPA 89
Levin, Fred Michael 1942- BiDrAPA 89
Levin, Fredrick 1944- WhoE 91
Levin, Gail 1948- WhoAmA 91
Levin, Gale Anne BiDrAPA 89
Levin, Gerald H. 1929- ConAu 33NR
Levin, Gerald M. 1939- St&PR 91
Levin, Gerald Manuel 1939- WhoAm 90
Levin, Gilbert Victor 1924- St&PR 91, WhoAm 90
Levin, Harold Alan BiDrAPA 89
Levin, Harriet ODwPR 91
Levin, Harry 1912- WhoAm 90
Levin, Harry 1925- WhoAm 90
Levin, Harry 1946- BiDrAPA 89
Levin, Herbert Allen 1943- BiDrAPA 89
Levin, Herman BioIn 16, NewYTBS 90 [port], -90
Levin, Howard S. BioIn 16
Levin, Howard S. 1924- St&PR 91
Levin, Hugh Lauter 1951- WhoAmA 91, WhoE 91
Levin, Ira 1929- MajTwCW, TwCCr&M 91, WhoAm 90, WhoWrEP 89, WorAlBi
Levin, Irene Staub 1928- WhoAmW 91
Levin, Jack 1932- WhoAm 90
Levin, Jack G. 1947- St&PR 91
Levin, Jack S. 1936- WhoAm 90
Levin, Jacob Joseph 1926- WhoAm 90
Levin, Jane Susan 1948- WhoAmW 91, WhoEmL 91
Levin, Jeffrey Scott BiDrAPA 89
Levin, Jeffrey Steven 1953- WhoEmL 91
Levin, Jennifer Dawn BioIn 16
Levin, Jeremy BioIn 16
Levin, Jerry Wayne 1944- St&PR 91, WhoAm 90, WhoSSW 91
Levin, Jonathan Vigdor 1927- WhoE 91
Levin, Jules Fred 1940- WhoAm 90
Levin, Kenneth BiDrAPA 89
Levin, Kenneth 1949- BiDrAPA 89
Levin, Kenneth Sherman 1937- St&PR 91
Levin, Kim WhoAmA 91
Levin, Laurence Louis 1959- WhoE 91
Levin, Lawrence D. 1952- St&PR 91
Levin, Leon A 1930- BiDrAPA 89
Levin, Lesley Jeanne 1946- WhoEmL 91
Levin, Lois Ann 1941- WhoAmW 91
Levin, M. Penny 1956- WhoAmW 91
Levin, Marcia Lee Meyers 1939- WhoE 91
Levin, Marcia Obrasky 1918- AuBYP 90
Levin, Mark Jay 1957- WhoEmL 91
Levin, Marlene 1934- WhoAmW 91
Levin, Marshall Abbott 1920- WhoE 91, WhoWor 91
Levin, Martin Paul 1918- WhoAm 90
Levin, Michael David 1943- WhoWor 91
Levin, Michael Eric 1943- ConAu 131
Levin, Michael H 1943- BiDrAPA 89
Levin, Michael I. 1950- WhoEmL 91
Levin, Michael Joseph 1943- WhoE 91
Levin, Michael Moshe 1955- WhoEmL 91
Levin, Michael S. 1950- St&PR 91
Levin, Michael Stuart 1950- WhoAm 90
Levin, Michael Sumner 1954- WhoEmL 91
Levin, Mitchell Allan 1944- St&PR 91
Levin, Morton D 1923- WhoAmA 91
Levin, Morton David 1923- WhoAm 90
Levin, Morton Harry 1922- WhoE 91
Levin, Murray Simon 1943- WhoAm 90
Levin, Nathan W. 1904-1988 BioIn 16
Levin, Neil W. 1946- IntWWM 90
Levin, Nina Mathay N 1922- BiDrAPA 89
Levin, Nora 1916-1989 BioIn 16, ConAu 130
Levin, Norman Cyril 1949- WhoE 91
Levin, Norman Lewis 1924- WhoE 91
Levin, Patricia Oppenheim 1932- WhoWor 91
Levin, Paul Frederick 1947- WhoEmL 91
Levin, Peter J. 1939- WhoAm 90
Levin, Rachel BioIn 16
Levin, Rami Yona 1954- IntWWM 90
Levin, Richard Aaron 1932-1990 BioIn 16
Levin, Richard Alan 1949- WhoE 91
Levin, Richard Barry 1956- WhoEmL 91
Levin, Richard Charles 1947- WhoE 91
Levin, Richard I. 1948- St&PR 91
Levin, Richard Louis 1922- WhoAm 90
Levin, Richard W 1948- BiDrAPA 89
Levin, Robert St&PR 91, WhoAm 90
Levin, Robert Alan 1957- WhoWor 91
Levin, Robert Bennett BiDrAPA 89
Levin, Robert D. 1947- IntWWM 90
Levin, Robert Daniel 1930- WhoAm 90
Levin, Robert David 1947- WhoEmL 91
Levin, Robert Joseph 1928- St&PR 91, WhoAm 90
Levin, Robert Marc 1951- BiDrAPA 89
Levin, Robert Randall BiDrAPA 89
Levin, Roger Phillip 1956- WhoEmL 91
Levin, Ronald W 1945- BiDrAPA 89
Levin, Samuel 1929- St&PR 91
Levin, Sander 1931- WhoAm 90
Levin, Saul Marc 1957- BiDrAPA 89
Levin, Sheldon L. 1935- St&PR 91
Levin, Sidney H. 1935- WhoSSW 91
Levin, Simon Asher 1941- WhoAm 90
Levin, Sis BioIn 16
Levin, Solomon A 1935- BiDrAPA 89
Levin, Stephen Dean 1955- WhoEmL 91
Levin, Steve WhoWrEP 89
Levin, Terry Larice 1959- WhoE 91
Levin, Theodore M 1946- BiDrAPA 89
Levin, Tobe 1948- WhoWor 91
Levin, Veda Mara 1949- WhoAmW 91
Levin, Walter PenDiMP
Levin, William Cohn 1917- WhoAm 90
Levin, Yale 1940- St&PR 91
LeVind, R. George BioIn 16
Levine, Aaron 1917- WhoAm 90
Levine, Abby BioIn 16
Levine, Alan J. 1947- WhoAm 90
Levine, Alan Jon BiDrAPA 89
Levine, Albert Bernard 1922- St&PR 91
Levine, Allan St&PR 91
Levine, Allen 1929- WhoAm 90
Levine, Allen A. 1912- St&PR 91
Levine, Allwyn Joseph 1941- BiDrAPA 89
Levine, Alvah Marc 1952- WhoEmL 91
Levine, Alvin L. 1917- St&PR 91
Levine, Arnold Eugene 1921- St&PR 91
Levine, Arnold Leslie 1948- WhoAm 90
Levine, Arthur Elliott 1948- WhoAm 90, WhoE 91
Levine, Arthur Samuel 1936- WhoAm 90
Levine, Bambe ODwPR 91
Levine, Barrett G 1949- BiDrAPA 89
Levine, Barry R. 1953- WhoEmL 91, WhoWor 91
Levine, Benjamin 1931- WhoE 91, WhoWor 91
Levine, Bernard 1918- WhoE 91
Levine, Bernard B. 1918- St&PR 91
Levine, Beryl Joyce 1935- WhoAm 90, WhoAmW 91
Levine, Betty K. 1933- AuBYP 90
Levine, Beverly Pomerantz 1937- WhoE 91
LeVine, Bill 1920- St&PR 91
LeVine, Bona Kellman 1923- St&PR 91
Levine, Bruce Clyde 1949- WhoE 91
Levine, Carl Morton 1931- WhoE 91
Levine, Charles Ellis 1953- WhoEmL 91
Levine, Charles H. 1939-1988 BioIn 16
Levine, Curtis Gilbert 1947- WhoEmL 91
Levine, Daniel 1934- WhoAm 90
Levine, Daniel J 1954- BiDrAPA 89
Levine, David BioIn 16
Levine, David 1926- WhoAm 90, WhoAmA 91
Levine, David Barry 1932- WhoAm 90
Levine, David Barry 1939- St&PR 91
Levine, David Ethan 1955- WhoEmL 91
Levine, David George 1943- BiDrAPA 89
Levine, David Israel 1953- WhoEmL 91
Levine, David L BiDrAPA 89
Levine, David Lawrence 1919- WhoAm 90
Levine, David M. 1949- WhoE 91
Levine, David Michael 1950- St&PR 91
Levine, David Roger 1952- BiDrAPA 89
Levine, David Yale 1934- BiDrAPA 89
Levine, Diana Maisel 1914- WhoAmW 91
Levine, Donald Nathan 1931- WhoAm 90
Levine, Douglas Stewart 1952- WhoEmL 91
Le Vine, Duane Gilbert 1933- WhoAm 90, WhoWor 91
Levine, Edward 1928- WhoAmA 91
Levine, Edward C. 1927- St&PR 91
Levine, Edwin Burton 1920- WhoAm 90
Levine, Eileen Blanche 1934- WhoAmW 91
Levine, Elizabeth P. 1954- WhoAmW 91
Levine, Ellen 1939- WhoWrEP 89
Levine, Ellen G 1941- BiDrAPA 89
Levine, Ellen Gail 1961- WhoAmW 91
Levine, Ellen R. 1943- WhoAm 90
Levine, Ellis B. 1938- St&PR 91
Levine, Ely Z. 1952- WhoWor 91
Levine, Erik BioIn 16
Levine, Erik 1960- WhoAmA 91
Levine, Ernest Stephen 1944- St&PR 91
Levine, Faith Laurel 1939- WhoAmW 91, WhoE 91
Levine, George Arthur 1935- WhoSSW 91
Levine, George H. 1928- St&PR 91
Levine, George Lewis 1931- WhoAm 90
Levine, George Richard 1929- WhoAm 90
Levine, Gerald Richard 1936- WhoE 91
Levine, Gilbert 1927- WhoE 91
Levine, Gilbert 1948- IntWWM 90
Levine, Gwenn Karel 1945- WhoEmL 91
Levine, Harold 1931- WhoSSW 91, WhoWor 91
Levine, Harold Grumet 1931- WhoSSW 91
Levine, Harold Norman 1912- BiDrAPA 89
Levine, Harriette BioIn 16
Levine, Harry 1922- WhoAm 90
Levine, Henry Samuel 1947- BiDrAPA 89
Levine, Herbert Malcolm 1933- WhoWrEP 89
Levine, Herbert Samuel 1928- WhoE 91
Levine, Howard Arnold 1932- WhoAm 90
Levine, Howard B 1943- BiDrAPA 89
Levine, Howard Harris 1949- WhoAm 90
Levine, Howard L. ODwPR 91
Levine, I. Robert 1932- St&PR 91
Levine, I. Stanley 1928- WhoAm 90
Levine, Ira Richard BiDrAPA 89
Levine, Irvin 1921- St&PR 91
Levine, Irving J. ODwPR 91
Levine, Irving M 1912- BiDrAPA 89
Levine, Irving Raskin WhoAm 90, WhoE 91
Levine, Irwin Lester BiDrAPA 89
Levine, Israel E. 1923- AuBYP 90
Levine, Jack 1915- WhoAmA 91
Levine, Jack 1932- St&PR 91
Levine, Jack B. 1941- St&PR 91
Levine, James 1943- IntWWM 90, PenDiMP, WhoAm 90, WhoE 91, WhoWor 91, WorAlBi
Levine, Jane Sheila 1946- WhoEmL 91
Levine, Janet 1945- BioIn 16, WhoWrEP 89
Levine, Janis E. 1953- WhoAmW 91
Levine, Jeffrey Mark BiDrAPA 89
Levine, Jerome 1934- BiDrAPA 89
Le Vine, Jerome Edward 1923- WhoSSW 91, WhoWor 91
Levine, Jerome Fredric 1949- WhoE 91
Levine, Jerome M BiDrAPA 89
Levine, Jerome Paul 1937- WhoAm 90
Levine, Joel 1930- St&PR 91
Levine, Joel 1945- WhoEmL 91
Levine, John David 1936- WhoAm 90
Levine, Jon M. 1958- St&PR 91
Levine, Jonathan B. 1943- St&PR 91
Levine, Joseph 1910- AuBYP 90
Levine, Joseph 1912- IntWWM 90, WhoAm 90
Levine, Joseph Allan 1962- BiDrAPA 89
Levine, Joseph I. 1926-1989 BioIn 16
Levine, Joshua 1916- St&PR 91
Levine, Julian Robert 1933- St&PR 91
Levine, Ken BioIn 16
Levine, Lainie 1942- WhoAm 90
Levine, Larry 1933- St&PR 91
Levine, Laurence E. 1941- WhoE 91
Levine, Laurence Eliott BiDrAPA 89
Levine, Laurence William 1931- WhoAm 90
Levine, Lawrence J. St&PR 91
Levine, Lawrence Steven 1934- WhoAm 90
Levine, Lawrence W. BioIn 16
Levine, Lawrence William 1933- WhoAm 90
Levine, Leo 1930- ODwPR 91
Levine, Leo M. 1930- St&PR 91
Levine, Leon 1937- WhoAm 90, WhoSSW 91
Levine, Leonard 1924- BiDrAPA 89
Levine, Leonard S. 1931- WhoE 91
Levine, Les 1935- WhoAmA 91
Levine, Lindsay Ann 1952- BiDrAPA 89
Levine, Louis BiDrAPA 89
Levine, Louis BioIn 16

Levine, Lowell J. 1937- *WhoAm 90*
Levine, Madeline Geltman 1942- *WhoAm 90*
Levine, Marc M. 1947- *WhoEmL 91*
Levine, Marc Steven 1957- *BiDrAPA 89*
Levine, Marilyn Anne 1935- *WhoAmA 91*
Levine, Marilyn Markovich 1930- *WhoAmW 91, WhoE 91, WhoWor 91*
Levine, Marion Lerner 1931- *WhoAmA 91*
Levine, Mark Leonard 1945- *WhoWrEP 89*
Levine, Martha Peaslee *BiDrAPA 89*
Levine, Martin 1944- *WhoAm 90*
Levine, Martin 1945- *WhoAmA 91*
Levine, Martin David 1938- *WhoAm 90*
Levine, Martin Robert 1943- *WhoAm 90*
Levine, Mary Elizabeth 1924- *IntWWM 90*
Levine, Meldon Edises 1943- *WhoAm 90*
Levine, Melinda 1947- *WhoAmA 91*
Levine, Melvin 1936- *BiDrAPA 89*
Levine, Melvin Charles 1930- *WhoE 91, WhoWor 91*
Levine, Melvin S *BiDrAPA 89*
Levine, Michael *BioIn 16, ODwPR 91*
Levine, Michael 1954- *ODwPR 91, WhoEmL 91*
Levine, Michael 1961- *OxCCanT*
Levine, Michael David 1955- *St&PR 91*
Levine, Michael E. 1941- *BioIn 16*
Levine, Michael Elias 1941- *WhoAm 90*
Levine, Michael Jay *BiDrAPA 89*
Levine, Michael Joseph 1945- *WhoEmL 91, WhoWor 91*
Levine, Milton A. 1925- *St&PR 91*
Levine, Miriam K 1950- *BiDrAPA 89*
Levine, Murray 1926- *St&PR 91*
Levine, Murray 1928- *BioIn 16*
Levine, Myron 1926- *WhoAm 90*
Levine, Naomi Bronheim 1923- *WhoAm 90*
Levine, Nathan *BioIn 16*
Levine, Neal T. 1952- *St&PR 91*
Levine, Noel 1920- *St&PR 91*
Levine, Norman Dion 1912- *WhoAm 90*
Levine, Norman Gene 1926- *WhoAm 90*
Levine, Pamela Gail 1942- *WhoE 91*
LeVine, Patti *ODwPR 91*
Levine, Paul George 1935- *BiDrAPA 89*
Levine, Paul J. 1936- *St&PR 91*
Levine, Paul Michael 1934- *WhoAm 90*
Levine, Peter Michael 1948- *BiDrAPA 89*
Levine, Philip 1922- *WhoAm 90*
Levine, Philip 1928- *WhoAm 90, WhoWrEP 89*
Levine, Philip 1947- *St&PR 91*
Levine, Philip Eliezer 1949- *BiDrAPA 89*
Levine, Rachmiel 1910- *WhoAm 90*
Levine, Ralph 1936- *St&PR 91*
Levine, Randy Lewis 1955- *WhoAm 90*
Levine, Raphael D. *BioIn 16*
Levine, Raphael David 1938- *WhoAm 90, WhoWor 91*
Levine, Rhea Joy Cottler 1939- *WhoAm 90, WhoAmW 91, WhoE 91*
Levine, Rhoda *AuBYP 90*
Levine, Rhoda J. *IntWWM 90*
Levine, Richard A. 1955- *BiDrAPA 89*
Levine, Richard Albert 1935- *St&PR 91*
Levine, Richard H 1954- *BiDrAPA 89*
Levine, Richard James 1942- *WhoAm 90*
Levine, Richard Lawrence 1949- *WhoE 91*
Levine, Richard Steven 1947- *WhoEmL 91*
LeVine, Robert Alan 1932- *WhoAm 90*
Levine, Robert Arthur 1930- *WhoAm 90*
Levine, Robert Bernard 1933- *St&PR 91*
Levine, Robert Howard *BiDrAPA 89*
Levine, Robert John 1934- *WhoAm 90*
Levine, Robert N. *WhoAm 90*
Levine, Robert Sidney 1921- *WhoAm 90*
Levine, Robert Sidney 1944- *St&PR 91*
Levine, Robert T 1943- *BiDrAPA 89*
Levine, Roger A. 1956- *St&PR 91*
Levine, Roger Gary 1950- *BiDrAPA 89*
Levine, Ronald H. 1935- *WhoAm 90*
Levine, Ronald Jay 1953- *WhoAm 90, WhoE 91, WhoEmL 91, WhoWor 91*
Levine, Ruth Rothenberg *WhoAm 90*
Levine, Samson Philip *WhoE 91*
Levine, Samuel *BioIn 16*
Levine, Samuel Gale 1928- *WhoAm 90*
Levine, Samuel Paul 1911- *WhoWrEP 89*
Levine, Sandra Joy 1937- *WhoAmW 91*
Levine, Sandra Mary 1935- *WhoAmW 91*
Levine, Sarah 1970- *BioIn 16*
Levine, Saul 1938- *BiDrAPA 89*
Levine, Seymour *St&PR 91*
Levine, Seymour *BioIn 16*
Levine, Seymour 1924- *WhoAm 90*
Levine, Seymour 1925- *WhoAm 90*
Levine, Seymour R 1906- *WhoAmA 91*
Levine, Shepard 1922- *WhoAmA 91*
Levine, Sol 1922- *WhoAm 90*
Levine, Sol 1928- *WhoAm 90*
Levine, Solomon Bernard 1920- *WhoAm 90*
Levine, Stanley M. *BioIn 16*
Levine, Stephen B 1942- *BiDrAPA 89*
Levine, Steven Alan 1951- *WhoEmL 91, WhoWor 91*
Levine, Steven Lance 1951- *WhoE 91*
Levine, Steven Roy 1951- *WhoE 91*
Levine, Stewart Barry *BiDrAPA 89*
Levine, Stuart George 1932- *WhoAm 90*
Levine, Stuart Howard 1953- *BiDrAPA 89*
Levine, Sumner Norton 1923- *WhoAm 90*
Levine, Susan P 1934- *BiDrAPA 89*
Levine, Suzanne Braun 1941- *WhoAm 90*
Levine, Suzanne Jill 1946- *ConAu 31NR*
Levine, Ted M. 1927- *ODwPR 91*
Levine, Tomar 1945- *WhoAmA 91*
Levine, Tony *BioIn 16*
Levine, Vicki Lucille 1927- *WhoWrEP 89*
Le Vine, Victor Theodore 1928- *WhoAm 90*
Levine, Walter Martin 1946- *WhoSSW 91*
Le Vine, William R 1942- *BiDrAPA 89*
Levine, Yari *WhoAmW 91*
Levine-Goffman, Laura Amy 1959- *WhoAmW 91*
Levinger, Elma Ehrlich 1887- *AuBYP 90*
Levinger, Jack 1922- *St&PR 91*
Levinger, Joseph Solomon 1921- *WhoAm 90*
Levinger, Samuel 1945- *St&PR 91*
Levings, Charles Sandford, III 1930- *WhoAm 90*
Levingston, Anne 1625?- *BiDEWW*
Levingston, Anne G *BiDrAPA 89*
Levingston, Ernest Lee 1921- *St&PR 91, WhoSSW 91*
Levingston, Jon Stuart 1958- *WhoSSW 91, WhoWor 91*
Levins, Ilyssa *ODwPR 91*
Levins, Ilyssa 1958- *WhoAmW 91*
Levins, Patrick James 1945- *WhoAm 90*
Levins, Richard 1930- *WhoAm 90*
Levinsky, Arkady P *BiDrAPA 89*
Levinsky, Norman George 1929- *WhoAm 90*
Levinsohn, Florence H 1926- *ConAu 132*
Levinsohn, Florence Hamlish *WhoWrEP 89*
Levinsohn, Ross 1963- *ODwPR 91*
Levinson, Anne 1958- *WhoAmW 91*
Levinson, Arthur David 1950- *WhoEmL 91*
Levinson, Barry *BioIn 16, NewYTBS 90 [port]*
Levinson, Barry 1942- *CurBio 90 [port]*
Levinson, Barry L. 1932- *WhoAm 90*
Levinson, Burton S. *WhoAm 90, WhoE 91*
Levinson, Charles 1916- *St&PR 91*
Levinson, Charles Bernard 1912- *WhoWor 91*
Levinson, Daniel Ronald 1949- *WhoAm 90, WhoEmL 91*
Levinson, David Judah 1934- *St&PR 91*
Levinson, Donald M. *BioIn 16*
Levinson, Douglas F 1949- *BiDrAPA 89*
Levinson, Edward D *BiDrAPA 89*
Levinson, Fred 1928- *St&PR 91*
Levinson, Gary Allen 1940- *BiDrAPA 89*
Levinson, Harlan Shaw 1961- *WhoE 91*
Levinson, Harold N *BiDrAPA 89*
Levinson, Harry 1922- *WhoAm 90*
Levinson, Harvey 1929- *St&PR 91*
Levinson, Jerome H. 1943- *ODwPR 91*
Levinson, Joel D 1953- *WhoAmA 91*
Levinson, Julius 1925- *St&PR 91*
Levinson, Lawrence Edward 1930- *St&PR 91, WhoAm 90*
Levinson, Lawrence M. 1918- *St&PR 91*
Levinson, Lawrence Stephen 1950- *WhoSSW 91*
Levinson, Leonard 1935- *ConAu 31NR*
Levinson, Leslie Harold 1929- *WhoAm 90*
Levinson, Mark Bradley 1956- *WhoEmL 91*
Levinson, Max L. 1915- *St&PR 91*
Levinson, Michael Howard 1951- *BiDrAPA 89*
Levinson, Mimi 1940- *WhoAmA 91*
Levinson, Mon *WhoE 91*
Levinson, Mon 1926- *WhoAmA 91*
Levinson, Morton I. 1930- *St&PR 91*
Levinson, Norman 1912-1975 *DcScB S2*
Levinson, Paul Howard 1952- *WhoEmL 91*
Levinson, Percival P *BiDrAPA 89*
Levinson, Peritz H 1928- *BiDrAPA 89*
Levinson, Peter Joseph 1943- *WhoWor 91*
Levinson, Rabiah 1952- *WhoAmW 91*
Levinson, Ralph 1948- *WhoEmL 91*
Levinson, Richard Stanley 1934- *WhoAm 90*
Levinson, Riki *BioIn 16, WhoAmW 91*
Levinson, Robert A. 1925- *St&PR 91*
Levinson, Robert Alan 1925- *WhoAm 90*
Levinson, Robert E. 1925- *ConAu 132*
Levinson, Robert S. *ODwPR 91*
Levinson, Rochelle Fox 1949- *WhoAmW 91*
Levinson, Salmon Oliver 1865-1941 *BioIn 16*
Levinson, Samuel E. 1951- *St&PR 91*
Levinson, Sanford Victor 1941- *WhoAm 90*
Levinson, Stephen Eliot 1944- *WhoAm 90*
Levinson, Sunni Roberta 1949- *WhoAmW 91*
Levinstein, Leon *BioIn 16*
Levinthal, Bernard L. 1864-1952 *BioIn 16*
Levinthal, Cyrus *NewYTBS 90*
Levinthal, Elliott Charles 1922- *WhoAm 90*
Levinthal, Israel Herbert 1888-1982 *BioIn 16*
Levinton, Jeffrey S. 1946- *WhoAm 90*
Levintow, Leon 1921- *WhoAm 90*
Levinzon, Rina 1945- *EncCoWW*
Levis, Albert J 1937- *BiDrAPA 89*
Levis, Alexander Henry 1940- *WhoAm 90, WhoE 91*
Levis, Donald James 1936- *WhoAm 90*
Levis, Eileen Ann 1950- *WhoE 91*
Levison, Henry W. 1906-1988 *BioIn 16*
Levison, Robert Irwin 1918- *WhoSSW 91*
Levit, Alla 1935- *BiDrAPA 89*
Levit, Edithe Judith 1926- *WhoAm 90, WhoAmW 91, WhoE 91*
Levit, Herschel 1912-1986 *WhoAmA 91N*
Levit, Milton 1924- *WhoAm 90*
Levit, Solomon Grigorevich 1894-1938 *DcScB S2*
Levit, Victor Bert 1930- *WhoAm 90, WhoWor 91*
Levit, Vladimir G 1923- *BiDrAPA 89*
Levit, William Harold, Jr. 1938- *WhoAm 90*
Levitan, Aida Tomas 1948- *WhoHisp 91*
Levitan, David Maurice 1915- *WhoAm 90*
Levitan, Harold L *BiDrAPA 89*
Levitan, Kenneth Mark 1946- *BiDrAPA 89*
Levitan, Laurence 1933- *WhoE 91*
Levitan, Robert Eugene 1933- *St&PR 91*
Levitan, Sar A. 1914- *WhoAm 90*
Levitan, Stephan J 1941- *BiDrAPA 89*
Levitas, Andrew S 1948- *BiDrAPA 89*
Levitas, Gloria B. 1931- *WhoWrEP 89*
Levitas, Miriam C. Strickman 1936- *WhoAmW 91*
Levitas, Mitchel Ramsey 1929- *WhoAm 90*
Levitas, Tamara B. 1948- *WhoAmW 91*
Levitch, Harry Herman 1918- *WhoSSW 91, WhoWor 91*
Levitch, Melvyn A 1937- *BiDrAPA 89*
Levite, Laurence Allen 1940- *WhoE 91*
Levite, Maurice Rudolph 1941- *WhoE 91*
Levites, Gail Carol 1943- *St&PR 91*
Levites, Miles F. 1944- *St&PR 91*
Levitin, Bruce Jay 1956- *St&PR 91*
Levitin, Lloyd Alan 1932- *St&PR 91*
Levitin, Sonia 1934- *AuBYP 90, BioIn 16, ConAu 32NR*
Levitine, George 1916- *WhoAmA 91*
Levitis, Gerald Martin 1941- *BiDrAPA 89*
Leviton, Adina Platt 1962- *WhoAmW 91*
Leviton, Alan Edward 1930- *WhoAm 90*
Leviton, Jay Bennet 1923- *WhoSSW 91*
Leviton, Ralph *ODwPR 91*
Levitskii, Grigorii Andreevich 1878-1942 *DcScB S2*
Levitsky, Asher S. 1943- *St&PR 91*
Levitsky, Louis Moses 1897-1975 *BioIn 16*
Levitsky, Melvyn 1938- *WhoAm 90*
Levitsky, Neil Stewart 1963- *BiDrAPA 89*
Levitt, Alfred 1894- *WhoAmA 91*
Levitt, Anthony Joseph *BiDrAPA 89*
Levitt, Arthur, Jr. 1931- *St&PR 91, WhoAm 90*
Levitt, Daniel Philip 1936- *WhoAm 90*
Levitt, Geoffrey Martin 1955- *WhoE 91*
Levitt, Gerald Steven 1944- *WhoAm 90*
Levitt, Geraldine L 1928- *BiDrAPA 89*
Levitt, Helen 1918- *WhoAmA 91*
Levitt, Irving Francis 1915- *WhoAm 90*
Levitt, Israel Monroe 1908- *WhoAm 90, WhoE 91*
Levitt, James J. *BiDrAPA 89*
Levitt, Jaren 1946- *WhoEmL 91*
Levitt, Katharine Rexroth 1954- *BiDrAPA 89*
Levitt, Lawrence I 1934- *BiDrAPA 89*
Levitt, LeRoy P *BiDrAPA 89*
Levitt, Leroy Paul 1918- *WhoAm 90*
Levitt, Mark Howard 1952- *WhoE 91*
Levitt, Michael Kent *BiDrAPA 89*
Levitt, Miriam 1946- *WhoAmW 91*
Levitt, Mortimer 1907- *St&PR 91*
Levitt, Nancy Gail 1954- *WhoAmW 91*
Levitt, Peter 1946- *WhoWrEP 89*
Levitt, Raymond Elliot 1949- *WhoEmL 91*
Levitt, Richard H. 1936- *St&PR 91*
Levitt, Richard S. 1930- *St&PR 91*
Levitt, Ronald L. 1931- *ODwPR 91*
Levitt, Seymour Herbert 1928- *WhoAm 90, WhoWor 91*
Levitt, Stephen R 1942- *BiDrAPA 89*
Levitt, Susan B. 1953- *WhoWrEP 89*
Levitt, Theodore 1925- *St&PR 91, WhoAm 90*
Levitt, William *BioIn 16*
Levitt, William J. 1907- *WorAlBi*
Levitte, Simon 1912-1970 *BioIn 16*
Levitz, Gary *BioIn 16*
Levitz, Paul Elliot 1956- *WhoAm 90, WhoE 91*
Levitz, Richard Jay 1946- *St&PR 91*
Levitz, William Lawrence 1943- *WhoAm 90*
Levitzky, Michael Gordon 1947- *WhoSSW 91*
Levkoff, Henry S. 1923- *St&PR 91*
Levkovitz, Michael 1947- *St&PR 91*
Levner, Louis Jules 1951- *WhoE 91*
Levonen, Juha Kalle Olavi 1952- *WhoWor 91*
Levos, Robert Wayne 1943- *St&PR 91*
Le Vot, Andre 1921- *ConAu 130*
Levovitz, Pesach Zechariah 1922- *WhoAm 90*
Levow, Melissa J. *ODwPR 91*
Levowitz, Herbert J 1934- *BiDrAPA 89*
Levoy, David Henry *BiDrAPA 89*
Levoy, Gregg *BioIn 16*
Levoy, Myron *AuBYP 90, BioIn 16*
Levreault, Rosemary Bowers 1927- *WhoAmW 91*
Levsen, Dutch 1898-1972 *Ballpl 90*
Levy, Alan B 1938- *BiDrAPA 89*
Levy, Alan Bruce 1953- *BiDrAPA 89*
Levy, Alan D. 1938- *St&PR 91*
Levy, Alan Joel 1937- *WhoAm 90*
Levy, Alan Joseph 1932- *WhoWrEP 89*
Levy, Alan Marcus 1925- *BiDrAPA 89*
Levy, Alfred W. 1919- *St&PR 91*
Levy, Allan 1925- *BiDrAPA 89*
Levy, Allan Lloyd 1951- *BiDrAPA 89*
Levy, Amnon 1950- *WhoWor 91*
Levy, Amy 1861-1889 *BioIn 16, FemiCLE*
Levy, Andrew P. 1951- *St&PR 91*
Levy, Andrew S. 1949- *St&PR 91*
Levy, Ann Porter Hellebusch 1925- *WhoAm 90*
Levy, Arnold Paul 1943- *BiDrAPA 89*
Levy, Arnold Stuart 1941- *WhoAm 90*
Levy, Arthur James 1947- *WhoE 91, WhoWor 91*
Levy, Arthur Theodore 1956- *WhoE 91*
Levy, Barnet M. 1917- *WhoAm 90*
Levy, Beatrice S 1892-1974 *WhoAmA 91N*
Levy, Benjamin 1940- *WhoAm 90*
Levy, Benjamin F, III 1945- *BiDrAPA 89*
Levy, Bennett S. 1929- *St&PR 91*
Levy, Bernard 1917- *WhoAmA 91*
Levy, Bernard G *BiDrAPA 89*
Levy, Bernard Henri *BioIn 16*
Levy, Bernard S 1936- *BiDrAPA 89*
Levy, Birdie 1918- *St&PR 91*
Levy, Bruce Howard *BiDrAPA 89*
Levy, Bruce Norman 1951- *WhoE 91*
Levy, Bruce Richard 1946- *BiDrAPA 89*
Levy, Burton 1912- *WhoAm 90*
Levy, Carol 1931- *WhoAm 90, WhoWrEP 89*
Levy, Carol Spiegel 1937- *BiDrAPA 89*
Levy, Charles Earl 1939- *BiDrAPA 89*
Levy, Claude 1924- *ConAu 129*
Levy, Cornelia Y. 1939- *WhoAmW 91*
Levy, Dan 1936- *WhoWor 91*
Levy, David *WhoAm 90, WhoWor 91*
Levy, David 1937- *St&PR 91, WhoAm 90*
Levy, David 1938- *BioIn 16*
Levy, David Alfred 1930- *WhoAm 90*
Levy, David Corcos 1938- *WhoAm 90, WhoAmA 91*
Levy, David E. 1935- *ODwPR 91*
Levy, David Lawrence 1936- *WhoE 91*
Levy, David Robert *BiDrAPA 89*
Levy, David Theodore 1952- *WhoE 91*
Levy, Deborah 1959- *FemiCLE*
Levy, Donald 1935- *WhoWor 91*
Levy, Donald Harris 1939- *WhoAm 90*
Levy, Donald S. 1943- *St&PR 91*
Levy, Dora Collazo- *BioIn 16*
Levy, Edward C., Jr. 1931- *St&PR 91*
Levy, Edward Charles, Jr. 1931- *WhoAm 90*
Levy, Edward D, Jr. 1937- *BiDrAPA 89*
Levy, Edwin Z 1929- *BiDrAPA 89*
Levy, Elaine Grace 1957- *WhoAmW 91*
Levy, Elinor Miller 1942- *WhoAmW 91*
Levy, Elizabeth 1942- *AuBYP 90*
Levy, Elizabeth H *BiDrAPA 89*
Levy, Elliot M *BiDrAPA 89*
Levy, Ellis Herbert *BiDrAPA 89*
Levy, Erwin *BiDrAPA 89*
Levy, Eugene *NewYTBS 90*
Levy, Eugene Howard 1944- *WhoAm 90*
Levy, Eugene Pfeifer 1936- *WhoAm 90*
Levy, Florence 1937- *BiDrAPA 89*
Levy, Florence N 1870-1947 *WhoAmA 91N*
Levy, Francis Alain 1940- *WhoWor 91*
Levy, Franklin I. 1944- *WhoAm 90*
Levy, Fred 1914- *BiDrAPA 89*
Levy, Fredric J 1946- *BiDrAPA 89*
Levy, Gaston R. 1928- *WhoAm 90*
Levy, Gaston Raymond 1928- *St&PR 91*
Levy, Geoffrey L 1924- *BiDrAPA 89*
Levy, George Charles 1944- *WhoAm 90*
Levy, Gerald Arnold 1933- *St&PR 91*
Levy, Gerard G. 1939- *St&PR 91*
Levy, Gerardo 1924- *IntWWM 90*
Levy, Gerhard 1928- *WhoAm 90*
Levy, Harold J 1925- *BiDrAPA 89*
Levy, Harold Louis 1958- *WhoSSW 91*

Levy, Harry Dale 1923- St&PR 91
Levy, Herbert Joel 1949- WhoSSW 91
Levy, Herbert Monte 1923- WhoE 91, WhoWor 91
Levy, Hilda WhoAmA 91
Levy, Hilton Bertram 1916- WhoE 91
Levy, Howard I. 1939- WhoSSW 91
Levy, Howard Ira 1945- BiDrAPA 89
Levy, Hyman 1889-1975 BioIn 16
Levy, Irvin L. 1929- St&PR 91, WhoSSW 91
Levy, Irwin Bertram 1933- BiDrAPA 89
Levy, Jack J 1940- BiDrAPA 89
Levy, Jacques BiDrAPA 89
Levy, James A. 1939- St&PR 91
Levy, James Peter 1940- WhoAm 90
Levy, Janet Caplan 1936- WhoAmW 91
Levy, Janet Sara 1959- WhoE 91
Levy, Janice Cohen 1936- BiDrAPA 89
Levy, Jeffrey Michael 1954- WhoWor 91
Levy, Jerre Marie 1938- WhoAm 90, WhoAmW 91
Levy, Joanna Sue 1951- WhoAmW 91
Levy, Joel 1935- WhoE 91
Levy, Joel Howard 1938- WhoE 91, WhoWor 91
Levy, Joel N. 1941- St&PR 91
Levy, John 1941- St&PR 91
Levy, John Feldberg 1947- WhoAm 90
Levy, John S. 1935- St&PR 91
Levy, John Stuart 1946- WhoWor 91
Levy, Jordan 1943- St&PR 91, WhoE 91
Levy, Joseph 1928- St&PR 91, WhoAm 90
Levy, Joseph P. BioIn 16
Levy, Joseph W. 1932- St&PR 91
Levy, Judd Seth BiDrAPA 89
Levy, Julia 1935- WhoAmW 91
Levy, Julien 1906-1981 WhoAmA 91N
Levy, Kathy Ann 1951- WhoAmW 91
Levy, Keith C 1949- BiDrAPA 89
Levy, Kenneth 1927- WhoAm 90
Levy, Kenneth James 1949- WhoAm 90
Levy, Kenneth Jay 1946- WhoAm 90
Levy, Larry 1947- WhoWrEP 89
Levy, Lawrence Edwin 1941- BiDrAPA 89
Levy, Leon BioIn 16
Levy, Leon 1925- St&PR 91, WhoAm 90
Levy, Leonard Williams 1923- WhoAm 90, WhoWrEP 89
Levy, Lester A. 1922- St&PR 91, WhoSSW 91
Levy, Lewis 1938- St&PR 91
Levy, Lou 1910- BioIn 16
Levy, Louis 1921- WhoAm 90
Levy, Louis Edward 1932- WhoAm 90
Levy, Louise Rachael 1950- WhoE 91
Levy, Margaret Wasserman 1899- WhoAmA 91
Levy, Mark 1947- WhoAmA 91
Levy, Mark A. 1952- St&PR 91
Levy, Mark Allan 1939- WhoAm 90
Levy, Mark Barry 1948- St&PR 91
Levy, Mark F. 1955- St&PR 91
Levy, Mark Ivan 1946- BiDrAPA 89
Levy, Mark Robert 1943- WhoE 91
Levy, Mark S. 1948- St&PR 91
Levy, Marvin B. 1935- St&PR 91
Levy, Marvin Daniel 1929- WhoAm 90, WhoE 91
Levy, Marvin David 1932- IntWWM 90, PenDiMP A, WhoAm 90
Levy, Mary Ann 1940- BiDrAPA 89
Levy, Matthew Nathan 1922- WhoAm 90
Levy, Max M. 1926- St&PR 91, WhoAm 90
Levy, Michael 1946- St&PR 91
Levy, Michael A 1946- BiDrAPA 89
Levy, Michael Howard 1947- WhoSSW 91
Levy, Michael I 1952- BiDrAPA 89
Levy, Michael Richard 1946- WhoAm 90
Levy, Michael Scott 1953- WhoEmL 91
Levy, Michael Sigmund 1945- IntWWM 90
Levy, Michael T 1945- BiDrAPA 89
Levy, Milton P., Jr. 1925- St&PR 91
Levy, Mitchel 1961- WhoSSW 91
Levy, Morris BioIn 16
Levy, Morris NewYTBS 90
Levy, Morris S 1936- BiDrAPA 89
Levy, Murray BioIn 16
Levy, Nathan 1945- SmATA 63 [port]
Levy, Nessim 1942- St&PR 91
Levy, Norman A BiDrAPA 89
Levy, Norman B 1931- BiDrAPA 89, WhoAm 90
Levy, Norman F. 1912- St&PR 91
Levy, Norman J 1919- BiDrAPA 89
Levy, Norman Jay 1942- WhoAm 90
Levy, Norman M 1926- BiDrAPA 89
Levy, Olivier 1949- WhoWor 91
Levy, Paul BiDrAPA 89
Levy, Paul 1941- WhoWor 91
Levy, Paul Gary BiDrAPA 89
Levy, Phyllis Houser 1927- WhoAmA 91
Levy, Ralph 1932- St&PR 91, WhoAm 90
Levy, Richard C. 1947- WhoE 91
Levy, Richard D. 1930- St&PR 91
Levy, Richard J 1931- BiDrAPA 89
Levy, Richard Philip 1923- WhoAm 90
Levy, Robert 1926- WhoAm 90, WhoWrEP 89
Levy, Robert Alan 1946- WhoWor 91
Levy, Robert B. 1911- St&PR 91
Levy, Robert Drew 1946- BiDrAPA 89
Levy, Robert E. 1939- St&PR 91
Levy, Robert Edward 1939- WhoAm 90
Levy, Robert Halle 1953- St&PR 91
Levy, Robert I BiDrAPA 89
Levy, Robert I. 1912- WhoWor 91
Levy, Robert Jeffrey 1956- WhoWrEP 89
Levy, Robert Joseph 1931- WhoAm 90
Levy, Robert Marquis 1949- WhoSSW 91
Levy, Rochelle Feldman 1937- WhoAmW 91, WhoE 91, WhoWor 91
Levy, Roland 1924- BiDrAPA 89
Levy, Ronald WhoAm 90
Levy, Ronald Melvyn BiDrAPA 89
Levy, Ronald Stewart 1948- St&PR 91
Levy, Ruth Elen 1952- WhoSSW 91
Levy, S Dean 1942- WhoAmA 91
Levy, S. William 1920- WhoAm 90
Levy, Salomon 1926- WhoAm 90
Levy, Samuel K. 1894-1989 BioIn 16
Levy, Sandy Lynn 1949- ODwPR 91
Levy, Sherrie D M 1951- BiDrAPA 89
Levy, Sidney 1909- WhoE 91
Levy, Sidney Jay 1921- WhoAm 90
Levy, Stanley H. 1922- St&PR 91
Levy, Stanley Herbert 1922- WhoAm 90
Levy, Stephen 1947- WhoWrEP 89
Levy, Stephen Anthony BiDrAPA 89
Levy, Stephen Raymond 1940- St&PR 91, WhoAm 90
Levy, Steven T 1945- BiDrAPA 89
Levy, Stewart Rich 1958- WhoE 91
Levy, Stuart David 1946- BiDrAPA 89
Levy, Susan 1949- WhoAmW 91, WhoE 91, WhoEmL 91
Levy, Susan Rae BiDrAPA 89
Levy, Sy 1929- WhoAm 90
Levy, Terri ODwPR 91
Levy, Tibbie 1908- WhoAmA 91
Levy, Tracy WhoSSW 91
Levy, Viviane 1932- WhoWor 91
Levy, Walter J., Jr. EncO&P 3
Levy, Walter James 1911- WhoAm 90
Levy, Warren P. 1952- St&PR 91
Levy, Wayne David BiDrAPA 89
Levy, William 1924- BiDrAPA 89
Levy, William G. 1912- St&PR 91
Levy, William H BiDrAPA 89
Levy, Yacov 1945- WhoE 91
Levy, Yeshayahou 1949- WhoWor 91
Levy-Spira, Eduardo BioIn 16
Levys, Isaac A. 1911- St&PR 91
Lew, Arthur BiDrAPA 89
Lew, Arthur 1944- WhoE 91
Lew, Edwin Wayne 1950- WhoSSW 91
Lew, Fran WhoAmA 91
Lew, Ira Eugene 1943- BiDrAPA 89
Lew, Karen Leslie 1942- WhoAmW 91
Lew, Roger A. 1941- St&PR 91
Lew, Roger Alan 1941- WhoAm 90
Lew, Salvador 1929- WhoHisp 91, WhoSSW 91
Lew, Weyman 1935- WhoAmA 91
Lewallen, Lynne Porter 1959- WhoSSW 91
Lewan, Roland, Jr. 1930- WhoAm 90
Lewando, Alfred Gerard, Jr. 1945- WhoSSW 91
Lewandoski, David John 1951- St&PR 91
Lewandowska, Barbara Ewa 1959- WhoAmW 91
Lewandowska, Stanislawa Slawomira 1924- WhoWor 91
Lewandowski, Andrew Anthony 1946- WhoE 91
Lewandowski, Bohdan 1926- WhoWor 91
Lewandowski, Chester T. 1948- St&PR 91
Lewandowski, Edmund D 1914- WhoAmA 91
Lewandowski, John Joseph 1956- WhoEmL 91
Lewandowski, Kate ODwPR 91
Lewandowski, Lucille M BiDrAPA 89
Lewandowski, Lynne 1953- IntWWM 90
Lewandowski, Victoria Theresa 1935- WhoAmW 91
Lewbel, Arthur Harris 1956- WhoE 91
Lewcock, Ronald Bentley 1929- WhoAm 90, WhoWor 91
Lewczuk, Margrit WhoAmA 91
Lewek, William T 1952- BiDrAPA 89
Lewellen, John Bryan 1910-1956 AuBYP 90
Lewellen, Wilbur Garrett 1938- WhoAm 90
Lewellen, William E. 1925- St&PR 91
Lewenstein, Leonard Norman BiDrAPA 89
Lewent, Judy C. 1949- WhoAmW 91
Lewenthal, Raymond 1926- PenDiMP
Lewenthal, Raymond 1926-1988 BioIn 16
Lewers, Leigh Edward 1927- St&PR 91
Lewes, George Henry 1817-1878 BioIn 16
Lewicke, Catherine Pearl 1917- WhoE 91
Lewicki, Ann Maria WhoAm 90
Lewicki, Lynne Powers 1952- ODwPR 91
Lewicki, Matthew Edward 1948- WhoE 91
Lewicky, George I. 1933- St&PR 91
Lewin, Alan Charles 1945- St&PR 91
Lewin, Andre Roderich 1934- WhoWor 91
Lewin, Arie Yehuda 1935- WhoSSW 91
Lewin, Bernard WhoAmA 91
Lewin, Bruce Roger 1947- St&PR 91
Lewin, Dasha 1929- St&PR 91
Lewin, Elizabeth Samelson 1938- WhoAmW 91
Lewin, George Forest 1916- WhoAm 90
Lewin, Jack 1932- WhoE 91
Lewin, James Davies 1812-1900 DcCanB 12
Lewin, Jan Landau ODwPR 91
Lewin, Jeff Lee 1951- WhoEmL 91
Lewin, John Calvert 1946- WhoAm 90
Lewin, John Henry, Jr. 1939- WhoAm 90
Lewin, Lawrence Stephen 1938- WhoAm 90
Lewin, Leonard 1919- WhoAm 90
Lewin, Leonard C. 1916- WhoWrEP 89
Lewin, Marian Eva 1954- WhoE 91
Lewin, Michael 1948- IntWWM 90
Lewin, Michael Z 1942- TwCCr&M 91
Lewin, Milton J 1929-1979 WhoAmA 91N
Lewin, Moshe 1921- WhoAm 90
Lewin, Nathan 1936- BioIn 16
Lewin, Pearl Goldman 1923- WhoAmW 91
Lewin, Philip Martin 1935- WhoAm 90
Lewin, Ralph Arnold 1921- WhoAm 90
Lewin, Rebecca 1954- WhoWrEP 89
Lewin, Roger Amos BiDrAPA 89
Lewin, Ronald 1914-1984 DcNaB 1981
Lewin, Sara BiDrAPA 89
Lewin, Seymour Zalman 1921- WhoAm 90
Lewin, Susan Grant 1939- WhoAmW 91
Lewin, Walter 1930- BiDrAPA 89
Lewin-Fetter, Victoria 1941- BiDrAPA 89
Lewin-Richter, Andres 1937- IntWWM 90
Lewinbuk, Joseph 1935- BiDrAPA 89
Lewine, Peter Emmett 1947- WhoE 91
Lewine, Richard 1910- WhoAm 90
Lewine, Robert F. 1913- WhoAm 90
Lewins, Steven 1943- WhoWor 91
Lewinsky, Herbert Christian 1928- WhoWor 91
Lewinsohn, Hilton Cecil 1928- WhoE 91
Lewinson, Sam 1914- St&PR 91
Lewinstein, Stephen R. 1941- St&PR 91
Lewinter, Donna Ellen BiDrAPA 89
Lewinter, Philippe Maurice 1956- BiDrAPA 89
Lewis, Aaron Bryce 1965- WhoE 91
Lewis, Abdon BioIn 16
Lewis, Ada St&PR 91
Lewis, Adele ConAu 131
Lewis, Adele Beatrice 1927-1990 BioIn 16
Lewis, Al BioIn 16
Lewis, Al 1923- ConTFT 8 [port]
Lewis, Alan Gerber 1946- St&PR 91
Lewis, Alethea 1750-1827 FemiCLE
Lewis, Alexander, Jr. 1916- St&PR 91, WhoAm 90
Lewis, Alexander C. 1932- St&PR 91
Lewis, Alfred B 1928- BiDrAPA 89
Lewis, Alfred Baker, III 1956- WhoEmL 91
Lewis, Alfred E. 1912-1968 AuBYP 90
Lewis, Alice Hudson 1895?-1971 AuBYP 90
Lewis, Allan 1905- WhoAm 90
Lewis, Allen 1873-1957 WhoAmA 91N
Lewis, Allen 1909- WhoWor 91
Lewis, Allen 1916- Ballpl 90
Lewis, Alvin Bower, Jr. 1932- WhoE 91, WhoWor 91
Lewis, Andrew 1720-1781 WhNaAH
Lewis, Andrew 1931- BiDrUSE 89
Lewis, Andrew L. BioIn 16
Lewis, Andrew Lindsay, Jr. 1931- St&PR 91, WhoAm 90
Lewis, Ann WhoWrEP 89
Lewis, Ann Frank 1937- WhoAm 90
Lewis, Anna WhoWrEP 89
Lewis, Anne Coleman 1945- BiDrAPA 89, WhoE 91
Lewis, Anne McCutcheon 1943- WhoAmW 91
Lewis, Annebel Victoria 1935- WhoAmW 91
Lewis, Anthony PenDiMP
Lewis, Anthony 1915-1983 PenDiMP
Lewis, Anthony 1927- BioIn 16, WhoAm 90, WhoE 91, WorAlBi
Lewis, Anthony Carey 1915-1983 DcNaB 1981
Lewis, Anthony Hugh Cassidy 1930- WhoAm 90
Lewis, Antoinette M BiDrAPA 89
Lewis, Archibald Ross NewYTBS 90
Lewis, Archibald Ross 1914-1990 BioIn 16, ConAu 130
Lewis, Argus W 1943- BiDrAPA 89
Lewis, Arlene Jane Quiring 1934- WhoAmW 91
Lewis, Arnold Marcus 1938- BiDrAPA 89
Lewis, Arthur Dee 1918- WhoAm 90
Lewis, Arthur J. 1946- St&PR 91
Lewis, Arthur Raymond 1933- WhoWor 91
Lewis, Aubrey 1935- St&PR 91
Lewis, Barbara ODwPR 91
Lewis, Barbara 1954- WhoAmW 91
Lewis, Barbara Ann 1945- WhoAmW 91, WhoEmL 91, WhoWor 91
Lewis, Barbara Ann 1953- WhoAmW 91
Lewis, Barbara Connolly 1927- IntWWM 90
Lewis, Barbara Jimmie 1932- WhoAmW 91
Lewis, Barbara S 1956- BiDrAPA 89
Lewis, Barton Lee BiDrAPA 89
Lewis, Benjamin Morgan 1920- WhoAm 90
Lewis, Bernard 1916- WhoAm 90
Lewis, Bernard Leroy 1923- WhoAm 90
Lewis, Boyd De Wolf 1905- WhoAm 90
Lewis, Bradley Eugene BiDrAPA 89
Lewis, Brenda 1920- IntWWM 90
Lewis, Brent Renault 1958- WhoEmL 91, WhoWor 91
Lewis, Brian 1958- ODwPR 91
Lewis, Brian William 1959- WhoEmL 91
Lewis, Buddy 1916- Ballpl 90
Lewis, Byron Eugene 1931- WhoAm 90
Lewis, C. Day TwCCr&M 91
Lewis, C. S. 1898-1963 BioIn 16
Lewis, C.S. 1898-1963 ConAu 33NR, DcLB 100 [port], MajTwCW
Lewis, C. S. 1898-1963 WorAlBi
Lewis, C S 1898-1963 WrPh
Lewis, Calvin Fred 1946- WhoEmL 91
Lewis, Carl BioIn 16
Lewis, Carl 1961- WorAlBi
Lewis, Carlos BioIn 16
Lewis, Carol Ann 1945- BiDrAPA 89
Lewis, Carol Ann 1946- WhoSSW 91
Lewis, Carol Reichel 1956- WhoEmL 91
Lewis, Carole 1934- WhoAmA 91
Lewis, Cary 1942- IntWWM 90
Lewis, Cary Blackburn, Jr. 1921- WhoAm 90
Lewis, Cecil Day 1904-1972 WorAlBi
Lewis, Cecil Paul WhoWrEP 89
Lewis, Celian H. 1914- WhoAm 90
Lewis, Ceylon Smith, Jr. 1920- WhoAm 90
Lewis, Chantee 1926- WhoE 91
Lewis, Charles A. 1942- WhoAm 90
Lewis, Charles Edwin 1928- WhoAm 90
Lewis, Charles J. 1927- St&PR 91
Lewis, Charles John 1927- WhoAm 90
Lewis, Charles Joseph 1940- WhoAm 90, WhoE 91
Lewis, Charles Leonard 1926- WhoAm 90
Lewis, Charles MacDonald 1941- WhoSSW 91
Lewis, Charles Thomas 1956- WhoE 91
Lewis, Chas Leon 1940- BiDrAPA 89
Lewis, Cheryl Denise 1954- WhoE 91
Lewis, Chester 1914-1990 BioIn 16
Lewis, Chester M. NewYTBS 90
Lewis, Chester M 1914-1990 CurBio 90N
Lewis, Christopher Alan 1955- WhoE 91, WhoEmL 91
Lewis, Christopher Terence 1944- WhoWor 91
Lewis, Clark Quincy 1919- WhoAm 90
Lewis, Claude, Jr. 1924- WhoAm 90
Lewis, Claude Aubrey 1936- WhoAm 90
Lewis, Claude H. 1943- St&PR 91
Lewis, Claudia 1907- AuBYP 90
Lewis, Clidie Rebecca Harvey 1947- WhoAmW 91
Lewis, Clifford, III 1904- WhoE 91, WhoWor 91
Lewis, Clifford Fuller 1955- WhoWrEP 89
Lewis, Clive Staples 1898-1963 AuBYP 90, BioIn 16
Lewis, Clyde 1911-1976 EncACom
Lewis, Clyde A. 1913- WhoWor 91
Lewis, Collins E 1945- BiDrAPA 89
Lewis, Craig 1930- ODwPR 91
Lewis, Craig A. 1955- ConAu 132
Lewis, Craig Graham David 1930- WhoAm 90
Lewis, Craig Meredith 1956- WhoSSW 91
Lewis, Cynthia Lynne 1962- WhoAmW 91
Lewis, Dale Kenton 1937- WhoAm 90
Lewis, Daniel 1925- IntWWM 90
Lewis, Daniel Day- BioIn 16
Lewis, Daniel Day 1958- WorAlBi
Lewis, Daniel Frederick 1954- WhoSSW 91
Lewis, Darlene D. 1938- WhoAmW 91
Lewis, Darrell L. 1931- WhoAm 90
Lewis, David 1917- BioIn 16
Lewis, David 1929- WhoE 91
Lewis, David 1944- WhoAm 90
Lewis, David A. 1937- WhoAm 90
Lewis, David Alan BiDrAPA 89
Lewis, David B. 1947- St&PR 91
Lewis, David Carleton 1935- WhoAm 90
Lewis, David Dan 1919- St&PR 91
Lewis, David Eldridge 1924- WhoAm 90
Lewis, David J 1920- BiDrAPA 89
Lewis, David John 1948- WhoE 91

Lewis, David Kellogg 1941- *ConAu 33NR, WhoAm 90*
Lewis, David Lanier 1927- *WhoAm 90, WhoWrEP 89*
Lewis, David Michael 1951- *BiDrAPA 89*
Lewis, David Olin 1956- *WhoEmL 91*
Lewis, David Sheldon 1929- *IntWWM 90*
Lewis, David Sloan, Jr. 1917- *St&PR 91*
Lewis, David Wayne 1955- *WhoEmL 91*
Lewis, Dawnn *BioIn 16*
Lewis, Dean Sumter 1933- *WhoAm 90*
Lewis, Del F. 1937- *WhoWor 91*
Lewis, Dennis 1940- *ODwPR 91*
Lewis, Dennis Carroll 1940- *WhoAm 90*
Lewis, Denny Clarke 1938- *St&PR 91*
Lewis, Diane 1936- *ConAu 129, WhoAmW 91*
Lewis, Diane Patricia 1956- *WhoAmW 91*
Lewis, Dickson W. 1948- *St&PR 91*
Lewis, Don S, Sr 1919- *WhoAmA 91*
Lewis, Donald *BioIn 16*
Lewis, Donald C. 1942- *St&PR 91*
Lewis, Donald Emerson 1950- *WhoAm 90, WhoE 91*
Lewis, Donald Ernest 1943- *WhoE 91*
Lewis, Donald Joseph 1922- *WhoAm 90*
Lewis, Donald Sykes, Jr 1947- *WhoAmA 91*
Lewis, Donna Cunningham 1945- *WhoE 91*
Lewis, Dorothy Otnow *BiDrAPA 89*
Lewis, Douglas 1938- *WhoAm 90, WhoAmA 91, WhoWrEP 89*
Lewis, Douglas Grinslade 1938- *WhoAm 90, WhoE 91*
Lewis, Drew *BioIn 16, WhoE 91*
Lewis, Duane L. 1934- *St&PR 91*
Lewis, Duffy 1888-1979 *Ballpl 90*
Lewis, Edith Patton 1914- *WhoAm 90*
Lewis, Edmonia 1843?-1900? *BioIn 16*
Lewis, Edmonia 1845-1911? *BiDWomA*
Lewis, Edmund 1959- *ConTFT 8 [port]*
Lewis, Edna *BioIn 16*
Lewis, Edward 1940- *WhoAm 90*
Lewis, Edward Alan 1942- *St&PR 91*
Lewis, Edward Alan 1946- *WhoEmL 91*
Lewis, Edward B. 1918- *WhoAm 90*
Lewis, Edward David 1953- *WhoE 91*
Lewis, Edward Earl 1926- *WhoAm 90, WhoWor 91*
Lewis, Edward M. 1923- *St&PR 91*
Lewis, Edward Sheldon 1920- *WhoAm 90*
Lewis, Edward T. 1940- *ConAmBL*
Lewis, Edward Van Vliet 1914- *WhoAm 90*
Lewis, Edwin Alvin 1942- *St&PR 91*
Lewis, Edwin Reynolds 1934- *WhoAm 90*
Lewis, Elizabeth *WhoAmA 91*
Lewis, Elizabeth Foreman 1892- *AuBYP 90*
Lewis, Elizabeth M 1947- *BiDrAPA 89*
Lewis, Elizabeth Matthew *WhoAmA 91*
Lewis, Ellen 1948- *BiDrAPA 89, WhoAmW 91*
Lewis, Ellen Terry 1959- *WhoAmW 91*
Lewis, Elliot Aubrey 1953- *St&PR 91*
Lewis, Elliott 1917- *WhoWrEP 89*
Lewis, Elliott 1917-1990 *ConAu 131*
Lewis, Elma I. 1921- *WhoAm 90*
Lewis, Elma Ina 1921- *WhoAmA 91*
Lewis, Emanuel Raymond 1928- *WhoAm 90*
Lewis, Emmanuel 1971- *DrBlPA 90*
Lewis, Ervin Walter *BiDrAPA 89*
Lewis, Evelyn 1946- *ODwPR 91, WhoAmW 91, WhoEmL 91*
Lewis, Flora *BioIn 16, WhoAm 90, WhoAmW 91*
Lewis, Florence M 1926- *BiDrAPA 89*
Lewis, Florence Wirsching 1924- *WhoAmW 91*
Lewis, Floyd Wallace 1925- *WhoAm 90*
Lewis, Frances Aaronson 1922- *WhoSSW 91*
Lewis, Francis 1713-1802 *EncCRAm*
Lewis, Francis James 1930- *WhoAm 90*
Lewis, Frank Harlan 1919- *WhoAm 90*
Lewis, Frank J. 1930- *St&PR 91*
Lewis, Frank Leroy 1949- *WhoEmL 91*
Lewis, Frank Ross 1931- *WhoSSW 91*
Lewis, Frederick A, Jr. 1927- *BiDrAPA 89*
Lewis, Frederick Carlton 1961- *WhoAm 90*
Lewis, Frederick Thomas *BiDrAPA 89*
Lewis, Fulton 1903-1966 *BioIn 16*
Lewis, Gail Dianne 1956- *WhoAmW 91*
Lewis, Gary 1946- *EncPR&S 89*
Lewis, Gene Dale 1931- *WhoAm 90*
Lewis, Gene E. 1928- *St&PR 91*
Lewis, Gene Evans 1928- *WhoAm 90*
Lewis, George 1900-1968 *OxCPMus*
Lewis, George Knowlton 1923- *WhoAm 90*
Lewis, George Orin 1928- *WhoSSW 91*
Lewis, George R. *BioIn 16*
Lewis, George Ralph 1941- *WhoAm 90*
Lewis, George Sherman 1916- *WhoAm 90*
Lewis, George Stephen 1908- *WhoAm 90*
Lewis, George Withrow 1929- *WhoAm 90*
Lewis, Gerald 1924- *St&PR 91*
Lewis, Gerald A. 1934- *WhoAm 90, WhoSSW 91*
Lewis, Gibson Donald 1936- *WhoSSW 91*
Lewis, Gladys Sherman 1933- *WhoAmW 91, WhoSSW 91*
Lewis, Glenn A 1935- *WhoAmA 91*
Lewis, Glenn M, Jr. 1931- *BiDrAPA 89*
Lewis, Golda *WhoAmA 91*
Lewis, Goldy S. *BioIn 16*
Lewis, Goldy S. 1921- *St&PR 91*
Lewis, Goldy Sarah 1921- *WhoAm 90*
Lewis, Gordon F *BiDrAPA 89*
Lewis, Graceanna 1821-1912 *WomFie*
Lewis, Gregg Allan 1951- *WhoAm 90, WhoWrEP 89*
Lewis, Gwen Ann 1941- *WhoAmW 91*
Lewis, H. Nelson, Jr. 1934- *St&PR 91*
Lewis, H. Spencer *NewAgE 90*
Lewis, H Spencer 1883-1939 *EncO&P 3*
Lewis, Hanna Ballin 1931- *WhoSSW 91*
Lewis, Harmon Stanton 1947- *St&PR 91*
Lewis, Harold Alexander 1953- *WhoE 91*
Lewis, Harold Allen 1945- *WhoE 91*
Lewis, Harold Gregg 1914- *WhoAm 90*
Lewis, Harold Walter 1917- *WhoAm 90*
Lewis, Harold Warren 1923- *WhoAm 90*
Lewis, Harrie F. 1917- *St&PR 91*
Lewis, Harriet 1905- *WhoWrEP 89*
Lewis, Harriet Gerber 1919- *St&PR 91*
Lewis, Harry 1942- *WhoWrEP 89*
Lewis, Harry Garnet *BiDrAPA 89*
Lewis, Harvey Dellmond, Jr. 1918- *WhoWor 91*
Lewis, Helen Elizabeth 1951- *WhoAmW 91*
Lewis, Helen Natalie 1946- *WhoAmW 91*
Lewis, Helen Phelps Hoyt 1902- *WhoAm 90, WhoAmW 91, WhoWor 91*
Lewis, Henry 1932- *DrBlPA 90, IntWWM 90, PenDiMP*
Lewis, Henry Donald 1941- *WhoE 91*
Lewis, Henry Ervin, Sr. 1936- *IntWWM 90*
Lewis, Henry Hicks 1940- *St&PR 91*
Lewis, Henry R. 1925- *St&PR 91*
Lewis, Henry Rafalsky 1925- *WhoAm 90*
Lewis, Henry Wilkins 1916- *WhoAm 90*
Lewis, Herbert Samuel 1934- *WhoAm 90*
Lewis, Hester T *BiDrAPA 89*
Lewis, Hope Boonshaft- *BioIn 16*
Lewis, Horacio Delano 1944- *WhoHisp 91*
Lewis, Huey *BioIn 16, EncPR&S 89*
Lewis, Huey 1951- *WorAlBi*
Lewis, Huey, and the News *EncPR&S 89*
Lewis, Hunter 1947- *WhoAm 90*
Lewis, Ida 1842-1911 *BioAmW*
Lewis, Irwin A. *NewYTBS 90*
Lewis, J. James 1939- *St&PR 91*
Lewis, J. Reilly 1944- *IntWWM 90*
Lewis, J.T. 1937- *St&PR 91*
Lewis, Jack 1924- *WhoAm 90, WhoWrEP 89*
Lewis, Jack Dinwiddie 1923- *WhoSSW 91*
Lewis, Jack K 1924- *BiDrAPA 89*
Lewis, Jack N. 1947- *St&PR 91*
Lewis, James B. 1947- *WhoAm 90*
Lewis, James Berton 1911- *WhoAm 90, WhoWor 91*
Lewis, James Bryan 1945- *WhoEmL 91*
Lewis, James Clarence 1945- *WhoEmL 91*
Lewis, James Edward *BiDrAPA 89*
Lewis, James Edward 1927- *WhoAm 90*
Lewis, James Eldon 1938- *WhoAm 90*
Lewis, James Histed 1912- *WhoAm 90*
Lewis, James Otto 1799-1858 *WhNaAH*
Lewis, James Pettis 1933- *WhoSSW 91*
Lewis, James Richard 1950- *St&PR 91*
Lewis, James Ross, Sr. 1919- *WhoSSW 91*
Lewis, Janet *WhoWrEP 89*
Lewis, Janet 1899- *FemiCLE*
Lewis, Janet Lisa *BiDrAPA 89*
Lewis, Janet Ruth 1952- *WhoAmW 91*
Lewis, Jason Alvert, Jr. 1941- *WhoWor 91*
Lewis, Jay Warren 1946- *St&PR 91*
Lewis, Jean 1924- *SmATA 61*
Lewis, Jeffrey 1942- *IntWWM 90*
Lewis, Jeffrey Michael Owen 1953- *WhoSSW 91*
Lewis, Jerald Paul 1938- *St&PR 91*
Lewis, Jerome A. 1927- *WhoAm 90*
Lewis, Jerrold 1928- *WhoAm 90*
Lewis, Jerry 1926- *BioIn 16, WhoAm 90, WhoWor 91, WorAlBi*
Lewis, Jerry 1934- *WhoAm 90*
Lewis, Jerry Lee *BiDrAPA 89, BioIn 16*
Lewis, Jerry Lee 1935- *EncPR&S 89, IntWWM 90, OxCPMus, WhoAm 90, WorAlBi*
Lewis, Jerry M 1924- *BiDrAPA 89, WhoAm 90*
Lewis, Jerry Mermod, III 1951- *BiDrAPA 89*
Lewis, Jessica Helen 1917- *WhoAm 90*
Lewis, Jill 1949- *ODwPR 91*
Lewis, Joan Joel 1957- *St&PR 91*
Lewis, Joan Mendenhall 1929- *WhoAmW 91, WhoWor 91*
Lewis, Joe E. 1902-1971 *WorAlBi*
Lewis, Joe Ollin 1935- *WhoSSW 91*
Lewis, Joe T. 1958- *WhoEmL 91*
Lewis, John 1920- *BioIn 16, DrBlPA 90, OxCPMus*
Lewis, John Blagdon 1928- *WhoWor 91*
Lewis, John Bradley 1925- *WhoAm 90*
Lewis, John Bruce 1947- *WhoEmL 91*
Lewis, John Chapman 1920- *WhoAmA 91*
Lewis, John Clark, Jr. 1935- *WhoAm 90*
Lewis, John Conard 1942- *WhoAmA 91*
Lewis, John Dale 1944- *WhoSSW 91*
Lewis, John Earl 1931- *WhoWrEP 89*
Lewis, John Elliott 1953- *St&PR 91*
Lewis, John Francis 1932- *WhoAm 90*
Lewis, John Furman 1934- *WhoAm 90*
Lewis, John Hardy, Jr. 1936- *WhoAm 90*
Lewis, John J. 1948- *ODwPR 91*
Lewis, John L. 1880-1969 *BioIn 16, WorAlBi*
Lewis, John Leeman, Jr. 1929- *WhoAm 90*
Lewis, John Milton 1931- *WhoAm 90*
Lewis, John Prior 1921- *WhoAm 90, WhoE 91*
Lewis, John R. 1940- *BlkAmsC [port], WhoAm 90, WhoSSW 91*
Lewis, John Samuel 1929- *WhoSSW 91*
Lewis, John Stuart 1946- *St&PR 91*
Lewis, John Wiley, III 1945- *WhoEmL 91*
Lewis, John Wilson 1930- *WhoAm 90*
Lewis, Johnny 1939- *Ballpl 90*
Lewis, Jon Richard 1947- *WhoSSW 91*
Lewis, Jonathan D 1943- *BiDrAPA 89*
Lewis, Jordan David 1937- *WhoAm 90*
Lewis, Joseph Brady 1946- *WhoSSW 91*
Lewis, Joseph W. 1918- *St&PR 91*
Lewis, Josephine Victoria 1936- *WhoAmW 91*
Lewis, Joy *BioIn 16*
Lewis, Joyce Marie Kienzle 1926- *WhoAmW 91*
Lewis, Joyce S, Jr. *BiDrAPA 89*
Lewis, Joyce Staat 1952- *WhoAmW 91*
Lewis, Judith Mary *AuBYP 90*
Lewis, Judy Jones 1956- *WhoWrEP 89*
Lewis, Julian B. 1932- *St&PR 91*
Lewis, Julianne 1949- *WhoAmW 91*
Lewis, Julius 1931- *WhoAm 90*
Lewis, Karen Callis 1951- *WhoAmW 91*
Lewis, Kathleen L. 1951- *St&PR 91*
Lewis, Kathryn Monica 1936- *WhoAmW 91, WhoWor 91*
Lewis, Keith 1950- *IntWWM 90*
Lewis, Kenneth 1934- *WhoWor 91*
Lewis, Kenneth D. 1947- *WhoAm 90, WhoSSW 91*
Lewis, Kenneth Edward 1929- *WhoAm 90*
Lewis, Kristin Anitra 1949- *WhoAmW 91*
Lewis, Larry N. 1941- *St&PR 91*
Lewis, Lawrence J *BiDrAPA 89*
Lewis, Lawrence Wickham 1947- *WhoE 91*
Lewis, Leland 1946- *St&PR 91*
Lewis, Lena Morrow 1868-1950 *EncAL*
Lewis, Lennox *BioIn 16*
Lewis, Leonard D. 1910- *St&PR 91*
Lewis, Leonard J. 1923- *WhoAm 90*
Lewis, Leroy L., Jr. 1929- *St&PR 91*
Lewis, Lester 1912-1988 *BioIn 16*
Lewis, Lillian Alberta 1861- *BioIn 16*
Lewis, Lillian Tucker *HarlReB*
Lewis, Linda Christine 1949- *St&PR 91, WhoEmL 91*
Lewis, Linda Ellen 1958- *WhoAmW 91*
Lewis, Linda Maureen 1948- *WhoAmW 91*
Lewis, Linda Ward 1945- *WhoAm 90, WhoWrEP 89*
Lewis, Lionel Stanley 1933- *WhoAm 90*
Lewis, Lois Fuller 1930- *WhoWrEP 89*
Lewis, Lorenzo, Jr. *BiDrAPA 89*
Lewis, Lucie Kaye 1951- *WhoAmW 91, WhoE 91*
Lewis, Lynn Owens 1957- *WhoSSW 91*
Lewis, Lynn Wirthlin *WhoSSW 91*
Lewis, M David 1946- *BiDrAPA 89*
Lewis, M.G. 1903- *St&PR 91*
Lewis, M. Leonard 1928- *St&PR 91*
Lewis, Marcia *WhoAmA 91*
Lewis, Margaret Mary 1959- *WhoAmW 91*
Lewis, Margaret Reddick 1930- *St&PR 91*
Lewis, Margaret Shively 1925- *WhoAm 90*
Lewis, Marian V. 1929- *WhoAmW 91*
Lewis, Marilyn W. 1944- *WhoAm 90*
Lewis, Marilyn Walsh 1956- *WhoSSW 91*
Lewis, Marilyn Ware 1943- *St&PR 91*
Lewis, Marion W., III 1922- *St&PR 91*
Lewis, Marjorie 1929- *WhoWrEP 89*
Lewis, Marjorie Herrera 1957- *WhoHisp 91*
Lewis, Mark *BioIn 16*
Lewis, Mark Edgar 1960- *WhoSSW 91*
Lewis, Mark Eliot 1926- *St&PR 91*
Lewis, Marshall C. 1925- *ODwPR 91*
Lewis, Marshall Edward 1950- *BiDrAPA 89*
Lewis, Martha Anne 1942- *WhoAmW 91*
Lewis, Martha Hamm 1831-1892 *DcCanB 12*
Lewis, Martin 1883-1962 *WhoAmA 91N*
Lewis, Martin Edward 1941- *St&PR 91*
Lewis, Martin Edward 1958- *WhoEmL 91, WhoWor 91*
Lewis, Martin R. 1929- *St&PR 91, WhoAm 90*
Lewis, Martin R., Jr. 1938- *St&PR 91*
Lewis, Mary 1907-1988 *SmATA 64*
Lewis, Mary 1926- *WhoAmA 91*
Lewis, Mary Christianna Milne 1907-1988 *BioIn 16*
Lewis, Mary Etta 1928- *WhoAmW 91, WhoWor 91*
Lewis, Mary Frances 1956- *WhoAmW 91*
Lewis, Mary Rio *DrBlPA 90*
Lewis, Mary Therese 1951- *WhoEmL 91*
Lewis, Matthew Gregory 1775-1818 *EncO&P 3, WorAlBi*
Lewis, Maymo Beryl 1931- *WhoAmW 91*
Lewis, Meade 1905-1964 *DrBlPA 90, OxCPMus*
Lewis, Mel *BioIn 16*
Lewis, Mel *NewYTBS 90 [port]*
Lewis, Melanie Mann 1954- *WhoSSW 91*
Lewis, Melvin *BiDrAPA 89*
Lewis, Melvin 1926- *WhoAm 90, WhoE 91*
Lewis, Melvin Wayne 1950- *St&PR 91*
Lewis, Meriwether 1774-1809 *BioIn 16, WhNaAH [port], WorAlBi*
Lewis, Mervyn *AuBYP 90*
Lewis, Michael *BioIn 16, ConAu 31NR*
Lewis, Michael A. 1939- *St&PR 91*
Lewis, Michael H 1941- *WhoAmA 91*
Lewis, Michael John 1944- *WhoAm 90*
Lewis, Michael Paul 1961- *WhoSSW 91*
Lewis, Michael Seth 1953- *WhoE 91*
Lewis, Mildred *AuBYP 90*
Lewis, Mildred D. 1912- *AuBYP 90*
Lewis, Milton *AuBYP 90*
Lewis, Milton F. 1913- *St&PR 91*
Lewis, Milton S. 1922- *St&PR 91*
Lewis, Monte Ross 1937- *WhoWrEP 89*
Lewis, Morgan 1906- *OxCPMus*
Lewis, Morris, Jr. 1911- *WhoAm 90*
Lewis, Murray D *BiDrAPA 89*
Lewis, Myra *BioIn 16*
Lewis, N. Richard 1925- *ODwPR 91*
Lewis, Nancy Ann 1950- *WhoE 91*
Lewis, Nancy Patricia 1956- *WhoEmL 91*
Lewis, Nancy Whyte 1937- *WhoAmW 91*
Lewis, Naomi *AuBYP 90*
Lewis, Nat Brush 1925- *WhoAmA 91, WhoE 91*
Lewis, Neville *BioIn 16*
Lewis, Norma J. *BioIn 16*
Lewis, Norman 1909-1979 *BioIn 16*
Lewis, Norman 1912- *WhoAm 90, WhoWor 91*
Lewis, Norman 1918- *ConAu 129, MajTwCW*
Lewis, Norman Albert 1936- *St&PR 91*
Lewis, Norman James 1918- *WhoSSW 91*
Lewis, Norman Wilfred *WhoAmA 91N*
Lewis, Orme 1903- *WhoAm 90*
Lewis, Orme, Jr. 1935- *WhoAm 90*
Lewis, Oscar 1914-1970 *WorAlBi*
Lewis, Owen Donald 1925- *WhoSSW 91*
Lewis, Owen Holt 1926- *St&PR 91*
Lewis, Owen W 1951- *BiDrAPA 89*
Lewis, P. Helen 1930- *WhoAmW 91*
Lewis, Paddy Sandra 1945- *WhoAmW 91*
Lewis, Patricia Fields 1946- *WhoAmW 91*
Lewis, Patty Jean 1952- *WhoAmW 91*
Lewis, Paul *AuBYP 90*
Lewis, Paul 1914-1988 *SmATA X*
Lewis, Paul, Jr. 1939- *WhoSSW 91*
Lewis, Paul Le Roy 1925- *WhoE 91*
Lewis, Peirce Fee 1927- *WhoAm 90*
Lewis, Percy Wyndham 1882-1957 *BioIn 16*
Lewis, Perry Joshua 1938- *WhoAm 90*
Lewis, Peter A. 1938- *WhoAm 90, WhoE 91*
Lewis, Peter B. 1933- *St&PR 91*
Lewis, Peter Benjamin 1933- *WhoAm 90*
Lewis, Peter Cushman 1934- *St&PR 91*
Lewis, Peter John 1944- *WhoWor 91*
Lewis, Phil 1883-1959 *Ballpl 90*
Lewis, Philip 1913- *WhoAm 90*
Lewis, Philip C 1942- *BiDrAPA 89*
Lewis, Philip M. 1931- *WhoAm 90*
Lewis, Phillip Harold 1922- *WhoAm 90, WhoAmA 91*
Lewis, R. Gregory 1952- *St&PR 91*
Lewis, R. W. B. *BioIn 16*
Lewis, Ralph Jay, III 1942- *WhoWor 91*
Lewis, Ralph M. *BioIn 16*
Lewis, Ralph M. 1919- *St&PR 91*
Lewis, Ralph Milton 1919- *WhoAm 90, WhoWor 91*
Lewis, Ramsey 1935- *DrBlPA 90, EncPR&S 89, WorAlBi*
Lewis, Ramsey Emanuel, Jr. 1935- *WhoAm 90*
Lewis, Randall W. 1951- *St&PR 91*
Lewis, Randi J. 1955- *St&PR 91*
Lewis, Randolph Vance 1950- *WhoEmL 91*
Lewis, Ray *ODwPR 91*
Lewis, Ray 1924- *BiDrAPA 89*

Lewis, Raymond Daniel, Jr. 1930- *St&PR 91*
Lewis, Rebecca L. 1938- *WhoAmW 91*
Lewis, Regina Marie 1954- *WhoAmW 91*
Lewis, Reginald F. *BioIn 16*
Lewis, Reginald F. 1942- *ConAmBL, WhoAm 90*
Lewis, Richard *BioIn 16*
Lewis, Richard 1914- *IntWWM 90, PenDiMP*
Lewis, Richard 1914-1990 *NewYTBS 90 [port]*
Lewis, Richard 1935- *AuBYP 90*
Lewis, Richard A. 1944- *St&PR 91*
Lewis, Richard Allan 1952- *WhoE 91*
Lewis, Richard Burnett, II 1941- *WhoSSW 91*
Lewis, Richard C 1928- *BiDrAPA 89*
Lewis, Richard David 1929- *WhoAm 90*
Lewis, Richard Jay 1933- *WhoAm 90*
Lewis, Richard Kent *BiDrAPA 89*
Lewis, Richard Knox 1946- *WhoSSW 91*
Lewis, Richard Lafayette 1923- *St&PR 91*
Lewis, Richard Neil 1953- *St&PR 91*
Lewis, Richard Phelps 1936- *WhoAm 90*
Lewis, Richard S. 1946- *ODwPR 91*
Lewis, Richard Stanley 1916- *WhoAm 90, WhoWrEP 89*
Lewis, Richard Warrington Baldwin *BioIn 16*
Lewis, Richard Warrington Baldwin 1917- *WhoWrEP 89*
Lewis, Ricki 1954- *WhoWrEP 89*
Lewis, Rita Hoffman 1947- *St&PR 91, WhoAmW 91, WhoE 91, WhoEmL 91, WhoWor 91*
Lewis, Robert Alan *BiDrAPA 89*
Lewis, Robert Alan 1933- *WhoAm 90*
Lewis, Robert C. 1916- *St&PR 91*
Lewis, Robert E. 1921- *ODwPR 91*
Lewis, Robert E. 1945- *St&PR 91*
Lewis, Robert Edwin, Jr. 1947- *WhoEmL 91, WhoSSW 91, WhoWor 91*
Lewis, Robert Enzer 1934- *WhoAm 90*
Lewis, Robert G. 1916- *St&PR 91*
Lewis, Robert George 1919- *WhoAm 90*
Lewis, Robert Hall 1926- *IntWWM 90*
Lewis, Robert Henry 1949- *WhoE 91*
Lewis, Robert J. 1946- *St&PR 91*
Lewis, Robert John Cornelius Koons 1938- *WhoWor 91*
Lewis, Robert K. *BioIn 16*
Lewis, Robert L 1922- *BiDrAPA 89*
Lewis, Robert L. 1947- *St&PR 91*
Lewis, Robert Lawrence 1919- *WhoAm 90*
Lewis, Robert Lee, III 1949- *WhoEmL 91*
Lewis, Robert Miller 1937- *WhoAm 90*
Lewis, Robert Owen 1927- *WhoAm 90*
Lewis, Robert Turner 1923- *WhoWor 91*
Lewis, Roger *AuBYP 90*
Lewis, Roger 1912-1987 *BioIn 16*
Lewis, Roger F. 1936- *ODwPR 91*
Lewis, Roger Franklin 1936- *St&PR 91*
Lewis, Roger G. 1948- *St&PR 91*
Lewis, Roger Kutnow 1941- *WhoAm 90*
Lewis, Ronald *WhoSSW 91*
Lewis, Ronald Loren 1946- *WhoEmL 91*
Lewis, Ronald Walter 1945- *WhoAmA 91*
Lewis, Rone 1944- *St&PR 91*
Lewis, Ronel Lee 1941- *BiDrAPA 89*
Lewis, Roy 1933- *TwCCr&M 91*
Lewis, Roy A. 1922-1988 *BioIn 16*
Lewis, Russell Baugh 1926- *St&PR 91*
Lewis, Ruth P *BiDrAPA 89*
Lewis, Sabrina LaVerne 1963- *WhoAmW 91*
Lewis, Sally Sirkin *BioIn 16*
Lewis, Sam M. 1885-1959 *OxCPMus*
Lewis, Samella Sanders 1924- *WhoAm 90, WhoAmA 91*
Lewis, Samuel W. *BioIn 16*
Lewis, Samuel Winfield 1930- *WhoAm 90*
Lewis, Sandra Combs 1939- *WhoAmW 91*
Lewis, Sean Day *ConAu 132*
Lewis, Shari 1934- *AuBYP 90, WhoAm 90, WorAlBi*
Lewis, Sharon Janicet 1960- *WhoSSW 91*
Lewis, Sheila Ellian 1958- *WhoAmW 91*
Lewis, Shelby Lynn 1945- *BiDrAPA 89*
Lewis, Sheldon Noah 1934- *St&PR 91, WhoAm 90*
Lewis, Sherman Richard 1936- *St&PR 91*
Lewis, Sherman Richard, Jr. 1936- *WhoAm 90, WhoWor 91*
Lewis, Sidney A. 1917- *St&PR 91*
Lewis, Sinclair 1885-1951 *DcLB 102 [port], MajTwCW, TwCLC 39 [port], WorAlBi*
Lewis, Stanley 1930- *WhoAmA 91*
Lewis, Stanley Xerxes, Jr. 1947- *WhoEmL 91*
Lewis, Stephen *AuBYP 90, BioIn 16*
Lewis, Stephen Richmond, Jr. 1939- *WhoAm 90*
Lewis, Steven Craig 1943- *WhoE 91*
Lewis, Steven Richard 1953- *WhoWrEP 89*
Lewis, Susan Vaughan 1948- *BiDrAPA 89*
Lewis, Sydney 1919- *St&PR 91, WhoAm 90*
Lewis, Sylvia 1945- *WhoWrEP 89*
Lewis, Sylvia Gail 1945- *WhoAmW 91*
Lewis, Ted 1872-1936 *Ballpl 90*
Lewis, Ted 1892-1971 *OxCPMus, WorAlBi*
Lewis, Terry *BioIn 16*
Lewis, Thomas Anthony 1946- *WhoEmL 91*
Lewis, Thomas B. 1938- *St&PR 91, WhoAm 90*
Lewis, Thomas F., Jr. 1924- *WhoAm 90, WhoSSW 91*
Lewis, Thomas H. A. 1902-1988 *BioIn 16*
Lewis, Thomas Knight, Jr. 1922- *BiDrAPA 89*
Lewis, Thomas Proctor 1930- *WhoAm 90*
Lewis, Thomas S W 1942- *ConAu 31NR*
Lewis, Thomas Skipwith 1936- *WhoAm 90*
Lewis, Thomasine Elizabeth 1958- *WhoWrEP 89*
Lewis, Tola Ethridge, Jr. 1945- *WhoEmL 91, WhoSSW 91*
Lewis, Tom 1940- *WhoE 91*
Lewis, Tyrone Steven 1955- *WhoSSW 91*
Lewis, Vernita Ann Wickliffe 1955- *WhoAmW 91*
Lewis, Vic 1919- *OxCPMus*
Lewis, Vicki *BioIn 16*
Lewis, Vincent Joseph 1944- *St&PR 91*
Lewis, Virginia Elnora 1907- *WhoAm 90, WhoAmA 91*
Lewis, Virginia Marie 1942- *WhoAmW 91*
Lewis, W. Arthur 1915- *WorAlBi*
Lewis, W. Deming 1915-1989 *BioIn 16*
Lewis, W. H. 1895-1973 *BioIn 16*
Lewis, W. Walker 1944- *St&PR 91*
Lewis, Wade H 1925- *BiDrAPA 89*
Lewis, Wally 1959- *BioIn 16*
Lewis, Walter David 1931- *WhoAm 90*
Lewis, Walter Laughn 1924- *WhoSSW 91*
Lewis, Warren Hamilton 1895-1973 *BioIn 16*
Lewis, Wassel A. 1943- *BiDrAPA 89*
Lewis, Welbourne Walker, Jr. 1915- *WhoAm 90*
Lewis, Wilbur Curtis 1930- *WhoAm 90, WhoSSW 91*
Lewis, Wilbur H. 1930- *WhoAm 90*
Lewis, William 1935- *IntWWM 90*
Lewis, William 1950- *WhoEmL 91*
Lewis, William A.J., III 1950- *St&PR 91*
Lewis, William Arthur 1915- *WhoAm 90, WhoE 91, WhoWor 91*
Lewis, William Arthur 1918- *WhoAmA 91*
Lewis, William Bryant 1931- *WhoAm 90*
Lewis, William Headley, Jr. 1934- *WhoSSW 91, WhoWor 91*
Lewis, William J. 1947- *St&PR 91*
Lewis, William Mark 1952- *WhoE 91*
Lewis, William R 1920- *WhoAmA 91*
Lewis, William Raymond 1934- *WhoSSW 91*
Lewis, William Scheer 1927- *WhoE 91, WhoWor 91*
Lewis, William Walker 1942- *WhoAm 90, WhoE 91*
Lewis, Woodrow T. 1916-1989 *BioIn 16*
Lewis, Wyndham 1882-1957 *BioIn 16, WorAlBi, WrPh*
Lewis, Yvonne Fay 1946- *WhoAmW 91*
Lewis-Brent, Lana Jane *BioIn 16*
Lewis-Brent, Lana Jane 1946- *St&PR 91*
Lewis Congdon, Rebecca Ann 1942- *WhoAmW 91*
Lewis-Fernandez, Roberto *BiDrAPA 89*
Lewis-Hall, Freda Colette 1955- *BiDrAPA 89*
Lewis-Jenson, Sandra M. 1950- *WhoAmW 91*
Lewis-Kolbus, Melinda Anne 1958- *WhoAmW 91, WhoWor 91*
Lewisohn, Adolph 1849-1938 *WorAlBi*
Lewisohn, Alice 1883-1972 *BioIn 16, NotWoAT*
Lewisohn, Irene 1892-1944 *BioIn 16, NotWoAT*
Lewisohn, Ludwig 1882-1955 *BioIn 16, DcLB 102 [port]*
Lewisohn, Mark 1958- *ConAu 130*
Lewisohn, Richard 1916-1988 *BioIn 16*
Lewison, J.E. Paul 1936- *St&PR 91*
Lewit, Eugene Myron 1946- *WhoE 91*
Lewit, Robert Todd 1937- *BiDrAPA 89*
Lewit, William V 1931- *BiDrAPA 89*
Lewitch, Joseph 1926- *BioIn 16*
Lewitin, Landes *WhoAmA 91N*
Lewiton, Mina 1904-1970 *AuBYP 90*
Le Witt, Jan 1907- *AuBYP 90, ConDes 90*
Lewitt, Maurice 1931- *St&PR 91, WhoAm 90*
Lewitt, Miles Martin 1952- *WhoEmL 91, WhoWor 91*
LeWitt, Sol 1928- *WhoAm 90*
Le Witt, Sol 1928- *WhoAmA 91*
Lewittes, Don Jordan 1950- *WhoWor 91*
Lewitzky, Bella 1916- *WhoAm 90, WhoAmW 91*
Lewkovitch, Bernhard 1927- *IntWWM 90*
Lewnes, Peter A. 1929- *WhoE 91*
Lewnes, Tula 1921- *WhoAmW 91*
Lewontin, Timothy 1955- *ConAu 130*
Lewter, Billy Ray 1936- *WhoSSW 91*
Lewton, Kathleen Larey 1948- *ODwPR 91*
Lewton, Val Edwin 1937- *WhoAmA 91, WhoE 91*
Lewy, Alfred James 1945- *BiDrAPA 89*
Lewy, Guenter 1923- *WhoE 91, WhoWrEP 89*
Lewy, Hans 1904-1988 *BioIn 16*
Lewy, Michael Morris 1943- *WhoE 91*
Lewy, Ralph I. 1931- *St&PR 91, WhoAm 90*
Lewy, Robert Max 1945- *WhoE 91*
Lewyn, Thomas Mark 1930- *WhoAm 90*
Lewyt, Alexander M. 1908-1988 *BioIn 16*
Lex, George James, III 1954- *WhoSSW 91*
Lex, William Joseph 1944- *WhoE 91*
Lexau, Henry 1928- *WhoAm 90, WhoWrEP 89*
Lexau, Joan M. *AuBYP 90*
Lexier, Lenard Jay *BiDrAPA 89*
Ley, Bruce M. 1951- *St&PR 91*
Ley, Herbert Leonard, Jr. 1923- *WhoAm 90*
Ley, James M. 1958- *WhoWrEP 89*
Ley, Margaretha *BioIn 16*
Ley, Rick 1948- *WhoAm 90, WhoE 91*
Ley, Robert 1890-1945 *BioIn 16*
Ley, Willy 1906-1969 *AuBYP 90, WorAlBi*
Ley, Wolfgang *BioIn 16*
Ley Koo, Jorge 1936- *WhoWor 91*
Leybourne, George 1842-1884 *OxCPMus*
Leyda, Jay 1910-1988 *BioIn 16*
Leyda, Margaret Larue 1923- *WhoAmW 91*
Leyden, Dennis Roger 1933- *WhoAm 90*
Leyden, Donald Elliott 1938- *WhoAm 90, WhoSSW 91*
Leyden, Ernst Oscar Mauritz van 1892-1969 *BioIn 16*
Leyden, Joan Marie 1944- *WhoWrEP 89*
Leyden, John T. 1943- *St&PR 91*
Leyden, Margaret M. 1962- *ODwPR 91*
Leydenfrost, Alexander 1889-1961 *WhoAmA 91N*
Leydet, Francois Guillaume 1927- *WhoWor 91*
Leydorf, Frederick Leroy 1930- *WhoAm 90, WhoWor 91*
Leyendecker, Joseph C 1874-1951 *WhoAmA 91N*
Leyetchkiss, Vladimir *BioIn 16*
Leygues, Jean-Claude Georges 1857-1933 *BiDFrPL*
Leyh, George Francis 1931- *WhoAm 90*
Leyh, Richard Edmund, Sr. 1930- *WhoAm 90*
Leyhausen, Paul Josef 1916- *WhoWor 91*
Leyland, James Richard 1944- *WhoAm 90, WhoE 91*
Leyland, Jim 1944- *Ballpl 90*
Leymaster, Glen R. 1915- *WhoAm 90*
Leyne, Sheila *ODwPR 91*
Leypoldt, Donald F. 1932- *St&PR 91*
Leypoldt, Frederick, III 1929- *St&PR 91*
Leys, Dale Daniel 1952- *WhoAmA 91*
Leys, Dirk Jan Gilbert 1955- *WhoWor 91*
Leys, Donald M. 1930- *St&PR 91*
Leyse, Walter Carlton 1932- *St&PR 91*
Leyson, Burr Watkins 1898- *AuBYP 90*
Leyson, Dativo Borces 1930- *WhoWor 91*
Leyster, Judith 1609-1660 *BioIn 16*
Leytens, Luc M. E. L. 1936- *IntWWM 90*
Leyton, Israel 1927- *WhoHisp 91*
Leyva, Jason Fernand 1953- *WhoWor 91*
Leyva, Jose J 1932- *BiDrAPA 89*
Leyva, Nick 1953- *WhoE 91*
Leyva, Nick Tom 1953- *WhoHisp 91*
Lezak, Cheryl C. 1950- *St&PR 91*
Lezak, Daniel S. 1933- *St&PR 91*
Lezak, Edward Herman 1939- *St&PR 91*
Lezama Lima, Jose 1910-1976 *BioIn 16, HispWr 90*
Lezcano, Sixto 1953- *Ballpl 90*
Lhamon, William T *BiDrAPA 89*
Lhermitte, Jacques Jean 1877-1959 *EncO&P 3*
L'Heureux, John Clarke 1934- *WhoAm 90, WhoWrEP 89*
L'Heureux, Willard John 1947- *WhoAm 90*
L'Heureux-Dube, Claire 1927- *WhoAm 90, WhoAmW 91*
Lhevine, Dave Bernard 1922- *St&PR 91, WhoSSW 91*
Lhevinne, Josef 1874-1944 *BioIn 16, PenDiMP*
Lhevinne, Rosina 1880-1976 *PenDiMP*
L'Hoir, Jean-Xavier 1941- *WhoWor 91*
L'Homme, Pierre Louis 1929- *WhoWor 91*
L'Hommedieu, Dorothy 1885-1961 *AuBYP 90*
L'Hommedieu, Toni Robin 1942- *WhoAmW 91*
Lhota, William J. *WhoAm 90*
Lhotka, Bonny Pierce 1942- *WhoAmA 91*
Lhotka, John Francis 1921- *WhoAm 90, WhoSSW 91*
Li Dazhao 1889-1927 *BioIn 16*
Li Guixian 1938- *WhoWor 91*
Li Hung-Chang 1823-1901 *WorAlBi*
Li Lan 1943- *WhoAmA 91*
Li Peng 1928- *BioIn 16, WhoWor 91, WorAlBi*
Li Po 701-762 *WorAlBi*
Li Quan Bang *BioIn 16*
Li Shuoxun 1903-1931 *BioIn 16*
Li Siguang 1889-1971 *DcScB S2*
Li Tieying 1936- *WhoWor 91*
Li Xiannian *BioIn 16*
Li Xiannian 1909- *WhoWor 91*
Li Yining *BioIn 16*
Li Zhen *BioIn 16, NewYTBS 90*
Li, Anne S. 1952- *St&PR 91*
Li, Bing Xi 1934- *WhoWor 91*
Li, Chi 1956- *WhoEmL 91*
Li, Chia-Chuan 1946- *WhoEmL 91*
Li, Ching-Chung 1932- *WhoAm 90*
Li, Choh-hao 1913-1987 *BioIn 16*
Li, Chu-Tsing 1920- *WhoAm 90, WhoAmA 91*
Li, Delun 1917- *IntWWM 90*
Li, Fang-kuei 1902-1987 *BioIn 16*
Li, Hanna Wu 1934- *IntWWM 90*
Li, Hui-Lin 1911- *WhoAm 90*
Li, James Chen Min 1925- *WhoAm 90*
Li, James Chien-chung 1931- *WhoE 91*
Li, Jane-Yu Ho 1946- *WhoE 91*
Li, Jun Hua 1962- *WhoEmL 91*
Li, Ka-shing *BioIn 16*
Li, Kui Wai 1952- *WhoWor 91*
Li, Lehmann K. *WhoAm 90*
Li, Luye 1925- *WhoWor 91*
Li, Ning *BioIn 16*
Li, Norman Chung 1913- *WhoAm 90*
Li, Norman L. 1947- *WhoWor 91*
Li, P'eng 1928- *BioIn 16*
Li, Philip Wing Kuen 1949- *WhoWor 91*
Li, Rebecca Mei-Huey 1942- *WhoAmW 91*
Li, Shihai 1963- *WhoEmL 91*
Li, Shude 1927- *WhoWor 91*
Li, Tian-sheng 1948- *IntWWM 90*
Li, Tien-yi 1915- *WhoAm 90*
Li, Tingye 1931- *WhoAm 90*
Li, Tu Leung 1948- *WhoAmW 91*
Li, Tze-chung 1927- *WhoAm 90*
Li, Wu 1958- *WhoWor 91*
Li, Yongxin 1930- *WhoWor 91*
Li, Yuan Zu 1923- *WhoWor 91*
Lia, Gary Peter 1941- *St&PR 91, WhoAm 90*
Liabo, Leslie Carl *WhoAm 90*
Liacos, Paul Julian 1929- *WhoAm 90, WhoE 91*
Liacouras, Peter James 1931- *WhoAm 90*
Liadra Kis, Florence 1914- *WhoAmW 91*
Liakopoulou, Magdalen *BiDrAPA 89*
Liakos, Shirley Atchison 1953- *WhoAmW 91*
Liakounakos, Thomas N. 1948- *WhoWor 91*
Lian, Teck Seng 1933- *BiDrAPA 89*
Liang *WomWR*
Liang, Edward Y 1926- *BiDrAPA 89*
Liang, Elisa Lee 1961- *WhoAmW 91*
Liang, Hung 1920- *St&PR 91*
Liang, Jason Chia 1935- *WhoWor 91*
Liang, Jeffrey Der-Shing 1915- *WhoWor 91*
Liang, Kuo-Shu 1930- *WhoWor 91*
Liang, Raymond Ambrose *BiDrAPA 89*
Liang, Robert 1947- *WhoWor 91*
Liang, Shu-ming 1893-1988 *BioIn 16*
Liang, Thomas C.B. 1947- *WhoWor 91*
Liang, Vera B Tsai 1946- *BiDrAPA 89*
Liang, Vera Beh-Yuin Tsai 1946- *WhoE 91*
Liang, Warren Min 1951- *BiDrAPA 89*
Lianides, Leon *BioIn 16*
Lianos, William P. 1936- *St&PR 91*
Liantonio, Julia Ann Mary 1950- *WhoAmW 91*
Liao 1936- *WhoAmA 91*
Liao, Elizabeth *BiDrAPA 89*
Liao, Eric Nan-Kang 1938- *WhoWor 91*
Liao, Keren 1932- *WhoWor 91*
Liao, Naixiong 1933- *IntWWM 90*
Liao, Paul Foo-Hung 1944- *WhoAm 90*
Liao, Shutsung 1931- *WhoAm 90*
Liao, Tony Tung Lin 1929- *WhoWor 91*
Liapakis, Pamela Anagnos 1947- *WhoAmW 91*
Lias, Bernard *BioIn 16*
Lias, Thomas L. *BioIn 16*
Lias, Thomas R *WhoAmA 91N*
Liau, Mary Chong-Chin *WhoE 91*
Liautaud, Georges *BioIn 16*
Liautaud, Georges 1899- *ArtLatA*
Liautaud, Theodore R *BiDrAPA 89*
Libassi, F. Peter 1930- *ODwPR 91, St&PR 91*
Libassi, Frank Peter 1930- *WhoAm 90*

Libbach, Roland Anton Bruno Friederich 1914- *IntWWM 90*
Libbey, Laura Jean 1862-1925 *FemiCLE*
Libbin, Anne Edna 1950- *WhoAm 90*
Libbon, Joseph A 1924- *BiDrAPA 89*
Libby, Bill *AuBYP 90*
Libby, Gary Russell 1944- *WhoAm 90, WhoAmA 91, WhoSSW 91*
Libby, Gwynne Margaret 1958- *WhoAmW 91*
Libby, John Douglass 1938- *WhoAm 90, WhoSSW 91*
Libby, John Kelway 1926- *WhoAm 90, WhoE 91, WhoWor 91*
Libby, Julianna 1956- *WhoAmW 91, WhoE 91*
Libby, Pamela Joanne 1955- *WhoAmW 91*
Libby, Peter 1947- *WhoAm 90*
Libby, Robert *WhoAm 90*
Libby, Sandra Chiavaras 1949- *WhoAmW 91*
Libby, Theodore Israel 1920- *St&PR 91*
Libby, Willard F. 1908-1980 *WorAlBi*
Libby, William C 1919- *WhoAmA 91N*
Libby, William M. 1927-1984 *AuBYP 90*
Libchaber, Albert Joseph 1934- *WhoAm 90*
Liben, Florence G *BiDrAPA 89*
Liber, Hillary Selese Jacobs 1953- *WhoAmW 91*
Liber, Jeffrey Mark 1952- *St&PR 91*
Liberace 1919-1987 *BioIn 16, OxCPMus, WorAlBi*
Liberace, Walter 1919-1987 *PenDiMP*
Liberakis, Eustace A 1930- *BiDrAPA 89*
Liberale, da Verona 1445-1526? *BioIn 16*
Liberati, Shari Lynn 1961- *WhoAmW 91*
Liberato, Jose Nunes 1951- *WhoWor 91*
Liberatore, Ed 1913- *BioIn 16*
Liberatore, James Howard 1933- *St&PR 91*
Liberatore, Marcia Antoinette 1954- *WhoAmW 91*
Liberatore, Nicholas Alfred 1916- *WhoAm 90*
Liberatori, Ronald Peter 1938- *St&PR 91*
Liberi, Dante 1919- *WhoAmA 91*
Liberia-Peters, Maria *WhoWor 91*
Liberia-Peters, Maria 1942- *BioIn 16*
Liberman, Alberto J. 1942- *WhoSSW 91*
Liberman, Alexander 1912- *BioIn 16, WhoAm 90, WhoAmA 91, WhoWrEP 89*
Liberman, Alvin Meyer 1917- *WhoAm 90*
Liberman, Gail Jeanne 1951- *WhoAmW 91*
Liberman, Ira L. 1926- *WhoAm 90*
Liberman, Isabelle *NewYTBS 90*
Liberman, Isabelle Y. *BioIn 16*
Liberman, Lee Marvin 1921- *St&PR 91, WhoAm 90*
Liberman, Lee Sarah 1956- *WhoAmW 91*
Liberman, Michael Ira 1944- *St&PR 91*
Liberman, Robert Paul 1937- *BiDrAPA 89, WhoAm 90*
Liberman, Samuel 1926- *St&PR 91, WhoAm 90*
Liberson, Wladimir T *BiDrAPA 89*
Libert, Donald Joseph 1928- *WhoAm 90*
Libert, Samuel A *BiDrAPA 89*
Liberte, Jean 1896-1965 *WhoAmA 91N*
Liberti, Kelly S. 1967- *WhoAmW 91*
Libertiny, Attila G. 1948- *St&PR 91*
Libertiny, George Zoltan 1934- *WhoAm 90*
Liberto, John Anthony 1960- *BiDrAPA 89*
Liberto, Joseph Gregory *BiDrAPA 89*
Liberto, Joseph Salvatore 1929- *WhoAm 90*
Liberto, Vincent 1949- *BiDrAPA 89*
Liberts, Ludolfs 1895-1959 *WhoAmA 91N*
Libertson, William 1907- *BiDrAPA 89*
Liberty, Arthur Lasenby 1843-1917 *PenDiDA 89*
Liberty, Jesse Levine 1955- *WhoE 91*
Liberty, Maria *WhoE 91*
Libhart, Bonni 1935- *WhoWrEP 89*
Libhart, Bonnie L. 1935- *WhoSSW 91*
Libhart, Myles Laroy 1931- *WhoAmA 91*
Libin, Jerome B. 1936- *WhoAm 90*
Libin, Laurence Elliot 1944- *IntWWM 90, WhoAm 90*
Libin, Paul 1930- *WhoAm 90*
Libke, Al 1918- *Ballpl 90*
Libman, Alan David 1943- *WhoWor 91*
Libman, Stuart 1952- *BiDrAPA 89*
Liboff, Richard Lawrence 1931- *WhoAm 90*
Libonati, Michael Ernest 1944- *WhoAm 90*
Libous, Thomas W. 1953- *WhoE 91*
Libove, Charles 1923- *WhoE 91*
Libove, Joel Michael 1954- *WhoEmL 91*
Libowitz, Richard Lawrence 1948- *WhoEmL 91*
Libros, John F. 1954- *St&PR 91*
Libros, Maxine 1924- *WhoAmW 91*
Libsch, Joseph Francis 1918- *WhoAm 90*
Liburdi, Lillian C. *BioIn 16*
Licamele, William Louis 1947- *BiDrAPA 89*
Licari, Louis 1951- *BioIn 16*
Licastri, Joseph Michael 1950- *St&PR 91*
Licata, Antonio Samuel 1937- *WhoSSW 91*
Licata, Arthur Frank 1947- *WhoEmL 91*
Licata, David Paul 1954- *WhoE 91*
Licata, Robert M 1942- *BiDrAPA 89*
Licata, Salvatore J. *BioIn 16, NewYTBS 90*
Licata-Facciodi, Orsola 1826- *BiDWomA*
Liccardo, John J *BiDrAPA 89*
Liccione, Alexander 1948- *WhoAmA 91*
Liccione, Stephen John 1955- *WhoEmL 91*
Licea, Rafael V. 1943- *WhoHisp 91*
Licette, Miriam 1882-1969 *PenDiMP*
Lich, Glen Ernst 1948- *WhoSSW 91, WhoWor 91*
Lichacz, Sheila Enit 1942- *WhoAmA 91*
Lichal, Robert 1932- *WhoWor 91*
Lichauer, Robert William 1947- *St&PR 91*
Lichaw, Pessia *WhoAmA 91*
Lichello, Robert 1926- *AuBYP 90*
Lichem, Walther G. 1940- *WhoWor 91*
Lichine, Alexis 1913-1989 *AnObit 1989, BioIn 16*
Lichman, Jacob 1913- *St&PR 91*
Lichnowsky, Mechthild von 1879-1958 *EncCoWW*
Lichota, Edith Fischer 1928- *St&PR 91*
Lichstein, Edgar 1936- *WhoE 91, WhoWor 91*
Lichstein, Herman Carlton 1918- *WhoAm 90*
Lichstein, Jacob 1908- *WhoAm 90*
Licht, Arnold L 1943- *BiDrAPA 89*
Licht, Evelyn M 1905- *WhoAmA 91*
Licht, Janice B. 1954- *WhoAmW 91*
Licht, Jeremy *BioIn 16*
Licht, Jeremy 1971- *ConTFT 8 [port]*
Licht, John M. 1947- *St&PR 91*
Licht, Lilla Giles McKnight *WhoWrEP 89*
Licht, Paul 1938- *WhoAm 90*
Licht, Richard A. 1948- *WhoAm 90*
Lichtblau, John H. 1921- *WhoAm 90*
Lichtblau, Myron Ivor 1925- *WhoAm 90*
Lichten, Frances 1889-1961 *WhoAmA 91N*
Lichten, Steven Michael 1959- *WhoEmL 91*
Lichtenauer, Dixon Ann 1934- *WhoAmW 91*
Lichtenberg, Bernhard 1875-1943 *BioIn 16*
Lichtenberg, Byron K. 1948- *WhoAm 90*
Lichtenberg, Georg Christoph 1742-1799 *DcLB 94 [port]*
Lichtenberg, James 1941- *ODwPR 91*
Lichtenberg, Joseph D 1925- *BiDrAPA 89*
Lichtenberg, Manes *WhoAmA 91*
Lichtenberg, Margaret Klee 1941- *WhoAm 90*
Lichtenberger, Arthur T. 1928- *St&PR 91*
Lichtenberger, Doris L. 1925- *WhoAmW 91*
Lichtenberger, Frank H. 1937- *St&PR 91*
Lichtenberger, Horst William 1935- *WhoAm 90*
Lichtenberger, Robert 1945- *St&PR 91*
Lichtenfeld, Sam Jacob 1948- *WhoE 91*
Lichtenfels, Joanna Loraine 1940- *WhoWrEP 89*
Lichtenheld, Frank Robert 1923- *WhoWor 91*
Lichtenstein, Bertram *BioIn 16*
Lichtenstein, Gary 1953- *WhoAmA 91*
Lichtenstein, Harvey 1929- *WhoAm 90*
Lichtenstein, Heinz *BiDrAPA 89*
Lichtenstein, Jacqueline W *BiDrAPA 89*
Lichtenstein, James Marshall 1943- *WhoSSW 91*
Lichtenstein, Judith Sara *BiDrAPA 89*
Lichtenstein, Lawrence Mark 1934- *WhoAm 90*
Lichtenstein, Natalie G. 1953- *WhoEmL 91*
Lichtenstein, Roy 1923- *IntDcAA 90, WhoAm 90, WhoAmA 91, WorAlBi*
Lichtenstein, Sara 1929- *WhoAmA 91N*
Lichtenstein, Sarah Carol 1953- *WhoEmL 91*
Lichtenstein, Seymour 1926- *St&PR 91*
Lichtenstein, Walter 1880-1964 *BioIn 16*
Lichtenthaler, Hartmut Karl 1934- *WhoWor 91*
Lichtenwalter, Michael David 1953- *St&PR 91*
Lichter, Edward Arthur 1928- *WhoAm 90*
Lichter, Paul Richard 1939- *WhoAm 90*
Lichter-Heath, Laurie Jean 1951- *WhoEmL 91*
Lichterman, Brian 1955- *WhoSSW 91*
Lichterman, Martin 1918- *WhoAm 90*
Lichti, Allan *WhoWrEP 89*
Lichti, Barbara Jean 1942- *WhoAmW 91*
Lichtiger, Monte 1939- *WhoSSW 91*
Lichtin, J. Leon 1924- *WhoAm 90*
Lichtin, Norman Nahum 1922- *WhoAm 90*
Lichtman, Cecil 1913- *St&PR 91*
Lichtman, Craig V *BiDrAPA 89*
Lichtman, Donna J. 1963- *ODwPR 91*
Lichtman, Howard 1955- *St&PR 91*
Lichtman, Judith *WhoAmW 91*
Lichtman, Kenneth J 1942- *BiDrAPA 89*
Lichtman, L. Savannah 1949- *St&PR 91*
Lichtmann, Theodor David 1938- *IntWWM 90*
Lichtner, Schomer Frank 1905- *WhoAmA 91*
Lichtor, David T. 1956- *WhoEmL 91*
Lichtsinn, Robert W. 1929- *St&PR 91*
Lichty, George 1905-1983 *EncACom*
Lichty, George M 1905- *WhoAmA 91N*
Lichty, Mark Edward 1949- *St&PR 91*
Licinio, Julio 1958- *BiDrAPA 89, WhoEmL 91*
Lick, Dale Wesley 1938- *WhoAm 90, WhoE 91*
Lick, James Samuel 1937- *WhoSSW 91*
Lick, Sherry Lee 1940- *WhoAmW 91*
Lick, Thomas Artz 1940- *WhoSSW 91*
Lick, Wilbert James 1933- *WhoAm 90*
Lickbarrow, Isabella *FemiCLE*
Licke, W. John 1945- *St&PR 91*
Lickenbrock, Kevin James *BiDrAPA 89*
Licker, Kenneth Ira 1944- *WhoSSW 91*
Lickerman, Howard Wayne 1927- *St&PR 91*
Lickle, William C. 1929- *St&PR 91*
Lickle, William Cauffiel 1929- *WhoAm 90, WhoWor 91*
Licklider, Joseph C. R. *NewYTBS 90 [port]*
Licklider, Karen Lee 1935- *WhoSSW 91*
Licko, Zuzana *BioIn 16*
Lickteig, David Leo 1943- *WhoSSW 91*
Licup-Ante, Gloria G *BiDrAPA 89*
Licursi, Joan Roeben 1943- *ODwPR 91*
Lidchi, Maggi *ConAu 132*
Lidchi Grass, Maggi 1930- *ConAu 132*
Liddell, Cynthia Ann 1951- *WhoAmW 91*
Liddell, Donald Macy, Jr. 1907- *WhoAm 90*
Liddell, Edward George Tandy 1895-1981 *DcNaB 1981*
Liddell, Gary W. 1950- *St&PR 91*
Liddell, James W. 1918- *St&PR 91*
Liddell, James Walter 1931- *St&PR 91*
Liddell, Jane Hawley Hawkes 1907- *WhoAmW 91, WhoWor 91*
Liddell, Kenneth 1912-1975 *SmATA 63*
Liddell, Leon Morris 1914- *WhoAm 90, WhoWor 91*
Liddell, Nona Patricia 1927- *IntWWM 90*
Liddell, Peter Richard 1947- *WhoWor 91*
Liddell, Robert 1908- *WorAu 1980 [port]*
Liddell, Sharen 1945- *WhoWrEP 89*
Liddell, W. Kirk 1949- *St&PR 91, WhoAm 90*
Liddell Hart, B. H. 1895-1970 *WorAlBi*
Liddiard, J. S. Anna *FemiCLE*
Liddicoat, Richard Thomas, Jr. 1918- *WhoAm 90*
Liddicoat, Roger H. 1943- *St&PR 91*
Liddle, Alan Curtis 1922- *WhoAm 90*
Liddle, Catherine Diane 1952- *WhoWrEP 89*
Liddle, Don *BioIn 16*
Liddle, Don 1925- *Ballpl 90*
Liddle, George R. 1927- *St&PR 91*
Liddle, Larry Brook 1935- *WhoE 91*
Liddle, Nancy Hyatt 1931- *WhoAmA 91*
Liddle, William David 1937- *WhoSSW 91*
Liddon, Sim Clark 1935- *BiDrAPA 89*
Liddy, Edward M. 1945- *WhoAm 90*
Liddy, G. Gordon *BioIn 16*
Liddy, G. Gordon 1930- *WorAlBi*
Liddy, Gordon Battle 1930- *SpyFic*
Liddy, James 1934- *WhoWrEP 89*
Liddy, Marie Therese 1932- *WhoWor 91*
Liddy, Terence Cullerton 1944- *St&PR 91*
Lide, Alice *AuBYP 90*
Lide, Mary *ConAu 132*
Lide, Neoma Jewell Lawhon 1926- *WhoAmW 91*
Lide, Theodore Ellis, Jr. 1926- *WhoAm 90*
Lidell, Alvar 1908-1981 *DcNaB 1981*
Lidestri, Paula Ann 1965- *WhoAmW 91*
Lidge, Douglas Christian 1958- *BiDrAPA 89*
Lidicker, William Zander, Jr. 1932- *WhoAm 90*
Lidke, Wilmer, II 1950- *St&PR 91*
Lidl, Vaclav 1922- *IntWWM 90*
Lidman, Sara 1921- *DcScanL*
Lidman, Sara Adela 1923- *EncCoWW*
Lidoff, Joan 1944-1989 *ConAu 130*
Lidon, Jean Sih 1961- *WhoAmW 91*
Li Donnici, Kenneth 1925- *St&PR 91*
Lidow, Alan E. 1942- *St&PR 91*
Lidow, Eric 1912- *St&PR 91, WhoAm 90*
Lidstone, Herrick Kenley, Jr. 1949- *WhoEmL 91, WhoWor 91*
Lidstone, John *AuBYP 90*
Lidstrom, Carol Weisgerber *BiDrAPA 89*
Lidstrom, Paul Donley *BiDrAPA 89*
Lidtke, Doris Keefe 1929- *WhoAmW 91*
Lidtke, Vernon LeRoy 1930- *WhoAm 90*
Lidz, Charles Wilmanns 1946- *WhoE 91*
Lidz, Edward 1936- *St&PR 91*
Lidz, Ruth W 1910- *BiDrAPA 89*
Lidz, Theodore 1910- *BiDrAPA 89*
Lie, Alvin Lingpiao 1961- *WhoWor 91*
Lie, Arne Brun 1925- *BioIn 16*
Lie, Jonas 1833-1908 *DcScanL*
Lie, Trygve 1896-1968 *WorAlBi*
Lie-Ingo, Luang Eng 1918-1989 *BioIn 16*
Lie-Injo, Luan Eng 1918- *WhoAm 90*
Lieb, Elliott Hershel 1932- *WhoAm 90*
Lieb, Eugene William 1938- *St&PR 91*
Lieb, Fred 1888-1980 *Ballpl 90*
Lieb, Frederick George 1888-1980 *AuBYP 90*
Lieb, Hans-Heinrich 1936- *WhoWor 91*
Lieb, Irwin Chester 1925- *WhoAm 90*
Lieb, Jeffrey Alan 1951- *BiDrAPA 89*
Lieb, Julian *BiDrAPA 89*
Lieb, Mark 1950- *St&PR 91*
Lieb, Robert C *BiDrAPA 89*
Lieban, Irene Stahovich 1942- *WhoAmW 91*
Liebbe, William Howard 1953- *WhoEmL 91*
Liebehenschel, Arthur 1901-1948 *BioIn 16*
Liebel-Weckowicz, Helen Pauline Grit 1930- *WhoAm 90, WhoAmW 91*
Liebeler, Susan Wittenberg 1942- *WhoAm 90, WhoAmW 91*
Liebeler, Virginia Mary Mayer 1900- *WhoAmW 91*
Liebeler, Wesley J. 1931- *WhoAm 90*
Liebelt, Lothar 1940- *WhoWor 91*
Lieben, Samuel 1909- *St&PR 91*
Liebenow, J. Gus 1925- *WhoAm 90*
Liebenow, Larry A. 1943- *St&PR 91*
Liebenow, Larry Albert 1943- *WhoE 91*
Liebenson, Herbert 1920- *WhoAm 90*
Lieber, Adele *BiDrAPA 89*
Lieber, Anna 1947- *WhoE 91*
Lieber, Arnold 1935- *BiDrAPA 89*
Lieber, Arnold L 1937- *BiDrAPA 89*
Lieber, Baruch Barry 1952- *WhoE 91*
Lieber, Charles Donald 1921- *WhoAm 90*
Lieber, Charles Saul 1931- *WhoAm 90, WhoWor 91*
Lieber, David Leo 1925- *BioIn 16, WhoAm 90*
Lieber, David Leslie 1957- *WhoAm 90*
Lieber, Edvard 1948- *IntWWM 90*
Lieber, Edward Joseph 1921- *St&PR 91*
Lieber, France *WhoAmA 91N*
Lieber, Francis 1800-1872 *BioIn 16*
Lieber, Franz 1800-1872 *BioIn 16*
Lieber, Gary L. 1949- *WhoEmL 91*
Lieber, Hank 1911- *Ballpl 90*
Lieber, Harvey 1937- *WhoE 91*
Lieber, Jerome B. 1920- *St&PR 91*
Lieber, John Howard 1953- *WhoEmL 91*
Lieber, Michael W. 1940- *St&PR 91*
Lieber, Perry 1905-1988 *BioIn 16*
Lieber, Richard Louis 1956- *WhoEmL 91*
Lieber, Robert J 1941- *ConAu 30NR*
Lieber, Thomas Alan 1949- *WhoAmA 91*
Lieber, Todd Michael 1944- *WhoWrEP 89*
Lieberfarb, D.L. 1916- *St&PR 91*
Lieberg, Gabriele Karin *BiDrAPA 89*
Lieberman, Alan A *BiDrAPA 89*
Lieberman, Anne Marie 1946- *WhoAmW 91*
Lieberman, Archie 1926- *WhoAm 90*
Lieberman, Barry Sherwin *BiDrAPA 89*
Lieberman, Beth Weinstein 1947- *WhoAmW 91*
Lieberman, Bruce Alan *BiDrAPA 89*
Lieberman, Burton Barnet 1938- *WhoE 91*
Lieberman, Carol 1943- *IntWWM 90*
Lieberman, Carole Ilene *BiDrAPA 89*
Lieberman, Dana Kaplan 1964- *WhoAmW 91*
Lieberman, Daniel 1919- *BiDrAPA 89*
Lieberman, Daniel 1949- *BiDrAPA 89*
Lieberman, David I. 1941- *WhoE 91*
Lieberman, David Joseph 1928- *WhoAm 90*
Lieberman, Dorothy 1930- *BiDrAPA 89*
Lieberman, E James 1934- *SmATA 62 [port]*
Lieberman, E. James 1934- *WhoWrEP 89*
Lieberman, Edwin James 1934- *BiDrAPA 89*
Lieberman, Ernest David 1945- *WhoE 91*
Lieberman, Eugene 1918- *WhoWor 91*
Lieberman, Fredric 1940- *IntWWM 90, WhoAm 90*
Lieberman, Gail Forman 1943- *WhoAm 90, WhoAmW 91*
Lieberman, Gary A. *BioIn 16*
Lieberman, Gerald J. 1925- *WhoAm 90*
Lieberman, Harry 1876-1983 *MusmAFA, WhoAmA 91N*
Lieberman, Harvey 1945- *St&PR 91*
Lieberman, Helen S *BiDrAPA 89*
Lieberman, Herbert H. 1933- *WhoWrEP 89*
Lieberman, Hillel 1942- *St&PR 91, WhoAm 90, WhoE 91*

Lieberman, Ilene 1956- WhoAmW 91
Lieberman, Jeffrey Alan 1948- BiDrAPA 89
Lieberman, Joe BioIn 16
Lieberman, Joseph I. 1942- WhoAm 90, WhoE 91, WhoWor 91
Lieberman, Judith Mazor 1932- WhoE 91
Lieberman, Julie 1960- BioIn 16
Lieberman, Laura Crowell 1952- WhoAmA 91
Lieberman, Laurence 1935- WhoAm 90, WhoWrEP 89
Lieberman, Leonard 1929- WhoAm 90
Lieberman, Lester Zane 1930- St&PR 91, WhoAm 90
Lieberman, Louis 1944- WhoAm 90, WhoAmA 91, WhoE 91
Lieberman, Melvyn 1938- WhoAm 90
Lieberman, Meyer Frank 1923- WhoAmA 91
Lieberman, Morris Baruch 1925- WhoAm 90
Lieberman, Murray BiDrAPA 89
Lieberman, Paul Benjamin 1949- BiDrAPA 89
Lieberman, Philip Alden 1948- WhoWrEP 89
Lieberman, Richard B 1928- BiDrAPA 89
Lieberman, Richard S 1944- BiDrAPA 89
Lieberman, Robert I. 1954- St&PR 91
Lieberman, Rosemarie C. 1948- WhoHisp 91
Lieberman, Saul 1898-1983 BioIn 16
Lieberman, Seymour 1916- WhoAm 90
Lieberman, Shari 1958- WhoAmW 91
Lieberman, Stuart T. 1952- St&PR 91
Lieberman, William S 1924- WhoAmA 91
Lieberman-Nissen, Karen 1950- WhoAmW 91
Liebermann, Joan Vera BiDrAPA 89
Liebermann, Lowell 1961- IntWWM 90
Liebermann, Max 1847-1935 WorAlBi
Liebermann, Philip 1934- WhoAmA 91
Liebermann, Rolf 1910- IntWWM 90, PenDiMP A
Lieberson, Jonathan BioIn 16
Lieberson, Stanley 1933- WhoAm 90, WhoWrEP 89
Lieberstein, Edward 1938- St&PR 91
Liebert, Frederick Pierson 1941- St&PR 91
Liebert, John Arthur 1937- BiDrAPA 89
Liebert, Robert S. 1930-1988 BioIn 16
Lieberthal, Kenneth G. 1943- ConAu 130
Liebes, Dorothy 1899-1972 WhoAmA 91N
Liebes, Raquel 1938- WhoAmW 91, WhoE 91, WhoWor 91
Liebeskind, Aharon 1912-1942 BioIn 16
Liebeskind, Arthur S BiDrAPA 89
Liebeskind, Donald R. 1931- St&PR 91
Liebeskind, Herbert 1921- WhoAm 90
Liebeskind, Richard L. BioIn 16
Liebhafsky, Erwin Eugene 1922- WhoSSW 91
Liebhardt, Glenn 1883-1956 Ballpl 90
Liebhauser, Catherine A. BiDrAPA 89
Liebhauser, Wilfrid A 1929- BiDrAPA 89
Liebi, Mark David 1946- St&PR 91
Liebich, Marcia Trathen 1942- WhoAmW 91
Liebig, Richard Arthur 1923- WhoAm 90
Liebig, Siegfried 1938- WhoWor 91
Liebing, Howard C. 1921- St&PR 91
Liebknecht, Karl 1871-1919 WorAlBi
Liebl, Arthur Fredrick 1928- St&PR 91
Liebl, Karl 1915- IntWWM 90
Liebl, Thomas A. 1960- St&PR 91
Lieblein, Seymour 1923- WhoAm 90
Liebling, A. J. 1904-1963 BioIn 16
Liebling, Abbott Joseph 1904-1963 BioIn 16
Liebling, David Seth BiDrAPA 89
Liebling, Jerome 1924- WhoAm 90, WhoAmA 91
Liebling, Norman Robert 1917- WhoWor 91
Liebman, Jerome 1927- WhoAm 90
Liebman, Jon Charles 1934- WhoAm 90
Liebman, Lance Malcolm 1941- WhoAm 90
Liebman, Lawrence M. 1930- St&PR 91
Liebman, Leila BiDrAPA 89
Liebman, Mayer C 1934- BiDrAPA 89
Liebman, Milton 1928- WhoAm 90
Liebman, Norman S. 1928- St&PR 91
Liebman, Ronald 1940- BiDrAPA 89
Liebman, Ronald Stanley 1943- WhoAm 90, WhoE 91, WhoWor 91
Liebman, Sarah WhoAmA 91
Liebman, Theodore 1939- WhoAm 90
Liebmann, George William 1939- WhoAm 90
Liebmann, Herman 1918- St&PR 91
Liebmann, Karl-Otto 1933- BiDrAPA 89
Liebmann, Lee 1923- St&PR 91
Liebmann, Richard 1950- St&PR 91
Liebmann, Seymour W. 1928- WhoSSW 91, WhoWor 91
Liebovich, Carl Victor 1916- St&PR 91
Liebovich, Samuel David 1946- St&PR 91
Liebovich, Sheldon Bernard 1937- St&PR 91, WhoAm 90
Liebowitz, Alan F. 1948- St&PR 91
Liebowitz, Janet WhoAmA 91
Liebowitz, Jerome Harvey 1943- BiDrAPA 89
Liebowitz, Larry Arnold 1941- WhoWor 91
Liebowitz, Leo 1926- WhoAm 90, WhoE 91
Liebowitz, Leo 1927- St&PR 91
Liebowitz, Michael R 1945- BiDrAPA 89
Liebowitz, Neil Robert 1956- BiDrAPA 89, WhoE 91
Liebowitz, Shelly B. 1946- WhoSSW 91
Liebreich, Brian Scott 1958- BiDrAPA 89
Liebson, Elizabeth S BiDrAPA 89
Liebson, Ira Allen BiDrAPA 89
Liebtag, Benford Gustav, III 1941- WhoSSW 91
Liebzeit, Andrea Clara 1960- WhoAmW 91
Liechty, Jon D. 1949- St&PR 91
Lied, Erik Robert 1953- WhoEmL 91
Lied, Michael Robert 1953- WhoEmL 91
Lieder, Allan R. 1953- WhoEmL 91
Liederman, Al 1911- WhoAm 90
Liederman, David Samuel 1935- WhoAm 90
Liederman, Paul C 1935- BiDrAPA 89
Liedholm, Carl Edward 1940- WhoAm 90
Liedle, James Michael 1955- WhoEmL 91, WhoWor 91
Liedtke, Guenter J. 1941- St&PR 91
Liedtke, J. Hugh 1922- St&PR 91
Liedtke, Jane A. BioIn 16
Liedtke, John Hugh 1922- WhoAm 90, WhoSSW 91
Liedtke, Russell Charles 1945- St&PR 91
Lief, Bruce A 1941- BiDrAPA 89
Lief, Harold I 1917- BiDrAPA 89
Lief, Harold Isaiah 1917- WhoAm 90
Lief, Leonard 1924- WhoAm 90, WhoE 91
Lief, Lilli ODwPR 91
Lief, Nina R 1907- BiDrAPA 89
Lief, Nina Rayersky 1907- WhoE 91
Lieff, Ann Spector 1952- St&PR 91
Lieff, Erwin 1926- St&PR 91
Lieff, Jonathan D BiDrAPA 89
Lieftinck, Pieter 1902-1989 BioIn 16
Liegel, Reinald David 1942- St&PR 91
Liegghio, Nazzareno E. BiDrAPA 89
Liegi, Ulvi 1859-1939 BioIn 16
Liegl, Joseph Leslie 1948- WhoEmL 91
Liehm, Antonin J. 1924- BioIn 16
Lielbriedis, George L BiDrAPA 89
Liem, Annie 1941- WhoAmW 91
Liem, Channing 1909- WhoAm 90, WhoWor 91
Liem, Han 1929- BiDrAPA 89, WhoE 91
Liem, Khian Kioe 1942- WhoWor 91
Lien, Brustuen Hawkins 1927- St&PR 91
Lien, Charles H. 1925- St&PR 91
Lien, Dallas Gene 1938- St&PR 91
Lien, Eric Jung-chi 1937- WhoAm 90
Lien, Jere H. 1932- St&PR 91
Lien, Neil 1925- St&PR 91
Lien, Peter C. 1958- St&PR 91
Lien, Warren H. 1935- St&PR 91
Lienard, Jean-Luc B. 1951- WhoWor 91
Lienard, Michel-Joseph Napoleon PenDiDA 89
Lienardy, Pierre Marie Constant Delphin 1952- WhoWor 91
Lienau, Henry N. W. 1935- ODwPR 91
Liendecker, Edgar Merrill 1925- St&PR 91
Liendo, Hector Javier 1950- WhoHisp 91
Lienenbrugger, Herbert Gene 1942- St&PR 91, WhoAm 90
Liener, Irvin Ernest 1919- WhoAm 90
Lienert, Robert M. 1926-1988 BioIn 16
Lienhard, John Henry 1930- WhoAm 90
Lienhart, David Arthur 1939- WhoAm 90
Lienhart, James L. 1935- WhoAm 90
Liepa, Andris BioIn 16
Liepa, Maris 1936-1989 AnObit 1989, BioIn 16
Liepman, Michael Roger 1946- BiDrAPA 89
Liepmann, Hans Wolfgang 1914- WhoAm 90
Liepmann, Klaus 1907- WhoAm 90
Lieppe, Charles Andrew 1944- St&PR 91
Lierley, Earl 1917- St&PR 91
Liers, Emil Ernest 1890-1975 AuBYP 90
Lies, Richard Lorenz, Jr. 1945- WhoAm 90
Liesenfeld, Vincent Joseph 1947- WhoSSW 91
Liester, Mitchell Brent 1959- BiDrAPA 89
Lieteau, Sharon Lewis BiDrAPA 89
Lietz, Gerald S. 1918- AuBYP 90
Lietz, Jeremy Jon 1933- WhoWor 91
Lietz, Marlys ODwPR 91
Lietz, William BioIn 16
Lietzke, Milton Henry 1920- WhoAm 90
Lieu, Hou-Shun 1921- WhoAm 90
Lieu, Winston Hong BioIn 16
Lieurance, Floyd Oscar 1939- St&PR 91
Lieutaud, Balthazar PenDiDA 89
Lieuwen, Edwin 1923-1988 BioIn 16
Lievano, Jaime BiDrAPA 89
Lievano, Joaquin NewAgMG
Lievano, Jorge E BiDrAPA 89
Lievens, Stefan Rene Jozef 1940- WhoWor 91
Lievense, William C. 1947- St&PR 91
Lievonen, Eve Elizabeth 1949- WhoSSW 91
Liew, Fah Pow 1960- WhoE 91
Lifchitz, Max 1948- IntWWM 90, WhoHisp 91
Liff, Adam Joseph 1960- St&PR 91
Liff, Noah 1929- St&PR 91
Liffers, William A. 1929- St&PR 91
Liffers, William Albert 1929- WhoAm 90
Liffick, Thomas Ford 1951- BiDrAPA 89, WhoEmL 91
Lifgren, Derwood Keith 1927- St&PR 91
Lifgren, Martin William 1953- WhoE 91
Lifka, Mary Lauranne 1937- WhoAmW 91
Lifka, William Joseph 1929- St&PR 91
Lifland, William Thomas 1928- WhoAm 90
Lifrak, Patricia Dina BiDrAPA 89
Lifschutz, David H 1942- BiDrAPA 89
Lifschutz, Joseph E 1924- BiDrAPA 89
Lifshin, Lyn Diane 1949- WhoWrEP 89
Lifshin, Ronald J. St&PR 91
Lifshits, Il'ia Mikhailovich 1917-1982 DcScB S2
Lifshitz, Chava 1936- WhoWor 91
Lifshitz, Kenneth 1930- BiDrAPA 89
Lifshitz, Leatrice H. 1933- WhoWrEP 89
Lifshutz, Susan D. BiDrAPA 89
Lifson, Bernard I 1923- BiDrAPA 89
Lifson, Burton S. 1923- St&PR 91
Lifson, David S. 1908- ConAu 32NR
Lifson, Edward Albert 1928- WhoE 91
Lifson, Hugh Anthony 1937- WhoAmA 91
Lifson, Kalman A. 1926- St&PR 91
Lifson, Lawrence E 1941- BiDrAPA 89
Lifson, Ludmilla V. 1945- IntWWM 90
Liftin, John Matthew 1943- WhoAm 90
Lifton, Betty Jean 1926- AuBYP 90
Lifton, Robert Jay BiDrAPA 89
Lifton, Robert Jay 1926- BioIn 16, WhoAm 90, WhoWrEP 89, WorAlBi
Lifton, Robert K. 1928- St&PR 91
Lifton, Robert Kenneth 1928- WhoAm 90, WhoE 91
Lifton, Walter M. 1918- WhoAm 90
Ligabue, Ilva 1932- IntWWM 90
Ligachev, Yegor 1920- CurBio 90 [port]
Ligachov, Egor Kuzmich 1920- WhoWor 91
Ligare, Kathleen Meredith 1950- WhoAm 90
Ligas, Henry W. 1936- St&PR 91
Lige, Peter 1941- WhoAm 90
Ligendza, Catarina 1937- IntWWM 90, PenDiMP
Ligendza, Peter 1943- IntWWM 90
Ligenza, Andrea Angela 1952- WhoAmW 91
Ligeti, Gyorgy 1923- PenDiMP A
Ligeti, Gyorgy Sandor WhoWor 91
Ligeti, Gyorgy Sandor 1923- IntWWM 90
Ligett, Waldo Buford 1916- WhoAm 90
Liggett, Darwin Sligar 1916- WhoAm 90
Liggett, Hiram Shaw, Jr. 1932- WhoAm 90
Liggett, Hunter ConAu 31NR
Liggett, James David 1946- WhoEmL 91
Liggett, Lawrence Melvin 1917- WhoAm 90
Liggett, Malcolm Hugh 1929- WhoE 91
Liggett, Thomas Jackson 1919- WhoAm 90
Liggins, Isabelle G. 1928- WhoAmW 91
Liggio, Carl Donald 1943- WhoAm 90
Liggio, Jean Vincenza 1927- WhoAmW 91
Light, Albert 1927- WhoAm 90
Light, Alexander Luders 1822?-1894 DcCanB 12
Light, Arnold H. 1940- WhoE 91
Light, Arthur Heath WhoAm 90, WhoSSW 91
Light, Betty Jensen Pritchett 1924- WhoAm 90
Light, Bryan Dempsey 1949- St&PR 91
Light, Christopher Upjohn 1937- WhoAm 90, WhoWor 91
Light, Donald Eugene 1933- St&PR 91
Light, Dorothy K. 1937- St&PR 91
Light, Duane R. BioIn 16
Light, James Forest 1921- WhoAm 90
Light, Jerome Elliott 1928- WhoAm 90
Light, Joe Louis 1934- MusmAFA
Light, John Caldwell 1934- WhoAm 90
Light, John Henry 1855- AmLegL
Light, Judith BioIn 16
Light, Judith 1949- WorAlBi
Light, Ken 1951- WhoAmA 91
Light, Kenneth B. 1932- St&PR 91, WhoAm 90
Light, Kenneth Freeman 1922- WhoAm 90
Light, Lawrence 1941- WhoAm 90
Light, Marion Jessel 1915- WhoAmW 91
Light, Marvin Lawrence 1941- St&PR 91
Light, Morton J 1936- BiDrAPA 89
Light, Murray Benjamin 1926- St&PR 91, WhoAm 90
Light, Nancy A. ODwPR 91
Light, Pamela Delamaide 1950- WhoEmL 91
Light, Patricia Kahn 1939- WhoAmW 91
Light, Richard Gerald 1931- St&PR 91
Light, Richard Jay 1942- WhoAm 90
Light, Robley Jasper 1935- WhoAm 90
Light, Terry Richard 1947- WhoEmL 91
Light, Timothy 1938- WhoAm 90
Light, Walter Frederick 1923- St&PR 91, WhoAm 90
Light, Will WhoWrEP 89
Lightall, Duane G. 1935- St&PR 91
Lightbody, James Davies 1918- St&PR 91
Lightbourne, Robert Edward Arthur 1944- WhoE 91
Lightburn, Jeffrey Caldwell 1947- WhoWrEP 89
Lightburn, John L 1921- BiDrAPA 89
Lightcap, Kenneth R. 1938- ODwPR 91, St&PR 91
Lightcap, Royal Mansfield 1927- St&PR 91
Lightcap, Shirley M. 1927- St&PR 91
Lightcap, William T. 1937- St&PR 91
Lighter, Eric Aaron 1950- WhoWor 91
Lightfeather, Melody BioIn 16
Lightfeather, Melody 1951- WhoAmW 91
Lightfoot, David William 1945- WhoAm 90
Lightfoot, Gordon 1938- BioIn 16, EncPR&S 89, WorAlBi
Lightfoot, Gordon Meredith 1938- WhoAm 90
Lightfoot, James Ross 1938- WhoAm 90
Lightfoot, Jan Linda 1949- WhoAmW 91
Lightfoot, Luke 1722?-1789 PenDiDA 89
Lightfoot, Mark Francis 1958- St&PR 91
Lightfoot, Orlando B 1937- BiDrAPA 89
Lightfoot, Ralph Butterworth 1913- WhoE 91
Lightfoot, Sara Lawrence BioIn 16
Lightfoot, Teddi 1946- WhoAmW 91
Lightfoote-Young, Brenda Jo BiDrAPA 89
Lighthall, David William 1958- WhoSSW 91
Lighthall, William Douw 1857-1954 DcLB 92 [port]
Lightheart, Kim WhoAm 90
Lightholder, Alan William 1945- WhoSSW 91
Lightman, David Abbott 1953- WhoE 91
Lightman, H. Allen 1925- WhoE 91
Lightman, Harold Allen 1925- WhoWor 91
Lightman, Stafford Louis 1948- WhoWor 91
Lightner, A. M. AuBYP 90
Lightner, Ardyce Leah Stevens 1932- WhoE 91
Lightner, Candy BioIn 16
Lightner, Candy Lynne 1946- WhoAm 90, WhoAmW 91
Lightner, Edwin Allan, Jr. NewYTBS 90
Lightner, James Richmond 1922- St&PR 91
Lightner, Jeffrey Kass BiDrAPA 89
Lightner, Kevin Wayne 1954- St&PR 91
Lightner, Merrie Elizabeth Turner 1956- WhoEmL 91
Lightner, Richard E. 1941- ODwPR 91
Lightner, Ruth H. 1940- WhoAmW 91
Lighton, Linda 1948- WhoAmA 91
Lights, Frederick L. EarBlAP
Lightsey, Harry McKinley, Jr. 1931- WhoSSW 91
Lightsey, Johnnie Mack 1932- St&PR 91
Lightstone, Marilyn 1941- OxCCanT
Lightstone, Ronald 1938- St&PR 91, WhoAm 90
Lightstone, Stephen A. 1945- St&PR 91
Lightwood, Carol Wilson 1941- WhoAmW 91
Lighty, Paul Bruce 1944- St&PR 91
Ligler, Frances Smith 1951- WhoAmW 91
Lignarolo, Fini 1950- WhoHisp 91
Ligneel, Sandra Kamil BiDrAPA 89
Lignelli, Elena Maria 1958- WhoAmW 91
Ligomenides, Panos Aristides 1928- WhoAm 90
Ligon, Betty Joyce 1923- WhoSSW 91
Ligon, Champ BiDrAPA 89
Ligon, Ed D., Jr. 1933- St&PR 91
Ligon, J.D. 1929- St&PR 91
Ligon, Patti-Lou Elsie 1953- WhoAmW 91
Ligon, Thomas Paul, Jr. 1939- WhoSSW 91
Ligorski, Mark W L 1956- BiDrAPA 89
Ligorski, Mark William Lloyd 1956- WhoE 91
Ligotti, Eugene Ferdinand 1936- WhoE 91
Ligozzi, Giacomo PenDiDA 89
Liguori, Frank Nicholas 1946- St&PR 91

Liguori, Fred 1930- *WhoAm 90*
Liguori, James Joseph 1948- *St&PR 91*
Liguori, Jennifer Gardiner 1961- *WhoE 91*
Liguori, Ralph Rocco 1945- *St&PR 91*
Lihn, Enrique 1929-1988 *ConAu 32NR, HispWr 90*
Lihota, G.M. 1948- *St&PR 91*
Liikane, Juhan 1931- *BiDrAPA 89*
Liimatainen, Bruce Carl 1956- *St&PR 91*
Liiv, H. Henry 1933- *St&PR 91*
Liiv, Karin Eve 1962- *WhoE 91*
Liiv, Tiina M. 1937- *St&PR 91*
Lijinsky, William 1928- *WhoAm 90*
Lijn, Liliane 1939- *BiDWomA, WhoAmA 91*
Lijoi, Angela Marie 1959- *WhoSSW 91*
Lijoi, Peter Bruno 1953- *WhoE 91*
Likan, Gustav 1912- *WhoAmA 91*
Likens, Gene Elden 1935- *WhoAm 90*
Likens, Suzanne Alicia 1945- *WhoEmL 91*
Liker, Jack 1926- *WhoE 91*
Likes, Pat *BioIn 16*
Likhachev, Dmitriy Sergeyevich 1906- *WhoWor 91*
Likins, Jeanne Marie 1953- *WhoAmW 91*
Likins, Peter William 1936- *WhoAm 90*
Likkel, Craig Francis 1953- *St&PR 91*
Likness, Lawrence Richard 1929- *WhoAm 90*
Lilagan-Schaedel, Maria Nieves *WhoAmW 91, WhoWor 91*
Li-Lan 1943- *WhoE 91*
Li-Lancaster, Sharon 1949- *St&PR 91*
Lilar, Francois *EncCoWW*
Lilar, Francoise 1930- *WhoWor 91*
Lilar, Suzanne 1901- *EncCoWW*
Lilavati *WomWR*
Lilburn, Douglas Gordon 1915- *IntWWM 90*
Lilburne, Elizabeth *BiDEWW*
Lileika, Laima T. 1947- *WhoAmW 91*
Liles, Allen C. *ODwPR 91*
Liles, James Maurice, Jr. 1942- *WhoSSW 91*
Liles, James Raymond *BiDrAPA 89*
Liles, John Henry, Jr. 1947- *WhoEmL 91*
Liles, Raeford Bailey 1923- *WhoAmA 91*
Liles, William Jackson, Jr. 1925- *WhoAm 90, WhoSSW 91*
Liley, Arthur 1924- *St&PR 91*
Liley, Peter Edward 1927- *WhoAm 90*
Lilien, Anita Rose 1929- *WhoE 91*
Lilien, Copie *BioIn 16*
Lilien, Linda H. 1947- *St&PR 91*
Lilien, Mark Ira 1953- *WhoAm 90*
Lilienfeld, Alfred 1906- *BiDrAPA 89*
Lilienfeld, David Eugene 1957- *WhoE 91*
Lilienfeld, Georg von 1912-1989 *BioIn 16*
Lilienfeld, Julius Edgar *BioIn 16*
Lilienfeld, Semon M 1920- *BiDrAPA 89*
Lilienfield, Karl *WhoAmA 91N*
Lilienstern, O. Clayton 1943- *WhoAm 90*
Lilienthal, Alfred M. 1915- *WhoAm 90*
Lilienthal, Felix R., Jr. 1919- *St&PR 91*
Lilienthal, James Richard 1916- *WhoAm 90*
Lilienthal, John G. 1947- *ODwPR 91*
Lilienthal, Max 1815-1882 *BioIn 16*
Lilienthal, Meta Stern *EncAL*
Liliuokalani 1838-1917 *BioAmW, WomWR*
Liljebeck, Roy C. 1937- *WhoAm 90*
Liljebeck, Roy C., Jr. 1937- *St&PR 91*
Liljegren, Frank 1930- *WhoAmA 91*
Liljegren, Frank Sigfrid 1930- *WhoAm 90*
Liljegren, Gus *BioIn 16*
Liljegren, Jan Ragnar Gustaf 1929- *WhoWor 91*
Liljestrand, Ake 1917- *WhoWor 91*
Liljestrand, Kathryn Eileen 1956- *WhoAmW 91*
Lill, John 1944- *PenDiMP*
Lill, John Richard 1944- *BioIn 16, IntWWM 90*
Lill, John William 1951- *St&PR 91*
Lillard, Bill J. *WhoAm 90, WhoSSW 91*
Lillard, Richard D. 1928- *St&PR 91*
Lillard, Richard G 1909-1990 *ConAu 131*
Lillard, Ross W. 1931- *WhoAm 90*
Lillehaug, David Lee 1954- *WhoEmL 91*
Lillehei, Clarence Walton 1918- *WhoAm 90*
Lillelund, Kurt Werner Andersen 1922- *WhoWor 91*
Lillemoe, Kent O. 1958- *St&PR 91*
Lillesand, John Walter 1938- *St&PR 91*
Lilleskov, Roy K 1927- *BiDrAPA 89*
Lillestol, Jane Marie 1936- *WhoAm 90*
Lillevang, Omar Johansen 1914- *WhoAm 90*
Lilley, Albert Frederick 1932- *WhoAm 90*
Lilley, Brian Ward *BioIn 16*
Lilley, Cheryl 1953- *WhoE 91*
Lilley, James Roderick 1928- *WhoAm 90, WhoWor 91*
Lilley, John Mark 1939- *WhoAm 90*
Lilley, John Robert, II 1929- *WhoAm 90*
Lilley, Mili Della *WhoAmW 91, WhoSSW 91*
Lilley, Peter Bruce 1943- *WhoWor 91*
Lilley, Robert D. 1912- *St&PR 91*
Lilley, Robert Francis 1939- *WhoAm 90*
Lilley, Sandra 1963- *WhoHisp 91*
Lilley, Theodore Robert 1923- *WhoAm 90*
Lilley, Thomas William 1924-1989 *SpyFic*
Lilley, William, III 1938- *WhoAm 90*
Lillibridge, J.L. 1939- *St&PR 91*
Lillibridge, John Lee 1924- *WhoAm 90*
Lillibridge, Rhoal Duane 1929- *St&PR 91*
Lillibridge, Thomas L. *BioIn 16*
Lillicrop, John Fredrick 1935- *St&PR 91*
Lillie, Amy Morris *AuBYP 90*
Lillie, Beatrice 1894-1989 *AnObit 1989, BioIn 16, OxCCanT, OxCPMus, WorAlBi*
Lillie, Charisse Ranielle 1952- *WhoAmW 91*
Lillie, Edwin William 1926- *WhoWor 91*
Lillie, Glenn 1948- *ODwPR 91*
Lillie, John Mitchell 1937- *WhoAm 90*
Lillie, Richard Horace 1918- *WhoWor 91*
Lillie, Thomas Henry 1954- *WhoSSW 91*
Lillienstein, Maxwell Julius 1927- *WhoAm 90*
Lilliestrom Tjus, Bo 1922- *WhoWor 91*
Lilliott, Richard W., III 1941- *St&PR 91*
Lilliquist, Derek 1966- *Ballpl 90*
Lillis, Arline 1935- *St&PR 91*
Lillis, Bob 1930- *Ballpl 90*
Lillis, Charles M. *St&PR 91*
Lillis, William G. 1930- *St&PR 91, WhoAm 90*
Lillo, Lawrence Edward 1946- *WhoAm 90*
Lillquist, Patricia A *BiDrAPA 89*
Lilly, Ben *BioIn 16*
Lilly, Bob 1939- *WorAlBi*
Lilly, Charles *BioIn 16*
Lilly, Doris 1930- *WhoAm 90, WhoWrEP 89*
Lilly, Douglas K. 1929- *WhoAm 90*
Lilly, Edward G., Jr. 1925- *St&PR 91*
Lilly, Edward Guerrant, Jr. 1925- *WhoAm 90*
Lilly, Edward Paul, Jr. 1940- *St&PR 91*
Lilly, Eli 1885-1977 *BioIn 16, WorAlBi*
Lilly, Elizabeth Ann 1936- *BiDrAPA 89, WhoE 91*
Lilly, Elizabeth Giles 1916- *WhoAmW 91*
Lilly, George David 1934- *St&PR 91, WhoAm 90*
Lilly, John 1915- *NewAgE 90*
Lilly, John Cunningham 1915- *BioIn 16, WhoAm 90*
Lilly, John Haskins, III 1949- *WhoSSW 91*
Lilly, John R. 1928- *St&PR 91*
Lilly, John Russell 1929- *WhoAm 90*
Lilly, Joy K *BiDrAPA 89*
Lilly, Leslie Bjerg 1953- *WhoAmW 91*
Lilly, Lynn L. 1926- *St&PR 91*
Lilly, Mari Lynn 1953- *BiDrAPA 89*
Lilly, Martin Stephen 1944- *WhoAm 90*
Lilly, Michael Alexander 1946- *WhoAm 90*
Lilly, Nancy Cobb 1930- *WhoSSW 91*
Lilly, Peter Byron 1948- *WhoAm 90, WhoSSW 91*
Lilly, Richard J 1922- *BiDrAPA 89*
Lilly, Steven Jay 1952- *WhoSSW 91*
Lilly, Thomas Gerald 1933- *WhoAm 90, WhoSSW 91*
Lilly, Thomas More 1942- *WhoE 91*
Lilly, Virgil Greene 1900-1988 *BioIn 16*
Lilly, William 1602-1681 *EncO&P 3*
Lilly, William Eldridge 1921- *WhoAm 90*
Lillya, Clifford Peter 1910- *WhoAm 90*
Lillydahl, Earl D., Jr. 1930- *St&PR 91*
Lillyman, William Brendan, Sr. 1928- *St&PR 91*
Lillyman, William John 1937- *WhoAm 90*
Lillywhite, Harvey Burr 1943- *WhoSSW 91*
Lilov, Alexander Vassilev 1933- *WhoWor 91*
Liluokalani, Lydia Kamekeha 1838-1917 *WorAlBi*
Lilyquist, Christine 1940- *WhoAmA 91*
Lim, Anita T 1941- *BiDrAPA 89*
Lim, Byung Hoon 1935- *BiDrAPA 89*
Lim, Catherine 1943- *FemiCLE*
Lim, David Jang Jai 1935- *WhoAm 90*
Lim, Dominic 1909- *BiDrAPA 89*
Lim, Eng-Cheng Alan 1956- *WhoWor 91*
Lim, Esteban Lim, Jr. 1958- *BiDrAPA 89*
Lim, Jimmy Keng-Teet 1926- *WhoWor 91*
Lim, Keun Hee 1946- *BiDrAPA 89*
Lim, Lynette Lina 1963- *IntWWM 90*
Lim, Meng Eng *BiDrAPA 89*
Lim, Ooi-Kong 1950- *WhoWor 91*
Lim, Prospero Alcido *BiDrAPA 89*
Lim, Robert Cheong, Jr. 1933- *WhoAm 90*
Lim, Shun Ping 1947- *WhoEmL 91, WhoWor 91*
Lim, Sonia 1955- *BiDrAPA 89*
Lim, Sook Hee *BiDrAPA 89*
Lim, Stephen 1949- *WhoWor 91*
Lim, Terry 1959- *WhoAmW 91*
Lim, Thuan Woon John 1946- *WhoWor 91*
Lim, William 1928- *BiDrAPA 89*
Lima, Albert J. *BioIn 16*
Lima, Alceu Amoroso 1893-1983 *BioIn 16*
Lima, Bruno R D M 1951- *BiDrAPA 89*
Lima, Bruno Russomano 1951- *WhoE 91*
Lima, Facundo P *BiDrAPA 89*
Lima, Gustavo Raul *WhoHisp 91*
Lima, Jacqueline 1949- *WhoAmA 91*
Lima, Jorge de 1893-1953 *BioIn 16*
Lima, Jose Lezama *HispWr 90*
Lima, Jose Lezama 1910-1976 *BioIn 16*
Lima, Jose T *BiDrAPA 89*
Lima, Joseph A. 1940- *St&PR 91*
Lima, Luis 1948- *IntWWM 90*
Lima, Luis Eduardo 1950- *WhoAm 90*
Lima, Richard M. 1940- *St&PR 91*
Lima, Robert 1935- *WhoAm 90, WhoWrEP 89*
Lima, Robert F., Jr. 1935- *WhoHisp 91*
Lima Barreto, Afonso Henrique de 1881-1922 *BioIn 16*
Liman, Arthur L. *BioIn 16*
Liman, Arthur L. 1932- *WhoAm 90*
Liman, Ellen 1936- *AuBYP 90*
Limantour, Jean Francois Pierre 1942- *WhoWor 91*
Limardo, Felix R. 1952- *WhoHisp 91*
Li Marzi, Joseph *WhoAmA 91*
LiMarzi, Joseph 1907- *WhoE 91*
Limbach, E.W. 1939- *St&PR 91*
Limbach, Karl Averell 1932- *WhoAm 90*
Limbach, Walter F. 1924- *WhoAm 90*
Limbacher, James Louis 1926- *WhoWor 91*
Limbaugh, Rush *NewYTBS 90 [port]*
Limbaugh, Rush Hudson 1891- *WhoAm 90*
Limbaugh, Stephen Nathaniel 1927- *WhoAm 90*
Limbert, David Edwin 1942- *WhoE 91*
Limbert, John William 1943- *WhoE 91*
Limbert, Paul Mark 1947- *St&PR 91*
Limbocker, Derek L. 1940- *St&PR 91*
Limbourg Brothers *IntDcAA 90*
Limbourg, Hermann de *IntDcAA 90*
Limbourg, Johan de *IntDcAA 90*
Limbourg, Paul de *IntDcAA 90*
Limentani, Davide *BiDrAPA 89*
Limentani, Uberto 1913-1989? *ConAu 129*
Limerick, Countess Of 1897-1981 *DcNaB 1981*
Limhaisen, Mohammed Abdulraham 1949- *WhoEmL 91, WhoWor 91*
Liming, George Francis 1923- *St&PR 91*
Limkemann, Margaret Alice 1941- *IntWWM 90, WhoAmW 91*
Limmer, Lou 1925- *Ballpl 90*
Limmroth, Karin Leigh 1949- *WhoAmW 91*
Limodin, M. Daniel *WhoWor 91*
Limoges, Richard F 1938- *BiDrAPA 89*
Limon, Jose 1908-1972 *BioIn 16, WorAlBi*
Limon, Otilio 1933- *St&PR 91*
Limoncelli, Barbara Marie 1936- *WhoAmW 91*
Limondin, Jacques 1928- *St&PR 91*
Limone, Frank 1938- *WhoAmA 91*
Limongelli, Enzo *BioIn 16*
Limoni, Uri *St&PR 91*
Limont, Naomi Charles *WhoAmA 91*
Limosin, Leonard 1515?-1576? *PenDiDA 89*
Limousin, Jean *PenDiDA 89*
Limousin, Leonard 1515?-1576? *PenDiDA 89*
Limper, Mary Gretchen 1943- *WhoE 91*
Limpert, John Arthur 1934- *WhoAm 90*
Limpert, Robert James 1939- *St&PR 91*
Limpitlaw, John Donald 1935- *WhoAm 90*
Limprecht, Hollis Joyce 1920- *WhoAm 90*
Limpus, Jane E. 1945- *St&PR 91*
Limpus, Sharon Lynn 1954- *WhoSSW 91*
Limsiaco, Marciano Salvio *BiDrAPA 89*
Limtao, D Cecilia Chan *BiDrAPA 89*
Lin Piao 1907-1971 *WorAlBi*
Lin, Alice Lee Lan 1937- *WhoAmW 91, WhoE 91*
Lin, Alice Murong Pu *BioIn 16*
Lin, Avi 1952- *WhoE 91*
Lin, Chin-Cheng 1959- *WhoEmL 91*
Lin, Chin-Chu 1935- *WhoAm 90, WhoWor 91*
Lin, Cho-Liang 1960- *IntWWM 90*
Lin, Cho-Liang Taiwanese *BioIn 16*
Lin, Chu-chia Steve 1956- *WhoWor 91*
Lin, Chwen-Hao Francis 1949- *WhoEmL 91*
Lin, Clifton 1857-1941? *BioIn 16*
Lin, Donald J.L. 1924- *St&PR 91*
Lin, Eric Y L *BiDrAPA 89*
Lin, Eva 1958- *St&PR 91*
Lin, Ih Foo 1942- *BiDrAPA 89*
Lin, Jack 1932- *St&PR 91*
Lin, James Chih-I 1942- *WhoAm 90*
Lin, Jen-Kun 1935- *WhoWor 91*
Lin, Joseph Pen-Tze 1932- *WhoAm 90*
Lin, Keh-Ming 1946- *BiDrAPA 89*
Lin, Lucia 1962- *WhoE 91*
Lin, Maya 1959- *WhoAmW 91*
Lin, Maya 1960?- *News 90 [port], -90-3 [port]*
Lin, Maya Y *WhoAmA 91*
Lin, Maya Ying *BioIn 16*
Lin, Min-Chung 1944- *WhoE 91*
Lin, Newman Kunti 1951- *WhoSSW 91*
Lin, Paul Y. 1942- *St&PR 91*
Lin, Pen-Min 1928- *WhoAm 90*
Lin, Shin 1945- *WhoAm 90*
Lin, Siong-Chi 1947- *BiDrAPA 89*
Lin, Su-Yi *BiDrAPA 89*
Lin, Tao 1958- *WhoWor 91*
Lin, Tsung-Yi 1920- *BiDrAPA 89, WhoAm 90*
Lin, Tung Hua 1911- *WhoAm 90*
Lin, Tung Yen 1911- *WhoAm 90, WhoWor 91*
Lin, Wen-Yeh 1931- *WhoWor 91*
Lin, William Wen-Rong 1942- *WhoAm 90*
Lin, Wuu-Long 1939- *WhoAm 90*
Lin, Y. K. 1923- *WhoAm 90*
Lin, Yang-Kang 1927- *WhoWor 91*
Lin, Yi 1959- *WhoE 91*
Linaburg, Barbara Jean 1941- *WhoWrEP 89*
Linabury, Virginia M 1957- *BiDrAPA 89*
Linan, Francisco S. 1948- *WhoHisp 91*
Linan-Gervacio, Lydia *BiDrAPA 89*
Linane, William Edward 1928- *WhoWor 91*
Linares, Julio *WhoWor 91*
Linares, Leonor Diana 1961- *WhoEmL 91*
Linares, Luisa-Maria 1915- *EncCoWW*
Linares, Nora Alicia 1954- *WhoSSW 91*
Linares, Rufino 1955- *Ballpl 90*
Linares-Flor, Jesus E. 1958- *BiDrAPA 89*
Linati, Claudio 1790-1832 *ArtLatA*
Linburn, Geoffrey E *BiDrAPA 89*
Linchitz, Richard Michael 1947- *BiDrAPA 89, WhoAm 90*
Lincicome, Bernard Wesley 1941- *WhoAm 90*
Linck, Albert J. *WhoAm 90*
Linck, Franz Konrad 1730-1793 *PenDiDA 89*
Lincke, Joseph 1783-1837 *PenDiMP*
Lincke, Lester Walter 1933- *St&PR 91*
Lincke, Paul 1866-1946 *OxCPMus*
Lincks, Stephen T *BiDrAPA 89*
Lincoln, Abbey 1930- *DrBIPA 90*
Lincoln, Abraham 1809-1865 *BiDrUSE 89, BioIn 16, EncO&P 3, EncPaPR 91, WhNaAH, WorAlBi*
Lincoln, Alexander, III 1943- *WhoWor 91*
Lincoln, Benjamin 1733-1810 *EncCRAm*
Lincoln, Bruce 1948- *WhoWrEP 89*
Lincoln, C. Eric 1924- *WhoWrEP 89*
Lincoln, Carl Clifford, Jr. 1928- *WhoE 91*
Lincoln, Carol Ann 1949- *WhoSSW 91*
Lincoln, Charles Eric 1924- *WhoAm 90*
Lincoln, Christopher Scott 1956- *WhoE 91*
Lincoln, Crawford 1928- *St&PR 91, WhoE 91*
Lincoln, David C. 1925- *St&PR 91*
Lincoln, Edmond Lynch 1949- *WhoAm 90*
Lincoln, Edward John 1949- *WhoE 91*
Lincoln, Elizabeth, Countess of *BiDEWW*
Lincoln, Elizabeth, Countess of 1574?-1630? *FemiCLE*
Lincoln, Elizabeth Clinton, Countess of 1574-1630 *BioIn 16*
Lincoln, Flynt Colby 1957- *St&PR 91*
Lincoln, Franklin Benjamin, Jr. 1908- *WhoAm 90*
Lincoln, Gordon A. 1928- *St&PR 91*
Lincoln, Ignatius Timothy Trebitsch- 1879-1943 *BioIn 16*
Lincoln, Jeannette Virginia 1915- *WhoAm 90*
Lincoln, John B. 1942- *St&PR 91*
Lincoln, John Francis 1916- *WhoWor 91*
Lincoln, Levi 1749-1820 *BiDrUSE 89, BioIn 16, EncCRAm*
Lincoln, Levi 1782-1868 *BioIn 16*
Lincoln, Lucian Abraham 1926- *WhoAm 90*
Lincoln, Lucy 1934- *WhoSSW 91*
Lincoln, Mary Anna *BiDrAPA 89*
Lincoln, Mary Johnson 1844-1921 *WorAlBi*
Lincoln, Mary Todd 1818-1882 *BioAmW, BioIn 16*
Lincoln, Nancy Hanks 1784-1818 *BioAmW*
Lincoln, Raynard C., Jr. 1934- *St&PR 91, WhoAm 90*
Lincoln, Richard Mather 1929- *WhoAmA 91*
Lincoln, Robert Adams 1921- *WhoAm 90*
Lincoln, Robert Allen 1946- *St&PR 91*
Lincoln, Robert D 1921- *BiDrAPA 89*
Lincoln, Robert Dix 1929- *IntWWM 90*
Lincoln, Robert Todd 1843-1926 *BiDrUSE 89, BioIn 16*
Lincoln, Sandy 1945- *WhoAm 90*
Lincoln, Victor D. 1941- *St&PR 91*
Lincoln, Wayne Kaui 1946- *St&PR 91*
Lincoln, Yvonna Sessions 1944- *WhoAmW 91*

Lind, Carl 1904-1946 Ballpl 90
Lind, Carl G. 1933- St&PR 91
Lind, Chester Carl 1918- WhoAm 90
Lind, Deborah Stoeppelwerth 1943- WhoAmW 91
Lind, Dennis Barry 1940- BiDrAPA 89
Lind, Esko Antero 1929- WhoWor 91
Lind, Gerard Garrett 1936- St&PR 91
Lind, James Forest 1925- WhoAm 90
Lind, James Peter 1932- WhoSSW 91, WhoWor 91
Lind, Jenny 1820-1887 BioIn 16, PenDiMP, WorAlBi
Lind, Jose 1964- Ballpl 90, WhoHisp 91
Lind, Kendra Johnson 1947- WhoAmW 91, WhoWor 91
Lind, Levi Robert 1906- WhoAm 90
Lind, Magnus Gosta 1939- WhoWor 91
Lind, Marshall L. WhoAm 90
Lind, Maurice David 1934- WhoWor 91
Lind, Maurice Duane 1932- WhoSSW 91
Lind, Niels Christian 1930- WhoAm 90
Lind, Robert G. 1927- St&PR 91
Lind, Robert Jeffrey 1953- WhoE 91
Lind, Sven-Gunnar 1954- WhoWor 91
Lind, Thomas Otto 1937- St&PR 91, WhoAm 90
Lind, Viviane BiDrAPA 89
Linda, Gerald 1946- WhoAm 90, WhoEmL 91
Linda, Gustav 1937- St&PR 91
Lindahl, Charles E. 1935- IntWWM 90
Lindahl, David Michael 1944- WhoE 91
Lindahl, Helen Gertrude 1917- WhoWrEP 89
Lindahl, Herbert Winfred 1927- WhoAm 90
Lindahl, Roger Mathews 1955- WhoEmL 91, WhoWrEP 89
Lindal, Douglas Frederick 1950- St&PR 91
Lindal, Robert Walter 1947- St&PR 91
Lindal, Walter Walter 1919- St&PR 91
Lindaman, Lois Jane 1940- WhoAmW 91
Lindaman, Vive 1877-1927 Ballpl 90
Lindamood, Judy Beth 1948- WhoAmW 91
Lindars, Laurence Edward 1922- St&PR 91, WhoAm 90
Lindau, Borge 1932- ConDes 90
Lindau, James H. 1933- St&PR 91, WhoAm 90
Lindau, Jules W. 1909- St&PR 91
Lindau, Philip J. 1936- St&PR 91
Lindauer, John Howard, II 1937- WhoAm 90
Lindauer, Kenneth Elliot 1950- WhoEmL 91
Lindauer, Lois Lyons 1933- WhoAmW 91
Lindauer, Theodore 1935- BiDrAPA 89
Linday, Linda Anne 1949- WhoE 91
Lindberg, Carol Anne BiDrAPA 89
Lindberg, Charles David 1928- WhoAm 90
Lindberg, Donald Allan Bror 1933- WhoAm 90
Lindberg, Edwin Howard 1948- WhoEmL 91
Lindberg, Francis Laurence, Jr. 1948- WhoSSW 91
Lindberg, Gail Bowman 1959- WhoAmW 91
Lindberg, Garry Martin 1941- WhoAm 90
Lindberg, Gladys 1905?-1990 ConAu 131
Lindberg, Gosta Carl Herbert 1927- St&PR 91
Lindberg, Helge 1926- WhoWor 91
Lindberg, J. Mark 1950- St&PR 91
Lindberg, Jean Melville 1918- WhoAm 90
Lindberg, Jeffrey 1954- IntWWM 90
Lindberg, Karl-Egon 1927- WhoWor 91
Lindberg, Kenneth Ames 1957- WhoE 91
Lindberg, Leif Erik 1944- WhoWor 91
Lindberg, Michael Charles 1951- WhoEmL 91
Lindberg, Nils Per Olof 1933- IntWWM 90
Lindberg, Orrin Henry 1955- BiDrAPA 89
Lindberg, R.E. 1924- St&PR 91
Lindberg, Ralph D. 1921- St&PR 91
Lindberg, Rosemarie 1925- St&PR 91
Lindberg, Soren V. 1945- ODwPR 91
Lindberg, Stanley William 1939- WhoAm 90, WhoWrEP 89
Lindberg, Stig PenDiDA 89
Lindberg, Stig 1916-1982 ConDes 90
Lindberg, Tod Marshall 1960- WhoAm 90
Lindbergh, Ann Morrow 1906- WorAlBi
Lindbergh, Anne BioIn 16
Lindbergh, Anne 1906- FemiCLE
Lindbergh, Anne Morrow 1906- BioAmW, BioIn 16, MajTwCW
Lindbergh, Anne Spencer Morrow 1906- WhoAm 90
Lindbergh, Charles 1902-1974 BioIn 16
Lindbergh, Charles A. 1902-1974 WorAlBi
Lindbergh, Charles A., Sr. 1859-1924 EncABHB 7 [port]
Lindbergh, Diana St. Leger 1957- WhoWor 91
Lindbergh, Reeve AuBYP 90
Lindblad, Paul 1941- Ballpl 90
Lindblad, Richard Arthur 1937- WhoAm 90
Lindblad, William John 1929- St&PR 91, WhoAm 90
Lindblade, Robert O. 1940- St&PR 91
Lindblom, Lance Edmund 1948- WhoWor 91
Lindblom, Ronald Carl 1942- St&PR 91
Lindbo, Larry Allen 1947- St&PR 91
Lindbom, Dixie Darlene 1939- WhoAmW 91
Lindburg, Merl J. 1926- St&PR 91
Linde, Gunnel 1924- AuBYP 90
Linde, Hans Arthur 1924- WhoAm 90
Linde, Hans-Martin 1930- IntWWM 90
Linde, Karl P. G. Von 1842-1934 WorAlBi
Linde, Lucille Mae 1919- WhoAmW 91
Linde, Maxine Helen 1939- WhoAm 90
Linde, Nancy 1949- WhoE 91
Linde, Paul Ruhr BiDrAPA 89
Linde, Robert Hermann 1944- WhoWor 91
Linde, Ronald Keith 1940- WhoAm 90
Lindeburg, Franklin A. 1918- AuBYP 90
Lindeen, Nils Folke 1948- WhoE 91
Lindegaard, Hans 1934- WhoWor 91
Lindegard, Janice ODwPR 91
Lindegren, Amalia Euphrosyne 1814-1891 BiDWomA
Lindegren, Cecile Keyser 1946- WhoAmW 91
Lindegren, Erik 1910-1968 DcScanL
Lindekrantz, Bo 1932- ConDes 90
Lindell, Andrea Regina 1943- WhoAmW 91, WhoWor 91
Lindell, Deborah Kay 1959- WhoAmW 91
Lindell, Edward Albert 1928- WhoAm 90
Lindell, Jan 1939- WhoWor 91
Lindell, John G. 1932- St&PR 91
Lindell, Johnny 1916-1986 Ballpl 90
Lindell, Kai Lasse 1954- WhoWor 91
Lindell, Marion 1926- ODwPR 91
Lindell, Richard Thomas 1934- WhoSSW 91
Lindelof, William Christian, Jr. 1946- WhoSSW 91
Lindem, Thomas Jules 1928- St&PR 91
Lindeman, Bard BioIn 16
Lindeman, Carolynn A. 1940- IntWWM 90
Lindeman, Janet Claire 1941- WhoAmW 91
Lindeman, Warren Charles 1924- St&PR 91
Lindemann, A. Bernard St&PR 91
Lindemann, Daryl R. 1954- St&PR 91
Lindemann, Donald Lee 1936- St&PR 91
Lindemann, Edna M WhoAmA 91
Lindemann, Edward AuBYP 90
Lindemann, Glen 1939- St&PR 91
Lindemann, James Arthur 1942- WhoWrEP 89
Lindemann, Lillian C 1922- BiDrAPA 89
Lindemer, George Geoffrey 1953- WhoE 91
Lindemer, Lawrence Boyd 1921- WhoAm 90
Linden, Brayden BioIn 16
Linden, Christopher 1950- St&PR 91
Linden, David Earl BiDrAPA 89
Linden, David Lee 1952- St&PR 91
Linden, Dennis Alan 1957- WhoEmL 91
Linden, Hal BioIn 16
Linden, Hal 1931- WorAlBi
Linden, Harold Arthur 1941- WhoE 91
Linden, Henry Robert 1922- St&PR 91, WhoAm 90
Linden, Herbert BiDrAPA 89
Linden, Jay Lawrence 1950- WhoE 91
Linden, Lars Arne Kent 1949- WhoWor 91
Linden, Oliver ConAu 129
Linden, Patricia ConAu 129
Linden, Patricia 1955- WhoAmW 91
Linden, Robert David 1952- BiDrAPA 89
Linden, Robert E 1935- BiDrAPA 89
Linden, Ronald A. 1948- St&PR 91
Linden, Thomas Milton 1943- WhoAm 90
Linden, Thomas T 1948- BiDrAPA 89
Linden, Trevor BioIn 16
Lindenast, Sebastian 1460?-1526 PenDiDA 89
Lindenau, Judith Wood 1941- WhoWrEP 89
Lindenbaum, Richard L BiDrAPA 89
Lindenbaum, Seymour Joseph 1925- WhoAm 90, WhoWor 91
Lindenberg, Arthur Jay 1942- WhoWrEP 89
Lindenberg, Mary K 1921- WhoAmA 91
Lindenberg, Sherri Korfin 1962- WhoSSW 91
Lindenberger, George Ferdinand 1924- WhoE 91
Lindenberger, Herbert Samuel 1929- WhoAm 90, WhoWrEP 89
Lindenburg, Keith J. 1960- ODwPR 91
Lindenfeld, Arthur BiDrAPA 89
Lindenfeld, Lore 1921- WhoAmW 91
Lindenfeld, Peter 1925- WhoAm 90
Lindenlaub, Dieter 1937- WhoWor 91
Lindenmann, Walter K. 1936- ODwPR 91
Lindenmayer, Jean-Pierre 1942- BiDrAPA 89, WhoE 91
Lindenmuth, Leonard Jerry, Jr. 1955- WhoE 91
Lindenmuth, Noel Charles 1940- WhoWor 91
Lindenmuth, Richard Alan 1944- WhoSSW 91, WhoWor 91
Lindenstein, Joan Kathryn 1953- WhoAmW 91
Linder, Allan David 1925- WhoAm 90
Linder, Bruno 1924- WhoAm 90
Linder, Forrest E. 1906-1988 BioIn 16
Linder, Harvey Ronald 1949- WhoSSW 91
Linder, Hilary F, III 1935- BiDrAPA 89
Linder, James Benjamin 1925- WhoAm 90
Linder, Jill Robin BiDrAPA 89
Linder, Joseph 1918- St&PR 91
Linder, Kate BioIn 16
Linder, Leslie AuBYP 90
Linder, Lionel 1932- WhoAm 90
Linder, Maurice BioIn 16
Linder, Paul Scott 1921- St&PR 91
Linder, Richard M. 1931- St&PR 91
Linder, Robert Eric 1949- BiDrAPA 89
Linder, Robert J. 1937- IntWWM 90
Linder, Roger Walter 1936- WhoAm 90
Linder, Theodore Marie Bernard 1931- WhoWor 91
Linder, William H. ODwPR 91
Linder-Victor, Mira 1921- WhoAmW 91
Linderberg, Jan Erik 1934- WhoWor 91
Linderholm, Carl E. 1937- WhoSSW 91
Linderman, Earl William 1931- WhoAmA 91
Linderman, Jeanne Herron 1931- WhoAmW 91
Linderman, Robert 1952- St&PR 91
Linders, Howard D. 1932- St&PR 91
Linders, Paul 1948- WhoWor 91
Linderski, Jerzy 1934- WhoAm 90
Linderstrom-Lang, Kaj Ulrik 1896-1959 DcScB S2
Lindfors, Viveca 1920- WhoWrEP 89
Lindgren, Arne Sigfrid 1932- WhoAm 90
Lindgren, Astrid 1907- AuBYP 90, DcScanL, EncCoWW
Lindgren, Barbro 1937- AuBYP 90, BioIn 16, SmATA 63
Lindgren, Bernard William 1924- WhoAm 90
Lindgren, Bjorn Frank 1943- WhoAmA 91
Lindgren, Carleton 1934- BiDrAPA 89
Lindgren, Charlotte 1931- WhoAmA 91
Lindgren, Charlotte Holt 1924- WhoWrEP 89
Lindgren, Derbin Kenneth, Jr. 1932- WhoAm 90
Lindgren, Donald R. 1933- St&PR 91
Lindgren, Ethel John BioIn 16
Lindgren, Ingvar Per 1931- WhoWor 91
Lindgren, John Ralph 1933- WhoAm 90
Lindgren, John Raymond, Jr. 1935- St&PR 91
Lindgren, Richard Thomas 1927- St&PR 91
Lindgren, Robert Kemper 1939- WhoWor 91
Lindgren, Timothy Joseph 1937- St&PR 91, WhoAm 90
Lindgren, Tore A. 1941- St&PR 91
Lindgren-Utsi, E. J. 1905-1988 AnObit 1988
Lindh, Erik Gunnar 1948- WhoWor 91
Lindh, Gunnar Ernst 1922- WhoWor 91
Lindh, Henry C.B. 1930- St&PR 91
Lindh, Patricia S. ODwPR 91
Lindh, Patricia Sullivan 1928- WhoAm 90
Lindhard, Jens 1922- WhoWor 91
Lindheim, James B. 1945- ODwPR 91
Lindheim, James Bruce 1945- WhoAm 90, WhoWor 91
Lindheim, Richard David 1939- WhoAm 90
Lindheimer, Jack H BiDrAPA 89
Lindhjem, Jon Alan 1946- St&PR 91
Lindholm, Berit Maria 1934- IntWWM 90
Lindholm, Carl Edward 1929- St&PR 91, WhoAm 90
Lindholm, Clifford F., II 1930- St&PR 91
Lindholm, Devern Wayne 1948- St&PR 91
Lindholm, Dwight Henry 1930- WhoAm 90, WhoWor 91
Lindholm, John Victor 1934- WhoAm 90
Lindholm, Ralf Valdemar 1924- WhoWor 91
Lindholm, Richard Theodore 1960- WhoWor 91
Lindholm, Ulric Svante 1931- St&PR 91, WhoAm 90
Lindig, Bill M. 1936- WhoAm 90, WhoSSW 91
Lindig, Otto 1895-1966 PenDiDA 89
Lindlahr, Henry 1853- NewAgE 90
Lindland, Roger K. 1932- WhoAm 90
Lindland, Roger Kyle 1932- St&PR 91
Lindlau, Douglas W. 1946- St&PR 91
Lindley, Charles Robert BiDrAPA 89
Lindley, David BioIn 16
Lindley, Francis Haynes, Jr. 1945- WhoEmL 91
Lindley, Geoffrey Kenneth 1940- WhoWor 91
Lindley, H Wain 1951- BiDrAPA 89
Lindley, Harry 1839-1913 OxCCanT
Lindley, James G. 1931- EncABHB 7 [port]
Lindley, James Gunn 1931- St&PR 91, WhoAm 90, WhoSSW 91
Lindley, Mary 1652- BiDEWW
Lindley, Norman Dale 1937- WhoWor 91
Lindley, Robert 1776-1855 PenDiMP
Lindley, Robert Roling 1940- WhoAm 90
Lindley, Ronald David 1954- St&PR 91
Lindley, Simon Geoffrey 1948- IntWWM 90
Lindman, Maj Jan 1886-1972 AuBYP 90
Lindmark, Arne 1929- WhoAmA 91
Lindner, Carl H. BioIn 16, St&PR 91
Lindner, Carl Henry 1919- WhoAm 90, WhoSSW 91
Lindner, Charlotte K. 1922- WhoE 91
Lindner, Don B. 1948- St&PR 91
Lindner, Doris PenDiDA 89
Lindner, Elizabeth M. 1951- St&PR 91
Lindner, Eric John 1958- WhoE 91
Lindner, Erna Caplow 1928- WhoAmW 91
Lindner, Joseph, Jr. 1929- WhoAm 90
Lindner, Keith E. WhoAm 90
Lindner, Kenneth Edward 1922- WhoAm 90
Lindner, Kurt Julius 1922- WhoAm 90
Lindner, Luther Edward 1942- WhoSSW 91
Lindner, Mary John 1923- WhoAmW 91
Lindner, Philip G. 1943- St&PR 91
Lindner, Richard 1901-1978 WhoAmA 91N
Lindner, Robert David 1920- St&PR 91, WhoAm 90
Lindner, Robert William, Jr. 1961- WhoE 91
Lindner, William R. 1945- St&PR 91
Lindo, David Kenneth 1936- WhoWrEP 89
Lindo, Donald John 1944- St&PR 91
Lindo, J Trevor 1925- BiDrAPA 89
Lindo-Drusch, Nancy Jo 1954- WhoEmL 91
Lindon, Jerome 1925- WhoWor 91
Lindon, John A 1924- BiDrAPA 89
Lindon, John Arnold 1924- WhoAm 90
Lindop, Edmund 1925- AuBYP 90
Lindow, Donald A. 1916- St&PR 91
Lindow, Donald August 1916- WhoAm 90
Lindow, John Wesley 1910- WhoAm 90
Lindow, Lester William 1913- WhoSSW 91, WhoWor 91
Lindow, Wayne Edwin 1926- St&PR 91
Lindow, Wesley 1910- St&PR 91
Lindquist, Barbara Louise 1930- WhoWrEP 89
Lindquist, Carl 1938- WhoWor 91
Lindquist, Emory Kempton 1908- ConAu 31NR
Lindquist, Evan 1936- WhoAmA 91
Lindquist, Everett Carlton 1912- WhoWor 91
Lindquist, Fred H. 1926- St&PR 91
Lindquist, Jack B. 1927- St&PR 91
Lindquist, Jane Ingrid 1953- WhoAmW 91
Lindquist, Jennie Dorothea 1899-1977 AuBYP 90
Lindquist, John A. BioIn 16
Lindquist, John A. 1919- St&PR 91, WhoAm 90
Lindquist, John Theodore, II 1950- WhoWor 91
Lindquist, Linda Janette 1951- WhoAmW 91
Lindquist, Margaret Charlotte 1917- WhoAmW 91
Lindquist, Mark 1949- WhoAmA 91
Lindquist, Peter Arthur 1957- St&PR 91
Lindquist, Raymond Irving 1907- WhoAm 90
Lindquist, Robert John 1948- WhoSSW 91
Lindquist, William Brent 1953- WhoE 91
Lindquist, Willis 1908- AuBYP 90
Lindqvist, Gunnar Jan 1950- WhoEmL 91
Lindroos, Peter 1944- IntWWM 90
Lindros, Eric BioIn 16
Lindros, John Edward 1949- WhoWor 91
Lindroth, Linda 1946- WhoAmA 91
Lindsay Quartet PenDiMP
Lindsay, The Master of 1847-1913 EncO&P 3
Lindsay, Alan C. 1932- St&PR 91
Lindsay, Arturo 1946- WhoAmA 91
Lindsay, Arturo Wesley 1946- WhoE 91
Lindsay, Bertha NewYTBS 90
Lindsay, Bruce George 1947- WhoE 91
Lindsay, Bryan Eugene 1931- WhoAm 90
Lindsay, Caroline 1844-1912 FemiCLE
Lindsay, Carolyn Patricia 1953- WhoAmW 91
Lindsay, Charles John 1953- WhoAm 90

Lindsay, Charles Joseph 1924- *WhoAm 90*
Lindsay, Charles W *BiDrAPA 89*
Lindsay, Dale Richard 1913- *WhoAm 90*
Lindsay, David Breed, Jr. 1922- *WhoAm 90*
Lindsay, Delroy Fitzherbert 1951- *WhoWor 91*
Lindsay, Dianna Marie 1948- *WhoAmW 91*
Lindsay, Donald Gene 1922- *WhoAm 90*
Lindsay, Donald J. 1941- *WhoE 91*
Lindsay, Donald Parker 1915- *WhoAm 90*
Lindsay, Edward Williams 1950- *St&PR 91*
Lindsay, Elena Margaret 1941- *WhoAmW 91*
Lindsay, Franklin Anthony 1916- *WhoAm 90*
Lindsay, Franklin Daniel 1929- *St&PR 91*
Lindsay, George Carroll 1928- *WhoAm 90*
Lindsay, George Edmund 1916- *WhoAm 90*
Lindsay, George Nelson 1919- *WhoAm 90*
Lindsay, Gilbert W. 1900-1990 *NewYTBS 90*
Lindsay, Herbert McKoy 1956- *WhoSSW 91*
Lindsay, Howard 1889-1968 *OxCPMus, WorAlBi*
Lindsay, Hugh *BioIn 16*
Lindsay, J. Arthur 1930- *St&PR 91*
Lindsay, Jack 1900-1990 *ConAu 131*
Lindsay, Jacqueline Mae 1959- *WhoAmW 91*
Lindsay, James Wiley 1934- *WhoAm 90*
Lindsay, Joan 1896-1984 *FemiCLE*
Lindsay, John J. *BioIn 16*
Lindsay, John Kennedy 1924- *WhoWor 91*
Lindsay, John Maurice 1918- *IntWWM 90*
Lindsay, John Robert, Jr. 1925- *WhoE 91*
Lindsay, John V. 1921- *WorAlBi*
Lindsay, John Vliet 1921- *WhoAm 90, WhoE 91*
Lindsay, John W. 1926- *St&PR 91*
Lindsay, Joseph H 1919- *BiDrAPA 89*
Lindsay, June Campbell McKee 1920- *WhoWor 91*
Lindsay, Karen *BioIn 16*
Lindsay, Katherine Ann 1946- *WhoAmW 91*
Lindsay, Kenneth C 1919- *WhoAmA 91*
Lindsay, L. Christeene 1951- *IntWWM 90*
Lindsay, Leslie 1960- *WhoAmW 91*
Lindsay, Maria Theresa 1950- *WhoAmW 91*
Lindsay, Martin Alexander 1905-1981 *DcNaB 1981*
Lindsay, Maud McKnight 1874- *AuBYP 90*
Lindsay, Nancy A. 1943- *St&PR 91*
Lindsay, Nancy L. 1949- *St&PR 91*
Lindsay, Philip G *BiDrAPA 89*
Lindsay, Powell *EarBlAP*
Lindsay, Rebecca Jane 1954- *BiDrAPA 89*
Lindsay, Richard Clark *NewYTBS 90*
Lindsay, Richard Paul 1934- *WhoAm 90*
Lindsay, Richard Paul 1945- *WhoWor 91*
Lindsay, Robert 1924- *WhoAm 90*
Lindsay, Robert V. 1926- *St&PR 91*
Lindsay, Robert Van Cleef 1926- *WhoAm 90*
Lindsay, Roger Alexander 1941- *WhoAm 90*
Lindsay, Scott *BioIn 16*
Lindsay, Ted 1925- *WorAlBi*
Lindsay, Vachel 1879-1931 *BioIn 16, WorAlBi*
Lindsay, William A. 1795-1876 *BioIn 16*
Lindsay, William Kerr 1920- *WhoAm 90*
Lindsell, Harold 1913- *WhoWor 91*
Lindseth, Richard Emil 1935- *WhoAm 90*
Lindseth, Roy Oliver 1925- *WhoAm 90*
Lindsey, Ada Marie 1937- *WhoAm 90*
Lindsey, Alton A 1907- *ConAu 131*
Lindsey, Ann Kendrick 1945- *WhoAmW 91*
Lindsey, Barbara Ann 1940- *WhoAmW 91*
Lindsey, Beth H. *BiDrAPA 89*
Lindsey, Bill *BioIn 16*
Lindsey, Bonnie Joan 1935- *WhoAmW 91*
Lindsey, Byron Anthony *BiDrAPA 89*
Lindsey, Casimir Charles 1923- *WhoAm 90*
Lindsey, Cisco Hembry 1931- *St&PR 91*
Lindsey, D. Ruth 1926- *WhoAmW 91*
Lindsey, David 1951- *ODwPR 91*
Lindsey, David Hosford 1950- *WhoAm 90*
Lindsey, Dottye Jean 1929- *WhoAmW 91*
Lindsey, Elizabeth 1586-1654 *BiDEWW*
Lindsey, Frank Irwin 1947- *St&PR 91*
Lindsey, H. Edward, Jr. 1926- *WhoSSW 91, WhoWor 91*
Lindsey, Hank 1943- *WhoSSW 91*
Lindsey, Jake W. *BioIn 16*
Lindsey, James Darryl 1944- *St&PR 91*
Lindsey, James L. 1940- *St&PR 91*
Lindsey, James Norris 1938- *BiDrAPA 89*
Lindsey, James Russell 1933- *WhoAm 90*
Lindsey, Jim 1898-1963 *Ballpl 90*
Lindsey, Johanna 1952- *WhoWrEP 89*
Lindsey, John Horace 1922- *WhoAm 90*
Lindsey, John M. 1931- *ODwPR 91*
Lindsey, John Morton 1930- *St&PR 91, WhoAm 90*
Lindsey, John Russell 1947- *IntWWM 90*
Lindsey, Jonathan Asmel 1937- *WhoAm 90*
Lindsey, Kenneth Ray 1937- *St&PR 91*
Lindsey, Lawrence Benjamin 1954- *WhoE 91*
Lindsey, Lowell L. *WhoSSW 91*
Lindsey, Margaret Ann 1949- *BiDrAPA 89*
Lindsey, Melvin G. 1939- *St&PR 91*
Lindsey, Mort 1923- *IntWWM 90*
Lindsey, Oliver *AmLegL*
Lindsey, Paul Scott 1945- *St&PR 91*
Lindsey, Riki Sue 1953- *WhoAmW 91*
Lindsey, Robert 1935- *WhoWrEP 89*
Lindsey, Robert Sours 1913- *WhoAm 90*
Lindsey, William Fuselle 1923- *WhoWrEP 89*
Lindsey, William H. *BioIn 16*
Lindskog, David Richard 1936- *WhoAm 90*
Lindskog, Karl Bertil 1936- *WhoWor 91*
Lindskog, Marjorie Otilda 1937- *WhoAmW 91, WhoWor 91*
Lindskog, Norbert F. 1932- *WhoWor 91*
Lindskog, Per Folke 1937- *WhoWor 91*
Lindslee, Thomas *PenDiDA 89*
Lindsley, Cynthia Woods 1962- *WhoAmW 91*
Lindsley, Donald Benjamin 1907- *WhoAm 90*
Lindsley, Julie Lynn 1959- *WhoAmW 91*
Lindsley, Mary F *ConAu 30NR*
Lindsley, Van Sinderen *BioIn 16*
Lindsley, William B. 1947- *WhoSSW 91*
Lindstedt-Siva, June 1941- *WhoAm 90, WhoAmW 91*
Lindsten, Jan Eric 1935- *WhoWor 91*
Lindstrand, Vicke 1904-1983 *ConDes 90*
Lindstrand, Viktor Emanuel 1904-1983 *PenDiDA 89*
Lindstrom, Eric Everett 1936- *WhoSSW 91*
Lindstrom, Ernest Algot 1931- *WhoAm 90*
Lindstrom, Eugene Shipman 1923- *WhoAm 90*
Lindstrom, Fred 1905-1981 *BioIn 16*
Lindstrom, Freddie 1905-1981 *Ballpl 90 [port]*
Lindstrom, Gaell 1919- *WhoAmA 91*
Lindstrom, Greg Mark 1957- *WhoSSW 91*
Lindstrom, John A. 1953- *St&PR 91*
Lindstrom, Joyce Leah Evans 1931- *WhoWrEP 89*
Lindstrom, Karl *PenDiDA 89*
Lindstrom, Lydia Salucka 1960- *WhoAmW 91*
Lindstrom, Mary Lou 1928- *WhoAmW 91*
Lindstrom, Naomi 1950- *ConAu 30NR*
Lindstrom, Nina Lucille 1940- *WhoAmW 91*
Lindstrom, Olle Birger 1924- *WhoWor 91*
Lindstrom, Philip Martin 1917- *St&PR 91*
Lindstrom, Raimo Matti 1943- *WhoWor 91*
Lindstrom, Ralph Emil 1925- *WhoAm 90*
Lindstrom, Robert Bruce 1942- *St&PR 91*
Lindstrom, Robert J. 1918- *St&PR 91*
Lindstrom, Sanford John 1957- *St&PR 91*
Lindstrom, Solveig Yvonne Louise *WhoWor 91*
Linduska, Joseph Paul 1913- *WhoAm 90*
Lindvall, Michael Lloyd 1947- *WhoE 91*
Lindy, David Charles 1952- *BiDrAPA 89, WhoE 91*
Lindy, Jacob David *BiDrAPA 89*
Lindzen, Richard Siegmund 1940- *WhoAm 90*
Lindzey, Gardner *BioIn 16*
Lindzey, Gardner 1920- *WhoAm 90*
Line, Kimberly Campbell 1961- *WhoAmW 91*
Line-Esker, Cathy Kaye 1957- *WhoEmL 91*
Lineback, Harvey Lee 1946- *WhoE 91, WhoWor 91*
Lineback, Lowell Kent 1943- *WhoE 91*
Lineback, Richard H 1936- *ConAu 31NR*
Linebarger, James Morris 1934- *WhoSSW 91, WhoWrEP 89*
Linebaugh, James Rhodes 1929- *St&PR 91*
Linebaugh, Mack Starks, Jr. 1938- *St&PR 91*
Lineberger, Brade Keener, Jr. 1932- *St&PR 91*
Lineberger, Donald R. 1933- *St&PR 91*
Lineberger, Herman Propst 1928- *BiDrAPA 89*
Lineberger, James R. 1946- *St&PR 91*
Lineberger, Larry Watson 1943- *St&PR 91*
Lineberger, Walter F., Jr. 1913- *St&PR 91*
Lineberger, William Carl 1939- *WhoAm 90*
Lineberry, Gary E. 1950- *St&PR 91*
Linehan, Earl L. 1941- *St&PR 91*
Linehan, Helen M. 1939- *WhoAmW 91*
Linehan, John Charles 1939- *St&PR 91*
Linehan, Thomas A. 1947- *ODwPR 91*
Linen, James A. 1938-1989 *BioIn 16*
Linen, Jonathan S. *WhoAm 90*
Linenthal, Edward Tabor 1947- *ConAu 30NR*
Linert, Susan Marie 1949- *WhoAmW 91*
Lines, Colleen Jessen *BioIn 16*
Lines, Dick 1938- *Ballpl 90*
Lines, Kathleen *AuBYP 90*
Lines, Kathleen 1902-1988 *AnObit 1988*
Lines, Kathleen Mary 1902-1988 *SmATA 61*
Lines, Laurence Richard 1949- *WhoSSW 91*
Lines, Richard Stuart 1936- *WhoWor 91*
Linet, Beverly 1929- *WhoWrEP 89*
Linet, Leslie Sidney 1942- *BiDrAPA 89*
Linett, Deena 1938- *WhoWrEP 89*
Linett, Robert Allen 1947- *St&PR 91*
Linette, Boguslaw 1926- *IntWWM 90*
Lineweaver, Paul Kelton 1925- *WhoE 91*
Linfante, Charles Vincent 1939- *WhoAm 90*
Linfield, James Clark Taylor 1955- *WhoEmL 91*
Linfield, Louis S *BiDrAPA 89*
Linford, Mary Suzanne 1935- *WhoAmW 91*
Ling, Daniel 1926- *WhoAm 90*
Ling, Dwight L. 1923- *WhoAm 90*
Ling, Edwin Rodger 1931- *WhoWrEP 89*
Ling, Fuyun 1944- *WhoE 91*
Ling, Jahja Wang-Chieh 1951- *WhoAm 90*
Ling, James J. *WhoAm 90*
Ling, Jan Nils 1934- *IntWWM 90*
Ling, Joseph Tso-Ti 1919- *WhoAm 90*
Ling, Julia K-F 1924- *BiDrAPA 89*
Ling, Julia Kuofang 1924- *WhoE 91*
Ling, Kathryn Wrolstad 1943- *WhoAmW 91*
Ling, Kwong Ung 1946- *WhoWor 91*
Ling, Lily Hsu-Chiang 1952- *WhoSSW 91*
Ling, Mae J. *BioIn 16*
Ling, Marian Ming Ho 1930- *WhoAmW 91*
Ling, Matthew S. 1963- *St&PR 91*
Ling, Per Henrik 1776-1839 *NewAgE 90*
Ling, Robert F. 1939- *WhoSSW 91*
Ling, Suilin 1930- *WhoE 91, WhoWor 91*
Ling, William H. *St&PR 91*
Lingafelter, Edward Clay, Jr. 1914- *WhoAm 90*
Lingam, Venkataramana S 1954- *BiDrAPA 89*
Lingam, Vijayalakshmi *BiDrAPA 89*
Lingamneni, Jaganmohan Rao 1942- *WhoAm 90*
Lingan, Alfonso Barrantes 1928- *BioIn 16*
Lingard, Joan *AuBYP 90, BioIn 16*
Lingas, John *BiDrAPA 89*
Lingbeck, Gary L. 1955- *St&PR 91*
Linge, Ruth 1927- *IntWWM 90*
Lingelbach, David Charles 1961- *WhoE 91*
Lingeman, Richard Roberts 1931- *WhoAm 90*
Lingen, Thekla 1866-1931 *EncCoWW*
Lingenfelser, Catherine Theresa 1952- *WhoAmW 91, WhoSSW 91*
Lingenfelter, Charles Wesley 1933- *St&PR 91*
Lingenfelter, Kenneth Albert 1944- *WhoSSW 91*
Lingenfelter, R. Brian 1944- *St&PR 91*
Lingenfelter, Sherwood Galen 1941- *WhoAm 90*
Lingens, Franz 1925- *WhoWor 91*
Linger, Gerald H. 1937- *St&PR 91*
Lingg, Joseph Frederick 1945- *St&PR 91*
Lingl, Friedrich A 1927- *BiDrAPA 89*
Lingl, Friedrich Albert 1927- *WhoAm 90*
Lingl, James Peter 1946- *WhoEmL 91*
Lingle, Kathleen McCall 1944- *WhoAmW 91*
Lingle, Marilyn Felkel 1932- *WhoAmW 91*
Lingle, Muriel E. *WhoAmW 91*
Lingle, Robert Christopher 1948- *WhoWor 91*
Lingle, Sarah Elizabeth 1955- *WhoSSW 91*
Lingman, Goran Krispin 1949- *WhoWor 91*
Lingnell, A. William 1942- *St&PR 91*
Lingo, Hazel Isabel 1911- *WhoAmW 91*
Lingo, Patricia Marie Sawyer 1950- *WhoAmW 91*
Lingoes, James Charles 1923- *WhoAm 90*
Lingris, John 1923- *St&PR 91*
Linhares, Judith 1940- *WhoAmA 91*
Linhares, Philip E 1939- *WhoAmA 91*
Linhart, Diane Sue 1953- *WhoAmW 91*
Linhart, Judy Kay 1958- *WhoEmL 91*
Linhart, Robert 1944- *ConAu 130*
Linhartova, Vera 1938- *EncCoWW*
Lini, Walter Hadye 1942- *WhoWor 91*
Lining, John 1708-1760 *EncCRAm*
Lininger, Mary Charlotte 1949- *WhoE 91*
Linington, Elizabeth *FemiCLE*
Linington, Elizabeth 1921-1988 *TwCCr&M 91*
Linjama, Jouko 1934- *IntWWM 90*
Link, Antony Cole 1947- *WhoEmL 91*
Link, Arthur Stanley 1920- *WhoAm 90*
Link, Bobby *BioIn 16*
Link, Christoph 1933- *WhoWor 91*
Link, Conrad Barnett 1912- *WhoE 91*
Link, David M. 1930- *St&PR 91, WhoAm 90*
Link, David Thomas 1936- *WhoAm 90*
Link, Deborah Shaw 1933- *BiDrAPA 89, WhoAmW 91*
Link, Frank Albert 1930- *WhoWor 91*
Link, Franz 1924- *WhoWor 91*
Link, Franz-Josef 1962- *WhoWor 91*
Link, Fred A. 1918- *St&PR 91*
Link, Fred Motter 1904- *WhoAm 90*
Link, George Hamilton 1939- *WhoAm 90*
Link, Howard Anthony 1934- *WhoAmA 91*
Link, James E. 1943- *St&PR 91*
Link, Jerome Edward 1931- *WhoE 91*
Link, Joseph E. 1942- *St&PR 91*
Link, Lawrence John 1942- *WhoAmA 91*
Link, Mae Mills 1915- *WhoAm 90, WhoAmW 91, WhoWor 91*
Link, Margaret Ann 1934- *WhoSSW 91*
Link, Nan Abra *BiDrAPA 89*
Link, Nina Beth 1943- *WhoAm 90*
Link, Norman 1908- *St&PR 91*
Link, O. Winston 1911- *BioIn 16*
Link, Paul Anthony 1951- *WhoEmL 91*
Link, Perry 1931- *St&PR 91*
Link, Peter Karl 1930- *WhoSSW 91*
Link, Raymond Roger 1943- *WhoSSW 91*
Link, Richard Edward 1961- *WhoE 91*
Link, Robert Allen 1932- *St&PR 91, WhoAm 90*
Link, Robert James 1950- *WhoEmL 91*
Link, Robert U. 1920- *St&PR 91*
Link, Rudolf W *BiDrAPA 89*
Link, Stanley 1894-1957 *EncACom*
Link, Thomas 1946- *St&PR 91*
Link, Val James 1940- *WhoAmA 91*
Link, Wendell H. 1922- *St&PR 91*
Link, William P. 1947- *St&PR 91*
Link, William Theodore 1933- *WhoAm 90*
Link Vorel, Bonnie 1949- *WhoE 91*
Linke, Curtis G. 1942- *ODwPR 91*
Linke, Ed 1911- *Ballpl 90*
Linke, Francesca *BioIn 16*
Linke, Fritz 1923- *IntWWM 90*
Linke, Hansjurgen 1928- *WhoWor 91*
Linke, Paul *BioIn 16*
Linkenauger, James Edward 1944- *St&PR 91*
Linker, Betty B. *BioIn 16*
Linker, David *BioIn 16*
Linker, Jonathan Steven 1949- *WhoAm 90*
Linker, Wendy Jane *BiDrAPA 89*
Linkey, Helen Elinor 1938- *WhoAmW 91*
Linkin, Robert Edward 1952- *St&PR 91*
Linklater, Kristin 1936- *BioIn 16, NotWoAT*
Linklater, Magnus 1942- *ConAu 131*
Linklater, William Joseph 1942- *WhoAm 90*
Linkletter, Art 1912- *WorAlBi*
Linkletter, Arthur Gordon 1912- *WhoAm 90*
Linko, Lauri Tapani 1931- *WhoWor 91*
Linkous, Stanley Michael 1950- *WhoSSW 91*
Linkous, William Joseph, Jr. 1929- *WhoAm 90*
Links, J. G. 1904- *BioIn 16*
Linksz, Arthur 1900-1988 *BioIn 16*
Linley, David Armstrong-Jones, Viscount 1961- *BioIn 16*
Linley, Elizabeth Ann 1754-1792 *PenDiMP*
Linley, George 1798-1865 *OxCPMus*
Linley, Thomas 1733-1795 *PenDiMP A*
Linley, Thomas 1756-1778 *PenDiMP A*
Linman, James William 1924- *WhoAm 90*
Linn, Abraham S 1930- *BiDrAPA 89*
Linn, Ann Marie 1937- *WhoE 91*
Linn, Anthony Blane 1951- *WhoE 91*
Linn, Carole Anne 1945- *WhoAmW 91, WhoEmL 91, WhoWor 91*
Linn, Charle F. 1930- *AuBYP 90*
Linn, Dennis L. *BioIn 16*
Linn, Edward Allen 1922- *WhoAm 90, WhoWrEP 89*
Linn, James Herbert 1925- *St&PR 91, WhoAm 90*
Linn, Jan M. *ODwPR 91*
Linn, Jay George, Jr. 1916- *WhoAm 90*
Linn, Jo White 1930- *WhoAmW 91*
Linn, John L 1925- *BiDrAPA 89*
Linn, John William 1936- *WhoAmA 91*
Linn, Judy 1947- *WhoAmA 91*
Linn, Karen Elizabeth 1957- *IntWWM 90*
Linn, Louis *BiDrAPA 89*
Linn, Milman H., III 1931- *St&PR 91*
Linn, Robert A. 1931- *St&PR 91*
Linn, Robert Allen 1932- *WhoE 91*
Linn, Robert Joseph 1926- *WhoSSW 91*
Linn, Stanley 1918- *WhoE 91*
Linn, Steven Allen 1943- *WhoAmA 91*

Linn, Stuart Michael 1940- *WhoAm 90*
Linn-Baker, Mark 1953- *WorAlBi*
Linna, Timo Juhani 1937- *WhoAm 90*
Linna, Vaino 1920- *DcScanL*
Linnaeus, Carolus 1707-1778 *EncPaPR 91, WorAlBi*
Linnainmaa, Terhikki 1942- *WhoWor 91*
Linnane, James Joseph 1941- *WhoE 91*
Linnankoski, Johannes 1869-1913 *DcScanL*
Linnansalo, Vera 1950- *WhoAmW 91*
Linne, Carl von 1707-1778 *DcScanL*
Linnea *ConTFT 8*
Linnehan, Joseph Arthur, Jr. 1953- *WhoEmL 91*
Linnell, Albert Paul 1922- *WhoAm 90*
Linnell, James Edward 1931- *St&PR 91*
Linnell, John *BioIn 16*
Linnell, John 1729-1796 *PenDiDA 89*
Linnell, Robert Hartley 1922- *WhoAm 90*
Linnell, William *PenDiDA 89*
Linnell, Zenos M 1925- *BiDrAPA 89*
Linneman, Jerome Robert 1941- *St&PR 91*
Linnemann, Hans 1931- *WhoWor 91*
Linnemann, Roger E. 1931- *St&PR 91*
Linnemeier, Thomas Jay 1936- *St&PR 91*
Linnen, Thomas Francis 1925- *WhoE 91*
Linnenberg, Clem Charles, Jr. 1912- *WhoE 91*
Linnert, Terrence Gregory 1946- *WhoEmL 91*
Linney, Beverly 1923- *WhoAm 90*
Linney, Romulus 1930- *WhoWrEP 89*
Linnik, Iurii Vladimirovich 1915-1972 *DcScB S2*
Linnoila, Veli Markku I *BiDrAPA 89*
Linnolt, Erik *BiDrAPA 89*
Linoff-Thornton, Marian Gottlieb 1937- *WhoAmW 91*
Linomarl *WhoWrEP 89*
Linos, Glenys 1941- *IntWWM 90*
Linowes, David F. 1917- *St&PR 91*
Linowes, David Francis 1917- *WhoAm 90, WhoWor 91*
Linowes, Harry Michael 1928- *WhoAm 90*
Linowes, Richard Gary 1951- *WhoEmL 91*
Linowitz, Sol Myron 1913- *WhoAm 90, WhoWor 91*
Linquist, Cindy Raye 1955- *WhoAmW 91*
Linquist, Ona *BioIn 16*
Lins, Delbert Edwin 1933- *WhoAm 90*
Lins Da Silva, Carlos Eduardo 1952- *WhoWor 91*
Linschitz, Henry 1919- *WhoAm 90*
Linsenbuehler, Georg Wilhelm 1955- *WhoWor 91*
Linsenmann, William Michael 1919- *St&PR 91, WhoAm 90*
Linsenmeyer, John Michael 1940- *WhoAm 90*
Linser, Paul William 1939- *WhoWrEP 89*
Linsk, Michael Stephen 1940- *WhoAm 90*
Linsley, Earle Gorton 1910- *WhoAm 90*
Linsley, Julia W. *St&PR 91*
Linsley, Ray Keyes 1917- *WhoAm 90*
Linsley, Robert Martin 1930- *WhoAm 90*
Linsmayer, J. Nicholas 1950- *St&PR 91*
Linsmayer, Robert Michael 1922- *St&PR 91*
Linsmeier, Mary Therese 1928- *WhoAmW 91*
Linson, William K *BiDrAPA 89*
Lintault, Roger Paul 1938- *WhoAmA 91*
Linthicum, James Harold 1944- *WhoSSW 91*
Linton, Alfred James 1925- *WhoSSW 91*
Linton, Charles *EncO&P 3*
Linton, Douglas Edward 1947- *St&PR 91*
Linton, Eliza 1822-1898 *FemiCLE*
Linton, Elizabeth Lynn 1822-1898 *BioIn 16*
Linton, F. Leroy 1937- *St&PR 91*
Linton, Fred Ernest Julius 1938- *WhoE 91*
Linton, Frederick M. 1932- *WhoAm 90*
Linton, George Howard 1924- *St&PR 91*
Linton, Janet Lynn *BiDrAPA 89*
Linton, Michael Manley *BioIn 16*
Linton, Michael Roy 1952- *IntWWM 90*
Linton, Patricia Ann 1942- *WhoE 91*
Linton, Patrick H *BiDrAPA 89*
Linton, Renee *BioIn 16*
Linton, Richard M. 1927- *St&PR 91*
Linton, Richard Murdoch 1927- *WhoAm 90*
Linton, Robert *BioIn 16*
Linton, Robert David 1954- *WhoE 91*
Linton, Roy N. 1918- *St&PR 91*
Linton, Roy Nathan 1918- *WhoAm 90*
Linton, William James 1812-1897 *BioIn 16*
Lintott, Edward Barnard 1875-1951 *WhoAmA 91N*
Lintz, Larry 1949- *Ballpl 90*
Lintz, Robert C. 1933- *St&PR 91*
Lintz, Robert Carroll 1933- *WhoAm 90*
Lintz, Robert Harry 1927- *St&PR 91*
Linvill, John Grimes 1919- *WhoAm 90*
Linville, Joanne 1926?- *ConTFT 8*
Linville, Lewis Frederick 1935- *St&PR 91*
Linville, Thomas Merriam 1904- *WhoAm 90, WhoWor 91*
Linwick, Phillip C. 1931- *St&PR 91*
Linxe, Robert *BioIn 16*
Linz, Anthony James 1948- *WhoEmL 91, WhoWor 91*
Linz, Arthur 1938- *St&PR 91*
Linz, Gerhard David 1927- *WhoSSW 91*
Linz, Phil 1939- *Ballpl 90*
Linz, Werner Mark 1935- *WhoAm 90*
Linzer, Estelle *WhoAmW 91*
Linzer, Harry 1917- *St&PR 91*
Linzer, Morton A. 1924- *St&PR 91*
Linzer, Ruth 1921- *St&PR 91*
Linzer, Wladimir Hermann 1936- *WhoWor 91*
Linzey, Andrew *BioIn 16*
Linzner, Gordon 1949- *WhoWrEP 89*
Linzy, Frank 1940- *Ballpl 90*
Lio, Augie *BioIn 16*
Lion, Donor Mitchell 1924- *WhoAm 90*
Lion, Flora 1876-1958 *BiDWomA*
Lion, John R 1938- *BiDrAPA 89*
Lion, Keith Louis 1950- *WhoE 91*
Lion, Margaret Joyce 1951- *IntWWM 90*
Lion, Paul Michel, III 1934- *WhoAm 90*
Lion, Stephanie Ann 1937- *WhoAmW 91*
Lion Cachet, Carel Adolph 1864-1945 *PenDiDA 89*
Lionakis, George 1924- *WhoAm 90*
Lionberger, John Shepley, Jr. 1927- *St&PR 91*
Lionberger, Lyle Jene 1948- *WhoSSW 91*
Lione, Chris *BioIn 16*
Lionel, Robert *ConAu 32NR*
Lionette, Dominick John 1922- *St&PR 91*
Lionetti, Frank Carmine 1947- *WhoEmL 91*
Lionni, Leo 1910- *AuBYP 90, BioIn 16, ConDes 90, WhoAm 90, WhoAmA 91*
Liontos, Anthea Linda 1961- *WhoAmW 91*
Lior, Gedalyahu 1931- *BiDrAPA 89*
Liotta, Grace Bellezza *BioIn 16*
Liotta, Louie *BioIn 16*
Liotta, Peter Hearns 1956- *WhoWrEP 89*
Liotta, Ray *BioIn 16*
Liotta, Tony *BioIn 16*
Liou, Ming-Lei 1935- *WhoAm 90*
Lioz, Lawrence Stephen 1945- *WhoE 91*
Lipari, Paul A. 1947- *St&PR 91*
Lipatti, Dinu 1917-1950 *PenDiMP*
Lipchitz, Jacques 1891-1973 *IntDcAA 90, WhoAmA 91N*
Lipe, Charles Grant 1932- *WhoSSW 91*
Lipe, Linda Bon 1948- *WhoAmW 91*
Lipe, Michael Alexander 1944- *WhoWrEP 89*
Lipeles, Maxine Ina 1953- *WhoEmL 91*
Lipely, Gary B. 1954- *St&PR 91*
Lipely, Kim Renee 1955- *WhoAmW 91*
Lipetzky, Paul A. 1946- *St&PR 91*
Lipford, John V. 1940- *St&PR 91*
Lipford, Rocque Edward 1938- *WhoAm 90*
Lipham, Mary Catherine 1947- *WhoAmW 91, WhoE 91*
Lipian, Mark Steven 1957- *BiDrAPA 89*
Lipic, Joseph G. 1935- *St&PR 91*
Lipin, Joan Carol 1947- *WhoE 91*
Lipin, S. Barry 1920- *WhoWor 91*
Lipin, Theodore 1920- *BiDrAPA 89*
Lipinski, Ann Marie *WhoAm 90, WhoAmW 91*
Lipinski, Edouard 1930- *WhoWor 91*
Lipinski, Jane Lynn 1953- *WhoAmW 91*
Lipinski, Joseph F, Jr. 1940- *BiDrAPA 89*
Lipinski, Joseph Floyd, Jr. 1940- *WhoE 91*
Lipinski, Karol Jozef 1790-1861 *PenDiMP*
Lipinski, Tomek 1955- *IntWWM 90*
Lipinski, William Oliver 1937- *WhoAm 90*
Lipinsky, Carol Debra 1957- *WhoSSW 91*
Lipinsky, Edward Solomon 1929- *WhoAm 90*
Lipinsky de Orlov, Lino Sigismondo 1908-1988 *BioIn 16*
Lipinsky de Orlov, Lucian Christopher 1962- *WhoE 91, WhoEmL 91*
Lipira, Robert D. 1946- *ODwPR 91*
Lipira, Robert Dominic 1946- *St&PR 91, WhoE 91*
Lipka, David H. *St&PR 91*
Lipka, David H. 1929- *WhoAm 90*
Lipka, James B. 1949- *WhoEmL 91*
Lipka, James Joseph 1954- *WhoEmL 91*
Lipka, Judy Ann 1960- *WhoSSW 91*
Lipka, Leonard Norman 1932- *WhoSSW 91*
Lipka, Leonhard 1938- *WhoWor 91*
Lipkaman, Christian F. 1950- *St&PR 91, WhoAm 90*
Lipke, Brian Jeffery 1951- *St&PR 91*
Lipke, Janis *BioIn 16*
Lipke, Ken 1929- *St&PR 91*
Lipker, Ronald Jude 1945- *WhoSSW 91*
Lipkin, David 1913- *WhoAm 90*
Lipkin, David Michael 1950- *BiDrAPA 89*
Lipkin, Edward Walter 1949- *WhoEmL 91*
Lipkin, Gary Dennis 1952- *WhoEmL 91*
Lipkin, Gerald H. *BioIn 16*
Lipkin, Gerald Howard 1941- *St&PR 91*
Lipkin, Jerome J. 1933- *St&PR 91*
Lipkin, John Osmond 1939- *BiDrAPA 89*
Lipkin, K Michael 1935- *BiDrAPA 89*
Lipkin, Mack 1907-1989 *BioIn 16*
Lipkin, Mack, Jr. 1943- *WhoAm 90, WhoE 91*
Lipkin, Malcolm Leyland 1932- *IntWWM 90*
Lipkin, Martin 1926- *WhoAm 90*
Lipkin, Mary Castleman Davis 1907- *WhoAmW 91, WhoWor 91*
Lipkin, Samuel J *BiDrAPA 89*
Lipkin, Seymour 1927- *WhoAm 90*
Lipkind, Marvin Lee 1926- *St&PR 91*
Lipkind, William 1904-1974 *AuBYP 90*
Lipking, Lawrence 1934- *ConAu 130, WhoAm 90, WhoWrEP 89*
Lipkovic, Peter 1934- *WhoSSW 91*
Lipkowitz, Marvin H 1928- *BiDrAPA 89*
Lipkowitz, Ronald Lee *BiDrAPA 89*
Lipkowitz, Zena *St&PR 91*
Lipman, Allan M., Jr. 1934- *WhoAm 90*
Lipman, Bernard 1920- *WhoAm 90*
Lipman, Burton E. 1931- *WhoWrEP 89*
Lipman, Daniel G *BiDrAPA 89*
Lipman, Daniel Gordon 1912- *WhoWor 91*
Lipman, David 1931- *AuBYP 90, WhoAm 90, WhoWrEP 89*
Lipman, Ellen Louise *BiDrAPA 89*
Lipman, Eugene Jay 1919- *WhoAm 90, WhoE 91*
Lipman, Frederick D. 1935- *WhoAm 90*
Lipman, Howard W 1905- *WhoAmA 91*
Lipman, Ira A. 1940- *St&PR 91*
Lipman, Ira Ackerman 1940- *WhoAm 90, WhoE 91, WhoSSW 91*
Lipman, Jean 1909- *BioIn 16*
Lipman, Joel Abelman 1942- *WhoWrEP 89*
Lipman, Kenneth M *BiDrAPA 89*
Lipman, Matthew 1923- *ConAu 32NR, WhoE 91*
Lipman, Michael 1934- *St&PR 91*
Lipman, Michael 1954- *IntWWM 90*
Lipman, Richard Paul 1935- *WhoE 91, WhoWor 91*
Lipman, Samuel 1934- *WhoAm 90*
Lipman, Vivian David 1921-1990 *ConAu 131*
Lipman, Wynona M. *WhoAmW 91*
Lipman-Wulf, Peter 1905- *WhoAmA 91, WhoE 91*
Lipmann, Fritz A. 1899-1986 *WorAlBi*
Lipmanowicz, Henri 1938- *St&PR 91*
Lipner, Harry 1922- *WhoAm 90*
Lipof, Irene Doris 1946- *WhoSSW 91*
Lipoff, Alvin 1930- *St&PR 91*
Lipofsky, Marvin B 1938- *WhoAmA 91*
Lipon, Johnny 1922- *Ballpl 90*
Liponis, Kim *BiDrAPA 89*
Lipovetsky, Leonidas 1937- *IntWWM 90*
Lipovitch, Fred Barnett 1937- *BiDrAPA 89*
Lipovitz, Joseph Zev 1889-1962 *BioIn 16*
Lipowski, Zbigniew J 1924- *BiDrAPA 89*
Lipowski, Zbigniew Jerzy 1924- *WhoAm 90*
Lipp, Donald Ralph 1935- *St&PR 91*
Lipp, Norma 1938- *WhoWor 91*
Lipp, Robert I. 1938- *WhoAm 90*
Lipp, Wilma 1925- *IntWWM 90, PenDiMP*
Lippa, Linda Susan Mottow 1951- *WhoAmW 91, WhoE 91*
Lippard, Lucy Rowland 1937- *WhoAmA 91, WhoWrEP 89*
Lippard, Stephen James 1940- *WhoAm 90*
Lippe, Aschwin 1914-1988 *BioIn 16*
Lippe, Melvin Karl 1933- *WhoAm 90*
Lippe, Pamela Towen 1952- *WhoAmW 91*
Lippe, Philipp Maria 1929- *WhoAm 90, WhoWor 91*
Lippe, Rudolf Zur 1937- *WhoWor 91*
Lipper, Arthur, III 1931- *St&PR 91*
Lipper, Clemens 1742-1813 *PenDiDA 89*
Lipper, Kenneth 1941- *WhoAm 90, WhoWor 91*
Lipper, Steven 1943- *BiDrAPA 89*
Lipper, Wilhelm Ferdinand 1742?-1800 *PenDiDA 89*
Lipperheide, Federico 1928- *WhoWor 91*
Lippershey, Hans 1587?-1619? *WorAlBi*
Lippert, Albert 1925- *St&PR 91, WhoAm 90*
Lippert, Christopher Nelson 1952- *WhoEmL 91*
Lippert, Felice Sally 1930- *St&PR 91*
Lippert, George Richard 1922- *St&PR 91*
Lippert, Herbert 1930- *WhoWor 91*
Lippert, Jack K. *BioIn 16*
Lippert, Lawrence Dennis 1947- *WhoSSW 91*
Lippert, Lawrence John 1937- *St&PR 91*
Lippert, Leon *WhoAmA 91N*
Lippert, Marion 1939- *IntWWM 90*
Lippert, Richard J. 1935- *St&PR 91*
Lippert, Robert 1914- *BiDrAPA 89*
Lippert, Ronald Steven 1949- *WhoWrEP 89*
Lippert, Thomas Joseph 1932- *St&PR 91*
Lippes, Richard James 1944- *WhoWor 91*
Lippi, D.M. 1914- *St&PR 91*
Lippi, Filippino 1457?-1504 *IntDcAA 90*
Lippi, Filippo 1402?-1469 *WorAlBi*
Lippi, Filippo 1406?-1469 *IntDcAA 90*
Lippi, Laura Anne 1952- *WhoEmL 91*
Lippin, Richard B. 1946- *ODwPR 91*
Lippincott & Margulies *PenDiDA 89*
Lippincott, Barbara Barnes 1934- *WhoAmW 91*
Lippincott, Barton Hirst 1925- *St&PR 91*
Lippincott, Charles Kenneth 1954- *BiDrAPA 89*
Lippincott, Gene L. 1944- *St&PR 91*
Lippincott, Gordon 1909- *PenDiDA 89*
Lippincott, James Andrew 1930- *WhoAm 90*
Lippincott, Janet 1918- *WhoAmA 91, WhoAmW 91*
Lippincott, Joseph Wharton 1887-1976 *AuBYP 90*
Lippincott, Marty *BioIn 16*
Lippincott, Philip *BioIn 16*
Lippincott, Philip Edward 1935- *St&PR 91, WhoAm 90, WhoE 91*
Lippincott, Richard *BiDrAPA 89*
Lippincott, Sara Jane Clarke 1823-1904 *BioIn 16*
Lippincott, Sarah Lee 1920- *WhoAm 90*
Lippincott, Walter Heulings, Jr. 1939- *WhoAm 90*
Lipping, Alar *WhoSSW 91*
Lippitt, Alexander F. 1923- *St&PR 91*
Lippitt, Elizabeth Charlotte *WhoAmW 91, WhoWor 91*
Lippitt, Ronald *BioIn 16*
Lippitz, Richard Allen, Sr. 1936- *St&PR 91*
Lippman, Abbott A 1907- *BiDrAPA 89*
Lippman, Alfred Julian 1900- *WhoSSW 91, WhoWor 91*
Lippman, Barry 1949- *WhoAm 90, WhoE 91*
Lippman, Bernard A. *BioIn 16*
Lippman, Cathie-Ann *BiDrAPA 89*
Lippman, David Harris *BiDrAPA 89*
Lippman, Ellen Marks 1943- *BiDrAPA 89*
Lippman, Glenn 1953- *BiDrAPA 89*
Lippman, John A. 1949- *St&PR 91*
Lippman, Judith 1929- *WhoAmA 91*
Lippman, Lee 1937- *St&PR 91*
Lippman, Sid 1914- *BioIn 16*
Lippman, Stacey *BioIn 16*
Lippman, William Jennings 1925- *WhoAm 90*
Lippman, William O., Jr. *St&PR 91*
Lippmann, Friedrich 1932- *IntWWM 90*
Lippmann, Janet 1936- *BioIn 16*
Lippmann, Janet Gurian 1936- *WhoAmA 91*
Lippmann, Michael 1944- *WhoE 91*
Lippmann, Steven B 1943- *BiDrAPA 89*
Lippmann, Walter 1889-1974 *BioIn 16, MajTwCW, WorAlBi*
Lippner, Alicejane 1944- *WhoE 91*
Lippo, Tom A. 1955- *WhoEmL 91*
Lippold, Richard 1915- *WhoAm 90, WhoAmA 91*
Lipps, Carolyn S. 1943- *WhoAmW 91*
Lipps, Raymond Edward 1960- *WhoE 91*
Lippsett, Paula Barbara *BiDrAPA 89*
Lipschitz, Alan 1951- *BiDrAPA 89, WhoE 91*
Lipschitz, Ervin 1926- *BiDrAPA 89*
Lipschultz, Frederick Phillip 1937- *WhoE 91*
Lipschultz, M. Richard 1913- *WhoWor 91*
Lipschultz, Maurice A 1912- *WhoAmA 91*
Lipschultz, William H. 1930- *St&PR 91*
Lipschutz, Ilse Hempel 1923- *WhoAm 90*
Lipschutz, Louis Barry 1954- *BiDrAPA 89*
Lipschutz, Marc Harris 1948- *BiDrAPA 89*
Lipschutz, Martin S. 1954- *BiDrAPA 89*
Lipschutz, Michael Elazar 1937- *WhoAm 90*
Lipschutz-Yevick, Miriam Amalie 1924- *WhoE 91*
Lipscomb, Anna Rose Feeny 1945- *WhoAmW 91, WhoWor 91*
Lipscomb, Aquila Rudolph 1949- *WhoE 91*
Lipscomb, Belinda *BioIn 16*
Lipscomb, G. D. 1898- *EarBlAP*
Lipscomb, Guy Fleming, Jr 1917- *WhoAmA 91, WhoSSW 91*
Lipscomb, John Bailey 1950- *WhoSSW 91*
Lipscomb, Oscar Hugh 1931- *WhoAm 90, WhoSSW 91*
Lipscomb, Patricia Anne 1948- *BiDrAPA 89*
Lipscomb, Paul Rogers 1914- *WhoAm 90*
Lipscomb, Sally T. 1948- *WhoAmW 91*
Lipscomb, Thomas Heber, III 1938- *WhoAm 90*
Lipscomb, Thomas Joseph 1946- *WhoEmL 91*
Lipscomb, Wendell R 1920- *BiDrAPA 89*

Lipscomb, William Nunn, Jr. 1919- *WhoAm 90, WhoE 91, WhoWor 91*
Lipscomb, William O., Jr. 1939- *St&PR 91*
Lipscomb, Willis Grandy 1901-1988 *BioIn 16*
Lipscomb-Brown, Edra Evadean 1919- *WhoAm 90*
Lipscombe, Clarence Douglas, Jr. 1925- *St&PR 91*
Lipset, David 1951- *ConAu 129*
Lipset, Seymour Martin 1922- *WhoAm 90, WhoWrEP 89*
Lipsett, Julius *NewYTBS 90*
Lipsett, Melvin M *BiDrAPA 89*
Lipsett, Suzanne 1943- *ConAu 132*
Lipsett, Valerie Alayne 1937- *WhoE 91*
Lipsey, David 1948- *ConAu 130*
Lipsey, John C. 1930- *WhoAm 90*
Lipsey, Richard Allan 1930- *WhoWor 91*
Lipsey, Richard George 1928- *WhoAm 90*
Lipsey, Robert Edward 1926- *WhoAm 90*
Lipsey, Stanford 1927- *St&PR 91, WhoAm 90, WhoE 91*
Lipshie, Joseph 1911- *WhoAm 90*
Lipshie, Tamara Leah *BiDrAPA 89*
Lipshutz, Daniel 1906- *BiDrAPA 89*
Lipshutz, Laurel Sprung *BiDrAPA 89*
Lipshutz, Robert Jerome 1921- *WhoAm 90*
Lipsig, Ethan 1948- *WhoEmL 91*
Lipsig, Harry 1901- *BioIn 16*
Lipsig, Robert J. 1942- *St&PR 91*
Lipsig, Stephen *BiDrAPA 89*
Lipsitch, Ian Irving 1942- *BiDrAPA 89*
Lipsitt, Don R 1927- *BiDrAPA 89*
Lipsitt, Lewis Paeff 1929- *WhoAm 90, WhoE 91*
Lipsitt, Martin Frederic 1934- *WhoAm 90, WhoE 91*
Lipsitz, George R 1947- *ConAu 32NR*
Lipsitz, Robert Joel 1949- *WhoE 91*
Lipsius, Steven H 1939- *BiDrAPA 89*
Lipska, Eva 1945- *ConAu 132*
Lipsker, Eileen Franklin- *BioIn 16*
Lipski, C. J. 1943- *WhoAmW 91*
Lipski, Donald G 1947- *WhoAmA 91*
Lipski, John Gabriel *BiDrAPA 89*
Lipski, Sharyn Ann 1945- *WhoE 91*
Lipski, Wayne Edward 1956- *WhoEmL 91*
Lipskin, Bernard *ODwPR 91*
Lipsky, David Bruce 1939- *WhoAm 90*
Lipsky, Lawrence J. 1926- *St&PR 91*
Lipsky, Leonard 1936- *WhoE 91*
Lipsky, Linda Ethel 1939- *WhoAmW 91*
Lipsky, Michael 1940- *WhoAm 90*
Lipsky, Richard Ronan 1936- *St&PR 91*
Lipsky, Robert David 1956- *St&PR 91*
Lipsky, Stephen Edward 1932- *St&PR 91, WhoAm 90*
Lipsman, Paulee 1947- *WhoAmW 91*
Lipsman, Richard Marc 1946- *WhoE 91, WhoEmL 91, WhoWor 91*
Lipsman, William Stuart 1949- *WhoEmL 91*
Lipson, Allen S. 1942- *St&PR 91*
Lipson, Avis Ruth 1951- *WhoAmW 91*
Lipson, Bernice B. 1933- *St&PR 91*
Lipson, Channing T *BiDrAPA 89*
Lipson, Goldie 1905- *WhoAm 90, WhoAmA 91*
Lipson, Herbert Harold 1924- *St&PR 91*
Lipson, Jack 1943-1989 *BioIn 16*
Lipson, Jack Louis 1932- *WhoAm 90*
Lipson, Leslie Michael 1912- *WhoAm 90*
Lipson, Leslie P *BiDrAPA 89*
Lipson, Marshall David 1946- *WhoE 91*
Lipson, Melvin Alan 1936- *WhoAm 90*
Lipson, Milton *BiDrAPA 89*
Lipson, Paul S. 1915- *WhoAm 90*
Lipson, Rachel Elizabeth *BiDrAPA 89*
Lipson, Sheldon Robert 1932- *WhoE 91*
Lipstate, Jo Ann 1930- *WhoAmW 91*
Lipstone, Howard Harold 1928- *St&PR 91, WhoAm 90*
Lipstone, Jane N. 1931- *WhoAmW 91*
Lipsyte, Robert *BioIn 16*
Lipsyte, Robert 1938- *AuBYP 90, ChlLR 23 [port]*
Liptak, David 1949- *IntWWM 90*
Liptak, Gregory J. *BioIn 16*
Liptak, Gregory J. 1940- *St&PR 91*
Liptak, Irene Frances 1926- *WhoAmW 91*
Liptak, John Frank 1945- *St&PR 91*
Liptak, Robert William 1939- *WhoAm 90*
Lipthratt, Charles Vernon 1937- *St&PR 91*
Lipton, Alan 1938- *St&PR 91*
Lipton, Alan A 1928- *BiDrAPA 89*
Lipton, Allan 1938- *WhoAm 90*
Lipton, Allen David 1940- *WhoSSW 91*
Lipton, Alvin Elliot 1945- *WhoEmL 91*
Lipton, Barbara *WhoAmW 91*
Lipton, Barbara B *WhoAmA 91*
Lipton, Barbara S 1919- *BiDrAPA 89*
Lipton, Brian Paul *BiDrAPA 89*
Lipton, Bronna *ODwPR 91*
Lipton, Bronna Jane 1951- *WhoE 91*
Lipton, Charles 1928- *ODwPR 91, St&PR 91, WhoAm 90*
Lipton, Daniel B. *IntWWM 90*
Lipton, Dean 1919- *ConAu 31NR*
Lipton, Edgar Louis *BiDrAPA 89*
Lipton, Edmond 1910- *BiDrAPA 89*
Lipton, Frank Robert *BiDrAPA 89*
Lipton, George Lucien 1936- *BiDrAPA 89*
Lipton, Harvey L. 1925- *St&PR 91*
Lipton, Howard Lee *WhoAm 90*
Lipton, Ira David *BiDrAPA 89*
Lipton, Jeffrey *BioIn 16*
Lipton, Jeffrey M. 1942- *St&PR 91*
Lipton, Jeffrey Marc 1942- *WhoAm 90, WhoE 91*
Lipton, Joan Elaine *WhoAm 90*
Lipton, Judith Eve 1951- *BiDrAPA 89*
Lipton, Leah *WhoAmA 91*
Lipton, Leah 1928- *WhoAmW 91, WhoE 91*
Lipton, Lester 1936- *WhoWor 91*
Lipton, Lorian 1957- *WhoAmW 91*
Lipton, Mark K. *St&PR 91*
Lipton, Martha 1916- *IntWWM 90*
Lipton, Martin 1931- *BioIn 16, WhoAm 90*
Lipton, Merrill I 1924- *BiDrAPA 89*
Lipton, Mildred Ceres 1921- *WhoAmW 91*
Lipton, Morris A *BiDrAPA 89*
Lipton, Morris A. 1915-1989 *BioIn 16*
Lipton, Peggy *BioIn 16*
Lipton, Sidney 1906- *OxCPMus*
Lipton, Simon M *BiDrAPA 89*
Lipton, Sondra *WhoAmA 91*
Lipton, Stuart Arthur 1950- *WhoAm 90*
Lipton, Sydney 1926- *WhoE 91*
Lipton, Terry David *BiDrAPA 89*
Lipton, Thomas J. 1850-1931 *WorAlBi*
Lipton, William Lawrence 1944- *WhoWrEP 89*
Lipton, Zelda 1923- *St&PR 91*
Liptzin, Benjamin 1945- *BiDrAPA 89, WhoAm 90, WhoE 91*
Liptzin, Myron B *BiDrAPA 89*
Liptzin, Sol 1901- *WhoWor 91*
Lipworth, Stephen 1939- *St&PR 91*
Lipzin, Janis Crystal 1945- *WhoAmA 91*
Liquori, Martin William, Jr. 1949- *ConAu 130, WhoAm 90*
Liquori, Marty *ConAu 130*
Liquori, Marty 1949- *WorAlBi*
Lira, Jose Arturo 1950- *WhoHisp 91*
Lira, Manoel Bastos 1913- *WhoWor 91*
Lira, Patrick 1937- *WhoSSW 91*
Lira-Powell, Julianne Hortensia 1945- *WhoHisp 91*
Lirette, Jerry Robert 1948- *WhoAm 90*
Liriano, Nelson 1964- *Ballpl 90*
Liriano, Nelson Arturo 1964- *WhoHisp 91*
Lirosi, Joseph A. 1949- *St&PR 91*
Lis, Anthony Stanley 1918- *WhoAm 90, WhoSSW 91, WhoWor 91*
Lis, Anthony Stanley 1956- *IntWWM 90*
Lis, Daniel T. 1946- *St&PR 91*
Lis, Edward Francis 1918- *WhoAm 90*
Lis, Janet Chapman 1943- *WhoAmA 91*
Lis, Joe 1946- *Ballpl 90*
Lisa Lisa *BioIn 16*
Lisa, Isabelle O'Neill 1934- *WhoAmW 91*
Lisa, Joseph Paul 1932- *St&PR 91*
Lisa, Manuel 1772-1820 *WhNaAH*
Lisagor, Peter Irvin 1915-1976 *BioIn 16*
Lisan, Amha Tume 1949- *WhoSSW 91*
Lisanby, James Walker 1928- *WhoAm 90*
Lisansky, Edgar Jonathan 1950- *BiDrAPA 89*
Lisansky, Ephraim T 1912- *BiDrAPA 89*
Lisardi, Andrew H. *WhoHisp 91*
Lisauskas, Anthony J. 1940- *St&PR 91*
Lisboa, Irene 1892-1958 *EncCoWW*
Lisboa-Farrow, Elizabeth Oliver 1947- *WhoAmW 91*
Lisby, Gregory Carroll 1952- *WhoSSW 91*
Lisch, Howard 1950- *WhoE 91, WhoEmL 91, WhoWor 91*
Lischer, Ludwig Frederick 1915- *WhoAm 90*
Lischewski, Hans-Christian 1944- *WhoE 91*
Lischke, Gottfried 1938- *WhoWor 91*
Liscom, Clayton Lee 1947- *St&PR 91, WhoEmL 91*
Liscombe, R. W. *ConAu 129*
Liscow, Andrew S. 1956- *St&PR 91*
Liscow, Christian Ludwig 1701-1760 *DcLB 97 [port]*
Lisec, Kenneth John 1942- *WhoE 91*
Lisenbee, Alvis Lee 1940- *WhoAm 90*
Lisenbee, Hod 1898-1987 *Ballpl 90*
Lisenby, Dorrece Edenfield 1942- *WhoSSW 91*
Lish, Gordon *BioIn 16*
Lish, Gordon 1934- *WhoAm 90*
Lish, Gordon Jay 1934- *WhoWrEP 89*
Lisher, John Leonard 1950- *WhoEmL 91*
Lishka, Edward Joseph 1949- *WhoEmL 91, WhoWor 91*
Lisi, Penelope Leitner 1951- *WhoAmW 91*
Lisi, Virna 1937- *BioIn 16*
Lisiak, Elena 1951- *BiDrAPA 89*
Lisicki, Bernice Marie 1963- *WhoAmW 91*
Lising, Jose Virtucio 1947- *WhoWor 91*
Lisio, Donald John 1934- *WhoAm 90*
Lisitski, Jon Louis 1939- *St&PR 91*
Lisitzky, Charles Edward *St&PR 91N*
Lisk, Joanne Estelle Jackson 1933- *WhoAmW 91*
Lisk, Penelope E Tsaltas 1959- *WhoAmA 91*
Lisk, Robert Douglas 1934- *WhoAm 90*
Liska, Ad 1906- *Ballpl 90*
Liska, Edward S *BiDrAPA 89*
Liska, Eileen Marguerite 1948- *WhoAmW 91*
Liska, George 1922- *WhoAm 90*
Liska, Ivan *WhoWor 91*
Liska, Ivan 1950- *BioIn 16*
Liska, Steven *BioIn 16*
Lisker, Arthur 1929- *St&PR 91*
Lisker, Harvey 1955- *St&PR 91*
Lisker, Larry 1927- *St&PR 91*
Lisker, Martin 1951- *St&PR 91*
Lisker, Sara 1918- *WhoAmA 91*
Lisker, Sonia 1933- *AuBYP 90*
Liskey, A. Keith 1944- *St&PR 91*
Liskin, Barbara Ann 1952- *BiDrAPA 89, WhoAmW 91, WhoE 91*
Liskov, Barbara Huberman 1939- *WhoAm 90, WhoAmW 91*
Liskov, David Michael *BiDrAPA 89*
Liskow, Barry I 1943- *BiDrAPA 89*
Lisle, Janet Taylor 1947- *BioIn 16*
Lisle, John C. 1941- *St&PR 91*
Lisle, Robert Walton 1927- *WhoAm 90*
Lisman, Bernard 1918- *WhoE 91*
Lisman, Elias 1919- *WhoE 91*
Lisman, William Franklyn 1903- *St&PR 91*
Lisnek, Paul Michael 1958- *WhoWor 91*
Lisnianskaia, Inna L'vovna 1928- *EncCoWW*
Lisoni, Gail Marie Landtbom 1949- *WhoAmW 91*
Lisovska, Olga 1928- *EncCoWW*
Lisowitz, Gerald M 1930- *BiDrAPA 89*
Lisowski, Gabriel 1946- *BioIn 16*
Lisowski, Joseph Anthony 1944- *WhoWrEP 89*
Lispector, Clarice 1924-1977 *BioIn 16*
Lispector, Clarice 1925-1977 *FemiCLE, WorAlBi, WorAu 1980 [port]*
Liss, Dorson Norman 1941- *BiDrAPA 89*
Liss, Herbert Myron 1931- *WhoAm 90, WhoWor 91*
Liss, Howard 1922- *AuBYP 90*
Liss, Jay Lawrence 1941- *BiDrAPA 89*
Liss, Norman 1932- *WhoWor 91*
Liss, Victor 1937- *St&PR 91*
Lissant, Ellen Marie 1922- *WhoAmW 91*
Lissauer, Ernst *BioIn 16*
Lissauer, Michael 1947- *ODwPR 91*
Lisse, Allan 1926- *St&PR 91*
Lisser, Amy *BiDrAPA 89*
Lisses, Larry Joel 1947- *WhoAm 90*
Lissim, Simon 1900-1981 *WhoAmA 91N*
Lissinna, Manfred *St&PR 91*
Lissitsky, Eleazar Markevich 1890-1941 *PenDiDA 89*
Lissitz, Robert Wooster 1941- *WhoAm 90*
Lissman, Barry Alan 1952- *WhoAm 90*
Lissner, John *ODwPR 91*
List, Andre *BioIn 16*
List, Anthony Francis 1942- *WhoE 91*
List, Birgit *BioIn 16*
List, Clair Z 1953- *WhoAmA 91*
List, David Patton 1920- *WhoAm 90*
List, Diane Ruth 1948- *WhoAmW 91*
List, Douglass William 1955- *WhoE 91*
List, Ericson John 1939- *WhoAm 90*
List, Eugene 1918- *PenDiMP*
List, Friedrich 1789-1846 *BioIn 16*
List, Guido von 1848-1919 *EncO&P 3*
List, Irwin 1932- *St&PR 91*
List, J.G. *PenDiDA 89*
List, Johann Georg Friedrich *PenDiDA 89*
List, John DeWitt 1935- *WhoAm 90*
List, John E. 1925?- *BioIn 16*
List, Phillip L. 1953- *St&PR 91*
List, Raymond Edward 1944- *WhoAm 90*
List, Stephen Joel *BiDrAPA 89*
List, Thomas *BioIn 16*
List, Vera G 1908- *WhoAmA 91*
Lister, Anne 1791-1840 *FemiCLE*
Lister, Ardele Diane 1950- *WhoAmA 91*
Lister, Elena Goldstein *BiDrAPA 89*
Lister, Elena Goldstein 1957- *WhoE 91*
Lister, Eric David 1948- *BiDrAPA 89*
Lister, Harry Joseph 1936- *St&PR 91, WhoAm 90*
Lister, Herbert Earl 1929- *St&PR 91*
Lister, Joseph 1827-1912 *BioIn 16, WorAlBi*
Lister, Louis 1914- *WhoAm 90*
Lister, Philip Nathaniel 1953- *BiDrAPA 89*
Lister, Priscilla M. 1949- *WhoAmW 91*
Lister, Stephen Anthony 1942- *St&PR 91*
Lister, Stephen L. 1942- *St&PR 91*
Lister, Sue Ann 1950- *WhoAmW 91*
Lister, Thomas Mosie 1921- *WhoAm 90*
Listerud, Mark Boyd 1924- *WhoWor 91*
Listfield, Emily *BioIn 16*
Listgarten, Max Albert 1935- *WhoAm 90*
Listi, Frank Joseph 1945- *St&PR 91*
Listinsky, Jay John 1951- *WhoSSW 91*
Listl, Joseph 1929- *WhoWor 91*
Listokin, Robert 1933- *IntWWM 90*
Liston, Alan A. 1946- *WhoAm 90*
Liston, Dennis Michael *BiDrAPA 89*
Liston, Florence Cary *WhoAmA 91N*
Liston, Harry 1843-1929 *OxCPMus*
Liston, Mary Frances 1920- *WhoAm 90*
Liston, Melba *BioIn 16*
Liston, Robert A. 1927- *AuBYP 90, ConAu 30NR*
Liston, Timothy Michael 1931- *St&PR 91*
Liszt, Ferenc 1811-1886 *PenDiMP, -A*
Liszt, Franz 1811-1886 *BioIn 16, WorAlBi*
Litaker, Dianne Smith *BiDrAPA 89*
Litaker, Thomas 1904-1976 *WhoAmA 91N*
Litan, Michael Morris *BiDrAPA 89*
Litan, Robert E 1950- *ConAu 131*
Litan, Robert Eli 1950- *WhoAm 90*
Litchard, Mary Jane 1951- *WhoAmW 91*
Litchfield, Ada Bassett 1916- *WhoWrEP 89*
Litchfield, Jean Anne 1942- *WhoAmW 91, WhoWor 91*
Litchfield, John Thomas, Jr. 1912- *WhoAm 90*
Litchfield, Lawrence H. *ODwPR 91*
Litchfield, Paul W. 1875-1959 *WorAlBi*
Litchfield, Richard William 1944- *WhoE 91*
Litchfield, Thompson Dumont 1917- *St&PR 91*
Litchman, Joseph F. 1927- *St&PR 91*
Lite, Victor 1939- *St&PR 91*
Liteanu, Eugeniu *BiDrAPA 89*
Liteanu, Ronald Radu *BiDrAPA 89*
Lites, James *WhoAm 90*
Litewka, Albert Bernard 1942- *WhoAm 90*
Litewka, Jack 1945- *WhoWrEP 89*
Litfin, Karen *BioIn 16*
Litfin, Richard Albert 1918- *WhoAm 90*
Litherland, Albert Edward 1928- *WhoAm 90*
Lithgoe, Thomas James, Jr. 1947- *St&PR 91*
Lithgow, John *BioIn 16*
Lithgow, John 1945- *WorAlBi*
Lithgow, John Arthur 1945- *WhoAm 90*
Lithiby, Beatrice Ethel 1889- *BiDWomA*
Lithman, Jerry Richard 1948- *BiDrAPA 89*
Lithman, Yngve Georg 1943- *ConAu 132*
Lithwick, Norman Harvey 1938- *WhoAm 90*
Litin, Donald E. 1919- *St&PR 91*
Litke, Arthur Ludwig 1922- *WhoAm 90*
Litke, Bruce William 1928- *St&PR 91*
Litke, Donald Paul 1934- *WhoAm 90*
Litke, James W. 1955- *St&PR 91*
Litke, Jean A. 1929- *St&PR 91*
Litke, Steven H. 1955- *St&PR 91*
Litle, Robert Forgie 1924- *WhoSSW 91*
Litman, Bernard 1920- *WhoAm 90*
Litman, Bert 1917- *St&PR 91*
Litman, George Irving 1939- *WhoAm 90*
Litman, James L. 1936- *St&PR 91*
Litman, Raymond S. 1936- *St&PR 91*
Litman, Robert Barry 1947- *WhoAm 90, WhoE 91, WhoEmL 91, WhoWor 91, WhoWrEP 89*
Litman, Robert E *BiDrAPA 89*
Litman, Roslyn Margolis 1928- *WhoAm 90*
Litman, Ruth Ann 1959- *WhoAmW 91*
Litoff, Judy Barrett 1944- *WhoE 91*
Litolff, Henry Charles 1818-1891 *PenDiMP A*
Litovitz, Gary Lane 1953- *BiDrAPA 89*
Litow, Joel David 1947- *WhoAm 90*
Litrenta, Frances *BiDrAPA 89*
Litrenta, Frances Marie 1928- *WhoAmW 91, WhoE 91*
Litrides, Lindy 1952- *WhoAmW 91*
Litrownik, Alan Jay 1945- *WhoAm 90*
Litschauer, Charles A. 1928- *St&PR 91*
Litschgi, A. Byrne 1920- *St&PR 91, WhoAm 90*
Litschgi, Richard John 1937- *WhoAm 90*
Litsey, Edwin Carlile 1874-1970 *LiHiK*
Litsey, Sarah *WhoWrEP 89*
Litsey, Sarah 1903- *LiHiK*
Litsinger, Richard Calvin 1934- *WhoAm 90*
Litsky, Andrew L. *ODwPR 91*
Litsky, Warren 1924- *WhoAm 90*
Litster, James David 1938- *WhoAm 90*
Litt, Iris 1928- *WhoWrEP 89*
Litt, Iris F. 1940- *WhoAm 90*
Litt, Mitchell 1932- *WhoAm 90*
Litt, Morton Herbert 1926- *WhoAm 90*
Litt, Nahum 1935- *WhoAm 90*
Littauer, Paula *BioIn 16*
Littauer, Vladimir S. *BioIn 16*
Littauer, Vladimir S. 1893-1989 *ConAu 129*
Litteken, John Dan 1948- *St&PR 91*
Littel, Mark 1953- *Ballpl 90*

Littell, Danny Lane 1941- St&PR 91
Littell, Franklin Hamlin 1917- WhoAm 90
Littell, Gaycelin Gray 1961- WhoAmW 91
Littell, Michael John 1960- WhoSSW 91
Littell, Norman Mather 1899- BioIn 16
Littell, Patricia L. 1954- WhoAmW 91
Littell, Robert AuBYP 90
Littell, Robert 1935- BioIn 16, SpyFic, TwCCr&M 91
Littell, Vicki C. 1946- WhoAmW 91
Littell, Wallace William 1922- WhoAm 90
Littell, Walter Damrosch 1932- ODwPR 91
Littell, William 1768-1824 LiHiK
Litten, C. Scott 1949- St&PR 91
Litten, Frederic Nelson 1885- AuBYP 90
Litten, H. Randall 1937- St&PR 91
Litterer, Karen Sue 1962- WhoAmW 91
Littig, Lawrence William 1927- WhoAm 90
Littke, Lael BioIn 16
Littke, Lael J. 1929- ConAu 33NR
Littky, Dennis BioIn 16
Little Abraham WhNaAH
Little Anthony 1940- DrBlPA 90
Little Anthony and the Imperials EncPR&S 89
Little Crow 1810?-1863 WhNaAH
Little Feat ConMus 4 [port], EncPR&S 89
Little Mountain 1805?-1866 WhNaAH
Little Paul WhNaAH
Little Priest WhNaAH
Little Raven 1820?-1889 WhNaAH
Little Richard BioIn 16
Little Richard 1935- DrBlPA 90, EncPR&S 89, OxCPMus, WorAlBi
Little Ricky Rocko BioIn 16
Little Robe 1828-1886 WhNaAH
Little Turtle 1752-1812 WhNaAH
Little Warrior WhNaAH
Little Wolf 1820?-1904 WhNaAH [port]
Little, Alan Brian 1925- WhoAm 90
Little, Angela Capobianco 1920- WhoAmW 91
Little, Anna Denise 1954- WhoAmW 91, WhoWor 91
Little, Anthony Andron 1963- WhoSSW 91
Little, Araminta BioIn 16
Little, Arthur Dehon 1944- St&PR 91, WhoAm 90
Little, Brenda Joyce 1945- WhoSSW 91
Little, Brian F. 1943- St&PR 91, WhoAm 90
Little, Brian Paul 1943- WhoE 91
Little, Bryan 1959- Ballpl 90
Little, C. Bailey, Jr. 1937- St&PR 91
Little, Carl Eugene 1927- St&PR 91
Little, Carl Maurice 1924- WhoAm 90
Little, Cervera Rochester, Jr. 1942- WhoE 91
Little, Charles Edward 1926- WhoAm 90, WhoWor 91
Little, Charles Edward, Sr. 1923- WhoAm 90
Little, Christopher Mark 1941- St&PR 91
Little, Clarence Cook 1888-1971 DcScB S2
Little, Cleavon 1939- DrBlPA 90, WorAlBi
Little, Cleavon Jake 1939- WhoAm 90
Little, Cyrus Harvey 1859-1926 AmLegL
Little, Debra Krueger 1960- WhoAmW 91
Little, Dennis Gage 1935- St&PR 91, WhoAm 90
Little, Diane M BiDrAPA 89
Little, Donald Alan 1935- St&PR 91
Little, Elbert Luther, Jr. 1907- WhoAm 90
Little, Elizabeth Chapman BioIn 16
Little, Emily Browning 1951- WhoAmW 91
Little, Francis J. 1934-1990 NewYTBS 90
Little, Frank 1879-1917 EncAL
Little, Fred A., Jr. 1936- WhoAm 90, WhoSSW 91
Little, Freed Sebastian 1926- WhoSSW 91
Little, George Daniel 1929- WhoAm 90
Little, Geraldine Clinton 1923- WhoWrEP 89
Little, H. Ganse BioIn 16, NewYTBS 90
Little, Hazel Marie 1934- WhoAmW 91
Little, Henri Bayliffe 1924- St&PR 91, WhoAm 90
Little, Ian Donald 1953- IntWWM 90
Little, Jack Edward 1938- St&PR 91, WhoAm 90
Little, James 1952- WhoAmA 91
Little, James A. 1933- ODwPR 91
Little, James B. 1935- St&PR 91
Little, James Hart 1956- BiDrAPA 89
Little, James S. 1941- St&PR 91
Little, Jan Nielsen 1958- WhoEmL 91
Little, Janet 1759-1813 FemiCLE
Little, Janice Raye 1940- WhoSSW 91
Little, Jean 1932- AuBYP 90, FemiCLE
Little, John 1907- WhoAmA 91N
Little, John Alexander 1935- WhoSSW 91
Little, John Andrew 1937- St&PR 91
Little, John Bertram 1929- WhoAm 90
Little, John Dozier 1871- AmLegL
Little, John Dutton Conant 1928- WhoAm 90, WhoWor 91
Little, John Reveley 1946- WhoAm 90
Little, John Sebastian 1851-1916 BioIn 16
Little, John Stanley 1931- St&PR 91
Little, John Wesley 1935- WhoAm 90
Little, John William, III 1944- WhoAm 90
Little, Jon Warren 1952- WhoSSW 91
Little, Josiah Storer 1801-1862 AmLegL
Little, Judith Ann 1944- St&PR 91
Little, Julia Elizabeth 1932- WhoAmW 91
Little, Ken Dawson 1947- WhoAmA 91
Little, Kenneth E. 1929- St&PR 91
Little, Kerry WhoWrEP 89
Little, Lessie Jones 1906-1986 BioIn 16, SmATA 60 [port]
Little, Lester Knox 1935- WhoAm 90
Little, Lewis Auburn 1933- WhoE 91
Little, Loren Everton 1941- WhoWor 91
Little, Loyd Harry, Jr. 1940- WhoAm 90, WhoWrEP 89
Little, Lucretia Ann BiDrAPA 89
Little, Malcolm 1925-1965 BioIn 16, MajTwCW
Little, Margaret L. 1952- BiDrAPA 89
Little, Martha Jane 1951- BiDrAPA 89
Little, Mary E. 1912- AuBYP 90
Little, Matthias 1913- St&PR 91
Little, Michael Alan 1937- WhoE 91
Little, Michael F. 1943- St&PR 91
Little, Michael Frederick 1943- WhoSSW 91
Little, Ned Allen 1940- WhoE 91
Little, Olga A G BiDrAPA 89
Little, Pamela Anne 1954- St&PR 91
Little, Philip Francis 1824-1897 DcCanB 12
Little, Polly A 1954- WhoAmA 91
Little, R. Donald 1937- WhoE 91, WhoWor 91
Little, Rich 1938- WorAlBi
Little, Richard Allen 1939- WhoWor 91
Little, Richard Caruthers 1938- WhoAm 90
Little, Richard Le Roy 1944- WhoAm 90
Little, Robert Andrews 1915- WhoAm 90
Little, Robert Carter 1925- WhoAm 90
Little, Robert Colby 1920- WhoAm 90
Little, Robert David 1937- WhoAm 90
Little, Robert Eugene 1933- WhoAm 90
Little, Royal 1896-1989 BioIn 16
Little, Sian C BiDrAPA 89
Little, Sophia 1799- FemiCLE
Little, Sylvia Ford WhoAmW 91
Little, Teruko O BiDrAPA 89
Little, Thomas Allyn 1947- WhoEmL 91
Little, Thomas M. 1935- ODwPR 91
Little, Thomas Malcolm 1932- St&PR 91
Little, Thomas Mayer 1935- WhoAm 90
Little, Thomas Nelson 1935- WhoSSW 91
Little, Vera 1928- IntWWM 90
Little, Vernon Lee BiDrAPA 89
Little, William Arthur 1930- WhoAm 90
Little, William Augustus 1838-1924 AmLegL
Little, William G. 1942- St&PR 91
Little, William John 1810-1894 BioIn 16
Little, William Norris 1931- St&PR 91
Little Chief, Barthell 1941- WhoAmA 91
Little-Marenin, Irene Renate 1941- WhoAmW 91
Little-Remington, Jo Ann ODwPR 91
Little Thunder, Merlin BioIn 16
Littlechild, Stephen C. 1943- WhoWor 91
Littledale, Freya Lota WhoWrEP 89
Littledale, Freya Lota Brown WhoAm 90, WhoAmW 91, WhoE 91
Littlefield, Baker R. 1907- St&PR 91
Littlefield, Bill 1948- WhoWrEP 89
Littlefield, Charles Edgar 1851-1915 AmLegL
Littlefield, Danielle Joan 1952- WhoE 91
Littlefield, David H. 1944- St&PR 91
Littlefield, Dick 1926- Ballpl 90
Littlefield, Donald Bruce 1946- St&PR 91
Littlefield, Edmund Wattis 1914- WhoAm 90
Littlefield, Joan Kohler 1936- WhoAmW 91
Littlefield, John 1954- Ballpl 90
Littlefield, John Walley 1925- WhoAm 90
Littlefield, Lawrence Crosby, Jr. 1938- St&PR 91, WhoAm 90, WhoWor 91
Littlefield, Paul Damon 1920- St&PR 91, WhoAm 90
Littlefield, Raymond S. 1945- St&PR 91
Littlefield, Roy Everett, III 1952- WhoE 91, WhoWor 91
Littlefield, Vivian Moore 1938- WhoAm 90, WhoAmW 91
Littleford, Jacqueline Reents 1934- WhoSSW 91
Littleford, Julian BioIn 16
Littleford, William BioIn 16
Littleford, William D. 1914- St&PR 91
Littlehale, John D. 1954- St&PR 91
Littlejohn, Angus Chisholm 1916- WhoAm 90
Littlejohn, Broadhus Richard 1960- St&PR 91
Littlejohn, David 1937- WhoAm 90
Littlejohn, Dewitt Clinton 1818-1892 AmLegL
Littlejohn, Joan Anne 1937- IntWWM 90
Littlejohn, Linda Lou 1952- WhoAmW 91
Littlejohn, Mark Hays 1936- WhoSSW 91
Littlejon, Jon WhoWrEP 89
Littler, Charles Armstrong WhoAmA 91
Littler, Gene Alec 1930- WhoAm 90
Littler, Mark Dunham 1911- WhoAm 90
Littler, William 1724-1784 PenDiDA 89
Littles, Gene WhoAm 90
Littleton, Arnold Benjamin 1919- St&PR 91
Littleton, Arthur Richard 1926- WhoAm 90
Littleton, Darryl 1949- St&PR 91
Littleton, Frank Leslie 1868-1935 AmLegL
Littleton, Harvey K. 1922- PenDiDA 89, WhoAmA 91
Littleton, Harvey Kline 1922- WhoAm 90, WhoE 91
Littleton, Isaac Thomas, III 1921- WhoAm 90
Littleton, Jeffre BioIn 16
Littleton, John Edward 1943- WhoSSW 91
Littleton, Joseph Cook 1920- WhoE 91
Littleton, Taylor Dowe 1930- WhoAm 90
Littlewit, Humphrey MajTwCW
Littlewood, Douglas Burden 1922- WhoAm 90
Littlewood, John Edensor 1885-1977 DcScB S2
Littlewood, Thomas Benjamin 1928- WhoAm 90
Littman, Andrew Bruce 1954- BiDrAPA 89
Littman, David Bernard 1949- WhoEmL 91
Littman, Earl 1927- St&PR 91
Littman, Howard 1927- WhoAm 90
Littman, Irving 1940- ODwPR 91, WhoAm 90
Littman, Jules Sanford 1946- WhoE 91
Littman, Lawrence, Jr. 1937- St&PR 91
Littman, Lynne 1941- WhoAmW 91
Littman, Mark 1920- WhoWor 91
Littman, Richard Anton 1919- WhoAm 90
Littman, Richard G. St&PR 91
Littman, Robert Leslie 1951- BiDrAPA 89
Littman, Robert Michael BiDrAPA 89
Littman, Sherwin A. 1936- St&PR 91
Littman, Solomon I BiDrAPA 89
Littman, Wendy P. 1946- WhoAmW 91
Littmann, Ernst-Ludwig 1936- WhoWor 91
Littmann, Mark Evan 1939- WhoE 91
Littner, Ner 1915- BiDrAPA 89, WhoAm 90
Litton, Andrew PenDiMP
Litton, Andrew 1959- IntWWM 90
Litton, James Howard 1934- IntWWM 90
Litton, Martin BioIn 16
Litton, Robert Clifton 1934- WhoSSW 91
Littrell, Doris Marie 1928- WhoAmA 91
Littunen, Kari Eino Antero 1948- WhoWor 91
Lituchy, Beverly Hope BiDrAPA 89
Litvack, Sanford Martin 1936- WhoAm 90
Litvak, King Jaime 1933- WhoWor 91
Litvak, Leonard L. 1922- St&PR 91
Litvak, Ronald 1938- BiDrAPA 89
Litvan, Leonard J., Jr. 1941- St&PR 91
Litvin, Henry 1923- BiDrAPA 89
Litvinne, Felia 1861-1936 PenDiMP
Litvinoff, Emanuel 1915- ConAu 129
Litvinov, Maxim Maximovich 1876-1951 BioIn 16
Litvinova, Felya 1861-1936 PenDiMP
Litwack, Arlene Debra 1945- WhoAmW 91
Litwack, Leon Frank 1929- WhoAm 90, WhoWrEP 89
Litwak, Leo 1924- WhoWrEP 89
Litweiler, John Berkey 1940- WhoAm 90, WhoWrEP 89
Litwhiler, Danny 1916- Ballpl 90
Litwiller, Malcolm Rex BiDrAPA 89
Litwiller, Michael Alan 1959- BiDrAPA 89
Litwin, Burton Lawrence 1931- WhoE 91, WhoWor 91
Litwin, Donald L. 1934- St&PR 91
Litwin, Harry 1907- St&PR 91
Litwin, Lawrence Theodore 1927- St&PR 91
Litwin, Martin Stanley 1930- WhoSSW 91
Litwin, Michael J. 1947- St&PR 91
Litwin, Michael Joseph 1947- WhoAm 90
Litwin, Ruth Forbes 1933- WhoAmA 91
Litz, Arthur Walton, Jr. 1929- WhoAm 90, WhoWrEP 89
Litz, Francis J. BioIn 16
Litz, Gisela 1922- IntWWM 90
Litz, James C 1948- WhoAmA 91
Litz, James Charles 1948- WhoE 91
Litzenberger, Robert Hermann 1943- WhoAm 90
Litzenboerger, Wolfgang 1935- WhoWor 91
Litzky, Michele C. 1954- ODwPR 91
Litzsinger, Paul Richard 1932- WhoAm 90
Liu Binyan 1925- BioIn 16, WorAu 1980 [port]
Liu En-buo 1931- WhoWor 91
Liu Huaqing 1916- BioIn 16
Liu Pin-Yen 1925- WorAu 1980 [port]
Liu Xiao Qing BioIn 16
Liu Xiaobo BioIn 16
Liu Yong BioIn 16
Liu, Alice Yee-Chang 1948- WhoAmW 91
Liu, Bede 1934- WhoAm 90
Liu, Ben-chieh 1938- WhoAm 90
Liu, Benjamin Young-hwai 1934- WhoAm 90
Liu, Binyan 1925- WhoE 91
Liu, Chao-Han 1939- WhoAm 90
Liu, Charles Chung-Cha 1953- WhoE 91
Liu, Chung-Chiun 1936- WhoAm 90
Liu, David C. 1920- St&PR 91
Liu, Edmund Kin 1951- WhoEmL 91
Liu, Ernest K. H. 1950- WhoAm 90
Liu, Ernest Sho-hua 1942- WhoAm 90
Liu, Fong Yu Mary 1948- WhoAmW 91
Liu, Hai-Sou 1896- WhoWor 91
Liu, Han-Shou 1930- WhoWor 91
Liu, Hao-wen 1926- WhoAm 90
Liu, Ho 1917- WhoAmA 91
Liu, Hung 1948- WhoAmA 91
Liu, Jinn-Liang 1957- WhoE 91
Liu, John Kung-Fu BioIn 16
Liu, John Kung-fu 1930- WhoE 91
Liu, Joseph T. C. 1934- WhoAm 90
Liu, Katherine Chang WhoAmA 91, WhoWor 91
Liu, Khang-Lee 1939- WhoWor 91
Liu, Lai Ching 1955- WhoSSW 91
Liu, Lee 1933- St&PR 91, WhoAm 90
Liu, Leonard 1958- WhoE 91
Liu, Ming-Wood 1947- WhoWor 91
Liu, Patricia Kay 1955- WhoE 91
Liu, Paul Yan 1951- BiDrAPA 89
Liu, Peter Chi-Lin 1925- BiDrAPA 89
Liu, Peter Yi-chih 1923- WhoWor 91
Liu, Philip M BiDrAPA 89
Liu, Pin-yen 1925- BioIn 16
Liu, Pung Show 1928- BiDrAPA 89
Liu, Qizhong 1938- WhoWor 91
Liu, Ralph Yieh-Min 1958- WhoE 91
Liu, Ray H. 1942- WhoSSW 91
Liu, Richard Kao 1964- BiDrAPA 89
Liu, Roger Kim Sing 1934- WhoWor 91
Liu, Roy Yoaning 1960- WhoE 91
Liu, Ruey-Wen 1930- WhoAm 90
Liu, Shan 1927- WhoWor 91
Liu, Shi-Yue 1935- IntWWM 90
Liu, Shing Kin Francis 1953- WhoEmL 91
Liu, Stephen Shu-Ning 1930- WhoWrEP 89
Liu, Tally C. 1950- St&PR 91
Liu, Vi-Cheng 1917- WhoAm 90
Liu, Wai To 1928- BiDrAPA 89
Liu, Yazhou 1953- WhoWor 91
Liu, Yick Wah Edmund 1953- WhoWor 91
Liu, Young King 1934- WhoAm 90
Liubimov, IUrii BioIn 16
Liuzzi, Dominic E. 1932- St&PR 91
Liuzzi, Robert C. 1944- St&PR 91, WhoAm 90
Liuzzo, Joseph Anthony 1926- WhoAm 90
Livasy, Ray G. 1929- St&PR 91
Livaudais, Herbert Syme 1917- St&PR 91
Livaudais, Marcel, Jr. 1925- WhoAm 90
Live, Israel 1907- WhoAm 90
Lively, Bud 1925- Ballpl 90
Lively, Carol A. 1935- WhoAm 90, WhoAmW 91
Lively, Danita Lynn BiDrAPA 89
Lively, David 1953- IntWWM 90
Lively, Donald Earl 1947- WhoEmL 91
Lively, Edwin Lester 1930- WhoAm 90
Lively, Edwin Lowe 1920- WhoAm 90
Lively, John K. 1933- ODwPR 91
Lively, John Pound 1945- WhoAm 90
Lively, Michael Eric 1923- WhoAm 90
Lively, Penelope 1933- AuBYP 90, BioIn 16, FemiCLE, MajTwCW, SmATA 60 [port]
Lively, Penelope Margaret 1933- WhoWor 91
Lively, Pierce 1921- WhoAm 90
Livergant, Harold Leonard 1924- St&PR 91
Liverman, Raymond E BiDrAPA 89
Livermore, Harriet 1788-1868 BioAmW
Livermore, Jeanne M. 1948- St&PR 91
Livermore, Joseph McMaster 1937- WhoAm 90
Livermore, Mary Ashton Rice 1820-1905 BioIn 16
Livermore, Norman 1911- BioIn 16
Livermore, Samuel 1732-1803 BioIn 16
Livers, Jon Michael 1940- St&PR 91
Liversage, Richard Albert 1925- WhoAm 90
Liverziani, Filippo 1926- EncPaPR 91

Livesay, Dorothy 1909- BioIn 16, FemiCLE, MajTwCW
Livesay, Florence 1874-1953 FemiCLE
Livesay, Florence Randal 1874-1953 DcLB 92 [port]
Livesay, John AuBYP 90
Livesay, Thomas Andrew 1945- WhoAm 90, WhoAmA 91, WhoEmL 91
Livesey, Michael J. BioIn 16, NewYTBS 90
Livesey, William D. BioIn 16
Livesey, William P. 1952- WhoE 91
Livet, Anne Hodge 1941- WhoAmA 91, WhoE 91
Livi, Yvo 1921- WhoWor 91
Livick, Malcolm Harris 1929- WhoAm 90
Livick, Stephen 1945- WhoAmA 91
Livigni, Margaret Veronica Shana 1953- WhoEmL 91
Livijn, Claes-Olof Einar 1923- WhoWor 91
Livingood, Clarence S. 1911- WhoAm 90, WhoWor 91
Livingood, James W 1910- ConAu 32NR
Livingood, John Michael 1940- BiDrAPA 89
Livingood, Suzanne Hubbuch 1948- WhoSSW 91
Livingston, Alan Lobell 1936- WhoSSW 91
Livingston, Ann Chambliss 1952- WhoEmL 91
Livingston, Boynton Parker 1913- WhoAm 90
Livingston, C.R. 1948- St&PR 91
Livingston, Colleen 1946- BiDrAPA 89
Livingston, Colleen M. 1946- WhoE 91
Livingston, Cynthia Errol 1946- WhoE 91
Livingston, Cynthia McClendon 1941- WhoE 91
Livingston, Don R. St&PR 91
Livingston, E Arthur BiDrAPA 89
Livingston, Edmund W., Jr. 1943- St&PR 91
Livingston, Edward 1764-1836 BiDrUSE 89, BioIn 16
Livingston, Edward Walter 1932- St&PR 91
Livingston, F. L. WhoAm 90
Livingston, Gordon Stuart 1938- BiDrAPA 89, WhoE 91
Livingston, Helen BiDEWW
Livingston, Homer J., Jr. 1935- St&PR 91
Livingston, J.A. 1905- WhoWrEP 89
Livingston, J A 1905-1989 ConAu 130
Livingston, J. Sterling 1916- WhoAm 90
Livingston, James Archibald, Jr. 1918- St&PR 91
Livingston, James Craig 1930- WhoAm 90, WhoWrEP 89
Livingston, James L. 1954- St&PR 91
Livingston, Jane S 1944- WhoAmA 91
Livingston, Jane Shelton 1944- WhoAm 90
Livingston, Jay 1915- OxCPMus
Livingston, Jay Carl WhoWrEP 89
Livingston, Jay Harold 1915- BioIn 16, WhoAm 90
Livingston, Jerry 1909- OxCPMus
Livingston, John 1837-1894 DcCanB 12
Livingston, John A. 1902-1988 BioIn 16
Livingston, John Gary BiDrAPA 89
Livingston, Johnston R. 1923- WhoAm 90
Livingston, Joseph A. 1905-1989 BioIn 16
Livingston, Julian Richard 1932- IntWWM 90
Livingston, Karen Dean 1948- WhoWrEP 89
Livingston, Laurie Anne 1951- WhoAmW 91
Livingston, Lee Franklin 1942- WhoE 91
Livingston, Leo L. BioIn 16
Livingston, Lorton Stoy, Jr. 1942- St&PR 91
Livingston, Margaret Gresham 1924- WhoAmA 91
Livingston, Margaret Morrow Gresham 1924- WhoAmW 91
Livingston, Marjorie EncO&P 3
Livingston, Mark A. BiDrAPA 89
Livingston, Mickey 1914-1983 Ballpl 90
Livingston, Myra 1926- AuBYP 90
Livingston, Myra Cohn BioIn 16
Livingston, Myra Cohn 1926- ConAu 33NR, WhoAm 90, WhoAmW 91, WhoWrEP 89
Livingston, Myran Jabez, Jr. 1934- WhoWrEP 89
Livingston, Myrtle Athleen Smith 1902-1973 HarlReB
Livingston, Myrtle Smith 1902-1974 EarBlAP
Livingston, Nancy 1935- TwCCr&M 91
Livingston, Nancy Tribley 1946- BiDrAPA 89
Livingston, Pamela Anna 1930- WhoAmW 91
Livingston, Patricia Ann 1954- WhoEmL 91
Livingston, Patrick Murray 1920- WhoAm 90, WhoWrEP 89
Livingston, Peter AuBYP 90
Livingston, Peter Van Brugh 1710-1792 EncCRAm
Livingston, Philip 1716-1778 EncCRAm, WorAlBi
Livingston, Richard Lee 1949- BiDrAPA 89
Livingston, Robert BioIn 16
Livingston, Robert 1654-1728 EncCRAm
Livingston, Robert Burr 1918- WhoAm 90
Livingston, Robert Gerald 1927- WhoE 91
Livingston, Robert I. 1937- St&PR 91
Livingston, Robert Jean 1932- St&PR 91
Livingston, Robert Linlithgow, Jr. 1943- WhoAm 90, WhoSSW 91
Livingston, Robert R. 1654-1728 WhNaAH
Livingston, Robert R. 1718-1775 EncCRAm
Livingston, Robert R. 1746-1813 BioIn 16, EncCRAm [port]
Livingston, Samuel Henry Harkwood 1831-1897 DcCanB 12
Livingston, Sidnee WhoAmA 91, WhoE 91
Livingston, Thomas Eugene 1948- WhoAm 90
Livingston, William 1723-1790 BioIn 16, EncCRAm
Livingston, William M. 1913- St&PR 91
Livingston, William M., Jr. 1946- St&PR 91
Livingston, William Samuel 1920- WhoAm 90
Livingston-White, Deborah Joyce Halemah 1947- WhoWrEP 89
Livingstone, Biganess WhoAmA 91
Livingstone, Bruce Leffler BiDrAPA 89
Livingstone, Charleen Thompson 1929- WhoAmW 91
Livingstone, Daniel Archibald 1927- WhoAm 90
Livingstone, David 1813-1873 BioIn 16, WorAlBi
Livingstone, Dinah 1940- FemiCLE
Livingstone, Ernest Felix 1915- IntWWM 90
Livingstone, Frank Brown 1928- WhoAm 90
Livingstone, Gary K. 1945- WhoAm 90
Livingstone, Harrison Edward 1937- WhoWrEP 89
Livingstone, Joan 1948- WhoAmA 91
Livingstone, John B 1932- BiDrAPA 89
Livingstone, John Leslie 1932- WhoAm 90
Livingstone, Kathleen Mary 1951- IntWWM 90
Livingstone, Ken BioIn 16
Livingstone, Susan Morrisey 1946- WhoAm 90
Livingstone, Trudy Dorothy Zweig 1946- WhoAmW 91, WhoE 91, WhoEmL 91, WhoWor 91
Livingstone, William Orr, Jr. 1927- WhoAm 90
Livinston, Robert R. 1746-1813 WorAlBi
Livio, Anne Marie Sullivan Reher 1915- WhoAmW 91
Livolsi, Santo 1938- WhoWor 91
Livornese, Thomas J. BioIn 16
Livous-McDowell, Karen Michelle 1956- WhoAmW 91
Livsey, Clara G BiDrAPA 89
Livsey, Robert Callister 1936- WhoAm 90
Livy 59?BC-17AD WorAlBi
Lix, Terry J. 1951- St&PR 91
Lixl-Purcell, Andreas 1951- WhoSSW 91
Liyanage, Amarasiri de Silva 1941- WhoWor 91
Lizardi, Jose Joaquin Fernandez de 1776-1827 BioIn 16, NinCLC 30
Lizardi, Joseph 1941- ConAu 129, HispWr 90, WhoHisp 91
Lizardo, Elias 1963- WhoE 91
Lizarraga, David C. WhoHisp 91
Lizarraga, Jose Ramon 1955- WhoWor 91
Lizars, Kathleen FemiCLE
Lizenby, Linda Lee 1956- WhoAmW 91
Lizer, James Robert BiDrAPA 89
Lizio, Celeste 1908-1988 BioIn 16
Lizotte, Mary C. BioIn 16
Lizotte, Shirley Guice 1935- WhoAmW 91
Lizut, Nona Moore Price 1923- WhoAmW 91
Ljaljevic, Zorica Milojko 1961- BiDrAPA 89
Ljubenko, Dusan J. 1927- St&PR 91
Ljubicic, Nikola 1916- WhoWor 91
Ljubicic Drozdowski, Miladin Peter 1921- WhoWor 91
Ljung, Greta Marianne WhoAmW 91
Ljung, Viveka 1935- WhoWor 91
Ljungh, Anders Erik Erland 1942- WhoWor 91
Ljungh, Esse W 1904- OxCCanT
Ljungsaeter, Ove Leif 1944- WhoWor 91
Ljungstrom, Goran 1933- WhoWor 91
Llado, Victor J BiDrAPA 89
Llaguno, Caesar Carpio 1931- WhoWor 91
Llaguno, Solita R BiDrAPA 89
Llamas, Carlos Fernandez BioIn 16
Lland, Michael BioIn 16
Llangollen, Ladies of FemiCLE
Llau, Pierre 1934- WhoWor 91
Llaurado, Josep G. 1927- WhoAm 90
Lledo, Alberto 1956- WhoWor 91
Llenas, Winston 1943- Ballpl 90
Llera, Rene Antonio 1918- BiDrAPA 89
Llerandi, Edward X. 1962- WhoHisp 91
Llerandi, Manuel WhoHisp 91
Llerandi, Richard Henry 1963- WhoHisp 91
Lleras Camargo, Alberto 1906-1990 BioIn 16, CurBio 90N, NewYTBS 90 [port]
Lleras Restrepo, Carlos 1908- BioIn 16
Llewellen, Betty Halff 1911- WhoAmW 91, WhoWor 91
Llewellen, Charles Elroy, Jr. 1922- BiDrAPA 89
Llewellyn, David Walter 1930- WhoWor 91
Llewellyn, Ensley M. BioIn 16
Llewellyn, Frederick Eaton 1917- St&PR 91, WhoWor 91
Llewellyn, Grant 1960- IntWWM 90
Llewellyn, Irene Beatrice 1940- WhoE 91
Llewellyn, James Bruce 1927- ConAmBL
Llewellyn, John 1915-1988 AnObit 1988
Llewellyn, John Schofield, Jr. 1935- St&PR 91, WhoAm 90, WhoE 91
Llewellyn, Julia Ann Wagner 1950- WhoAmW 91, WhoE 91
Llewellyn, Kate 1940- FemiCLE
Llewellyn, Leonard Frank 1933- WhoWor 91
Llewellyn, Martin BioIn 16
Llewellyn, Norman W. WhoAm 90
Llewellyn, Ralph Alvin 1933- WhoAm 90
Llewellyn, Richard DcNaB 1981
Llewellyn, Richard 1906-1983 WorAlBi
Llewellyn, Richard Kennedy 1951- WhoWor 91
Llewellyn, Thomas H 1913- BiDrAPA 89
Llewellyn, Thomas Sylvester, III 1936- WhoSSW 91
Llewellyn, William Alfred 1934- WhoAm 90
Llewellyn, William Benjamin James 1925- IntWWM 90
Llewelyn Davies, Richard 1912-1981 DcNaB 1981
Llewllyn, William Henry Harrison 1854-1927 AmLegL
Llinas, Joseph Francisco 1955- BiDrAPA 89
Llinas, Joseph J 1928- BiDrAPA 89
Llinas, Rodolfo Riascos 1934- WhoAm 90
Llompart, Jose 1930- WhoWor 91
Llona, Antonio BiDrAPA 89
Llorens, Marcelo Gustavo 1957- WhoHisp 91
Llorens, Washington 1900- HispWr 90
Llorens Torres, Luis 1876-1944 BioIn 16
Llorente, Luis WhoAmA 91
Llorente, Maria D D BiDrAPA 89
Llorente, Rigoberto Lino 1956- WhoHisp 91
Llosa, Mario Vargas HispWr 90, MajTwCW
Llosa, Mario Vargas 1936- BioIn 16
Lloyd, A. L. 1908-1982 OxCPMus
Lloyd, Alan T. BiDrAPA 89
Lloyd, Albert Lawrence, Jr. 1930- WhoAm 90
Lloyd, Arthur 1840-1904 OxCPMus
Lloyd, Arthur Leonard 1925- St&PR 91
Lloyd, Brian Emory 1941- BiDrAPA 89
Lloyd, Carolyn Provan 1936- WhoAmW 91
Lloyd, Cecil Rhodes 1930- WhoSSW 91
Lloyd, Charles NewAgMG
Lloyd, Charles Hudson 1950- WhoAm 90
Lloyd, Charles R. 1932- St&PR 91
Lloyd, Christine 1949- BiDrAPA 89
Lloyd, Christopher 1938- BioIn 16, WhoAm 90, WorAlBi
Lloyd, Christopher S. 1940- St&PR 91
Lloyd, Darryl 1941- ODwPR 91
Lloyd, David 1656-1731 EncCRAm
Lloyd, David 1920- IntWWM 90
Lloyd, David Bellamy 1937- IntWWM 90
Lloyd, David Hubert 1948- WhoWrEP 89
Lloyd, Don Keith 1944- St&PR 91, WhoAm 90
Lloyd, Douglas Seward 1939- WhoAm 90
Lloyd, Edward 1845-1927 PenDiMP
Lloyd, Eleanor L. 1927- St&PR 91
Lloyd, Elizabeth Ellen 1949- WhoAmW 91
Lloyd, Elizabeth Jeanine 1936- WhoAmW 91
Lloyd, Emily BioIn 16
Lloyd, Emily 1979- WorAlBi
Lloyd, Errol 1943- BioIn 16
Lloyd, Eugene Walter 1943- St&PR 91, WhoAm 90
Lloyd, Eva Mae BioIn 16
Lloyd, Francis Vernon, Jr. 1908- WhoAm 90
Lloyd, Fredric Reynolds 1923- WhoAm 90
Lloyd, Gary Arthur 1934- WhoAm 90
Lloyd, Gary E. St&PR 91
Lloyd, Gary Evan 1936- WhoE 91
Lloyd, George Walter Selwyn 1913- IntWWM 90
Lloyd, Harold 1893-1971 WorAlBi
Lloyd, Harold 1894-1971 BioIn 16
Lloyd, Harold Sidney 1953- St&PR 91
Lloyd, Harris Horton 1937- WhoSSW 91
Lloyd, Hortense Collins WhoAmW 91, WhoSSW 91
Lloyd, Hugh Adams 1918- WhoAm 90
Lloyd, Hugh Pughe 1894-1981 DcNaB 1981
Lloyd, James A. 1946- St&PR 91
Lloyd, John A. 1911- St&PR 91
Lloyd, John Raymond 1942- WhoAm 90
Lloyd, John Selwyn Brooke Selwyn- 1904-1978 BioIn 16
Lloyd, John Stoddard 1914- WhoWor 91
Lloyd, John Uri 1849-1936 LiHiK
Lloyd, Jonathan 1948- IntWWM 90
Lloyd, Jonathan David 1952- St&PR 91
Lloyd, Joseph D 1927- BiDrAPA 89
Lloyd, Judith 1940- ODwPR 91
Lloyd, Kate Rand 1923- WhoAm 90
Lloyd, Kenneth D., Jr. 1932- St&PR 91
Lloyd, Kent 1931- WhoAm 90
Lloyd, Leona Loretta 1949- WhoEmL 91
Lloyd, Lewis Keith, Jr. 1941- WhoAm 90
Lloyd, Linda Marie 1941- WhoWrEP 89
Lloyd, Malcolm Russell 1939- St&PR 91, WhoAm 90
Lloyd, Margaret Ann 1942- WhoSSW 91
Lloyd, Margaret Glynne 1946- ConAu 130
Lloyd, Marie 1870-1922 BioIn 16, OxCPMus
Lloyd, Marilyn WhoAm 90, WhoAmW 91, WhoSSW 91
Lloyd, Michael 1947- ODwPR 91
Lloyd, Michael Jeffrey 1948- WhoAm 90
Lloyd, Morris, Jr. 1937- St&PR 91
Lloyd, Nelson 1851-1925 Ballpl 90
Lloyd, Norman 1909-1980 AuBYP 90
Lloyd, Peter John 1937- WhoWor 91
Lloyd, Peter William 1929- WhoAm 90
Lloyd, Pop 1884-1964 Ballpl 90 [port]
Lloyd, Raymond Grann WhoAm 90
Lloyd, Raymond Joseph 1942- St&PR 91
Lloyd, Raymond Thomas 1925- St&PR 91
Lloyd, Richard Alan 1939- BiDrAPA 89
Lloyd, Richard Dafydd Vivian Llewellyn 1906-1983 DcNaB 1981
Lloyd, Richard E. 1954- St&PR 91
Lloyd, Richard Wingate BiDrAPA 89
Lloyd, Robert 1940- PenDiMP
Lloyd, Robert Albert 1930- WhoE 91
Lloyd, Robert Andrew 1940- IntWWM 90, WhoWor 91
Lloyd, Robert Jabez 1918- St&PR 91
Lloyd, Robert Michael 1945- WhoSSW 91
Lloyd, Robert V. 1938- St&PR 91
Lloyd, Robert William 1954- St&PR 91
Lloyd, Seton 1902- ConAu 132
Lloyd, Trevor Owen 1934- WhoWrEP 89
Lloyd, Wanda Smalls 1949- WhoAm 90
Lloyd, William Hunter, Sr. 1948- WhoSSW 91
Lloyd, Wingate 1931- WhoE 91
Lloyd-Caldwell, Marian Jean 1942- WhoAmW 91
Lloyd-Davies, Peter R. 1943- WhoE 91
Lloyd George, David 1863-1945 WorAlBi
Lloyd-Howells, David 1942- IntWWM 90
Lloyd-Jones, David 1934- PenDiMP
Lloyd-Jones, David Mathias 1934- IntWWM 90, WhoWor 91
Lloyd-Jones, Donald J. 1931- WhoE 91
Lloyd-Jones, Esther McDonald 1901- WhoE 91
Lloyd-Jones, Hugh 1922- WhoWor 91
Lloyd-Jones, Jean 1929- WhoAmW 91
Lloyd-Jones, Mary 1934- BiDWomA
Lloyd-Morgan, Glenys 1945- WhoWor 91
Lloyd-Murie, Rosemarie 1960- WhoAmW 91
Lloyd of Dolobran, Baron 1879-1941 BioIn 16
Lloyd Webber, Andrew 1948- BioIn 16, IntWWM 90, OxCPMus, WhoAm 90, WhoWor 91, WorAlBi
Lloyd Webber, Julian 1951- IntWWM 90, PenDiMP
Lluch, Myrna 1950- WhoHisp 91
Lluch, Roberto S 1959- BiDrAPA 89
Lo, Andrew W. 1960- WhoE 91
Lo, Eddy Kong Chuan 1937- WhoWor 91
Lo, Elizabeth Shen 1926- WhoAmW 91
Lo, Fu-lang BioIn 16
Lo, Gustav M 1936- BiDrAPA 89
Lo, Joseph Kong 1964- WhoSSW 91
Lo, Lawrence Naai-Lei 1941- IntWWM 90
Lo, Quinn WhoWrEP 89
Lo, Ron 1956- WhoE 91
Lo, Ronald Ping Wong 1936- WhoAm 90, WhoWor 91
Lo, Steven C. 1949- ConAu 132
Lo, Theresa Nong 1945- WhoAmW 91
Lo, Victor Tang Seong 1915- WhoWor 91

Lo, Yuen-Tze 1920- WhoAm 90
Loach, Ken BioIn 16
Loach, Kenneth W BiDrAPA 89
Loach, Paul Allen 1934- WhoAm 90
Loader, David Norman 1941- WhoWor 91
Loader, Jay Gordon 1923- WhoAm 90
Loan, Richard Keith 1936- St&PR 91
Loar, Peggy A 1948- WhoAmA 91
Loasby, Brian John 1930- WhoWor 91
Lobalbo, Anthony Charles 1949- IntWWM 90
Lobanov-Rostovsky, Nikita D. BioIn 16
Lobanov-Rostovsky, Oleg 1934- IntWWM 90, WhoAm 90
Lobato, Arthur Sayao 1966- WhoEmL 91
Lobato, Francesca WhoHisp 91
Lobato, Toribio Q. 1954- WhoHisp 91
Lobaugh, Bruce 1953- WhoSSW 91
Lobb, James W. 1932- St&PR 91
Lobb, John 1840-1921 EncO&P 3
Lobb, John C. NewYTBS 90
Lobb, John C. 1914-1990 BioIn 16
Lobbia, John E. 1941- WhoAm 90
Lobdell, Charles E. 1861-1949 AmLegL
Lobdell, Frank 1921- WhoAm 90, WhoAmA 91
Lobdell, Leighton M. 1927- St&PR 91
Lobdell, Robert Charles 1926- WhoAm 90
Lobeck, Daniel John 1951- WhoSSW 91
Lobel, Anita 1934- BioIn 16, ConAu 33NR
Lobel, Arnold BioIn 16
Lobel, Arnold 1933-1987 ConAu 33NR
Lobel, Arnold Stark 1933- WhoWrEP 89
Lobel, Arnold Stark 1933-1987 AuBYP 90
Lobel, Edgar 1888-1982 DcNaB 1981
Lobel, Henry Kenneth 1913- St&PR 91
Lobel, Irving 1917- WhoE 91
Lobel, Jules Loren 1951- WhoE 91
Lobel, Leonard J. 1940- St&PR 91
Lobel, Martin 1941- WhoWor 91
Lo Bello, Anthony Joseph 1947- WhoE 91
Lo Bello, Joseph D. 1940- St&PR 91
Lobello, Peter 1935- WhoAmA 91
Lobene, Joyce Anne 1939- WhoAmW 91
Lobenherz, William Ernest 1949- WhoEmL 91
Lober, Georg J 1892-1961 WhoAmA 91N
Lober, Holly Henderson 1951- WhoAmW 91
Lober, Irene Moss 1927- WhoE 91
Lober, Paul Hallam 1919- WhoAm 90
Lober, Richard O. 1932- St&PR 91
Loberg, Robert Warren 1927- WhoAmA 91
Lobert, Hans 1881-1968 Ballpl 90 [port]
Lobig, Janie Howell 1945- WhoAmW 91
Lobingier, John Huston 1939- WhoSSW 91, WhoWor 91
Lobis, Robert Alan 1942- BiDrAPA 89, WhoE 91
Lobisser, George J. 1927- St&PR 91
Lobitz, Walter Charles, Jr. 1911- WhoAm 90
Lobkowicz, Nicholas 1931- ConAu 32NR, WhoWor 91
Lobkowicz, Robert de BioIn 16
Lobl, Herbert Max 1932- WhoAm 90
Lobl, Joseph George BiDrAPA 89
Lobl, Lawrence T 1939- BiDrAPA 89
Loble, Lester H., II 1941- St&PR 91
Lobley, Alan Haigh 1927- WhoAm 90
Lobley, James D. 1946- St&PR 91
Lobley, James Richard 1932- St&PR 91
Lobliner, Sanford M. 1936- St&PR 91
Lobman, Harry L. 1920- St&PR 91
Lobmeyr, Josef 1792-1855 PenDiDA 89
Lobmeyr, Josef 1828-1864 PenDiDA 89
Lobmeyr, Ludwig 1829-1917 PenDiDA 89
Lobner, Kneeland Harkness 1919- WhoAm 90
Lobner, Kurt Edmund Gunther 1935- WhoWor 91
Lobo, Antonio BiDrAPA 89
Lobo, Luiza Leite Bruno 1948- WhoWor 91
Lobo, Pio Caetano 1936- WhoWor 91
Lobo, Richard M. 1936- WhoHisp 91
Lobo, Suely Maria de Paula e Silva WhoWor 91
Lobos, Heitor Villa- BioIn 16
Lobosco, Louis William 1952- WhoE 91
Lobotkova, Jana 1933- WhoWor 91
Loboz-Grudzien, Krystyna 1946- WhoWor 91
Lobsenz, Amelia ODwPR 91, WhoAm 90
Lobsenz, Amelia Freitag AuBYP 90
Lobsenz, Herbert M. 1932- St&PR 91
Lobsenz, Herbert Munter 1932- WhoAm 90
Lobue, Ange 1937- BiDrAPA 89
Lo Buglio, Rudecinda Ann 1934- WhoHisp 91
Locadia, Alex BioIn 16
Localio, Arthur 1911- WhoAm 90
LoCasale, Edward Joseph 1947- St&PR 91
LoCascio, James Edward 1955- WhoWor 91
LoCascio, Joseph Peter 1947- WhoE 91
Locastro, Dominic James 1941- WhoSSW 91
Locatelli, Lucy Ellen 1945- St&PR 91
Locatelli, Paul Leo 1938- WhoAm 90
Locati, Andrew James 1964- WhoEmL 91
Loch, Edward James 1939- WhoSSW 91
Lochan, F.N.C. 1940- St&PR 91
Locher, Edward P. 1951- St&PR 91
Locher, Gottfried Wilhelm 1911- WhoWor 91
Locher, Marianne 1959- WhoE 91
Locher, Paul Raymond, Jr. 1957- WhoE 91
Locher, Ralph S. 1915- WhoAm 90
Locher, Richard Earl 1929- WhoAm 90
Locher, Theo 1921- EncPaPR 91
Lochhead, Douglas Grant 1922- WhoAm 90
Lochhead, Jack Van Slyke 1944- WhoE 91
Lochhead, Liz 1947- FemiCLE
Lochhead, Louise P. 1940- WhoAmW 91
Lochhead, Robert Bruce 1952- WhoEmL 91
Lochlons, Colin AuBYP 90
Lochman, William H., Jr. 1947- St&PR 91
Lochmiller, Jim 1957- ODwPR 91
Lochmiller, Kurtis L. 1952- WhoEmL 91, WhoWor 91
Lochnan, Katharine A 1946- WhoAmA 91
Lochner, John M. 1946- St&PR 91
Lochner, Louis Paul 1887-1975 BioIn 16
Lochner, Stefan 1400?-1451? IntDcAA 90
Lochridge, John B 1952- BiDrAPA 89
Lochridge, Katherine 1946- WhoE 91
Lochridge, Thomas Newton, Jr. 1925- WhoSSW 91
Lochrie, Elizabeth Davey 1890-1981 WhoAmA 91N
Lochte, Dick 1944- TwCCr&M 91
Lochtenberg, Bernard Hendrik 1931- St&PR 91, WhoAm 90, WhoE 91
Lock, Aaron Charles, Jr. 1925- WhoSSW 91
Lock, Albert Larry, Jr. 1947- WhoEmL 91
Lock, Dennis 1929- ConAu 32NR
Lock, Don 1936- Ballpl 90
Lock, Gerald Seymour Hunter 1935- WhoAm 90
Lock, Grahame Edwin 1946- WhoWor 91
Lock, James D BiDrAPA 89
Lock, Joan 1933- ConAu 132
Lock, Joseph Henry 1932- St&PR 91
Lock, Matthias 1710?-1765 PenDiDA 89
Lock, Richard William 1931- St&PR 91, WhoAm 90
Lock, Robert Joseph 1955- WhoEmL 91
Lock, Thomas Graham 1931- WhoWor 91
Lock, William Rowland 1932- IntWWM 90
Lockard, James Allen 1945- WhoEmL 91
Lockard, Peggy Lou 1931- WhoAmW 91
Lockard, Raymond Gilbert 1925- WhoE 91
Locke, Anne BioIn 16
Locke, Anne 1530?- FemiCLE
Locke, Annie NewAgMG
Locke, Brian 1924- WhoWor 91
Locke, Carl Edwin, Jr. 1936- WhoAm 90
Locke, Carol Anne BiDrAPA 89
Locke, Charles Stanley 1929- St&PR 91, WhoAm 90
Locke, Charmaine BioIn 16
Locke, David Ross 1833-1888 BioIn 16
Locke, Donald BioIn 16
Locke, Edward 1928- WhoWrEP 89
Locke, Edwin Allen, III 1938- WhoAm 90
Locke, Edwin Allen, Jr. 1910- WhoAm 90
Locke, Gordon 1938- St&PR 91
Locke, James Craig 1951- St&PR 91
Locke, Jane 1805-1859 FemiCLE
Locke, Joan Neuhaus 1958- WhoSSW 91
Locke, John 1632-1702 EncCRAm
Locke, John 1632-1704 BioIn 16, DcLB 101 [port], WorAlBi, WrPh P
Locke, John Robinson 1894- WhoAm 90
Locke, John Whiteman, III 1936- WhoAm 90
Locke, Joseph 1846-1936 PenDiDA 89
Locke, Kevin NewAgMG
Locke, L.W. 1934- St&PR 91
Locke, Larry 1934- Ballpl 90
Locke, Lawrence 1943- ODwPR 91
Locke, Matthew 1621?-1677 PenDiMP A
Locke, Michael 1929- WhoAm 90
Locke, Michelle Wilson 1947- WhoAmA 91
Locke, Murray S BiDrAPA 89
Locke, Nicke C. St&PR 91
Locke, Norton 1927- WhoAm 90
Locke, Peter 1937- IntWWM 90
Locke, Ralph P. 1949- IntWWM 90
Locke, Randy Lee 1944- WhoWor 91
Locke, Richard Adams 1800-1871 BioIn 16
Locke, Richard S. 1937- St&PR 91
Locke, Robert 1944- ConAu 129, SmATA 63 [port]
Locke, Robert Albert 1940- St&PR 91
Locke, Robert O. 1918- St&PR 91
Locke, Sondra BioIn 16
Locke, Sondra 1947- WhoAm 90
Locke, Stephen Charles 1953- WhoSSW 91
Locke, Steven Elliot 1945- BiDrAPA 89, WhoAm 90, WhoE 91
Locke, Sumner Helena 1881-1917 FemiCLE
Locke, Thomas Bernard 1948- WhoSSW 91
Locke, Virginia Otis 1930- WhoAmW 91
Locke, W. Timothy 1955- WhoAm 90
Locke, Wendell Vernon 1924- WhoAm 90
Locke, William H. 1869-1913 Ballpl 90
Locke, William Wesley 1935- St&PR 91, WhoAm 90
Lockemann, June Elaine Loughridge 1969- IntWWM 90
Locker, Bob 1938- Ballpl 90
Locker, J. Gary 1937- WhoAm 90
Locker, Laurence David 1940- WhoSSW 91
Locker, Lois Serota 1960- WhoE 91
Locker, Thomas 1937- AuBYP 90, BioIn 16
Lockert-Daniels, Cheryl Lynne BiDrAPA 89
Lockett, Barbara Ann 1936- WhoAm 90, WhoAmW 91
Lockett, David Robert 1951- IntWWM 90
Lockett, Donna Alcorn 1941- St&PR 91
Lockett, Harold J 1924- BiDrAPA 89
Lockett, James L. 1930- St&PR 91
Lockett, Mary 1872- FemiCLE
Lockett, Reginald Franklin 1947- WhoWrEP 89
Lockett, Ronald 1965- MusmAFA
Lockett, Tyler C. 1932- WhoAm 90
Lockett, William Alexander 1949- WhoEmL 91
Lockett-Egan, Marian Workman 1931- WhoAmW 91
Locketz, Harold David 1925- BiDrAPA 89
Lockey, Anne Elizabeth 1939- BiDrAPA 89
Lockey, Charles 1820-1901 PenDiMP
Lockey, Mary BiDEWW
Lockey, Richard Funk 1940- WhoAm 90
Lockhart, Aileene Simpson 1911- WhoAm 90
Lockhart, Anita May 1934- WhoWrEP 89
Lockhart, Ann June 1945- WhoAmW 91
Lockhart, Anne Ivey 1943- WhoAmA 91
Lockhart, Araby 1926- OxCCanT
Lockhart, Bette Jayne 1936- St&PR 91
Lockhart, Brooks Javins 1920- WhoAm 90
Lockhart, Calvin 1934- DrBIPA 90
Lockhart, Charles David 1953- St&PR 91
Lockhart, Colleen Marie 1964- WhoAmW 91
Lockhart, Frank BioIn 16
Lockhart, James 1930- IntWWM 90, PenDiMP
Lockhart, James Blakely 1936- WhoAm 90
Lockhart, James Blakley 1936- St&PR 91
Lockhart, James Kenneth 1935- St&PR 91
Lockhart, John 1928- BiDrAPA 89
Lockhart, John M. 1911- St&PR 91
Lockhart, John Mallery 1911- WhoAm 90
Lockhart, Keith Alan 1959- IntWWM 90
Lockhart, Linda BioIn 16
Lockhart, Madge Clements 1920- WhoAmW 91
Lockhart, Mary Guy 1947- WhoAmW 91
Lockhart, Paula Jones BiDrAPA 89
Lockhart, Richard David 1936- St&PR 91
Lockhart, Robert John McLean BiDrAPA 89
Lockhart, Robert Ray, III 1939- St&PR 91
Lockhart, Ronald Wayne 1931- St&PR 91
Lockhart, Rosalie Pergantis 1938- WhoSSW 91
Lockhart, Russel A. 1938- WhoWrEP 89
Lockhart, Thelma 1942- WhoAmW 91
Lockhart, Wayne BiDrAPA 89
Lockhead, Gregory Roger 1931- WhoAm 90
Locklair, Dale Lewis 1955- WhoSSW 91
Locklair, Dan Steven 1949- IntWWM 90, WhoSSW 91
Locklear, Clisby Rene 1963- WhoSSW 91
Locklear, Freda Porter 1957- WhoSSW 91
Locklear, Gene 1949- Ballpl 90
Locklear, Heather BioIn 16
Locklear, Heather 1961- WorAlBi
Locklear, Jeanne Marie 1953- WhoAmW 91
Locklin, Allen C. 1929- St&PR 91
Locklin, Gerald 1941- ConAu 32NR
Locklin, Wilbert Edwin 1920- St&PR 91, WhoAm 90
Lockman, Norman Alton 1938- WhoAm 90
Lockman, Whitey 1926- Ballpl 90
Lockman-Brooks, Linda BioIn 16
Lockmiller, Carlotta Elizabeth 1942- WhoSSW 91
Lockmiller, David Alexander 1906- WhoAm 90
Lockridge, Ernest Hugh 1938- WhoAm 90, WhoWrEP 89
Lockridge, Frances 1896-1963 TwCCr&M 91
Lockridge, Laurence 1942- WhoE 91
Lockridge, Laurence S 1942- ConAu 130
Lockridge, Patricia BioIn 16
Lockridge, Richard 1898-1982 TwCCr&M 91, WorAlBi
Lockridge, Robert Lynn 1944- WhoSSW 91
Lockroy, Edouard Etienne Antoine Simon 1840-1913 BiDFrPL
Locks, Marian WhoAmA 91
Locksmith, Joseph Louis 1926- WhoWrEP 89
Lockwood, A. Douglas 1923- St&PR 91
Lockwood, Annea Ferguson 1939- IntWWM 90
Lockwood, Brocton BioIn 16
Lockwood, Bruce Hamilton BiDrAPA 89
Lockwood, Carol Luan 1945- WhoEmL 91
Lockwood, Courtney 1951- ODwPR 91
Lockwood, David W 1934- BiDrAPA 89
Lockwood, Don L. 1932- St&PR 91
Lockwood, Doris Hoffmann 1931- WhoAmW 91
Lockwood, Dorothy Pyle C.H. St&PR 91
Lockwood, Eileen Chamberlain 1934- WhoWrEP 89
Lockwood, Frances Ellen 1950- WhoAm 90
Lockwood, Frank James 1931- WhoWor 91
Lockwood, Gerald A. 1946- St&PR 91
Lockwood, Glenn Edwin 1947- WhoSSW 91
Lockwood, Helshi 1941- WhoE 91
Lockwood, John Alexander 1919- WhoAm 90
Lockwood, John LeBaron 1924- WhoAm 90
Lockwood, Kenneth Paul 1942- St&PR 91
Lockwood, Kent 1960- St&PR 91
Lockwood, Lewis Henry 1930- WhoAm 90
Lockwood, Margaret 1916-1990 CurBio 90N, NewYTBS 90 [port]
Lockwood, Molly Ann 1936- WhoE 91, WhoWor 91
Lockwood, Myna AuBYP 90
Lockwood, Normand 1906- IntWWM 90
Lockwood, Pamela Jane BiDrAPA 89
Lockwood, Patricia Margaret 1953- WhoE 91
Lockwood, Paul W. 1951- St&PR 91
Lockwood, Ralph Gregory 1942- IntWWM 90
Lockwood, Ralph Harold 1929- St&PR 91
Lockwood, Rhodes Greene 1919- WhoAm 90
Lockwood, Robert Philip 1949- WhoAm 90
Lockwood, Robert W. 1924- WhoAm 90
Lockwood, Skip 1946- Ballpl 90
Lockwood, Stephen Chapman 1941- WhoE 91
Lockwood, Theodore Davidge 1924- WhoAm 90
Lockwood, Victoria BioIn 16
Lockwood, Ward 1894-1963 WhoAmA 91N
Lockwood, Warren S. BioIn 16
Lockwood, Willard Atkinson 1924- WhoAm 90
Lockwood, William A. 1923- St&PR 91
Lockyer, Charles Warren, Jr. 1944- St&PR 91, WhoAm 90
Lockyer, John A. 1934- St&PR 91
Lockyer, Joseph Norman 1836-1920 WorAlBi
Loco WhNaAH
Locock, Victoria Jane 1953- IntWWM 90
LoConto, Peter R. 1942- St&PR 91
Locre, Peter E ConAu 31NR
Locuratolo, Luis Rolando BiDrAPA 89
Lodder, Adrianus 1939- WhoWor 91
Lodder, Bryan E. 1944- St&PR 91
Lodder, Robert Andrew 1959- WhoSSW 91
Loden, Harold Dickson 1918- WhoAm 90
Loder, Edward James 1813-1865 BioIn 16
Loder, James Edwin WhoAm 90
Loder, John 1897-1988 AnObit 1988
Loder, John 1898-1988 BioIn 16
Loder, Kate 1825-1904 PenDiMP
Loder, Marc 1919- St&PR 91
Loderstedt, Robert L. St&PR 91
Lodewick, Philip Hughes 1944- WhoE 91
Lodewyk, Eric 1940- WhoAm 90
Lodge, Arthur John 1918- WhoE 91
Lodge, Arthur Scott 1922- WhoAm 90
Lodge, David 1935- BioIn 16, MajTwCW
Lodge, David John 1935- WhoWor 91
Lodge, David Williams 1941- St&PR 91, WhoAm 90
Lodge, Henry Cabot 1850-1924 BioIn 16, WorAlBi
Lodge, Henry Cabot 1902-1985 BioIn 16
Lodge, Henry Cabot, Jr. 1902-1985 WorAlBi
Lodge, Jack W., Jr. 1912- St&PR 91

Lodge, James Robert 1925- WhoAm 90
Lodge, John W., III 1947- St&PR 91
Lodge, Michelle WhoAmW 91
Lodge, Oliver 1851-1940 EncO&P 3
Lodge, Oliver Joseph 1851-1940 EncPaPR 91
Lodge, Patricia Grace 1934- WhoAmW 91, WhoWor 91
Lodge, Thomas Russell, Sr. 1943- WhoE 91
Lodhia, Anil J. 1949- St&PR 91
Lodica, Maria Francesca 1967- St&PR 91
Lodigensky, AlexisAlexandrovitch 1916- WhoWor 91
Lodigiani, Dario 1916- Ballpl 90
Lodish, Harvey Franklin 1941- WhoAm 90
Lodish, Leonard Melvin 1943- WhoAm 90
Lodmell, Dean Walter 1959- WhoE 91
Lodmell, Marilyn Maki 1937- WhoAmW 91
Lodovico, Maestro PenDiDA 89
Lodowski, Ruth Ellen 1951- WhoAmW 91, WhoSSW 91
Lo Duca, Gerard C. 1954- St&PR 91
Lodwick, Gwilym Savage 1917- WhoAm 90, WhoWor 91
Lodwick, Michael Wayne 1946- WhoEmL 91
Lodwick, Sheila Anne Ramerman 1956- WhoAmW 91
Lodwick, Teresa Jane 1959- WhoWrEP 89
Lodynsky, Jerry Roman 1951- WhoE 91
Loe, Brian Robert 1954- WhoEmL 91
Loe, Donn E. 1935- St&PR 91
Loe, Emmett Baxter 1924- WhoSSW 91
Loe, Harald 1926- WhoAm 90
Loe, James W 1929- BiDrAPA 89
Loe, Raymond A. 1931- St&PR 91
Loeb, Andrew Gothard 1944- St&PR 91
Loeb, Arthur L. 1923- IntWWM 90
Loeb, Ben Fohl, Jr. 1932- WhoAm 90
Loeb, Benjamin S. 1914- WhoE 91
Loeb, Carl M. 1875-1955 WorAlBi
Loeb, David S. 1924- St&PR 91
Loeb, Estelle S 1928- BiDrAPA 89
Loeb, Eva Gomez BiDrAPA 89
Loeb, Felix F, Jr. 1930- BiDrAPA 89
Loeb, Frances Lehman 1906- WhoAmW 91, WhoE 91, WhoWor 91
Loeb, Harvey 1952- WhoE 91
Loeb, Jacques 1859-1924 BioIn 16
Loeb, Jane Rupley 1938- WhoAmW 91
Loeb, Jeff AuBYP 90
Loeb, Jeffrey 1946- BioIn 16
Loeb, Jerome T. 1940- St&PR 91
Loeb, Jerome Thomas 1940- WhoAm 90
Loeb, John L. 1902- St&PR 91
Loeb, John L., Jr. 1930- St&PR 91
Loeb, John Langeloth 1902- WhoAm 90
Loeb, John Langeloth, Jr. 1930- WhoAm 90, WhoE 91
Loeb, Joyce Lichtgarn 1936- WhoAmW 91
Loeb, Larry Morris 1940- WhoAm 90, WhoE 91
Loeb, Laurence 1929- BiDrAPA 89, WhoE 91
Loeb, Loretta R 1932- BiDrAPA 89
Loeb, Marcel BioIn 16
Loeb, Marcia Joan 1933- WhoAmW 91
Loeb, Margaret Ann 1940- WhoAmW 91
Loeb, Marshall Robert 1929- WhoAm 90
Loeb, Marvin Phillip 1926- St&PR 91
Loeb, Nackey S. 1924- St&PR 91
Loeb, Nackey Scripps 1924- WhoAmW 91
Loeb, Nancy Hill 1949- WhoAmW 91
Loeb, Peter Kenneth 1936- WhoAm 90
Loeb, Richard 1906?-1936 WorAlBi
Loeb, Robert J. 1948- WhoEmL 91
Loeb, Ronald Marvin 1932- WhoAm 90
Loeb, Sheldon 1926- BiDrAPA 89
Loeb, Stephen H. 1931- St&PR 91
Loeb, Stuart Larry BiDrAPA 89
Loeb, Timothy Allan 1950- St&PR 91, WhoWrEP 89
Loeb, Virgil, Jr. 1921- WhoAm 90
Loebach, Michael Claud 1946- WhoEmL 91
Loebbecke, Ernest J. 1911- St&PR 91
Loebel, David 1950- IntWWM 90
Loebel, Jean Pierre 1935- BiDrAPA 89
Loebel, Kurt 1921- IntWWM 90
Loeben, Arthur Francis 1919- WhoE 91
Loeber, Lou 1894-1983 BiDWomA
Loebl, Ernest Moshe 1923- WhoAm 90
Loebl, Suzanne AuBYP 90
Loeblich, Helen Nina Tappan 1917- WhoAm 90
Loedding, Peter Alfred 1934- WhoE 91
Loedy, Ann 1941- WhoAmW 91
Loeff, Phyllis Saxon 1927- BiDrAPA 89
Loeffel, Bruce 1943- WhoE 91, WhoWor 91
Loeffel, Robert L. 1926- St&PR 91
Loeffelholz, Paul L BiDrAPA 89
Loeffler, Carl Eugene 1946- WhoAmA 91, WhoWrEP 89
Loeffler, Cheryl 1944- WhoAmW 91
Loeffler, David E. 1946- St&PR 91
Loeffler, David Karl 1959- WhoSSW 91
Loeffler, Ernst Wolfgang 1939- WhoWor 91
Loeffler, Frank Joseph 1928- WhoAm 90
Loeffler, Heinrich 1938- WhoWor 91
Loeffler, James Joseph 1931- WhoAm 90
Loeffler, Richard Harlan 1932- WhoAm 90
Loeffler, Roy J. 1942- St&PR 91
Loeffler, William George, Jr. 1939- WhoSSW 91
Loeffler, William R. 1914- St&PR 91
Loeffler, William Robert 1949- WhoWor 91
Loefgren, Gail Pitchford 1942- WhoAmW 91
Loegering, William Q. 1912-1987 BioIn 16
Loeh, Herbert W. 1932- St&PR 91
Loehle, Betty Barnes 1923- WhoAm 90, WhoAmA 91
Loehle, Richard E 1923- WhoAmA 91
Loehlin, John Clinton 1926- WhoAm 90
Loehr, Dean Verner 1952- St&PR 91
Loehr, Franklin 1912- EncO&P 3
Loehr, Gerald G. 1929- WhoAm 90
Loehr, Marla 1937- WhoAm 90, WhoAmW 91
Loehr, Max 1903-1988 BioIn 16, WhoAmA 91N
Loehrke, Christine Carol 1950- WhoAmW 91
Loehwing, William H. 1934- St&PR 91
Loeken, Janiese Ann 1939- BiDrAPA 89
Loenen, Gabrielle van EncCoWW
Loengard, John Borg 1934- WhoAm 90
Loening, Peter B. 1957- St&PR 91
Loening, Sarah Larkin 1896- WhoWrEP 89
Loeper, F. Joseph 1944- WhoE 91
Loepp, Fred Edward 1940- St&PR 91
Loeppert, H. Verne 1921- St&PR 91
Loeppert, Richard Henry, Jr. 1944- WhoSSW 91
Loeppke, Larry Dean 1950- WhoEmL 91
Loera, George WhoHisp 91
Loerakker, Jo Ann Katherine 1941- WhoSSW 91
Loerch, Russel D. 1926- St&PR 91
Loerke, William Carl 1920- WhoAm 90, WhoE 91
Loertscher, Alfred 1915- WhoWor 91
Loes, Billy 1929- Ballpl 90
Loes, David Anthony 1927- St&PR 91
Loesberg, Lance David 1956- St&PR 91
Loesberg, Richard Scott 1953- St&PR 91
Loesch, Harold C. 1926- WhoSSW 91
Loesch, Harrison 1916- WhoAm 90
Loesch, John George BiDrAPA 89
Loesch, Judith Ann 1946- WhoAmW 91
Loesch, Margaret BioIn 16
Loesch, Uwe 1943- BioIn 16
Loesche, Walter Joseph 1935- WhoAm 90
Loescher, Barbara Ann 1953- WhoAmW 91
Loescher, Edward M. 1943- St&PR 91
Loescher, Robert Wayne 1947- WhoAm 90
Loeschner, Ray B. 1931- WhoAm 90
Loeser, Hans F. 1920- St&PR 91
Loeser, Hans Ferdinand 1920- WhoAm 90
Loeser, John David 1935- WhoAm 90
Loeser, Lucille K BiDrAPA 89
Loeser, Norma Maine 1922- WhoAm 90
Loeser, Thomas 1956- WhoAmA 91
Loess, Henry Bernard 1924- WhoAm 90
Loesser, Frank 1910-1969 BioIn 16, OxCPMus, WorAlBi
Loetz, Johann PenDiDA 89
Loetz, Johann, Mrs. PenDiDA 89
Loev, Bernard 1928- WhoE 91
Loev, Gerald 1947- St&PR 91
Loevi, Francis Joseph, Jr. 1945- WhoE 91, WhoEmL 91
Loevinger, Barbara Lee BiDrAPA 89
Loevinger, Lee 1913- WhoAm 90, WhoE 91, WhoWor 91
Loevy, Sandor A. 1940- St&PR 91
Loew, Charles Elwood 1913- St&PR 91
Loew, Charles Williams 1953- St&PR 91
Loew, David N. 1949- WhoWor 91
Loew, Franklin Martin 1939- WhoAm 90
Loew, Mildred Falk NewYTBS 90
Loew, Patricia Ann 1943- WhoAmW 91
Loew, Ralph William 1907- WhoAm 90
Loew, Thomas Ward 1954- WhoE 91
Loewald, Elizabeth L BiDrAPA 89
Loewald, Hans W BiDrAPA 89
Loewe, Elaine Hilda 1955- WhoE 91
Loewe, Frederick 1901-1988 AnObit 1988, OxCPMus, WorAlBi
Loewe, Frederick 1904-1988 BioIn 16
Loewe, Leslie F. 1921- St&PR 91, WhoAm 90
Loewen, Erwin G. 1921- WhoAm 90
Loewen, Irene Leona 1945- WhoAmW 91
Loewen, Peter Cecil 1946- WhoAm 90
Loewenbaum, G. Walter, II 1945- WhoSSW 91
Loewenberg, Gerhard 1928- WhoAm 90
Loewenberg, John Dieter 1940- St&PR 91
Loewenguth Quartet PenDiMP
Loewenguth, Alfred PenDiMP
Loewenguth, Roger PenDiMP
Loewenstein, Benjamin S. 1912- St&PR 91
Loewenstein, Benjamin Steinberg 1912- WhoAm 90
Loewenstein, George Wolfgang 1890- WhoSSW 91
Loewenstein, Gerard 1930- St&PR 91
Loewenstein, Gustav 1899- BiDrAPA 89
Loewenstein, Martha Josephine 1913- WhoAmW 91
Loewenstein, Richard Joseph BiDrAPA 89
Loewenstein, Ruth WhoAmW 91
Loewenstein, Werner Randolph 1926- WhoAm 90
Loewenthal, Arthur Monroe 1941- St&PR 91
Loewenthal, Nessa Parker 1930- WhoAmW 91
Loewentheil, Albert BioIn 16
Loewer, Henry Peter 1934- WhoAmA 91, WhoSSW 91
Loewi, Andrew William 1950- WhoEmL 91
Loewi, Otto 1873-1961 WorAlBi
Loewi, Pat ODwPR 91
Loewinger, Kenneth Jeffery 1945- WhoEmL 91, WhoWor 91
Loewy, Arthur F. 1929- St&PR 91, WhoAm 90
Loewy, David Michael 1955- WhoSSW 91
Loewy, Henry M. 1910- St&PR 91
Loewy, Joanne Victoria 1961- WhoAmW 91
Loewy, Raymond 1893-1986 ConDes 90, PenDiDA 89
Loewy, Robert Gustav 1926- WhoAm 90, WhoE 91
Loewy, Steven A. 1952- WhoE 91
Lof, Carol Muriel 1941- WhoAmW 91, WhoE 91
Lofaro, Raymond Anthony 1936- WhoE 91
Lofaro, Rocco, Jr. 1950- WhoE 91
Lo Faso, Fred Joseph 1932- WhoE 91
Lofberg, Per G.H. 1947- St&PR 91
Lofchy, Jodi S BiDrAPA 89
Loferski, Joseph John 1925- WhoAm 90
Loff, Betty Garland 1932- WhoAmW 91
Loffer, Robert F. 1921- St&PR 91
Lofficier, Randy Joanne 1953- WhoAmW 91
Loffler, Berthold PenDiDA 89
Loffler, Leonard L. 1924- St&PR 91
Loffler, Pedro Max 1942- BiDrAPA 89
Loffredo, John Michael 1963- WhoE 91
Lofft, Thomas F 1935- BiDrAPA 89
Lofgren, Charles Augustin 1939- WhoAm 90
Lofgren, Karl Adolph 1915- WhoAm 90
Lofgren, Lars B BiDrAPA 89
Lofgren, Nils 1950?- EncPR&S 89
Lofgren, Norman Randolph 1940- WhoSSW 91
Lofgren, Sten Borje BiDrAPA 89
Lofgren-Laudenschlager, Sandra 1937- WhoAmW 91
Lofland, John Franklin 1936- WhoAm 90
Lofland, Lyn Hebert 1937- WhoAm 90
Loflin, Alan Russell 1947- WhoE 91
Lo Forti, Vernon Allen 1953- St&PR 91
Lofquist, Les BioIn 16
Lofquist, William Spencer 1936- WhoE 91
Lofstedt, Bengt Torkel Magnus 1931- WhoAm 90
Lofstrom, Donald J. 1948- St&PR 91
Lofstrom, Mark D. 1953- WhoEmL 91
Loft, Jep 1949- WhoWor 91
Loftfield, Robert Berner 1919- WhoAm 90
Lofthouse, Robert Ellis 1950- WhoE 91
Lofthouse, William 1934- BiDrAPA 89
Loftin, Judy Hill 1946- WhoSSW 91
Loftin, Marion Theo 1915- WhoAm 90
Loftin, Michael L. 1941- St&PR 91
Loftin, Nancy Carol 1954- St&PR 91
Lofting, Hugh 1886-1947 AuBYP 90, WorAlBi
Loftis, Curtis Bryant 1952- WhoSSW 91
Loftis, John 1919- WhoAm 90
Loftis, Joseph Michael 1941- St&PR 91
Lofton, James David 1956- WhoAm 90
Lofton, Michael W. 1946- St&PR 91
Lofton, Otmara 1959- WhoAmW 91
Lofton, Randall Hampton 1947- WhoSSW 91
Lofts, Nora 1904-1983 AuBYP 90
Lofts, Norah 1904-1983 FemiCLE
Loftus, Anne S. BioIn 16
Loftus, Joseph A NewYTBS 90
Loftus, Joseph A. 1907-1990 BioIn 16
Loftus, Joseph Philip, Jr. 1930- WhoSSW 91
Loftus, Michael J. 1928- St&PR 91
Loftus, Peter G. 1940- St&PR 91
Loftus, Peter M 1948- WhoAmA 91
Loftus, Rita Celestine 1938- WhoAmW 91
Loftus, Robert Gordon 1930- WhoWor 91
Loftus, Thomas A BiDrAPA 89
Loftus, Thomas Adolph 1945- WhoAm 90
Loftus, Tom 1856-1910 Ballpl 90
Loftus, William 1927- St&PR 91
Loftus, William Frederick 1938- St&PR 91, WhoAm 90
Loftus, William George 1926- St&PR 91, WhoSSW 91
Lofty, Charles F. 1945- St&PR 91
Loga, John 1926- WhoAm 90
Loga, Sanda 1932- WhoAm 90
Logalbo, Michael 1955- St&PR 91
Logan 1725?-1780 WhNaAH
Logan the Mingo 1725?-1780 WhNaAH
Logan, Alexander 1841-1894 DcCanB 12
Logan, Barbara Aimar 1941- WhoAmW 91
Logan, Bob 1910-1978 Ballpl 90
Logan, Carolyn Elizabeth 1943- WhoSSW 91
Logan, Charles Harper 1955- WhoSSW 91
Logan, Christine Lynne 1961- WhoAmW 91
Logan, Cornelius Ambrose 1832-1899 BioIn 16
Logan, Dan 1946- WhoE 91, WhoWor 91
Logan, Daniel 1936- EncO&P 3
Logan, David BiDrAPA 89
Logan, David George 1937- WhoAmA 91
Logan, David Gill 1935- BiDrAPA 89
Logan, David J. 1933- St&PR 91
Logan, David Samuel 1918- WhoWor 91
Logan, Debora Lynn 1962- WhoSSW 91
Logan, Deborah 1761-1839 FemiCLE
Logan, Denise Patricia 1958- WhoE 91
Logan, Devere E. 1934- ODwPR 91
Logan, Ella 1913-1969 OxCPMus
Logan, Francis D., Jr. 1945- St&PR 91
Logan, Francis Dummer 1931- WhoAm 90
Logan, Frank Anderson 1924- WhoAm 90
Logan, Frank Henderson 1936- WhoAm 90
Logan, Frederick Knight 1871-1928 OxCPMus
Logan, Gene Adams 1922- WhoAmA 91
Logan, George BioIn 16
Logan, George H. 1916- St&PR 91
Logan, George M 1941- ConAu 131
Logan, Gordon Baker 1946- WhoSSW 91
Logan, Grace Eleanor Miller 1908- WhoAmW 91, WhoE 91, WhoWor 91
Logan, Harold Roy 1921- WhoAm 90
Logan, Harry A. 1924-1989 BioIn 16
Logan, Henry Vincent 1942- St&PR 91, WhoAm 90
Logan, Howard M. 1925- St&PR 91
Logan, Ian 1939- ConDes 90
Logan, James 1674-1751 EncCRAm, WhNaAH
Logan, James 1725?-1780 EncCRAm
Logan, James Addison 1879-1930 BioIn 16
Logan, James C. 1914- WhoAm 90
Logan, James Kenneth 1929- WhoAm 90
Logan, Janet Ruth 1941- WhoAmW 91
Logan, Jean Shipley 1943- WhoAmW 91
Logan, Jerome A 1929- BiDrAPA 89
Logan, John A. WhoSSW 91
Logan, John Arthur, Jr. 1923- WhoAm 90
Logan, John F. 1938- St&PR 91
Logan, John Francis 1938- WhoE 91
Logan, Johnny 1927- Ballpl 90
Logan, Joseph Granville, Jr. 1920- WhoAm 90
Logan, Joshua BioIn 16
Logan, Joshua 1908-1988 AnObit 1988, OxCPMus, WorAlBi
Logan, Joyce Polley 1935- WhoSSW 91
Logan, Judith Manss 1945- WhoSSW 91
Logan, Kathleen BiDrAPA 89
Logan, Kathryn Vance 1946- WhoAmW 91, WhoSSW 91
Logan, Lacey Alexis 1958- WhoAmW 91
Logan, Langston Duvall 1951- WhoSSW 91
Logan, Larry Glenn 1927- IntWWM 90
Logan, Laura Robekah 1879-1974 BioIn 16
Logan, Liz 1957- WhoAmW 91
Logan, Lowell Alvin 1921- WhoAm 90
Logan, Lowell Arthur 1929- St&PR 91
Logan, Lox Albert, Jr. 1954- WhoAm 90
Logan, Margaret Colston 1942- WhoSSW 91
Logan, Mark Gooch 1950- WhoSSW 91
Logan, Martha Daniell 1704-1779 EncCRAm
Logan, Mathew Kuykendall 1933- WhoAm 90
Logan, Maurice 1886-1977 WhoAmA 91N
Logan, Michael J 1939- BiDrAPA 89
Logan, Nedda BioIn 16
Logan, Nedda Harrigan 1900-1989 ConTFT 8
Logan, Nesta Adean 1951- WhoAmW 91
Logan, Olive 1836-1909 NotWoAT
Logan, Olive 1839-1909 BioIn 16, FemiCLE
Logan, Onnie Lee BioIn 16
Logan, Oran F. 1943- St&PR 91
Logan, Peter Stephen, Sr. 1925- St&PR 91
Logan, Rae W. 1942- St&PR 91

Logan, Ralph Andre 1926- *WhoAm 90*
Logan, Raymond F. 1923- *St&PR 91*
Logan, Richard Fink 1914- *WhoAm 90*
Logan, Richard Leo 1941- *St&PR 91*
Logan, Richard Walter 1950- *WhoEmL 91*
Logan, Rodman Emmason 1922- *WhoAm 90*
Logan, Sandra Jean 1940- *WhoAmW 91*
Logan, Scott Allen 1957- *WhoSSW 91*
Logan, Sharon Brooks 1945- *WhoAmW 91*
Logan, Stanley Nicholas 1954- *WhoEmL 91*
Logan, Stephen Bean, III 1932- *WhoSSW 91*
Logan, Terence Patrick 1936- *WhoAm 90*
Logan, Terry Lynn 1955- *WhoSSW 91*
Logan, Thomas Joseph 1951- *WhoEmL 91*
Logan, Veryle Jean *WhoAmW 91*
Logan, W.A. 1903- *St&PR 91*
Logan, W. Miller 1959- *BiDrAPA 89*
Logan, Walter C., II *St&PR 91*
Logan, William Bryant *BioIn 16*
Logan, William E 1942- *BiDrAPA 89*
Logan, William Searle 1949- *BiDrAPA 89*
Loganbill, G. Bruce 1938- *WhoAm 90*
Loge, Dan *BioIn 16*
Loge, Frank Jean, II 1945- *WhoAm 90, WhoEmL 91*
Logemann, Jane Marie 1942- *WhoAmA 91*
Logemann, Jerilyn Ann 1942- *WhoAm 90*
Loggans, Susan Elizabeth 1949- *WhoAm 90*
Loggia, Robert *BioIn 16*
Loggia, Robert 1930- *WhoAm 90, WorAlBi*
Loggie, Helen A *WhoAmA 91N*
Loggie, Jennifer Mary Hildreth 1936- *WhoAm 90*
Loggins and Messina *EncPR&S 89*
Loggins, Bobby Gene 1955- *WhoEmL 91*
Loggins, Kenny 1947- *WhoAm 90*
Loggins, Kenny 1948- *EncPR&S 89, WorAlBi*
Loghry, Gerald Jay 1937- *St&PR 91*
Logie, Nicholas 1950- *IntWWM 90*
Login, Ivan Stewart 1946- *WhoSSW 91*
Logli, Paolo 1937- *WhoWor 91*
Logothetis, Anestis 1921- *IntWWM 90*
Logothetis, E.N. *St&PR 91*
Logothetis, Steven 1955- *St&PR 91*
Logreco, Gerard Ernest 1951- *WhoSSW 91*
Logsdon, John Mortimer, III 1937- *WhoE 91*
Logsdon, Kay Lynne 1955- *WhoWrEP 89*
Logsdon, Linda 1940- *BiDrAPA 89*
Logsdon, Lois Irene *AuBYP 90*
Logsdon, Richard Henry 1912- *AuBYP 90, WhoAm 90*
Logsdon, Thomas S. 1937- *WhoWrEP 89*
Logue, A Douglas 1938- *BiDrAPA 89*
Logue, A. Douglas 1938- *WhoE 91*
Logue, Dennis Emhardt 1944- *WhoAm 90*
Logue, Dora D *BiDrAPA 89*
Logue, Edward Joseph 1921- *WhoAm 90, WhoE 91*
Logue, Frank 1924- *WhoAm 90*
Logue, Harry Edward 1934- *BiDrAPA 89*
Logue, J. Gordon 1922- *St&PR 91*
Logue, James Allen 1947- *WhoE 91*
Logue, Joseph Carl 1920- *WhoAm 90*
Logue, Peggy King 1958- *WhoAmW 91*
Logue-Kinder, Joan 1943- *WhoAmW 91, WhoE 91*
Loh, Anton *PenDiMP*
Loh, Arthur Tsung Yuan 1923- *WhoE 91*
Loh, Morag *AuBYP 90*
Loh, Robert Daniel, Jr. 1951- *WhoEmL 91*
Loh, Robert Nan-Khang *WhoAm 90*
Loh, Toon Seng Michael 1957- *WhoWor 91*
Lohafer, Douglas Allen 1949- *WhoWor 91*
Lohan, William Denis 1931- *WhoWrEP 89*
Lohden, William P. 1932- *St&PR 91*
Lohf, Kenneth A. 1925- *BioIn 16, WhoAm 90*
Lohia, Renagi Renagi 1945- *WhoWor 91*
Lohman, Ann S. 1812-1878 *BioAmW*
Lohman, Catherina Anna Maria de Savornin 1868-1930 *EncCoWW*
Lohman, Gordon Russell 1934- *St&PR 91*
Lohman, John Frederick 1935- *WhoAm 90*
Lohman, Loretta Cecellia 1944- *WhoAmW 91*
Lohman, Maurice Anatole 1921- *WhoE 91*
Lohman, Walter Rearick 1917- *WhoAm 90*
Lohman, William Francis 1948- *St&PR 91, WhoAm 90*
Lohmann, Donald Gene 1940- *St&PR 91, WhoAm 90*
Lohmann, Janet Cynthia 1939- *St&PR 91*
Lohmann, Jeanne Ruth Ackley 1923- *WhoWrEP 89*
Lohmann, Keith Henry 1955- *WhoE 91*
Lohmann, Wolfgang Hans-Joachim 1930- *WhoWor 91*
Lohmeier, Stanley F. 1951- *St&PR 91*
Lohmeyer, Lyle S. 1953- *St&PR 91*
Lohmuller, Martin Nicholas 1919- *WhoAm 90*
Lohner, Luisa Maria 1954- *BiDrAPA 89*
Lohnes, Walter F. W. 1925- *WhoAm 90*
Lohr, Benjamin Franklin, Mrs. *WhoAmW 91, WhoSSW 91, WhoWor 91*
Lohr, Donald Russell 1933- *St&PR 91, WhoAm 90*
Lohr, George E. 1931- *WhoAm 90*
Lohr, Harold Russell 1922- *WhoAm 90*
Lohr, James B 1955- *BiDrAPA 89*
Lohr, John William 1947- *St&PR 91*
Lohr, Judith Kaufer 1944- *WhoAmW 91*
Lohr, Mary Margaret *WhoAm 90*
Lohr, Richard Theodore 1941- *St&PR 91*
Lohr, Theodore R. 1911- *St&PR 91*
Lohrer, Richard Baker 1932- *St&PR 91, WhoAm 90*
Lohrke, Lucky 1924- *Ballpl 90*
Lohrman, Bill 1913- *Ballpl 90*
Lohrman, George H *BiDrAPA 89*
Lohrman, John J. 1920- *St&PR 91, WhoAm 90*
Lohrman, William Walter 1954- *WhoSSW 91*
Lohry, Janet Sue 1941- *WhoAmW 91*
Lohse, Austin Webb 1926- *WhoAm 90*
Lohse, Bernhard 1928- *WhoWor 91*
Lohse, Fred 1908- *IntWWM 90*
Lohse, Heinrich 1896-1964 *BioIn 16*
Lohse, Richard Paul 1902-1988 *BioIn 16*
Lohse, William 1952- *St&PR 91*
Lohsen, Robert A. 1955- *St&PR 91*
Lohuizen-De Leeuw, Johanna E van 1919-1983 *BioIn 16*
Loiello, John Peter 1943- *WhoE 91*
Loigman, Harold 1930- *St&PR 91, WhoAm 90*
Loigman, Larry Scott 1954- *WhoEmL 91*
Loir, Alexis 1640-1713 *PenDiDA 89*
Lois, George 1931- *ConDes 90, St&PR 91, WhoAm 90*
Loiseaux, Pierre Roland 1925- *WhoAm 90*
Loiselle, Bernard Roger 1919- *WhoAmA 91*
Loiselle, Gilles 1929- *WhoAm 90, WhoE 91*
Loiselle, Helene 1928- *OxCCanT [port]*
Loisy, Jeanne 1913- *AuBYP 90*
Loizzo, Joseph John *BiDrAPA 89*
Loizzo, Marius J *BiDrAPA 89*
Lo-Johansson, Ivar 1901- *DcScanL*
Lo-Johansson, ivar 1901-1990 *ConAu 131*
L'Okanga La Ndju Pene Luambo Makiadi *BioIn 16*
Loken, Merle Kenneth 1924- *WhoAm 90*
Loken, Michael Edwin 1942- *St&PR 91*
Loken-Egdahl, Elizabeth P *BiDrAPA 89*
Lokesh, C. B. *BiDrAPA 89*
Lokey, Hamilton 1910- *WhoAm 90*
Lokey, Irene Raye 1946- *WhoAmW 91*
Lokhandwala, Fakhrudin Akberali 1932- *St&PR 91*
Lokhorst, Jonathan Robert 1962- *WhoEmL 91*
Lokhvitskaia, Mirra Aleksandrovna 1869-1905 *EncCoWW*
Lokin, D.H.A.C. *WhoWor 91*
Lokke, Stephen Warren 1953- *BiDrAPA 89*
Lokken, Eva Tryti 1964- *WhoAmW 91*
Lokmer, Stephanie Ann 1957- *WhoWor 91*
Lola, Mama *EncCoWW*
Lolich, Mickey 1940- *Ballpl 90 [port]*
Lolich, Mickey Stephen 1940- *WhoAm 90*
Lolla, John Joseph 1953- *WhoE 91*
Lollar, Coleman Aubrey 1946- *WhoWrEP 89*
Lollar, Coleman Aubrey, Jr. 1946- *WhoAm 90*
Lollar, Deborah Yepsen 1953- *WhoSSW 91*
Lollar, John H. 1938- *St&PR 91*
Lollar, John Henry, III 1938- *WhoAm 90*
Lollar, Robert Miller 1915- *WhoWor 91*
Lollar, Sherm 1924-1977 *Ballpl 90 [port]*
Lollar, Thurman Ray 1940- *St&PR 91, WhoAm 90*
Lollar, Tim 1956- *Ballpl 90*
Lolley, William Randall 1931- *WhoAm 90*
Lolli, Don Ray 1949- *WhoEmL 91*
Lollobrigida, Gina 1927- *WhoWor 91*
Lollobrigida, Gina 1928- *WorAlBi*
Loloma, Charles 1921- *WhoAmA 91*
Lolwing, Alfred James 1929- *St&PR 91*
Lom, Herbert 1917- *ConTFT 8 [port], WorAlBi*
Lomahaftewa, Linda 1947- *WhoAmA 91*
Lomakoski, Stephen M. 1926- *St&PR 91*
Loman, Diane Louise Moore 1948- *WhoAmW 91*
Loman, Julius *BiDrAPA 89*
Loman, M. Laverne 1928- *WhoAmW 91, WhoSSW 91*
Lomas, Ben 1936- *BiDrAPA 89*
Lomas, Bernard Tagg 1924- *WhoAm 90, WhoWor 91*
Lomask, Milton 1909- *AuBYP 90*
Lomask, Milton Nachman 1909- *WhoAm 90, WhoWrEP 89*
Lomasney, Mary T. 1957- *St&PR 91*
Lomason, Harry Austin, II 1934- *St&PR 91, WhoAm 90*
Lomason, William Keithledge 1910- *St&PR 91, WhoAm 90*
Lomax, Adrian *BioIn 16*
Lomax, Alan 1915- *OxCPMus*
Lomax, Derek W 1933- *ConAu 130*
Lomax, Donald P. 1934- *St&PR 91*
Lomax, Gary T. 1951- *St&PR 91*
Lomax, Harvard 1922- *WhoAm 90*
Lomax, James Welton, II 1944- *BiDrAPA 89*
Lomax, John 1867-1948 *OxCPMus*
Lomax, John Frank 1939- *St&PR 91*
Lomax, John H. 1924- *St&PR 91, WhoAm 90, WhoSSW 91*
Lomax, Michael L. *BioIn 16*
Lomax, Peggy Jean *BiDrAPA 89*
Lomax, Peggy Jean 1960- *WhoE 91*
Lomax, Stan 1899-1988 *Ballpl 90*
Lomax, Susan Mary *BiDrAPA 89*
Lomax, Wesley James 1929- *St&PR 91*
Lombard, Alain 1940- *IntWWM 90, PenDiMP*
Lombard, Annette 1929- *WhoAmA 91*
Lombard, Carole 1908-1942 *BioIn 16*
Lombard, Carole 1909-1942 *BioAmW, WorAlBi*
Lombard, Elna A *BiDrAPA 89*
Lombard, F. Ernest 1947- *St&PR 91*
Lombard, James Anthony, III 1955- *WhoE 91*
Lombard, James Raymond 1942- *WhoE 91*
Lombard, Jay Leslie *BiDrAPA 89*
Lombard, John Francis 1929- *St&PR 91*
Lombard, Michael Joseph 1930- *St&PR 91*
Lombard, Mitchell Monte 1951- *WhoSSW 91*
Lombard, Nap *MajTwCW*
Lombard, Peter 1100?-1160 *WorAlBi*
Lombard, Richard D. *BioIn 16*
Lombard, Richard S. 1928- *St&PR 91*
Lombard, Richard Spencer 1928- *WhoAm 90*
Lombarda *EncCoWW*
Lombardi, Angelo Rocco 1923- *WhoAm 90*
Lombardi, Carl A. 1943- *St&PR 91*
Lombardi, Carole *ODwPR 91*
Lombardi, Cornelius Ennis, Jr. 1926- *WhoAm 90*
Lombardi, David Ennis, Jr. 1940- *WhoWor 91*
Lombardi, Ernie 1908-1977 *Ballpl 90 [port]*
Lombardi, Eugene Patsy 1923- *IntWWM 90, WhoAm 90*
Lombardi, Giancarlo 1937- *WhoWor 91*
Lombardi, Jeffrey 1962- *St&PR 91*
Lombardi, John Barba-Linardo 1915- *WhoAm 90*
Lombardi, John Joseph 1940- *St&PR 91*
Lombardi, John V. 1942- *WhoAm 90*
Lombardi, Louis, Jr. 1946- *St&PR 91*
Lombardi, Richard M. 1956- *St&PR 91*
Lombardi, Richard Thomas 1946- *WhoAm 90*
Lombardi, Vic 1922- *Ballpl 90*
Lombardi, Vince *BioIn 16*
Lombardi, Vince 1913-1970 *WorAlBi*
Lombardi, Vincent A *BiDrAPA 89*
Lombardo, Anthony Lawrence 1927- *St&PR 91*
Lombardo, Bonnie Jane 1941- *WhoAmW 91*
Lombardo, Carmen 1903-1971 *OxCPMus*
Lombardo, Charles J. 1943- *St&PR 91*
Lombardo, David Albert 1947- *WhoWor 91*
Lombardo, Gaetano 1940- *WhoAm 90*
Lombardo, Gary Anthony 1948- *WhoE 91*
Lombardo, Gregory Thomas *BiDrAPA 89*
Lombardo, Guy 1902-1977 *BioIn 16, OxCPMus, WorAlBi*
Lombardo, Irene E. 1944- *WhoWrEP 89*
Lombardo, Jay Frank 1963- *WhoSSW 91*
Lombardo, John Richard 1933- *St&PR 91*
Lombardo, Josef Vincent 1908- *WhoAm 90, WhoAmA 91*
Lombardo, Joseph J. 1914-1990 *BioIn 16*
Lombardo, Michael John 1927- *WhoE 91, WhoWor 91*
Lombardo, Philip Joseph 1935- *WhoAm 90, WhoE 91, WhoWor 91*
Lombardo Toledano, Vicente 1894-1968 *BioIn 16*
Lombardozzi, Steve 1960- *Ballpl 90*
Lombardy, Ross David 1920- *St&PR 91*
Lombillo, Jose R 1937- *BiDrAPA 89*
Lombra, Raymond Eugene 1946- *WhoAm 90*
Lombroso, Cesare 1835-1909 *EncPaPR 91*
Lombroso, Cesare 1836-1909 *EncO&P 3*
Lombroso, Paul Jan 1950- *BiDrAPA 89*
Lo Medico, Thomas Gaetano 1904-1985 *WhoAmA 91N*
Lomeli, Francisco A. 1947- *WhoHisp 91*
Lomeli, Marta 1952- *WhoAmW 91*
Lomer, Mary *ConAu 132*
Lomerson, Edwin Orville, Jr. 1928- *WhoE 91*
Lomerson, James Dale, Jr. 1956- *WhoE 91*
Lomicka, William Henry 1937- *St&PR 91, WhoAm 90*
Lomma, Anthony C. 1958- *St&PR 91*
Lomma, Ralph J. 1926- *St&PR 91*
Lommatzsch, Ruth Myrtle 1913- *WhoWrEP 89*
Lomnicki, Tadeusz Jan 1927- *WhoWor 91*
Lomo, Leif 1929- *St&PR 91, WhoAm 90*
Lomon, Earle Leonard 1930- *WhoAm 90*
Lomon, Kevin *BioIn 16*
Lomon, Ruth 1930- *IntWWM 90*
Lomonaco, Robert Anthony 1940- *St&PR 91*
Lomonaco, Salvatore 1940- *BiDrAPA 89*
Lomonaco, Vito Paul 1948- *St&PR 91*
Lomonosoff, James Marc 1951- *WhoAm 90, WhoEmL 91*
Lomonosov, Mikhail 1711-1765 *WorAlBi*
Lomonosov, Mikhail Vasilievich 1711-1765 *BioIn 16*
Lo Monte, John 1947- *WhoE 91*
Lomov', Georgii Ippolitovich 1888-1938 *BioIn 16*
Lomova, Charlotte *BiDrAPA 89*
Lompa, Susan Joyce 1941- *WhoAmW 91*
LoMurro, Dominic Dennis 1929- *WhoSSW 91*
Lona Reyes, Arturo 1925- *WhoAm 90*
Lonati, John, Jr. 1933- *St&PR 91*
Lonborg, James Reynold 1942- *WhoAm 90*
Lonborg, Jim 1942- *Ballpl 90*
Loncar, Budimir 1925- *WhoWor 91*
Loncaric, Josip 1958- *WhoE 91*
Lond, Harley Weldon 1946- *WhoWrEP 89*
Londborg, Peter D. *BiDrAPA 89*
Londen, William Howard 1927- *St&PR 91*
Londin, Barbara 1931- *WhoAmA 91*
Londkuist, Resa Ann 1960- *St&PR 91*
London String Quartet *PenDiMP*
London, Alexander *WhoAmA 91*
London, Anna 1913- *WhoAmA 91*
London, Barbara 1946- *WhoAmA 91*
London, Barry Joseph 1946- *WhoAm 90*
London, Bobby 1950- *EncACom*
London, Carol Allen 1945- *WhoSSW 91*
London, Charles Stuart 1946- *WhoE 91*
London, Charlotte Isabella 1946- *WhoEmL 91*
London, Charmian K. 1870-1955 *BioAmW*
London, Cheryl Ann 1957- *WhoAmW 91*
London, David B 1948- *BiDrAPA 89, WhoE 91*
London, Debra S *BiDrAPA 89*
London, Elca 1930- *WhoAmA 91*
London, Eleanor 1955- *WhoE 91*
London, Emanuel *BioIn 16*
London, Ephraim *NewYTBS 90 [port]*
London, Ephraim 1911-1990 *BioIn 16, ConAu 131*
London, Eric Bart 1952- *BiDrAPA 89*
London, Eric S. 1952- *St&PR 91*
London, Gabrielle *BioIn 16*
London, George 1919-1985 *PenDiMP*
London, Herbert Ira 1939- *WhoAm 90*
London, Irving Myer 1918- *WhoAm 90*
London, J. Phillip 1937- *WhoAm 90, WhoSSW 91*
London, Jack *MajTwCW*
London, Jack 1876-1916 *AuBYP 90, BioIn 16, EncAL, EncPaPR 91, TwCLC 39 [port], WorAlBi, WrPh*
London, Jack 1915- *WhoWrEP 89*
London, Jack Edward 1949- *WhoEmL 91*
London, Jacqueline 1943- *WhoWor 91*
London, Jeffrey Arthur 1948- *BiDrAPA 89*
London, Jill Abbey 1953- *WhoAmW 91*
London, John Griffith *AuBYP 90*
London, John Griffith 1876-1916 *MajTwCW*
London, Jonathan Paul 1947- *WhoWrEP 89*
London, Julie 1926- *OxCPMus, WorAlBi*
London, Leslie H. 1945- *St&PR 91*
London, Liz E. *WhoWrEP 89*
London, Lloyd Llewellyn 1920- *St&PR 91, WhoSSW 91*
London, Marina 1956- *WhoAmW 91*
London, Martin 1934- *WhoAm 90*
London, Meyer 1871-1926 *EncAL*
London, Michael J. 1952- *ODwPR 91*
London, Michael Jeffrey 1952- *WhoE 91*
London, Nathaniel J 1927- *BiDrAPA 89*
London, Peter 1939- *WhoAmA 91*
London, Philip 1932- *St&PR 91*
London, Rachel *BioIn 16*
London, Ray William 1943- *WhoWor 91*
London, Robert T *BiDrAPA 89*
London, Robin Sigman 1963- *WhoAmW 91*
London, Sheri Faith 1955- *WhoAmW 91*
London, Sherri Sue 1960- *WhoAmW 91*
London, Theodore 1933- *St&PR 91*
London, W. Boyd, Jr. 1952- *St&PR 91*

London, W. Thomas 1944- *St&PR 91*
London, Wayne Paul 1938- *BiDrAPA 89*
Londoner, David Jay 1937- *WhoAm 90*
Londono Arango, Jairo 1941- *WhoWor 91*
Londono Peredes, Julio *WhoWor 91*
Londre, Felicia Hardison 1941- *WhoWrEP 89*
Londre, Larry S. *ODwPR 91*
Londroche, Gerald Clifford 1938- *WhoSSW 91*
Lone Justice *EncPR&S 89*
Lone Wolf 1820?-1879 *WhNaAH*
Lone, John *BioIn 16*
Lone, Mohammed Salim 1943- *WhoE 91*
Lonegan, Thomas Lee 1932- *WhoWor 91*
Lonergan, James D. 1925- *St&PR 91*
Lonergan, Joy 1909- *AuBYP 90*
Lonergan, Marc 1949- *BiDrAPA 89*
Lonergan, Pierce James 1931- *St&PR 91*
Lonergan, Thomas Francis, III 1941- *WhoWor 91*
Lonergan, Thomas W. *St&PR 91*
Lonewolf, Rosemary 1953- *BioIn 16*
Loney, George Edward 1946- *WhoAm 90*
Loney, Glenn Meredith 1928- *WhoAm 90*
Loney, Robert Treulieb 1932- *St&PR 91*
Loney Gallegos, Jacqueline A. 1961- *WhoAmW 91*
Long, Alfred B. 1909- *WhoSSW 91*
Long, Alvin W. 1923- *St&PR 91*
Long, Alvin William 1923- *WhoAm 90*
Long, Anne 1681?-1711 *BiDEWW*
Long, Anne Williams 1943- *WhoAmW 91*
Long, Anthony Arthur 1937- *WhoAm 90*
Long, Armistead Hunter 1938- *St&PR 91*
Long, Arthur Dennis 1952- *WhoE 91*
Long, Arthur F. *BioIn 16*
Long, Avon 1910-1984 *DrBlPA 90*
Long, Barbara 1951- *BiDrAPA 89*
Long, Bernard Jackson 1941- *St&PR 91*
Long, Bernard Robert 1929- *WhoWor 91*
Long, Beverly Glenn 1923- *WhoAm 90*
Long, Bill 1960- *Ballpl 90*
Long, Boaz Walton 1876-1962 *BioIn 16*
Long, Brian Kenneth 1958- *BiDrAPA 89*
Long, Bruce C. 1945- *St&PR 91*
Long, C Chee 1942- *WhoAmA 91N*
Long, Carl Ferdinand 1928- *WhoAm 90*
Long, Cecil Lanier 1938- *WhoSSW 91*
Long, Charles F. 1938- *ODwPR 91*
Long, Charles Farrell 1933- *WhoSSW 91*
Long, Charles Franklin 1938- *WhoAm 90, WhoWrEP 89*
Long, Charles Houston 1926- *WhoAm 90*
Long, Charles W *BiDrAPA 89*
Long, Cheryl Lynn 1946- *WhoAmW 91*
Long, Chin-san 1892- *BioIn 16*
Long, Christine Mathews 1953- *WhoEmL 91*
Long, Christopher Francis 1955- *WhoEmL 91*
Long, Clarence E., III 1943- *St&PR 91*
Long, Clarence William 1917- *WhoAm 90*
Long, Cynthia Ann 1961- *WhoAmW 91*
Long, Cyril Norman Hugh 1901-1970 *DcScB S2*
Long, Dale 1926- *Ballpl 90*
Long, Dale Hawkins 1952- *WhoSSW 91*
Long, Daniel James 1954- *WhoEmL 91*
Long, David Gordon 1952- *WhoEmL 91*
Long, David Ricard 1943- *St&PR 91*
Long, David Russell 1942- *WhoE 91*
Long, Debra Jean 1956- *WhoEmL 91*
Long, Dennis Arnold *BiDrAPA 89*
Long, Dennis Patrick 1935- *St&PR 91*
Long, Donald Charles 1923- *St&PR 91*
Long, Donald E. *St&PR 91*
Long, Donald Gregory 1937- *WhoE 91*
Long, Donlin Martin 1934- *WhoAm 90*
Long, Dorothy Valjean 1928- *WhoAmW 91*
Long, Douglas 1925-1990 *BioIn 16*
Long, Douglas Clark 1932- *WhoAm 90*
Long, Douglas Paul 1954- *WhoEmL 91*
Long, Dreama Ann 1959- *WhoSSW 91*
Long, Durward 1930- *WhoAm 90*
Long, Dwight William 1928- *St&PR 91*
Long, Earl 1895-1960 *WorAlBi*
Long, Earl K. *BioIn 16*
Long, Earlene 1938- *BioIn 16*
Long, Earlene Roberta 1938- *WhoWrEP 89*
Long, Edward A. 1927- *St&PR 91*
Long, Edward Arlo 1927- *WhoAm 90*
Long, Edward G *BiDrAPA 89*
Long, Eleanor Pauline 1942- *WhoSSW 91*
Long, Electra 1943- *WhoAmA 91*
Long, Erik L. 1951- *WhoSSW 91*
Long, Ernestine Martha Joullian 1906- *WhoAmW 91*
Long, Eugene Hudson 1908- *WhoAm 90, WhoWrEP 89*
Long, Eugene Thomas, III 1935- *WhoAm 90*
Long, Eva Marie 1944- *St&PR 91*
Long, Evelyn Margaret 1964- *WhoAmW 91, WhoE 91*
Long, Francis Mark 1929- *WhoAm 90*
Long, Frank Weathers 1906- *WhoAmA 91, WhoWrEP 89*
Long, Franklin A. 1910- *WhoAm 90*
Long, G. Donald *BioIn 16*
Long, G.E. 1944- *St&PR 91*
Long, G. Gordon 1953- *WhoWrEP 89*
Long, Gary L. 1942- *St&PR 91*
Long, Gary Marvin 1949- *WhoSSW 91*
Long, Gerald H. 1928- *WhoSSW 91*
Long, Gilles 1940- *WhoWor 91*
Long, Gretchen 1937- *St&PR 91*
Long, Helen Halter *WhoAm 90*
Long, Helen Halter 1906- *WhoWrEP 89*
Long, Henry K., Jr. 1936- *St&PR 91*
Long, Henry Martyn 1836- *AmLegL*
Long, Herbert Strainge 1919- *WhoAm 90*
Long, Herman 1866-1909 *Ballpl 90 [port]*
Long, Howard Charles 1918- *WhoAm 90*
Long, Howie 1960- *WorAlBi*
Long, Hubert 1907- *WhoAmA 91*
Long, Huey P. 1893-1935 *WorAlBi*
Long, I. A. *WhoAm 90*
Long, I.A. 1899- *St&PR 91*
Long, Jackie B. 1956- *St&PR 91*
Long, James A. 1942- *St&PR 91*
Long, James Duncan 1925- *WhoSSW 91*
Long, James T 1940- *BiDrAPA 89*
Long, Jefferson Franklin 1836-1901 *BlkAmsC [port]*
Long, Jenny 1955- *WhoAmA 91*
Long, Jill 1952- *WhoAm 90, WhoAmW 91*
Long, Joan Hazel 1952- *WhoE 91*
Long, Joanna Ormiston 1922- *WhoWrEP 89*
Long, John Allen 1919- *St&PR 91*
Long, John Aloysius, Jr. 1947- *WhoE 91*
Long, John Broaddus, Jr. 1944- *WhoAm 90*
Long, John C. *ODwPR 91*
Long, John Chancellor 1953- *WhoE 91*
Long, John D. 1920- *WhoAm 90*
Long, John Davis 1838-1915 *AmLegL, BiDrUSE 89*
Long, John Maloy 1925- *WhoAm 90*
Long, John Paul 1926- *WhoAm 90*
Long, John Walter *BiDrAPA 89*
Long, Joseph F. 1940- *St&PR 91*
Long, Joseph K., III 1937- *WhoE 91*
Long, Joseph M. *NewYTBS 90*
Long, Joseph M. 1912- *St&PR 91, WhoAm 90*
Long, Kathleen Pettebone 1945- *WhoAmW 91*
Long, Kenneth Robert 1940- *St&PR 91, WhoAm 90*
Long, Kerry Jean 1948- *WhoAmW 91*
Long, Kim 1949- *ConAu 129*
Long, Larry Clark 1950- *St&PR 91*
Long, Larry E. 1940- *St&PR 91*
Long, Laura Louise 1951- *WhoSSW 91*
Long, Linda Ann 1952- *WhoEmL 91*
Long, Linda Ann 1953- *WhoAmW 91*
Long, Linda Jean 1953- *WhoAmW 91*
Long, Lorna E. 1944- *St&PR 91*
Long, Lorna Erickson 1944- *WhoAm 90, WhoAmW 91*
Long, Lucinda Herron 1946- *WhoAmW 91*
Long, Madalyn Shannon 1938- *WhoSSW 91*
Long, Madeleine J. *WhoAm 90*
Long, Margaret S. 1947- *St&PR 91*
Long, Margaret Wick 1950- *WhoEmL 91*
Long, Marguerite 1874-1966 *PenDiMP*
Long, Marilyn *WhoWrEP 89*
Long, Marion Wilson 1934- *BiDrAPA 89*
Long, Marjorie Jean 1950- *WhoAmW 91*
Long, Martha Ardelia 1913- *WhoWrEP 89*
Long, Max Freedom 1890-1971 *EncO&P 3*
Long, Meredith J. 1928- *St&PR 91, WhoAm 90, WhoAmA 91*
Long, Michael Eldon 1950- *WhoSSW 91*
Long, Michael Howard 1956- *WhoE 91*
Long, Michael Thomas 1942- *St&PR 91, WhoAm 90*
Long, Molly A. 1945- *St&PR 91*
Long, Monroe W. 1921- *St&PR 91*
Long, Nancy K. 1938- *WhoAmW 91*
Long, Nancy Suttle 1935- *WhoSSW 91*
Long, Nichola Y. 1955- *WhoAmW 91*
Long, Norris Franklin, Jr. 1958- *WhoSSW 91*
Long, Norton E. 1910- *WhoAm 90*
Long, Patricia D. 1925- *St&PR 91*
Long, Patrick Brien 1943- *St&PR 91, WhoAm 90*
Long, Patrick Cahill 1946- *WhoAm 90, WhoSSW 91*
Long, Patrick Kevin 1950- *St&PR 91*
Long, Peter *BioIn 16*
Long, Peter P. 1928- *St&PR 91*
Long, Phillip Clifford 1942- *St&PR 91, WhoAm 90*
Long, Phillip William 1944- *BiDrAPA 89*
Long, R. Kenneth 1922- *St&PR 91*
Long, Randall G. 1958- *St&PR 91*
Long, Richard E. 1947- *St&PR 91*
Long, Richard John 1942- *St&PR 91*
Long, Richard Louis, Jr. 1947- *WhoEmL 91*
Long, Richard Paul 1934- *WhoAm 90*
Long, Rick David 1953- *WhoSSW 91*
Long, Robert 1954- *ConAu 30NR, WhoWrEP 89*
Long, Robert Alexander 1850-1934 *BioIn 16*
Long, Robert Emmet 1934- *WhoAm 90*
Long, Robert Eugene 1931- *WhoAm 90*
Long, Robert G. 1912- *St&PR 91*
Long, Robert Hill 1952- *WhoWrEP 89*
Long, Robert J. 1927- *St&PR 91*
Long, Robert L. 1937- *St&PR 91*
Long, Robert Livingston 1937- *WhoAm 90*
Long, Robert Lyman John 1920- *WhoAm 90*
Long, Robert McLin *BiDrAPA 89*
Long, Robert Merrill 1938- *St&PR 91, WhoAm 90*
Long, Robert Radcliffe 1919- *WhoAm 90*
Long, Robert William 1928- *St&PR 91*
Long, Roland John 1921- *WhoWor 91*
Long, Ronald Alex 1948- *WhoE 91, WhoEmL 91*
Long, Rose-Carol Washton 1938- *WhoAmA 91*
Long, Russell B. 1918- *WorAlBi*
Long, Russell Billiu 1918- *WhoAm 90*
Long, Russell E. 1959- *St&PR 91*
Long, Ruth F. 1926- *St&PR 91*
Long, S Eugene *BiDrAPA 89*
Long, Samuel Byron 1951- *WhoSSW 91*
Long, Sarah Ann 1943- *WhoAm 90, WhoAmW 91*
Long, Scott 1917- *WhoAmA 91*
Long, Shelley *BioIn 16, WhoAm 90, WhoAmW 91*
Long, Shelley 1949- *WorAlBi*
Long, Shirley Dobbins 1943- *WhoSSW 91, WhoWrEP 89*
Long, Stanley M 1892-1972 *WhoAmA 91N*
Long, Stephen Harriman 1784-1864 *WhNaAH*
Long, Susan Grafeld 1951- *WhoWrEP 89*
Long, Susan Webb 1946- *WhoAmW 91, WhoSSW 91*
Long, Tania 1913- *BioIn 16*
Long, Thomas G. 1935- *St&PR 91*
Long, Thomas J. 1910- *St&PR 91*
Long, Thomas J. 1915- *St&PR 91*
Long, Thomas Leslie 1951- *WhoEmL 91*
Long, Thomas Michael 1943- *WhoAm 90*
Long, Thomas R. 1930- *St&PR 91*
Long, Tom 1932- *St&PR 91, WhoAm 90*
Long, Tommy 1890-1972 *Ballpl 90*
Long, Tony *BioIn 16*
Long, Virginia M. 1935- *ODwPR 91*
Long, Walter Edward 1935- *WhoE 91*
Long, Walter Kinscella 1904-1986 *WhoAmA 91N*
Long, William A. *PenDiDA 89*
Long, William A. 1950- *St&PR 91*
Long, William Allan 1928- *St&PR 91, WhoAm 90*
Long, William B *BiDrAPA 89*
Long, William Everett, Jr. 1919- *WhoAm 90*
Long, William Ivey *ConTFT 8*
Long, William Joseph 1946- *WhoSSW 91*
Long, William Michael 1952- *St&PR 91*
Long, William Penuel, Jr. 1944- *WhoE 91*
Long, William Robert 1961- *WhoEmL 91*
Long-Tims, Marilyn Virginia 1940- *WhoWrEP 89*
Longacre, Carolyn *BiDrAPA 89*
Longacre, David Evans 1958- *WhoSSW 91*
Longacre, Lilian T. 1928- *WhoAmW 91*
Longacre, Lydia E 1870-1951 *WhoAmA 91N*
Longacre, Margaret Gruen 1910-1976 *WhoAmA 91N*
Longair, Malcolm Sim 1941- *WhoWor 91*
Longaker, Abraham Brower 1828-1915? *AmLegL*
Longaker, Jon Dasu 1920- *WhoAmA 91*
Longaker, Richard Pancoast 1924- *WhoAm 90*
Longaker, William D 1920- *BiDrAPA 89*
Longan, Robert C, Jr. 1914- *BiDrAPA 89*
Longano, Madeleine McLean 1954- *WhoE 91*
Longbons, James Leland 1941- *WhoAm 90*
Longbrake, William A. 1943- *St&PR 91*
Longbrake, William Arthur 1943- *WhoAm 90*
Longchampt, Michel 1934- *WhoAm 90*
Longchampt, Michel Jean-Marie 1934- *St&PR 91*
Longden, Albert Teshon 1946- *St&PR 91*
Longdon, William Henry *BiDrAPA 89*
Longe, Kevin Thomas 1959- *St&PR 91*
Longenbach, James L. 1948- *St&PR 91*
Longenecker, Herbert Eugene 1912- *WhoAm 90*
Longer, Janice Martino 1955- *St&PR 91*
Longer, Joan *BioIn 16*
Longer, Joan Donna *BiDrAPA 89*
Longer, William John 1951- *WhoEmL 91*
Longest-Slaughter, Helen Vezelma 1944- *WhoSSW 91*
Longeteig, Iver J. 1941- *WhoWrEP 89*
Longfellow, Henry Wadsworth 1807-1882 *AuBYP 90, BioIn 16, WhNaAH, WorAlBi*
Longfield, Craig N. *St&PR 91*
Longfield, Ross Nicol 1940- *St&PR 91*
Longfield, Samuel Mountifort 1802-1884 *BioIn 16*
Longfield, William Herman 1938- *WhoAm 90*
Longford, Francis A Pakenham, Earl of 1905- *BioIn 16*
Longhi, Lucia Lopresti *EncCoWW*
Longhi, Pietro 1702-1785 *IntDcAA 90*
Longhitano, Maria *BiDrAPA 89*
Longhofer, Ronald Stephen 1946- *WhoEmL 91*
Longhouser, Michael Douglas 1950- *WhoAm 90*
Longhurst, Robert R., III 1927- *St&PR 91*
Longhurst, Robert Russell 1921- *WhoSSW 91, WhoWor 91*
Longhurst, Robert Russell, III 1927- *WhoSSW 91*
Longhurst, Suzanne Elizabeth 1958- *WhoWrEP 89*
Longin, Thomas Charles 1939- *WhoAm 90*
Longinovic, Tomislav Z. 1955- *WhoWrEP 89*
Longland, Jean Rogers 1913- *WhoWrEP 89*
Longley, Bernique *WhoAmA 91*
Longley, Bernique 1923- *WhoAm 90*
Longley, Diane Gene 1937- *WhoWrEP 89*
Longley, Evelyn Louise 1921-1959 *WhoAmA 91N*
Longley, Jack Winston 1941- *St&PR 91*
Longley, James Wildon 1913- *WhoE 91*
Longley, Laura Ann 1948- *WhoWrEP 89*
Longley, Marjorie Watters 1925- *WhoAm 90*
Longley, Michael 1939- *WorAu 1980*
Longley, Robert Preston 1851- *BioIn 16*
Longman, Donald R. *BioIn 16*
Longman, Evelyn Beatrice 1874-1954 *BiDWomA*
Longman, Gary Lee 1948- *WhoAm 90*
Longman, Phillip *BioIn 16*
Longman, Richard Winston 1943- *WhoAm 90*
Longmire, William Polk, Jr. 1913- *WhoAm 90*
Longmoore, John T. 1934- *St&PR 91*
Longmore, George 1793?-1867 *DcLB 99*
Longnaker, John L. 1926- *St&PR 91*
Longnaker, John Leonard 1926- *WhoAm 90*
Longnecker, Beth Anne 1956- *WhoAmW 91*
Longnecker, David E. 1939- *WhoAm 90*
Longo, Al 1919- *ODwPR 91*
Longo, Anthony 1930- *ODwPR 91*
Longo, Charles Michael 1942- *St&PR 91*
Longo, Dennis 1945- *St&PR 91*
Longo, Diane 1957- *WhoAmW 91*
Longo, Edward Charles, III 1959- *BiDrAPA 89*
Longo, Jeannie *BioIn 16*
Longo, Joseph Thomas 1942- *WhoAm 90*
Longo, Kathryn Milani 1946- *WhoE 91*
Longo, Lawrence Daniel 1926- *WhoAm 90*
Longo, Michael Clovis 1952- *WhoEmL 91*
Longo, Michael Joseph 1935- *WhoAm 90*
Longo, Nicholas V. *BioIn 16*
Longo, Patricia Lacy 1927- *WhoAmW 91*
Longo, Patti Jean 1954- *WhoSSW 91*
Longo, Robert *BioIn 16*
Longo, Robert 1953- *CurBio 90 [port], News 90 [port], WhoAmA 91*
Longo, Tony *BioIn 16*
Longo, Vincent 1923- *WhoAmA 91*
Longo-Muth, Linda L 1948- *WhoAmA 91*
Longobardi, AnitaRose Teresa 1961- *WhoAmW 91*
Longobardi, Giuseppe 1955- *WhoWor 91*
Longobardi, Laura Elizabeth 1962- *WhoAmW 91*
Longobardi, Pam 1958- *WhoAmA 91*
Longobardo, Anna Kazanjian *WhoE 91*
Longone, Daniel Thomas 1932- *WhoAm 90*
Longood, Robert James *BioIn 16*
Longoria, Felix *BioIn 16*
Longoria, Frank A. 1935- *WhoHisp 91*
Longoria, Jose L. 1947- *WhoHisp 91*
Longoria, Leovaldo Carol 1927- *WhoHisp 91*
Longoria, Roberto 1963- *WhoHisp 91*
Longoria, Salvador Gonzalez, Jr. 1958- *WhoHisp 91*
Longrigg, Paul 1927- *WhoWor 91*
Longrigg, Roger *TwCCr&M 91*
Longsderff, Richard William 1934- *St&PR 91*
Longshore, Carrol Timothy *BiDrAPA 89*
Longshore, June Usry 1934- *WhoSSW 91*

Longshore, Marsha *ODwPR 91*
Longstaff, John P 1930- *BiDrAPA 89*
Longstaff, Patricia Hirl 1948- *WhoEmL 91*
Longstaffe, John Ronald 1934- *WhoAm 90, WhoAmA 91*
Longstreet, Donna Mae 1937- *WhoAmW 91*
Longstreet, James 1821-1904 *BioIn 16, WorAlBi*
Longstreet, Stephen 1907- *WhoAm 90, WhoAmA 91*
Longstreth, Joseph 1920- *AuBYP 90*
Longstreth, Richard 1946- *ConAu 132*
Longstreth, Susan 1946- *WhoAmW 91*
Longstreth, Thomas Morris 1886- *AuBYP 90*
Longstreth, William Thacher 1920- *St&PR 91*
Longsworth, Charles R. 1929- *WhoAm 90*
Longsworth, Charles Robert 1929- *St&PR 91*
Longsworth, Eileen Catherine 1950- *WhoAmW 91*
Longsworth, Ellen Louise 1949- *WhoAmW 91*
Longsworth, Gerald Grant 1959- *WhoEmL 91*
Longsworth, Polly Ormsby 1933- *AuBYP 90*
Longtin, Cheryl Joy 1948- *St&PR 91*
Longtin, Michel 1946- *IntWWM 90*
Longto, Frank J. 1940- *St&PR 91*
Longuet, Gregory Arthur 1945- *WhoSSW 91*
Longuet, Jean Frederic Laurent 1876-1938 *BiDFrPL*
Longueuil, Charles Le Moyne, Baron De 1656-1729 *WhNaAH*
Longueval, Georg Franz August *PenDiDA 89*
Longueville, comte de 1320?-1380 *BioIn 16*
Longueville, Penelope Victoria 1648-1674 *BiDEWW*
Longus *WorAlBi*
Longval, Gloria 1931- *WhoAmA 91*
Longwell, Dennis Charles 1941- *St&PR 91, WhoAm 90*
Longwell, John Ploeger 1918- *WhoAm 90*
Longworth, Alice Roosevelt 1884-1980 *BioAmW, BioIn 16*
Longworth, Maria Theresa 1832?-1881 *FemiCLE*
Longworth, Richard Cole 1935- *WhoAm 90*
Longworth, Ruskin 1927- *WhoE 91*
Longyear, Barry Brookes 1942- *RGTwCSF*
Longyear, John Munro, III 1914- *WhoAm 90*
Longyear, Russell Hammond 1935- *WhoAm 90*
Lonidier, Fred Spencer 1942- *WhoAmA 91*
Lonigan, Paul Raymond 1935- *WhoWrEP 89*
Lonkart, Georgia Faith 1947- *WhoAmW 91, WhoE 91*
Lonker, Arthur 1917- *St&PR 91*
Lonn, Donald Warner 1926- *St&PR 91*
Lonnbohm, Armas Eino Leopold *DcScanL*
Lonnebotn, Trygve 1937- *WhoAm 90*
Lonneke, Michael Dean 1943- *WhoAm 90*
Lonner, Joseph 1928- *St&PR 91*
Lonner, Thomas Dunstan 1942- *WhoAm 90*
Lonngren, Karl Erik 1938- *WhoAm 90*
Lonning, Inge Johan 1938- *WhoWor 91*
Lonnquist, George Eric 1946- *WhoAm 90*
Lonnqvist, Berit Elisabet 1935- *WhoWor 91*
Lonnqvist, Jouko K 1943- *BiDrAPA 89*
Lonoff, Marc Joshua 1952- *WhoEmL 91*
Lonquist, Bert Arthur 1926- *WhoAm 90*
Lonsdale, G.F. 1932- *St&PR 91*
Lonsdale, Hugh Cecil Lowther, Earl of 1857-1944 *BioIn 16*
Lonsdale, Jeffrey James 1948- *St&PR 91*
Lonsdale, Kathleen 1903-1971 *BioIn 16*
Lonsdale, Michael *ConTFT 8*
Lonsdale, Michel 1931- *ConTFT 8*
Lonsdale, Richard 1914?-1988 *AnObit 1988*
Lonsdale-Hands, Richard de Prilleux 1953- *WhoWor 91*
Lonsdorf, John P. 1956- *ODwPR 91*
Lonsdorf, Joseph Charles 1937- *WhoSSW 91*
Lonsdorf, Richard G 1922- *BiDrAPA 89*
Lonsford, Florence Elizabeth Hutchinson 1914- *WhoE 91*
Lonson, Thomas J. 1937- *St&PR 91*
Loo, Beverly Jane 1931- *WhoAm 90*
Loo, Carl Arthur K.-H. 1958- *WhoWor 91*
Loo, Tsu Teng 1936- *BiDrAPA 89, WhoE 91*
Loof, Jan 1940- *AuBYP 90*
Looff, David H 1928- *BiDrAPA 89*
Looft, Walter Gene 1938- *St&PR 91*
Look, Dona 1948- *WhoAmA 91*
Look, Vivian Ann *WhoAmW 91*
Look Hong, William Andrew 1942- *BiDrAPA 89*
Lookabaugh, Cindy Kaye *BiDrAPA 89*
Lookabill, Reid Davis 1949- *St&PR 91*
Lookebill, Gaylene Lucile 1941- *WhoAmW 91*
Looker, Andrew Noah 1942- *BiDrAPA 89*
Looker, Brian Budd 1941- *WhoSSW 91*
Looking Glass 1823?-1877 *WhNaAH*
Loomans, Leslie Louis 1943- *St&PR 91*
Loomer, Frank Stephen 1951- *BiDrAPA 89*
Loomer, Harry P *BiDrAPA 89*
Loomes, Brian 1938- *ConAu 30NR*
Loomie, Leo S 1916- *BiDrAPA 89*
Loomie, Leo Stephen 1916- *WhoE 91*
Loomis, Alfred Lee, Jr. 1913- *St&PR 91*
Loomis, Amy Brown *NewAgE 90*
Loomis, Arthur H. 1938- *St&PR 91*
Loomis, Bernard 1923- *St&PR 91*
Loomis, Burdett A. 1945- *ConAu 129*
Loomis, Carol J. 1929- *WhoAmW 91*
Loomis, Carol Junge *BioIn 16*
Loomis, Christopher Knapp 1947- *WhoEmL 91, WhoWor 91*
Loomis, Craig Alan 1952- *St&PR 91*
Loomis, Earl A, Jr. 1921- *BiDrAPA 89*
Loomis, Francis Butler 1861-1948 *BioIn 16*
Loomis, Gaston Plantiff *BiDrAPA 89*
Loomis, Henry 1919- *WhoAm 90*
Loomis, Howard Krey 1927- *WhoAm 90, WhoWor 91*
Loomis, J. Paul *AuBYP 90*
Loomis, Jacqueline Chalmers 1930- *WhoAmW 91, WhoWor 91*
Loomis, James Richard 1926- *St&PR 91*
Loomis, Jan 1944- *WhoWrEP 89*
Loomis, John N 1933- *BiDrAPA 89*
Loomis, John Norman 1933- *WhoWor 91*
Loomis, Kathleen Arnold 1945- *WhoSSW 91*
Loomis, Margaret Anne *BiDrAPA 89*
Loomis, Philip Clark 1926- *WhoE 91*
Loomis, Robert D. *AuBYP 90*
Loomis, Robert Duane 1926- *WhoAm 90*
Loomis, Robert Strother 1955- *St&PR 91*
Loomis, S Dale 1930- *BiDrAPA 89*
Loomis, Sabra 1937- *WhoWrEP 89*
Loomis, Wesley Horace, III 1913- *WhoAm 90*
Loomis, Worth 1923- *St&PR 91*
Looney, Anthony Glen 1949- *St&PR 91, WhoAm 90*
Looney, Cullen Rogers 1946- *WhoSSW 91*
Looney, H. Ray 1935- *St&PR 91, WhoAm 90*
Looney, J. Anna 1951- *WhoAmW 91*
Looney, Joe Don 1942-1988 *BioIn 16*
Looney, John Guy *BiDrAPA 89*
Looney, John Joseph *St&PR 91*
Looney, Marlene de Jesus 1959- *WhoAmW 91*
Looney, Norman 1942- *WhoAmA 91*
Looney, Paul Alan *BiDrAPA 89*
Looney, Ralph 1927- *St&PR 91*
Looney, Ralph Edwin 1924- *WhoAm 90, WhoWor 91*
Looney, Richard Carl 1934- *WhoAm 90*
Looney, Robert Fain 1925- *WhoAmA 91*
Looney, Ronald Lee 1956- *WhoSSW 91*
Looney, William Boyd 1922- *WhoAm 90*
Looney, William Francis, Jr. 1931- *WhoE 91, WhoWor 91*
Looney, Wilton D. 1919- *WhoSSW 91*
Loonnroth, Lars Christoffer 1935- *WhoWor 91*
Loop, Floyd D. 1936- *WhoAm 90*
Loop, John Wickwire 1924- *WhoAm 90*
Looper, Charles B. 1931- *St&PR 91*
Looper, Charles Eugene 1920- *WhoAm 90*
Looper, Donald Ray 1952- *WhoEmL 91*
Looper, John Stuart *BiDrAPA 89*
Loory, Stuart Hugh 1932- *WhoAm 90*
Loos, A.W. 1928- *St&PR 91*
Loos, Adolf 1870-1933 *PenDiDA 89*
Loos, Amandus William 1908- *WhoAm 90*
Loos, Anita 1888-1981 *BioAmW, FemiCLE, NotWoAT*
Loos, Anita 1893-1981 *WorAlBi*
Loos, Anita 1894-1981 *BioIn 16*
Loos, Carole Marie 1946- *St&PR 91*
Loos, Cecile Ines 1883-1959 *EncCoWW*
Loos, Jackie Jaynine 1960- *WhoAmW 91*
Loos, John Louis 1918- *WhoAm 90*
Loos, John T. 1947- *WhoSSW 91*
Loos, Karl D. 1950- *St&PR 91*
Loose Tubes *OxCPMus*
Loose, John W. 1942- *St&PR 91*
Loose, John Ward Willson 1925- *WhoE 91*
Loose, Thomas Arthur 1932- *St&PR 91*
Loosemore, Craig Steven 1947- *St&PR 91*
Loosemore, Kevin Michael 1952- *St&PR 91*
Loosen, Peter Thomas 1944- *BiDrAPA 89*
Looser, Donald William 1939- *WhoSSW 91*
Loosley, Janine Elisabeth 1962- *WhoAmW 91*
Loosli, Arthur 1926- *IntWWM 90*
Lootens, Lena 1959- *IntWWM 90*
Loots, Barbara Kunz 1946- *WhoAmW 91*
Loots, James Mason 1958- *WhoE 91*
Lopach, James Joseph 1942- *WhoAm 90*
Lopacki, Edward Joseph, Jr. 1947- *WhoSSW 91*
Lopacki, Joan Marie 1957- *WhoAmW 91*
Lopardo, Donald Leonard 1947- *St&PR 91*
Lopat, Ed 1918- *Ballpl 90*
Lopat, Eddie 1918- *BioIn 16*
Lopata, Edwin L. 1909- *St&PR 91*
Lopata, Helena Znaniecka 1925- *WhoAm 90*
Lopata, James Randolph 1945- *St&PR 91*
Lopata, Martin Barry 1939- *WhoWor 91*
Lopata, Stan 1925- *Ballpl 90*
Lopata, Stanley L. 1914- *St&PR 91*
Lopate, Phillip 1943- *BioIn 16, WorAu 1980 [port]*
Lopategui, Eduardo M. 1949- *St&PR 91*
Lopatin, Alan G. 1956- *WhoEmL 91*
Lopatin, Judy 1954- *WhoWrEP 89*
Lopatka, Adam 1928- *WhoWor 91*
Lopatka, Kenneth Thaddeus 1947- *WhoEmL 91*
Lopato, David 1911- *EncO&P 3*
Lopato, Esther Wolf 1920- *WhoAmW 91*
Lopato, Leslie M *BiDrAPA 89*
Lopdrup, Kjeld Emil 1927- *WhoSSW 91*
Loper, Candice Kay 1953- *WhoAmW 91*
Loper, Carl Richard, Jr. 1932- *WhoAm 90*
Loper, Charlene M. 1958- *WhoAmW 91*
Loper, Herbert B. 1896-1989 *BioIn 16*
Loper, James Leaders 1931- *WhoAm 90*
Loper, Janet Swanson 1934- *WhoAmW 91*
Loper, Mark Warren 1954- *St&PR 91*
Loper, Merle William 1940- *WhoAm 90*
Loper, Robert Bruce 1925- *WhoAm 90*
Lopes, Antonio Simoes 1934- *WhoWor 91*
Lopes, Davey 1946- *Ballpl 90 [port]*
Lopes, Henri 1937- *ConAu 132*
Lopes, James Joseph 1952- *St&PR 91*
Lopes, Jose Leme *BiDrAPA 89*
Lopes, Joseph Francis 1925- *St&PR 91*
Lopes, Lola Lynn 1941- *WhoAm 90*
Lopes, Myra Amelia 1931- *WhoAmW 91*
Lopes, Peter Francis 1949- *WhoE 91*
Lopes, Rob *BioIn 16*
Lopes-Graca, Fernando 1906- *IntWWM 90*
Lopez, Aaron Galicia 1933- *WhoHisp 91*
Lopez, Adalberto 1943- *WhoHisp 91*
Lopez, Adolfo Danilo 1954- *WhoSSW 91*
Lopez, Agustin D *BiDrAPA 89*
Lopez, Al 1908- *Ballpl 90 [port]*
Lopez, Alberto Gerardo 1952- *BiDrAPA 89*
Lopez, Alfonso 1886-1959 *BioIn 16*
Lopez, Alfred L. 1931- *St&PR 91*
Lopez, Alfred R. *WhoAm 90*
Lopez, Alvaro Benito *BiDrAPA 89*
Lopez, Amalia Rebecca 1963- *WhoHisp 91*
Lopez, Amando *BioIn 16*
Lopez, Ana M. 1956- *WhoHisp 91*
Lopez, Andres *EncCRAm*
Lopez, Angel Andres 1943- *WhoHisp 91*
Lopez, Ann Aurelia 1945- *WhoHisp 91*
Lopez, Anna B. 1962- *WhoHisp 91*
Lopez, Antonio 1934- *WhoHisp 91*
Lopez, Antonio Manuel, Jr. 1949- *WhoHisp 91*
Lopez, Antony Carlos 1950- *WhoWor 91*
Lopez, Armando X. 1958- *WhoHisp 91*
Lopez, Aura A. 1933- *WhoHisp 91*
Lopez, Aurelio 1948- *Ballpl 90*
Lopez, Barry Holstun 1945- *MajTwCW, WhoAm 90, WhoWrEP 89, WorAu 1980 [port]*
Lopez, Benito Moleiro, Jr. 1933- *WhoAm 90*
Lopez, Bernard Ronald *BiDrAPA 89*
Lopez, Carlos 1950- *Ballpl 90*
Lopez, Carlos Antonio 1792-1862 *BioIn 16*
Lopez, Carlos Jose 1949- *WhoHisp 91*
Lopez, Carlos Urrutia 1932- *WhoHisp 91*
Lopez, Carolyn Catherine 1951- *WhoEmL 91*
Lopez, David Barwis 1938- *St&PR 91*
Lopez, David Tiburcio 1939- *WhoSSW 91, WhoWor 91*
Lopez, Debra Alice 1953- *BiDrAPA 89*
Lopez, Diana 1948- *HispWr 90*
Lopez, Eddie *WhoHisp 91*
Lopez, Eddie 1929- *WhoHisp 91*
Lopez, Edward Alexander 1954- *WhoHisp 91*
Lopez, Elizabeth Jeannette 1958- *WhoAmW 91*
Lopez, Enrique Angel 1940- *St&PR 91, WhoHisp 91*
Lopez, Felix A. 1942- *MusmAFA*
Lopez, Felix Caridad *WhoHisp 91*
Lopez, Fernando 1930- *BiDrAPA 89*
Lopez, Francis 1916- *OxCPMus*
Lopez, Francisco Solano 1826?-1870 *BioIn 16*
Lopez, Frank W. *ODwPR 91*
Lopez, Franklin A. 1942- *WhoHisp 91*
Lopez, Genaro 1947- *WhoHisp 91*
Lopez, George Mario 1967- *WhoE 91*
Lopez, George T. 1900- *MusmAFA*
Lopez, Geraldine Jean 1968- *WhoAmW 91*
Lopez, Gerard F. *WhoHisp 91*
Lopez, German 1933- *St&PR 91*
Lopez, Gloria Berta-Cruz 1937- *WhoHisp 91*
Lopez, Gloria E. 1951- *WhoHisp 91*
Lopez, Gloria Margarita 1948- *WhoHisp 91*
Lopez, Gualberto Villarroel 1908-1946 *BioIn 16*
Lopez, Hector 1932- *Ballpl 90*
Lopez, Hector 1947- *WhoHisp 91*
Lopez, Humberto *WhoHisp 91*
Lopez, Humberto Salazar 1944- *WhoHisp 91*
Lopez, Ignacio 1908- *BioIn 16*
Lopez, Ignacio Javier 1956- *WhoHisp 91*
Lopez, Israel 1922- *WhoWor 91*
Lopez, Jack, Jr. 1953- *WhoSSW 91*
Lopez, Joanne Carol 1952- *WhoHisp 91*
Lopez, Joaquin Lopez y *BioIn 16*
Lopez, John J. 1947- *WhoHisp 91*
Lopez, John William 1957- *WhoHisp 91*
Lopez, Jorge Luis *BiDrAPA 89*
Lopez, Jose Dolores 1868-1937 *MusmAFA*
Lopez, Jose Ignacio, Sr. 1932- *WhoHisp 91*
Lopez, Jose M. 1947- *WhoHisp 91*
Lopez, Jose M., Jr. 1949- *WhoHisp 91*
Lopez, Jose R. 1940- *WhoHisp 91*
Lopez, Jose R. 1945- *WhoHisp 91*
Lopez, Jose Rafael 1957- *WhoHisp 91*
Lopez, Jose Tomas 1949- *WhoHisp 91*
Lopez, Joseph 1952- *WhoHisp 91*
Lopez, Joseph Anthony 1951- *St&PR 91, WhoHisp 91*
Lopez, Juan Francisco 1958- *BiDrAPA 89*
Lopez, Juan Manuel *BiDrAPA 89*
Lopez, Kathleen Anne 1957- *WhoAmW 91*
Lopez, Kay Strickland 1946- *WhoAmW 91*
Lopez, Ken *BioIn 16*
Lopez, Lino M. 1910-1978 *BioIn 16*
Lopez, Louis Rey 1946- *WhoHisp 91*
Lopez, Lourdes 1958- *WhoHisp 91*
Lopez, Luz E. *WhoHisp 91*
Lopez, Lydia 1943- *WhoSSW 91*
Lopez, Manuel, Sr. 1950- *WhoHisp 91*
Lopez, Manuel Dennis 1934- *WhoWrEP 89*
Lopez, Manuel Isaias 1941- *BiDrAPA 89*
Lopez, Marcelino 1943- *Ballpl 90*
Lopez, Marciano 1934- *WhoHisp 91*
Lopez, Marco Antonio 1957- *WhoHisp 91*
Lopez, Marcus C. 1934- *WhoHisp 91*
Lopez, Mario *WhoHisp 91*
Lopez, Marisela 1956- *WhoHisp 91*
Lopez, Marvin J. 1937- *WhoHisp 91*
Lopez, Mary Frances 1955- *WhoE 91*
Lopez, Michael J. 1937- *BioIn 16*
Lopez, Michael John 1937- *WhoAmA 91*
Lopez, Micheline Brierre 1943- *WhoAmW 91*
Lopez, Nancy 1957- *BioIn 16, WhoAm 90, WhoAmW 91, WhoHisp 91, WorAlBi*
Lopez, Nicolas *EncCRAm*
Lopez, Norberto H. 1938- *WhoHisp 91*
Lopez, Oscar S *BiDrAPA 89*
Lopez, Pablo Vincent 1964- *WhoHisp 91*
Lopez, Pedro Ramon *WhoHisp 91*
Lopez, Peter Dickson 1950- *IntWWM 90*
Lopez, Pia 1937- *WhoAmW 91*
Lopez, Priscilla 1948- *WhoAm 90, WhoHisp 91*
Lopez, Rafael 1929- *WhoHisp 91*
Lopez, Rafael C. 1931- *WhoHisp 91*
Lopez, Rafael Tobias *BiDrAPA 89*
Lopez, Ramon Moleiro 1937- *St&PR 91*
Lopez, Ray *St&PR 91*
Lopez, Raymond Michael 1959- *WhoWrEP 89*
Lopez, Raymond Valencia 1921- *IntWWM 90*
Lopez, Remi 1939- *WhoWor 91*
Lopez, Rhoda Le Blanc 1912- *WhoAmA 91*
Lopez, Ricardo Rafael 1957- *WhoHisp 91*
Lopez, Richard 1943- *WhoHisp 91*
Lopez, Richard E. 1945- *WhoHisp 91*
Lopez, Richard G. 1934- *WhoHisp 91*
Lopez, Rigoberto Adolfo 1957- *WhoHisp 91*
Lopez, Robert 1940- *WhoHisp 91*
Lopez, Robert Sabatino 1910-1986 *BioIn 16*
Lopez, Rosemary 1963- *WhoAmW 91, WhoHisp 91*
Lopez, Roy George *BiDrAPA 89*
Lopez, Rubin R. 1947- *WhoHisp 91*
Lopez, Steven Regeser 1953- *WhoHisp 91*
Lopez, Trini 1937- *BioIn 16, WhoAm 90, WhoHisp 91*
Lopez, Ubaldo P, Jr. 1930- *BiDrAPA 89*
Lopez, Vidal N *BiDrAPA 89*
Lopez, Vincent 1894-1975 *OxCPMus*
Lopez, Vincent Joseph Michael 1953- *St&PR 91*
Lopez, Virgilio D 1944- *BiDrAPA 89*
Lopez, Welquis Raimundo 1954- *WhoHisp 91*

Lopez, Wilma Ida 1938- WhoAmW 91, WhoSSW 91
Lopez, Xavier 1964- WhoWor 91
Lopez Adorno, Pedro J. 1954- WhoHisp 91
Lopez-Alves, Fernando 1950- WhoHisp 91
Lopez Arellano, Oswaldo 1921- BioIn 16
Lopez-Avila, Viorica 1949- WhoEmL 91
Lopez Avina, Antonio 1915- WhoAm 90
Lopez-Baez, Sandra Ivelisse 1952- WhoEmL 91
Lopez-Bayron, Juan L. 1955- WhoHisp 91
Lopez-Calderon, Jose Luis 1948- WhoHisp 91
Lopez-Carmona, Antonio 1954- WhoWor 91
Lopez-Cepero, Robert Michael 1943- WhoHisp 91
Lopez-Cobos, Jesus 1940- IntWWM 90, PenDiMP, WhoAm 90, WhoWor 91
Lopez Contreras, Carlos 1942- WhoWor 91
Lopez Contreras, Eleazar 1883-1973 BioIn 16
Lopez de Cordoba, Leonor 1362?-1412? EncCoWW
Lopez de Gamero, Iliana Veronica 1963- WhoHisp 91
Lopez de Lacarra, Amalia 1956- WhoHisp 91
Lopez de Victoria, Juan de Dios WhoAm 90
Lopez-Falkowski, Sonia Milagros 1942- WhoAmW 91
Lopez-Gomez, Susana 1955- WhoAmW 91
Lopez-Gonzalez, Margarita Maria 1947- WhoHisp 91
Lopez-Heredia, Jose 1922- WhoHisp 91
Lopez-Ibor, Juan J 1907- BiDrAPA 89
Lopez Laguerre, Maria Monserrate 1938- WhoSSW 91
Lopez-Lopez, Fernando Jose WhoHisp 91
Lopez-Loucel, Alberto BiDrAPA 89
Lopez Mateos, Adolfo 1910-1969 BioIn 16
Lopez-Mayhew, Barbara D. 1959- WhoHisp 91
Lopez-McKnight, Gloria 1937- WhoHisp 91
Lopez Michelsen, Alfonso 1913- BioIn 16
Lopez-Morales, Stephen BiDrAPA 89
Lopez-Morillas, Juan 1913- WhoAm 90, WhoHisp 91
Lopez-Munoz, Maria Rosa P. 1938- WhoAmW 91
Lopez Nieves, Carlos Juan 1948- WhoHisp 91
Lopez-Oliver, Rosa Maria 1963- WhoWor 91
Lopez-Otin, Maria E. 1950- WhoHisp 91
Lopez-Permouth, Sergio Roberto 1957- WhoHisp 91
Lopez-Pina, Antonio 1937- WhoWor 91
Lopez Portillo, Jose BioIn 16
Lopez Portillo, Jose 1920- ConAu 129, HispWr 90
Lopez Portillo y Pacheco, Jose 1920- HispWr 90
Lopez Rega, Jose 1916-1989 BioIn 16
Lopez-Revilla, Ruben 1942- WhoWor 91
Lopez-Rivera, Anabel BiDrAPA 89
Lopez-Sanabria, Sixto 1928- WhoHisp 91
Lopez Sanchez, Maria del Pilar 1949- WhoHisp 91
Lopez-Sanz, Mariano 1931- WhoHisp 91
Lopez-Sotomayor, Manuel A BiDrAPA 89
Lopez Suria, Violeta 1926- HispWr 90
Lopez Trujillo, Alfonso 1935- WhoWor 91
Lopez Uzcategui, Filmo WhoWor 91
Lopez Velarde, Ramon 1888-1921 BioIn 16
Lopez-Videla G., Ana Doris 1934- WhoHisp 91
Lopez-Woodward, Dina 1956- WhoHisp 91
Lopez y Fuentes, Gregorio 1897?-1966 ConAu 131, HispWr 90
Lopez y Lopez, Joaquin BioIn 16
Lo Piccolo, Charles Joseph 1954- BiDrAPA 89, WhoE 91
LoPiccolo, Joseph 1943- WhoAm 90
Lopina, Lawrence Thomas 1930- St&PR 91, WhoAm 90
Lopina, Louise Carol 1936- WhoAmA 91
Lopker, Anita M BiDrAPA 89
Lopker, Anita Mae 1955- WhoAmW 91, WhoE 91
Lopo, Alina Concepcion 1951- WhoAmW 91
Lopokov, Fyodor Vasilievich 1887?-1973 BioIn 16
Lopokova, Lydia Vasilievna 1892-1981 DcNaB 1981
Lopp, G. Raymond 1930- St&PR 91
Lopp, Walter James, II NewYTBS 90
Loppinet, Alain Louis 1940- WhoWor 91
Loppnow, Milo Alvin 1914- WhoAm 90
Lopreato, Joseph 1928- WhoAm 90, WhoWor 91
Lopresti, Philip Vincent 1932- WhoAm 90
LoPrete, James Hugh 1929- WhoAm 90
Lopshire, Robert M 1927- ConAu 30NR
Lopshire, Robert Martin 1927- AuBYP 90
Lopukhin, I. V. 1756-1816 EncO&P 3
Lopukhov, Fyodor Vasilievich 1887?-1973 BioIn 16
Loquasto, Santo WhoAm 90
Loquasto, Santo 1944- ConDes 90
Lora, Guillermo 1924- BioIn 16
Lorac, E. C. R. TwCCr&M 91
Lorah, Clay L. 1935- St&PR 91
Lorah, Joanne Margaret 1938- WhoE 91
Loraine, Philip TwCCr&M 91
Loraine, Violet 1886-1956 OxCPMus
Loran, Erle 1905- WhoAm 90, WhoAmA 91
Loran, Haim 1932- St&PR 91
Loran, Jason D. WhoWrEP 89
Lorand, Colette 1923- IntWWM 90
Lorand, Laszlo 1923- WhoAm 90
Loranger, Francoise 1913- OxCCanT
Loranger, George Peter 1946- St&PR 91
Loranger, J. Albert 1943- St&PR 91
Loranger, Jean-Aubert 1896-1942 DcLB 92 [port]
Loranger, Leo Joseph 1949- St&PR 91
Loranger, Richard Leo 1936- St&PR 91
Lorant, Reginald James 1937- WhoE 91
Lorant, Stefan 1901- BioIn 16, WhoAm 90
Lorber, Barbara H. ODwPR 91
Lorber, Charlotte Laura 1952- WhoAmW 91
Lorber, D Martin H B 1943- WhoAmA 91
Lorber, Richard 1946- WhoAmA 91
Lorber, Richard Jan 1946- WhoE 91
Lorber, Richard Paul 1924- St&PR 91
Lorber, Stephen Neil 1943- WhoAmA 91
Lorber, Victor 1912- WhoAm 90
Lorca, Federico Garcia ConAu 131, HispWr 90, MajTwCW
Lorca, Federico Garcia 1898-1936 BioIn 16
Lorcee, Peter WhoWrEP 89
Lorch, Edgar R 1907-1990 ConAu 131
Lorch, Edgar Raymond NewYTBS 90
Lorch, Edgar Raymond 1907-1990 BioIn 16
Lorch, George A. 1941- St&PR 91, WhoAm 90
Lorch, Maristella De Panizza 1919- WhoAm 90
Lorch, Robert Frederick, Jr. 1952- WhoSSW 91
Lorcini, Gino 1923- WhoAmA 91
Lorcini, Marie Losch 1930- IntWWM 90
Lord Observer 1937- DrBIPA 90
Lord Rothschild ConAu 131
Lord, Anthony 1900- WhoAm 90
Lord, Bemen 1924- AuBYP 90
Lord, Bette Bao BioIn 16
Lord, Bette Bao 1938- BestSel 90-3 [port], WhoAmW 91
Lord, Bris 1883-1964 Ballpl 90
Lord, Charles J 1944- BiDrAPA 89
Lord, Chester Sanders 1850-1933 BioIn 16
Lord, Claude Franklin, Jr. 1921- WhoSSW 91
Lord, David Malcolm 1944- IntWWM 90
Lord, Douglas ConAu 130
Lord, Ernest Raymond 1930- St&PR 91
Lord, Farrell 1938- St&PR 91
Lord, Fonchen Usher 1926- WhoAm 90
Lord, Frederic M. 1912- BioIn 16
Lord, Gabrielle 1946- FemiCLE
Lord, Guy Russell, Jr. 1943- BiDrAPA 89
Lord, Harold Wilbur 1905- WhoAm 90, WhoWor 91
Lord, Harriet 1879-1958 WhoAmA 91N
Lord, Harry 1882-1948 Ballpl 90
Lord, Henry 1847- AmLegL
Lord, Henry Robbins 1939- WhoAm 90
Lord, Herbert Mathew 1917- WhoAm 90
Lord, Jack 1930- WhoAm 90, WorAlBi
Lord, Jacqueline Ward 1936- WhoAmW 91
Lord, Jenny EncO&P 3
Lord, Jere Johns 1922- WhoAm 90
Lord, Jerome Edmund 1935- WhoAm 90, WhoWor 91
Lord, John H. 1932- St&PR 91
Lord, John Keast 1818-1872 DcLB 99 [port]
Lord, John Wesley 1902-1989 BioIn 16, CurBio 90N
Lord, Jonathan Peter 1952- WhoSSW 91
Lord, Joseph Simon, III 1912- WhoAm 90
Lord, M. G. 1955- WhoAm 90
Lord, Marguerite Davenport 1934- WhoSSW 91
Lord, Marjorie BioIn 16
Lord, Marvin 1937- WhoAm 90
Lord, Maud E. 1852-1924 EncO&P 3
Lord, Michael Harry 1954- WhoAmA 91
Lord, Miles W. BioIn 16
Lord, Morton A. 1938- St&PR 91
Lord, N. Philip 1925- St&PR 91
Lord, Nancy ConAu 30NR
Lord, Nancy Joan 1967- WhoEmL 91
Lord, Otis Phillips 1812-1884 AmLegL
Lord, Pamela Ann 1951- WhoSSW 91
Lord, Patricia C. 1927-1988 BioIn 16
Lord, Pauline 1890-1950 BioIn 16, NotWoAT
Lord, Peter 1929- ConDes 90
Lord, Priscilla Sawyer WhoWor 91
Lord, Raymond Morrieson 1930- St&PR 91
Lord, Richard C. 1910-1989 BioIn 16
Lord, Richard J. BioIn 16
Lord, Robert Sutherland 1930- IntWWM 90
Lord, Robert Wilder 1917- WhoWrEP 89
Lord, Robin M. 1957- WhoE 91
Lord, Roy Alvin 1918- WhoAm 90
Lord, Ruth M 1900- BiDrAPA 89
Lord, Sally Ann 1966- WhoAmW 91
Lord, Thomas St&PR 91N
Lord, Todd Michael 1957- WhoE 91
Lord, Walter 1917- WhoAm 90
Lord, Wesley Kenneth 1950- WhoE 91
Lord, William Adams 1849- AmLegL
Lord, William E. WhoAm 90
Lord, William Grogan 1914- WhoAm 90
Lord, William Jackson, Jr. 1926- WhoAm 90
Lord, Winston BioIn 16
Lord, Winston 1937- WhoAm 90, WhoWor 91
Lord Bridges, Thomas Edward 1927- WhoWor 91
Lordan, Beth 1948- ConAu 130
Lorde, Audre BioIn 16
Lorde, Audre 1934- FemiCLE, MajTwCW
Lorde, Audre Geraldin 1934- WhoWrEP 89
Lorden, John Joseph 1944- St&PR 91
Lordi, Katherine Mary 1949- WhoEmL 91
Lordi, Peter 1943- St&PR 91
Lordi, Susan Louise 1937- WhoAmW 91
Lordi, William M 1923- BiDrAPA 89
Lords, Steven DeMar 1953- St&PR 91
Lords, Traci BioIn 16
Lore, Charles Eli 1934- WhoSSW 91
Lore, Ludwig 1875-1942 EncAL
Lore, Martin Maxwell 1914- WhoAm 90
Loredano, Cassio 1948- BioIn 16
Lorefice, Laurence S, Jr. 1950- BiDrAPA 89
Lorefice, Laurence Santo 1950- WhoE 91
Lorek, Daniel Joseph 1959- WhoE 91
Lorek, Kenneth J. 1946- WhoAm 90
Lorelli, Charles A. 1953- St&PR 91
Lorelli, Elvira Mae 1927- WhoAmA 91
Lorelli, Michael BioIn 16
Lorelli, Michael Kevin 1950- WhoAm 90, WhoWor 91
Loren, Barbara BioIn 16
Loren, John David BiDrAPA 89
Loren, Joseph Louis 1950- WhoE 91
Loren, Leonard M BiDrAPA 89
Loren, Pamela 1944- WhoE 91, WhoWor 91
Loren, Sophia 1934- BioIn 16, WhoAm 90, WhoWor 91, WorAlBi
Lorena, Inmaculada de Habsburgo- BioIn 16
Lorenc, Jan 1954- WhoSSW 91
Lorenceau, Bernard Jean 1947- WhoWor 91
Lorengar, Pilar 1921- IntWWM 90, PenDiMP
Loreno, Pamela Kathleen 1958- WhoE 91
Lorenson, Harold Walfred 1928- St&PR 91
Lorente, Guido Oscar 1923- BiDrAPA 89
Lorente, Hector F BiDrAPA 89
Lorente, Roderick Dana 1949- WhoE 91
Lorente de No, Rafael NewYTBS 90
Lorente de No, Rafael 1902-1990 BioIn 16
Lorentson, Holly Jean 1956- WhoAmW 91
Lorentz, Hendrik A. 1853-1928 WorAlBi
Lorentz, John A. 1927- St&PR 91
Lorentz, Pauline WhoAmA 91
Lorentz, William Beall 1937- WhoSSW 91
Lorentzen, Bent 1935- IntWWM 90
Lorentzen, Carl W. 1929- St&PR 91
Lorentzen, Carl Warren 1929- WhoAm 90
Lorentzen, James Clifford 1957- WhoSSW 91
Lorentzen, Marianne Louise 1949- WhoAmW 91
Lorentzen, Robert R. 1935- St&PR 91
Lorentzsen, Norman Martin 1916- St&PR 91, WhoAm 90
Lorenz, Albert A BiDrAPA 89
Lorenz, Alfred Lawrence 1937- WhoSSW 91
Lorenz, Andrew Bela 1951- IntWWM 90
Lorenz, Brian E. 1939- St&PR 91
Lorenz, Carl Edward 1933- WhoAm 90
Lorenz, Carol Elaine 1946- WhoAmW 91
Lorenz, Charlotte Reinhold 1923- St&PR 91
Lorenz, Daniel Christopher 1954- WhoEmL 91
Lorenz, Donald Norman 1935- St&PR 91
Lorenz, Gary W. 1949- St&PR 91
Lorenz, Geoffrey R. 1943- St&PR 91
Lorenz, Hans Ernest 1940- WhoSSW 91
Lorenz, Hans-Walter 1951- WhoWor 91
Lorenz, Hugo Albert 1926- WhoAm 90
Lorenz, John George 1915- WhoAm 90
Lorenz, Jonathan Charles 1951- St&PR 91
Lorenz, Katherine Mary 1946- WhoAmW 91
Lorenz, Konrad BioIn 16
Lorenz, Konrad 1903-1989 AnObit 1989, WorAlBi
Lorenz, Konrad Zacharias 1903- MajTwCW
Lorenz, Kuno 1932- WhoWor 91
Lorenz, Lee Sharp 1932- WhoAm 90
Lorenz, Maria BiDrAPA 89
Lorenz, Max 1901-1975 BioIn 16, PenDiMP
Lorenz, Max Paul 1936- WhoSSW 91
Lorenz, Michael Duane WhoAm 90
Lorenz, Patrick Casey BiDrAPA 89
Lorenz, Richard Theodore, Jr. 1931- WhoAm 90
Lorenz, Robert Paul 1946- WhoEmL 91
Lorenz, Ronald Theodore 1936- WhoWor 91
Lorenz, Ruediger 1932- WhoWor 91
Lorenz, Sarah E. WhoWrEP 89
Lorenz, Walter A 1919- BiDrAPA 89
Lorenz, Wendy Joy 1950- IntWWM 90
Lorenzani, Arthur Emanuele 1886-1986 WhoAmA 91N
Lorenze, George Doubleday 1925- St&PR 91
Lorenzen, Heidi Christine 1963- WhoAmW 91
Lorenzen, Myron L. 1925- St&PR 91
Lorenzen, Philip A. 1942- St&PR 91
Lorenzen, Robert Frederick 1924- WhoAm 90
Lorenzetti, Ambrogio 129-?-1348 IntDcAA 90
Lorenzetti, Maureen Shields 1965- WhoE 91
Lorenzetti, Pietro IntDcAA 90
Lorenzi, Armandina 1947- WhoHisp 91
Lorenzi, Raymond James 1954- WhoSSW 91
Lorenzini, Carlo 1826-1890 AuBYP 90
Lorenzini, Kathryn Marie 1953- WhoSSW 91
Lorenzini, Robert Ernest 1936- St&PR 91
Lorenzl, Gunter 1937- WhoWor 91
Lorenzo, di Pietro 1412?-1480 BioIn 16
Lorenzo Monaco 1370?-1423? IntDcAA 90
Lorenzo, Edgardo De Dios 1956- BiDrAPA 89
Lorenzo, Francisco A. BioIn 16
Lorenzo, Francisco A. 1940- St&PR 91, WhoAm 90, WhoSSW 91
Lorenzo, Francisco Anthony 1940- ConAmBL
Lorenzo, Frank BioIn 16
Lorenzo, Frank 1940- WorAlBi
Lorenzo, Frank A. 1940- WhoHisp 91
Lorenzo, Heberto Padilla ConAu 131, HispWr 90
Lorenzo, Isabel Caridad BiDrAPA 89
Lorenzo, Lynn Robin 1966- WhoHisp 91
Lorenzo, Michael 1920- WhoAm 90, WhoWor 91
Lorenzo, Roberto 1944- WhoE 91
Loreto, Charles A. 1903?-1990 ConAu 132
Loretoni, Richard Stephen 1955- WhoE 91
Loretto, Judith BioIn 16
Lorey, Frank William 1929- St&PR 91
Lori, Anthony John 1937- WhoE 91
Loria, Martin A. 1951- WhoEmL 91
Loria, Robert Claude 1962- WhoHisp 91
Loriaux, Maurice Lucien 1909- WhoAm 90
Lorick, Herbert C., III 1940- St&PR 91
Lorie, James Hirsch 1922- WhoAm 90
Lorimer, Amy McClellan WhoAmA 91N
Lorimer, David 1952- EncPaPR 91
Lorimer, Frank M BiDrAPA 89
Lorimer, George H. 1867-1937 WorAlBi
Lorimer, George Horace BioIn 16
Lorimer, George Horace 1867-1937 LiHiK
Lorimer, James Jasper 1926- WhoAm 90
Lorimer, Janet 1941- SmATA 60 [port]
Lorimer, Linda Koch WhoAm 90, WhoAmW 91, WhoSSW 91
Lorimer, Maxwell George 1908-1990 BioIn 16
Lorimer, Michael George 1946- IntWWM 90
Lorimer, Rodric Alan 1936- St&PR 91
Lorimer, Scat WhoWrEP 89
Lorimer, Sue 1959- WhoE 91
Lorincz, Albert Bela 1922- WhoAm 90
Lorincz, Louis 1965- WhoEmL 91
Lorinczi, George Gabriel 1929- WhoAm 90
Loring, Arthur 1947- WhoAm 90, WhoEmL 91
Loring, Arthur Stanley 1947- St&PR 91
Loring, Caleb, Jr. 1921- St&PR 91, WhoE 91
Loring, Dagmar BioIn 16
Loring, Emilie Baker BioIn 16
Loring, Eugene BioIn 16

Loring, Gloria Jean 1946- *WhoAm 90*
Loring, John 1939- *WhoAmA 91*
Loring, John Robbins 1939- *St&PR 91, WhoAm 90*
Loring, Kimball A., Jr. 1918- *St&PR 91*
Loring, Meredith Susan Elliott 1945- *WhoAmW 91*
Loring, Murray 1917- *WhoWrEP 89*
Loring, Richard William 1928- *WhoE 91*
Loring, Selden M. *AuBYP 90*
Loring, William D. 1928- *St&PR 91*
Lorini, John C. 1924- *St&PR 91*
Lorino, Philippe Andre' 1950- *WhoWor 91*
Lorio, Kathryn Venturatos 1949- *WhoEmL 91*
Loriod, Jeanne 1928- *PenDiMP*
Loriod, Yvonne 1924- *IntWWM 90, PenDiMP*
Lorist, Rudy Gerard 1936- *WhoWor 91*
Loritz, Hans 1895-1946 *BioIn 16*
Lorman, Barbara K. 1932- *WhoAmW 91*
Lorman, William Rudolph 1910- *WhoAm 90, WhoWor 91*
Lorne, David *WhoWrEP 89*
Lorne, Simon Michael 1946- *WhoWor 91*
Lorona, Marie A. 1938- *WhoHisp 91*
Lorquet, Jean Claude 1935- *WhoWor 91*
Lorrah, Jean *WhoWrEP 89*
Lorrain, Denis 1948- *IntWWM 90*
Lorraine, Eva *IntWWM 90*
Lorraine, Lillian 1892-1955 *OxCPMus*
Lorraine, Richard A. 1945- *St&PR 91*
Lorrance, Arleen 1939- *WhoWrEP 89*
Lorre, Peter 1904-1964 *WorAlBi*
Lorry, Wilfred Fleet 1934- *WhoAm 90*
Lorscheider, Aloisio 1924- *WhoWor 91*
Lortel, Lucille 1902?- *BioIn 16, NotWoAT*
Lortel, Lucille 1905- *WhoAm 90*
Lortie, John William 1920- *WhoWor 91*
Lortie, Pierre 1947- *WhoAm 90*
Lortie, Sylvie Marie *BiDrAPA 89*
Lorton, Donald 1930- *St&PR 91*
Lorton, Lewis 1939- *WhoAm 90, WhoE 91*
Lorton, Mary Manning 1948- *WhoAmW 91*
Lorton, William L *BiDrAPA 89*
Lorts, Jack E. 1940- *WhoWrEP 89*
Lortscher, Loren C *BiDrAPA 89*
Lortz, Charles William, Jr. 1941- *St&PR 91*
Lortz, Don 1916- *St&PR 91*
LoRusso, Lawrence R. 1940- *St&PR 91*
Lorwin, Boris S. 1921- *ODwPR 91*
Lory, Marc H. 1948- *WhoAm 90*
Los Lobos *EncPR&S 89*
Los, Cornelis Albertus 1951- *WhoEmL 91*
Losacco, Dominic *BiDrAPA 89*
Losack, Glenn Mark *BiDrAPA 89*
Losada, Jorge *WhoHisp 91*
Losada-Paisey, Gloria 1957- *WhoAmW 91*
Losambe, Lokangaka 1952- *WhoWor 91*
Los Angeles, Victoria de 1923- *PenDiMP*
Losanno, Carmen 1938- *St&PR 91*
LoSapio, Kathleen 1955- *WhoAmW 91, WhoE 91, WhoWor 91*
Losavio, Samuel 1952- *WhoAmA 91*
Loscalzo, Anthony Joseph 1946- *WhoEmL 91*
Loscalzo, Frank E. *St&PR 91*
Loscavio, Frank John 1949- *WhoAm 90*
.osch, Tilly 1904-1975 *WhoAmA 91N*
.oschen, Earl Lee 1944- *BiDrAPA 89*
.o Schiavo, John Joseph 1925- *WhoAm 90*
.oSchiavo, Joseph James 1927- *St&PR 91*
.oschiavo, Linda Ann *WhoWrEP 89*
.osching, B.H. 1917- *St&PR 91*
.osco, John Joseph 1944- *St&PR 91*
.oscutoff, Lynn Leon 1934- *WhoE 91*
.ose, George W *BiDrAPA 89*
.oseby, Margaret 1939- *WhoWor 91*
.oSecco, John M. 1950- *WhoEmL 91*
.osee, John Frederick, Jr. 1951- *WhoEmL 91, WhoWor 91*
.osee, Thomas Penny, Jr. 1940- *WhoAm 90*
.osener, Bernard 1890-1952 *BioIn 16*
.oser, Ernest L. 1926- *St&PR 91, WhoAm 90*
.osev, Sergei A. 1927-1988 *BioIn 16*
.osey, Debra Ann 1958- *WhoEmL 91*
.osey, Jeanne K. 1925- *WhoWrEP 89*
.osey, Joseph 1909-1984 *BioIn 16*
.osey, Michael Robert 1938- *WhoE 91*
.osh, J. Michael *BioIn 16*
.osh, J. Michael 1946- *WhoAm 90*
.osi, Maxim John 1939- *WhoE 91, WhoWor 91*
.osice, Abraham S. 1960- *St&PR 91*
.sier, Gaetan 1934- *St&PR 91*
.osoncy, Lawrence J. 1941- *ConAu 32NR*
.sordo, Matthew D. *ODwPR 91*
.sowsky, Monty Seymour 1931- *WhoWor 91*
.ss, Joe 1909-1990 *OxCPMus*
.ss, Joe 1910-1990 *BioIn 16*
.ss, John C. 1931- *WhoAm 90*
ss, Louis 1914- *WhoAm 90*
ss, Margaret Ruth 1946- *WhoAm 90, WhoEmL 91*

Loss, Z. Alan 1929- *St&PR 91*
Losse, Arlyle Mansfield 1917- *WhoAmW 91*
Losse, John W., Jr. 1916- *St&PR 91*
Losse, John William, Jr. 1916- *WhoAm 90*
Lossing, Frederick Pettit 1915- *WhoAm 90*
Lossy, Frank T 1924- *BiDrAPA 89*
Losten, Basil Harry 1930- *WhoAm 90*
Lostetter, Al *BioIn 16*
Losty, Barbara Paul 1942- *WhoAmW 91*
Lo Surdo, Antonio 1943- *WhoAm 90*
Losure, Joyce Nelma 1928- *WhoWrEP 89*
Loszak, Karl George *BiDrAPA 89*
Lota, Conrado Santos, Jr. *BiDrAPA 89*
Lotas, Judith Patton 1942- *WhoAm 90, WhoAmW 91*
LoTempio, Julia Matild 1934- *WhoAmW 91, WhoE 91, WhoWor 91*
Lotesta, Pasquale D 1913- *BiDrAPA 89*
Lotfi, Mohamad A 1931- *BiDrAPA 89*
Loth, David *AuBYP 90*
Loth, David 1899-1988 *BioIn 16*
Loth, Eric 1958- *WhoWor 91*
Loth, Gerald Lawrence 1936- *St&PR 91*
Loth, Jerry R. 1929- *St&PR 91*
Loth, Stanislaw Jerzy 1929- *WhoWor 91*
Lothane, Henry Zvi 1934- *WhoE 91*
Lothane, Zvi 1934- *BiDrAPA 89*
Lotharius, Susan Moecker 1950- *WhoAmW 91*
Lothholz, Klaus 1932- *WhoWor 91*
Lothian, Jennifer Brooks *BiDrAPA 89*
Lothian, Roxburghe 1818?-1876 *FemiCLE*
Lothringer, Harvey Norman 1921- *BiDrAPA 89*
Lothrop, George Edwin 1867-1939 *MusmAFA*
Lothrop, Harriet 1844-1924 *WorAlBi*
Lothrop, Harriet Mulford 1844-1924 *AuBYP 90*
Lothrop, Howard John 1957- *WhoSSW 91*
Lothrop, Kristin Curtis 1930- *WhoAm 90, WhoAmA 91*
Lothson, David J. 1945- *WhoAm 90*
Lotkin, Ralph Louis 1946- *WhoEmL 91*
Lotochinski, Eugene B. 1938- *St&PR 91*
Lotocky, Innocent H. 1915- *WhoAm 90*
Lotringer, Sylvere 1938- *WhoAm 90*
Lotspeich, George Oscar 1926- *St&PR 91*
Lotstein, James I. 1944- *WhoAm 90*
Lotstein, Ralph 1927- *St&PR 91*
Lott, Brenda Louise 1955- *WhoAmW 91*
Lott, Bret 1958- *WhoWrEP 89*
Lott, Clarinda Harriss 1939- *WhoWrEP 89*
Lott, Dillon 1924- *WhoWor 91*
Lott, Felicity 1947- *PenDiMP*
Lott, Felicity Ann 1947- *IntWWM 90, WhoWor 91*
Lott, Kench Lee 1920- *St&PR 91*
Lott, Kench Lee, Jr. 1920- *WhoAm 90*
Lott, Michael Blan 1951- *WhoSSW 91*
Lott, Michael Hughes 1956- *BiDrAPA 89*
Lott, Peter DeForest 1933- *St&PR 91*
Lott, R. Allen 1956- *IntWWM 90*
Lott, Richard Norman 1930- *St&PR 91*
Lott, Rick 1950- *WhoWrEP 89*
Lott, Ronnie 1959- *BioIn 16*
Lott, Thomas Luther 1946- *WhoSSW 91*
Lott, Trent *BioIn 16*
Lott, Trent 1941- *WhoAm 90, WhoSSW 91*
Lott, William Cato 1914- *WhoAm 90*
Lotta, Tom 1924- *WhoE 91*
Lotter, John George 1925- *St&PR 91*
Lotter, William H., Jr. 1934- *St&PR 91*
Lotterman, Andrew Clifford 1950- *BiDrAPA 89*
Lotterman, Hal 1920- *WhoAm 90, WhoAmA 91*
Lottes, John William 1934- *WhoAmA 91*
Lottes, Ronald L. 1945- *St&PR 91*
Lotti, Leila Kyllikki 1945- *WhoWor 91*
Lotti, Marcello 1949- *WhoE 91*
Lottinger, Morris Albert, Jr. 1937- *WhoSSW 91*
Lottman, Eileen 1927- *ConAu 30NR*
Lottman, Herbert R 1927- *ConAu 12AS [port]*
Lotto, Lorenzo 1480?-1556? *IntDcAA 90*
Lotton, Donald R. 1940- *St&PR 91*
Lotts, Gordon R. 1923- *St&PR 91*
LoTurco, Ed *BioIn 16*
Lotz, Arthur William 1927- *St&PR 91, WhoAm 90*
Lotz, Benno Paul 1931- *St&PR 91*
Lotz, George Michael 1928- *WhoE 91*
Lotz, Jack Coldwell 1929- *St&PR 91*
Lotz, James Robert 1929- *ConAu 31NR*
Lotz, Jim *ConAu 31NR*
Lotz, Joan Theresa 1948- *WhoAmW 91*
Lotz, John Jacob 1922- *WhoE 91, WhoWor 91*
Lotz, Steven Darryl 1938- *WhoAmA 91*
Lotz, Vivian Evelyn 1943- *WhoAmW 91*
Lotze, Barbara 1924- *WhoAmW 91, WhoWor 91*
Lotze, Dieter P 1933- *ConAu 132*
Lou 1898-1968 *EncO&P 3*
Lou, Peter Louis 1945- *WhoE 91*

Loube, Samuel Dennis 1921- *WhoAm 90*
Loubeau, Micheline O *BiDrAPA 89*
Loubere, Leo A 1923- *ConAu 130*
Loubet, Emile 1838-1929 *BiDFrPL*
Loucas, Spiro Paul 1929- *WhoE 91*
Louch, Alfred Richard 1927- *WhoAm 90*
Loucheur, Louis Albert Joseph 1872-1931 *BiDFrPL*
Louchheim, Donald Harry 1937- *WhoAm 90*
Louchheim, Frank P. *St&PR 91*
Louchheim, Frank Pfeifer 1923- *WhoAm 90*
Louchheim, Mark S. *St&PR 91*
Louchheim, William S. 1904- *St&PR 91*
Louchheim, William Sandel, Jr. 1930- *St&PR 91*
Louckes, Theodore Nicholas 1930- *St&PR 91*
Loucks, Daniel Peter 1932- *WhoAm 90, WhoE 91*
Loucks, Nancy J. 1957- *WhoAmW 91*
Loucks, Thomas Alexander 1949- *St&PR 91*
Loucks, Vernon R. 1934- *St&PR 91*
Loucks, Vernon R., Jr. 1934- *WhoAm 90, WhoWor 91*
Loud, Franck Bjorn 1947- *WhoWor 91*
Loud, James John 1946- *WhoSSW 91*
Loud, Karen A. G. 1935- *WhoAm 90*
Loud, Nelson M. 1914- *St&PR 91*
Loud, Warren Simms 1921- *WhoAm 90*
Louden, Baldy 1885-1935 *Ballpl 90*
Louden, J Keith 1905- *ConAu 132*
Louden, J. Keith 1905- *St&PR 91*
Louden, James A., Jr. 1937- *St&PR 91*
Louden, James Keith 1905- *WhoAm 90*
Louden, Joan Karen 1947- *WhoSSW 91*
Louden, Thomas A. 1919- *St&PR 91*
Louden, William G. 1921- *St&PR 91*
Loudenslager, Larry Neal 1949- *WhoEmL 91*
Louderback, Truman Eugene 1946- *WhoEmL 91*
Loudermilk, R. Charles 1927- *WhoAm 90*
Loudermilk, Robert Charles, Sr. 1927- *St&PR 91*
Loudin, David Earnest 1947- *St&PR 91*
Loudon, Aarnout Alexander 1936- *WhoWor 91*
Loudon, Craig Michael 1950- *WhoWor 91*
Loudon, Dorothy 1933- *WhoAm 90, WorAlBi*
Loudon, George *BioIn 16*
Loudon, J. C. 1783-1843 *BioIn 16*
Loudon, James A. 1944- *St&PR 91*
Loudon, John Campbell, Earl of 1705-1782 *EncCRAm*
Loudon, John Claudius 1783-1843 *BioIn 16, PenDiDA 89*
Loudova, Ivana 1941- *IntWWM 90*
Louer, Melissa Heyward 1953- *WhoE 91*
Louganis, Greg *BioIn 16*
Louganis, Greg 1960?- *WorAlBi*
Louganis, Greg E. 1960- *WhoAm 90*
Lougee, Alan T. 1953- *St&PR 91*
Lougee, David Louis 1940- *WhoWor 91*
Lougee, Robert W., Jr. 1945- *ODwPR 91*
Lougee, Robert Wayne 1919- *WhoAm 90*
Lougee, Robert Wayne 1945- *WhoE 91*
Lougee, Robert Wayne, Jr. 1945- *St&PR 91*
Lough, Ernest 1911- *PenDiMP*
Lough, John David 1926- *St&PR 91*
Loughary, Thomas Michael 1959- *WhoEmL 91*
Lougheed, Peter 1928- *BioIn 16, WhoAm 90*
Loughlin, Beverly Anne 1944- *WhoAmW 91*
Loughlin, Donald Alexander 1926- *WhoE 91*
Loughlin, John *BioIn 16*
Loughlin, John Leo 1931- *WhoAmA 91, WhoE 91*
Loughlin, Kathi Puglise 1958- *WhoAmW 91*
Loughlin, Lawrence *BiDrAPA 89*
Loughlin, Lawrence Joseph, Jr. 1932- *St&PR 91*
Loughlin, Lori *ConTFT 8*
Loughlin, Martin Francis 1923- *WhoAm 90*
Loughlin, Mary Anne Elizabeth 1956- *WhoAm 90*
Loughlin, Richard J. 1932- *WhoAm 90*
Loughlin, Richard L. 1907- *WhoWrEP 89*
Loughman, Aleda P. 1932- *St&PR 91*
Loughmiller, Bert Edward 1942- *St&PR 91*
Loughmiller, Robert Alden 1931- *St&PR 91*
Loughnane, Lee David 1946- *WhoAm 90*
Loughran, James 1931- *IntWWM 90, PenDiMP*
Loughran, James Newman 1940- *WhoAm 90*
Loughran, John Francis 1932- *WhoAm 90*
Loughran, Judy D. 1947- *St&PR 91*
Loughran, Robert Hall 1916- *WhoAm 90*

Loughran, Thomas Joseph 1929- *St&PR 91*
Loughran, Thomas Patrick, Jr. 1953- *WhoEmL 91*
Loughrey, Sean David 1964- *WhoWor 91*
Loughridge, Dennis Wayne 1947- *St&PR 91*
Loughridge, Edward K. *ODwPR 91*
Loughridge, Robert F. 1935- *St&PR 91*
Loughridge, Robert Foster, Jr. 1935- *WhoAm 90*
Loughridge, Robert Foster, Sr. 1906- *St&PR 91*
Louie, Alan Kuo-Hin *BiDrAPA 89*
Louie, Alexina Diane 1949- *WhoAmW 91*
Louie, David Mark 1951- *WhoEmL 91*
Louie, Donald F *BiDrAPA 89*
Louie, Edward *BioIn 16, NewYTBS 90*
Louie, Kwok Ying 1953- *WhoE 91*
Louie, Richard *NewYTBS 90*
Louie, Theodore Y. 1956- *St&PR 91*
Louiguy, Louis Guiglielmi 1916- *OxCPMus*
Louineau, Michel-Yves 1955- *WhoWor 91*
Louis XIV *PenDiDA 89*
Louis XIV 1638-1715 *WorAlBi*
Louis XV *PenDiDA 89*
Louis XVI *PenDiDA 89*
Louis XVI 1754-1793 *WorAlBi*
Louis, Father 1915-1968 *BioIn 16*
Louis Francis, Prince of Battenberg 1900-1979 *BioIn 16*
Louis VIII, King of France 1601-1643 *BioIn 16*
Louis XIV, King of France 1638-1715 *BioIn 16*
Louis XVI, King of France 1754-1793 *BioIn 16*
Louis Philippe, King of the French 1773-1850 *BioIn 16*
Louis, Barbra Schantz 1940- *WhoE 91*
Louis, David *ConAu 129*
Louis, Ernest G. 1923- *St&PR 91*
Louis, Eugenia *BioIn 16*
Louis, Francois Pierre 1929- *WhoE 91*
Louis, Henry 1927- *St&PR 91*
Louis, Jean-Jacob *PenDiDA 89*
Louis, Joe 1914-1981 *BioIn 16, WorAlBi*
Louis, John, Jr. 1925- *WhoAm 90*
Louis, John Jeffry, Jr. *BioIn 16*
Louis, Leslie Bertram 1948- *WhoWor 91*
Louis, Lester 1928- *WhoAm 90*
Louis, Louis F. 1955- *St&PR 91*
Louis, M. *MajTwCW*
Louis, Marian *BiDrAPA 89*
Louis, Martin Bernard 1934- *WhoAm 90*
Louis, Morris 1912-1962 *IntDcAA 90*
Louis, Morris 1912-1963 *WhoAmA 91N*
Louis, Paul Adolph 1922- *WhoAm 90*
Louis, Rene Paul 1933- *WhoWor 91*
Louis, Robert Henry 1947- *WhoEmL 91*
Louis, William Roger 1936- *WhoAm 90, WhoWrEP 89*
Louis-Dreyfus, Julia *BioIn 16*
Louis-Dreyfus, Robert *BioIn 16*
Louis-Dreyfus, Robert 1946- *WhoAm 90*
Louis-Philippe *PenDiDA 89*
Louise *EncCoWW*
Louise Caroline Alberta 1848-1939 *BiDWomA*
Louise de Savoy 1476-1531 *WomWR*
Louise Hippolyte 1697-1731 *WomWR*
Louise, Queen 1776-1810 *BioIn 16*
Louise, Tina 1934- *BioIn 16*
Louison, Deborah Finley 1951- *WhoAmW 91*
Louisot, Pierre Auguste Alphonse 1933- *WhoWor 91*
Louisy, Allan *BioIn 16*
Louka, Alain 1952- *WhoSSW 91*
Louke, Samuel Franklin 1956- *WhoEmL 91*
Loukidis, Dimitris K. 1936- *St&PR 91*
Loundy, Mason A. 1906- *St&PR 91*
Loundy, Richard A. *St&PR 91*
Lounge, John M. 1946?- *BioIn 16*
Lounsberry, Clement Augustus 1843-1926 *BioIn 16*
Lounsbury, Charles B. 1942- *St&PR 91*
Lounsbury, Floyd Glenn 1914- *WhoAm 90*
Lounsbury, John Frederick 1918- *WhoAm 90*
Loup, Francois Bernard 1940- *WhoAm 90*
Loup, Jean L. 1941- *WhoAmW 91*
Loupard, Marie Claire *EncCoWW*
Lourdet, Simon *PenDiDA 89*
Lourdusamy, Simon 1924- *WhoWor 91*
Lourenco, Antonio Filipe 1934- *BiDrAPA 89*
Lourenco, Ruy Valentim 1929- *WhoAm 90*
Loures, Constantine 1918- *BiDrAPA 89*
Loures, Constantine Demetrios 1918- *WhoE 91*
Lourey, Joseph R. 1940- *St&PR 91*
Louria, Felice Jarecky *BioIn 16*
Lourido-Ferrer, Heriberto D *BiDrAPA 89*
Lourie, Alan David 1935- *WhoAm 90*
Lourie, Daniel Norman 1928- *WhoE 91*
Lourie, Dick 1937- *WhoWrEP 89*

Lourie, Donold B. *NewYTBS 90*
Lourie, Donold B. 1899-1990 *BioIn 16*
Lourie, Eugene 1905- *ConDes 90*
Lourie, Helen *AuBYP 90*
Lourie, Herbert S 1923-1981 *WhoAmA 91N*
Lourie, Ira Sanders 1941- *BiDrAPA 89, WhoE 91*
Lourie, Iven B. 1946- *WhoWrEP 89*
Lourie, Norman V 1912- *BiDrAPA 89*
Lourie, Norman Victor 1912- *WhoAm 90*
Lourie, Reginald S. 1908-1988 *BioIn 16*
Lourie, Richard 1940- *ConAu 131*
Lourie, Roger H. 1941- *St&PR 91*
Lous, Per 1914- *WhoWor 91*
Lousberg, Peter Herman 1931- *WhoAm 90*
Loustunau-Lacau, Georges 1894-1955 *BiDFrPL*
Loutfy, Aly 1935- *WhoWor 91*
Louth, William T. 1926- *St&PR 91*
Loutrel, Claude Yves 1930- *WhoAm 90*
Loutsch, Enrique H 1932- *BiDrAPA 89*
Loutsch, Erica M K 1937- *BiDrAPA 89*
Louttit, Gordon James 1947- *St&PR 91*
Louttit, James Russell 1924- *WhoAm 90*
Louttit, Richard Talcott 1932- *WhoAm 90*
Louttit, William A. 1946- *WhoAm 90*
Loutzenheiser, Edwin J., Jr. 1917- *St&PR 91*
Loutzenhiser, James K 1931- *BiDrAPA 89*
Loutzenhiser, Jan S. 1937- *WhoAm 90*
Louvain, Michel Rene *BiDrAPA 89*
Louviere, Nadine *BioIn 16*
Louvin Brothers, The *WhoNeCM C*
Louvin, Charlie *WhoNeCM C [port]*
Louvin, Ira *WhoNeCM C*
Louw, Antoni Alexander *WhoE 91*
Louw, Jan Cornelius 1933- *BiDrAPA 89*
Louw, N. P. Van Wyk 1906-1970 *WorAlBi*
Loux, Joseph Anthony, Jr. 1945- *WhoWor 91*
Loux, Lloyd Fox, Jr. 1929- *WhoAm 90*
Loux, Michael Joseph 1942- *WhoAm 90*
Loux, Norman L 1919- *BiDrAPA 89*
Loux, Norman Landis 1919- *WhoAm 90, WhoE 91*
Lovaas, M. John 1936- *St&PR 91*
Lovallo, Patricia Gaffney 1957- *WhoAmW 91, WhoE 91*
Lovan, Joan Denise 1954- *WhoAmW 91*
Lovatelli, Roberta Maria 1954- *WhoE 91*
Lovato, Charles Frederic 1937-1988 *WhoAmA 91N*
Lovato, Eugene Daniel 1951- *WhoHisp 91*
Love *OxCPMus*
Love, Alfred Henry 1830-1913 *WhNaAH*
Love, Allan Walter 1916- *WhoAm 90*
Love, Ann *BioIn 16*
Love, Ann Purcell *WhoE 91*
Love, Arthur MacDougall, III 1947- *WhoAm 90*
Love, Arthur Richard 1945- *St&PR 91*
Love, Ben F. 1924- *St&PR 91, WhoAm 90, WhoSSW 91*
Love, Ben Howard 1930- *WhoAm 90*
Love, Bob *BioIn 16*
Love, Bonnie 1948- *WhoAmW 91*
Love, Cathleen T. *BioIn 16*
Love, Clinton Kenneth 1952- *WhoAm 90*
Love, Cynthia Wallace *BioIn 16*
Love, David 1935- *WhoAm 90*
Love, Edith Holmes 1950- *WhoAmW 91, WhoSSW 91*
Love, Edmund G. *NewYTBS 90 [port]*
Love, Edmund G 1912-1990 *ConAu 132*
Love, Edward Willis, Jr. *BiDrAPA 89*
Love, Emma Louise 1944- *WhoAmW 91*
Love, Frances Taylor 1926- *WhoAmA 91*
Love, Frank, Jr. 1927- *WhoAm 90*
Love, Franklin Sadler 1915- *WhoAm 90*
Love, George C. 1928- *St&PR 91*
Love, George Hayward 1924- *WhoE 91*
Love, Harold Sanford 1939- *WhoSSW 91*
Love, Harold Timothy 1953- *WhoSSW 91*
Love, Hortense 1910- *DcAfAmP*
Love, Howard McClintic 1930- *St&PR 91, WhoAm 90, WhoE 91*
Love, Iris *BioIn 16*
Love, James Oliver 1938- *St&PR 91*
Love, James S. 1896-1962 *WorAlBi*
Love, Jane Hazelton 1931-1988 *BioIn 16*
Love, Jerry Bert 1950- *WhoEmL 91*
Love, Jim 1927- *WhoAmA 91*
Love, John, Jr. 1916- *WhoAm 90*
Love, John Edward 1932- *St&PR 91*
Love, John Wesley, Jr. 1932- *WhoSSW 91*
Love, John William, Jr. *BiDrAPA 89*
Love, Keith Sinclair 1947- *WhoAm 90*
Love, Kenneth E. 1932- *St&PR 91*
Love, L. Ross *BioIn 16*
Love, Laurie Miller 1960- *WhoEmL 91*
Love, Lenore *BioIn 16*
Love, Lisa *BioIn 16*
Love, Lois H *BiDrAPA 89*
Love, Lois Marie 1931- *WhoAmW 91*
Love, Lynette *BioIn 16*
Love, Malcolm A. 1904-1990 *BioIn 16*
Love, Mary *BiDEWW, FemiCLE*
Love, Mildred Allison 1915- *WhoAmW 91*
Love, Mildred Lois 1928- *WhoAmW 91*
Love, Nancy 1927- *WhoAm 90, WhoWrEP 89*
Love, Nat 1854- *WhNaAH*
Love, Nick *BioIn 16*
Love, Richard Emerson 1926- *WhoAm 90*
Love, Richard Harvey 1915- *WhoAm 90*
Love, Richard Henry 1939- *WhoAm 90, WhoAmA 91*
Love, Richard M. 1946- *St&PR 91*
Love, Robert Alonzo 1898- *WhoAm 90*
Love, Robert L 1929- *BiDrAPA 89*
Love, Robert Lyman 1925- *WhoAm 90*
Love, Robert Merton 1909- *WhoAm 90*
Love, Robert William, Jr. 1929- *WhoAm 90*
Love, Robin Fern 1959- *WhoE 91*
Love, Rodney Marvin 1908- *WhoAm 90*
Love, Ronald Jackson 1943- *WhoSSW 91*
Love, Rose Leary 1898-1969 *HarlReB*
Love, Samuel B. *AmLegL*
Love, Sandra Rae 1947- *WhoAmW 91*
Love, Shirley 1940- *IntWWM 90*
Love, Slim 1890-1942 *Ballpl 90*
Love, Stanley 1926- *St&PR 91*
Love, Susan Denise 1954- *WhoAmW 91*
Love, Sydney Charles 1930- *WhoSSW 91*
Love, Thomas Bell 1870-1948 *AmLegL*
Love, Tom Jay, Jr. 1923- *WhoAm 90*
Love, Victor 1957?- *DrBIPA 90*
Love, Virginia M *BiDrAPA 89*
Love, Walter Bennett, Jr. 1921- *WhoWor 91*
Love, Warner Bruce 1932- *St&PR 91*
Love, William Edward 1926- *WhoAm 90*
Love, William F. 1932- *ConAu 132*
Love, William T *BiDrAPA 89*
Love, William Wray 1936- *St&PR 91*
Love-Hoekstra, Wendy 1956- *ODwPR 91*
Lovec, Rosita Borunda 1935- *WhoAmW 91*
Lovecky, Deirdre Vally 1945- *WhoE 91*
Lovecraft, H P 1890-1937 *EncO&P 3, MajTwCW*
Lovecraft, H. P. 1890-1937 *RGTwCSF, WorAlBi*
Loveday, Alan 1928- *IntWWM 90*
Loveid, Cecilie 1951- *DcScanL, EncCoWW*
Lovejoy, Allen Fraser 1919- *WhoAm 90*
Lovejoy, Bahija Fattouhi 1914- *AuBYP 90*
Lovejoy, Barbara Campbell 1919- *WhoAm 90*
Lovejoy, David R. 1948- *St&PR 91*
Lovejoy, David William 1942- *St&PR 91*
Lovejoy, Elijah Parish 1802-1837 *BioIn 16*
Lovejoy, Howard E. 1916- *St&PR 91*
Lovejoy, Jean Hastings 1913- *WhoAmW 91*
Lovejoy, Joseph Ensign 1940- *St&PR 91*
Lovejoy, L. James 1931- *ODwPR 91*
Lovejoy, Margot R 1930- *WhoAmA 91*
Lovejoy, Morris Lester 1955- *BiDrAPA 89*
Lovejoy, Patricia T. 1954- *St&PR 91*
Lovejoy, Robert B. 1937- *St&PR 91*
Lovejoy, Robert C. *St&PR 91N*
Lovejoy, Rosie *NewAgMG*
Lovejoy, Susann Lea *BiDrAPA 89*
Lovejoy, Thomas E. *BioIn 16*
Lovejoy, Thomas E. 1941- *St&PR 91*
Lovejoy, Thomas Eugene 1941- *WhoAm 90, WhoWor 91*
Lovejoy, William Joseph 1940- *St&PR 91, WhoAm 90*
Lovekamp, Glen Hugo 1925- *St&PR 91*
Lovelace, Alan Mathieson 1929- *St&PR 91, WhoAm 90*
Lovelace, Augusta A B King, Countess of 1815-1852 *BioIn 16*
Lovelace, Carey 1952- *WhoWrEP 89*
Lovelace, Delos Wheeler 1894-1967 *AuBYP 90*
Lovelace, Donna Landon 1947- *WhoAmW 91, WhoSSW 91*
Lovelace, Earl 1935- *MajTwCW*
Lovelace, Eldridge Hirst 1913- *WhoAm 90*
Lovelace, Ella *BioIn 16*
Lovelace, Francis 1621?-1675 *EncCRAm*
Lovelace, George David, Jr. 1952- *WhoSSW 91*
Lovelace, Jon B. 1927- *WhoAm 90*
Lovelace, Jon B., Jr. 1927- *St&PR 91*
Lovelace, Keith 1935- *WhoSSW 91*
Lovelace, Leopoldo Guisasola 1950- *WhoWor 91*
Lovelace, Linda *ConAu 129*
Lovelace, Maud Hart 1892-1980 *AuBYP 90*
Lovelace, Richard 1618?-1656? *WorAlBi*
Lovelace, Robert Edward 1929- *BiDrAPA 89*
Lovelace, Robert Frank 1950- *WhoAm 90*
Lovelace, Stewart W *BiDrAPA 89*
Lovelace, Walter L. 1831-1866 *AmLegL*
Lovelady, Carolyn Moore 1952- *WhoSSW 91*
Lovelady, Steven M. 1943- *WhoAm 90*
Loveland, Charles E. 1916- *St&PR 91*
Loveland, Donald William 1934- *WhoAm 90, WhoSSW 91*
Loveland, Edward Henry 1922- *WhoAm 90*
Loveland, Eugene Franklin 1920- *WhoAm 90*
Loveland, Holly Standish 1947- *WhoAmW 91*
Loveland, James A. 1941- *St&PR 91*
Loveland, James Lee 1951- *WhoE 91*
Loveland, Joseph Albert, Jr. 1932- *WhoAm 90*
Loveland, Kenneth 1915- *IntWWM 90*
Loveland, Olga Helen 1920- *IntWWM 90*
Loveland, Peter Graham 1926- *St&PR 91*
Loveless, Edward Eugene 1919- *WhoAm 90*
Loveless, Herschel Cellel 1911-1989 *BioIn 16*
Loveless, Homer Jackson, Jr. 1931- *St&PR 91*
Loveless, Howard William 1927- *St&PR 91*
Loveless, Jim 1935- *WhoAmA 91*
Loveless, Jon Alfred 1942- *St&PR 91*
Loveless, Patty *BioIn 16, WhoNeCM [port]*
Loveless, Patty 1957- *ConMus 5 [port]*
Loveless, William Edward 1951- *WhoWrEP 89*
Loveling, Rosalie 1834-1875 *EncCoWW*
Loveling, Virginie 1836-1923 *EncCoWW*
Lovell, Alfred C. B. 1913- *WorAlBi*
Lovell, Arnold Buffum 1937- *WhoAm 90*
Lovell, Bernard 1913- *WhoWor 91*
Lovell, Charles V *BiDrAPA 89*
Lovell, Cyrus 1804- *AmLegL*
Lovell, Edward George 1939- *WhoAm 90*
Lovell, Emily Kalled 1920- *WhoAmW 91, WhoWor 91*
Lovell, Francis Joseph, III 1949- *WhoE 91, WhoWor 91*
Lovell, Frederick S. 1815-1878 *AmLegL*
Lovell, Gerald Donald *St&PR 91*
Lovell, Harold W *BiDrAPA 89*
Lovell, J. Byron 1927- *WhoE 91*
Lovell, James 1737-1814 *BioIn 16*
Lovell, James A., Jr. 1928- *WhoAm 90, WorAlBi*
Lovell, James Arthur 1928- *St&PR 91*
Lovell, James Barton 1928- *St&PR 91*
Lovell, James C. 1926- *St&PR 91, WhoAm 90, WhoE 91*
Lovell, James Frederick 1934- *WhoAm 90*
Lovell, James Riley 1927- *WhoSSW 91*
Lovell, John 1810-1893 *DcCanB 12*
Lovell, Malcolm Read, Jr. 1921- *WhoAm 90*
Lovell, Marc *TwCCr&M 91*
Lovell, Margaretta Markle 1944- *WhoAmA 91*
Lovell, Martin H. 1894- *BioIn 16*
Lovell, Michael C. 1930- *WhoAm 90, WhoE 91*
Lovell, Percy Albert 1919- *IntWWM 90*
Lovell, Robert Gibson 1920- *WhoAm 90*
Lovell, Robert Marlow, Jr. 1930- *St&PR 91, WhoAm 90, WhoE 91*
Lovell, Stephen S. 1941- *St&PR 91*
Lovell, Tom 1909- *WhoAmA 91*
Lovell, Walter Carl 1934- *WhoE 91, WhoWor 91*
Lovell, William George 1939- *St&PR 91*
Lovely, Candace Whittemore 1953- *WhoAmW 91*
Lovely, Jack *St&PR 91*
Lovely, Mary Ruth 1961- *WhoAmW 91*
Lovely, Thomas Dixon 1930- *WhoAm 90, WhoWor 91*
Lovely, Thomas Dixon 1931- *St&PR 91*
Loveman, David Bernard 1942- *St&PR 91*
Loveman, Gail J. 1949- *St&PR 91*
Loveman, Gail Jean 1949- *WhoAm 90*
Loveman, Marc 1938- *St&PR 91*
Loven, Andrew Witherspoon 1935- *WhoAm 90*
Loven, Dana Ellen 1950- *BiDrAPA 89*
Lovenbach, Thierry Jacques 1946- *WhoWor 91*
Loventhal, Milton 1923- *WhoWor 91*
Loveras, Joseph J. *BioIn 16*
Loverboy *EncPR&S 89*
Loverd, Robert L. 1942- *St&PR 91*
Loverd, William N. 1911- *St&PR 91, WhoAm 90*
Loveridge, James William 1947- *St&PR 91*
Lovering, Loreli 1934- *WhoAmW 91*
Loversky, Frank G. 1934- *St&PR 91*
Lovesey, Peter 1936- *MajTwCW, TwCCr&M 91*
Lovesky, Jerome 1930- *WhoAm 90*
Lovestone, Jay 1898-1990 *BioIn 16, NewYTBS 90 [port]*
Lovet-Lorski, Boris 1894-1973 *WhoAmA 91N*
LoVetere, Arthur J. 1939- *St&PR 91*
Lovetri, Jeannette Louise 1949- *WhoAmW 91*
Lovett, Brent Roger *BiDrAPA 89*
Lovett, Carlus L. 1944- *St&PR 91*
Lovett, Clara Maria 1939- *WhoAm 90*
Lovett, David F.G. 1942- *St&PR 91*
Lovett, Eddie *BioIn 16*
Lovett, Gail Ellison 1951- *WhoSSW 91*
Lovett, Henry Malcolm 1902- *WhoAm 90*
Lovett, James Everett 1930- *WhoSSW 91*
Lovett, John Robert 1931- *St&PR 91*
Lovett, Juanita Pelletier 1937- *WhoAmW 91*
Lovett, Laurence Dow 1930- *WhoAm 90*
Lovett, Lyle *BioIn 16, WhoNeCM [port]*
Lovett, Lyle 1958?- *ConMus 5 [port]*
Lovett, Martin *PenDiMP*
Lovett, Mary Deloache 1909- *St&PR 91*
Lovett, Radford Dow 1933- *WhoAm 90*
Lovett, Raymond E. *BioIn 16*
Lovett, Robert A. 1895-1986 *BioIn 16*
Lovett, Robert Abercrombie 1895-1986 *BiDrUSE 89*
Lovett, Rosalee 1949- *St&PR 91*
Lovett, Shirley Morris *BiDrAPA 89*
Lovett, Terence George 1922- *IntWWM 90*
Lovett, Wendell Harper 1922- *WhoAm 90*
Lovett, William 1800-1877 *BioIn 16*
Lovett, William Anthony 1934- *WhoSSW 91*
Lovette, Blake Duane 1942- *WhoAm 90, WhoSSW 91*
Lovette, Bonnie *BioIn 16*
Lovette, Louise J. *EarBIAP*
Lovewell, Hubart Stonex, Jr. 1936- *WhoSSW 91*
Lovewell, Paul Joseph 1915- *WhoAm 90*
Lovig, Lawrence, III 1942- *WhoE 91*
Lovin' Spoonful, The *EncPR&S 89, OxCPMus*
Lovin, Keith Harold 1943- *WhoAm 90*
Lovinescu, Monica 1923- *EncCoWW*
Loving, Al 1935- *WhoAmA 91*
Loving, Dabney Carr 1929- *St&PR 91*
Loving, George Gilmer, Jr. 1923- *WhoAm 90*
Loving, Jerome MacNeill 1941- *ConAu 30NR*
Loving, Richard Maris 1924- *WhoAmA 91*
Loving, William M 1947- *BiDrAPA 89*
Lovinger, Richard Ralph 1927- *St&PR 91*
Lovinger, Sophie Lehner 1932- *WhoAmW 91*
Lovinger, Warren Conrad 1915- *WhoAm 90*
Lovingheart, Dr. *DcCanB 12*
Lovingood, Rebecca Britten 1939- *WhoE 91*
Lovins, Amory B 1947- *ConAu 32NR*
Lovins, Amory Bloch 1947- *WhoAm 90*
Lovins, Sharron Joyce 1946- *WhoAmW 91*
Lovis, William Anthony 1948- *WhoAm 90*
Lovisi, Arthur Anthony 1954- *WhoSSW 91*
Lovitt, George Harold 1922- *WhoAm 90*
Lovitto, Joe 1951- *Ballpl 90*
Lovitz, Alix Jean *BiDrAPA 89*
Lovitz, David D. 1920- *St&PR 91*
Lovitz, Jon 1957- *WorAlBi*
Lovkay, John 1937- *St&PR 91*
Lovko, Kenneth Ray *BiDrAPA 89*
Lovoos, Janice *AuBYP 90, BioIn 16*
Lovretin, Andrew, Jr. 1925- *WhoE 91*
Lovrien, Phyllis Ann 1941- *St&PR 91*
Lovsky, Fay 1955- *WhoWor 91*
Lovvorn, Dixon Cannon 1925- *St&PR 91*
Lovvorn, Joella 1934- *WhoAmW 91*
Lovvorn, John Ridley 1934- *BiDrAPA 89*
Lovvorn, Roy Lee 1910- *WhoAm 90*
Lovy, Andrew 1935- *BiDrAPA 89, WhoWor 91*
Low, Alice 1926- *AuBYP 90, BioIn 16*
Low, Anthony 1935- *WhoAm 90, WhoWrEP 89*
Low, Barbara Wharton 1920- *WhoAm 90*
Low, Bet 1924- *BiDWomA*
Low, Bobbi S. 1942- *WhoAmW 91*
Low, Carl 1916-1988 *BioIn 16*
Low, Dana E. 1932- *St&PR 91*
Low, David A. 1939- *St&PR 91*
Low, David B. 1942- *St&PR 91*
Low, Denise Lea 1949- *WhoWrEP 89*
Low, Donald Gottlob 1925- *WhoAm 90*
Low, E. Herrick *BioIn 16*
Low, Edward E *BiDrAPA 89*
Low, Elizabeth Hammond 1898- *AuBYP 90*
Low, Emmet Francis, Jr. 1922- *WhoAm 90*
Low, Francis Eugene 1921- *WhoAm 90*
Low, Frank James 1933- *WhoAm 90*
Low, Frank Norman 1911- *WhoAm 90*
Low, Frederick Ferdinand 1828-1894 *BioIn 16*
Low, H. Burton 1929- *St&PR 91*
Low, Harry William 1931- *WhoAm 90*
Low, Jaclyn Faglie 1941- *WhoSSW 91*
Low, James A. 1925- *WhoAm 90*
Low, James Patterson 1927- *WhoAm 90, WhoWor 91*
Low, John Henry 1954- *WhoE 91*
Low, John Wayland 1923- *WhoAm 90*

Low, Joseph 1911- AuBYP 90, WhoAm 90, WhoAmA 91, WhoE 91, WhoSSW 91
Low, Julie Ann 1954- BiDrAPA 89
Low, Juliette Gordon 1860-1927 BioAmW, BioIn 16
Low, Kathleen 1956- WhoEmL 91
Low, Linda BiDrAPA 89
Low, Madeleine M. BioIn 16
Low, Marissa Eva 1960- WhoAmW 91
Low, Mary 1858-1946 BiDWomA
Low, Max M. 1901-1989 BioIn 16
Low, Merry Cook 1925- WhoAmW 91
Low, Morton David 1935- WhoAm 90
Low, Paul M. 1930- St&PR 91, WhoAm 90
Low, Peter W. 1937- WhoAm 90
Low, Philip Funk 1921- WhoAm 90
Low, Remington 1911- St&PR 91
Low, Richard H. 1927- WhoAm 90, WhoWor 91
Low, Sanford 1905-1964 WhoAmA 91N
Low, Stephen 1927- WhoAm 90
Low, Stuart M. 1917- St&PR 91
Low, Teresa Lingchun Kao 1941- WhoWor 91
Low, Walter Cheney 1950- WhoWor 91
Low, William H. 1926- St&PR 91
Low-Beer, Thomas Stephen 1932- WhoWor 91
Lowd, Catherine Ann 1943- WhoAmW 91
Lowd, Judson Dean 1918- WhoAm 90
Lowden, Cynthia Gail 1958- WhoE 91
Lowden, Gordon 1927- BioIn 16
Lowden, John L. 1921- WhoAm 90
Lowden, Robert Davidson 1937- St&PR 91
Lowden, Robert William 1920- IntWWM 90
Lowden, Scott Richard 1940- WhoAm 90
Lowdermilk, Grover 1885-1968 Ballpl 90
Lowdermilk, Walter 1888-1974 BioIn 16
Lowdin, William PenDiDA 89
Lowe, Adele Virginia 1919- WhoAmW 91
Lowe, Adolph 1893- WhoWor 91
Lowe, Alfred Mifflin, III 1948- WhoE 91
Lowe, Bobby 1868-1951 Ballpl 90[port]
Lowe, Brian 1935- St&PR 91
Lowe, Caroline A. 1874-1933 EncAL
Lowe, Chris BioIn 16
Lowe, D. Nelson 1938- St&PR 91
Lowe, Daniel 1932- St&PR 91
Lowe, David 1933- WhoWrEP 89
Lowe, David Jon 1949- St&PR 91
Lowe, Donald C. 1932- St&PR 91
Lowe, Donald Cameron 1932- WhoAm 90
Lowe, Douglas Hayse 1952- WhoWrEP 89
Lowe, Douglas Howard 1952- WhoSSW 91
Lowe, Douglass Arnold 1932- BiDrAPA 89
Lowe, Eaph St&PR 91
Lowe, Edward 1921- News 90[port]
Lowe, Edwin Nobles 1912- WhoAm 90, WhoWor 91
Lowe, Emily WhoAmA 91N
Lowe, Ethel Black 1904- WhoAmW 91, WhoE 91, WhoWor 91
Lowe, Felix Caleb 1933- WhoAm 90
Lowe, Ferdinand 1865-1925 PenDiMP
Lowe, Florence Leontine 1901-1975 BioIn 16
Lowe, Florence Segal WhoAmW 91, WhoE 91
Lowe, Franklyn Rudolph A. 1942- WhoWor 91
Lowe, G. Nelson 1929- St&PR 91
Lowe, G. Ralph 1916- St&PR 91
Lowe, George Ralph, III 1941- St&PR 91
Lowe, Harry 1922- WhoAm 90, WhoAmA 91
Lowe, Henry Paget MajTwCW
Lowe, Henry Thomas 1925- WhoAm 90
Lowe, J Michael 1942- WhoAmA 91
Lowe, J. Michael 1942- WhoE 91
Lowe, James Allison 1945- WhoEmL 91
Lowe, James B 1880?-1963 DrBlPA 90
Lowe, James J. 1915- St&PR 91
Lowe, James Lewis 1929- WhoE 91
Lowe, Jamie BioIn 16
Lowe, Janet 1940- WhoAmW 91
Lowe, Jeanne Catherine 1942- IntWWM 90
Lowe, Jewell Parkerson WhoSSW 91
Lowe, Joe 1842-1899 BioIn 16
Lowe, John, III 1916- WhoAm 90
Lowe, John Hugh, III 1941- BiDrAPA 89
Lowe, John Richard BiDrAPA 89
Lowe, John William 1945- WhoE 91
Lowe, Jonathan F. 1953- WhoWrEP 89
Lowe, Judah ConAu 132
Lowe, Justus Frederick 1927- St&PR 91
Lowe, Justus Frederick, Jr. 1927- WhoAm 90
Lowe, Kathleen Orban 1947- WhoAmW 91
Lowe, Kenneth Stephen 1921- WhoAm 90, WhoWrEP 89
Lowe, Lester Vincent, Jr. 1936- St&PR 91
Lowe, Liz 1956- BioIn 16
Lowe, Margaret B. 1927- WhoAmW 91
Lowe, Marvin 1922- WhoAm 90
Lowe, Marvin 1927- WhoAmA 91
Lowe, Marvin Duke 1929- St&PR 91
Lowe, Mary Frances 1952- WhoAm 90
Lowe, Mary Johnson 1924- WhoAm 90, WhoAmW 91
Lowe, Max Alan 1948- St&PR 91, WhoSSW 91
Lowe, Michael Craig 1942- WhoE 91, WhoWor 91
Lowe, Michael Graeme 1947- IntWWM 90
Lowe, Mildred 1927-1988 BioIn 16
Lowe, Nick 1949- EncPR&S 89
Lowe, Paul Phillip BiDrAPA 89
Lowe, Raymond Wayne 1922- St&PR 91
Lowe, Richard Gerald, Jr. 1960- WhoEmL 91, WhoWor 91
Lowe, Richard Grady 1942- WhoSSW 91
Lowe, Richard L. 1928- St&PR 91
Lowe, Rita K. 1966- WhoAmW 91
Lowe, Rob BioIn 16
Lowe, Rob 1964?- News 90[port], WorAlBi
Lowe, Robert Charles 1927- WhoAm 90
Lowe, Robert Charles 1949- WhoSSW 91, WhoWor 91
Lowe, Robert Stanley 1923- WhoAm 90
Lowe, Ruthe Meekins 1945- WhoAmW 91
Lowe, Sam Jack ConAu 132
Lowe, Sheldon 1926- WhoAm 90
Lowe, Steven Warren 1948- St&PR 91
Lowe, Sue Esther 1954- WhoAmW 91
Lowe, Thomas L BiDrAPA 89
Lowe, Timothy 1953- IntWWM 90
Lowe, Todd Parker 1959- WhoSSW 91
Lowe, Valerie Ann 1963- WhoE 91
Lowe, Victor 1907-1988 BioIn 16
Lowe, William C. BioIn 16, WhoAm 90
Lowe, Winston I. 1951- St&PR 91
Lowell, Alan F. 1925- St&PR 91
Lowell, Alan I. 1939- St&PR 91
Lowell, Amy 1874-1925 BioAmW, EncPaPR 91, FemiCLE
Lowell, Amy Lawrence 1874-1925 WorAlBi
Lowell, Arthur Harold 1928- WhoAm 90
Lowell, Carey BioIn 16
Lowell, Charles W. AmLegL
Lowell, Edward H 1929- BiDrAPA 89
Lowell, Edward Herbert 1929- WhoE 91
Lowell, Frank 1960- WhoE 91
Lowell, Fred Milton 1932- BiDrAPA 89
Lowell, Howard Parsons 1945- WhoAm 90
Lowell, Jacqueline Peters WhoAmW 91
Lowell, James Russell 1819-1891 BioIn 16, WorAlBi
Lowell, John 1919- St&PR 91
Lowell, John Keith 1950- WhoSSW 91
Lowell, Josephine S. 1843-1905 BioAmW
Lowell, Juliet 1901- WhoAm 90
Lowell, Orson Byron 1871-1956 WhoAmA 91N
Lowell, Payson W. 1932- St&PR 91
Lowell, Percival 1855-1916 WorAlBi
Lowell, Robert 1917-1977 BioIn 16, MajTwCW, WorAlBi, WrPh
Lowell, Robert Traill Spence 1816-1891 DcCanB 12
Lowell, Ronald J BiDrAPA 89
Lowell, Stanley Edgar 1923- WhoE 91
Lowell, Stanley Herbert 1919- WhoE 91
Lowell, Stephen Craig 1953- WhoSSW 91
Lowell, Wayne Brian 1955- WhoAm 90
Lowen, Allen Wayne 1946- WhoSSW 91
Lowen, Gerard Gunther 1921- WhoAm 90
Lowen, Irwin 1923- St&PR 91
Lowen, Theodore ODwPR 91
Lowen, Walter 1921- WhoAm 90
Lowenberg, John David 1942- St&PR 91
Lowenberg, Kenneth Dale 1939- IntWWM 90
Lowenberg, Robert Ira WhoSSW 91
Lowenbraun, Leslie 1953- St&PR 91
Lowenfeld, Andreas Frank 1930- WhoAm 90, WhoE 91
Lowenfeld, Viktor BioIn 16
Lowenfeld, Viktor 1903-1960 WhoAmA 91N
Lowenfels, Fred M. 1944- St&PR 91, WhoAm 90
Lowenfels, Jeff BioIn 16
Lowenfels, Walter 1897-1976 AuBYP 90, BioIn 16
Lowenfinck, Adam Friedrich von 1714-1754 PenDiDA 89
Lowengard, Mary Bear 1953- WhoAmW 91
Lowengrund, Margaret 1905-1957 WhoAmA 91N
Lowenhaupt, Charles Abraham 1947- WhoEmL 91
Lowenhaupt, Elizabeth BiDrAPA 89
Lowenheim, Leopold 1878-1957 DcScB S2
Lowenherz, Josef 1884-1946? BioIn 16
Lowenhjelm, Harriet Augusta Dorotea 1887-1918 DcScanL
Lowenick, Peter PenDiDA 89
Lowenkamp, William Charles, Jr. 1941- WhoWrEP 89
Lowenkopf, Eugene L 1934- BiDrAPA 89
Lowenkron, Michael 1943- St&PR 91
Lowensburg, Verena 1912- BiDWomA
Lowenstam, Susan Guggenheim 1942- St&PR 91
Lowenstein, Alan Victor 1913- WhoAm 90
Lowenstein, Alexander BioIn 16
Lowenstein, David Carl 1945- St&PR 91
Lowenstein, Derek Irving 1943- WhoAm 90
Lowenstein, Glenn Walker 1943- St&PR 91
Lowenstein, Irwin L. 1935- St&PR 91
Lowenstein, Irwin Lang 1935- WhoAm 90
Lowenstein, Jack Gert 1927- WhoAm 90
Lowenstein, John 1947- Ballpl 90
Lowenstein, Keith Grey BiDrAPA 89
Lowenstein, Louis BioIn 16
Lowenstein, Louis 1925- WhoAm 90
Lowenstein, Mark G. 1937- St&PR 91
Lowenstein, Michael Thomas BiDrAPA 89
Lowenstein, Peter David 1935- WhoAm 90
Lowenstein, Ralph Lynn 1930- WhoAm 90
Lowenstein, Richard BioIn 16
Lowenstein, Robert A 1940- BiDrAPA 89
Lowenstein, Roy Sidney 1944- BiDrAPA 89
Lowenstein, Suse BioIn 16
Lowenstine, James R. 1923- WhoAm 90
Lowenstine, Maurice Richard, Jr. 1910- WhoAm 90
Lowenthal, Abraham Frederic 1941- WhoAm 90
Lowenthal, Alexander BioIn 16
Lowenthal, Armand 1919- WhoWor 91
Lowenthal, Constance 1945- WhoAm 90, WhoAmA 91
Lowenthal, Henry 1931- St&PR 91, WhoAm 90
Lowenthal, Jack St&PR 91
Lowenthal, Jerome 1932- IntWWM 90
Lowenthal, Judith Nelson 1945- WhoAmW 91
Lowenthal, Malcolm Paul 1935- St&PR 91
Lowenthal, Mort 1931- St&PR 91, WhoAm 90
Lowenthal, Paul 1936- WhoWor 91
Lowenthal, Richard L. 1952- St&PR 91
Lowenthal, Susan 1946- WhoAmW 91
Lower, Arthur 1889-1988 AnObit 1988
Lower, Arthur Reginald Marsden 1889-1988 BioIn 16
Lower, Dorothy Margaret 1914- WhoAmW 91
Lower, Elmer W. 1913- BioIn 16
Lower, Frederick Joseph, Jr. 1935- WhoAm 90
Lower, James Brian 1949- WhoSSW 91
Lower, Joyce Q. 1943- WhoAm 90
Lower, Louis Gordon, II 1945- WhoAm 90
Lower, Martin Avery 1938- St&PR 91
Lower, Mary 1644?-1719 BiDEWW
Lower, Richard Lawrence 1935- WhoAm 90
Lowers, Gina Cattani 1961- WhoAmW 91
Lowery, Major WhNaAH
Lowery, Ann Ward 1948- WhoSSW 91
Lowery, Bill 1924- WhoAm 90
Lowery, Bruce Arlie 1931- WhoAm 90
Lowery, Charles Douglas 1937- WhoAm 90
Lowery, Clinton Hershey 1929- WhoAm 90
Lowery, Dennis Joseph 1933- St&PR 91
Lowery, Floyd Lynn, Jr. 1940- WhoSSW 91
Lowery, James Stephan 1947- IntWWM 90
Lowery, Jeremy BioIn 16
Lowery, Jimmy Dale BiDrAPA 89
Lowery, Joseph E. WhoAm 90
Lowery, Joseph Echols WhoSSW 91
Lowery, Lee Leon, Jr. 1938- WhoAm 90
Lowery, Marcella 1946- DrBlPA 90
Lowery, Robert E. AmLegL
Lowery, Robert G. 1941- ConAu 130
Lowery, Sharon A. 1943- WhoAmW 91
Lowery, Vernado Bene 1963- WhoSSW 91
Lowery, William David 1947- WhoAm 90
Lowery, William Herbert 1925- WhoAm 90
Lowery-Payntter, Marion Margaret 1934- WhoAmW 91
Lowes, Gary H. 1951- St&PR 91
Lowey, Nita M. 1937- BioIn 16, WhoAm 90, WhoAmW 91, WhoE 91
Lowi, Theodore Jay 1931- WhoAm 90, WhoE 91, WhoWor 91
Lowin, John 1576-1653 BioIn 16
Lowinger, Daniel 1935- WhoWor 91
Lowinger, Paul L 1923- BiDrAPA 89
Lowinger, Robert BiDrAPA 89
Lowinsky, Joshua Michael 1960- BiDrAPA 89
Lowinson, Joyce H BiDrAPA 89
Lowish, Michael David 1950- WhoSSW 91
Lowitt, Richard 1922- WhoAm 90
Lowman, George Frederick 1916- St&PR 91, WhoAm 90
Lowman, George S. 1944- ODwPR 91
Lowman, James 1947- St&PR 91
Lowman, Mary Bethena Hemphill 1922- WhoAmW 91
Lowman, Meredith Ann 1950- WhoAmW 91
Lowman, Patricia J. 1941- WhoAmW 91
Lowman, Samuel James 1939- St&PR 91
Lown, Bernard 1921- WhoAm 90
Lown, David Jolley 1948- WhoWor 91
Lown, Turk 1924- Ballpl 90
Lowndes, Gillian BioIn 16
Lowndes, Marie Belloc 1868-1947 BioIn 16, TwCCr&M 91
Lowndes, William 1782-1822 BioIn 16
Lowndes-Rosen, Dyana 1942- BiDrAPA 89
Lowney, Bruce Stark 1937- WhoAm 90, WhoAmA 91
Lownsbury, M.H., Jr. 1932- St&PR 91
Lowrance, Bobby Roy 1942- BiDrAPA 89
Lowrance, Judith Manss 1945- WhoSSW 91
Lowrance, Muriel Edwards 1922- WhoAmW 91
Lowrey, Charles Boyce 1941- WhoSSW 91
Lowrey, Edwin Joseph 1926- St&PR 91
Lowrey, Ernest James 1928- St&PR 91
Lowrey, Janette 1892- AuBYP 90
Lowrey, Joseph Patrick 1945- St&PR 91
Lowrey, Judith Gale 1939- WhoSSW 91
Lowrey, Peter Doran 1941- St&PR 91
Lowrey, Richard William 1938- WhoE 91, WhoWor 91
Lowrey, Robert Edward 1940- WhoSSW 91
Lowrie, Gerald M. 1936- ODwPR 91
Lowrie, Gerald Marvin 1935- St&PR 91
Lowrie, Herbert Stanford 1941- WhoSSW 91
Lowrie, Jean Elizabeth 1918- WhoAm 90
Lowrie, John M. 1940- St&PR 91
Lowrie, Kathryn Yanacek 1958- WhoAmW 91
Lowrie, W.G. 1943- St&PR 91
Lowrie, Walter Olin 1924- WhoAm 90
Lowrie, William G. 1943- WhoAm 90
Lowry, A. Robert 1919- WhoAm 90
Lowry, Albert J 1927- ConAu 129
Lowry, Alfred WhoAm 90
Lowry, Bates 1923- WhoAmA 91, WhoSSW 91
Lowry, Charles Bryan 1942- WhoSSW 91
Lowry, Charles Wesley 1905- WhoAm 90
Lowry, Constance Keenan 1956- WhoAmW 91
Lowry, Craig R. 1950- St&PR 91
Lowry, Dennis Martin 1953- WhoWor 91
Lowry, Donald Michael 1929- St&PR 91
Lowry, Edward Francis, Jr. 1930- WhoAm 90
Lowry, Gary William 1936- St&PR 91
Lowry, George WhNaAH
Lowry, George Eugene BiDrAPA 89
Lowry, George W. 1913- St&PR 91
Lowry, Henry Berry 1856?-1872 WhNaAH
Lowry, Houston Putnam 1955- WhoE 91, WhoEmL 91
Lowry, J. F. AmLegL
Lowry, James David 1942- WhoAm 90, WhoWor 91
Lowry, James H. 1923- St&PR 91
Lowry, James V BiDrAPA 89
Lowry, Jean 1921- WhoAmW 91
Lowry, Joan Marie Dondrea 1935- WhoAmW 91
Lowry, John WhNaAH
Lowry, Larry L. 1947- St&PR 91
Lowry, Larry Lorn 1947- WhoAm 90
Lowry, Leo Elmo 1916- WhoSSW 91
Lowry, Lois 1937- Au&Arts 5[port], AuBYP 90
Lowry, Malcolm 1909-1957 BioIn 16, ConAu 131, MajTwCW, TwCLC 40[port], WorAlBi
Lowry, Margerie Bonner BioIn 16
Lowry, Marilyn Jean 1932- WhoE 91
Lowry, Marlene Faye 1950- WhoAmW 91
Lowry, Michael Roy BiDrAPA 89
Lowry, Patricia 1927- WhoAmW 91
Lowry, Patrick Joseph 1956- BiDrAPA 89
Lowry, Peanuts 1918-1986 Ballpl 90
Lowry, Peter 1953- AuBYP 90
Lowry, Ralph Addison 1926- WhoAm 90
Lowry, Ralph James, Sr. 1928- WhoSSW 91
Lowry, Richard William 1937- WhoSSW 91
Lowry, Robert Dudley 1949- WhoEmL 91
Lowry, Robert E. 1926- ODwPR 91
Lowry, Robert James 1919- WhoAm 90
Lowry, Robert Lynd Erskine 1919- WhoWor 91
Lowry, Sheldon Gaylon 1924- WhoAm 90
Lowry, Thomas Hastings 1938- WhoAm 90
Lowry, William Ketchin, Jr. 1951- WhoE 91, WhoWor 91
Lowry, Wilson McNeil 1913- WhoAm 90
Lowson, Kathleen 1953- WhoAmW 91
Lowstuter, William R. St&PR 91

Lowther, Elizabeth *BiDEWW*
Lowther, Frank Eugene 1929- *WhoSSW 91, WhoWor 91*
Lowther, Gerald Halbert 1924- *WhoAm 90*
Lowther, Hugh Cecil 1857-1944 *BioIn 16*
Lowther, Pat 1935-1975 *FemiCLE*
Lowum, David Donald 1932- *St&PR 91*
Lowy, Frederick H 1933- *BiDrAPA 89*
Lowy, Frederick Hans 1933- *WhoAm 90*
Lowy, Jay Stanton 1935- *WhoAm 90*
Lowy, Louis 1920- *WhoAm 90*
Lowy, Sam Joseph 1949- *BiDrAPA 89*
Lowy, Steven R. 1946- *St&PR 91*
Lowy, Steven Robert 1951- *WhoEmL 91*
Lowy, Steven Rudolf 1946- *WhoAm 90*
Lowys, Elizabeth 1525?-1565 *BioIn 16*
Loxley, John 1942- *WhoAm 90*
Loxsmith, John *MajTwCW*
Loxton, David *BioIn 16*
Loy, Frank Ernest 1928- *WhoAm 90, WhoE 91*
Loy, James Willard 1925- *WhoSSW 91*
Loy, John Sheridan 1930- *WhoAmA 91*
Loy, Michael Warren 1949- *St&PR 91*
Loy, Mina *BioIn 16*
Loy, Mina 1882-1966 *BioAmW, FemiCLE*
Loy, Myrna *BioIn 16*
Loy, Myrna 1905- *WhoAm 90, WhoAmW 91, WorAlBi*
Loy, Richard Nelson 1945- *St&PR 91*
Loya, Ofelia Olivares 1929- *WhoHisp 91*
Loya, Richard *BioIn 16*
Loyal, Charles *PenDiDA 89*
Loyd, Doyne W. Jr. 1945- *BiDrAPA 89*
Loyd, James Leonard 1948- *St&PR 91*
Loyd, Jan Brooks 1950- *WhoAmA 91*
Loyd, John Francis, Jr. 1948- *WhoSSW 91*
Loyd, Loye Carroll 1926- *WhoSSW 91*
Loyd, Randall M. 1957- *St&PR 91*
Loyd, Robert W. 1936- *St&PR 91*
Loyd, Thomas Carter 1952- *WhoSSW 91*
Loye, Dieter Zur 1928- *St&PR 91*
Loyet, Gerard *PenDiDA 89*
Loyless, Bonnie Wainright 1954- *WhoAmW 91*
Loyless, P. Edward, Jr. 1949- *WhoSSW 91*
Loyn Moon, Yusef Noman 1929- *WhoWor 91*
Loynd, Mike 1964- *Ballpl 90*
Loynd, Richard B. 1927- *St&PR 91*
Loynd, Richard Birkett 1927- *WhoAm 90*
Loynes, John Hamilton 1933- *St&PR 91, WhoAm 90*
Loyola *WhNaAH*
Loyonnet, Paul Louis 1889- *IntWWM 90*
Loza, Enrique *WhoHisp 91*
Lozada-Rossy, Joyce 1952- *WhoHisp 91*
Lozano, Antonio, Jr. 1914- *WhoHisp 91*
Lozano, Cosme Ozich, Jr. *BiDrAPA 89*
Lozano, Denise M. 1951- *WhoHisp 91*
Lozano, Efrain, Jr. 1925- *WhoE 91*
Lozano, Frank Philip 1924- *WhoHisp 91*
Lozano, Fred C. 1949- *WhoHisp 91*
Lozano, Ignacio E. 1886?-1953 *BioIn 16*
Lozano, Ignacio E. 1927- *BioIn 16*
Lozano, Ignacio Eugenio, Jr. 1927- *WhoHisp 91*
Lozano, John Manuel 1930- *WhoHisp 91*
Lozano, Jorge Anthony 1962- *WhoHisp 91*
Lozano, Jose Carlos 1958- *WhoHisp 91*
Lozano, Julian 1900- *BioIn 16*
Lozano, Leonard J. 1935- *WhoHisp 91*
Lozano, Maria J *BiDrAPA 89*
Lozano, Robert 1918- *WhoHisp 91*
Lozano, Wilfredo 1946- *WhoHisp 91*
Lozanovskaya, Rita *BiDrAPA 89*
Lozansky, Edward D 1941- *SmATA 62*
Lozaw, Clarence B. 1931- *St&PR 91*
Lozeau, Albert 1878-1924 *DcLB 92 [port]*
Lozeau, Roland U. 1941- *St&PR 91*
Lozier, Allan G. 1933- *St&PR 91*
Lozoff, Milton 1914- *BiDrAPA 89*
Lozowick, Louis 1892-1973 *WhoAmA 91N*
Lozowski, James Michael 1946- *WhoE 91*
Lozyniak, Andrew 1931- *St&PR 91, WhoAm 90*
Lozza, Raul 1911- *ArtLatA*
Lozzi, Virginia 1932- *BiDrAPA 89*
Lphia Pa 1910 *WhoAmA 91*
Lu Chengxin 1938- *WhoWor 91*
Lu Hou *WomWR*
Lu Wenfu 1928- *WorAu 1980*
Lu, Allena Fong 1941- *WhoAmW 91*
Lu, David John 1928- *WhoAm 90, WhoWrEP 89*
Lu, Francis G 1949- *BiDrAPA 89*
Lu, Frank Kerping 1954- *WhoSSW 91*
Lu, Janny M. 1958- *St&PR 91*
Lu, Keh-Ming 1949- *WhoE 91*
Lu, Leighmin J 1934- *BiDrAPA 89*
Lu, Mary Chao 1935- *WhoAmW 91*
Lu, Milton Ming-Deh 1919- *WhoE 91, WhoWor 91*
Lu, Pang-Chia 1949- *WhoE 91*
Lu, Ponzy 1942- *WhoAm 90*
Lu, Tzu-Chiau 1937- *BiDrAPA 89*
Lu, Ya Yan 1963- *WhoE 91*
Lu, Yimin 1935- *WhoWor 91*
Luallen, Sally Carol Shank 1938- *WhoAmW 91*
Luard, Nicholas 1937- *TwCCr&M 91*
Luard, Nicholas Lambert 1937- *SpyFic*
Luard, Richard George Amherst 1827-1891 *DcCanB 12*
Luba, R.W. 1942- *St&PR 91*
Lubachivsky, Myroslav Ivan 1914- *WhoWor 91*
Lubalin, Herbert 1918-1981 *ConDes 90*
Lubalin, Irwin 1918- *St&PR 91*
Lubalin, Peter *BioIn 16, WhoAm 90*
Luban, Arthur *BiDrAPA 89*
Lubansky, Harry John 1949- *WhoSSW 91*
Lubar, Bernard *BioIn 16*
Lubar, Jeffrey Stuart 1947- *WhoAm 90*
Lubar, Joel F. 1938- *WhoSSW 91*
Lubar, Robert 1920- *WhoWrEP 89*
Lubart, David 1915- *St&PR 91*
Lubart, Henriette d'Arlin 1915- *WhoE 91*
Lubasch, Richard J. 1946- *St&PR 91*
Lubatti, Henry Joseph 1937- *WhoAm 90*
Lubbe, Hermann Gottfried 1926- *WhoWor 91*
Lubbe, Willem Johannes 1947- *WhoWor 91*
Lubben, Lynn-Alison 1964- *WhoAmW 91*
Lubbers, Arend Donselaar 1931- *WhoAm 90*
Lubbers, Bob 1922- *EncACom*
Lubbers, Georg Nicolaus *PenDiDA 89*
Lubbers, Laura Lee 1962- *WhoAmW 91*
Lubbers, Leland Eugene 1928- *WhoAmA 91*
Lubbers, Rudolphus *BioIn 16*
Lubbers, Ruud 1939- *WhoWor 91*
Lubbock, Fiona Constance 1957- *WhoE 91*
Lubbock, Mark 1898-1986 *OxCPMus*
Lubcker, Robert L. 1937- *St&PR 91*
Lube, Frank H 1938- *WhoWor 91*
Lubeck, Benjamin B 1942- *BiDrAPA 89*
Lubeck, Doreen *ODwPR 91*
Lubeck, Jackie *BioIn 16*
Lubeck, Marvin Jay 1929- *WhoAm 90, WhoWor 91*
Lubeck, Sally 1945- *WhoAmW 91*
Lubeck, Stanley 1935- *WhoE 91*
Lubell, Cecil 1912- *AuBYP 90*
Lubell, Ellen 1950- *WhoAmA 91, WhoE 91*
Lubell, Harold 1925- *WhoAm 90*
Lubell, Michael Stephen 1943- *WhoE 91*
Lubell, Richard M. *BioIn 16*
Lubell, Samuel 1911-1987 *BioIn 16*
Lubell, Winifred 1914- *AuBYP 90*
Lubelski, Ruth *BiDrAPA 89*
Lubenow, Gerald Charles 1939- *WhoAm 90*
Lubenow, Larry R. 1936- *ODwPR 91*
Lubensky, Lloyd C. 1922- *St&PR 91*
Luber, Elliot B. 1959- *WhoWrEP 89*
Luber, Frederick George 1925- *St&PR 91*
Luber, M Philip *BiDrAPA 89*
Luber, Thomas Julian 1949- *WhoEmL 91, WhoWor 91*
Luberoff, Benjamin J. 1925- *WhoWrEP 89*
Lubers, Harry Lauritz 1859- *AmLegL*
Lubert, Ira Mark 1950- *WhoAm 90*
Lubertazzi, Paul Patrick 1935- *St&PR 91*
Lubet, Alex Jeffery 1954- *IntWWM 90*
Lubetkin, Alvin Nat 1933- *St&PR 91, WhoAm 90*
Lubetkin, Berthold *NewYTBS 90*
Lubetkin, Charles Schiller 1932- *St&PR 91*
Lubetkin, James G. *ODwPR 91*
Lubetkin, Steven L. 1957- *ODwPR 91*
Lubetkin, Zivia 1914-1976 *BioIn 16*
Lubetski, Edith Esther 1940- *WhoE 91*
Lubetsky, Elsie 1917- *WhoWrEP 89*
Lubetsky, Martin Joel 1955- *BiDrAPA 89*
Lubic, Ruth Watson 1927- *WhoAm 90, WhoAmW 91*
Lubick, Donald Cyril 1926- *WhoAm 90*
Lubin, Albert Joseph *BiDrAPA 89*
Lubin, Benjamin L. 1934- *St&PR 91*
Lubin, Benjamin Livingston 1934- *WhoAm 90*
Lubin, Bernard 1923- *WhoAm 90*
Lubin, Bruce S. 1953- *St&PR 91*
Lubin, Charles W. *BioIn 16*
Lubin, Diane *BioIn 16*
Lubin, Donald G. 1934- *WhoAm 90*
Lubin, Frantz Hernould *BiDrAPA 89*
Lubin, Gerald I 1928- *BiDrAPA 89*
Lubin, Germaine 1890-1979 *PenDiMP*
Lubin, Harold 1924- *BiDrAPA 89*
Lubin, Henry 1944-1989 *BioIn 16*
Lubin, Howard Jay 1957- *WhoEmL 91*
Lubin, Jack 1931- *St&PR 91, WhoAm 90, WhoSSW 91*
Lubin, Jim *BioIn 16*
Lubin, Joy Kathleen 1943- *WhoAmW 91*
Lubin, Leonard B. 1943- *BioIn 16*
Lubin, Martin 1923- *WhoAm 90*
Lubin, Martin I 1929- *BiDrAPA 89*
Lubin, Michael Frederick 1947- *WhoAm 90, WhoSSW 91*
Lubin, Steven *BioIn 16*
Lubin, Steven 1942- *IntWWM 90, PenDiMP, WhoAm 90*
Lubin, Susan Trepel *BiDrAPA 89*
Lubiner, Elaine Davis 1937- *WhoE 91*
Lubing, Harold N *BiDrAPA 89*
Lubinski, Arthur 1910- *WhoAm 90*
Lubinsky, Leonard Jay 1941- *WhoE 91*
Lubit, Roy Howard 1953- *BiDrAPA 89, WhoE 91*
Lubitsch, Ernst 1892-1947 *WorAlBi*
Lubizka, Alexandra 1918- *BiDrAPA 89*
Lubker, John William, II 1943- *WhoSSW 91*
Lubkin, Gloria Becker 1933- *WhoAm 90, WhoAmW 91*
Lublin, Andre 1940- *WhoWor 91*
Lublin, Eliane 1938- *IntWWM 90*
Lublin, Irving *St&PR 91*
Lublin, Lucien 1909- *BioIn 16*
Lubliner, Murray J. *ODwPR 91*
Lubman, Stanley Bernard 1934- *WhoAm 90*
Luboff, Marvin 1939- *St&PR 91*
Luborsky, Ellen B. 1948- *WhoAmW 91*
Luborsky, Fred Everett 1923- *WhoAm 90*
Lubotsky, Mark 1931- *IntWWM 90*
Lubovitch, Lar *WhoAm 90*
Lubow, Robert Edward 1939- *BiDrAPA 89*
Lubowe, Irwin Irville 1905-1989 *BioIn 16*
Lubowski, Anton *BioIn 16*
Lubowsky, Susan 1949- *WhoAmA 91*
Lubrano, Al Thomas 1950- *WhoE 91*
Lubrano, Alfred *BioIn 16*
Lubrano, Mike 1961- *WhoE 91*
Lubrano, Vincent P. 1941- *St&PR 91*
Lubrecht, Heinz D. 1908- *WhoWor 91*
Lubs, Herbert Augustus 1929- *WhoAm 90*
Lubs, James D. 1925- *St&PR 91*
Luby, Elliot D 1924- *BiDrAPA 89*
Luby, Elliot Donald 1924- *WhoAm 90*
Luby, George James 1931- *St&PR 91*
Luby, Joan Lida *BiDrAPA 89*
Luby, Patrick Joseph 1930- *St&PR 91*
Luc, Richard August 1946- *BiDrAPA 89*
Luca Della Robbia 1399?-1482 *IntDcAA 90*
Luca, Giuseppe De *PenDiMP*
Luca, Mark 1918- *WhoAmA 91*
Luca, Raymond Joseph 1941- *St&PR 91*
Luca, Sergiu 1944- *BioIn 16*
Lucadello, Tony *Ballpl 90*
Lucadello, Tony 1913-1989 *BioIn 16*
Lucado, F. Greg, Jr. 1954- *St&PR 91*
Lucadou, Walter von 1945- *EncPaPR 91*
Lucan, Margaret *FemiCLE*
Lucan, Matej 1928- *WhoWor 91*
Lucander, Anitra Maria Ingeborg 1918- *BiDWomA*
Lucander, Nils 1924- *WhoWrEP 89*
Lucarelli, Benjamin J. *BioIn 16*
Lucas van Leyden 1489?-1533 *IntDcAA 90*
Lucas, Adetokunbo Olumide Oluwole 1931- *WhoAm 90*
Lucas, Alec 1913- *WhoWrEP 89*
Lucas, Alexander R 1931- *BiDrAPA 89*
Lucas, Alexander Ralph 1931- *WhoAm 90*
Lucas, Alfred Winslow, Jr. 1950- *WhoE 91*
Lucas, Allene S. *WhoAm 90*
Lucas, Andre 1927- *WhoWor 91*
Lucas, Anthony S. 1933- *St&PR 91*
Lucas, Arthur Clay 1931- *St&PR 91*
Lucas, Aubrey Keith 1934- *WhoAm 90, WhoSSW 91*
Lucas, Barbara B. 1945- *St&PR 91, WhoAmW 91*
Lucas, Bert A. 1933- *WhoWor 91*
Lucas, Bill L. 1940- *St&PR 91*
Lucas, Billy Joe 1942- *WhoE 91*
Lucas, Bonnie Lynn 1950- *WhoAmA 91, WhoE 91*
Lucas, Brenda *PenDiMP*
Lucas, Carol Ann 1941- *WhoAmW 91*
Lucas, Carol Lee 1940- *WhoAm 90*
Lucas, Charlie 1951- *MusmAFA*
Lucas, Christopher 1958- *WhoAmA 91*
Lucas, Claude Paul 1945- *St&PR 91*
Lucas, Craig 19--?- *ConLC 64*
Lucas, Daniel Joe 1947- *WhoSSW 91*
Lucas, David *ODwPR 91*
Lucas, Donald L. 1930- *St&PR 91*
Lucas, Donald Leo 1930- *WhoAm 90*
Lucas, E V 1868-1938 *DcLB 98 [port]*
Lucas, Elihu Root, Jr. 1925- *St&PR 91*
Lucas, Elizabeth Coughlin 1918- *WhoAmW 91*
Lucas, Elizabeth Helene 1936- *WhoAmW 91*
Lucas, Fred Vance 1922- *WhoAm 90*
Lucas, Gary 1954- *Ballpl 90*
Lucas, George *BioIn 16*
Lucas, George 1944- *ConAu 30NR*
Lucas, George, Jr. 1944- *WorAlBi*
Lucas, George Ramsdell, Jr. 1949- *WhoSSW 91*
Lucas, George W., Jr. 1944- *WhoAm 90*
Lucas, Georges 1915- *WhoWor 91*
Lucas, Georgetta Marie Snell 1920- *WhoAmW 91, WhoWor 91*
Lucas, Harry Edward, Jr. 1947- *WhoAm 90*
Lucas, Henry Cameron, Jr. 1944- *WhoAm 90*
Lucas, Hugh H. 1937- *St&PR 91*
Lucas, Hugh Hampton 1937- *WhoAm 90*
Lucas, J K *ConAu 31NR*
Lucas, J. Richard 1929- *WhoAm 90*
Lucas, James Dornan 1932- *St&PR 91*
Lucas, James Evans 1933- *WhoAm 90*
Lucas, James Raymond 1950- *WhoEmL 91, WhoWor 91*
Lucas, James Roberts 1942- *WhoE 91*
Lucas, James Walter 1940- *WhoAm 90*
Lucas, Jeffrey David 1948- *WhoE 91*
Lucas, Jeffrey Wayne 1951- *WhoEmL 91, WhoWor 91*
Lucas, John 1937- *ConAu 32NR*
Lucas, John, Jr. 1930- *St&PR 91*
Lucas, John E. 1953- *ODwPR 91*
Lucas, John Hume, III 1967- *WhoEmL 91*
Lucas, John Joseph, Jr. *BiDrAPA 89*
Lucas, John Kenneth 1946- *WhoAm 90, WhoEmL 91*
Lucas, John Michael 1951- *St&PR 91*
Lucas, John Robert *PenDiDA 89*
Lucas, John Roy 1935- *WhoE 91*
Lucas, John Wayne 1904- *WhoAm 90*
Lucas, Klaus 1943- *WhoWor 91*
Lucas, Larry Donnell 1951- *WhoSSW 91*
Lucas, Lawrence Newton 1906- *WhoAm 90*
Lucas, Luke Wilson *BiDrAPA 89*
Lucas, Malcolm Millar 1927- *WhoAm 90*
Lucas, Margaret 1701-1769 *FemiCLE*
Lucas, Mark Thornton 1953- *WhoSSW 91*
Lucas, Michael Leslie 1948- *WhoWor 91*
Lucas, Ouida La Forrest 1915- *WhoWrEP 89*
Lucas, Paul Martin 1926- *BiDrAPA 89*
Lucas, Peter Brown 1954- *BiDrAPA 89*
Lucas, Prudence W. 1954- *St&PR 91*
Lucas, Red 1902-1986 *Ballpl 90*
Lucas, Richard Charles 1947- *BiDrAPA 89*
Lucas, Robbie Diane 1963- *WhoSSW 91*
Lucas, Robert Elmer 1916- *WhoAm 90*
Lucas, Robert Scott 1961- *WhoEmL 91*
Lucas, Sam 1840-1916 *DrBlPA 90*
Lucas, Sharron Riessinger 1961- *WhoAmW 91*
Lucas, Shirley Agnes Hoyt 1921- *WhoAmW 91*
Lucas, Snell Georgetta 1920- *WhoAmA 91*
Lucas, Stanley Jerome 1929- *WhoAm 90*
Lucas, Steven Mitchell 1948- *WhoEmL 91*
Lucas, Steven Robert 1959- *WhoSSW 91*
Lucas, Stuart Mitchell 1952- *St&PR 91*
Lucas, Thomas 1924- *BiDrAPA 89*
Lucas, Thomas George 1954- *BiDrAPA 89*
Lucas, Thomas W 1944- *BiDrAPA 89*
Lucas, Valerie Patricia 1951- *WhoAmW 91*
Lucas, Vane Thomas 1961- *WhoE 91*
Lucas, Victoria *MajTwCW*
Lucas, William *BioIn 16*
Lucas, William Blair 1925- *St&PR 91*
Lucas, William Campbell, Jr. 1932- *WhoE 91*
Lucas, William John 1940- *St&PR 91*
Lucas, William Joseph 1947- *WhoE 91*
Lucas, William Max, Jr. 1934- *WhoAm 90*
Lucas, William Nelson 1941- *St&PR 91*
Lucas, William Ray 1922- *WhoAm 90*
Lucas, Wingate H. 1908-1989 *BioIn 16*
Lucas-Medina, Romeo *BiDrAPA 89*
Lucash, Peter David 1953- *WhoE 91*
Lucca, John James 1921- *WhoAm 90*
Lucca, Pauline 1841-1908 *PenDiMP*
Lucca, Thomas George 1938- *St&PR 91*
Lucchese, Gaetano 1900-1967 *WorAlBi*
Lucchesi, Bruno 1926- *WhoAmA 91*
Lucchesi, Donald Albert 1950- *WhoE 91*
Lucchesi, Donna Lyn 1963- *WhoSSW 91*
Lucchesi, Frank 1926- *Ballpl 90*
Lucchesi, John C. *WhoAm 90*
Lucchesi, Nello William 1955- *WhoEmL 91*
Lucchetti, Lynn L. 1939- *WhoAmW 91*
Lucchetti, Vincent Anton 1954- *WhoSSW 91*
Lucchino, Lawrence 1945- *WhoAm 90, WhoE 91*
Lucchitta, Baerbel Koesters 1938- *WhoAmW 91*
Lucci, Guy Daniel, Jr. 1929- *St&PR 91*
Lucci, Susan *BioIn 16, WhoAm 90*
Lucci, Susan 1949- *WorAlBi*
Luce, Bill J. 1946- *St&PR 91*
Luce, C 1947- *WhoAmA 91*
Luce, Charles Franklin 1917- *St&PR 91, WhoAm 90*
Luce, Claire *BioIn 16*
Luce, Claire 1904-1989 *AnObit 1989*
Luce, Clare 1903-1987 *FemiCLE*
Luce, Clare Boothe 1903-1987 *BioAmW, BioIn 16, NotWoAT, WorAlBi*
Luce, D. Gregory *St&PR 91*
Luce, Eleanor M 1929- *BiDrAPA 89*
Luce, Gordon Coppard 1925- *WhoAm 90*

Luce, Henry, III 1925- St&PR 91, WhoAm 90
Luce, Henry, III, Mrs. 1925- WhoAmW 91, WhoWor 91
Luce, Henry R 1898-1967 MajTwCW, WorAlBi
Luce, Henry Robinson 1898-1967 BioIn 16
Luce, James A. 1940- WhoWrEP 89
Luce, Jean 1895-1964 PenDiDA 89
Luce, John Thomas 1946- St&PR 91
Luce, Kenneth Warren 1961- WhoSSW 91
Luce, Michael Wayne 1950- St&PR 91
Luce, Molly 1896-1986 BiDWomA
Luce, Peggy BioIn 16
Luce, Ralph A. Jr. BiDrAPA 89
Luce, Richard Napier 1936- BioIn 16
Luce, Robert Duncan 1925- WhoAm 90
Luce, T James 1932- ConAu 129
Luce, Thomas A. 1956- St&PR 91
Lucente, Edward E. 1939- St&PR 91
Lucente, Rosemary Dolores 1935- WhoAmW 91
Lucero, Alvin K. WhoHisp 91
Lucero, C. Steven 1967- WhoHisp 91
Lucero, Carlos Estanislao 1940- WhoSSW 91
Lucero, Frank Anthony 1935- St&PR 91
Lucero, Helen R. 1943- WhoHisp 91
Lucero, Michael 1953- WhoAmA 91
Lucero, Michael L. 1953- WhoHisp 91
Lucero, Rosalba 1964- WhoHisp 91
Lucero, Stephanie Denise 1957- WhoHisp 91
Lucero, Stephen Paul 1955- WhoHisp 91
Lucero, Wendy 1964- WhoHisp 91
Lucey, Charles Timothy 1905- WhoAm 90
Lucey, Douglas Michael 1947- St&PR 91
Lucey, Eileen Alida BiDrAPA 89
Lucey, Jack 1929- WhoAmA 91
Lucey, Kevin Paul 1950- WhoE 91
Lucey, Patrick J. 1918- BioIn 16
Lucey, Thomas J. BioIn 16
Lucey, Thomas Joseph 1943- St&PR 91, WhoAm 90
Lucey, William F., Jr. 1935- St&PR 91
Luchak, Frank Alexander 1950- WhoEmL 91
Luchansky, Mitchell Alan BiDrAPA 89
Luchetti, Raymond 1944- St&PR 91
Luchetti, Veriano 1939- IntWWM 90
Luchins, Daniel J 1948- BiDrAPA 89
Luchs, Alison 1948- WhoAmA 91
Luchsinger, Daniel J. 1936- ODwPR 91
Luchsinger, John Francis 1920- St&PR 91
Luchsinger, Ronald 1940- IntWWM 90
Luchsinger, Vincent Peter, Jr. 1929- WhoAm 90
Luchsinger, Wayne Wesley 1924- WhoAm 90
Lucht, David Lee 1943- WhoSSW 91
Lucht, John Charles 1933- St&PR 91, WhoAm 90
Lucht, Sondra Moore 1942- WhoAmW 91
Luchte, Charles Eugene 1926- St&PR 91
Luchterhand, Ralph Edward 1952- WhoWor 91
Luci, James S. 1937- St&PR 91
Lucia WomWR
Lucia, Ellis 1922- WhoWrEP 89
Lucia, Fernando De PenDiMP
Lucia, Marilyn Reed BiDrAPA 89
Lucia, Philip John 1928- St&PR 91
Lucian 120-180? WorAlBi
Luciana, Eugene D. 1941- St&PR 91
Luciani, Albino 1912-1978 BioIn 16
Luciano, Alfred J. 1931- St&PR 91
Luciano, Charles 1896-1962 WorAlBi
Luciano, Jeannie 1952- St&PR 91
Luciano, Lucky 1897-1962 BioIn 16
Luciano, Mark R. 1959- St&PR 91
Luciano, Robert Peter 1933- St&PR 91, WhoE 91
Luciano, Ron 1937- Ballpl 90
Lucid, Robert Francis 1930- WhoAm 90
Lucid, Shannon BioIn 16
Lucid, Shannon W. 1943- WhoAmW 91
Lucido, Chester Charles, Jr. 1939- WhoAm 90
Lucido, Frank Cesare 1937- St&PR 91
Lucido, John Anthony 1952- St&PR 91
Lucido, Louis Charles 1948- WhoAm 90
Lucidor 1638-1674 DcScanL
Lucie, Edwin James 1931- WhoE 91
Lucie, Stephanie Alyce 1962- WhoE 91
Lucien, Jon DrBlPA 90
Lucienne WomWR
Lucientes, Francisco Jose de Goya y 1746-1828 BioIn 16
Lucier, Alvin NewAgMG
Lucier, Alvin 1931- IntWWM 90
Lucier, Francis Paul 1927- WhoAm 90
Lucier, James Alfred 1920- WhoSSW 91
Lucier, Mary 1944- WhoAmA 91
Lucier, P. Jeffrey 1941- St&PR 91, WhoAm 90
Lucier, Ralph Arthur 1921- St&PR 91
Lucila, Danilo V BiDrAPA 89
Lucinda, Camila 157-?-1612? EncCoWW
Lucindo-Del Rosario, Alice 1952- BiDrAPA 89
Lucio, Eduardo A. 1946- WhoHisp 91
Lucioni, Luigi 1900-1988 BioIn 16
Luciuk, Juliusz Mieczyslaw 1927- IntWWM 90
Luciuk, Lubomyr Y 1953- ConAu 132
Lucius, Ernette Kay 1944- WhoAmW 91
Luck, Allan 1938- BiDrAPA 89
Luck, Andrew Peter 1960- WhoE 91
Luck, David Jonathan Lewis 1929- WhoAm 90
Luck, Edward Carmichael 1948- WhoAm 90
Luck, Georg Hans Bhawani 1926- WhoAm 90
Luck, Gilbert Clayton 1935- St&PR 91
Luck, Helmut Ekkehart 1941- WhoWor 91
Luck, Herman David 1925- WhoSSW 91
Luck, James I. 1945- WhoAm 90, WhoEmL 91
Luck, Johann Christoph Ludwig von 1703?-1780 PenDiDA 89
Luck, Johann Friedrich von PenDiDA 89
Luck, Karl Gottlieb von PenDiDA 89
Luck, Michael Frederick 1947- WhoWor 91
Luck, Ray Egan 1942- IntWWM 90
Luck, Robert 1921- WhoAmA 91
Luck, Werner Albrecht Paul 1922- WhoWor 91
Luck, William Clifton 1943- St&PR 91
Lucke, Johann Christoph Ludwig von 1703?-1780 PenDiDA 89
Lucke, Loren Ernest 1930- St&PR 91
Lucke, Wolfgang Robert W. 1926- WhoWor 91
Luckel, Lucien J. 1921- St&PR 91
Lucken, Gary James 1943- WhoAm 90
Luckenbach, Carl Albert 1945- WhoSSW 91
Luckenbach, Thomas Alexander 1933- WhoE 91
Luckenbaugh, Richard Lee 1937- St&PR 91
Lucker, Jay K. 1930- WhoAm 90
Lucker, Raymond Alphonse 1927- WhoAm 90
Luckett, Hubert P. 1916-1988 BioIn 16
Luckett, Jack Cooper 1932- St&PR 91
Luckett, Karen Beth WhoWrEP 89
Luckett, Paul H., III 1935- St&PR 91
Luckey, Alice Davison 1930- WhoAmW 91
Luckey, Egbert Hugh 1920-1989 BioIn 16
Luckey, Ellen Jane 1951- WhoSSW 91
Luckey, Irene 1949- WhoAmW 91
Luckey, Joseph Frank 1936- St&PR 91
Luckey, Laura Colby WhoAm 90, WhoE 91
Luckey, Richard Roy 1945- WhoEmL 91
Luckey, Robert Reuel Raphael 1917- WhoAm 90
Luckham, Claire 1944- FemiCLE
Luckham, Cyril 1907-1989 AnObit 1989, ConTFT 8
Luckhardt, Mildred Corell 1898- AuBYP 90
Luckie, David Marshal 1948- WhoSSW 91
Luckie, Nancy Carol 1954- BiDrAPA 89
Luckie, Robert Ervin, Jr. 1917- WhoAm 90
Luckinbill, Laurence 1934- ConTFT 8, WorAlBi
Luckinbill, Laurence George 1934- WhoAm 90
Lucking, Peter Stephen 1945- WhoEmL 91, WhoWor 91
Lucking, Robert George, Jr. 1951- BiDrAPA 89
Luckman, Charles 1909- BioIn 16, St&PR 91, WhoAm 90
Luckman, James McElroy 1935- St&PR 91
Luckman, Sid 1916- WorAlBi
Luckmann, William Henry 1926- WhoAm 90
Luckner, Herman Richard, III 1933- WhoWor 91
Luckner, Kurt T 1945- WhoAmA 91
Luckock, Elizabeth 1914- AuBYP 90
Lucks, Julius Jack 1928- St&PR 91
Lucktenberg, Kathryn 1958- WhoAm 90
Lucky, Robert Wendell 1936- WhoAm 90
Lucky, Stepan 1919- IntWWM 90
Lucky, William Artmer, III 1955- WhoSSW 91
Luckyn-Malone, Laura Elizabeth 1952- St&PR 91, WhoAm 90
Luco, Ramon Barros 1835-1919 BioIn 16
Lucore, Wayne E. 1927- St&PR 91
Lucow, Milton 1924- WhoAm 90
Lucretius 98?BC-55BC WorAlBi
Lucretius 99?BC-55BC WrPh P
Lucretius Carus, Titus 99?BC-55BC WrPh P
Lucus, William Roy 1953- St&PR 91
Lucy, Autherine BioIn 16
Lucy, Dennis Durwood, Jr. 1934- WhoAm 90
Lucy, Kavaler E. St&PR 91
Lucy, Paul Edward 1936- St&PR 91, WhoAm 90
Lucy, Robert Meredith 1926- WhoAm 90
Luczak, Holger Theodor 1943- WhoWor 91
Luczak, Janet Williams 1955- WhoAmW 91
Luczek, Philomena I 1930- BiDrAPA 89
Luczkowski, Barbara Jean 1958- WhoAmW 91
Lucznikowska, Valerie ODwPR 91
Luczun, Mary Ellen Teresa 1951- WhoWrEP 89
Luczy, Leslie M 1919- BiDrAPA 89
Ludat, Herbert 1910- WhoWor 91
Ludatscher, Jack I 1924- BiDrAPA 89
Ludden, George Clemens 1945- WhoSSW 91
Ludden, John Dwight 1819-1907 AmLegL
Ludden, John Marten 1940- BiDrAPA 89
Ludden, Timothy Wayne 1940- St&PR 91
Luddie, Walter Joseph 1917- WhoWrEP 89
Ludeking, Judson Scott 1951- WhoE 91
Ludel, Jacqueline 1945- SmATA 64, WhoAmW 91
Ludeman, Kate 1946- WhoEmL 91
Ludeman, Robert Ervin 1929- St&PR 91
Ludemann, Winfried August 1951- IntWWM 90
Ludendorff, Erich 1865-1937 BioIn 16, WorAlBi
Luder, Everett Kirk BiDrAPA 89
Luder, Owen 1928- WhoWor 91
Luderitz, Berndt 1940- WhoWor 91
Luders, Adam 1950- WhoAm 90, WhoE 91
Luders, Gustav 1865-1913 OxCPMus
Luderus, Fred 1885-1961 Ballpl 90
Ludes, J.E. 1938- St&PR 91
Ludewig, Robert Morris 1940- WhoE 91
Ludgin, Chester 1925- IntWWM 90
Ludgin, Chester Hall 1925- WhoAm 90
Ludgin, Donald Hugh 1929- WhoE 91
Ludgin, Earle 1898-1981 WhoAmA 91N
Ludi, Kirk Michael 1961- WhoEmL 91
Ludicke, Karl Friedrich PenDiDA 89
Ludicke, Robert E 1935- BiDrAPA 89
Ludin, Albert P BiDrAPA 89
Ludin, Hans Elard 1905-1946 BioIn 16
Ludington, Charles Townsend, Jr. 1936- WhoAm 90
Ludington, Christopher P. 1953- St&PR 91
Ludington, Francis Henry, Jr. 1923- St&PR 91, WhoAm 90
Ludington, John Samuel 1928- St&PR 91, WhoAm 90
Ludington, William F. 1935- St&PR 91
Ludlam, Charles BioIn 16
Ludlam, Chester A. 1924- St&PR 91
Ludlam, Eugenie Shonnard 1936-1978 WhoAmA 91N
Ludlam, James Edward, III 1943- WhoAm 90
Ludlam, Roger James 1942- St&PR 91
Ludlow, Charles H. 1923- St&PR 91
Ludlow, Christy Leslie 1944- WhoAmW 91
Ludlow, Geoffrey 1899-1989 SmATA X
Ludlow, Jean W. 1935- WhoSSW 91
Ludlow, Michael Alan 1951- WhoWor 91
Ludlow, Roger EncCRAm
Ludlow, William Handy 1821-1890 AmLegL
Ludlum, David Blodgett 1929- WhoAm 90
Ludlum, John Charles 1913- WhoSSW 91
Ludlum, Robert BestSel 90-3 [port]
Ludlum, Robert 1927- MajTwCW, SpyFic, TwCCr&M 91, WhoAm 90, WhoWrEP 89, WorAlBi, WorAu 1980 [port]
Ludman, Joan Hurwitz 1932- WhoAmA 91
Ludmer, Charles Henry 1948- BiDrAPA 89
Ludmer, Irving 1935- WhoAm 90
Ludmer, Joyce Pellerano WhoAmA 91
Ludmer, Raul Isidro BiDrAPA 89
Ludmila 860?-921 WomWR
Ludolph, Robert Charles 1948- WhoEmL 91
Ludorf, Carol A. ODwPR 91
Ludorf, Patricia Joan WhoE 91
Ludovici, Anthony 1927- WhoE 91
LuDovico, Robert Donald 1937- St&PR 91
Ludtke, James Buren 1924- WhoAm 90
Ludtke, Jens-Ulrich Holger 1941- WhoWor 91
Ludtke, John LeRoy 1950- WhoE 91
Ludtke, Lawrence Monroe 1929- WhoAmA 91
Ludtke, Mary Alice 1950- WhoAmW 91
Ludutsky, John M. 1943- St&PR 91
Ludvigsen, Frants Josef Bernhard Thoger 1923- WhoSSW 91
Ludvigson, David L. 1938- St&PR 91
Ludvigson, Neil A. 1935- St&PR 91
Ludvigson, Susan Gayle 1942- WhoWrEP 89
Ludwick, Andrea Marie 1962- WhoAmW 91
Ludwick, John D. 1941- St&PR 91
Ludwig II, King of Bavaria 1845-1886 BioIn 16
Ludwig Rudolph, of Hanover BioIn 16
Ludwig, Allan I 1933- WhoAmA 91
Ludwig, Allan Ira 1933- WhoAm 90
Ludwig, Arnold M BiDrAPA 89
Ludwig, Charles Fine 1931- St&PR 91
Ludwig, Christa WhoAm 90, WhoWor 91
Ludwig, Christa 1924- PenDiMP
Ludwig, Christa 1928- IntWWM 90, WorAlBi
Ludwig, Daniel Keith BioIn 16
Ludwig, David Steven BiDrAPA 89
Ludwig, David Willard 1926- WhoWor 91
Ludwig, Dorothy 1909- BiDrAPA 89
Ludwig, Douglas Leroy 1953- St&PR 91
Ludwig, Edmund David 1940- St&PR 91
Ludwig, Edmund Vincent 1928- WhoAm 90, WhoWor 91
Ludwig, Edward B. 1930- St&PR 91
Ludwig, Eva 1923- WhoAmA 91, WhoE 91
Ludwig, Frederick J. BioIn 16
Ludwig, George Harry 1927- WhoAm 90
Ludwig, Harvey Fred 1916- WhoAm 90
Ludwig, Hermann-Henry 1954- WhoSSW 91
Ludwig, Irene BioIn 16
Ludwig, Irene Helen 1954- WhoE 91
Ludwig, Jack 1922- BioIn 16
Ludwig, James C. St&PR 91
Ludwig, John Howard 1913- WhoAm 90
Ludwig, John McKay 1935- WhoAm 90
Ludwig, John William 1949- St&PR 91
Ludwig, Judith K. ODwPR 91
Ludwig, Karl David 1930- BiDrAPA 89
Ludwig, Ken 19--?- ConLC 60 [port]
Ludwig, Kenneth J. 1922- St&PR 91
Ludwig, Lloyd, Jr. 1944- St&PR 91
Ludwig, Lyndell 1923- SmATA 63 [port]
Ludwig, Margaret G. WhoAmW 91
Ludwig, Marvin J. 1926- WhoAm 90
Ludwig, Ora Lee J. 1919- St&PR 91
Ludwig, Patricia A. 1949- WhoE 91
Ludwig, Paul Lou 1934- St&PR 91
Ludwig, Paula 1900-1974 EncCoWW
Ludwig, Peter 1925- BioIn 16
Ludwig, Richard 1930- WhoE 91
Ludwig, Richard Joseph 1937- WhoAm 90
Ludwig, Richard Marshall 1931- St&PR 91
Ludwig, Richard Milton 1920- WhoAm 90
Ludwig, Robert Cleo 1931- St&PR 91
Ludwig, Robert Sanford WhoSSW 91
Ludwig, Rolf Martin 1924- WhoWor 91
Ludwig, Vernell P. 1944- St&PR 91
Ludwig, Vernell Patrick 1944- WhoAm 90
Ludwig, Walther 1929- WhoWor 91
Ludwig, William 1912- WhoAm 90
Ludwig, William D. 1938- St&PR 91
Ludwig, William O. 1931- St&PR 91
Ludwig, William Orland 1931- WhoAm 90
Ludwiga EncCoWW
Ludwigson, John Ormont 1938- WhoAm 90
Ludwikowski, Rett Ryszard 1943- WhoE 91
Ludy, Andrew William 1947- WhoWrEP 89
Ludy, Kenneth John 1945- St&PR 91
Lueb, Louise Estelle 1947- WhoAmW 91
Luebber, Steve 1949- Ballpl 90
Luebbert, James Francis BiDrAPA 89
Luebbert, Jens Ingwer Adolf 1928- WhoWor 91
Luebke, Neil Robert 1936- WhoAm 90
Luebs, August A. 1889-1989 BioIn 16
Lueck, Therese Louise 1956- WhoAmW 91
Luecke, Carl William 1943- St&PR 91
Luecke, David A. 1948- St&PR 91
Luecke, John D. 1922- St&PR 91
Luecke, Joseph E. 1927- WhoAm 90
Luecke, Percy Edgar, Jr. 1926- WhoSSW 91
Luecke, Richard Harry 1930- WhoAm 90
Luecke, Richard William 1917- WhoAm 90
Lueckel, Earl R. 1923- St&PR 91
Luecking, Stephen Joseph 1948- WhoAmA 91
Luedde, Charles Edwin Howell 1944- WhoAm 90
Lueder, Robert Gregg 1922- St&PR 91
Luederitz, Alexander Wilhelm 1932- WhoWor 91
Lueders, Edward George 1923- AuBYP 90, WhoAm 90, WhoWrEP 89
Lueders, Jimmy C 1927- WhoAmA 91
Lueders, Kurt Demaree 1950- IntWWM 90
Lueders, W.M. 1951- St&PR 91
Luedke, George William 1945- BiDrAPA 89
Luedke, Janet Louise 1962- WhoAmW 91
Luedke, Keith Alan 1949- St&PR 91
Luedtke, Karl Elroy 1930- St&PR 91
Luedtke, Roland Alfred 1924- WhoAm 90
Luedy, Laurence Glenn 1940- St&PR 91
Lueger, Karl 1844-1910 BioIn 16

Lueger, Susan Ann 1953- *WhoAmW 91*
Luehr, John Gregory 1957- *BiDrAPA 89*
Lueken, John Joseph 1964- *WhoWor 91*
Lueken, Mary Judeann 1942- *WhoAmW 91*
Lueking, Herman August, Jr. 1930- *St&PR 91*
Luellen, Charles J. 1929- *St&PR 91*, *WhoAm 90*, *WhoSSW 91*, *WhoWor 91*
Luellen, Valentina *ConAu 129*
Luenberger, David Gilbert 1937- *WhoAm 90*
Luening, Otto *BioIn 16*
Luening, Otto 1900- *IntWWM 90*, *WhoAm 90*
Luening, Robert Adami 1924- *WhoAm 90*
Luenn, Nancy 1954- *BioIn 16*
Luenz, Pamela Marie 1947- *WhoAmW 91*
Luepke, Gretchen 1943- *WhoAmW 91*
Lueptow, Diana *ODwPR 91*
Luer, Charlotte *ODwPR 91*
Luera, Anita Favela 1955- *WhoHisp 91*
Luers, Wendy Wilson Woods 1940- *WhoAmW 91*
Luers, William H. 1929- *BioIn 16*
Luers, William Henry 1929- *WhoAm 90*, *WhoE 91*, *WhoWor 91*
Luerssen, Frank Wonson 1927- *St&PR 91*, *WhoAm 90*
Lueth, Faith M. 1943- *WhoAmW 91*
Lueth, Shirley 1930- *WhoWrEP 89*
Luethy, Hans Armin 1932- *WhoWor 91*
Luetke, Philip A. 1922- *ODwPR 91*
Luetkemeyer, Mary Jane 1951- *WhoAmW 91*
Luevano, Rosalva 1959- *WhoHisp 91*
Luff, Carl Richard 1954- *St&PR 91*
Luff, Enid 1935- *IntWWM 90*
Luff, Gerald Meredith, Jr. 1937- *WhoE 91*
Luffsey, Walter Stith 1934- *WhoAm 90*
Luffy, Robert H. 1947- *WhoAm 90*
Lufi, Dubi 1948- *WhoWor 91*
Lufkin, Joseph Charles Francis 1955- *WhoEmL 91*
Luft, Harold S. 1947- *WhoAm 90*
Luft, Rene W. 1943- *St&PR 91*
Luft, Roberta Moloff *BiDrAPA 89*
Luft, Roberta Moloff 1957- *WhoE 91*
Luftglass, Murray A. 1931- *St&PR 91*
Luftglass, Murray Arnold 1931- *WhoAm 90*, *WhoWor 91*
Luftig, David 1916- *St&PR 91*
Luftman, Michael 1946- *ODwPR 91*
Lugar, Richard G. *BioIn 16*
Lugar, Richard G. 1932- *WorAlBi*
Lugar, Richard Green 1932- *NewYTBS 90*, *WhoAm 90*, *WhoWor 91*
Lugbauer, Catherine A. *ODwPR 91*
Lugbill, Jon *BioIn 16*
Lugenbeel, Edward Elmer 1932- *WhoAm 90*
Luger, Donald R. 1938- *WhoAm 90*, *WhoSSW 91*
Luger, Donald Richard 1938- *St&PR 91*
Luger, George P. 1932- *St&PR 91*
Lughes, Joseph Albert 1928- *St&PR 91*
Luginbuhl, Edna *AuBYP 90*
Luginbuhl, William Hossfeld 1929- *WhoAm 90*
Lugo, Adrian C. 1947- *WhoHisp 91*
Lugo, Fabio H *BiDrAPA 89*
Lugo, Gail Maxson 1943- *WhoSSW 91*
Lugo, Hector M. 1938- *St&PR 91*
Lugo, Irving A *BiDrAPA 89*
Lugo, John Philip, Sr. 1930- *WhoHisp 91*
Lugo, Robert M. 1933- *WhoHisp 91*
Lugo, Urbano 1962- *Ballpl 90*
Lugo-Caceres, Carmelo *BiDrAPA 89*
Lugo-Juan, Marisol 1965- *WhoEmL 91*
Lugones, Leopoldo 1874-1938 *BioIn 16*, *ConAu 131*, *HispWr 90*
Lugosi, Bela 1882-1956 *BioIn 16*, *WorAlBi*
Lugossy, Maria 1950- *BiDWomA*
Luh, Jiang 1932- *WhoSSW 91*
Luhan, Joseph A *BiDrAPA 89*
Luhan, Mabel Dodge 1879-1962 *BioAmW*, *FemiCLE*
Luhmann, Niklas 1927- *WhoWor 91*
Luhmer, Klaus 1916- *WhoWor 91*
Luhring, John William 1912- *WhoAm 90*
Luhring, R.A. 1947- *St&PR 91*
Luhrman, Henry *BioIn 16*
Luhrman, Louella 1881-1990 *BioIn 16*
Luhrmann, George W 1934- *BiDrAPA 89*
Luhrmann, T M 1959- *ConAu 130*
Luhrs, H. Ric 1931- *St&PR 91*, *WhoAm 90*, *WhoE 91*, *WhoWor 91*
Luhrs, James Everett 1934- *St&PR 91*
Luhrs, Stephen F. 1952- *St&PR 91*
Lui, Dennis Pok-Man 1951- *WhoWor 91*
Lui, Ming Wah 1938- *WhoWor 91*
Lui, Tien *BioIn 16*
Luick, Earl *BioIn 16*
Luick, Gary L. 1940- *St&PR 91*
Luick, Robert B. 1911- *St&PR 91*
Luick, Robert Burns 1911- *WhoAm 90*
Luigs, Charles Russell 1933- *St&PR 91*, *WhoAm 90*
Luik, Lauren *ODwPR 91*
Luikart, Fordyce Whitney 1910- *WhoAm 90*
Luikart, John F. 1949- *St&PR 91*
Luikart, John Ford 1949- *WhoAm 90*
Luikart, Walter P 1926- *BiDrAPA 89*
Luikart, William McCollam 1921- *WhoSSW 91*
Luing, Gary Alan 1937- *WhoAm 90*
Luino, Bernardino 1951- *WhoAmA 91*
Luis Oacpicagigua *BioIn 16*
Luis, Antonio *BiDrAPA 89*
Luis, Cambronero Artes 1940- *WhoWor 91*
Luis, Juan 1940- *BioIn 16*
Luis, Juanita Bolland 1950- *St&PR 91*, *WhoAm 90*
Luis, Olga Maria 1958- *WhoHisp 91*
Luis, Washington 1869-1957 *BioIn 16*
Luis-Deza, Ramon *BiDrAPA 89*
Luisa 1782-1824 *WomWR*
Luisa Maria de Guzman *WomWR*
Luise *EncCoWW*
Luise 1776-1810 *BioIn 16*
Luise-Marie 1819-1864 *WomWR*
Luisi, Hector *WhoWor 91*
Luisi, Jerry 1939- *WhoAmA 91*
Luiskutty, Cheriyakalathil Thomas 1944- *WhoSSW 91*
Luiso, Anthony 1944- *St&PR 91*, *WhoAm 90*
Luitjens, Helen Anita *WhoAmA 91*
Luitz, Josef 1934- *IntWWM 90*
Luiz, Albert H. 1942- *St&PR 91*
Luiz, Douglas Edmund 1934- *St&PR 91*
Luiza-Forest, Peggy Ann 1948- *WhoSSW 91*
Lujan, Cleo Charlotte 1946- *WhoAmW 91*
Lujan, David 1953- *WhoSSW 91*
Lujan, Edward L. 1932- *WhoHisp 91*
Lujan, Leonard 1948- *WhoWor 91*
Lujan, Manuel, Jr. *BioIn 16*
Lujan, Manuel, Jr. 1928- *BiDrUSE 89*, *WhoAm 90*, *WhoE 91*, *WhoHisp 91*, *WhoWor 91*
Luk, Charles 1898- *EncO&P 3*
Luk, John Wang Kwong 1944- *WhoWor 91*
Luk, King Sing 1932- *WhoAm 90*
Luka, Concetta Gertrude 1939- *WhoAmW 91*
Luka, Thomas Phillip 1946- *St&PR 91*
Lukac, Carlos N. 1950- *St&PR 91*
Lukach, Arthur S., Jr. 1935- *St&PR 91*
Lukachko, William B 1929- *BiDrAPA 89*
Lukacs, Bela Bernard 1915- *St&PR 91*
Lukacs, Ervin 1928- *IntWWM 90*
Lukacs, Georg *MajTwCW*
Lukacs, George *MajTwCW*
Lukacs, Gyorgy 1885-1971 *MajTwCW*
Lukacs, John 1924- *BioIn 16*
Lukacs, John Adalbert 1924- *WhoAm 90*, *WhoWrEP 89*
Lukacs, Michael Edward 1946- *WhoE 91*, *WhoEmL 91*
Lukanov, Andrey Karlov 1938- *WhoWor 91*
Lukas, D. Wayne *BioIn 16*
Lukas, Dennis Brian 1947- *WhoAmA 91*
Lukas, Elaine Kozlowicz 1954- *WhoAmW 91*
Lukas, Elsa Victoria 1927- *WhoWor 91*
Lukas, Gaze Elmer 1907- *WhoSSW 91*, *WhoWor 91*
Lukas, J. Anthony 1933- *AuBYP 90*
Lukas, J Anthony 1933- *MajTwCW*
Lukas, J. Anthony 1933- *WhoAm 90*, *WhoE 91*
Lukas, Paul 1894-1971 *WorAlBi*
Lukas, Seth M. *St&PR 91*
Lukas, Susan 1940- *WhoWrEP 89*
Lukas, Viktor 1931- *IntWWM 90*
Lukas, Zdenek 1928- *IntWWM 90*
Lukasiewicz, Ronald Joseph 1943- *WhoAmA 91*
Lukasik, Stephen Joseph 1931- *WhoAm 90*
Lukaszewski, James Edmund 1942- *ODwPR 91*, *WhoE 91*
Lukatch, Edward 1954- *St&PR 91*
Lukatch, Susan Vikstrom 1951- *St&PR 91*
Luke, Alexandra 1901- *WhoAmA 91N*
Luke, Bernardita A *BiDrAPA 89*
Luke, Brian Thomas 1953- *WhoE 91*, *WhoEmL 91*
Luke, Claude Michael *BiDrAPA 89*
Luke, Cornelius *NewYTBS 90*
Luke, David L., III 1923- *St&PR 91*
Luke, David Lincoln, III 1923- *WhoAm 90*, *WhoE 91*
Luke, Dorothy Rawls 1907- *WhoWrEP 89*
Luke, Douglas Sigler, Jr. 1941- *WhoAm 90*, *WhoE 91*
Luke, Eben Livesey 1930- *WhoWor 91*
Luke, Edward Albert, Jr. *BiDrAPA 89*
Luke, Frank 1897-1918 *BioIn 16*
Luke, Hugh Jay 1932-1988 *BioIn 16*
Luke, James Phillip 1942- *St&PR 91*
Luke, John A., Jr. 1948- *St&PR 91*
Luke, John Anderson 1925- *St&PR 91*, *WhoAm 90*, *WhoE 91*
Luke, Keye 1904- *ConTFT 8*, *WorAlBi*
Luke, Norman J. 1921- *St&PR 91*
Luke, Norman John, Jr. 1955- *WhoE 91*
Luke, Patricia Ann 1934- *WhoAmW 91*
Luke, Peter B *BiDrAPA 89*
Luke, Randall Dan 1935- *St&PR 91*, *WhoAm 90*
Luke, Ray 1926- *IntWWM 90*
Luke, Robert Alfred 1914- *WhoAm 90*
Luke, Robert George 1935- *WhoAm 90*
Luke, Robert Phillips 1940- *St&PR 91*
Luke, Victor Stirling 1927- *St&PR 91*
Luke, Warren K. K. 1944- *WhoWor 91*
Lukeman, Karen Calmon 1953- *WhoAmW 91*
Luken, Thomas A. 1925- *WhoAm 90*
Lukenbill, Gregg *WhoAm 90*
Lukens, Alan Wood 1924- *WhoAm 90*
Lukens, Barbara 1930- *St&PR 91*
Lukens, Donald E. 1931- *WhoAm 90*
Lukens, Mary Brennan 1952- *WhoE 91*
Lukens, Norman G. 1926- *WhoE 91*
Lukens, Paul Bourne 1934- *WhoAm 90*
Lukens, T John 1920- *BiDrAPA 89*
Lukens, Walter Patrick 1924- *St&PR 91*, *WhoAm 90*
Lukensmeyer, William W 1943- *BiDrAPA 89*
Luker, James S. 1926- *St&PR 91*
Luker, Jeffrey Paul 1954- *WhoE 91*
Luker, Kristin 1946- *WhoAm 90*
Luker, Lynn Michael 1953- *WhoEmL 91*
Luker, Nicholas 1945- *ConAu 130*
Luker, Robert Charles 1927- *St&PR 91*
Lukes, Richard Elwood 1919- *WhoE 91*, *WhoWor 91*
Lukin, Philip 1903- *WhoAm 90*
Lukin, Sven 1934- *WhoAmA 91*
Lukins, Scott B. 1929- *St&PR 91*
Lukirskii, Petr Ivanovich 1894-1954 *DcScB S2*
Lukman, John C. 1922- *St&PR 91*
Lukman, Rilwanu 1937- *WhoWor 91*
Lukoff, Young-Soon *BiDrAPA 89*
Lukomska, Halina 1929- *IntWWM 90*, *PenDiMP*
Lukosius, Richard Benedict 1918- *WhoAmA 91*
Lukowiak, Joan Ann 1946- *WhoE 91*
Luks, George 1867-1933 *BioIn 16*
Luksch, James A. 1930- *St&PR 91*
Luksic, Cynthia Lee 1965- *WhoAmW 91*
Lukstat, Richard *ODwPR 91*
Luk'yanenko, Vladimir Matveyevich 1927- *WhoWor 91*
Luk'yanov, Anatoliy Ivanovich 1930- *WhoWor 91*
Lukyanov, Anatoly I. 1930- *BioIn 16*
Lulham, Stella 1933- *WhoSSW 91*
Lull, Ramon 1232?-1315 *EncO&P 3*
Lull, Robert Adelbert 1931- *St&PR 91*
Lulla, Jack 1929- *St&PR 91*
Lully, Jean-Baptiste 1632-1687 *PenDiMP A*, *WorAlBi*
Lully, Raymond 1232?-1315 *EncO&P 3*
Lulof, Fred W.Z. 1938- *St&PR 91*
Luloff, Harry 1911- *BiDrAPA 89*
Luloff, Philip Barrie *BiDrAPA 89*
Lulu 1948- *OxCPMus*
Lulu, Donald James 1926- *WhoAm 90*
Lulves, William Joseph 1945- *WhoEmL 91*
Lum, Darrell H.Y. 1950- *WhoWrEP 89*
Lum, Herman Tsui Fai 1926- *WhoAm 90*
Lum, Hubert J. 1953- *St&PR 91*
Lum, Jean Loui Jin 1938- *WhoAm 90*, *WhoAmW 91*
Lum, Kwong Yen 1926- *BiDrAPA 89*
Lum, Linda Li Ching 1957- *WhoAmW 91*
Lum, Mike 1945- *Ballpl 90*
Lum, Peter 1911- *AuBYP 90*
Lum, Rita Kaye *BiDrAPA 89*
Lumadue, Donald Dean 1938- *WhoE 91*
Lumadue, Joyce Ann 1941- *WhoAmW 91*
Lumapas, Arturo R 1943- *BiDrAPA 89*
Lumb, Geoffrey Norman 1925- *WhoWor 91*
Lumba, Gracia Navarro *WhoAmW 91*
Lumbard, Eliot Howland 1925- *WhoE 91*, *WhoWor 91*
Lumbard, Jean Ashmore *WhoAmA 91*
Lumbard, Joseph Edward, Jr. 1901- *WhoAm 90*
Lumbers, James Richard 1929- *WhoAmA 91*
Lumbly, Carl *BioIn 16*, *DrBIPA 90*
Lumbra, Reuben W. 1931- *St&PR 91*
Lumbye, Hans Christian 1810-1874 *OxCPMus*
Lumello, Giovanni *PenDiDA 89*
Lumenganeso, Kiobe 1943- *WhoWor 91*
Lumet, Sidney *BioIn 16*
Lumet, Sidney 1924- *WhoAm 90*, *WorAlBi*
Lumiansky, R. M. 1913-1987 *BioIn 16*
Lumiansky, Robert Mayer 1913-1987 *BioIn 16*
Lumingkewas, Stefanus Buang 1937- *WhoWor 91*
Lumley, Brian 1937- *ConAu 132*
Lumley, Harry 1880-1938 *Ballpl 90*
Lumley, Jane 1537-1576 *BioIn 16*, *FemiCLE*
Lumley, John Leask 1930- *WhoAm 90*, *WhoE 91*
Lumley, John Savile 1818-1896 *BioIn 16*
Lumley, Robert Alan 1936- *St&PR 91*
Lumm, Randolph Stephen 1949- *WhoHisp 91*
Lummis, Charles Fletcher 1859-1928 *BioIn 16*, *WhNaAH*
Lummis, William R. 1929- *WhoAm 90*
Lummus, Carol Travers 1937- *WhoAmA 91*
Lummus, Marion Morris 1934- *WhoWrEP 89*
Lumn, Peter *AuBYP 90*
Lumpe, Adolf Ingo 1927- *WhoWor 91*
Lumpe, Jerry 1933- *Ballpl 90*
Lumpkin, Alva Moore, III 1948- *WhoSSW 91*
Lumpkin, Angela 1950- *ConAu 32NR*
Lumpkin, Anne Craig 1919- *WhoAmW 91*, *WhoSSW 91*
Lumpkin, Bruce Keyser 1944- *WhoE 91*
Lumpkin, Dennis Lee 1952- *WhoE 91*
Lumpkin, Grace 1903?- *FemiCLE*
Lumpkin, James Robert 1950- *WhoAm 90*
Lumpkin, John Henderson 1916- *St&PR 91*
Lumpkin, Joseph Burton 1955- *WhoSSW 91*
Lumpkin, Kenneth Charles 1951- *WhoWrEP 89*
Lumpkin, Lee Roy 1925- *WhoAm 90*
Lumpkin, Peggy Ann Lanza 1948- *WhoEmL 91*
Lumpkin, R.A. *St&PR 91N*
Lumpkin, Thomas Dunlap 1914- *St&PR 91*
Lumpp, Karen Eve 1951- *WhoAmW 91*
Lumry, Rufus Worth, II 1920- *WhoAm 90*
Lumsdaine, Arthur Allen 1913- *WhoWrEP 89*
Lumsdaine, David 1931- *IntWWM 90*
Lumsdaine, Edward 1937- *WhoAm 90*
Lumsden, Andrew Michael 1962- *IntWWM 90*
Lumsden, David James 1928- *IntWWM 90*
Lumsden, Ian Gordon 1945- *WhoAm 90*, *WhoAmA 91*, *WhoE 91*
Lumsden, Lynne A. *BioIn 16*
Lumsden, Lynne Ann 1947- *WhoAm 90*
Lumsden, Robert William 1921- *WhoE 91*
Lumsden, Roy Stewart 1930- *WhoAm 90*
Lumumba, Patrice 1925-1961 *WorAlBi*
Luna 1910-1984 *WhoAmA 91N*
Luna, Albert *WhoHisp 91*
Luna, Carmen E. 1959- *WhoHisp 91*
Luna, Carolyn F. 1945- *WhoAmW 91*
Luna, Casey E. 1931- *WhoHisp 91*
Luna, Dennis R. 1946- *WhoHisp 91*, *WhoWor 91*
Luna, Elizabeth Jean 1951- *WhoAmW 91*
Luna, Fred 1931- *WhoHisp 91*
Luna, Gregory 1932- *WhoHisp 91*
Luna, Hugh A. *WhoSSW 91*
Luna, Maximiliano 1870-1899 *AmLegL*
Luna, Mickie Solorio 1945- *WhoHisp 91*
Luna, Nidia Casilda R. 1926- *WhoHisp 91*
Luna, Pablo 1880-1942 *OxCPMus*
Luna, Patricia Adele 1956- *WhoAmW 91*, *WhoEmL 91*, *WhoSSW 91*, *WhoWor 91*
Luna, Pedro A 1917- *BiDrAPA 89*
Luna, Rodrigo F. 1940- *WhoHisp 91*
Luna, Solomon 1858-1912 *BioIn 16*
Luna, Vickie Guzman de *BioIn 16*
Luna, William 1936- *WhoHisp 91*
Luna-Caro, Roberto 1941- *BiDrAPA 89*
Luna Padilla, Nitza Enid 1959- *WhoAmW 91*
Luna Smith, Carla Marie 1960- *WhoAmW 91*
Luna Solorzano, Maria Isela 1964- *WhoHisp 91*
Luna Y Arellano, Tristan De 1510-1573 *EncCRAm*
Lunacharsky, Anatoly Vasilievich 1875-1933 *BioIn 16*
Lunburg, Debra Ann 1952- *WhoAmW 91*
Lunceford, Jimmie 1902-1947 *BioIn 16*, *DrBIPA 90*, *OxCPMus*, *WorAlBi*
Lunceford, Laura 1954- *WhoAmW 91*
Lund, Alan Howard 1949- *St&PR 91*
Lund, Allan 1927- *OxCCanT*
Lund, Art *NewYTBS 90 [port]*
Lund, Art 1915-1990 *BioIn 16*
Lund, Beatrice B. 1945- *ODwPR 91*
Lund, Benjamin *PenDiDA 89*
Lund, Bert O. 1920- *St&PR 91*
Lund, Bert Oscar, Jr. 1920- *WhoAm 90*
Lund, Candida *WhoAm 90*
Lund, Charles L. *St&PR 91*
Lund, Daniel Peter 1940- *St&PR 91*
Lund, David 1925- *WhoAmA 91*
Lund, David H. 1927- *St&PR 91*
Lund, David Harrison 1927- *WhoAm 90*

Lund, David Nathan 1925- *WhoAm 90*
Lund, Don 1923- *Ballpl 90*
Lund, Edward *BioIn 16*
Lund, Frederick Henry 1929- *WhoSSW 91*
Lund, George Edward 1925- *WhoAm 90, WhoE 91*
Lund, Gunnar 1918- *St&PR 91*
Lund, Hal J. 1930- *St&PR 91*
Lund, Hans Bruno 1933- *WhoWor 91*
Lund, Harold Howard 1928- *St&PR 91*
Lund, Harry James 1931- *St&PR 91*
Lund, Henning 1929- *WhoWor 91*
Lund, Jane *WhoAmA 91*
Lund, Jo Lynn 1954- *WhoAmW 91*
Lund, Joseph John 1937- *St&PR 91*
Lund, Joshua B 1914- *BiDrAPA 89*
Lund, Lois Ann 1927- *WhoAm 90, WhoAmW 91*
Lund, Lyle D. 1925- *St&PR 91*
Lund, Martin Allan 1936- *WhoE 91*
Lund, Mireya Valencia 1936- *WhoAmW 91*
Lund, Oeivind 1945- *WhoWor 91*
Lund, Orval A., Jr. 1940- *WhoWrEP 89*
Lund, Paul A. 1938- *St&PR 91*
Lund, Pauline Kay 1955- *WhoAmW 91*
Lund, Peter Anthony 1941- *WhoAm 90*
Lund, Richard A. 1951- *St&PR 91*
Lund, Rita Pollard 1950- *WhoAmW 91*
Lund, Stephen D. *St&PR 91*
Lund, Stevan Robert 1946- *BiDrAPA 89*
Lund, Steve 1923- *WhoAm 90*
Lund, Victor L. 1947- *WhoAm 90*
Lund, Victor Lynn 1947- *St&PR 91*
Lund, Wendell Luther 1905- *WhoAm 90*
Lund, William Boyce 1959- *WhoEmL 91*
Lunda, Donald L. 1923- *St&PR 91*
Lunda-Bululu *WhoWor 91*
Lundahl, Steven Mark 1955- *WhoE 91*
Lundberg, Ante Sven A *BiDrAPA 89*
Lundberg, Barbara Jean 1952- *WhoAmW 91*
Lundberg, Ferdinand Edgar 1902- *WhoAm 90, WhoWrEP 89*
Lundberg, George David, II 1933- *WhoAm 90*
Lundberg, Hans Olof 1935- *WhoWor 91*
Lundberg, Jeanne Leighton- *BioIn 16*
Lundberg, John Kessander 1934- *WhoAm 90*
Lundberg, Lance B. 1956- *St&PR 91*
Lundberg, Larry Thomas 1938- *St&PR 91*
Lundberg, Lars Rune 1955- *WhoWor 91*
Lundberg, Lawrence Laska 1927- *St&PR 91*
Lundberg, Lois Ann 1928- *WhoAmW 91*
Lundbergh, Holger *AuBYP 90*
Lundblad, Roger Lauren 1939- *WhoSSW 91*
Lundborg, Erik 1948- *IntWWM 90*
Lundborg, Florence *WhoAmA 91N*
Lundbye, Eyvind Johan 1928- *WhoWor 91*
Lunde, Asbjorn Rudolph 1927- *WhoE 91, WhoWor 91*
Lunde, Charles A. 1940- *St&PR 91*
Lunde, David Eric 1941- *WhoWrEP 89*
Lunde, Diane S. 1942- *WhoWrEP 89*
Lunde, Dolores Benitez 1929- *WhoAmW 91*
Lunde, Donald T 1937- *BiDrAPA 89*
Lunde, Ellen B. 1952- *WhoWor 91*
Lunde, Emily 1914- *MusmAFA*
Lunde, Finn 1928- *BiDrAPA 89*
Lunde, Harold Irving 1929- *WhoAm 90*
Lunde, Henning Kanstrup 1935- *WhoWor 91*
Lunde, Henry B. 1943- *St&PR 91*
Lunde, Joan 1939- *IntWWM 90*
Lunde, Karl Roy 1931- *WhoAmA 91*
Lunde, Katherine L. 1947- *WhoAmW 91*
Lunde, Marvin C., Jr. 1936- *St&PR 91*
Lunde, Nanette Gomory 1943- *IntWWM 90*
Lundeberg, Helen 1908- *BiDWomA, WhoAmA 91*
Lundeberg, Philip Karl 1923- *WhoAm 90*
Lundeen, George Wayne 1948- *WhoAmA 91*
Lundeen, John Anton 1952- *WhoE 91*
Lundeen, Robert W. 1921- *St&PR 91*
Lundeen, Robert West 1921- *WhoAm 90, WhoWor 91*
Lundegaard, Robert Anton 1932- *WhoAm 90*
Lundegard, John Thomas 1931- *St&PR 91, WhoAm 90*
Lundelius, Ernest Luther, Jr. 1927- *WhoAm 90*
Lundell, Frederick *BiDrAPA 89*
Lundell, Nancy *ODwPR 91*
Lunden, Joan *BioIn 16*
Lunden, Joan 1950- *WhoAm 90, WhoAmW 91, WhoEmL 91*
Lunden, Samuel Eugene 1897- *WhoAm 90*
Lunder, Peter Harold 1933- *St&PR 91*
Lundergan, Barbara Keough 1938- *WhoAm 90*
Lundergan, Meredith 1957- *BiDrAPA 89*
Lunderman, Jack C. 1945- *BiDrAPA 89*
Lundgaard, L.L. 1924- *St&PR 91*
Lundgren, Carl 1880-1934 *Ballpl 90*
Lundgren, Clara Eloise 1951- *WhoAmW 91, WhoSSW 91, WhoWor 91*
Lundgren, Donald J. 1948- *St&PR 91*
Lundgren, John Thornton 1942- *BiDrAPA 89*
Lundgren, Kenneth B. 1948- *St&PR 91*
Lundgren, Lawrence Elmer 1952- *WhoE 91*
Lundgren, Lennart Stig Ake 1944- *WhoWor 91*
Lundgren, Robert Wayne 1917- *WhoAm 90*
Lundgren, Ruth Williamson Wood *WhoAmW 91, WhoWor 91*
Lundgren, Tyra 1897-1979 *BiDWomA*
Lundgren-Weber, Gail 1955- *WhoAmW 91*
Lundhagen, Edwin Wayne 1937- *St&PR 91*
Lundie, Edwin Hugh 1886-1972 *WhoAmA 91N*
Lundin, Adolf Henrik 1932- *WhoWor 91*
Lundin, Bruce Theodore 1919- *WhoAm 90*
Lundin, David Erik 1949- *WhoEmL 91*
Lundin, Linda Shacter 1951- *BiDrAPA 89*
Lundin, Norman K 1938- *WhoAmA 91*
Lundin, Roger E. 1944- *St&PR 91*
Lundin, Stacy Donald *BiDrAPA 89*
Lundin, Vernard E. *BioIn 16*
Lundine, Stanley Nelson 1939- *WhoAm 90, WhoE 91*
Lundkvist, Artur 1906- *DcScanL*
Lundlam, Roger 1942- *St&PR 91*
Lundman, Richard Jack 1944- *WhoAm 90*
Lundquist, Bruce G. 1956- *St&PR 91*
Lundquist, Carl 1913- *WhoWrEP 89*
Lundquist, Carl Harold 1916- *WhoAm 90*
Lundquist, Charles Arthur 1928- *WhoAm 90*
Lundquist, Christie Renis 1946- *IntWWM 90*
Lundquist, Dana Richard 1941- *WhoE 91*
Lundquist, David John 1942- *St&PR 91*
Lundquist, David Robert 1950- *WhoSSW 91*
Lundquist, Gene Alan 1943- *St&PR 91*
Lundquist, James Harold 1931- *WhoAm 90*
Lundquist, Linda Ann Johnson 1945- *WhoAmW 91*
Lundquist, Mary Elizabeth 1954- *WhoAmW 91*
Lundquist, Richard D. 1947- *WhoWrEP 89*
Lundquist, Violet Elvira 1912- *WhoAmW 91, WhoWor 91*
Lundquist, Weyman Ivan 1930- *WhoAm 90*
Lundqvist, Lennart J. 1939- *ConAu 129*
Lundry, Viola Delight 1924- *WhoAmW 91*
Lundsgaarde, Henry Peder 1938- *WhoAm 90*
Lundstedt, Peter Sanford 1958- *WhoE 91*
Lundstedt, Sven Bertil 1926- *WhoAm 90*
Lundsten, Ralph 1936- *IntWWM 90*
Lundsten, S. R. Henrik 1934- *WhoWor 91*
Lundstrom, Frank E. 1930- *St&PR 91*
Lundstrom, Hans Olof 1927- *WhoWor 91*
Lundstrom, Jarl Olof 1933- *WhoWor 91*
Lundstrom, Nils Erik *PenDiDA 89*
Lundstrom, William John 1944- *WhoSSW 91*
Lundvall, Bruce *BioIn 16*
Lundy, Audie Lee, Jr. 1943- *St&PR 91, WhoAm 90*
Lundy, Benjamin 1789-1839 *BioIn 16*
Lundy, Daniel F. 1930- *St&PR 91*
Lundy, Daniel Francis 1930- *WhoAm 90*
Lundy, Dick 1899-1965 *Ballpl 90*
Lundy, Edward D. 1926- *St&PR 91*
Lundy, Francis E. 1937- *St&PR 91*
Lundy, Gerald 1936- *ODwPR 91*
Lundy, J. Edward *BioIn 16*
Lundy, J. Edward 1915- *St&PR 91*
Lundy, Joseph Edward 1915- *WhoAm 90, WhoWor 91*
Lundy, Kathryn Renfro 1918- *WhoAmW 91*
Lundy, Larry E. 1950- *St&PR 91*
Lundy, Lisa Gail 1962- *WhoAmW 91*
Lundy, Mary Aletha 1965- *WhoSSW 91*
Lundy, Matt *ODwPR 91*
Lundy, Michael Stephen 1953- *BiDrAPA 89*
Lundy, Richard Alan 1934- *WhoAm 90*
Lundy, Richard Bruce 1941- *St&PR 91*
Lundy, Robert Benjamin *BiDrAPA 89*
Lundy, Robert Donald 1926- *St&PR 91*
Lundy, Sadie Allen 1918- *WhoAmW 91, WhoWor 91*
Lundy, William Howard *BiDrAPA 89*
Luneau, Claude 1935- *WhoAmA 91*
Luney, Percy Robert, Jr. 1949- *WhoEmL 91*
Luney, William Ross 1930- *St&PR 91*
Lung, Chang *WhoWrEP 89*
Lung, David Edward 1936- *St&PR 91*
Lung, Mervin Dean 1928- *St&PR 91*
Lung, Raymond H. 1926- *WhoAm 90*
Lung, Raymond Henry 1926- *St&PR 91*
Lung, William Dale 1941- *St&PR 91*
Lunger, Charles William 1927- *WhoAm 90*
Lunger, Gary Edward 1942- *St&PR 91*
Lunger, Irvin Eugene 1912- *WhoAm 90*
Lungerhausen, Richard Earle 1952- *WhoEmL 91*
Lunghi, Cherie 1953- *ConTFT 8*
Lunghino, Donald Joseph 1921- *WhoAm 90*
Lungren, Daniel Edward 1946- *WhoAm 90*
Lungren, Grant Preston 1952- *St&PR 91*
Lungren, Stefan 1949- *IntWWM 90*
Luniak, Rhonda Jean 1965- *WhoAmW 91*
Lunianski, Irwin L 1937- *BiDrAPA 89*
Luniewski, Allen William 1952- *WhoEmL 91*
Lunin, Lois Frumkin *WhoAmW 91*
Lunin, Martin 1917- *WhoAm 90*
Lunine, Jonathan Irving 1959- *WhoEmL 91*
Lunkley, Bruce Glenn 1929- *IntWWM 90*
Lunn, Harry 1934- *BioIn 16*
Lunn, James Snow 1909- *St&PR 91*
Lunn, Janet 1928- *SmATA 12AS [port], WhoWrEP 89*
Lunn, Janet Louise Swoboda 1928- *BioIn 16*
Lunn, Jean 1933- *WhoWrEP 89*
Lunn, Jeneane *BioIn 16*
Lunn, Villars *BiDrAPA 89*
Lunny, Robert Miller *BioIn 16*
Luns, Joseph Marie Antoine Hubert 1911- *WhoWor 91*
Lunsford, David H. 1956- *WhoEmL 91*
Lunsford, Donald Wayne 1938- *WhoSSW 91*
Lunsford, Everett Pollard, Jr. 1949- *WhoSSW 91*
Lunsford, John 1933- *WhoAmA 91*
Lunsford, Julia Ogden *BiDrAPA 89*
Lunsford, Julius R., Jr. 1915- *WhoSSW 91*
Lunsford, M. Rosser 1922- *WhoWrEP 89*
Lunsky, Louis 1923- *BiDrAPA 89*
Lunt, Alfred 1893-1977 *WorAlBi*
Lunt, Denham C., Jr. 1926- *St&PR 91*
Lunt, Horace Gray 1918- *WhoAm 90*
Lunt, Jack 1944- *St&PR 91*
Lunt, Paula *BiDrAPA 89*
Luntey, Donald Rae 1945- *WhoSSW 91*
Luntz, Gregory William 1952- *St&PR 91*
Luntz, Irving 1929- *WhoAmA 91*
Luntz, Perry 1927- *WhoWrEP 89*
Luntz, Theodore M. 1926- *St&PR 91*
Luntz, William L. 1924- *St&PR 91*
Lunz, William Edward 1952- *WhoSSW 91*
Lunzer, Richard G *BiDrAPA 89*
Luo Qianglie *BioIn 16*
Luo, Ren-Chyuan 1949- *WhoWor 91*
Luolajan-Mikkola, Vilho Rafael 1911- *IntWWM 90*
Luong, My Thi *BiDrAPA 89*
Luongo, C. Paul 1930- *ODwPR 91, WhoAm 90*
Luongo, Janet Duffy 1949- *WhoE 91*
Luongo, John Patrick 1949- *WhoE 91*
Luongo, Lucille Francesca 1948- *WhoAmW 91, WhoE 91*
Luongo, Pino *BioIn 16*
Luparello, Thomas J *BiDrAPA 89*
Lupas, Roland Patrick 1929- *WhoE 91*
Lupberger, Edwin Adolph 1936- *St&PR 91, WhoAm 90, WhoSSW 91*
Lupe, John E. *St&PR 91N*
Luper, Edna Lane 1942- *WhoSSW 91*
Luper, William Donald, Sr. 1933- *St&PR 91*
Lupert, Leslie Allan 1946- *WhoE 91, WhoEmL 91, WhoWor 91*
Lupi, Robert S 1946- *BiDrAPA 89*
Lupia, Harry E. 1925- *St&PR 91*
Lupien, Charles Alfred 1935- *St&PR 91*
Lupien, Tony 1917- *Ballpl 90*
Lupin, Ellis Ralph 1931- *WhoAm 90, WhoSSW 91*
Lupino, Ida 1918- *BioIn 16, WhoAm 90, WorAlBi*
Lupino, Stanley 1894-1942 *OxCPMus*
Lupinski, Thomas Marion 1952- *St&PR 91*
Lupis, G. Massimo 1954- *WhoWor 91*
Luplow, Al 1939- *Ballpl 90*
Lupo, Alan Isaac 1938- *WhoE 91*
Lupo, Andrew Britton 1944- *WhoSSW 91*
Lupo, Benedetto 1963- *IntWWM 90*
Lupo, Joseph F 1933- *BiDrAPA 89*
Lupo, Joseph Vincent *St&PR 91*
Lupo, Margaret Kennon 1919- *WhoSSW 91*
Lupo, Michael A. 1932- *WhoAm 90*
Lupo, Michael Anthony 1932- *St&PR 91*
Lupo, Perry Irvine 1948- *BiDrAPA 89*
Lupo, Robert Edward Smith 1953- *WhoSSW 91, WhoWor 91*
Lupo, Samuel Eldred 1933- *WhoAm 90, WhoWor 91*
Lupo, Thomas A. 1948- *St&PR 91*
Lupoff, Dick 1935- *SmATA X*
Lupoff, Richard A 1935- *SmATA 60*
LuPone, Patti *BioIn 16*
LuPone, Patti 1949- *WhoAm 90, WhoAmW 91, WorAlBi*
Lupori, Peter John 1918- *WhoAmA 91*
Lupovici, Marius 1931- *WhoWor 91*
Lupp, Joerg Stefan 1955- *WhoSSW 91*
Luppen, Yvonne Faith 1965- *WhoEmL 91*
Luppens, Carl Henry 1952- *WhoEmL 91*
Lupper, Edward 1936- *WhoAmA 91*
Luprecht, Geri Lyn *BiDrAPA 89*
Lupton, Charles Hamilton, Jr. 1919- *WhoAm 90*
Lupton, Debbie Ann 1962- *WhoAmW 91*
Lupton, Jeanne Traphagen 1923- *WhoAm 90*
Lupton, Mary Hosmer 1914- *WhoAmW 91*
Lupton, Thomas Ray 1932- *WhoSSW 91*
Lupton, Whitney Blair 1965- *WhoSSW 91*
Lupu, Marian Florentin 1935- *BiDrAPA 89*
Lupu, Radu 1945- *IntWWM 90, PenDiMP, WhoAm 90*
Lupulescu, Aurel Peter 1923- *WhoWor 91*
Luque, Dolf 1890-1957 *Ballpl 90 [port]*
Luquiens, Huc-Mazelet 1882-1961 *WhoAmA 91N*
Luquire, Hans 1958- *St&PR 91*
Luray, J 1939- *WhoAmA 91*
Lurcat, Jean 1892-1965 *PenDiDA 89*
Lurensky, Robert Lee 1928- *WhoE 91*
Lurey, Alfred Saul 1942- *WhoAm 90*
Luria, Alexander R. 1902-1977 *ConAu 33NR, MajTwCW*
Luria, Buck 1912- *BiDrAPA 89*
Luria, Gloria *WhoAmA 91*
Luria, Gloria 1925- *St&PR 91*
Luria, Isaac ben Solomon 1534-1572 *BioIn 16*
Luria, Leonard 1923- *St&PR 91*
Luria, Mary M. 1942- *WhoAm 90*
Luria, Peter P. 1952- *St&PR 91*
Luria, Richard E 1943- *BiDrAPA 89*
Luria, S. E. 1912- *BioIn 16*
Luria, Salvador 1912- *WorAlBi*
Luria, Salvador Edward 1912- *BioIn 16, WhoAm 90, WhoE 91, WhoWor 91*
Luria, Zella 1924- *WhoAm 90*
Lurie, Alison 1926- *FemiCLE, MajTwCW, WhoAm 90, WhoAmW 91, WhoWrEP 89, WorAlBi*
Lurie, Alvin David 1923- *WhoAm 90*
Lurie, Bob *BioIn 16*
Lurie, Boris 1924- *WhoAmA 91*
Lurie, Deborah Gail 1957- *WhoEmL 91*
Lurie, Harold 1919- *WhoAm 90*
Lurie, Howard Ray 1938- *WhoE 91*
Lurie, Hugh James 1935- *BiDrAPA 89*
Lurie, Jerome B. 1917-1988 *BioIn 16*
Lurie, Jonathan 1939- *ConAu 132*
Lurie, Lawrence B 1934- *BiDrAPA 89*
Lurie, Max L *BiDrAPA 89*
Lurie, Maxine Neustadt 1940- *WhoAmW 91*
Lurie, Melvyn Louis 1943- *BiDrAPA 89*
Lurie, Michael Edward 1943- *St&PR 91*
Lurie, Nancy Oestreich 1924- *WhoAm 90*
Lurie, Ranan Raymond 1932- *WhoAm 90*
Lurie, Robert *WhoAm 90*
Lurie, Ron *WhoAm 90*
Lurie, Scott N 1960- *BiDrAPA 89*
Lurie, Sheldon M 1942- *WhoAmA 91*
Lurie, Susan 1958- *BiDrAPA 89*
Lurie, Toby 1925- *WhoWrEP 89*
Lurie, William L. 1931- *St&PR 91, WhoAm 90*
Lurie, William V. 1903- *St&PR 91*
Lurin, Mitch 1941- *St&PR 91*
Lurix, Paul Leslie, Jr. 1949- *WhoSSW 91, WhoWor 91*
Lurton, Ernest Lee 1944- *WhoWor 91*
Lurton, H. William 1929- *St&PR 91, WhoAm 90*
Lurton, Horace Van Deventer 1941- *St&PR 91*
Lurton, Horace VanDeventer 1941- *WhoE 91*
Lurvey, Ira Harold 1935- *WhoWor 91*
Lusaka, Paul John Firmino 1935- *WhoWor 91*
Lusardi, Lawrence Mario 1952- *WhoE 91*
Lusby, George C. 1943- *St&PR 91*
Lusby, Thomas Reed 1954- *St&PR 91*
Lusch, Charles Jack 1936- *WhoE 91*
Lusch, Frans Ernest 1925- *St&PR 91*
Lusche, Peter Jay 1956- *BiDrAPA 89*
Luscinski, Steven Michael 1951- *St&PR 91, WhoE 91*
Luscomb, Karen Marie 1942- *WhoAmW 91*
Luscomb, Robert Charles, Jr. 1936- *WhoWor 91*
Luscombe, George 1926- *OxCCanT*
Luscombe, Herbert Alfred 1916- *WhoAm 90*
Luscombe, Tim 1960- *ConTFT 8 [port]*

Luscombe, Wendy 1951- *St&PR 91*
Lush, Billy 1873-1951 *Ballpl 90*
Lush, Ernest 1908-1988 *AnObit 1988, PenDiMP*
Lush, Johnny 1885-1946 *Ballpl 90*
Lushbough, Channing H. 1929- *St&PR 91*
Lusher, Robert William 1923- *St&PR 91*
Lushing, Gloria *BioIn 16*
Lushing, Jerry *BioIn 16*
Lushis, John Francis, Jr. 1955- *WhoEmL 91*
Lushis, Stella Anne 1958- *WhoAmW 91*
Lusic, Judith Ruth *BiDrAPA 89*
Lusic, Ronald R. 1947- *WhoAm 90*
Lusinchi, Jaime *BioIn 16*
Lusinchi, Jaime 1924- *WhoWor 91*
Lusk, Charles Michael, III 1948- *WhoSSW 91*
Lusk, Glenna Rae Knight 1935- *WhoAmW 91, WhoSSW 91*
Lusk, Harlan Gilbert 1943- *WhoAm 90*
Lusk, John William *BioIn 16*
Lusk, Martha Larche 1925- *WhoWrEP 89*
Lusk, Patricia A 1945- *WhoAmA 91*
Lusk, Patricia Jane 1945- *WhoSSW 91*
Lusk, Samuel Gary *BiDrAPA 89*
Lusk, William Edward 1916- *WhoAm 90*
Lusker, Ron 1937- *WhoAmA 91*
Luskey, Louis 1920- *St&PR 91*
Luskin, Bernard 1925- *St&PR 91*
Luskin, Evan Ross 1946- *IntWWM 90*
Luskin, Jack 1928- *St&PR 91*
Luskin, Meyer 1925- *St&PR 91*
Lusky, Larry E. 1949- *St&PR 91*
Lusky, Lois Freese 1931- *ODwPR 91*
Lusky, Louis 1915- *WhoAm 90*
Lusky, Monnie L., Jr. 1921- *St&PR 91*
Luss, Dan 1938- *WhoAm 90*
Luss, Gerald 1926- *ConDes 90*
Lussato, Bruno 1932- *WhoWor 91*
Lussen, John F. 1942- *St&PR 91*
Lussen, John Frederick 1942- *WhoAm 90*
Lussi, Caroline Frances Draper 1939- *WhoE 91, WhoWor 91*
Lussier, Gaetan 1941- *WhoAm 90*
Lussier, Georges H *BiDrAPA 89*
Lussier, Jacques 1941- *WhoAm 90*
Lussier, Jean-Paul 1917- *WhoAm 90*
Lussier, John H. 1927- *St&PR 91*
Lussier, Rene *BioIn 16*
Lussier, Robert George 1956- *BiDrAPA 89*
Lussky, Warren Alfred 1919- *WhoSSW 91*
Lusso, Del Patrick 1954- *St&PR 91*
Lust, Benedict 1872-1945 *NewAgE 90*
Lust, Elenore *WhoAmW 91*
Lust, Herbert Cohnfeldt, II 1926- *WhoE 91*
Lustbader, Philip Lawrence 1949- *St&PR 91*
Lustbader, Robert *St&PR 91*
Lustberg, Eugene Joseph 1923- *St&PR 91*
Lustberg, Thomas Joseph *BiDrAPA 89*
Luste, Joseph Francis, Jr. 1940- *WhoE 91*
Luster, George Orchard 1921- *WhoAm 90*
Luster, Linda 1940- *BiDrAPA 89*
Luster, Mark Richard 1944- *St&PR 91*
Luster, Michelle 1955- *WhoAmW 91*
Lustgarten, Baier *BioIn 16*
Lustgarten, Edgar 1907-1978 *TwCCr&M 91*
Lustgarten, Marc A. *BioIn 16*
Lustgarten, Maurice V 1940- *BiDrAPA 89*
Lustgarten, Stewart J. 1943- *WhoE 91*
Lustick, Michael Jay *BiDrAPA 89*
Lustig, Arnost *BioIn 16*
Lustig, Arnost 1926- *WhoWor 91*
Lustig, David Vernon 1947- *ODwPR 91*
Lustig, Ernst 1921- *WhoWor 91*
Lustig, Harry 1925- *WhoAm 90*
Lustig, Herbert S 1943- *BiDrAPA 89*
Lustig, Ilana Denise 1951- *WhoAmW 91*
Lustig, Noel *BiDrAPA 89*
Lustig, Theodore *ODwPR 91*
Lustiger, Jean-Marie 1926- *WhoWor 91*
Lustre, Redencion Bote 1937- *BiDrAPA 89*
Lusztig, Peter Alfred 1930- *WhoAm 90*
Lutali, A. P. 1919- *WhoWor 91*
Lutas, Elizabeth Mary 1951- *WhoE 91*
Lutcher, Nellie 1915- *DrBIPA 90, OxCPMus*
Lutchi, Doina Peana 1967- *WhoAmW 91*
Lutchmeenaraidoo, Seetanah 1944- *WhoWor 91*
Lutenbacher, Mark Gerard 1953- *WhoSSW 91*
Lutens, Serge *BioIn 16*
Luter, Carol E. *St&PR 91*
Luter, John 1919- *WhoAm 90, WhoWor 91*
Luter, Joseph Williamson, III 1939- *St&PR 91, WhoAm 90, WhoSSW 91*
Luterman, Arnold 1946- *WhoSSW 91*
Luters, Aina 1944- *WhoAmW 91*
Lutes, Donald Henry 1926- *WhoAm 90*
Lutes, Jim 1955- *WhoAmA 91*
Lutes, Joseph W. 1950- *St&PR 91*
Lutes, Joseph Wycoff 1950- *WhoE 91*
Lutfi, Najib 1941- *WhoE 91*
Lutgen, Kurt 1911- *AuBYP 90*
Lutgens, Harry Gerardus *WhoAm 90*
Luther, Andrew C. 1942- *St&PR 91*
Luther, Anne 1948- *ODwPR 91*
Luther, Clark Edward 1924- *WhoAm 90*
Luther, D. Joseph 1947- *St&PR 91*
Luther, David B. 1936- *St&PR 91*
Luther, David Byron 1936- *WhoAm 90*
Luther, Doris Evelyn 1933- *WhoAmW 91*
Luther, Florence Joan 1928- *WhoAmW 91*
Luther, George Aubrey 1933- *WhoAm 90*
Luther, James E. 1940- *St&PR 91*
Luther, James H. 1928- *St&PR 91*
Luther, James H. 1929- *St&PR 91*
Luther, James Howard 1928- *WhoAm 90*
Luther, John Michael 1952- *IntWWM 90*
Luther, John Wayne 1938- *WhoAm 90*
Luther, Louise Ellen 1943- *WhoAmW 91*
Luther, Luana Mae 1939- *WhoAmW 91*
Luther, Martin 1483-1546 *BioIn 16, EncPaPR 91, WorAlBi*
Luther, Martin Franz Julius 1895-1945 *BioIn 16*
Luther, Paul Kenneth *BiDrAPA 89*
Luther, Raymond J. 1946- *St&PR 91*
Luther, Robert C 1934- *BiDrAPA 89*
Luther, Robert Karl, Jr. 1954- *St&PR 91*
Luther, Robert W. *St&PR 91*
Luther, Ron B. 1932- *St&PR 91*
Luther, Susan Militzer 1946- *WhoWrEP 89*
Luther, Wallace John 1947- *St&PR 91*
Luther, William Lee 1952- *WhoE 91*
Luther-Lemmon, Carol Len 1955- *WhoAmW 91*
Luthey, Graydon Dean, Jr. 1955- *WhoEmL 91, WhoSSW 91, WhoWor 91*
Luthringshauser, Daniel Rene 1935- *WhoAm 90*
Luthro, John O. 1937- *St&PR 91*
Luthuli, Albert 1898-1967 *WorAlBi*
Luthy, Chella *WhoHisp 91*
Luthy, Richard Godfrey 1945- *WhoAm 90*
Lutjeharms, Joseph Earl 1933- *WhoAm 90*
Lutken, Donald C. 1924- *St&PR 91, WhoAm 90, WhoSSW 91*
Lutkenhouse, Anne 1957- *WhoAmW 91*
Lutkins, William Burgess 1926- *St&PR 91*
Lutkowitz, Mark 1960- *WhoSSW 91*
Lutkowski, Noel J. 1944- *St&PR 91*
Lutley, John H. 1935- *WhoAm 90*
Lutma, Johannes 1587?-1669 *PenDiDA 89*
Lutoborski, Adam 1951- *WhoE 91*
Lutomski, Dorothy Odile 1920- *WhoWrEP 89*
Luton, Mary Kathryn *WhoSSW 91*
Luton, W.C. 1923- *St&PR 91*
Lutoslawski, Wincenty 1863-1954 *EncO&P 3*
Lutoslawski, Witold 1913- *IntWWM 90, PenDiMP A, WhoWor 91*
Lutovich, Gerald 1931- *BiDrAPA 89*
Lutrick, Charles Gary 1955- *WhoSSW 91*
Lutter, Joseph *BioIn 16*
Lutterbach, Rick Steven 1949- *St&PR 91*
Luttermoser, Donald Louis 1941- *St&PR 91*
Luttmann, Gail Jane 1944- *WhoWrEP 89*
Lutto, Karen *ODwPR 91*
Luttrell, Arvell S *BiDrAPA 89*
Luttrell, Everett Stanley 1916-1988 *BioIn 16*
Luttrell, Gregory Brent 1962- *WhoE 91*
Luttrell, John W. 1931- *St&PR 91*
Luttrell, Michael C. 1950- *St&PR 91*
Luttrell, Michael Joseph 1948- *WhoEmL 91*
Luttrell, Nancy Kay Border 1946- *IntWWM 90*
Luttrell, Robert Grant 1937- *St&PR 91*
Luttrell, Robert R 1921- *BiDrAPA 89*
Luttrell, Robert Samuel 1944- *St&PR 91*
Luttrell, Robert Stephens 1933- *WhoSSW 91*
Lutts, Ralph Herbert 1944- *WhoE 91*
Luttwak, Edward Nicolae 1942- *WhoAm 90*
Lutvak, Mark Allen 1939- *WhoWor 91*
Lutwak, Leo 1928- *WhoAm 90*
Lutwiniak, William *BioIn 16*
Luty, Fritz 1928- *WhoAm 90*
Lutyens, Edwin Landseer 1869-1944 *BioIn 16*
Lutyens, Elisabeth 1906-1983 *BioIn 16, DcNaB 1981, PenDiMP A*
Lutynski, Adam M. 1942- *St&PR 91*
Lutz, Alma 1890-1973 *FemiCLE*
Lutz, Andrew S. 1927- *St&PR 91*
Lutz, Carl 1895-1975 *BioIn 16*
Lutz, Carl Frederick 1917- *WhoWor 91*
Lutz, Carl Freiheit 1934- *WhoAm 90*
Lutz, Christian Armin 1919- *WhoWor 91*
Lutz, Dan S 1906-1978 *WhoAmA 91N*
Lutz, David S. 1945- *St&PR 91*
Lutz, Edward Oscar 1919- *WhoWor 91*
Lutz, Elizabeth May 1928- *St&PR 91*
Lutz, Elmar G 1928- *BiDrAPA 89*
Lutz, Felix Philipp 1958- *WhoWor 91*
Lutz, Francis Charles 1944- *WhoAm 90*
Lutz, Frank Wenzel 1928- *WhoSSW 91*
Lutz, Frederick E. 1915- *St&PR 91*
Lutz, George D. 1941- *St&PR 91*
Lutz, Gregory Elmar *BiDrAPA 89*
Lutz, Hans-Rudolf 1939- *ConDes 90*
Lutz, Hartwell Borden 1932- *WhoAm 90*
Lutz, Jeffrey Christian 1959- *WhoEmL 91*
Lutz, Jeffry R. *St&PR 91*
Lutz, Jessie Gregory 1925- *WhoE 91*
Lutz, John 1939- *TwCCr&M 91*
Lutz, John N. 1926- *St&PR 91*
Lutz, John Sammel 1946- *WhoSSW 91*
Lutz, Joseph Philip 1951- *WhoE 91*
Lutz, Julie Haynes 1944- *WhoAmW 91*
Lutz, Karl Evan 1949- *WhoEmL 91*
Lutz, Marjorie Brunhoff 1933- *WhoAmA 91*
Lutz, Matthew Charles 1934- *WhoAm 90*
Lutz, Meyer 1822-1903 *OxCPMus*
Lutz, Nicholas *PenDiDA 89*
Lutz, Raymond Price 1935- *WhoAm 90, WhoSSW 91*
Lutz, Robert A. *BioIn 16*
Lutz, Robert A 1932- *News 90 [port]*
Lutz, Robert Anthony 1932- *WhoAm 90*
Lutz, Robert Brady, Jr. 1944- *WhoSSW 91*
Lutz, Robert Philip, Jr. 1963- *WhoE 91*
Lutz, Verena 1941- *IntWWM 90*
Lutz, Wilbur M 1915- *BiDrAPA 89*
Lutz, William Andrew 1944- *WhoE 91, WhoWor 91*
Lutz, Winifred Ann 1942- *WhoAmA 91*
Lutz, Zoi Douca *BiDrAPA 89*
Lutze, Frederick Henry, Jr. 1937- *WhoSSW 91*
Lutze, Gert 1917- *IntWWM 90*
Lutze, P. Michael 1944- *St&PR 91*
Lutze, Ruth Louise 1917- *WhoE 91*
Lutzeier, Dan P. 1928- *ODwPR 91*
Lutzeier, Peter Rolf 1948- *WhoWor 91*
Lutzer, David John 1943- *WhoAm 90*
Lutzer, Gerald Marc 1941- *BiDrAPA 89*
Lutzke, Arthur Saul 1945- *WhoAm 90*
Lutzke, Rube 1897-1938 *Ballpl 90*
Lutzker, Paul *ODwPR 91*
Lutzky, Frank Joseph, Jr. 1934- *WhoE 91*
Lutzky, Maya 1947- *BiDrAPA 89*
Lutzwick, Steven Henry 1959- *BiDrAPA 89*
Luu, Chi *BioIn 16*
Luu, Le *BioIn 16*
Luukka, Pisa Pirkko-Liisa 1954- *WhoWor 91*
Luukkainen, Timo Risto 1954- *WhoWor 91*
Luvisi, Fred Paul 1937- *St&PR 91*
Luvisi, Lee 1937- *WhoAm 90*
Luwisch, Joachim *BiDrAPA 89*
Lux, Ann Mary 1938- *BiDrAPA 89*
Lux, C.L. 1914- *St&PR 91*
Lux, Donna Marie 1945- *WhoEmL 91*
Lux, Gladys M 1899- *WhoAmA 91*
Lux, Guillermo 1938- *WhoHisp 91*
Lux, John Ernst 1946- *WhoSSW 91*
Lux, John H. 1918- *St&PR 91, WhoAm 90*
Lux, Paul S. 1950- *St&PR 91*
Lux, Philip Gordon 1928- *St&PR 91*
Luxborough, Henrietta 1700?-1756 *FemiCLE*
Luxemburg, Jack Alan 1949- *WhoE 91*
Luxemburg, Philip Irwin 1945- *WhoE 91*
Luxemburg, Rosa 1871-1919 *BioIn 16, EncCoWW, WorAlBi*
Luxemburg, Wilhelmus Anthonius Josephus 1929- *WhoAm 90*
Luxenberg, Alan Henry 1954- *WhoE 91*
Luxenberg, Malcolm Neuwahl 1935- *WhoAm 90, WhoSSW 91*
Luxenberg, Michael Gary 1949- *WhoEmL 91*
Luxenberg, Reva 1930- *St&PR 91*
Luxmoore, Robert John 1940- *WhoAm 90*
Luxner, Morton Bennett 1917- *WhoWrEP 89*
Luxon, Benjamin 1937- *PenDiMP*
Luxon, Benjamin Matthew 1937- *IntWWM 90*
Luxton, Richard N. 1950- *WhoEmL 91*
Luye, Li *WhoE 91*
Luz, Eberhard Ludwig 1933- *WhoWor 91*
Luz, Herbert M. 1931- *St&PR 91*
Luz, Silvino Manuel da *WhoWor 91*
Luz, Virginia 1911- *WhoAmA 91*
Luza, Radomir Vaclav 1922- *WhoAm 90, WhoSSW 91*
Luzader, S. D. *WhoWrEP 89*
Luzanovski-Marinesco, Lydia 1899- *BiDWomA*
Luzinski, Greg 1950- *Ballpl 90*
Luzio, Leon R. 1946- *St&PR 91*
Luzma *HispWr 90*
Luzum, James Aloysius 1940- *St&PR 91*
Luzuriaga, Adel 1949- *WhoAmW 91*
Luzzati, Emanuele 1921- *ConDes 90*
Luzzatto, Ephraim 1729-1792 *BioIn 16*
Luzzi, Louis Anthony 1932- *WhoAm 90*
L'vov, Georgii Evgenievich 1861-1925 *BioIn 16*
Lwoff, Andre 1902- *WorAlBi*
Lwoff, Andre Michel 1902- *WhoAm 90, WhoWor 91*
Ly, Raymond Hoa Binh 1943- *WhoSSW 91*
Lyall, Edna 1857-1903 *BioIn 16, FemiCL*
Lyall, Gavin 1932- *TwCCr&M 91, WorAu 1980 [port]*
Lyall, Gavin Tudor 1932- *SpyFic*
Lyall, George Albert 1924- *St&PR 91*
Lyall, Katharine Culbert 1941- *WhoAm 9*
Lyall, Robert 1948- *IntWWM 90*
Lyall, Tony Allen 1949- *St&PR 91, WhoSSW 91*
Lyautey, Henry Jules 1959- *WhoSSW 91*
Lyautey, Louis Hubert Gonsalve 1854-1934 *BiDFrPL*
Lybarger, Adrienne Reynolds 1926- *WhoAmW 91, WhoE 91*
Lybarger, Lee Hartshorne 1934- *WhoE 91*
Lybbert, Dan B. 1944- *St&PR 91*
Lybecker, Martin Earl 1945- *WhoEmL 91*
Lyberaki, Margarita 1910- *EncCoWW*
Lyberopoulos, Athanasios Nikolaos 1959- *WhoEmL 91*
Lybrook, Charles W. 1939- *WhoAm 90*
Lybrook, Charles William 1939- *St&PR 9*
Lycan, Kelly G. 1958- *WhoWrEP 89*
Lycan, Rebecca Tatum 1960- *WhoAmW 91, WhoSSW 91*
Lychak, John C *BiDrAPA 89*
Lycouris, Steve G. 1957- *WhoSSW 91*
Lyczko, Judith Elizabeth 1947- *WhoAmW 91*
Lyday-Lee, Kathy June 1953- *WhoSSW 9*
Lydden, Phillip Schuyler 1932- *St&PR 91*
Lyddon, Jan Wendee 1951- *WhoEmL 91*
Lyddon, William John 1951- *WhoSSW 91*
Lydecker, Beatrice *BioIn 16*
Lydecker, Richard Ackerman 1944- *St&PR 91*
Lyden, Fremont James 1926- *WhoAm 90*
Lyden, W.G., III 1952- *St&PR 91*
Lyden, William G., Jr. 1926- *St&PR 91*
Lyders, William Oscar 1927- *St&PR 91*
Lydgate, William A. 1909- *ODwPR 91*
Lydiard, Robert Bruce *BiDrAPA 89*
Lydic, Frank Aylsworth 1909- *WhoWor 9*
Lydick, J. Lee 1939- *St&PR 91*
Lydick, Lawrence Tupper 1916- *WhoAm 90, WhoWor 91*
Lydis, Marietta 1894- *BiDWomA*
Lydolph, Paul Edward 1924- *WhoAm 90*
Lydon, James M. 1928- *St&PR 91*
Lydon, Patrick Robert 1943- *BiDrAPA 89*
Lydon, Patrick S. 1942- *St&PR 91*
Lydon, Philip F. 1931- *St&PR 91*
Lydon, Thomas Michael 1923- *St&PR 91*
Lye, Benjamin 1945- *BiDrAPA 89*
Lye, Len 1901-1980 *BioIn 16*
Lye, Len 1901-1981 *WhoAmA 91N*
Lye, Veronica *BiDrAPA 89*
Lyell, Charles 1797-1875 *BioIn 16, WorAlBi*
Lyell, Edward Harvey 1944- *WhoWor 91*
Lyerly, Elaine M. 1951- *ODwPR 91*
Lyerly, Melia Lynn 1956- *WhoAmW 91*
Lyerly, William Voigt 1928- *St&PR 91*
Lyford, Cabot 1925- *WhoAmA 91, WhoE 91*
Lyford, Carol Gray 1956- *WhoAmW 91*
Lyford, Fred S. 1928- *St&PR 91*
Lyford, Joseph Philip 1918- *WhoWrEP 89*
Lyghte *NewAgMG*
Lyhne, H. M. *EncCoWW*
Lyke, James Patterson 1939- *WhoAm 90*
Lyke, Marguerite Richard 1929- *WhoSSW 91*
Lykes, Joseph T., III 1948- *WhoEmL 91*
Lykes, Joseph T., Jr. 1918- *St&PR 91*
Lyketsos, George C *BiDrAPA 89*
Lykins, Jay Arnold 1947- *WhoEmL 91*
Lykins, Marshall Herbert 1944- *St&PR 91, WhoAm 90*
Lykke, Jorgen 1939- *WhoWor 91*
Lyklema, Johannes 1930- *WhoWor 91*
Lykos, Peter George 1927- *WhoAm 90*
Lykoudis, Michael Nikephoros 1954- *WhoE 91*
Lykoudis, Paul S. 1926- *WhoAm 90*
Lyle, Aaron Kerr, III 1929- *WhoSSW 91*
Lyle, Carlene Williams *BiDrAPA 89*
Lyle, Carol Ann 1955- *BiDrAPA 89*
Lyle, Charles Thomas 1946- *WhoAm 90, WhoAmA 91*
Lyle, Claude Weiss 1932- *St&PR 91*
Lyle, Henry Richard Philip 1954- *WhoE 91*
Lyle, Idalee Martin 1907- *WhoWrEP 89*
Lyle, James Arthur 1945- *WhoSSW 91*
Lyle, John Donald 1933- *St&PR 91*
Lyle, John Robert, Jr. *BiDrAPA 89*
Lyle, Joseph M. 1912-1990 *BioIn 16*
Lyle, Joseph Melvin *NewYTBS 90*
Lyle, Katie Letcher 1938- *BioIn 16*
Lyle, Kevin R. 1960- *St&PR 91*
Lyle, Quentin Ernest 1958- *WhoE 91*
Lyle, Robert Edward 1926- *St&PR 91, WhoAm 90*
Lyle, Robert G. 1929- *St&PR 91*

Lyle, Sandy BioIn 16
Lyle, Sparky 1944- Ballpl 90 [port], BioIn 16
Lyle, Virginia Reavis 1926- WhoAm 90, WhoSSW 91
Lyle, William David 1950- WhoWrEP 89
Lyles, Aubrey EarBlAP
Lyles, Aubrey L 1884?-1932 DrBlPA 90
Lyles, John Oliver 1945- St&PR 91
Lyles, Marjorie Appleman 1946- WhoEmL 91
Lyles, Michael Roy 1955- BiDrAPA 89
Lyles, Virginia Henninger 1953- WhoSSW 91
Lyles, W. Bradford 1959- BiDrAPA 89
Lyles-Anderson, Barbara Dunbar 1954- WhoAmW 91
Lyly, John 1554?-1606 BioIn 16
Lyman, Abe 1897-1957 OxCPMus
Lyman, Arthur Joseph 1953- WhoAm 90
Lyman, Charles Peirson 1912- WhoAm 90
Lyman, David 1936- WhoWor 91
Lyman, Edward Wells, Jr. 1942- St&PR 91
Lyman, Elisabeth Reed 1912- WhoAmW 91
Lyman, Ellyn Elizabeth 1951- WhoAmW 91
Lyman, Ernestine Mosman 1932- WhoE 91
Lyman, Francis Marion 1840- AmLegL
Lyman, Frederic A. 1934- WhoAm 90
Lyman, Harold S. 1935- St&PR 91
Lyman, Henry 1915- WhoAm 90
Lyman, Jerry Ross 1941- St&PR 91
Lyman, John WhoAmA 91N
Lyman, John 1921- WhoAm 90
Lyman, John Root 1939- St&PR 91, WhoAm 90
Lyman, Peggy 1950- WhoAm 90, WhoAmW 91
Lyman, Princeton Nathan 1935- WhoAm 90, WhoWor 91
Lyman, Ransom Huffman, Jr. 1924- St&PR 91
Lyman, Richard Jeffrey 1963- WhoE 91
Lyman, Richard Wall 1923- WhoAm 90
Lyman, Robert Curtis 1959- BiDrAPA 89
Lyman, Ronald T. BioIn 16
Lyman, Stanford M 1933- ConAu 32NR
Lyman, Stephen Wesley 1945- WhoSSW 91
Lyman, Susan E. 1906-1976 AuBYP 90
Lyman, Thomas William 1926- WhoAmA 91
Lyman, William W., Jr. 1916- WhoE 91
Lymberis, Maria T 1938- BiDrAPA 89
Lymon, Frankie EncPR&S 89
Lymon, Frankie 1942-1968 DrBlPA 90
Lympany, Moura 1916- IntWWM 90, PenDiMP, WhoWor 91
Lyn, Wei-Tze 1917- St&PR 91
Lynam, C. David 1953- BiDrAPA 89
Lynam, Jill A. 1958- WhoAmW 91
Lynam, Jim 1941- WhoAm 90, WhoE 91
Lynam, Margaret FemiCLE
Lynam, Margaret BiDEWW
Lynam, Nicholas E. 1946- St&PR 91
Lynass, Jack 1933- St&PR 91
Lynch, Alexander P. 1952- St&PR 91
Lynch, Alison Marah BiDrAPA 89
Lynch, Annette Kay 1958- WhoAmW 91
Lynch, B. Quinton 1941- WhoE 91, WhoWor 91
Lynch, B. Suarez HispWr 90, MajTwCW
Lynch, Ben E. 1937- St&PR 91
Lynch, Benito 1885-1951 BioIn 16, HispWr 90
Lynch, Benjamin Leo 1923- WhoAm 90
Lynch, Bernard Joseph 1935- St&PR 91
Lynch, Betty WhoAmA 91
Lynch, Beverly Pfeifer 1935- WhoAm 90, WhoAmW 91
Lynch, Bill BioIn 16
Lynch, Brian BioIn 16
Lynch, Brian 1945- WhoE 91
Lynch, Candace Krafft 1952- WhoAmW 91
Lynch, Carole Lou 1935- WhoSSW 91
Lynch, Carole Yard 1951- WhoEmL 91, WhoSSW 91
Lynch, Catherine Gores 1943- WhoAmW 91, WhoSSW 91
Lynch, Charles Allen 1927- WhoAm 90
Lynch, Charles Thomas 1918- WhoAm 90
Lynch, D.R., Jr. 1922- St&PR 91
Lynch, Daniel J. 1930- St&PR 91
Lynch, Daniel O 1900- BiDrAPA 89
Lynch, Daniel Patrick 1949- WhoEmL 91
Lynch, David BioIn 16
Lynch, David 1946- ConAu 129, NewYTBS 90 [port], News 90 [port]
Lynch, David K. 1946- WhoAm 90
Lynch, David William 1932- WhoAm 90
Lynch, Dennis 1952- ODwPR 91
Lynch, Dennis L. 1952- St&PR 91
Lynch, Derrell Sevier 1935- WhoAm 90
Lynch, Donald Francis, Jr. 1946- WhoSSW 91
Lynch, Dorsey Henry 1947- St&PR 91
Lynch, Douglas Percy 1927- WhoWor 91
Lynch, Ed 1956- Ballpl 90
Lynch, Edward Francis 1945- WhoE 91
Lynch, Edward John 1933- WhoE 91
Lynch, Edward Stephen 1911- WhoAm 90
Lynch, Elizabeth Ann 1965- WhoAmW 91
Lynch, Erin Yvette 1963- WhoAmW 91
Lynch, Etta Lee 1924- WhoWrEP 89
Lynch, Fran J. 1948- WhoAmW 91, WhoE 91, WhoWor 91
Lynch, Fran Jackie 1948- WhoEmL 91
Lynch, Francis Charles 1944- WhoAm 90
Lynch, Francis Michael 1956- WhoEmL 91
Lynch, Francis Xavier 1918- WhoE 91
Lynch, Frank J. St&PR 91
Lynch, Frank W. 1921- St&PR 91
Lynch, Frank William 1921- WhoAm 90
Lynch, Frederick C., Jr. 1944- St&PR 91
Lynch, Gary Christopher 1947- WhoWor 91
Lynch, George B. 1920- St&PR 91
Lynch, Gerald 1944- WhoAmA 91
Lynch, Gerald John 1906- WhoAm 90
Lynch, Gerald Weldon 1937- WhoAm 90, WhoE 91
Lynch, Gregory Robert 1937- St&PR 91
Lynch, Hannah 1859-1904 FemiCLE
Lynch, Howard William 1947- St&PR 91
Lynch, J. Robert 1943- St&PR 91
Lynch, Jack BioIn 16
Lynch, James Bernard, Jr. 1933- St&PR 91
Lynch, James Brendan BiDrAPA 89
Lynch, James H. ODwPR 91
Lynch, James Henry, Jr. 1931- WhoAm 90
Lynch, James M. 1930- St&PR 91
Lynch, James Patrick 1952- WhoSSW 91
Lynch, James Terry 1946- WhoSSW 91
Lynch, James W. 1932- St&PR 91
Lynch, Jayne Thorner ODwPR 91
Lynch, Jerry 1930- Ballpl 90
Lynch, Joan Patricia 1956- BiDrAPA 89
Lynch, John A. 1938- WhoE 91
Lynch, John Andrew 1917- St&PR 91
Lynch, John Brown 1929- WhoAm 90, WhoWor 91
Lynch, John C. 1851-1941 AmLegL
Lynch, John D. 1926- St&PR 91
Lynch, John Henry 1938- St&PR 91
Lynch, John Joseph 1931- WhoAm 90
Lynch, John Joseph 1947- St&PR 91
Lynch, John Patrick 1943- WhoAm 90
Lynch, John Roy 1847-1939 AmLegL, BlkAmsC [port]
Lynch, John Thomas 1923- St&PR 91
Lynch, Joseph John 1949- WhoE 91
Lynch, Joseph Patrick 1926- St&PR 91
Lynch, Joyce BioIn 16
Lynch, Karen Emery 1958- WhoE 91
Lynch, Karen Renzulli 1946- WhoAmW 91
Lynch, Kelle Elizabeth 1966- WhoAmW 91
Lynch, Kelly BioIn 16
Lynch, Kenneth J. BioIn 16
Lynch, Kerry BioIn 16
Lynch, Kevin 1948- ODwPR 91
Lynch, Larry Allen 1947- WhoSSW 91
Lynch, Lee 1945- BioIn 16
Lynch, Leo A. 1926- St&PR 91
Lynch, Leslie O. 1946- St&PR 91
Lynch, Linda La Reau 1947- WhoAmW 91
Lynch, Linda Zanetti 1933- WhoE 91
Lynch, Lorenzo 1932- BioIn 16
Lynch, M. Teri 1952- St&PR 91
Lynch, Margaret Comard 1956- WhoEmL 91
Lynch, Margaret Teri 1952- WhoAm 90
Lynch, Maria Rosaria 1962- WhoE 91
Lynch, Mark Francis 1954- WhoWor 91
Lynch, Martha Schiesz 1962- WhoAmW 91
Lynch, Martin Andrew 1937- St&PR 91
Lynch, Mary Britten 1932- WhoAmA 91
Lynch, Mary Dennis 1920- WhoAmW 91
Lynch, Mary Patricia 1932- WhoAmW 91
Lynch, Michael D. 1947- St&PR 91
Lynch, Michael Eugene 1962- WhoSSW 91
Lynch, Michael H.T. 1944- St&PR 91
Lynch, Michael J. BioIn 16
Lynch, Michael J 1932- BiDrAPA 89
Lynch, Mike 1880-1927 Ballpl 90
Lynch, Mildred Virginia 1928- WhoSSW 91
Lynch, Milton Terrence 1931- WhoAm 90
Lynch, Monika Fehrmann 1932- WhoAmW 91
Lynch, Nancy Ann 1948- WhoAm 90
Lynch, Neil Lawrence 1930- WhoAm 90, WhoE 91
Lynch, Nnenna BioIn 16
Lynch, Owen Martin 1931- WhoAm 90
Lynch, Patricia A. 1958- WhoAmW 91
Lynch, Patricia Gates 1926- WhoAm 90, WhoAmW 91, WhoWor 91
Lynch, Patrick 1937- WhoAm 90
Lynch, Patrick David 1933- St&PR 91
Lynch, Patrick J. 1937- St&PR 91
Lynch, Paul Edward BiDrAPA 89
Lynch, Paul Vincent 1932- WhoE 91, WhoWor 91
Lynch, Paula Marie BiDrAPA 89
Lynch, Pauline Ann 1939- WhoAmW 91
Lynch, Peter BioIn 16
Lynch, Peter 1944- WhoWor 91
Lynch, Peter John 1936- WhoAm 90, WhoWor 91
Lynch, Peter Michael 1925- St&PR 91
Lynch, Podie BioIn 16
Lynch, Priscilla WhoE 91
Lynch, Ray NewAgMG
Lynch, Richard BioIn 16
Lynch, Richard William 1936- St&PR 91
Lynch, Robert Dubois BiDrAPA 89
Lynch, Robert J. BioIn 16
Lynch, Robert John 1937- St&PR 91
Lynch, Robert L. 1918- St&PR 91
Lynch, Robert Martin 1950- WhoEmL 91
Lynch, Robert Merrill 1919- St&PR 91
Lynch, Robyn Delphine 1960- WhoAmW 91
Lynch, Ronald P. 1935- St&PR 91
Lynch, Rose Peabody 1949- WhoE 91, WhoEmL 91
Lynch, Sean Dennis 1957- WhoE 91
Lynch, Sheila 1958- ODwPR 91
Lynch, Sherry Kay 1957- WhoAmW 91
Lynch, Sonia 1938- WhoAmW 91, WhoE 91, WhoWor 91
Lynch, Stephanie Nadine 1951- WhoAmW 91
Lynch, Thomas 1749-1779 EncCRAm
Lynch, Thomas 1922- BiDrAPA 89
Lynch, Thomas Dexter 1942- WhoSSW 91
Lynch, Thomas Francis 1938- WhoAm 90
Lynch, Thomas Gregory 1954- WhoE 91
Lynch, Thomas J. 1859-1924 Ballpl 90
Lynch, Thomas M. 1926- St&PR 91
Lynch, Thomas Peter 1924- WhoAm 90
Lynch, Thomas W. 1930- St&PR 91
Lynch, Thomas Wimp 1930- WhoAm 90
Lynch, Timothy Edward 1948- IntWWM 90
Lynch, Timothy Jeremiah-Mahoney 1952- WhoEmL 91
Lynch, Timothy John 1941- St&PR 91
Lynch, Tom 1950- WhoAmA 91
Lynch, Vivian Elizabeth 1940- WhoAmW 91
Lynch, W. Ware BioIn 16
Lynch, Walter Francis, Jr. 1926- WhoSSW 91
Lynch, Wendell A. 1951- St&PR 91
Lynch, William Dennis, Jr. 1945- WhoAm 90
Lynch, William F BiDrAPA 89
Lynch, William F. 1952- St&PR 91
Lynch, William L., Jr. 1932- St&PR 91
Lynch, William Raymond BiDrAPA 89
Lynch, William Redington 1928- WhoAm 90
Lynch, William Thomas, Jr. 1942- WhoAm 90
Lynch, William Walker 1926- WhoAm 90
Lynch, William Wright, Jr. 1936- WhoSSW 91
Lynch-Brennan, Margaret Elizabeth 1950- WhoAmW 91
Lynch Davis, B. ConAu 33NR, HispWr 90, MajTwCW
Lynch-Nakache, Margaret 1932- WhoAmA 91
Lyncker, Anton PenDiDA 89
Lynd, Jeffrey Lee 1952- WhoSSW 91
Lynd, Robert 1879-1949 DcLB 98 [port]
Lynd, Sylvia 1888-1952 FemiCLE
Lynde, Paul 1926-1982 WorAlBi
Lynde, Stan 1931- EncACom, WhoAm 90, WhoAmA 91
Lynden-Bell, Donald 1935- WhoWor 91
Lyndon, Amy WhoWrEP 89
Lyndon, Keith 1941- WhoSSW 91
Lyndon, Maynard 1907- WhoAm 90
Lynds, Beverly Turner 1929- WhoAm 90
Lynds, Clyde 1936- WhoAmA 91
Lynds, Dennis TwCCr&M 91
Lynds, Dennis 1924- BioIn 16, WhoWrEP 89
Lynds, Jeffrey Clark BiDrAPA 89
Lyne, Adrian BioIn 16
Lyne, Austin Francis 1927- WhoAm 90
Lyne, Dorothy-Arden 1928- WhoAmW 91, WhoE 91
Lyne, Fritz Lanham, Jr. 1955- WhoEmL 91
Lyne, Kerry Richard 1930- WhoAm 90
Lyne, Michael 1912-1989 AnObit 1989
Lyne, Richard Clement 1948- IntWWM 90
Lynes, Russell 1910- WhoAmA 91, WhoWrEP 89
Lynes, Russell, Jr. 1910- WhoAm 90
Lyness, Jeffrey Marc 1960- BiDrAPA 89
Lynett, George Vincent 1943- WhoAm 90
Lynett, Lawrence Wilson 1921- WhoAm 90, WhoWor 91
Lynett, Matthew Joseph 1948- St&PR 91, WhoAm 90
Lynett, William R. 1947- St&PR 91
Lyng, Richard Edmund 1918- BiDrUSE 89, WhoAm 90, WhoWor 91
Lyngberg, Bent Soren 1942- WhoWor 91
Lyngso, Jakob Buus 1947- WhoWor 91
Lyngved, Viggo R. 1945- St&PR 91
Lynham, C. Richard 1942- St&PR 91
Lynham, Charles Richard 1942- WhoAm 90
Lynk, Stanley Mark BiDrAPA 89
Lynley, Carol 1942- BioIn 16
Lynn, Amy BioIn 16
Lynn, Arthur B. 1947- St&PR 91
Lynn, Arthur Dellert, Jr. 1921- WhoAm 90
Lynn, Barry X. 1951- WhoAm 90
Lynn, C. Stephen 1947- St&PR 91
Lynn, Charles Stephen 1947- WhoAm 90
Lynn, Christine Wood 1955- WhoSSW 91
Lynn, Clabe W, Jr. 1932- BiDrAPA 89
Lynn, Clarence E. 1928- St&PR 91
Lynn, Cynthia Schumo 1951- St&PR 91
Lynn, David Ayers 1936- St&PR 91
Lynn, David John 1948- BiDrAPA 89
Lynn, Dennis Brown 1946- St&PR 91
Lynn, Donna M. 1945- ODwPR 91
Lynn, Donna Maria 1945- WhoAmW 91, WhoE 91
Lynn, Donna Marie 1960- WhoAmW 91
Lynn, E.M. 1918- St&PR 91
Lynn, Edward Joseph 1938- BiDrAPA 89
Lynn, Eugene Matthew 1918- WhoWor 91
Lynn, Evelyn Joan 1930- WhoSSW 91
Lynn, Fred BioIn 16
Lynn, Fred 1952- Ballpl 90 [port]
Lynn, Fredric Michael 1952- WhoAm 90
Lynn, Gene E 1931- BiDrAPA 89
Lynn, George 1915-1989 BioIn 16
Lynn, Harold P 1915- BiDrAPA 89
Lynn, James Dougal 1934- WhoAm 90
Lynn, James F. WhoAm 90
Lynn, James Joseph 1947- WhoSSW 91
Lynn, James N ODwPR 91
Lynn, James T. 1927- WhoAm 90, WhoE 91
Lynn, James Thomas 1927- BiDrUSE 89
Lynn, James William 1949- WhoE 91
Lynn, Janet 1953- WhoAm 90
Lynn, Joe Joshua 1931- St&PR 91
Lynn, John Daniel 1915- WhoE 91
Lynn, John Warren 1921- St&PR 91, WhoAm 90
Lynn, Kathryn Louise 1953- WhoAmW 91
Lynn, Kenneth Clyde 1924- WhoE 91
Lynn, Kenneth Schuyler 1923- WhoAm 90
Lynn, Laurence Edwin, Jr. 1937- WhoAm 90
Lynn, Linda Solter BiDrAPA 89
Lynn, Loretta BioIn 16, WhoNeCM C [port]
Lynn, Loretta 1935- OxCPMus, WorAlBi
Lynn, Loretta Webb 1935- WhoAm 90, WhoAmW 91
Lynn, Lynn Marie 1961- ODwPR 91
Lynn, Margaret E. 1924- BioIn 16, NotWoAT
Lynn, Mary 1951- WhoAmW 91
Lynn, Merrill 1930- WhoE 91
Lynn, Michael E., III BioIn 16
Lynn, Michael Edward, III 1936- WhoAm 90
Lynn, Michael Francis 1947- St&PR 91
Lynn, Milton B. 1918- St&PR 91
Lynn, Mitchell Gordon 1948- WhoAm 90
Lynn, Nanci C. Koperski 1962- WhoAmW 91
Lynn, Nanne Joyce 1938- WhoAmW 91
Lynn, Naomi B. 1933- WhoAm 90
Lynn, Otis Clyde 1927- WhoAm 90
Lynn, Patricia AuBYP 90
Lynn, Patricia Anita 1943- WhoAmW 91
Lynn, Pauline Judith Wardlow 1920- WhoAmW 91
Lynn, Robert 1933- BiDrAPA 89
Lynn, Robert G. 1950- WhoAm 90
Lynn, Robert Lilburn 1937- St&PR 91
Lynn, Robert R. 1926- St&PR 91
Lynn, Robert T. St&PR 91N
Lynn, Robert T. 1937- WhoAm 90, WhoE 91
Lynn, Robert Wood BioIn 16
Lynn, Robert Wood 1925- WhoAm 90
Lynn, Sam WhoSSW 91
Lynn, Sandra Dykes 1944- WhoWrEP 89
Lynn, Sheilah Ann 1947- WhoAmW 91, WhoSSW 91
Lynn, Stephen Allen 1945- WhoWor 91
Lynn, Steven Marc 1953- BiDrAPA 89
Lynn, Storme BiDrAPA 89
Lynn, Sylvia Krein 1944- WhoAmW 91
Lynn, Theodore Stanley 1937- WhoAm 90, WhoE 91
Lynn, Thomas EncO&P 3
Lynn, Thomas Edward 1930- WhoWrEP 89
Lynn, Thomas Neil, Jr. 1930- WhoAm 90
Lynn, Thomas W. 1941- St&PR 91
Lynn, Tony Lee 1939- WhoSSW 91
Lynn, Vera 1917- IntWWM 90, OxCPMus
Lynn, Walter Royal 1928- WhoAm 90
Lynn, Wayne Reed 1944- WhoSSW 91

Lynn, William B. 1945- *St&PR 91*
Lynn, William Brian 1945- *WhoAm 90*
Lynn, William Max 1927- *WhoWor 91*
Lynne, Andree *EncCoWW*
Lynne, Gillian *BioIn 16*
Lynne, Gillian Barbara *WhoAm 90, WhoWor 91*
Lynne, Janice C. 1954- *WhoAmW 91*
Lynne, Jeff 1942- *WhoAm 90*
Lynne, Jeff 1947- *ConMus 5 [port]*
Lynne, Seybourn Harris 1907- *WhoAm 90*
Lynne, Shelby *WhoNeCM [port]*
Lynne, Shelby 1968- *ConMus 5*
Lynott, John Anthony 1936- *St&PR 91, WhoAm 90*
Lynskey, Edward Charles 1956- *WhoWrEP 89*
Lynton, Ann *ConAu 30NR*
Lynton, Edith F. *BioIn 16*
Lynton, Ernest Albert 1926- *WhoAm 90*
Lynum, Curtis O. 1917- *BioIn 16*
Lynwander, Peter 1936- *St&PR 91*
Lynx *MajTwCW*
Lynyak, Robert M. 1942- *St&PR 91*
Lynyrd Skynyrd *EncPR&S 89*
Lyon, Agnes 1762-1840 *FemiCLE*
Lyon, Benjamin Noel 1945- *WhoSSW 91*
Lyon, Berenice Iola Clark 1920- *WhoAmW 91*
Lyon, Birgit Blatt 1933- *WhoWor 91*
Lyon, Bryce Dale 1920- *WhoAm 90*
Lyon, Buck *ConAu 31NR*
Lyon, C. Dale 1923- *St&PR 91*
Lyon, C.H. Randolph 1943- *St&PR 91*
Lyon, Carl Francis, Jr. 1943- *WhoAm 90*
Lyon, Cecil Burton 1903- *BioIn 16, WhoAm 90*
Lyon, Charles P. 1934- *St&PR 91*
Lyon, Charles Stuart *BioIn 16*
Lyon, Cheryl *BioIn 16*
Lyon, Christopher 1949- *ConAu 132*
Lyon, Constance Cherie 1949- *WhoSSW 91*
Lyon, David B *BiDrAPA 89*
Lyon, David Norman 1938- *IntWWM 90*
Lyon, David William 1941- *St&PR 91, WhoAm 90*
Lyon, David William 1949- *WhoWrEP 89*
Lyon, E. Wilson 1904-1989 *BioIn 16*
Lyon, Frank Emery, Jr. 1928- *St&PR 91*
Lyon, Fred W. 1929-1989 *BioIn 16*
Lyon, Gary Keith 1959- *WhoSSW 91*
Lyon, Geoffrey Dale 1945- *St&PR 91*
Lyon, George Ella 1949- *AuBYP 90, LiHiK, WhoWrEP 89*
Lyon, George R. 1923- *St&PR 91*
Lyon, George Robert *NewYTBS 90*
Lyon, George Robert 1923-1990 *BioIn 16*
Lyon, Harllee Wingate 1935- *St&PR 91*
Lyon, Harold Clifford, Jr. 1935- *WhoWrEP 89*
Lyon, Harvey T. 1927- *St&PR 91*
Lyon, Hugh C. 1931- *St&PR 91*
Lyon, James Burroughs 1930- *WhoAm 90, WhoE 91, WhoWor 91*
Lyon, James Karl 1934- *WhoAm 90*
Lyon, James McDonald 1952- *WhoAm 90*
Lyon, James Robert 1927- *WhoAm 90*
Lyon, James Travers 1922- *WhoAm 90*
Lyon, Jeff 1943- *ConAu 130*
Lyon, Jeffrey 1943- *WhoAm 90*
Lyon, Jessica *AuBYP 90*
Lyon, Kathleen Anne *BiDrAPA 89*
Lyon, Keith Geoffrey 1951- *WhoEmL 91*
Lyon, Lawrence Bruce 1947- *WhoAm 90*
Lyon, Lilian Bowes 1895-1949 *FemiCLE*
Lyon, Linda Gale *ConAu 129*
Lyon, Lyman R. *AuBYP 90*
Lyon, Martha Sue 1935- *WhoAmW 91*
Lyon, Mary 1797-1849 *BioAmW, BioIn 16, WorAlBi*
Lyon, Mary F. *BioIn 16*
Lyon, Matthew 1749-1822 *BioIn 16*
Lyon, Michael 1943- *St&PR 91*
Lyon, Norma Duffield 1929- *WhoAmW 91*
Lyon, Philip Kirkland 1944- *WhoWor 91*
Lyon, Randolph Matthew 1955- *WhoE 91*
Lyon, Richard 1923- *WhoAm 90*
Lyon, Richard 1936- *St&PR 91*
Lyon, Richard Eugene, Jr. 1932- *WhoAm 90*
Lyon, Richard Harold 1929- *WhoAm 90*
Lyon, Robert 1810-1858 *BioIn 16*
Lyon, Robert F 1952- *WhoAmA 91*
Lyon, Robert Louis 1906- *WhoE 91, WhoWor 91*
Lyon, Russell Thomas 1940- *St&PR 91*
Lyon, Samuel C. 1932- *St&PR 91*
Lyon, Sherman Orwig 1939- *WhoAm 90, WhoSSW 91*
Lyon, Sterling 1927- *WhoAm 90*
Lyon, Steven William 1963- *WhoE 91*
Lyon, Sue 1946- *BioIn 16*
Lyon, Ted 1939- *WhoWrEP 89*
Lyon, Trent W. *St&PR 91*
Lyon, Virginia Rose 1928- *WhoAmW 91*
Lyon, Waldo Kampmeier 1914- *WhoAm 90*
Lyon, Wayne Barton 1932- *St&PR 91, WhoAm 90*
Lyon, Wilford Charles, Jr. 1935- *St&PR 91, WhoAm 90, WhoSSW 91*
Lyon, William C 1915- *BiDrAPA 89*
Lyon, William Carl 1938- *WhoAm 90, WhoE 91*
Lyon, William Penn 1822-1913 *AmLegL*
Lyons, Allan Stuart 1929- *WhoE 91*
Lyons, Arthur 1946- *TwCCr&M 91*
Lyons, Barry 1960- *Ballpl 90*
Lyons, Beauvais 1958- *WhoAmA 91*
Lyons, Beth 1960- *ODwPR 91*
Lyons, Champ, Jr. 1940- *WhoAm 90*
Lyons, Charles R. 1933- *WhoAm 90*
Lyons, Cherie Ann 1948- *WhoEmL 91*
Lyons, Chopeta C. 1949- *WhoWrEP 89*
Lyons, Daniel Joseph, Jr. 1937- *WhoE 91*
Lyons, David Alexander 1954- *BiDrAPA 89*
Lyons, David Barry 1935- *WhoAm 90*
Lyons, David F. 1947- *St&PR 91*
Lyons, Dennis G. 1931- *St&PR 91*
Lyons, Dennis Gerald 1931- *WhoAm 90*
Lyons, Denny 1866-1929 *Ballpl 90*
Lyons, Don *BioIn 16*
Lyons, Edward 1920- *WhoWor 91*
Lyons, Edward Timothy 1946- *WhoWrEP 89*
Lyons, Elaine Turner *WhoE 91*
Lyons, Ellis 1915- *WhoAm 90*
Lyons, Francis Joseph 1921- *WhoAm 90*
Lyons, Franics E, Jr 1943- *WhoAmA 91*
Lyons, Frank J. 1926- *St&PR 91*
Lyons, Frederick William, Jr. 1935- *WhoAm 90*
Lyons, Gene Martin 1924- *WhoAm 90*
Lyons, George Sage 1936- *WhoAm 90*
Lyons, Heidi Held 1962- *WhoAmW 91*
Lyons, Helen Hadassah *BioIn 16*
Lyons, Henry R *BiDrAPA 89*
Lyons, Henry Warren 1924- *St&PR 91*
Lyons, James David 1935- *St&PR 91*
Lyons, James Edward 1952- *WhoAm 90, WhoE 91*
Lyons, James Francis 1934- *WhoAm 90, WhoE 91*
Lyons, James Stephen 1941- *WhoAm 90*
Lyons, Jerry Lee 1939- *WhoAm 90, WhoWor 91*
Lyons, Jim *BioIn 16*
Lyons, Jimmy *Ballpl 90*
Lyons, Joan 1937- *WhoAmA 91*
Lyons, John 1932- *ConAu 132*
Lyons, John Bartholomew 1916- *WhoAm 90*
Lyons, John David 1946- *WhoAm 90*
Lyons, John Edward *WhoAm 90*
Lyons, John Edward 1926- *St&PR 91*
Lyons, John Matthew 1948- *WhoE 91, WhoWor 91*
Lyons, John Ormsby 1927- *WhoAm 90*
Lyons, John Winship 1930- *WhoAm 90*
Lyons, Joseph Chisholm 1927- *St&PR 91, WhoAm 90*
Lyons, Joseph Norman 1901- *WhoAm 90, WhoWor 91*
Lyons, Larry D. *BioIn 16*
Lyons, Laurence 1911- *St&PR 91, WhoAm 90*
Lyons, Laurie Wilkinson 1954- *WhoEmL 91*
Lyons, Lawrence Ernest 1922- *WhoWor 91*
Lyons, Lawrence Michael 1919- *St&PR 91*
Lyons, Leland 1923-1983 *DcNaB 1981*
Lyons, Linda Mary 1949- *WhoAmW 91*
Lyons, Lisa 1950- *WhoAmA 91*
Lyons, Lloyd Carson 1942- *St&PR 91*
Lyons, Marcus *MajTwCW*
Lyons, Margaret J. 1964- *WhoAmW 91*
Lyons, Margaret V. 1942- *WhoAmW 91*
Lyons, Michael Henry, II 1936- *St&PR 91*
Lyons, Michael John 1952- *WhoE 91*
Lyons, Michael T. 1934- *St&PR 91*
Lyons, Orville Richard 1942- *St&PR 91*
Lyons, Paul Edward 1935- *WhoE 91*
Lyons, Paul Michael 1932- *WhoAm 90*
Lyons, Paul Vincent 1939- *WhoAm 90*
Lyons, Phillip Michael, Sr. 1941- *WhoSSW 91, WhoWor 91*
Lyons, Phyllis Ilona 1942- *WhoWrEP 89*
Lyons, Renee C. *BiDrAPA 89*
Lyons, Richard Chapman 1919- *WhoAm 90, WhoWor 91*
Lyons, Richard E. 1920- *WhoWrEP 89*
Lyons, Richard Kent 1961- *WhoE 91*
Lyons, Richard M. 1935- *WhoWrEP 89*
Lyons, Robert E. *St&PR 91*
Lyons, Robert John 1954- *St&PR 91*
Lyons, Robert P. 1912- *BioIn 16*
Lyons, Robert R. 1944- *St&PR 91*
Lyons, Roger *BioIn 16*
Lyons, Stephen Michael, II 1931- *St&PR 91*
Lyons, Steve 1960- *Ballpl 90*
Lyons, Steven A. *ODwPR 91*
Lyons, Ted 1900-1986 *Ballpl 90 [port]*
Lyons, Terrence Allan 1949- *WhoEmL 91*
Lyons, Terry A. 1949- *St&PR 91*
Lyons, Thomas J. 1928- *St&PR 91*
Lyons, Victoria Mary 1953- *WhoAmW 91*
Lyons, William 1901-1985 *DcNaB 1981*
Lyons, William Drewry 1927- *St&PR 91*
Lyons, William H 1914- *BiDrAPA 89*
Lyons, William P. 1941- *St&PR 91*
Lyons, William W. 1935- *St&PR 91*
Lyou, Keith Weeks 1930- *WhoAmW 91*
Lyou-Kim, Chung Hi *BiDrAPA 89*
Lyre, Pinchbeck *MajTwCW*
Lyrene, Stephen Arthur *BiDrAPA 89*
Lyrintzis, Anastasios Sotirios 1959- *WhoE 91*
Lysak, George Julian 1943- *St&PR 91*
Lysander, Rick 1953- *Ballpl 90*
Lysaught, Jerome Paul 1930- *WhoE 91*
Lysaught, Thomas Francis 1936- *St&PR 91, WhoAm 90, WhoSSW 91*
Lyseight, Cynthia Anna Maria 1950- *WhoAmW 91*
Lysen, Edward John 1937- *St&PR 91*
Lysenko, Trofim 1898-1976 *WorAlBi*
Lysenko, Trofim Denisovich 1898-1976 *DcScB S2*
Lysenko, Vera 1910-1975 *FemiCLE*
Lysinger, Rex Jackson 1937- *St&PR 91, WhoAm 90, WhoSSW 91*
Lyskowski, John Casimir 1951- *BiDrAPA 89*
Lyskowski, Maria M 1922- *BiDrAPA 89*
Lysne, Douglas L. 1944- *St&PR 91*
Lysne, Dwight Howard 1955- *BiDrAPA 89*
Lysons, Kenneth 1923- *ConAu 33NR*
Lystad, Mary Hanemann 1928- *WhoAm 90, WhoWrEP 89*
Lystad, Robert Arthur Lunde 1920- *WhoAm 90*
Lyster, Shirley Ann 1929- *WhoAmW 91*
Lystra, Helen Percy 1939- *WhoWrEP 89*
Lysun, Gregory 1924- *WhoAmA 91, WhoWor 91*
Lysy, Alberto 1935- *IntWWM 90, PenDiMP*
Lysy, Antonio 1963- *IntWWM 90*
Lysyk, Kenneth Martin 1934- *WhoAm 90*
Lytle, Andrew Nelson 1902- *WhoAm 90*
Lytle, Cecil *NewAgMG*
Lytle, J. Ellen 1956- *WhoEmL 91*
Lytle, John Stephen 1951- *WhoSSW 91*
Lytle, Michael Allen 1946- *WhoE 91, WhoEmL 91, WhoWor 91*
Lytle, Mike 1948- *St&PR 91*
Lytle, Richard 1935- *WhoAmA 91*
Lytle, Richard Harold 1937- *WhoAm 90*
Lytle, Victoria Elizabeth 1951- *WhoAmW 91*
Lytras, Panayiotis 1947- *WhoWor 91*
Lyttelton, Christopher Charles 1947- *WhoWor 91*
Lyttelton, Edith 1865?-1948 *EncPaPR 91*
Lyttelton, Edith 187-?-1948 *EncO&P 3*
Lyttelton, Humphrey 1921- *BioIn 16, ConAu 129, OxCPMus*
Lyttelton, Humphrey Richard Adeane 1921- *IntWWM 90, WhoWor 91*
Lyttle, Cosima Venet 1948- *WhoSSW 91*
Lyttle, Douglas Alfred 1919- *WhoAm 90*
Lyttle, Jim 1946- *Ballpl 90*
Lyttle, Richard B. 1927- *AuBYP 90*
Lyttle, Thomas Peyton 1947- *WhoSSW 91*
Lytton, Bart *WhoAmA 91N*
Lytton, Bulwer 1803-1873 *EncO&P 3*
Lytton, Constance B *WhoAmA 91*
Lytton, Edith, Countess of 1841-1936 *BioIn 16*
Lytton, Edward Bulwer 1803-1873 *BioIn 16*
Lytton, George J 1915- *BiDrAPA 89*
Lytton, Henry 1865-1936 *PenDiMP*
Lytton, Henry A. 1860-1936 *OxCPMus*
Lytton, Rosina Bulwer- 1802-1882 *BioIn 16, FemiCLE*
Lytton, Sidney M 1927- *BiDrAPA 89*
Lytton, William B. 1948- *WhoAm 90*
Lyubimov, Yuri *BioIn 16*

M

M, A *BiDEWW*
M., Earle *BioIn 16*
M, M *BiDEWW*
M., Terezka *EncCoWW*
M, W *BiDEWW*
M. A., Oxon *EncO&P 3*
M.C. *EncCoWW*
M-Roblin, John 1958- *WhoE 91*
M.-V., Marg. *EncCoWW*
Ma, Guru *BioIn 16*
Ma Haide 1910-1988 *BioIn 16*
Ma Tongchang *BioIn 16*
Ma, Fai 1954- *WhoEmL 91*
Ma, John T 1920- *ConAu 31NR*
Ma, Jun Sheng *BiDrAPA 89*
Ma, Pearl 1928-1989 *BioIn 16, ConAu 130*
Ma, Shui-Long 1939- *WhoWor 91*
Ma, Trang To 1947- *BiDrAPA 89*
Ma, Tsu Sheng 1911- *WhoWor 91*
Ma, Xiaoyun 1945- *WhoEmL 91*
Ma, Yo Yo *WhoAm 90, WhoWor 91*
Ma, Yo-Yo 1955- *BioIn 16, IntWWM 90, PenDiMP*
Ma, Yuan Yuan 1952- *WhoE 91*
Ma Hood, James Herbert 1937- *WhoWrEP 89*
Maag, John C. 1949- *St&PR 91*
Maag, Peter 1919- *IntWWM 90, PenDiMP, WhoWor 91*
Maag, Urs Richard 1938- *WhoAm 90*
Maany, Iradj 1941- *BiDrAPA 89*
Maarbjerg, Mary Penzold 1943- *St&PR 91*
Maart, Rozena *BioIn 16*
Maas, Albert L. 1926- *St&PR 91*
Maas, Curtis N. 1955- *St&PR 91*
Maas, Darryl Wayne 1960- *WhoEmL 91*
Maas, Duane Harris 1927- *WhoAm 90*
Maas, Duke 1929- *Ballpl 90*
Maas, Gary William 1945- *WhoSSW 91*
Maas, Gerald L. 1937- *St&PR 91*
Maas, Gerald Lee 1937- *WhoAm 90*
Maas, James Beryl 1938- *WhoAm 90, WhoWor 91*
Maas, James W *BiDrAPA 89*
Maas, Jane Brown *WhoAm 90, WhoAmW 91*
Maas, Jeremy 1928- *ConAu 32NR*
Maas, Margaret Ellen 1949- *BiDrAPA 89*
Maas, Marion Elizabeth 1930- *WhoAmA 91*
Maas, Michael 1931- *WhoAm 90*
Maas, Peter 1929- *WhoAm 90, WhoWrEP 89*
Maas, Richard Theodore 1957- *WhoSSW 91*
Maas, Robert *PenDiMP*
Maas, Utz 1942- *WhoWor 91*
Maas, Werner Karl 1921- *WhoAm 90*
Maasha, Ntungwa 1941- *WhoSSW 91*
Maasik, Rein 1942- *St&PR 91*
Maasilta, Timo Tuomas Mikael 1954- *WhoWor 91*
Maasoumi, Esfandiar 1950- *WhoSSW 91*
Maass, Arthur 1917- *WhoAm 90*
Maass, Clara Louise 1876-1901 *BioIn 16*
Maass, James Eric 1942- *St&PR 91*
Maass, R. Andrew 1946- *WhoAm 90, WhoSSW 91*
Maass, Richard Andrew 1946- *WhoAmA 91*
Maass, Siegrfried Lothar 1937- *WhoWor 91*
Maass, Vera Sonja 1931- *WhoAmW 91*
Maass-Robinson, Saundra Ann *BiDrAPA 89*
Maat, Benjamin 1947- *WhoWor 91*
Maatman, Gerald Leonard 1930- *St&PR 91, WhoAm 90*
Maazel, Lorin 1930- *BioIn 16, IntWWM 90, PenDiMP, WhoAm 90, WhoE 91, WhoWor 91, WorAlBi*
Mabbs, Edward Carl 1921- *St&PR 91, WhoAm 90*
Mabe, Bob 1929- *Ballpl 90*
Mabe, Chauncey 1955- *WhoWrEP 89*
Mabe, Donald W. *WhoAm 90*
Mabee, Bruce Orland 1950- *WhoEmL 91*
Mabee, Carleton 1914- *WhoAm 90, WhoWrEP 89*
Mabee, Gwynne 1924- *WhoWor 91*
Mabee, Keith 1947- *ODwPR 91*
Mabee, Keith Vance 1947- *St&PR 91*
Mabee, Sandra Ivonne Noriega 1955- *IntWWM 90*
Mabery, D. L. 1953- *BioIn 16*
Mabie, Gifford M. 1940- *St&PR 91*
Mabie, Marshall Lewis 1936- *St&PR 91*
Mabie, Ruth Marie *WhoAmW 91*
Mabileau, Albert 1927- *WhoWor 91*
Mabley, Edward T. *BioIn 16*
Mabley, Jack 1915- *WhoAm 90*
Mabley, Jackie 1897-1975 *DrBlPA 90*
Mabley, Moms 1897-1975 *BioIn 16*
Mabomba, Rodrick Samson 1948- *WhoWor 91*
Mabrey, Harold Richard 1927- *St&PR 91*
Mabrey, Thomas W. 1862- *AmLegL*
Mabrouk, Sarah Lou 1962- *WhoE 91*
Mabry, Donald R. 1933- *St&PR 91*
Mabry, Drake 1928- *WhoAm 90*
Mabry, Edward L. 1897-1989 *BioIn 16*
Mabry, George L., Jr. *NewYTBS 90*
Mabry, Guy O. 1926- *WhoAm 90*
Mabry, Guy Orrin 1926- *St&PR 91*
Mabry, James C. 1937- *ODwPR 91*
Mabry, Michael *BioIn 16*
Mabry, Nelloise Johnson 1921- *WhoSSW 91, WhoWor 91*
Mabry, Raymond Edward 1938- *IntWWM 90*
Mabry, Sharon Cody 1945- *WhoSSW 91*
Mabry, Wilson Drake 1950- *IntWWM 90*
Mabus, Raymond Edwin, Jr. 1948- *WhoAm 90, WhoSSW 91, WhoWor 91*
Mac, Daljit Singh *BiDrAPA 89*
Mac, Paula Marie 1961- *WhoAmW 91*
Maca, Allan Leigh 1934- *St&PR 91*
MacAdam, Preston *ConAu 130*
MacAdam, Walter Kavanagh 1913- *WhoAm 90*
Macadam, William Foster, Jr. 1942- *St&PR 91*
Macadams, John David 1933- *St&PR 91*
Macado, Mary Stanley 1912- *WhoWrEP 89*
Mac Afee, Norman 1943- *WhoWrEP 89*
MacAgy, Douglas G 1913-1973 *AuBYP 90*
Macagy, Douglas Guernsey 1913-1973 *WhoAmA 91N*
Macagy, Jermayne *WhoAmA 91N*
Macak, Ivan 1935- *IntWWM 90*
Macal, Zdenek *PenDiMP*
Macal, Zdenek 1936- *IntWWM 90*
Macaleer, Richard James 1934- *St&PR 91*
Macaleese, John Elmer 1932- *St&PR 91*
MacAlister, Ian *ConAu 30NR, TwCCr&M 91*
Macalister, Kim Porter 1954- *WhoAm 90, WhoAmW 91*
Macalister, Paul Ritter 1901- *WhoAmA 91*
Macalister-Smith, Peter Nigel Edward 1951- *WhoWor 91*
Mac Allister, Fern Esther *BiDrAPA 89*
Macallister, Jack A. 1927- *St&PR 91*
MacAllister, Jack Alfred 1927- *WhoAm 90*
MacAlpine, Loretta 1960- *WhoAmW 91*
Macaluso, Charles A. 1928- *St&PR 91*
Macaluso, James 1943- *WhoSSW 91*
Macaluso, Vincent 1937- *St&PR 91*
Macam, Ester S *BiDrAPA 89*
Macan, William Alexander, IV 1942- *WhoAm 90*
Macandrew, E. Gail *BioIn 16*
Macann, Rodney 1950- *IntWWM 90*
Mac Aonghusa, Proinsias Sean 1933- *WhoWor 91*
Macaray, Lawrence Richard 1921- *WhoAmA 91*
Macario, Alberto Juan Lorenzo 1935- *WhoAm 90*
Macarthur, Arthur 1845-1912 *WorAlBi*
MacArthur, Brian Henry 1949- *WhoE 91, WhoEmL 91*
MacArthur, Charles 1895-1956 *BioIn 16, WorAlBi*
MacArthur, Diana Taylor 1933- *WhoAmW 91, WhoWor 91*
MacArthur, Donald 1901-1990 *BioIn 16*
MacArthur, Douglas 1880-1964 *BioIn 16, EncJap, WorAlBi*
MacArthur, Douglas 1909- *BioIn 16*
MacArthur, Douglas, II 1909- *WhoE 91*
Macarthur, Elizabeth 1769-1850 *FemiCLE*
Macarthur, Gloria 1924- *WhoWrEP 89*
MacArthur, James 1937- *WhoAm 90, WorAlBi*
Macarthur, James Y. 1938- *St&PR 91*
Macarthur, John Daniel 1930- *St&PR 91*
MacArthur, John Roderick 1956- *WhoAm 90, WhoE 91*
Mac Arthur, Loren 1935- *WhoWrEP 89*
MacArthur, Robert Helmer 1930-1972 *DcScB S2*
MacArthur, Sandra Lea 1946- *WhoAmW 91*
Mac Arthur, William Henry 1936- *WhoSSW 91*
Macarthur-Onslow, Annette 1933- *AuBYP 90*
Macartney, Frank P. 1931- *St&PR 91*
Macartney, Michelle Lynn 1963- *WhoAmW 91*
Macasaet, Joanne Julia M 1950- *BiDrAPA 89*
Macatangay, Cesar Torres *BiDrAPA 89*
Macatangay, Nelson M 1939- *BiDrAPA 89*
Macatee, Bill *BioIn 16*
Macaulay, Alice Ittner *WhoAmW 91*
Macaulay, Ann Saunders 1958- *WhoAmW 91*
Macaulay, Catharine 1731-1791 *FemiCLE*
Macaulay, Catherine 1731-1791 *DcLB 104 [port]*
Macaulay, Catherine Sawbridge 1731-1791 *BioIn 16*
Macaulay, Colin A. 1931- *St&PR 91*
Macaulay, Colin Alexander 1931- *WhoAm 90*
Macaulay, David 1946- *BioIn 16*
Macaulay, David Alexander 1946- *WhoAmA 91*
Macaulay, Emilie Rose 1881-1958 *BioIn 16*
Macaulay, Fannie Caldwell 1863-1941 *LiHiK*
Macaulay, H.L. 1925- *St&PR 91*
Macaulay, Hugh L. 1925- *WhoAm 90*
Macaulay, J. Blair 1934- *St&PR 91*
Macaulay, Ronald Kerr Steven 1927- *WhoAm 90*
Macaulay, Rose 1881-1958 *BioIn 16, FemiCLE*
Macaulay, Thomas B. 1800-1859 *WorAlBi*
Macaulay, Thomas Babington 1800-1859 *BioIn 16*
Macaulay, Thomas S 1946- *WhoAmA 91*
Macaulay, William Edward 1945- *WhoAm 90*
Macauley, David Alexander 1946- *AuBYP 90*
Macauley, Jack 1952- *ODwPR 91*
Macauley, James Alvan 1872-1952 *EncABHB 5 [port]*
Macauley, Robert Conover *BioIn 16*
Macauley, Robert Conover 1923- *St&PR 91*
Macauley, Robie Mayhew 1919- *WhoAm 90, WhoWrEP 89*
Macavinta-Tenazas, Gemorsita 1938- *WhoAmW 91*
MacAvoy, Paul Webster 1934- *WhoAm 90*
Mac Avoy, Thomas Coleman 1928- *WhoAm 90, WhoSSW 91*
MacBain, William Halley 1916- *WhoAm 90*
MacBean, Dilla Whittemore 1895- *AuBYP 90*
MacBeth, George *BioIn 16*
Macbeth, George 1932- *AuBYP 90, MajTwCW*
Macbeth, Hugh James 1947- *WhoEmL 91, WhoSSW 91, WhoWor 91*
Macbeth, Madge 1880-1965 *DcLB 92 [port]*
MacBeth, Madge Hamilton 1881?-1965 *FemiCLE*
Macbeth, William *St&PR 91*
Macbird, Rosemary 1921- *WhoAmA 91*
Macbride, John J 1919- *BiDrAPA 89*
MacBride, Karin Lee 1960- *WhoE 91*
MacBride, Maud Gonne 1866-1953 *BioIn 16*
MacBride, Roger Lea 1929- *AuBYP 90*
MacBride, Sean *BioIn 16*
MacBride, Sean 1904-1988 *AnObit 1988, WorAlBi*
MacBride, Teri J. 1957- *WhoAmW 91*
MacBride, Thomas Jamison 1914- *WhoAm 90*
Macca, Nancy Lucia 1940- *WhoE 91*
MacCabe, Bernard S., Jr. 1927- *St&PR 91*
Maccabe, Frederic, Jr. *BiDrAPA 89*
MacCabe, Ian 1934- *WhoWor 91*
MacCaffrey, Wallace Trevethic 1920- *WhoAm 90*
Maccallan, W. David 1927- *St&PR 91*
MacCallan, William David 1927- *WhoAm 90*

Mac Callum, John Patrick 1944- *BiDrAPA 89*
MacCallum, Laurie Ann 1958- *WhoE 91*
MacCallum, Lorene 1928- *WhoAmW 91*
MacCallum, Robert Alexander 1943- *WhoWor 91*
Mac Cannel, W A *BiDrAPA 89*
MacCannell, Dean 1940- *BioIn 16*
Maccarini, Anthony George 1948- *WhoEmL 91*
Maccarini, Pier Andrea 1926- *WhoWor 91*
Maccario, Maurice Malcolm 1942- *WhoE 91*
Maccaro, Peter Anthony 1948- *St&PR 91*
Maccarone, Joseph Thomas 1952- *WhoE 91*
MacCarron, Damien *BiDrAPA 89*
Maccarrone, Harry Vincent 1947- *St&PR 91*
MacCarthy, Jerome 1952-1988 *BioIn 16*
Maccarthy, John Peters 1933- *St&PR 91*
MacCarthy, Mark Michael *BioIn 16*
MacCarthy, Terence 1934- *WhoAm 90*
Mac Cartney, John William 1945- *St&PR 91*
Maccaul, Bruce Gordon 1936- *St&PR 91*
MacCauley, Hugh Bournonville 1922- *WhoWor 91*
MacCausland, Paul Joseph 1965- *WhoEmL 91*
Maccecchini, Maria-Luisa 1951- *WhoE 91*
MacChesney, John Burnette 1929- *WhoAm 90*
Macchi, Eugene Edward 1926- *WhoE 91*
Macchia, Donald Dean 1948- *WhoWrEP 89*
Macchia, Joseph Dominick 1935- *St&PR 91*
Macchia, Marilyn Felecia 1937- *WhoE 91*
Macchia, Richard 1951- *St&PR 91*
Macchiarini, Peter 1909- *BioIn 16*
Macchiarola, Frank Joseph 1941- *WhoAm 90*
Macchio, Ralph *BioIn 16*
Maccini, Margaret Agatha 1931- *WhoAmW 91*
MacClintock, Dorcas 1932- *AuBYP 90, WhoAmA 91*
MacClintock, Stuart *NewYTBS 90*
MacClintock, Stuart 1919-1990 *BioIn 16*
Maccluggage, Reid 1938- *St&PR 91, WhoAm 90*
Maccoby, Eleanor E. 1917- *BioIn 16*
Maccoby, Eleanor Emmons 1917- *WhoAm 90, WhoAmW 91*
Maccoby, Michael 1933- *WhoE 91*
MacColl, Evan 1808-1898 *DcCanB 12*
MacColl, Ewan 1915-1989 *AnObit 1989, BioIn 16, OxCPMus*
MacCollam, Joel Allan 1946- *WhoEmL 91*
MacCombie, Bruce Franklin 1943- *WhoAm 90*
MacConkey, Dorothy I. *WhoAm 90, WhoAmW 91*
MacCord, Howard Arthur, Jr. 1950- *WhoEmL 91*
MacCormick, Neil 1941- *ConAu 129*
MacCoun, Catherine 1953- *ConAu 131*
Maccracken, Mark Mitchell 1954- *St&PR 91*
MacCracken, Mary 1926- *ConAu 30NR*
MacCracken, Mary Jo 1943- *WhoAmW 91*
MacCracken, Peter James *ODwPR 91*
MacCrate, Robert 1921- *WhoAm 90, WhoE 91*
MacCrea, Jane 1757-1777 *WhNaAH*
MacCready, Paul B. *BioIn 16*
Mac Cready, Paul Beattie 1925- *WhoAm 90*
MacCrimmon, Kenneth Robert 1937- *WhoAm 90*
Maccubbin, Emmett C. 1909- *St&PR 91*
Mac Cuish, James Allan *BiDrAPA 89*
MacCurdy, John A. 1947- *WhoSSW 91*
MacCurdy, Raymond Ralph, Jr. 1916- *WhoAm 90*
MacCutcheon, Edward Mackie 1915- *WhoE 91, WhoWor 91*
Macdaid, Gerald Philip 1954- *WhoSSW 91*
Macdaniel, Gibbs, Jr. 1937- *WhoAm 90*
MacDermot, Galt 1928- *OxCPMus*
Macdermott, G. H. 1845-1901 *OxCPMus*
MacDiarmid, Hugh *ConAu 33NR, MajTwCW*
MacDiarmid, Hugh 1892-1978 *BioIn 16, ConLC 63 [port], WorAlBi*
Mac Diarmid, William Donald 1926- *WhoAm 90*
Mac Donald, A. Ewan 1941- *St&PR 91*
Mac Donald, Alan Douglas 1939- *St&PR 91, WhoAm 90*
Macdonald, Alan G. 1944- *WhoE 91*
MacDonald, Alan Hugh 1943- *WhoAm 90*
MacDonald, Alan V. *BioIn 16*
Macdonald, Alexander Plath 1929- *WhoAm 90*
MacDonald, Anna Kay 1950- *WhoAmW 91*
MacDonald, Anson *AuBYP 90, MajTwCW*
Mac Donald, Barbara A 1953- *BiDrAPA 89*
Macdonald, Barbara Elizabeth 1955- *WhoE 91*
Macdonald, Benjamin F 1930- *BiDrAPA 89*
Mac Donald, Bernard Callaghan 1927- *St&PR 91*
MacDonald, Betty 1908- *AuBYP 90*
MacDonald, Betty 1908-1958 *FemiCLE*
Macdonald, Betty Ann 1936- *WhoAmA 91*
Macdonald, Bill 1929- *Ballpl 90*
Macdonald, Brian 1928- *OxCCanT*
MacDonald, Brian Scott 1939- *WhoAm 90*
MacDonald, Bruce G. *ODwPR 91*
Macdonald, Bruce K *WhoAmA 91*
MacDonald, Bruce Kenneth 1933- *WhoE 91*
MacDonald, Caleb Alan 1933- *WhoAm 90*
MacDonald, Charles Brown *NewYTBS 90*
Macdonald, Clifford Palmer 1919- *WhoAm 90*
Macdonald, Clyde V. 1909- *St&PR 91*
Macdonald, Colin Somerled 1925- *WhoAmA 91*
MacDonald, Cordelia Howard 1848-1941 *BioIn 16*
MacDonald, Craig Curry 1949- *WhoEmL 91*
Macdonald, Cynthia 1928- *DcLB 105 [port], WhoWrEP 89*
Mac Donald, David M 1923- *BiDrAPA 89*
Macdonald, David Robert 1930- *WhoAm 90, WhoWor 91*
Macdonald, Donald Alexander 1817-1896 *DcCanB 12*
Macdonald, Donald E 1926- *BiDrAPA 89*
Macdonald, Donald Ian 1931- *WhoAm 90*
Macdonald, Donald Stovel 1932- *WhoAm 90*
MacDonald, Donald William 1935- *WhoAm 90*
Macdonald, Douglas Kent 1929- *St&PR 91*
Macdonald, Dwight 1906-1982 *EncAL*
Mac Donald, Edward King 1929- *St&PR 91*
MacDonald, Elizabeth *BioIn 16*
MacDonald, Elizabeth 1864-1922 *FemiCLE*
Macdonald, Erin *St&PR 91*
Macdonald, Finlay J. 1925- *ConAu 132*
MacDonald, Frances 1874-1921 *BiDWomA, PenDiDA 89*
Macdonald, Frederick H. 1934- *St&PR 91*
MacDonald, George 1824-1905 *AuBYP 90, BioIn 16*
MacDonald, Gerald V. 1938- *WhoAm 90*
MacDonald, Golden *AuBYP 90*
MacDonald, Golden 1910-1952 *BioIn 16*
MacDonald, Gordon *BioIn 16*
Macdonald, Gordon C. 1928- *St&PR 91*
MacDonald, Gordon Chalmers 1928- *WhoAm 90*
Macdonald, Gordon James 1929- *St&PR 91*
Mac Donald, Gordon James Fraser 1929- *WhoAm 90*
MacDonald, Gordon L. *WhoAm 90*
MacDonald, Grant 1909-1987 *WhoAmA 91N*
Macdonald, H. Malcolm 1914- *WhoAm 90*
Macdonald, Helen L. 1910- *St&PR 91*
MacDonald, Herbert 1898-1972 *WhoAmA 91N*
Macdonald, Howard Goodwin 1928- *St&PR 91*
Macdonald, Hugh 1940- *IntWWM 90*
Macdonald, Hugh Ian 1929- *WhoAm 90*
Macdonald, Ian 1929- *St&PR 91*
MacDonald, J. Fred 1941- *ConAu 130*
Mac Donald, James Gordon 1925- *St&PR 91*
MacDonald, James Ramsay 1866-1937 *BioIn 16*
Macdonald, James Ross 1923- *WhoAm 90*
MacDonald, James W A 1824-1908 *WhoAmA 91N*
MacDonald, Jeanette 1903-1965 *OxCPMus, WorAlBi*
MacDonald, Jeanette 1907-1965 *BioAmW, PenDiMP*
MacDonald, Jeffrey R. *BioIn 16*
MacDonald, Jerome Edward 1925- *WhoE 91, WhoWor 91*
Macdonald, John *MajTwCW*
Macdonald, John 1815-1891 *WorAlBi*
Macdonald, John 1930- *St&PR 91*
Macdonald, John Alexander 1815-1891 *DcCanB 12, WhNaAH*
Macdonald, John Barfoot 1918- *WhoAm 90*
Macdonald, John Coury 1966- *WhoEmL 91*
MacDonald, John D 1916-1986 *MajTwCW, TwCCr&M 91, WorAlBi*
MacDonald, John Dann 1916-1986 *SpyFic*
Macdonald, John M 1920- *BiDrAPA 89*
Macdonald, John Ross *MajTwCW, TwCCr&M 91*
Macdonald, John Stephen 1943- *WhoAm 90*
MacDonald, John Thomas 1932- *WhoAm 90, WhoE 91*
Macdonald, Joseph *St&PR 91*
Macdonald, Joseph Albert Friel 1942- *WhoAm 90*
MacDonald, Joseph Faber 1932- *WhoAm 90*
Macdonald, Karen Crane 1955- *WhoAmW 91, WhoE 91, WhoEmL 91, WhoWor 91*
Macdonald, Katharine March 1949- *WhoAmW 91*
Macdonald, Kathryn Elizabeth 1948- *WhoWrEP 89*
MacDonald, Kenneth 1905- *WhoAm 90*
Macdonald, Kevin John 1946- *WhoAmA 91*
Macdonald, Lenna Ruth 1962- *WhoE 91*
Macdonald, Leo T. *St&PR 91*
Macdonald, Linda Gail 1954- *WhoEmL 91*
Macdonald, Malcolm Calum 1948- *IntWWM 90*
MacDonald, Malcolm John 1901-1981 *DcNaB 1981*
Mac Donald, Malcolm Murdoch 1935- *WhoAm 90*
MacDonald, Malcolm Murdoch 1935- *WhoWrEP 89*
MacDonald, Margaret 1865-1933 *BiDWomA, BioIn 16, PenDiDA 89*
MacDonald, Margaret Mary 1920- *WhoAm 90*
MacDonald, Maril Gagen 1956- *ODwPR 91, WhoE 91*
MacDonald, Mark Edward 1943- *WhoAm 90*
Macdonald, Martha Wilson *BiDrAPA 89*
MacDonald, Mary Edith *BiDrAPA 89*
Mac Donald, Matthew Anita 1938- *WhoAm 90, WhoAmW 91*
Macdonald, Norman Malcolm 1927- *ConAu 130*
MacDonald, Peter *BioIn 16*
MacDonald, Peter, Sr. 1928- *WhoAm 90*
Macdonald, Peter McIntyre 1916- *WhoAm 90*
MacDonald, Philip 1899-1981 *TwCCr&M 91*
MacDonald, R. Fulton 1940- *WhoE 91, WhoWor 91*
Macdonald, Ralph Lewis, Jr. 1942- *St&PR 91, WhoAm 90*
Macdonald, Ranald 1824-1894 *DcCanB 12*
Macdonald, Ranald H., Jr. 1923- *St&PR 91*
Macdonald, Ranald Hugh *BioIn 16*
Macdonald, Reynold C. 1918- *St&PR 91*
MacDonald, Richard Annis 1928- *WhoAm 90, WhoWor 91*
MacDonald, Richard Barry 1950- *WhoEmL 91*
MacDonald, Richard J. *BioIn 16*
Mac Donald, Richard M 1940- *BiDrAPA 89*
MacDonald, Robert Bruce 1930- *WhoE 91*
MacDonald, Robert James 1939- *BiDrAPA 89*
Mac Donald, Robert Ley 1947- *St&PR 91*
Macdonald, Robert R 1942- *WhoAmA 91*
Macdonald, Robert Rigg, Jr. 1942- *WhoAm 90, WhoE 91*
MacDonald, Robert Taylor 1930- *WhoAm 90*
MacDonald, Robert Upton 1946- *WhoSSW 91*
MacDonald, Robert W. *BioIn 16*
Mac Donald, Robert William 1922- *WhoWrEP 89*
Macdonald, Robert William 1943- *St&PR 91, WhoAm 90*
Macdonald, Robin Alisdair Stuart 1944- *WhoWor 91*
MacDonald, Rod *ODwPR 91*
MacDonald, Roderick 1931- *WhoAm 90*
Macdonald, Roderick Alexander 1948- *WhoAm 90*
MacDonald, Rodney Douglas 1942- *WhoE 91*
MacDonald, Ronald Angus Neil 1935- *WhoAm 90*
Macdonald, Ronald F. 1930- *St&PR 91*
Macdonald, Ross *MajTwCW*
Macdonald, Ross 1915-1983 *TwCCr&M 91, WorAlBi*
Macdonald, Scott 1942- *WhoAmA 91*
MacDonald, Sharon Ethel 1952- *WhoAmW 91, WhoE 91, WhoWor 91*
Macdonald, Sheila de Marillac 1952- *WhoAmW 91*
MacDonald, Steve *BioIn 16*
Macdonald, Stewart Robert 1925- *WhoSSW 91*
MacDonald, Suse *AuBYP 90*
Macdonald, Suse 1940- *BioIn 16*
MacDonald, Theresa Pellegrino 1927- *WhoAmW 91*
MacDonald, Thomas 1784?-1862 *BioIn 16*
MacDonald, Thomas Cook, Jr. 1929- *WhoAm 90*
Macdonald, Thomas J. 1940- *St&PR 91*
MacDonald, Thomas Reid 1908- *WhoAmA 91N*
Macdonald, Thomas S. 1952- *St&PR 91*
MacDonald, Timothy Lee 1948- *WhoSSW 91*
Macdonald, Victor Roderick 1930- *WhoAm 90*
Macdonald, Virginia B. 1920- *WhoAmW 91*
MacDonald, Walter E. 1926- *WhoAm 90*
MacDonald, Walter Howard 1920- *WhoAm 90*
MacDonald, Wesley Angus Reginald 1932- *WhoAm 90*
Macdonald, William A. *BioIn 16*
MacDonald, William Brien 1935- *WhoAm 90*
MacDonald, William David 1937- *WhoE 91*
Mac Donald, William Francis, Jr. 1944- *St&PR 91*
Mac Donald, William Irving 1928- *St&PR 91*
Macdonald, William L 1921- *WhoAmA 91*
MacDonald, William Lloyd 1921- *WhoAm 90, WhoWrEP 89*
MacDonald, Wilson 1880-1967 *DcLB 92 [port]*
MacDonald, Zillah Katherine 1885- *AuBYP 90*
MacDonald-Wright, Stanton 1890-1973 *WhoAmA 91N*
MacDonell, Bruce R. 1938- *WhoWor 91*
Macdonell, Cameron 1938- *WhoAmA 91*
Macdonnell, Daniel James 1843-1896 *DcCanB 12*
MacDonnell, Joanne Theresa 1937- *WhoAmW 91*
MacDonnell, Kevin 1919- *ConAu 31NR*
MacDonogh, Giles 1955- *ConAu 132*
Macdonough, John N. 1943- *St&PR 91*
Macdougal, Gary Edward 1936- *St&PR 91, WhoAm 90*
MacDougal, John *MajTwCW*
Macdougald, James A. 1928- *St&PR 91*
MacDougall, A. Kent *BioIn 16*
Macdougall, Alan 1842-1897 *DcCanB 12*
MacDougall, Alexander 1732-1786 *EncCRAm*
Macdougall, Anne 1944- *WhoAmA 91*
MacDougall, Donald 1912- *WhoWor 91*
MacDougall, Genevieve Rockwood 1914- *WhoAmW 91*
MacDougall, Hartland Molson 1931- *WhoAm 90*
Macdougall, Iver Cameron 1926- *WhoAm 90*
MacDougall, Malcolm D. *WhoAm 90*
MacDougall, Mary Katherine *WhoAmW 91*
Mac Dougall, Mary Katherine *WhoWrEP 89*
Mac Dougall, Monica Kathleen *BiDrAPA 89*
MacDougall, Patrick Leonard 1819-1894 *DcCanB 12*
MacDougall, Peter 1937- *WhoAm 90*
Macdougall, Peter Steven 1951- *WhoAmA 91*
Macdougall, Roderick M. 1926- *St&PR 91*
MacDougall, Roderick M. 1926-1988 *BioIn 16*
Mac Dougall, William Lowell 1931- *WhoAm 90*
MacDougall, William Lowell 1931- *WhoWrEP 89*
MacDowell, Andie *BioIn 16*
MacDowell, Anne Katherine 1956- *WhoAmW 91*
Mac Dowell, David Dawson 1937- *St&PR 91*
Macdowell, Edward 1860-1908 *PenDiMPA*
MacDowell, John *ConAu 131*
MacDowell, Katherine *BioAmW*
Mac Dowell, Lawrence James 1951- *St&PR 91*
Macdowell, Roland H. 1929- *St&PR 91*
MacDuffee, Robert Colton 1923- *WhoSSW 91*
Mace, David Kendrew 1951- *SpyFic*
Mace, David M. 1938- *WhoAm 90*
Mace, David Robert 1907- *WhoAm 90*
Mace, Dean Tolle 1922- *WhoAm 90*
Mace, Edgar G. 1929- *St&PR 91*
Mace, Flora Carrie *BioIn 16*
Mace, Georgia M. 1949- *St&PR 91*
Mace, James Patrick 1949- *WhoEmL 91*
Mace, Jean 1602?-1672 *PenDiDA 89*
Mace, John Weldon 1938- *WhoAm 90*
Mace, Katherine 1921- *AuBYP 90*
Mace, Mary Alice 1949- *WhoAmW 91*

Mace, Richard L. 1929- *St&PR 91*
Mace, Robert Rhoton 1930- *St&PR 91*
Mace, Terence Richard 1956- *St&PR 91*
Mace, Varian 1938- *BioIn 16*
Mace, William L. 1924- *ODwPR 91*
Mace, Wynn *AuBYP 90*
MacEachen, Allan Joseph *BioIn 16*
MacEachen, Allan Joseph 1921- *WhoAm 90*
MacEachern-Condon, Laura 1954- *WhoAmW 91*
MacEachron, David W. *BioIn 16*
MacEachron, David Wells *NewYTBS 90 [port]*
Macebuh, Sandy *WhoWrEP 89*
Macedo, Antonio *BioIn 16*
Macedo, Carlos A 1943- *BiDrAPA 89*
Macedo, Cheryl A. 1964- *WhoAmW 91*
Macedo, Richard Stanley 1941- *WhoAm 90*
Macedonia, Margaret Anne 1955- *WhoAmW 91, WhoWor 91*
Macenko, Mike *BioIn 16*
Macenko, Nancy A. 1947- *ODwPR 91*
MacEntee, George *EarBlAP*
Maceo, Antonio 1845-1896 *BioIn 16*
Macer, Dan Johnstone 1917- *WhoAm 90*
Macer-Story, Eugenia Ann 1945- *WhoAmW 91, WhoE 91, WhoEmL 91, WhoWor 91*
Macera, Salvatore 1931- *WhoAm 90*
Macero, Jeanette DiRusso 1931- *WhoAmW 91*
Macerola, Francois N. 1942- *WhoAm 90*
Macesic, Nedeljko 1956- *WhoWor 91*
Macesich, George 1927- *WhoWrEP 89*
MacEvoy, Brendan Patrick 1942- *WhoWor 91*
Mac Ewan, Gordon W *BiDrAPA 89*
Macewan, Nigel Savage 1933- *St&PR 91, WhoAm 90*
MacEwen, Edward C. *ODwPR 91*
Macewen, Edward C. 1938- *St&PR 91*
MacEwen, Edward Carter 1938- *WhoAm 90*
Mac Ewen, George Dean 1927- *WhoAm 90*
MacEwen, Gwendolyn 1941-1987 *BioIn 16, FemiCLE, WorAu 1980 [port]*
Macewen, Thomas V. 1946- *St&PR 91*
Macey, Chester O. 1938- *St&PR 91*
Macey, Morris William 1922- *WhoAm 90*
Macey, William Blackmore 1920- *WhoAm 90*
Macfadden, Bernarr 1868-1955 *BioIn 16*
MacFadden, Clifford Herbert 1908- *WhoAm 90*
MacFadden, John Edward 1942- *WhoE 91*
Macfadden, William Semple, Jr. 1928- *St&PR 91*
MacFadyen, Alexander Hugh 1931- *WhoWor 91*
MacFadyen, David Jerry 1940- *WhoAm 90*
Mac Fadyen, James *BiDrAPA 89*
Macfarlan, Allan A. 1892-1982 *AuBYP 90*
Macfarland, Robert Fredrick 1931- *St&PR 91*
Macfarlane, Alastair Iain Robert 1940- *WhoAm 90, WhoSSW 91*
MacFarlane, Andrew Walker 1928- *WhoAm 90*
Macfarlane, Bruce A. 1952- *St&PR 91*
Macfarlane, Gordon F. 1925- *St&PR 91*
MacFarlane, Gordon Frederick 1925- *WhoAm 90*
Macfarlane, Gwyn 1907-1987 *ConAu 131*
MacFarlane, James Douglas 1916- *ConAu 132*
Macfarlane, Jean Walker 1894-1989 *BioIn 16*
Macfarlane, Jeptha Robert *BiDrAPA 89*
Macfarlane, John 1942- *St&PR 91*
Macfarlane, John C. *St&PR 91*
Macfarlane, John Charles 1939- *St&PR 91*
Macfarlane, John Craig 1947- *St&PR 91*
Macfarlane, M. David 1940- *St&PR 91*
MacFarlane, Malcolm David 1940- *WhoAm 90*
Mac Farlane, Mark Raymond Thor 1953- *WhoWor 91*
Macfarlane, Mike 1964- *Ballpl 90*
Macfarlane, Robert Bruce 1896- *WhoSSW 91*
MacFarlane, Robert Bruce 1947- *WhoEmL 91*
Macfarlane, Samuel Graham 1931- *St&PR 91*
MacFarlane, Stephen *AuBYP 90*
MacFarren, George Alexander 1813-1887 *BioIn 16*
MacFayden, Danny 1905-1972 *Ballpl 90*
Macfie, Clyde Allen 1922- *St&PR 91*
MacGaffey, Wyatt 1932- *WhoAm 90*
MacGahan, Januarius Aloysius 1844-1878 *BioIn 16*
Macgaw, Wendy 1955- *WhoAmA 91*
MacGibbon, Jean 1913- *AuBYP 90*
Macgill, Richard G. 1910-1989 *BioIn 16*
Macgill, Richard Gambrill, Jr. 1932- *St&PR 91*
Macgillis, Robert Donald 1936- *WhoAmA 91*
MacGillivray, Lois Ann 1937- *WhoAm 90, WhoAmW 91*
Macgillivray, Lorna D. 1951- *St&PR 91*
MacGillivray, MaryAnn Leverone 1947- *WhoAmW 91*
MacGilvary, Norwood 1874-1949 *WhoAmA 91N*
MacGimsey, Robert 1898-1979 *OxCPMus*
MacGinitie, Harry D. 1896-1987 *BioIn 16*
MacGinitie, Walter Harold 1928- *WhoAm 90*
MacGinty, Francis Marius 1953- *WhoWor 91*
MacGiolla Bhrighde, Maud 1866-1953 *BioIn 16*
MacGowan, Charles Frederic 1918- *WhoAm 90*
Macgowan, Kenneth Owen 1921- *St&PR 91*
Mac Gowan, Mary Eugenia 1928- *WhoAm 90, WhoWor 91*
Macgoye, Marjorie 1928- *FemiCLE*
MacGrath, C. Richard 1921- *WhoAm 90*
MacGraw, Ali *BioIn 16*
MacGraw, Ali 1939- *WhoAm 90, WorAlBi*
MacGregor, Bonnie Lynn 1948- *WhoAmW 91*
MacGregor, Clark 1922- *WhoAm 90*
Macgregor, David C. 1937- *St&PR 91*
MacGregor, David Lee 1932- *WhoAm 90*
Macgregor, Donald L., Jr. 1930- *St&PR 91*
MacGregor, Donald Lane, Jr. 1930- *WhoAm 90*
MacGregor, Ellen 1906-1954 *AuBYP 90*
MacGregor, Geddes 1909- *WhoAm 90*
MacGregor, George Lescher, Jr. 1936- *WhoAm 90*
Macgregor, Gregory Allen 1941- *WhoAmA 91*
Macgregor, Ian K. 1912- *St&PR 91*
MacGregor, Jackie Donald 1940- *WhoE 91*
MacGregor, James Grierson 1934- *WhoAm 90*
Mac Gregor, James P. 1932- *St&PR 91*
MacGregor, Jeff *BioIn 16*
MacGregor, Jessie 1846?-1919 *BiDWomA*
MacGregor, Kenneth Robert 1906- *WhoAm 90*
MacGregor, Mary Esther 1876-1961 *FemiCLE*
MacGregor, Melissa Ann 1959- *WhoAmW 91*
MacGregor, Neil *NewYTBS 90*
MacGregor, Neil 1946- *WhoWor 91*
MacGregor, Robert Ken 1922- *WhoAm 90*
MacGregor, Thomas H. 1933- *WhoE 91*
MacGregor, Trish Janeshutz *BioIn 16*
Macgregor, Wallace 1917- *WhoAm 90, WhoWor 91*
MacGregor-Hastie, Roy 1929- *AuBYP 90*
Mac Guigan, Mark R. 1931- *WhoAm 90, WhoE 91*
MacGuire, Henrietta *BioIn 16*
Mach, Alexander 1902- *BioIn 16*
Mach, Elyse 1941- *ConAu 131, IntWWM 90*
Mach, Ernst 1838-1916 *WorAlBi*
Mach, Raymond Scott 1956- *St&PR 91*
Macha, Ken 1950- *Ballpl 90*
Macha, Otmar 1922- *IntWWM 90*
Machac, Jarmilla A S *BiDrAPA 89*
Machado de Assis 1839-1908 *BioIn 16*
Machado, Alfredo C. 1922- *WhoWor 91*
Machado, Antonio 1875-1939 *BioIn 16*
Machado, David 1938- *WhoWor 91*
Machado, Eduardo 1931- *BiDrAPA 89*
Machado, Eduardo 1953- *ConAu 131, HispWr 90*
Machado, Gus *WhoHisp 91*
Machado, Gustavo 1898-1983 *BioIn 16*
Machado, Hector Antonio 1960- *WhoHisp 91*
Machado, Jeffrey D. 1953- *St&PR 91*
Machado, Joao 1942- *BioIn 16*
Machado, Jose Luis 1951- *WhoHisp 91*
Machado, Julio Cesar, Jr. *BiDrAPA 89*
Machado, Manuel Antonio, Jr. 1939- *WhoHisp 91*
Machado, Melinda 1961- *WhoHisp 91*
Machado, Raul L 1918- *BiDrAPA 89*
Machado De Assis, Joachim Maria 1839-1908 *WorAlBi*
Machado y Morales, Gerardo 1871-1939 *BioIn 16*
Machado Y Ruiz, Antonio 1875-1939 *WorAlBi*
Machaj-Schutz, Janice Lynn 1953- *WhoAmW 91*
Machajski, Jan Waclaw *BioIn 16*
Machale, Sean 1936- *St&PR 91*
Machamer, Jefferson 1900-1960 *EncACom, WhoAmA 91N*
Machamer, Peter Kennedy 1942- *WhoE 91*
Machan, Myrle Bernice 1927- *WhoWrEP 89*
Machanic, Harmon Jack 1923- *WhoE 91*
Machanic, Roger 1933- *WhoSSW 91*
Machann, Clinton 1947- *ConAu 131*
Machar, Agnes Maule 1837-1927 *DcLB 92 [port], FemiCLE*
MacHarg, William *TwCCr&M 91*
Macharski, Franciszek 1927- *WhoWor 91*
Machas, Richard Frank 1940- *St&PR 91*
Machat, Allan Richard 1946- *St&PR 91*
Machate, Robert E. *BioIn 16*
Machatschki, Felix Karl Ludwig 1895-1970 *DcScB S2*
Machatzke, Heinz Wilhelm 1932- *WhoAm 90*
Machel, Samora *BioIn 16*
Macheleid, Georg Heinrich *PenDiDA 89*
Machemer, Christine Ann *BiDrAPA 89*
Machemer, Robert 1933- *WhoAm 90*
Machen, Arthur 1863-1947 *BioIn 16, EncO&P 3*
Machen, Arthur Webster, Jr. 1920- *WhoAm 90*
Mac Hendrie, Will Lindsay 1940- *BiDrAPA 89*
Machenschalk, Ruddolf A. 1928- *WhoWor 91*
Macher, Jean-Paul 1946- *BiDrAPA 89*
Machetanz, Fred 1908- *WhoAmA 91*
Machi, Anthony T *BiDrAPA 89*
Machiavelli, Niccolo 1469-1527 *BioIn 16, WorAlBi*
Machida, Curtis A. 1954- *WhoEmL 91*
Machida, Ken Jyoso 1955- *St&PR 91*
Machida, Susumu 1936- *WhoWor 91*
Machin, John Donald Ray 1932- *WhoAm 90*
Machin, Roger 1955- *WhoAmA 91*
Machin, Timothy Nostran 1822?-1905 *AmLegL*
Machinski, Michael Francis 1950- *WhoE 91*
Machir, John Lewis 1949- *WhoE 91*
Machisko, Diana S. 1961- *WhoEmL 91*
Machiz, Leon 1924- *WhoAm 90, WhoE 91*
Machl, Tadeusz 1922- *IntWWM 90*
Machle, Edward Johnstone 1918- *WhoAm 90*
Machler, Theodore J, Jr. 1930- *BiDrAPA 89*
Machlin, Eugene Solomon 1920- *WhoAm 90*
Machlin, Milton Robert 1924- *WhoAm 90, WhoWrEP 89*
Machlin, Robert N. 1957- *St&PR 91*
Machlin, Sheldon M 1918-1975 *WhoAmA 91N*
Machlin, Stanley D 1930- *BiDrAPA 89*
Machlis, Joseph 1906- *IntWWM 90*
Machlis, Oscar 1930- *St&PR 91*
Machnik, Joseph Andrew 1943- *WhoE 91*
Machol, Robert E. 1917- *WhoE 91*
Machold, William F. 1906- *St&PR 91*
Machonga, John Anthony 1957- *WhoEmL 91*
Machover, Carl 1927- *WhoE 91, WhoWor 91*
Machover, Tod 1953- *IntWWM 90*
Machover, Wilma Simon 1929- *IntWWM 90*
Machson, Marvin S. 1915-1989 *BioIn 16*
Macht, Carol Malisoff *WhoAm 90*
Macht, Norman L. 1929- *Ballpl 90*
Macht, Stuart Martin *St&PR 91N*
Macht, Stuart Martin 1930- *WhoAm 90, WhoE 91, WhoWor 91*
Machtiger, Harriet Gordon 1927- *WhoAmW 91, WhoE 91*
Machtley, Ronald K. 1948- *BioIn 16*
Machtley, Ronald Keith 1948- *WhoAm 90, WhoE 91*
Machulak, Edward A. 1951- *St&PR 91*
Machulak, Edward L. 1926- *St&PR 91*
Machulak, Edward Leon 1926- *WhoAm 90, WhoWor 91*
Machungo, Mario da Graca *WhoWor 91*
Machurek, Joseph Edward 1926- *WhoE 91*
Macia, Francesc 1859-1933 *BioIn 16*
Macia, Sylvia 1964- *WhoAmW 91*
Macia y Llusa, Francisco 1859-1933 *BioIn 16*
Maciag, Anthony Edward 1928- *St&PR 91*
Maciag, John Andrew, Jr. 1953- *WhoE 91*
MacIan, Fanny 1814-1897 *BiDWomA*
Macias, Edward S. 1944- *WhoAm 90*
Macias, Fernando R. 1952- *WhoHisp 91*
Macias, Jose Miguel *WhoHisp 91*
Macias, Reynaldo Flores *WhoHisp 91*
Macias, Veronica Denise 1958- *WhoAmW 91*
Macielag, Michael 1949- *WhoE 91*
Macier, Karen Annette 1954- *WhoE 91*
MacIlroy, John Whittington 1946- *WhoEmL 91, WhoSSW 91*
MacIlvaine, Chalmers Acheson 1921- *WhoAm 90*
Macilwham, George 1926- *IntWWM 90*
Macindoe, Thomas Hunter 1924- *St&PR 91*
MacInnes, Colin 1914-1976 *MajTwCW*
MacInnes, Donald 1824?-1900 *DcCanB 12*
MacInnes, Helen 1907-1985 *FemiCLE, MajTwCW, TwCCr&M 91*
MacInnes, Helen Clark 1907-1985 *SpyFic, WorAlBi*
MacInnes, Margo *WhoAmW 91*
Macinnis, Al 1963- *WorAlBi*
MacInnis, Frank T. 1946- *WhoAm 90*
MacInnis, Linda Frances 1938- *WhoE 91*
Mac Innis, Ronald 1943- *St&PR 91*
MacIntosh, Alexander John 1921- *WhoAm 90*
Macintosh, Douglas Clyde 1877-1948 *BioIn 16*
MacIntosh, Frank Campbell 1909- *WhoAm 90*
Mac Intosh, Houston 1936- *BiDrAPA 89*
MacIntosh, Houston Hood 1936- *WhoE 91*
MacIntosh, Joan 1945- *ConTFT 8*
MacIntosh, Llewellyn *BioIn 16*
MacIntosh, Monica Bernadette 1957- *WhoE 91*
Macintosh, Robert 1897-1989 *AnObit 1989*
Macintosh, Robert Mallory 1923- *St&PR 91, WhoAm 90*
MacIntosh, W. James *St&PR 91N*
MacIntosh, William James 1901-1989 *BioIn 16*
MacIntyre, Alasdair Chalmers 1929- *WhoAm 90*
MacIntyre, Alexander Cringan 1931- *WhoSSW 91*
MacIntyre, Alfonso Everette 1901- *WhoAm 90*
Macintyre, Donald George Frederick W 1904-1981 *DcNaB 1981*
Mac Intyre, Donald John 1939- *WhoAm 90*
Macintyre, George W. 1945- *St&PR 91*
Mac Intyre, James Campbell, II 1946- *BiDrAPA 89*
Macintyre, John Alexander 1939- *St&PR 91*
MacIntyre, Malcolm Ames 1908- *WhoAm 90*
Macintyre, Margaret 1865?-1943 *PenDiMP*
MacIntyre, Michael 1939- *ConAu 131*
Macintyre, Pamela J. *St&PR 91*
MacIntyre, R. Douglas 1951- *WhoAm 90, WhoEmL 91*
Mac Intyre, Regina *WhoWrEP 89*
Macintyre, Robert Charles 1926- *St&PR 91*
MacIntyre, Rod 1947- *ConAu 132*
Macintyre, Stuart 1947- *ConAu 131*
Macioce, Frank Michael, Jr. 1945- *WhoEmL 91*
Macioce, Thomas M. *NewYTBS 90 [port]*
Macioce, Thomas M. 1919- *St&PR 91*
Macioce, Thomas Matthew 1919- *WhoAm 90*
Maciolek, John L. 1936- *St&PR 91*
Maciolka, Michal Eugeniusz 1936- *WhoWor 91*
MacIsaac, David 1935- *ConAu 31NR*
Maciunas, George 1931-1978 *WhoAmA 91N*
Maciuszko, Kathleen Lynn 1947- *WhoAmW 91*
Mac Iver, John *BiDrAPA 89*
MacIver, Loren 1909- *BiDWomA, WhoAmA 91*
MacIver Rodriguez, Enrique 1845-1922 *BioIn 16*
MacIvor, Hazel Judith Arnold 1921- *WhoAmW 91*
Mack, Alan Wayne 1947- *WhoEmL 91, WhoWor 91*
Mack, Anthony A. 1949- *St&PR 91*
Mack, Augustus F *EncABHB 4*
Mack, Brenda Lee 1940- *WhoAmW 91*
Mack, Carol K *ConAu 130*
Mack, Cathy 1955- *WhoWor 91*
Mack, Cecil *EarBlAP*
Mack, Charles Randall 1940- *WhoAmA 91*
Mack, Clifford Glenn 1927- *WhoAm 90*
Mack, Connie 1862-1956 *Ballpl 90 [port], BioIn 16, WorAlBi*
Mack, Connie 1940- *BioIn 16*
Mack, Connie, III 1940- *WhoAm 90, WhoSSW 91, WhoWor 91*
Mack, Conrad John 1936- *St&PR 91*
Mack, Cristina Iannone 1940- *WhoAmW 91*
Mack, Daniel R 1947- *WhoAmA 91*
Mack, David J. 1947- *St&PR 91*
Mack, David L. 1940- *WhoAm 90, WhoWor 91*
Mack, Debra Kaye 1955- *WhoAmW 91, WhoE 91*
Mack, Dennis Wayne 1943- *St&PR 91, WhoAm 90*

Mack, Earle Irving 1939- *WhoAm 90, WhoE 91, WhoWor 91*
Mack, Edward Gibson 1917- *WhoAm 90*
Mack, Edward John 1916- *WhoAm 90*
Mack, Elsie Frances 1909-1967 *FemiCLE*
Mack, Eugene K. 1922- *St&PR 91*
Mack, Eugene Kevin 1922- *WhoAm 90*
Mack, Evelyn Walker 1930- *St&PR 91*
Mack, Garnett Lloyd 1931- *WhoWor 91*
Mack, Gene *Ballpl 90*
Mack, Gerstle 1894-1983 *ConAu 129*
Mack, J. Curtis, II 1944- *WhoAm 90*
Mack, James Edgar 1934- *St&PR 91*
Mack, James Edward 1920- *WhoE 91*
Mack, James Franklin 1924- *St&PR 91*
Mack, James Melvin 1947- *WhoWrEP 89*
Mack, Jeremy Roger *BiDrAPA 89*
Mack, Jerome D. 1920- *WhoAm 90*
Mack, Jillie *BioIn 16*
Mack, Jim *St&PR 91*
Mack, John Duncan 1924- *St&PR 91*
Mack, John E *BiDrAPA 89*
Mack, John Edward, III 1934- *St&PR 91, WhoAm 90, WhoE 91*
Mack, John M *EncABHB 4*
Mack, John Parker 1926- *St&PR 91*
Mack, John Paul *BioIn 16*
Mack, Joseph P. 1939- *WhoE 91*
Mack, Joseph S *EncABHB 4*
Mack, Joseph S. 1870-1953 *WorAlBi*
Mack, Julia Cooper 1920- *WhoAm 90, WhoAmW 91, WhoE 91*
Mack, Karin F *BiDrAPA 89*
Mack, L. V. *WhoWrEP 89*
Mack, Lawrence Allen 1955- *WhoEmL 91*
Mack, Lorraine Ann 1942- *St&PR 91*
Mack, Louise 1870-1935 *FemiCLE*
Mack, Lynn 1933- *ODwPR 91*
Mack, Marion *BioIn 16*
Mack, Marion Pierce *BioIn 16*
Mack, Marjorie *AuBYP 90*
Mack, Mark Philip 1950- *WhoSSW 91*
Mack, Mary Elizabeth *WhoAmW 91*
Mack, Mary Margaret 1955- *WhoWor 91*
Mack, Maynard 1909- *WorAu 1980 [port]*
Mack, Melissa Lee 1963- *WhoE 91*
Mack, Molly Ann 1950- *WhoAmW 91*
Mack, Patrice C 1942- *BiDrAPA 89*
Mack, Paul Frederick 1932- *St&PR 91*
Mack, Ray 1916-1969 *Ballpl 90*
Mack, Raymond Francis 1912- *WhoAm 90*
Mack, Raymond Phillip 1940- *St&PR 91*
Mack, Raymond Wright 1927- *WhoAm 90*
Mack, Rene Allen 1959- *ODwPR 91*
Mack, Richard N *BiDrAPA 89*
Mack, Robert Emmet 1924- *WhoAm 90*
Mack, Robert N. 1952- *St&PR 91*
Mack, Rodger Allen 1938- *WhoAmA 91*
Mack, Russell R., Jr. 1951- *ODwPR 91*
Mack, Sara Rohrbach 1921- *WhoAmW 91*
Mack, Shane 1963- *Ballpl 90*
Mack, Stanley 1936- *EncACom*
Mack, Steven Philp 1951- *St&PR 91*
Mack, Thomas H. 1942- *St&PR 91*
Mack, Walter *BioIn 16*
Mack, Walter S. 1895-1990 *NewYTBS 90 [port]*
Mack, Walter S., Jr. 1895-1990 *CurBio 90N*
Mack, Wayne *WhoWrEP 89*
Mack, William *EncABHB 4*
Mack, William Gray 1827-1898 *AmLegL*
Mack Smith, Denis 1920- *WorAu 1980 [port]*
Mack-Toner, Patricia E *BiDrAPA 89*
Mackal, Roy Paul 1925- *WhoAm 90*
Mackall, Henry Clinton 1927- *WhoWor 91*
Mackall, Jane Friedman 1949- *WhoAm 90*
Mackall, Laidler Bowie 1916- *WhoAm 90*
Mackaman, Donald Hayes 1912- *St&PR 91*
Mackaness, George Bellamy 1922- *WhoAm 90*
Mackanin, Pete 1951- *Ballpl 90*
MacKaronis, Gregory Constantine 1941- *WhoE 91*
Mackasey, Michael P. 1954- *St&PR 91*
Mackavey, William Raymond 1932- *WhoAm 90*
Mackay, Lord 1927- *WhoWor 91*
Mackay, Alexander Russell 1911- *WhoWor 91*
MacKay, Andrew Dougal 1946- *WhoEmL 91, WhoSSW 91*
MacKay, Angus 1836-1897? *DcCanB 12*
Mackay, Ann 1956- *IntWWM 90*
MacKay, Buddy *BioIn 16*
Mackay, Claire 1930- *WhoWrEP 89*
Mackay, David *AuBYP 90*
MacKay, Donald Cameron 1906-1979 *WhoAmA 91N*
Mac Kay, Donald MacGregor 1935- *WhoE 91*
Mackay, Douglas McDuff 1948- *WhoEmL 91*
Mackay, Edward F. 1942- *St&PR 91*
MacKay, Elmer MacIntosh 1936- *WhoAm 90, WhoE 91*
MacKay, Gordon 1878-1941 *Ballpl 90*
Mackay, H.H. 1940- *St&PR 91*
MacKay, Harold Hugh 1940- *WhoAm 90*
Mackay, Harvey 1933?- *ConAu 130*
MacKay, Isabel 1875-1928 *FemiCLE*
MacKay, Isabel Ecclestone 1875-1928 *DcLB 92 [port]*
Mackay, Jacqueline E. 1958- *ODwPR 91*
Mackay, James G. 1934- *St&PR 91*
Mackay, James Lyle 1852-1932 *BioIn 16*
Mackay, Jessie 1864-1938 *FemiCLE*
MacKay, John Norman 1946- *WhoEmL 91*
Mac Kay, John Robert 1945- *St&PR 91*
Mackay, John S. 1943- *ODwPR 91*
Mackay, Joseph William 1829-1900 *DcCanB 12*
Mackay, Kenneth Donald 1942- *WhoAm 90*
Mackay, Malcolm 1940- *St&PR 91, WhoAm 90*
MacKay, Marie L. 1843-1928 *BioAmW*
Mackay, Mary 1855-1924 *BioIn 16*
Mac Kay, Mary Calder *BiDrAPA 89*
Mackay, Patricia McIntosh 1922- *WhoAmW 91*
Mackay, Paul 1932- *St&PR 91*
Mackay, Penelope Judith 1943- *IntWWM 90*
Mac Kay, Pierre Antony 1933- *WhoAm 90*
Mackay, Shena 1945- *FemiCLE*
MacKay, William Andrew 1929- *WhoAm 90*
Mackay, William Brydon Fraser 1914- *WhoAm 90*
Mackay, William Reay 1943- *St&PR 91*
MacKaye, Benton 1879-1975 *BioIn 16*
MacKaye, William Ross 1934- *WhoAm 90*
Macke, August 1887-1914 *IntDcAA 90*
Macke, David H. 1928- *St&PR 91*
Macke, Donald L. 1937- *St&PR 91*
Macke, Donald LaVerne 1937- *WhoAm 90*
Macke, Julia Edelweiss 1961- *WhoSSW 91*
Macke, Kenneth A. 1938- *WhoAm 90*
Mackechnie, Linda Allen 1950- *WhoAmW 91*
MacKeigan, Ian Malcolm 1915- *WhoAm 90*
Mackellar, Dorothea 1885-1968 *FemiCLE*
MacKellar, William 1914- *AuBYP 90*
Macken, Daniel E. 1905-1989 *BioIn 16*
Macken, Joseph Sylvester, III 1951- *WhoE 91*
Macken, Walter 1915-1967 *AuBYP 90*
Mackendrick, Alexander 1912- *BioIn 16*
MacKendrick, Paul Lachlan 1914- *WhoAm 90*
Mackenna, Benjamin Vicuna 1831-1886 *BioIn 16*
Mackenna, Luis Fernando 1940- *WhoWor 91*
Mackenstadt, Robert Clay *BiDrAPA 89*
Mackenzie, A.M. 1929- *St&PR 91*
Mackenzie, Alexander 1755?-1820 *BioIn 16, WorAlBi*
Mackenzie, Alexander 1763-1820 *DcLB 99 [port]*
Mackenzie, Alexander 1764-1820 *EncCRAm, WhNaAH*
Mackenzie, Alexander 1822-1892 *DcCanB 12*
Mackenzie, Alexander 1847-1935 *PenDiMP A, WorAlBi*
Mackenzie, Alexander Campbell 1847-1935 *BioIn 16*
MacKenzie, Alistair MacIntosh 1929- *WhoAm 90*
MacKenzie, Andrew 1911- *EncPaPR 91*
MacKenzie, Andrew Ross 1934- *WhoAm 90*
Mackenzie, Anna Maria *FemiCLE*
Mackenzie, Brian S. 1951- *St&PR 91*
Mackenzie, Carolyn Kay 1941- *St&PR 91*
Mackenzie, Charles Edward 1943- *WhoE 91*
MacKenzie, Charles Sherrard 1924- *WhoAm 90*
Mackenzie, Charles Westlake, III 1946- *WhoAm 90*
Mackenzie, Clara Childs 1931- *WhoWrEP 89*
Mackenzie, Compton 1883-1972 *AuBYP 90, BioIn 16, DcLB 100 [port]*
Mackenzie, Compton 1883-1973 *SpyFic*
Mackenzie, Cosmo Glenn 1907- *WhoAm 90*
MacKenzie, David, IV 1942- *WhoAmA 91*
Mackenzie, Dianne Veronica 1947- *WhoAmW 91*
MacKenzie, Donald 1918- *TwCCr&M 91, WhoWrEP 89*
Mac Kenzie, Ellen Pickard 1920- *BiDrAPA 89*
Mackenzie, Fred Hartsell 1950- *St&PR 91*
Mackenzie, G. Allan 1931- *St&PR 91*
Mackenzie, George 1949- *St&PR 91, WhoAm 90*
MacKenzie, George Allan 1931- *WhoAm 90*
MacKenzie, Ginny Lee 1945- *WhoWrEP 89*
MacKenzie, Hugh Seaforth 1928- *WhoAmA 91*
Mackenzie, Hugh Sinclair 1911- *St&PR 91*
Mackenzie, Jack *BioIn 16*
Mackenzie, James 1933- *WhoE 91*
MacKenzie, James Cameron 1852-1931 *WorAlBi*
Mac Kenzie, James Donald 1924- *WhoSSW 91*
Mackenzie, James William, IV 1947- *St&PR 91*
MacKenzie, Janis R. 1953- *ODwPR 91*
Mackenzie, Jeanette Brown *AuBYP 90*
MacKenzie, Jeanne 1922-1986 *ConAu 130*
Mac Kenzie, Joan H *BiDrAPA 89*
Mackenzie, John 1803-1866 *BioIn 16*
MacKenzie, John Douglas 1926- *WhoAm 90*
Mac Kenzie, John Edward 1934- *St&PR 91*
Mackenzie, John M *BiDrAPA 89*
MacKenzie, John Pettibone 1930- *WhoAm 90*
Mackenzie, Joseph Wilkes 1924- *St&PR 91*
Mackenzie, Julianne Schlass 1953- *WhoAmW 91*
Mackenzie, K. Colin 1933- *St&PR 91*
Mac Kenzie, K Roy 1937- *BiDrAPA 89*
MacKenzie, Karen G. *ODwPR 91*
MacKenzie, Ken 1934- *Ballpl 90*
Mackenzie, Kenneth 1797-1861 *WhNaAH*
Mackenzie, Kenneth Donald 1937- *WhoAm 90*
Mackenzie, Kenneth R H 1833-1886 *EncO&P 3*
Mackenzie, Kenneth Victor 1911- *WhoAm 90, WhoWor 91*
Mackenzie, Lennox *PenDiMP*
MacKenzie, Lewis Wharton 1940- *WhoAm 90*
Mackenzie, Linda Alice 1949- *WhoAmW 91*
Mackenzie, Malcolm George 1938- *St&PR 91*
Mackenzie, Malcolm Lewis 1926- *WhoAm 90*
Mac Kenzie, Malcolm Robert 1924- *WhoSSW 91, WhoWor 91*
MacKenzie, Mark Scott 1959- *WhoE 91*
MacKenzie, Mary Hawkins 1936- *WhoAmW 91*
MacKenzie, Norman 1921- *ConAu 130*
Mac Kenzie, Norman Hugh 1915- *WhoAm 90*
MacKenzie, Norman Hugh 1915- *WhoWrEP 89*
MacKenzie, Philip Charles *ConTFT 8*
MacKenzie, Ralph Sidney 1934- *WhoAm 90*
Mackenzie, Ranald Slidell 1840-1889 *WhNaAH [port]*
Mackenzie, Richard D. 1943- *St&PR 91*
MacKenzie, Robert Bruce 1927- *WhoAm 90*
Mackenzie, Robert Fraser 1910-1987 *BioIn 16*
MacKenzie, Robert Peck 1945- *WhoEmL 91*
MacKenzie, Roland Redus 1907- *BioIn 16*
Mackenzie, Scott James 1937- *WhoWor 91*
Mackenzie, Thayer M *BiDrAPA 89*
MacKenzie, Thomas Brooke 1944- *BiDrAPA 89*
MacKenzie, Warren 1924- *BioIn 16*
Mackenzie, William 1877- *EncO&P 3*
Mackenzie, William J M 1923- *BiDrAPA 89*
Mackenzie-Forbes, Kenneth 1944- *IntWWM 90*
MacKenzie-Smith, Sydney 1937- *WhoWor 91*
Mackeown, Hugh Neil 1941- *WhoWor 91*
MacKeown, Ida C *WhoAmA 91N*
Mackercher, Peter Angus, II 1946- *WhoSSW 91*
MacKerell, Kerry 1959- *WhoAmW 91*
Mackerodt, Fred 1938- *ODwPR 91, WhoAm 90*
Mackerras, Charles 1925- *PenDiMP, WhoWor 91, WorAlBi*
Mackerras, Charles MacLaurin 1925- *IntWWM 90*
Mackerras, Colin Patrick 1939- *ConAu 33NR, WhoWor 91*
Mackesy, Jerome C. 1934- *St&PR 91*
Mackett, Ann 1643-1691 *BiDEWW*
Mackety, Carolyn J. 1932- *WhoAmW 91*
Mackey, Albert Gallatin 1807-1881 *EncO&P 3*
Mackey, Biz 1897-1959 *Ballpl 90*
Mackey, Bruce Q. 1945- *WhoAm 90*
Mackey, Clarence L. 1932- *St&PR 91*
Mackey, Curtis Thelbert 1927- *WhoSSW 91*
Mackey, Dallas L. 1920- *WhoWor 91*
Mackey, David 1942- *ODwPR 91*
Mackey, David Clark 1955- *WhoEmL 91*
Mackey, Dorothea Margarette 1925- *WhoAmW 91*
Mackey, Elizabeth Jocelyn 1927- *IntWWM 90*
Mackey, Eugene J. 1938- *BioIn 16*
Mackey, Howard Hamilton, Jr. 1926- *WhoWrEP 89*
Mackey, James A., Mrs. 1932- *WhoAmW 91, WhoE 91*
Mackey, James Ethan 1947- *St&PR 91*
Mackey, John E. 1946- *St&PR 91*
Mackey, Lenora Jarvis 1944- *WhoAmW 91*
Mackey, Leonard B. 1925- *St&PR 91*
Mackey, Leonard Bruce 1925- *WhoAm 90*
Mackey, Louis Henry 1926- *WhoAm 90*
Mackey, Mary 1945- *WhoWrEP 89*
Mackey, Mary Lou 1945- *WhoEmL 91*
Mackey, Maurice Cecil 1929- *WhoAm 90, WhoWor 91*
Mackey, Patrick Glenn 1946- *WhoAm 90*
Mackey, Randall Aubrey 1945- *WhoEmL 91*
Mackey, Richard Charles 1927- *St&PR 91*
Mackey, Richard James 1931- *St&PR 91*
Mackey, Robert Joseph 1946- *WhoAm 90*
Mackey, Sandra 1951- *St&PR 91*
Mackey, Sheldon Elias 1913- *WhoAm 90*
Mackey, Steve R. 1950- *St&PR 91*
Mackey, Timothy Shaun 1963- *WhoSSW 91*
Mackey, Vaino Ilmar 1911- *WhoWrEP 89*
Mackey, Warren Cornell 1950- *WhoSSW 91*
Mackey, Willia W. 1934- *WhoSSW 91*
Mackey, William Arthur Godfrey 1946- *WhoE 91*
Mackey, William F. Jr. *BiDrAPA 89*
Mackey, William Sturges, Jr. 1921- *WhoAm 90*
Mackey, William Wellington *DrBlPA 90*
Mackichan, Robin Kenneth 1935- *WhoWor 91*
Mackie, Bob *BioIn 16*
Mackie, Carolyn Lee 1962- *WhoAmW 91*
Mackie, David 1943- *IntWWM 90*
Mackie, David F. 1937- *WhoSSW 91*
Mackie, Dian Boyce 1950- *WhoAmW 91*
Mackie, Diana Jane 1946- *WhoAmW 91*
Mackie, Donald John, Jr. 1944- *WhoSSW 91, WhoWor 91*
Mackie, Frederick David 1910- *WhoAm 90*
Mackie, James L. 1944- *St&PR 91*
Mackie, Jean 1920- *IntWWM 90*
Mackie, John *ConAu 31NR*
Mackie, Neil 1946- *IntWWM 90*
Mackie, Pauline Bradford 1874- *FemiCLE*
Mackie, Robert Gordon 1940- *WhoAm 90, WhoWor 91*
Mackie, Shirley M. 1929- *IntWWM 90, WhoAmW 91*
Mackiewicz, Anne Lisa 1950- *WhoAmW 91*
Mackiewicz, Edward Robert 1951- *WhoEmL 91*
Mackiewicz, Felix 1917- *Ballpl 90*
MacKiewicz, Laura *WhoAmW 91*
Mackil, Joseph D. 1945- *St&PR 91*
MacKimm, James Bradley 1932- *WhoAm 90*
Mackimm, Margaret P. 1933- *St&PR 91*
Mac Kimm, Margaret Pontius 1933- *WhoAmW 91*
Mackin, Bernard John 1917- *St&PR 91*
Mackin, Cooper Richerson 1933- *WhoAm 90*
Mackin, H. Carroll 1940- *St&PR 91*
Mackin, Jeanne A. 1948- *WhoWrEP 89*
Mackin, Michael Dunne 1950- *WhoSSW 91*
Mackin, Thomas H. 1929- *St&PR 91*
MacKinlay, Jean Sterling *PenDiMP*
Mac Kinney, Archie Allen, Jr. 1929- *WhoAm 90*
MacKinney, Arthur Clinton, Jr. 1928- *WhoAm 90*
Mackinnon, Aleck M. 1924- *St&PR 91*
MacKinnon, Catharine A. 1946- *ConAu 132*
Mackinnon, Colin *SpyFic*
MacKinnon, Cyrus Leland 1916- *WhoAm 90*
Mackinnon, Donald Sargent 1942- *St&PR 91*
MacKinnon, Donald W. 1903-1987 *BioIn 16*
MacKinnon, George E. 1906- *WhoAm 90, WhoE 91*
Mac Kinnon, Gregory Aloysius 1925- *WhoAm 90*
Mac Kinnon, Harry L 1912- *BiDrAPA 89*
Mackinnon, J. Allan 1944- *IntWWM 90*
Mackinnon, Larry D. 1949- *St&PR 91*

Mackinnon, M.C. 1934- *St&PR 91*
MacKinnon, Marion Elizabeth 1952- *WhoAmW 91*
MacKinnon, Maureen Elizabeth 1966- *WhoAmW 91*
MacKinnon, Nancy Williams 1925- *WhoAmW 91*
Mackinnon, Paul Joseph 1949- *St&PR 91*
Mackinnon, Peggy L. *ODwPR 91*
Mackinnon, Peggy Louise 1945- *WhoEmL 91*
MacKinnon, R. Peter 1947- *WhoAm 90*
Mac Kinnon, Roger A 1927- *BiDrAPA 89*
MacKinnon, Roger Alan 1927- *WhoE 91*
MacKinnon, Ross Douglas 1942- *WhoAm 90*
MacKinnon, Sally Anne 1938- *WhoAm 90*
Mackinnon, W.G. *St&PR 91*
MacKinnon, Walter Allan 1929- *WhoE 91*
MacKinnon Groomer, Vera 1915- *BioIn 16*
MacKintosh, Cameron *BioIn 16, NewYTBS 90 [port]*
Mackintosh, Cameron 1946- *WhoAm 90*
Mackintosh, Charles Rennie 1868-1928 *BioIn 16, PenDiDA 89*
Mackintosh, Elizabeth 1896-1952 *BioIn 16*
MacKintosh, Frederick Roy 1943- *WhoWor 91*
MacKintosh, Graham 1951- *ConAu 132*
Mackintosh, M. *BiDWomA*
Mackintosh, Margaret Macdonald 1865-1933 *BioIn 16*
Mackintosh, Sandra 1944- *WhoAmA 91, WhoE 91*
Mackiw, Vladimir Nicholaus 1923- *WhoAm 90*
Mackland, Charles Raymond *BioIn 16*
Mackle, Francis Elliott, Jr. 1916- *WhoAm 90*
Mackle, Frank E., Jr. 1916- *St&PR 91*
Macklem, Michael Kirkpatrick 1928- *WhoAm 90*
Macklem, Peter Tiffany 1931- *WhoAm 90*
Mackler, Judith Ann 1945- *WhoAmW 91*
Mackler, Tina *WhoAm 90*
Mackles, Lawrence F *BiDrAPA 89*
Macklin, Edgar Augustus *BioIn 16*
Macklin, Gordon S. 1928- *St&PR 91*
Macklin, Gordon Stanley 1928- *WhoAm 90*
Macklin, John Edward 1936- *St&PR 91*
Macklin, Martin 1934- *BiDrAPA 89*
Macklin, Michael Neal 1953- *BiDrAPA 89*
Macklin, Philip Alan 1925- *WhoAm 90*
Macklin, Ruth *NewYTBS 90*
Macklowe, Barbara *BioIn 16*
Macklowe, Lloyd *BioIn 16*
Mackmurdo, Arthur Heygate 1851-1942 *BioIn 16, PenDiDA 89*
Mackney, Richard 1953- *St&PR 91*
MacKnight, Carol Bernier 1938- *WhoAmW 91*
MacKnight, William John 1936- *WhoAm 90, WhoWor 91*
Macknin, Carol Hyman *BiDrAPA 89*
Macko, Helen Ann 1937- *WhoAmW 91*
Macko, John 1947- *WhoE 91*
Macko, Lesia L. 1958- *WhoE 91*
Mackorell, James Theodore, Jr. 1959- *WhoEmL 91, WhoSSW 91*
Mackoul, Sabry Joseph 1940- *St&PR 91, WhoAm 90*
Mackovic, John 1943- *WhoAm 90*
Mackowiak, Elaine DeCusatis 1940- *WhoAmW 91*
MacKown, Diana *BioIn 16*
Mackowski, J. Matthew 1954- *St&PR 91*
MacKowski, John Joseph 1926- *WhoAm 90*
Macksey, K J *ConAu 30NR*
Macksey, Kenneth J 1923- *ConAu 30NR*
Mackta, Barnett 1935- *St&PR 91*
Mackuse, Donna Marie 1957- *BiDrAPA 89*
Mackworth, Alan Keith 1945- *WhoAm 90*
Mackworth, Cecily 1911- *FemiCLE*
Mackworth-Young, Lucinda Jane 1957- *IntWWM 90*
Macky, Spencer 1880-1958 *WhoAmA 91N*
Mac Lachlan, Alexander 1933- *St&PR 91*
MacLachlan, Alexander 1933- *WhoAm 90*
MacLachlan, Douglas Lee 1940- *WhoAm 90*
Maclachlan, Gordon Alistair 1930- *WhoAm 90*
MacLachlan, Janet *DrBlPA 90*
MacLachlan, Kyle *BioIn 16*
MacLachlan, Patricia *AuBYP 90, BioIn 16, WhoAmW 91*
MacLachlan, Patricia 1938- *SmATA 62 [port]*
Maclachlan, Robert H. 1925- *St&PR 91*
Mac Lachlan, Robert Taylor *BiDrAPA 89*
Maclagan, John Lyall 1929- *WhoAm 90*
MacLagger, Richard Joseph 1947-1989 *WhoAmA 91N*
MacLaine, Allan Hugh 1924- *WhoAm 90*
MacLaine, Shirley *BioIn 16*
MacLaine, Shirley 1934- *ConAu 32NR, EncO&P 3, EncPaPR 91, NewAgE 90, OxCPMus, WhoAm 90, WhoAmW 91, WhoWrEP 89, WorAlBi*
MacLane, Jack *ConAu 30NR*
MacLane, Jean 1878-1964 *WhoAmA 91N*
MacLane, Saunders 1909- *BioIn 16, WhoAm 90*
Maclaren, David S. 1931- *St&PR 91*
Mac Laren, David Sergeant 1931- *WhoAm 90, WhoWor 91*
MacLaren, James *ConAu 33NR, MajTwCW*
Maclaren, James 1818-1892 *DcCanB 12*
Maclaren, Jeff 1951- *St&PR 91*
MacLaren, Mary 1900-1985 *BioIn 16*
Maclaren, Ronny K. 1939- *St&PR 91*
MacLaren, Roy 1934- *WhoAm 90*
Maclaskey, Steven Roy 1945- *WhoSSW 91*
Maclaughlin, Donald C. 1925- *St&PR 91*
Maclaughlin, Douglas Earl 1938- *WhoAm 90*
MacLaughlin, Francis Joseph 1933- *WhoAm 90*
MacLaughlin, Harry Hunter 1927- *WhoAm 90*
MacLaurin, William 1941- *ODwPR 91*
MacLaury, Bruce King 1931- *WhoAm 90*
MacLaury, Richard Joyce 1918- *WhoAm 90*
Maclay, Archibald 1776-1860 *BioIn 16*
Maclay, Donald Merle 1934- *WhoAm 90*
Maclay, Robert Samuel 1824-1907 *BioIn 16*
Maclay, William Nevin 1924- *WhoAm 90*
Maclean, Lord *NewYTBS 90*
MacLean, Alan Scott 1940- *WhoSSW 91*
MacLean, Alex Stokes 1947- *WhoE 91*
MacLean, Alistair 1922- *AuBYP 90, WorAlBi*
MacLean, Alistair 1922-1987 *BioIn 16, ConLC 63 [port], MajTwCW, TwCCr&M 91*
Maclean, Alistair Stuart 1923-1987 *SpyFic*
Maclean, Barry L. 1938- *St&PR 91, WhoAm 90*
MacLean, Carolyn *BioIn 16*
Maclean, Charles 1945- *WhoAm 90*
Maclean, Charles 1946- *BioIn 16*
Maclean, Charles Hector Fitzroy 1916-1990 *BioIn 16*
Maclean, Daniel Crawford, III 1942- *St&PR 91, WhoAm 90*
MacLean, David Bailey 1923- *WhoAm 90*
Mac Lean, Donald *BiDrAPA 89*
Maclean, Donald Duart 1913-1983 *BioIn 16, DcNaB 1981*
MacLean, Donald I. 1929-1989 *BioIn 16*
MacLean, Effie *BioIn 16*
Maclean, Fitzroy 1911- *ConAu 31NR*
MacLean, Guy Robertson 1929- *WhoAm 90*
MacLean, Harry N 1942- *BestSel 90-3 [port], ConAu 130*
MacLean, Hector 1920- *WhoAm 90*
Maclean, J.B. 1946- *St&PR 91*
MacLean, Janet Rockwood 1917- *WhoAm 90*
MacLean, John Angus 1914- *WhoAm 90*
MacLean, John Ronald 1938- *WhoAm 90*
Maclean, John Torry 1933- *IntWWM 90*
MacLean, John W. 1940- *WhoE 91*
MacLean, Katherine Anne 1925- *RGTwCSF*
Mac Lean, Lloyd Douglas 1924- *WhoAm 90*
MacLean, Malcolm Alexander 1844-1895 *DcCanB 12*
Maclean, Malcolm Roderick, Jr. 1919- *WhoSSW 91*
Maclean, Norman *NewYTBS 90*
Maclean, Norman 1902-1990 *ConAu 132, WorAu 1980 [port]*
Maclean, Norman Fitzroy 1902- *WhoAm 90*
MacLean, Paul Donald 1913- *WhoAm 90*
MacLean Beaty, Shirley 1934- *EncO&P 3*
Maclean-Smith, Elizabeth 1916- *WhoAmA 91*
Maclear, Thomas 1815-1898 *DcCanB 12*
Macleay, Donald 1908- *WhoAm 90*
MacLeish, Archibald 1892-1982 *BioIn 16, ConAu 33NR, MajTwCW, WorAlBi*
MacLeish, William H. 1928- *BioIn 16*
MacLeish, William Hitchcock 1928- *WhoE 91*
Maclellan, Hugh O. 1912- *St&PR 91*
MacLennan, Beryce W. 1920- *WhoAm 90*
Mac Lennan, David Herman 1937- *WhoAm 90*
MacLennan, Hugh *NewYTBS 90 [port]*
MacLennan, Hugh 1907- *MajTwCW, WhoAm 90*
MacLennan, Hugh 1907-1990 *ConAu 33NR*
Maclennan, Robert Douglas 1932- *St&PR 91*
Mac Leod, Alastair W *BiDrAPA 89*
MacLeod, Alistair *BioIn 16*
Macleod, Alistair 1939- *WhoWor 91*
Macleod, Anthony Michael 1947- *St&PR 91, WhoAm 90*
MacLeod, Beatrice 1910- *AuBYP 90*
MacLeod, Charlotte 1922- *TwCCr&M 91, WhoAmW 91*
MacLeod, Colin Munro 1909-1972 *DcScB S2*
Macleod, Daniel Broyles 1941- *St&PR 91*
Macleod, David E. 1924- *St&PR 91*
MacLeod, Denis Frederick 1954- *WhoWor 91*
Macleod, Donald 1913- *WhoAm 90*
Macleod, Donald G. 1930- *St&PR 91*
Macleod, Donald Goulding 1928- *St&PR 91*
MacLeod, Donald Martin 1929- *WhoSSW 91*
MacLeod, Donald W. 1925- *St&PR 91*
MacLeod, Doug 1959- *SmATA 60 [port]*
MacLeod, Douglas Donald 1930- *WhoE 91*
MacLeod, Edward James Waring 1950- *WhoE 91*
MacLeod, Fiona 1856-1905 *EncO&P 3*
Macleod, Fred Lawrence 1926- *St&PR 91*
Macleod, Gavin 1930- *WorAlBi*
MacLeod, Gavin 1931- *WhoAm 90*
MacLeod, Gordon Kenneth 1929- *WhoAm 90*
Mac Leod, Ian Roberts 1931- *St&PR 91*
MacLeod, Ian Roberts 1931- *WhoAm 90, WhoEmL 91*
Macleod, Iris Jean 1927- *IntWWM 90*
MacLeod, Jack 1931- *WhoAm 90*
Macleod, James Farquharson 1836?-1894 *DcCanB 12, WhNaAH*
Mac Leod, John A 1925- *BiDrAPA 89*
Macleod, John A., Jr. 1951- *St&PR 91*
Macleod, John Amend 1942- *WhoAm 90, WhoWor 91*
MacLeod, John Daniel, Jr. 1922- *WhoAm 90, WhoSSW 91*
Macleod, John Graeme 1930- *WhoSSW 91, WhoWor 91*
Macleod, John J. R. 1876-1935 *WorAlBi*
Macleod, Kathi Ann 1960- *St&PR 91*
MacLeod, Kenneth Authier 1934- *WhoAm 90*
Macleod, Malcolm W. *St&PR 91*
Macleod, Millie Evelyn 1933- *WhoAmW 91*
MacLeod, Norman Cloud 1931- *WhoWor 91*
MacLeod, Pegi Nichol *WhoAmA 91N*
MacLeod, Robert *TwCCr&M 91*
MacLeod, Robert Angus 1921- *WhoAm 90*
MacLeod, Robert Fredric 1917- *WhoAm 90*
MacLeod, Stuart Maxwell 1943- *WhoAm 90*
MacLeod, Thomas D. *WhoAm 90*
MacLeod, Yan 1889-1978 *WhoAmA 91N*
Macletchie, J. Graeme, III 1937- *St&PR 91*
Maclin, Ernest 1931- *St&PR 91, WhoAm 90*
Maclin, Samuel Earl 1929- *St&PR 91*
Maclure, Samuel 1860-1929 *BioIn 16*
Maclure, William 1763-1840 *BioIn 16*
MacLurg, B. Jason 1952- *BiDrAPA 89*
MacMahon, Brian 1923- *WhoAm 90*
MacMahon, Charles Hutchins, Jr. 1918- *WhoAm 90*
Macmahon, Harold Bernard 1917- *St&PR 91*
MacMahon, John 1935- *BiDrAPA 89*
MacMahon, Lloyd F. 1912-1989 *BioIn 16*
Macmahon, Marie Edme Patrice Maurice De 1808-1893 *WorAlBi*
MacMahon, Marie-Edmonde P M, comte de 1808-1893 *BiDFrPL*
Macmannis, Kenneth Lawrence 1925- *St&PR 91*
MacManus, Declan Patrick Aloysius *BioIn 16*
MacManus, James *AuBYP 90*
Macmanus, L. 1850?-1941 *FemiCLE*
MacManus, Quentin 1944- *WhoSSW 91*
MacManus, Seumas 1869-1960 *AuBYP 90*
MacManus, Susan Ann 1947- *WhoAmW 91, WhoSSW 91, WhoWor 91*
MacManus, Yvonne Cristina 1931- *WhoWrEP 89*
MacMaster, Daniel Miller 1913- *WhoAm 90*
Macmaster, Douglas Joseph, Jr. 1930- *St&PR 91, WhoAm 90*
Mac Master, Duncan R *BiDrAPA 89*
MacMaster, Duncan Raymond 1934- *WhoE 91*
MacMaster, Lori Fritze 1956- *WhoSSW 91*
MacMaster, Patricia Ruth Hughes 1940- *WhoSSW 91*
MacMaster, Robert Ellsworth 1919- *WhoAm 90*
Mac Master, William R 1938- *BiDrAPA 89*
Macmeeken, John Peebles 1924- *WhoAm 90*
MacMeekin, Donald Markell 1947- *WhoE 91*
Macmillan, Alexander Daniel Alan 1943- *WhoWor 91*
MacMillan, Catherine Cope 1947- *WhoAmW 91*
MacMillan, David Wishart 1937- *WhoSSW 91*
Macmillan, Diane Frances 1938- *St&PR 91*
Macmillan, Donald B. 1874-1970 *WorAlBi*
MacMillan, Douglas Clark 1912- *WhoAm 90*
Macmillan, Douglas Hathaway 1946- *St&PR 91, WhoAm 90*
Macmillan, Ernest 1893-1973 *PenDiMP*
Macmillan, Harold 1894-1986 *BioIn 16, WorAlBi*
Macmillan, J. Graham 1941- *St&PR 91*
MacMillan, Jake 1924- *WhoWor 91*
Macmillan, James *ConAu 129*
Macmillan, James 1959- *IntWWM 90*
Mac Millan, James Edmund 1953- *BiDrAPA 89*
Macmillan, Jennifer-Anne 1956- *IntWWM 90*
MacMillan, Joann Lawler 1926- *WhoAmW 91*
MacMillan, John Hugh, Jr. 1895-1960 *ConAmBL*
MacMillan, Kenneth 1929- *WhoAm 90, WhoWor 91, WorAlBi*
MacMillan, Kip Van Metre 1937- *WhoWor 91*
MacMillan, Tracy Marie 1953- *WhoAmW 91*
MacMillan, Whitney 1929- *ConAmBL*
Macmillan, William Hooper 1923- *WhoAm 90*
MacMillan, William Leedom, Jr. 1913- *WhoAm 90*
MacMillan, Yolanda *BioIn 16*
MacMillen, William Charles, Jr. 1913- *WhoAm 90*
MacMinn, Aleene Merle Barnes 1930- *WhoAm 90*
Macmonnies, M. *BiDWomA*
MacMullen, Jean Alexandria Stewart 1945- *WhoAmW 91, WhoSSW 91*
MacMullen, Neil Harvard 1938- *WhoAm 90*
MacMullen, Ramsay 1928- *WhoAm 90*
MacMurchy, Marjory *FemiCLE*
Macmurray, Fred 1908- *WorAlBi*
MacMurray, Frederick Martin 1908- *WhoAm 90*
Macmurray, James A. 1925- *St&PR 91*
MacMurren, Harold Henry, Jr. 1942- *WhoE 91*
Macnabb, W.V. 1937- *St&PR 91*
MacNair, Andrew Pierce 1946- *WhoE 91*
MacNair, Donald Shaw 1928- *WhoSSW 91*
Macnair, F. *BiDWomA*
Mac Namara, Donal E.J. 1916- *WhoWrEP 89*
Mac Namara, Donal Eoin Joseph 1916- *WhoAm 90*
Macnamara, John 1925- *St&PR 91, WhoAm 90*
Macnamara, Susan Elizabeth 1955- *WhoAmW 91*
Macnamara, Thomas Edward 1929- *WhoAm 90*
MacNaughtan, Sarah 1864-1916 *FemiCLE*
MacNaughton, Alexander Douglas 1913- *WhoAm 90*
MacNaughton, Angus Athole 1931- *WhoAm 90, WhoWor 91*
Mac Naughton, Anne L. 1945- *WhoWrEP 89*
Macnaughton, Bruce A. 1930- *St&PR 91*
Mac Naughton, D. Bruce *St&PR 91*
Mac Naughton, David Victor, Jr. *BiDrAPA 89*
Macnaughton, Donald S. 1917- *St&PR 91*
MacNaughton, Donald Sinclair 1917- *WhoAm 90*
MacNaughton, John David Francis 1932- *WhoAm 90*
Macnaughton, Malcolm, Jr. 1938- *St&PR 91*
Macnaughton, Robert *BioIn 16*
MacNeal, Edward Arthur 1925- *WhoE 91, WhoWor 91*
Macnee, Alan Breck 1920- *WhoAm 90*
MacNee, Patrick *BioIn 16*
Macnee, Patrick 1922- *WhoAm 90, WorAlBi*
MacNeice, Louis 1907-1963 *MajTwCW*
MacNeil, Catherine 1936- *WhoSSW 91*
Macneil, Cornell 1922- *IntWWM 90, PenDiMP*
MacNeil, Duncan *TwCCr&M 91*

MacNeil, Grace M. S. McKittrick 1907- WhoAm 90
Macneil, Ian Roderick 1929- WhoAm 90
Mac Neil, Joseph Neil 1924- WhoAm 90
Mac Neil, Melinda Sopher 1957- WhoSSW 91
MacNeil, Neil TwCCr&M 91
MacNeil, Rita BioIn 16
MacNeil, Robert 1931- BioIn 16, WorAlBi
MacNeil, Robert Breckenridge Ware 1931- WhoAm 90
MacNeill, Alastair 1960- ConAu 130
Macneill, D. Gilmore 1931- St&PR 91
Macneill, Frederick Douglas 1929- WhoAmA 91
Macneill, H.G. 1925- St&PR 91
MacNeill, Hugh Gordon 1925- WhoAm 90
Mac Neill, James William 1928- WhoAm 90
Macneill, Robert Charles 1946- St&PR 91
Macneill, William E. 1941- St&PR 91
Macneill, William Eric 1941- WhoAm 90
Mac Neish, Richard Stockton 1918- WhoAm 90
MacNelly, Jeff BioIn 16
MacNelly, Jeff 1947- EncACom
Mac Nelly, Jeffrey Kenneth 1947- WhoAm 90
Macnelly, Jeffrey Kenneth 1947- WhoAmA 91
MacNichol, Edward Ford, Jr. 1918- WhoAm 90
MacNichol, George Pope 1899-1989 BioIn 16
MacNicol, Peter BioIn 16
Macnider, Jack 1927- St&PR 91, WhoAm 90
MacNow, Alan 1932- ODwPR 91
MacNutt, Glenn Gordon 1906-1987 WhoAmA 91N
Maco, Paul Stephen, Jr. 1952- WhoEmL 91
Maco, Teri R. 1953- WhoAmW 91
Macom, John Morgan, III 1965- St&PR 91
Macomber, Allison 1916-1979 WhoAmA 91N
Macomber, George 1927- St&PR 91, WhoAm 90
Macomber, J. Locke 1923- St&PR 91
Macomber, John D. 1928- WhoAm 90
Macon, Dave 1870-1952 OxCPMus
Macon, Irene Elizabeth 1935- WhoAmW 91, WhoWor 91
Macon, Max 1915- Ballpl 90
Macon, Myra Faye 1937- WhoAmW 91
Macon, Seth Craven 1919- WhoAm 90
Maconchy, Elizabeth 1907- IntWWM 90
Macovski, Albert 1929- WhoAm 90
MacPeek, Walter G. 1902-1973 AuBYP 90
Macphail, Andrew 1864-1938 DcLB 92 [port]
MacPhail, Andy WhoAm 90
MacPhail, Larry 1890-1975 Ballpl 90 [port], BioIn 16
MacPhail, Lee 1917- Ballpl 90, BioIn 16
MacPhail, Lloyd George 1920- WhoAm 90, WhoE 91
Macphail, Moray St. John 1912- WhoAm 90
MacPhearson, James ConAu 131
MacPhee, Allan Alexander 1941- WhoSSW 91
MacPhee, Donald Albert 1928- WhoAm 90
MacPhee, Gordon W. 1941- WhoE 91
Macphee, John 1928- St&PR 91
MacPherson, Alexa Zivley Binnion 1956- WhoAmW 91
Macpherson, Craig 1944- St&PR 91
Macpherson, David Lewis 1818-1896 DcCanB 12
Macpherson, Duncan Ian 1924- WhoAm 90
Macpherson, Elle BioIn 16
MacPherson, Frank Becker, III 1948- WhoE 91
Macpherson, George W. 1856-1943 AmLegL
Macpherson, Gordon Clarke 1924- IntWWM 90
MacPherson, Herbert Grenfell 1911- WhoAm 90
Macpherson, Jay 1931- FemiCLE
MacPherson, Jill Aaron 1960- WhoE 91
Macpherson, Kevin BioIn 16, WhoAmA 91
MacPherson, Margaret L. AuBYP 90
MacPherson, Robert B. 1928- ODwPR 91
MacPherson, Robert Duncan 1944- WhoE 91
Macpherson, Robert W. 1924- St&PR 91
MacPherson, Thomas George 1915-1976 AuBYP 90
Macpherson, Trevor Andrew 1946- WhoE 91
Macquarre, John F., Sr. 1943- St&PR 91
Macquarrie, Heath Nelson 1919- WhoAm 90
MacQueen, Angus James 1912- WhoAm 90
MacQueen, Elizabeth BioIn 16
MacQueen, James Henry 1962- WhoSSW 91
MacQueen, Jane W. ODwPR 91
Mac Queen, Robert Mitchell 1939- St&PR 91
MacQueen, Robert Moffat 1938- WhoAm 90
Macquet, Michel-Guy Francois 1957- WhoWor 91
MacQuiddy, Jean Elizabeth 1943- WhoE 91
MacQuitty, Jonathan James 1952- WhoEmL 91
Macquoid, Alan P. 1935- St&PR 91
Macquoid, Katharine S. 1824-1917 FemiCLE
Macquown, David K. 1948- St&PR 91
Macquown, Richard Sladden 1919- St&PR 91
Mac Rae, Alfred Urquhart 1932- WhoAm 90
MacRae, Allison BioIn 16
MacRae, C. Duncan 1940- WhoAm 90
MacRae, Cameron Farquhar 1905- WhoAm 90
MacRae, Cameron Farquhar, III 1942- WhoAm 90
MacRae, Donald Alexander 1916- WhoAm 90
Mac Rae, Donald Keith BiDrAPA 89
MacRae, Duncan, Jr. 1921- WhoAm 90
Macrae, Duncan A. 1943- St&PR 91
MacRae, Edith Krugelis 1919- WhoAm 90
MacRae, Elisabeth L BiDrAPA 89
Macrae, Gordon 1921-1986 WorAlBi
Mac Rae, Herbert Farquhar 1926- WhoAm 90
MacRae, Mary Jenkins 1954- WhoAmW 91
MacRae, Meredith BioIn 16
Macrae, Travis AuBYP 90
Mac Rane, Buick WhoWrEP 89
Macready, William Charles 1793-1873 BioIn 16
Macri, Francisco 1930- WhoWor 91
Macri, Theodore William 1937- WhoAm 90
Macridis, Roy Constantine 1918- WhoAm 90
Macro, Eric 1920- ConAu 32NR
Mac Robbie, D Stuart 1924- BiDrAPA 89
MacRobert, Russell Galbraith 1890- EncO&P 3
Macroe-Wiegand, Viola Lucille 1920- WhoAmW 91, WhoE 91, WhoWor 91
Macrory, Patrick Francis John 1941- WhoAm 90
Macrum, Joseph M. 1938- ODwPR 91
MacRury, King 1915- WhoAm 90, WhoE 91, WhoWor 91
Macsai, John 1926- WhoAm 90
MacShane, Frank 1927- ConAu 33NR
MacTaggart, Terrence Joseph 1946- WhoAm 90
MacTaggart, William 1903-1981 DcNaB 1981
Mac Tavish, John Newton 1936- BiDrAPA 89
Mactye, David Craig 1930- BiDrAPA 89
Macuch, Rudolf 1919- WhoWor 91
Maculaitis, Jean D'Arcy WhoAmW 91, WhoE 91
Macune, Mary Julia 1956- St&PR 91
Macur, Patricia A. WhoAmW 91
Macurdy, John 1929- IntWWM 90
Macurdy, John Edward 1929- WhoAm 90
Macut, Sharon Nickolene 1951- WhoAmW 91
Macvaugh, Gilbert S 1902-1990 ConAu 131
MacVeagh, Charles 1860-1931 BioIn 16
MacVeagh, Franklin 1837-1934 BiDrUSE 89
MacVeagh, Lincoln 1890-1972 BioIn 16
MacVeagh, Wayne 1833-1917 BiDrUSE 89
MacVean, Jean ConAu 131
MacVicar, Angus 1908- ConAu 30NR
Mac Vicar, Margaret Love Agnes 1943- WhoAm 90
Mac Vicar, Mary K BiDrAPA 89
Mac Vicar, Robert William 1918- WhoAm 90
Mac Vittie, Robert William 1920- WhoAm 90
MacWatters, Virginia BioIn 16
Mac Watters, Virginia Elizabeth WhoAm 90
MacWeeney, Alen Brazil 1939- WhoAmA 91
Mac Whinnie, John Vincent 1945- WhoAmA 91, WhoWor 91
MacWhorter, Robert Bruce 1930- WhoAm 90
MacWilliams, Florence Jessie 1917-1990 BioIn 16
Macwilliams, Kenneth Edward 1936- St&PR 91, WhoE 91
MacWilliams, Richard Kent 1952- WhoAm 90
Macy, Anne Sullivan 1866-1936 BioAmW, WorAlBi
Macy, Bruce Wendell 1930- St&PR 91
Macy, Carleton 1944- IntWWM 90
Macy, Dayna Alison 1960- WhoAmW 91
Macy, Henrietta Gardner 1854-1927 BioAmW
Macy, Icie Gertrude 1892-1984 BioIn 16
Macy, Mark H. 1949- WhoWrEP 89
Macy, Richard J. WhoAm 90
Macy, Terrence William 1946- WhoE 91
Macy Marcy, Suzanne Kay 1951- WhoAmW 91
Maczaj, Marta BiDrAPA 89
Maczka, Jan H. 1948- ODwPR 91
Maczko, Karen M BiDrAPA 89
Maczulski, Margaret Louise 1949- WhoAmW 91, WhoEmL 91
Mad Mike WhoWrEP 89
Madach, Michael Jay 1927- WhoSSW 91
Madah, Anna BioIn 16
Madaiah, Madappa 1936- WhoWor 91
Madakasira, Sudhakar 1951- BiDrAPA 89
Madama, Patrick Stephen 1951- WhoE 91
Madamala, Thakshaka M BiDrAPA 89
Madame de BAAAs EncCoWW
Madame d'Orleans EncCoWW
Madame la baronne Caroline A. EncCoWW
Madan, Judith 1702-1781 FemiCLE
Madan, Rafael Alberto 1962- WhoE 91
Madan-Shotkin, Rhoda WhoAmA 91
Madansky, Albert 1934- WhoAm 90
Madansky, Leon 1923- WhoAm 90
Madar, Jean 1961- St&PR 91
Madar, William P. 1939- St&PR 91
Madaras, Thomas Patrick 1958- WhoE 91
Madaras, William 1957- ODwPR 91
Madariaga, Salvador de 1886-1978 ConAu 32NR, HispWr 90
Madariaga y Rojo, Salvador de 1886-1978 ConAu 32NR, HispWr 90
Maday, Clifford Ronald 1947- WhoSSW 91
Madda, Carl J. 1936- St&PR 91
Maddaiah, Shaila 1957- BiDrAPA 89
Maddalena, Frank Joseph 1941- WhoAm 90
Maddalena, Lucille Ann 1948- WhoAm 90, WhoAmW 91
Madden, Bartley Joseph 1943- WhoWor 91
Madden, Bert Conger 1932- St&PR 91
Madden, Betty Campbell 1942- St&PR 91
Madden, Brian Brendan 1937- WhoE 91
Madden, Dann Michael 1932- St&PR 91
Madden, David 1933- LiHiK, MajTwCW, WhoAm 90, WhoWrEP 89
Madden, Dean E. 1921- St&PR 91
Madden, Denis BioIn 16
Madden, Donald Paul 1933- WhoAm 90
Madden, Edward Harry 1925- WhoAm 90
Madden, Emma Fae 1931- WhoAmW 91
Madden, Eva 1863-1958 LiHiK
Madden, G. William 1925- St&PR 91
Madden, Gerald Patrick 1942- WhoE 91
Madden, Ian Beresford 1931- WhoWor 91
Madden, James Anthony 1940- BiDrAPA 89
Madden, Janice Fanning 1947- WhoE 91
Madden, Jerome Anthony 1948- WhoEmL 91
Madden, Joan Mayne 1932- St&PR 91
Madden, John BioIn 16
Madden, John 1936- WhoAm 90
Madden, John, Jr. 1929- St&PR 91
Madden, John Joseph 1946- WhoEmL 91
Madden, John Kevin 1938- WhoAm 90
Madden, John Stephen 1937- WhoAm 90, WhoSSW 91
Madden, Joseph Daniel 1921- WhoAm 90
Madden, Joseph R. 1919- St&PR 91
Madden, Kenneth Cromwell, Jr. 1950- WhoE 91
Madden, Laurence Vincent 1953- WhoEmL 91
Madden, Lawrence J. St&PR 91
Madden, Leo James 1932- St&PR 91
Madden, Lloyd Willis 1918- WhoWor 91
Madden, Margaret Ruth BiDrAPA 89
Madden, Marie Frances 1928- WhoSSW 91
Madden, Marsha Louise 1952- WhoAmW 91
Madden, Martin WhoAm 90
Madden, Michael Daniel 1949- WhoAm 90
Madden, Michael E. BioIn 16
Madden, Mike 1957- Ballpl 90
Madden, Murdaugh Stuart 1922- WhoAm 90
Madden, Patrick M. ODwPR 91
Madden, Peter E. 1942- WhoAm 90
Madden, Richard B. 1929- St&PR 91
Madden, Richard Blaine 1929- WhoAm 90
Madden, Richard Lewis 1951- WhoSSW 91
Madden, Richard Othick 1948- St&PR 91
Madden, Robert T. 1922- St&PR 91
Madden, Ronald Rex 1956- WhoWor 91
Madden, Thomas J. 1947- St&PR 91
Madden, Thomas J., III 1947- WhoAm 90
Madden, Thomas James 1941- WhoAm 90
Madden, Wales Hendrix, Jr. 1927- St&PR 91, WhoAm 90
Madden-Work, Betty I 1915- WhoAmA 91
Maddern, Al MajTwCW
Maddern, Bruce Robert 1954- WhoEmL 91, WhoSSW 91
Maddex, Myron Brown 1924- WhoAm 90
Maddicks, Nona Mihr 1942- WhoAmW 91
Maddie, John E. 1934- St&PR 91
Maddison, Angus 1926- WhoWor 91
Maddison, Dorothy 1956- IntWWM 90
Maddock, Reginald 1912- AuBYP 90
Maddock, Richard John BiDrAPA 89
Maddock, Rosemary Schroer 1919- WhoAmW 91, WhoWor 91
Maddock, Thomas Smothers 1928- WhoAm 90
Maddocks, James 1919- IntWWM 90
Maddocks, John H. St&PR 91
Maddocks, Robert Allen 1933- St&PR 91, WhoAm 90
Maddow, Ben 1909- BioIn 16
Maddox, Alva Hugh 1930- WhoAm 90
Maddox, C. Brian 1957- ODwPR 91
Maddox, Catharine Patrick 1948- WhoAmW 91
Maddox, Dan W. 1909- St&PR 91
Maddox, Edwin Thomas, Jr. 1941- WhoSSW 91
Maddox, Elliott 1947- Ballpl 90
Maddox, Garry 1949- Ballpl 90
Maddox, Gloria Denby EarBlAP
Maddox, Jay R. 1936- St&PR 91
Maddox, Jerald Curtis 1933- WhoAmA 91
Maddox, Jerrold Warren 1932- WhoAmA 91
Maddox, Jesse Cordell 1931- WhoAm 90
Maddox, Lester 1915- WorAlBi
Maddox, Michele 1946- WhoAmW 91
Maddox, Milton Roland 1937- St&PR 91
Maddox, Nick 1886-1954 Ballpl 90
Maddox, Randall Bert 1959- WhoSSW 91
Maddox, Robert Alan 1944- WhoAm 90
Maddox, Robert L. 1935- IntWWM 90
Maddox, Robert Nott 1925- WhoAm 90
Maddox, Truett Layton, Jr. BiDrAPA 89
Maddox, William C. 1938- St&PR 91
Maddrey, E. E., II WhoSSW 91
Maddrey, Willis Crocker 1939- WhoAm 90
Maddux, Deborah BioIn 16
Maddux, Greg 1966- Ballpl 90
Maddux, Holly BioIn 16
Maddux, James F 1916- BiDrAPA 89
Maddux, Mike 1961- Ballpl 90
Maddux, Robert F BiDrAPA 89
Madeira, Edward Walter, Jr. 1928- WhoAm 90
Madeira, Francis King Carey 1917- WhoAm 90
Madeira, Jean 1918-1972 PenDiMP
Madeira, Robert Lehman 1915- WhoAm 90
Madeleva, Mary 1887-1964 FemiCLE
Maden, William Leroy, Jr. 1931- BiDrAPA 89
Madeo, Elfriede M BiDrAPA 89
Madeo, Elfriede M. 1934- WhoE 91
Mader, Jon Terry 1944- WhoWor 91
Mader, Pamela Beile 1939- WhoAmW 91
Mader, Sheldon George 1929- St&PR 91
Mader, William 1934- WhoWor 91
Madera, Asuncion 1901- EncCoWW
Madera, Chona EncCoWW
Madera, Cornelius J. J., Jr. 1949- WhoAm 90
Madera, Joseph J. 1927- WhoAm 90
Madera, Maria S. 1953- WhoHisp 91
Madera, Marie Louise 1955- WhoAmW 91
Maderna, Bruno 1920-1973 PenDiMP, -A
Madero, Francisco I. 1873-1913 BioIn 16
Madewell, D'Ann 1945- WhoSSW 91
Madey, Candice Whitmore 1958- WhoAmW 91
Madey, Ronald Eliot 1959- WhoE 91
Madge, Nicola 1949- ConAu 130
Madgett, Naomi Long 1923- WhoWrEP 89
Madhavan, Jaya K 1941- BiDrAPA 89
Madhere, Marie Immaculee Magaly 1953- WhoAmW 91
Madhubuti, Haki R. 1942- DcLB DS8 [port]
Madhusoodanan, Subramoniam 1947- BiDrAPA 89
Madia, Sandra 1943- St&PR 91
Madia, William Juul 1947- St&PR 91, WhoAm 90
Madian, Jon 1941- AuBYP 90

Madigan, Amy 1957- WhoAmW 91
Madigan, Daniel Paul 1956- St&PR 91
Madigan, Doris Mary St&PR 91
Madigan, Edward R. 1936- WhoAm 90
Madigan, Grace Evelyn 1902- WhoWrEP 89
Madigan, James D. 1951-1988 BioIn 16
Madigan, James E. 1923- St&PR 91
Madigan, Janet Ann 1952- BiDrAPA 89
Madigan, Jeanne Marie 1958- WhoEmL 91, WhoSSW 91
Madigan, John BioIn 16
Madigan, John William 1937- St&PR 91, WhoAm 90
Madigan, Joseph Edward 1932- WhoAm 90
Madigan, Joseph V. 1933- ODwPR 91
Madigan, Mary Ann BioIn 16
Madigan, Mary Jean Smith WhoAmA 91
Madigan, Michael Joseph 1942- WhoAm 90
Madigan, Michael Joseph 1946- BiDrAPA 89
Madigan, Richard Allen 1937- WhoAm 90, WhoAmA 91
Madigan, Richard Edward 1941- WhoAm 90
Madigan, William Michael 1925- St&PR 91
Madis, Voldemar 1941- St&PR 91, WhoE 91
Madisetty, Sasi 1947- BiDrAPA 89
Madison, Alfreda Louise 1911-1989 ConAu 129
Madison, Arnold 1937- AuBYP 90
Madison, Bernard L. 1941- WhoAm 90
Madison, Dave 1921-1985 Ballpl 90
Madison, Dolley 1768-1849 BioIn 16, WorAlBi
Madison, Dolly 1768-1849 FemiCLE
Madison, Dolly Payne 1768-1849 BioAmW
Madison, Douglas H. 1950- St&PR 91
Madison, Gary 1940- ConAu 131
Madison, James 1751-1836 BiDrUSE 89, BioIn 16, EncCRAm [port], WorAlBi
Madison, James Raymond 1931- WhoAm 90
Madison, James S. 1834- AmLegL
Madison, Robert Prince 1923- WhoAm 90
Madison, Roberta Eleanor 1932- WhoAmW 91
Madison, Thomas F. 1936- WhoAm 90
Madison, Thomas Frederick 1936- St&PR 91
Madison, Vivian L. 1956- WhoEmL 91
Madison-Glover, Carol BiDrAPA 89
Madjeski, Ed 1909- Ballpl 90
Madla, Frank 1937- WhoHisp 91
Madle, Robert Albert 1920- WhoE 91, WhoWor 91
Madlee, Dorothy 1917-1980 AuBYP 90
Madlener, Elizabeth W. 1941- WhoAmW 91
Madler, Paul W. 1929- St&PR 91
Madley, Maurice Andrew 1936- St&PR 91
Madlock, Bill BioIn 16
Madlock, Bill 1951- Ballpl 90 [port], WorAlBi
Madness OxCPMus
Madni, Asad Mohamed 1947- WhoEmL 91
Madni, Azad M. 1945- St&PR 91
Madokawando 1630?-1698 WhNaAH
Madonia, Ann C WhoAmA 91
Madonick, Moses J 1907- BiDrAPA 89
Madonna BioIn 16
Madonna 1958- ConMus 4 [port], OxCPMus, WhoAm 90
Madonna 1959- EncPR&S 89, WorAlBi
Mador, Joseph Alan 1957- BiDrAPA 89
Mador, Joseph F. 1940- St&PR 91
Madore, Bernadette 1918- WhoAmW 91
Madorsky, Harold A. 1950- St&PR 91
Madory, Marticia 1941- ODwPR 91
Madow, Leo 1915- BiDrAPA 89, WhoAm 90, WhoE 91
Madow, Michael R BiDrAPA 89
Madras, Michael J. 1950- WhoSSW 91
Madrazo, Aurelio 1935- St&PR 91
Madrazo y Kuntz, Federico de 1815-1894 BioIn 16
Madresehee, Mehrdad 1948- WhoE 91
Madresh, Richard 1945- St&PR 91
Madri, Alberta Maria 1924- WhoWrEP 89
Madrid, Arnulfo Arias BioIn 16
Madrid, Arturo WhoHisp 91
Madrid, Chilo L. 1945- WhoHisp 91
Madrid, Donna Kay 1937- WhoAmW 91
Madrid, Harmodio Arias 1886-1962 BioIn 16
Madrid, Jay Joseph 1942- WhoAm 90
Madrid, Jose Saul 1956- WhoHisp 91
Madrid, Leasher Dennis 1949- WhoHisp 91
Madrid-Barela, Arturo 1939- BioIn 16
Madrid Hurtado, Miguel de la BioIn 16
Madridejos, Sol 1958- WomArch [port]
Madrigal, Ray 1944- WhoHisp 91
Madrigal, Vicente 1880-1972 BioIn 16
Madrigal-Nieto, Rodrigo 1924- WhoWor 91
Madris, Russell L. 1957- St&PR 91
Madron, Beverly Brown 1937- WhoAmW 91
Madry, Maude Holt 1949- WhoSSW 91
Madsen, Adam M. 1936- St&PR 91
Madsen, Arch Leonard 1913- WhoAm 90
Madsen, Axel 1930- ConAu 33NR
Madsen, Bent 1928- WhoWor 91
Madsen, Brigham Dwaine 1914- WhoAm 90
Madsen, Carlos N BiDrAPA 89
Madsen, Charles Clifford 1908- WhoAm 90
Madsen, Claus 1950- WhoWor 91
Madsen, Clifford K. 1937- IntWWM 90
Madsen, David William 1943- WhoE 91
Madsen, Dennis G. 1943- St&PR 91
Madsen, Don Ray 1946- WhoSSW 91
Madsen, Donald Howard 1922- WhoAm 90
Madsen, Dorothy Louise WhoAmW 91
Madsen, Douglas Fred 1942- WhoAm 90
Madsen, Douglas Thor 1935- St&PR 91
Madsen, Erik Strojer 1950- WhoWor 91
Madsen, Finn Toft 1947- WhoWor 91
Madsen, Hans 1949- WhoWor 91
Madsen, Hans Berg 1939- WhoWor 91
Madsen, Henrik, II 1929- WhoSSW 91
Madsen, Henry Stephen 1924- WhoAm 90
Madsen, Jan Birger Lovgren 1944- WhoWor 91
Madsen, Knud Borge 1939- WhoWor 91
Madsen, Linda Lorraine 1957- IntWWM 90
Madsen, Loren Wakefield 1943- WhoAm 90, WhoAmA 91
Madsen, Mette B 1955- WhoAmA 91
Madsen, Peter Eric 1945- WhoAm 90
Madsen, Richard Wellington 1938- WhoAm 90
Madsen, Rud Frik 1930- WhoWor 91
Madsen, Stephen Stewart 1951- WhoEmL 91
Madsen, T.C. PenDiDA 89
Madsen, Ted Alan 1953- St&PR 91
Madsen, Viggo Holm 1925- WhoAmA 91
Madsen, Virginia BioIn 16
Madsen, Willard R. 1932- St&PR 91
Madson, Jerry 1948- WhoWrEP 89
Madson, Paul 1944- St&PR 91
Maduakor, Obiajuru 1942- WhoWor 91
Madura, Jack Joseph 1941- WhoAmA 91
Madva, Stephen Alan 1948- WhoEmL 91
Maebori, Stanley T. 1943- St&PR 91
Maechler, Erwin 1925- St&PR 91, WhoAm 90, WhoWor 91
Maechling, Charles, Jr. 1920- WhoAm 90, WhoE 91
Maeda Clan EncJap
Maeda Toshiie 1538?-1599 EncJap
Maeda, Hiroshi 1919- WhoWor 91
Maeda, Hiroshi 1938- WhoWor 91
Maeda, J. A. 1940- WhoAmW 91
Maeda, Takayuki 1927- St&PR 91
Maeda, Yukio 1922- WhoWor 91
Maeder, Hans K. 1909-1988 BioIn 16
Maeder, Jean-Bernard 1949- WhoWor 91
Maeder, Kurt Arthur 1925- WhoWor 91
Maeder, Paul Albert 1954- WhoE 91
Maeder, Thomas 1951- ConAu 132
Maegaard, Jan Carl Christian 1926- IntWWM 90
Maegraith, Brian 1907-1989 AnObit 1989
Maehl, Audrey Ellsworth 1930- WhoAmW 91
Maehl, William Harvey 1915- WhoWor 91
Maehl, William Henry 1930- WhoAm 90
Maehr, Martin Louis 1932- WhoAm 90
Maejima, Noboru 1939- St&PR 91
Maekawa, Taijiro 1925- WhoWor 91
Maekawa, Zyun-iti 1925- WhoWor 91
Mael, Bobbie Louise 1955- WhoAmW 91
Maenpaa, Pekka Heikki 1939- WhoWor 91
Maenza, Lisa 1960- WhoE 91
Maenza, Philip Joseph 1950- WhoE 91
Maer, Claude McCabe, Jr. 1919- WhoAm 90
Maerker, Richard Erwin 1928- WhoSSW 91
Maeroff, Gene I. 1939- WhoAm 90
Maerov, Arnold S 1937- BiDrAPA 89
Maes, James Alfredo 1947- WhoHisp 91
Maes, Petra Jimenez 1947- WhoHisp 91
Maes, Robert A. 1937- WhoWor 91
Maes, Roman M. 1943- WhoHisp 91
Maese, Carlos Octavio, Jr. 1946- WhoSSW 91
Maesen, William August 1939- WhoWor 91
Maestre, Joaquin 1927- ODwPR 91
Maestro, Betsy 1944- AuBYP 90, BioIn 16
Maestro, Giulio 1942- AuBYP 90, BioIn 16
Maeterlinck, Maurice 1862-1949 EncO&P 3, EncPaPR 91, WorAlBi
Maetozo, Matthew G. BioIn 16
Maez, Yvette Georgina 1965- WhoHisp 91
Maeztu, Ramiro de 1875-1936 BioIn 16
Mafai, Antonietta Raphael 1900-1975 BioIn 16
Maffei, Charles Michael 1952- WhoSSW 91
Maffei, Dorothy J. 1951- WhoAmW 91
Maffei, Paolo 1926- WhoWor 91
Maffei, Paul R. 1936- St&PR 91
Maffei, Stephen R. 1939- St&PR 91
Maffeo, Elaine P. 1935- St&PR 91
Maffeo, Neil T. BioIn 16
Maffett, Dan Wesley 1929- St&PR 91
Maffett, Phillip Wayne 1924- St&PR 91
Maffezzoli, Giovanni PenDiDA 89
Maffie, Adolph BioIn 16
Maffie, Michael Otis 1948- St&PR 91, WhoAm 90
Maffly, Roy Herrick 1927- WhoAm 90
Mag, Morton 1903- St&PR 91
Magad, Linda Maureen 1940- WhoAmW 91
Magad, Samuel 1932- WhoAm 90
Magadan, Dave 1962- Ballpl 90
Magafan, Ethel WhoAmA 91
Magafan, Ethel 1916- WhoAm 90, WhoAmW 91
Magafan, Jennie 1916- WhoAmA 91N
Magalhaes, Benjamin Constant Botelho de 1836-1891 BioIn 16
Magalhaes, Thomaz Pompeu Pires 1954- WhoWor 91
Magallanes, Deborah Jean 1951- WhoAmW 91, WhoWor 91
Magaloff, Nikita 1912- IntWWM 90, PenDiMP
Magalska, James M. 1942- St&PR 91
Magana, Ignacio 1928- BiDrAPA 89
Magana, Raoul Daniel 1911- WhoHisp 91
Magana Garcia, Sabas 1921- WhoAm 90
Maganzini, Teresa Aversa 1951- WhoEmL 91
Magarian, Elizabeth Ann 1940- WhoSSW 91
Magarian, Robert Armen 1930- WhoAm 90
Magarity, Russell Lynn 1946- WhoAm 90
Magarrell, Elaine 1928- WhoWrEP 89
Magary, Alan Bruce 1942- WhoAm 90
Magary, Alan K. BioIn 16
Magary, Richard 1940- St&PR 91
Magasanik, Boris 1919- WhoAm 90
Magasiny, Irving Pincus 1925- WhoE 91
Magassy, Gabriel L BiDrAPA 89
Magat, Richard 1927- WhoE 91
Magaw, Susan G. ODwPR 91
Magazine, Alan Harrison 1944- WhoWor 91
Magaziner, Elliot A. 1921- IntWWM 90
Magaziner, Elliot Albert 1921- WhoE 91
Magaziner, Henry Jonas 1911- WhoAm 90
Magazzini, Gene 1914- WhoAmA 91
Magda EncCoWW
Magdales, Maria Erlinda Floro 1952- WhoWor 91
Magdeburg, Mechthild von 1210?-1282? EncCoWW
Magdol, Michael O. 1937- St&PR 91
Magdol, Michael Orin 1937- WhoE 91
Magdovitz, Earl J. 1943- St&PR 91
Magdovitz, Lawrence Maynard 1937- WhoSSW 91
Mageau, Mary Jane Magdalen 1934- IntWWM 90
Magee, A. Alan 1947- WhoE 91
Magee, Alan Arthur 1947- WhoAmA 91
Magee, Alderson 1929- WhoAmA 91
Magee, Bill 1864-1922 Ballpl 90
Magee, Charles L. 1943- St&PR 91
Magee, Charles Thomas 1932- WhoE 91
Magee, David B. 1925- St&PR 91
Magee, David Backhouse 1925- WhoE 91
Magee, Denis M. 1929- WhoWor 91
Magee, Forrest Craig 1943- WhoAm 90
Magee, Frank W. 1926- St&PR 91
Magee, John Adams 1946- St&PR 91
Magee, John Francis 1926- St&PR 91, WhoAm 90
Magee, Lee 1889-1966 Ballpl 90 [port]
Magee, M. Ann Sheen 1939- WhoAmW 91
Magee, Marshall R. 1946- WhoAm 90
Magee, Paul Terry 1937- WhoAm 90
Magee, Robert Paul 1947- WhoAm 90
Magee, Sharon Lynn 1952- WhoAmW 91
Magee, Sherry 1884-1929 Ballpl 90
Magee, Stephen Pat 1943- WhoAm 90
Magee, Thomas P. 1956- WhoE 91
Magee, Timothy M 1936- BiDrAPA 89
Magee, Wayne Edward 1929- WhoAm 90
Magee, Wes 1939- SmATA 64
Magel, Catherine Anne 1956- WhoAmA 91
Magellan, Ferdinand 1480?-1521 BioIn 16, EncCRAm, WorAlBi
Magelli, Paul John 1931- WhoAm 90
Magen, Jed Gary 1953- BiDrAPA 89, WhoEmL 91
Magen, Myron Shimin 1926- WhoAm 90
Magendie, Francois 1783-1855 WorAlBi
Magenheim, Michael Joseph 1941- St&PR 91, WhoAm 90
Magenheimer, Fred E. 1939- St&PR 91
Magenta, Muriel 1932- WhoAmA 91
Mager, Artur 1919- St&PR 91, WhoAm 90
Mager, Donald Northrop 1942- WhoWrEP 89
Mager, Ezra Pascal 1941- St&PR 91, WhoAm 90
Mager, Gus 1878-1956 EncACom
Mager, Harold BioIn 16
Mager, Howard M. St&PR 91
Mager, Howard M. 1948- WhoAm 90, WhoE 91
Magerkurth, George 1888-1966 Ballpl 90
Magers, Jane F. 1943- WhoAmW 91
Mages, Norman L 1935- BiDrAPA 89
Maggal, Moshe Morris 1908- WhoAm 90
Maggard, Marjorie Louise 1939- WhoE 91
Maggard, Sarah Elizabeth 1948- WhoEmL 91
Maggard, Woodrow Wilson, Jr. 1947- WhoWor 91
Maggart, Brandon 1933- ConTFT 8
Maggart, Thomas Allen 1946- WhoEmL 91
Maggiacomo, Joseph, Jr. 1930- St&PR 91
Maggin, Bruce 1943- St&PR 91
Maggio, Antonio Michelino BioIn 16
Maggio, Carmen J. 1925- St&PR 91
Maggio, Edward P. 1949- St&PR 91
Maggio, Henry Anthony BiDrAPA 89
Maggio, Joe 1938- SpyFic
Maggio, Joseph P. BioIn 16
Maggio, Loida Weber 1919- WhoWrEP 89
Maggio, Michael BioIn 16, ODwPR 91
Maggio, Michel G., Jr. 1956- WhoSSW 91
Maggio, Rosalie 1943- ConAu 130, WhoWrEP 89
Maggio, Salvatore A. 1931- ODwPR 91
Maggio, Thomas Edward 1935- St&PR 91
Maggiolini, Carlo Francesco 1758-1834 PenDiDA 89
Maggiolini, Giuseppe 1738-1814 PenDiDA 89
Maggiolo, Allison Joseph 1943- WhoWor 91
Maggiolo, Marcio E. Veloz HispWr 90
Maggiore, Susan 1957- WhoAmW 91
Maggipinto, V. Anthony 1943- WhoE 91
Maggs, Arnaud 1926- WhoAmA 91
Maggs, D.T. St&PR 91
Maggs, Louis Michael 1942- St&PR 91
Maggs, Peter Blount 1936- WhoAm 90
Maggs, Robert W., Jr. 1944- St&PR 91
Maggs, Robert William, Jr. 1944- WhoAm 90
Maggs, Roger John 1946- St&PR 91
Maghami, Mahmood Ghaem 1960- WhoEmL 91
Magharious, William D BiDrAPA 89
Maghazaji, Haider Ismail BiDrAPA 89
Magher, Craig Francis 1942- St&PR 91
Maghielse, Craig 1949- St&PR 91
Maghielse, Steve 1952- St&PR 91
Maghir, Rim BiDrAPA 89
Maghopoy, Felicitas 1948- St&PR 91
Magi, Enn 1943- BiDrAPA 89
Magical Strings NewAgMG
Magid, Boris BiDrAPA 89
Magid, David H. 1916- St&PR 91
Magid, Gail Avrum 1934- WhoAm 90
Magid, Gary Steven BiDrAPA 89
Magid, Per 1943- WhoWor 91
Magid, Samuel E. St&PR 91
Magid, Zalman BiDrAPA 89
Magida, Arthur Jay 1945- WhoAm 90
Magida, Nathan H. 1928- St&PR 91
Magida, Phyllis 1936- WhoWrEP 89
Magidson, Micki ODwPR 91
Magie, Patricia Crane 1961- WhoAmW 91
Magie, William A., Jr. 1931- St&PR 91
Magie, William Ashley, Jr. 1931- WhoAm 90
Magier, Igor BiDrAPA 89
Magier, Nina G 1910- BiDrAPA 89
Magiera, Estelle A BiDrAPA 89
Magill, Charles W. 1937- St&PR 91
Magill, Dan BioIn 16
Magill, Frank John 1927- WhoAm 90
Magill, Ian David BiDrAPA 89
Magill, J. Patrick 1953- St&PR 91
Magill, James Marion 1921- WhoAm 90
Magill, John 1949- St&PR 91
Magill, Kenneth Derwood, Jr. 1933- WhoE 91
Magill, Lawrence J. 1954- St&PR 91
Magill, Michael D. 1948- St&PR 91
Magill, Michael James Ponsonby 1942- WhoAm 90
Magill, Nathan BioIn 16
Magill, Robert F. 1917- ODwPR 91
Magill, Robert Francis 1917- St&PR 91
Magill, Samuel Hays 1928- WhoAm 90

Magill, Saraswathi Subbiah 1929- WhoE 91
Magill, William Davies, Jr. 1950- WhoSSW 91
Magill, William Sharp, III 1947- WhoSSW 91
Magin, Larry BiDrAPA 89
Maginn, John L. 1940- St&PR 91
Maginn, Raymond Graham 1925- St&PR 91
Maginn, William 1793-1842 BioIn 16
Maginnes, Agnes C. BioIn 16
Maginnis, Corinne F. 1948- St&PR 91
Maginnis, Steven Glen 1958- WhoSSW 91
Maginot, Adele EncO&P 3
Maginot, Andre 1877-1932 BiDFrPL, WorAlBi
Magistrali, Giovanni 1936- St&PR 91
Magistretti, Adriano BioIn 16
Magistretti, Vico 1920- ConDes 90, PenDiDA 89
Magistro, Charles John 1941- WhoAmA 91
Magitsky, Yefim BiDrAPA 89
Maglathlin, Leon Edward, Jr. 1926- St&PR 91
Magleby, Frank 1928- WhoAmA 91
Magley, Dennis Paul 1941- WhoSSW 91
Magliano, John V. 1945- St&PR 91
Maglich, Bogdan C 1928- News 90 [port]
Maglich, Bogdan C. 1934- WhoAm 90
Maglie, Sal 1917- Ballpl 90 [port]
Magliocco, E Bruno 1928- BiDrAPA 89
Magliola, Gertrude Louise 1933- WhoAmW 91
Magliola, Robert Rino-Thomas 1940- WhoWor 91
Magliolo, Joseph Salvatore 1947- St&PR 91
Magliozzi, Ray BioIn 16
Magliozzi, Tom BioIn 16
Magloire, Paul Eugene 1907- BioIn 16
Magman, Larry WhoAm 90
Magnan, Oscar Gustav 1937- WhoAmA 91
Magnani, Anna 1908-1973 WorAlBi
Magnani, Bruno 1926- WhoWor 91
Magnani, Livio Enrico 1920- WhoWor 91
Magnano, Louis A. St&PR 91
Magnano, Louis M. St&PR 91
Magnano, Salvatore Paul 1934- St&PR 91
Magnasco, Alessandro 1667-1749 IntDcAA 90
Magnatta, Ralph Andrew 1955- WhoE 91
Magneli, Arne 1914- WhoWor 91
Magnell, Steffen Inguar 1945- St&PR 91
Magnelli, Andrea Dale 1959- WhoAmW 91
Magner, Frederic 1950- St&PR 91
Magner, Fredric Michael 1950- WhoAm 90
Magner, George William 1927- WhoAm 90
Magner, James Edmund, Jr. 1928- WhoWrEP 89
Magner, Jerome Allen 1929- WhoAm 90, WhoE 91
Magner, Martin 1900- WhoAm 90
Magner, Rachel Harris WhoAmW 91
Magness, Bob John 1924- St&PR 91, WhoAm 90
Magness, Carla Louise 1957- WhoAmW 91
Magness, Howard Albert 1945- St&PR 91
Magness, Jacquelyn Mary 1957- WhoE 91
Magness, Michael Kenneth 1948- WhoEmL 91
Magness, Milton S. 1952- WhoSSW 91
Magnet, Myron 1944- WhoE 91
Magni, Giulio 1940- WhoWor 91
Magnier, Philippe 1930- St&PR 91
Magnier, Philippe Jean Marie 1930- WhoAm 90
Magnificent Lafayette 1871-1911 BioIn 16
Magnin, Cyril 1899-1988 BioIn 16
Magnissalis, Kostas Georges 1934- WhoWor 91
Magnoli, Michael A. WhoAm 90
Magnon, Alberto H., Jr. 1934- St&PR 91
Magnor, William T. 1915- St&PR 91
Magnotta, Dennis Phillip 1950- WhoE 91
Magnotta, John R. 1950- WhoE 91
Magnum, Wyatt D. 1961- WhoSSW 91
Magnus WhNaAH
Magnus, Frederick Samuel 1932- St&PR 91, WhoE 91
Magnus, Philip Douglas WhoAm 90
Magnus-Allcroft, Philip 1906-1988 AnObit 1988
Magnus-Levy, Adolf 1865-1955 DcScB S2
Magnusen, Donald Walter 1942- St&PR 91
Magnuson, Clyde R. 1928- St&PR 91
Magnuson, Donald Lee 1949- WhoAm 90
Magnuson, Donald V. 1925- St&PR 91
Magnuson, Gerald E. 1930- St&PR 91
Magnuson, Gerald Edward 1930- WhoAm 90
Magnuson, Harold Joseph 1913- WhoAm 90
Magnuson, James Vernon 1941- BiDrAPA 89
Magnuson, Jerry Ross 1943- St&PR 91
Magnuson, Jim 1946- Ballpl 90
Magnuson, Keith B. 1942- St&PR 91
Magnuson, Nancy 1944- WhoAm 90
Magnuson, Paul Arthur 1937- WhoAm 90
Magnuson, Robert John 1943- St&PR 91
Magnuson, Robert Martin 1927- WhoAm 90
Magnuson, Warren 1905-1989 BioIn 16
Magnuson, Warren G. 1905-1989 WorAlBi
Magnussen, Daniel Osar 1919- WhoWrEP 89
Magnussen, Erik PenDiDA 89
Magnussen, Erik 1940- ConDes 90
Magnussen, Gudmund 1908- BiDrAPA 89
Magnusson, Barney 1951- St&PR 91
Magnusson, Bernt Erland 1941- WhoWor 91
Magnusson, Gudmar Eyjolfur 1941- WhoWor 91
Magnusson, Gudmundur 1873-1918 DcScanL
Magnusson, Kathy Ruth 1957- WhoAmW 91
Magnusson, Magnus 1954- WhoWor 91
Magoffin, Richard I. 1939- St&PR 91
Magon, Ricardo Flores 1873-1922 BioIn 16
Magon, Ricardo Flores 1874-1922 EncAL [port]
Magoon, Charles Edward 1861-1920 BioIn 16
Magoon, Duncan J J 1933- BiDrAPA 89
Magoon, George 1851-1929 BioIn 16
Magoon, George 1875-1943 Ballpl 90
Magoon, John Bruce 1960- WhoE 91
Magoon, John Henry, Jr. 1915- WhoAm 90
Magoon, Linda J. 1950- St&PR 91
Magor, Howard 1922- St&PR 91
Magor, Louis Roland 1945- WhoAm 90
Magorian, James Irvin 1942- WhoWrEP 89
Magorian, Michelle 1947- BioIn 16
Magoteaux, Cheryl Ann 1955- WhoWrEP 89
Magouirk, Conrad W. 1931- St&PR 91
Magovern, Thomas J. 1942- St&PR 91
Magowan, Peter Alden 1942- St&PR 91, WhoAm 90
Magran, Leonardo BiDrAPA 89
Magrane, Joe BioIn 16
Magraner-Folch, Gabriel A BiDrAPA 89
Magrans, Berta 1958- WhoEmL 91, WhoSSW 91
Magrans, Ralph 1947- St&PR 91
Magrath, C. Peter 1933- WhoAm 90
Magrath, Geoffrey Thompson 1944- St&PR 91
Magraw, Charles E BiDrAPA 89
Magraw, Richard M 1919- BiDrAPA 89
Magree, Montie 1916- BiDrAPA 89
Magriel, Paul NewYTBS 90
Magriel, Paul 1906?-1990 ConAu 132
Magrinat, Gaston S 1915- BiDrAPA 89
Magrini, Tullia 1950- IntWWM 90
Magrino, Michael J. 1922- St&PR 91
Magrino, Peter Frank 1952- WhoSSW 91
Magritte, Rene 1898-1967 BioIn 16, IntDcAA 90, ModArCr 1 [port], WorAlBi
Magro, Anthony John 1954- St&PR 91
Magro, John L. 1907- IntWWM 90
Magrone, Joe 1964- Ballpl 90
Magruder, Alexander Leonard C. 1934- St&PR 91
Magruder, Jeb Stuart 1934- BioIn 16, WorAlBi
Magruder, Joseph H. BioIn 16
Magruder, Marion Reiley 1918- WhoAmW 91
Magruder, Munro 1953- WhoAm 90
Magruder, Samuel H.S. 1945- St&PR 91
Magruder, William W BiDrAPA 89
Magub, Roshan 1941- IntWWM 90
Magubane, Peter 1932- BioIn 16
Maguigad, Leonardo C 1933- BiDrAPA 89
Maguire, Bassett 1904- WhoAm 90, WhoE 91, WhoWor 91
Maguire, Bruce W. ODwPR 91
Maguire, Cary M. 1928- St&PR 91
Maguire, Cary McIlwaine 1928- WhoSSW 91
Maguire, Charlotte Edwards 1918- WhoAm 90, WhoWor 91
Maguire, Daniel Charles 1931- ConAu 32NR
Maguire, David Edward 1938- WhoAm 90
Maguire, Denise 1956- ODwPR 91
Maguire, Freddie 1899-1961 Ballpl 90
Maguire, Henry Clinton, Jr. 1928- WhoAm 90
Maguire, Henry Pownall 1943- WhoAmA 91
Maguire, Hugh PenDiMP
Maguire, Hugh 1927- IntWWM 90
Maguire, Jack Russell 1920- WhoWor 91
Maguire, John Clark 1951- WhoEmL 91
Maguire, John David 1932- WhoAm 90
Maguire, John Francis 1951- WhoSSW 91
Maguire, John Gordon BiDrAPA 89
Maguire, John J. 1904-1989 BioIn 16
Maguire, John P. 1917- St&PR 91
Maguire, John Patrick 1917- WhoAm 90
Maguire, Joseph 1931?- EncO&P 3
Maguire, Joseph F. 1919- WhoAm 90, WhoE 91
Maguire, Kathleen BioIn 16
Maguire, Kevin 1951- WhoSSW 91
Maguire, Mary F. ODwPR 91
Maguire, Michael Francis 1937- St&PR 91
Maguire, Michael M. 1925- WhoAm 90
Maguire, Robert Alan 1930- WhoAm 90
Maguire, Robert Edward 1928- St&PR 91, WhoAm 90
Maguire, Robert Francis, III 1935- WhoAm 90
Maguire, Robert Wyman, Jr. 1944- WhoE 91
Maguire, Shirley Elizabeth 1948- WhoEmL 91
Maguire-Krupp, Marjorie Anne 1955- WhoAmW 91
Maguire-Zinni, Deirdre 1954- WhoAmW 91, WhoE 91, WhoWor 91
Magulac, Mark Lyman 1957- BiDrAPA 89
Magurno, Richard Peter 1943- St&PR 91, WhoE 91
Maguth, Frank Joseph 1916- St&PR 91
Magyar, Gabriel PenDiMP
Magyar, Gabriel 1914- IntWWM 90, WhoAm 90
Magyar, Mary Kay 1951- St&PR 91
Mah, Feng-hwa 1922- WhoAm 90
Mah, Richard Sze Hao 1934- WhoAm 90
Mah, Sy BioIn 16
Maha, George Edward 1924- WhoAm 90, WhoSSW 91
Maha, Richard Damian 1955- St&PR 91
Mahableshwarkar, Atul R 1956- BiDrAPA 89
Mahadeva, Manoranjan 1955- WhoSSW 91
Mahadeva, Wijeyaraj Anandakumar 1952- WhoE 91
Mahadevan, Kumar 1948- WhoAm 90
Mahadevan, Rajan BioIn 16
Mahady, Frank G. 1939- WhoAm 90
Mahaffay, William Edward WhoAm 90
Mahaffey, Art 1938- Ballpl 90
Mahaffey, Dick Dysart, Jr. 1948- WhoSSW 91
Mahaffey, Joan 1926- WhoWor 91
Mahaffey, John 1948- WhoAm 90
Mahaffey, Marcia Jeanne Hixson• WhoAmW 91, WhoWor 91
Mahaffey, Merrill Dean 1937- WhoAmA 91
Mahaffey, Redge Allan 1949- WhoAm 90, WhoEmL 91
Mahaffey, Robert L. 1934- St&PR 91
Mahaffey, Roy 1903-1969 Ballpl 90
Mahaffey, Susette Fischer 1950- WhoSSW 91
Mahaffey, Wilton Larron 1942- St&PR 91
Mahaffy, Christopher Adams Lamont 1952- WhoSSW 91
Mahaffy, John H BiDrAPA 89
Mahaffy-Berman, Anne R. 1948- St&PR 91
Mahajan, Anant Onkar 1956- WhoWor 91
Mahakian, Charles G 1940- BiDrAPA 89
Mahakkanukrauh, Chanintr Siam 1936- WhoWor 91
Mahal, Surjit Singh 1952- BiDrAPA 89
Mahal, Taj 1942- DrBIPA 90, WhoAm 90
Mahalingaiah, Halevoor B BiDrAPA 89
Mahalingaiah, Halevoor Boralingaiah 1947- WhoE 91
Mahalingam, Padmanabhan 1954- WhoWor 91
Mahalov, Alex Semyon 1960- WhoEmL 91
Maham Anga WomWR
Mahamat, Soumaila BioIn 16
Mahan, A. T. 1840-1914 BioIn 16
Mahan, Alexis Armstrong, Jr. 1920- WhoE 91
Mahan, Alfred Thayer 1840-1914 BioIn 16, WorAlBi
Mahan, Clare Maureen 1941- WhoAmW 91
Mahan, Danny Milton 1963- WhoSSW 91
Mahan, Dulany, Jr. 1914- WhoE 91, WhoWor 91
Mahan, Eileen BioIn 16
Mahan, Gerald Dennis 1937- WhoAm 90
Mahan, Harold Dean 1931- WhoAm 90
Mahan, John Allen 1934- St&PR 91
Mahanaim, Anna WhoWrEP 89
Mahanes, David James 1923- St&PR 91
Mahanes, David James, Jr. 1923- WhoAm 90
Mahanes, Michael Wayne 1956- WhoSSW 91, WhoWor 91
Mahanes, Walter J. 1935- WhoAm 90
Mahaney, Elizabeth Florence 1962- WhoAmW 91
Mahaney, Joe Temple BiDrAPA 89
Mahaney, Mark Stephen Finbar 1965- WhoE 91
Mahannah, Harry A 1937- BiDrAPA 89
Mahanthappa, Kalyana Thipperudraiah 1934- WhoAm 90
Mahapatra, Jayanta 1928- ConAu 33NR, WorAu 1980 [port]
Mahar, Harold W., Jr. 1943- St&PR 91
Mahar, Sherry Lynn 1954- WhoAmW 91
Maharam, Benita 1935- St&PR 91
Maharam, Donald H. 1931- St&PR 91
Mahard, Richard Harold 1915- WhoAm 90
Maharg, Meredith McClintock 1938- WhoSSW 91
Maharidge, Dale Dimitro 1956- WhoAm 90
Maharishi Mahesh Yogi 1918?- EncO&P 3
Maharry, Sharon Scott 1949- WhoAmW 91, WhoEmL 91
Mahaska 1785?-1834 WhNaAH
Mahaskah 1785?-1834 WhNaAH
Mahathero, Visuddhananda 1909- WhoWor 91
Mahathir bin Mohamad BioIn 16
Mahathir Bin Mohamad 1925- WhoWor 91
Mahaut I WomWR
Mahaut de Boulogne WomWR
Mahaut de Courtenay WomWR
Mahaut de Dammaratin WomWR
Mahaut II de Dampierre WomWR
Mahavira 599?BC-527BC WorAlBi
Mahdavi, Rafael Sinclair 1946- WhoAmA 91
Mahdi, Sadiq Al- 1936- PolLCME, WhoWor 91
Mahelsky, Michael Joseph 1962- BiDrAPA 89
Mahendra, Balram Kumar 1927- WhoWor 91
Maher, Alice Lombardo BiDrAPA 89
Maher, Brendan Arnold 1924- WhoAm 90
Maher, Brian D BiDrAPA 89
Maher, Chauncey C, III BiDrAPA 89
Maher, Daniel BioIn 16
Maher, Daniel Francis, Jr. 1956- WhoEmL 91
Maher, Daniel J. 1946- St&PR 91
Maher, David Willard 1934- WhoAm 90
Maher, Fran 1938- WhoAmW 91
Maher, Frank Aloysius 1941- WhoWor 91
Maher, Frank Thomas 1909- WhoAm 90
Maher, George F. 1929- WhoE 91
Maher, James L, Jr. BiDrAPA 89
Maher, Jean Elizabeth 1953- WhoAmW 91
Maher, John BioIn 16
Maher, John A. 1930- WhoE 91
Maher, John Edward 1925- WhoE 91
Maher, John F. 1943- WhoSSW 91
Maher, John Francis 1943- WhoAm 90
Maher, John Joseph 1954- WhoSSW 91
Maher, John Richard 1932- St&PR 91
Maher, Joseph 1933- ConTFT 8 [port]
Maher, Kim Leverton 1946- WhoAm 90, WhoAmW 91, WhoSSW 91
Maher, Laurence James 1926- St&PR 91
Maher, Leo Thomas 1915- WhoAm 90
Maher, Lisa ODwPR 91
Maher, Louis J. 1922- St&PR 91
Maher, Louis James, Jr. 1933- WhoAm 90
Maher, Marina 1945- ODwPR 91
Maher, Mary Ann 1949- WhoAmW 91
Maher, Michael Scott 1952- BiDrAPA 89
Maher, Patricia Marie 1954- WhoAmW 91
Maher, Patrick J. 1936- St&PR 91
Maher, Patrick Joseph 1936- WhoAm 90
Maher, Peter Michael 1940- WhoAm 90
Maher, Peter Robert 1952- St&PR 91
Maher, Raymond Leroy 1923- St&PR 91
Maher, Robert Edward 1929- St&PR 91
Maher, Robert Thomas 1951- WhoE 91
Maher, Stephen Albert 1944- St&PR 91, WhoAm 90
Maher, Sylvia Arlene 1946- WhoAmW 91
Maher, Trafford Patrick 1914- WhoAm 90
Maher, William James 1937- WhoSSW 91, WhoWor 91
Maher, William Lawrence 1928- St&PR 91
Maher, William Michael 1947- WhoE 91
Maher, William T., Jr. 1931- St&PR 91
Mahesh, Virendra Bhushan 1932- WhoAm 90
Maheshwari, Arun Kumar 1944- St&PR 91, WhoE 91
Maheshwari, Bhanwar Lal 1934- WhoWor 91
Maheshwari, Shriram 1931- ConAu 30NR
Maheswaranathan, Ponn 1954- WhoSSW 91

Maheu, Jean 1931- WhoWor 91
Maheu, Marlene Muriel 1954- WhoEmL 91
Maheu, Shirley 1931- WhoAmW 91
Maheux-Forcier, Louise 1929- BioIn 16
Mahey, John A 1932- WhoAmA 91
Mahfood, Stephen Michael 1949- WhoEmL 91, WhoWor 91
Mahfoozi, Hassan M BiDrAPA 89
Mahfouz, Naguib 1911?- MajTwCW, NewYTBS 90 [port], WhoWor 91, WorAlBi
Mahfouz, Naguib 1912- BioIn 16
Mahfuz, Najib MajTwCW
Mahfuz, Najib 1912- BioIn 16
Mahibullah, Abul Hashem Mohammad 1953- WhoWor 91
Mahin, Charles D. 1940- St&PR 91
Mahin, Charles Douglas 1940- WhoE 91
Mahkee, Wells BioIn 16
Mahl, George Franklin 1917- WhoAm 90
Mahl, Michael 1952- BiDrAPA 89
Mahl, Olga Berde 1946- WhoAmW 91
Mahla, Edward H. 1914-1989 BioIn 16
Mahlberg, Arden Franklin 1948- WhoEmL 91
Mahler, Alan E. 1942- St&PR 91
Mahler, Alma 1879-1964 BioIn 16
Mahler, Anna 1904-1988 AnObit 1988
Mahler, David 1911- WhoWor 91
Mahler, Elizabeth J BiDrAPA 89
Mahler, Ella Swartz Zonis 1936- WhoAmW 91
Mahler, Ernestine Friederike Elisabeth EncCoWW
Mahler, Gustav 1860-1911 BioIn 16, PenDiMP, -A, WorAlBi
Mahler, Halfdan BioIn 16
Mahler, Halfdan Theodor 1923- WhoAm 90, WhoWor 91
Mahler, Harry Bez 1928- WhoAm 90
Mahler, Howard Samuel 1952- BiDrAPA 89, WhoE 91
Mahler, John Chetwood, Jr. BiDrAPA 89
Mahler, Margaret S. 1897-1985 BioIn 16
Mahler, Michael David 1936- St&PR 91
Mahler, Mickey 1952- Ballpl 90
Mahler, Rick 1953- Ballpl 90
Mahler, Stephanie Irene 1952- WhoEmL 91
Mahler, Thomas Richard 1945- St&PR 91
Mahler, W. Keith 1942- St&PR 91
Mahler-Sussman, Leona Julia 1926- WhoWrEP 89
Mahlert, Ulrich 1950- WhoWor 91
Mahlke, Ernest D 1930- WhoAmA 91
Mahlman, Harvey Arthur 1923- WhoSSW 91
Mahlman, Jerry David 1940- WhoAm 90
Mahlman, Kent Earl 1928- St&PR 91
Mahlman, Nancy Deering 1934- St&PR 91
Mahlmann, John James 1942- WhoAm 90, WhoAmA 91
Mahlmann, Karsten BioIn 16, WhoAm 90
Mahlmann, Lewis AuBYP 90
Mahlmeister, Joseph E. 1945- St&PR 91
Mahlstedt, Robert A. 1941- ODwPR 91
Mahlum-Henegar, Rhonda Lynn 1959- WhoAmW 91
Mahmood Iskandar Ibni Sultan Ismail 1932- WhoWor 91
Mahmood, Fauzia 1953- BiDrAPA 89
Mahmoody, Betty BioIn 16
Mahmoud, Adel Abdel Fattah 1941- WhoAm 90
Mahmoud, Aly Ahmed 1935- WhoAm 90
Mahmoud, Ben 1935- WhoAmA 91
Mahmoud, Issa Said 1942- WhoSSW 91
Mahmud al-Kurdi PenDiDA 89
Mahmud, Anisul Islam 1947- WhoWor 91
Mahmud, Ibni Al-Marhum Tuanku 1930- WhoWor 91
Mahmud, Rehan 1952- WhoSSW 91
Mahn Win Maung 1916-1989 BioIn 16
Mahnke, Mark William BiDrAPA 89
Mahnke, Roger William 1938- St&PR 91
Maholick, Leonard T BiDrAPA 89
Mahomet BioIn 16
Mahon, Annette ODwPR 91
Mahon, Arthur Joseph 1934- WhoAm 90, WhoE 91
Mahon, Christopher B BiDrAPA 89
Mahon, Eldon Brooks 1918- WhoAm 90
Mahon, Florence Lucy WhoAmW 91
Mahon, John Keith 1912- WhoAm 90
Mahon, Joseph Bond, Jr. 1965- WhoSSW 91
Mahon, Julia C. 1916- AuBYP 90
Mahon, Malachy Thomas 1934- WhoAm 90
Mahon, Mary Brogan 1924- WhoE 91
Mahon, Rita 1949- WhoAmW 91
Mahon, Robert 1949- WhoAmA 91, WhoE 91
Mahon, Sal 1941- St&PR 91
Mahon, Tom 1944- ODwPR 91
Mahone, Barbara Jean 1946- WhoAm 90
Mahone, Cathy BioIn 16
Mahone, William L. 1951- St&PR 91
Mahoney, Beth Neville 1947- WhoE 91
Mahoney, Daniel Dennis 1943- St&PR 91
Mahoney, David 1923- WhoAm 90
Mahoney, Dorothy Reed 1919- WhoAmW 91
Mahoney, Edward Alexander 1919- St&PR 91
Mahoney, Edward M. 1930- St&PR 91
Mahoney, Edward Maurice 1930- WhoAm 90
Mahoney, Elizabeth Anne 1942- WhoE 91
Mahoney, Eugene Frederick 1923- WhoWrEP 89
Mahoney, Francis Xavier 1931- WhoWor 91
Mahoney, George LeFevre 1952- WhoEmL 91
Mahoney, George Perry 1901-1989 BioIn 16
Mahoney, George Robert, Jr. 1942- St&PR 91
Mahoney, Gerald F. 1943- St&PR 91
Mahoney, Gerald Francis 1943- WhoAm 90
Mahoney, Irene Jacobson 1954- WhoAmW 91
Mahoney, J. Daniel 1931- WhoAm 90
Mahoney, James Anthony, Jr. 1935- St&PR 91, WhoAm 90
Mahoney, James P. 1927- WhoAm 90
Mahoney, James Patrick 1925- WhoAm 90
Mahoney, Jane W. St&PR 91
Mahoney, Jock 1919-1989 BioIn 16
Mahoney, Joella Jean 1933- WhoAmA 91
Mahoney, John BioIn 16
Mahoney, John Francis 1953- WhoEmL 91
Mahoney, John J. 1931- St&PR 91
Mahoney, John L. 1928- WhoAm 90
Mahoney, John Marquis 1935- WhoWrEP 89
Mahoney, John Thomas BiDrAPA 89
Mahoney, John Thomas Fitzsimmons 1941- WhoWrEP 89
Mahoney, John William 1942- St&PR 91
Mahoney, Karen Renee 1960- WhoAmW 91
Mahoney, Katherine Hanora 1964- WhoE 91
Mahoney, Larry BioIn 16
Mahoney, Laura Stepeck 1926- WhoAmW 91
Mahoney, Louis Emmet 1939- WhoWor 91
Mahoney, Margaret Ann 1949- WhoAmW 91
Mahoney, Margaret Ellerbe 1924- WhoAm 90, WhoAmW 91
Mahoney, Margaret Ellis 1929- WhoAmW 91
Mahoney, Mary Dzurko 1946- WhoAmW 91
Mahoney, Mary Eliza 1845-1926 BioIn 16
Mahoney, Michael James 1960- WhoE 91
Mahoney, Michael Joseph 1950- WhoE 91
Mahoney, Michael R T 1935- WhoAmA 91
Mahoney, Michael Robert Taylor 1935- WhoAm 90
Mahoney, Michael Sean 1939- WhoAm 90
Mahoney, Neil Ballpl 90
Mahoney, Patrick A. 1951- St&PR 91
Mahoney, Patrick Morgan 1929- WhoAm 90, WhoE 91
Mahoney, Paul George 1937- St&PR 91
Mahoney, Peter Edward 1951- St&PR 91
Mahoney, Richard John BioIn 16
Mahoney, Richard John 1934- St&PR 91, WhoAm 90
Mahoney, Robert C. 1926- St&PR 91
Mahoney, Robert Charles 1926- WhoAm 90
Mahoney, Robert W. 1936- St&PR 91
Mahoney, Robert William 1936- WhoAm 90
Mahoney, Stephen Joseph 1934- St&PR 91
Mahoney, Suzanne Matthews 1963- WhoAmW 91
Mahoney, Thomas Arthur 1928- WhoSSW 91
Mahoney, Thomas Henry 1952- WhoWor 91
Mahoney, Thomas Henry Donald 1913- WhoAm 90, WhoE 91
Mahoney, Thomas Wren 1928- St&PR 91
Mahoney, Vincent P BiDrAPA 89
Mahoney, William E. 1939- St&PR 91
Mahoney, William F. 1955- ODwPR 91
Mahoney, William Francis 1935- WhoE 91, WhoWrEP 89
Mahoney, William Grattan 1925- WhoAm 90
Mahony, Devin 1963- ConAu 130
Mahony, Elizabeth Alsop WhoWrEP 89
Mahony, Elizabeth Winthrop AuBYP 90
Mahony, Pat 1951- WhoAmA 91
Mahony, Phillip 1955- BioIn 16
Mahony, Roger Michael 1936- WhoAm 90
Mahony, Terence St&PR 91
Mahood, Helen Maynard 1953- WhoAmW 91
Mahood, Janice H. 1940- WhoAmW 91
Mahood, Ramona Madson 1933- WhoSSW 91
Mahorn, Rick BioIn 16
Mahorney, Steven Louis BiDrAPA 89
Mahorney, William Richard 1930- St&PR 91
Mahovlic, Joseph John 1942- St&PR 91
Mahowald, Anthony Peter 1932- WhoAm 90
Mahowald, Mark Edward 1931- WhoAm 90
Mahr, George Joseph 1947- St&PR 91
Mahr, George Joseph, Jr. 1947- WhoAm 90
Mahr, Gregory Conrad 1957- BiDrAPA 89
Mahre, Phil BioIn 16
Mahre, Phil 1957- WhoAm 90
Mahre, Steve BioIn 16
Mahrous, Ahmed Ali 1946- WhoSSW 91
Mahurin, Matt 1959?- BioIn 16
Mahy, Cristopher Carl 1958- St&PR 91
Mahy, Margaret 1936- AuBYP 90, ConAu 30NR, FemiCLE
Mai, Chao C. 1936- St&PR 91
Mai, Kenneth William 1963- WhoEmL 91
Mai, Klaus L. 1930- WhoAm 90, WhoSSW 91
Mai, William Frederick 1916- WhoAm 90, WhoWor 91
Maia EncCoWW
Maiakovsky, Vladimir 1894-1930 BioIn 16
Maibach, Ben C., III 1946- WhoAm 90
Maibach, Ben C., Jr. 1920- St&PR 91, WhoAm 90
Maibach, Howard I. 1929- WhoAm 90
Maiberger, Richard L 1943- BiDrAPA 89
Maich, Robert Samuel 1941- WhoAm 90
Maichel, Joseph Raymond 1934- St&PR 91, WhoAm 90
Maickel, Roger Philip 1933- WhoAm 90
Maida, Adam J. 1930- WhoAm 90
Maiden, Cecil 1902-1981 BioIn 16
Maiden, Jennifer 1949- FemiCLE
Maidenberg, Reed NewAgMG
Maidin, Zainuddin 1939- WhoWor 91
Maidique, Modesto A. 1940- WhoHisp 91
Maidique, Modesto Alex, Jr. 1940- WhoAm 90, WhoSSW 91
Maidlow, Dolores Mary 1934- WhoAmW 91
Maidman, Richard Harvey Mortimer 1933- WhoAm 90
Maidman, Stephen Paul 1954- WhoEmL 91
Maidon, Carolyn Howser 1946- WhoAmW 91
Maidt, David Frederick 1955- WhoE 91
Maienschein, Fred C. 1925- WhoAm 90
Maier, Alfred 1929- WhoSSW 91
Maier, Charles Steven 1939- WhoAm 90
Maier, Cornell C. 1925- St&PR 91, WhoAm 90
Maier, Craig F. 1949- St&PR 91
Maier, Dianne Barbara BiDrAPA 89
Maier, Donna Jane-Ellen 1948- WhoAmW 91
Maier, Edward Handy 1944- St&PR 91
Maier, Edward Louis, Jr. 1955- WhoE 91
Maier, Frank BioIn 16
Maier, Franz Georg 1926- WhoWor 91
Maier, Franzjosef PenDiMP
Maier, Gary J 1943- BiDrAPA 89
Maier, Gary S. 1953- ODwPR 91
Maier, Gerald James 1928- St&PR 91, WhoAm 90
Maier, Harold Geistweit 1937- WhoAm 90
Maier, Henry W. BioIn 16
Maier, Jack C. 1925- St&PR 91
Maier, James H BiDrAPA 89
Maier, John Raymond 1943- WhoE 91
Maier, Karl George 1937- WhoSSW 91
Maier, Maryanne E WhoAmA 91
Maier, Michael 1568?-1622 EncO&P 3
Maier, Paul Luther 1930- WhoAm 90
Maier, Paul Victor 1947- St&PR 91, WhoAm 90, WhoEmL 91
Maier, Pauline 1938- WhoAm 90
Maier, Peter Klaus 1929- WhoAm 90
Maier, Robert Hawthorne 1927- WhoAm 90, WhoSSW 91
Maier, Robert Henry 1932- WhoSSW 91
Maier, Theresa F. 1964- WhoEmL 91
Maier, Thomas 1934- BiDrAPA 89
Maier, Thomas James 1948- St&PR 91
Maier, Waldemar C. 1939- St&PR 91
Maier, William John BiDrAPA 89
Maierhofer, Ronald Paul 1935- WhoAm 90
Maihafer, Harry James 1924- St&PR 91, WhoAm 90
Maihle, Nita Jane 1955- WhoEmL 91
Maikish, Charles John 1946- WhoE 91
Mailand, Walter Carl 1924- St&PR 91
Mailander, Cat Margaret 1957- WhoAmW 91
Mailepors, Victoria 1905- BiDrAPA 89
Mailer, Kate BioIn 16
Mailer, Norman BioIn 16
Mailer, Norman 1923- MajTwCW, WhoWrEP 89, WorAlBi
Mailhot, Terrie Annette 1951- BiDrAPA 89
Maillart, Ella 1903- EncCoWW
Maillart, Ella Kini 1903- FemiCLE
Maillat, Denis 1940- WhoWor 91
Mailler, William M. 1944- St&PR 91
Maillet, Antonine 1923- OxCCanT [port]
Maillet, Antonine 1929- BioIn 16, FemiCLE
Maillet, Lee E. 1950- St&PR 91
Maillet, Lucienne 1934- WhoAm 90
Maillet, Martin Joseph 1933- WhoE 91
Maillet, Wasim BioIn 16
Maillian, LeAnne Elizabeth 1952- WhoEmL 91
Mailliard, Anna W. BioAmW
Mailliard, John Ward, III 1914- St&PR 91
Maillol, Aristide 1861-1944 IntDcAA 90
Mailloux, Noel 1909- WhoAm 90
Mailloux, Robert Joseph 1938- WhoAm 90
Mailman, Charles 1931- St&PR 91
Mailman, Cynthia 1942- WhoAmA 91
Mailman, Cynthia Marcia 1942- WhoE 91
Mailman, Joseph L. NewYTBS 90 [port]
Mailman, Martin 1932- IntWWM 90
Mails, Duster 1895-1974 Ballpl 90
Maiman, Dana Robin 1960- WhoE 91
Maiman, Theodore Harold 1927- WhoAm 90, WhoWor 91
Maimin, David Sidney, Jr. 1928- St&PR 91
Maimin, Joseph 1920- St&PR 91
Maimonides, Moses 1135-1204 EncO&P 3, WorAlBi
Main, Alice Lee 1941- WhoAmW 91
Main, Bart Louis, Jr. BiDrAPA 89
Main, Bert 1919 BioIn 16
Main, Bruce Lee 1939- St&PR 91
Main, David D. 1956- St&PR 91
Main, Edna Dewey 1940- WhoAmW 91, WhoSSW 91
Main, Guy F. 1919- St&PR 91
Main, Jackson Turner 1917- WhoAm 90
Main, Janalyn Irene 1956- WhoWrEP 89
Main, John G. BioIn 16
Main, Lisa Marie 1963- BiDrAPA 89
Main, Marjorie 1890-1975 WorAlBi
Main, Mary Gale Saxon WhoSSW 91
Main, Miles 1884-1965 Ballpl 90
Main, Nancy Lillian 1946- WhoAmW 91
Main, Robert Gail 1932- WhoWor 91
Main, Roger Paul 1939- WhoWor 91
Main, Woody 1922- Ballpl 90
Maina wa Kinyatti BioIn 16
Mainardi, Dominic 1914- St&PR 91
Mainardi, Enrico 1897-1976 PenDiMP
Mainardi, Patricia M 1942- WhoAmA 91
Mainbocher 1890- BioIn 16
Mainbocher 1890-1976 ConDes 90
Mainbocher 1891-1976 WorAlBi
Mainella, Anthony John 1919- St&PR 91
Mainella, Lee Francis 1945- WhoSSW 91
Mainelli, Michael R. 1935- St&PR 91
Mainer, Robert 1927- St&PR 91
Maines, Clifford Bruce 1926- St&PR 91, WhoAm 90
Maines, James Allen 1951- WhoSSW 91
Mainfort, Jack BiDrAPA 89
Maini, Paolo 1939- WhoWor 91
Mainieri, Mike BioIn 16
Mainieri, Roberto C. 1949- EncPaPR 91
Mainka, Albert Pierre 1947- St&PR 91
Maino, Juan Bautista 1578-1649 IntDcAA 90
Maino, Michael S. 1941- St&PR 91
Mainone, Robert Franklin 1929- WhoWrEP 89
Mainor, Gary Alan 1950- St&PR 91
Mainor, James Horace 1928- St&PR 91
Mainor, Robert Perez 1953- WhoE 91
Mainous, Arch G., Jr. 1933- St&PR 91
Mainous, Bruce Hale 1914- WhoAm 90
Mains, Donald Allen 1928- St&PR 91
Mains, Gilbert Joseph 1929- WhoAm 90
Mainster, Donna Marie 1954- WhoWrEP 89
Maintenon, Marquise de 1635-1719 EncCoWW
Mainthia, Jay 1949- WhoEmL 91
Mainusch, Herbert Johannes 1929- WhoWor 91
Mainwaring, A. Bruce 1927- St&PR 91
Mainwaring, Daniel TwCCr&M 91
Mainwaring, Thomas Lloyd 1928- WhoAm 90
Mainwaring, William Lewis 1935- WhoAm 90, WhoWrEP 89
Mainwaring, William R. 1943- St&PR 91
Mainwaring, William Robert 1943- WhoAm 90
Mainzer, Barry 1958- St&PR 91
Mainzer, Ronald O. 1931- St&PR 91
Maio, Thomas Anthony 1936- St&PR 91

Maiocchi, Christine 1949- *WhoAmW 91, WhoE 91*
Maiolo, Joseph 1938- *WhoWrEP 89*
Maiorana, Ronald 1930- *WhoWrEP 89*
Maiorano, Isabelle J. 1922- *WhoAmW 91*
Maiorella, Marc Anthony 1957- *St&PR 91*
Maioriello, Richard Patrick 1936- *WhoWor 91*
Maiotti, Dennis Paul 1950- *WhoEmL 91*
Mair, Charles 1838-1927 *DcLB 99 [port], OxCCanT*
Mair, George L. 1929- *ConAu 129*
Mair, Joel *St&PR 91*
Mair, Victor H 1943- *ConAu 32NR*
Maira, Arthur Francis 1943- *St&PR 91*
Mairants, Ivor 1908- *IntWWM 90*
Maire, Barbara Jean 1932- *WhoSSW 91*
Maire, Edmond Louis 1931- *BiDFrPL*
Mairose, Paul Timothy 1956- *WhoWor 91*
Mairs, Candyce Wenborg 1958- *WhoAmW 91*
Mairs, Nancy *BioIn 16*
Mairs, Nancy Pedrick 1943- *WhoWrEP 89*
Mais, Roger 1905-1955 *MajTwCW*
Mais, Walter Henry 1907-1989 *BioIn 16*
Maisami, Mohammad 1943- *BiDrAPA 89*
Maisano, Phillip Nicholas 1947- *WhoE 91*
Maise, Ray E. 1933- *St&PR 91*
Maisel, Alan Neil 1945- *WhoE 91*
Maisel, Eric Richard 1947- *WhoWrEP 89*
Maisel, Fritz 1889-1967 *Ballpl 90*
Maisel, George 1892-1968 *Ballpl 90*
Maisel, Herbert 1930- *WhoAm 90*
Maisel, Josh *BioIn 16*
Maisel, Melvin Leo 1924- *WhoE 91*
Maisel, Michael 1947- *WhoE 91, WhoEmL 91*
Maisel, Sherman Joseph 1918- *WhoAm 90*
Maiser, David Francis 1945- *WhoEmL 91*
Maish, James A. 1932- *St&PR 91*
Maisky, Mischa 1948- *IntWWM 90, PenDiMP*
Maislin, Isidore 1919- *WhoAm 90*
Maisner, Bernard Lewis 1954- *WhoAmA 91*
Maison, George L. 1911- *WhoAm 90*
Maisonrouge, Jacques Gaston 1924- *St&PR 91*
Maissel, Leon Israel 1930- *WhoAm 90*
Maister, David Hilton 1947- *WhoWor 91*
Mait, Ellen *ODwPR 91*
Maital, Sharone L 1947- *ConAu 131*
Maitani, Lorenzo 1270?-1330? *IntDcAA 90*
Maitheny, Paul Lester 1926- *BiDrAPA 89*
Maitin, Sam 1928- *WhoAmA 91*
Maitinsky, Steven 1926- *BiDrAPA 89*
Maitland, Edward 1824-1897 *EncO&P 3*
Maitland, Guy Edison Clay 1942- *WhoE 91, WhoWor 91*
Maitland, James 1759-1839 *BioIn 16*
Maitland, James Dean 1960- *WhoWor 91*
Maitland, Lester J. 1899-1990 *BioIn 16, NewYTBS 90 [port]*
Maitland, Sara 1950- *BioIn 16, FemiCLE*
Maitlis, Peter Michael 1933- *WhoWor 91*
Maitner, Robert Emil 1948- *St&PR 91*
Maitre, Patrick Jean 1951- *WhoWor 91*
Maitreya *NewAgMG*
Maitrigupta *BioIn 16*
Maitripa *BioIn 16*
Maivald, James John 1956- *WhoWrEP 89*
Maiwurm, James John 1948- *WhoE 91, WhoEmL 91*
Maiz, Marta 1959- *WomArch*
Maizner, Janet P. 1944- *ODwPR 91*
Majakowskij, Wladimir 1894-1930 *BioIn 16*
Majali, Abdul Salam Attalah 1925- *WhoWor 91*
Majarakis, James D. 1915-1988 *BioIn 16*
Majauskas, Vytautas E 1918- *BiDrAPA 89*
Majcher, Diane *BiDrAPA 89*
Majchrzak, David Joseph 1936- *WhoE 91*
Majdrakoff, Ivan 1927- *WhoAmA 91*
Majerova, Marie 1882-1967 *EncCoWW*
Majerus, Michael Gerard 1956- *WhoEmL 91*
Majerus, Philip Warren 1936- *WhoAm 90*
Majeski, Anthony Chester 1931- *St&PR 91*
Majeski, Hank 1916- *Ballpl 90*
Majeski, Thomas H. 1933- *WhoAm 90, WhoAmA 91*
Majete, Clayton Aaron 1941- *WhoWor 91*
Majev, Howard Rudolph 1952- *WhoE 91*
Majewski, Frank 1941- *WhoWor 91*
Majewski, Patricia Ann *BiDrAPA 89*
Majgaard, Jens 1938- *WhoWor 91*
Majid, Ekbal Basith 1929- *BiDrAPA 89*
Majidi-Mashhadi, Mahmoud 1953- *WhoSSW 91*
Majka, Frank A 1910- *BiDrAPA 89*
Majka, Richard *St&PR 91*
Majkowski, E. Jon 1942- *St&PR 91*
Major, Andre 1942- *BioIn 16*
Major, Andre Wilfrid 1942- *WhoAm 90*
Major, Clare Tree 1880?-1954 *BioIn 16, NotWoAT*
Major, Clarence *BioIn 16*
Major, Clarence Lee 1936- *WhoAm 90, WhoWrEP 89*
Major, Coleman Joseph 1915- *WhoAm 90*
Major, Edward A 1938- *BiDrAPA 89*
Major, Elizabeth *BiDEWW, FemiCLE*
Major, James Russell Richards 1921- *WhoAm 90, WhoWrEP 89*
Major, Jean-Louis 1937- *WhoAm 90, WhoWrEP 89*
Major, John 1943- *CurBio 90 [port], NewYTBS 90 [port], News 91-2 [port], WhoWor 91*
Major, John Keene 1924- *WhoAm 90*
Major, John R. 1944- *St&PR 91*
Major, John Stephen 1942- *WhoE 91*
Major, Kevin 1949- *BioIn 16*
Major, Kevin Gerald 1949- *WhoAm 90, WhoWrEP 89*
Major, Leon 1933- *OxCCanT*
Major, Leslie F 1945- *BiDrAPA 89*
Major, Malvina Lorraine 1943- *IntWWM 90*
Major, Margaret *PenDiMP*
Major, Margaret 1932- *IntWWM 90*
Major, Richard Demarest 1935- *WhoAm 90*
Major, Stephen 1904- *BiDrAPA 89*
Major, Tony 1939- *DrBIPA 90*
Major, Vilmos *BiDrAPA 89*
Major, Warren R. 1947- *St&PR 91*
Major, William Alexander, Jr. 1942- *WhoAm 90*
Major, Winfield Watson 1925- *WhoAm 90*
Majorano, Gaetano *PenDiMP*
Majorelle, Auguste *PenDiDA 89*
Majorelle, Louis 1859-1926 *PenDiDA 89*
Majors, Lee 1940- *WhoAm 90, WorAlBi*
Majors, Nelda Faye 1938- *WhoSSW 91*
Majors, Robin LaRue 1955- *WhoSSW 91*
Majors, Shirley Fanelle 1934- *WhoAmW 91*
Majower, Herbert 1930- *WhoE 91*
Majumdar, Asit B. 1941- *St&PR 91*
Majumdar, Lisa Ann 1955- *BiDrAPA 89*
Majumdar, Milon Mohan *BiDrAPA 89*
Majumdar, Mukul Kumar 1944- *WhoAm 90*
Majumdar, Radha Arun *BiDrAPA 89*
Majumdar, Sharmila 1961- *WhoAmW 91*
Majure, James T. 1924- *St&PR 91*
Mak, A 1914- *EncO&P 3*
Mak, Alexander Kwai-Wing 1950- *WhoWor 91*
Mak, Jacques Chak-Cheong 1937- *WhoWor 91*
Mak, Joon Jun 1937- *WhoWor 91*
Mak, Kai-Kwong 1948- *WhoSSW 91*
Mak, Oi-Tong 1955- *WhoWor 91*
Mak, Reginald W. 1940- *St&PR 91*
Mak, Tak Wah 1946- *WhoAm 90*
Makabe, Osamu *St&PR 91*
Makadok, Stanley 1941- *WhoWor 91*
Makalou, Oumar 1934- *WhoAm 90, WhoE 91*
Makanoff, Lon David 1948- *St&PR 91*
Makapugay, Gloria Q *BiDrAPA 89*
Makar, Arthur Dennis 1950- *WhoE 91*
Makarem, Essam Faiz 1936- *WhoWor 91*
Makarem, Samir Said 1957- *WhoWor 91*
Makarenko, Anton Semenovich 1888-1939 *BioIn 16*
Makari, George Jack *BiDrAPA 89*
Makarios III 1913-1977 *WorAlBi*
Makarov, Askold Anatolevich 1925- *IntWWM 90*
Makarov, Nikolay 1810-1890 *PenDiMP*
Makarova, Elena 195-?- *EncCoWW*
Makarova, Natalia 1940- *BioIn 16, WhoAmW 91, WhoWor 91, WorAlBi*
Makarowski, William Stephen 1948- *WhoE 91*
Makarowsky, Eugene *BiDrAPA 89*
Makasiar, Gary Santos 1947- *WhoWor 91*
Makatini, Mfanafuthi *BioIn 16*
Makavejev, Dusan *BioIn 16*
Makavejev, Dusan 1932- *ConTFT 8*
Make-Peace, Mary *BiDEWW*
Makeba, Miriam 1932- *BioIn 16*
Makeba, Miriam 1934- *DrBIPA 90*
Makeda *WomWR [port]*
Makela, Benjamin R. 1922- *WhoAm 90*
Makela, Jyrki Tapani 1953- *WhoWor 91*
Makemie, Francis 1658?-1708 *EncCRAm*
Makepeace, Coline M. 1929- *WhoE 91*
Makepeace, Darryl Lee 1941- *WhoWor 91*
Makepeace, John *PenDiDA 89*
Maker, Janet Anne 1942- *WhoAmW 91*
Makey, Arthur Robertson 1922- *WhoWor 91*
Makhani, Madan P. 1937- *St&PR 91*
Makhija, Vasudev N *BiDrAPA 89*
Makhno, Nestor Ivanovich 1889-1934 *BioIn 16*
Makhoere, Caesarina Kona 1955- *BioIn 16*
Makholm, Mark Henry 1915- *WhoAm 90*
Makhoul, John Ibrahim 1942- *WhoAm 90*
Maki, Allan Abel 1922- *St&PR 91*
Maki, Atsushi 1948- *WhoWor 91*
Maki, Charles E. 1928- *St&PR 91*
Maki, Dennis G. 1940- *WhoAm 90*
Maki, Fumihiko 1928- *BioIn 16, WhoWor 91*
Maki, Jerrold Alan 1947- *WhoEmL 91*
Maki, Kazumi 1936- *WhoAm 90*
Maki, Robert Richard 1938- *WhoAmA 91*
Maki, Ronald Scott *BiDrAPA 89*
Maki, Sheila Anne 1932- *WhoAmA 91*
Maki, Susan Kay 1947- *WhoEmL 91*
Makielski, Stanislaw John, Jr. 1935- *WhoAm 90*
Makihara, Minoru *WhoE 91*
Makim, Alex *BioIn 16*
Makim, Jane Ferguson *BioIn 16*
Makin, Bathsua *BioIn 16*
Makin, Bathsua 1600- *FemiCLE*
Makin, Bathsua 1600-1674? *BiDEWW*
Makinen, Marvin William 1939- *WhoAm 90*
Makinen, Matti Kalervo 1932- *WhoWor 91*
Makino, Ryoji 1944- *BiDrAPA 89*
Makino, Shojiro 1929- *WhoWor 91*
Makins, Clifford 1924-1990 *ConAu 132*
Makins, James Edward 1923- *WhoWor 91*
Makinson, Robert Bruce 1929- *WhoE 91*
Makios, Vasilios 1938- *WhoWor 91*
Makita, Akira 1931- *WhoWor 91*
Makkapati, Rao B P 1940- *BiDrAPA 89*
Makki, Neosha 1957- *WhoSSW 91*
Makki, Syed A *BiDrAPA 89*
Maklakiewicz, Tadeusz Wojciech 1922- *IntWWM 90*
Maklakov, Vasilii Alekeseevich 1870-1957 *BioIn 16*
Makler, Hope Welsh 1924- *WhoAmA 91*
Maklin, Mickey 1942- *St&PR 91*
Makman, Marianne W 1936- *BiDrAPA 89*
Makman, Richard S 1936- *BiDrAPA 89*
Mako 1932- *ConTFT 8 [port]*
Mako, Anthony 1921-1988 *BioIn 16*
Mako, William Lawrence 1958- *WhoEmL 91, WhoWor 91*
Makos, James Brendan 1943- *WhoAm 90*
Makoski, Milton J. 1946- *St&PR 91*
Makoti, Edwin Letsholo *BioIn 16*
Makous, Walter Leon *WhoAm 90*
Makover, Richard B *BiDrAPA 89*
Makovich, Carol J. *ODwPR 91*
Makovsky, David 1960- *WhoWor 91*
Makovsky, Kenneth D. 1940- *ODwPR 91*
Makovsky, Kenneth Dale 1940- *WhoAm 90*
Makower, Joel 1952- *WhoE 91*
Makowicz, Adam *BioIn 16*
Makowski, Edgar Leonard 1927- *WhoAm 90*
Makowski, Karen R. 1956- *St&PR 91*
Makowski, Karen Raechal 1956- *WhoAmW 91*
Makowski, M. Paul 1922- *St&PR 91, WhoAm 90*
Makowski, Thomas Anthony 1952- *WhoEmL 91*
Makowski, Wayne Robert *BiDrAPA 89*
Makrianes, James Konstantin, Jr. 1925- *WhoAm 90*
Makris, Andreas 1930- *IntWWM 90, WhoAm 90, WhoWor 91*
Makris, Constantine John 1927- *WhoE 91*
Maksimon, Carol Wintrode 1959- *WhoE 91*
Maksimovic, Desanka 1898- *EncCoWW*
Maksymiuk, Jerzy *WhoWor 91*
Maksymiuk, Jerzy 1936- *IntWWM 90, PenDiMP*
Maksymowicz, Gregory John 1946- *BiDrAPA 89*
Maktum bin Rashid Al-Maktum, Sheikh 1940- *WhoWor 91*
Makuch, Stefan 1953- *WhoE 91*
Makuck, Peter 1940- *WhoWrEP 89*
Makupson, Amyre Porter 1947- *WhoAmW 91*
Mala, Theodore Anthony 1946- *WhoEmL 91, WhoWor 91*
Malabaila, Damiano *ConAu 33NR, MajTwCW*
Malabanan, Ernesto Herella 1919- *WhoWor 91*
Malabarba, Dale 1953- *WhoE 91*
Malabre, Alfred Leopold, Jr. 1931- *WhoAm 90*
Malaca *WhNaAH*
Malacarne, C. John 1941- *St&PR 91, WhoAm 90*
Malach, Herbert John 1922- *WhoE 91, WhoWor 91*
Malach, Janice Toni 1959- *WhoAmW 91*
Malach, Monte 1926- *WhoAm 90, WhoWor 91*
Malachowski, Carla 1953- *WhoAmW 91, WhoWor 91*
Malachowski, Ernest S. 1946- *St&PR 91*
Malachowski, Jerome Alfred 1942- *St&PR 91*
Malachuk, Allan F. 1940- *St&PR 91*
Malachy, St. 1095- *EncO&P 3*
Maladwala, Laila Shiraz *BiDrAPA 89*
Malafronte, Donald 1931- *WhoAm 90*
Malagodi, Giovanni Battista 1729-1797 *PenDiDA 89*
Malagon-Barcelo, Javier 1911- *WhoWor 91*
Malagu, Stefania 1933- *IntWWM 90*
Malai, Serve Ambrose 1946- *WhoWor 91*
Malaker, Stephen F. 1922- *St&PR 91*
Malakhov, Vladimir *BioIn 16*
Malakoff, James Leonard 1933- *St&PR 91*
Malamed, Lionel *BioIn 16*
Malamed, Seymour H. 1921- *St&PR 91, WhoAm 90*
Malamood, Herman *BioIn 16*
Malamud, Bernard 1914-1986 *BioIn 16, MajTwCW, WorAlBi, WrPh*
Malamud, Daniel 1939- *WhoAm 90*
Malamud, Judith Reva 1940- *WhoAmW 91*
Malamud, Michael H 1933- *BiDrAPA 89*
Malamud, Nathan *BiDrAPA 89*
Malamud, Phyllis Carole 1938- *WhoAmW 91*
Malamud, William I, Jr. *BiDrAPA 89*
Malamy, Michael Howard 1938- *WhoAm 90*
Malan, Dean Tracy 1926- *St&PR 91*
Malan, Magnus Andre de Merindol 1930- *WhoWor 91*
Malan, Rian 1954- *BestSel 90-3 [port]*
Malana, Danilo Lengyel 1946- *WhoWor 91*
Malanaphy-Sorg, Marie A 1955- *WhoAmW 91*
Maland, Tim 1953- *St&PR 91*
Malaney, Sara A. 1961- *ODwPR 91*
Malanga, Gerard Joseph 1943- *WhoWrEP 89*
Malangatana, Valente 1936- *BioIn 16*
Malani, Surendar C 1948- *BiDrAPA 89*
Malaniuk, Ira 1923- *IntWWM 90*
Malara, Tony C. 1936- *St&PR 91*
Malarcher, Dave 1894-1982 *Ballpl 90*
Malarchuk, Clint *BioIn 16*
Malaret, Marisol *BioIn 16*
Malarkey, John 1872-1949 *Ballpl 90*
Malarkey, Martin Francis, Jr. 1918- *WhoAm 90*
Malarkey, Thomas B., Jr. 1928- *WhoAm 90*
Malas, Kenneth Lee 1947- *BiDrAPA 89*
Malas, Mohannad Said 1953- *WhoSSW 91*
Malas, Spiro 1933- *IntWWM 90*
Malaschak, Dolores Boyer 1923- *WhoWrEP 89*
Malashevich, Bruce Peter 1952- *WhoAm 90*
Malasky, Paul Michael 1927- *WhoSSW 91*
Malaspina, Alejandro 1755?-1810 *WhNaAH*
Malaspina, Alex 1931- *St&PR 91, WhoAm 90*
Malaspina, Dolores *BiDrAPA 89*
Malat, Alan 1944- *St&PR 91*
Malatesta, Peter *BioIn 16*
Malatesta, Peter J *NewYTBS 90*
Malatesta, Peter J. 1932-1990 *ConAu 130*
Malatin, James A. 1942- *St&PR 91*
Malatino, Anthony Michael 1944- *WhoSSW 91*
Malaty, Violet Louis *BiDrAPA 89*
Malavaud, Andre Pierre 1928- *WhoWor 91*
Malave, Ronald 1957- *BiDrAPA 89*
Malave-Colon, Eddie G. 1963- *WhoHisp 91*
Malawer, Irving 1917- *St&PR 91*
Malawski, Louis 1934- *WhoE 91*
Malaya, Ronald Penha 1951- *WhoAm 90*
Malayeri, Mahmoud *BiDrAPA 89*
Malayil, Michael Thomas 1941- *BiDrAPA 89*
Malaysian Pale *NewAgMG*
Malbin, Lydia W 1897-1989 *WhoAmA 91N*
Malbin, Lydia Winston *BioIn 16*
Malboeuf, John Alfred 1961- *WhoE 91*
Malbon, Craig Curtis 1950- *WhoE 91*
Malbon, Robert M. 1942- *St&PR 91*
Malbone, Edward Greene 1777-1807 *BioIn 16*
Malbrough, Bobby Ray Thomas 1951- *WhoSSW 91*
Malbrough, Ray Thomas 1952- *WhoWrEP 89*
Malby, George Roland 1857-1912 *AmLegL*
Malcarney, Arthur Edward 1942- *St&PR 91*
Malce, Michael *BioIn 16*
Malchon, Jeanne Keller 1923- *WhoAmW 91*
Malcohn, Elissa *WhoWrEP 89*
Malcolm X *EncAL, MajTwCW*
Malcolm X 1925-1965 *BioIn 16, WorAlBi*
Malcolm, Andrew H. 1943- *BioIn 16*
Malcolm, Beatrice Bowles *BioIn 16*

Malcolm, Boyd Gerneaux 1937- WhoSSW 91
Malcolm, Bruce Gordon 1947- WhoSSW 91
Malcolm, Carlos Edmond 1945- IntWWM 90
Malcolm, Christine BioIn 16
Malcolm, Dan MajTwCW
Malcolm, Derek BioIn 16
Malcolm, Gail Baumgaertel 1954- WhoAmW 91
Malcolm, George 1917- IntWWM 90, PenDiMP
Malcolm, Howard 1799-1879 BioIn 16
Malcolm, J. Parke 1940- St&PR 91
Malcolm, Janet 193-?- WorAu 1980 [port]
Malcolm, John 1936- TwCCr&M 91
Malcolm, John A BiDrAPA 89
Malcolm, Koressa Kutsick 1957- WhoSSW 91
Malcolm, Norman 1911-1990 ConAu 132
Malcolm, Paul Jennings 1922- St&PR 91
Malcolm, Robert J, Jr. 1943- BiDrAPA 89
Malcolm, Robert L. 1927- St&PR 91
Malcolm, Ronald Paul 1941- St&PR 91
Malcolm, Wesley R. 1934- St&PR 91
Malcolmson, Anne 1910- AuBYP 90
Malcolmson, Harry BioIn 16
Malcomson, Alexander Young 1865-1923 EncABHB 4 [port]
Malcuzynski, Witold 1914-1977 PenDiMP
Maldarelli, Oronzio 1892-1963 WhoAmA 91N
Malden, Joan Williams 1931- WhoAmW 91
Malden, Karl 1913- WorAlBi
Malden, Karl 1916- WhoAm 90
Maldjian, Vartavar B 1918- WhoAmA 91
Maldonado, Adal Alberto 1947- WhoHisp 91
Maldonado, Alexander A. 1901-1989 BioIn 16, MusmAFA
Maldonado, Alfonso Javier 1960- WhoHisp 91
Maldonado, Candy 1960- Ballpl 90, WhoHisp 91
Maldonado, Che 1954- WhoHisp 91
Maldonado, Daniel Chris 1942- WhoHisp 91
Maldonado, Frank Parker 1938- WhoAm 90
Maldonado, Gilbert G BiDrAPA 89
Maldonado, Irma 1946- WhoHisp 91
Maldonado, Jose 1904- WhoHisp 91
Maldonado, Juan Jose 1946- WhoHisp 91
Maldonado, Juan R. 1938- WhoHisp 91
Maldonado, Lisa M 1960- BiDrAPA 89
Maldonado, Macario Olivarez 1944- WhoHisp 91
Maldonado, Marianna BiDrAPA 89
Maldonado, Michael Mark 1952- WhoHisp 91
Maldonado, Norman I. 1935- WhoHisp 91
Maldonado, Otmara Lina 1944- WhoSSW 91
Maldonado, Tomas PenDiDA 89
Maldonado, Tomas 1922- ConDes 90
Maldonado-Bear, Rita Marinita 1938- WhoAmW 91, WhoHisp 91
Maldonado-Chinea, Carmen BiDrAPA 89
Maldonado-Denis, Manuel 1933- ConAu 131, HispWr 90
Maldonado-Rivera, Felix BiDrAPA 89
Maldonado-Rodriquez, Orlando BiDrAPA 89
Maldre, Mati 1947- WhoAmA 91
Male, Belkis Cuza ConAu 131, HispWr 90
Male, Kenneth James 1923- St&PR 91
Male, Roy Raymond 1919- WhoAm 90, WhoWrEP 89
Malea, Olga 1960- WhoWor 91
Malec, John 1944- WhoAm 90
Malec, John William 1941- St&PR 91
Malec, Joseph, III St&PR 91
Malec, Joseph, Jr. 1931- St&PR 91
Malec, Judith Mary 1955- WhoAmW 91
Malec, William Frank 1940- St&PR 91, WhoAm 90
Malecha, Myron BiDrAPA 89
Malecki, Edward Stanley, Jr. 1938- WhoAm 90
Malecki, Henry Raymond 1922- WhoAm 90
Malecki, Jean Marie 1953- WhoAmW 91
Maleczech, Ruth 1938- BioIn 16, NotWoAT
Maledy, Linda Kay 1955- WhoEmL 91
Maleeva, Katerina BioIn 16
Maleeva, Manuela BioIn 16
Malefakis, Edward E. 1932- WhoAm 90, WhoWrEP 89
Maleh, Edward B. 1951- St&PR 91
Maleh, Sam 1926- St&PR 91
Malek, Diana Gail 1953- WhoAmW 91
Malek, Frederic Vincent 1936- WhoAm 90
Malek, Garey Andrew BiDrAPA 89
Malek, Haleh Fatemeh 1958- WhoEmL 91
Malek, James Stanley 1941- WhoAm 90
Malek, Marlene Anne 1939- WhoAmW 91, WhoWor 91
Malek, Richard Allen 1940- BiDrAPA 89
Malek-Ahmadi, Parviz 1943- BiDrAPA 89
Maleki, Nahid 1945- WhoE 91
Malekpour, Bahman 1937- BiDrAPA 89
Malempati, Narasimha Rao 1951- BiDrAPA 89
Malemud, Lee L. 1948- WhoAmW 91
Malen, David Guy 1953- BiDrAPA 89
Malen, Richard Lewis 1944- BiDrAPA 89, WhoE 91
Malenbaum, Roxanne Fay 1953- BiDrAPA 89
Malenbaum, Wilfred 1913- WhoAm 90
Malenda, James William 1946- WhoAmA 91
Malenich, Linda Lou 1951- WhoWrEP 89
Malenick, Donal H. 1939- WhoAm 90
Malenka, Bertram Julian 1923- WhoAm 90
Malenkov, Georgi M. 1902-1988 BioIn 16
Malenkov, Georgiy 1902-1988 AnObit 1988
Malerba, Franco G. 1950- WhoWor 91
Malerba, Luigi 1927- WhoWor 91
Malerba, Robert F.S., II BiDrAPA 89
Maleriat, Leopold PenDiDA 89
Malernee, James Kent, Jr. 1947- WhoWor 91
Malerstein, Abraham J 1924- BiDrAPA 89
Males, R.H. 1932- St&PR 91
Males-Madrid, Sandra Kay 1942- WhoAmW 91
Maleska, Eugene T. BioIn 16
Maleska, Eugene T. 1916- WhoAm 90
Maleska, Martin Edmund 1944- WhoAm 90, WhoE 91, WhoWor 91
Maleski, Cynthia Maria 1951- WhoAmW 91
Maleson, Franklin George 1940- BiDrAPA 89
Malespin, Francisco 1806-1846 BioIn 16
Malet, Lucas 1852-1931 BioIn 16, FemiCLE
Maletta, Gabe Joseph BiDrAPA 89
Maletta, Thomas Peter 1941- WhoAm 90
Maletz, Herbert Naaman 1913- WhoAm 90
Maletzky, Barry Michael 1941- BiDrAPA 89
Malev, Jonathan S BiDrAPA 89
Malev, Milton 1900- BiDrAPA 89
Malev, William S. 1898-1973 BioIn 16
Malevich, Kasimir PenDiDA 89
Malevich, Kasimir 1878-1935 IntDcAA 90
Malewitz, Bernard G. 1927- St&PR 91
Malewska, Hanna 1911- EncCoWW
Malewski, Ralph Stanley 1950- WhoSSW 91
Maley, Donald 1918- WhoAm 90
Maley, Henry C. 1942- St&PR 91
Maley, Patricia Ann 1955- WhoAmW 91, WhoE 91
Maley, Patrick J. 1949- St&PR 91
Maley, Samuel Wayne 1928- WhoAm 90
Maley, Thomas Charles 1952- WhoSSW 91
Maley, William B. 1924- St&PR 91
Malezieux, Marie EncCoWW
Malfa, Horace M. 1933- St&PR 91
Malfas, Nicholas E., Jr. 1935- St&PR 91
Malfatti, Anita 1889-1964 ArtLatA
Malfitano, Catherine 1948- IntWWM 90
Malgieri, Kathryn Driscoll 1951- WhoAmW 91
Malgoire, Jean-Claude 1940- IntWWM 90, PenDiMP
Malham, Nicholas Zachary 1937- St&PR 91
Malhan, Prem Sheel 1933- WhoWor 91
Malherbe, Abraham Johannes, VI 1930- WhoAm 90
Malherbe, Bernard 1930- WhoWor 91
Malherbe, Dianne St&PR 91
Malherbe, Earl F. 1933- St&PR 91
Malhi, Balwinder Singh 1944- WhoE 91
Malhotra, Harish Kumar 1945- BiDrAPA 89, WhoE 91
Malhotra, Jagadish C 1916- BiDrAPA 89
Malhotra, Mahamaya BiDrAPA 89
Malhotra, Naresh Kumar 1949- WhoEmL 91
Malhotra, Rashpal 1936- WhoWor 91
Malhotra, Surin M. 1948- WhoE 91
Mali, Jane Lawrence 1937- BioIn 16
Malia, Patrick Anthony 1939- St&PR 91
Malia, Thomas J. 1950- St&PR 91
Maliakas, Mihalis Pan 1961- WhoEmL 91
Maliakkal, Dominic Joseph BiDrAPA 89
Malibran, Maria 1808-1836 BioIn 16, PenDiMP
Malich, Kenneth Antone 1946- WhoEmL 91
Malick, Howard Morgan 1917- St&PR 91
Malick, Terrence 1943- BioIn 16
Malicky, Neal 1934- WhoAm 90
Malicoat, Jean Ann 1935- St&PR 91
Malicoat, Philip Cecil 1908-1981 WhoAmA 91N
Malieckal, Stephen 1942- BiDrAPA 89
Malietoa Tanumafili 1913- WhoWor 91
Maliff, John St&PR 91
Malihan, Amie A. 1950- WhoE 91
Malik, Abdul BiDrAPA 89
Malik, Azfar BiDrAPA 89
Malik, Charles Habib 1906-1987 BioIn 16
Malik, Gerald I. 1941- St&PR 91
Malik, Gerald Irwin 1941- WhoAm 90
Malik, Helen T. 1943- St&PR 91
Malik, Helen Theresa 1943- WhoAmW 91, WhoWor 91
Malik, Josie M. Meza 1947- WhoAmW 91
Malik, Muhammad Aslam 1951- BiDrAPA 89
Malik, Raymond Howard 1933- WhoAm 90
Malik, Robert Kevin 1942- WhoWor 91
Malile, Reiz WhoWor 91
Malimoto ConAu 130
Malin, Arthur 1925- BiDrAPA 89
Malin, Barnet David 1954- BiDrAPA 89
Malin, Evangeline May 1928- WhoAmW 91
Malin, Howard Gerald 1941- WhoAm 90
Malin, Irving 1934- WhoAm 90, WhoWrEP 89
Malin, Patrick J. 1935- St&PR 91
Malin, Randall 1937- St&PR 91, WhoAm 90
Malin, Robert A. 1931- St&PR 91
Malin, Robert Abernethy 1931- WhoAm 90
Malin, Roni Sue 1939- WhoAmW 91
Malina, Frank Joseph 1912-1981 BioIn 16, WhoAmA 91N
Malina, Judith 1926- BioIn 16, NotWoAT, WhoAm 90
Malina, Michael 1936- WhoAm 90
Malina-Maxwell, Christine Yvonne 1950- WhoAmW 91, WhoWor 91
Malinak, David 1955- ODwPR 91
Malinak, Dennis Paul BiDrAPA 89
Malinas, Philip David BiDrAPA 89
Malinche EncCRAm
Malinconico, S. Michael 1941- WhoSSW 91
Maling, Arthur 1923- TwCCr&M 91, WhoWrEP 89
Maling, C.T. PenDiDA 89
Maling, George C., Jr. 1931- WhoWrEP 89
Maling, George Croswell, Jr. 1931- WhoAm 90
Maling, William Bell 1933- St&PR 91
Malini, Max 1873-1942 BioIn 16
Malinick, Charles David BiDrAPA 89
Malino, Jerome R. 1911- WhoAm 90
Malino, John G. 1939- St&PR 91
Malino, John Gray 1939- WhoAm 90
Malinoski, Frank J. 1954- WhoE 91
Malinow, Kenneth Leslie BiDrAPA 89
Malinowski, Bronislaw 1884-1942 BioIn 16
Malinowski, Doris Sebring 1934- WhoE 91
Malinowski, Edmund Robert 1932- WhoE 91
Malipiero, Gian Francesco 1882-1973 PenDiMP A
Malipiero, Riccardo 1914- IntWWM 90
Maliponte, Adriana 1938- IntWWM 90
Malirova, Helena 1877-1940 EncCoWW
Malis, Louise 1921- WhoAm 90
Malison, Robert Thomas BiDrAPA 89
Maliszewski, R.M. 1934- St&PR 91
Malitz, Eugene BiDrAPA 89
Malitz, Sidney BiDrAPA 89
Malitz, Sidney 1923- WhoAm 90
Maliyekkel, Ittoop Thomas 1946- BiDrAPA 89
Malkames, Don 1904-1986 BioIn 16
Malkames, James Patterson, III 1950- St&PR 91
Malkani, Gopal St&PR 91
Malkani, Mohan Jethmal 1933- WhoSSW 91
Malkasian, George Durand, Jr. 1927- WhoAm 90, WhoWor 91
Malkasian, Henry Aram 1917- WhoE 91
Malkemes, Lois Constance 1940- WhoSSW 91
Malki, Debra Block 1951- WhoEmL 91
Malkiel, Burton Gordon 1932- ConAu 31NR, St&PR 91, WhoAm 90
Malkiel, Nancy Weiss 1944- WhoAm 90
Malkiel, Theresa Serber 1874-1949 EncAL, FemiCLE
Malkiel, Yakov 1914- WhoAm 90
Malkin, Bill 1908- WhoSSW 91
Malkin, J.E. 1946- St&PR 91
Malkin, Jocelyn S BiDrAPA 89
Malkin, Michael D 1942- BiDrAPA 89
Malkin, Michael R 1943- ConAu 129
Malkin, Moses Montefiore 1919- WhoE 91
Malkin, Myron Samuel 1924- WhoAm 90, WhoE 91
Malkin, Peter Laurence 1934- WhoAm 90
Malkin, Roger David 1931- St&PR 91
Malkin, Shmuel 1934- WhoWor 91
Malkin, Stanley Lee 1942- WhoAm 90, WhoE 91
Malkinson, Frederick David 1924- WhoAm 90
Malko, Nikolay 1883-1961 PenDiMP
Malko, Richard W. 1937- St&PR 91
Malkoff, Alan Richard 1946- WhoE 91
Malkoff, Eileen Weider 1954- WhoAmW 91
Malkovich, John BioIn 16
Malkovich, John 1953- WhoAm 90, WorAlBi
Malkovich, Mark Paul 1930- IntWWM 90
Malkovich, Mark Paul, III 1930- WhoAm 90
Malkowicz, Matthew 1939- St&PR 91
Malkowicz, Stanley Bruce WhoE 91
Malkus, Alida Wright 1899- AuBYP 90
Malkus, Willem Van Rensselaer 1923- WhoAm 90
Mall, Margaret Darphin 1943- WhoWrEP 89
Mall, Myron Merriell 1940- WhoSSW 91
Mall, Scott ODwPR 91
Mall, William John, Jr. 1933- WhoAm 90
Mallakh, Kamal el BioIn 16
Mallalieu, John Percival William 1908-1980 ConAu 129
Mallard, Henry Clay, Jr. BiDrAPA 89
Mallard, Jon L. 1936- St&PR 91
Mallard, Prudent 1809-1879 PenDiDA 89
Mallard, Stephen Anthony 1924- WhoAm 90
Mallardi, Michael Patrick 1934- St&PR 91, WhoE 91
Mallare, Lydia O. BiDrAPA 89
Mallarme, Stephane 1842-1898 BioIn 16, WorAlBi
Mallary, Gertrude Robinson 1902- WhoAmW 91, WhoE 91
Mallary, Raymond DeWitt 1898- WhoAm 90, WhoWor 91
Mallary, Richard Walker 1929- WhoAm 90
Mallary, Robert 1917- WhoAm 90
Mallary, Robert W 1917- WhoAmA 91
Mallary, Stephen D 1953- BiDrAPA 89
Mallatt, Keith Allen 1956- WhoEmL 91
Malle, Louis 1932- BioIn 16, WhoAm 90, WhoWor 91, WorAlBi
Mallea, Eduardo 1903-1982 BioIn 16, HispWr 90
Mallebranche EncO&P 3
Malleck, Diane Elizabeth 1954- WhoAmW 91
Mallen, David BioIn 16
Mallen, Ronald Edward 1942- WhoAm 90, WhoWrEP 89
Mallender, Fred, II 1931- WhoAm 90
Mallender, William Harry 1935- St&PR 91, WhoAm 90
Mallendick, Robert Jacob 1943- St&PR 91
Maller, Dennis Allen 1953- St&PR 91
Maller, Michael Joseph 1944- WhoE 91
Maller, Robert Russell 1928- WhoAm 90
Mallerdino, Anthony Michael 1959- WhoEmL 91
Mallers, George Peter 1928- WhoAm 90
Mallery, Richard 1937- WhoAm 90, WhoWor 91
Malless, Stanley 1914- St&PR 91
Mallet, Alexis, Jr. 1951- WhoSSW 91
Mallet, Jacques Robert 1945- WhoE 91, WhoWor 91
Mallet, Laurie BioIn 16
Mallet, Michel Marie-Joseph 1934- WhoWor 91
Mallet, Pierre Antoine 1700-1751? WhNaAH
Mallet, Rosalyn Theresa 1955- WhoSSW 91
Mallet-Joris, Francoise 1930- EncCoWW, WhoWor 91
Mallet-Stevens, Robert 1886-1945 PenDiDA 89
Mallett, A.W. 1917- St&PR 91
Mallett, Jane 1899-1984 OxCCanT
Mallett, Molly Gayle 1966- WhoSSW 91
Mallett, Russell Ballou, Jr. 1934- St&PR 91
Mallette, Eugene Robert 1949- WhoEmL 91
Mallette, Gertrude 1887- FemiCLE
Mallette, Lila Mohler 1931- WhoWor 91
Mallette, Malcolm Francis 1922- WhoAm 90
Malley, Joseph Hanson 1956- WhoSSW 91
Malley, Robert Joseph 1923- WhoAm 90
Malley, Walter BioIn 16
Mallhi, Nirmal Singh BiDrAPA 89
Mallia, Robert Michael 1944- WhoE 91
Mallick, Earl W. 1926- ODwPR 91
Mallick, Earl William 1926- St&PR 91, WhoAm 90
Mallick, George A. BioIn 16
Mallick, Mohammad Sultan Ahmad BiDrAPA 89

Mallicoat, Frank H. 1925- *St&PR 91*
Malliet, James W. *St&PR 91*
Mallik, Balwant Singh *BiDrAPA 89*
Mallin, Dea Adria 1942- *WhoWrEP 89*
Mallin, Dea Zuckerman 1942- *WhoAmW 91, WhoE 91*
Mallin, Jay 1927- *WhoE 91*
Mallin, John Ronald 1950- *WhoE 91*
Mallin, Judith Young *WhoAmA 91*
Mallin, Sam 1923- *St&PR 91*
Mallinckrodt, George W. 1930- *WhoAm 90, WhoWor 91*
Mallinen, Teuvo Sakari 1940- *WhoWor 91*
Malling, Mathilda 1864-1942 *EncCoWW*
Mallinson, George Greisen 1917- *WhoAm 90*
Mallion, Richard James 1940- *WhoAm 90*
Mallison, Thomas C. 1941- *St&PR 91*
Mallo-Garrido, Josephine Ann 1955- *WhoAm 90*
Mallock, William Hurrell 1849-1923 *BioIn 16*
Mallon, Edward John 1944- *St&PR 91*
Mallon, Florencia Elizabeth 1951- *WhoHisp 91*
Mallon, J.H. 1933- *St&PR 91*
Mallon, Jack 1925- *St&PR 91*
Mallon, John C. 1939- *St&PR 91*
Mallon, Kevin J. *ODwPR 91*
Mallon, Les 1905- *Ballpl 90*
Mallon, Mark 1951- *St&PR 91*
Mallon, Mary *BioIn 16*
Mallon, Mary 1870-1938 *WorAlBi*
Mallon, Maurus Edward 1932- *WhoWrEP 89*
Mallon, Paul F. 1925- *St&PR 91*
Mallon, Paul Frank 1925- *WhoAm 90*
Mallon, Richard Dicks 1926- *WhoE 91*
Mallon, Vincent P. *BioIn 16*
Mallon, William George 1946- *St&PR 91*
Mallonee, Bruce Ervin 1918- *St&PR 91*
Mallory, Aileen Lucile 1917- *WhoWrEP 89*
Mallory, Alvin O. 1908- *St&PR 91*
Mallory, Arthur Lee 1932- *WhoAm 90*
Mallory, Carole *BioIn 16*
Mallory, Charles King, III 1936- *WhoAm 90*
Mallory, Charles Shannon *WhoAm 90*
Mallory, Frank Bryant 1933- *WhoAm 90*
Mallory, Frank Linus 1920- *WhoAm 90*
Mallory, George L *BiDrAPA 89*
Mallory, James D., Jr. 1932- *BiDrAPA 89*
Mallory, James Russell 1916- *WhoAm 90*
Mallory, John Michael 1951- *St&PR 91*
Mallory, John Wickliffe 1912- *St&PR 91*
Mallory, Joseph Samuel 1937- *St&PR 91*
Mallory, Lee W., III 1946- *WhoWrEP 89*
Mallory, Margaret 1911- *WhoAmA 91*
Mallory, Nina Ayala *WhoAmA 91*
Mallory, Ray D. 1937- *St&PR 91*
Mallory, Robert Mark 1950- *WhoAm 90*
Mallory, Ronald 1945- *WhoAmA 91*
Mallory, Rufus 1831-1914 *AmLegL*
Mallory, Stanley O. 1938- *St&PR 91*
Mallory, Troy L. 1923- *WhoWor 91*
Mallory, Veston H. 1935- *St&PR 91*
Mallory, Virgil Standish 1919- *WhoAm 90, WhoWor 91*
Mallory, Wilhelm A. 1929- *St&PR 91*
Mallory, Wilhelm Antriller 1929- *WhoAm 90*
Mallory, William Barton, III 1944- *WhoAm 90*
Mallory, William Palmer 1925- *St&PR 91*
Mallory Silliere, Judith Esther 1961- *WhoAmW 91*
Mallott, Byron Ivar 1943- *St&PR 91, WhoAm 90*
Mallott, David Bruce 1953- *BiDrAPA 89*
Mallott, I Floyd 1922- *BiDrAPA 89*
Mallouk, Ann Marmon 1923- *WhoAmW 91*
Mallow, Marisa Gale 1959- *WhoAmW 91*
Mallowan, Agatha Christie *MajTwCW*
Malloy, Ann Marie 1951- *WhoSSW 91*
Malloy, Bernard M 1928- *BiDrAPA 89*
Malloy, Bernard Mathis 1928- *WhoE 91*
Malloy, Betsy Brownrigg 1952- *WhoAmW 91*
Malloy, Dale R. 1945- *WhoAm 90*
Malloy, Dennis Edward 1953- *WhoE 91*
Malloy, Edward Aloysius *BioIn 16*
Malloy, Edward Aloysius 1941- *WhoAm 90, WhoWor 91*
Malloy, Edwin Arthur 1926- *St&PR 91*
Malloy, Fred P. 1934- *St&PR 91*
Malloy, Grace Louise 1959- *WhoAmW 91*
Malloy, James B. 1927- *St&PR 91, WhoAm 90*
Malloy, James David 1955- *WhoE 91*
Malloy, James Matthew 1939- *WhoAm 90*
Malloy, John Atherton *BiDrAPA 89*
Malloy, John Francis 1945- *WhoE 91*
Malloy, John Michael 1918- *WhoAm 90*
Malloy, John R. 1932- *St&PR 91*
Malloy, John R. 1933- *ODwPR 91*
Malloy, John Richard 1932- *WhoAm 90*
Malloy, Johnn Edward 1940- *WhoWor 91*
Malloy, Joseph Thomas 1950- *WhoE 91*
Malloy, Kathleen Sharon 1948- *WhoAmW 91, WhoEmL 91*
Malloy, Margaret Ann Peters 1956- *WhoEmL 91*
Malloy, Michael Terrence 1936- *WhoAm 90*
Malloy, Pheobe Smalls 1954- *WhoAmW 91, WhoSSW 91*
Malloy, Ruth Lor 1932- *WhoWrEP 89*
Malloy, Tom 1950- *WhoSSW 91*
Malloy, William Manning 1922- *St&PR 91*
Mallozzi, Cos M. 1951- *ODwPR 91*
Malluche, Hartmut Horst 1943- *WhoWor 91*
Mallum, Daniel William 1940- *WhoAm 90*
Mallya, Ashok R 1950- *BiDrAPA 89*
Mallya, Gopinath K *BiDrAPA 89*
Mallya, Ullal Laxman *BiDrAPA 89*
Malm, David G. *St&PR 91*
Malm, E. Gustav 1946- *St&PR 91*
Malm, James Royal 1925- *WhoAm 90*
Malm, Richard Lewis 1948- *WhoSSW 91*
Malm, Rita P. 1932- *WhoAmW 91*
Malm, William Paul 1928- *IntWWM 90*
Malman, Bernard D. 1936- *St&PR 91*
Malman, Christina 1912-1958 *WhoAmA 91N*
Malmberg, David Curtis 1943- *St&PR 91*
Malmberg, James C. 1937- *St&PR 91*
Malmberg, John Holmes 1927- *WhoAm 90*
Malmborg, Gunila 1933- *IntWWM 90*
Malmer, Reynold W. 1929- *ODwPR 91*
Malmgren, Anders Helge Mikael 1945- *WhoWor 91*
Malmgren, Harald Bernard 1935- *WhoE 91*
Malmgren, Rene Louise 1938- *WhoAmW 91*
Malmgren, Richard Clifford 1933- *St&PR 91*
Malmierca Peoli, Isidoro Octavio *WhoWor 91*
Malmquist, Carl P 1933- *BiDrAPA 89*
Malmros, Lars 1927- *WhoWor 91*
Malmstadt, Howard V. 1922- *BioIn 16*
Malmsten, Carl 1888- *PenDiDA 89*
Malmsten, Carl 1888-1972 *ConDes 90*
Malmstrom, Eric Martin 1933- *BiDrAPA 89*
Malmstrom, Vincent Herschel 1926- *WhoAm 90*
Malnati, George Anthony 1946- *WhoSSW 91*
Malnati, Giovanni 1947- *WhoWor 91*
Malnati, Peggy S. 1960- *ODwPR 91*
Malneck, Matty 1903- *OxCPMus*
Malnes, Carolyn Kay Burke 1937- *IntWWM 90*
Malo, Teri 1954- *WhoAmA 91*
Maloch, W.H., Jr. 1925- *St&PR 91*
Malock, Ronald Anthony 1944- *St&PR 91*
Maloff, Chalda 1946- *ConAu 129*
Maloff, Perry Arlen *BiDrAPA 89*
Maloff, Saul 1922- *WhoWrEP 89*
Maloley, Nancy A. 1946- *ODwPR 91*
Malone, Alan Wayne 1951- *St&PR 91*
Malone, Barbara E. 1930- *St&PR 91*
Malone, Bette June 1950- *WhoAmW 91*
Malone, Carol Cross 1941- *WhoSSW 91*
Malone, Charles A 1927- *BiDrAPA 89*
Malone, Claudine Berkeley 1936- *St&PR 91*
Malone, Colonel Dick *ConAu 129*
Malone, Creighton Paul 1933- *WhoE 91*
Malone, Donald Anthony, Jr. *BiDrAPA 89*
Malone, Dorothy Ann 1931- *WhoAmW 91*
Malone, Dudley Field 1931-1990 *BioIn 16*
Malone, Dumas *BioIn 16*
Malone, Edward H 1917- *BiDrAPA 89*
Malone, Edward H. 1924- *WhoAm 90*
Malone, Edwin Scott, III 1938- *WhoAm 90*
Malone, Eileen *IntWWM 90*
Malone, Eleanor Wallace 1945- *WhoSSW 91*
Malone, Elmer Taylor, Jr. 1943- *WhoWrEP 89*
Malone, Elquin Lea 1956- *WhoAmW 91*
Malone, Francis Joseph 1937- *St&PR 91, WhoAm 90*
Malone, Gary Louis 1953- *BiDrAPA 89*
Malone, George Woodley 1943- *WhoE 91*
Malone, Harry N. *ODwPR 91*
Malone, James 1942- *WhoAm 90, WhoSSW 91*
Malone, James Hiram 1930- *WhoAmA 91*
Malone, James Louis 1931- *WhoAm 90*
Malone, James Patrick 1942- *St&PR 91*
Malone, James Perry 1937- *WhoSSW 91*
Malone, James R. 1942- *St&PR 91*
Malone, James William 1920- *WhoAm 90*
Malone, Jan J. 1956- *St&PR 91*
Malone, Jean Hambidge 1954- *WhoAmW 91*
Malone, John E. 1943- *St&PR 91*
Malone, John J. 1924- *St&PR 91*
Malone, Joseph James 1932- *WhoAm 90*
Malone, Joseph Lawrence 1937- *WhoAm 90*
Malone, Julia Louise 1947- *WhoE 91*
Malone, Karen Sellars 1951- *WhoAmW 91*
Malone, Karl *BioIn 16*
Malone, Karl 1963- *News 90 [port], WorAlBi*
Malone, Keith Paul 1957- *St&PR 91*
Malone, Lee H B 1913- *WhoAmA 91*
Malone, Leslie Richard 1923- *St&PR 91*
Malone, Linda Sue 1944- *WhoAmW 91*
Malone, Louis *MajTwCW*
Malone, Lucy Waggoner 1947- *WhoAmW 91*
Malone, Mary *AuBYP 90*
Malone, Mary Frances Alicia 1946- *WhoAmW 91*
Malone, Michael 1942- *ConAu 32NR*
Malone, Michael Christopher 1942- *WhoWrEP 89*
Malone, Michael Patrick 1951- *WhoWrEP 89*
Malone, Monica 1953- *WhoAmW 91*
Malone, Moses 1955- *WorAlBi*
Malone, Nola Langner 1930- *WhoAmA 91*
Malone, Pamela Altfeld 1943- *WhoWrEP 89*
Malone, Pat 1902-1943 *Ballpl 90*
Malone, Patricia Lynn 1930- *WhoAmA 91*
Malone, Patrick R. 1953- *IntWWM 90*
Malone, Perrillah Atkinson 1922- *WhoAmW 91, WhoSSW 91, WhoWor 91*
Malone, R. S. *ConAu 129*
Malone, Richard 1937- *WhoE 91*
Malone, Richard Patrick 1952- *BiDrAPA 89*
Malone, Richard S 1909-1985 *ConAu 129*
Malone, Richard Wayne 1951- *WhoSSW 91*
Malone, Robert B. *WhoSSW 91*
Malone, Robert R 1933- *WhoAmA 91*
Malone, Robert Roy 1933- *WhoAm 90*
Malone, Ruth *TwCCr&M 91*
Malone, Ruth Moore *WhoWor 91*
Malone, Sue Anderson 1930- *WhoAmW 91*
Malone, Ted *BioIn 16*
Malone, Thomas Francis 1917- *WhoAm 90*
Malone, Thomas P. 1956- *St&PR 91*
Malone, Vincent T. *BioIn 16*
Malone, Wallace D., Jr. 1936- *St&PR 91, WhoAm 90, WhoSSW 91*
Malone, William Grady 1915- *WhoAm 90, WhoSSW 91*
Maloney, Barry Charles 1942- *WhoE 91*
Maloney, Bill 1878-1960 *Ballpl 90*
Maloney, Brian M. 1943- *St&PR 91*
Maloney, Clement Garland 1917- *WhoWor 91*
Maloney, Dennis Michael 1942- *St&PR 91*
Maloney, Dennis Michael 1951- *WhoWrEP 89*
Maloney, Dorothy Ann Gose 1933- *WhoAmW 91*
Maloney, Edward Thomas 1943- *St&PR 91*
Maloney, George 1928- *Ballpl 90*
Maloney, George Thomas 1932- *St&PR 91, WhoAm 90*
Maloney, Gerald P. 1933- *St&PR 91, WhoAm 90*
Maloney, James Joseph 1941- *WhoE 91*
Maloney, Jim 1940- *Ballpl 90*
Maloney, Joan Ann 1942- *WhoAmW 91*
Maloney, John Alexander 1927- *WhoAm 90*
Maloney, John C. 1943- *St&PR 91*
Maloney, John Frederick 1913- *WhoAm 90*
Maloney, John J. 1929- *ODwPR 91*
Maloney, John R. *BiDrAPA 89*
Maloney, John Timothy 1943- *St&PR 91*
Maloney, Joseph H. 1927- *St&PR 91*
Maloney, Joseph Henry 1927- *WhoAm 90*
Maloney, Kevin Howard 1958- *IntWWM 90*
Maloney, Lucille Tinker 1920- *WhoAmW 91, WhoSSW 91*
Maloney, Mary Margaret 1956- *BiDrAPA 89*
Maloney, Michael J 1944- *BiDrAPA 89*
Maloney, Michael Patrick 1944- *St&PR 91, WhoAm 90*
Maloney, Milford Charles 1927- *WhoE 91*
Maloney, Nathan Alexander 1963- *WhoSSW 91*
Maloney, Pat *AuBYP 90*
Maloney, Patricia M. 1950- *St&PR 91*
Maloney, Paul 1942- *St&PR 91*
Maloney, Peter *ConTFT 8*
Maloney, Philip Dennis 1947- *WhoEmL 91*
Maloney, Richard Gerard 1925- *St&PR 91*
Maloney, Richard H 1924- *BiDrAPA 89*
Maloney, Susan Yacher 1954- *WhoAmW 91*
Maloney, Therese Adele 1929- *St&PR 91, WhoAm 90, WhoAmW 91*
Maloney, Toni *WhoAmW 91*
Maloney, Toni 1949- *ODwPR 91*
Maloney, Walter E. 1911- *WhoAm 90*
Maloney, William Gerard 1917- *WhoAm 90*
Maloni, William R. 1944- *St&PR 91*
Maloof, Farahe Paul 1950- *WhoEmL 91, WhoWor 91*
Maloof, James Aloysius 1919- *WhoAm 90*
Maloof, Richard C. 1945- *St&PR 91*
Maloof, Sam *PenDiDA 89*
Malooly, William Joseph 1942- *St&PR 91*
Maloon, James Harold 1926- *WhoAm 90*
Malory, Thomas *BioIn 16*
Malory, Thomas *WorAlBi*
Malosky, S.S. 1923- *St&PR 91*
Malot, Hector Henri 1830-1907 *AuBYP 90*
Malott, Adele Renee 1935- *WhoAm 90, WhoWrEP 89*
Malott, B.N. 1913- *St&PR 91*
Malott, Dwight Ralph 1947- *WhoEmL 91*
Malott, James Raymond, Jr. 1917- *WhoAm 90*
Malott, Mary *WhoAmA 91*
Malott, Ralph J 1923- *BiDrAPA 89*
Malott, Robert Harvey 1926- *St&PR 91, WhoAm 90*
Malott, Thomas J. 1937- *WhoAm 90*
Malouf, George S. 1942- *St&PR 91*
Malouf, Peter Joseph 1952- *St&PR 91*
Malouf-Cundy, Pamela Bonnie 1956- *WhoAmW 91*
Malouin, Jean-Louis 1943- *WhoAm 90*
Maloy, James G. 1921- *St&PR 91*
Maloy, Paul J. 1947- *St&PR 91*
Malozemoff, Plato 1909- *St&PR 91, WhoAm 90*
Malpas, Robert 1927- *St&PR 91, WhoAm 90, WhoWor 91*
Malpass, Leslie Frederick 1922- *WhoAm 90*
Malpass, Michael Allen 1946- *WhoAmA 91*
Malpede, Karen *BioIn 16*
Malpede, Karen 1945- *FemiCLE, NotWoAT*
Malphurs, Roger Edward 1933- *WhoWor 91*
Malpighi, Marcello 1628-1694 *WorAlBi*
Malquiades *ConAu 130*
Malraux, Andre 1901-1976 *BioIn 16, EuWr 12, MajTwCW, WhoAmA 91N, WorAlBi, WrPh*
Malraux, Clara *BioIn 16*
Malraux, Georges Andre 1901-1976 *BiDFrPL, BioIn 16*
Malroney, Robin *NewAgE 90*
Malsack, James Thomas 1921- *WhoAm 90*
Malsbury, Angela Mary 1945- *IntWWM 90*
Malsch, Craig B. 1940- *St&PR 91*
Malsch, Ellen L *WhoAmA 91N*
Malsky, Stanley Joseph 1925- *WhoAm 90, WhoE 91, WhoWor 91*
Malson, John Raymond, Sr. 1911- *WhoSSW 91*
Malson, Rex Richard 1931- *WhoAm 90*
Malson, Robert Allen 1944- *WhoAm 90*
Malsop, Verna Lee 1937- *WhoAmW 91*
Malt, Carol Nora 1942- *WhoSSW 91*
Malt, Harold Lewis 1918- *WhoWor 91*
Malt, Ronald Bradford 1954- *WhoWor 91*
Malta, Alexander 1942- *IntWWM 90*
Malta, Demetrio Aguilera *HispWr 90*
Malta, Victor Guillermo 1928- *WhoHisp 91*
Malta, Vincent 1922- *WhoAmA 91*
Maltbie, Allan A 1943- *BiDrAPA 89*
Maltby, Jack Allen *St&PR 91*
Maltby, John Newcombe 1928- *WhoWor 91*
Maltby, Richard Eldridge, Jr. 1937- *WhoAm 90*
Malter, Alan Steven *BiDrAPA 89*
Maltese, George John 1931- *WhoAm 90*
Maltese, Louis *BioIn 16, NewYTBS 90*
Malthus, T. R. 1766-1834 *BioIn 16*
Malthus, Thomas R. 1766-1834 *WorAlBi*
Malthus, Thomas Robert 1766-1834 *BioIn 16*
Maltin, Lawrence Joel 1937- *BiDrAPA 89*
Maltos, Charles Michael 1961- *St&PR 91*
Maltsberger, John Terry 1933- *BiDrAPA 89, WhoE 91*
Maltz, Albert 1908-1985 *BioIn 16, DcLB 102 [port]*
Maltz, Herschel 1929- *St&PR 91*
Maltz, J Herbert 1920- *BiDrAPA 89*
Maltz, J. Herbert 1920- *WhoAm 90*
Maltz, Jules 1918- *St&PR 91*
Maltz, Michael David 1938- *WhoAm 90*
Maltz, Milton 1930- *St&PR 91*
Maltzman, Irving Myron 1924- *WhoAm 90*

Maltzman, Marvin Stephen 1936- *St&PR 91*
Maltzman, Stanley 1921- *WhoAmA 91, WhoE 91*
Malueg, Thomas John 1935- *BiDrAPA 89*
Malugen, Louise D. 1945- *WhoAmW 91*
Malula, Joseph 1917-1989 *AnObit 1989*
Malula, Joseph-Albert 1917-1989 *BioIn 16*
Maluquer i Gonzalez, Concepcio 1918- *EncCoWW*
Malura, Oswald 1906- *WhoWor 91*
Malvasio, Paul John *St&PR 91*
Malveaux, Julianne Marie 1953- *WhoAmW 91, WhoEmL 91*
Malvern, Corinne *WhoAmA 91N*
Malvern, Donald 1921- *WhoAm 90*
Malvern, Gladys *AuBYP 90*
Malvern, Lawrence Earl 1916- *WhoAm 90*
Malves, Herman *BiDrAPA 89*
Malvestiti, Abel Orlando 1913- *WhoHisp 91*
Malvin, Frederick Bage 1932- *WhoSSW 91*
Malwitz, Donald Walter 1943- *St&PR 91*
Maly, George Joseph, Jr. 1933- *St&PR 91, WhoAm 90*
Maly, Kurt John 1944- *WhoAm 90*
Maly, Radek 1964- *WhoSSW 91*
Malyan-Wilson, Peter John 1933- *WhoWor 91*
Malycke, Steven 1920- *IntWWM 90*
Malz, Betty 1929- *ConAu 32NR*
Malzahn, Ray Andrew 1929- *WhoAm 90*
Malzberg, Barry 1939- *AuBYP 90*
Malzberg, Barry N. 1939- *RGTwCSF, TwCCr&M 91*
Malzberger, Gordon 1912-1974 *Ballpl 90*
Malzone, Frank 1930- *Ballpl 90*
Mamaloi *EncO&P 3*
Mamaloni, Solomon *WhoWor 91*
Maman, Maurice 1936- *WhoWor 91*
Maman, Robert *BiDrAPA 89*
Mamana, Joseph 1909- *WhoE 91*
Mamani, Manuel M. 1936- *IntWWM 90*
Maman'te *WhNaAH*
Mamanti *WhNaAH*
Mamantov, Gleb 1931- *WhoAm 90, WhoSSW 91*
Mamary, Abraham 1933- *WhoE 91*
Mamas and the Papas, The *EncPR&S 89, OxCPMus*
Mamat, Frank Trustick 1949- *WhoEmL 91, WhoWor 91*
Mamaux, Al 1894-1963 *Ballpl 90*
Mamba, Enoch 1861?- *BioIn 16*
Mamba, George Mbikwakhe 1932- *WhoWor 91*
Mambakkam, Balakrishnan Narayan 1949- *WhoWor 91*
Mamberg, David *ODwPR 91*
Mamelok, Alfred Edgar 1924- *WhoE 91*
Mamer, Stuart Mies 1921- *WhoAm 90*
Mamet, David *BioIn 16*
Mamet, David 1947- *ConTFT 8, MajTwCW, WorAlBi*
Mamet, David Alan 1947- *WhoAm 90, WhoE 91, WhoWrEP 89*
Mamlet, Laurence N *BiDrAPA 89*
Mamlok, Erich R *BiDrAPA 89*
Mamlok, Ursula 1928- *WhoAm 90*
Mammel, Clayton Gary 1947- *St&PR 91*
Mammel, Russell N. 1926- *St&PR 91*
Mammel, Russell Norman 1926- *WhoAm 90*
Mammen, Edward William 1907- *AuBYP 90*
Mammen, Jeanne 1890-1976 *BiDWomA, BioIn 16*
Mammen, Joy 1937- *IntWWM 90*
Mammen, Mariam *BiDrAPA 89*
Mammen, Oommen K 1959- *BiDrAPA 89*
Mammola, George C. 1940- *St&PR 91*
Mammone, Richard James 1953- *WhoEmL 91, WhoWor 91*
Mammoser, Thomas L. 1939- *ODwPR 91*
Mammoser, William Joseph 1932- *St&PR 91*
Mamo, George Elias 1935- *WhoE 91*
Mamoulian, Rouben 1897-1987 *BioIn 16*
Mamouris, Constant *BiDrAPA 89*
Mampre, Virginia Elizabeth 1949- *WhoAmW 91*
Mamrak, Sandra Ann 1944- *WhoAmW 91*
Man O'War 1917-1947 *WorAlBi*
Man Ray 1890-1976 *BioIn 16*
Man Xibo *ConAu 131*
Man, Cameron Robert James 1935- *WhoAm 90*
Man, Eugene Herbert 1923- *WhoAm 90*
Man, Evelyn Brower 1904- *WhoAmW 91*
Man, Judith *BiDEWW*
Man, Judith 1622?- *FemiCLE*
Man, Pang-Ling 1934- *BiDrAPA 89*
Man, Sai Chuen Kelvin 1959- *WhoWor 91*
Man, Wai-Cheong 1955- *St&PR 91*
Man-Afraid-of-His-Horses 1830?-1900 *WhNaAH*
Manabat, Conchita Labao 1946- *WhoWor 91*
Manabe, Kazufumi 1942- *WhoWor 91*
Manabu, Mabe 1924- *WhoAmA 91*
Manach, Jorge 1898-1961 *BioIn 16*
Manacka-Huk, Maria A 1925- *BiDrAPA 89*
Manaker, Arnold Martin 1947- *WhoSSW 91*
Manalac, Fernando J *BiDrAPA 89*
Manalastas, Ruby De Guzman *BiDrAPA 89*
Manalis, Sylvia Anne 1942- *BiDrAPA 89*
Manara, Baldassare *PenDiDA 89*
Manaray, Thelma Alberta 1913- *WhoAmA 91N*
Manasc, Vivian 1956- *WhoAmW 91*
Manaser, Karo 1933- *BiDrAPA 89*
Manasrah, Mustafa Moh'd 1940- *WhoWor 91*
Manassah, Jamal Tewfek 1945- *WhoWor 91*
Manasse, Adrienne Lorri 1941- *WhoAmW 91, WhoE 91*
Manasse, Gabriel Otto 1942- *BiDrAPA 89, WhoE 91*
Manasse, Henri Richard, Jr. 1945- *WhoAm 90, WhoEmL 91*
Manasse, Peter 1939- *St&PR 91*
Manasseh, Leonard 1916- *ConDes 90*
Manassen, Alex Jacques 1950- *IntWWM 90*
Manassero, Henri J. P. 1932- *WhoAm 90*
Manaster, Melvyn Lee 1937- *St&PR 91*
Manatos, Andrew Emanuel 1944- *WhoAm 90, WhoE 91*
Manatt, Richard 1931- *WhoAm 90*
Manausa, Terry E. 1940- *St&PR 91*
Manay, R. Jayanth 1944- *St&PR 91*
Manazar *BioIn 16*
Manberg, Richard I. 1938- *St&PR 91*
Manburg, Barbara Ruth 1953- *WhoAmW 91*
Manburg, Edwin 1924- *St&PR 91*
Manca, Gianni 1924- *WhoWor 91*
Mancall, Elliott Lee 1927- *WhoAm 90*
Mance, Rosalind Mary *BiDrAPA 89*
Manceaux, Michele 1928- *EncCoWW*
Mancel, Claude P. 1942- *St&PR 91*
Mancel, Claude Paul 1942- *WhoWor 91*
Manchel, Frank 1935- *AuBYP 90*
Mancher, Harry R. 1917-1988 *BioIn 16*
Mancher, Rhoda Ross 1935- *WhoAm 90*
Mancheski, Frederick J. 1926- *St&PR 91*
Mancheski, Frederick John 1926- *WhoAm 90, WhoE 91*
Manchester, Alden Coe 1922- *WhoE 91*
Manchester, David Fuller 1942- *St&PR 91*
Manchester, Diana 1955- *WhoE 91*
Manchester, Gilbert Mott 1944- *St&PR 91*
Manchester, Kenneth Edward 1925- *WhoAm 90*
Manchester, Melissa *BioIn 16*
Manchester, Melissa 1951- *EncPR&S 89, WorAlBi*
Manchester, Melissa Toni 1951- *WhoAmW 91*
Manchester, P. W. *BioIn 16*
Manchester, Paul Brunson 1942- *WhoE 91*
Manchester, Phyllis Winifred *BioIn 16*
Manchester, Robert D. 1942- *St&PR 91, WhoAm 90*
Manchester, Scott Owen 1951- *WhoEmL 91*
Manchester, Susan Jan 1945- *St&PR 91*
Manchester, William 1922- *ConAu 31NR, MajTwCW, WhoAm 90, WhoWrEP 89, WorAlBi*
Manchin, A. James 1927- *WhoSSW 91*
Mancina, David James 1956- *St&PR 91*
Mancinelli, Aldo 1928- *IntWWM 90*
Mancinelli, Bruce Regis 1946- *WhoSSW 91, WhoWor 91*
Mancinelli, Luigi 1848-1921 *PenDiMP*
Mancinelli, Victor A. 1943- *St&PR 91*
Mancini, Brooks Thomas 1940- *St&PR 91*
Mancini, Catherine *BiDrAPA 89*
Mancini, Dawn *St&PR 91*
Mancini, Elaine 1953- *ODwPR 91*
Mancini, Eva Cattermole 1849-1896 *EncCoWW*
Mancini, Henry 1924- *BioIn 16, IntWWM 90, OxCPMus, WhoAm 90, WorAlBi*
Mancini, John 1925- *WhoAmA 91*
Mancini, Louis Joseph 1950- *WhoWor 91*
Mancini, Thomas C. 1926- *St&PR 91*
Mancino, John Gregory 1946- *WhoEmL 91, WhoWor 91*
Mancke, Richard Bell 1943- *WhoE 91*
Mancoba, Sonja Ferlov 1911- *BiDWomA*
Mancoff, Neal Alan 1939- *WhoAm 90*
Mancusi, Vincent Dominick 1948- *WhoSSW 91*
Mancuso, A.R. 1937- *St&PR 91*
Mancuso, Anthony J. 1941- *St&PR 91*
Mancuso, Dawn Marie 1959- *WhoE 91*
Mancuso, Donna Mariene *BiDrAPA 89*
Mancuso, Frank 1918- *Ballpl 90*
Mancuso, Frank G. *St&PR 91*
Mancuso, Frank G. 1933- *WhoAm 90*
Mancuso, Gus 1905-1984 *Ballpl 90 [port]*
Mancuso, James Vincent 1918- *WhoWrEP 89*
Mancuso, Leni *WhoAmA 91*
Mancuso, Michele Geryl 1956- *WhoAmW 91*
Mancuso, Nancy J. 1957- *WhoAmW 91*
Mancuso, Robert James 1949- *WhoE 91*
Mancuso, Ronald 1946- *St&PR 91*
Mancuso, Sam 1928- *St&PR 91*
Mand, Martin G. 1936- *St&PR 91, WhoAm 90*
Mandac, Evelyn 1945- *IntWWM 90*
Mandalos, George Elias *BiDrAPA 89*
Mandanici, Marcella 1958- *IntWWM 90*
Mandanis, Alice S. *WhoAm 90*
Mandanis, George P. 1927- *St&PR 91*
Mandarich, Tony *BioIn 16*
Mandart, Tracy Joseph, Jr. 1936- *St&PR 91*
Mandel, Alan Roger 1935- *IntWWM 90*
Mandel, Allan Lee 1939- *WhoSSW 91*
Mandel, Barry Irving 1943- *WhoE 91*
Mandel, Carola Panerai 1920- *WhoAmW 91, WhoWor 91*
Mandel, Charlotte *WhoWrEP 89*
Mandel, Dorothy *WhoAmA 91*
Mandel, Eli 1922- *WorAu 1980*
Mandel, Georges Louis Rothschild 1885-1944 *BiDFrPL*
Mandel, Harold George 1924- *WhoAm 90*
Mandel, Harry *BioIn 16*
Mandel, Harvey I 1928- *BiDrAPA 89*
Mandel, Herbert Maurice 1924- *WhoE 91*
Mandel, Howard 1917- *WhoAmA 91*
Mandel, Howie 19--?- *WorAlBi*
Mandel, Irwin Daniel 1922- *WhoAm 90*
Mandel, Jack N. 1911- *St&PR 91, WhoAm 90*
Mandel, Jeff 1952- *WhoEmL 91*
Mandel, Jeffrey T. 1948- *St&PR 91*
Mandel, Jerome 1937- *WhoWor 91*
Mandel, John 1941- *WhoAmA 91*
Mandel, Johnny 1925- *OxCPMus*
Mandel, Jon 1944- *St&PR 91*
Mandel, Joseph C. 1913- *St&PR 91*
Mandel, Joseph David 1940- *WhoAm 90*
Mandel, Karyl Lynn 1935- *WhoAmW 91, WhoWor 91*
Mandel, Leonard *WhoAm 90*
Mandel, Leslie Ann 1945- *WhoAmW 91, WhoE 91, WhoWor 91*
Mandel, Maurice, II *WhoWor 91*
Mandel, Max A. 1914- *St&PR 91*
Mandel, Melvin 1923- *BiDrAPA 89*
Mandel, Michael G *BiDrAPA 89*
Mandel, Michael Ross *BiDrAPA 89*
Mandel, Miriam 1930-1982 *FemiCLE*
Mandel, Morton L. 1921- *St&PR 91*
Mandel, Morton Leon 1921- *WhoAm 90*
Mandel, Murray 1930- *St&PR 91*
Mandel, Newton W. 1926- *WhoWor 91*
Mandel, Oscar 1926- *WhoWrEP 89*
Mandel, Richard E. 1958- *St&PR 91*
Mandel, Robert C. 1926- *St&PR 91*
Mandel, Robert Jay 1926- *St&PR 91*
Mandel, Sally 1944- *SmATA 64*
Mandel, Sandra *BiDrAPA 89*
Mandel, Saul 1926- *WhoAmA 91*
Mandel, Siegfried 1922- *WhoAm 90, WhoWrEP 89*
Mandel, Stanley Wayne 1942- *St&PR 91*
Mandel, William E. 1953- *St&PR 91*
Mandel, William Kurt 1948- *WhoAm 90*
Mandela, Josette 1960- *WhoE 91*
Mandela, Nelson *BioIn 16*
Mandela, Nelson 1918- *NewYTBS 90 [port], News 90 [port], -90-3 [port], WorAlBi*
Mandela, Nelson Rolihlahia 1918- *WhoWor 91*
Mandela, Nomzamo Winnie 1934- *WhoWor 91*
Mandela, Winnie *BioIn 16*
Mandelbaum, Bernard 1922- *BioIn 16, ConAu 130, WhoAm 90*
Mandelbaum, David Goodman 1911-1987 *BioIn 16*
Mandelbaum, Dorothy Rosenthal 1935- *WhoAmW 91, WhoE 91*
Mandelbaum, Ellen 1938- *WhoAmA 91*
Mandelbaum, Frank 1934- *St&PR 91, WhoWor 91*
Mandelbaum, Fredericka 1818-1889 *WorAlBi*
Mandelbaum, Gary 1949- *St&PR 91*
Mandelbaum, Howard Arnold 1941- *WhoAm 90*
Mandelbaum, Jonna Lynn Knauer 1946- *WhoAmW 91*
Mandelbaum, Kathy Coons 1958- *WhoAmW 91*
Mandelbaum, Ken *BioIn 16*
Mandelbaum, Lyn 1950- *WhoAmA 91*
Mandelbaum, Maurice 1908-1987 *ConAu 131*
Mandelblatt, Jeanne Susan 1951- *WhoAmW 91*
Mandelbrot, Benoit B. 1924- *WhoAm 90*
Mandelert, Hugh *BioIn 16*
Mandelert, Joseph C. 1925- *St&PR 91*
Mandelker, Daniel Robert 1926- *WhoAm 90*
Mandelker, Gershon Nachman *WhoE 91*
Mandelkern, David 1959- *WhoEmL 91*
Mandelkern, Emanuel 1922- *St&PR 91*
Mandelkern, Leo 1922- *WhoAm 90, WhoSSW 91*
Mandelkern, Marshal 1953- *BiDrAPA 89*
Mandelkorn, Eugenia Miller *AuBYP 90*
Mandell, Allan Martin 1942- *St&PR 91*
Mandell, Arlene Linda 1941- *WhoAmW 91*
Mandell, Arnold Joseph *BiDrAPA 89*
Mandell, Betty Ellen 1936- *WhoAmW 91*
Mandell, Gordon Keith 1947- *WhoEmL 91*
Mandell, Harry *BiDrAPA 89*
Mandell, Harry J. *St&PR 91*
Mandell, Herbert E *BiDrAPA 89*
Mandell, James 1945- *WhoE 91*
Mandell, Lewis 1943- *WhoE 91*
Mandell, Mark Steven 1949- *WhoEmL 91*
Mandell, Mel 1926- *WhoWrEP 89*
Mandell, Muriel 1921- *SmATA 63*
Mandell, Patricia Athena 1952- *WhoWrEP 89*
Mandell, Ralph B. 1941- *St&PR 91*
Mandell, Richard M. 1930- *St&PR 91*
Mandell, Richard S. 1953- *WhoWrEP 89*
Mandell, Todd *BiDrAPA 89*
Mandell, Walter Alan *BiDrAPA 89*
Mandelli, Mariuccia 1933- *ConDes 90*
Mandelman, Beatrice M 1912- *WhoAmA 91*
Mandelshtam, Nadezhda 1899-1980 *EncCoWW*
Mandelstam, Arnold 1953- *BiDrAPA 89*
Mandelstam, Charles Lawrence 1927- *WhoAm 90*
Mandel'stam, Nadezhda 1899-1980 *BioIn 16*
Mandelstam, Osip 1891-1938? *WorAlBi*
Mandelstamm, Jerome Robert 1932- *WhoAm 90*
Mandeltort, Stanley T. 1934- *St&PR 91*
Mander, Jane 1877-1949 *FemiCLE*
Mander, Karel van 1610-1670 *BioIn 16*
Manderfield, G.J. 1933- *St&PR 91*
Manderino, James J. *BioIn 16*
Manders, Karl Lee 1927- *WhoAm 90, WhoWor 91*
Manderscheid, Lester V. *BioIn 16*
Manderscheid, Lester Vincent 1930- *WhoAm 90*
Manderscheid, Robert Kenneth 1955- *WhoE 91*
Manderscheid, Ronald William 1943- *WhoE 91*
Mandes, Ellen A. 1936- *WhoAmW 91*
Mandeville, Bernard 1670-1733 *BioIn 16, DcLB 101*
Mandeville, C. Robert 1933- *St&PR 91*
Mandeville, Gilbert Harrison 1910- *WhoAm 90*
Mandeville, Gregory W. 1922- *St&PR 91*
Mandeville, Mark David 1958- *WhoSSW 91*
Mandeville, Robert Clark, Jr. 1927- *WhoAm 90*
Mandeville, Robert R. 1943- *St&PR 91*
Mandia, Eglantina 1936- *EncCoWW*
Mandic, Borislava 1946- *BiDrAPA 89*
Mandich, Donald Ralph 1925- *St&PR 91*
Mandicott, Grace Marie 1942- *WhoAmW 91*
Mandigo, Theodore R. *BioIn 16*
Mandil, I. Harry 1919- *WhoAm 90*
Mandini, Maria *PenDiMP*
Mandini, Paolo 1757-1842 *PenDiMP*
Mandini, Stefano 1750?-1810? *PenDiMP*
Mandino, Og 1923- *WhoAm 90, WhoWrEP 89*
Mandl, Alex J. 1943- *St&PR 91*
Mandl, Alex Johann 1943- *WhoAm 90*
Mandl, Alexander J. *BioIn 16*
Mandl, David 1953- *WhoE 91, WhoEmL 91*
Mandl, Heinz 1937- *WhoWor 91*
Mandl, Scott Carlton 1961- *WhoSSW 91*
Mandle, Earl Roger 1941- *WhoAm 90, WhoAmA 91, WhoE 91*
Mandle, Richard Max 1921- *St&PR 91*
Mandle, William Dee 1928- *IntWWM 90*
Mandlebaum, D. Allen 1942- *WhoSSW 91*
Mandler, George 1924- *WhoAm 90*
Mandler, Jean Matter 1929- *WhoAm 90*
Mandler, John Irvin 1930- *WhoE 91*
Mandler, Susan Ruth 1949- *WhoAmW 91*
Mandlikova, Hana 1962- *WhoWor 91*
Mando, Raymond A. 1935- *St&PR 91*
Mandody, Julian W. 1949- *WhoSSW 91*
Mandoki, Miguel 1950- *BiDrAPA 89*
Mandolini, Anthony Mario 1933- *WhoAm 90*
Mandra, York T. 1922- *WhoAm 90*
Mandravelis, Patricia Jean 1938- *WhoAmW 91*
Mandrell, Barbara *BioIn 16*

Mandrell, Barbara 1948- *ConMus 4 [port], OxCPMus, WorAlBi*
Mandrell, Barbara Ann 1948- *WhoAm 90, WhoAmW 91*
Mandri, Daniel F 1950- *BiDrAPA 89*
Mandry, George Gilbert, Sr. 1926- *WhoSSW 91*
Mandry, Kathy *AuBYP 90*
Manduell, John 1928- *IntWWM 90*
Mandughai *WomWR*
Manduke, Rhonda Carol 1955- *WhoAmW 91*
Mandula, Jeffrey Ellis 1941- *WhoAm 90*
Manduley, Jose Carlos 1944- *WhoAm 90*
Mandy, Ivan 1918- *WorAu 1980 [port]*
Mandziuk, Michael Dennis 1942- *WhoAmA 91*
Mane, Jorge Ignacio Rubio *BioIn 16*
Manear, John L. 1941- *WhoE 91*
Maneely, Joe 1926-1958 *EncACom*
Maneepairoj, Paitoon 1956- *WhoWor 91*
Manegold, Deborah Ketchum *BiDrAPA 89*
Manejias, Sergio 1909- *WhoWrEP 89*
Manejwala, Hameed 1953- *St&PR 91*
Manek, Ravindra M 1938- *BiDrAPA 89*
Maneker, Morton M. 1932- *WhoAm 90*
Maneker, Roberta S. 1937- *ODwPR 91*
Maneli, Mieczyslaw 1924- *WhoE 91*
Manell, Abram E. 1912- *WhoAm 90*
Manelli, Daniel A *BiDrAPA 89*
Manelli, Donald Dean 1936- *WhoAm 90*
Manepalli, Jothika Narayan *BiDrAPA 89*
Maner, Charlotte Fawn 1951- *WhoSSW 91*
Manera, Enrico Orlando 1947- *WhoAmA 91*
Maneri, K. Peter 1945- *ODwPR 91*
Maneri, Remo R. 1928- *WhoAm 90*
Manero, Tony 1905-1989 *BioIn 16*
Manero, Victoria 1942- *WhoAmW 91*
Manes, Belle *WhoAmA 91*
Manes, Carl 1918- *St&PR 91*
Manes, Jack L., Jr. 1938- *St&PR 91*
Manes, John Dalton 1920- *WhoAm 90*
Manes, Michael Gerard 1947- *WhoSSW 91*
Manes, Michael Lewis 1946- *St&PR 91*
Manes, Milton 1918- *WhoAm 90*
Manes, Nella Cellini 1920- *St&PR 91, WhoAm 90*
Manes, Paul 1948- *WhoAmA 91*
Manes, Peter Rolf 1930- *BiDrAPA 89*
Manes, Stephen 1949- *AuBYP 90*
Manes, Stephen Gabriel 1940- *WhoAm 90*
Maness, John D. 1920- *St&PR 91*
Maness, Sam A. 1907- *St&PR 91*
Manesse, Daniel Arthur 1921- *WhoWrEP 89*
Manessiotis, Basil 1946- *WhoWor 91*
Manet, Edouard 1832-1883 *BioIn 16, IntDcAA 90, WorAlBi*
Manetta, Edward J 1925- *WhoAmA 91*
Manetta, Edward J., Jr. *ODwPR 91*
Manetti, Antonio *PenDiDA 89*
Manetti, Vincent Blaze 1953- *BiDrAPA 89*
Manevitz, Alan Z A *BiDrAPA 89*
Manewitz, Sharon F. 1948- *WhoAmW 91*
Maney, Michael Mason 1936- *WhoAm 90*
Maney, Thomas P. 1932- *St&PR 91*
Manford, Barbara Ann 1929- *IntWWM 90, WhoAmW 91*
Manfra-Marretta, Sandra 1949- *WhoAmW 91*
Manfred, Carl Lawrence 1918- *WhoAm 90*
Manfred, Frederick Feikema 1912- *WhoAm 90, WhoWrEP 89*
Manfreda, Michael Joseph 1951- *WhoWor 91*
Manfredi, Harold M 1925- *BiDrAPA 89*
Manfredi, John F. *ODwPR 91*
Manfredi, Joseph Francis 1935- *St&PR 91*
Manfredi, Nino 1921- *ConTFT 8*
Manfredi, Rocco Louis 1957- *BiDrAPA 89*
Manfredini, Luigi 1771-1840 *PenDiDA 89*
Manfredonia, Catherine Carmela Bernitt 1946- *WhoAmW 91*
Manfrey, Barbara L. *WhoE 91*
Manfro, Patrick James 1947- *WhoEmL 91*
Mang, Karl 1922- *ConDes 90*
Mang, Warren George 1928- *St&PR 91*
Mangan, F. Lee *BioIn 16*
Mangan, Gordon Lavelle 1924- *EncO&P 3*
Mangan, James Clarence 1803-1849 *NinCLC 27 [port]*
Mangan, Jean 1934- *WhoWrEP 89*
Mangan, John 1908-1988 *BioIn 16*
Mangan, John Joseph 1939- *St&PR 91*
Mangan, John Leo 1920- *WhoAm 90*
Mangan, Patricia Ann Pritchett 1953- *WhoAmW 91*
Mangan, Patrick Joseph 1958- *WhoSSW 91*
Manganaro, Francis Ferdinand 1925- *WhoAm 90*
Manganas, Antoun C 1950- *BiDrAPA 89*
Manganas, Nelly Mahrous *BiDrAPA 89*
Manganello, James Angelo 1944- *WhoE 91*
Manganello, Joseph James 1949- *WhoSSW 91*
Mangano, James V. *BioIn 16*
Mangano, Joseph 1943- *WhoE 91*
Mangano, Silvana *BioIn 16*
Mangano, Sylvana 1930-1989 *AnObit 1989*
Mangapit, Conrado, Jr. 1946- *WhoSSW 91*
Mangarella, James 1962- *WhoE 91*
Mangarelli, George E. 1943- *St&PR 91*
Mangas Coloradas 1797?-1863 *WhNaAH*
Mangat, Balminder S 1949- *BiDrAPA 89*
Mange, Franklin Edwin 1928- *St&PR 91*
Mangel, Benjamin 1925- *WhoAmA 91*
Mangel, LeRoy Dwight 1945- *WhoEmL 91*
Mangel, Solomon Z. 1916- *St&PR 91*
Mangels, Barbara Jean 1947- *WhoEmL 91*
Mangels, John Donald 1926- *St&PR 91, WhoAm 90*
Mangelsdorf, Albert 1928- *BioIn 16*
Mangelsdorf, Jenny Lynn Moffitt 1957- *WhoAmW 91*
Mangelsdorf, Paul Christoph *BioIn 16*
Mangelsdorf, Thomas K *BiDrAPA 89*
Mangelsdorff, Arthur *NewYTBS 90*
Mangelsen, William Paul 1943- *St&PR 91*
Mangen, Lawrence Raymond 1927- *WhoE 91*
Mangen, Marcel 1945- *WhoWor 91*
Mangen, Mary Jane *BiDrAPA 89*
Manger, William Muir 1920- *WhoAm 90, WhoE 91*
Manges, James H. 1927- *St&PR 91*
Manges, James Horace 1927- *WhoAm 90, WhoE 91, WhoWor 91*
Manget, Frederic Fairfield 1951- *WhoEmL 91*
Mangham, Charles A, Sr. 1919- *BiDrAPA 89*
Manghirmalani, Ramesh 1953- *WhoEmL 91*
Mangia, Angelo James 1954- *WhoEmL 91*
Mangiafico, Josephine Mary 1916- *St&PR 91*
Mangiafico, Paul S. 1936- *St&PR 91*
Mangiaracina, Leonard 1939- *WhoE 91*
Mangiarotti, Angelo 1921- *ConDes 90*
Mangieri, John Nicholas 1946- *WhoAm 90*
Mangillani, Ada 1863- *BiDWomA*
Mangin, Marie-France 1940- *BioIn 16*
Mangin, Noel 1932- *IntWWM 90*
Mangino, Angie Theresa 1949- *WhoAmW 91*
Mangino, Kristin Mikalson 1939- *WhoAmW 91*
Mangion, Carmen Margaret 1962- *WhoAmW 91*
Mangione, Chuck 1940- *EncPR&S 89, WorAlBi*
Mangione, Jerre Gerlando 1909- *BioIn 16, WhoAm 90, WhoWrEP 89*
Mangione, Patricia Anthony *WhoAmA 91*
Manglapus, Raul S. 1918- *WhoWor 91*
Manglona, Benjamin T. 1938- *WhoWor 91*
Mango, Joseph Robert 1923- *WhoAm 90*
Mango, Karin N *AuBYP 90*
Mango, Karin N. 1936- *BioIn 16*
Mango, Wilfred G., Jr. 1940- *St&PR 91*
Mango, Wilfred Gilbert, Jr. 1940- *WhoAm 90*
Mangol, Leona Alvina 1942- *WhoE 91*
Mangold, Glenn E. 1942- *St&PR 91*
Mangold, John Frederic 1927- *St&PR 91, WhoAm 90*
Mangold, Margaret M. *BioIn 16*
Mangold, Martin Clarence 1952- *IntWWM 90*
Mangold, Robert Peter 1937- *WhoAmA 91*
Mangold, Sylvia Plimack 1938- *WhoAm 90, WhoAmA 91*
Mangoldt, Hans Karl Emil von 1824-1868 *BioIn 16*
Mangolte, Babette M 1941- *WhoAmA 91*
Mangone, Dominic M. 1950- *St&PR 91*
Mangone, Dominic Merle 1950- *WhoAm 90*
Mangone, Gerard J. 1918- *WhoAm 90*
Mangope, Lucas Manyane 1927- *WhoWor 91*
Mangos 1797?-1863 *WhNaAH*
Mangoubi, Elie K *BiDrAPA 89*
Mangoubi, Nabih *St&PR 91*
Mangouni, Norman 1932- *WhoAm 90*
Mangravite, Peppino Gino 1896-1978 *WhoAmA 91N*
Mangrola, Raju Prabhatsinh *BiDrAPA 89*
Mangrum, Franklin Mayer 1925- *WhoSSW 91*
Mangrum, Tomontra *BioIn 16*
Mangual, Angel 1947- *Ballpl 90*
Mangual, Pepe 1952- *Ballpl 90*
Mangual, Theresa Y. 1958- *WhoHisp 91*
Manguel, Alberto 1948- *ConAu 131, HispWr 90*
Mangulabnan, Lilia Serrano *BiDrAPA 89*
Mangum, Leo 1896-1974 *Ballpl 90*
Mangum, Walter Curtis 1923- *St&PR 91*
Mangum, William *WhoAmA 91*
Mangunay, Nora Ramos *BiDrAPA 89*
Mangus *WhNaAH*
Mangus 1797?-1863 *WhNaAH*
Mangus, Carl William 1930- *WhoSSW 91*
Mangus, Debbie Dee 1955- *WhoAmW 91*
Mangus, Patrick T. 1949- *ODwPR 91*
Mangwende, Witness 1946- *WhoWor 91*
Manhart, Marcia Y 1943- *WhoAmA 91*
Manhart, Marcia Yockey 1943- *WhoAm 90, WhoAmW 91, WhoSSW 91*
Manhart, Thomas Arthur 1937- *WhoAmA 91*
Manhattan Transfer *EncPR&S 89, OxCPMus*
Manhattan, Avro 1914- *ConAu 30NR*
Manheim, Emmanuel *BioIn 16*
Manheim, Jarol B. 1946- *WhoWrEP 89*
Manheim, Marvin Lee 1937- *WhoAm 90*
Manheim, Michael 1928- *WhoAm 90*
Manheim, Paul E. 1905- *St&PR 91*
Manheimer, Alan Robert 1945- *St&PR 91*
Manheimer, Arnold L. 1945- *St&PR 91*
Manheimer, Bruce S. 1939- *St&PR 91*
Manheimer, Martha L. 1921-1989 *BioIn 16*
Manheimer, Stephen R. 1941- *St&PR 91*
Manhertz, Huntley George 1938- *WhoWor 91*
Manhold, John Henry 1919- *WhoAmA 91, WhoWor 91*
Mani 216-274? *WorAlBi*
Mani, Matharbootham 1945- *WhoEmL 91*
Mani, Swarnambal *BiDrAPA 89*
Maniaci, Elizabeth Hoffer 1955- *WhoAmW 91*
Manian, Janaki Venkat 1944- *BiDrAPA 89*
Maniar, Rajeshkumar C 1953- *BiDrAPA 89*
Maniates, Maria Rika 1937- *IntWWM 90*
Maniatis, Paraschos 1957- *IntWWM 90*
Maniatty, Philip Ward 1952- *WhoEmL 91*
Manichello, Richard 1947- *WhoE 91*
Manickavasagam, Joe 1942- *WhoE 91*
Manicus, Frederick 1740-1785 *PenDiDA 89*
Manigat, Leslie F. 1930- *WhoWor 91*
Manigault, Peter 1927- *WhoAm 90*
Manikas, William T. 1938- *WhoSSW 91*
Manikhao, Narong 1930- *IntWWM 90*
Maniktala, Kalpana 1954- *BiDrAPA 89*
Manilla, Jack 1941- *St&PR 91*
Manilla, Manuel 1830-1895 *ArtLatA*
Manilla, Tess *WhoAmA 91*
Maniloff, Jack 1938- *WhoAm 90*
Manilow, Barry 1946- *EncPR&S 89, OxCPMus, WhoAm 90, WorAlBi*
Manilow, Lewis 1927- *WhoAmA 91*
Manin, Mitchell *BiDrAPA 89*
Maninger, Ralph Carroll 1918- *WhoAm 90*
Manio, Jack de 1914-1988 *AnObit 1988*
Manion, Clyde 1896-1967 *Ballpl 90*
Manion, Daniel Anthony 1942- *WhoAm 90*
Manion, John Richard 1933- *St&PR 91*
Manion, Kernan Thomas 1950- *BiDrAPA 89*
Manion, Maria Elena *BiDrAPA 89*
Manion, Michael Lawrence 1952- *IntWWM 90*
Manion, Thomas A. 1934- *WhoAm 90*
Manion, William Joseph 1929- *St&PR 91*
Manire, George Philip 1919- *WhoAm 90*
Manire, James McDonnell 1918- *WhoAm 90*
Manis, Jimmy E. 1936- *St&PR 91*
Manis, Marc David 1955- *WhoSSW 91*
Manis, Melvin 1931- *WhoAm 90*
Maniscalco, Anthony E 1911- *BiDrAPA 89*
Maniscalco, Joseph Stephen 1936- *St&PR 91, WhoAm 90*
Maniscalco, Rosemary *BioIn 16*
Manischewitz, Bernard 1913- *St&PR 91, WhoAm 90*
Manischewitz, D. Beryl *St&PR 91N*
Manischewitz, David M. 1938- *St&PR 91*
Manisto'kos *DcCanB 12*
Manitius, Andrzej Zdzislaw 1938- *WhoAm 90*
Manitsas, Nikitas Constantin 1923- *St&PR 91*
Maniwa, Mitsuyuki 1934- *WhoWor 91*
Manix, John C. 1918- *St&PR 91*
Manizade, Ali *BiDrAPA 89*
Manjos, Peter 1909- *BiDrAPA 89*
Manjos, Robert Michael 1944- *St&PR 91*
Manjura, Bonnie Doreen 1956- *WhoSSW 91*
Mankamyer, Jack L. 1931- *St&PR 91*
Mankato *WhNaAH*
Manke, Dean Joseph 1949- *WhoE 91*
Manke, Dean V. 1949- *St&PR 91*
Mankiewicz, Frank 1924- *ODwPR 91*
Mankiewicz, Frank F. 1924- *WhoAm 90*
Mankiewicz, Joseph L. 1909- *WorAlBi*
Mankiewicz, Joseph Leo 1909- *WhoAm 90, WhoE 91*
Mankiller, Wilma *BioIn 16*
Mankiller, Wilma Pearl 1945- *WhoAmW 91*
Mankiller, Wilma T. 1944- *WomWR*
Mankin, Charles John 1932- *WhoAm 90*
Mankin, Hart Tiller 1933- *WhoAm 90*
Mankin, Helen Douglas 1896-1956 *BioAmW*
Mankin, Henry Jay 1928- *WhoAm 90*
Mankin, Robert Stephen 1939- *WhoAm 90, WhoE 91*
Mankins, John Carlton 1956- *WhoEmL 91*
Mankiw, Gregory *BioIn 16*
Mankiw, Nicholas Gregory 1958- *WhoE 91*
Manko, Ida *BioIn 16*
Manko, Joseph Martin, Sr. 1939- *WhoAm 90*
Manko, Kenneth *BioIn 16*
Mankodi, Rashmi *BiDrAPA 89*
Mankoff, Alan Howard 1933- *St&PR 91*
Mankoff, Ronald Morton 1931- *WhoAm 90*
Mankowski, Bruno 1902- *WhoAm 90*
Mankowski, Bruno 1902-1990 *WhoAmA 91N*
Mankowski, Phil 1953- *Ballpl 90*
Manlavi, Thelma Sempio *BiDrAPA 89*
Manley, Albert Edward 1908- *WhoAm 90*
Manley, Audrey Forbes 1934- *WhoAm 90, WhoAmW 91*
Manley, Barbara Lee Dean 1946- *WhoAmW 91*
Manley, Cathey Neracker 1951- *WhoAmW 91, WhoEmL 91, WhoWor 91*
Manley, Charles G. 1944- *St&PR 91*
Manley, Delarivier 1663?-1724 *BiDEWW, FemiCLE*
Manley, Delariviere 1672?-1724 *BioIn 16*
Manley, Dexter *BioIn 16*
Manley, Douglas Rempet 1952- *WhoEmL 91*
Manley, Effa 1897?-1981 *Ballpl 90*
Manley, Elizabeth *BioIn 16*
Manley, Frank 1930- *WhoAm 90*
Manley, Harry Stockwell 1920- *WhoAm 90*
Manley, Helen 1894-1987 *BioIn 16*
Manley, Joan Adele Daniels 1932- *WhoAm 90*
Manley, Joan Marie 1955- *WhoAmW 91*
Manley, John Frederick 1939- *WhoAm 90*
Manley, John H. *NewYTBS 90*
Manley, John H. 1907-1990 *BioIn 16*
Manley, John Hugo 1932- *WhoE 91*
Manley, John Joseph 1954- *WhoEmL 91*
Manley, Joseph Homan 1842-1905 *AmLegL*
Manley, Kim 1943- *WhoAmW 91*
Manley, Lance Filson 1945- *WhoSSW 91*
Manley, Louis V *BiDrAPA 89*
Manley, Marshall 1940- *St&PR 91, WhoAm 90, WhoE 91*
Manley, Michael 1924- *BioIn 16*
Manley, Michael Norman 1924- *WhoWor 91*
Manley, Myrl Ray Stephen 1947- *BiDrAPA 89*
Manley, Nancy Jane 1951- *WhoAmW 91*
Manley, Norman Washington 1893-1969 *BioIn 16*
Manley, Richard D. 1938- *St&PR 91*
Manley, Richard Shannon 1932- *WhoSSW 91*
Manley, Robert Edward 1935- *WhoAm 90*
Manley, Robert Merrill, Jr. 1947- *WhoWrEP 89*
Manley, Seon 1921- *AuBYP 90*
Manley, William Tanner 1929- *WhoAm 90*
Manlove, Colin Nicholas 1942- *ConAu 32NR*
Manlove, Francis R *BiDrAPA 89*
Manlove, John Gregory 1952- *WhoSSW 91*
Manlove, Robert Scott 1921- *St&PR 91*
Manlove, Stephen Paul 1955- *BiDrAPA 89*
Manly, David T 1957- *BiDrAPA 89*
Manly, Douglas H. 1927- *St&PR 91*
Manly, Marc Edward 1952- *WhoEmL 91*
Manly, Samuel 1945- *WhoSSW 91, WhoWor 91*
Manly, William Donald 1923- *WhoAm 90*
Mann, Abel *MajTwCW, TwCCr&M 91*
Mann, Alfred 1917- *IntWWM 90, WhoAm 90*
Mann, Andrew David *BiDrAPA 89*
Mann, Andrew Hudson, Jr. 1947- *WhoE 91*
Mann, Arthur 1922- *WhoAm 90, WhoWor 91, WhoWrEP 89*
Mann, Avery *AuBYP 90*
Mann, Barry 1939- *OxCPMus*
Mann, Benjamin Howard 1958- *WhoEmL 91, WhoWor 91*
Mann, Bernie *WhoAm 90*
Mann, Carroll Wesley 1927- *St&PR 91*
Mann, Cecil 1923- *St&PR 91*

Mann, Cedric Robert 1926- WhoAm 90
Mann, Charles J. 1945- St&PR 91
Mann, Charles Kellogg 1934- WhoE 91, WhoWor 91
Mann, Chelsea 1961- WhoAmW 91
Mann, Dale BioIn 16
Mann, David Scott 1939- WhoAm 90
Mann, David W 1950- BiDrAPA 89
Mann, David Wayne 1950- WhoE 91
Mann, Delbert 1920- BioIn 16, WhoAm 90
Mann, Dennis Lee 1949- St&PR 91
Mann, Dick WhoWrEP 89
Mann, Duncan Paulson 1953- WhoE 91
Mann, Eddie 1951- WhoE 91
Mann, Edith Kerby 1946- WhoAmW 91
Mann, Elizabeth Brown 1924- WhoAmW 91
Mann, Emily BioIn 16
Mann, Emily 1952- ConAu 130, FemiCLE, NotWoAT
Mann, Emily Betsy 1952- WhoAm 90
Mann, Erika 1905-1969 EncCoWW
Mann, Eugene T. St&PR 91
Mann, Genevieve Coratti 1958- WhoAmW 91
Mann, George Stanley 1932- St&PR 91, WhoAm 90
Mann, Gerald Arthur 1932- WhoE 91
Mann, Golo 1909- WhoWor 91
Mann, Gordon Hossley 1928- WhoSSW 91
Mann, Gordon Tyler 1936- St&PR 91
Mann, Harold A. 1938- St&PR 91
Mann, Harold E 1920- BiDrAPA 89
Mann, Harvey Blount 1930- WhoSSW 91
Mann, Heinrich 1871-1950 BioIn 16, WorAlBi
Mann, Henry Brower 1937- BiDrAPA 89
Mann, Herbie 1930- OxCPMus, WhoAm 90, WorAlBi
Mann, Horace 1796-1859 WorAlBi
Mann, Hosea, Jr. 1858- AmLegL
Mann, Iurii Vladimirovich 1929- WhoWor 91
Mann, J.M. St&PR 91
Mann, J. Robert, Jr. 1930- St&PR 91
Mann, Jacinta 1925- WhoAmW 91
Mann, Jack Matthewson 1932- WhoSSW 91
Mann, Jacques R. St&PR 91N
Mann, James 1913- BiDrAPA 89
Mann, James E. 1943- WhoAm 90
Mann, James Howell, III 1952- WhoSSW 91
Mann, James Lee 1926- St&PR 91
Mann, James Robert 1920- WhoAm 90
Mann, Jessica 1937- TwCCr&M 91
Mann, Jim 1919- WhoE 91, WhoWrEP 89
Mann, John 1798-1891 DcCanB 12
Mann, John Hatch 1940- BiDrAPA 89
Mann, John Michael 1946- WhoAm 90
Mann, Jonathan Max 1947- WhoWor 91
Mann, Jonnie Yvonne 1939- WhoAmW 91
Mann, Joseph 1918- BiDrAPA 89
Mann, Joseph John 1948- BiDrAPA 89
Mann, Julia Ann 1959- WhoSSW 91
Mann, Karen 1942- WhoAmW 91
Mann, Katinka 1925- WhoAmA 91
Mann, Kenneth Gerard 1941- WhoAm 90
Mann, Kenneth Henry 1923- WhoAm 90
Mann, Kenneth Walker 1914- WhoAm 90
Mann, Klaus 1906-1949 BioIn 16
Mann, Klaus 1945- WhoWor 91
Mann, Larry Norbert 1934- WhoE 91
Mann, Lawrence Langston 1935- St&PR 91
Mann, Les 1893-1962 Ballpl 90
Mann, Lisa 1953- WhoAmW 91
Mann, Lowell Dean BiDrAPA 89
Mann, Lowell Kimsey 1917- St&PR 91, WhoAm 90
Mann, Manfred 1940- EncPR&S 89, OxCPMus
Mann, Margery 1919-1977 WhoAmA 91N
Mann, Marion 1920- WhoAm 90
Mann, Marty BiDrAPA 89
Mann, Marvin L. 1933- St&PR 91, WhoAm 90
Mann, Mary Peabody 1806-1887 BioAmW
Mann, Marylen 1937- WhoAmW 91
Mann, Maurice NewYTBS 90
Mann, Maurice 1929- St&PR 91, WhoAm 90
Mann, Maybelle 1915- WhoAmA 91
Mann, Michael BioIn 16
Mann, Michael 1903-1989 BioIn 16
Mann, Michael Martin 1939- St&PR 91, WhoAm 90, WhoWor 91
Mann, Milton B 1931- BiDrAPA 89
Mann, Monroe Yale 1922- WhoWor 91
Mann, Morris B BiDrAPA 89
Mann, Ned 1955- WhoWrEP 89
Mann, Norman 1930- St&PR 91
Mann, Oscar 1934- WhoE 91
Mann, Peggy WhoAmW 91
Mann, Peter C. 1942- St&PR 91
Mann, Philip Roy 1948- WhoEmL 91, WhoWor 91
Mann, Polly BioIn 16
Mann, Prem Singh 1947- WhoE 91
Mann, Richard Allan 1946- WhoEmL 91
Mann, Richard D. 1935- St&PR 91
Mann, Richard Dale 1931- WhoWrEP 89
Mann, Richard E 1931- BiDrAPA 89
Mann, Richard Edward 1943- WhoSSW 91
Mann, Richard O. 1933- ODwPR 91
Mann, Richard Otto 1933- WhoE 91
Mann, Robert PenDiMP
Mann, Robert 1920- IntWWM 90
Mann, Robert A. 1926- St&PR 91
Mann, Robert Allen 1931- WhoAm 90
Mann, Robert E. 1954- St&PR 91
Mann, Robert Henry 1935- St&PR 91, WhoAm 90
Mann, Robert Nathaniel 1920- WhoAm 90
Mann, Robert W., Jr. 1953- St&PR 91
Mann, Robert Wellesley 1924- WhoAm 90
Mann, Robert Wellesley, Jr. 1953- WhoE 91
Mann, Roger Ellis 1948- WhoE 91
Mann, Roger Mowry 1944- WhoE 91
Mann, Roland 1926- WhoWor 91
Mann, Rusten C. 1951- St&PR 91
Mann, Sally WhoAmA 91
Mann, Sally 1951- BioIn 16
Mann, Sandra Peete 1948- WhoAmW 91
Mann, Seymour BioIn 16
Mann, Seymour St&PR 91N
Mann, Seymour Zalmon 1921- WhoAm 90
Mann, Sheldon S. 1927- St&PR 91
Mann, Stephan C BiDrAPA 89
Mann, Stephen Ashby 1947- WhoSSW 91
Mann, Stephen L. 1938- St&PR 91
Mann, Steven William 1949- St&PR 91
Mann, Theodore 1924- WhoAm 90
Mann, Theodore R. 1928- WhoAm 90
Mann, Thomas 1875-1955 BioIn 16, EncPaPR 91, MajTwCW, WorAlBi, WrPh
Mann, Thomas Clifton 1912- BioIn 16
Mann, Thomas Edward 1944- WhoAm 90
Mann, Timothy 1942- WhoAm 90
Mann, Ward Palmer WhoAmA 91
Mann, William 1924-1989 BioIn 16
Mann, William Frederick 1917- St&PR 91
Mann, William Houston 1926- St&PR 91
Mann, William J.C. 1942- St&PR 91
Mann, William M, Jr. 1931- BiDrAPA 89
Mann, William S 1924-1989 ConAu 129
Mann, Wm.F. 1949- St&PR 91
Mann Amirsoleimani, Mali A BiDrAPA 89
Mann-Lambert, Sandra Marie 1946- WhoEmL 91
Manna, Daniel Carl 1947- St&PR 91
Manna, Frank J. 1935- St&PR 91
Mannan, Abdul 1938- WhoWor 91
Mannausa, Thomas James 1957- WhoSSW 91
Mannava, Uma BiDrAPA 89
Manne, Beryl H. BioIn 16
Manne, Henry Girard 1928- WhoAm 90
Manne, Shelly 1920- WorAlBi
Manne, Shelly 1920-1984 OxCPMus
Mannelli, Italo Marcello 1933- WhoWor 91
Manner, Eeva-Liisa 1921- DcScanL, EncCoWW
Manner, Maurice Richard 1930- WhoE 91
Manner, Wendell A. 1924- St&PR 91
Mannerheim, Carl, Baron Von 1867-1951 WorAlBi
Mannering, Jerry Vincent 1929- WhoAm 90
Manners, Charles PenDiMP
Manners, David X. 1912- ODwPR 91
Manners, Frances BiDEWW
Manners, George Emanuel 1910- WhoAm 90
Manners, Nancy WhoAmW 91
Manners, Paul E. 1918- St&PR 91
Manners, Robert Alan 1913- WhoAm 90
Manners, Timothy G. 1957- ODwPR 91
Manners, Timothy George 1957- WhoE 91
Mannes, Barry Leonard 1939- St&PR 91
Mannes, Elena Sabin 1943- WhoAm 90, WhoAmW 91
Mannes, Marya 1904- FemiCLE
Mannes, Marya 1904-1990 ConAu 132, NewYTBS 90 [port]
Mannetti, Lisa 1953- BioIn 16
Manney, Henry N. 1922-1988 BioIn 16
Manney, Jimmy Darrell 1957- WhoSSW 91
Manney, Richard 1936- WhoE 91
Mannheim Steamroller NewAgMG
Mannheim, Hermann 1889-1974 BioIn 16
Mannheim, Karl 1893-1947 BioIn 16
Mannheim, Walter 1930- WhoWor 91
Mannheimer, Jack BiDrAPA 89
Mannheimer, Renato 1947- WhoWor 91
Manni, Victor Macedonio 1940- WhoHisp 91
Mannick, John Anthony 1928- WhoAm 90
Mannikainen, Osmo Tapio 1944- WhoWor 91
Mannin, Ethel 1900-1984 BioIn 16, FemiCLE
Mannin, Ethel Edith 1900-1984 DcNaB 1981
Manninen, Otto 1872-1950 DcScanL
Manninen, Raimo Kalevi 1939- WhoWor 91
Manning, Anne 1807-1879 BioIn 16, FemiCLE
Manning, Arthur Brewster 1913- WhoAm 90
Manning, Bonnie Lee 1958- WhoAmW 91
Manning, Brent V. 1950- WhoEmL 91
Manning, Burt WhoAm 90, WhoE 91
Manning, Burt 1931- St&PR 91
Manning, Burton J. BioIn 16
Manning, Catherine Marie 1938- WhoAmW 91
Manning, Charles Terrill 1925- WhoAm 90
Manning, Christopher Ashley 1945- WhoWor 91
Manning, Cynthia Riette 1925- WhoAmW 91
Manning, Daniel 1831-1887 BiDrUSE 89
Manning, David Bryan 1961- BiDrAPA 89
Manning, Donald E 1945- BiDrAPA 89
Manning, Donald S. 1922- St&PR 91
Manning, Donald W. 1927- St&PR 91
Manning, Donna West 1950- BiDrAPA 89
Manning, Ellis E. 1933- WhoAm 90
Manning, Eugene Baines 1940- WhoAm 90
Manning, Eugene Randolph 1942- St&PR 91
Manning, Farley 1909- WhoAm 90, WhoWor 91
Manning, Foster Thomas 1930- WhoWor 91
Manning, Frank Arthur 1946- WhoAm 90
Manning, Frank E. 1919- St&PR 91
Manning, Frederic 1887?-1935 BioIn 16
Manning, Frederick James 1947- WhoEmL 91
Manning, Frederick William 1924- WhoAm 90
Manning, George Weston 1947- BiDrAPA 89
Manning, Harry Bradley, Jr. 1934- WhoE 91
Manning, Harvey 1925- ConAu 30NR
Manning, Helen Harton 1921- WhoAmW 91
Manning, Henry Edward 1808-1892 BioIn 16
Manning, Henry Eugene 1935- WhoAm 90
Manning, Hilda Scudder WhoAmA 91N
Manning, Jack 1920- WhoAm 90
Manning, Jack J. 1931- St&PR 91
Manning, Jack Robert 1921- St&PR 91
Manning, James 1738-1791 BioIn 16
Manning, James David 1957- BiDrAPA 89
Manning, James Forrest 1929- WhoAm 90
Manning, Jane 1938- PenDiMP
Manning, Jane Marian 1938- IntWWM 90
Manning, Jeannene Seeger ODwPR 91
Manning, Jerome Alan 1929- WhoAm 90
Manning, Jo 1923- WhoAmA 91
Manning, Joan Elizabeth 1953- WhoAmW 91
Manning, John J. BioIn 16
Manning, John Joseph 1930- WhoE 91
Manning, John Patrick, V 1956- WhoEmL 91
Manning, John Thomas 1921- WhoAm 90
Manning, Joseph A., III 1946- St&PR 91
Manning, Judith Susan 1941- WhoAmW 91
Manning, Kathryn Ann 1958- WhoAmW 91
Manning, Kenneth Alan 1951- WhoEmL 91
Manning, Lillian O'Neal 1956- WhoWrEP 89
Manning, Lydia 1948- WhoAmW 91
Manning, Marguerite WhoWor 91
Manning, Marie 1873?-1945 BioIn 16
Manning, Martha E. BioIn 16
Manning, Mary 1947- WhoAmW 91
Manning, Matthew 1955- EncO&P 3, EncPaPR 91
Manning, Maxwell Cornelius 1948- WhoE 91
Manning, Mervyn H. 1932- WhoAm 90
Manning, Michael P. 1943- St&PR 91
Manning, Myrtle Marion 1921- St&PR 91
Manning, Noel Thomas 1939- WhoAm 90
Manning, Olivia BioIn 16
Manning, Olivia 1908-1980 FemiCLE
Manning, Olivia 1915-1980 MajTwCW
Manning, Patricia Kamaras 1953- WhoAmW 91, WhoWor 91
Manning, Peter 1956- IntWWM 90
Manning, Peter Kirby 1940- WhoAm 90
Manning, Ralph Fabian 1945- WhoAm 90
Manning, Randolph H. 1947- WhoE 91
Manning, Raymond A BiDrAPA 89
Manning, Reg 1905-1986 WhoAmA 91N
Manning, Rick 1954- Ballpl 90
Manning, Robert 1953- IntWWM 90
Manning, Robert E. 1936- St&PR 91
Manning, Robert Edward 1946- St&PR 91
Manning, Robert John 1942- St&PR 91
Manning, Robert Joseph 1919- WhoAm 90
Manning, Robert Thomas 1927- WhoAm 90
Manning, Roberta Thompson 1940- ConAu 130
Manning, Rosemary 1911- AuBYP 90
Manning, Rosemary 1911-1988 FemiCLE
Manning, Rube 1883-1930 Ballpl 90
Manning, Sam EarBlAP
Manning, Sandra Kay 1951- WhoAmW 91
Manning, Stephen D. 1949- ODwPR 91
Manning, Sylvia 1943- WhoAm 90
Manning, Thomas K. 1953- St&PR 91
Manning, Thomas Michael 1939- St&PR 91
Manning, Timothy BioIn 16
Manning, Toni Ruth 1946- WhoAmW 91
Manning, Travis Warren 1921- WhoAm 90
Manning, V. C. 1947- WhoSSW 91
Manning, Victor Patrick 1945- St&PR 91
Manning, Walter Scott 1933- WhoSSW 91, WhoWor 91
Manning, Walter Scott, Jr. 1945- WhoSSW 91, WhoWor 91
Manning, William Dudley, Jr. 1934- WhoAm 90
Manning, William Frank, Jr. 1965- St&PR 91
Manning, William Frederick 1920- WhoAm 90
Manning, William George 1923- WhoE 91
Manning, William Joseph 1926- WhoAm 90
Manning, William Meredith 1933- IntWWM 90
Manning, William Raymond 1920- WhoAm 90
Manning, William Sinkler 1925- St&PR 91
Manning, Winton Howard 1930- WhoE 91
Manning-Mims, Madeline BioIn 16
Manning Russell, Marlou 1956- WhoAmW 91, WhoEmL 91
Manning-Sanders, Ruth 1888-1988 AnObit 1988, FemiCLE
Manning-Sanders, Ruth 1895- AuBYP 90
Manning-Sanders, Ruth 1895-1988 BioIn 16
Manningham, John BioIn 16
Mannino, Edward Francis 1941- WhoAm 90
Mannino, Franco 1924- IntWWM 90, PenDiMP A
Mannino, J. Davis 1949- WhoEmL 91
Mannion, Ellen Carol 1964- WhoE 91
Mannion, John F.X. 1932- St&PR 91
Mannion, John Francis Xavier 1932- WhoE 91
Mannion Peer, Gail Margaret 1953- WhoE 91
Mannis, Bob Davis 1949- WhoEmL 91
Mannis, Kent S 1935- BiDrAPA 89
Mannix, Arthur J. 1922-1989 BioIn 16
Mannix, Daniel P. AuBYP 90
Mannix, Edgar P. 1913-1989 BioIn 16
Mannix, Frederick Phillip 1942- St&PR 91
Mannix, Henry 1927-1989 BioIn 16
Mannix, James G. 1941- St&PR 91
Mannix, James J. BioIn 16
Mannix, James J. 1939- St&PR 91
Mannix, Kevin Leese 1949- WhoEmL 91
Mannix, Mary Katherine 1960- WhoE 91
Mannlein, William John 1935- St&PR 91
Mannlich, Daniel 1625-1701 PenDiDA 89
Mannlich, Heinrich, I 1625?-1698 PenDiDA 89
Mannlich, Heinrich, II PenDiDA 89
Mannlich, Jacob PenDiDA 89
Mannlich, Johann Heinrich 1660-1718 PenDiDA 89
Mannlich, Otto PenDiDA 89
Manno di Bastiano Sbarri PenDiDA 89
Manno, Joseph A BiDrAPA 89
Manno, Joseph Eugene 1942- WhoSSW 91
Manno, M.V. 1926- St&PR 91
Manno, Ned C. 1932- St&PR 91
Manno, Samuel F. 1940- St&PR 91
Mannon, William H. 1921- St&PR 91
Mannoni, Raymond 1921- WhoAm 90
Manns, August 1825-1907 PenDiMP
Manns, Lindsey Regan BioIn 16
Mannsfeld, Sven Peter 1935- St&PR 91
Mannucci, Mannuccio 1926- BiDrAPA 89
Manny, Carter Hugh, Jr. 1918- WhoAm 90
Mano, D. Keith BioIn 16
Mano, D. Keith 1942- WhoAm 90, WhoWrEP 89, WorAu 1980 [port]
Mano, Toru 1945- WhoAmA 91
Manobianco, Patricia Ann 1959- WhoAmW 91
Manobianco, Vincent J. 1928- St&PR 91
Manoff, Dinah BioIn 16

Manoff, Dinah 1958- *WorAlBi*
Manoff, Dinah Beth *WhoAmW 91*
Manoff, Michelle 1958- *ODwPR 91*
Manoff, Richard Kalman 1916- *WhoAm 90*
Manogue, Helen Smith 1931- *St&PR 91, WhoAmW 91*
Manohar, Kaup Anthappa 1931- *BiDrAPA 89*
Manohar, Velandy 1942- *BiDrAPA 89*
Manohara, Sakrepatna A *BiDrAPA 89*
Manoharan, Nachiyappan *BiDrAPA 89*
Manolakas, Stanton Peter 1946- *WhoAmA 91*
Manoleehagul, Pisarn 1949- *WhoWor 91*
Manolis, Deane C 1936- *BiDrAPA 89*
Manolov, Stephen Assenov 1925- *WhoWor 91*
Manolukas, Paul A 1928- *BiDrAPA 89*
Manon, Violet *ODwPR 91*
Manone, Wingy 1900-1982 *OxCPMus*
Manone, Wingy 1904- *BioIn 16*
Manongdo, Ernesto M *BiDrAPA 89*
Manoogian, Richard *BioIn 16*
Manoogian, Richard 1936- *St&PR 91*
Manoogian, Richard Alexander 1936- *WhoAm 90*
Manoogian, Torkom *WhoAm 90*
Manor, Philip Craig 1944- *WhoE 91*
Manos, John T 1924- *BiDrAPA 89*
Manos, Nikolas 1941- *BiDrAPA 89*
Manos, Paul William 1949- *WhoEmL 91*
Manos, Pete Lazaros 1936- *St&PR 91, WhoE 91*
Manos, Peter James *BiDrAPA 89*
Manosevitz, Martin 1938- *WhoAm 90*
Manoukian, Noel Edwin 1938- *WhoAm 90*
Manoushagian, Berj 1947- *WhoE 91*
Manousos, James William 1919- *WhoAm 90, WhoWrEP 89*
Manoux, Dominique 1950- *WhoWor 91*
Manov, Gregory A 1942- *BiDrAPA 89*
Manray 1890-1976 *WhoAmA 91N*
Manring, John Michael, Jr. 1948- *BiDrAPA 89*
Manring, Michael *NewAgMG*
Manrique, Carlos D. 1945- *St&PR 91*
Manrique, Fred 1961- *Ballpl 90*
Manrique, Jaime 1949- *WhoE 91, WhoHisp 91*
Manrodt, W.H. 1948- *St&PR 91*
Manry, Larry Alan 1947- *St&PR 91*
Mansager, Erik Donn 1955- *WhoEmL 91*
Mansaram, P 1934- *WhoAmA 91*
Mansbach, Robert Earl, Jr. 1957- *WhoEmL 91*
Mansberg, Ruth 1924- *ConAu 130*
Mansberger, Arlie Roland, Jr. 1922- *WhoAm 90*
Mansbridge, Albert *BioIn 16*
Manschreck, Theo C 1945- *BiDrAPA 89*
Manschreck, Theo Clyde 1945- *WhoE 91*
Manseau, Melissa Marie 1962- *WhoAmW 91*
Manselian, Harold S. 1918- *St&PR 91*
Mansell, Darrel Lee, Jr. 1934- *WhoAm 90*
Mansell, Frank Luther 1922- *WhoAm 90*
Mansell, Gerard 1921- *ConAu 130*
Mansell, James R. 1929- *St&PR 91*
Mansell, Thomas S. 1939- *St&PR 91*
Manser, George Robert 1931- *St&PR 91*
Manses, Simon Louis 1953- *WhoEmL 91*
Manset, Edouard Miguel 1943- *WhoWor 91*
Mansfield, Arthur Rulon, Jr. 1926- *St&PR 91*
Mansfield, Carl Mansfield 1928- *WhoAm 90*
Mansfield, Christopher Charles 1950- *St&PR 91, WhoAm 90*
Mansfield, David Kay 1947- *WhoSSW 91*
Mansfield, Edwin 1930- *WhoAm 90*
Mansfield, Fred W. 1928- *St&PR 91*
Mansfield, Harvey Claflin 1905-1988 *BioIn 16*
Mansfield, Irving *BioIn 16*
Mansfield, J. V. *EncO&P 3*
Mansfield, James Norman, III 1951- *WhoEmL 91*
Mansfield, Jayne 1932-1967 *BioAmW*
Mansfield, Jayne 1933-1967 *BioIn 16, WorAlBi*
Mansfield, Joseph John 1938- *WhoE 91*
Mansfield, Karen Lee 1942- *WhoWor 91*
Mansfield, Karla Jean 1950- *St&PR 91*
Mansfield, Katherine 1888-1923 *BioIn 16, FemiCLE, TwCLC 39 [port], WorAlBi*
Mansfield, Kathleen Beauchamp 1888-1923 *BioIn 16*
Mansfield, Kenneth Eugene 1946- *WhoAm 90*
Mansfield, Marc Lewis 1955- *WhoAm 90*
Mansfield, Margo 1947- *WhoAmW 91*
Mansfield, Mike *BioIn 16*
Mansfield, Mike 1903- *WorAlBi*
Mansfield, Norman Connie 1916- *WhoSSW 91*
Mansfield, Norman Jerome 1952- *WhoSSW 91*
Mansfield, Portia 1887-1979 *BioIn 16, NotWoAT*
Mansfield, Richard Thomas 1944- *St&PR 91*
Mansfield, Robert Adams 1942- *WhoAmA 91*
Mansfield, Stephen Scott 1942- *WhoSSW 91*
Mansfield, Tobi Ellen 1949- *WhoAmW 91*
Manshadi, Manoochehr Sharifolatebba 1941- *BiDrAPA 89*
Manshardt, Clifford 1897- *WhoAm 90*
Manshardt, Thomas 1927- *IntWWM 90*
Mansheim, Paul Adolph 1945- *BiDrAPA 89*
Manshel, Andrew Maximilian 1956- *WhoEmL 91*
Manshel, Warren D. *NewYTBS 90*
Manshel, Warren D. 1924-1990 *BioIn 16*
Manship, Charles P., Jr. 1908- *St&PR 91*
Manship, Charles Phelps, Jr. 1908- *WhoAm 90*
Manship, Douglas 1918- *WhoAm 90*
Manship, John Paul 1927- *WhoAmA 91*
Manship, Paul 1885-1966 *WhoAmA 91N*
Mansi, Joseph A. 1935- *ODwPR 91*
Mansi, Joseph Anneillo 1935- *WhoAm 90*
Mansion, Gracie 1946- *WhoAmA 91*
Mansk, Sharon Sue 1948- *WhoAmW 91*
Manske, John *St&PR 91*
Manske, Paul Robert 1938- *WhoAm 90*
Manski, Wladyslaw Julian 1915- *WhoAm 90*
Mansky, Peter Alan 1943- *BiDrAPA 89*
Mansmann, Carol Los 1942- *WhoAmW 91*
Mansmann, Herbert C., Jr. 1924- *WhoAm 90*
Manso, Gilbert 1942- *WhoWor 91*
Manso, Leo 1914- *WhoAmA 91*
Mansolino, Barbara Ann 1947- *WhoAmW 91*
Manson, Beverlie 1945- *BioIn 16*
Manson, Bruce Malcolm 1944- *St&PR 91, WhoAm 90*
Manson, Carolyn Sue 1951- *BiDrAPA 89*
Manson, Charles 1934- *BioIn 16, WorAlBi*
Manson, Charles M. 1934- *EncO&P 3*
Manson, Eddy Lawrence *IntWWM 90, WhoAm 90*
Manson, James H. 1842-1901 *AmLegL*
Manson, Jeane Ann 1950- *WhoWor 91*
Manson, Joseph R 1925- *BiDrAPA 89*
Manson, Paul David 1934- *WhoAm 90*
Manson, Robert Hunter 1941- *St&PR 91*
Manson, Samuel Stanford 1919- *WhoAm 90*
Manson, Simon Verril 1921- *WhoE 91*
Manson-Hing, Lincoln Roy 1927- *WhoAm 90*
Mansoor, Lutfi Gabrie, Jr. 1941- *WhoHisp 91*
Mansoor, Menahem 1911- *WhoAm 90*
Mansour, George P. 1939- *WhoAm 90*
Mansour, Kamal A. 1929- *WhoSSW 91*
Mansour, Maguid Nosshi 1943- *BiDrAPA 89*
Mansour, Maher Monir *BiDrAPA 89*
Mansour, Tag Eldin 1924- *WhoAm 90*
Mansouri, Jaleh 1967- *WhoEmL 91*
Mansouri, Lotfi *BioIn 16*
Mansouri, Lotfi 1929- *CurBio 90 [port]*
Mansouri, Lotfollah 1929- *WhoAm 90*
Manspeizer, Susan R *WhoAmA 91*
Mansson, Bengt Ake 1953- *WhoWor 91*
Manstein, Erich von 1887-1973 *BioIn 16*
Mansueti, Albert E. 1924- *St&PR 91*
Mansur, Albert 1939- *WhoWor 91*
Mansur, Bernadette *ODwPR 91*
Mansur, Juliane Louise 1957- *WhoAmW 91*
Mansur, Paul Max 1926- *IntWWM 90, WhoSSW 91*
Mansuy, Jane Webster 1951- *WhoAmW 91*
Mantas, Santiago 1949- *IntWWM 90*
Mantay, Werener Rudy 1957- *St&PR 91*
Mantecon, Juan Jimenez *ConAu 131, HispWr 90, MajTwCW*
Mantegna, Andrea 1430?-1506 *IntDcAA 90*
Mantegna, Andrea 1431-1506 *BioIn 16, WorAlBi*
Mantegna, Joe 1948?- *BioIn 16*
Mantegna, Joe Anthony 1947- *WhoAm 90*
Mantel, Gerhard Friedrich 1930- *IntWWM 90*
Mantel, Kenneth Haskell 1927- *WhoE 91*
Mantel, Mark D. 1961- *IntWWM 90*
Mantel, S. G. *AuBYP 90*
Mantel, Samuel Joseph, Jr. 1921- *WhoAm 90*
Mantel, Wendy Luise 1954- *WhoAmW 91*
Mantell, Cecil 1914-1989 *BioIn 16*
Mantell, Lester J. 1937- *St&PR 91, WhoAm 90*
Mantell, Suzanne 1944- *WhoAm 90, WhoWrEP 89*
Manteo, Mike *BioIn 16*
Manter, Margaret C 1923- *WhoAmA 91*
Mantey, Elmer Martin 1926- *WhoSSW 91*
Mantey, James R. 1941- *St&PR 91*
Manthe, Cora De Munck 1928- *WhoAmW 91*
Manthei, Lydia *BiDrAPA 89*
Manthei, Richard D. 1935- *St&PR 91*
Manthei, Richard Dale 1935- *WhoAm 90*
Manthei, Robin Dickey 1956- *WhoEmL 91*
Manthey, Frank Anthony 1933- *WhoSSW 91, WhoWor 91*
Manthey, Mary Ellen N. 1950- *St&PR 91*
Manthey, Robert Wendelin 1935- *WhoE 91*
Manthey, Roberta Raye 1959- *St&PR 91*
Manthey, William Armand 1949- *St&PR 91*
Manthorne, Jackie Ann 1946- *WhoAmW 91*
Manthos, A.J. 1926- *St&PR 91*
Mantica, Pamela Ann 1956- *WhoAmW 91*
Mantice, Tom G. 1926- *St&PR 91*
Mantilla, Felix 1934- *Ballpl 90*
Mantilla, Felix 1955- *WhoHisp 91*
Mantilla, Nectario Ruben 1940- *WhoWor 91*
Mantione, Sandra Marie *WhoAmW 91*
Mantle, John Edward 1940- *WhoAm 90*
Mantle, Jonathan 1954- *ConAu 129*
Mantle, Lee 1851-1934 *AmLegL*
Mantle, Mickey 1931- *Ballpl 90 [port], BioIn 16, WorAlBi*
Mantle, Mickey Charles 1931- *WhoAm 90*
Mantle, Neil Christopher 1951- *IntWWM 90*
Mantle, Raymond Allan 1937- *WhoWor 91*
Mantley, John *BioIn 16*
Manton, E.A.G. 1909- *St&PR 91*
Manton, J Herbert *BiDrAPA 89*
Manton, Jo 1919- *AuBYP 90*
Manton, Peter *MajTwCW, TwCCr&M 91*
Manton, Thomas Joseph 1932- *WhoAm 90, WhoE 91*
Mantonya, John Butcher 1922- *WhoAm 90*
Mantooth, John Albert 1947- *WhoEmL 91*
Mantor, P. David 1936- *St&PR 91*
Mantor, Philip David 1936- *WhoAm 90*
Mantovani 1905-1980 *OxCPMus*
Mantovani, Annunzio 1905-1980 *WorAlBi*
Mantovani, Annunzio Paolo 1905-1980 *PenDiMP*
Mantovani, Mark Peter 1954- *WhoEmL 91*
Mantravadi, Murty V. 1929- *WhoWor 91*
Mantsch, Henry Horst 1935- *WhoAm 90*
Mantu, Lucia 1888-1971 *EncCoWW*
Mantyla, Joyce *ODwPR 91*
Mantyla, Karen 1944- *WhoAmW 91*
Mantzavinos, Anthony George 1928- *St&PR 91*
Mantzoros, Anne 1920- *St&PR 91*
Manucci, Daniel Joseph 1930- *St&PR 91*
Manuel, Don Juan 1281- *AuBYP 90*
Manuel, Ernest James *BiDrAPA 89*
Manuel, Frank Edward 1910- *WhoWrEP 89*
Manuel, Jimmy Lee 1934- *St&PR 91*
Manuel, K. Lee *BioIn 16*
Manuel, Kathryn Lee *WhoAmA 91*
Manuel, Lau-Rene Anntwan 1964- *WhoE 91*
Manuel, Monte Morgan 1925- *St&PR 91*
Manuel, Ralph Nixon 1936- *WhoAm 90*
Manuel, Robert 1916- *WhoWor 91*
Manuel, Vivian 1941- *ODwPR 91, WhoE 91*
Manuele, John Nicholas 1954- *WhoE 91*
Manuelito 1818?-1894 *WhNaAH*
Manuell, Lynn Marie 1961- *WhoAmW 91*
Manuella, Frank R *WhoAmA 91*
Manuguerra, Matteo 1924- *IntWWM 90*
Manulis, Martin 1915- *WhoAm 90*
Manulkin, Dena J. 1947- *WhoWrEP 89*
Manus, Connie Sandage *WhoAmA 91*
Manus, Jane Elizabeth 1951- *WhoAmA 91*
Manush, Heinie 1901-1971 *Ballpl 90 [port]*
Manushkin, Fran *BioIn 16*
Manuso, James S. J. 1948- *WhoEmL 91*
Manuso, Susan Alexander 1952- *WhoEmL 91*
Manuszak, George Daniel 1926- *St&PR 91*
Manuti, Annabelle Theresa 1928- *WhoAmW 91*
Manutius, Aldus Pius 1449?-1515 *BioIn 16*
Manuzio, Aldo Pio 1449?-1515 *BioIn 16*
Manvi, Ramachandra 1939- *WhoAm 90*
Manvill, P. D. *FemiCLE*
Manville, Alfred Rollin 1917-1989 *BioIn 16*
Manville, Ella Viola Grainger 1889-1979 *WhoAmA 91N*
Manville, Elsie 1922- *WhoAmA 91*
Manville, Richard W. 1926- *St&PR 91*
Manville, Stewart Roebling 1927- *IntWWM 90, WhoE 91, WhoWor 91*
Manwaring, Kirt 1965- *Ballpl 90*
Manwaring, Michael 1942- *ConDes 90*
Manwaring, Robert *PenDiDA 89*
Manwaring, Teri Marie 1957- *WhoSSW 91*
Manwell, Edmund Ray 1942- *St&PR 91*
Manwell, Philip 1946- *IntWWM 90*
Many Horses *WhNaAH*
Many, Cecile L 1954- *BiDrAPA 89*
Manyen, Susan Mary Gager 1956- *WhoAmW 91*
Manygoats, Betty 1945- *MusmAFA*
Manypenny, George W. 1808-1892 *WhNaAH*
Manz, Andre 1942- *IntWWM 90*
Manz, Betty Ann 1935- *WhoAmW 91, WhoE 91*
Manz, Friedrich 1941- *WhoWor 91*
Manz, Wolfgang 1960- *IntWWM 90*
Manzana-Pissarro, Georges 1871-1961 *PenDiDA 89*
Manzanares, Francisco Antonio 1843-1904 *BioIn 16*
Manzanares, Juan Manuel 1953- *WhoHisp 91*
Manzanero, Bienvenido 1954- *BiDrAPA 89*
Manzano, J. Mia 1952- *WhoAmW 91*
Manzano, Jesus Carretero 1954- *WhoWor 91*
Manzano, Nevilla P *BiDrAPA 89*
Manzano, Sonia *WhoHisp 91*
Manzarek, Ray 1935- *WorAlBi*
Manzer, Virginia Lee 1951- *St&PR 91*
Manzi, Albert Peter 1917- *WhoE 91*
Manzi, Giuseppina *BioIn 16*
Manzi, Jim P. *BioIn 16*
Manzi, Jim P. 1951- *St&PR 91*
Manzi, Joseph Edward 1945- *WhoWor 91*
Manziel, Dorothy Nolan 1920- *WhoAmW 91*
Manzini, Gianna 1896-1974 *EncCoWW*
Manzini, Mavivi 1956- *BioIn 16*
Manzione, H.J. 1924- *St&PR 91*
Manzo, Anthony Joseph *WhoAmA 91*
Manzo, Peter Thomas 1947- *WhoE 91*
Manzo, Salvatore Edward 1917- *WhoSSW 91*
Manzoni, Alessandro 1785-1873 *NinCLC 29 [port]*
Manzoni, Allesandro 1785-1873 *WorAlBi*
Manzoni, Giacomo 1932- *IntWWM 90*
Manzu, Giacomo 1908- *BioIn 16*
Mao, Madame 1910- *BioIn 16*
Mao Tse-tung 1893-1976 *MajTwCW, WorAlBi*
Mao Zedong 1893-1976 *BioIn 16*
Mao, Tse-tung 1893-1976 *BioIn 16*
Maoate, Terepai 1934- *WhoWor 91*
Maouad, Joseph 1939- *WhoWor 91*
Mapa, Domingo Ongpin, II 1962- *WhoWor 91*
Mape, Avelino M *BiDrAPA 89*
Mapel, William Marlen Raines 1931- *WhoAm 90*
Mapelli, Roland L. 1922- *St&PR 91*
Mapelli, Roland Lawrence 1922- *WhoAm 90*
Mapelli, Stephanie D. 1953- *WhoAmW 91*
Mapes, Cliff 1922- *Ballpl 90*
Mapes, Doris Williamson 1920- *WhoAmA 91*
Mapes, Gene E., Jr. 1959- *St&PR 91*
Mapes, Glynn Dempsey 1939- *WhoAm 90, WhoWor 91*
Mapes, James Jay 1806-1866 *EncO&P 3*
Mapes, John G. 1906-1989 *BioIn 16*
Mapes, Lynn Calvin 1928- *WhoAm 90, WhoE 91*
Mapes, Paul 1953- *WhoSSW 91*
Mapes, Pierson *WhoAm 90*
Mapes, Steven Gregory 1964- *WhoSSW 91*
Mapes, William E. 1934- *St&PR 91*
Maple, Eric 1915- *EncO&P 3*
Maple, Marilyn Jean 1931- *WhoAmW 91*
Maple, Opal Lucille 1935- *WhoAmW 91*
Maple, Timothy Michael 1936- *WhoSSW 91*
Maples, Dillard Ray 1946- *WhoSSW 91*
Maples, Jimmie Kay 1940- *WhoWor 91*
Maples, Larry Dean 1946- *St&PR 91*
Maples, William Ross 1937- *WhoSSW 91*
Maples-Pacheco, Elizabeth Mae 1941- *WhoAmW 91*
Maplesden, Douglas Cecil 1919- *WhoSSW 91*
Mapletoft, Kenneth E 1920- *BiDrAPA 89*
Mapother, Dillon Edward 1921- *WhoAm 90*
Mapp, Alf Johnson, Jr. 1925- *WhoAm 90, WhoWor 91, WhoWrEP 89*
Mapp, Frederick Everett 1910- *WhoSSW 91*
Mapp, Janis Dianne Guy 1946- *WhoSSW 91*
Mapp, Jim E *DrBlPA 90*
Mapp, William Ernest, III 1959- *WhoSSW 91*
Mappes, Richard Louis 1928- *St&PR 91*
Mappes, William Patrick *BiDrAPA 89*
Mapplethorpe, Robert *BioIn 16*

Mapplethorpe, Robert 1946-1989 AnObit 1989, WhoAmA 91N
Mapula, Olga 1938- WhoHisp 91
Maquet, Jacques Jerome Pierre 1919- WhoAm 90
Maquet, Paul-Germain 1928- WhoWor 91
Maquinna WhNaAH
Mar, Maria WhoHisp 91
Mar, Norman Del PenDiMP
Mara, Barney AuBYP 90
Mara, Edward James, Jr. 1929- St&PR 91
Mara, George Edward 1921- WhoAm 90
Mara, Gertrud Elisabeth 1749-1833 PenDiMP
Mara, Jeanette ConAu 30NR
Mara, John Lawrence 1924- WhoE 91
Mara, Kamisese Kapaiwai Tuimacilai 1920- WhoWor 91
Mara, Sally ConAu 32NR, MajTwCW
Mara, Vincent Joseph 1930- WhoAm 90, WhoE 91
Mara, Wellington T. 1916- WhoAm 90, WhoE 91
Marabella, Madeline AuBYP 90
Marabini, Enrico 1923- EncO&P 3
Marable, Fate 1890-1947 BioIn 16, OxCPMus
Marable, Manning 1950- WhoAm 90
Marable, Simeon-David 1948- WhoE 91, WhoEmL 91, WhoWor 91
Marachi, Jean Paul 1949- BiDrAPA 89
Maracle, David Earl 1948- WhoEmL 91, WhoWor 91
Maracle, John E. BioIn 16
Maradiaga, Ralph 1934-1985 WhoAmA 91N
Maradona, Diego BioIn 16
Maradona, Diego 1960- CurBio 90 [port]
Marafino, Vincent Norman 1930- St&PR 91, WhoAm 90
Maraghi, Mustafa al- 1881-1945 BioIn 16
Maragliotti, Vincent 1888-1978 WhoAmA 91N
Maragoudakis, Michael Emmanuel 1932- WhoWor 91
Maraini, Adelaide 1843- BiDWomA
Maraini, Dacia 1936- EncCoWW
Marais WhoAmA 91
Marais, Josef 1905-1978 AuBYP 90, OxCPMus
Marais, Marin 1656-1728 PenDiMP
Maraj, Bhadase Sagan 1919-1971 BioIn 16
Marak, Louis Bernard 1942- WhoAmA 91
Marak, Randy Barton 1962- WhoSSW 91
Marakas, George Michael 1953- WhoSSW 91
Marakas, John Lambros 1926- St&PR 91, WhoAm 90
Maraldo, John Charles 1942- WhoSSW 91
Maraldo, Pamela Jean 1947- WhoAm 90
Maraldo, Ushanna F WhoAmA 91
Maraman, Grady Vancil 1936- WhoSSW 91
Marames, William Etheme 1955- WhoEmL 91
Maramorosch, Karl 1915- WhoAm 90
Maran, Charles 1907- WhoE 91
Maran, Gene Ira BiDrAPA 89
Maran, Joe 1933- WhoE 91
Maran, Stephen Paul 1938- WhoAm 90
Maranda, Georges 1932- Ballpl 90
Maranda, Pierre Jean 1930- WhoAm 90
Marandi, Morteza 1949- BiDrAPA 89
Marangell, Lauren Beth BiDrAPA 89
Marangell, Robert P. 1949- St&PR 91
Marangiello, Betty Ann 1942- WhoAmW 91
Marangos, Akis 1940- WhoWor 91
Marani, Jean Victoria 1924- WhoSSW 91
Marano, Anthony Joseph 1934- WhoAm 90, WhoE 91
Marano, David Francis 1945- St&PR 91
Marano, John Paul, Jr. 1942- WhoAm 90
Marano, R.J. 1928- St&PR 91
Marano, Richard Michael 1960- WhoE 91
Marans, Allen Elias 1926- BiDrAPA 89
Marans, J. Eugene 1940- WhoAm 90
Marans, Jane Susan BiDrAPA 89
Marans, Moissaye 1902-1977 WhoAmA 91N
Marantette, David Theodore, III 1941- St&PR 91
Maranto, Paul A. 1938- St&PR 91
Marantz, Irving 1912-1972 WhoAmA 91N
Marantz, Robert 1941- BiDrAPA 89
Maranville, Rabbit 1891-1954 Ballpl 90 [port]
Marasco, Amy L. 1954- St&PR 91
Marasco, Frank St&PR 91
Marasco, Rose 1948- WhoAmA 91
Marasco, Rose Marie 1929- St&PR 91
Marash, David 1942- WhoAm 90
Marash, Marge L BiDrAPA 89
Marash, Stanley Albert 1938- WhoE 91, WhoWor 91
Marasovich, Gary Michael 1958- WhoEmL 91
Marasse, Henry F. 1920- BiDrAPA 89
Marat, Jean Paul 1743-1793 BioIn 16, WorAlBi
Marat-Mendes, Jose Narciso 1939- WhoWor 91
Maratta, Grace Elvira 1922- WhoAmW 91
Maravel, Patricia 1949- WhoAmW 91
Maravelas, Paul 1956- WhoWrEP 89
Maravich, Mary Louise 1951- WhoAmW 91
Maravich, Pete 1948-1988 BioIn 16
Maravich, Peter 1948-1988 WorAlBi
Maraynes, Allan Lawrence 1950- WhoE 91
Marazita, Eleanor Marie Harmon 1933- WhoAmW 91
Marazzi, William 1947- WhoAmA 91
Marbach, Lois Betty 1946- WhoAmW 91
Marbe, Myriam-Lucia 1931- IntWWM 90
Marber, Scott 1956- WhoE 91
Marberger, A. Aladar 1947-1988 BioIn 16
Marberger, A Aldar 1947-1988 WhoAmA 91N
Marberry, David George 1950- St&PR 91
Marberry, Firpo 1898-1976 Ballpl 90 [port]
Marbert, Larry David 1953- WhoAm 90
Marble, Alice 1913- WorAlBi
Marble, Alice 1913-1990 NewYTBS 90 [port]
Marble, Manton 1834-1917 BioIn 16
Marble, Samuel Davey 1915- WhoAm 90
Marburger, John Harmen, III 1941- WhoAm 90, WhoWor 91
Marburger, Ronald Ross 1943- St&PR 91
Marbury, Benjamin Edward 1914- WhoAm 90
Marbury, Elisabeth 1856-1933 BioIn 16, NotWoAT
Marbury, Virginia Lomax 1918- WhoSSW 91
Marbury, William L. 1901-1988 BioIn 16
Marbut, Robert Gordon 1935- St&PR 91, WhoSSW 91
Marc, Alessandra BioIn 16
Marc, Franz 1880-1916 BioIn 16, IntDcAA 90
Marc, Simon 1962- WhoWor 91
Marca, Sulpicia Ytis BiDrAPA 89
Marca-Relli, Conrad 1913- WhoAm 90, WhoAmA 91
Marcano Duerto, Serapio Jose BiDrAPA 89
Marcantel, Silva Cooper 1940- WhoAmW 91
Marcantonio, Vito 1902-1954 BioIn 16, EncAL
Marcarelli, Dean Paul 1961- WhoSSW 91
Marcarelli, Louis G. 1942- St&PR 91
Marcasiano, Mary Jane BioIn 16
Marcasiano, Mary Jane 1955- WhoAmW 91
Marcatante, John Joseph 1930- WhoE 91, WhoWor 91
Marceau, Marcel BioIn 16
Marceau, Marcel 1923- WhoAm 90, WhoWor 91, WorAlBi
Marceau, R Fred 1913- BiDrAPA 89
Marceau, Richard E. 1926- WhoAm 90
Marceau, Sophie BioIn 16
Marceau-Crooks, Helene BiDrAPA 89
Marcel, Gabriel Honore 1889-1973 MajTwCW
Marcel, Georges Anthony 1940- WhoWor 91
Marcel, Leonard J 1942- BiDrAPA 89
Marceleno, Troy 1937- WhoHisp 91
Marcell, David Wyburn 1937- WhoAm 90
Marcella, Carole A. 1945- ODwPR 91
Marcella, Joseph 1948- St&PR 91
Marcelle, Ghost 1897-1949 Ballpl 90
Marcellin, Raymond 1914- BiDFrPL
Marcellino, Jeanne BioIn 16
Marcello 1836-1879 BiDWomA
Marcello, Amedeo Alfred 1904- WhoAm 90
Marcello, Carlos BioIn 16
Marcello, Jody Smothers 1956- WhoAmW 91
Marcello, Linda Susan 1949- WhoAmW 91
Marcello, Robert S 1953- BiDrAPA 89
Marcellus Empiricus EncO&P 3
Marcellus, David Ward 1942- St&PR 91
Marcellus, John Robert, III 1939- WhoAm 90
Marcelo, Charito-Quiambao 1940- BiDrAPA 89
Marcelo, Marina Salem 1939- WhoWor 91
Marcet, Jane 1769-1858 FemiCLE
Marcet, Jane Haldimand 1769-1858 BioIn 16
March, Babette BioIn 16
March, Beryl Elizabeth 1920- WhoAm 90, WhoAmW 91
March, Bill ConAu 132
March, Brookman P. 1945- St&PR 91
March, Donald E. 1948- St&PR 91
March, Fredric 1897-1975 WorAlBi
March, George Patrick 1924- WhoAm 90
March, Herbert 1913- EncAL
March, Jacqueline Front WhoAmW 91
March, James Gardner 1928- WhoAm 90
March, Jim BioIn 16
March, John P. 1941- St&PR 91
March, John Quarles 1949- IntWWM 90
March, John Steven BiDrAPA 89
March, John William 1923- WhoAm 90
March, Juan 1880-1962 BioIn 16
March, Maxwell TwCCr&M 91
March, Michael Richard 1956- WhoE 91
March, Ralph Burton 1919- WhoAm 90
March, Robert Lee BiDrAPA 89
March, Susana 1918- EncCoWW
March, Thomas A BiDrAPA 89
March, William Joseph 1941-1990 ConAu 132
March, William Victor 1935- St&PR 91
Marc'Hadour, Germain Pierre 1921- WhoWor 91
Marchais, Georges 1920- WhoWor 91
Marchais, Georges Rene Louis 1920- BiDFrPL
Marchais, Pierre Julien 1924- WhoWor 91
Marchak, Betty J. 1926- St&PR 91
Marchak, Frank James 1923- St&PR 91
Marchak, Maureen Patricia 1936- WhoAmW 91
Marchal, A.W. 1942- St&PR 91
Marchal, Andre 1894-1980 PenDiMP
Marchalonis, John Jacob 1940- WhoAm 90, WhoWor 91
Marcham, Timothy Victor 1943- WhoE 91
Marchand, A. Whitman 1936- WhoAm 90
Marchand, Cecelia Gloria 1933- WhoWrEP 89
Marchand, Donat C. 1934- WhoE 91
Marchand, Douglas James 1947- St&PR 91
Marchand, Felix-Gabriel 1832-1900 DcCanB 12, OxCCanT
Marchand, J. C. de Montigny 1936- WhoAm 90
Marchand, James PenDiDA 89
Marchand, Jean 1918-1988 BioIn 16
Marchand, Jorge E. 1953- St&PR 91
Marchand, Leslie A. 1900- DcLB 103 [port]
Marchand, Leslie Alexis 1900- WhoAm 90
Marchand, Nancy 1928- WhoAm 90, WhoAmW 91
Marchand, Nathan 1916- WhoAm 90
Marchand, Philip 1946- ConAu 130
Marchand, Raphael BioIn 16
Marchand, William Rush 1956- BiDrAPA 89
Marchant, Bessie 1862-1941 FemiCLE
Marchant, Catherine MajTwCW
Marchant, G. Todd 1938- St&PR 91
Marchant, Hugh 1916- IntWWM 90
Marchant, Maurice Peterson 1927- WhoAm 90
Marchant, Murray Scott 1940- St&PR 91
Marchant, Philip Louis 1922- St&PR 91
Marchant, Stephen K. 1940- St&PR 91
Marchant, Trelawney Eston 1920- WhoAm 90, WhoSSW 91
Marchbanks, Samuel MajTwCW
Marchello, Joseph Maurice 1933- WhoAm 90
Marchelos, George Franklin 1937- WhoAm 90, WhoE 91
Marcheschi, Cork 1945- WhoAmA 91
Marchese, John Carmine 1954- WhoE 91
Marchese, John Lloyd 1931- St&PR 91
Marchese, Joseph Francis 1934- WhoE 91
Marchese, Michael, Jr. 1928- St&PR 91
Marchese, Michael John BiDrAPA 89
Marchese, Nicholas A 1923- BiDrAPA 89
Marchese, Paul J. 1955- St&PR 91
Marchese, Paul Stephan 1945- WhoE 91, WhoWor 91
Marchese, Ronald Thomas 1947- WhoAm 90
Marchesi, Blanche 1863-1940 PenDiMP
Marchesi, Guy Anthony 1950- St&PR 91
Marchesi, Mathilde 1821-1913 PenDiMP
Marchesi, Salvatore 1822-1908 PenDiMP
Marchessault, Jovette 1938- BioIn 16, FemiCLE, OxCCanT
Marchessault, Thomas Edward 1948- WhoE 91
Marcheteau, Michel Gilbert 1938- WhoWor 91
Marchetta, Russell ODwPR 91
Marchette, Ann BioIn 16
Marchette, Elizabeth Quincy BiDrAPA 89
Marchetti, Emerino John 1929- St&PR 91
Marchetti, Joseph Peter, Jr. 1956- WhoSSW 91
Marchetti, Kimberly 1958- WhoAmW 91
Marchetti, Richard J. 1930- St&PR 91
Marchetti, Victor SpyFic
Marchi, Giacomo ConAu 33NR, MajTwCW
Marchi, Jason J. 1960- WhoWrEP 89
Marchi, John Joseph 1921- WhoE 91
Marchi, Rosemarie 1927- WhoAmW 91
Marchi, Teresa 1962- WhoAmW 91
Marchiano, Linda Boreman 1949?- ConAu 129
Marchiano, Sue BioIn 16
Marchildon, Jean 1934- St&PR 91
Marchildon, Phil 1913- Ballpl 90
Marchington, Anthony David 1934- St&PR 91
Marchiol, Gilbert G. 1942- WhoWor 91
Marchionna-Fare, Alejandro Emilio 1957- WhoWor 91
Marchioro, Thomas Louis 1928- WhoAm 90
Marchisio, Barbara 1833-1919 PenDiMP
Marchisio, Carlotta 1835-1872 PenDiMP
Marchisotto, Alan 1949- St&PR 91
Marchitti, Elizabeth Van Houten 1931- WhoWrEP 89
Marchitto, Alfred Joseph 1941- St&PR 91
Marchlewski, Anthony Joseph 1962- BiDrAPA 89
Marchman, Dennis LeRoy 1915- WhoSSW 91
Marchman, Ray E., Jr. 1933- St&PR 91
Marchman, Robert L., III 1925- St&PR 91, WhoAm 90
Marchman, Robert Lee, III 1925- WhoSSW 91
Marchment, Alan Roy 1927- St&PR 91
Marchuk, Raymond 1951- St&PR 91
Marcial, Edwin 1940- WhoHisp 91
Marciani, Dante J. 1939- St&PR 91
Marciano, Richard Alfred 1934- WhoAm 90
Marciano, Rocky 1923-1969 WorAlBi
Marciano, Rocky 1924-1969 BioIn 16
Marcicano, Gary Robert 1959- WhoEmL 91
Marcie-Riviere, Jean-Pierre BioIn 16
Marcie-Riviere, Rosemarie BioIn 16
Marcil, Benoit 1963- St&PR 91
Marcil, Denise Mary WhoAmW 91
Marcil, Denise Mary 1952- WhoWrEP 89
Marcil, Monique 1934- IntWWM 90
Marcil, William Albert BiDrAPA 89
Marcil, William Christ 1936- St&PR 91, WhoAm 90
Marcillo, Carlos E. 1939- WhoHisp 91
Marcinek, Joyce E. 1930- WhoAmW 91
Marcinek, Margaret Ann 1948- WhoAmW 91
Marciniak, Richard Dwight BiDrAPA 89
Marcinkowski, Marion John 1931- WhoAm 90
Marcion, of Sinope BioIn 16
Marcion, Pierre-Benoit 1769-1840 PenDiDA 89
Marcis, Richard G. 1940- WhoE 91
Marciulionis, Sarunas BioIn 16
Marck, Jan Van Der 1929- WhoAmA 91
Marcks, Gerhard 1889-1981 PenDiDA 89
Marco ConAu 31NR
Marco, Carol Lenore 1960- WhoWrEP 89
Marco, Concha de 1916- EncCoWW
Marco, Emilio Jose 1948- WhoWor 91
Marco, Guy Anthony 1927- IntWWM 90, WhoAm 90, WhoWor 91
Marco, Luis Alaman BiDrAPA 89
Marco, Paul BioIn 16
Marcoccia, Louis Gary 1946- WhoAm 90
Marcolini, Camillo 1736-1814 PenDiDA 89
Marcolini, Marietta 1780?- PenDiMP
Marcolini, Richard Charles BiDrAPA 89
Marcon, Elio L. 1934- St&PR 91
Marcon, Giovanni PenDiDA 89
Marconi, Diego 1947- WhoWor 91
Marconi, Guglielmo 1874-1937 BioIn 16, WorAlBi
Marconis, Carolyn Mary 1957- WhoE 91
Marconnet, Roger Andre Charles 1931- WhoWor 91
Marcopulos, Bernice Anne 1958- WhoAmW 91
Marcos, Ferdinand 1907-1989 AnObit 1989
Marcos, Ferdinand 1917-1989 News 90
Marcos, Ferdinand E. 1917-1989 BioIn 16, ConAu 130, WorAlBi
Marcos, Imelda BioIn 16
Marcos, Imelda 1931- WorAlBi
Marcos, Josefa Edralin BioIn 16
Marcos, Luis Rojas 1943- BiDrAPA 89, WhoE 91
Marcos-Marin, Francisco 1946- WhoWor 91
Marcosson, Isaac Frederick 1876-1961 BioIn 16
Marcosson, Thomas I. 1936- WhoAm 90
Marcot, Neal A BiDrAPA 89
Marcotte, Brian Michael 1949- WhoE 91
Marcotte, David B 1936- BiDrAPA 89
Marcotte, Frank Basil 1923- WhoAm 90, WhoE 91
Marcotte, Joseph B., Jr. 1934- St&PR 91
Marcotte, Joseph Bernard, Jr. 1934- WhoAm 90
Marcotte, Leon 1824-1891 PenDiDA 89
Marcotte, Michael J. 1943- ODwPR 91

Marcotte, Michael Steven 1951- *WhoSSW 91*
Marcotte, Robert S. 1932- *St&PR 91*
Marcotte, Ronald P. 1945- *St&PR 91*
Marcotty, Andreas A 1923- *BiDrAPA 89*
Marcoux, Carl Henry 1927- *WhoAm 90*
Marcoux, Craig 1949- *St&PR 91*
Marcoux, George 1896-1946 *EncACom*
Marcoux, Jules Edouard 1924- *WhoAm 90*
Marcoux, Lee C. 1951- *St&PR 91*
Marcoux, Marie Celeste 1951- *WhoAmW 91*
Marcoux, Vanni 1877-1962 *PenDiMP*
Marcoux, William Joseph 1927- *WhoAm 90*
Marcovicci, Andrea *BioIn 16*
Marcovich, Miroslav 1919- *WhoAm 90*
Marcovici, Guillermo D 1953- *BiDrAPA 89*
Marcovici, Martin *BiDrAPA 89*
Marcovici, Mia *BiDrAPA 89*
Marcovici, Sorin 1948- *St&PR 91*
Marcovitz, Leonard Edward 1934- *WhoAm 90, WhoWor 91*
Marcricostas, Constantine *St&PR 91*
Marcucci, Frank James 1940- *St&PR 91*
Marcucci, Louis Leo 1914- *St&PR 91*
Marcucci, Nicholas John 1956- *WhoEmL 91*
Marcuccio, Phyllis Rose 1933- *WhoAm 90*
Marcum, Billye Jean 1946- *WhoEmL 91*
Marcum, Gordon George, II 1942- *WhoSSW 91*
Marcum, Harold Anthony 1934- *St&PR 91*
Marcum, James Benton 1938- *WhoAm 90*
Marcum, James Michael 1947- *BiDrAPA 89*
Marcum, Jerry Dean 1931- *St&PR 91*
Marcum, Johnny 1909-1984 *Ballpl 90*
Marcum, Joseph L. 1923- *St&PR 91*
Marcum, Joseph LaRue 1923- *WhoAm 90*
Marcum, Kenneth William 1939- *St&PR 91*
Marcum, Walter Phillip 1944- *St&PR 91*
Marcum, William I. 1950- *WhoSSW 91*
Marcus Aurelius 121-180 *WorAlBi*
Marcus, A Martin 1929- *BiDrAPA 89*
Marcus, Ada Belle Gross 1929- *IntWWM 90*
Marcus, Adrianne Maris 1935- *WhoWrEP 89*
Marcus, Alan C. 1947- *ODwPR 91*
Marcus, Alexander 1913- *St&PR 91*
Marcus, Angelo P *WhoAmA 91*
Marcus, Arthur 1926- *St&PR 91*
Marcus, Barbara *ODwPR 91*
Marcus, Becca Nimmer 1948- *WhoEmL 91*
Marcus, Ben 1911- *St&PR 91*
Marcus, Bernard 1924- *WhoAm 90*
Marcus, Bernard 1929- *WhoAm 90, WhoSSW 91*
Marcus, Bernard P. 1922- *St&PR 91*
Marcus, Bruce William 1925- *WhoE 91*
Marcus, Carl 1943- *St&PR 91*
Marcus, Chester L. 1917-1989 *BioIn 16*
Marcus, Claude 1924- *WhoWor 91*
Marcus, Constance Washburn 1951- *WhoE 91*
Marcus, David 1939- *WhoAm 90*
Marcus, David A *BiDrAPA 89*
Marcus, David Donald 1943- *WhoSSW 91*
Marcus, David M. 1942- *St&PR 91*
Marcus, Donald Howard 1916- *WhoAm 90*
Marcus, Donald M 1924- *BiDrAPA 89*
Marcus, Douglas Alan 1947- *BiDrAPA 89*
Marcus, Edward 1918- *WhoAm 90*
Marcus, Edward S 1910-1972 *WhoAmA 91N*
Marcus, Egerton *BioIn 16*
Marcus, Ellis 1918?-1990 *ConAu 132*
Marcus, Eric Robert 1944- *BiDrAPA 89, WhoE 91*
Marcus, Francine Lee *BiDrAPA 89*
Marcus, Frank 1933- *WhoAm 90*
Marcus, Frank Isadore 1928- *WhoAm 90*
Marcus, Frank W. 1914- *St&PR 91*
Marcus, Fred 1933- *St&PR 91*
Marcus, Gail Boxer 1956- *WhoE 91*
Marcus, Gerald R 1946- *WhoAmA 91*
Marcus, Greil Gerstley 1945- *WhoAm 90*
Marcus, Guy Taylor 1938- *St&PR 91*
Marcus, Harold *BiDrAPA 89*
Marcus, Harold S. 1905- *WorAlBi*
Marcus, Harriet 1917- *St&PR 91*
Marcus, Harris Leon 1931- *WhoAm 90, WhoSSW 91*
Marcus, Hershey 1928- *BiDrAPA 89*
Marcus, Hyman 1914- *WhoAm 90*
Marcus, Irving E 1929- *WhoAmA 91*
Marcus, Irwin M *BiDrAPA 89*
Marcus, Jacob Rader 1896- *WhoAm 90*
Marcus, James S. *BioIn 16*
Marcus, James S. 1929- *St&PR 91*
Marcus, James Stewart 1929- *WhoAm 90*
Marcus, Jay 1939- *St&PR 91*
Marcus, Jeff *BioIn 16*
Marcus, Jeffrey Arthur 1953- *WhoE 91*
Marcus, Jeffrey Howard 1950- *WhoEmL 91*
Marcus, Joel I 1958- *BiDrAPA 89*
Marcus, Joseph 1928- *BiDrAPA 89, WhoAm 90*
Marcus, Judith A *BiDrAPA 89*
Marcus, Junis Roberts 1935- *WhoE 91*
Marcus, Kenneth M 1949- *BiDrAPA 89*
Marcus, Kenneth Neal 1941- *St&PR 91*
Marcus, Lawrence I 1937- *BiDrAPA 89*
Marcus, Leah 1936- *WhoAmW 91*
Marcus, Lee Evan 1953- *WhoSSW 91*
Marcus, Leonard S *BiDrAPA 89*
Marcus, Linda 1952- *ODwPR 91*
Marcus, Marcia *WhoE 91*
Marcus, Marcia 1928- *WhoAmA 91*
Marcus, Marshall Matthew 1933- *St&PR 91*
Marcus, Marvin 1927- *WhoAm 90*
Marcus, Maurice G 1934- *BiDrAPA 89*
Marcus, Michael Neuman 1946- *WhoE 91*
Marcus, Michael W 1942- *BiDrAPA 89*
Marcus, Michael William 1942- *WhoE 91*
Marcus, Morton Jay 1936- *WhoWrEP 89*
Marcus, Nancy Helen 1950- *WhoAmW 91*
Marcus, Ned Nathaniel 1935- *BiDrAPA 89*
Marcus, Norman 1932- *WhoAm 90*
Marcus, Norman J 1941- *BiDrAPA 89*
Marcus, Norman Jay 1941- *WhoE 91*
Marcus, Paul 1946- *WhoAm 90*
Marcus, Paula *BiDrAPA 89*
Marcus, Philip Irving 1927- *WhoAm 90*
Marcus, Phillip Ronald 1947- *WhoE 91*
Marcus, Rebecca 1907- *AuBYP 90*
Marcus, Richard Alan 1933- *WhoAm 90*
Marcus, Richard Greenwald 1947- *St&PR 91, WhoAm 90*
Marcus, Richard Leon 1948- *WhoEmL 91*
Marcus, Richard Sheldon 1932- *St&PR 91*
Marcus, Robert 1925- *St&PR 91, WhoAm 90*
Marcus, Robert D. 1936- *WhoAm 90*
Marcus, Robert G. 1908- *St&PR 91*
Marcus, Robert L 1925- *BiDrAPA 89*
Marcus, Robert P 1923- *WhoAmA 91*
Marcus, Ronald Alan *BiDrAPA 89*
Marcus, Ronald Nathaniel 1957- *BiDrAPA 89*
Marcus, Rudolph A. *BioIn 16*
Marcus, Rudolph Arthur 1923- *WhoAm 90*
Marcus, Ruth Barcan *WhoAm 90*
Marcus, Samuel S. 1927- *St&PR 91*
Marcus, Seymour 1912- *St&PR 91*
Marcus, Sheila Marie *BiDrAPA 89*
Marcus, Sheldon 1937- *WhoAm 90*
Marcus, Spencer D 1946- *BiDrAPA 89*
Marcus, Stanley 1905- *ConAmBL, St&PR 91, WhoAm 90, WhoAmA 91, WhoSSW 91, WhoWrEP 89*
Marcus, Stephen Cecil 1932- *St&PR 91*
Marcus, Stephen H. 1935- *St&PR 91*
Marcus, Stephen Howard 1935- *WhoAm 90*
Marcus, Steven 1928- *WhoAm 90, WhoWrEP 89*
Marcus, Steven Ezra 1946- *WhoEmL 91*
Marcus, Steven Irl 1949- *WhoAm 90*
Marcus, Warren 1929- *St&PR 91*
Marcus, William M. 1938- *St&PR 91*
Marcus, William Michael 1938- *WhoAm 90*
Marcuse, Dietrich 1929- *WhoAm 90*
Marcuse, Donald J 1936- *BiDrAPA 89*
Marcuse, Erica Sherover- *BioIn 16*
Marcuse, Herbert 1898-1979 *EncAL, WorAlBi, WrPh P*
Marcuss, Stanley Joseph 1942- *WhoAm 90, WhoWor 91*
Marcussen, Arthur James 1925- *St&PR 91*
Marcuvitz, Nathan 1913- *WhoAm 90*
Marcy, Carl M. *NewYTBS 90 [port]*
Marcy, Carl Milton 1913- *WhoAm 90*
Marcy, Dwight 1840-1887 *AmLegL*
Marcy, Elona G. 1941- *WhoAmW 91*
Marcy, Henry O., III 1915- *St&PR 91*
Marcy, John Allen 1952- *WhoSSW 91*
Marcy, Mary Edna 1866-1922 *EncAL*
Marcy, William L. 1786-1857 *WorAlBi*
Marcy, William Learned 1786-1857 *BiDrUSE 89, BioIn 16*
Marcyn, Edward J. 1949- *WhoEmL 91*
Marcz, Roland Paul 1954- *WhoWor 91*
Marczynski, Karen Kathryn 1943- *WhoAmW 91*
Marda, Rama Shankar 1949- *WhoE 91*
Mardas, Dimitri Chrisovergis 1955- *WhoWor 91*
Mardell, Fred Robert 1934- *St&PR 91, WhoAm 90*
Mardelli, Paul *BiDrAPA 89*
Marden, Brice 1938- *BioIn 16, CurBio 90 [port], WhoAmA 91*
Marden, George Augustus 1839- *AmLegL*
Marden, Kenneth Allen 1928- *WhoAm 90*
Marden, Orison S. 1931- *St&PR 91*
Marden, Orison Swett *NewAgE 90*
Marden, Philip Ayer 1911- *WhoAm 90*
Marden, Philip Snyder 1955- *WhoE 91*
Marden, Robert Allen 1927- *St&PR 91*
Marder, Daniel 1923- *WhoWrEP 89*
Marder, Dorie *WhoAmA 91, WhoE 91*
Marder, Howard 1943- *ODwPR 91*
Marder, John G. 1926- *WhoAm 90*
Marder, Julian B 1934- *BiDrAPA 89*
Marder, Leon *BiDrAPA 89*
Marder, Michael Zachary 1938- *WhoAm 90*
Marder, Samuel H *BiDrAPA 89*
Marder, Stephen R 1945- *BiDrAPA 89*
Marder, William Zev 1947- *WhoWor 91*
Mardersteig, Giovanni 1892-1977 *ConDes 90*
Mardian, Samuel, Jr. 1919- *WhoAm 90*
Mardie 1933- *WhoAmW 91*
Mardiks, Ellen Ryan 1959- *ODwPR 91*
Mardirossian, Armenak *BioIn 16*
Mardis, Linda Keiser 1937- *WhoAmW 91*
Mardock, John F 1933- *BiDrAPA 89*
Mardock, Ruth Anne *BiDrAPA 89*
Mardosz, Chuck 1951- *BioIn 16*
Mardrus de Mingrelie, Raymond Cecil 1937- *WhoWor 91*
Mardy, Michael J. 1949- *St&PR 91*
Mare, Andre *PenDiDA 89*
Mare, Gina 1952- *WhoE 91*
Mare, Robert V. 1928- *St&PR 91*
Maready, William Frank 1932- *WhoWor 91*
Marechal, Leopoldo 1900-1970 *BioIn 16, HispWr 90*
Marechal, Louis-Delphis-Adolphe 1824-1892 *DcCanB 12*
Marechera, Dambudzo *BioIn 16*
Marechera, Dambudzo 1952-1987 *WorAu 1980*
Maree, Andrew Morgan, III 1927- *WhoWor 91*
Maree, Wendy P 1938- *WhoAmA 91*
Marees, Hans von 1837-1887 *IntDcAA 90*
Marek, Alan J. *St&PR 91*
Marek, Charles Robert 1940- *WhoSSW 91*
Marek, George R. 1902- *AuBYP 90*
Marek, Larry Ted 1955- *St&PR 91*
Marek, Margot *BioIn 16*
Marek, Paul Michael 1942- *WhoSSW 91*
Marek, Richard William 1933- *St&PR 91, WhoAm 90*
Marek, Stephen Edward 1942- *WhoE 91*
Marek, Vladimir 1928- *WhoAm 90*
Marella, Philip Daniel 1929- *WhoAm 90, WhoWor 91*
Maremont, Arnold H 1904-1978 *WhoAmA 91N*
Marenbon, John 1955- *ConAu 131*
Marencic, Richard John 1927- *St&PR 91*
Marencik, James Gregory 1948- *BiDrAPA 89*
Marengo, Lou *BioIn 16*
Marengo, Paul Bart 1947- *WhoEmL 91*
Marengo, Pierre Michel 1942- *WhoWor 91*
Marentette, Navarre A. 1925- *St&PR 91*
Mares, Donald J. *WhoHisp 91*
Mares, Frank James 1951- *WhoWor 91*
Mares, Michael Allen 1945- *WhoSSW 91*
Mares, Paul 1900-1949 *OxCPMus*
Maresca, Eugene Merrill 1944- *St&PR 91*
Maresca, Giuseppe 1926- *BiDrAPA 89*
Maresca, Maria 1951- *WhoE 91*
Maresca, Rosalia *IntWWM 90*
Maresh, Franklin W. 1938- *WhoAm 90*
Maresh, Nancy 1946- *WhoEmL 91*
Maresh, Robert David *BiDrAPA 89*
Mareth, Thomas Ray 1949- *BiDrAPA 89*
Maretz, Fred Robert 1924- *WhoE 91*
Marevna 1892-1983? *BiDWomA*
Marez, Jesus M. 1963- *WhoHisp 91*
Marez Oyens, Tera de 1932- *IntWWM 90*
Marfaing, Andre 1925- *BioIn 16*
Marfori, Beatriz L B *BiDrAPA 89*
Marg, Caroline Catherine 1962- *WhoWrEP 89*
Margalit, Israela *PenDiMP*
Margalith, Ethan Harold 1955- *WhoEmL 91*
Margall, Francisco Pi y 1824-1901 *BioIn 16*
Margaret 1200?-1280 *WomWR*
Margaret 1318-1369 *WomWR*
Margaret 1350-1405 *WomWR*
Margaret 1353-1412 *WomWR*
Margaret, Duchess of Burgundy 1446-1503 *BioIn 16*
Margaret, Duchess of Newcastle 1624?-1674 *BioIn 16*
Margaret of Anjou 1430-1482 *WomWR*
Margaret of Antioch-Lusignan *WomWR*
Margaret of Austria 1480-1530 *EncCoWW, WomWR*
Margaret of Austria 1522-1586 *WomWR*
Margaret of Navarre *WomWR*
Margaret of Norway 1282?-1290 *WomWR*
Margaret, of York 1446-1503 *BioIn 16*
Margaret Rose, Princess 1930- *WhoWor 91*
Margaret Tudor 1489-1541 *FemiCLE, WomWR*
Margareta *WomWR*
Margaretha *WomWR*
Margaretten, Michael Elliot 1937- *WhoWor 91*
Margarita Maria, Mother *BioIn 16*
Margarita, of Cascia 1381?-1457 *BioIn 16*
Margaritis, John P. 1949- *ODwPR 91*
Margaritis, John Paul 1949- *WhoAm 90*
Margaritoff, Dimitri Andrej 1947- *WhoWor 91*
Marge, Michael 1928- *WhoAm 90*
Marged, Judith Michele 1954- *WhoAmW 91, WhoSSW 91*
Margel, Bernadette 1953- *WhoE 91*
Margenat, Hugo 1933-1957 *BioIn 16*
Margeot, Jean 1916- *WhoWor 91*
Margeotes, John 1924- *WhoE 91*
Margerison, Richard W. 1948- *St&PR 91*
Margerison, Richard Wayne 1948- *WhoAm 90*
Margerum, Dale William 1929- *WhoAm 90*
Margerum, Fred M. 1953- *St&PR 91*
Margerum, John David 1929- *WhoAm 90*
Margerum, Roger Williams, Jr. 1930- *WhoAm 90*
Margery *EncPaPR 91*
Margery 189-?-1941 *EncO&P 3*
Margeson, Albert R. 1933- *St&PR 91*
Margeson, Hector 1924- *WhoWrEP 89*
Margesson, Maxine Edge 1933- *WhoSSW 91*
Marget, Madeline *BioIn 16*
Margeton, Stephen George 1945- *WhoAm 90, WhoEmL 91*
Margetson, Edward H 1892-1962 *DrBlPA 90*
Margetts, Edward Lambert 1920- *BiDrAPA 89*
Margetts, Josephine S. *BioIn 16*
Margetts, Mark J. 1938- *St&PR 91*
Margetts, W. Thomas 1936- *St&PR 91, WhoAm 90*
Marggraf, Wolfgang 1933- *IntWWM 90*
Margherio, Martin John 1945- *St&PR 91*
Marghieri, Clotilde *BioIn 16*
Marghiloman, Alexandru 1854-1925 *BioIn 16*
Margie, Joyce Daly 1940- *WhoWrEP 89*
Margileth, Andrew Menges 1920- *WhoAm 90*
Margileth, Lynn 1945- *WhoE 91*
Margini, Lorenzo M 1943- *BiDrAPA 89*
Margiotta, Daniel M. 1949- *St&PR 91*
Margiotta, Domenico *EncO&P 3*
Margiotta, Mary-Lou Ann 1956- *WhoAmW 91*
Margiotta, William Thomas, Jr. 1937- *St&PR 91*
Margittai, Katalin Judit 1960- *BiDrAPA 89*
Margly, Violet R. 1931- *WhoAmW 91*
Margo, Boris 1902- *WhoAmA 91*
Margo, Geoffrey Myles 1946- *BiDrAPA 89*
Margol, Irving 1930- *St&PR 91*
Margoliash, Emanuel 1920- *WhoAm 90*
Margolies, Ethel Polacheck 1907- *WhoAmA 91*
Margolies, George Howard 1948- *WhoE 91*
Margolies, Joel 1934- *St&PR 91, WhoAm 90*
Margolies, John *BioIn 16*
Margolies, Luise 1947- *WhoWrEP 89*
Margolies, Matthew Eric 1948- *St&PR 91*
Margolies, Raymond 1920- *WhoAm 90*
Margolin, Arthur Stanley 1936- *St&PR 91, WhoAm 90*
Margolin, Carl M. 1939- *WhoE 91*
Margolin, Charles H. 1927- *St&PR 91*
Margolin, Ephraim 1926- *WhoAm 90*
Margolin, Eric Mitchell 1953- *WhoAm 90*
Margolin, Harold 1922- *WhoAm 90*
Margolin, Jean Maday 1937- *WhoE 91*
Margolin, Jeanette R 1938- *BiDrAPA 89*
Margolin, Milton 1930- *WhoE 91*
Margolin, Morris *BioIn 16*
Margolin, N Lionel 1933- *BiDrAPA 89*
Margolin, Paul 1923-1989 *BioIn 16*
Margolin, Richard Alan *BiDrAPA 89*
Margolis, Aaron E. 1943- *St&PR 91*
Margolis, Alan 1949- *WhoE 91*
Margolis, Bernard Allen 1948- *WhoAm 90*
Margolis, Carl Ira *BiDrAPA 89*
Margolis, Daniel Herbert 1926- *WhoAm 90*
Margolis, David 1911- *WhoAmA 91*
Margolis, David I. 1930- *St&PR 91*
Margolis, David Israel 1930- *WhoAm 90, WhoE 91*
Margolis, Elias 1880-1946 *BioIn 16*
Margolis, Esther Luterman 1939- *WhoAmW 91*
Margolis, Eugene 1935- *WhoAm 90, WhoE 91*
Margolis, Gary Francis 1945- *WhoWrEP 89*
Margolis, George 1914- *WhoAm 90*

Margolis, Gerald Hersch 1942- BiDrAPA 89
Margolis, Gerald J 1935- BiDrAPA 89
Margolis, Gerald Joseph 1935- WhoE 91
Margolis, Gwen Liedman 1934- WhoAmW 91, WhoSSW 91
Margolis, Harold Allen 1943- St&PR 91
Margolis, Harry W. 1943- St&PR 91
Margolis, Henry Melville 1909-1989 BioIn 16
Margolis, Howard 1932- ConAu 130
Margolis, Irving Bernard 1930- WhoE 91
Margolis, James Alan 1939- BiDrAPA 89
Margolis, Jay M. 1949- WhoAm 90
Margolis, John Gilbert 1947- WhoEmL 91
Margolis, Jon BioIn 16
Margolis, Jonathan J. 1945- WhoEmL 91
Margolis, Joseph 1924- WhoWrEP 89
Margolis, Julius 1920- WhoAm 90
Margolis, Lawrence Allen 1947- St&PR 91
Margolis, Lawrence Stanley 1935- WhoAm 90
Margolis, Leo 1927- WhoAm 90
Margolis, Leon St&PR 91
Margolis, Lester H BiDrAPA 89
Margolis, Margo 1947- WhoAmA 91
Margolis, Marvin O 1927- BiDrAPA 89
Margolis, Max Leopold 1866-1932 BioIn 16
Margolis, Milton Joseph St&PR 91
Margolis, Milton Joseph 1925- WhoAm 90, WhoE 91
Margolis, Norman M BiDrAPA 89
Margolis, Oscar St&PR 91
Margolis, Philip M 1925- BiDrAPA 89
Margolis, Philip Marcus 1925- WhoAm 90
Margolis, Richard Craig BiDrAPA 89
Margolis, Richard D. 1938- St&PR 91
Margolis, Richard J. 1929- AuBYP 90
Margolis, Richard M 1943- WhoAmA 91
Margolis, Richard Martin 1943- WhoAm 90
Margolis, Sidney O. 1925- St&PR 91, WhoAm 90, WhoE 91
Margolis, Tina Louise WhoAmW 91
Margon, Bruce Henry 1948- WhoAm 90, WhoEmL 91
Margon, Marilyn Simon 1947- WhoAmW 91
Margoneri, Joe 1930- Ballpl 90
Margosian, Lucille K. Manougian 1935- WhoAmW 91
Margot, Leslie WhoWrEP 89
Margouleff, Robert NewAgMG
Margowski, Janusz 1929- WhoWor 91
Margowski, Marilyn Joyce 1949- WhoAmW 91
Margrave, John Lee 1924- WhoAm 90
Margrethe II 1940- WhoWor 91, WomWR
Margrethe I, Queen of Denmark 1353-1412 BioIn 16
Margrethe II, Queen of Denmark 1940- BioIn 16
Margrett, John G 1926- BiDrAPA 89
Marguard, Charles St&PR 91
Marguerite WomWR
Marguerite WomWR
Marguerite de Thouars WomWR
Marguerite, Carl A. 1935- St&PR 91
Margules, Dehirsh 1899-1965 WhoAmA 91N
Margules, Gabriele Ella 1927- WhoAmA 91
Margules, Matthew BioIn 16
Margulies, Alfred Irwin BiDrAPA 89
Margulies, Alfred Salsbury 1948- BiDrAPA 89, WhoE 91
Margulies, Fred 1924- St&PR 91
Margulies, Herman 1922- WhoAmA 91, WhoE 91
Margulies, Irving 1934- St&PR 91
Margulies, Isidore 1921- WhoAmA 91
Margulies, James Howard 1951- WhoSSW 91
Margulies, Jerome 1914- St&PR 91
Margulies, Joseph 1896-1986 WhoAmA 91N
Margulies, Martin B. 1940- WhoAm 90
Margulies, Newton WhoAm 90
Margulies, Todd David 1959- WhoEmL 91
Margulies, William 1906-1988 BioIn 16
Margulis, Alan D. 1937- St&PR 91
Margulis, Alexander Rafailo 1921- WhoAm 90
Margulis, Jerry 1929- WhoWrEP 89
Margulis, Lynn 1938- BioIn 16, WhoAm 90, WhoAmW 91
Margulis, Martha 1928- WhoAmA 91
Margulis, Martha Boyer 1928- WhoE 91
Margulois, David 1912- WhoE 91
Margus, Edward A. 1920- St&PR 91
Marhatta, Hari Prasad 1945- WhoE 91
Marhenke, Jon David 1943- BiDrAPA 89
Marhic, Michel Edmond 1945- WhoAm 90
Marholm, Leonhard EncCoWW
Marholm-Hansson, Laura 1854-1928 EncCoWW
Mari WhoAmA 91
Mari, Enzo PenDiDA 89
Mari, Enzo 1932- ConDes 90
Mari, Maria Del Carmen 1959- WhoHisp 91
Maria WomWR
Maria Adelaide 1894-1924 WomWR
Maria Anna of Austria 1634-1696 WomWR
Maria Anna of Spain 1718- WomWR
Maria Carolina 1752-1814 WomWR
Maria Christina 1742-1798 WomWR
Maria Christina of Austria 1858-1929 WomWR
Maria Christina I of Naples 1806-1878 WomWR
Maria Cristina, Queen 1806-1878 BioIn 16
Maria Cristina, Queen 1858-1929 BioIn 16
Maria II da Gloria 1819-1853 WomWR
Maria de Jesus 1602-1665 EncO&P 3
Maria de la Mercedes 1880-1904 WomWR
Maria Estela Martinez de Peron WomWR
Maria of Anjou 1370-1395 WomWR
Maria of Austria WomWR
Maria I of Braganza 1734-1816 WomWR
Maria, Queen of Hungary 1370?-1395 BioIn 16
Maria I, Queen of Portugal 1734-1816 BioIn 16
Maria II, Queen of Portugal 1819-1853 BioIn 16
Maria Theresa 1717-1780 WomWR [port], WorAlBi
Maria Theresa, Empress of Austria 1717-1780 BioIn 16
Maria, Joseph Mario 1935- St&PR 91
Mariah, Paul WhoWrEP 89
Mariam, Mengistu Haile 1937- WhoWor 91
Mariam, Thomas 1957- ODwPR 91
Marian, Teresa 1955- WhoEmL 91
Mariana AuBYP 90
Marianes, William Byron 1955- WhoEmL 91
Mariani, David Frank 1942- WhoE 91
Mariani, Giuseppe Mario 1926- WhoWor 91
Mariani, Michael Matthew 1950- WhoEmL 91
Mariani, Paul Louis 1940- WhoWrEP 89
Mariani, Robert K. 1934- St&PR 91
Mariani, Theodore Frank 1931- WhoAm 90
Mariani, Veronica Joan 1960- WhoAmW 91
Marianik, Charles Gabor 1946- WhoEmL 91
Marianne 1941- WhoAmA 91
Mariano, Pellegrino di BioIn 16
Mariante, Benjamin Robert 1934- WhoE 91
Mariaschin, Mark Arthur 1953- WhoE 91
Mariategui, Jose Carlos 1894-1930 BioIn 16
Maribona, Ricardo P BiDrAPA 89
Maric, Jovan K BiDrAPA 89
Maric, Ljubica 1909- IntWWM 90
Marichal, Juan 1937- Ballpl 90 [port]
Marichal, Juan 1938- WhoHisp 91
Maricich, Suzanne 1941- ODwPR 91
Marick, Michael Miron 1957- WhoEmL 91
Maricle, Robert Alan BiDrAPA 89
Marie WomWR
Marie WomWR
Marie 1192?-1212 WomWR
Marie Adelaide 1894-1924 BioIn 16
Marie Antoinette 1755-1793 WorAlBi
Marie Antoinette, Queen 1755-1793 BioIn 16
Marie de Bourbon Montpensier 1606-1627 WomWR
Marie de Chatillon WomWR
Marie, de France BioIn 16
Marie de France EncCoWW, FemiCLE
Marie de l'Incarnation EncCoWW, WhNaAH
Marie de Medicis 1573-1642 WomWR [port]
Marie de Romieu 1556?- EncCoWW
Marie Des Sept-Douleurs DcCanB 12
Marie d'Savoy-Nemours WomWR
Marie of Agreda 1602-1665 EncO&P 3
Marie, Queen 1875-1938 BioIn 16
Marie, Andre Desire Paul 1897-1979 BiDFrPL
Marie, Geraldine 1949- SmATA 61 [port]
Marie, Janet WhoWrEP 89
Marie, Kathy Louise 1953- WhoAmW 91
Marie, Lisa BioIn 16
Marie-Angele DcCanB 12
Marie-Angele Gauthier DcCanB 12
Marie-Louise 1791-1847 WomWR
Marie-Victorin, Frere 1885-1944 DcLB 92 [port]
Mariella, Raymond P. 1919- WhoAm 90
Marienchild, Eva 1957- WhoAmW 91
Marienthal, George 1938- St&PR 91, WhoAm 90
Marier, Jean-Jacques BiDrAPA 89
Marier, Paul A. 1928- St&PR 91
Mariia, Mat 1891-1945 EncCoWW
Marijnissen, Roger H. BioIn 16
Marik, Jan 1920- WhoAm 90
Marik, Raymond Lewis 1932- WhoWrEP 89
Marikos, Kathryn Ann 1947- WhoAmW 91
Maril, Elizabeth Joan 1943- WhoAmW 91
Maril, Herman 1908-1986 WhoAmA 91N
Marill, Irwin H BiDrAPA 89
Marillac, Louise de 1591-1660 EncCoWW
Marimow, William Kalmon 1947- WhoAm 90
Marin WhNaAH
Marin, Carole J 1942- BiDrAPA 89
Marin, Cella EncCoWW
Marin, Cheech BioIn 16
Marin, Cheech 1946- WhoHisp 91, WorAlBi
Marin, Connie 1939- WhoAmW 91
Marin, Connie Flores 1939- WhoHisp 91
Marin, Emilio 1951- WhoWor 91
Marin, Frank 1940- WhoHisp 91
Marin, Gerardo 1947- WhoHisp 91
Marin, John BioIn 16
Marin, John BioIn 16
Marin, John 1870-1953 BioIn 16, WhoAmA 91N
Marin, Louis 1871-1960 BiDFrPL
Marin, Luis Munoz HispWr 90
Marin, Luis Munoz 1898-1980 BioIn 16
Marin, Michelle J. 1956- ODwPR 91
Marin, Myra 1964- WhoHisp 91
Marin, Richard Anthony 1946- WhoAm 90
Marin, Robert S 1946- BiDrAPA 89
Marin, Rosaura 1952- WhoHisp 91
Marin, Vincent Arul 1959- WhoEmL 91, WhoWor 91
Marin Canas, Jose 1904-1980 BioIn 16
Marina, Duchess of Kent 1906-1968 BioIn 16
Marinacci, Alberto A BiDrAPA 89
Marinacci, Michael Anthony 1960- WhoWrEP 89
Marinaccio, Alexander Teresio 1912- WhoSSW 91
Marinaccio, Charles Lindbergh 1933- WhoAm 90
Marinaccio, Jim BioIn 16
Marinaccio, Marilyn BioIn 16
Marinak, Kathleen Louise 1957- WhoAmW 91
Marinaro, Ed BioIn 16
Marinaro, Edward Francis 1950- WhoAm 90
Marinas, Manuel G BiDrAPA 89
Marinatos, Anthony 1946- St&PR 91
Marinchak, Pamela Anne BiDrAPA 89
Marincola, Dian Angela 1954- WhoAmW 91
Marine, Clyde Lockwood 1936- St&PR 91, WhoAm 90
Marine, Gene 1926- WhoAm 90, WhoWrEP 89
Marine, Jack J. 1955- St&PR 91
Marine, Michael Ray 1954- WhoWrEP 89
Marineau, Philip Albert 1946- WhoAm 90
Marinelli, Ada Santi 1942- WhoAmW 91
Marinelli, Carlo 1926- IntWWM 90
Marinelli, Joseph Marcello 1948- WhoE 91
Marinello, Juan 1898-1977 BioIn 16
Mariner, Allen S BiDrAPA 89
Mariner, Donna M 1934- WhoAmA 91
Mariner, Martin Romig 1939- WhoE 91
Mariner, Scott MajTwCW
Mariner, William Martin 1949- WhoWor 91
Marines, Louis Lawrence 1942- WhoAm 90
Marinescu, John 1940- WhoWor 91
Marinescu, Mihaela 1951- IntWWM 90
Marinetti, B. BiDWomA
Marinetti, Benedetta Cappa 1899-1980 EncCoWW
Marinetti, Filippo Tommaso 1876-1944 WorAlBi
Marinetti, Guido V. 1918- WhoAm 90
Maring, Norma Ann 1933- WhoAmW 91
Marinho, Roberto BioIn 16
Marinho, Roberto 1904- WhoWor 91
Marini, Frank 1935- WhoAm 90
Marini, Guido A. 1929- St&PR 91
Marini, Guy L. 1956- St&PR 91
Marini, Manuel Augusto 1939- WhoHisp 91
Marini, Marino 1901-1980 IntDcAA 90
Marini, Robert Charles 1931- WhoAm 90
Marini Bettolo, Giovanni Battista 1915- WhoWor 91
Marini-Roig, Luis E. 1949- WhoHisp 91
Marinis, Thomas Paul, Jr. 1943- WhoSSW 91
Marinko, Monica Marie 1948- WhoAmW 91
Marino, Albert Joseph 1899-1975 WhoAmA 91N
Marino, Anthony, Jr. 1953- BiDrAPA 89
Marino, Arthur J., Jr. 1936- ODwPR 91
Marino, Arthur Joseph, Jr. 1936- WhoE 91
Marino, Dan BioIn 16
Marino, Dan 1961- WorAlBi
Marino, Daniel Constantine 1961- WhoAm 90, WhoSSW 91
Marino, Dorothy 1912- AuBYP 90
Marino, Eugene A. BioIn 16
Marino, Eugene Antonio 1934- WhoSSW 91
Marino, Eugene B. 1946- WhoE 91
Marino, Eugene Louis 1929- WhoAm 90
Marino, Francis J. 1943- St&PR 91
Marino, Frank 1942- WhoAmA 91
Marino, Frank Anthony 1947- WhoSSW 91
Marino, Frederick M. 1946- St&PR 91
Marino, Gary O. 1944- St&PR 91
Marino, James Francis 1943- St&PR 91
Marino, Joanne Marie 1951- WhoAmW 91
Marino, Joseph 1943- St&PR 91
Marino, Joseph Anthony 1932- St&PR 91, WhoAm 90
Marino, Joseph Frank 1933- St&PR 91
Marino, Joseph William 1939- St&PR 91
Marino, Kenneth K. 1946- St&PR 91
Marino, Louis John 1949- WhoSSW 91
Marino, Nick TwCCr&M 91
Marino, Peter BioIn 16
Marino, Peter A. 1942- St&PR 91
Marino, Peter Andrew 1942- WhoAm 90
Marino, Ralph J. 1928- WhoE 91
Marino, Richard John 1950- St&PR 91
Marino, Robert J. 1893-1973 MusmAFA
Marino, Robert James 1947- WhoAm 90
Marino, Roger M. BioIn 16
Marino, Rose Linda 1950- WhoHisp 91
Marino, Ruth Elizabeth Reiff 1924- IntWWM 90
Marino, Sal F. 1920- St&PR 91, WhoAm 90
Marino, Santiago 1788-1854 BioIn 16
Marino, Sheila Burris 1947- WhoAmW 91
Marino, Virgil John 1945- WhoE 91
Marino-Merlo, Joseph 1906-1956 WhoAmA 91N
Marinos, Elia Peter 1941- WhoAm 90
Marinot, Maurice 1882-1962 PenDiDA 89
Marinovich, Todd BioIn 16
Marinsky, Harry 1909- WhoAmA 91
Mario, Ernest 1938- BioIn 16, WhoAm 90
Mario, Giovanni 1810-1883 PenDiMP
Mario, Jessie White 1832-1906 FemiCLE
Marion, Andre F. 1935- St&PR 91
Marion, Andrew Burnet 1919- WhoAm 90
Marion, Beverly Ann 1962- WhoAmW 91
Marion, Douglas Welch 1944- WhoWrEP 89
Marion, Frances 1886-1973 FemiCLE
Marion, Francis 1732-1795 BioIn 16, EncCRAm [port], WorAlBi
Marion, Frederick 1892- EncO&P 3
Marion, Georgette A. 1927- WhoAmW 91
Marion, Henry MajTwCW
Marion, John Francis 1922- WhoAm 90, WhoWrEP 89
Marion, John L. 1933- BioIn 16
Marion, John Louis 1933- St&PR 91, WhoAm 90
Marion, Marjorie Anne 1935- WhoAm 90
Marion, Marty 1917- Ballpl 90 [port]
Marion, Patrice Jules Jean 1949- WhoWor 91
Marion, Robert W. 1952- ConAu 130
Marion, Thomas D. 1946- St&PR 91
Marion, Wade Hampton, Jr. 1947- WhoSSW 91
Marioni, Paul 1941- WhoAmA 91
Marioni, Tom 1937- WhoAmA 91
Mariotti, John Louis 1941- St&PR 91
Maris, Albert B. 1893-1989 BioIn 16
Maris, Roger 1934-1985 Ballpl 90 [port], BioIn 16, WorAlBi
Maris, Ron AuBYP 90
Mariscal, Javier 1950- ConDes 90
Mariscalo, Rosemary Jean 1939- WhoE 91
Mariscotti, John A. 1933- St&PR 91
Marishall, Jean FemiCLE
Mariska, Mark D. 1944- St&PR 91
Marisol 1930- BiDWomA, BioIn 16, WhoAm 90, WhoAmA 91, WhoAmW 91
Maritain, Jacques 1882-1973 BioIn 16, WorAlBi, WrPh P
Maritain, Raissa Oumansoff 1883-1960 EncCoWW
Maritato, Victor BioIn 16
Maritzen, Lynn Marie 1958- WhoAmW 91
Mariucci, Anne L. 1957- St&PR 91
Mariwalla, Gopal Chetanram 1944- WhoE 91, WhoWor 91
Marjama, Jill Marie BiDrAPA 89
Mark Twain 1835-1910 EncO&P 3

Mark, Alan A BiDrAPA 89
Mark, Albert L. 1926- ODwPR 91
Mark, Andrew R. 1952- WhoE 91
Mark, Angela S. 1960- WhoWrEP 89
Mark, Arlene Joan 1940- WhoAmW 91
Mark, Bendor 1912- WhoAmA 91
Mark, Betsy Yvonne 1947- WhoAmW 91
Mark, Burton Thomas BiDrAPA 89
Mark, Cecil James 1926- St&PR 91
Mark, Dewey 1927- St&PR 91, WhoAm 90, WhoSSW 91
Mark, Enid 1932- WhoAmA 91
Mark, Enid Epstein 1932- WhoE 91
Mark, H. F. 1895- BioIn 16
Mark, Hans Michael 1929- WhoAm 90, WhoSSW 91, WhoWor 91
Mark, Herman Francis 1895- BioIn 16, WhoAm 90
Mark, James B. D. 1929- WhoAm 90
Mark, James Leland 1933- WhoAm 90
Mark, Jan 1943- AuBYP 90
Mark, Jane Anne 1945- WhoAmW 91
Mark, Janet Lee 1946- BiDrAPA 89
Mark, Joan 1937- ConAu 130
Mark, Jonathan Greenfield 1948- WhoEmL 91
Mark, Kathleen Mary 1951- WhoAmW 91
Mark, Laura J BiDrAPA 89
Mark, Laurence Peter 1953- WhoE 91
Mark, Leighton BioIn 16
Mark, Leslie Dean 1961- WhoAmW 91
Mark, Lillian Gee 1932- WhoAmW 91
Mark, Margaret B. NewYTBS 90
Mark, Marilyn WhoAmA 91
Mark, Mary Ellen 1940- BioIn 16, WhoAm 90, WhoAmA 91, WhoE 91
Mark, Mary L. St&PR 91
Mark, Melvin 1922- WhoAm 90
Mark, Michael L. 1936- IntWWM 90
Mark, Michael Laurence 1936- WhoAm 90
Mark, Morris BioIn 16
Mark, Norman BioIn 16
Mark, Peter 1940- IntWWM 90, WhoAm 90, WhoSSW 91
Mark, Phyllis WhoAmA 91
Mark, Reuben BiDrAPA 89
Mark, Reuben 1939- WhoAm 90
Mark, Richard Allen 1953- WhoAm 90
Mark, Ronnie Joan 1941- WhoAmW 91
Mark, Samuel 1951- WhoHisp 91
Mark, Shelley Muin 1922- WhoAm 90
Mark, Shew-Kuey Tommy 1936- WhoAm 90
Mark, Stewart Winston 1915- WhoAm 90
Markand, Narendra Nath BiDrAPA 89
Markandaya, Kamala 1924- FemiCLE
Markarian, Alexia WhoAmA 91
Markaryants, Vladimir Siremo WhoWor 91
Markbein, Gilbert 1944- St&PR 91
Markbreit, Jerry BioIn 16
Markby, Ronald Thomas BiDrAPA 89
Marke, Jane Elizabeth BiDrAPA 89
Marke, Julius Jay 1913- WhoAm 90, WhoE 91
Markee, Katherine Madigan 1931- WhoAmW 91
Markel, Bennett F 1931- BiDrAPA 89
Markel, David 1934- BiDrAPA 89
Markel, Geraldine 1939- WhoAmW 91
Markel, Gregory Arthur 1945- WhoE 91, WhoEmL 91, WhoWor 91
Markel, Helen BioIn 16, NewYTBS 90
Markel, Helen 1919?-1990 ConAu 130
Markel, Janet L. 1937- St&PR 91
Markel, John Dundas 1943- WhoAm 90
Markel, Kathryn E 1946- WhoAmA 91
Markel, Robert Edwin 1957- WhoEmL 91
Markel, Scott Alan 1959- WhoE 91
Markel, Steven A. 1948- St&PR 91
Markell, Alan William 1933- WhoE 91
Markell, Eric M. 1951- St&PR 91
Markell, George Alexander 1925- St&PR 91
Markello, Anthony P BiDrAPA 89
Markellos, Theodore G 1925- BiDrAPA 89
Markels, Michael, Jr. 1926- St&PR 91, WhoAm 90
Marken, Gideon Andrew, III 1940- ODwPR 91
Marken, Jack W 1922- ConAu 31NR
Marken, William Riley 1942- WhoAm 90
Marker, Chris 1921- BioIn 16
Marker, David G. 1937- WhoAm 90
Marker, Jamsheed K. A. BioIn 16
Marker, Leonard K. IntWWM 90
Marker, Leonard K. 1913- WhoE 91, WhoWor 91
Marker, Linda ODwPR 91
Marker, Marc Linthacum 1941- WhoAm 90, WhoWor 91
Marker, Mariska Pugsley WhoAmA 91
Marker, Robert K. 1932- ODwPR 91
Marker, Robert Sydney 1922- WhoAm 90
Marker, Victor E. 1916- St&PR 91
Markert, Clement Lawrence 1917- WhoAm 90
Markert, James Macdowell 1934- St&PR 91, WhoAm 90
Markert, John William 1947- St&PR 91
Markert, Leonard P., Jr. 1926- St&PR 91
Markert, Russell 1899-1990 NewYTBS 90
Markert, Wallace, Jr. 1924- WhoAm 90
Markesbery, William R. 1932- WhoAm 90
Markessini, Joan 1942- WhoAmW 91
Marketti, Louis Lawrence 1927- St&PR 91
Markevitch, Igor 1912-1983 PenDiMP
Markewich, Maurice Elish 1936- BiDrAPA 89
Markey, Andrew J. 1931- St&PR 91
Markey, Andrew Joseph 1931- WhoAm 90
Markey, Arthur Andrew 1946- WhoE 91
Markey, Daniel Peter 1857- AmLegL
Markey, Edward John 1946- WhoAm 90, WhoE 91
Markey, Gene 1895-1980 LiHiK
Markey, Howard Thomas 1920- WhoAm 90
Markey, James Kevin 1956- WhoEmL 91
Markey, Joanne Zink 1941- WhoAmW 91
Markey, John Allen 1934- WhoAm 90
Markey, Joseph H., Jr. 1945- St&PR 91
Markey, Michael J. 1932- St&PR 91
Markey, Oscar B BiDrAPA 89
Markey, Richard B BiDrAPA 89
Markey, Robert Guy 1939- St&PR 91, WhoAm 90
Markey, William Alan 1927- WhoAm 90
Markey, William C. 1906- St&PR 91
Markey, William F. WhoAm 90
Markey, William Francis, Jr. 1939- WhoE 91
Markey, Winston Roscoe 1929- WhoAm 90
Markfort, Anne Marie 1950- WhoWrEP 89
Markgraf, Carl 1928- ConAu 31NR
Markgraf, John Hodge 1930- WhoAm 90
Markgraf, Rosemarie 1934- WhoAmW 91
Markham, Beryl 1902-1986 BioIn 16
Markham, Charles Buchanan 1926- WhoAm 90, WhoSSW 91
Markham, Charles Rinklin 1959- WhoE 91, WhoEmL 91
Markham, Claire Agnes 1919- WhoE 91
Markham, Dewey 1906-1981 DrBlPA 90
Markham, Edward Murphy, III 1930- St&PR 91
Markham, Edwin 1852-1940 WorAlBi
Markham, Elizabeth Jane 1952- IntWWM 90
Markham, Elizabeth Mary 1929- WhoAmW 91
Markham, George BioIn 16
Markham, Gregory H. 1951- St&PR 91
Markham, Jacqueline ODwPR 91
Markham, James M. 1943-1989 BioIn 16, ConAu 129
Markham, Jane BiDEWW
Markham, Jerome David 1917- WhoSSW 91
Markham, John Steven 1930- St&PR 91
Markham, Jordan J. 1916- WhoAm 90
Markham, Marion M. 1929- ConAu 129, SmATA 60[port], WhoAmW 91, WhoWrEP 89
Markham, Mary Headlee 1908-1990 BioIn 16
Markham, Richard 1952- IntWWM 90
Markham, Robert MajTwCW
Markham, Robert 1922- BioIn 16
Markham, Roy 1916-1979 BioIn 16
Markham, Sara Frances Norris 1947- WhoAmW 91
Markham, Thomas N. 1934- St&PR 91
Markie, Peter Joseph 1950- WhoAm 90
Markiewicz, James Edward 1932- St&PR 91
Markiewicz, John Michael 1953- WhoWor 91
Markiewicz, Wladyslaw 1920- WhoWor 91
Markijohn, Judy Ann 1956- WhoAmW 91
Markim, Alfred 1927- St&PR 91
Markin, Rom J. 1932- WhoAm 90
Markins, W. S. AuBYP 90
Markkula, A. C., Jr. WhoAm 90
Markl, Hubert 1938- WhoWor 91
Markl, Josef 1928- IntWWM 90
Markland, Bjorn Walter 1943- WhoWor 91
Markland, Francis Swaby, Jr. 1936- WhoAm 90
Markland, Judith 1944- St&PR 91, WhoAm 90
Markle, Ann Elizabeth 1952- WhoAmW 91
Markle, Cliff 1894-1974 Ballpl 90
Markle, George Bushar, IV 1921- WhoAm 90
Markle, Greer 1946- WhoAmA 91
Markle, Jack M 1939- WhoAmA 91
Markle, John, Jr. 1931- WhoAm 90
Markle, Joseph 1900-1989 BioIn 16
Markle, Rae Lynn BiDrAPA 89
Markle, Robert N. 1951- WhoSSW 91
Markle, Roger A. 1933- St&PR 91
Markle, Roger Allan 1933- WhoAm 90
Markle, Sam 1933- WhoAmA 91
Markle, Sandra 1946- BioIn 16
Markle, Susan Meyer 1928- WhoAm 90
Markley, Doris Yocum 1921- WhoAmA 91
Markley, John R. 1934- WhoAm 90
Markley, Keith Michael 1954- BiDrAPA 89
Markley, Lynn McMaster 1938- WhoWor 91
Markley, Nelson G. 1940- WhoAm 90
Markley, Rodney W. 1912-1988 BioIn 16
Markley, Thomas R. 1940- St&PR 91
Markman, Henry C 1951- BiDrAPA 89
Markman, Raymond Jerome 1927- WhoAm 90
Markman, Ronald 1931- WhoAm 90, WhoAmA 91
Markman, Ronald A 1936- BiDrAPA 89
Markman, Sherman 1920- WhoWor 91
Markman, Sherwin J. 1929- WhoAm 90
Markman, Sidney David 1911- WhoAmA 91
Markman, Stephen J. 1949- WhoAm 90
Markman-Reubins, Beatriz BiDrAPA 89
Marko, Harold 1925- St&PR 91
Marko, Harold Meyron 1925- WhoAm 90
Marko, Marlene 1945- BiDrAPA 89
Marko, Szilard Szaniszlo 1934- WhoWor 91
Markoe, Arnold Michael 1942- WhoE 91, WhoSSW 91
Markoe, Frank, Jr. 1923- WhoAm 90
Markoe, Guy Leigh 1953- St&PR 91
Markoe, M.A. 1927- St&PR 91
Markoe, M. Allen 1927- WhoWor 91
Markoe, Merrill BioIn 16
Markoff, Elliott L 1932- BiDrAPA 89
Markoff, Gary David 1956- WhoE 91
Markoff, Richard A 1929- BiDrAPA 89
Markolf, Ada Mayo Stewart 1870-1945 BioIn 16
Markoosie 1942- ChILR 23
Markopoulos, Andrew John 1931- WhoWor 91
Markos, Dennis Ray 1947- WhoSSW 91
Markou, Peter John 1940- WhoE 91
Markov, Albert 1933- IntWWM 90
Markov, Georgi 1929-1978 BioIn 16
Markova, Alicia 1910- WorAlBi
Markova, Juliana 1945- IntWWM 90
Markovic, Ante 1924- WhoWor 91
Markovic, Mihailo 1923- ConAu 131
Markovich, Ann Marie 1948- WhoAmA 91
Markovich, Ched J. 1942- St&PR 91
Markovich, Dejan 1932- BiDrAPA 89
Markovich, John M. 1956- St&PR 91
Markovich, Lois Ann Gimondo 1947- WhoAmW 91
Markovich, Olga 1940- WhoAmW 91
Markovich-Treece, Patricia Helen 1941- WhoAmW 91, WhoWor 91
Markovits, Andrei Steven 1948- WhoE 91, WhoEmL 91, WhoWor 91
Markovits, Paul B. 1943- St&PR 91, WhoAm 90
Markovits, Ronald D. 1943- St&PR 91
Markovitz, Alvin 1929- WhoAm 90
Markow, Harry Gregory BiDrAPA 89
Markow, Jack 1905-1983 WhoAmA 91N
Markowich, Michael A. 1948- St&PR 91
Markowicz, Victor 1944- St&PR 91
Markowitz, Arthur Donald 1940- WhoE 91
Markowitz, David 1923- St&PR 91
Markowitz, David Jeffrey 1953- BiDrAPA 89
Markowitz, Edwin R. 1930- St&PR 91
Markowitz, Harry M. 1927- WhoAm 90
Markowitz, Irving 1914- BiDrAPA 89
Markowitz, Joel 1927- BiDrAPA 89
Markowitz, John C 1954- BiDrAPA 89, WhoE 91
Markowitz, Lewis Harrison 1933- WhoE 91
Markowitz, Marilyn WhoAmA 91
Markowitz, Mark Joel 1951- St&PR 91
Markowitz, Max BiDrAPA 89
Markowitz, Michael BioIn 16
Markowitz, Victor 1887-1979 BioIn 16
Markowski, Benedict Stephen 1932- WhoWrEP 89
Markowski, Eugene David 1931- WhoAmA 91, WhoE 91
Markowski, Michael A. 1947- WhoWrEP 89
Markowski, Michael Anthony 1947- WhoEmL 91
Markowsky, James J. St&PR 91
Marks Brothers, The OxCCanT
Marks, Ada Greiner 1896- WhoWrEP 89
Marks, Alan D. 1955- St&PR 91
Marks, Alan Norman BiDrAPA 89
Marks, Albert Aubrey, Jr. BioIn 16
Marks, Albert Aubrey, Jr. 1912- St&PR 91
Marks, Arnold 1912- WhoAm 90
Marks, Arthur 1920- WhoE 91, WhoWor 91
Marks, Barbara Hannah 1956- WhoAmW 91
Marks, Barbara Hanzel 1955- St&PR 91, WhoAm 90
Marks, Beatrice Glass WhoAmW 91
Marks, Ben 1907- BiDrAPA 89
Marks, Bernard Bailin 1917- WhoAm 90
Marks, Bruce 1937- WhoAm 90, WhoE 91
Marks, Burton 1930- BioIn 16
Marks, C. Caldwell 1921- St&PR 91
Marks, Carolyn Ann 1945- WhoAmW 91
Marks, Cedric H WhoAmA 91
Marks, Cedric H, Mrs WhoAmA 91
Marks, Charles 1922- WhoAm 90
Marks, Charles Caldwell 1921- WhoAm 90
Marks, Charles Preston 1941- WhoSSW 91
Marks, Claude 1915- WhoAmA 91, WhoE 91
Marks, Craig 1929- WhoAm 90
Marks, David 1945- ConAu 132
Marks, David Hunter 1939- WhoAm 90
Marks, David Jackson 1951- WhoSSW 91
Marks, David Michael 1961- WhoE 91
Marks, Dennis Howard BioIn 16
Marks, Dorothy Lind 1900- WhoAmW 91, WhoWor 91
Marks, Dorothy Louise Ames 1919- WhoAm 90
Marks, Edward B. 1865-1944 BioIn 16
Marks, Edwin S. 1926- WhoAm 90
Marks, Elaine 1930- WhoAm 90
Marks, Elizabeth L 1952- BiDrAPA 89
Marks, Frances 1956- WhoE 91
Marks, Francis A. 1934- St&PR 91
Marks, Frank Henry 1898- WhoWrEP 89
Marks, Gary 1948- St&PR 91
Marks, Geoffrey 1906- AuBYP 90
Marks, George B 1923-1983 WhoAmA 91N
Marks, Gerald 1925- WhoAm 90, WhoE 91
Marks, Gordon William 1944- St&PR 91
Marks, Graham PenDiDA 89
Marks, Hayley BiDrAPA 89
Marks, Henry M. 1938- WhoSSW 91
Marks, Henry Thomas 1908- WhoAm 90
Marks, Herbert Edward 1935- WhoAm 90
Marks, Howard Lee 1929- WhoE 91
Marks, Ila Circle 1932- WhoSSW 91
Marks, Jack A 1926- BiDrAPA 89
Marks, James MacDonald 1921- AuBYP 90
Marks, Jane S 1945- BiDrAPA 89
Marks, Janet Lynn 1963- WhoAmW 91
Marks, Janice Elizabeth 1960- WhoAmW 91
Marks, Jeannette A. 1875-1964 BioAmW
Marks, Jerome 1931- WhoAm 90
Marks, Joan 1932- St&PR 91
Marks, Joel E. 1956- St&PR 91
Marks, John Henry 1923- WhoAm 90
Marks, John Henry 1925- WhoWor 91
Marks, Johnny 1909- IntWWM 90
Marks, Johnny 1909-1985 OxCPMus
Marks, Jonathan Paul 1958- WhoWor 91
Marks, Judith Francine 1947- WhoAmW 91
Marks, Kenneth Jay 1957- BiDrAPA 89
Marks, Lawrence BioIn 16
Marks, Leonard, Jr. 1921- WhoAm 90
Marks, Leonard Harold 1916- WhoAm 90
Marks, Lillian Shapiro 1907- WhoAmW 91
Marks, Lynn Wilson 1955- WhoAmW 91
Marks, Malvin 1931- St&PR 91
Marks, Marjorie ConAu 132
Marks, Matthew Stuart 1962- WhoAmA 91, WhoE 91
Marks, Meyer Benjamin 1907- WhoAm 90, WhoSSW 91, WhoWor 91
Marks, Michael G. 1931- St&PR 91
Marks, Michael George 1931- WhoAm 90
Marks, Michael J. 1938- WhoAm 90
Marks, Michel David 1949- WhoAm 90
Marks, Mickey Klar 1914- AuBYP 90
Marks, Mitchell 1940- St&PR 91
Marks, Morton 1918- BiDrAPA 89
Marks, Neville Sydney 1939- BiDrAPA 89
Marks, Paul 1920- St&PR 91
Marks, Paul Alan 1926- WhoAm 90, WhoWor 91
Marks, Peter AuBYP 90
Marks, Peter C. 1942- St&PR 91
Marks, Ramon Paul 1948- WhoEmL 91
Marks, Randolph Anthony 1935- St&PR 91
Marks, Raymond H. 1922- WhoAm 90
Marks, Richard C. 1937- St&PR 91
Marks, Richard M 1935- BiDrAPA 89
Marks, Richard Samuel 1937- St&PR 91
Marks, Rita 1938- BioIn 16
Marks, Robert Bosler 1953- WhoE 91
Marks, Robert Carl 1948- BiDrAPA 89
Marks, Roberta Barbara WhoAmA 91, WhoAmW 91

Marks, Royal S 1927-1987 *WhoAmA 91N*
Marks, Russell Edward, Jr. 1932- *WhoAm 90*
Marks, Russell Howard *BiDrAPA 89*
Marks, Ruth Antoinette 1920- *WhoWrEP 89*
Marks, Sheila Hoffman *WhoAmW 91*
Marks, Sherwin J. 1948- *St&PR 91*
Marks, Stan *ConAu 31NR*
Marks, Stan M. 1946- *St&PR 91*
Marks, Stephanie Lyn 1958- *WhoAmW 91*
Marks, Stephen Paul 1943- *WhoE 91*
Marks, Steven L. 1935- *St&PR 91*
Marks, Susan Jane 1954- *WhoAmW 91*
Marks, Tamara Elizabeth 1962- *WhoAmW 91*
Marks, Theodore Lee 1935- *WhoE 91, WhoWor 91*
Marks, Thomas 1834-1900 *DcCanB 12*
Marks, Tobin Jay 1944- *WhoAm 90*
Marks, Victoria *BioIn 16*
Marks, William Louis 1933- *St&PR 91*
Marks-Brown, Shirley F *BiDrAPA 89*
Marksheid, Jay Dennis 1946- *WhoE 91*
Markson, David M. 1927- *WhoWrEP 89*
Markson, Eileen 1939- *WhoAmA 91*
Markson, John W 1919- *BiDrAPA 89*
Markson, Mitchell *ODwPR 91*
Markson, Peter 1962- *St&PR 91*
Markstein, George 1929-1987 *SpyFic*
Markstrom, Wilbur Jack 1930- *WhoAm 90*
Markum, Louise Steele 1937- *WhoSSW 91*
Markun, Frank O. 1947- *WhoEmL 91, WhoSSW 91*
Markun, Patricia 1924- *AuBYP 90*
Markun, Patricia Maloney 1924- *WhoAm 90, WhoWrEP 89*
Markus, David 1942- *St&PR 91*
Markus, Fred H. 1927- *St&PR 91*
Markus, Henry A *WhoAmA 91N*
Markus, James S. 1947- *St&PR 91*
Markus, Joel Seth 1950- *WhoEmL 91*
Markus, Joseph Francis 1952- *WhoEmL 91, WhoSSW 91, WhoWor 91*
Markus, Julia *WhoWrEP 89*
Markus, Lawrence 1922- *WhoAm 90*
Markus, Manfred Wilhelm 1941- *WhoWor 91*
Markus, N.W., Jr. 1925- *St&PR 91*
Markus, Norbert Williams, Jr. 1925- *WhoAm 90*
Markus, Richard M. 1930- *WhoAm 90*
Markus, Robert Michael 1934- *WhoAm 90*
Markusen, Thomas Roy 1940- *WhoAmA 91*
Markusson, Sigthor Halldor 1965- *WhoEmL 91*
Markuszka, Nancy Ann 1951- *WhoAmW 91*
Markwald, Roger R. 1943- *WhoAm 90*
Markward, Charles Gale 1924- *BiDrAPA 89*
Markward, Edward Walter 1944- *IntWWM 90*
Markwardt, Kenneth M. 1928- *St&PR 91*
Markwardt, Kenneth Marvin 1928- *WhoAm 90*
Markwell, Dick Robert 1925- *WhoSSW 91*
Markwell, Kenneth, Jr. 1923- *St&PR 91*
Markwick, Betty 1933- *EncPaPR 91*
Marla, Rozka Korczak- 1921-1988 *BioIn 16*
Marlan, Lori J. 1957- *WhoAmW 91*
Marland, Alkis Joseph 1943- *WhoE 91, WhoWor 91*
Marland, Dorothy Margaret *WhoAmW 91*
Marlar, John Thomas 1939- *WhoSSW 91*
Marlas, James C. 1937- *St&PR 91*
Marlas, James Constantine 1937- *WhoAm 90, WhoWor 91*
Marlatt, Daphne 1942- *BioIn 16, FemiCLE*
Marlatt, Edward Thomas 1941- *St&PR 91*
Marlatt, Jerry Ronald 1942- *WhoSSW 91*
Marlborough, Donald John 1936- *St&PR 91*
Marlborough, Sarah, Duchess of 1660-1744 *FemiCLE*
Marlborough, Sarah Churchill, Duchess of 1660-1744 *BioIn 16*
Marleau, Diane 1943- *WhoAmW 91*
Marleau, Guy Georges 1951- *St&PR 91*
Marleau, Robert 1948- *WhoAm 90*
Marlef, Claude 1864-1922? *BiDWomA*
Marlen, James S. 1941- *WhoAm 90*
Marlenee, Ronald Charles 1935- *WhoAm 90*
Marler, Bob, Jr. 1942- *St&PR 91*
Marler, Kerry Francis 1948- *WhoWor 91*
Marler, Linda Susan 1951- *WhoAmW 91*
Marler, Timothy Greville 1957- *WhoE 91*
Marlett, Charles D. 1954- *St&PR 91*
Marlett, De Otis Loring 1911- *WhoAm 90, WhoWor 91*
Marlett, Eugene Byrns 1927- *St&PR 91*
Marlett, Judith Ann *WhoAmW 91*
Marlette, Doug 1949- *BioIn 16, EncACom*
Marlette, Douglas Nigel 1949- *WhoAm 90, WhoE 91*
Marletto, Janet Cheryl 1946- *WhoAmW 91*
Marley, Anne Harder 1959- *WhoEmL 91*
Marley, Bob 1945-1981 *DrBIPA 90, EncPR&S 89, OxCPMus, WorAlBi*
Marley, David Alexander 1941- *WhoSSW 91*
Marley, Elfriede 1943- *WhoAmW 91*
Marley, Everett Armistead, Jr. 1933- *WhoAm 90, WhoSSW 91*
Marley, James Earl 1935- *St&PR 91, WhoAm 90, WhoE 91*
Marley, Kemper, Sr. *NewYTBS 90*
Marley, Mary Louise 1923- *WhoAmW 91, WhoE 91, WhoWor 91*
Marley, Ziggy *BioIn 16, EncPR&S 89*
Marley, Ziggy 1968- *News 90 [port]*
Marlin, Joanne 1955- *ODwPR 91*
Marlin, John Tepper 1942- *WhoE 91, WhoWor 91*
Marlin, Kenneth Brian 1950- *St&PR 91*
Marlin, Richard 1933- *WhoAm 90, WhoWor 91*
Marlin, Robert M. *St&PR 91*
Marlin, Therese Rose 1938- *WhoAmW 91*
Marling, Jack *BioIn 16*
Marling-George, Lisa 1964- *WhoAmW 91*
Marlink, Pamela Reeves *BiDrAPA 89*
Marlitt, Eugenie 1825-1887 *EncCoWW*
Marlor, Clark Strang 1922- *WhoAmA 91, WhoE 91*
Marlow, Bruce W. 1949- *WhoAm 90*
Marlow, Christopher 1564-1593 *WorAlBi*
Marlow, Herbert David, Jr. 1955- *St&PR 91*
Marlow, Michael F. 1947- *St&PR 91*
Marlow, Orval Lee, II 1956- *WhoEmL 91*
Marlow, Richard 1921- *St&PR 91*
Marlow, Robert Weyburn 1952- *St&PR 91*
Marlow, Thomas A., II 1933- *St&PR 91*
Marlowe, Christopher 1564-1593 *BioIn 16*
Marlowe, Dan J 1914- *TwCCr&M 91*
Marlowe, Derek 1938- *TwCCr&M 91*
Marlowe, Dick 1929-1968 *Ballpl 90*
Marlowe, Edward 1935- *St&PR 91, WhoAm 90*
Marlowe, Howard David 1943- *WhoAm 90*
Marlowe, Hugh *ConAu 33NR, MajTwCW, TwCCr&M 91*
Marlowe, Jeanne 1942- *WhoWrEP 89*
Marlowe, Julia 1865?-1950 *BioIn 16*
Marlowe, Julia 1866-1950 *BioAmW, NotWoAT*
Marlowe, Nina D *BiDrAPA 89*
Marlowe, Stephen *AuBYP 90*
Marlowe, Stephen 1928- *TwCCr&M 91*
Marlowe, Theresa 1957- *ConTFT 8 [port]*
Marmaduke, John H. 1947- *WhoSSW 91*
Marmanda, Marvin V. 1929- *WhoSSW 91*
Marmas, James Gust 1929- *WhoAm 90*
Marmash, B.V. 1937- *St&PR 91*
Marmaud, John Edmund 1961- *WhoE 91*
Marmer, Ellen Lucille 1939- *WhoAmW 91, WhoE 91*
Marmer, Stephen Seth *BiDrAPA 89*
Marmet, Gottlieb John 1946- *WhoWor 91*
Marmet, Paul 1932- *WhoAm 90*
Marmey, Jacques 1906-1988 *BioIn 16*
Marmion, Columba 1858-1923 *BioIn 16*
Marmion, Shackerley 1603-1639 *BioIn 16*
Marmion, Sheila *ODwPR 91*
Marmion, William Henry 1907- *WhoAm 90*
Marmitt, William E. *St&PR 91*
Marmo, Joseph 1931- *St&PR 91*
Marmol, Jose 1817-1871 *BioIn 16*
Marmol, Miguel 1905- *BioIn 16*
Marmon, Dennis Carl 1949- *WhoEmL 91, WhoSSW 91*
Marmon, Owen H. 1923- *St&PR 91*
Marmon, Owen Holloway 1923- *WhoAm 90*
Marmon, Robert Allen 1944- *St&PR 91*
Marmor, Debra Susan 1958- *WhoAmW 91*
Marmor, Judd 1910- *BiDrAPA 89, WhoAm 90*
Marmor, Michael Franklin 1941- *WhoAm 90*
Marmor, Robert R. 1926- *St&PR 91*
Marmorstein, Harry John 1954- *WhoE 91*
Marnell, Anthony Austin, II 1949- *WhoAm 90*
Marnell, Joseph Philip 1948- *BiDrAPA 89*
Marnell, Marjorie Ann 1954- *WhoAmW 91*
Marner, Eugene 1936- *WhoE 91*
Marnhout, Michael 1950- *WhoSSW 91*
Marnitz, Bradley Lloyd 1953- *WhoSSW 91*
Marohn, Ann Elizabeth 1946- *WhoAmW 91*
Marohn, Richard C 1934- *BiDrAPA 89*
Marohn, William D. 1940- *St&PR 91*
Marois, Harriet Sukoneck 1945- *WhoAmW 91*
Marokvia, Mireille 1918- *AuBYP 90*
Marol, Jean-Claude 1946- *ConAu 130*
Marolakos, Laura *BioIn 16*
Marold, Allen D. 1940- *St&PR 91*
Marold, David William 1947- *WhoEmL 91*
Marold, F. 1925- *St&PR 91*
Marolda, Anthony Joseph 1939- *St&PR 91*
Marolda, Robert L. 1950- *St&PR 91*
Marolen, Daniel *BioIn 16*
Maron, Jeffrey 1949- *WhoAmA 91*
Maron, Melvin Earl 1924- *WhoAm 90*
Maron, Monika 1941- *EncCoWW*
Maronde, Robert Francis 1920- *WhoAm 90, WhoWor 91*
Maroney, Dalton 1947- *WhoAmA 91*
Maroney, Denman Fowler 1949- *IntWWM 90*
Maroney, James H, Jr 1943- *WhoAmA 91*
Maroni, Paul L. 1947- *St&PR 91*
Maroof, Shaheda Fatima *BiDrAPA 89*
Maroon, Fred J. 1924- *ConAu 132*
Maros, Miklos 1943- *IntWWM 90*
Maroscher, Betty Jean 1934- *WhoAmW 91*
Marosits, Robert J. 1942- *St&PR 91*
Marot, Daniel 1663?-1752 *BioIn 16, PenDiDA 89*
Marothy, Janos 1925- *IntWWM 90*
Marothy-Soltesova, Elena 1855-1939 *EncCoWW*
Marotta, Carmine A. 1927- *St&PR 91*
Marotta, Charles Anthony *BiDrAPA 89*
Marotta, George 1926- *ODwPR 91*
Marotta, Joseph Thomas 1926- *WhoAm 90*
Marotta, Lynne Marie 1959- *WhoE 91*
Marotta, Nicholas Gene 1929- *St&PR 91*
Marotta, Priscilla Valerie 1946- *WhoAmW 91*
Marotta, Richard Nathan 1941- *WhoWor 91*
Marotta, Robert Paul 1956- *WhoE 91*
Marotta, Rocco F. *BiDrAPA 89*
Marotta, Thomas S. 1943- *St&PR 91*
Marotz, Guenter Werner 1930- *WhoWor 91*
Marouf, Taha Muhyiddin 1924- *WhoWor 91*
Maroulis, Seung S Han 1933- *BiDrAPA 89*
Maroun, Joseph Ernest 1929- *St&PR 91*
Marous, John C. *BioIn 16*
Marous, John Charles, Jr. 1925- *WhoAm 90, WhoE 91*
Marovitz, Abraham Lincoln 1905- *WhoAm 90*
Marovitz, James Lee 1939- *WhoAm 90*
Marozas, Robert J 1935- *BiDrAPA 89*
Marozia Crescentii *WomWR*
Marozsan, John Robert 1941- *WhoAm 90*
Marozzi, Eli Raphael 1913- *WhoAmA 91*
Marple, Dorothy Jane 1926- *WhoAm 90*
Marple, Elaine Noel 1951- *WhoAmW 91*
Marple, Gary Andre 1937- *WhoE 91*
Marple, Mary Lynn 1951- *WhoSSW 91*
Marquand, J. P. 1893-1960 *WorAlBi*
Marquand, John P 1893-1960 *DcLB 102 [port], TwCCr&M 91*
Marquand, John Phillips 1893-1960 *SpyFic*
Marquard, Jean 1942-1984 *FemiCLE*
Marquard, Michael John 1948- *WhoE 91*
Marquard, Rube 1889-1980 *Ballpl 90 [port], BioIn 16*
Marquard, William A., Jr. 1920- *St&PR 91*
Marquard, William Albert 1920- *WhoSSW 91*
Marquardt, Christel Elisabeth 1935- *WhoAm 90, WhoAmW 91*
Marquardt, Diana Lee 1954- *WhoAmW 91*
Marquardt, Frederic Sylvester 1905- *WhoAm 90*
Marquardt, James Edward 1935- *BiDrAPA 89*
Marquardt, Kathleen Patricia 1944- *WhoAmW 91, WhoWor 91*
Marquardt, Richard George 1935- *WhoAm 90*
Marquardt, Terry Tyrone 1949- *WhoWor 91*
Marquardt, Thomas E. *St&PR 91*
Marquardt, Thomas James 1945- *WhoEmL 91*
Marquardt, Wendy M. *BioIn 16*
Marquart, Robert Donald 1953- *St&PR 91*
Marquart, Stephen W. *ODwPR 91*
Marques, Diane Marie 1958- *WhoAmW 91*
Marques, Jose Ferreira 1936- *WhoWor 91*
Marques, Rene 1919-1979 *BioIn 16, HispWr 90*
Marques, Walter Waldemar Pego 1936- *WhoWor 91*
Marques Mendes, Antonio Jose 1952- *WhoWor 91*
Marquess, Lawrence Wade 1950- *WhoEmL 91*
Marquess, William H. 1918- *St&PR 91*
Marquet, Adrien Theodore Ernest 1884-1955 *BiDFrPL*
Marquet, Louis C. 1936- *St&PR 91*
Marquets, Anne de 1533-1588 *EncCoWW*
Marquette, Jacques 1637-1675 *EncCRAm [port], WhNaAH, WorAlBi*
Marquette, Robert, Jr. 1931- *St&PR 91*
Marquez, Alfredo C. 1922- *WhoAm 90*
Marquez, Camilo Raoul 1942- *BiDrAPA 89*
Marquez, Enrique 1952- *WhoHisp 91*
Marquez, Francisco Javier *BiDrAPA 89*
Marquez, Francisco Javier 1947- *WhoHisp 91*
Marquez, Gabriel Garcia *HispWr 90*
Marquez, Gabriel Garcia 1928- *BioIn 16*
Marquez, Jesus N. 1950- *WhoAm 90*
Marquez, Leo 1932- *BioIn 16, WhoHisp 91*
Marquez, Lorenzo Antonio, Jr. 1940- *WhoHisp 91*
Marquez, Maria D. 1931- *WhoHisp 91*
Marquez, Pascual Gregory 1937- *WhoHisp 91*
Marquez, Rafael Benito 1938- *WhoSSW 91*
Marquez, Synthia Laura 1963- *WhoAmW 91*
Marquez-Cuervo, Jose A. *BiDrAPA 89*
Marquez-Floyd, Estelita P *BiDrAPA 89*
Marquez-Villanueva, Francisco 1931- *WhoHisp 91*
Marquinez-Castellanos, Ana *BiDrAPA 89*
Marquirt, Franz *PenDiDA 89*
Marquis, Don 1878-1937 *BioIn 16*
Marquis, Donald 1878-1937 *WorAlBi*
Marquis, Elizabeth *BiDrAPA 89*
Marquis, Geraldine Mae Hildreth *WhoWor 91*
Marquis, Harold Holliday, Jr. 1928- *WhoAm 90*
Marquis, Henrietta L 1907- *BiDrAPA 89*
Marquis, Janet 1948- *WhoAmW 91*
Marquis, Jeanne Lorraine 1953- *WhoAmW 91*
Marquis, Joshua Kai 1952- *WhoEmL 91*
Marquis, Ken *BioIn 16*
Marquis, Maynard Laurier *BiDrAPA 89*
Marquis, Richard 1945- *BioIn 16, WhoAmA 91*
Marquis, Robert 1944- *ODwPR 91*
Marquis, Robert B. 1927- *WhoAm 90*
Marquis, Robert William 1949- *BiDrAPA 89*
Marquis, Rollin Park 1925- *WhoAm 90*
Marr, Carmel Carrington 1921- *WhoAm 90*
Marr, Clinton, Jr. 1925- *WhoAm 90*
Marr, Daniel F., Jr. 1931- *St&PR 91*
Marr, David Francis 1933- *WhoAm 90*
Marr, David Franklin 1953- *WhoEmL 91, WhoSSW 91*
Marr, Donald W. 1948- *St&PR 91*
Marr, John Albert 1931- *WhoSSW 91*
Marr, John S. 1940- *BioIn 16*
Marr, Luther R. 1925- *St&PR 91*
Marr, Luther Reese 1925- *WhoAm 90*
Marr, Patricia *BioIn 16*
Marr, Peter 1936- *IntWWM 90*
Marr, Richard Arnold 1936- *St&PR 91*
Marr, Robert Bruce 1932- *WhoAm 90*
Marr, Robert L. 1936- *St&PR 91*
Marr, Rose Marie 1943- *WhoAmW 91*
Marr, Walter L. 1865-1941 *EncABHB 4 [port]*
Marra, Dorothea Catherine 1922- *WhoAmW 91*
Marra, Frank S. 1927- *St&PR 91*
Marra, Michael Robert 1933- *St&PR 91*
Marra, Peter Gerald 1940- *WhoWor 91*
Marra, Ralph Vincent 1937- *St&PR 91*
Marrable, Madeline Frances 1833?-1916 *BiDWomA*
Marrack, John Richardson 1886-1976 *DcScB S2*
Marran, James Emery 1940- *St&PR 91*
Marran, Ray J. *AuBYP 90*
Marranca, Bonnie *BioIn 16*
Marranca, Bonnie 1947- *NotWoAT*
Marrano, Anthony B. 1947- *St&PR 91*
Marrazzo, William J. 1949- *St&PR 91*
Marren, Bernard T. 1935- *St&PR 91*
Marrero, Ana R 1913- *BiDrAPA 89*
Marrero, Charles A. 1942- *WhoHisp 91*
Marrero, Connie 1917- *Ballpl 90*
Marrero, Dilka E. 1961- *WhoHisp 91*
Marrero, Ernesto Rafael *BiDrAPA 89*
Marrero, Magaly Victoria 1952- *WhoAmW 91*
Marrero, Manuel 1954- *WhoHisp 91*
Marrero, Robert Lucien 1953- *WhoSSW 91*
Marrero-Favreau, Gloria 1948- *WhoHisp 91*
Marrero-Figarella, Arturo L 1953- *BiDrAPA 89*
Marrian, Guy Frederic 1904-1981 *DcNaB 1981*
Marric, J.J. *MajTwCW*

Marric, J. J. *TwCCr&M 91*
Marrie, Thomas Phillip 1938- *St&PR 91*
Marrin, Albert 1936- *BioIn 16, ConAu 30NR*
Marrinan, Susan Faye 1948- *WhoAmW 91*
Marrinan, William Keating 1925- *St&PR 91*
Marriner, David R. 1934- *St&PR 91*
Marriner, David Richard 1934- *WhoAm 90*
Marriner, Neville 1924- *BioIn 16, IntWWM 90, PenDiMP, WhoAm 90, WhoWor 91*
Marringa, Jacques Louis 1928- *St&PR 91, WhoAm 90*
Marriot, Emil *EncCoWW*
Marriott Family *BioIn 16*
Marriott, Alice Lee 1910- *AuBYP 90*
Marriott, Alice Sheets 1907- *St&PR 91, WhoAm 90*
Marriott, Bill 1893-1969 *Ballpl 90*
Marriott, Bubba 1938- *St&PR 91*
Marriott, Charles Handel Rand 1831-1889 *OxCPMus*
Marriott, David M. 1943- *ODwPR 91*
Marriott, J. Willard 1932- *BioIn 16*
Marriott, J. Willard, Jr. 1932- *St&PR 91*
Marriott, John 1893-1977 *DrBIPA 90*
Marriott, John W. 1900-1985 *WorAlBi*
Marriott, John W., Jr. 1932- *WhoAm 90, WhoE 91*
Marriott, Joyce Anne 1913- *FemiCLE*
Marriott, Richard Edwin 1939- *St&PR 91, WhoAm 90*
Marriott, Terrez S. 1961- *WhoAmW 91*
Marriott, William Allen 1942- *WhoAmA 91*
Marriott, William S. *EncO&P 3*
Marro, Anthony James 1942- *WhoE 91*
Marro, Joseph R. *BioIn 16*
Marro, Stephen R. 1947- *St&PR 91*
Marrocco, William Thomas 1909- *IntWWM 90*
Marron, Catie *BioIn 16*
Marron, Darlene Lorraine 1946- *WhoAmW 91*
Marron, Donald B. *BioIn 16*
Marron, Donald B. 1934- *St&PR 91, WhoAmA 91*
Marron, Donald Baird 1934- *WhoE 91*
Marron, Joan 1934- *WhoAmA 91*
Marrone, Daniel Scott 1950- *WhoE 91*
Marrone, Michael John 1942- *St&PR 91*
Marrone, Steven P 1947- *ConAu 130*
Marroquin, Armando, Jr. 1940- *WhoSSW 91*
Marroquin, Patricia *AuBYP 90*
Marroquin, Patricia 1957- *WhoHisp 91*
Marroquin, Samuel Najar 1932- *WhoHisp 91*
Marrow, Dorothy Combellack 1937- *WhoAmW 91, WhoE 91*
Marrow, Elizabeth *BiDEWW*
Marrow, James Henry 1941- *WhoAmA 91*
Marrow, Marva Jan 1948- *WhoEmL 91*
Marrow, Patricia L *BiDrAPA 89*
Marrs, Barbara Jeanne 1943- *WhoAmW 91*
Marrs, Dean Jeffery 1956- *WhoSSW 91*
Marrs, Doyle G. *WhoAm 90*
Marrs, Richard E. *WhoAm 90*
Marrs, Richard Preston 1947- *WhoAm 90*
Marrs, Stella 1932- *DrBIPA 90*
Marrujo, Ralph *WhoHisp 91*
Marrus, Allan J. *WhoE 91*
Marrus, Rick 1915- *St&PR 91*
Marryat, Florence 1837-1899 *EncO&P 3*
Marryat, Florence 1838-1899 *BioIn 16, FemiCLE*
Marryat, Frederick 1792-1848 *BioIn 16*
Marryshow, Terry *BioIn 16*
Marryshow, Theophilus Albert 1887-1958 *BioIn 16*
Mars, Audrey *BioIn 16*
Mars, Ethel 1876-1956? *BiDWomA*
Mars, Forrest E., Sr. *WhoSSW 91*
Mars, Forrest Edward, Sr. 1904- *ConAmBL*
Mars, Gerald 1933- *ConAu 132*
Mars, Henri-Claude 1925- *WhoWor 91*
Mars, Jacques 1926- *IntWWM 90*
Mars, Louis *BiDrAPA 89*
Mars, Louis 1906- *EncO&P 3*
Mars, Robert S., Jr. 1926- *St&PR 91*
Marsac, Peter L. 1943- *St&PR 91*
Marsal, Bryan P. *WhoSSW 91*
Marsal, Jacques *BioIn 16*
Marsalek, Lawrence Fredrick 1938- *St&PR 91*
Marsalis, Branford *BioIn 16*
Marsalis, Branford 1960- *DrBIPA 90, PenDiMP, WhoAm 90*
Marsalis, Wynton *BioIn 16*
Marsalis, Wynton 1961- *DrBIPA 90, IntWWM 90, OxCPMus, PenDiMP, WhoAm 90, WorAlBi*
Marsan, Jean-Claude 1938- *WhoAm 90*
Marsans, Armando 1887-1960 *Ballpl 90*
Marsar, Joseph R., Jr. 1953- *St&PR 91*
Marschalk, William John 1944- *St&PR 91*
Marschall, Charles J. 1939- *St&PR 91*
Marschel, C. Thomas 1945- *St&PR 91*
Marsching, Ronald 1927- *St&PR 91*
Marsching, Ronald Lionel 1927- *WhoAm 90*
Marschner, Heinrich August 1795-1861 *PenDiMP A*
Marschner, Wolfgang 1926- *IntWWM 90*
Marscot, Ann *WhoWrEP 89*
Marsden, Brian Geoffrey 1937- *WhoAm 90*
Marsden, Brian William H. 1932- *St&PR 91*
Marsden, Charles Joseph 1940- *St&PR 91, WhoAm 90*
Marsden, Ernest 1889-1970 *DcScB S2*
Marsden, Guy Talbot 1955- *WhoEmL 91*
Marsden, Herci Ivana 1937- *WhoE 91*
Marsden, James *MajTwCW*
Marsden, Lawrence Albert 1919- *WhoAm 90*
Marsden, Michael H E 1904- *WhoAmA 91*
Marsden, Richard Anton 1966- *WhoE 91*
Marsden Thomas, Anne 1948- *IntWWM 90*
Marse, Juan 1933- *IntvSpW [port]*
Marsee, Stuart 1917- *WhoAm 90*
Marsee, Susanne Irene 1941- *WhoAm 90*
Marseen, Ulrike 1912- *BiDWomA*
Marsella, Donna Laura 1952- *St&PR 91*
Marsella, Gregory Quentin *BiDrAPA 89*
Marsh & Jones *PenDiDA 89*
Marsh, Alan Christopher 1948- *St&PR 91*
Marsh, Alfred F. 1930- *St&PR 91*
Marsh, Alvin 1834- *AmLegL*
Marsh, Alvin Charles, Jr. 1925- *St&PR 91*
Marsh, Anna Louise 1952- *WhoE 91*
Marsh, Anne 1791-1874 *FemiCLE*
Marsh, Anne Steele 1901- *WhoAmA 91*
Marsh, Archaleus D. 1844- *AmLegL*
Marsh, Benjamin Franklin 1927- *WhoAm 90*
Marsh, Brian Richard 1948- *WhoE 91*
Marsh, Bruce David 1947- *WhoE 91*
Marsh, Burton Wallace 1898-1988 *BioIn 16*
Marsh, Carole 1946- *WhoWrEP 89*
Marsh, Caryl Amsterdam 1923- *WhoAm 90*
Marsh, Chares Russell, Jr. 1924- *St&PR 91*
Marsh, Charles Alan 1941- *St&PR 91, WhoAm 90*
Marsh, Charles F *BiDrAPA 89*
Marsh, Cheryl Lynn 1950- *St&PR 91*
Marsh, Claire Coverdale *BiDrAPA 89*
Marsh, Clare Teitgen 1934- *WhoAmW 91*
Marsh, Colleen Beth Meylor 1957- *WhoAmW 91*
Marsh, Connie M 1947- *BiDrAPA 89*
Marsh, Corinna *AuBYP 90*
Marsh, Corinna 1891-1990 *ConAu 132*
Marsh, Corinna Reiman 1891-1990 *NewYTBS 90*
Marsh, Dave Rodney 1950- *WhoAm 90*
Marsh, David 1945- *WhoSSW 91*
Marsh, David Foster 1926- *WhoAmA 91*
Marsh, David John 1950- *BiDrAPA 89*
Marsh, David O. 1927- *WhoAm 90*
Marsh, Don E. 1938- *St&PR 91, WhoAm 90*
Marsh, Don Seagle 1927- *WhoAm 90*
Marsh, Donald B. 1950- *St&PR 91*
Marsh, Donald Jay 1934- *WhoAm 90*
Marsh, Dorothy Jane 1915- *WhoAmW 91*
Marsh, Douglas Dean 1941- *St&PR 91*
Marsh, Dwight Chaney 1932- *WhoWrEP 89*
Marsh, Earle Milliard 1911- *BiDrAPA 89*
Marsh, Elias J 1915- *BiDrAPA 89*
Marsh, Estel V. 1912- *St&PR 91*
Marsh, Florence Gertrude 1916- *WhoAm 90, WhoWrEP 89*
Marsh, Francis Patrick 1936- *WhoWor 91*
Marsh, Frank 1924- *WhoAm 90*
Marsh, Fred Dana 1872-1961 *WhoAmA 91N*
Marsh, Freddie 1924- *Ballpl 90*
Marsh, Frederick E *BiDrAPA 89*
Marsh, George Perkins 1801-1882 *BioIn 16*
Marsh, Georgia *WhoAmA 91*
Marsh, Gilbert Reid 1946- *St&PR 91*
Marsh, Harry Dean 1928- *WhoAm 90*
Marsh, Hugh *BioIn 16*
Marsh, Hugh L. *BioIn 16*
Marsh, J.J., Jr. 1925- *St&PR 91*
Marsh, James 1794-1842 *BioIn 16*
Marsh, James P. 1938- *St&PR 91*
Marsh, James W. 1947- *St&PR 91*
Marsh, Jane 1945- *IntWWM 90*
Marsh, Jean 1934- *WorAlBi*
Marsh, Jean Lyndsey Torren 1934- *WhoAm 90*
Marsh, Jeremiah 1933- *WhoAm 90*
Marsh, Jeri 1940- *SmATA X*
Marsh, Jesse 1907-1966 *EncACom*
Marsh, Joan Knight 1934- *WhoAmW 91*
Marsh, John *PenDiDA 89*
Marsh, John O., Jr. *BioIn 16*
Marsh, John Otho, Jr. 1926- *WhoAm 90*
Marsh, John Richard 1935- *St&PR 91*
Marsh, Joseph Franklin, Jr. 1925- *WhoAm 90*
Marsh, Joseph Virgil 1952- *WhoEmL 91, WhoSSW 91, WhoWor 91*
Marsh, Judith Ann 1941- *WhoWrEP 89*
Marsh, Kerry Daniel 1944- *WhoE 91*
Marsh, Kevin B. 1955- *St&PR 91*
Marsh, Laura 1959- *BiDrAPA 89*
Marsh, Leonard W. 1945- *St&PR 91*
Marsh, Loralee *BiDrAPA 89*
Marsh, Malcolm Roy, Jr. 1932- *WhoSSW 91*
Marsh, Marcus Marlene 1948- *WhoEmL 91*
Marsh, Marianne *BiDrAPA 89*
Marsh, Marvin I *BiDrAPA 89*
Marsh, Mary Elizabeth 1949- *WhoAmW 91*
Marsh, Mary Val 1925- *IntWWM 90*
Marsh, Maurice Clement 1922- *EncO&P 3*
Marsh, Melinda Ray 1943- *WhoE 91*
Marsh, Michele Robin *BiDrAPA 89*
Marsh, Miles L. *WhoAm 90*
Marsh, Milton R. W. 1945- *IntWWM 90*
Marsh, Nelson Leroy 1937- *WhoSSW 91*
Marsh, Ngaio 1895-1982 *TwCCr&M 91*
Marsh, Ngaio 1899-1982 *AuBYP 90, BioIn 16, DcNaB 1981, FemiCLE, MajTwCW, WorAlBi*
Marsh, Norman James 1936- *St&PR 91*
Marsh, Othniel C. 1831-1899 *WorAlBi*
Marsh, Pamela Alison 1954- *WhoEmL 91*
Marsh, Peter William 1945- *WhoE 91*
Marsh, Quinton Neely 1915- *WhoAm 90*
Marsh, R. Bruce 1929- *WhoAm 90*
Marsh, Ralph 1928- *St&PR 91*
Marsh, Reginald 1898-1954 *WhoAmA 91N*
Marsh, Richard B. 1926- *St&PR 91*
Marsh, Richard Ken 1945- *WhoSSW 91*
Marsh, Richard Philip 1961- *WhoWrEP 89*
Marsh, Robert Charles 1924- *IntWWM 90, WhoAm 90, WhoWor 91*
Marsh, Robert James 1954- *WhoEmL 91*
Marsh, Robert Mortimer 1931- *WhoAm 90*
Marsh, Robert Wayne 1956- *IntWWM 90*
Marsh, Roger Michael 1949- *IntWWM 90*
Marsh, Rosalind *ConAu 132*
Marsh, Rosalind J 1950- *ConAu 132*
Marsh, Royden W *BiDrAPA 89*
Marsh, Ruth Lorraine 1927- *WhoE 91*
Marsh, Shepherd R. 1946- *St&PR 91, WhoSSW 91*
Marsh, Sherry S. *BioIn 16*
Marsh, Thomas 1934- *WhoAmA 91*
Marsh, Thomas A 1951- *WhoAmA 91*
Marsh, Thomas R. 1946- *St&PR 91*
Marsh, Verdell 1952- *WhoSSW 91*
Marsh, Wayne C. 1936- *St&PR 91*
Marsh, William *PenDiDA 89*
Marsh, William T. 1932- *St&PR 91*
Marsh, William W. 1915- *ODwPR 91*
Marsh-Caldwell, Anne 1791-1874 *BioIn 16*
Marsh-Edwards, Michael Richard 1928- *IntWWM 90*
Marshak, Alan Howard 1938- *WhoAm 90*
Marshak, Hilary Wallach 1950- *WhoAmW 91*
Marshak, Ilia IAkolevich 1895- *AuBYP 90*
Marshak, Marvin Lloyd 1946- *WhoAm 90*
Marshak, Robert Eugene 1916- *WhoAm 90*
Marshak, Robert Reuben 1923- *WhoAm 90*
Marshak, Rubin *BiDrAPA 89*
Marshal, Nellie Jean 1933- *WhoAmW 91*
Marshall, Al King *BiDrAPA 89*
Marshall, Alexander 1929- *St&PR 91*
Marshall, Alfred 1842-1924 *BioIn 16*
Marshall, Allen Wright, III 1941- *WhoSSW 91*
Marshall, Alton G. 1921- *St&PR 91*
Marshall, Alton Garwood 1921- *WhoAm 90*
Marshall, Alvin *BioIn 16*
Marshall, Andrew Walter 1921- *WhoE 91*
Marshall, Archibald 1866-1934 *AuBYP 90*
Marshall, Armina 1900?- *BioIn 16, NotWoAT*
Marshall, Arthur 1881-1968 *OxCPMus*
Marshall, Arthur 1910-1989 *AnObit 1989*
Marshall, Arthur K. 1911- *WhoAm 90*
Marshall, Barry James 1951- *WhoWor 91*
Marshall, Benton Hines 1923- *BiDrAPA 89*
Marshall, Beulah Marian 1929- *WhoAmW 91*
Marshall, Brenda Fran 1954- *WhoAmW 91*
Marshall, Brenda Joyce 1955- *WhoAmW 91*
Marshall, Brian Laurence 1941- *WhoE 91, WhoWor 91*
Marshall, Bruce 1929- *WhoAmA 91*
Marshall, Bryan Edward 1935- *WhoAm 90*
Marshall, Burke 1922- *St&PR 91*
Marshall, C. Travis 1926- *WhoAm 90*
Marshall, Cak 1943- *WhoAmW 91*
Marshall, Catherine *AuBYP 90*
Marshall, Catherine 1914- *WorAlBi*
Marshall, Cedric Russell 1936- *WhoWor 91*
Marshall, Charles 1929- *St&PR 91, WhoAm 90*
Marshall, Charles Burton 1908- *WhoAm 90, WhoWor 91*
Marshall, Charles Louis 1912- *WhoAm 90*
Marshall, Charles Noble 1942- *St&PR 91, WhoAm 90*
Marshall, Charlotte *ODwPR 91*
Marshall, Cheryl Lynn 1953- *St&PR 91*
Marshall, Chester R. 1952- *St&PR 91*
Marshall, Clarence Taylor 1926- *WhoAm 90*
Marshall, Claudia E. 1946- *St&PR 91*
Marshall, Clifford Wallace 1928- *WhoAm 90*
Marshall, Clyde S *BiDrAPA 89*
Marshall, Colin 1933- *WhoWor 91*
Marshall, Consuelo Bland 1936- *WhoAmW 91*
Marshall, Cuddles 1925- *Ballpl 90*
Marshall, Cynthia Louise 1956- *WhoAmW 91*
Marshall, Dana X. 1939- *WhoAm 90*
Marshall, Dave 1943- *Ballpl 90*
Marshall, David 1914- *WhoE 91, WhoWor 91*
Marshall, David Frederick 1948- *WhoE 91*
Marshall, David Lawrence 1939- *St&PR 91*
Marshall, Dean 1900- *AuBYP 90*
Marshall, Denise Jill 1965- *WhoAmW 91*
Marshall, Don 1934- *DrBIPA 90*
Marshall, Don Alfredo, Jr. *BiDrAPA 89*
Marshall, Donald Glenn 1943- *WhoAm 90*
Marshall, Donald S. 1938- *St&PR 91*
Marshall, Donald Tompkins 1933- *WhoAm 90*
Marshall, Douglas *AuBYP 90*
Marshall, Douglas A. 1948- *St&PR 91*
Marshall, E. G. 1910- *WhoAm 90, WorAlBi*
Marshall, Edison 1894-1967 *DcLB 102 [port]*
Marshall, Edmund 1938-1979 *WhoAmA 91N*
Marshall, Edward 1598-1675 *BioIn 16*
Marshall, Edward 1942- *BioIn 16*
Marshall, Elizabeth Eileen 1942- *WhoAmW 91*
Marshall, Ellen Ruth 1949- *WhoEmL 91*
Marshall, Emily *BioIn 16*
Marshall, Emma 1830-1899 *FemiCLE*
Marshall, F. Ray *WhoAm 90*
Marshall, Francis Joseph 1923- *WhoAm 90*
Marshall, Frank Lester *WhoSSW 91*
Marshall, Frank X. *St&PR 91*
Marshall, Franklin Nick 1933- *WhoAm 90*
Marshall, Freddie Ray 1928- *BiDrUSE 89*
Marshall, Frederick William, Jr. 1942- *St&PR 91*
Marshall, Garry 1934- *BioIn 16, SmATA 60 [port], WhoAm 90, WorAlBi*
Marshall, Gary Charles 1943- *WhoE 91*
Marshall, Geoffrey 1938- *WhoAm 90*
Marshall, George C. 1880-1959 *BioIn 16, WorAlBi*
Marshall, George Catlett 1880-1959 *BiDrUSE 89*
Marshall, George Dwire 1940- *St&PR 91*
Marshall, George Nichols 1920- *WhoWor 91*
Marshall, Gerald Francis 1929- *WhoAm 90*
Marshall, Gerald R. 1934- *St&PR 91*
Marshall, Gerald Robert 1934- *WhoAm 90*
Marshall, Gilly Anthony 1948- *WhoSSW 91*
Marshall, Gordon Bruce 1943- *St&PR 91, WhoAm 90*
Marshall, Greta *BioIn 16*
Marshall, Hannah *BiDEWW*
Marshall, Harold D. 1936- *WhoAm 90*
Marshall, Henry Wright 1865-1951 *AmLegL*
Marshall, Herbert 1890-1966 *WorAlBi*
Marshall, Herbert A. 1917- *WhoAm 90*
Marshall, Howard Andrew 1931- *St&PR 91*
Marshall, Howard Lowen 1931- *WhoSSW 91*
Marshall, Ingram *NewAgMG*
Marshall, Innes 1924- *WhoWor 91*

Marshall, Irl H., Jr. 1929- St&PR 91
Marshall, J D 1919- ConAu 31NR
Marshall, J. Howard, II 1905- WhoAm 90
Marshall, J. Howard, III 1936- St&PR 91
Marshall, J. Richard 1929- IntWWM 90
Marshall, Jack 1936- St&PR 91
Marshall, James AuBYP 90
Marshall, James 1941- IntWWM 90
Marshall, James 1942- AuBYP 90, BioIn 16, ChlLR 21 [port]
Marshall, James 1949- IntWWM 90
Marshall, James Arthur 1935- WhoAm 90
Marshall, James D. 1936- St&PR 91
Marshall, James Duard 1914- WhoAmA 91
Marshall, James Fowle Baldwin 1818-1891 BioIn 16
Marshall, James Kenneth 1952- WhoEmL 91
Marshall, James Sylvester 1937- WhoSSW 91
Marshall, James William 1822-1910 BiDrUSE 89
Marshall, Jay 1919- BioIn 16
Marshall, Jean McElroy 1922- WhoAm 90
Marshall, Jeanne 1945- WhoAmW 91
Marshall, Jeff AuBYP 90
Marshall, Jim 1932- Ballpl 90
Marshall, Jim 1936- BioIn 16
Marshall, Joan Holwell 1916- WhoWrEP 89
Marshall, Joanne Ellen 1954- WhoAmW 91
Marshall, John WhoAm 90, WhoSSW 91
Marshall, John BioIn 16
Marshall, John 1755-1835 BiDrUSE 89, BioIn 16, WorAlBi
Marshall, John 1913- WhoWrEP 89
Marshall, John 1957- WhoAmA 91
Marshall, John Aloysius 1928- WhoE 91
Marshall, John Carl 1936- WhoAmA 91
Marshall, John David 1940- WhoAm 90
Marshall, John E. 1945- St&PR 91
Marshall, John Elbert, III 1942- WhoAm 90
Marshall, John H. 1941- St&PR 91
Marshall, John H L BiDrAPA 89
Marshall, John Harris, Jr. 1924- WhoSSW 91, WhoWor 91
Marshall, John Henry 1949- WhoEmL 91
Marshall, John James 1955- WhoSSW 91
Marshall, John Jeffrey 1956- WhoSSW 91
Marshall, John Patrick 1950- WhoE 91, WhoWor 91
Marshall, John Paul WhoWor 91
Marshall, John Richard 1929- WhoE 91
Marshall, John Richard 1939- BiDrAPA 89
Marshall, John Treutlen 1934- WhoAm 90, WhoSSW 91
Marshall, John Wesley AmLegL
Marshall, Joseph H BiDrAPA 89
Marshall, Joseph Hartwell, III 1936- WhoSSW 91
Marshall, Joseph W. 1936- St&PR 91
Marshall, Joyce 1913- FemiCLE
Marshall, Julian Howard, Jr. 1922- WhoAm 90
Marshall, Karyn BioIn 16
Marshall, L F Woodward 1921- BiDrAPA 89
Marshall, Lane Lee 1937- WhoAm 90
Marshall, Leonard 1961- BioIn 16
Marshall, Leonard Briggs, Jr. 1932- St&PR 91
Marshall, Leslie B. 1943- WhoAmW 91
Marshall, Lester Bell 1928- WhoWor 91
Marshall, Linda Rae 1940- WhoAmW 91, WhoWor 91
Marshall, Lois 1925- IntWWM 90, PenDiMP
Marshall, Lonnie L 1953- BiDrAPA 89
Marshall, Loren Dean 1953- WhoWrEP 89
Marshall, Lowell Larry 1940- St&PR 91
Marshall, M. H. Shen 1946- WhoWor 91
Marshall, Mara 1926- WhoAmA 91
Marshall, Margaret 1949- PenDiMP
Marshall, Margaret Anne 1949- IntWWM 90
Marshall, Marguerite Mitchell 1911- WhoAmW 91
Marshall, Maria BioIn 16
Marshall, Marie Annette 1958- WhoAmW 91
Marshall, Mark S BiDrAPA 89
Marshall, Marlena BioIn 16
Marshall, Martin Vivan 1922- WhoAm 90
Marshall, Mary 1842-1884 EncO&P 3
Marshall, Mary Aydelotte 1921- WhoAmW 91
Marshall, Mary Gladys 1939- WhoSSW 91
Marshall, Mary Hewitt 1939- WhoAmW 91
Marshall, Mary Jones WhoAmW 91
Marshall, Maryan Lorraine 1940- WhoAmW 91
Marshall, Maryann Chorba 1952- WhoAmW 91
Marshall, Maryann Radke 1955- WhoSSW 91
Marshall, Maureen Greta 1921- WhoWor 91
Marshall, Max 1913- Ballpl 90
Marshall, Mel BioIn 16
Marshall, Meryl Corinblit 1949- WhoAmW 91
Marshall, Michael Borden 1957- WhoE 91
Marshall, Mike NewAgMG
Marshall, Mike 1943- Ballpl 90 [port]
Marshall, Mike 1960- Ballpl 90
Marshall, Mortimer Mercer, Jr. 1929- WhoAm 90
Marshall, Muriel WhoWrEP 89
Marshall, Myrna Estey 1938- WhoWrEP 89
Marshall, Myron H 1939- BiDrAPA 89
Marshall, Nancy Haig 1932- WhoAm 90
Marshall, Natalie Junemann 1929- WhoAm 90
Marshall, Navarre 1916- WhoAmW 91
Marshall, Nicholas 1942- IntWWM 90
Marshall, Norma Jean 1938- WhoSSW 91
Marshall, Norman Barry 1926- WhoAm 90
Marshall, Norman Sturgeon 1934- WhoAm 90
Marshall, Paul Macklin 1923- WhoAm 90
Marshall, Paule 1929- FemiCLE, MajTwCW
Marshall, Penny BioIn 16
Marshall, Penny 1943- WhoAm 90, WorAlBi
Marshall, Percy ConAu 31NR
Marshall, Peter 1902-1949 WorAlBi
Marshall, Philip Richard 1926- WhoAm 90
Marshall, Philips Williamson 1935- WhoE 91
Marshall, Philomena Ann WhoAmW 91
Marshall, Phyllis 1933- WhoAmW 91
Marshall, Phyllis Ellinwood 1929- WhoAmW 91, WhoE 91, WhoWor 91
Marshall, Quintin Gregory 1961- WhoE 91
Marshall, Ralph 1923-1984 WhoAmA 91N
Marshall, Raymond TwCCr&M 91
Marshall, Richard Carlson 1926- St&PR 91
Marshall, Richard Donald 1947- WhoAmA 91
Marshall, Richard Paul, Jr. 1949- WhoSSW 91
Marshall, Richard Treeger 1925- WhoWor 91
Marshall, Rita BioIn 16
Marshall, Rob BioIn 16
Marshall, Robert 1901-1939 BioIn 16
Marshall, Robert 1939- IntWWM 90
Marshall, Robert Charles 1931- St&PR 91, WhoAm 90
Marshall, Robert Creel 1921- WhoAm 90
Marshall, Robert Gerald 1919- WhoAm 90
Marshall, Robert Herman 1929- WhoAm 90
Marshall, Robert L. BioIn 16
Marshall, Robert Leroy 1944- WhoAmA 91
Marshall, Robert Lewis 1939- WhoAm 90
Marshall, Robert W BiDrAPA 89
Marshall, Roby BioIn 16
Marshall, Sally Ann 1942- WhoWrEP 89
Marshall, Samuel Lyman Atwood 1900-1977 AuBYP 90
Marshall, Scott WhoAm 90
Marshall, Sheila Hermes 1934- WhoAm 90
Marshall, Sherrie BioIn 16
Marshall, Shirley 1941- WhoAmW 91
Marshall, Stanley 1923- WhoAm 90
Marshall, Stirrat Andrew William Johnson 1912-1981 DcNaB 1981
Marshall, Stuart Alan 1946- WhoE 91
Marshall, Susan BioIn 16
Marshall, Susan Kay 1954- WhoSSW 91
Marshall, Susan Lockwood 1939- WhoAmW 91
Marshall, Sylvan Mitchell 1917- WhoAm 90
Marshall, Tari 1955- ODwPR 91
Marshall, Terrell 1908- WhoAm 90
Marshall, Terry Dean 1945- St&PR 91
Marshall, Theodore Henry 1902-1989 BioIn 16
Marshall, Theodore J 1930- BiDrAPA 89
Marshall, Theresa Hooper WhoE 91
Marshall, Thomas 1929- St&PR 91, WhoAm 90
Marshall, Thomas Carlisle 1935- WhoAm 90
Marshall, Thomas E 1941- WhoAmA 91
Marshall, Thomas Humphrey 1893-1981 DcNaB 1981
Marshall, Thomas Oliver, Jr. 1920- WhoAm 90, WhoSSW 91
Marshall, Thomas R. 1854-1925 WorAlBi
Marshall, Thomas Riley 1854-1925 BiDrUSE 89
Marshall, Thurgood BioIn 16
Marshall, Thurgood 1908- WhoAm 90, WhoE 91, WorAlBi
Marshall, Tom BioIn 16
Marshall, Valerie Ann 1954- WhoEmL 91
Marshall, Victor Fray 1913- WhoAm 90
Marshall, Victoria ODwPR 91
Marshall, Vincent de Paul 1943- WhoAm 90
Marshall, Vincent J 1938- BiDrAPA 89
Marshall, Wayne 1961- IntWWM 90
Marshall, Wayne Keith 1948- WhoE 91
Marshall, Wilber BioIn 16
Marshall, Willard 1921- Ballpl 90
Marshall, William BioIn 16
Marshall, William 1924- ConTFT 8, DrBlPA 90
Marshall, William 1944- TwCCr&M 91
Marshall, William, Jr. 1925- WhoAm 90
Marshall, William Edward 1925- WhoAm 90
Marshall, William Emmett 1935- WhoAm 90
Marshall, William Gene, Jr. 1953- WhoSSW 91
Marshall, William Gilbert 1946- St&PR 91, WhoAm 90
Marshall, William Jeffrey BiDrAPA 89
Marshall, William Lawrence, III 1937- St&PR 91
Marshall, William T. 1858- AmLegL
Marshall, Willis H 1936- BiDrAPA 89
Marshall, Zeenat Latif 1956- BiDrAPA 89
Marshall-Cornwall, James Handyside 1887-1985 DcNaB 1981
Marshall-Hall, Edward 1858-1927 BioIn 16
Marshall-Nadel, Nathalie 1932- WhoAmA 91, WhoAmW 91, WhoWrEP 89
Marshall-Reed, Diane 1950- WhoAmW 91
Marshall-Salomon, Gabrielle 1955- WhoE 91
Marshall-Salomon, Gabrielle S. 1955- BiDrAPA 89
Marsham, Tom 1923-1989 BioIn 16
Marshburn, Gary Howard 1952- St&PR 91
Marshman, Joan Anne 1939- WhoAm 90
Marshutz, James BioIn 16
Marsicano, Jon 1940- St&PR 91
Marsick, Martin 1848-1924 PenDiMP
Marsico, Leonard Joseph 1955- WhoEmL 91
Marsico, Theodore W. 1917- St&PR 91
Marsilius, Newman M., III 1946- St&PR 91
Marsilius, Newman M., Jr. 1918- St&PR 91
Marsilius, Philip Roger 1921- St&PR 91
Marsilius, Richard Alan 1947- St&PR 91
Marsin, M. FemiCLE
Marsini, Nicholas Michael, Jr. 1955- St&PR 91
Marso, Edward Raymond 1958- WhoEmL 91
Marsoli, Lisa Ann 1958- BioIn 16
Marson, Kenneth, Jr. 1954- St&PR 91
Marson, Kenneth Gordon, Sr. 1931- St&PR 91
Marson, Stephen Mark 1951- WhoSSW 91
Marson, Una 1905-1965 FemiCLE
Marsteller, Dudley Leonard, Jr. 1925- WhoSSW 91
Marsteller, Julie V. BioIn 16, NewYTBS 90
Marsteller, Thomas Franklin, Jr. 1951- WhoSSW 91
Marsteller, William A 1914- WhoAmA 91
Marsten, Richard MajTwCW, TwCCr&M 91
Marsters, Ann Pierce 1916- WhoAm 90
Marstiller, Phyllis 1947- St&PR 91
Marston, Alfred J. 1924-1988 BioIn 16
Marston, Alfred L. 1945- St&PR 91
Marston, Betsy BioIn 16
Marston, Charles Harold 1932- WhoE 91
Marston, Ed BioIn 16
Marston, Edgar Jean, III 1939- WhoAm 90, WhoSSW 91
Marston, Elsa 1933- ConAu 32NR
Marston, George White 1850-1946 BioIn 16
Marston, John 1575?-1634 BioIn 16
Marston, Michael 1936- WhoAm 90, WhoWor 91
Marston, Robert A. 1937- ODwPR 91
Marston, Robert Andrew 1937- WhoAm 90
Marston, Robert Quarles 1923- WhoAm 90
Marston, Ronald Clyde 1942- WhoSSW 91
Marston, William Moulton EncACom
Marston-Scott, Mary Vesta 1924- WhoAm 90
Marszalek, Georgia Ann 1946- WhoAmW 91
Marszowski, Bruno Anthony 1941- St&PR 91
Mart, Colette 1955- EncCoWW
Marta, Istvan 1952- IntWWM 90
Marta, Robert John 1949- St&PR 91
Martarella, Franc David WhoE 91
Martas, Julia Ann 1949- WhoAmW 91
Martchenko, Michael 1942- BioIn 16
Martchevski, Anatoli BioIn 16
Marte, Kenneth James 1951- St&PR 91
Marteka, Vincent James, Jr. 1936- WhoAm 90, WhoWrEP 89
Martel, Arlene BioIn 16
Martel, Bonnie Gillespie 1940- WhoAmW 91
Martel, Eugene Harvey 1934- St&PR 91, WhoAm 90
Martel, Eva Leona 1945- WhoAmW 91
Martel, John Sheldon 1931- WhoAm 90, WhoWor 91
Martel, Leon Charles 1933- WhoE 91
Martel, Linda 1956-1961 EncO&P 3
Martel, Patricia Callahan WhoE 91
Martel, Pierre 1801-1891 DcCanB 12
Martel, Richard 1950- WhoAmA 91
Martel, Richard P. BioIn 16
Martel, Tasha BioIn 16
Martel, William 1927- WhoAm 90
Martell, Arthur Earl 1916- WhoAm 90, WhoSSW 91
Martell, Barbara Bentley WhoAmA 91
Martell, Clare Eileen 1945- WhoAmW 91
Martell, Sarah Ann BiDrAPA 89
Martella, Janet Elaine 1956- WhoAmW 91
Martella, Joseph Edward, Jr. 1957- St&PR 91
Martelli, Christine Ann 1963- WhoE 91
Martelli, Claudio 1943- WhoWor 91
Martello, Benjamin F. 1940- St&PR 91
Martello, Leo Luis EncO&P 3
Martello, Lois Penn 1951- WhoAmW 91
Martellucci, Anthony 1930- St&PR 91, WhoE 91
Marten, George W BiDrAPA 89
Marten, Gordon Cornelius 1935- WhoAm 90
Marten, John Francis 1914- WhoAm 90
Marten, Mary BiDEWW
Marten, Michael 1947- ConAu 132
Marteney, Loire 1959- WhoAmW 91
Martenot, Maurice 1898-1980 PenDiMP
Martens, Barbara Colwell 1932- WhoAmW 91
Martens, David Baker 1942- St&PR 91
Martens, Donald G. 1932- St&PR 91
Martens, Elisabeth EncCoWW
Martens, Harry 1928- St&PR 91
Martens, Herbert Ralston, Jr. 1952- WhoAm 90
Martens, John Dale 1943- WhoE 91
Martens, Kurt 1870-1945 BioIn 16
Martens, Mary E. FemiCLE
Martens, Patricia Margaret 1962- WhoAmW 91
Martens, Robert Edmund 1945- St&PR 91
Martens, Robert John 1925- WhoAm 90
Martens, Roy Michael 1950- WhoEmL 91, WhoWor 91
Martens, Wilfried 1936- WhoWor 91
Martens, Yvonne S 1937- BiDrAPA 89
Martenson, Carroll Mooney 1921- St&PR 91
Martensson, Bengt Krister 1956- WhoWor 91
Marter, Allan J. 1947- St&PR 91
Marter, Joan 1946- WhoAmA 91, WhoE 91
Marterer, Gerald Charles 1945- St&PR 91
Marth, Dave S. 1929- St&PR 91
Marth, Elmer Herman 1927- WhoAm 90, WhoWrEP 89
Marth, Fritz Ludwig 1935- WhoE 91
Martha and the Vandellas EncPR&S 89, OxCPMus
Martha Louise, Princess 1971- BioIn 16
Marthinsen, John Edward 1949- WhoE 91
Marti, Bernabe PenDiMP
Marti, Gloria 1924- St&PR 91
Marti, Hans Rudolf 1922- WhoWor 91
Marti, Jose 1853-1895 BioIn 16, EncAL, WorAlBi
Marti, Kurt 1936- WhoAm 90
Marti, Lori Lee 1963- WhoAmW 91
Marti, Marian Jean 1946- WhoEmL 91
Marti de Cid, Dolores 1916- WhoHisp 91
Marti-Huang, Duen 1948- WhoWor 91
Martial 40-103? WorAlBi
Martial, Johanne 1960- BiDrAPA 89
Marticelli, Frank Anthony 1953- WhoE 91
Marticelli, Joseph John 1921- WhoAm 90
Martignette, Charles BioIn 16
Martika BioIn 16
Martika 1969- WhoHisp 91

Martikainen, Aune Helen 1916- *WhoAmW 91*
Martimucci, Richard Anthony 1934- *WhoE 91*
Martin, Mrs. *FemiCLE*
Martin, Saint 316?-400? *EncO&P 3*
Martin, Adeline W *BiDrAPA 89*
Martin, Agnes 1912- *BiDWomA, BioIn 16, WhoAm 90*
Martin, Agnes Bernice 1912- *WhoAmA 91*
Martin, Albert C. 1913- *St&PR 91*
Martin, Albert Carey 1913- *WhoAm 90*
Martin, Albert Charles 1928- *WhoAm 90*
Martin, Albert Sidney, Jr. 1930- *St&PR 91*
Martin, Albert V. J. 1920- *WhoWor 91*
Martin, Alejandro *WhoWrEP 89*
Martin, Alexander 1740-1807 *BioIn 16*
Martin, Alexander Stella 1929- *WhoWrEP 89*
Martin, Alexander Toedt 1931- *WhoAmA 91, WhoE 91*
Martin, Alfred 1919- *WhoAm 90*
Martin, Alfred Deloach, Jr. 1929- *St&PR 91*
Martin, Alfred Manuel 1928-1989 *ConAu 130*
Martin, Alicia Santiago *BiDrAPA 89*
Martin, Alisa *ODwPR 91*
Martin, Allen 1937- *WhoAm 90, WhoWor 91*
Martin, Alvin Charles 1933- *WhoAm 90*
Martin, Andrea *ODwPR 91*
Martin, Andrew K *BiDrAPA 89*
Martin, Angela 1959- *WhoE 91*
Martin, Angela Michiko 1957- *WhoAmW 91*
Martin, Anita Ellen 1925- *WhoAmW 91*
Martin, Ann 1955- *Au&Arts 6 [port]*
Martin, Ann M. 1955- *BioIn 16, ConAu 32NR*
Martin, Anne 1875-1951 *BioIn 16*
Martin, Anne H. 1875-1951 *BioAmW*
Martin, Anthony G. 1945- *WhoHisp 91*
Martin, Archer J. P. 1910- *WorAlBi*
Martin, Archer John Porter 1910- *WhoAm 90, WhoWor 91*
Martin, Argue 1898- *St&PR 91*
Martin, Art S. 1962- *WhoSSW 91*
Martin, Barbara A. 1942- *WhoAmW 91*
Martin, Barbara Bursa 1934- *WhoAmW 91*
Martin, Barbara Jo 1954- *WhoAmW 91*
Martin, Barbara Lee 1941- *WhoAmW 91*
Martin, Barbara Lynne 1943- *WhoAmW 91*
Martin, Bernard Lee 1923- *WhoAm 90*
Martin, Bernard Murray 1935- *WhoAmA 91*
Martin, Bernice Carey *BioIn 16*
Martin, Betty Clement 1938- *St&PR 91*
Martin, Bill *ConAu 130*
Martin, Bill 1916- *BioIn 16*
Martin, Bill 1943- *WhoAm 90, WhoAmA 91*
Martin, Bill, Jr. *ConAu 130*
Martin, Billy *ConAu 130*
Martin, Billy 1928-1989 *AnObit 1989, Ballpl 90 [port], BioIn 16, CurBio 90N, News 90, WorAlBi*
Martin, Bobby L. 1948- *WhoAm 90*
Martin, Boe Willis 1940- *WhoAm 90*
Martin, Boyce Ficklen, Jr. 1935- *WhoAm 90*
Martin, Boyd Archer 1911- *WhoAm 90, WhoWor 91*
Martin, Brett E. 1952- *St&PR 91*
Martin, Brian K. 1944- *St&PR 91*
Martin, Brian T. 1949- *ODwPR 91*
Martin, Bruce *ConAu 31NR*
Martin, Bruce Douglas 1934- *WhoAm 90*
Martin, C. Robert 1925- *St&PR 91*
Martin, Camilo A *BiDrAPA 89*
Martin, Carl *WhoAm 90*
Martin, Carol 1948- *DrBIPA 90*
Martin, Carol Ann *BiDrAPA 89*
Martin, Carol Ann 1941- *WhoAmW 91*
Martin, Carol Ann 1959- *WhoWrEP 89*
Martin, Carol Jacquelyn 1943- *WhoSSW 91*
Martin, Carolyn Stewart 1951- *WhoAmW 91*
Martin, Carroll Harris, Jr. 1928- *St&PR 91*
Martin, Catherine 1847-1937 *FemiCLE*
Martin, Catherine Anne 1952- *BiDrAPA 89*
Martin, Cecilia Ann 1934- *WhoAmW 91*
Martin, Celia Lopez 1946- *WhoHisp 91*
Martin, Charles A., Jr. 1927- *St&PR 91*
Martin, Charles Douglas 1846-1901 *PenDiDA 89*
Martin, Charles E 1910- *WhoAmA 91*
Martin, Charles Elmer 1910- *WhoAm 90*
Martin, Charles F., Jr. 1939- *St&PR 91*
Martin, Charles James 1866-1955 *DcScB S2*
Martin, Charles John 1935- *WhoSSW 91*
Martin, Charles Morris 1891- *AuBYP 90*
Martin, Charles Thomas 1940- *St&PR 91*
Martin, Charles Wallace 1916- *WhoAm 90*
Martin, Cheri Christian 1956- *WhoAmW 91*
Martin, Chester Y. 1934- *WhoAm 90*
Martin, Chris 1954- *WhoAmA 91*
Martin, Christian F. 1955- *St&PR 91*
Martin, Christopher 1942- *WhoAm 90*
Martin, Christopher Michael 1928- *WhoAm 90*
Martin, Christopher Sanford 1938- *IntWWM 90*
Martin, Claire *BioIn 16*
Martin, Claire 1914- *FemiCLE*
Martin, Clara Morris 1931- *WhoSSW 91*
Martin, Clarence Eugene, Jr. 1909- *WhoAm 90*
Martin, Clarence Terrell 1937- *WhoSSW 91*
Martin, Clarence William 1930- *St&PR 91*
Martin, Claude G. 1946- *St&PR 91*
Martin, Claude Raymond, Jr. 1932- *WhoAm 90, WhoWor 91*
Martin, Clyde Verne 1933- *BiDrAPA 89, WhoAm 90, WhoWor 91*
Martin, Connie Ruth 1963- *WhoAmW 91*
Martin, Constance Rigler 1923- *WhoE 91*
Martin, Craig Haden 1962- *WhoSSW 91*
Martin, Craig Harold 1943- *St&PR 91*
Martin, Craig Mell 1951- *BiDrAPA 89, WhoE 91*
Martin, Cynthia L. *ODwPR 91*
Martin, Cynthia Lea 1957- *WhoE 91*
Martin, Dale 1935- *WhoAmW 91*
Martin, Dale Floyd 1942- *St&PR 91*
Martin, Dale Richard 1936- *St&PR 91*
Martin, Daniel Joseph 1940- *BiDrAPA 89*
Martin, Daniel Lee 1955- *St&PR 91*
Martin, Daniel Richard 1937- *WhoE 91*
Martin, Daniel W. 1918- *BioIn 16*
Martin, Daniel William 1918- *WhoAm 90*
Martin, Dannie *BioIn 16*
Martin, David *PenDiMP*
Martin, David Allan 1937- *WhoAm 90*
Martin, David Allan 1939- *St&PR 91*
Martin, David B. 1947- *St&PR 91*
Martin, David Edward 1939- *WhoAm 90*
Martin, David Lee 1938- *St&PR 91*
Martin, David Leo 1945- *WhoWor 91*
Martin, David Lloyd 1934- *IntWWM 90*
Martin, David Nathan 1930- *WhoAm 90*
Martin, David O'Brien 1944- *WhoAm 90, WhoE 91*
Martin, David Robert 1936- *WhoWor 91*
Martin, David Standish 1937- *WhoE 91*
Martin, David Stone 1913- *WhoAm 90*
Martin, David Stuart 1948- *WhoEmL 91*
Martin, David Uhl 1947- *WhoEmL 91*
Martin, David Wallace 1938- *St&PR 91*
Martin, David William, Jr. 1941- *WhoAm 90*
Martin, Dean *BioIn 16*
Martin, Dean 1917- *ConTFT 8 [port], OxCPMus, WhoAm 90, WorAlBi*
Martin, Dean Erwin 1953- *BiDrAPA 89*
Martin, Dean Frederick 1933- *WhoAm 90, WhoWrEP 89*
Martin, Dean Paul *BioIn 16*
Martin, Deborah Jones 1956- *WhoAmW 91*
Martin, Debra Z 1951- *BiDrAPA 89*
Martin, Denise Belisle 1940- *WhoWrEP 89*
Martin, Dennis Charles 1960- *WhoWor 91*
Martin, Denny Ross 1952- *WhoSSW 91*
Martin, Derek 1923- *WhoAm 90*
Martin, Diane D. *WhoWrEP 89*
Martin, Dianne *BiDrAPA 89*
Martin, Dianne L 1940- *WhoAmA 91*
Martin, Dick 1923- *BioIn 16, WorAlBi*
Martin, Don R. 1938- *St&PR 91*
Martin, Donald Carter 1944- *St&PR 91*
Martin, Donald Leon 1920- *WhoSSW 91*
Martin, Donald R. 1948- *St&PR 91*
Martin, Donald Ray 1915- *WhoAm 90*
Martin, Donald Victor 1929- *St&PR 91*
Martin, Donald W 1921- *BiDrAPA 89*
Martin, Donald William 1921- *WhoAm 90*
Martin, Donna Lee 1935- *WhoAm 90*
Martin, Donnan 1932- *WhoE 91*
Martin, Doris-Marie Constable 1941- *WhoAmA 91*
Martin, Dorothy 1921- *BioIn 16*
Martin, Dorothy Anne 1938- *WhoAmW 91*
Martin, Dorothy R 1912- *EncO&P 3*
Martin, Dorothy Woods *BioIn 16*
Martin, Doug 1947- *WhoAmA 91*
Martin, Douglas Dale 1943- *WhoE 91*
Martin, Duane Greer 1953- *WhoAm 90*
Martin, D'Urville 1939-1984 *DrBIPA 90*
Martin, E.A., Jr. 1907- *St&PR 91*
Martin, Earl L. *St&PR 91*
Martin, Eddie Owens 1908-1986 *MusmAFA*
Martin, Edgar *EncACom*
Martin, Edgar Bertram 1939- *St&PR 91*
Martin, Edgar Thomas 1918- *WhoAm 90*
Martin, Edith Kingdon Gould 1920- *WhoAmW 91*
Martin, Edith Park *BioIn 16*
Martin, Edith Waisbrot 1945- *WhoAm 90, WhoAmW 91*
Martin, Edley Wainright, Jr. 1927- *WhoAm 90*
Martin, Edward B. 1951- *St&PR 91*
Martin, Edward Curtis, Jr. 1928- *WhoAm 90, WhoSSW 91*
Martin, Edward Fontaine 1942- *WhoAm 90*
Martin, Edward Francis 1936- *St&PR 91*
Martin, Edward Gabriel 1932- *St&PR 91*
Martin, Edward L. 1954- *St&PR 91*
Martin, Edwin 1934- *WhoAm 90*
Martin, Edwin Bruce 1860-1915 *PenDiDA 89*
Martin, Edwin Dennis 1920- *WhoSSW 91*
Martin, Edwin McCammon, Jr. 1942- *St&PR 91*
Martin, Edwin Pruitt 1938- *WhoSSW 91*
Martin, Elizabeth A 1945- *ConAu 132*
Martin, Elizabeth A. 1953- *ODwPR 91*
Martin, Ellen Fishwick 1948- *WhoAmW 91*
Martin, Elliot Edwards 1924- *WhoAm 90, WhoWor 91*
Martin, Enos Daniel 1944- *BiDrAPA 89*
Martin, Eric Lewis 1953- *WhoSSW 91*
Martin, Ernest H. 1919- *WhoAm 90*
Martin, Ernie *BioIn 16*
Martin, Etienne-Simon *PenDiDA 89*
Martin, Everett Anthony 1935- *St&PR 91*
Martin, F X 1922- *ConAu 30NR*
Martin, Felix Breaux *BiDrAPA 89*
Martin, Fletcher 1904-1979 *WhoAmA 91N*
Martin, Francine Renee 1948- *WhoAmW 91*
Martin, Francis David 1920- *WhoAm 90*
Martin, Francis Gerard 1942- *WhoE 91*
Martin, Francois-Xavier 1762-1846 *BioIn 16*
Martin, Frank 1890-1974 *PenDiMP A*
Martin, Frank James, Jr. 1931- *WhoE 91*
Martin, Fred 1925- *WhoAm 90*
Martin, Fred 1927- *WhoAm 90*
Martin, Fred Kenneth, Jr. 1942- *WhoWor 91*
Martin, Fred Thomas 1927- *WhoAmA 91*
Martin, Freddie 1915-1979 *Ballpl 90*
Martin, Freddie Anthony 1945- *WhoSSW 91*
Martin, Freddy 1906-1983 *OxCPMus*
Martin, Frederick *BioIn 16*
Martin, Frederick 1908- *St&PR 91*
Martin, Frederick H. 1912- *St&PR 91*
Martin, Frederick Noel 1931- *WhoAm 90*
Martin, Fredric *AuBYP 90*
Martin, G.M. *St&PR 91*
Martin, Gary C. 1935- *St&PR 91*
Martin, Gary Cabot 1941- *BiDrAPA 89*
Martin, Gary L. 1946- *St&PR 91*
Martin, Gaylon E. 1946- *St&PR 91*
Martin, Geoffrey Haward 1928- *WhoWor 91*
Martin, George 1926- *AuBYP 90, ConTFT 8, OxCPMus, WhoWrEP 89*
Martin, George Coleman 1910- *WhoAm 90*
Martin, George Edward 1932- *WhoE 91*
Martin, George J *BiDrAPA 89*
Martin, George Madden 1866-1946 *FemiCLE*
Martin, George Madden, Mrs. 1866-1946 *LiHiK*
Martin, George Maybee 1906- *WhoAm 90, WhoWor 91*
Martin, George Paul 1946- *St&PR 91*
Martin, George R. R. 1948- *RGTwCSF*
Martin, George Raymond Richard 1948- *WhoWrEP 89*
Martin, George Reilly 1933- *WhoAm 90*
Martin, George Robert 1931- *WhoSSW 91*
Martin, George Whitney 1926- *IntWWM 90*
Martin, George Wilbur 1930- *WhoAm 90*
Martin, George William 1924- *WhoAm 90*
Martin, Gerald Edward 1926- *St&PR 91*
Martin, Glenn Andrew 1956- *BiDrAPA 89*
Martin, Glenn L. 1886-1955 *WorAlBi*
Martin, Glenn Michael 1950- *WhoE 91*
Martin, Gordon Mather 1915- *WhoAm 90*
Martin, Grace Burkett 1939- *WhoWor 91*
Martin, Graham A. 1912-1990 *NewYTBS 90 [port]*
Martin, Graham Anderson 1912-1990 *BioIn 16*
Martin, Greg L. 1952- *WhoSSW 91*
Martin, Gregory Allan 1950- *WhoE 91*
Martin, Gregory Keith 1956- *WhoSSW 91*
Martin, Gregory Sharp 1957- *WhoSSW 91*
Martin, Guillaume *PenDiDA 89*
Martin, Guillermo Joaquin 1942- *WhoHisp 91*
Martin, Guy 1911- *WhoAm 90*
Martin, Hans 1945- *WhoWor 91*
Martin, Harold 1918-1988 *AnObit 1988, BioIn 16*
Martin, Harold Clark 1917- *WhoAm 90*
Martin, Harold Eugene 1923- *WhoAm 90*
Martin, Harold Harber 1910- *WhoAm 90, WhoWrEP 89*
Martin, Harold R 1919- *BiDrAPA 89*
Martin, Harrold Bert 1916- *WhoE 91*
Martin, Harry Stratton, III 1943- *WhoAm 90*
Martin, Harvey *BioIn 16*
Martin, Harvey Connett *BiDrAPA 89*
Martin, Helen *BioIn 16, ConTFT 8, DrBIPA 90*
Martin, Helen 1868-1939 *FemiCLE*
Martin, Helen Elizabeth 1945- *WhoAmW 91, WhoE 91*
Martin, Helene Ariane *BiDrAPA 89*
Martin, Helene Getter 1940- *WhoAmW 91*
Martin, Henry Alan 1949- *WhoEmL 91*
Martin, Henry Bradley *BioIn 16*
Martin, Henry Read 1925- *WhoE 91*
Martin, Herbert *BioIn 16*
Martin, Herbert Wayne 1929- *St&PR 91*
Martin, Herbert Woodward 1933- *WhoWrEP 89*
Martin, Hernando *EncCRAm*
Martin, Herschel 1909-1980 *Ballpl 90*
Martin, Hillary *ODwPR 91*
Martin, Hodges Lee *BiDrAPA 89*
Martin, Holger 1942- *WhoWor 91*
Martin, Homer 1901-1968 *EncABHB 5*
Martin, Homer B 1924- *BiDrAPA 89*
Martin, Howard B. *St&PR 91*
Martin, Hugh 1830-1893 *AmLegL*
Martin, Hugh 1914- *OxCPMus*
Martin, Hugh Jack, Jr. 1926- *WhoAm 90*
Martin, Ian *BioIn 16*
Martin, Ian 1946- *WhoWor 91*
Martin, Ian A. 1935- *St&PR 91*
Martin, Ian Alexander 1935- *WhoAm 90*
Martin, Ignacio 1928- *WhoHisp 91*
Martin, Ignacio Baro- *BioIn 16*
Martin, Iva Berniece 1929- *WhoAmW 91*
Martin, J. C. 1936- *Ballpl 90*
Martin, J. G. 1931- *WhoSSW 91*
Martin, J. Landis 1945- *WhoAm 90, WhoSSW 91*
Martin, Jack 1927- *BiDrAPA 89*
Martin, Jack D. *BioIn 16*
Martin, Jacqueline Byrd *WhoAmW 91*
Martin, Jacques 1908- *WhoWor 91*
Martin, James Alfred, Jr. 1917- *WhoAm 90*
Martin, James Cullen 1928- *WhoAm 90*
Martin, James Edward 1926- *St&PR 91*
Martin, James Everett 1932- *WhoAm 90, WhoSSW 91*
Martin, James Gilbert 1926- *WhoAm 90*
Martin, James Grubbs 1935- *WhoAm 90, WhoSSW 91, WhoWor 91*
Martin, James Hanley 1960- *WhoE 91*
Martin, James J *BiDrAPA 89*
Martin, James John, Jr. 1936- *WhoAm 90*
Martin, James Kirby 1943- *WhoAm 90*
Martin, James L. *BioIn 16*
Martin, James Loren 1846-1915 *AmLegL*
Martin, James Luther, Jr. 1917- *WhoAm 90*
Martin, James Patrick 1946- *WhoWor 91*
Martin, James R. 1941- *WhoHisp 91*
Martin, James Royer 1946- *WhoAm 90*
Martin, James Smith 1936- *St&PR 91, WhoAm 90*
Martin, James Victor, Jr. 1916- *WhoE 91*
Martin, James W. 1927- *St&PR 91*
Martin, James William *BiDrAPA 89*
Martin, James William 1949- *WhoEmL 91*
Martin, Jamie Lou *BioIn 16*
Martin, Jane 1943- *WhoAmA 91*
Martin, Jane Ann 1931- *WhoSSW 91*
Martin, Janet M. Daddino 1954- *WhoE 91*
Martin, Janette Gould 1957- *WhoWrEP 89*
Martin, Janice Anita Elrod 1952- *WhoSSW 91*
Martin, Janie Mary 1958- *WhoWor 91*
Martin, Janis 1939- *IntWWM 90*
Martin, Jay 1935- *WhoWrEP 89*
Martin, Jay Herbert 1935- *WhoAm 90*
Martin, Jean-Alexandre 1739-1791? *PenDiDA 89*
Martin, Jean Ann 1942- *WhoAmW 91, WhoSSW 91*
Martin, Jean Claude 1929- *WhoAm 90*
Martin, Jean Mc Fall 1955- *WhoWrEP 89*
Martin, Jeffrey Lynn 1951- *WhoE 91*
Martin, Jennifer Miller 1962- *WhoAmW 91*
Martin, Jerome *AuBYP 90*
Martin, Jerri Whan 1931- *WhoAmW 91*
Martin, Jerry 1949- *Ballpl 90*
Martin, Jerry C. 1932- *WhoAm 90*
Martin, Jerry Calhoun 1932- *St&PR 91*
Martin, Jerry Patrick 1943- *BiDrAPA 89*
Martin, Jim 1939- *WhoWrEP 89*
Martin, Jimmy 1927- *ConMus 5*
Martin, Joan Louise *BiDrAPA 89*
Martin, Joan Marie 1938- *St&PR 91*
Martin, Joann Fleischmann 1954- *WhoE 91*
Martin, Joann Speer 1955- *WhoAmW 91*

Martin, Joe M *BiDrAPA 89*
Martin, John 1956- *Ballpl 90*
Martin, John Bruce 1922- *WhoAm 90*
Martin, John C., III 1952- *St&PR 91*
Martin, John E. 1947- *St&PR 91*
Martin, John Gerard 1944- *BiDrAPA 89*
Martin, John Gustin 1928- *St&PR 91, WhoAm 90*
Martin, John H. 1922- *BioIn 16*
Martin, John Hugh 1918- *WhoAm 90*
Martin, John Joseph 1931- *St&PR 91, WhoAm 90*
Martin, John Joseph 1938- *WhoAm 90*
Martin, John Joseph 1956- *WhoE 91, WhoEmL 91*
Martin, John L. 1941- *WhoAm 90, WhoE 91*
Martin, John M. *St&PR 91N*
Martin, John M. *NewYTBS 90*
Martin, John M. 1913-1990 *BioIn 16*
Martin, John Michael 1947- *WhoE 91*
Martin, John P. 1939- *St&PR 91*
Martin, John R., Jr. 1941- *ODwPR 91*
Martin, John Richard, Jr. 1941- *WhoSSW 91*
Martin, John Rupert 1916- *WhoAm 90, WhoAmA 91, WhoWrEP 89*
Martin, John Thomas 1924- *WhoWor 91*
Martin, John William 1946- *WhoEmL 91, WhoWor 91*
Martin, John William, Jr. 1936- *WhoAm 90*
Martin, Johnny Benjamin 1947- *WhoEmL 91*
Martin, Jorge Luis 1953- *WhoHisp 91*
Martin, Jose L 1921- *HispWr 90*
Martin, Joseph, Jr. 1915- *WhoAm 90, WhoWor 91*
Martin, Joseph Boyd 1938- *WhoAm 90, WhoWor 91*
Martin, Joseph Eugene 1936- *WhoSSW 91*
Martin, Joseph Ramsey 1930- *WhoAm 90*
Martin, Josephine D *BiDrAPA 89*
Martin, Josiah 1737-1786 *EncCRAm*
Martin, Joyce M. *ODwPR 91*
Martin, Judi *ODwPR 91*
Martin, Judith *AuBYP 90*
Martin, Judith 1918- *BioIn 16, NotWoAT*
Martin, Judith 1938- *BioIn 16, WhoWrEP 89, WorAlBi*
Martin, Judith Sylvia 1938- *WhoAm 90, WhoE 91*
Martin, Judson Phillips 1921- *WhoAm 90*
Martin, Julia *BiDrAPA 89*
Martin, Julian *BioIn 16*
Martin, Julian *PenDiDA 89*
Martin, Julian S. 1929- *WhoAm 90*
Martin, Julian S. S. 1929- *WhoWrEP 89*
Martin, June Johnson Caldwell *WhoAmW 91*
Martin, Justus Carlile, Jr. 1925- *St&PR 91*
Martin, Karen 1959- *ODwPR 91*
Martin, Karen Krausche 1947- *WhoAmW 91, WhoE 91*
Martin, Katharine Hawley 1916- *BiDrAPA 89*
Martin, Kathleen Ann 1944- *WhoAmW 91*
Martin, Kathleen Anne 1942- *WhoAmW 91*
Martin, Kathleen Suzanne 1950- *WhoE 91*
Martin, Kathryn A. *WhoAm 90*
Martin, Keith Douglas 1953- *WhoEmL 91*
Martin, Keith Morrow 1911-1983 *WhoAmA 91N*
Martin, Kellie Sue 1961- *WhoAmW 91*
Martin, Kendra Leigh 1961- *WhoAmW 91*
Martin, Kenneth Albert 1940- *WhoE 91*
Martin, Kenneth Douglas 1940- *WhoAm 90*
Martin, Kenneth Ray 1953- *WhoSSW 91*
Martin, Kevin Preston *BiDrAPA 89*
Martin, Kiel *WhoAm 90*
Martin, Kim Irene 1952- *WhoSSW 91*
Martin, Knox 1923- *WhoAmA 91*
Martin, Larry Kenneth 1939- *WhoAmA 91*
Martin, Larry Ross 1949- *St&PR 91*
Martin, Laura Belle 1915- *WhoAmW 91, WhoWor 91*
Martin, Lawrence J. 1923- *St&PR 91*
Martin, Lawrence M *BiDrAPA 89*
Martin, Lee *WhoWrEP 89*
Martin, Lee 1920- *St&PR 91, WhoAm 90*
Martin, Leland Morris 1930- *WhoSSW 91*
Martin, Leon Jean 1927- *WhoWor 91*
Martin, Leslie Kay 1958- *WhoAmW 91*
Martin, Leslie Paul 1920- *WhoAm 90*
Martin, Lillien J. 1851-1943 *BioAmW*
Martin, Lincoln A. 1912- *St&PR 91*
Martin, Linda Rickson 1947- *WhoSSW 91*
Martin, Lisa Ann 1961- *WhoAmW 91*
Martin, Lisa Diane 1957- *WhoWor 91*
Martin, Lois Christine *St&PR 91*
Martin, Loretta Marsh 1933- *WhoAmA 91*
Martin, Lorraine B. 1940- *WhoAmW 91, WhoE 91*
Martin, Louis C 1928- *BiDrAPA 89*
Martin, Louis Edward 1928- *WhoAm 90*
Martin, Lucille Caiar 1918- *WhoAmA 91*
Martin, Lucy Z. 1941- *WhoAm 90, WhoAmW 91*
Martin, Luis 1927- *ConAu 131, HispWr 90, WhoHisp 91*
Martin, Luther 1744-1826 *BioIn 16*
Martin, Luther 1748-1826 *EncCRAm*
Martin, Lynda K *WhoAmA 91*
Martin, Lynn Morley 1939- *BioIn 16, WhoAm 90, WhoAmW 91*
Martin, Lynne 1923- *AuBYP 90*
Martin, Mahlon *BioIn 16*
Martin, Malachi *AmLegL*
Martin, Malcolm Elliot 1935- *WhoAm 90*
Martin, Malcolm Woods 1912- *WhoAm 90*
Martin, Manuel, Jr. 1934- *WhoHisp 91*
Martin, Marcia *AuBYP 90*
Martin, Margaret M 1940- *WhoAmA 91, WhoE 91*
Martin, Maria *WomFie*
Martin, Maria Sonia 1951- *WhoHisp 91*
Martin, Marie Young 1908- *WhoAm 90*
Martin, Marilyn Lydia 1957- *BiDrAPA 89*
Martin, Mark 1914- *WhoAm 90*
Martin, Marsha Ann 1952- *WhoAmW 91*
Martin, Martha *BiDrAPA 89*
Martin, Martha Brown 1954- *BiDrAPA 89*
Martin, Marvis *BioIn 16*
Martin, Mary 1815-1850 *FemiCLE*
Martin, Mary 1913- *BioIn 16, NotWoAT, WhoAm 90, WorAlBi*
Martin, Mary 1913?-1990 *ConAu 132, NewYTBS 90 [port], News 91-2, OxCPMus*
Martin, Mary Adela 1907-1969 *BiDWomA*
Martin, Mary Belle 1932- *WhoSSW 91*
Martin, Mary Evelyn 1958- *WhoAmW 91*
Martin, Mary Finch 1916- *WhoAmA 91*
Martin, Mary Lee 1938- *WhoAmW 91*
Martin, Mary Lou 1953- *WhoAmW 91*
Martin, Mary Ruth 1926- *St&PR 91*
Martin, Maryanne *BiDrAPA 89*
Martin, Maud *PenDiMP*
Martin, Maurice J 1929- *BiDrAPA 89*
Martin, Maurice John 1929- *WhoAm 90*
Martin, Michael 1943- *WhoAm 90*
Martin, Michael Alexander 1939- *St&PR 91*
Martin, Michael David 1927- *St&PR 91*
Martin, Michael Frederick 1957- *WhoE 91*
Martin, Michael L. 1949- *St&PR 91*
Martin, Michael McCulloch 1935- *WhoAm 90*
Martin, Michael S. 1946- *St&PR 91*
Martin, Michael Townsend 1941- *WhoE 91, WhoWor 91*
Martin, Miguel D. 1949- *WhoHisp 91*
Martin, Millicent 1934- *OxCPMus*
Martin, Milton T., Jr. 1939- *WhoAm 90*
Martin, Mona Helen 1951- *WhoAmW 91*
Martin, Morgan G 1921- *BiDrAPA 89*
Martin, Morrie 1922- *Ballpl 90*
Martin, Murray Simpson 1928- *WhoAm 90*
Martin, Nancy A. 1943- *St&PR 91*
Martin, Nancy Jean Van Dervoort 1928- *WhoWor 91*
Martin, Nancy Lee 1962- *WhoAmW 91*
Martin, Ned *Ballpl 90*
Martin, Ned Harold 1945- *WhoSSW 91*
Martin, Noel 1922- *ConDes 90, WhoAm 90*
Martin, Norman K. 1926- *St&PR 91*
Martin, Norman Keith 1930- *WhoAm 90*
Martin, Norman Marshall 1924- *WhoAm 90*
Martin, Oscar Thaddeus 1908- *WhoAm 90*
Martin, Pamela Ann *BiDrAPA 89*
Martin, Paris Leveret 1944- *WhoSSW 91*
Martin, Patricia Miles 1899-1986 *AuBYP 90*
Martin, Patricia Stone 1931- *WhoWrEP 89*
Martin, Patrick 1941- *WhoAm 90*
Martin, Patrick David 1948- *BiDrAPA 89*
Martin, Patrick Donald 1958- *WhoSSW 91*
Martin, Paul 1903- *BioIn 16*
Martin, Paul 1920- *St&PR 91*
Martin, Paul 1938- *BioIn 16, WhoAm 90*
Martin, Paul Cecil 1931- *WhoAm 90*
Martin, Paul Edward 1914- *WhoAm 90*
Martin, Paul Edward 1928- *WhoSSW 91, WhoWor 91*
Martin, Paul Joseph 1936- *WhoAm 90*
Martin, Paul M. 1915- *St&PR 91*
Martin, Paul Rene 1940- *WhoWor 91*
Martin, Paul Simeon 1914- *WhoAm 90*
Martin, Paula Jean 1947- *WhoAmW 91*
Martin, Pepper 1904-1965 *Ballpl 90 [port]*
Martin, Pete *WhoHisp 91*
Martin, Peter *ODwPR 91*
Martin, Peter A 1916- *BiDrAPA 89*
Martin, Peter Gerard 1952- *WhoEmL 91*
Martin, Peter John 1949- *IntWWM 90*
Martin, Peter M. 1937- *St&PR 91*
Martin, Peter Robert 1949- *BiDrAPA 89, WhoSSW 91*
Martin, Peter William 1939- *WhoAm 90*
Martin, Philip James 1947- *IntWWM 90*
Martin, Philip Lee, Jr. 1956- *WhoE 91*
Martin, Phyllis R *ConAu 130*
Martin, Pierre 1938- *WhoAm 90*
Martin, Preston 1923- *WhoAm 90*
Martin, Quinn William 1948- *WhoEmL 91*
Martin, R.B. 1934- *St&PR 91*
Martin, R. Keith 1933- *WhoAm 90*
Martin, R. William 1943- *WhoWrEP 89*
Martin, Ralph Arthur 1927- *St&PR 91*
Martin, Ralph G. 1920- *AuBYP 90*
Martin, Ralph Guy 1920- *WhoAm 90, WhoWrEP 89*
Martin, Ray 1918- *OxCPMus*
Martin, Ray D. 1927- *St&PR 91*
Martin, Raymond Edward 1957- *WhoEmL 91*
Martin, Regina Maria Anita 1950- *WhoAmW 91*
Martin, Renee Angela 1963- *WhoEmL 91*
Martin, Renie 1955- *Ballpl 90*
Martin, Richard *MajTwCW, TwCCr&M 91*
Martin, Richard 1946- *WhoAmA 91*
Martin, Richard A. 1934- *St&PR 91*
Martin, Richard Blazo 1917- *WhoWor 91*
Martin, Richard Carlton 1939- *WhoSSW 91*
Martin, Richard Francis 1920- *St&PR 91, WhoAm 90*
Martin, Richard Harrison 1946- *WhoAm 90, WhoE 91, WhoWor 91*
Martin, Richard Jay 1946- *WhoAm 90*
Martin, Richard L. 1932- *WhoE 91*
Martin, Richard L. 1933- *St&PR 91*
Martin, Richard Otto 1940- *WhoAm 90*
Martin, Richard Theodore 1925- *WhoE 91*
Martin, Robert 1706-1766 *PenDiDA 89*
Martin, Robert A. *WhoAm 90*
Martin, Robert Allan 1948- *St&PR 91*
Martin, Robert Alphonse 1946- *WhoEmL 91*
Martin, Robert B. 1933- *St&PR 91*
Martin, Robert Bernard 1918- *WhoWrEP 89*
Martin, Robert Blair 1950- *WhoEmL 91*
Martin, Robert Bruce 1929- *WhoAm 90*
Martin, Robert David 1939- *BiDrAPA 89*
Martin, Robert Donald 1943- *WhoWor 91*
Martin, Robert Earnshaw 1909- *WhoSSW 91*
Martin, Robert Edward 1928- *WhoWor 91*
Martin, Robert Edward, Jr. 1931- *WhoAm 90*
Martin, Robert Eugene *BiDrAPA 89*
Martin, Robert F. 1923- *St&PR 91*
Martin, Robert Finlay, Jr. 1925- *WhoAm 90*
Martin, Robert G. 1945- *St&PR 91*
Martin, Robert G. 1954- *ODwPR 91*
Martin, Robert Gregory 1959- *WhoEmL 91*
Martin, Robert Huxley 1916- *St&PR 91*
Martin, Robert Joseph, Sr. 1931- *WhoSSW 91*
Martin, Robert K. *ODwPR 91*
Martin, Robert Richard 1910- *WhoAm 90*
Martin, Robert Roy 1927- *St&PR 91, WhoAm 90*
Martin, Robert Sacks *BiDrAPA 89*
Martin, Robert V., Jr. 1915- *St&PR 91*
Martin, Robert Wallace 1843-1923 *PenDiDA 89*
Martin, Robert William 1936- *WhoAm 90*
Martin, Roblee B. 1922- *St&PR 91*
Martin, Roblee Boettcher 1922- *WhoAm 90*
Martin, Roger *WhoHisp 91*
Martin, Roger 1925- *WhoAmA 91*
Martin, Roger Bond 1936- *WhoAm 90*
Martin, Roger F. 1927- *St&PR 91*
Martin, Roger H 1943- *ConAu 132*
Martin, Roger Harry 1943- *WhoAm 90*
Martin, Roger Lawrence 1958- *WhoAm 90*
Martin, Roger Lloyd 1956- *WhoWor 91*
Martin, Rogers William 1956- *WhoSSW 91*
Martin, Ron *BioIn 16*
Martin, Ronald Ellis 1944- *WhoE 91*
Martin, Ronald Joseph 1949- *St&PR 91*
Martin, Ronald L 1945- *BiDrAPA 89*
Martin, Ronald Lavern 1922- *WhoAm 90*
Martin, Ronald Michael 1948- *WhoEmL 91*
Martin, Rose Kocsis 1928- *WhoAmW 91, WhoE 91, WhoWor 91*
Martin, Rosemary Scarbrough 1935- *WhoAm 90*
Martin, Rosy 1946- *WhoWor 91*
Martin, Russell D 1935- *BiDrAPA 89*
Martin, Russell Goodale 1949- *WhoE 91*
Martin, Ruth *ConAu 30NR*
Martin, Ruth Held 1953- *BiDrAPA 89*
Martin, Ruth Kelley 1914- *IntWWM 90*
Martin, Ruth M. *BioIn 16, NewYTBS 90*
Martin, Ruth Swimmer 1946- *BiDrAPA 89*
Martin, Sallie *BioIn 16*
Martin, Sally Nan 1947- *WhoAmW 91*
Martin, Sally Sue Johnson 1945- *WhoSSW 91*
Martin, Sally Sykes 1953- *WhoAmW 91*
Martin, Sam 1920- *WhoAm 90*
Martin, Samuel Albert 1945- *St&PR 91*
Martin, Samuel Elmo 1924- *WhoAm 90*
Martin, Samuel Preston, III 1916- *WhoAm 90*
Martin, Sandra Archer 1945- *WhoAmW 91*
Martin, Sandra Louise 1956- *WhoAmW 91*
Martin, Sara 1884-1955 *BioIn 16*
Martin, Saul Avrum 1932- *BiDrAPA 89*
Martin, Sharon Jaffe 1944- *WhoAmW 91*
Martin, Shelly Jo 1957- *WhoAmW 91*
Martin, Sherri 1950- *WhoSSW 91*
Martin, Shirley 1932- *WhoAm 90, WhoAmW 91, WhoE 91*
Martin, Shirley Marie 1944- *WhoAmW 91*
Martin, Simone *BioIn 16*
Martin, Speed 1893-1983 *Ballpl 90*
Martin, Stacey Lynn 1951- *WhoAmW 91, WhoSSW 91*
Martin, Stefan 1936- *WhoAmA 91*
Martin, Stella *MajTwCW*
Martin, Stephanie *BioIn 16*
Martin, Stephen 1948- *WhoWor 91*
Martin, Stephen George 1941- *St&PR 91*
Martin, Stephen-Paul 1949- *WhoWrEP 89*
Martin, Steve *WhoAm 90*
Martin, Steve 1945?- *BioIn 16, ConAu 30NR, MajTwCW, WorAlBi*
Martin, Steven Dana 1949- *BiDrAPA 89*
Martin, Steven Dee 1958- *WhoSSW 91*
Martin, Stu 1913- *Ballpl 90*
Martin, Stuart *EncO&P 3*
Martin, Sue Wilma Vern 1926- *WhoSSW 91*
Martin, Susan Katherine 1942- *WhoAm 90, WhoAmW 91*
Martin, Susan Lorde 1943- *WhoAmW 91*
Martin, Sylvia Cooke 1938- *WhoAmW 91*
Martin, Sylvia Parsons *AuBYP 90*
Martin, Tamela Sheree 1962- *WhoAmW 91*
Martin, Teresa G. 1958- *WhoSSW 91*
Martin, Terri Tolleson 1954- *WhoSSW 91*
Martin, Theodore Krinn 1915- *WhoAm 90*
Martin, Thomas 1943- *WhoAmA 91*
Martin, Thomas Allen, III 1947- *BiDrAPA 89*
Martin, Thomas Brooks 1935- *St&PR 91*
Martin, Thomas Brooks, Jr. 1955- *WhoEmL 91*
Martin, Thomas Edward 1942- *St&PR 91*
Martin, Thomas Lyle 1921- *St&PR 91*
Martin, Thomas Lyle, Jr. 1921- *WhoAm 90*
Martin, Thomas Stephen 1946- *WhoAm 90*
Martin, Thomas Victor *BiDrAPA 89*
Martin, Timothy *BioIn 16*
Martin, Tom *ConAu 31NR*
Martin, Tony 1912- *OxCPMus*
Martin, Tony 1913- *WhoAm 90, WorAlBi*
Martin, Valerie *BioIn 16*
Martin, Valerie Metcalf 1948- *WhoWrEP 89*
Martin, Velma A *BiDrAPA 89*
Martin, Vernon 1929- *IntWWM 90*
Martin, Vertel *BioIn 16*
Martin, Vicki Jean 1954- *WhoAmW 91*
Martin, Victoria Bills 1948- *BiDrAPA 89*
Martin, Victoria Claflin Woodhull 1838-1927 *BioIn 16*
Martin, Vincent George 1922- *WhoAm 90*
Martin, Vincent Lionel 1939- *St&PR 91, WhoAm 90*
Martin, Violet Florence 1862-1915 *BioIn 16*
Martin, Virve Paul 1928- *WhoAmW 91*
Martin, Vivian *IntWWM 90*
Martin, Walter Edwin 1908- *WhoAm 90*
Martin, Walter Frazer 1859-1912 *PenDiDA 89*
Martin, Walter L., Jr. *WhoAm 90*
Martin, Walter Larry 1949- *BiDrAPA 89*
Martin, Walter Patrick 1912- *WhoAm 90*
Martin, Walter Ralston 1928-1989 *ConAu 129*
Martin, Warren H. 1956- *St&PR 91*
Martin, Warren O. 1917- *St&PR 91*
Martin, Wayne Harvey 1945- *WhoEmL 91*
Martin, Wayne Joseph 1939- *St&PR 91*
Martin, Wayne Stanley 1937- *St&PR 91*
Martin, Webb Franklin 1944- *St&PR 91*
Martin, Webber *MajTwCW*
Martin, Wendell 1947- *WhoSSW 91*
Martin, Wendy Lynn *WhoSSW 91*
Martin, Wesley George 1946- *WhoEmL 91*
Martin, William A. 1941- *St&PR 91*
Martin, William Bryan 1938- *WhoAm 90*
Martin, William Burgard 1927- *WhoE 91*
Martin, William Charles 1930- *WhoSSW 91*

Martin, William Frederick 1917- St&PR 91, WhoAm 90
Martin, William G. AuBYP 90
Martin, William George 1923- St&PR 91
Martin, William Ivan 1916- BioIn 16, ConAu 130
Martin, William Joseph 1935- St&PR 91
Martin, William Logan 1850-1907 AmLegL
Martin, William McChesney 1906- EncABHB 7 [port]
Martin, William McChesney, Jr. 1906- WorAlBi
Martin, William Raymond 1939- WhoWor 91
Martin, William Robert 1921- WhoAm 90
Martin, William Royall, Jr. 1926- WhoAm 90, WhoSSW 91
Martin, William Russell, Jr. 1939- St&PR 91
Martin, William Ted 1911- WhoAm 90
Martin, William Vandever 1944- St&PR 91
Martin, William Walker 1925- St&PR 91
Martin, Winslow BioIn 16
Martin, Yvonne Connolly 1936- WhoAmW 91
Martin-Alonso, Olga 1959- WhoWor 91
Martin-Baro, Ignacio BioIn 16
Martin-Bowen, Lindsey 1949- WhoWor 91
Martin del Campo, Diego Ramiro 1929- WhoWor 91
Martin Del Campo, Enrique BiDrAPA 89
Martin du Gard, Roger 1881-1958 BioIn 16, WorAlBi
Martin-Gaite, Carmen 1925- EncCoWW, IntvSpW [port]
Martin-Gerhards, Rebecca Ann 1949- WhoAmW 91
Martin-Lof, Per Erik Rutger 1942- WhoWor 91
Martin-Lof, Sverker Knut Ture 1943- WhoWor 91
Martin-Pelaez, Alberto 1939- WhoSSW 91
Martin-Pitman, Kari Lisa 1958- WhoWrEP 89
Martin Sanchez, Juan Antonio 1940- WhoWor 91
Martina, Don WhoWor 91
Martina, Joe 1889-1962 Ballpl 90
Martinak, Rosemary 1954- WhoAmW 91
Martinazzo-Dunn, Anna Rosa BiDrAPA 89
Martinazzoli Fermo, Mino 1931- WhoWor 91
Martincek, Dusan 1936- IntWWM 90
Martincic, Joseph Anton 1941- St&PR 91
Martindale, Cameron Joan 1946- WhoSSW 91
Martindale, Lucy Gene 1954- WhoAmW 91
Martindale, Peter Craig BiDrAPA 89
Martindale, Robert H. 1919- St&PR 91
Martindale, Steven BioIn 16
Martindale, Steven Addington 1944- WhoE 91
Martindall, Anne 1659- BiDEWW
Martindell, Jackson NewYTBS 90
Martindell, Jackson 1900-1990 BioIn 16
Martine, Jack A. 1949- St&PR 91
Martineau, Bolivar P 1929- BiDrAPA 89
Martineau, Denise Cory 1954- WhoAmW 91
Martineau, Donald Jean 1943- St&PR 91
Martineau, Francis Edward 1921- WhoWrEP 89
Martineau, Harriet 1802-1876 BioIn 16, FemiCLE
Martineau, James 1805-1900 BioIn 16
Martineau, James Louis 1940- St&PR 91
Martineau, John Ellis 1873-1937 BioIn 16
Martineau, Thomas Richard 1946- WhoSSW 91, WhoWor 91
Martinelli, A.W. 1928- St&PR 91
Martinelli, Alfred Walter 1928- WhoAm 90
Martinelli, Ezio 1913- WhoAmA 91N
Martinelli, Gary Robert 1950- WhoE 91
Martinelli, Giovanni 1885-1969 PenDiMP
Martinelli, Joseph John, Jr. 1953- St&PR 91
Martinelli, Louis Adrio 1933- St&PR 91
Martinelli, Robert Owens 1924- St&PR 91
Martinelli, Rosemary 1957- WhoAmW 91, WhoE 91
Martinello, Marty E. 1931- St&PR 91
Martinen, John A. 1938- WhoE 91
Martinengou, Elisavet Moutzan EncCoWW
Martines, Julia MajTwCW
Martines, Lauro 1927- WhoWrEP 89
Martines, Lauro Rene 1927- WhoAm 90
Martines, Steven L. WhoHisp 91
Martinet, Marjoried 1886-1981 WhoAmA 91N
Martinetti, Ronald Anthony 1945- WhoEmL 91
Martinez, A. BioIn 16, WhoHisp 91
Martinez, Abigail 1953- WhoAmW 91
Martinez, Al 1929- WhoAm 90, WhoHisp 91
Martinez, Alejandro Macias 1951- WhoHisp 91
Martinez, Alejandro N BiDrAPA 89
Martinez, Alex G. WhoHisp 91
Martinez, Alex J. 1951- WhoHisp 91
Martinez, Alfred 1944- WhoAmA 91
Martinez, Alfred P. 1939- WhoHisp 91
Martinez, Alice Conde 1946- WhoAm 90, WhoHisp 91
Martinez, Ana F BiDrAPA 89
Martinez, Andres A. 1947- St&PR 91
Martinez, Antonio Jose 1793-1867 BioIn 16
Martinez, Aristides 1939- WhoHisp 91
Martinez, Arlene M 1958- BiDrAPA 89
Martinez, Armando 1938- WhoHisp 91
Martinez, Augusto Julio 1930- WhoHisp 91
Martinez, Ben WhoHisp 91
Martinez, Betty Elnora 1947- WhoAmW 91
Martinez, Blas M. 1935- WhoHisp 91
Martinez, Bob 1934- WhoAm 90, WhoHisp 91, WhoSSW 91, WhoWor 91
Martinez, Buck 1948- Ballpl 90
Martinez, Camilo Amado, Jr. 1935- WhoHisp 91
Martinez, Carlos Alberto 1965- WhoHisp 91
Martinez, Carlos Serafin 1932- BiDrAPA 89
Martinez, Carmelo 1960- Ballpl 90
Martinez, Cecilia Gonzalez 1958- WhoHisp 91
Martinez, Celestino 1945- WhoHisp 91
Martinez, Cesar Augusto 1944- WhoHisp 91
Martinez, Charles 1953- WhoHisp 91
Martinez, Cindy Lee 1952- WhoAmW 91
Martinez, Cleopatria 1948- WhoHisp 91
Martinez, Daniel J 1957- WhoAmA 91
Martinez, Danny 1948- WhoHisp 91
Martinez, Dave 1964- Ballpl 90, WhoHisp 91
Martinez, David Herrera 1937- WhoHisp 91
Martinez, David Roger 1954- WhoSSW 91
Martinez, Dennis 1955- Ballpl 90, WhoHisp 91
Martinez, Diane Lawson 1950- BiDrAPA 89
Martinez, Diego Gutierrez 1948- WhoHisp 91
Martinez, Dionisio D. 1956- WhoHisp 91
Martinez, Donna Lynn 1952- WhoAmW 91
Martinez, Edgar 1963- WhoHisp 91
Martinez, Edie BioIn 16
Martinez, Elena 1940- WhoAmW 91
Martinez, Eliana BioIn 16
Martinez, Elmer 1933- WhoHisp 91
Martinez, Eloise Fontanet 1931- WhoHisp 91
Martinez, Enrique Gonzalez HispWr 90
Martinez, Eric Scott 1966- WhoE 91
Martinez, Erminio E. 1943- WhoHisp 91
Martinez, Ernest Alcario, Jr. 1941- WhoHisp 91
Martinez, Ernesto 1941- WhoSSW 91
Martinez, Ernesto, III 1953- WhoSSW 91
Martinez, Ernesto Pedregon 1926- WhoAmA 91
Martinez, Esteban Conde 1932- WhoHisp 91
Martinez, Felix 1857-1916 BioIn 16
Martinez, Frank Augustine 1943- WhoSSW 91
Martinez, Fred 1957- Ballpl 90
Martinez, Gabriel Guerrero, Jr. 1951- WhoHisp 91
Martinez, Gary Wayne 1950- St&PR 91
Martinez, George 1955- WhoHisp 91
Martinez, Georgina V. 1953- WhoWrEP 89
Martinez, Gerald Lafayette 1939- WhoHisp 91
Martinez, Gina Amelia 1960- WhoHisp 91
Martinez, Guillermo Ignacio 1941- WhoSSW 91, WhoWor 91
Martinez, Guillermo Ivan 1962- WhoSSW 91
Martinez, Gustave WhoAm 90
Martinez, Harold Joseph 1959- WhoHisp 91
Martinez, Hector 1962- WhoSSW 91
Martinez, Hector Arteche WhoAmA 91
Martinez, Herminia S. WhoAmW 91
Martinez, Humberto L. 1944- BiDrAPA 89, WhoHisp 91
Martinez, Ignacio Gonzalo BiDrAPA 89
Martinez, Irene B. 1944- WhoHisp 91
Martinez, Jeordano Severo 1946- WhoHisp 91
Martinez, Jesus M. WhoHisp 91
Martinez, Jo Ann 1950- WhoAmW 91
Martinez, Joaquin Costa Y 1846-1911 BioIn 16
Martinez, Joe L. 1944- WhoHisp 91
Martinez, John Stanley 1930- WhoWor 91
Martinez, Jorge 1940- WhoHisp 91
Martinez, Jose 1942- WhoHisp 91
Martinez, Jose 1950- WhoHisp 91
Martinez, Jose Angel 1946- WhoHisp 91
Martinez, Jose E. 1954- WhoHisp 91
Martinez, Jose Leonor 1939- BiDrAPA 89
Martinez, Joseph 1941- WhoHisp 91
Martinez, Joseph V. WhoHisp 91
Martinez, Juan J. 1908- St&PR 91
Martinez, Judith 1955- WhoHisp 91
Martinez, Julia Jaramillo 1926- WhoHisp 91
Martinez, Julio A 1931- HispWr 90
Martinez, Julio Enrique, Jr. 1943- WhoHisp 91
Martinez, Kenneth A. WhoHisp 91
Martinez, Lee William 1953- WhoHisp 91
Martinez, Lilliam WhoHisp 91
Martinez, Louis EncO&P 3
Martinez, Luis 1898-1973 EncPaPR 91
Martinez, Luis Antonio Sanchez 1959- WhoWor 91
Martinez, Luis Osvaldo 1927- WhoSSW 91
Martinez, Lupe 1945- WhoHisp 91
Martinez, M. A. Laura 1960- WhoHisp 91
Martinez, Manuel Albert 1959- WhoSSW 91
Martinez, Manuel C. 1945- WhoHisp 91
Martinez, Manuel Guiang BiDrAPA 89
Martinez, Manuel S. WhoHisp 91
Martinez, Maria 1887-1980 MusmAFA
Martinez, Maria J. 1951- WhoHisp 91
Martinez, Maria Leonor 1948- WhoAmW 91
Martinez, Maria M. 1887-1980 BioAmW
Martinez, Maria Montoya 1887-1980 BioIn 16
Martinez, Marlo R. 1957- WhoHisp 91
Martinez, Martin WhoHisp 91
Martinez, Marty 1941- Ballpl 90
Martinez, Matt G., Sr. 1917- WhoHisp 91
Martinez, Matthew G. 1929- WhoHisp 91
Martinez, Matthew Gilbert 1929- WhoAm 90
Martinez, Max 1943- ConAu 131, HispWr 90
Martinez, Maximiliano Hernandez 1882-1966 BioIn 16
Martinez, Michael C. 1954- WhoHisp 91
Martinez, Michael N. 1949- WhoHisp 91
Martinez, Miguel A. 1930- WhoHisp 91
Martinez, Miguel Agustin 1937- WhoHisp 91
Martinez, Nabar Enrique 1946- WhoHisp 91
Martinez, Narciso 1911- WhoHisp 91
Martinez, Octavio Nestor, Jr. 1961- WhoHisp 91
Martinez, Octavio Vincent 1947- WhoHisp 91
Martinez, Odaline De La 1949- IntWWM 90, PenDiMP
Martinez, Oscar J. 1943- BioIn 16, WhoHisp 91
Martinez, Patricia Hincapie 1959- WhoHisp 91
Martinez, Paul Edward 1952- WhoHisp 91
Martinez, Pedro 1924- WhoHisp 91
Martinez, Pedro Enrique BiDrAPA 89
Martinez, Pete R. 1937- WhoHisp 91
Martinez, Rafael Arevalo HispWr 90
Martinez, Ralph T. WhoHisp 91
Martinez, Ramon 1968- Ballpl 90
Martinez, Ramon Anthony 1966- WhoEmL 91
Martinez, Ramon Jaime 1968- WhoHisp 91
Martinez, Ramon O BiDrAPA 89
Martinez, Raul Cisneros 1942- WhoHisp 91
Martinez, Raul L. 1949- WhoAm 90, WhoSSW 91
Martinez, Ricardo Pedro 1945- WhoHisp 91
Martinez, Ricardo Salazar 1951- WhoHisp 91
Martinez, Rich 1950- WhoHisp 91
Martinez, Richard WhoHisp 91
Martinez, Richard 1952- WhoHisp 91
Martinez, Richard Isaac 1944- WhoHisp 91
Martinez, Richard P. BiDrAPA 89
Martinez, Rick A. BiDrAPA 89
Martinez, Robert 1943- WhoHisp 91
Martinez, Robert 1949- WhoHisp 91
Martinez, Robert A. 1943- WhoHisp 91
Martinez, Robert Manuel 1943- WhoE 91
Martinez, Rolando 1954- WhoSSW 91
Martinez, Roman Octaviano 1958- WhoHisp 91
Martinez, Rosa Borrero 1956- WhoHisp 91
Martinez, Ruben Martin 1948- WhoWor 91
Martinez, Ruben O. 1952- WhoHisp 91
Martinez, Sally Verdugo 1934- WhoHisp 91
Martinez, Salome 1947- WhoHisp 91
Martinez, Salutario 1935- WhoHisp 91
Martinez, Salvador M BiDrAPA 89
Martinez, Seledon C., Sr. 1921- WhoHisp 91
Martinez, Serge Anthony 1942- WhoHisp 91
Martinez, Sergio E. 1919- WhoHisp 91
Martinez, Sergio Ernesto 1919- WhoSSW 91
Martinez, Silvia Jacinta 1955- WhoE 91
Martinez, Silvio 1955- Ballpl 90
Martinez, Sylvia Ann 1951- WhoHisp 91
Martinez, Teddy 1947- Ballpl 90
Martinez, Teresa Virginia Dant 1959- WhoWor 91
Martinez, Tino BioIn 16
Martinez, Tippy 1950- Ballpl 90
Martinez, Tomas Eloy ConAu 131, HispWr 90
Martinez, Tomas Eugene 1949- WhoHisp 91
Martinez, Victor Hipolito 1924- WhoWor 91
Martinez, Victor Sanabria 1899-1952 BioIn 16
Martinez, Vilma BioIn 16
Martinez, Vilma S. 1943- WhoHisp 91
Martinez, Virginia 1949- WhoHisp 91
Martinez, Walter 1951- WhoHisp 91
Martinez, Walter Baldomero 1937- WhoAm 90
Martinez, Walter Kenneth, Jr. 1959- WhoHisp 91
Martinez, Xavier 1869-1943 BioIn 16
Martinez, Yolanda R. 1936- WhoAmW 91
Martinez, Yvette 1954- WhoHisp 91
Martinez, Zobeida Enid BiDrAPA 89
Martinez-Boue, Manuel Guillermo BiDrAPA 89
Martinez-Burgoyne, Toni 1943- WhoHisp 91
Martinez-Canas, Maria 1960- WhoAmA 91
Martinez-Carrion, Marino 1936- WhoAm 90
Martinez-Chavez, Diana 1955- WhoHisp 91
Martinez de Aragon, Antonio 1952- WhoWor 91
Martinez-De La Cruz, Francisco J BiDrAPA 89
Martinez de la Rosa, Francisco 1787-1862 BioIn 16
Martinez De Peron, Maria Estela 1931- WhoWor 91
Martinez de Pinillos, Joaquin Victor 1941- WhoHisp 91
Martinez Dominguez, Guillermo 1923- WhoWor 91
Martinez Estrada, Ezequiel 1895-1964 BioIn 16
Martinez-Fonts, Alberto, Jr. 1943- WhoHisp 91
Martinez-Garduno, Beatriz 1940- WhoHisp 91
Martinez-Hernandez, Antonio 1944- WhoE 91
Martinez-Lanza, Mario 1929- BiDrAPA 89
Martinez-Lopez, Norman P. WhoHisp 91
Martinez-Maldonado, Manuel 1937- WhoAm 90, WhoHisp 91
Martinez-Miranda, Luz Josefina 1956- WhoHisp 91
Martinez Moreno, Carlos 1917-1986 ConAu 131, HispWr 90
Martinez-Paula, Emilio WhoHisp 91
Martinez-Pico, Jose L. 1918- WhoAm 90
Martinez-Purson, Rita 1955- WhoHisp 91
Martinez-Ramirez, Jose Roberto 1954- WhoHisp 91
Martinez-Roach, N. Patricia 1949- WhoHisp 91
Martinez-Rodgers, Victoria BioIn 16
Martinez-Romero, Sergio 1936- WhoHisp 91
Martinez Ruiz, Jose 1873-1967 HispWr 90
Martinez Sierra, Maria 1874-1974 EncCoWW
Martinez Somalo, Eduardo 1927- WhoWor 91
Martinez-Tejeda, Juan J. 1908- WhoAm 90
Martinez Toro, Vilma 1959- WhoHisp 91
Marting, Leeda Pollock 1945- WhoE 91
Marting, Walter A. 1946- St&PR 91
Marting, William Locke 1936- St&PR 91
Martini, Arthur Pete 1943- WhoWor 91
Martini, Arturo 1889-1947 PenDiDA 89
Martini, Carlo Maria 1927- WhoWor 91
Martini, D. Richard BiDrAPA 89
Martini, Emil P., Jr. 1928- St&PR 91, WhoAm 90
Martini, Federico BioIn 16
Martini, Francesco Di Giorgio 1439-1501? BioIn 16

Martini, James J. 1910- St&PR 91
Martini, Luciano 1927- WhoWor 91
Martini, Maureen Anne 1950- WhoE 91
Martini, R.E. 1932- St&PR 91
Martini, Robert E. 1932- WhoAm 90
Martini, Simone 1284?-1344 IntDcAA 90
Martini, Teri 1930- AuBYP 90
Martinic, Leo Daniel 1958- St&PR 91
Martinich, Aloysius Patrick 1946- WhoSSW 91
Martinie, Steven 1954- WhoEmL 91
Martinis, Carla 1921- IntWWM 90
Martinis, William J. 1941- St&PR 91
Martinko, Mark James 1949- WhoSSW 91
Martinkus, Stanley J. 1947- St&PR 91
Martino, A. BiDWomA
Martino, Babette WhoAmA 91
Martino, Babette 1956- WhoE 91
Martino, Donald James 1931- IntWWM 90, WhoAm 90
Martino, Eva E WhoAmA 91
Martino, Eva Ellena 1926- WhoE 91
Martino, Frank 1937- WhoAm 90
Martino, Frank Dominic 1919- WhoAm 90
Martino, Frank N. 1929- St&PR 91
Martino, Giovanni 1908- WhoAmA 91
Martino, James B. 1951- St&PR 91
Martino, John E. 1936- St&PR 91
Martino, Joseph BioIn 16
Martino, Joseph Paul 1931- WhoAm 90
Martino, Maria Linda 1962- WhoWrEP 89
Martino, Marie G. St&PR 91
Martino, Mary Louise Dolinar 1930- WhoE 91
Martino, Michael Felix 1946- WhoE 91
Martino, Nina F WhoAmA 91
Martino, Nina Florence 1952- WhoE 91
Martino, Pat 1944- BioIn 16
Martino, Rezan Solmaz 1961- WhoAmW 91
Martino, Richard L. 1930- St&PR 91
Martino, Robert Francis 1944- WhoE 91
Martino, Rocco Leonard 1929- WhoE 91, WhoWor 91
Martinon, Jean 1910-1976 PenDiMP
Martinovsky, Eugene BiDrAPA 89
Martins, Americo Antunes 1926- WhoWor 91
Martins, Anna W BiDrAPA 89
Martins, Antonio Gentil 1930- WhoWor 91
Martins, Clovis 1920- BiDrAPA 89
Martins, Heitor Miranda 1933- WhoAm 90
Martins, Joao R. 1938- St&PR 91
Martins, Joseph 1953- St&PR 91
Martins, Maria De Lourdes 1926- IntWWM 90
Martins, Orlando 1900-1985 DrBIPA 90
Martins, Peter 1946- WhoAm 90, WhoE 91, WorAlBi
Martinsen, Ivar Richard 1922- WhoAmA 91
Martinsen, Keith Alan 1965- WhoEmL 91
Martinsen, Martin ConAu 33NR, MajTwCW
Martinson, A. Denise 1947- WhoWrEP 89
Martinson, Charles F BiDrAPA 89
Martinson, David John 1942- St&PR 91
Martinson, David Keith 1946- WhoWrEP 89
Martinson, Earl Merrill 1924- St&PR 91
Martinson, Fred L. 1921- St&PR 91
Martinson, Genevieve L. 1923- WhoAmW 91
Martinson, Harry 1904-1978 DcScanL
Martinson, Harry Edmund 1904-1978 WorAlBi
Martinson, Helen Delabar 1939- WhoAmW 91, WhoSSW 91
Martinson, Helga Maria 1890- DcScanL
Martinson, Helga Maria 1890-1964 EncCoWW
Martinson, Ida Marie 1936- WhoAm 90, WhoAmW 91
Martinson, Jacob Christian, Jr. 1933- WhoAm 90
Martinson, Jeanne Angelo 1962- WhoWrEP 89
Martinson, Judith Ann 1951- WhoAmW 91
Martinson, Moa DcScanL
Martinson, William Henry 1926- St&PR 91
Martinu, Bohuslav 1890-1959 PenDiMP A
Martinucci, Nicola 1941- IntWWM 90
Martinuzzi, Leo S. 1928- St&PR 91
Martinuzzi, Leo Sergio, Jr. 1928- WhoAm 90
Martiny, M 1897- EncO&P 3
Martio, Olli Tapani 1941- WhoWor 91
Martirena-Mantel, Ana Maria 1935- WhoWor 91
Martland, Steve 1958- IntWWM 90
Martmer, William Philip 1939- WhoAmA 91
Martocchio, Emilio F. 1927- St&PR 91
Martocci, Angeline Anne 1930- St&PR 91
Martoche, Salvatore Richard 1940- WhoAm 90
Martoff, Charles Jeff 1954- WhoE 91
Martoglio, Alberta Margaret 1932- WhoAmW 91
Marton, Emery 1922- WhoAm 90
Marton, Eva 1943- PenDiMP
Marton, Eva Heinrich 1943- IntWWM 90, WhoAm 90, WhoWor 91
Marton, G.E. 1940- St&PR 91
Marton, Laurence Jay 1944- WhoAm 90
Marton, Pier 1950- WhoAmA 91
Marton, Tutzi 1936- WhoAmA 91
Martone, Christine Anne 1945- BiDrAPA 89
Martone, Michael 1941- WhoAmA 91
Martone, Michael 1955- WhoWrEP 89
Martone, William Robert 1945- WhoAmA 91
Martoni, Charles J. 1936- WhoE 91, WhoWor 91
Martonmere, John Roland Robinson, Baron 1907-1989 BioIn 16
Martonosi, Anthony Nicholas 1928- WhoAm 90
Martorana, Andrew BiDrAPA 89
Martorana, Sebastian Vincent 1919- WhoAm 90
Martorell, Joseph Anthony 1939- WhoHisp 91
Martorelli, Louis, Jr. 1949- St&PR 91
Martosella, Peter Anthony, Jr. 1936- WhoAm 90
Martov, IUrii Osipovich 1873-1923 BioIn 16
Martov, L. 1873-1923 BioIn 16
Martres, Ruben Walter 1933- WhoWor 91
Martschink, Sherry Shealy 1949- WhoAmW 91, WhoSSW 91
Marttila, James Konstantin 1948- WhoEmL 91
Marttin, Paul WhoWrEP 89
Marttinen, Tauno 1912- IntWWM 90
Martucci, Gloria Martha 1934- WhoWor 91
Martucci, Sheryl Lee 1962- WhoAmW 91
Martucci, William Christopher 1952- WhoEmL 91
Marturana, Louis 1932- St&PR 91
Martus, Ida Davidoff BioIn 16
Martuscello, Diane Mataraza 1952- WhoE 91
Marty, Andre Pierre 1886-1956 BiDFrPL
Marty, Francis 1942- WhoWor 91
Marty, Francois 1904- WhoWor 91
Marty, Georganne Spurling 1933- WhoAmW 91
Marty, Joe 1913-1984 Ballpl 90
Marty, Julio E. WhoHisp 91
Marty, Martin E. 1928- BioIn 16
Marty, Martin Emil 1928- WhoAm 90
Marty, Raymond 1929- WhoWor 91
Marty, Robert S. 1944- St&PR 91
Marty, Samuel C., Jr. 1928- BiDrAPA 89
Martyak, Joseph J. WhoAm 90
Martyl 1918- WhoAm 90, WhoAmA 91
Martyn, David Forbes 1906-1970 DcScB S2
Martyn, Howe 1906-1989 ConAu 129
Martyn, James Louis 1925- WhoAm 90
Martyn, Pamela Pagones 1949- WhoAmW 91
Martyniak, Kay BioIn 16
Martyniuk, John William 1957- BiDrAPA 89
Martyr, Crista L. 1946- St&PR 91
Martz, Cindy Lynne 1965- WhoAmW 91
Martz, Clyde Ollen 1920- WhoAm 90
Martz, Donna Kay 1959- WhoAmW 91
Martz, Gary 1955- BiDrAPA 89
Martz, John Danhouse, III 1934- WhoAm 90, WhoE 91
Martz, Karl BioIn 16
Martz, Karl 1912- WhoAmA 91
Martz, Randy 1956- Ballpl 90
Martz, Robert L. 1930- St&PR 91
Martz, Stephen 1942- St&PR 91
Martz, Walter Atlee 1923- WhoAm 90, WhoSSW 91
Maruki, Toshi 1912- BioIn 16
Marullo, Michael Anthony 1947- WhoSSW 91
Marumoto, Katsuhiko 1940- St&PR 91
Marumoto, Therese M 1950- BiDrAPA 89
Marumoto, William Hideo 1934- WhoAm 90
Marusak, Carl Edward BiDrAPA 89
Marushack, Andrew Joseph 1935- St&PR 91
Maruska, Edward Joseph 1934- WhoAm 90
Maruskin Mott, Joan 1944- WhoAmW 91
Marut, Edward Lawrence 1949- WhoEmL 91
Marut, Ret BioIn 16, MajTwCW
Maruta, Toshihiko 1946- BiDrAPA 89, WhoEmL 91
Maruvada, Pereswara Sarma 1938- WhoAm 90
Maruvada, Umamahesara Rao BiDrAPA 89
Maruyama, Magoroh 1929- WhoWor 91
Maruyama, Masao 1914- WhoWor 91
Maruyama, Wendy 1952- WhoAmA 91
Maruyama, Yosh 1930- WhoAm 90, WhoSSW 91
Marval, Jacqueline 1866-1932 BiDWomA
Marvan, George Jan 1936- WhoWor 91
Marvasti, Jamshid Alem 1946- BiDrAPA 89
Marvasti, Mariam A BiDrAPA 89
Marvel, Andrew Scott 1961- WhoE 91
Marvel, Carl S. BioIn 16
Marvel, Carl Shipp 1894-1988 DcScB S2
Marvel, David T. 1906-1988 BioIn 16
Marvel, Douglas James 1944- WhoSSW 91
Marvel, John A. 1922- WhoAm 90
Marvel, Nathaniel T BiDrAPA 89
Marvel, Thomas Stahl 1935- WhoAm 90
Marvelettes, The EncPR&S 89
Marvell, Andrew 1621-1678 WorAlBi
Marvelley, Brian 1947- St&PR 91
Marvenko-Smith, Patricia Ann 1947- WhoE 91
Marver, James D. 1950- St&PR 91
Marvi, David D BiDrAPA 89
Marvia, Einari 1915- IntWWM 90
Marvil, Patricia De L. WhoHisp 91
Marvil, Richard A. 1938- St&PR 91
Marvin, Daniel E., Jr. 1938- St&PR 91
Marvin, David Keith 1921- WhoAm 90
Marvin, Douglas Raymond 1947- WhoAm 90
Marvin, Earl 1918- St&PR 91
Marvin, Elizabeth West 1955- IntWWM 90
Marvin, Frederick 1923- IntWWM 90
Marvin, Guy, III 1941- St&PR 91
Marvin, H.A. St&PR 91
Marvin, Helen Rhyne 1917- WhoAmW 91, WhoSSW 91
Marvin, James Conway 1927- WhoAm 90
Marvin, John George 1912- WhoE 91, WhoWor 91
Marvin, Ken St&PR 91
Marvin, Kurt St&PR 91
Marvin, Lee 1924-1987 WorAlBi
Marvin, Levi Chandler 1807-1873 AmLegL
Marvin, Marajean L. 1933- IntWWM 90
Marvin, Mel 1941- IntWWM 90
Marvin, Oscar McDowell 1924- WhoAm 90
Marvin, Philip 1916- WhoE 91
Marvin, Robert L 1925- BiDrAPA 89
Marvin, Roy Mack 1931- St&PR 91, WhoAm 90
Marvin, Susan Isabelle 1954- WhoAmW 91
Marvin, Ursula Bailey 1921- WhoAmW 91
Marvin, William Glenn, Jr. 1920- WhoAm 90
Marvit, Robert C 1938- BiDrAPA 89
Marvit, Robert Charles 1938- WhoAm 90
Marwell, Edward M. 1922- St&PR 91
Marwell, Emily 1950- WhoE 91
Marwell, Gerald 1937- WhoAm 90
Marwick, Arthur 1936- ConAu 30NR
Marwood, Mary Teresa 1958- WhoE 91
Marx Brothers BioIn 16
Marx, Alan Harvey 1946- BiDrAPA 89
Marx, Alexander 1878-1953 BioIn 16
Marx, Anne ConAu 30NR, WhoAm 90
Marx, Arthur 1888-1964 WorAlBi
Marx, Arthur 1921- WhoAm 90
Marx, Barbara Kaye 1949- ODwPR 91
Marx, David L. 1952- St&PR 91
Marx, Eleanor 1855-1898 BioIn 16
Marx, Elizabeth Ellen 1945- WhoE 91
Marx, Enid 1902- ConDes 90
Marx, Evelyn WhoAmA 91
Marx, Frederick Henry 1942- St&PR 91
Marx, Gary 1938- ODwPR 91
Marx, Gary T. BioIn 16
Marx, Gary T. 1938- ConAu 32NR
Marx, George L. 1932- WhoAm 90
Marx, Gerald A. 1930-1988 BioIn 16
Marx, Gertie Florentine 1912- WhoAm 90
Marx, Groucho 1891-1977 BioIn 16
Marx, Herbert 1901-1979 WorAlBi
Marx, Herbert 1932- WhoAm 90
Marx, James Henry 1925- WhoE 91
Marx, Jay Neil 1945- WhoEmL 91
Marx, Joe E., III 1947- St&PR 91
Marx, Johann R BiDrAPA 89
Marx, Julius 1890-1977 WorAlBi
Marx, Julius H. 1891-1977 BioIn 16
Marx, Karl 1818-1883 BioIn 16, WorAlBi, WrPh P
Marx, Larry Steven BiDrAPA 89
Marx, Leo 1919- WhoAm 90
Marx, Leo A., Jr. 1946- St&PR 91
Marx, Leonard 1887-1961 WorAlBi
Marx, Leonard, Jr. 1932- St&PR 91
Marx, Marilyn ODwPR 91
Marx, Michael H. St&PR 91
Marx, Milton 1897-1977 WorAlBi
Marx, Morris L. WhoAm 90, WhoSSW 91
Marx, Nikolaus 1938- WhoWor 91
Marx, Nolan Jay 1928- BiDrAPA 89
Marx, Otto, Jr. 1909- WhoAm 90, WhoE 91
Marx, Paula Jeannette 1956- WhoEmL 91
Marx, Peter Jay 1955- WhoE 91
Marx, Randall P. St&PR 91
Marx, Richard BioIn 16
Marx, Robert 1928- WhoWor 91
Marx, Robert Ernst 1925- WhoAmA 91
Marx, Robert Frank 1936- AuBYP 90
Marx, Roberto Burle- BioIn 16
Marx, Russell David BiDrAPA 89
Marx, Thomas Antonius 1960- WhoE 91
Marx, Thomas George 1943- WhoAm 90
Marx, Walter D. 1918- St&PR 91
Marx, Walter Herbert 1926- St&PR 91
Marx, William 1920- St&PR 91
Marx, William B., Jr. 1939- WhoAm 90
Marxer, John A. 1943- WhoAm 90
Marxsen, Willi 1919- WhoWor 91
Mary WomWR, WorAlBi
Mary 1457-1482 WomWR
Mary I 1516- WomWR [port]
Mary I 1516-1558 WorAlBi
Mary II 1662-1694 WomWR [port]
Mary Agnes 1928- FemiCLE
Mary Ann BioIn 16
Mary Benedicta DcCanB 12
Mary, Blessed Virgin BioIn 16
Mary Bosomworth WomWR
Mary of Antioch WomWR
Mary of Guise 1515-1560 WomWR
Mary of Lorraine WomWR
Mary I, Queen of England 1516-1558 BioIn 16
Mary II, Queen of England 1662-1694 BiDEWW
Mary II, Queen of Great Britain 1662-1694 BioIn 16
Mary, Queen of Hungary 1370?-1395 BioIn 16
Mary, Queen of Scots 1542-1587 BioIn 16, WorAlBi
Mary, Saint EncPaPR 91
Mary Stuart 1542-1586 WomWR [port]
Mary Vincent DcCanB 12
Mary, John St&PR 91
Maryan, Maryan S 1927-1977 WhoAmA 91N
Marye, George Thomas 1849-1933 BioIn 16
Marylebone, Quintin Hogg Hailsham of St. BioIn 16
Marzan, Gregorio 1906- MusmAFA
Marzan, Julio 1946- ConAu 131, HispWr 90
Marzani, Valerie June 1958- WhoE 91
Marzano, A.M. 1929- St&PR 91
Marzano, Albert 1919- WhoAmA 91
Marziale, Antonio 1959- WhoSSW 91
Marzilli, Mario 1947- WhoWor 91
Marzio, Peter Cort 1943- WhoAm 90, WhoAmA 91, WhoSSW 91
Marzke, David Wayne 1956- WhoEmL 91
Marzloff, George Ernest 1950- WhoEmL 91
Marzluf, George Austin 1935- WhoAm 90
Marzollo, Claudio 1938- WhoAmA 91
Marzollo, Jean BioIn 16
Marzuk, Peter Michael 1956- BiDrAPA 89
Marzullo, Vito 1897-1990 BioIn 16
Mas, Francis G 1939- BiDrAPA 89
Mas, Jorge BioIn 16
Mas, Luis Pablo 1924- WhoHisp 91
Mas Canosa, Jorge L. 1939- WhoHisp 91
Masaccio 1401-1428 IntDcAA 90
Masaccio, Guidi 1401-1428 WorAlBi
Masai, Mitsuo 1932- WhoWor 91
Masaki, Yoshiki 1934- St&PR 91
Masamune, Satoru 1928- WhoAm 90
Masand, Prakash S BiDrAPA 89
Masangkay, Generoso Pedro BiDrAPA 89
Masani, Shakuntala AuBYP 90
Masaoka, Shiki 1867-1902 BioIn 16
Masarik, Albert E. 1943- WhoWrEP 89
Masaryk, Jan Garrigue 1886-1948 WorAlBi
Masaryk, T.G. 1850-1937 BioIn 16
Masaryk, Tomas Garrigue 1850-1937 WorAlBi
BioIn 16
Masaschi, John E. 1933- St&PR 91
Masatsugu, Mitsuyuki 1924- ConAu 129
Masbaum, Ned Paul BiDrAPA 89
Masbruch, Randal J. 1954- St&PR 91
Mascagni, Pietro 1863-1945 PenDiMP A, WorAlBi
Mascarello, Henry J. BioIn 16
Mascarenhas, Alipio Barros 1948- BiDrAPA 89
Mascarenhas, Cela Margaret 1935- WhoAmW 91
Mascarenhas, Maritza Helmen Freda 1956- WhoSSW 91
Mascarenhas, Mary-Ann Helen 1961- WhoAmW 91
Mascari, Joseph C. 1922- St&PR 91

Mascayano, Jose Joaquin Perez 1801-1889 *BioIn 16*
Masch, Frank Dewey, Jr. 1933- *WhoSSW 91*
Maschal, Charles Emerson, Jr. 1945- *WhoE 91*
Mascheroni, Aldo 1954- *St&PR 91*
Mascheroni, Edoardo 1852-1941 *PenDiMP*
Mascherpa, Antonio 1908- *WhoWor 91*
Maschin, Douglas Raymond 1950- *WhoE 91*
Maschmann, Michael Wayne 1949- *St&PR 91*
Maschmeyer, Robert 1914- *BiDrAPA 89*
Mascho, George Leroy 1925- *WhoAm 90*
Maschwitz, Eric 1901-1969 *OxCPMus*
Masci, Carmela 1964- *WhoAmW 91*
Mascia, Armond Vincent 1921-1990 *BioIn 16*
Masciantonio, Philip Xavier 1929- *St&PR 91, WhoAm 90*
Mascilak, Joei Janna 1955- *WhoSSW 91*
Masciole, Denis Michael 1941- *St&PR 91*
Mascioli, Mario V. 1921- *St&PR 91*
Mascioli-Charlton, Maria C. 1956- *St&PR 91*
Masclee, Kent Ivan 1943- *WhoE 91*
Masco, Howard Leslie 1940- *BiDrAPA 89*
Masco, Matt Schelb 1940- *St&PR 91*
Mascoll, Doris Walker 1936- *WhoAmW 91*
Mascolo, Donna Marie 1955- *WhoAmW 91*
Mascort, Juan A *BiDrAPA 89*
Mascotte, John P. *St&PR 91*
Mascotte, John Pierre 1939- *WhoAm 90, WhoE 91*
Mascovich, Paul Richard 1948- *BiDrAPA 89*
Masden, Deborah Cheryl 1953- *WhoSSW 91*
Mase, Barbara Ann 1950- *WhoAmW 91*
Mase, Raymond James 1951- *IntWWM 90*
Masecampo, Alfe Aguirre *BiDrAPA 89*
Masefield, John 1878-1967 *AuBYP 90, BioIn 16, ConAu 33NR, MajTwCW, WorAlBi*
Masefield, John 1933- *St&PR 91*
Masek, Barry Michael 1955- *WhoEmL 91, WhoWor 91*
Masek, Joseph Peter 1947- *St&PR 91*
Masekela, Hugh 1939- *DrBlPA 90*
Maselli, Joe *BioIn 16*
Maselli, John Anthony 1929- *WhoAm 90*
Masemola, Jafta *BioIn 16, NewYTBS 90*
Masemore, Gerald L. 1938- *St&PR 91*
Masencup, Mary Elizabeth 1954- *WhoSSW 91*
Maseng, Mari 1954- *WhoAm 90*
Masengill, Robert G. 1942- *WhoSSW 91*
Masenheimer, Ned A. 1928- *St&PR 91*
Maser, Chris 1938- *ConAu 132*
Maser, Edward Andrew 1923-1988 *WhoAmA 91N*
Maser, Frederick Ernest 1908- *WhoAm 90, WhoWor 91*
Maser, James Ellison 1938- *St&PR 91*
Maser, John *PenDiDA 89*
Maser, Karl A. 1937- *St&PR 91*
Maserati, Ettore *NewYTBS 90*
Maseri, Attilio 1935- *WhoWor 91*
Masey, Jack 1924- *WhoAm 90*
Masey, Mary Lou 1932- *AuBYP 90*
Masey-Ayub, Mary Oma 1952- *WhoAmW 91*
Masferrer, Maria E 1952- *BiDrAPA 89*
Masferrer, Mauricio 1950- *BiDrAPA 89*
Mash, Donald J. *WhoAm 90*
Masham, Damaris *BiDEWW*
Masham, Damaris 1658-1708 *FemiCLE*
Mashariqa, Muhammad Zuhayr *WhoWor 91*
Mashaw, Jerry L. 1941- *WhoAm 90*
Mashbern, William Allen 1947- *IntWWM 90*
Mashburn, Guerry Leonard 1952- *WhoSSW 91*
Mashburn, Judith Marie 1942- *WhoE 91*
Mashburn, Kimberly Joy Needham 1957- *WhoAmW 91*
Mashburn, Lillian Tauxe 1943- *WhoAmW 91*
Mashburn, Thomas Matthew 1960- *WhoSSW 91*
Masheck, Joseph Daniel 1942- *WhoAm 90*
Masheck, Joseph Daniel Cahill 1942- *WhoAmA 91*
Mashek, Carol Ann Martin 1937- *WhoAmW 91*
Mashek, Robert William 1936- *WhoAm 90*
Masheke, Malimba 1941- *WhoWor 91*
Mashikian, Hagop S *BiDrAPA 89*
Mashiko, Toru 1948- *WhoWor 91*
Mashimo, Paul Akira 1926- *WhoE 91*
Mashin, Jacqueline Ann Cook 1941- *WhoAmW 91, WhoE 91, WhoWor 91*
Mashinini, Emma 1929- *BioIn 16*
Masi, Alfonse Thomas 1930- *WhoAm 90*
Masi, Dale A. *WhoAm 90*
Masi, Enrico *PenDiMP*
Masi, J. Roger 1954- *WhoE 91*
Masi, Jane Virginia 1947- *WhoEmL 91, WhoWor 91*
Masi, Phil 1917- *Ballpl 90*
Masiar, Stephen J. *BiDrAPA 89*
Masica, James Gerald 1943- *St&PR 91*
Masie, Elliott 1950- *WhoE 91*
Masiello, Richard James 1965- *WhoE 91*
Masiello, Rocco Joseph 1922- *WhoAm 90*
Masilla, Thomas Anthony, Jr. 1946- *St&PR 91, WhoAm 90*
Masilotti, Sharyn Rose 1956- *WhoAmW 91*
Masin, Leo 1916- *St&PR 91*
Masin, Ronald 1937- *IntWWM 90*
Masina, Giulietta 1921- *ConTFT 8*
Masington, Nicholas Joseph, Jr. 1941- *St&PR 91*
Masini, Alfred M. *BioIn 16*
Masini, Donald Joseph 1935- *St&PR 91*
Masini, Eleonora Barbieri 1928- *ConAu 130*
Masini, Gerardo 1920- *WhoWor 91*
Masinter, Edgar M. 1931- *St&PR 91*
Masinter, Edgar Martin 1931- *WhoAm 90*
Masinter, Thomas Alan 1950- *IntWWM 90*
Masire, Quett 1925- *WhoWor 91*
Masironi, Roberto 1931- *WhoWor 91*
Maskall, Martha Josephine 1945- *WhoAmW 91, WhoEmL 91*
Maskelyne, John Nevil 1839-1917 *BioIn 16, EncO&P 3*
Maskelyne, Nevil 1732-1811 *BioIn 16*
Masket, Edward Seymour 1923- *WhoAm 90*
Maskin, Eric Stark 1950- *WhoE 91*
Masko, John J *BiDrAPA 89*
Maskrey, Joseph *St&PR 91*
Maslach, Christina 1946- *WhoAm 90*
Maslach, George James 1920- *WhoAm 90*
Maslan, John Patrick 1939- *St&PR 91*
Maslan, Lawrence 1926- *St&PR 91*
Masland, Frank E., III 1921- *St&PR 91*
Masland, William S. 1921- *St&PR 91*
Maslanka, John A. 1944- *St&PR 91*
Maslanka, Stanislaw A 1922- *BiDrAPA 89*
Maslansky, Paul *BioIn 16*
Maslen, Neil Leonard 1933- *St&PR 91*
Maslen, Stephen Harold 1926- *WhoAm 90*
Masler, Ernest G 1923- *BiDrAPA 89*
Masliah, Leo 1954- *IntWWM 90*
Masliah, Michele Irene 1951- *BiDrAPA 89*
Maslinoff, Jane Rona 1948- *WhoE 91*
Maslo, Hans Joseph 1951- *WhoSSW 91*
Masloff, Sophie 1917- *WhoAm 90, WhoAmW 91, WhoE 91*
Maslow, Abraham H 1908-1970 *MajTwCW*
Maslow, Abraham Harold *BioIn 16*
Maslow, David Ezra 1943- *WhoE 91*
Maslow, Will 1907- *WhoAm 90, WhoE 91*
Maslyk, Cheri Ann 1949- *WhoAmW 91*
Maslyn, Michael E. 1940- *St&PR 91*
Maslyukov, Yuri 1937- *BioIn 16*
Maslyukov, Yuriy Dmitrievich 1937- *WhoWor 91*
Masnari, Nino Antonio 1935- *WhoSSW 91*
Maso Di Banco *IntDcAA 90*
Masol, Vitaly Andriovych 1928- *WhoWor 91*
Masolino da Panicale 1383?-1440? *IntDcAA 90*
Masoliver, Liberata 1911- *EncCoWW*
Masom, Dorothy Shirley 1930- *WhoE 91*
Mason, A E W 1865-1948 *TwCCr&M 91*
Mason, Aaron S 1912- *BiDrAPA 89, WhoAm 90*
Mason, Aimee Hunnicutt Romberger 1918- *WhoAmW 91, WhoSSW 91, WhoWor 91*
Mason, Albert A *BiDrAPA 89*
Mason, Alden C 1919- *WhoAmA 91*
Mason, Alfred Edward Woodley 1865-1948 *SpyFic*
Mason, Alice 1904-1971 *BiDWomA*
Mason, Alice Frances 1895- *WhoAmA 91N*
Mason, Alice Trumball 1904-1971 *WhoAmA 91N*
Mason, Alpheus Thomas 1899- *ConAu 32NR*
Mason, Alpheus Thomas 1899-1989 *BioIn 16, ConAu 130*
Mason, Anthony Halstead 1938- *WhoAm 90, WhoWor 91*
Mason, Barbara Ellen 1945- *WhoAmW 91*
Mason, Barbara Lynn *BiDrAPA 89*
Mason, Barbara Mentzer 1937- *WhoAmW 91*
Mason, Barry 1947- *IntWWM 90*
Mason, Barry Jean 1930- *WhoAm 90*
Mason, Belinda *BioIn 16*
Mason, Benedict 1954- *IntWWM 90*
Mason, Benjamin Lincoln 1940- *WhoAm 90*
Mason, Bessie Marlin 1899- *BioIn 16*
Mason, Betty Gwendolyn 1928- *WhoAmW 91*
Mason, Bobbie Ann *BioIn 16*
Mason, Bobbie Ann 1940- *Au&Arts 5 [port], ConAu 31NR, LiHiK, MajTwCW, WhoAmW 91, WhoWrEP 89, WorAu 1980 [port]*
Mason, Brian Harold 1917- *WhoAm 90*
Mason, Bruce 1939- *WhoAm 90*
Mason, Bruce Edward George 1921-1982 *ConAu 129*
Mason, Bryan St. Clair 1963- *WhoSSW 91*
Mason, Carlos Guillermo Suarez *BioIn 16*
Mason, Caroline Faith Vibert 1942- *WhoAmW 91*
Mason, Charles Ellis, III 1938- *WhoAm 90, WhoWrEP 89*
Mason, Charles J. *BioIn 16*
Mason, Charles James 1791-1856 *PenDiDA 89*
Mason, Cherie *BioIn 16*
Mason, Christopher *BioIn 16*
Mason, Clifford 1932- *DrBlPA 90*
Mason, Craig Watson 1954- *WhoE 91, WhoEmL 91*
Mason, Daniel Evan *BiDrAPA 89*
Mason, Daniel Evan 1953- *WhoE 91*
Mason, Dave 1946- *EncPR&S 89*
Mason, David Aaron 1940- *St&PR 91*
Mason, David Dickenson 1917- *WhoAm 90*
Mason, David Ernest 1928- *WhoAm 90*
Mason, David Stewart 1947- *WhoWrEP 89*
Mason, Dean Towle 1932- *WhoAm 90, WhoWor 91*
Mason, Don 1944- *Ballpl 90*
Mason, Douglas L. *St&PR 91*
Mason, Edward 1925- *BiDrAPA 89*
Mason, Edward A 1919- *BiDrAPA 89*
Mason, Edward Allen 1926- *WhoAm 90*
Mason, Edward Archibald 1924- *St&PR 91, WhoAm 90*
Mason, Edward Eaton 1920- *WhoAm 90*
Mason, Elizabeth 1919- *WhoAmW 91*
Mason, Ellsworth Goodwin 1917- *WhoAm 90*
Mason, Emma Newby 1937- *St&PR 91*
Mason, Eric Morris 1925- *IntWWM 90*
Mason, Ernst *MajTwCW*
Mason, F. Eugenia 1947- *St&PR 91*
Mason, F Van Wyck 1901-1978 *TwCCr&M 91*
Mason, Floyd E. 1932- *St&PR 91*
Mason, Ford 1893-1989 *BioIn 16*
Mason, Francis Scarlett, Jr 1921- *WhoAmA 91*
Mason, Francis van Wyck *AuBYP 90*
Mason, Francis Van Wyck 1901-1978 *SpyFic*
Mason, Frank H. 1936- *St&PR 91*
Mason, Frank Herbert 1921- *WhoAmA 91*
Mason, Frank W. 1901-1978 *AuBYP 90, SpyFic*
Mason, Franklin Rogers 1936- *WhoAm 90, WhoSSW 91*
Mason, George *BioIn 16*
Mason, George 1725-1792 *BioIn 16, EncCRAm*
Mason, George E 1932- *ConAu 30NR*
Mason, George Frederick 1904- *AuBYP 90*
Mason, George L. 1946- *St&PR 91*
Mason, George Miles 1789-1859 *PenDiDA 89*
Mason, George Perry, Jr. 1942- *WhoSSW 91*
Mason, George Robert 1932- *WhoAm 90*
Mason, George Walter 1891-1954 *EncABHB 5 [port]*
Mason, H. Griff 1944- *St&PR 91*
Mason, Harold 1937- *WhoAmA 91*
Mason, Harold Jesse 1926- *WhoAm 90*
Mason, Harry C. 1867- *AmLegL*
Mason, Helen Ringer 1937- *BiDrAPA 89*
Mason, Henry Lloyd 1921- *WhoAm 90*
Mason, Henry Lowell, III 1941- *WhoAm 90*
Mason, Herbert Warren, Jr. 1932- *WhoAm 90*
Mason, Howard E. 1932- *St&PR 91*
Mason, Howard Keith *BiDrAPA 89*
Mason, Jack F. 1940- *St&PR 91*
Mason, Jackie *BioIn 16*
Mason, Jackie 1931- *WorAlBi*
Mason, James 1909-1984 *WorAlBi*
Mason, James Albert 1929- *WhoAm 90*
Mason, James Boyd 1941- *WhoAm 90*
Mason, James Carlan 1944- *WhoAm 90*
Mason, James D. 1944- *WhoSSW 91*
Mason, James F. 1942- *St&PR 91*
Mason, James Lee 1938- *BiDrAPA 89*
Mason, James Murray 1798-1871 *BioIn 16*
Mason, James Neville 1909-1984 *DcNaB 1981*
Mason, James Ostermann 1930- *WhoAm 90*
Mason, James Tate 1913- *WhoAm 90*
Mason, James W. 1929- *St&PR 91*
Mason, Jean K. *BioIn 16*
Mason, Jeffrey V. 1956- *St&PR 91*
Mason, Jerry 1913- *WhoWrEP 89*
Mason, Jim 1950- *Ballpl 90*
Mason, John 1600?-1672 *EncCRAm, WhNaAH*
Mason, John 1927- *WhoAmA 91*
Mason, John 1935- *WhoSSW 91*
Mason, John Allen 1944- *St&PR 91*
Mason, John Bell 1928- *St&PR 91*
Mason, John Dudley 1949- *WhoEmL 91*
Mason, John F, Jr. 1935- *BiDrAPA 89*
Mason, John Frederick 1913- *WhoE 91*
Mason, John H. 1936- *St&PR 91*
Mason, John Hayes 1950- *WhoE 91*
Mason, John Latimer 1923- *WhoAm 90*
Mason, John Lemear 1921- *St&PR 91*
Mason, John Milton 1938- *WhoAm 90*
Mason, John Murwyn, Jr. 1940- *WhoAm 90, WhoE 91*
Mason, John Young 1799-1859 *BiDrUSE 89, BioIn 16*
Mason, Jonathan 1916- *St&PR 91, WhoAm 90*
Mason, Joseph 1932- *WhoAm 90*
Mason, Joseph Thomas *BiDrAPA 89*
Mason, Joseph Thomas 1954- *BiDrAPA 89*
Mason, Joyce W *BiDrAPA 89*
Mason, Judi Ann *BioIn 16*
Mason, Judith Ann 1945- *WhoAmW 91*
Mason, Karen A. *ODwPR 91*
Mason, Kenneth Robert 1933- *WhoAm 90*
Mason, Lee W. *TwCCr&M 91*
Mason, Linda Ann 1947- *WhoAmW 91*
Mason, Louise Orazio 1953- *WhoEmL 91*
Mason, Lowell 1792-1872 *BioIn 16, WorAlBi*
Mason, Lucile Gertrude 1925- *WhoAmW 91, WhoE 91*
Mason, Lucy Randolph 1882-1959 *BioAmW*
Mason, Luther Whiting 1828-1896 *BioIn 16*
Mason, Marilyn Gell 1944- *WhoAm 90, WhoAmW 91*
Mason, Marsha *BioIn 16, WhoAm 90, WhoAmW 91*
Mason, Marsha 1942- *WorAlBi*
Mason, Marshall W. 1940- *WhoAm 90*
Mason, Martha 1931- *WhoAmW 91*
Mason, Maude M 1867-1956 *WhoAmA 91N*
Mason, Michael E. 1929- *WhoAm 90*
Mason, Mike 1958- *Ballpl 90*
Mason, Miriam Evangeline 1900-1973 *AuBYP 90*
Mason, Molly Ann 1953- *WhoAmA 91*
Mason, Myrtle H R *BiDrAPA 89*
Mason, Nancy Tolman 1933- *WhoAmW 91*
Mason, Novem M 1942- *WhoAmA 91*
Mason, Orley B. 1908- *St&PR 91*
Mason, Otis Tufton 1838-1908 *WhNaAH*
Mason, Pamela Helen 1922- *WhoAm 90*
Mason, Paul 1920- *St&PR 91*
Mason, Percy *BiDrAPA 89*
Mason, Perry Carter 1939- *WhoAm 90*
Mason, Phillip Howard 1932- *WhoAm 90, WhoE 91*
Mason, R. H. *BioIn 16*
Mason, Ralph Edward 1919- *WhoAm 90*
Mason, Ralph L. 1932- *St&PR 91*
Mason, Rausey Wood 1937- *St&PR 91*
Mason, Raymond A. 1936- *St&PR 91*
Mason, Raymond Adams 1936- *WhoAm 90*
Mason, Raymond Edward, Jr. 1920- *St&PR 91*
Mason, Richard Gordon 1930- *St&PR 91, WhoAm 90*
Mason, Robert Allan 1943- *WhoE 91*
Mason, Robert F. 1927- *St&PR 91*
Mason, Robert Francis 1927- *WhoSSW 91*
Mason, Robert Joseph 1918- *WhoAm 90*
Mason, Robert Lester 1945- *WhoSSW 91*
Mason, Robert Roy 1954- *WhoEmL 91*
Mason, Robert Shephard 1943- *St&PR 91*
Mason, Robert Steven 1930- *WhoAm 90*
Mason, Roger 1958- *Ballpl 90*
Mason, Roger LeRoy 1952- *St&PR 91*
Mason, Ronald 1930- *WhoWor 91*
Mason, Ronald L., Sr. 1928- *St&PR 91*
Mason, Roy Martell 1886-1972 *WhoAmA 91N*
Mason, Scott Aiken 1951- *WhoEmL 91*
Mason, Sharon Ann 1949- *WhoAmW 91*
Mason, Shipley Childs 1946- *St&PR 91*
Mason, Stephen C, III *BiDrAPA 89*
Mason, Stephen Olin 1952- *WhoSSW 91*
Mason, Steven Charles 1936- *St&PR 91, WhoAm 90*
Mason, Steven Jude 1944- *St&PR 91, WhoAm 90*
Mason, Tally *AuBYP 90*
Mason, Terence Harold 1941- *WhoWor 91*
Mason, Theodore Toner 1935- *St&PR 91*

Mason, Thomas Albert 1936- *WhoAm 90*
Mason, Thomas Lyle 1927- *St&PR 91*
Mason, Thomas Paul 1930- *WhoE 91*
Mason, Timothy Patrick 1940- *St&PR 91*
Mason, Tommy Ray *BioIn 16*
Mason, Trudy L. *BioIn 16*
Mason, William Alvin 1926- *WhoAm 90*
Mason, William Cordell, III 1938- *WhoAm 90*
Mason-Bell, Sharon E *BiDrAPA 89*
Mason-O'Neal, Beth Barwick 1939- *WhoSSW 91*
Masoner, Paul Henry 1908- *WhoAm 90*
Masoro, Edward Joseph, Jr. 1924- *WhoAm 90*
Masotti, Ada *BioIn 16*
Masotti, Alberto *BioIn 16*
Masotti, George M *BiDrAPA 89*
Masotti, Lewis Richard 1933- *St&PR 91, WhoE 91*
Masotti, Louis Henry 1934- *WhoAm 90*
Masotti, Olga *BioIn 16*
Masotto, Guido Giovanni 1938- *WhoWor 91*
Masoudi, Sherry Sharbanue 1963- *WhoEmL 91*
Masquelier, John Roger 1947- *WhoE 91*
Masquelier, Sibyl W. 1946- *WhoAmW 91*
Masquerier, Lewis 1802- *BioIn 16*
Masreliez, Louis Adrien 1748-1810 *PenDiDA 89*
Masri, Asad M *BiDrAPA 89*
Masri, Munib al- *BioIn 16*
Masri, Sami Faiz 1939- *WhoAm 90*
Masri, Taher Nashat 1942- *WhoWor 91*
Mass, Donna Marie 1954- *WhoAmW 91*
Mass, Edward R. 1926- *St&PR 91*
Mass, Haim 1921- *WhoWor 91*
Mass, Paul *PenDiMP*
Massa, Conrad Harry 1927- *WhoAm 90*
Massa, Don Joseph 1923- *St&PR 91*
Massa, Donald Patrick 1946- *St&PR 91*
Massa, Emilio 1938- *BiDrAPA 89*
Massa, Frank *St&PR 91N*
Massa, Harold A. 1938- *St&PR 91*
Massa, Miguel Souza, III 1950- *WhoE 91*
Massa, Paul Peter 1940- *WhoAm 90*
Massa, Peter 1926- *St&PR 91*
Massa, Robert P. 1947- *St&PR 91*
Massa, Salvatore Peter 1955- *WhoAm 90, WhoE 91*
Massad, Carolyn Emrick 1935- *WhoE 91*
Massad, Gary Lloyd 1946- *BiDrAPA 89*
Massad, John Benedict 1956- *WhoE 91*
Massad, Susan *BioIn 16*
Massagee, Deanie Herman 1947- *WhoSSW 91*
Massai *WhNaAH*
Massalska, Appolline-Helene 1763-1815 *EncCoWW*
Massalski, Thaddeus Bronislaw 1926- *WhoAm 90*
Massana, Juan *BiDrAPA 89*
Massar, Jack 1925- *St&PR 91*
Massar, Ruth Lisa 1962- *WhoAmW 91*
Massara, Aldo 1935- *St&PR 91*
Massarano, John R. 1933- *St&PR 91*
Massard, Robert 1925- *IntWWM 90*
Massarelli, Stanley Myron 1933- *St&PR 91*
Massaro, Karen Thuesen 1944- *WhoAmA 91*
Massaro, Louis L. 1946- *St&PR 91*
Massary, Fritzi *BioIn 16*
Massary, Fritzi 1882-1969 *PenDiMP*
Massaryk, Friederike 1882-1969 *PenDiMP*
Massasoit 1580?-1661 *WhNaAH*
Massasoit 1580?-1662? *EncCRAm*
Massassoit 1580?-1661 *WhNaAH*
Massaua, John Roger 1947- *WhoE 91*
Massaux, Yves M. 1948- *WhoWor 91*
Masse, Ernest J. 1944- *St&PR 91*
Masse, Francois 1891- *EncO&P 3*
Masse, Jean Pierre 1944- *St&PR 91*
Masse, Laurence Raymond 1926- *St&PR 91*
Masse, Marcel 1936- *WhoAm 90, WhoWor 91*
Masse, Marcel 1940- *WhoAm 90, WhoE 91*
Masse, Mark H. 1952- *ODwPR 91*
Masse, Peggy Hart 1925- *WhoWrEP 89*
Masse, Victor 1822-1884 *OxCPMus*
Masse, Yvon H. 1935- *WhoAm 90*
Masse, Yvon Henri 1935- *St&PR 91*
Massee, David Lurton, Jr. 1936- *WhoAm 90*
Massel, Elihu Saul 1940- *WhoE 91*
Massel, Paul Martin 1953- *IntWWM 90*
Masselink, Carla Ann 1943- *WhoAmW 91*
Masselink, John P. 1931- *St&PR 91*
Masselli, Michael A. 1938- *St&PR 91*
Masselos, William 1920- *IntWWM 90*
Massena, Andre 1758-1817 *WorAlBi*
Massenburg, Jerome D 1946- *BiDrAPA 89*
Massenet, Jules 1842-1912 *BioIn 16, PenDiMP A, WorAlBi*
Massengale, James Edward 1948- *St&PR 91*
Massengale, John E. 1921-1988 *BioIn 16*
Massengale, Martin Andrew 1933- *WhoAm 90*
Massengale, Shari Louise 1958- *WhoAmW 91*
Massengill, Dennis Alan 1946- *St&PR 91*
Massengill, Robert Virgil 1939- *WhoSSW 91*
Masser, Ian 1937- *WhoWor 91*
Masser, Michael Rodney 1948- *WhoWor 91*
Masser, William J. 1937- *St&PR 91*
Masserman, Jules H 1905- *BiDrAPA 89*
Masserman, Jules Homan 1905- *WhoAm 90*
Masseus, Jan 1913- *IntWWM 90*
Massey, Andrew John 1946- *IntWWM 90*
Massey, Burnard F. 1938- *St&PR 91*
Massey, Charles Carleton 1838-1905 *EncPaPR 91*
Massey, Charles Knox, Jr. 1936- *WhoAm 90*
Massey, Charles L. 1922- *WhoAm 90*
Massey, Charles Wesley, Jr 1942- *WhoAmA 91*
Massey, Clinton Edward 1947- *WhoSSW 91*
Massey, Daniel Wayne 1949- *WhoSSW 91*
Massey, David Eugene 1938- *WhoSSW 91*
Massey, Deobrah Prescott 1956- *WhoSSW 91*
Massey, Donald F. 1945- *ODwPR 91*
Massey, Donald Terhune 1951- *WhoEmL 91*
Massey, Donald Wayne 1938- *WhoSSW 91*
Massey, Dorothy Butler *WhoAmW 91*
Massey, E. Morgan *St&PR 91*
Massey, E. Morgan 1926- *WhoAm 90, WhoSSW 91*
Massey, Ellen Gray 1921- *WhoWrEP 89*
Massey, George 1947- *IntWWM 90*
Massey, Gerald 1828-1907 *EncO&P 3*
Massey, Harold Wallace 1914- *WhoAm 90*
Massey, Harrie Stewart Wilson 1908-1983 *DcNaB 1981*
Massey, Hart Almerrin 1823-1896 *DcCanB 12*
Massey, Henry Heath, Jr. 1935- *St&PR 91*
Massey, Jack C. *NewYTBS 90 [port]*
Massey, Jack C. 1904- *St&PR 91*
Massey, Jack C. 1904-1990 *BioIn 16*
Massey, Jack T. 1927- *St&PR 91*
Massey, James D. *WhoAm 90*
Massey, James D. 1935- *St&PR 91*
Massey, James E. 1951- *St&PR 91*
Massey, James L. *St&PR 91*
Massey, James L. 1943- *WhoAm 90*
Massey, Janice Gayle 1955- *WhoSSW 91*
Massey, John 1931- *ConDes 90*
Massey, Joseph T. *BioIn 16*
Massey, Julia England 1942- *WhoSSW 91*
Massey, Kathleen Marie Oates 1955- *WhoEmL 91*
Massey, Kathy Diane 1964- *WhoAmW 91*
Massey, Leon R. 1930- *WhoAm 90*
Massey, Morris R. 1931- *St&PR 91*
Massey, Nathan Reuel 1951- *BiDrAPA 89*
Massey, Patti Chryl 1952- *WhoSSW 91*
Massey, R. Daniel 1942- *St&PR 91*
Massey, Raymond 1896-1983 *WorAlBi*
Massey, Raymond Hart 1896-1983 *OxCCanT*
Massey, Richard R. 1941- *St&PR 91*
Massey, Richard Walter, Jr. 1917- *WhoAm 90*
Massey, Robert John 1945- *WhoAm 90*
Massey, Robert Joseph 1921- *WhoAmA 91*
Massey, Robert L. 1934- *St&PR 91*
Massey, Robert Unruh 1922- *WhoAm 90*
Massey, Ronald Charles 1933- *WhoWor 91*
Massey, Roy Cyril 1934- *IntWWM 90*
Massey, Samuel 1817-1897 *DcCanB 12*
Massey, Shelby D. 1933- *St&PR 91*
Massey, Stephen Charles 1946- *WhoAm 90*
Massey, Stephen Walter 1956- *WhoSSW 91*
Massey, Steven James 1959- *WhoEmL 91*
Massey, Thomas Benjamin 1926- *WhoAm 90, WhoE 91*
Massey, Vincent 1887-1967 *BioIn 16, OxCCanT [port]*
Massey, Vincent 1926- *WhoAm 90*
Massey, Wallace W. 1924- *St&PR 91*
Massey, Walter E. *BioIn 16*
Massey, Walter Eugene 1938- *WhoAm 90*
Massey, William S. 1920- *WhoAm 90, WhoE 91*
Massey, Willie 1910-1990 *MusmAFA*
Massiano, Michael Francis 1934- *St&PR 91*
Massicott, Andre Jean 1937- *St&PR 91*
Massicotte, Jacques 1940- *St&PR 91*
Massicotte, Joseph H. 1923- *St&PR 91*
Massie, David Walter *BiDrAPA 89*
Massie, Diane Redfield *AuBYP 90*
Massie, Edward *NewYTBS 90*
Massie, Edward 1910-1990 *BioIn 16*
Massie, Edward Lindsey 1929- *St&PR 91*
Massie, Edward Lindsey, Jr. 1929- *WhoAm 90*
Massie, Elaine Catherine 1944- *WhoAmW 91*
Massie, Henry Norton 1941- *BiDrAPA 89*
Massie, James William, III 1949- *St&PR 91*
Massie, John A. 1944- *St&PR 91*
Massie, Lorna 1938- *WhoAmA 91*
Massie, Mary Jane *BiDrAPA 89*
Massie, Robert J. 1949- *St&PR 91*
Massie, Robert Kinloch 1929- *WhoAm 90*
Massie, Suzanne Rohrbach 1931- *WhoE 91*
Massie, Walter Arthur 1922- *BiDrAPA 89*
Massier, Clement 1845?-1917 *PenDiDA 89*
Massieu, Jean 1772-1846 *BioIn 16*
Massigli, Rene 1888-1988 *AnObit 1988*
Massignon, Daniel 1919- *WhoWor 91*
Massignon, Louis 1883-1962 *BioIn 16*
Massillo, Joseph Richard 1943- *St&PR 91*
Massimino, John H R *BiDrAPA 89*
Massimino, Roland V. 1934- *WhoAm 90*
Massimo, Joseph Thomas 1930-1987 *BioIn 16*
Massin, Eugene Max 1920- *WhoAmA 91*
Massin, Robert 1925- *ConDes 90*
Massina, Vincent M. 1932- *St&PR 91*
Massine, Leonide 1896-1979 *WorAlBi*
Massing, Bertram K. 1933- *St&PR 91*
Massing, Dale F. 1944- *St&PR 91*
Massinger, Philip 1583-1640 *BioIn 16*
Massino, Anthony Chester 1923- *St&PR 91*
Massion-Verniory, L *BiDrAPA 89*
Massler, Chris *BioIn 16*
Massler, Dennis Joel 1945- *BiDrAPA 89, WhoE 91*
Massler, Howard Arnold 1946- *WhoE 91, WhoEmL 91, WhoWor 91*
Massman, Virgil Frank *WhoAm 90*
Massnick, Forler 1931- *ODwPR 91*
Massolo, Arthur James 1942- *WhoAm 90*
Masson, Andre 1896-1987 *BioIn 16, IntDcAA 90*
Masson, Andre Emile 1921- *WhoWor 91*
Masson, Askell 1953- *IntWWM 90*
Masson, Claude *St&PR 91*
Masson, Diego 1935- *IntWWM 90, PenDiMP*
Masson, Gayl Angela 1951- *WhoAmW 91*
Masson, Gerard 1936- *IntWWM 90*
Masson, Pierre 1928- *St&PR 91*
Masson, Robert Henry 1935- *St&PR 91*
Massonneau, Robert L, III 1924- *BiDrAPA 89*
Massopust, Peter Robert 1958- *WhoSSW 91*
Massoth, Sue Virginia *BiDrAPA 89*
Massoubre, Jean-Marie 1921- *BioIn 16*
Massoud, Ahmed Shah *BioIn 16*
Massoud, Joseph D 1929- *BiDrAPA 89*
Massouda, Robert A *BiDrAPA 89*
Massu, Jacques Emile Charles-Marie 1908- *BiDFrPL*
Massullo, Anne-Christine *BioIn 16*
Massullo, Celeste *BioIn 16*
Massullo, Lucy *BioIn 16*
Massullo, Mary-Helene *BioIn 16*
Massullo, Michele *BioIn 16*
Massura, Edward Anthony 1938- *WhoAm 90*
Massura, Eileen Kathleen 1925- *WhoWor 91*
Massy, Patricia Graham Bibbs 1918- *WhoAmW 91*
Massy, William Francis 1934- *WhoAm 90*
Massys, Quentin 1465?-1530 *IntDcAA 90*
Massys, Quentin 1466?-1530 *WorAlBi*
Mast, Frank 1927- *WhoE 91*
Mast, Frederick William 1910- *WhoAm 90*
Mast, Gerald 1908-1971 *WhoAmA 91N*
Mast, Gerald 1940-1988 *BioIn 16*
Mast, Gifford Morrison 1943- *St&PR 91*
Mast, Ken W. 1944- *St&PR 91*
Mast, Richard Melvin 1934- *St&PR 91*
Mast, Stanley I. 1931- *WhoE 91*
Mast, Stewart Dale 1924- *WhoAm 90, WhoSSW 91*
Mast, Truman E 1932- *BiDrAPA 89*
Mastbaum, William Edward 1923- *St&PR 91*
Masteller, Barry 1945- *WhoAmA 91*
Masteller, Edwin Charles 1934- *WhoE 91*
Masten, Ann Stringfellow 1951- *WhoAmW 91*
Masten, Elizabeth R. 1947- *St&PR 91*
Masten, Helen Adams *BioIn 16*
Master of the Amsterdam Cabinet 1445?-1505? *IntDcAA 90*
Master of the Housebook 1445?-1505? *IntDcAA 90*
Master of the Osservanza *BioIn 16*
Master Therion 1875-1947 *BioIn 16*
Master, Franklin D *BiDrAPA 89*
Master, Lori Elizabeth 1962- *WhoAmW 91*
Master, Roshen Sohrab 1923- *BiDrAPA 89*
Master, Sheridan F. *AmLegL*
Master, Sherman *BiDrAPA 89*
Master-Karnik, Paul 1948- *WhoAmA 91*
Masterfield, Maxine 1933- *WhoAmA 91*
Masterman, Jack Verner 1930- *St&PR 91, WhoAm 90*
Masterman, John 1891-1977 *TwCCr&M 91*
Masterman, John Cecil 1891-1977 *SpyFic*
Masterman-Smith, Virginia 1937- *WhoWrEP 89*
Masters, Beda Doris 1942- *WhoAmW 91*
Masters, Bettie Sue Siler 1937- *WhoAm 90*
Masters, Bruce Allen 1936- *WhoSSW 91, WhoWor 91*
Masters, Charles Day 1929- *WhoAm 90*
Masters, David M *BiDrAPA 89*
Masters, David Romey 1947- *WhoSSW 91*
Masters, Dexter 1908-1989 *BioIn 16*
Masters, Edgar Lee 1868-1950 *MajTwCW, PoeCrit 1 [port]*
Masters, Edgar Lee 1869-1950 *WorAlBi, WrPh*
Masters, Edward E. 1924- *WhoAm 90*
Masters, Elaine Therese 1951- *WhoAmW 91*
Masters, G. *PenDiDA 89*
Masters, Gary Everett 1941- *WhoE 91*
Masters, George William 1940- *St&PR 91*
Masters, Hilary Thomas 1928- *WhoWrEP 89*
Masters, John 1914-1983 *DcNaB 1981*
Masters, John Christopher 1941- *WhoAm 90*
Masters, John D. 1924- *St&PR 91*
Masters, Jon Joseph 1937- *WhoAm 90*
Masters, Kelly Ray 1897- *AuBYP 90*
Masters, Lee *ODwPR 91*
Masters, Mary 1694?-1771 *FemiCLE*
Masters, Olga 1919-1986 *FemiCLE*
Masters, Rachel 1958- *IntWWM 90*
Masters, Richard L. 1954- *WhoEmL 91*
Masters, Robert 1917- *IntWWM 90*
Masters, Robert E. L. *EncO&P 3*
Masters, Roger Davis 1933- *WhoAm 90*
Masters, Sybilla *EncCRAm*
Masters, William H. 1915- *WorAlBi*
Masterson, Bat 1853-1921 *BioIn 16*
Masterson, Brian Joseph *BiDrAPA 89*
Masterson, Byron Jackson 1933- *WhoAm 90*
Masterson, Carlin 1940- *WhoAm 90*
Masterson, Charles Francis 1917- *WhoAm 90*
Masterson, Deborah 1953- *WhoAmW 91*
Masterson, Donald Earl, Jr. 1932- *St&PR 91*
Masterson, Gilbert Al *BiDrAPA 89*
Masterson, James Francis 1926- *BiDrAPA 89, WhoAm 90*
Masterson, James Joseph 1958- *WhoE 91*
Masterson, Joe A. 1943- *St&PR 91, WhoAm 90*
Masterson, John Patrick 1925- *WhoAm 90*
Masterson, Joseph Gerard 1930- *St&PR 91*
Masterson, Kenneth Rhodes 1944- *St&PR 91, WhoAm 90*
Masterson, Kleber Sandlin 1908- *WhoAm 90, WhoWor 91*
Masterson, Mary Stuart *BioIn 16*
Masterson, Michael Rue 1946- *WhoAm 90*
Masterson, Nola *BioIn 16*
Masterson, Patricia O'Malley 1952- *WhoAmW 91, WhoE 91, WhoWrEP 89*
Masterson, Patrick 1936- *WhoWor 91*
Masterson, Peter 1934- *WhoAm 90*
Masterson, Valerie *IntWWM 90*
Masterson, Valerie 1937- *PenDiMP*
Masterson, Walt 1920- *Ballpl 90*
Masterson, William A. 1931- *WhoAm 90*
Masterton, Whit *TwCCr&M 91*
Masterton, William Lewis 1927- *WhoAm 90*
Mastick, Seabury Cone, Mrs. 1895- *WhoE 91*
Mastilovic, Daniza 1933- *IntWWM 90*
Mastin, Peter Blackwell, Jr. 1842- *AmLegL*
Mastin, Robert Eldon 1940- *WhoSSW 91*
Mastin, Thomas William 1913- *St&PR 91*
Masto, Howard T. 1952- *ODwPR 91*
Maston, T. B. 1897-1988 *BioIn 16*
Maston, Thomas Bufford 1897-1988 *BioIn 16*
Mastor, George Constandine 1925- *WhoAm 90*
Mastorake, Jenny *EncCoWW*
Mastoraki, Jenny 1949- *EncCoWW*
Mastos, Louis T. 1921- *St&PR 91*

Mastrangelo, Bobbi A 1937- *WhoAmA 91*
Mastrangelo, Marygrace 1963- *WhoE 91*
Mastrantonio, Mary Elizabeth *BioIn 16*
Mastrantonio, Mary Elizabeth 1958- *WorAlBi*
Mastrianni, Alfred J. *St&PR 91*
Mastrianni, Xavier 1934- *BiDrAPA 89*
Mastrini, Jane Reed 1948- *WhoEmL 91*
Mastrino, Millard Michael 1941- *WhoE 91*
Mastro, A. F. 1939- *WhoAm 90*
Mastro, John M. 1950- *St&PR 91*
Mastroberte, Violet Marie 1932- *WhoAmW 91*
Mastrobuono, Amedeo 1904- *BiDrAPA 89*
Mastrodonato, Richard A *BiDrAPA 89*
Mastrogiovanni, Raymond Vincent 1941- *WhoE 91*
Mastroianni, Luigi, Jr. 1925- *WhoAm 90, WhoE 91*
Mastroianni, Marcello 1924- *BioIn 16, WhoWor 91, WorAlBi*
Mastroianni, Thomas O. 1934- *IntWWM 90*
Mastromonico, Arnold Michael 1933- *St&PR 91*
Mastrosimone, Claude Anthony 1937- *WhoE 91*
Mastrosimone, William 1947- *ConTFT 8*
Mastrovito, Rene C 1924- *BiDrAPA 89*
Mastry, Nicholas Joseph, III 1947- *St&PR 91*
Masubuchi, Koichi 1924- *WhoAm 90, WhoE 91, WhoWor 91*
Masucci, Christina Marie 1958- *WhoE 91*
Masucci, Richard Paul 1947- *St&PR 91*
Masucci, Robert N. 1937- *St&PR 91*
Masud, Khawaja Daud 1946- *WhoWor 91*
Masuda, Gohta 1940- *WhoWor 91*
Masuda, Sueo Suto 1926- *WhoWor 91*
Masuda, Sumiko 1930- *WhoWor 91*
Masuda, Yuji 1938- *WhoWor 91*
Masumoto, David Mas 1954- *WhoWrEP 89*
Masuo, Ryuichi 1928- *WhoWor 91*
Masur, Harold Q. 1909- *TwCCr&M 91*
Masur, Kurt 1927- *BioIn 16, CurBio 90 [port], IntWWM 90, PenDiMP, WhoWor 91, WorAlBi*
Masurel, Jean-Louis Antoine Nicolas 1940- *WhoAm 90*
Masurok, Yuri 1931- *IntWWM 90, PenDiMP*
Masurovsky, Gregory 1929- *WhoAmA 91*
Masursky, Harold *NewYTBS 90*
Masursky, Harold 1923- *WhoAm 90*
Masursky, Harold 1923-1990 *CurBio 90N*
Masury, Julia Anne 1962- *WhoAmW 91*
Maszak, Aladar Szegedy- *BioIn 16*
Maszkiewicz, Ruth Agnes 1928- *WhoAmW 91*
Mata Hari 1876-1917 *WorAlBi*
Mata, Eduardo 1942- *IntWWM 90, PenDiMP, WhoAm 90, WhoHisp 91, WhoSSW 91*
Mata, Elizabeth Adams 1946- *WhoSSW 91*
Mata, Fernando V *BiDrAPA 89*
Mata, Marina Martha 1966- *WhoHisp 91*
Mata, Pedro F. 1944- *St&PR 91, WhoHisp 91*
Mata, Pedro Francisco 1944- *WhoAm 90*
Mata, Zenaida M 1945- *BiDrAPA 89*
Matacic, Lovro von 1899-1985 *PenDiMP*
Mataga, Noboru 1927- *WhoWor 91*
Mataja, Emilie 1855-1938 *EncCoWW*
Matalamaki, Margaret Marie 1921- *WhoAmW 91, WhoWor 91*
Matalon, Norma 1949- *WhoWor 91*
Matalon, Vivian 1929- *WhoAm 90, WhoE 91*
Matamoros, Lourdes M. 1963- *WhoHisp 91*
Matanky, Robert William 1955- *WhoEmL 91*
Matano, Tsuneo 1924- *WhoWor 91*
Matanoski, Genevieve Murray 1930- *WhoAm 90, WhoAmW 91*
Mataraso, M.H. 1929- *St&PR 91*
Matarasso, Alan 1953- *WhoE 91*
Matarazzo, Joseph Dominic 1925- *WhoAm 90*
Matarazzo, Ruth Gadbois 1926- *WhoAm 90*
Matarese, James M. 1930- *St&PR 91*
Matas, Carol 1949- *BioIn 16*
Matas, Julio 1931- *BioIn 16*
Matas, Manuel 1945- *BiDrAPA 89*
Matas, Myra Dorothea 1938- *WhoWor 91*
Matas, Raquel M. 1956- *WhoHisp 91*
Matasar, Ann B. 1940- *WhoAm 90, WhoAmW 91*
Matasovic, Marilyn Estelle 1946- *WhoAmW 91, WhoEmL 91, WhoWor 91*
Matassa, John P 1945- *WhoAmA 91*
Matatia, Michael Robin 1959- *WhoE 91*
Matatu, Michael *ConAu 130*
Mataxis, Theodore Christopher 1917- *WhoAm 90, WhoWor 91*
Matcha, Jack 1919- *WhoWrEP 89*
Matchar, David Bruce 1955- *WhoSSW 91*
Matcher, Rita Harriet 1943- *WhoE 91*
Matchett, Myrtle O *BiDrAPA 89*
Matchett, William F 1937- *BiDrAPA 89*
Matchett, William Hayes 1932- *WhoAm 90*
Matchett, William Henry 1923- *WhoAm 90*
Matchette, Phyllis Lee 1921- *WhoAmW 91*
Matchick, Tommy 1943- *Ballpl 90*
Mate, Janos 1934- *IntWWM 90*
Mate, Leslie L 1934- *BiDrAPA 89*
Mateczun, John Matthew 1946- *BiDrAPA 89*
Mateer, David Gordon 1946- *IntWWM 90*
Mateer, Don Metz 1945- *WhoEmL 91, WhoWor 91*
Mateer, Donald D. 1927- *St&PR 91*
Mateja, Michael E. 1938- *St&PR 91*
Matejic, Mateja 1924- *ConAu 30NR*
Matejka, Michael G. 1953- *WhoEmL 91*
Mateju, Joseph Frank 1927- *WhoAm 90*
Matek, Deborah Hope 1954- *BiDrAPA 89*
Mateker, Emil Joseph, Jr. 1931- *St&PR 91, WhoSSW 91*
Matel, Daniel F. 1959- *WhoAm 90*
Matelan, Mathew Nicholas 1945- *St&PR 91*
Mateles, Richard Isaac 1935- *WhoAm 90*
Matell, Robin M. 1934- *ODwPR 91*
Maten, Mark James 1957- *St&PR 91*
Mateo, Bayoan C 1937- *BiDrAPA 89*
Mateo, Julio 1951- *WhoAmA 91*
Mateo-Bermudez, Jose Manuel *BiDrAPA 89*
Mateos, Adolfo Lopez 1910-1969 *BioIn 16*
Mateos, Manuel 1928- *WhoWor 91*
Mater, Gene P. 1926- *WhoAm 90*
Mater, Jonathan W. 1949- *St&PR 91*
Matera, Jack John 1940- *St&PR 91*
Matera, Raymond Ambrose 1925- *WhoAm 90*
Matera, Victor Dominic 1957- *WhoEmL 91*
Materas, Alfred Patrick, Jr. 1938- *St&PR 91*
Materazzi, Miguel Angel 1935- *BiDrAPA 89*
Materazzo, Patrick R. 1934- *St&PR 91*
Materia, Kathleen Patricia Ayling 1954- *WhoAmW 91*
Matern, Rosina *BiDEWW*
Materna, Amalie 1844-1918 *PenDiMP*
Materson, Richard Stephen 1941- *WhoSSW 91, WhoWor 91*
Mates, Jacob William *BiDrAPA 89*
Mates, Julian 1927- *ConAu 31NR*
Matesic, Michael Mark 1965- *WhoE 91*
Mateus, Francy M 1943- *BiDrAPA 89*
Mateus, Rui Fernando 1944- *WhoWor 91*
Matevich, Branislava 1949- *WhoAmW 91*
Mateyo, George R. 1942- *St&PR 91*
Matez, Jerry *St&PR 91*
Matflerd, Carolynn Ann 1958- *BiDrAPA 89*
Mathabane, Mark *BioIn 16*
Mathai, Chirathalakal Varughese 1945- *WhoWor 91*
Mathai, Rachel 1947- *BiDrAPA 89*
Mathalon, Charles 1925- *St&PR 91*
Matharu, Harcharanjit Singh 1958- *WhoWor 91*
Mathe, Albert *MajTwCW*
Mathe, Aleksander Arie 1934- *BiDrAPA 89*
Mathe, Lynda Anne Paloma 1948- *WhoAmW 91*
Mathe, Mirjam Reiner *BiDrAPA 89*
Matheiu, Raymond Maurice 1947- *St&PR 91*
Matheny, Charles Woodburn, Jr. 1914- *WhoWor 91*
Matheny, Donald R. 1942- *St&PR 91*
Matheny, Edward Taylor, Jr. 1923- *WhoAm 90*
Matheny, Jo Ann 1953- *BiDrAPA 89*
Matheny, Paul Edward, Jr. 1947- *WhoSSW 91*
Matheny, Raymond Thomas 1925- *WhoAm 90*
Matheny, Robert Duane 1924- *WhoSSW 91*
Matheny, Robert Lavesco 1933- *WhoAm 90*
Matheny, Ruth Ann 1918- *WhoAm 90*
Matheny, Thomas Richard 1955- *WhoEmL 91*
Matheny, Timothy Earl 1952- *WhoSSW 91*
Matheny, Tom Harrell *WhoAm 90, WhoSSW 91, WhoWor 91*
Mather, Allen Frederick 1922- *WhoAm 90*
Mather, Berkely *TwCCr&M 91*
Mather, Betty Bang 1927- *IntWWM 90, WhoAm 90*
Mather, Bryant 1916- *WhoAm 90*
Mather, Charles E., III 1934- *St&PR 91*
Mather, Cotton 1662-1728 *EncO&P 3*
Mather, Cotton 1663-1728 *BioIn 16, EncCRAm, WhNaAH, WorAlBi*
Mather, Gary Douglas 1944- *St&PR 91*
Mather, Herbert 1934- *WhoSSW 91*
Mather, Increase 1639-1723 *BioIn 16, EncCRAm, EncO&P 3, WorAlBi*
Mather, Jay B. 1946- *WhoAm 90*
Mather, Jean Paul 1914- *WhoAm 90*
Mather, Jennie Powell 1948- *WhoAmW 91*
Mather, John B 1845?-1892 *DcCanB 12*
Mather, John Norman 1942- *WhoAm 90*
Mather, John Russell 1923- *WhoAm 90*
Mather, Katharine 1916- *WhoAm 90*
Mather, Kenneth 1911- *WhoWor 91*
Mather, Kenneth 1911-1990 *ConAu 131*
Mather, Kirtley F. 1888-1978 *BioIn 16*
Mather, Kirtley Fletcher 1888-1978 *DcScB S2*
Mather, Margaret *DcCanB 12*
Mather, Mildred Eunice 1922- *WhoAm 90*
Mather, Patricia Lynn 1950- *WhoAmW 91*
Mather, Richard 1596-1669 *BioIn 16*
Mather, Richard Burroughs 1913- *WhoAm 90*
Mather, Roger Frederick 1917- *IntWWM 90, WhoWor 91*
Mather, Stephen *BioIn 16*
Mather, William L. *BioIn 16*
Matherne, J. Marion 1924- *WhoSSW 91*
Matherne, Louis K. 1951- *St&PR 91*
Mathers, Helen 1853-1920 *FemiCLE*
Mathers, Kris Lee 1951- *WhoEmL 91*
Mathers, Margaret 1929- *WhoAmW 91*
Mathers, Peter 1931- *ConAu 130*
Mathers, Peter Robert 1955- *WhoEmL 91*
Mathers, S L MacGregor 1854-1918 *EncO&P 3*
Mathers, Stephen Charles 1946- *WhoEmL 91*
Mathers, T.G. 1938- *St&PR 91*
Mathers, Thomas Nesbit 1914- *WhoAm 90*
Mathers, William Dean 1947- *WhoE 91*
Mathers, William Harris 1914- *St&PR 91, WhoAm 90*
Mathes, Charles Elliott 1949- *WhoE 91*
Mathes, Donald Ely 1933- *WhoE 91*
Mathes, Edward Conrad 1943- *WhoSSW 91*
Mathes, Elizabeth M. *ODwPR 91*
Mathes, Joe 1891-1978 *Ballpl 90*
Mathes, John Charles 1931- *WhoAm 90*
Mathes, Mary Louise 1919- *WhoAmW 91*
Mathes, Rachel 1941- *IntWWM 90*
Mathes, Stephen Jon 1945- *WhoE 91, WhoWor 91*
Matheson, Alan Adams 1932- *WhoAm 90*
Matheson, Alastair Taylor 1929- *WhoAm 90*
Matheson, Alex 1951- *St&PR 91*
Matheson, Annie 1853-1924 *FemiCLE*
Matheson, David Stewart 1945- *WhoAm 90*
Matheson, Hugh J. 1928- *St&PR 91*
Matheson, Ian M. 1944- *St&PR 91*
Matheson, Jane Gesell 1955- *WhoAmW 91*
Matheson, Linda 1918- *WhoAmW 91, WhoE 91, WhoWor 91*
Matheson, Robert Stuart 1919- *St&PR 91*
Matheson, Scott M. *NewYTBS 90*
Matheson, Scott Milne 1929- *WhoAm 90*
Matheson, Stephen H. 1946- *St&PR 91*
Matheson, Tim Lewis 1947- *St&PR 91*
Matheson, W.A., Jr. 1919- *St&PR 91*
Matheson, Wayne Malcolm, Jr. 1929- *WhoWrEP 89*
Matheson, William Lyon 1924- *WhoAm 90, WhoWor 91*
Matheson-Bruce, Graeme 1949- *IntWWM 90*
Matheu, Federico Manuel 1941- *WhoAm 90*
Matheu, Manuel de Falla y 1876-1946 *BioIn 16*
Matheus, John Frederick 1887-1983 *EarBlAP*
Mathew, Aleyamma *BiDrAPA 89*
Mathew, Cyril *BioIn 16*
Mathew, K Varkey *BiDrAPA 89*
Mathew, Kizhake-Kachukuzhiyil Cherian 1951- *WhoWor 91*
Mathew, Koshy 1954- *WhoWor 91*
Mathew, Maleakal S *BiDrAPA 89*
Mathew, Poyanil M 1930- *BiDrAPA 89*
Mathew, Roy Jacob 1945- *BiDrAPA 89*
Mathew, Shila Jacob *BiDrAPA 89*
Mathew, Thankamma *BiDrAPA 89*
Mathew, Thomas 1940- *BiDrAPA 89*
Mathews, Arthur F. 1938- *BioIn 16*
Mathews, Arthur Francis 1938- *WhoAm 90*
Mathews, Arthur Frank 1860-1945 *PenDiDA 89*
Mathews, Barbara Edith 1946- *WhoAmW 91*
Mathews, Beverly 1928- *WhoWrEP 89*
Mathews, Bobby 1851-1898 *Ballpl 90*
Mathews, Carmen Sylva 1918- *WhoAm 90*
Mathews, Charles Anderson 1938- *St&PR 91*
Mathews, Christopher King 1937- *WhoAm 90*
Mathews, Cornelius 1817-1889 *BioIn 16*
Mathews, Curtis Joseph 1938- *WhoSSW 91*
Mathews, David 1935- *WhoAm 90*
Mathews, David L. 1947- *St&PR 91*
Mathews, Donald G. 1932- *WhoAm 90*
Mathews, Eddie 1931- *Ballpl 90 [port], BioIn 16, WorAlBi*
Mathews, Edward E. 1926- *St&PR 91*
Mathews, Eliza Kirkham 1772-1802 *FemiCLE*
Mathews, Everette *BioIn 16*
Mathews, Fred Leroy 1938- *WhoSSW 91*
Mathews, George W., Jr. 1927- *WhoAm 90*
Mathews, Greg 1962- *Ballpl 90*
Mathews, Harlan *WhoAm 90*
Mathews, Harry *BioIn 16*
Mathews, Harry 1930- *WorAu 1980 [port]*
Mathews, Hugh M *BiDrAPA 89*
Mathews, Ian Richard 1933- *WhoWor 91*
Mathews, J Wayne 1940- *BiDrAPA 89*
Mathews, Jean Ann H. 1941- *WhoAmW 91*
Mathews, Jessica Tuchman 1946- *WhoAm 90, WhoEmL 91*
Mathews, Judith Ann 1947- *WhoE 91*
Mathews, Keith Rowland 1934- *WhoWrEP 89*
Mathews, Kenneth A. 1929- *St&PR 91*
Mathews, Kenneth Pine 1921- *WhoAm 90*
Mathews, Larry R. *WhoSSW 91*
Mathews, Linda McVeigh 1946- *WhoAm 90*
Mathews, Marion W 1913- *BiDrAPA 89*
Mathews, Marsha 1952- *WhoWrEP 89*
Mathews, Marvin G *BiDrAPA 89*
Mathews, Mary Alice 1929- *BiDrAPA 89*
Mathews, Mary Kathryn 1948- *WhoAmW 91, WhoE 91*
Mathews, Max V. *BioIn 16*
Mathews, Nancy Mowll 1947- *WhoAmA 91*
Mathews, Nelson 1941- *Ballpl 90*
Mathews, Patricia Ann 1945- *WhoAmW 91*
Mathews, Raymond S. 1902- *St&PR 91*
Mathews, Ressy *BiDrAPA 89*
Mathews, Richard Barrett 1944- *WhoSSW 91*
Mathews, Richard Stewart M. 1946- *St&PR 91*
Mathews, Richard Stewart Monteague 1946- *WhoE 91*
Mathews, Rita A. 1939- *WhoAmW 91*
Mathews, Robert D., Jr. *WhoSSW 91*
Mathews, Robert Daniel 1928- *St&PR 91, WhoAm 90*
Mathews, Robert E. 1940- *St&PR 91*
Mathews, Robert Edward 1909- *WhoAm 90*
Mathews, Robert Paul 1953- *IntWWM 90*
Mathews, Roderick Bell 1941- *WhoSSW 91*
Mathews, Shailer 1863-1941 *BioIn 16*
Mathews, Sharon Walker 1947- *WhoAm 90, WhoAmW 91*
Mathews, Stella S. 1868-1949 *BioIn 16*
Mathews, Susan McKiernan 1946- *WhoAmW 91*
Mathews, Thomas A 1927- *BiDrAPA 89*
Mathews, William Alwood 1947- *WhoSSW 91*
Mathews, Wilma 1945- *WhoAmW 91*
Mathewson, Charles Payson 1848-1941 *AmLegL*
Mathewson, Christopher Colville 1941- *WhoSSW 91*
Mathewson, Christy 1878-1925 *Ballpl 90 [port]*
Mathewson, Christy 1880-1925 *BioIn 16, WorAlBi*
Mathewson, Hugh Spalding 1921- *WhoAm 90, WhoWor 91*
Mathewson, Rufus 1920- *WhoE 91*
Mathewson, William Donald 1937- *St&PR 91*
Matheyka, James Allan 1942- *St&PR 91*
Mathias, Alice Irene 1949- *WhoAmW 91, WhoWor 91*
Mathias, Alyce 1947- *WhoEmL 91, WhoSSW 91*
Mathias, Betty Jane 1923- *WhoAmW 91*
Mathias, Bob *BioIn 16*
Mathias, Charles Bulmer 1940- *WhoAm 90*
Mathias, Charles McCurdy, Jr. 1922- *WhoE 91*
Mathias, Edward Joseph 1941- *WhoAm 90*
Mathias, Gerald Dodson 1930- *St&PR 91, WhoAm 90, WhoSSW 91*

Mathias, James Herman 1913- WhoAm 90
Mathias, James Marion 1944- BiDrAPA 89
Mathias, James P. 1950- St&PR 91
Mathias, John H. 1946- St&PR 91
Mathias, John Stephen 1948- WhoSSW 91
Mathias, Joseph Simon 1925- WhoAm 90
Mathias, Lynda Rowell 1943- WhoAmW 91, WhoSSW 91
Mathias, Margaret Grossman 1928- WhoAmW 91, WhoWor 91
Mathias, Mildred Esther 1906- WhoAm 90
Mathias, Reuben Victor 1926- WhoAm 90
Mathias, Richard Douglas 1940- St&PR 91
Mathias, Rob St&PR 91
Mathias, William 1934- IntWWM 90, PenDiMP A
Mathias, William G. AmLegL
Mathias, William J. 1934- WhoWor 91
Mathiasen, Geneva NewYTBS 90
Mathiasen, Geneva 1899-1990 BioIn 16
Mathies, Allen Wray, Jr. 1930- WhoAm 90
Mathiesen, Pat Harmon 1934- WhoAmW 91
Mathiesen, Thomas James 1947- IntWWM 90
Mathieson, Andrew Wray 1928- St&PR 91, WhoAm 90
Mathieson, Douglas George 1942- St&PR 91
Mathieson, Malcolm B. St&PR 91
Mathieson, Michael Raymond 1952- WhoE 91
Mathieson, Muir 1911-1975 PenDiMP
Mathieu, Allaudin NewAgMG
Mathieu, Bertrand M. 1936- WhoWor 91
Mathieu, Donald Roland 1929- WhoAm 90
Mathieu, Georges Victor Adolphe 1921- WhoWor 91
Mathieu, Hans Jorg 1942- WhoWor 91
Mathieu, Henri Donat 1936- WhoWor 91
Mathieu, Noel Jean 1916-1984 ConAu 130
Mathieu, Patrick 1953- WhoWor 91
Mathieu, Paul BioIn 16
Mathieu, Raymond Maurice 1947- WhoEmL 91
Mathieu, Robert J. 1935- St&PR 91
Mathieu, Thomas Joseph 1961- WhoE 91
Mathieu-Harris, Michele Suzanne 1950- WhoAmW 91, WhoWor 91
Mathilde WomWR
Mathile, Clayton Lee 1941- WhoAm 90
Mathis, Aaron L. 1933- St&PR 91
Mathis, Allen W., Jr. 1920- St&PR 91
Mathis, Betty 1918- WhoAmW 91
Mathis, Billie F 1936- WhoAmA 91
Mathis, Carolyn Ayers 1950- WhoSSW 91
Mathis, Clyde Henry 1913- WhoSSW 91
Mathis, David Montanus 1946- WhoSSW 91
Mathis, Edith 1938- IntWWM 90, PenDiMP
Mathis, Elizabeth James 1955- WhoSSW 91
Mathis, Emile Henry, II 1946- WhoAmA 91
Mathis, F. John 1941- St&PR 91
Mathis, George Russell 1926- WhoSSW 91
Mathis, Jack David 1931- WhoWor 91
Mathis, James L 1925- BiDrAPA 89
Mathis, Joel H. 1939- St&PR 91
Mathis, John Samuel 1931- WhoAm 90
Mathis, Johnny 1935- DrBIPA 90, OxCPMus, WhoAm 90, WorAlBi
Mathis, Judy Moore 1951- St&PR 91
Mathis, June Green 1941- WhoAmW 91
Mathis, Laurelle Sheedy 1948- WhoAmW 91
Mathis, Louis Edwin, Jr. 1949- WhoSSW 91
Mathis, Luster Doyle 1936- WhoAm 90
Mathis, Margaret E. Myrick 1932- WhoAmW 91
Mathis, Marilyn Kelty 1958- WhoAmW 91
Mathis, Mark Jay 1947- WhoAm 90
Mathis, Marsha Debra 1953- WhoAmW 91, WhoSSW 91
Mathis, Paul Carl, III 1948- WhoSSW 91
Mathis, Peyton S. 1949- St&PR 91
Mathis, Philip Monroe 1942- WhoSSW 91
Mathis, Ray 1937-1981 ConAu 31NR
Mathis, Sharon Ann 1957- WhoAmW 91
Mathis, Sharon Bell 1937- AuBYP 90, BioIn 16, WhoAm 90, WhoWrEP 89
Mathis, Thelma Atwood WhoAmW 91
Mathis, Valerie Elaine BiDrAPA 89
Mathis, Verdell 1913- Ballpl 90
Mathis, Warner Livingston 1926- St&PR 91
Mathis, William David 1947- WhoEmL 91
Mathis, William E. 1931- IntWWM 90
Mathis, William Edward 1948- WhoE 91
Mathis, William Hubert 1933- St&PR 91
Mathis, William Lowrey 1926- WhoAm 90
Mathis-Eddy, Darlene Fern 1937- WhoWrEP 89
Mathisen, Harold Clifford 1924- WhoE 91, WhoWor 91
Mathisen, Irwin Wald, Jr. 1928- St&PR 91
Mathisen, Jane M BiDrAPA 89
Mathisen, Lillian Alice 1941- WhoAmW 91
Mathisen, Rhoda Sharon 1942- WhoAmW 91, WhoWor 91
Mathison, Ian William 1938- WhoAm 90
Mathsson, Bruno 1907-1988 AnObit 1988, ConDes 90
Mathsson, Karl Bruno 1907- PenDiDA 89
Mathues, Thomas Oliver 1923- WhoAm 90
Mathuny, Robert Stephen 1959- St&PR 91
Mathur, Anil Chand 1957- WhoWor 91
Mathur, Ashok WhoWor 91
Mathur, Pradeep 1958- BiDrAPA 89
Mathur, Raghuvansh B 1918- EncO&P 3
Mathur, Suresh B 1933- BiDrAPA 89
Mathur, Usha BiDrAPA 89
Mathur, Vinod Raj 1943- WhoSSW 91
Mathur, Vishnu Sahai 1934- WhoAm 90
Mathurin, Trevor 1946- St&PR 91
Mathwich, Dale F. 1934- St&PR 91
Mathys, Gertrud E. 1939- St&PR 91
Matias, Antonio Cabrita 1928- WhoWor 91
Matic, Vojin 1911- BiDrAPA 89
Matiella, Ana Consuelo 1951- WhoHisp 91
Matienzo, Peter WhoHisp 91
Matier, William L. 1939- St&PR 91
Matijevic, Egon 1922- WhoAm 90
Matilainen, Riitta Marja 1948- WhoWor 91
Matilal, Bimal Krishna 1935- ConAu 30NR
Matilda WomWR
Matilda 1102-1167 WomWR
Matilda of Flanders WomWR
Matilda, of Tuscany 1046-1115 BioIn 16
Matilda of Tuscany 1046-1115 WomWR [port]
Matilda, Princess of England 1102-1167 BioIn 16
Matilde, di Canossa 1046-1115 BioIn 16
Matilla, Alfredo 1937- WhoHisp 91
Matin, Khan M A BiDrAPA 89
Matin, M. A. 1937- WhoWor 91
Matin, Razia Qureshi BiDrAPA 89
Matinale, Richard Joseph 1947- St&PR 91
Matinkhou, Einollah 1932- St&PR 91
Matis, Howard Scott 1948- WhoEmL 91
Matise, Salvatore Anthony 1945- St&PR 91
Matisi, Catherine Rose BiDrAPA 89
Matisse, Henri BioIn 16
Matisse, Henri 1869-1954 IntDcAA 90, WorAlBi
Matisse, Pierre BioIn 16
Matisse, Pierre 1900-1989 AnObit 1989, WhoAmA 91N
Matius, Cynthia Kay 1956- St&PR 91
Matjasich, Carol Ann 1955- WhoEmL 91
Matkins, Robert Edwin 1934- St&PR 91
Matkovic, Thomas V 1928- BiDrAPA 89
Matkovich, Vlado I. 1924- St&PR 91
Matkowsky, Bernard Judah 1939- WhoAm 90
Matlack, George Miller 1921- WhoAm 90
Matlack, Jon 1950- Ballpl 90
Matlack, Rex William 1957- St&PR 91
Matlack, William Ernest 1951- St&PR 91
Matlaga, Joan 1942- WhoWrEP 89
Matlaga, Richard Allen 1944- St&PR 91
Matlaw, Myron 1924-1990 BioIn 16
Matlaw, Ralph NewYTBS 90
Matlaw, Ralph E. 1927-1990 BioIn 16, ConAu 131
Matles, Harold Bernard 1936- St&PR 91
Matlick, Gerald Allen 1947-1988 WhoAmA 91N
Matlin, Eric S. 1941- St&PR 91
Matlin, Marlee BioIn 16
Matlin, Marlee 1965- WhoAmW 91
Matlin, Stephen A 1940- BiDrAPA 89
Matlins, Stuart M. 1940- WhoE 91, WhoWor 91
Matlock, Clifford Charles 1909- WhoAm 90, WhoWor 91
Matlock, Hudson 1919- WhoAm 90
Matlock, Jack Foust, Jr. 1929- WhoAm 90, WhoWor 91
Matlock, John F., Jr. BioIn 16
Matlock, Kenneth Jerome 1928- St&PR 91, WhoAm 90
Matlock, Norman DrBIPA 90
Matlock, Stephen J. St&PR 91
Matloff, Lawrence BioIn 16
Matloff, Maurice 1915- WhoAm 90
Matlon, Chris John 1943- St&PR 91
Matlon, Ronald J. 1938- WhoE 91
Matlovich, Leonard BioIn 16
Matlow, Linda Monique 1955- WhoAmW 91
Matlow, Stuart A. 1950- ODwPR 91
Matney, David Earl 1928- St&PR 91
Matney, Marjorie Maye 1931- WhoAmW 91
Matney, Stephen Lewis BiDrAPA 89
Mato, Christine Yuriko 1950- WhoAmW 91
Mato-Tope 1800-1837 WhNaAH [port]
Matocha, Gary Paul 1958- St&PR 91
Matola, Laurence Frank 1955- WhoEmL 91
Maton, Paul Nicholas 1947- WhoWor 91
Matonabbee 1736?-1782 WhNaAH
Matos, Abilio Rogerio Barbosa 1948- WhoWor 91
Matos, Gregorio de 1636-1695 BioIn 16
Matos, Israel 1954- WhoHisp 91
Matos, John WhoAmA 91
Matos, Luis Pales HispWr 90
Matos, Luis Pales 1898-1959 BioIn 16
Matos, Maria M. 1950- WhoHisp 91
Matos, Otsenre E BiDrAPA 89
Matos, Philip Waite 1936- WhoAm 90
Matos, Wilfredo 1940- WhoHisp 91
Matos Paoli, Francisco 1915- BioIn 16, ConAu 131, HispWr 90
Matousek, Lukas 1943- IntWWM 90
Matovina, John Michael 1954- St&PR 91, WhoAm 90
Matraini, Chiara 1515-1604? EncCoWW
Matranga, Frances Carfi 1922- WhoWrEP 89
Matranga, Roman J. 1939- St&PR 91
Matras, Christian 1900- DcScanL
Matrazzo, Donna J. 1948- WhoWrEP 89
Matre, Susan Jane 1952- WhoAmW 91
Matsa, Loula Zacharoula 1935- WhoAmW 91, WhoE 91, WhoWor 91
Matsch, Richard P. 1930- WhoAm 90
Matschulat, Natel Kypriotou 1944- WhoAm 90
Matschulat, Walter Roy 1921- St&PR 91
Matsen, Frederick Albert, III 1944- WhoAm 90
Matsikenyiri, Patrick 1937- IntWWM 90
Matsikoudis, Philip John Paul 1953- WhoE 91
Matsler, Edward Jay 1939- St&PR 91
Matsler, Franklin Giles 1922- WhoAm 90
Matson, A. James 1934- St&PR 91
Matson, Albert Thomas 1915-1987 BioIn 16
Matson, Arlene Mae 1926- WhoAmW 91
Matson, Clive 1941- ConAu 129
Matson, Frances Shober 1921- WhoAmW 91
Matson, Greta WhoAmA 91
Matson, James Herbert 1940- St&PR 91, WhoAm 90
Matson, John William, II 1944- WhoWrEP 89
Matson, Mariechen Anne 1957- WhoAmW 91, WhoWrEP 89
Matson, Merridee Lynn WhoAmW 91
Matson, Patricia J. ODwPR 91
Matson, Robert Edward 1930- WhoAm 90
Matson, Robert J. 1942- St&PR 91
Matson, Sigfred Christian 1917- WhoAm 90
Matson, Wallace I. 1921- WhoAm 90
Matson, Wayne R. 1942- St&PR 91
Matson, Wesley Jennings 1924- WhoAm 90
Matsuba, Minoru 1929- ConDes 90
Matsubara, Naoko 1937- WhoAmA 91
Matsuda, Fujio 1924- WhoAm 90
Matsuda, Henry Komei 1936- St&PR 91
Matsuda, Itaru 1951- WhoWor 91
Matsuda, Masayuki Morris 1933- WhoWor 91
Matsuda, Minoru 1933- WhoWor 91
Matsuda, Yusaku BioIn 16
Matsudaira, Kazuaki 1927- WhoWor 91
Matsudaira, Renko 1928- IntWWM 90
Matsui, Dorothy Nobuko 1954- WhoAmW 91
Matsui, Eiichi 1925- WhoWor 91
Matsui, Kengo 1931- WhoWor 91
Matsui, Robert Takeo 1941- WhoAm 90
Matsui, Yoshihiko 1921- WhoWor 91
Matsukata Masayoshi 1835-1924 EncJap
Matsukata, Tane BioIn 16
Matsukawa, Leslie Ann BiDrAPA 89
Matsukawa, Michiya 1924- WhoWor 91
Matsumoto, Franklin M 1929- BiDrAPA 89
Matsumoto, George 1922- WhoAm 90
Matsumoto, Hiroshi 1948- WhoWor 91
Matsumoto, Kihachiro 1937- St&PR 91
Matsumoto, Seicho 1909- TwCCr&M 91B
Matsumoto, Shigeharu 1899-1989 BioIn 16
Matsumoto, Shigemi IntWWM 90
Matsumoto, Takaaki 1954- ConDes 90
Matsumoto, Teruo 1929- WhoAm 90
Matsumoto, Yasuo 1954- WhoWor 91
Matsumoto, Yukimichi 1937- WhoWor 91
Matsumura, Hideyuki 1930- WhoWor 91
Matsumura, Kenichi 1942- WhoWor 91
Matsumura, Lane Doro BiDrAPA 89
Matsumura, Takao 1942- ConAu 132
Matsumura, Vera Yoshi IntWWM 90, WhoAmW 91
Matsunaga, Don William 1948- BiDrAPA 89
Matsunaga, Fumio 1921- WhoWor 91
Matsunaga, Ichiro 1928- WhoWor 91
Matsunaga, Spark M. BioIn 16
Matsunaga, Spark M 1916-1990 ConAu 131, NewYTBS 90 [port]
Matsunaka, Shooichi 1927- WhoWor 91
Matsuno, Masako ConAu 31NR
Matsuno, Masako 1935- AuBYP 90
Matsuno, Ryuichi 1939- WhoWor 91
Matsuo Basho EncJap
Matsuo Basho 1644-1694 WorAlBi
Matsuo, Akira 1948- WhoWor 91
Matsuo, Basho 1644-1694 BioIn 16
Matsuo, Kazuyuki Joseph 1941- WhoWor 91
Matsuoka, Mikihiro 1962- WhoWor 91
Matsuoka, Seijiro BioIn 16
Matsuoka, Shiro 1930- WhoAm 90
Matsushige, Cary Shigeru 1953- WhoEmL 91
Matsushima, Akira Paul 1937- St&PR 91, WhoWor 91
Matsushima, Kozo 1929- WhoWor 91
Matsushima, Satoshi 1923- WhoAm 90
Matsushima, Shisho 1934- WhoWor 91
Matsushita, Keiichiro 1953- WhoWor 91
Matsushita, Konosuke 1894-1989 AnObit 1989, BioIn 16
Matsushita, Masaharu 1912- WhoWor 91
Matsushita, Shigenori 1936- WhoWor 91
Matsutani, Osamu Harold 1942- BiDrAPA 89
Matsuura, Takanori 1940- WhoWor 91
Matsuyama, Brian St&PR 91
Matsuzaka, Hirozo 1920- BiDrAPA 89
Matsuzaki, Isao 1930- WhoWor 91
Matt, Calman David 1887-1951 BioIn 16
Matt, Francis X. 1933- St&PR 91
Matt, Linda Ann 1952- WhoWrEP 89
Matt, Nicholas O. WhoE 91
Matt, Paul 1901-1987 BioIn 16
Matt, Toni BioIn 16
Matta ArtLatA
Matta 1911- ModArCr 1 [port]
Matta, David Lyles 1945- WhoHisp 91
Matta, Nadim Fadel 1958- WhoE 91
Matta, Ram Kumar 1946- WhoAm 90
Matta-Armanious, Shoukry BiDrAPA 89
Matta-Clark, Gordon 1945-1978 WhoAmA 91N
Mattal, Alan Jean 1930- St&PR 91
Mattar, Ahmad 1936- WhoWor 91
Mattar, Farres P. 1947-1989 BioIn 16
Mattason, Donald J. 1931- St&PR 91
Mattauch, Robert Joseph 1940- WhoAm 90
Mattausch, Thomas E. 1944- ODwPR 91
Mattausch, Thomas Edward 1944- WhoAm 90
Matte, Gilbert 1946- BiDrAPA 89
Matte, Harry 1931- ODwPR 91, St&PR 91
Matte, James Allan 1931- WhoWrEP 89
Matte-Blanco, Ignacio 1908- BiDrAPA 89
Mattea, Kathy ConMus 5 [port], WhoAmW 91, WhoNeCM [port]
Mattei, C. A. WhoAm 90
Mattei, Loren Neal 1949- WhoWrEP 89
Matteis, Joseph Theodore, Jr. 1947- WhoEmL 91
Matteis, Nicola 1707?- PenDiMP
Mattenklott, Gert 1942- WhoWor 91
Matteo, da Siena 1430?-1495 BioIn 16
Matteo, di Giovanni di Bartolo 1430?-1495 BioIn 16
Matteo, Vittucci 1919- IntWWM 90
Matter, David 1925- St&PR 91
Matter, Gary L. 1945- St&PR 91
Matter, Herbert 1907-1984 ConDes 90
Matter, John P. 1952- St&PR 91
Matter, LeRoy Robert 1932- St&PR 91
Mattera, Anthony F. 1954- ODwPR 91
Mattera, Don 1935- BioIn 16
Mattera, John 1953- ConAu 131
Mattern, Al 1883-1958 Ballpl 90
Mattern, Bruce William 1943- St&PR 91
Mattern, Carl Maximilian 1705-1774 PenDiDA 89
Mattern, Donald Eugene 1930- WhoAm 90
Mattern, Douglas James 1933- WhoWor 91
Mattern, Gerry A. 1935- WhoE 91
Mattern, Karl 1892-1969 WhoAmA 91N
Mattern, Keith Edward 1931- WhoAm 90
Mattern, Patricia Ann 1950- WhoEmL 91
Mattern, Perry Chalmers 1950- WhoEmL 91
Mattern, Robert Franklin 1921- St&PR 91
Mattern, Walter Gray, Jr. 1926- WhoAm 90
Matternes, Jay Howard 1933- WhoAmA 91

Matters, Arnold 1904- *IntWWM 90*
Matters, Clyde Burns 1924- *WhoAm 90*
Matterson, Joan McDevitt 1949- *WhoAmW 91*
Mattes, Hans George 1943- *WhoE 91*
Mattes, Jeffrey Allan 1948- *BiDrAPA 89*
Mattes-Kulig, Debra Ann 1954- *WhoAmW 91*
Matteson, E. David 1939- *St&PR 91*
Matteson, Frederick Edgar 1956- *WhoE 91*
Matteson, Ira 1917- *WhoAmA 91*
Matteson, Jack E. *BiDrAPA 89*
Matteson, Lawrence James 1939- *St&PR 91, WhoAm 90*
Matteson, Mary L. 1935- *WhoSSW 91*
Matteson, Patricia Ely 1945- *WhoAmW 91*
Matteson, Robert Eliot 1914- *WhoAm 90*
Matteson, Sumner W. 1867-1920 *BioIn 16, WhNaAH*
Matteson, Thomas T. *WhoAm 90*
Mattessich, Martin John 1958- *St&PR 91*
Mattessich, Richard Victor 1922- *WhoAm 90*
Matteucci, Margaret Mary 1940- *WhoAmW 91*
Mattey, John Joseph 1927- *WhoE 91*
Mattfeld, Jacquelyn A 1925- *WhoAm 90*
Mattfolk, Nils Goran 1951- *WhoWor 91*
Matthaei, Charles W.H. 1920- *St&PR 91*
Matthaei, Frederick C., Jr. 1925- *St&PR 91*
Matthaei, Pearl V *BiDrAPA 89*
Matthau, Walter 1920- *BioIn 16, WhoAm 90, WorAlBi*
Matthay, Tobias 1858-1945 *PenDiMP*
Matthei, Edward Hodge 1927- *WhoAm 90*
Matthei, Warren Douglas 1951- *WhoE 91*
Matthei Aubel, Fernando 1925- *WhoWor 91*
Matthes, John Jay 1952- *WhoEmL 91*
Matthes, Steven Allen 1950- *WhoEmL 91*
Mattheson, Rodney *MajTwCW*
Matthew, Christopher C F 1939- *ConAu 129*
Matthew, David Vandlan 1935- *St&PR 91*
Matthew, Eunice *BioIn 16, NewYTBS 90*
Matthew, Eunice S. *AuBYP 90*
Matthew, Lyn 1936- *WhoAmW 91, WhoWor 91*
Matthew, Thomas Cyril 1936- *WhoWor 91*
Matthew, William Henry 1943- *BiDrAPA 89*
Matthews, A. Bruce 1909- *St&PR 91*
Matthews, Agnes Cynthia 1924- *WhoAmW 91, WhoE 91*
Matthews, Albert E., Jr. 1935- *St&PR 91*
Matthews, Alexander George 1935- *St&PR 91*
Matthews, Allan Freeman 1916- *WhoWrEP 89*
Matthews, Andrea 1956- *IntWWM 90*
Matthews, Anne Lamb 1942- *WhoAmW 91*
Matthews, Anthony *TwCCr&M 91*
Matthews, Arthur Conrad *BiDrAPA 89*
Matthews, Arthur Morris, Jr. 1946- *WhoSSW 91*
Matthews, Asa Carrington 1838-1908 *AmLegL*
Matthews, Barbara Ann 1951- *WhoAmW 91*
Matthews, Barbara Jean 1936- *WhoAmW 91*
Matthews, Bernard S 1918- *BiDrAPA 89*
Matthews, Beverley 1905- *St&PR 91*
Matthews, Brander 1852-1929 *BioIn 16*
Matthews, Brian W. 1938- *WhoAm 90*
Matthews, Burnita Shelton 1894-1988 *BioIn 16*
Matthews, Cameron 1884-1958 *OxCCanT*
Matthews, Carolyn Croker 1938- *WhoAmW 91*
Matthews, Charles A. *BioIn 16*
Matthews, Charles David 1946- *WhoEmL 91*
Matthews, Charles Sedwick 1920- *WhoAm 90*
Matthews, Clark J., II 1936- *St&PR 91*
Matthews, Clark Jio, II 1936- *WhoAm 90*
Matthews, Colin 1946- *IntWWM 90*
Matthews, Craig G. 1943- *St&PR 91*
Matthews, Craig Gerard 1943- *WhoAm 90*
Matthews, Dan Gus 1939- *WhoSSW 91*
Matthews, Daniel George 1932- *WhoAm 90, WhoE 91, WhoWor 91*
Matthews, Darlene Theresa 1953- *WhoAmW 91*
Matthews, Daryl Bruce 1947- *BiDrAPA 89, WhoEmL 91*
Matthews, David *PenDiMP*
Matthews, David 1920- *WhoAm 90*
Matthews, David John 1943- *IntWWM 90*
Matthews, Dean 1934- *ODwPR 91*
Matthews, Denis 1919-1988 *AnObit 1988, PenDiMP*
Matthe•s, Denise *BioIn 16*
Matthews, Domina Marvyl 1947- *WhoAmW 91*
Matthews, Donald John 1933- *WhoE 91*
Matthews, Donald Rowe 1925- *WhoAm 90*
Matthews, Douglas Alan 1955- *WhoWor 91*
Matthews, Douglas Gary 1945- *BioIn 16, St&PR 91*
Matthews, Drexel Gene 1952- *WhoSSW 91, WhoWor 91*
Matthews, Duane Ellison 1929- *WhoAm 90*
Matthews, Dwight Earl 1951- *WhoE 91*
Matthews, Earnestine Stroud 1943- *WhoAmW 91*
Matthews, Edward 1904-1954 *DcAfAmP*
Matthews, Edward 1955- *WhoE 91*
Matthews, Edward Easton 1931- *St&PR 91*
Matthews, Edwin Spencer, Jr. 1934- *WhoAm 90*
Matthews, Elizabeth Woodfin 1927- *WhoAmW 91*
Matthews, Ellen *ConAu 129, WhoWrEP 89*
Matthews, Eugene Edward 1931- *WhoAm 90*
Matthews, Eugene S. 1872- *AmLegL*
Matthews, F.P. 1921- *St&PR 91*
Matthews, Florence *BiDrAPA 89*
Matthews, Ford *WhoWrEP 89*
Matthews, Forrest David 1935- *BiDrUSE 89*
Matthews, Francis Richard 1920- *St&PR 91, WhoAm 90*
Matthews, Frank 1931- *WhoSSW 91*
Matthews, Gareth Blanc 1929- *WhoAm 90*
Matthews, Gary 1950- *Ballpl 90 [port]*
Matthews, Gene 1931- *WhoAmA 91*
Matthews, George A., Jr. 1934- *St&PR 91*
Matthews, George Hubert 1930- *WhoAm 90*
Matthews, George Tennyson 1917- *WhoAm 90*
Matthews, George William 1949- *WhoSSW 91*
Matthews, Gerald Lester 1928- *WhoSSW 91*
Matthews, Gilbert Elliott 1930- *St&PR 91, WhoAm 90*
Matthews, Gillian Rachel 1962- *IntWWM 90*
Matthews, Glenn Edward 1951- *WhoSSW 91*
Matthews, Harriett 1940- *WhoAmA 91*
Matthews, Harrison Freeman, Jr. 1927- *WhoE 91*
Matthews, Herbert L. 1900-1977 *BioIn 16*
Matthews, Herbert Lionel 1900-1977 *AuBYP 90*
Matthews, Ian *EncPR&S 89, NewAgMG*
Matthews, Inez 1917- *BioIn 16, DcAfAmP*
Matthews, Jack 1917- *WhoAm 90*
Matthews, Jack 1925- *WhoAm 90, WhoWrEP 89*
Matthews, Jack Beverly, Jr. 1951- *WhoSSW 91*
Matthews, Jack Edward 1928- *WhoAm 90*
Matthews, James Benning 1933- *WhoAm 90*
Matthews, James Bernard 1950- *WhoSSW 91*
Matthews, James Fredrick 1947- *WhoSSW 91*
Matthews, James Michael 1948- *WhoEmL 91*
Matthews, James Shadley 1951- *St&PR 91*
Matthews, Jana B. 1940- *WhoAmW 91*
Matthews, Jessie 1907-1981 *OxCPMus*
Matthews, Jessie Margaret 1907-1981 *DcNaB 1981*
Matthews, John David *BiDrAPA 89*
Matthews, John Edward 1941- *WhoSSW 91*
Matthews, John Floyd 1919- *WhoAm 90, WhoWrEP 89*
Matthews, John K., Jr. 1929- *St&PR 91*
Matthews, John L. 1914- *St&PR 91*
Matthews, John Louis 1932- *WhoAm 90*
Matthews, John T. 1946- *WhoSSW 91*
Matthews, Joseph E. 1938- *St&PR 91*
Matthews, Joseph Ronald 1942- *WhoE 91*
Matthews, Justus 1945- *IntWWM 90*
Matthews, Kathleen *BiDrAPA 89*
Matthews, Kay Ann Bean 1955- *WhoAmW 91*
Matthews, Kelly K. 1944- *St&PR 91*
Matthews, Kelly King 1944- *WhoAm 90*
Matthews, Kenneth Lee 1944- *BiDrAPA 89*
Matthews, L. White, III 1945- *St&PR 91, WhoAm 90, WhoEmL 91*
Matthews, Lemuel Hatch 1909- *WhoAm 90*
Matthews, Leonard Sarver 1922- *St&PR 91, WhoAm 90*
Matthews, Lester G 1930- *BiDrAPA 89*
Matthews, Linda Llewellyn Fink 1950- *WhoAmW 91*
Matthews, Margaret Ellen 1951- *WhoE 91*
Matthews, Marilyn L 1939- *BiDrAPA 89*
Matthews, Mary Lathrop Wright 1891-1955 *BioIn 16*
Matthews, Michael A. G. 1940- *WhoWor 91*
Matthews, Michael Gough 1931- *IntWWM 90*
Matthews, Mike *WhoWrEP 89*
Matthews, Norman Stuart 1933- *St&PR 91, WhoAm 90*
Matthews, Pamela Thornton 1954- *WhoAmW 91*
Matthews, Patricia 1927- *MajTwCW*
Matthews, Patrick J. 1942- *St&PR 91*
Matthews, Patrick John 1942- *WhoAm 90*
Matthews, Paul A. *BioIn 16*
Matthews, Paul D. 1929- *St&PR 91*
Matthews, Paul Deacon 1929- *WhoAm 90*
Matthews, Paul William 1954- *WhoEmL 91*
Matthews, Pearl Parkerson 1941- *WhoWrEP 89*
Matthews, Ralph 1939- *WhoSSW 91*
Matthews, Randall 1945- *BiDrAPA 89*
Matthews, Richard G. 1959- *St&PR 91*
Matthews, Robert C., Jr. 1947- *St&PR 91*
Matthews, Robert Charles Oliver 1927- *WhoWor 91*
Matthews, Robert L. 1937- *St&PR 91*
Matthews, Robert Leon 1946- *WhoE 91*
Matthews, Robert Lloyd 1937- *WhoAm 90*
Matthews, Robert Orin 1925- *WhoAm 90*
Matthews, Robert R 1929- *BiDrAPA 89*
Matthews, Ronald Alan 1952- *IntWWM 90*
Matthews, Ronald W. 1940- *St&PR 91*
Matthews, Rowena Green 1938- *WhoAmW 91*
Matthews, Roy S. 1945- *St&PR 91*
Matthews, Rupert Oliver 1961- *AuBYP 90*
Matthews, Stephen George 1932- *St&PR 91*
Matthews, Steve Allen 1955- *WhoAm 90*
Matthews, Stuart 1936- *WhoSSW 91*
Matthews, Susan F. 1957- *ODwPR 91*
Matthews, T.K., II 1926- *St&PR 91*
Matthews, Thomas *AmLegL*
Matthews, Thomas Michael 1943- *WhoSSW 91*
Matthews, Thomas W. 1934- *St&PR 91*
Matthews, Valerie Jo 1947- *WhoAmW 91*
Matthews, Wanda Miller 1930- *WhoAm 90, WhoAmA 91*
Matthews, Warren Wayne 1939- *WhoAm 90*
Matthews, Washington 1843-1905 *WhNaAH*
Matthews, Westina *BioIn 16*
Matthews, Westina L. 1948- *WhoAmW 91*
Matthews, Wid 1896-1965 *Ballpl 90*
Matthews, Wilbur Lee 1903- *WhoAm 90*
Matthews, William 1942- *WhoWrEP 89, WorAu 1980 [port]*
Matthews, William Andrew 1934- *WhoSSW 91*
Matthews, William D. 1934- *St&PR 91*
Matthews, William Doty 1934- *WhoAm 90*
Matthews, William Elliott, IV 1929- *St&PR 91, WhoAm 90, WhoSSW 91*
Matthews, William H. 1919- *AuBYP 90*
Matthews, William J. 1950- *St&PR 91*
Matthews, William John 1919- *WhoWor 91*
Matthews, William McGill, V 1940- *WhoSSW 91*
Matthews, William Procter 1942- *WhoAm 90*
Matthews-Bellinger, Julia A *BiDrAPA 89*
Matthews-Brylski, Beverly Ann *BiDrAPA 89*
Matthews-Ferrari, Katina Argero 1954- *BiDrAPA 89*
Matthews-Johnson, Cynthia L. 1959- *WhoAmW 91*
Matthews-Simonton, Stephanie *NewAgE 90*
Matthews-Simonton, Stephanie 1947- *ConAu 132*
Matthey, William A. 1951- *WhoSSW 91*
Matthey de l'Endroit, Georges-Adrien 1929- *WhoWor 91*
Matthias Jochumsson *DcScanL*
Matthias Johannessen *DcScanL*
Matthias, C. David 1955- *St&PR 91*
Matthias, Fritz Reinhard 1938- *WhoWor 91*
Matthias, George Frank 1934- *WhoE 91*
Matthias, Russell Howard, Jr. 1934- *St&PR 91*
Matthias, Willard C. 1914- *WhoAm 90*
Matthiasson, Thorolfur 1953- *WhoWor 91*
Matthies, Duane Darwin 1960- *St&PR 91*
Matthies, Evelyn Fern 1936- *WhoAmW 91*
Matthies, Frederick John 1925- *WhoAm 90*
Matthies, Holger 1940- *ConDes 90*
Matthiesen, Garvin C. 1928- *WhoAm 90*
Matthiesen, Leroy Theodore 1921- *WhoAm 90, WhoSSW 91*
Matthiesen, Thomas *AuBYP 90*
Matthiessen, F. O. 1902-1950 *BioIn 16*
Matthiessen, Francis Otto 1902-1950 *BioIn 16, EncAL*
Matthiessen, Lars Overgaard 1930- *WhoWor 91*
Matthiessen, Peter *BioIn 16, NewYTBS 90 [port]*
Matthiessen, Peter 1927- *Au&Arts 6 [port], BestSel 90-4 [port], ConLC 64 [port], MajTwCW, WhoAm 90, WhoWrEP 89*
Matthis, Eva Mildred Boney 1927- *WhoAmW 91*
Matthus, Siegfried 1934- *IntWWM 90, PenDiMPA*
Matthys, Eric Francois 1956- *WhoEmL 91*
Matthys, Paul Lodewijk Juul 1949- *WhoWor 91*
Mattia, Thomas G. *ODwPR 91*
Mattiace, Michael 1944- *WhoSSW 91*
Mattice, Stanley E. 1945- *St&PR 91*
Mattich, Angelo 1936- *BiDrAPA 89*
Mattick, Bobby 1915- *Ballpl 90*
Mattiesen, Emil 1875-1939 *EncPaPR 91*
Mattila, Aarne Ilmari 1937- *WhoWor 91*
Mattila, Edward Charles 1927- *IntWWM 90*
Mattila, Karita 1960- *IntWWM 90*
Mattila, Lauri Lasse Juhani 1947- *WhoWor 91*
Mattill, A J, Jr. 1924- *ConAu 31NR*
Mattimore, Bryan William 1954- *WhoE 91*
Mattin, Harry E. 1896-1988 *BioIn 16*
Mattingly 1934- *WhoAmA 91*
Mattingly, Don *BioIn 16*
Mattingly, Don 1961- *Ballpl 90 [port], WorAlBi*
Mattingly, Donald Arthur 1961- *WhoAm 90, WhoE 91*
Mattingly, Helen Elizabeth 1939- *WhoSSW 91*
Mattingly, John H. 1950- *St&PR 91*
Mattingly, Larry Alan 1946- *WhoSSW 91*
Mattingly, Mack F. 1931- *WhoAm 90, WhoWor 91*
Mattingly, Paul H 1941- *ConAu 129*
Mattingly, Paul Havey 1941- *WhoE 91*
Mattingly, Richard E. 1950- *WhoWrEP 89*
Mattingly, Rita Patricia 1963- *WhoEmL 91*
Mattingly, Robert Kerker 1921- *WhoWor 91*
Mattingly, Robert Martin 1939- *WhoE 91*
Mattingly, Thomas K. 1936- *WhoAm 90*
Mattingly, William J. 1938- *St&PR 91*
Mattioli, Joseph Reginald 1925- *St&PR 91*
Mattioli, Joseph Reginald, Jr. 1925- *WhoE 91*
Mattis, Louis Price 1941- *WhoAm 90*
Mattis, Noemi Perelman 1936- *WhoAmW 91*
Mattison, Donald Mangus 1905-1975 *WhoAmA 91N*
Mattison, Harry D. 1936- *WhoSSW 91*
Mattison, Joel 1931- *WhoSSW 91*
Mattison, Priscilla Jane 1960- *WhoAmW 91*
Mattison, Richard E 1946- *BiDrAPA 89*
Mattison, Stanley Barron 1943- *St&PR 91*
Mattison-Earls, Donna Lynne 1949- *WhoE 91*
Mattke, Dunnley L. 1953- *St&PR 91*
Mattler, Rise B. *ODwPR 91*
Mattman, Lida Holmes 1912- *WhoAmW 91*
Mattmann, Eugen Anton 1935- *WhoWor 91*
Matto de Turner, Clorinda 1852-1909 *BioIn 16*
Mattola, Guy A. *St&PR 91*
Matton, Ida 1863-1940 *BiDWomA*
Matton, Roger 1929- *IntWWM 90*
Mattone, Irene *BioIn 16*
Mattone, Joseph Michael 1931- *WhoE 91, WhoWor 91*
Mattoon, Henry Amasa, Jr. 1914- *WhoAm 90*
Mattoon, Peter Mills 1931- *WhoAm 90*
Mattoon, Sara Halsey 1947- *WhoAmW 91*
Mattos, Gregorio de 1636-1695 *BioIn 16*
Mattos, Joseph Glenn 1953- *St&PR 91*
Mattos, William Joseph 1949- *WhoE 91*
Mattox, Gail Arie 1951- *BiDrAPA 89*
Mattox, James Albon 1943- *WhoAm 90, WhoSSW 91*
Mattox, James Dwight, Jr. *BiDrAPA 89*
Mattox, Joyce *BioIn 16*
Mattox, Kenneth Leon 1938- *WhoAm 90*
Mattran, Donald Albert 1934- *WhoAm 90*
Mattrella, Anne Laura 1954- *WhoE 91*
Matts, Carrie E. 1962- *St&PR 91*
Mattson, Ake Erik 1929- *BiDrAPA 89*
Mattson, Carol Linnette 1946- *WhoAmW 91*
Mattson, Clarence Russell 1924- *WhoE 91*
Mattson, Ellwood A. 1918- *St&PR 91*

Mattson, Eric Leonard 1951- *St&PR 91*
Mattson, Francis O. 1931- *WhoAm 90*
Mattson, Gail 1950- *WhoAmW 91*
Mattson, Harold Frazyer, Jr. 1930- *WhoE 91*
Mattson, Helmi *EncAL*
Mattson, Henry 1887-1971 *WhoAmA 91N*
Mattson, Janet Marie 1947- *WhoEmL 91*
Mattson, Jean Murphey 1926- *WhoAmW 91*
Mattson, John Andrew *BiDrAPA 89*
Mattson, Kay Roberta 1950- *WhoAmW 91*
Mattson, Lawrence Sigfrid 1931- *St&PR 91, WhoAm 90*
Mattson, Marcus 1904- *WhoAm 90*
Mattson, Marlin Roy Albin 1939- *BiDrAPA 89*
Mattson, Roger A 1938- *BiDrAPA 89*
Mattson, Roy Henry 1927- *WhoAm 90*
Mattson, Ursula Ingrid 1953- *WhoWrEP 89*
Mattson, Victor F. 1925- *St&PR 91*
Mattson, Victor Frank 1925- *WhoAm 90, WhoSSW 91*
Mattson, Walter *BioIn 16*
Mattson, Walter Edward 1932- *WhoAm 90, WhoWor 91*
Mattsson, Ake 1929- *WhoAm 90*
Mattsson, Bjorn Evert Alexander 1941- *WhoWor 91*
Mattsson, Donald Marvin 1923- *St&PR 91*
Mattsson, Nils Gosta 1938- *WhoWor 91*
Mattuchio, Frank Edward 1934- *St&PR 91*
Matuella, Lewis Joseph 1929- *St&PR 91*
Matuhasi, Tyoku 1922- *WhoWor 91*
Matula, Richard Allan 1939- *WhoAm 90*
Matula, Rick 1953- *Ballpl 90*
Matulich, Erika 1963- *WhoAmW 91*
Matulka, Jan 1890-1972 *WhoAmA 91N*
Matunas, Anthony *BiDrAPA 89*
Matune, Frank Joseph 1948- *WhoE 91*
Matunis, Frank X. 1941- *St&PR 91*
Matura, Robert Joseph 1933- *St&PR 91*
Matura, Thaddee 1922- *ConAu 132*
Maturana de Guitierrez, Vicenta 1793-1857 *EncCoWW*
Mature, Victor 1916- *WorAlBi*
Maturi, Raymond R. 1938- *St&PR 91, WhoAm 90*
Maturin, Edmund 1818?-1891 *DcCanB 12*
Maturo, James V. 1943- *St&PR 91*
Matus, Alicia Mercedes 1946- *BiDrAPA 89*
Matus, Barry 1949- *WhoE 91*
Matus, Irvin *BioIn 16*
Matus, Irvin Leigh 1941- *ConAu 129*
Matus, Wayne Charles 1950- *WhoE 91, WhoEmL 91*
Matusch, Johann *PenDiDA 89*
Matuschka, Albrecht *BioIn 16*
Matushek, Edward J., III 1954- *WhoEmL 91*
Matusiak, Thomas 1948- *St&PR 91*
Matusiewicz, Anna Holster *BiDrAPA 89*
Matusow, Allen Joseph 1937- *WhoAm 90*
Matuszak, Alice Jean Boyer 1935- *WhoAmW 91*
Matuszak, John *BioIn 16*
Matuszak, John 1950-1989 *ConAu 130*
Matuszek, Len 1954- *Ballpl 90*
Matuszewski, Stanley 1915- *WhoWor 91*
Matuszewski, Tadek I. 1925-1989 *BioIn 16*
Matuszko, Anthony Joseph 1926- *WhoAm 90*
Matute, Ana Maria 1925- *MajTwCW*
Matute, Ana Maria 1926- *IntvSpW [port]*
Matuz, Istvan 1947- *IntWWM 90*
Matuzak, Joseph Matthew 1955- *WhoWrEP 89*
Matuzas, William *BiDrAPA 89*
Matyas, Diane C 1961- *WhoAmA 91*
Matyas, Miroslav *PenDiMP*
Matyas, Robert Michael 1926- *WhoE 91*
Matychowiak, Francis A 1926- *BiDrAPA 89*
Matz, Glenn M. 1939- *St&PR 91*
Matz, Jerome Gershin 1927- *St&PR 91*
Matz, Joyce *ODwPR 91*
Matz, Kay Elaine 1946- *WhoAmW 91*
Matz, Merton J. 1922- *WhoAm 90*
Matz, Robert 1931- *WhoE 91*
Matz, Rodney S 1942- *BiDrAPA 89*
Matza, Bruce R. 1943- *St&PR 91*
Matzdorff, James Arthur 1956- *WhoWor 91*
Matzen, Lynn Robert 1938- *St&PR 91*
Matzen, Richard Norman, Jr. 1957- *WhoWrEP 89*
Matzen, Ted Andrew *BiDrAPA 89*
Matzenauer, Margarete 1881-1963 *PenDiMP*
Matzer, John W. 1945- *St&PR 91*
Matziorinis, Kenneth N. 1954- *WhoE 91, WhoWor 91*
Matzka, John 1924- *St&PR 91*
Matzke, Frank J. 1922- *WhoAm 90, WhoE 91*
Matzke, Gary Roger 1950- *WhoSSW 91*
Matzkin, William L *BiDrAPA 89*
Matzkin, William Lionel 1922- *WhoE 91*
Matzner, Frederick J 1953- *BiDrAPA 89*
Mau, Chuck 1907- *WhoAm 90*
Mau, Ernest Eugene 1945- *WhoWrEP 89*
Mau, James Anthony 1935- *WhoAm 90*
Mau, Richard R. 1931- *ODwPR 91*
Mau, Turia *BioIn 16*
Mau, William Koon-Hee 1913- *WhoAm 90*
Mau, William L. 1922- *St&PR 91*
Mauceri, Jennie *BiDrAPA 89*
Mauceri, John 1945- *PenDiMP*
Mauceri, John F. 1945- *IntWWM 90*
Mauceri, John Francis 1945- *WhoAm 90*
Mauch, Betty L. 1941- *WhoAmW 91*
Mauch, Douglas Bruce 1944- *St&PR 91*
Mauch, Gene 1925- *Ballpl 90 [port]*
Mauch, Gene W. 1925- *WhoAm 90*
Mauch, Robert Carl 1939- *St&PR 91*
Mauchahty-Ware, Tom *NewAgMG*
Maucher, Helmut *BioIn 16*
Maucher, Johann Michael 1645-1700 *PenDiDA 89*
Mauck, Elwyn Arthur 1910-1990 *WhoAm 90, WhoWor 91*
Mauck, Henry Page, Jr. 1926- *WhoAm 90*
Mauck, William M., Jr. 1938- *WhoSSW 91*
Maud *WomWR*
Maud 1102-1167 *BioIn 16*
Maud, John P. R. *ConAu 129*
Maud, John Primatt Redcliffe *ConAu 129*
Maud, John Primatt Redcliffe 1906-1982 *DcNaB 1981*
Maud, Ralph 1928- *ConAu 129*
Maude, Edward Joseph 1924- *WhoAm 90*
Maude, George 1931- *ConAu 33NR*
Mauderli, Walter 1924- *WhoAm 90*
Maudgal, Dharam Pal 1943- *WhoWor 91*
Maudlin, Robert V. 1927- *WhoE 91*
Maue, Frederick R 1949- *BiDrAPA 89*
Mauer, Alvin Marx 1928- *WhoAm 90*
Mauer, David Michael 1948- *WhoAm 90*
Mauer, Michael Leonard 1940- *WhoAm 90*
Mauet, Thomas Anton 1945- *WhoEmL 91*
Maugans, Edgar H. 1935- *St&PR 91*
Maugans, Edgar Hurley 1935- *WhoAm 90*
Mauge, Cecile A *BiDrAPA 89*
Mauger, Lee Fillmen 1956- *WhoEmL 91*
Mauger, Leonard Albert 1923- *WhoWor 91*
Mauger, Patricia Ann 1937- *WhoAm 90*
Mauger, Stephen John 1949- *St&PR 91*
Mauger, Theodore Fitch 1941- *BiDrAPA 89*
Maugeri, Sam J. 1933- *St&PR 91*
Maugham, Somerset 1874-1965 *BioIn 16*
Maugham, W. S. *MajTwCW*
Maugham, W Somerset *MajTwCW*
Maugham, W. Somerset 1874-1965 *BioIn 16*
Maugham, W Somerset 1874-1965 *DcLB 100 [port], TwCCr&M 91*
Maugham, W. Somerset 1874-1965 *WorAlBi*
Maugham, William Somerset 1874-1965 *BioIn 16, MajTwCW, SpyFic*
Maughan, Janet 1828-1926 *FemiCLE*
Maughelli, Mary L 1935- *WhoAmA 91*
Maughmer, Mark David 1950- *WhoE 91*
Maughn, James D. 1947- *St&PR 91*
Maughon, Bob R *BiDrAPA 89*
Maughs, Sydney B *BiDrAPA 89*
Mauk, Kenneth Leon 1945- *St&PR 91*
Mauk, Steven Glenn 1949- *IntWWM 90*
Mauke, Otto Russell 1924- *WhoAm 90*
Maul, Al 1865-1958 *Ballpl 90*
Maul, Arthur Benjamin 1924- *WhoWor 91*
Maulbetsch, Stephen Robert 1957- *St&PR 91*
Maulden, Jerry L. 1936- *St&PR 91, WhoAm 90, WhoSSW 91*
Maulden, John Harrison 1927- *WhoSSW 91*
Mauldin, Bill 1921- *BioIn 16, EncACom, WhoAmA 91*
Mauldin, Karen Singley 1964- *WhoWrEP 89*
Mauldin, Randolph *BioIn 16*
Mauldin, Robert Ray 1935- *WhoAm 90*
Mauldin, William H. 1921- *WhoAm 90*
Maulding, Barry Clifford 1945- *St&PR 91, WhoAm 90*
Maule, Cynthia Lea 1949- *WhoAmW 91*
Maule, Hamilton Bee 1915- *AuBYP 90, WhoWrEP 89*
Maule, James Edward 1951- *WhoEmL 91*
Maule, Tex *AuBYP 90*
Maulin, Jack Doolin 1934- *St&PR 91*
Maulion, Richard Peter 1949- *BiDrAPA 89*
Maull, Flora Davis 1904- *WhoAm 90*
Maull, George Marriner 1947- *WhoE 91*
Maull, Louis Thomas, IV 1944- *St&PR 91*
Maulnier, Thierry 1909-1988 *BiDFrPL*
Maulsby, Allen Farish 1922- *WhoAm 90*
Maultsby, Hubert Danford 1943- *WhoE 91*
Maultsby, Maxie C 1932- *BiDrAPA 89*
Maumenee, Alfred Edward 1913- *WhoAm 90*
Maumus, Craig W 1946- *BiDrAPA 89*
Maun, Joseph Angus 1909- *WhoAm 90*
Maun, Mary Ellen 1951- *WhoAmW 91, WhoE 91*
Maund, Timothy Faulk 1934- *WhoSSW 91*
Maunder, Addison Bruce 1934- *WhoAm 90*
Mauney, Dick 1920-1970 *Ballpl 90*
Mauney, John David, III 1942- *BiDrAPA 89*
Mauney, Keith James 1948- *WhoE 91*
Mauney, William Kemp, III 1951- *St&PR 91*
Mauney, William Kemp, Jr. 1917- *St&PR 91*
Maung Maung *BioIn 16*
Maung Maung 1925- *WhoWor 91*
Maung Maung Gyi *BioIn 16*
Maung Maung Kha 1917- *WhoWor 91*
Maung, Myint 1939- *WhoWor 91*
Maung-U, Edward *BiDrAPA 89*
Maunsbach, George Eric 1890- *WhoAmA 91N*
Maunsbach, Kay Benedicta 1933- *WhoAmW 91, WhoE 91*
Maupassant, Guy De 1850-1893 *WorAlBi*
Maupay, Walter R. 1939- *St&PR 91*
Maupin 1670?-1707 *PenDiMP*
Maupin, Armistead *BioIn 16*
Maupin, Armistead 1944- *ConAu 130*
Maupin, Armistead Jones 1914- *WhoAm 90*
Maupin, Armistead Jones, Jr. 1944- *WhoAm 90*
Maupin, Carol Grinstead 1936- *WhoAmW 91*
Maupin, Levi Pleasant 1924- *St&PR 91*
Maupin, Robert Wade 1932- *St&PR 91*
Maura, Antonio 1853-1925 *BioIn 16*
Maura, Carmen *BioIn 16*
Maura, Julia 1910-1970 *EncCoWW*
Mauran, Duncan H. 1926- *St&PR 91*
Maurano, Steven J. *ODwPR 91*
Maurel, Victor 1848-1923 *PenDiMP*
Maurer, Armand Augustine 1915- *WhoWrEP 89*
Maurer, Arthur Walter 1921- *St&PR 91*
Maurer, Carol N *BiDrAPA 89*
Maurer, Carol Nellis 1933- *WhoAmW 91, WhoE 91*
Maurer, Charles Frederick William, III 1939- *WhoWor 91*
Maurer, Claude Emile 1924- *WhoWor 91*
Maurer, Donald D. 1937- *St&PR 91*
Maurer, Eleanor Johnson 1914- *WhoSSW 91*
Maurer, Ely 1913- *WhoE 91*
Maurer, Evan Maclyn 1944- *WhoAmA 91*
Maurer, Evan Mallyn 1944- *WhoAm 90*
Maurer, Fred Dry 1909- *WhoAm 90*
Maurer, Frederic George, III 1952- *WhoEmL 91*
Maurer, Gernant Elmer 1949- *WhoAm 90*
Maurer, Gilbert Charles 1928- *WhoAm 90, WhoE 91*
Maurer, Harold Maurice 1936- *WhoAm 90*
Maurer, James Hudson 1864-1944 *EncAL*
Maurer, James R. 1939- *St&PR 91*
Maurer, Jeffrey S. 1947- *St&PR 91*
Maurer, JoAnn Denice 1951- *WhoAmW 91*
Maurer, John A. *BioIn 16*
Maurer, John Irving 1934- *BiDrAPA 89*
Maurer, John Sylvester 1938- *WhoAm 90*
Maurer, Jose Clemente 1900- *WhoWor 91*
Maurer, Joy Adelaide 1934- *St&PR 91*
Maurer, Laurie Mutchnik 1935- *WhoAm 90*
Maurer, Lucille Darvin 1922- *WhoAm 90, WhoAmW 91, WhoE 91*
Maurer, Marc *BioIn 16*
Maurer, Morris Lee 1951- *St&PR 91*
Maurer, Neil Douglas 1941- *WhoAmA 91*
Maurer, Norman 1926-1986 *EncACom*
Maurer, Patricia *BioIn 16*
Maurer, Paul Herbert 1923- *WhoAm 90, WhoE 91*
Maurer, Paul Reed 1937- *WhoWor 91*
Maurer, Pierre 1924- *St&PR 91*
Maurer, Ralph A. 1931- *St&PR 91*
Maurer, Ralph Gerald *BiDrAPA 89*
Maurer, Robert 1933- *WhoE 91, WhoWor 91*
Maurer, Robert Distler 1924- *WhoAm 90*
Maurer, Rosalie Grace 1945- *WhoAmW 91*
Maurer, Ruth Allene 1939- *WhoAmW 91*
Maurer, Sascha 1897-1961 *WhoAmA 91N*
Maurer, Susan L. 1959- *WhoSSW 91*
Maurer, Thomas James 1921- *St&PR 91*
Maurer, Tracey Lynn 1963- *WhoAmW 91*
Maurer, Virginia Gallaher 1946- *WhoSSW 91*
Maurer, Walter Harding 1921- *WhoAm 90*
Maurer, Walter John 1941- *St&PR 91*
Maurer, Wesley Henry 1897- *WhoWor 91*
Mauretti, Gerald Joseph 1943- *St&PR 91*
Maurhoff, William Howard 1936- *WhoE 91*
Mauri, Robert L. 1935- *St&PR 91*
Mauriac, Claude 1914- *WhoWor 91*
Mauriac, Francois 1885-1970 *BioIn 16, MajTwCW, WorAlBi*
Mauriac, Francois Charles 1885-1970 *BiDFrPL*
Maurice, Alfred Paul 1921- *WhoAm 90, WhoAmA 91*
Maurice, E Ingersoll 1901- *WhoAmA 91*
Maurice, Frederick Denison 1805-1872 *BioIn 16*
Maurice, Gerald D. 1933- *St&PR 91*
Maurice, Robert H *BiDrAPA 89*
Maurice, Samuel Joseph 1945- *St&PR 91*
Maurice, Thomas F. 1916- *St&PR 91*
Maurice, Wendy *ODwPR 91*
Mauricio, Cipriano G *BiDrAPA 89*
Maurin, Gayle Elizabeth 1950- *WhoAmW 91*
Maurin, Louis Felix 1869-1956 *BiDFrPL*
Maurin, Mario Leon 1928- *WhoAm 90*
Maurina, Zenta 1897-1978 *EncCoWW*
Maurissens, Marc 1949- *WhoWor 91*
Mauritzen, Joseph Howard *BiDrAPA 89*
Mauro, Albert P. 1929- *St&PR 91*
Mauro, Alexander 1921-1989 *BioIn 16*
Mauro, Anthony R. 1934- *St&PR 91*
Mauro, Arthur Valentine 1927- *St&PR 91*
Mauro, Carmen 1926- *Ballpl 90*
Mauro, Ermanno 1939- *IntWWM 90*
Mauro, John Baptist 1923- *WhoAm 90*
Mauro, Joseph William 1932- *St&PR 91*
Mauro, Raymond Vincent 1958- *WhoE 91*
Mauro, Richard Frank 1945- *WhoAm 90*
Mauro, Thomas Vincent 1939- *WhoAm 90*
Maurois, Andre 1885-1967 *AuBYP 90, BioIn 16, MajTwCW, WorAlBi*
Mauroner, Norman Lee 1922- *BiDrAPA 89*
Mauroner, Richard F *BiDrAPA 89*
Mauroy, Pierre 1928- *BiDFrPL*
Maurras, Charles Marie Photius 1868-1952 *BiDFrPL*
Maurstad, David Ingolf 1953- *WhoEmL 91*
Maurstad, Toralv 1926- *WhoWor 91*
Maury, Antonia Caetana de Paiva Pereira 1866-1952 *BioIn 16*
Maury, James *EncCRAm*
Maury, Marc A. 1938- *St&PR 91*
Maury, Mario A., Jr. 1936- *St&PR 91*
Maus, Catherine 1959- *St&PR 91*
Maus, Gerard Peter 1951- *St&PR 91*
Mausberg, Lionel N 1938- *BiDrAPA 89*
Mausel, Paul Warner 1936- *WhoAm 90*
Mauser, Patricia A. 1951- *St&PR 91*
Mauser, Patricia Rhoads 1943- *AuBYP 90*
Mausert, William H. 1940- *St&PR 91*
Mausi, Shahida *BioIn 16*
Mauskop, Alexander 1956- *WhoE 91*
Mauskopf, Seymour Harold 1938- *WhoAm 90*
Mausner, Dorothy *St&PR 91*
Mausner, Leonard F. *St&PR 91*
Mausner, Seymour *St&PR 91*
Mauss, Marcel 1872-1950 *BioIn 16*
Maussion, Pierre Eduoard *WhoAmA 91*
Mautner, Henry George 1925- *WhoAm 90*
Mautner, Irwin 1933- *St&PR 91*
Mautz, Bernhard Frederick 1936- *St&PR 91*
Mautz, Robert Barbeau 1915- *WhoAm 90*
Mauzerall, David Charles 1929- *WhoAm 90*
Mauzy, Michael Philip 1928- *St&PR 91*
Mauzy, Oscar Holcombe 1926- *WhoAm 90, WhoSSW 91*
Mavellia, Adriana 1949- *WhoWor 91*
Maverick, Samuel 1602?-1676? *EncCRAm*
Maves, David Walter 1937- *WhoSSW 91*
Maves, Paul Benjamin 1913- *WhoAm 90*
Mavia *WomWR*
Mavigliano, George Jerome 1941- *WhoAmA 91*
Mavignier, Almir 1925- *ConDes 90*
Mavis, Nancy Ann 1938- *BiDrAPA 89*
Mavissakalian, Matig Rouben 1943- *BiDrAPA 89*
Mavor, Elizabeth 1927- *BioIn 16*
Mavrides, Gregory 1955- *WhoSSW 91*
Mavris, G.S. 1956- *St&PR 91*
Mavritte, Harold E 1929- *BiDrAPA 89*
Mavrodin, Alice 1941- *IntWWM 90*
Mavroidis, Michael Louis 1948- *BiDrAPA 89*
Mavromatis, Mary Irene 1951- *BiDrAPA 89*
Mavros, Donald Odysseus 1927- *WhoAmA 91*

Mavros, George S. 1957- *WhoEmL 91, WhoSSW 91, WhoWor 91*
Mavroudis, Demetrios 1937- *WhoAmA 91*
Mavroules, Nicholas 1929- *WhoAm 90, WhoE 91*
Maw, Herbert B. 1893-1990 *NewYTBS 90*
Maw, James Gordon 1936- *WhoAm 90*
Maw, Nicholas 1935- *IntWWM 90, PenDiMP A*
Maw, Samuel H. *BioIn 16*
Maw, Samuel H. 1933- *St&PR 91*
Mawani, Al W. 1951- *St&PR 91*
Mawardi, Osman Kamel 1917- *WhoAm 90*
Mawardi, Youssef K 1913- *BiDrAPA 89*
Mawby, Colin 1936- *IntWWM 90*
Mawby, Russell George 1928- *WhoAm 90*
Mawdsley, William H. 1951- *St&PR 91*
Mawhinney, Eugene Alberto 1921- *WhoAm 90*
Mawhinney, Joseph Robert 1941- *BiDrAPA 89*
Mawhorter, Robert Lee 1939- *St&PR 91*
Mawia *WomWR*
Mawn, Paul Everett 1941- *WhoWor 91*
Max *ConAu 130, MajTwCW*
Max 1906-1989 *SmATA X*
Max, Carol Ann 1947- *WhoAmW 91*
Max, Claire Ellen 1946- *WhoAmW 91*
Max, Friedrich 1912- *WhoWor 91*
Max, Herbert B. 1931- *WhoAm 90*
Max, Jeffrey Edwin 1959- *BiDrAPA 89*
Max, Lope 1943- *WhoAmA 91*
Max, Peter 1937- *WhoAm 90, WhoAmA 91*
Max, Robert 1968- *IntWWM 90*
Max, Robert Jay 1957- *WhoSSW 91*
Max, Rodney Andrew 1947- *WhoEmL 91*
Max, Solomon Mannes 1935- *WhoE 91*
Maxa, Rudolph Joseph, Jr. 1949- *WhoAm 90*
Maxeiner, Clarence William 1914- *WhoAm 90*
Maxeiner, James Randolph 1952- *WhoEmL 91*
Maxey, Catherine Annette 1938- *WhoAmW 91, WhoSSW 91*
Maxey, James Robert 1923- *St&PR 91*
Maxey, Joy Ann 1958- *WhoSSW 91*
Maxey, Margaret Nan *WhoAm 90*
Maxey, Roberta Gay 1947- *WhoAmW 91*
Maxey, Thomas F. 1937- *St&PR 91*
Maxey, Thomas Fleming 1937- *WhoAm 90*
Maxfield, Allen Agnew, III 1948- *WhoE 91*
Maxfield, Doris Morris 1953- *ConAu 129*
Maxfield, James 1939- *ConTFT 8 [port]*
Maxfield, John Edward 1927- *WhoAm 90*
Maxfield, Kenneth Wayne 1924- *WhoAm 90*
Maxfield, Maria Ursula 1932- *WhoWrEP 89*
Maxfield, Michael G. 1949- *St&PR 91*
Maxfield, Michael Gerald 1954- *WhoAm 90*
Maxfield, Myles, Jr. 1947- *WhoE 91*
Maxfield, Roberta Masur 1952- *WhoAmA 91*
Maxfield, Steve *ODwPR 91*
Maxfield, Theda Mae 1929- *WhoSSW 91*
Maxfield, Wendell Dean 1919- *St&PR 91*
Maxfield, Wesley Burton, Jr. 1923- *BiDrAPA 89*
Maxheim, John Howard 1934- *St&PR 91, WhoAm 90, WhoSSW 91*
Maxim, Hiram Percy 1869-1936 *EncABHB 4 [port]*
Maxim, Hiram Stevens 1840-1916 *WorAlBi*
Maxim, James Andrew 1953- *WhoE 91*
Maxim, Peter Edward 1940- *BiDrAPA 89*
Maximilian 1832-1867 *WorAlBi*
Maximilian, Father 1894-1941 *BioIn 16*
Maximilian, Alexander Philipp 1782-1867 *WhNaAH*
Maximo, Antonieta Elizabeth 1942- *WhoHisp 91*
Maximova, Ekaterina 1939- *BioIn 16*
Maxman, Susan Abel 1938- *WhoAmW 91, WhoE 91*
Maxmen, Jerrold S *BiDrAPA 89*
Maxon, Don Carlton 1914- *WhoWor 91*
Maxon, Gene Harland 1932- *St&PR 91*
Maxon, John 1916-1977 *WhoAmA 91N*
Maxon, Rex 1892-1973 *EncACom*
Maxon, Robert John 1927- *St&PR 91*
Maxson, A.L. 1935- *St&PR 91*
Maxson, Albert Leroy 1935- *WhoAm 90*
Maxson, Linda Ellen 1943- *WhoAmW 91*
Maxson, Morris C. 1942- *St&PR 91*
Maxson, Noel Tope 1926- *WhoWrEP 89*
Maxson, Robert C. *WhoAm 90*
Maxvill, Dal 1939- *Ballpl 90, WhoAm 90*
Maxwell, Alice S. *WhoWrEP 89*
Maxwell, Allen R. 1939- *St&PR 91*
Maxwell, Anders John 1946- *WhoAm 90, WhoE 91*
Maxwell, Anna Caroline 1851-1929 *BioIn 16*
Maxwell, Arthur Graham 1921- *WhoAm 90*
Maxwell, Barbara Mary *BiDrAPA 89*
Maxwell, Barbara Sue 1950- *WhoAmW 91, WhoE 91*
Maxwell, Bruce David 1949- *WhoWrEP 89*
Maxwell, Bryce 1919- *WhoAm 90*
Maxwell, Carla Lena 1945- *WhoAm 90*
Maxwell, Charles Thoburn 1931- *St&PR 91*
Maxwell, Charlie 1927- *Ballpl 90*
Maxwell, Cheryl Nash 1945- *WhoSSW 91*
Maxwell, Chester Arthur 1930- *WhoAm 90*
Maxwell, Christine 1950- *WhoAm 90*
Maxwell, Colin 1956- *ConAu 132*
Maxwell, D. Malcolm 1934- *WhoAm 90*
Maxwell, Daphne *BioIn 16*
Maxwell, David E. 1944- *WhoAm 90*
Maxwell, David Ogden *BioIn 16*
Maxwell, David Ogden 1930- *St&PR 91, WhoAm 90*
Maxwell, David R. 1938- *St&PR 91*
Maxwell, Donald Robert 1929- *WhoAm 90*
Maxwell, Donald S. 1930- *St&PR 91*
Maxwell, Donald Stanley 1930- *WhoAm 90*
Maxwell, Douglas Irving, III 1958- *WhoSSW 91*
Maxwell, Earle W., Jr. 1939- *St&PR 91*
Maxwell, Edith 1923- *AuBYP 90*
Maxwell, Edward Nisbet, Jr. *BiDrAPA 89*
Maxwell, Florence Hinshaw 1914- *WhoAmW 91*
Maxwell, Florida Pier Scott- *BioIn 16*
Maxwell, Frank 1916- *WhoAm 90*
Maxwell, Gavin 1914-1969 *AuBYP 90, MajTwCW*
Maxwell, H. D., Jr. 1931- *WhoAm 90*
Maxwell, Hamish *BioIn 16*
Maxwell, Hamish 1926- *WhoAm 90, WhoE 91*
Maxwell, Ian Robert Charles 1956- *WhoAm 90, WhoWor 91*
Maxwell, J. Douglas, Jr. 1941- *WhoAm 90*
Maxwell, Jack E. 1926- *St&PR 91*
Maxwell, Jack Erwin 1926- *WhoAm 90*
Maxwell, James Clerk 1831-1879 *BioIn 16, WorAlBi*
Maxwell, James Leroy 1951- *St&PR 91*
Maxwell, Jane *WhoWrEP 89*
Maxwell, Jane Nobel *BiDrAPA 89*
Maxwell, Jay C 1922- *BiDrAPA 89*
Maxwell, Jerome E. 1944- *St&PR 91*
Maxwell, Jerome Eugene 1944- *WhoSSW 91*
Maxwell, Joanne Dutcher 1931- *WhoAmW 91*
Maxwell, John *WhoAmA 91*
Maxwell, John Crawford 1914- *WhoAm 90*
Maxwell, John Douglas, Jr. 1941- *St&PR 91*
Maxwell, John Raymond 1909- *WhoAm 90*
Maxwell, Jonathan Dixon 1864-1928 *EncABHB 4*
Maxwell, Joseph *EncO&P 3*
Maxwell, Judith 1943- *WhoAm 90, WhoAmW 91*
Maxwell, June Kay 1943- *WhoSSW 91*
Maxwell, Karen Oliver 1960- *WhoAmW 91*
Maxwell, Katherine Gant 1931- *WhoAmW 91*
Maxwell, Kenneth 1941- *ConAu 33NR*
Maxwell, Kevin F. H. 1959- *WhoAm 90, WhoE 91, WhoWor 91*
Maxwell, Lois 1927- *ConTFT 8*
Maxwell, Lorraine Edwyna 1946- *WhoAmW 91*
Maxwell, Marcia Gail 1948 *WhoAmW 91, WhoEmL 91*
Maxwell, Margaret Witmer 1918- *WhoAmW 91*
Maxwell, Mark William 1943- *BiDrAPA 89*
Maxwell, Marta Montidoro *WhoHisp 91*
Maxwell, Martha 1831-1881 *WomFie [port]*
Maxwell, Martha 1923- *BioAmW*
Maxwell, Mary Susanna 1948- *WhoEmL 91*
Maxwell, Melissa Faye 1939- *WhoAmW 91*
Maxwell, Milton A. *BioIn 16*
Maxwell, Nicholas 1937- *ConAu 132*
Maxwell, Olen Dale *BiDrAPA 89*
Maxwell, Otis Allen 1915- *WhoAm 90, WhoWrEP 89*
Maxwell, Owen Forest 1931- *St&PR 91*
Maxwell, Patricia Anne 1942- *WhoAmW 91*
Maxwell, Peter 1930- *WhoAmA 91*
Maxwell, Richard A. 1927- *St&PR 91*
Maxwell, Richard Anthony 1933- *WhoWor 91*
Maxwell, Richard Callender 1919- *WhoAm 90*
Maxwell, Robert *BioIn 16*
Maxwell, Robert 1923- *News 90 [port], WhoAm 90, WhoE 91, WhoWor 91, WorAlBi*
Maxwell, Robert Earl 1924- *WhoAm 90, WhoSSW 91*
Maxwell, Robert Edwin 1929- *WhoAmA 91*
Maxwell, Robert Lee 1933- *St&PR 91*
Maxwell, Robert Oliver 1940- *St&PR 91*
Maxwell, Robert Wallace, II 1943- *WhoAm 90*
Maxwell, Roberta 1942- *OxCCanT*
Maxwell, Robin Lee 1956- *WhoAmW 91*
Maxwell, Ruby Hoots 1924- *WhoAmW 91*
Maxwell, Sandra Rose 1945- *WhoAmW 91*
Maxwell, Sarz 1954- *BiDrAPA 89*
Maxwell, Sonia L. 1947- *WhoEmL 91*
Maxwell, Tiny 1884-1922 *Ballpl 90*
Maxwell, Vincent Oluoma 1926- *WhoWor 91*
Maxwell, Wilbur Richard 1920- *WhoAm 90*
Maxwell, William 1908- *AuBYP 90, WhoAm 90, WhoWrEP 89*
Maxwell, William C 1941- *WhoAmA 91*
Maxwell, William Jackson *WhoAmA 91*
Maxwell, William Joseph 1932- *WhoAm 90, WhoE 91*
Maxwell, William L. 1951- *St&PR 91*
Maxwell, William Laughlin 1934- *WhoAm 90*
Maxwell, William Stewart 1900-1989 *BioIn 16*
Maxwell, William Stirling 1922- *WhoAm 90*
Maxwell-Brogdon, Florence Morency 1929- *WhoAmW 91, WhoWor 91*
Maxwell-Timmins, Donald 1927- *IntWWM 90*
Maxworthy, Tony 1933- *WhoAm 90*
May, A. John 1928- *St&PR 91*
May, Addison Cushman 1933- *WhoAm 90*
May, Adolf Darlington 1927- *WhoAm 90*
May, Andrew P *BiDrAPA 89*
May, Anne Catherine 1940- *WhoAmW 91*
May, Anthony Shelby 1951- *WhoEmL 91*
May, Arthur W. 1937- *WhoAm 90*
May, Aviva Rabinowitz *WhoAmW 91*
May, Barbara L. 1937- *WhoWrEP 89*
May, Billy 1916- *OxCPMus*
May, Bruce R. 1942- *St&PR 91*
May, Carlos 1948- *Ballpl 90*
May, Catherine Stuart *BiDrAPA 89*
May, Charlene Pennell 1952- *WhoSSW 91*
May, Charles Kent 1939- *WhoAm 90, WhoWor 91*
May, Charles Paul 1920- *AuBYP 90*
May, Charles R 1958- *BiDrAPA 89*
May, Charles Robert 1941- *St&PR 91*
May, Clifford E. 1933- *St&PR 91*
May, Craig G. *BioIn 16*
May, Daniel F. 1930- *St&PR 91*
May, Daniel Striger 1942 *WhoAmA 91*
May, Dave 1943- *Ballpl 90*
May, Derald G 1925- *BiDrAPA 89*
May, Derwent James 1930- *WhoWor 91*
May, Edgar 1929- *WhoAm 90, WhoE 91*
May, Edna 1878-1948 *OxCPMus*
May, Edward Thomas 1962- *WhoE 91*
May, Elaine *BioIn 16*
May, Elaine 1932- *NotWoAT, WhoAm 90, WhoAmW 91, WorAlBi*
May, Elaine Tyler 1947- *ConAu 30NR*
May, Elizabeth Theresa 1935- *WhoAmW 91*
May, Elvira Margarite 1927- *WhoAmW 91*
May, Ernest Dewey 1942- *IntWWM 90, WhoE 91*
May, Ernest Max 1913 *WhoAm 90*
May, Ernest Richard 1928- *WhoWrEP 89*
May, Felton Edwin 1935- *WhoAm 90, WhoE 91*
May, Florence 1845-1923 *PenDiMP*
May, Florence Lewis *BioIn 16*
May, Francis Hart, Jr. 1917- *WhoAm 90*
May, Fritz G. 1925- *St&PR 91*
May, G. Lynwood 1927- *WhoE 91*
May, Genevieve M S 1909- *BiDrAPA 89*
May, George Walter 1926- *St&PR 91*
May, Georges 1920- *WhoAm 90*
May, Georgia *BioIn 16*
May, Gerald William 1941- *WhoAm 90*
May, Gita 1929- *WhoAm 90, WhoE 91*
May, Hans 1880-1959 *OxCPMus*
May, Harold Edward 1920- *WhoAm 90*
May, Harold V. 1924- *St&PR 91*
May, J. Joel 1935- *WhoE 91*
May, J. Peter 1939- *WhoAm 90*
May, Jack Garrett, II *BiDrAPA 89*
May, Jacqueline Marie 1961- *WhoAmW 91*
May, Jacques S. 1927- *WhoWor 91*
May, Jakie 1895-1970 *Ballpl 90*
May, James 1921- *WhoE 91*
May, James Collins 1946- *BioIn 16*
May, James L. 1947- *St&PR 91*
May, James M 1939- *BiDrAPA 89*
May, James S *BiDrAPA 89*
May, Jerry 1943- *Ballpl 90*
May, Jerry Russell 1942- *WhoAm 90*
May, John Lawrence 1922- *WhoAm 90*
May, John M. 1928- *St&PR 91*
May, John M. 1944- *WhoSSW 91*
May, John M. 1948- *WhoE 91*
May, John M. 1952- *WhoE 91*
May, John R. *BioIn 16*
May, Joseph Leserman 1929- *WhoSSW 91*
May, Joseph W. 1945- *St&PR 91*
May, Julian 1931- *AuBYP 90*
May, Julian 1932- *RGTwCSF*
May, Karl Friedrich 1842-1912 *WhNaAH*
May, Kenneth L. 1946- *St&PR 91*
May, Kenneth Nathaniel 1930- *St&PR 91, WhoAm 90, WhoSSW 91*
May, Kenneth R. *BioIn 16*
May, Lary L. 1944- *ConAu 130*
May, Laura Rose *WhoSSW 91*
May, Lee 1943- *Ballpl 90 [port]*
May, Lizzy Sara 1918- *EncCoWW*
May, Maben Floyd 1942- *St&PR 91*
May, Mary Diane 1930- *WhoAmW 91*
May, Mary Lil 1953- *St&PR 91*
May, Melanie Ann 1955- *WhoAmW 91*
May, Melvin Arthur 1940- *WhoAm 90*
May, Michael Andrew 1953- *BiDrAPA 89*
May, Michael Wayne 1949- *WhoWor 91*
May, Milt 1950- *Ballpl 90*
May, Peter William 1942- *WhoAm 90*
May, Phyllis Jean 1932- *WhoAmW 91, WhoWor 91*
May, Pinky 1911- *Ballpl 90*
May, Randolph Joseph 1946- *WhoWor 91*
May, Randy Lee 1957- *WhoSSW 91*
May, Richard Den 1952- *St&PR 91*
May, Richard Edward 1946- *WhoAm 90*
May, Richard H. 1933- *St&PR 91*
May, Richard L. 1956- *St&PR 91*
May, Richard Walter 1952- *WhoSSW 91*
May, Richard Warren 1944- *WhoE 91, WhoWor 91*
May, Robert *BioIn 16*
May, Robert A. 1911- *WhoAm 90*
May, Robert B *BiDrAPA 89*
May, Robert George 1943- *WhoAm 90*
May, Robert Lewis *BioIn 16*
May, Robert McCredie 1936- *WhoAm 90, WhoWor 91*
May, Robert Stephen 1929- *ConAu 30NR*
May, Robert V. 1943- *St&PR 91*
May, Robin *ConAu 30NR*
May, Roger *ODwPR 91*
May, Rollo *BioIn 16*
May, Rollo 1909- *WhoAm 90*
May, Ronald Alan 1928- *WhoAm 90, WhoSSW 91*
May, Rudy 1944- *Ballpl 90*
May, Rupert 1923- *BiDrAPA 89*
May, Stephen 1931- *WhoAm 90*
May, Stephen G *BiDrAPA 89*
May, Sterling Randolph 1946- *WhoAm 90*
May, Stuart L. 1920- *St&PR 91*
May, Thomas 1595-1650 *BioIn 16*
May, Thomas J. 1947- *St&PR 91*
May, Timothy James 1932- *WhoAm 90, WhoE 91, WhoWor 91*
May, Tom *BioIn 16*
May, Tony *BioIn 16*
May, Vern Tempest 1940- *WhoAm 90*
May, Walter Grant 1918- *WhoAm 90*
May, Walter Herbert, Jr. 1936- *St&PR 91*
May, Walter Ruch 1937- *WhoSSW 91*
May, William F. 1915- *St&PR 91*
May, William Frederick 1915- *WhoAm 90*
May, William P. 1946- *St&PR 91*
May, Wolfgang W 1932- *BiDrAPA 89*
Maya, William E. 1949- *St&PR 91*
Mayakovsky, Vladimir 1893-1930 *WorAlBi*
Mayakovsky, Vladimir 1894-1930 *BioIn 16*
Mayall, John 1933- *OxCPMus*
Mayall, John 1934- *EncPR&S 89*
Mayans, Steven Anthony 1956- *WhoEmL 91*
Mayaux, Daniel Henry 1931- *WhoWor 91*
Maybank, Joseph 1930- *WhoAm 90*
Maybank, Vanessa Turner- *BioIn 16*
Maybee, Joe Thomas 1954- *WhoEmL 91*
Mayberg, Donald MacMillan 1924- *BiDrAPA 89*
Mayberry, Alton Ray 1929- *BiDrAPA 89*
Mayberry, Andrew McNeely 1951- *St&PR 91*
Mayberry, Barbara Hurter 1942- *WhoE 91*
Mayberry, Janis Peterson 1957- *WhoAmW 91*
Mayberry, John 1949- *Ballpl 90*
Mayberry, John Francis 1951- *WhoWor 91*
Mayberry, Julius Eugene 1935- *WhoSSW 91*
Mayberry, Thomas Alfred, Jr. 1930- *WhoSSW 91*

Mayberry, William Eugene 1929- *WhoAm 90*
Maybin, John Edwin 1925- *St&PR 91*
Maybury, Edward A. 1939- *St&PR 91*
Maybury, James Richard 1944- *BiDrAPA 89*
Maybury, Paul Calvin 1924- *WhoSSW 91*
Maybury, Robert Harris 1923- *WhoSSW 91*
Maybury-Lewis, David Henry Peter 1929- *WhoAm 90*
Maycen, Dale Frank 1938- *St&PR 91*
Mayces, Adrian 1950- *St&PR 91*
Maycock, Ian David 1935- *St&PR 91, WhoAm 90*
Maycock, Joseph Farwell, Jr. 1930- *WhoAm 90*
Maycock, Lan L. 1939- *St&PR 91*
Mayda, Jaro 1918- *WhoAm 90*
Maydan, Dan *St&PR 91*
Maydew, Mary Jo 1949- *WhoEmL 91*
Maye, Lee 1934- *Ballpl 90*
Mayeda, Aimee Ruth 1954- *BiDrAPA 89*
Mayeda, Edward Yoshio 1931- *St&PR 91*
Mayefsky, Cheryl Joyce 1966- *WhoAmW 91*
Mayekar, Ruta U 1955- *BiDrAPA 89*
Mayekar, Ulhas Vasant 1951- *BiDrAPA 89*
Mayekawa, Seiro 1920- *WhoWor 91*
Mayell, Sharon Lee 1953- *WhoAmW 91*
Mayen, Paul 1918- *WhoAmA 91*
Mayer, Alain Laurent 1957- *WhoWor 91*
Mayer, Alfons 1927- *St&PR 91*
Mayer, Alfred 1921- *IntWWM 90*
Mayer, Ann Elizabeth 1945- *WhoE 91, WhoEmL 91*
Mayer, Anne Brestel 1935- *WhoAm 90*
Mayer, Arno Joseph 1926- *WhoAm 90*
Mayer, Beatrice Cummings 1921- *WhoAmW 91*
Mayer, Ben *BioIn 16*
Mayer, Bena Frank 1900- *WhoAmA 91*
Mayer, Bernard C. 1935- *St&PR 91*
Mayer, Billy 1953- *WhoAmA 91*
Mayer, Bruce Hillis 1945- *WhoSSW 91*
Mayer, C. H. *BioIn 16*
Mayer, Carey Charles *BiDrAPA 89*
Mayer, Carl Joseph 1959- *WhoE 91, WhoEmL 91*
Mayer, Catherine A *BiDrAPA 89*
Mayer, Charles James 1936- *WhoAm 90, WhoE 91*
Mayer, Charles Theodore 1924- *WhoE 91*
Mayer, Clara Woolie *BioIn 16*
Mayer, Clinton O. *BioIn 16*
Mayer, Cyrus Anderson 1924- *St&PR 91*
Mayer, Daniel 1909- *BiDFrPL*
Mayer, David Jonathan 1942- *WhoSSW 91*
Mayer, David L 1929- *BiDrAPA 89*
Mayer, David Louis 1927- *St&PR 91*
Mayer, Deborah Amy 1947- *WhoAmW 91*
Mayer, Dennis Thomas 1901- *WhoAm 90*
Mayer, Diana K. *St&PR 91*
Mayer, Dieter H. 1936- *St&PR 91*
Mayer, Donald L. 1947- *St&PR 91*
Mayer, Doris Y 1913- *BiDrAPA 89*
Mayer, Ed 1931- *BioIn 16*
Mayer, Edward Albert 1942- *WhoAmA 91*
Mayer, Elijah *PenDiDA 89*
Mayer, Erich Anton 1930- *WhoWor 91*
Mayer, Erskine 1891-1957 *Ballpl 90*
Mayer, Eugene Stephen 1938- *WhoAm 90*
Mayer, Foster Lee, Jr. 1942- *WhoAm 90*
Mayer, Francis Blackwell 1827-1899 *WhNaAH*
Mayer, Franz Ferdinand *PenDiDA 89*
Mayer, Fred Christian 1911- *WhoAm 90*
Mayer, Frederic David 1931- *IntWWM 90*
Mayer, Frederick Miller 1898- *WhoAm 90, WhoSSW 91*
Mayer, Frederick Rickard 1928- *St&PR 91*
Mayer, Gail Lynne 1952- *WhoAmW 91*
Mayer, George Louis 1929- *IntWWM 90*
Mayer, Gerda 1927- *FemiCLE*
Mayer, Gertrude Townshend 1839-1932 *FemiCLE*
Mayer, Grace M *WhoAmA 91*
Mayer, Grace Milly 1907- *WhoE 91*
Mayer, Gregg Lindstrom 1958- *St&PR 91*
Mayer, Haldane Robert 1941- *WhoAm 90*
Mayer, Harold Frederick 1929- *St&PR 91*
Mayer, Henry L. 1918- *St&PR 91*
Mayer, Henry Michael 1922- *WhoAm 90*
Mayer, Ira 1952- *WhoWrEP 89*
Mayer, Irwin 1934- *St&PR 91*
Mayer, J. Gerald 1908- *WhoAm 90*
Mayer, Jacob 1923- *BiDrAPA 89*
Mayer, James *BioIn 16*
Mayer, James Joseph 1938- *St&PR 91, WhoAm 90*
Mayer, James Lamoine 1951- *WhoEmL 91*
Mayer, James Walter 1930- *WhoAm 90*
Mayer, Jan Alan *BiDrAPA 89*
Mayer, Jane *BioIn 16*
Mayer, Jane 1903- *AuBYP 90*
Mayer, Jane S. 1929- *WhoWrEP 89*
Mayer, Jean 1920- *ConAu 129, WhoAm 90, WhoE 91, WhoWor 91*
Mayer, Jean-Ghislain-Joseph *PenDiDA 89*
Mayer, Jeffrey *BioIn 16*
Mayer, John 1930- *IntWWM 90*
Mayer, John 1948- *WhoSSW 91*
Mayer, John Anton, Jr. 1940- *WhoAm 90*
Mayer, Jonas 1929- *St&PR 91*
Mayer, Joseph C 1932- *BiDrAPA 89*
Mayer, Jules F. *BioIn 16*
Mayer, Julius Robert, Von 1814-1878 *WorAlBi*
Mayer, Karl Ulrich 1945- *WhoWor 91*
Mayer, Kathe 1940- *WhoAmW 91*
Mayer, Kathleen K. 1954- *St&PR 91*
Mayer, Lambert 1926- *ODwPR 91*
Mayer, Lothar L. 1939- *St&PR 91*
Mayer, Louis B. 1885-1957 *BioIn 16, WorAlBi*
Mayer, Lucille Mendenhall 1926- *WhoAmW 91*
Mayer, Marcia Kramer 1946- *St&PR 91*
Mayer, Margery Weil 1952- *WhoAm 90*
Mayer, Maria Goeppert- 1906-1972 *BioIn 16, DcScB S2*
Mayer, Marianna 1945- *AuBYP 90*
Mayer, Marilyn Gooder *WhoAmW 91*
Mayer, Martin Paul *BiDrAPA 89*
Mayer, Martin Prager 1928- *WhoAm 90, WhoWrEP 89*
Mayer, Mercer 1943- *AuBYP 90, BioIn 16*
Mayer, Michael Joseph 1944- *WhoSSW 91*
Mayer, Morris Lehman 1925- *WhoAm 90*
Mayer, Myra Lou 1944- *St&PR 91, WhoSSW 91*
Mayer, Nancy Jo Harmon 1950- *WhoAmW 91*
Mayer, Neil 1934- *St&PR 91*
Mayer, Oscar F. 1859-1955 *WorAlBi*
Mayer, Patricia Jayne 1950- *WhoAmW 91, WhoEmL 91, WhoWor 91*
Mayer, Paul Augustin 1911- *WhoWor 91*
Mayer, Paul D 1933- *BiDrAPA 89*
Mayer, Paul Joseph 1932- *St&PR 91*
Mayer, Paul L. 1931- *St&PR 91*
Mayer, Peter Arno 1929- *St&PR 91*
Mayer, Ralph 1895-1979 *WhoAmA 91N*
Mayer, Ramona Ann 1929- *WhoAmW 91*
Mayer, Raymond Richard 1924- *WhoAm 90*
Mayer, Rene Joel Simon 1895-1972 *BiDFrPL*
Mayer, Richard 1950- *BiDrAPA 89*
Mayer, Richard Allen 1927- *WhoE 91*
Mayer, Richard Dean 1930- *WhoAm 90*
Mayer, Richard Edwin 1947- *WhoAm 90*
Mayer, Richard Henry 1930- *WhoAm 90*
Mayer, Richard L. 1913- *St&PR 91*
Mayer, Richard P. 1940- *St&PR 91*
Mayer, Richard Philip 1940- *WhoAm 90, WhoE 91*
Mayer, Robert 1879-1985 *DcNaB 1981*
Mayer, Robert A. 1942- *St&PR 91*
Mayer, Robert Anthony 1933- *WhoAm 90, WhoAmA 91, WhoE 91*
Mayer, Robert E., Jr. 1947- *St&PR 91*
Mayer, Robert Glenn 1938- *BiDrAPA 89*
Mayer, Robert M. 1922- *St&PR 91*
Mayer, Robert Michael *BiDrAPA 89*
Mayer, Robert Wallace 1909- *WhoAm 90*
Mayer, Roger Laurance 1926- *St&PR 91*
Mayer, Rosemary 1943- *WhoAmA 91, WhoE 91*
Mayer, Ruth Ann 1951- *WhoAmW 91, WhoSSW 91*
Mayer, Ruth L *BiDrAPA 89*
Mayer, Saly 1882-1950 *BioIn 16*
Mayer, Sebastian *PenDiMP*
Mayer, Sheldon 1917- *EncACom*
Mayer, Sondra 1933- *WhoAmA 91*
Mayer, Stanley 1945- *St&PR 91*
Mayer, Stephen H. *BioIn 16, NewYTBS 90*
Mayer, Susan M. *WhoWrEP 89*
Mayer, Susan Martin 1931- *WhoAmA 91*
Mayer, Sydney L. 1937- *WhoE 91*
Mayer, Theodore Jack 1933- *WhoE 91*
Mayer, Thomas 1915- *IntWWM 90*
Mayer, Timothy S. *BioIn 16*
Mayer, Valerie *BioIn 16*
Mayer, Victor James 1933- *WhoAm 90*
Mayer, Virginia Anne 1929- *WhoAmW 91*
Mayer, William Dixon 1928- *WhoAm 90*
Mayer, William E. 1940- *St&PR 91*
Mayer, William Emilio 1940- *WhoAm 90, WhoE 91*
Mayer, William Ray 1935- *WhoAm 90*
Mayer, William V. *BioIn 16*
Mayer, Wolfgang Ulrich 1937- *WhoE 91*
Mayer-Koenig, Wolfgang 1946- *WhoWor 91*
Mayer-Kuckuk, Theo 1927- *WhoWor 91*
Mayer-Reinach, Ursula 1920- *IntWWM 90*
Mayerhofer, James T. 1944- *St&PR 91*
Mayerhofer, James Thomas 1944- *WhoAm 90*
Mayerhoff, David Isak 1958- *BiDrAPA 89, WhoE 91*
Mayeri, Beverly *WhoAmA 91*
Mayerl, Billy 1902-1959 *OxCPMus*
Mayers, Al 1960- *St&PR 91*
Mayers, Alan Elsas 1932- *WhoE 91*
Mayers, Bernard Gilbert 1943- *St&PR 91*
Mayers, Daniel E. *BioIn 16*
Mayers, Daniel E. 1933?-1988 *ConAu 129*
Mayers, Daniel Kriegsman 1934- *WhoAm 90*
Mayers, David 1936- *WhoAm 90*
Mayers, David 1951- *ConAu 131*
Mayers, David Wm. 1916- *St&PR 91*
Mayers, Eugene David 1915- *WhoAm 90*
Mayers, Howard Alex 1946- *St&PR 91*
Mayers, Jean 1920- *WhoAm 90*
Mayers, Lawrence Michael 1935- *St&PR 91*
Mayers, Leonard Warren 1950- *St&PR 91*
Mayers, Stanley Penrose, Jr. 1926- *WhoAm 90, WhoE 91*
Mayersohn, Robert Alan 1958- *St&PR 91*
Mayerson, Donald J 1938- *BiDrAPA 89*
Mayerson, Evelyn Wilde 1934- *BioIn 16*
Mayerson, Peter 1933- *BiDrAPA 89*
Mayerson, Philip 1918- *WhoAm 90, WhoWrEP 89*
Mayes, Alexander McDaniel 1946- *WhoE 91*
Mayes, Carl Douglas 1921- *WhoSSW 91*
Mayes, David Geoffrey 1946- *WhoWor 91*
Mayes, Elaine 1938- *WhoAmA 91, WhoE 91*
Mayes, Frank G. 1930- *St&PR 91*
Mayes, Helen 1918- *WhoSSW 91*
Mayes, Herbert Raymond 1900- *WhoWrEP 89*
Mayes, Kathleen 1931- *WhoWrEP 89*
Mayes, Kathryn 1949- *St&PR 91*
Mayes, Kathryn J. 1949- *St&PR 91*
Mayes, Lorene Anderson 1939- *WhoAmW 91*
Mayes, Richard F. 1941- *ODwPR 91, St&PR 91*
Mayes, Roy, Jr. 1934- *St&PR 91*
Mayes, Stella I. 1936- *St&PR 91*
Mayes, Steven Lee 1939- *WhoAmA 91*
Mayes, Wayne K. 1935- *St&PR 91*
Mayes, Wendell Wise, Jr. 1924- *WhoAm 90, WhoSSW 91*
Mayesh, Jay Philip 1947- *WhoEmL 91*
Mayeux, Herman Joseph 1949- *WhoSSW 91*
Mayfair, Bertha *WhoWrEP 89*
Mayfield, Curtis 1942- *BioIn 16, DrBIPA 90, EncPR&S 89, OxCPMus*
Mayfield, David Merkley 1942- *WhoAm 90*
Mayfield, Demmie G 1932- *BiDrAPA 89*
Mayfield, Edgar 1925- *WhoAm 90*
Mayfield, J. W. 1937- *WhoSSW 91*
Mayfield, James Theron 1931- *St&PR 91*
Mayfield, John Emory 1937- *WhoSSW 91*
Mayfield, Judith Ann 1946- *WhoAmW 91*
Mayfield, Julian 1928-1984 *DrBIPA 90*
Mayfield, Lori Jayne 1955- *WhoAmW 91*
Mayfield, Peggy Jordan 1934- *WhoAmW 91*
Mayfield, Percy 1920-1984 *OxCPMus*
Mayfield, Richard Heverin 1921- *WhoAm 90*
Mayfield, Rita *WhoWrEP 89*
Mayfield, Robert Charles 1928- *WhoAm 90*
Mayfield, Robert Edward 1946- *St&PR 91*
Mayfield, Sandra Jeanne 1942- *WhoAmW 91*
Mayfield, Thomas Brient, III 1919 *WhoAm 90*
Mayfield, William Cary 1958- *WhoSSW 91*
Mayfield, William Stephen 1919- *WhoAm 90*
Mayhall, Dorothy *WhoAmA 91*
Mayhall, Jane 1921- *LiHiK*
Mayhall, Jane Francis 1922- *WhoWrEP 89*
Mayhall, Michael Wayne 1953- *WhoSSW 91*
Mayhan, Thomas Michael 1958- *WhoEmL 91*
Mayher, Arnold J. 1919- *St&PR 91*
Mayher, Matt R. 1923- *St&PR 91*
Mayher, William Edgar, III 1938- *WhoSSW 91*
Mayhew, Alexander E. *AmLegL*
Mayhew, David L. 1951- *St&PR 91*
Mayhew, David Raymond 1937- *WhoAm 90*
Mayhew, Edgar De Noailles 1913- *WhoAmA 91, WhoE 91*
Mayhew, Elizabeth Whitehouse 1951- *WhoAmW 91, WhoE 91*
Mayhew, Elza *WhoAmA 91*
Mayhew, Gary George 1936- *St&PR 91*
Mayhew, Harry Eugene 1933- *WhoAm 90*
Mayhew, Henry 1812-1887 *BioIn 16*
Mayhew, John *PenDiDA 89*
Mayhew, Jonathan 1720-1766 *EncCRAm*
Mayhew, Kenneth E., Jr. 1934- *St&PR 91*
Mayhew, Kenneth Edwin, Jr. 1934- *WhoAm 90, WhoSSW 91*
Mayhew, Lawrence Lee 1933- *St&PR 91, WhoAm 90*
Mayhew, Lewis Baltzell 1916- *WhoAm 90*
Mayhew, Linda S. 1939- *St&PR 91*
Mayhew, Marce Paul 1925- *WhoAm 90*
Mayhew, Paul D. 1958- *WhoSSW 91*
Mayhew, Richard 1934- *WhoAmA 91*
Mayhew, Thomas 1621?-1657 *EncCRAm*
Mayhew, Thomas, Jr. 1621-1657 *WhNaAH*
Mayhew, William E. 1942- *St&PR 91*
Mayhew-Perez, Teresa Ann 1960- *WhoAmW 91*
Mayhue, W. Paul 1947- *WhoEmL 91*
Mayka, Daniel Stanley, Jr. 1948- *WhoE 91*
Mayka, Stephen Paul 1946- *WhoEmL 91*
Mayland, Kenneth T. 1951- *St&PR 91*
Mayland, Kenneth Theodore 1951- *WhoEmL 91*
Mayle, Peter *BioIn 16*
Mayle, Robert Edward 1938- *WhoAm 90*
Mayleas, Ruth 1925- *BioIn 16*
Mayleas, Ruth Rothschild 1925- *NotWoAT*
Maylor, Alan Ford 1935- *St&PR 91*
Mayman, Martin 1924- *WhoAm 90, WhoWrEP 89*
Maymi, Debra Ann 1957- *WhoSSW 91*
Maymon, Gilbert William 1927- *WhoE 91*
Maynadier, Alain De 1929- *St&PR 91*
Maynard, Anna Morse 1920- *WhoE 91*
Maynard, Charles Douglas 1934- *WhoAm 90*
Maynard, Charles N. 1936- *St&PR 91*
Maynard, Chris *BioIn 16*
Maynard, Clement T. *WhoWor 91*
Maynard, Curtis G. 1922- *St&PR 91*
Maynard, David W. 1943- *St&PR 91*
Maynard, Donald Nelson 1932- *WhoAm 90*
Maynard, George Fleming, III 1947- *WhoSSW 91*
Maynard, Harry Edgar 1918- *WhoE 91*
Maynard, Henrietta Sturdevant 1841-1892 *EncO&P 3*
Maynard, Horace 1814-1882 *BiDrUSE 89*
Maynard, Horace S. 1920- *St&PR 91*
Maynard, James G. 1926- *St&PR 91*
Maynard, James Joseph 1956- *BiDrAPA 89*
Maynard, Joan 1932- *WhoAmW 91*
Maynard, John Irwin 1954- *St&PR 91*
Maynard, John Ralph 1942- *WhoWor 91*
Maynard, John Rogers 1941- *WhoAm 90, WhoE 91*
Maynard, John Steven 1945- *St&PR 91*
Maynard, Joyce 1953- *AuBYP 90, ConAu 129*
Maynard, Kenneth Alan 1948- *St&PR 91*
Maynard, Leonard Amby 1887-1972 *BioIn 16*
Maynard, Luther Devere 1937- *WhoWor 91*
Maynard, Michael Anthony 1953- *WhoE 91*
Maynard, Nancy Gray 1941- *WhoAmW 91*
Maynard, Peter David 1950- *WhoE 91*
Maynard, Rex Alderman 1947- *St&PR 91*
Maynard, Robert *BioIn 16*
Maynard, Robert Clyve 1937- *WhoWrEP 89*
Maynard, Robert Edward, Jr. 1941- *St&PR 91*
Maynard, Robert M. *BioIn 16*
Maynard, Ronald C. 1944- *St&PR 91*
Maynard, Virginia Madden 1924- *WhoAmW 91*
Maynard, W. Neil 1942- *WhoSSW 91*
Maynard, William 1921- *WhoAmA 91, WhoE 91*
Mayne, Alan James 1927- *EncO&P 3, EncPaPR 91*
Mayne, Anne 1940- *BioIn 16*
Mayne, Clarice 1886-1966 *OxCPMus*
Mayne, Lucille Stringer 1924- *WhoAm 90*
Mayne, Randall Andrew 1947- *WhoSSW 91*
Mayne, Robert *ODwPR 91*
Mayne, Seymour 1944- *BioIn 16*
Mayne, W. Harry 1913- *BioIn 16*
Mayne, William 1928- *AuBYP 90, SmATA 11AS [port], WhoAm 90*
Maynes, Charles William 1938- *WhoAm 90*
Maynes, Charles William, Jr. 1938- *WhoE 91*
Maynes, E Scott 1922- *ConAu 30NR*
Maynes, E. Scott 1922- *WhoAm 90*
Maynes, Leo P. 1937- *St&PR 91*
Maynor, Dorothy 1909- *DcAfAmP*
Maynor, Dorothy 1910- *BioIn 16, DrBIPA 90*
Maynor, Kevin Elliott 1954- *IntWWM 90*
Mayo, Aryan R. 1926- *St&PR 91, WhoAm 90*

Mayo, Byron W. 1922- WhoAm 90
Mayo, Cathy Metcalf 1955- WhoAmW 91
Mayo, Charles H. 1865-1939 WorAlBi
Mayo, Charles Horace 1865-1939 BioIn 16
Mayo, Eddie 1910- Ballpl 90
Mayo, Eli 1933- WhoWor 91
Mayo, Frank 1901- St&PR 91
Mayo, Frank Joseph 1948- WhoE 91
Mayo, Gerald Edgar 1932- St&PR 91, WhoAm 90
Mayo, Isabella 1843-1914 FemiCLE
Mayo, J Richard BiDrAPA 89
Mayo, James TwCCr&M 91
Mayo, James Otis 1920- St&PR 91
Mayo, Janice 1952- WhoAmW 91
Mayo, Janice Lynne 1952- St&PR 91
Mayo, Jill Marie 1954- WhoSSW 91
Mayo, Jim MajTwCW
Mayo, Jim 1908-1988 BioIn 16
Mayo, John Sullivan 1930- St&PR 91, WhoAm 90
Mayo, Kim Pamela 1960- WhoSSW 91
Mayo, Leonard W 1899- BiDrAPA 89
Mayo, Louis Allen 1928- WhoE 91, WhoWor 91
Mayo, Margaret Ellen 1944- WhoAmA 91
Mayo, Marilyn BioIn 16
Mayo, Marti 1945- WhoAmA 91
Mayo, Michael George 1949- WhoE 91
Mayo, Pamela Elizabeth 1959- WhoAmA 91, WhoAmW 91
Mayo, Payton Colquitt 1926- St&PR 91
Mayo, Richard C. 1947- St&PR 91
Mayo, Richard Southwell Bourke, Earl of 1822-1872 BioIn 16
Mayo, Robert Aaron BioIn 16
Mayo, Robert Bowers 1933- WhoAmA 91
Mayo, Robert Porter 1916- WhoAm 90
Mayo, Stephen I. 1952- St&PR 91
Mayo, Virginia 1920- WorAlBi
Mayo, W Bruce BiDrAPA 89
Mayo, Walker Porter 1922- WhoSSW 91
Mayo, Wayne 1939- St&PR 91
Mayo, Whitman 1930- DrBIPA 90
Mayo, William J. 1861-1939 WorAlBi
Mayo, William James 1861-1939 BioIn 16
Mayo, William L. St&PR 91
Mayock, Robert Lee 1917- WhoAm 90, WhoWor 91
Mayol, Hector M., Jr. 1950- St&PR 91
Mayol, Jacques BioIn 16
Mayor, A Hyatt 1901-1980 WhoAmA 91N
Mayor, F. M. 1872-1932 BioIn 16, FemiCLE
Mayor, Flora Macdonald 1872-1932 BioIn 16
Mayor, Harriet 1933- WhoAmW 91, WhoE 91
Mayor, Heather Donald 1930- WhoSSW 91
Mayor, John Roberts 1906- WhoAm 90
Mayor, Richard Blair 1934- WhoAm 90
Mayor Zaragoza, Federico 1934- WhoWor 91
Mayoral, Guillermo Herrero 1924- WhoWor 91
Mayoral, Jose Angel BiDrAPA 89
Mayoral, Maria Elena BiDrAPA 89
Mayoral, Marina 1942- EncCoWW
Mayoras, Donald Eugene 1939- WhoAm 90, WhoE 91
Mayorga, Oscar Danilo 1949- WhoHisp 91
Mayorga, Rene N. 1956- WhoHisp 91
Mayorkas, Charles R. 1930- St&PR 91
Mayoski, Edward Joseph 1910- Ballpl 90
Mayotte, Tim BioIn 16
Mayou, Bryan Jonathan 1944- WhoWor 91
Maypole, John Floyd 1939- St&PR 91, WhoAm 90
Mayr, Ernst 1904- WhoAm 90
Mayr, Otto 1930- WhoWor 91
Mayr, Richard 1877-1935 PenDiMP
Mayr, Rupert Erich 1926- IntWWM 90
Mayrocker, Friederike 1924- EncCoWW
Mayron, Melanie BioIn 16
Mayron, Melanie 1952- WhoAmW 91
Mayrose, William C. 1942- St&PR 91
Mayrs, David Blair 1935- WhoAmA 91
Mays, Bowdre P. 1927- St&PR 91
Mays, Buddy 1943- ConAu 30NR
Mays, Carl 1891-1971 Ballpl 90 [port]
Mays, Charles A. 1939- St&PR 91
Mays, Chris BioIn 16
Mays, Clara Florence 1944- WhoAmW 91
Mays, Dannie Hill 1852-1930 AmLegL
Mays, David Vernon 1950- BiDrAPA 89
Mays, Gerald Anthony 1935- St&PR 91
Mays, Gerald Avery 1939- WhoAm 90
Mays, Jan F. 1938- St&PR 91
Mays, Janice Ann 1951- WhoAmW 91
Mays, John Anthony 1928- St&PR 91
Mays, John Hearn 1947- St&PR 91
Mays, Kimberly BioIn 16
Mays, L. Lowry 1935- WhoAm 90
Mays, Landis Rudolph 1932- WhoSSW 91
Mays, Lewis Victor, Jr. 1927- WhoE 91
Mays, Lucinda 1924- BioIn 16
Mays, Lyle NewAgMG
Mays, Norman Gerald, Jr. 1954- St&PR 91
Mays, Paul Kirtland 1887-1961 WhoAmA 91N
Mays, Penny Sandra 1940- WhoAmW 91
Mays, Robert W. BioIn 16
Mays, Sally Ann 1930- IntWWM 90
Mays, Victor 1927- WhoAmA 91
Mays, William Gay, II 1947- WhoEmL 91
Mays, Willie 1931- Ballpl 90, BioIn 16, WorAlBi
Mays, Willie Howard, Jr. 1931- WhoAm 90
Maysent, Harold Wayne 1923- WhoAm 90
Maysilles, Elizabeth WhoAmW 91
Maysles, Albert BioIn 16
Maysles, David 1932-1987 BioIn 16
Mayson, Betty Anne Peeples 1943- WhoAmW 91
Mayson, Sterrett 1948- BiDrAPA 89
Mayson, William Penland, Jr. 1930- WhoSSW 91
Maystadt, Philippe 1948- WhoWor 91
Maystead, Suzanne Rae 1955- WhoAmW 91
Maytag, Elmer H. 1883-1940 WorAlBi
Maytag, Frederick L. 1857-1937 WorAlBi
Maytag, Lewis B. NewYTBS 90 [port]
Maytham, Thomas Northrup 1931- WhoAmA 91
Mayton, John Pershing 1961- WhoSSW 91
Mayugba, Carmen P BiDrAPA 89
Mayuzumi, Toshiro 1929- PenDiMPA
Mayweather, Billie Jean Fields 1938- WhoAmW 91
Maywhort, William Walter 1946- WhoEmL 91
Maza, Penelope Lee 1946- WhoE 91
Maza Miquel, Ignacio Agustin 1956- WhoE 91
Mazabob, Janine Marie 1954- WhoE 91
Mazakutamane 1806?-1885 WhNaAH
Mazakutemani, Paul 1806?-1885 WhNaAH
Mazan, Walter Lawrence 1921- WhoAm 90
Mazankowski, Donald Frank 1935- WhoAm 90, WhoE 91, WhoWor 91
Mazaraki-Baltsavia, Phedon 1932- WhoWor 91
Mazarakis, Michael Gerassimos 1943- WhoWor 91
Mazarin, Jules 1602-1661 WorAlBi
Mazcuri, Riaz BiDrAPA 89
Mazda, Fred Rustom 1928- WhoWor 91
Maze Featuring Frankie Beverly EncPR&S 89
Maze, Clarence, Jr. 1931- WhoAm 90
Maze, Judah M 1934- BiDrAPA 89
Mazeiko, Peter John 1952- WhoE 91
Mazek, Warren Felix 1938- WhoAm 90
Mazel, Joseph Lucas 1939- WhoE 91, WhoWor 91
Mazenko, Gene Francis 1945- WhoAm 90
Mazeo, Jean 1934- WhoWor 91
Mazer, Harry 1925- Au&Arts 5 [port], BioIn 16, ConAu 32NR, SmATA 11AS [port]
Mazer, Harvey Etamar 1938- BiDrAPA 89
Mazer, Milton 1911- BiDrAPA 89, WhoE 91
Mazer, Norma Fox 1931- Au&Arts 5 [port], BioIn 16, ChILR 23 [port], ConAu 32NR, WhoAm 90
Mazer, Susan NewAgMG
Mazero, T. Jean Louise 1924- WhoE 91
Mazeroski, Bill 1936- Ballpl 90 [port], BioIn 16
Mazeski, Edward James, Jr. 1929- St&PR 91, WhoAm 90
Mazewski, Aloysius BioIn 16
Mazgaj, James Perry 1958- BiDrAPA 89
Mazlade, Michel 1949- BiDrAPA 89
Maziar, Harry 1934- St&PR 91
Maziar, Howard M 1946- BiDrAPA 89
Maziarz, Edward Anthony 1915- WhoAm 90
Mazie, Marvin E. 1930- St&PR 91
Mazie, Marvin Edward 1930- WhoAm 90
Mazik, Ronald R. 1943- St&PR 91
Mazin, Joseph 1946- St&PR 91
Mazique, Edward C. BioIn 16
Mazkalnins, Elga M 1923- BiDrAPA 89
Mazkalnins, John Hugo 1924- BiDrAPA 89
Mazlen, Roger Geoffrey 1937- WhoAm 90, WhoE 91, WhoWor 91
Mazlish, Bruce 1923- WhoAm 90, WhoWrEP 89
Mazloomdoost, Camelia S BiDrAPA 89
Mazmanian, Brian John BiDrAPA 89
Mazo, Earl 1919- WhoAm 90
Mazo, Mark Elliott 1950- WhoE 91, WhoEmL 91, WhoWor 91
Mazo, Robert Marc 1930- WhoAm 90
Mazol, Thomas George 1947- WhoE 91
Mazomani WhNaAH
Mazonkey, Robert Michael 1935- WhoE 91
Mazonson, Anne Clare BiDrAPA 89
Mazor, Miriam D 1940- BiDrAPA 89
Mazouni, Mohammed 1937- WhoWor 91
Mazowiecki, Tadeusz BioIn 16
Mazowiecki, Tadeusz 1927- CurBio 90 [port], WhoWor 91
Mazrui, Ali Al'Amin 1933- WhoAm 90, WhoWor 91
Mazumdar, Dipak 1935- WhoWor 91
Mazumdar, Shudha BioIn 16
Mazumder, Amitabha 1952- WhoEmL 91
Mazur, Allan Carl 1939- WhoAm 90
Mazur, Arnold S. 1942- St&PR 91
Mazur, Bernice C. St&PR 91
Mazur, David John 1947- BiDrAPA 89
Mazur, Edward John, Jr. 1948- WhoE 91
Mazur, Gail Beckwith 1937- WhoWrEP 89
Mazur, Jay J. WhoE 91
Mazur, Joseph A. 1938- St&PR 91
Mazur, Margie Ella Handley Meredith 1941- WhoWor 91
Mazur, Marilyn 1955- IntWWM 90
Mazur, Mark James 1956- WhoE 91
Mazur, Mark Steven 1955- WhoE 91
Mazur, Michael 1935- WhoAm 90, WhoAmA 91
Mazur, Peter 1928- WhoWor 91
Mazur, Rhoda Himmel 1929- WhoAm 90
Mazur, Stella Mary 1923- WhoAmW 91
Mazur, Wladyslaw P 1921- BiDrAPA 89
Mazur-Baker, Deborah Joan 1958- WhoEmL 91
Mazura, Adrianne C. 1951- WhoAmW 91
Mazura, Franz 1924- IntWWM 90
Mazurkevich, Yuri Nicholas 1941- IntWWM 90
Mazurki, Mike 1909- WorAlBi
Mazurkiewicz, Albert Joseph 1926- WhoE 91
Mazurkiewicz, Gregory A. 1950- ODwPR 91
Mazurkiewicz, Gregory Allen 1950- WhoEmL 91
Mazurok PenDiMP
Mazurov, Kirill T. 1914-1989 BioIn 16
Mazursky, Paul BioIn 16
Mazursky, Paul 1930- WhoAm 90, WorAlBi
Mazutis, Juris 1940- WhoWrEP 89
Mazyck, Reaven Elaine 1954- WhoE 91
Mazza, Arlene Joan 1944- WhoAmW 91
Mazza, Bob ODwPR 91
Mazza, Christine Elaine 1952- WhoAmW 91
Mazza, Cris 1956- ConAu 132
Mazza, Dominic Louis 1952- BiDrAPA 89
Mazza, John Gamble 1945- St&PR 91
Mazza, Terilyn McGovern 1952- WhoEmL 91
Mazzaferri, Ernest Louis 1936- WhoAm 90
Mazzaferri, Katherine Aquino 1947- WhoAm 90
Mazzaglia, Joseph Ronald BiDrAPA 89
Mazzanti, Vincent F 1917- BiDrAPA 89
Mazzarella, Mario Domenic 1941- WhoSSW 91
Mazzariol, Giuseppe 1922-1989 BioIn 16
Mazzaro, Jerome Louis 1934- WhoWrEP 89
Mazze, Edward Mark 1941- WhoAm 90
Mazze, Irving WhoAmA 91
Mazze, Roger Steven 1943- WhoAm 90
Mazzei, Augustine Anthony, Jr. 1936- St&PR 91, WhoAm 90
Mazzei, Doreen Cheryl 1956- WhoAmW 91
Mazzei, Philip 1730-1816 BioIn 16
Mazzeo, Joseph Anthony 1923- WhoAm 90
Mazzeo-Merkle, Linda L. 1947- WhoAmW 91, WhoE 91, WhoWor 91
Mazzia, Valentino Don Bosco 1922- WhoAm 90, WhoWor 91
Mazzie, Sandra Anne 1951- WhoE 91
Mazzilli, Lee 1955- Ballpl 90
Mazzilli, Paul John 1948- WhoAm 90
Mazzini, Giuseppe 1805-1872 WorAlBi
Mazzo, Kay 1946- WhoAm 90
Mazzocca, Gus 1940- WhoAmA 91
Mazzocco, Reynold Anthony 1957- St&PR 91
Mazzochette, John A BiDrAPA 89
Mazzola, Anthony Thomas 1923- WhoAm 90
Mazzola, Christian Larsen 1939- St&PR 91
Mazzola, John William 1928- WhoAm 90
Mazzola, Linda L. 1911-1989 BioIn 16
Mazzola, Mary Papakyrikos 1959- WhoAmW 91
Mazzola, Patrizio 1956- IntWWM 90
Mazzoli, Antoinette M. 1937- St&PR 91
Mazzoli, Romano Louis 1932- WhoAm 90, WhoSSW 91
Mazzoline, Pamela 1949- BiDrAPA 89
Mazzone, A. David 1928- WhoAm 90
Mazzone, Domenico 1927- WhoAmA 91
Mazzoni, Guido 1450?-1518 IntDcAA 90
Mazzoni, Michael James 1946- WhoAm 90
Mazzorana, Edward C. 1932- St&PR 91
Mazzotta, Dorothy 1933- WhoAmW 91
Mazzotta, Dorothy 1935- St&PR 91
Mazzotta, Robert J. 1954- St&PR 91
Mazzotta, Roberto BioIn 16
Mazzotta, Roberto 1940- WhoWor 91
Mazzuca, Robin Lynn 1958- WhoAmW 91
Mazzucotelli, Alessandro 1865-1938 PenDiDA 89
Mbabi-Katana, Solomon 1922- IntWWM 90
Mbah, Brian Chibuike 1956- WhoWor 91
Mbaye, Keba 1924- WhoWor 91
Mbaye, Saliou 1946- WhoWor 91
Mbonimpa, Cyprien 1946- WhoWor 91
Mboya, Tom 1930-1969 WorAlBi
Mbugguss, Anthony George 1936- WhoWor 91
McAbee, Jeffrey Deane 1957- WhoSSW 91
McAbee, Robin 1956- WhoAmW 91
Mc Abee, Thomas Allen 1949- WhoEmL 91, WhoSSW 91, WhoWor 91
McAbeer, Sara Carita 1906- WhoAmW 91
McAdam, Charles Vincent, Sr. 1892- WhoAm 90
McAdam, John St&PR 91N
McAdam, Will 1921- WhoAm 90
Mc Adams, Andrew Jack 1911- WhoAm 90
McAdams, Brian 1942- WhoAm 90
McAdams, Donald Ray 1941- WhoSSW 91
McAdams, Herbert H., II 1915- St&PR 91
McAdams, Herbert Hall, II 1915- WhoAm 90
McAdams, Jane Hulen 1946- WhoSSW 91
McAdams, John A. 1942- WhoAm 90
Mc Adams, John Michael 1952- WhoSSW 91
McAdams, Leonard I. 1943- St&PR 91
McAdams, Melinda Jeanne 1959- WhoAmW 91
McAdams, Patricia Daniels 1936- WhoAmW 91
McAdams, Richard S. 1945- St&PR 91
McAdams, Robert, Jr. 1939- St&PR 91, WhoAm 90
Mc Adams, Ronald Earl 1910- WhoAm 90
McAdams, Thomas P. 1919- St&PR 91
McAdams, Thomas P., Jr. 1919- WhoSSW 91
McAden, Rufus Yancey 1833-1889 AmLegL
McAdoo, Bob 1951- WorAlBi
McAdoo, Carol Westbrook 1937- WhoAmA 91, WhoSSW 91
McAdoo, Donald Eldridge 1929- WhoAmA 91N
McAdoo, Gayle A. 1947- WhoAmW 91
Mcadoo, Hosea W BiDrAPA 89
Mcadoo, Julia K BiDrAPA 89
McAdoo, Robert Dale 1934- St&PR 91
McAdoo, William G. 1863-1941 WorAlBi
McAdoo, William Gibbs 1863-1941 BiDrUSE 89, EncABHB 7 [port]
McAdory, Denise Davenporte 1947- WhoSSW 91
McAfee, Alexander 1927- St&PR 91
McAfee, Annalena AuBYP 90
McAfee, Barbara Ann 1937- WhoE 91
McAfee, Barbara Boyd 1957- WhoSSW 91
McAfee, Charles Francis 1932- WhoAm 90
McAfee, Deborah Yeldell 1952- WhoSSW 91
McAfee, Donald R. St&PR 91
Mc Afee, George Joseph 1943- BiDrAPA 89
McAfee, Horace J. 1905- WhoAm 90, WhoE 91
McAfee, James T., Jr. 1939- St&PR 91
Mc Afee, Jerry 1916- WhoAm 90
McAfee, John BioIn 16
McAfee, John A. 1809-1880 AmLegL
McAfee, John Andrew 1927- WhoE 91
McAfee, John Gilmour 1926- WhoE 91
Mc Afee, Joyce Janine 1958- WhoAmW 91
McAfee, Kathleen Crowe BioIn 16
McAfee, Larry BioIn 16
Mc Afee, Laurice L BiDrAPA 89
McAfee, Lawrance Wiley 1955- WhoAm 90
McAfee, Lawrence W. V. 1955- St&PR 91
McAfee, Loran 1923- St&PR 91
McAfee, Naomi Jones 1934- WhoAmW 91
McAfee, Paul 1948- St&PR 91
Mc Afee, R Gordon 1927- BiDrAPA 89
McAfee, Rhonda Jackson 1956- IntWWM 90
McAfee, Robert Harold 1921- St&PR 91
McAfee, Tracy Lee 1961- WhoSSW 91
McAfee, Virginia Thurston 1950- WhoWrEP 89

Mc Afee, William 1910- *WhoAm 90*
McAhren, Robert Willard 1935- *WhoAm 90*
McAlduff, John D. 1930- *St&PR 91*
McAlear, Robert T. 1942- *St&PR 91, WhoAm 90*
McAleavey, David Willard 1946- *WhoWrEP 89*
Mc Aleece, Donald John 1918- *WhoAm 90*
McAleer, Howard J. 1915- *St&PR 91*
McAleer, Jimmy 1864-1931 *Ballpl 90*
McAleer, Joseph Patrick 1929- *St&PR 91*
McAleer, Kevin William 1950- *St&PR 91*
McAleer, Raymond Allan 1938- *St&PR 91*
McAleer, Robert J. *St&PR 91*
McAleese, Dermot 1942- *WhoWor 91*
Mc Alester, Arcie Lee, Jr. 1933- *WhoAm 90, WhoSSW 91, WhoWor 91*
McAlester, Virginia Savage 1943- *WhoAm 90*
McAlevey, John Francis 1923- *WhoE 91*
McAlexander, Gary A. 1944- *St&PR 91*
McAlinden, Joseph J. 1943- *St&PR 91*
McAlindon, Mary Naomi 1935- *WhoAmW 91*
McAliskey, Bernadette Devlin 1947- *BioIn 16*
McAlister, Daniel K. 1938- *St&PR 91*
McAlister, E. Elmo, Jr. 1939- *WhoAm 90*
McAlister, John D. 1926- *St&PR 91*
McAlister, Kyle Ross 1967- *WhoSSW 91*
Mc Alister, Luther Durwood 1927- *WhoAm 90*
McAlister, Lydia Gale 1959- *IntWWM 90*
McAlister, Maurice L. 1925- *WhoAm 90*
McAlister, Philip Reagan 1963- *WhoE 91*
McAlister, Robert Beaton 1932- *WhoAm 90*
McAlister, Sidney Stinson 1924- *St&PR 91*
McAllster, Thomas Allen 1948- *WhoWrEP 89*
McAllan, Robert Edward 1946- *St&PR 91*
McAllaster, Claudia 1952- *WhoAmW 91*
McAllister, Antonia Dabbs 1948- *WhoSSW 91*
Mc Allister, Charles Kenneth 1944- *WhoAm 90, WhoSSW 91*
McAllister, Claude Huntley, Jr. 1930- *WhoSSW 91*
McAllister, Dianne Elaine 1951- *WhoAmW 91*
McAllister, Donal G. 1930- *St&PR 91*
McAllister, Donald 1902- *St&PR 91*
McAllister, Eugene J. 1952- *WhoAm 90*
McAllister, Ferdinand F. 1912-1989 *BioIn 16*
McAllister, Francis R. 1942- *St&PR 91*
McAllister, Francis Ralph 1942- *WhoAm 90*
McAllister, Geraldine E 1925- *WhoAmA 91*
McAllister, Helen B *BiDrAPA 89*
McAllister, James Addams 1915- *WhoWor 91*
McAllister, James Gray, III 1935- *BiDrAPA 89*
McAllister, James P. *BioIn 16*
Mc Allister, Joseph Charles 1928- *WhoWor 91*
McAllister, Julia Anne 1962- *WhoAmW 91*
Mc Allister, Kenneth D. 1943- *WhoSSW 91*
Mc Allister, Lester Belden 1921- *WhoAm 90*
McAllister, Lowell Arthur 1950- *WhoE 91*
McAllister, Mariana Kennedy *AuBYP 90*
Mc Allister, Michael Richard 1946- *BiDrAPA 89*
McAllister, Nancy Hardacre 1940- *WhoAmW 91*
McAllister, Reagin Scott 1946- *St&PR 91*
Mc Allister, Robert *BiDrAPA 89*
McAllister, Robert Cowden 1940- *St&PR 91, WhoAm 90*
McAllister, Robert H. 1916- *St&PR 91*
Mc Allister, Robert John 1919- *BiDrAPA 89*
McAllister, Robert John 1919- *WhoAm 90*
McAllister, Rometta 1948- *WhoAmW 91*
McAllister, Russell Greenway, Jr. 1941- *WhoSSW 91*
McAllister, Sport 1874-1962 *Ballpl 90*
McAllister, Susan A. *ODwPR 91*
McAllister, W. W., Jr. 1918- *St&PR 91*
McAllister, Ward *BioIn 16*
McAllister, William *BiDrAPA 89*
McAllister, William Howard, III 1941- *WhoAm 90*
McAllister, William Middleton 1933- *WhoAm 90*
McAlmon, Robert 1896-1956 *BioIn 16*
McAloon, Richard A. 1942- *St&PR 91*
McAlpin, Bruce Evans 1959- *WhoSSW 91*
McAlpin, David H. *BioIn 16*
McAlpin, David Mark 1955- *WhoE 91*
McAlpin, Kirk Martin 1923- *WhoAm 90*
Mc Alpine, Donald Eugene 1949- *BiDrAPA 89*
McAlpine, Douglas 1890-1981 *DcNaB 1981*
McAlpine, Marshall Edward 1948- *St&PR 91*
McAlpine, Rachel 1940- *FemiCLE*
McAlpine, Stephen A. 1949- *WhoAm 90*
McAlpine, William Ray 1931- *St&PR 91*
McAmis, Edwin Earl 1934- *WhoAm 90, WhoWor 91*
McAmis, Pauline Eula 1913- *WhoWrEP 89*
McAnally, Billie Hargis *BiDrAPA 89*
McAnally, Don 1913- *WhoWrEP 89*
McAnally, Ernie 1946- *Ballpl 90*
McAnally, Gene *BioIn 16*
McAnally, James Willard 1934- *St&PR 91*
McAnally, Mary E. 1939- *WhoWrEP 89*
McAnally, Ray 1926-1989 *AnObit 1989, BioIn 16*
McAndrew, Ben B., III *WhoAm 90*
McAndrew, Gordon Leslie 1926- *WhoAm 90*
McAndrew, Jim 1944- *Ballpl 90*
Mc Andrew, John Burton 1934- *BiDrAPA 89*
Mc Andrew, John J *BiDrAPA 89*
Mc Andrew, William 1957- *BiDrAPA 89*
McAndrews, Anita Grosvenor 1924- *WhoWrEP 89*
McAndrews, James Patrick 1929- *WhoAm 90*
McAndrews, John P. *BioIn 16*
McAndrews, John P. 1925- *St&PR 91*
McAndrews, Phillip James 1950- *St&PR 91*
McAnelly, George, II 1954- *BiDrAPA 89*
McAniff, John E. 1903-1989 *BioIn 16*
McAninch, Harold D. 1933- *WhoAm 90*
McAninch, Mary Kunkle 1935- *WhoAmW 91*
Mc Aninch, Robert Danford 1942- *WhoSSW 91*
McAninch, William Shepard 1940- *WhoSSW 91*
McAnuff, Des 1952- *OxCCanT, WhoAm 90*
Mc Anulty, Henry Joseph 1915- *WhoAm 90*
Mc Anulty, Mary Catherine Cramer 1908- *WhoAmW 91*
McArdle, Allan B. 1917- *St&PR 91*
McArdle, Dennis Edwin 1946- *St&PR 91*
McArdle, Francis T. *St&PR 91*
McArdle, Frank Brian 1946- *WhoE 91*
McArdle, Harry A. *BioIn 16*
McArdle, John Edward 1928- *St&PR 91*
McArdle, Joseph Withrow 1941- *St&PR 91*
McArdle, Karen 1936- *ConAu 129*
Mc Ardle, M Jacquelyn 1932- *BiDrAPA 89*
McArdle, Malcolm Robert 1920- *WhoSSW 91*
McArdle, Paul Francis 1918- *WhoAm 90*
McArdle, Phil 1939- *ConAu 129*
McArdle, Richard Joseph 1934- *WhoAm 90*
McAree, Bill 1935- *WhoSSW 91*
Mc Aree, Christopher P 1932- *BiDrAPA 89*
McArthur, Alexander 1839-1895 *DcCanB 12*
McArthur, Anson James *BioIn 16*
McArthur, Barbara Jean *WhoWrEP 89*
McArthur, Charlton Bryan 1937- *St&PR 91*
McArthur, Cheryl *BioIn 16*
McArthur, Clifton Nesmith 1879-1923 *AmLegL*
McArthur, Dale Kent 1934- *WhoE 91*
Mc Arthur, George 1924- *WhoAm 90*
Mc Arthur, Janet Ward 1914- *WhoAm 90, WhoAmW 91*
McArthur, John Alfred 1937- *WhoE 91*
McArthur, John Hector 1934- *WhoAm 90*
McArthur, John William, Jr. 1955- *WhoEmL 91, WhoSSW 91*
McArthur, Joseph B. 1928- *St&PR 91*
McArthur, Peter 1866-1924 *DcLB 92 [port]*
McArthur, Sara Dee 1948- *WhoAmW 91*
McArtor, T. Allan *BioIn 16*
McAtee, David Ray 1941- *WhoAm 90*
McAtee, James C. 1944- *St&PR 91*
McAtee, James Wayne 1945- *St&PR 91, WhoAm 90*
Mc Atee, Ott B *BiDrAPA 89*
McAtee, Patricia Anne Rooney 1931- *WhoAm 90*
McAtee, Waldo Lee 1883-1962 *DcScB S2*
McAteer, Deborah Grace 1950- *WhoAmW 91*
McAteer, John Joseph 1920- *St&PR 91*
McAteer, Mary Ian 1958- *WhoAmW 91*
McAulay, Sara W. 1940- *WhoWrEP 89*
Mc Auley, Arthur A *BiDrAPA 89*
McAuley, Charles G. 1950- *St&PR 91*
McAuley, Francis Desmond 1919- *WhoWor 91*
Mc Auley, George 1932- *BiDrAPA 89*
McAuley, Joanne Elaine 1932- *WhoSSW 91*
McAuley, John Thomas 1939- *St&PR 91*
McAuley, Kathleen Anne 1951- *WhoE 91*
McAuley, Milton Kenneth 1919- *WhoWrEP 89*
McAuley, P. Douglas 1940- *WhoAm 90*
McAuley, Patrick J. 1923- *St&PR 91*
McAuley, Skeet 1951- *WhoAmA 91*
McAuley, Van Alfon 1926- *WhoSSW 91*
McAuliff, Timothy M. *BioIn 16*
McAuliffe, Anthony C. 1898-1975 *WorAlBi*
McAuliffe, Christa *BioIn 16*
McAuliffe, Christa 1948-1986 *BioAmW*
McAuliffe, Clayton Doyle 1918- *WhoAm 90*
McAuliffe, David John 1924- *St&PR 91*
McAuliffe, Dennis Philip 1922- *WhoAm 90, WhoWor 91*
McAuliffe, Dick 1939- *Ballpl 90*
McAuliffe, Elizabeth Ann 1945- *WhoE 91*
McAuliffe, Eugene Vincent 1918- *WhoE 91*
McAuliffe, Frank 1926- *TwCCr&M 91*
McAuliffe, Frank Malachi 1926- *WhoWrEP 89*
McAuliffe, Jack *BioIn 16*
McAuliffe, James R. 1944- *St&PR 91*
Mc Auliffe, John 1943- *WhoAm 90*
McAuliffe, John F. 1932- *WhoE 91*
Mc Auliffe, Michael F. 1920- *WhoAm 90*
McAuliffe, Rosemary 1927- *WhoAmW 91, WhoE 91*
McAuliffe, Ruthie *BioIn 16*
McAurther, John 1934- *St&PR 91*
McAuslan, Mary Elizabeth Kane 1955- *WhoAmW 91*
McAusland, Randolph M. 1934- *WhoE 91*
McAvity, John Gillis 1950- *WhoAm 90*
McAvoy, Don L. 1942- *St&PR 91*
McAvoy, Doug *BioIn 16*
McAvoy, James E. 1955- *ODwPR 91*
McAvoy, John Joseph 1933- *WhoAm 90*
McAvoy, Katherine Turner 1925- *WhoWrEP 89*
McAvoy, Rogers 1927- *WhoSSW 91*
McAvoy, William Charles 1921- *WhoAm 90, WhoWrEP 89*
McAward, Patrick J., Jr. 1934- *St&PR 91*
McAward, Patrick Joseph, Jr. 1934- *WhoAm 90*
McBain, Ed *AuBYP 90, MajTwCW, WhoWrEP 89*
McBain, Ed 1926- *TwCCr&M 91*
McBane, Alan R. 1938- *St&PR 91*
McBarron, Charles *ODwPR 91*
Mc Bath, James Harvey 1922- *WhoAm 90*
McBath, Tim L 1958- *BiDrAPA 89*
McBay, Arthur John 1919- *WhoAm 90*
McBean, Al 1938- *Ballpl 90*
McBean, Angus 1904-1990 *BioIn 16, NewYTBS 90*
McBeath, Beverly Olena 1954- *WhoSSW 91*
McBeath, Michael Kevin 1955- *WhoEmL 91*
McBee, Denis 1952- *WhoWrEP 89*
McBee, Frank W., Jr. 1920- *St&PR 91*
McBee, Frank Wilkins, Jr. 1920- *WhoAm 90, WhoSSW 91*
McBee, Joe David 1947- *WhoSSW 91*
McBee, Susanna Barnes 1935- *WhoAmW 91, WhoWor 91*
McBennett, Robert J. 1942- *St&PR 91*
McBennett, Robert Joseph 1942- *WhoAm 90*
McBey, James 1884-1959 *WhoAmA 91N*
McBrady, William J. 1931- *St&PR 91*
McBrand, Quinten *WhoWrEP 89*
McBrayer, Nellie K. 1924- *WhoWrEP 89*
McBrearty, Robert Garner 1954- *WhoWrEP 89*
McBride, Algie 1869-1956 *Ballpl 90*
McBride, Bake 1949- *Ballpl 90*
McBride, Barry Clarke 1940- *WhoAm 90*
Mc Bride, Beverley Booth 1929- *WhoSSW 91*
McBride, Beverly Jean 1941- *WhoAmW 91*
McBride, Christian *BioIn 16*
McBride, Clifford 1901-1951 *EncACom*
McBride, Daniel A. 1922- *St&PR 91*
McBride, Daniel Joseph 1939- *St&PR 91*
McBride, Dennis Kessler 1953- *WhoE 91*
McBride, Edwin S. 1926- *St&PR 91*
McBride, Ella Andrepont 1919- *WhoWrEP 89*
McBride, F. Scott 1872-1955 *WorAlBi*
McBride, George 1880-1973 *Ballpl 90*
McBride, George Wickliffe 1854-1911 *AmLegL*
McBride, Guy Thornton, Jr. 1919- *St&PR 91*
Mc Bride, Guy Thornton, Jr. 1919- *WhoAm 90*
McBride, Henry 1867-1962 *WhoAmA 91N*
McBride, Herbert John 1938- *BiDrAPA 89*
McBride, Howard Earl 1932- *WhoWor 91*
McBride, James Charles 1943- *St&PR 91*
McBride, James E. 1911- *St&PR 91*
McBride, James Francis 1946- *WhoEmL 91*
McBride, Jim *BioIn 16*
McBride, Jim 1941- *ConTFT 8*
Mc Bride, John Alexander 1918- *WhoAm 90*
McBride, John Hyatt 1938- *St&PR 91*
McBride, Jon Andrew 1943- *WhoAm 90*
McBride, Jonathan Evans 1942- *WhoAm 90*
McBride, Joseph A. 1919- *St&PR 91*
McBride, Joyce Browning 1927- *WhoAmW 91*
McBride, Judith Ellen 1941- *WhoAmW 91*
McBride, Ken 1935- *Ballpl 90*
McBride, Kenneth Eugene 1948- *WhoEmL 91, WhoWor 91*
McBride, Mary Margaret 1899-1976 *WorAlBi*
McBride, Mary Margaret 1900-1976 *AuBYP 90*
McBride, Milford L., Jr. 1923- *St&PR 91*
McBride, Milford Lawrence, Jr. 1923- *WhoE 91*
McBride, P Anne *BiDrAPA 89*
McBride, Patricia *BioIn 16*
McBride, Patricia 1942- *WorAlBi*
McBride, Patricia Marie Burka 1955- *WhoSSW 91*
McBride, Paul L. 1929- *St&PR 91*
Mc Bride, Raymond Andrew 1927- *WhoAm 90*
Mc Bride, Robert Dana 1927- *WhoAm 90*
McBride, Robert John 1931- *St&PR 91*
McBride, Robert Terrence 1935- *WhoAm 90*
McBride, Rodney Lester 1941- *WhoE 91*
McBride, Stephen Paul 1957- *WhoWor 91*
McBride, Teresa 1962- *WhoHisp 91*
McBride, Thomas Francis 1935- *St&PR 91, WhoAm 90*
Mc Bride, Thomas Frederick 1929- *WhoAm 90*
McBride, Timothy Dominic 1959- *WhoE 91*
McBride, Tom 1914- *Ballpl 90*
Mc Bride, William A, Jr. 1921- *BiDrAPA 89*
McBride, William B., Jr. 1919- *St&PR 91*
McBride, William Bernard 1931- *WhoAm 90*
McBride, William Griffith 1927- *WhoWor 91*
Mc Bride, William Leon 1938- *WhoAm 90*
McBrien, Richard Peter 1936- *WhoAm 90*
McBrine, Ava Jean 1947- *WhoWrEP 89*
McBroom, John K. 1907- *St&PR 91*
McBroom, Marcia 1947- *DrBlPA 90*
McBroom, Mary Catherine 1923- *WhoWrEP 89*
McBroom, Mary J. 1913- *St&PR 91*
McBroom, Nancy Lee 1925- *WhoAmW 91*
McBrown, Gertrude Parthenia *EarBlAP*
McBrown, Gertrude Parthenia 1902- *HarlReB*
McBryan, John Paul 1948- *St&PR 91*
Mc Bryde, Felix Webster 1908- *WhoAm 90, WhoE 91, WhoWor 91*
McBryde, Michael P. 1945- *St&PR 91*
McBryde, Sarah Elva 1942- *WhoAmA 91, WhoE 91*
McBurnett, Terri Patricia 1956- *WhoSSW 91*
McBurney, Andrew Marvell 1913- *St&PR 91*
McBurney, Charles Walker, Jr. 1957- *WhoEmL 91*
McBurney, Edwin B. 1926- *St&PR 91*
McBurney, George William 1926- *WhoAm 90*
McBurney, Linda Lee 1942- *WhoAmW 91*
McBurney, Margot B. *WhoAm 90*
Mc Burney, P Louis 1938- *BiDrAPA 89*
McCabe, Anderson L. 1955- *St&PR 91*
Mc Cabe, Brian Francis 1926- *WhoAm 90*
McCabe, Brooks Fleming, Jr. 1949- *WhoSSW 91*
McCabe, Charles Law 1922- *WhoAm 90*
McCabe, Donald G. 1933- *St&PR 91*
McCabe, Edward Aeneas 1917- *WhoAm 90*
McCabe, Edward Arthur *BioIn 16*
McCabe, Edward Arthur 1938- *WhoAm 90*
McCabe, Francis Joseph 1936- *WhoWor 91*
McCabe, Frank Lacey 1943- *WhoE 91*
Mc Cabe, Gerard Benedict 1930- *WhoAm 90*
McCabe, Harry 1920-1988 *BioIn 16*
McCabe, James E. 1937- *St&PR 91*
McCabe, James J. 1929- *WhoAm 90*
Mc Cabe, James Michael *BiDrAPA 89*

McCabe, Jean Marie 1952- *WhoAmW 91*
McCabe, John 1939- *IntWWM 90, PenDiMP A*
Mc Cabe, John Charles, III 1920- *WhoAm 90*
McCabe, John Charles, III 1920- *WhoWrEP 89*
McCabe, John Henry 1947- *St&PR 91*
Mccabe, Joseph *BiDrAPA 89*
McCabe, Joseph P. 1948- *St&PR 91*
McCabe, Lance C. 1949- *St&PR 91*
McCabe, Laurence Jerome 1930- *St&PR 91*
McCabe, Lawrence J. 1935- *St&PR 91*
McCabe, Lawrence James 1935- *WhoAm 90*
Mc Cabe, Leo Orvine 1899- *WhoAm 90*
Mc Cabe, Mary Joan 1932- *BiDrAPA 89*
McCabe, Mary Williamson 1934- *WhoAmW 91*
McCabe, Maureen M *WhoAmA 91*
McCabe, Mike *ODwPR 91*
McCabe, Monica Petraglia 1959- *WhoEmL 91*
McCabe, Patrick 1955- *ConAu 130*
McCabe, Robert Albert 1914- *WhoAm 90*
McCabe, Robert F., Jr. 1936- *St&PR 91*
McCabe, Robin 1949- *IntWWM 90*
McCabe, Roger J. 1944- *St&PR 91*
McCabe, St. Clair Landerkin 1915- *St&PR 91*
McCabe, Thomas R. 1945- *St&PR 91*
McCabe, Tim Patrick 1957- *St&PR 91*
McCabe, Verne L. 1948- *St&PR 91*
McCabe, Victoria 1948- *WhoWrEP 89*
McCabe, William R. 1859- *AmLegL*
McCachren, Jo Renee 1955- *WhoAmW 91*
McCafferty, Barbara Jean 1940- *WhoAmW 91*
McCafferty, Barbara Taylor 1946- *WhoWrEP 89*
Mc Cafferty, Charles *BiDrAPA 89*
McCafferty, Charles T. 1934- *St&PR 91*
Mc Cafferty, Francis L 1934- *BiDrAPA 89*
McCafferty, James Arthur 1926- *WhoE 91, WhoWor 91*
McCafferty, Jay David 1948- *WhoAmA 91*
McCafferty, John Martin 1956- *WhoEmL 91*
McCafferty, Mary Jude *BiDrAPA 89*
McCafferty, Michael Gilbert 1938- *WhoAm 90*
McCafferty, Owen Edward 1952- *WhoEmL 91*
McCafferty, William 1937- *St&PR 91*
McCafferty, William 1938- *WhoAm 90*
McCaffery, Dan 1952- *ConAu 129*
McCaffery, Eileen Marie 1961- *WhoAmW 91*
McCaffree, Burnham Clough, Jr. 1931- *WhoAm 90*
McCaffree, William G. 1934- *WhoWor 91*
McCaffrey, Anne *BioIn 16*
McCaffrey, Anne 1926- *Au&Arts 6 [port], MajTwCW, RGTwCSF, SmATA 11AS [port]*
McCaffrey, Anne Inez 1926- *WhoAm 90*
McCaffrey, Barbara Jean 1963- *WhoAmW 91*
McCaffrey, Connie *ODwPR 91*
McCaffrey, Deborah 1941- *WhoE 91*
McCaffrey, Eileen *ODwPR 91*
McCaffrey, Francis J. 1917-1989 *BioIn 16*
McCaffrey, James P. *St&PR 91*
McCaffrey, John Anthony 1944- *WhoE 91*
McCaffrey, Judith Elizabeth 1944- *St&PR 91, WhoAm 90*
McCaffrey, Michael Duff 1940- *WhoE 91*
McCaffrey, Neil 1925- *WhoAm 90*
McCaffrey, Robert H. 1927- *St&PR 91*
McCaffrey, Robert Henry, Jr. 1927- *WhoAm 90, WhoE 91*
McCaffrey, Shellyn Gae 1957- *WhoAm 90*
McCaffrey, Thomas Michael 1933- *St&PR 91*
McCaffrey, William T. 1936- *St&PR 91*
McCaffrey, William Thomas 1936- *WhoAm 90*
McCaghren, Marty Don 1953- *WhoSSW 91*
McCaghy, Charles Henry 1934- *WhoAm 90*
McCague, James Daniel 1941- *WhoSSW 91*
McCague, William Langan, II 1945- *St&PR 91*
McCahan, Bill 1921-1986 *Ballpl 90*
McCahan, Walter K. 1935- *WhoAm 90*
McCahey, James Brady, Jr. 1920- *WhoAm 90*
McCahey, Jeanne *WhoWrEP 89*
McCahill, Barry Winslow 1947- *WhoE 91*
McCahill, Julie P. *ODwPR 91*
McCahill, Margaret E 1948- *BiDrAPA 89*
McCahill, William P. *AuBYP 90*
McCaig, Charles George 1943- *St&PR 91, WhoAm 90*
McCaig, Jeffery James 1951- *WhoAm 90*
McCaig, John Robert 1929- *St&PR 91*
McCaig, Joseph J. 1944- *WhoAm 90, WhoE 91*
McCaig, Joseph John 1944- *St&PR 91*
Mc Caig, Nancy Catherine *BiDrAPA 89*
McCaige, Daniel L. 1940- *St&PR 91*
McCain, Betty Landon Ray 1931- *WhoAmW 91*
McCain, Buck *BioIn 16*
McCain, Carter Braxton 1963- *WhoSSW 91*
McCain, George Wallace F. 1930- *WhoAm 90*
McCain, H. Harrison 1927- *WhoAm 90*
McCain, Hugh Boyd, Jr. 1945- *WhoSSW 91*
McCain, James Franklin 1943- *St&PR 91*
McCain, James Ross 1949- *WhoSSW 91*
McCain, John Burns 1937- *St&PR 91*
McCain, John S. 1936- *BioIn 16*
McCain, John Sidney, III 1936- *WhoAm 90, WhoWor 91*
McCain, Richard *St&PR 91*
McCain, Russell P. 1927- *St&PR 91*
McCain, Shirley Joyce 1943- *WhoAmW 91*
McCain, Warren Earl 1925- *St&PR 91, WhoAm 90*
McCain, William B. 1931- *St&PR 91*
McCairns, Ragina Carfagno 1951- *WhoAmW 91*
McCaldin, Denis 1933- *IntWWM 90*
McCaleb, Mary Anne 1940- *WhoAmW 91*
McCalendon, Zach 1937- *St&PR 91*
Mc Call, Abner Vernon 1915- *WhoAm 90*
McCall, Albert Burr 1929- *St&PR 91*
McCall, Alvin A., Jr. 1927- *St&PR 91*
McCall, Ann 1941- *WhoAmA 91*
McCall, Anthony *TwCCr&M 91*
McCall, Anthony 1946- *WhoAmA 91*
McCall, Billy Gene 1928- *WhoAm 90*
McCall, Catherine W *BiDrAPA 89*
Mc Call, Charles Barnard 1928- *WhoAm 90*
McCall, Charles W. 1944- *St&PR 91, WhoAm 90*
McCall, Clyde Samuel, Jr. 1931- *WhoSSW 91, WhoWor 91*
McCall, Daniel Thompson, Jr. 1909- *WhoAm 90, WhoSSW 91*
McCall, David Bruce 1928- *St&PR 91*
McCall, David W. 1928- *WhoAm 90, WhoE 91*
McCall, Debra Laurette Hansford 1958- *WhoAmW 91*
McCall, Donald Lee 1932- *St&PR 91*
McCall, Dorothy Kay 1948- *WhoAmW 91, WhoEmL 91, WhoWor 91*
McCall, Duke Kimbrough 1914- *WhoAm 90*
McCall, E. W. 1913- *St&PR 91*
McCall, Edith Sansom 1911- *AuBYP 90*
McCall, Gilbert D. 1942- *St&PR 91*
Mc Call, Hobby Halbert 1919- *WhoWor 91*
McCall, Howard W., Jr. 1907- *St&PR 91*
McCall, J. A. 1947- *St&PR 91*
Mc Call, Jerry Chalmers 1927- *WhoAm 90*
McCall, John Anthony 1940- *WhoAm 90*
McCall, John Patrick 1927- *WhoAm 90*
McCall, Judith Tate 1944- *WhoSSW 91*
McCall, Julien L. 1921- *St&PR 91*
Mc Call, Julien Lachicotte 1921- *WhoAm 90*
McCall, Linda Combs *WhoSSW 91*
McCall, Lorraine Ann 1955- *WhoE 91*
McCall, Louise Harrup 1925- *WhoAmW 91*
McCall, Mabel Bunny 1923- *WhoWrEP 89*
McCall, Merry Lyn 1955- *WhoSSW 91*
McCall, Nelda Dunn 1945- *WhoEmL 91*
McCall, Robert *BioIn 16*
McCall, Robert R. 1926- *St&PR 91*
Mc Call, Robert R. 1926- *WhoAm 90*
McCall, Robert Theodore 1919- *WhoAmA 91*
McCall, Ronald Henry 1946- *WhoE 91*
McCall, Ronald Leon 1941- *St&PR 91, WhoAm 90*
McCall, Russell Lowell 1945- *WhoSSW 91*
McCall, Shalane *BioIn 16*
McCall, Susan Elizabeth 1945- *WhoAmW 91*
McCall, Thomas Mark 1957- *WhoAm 90*
McCall, Vincent *TwCCr&M 91*
McCall, Virginia 1909- *AuBYP 90*
McCall, W. Calder 1906- *St&PR 91*
McCall, W. Kent 1940- *St&PR 91*
McCall, William Calder 1906- *WhoAm 90*
McCall, William Vaughn *BiDrAPA 89*
McCall, William Vaughn 1958- *WhoSSW 91*
McCall, Windy 1925- *Ballpl 90*
McCall-Simpson, Mary Muyelinda 1963- *WhoAmW 91*
McCalla, Alex F. 1937- *BioIn 16*
Mc Calla, Dennis Robert 1934- *WhoAm 90*
McCalla, Gary Edward 1931- *WhoWrEP 89*
McCalla, John F. 1941- *St&PR 91*
McCalla, Sandra Ann 1939- *WhoAmW 91, WhoSSW 91*
McCalla, William James 1943- *WhoAm 90*
McCalley, Robert Bruce, Jr. 1922- *WhoE 91*
McCalley-Whitters, Mona K. 1956- *WhoAmW 91*
McCallion, Hazel *WhoAm 90, WhoAmW 91*
McCallion, Jack *BiDrAPA 89*
McCallion, John James 1932- *WhoE 91*
McCallister, Ralph 1905-1988 *BioIn 16*
McCallum, Alex 1940- *ODwPR 91*
McCallum, Bennett Tarlton 1935- *WhoAm 90*
Mc Callum, Charles Alexander 1925- *WhoAm 90, WhoSSW 91*
Mc Callum, Charles Edward 1939- *WhoAm 90*
McCallum, Corrie 1914- *WhoAmA 91*
Mc Callum, David 1933- *WhoAm 90*
McCallum, David Kyle 1948- *IntWWM 90*
McCallum, Francis A. 1917- *WhoAm 90*
McCallum, G. W. 1945- *St&PR 91*
McCallum, Gloria Jean 1954- *WhoAmW 91*
McCallum, Ian *BioIn 16*
McCallum, Ian A. C. 1936- *St&PR 91*
McCallum, Jack 1949- *BioIn 16*
McCallum, James Scott 1950- *WhoAm 90*
McCallum, Jason *BioIn 16*
McCallum, Joanna *ConTFT 8 [port]*
McCallum, John *BioIn 16*
McCallum, John 1918- *ConTFT 8 [port]*
McCallum, John Charles 1946- *WhoWor 91*
McCallum, John Dennis 1924-1988 *BioIn 16*
McCallum, John Stuart 1944- *WhoAm 90*
McCallum, Kenneth James 1918- *WhoAm 90*
McCallum, Kimberli Etta 1959- *BiDrAPA 89*
McCallum, Louise 1947- *St&PR 91*
McCallum, Napoleon *BioIn 16*
McCallum, Peter Clark 1951- *St&PR 91*
McCallum, Richard Dee 1936- *St&PR 91*
McCallum, Richard Warwick 1945- *WhoAm 90*
McCallum, Valerie Lane 1957- *WhoSSW 91*
McCalmont, John Swayze 1822-1906 *AmLegL*
McCalpin, Francis William 1921- *WhoAm 90*
McCambridge, John James 1933- *WhoE 91*
McCambridge, Mercedes 1918- *WorAlBi*
Mc Cameron, Fritz Allen 1929- *WhoAm 90*
McCamley, Gordon Dale *BiDrAPA 89*
McCammon, Bob *WhoAm 90*
McCammon, David N. 1934- *St&PR 91*
Mc Cammon, David Noel 1934- *WhoAm 90*
McCammon, James Andrew 1947- *WhoAm 90*
McCammond, Donald B. 1915- *ODwPR 91*
McCammond, Donald Barr 1915- *WhoAm 90*
McCampbell, Eugene Wayne 1924- *St&PR 91*
Mc Camy, James Lucian 1906- *WhoAm 90*
McCamy, Sam C. 1930- *St&PR 91*
McCamy, W. R. 1930- *St&PR 91*
McCance, Andrew 1889-1983 *DcNaB 1981*
McCance-Katz, Elinore Frances 1956- *BiDrAPA 89*
McCance-Lowe, Jeannie M. *BiDrAPA 89*
Mc Candless, Alfred A. 1927- *WhoAm 90*
Mc Candless, Anna Loomis 1897- *WhoAmW 91, WhoE 91*
McCandless, Barbara J. 1931- *WhoAmW 91*
McCandless, Bruce 1937- *BioIn 16*
Mc Candless, Bruce, II 1937- *WhoAm 90*
McCandless, Carolyn Keller 1945- *St&PR 91, WhoAmW 91*
McCandless, Hugh *ODwPR 91*
McCandless, Hugh Douglas *BioIn 16*
McCandless, Peter L. *ODwPR 91*
McCandless, Stephen Porter 1941- *WhoAm 90*
Mc Candlish, Fairfax Sheild 1918- *WhoAm 90*
Mc Candlish, Robert John, Jr. 1909- *WhoAm 90, WhoSSW 91*
McCanham, Frank A. 1943- *WhoSSW 91*
McCanles, Michael Frederick 1936- *WhoAm 90*
McCann, Alexander P. 1929- *St&PR 91*
Mc Cann, Anthony *BiDrAPA 89*
McCann, Anthony F. 1940- *St&PR 91*
McCann, Arthur *MajTwCW*
McCann, Barbara Marie 1931- *WhoSSW 91*
McCann, Bridget Ann 1955- *WhoAmW 91*
McCann, Carol Cole 1945- *WhoAmW 91*
Mc Cann, Cecile Nelken *WhoAm 90*
McCann, Cecile Nelken *WhoAmA 91, WhoWrEP 89*
McCann, Clarence David, Jr. 1948- *WhoAm 90*
McCann, Daisy S. 1927- *WhoAmW 91*
McCann, David A. 1929- *St&PR 91*
McCann, David Anthony 1929- *WhoAm 90*
Mc Cann, David L *BiDrAPA 89*
McCann, Dean Merton 1927- *WhoAm 90*
McCann, Donald V. 1934- *St&PR 91*
McCann, Edson *MajTwCW*
McCann, Edward 1943- *WhoE 91*
McCann, Elizabeth I. 1931- *BioIn 16, NotWoAT*
McCann, Elizabeth Ireland 1931- *WhoAm 90*
Mc Cann, Frances Veronica 1927- *WhoAm 90, WhoAmW 91*
McCann, James P. 1930- *WhoAm 90*
McCann, Janet 1942- *WhoWrEP 89*
McCann, Joan Celia 1936- *WhoAmW 91*
McCann, John Francis 1937- *WhoAm 90, WhoWor 91*
Mc Cann, John Joseph 1937- *WhoAm 90*
McCann, John Patrick 1944- *St&PR 91*
McCann, Joseph F. 1941- *ODwPR 91*
McCann, Les 1935- *DrBIPA 90*
McCann, Mary Cheri 1956- *WhoAmW 91*
McCann, Maurice Joseph 1950- *WhoWor 91*
McCann, Merle C *BiDrAPA 89*
McCann, Michael F. 1943- *WhoE 91, WhoWrEP 89*
McCann, Michael Timothy 1951- *St&PR 91*
McCann, Mikel Bradshaw 1957- *WhoSSW 91*
McCann, Norman *IntWWM 90*
McCann, Owen 1907- *WhoWor 91*
McCann, R. Bruce 1948- *St&PR 91*
McCann, Raymond J. 1934- *WhoAm 90*
McCann, Raymond Joseph 1934- *St&PR 91*
McCann, S. Anthony 1943- *WhoAm 90*
Mc Cann, Samuel McDonald 1925- *WhoAm 90*
McCann, Sheila 1944- *ODwPR 91*
McCann, Thomas F. *WhoAm 90*
McCann, Una Deirdre 1958- *WhoE 91*
McCanna, William Joseph 1940- *St&PR 91, WhoAm 90*
McCanne, William G. 1939- *St&PR 91*
McCannel, Malcolm A, Mrs 1915- *WhoAmA 91*
McCannon, Dindga Fatima 1947- *BioIn 16*
McCants, David Arnold 1937- *WhoAm 90*
McCants, Renee Denise *WhoAmW 91*
McCants, Zauditu Esther 1944- *WhoAmW 91*
Mc Card, Ray H 1934- *BiDrAPA 89*
McCardell, James Elton 1931- *WhoAm 90*
McCardell, John Malcolm, Jr. 1949- *WhoAm 90*
McCardle, Robert William 1925- *St&PR 91*
McCarey, Leo 1898-1969 *WorAlBi*
McCargar, James Goodrich 1920- *WhoE 91*
McCarl, Foster James 1947- *St&PR 91*
McCarl, Henry N. 1941- *WhoSSW 91*
McCarl, Kevin A. 1956- *St&PR 91*
McCarley, Bobby Joe 1928- *St&PR 91*
McCarley, George David 1953- *WhoSSW 91*
McCarley, Joe Bruce 1931- *St&PR 91*
McCarley, Kenneth Wayne 1942- *St&PR 91*
Mc Carley, Robert W 1937- *BiDrAPA 89*
McCarley, Thomas David 1942- *WhoSSW 91*
Mc Carley, Tracey H *BiDrAPA 89*
McCarragher, Bernard John 1927- *St&PR 91, WhoAm 90*
McCarran, Patrick A. 1876-1954 *WorAlBi*
Mc Carrick, Richard G 1951- *BiDrAPA 89*
McCarrick, Richard Gaynor 1951- *WhoE 91*
Mc Carrick, Theodore Edgar 1930- *WhoAm 90, WhoE 91*
McCarriston, Linda 1943- *WhoWrEP 89*
McCarroll, Jesse Cornelius 1933- *IntWWM 90*
McCarroll, John R. 1940- *St&PR 91*
McCarroll, Michael Vincent 1952- *St&PR 91*
McCarroll, Orville W. 1920- *St&PR 91, WhoAm 90*
McCarron, John Francis 1949- *WhoAm 90*
McCarron, John R. 1940- *St&PR 91*
McCarron, Paul 1933- *WhoAmA 91*
McCarron, Vicki L. 1951- *St&PR 91*

McCarry, Charles *BioIn 16*
McCarry, Charles 1930- *SpyFic, TwCCr&M 91*
McCart, Harold Franklin, Jr. 1938- *St&PR 91*
McCart, Sharon Rae 1953- *WhoEmL 91*
McCartan, Lucy 1942- *WhoAmW 91*
McCartee, Divie Bethune 1820-1900 *BioIn 16*
McCarten, Paul Vincent 1949- *WhoEmL 91*
McCarter, Bobby G. 1935- *St&PR 91*
McCarter, Bobby Gene 1935- *WhoSSW 91*
McCarter, C. Ted *WhoAm 90*
McCarter, Charles Chase 1926- *WhoAm 90*
McCarter, Craig A. 1945- *St&PR 91*
McCarter, Francis E. P. 1917-1988 *BioIn 16*
McCarter, Gary 1936- *St&PR 91*
Mc Carter, John Alexander 1918- *WhoAm 90*
McCarter, John B. 1930- *St&PR 91*
McCarter, John Pringle 1929- *WhoAm 90*
McCarter, John Walter 1950- *St&PR 91*
McCarter, John Wilbur, Jr. 1938- *St&PR 91*
Mc Carter, John Wilbur, Jr. 1938- *WhoAm 90*
McCarter, Judy *ODwPR 91*
McCarter, Neely Dixon 1929- *BioIn 16*
McCarter, Pender M. 1946- *ODwPR 91*
McCarter, Pete Kyle, Jr. 1945- *WhoAm 90*
Mc Carter, Robert H 1916- *BiDrAPA 89*
Mc Carter, Thomas N., III 1929- *WhoAm 90, WhoE 91*
McCarters, The *WhoNeCM [port]*
McCarthey, Frank Nelson 1955- *WhoE 91*
McCarthey, Thomas Kearns 1950- *St&PR 91*
McCarthy, Alex 1888-1978 *Ballpl 90*
McCarthy, Arlene Theresa 1960- *WhoEmL 91*
McCarthy, Barry 1943- *ConAu 32NR*
McCarthy, Bettie S. 1948- *ODwPR 91*
McCarthy, Beverly Fitch 1933- *WhoAmW 91*
McCarthy, Bruce *ODwPR 91*
McCarthy, Burkley F. 1930- *St&PR 91*
McCarthy, Carol M. 1940- *WhoAm 90*
McCarthy, Catherine Frances 1921- *WhoAmW 91*
McCarthy, Charles J. *BioIn 16*
Mc Carthy, Charles Joseph 1907- *WhoAm 90*
McCarthy, Charles Justin 1937- *WhoAm 90*
McCarthy, Charles R., Jr. 1938- *St&PR 91*
McCarthy, Charlotte *FemiCLE*
McCarthy, Charlotte Colyer 1943- *WhoAmW 91*
McCarthy, Cornelius Stephen 1916- *WhoAm 90*
Mc Carthy, D. Justin *WhoAm 90*
McCarthy, D'Alton 1836-1898 *DcCanB 12*
McCarthy, Daniel *PenDiDA 89*
McCarthy, Daniel C. 1924- *St&PR 91*
Mc Carthy, Daniel Christopher, Jr. 1924- *WhoAm 90*
McCarthy, Daniel F. 1944- *St&PR 91*
Mc Carthy, David Edwin *BiDrAPA 89*
Mc Carthy, David Jerome, Jr. 1935- *WhoAm 90*
McCarthy, Denis 1935- *WhoAmA 91*
McCarthy, Denis M. 1942- *St&PR 91*
Mc Carthy, Denis Michael 1942- *WhoAm 90*
McCarthy, Denise Eileen 1941- *WhoAmW 91*
McCarthy, Dennis 1921- *WhoAmA 91*
McCarthy, Dennis 1924- *St&PR 91*
McCarthy, Dermott F. 1919-1988 *BioIn 16*
McCarthy, Dianne Elizabeth 1957- *WhoAmW 91*
McCarthy, Donald Wans 1922- *St&PR 91*
McCarthy, Doris Jean 1910- *WhoAmA 91*
Mc Carthy, Edward, Jr. 1931- *WhoSSW 91*
Mc Carthy, Edward A, Jr. 1941- *BiDrAPA 89*
McCarthy, Edward Anthony 1918- *WhoAm 90, WhoSSW 91*
Mc Carthy, Edward James 1914- *WhoAm 90*
McCarthy, Edwward Joseph 1942- *St&PR 91*
McCarthy, Emily J 1945- *ConAu 32NR*
McCarthy, Eugene 1916- *WorAlBi*
McCarthy, Eugene J. 1916- *BioIn 16*
McCarthy, Eugene John 1938- *St&PR 91*
Mc Carthy, Eugene Joseph 1916- *WhoAm 90*
McCarthy, Eugene Joseph 1916- *WhoWrEP 89*
McCarthy, Francis A. 1953- *St&PR 91*
McCarthy, Francis Xavier 1952- *St&PR 91*
McCarthy, Frank A., Jr. 1953- *St&PR 91*
Mc Carthy, Frank Martin 1924- *WhoAm 90*
McCarthy, Frederick William 1941- *WhoE 91, WhoWor 91*
Mc Carthy, Gerald C 1922- *BiDrAPA 89*
McCarthy, Gerald M. 1941- *St&PR 91*
McCarthy, Gerald Michael 1941- *WhoAm 90*
McCarthy, Gerald Patrick 1943- *WhoSSW 91*
McCarthy, Gerald T. *NewYTBS 90*
McCarthy, Glenn Herbert 1907-1988 *BioIn 16*
McCarthy, Grace *BioIn 16*
McCarthy, Grace Mary 1927- *WhoAmW 91*
McCarthy, Gregory Alan 1956- *BiDrAPA 89*
McCarthy, Gregory Joseph 1946- *WhoE 91*
Mc Carthy, Harold Charles 1926- *WhoAm 90*
McCarthy, Herbert R. *BioIn 16*
Mc Carthy, J Francis *BiDrAPA 89*
McCarthy, J. Thomas 1937- *WhoAm 90*
McCarthy, Jack 1869-1931 *Ballpl 90*
McCarthy, Jack D. 1943- *St&PR 91*
McCarthy, James A. 1927- *St&PR 91*
McCarthy, James Joseph 1944- *WhoAm 90, WhoE 91*
McCarthy, James M. 1922- *St&PR 91*
McCarthy, James P. 1935- *WhoAm 90*
McCarthy, James S. 1941- *St&PR 91*
McCarthy, Jerome F. 1907- *St&PR 91*
McCarthy, JoAnne Elizabeth 1943- *WhoAmW 91, WhoWor 91*
McCarthy, Joe 1887-1978 *Ballpl 90 [port], BioIn 16*
McCarthy, John *IntWWM 90*
McCarthy, John 1919- *PenDiMP*
McCarthy, John 1927- *WhoAm 90*
McCarthy, John Connell 1952- *WhoSSW 91*
McCarthy, John Donald 1935- *St&PR 91*
Mc Carthy, John Edward 1930- *WhoAm 90, WhoSSW 91*
McCarthy, John Francis, III 1947- *WhoE 91*
McCarthy, John J 1909- *ConAu 130*
Mc Carthy, John Michael 1927- *WhoAm 90*
McCarthy, John Michael 1946- *St&PR 91*
McCarthy, John Robert 1945- *WhoE 91*
McCarthy, John Russell 1931- *WhoAm 90*
McCarthy, John Thomas *BiDrAPA 89*
McCarthy, John Thomas 1929- *WhoE 91*
McCarthy, John Thomas 1939- *WhoAm 90, WhoWor 91*
McCarthy, Johnny 1910-1973 *Ballpl 90*
McCarthy, Jose E Campion 1938- *BiDrAPA 89*
McCarthy, Joseph 1908-1957 *BioIn 16*
McCarthy, Joseph Francis 1946- *St&PR 91*
McCarthy, Joseph Gerald 1938- *WhoAm 90*
McCarthy, Joseph Harold 1921- *St&PR 91, WhoAm 90*
McCarthy, Joseph M. 1935- *ODwPR 91*
Mc Carthy, Joseph Michael 1940- *WhoAm 90, WhoE 91, WhoWor 91*
McCarthy, Joseph R. 1908-1957 *WorAlBi*
McCarthy, Joseph W. *WhoAm 90*
McCarthy, Joseph Weston 1915-1980 *BioIn 16*
McCarthy, Joyce Ann 1960- *WhoAmW 91*
McCarthy, Justin 1892- *WhoAmA 91N*
McCarthy, Justin 1892-1977 *MusmAFA*
McCarthy, Justine Sarah *BiDrAPA 89*
Mc Carthy, Kathryn A. 1924- *WhoAm 90, WhoAmW 91*
McCarthy, Kevin 1914- *WorAlBi*
McCarthy, Kevin 1947- *WhoWor 91*
McCarthy, Kevin A. 1957- *St&PR 91*
McCarthy, Kevin Michael 1940- *WhoWrEP 89*
McCarthy, Leo Tarcisius 1930- *WhoAm 90*
McCarthy, Marina Chukayeff 1950- *WhoE 91*
McCarthy, Martha M 1945- *ConAu 31NR*
McCarthy, Mary 1912- *WhoWrEP 89*
McCarthy, Mary 1912-1989 *AnObit 1989, BioIn 16, ConAu 129, ConLC 59 [port], CurBio 90N, FemiCLE, MajTwCW, WorAlBi*
McCarthy, Mary Abigail *NewYTBS 90*
Mccarthy, Mary K *BiDrAPA 89*
McCarthy, Mary Lynn 1950- *WhoAm 90, WhoE 91*
McCarthy, Mary McCloskey 1923- *WhoAmW 91*
McCarthy, Mary T. 1912-1989 *BioAmW*
McCarthy, Maryanne 1960- *WhoAmA 91*
McCarthy, Matthew M. 1947- *St&PR 91*
McCarthy, Michael 1937- *St&PR 91*
Mc Carthy, Michael D *BiDrAPA 89*
Mccarthy, Michael John 1949- *BiDrAPA 89*
McCarthy, Michael Joseph 1944- *St&PR 91*
McCarthy, Michael W. 1941- *St&PR 91*
Mc Carthy, Nanette Mary 1949- *BiDrAPA 89*
Mc Carthy, Neal Edward *BiDrAPA 89*
McCarthy, Pamela Maffei 1952- *WhoAm 90, WhoE 91, WhoEmL 91*
Mc Carthy, Patricia Margaret 1943- *WhoAmW 91*
McCarthy, Patrick A. 1945- *WhoSSW 91*
Mc Carthy, Patrick Edward 1930- *WhoAm 90*
McCarthy, Patrick Francis *St&PR 91N*
McCarthy, Patrick Michael 1936- *St&PR 91*
McCarthy, Paul Fenton 1934- *WhoAm 90*
McCarthy, Paul Joseph 1937- *St&PR 91*
McCarthy, Paul W. 1951- *St&PR 91*
McCarthy, Peggy *ODwPR 91*
McCarthy, Peter J. 1943- *ODwPR 91*
McCarthy, Peter John 1943- *St&PR 91*
McCarthy, R. Patrick 1944- *ODwPR 91*
McCarthy, Raymond M. *St&PR 91N*
McCarthy, Raymond M. 1927-1989 *BioIn 16*
McCarthy, Richard H 1948- *BiDrAPA 89*
McCarthy, Robert E., Jr. 1931- *St&PR 91*
McCarthy, Robert Emmett 1951- *WhoEmL 91*
McCarthy, Robert Joseph *WhoE 91*
Mc Carthy, Robert Vincent 1921- *WhoAm 90*
McCarthy, Rosemary P. 1928- *WhoWrEP 89*
McCarthy, Sean Dennis *BiDrAPA 89*
McCarthy, Sharon Murphy 1956- *WhoAmW 91*
McCarthy, Shawna Lee 1954- *WhoAm 90*
McCarthy, Stephen A. *BioIn 16*
McCarthy, Terence Alan 1939- *ODwPR 91*
Mc Carthy, Thomas James 1941- *WhoAm 90*
Mc Carthy, Thomas Patrick 1928- *WhoAm 90*
McCarthy, Thomas Patrick 1954- *WhoSSW 91*
McCarthy, Timothy Michael 1954- *WhoEmL 91*
McCarthy, Tommy 1863-1922 *Ballpl 90 [port]*
McCarthy, Vern I., Jr. 1927- *St&PR 91*
McCarthy, Vincent Paul 1940- *WhoAm 90*
McCarthy, Walter John, Jr. 1925- *St&PR 91*
Mc Carthy, Walter John, Jr. 1925- *WhoAm 90*
McCarthy, William Bernard 1939- *WhoE 91*
McCarthy, William Daniel 1935- *WhoSSW 91*
McCarthy, William J. *BioIn 16*
McCarthy, William J. *BioIn 16*
McCarthy, William J. 1919- *WhoAm 90, WhoE 91*
McCarthy, William J. 1938- *St&PR 91*
Mc Carthy, William L 1927- *BiDrAPA 89*
McCarthy, Wilson 1930- *SpyFic*
McCartin, Thomas Ronald 1934- *WhoAm 90, WhoSSW 91, WhoWor 91*
McCartin, William Francis 1905- *WhoAmA 91*
McCartin, William Robert 1928- *St&PR 91*
McCartney, Alan Raymond 1947- *WhoE 91*
McCartney, Allen Papin 1940- *WhoAm 90*
McCartney, Bob *BioIn 16*
McCartney, Charles Price 1912- *WhoAm 90*
Mc Cartney, Cheryl F 1947- *BiDrAPA 89*
McCartney, Christine Maye 1949- *WhoAmW 91*
McCartney, Daniel Patrick 1951- *St&PR 91*
McCartney, Dorothy Wilson 1914- *WhoWrEP 89*
McCartney, Douglas 1938- *St&PR 91, WhoE 91*
McCartney, Forrest Striplin 1931- *WhoAm 90*
McCartney, James E. 1918- *St&PR 91*
Mc Cartney, James R 1932- *BiDrAPA 89*
McCartney, James Robert 1932- *WhoE 91*
McCartney, Jerry Thomas 1943- *St&PR 91*
McCartney, John Joseph 1943- *St&PR 91, WhoAm 90*
Mc Cartney, Kenneth Hall 1924- *WhoAm 90*
McCartney, Michael 1944- *BioIn 16*
McCartney, O. Kenton, III 1943- *St&PR 91*
McCartney, Paul *BioIn 16*
McCartney, Paul 1942- *ConMus 4 [port], EncPR&S 89, IntWWM 90, OxCPMus, WhoAm 90, WhoWor 91, WorAlBi*
McCartney, Robert Charles 1934- *St&PR 91*
Mc Cartney, Robert Charles 1934- *WhoAm 90, WhoE 91, WhoWor 91*
Mc Cartor, Harold Robert 1933- *BiDrAPA 89*
McCarty, Barbara Smith 1940- *WhoAmW 91*
Mc Carty, Bruce 1920- *WhoAm 90*
McCarty, C. Dwight 1957- *WhoSSW 91*
McCarty, Catherine *BiDEWW*
McCarty, Chester Earl 1905- *WhoAm 90, WhoWor 91*
McCarty, David *WhoSSW 91*
McCarty, David Lewis 1950- *WhoSSW 91*
McCarty, Donald James 1921- *WhoAm 90*
McCarty, Doran Chester 1931- *ConAu 31NR, WhoE 91*
McCarty, Elizabeth *BiDEWW*
McCarty, Emmit F. *St&PR 91*
McCarty, Harold Hull 1901-1987 *BioIn 16*
McCarty, Harry Downman 1946- *WhoE 91*
McCarty, Henry *BioIn 16*
McCarty, Horace G. 1924- *St&PR 91*
McCarty, James *NewAgMG*
McCarty, James Joseph 1930- *St&PR 91, WhoAm 90*
McCarty, Jesse Louis Henry 1941- *WhoWrEP 89*
McCarty, John B. 1944- *St&PR 91*
McCarty, John Bruce 1944- *WhoSSW 91*
McCarty, John S. *BioIn 16*
McCarty, Joseph C. 1942- *St&PR 91*
McCarty, Joseph William, Jr. 1944- *St&PR 91*
Mc Carty, Kathleen *BiDrAPA 89*
McCarty, L. Thomas 1940- *St&PR 91*
McCarty, Laura Smith 1967- *WhoAmW 91*
McCarty, Lew 1888-1930 *Ballpl 90*
McCarty, Lorraine Chambers *WhoAmA 91*
McCarty, Maclyn 1911- *WhoAm 90*
McCarty, Margaret *BiDEWW*
McCarty, Marvin Samuel 1939- *WhoSSW 91*
Mc Carty, Michael B *BiDrAPA 89*
McCarty, Michiel *BioIn 16*
McCarty, Michiel Cleve 1951- *WhoAm 90*
McCarty, Mosie *BioIn 16*
McCarty, Patricia 1954- *IntWWM 90*
Mc Carty, Perry Lee 1931- *WhoAm 90*
McCarty, Philip N. 1938- *St&PR 91*
McCarty, Philip Norman 1938- *WhoAm 90*
McCarty, Richard Earl 1938- *WhoAm 90*
Mc Carty, Robert Lee 1920- *WhoAm 90*
McCarty, Robert Lee 1934- *St&PR 91*
McCarty, Robert Marvin, Jr. 1926- *St&PR 91*
McCarty, Stuart 1923- *St&PR 91*
Mc Carty, Teresita Ann *BiDrAPA 89*
McCarty, Theodore Frederick 1937- *St&PR 91, WhoAm 90*
McCarty, Theodore M. 1909- *St&PR 91*
Mc Carty, Theodore Milson 1909- *WhoAm 90*
McCarty, Thomas J. 1938- *St&PR 91*
McCarty, Thomas Joseph 1938- *WhoAm 90*
McCarty, William Bonner, Jr. 1921- *St&PR 91, WhoAm 90*
Mc Carty, William Michael, Jr. 1938- *WhoWor 91*
McCarus, Ernest Nasseph 1922- *WhoAm 90*
McCarver, Betty Louise 1932- *WhoAmW 91*
McCarver, Frank 1941- *St&PR 91*
McCarver, James Timothy 1941- *WhoAm 90*
McCarver, Samuel C. *WhoAm 90*
McCarver, Samuel C. 1927- *St&PR 91*
McCarver, Tim 1941- *Ballpl 90 [port]*
McCarvill, Richard Lee 1946- *WhoE 91*
McCarville, Mark John 1946- *St&PR 91, WhoAm 90*
McCary, Deanna Brewer 1943- *WhoAmW 91*
McCary, Leon E. 1937- *St&PR 91*
Mc Cary, Roger Glynn 1942- *BiDrAPA 89*
McCashin, Arthur J. *BioIn 16*
McCaskey, Edward *WhoAm 90*
McCaskey, Michael 1943- *WhoAm 90*
McCaskill, Austin, Sr. 1920- *St&PR 91*
McCaskill, Beverly H *WhoAm 90*
McCaskill, Kirk 1961- *Ballpl 90*
McCaskill, Patricia Lorenz 1948- *WhoAmW 91*
McCaskill, Richard E. 1936- *St&PR 91*
McCasland, Thomas H., Jr. 1933- *St&PR 91*
McCaslin, F. Catherine 1947- *WhoAmW 91*
McCaslin, Nellie 1914- *BioIn 16, NotWoAT*
McCaslin, Peggy Ann Cagle 1934- *WhoSSW 91*

McCaslin, Rosemary 1948- *WhoEmL 91*
McCaslin, Teresa Eve 1949- *WhoAmW 91*
McCaslin, Thomas Wilbert 1947- *WhoE 91*
McCaslin, Walter Wright 1924- *WhoAmA 91N*
McCastlain, Hugh M. 1943- *St&PR 91*
McCathrin, E. Zoe *ODwPR 91*
McCatty, Steve 1954- *Ballpl 90*
McCaughan, James William 1950- *St&PR 91*
McCaughan, John F. 1935- *WhoAm 90*
McCaughan, John Forbes 1935- *St&PR 91*
McCaughey, Andrew G. 1922- *St&PR 91*
McCaughey, Arnold Patrick 1943- *WhoAmA 91*
McCaughey, John Willett 1936- *St&PR 91*
McCaughey, Lorraine B. 1950- *WhoAmW 91*
McCaughey, Patrick *WhoAm 90*
McCaughey, Patrick 1944- *BioIn 16*
McCaughey, William S. 1821-1889 *AmLegL*
McCaughrin, Wendy Bordoff 1944- *WhoAmW 91*
McCaul, Bruce W. 1939- *St&PR 91*
McCauley, Alberta 1905?-1988 *BioIn 16*
McCauley, Brenda Julia 1929- *WhoAmW 91, WhoE 91*
McCauley, Bruce D. 1936- *St&PR 91*
McCauley, Bruce Gordon *WhoAm 90*
McCauley, Carole Spearin 1939- *WhoWrEP 89*
McCauley, Cleyburn Lycurgus 1929- *WhoSSW 91, WhoWor 91*
McCauley, Daniel Joseph, Jr. 1917- *WhoAm 90*
McCauley, David F. 1925- *St&PR 91*
McCauley, David W. 1958- *WhoWor 91*
McCauley, Fay Shore 1960- *WhoSSW 91*
Mc Cauley, Floyce D *BiDrAPA 89*
McCauley, Floyce Reid 1933- *WhoE 91*
McCauley, Gardiner Rae 1933- *WhoAmA 91*
McCauley, Herbert Nicholas 1933- *St&PR 91*
Mc Cauley, Jacqueline Robinson 1950- *WhoSSW 91*
McCauley, James P. 1943- *St&PR 91*
McCauley, Janie Caves 1946- *WhoSSW 91*
McCauley, John *BioIn 16*
McCauley, John Edward 1946- *St&PR 91*
McCauley, John Francis 1932- *WhoAm 90*
McCauley, John J. 1937- *IntWWM 90*
McCauley, Lawrence H. 1922- *St&PR 91*
McCauley, Mary *EncCRAm*
McCauley, Mary 1754-1832 *WorAlBi*
McCauley, Norman A. 1953- *St&PR 91*
Mc Cauley, R. Paul 1943- *WhoAm 90, WhoWor 91*
McCauley, Richard Gray 1940- *St&PR 91, WhoAm 90*
McCauley, Robert Joseph 1933- *St&PR 91*
McCauley, Robert Neil 1952- *WhoSSW 91*
McCauley, Robert William 1926- *WhoAm 90*
Mc Cauley, Roger Lee *BiDrAPA 89*
Mc Cauley, Roy Barnard 1919- *WhoAm 90*
McCauley, Shirley Ann 1938- *WhoAmW 91*
McCauley, Stephen *BioIn 16*
McCauley, Sue 1941- *FemiCLE*
McCauley, William Alexander 1917- *IntWWM 90*
McCauley, William Patrick 1948- *St&PR 91*
McCaull, Julian Lincoln 1936- *WhoWrEP 89*
McCaulley, Glen L. 1942- *St&PR 91*
McCausland, Bruce Henderson 1931- *WhoE 91*
McCausland, Charles 1935- *WhoAm 90*
McCausland, Edwin Pugh 1945- *St&PR 91*
McCausland, Elizabeth 1899-1965 *WhoAmA 91N*
McCausland, George Jackson 1933- *St&PR 91*
McCausland, Thomas J., Jr. 1934- *St&PR 91*
McCausland, Thomas James, Jr. 1934- *WhoAm 90*
McCaw, Craig *BioIn 16*
Mc Caw, William W 1925- *BiDrAPA 89*
Mc Cawley, Austin 1925- *BiDrAPA 89*
McCawley, Austin 1925- *WhoE 91*
McCay, Thomas Walter 1943- *WhoSSW 91*
McCay, Winsor 1869?-1934 *EncACom*
McChesney, Cheryl *BiDrAPA 89*
McChesney, Clifton 1929- *WhoAmA 91*
McChesney, David Allen 1938- *St&PR 91*
McChesney, James 1941- *IntWWM 90*
McChesney, Mary Fuller *WhoAmA 91*
McChesney, Peter Brooks 1948- *WhoAm 90*
McChesney, Robert Michael, Sr. 1942- *WhoSSW 91*
Mc Chesney, Robert Pearson 1913- *WhoAm 90*
McChesney, Robert Pearson 1913- *WhoAmA 91*
McChesney, Samuel Parker, III 1945- *WhoEmL 91*
McChristy, Quentin L 1921- *WhoAmA 91*
McChristy, Thomas A. *St&PR 91*
McClafferty, John Joseph 1906- *WhoAm 90, WhoWor 91*
McClain, Charles James 1931- *WhoAm 90*
McClain, Dennis Douglas 1948- *WhoAm 90*
McClain, Francis Bernard 1864-1925 *AmLegL*
McClain, Jerome Gerald 1939- *St&PR 91*
McClain, Joe 1933- *Ballpl 90*
McClain, John David 1944- *St&PR 91*
McClain, John O 1942- *ConAu 30NR*
Mc Clain, John P *BiDrAPA 89*
McClain, John R. 1952- *St&PR 91*
McClain, Larry French 1937- *St&PR 91*
McClain, Lee Bert 1943- *St&PR 91, WhoAm 90*
McClain, Matthew 1956- *WhoAmA 91*
McClain, Robert W. 1919- *St&PR 91*
McClain, Terry James 1948- *St&PR 91*
McClain, Vickie S. 1959- *WhoSSW 91*
McClain, William Andrew 1913- *WhoWor 91*
Mc Clain, William Harold 1917- *WhoAm 90*
McClain, William K. *St&PR 91*
McClammy, Joseph C. 1934- *St&PR 91*
McClammy, Robert Karl 1942- *St&PR 91*
McClamroch, N. Harris 1942- *WhoAm 90*
McClanahan, Ed 1932- *LiHiK*
McClanahan, John D *WhoAmA 91*
McClanahan, Lowell P. 1943- *St&PR 91*
McClanahan, Rue *BioIn 16*
Mc Clanahan, Rue *WhoAm 90, WhoAmW 91, WhoWor 91*
McClanahan, Rue 1936- *WorAlBi*
McClane, Kenneth Anderson, Jr. 1951- *WhoWrEP 89*
McClane, Robert S. 1939- *St&PR 91*
McClane, Robert Sanford 1939- *WhoAm 90, WhoSSW 91*
Mc Clane, Thomas K 1936- *BiDrAPA 89*
McClannahan, Cindy Ann 1956- *WhoEmL 91*
McClaran, George Joseph 1924- *St&PR 91*
McClaran, George Joseph, Sr. 1924- *WhoAm 90*
McClard, Jack Edward 1946- *WhoEmL 91*
McClaren, Fred 1947- *St&PR 91*
Mc Clarren, Robert Royce 1921- *WhoAm 90*
Mc Clary, Allan R 1923- *BiDrAPA 89*
McClary, James Daly 1917- *WhoAm 90, WhoWor 91*
McClary, Jane McIlvaine *WhoWrEP 89*
McClary, Jane Stevenson *AuBYP 90*
McClary, Jane Stevenson 1919-1990 *ConAu 130, SmATA 64*
McClary, Jim Marston 1949- *WhoSSW 91*
McClary, Merle David 1958- *WhoSSW 91*
McClatchey, Devereaux F. 1906- *St&PR 91*
Mc Clatchey, Devereaux Fore 1906- *WhoAm 90*
McClatchey, John Francis 1929- *WhoAm 90*
McClatchey, Robert Alan 1938- *WhoE 91*
McClatchy, C. K. 1858-1936 *BioIn 16*
McClatchy, C. K. 1927-1989 *BioIn 16*
McClatchy, Charles Kenny 1858-1936 *BioIn 16*
McClatchy, Charles Kenny 1927-1989 *BioIn 16*
McClatchy, James *St&PR 91*
McClatchy, James B. *WhoAm 90*
McClatchy, Joseph Donald 1945- *WhoWrEP 89*
McClaugherty, Joe L. 1951- *WhoEmL 91*
McClaughry, John 1937- *WhoE 91*
McClave, Donald Silsbee 1941- *WhoAm 90*
McClave, James Cummins 1925- *St&PR 91, WhoAm 90*
McClave, William H., Jr. 1943- *ODwPR 91*
McClay, Randy A. 1949- *WhoSSW 91*
McClean, Celeita A. 1956- *WhoAmW 91*
McClean, Graham J. *WhoAm 90*
McClean, Henry Joseph 1941- *St&PR 91*
McClean-Rice, Nicholas T.C. *BiDrAPA 89*
McCleary, Benjamin W. 1944- *St&PR 91*
McCleary, Beryl Nowlin 1929- *WhoAmW 91*
McCleary, Henry Glen 1922- *WhoAm 90*
McCleary, Herbert Elwood 1931- *St&PR 91*
McCleary, James Kent 1941- *St&PR 91*
McCleary, John H. 1952- *WhoE 91*
McCleary, Ken Ward 1947- *WhoSSW 91*
McCleary, Lloyd Everald 1924- *WhoAm 90*
McCleary, Mary Fielding 1951- *WhoAmA 91*
McCleary, Mary Gilkeson 1920- *IntWWM 90*
McCleary, Monica Jean 1952- *WhoAmW 91*
McCleary, Paul Frederick 1930- *WhoWor 91*
McCleary, Robert D. *St&PR 91*
McCleary, Robert L. 1932- *St&PR 91*
McCleerey, Patricia Jean 1950- *WhoAmW 91*
Mc Cleery, William Thomas 1911- *WhoAm 90*
McCleery, William Thomas 1911- *WhoWrEP 89*
McCleese, Dale 1938- *St&PR 91*
McCleland, Desmond Geoffrey 1924- *WhoWor 91*
McClellan, Barbara Vogl 1945- *WhoSSW 91*
McClellan, Bruce 1924- *WhoAm 90*
Mc Clellan, Catharine 1921- *WhoAm 90*
McClellan, Charles Ellard 1936- *WhoAm 90*
McClellan, Charles Ross, Jr. 1932- *St&PR 91*
McClellan, Cindy *BioIn 16*
Mc Clellan, Clara Adams *BiDrAPA 89*
McClellan, Craig Rene 1947- *WhoWor 91*
McClellan, Dan *Ballpl 90*
McClellan, Douglas Eugene 1921- *WhoAmA 91*
Mc Clellan, Edwin 1925- *WhoAm 90*
McClellan, Ezra Ernest 1925- *St&PR 91*
McClellan, George B. 1826-1885 *WorAlBi*
McClellan, George Brinton 1826-1885 *BioIn 16*
McClellan, Harvey 1894-1925 *Ballpl 90*
McClellan, Irina *BioIn 16*
McClellan, James E. 1948- *St&PR 91*
Mc Clellan, James Edward, Jr. 1922- *WhoAm 90*
McClellan, James Harold 1947- *WhoAm 90*
McClellan, Joan C. 1934- *WhoAmW 91*
McClellan, John James, Jr. 1931- *St&PR 91*
McClellan, John L. 1896-1977 *WorAlBi*
McClellan, Jon Montgomery *BiDrAPA 89*
McClellan, Leo F. 1933- *St&PR 91*
McClellan, Lewis Reid 1930- *St&PR 91*
McClellan, Margaret N. *St&PR 91*
McClellan, Mike *BioIn 16*
McClellan, Mildred Nolte 1922- *WhoAmW 91*
McClellan, Richard Augustus 1930- *WhoSSW 91*
McClellan, Robert Edward 1922- *WhoWor 91*
McClellan, Roger O. 1937- *St&PR 91*
McClellan, Roger Orville 1937- *WhoAm 90, WhoWor 91*
McClellan, Sam *NewAgMG*
Mc Clellan, Samuel G *BiDrAPA 89*
McClellan, William Monson 1934- *IntWWM 90*
Mc Clellan, William Monson 1934- *WhoAm 90*
McClelland, Allan 1917-1989 *ConTFT 8*
McClelland, Bramlette 1920- *WhoAm 90*
McClelland, David Clarence *BioIn 16*
McClelland, Doug 1934- *ConAu 31NR*
McClelland, Edward Lee 1941- *WhoSSW 91*
McClelland, George D. 1946- *St&PR 91*
McClelland, Harold Franklin 1918- *WhoAm 90*
Mc Clelland, James Craig 1901- *WhoAm 90*
McClelland, James E., III 1943- *St&PR 91*
McClelland, James Farley, III 1948- *WhoE 91*
McClelland, James L. 1948- *WhoAm 90*
McClelland, James Morris 1943- *St&PR 91*
McClelland, James Ray 1946- *WhoSSW 91*
McClelland, Jean Elizabeth 1949- *WhoAmW 91*
McClelland, Jeanne C *WhoAmA 91*
McClelland, Jeffrey Wilson 1942- *St&PR 91*
McClelland, John P. 1933- *St&PR 91*
Mc Clelland, John Peter 1933- *WhoAm 90*
McClelland, Kerwin T. 1927- *St&PR 91*
McClelland, Michael D. 1938- *St&PR 91*
McClelland, Patricia G. 1944- *WhoAmW 91*
Mc Clelland, Paul A *BiDrAPA 89*
McClelland, Peter Dean 1934- *WhoE 91*
McClelland, Rex Arnold 1936- *St&PR 91, WhoAm 90*
McClelland, Richard Lee 1927- *WhoE 91*
McClelland, Robert 1807-1880 *BiDrUSE 89*
Mc Clelland, Robert Nelson 1929- *WhoAm 90, WhoWor 91*
McClelland, Shearwood, Jr. 1947- *WhoEmL 91*
McClelland, T. Bramlette 1920- *St&PR 91*
McClelland, Tommy Bennett, Jr. 1956- *WhoE 91*
McClelland, W. Clark 1939- *St&PR 91, WhoAm 90*
McClelland, W. Craig 1934- *St&PR 91*
McClelland, William Craig 1934- *WhoAm 90, WhoE 91*
McClements, Robert, Jr. 1928- *St&PR 91, WhoAm 90, WhoE 91, WhoWor 91*
McClenathan, John Leroy 1944- *St&PR 91*
McClenathen, William Richard 1915- *WhoSSW 91*
McClendon, Charles Y. *BioIn 16*
McClendon, Charles Youmans 1923- *WhoAm 90, WhoSSW 91*
McClendon, Cherisse Ella 1962- *WhoAmW 91*
McClendon, Edwin James 1921- *WhoAm 90*
McClendon, Ernestine 1918- *DrBlPA 90*
Mc Clendon, Fred Vernon *WhoSSW 91, WhoWor 91*
McClendon, James 1948- *BiDrAPA 89*
McClendon, Kathryn Joyce 1959- *WhoE 91*
McClendon, Lloyd 1959- *Ballpl 90*
McClendon, Mary Angie 1929- *St&PR 91*
McClendon, Maxine 1931- *WhoAmA 91, WhoAmW 91*
McClendon, Rose 1884?-1936 *BioIn 16, EarBlAP, NotWoAT*
McClendon, Rose 1885-1936 *DrBlPA 90*
McClendon, Sarah *BioIn 16*
Mc Clendon, Sarah Newcomb 1910- *WhoAm 90*
Mc Clendon, William Hutchinson, III 1933- *WhoAm 90*
McClendon, Zach, Jr. 1937- *St&PR 91*
McClennan, Mort C. 1945- *St&PR 91*
McClennen, George Michael 1943- *St&PR 91*
Mc Clennen, Louis 1912- *WhoAm 90*
McClennen, Miriam J. 1923- *WhoAmW 91*
Mc Clenney, Byron Nelson 1939- *WhoAm 90*
McClenney, Cheryl Ilene 1948- *WhoAmA 91*
McClenny, Dan Clark 1923- *St&PR 91*
McClenon, James 1947- *EncPaPR 91*
McClenon, John Raymond 1937- *WhoAm 90*
McClerklin, Ernest Nobin 1951- *WhoSSW 91*
McClernon, Crystal Dawn 1960- *WhoWrEP 89*
McCleskey, Melissa Dannelly 1959- *ODwPR 91*
McClester, John Richard 1923- *WhoAm 90*
McCliggott, Duane J. 1935- *St&PR 91*
McClintic, Howard Gresson 1951- *WhoE 91*
McClintic, Madison P. 1928- *St&PR 91*
McClintick, Robert Roy 1924- *St&PR 91*
Mc Clintock, Archie Glenn 1911- *WhoAm 90*
McClintock, Barbara *BioIn 16*
McClintock, Barbara 1902- *BioAmW, WhoAm 90, WhoAmW 91, WhoE 91, WhoWor 91, WorAlBi*
McClintock, Beatrice Kellogg *BioIn 16*
McClintock, Ernie *DrBlPA 90*
McClintock, George Dunlap 1920- *WhoAm 90*
McClintock, Janet Marie 1947- *WhoAmW 91*
McClintock, Jessica 1930- *WhoAm 90, WhoAmW 91*
McClintock, Laura Leigh *BiDrAPA 89*
McClintock, Marshall 1906-1967 *AuBYP 90*
McClintock, May Garelick *ConAu 130*
McClintock, Robert Bayles 1946- *IntWWM 90*
McClintock, Robert James *BiDrAPA 89*
McClintock, Robert L. 1926- *St&PR 91*
McClintock, Sandra Janise 1938- *WhoAmW 91*
McClintock, Simms 1927- *WhoSSW 91*
McClintock, Theodore 1902-1971 *AuBYP 90*
McClintock, Theodore E. 1940- *St&PR 91*
McClintock-Hernandez, Kenneth Davison 1957- *WhoHisp 91*
Mc Clinton, Donald G. 1933- *WhoAm 90*
McClinton, Robert 1950- *St&PR 91*
McClish, C. Polly 1933- *WhoAmW 91*
McClister, Debra L. 1954- *St&PR 91*
McClister, Debra Lynn 1954- *WhoAmW 91*
McClory, Robert N. 1908-1988 *BioIn 16*
McCloskey, Candice Joy 1953- *WhoSSW 91*
McCloskey, Daniel 1936- *St&PR 91*

McCloskey, Deborah Haywood 1952- *WhoAmW 91*
McCloskey, Donald N 1942- *ConAu 31NR*
McCloskey, Donald Nansen 1942- *WhoAm 90*
McCloskey, Downs, Jr. 1930- *St&PR 91*
McCloskey, Frank 1939- *WhoAm 90*
McCloskey, J. Michael *BioIn 16*
McCloskey, Jack *WhoAm 90*
McCloskey, James Boswell 1945- *WhoSSW 91*
McCloskey, James P. 1941- *St&PR 91*
McCloskey, James W. 1931- *St&PR 91*
McCloskey, John 1862-1940 *Ballpl 90*
McCloskey, John Michael *BioIn 16*
McCloskey, John Michael 1934- *WhoAm 90*
McCloskey, Mark 1938- *WhoWrEP 89*
McCloskey, Paul N. *BioIn 16*
Mc Closkey, Paul N., Jr. 1927- *WhoAm 90*
McCloskey, Paul N., Jr. 1927- *WorAlBi*
McCloskey, Pete *BioIn 16*
McCloskey, Peter Francis 1935- *WhoAm 90*
McCloskey, Robert 1914- *AuBYP 90*
Mc Closkey, Robert 1914- *WhoAm 90*
Mc Closkey, Robert James 1922- *WhoAm 90, WhoE 91*
McCloskey, William Joseph 1944- *WhoE 91*
McCloud, Anece Faison 1937- *WhoSSW 91*
McCloud, Lynn 1950- *WhoE 91*
McCloud, Raymond Ward 1955- *St&PR 91*
McCloud, Ronald Bernard 1948- *St&PR 91*
McCloud, Van *TwCCr&M 91*
McCloy, Helen 1904- *TwCCr&M 91*
McCloy, James F. 1941- *BioIn 16*
McCloy, John Jay 1895-1989 *AnObit 1989, BioIn 16*
McCloy, John Jay, II 1937- *WhoE 91*
McCloy, Kristin *BioIn 16*
McCloy, William Ashby 1913- *WhoAm 90*
McCluer, Daniel J. 1937- *St&PR 91, WhoAm 90*
McCluney, Gregory Day 1946- *WhoSSW 91*
McClung, A. Keith, Jr. 1934- *St&PR 91*
McClung, Christina June 1948- *WhoAmW 91*
McClung, David W. 1927- *St&PR 91*
McClung, James A. 1937- *St&PR 91*
McClung, James Allen 1937- *WhoAm 90*
McClung, Jim Hill 1936- *St&PR 91*
Mc Clung, Jim Hill 1936- *WhoSSW 91*
McClung, John Alexander 1804-1859 *LiHiK*
McClung, John Robinson, Jr. 1914- *WhoAm 90, WhoWor 91*
McClung, Kenneth Austin, Jr. 1947- *WhoE 91, WhoWor 91*
Mc Clung, Leland Swint 1910- *WhoAm 90*
McClung, Mark Richard *BiDrAPA 89*
McClung, Merle Steven 1943- *WhoWor 91*
McClung, Nellie 1873-1951 *FemiCLE*
McClung, Nellie Letitia 1873-1951 *DcLB 92 [port]*
McClung, Richard Goehring 1913- *WhoAm 90*
McClung, Robert Edward *BiDrAPA 89*
McClung, Robert M. 1916- *WhoWrEP 89*
McClung, Robert Marshall 1916- *AuBYP 90*
McClung, Robert Warren 1928- *WhoSSW 91*
McClure, Alan Campbell 1923- *WhoAm 90*
McClure, Alvin Bruce 1953- *WhoEmL 91*
McClure, Angeline Kitchens 1945- *WhoAmW 91*
McClure, Anna Jo 1928- *WhoAmW 91*
McClure, Betty Padgett 1929- *St&PR 91*
McClure, Bob 1952- *Ballpl 90*
McClure, Brooks 1919- *WhoAm 90*
McClure, Bruce Edward 1954- *WhoSSW 91*
McClure, Charles J. 1935- *St&PR 91*
McClure, Charles Stanton 1953- *WhoEmL 91*
McClure, Charlotte Swain 1921- *WhoSSW 91*
McClure, Christopher Ewart 1943- *WhoSSW 91*
McClure, Connie Diane 1956- *WhoSSW 91*
McClure, Constance 1934- *WhoAmA 91*
McClure, Darrell *EncACom*
McClure, David H. 1948- *WhoSSW 91*
Mc Clure, David J *BiDrAPA 89*
McClure, Donald G., Jr. 1943- *St&PR 91*
McClure, Donald J. 1940- *St&PR 91*
Mc Clure, Donald Stuart 1920- *WhoAm 90*
McClure, Doug 1935- *WhoAm 90*
McClure, Douglas Templeton 1924- *St&PR 91*
McClure, Florence Helen 1930- *WhoAmW 91*
McClure, Frederick Donald 1954- *WhoAm 90*
McClure, George R. 1921- *St&PR 91*
Mc Clure, George Tarrence 1928- *WhoAm 90*
McClure, Grover Benjamin 1918- *WhoAm 90*
McClure, Howard Gundry 1936- *St&PR 91*
McClure, James 1939- *TwCCr&M 91, WorAlBi*
McClure, James A. 1924- *WhoAm 90, WhoWor 91*
Mc Clure, James J., Jr. 1920- *WhoAm 90*
McClure, Janice Lee 1941- *WhoAmW 91*
McClure, Jessica *BioIn 16*
McClure, John A. 1945- *ConAu 132*
McClure, John Richard 1955- *WhoSSW 91*
McClure, Marilyn *BioIn 16*
McClure, Mary Anne 1939- *WhoAmW 91*
McClure, Michael DeStewart 1942- *WhoWor 91*
Mc Clure, Michael Thomas 1932- *WhoAm 90*
McClure, Michael Thomas 1932- *WhoWrEP 89*
McClure, Polley Ann 1943- *WhoAmW 91*
McClure, Rex 1931- *St&PR 91*
McClure, Richard Fowler 1927- *WhoAm 90*
Mc Clure, Robert M. *WhoSSW 91*
McClure, Roger John 1943- *WhoSSW 91*
McClure, Sam S. *BioIn 16*
Mc Clure, Samuel S *BiDrAPA 89*
McClure, Samuel S. 1857-1949 *WorAlBi*
Mc Clure, Scott Helm 1949- *BiDrAPA 89*
Mc Clure, Sharon W 1948- *BiDrAPA 89*
McClure, Thomas Edward 1954- *WhoEmL 91*
McClure, Thomas F 1920- *WhoAmA 91*
McClure, Thomas Lynn 1952- *WhoSSW 91*
McClure, Wesley Allan 1959- *WhoE 91*
McClure, Wesley C. *WhoAm 90*
McClure, William Earl 1946- *WhoEmL 91*
Mc Clure, William Pendleton 1925- *WhoAm 90*
McClure, William Robert 1941- *WhoE 91*
McClurg, Edie *BioIn 16, ConTFT 8*
McClurg, James 1746?-1823 *BioIn 16*
McClurg, James Edward 1945- *WhoAm 90*
McClurg, Ned S. 1945- *St&PR 91*
McClurg, Patricia A. 1939- *WhoAm 90, WhoAmW 91*
McClurkin, Iola Taylor 1930- *WhoAmW 91*
McCluskey, Annette *ODwPR 91*
McCluskey, Carolina Paciencia Salas 1949- *WhoAmW 91*
McCluskey, Edward Joseph 1929- *WhoAm 90, WhoWor 91*
McCluskey, Jean Louise 1947- *WhoE 91*
McCluskey, Michael 1951- *ODwPR 91*
McCluskey, Neil Gerard 1920- *WhoE 91*
McCluskey, Norman Dean 1952- *WhoSSW 91*
McCluskey, Richard Thomas 1943- *St&PR 91*
McCluskey, Robert A. 1917- *St&PR 91*
McCluskey, Stephen Christian 1942- *St&PR 91*
McCluskey, Walter H. 1939- *St&PR 91*
McClusky, William John, II 1960- *WhoE 91*
McClymond, J. L., Jr. 1928- *St&PR 91*
McClymonds, Jean Ellen *WhoAmW 91*
McClymonds, Marita Martha Petzoldt 1935- *IntWWM 90*
McClymont, Eleanor Jean 1938- *WhoE 91*
Mc Clymont, Hamilton 1944- *WhoAm 90*
McClymont, Kenneth Ross 1924- *WhoAm 90*
Mccoard, Barbar Fern *BiDrAPA 89*
McCobb, John Bradford, Jr. 1939- *WhoWor 91*
Mc Coin, John Mack 1931- *WhoWor 91*
McCole, Robert Richard 1939- *St&PR 91*
McColgan, Andree Lorraine Eliz 1925- *WhoE 91*
McColgan, John 1946- *ConAu 132*
McColl, Bill *BioIn 16*
McColl, Hugh L., Jr. *BioIn 16*
McColl, Hugh L., Jr. 1935- *St&PR 91*
McColl, Hugh Leon, Jr. 1935- *WhoAm 90, WhoSSW 91*
McColl, James George 1938- *St&PR 91*
McColl, John Angus 1928- *St&PR 91*
McColl, John Duncan 1925- *WhoAm 90, WhoSSW 91*
McColl, William Duncan 1933- *IntWWM 90*
McCollam, William, Jr. 1925- *St&PR 91, WhoAm 90*
McColley, Diane Kelsey 1934- *ConAu 130*
McColley, Robert McNair 1933- *WhoAm 90*
McColley, Susanna Antonia 1961- *WhoAmW 91*
McColley, Sutherland 1937- *WhoAmA 91, WhoE 91*
McCollister, George Maxwell 1928- *St&PR 91*
Mc Collister, John Charles 1935- *WhoAm 90*
McCollister, John S. *St&PR 91*
McCollister, Paul Wayne 1915- *St&PR 91*
McColloch, Murray M. 1926- *St&PR 91*
McCollom, Brian Edwin 1950- *WhoE 91*
Mc Collom, Kenneth Allen 1922- *WhoAm 90*
McCollough, Joseph R. 1943- *St&PR 91*
McCollough, Michael Leon 1953- *WhoWor 91*
Mc Collough, Newton Clark, III 1934- *WhoAm 90*
McCollough, W. H. 1928- *St&PR 91*
McCollough, W. Vance 1947- *WhoEmL 91*
McCollough, William Hugh 1928- *WhoAm 90*
McCollow, J. G. 1919- *St&PR 91*
McCollow, Thomas James 1925- *St&PR 91*
McCollum, Allan 1944- *WhoAmA 91*
McCollum, Clifford Glenn 1919- *WhoAm 90*
McCollum, Donna Jewell 1957- *WhoAmW 91*
Mc Collum, Ira William, Jr. 1944- *WhoAm 90, WhoSSW 91*
McCollum, James Fountain 1946- *WhoEmL 91, WhoSSW 91, WhoWor 91*
McCollum, John Morris 1922- *WhoAm 90*
McCollum, Julie M. 1946- *St&PR 91*
McCollum, Mack D. 1932- *St&PR 91*
McCollum, Mike L 1939- *WhoAmA 91*
McCollum, Randall Hampton 1944- *WhoE 91*
McCollum, Robert Wayne 1925- *WhoAm 90*
McCollum, Shaune *BioIn 16*
McCollum, Susan Hill 1955- *WhoEmL 91*
McCollum, William Bruce 1951- *St&PR 91*
McCollum, William Edward *BiDrAPA 89*
McCollum, William Henry 1930- *St&PR 91*
McColman, William Ernest 1947- *WhoWor 91*
McColough, C Peter 1922- *News 90 [port]*
McColough, C. Peter 1922- *St&PR 91*
Mc Colough, Charles Peter 1922- *WhoAm 90*
McColvin, Lionel Roy 1896-1976 *AuBYP 90*
McComas, James Douglas 1928- *WhoAm 90, WhoSSW 91*
McComas, Louis Gough, Jr. 1932- *St&PR 91*
McComas, Murray Knabb 1936- *St&PR 91, WhoAm 90*
McComb, Ray Buel, Jr. 1945- *WhoSSW 91, WhoWor 91*
McComber, Donald H. 1929- *St&PR 91*
Mc Combs, G. B. 1909- *WhoAm 90*
McCombs, Maxwell E 1938- *ConAu 31NR*
McCombs, Red *WhoAm 90*
Mc Comic, Robert Barry 1939- *WhoAm 90*
McComiskey, Bruce Thomas 1963- *WhoWrEP 89*
McCommon, Faye di Carla 1955- *WhoAmW 91*
McCommon, Hubert 1929- *WhoAm 90*
McCommon, Robert L., Jr. 1925- *St&PR 91*
McCommons, James V. 1859-1941 *AmLegL*
McComsey, Robert Ronald 1944- *WhoAm 90, WhoWor 91*
Mc Conagha, Glenn Lowery 1910- *WhoAm 90, WhoWor 91*
McConahey, Stephen George 1943- *WhoAm 90*
McConatha, Phillip Douglas 1948- *WhoE 91*
McConathy, Dale *BioIn 16*
McConaughy, David Francis 1932- *St&PR 91*
Mc Conaughy, Robert S 1946- *BiDrAPA 89*
McConaughy, Walter Patrick 1908- *BioIn 16*
McConchie, John Lewis 1938- *St&PR 91*
McCone, Susan Jonal 1949- *WhoE 91*
McConeghey, John Francis 1923- *St&PR 91*
McConkey, Dale Durant 1928- *WhoAm 90*
McConkey, David Lee 1948- *IntWWM 90*
McConkey, James R. 1921- *WhoAm 90, WhoWrEP 89*
Mc Conkie, George Wilson 1937- *WhoAm 90*
McConnaughey, George C., Jr. 1925- *St&PR 91*
Mc Connaughey, George Carlton, Jr. 1925- *WhoAm 90*
McConnaughey, Harlow 1911- *St&PR 91*
McConnaughey, James Walter 1951- *WhoE 91, WhoEmL 91, WhoWor 91*
McConnaughy, John E. 1929- *St&PR 91*
Mc Connaughy, John Edward, Jr. 1929- *WhoAm 90*
McConnaughy, Thomas Bowen, Jr. 1942- *WhoAm 90*
McConnel, James W. 1954- *WhoSSW 91*
McConnel, W. Bruce, III 1943- *St&PR 91*
McConnell, Addison Mitchell, Jr. 1942- *WhoAm 90, WhoSSW 91, WhoWor 91*
McConnell, Albert Lynn 1946- *WhoSSW 91*
McConnell, Alicia *BioIn 16*
McConnell, Amby 1883-1942 *Ballpl 90*
McConnell, Barbara 1943- *WhoAmW 91*
Mc Connell, Bruce Bower *BiDrAPA 89*
McConnell, Calvin Dale 1928- *WhoAm 90*
McConnell, Carl 1926- *BioIn 16*
McConnell, Charles Goodloe 1943- *St&PR 91, WhoAm 90*
McConnell, Charles Warren 1939- *WhoE 91*
McConnell, David Graham 1926- *WhoAm 90*
McConnell, David Moffatt 1912- *WhoAm 90*
McConnell, David Stuart 1935- *WhoAm 90*
McConnell, Dorothy *BioIn 16*
McConnell, Dorothy 1900?-1989 *ConAu 129*
McConnell, E. Hoy, II 1941- *St&PR 91, WhoAm 90*
McConnell, Eamonn Brian Patrick 1959- *WhoWor 91*
McConnell, Earl P. 1927- *St&PR 91*
Mc Connell, Edward Bosworth 1920- *WhoAm 90*
McConnell, Elliott Bonnell, Jr. 1928- *WhoAm 90*
McConnell, Florence Leonard 1931- *WhoAmW 91, WhoSSW 91*
Mc Connell, Freeman Erton 1914- *WhoAm 90*
McConnell, George 1877-1964 *Ballpl 90*
McConnell, Harden Marsden 1927- *WhoAm 90*
McConnell, Harry Cecil 1913- *IntWWM 90*
McConnell, J. Daniel 1944- *ODwPR 91*
McConnell, J. H. Tyler 1914-1989 *BioIn 16*
McConnell, J. R. *BioIn 16*
McConnell, Jack Lewis 1934- *St&PR 91*
McConnell, James 1915-1988 *BioIn 16*
McConnell, James David 1955- *WhoEmL 91*
McConnell, James Desmond 1930- *WhoWor 91*
McConnell, James F. 1933- *St&PR 91*
McConnell, James Guy 1947- *WhoWor 91*
McConnell, James V. 1925-1990 *BioIn 16, ConAu 131*
McConnell, James Whitney 1946- *WhoEmL 91*
McConnell, Jill Robb 1940- *WhoAmW 91*
Mc Connell, John Douglas 1932- *WhoAm 90*
McConnell, John Francis *BioIn 16*
McConnell, John H. 1923- *St&PR 91*
McConnell, John Henderson 1923- *WhoAm 90*
McConnell, John Howard 1933- *WhoE 91*
McConnell, John Thomas 1945- *WhoAm 90*
McConnell, John W. 1941- *St&PR 91*
Mc Connell, John Wilkinson 1907- *WhoAm 90*
McConnell, John William, Jr. 1921- *WhoAm 90*
McConnell, Joseph H. 1906- *St&PR 91*
McConnell, Kenneth J. 1926- *St&PR 91*
McConnell, Marie Andrews 1938- *WhoSSW 91, WhoWor 91*
McConnell, Melissa 1953- *WhoAmW 91*
McConnell, Michael 1954- *WhoAm 90*
McConnell, Michael Patrick 1948- *WhoAmA 91*
McConnell, Patricia Ann 1935- *WhoAmW 91*
McConnell, Paul Stewart 1955- *WhoEmL 91*
McConnell, R. A. 1914- *EncO&P 3*
McConnell, Robert A. *BioIn 16*
McConnell, Robert A. 1914- *EncPaPR 91*
Mc Connell, Robert Chalmers 1913- *WhoAm 90*
Mc Connell, Robert Eastwood 1930- *WhoAm 90*
McConnell, Robin Ellen 1954- *WhoAmW 91*
McConnell, Shirley Russell 1934- *WhoSSW 91*

McConnell, Stephen A. 1952- *St&PR 91, WhoAm 90*
Mc Connell, Stuart Bonau 1941- *BiDrAPA 89*
McConnell, Susan E. 1943- *St&PR 91*
McConnell, Thomas Lee 1937- *BiDrAPA 89*
McConnell, Thomas R. 1901-1989 *BioIn 16*
McConnell, Viola Carlberg 1903- *WhoAmW 91*
Mc Connell, Whitman Hurst *BiDrAPA 89*
McConnell, William Arthur 1918- *WhoAm 90*
McConnell, William Thompson 1933- *St&PR 91, WhoAm 90*
McConner, Dorothy 1929- *St&PR 91*
McConner, Ora B. 1929- *WhoAmW 91, WhoWor 91*
McConnico, Hilton *BioIn 16*
McConniel, Lynette *BioIn 16*
McConomy, James Herbert 1937- *WhoAm 90*
McConomy, Thomas Arthur 1933- *St&PR 91, WhoAm 90, WhoE 91*
McConvey, D'Arcy F. 1918- *St&PR 91*
Mc Conville, Brian John 1933- *BiDrAPA 89*
McConville, Clarence Joseph 1925- *St&PR 91*
McConville, John A. *WhoSSW 91*
McConville, John Mitchell 1931- *St&PR 91*
McConville, William *WhoAm 90*
McCoo, Edward J. *EarBlAP*
McCoo, Marilyn *BioIn 16, DrBlPA 90*
McCoo, Mary H. *BioIn 16*
McCooe, Terry Alan 1950- *WhoEmL 91*
McCoog, James H. 1931- *St&PR 91*
McCook, Allen W. 1947- *St&PR 91*
McCook, John S. 1913-1988 *BioIn 16*
McCook, Richard Paul 1953- *St&PR 91*
McCool, Billy 1944- *Ballpl 90*
Mc Cool, Dick C *BiDrAPA 89*
McCool, James F. *AmLegL*
McCool, Pamela Lynn Reed 1963- *WhoAmW 91*
McCool, Richard Bunch 1925- *WhoWor 91*
Mc Cool, Woodford B. 1915- *WhoAm 90*
McCoole, Robert F. 1950- *St&PR 91*
McCoppin, Peter *WhoAm 90*
McCord, Alice Bird *WhoE 91*
Mc Cord, Berry Lee 1940- *BiDrAPA 89*
McCord, Bert *BioIn 16*
McCord, Betty J. 1940- *WhoSSW 91*
McCord, Carol Finney 1951- *WhoSSW 91*
McCord, Carole Ann 1948- *WhoWrEP 89*
McCord, Catherine Gumm 1926- *WhoWrEP 89*
McCord, Christian *WhoWrEP 89*
McCord, Dale Lynn 1942- *WhoSSW 91*
McCord, David 1897- *AuBYP 90*
McCord, David Thompson Watson 1897- *BioIn 16*
McCord, Gary *BioIn 16*
McCord, George Edward 1938- *St&PR 91, WhoE 91*
Mc Cord, Guyte Pierce, Jr. 1914- *WhoSSW 91*
McCord, Howard Lawrence 1932- *WhoWrEP 89*
McCord, J. T. 1945- *MusmAFA*
McCord, James Iley *NewYTBS 90 [port]*
McCord, James Iley 1919-1990 *BioIn 16*
McCord, James W., Jr. 1924- *WorAlBi*
McCord, Joe Milton 1945- *WhoAm 90*
Mc Cord, John Harrison 1934- *WhoAm 90*
Mc Cord, Kenneth Armstrong 1921- *WhoAm 90*
McCord, Louisa 1810-1879 *FemiCLE*
Mc Cord, Marshal 1917- *WhoAm 90*
McCord, Patrick Joseph 1938- *St&PR 91*
McCord, Paul Mark 1950- *WhoSSW 91*
McCord, Ronald John 1938- *St&PR 91*
McCord, Steven Grant 1948- *St&PR 91*
McCord, Terry R. *ODwPR 91*
McCord, Wilfred Murray 1927- *St&PR 91*
McCord, William Charles 1928- *St&PR 91, WhoSSW 91, WhoWor 91*
McCord, William Maxwell 1930- *WhoAm 90, WhoE 91*
Mc Cord, William Mellen 1907- *WhoAm 90*
McCorduck, Pamela Ann 1940- *WhoE 91*
Mc Corison, Marcus Allen 1926- *WhoAm 90*
McCorison, Marcus Allen 1926- *WhoAmA 91*
Mc Corison, Marcus Allen 1926- *WhoE 91*
McCorkele, Pope, Jr. 1925- *St&PR 91*
McCorkell, Peter L. 1946- *St&PR 91*
McCorkindale, Douglas H. *BioIn 16*
McCorkindale, Douglas H. 1939- *St&PR 91*
McCorkindale, Douglas Hamilton 1939- *WhoAm 90*
McCorkle, Allan James *BiDrAPA 89*
McCorkle, Allan James 1931- *St&PR 91*
Mc Corkle, Allan James 1931- *WhoSSW 91, WhoWor 91*
McCorkle, Barry Scott 1961- *BiDrAPA 89*
McCorkle, Constance Marie 1948- *WhoAmW 91*
McCorkle, Dennis *NewAgMG*
McCorkle, Francis Williamson 1922- *WhoAm 90*
McCorkle, Horace Jackson 1905- *WhoAm 90*
McCorkle, Liza Louise 1961- *WhoAmW 91*
McCorkle, Michael 1944- *St&PR 91, WhoAm 90*
McCorkle, Michael 1957- *WhoSSW 91*
McCorkle, Susannah *BioIn 16*
McCorkle, William Dickins 1928- *St&PR 91*
McCormac, Billy Murray 1920- *WhoAm 90*
McCormac, John Simmen 1930- *St&PR 91*
Mc Cormac, John Waverly 1926- *WhoAm 90*
McCormack, Charles N. 1950- *St&PR 91*
McCormack, Donald Paul 1926- *WhoAm 90, WhoWor 91*
McCormack, Edward Joseph, Jr. 1923- *WhoE 91*
McCormack, Francis Xavier 1929- *St&PR 91*
Mc Cormack, Francis Xavier 1929- *WhoAm 90*
Mc Cormack, Fred Allen 1930- *WhoAm 90*
McCormack, Grace 1908- *WhoE 91*
McCormack, Grace Lynette 1928- *WhoAmW 91*
McCormack, James J. 1942- *St&PR 91*
McCormack, James Stuckey 1931- *WhoSSW 91*
McCormack, John *BioIn 16*
McCormack, John 1884-1945 *PenDiMP, WorAlBi*
Mc Cormack, John A *BiDrAPA 89*
McCormack, John A. 1936- *St&PR 91*
Mc Cormack, John C 1935- *BiDrAPA 89*
McCormack, John Joseph 1932- *WhoAm 90*
McCormack, John Joseph, Jr. 1944- *WhoAm 90*
McCormack, John W. 1891-1980 *WorAlBi*
McCormack, Joseph Andrew 1944- *WhoAm 90*
McCormack, Kimberly Robin 1960- *WhoAmW 91*
McCormack, Lowell Ray 1925- *WhoAmW 91, WhoWor 91*
McCormack, Marjorie Guth 1934- *WhoWor 91*
McCormack, Mark Hume 1930- *WhoAm 90*
McCormack, Mary Beatrice 1925- *St&PR 91, WhoAmW 91*
McCormack, Maryanne *BioIn 16*
McCormack, Mike *WhoAm 90*
McCormack, Olivia *WhoWrEP 89*
McCormack, Patricia Seger 1927- *WhoAm 90*
McCormack, Patty 1945- *ConTFT 8*
McCormack, Richard Austin *St&PR 91*
McCormack, Richard Thomas Fox 1941- *WhoAm 90*
McCormack, Robert Emmett, Jr. 1923- *St&PR 91*
McCormack, Sharon Renda 1961- *WhoWrEP 89*
McCormack, Thomas Joseph 1932- *St&PR 91*
Mc Cormack, Thomas Joseph 1932- *WhoAm 90*
McCormack, Veronica *WhoE 91*
McCormack, William Arthur 1951- *WhoSSW 91*
McCormack, William Charles 1929- *WhoAm 90*
McCormally, Kevin Jay 1950- *WhoE 91*
McCormick, Adele von Rust 1929- *WhoWor 91*
McCormick, Alma Heflin *AuBYP 90*
McCormick, Alma Heflin 1910- *WhoAmW 91*
McCormick, Anne 1880-1954 *FemiCLE*
McCormick, Anne O'Hare 1880-1954 *BioIn 16*
McCormick, Barnes Warnock 1926- *WhoAm 90*
McCormick, Barry 1874-1956 *Ballpl 90*
McCormick, Bill *AuBYP 90, Ballpl 90*
McCormick, Blake Eric 1964- *WhoE 91*
McCormick, Charles Clair 1946- *WhoE 91*
McCormick, Charles Perry, Jr. 1928- *St&PR 91, WhoAm 90, WhoE 91*
McCormick, Charles Tilford 1889-1963 *BioIn 16*
McCormick, Chris Weldon 1954- *WhoSSW 91*
McCormick, Clarence James 1925- *WhoAm 90*
McCormick, Clarence Okey 1925- *St&PR 91*
McCormick, Cyrus H. 1809-1884 *WorAlBi*
McCormick, David Clement 1930- *IntWWM 90*
McCormick, Dennis Ray 1942- *WhoAm 90*
McCormick, Denton E. 1943- *St&PR 91*
McCormick, Don 1940- *St&PR 91*
McCormick, Donald 1911- *ConAu 32NR*
Mc Cormick, Donald Bruce 1932- *WhoAm 90, WhoSSW 91*
McCormick, Donald Clayton 1934- *St&PR 91*
McCormick, Donald F. 1931- *WhoAm 90*
McCormick, Donna Lisa 1955- *WhoE 91*
McCormick, Edmund J. *St&PR 91*
McCormick, Edmund J. *BioIn 16*
Mc Cormick, Edward Allen 1925- *WhoAm 90*
McCormick, Elaine Alice 1943- *WhoAmW 91, WhoE 91*
McCormick, Floyd Guy, Jr. 1927- *WhoAm 90*
McCormick, Frank 1911-1982 *Ballpl 90*
McCormick, G. Roger 1940- *St&PR 91*
McCormick, Gedney John 1936- *St&PR 91*
McCormick, George Paul, Jr. 1947- *WhoEmL 91*
McCormick, Henry H. 1840-1885 *AmLegL*
Mc Cormick, Hope Baldwin 1919- *WhoAm 90*
McCormick, James C. 1938- *St&PR 91*
Mc Cormick, James Charles 1938- *WhoAm 90*
McCormick, James Clarence 1924- *WhoAm 90*
McCormick, James E. 1927- *St&PR 91*
McCormick, James Edward 1927- *WhoAm 90*
Mc Cormick, James Harold 1938- *WhoAm 90, WhoE 91*
McCormick, James Hillman 1921- *WhoSSW 91*
McCormick, James Loren 1926- *WhoAm 90*
McCormick, James M. 1925- *St&PR 91*
McCormick, James Michael 1947- *WhoAm 90*
McCormick, Jane Griffel 1939- *WhoAmW 91*
Mc Cormick, Jay E 1913- *BiDrAPA 89*
McCormick, Jill Marie 1959- *WhoAmW 91*
McCormick, Jim 1856-1918 *Ballpl 90*
McCormick, Joan A. 1938- *St&PR 91*
McCormick, John 1918- *BioIn 16*
McCormick, John Crimmins 1935- *WhoAm 90*
McCormick, John Francis 1933- *St&PR 91*
McCormick, John Hoyle 1933- *WhoSSW 91*
Mc Cormick, John Owen 1918- *WhoAm 90*
McCormick, John R. *BioIn 16*
McCormick, John R. 1942- *St&PR 91*
McCormick, Joseph Burke 1957- *WhoEmL 91*
McCormick, Katharine H 1882-1960 *WhoAmA 91N*
Mc Cormick, Kenneth Dale 1906- *WhoAm 90*
McCormick, Kenneth Dale 1906- *WhoWrEP 89*
McCormick, Leslie L. 1961- *WhoAmW 91*
McCormick, Leta Marie 1930- *St&PR 91*
McCormick, Louise L. 1942- *St&PR 91*
McCormick, Loyd Weldon 1928- *WhoAm 90*
McCormick, Lynellar Y 1955- *BiDrAPA 89*
McCormick, Mariann Honor 1942- *WhoAmW 91*
Mc Cormick, Mark Gerald F 1945- *BiDrAPA 89*
McCormick, Maureen Olivea 1956- *WhoAmW 91*
McCormick, Merle 1941- *St&PR 91*
McCormick, Michael Andrew 1939- *WhoE 91*
McCormick, Michael D. 1948- *St&PR 91*
McCormick, Mike 1917-1976 *Ballpl 90*
McCormick, Mike 1938- *Ballpl 90*
McCormick, Moose 1881-1962 *Ballpl 90*
McCormick, Nancy Jane 1935- *WhoAmW 91, WhoSSW 91*
McCormick, Pam 1946- *WhoAmA 91*
McCormick, Pamela Ann 1948- *WhoE 91*
McCormick, Pat *ODwPR 91*
McCormick, Patrick M.J. 1952- *WhoWrEP 89*
McCormick, Richard D. 1940- *St&PR 91*
McCormick, Richard David 1940- *WhoAm 90*
McCormick, Richard L. 1943- *St&PR 91*
Mc Cormick, Richard Patrick 1916- *WhoAm 90*
McCormick, Robert Junior 1929- *WhoAm 90*
McCormick, Robert Lee 1928- *St&PR 91*
McCormick, Robert Matthew, III 1938- *WhoAm 90*
McCormick, Robert Rutherford 1880-1955 *BioIn 16, WorAlBi*
McCormick, Robert Sanderson 1849-1919 *BioIn 16*
McCormick, Samuel Lewis, III 1949- *WhoSSW 91*
McCormick, Scott, III 1959- *BiDrAPA 89*
McCormick, Stephen Francis 1937- *St&PR 91*
McCormick, Steven Thomas 1955- *WhoEmL 91, WhoSSW 91*
McCormick, Stewart W. 1925- *St&PR 91*
McCormick, Susan Konn 1953- *St&PR 91, WhoAmW 91*
Mc Cormick, Thaddeus C, Jr. *BiDrAPA 89*
McCormick, Thomas Clark 1929- *St&PR 91*
Mc Cormick, Thomas E 1924- *BiDrAPA 89*
McCormick, Thomas Emerick 1953- *WhoE 91*
Mc Cormick, Thomas Francis 1929- *WhoAm 90*
McCormick, Thomas H. 1940- *St&PR 91*
McCormick, Thomas Jay 1946- *WhoE 91*
Mc Cormick, Thomas Julian 1925- *WhoAm 90*
McCormick, Thomas Patrick 1953- *St&PR 91*
Mc Cormick, Thomas Roy 1952- *BiDrAPA 89*
McCormick, Wanda Fay 1948- *WhoAmW 91*
McCormick, Wilfred 1903- *AuBYP 90*
McCormick, Willard Francis 1904-1989 *BioIn 16*
McCormick, William Edward 1912- *WhoAm 90, WhoWor 91*
Mc Cormick, William Frederick 1933- *WhoAm 90*
Mc Cormick, William Martin 1921- *WhoAm 90, WhoE 91*
McCormick, William T., Jr. 1944- *St&PR 91*
McCormick, William Thomas, Jr. 1944- *WhoAm 90*
Mc Cormick, Willie Mae Ward 1908- *WhoAmW 91, WhoSSW 91, WhoWor 91*
McCormick-Sakurai, Jo Mary 1918- *WhoE 91*
McCorquodale, Barbara *MajTwCW*
McCorquodale, Barbara Hamilton Cartland 1902- *BioIn 16*
McCorry, Mary Elenore 1925- *WhoAmW 91*
McCorry, Patrick George 1941- *St&PR 91*
McCorry, Vincent P *NewYTBS 90*
McCorry, Vincent P. 1909-1990 *BioIn 16, ConAu 131*
McCorvey, Norma *BioIn 16*
Mc Cory, Catherine L *BiDrAPA 89*
McCosh, David J 1903-1980 *WhoAmA 91N*
McCoskey, James John 1939- *St&PR 91*
McCosky, Barney 1918- *Ballpl 90*
McCotter, Burney Richard 1920- *St&PR 91*
McCotter, James Rawson 1943- *WhoAm 90*
McCoubrey, R. James 1944- *WhoAm 90*
McCoubrey, Sarah 1956- *WhoAmA 91*
McCouch, Gordon Mallet 1885-1962 *WhoAmA 91N*
McCoun, Gordon Wickersham 1952- *WhoEmL 91*
McCourt, David Jerome 1942- *St&PR 91*
McCourt, Mark Edward 1953- *WhoSSW 91*
McCourtie, Cheryl *BioIn 16*
McCovey, Willie *BioIn 16*
McCovey, Willie 1938- *Ballpl 90 [port], WorAlBi*
Mc Covey, Willie Lee 1938- *WhoAm 90*
McCowan, Lois Boyd *BioIn 16*
Mc Cowan, Robert Taylor 1928- *WhoAm 90*
McCowen, Alec *ConAu 129*
McCowen, Alec 1925- *ConTFT 8 [port], WhoWor 91*
McCowen, Alexander Duncan 1925- *ConAu 129*
McCowen, Max Creager 1915- *WhoAm 90*
McCown, David Layton 1949- *St&PR 91*
McCown, Frank J. 1940- *WhoWor 91*
McCown, Fred E. 1938- *St&PR 91*
McCown, George E. 1935- *WhoAm 90, WhoWor 91*
McCown, George Edwin 1935- *St&PR 91*
McCown, Hal Dale 1916- *WhoAm 90*
McCown, Hale 1914- *WhoAm 90*
McCown, John Clinton 1952- *WhoWrEP 89*
McCown, John D. 1954- *St&PR 91*

McCown, Judith Porter 1904- WhoAmW 91
McCoy, Ann 1946- WhoAmA 91
McCoy, Ann Brelsford 1940- WhoAmW 91
McCoy, Benny 1915- Ballpl 90
McCoy, Bowen Hadley 1937- WhoAm 90
McCoy, Carol P. 1948- WhoAmW 91
McCoy, Charles Allan 1928- WhoWor 91
McCoy, Charles Wallace 1920- WhoAm 90, WhoSSW 91
Mc Coy, Clarence John, Jr. 1935- WhoAm 90
McCoy, Clyde 1903- OxCPMus
McCoy, Daniel Eugene 1937- St&PR 91
McCoy, Dawn Crowley 1956- WhoAmW 91
McCoy, Debra J. 1958- St&PR 91
McCoy, Dennis C. 1942- WhoE 91
Mc Coy, Donald Richard 1928- WhoAm 90
McCoy, Donald Sanford 1930- St&PR 91
McCoy, Donald Y. BioIn 16
McCoy, Donna Carol 1952- WhoAmW 91
McCoy, Dorothy Eloise 1916- WhoAmW 91
McCoy, Easton Whitney 1918- WhoWrEP 89
McCoy, Edward Fitzgerald 1938- WhoAm 90
McCoy, Eileen Carey WhoE 91
McCoy, Elaine Jean 1946- WhoAmW 91
McCoy, Elmer C. 1936- St&PR 91
McCoy, Esther 1904?-1989 BioIn 16, ConAu 130
McCoy, Frank Ross 1874-1954 BioIn 16
Mc Coy, Frederick John 1916- WhoAm 90, WhoWor 91
Mc Coy, Georgia Anne 1936- BiDrAPA 89
McCoy, Gregory Allen 1954- WhoSSW 91
McCoy, Harold Vincent 1921- St&PR 91
McCoy, Henry Banks, Jr. 1928- St&PR 91
McCoy, Horace 1897-1955 TwCCr&M 91
McCoy, Isaac 1784-1846 BioIn 16, WhNaAH
McCoy, Jack Eugene 1957- WhoSSW 91
McCoy, James Andrew 1960- BiDrAPA 89
McCoy, James Freeman 1926- St&PR 91
McCoy, James Labon, Jr. 1948- WhoSSW 91
McCoy, James M. 1946- St&PR 91
McCoy, Janice Maxine 1945- WhoAmW 91
McCoy, Joenne Rae 1941- WhoAmW 91
McCoy, John Bonnet BioIn 16
McCoy, John Bonnet 1943- St&PR 91
Mc Coy, John Bonnet 1943- WhoAm 90
McCoy, John Gardner 1913- St&PR 91
Mc Coy, John Gardner 1913- WhoAm 90
McCoy, John Joseph 1934- St&PR 91
McCoy, John O. 1951- St&PR 91
McCoy, John W. 1910-1989 BioIn 16, WhoAmA 91N
McCoy, Joseph Jerome 1917- AuBYP 90
Mc Coy, Joseph Jerome, Jr. 1917- WhoWrEP 89
Mc Coy, Karen Kawamoto 1953- WhoWrEP 89
McCoy, Katherine 1945- BioIn 16
McCoy, Katherine Braden 1945- WhoAm 90, WhoAmA 91
McCoy, Kathleen 1945- WhoWrEP 89
McCoy, Kathleen Lynne 1945- WhoAmW 91
McCoy, Kevin 1942- St&PR 91
McCoy, Larry 1941- Ballpl 90
McCoy, Larry Dean 1938- WhoE 91
McCoy, Linda Jane 1951- WhoAmW 91
Mc Coy, Lois Clark 1920- WhoAmW 91, WhoWor 91
McCoy, Marilyn 1948- WhoAmW 91
McCoy, Mary Margaret 1948- WhoAmW 91
McCoy, Maureen Ellen WhoWrEP 89
McCoy, Michael Dale 1944- WhoAm 90, WhoAmA 91
McCoy, Michael James 1954- WhoSSW 91
Mc Coy, Miles Edward 1949- WhoWrEP 89
McCoy, Neal S. 1940- WhoAm 90
McCoy, Phyllistine 1943- WhoAmW 91
Mc Coy, Pressley Crane 1926- WhoAm 90
McCoy, Ralph R. 1909-1989 BioIn 16
McCoy, Raymond ODwPR 91
Mc Coy, Raymond F. 1913- WhoAm 90
McCoy, Reagan Scott 1945- WhoEmL 91
McCoy, Richard Hugh 1908- WhoAm 90
Mc Coy, Robert Baker 1916- WhoAm 90
McCoy, Robert S., Jr. 1938- WhoSSW 91
McCoy, Robert Smith, Jr. 1938- St&PR 91
Mc Coy, Robin Renee 1957- WhoWrEP 89
McCoy, Ronald Wayne 1940- WhoSSW 91
McCoy, Seth 1928- IntWWM 90
McCoy, Shirley Tutt 1937- WhoAmW 91
McCoy, Stephen Albert BioIn 16
McCoy, Stuart Sherman 1958- WhoSSW 91
McCoy, Suzanne Donavant 1957- WhoAmW 91
McCoy, Thomas G. 1943- St&PR 91
Mc Coy, Thomas LaRue 1933- WhoAm 90
McCoy, Thomas Raymond 1943- WhoAm 90
Mc Coy, Tidal Windham 1945- WhoAm 90
McCoy, Tom St&PR 91
McCoy, Van 1944-1979 DrBlPA 90
McCoy, Wanda Gay 1946- WhoSSW 91
McCoy, Wesley Lawrence 1935- WhoAm 90
Mc Coy, William Daniel 1929- WhoAm 90
McCoy, William O. 1933- St&PR 91
McCoy, Wilson 1902-1961 EncACom
McCoy, Wirth Vaughan 1913- WhoAmA 91, WhoE 91
McCoys, The EncPR&S 89
McCrabb, Les 1914- Ballpl 90
McCracken, Alan L. 1950- St&PR 91
McCracken, Caron Francis 1951- WhoAmW 91, WhoEmL 91
McCracken, Christopher Cornell 1951- WhoEmL 91
Mc Cracken, Daniel Delbert 1930- WhoAm 90, WhoWrEP 89
McCracken, Donna Lee 1954- WhoSSW 91
McCracken, Edward R. 1943- St&PR 91
McCracken, Ernest E. 1934- St&PR 91
McCracken, George Herbert 1899- St&PR 91
Mc Cracken, George Herbert 1899- WhoAm 90
McCracken, Harold 1894- AuBYP 90
McCracken, Ina 1939- WhoAmW 91
McCracken, James 1926-1988 AnObit 1988, BioIn 16, PenDiMP, WorAlBi
Mc Cracken, James Thomas 1954- BiDrAPA 89
McCracken, John Harvey 1934- WhoAm 90, WhoAmA 91
McCracken, John Walter 1944- St&PR 91
McCracken, L. S. 1928- St&PR 91
McCracken, Lawrence L. 1943- ODwPR 91
McCracken, Linda 1948- WhoAmW 91
McCracken, Michael BioIn 16
Mc Cracken, Paul Winston 1915- WhoAm 90
McCracken, Philip 1928- WhoAmA 91
Mc Cracken, Philip Trafton 1928- WhoAm 90
McCracken, Richard Allen 1939- IntWWM 90
McCracken, Robert David 1934- St&PR 91
McCracken, Sarah Elizabeth 1950- WhoEmL 91
McCracken, Thomas C. 1948- St&PR 91
McCracken, Thomas Charles 1948- WhoAm 90
McCracken, William Edward 1929- St&PR 91
McCracken, William Lobach 1937- WhoAm 90
McCrackin, Josephine 1838-1920 FemiCLE
McCrackin, William K. 1933- WhoAm 90
McCrady, Howard Clark 1931- St&PR 91
McCrady, James David 1930- WhoAm 90
McCrady, Kenneth Allen 1930- St&PR 91
McCrae, Charles A. 1928- WhoAm 90
McCrae, Charles Andrew 1928- St&PR 91
McCrae, John 1872-1918 DcLB 92 [port]
McCrae, Robert Fletcher 1945- St&PR 91
Mc Crae, Sharon Elizabeth 1955- WhoWrEP 89
Mc Cranie, E James BiDrAPA 89
McCranie, Ed 1948- St&PR 91
McCranie, Stephen C. 1945- St&PR 91
McCrary, Dennie L. 1938- St&PR 91
McCrary, Douglas L. 1929- WhoSSW 91
McCrary, Eugenia Lester 1929- WhoAmW 91, WhoE 91, WhoWor 91
McCrary, George Washington 1835-1890 BiDrUSE 89
McCrary, Larry Frank 1949- WhoSSW 91
McCrary, Leon E. 1937- St&PR 91
McCraven, Carl Clarke 1926- WhoWor 91
McCraven, Eva Stewart Mapes 1936- WhoWor 91
McCraven, Marcus Rollins 1923- St&PR 91
McCravy, C. Hearon 1941- St&PR 91
McCraw, David BioIn 16
McCraw, David Bruce 1942- WhoSSW 91
McCraw, Harris Lamar, III 1952- WhoSSW 91
McCraw, John Louis 1953- WhoE 91
McCraw, Leslie BioIn 16
McCraw, Leslie Gladstone 1934- St&PR 91, WhoAm 90
McCraw, Ronald Kent 1947- WhoWor 91
McCraw, Thomas Erwin 1948- St&PR 91
McCraw, Thomas Kincaid 1940- WhoAm 90
McCraw, Tom 1941- Ballpl 90
McCray, Bernard Winn, Jr. 1934- St&PR 91
McCray, Curtis Lee 1938- WhoAm 90
Mc Cray, David Steele 1940- BiDrAPA 89
Mc Cray, Evelina Williams 1932- WhoAmW 91, WhoWor 91
Mc Cray, Glen M BiDrAPA 89
McCray, Harry Claxton, Jr. 1933- St&PR 91
McCray, James 1939- IntWWM 90
Mc Cray, Katherine Lee 1961- WhoWrEP 89
McCray, Mike ConAu 130
McCray, Richard Alan 1937- WhoAm 90
McCray, Robert Cone 1926- St&PR 91
McCray, Ronald David 1957- WhoSSW 91
Mc Cray, William E BiDrAPA 89
McCray, Yvonne 1950- WhoSSW 91
Mc Crea, Frank William 1942- WhoWrEP 89
McCrea, Jane 1752-1777 EncCRAm
McCrea, Joel 1905- WorAlBi
McCrea, Joel 1905-1990 NewYTBS 90 [port], News 91-1
McCrea, John L. NewYTBS 90
McCrea, John L. 1891-1990 BioIn 16
McCrea, Joseph William 1946- St&PR 91
McCrea, Mary AuBYP 90
McCrea, Patricia Anne 1945- WhoAmW 91
McCrea, Peter Frederick 1942- St&PR 91
McCrea, Robert Barlow 1823-1897 DcCanB 12
McCrea, Robert Stanley 1948- WhoEmL 91
McCrea, Terri Lyn 1967- WhoAmW 91
McCrea, William Sloan 1913- St&PR 91
McCready, Eric Scott 1941- WhoAm 90, WhoAmA 91
McCready, Jack TwCCr&M 91
McCready, K. F. 1939- St&PR 91
McCready, Karen 1946- WhoAmA 91
McCready, Kenneth Frank 1939- WhoAm 90
McCready, Leo Stephen 1956- WhoEmL 91
McCready, Mark ODwPR 91
McCready, Richard French 1905- St&PR 91
McCreary, Alf 1940- ConAu 31NR
McCreary, Bill 1933- DrBlPA 90
McCreary, Dustin Campbell 1928- WhoAm 90
McCreary, Harry Clay 1926- St&PR 91
McCreary, James Bennett 1838-1918 AmLegL
Mc Creary, James Franklin 1942- WhoAm 90
McCreary, Jay Lee 1951- WhoEmL 91
McCreary, Judy Marian 1946- WhoAmW 91
McCreary, Robert Grosvenor, Jr. 1918- WhoAm 90
McCree, Floyd J. 1923-1988 BioIn 16
McCree, Jeanie Cole 1949- WhoAmW 91
McCree, Paul William, Jr. 1926- WhoE 91, WhoWor 91
McCreery, Franc Root WhoAmA 91N
McCreery, James Allan 1933- WhoSSW 91
Mc Creery, Joseph Michael BiDrAPA 89
McCreery, Lawrence Kip, Jr. 1948- WhoWor 91
McCreery, Robert D. 1917- St&PR 91
McCreery, Tom 1874-1941 Ballpl 90
McCreery, William C. 1896-1988 BioIn 16
McCreesh, Paul D. 1960- IntWWM 90
McCreigh, James MajTwCW
Mc Creight, David W BiDrAPA 89
McCrensky, Edward 1912- WhoAm 90
McCrery, Jim BioIn 16
McCrery, Jim 1949- WhoAm 90, WhoSSW 91
Mc Crie, Robert Delbert 1938- WhoAm 90, WhoWrEP 89
McCright, Gary James 1946- St&PR 91
McCrimmon, Barbara Smith 1918- WhoAmW 91
McCrimmon, James McNab 1908- WhoAm 90
Mc Crimmon, James McNab 1908- WhoWrEP 89
McCrimmon, Ronald L. 1947- St&PR 91
McCristal, J. Bruce ODwPR 91
McCron, Raymond C. 1921-1990 BioIn 16
Mc Crone, Alistair William 1931- WhoAm 90
McCrone, Kathleen E. 1941- ConAu 130
McCrone, Walter Cox 1916- WhoAm 90
Mc Crory, Dennis Joseph BiDrAPA 89
McCrory, Donald Brann 1946- St&PR 91
McCrory, Edward Lawrence 1921- St&PR 91
McCrory, Ellann 1936- WhoAmW 91, WhoWor 91
McCrory, James T. ODwPR 91
McCrory, John Brooks 1925- WhoAm 90
McCrory, Martha WhoSSW 91
McCrory, Moy 1953- ConAu 130
McCrory, Shirley Till 1935- WhoAmW 91
Mc Crory, Wallace Willard 1920- WhoAm 90
McCroskey, Lenora Estelle 1943- WhoSSW 91
Mc Croskey, William James 1937- WhoAm 90
Mc Crossan, John Anthony 1930- WhoAm 90
McCrossen, William WhoSSW 91
McCrosson, Andrew James, Jr. 1951- WhoE 91
McCrudden, Michael Joseph, III 1944- WhoAm 90
McCrudden, Stephen Worth 1949- WhoE 91
McCruden, Jane Evelyn BiDrAPA 89
McCrum, C. David 1946- WhoSSW 91
McCrum, Lindsay BioIn 16
McCrum, Michael William 1924- WhoWor 91
McCrum, Robert 1953- SpyFic
McCrummen, Norman H. WhoAm 90
Mc Crystal, Frank BiDrAPA 89
McCrystal, James Teevan 1916- WhoAm 90
McCubbin, Hamilton, II 1941- WhoAm 90
McCubbin, Horace W. 1931- St&PR 91
McCubbin, Susan Brubeck 1948- WhoAmW 91
McCudden, Bernard Joseph 1946- St&PR 91
McCue, Arthur Bernard 1926- WhoE 91
McCue, Arthur Harry 1944- WhoE 91
Mc Cue, Carolyn Moore 1916- WhoAm 90
McCue, Ching-Yi S. 1958- WhoSSW 91
McCue, Frank C., III 1931- WhoAm 90
McCue, George 1910- BioIn 16
McCue, Harry 1944- WhoAmA 91
McCue, Howard McDowell, III 1946- WhoAm 90
McCue, Kevin 1959- St&PR 91
McCue, Lillian Bueno AuBYP 90
McCue, Mary 1947- ODwPR 91
McCue, Mary Madeline 1947- WhoAm 90
McCue, Miriam Eugenia 1917- WhoAmW 91
McCue, Peter S. 1947- ODwPR 91
McCue, Robert Edward 1953- BiDrAPA 89, WhoE 91
McCue, Wolford ODwPR 91
McCuen, John Francis, Jr. 1944- WhoAm 90, WhoWor 91
McCuen, John Joachim 1926- WhoWor 91
McCuen, Phyllis Montaigne 1923- WhoE 91
McCuen, William James 1943- WhoAm 90, WhoSSW 91
McCuistion, Jack Haywood 1934- St&PR 91
McCuistion, Peg Orem 1930- WhoAmW 91
McCuistion, Robert Wiley 1927- WhoAm 90
McCulla, James Willard 1930- WhoE 91
McCullagh, Andrew M., Jr. 1948- St&PR 91
McCullagh, Grant Gibson 1951- WhoWor 91
McCullagh, James Charles 1941- WhoAm 90
Mc Cullagh, James Charles 1941- WhoWrEP 89
McCullagh, Joseph Burbridge 1842-1896 BioIn 16
McCullagh, Kevin Joseph 1945- St&PR 91
Mc Cullagh, William Henry BiDrAPA 89
McCullar, Bruce Hayden 1953- WhoSSW 91, WhoWor 91
McCullars, Denise Williams 1953- St&PR 91
Mc Cullars, Eva Helen 1948- BiDrAPA 89
McCullen, Michael John 1937- WhoE 91
McCullers, Carson 1917-1967 BioIn 16, FemiCLE, MajTwCW, NotWoAT, WorAlBi, WrPh
McCullers, Carson S. 1919-1967 BioAmW
McCullers, Lance 1964- Ballpl 90
McCulley, Sandra Kay 1957- WhoAmW 91
McCulley, Thomas Melvin 1947- St&PR 91, WhoSSW 91
McCullion, Michael Andrew 1959- WhoSSW 91
McCulloch, Albert Donald, Jr. BioIn 16
McCulloch, Anna Mary Knott 1964- WhoE 91
McCulloch, Catharine 1862-1945 FemiCLE
McCulloch, Cathy Marie 1954- WhoAmW 91
Mc Culloch, Ernest Armstrong 1926- WhoAm 90
McCulloch, Frank E 1930- WhoAmA 91
Mc Culloch, Frank W. 1905- WhoAm 90
McCulloch, Frank Walter, Jr. 1920- WhoAm 90
McCulloch, Hugh 1808-1895 BiDrUSE 89, EncABHB 6 [port]

McCulloch, James Callahan 1947- WhoAm 90, WhoE 91
McCulloch, Jenifer Susan 1957- IntWWM 90
McCulloch, John Ramsay 1789-1864 BioIn 16
McCulloch, John Tyler ConAu 132, MajTwCW
McCulloch, Joseph 1908-1990 ConAu 131
McCulloch, Kenneth John 1943- WhoAm 90
McCulloch, Norman E., Jr. 1926- St&PR 91
McCulloch, Rachel 1942- WhoAm 90, WhoE 91
McCulloch, Roderick Allister 1938- WhoAm 90
Mc Culloch, Samuel Clyde 1916- WhoAm 90
McCulloch, Thomas 1776-1843 DcLB 99 [port]
Mc Culloch, Thomas A BiDrAPA 89
McCulloch, William Leonard 1921- WhoAm 90
McCulloh, Evelyn Butler 1910- WhoSSW 91
McCulloh, Judith Marie 1935- IntWWM 90
McCulloh, Mark Lightner 1962- WhoE 91
McCullom, Cornell, Jr. 1932- WhoAm 90, WhoE 91
McCullough, Ann Elizabeth 1957- WhoEmL 91
McCullough, Barbara Anne Ferguson 1957- WhoAmW 91
McCullough, C. Hax St&PR 91N
McCullough, Charles David 1940- WhoSSW 91
McCullough, Clyde 1917-1982 Ballpl 90
McCullough, Colleen WhoAm 90
McCullough, Colleen 1937- FemiCLE, WorAlBi
McCullough, Colleen 1938?- MajTwCW
McCullough, David 1933- ConAu 31NR, SmATA 62 [port]
Mc Cullough, David 1933- WhoAm 90
McCullough, David William 1945- WhoAmA 91
McCullough, Donald F. 1925- St&PR 91
McCullough, Donald W. 1949- ConAu 130
McCullough, Edgar Joseph, Jr. 1931- WhoAm 90
Mc Cullough, Elizabeth Lane BiDrAPA 89
McCullough, Foy, Jr. 1927- WhoAm 90
Mc Cullough, Frances Monson 1938- WhoWrEP 89
McCullough, George Bierce 1925- WhoAm 90
McCullough, George R. 1929- St&PR 91
Mc Cullough, Helen Craig 1918- WhoAm 90
McCullough, Hester R. BioIn 16
McCullough, Hiram 1813-1885 AmLegL
Mc Cullough, J. Lee 1945- WhoWor 91
McCullough, James Armstrong 1934- St&PR 91
McCullough, John Jeffrey 1938- WhoAm 90
McCullough, John Norcott 1932- St&PR 91
Mc Cullough, John Price 1925- WhoAm 90
McCullough, Joseph 1922- WhoAm 90, WhoAmA 91
McCullough, Joseph E. 1942- St&PR 91
McCullough, Julie BioIn 16
Mc Cullough, Ken 1943- WhoWrEP 89
McCullough, Kimberly Anne 1956- WhoAmW 91, WhoSSW 91
Mc Cullough, Lawrence N BiDrAPA 89
McCullough, Norman John 1946- WhoE 91
McCullough, Oscar James 1922- IntWWM 90
McCullough, Phillip J. 1945- St&PR 91
Mc Cullough, Philip Kirk BiDrAPA 89
McCullough, R. Michael 1938- WhoAm 90
Mc Cullough, Ralph Clayton, II 1941- WhoAm 90
McCullough, Ray Daniel, Jr. 1938- WhoAm 90
McCullough, Richard Lawrence 1937- WhoAm 90
McCullough, Robert Willis 1920- WhoAm 90
McCullough, Samuel Alexander 1938- St&PR 91
Mc Cullough, Samuel Alexander 1938- WhoAm 90, WhoE 91
McCullough, Thomas Mark 1955- BiDrAPA 89
McCullough, Todd Alan 1962- WhoAm 90
Mc Cullough, William Earl BiDrAPA 89
McCullum, R. Gene 1934- St&PR 91
McCully, Clinton Paxton 1947- WhoE 91
McCully, Emily Arnold 1939- AuBYP 90
Mc Cully, Emily Arnold 1939- WhoWrEP 89
McCully, James Kimball 1958- IntWWM 90
McCully, L. D. 1929- St&PR 91
McCully, Newton Alexander BioIn 16
McCully, Ruth Alida 1933- WhoAmW 91
McCummings, LeVerne 1932- WhoAm 90
McCune, Albert L. 1932- St&PR 91
McCune, Amy Reed 1954- WhoAmW 91
McCune, Barbara Ann 1934- WhoSSW 91
Mc Cune, Barron Patterson 1915- WhoAm 90
McCune, Cecil Perry 1946- WhoSSW 91
McCune, Donald A. BioIn 16
McCune, Ellis E. 1921- WhoAm 90
McCune, James Augustus, III 1938- St&PR 91
McCune, John Conner 1936- St&PR 91
Mc Cune, John Francis, III 1921- WhoAm 90
McCune, Mary Joan Huxley 1932- WhoAmW 91
McCune, Nancy Bentley 1946- WhoAmW 91
McCune, Paul 1941- St&PR 91
McCune, R. G. St&PR 91
McCune, Samuel K. 1921- St&PR 91
McCune, Samuel Kirk 1921- WhoAm 90
Mc Cune, Shannon 1913- WhoAm 90
McCune, William James, Jr. 1915- St&PR 91
Mc Cune, William James, Jr. 1915- WhoAm 90, WhoE 91
McCune, William M. 1922- St&PR 91
McCune, William Minton 1922- WhoAm 90
McCunn, Ruthanne Lum 1946- SmATA 63
Mc Cunn, Ruthanne Lum 1946- WhoWrEP 89
McCurdy, Charles Gribbel 1955- St&PR 91
McCurdy, Clair Eugene 1931- WhoAm 90
McCurdy, Daniel T. 1933- St&PR 91
McCurdy, David Keith 1950- WhoAm 90, WhoSSW 91
McCurdy, Floyd A. St&PR 91
McCurdy, George Reese, III 1946- St&PR 91
McCurdy, Gilbert Geier 1922- St&PR 91
Mc Curdy, Gilbert Geier 1922- WhoAm 90
Mc Curdy, Harold Grier 1909- WhoAm 90
McCurdy, Harry 1900-1972 Ballpl 90
McCurdy, Harry Ward 1918- WhoAm 90
McCurdy, Horace Winslow St&PR 91N
McCurdy, Horace Winslowe 1899-1989 BioIn 16
Mc Curdy, James Rollin 1943- BiDrAPA 89
Mc Curdy, Jole E C 1939- BiDrAPA 89
McCurdy, Julius A. 1903- St&PR 91
McCurdy, Larry Wayne 1935- St&PR 91, WhoAm 90, WhoWor 91
Mc Curdy, Layton 1935- BiDrAPA 89
McCurdy, Mary Jacqueline 1933- WhoAmW 91
McCurdy, Michael Charles 1942- WhoAmA 91, WhoE 91
McCurdy, Michael J. ODwPR 91
Mc Curdy, Pamela Mary 1949- BiDrAPA 89
Mc Curdy, Patrick Pierre 1928- WhoAm 90, WhoWor 91, WhoWrEP 89
McCurdy, Richard Clark 1909- WhoAm 90, WhoWor 91
McCurley, Carl Michael 1946- WhoWor 91
Mc Curley, Robert Lee, Jr. 1941- WhoAm 90
McCurley, William S 1936- BiDrAPA 89
McCurn, Neal Peters 1926- WhoAm 90, WhoE 91
McCurrach, James Crampton 1934- WhoE 91
McCurry, Edward Norris 1952- WhoSSW 91
McCurry, Harr Orr 1889-1964 WhoAmA 91N
McCurry, John DrBlPA 90
Mc Curry, Paul D. 1903- WhoAm 90
McCurry, Virginia Marie 1928- WhoAmW 91
McCurry, William Jeffery 1947- St&PR 91
Mc Curtis, Henry Lloyd BiDrAPA 89
McCusker, Harold NewYTBS 90
McCusker, Harold 1940-1990 BioIn 16
McCusker, J. Stephen 1946- WhoAm 90
McCusker, John 1939- St&PR 91
McCusker, Mary Lauretta 1919- WhoAm 90
McCusker, Paul Donald 1921- WhoE 91
McCusker, William LaValle 1918- WhoWor 91
McCutchan, Gordon E. 1935- St&PR 91
McCutchan, Gordon Eugene 1935- WhoAm 90
Mc Cutchan, Kenneth Peva 1913- WhoWrEP 89
McCutchan, Philip 1920- TwCCr&M 91
McCutchan, Philip Donald 1920- SpyFic
McCutchan, William M. 1954- St&PR 91
McCutchen, Audrey Jean 1942- WhoAmW 91
McCutchen, Edna Elizabeth 1914- WhoAmW 91
McCutchen, James N. 1949- St&PR 91
McCutchen, Lisa Star BiDrAPA 89
McCutchen, William Walter, Jr. 1940- WhoE 91
McCutcheon, Andrew H. 1927- ODwPR 91
McCutcheon, Elsie 1937- SmATA 60 [port]
Mc Cutcheon, Frederic York 1940- WhoAm 90
McCutcheon, Holly Marie 1950- WhoEmL 91
McCutcheon, John Oliver 1924- St&PR 91
McCutcheon, John Tinney 1870-1949 BioIn 16
Mc Cutcheon, John Tinney, Jr. 1917- WhoAm 90
McCutcheon, Lynn Ellis 1944- WhoSSW 91
McCutcheon, Stephen Christian 1939- WhoSSW 91
Mc Cuthcheon, James F BiDrAPA 89
McDade, Herbert Hardinge 1927- St&PR 91
Mc Dade, Herbert Hardinge, Jr. 1927- WhoAm 90
McDade, James Russell 1925- WhoWor 91
Mc Dade, Joseph Michael 1931- WhoAm 90, WhoE 91
McDade, Sharon Ann 1952- WhoAmW 91
McDade, William Joseph 1937- WhoAm 90
McDade, William Robert 1936- St&PR 91
McDaid, Janet Litwinowich WhoAmW 91
Mc Danal, Clarence E, Jr. 1944- BiDrAPA 89
Mc Danald, Conway Lawrence BiDrAPA 89
Mc Danald, Eugene C, Jr. 1914- BiDrAPA 89
McDaniel, Armour G. BioIn 16
McDaniel, Audrey May 1908- WhoAmW 91
McDaniel, Barry 1930- IntWWM 90
McDaniel, Becky B 1953- SmATA 61 [port]
McDaniel, Bessie Lee 1937- WhoAmW 91
McDaniel, Betty Flowers 1940- WhoAmW 91
McDaniel, Bobby L. 1939- St&PR 91
Mc Daniel, Bonny Elizabeth 1936- WhoWrEP 89
McDaniel, Boyce Dawkins 1917- WhoAm 90
McDaniel, Charles-Gene 1931- WhoAm 90
Mc Daniel, Charles-Gene 1931- WhoWrEP 89
McDaniel, Charles Russell 1930- WhoSSW 91
McDaniel, D. Allen 1938- St&PR 91
McDaniel, David J. 1942- St&PR 91
McDaniel, David Jamison 1913- WhoAm 90
McDaniel, Diane O. 1950- St&PR 91
McDaniel, Dolan Kenneth 1935- WhoAm 90
Mc Daniel, Ellen Garb 1941- BiDrAPA 89
McDaniel, Etta 1890-1946 DrBlPA 90
McDaniel, Felix C. 1939- St&PR 91
McDaniel, Gary Allan 1931- WhoSSW 91
McDaniel, George H. 1931- St&PR 91
McDaniel, Gerald Green Goforth 1945- WhoSSW 91
McDaniel, Hattie 1895-1952 DrBlPA 90, WorAlBi
McDaniel, Hattie 1898-1952 BioIn 16
Mc Daniel, James Edwin 1931- WhoAm 90, WhoWor 91
McDaniel, James Mark, Jr. 1953- WhoSSW 91
McDaniel, Jarrel Dave 1930- WhoAm 90
McDaniel, John Perry 1942- WhoAm 90
McDaniel, John Stephen 1959- BiDrAPA 89
McDaniel, Larry Gray 1947- WhoSSW 91
McDaniel, Larry Scott 1953- WhoSSW 91
McDaniel, Lindy 1935- Ballpl 90
McDaniel, Lisa Mae 1964- WhoAmW 91
McDaniel, Mary Grace Coen 1958- WhoAmW 91
McDaniel, Mary Jane 1946- WhoAmW 91
McDaniel, Michael Conway Dixon 1929- WhoAm 90, WhoSSW 91
McDaniel, Michael John BiDrAPA 89
McDaniel, Michael Keith 1948- WhoEmL 91
McDaniel, Molly 1961- WhoE 91
McDaniel, Myra Atwell 1932- WhoAm 90, WhoAmW 91, WhoSSW 91
McDaniel, Neil W. 1916- St&PR 91
McDaniel, Norwood Allan 1928- WhoE 91
McDaniel, Ollie Frank, Jr. 1945- St&PR 91
McDaniel, Raymond Deal, Jr. 1950- WhoSSW 91
McDaniel, Raymond Lamar 1925- WhoAm 90
McDaniel, Reuben Roosevelt, Jr. 1936- WhoAm 90
Mc Daniel, Robbie Lee 1940- WhoWrEP 89
Mc Daniel, Roderick Rogers 1926- WhoAm 90
McDaniel, Sam 1896?-1962 DrBlPA 90
McDaniel, Sara A. 1949- ODwPR 91
McDaniel, Sara Sherwood 1943- WhoSSW 91
McDaniel, Susan Holmes 1951- WhoAmW 91
Mc Daniel, Thomas W, Jr. BiDrAPA 89
McDaniel, Virginia Lee 1937- WhoAmW 91
McDaniel, Von 1939- Ballpl 90
McDaniel, William J. 1943- WhoAm 90
McDaniel, William Jason, Jr. 1941- WhoSSW 91
McDaniel, William Patrick 1948- St&PR 91
Mcdaniel, William Windsor 1952- BiDrAPA 89, WhoSSW 91
McDaniels, David Martin 1962- WhoSSW 91
McDaniels, Delores Pauline 1941- WhoWor 91
McDaniels, Gene 1935- EncPR&S 89
McDaniels, John Francis 1935- WhoAm 90
Mc Dannald, Clyde Elliott, Jr. 1923- WhoWor 91
McDannald, Werner Bagwell 1943- St&PR 91
Mc Dargh-Elvins, Eileen 1948- WhoWrEP 89
McDarrah, Fred William 1926- WhoAm 90, WhoAmA 91, WhoE 91
Mc Darrah, Fred William 1926- WhoWrEP 89
McDarrah, Gloria Schoffel 1932- WhoAm 90, WhoE 91
Mc David, George Eugene 1930- WhoAm 90
McDavid, J. Gary 1947- WhoE 91
McDavid, James Evans, Jr. 1937- WhoSSW 91
McDavid, Joshua Dent BiDrAPA 89
McDavid, Ned 1927-1984 BioIn 16
McDavid, Samuel L. 1946- St&PR 91
Mc David, Virginia Glenn 1926- WhoAm 90
McDavid, William H. 1946- St&PR 91
McDearmon, Kay AuBYP 90
McDermid, Alice Marguerite Connell 1910- WhoAmW 91
McDermid, Edward J. 1908- St&PR 91
McDermid, John Horton 1940- WhoAm 90, WhoE 91
Mc Dermid, L David BiDrAPA 89
McDermit, Robert Edward 1932- WhoAm 90
McDermitt, Edward Vincent 1953- WhoEmL 91
McDermott, Agnes Charlene Senape 1937- WhoAm 90
Mc Dermott, Albert Leo 1923- WhoAm 90
McDermott, Arthur Dennis 1943- St&PR 91
McDermott, Beverly 1941- AuBYP 90
McDermott, Catherine Elizabeth WhoE 91
Mc Dermott, Charles E 1936- BiDrAPA 89
McDermott, Cheryl Lynn 1953- WhoAmW 91
McDermott, Daniel Joseph 1936- St&PR 91, WhoAm 90
McDermott, Deborah 1954- BioIn 16
McDermott, Dennis A. 1950- St&PR 91
McDermott, Dylan BioIn 16
McDermott, Edward Aloysious 1920- WhoAm 90
McDermott, Francis Owen 1933- WhoWor 91
McDermott, Frank A., Jr. 1918- St&PR 91
McDermott, Frank Clark 1926- WhoE 91
McDermott, Gerald BioIn 16
McDermott, Gerald 1941- AuBYP 90, WhoAmA 91
McDermott, Helen Crawford 1959- BiDrAPA 89
McDermott, Hugh 1960- WhoE 91
Mc Dermott, James A BiDrAPA 89
McDermott, James A. 1936- WhoAm 90
McDermott, James Alexander 1938- WhoAm 90
McDermott, James T. 1926- WhoAm 90, WhoE 91
McDermott, Jim 1936- BioIn 16
Mc Dermott, John F, Jr. 1929- BiDrAPA 89
Mc Dermott, John Francis, Jr. 1929- WhoAm 90

McDermott, John Henry 1931- *WhoAm 90*
Mc Dermott, John Joseph 1932- *WhoAm 90*
McDermott, Kevin L. 1954- *St&PR 91*
McDermott, Kevin M. 1950- *St&PR 91*
McDermott, Mary 1943- *St&PR 91*
Mc Dermott, Michael James 1952- *WhoWrEP 89*
McDermott, Michael James 1956- *WhoEmL 91*
McDermott, Mickey 1928- *Ballpl 90, BioIn 16*
McDermott, Nelson J. 1923- *St&PR 91*
McDermott, Norbert 1954- *St&PR 91*
McDermott, P. Michael 1945- *ODwPR 91*
McDermott, Pamela McClure 1938- *WhoE 91*
McDermott, Patricia Ann 1943- *WhoAmW 91*
McDermott, Patricia Louise *WhoAmW 91*
Mc Dermott, Philip Alan 1951- *WhoAm 90*
McDermott, Raymund Gerald 1927- *St&PR 91, WhoAm 90*
McDermott, Renee Rassler 1950- *WhoEmL 91*
McDermott, Richard T. 1940- *WhoE 91*
McDermott, Robert B. 1927- *WhoAm 90*
Mc Dermott, Robert Francis 1920- *WhoAm 90*
McDermott, Robert J. *ODwPR 91*
McDermott, Robert James *BioIn 16*
McDermott, Robert W. 1943- *St&PR 91*
Mc Dermott, Robert William *BiDrAPA 89*
McDermott, Stephen Patrick *BiDrAPA 89*
McDermott, Thomas Albert 1932- *St&PR 91*
McDermott, Thomas Albert, Jr. 1959- *St&PR 91*
McDermott, Thomas C. 1936- *St&PR 91*
McDermott, Thomas Curtis 1936- *WhoAm 90*
McDermott, Thomas J. *NewYTBS 90*
McDermott, Thomas Joseph 1915- *WhoSSW 91*
McDermott, Thomas Ward 1948- *St&PR 91*
McDermott, Vincent 1933- *IntWWM 90*
McDermott, William Thomas 1945- *WhoEmL 91, WhoSSW 91, WhoWor 91*
Mc Dermott, William Vincent, Jr. 1917- *WhoAm 90*
McDevitt, Dan *BioIn 16*
McDevitt, Danny 1932- *Ballpl 90*
McDevitt, Hugh O'Neill 1930- *WhoAm 90*
Mc Devitt, John Bourke 1917- *BiDrAPA 89*
Mc Devitt, Joseph Bryan 1918- *WhoAm 90*
McDevitt, Joyce Ann 1957- *WhoAmW 91*
McDevitt, Richard E. 1919- *St&PR 91*
McDevitt, Richard H. 1936- *St&PR 91*
Mc Devitt, Robert J 1928- *BiDrAPA 89*
McDevitt, Sheila Marie 1947- *WhoAmW 91*
McDilda, Wayne Allen 1960- *WhoSSW 91*
McDill, Robert Lee 1944- *WhoSSW 91, WhoWor 91*
McDill, Thomas Allison 1926- *WhoAm 90*
McDivitt, James A. 1929- *St&PR 91*
McDivitt, James Alton 1929- *WhoAm 90*
McDole, Carol *AuBYP 90*
Mc Donagh, Edward Charles 1915- *WhoAm 90*
McDonagh, Jan 1942- *WhoAmW 91*
McDonagh, Michael J. 1959- *St&PR 91*
Mc Donagh, Patrick H 1927- *BiDrAPA 89*
McDonagh, Thomas Joseph 1932- *WhoAm 90*
McDonagh-Coyle, Annmarie *BiDrAPA 89*
McDonald, Alexander David 1954- *WhoWor 91*
McDonald, Alice Coig 1940- *WhoAm 90, WhoAmW 91*
Mc Donald, Allan A *BiDrAPA 89*
McDonald, Allan James 1937- *WhoAm 90, WhoWor 91*
McDonald, Alonzo Lowry, Jr. 1928- *WhoAm 90*
McDonald, Alva Julian 1939- *WhoSSW 91*
Mc Donald, Andrew J. 1923- *WhoAm 90, WhoSSW 91*
McDonald, Andrew Jewett 1929- *St&PR 91*
Mc Donald, Andrew Jewett 1929- *WhoAm 90*
McDonald, Andrew Melvin, Jr. 1941- *WhoAm 90*
Mcdonald, Angus 1943- *BiDrAPA 89*
McDonald, Angus Henry 1904?-1990 *ConAu 130*
McDonald, Angus Wheeler 1927- *WhoSSW 91*
McDonald, Ann Margret *BiDrAPA 89*
McDonald, Arlys Lorraine 1932- *WhoAmW 91*
McDonald, Arthur Bruce 1943- *WhoAm 90*
Mc Donald, Barbara Ann 1932- *WhoAmW 91*
McDonald, Barbara Black Robertson 1951- *WhoEmL 91*
McDonald, Barbara Guthrie *AuBYP 90*
McDonald, Barbara Jean 1941- *WhoSSW 91*
McDonald, Barbara Jeannie B. *WhoAmW 91*
McDonald, Ben *BioIn 16*
McDonald, Bernard Robert 1940- *WhoE 91*
McDonald, Bonnie J. Sharp 1944- *WhoAmW 91*
McDonald, Brendan John 1930- *WhoAm 90*
McDonald, Brian M. 1947- *St&PR 91*
McDonald, Bruce Edward 1939- *St&PR 91*
McDonald, Carole Ann 947- *WhoAmW 91*
McDonald, Catherine A 1948- *BiDrAPA 89*
McDonald, Catherine Alice 1946- *WhoAmW 91*
McDonald, Charles Clarence 1933- *WhoAm 90*
McDonald, Charles F., Jr. 1955- *WhoSSW 91*
McDonald, Charles G. 1936- *St&PR 91*
McDonald, Charles H. 1938- *St&PR 91*
Mc Donald, Charles J. 1931- *WhoAm 90*
McDonald, Charles W. 1935- *WhoAm 90*
McDonald, Cheryl Lynn *BiDrAPA 89*
McDonald, Cheryl Lynn 1961- *WhoE 91*
McDonald, Clark Edward 1917- *WhoSSW 91*
McDonald, Cornelius Trawick, III 1955- *WhoEmL 91, WhoSSW 91*
McDonald, Country Joe 1942- *WorAlBi*
McDonald, Daniel Francis 1926- *St&PR 91*
McDonald, Darrel Lee 1950- *WhoSSW 91*
McDonald, Daryl Patrick 1950- *WhoEmL 91*
McDonald, David Edward 1958- *WhoSSW 91*
McDonald, David J. 1928- *WhoAm 90*
McDonald, David John 1928- *St&PR 91*
Mc Donald, David William 1923- *WhoAm 90*
McDonald, Desmond P. 1927- *St&PR 91, WhoAm 90*
McDonald, Donald 1930- *WhoAm 90*
McDonald, Donald Michael 1947- *WhoSSW 91*
McDonald, Dorothy Colette 1938- *WhoAmW 91*
McDonald, Dorothy Marie 1937- *WhoAmW 91*
McDonald, Eugene John 1948- *WhoE 91*
McDonald, Florence *BioIn 16*
McDonald, Forrest 1927- *AuBYP 90, WhoAm 90*
McDonald, Francis John 1815-1900 *DcCanB 12*
Mc Donald, Frank Bethune 1925- *WhoAm 90*
McDonald, Frank F., II 1951- *WhoAm 90*
McDonald, Frank J., Jr. 1924- *St&PR 91*
McDonald, Gabrielle Anne Kirk 1942- *WhoAmW 91*
McDonald, Gail Faber 1917- *IntWWM 90*
McDonald, George William, Jr. 1946- *St&PR 91*
McDonald, Gerald 1913- *IntWWM 90*
McDonald, Gloria Jeanette 1943- *WhoAmW 91*
McDonald, Gregory 1937- *TwCCr&M 91*
Mcdonald, Gregory Christopher 1937- *WhoAm 90*
McDonald, Harley C. 1941- *St&PR 91*
McDonald, Harold Franklin 1923- *St&PR 91*
McDonald, Henry Burnside, Jr. 1947- *WhoSSW 91*
Mc Donald, Henry Stanton 1927- *WhoAm 90*
Mc Donald, Ian M 1928- *BiDrAPA 89*
McDonald, Ian MacLaren 1928- *WhoAm 90*
McDonald, Irene Mary 1940- *WhoAmW 91*
Mc Donald, J Kenneth 1931- *BiDrAPA 89*
McDonald, Jack 1936- *WhoSSW 91*
McDonald, Jack Russell 1920- *St&PR 91*
McDonald, James A. 1962- *WhoE 91*
McDonald, James Charles 1925- *St&PR 91*
McDonald, James F. 1940- *St&PR 91*
McDonald, James Francis 1940- *WhoAm 90*
McDonald, James Grover 1886-1964 *BioIn 16*
Mc Donald, James Michael, Jr. 1924- *WhoAm 90*
McDonald, James P. *BioIn 16*
McDonald, James T. *BioIn 16*
Mc Donald, Jamie *WhoWrEP 89*
McDonald, Jane Frances 1940- *WhoAmW 91*
Mc Donald, Jeanette N *BiDrAPA 89*
McDonald, Jerry N 1944- *ConAu 31NR*
McDonald, Jim 1927- *Ballpl 90*
McDonald, Joanne 1947- *WhoAmW 91*
McDonald, John Cecil 1924- *WhoAm 90*
McDonald, John Charles 1936- *St&PR 91*
McDonald, John Clifton 1930- *WhoAm 90*
McDonald, John Edwin 1943- *St&PR 91*
McDonald, John Francis Patrick 1942- *WhoE 91, WhoWor 91*
McDonald, John Franklin, III 1950- *WhoEmL 91*
McDonald, John G. *WhoAm 90*
McDonald, John Gregory 1937- *WhoAm 90*
McDonald, John Harvey 1930- *St&PR 91*
Mc Donald, John Joseph 1930- *WhoAm 90, WhoE 91*
Mc Donald, John Richard 1933- *WhoAm 90*
McDonald, John Stanley 1943-1981 *WhoAmA 91N*
Mc Donald, John Warlick 1922- *WhoAm 90, WhoWor 91*
Mc Donald, Joseph Valentine 1925- *WhoAm 90*
Mc Donald, Julie J. 1929- *WhoWrEP 89*
McDonald, Karen Denise 1961- *WhoAmW 91*
McDonald, Kathleen Edna 1960- *WhoAmW 91*
McDonald, Kathryn Irene 1960- *WhoAmW 91*
McDonald, Kay 1952- *WhoAmW 91*
McDonald, Kay L. 1934- *BioIn 16*
McDonald, Kenneth John 1942- *St&PR 91*
Mc Donald, Lawrence F *BiDrAPA 89*
Mc Donald, Lee Cameron 1925- *WhoAm 90*
McDonald, Lewis Newton 1937- *WhoE 91*
McDonald, Lucile 1898- *AuBYP 90*
McDonald, Marguerite Fuller 1911- *WhoAmW 91*
McDonald, Marianne 1937- *WhoAmW 91, WhoWor 91*
McDonald, Marjorie 1898- *MusmAFA*
Mc Donald, Marshall 1918- *WhoAm 90*
McDonald, Martha Jane 1951- *WhoSSW 91*
McDonald, Mary Ann Melody 1944- *WhoAmW 91*
McDonald, Mary-Rea *BioIn 16*
McDonald, Marybeth 1955- *WhoAmW 91*
McDonald, Meg 1948- *ODwPR 91*
McDonald, Michael D. 1940- *St&PR 91*
McDonald, Michael James 1948- *St&PR 91*
McDonald, Michael L. 1946- *St&PR 91*
McDonald, Mike *BioIn 16*
Mc Donald, Miles Francis 1905- *WhoAm 90*
McDonald, Miller Baird 1920- *WhoAm 90, WhoSSW 91*
McDonald, Norman John 1926- *St&PR 91*
McDonald, O. V. 1922- *St&PR 91*
McDonald, Parker Lee 1924- *WhoAm 90, WhoSSW 91*
McDonald, Patrick 1956- *St&PR 91*
Mc Donald, Patrick Allen 1936- *WhoAm 90*
McDonald, Patrick Charles 1947- *St&PR 91*
McDonald, Patrick Hill, Jr. 1924- *WhoAm 90*
McDonald, Patti Ann *BioIn 16*
McDonald, Paul M. 1939- *St&PR 91*
McDonald, Peggy Ann Stimmel 1931- *WhoAmW 91*
McDonald, Ralph 1955- *IntWWM 90*
McDonald, Randal B. 1930- *St&PR 91, WhoAm 90*
McDonald, Raymond J. 1948- *St&PR 91*
McDonald, Rebecca Ann 1952- *WhoAmW 91*
McDonald, Richard E. 1933- *St&PR 91*
McDonald, Robert *BioIn 16*
McDonald, Robert 1933- *WhoAm 90*
McDonald, Robert B. 1936- *St&PR 91*
McDonald, Robert D. 1931- *St&PR 91*
McDonald, Robert Delos 1931- *WhoAm 90*
Mc Donald, Robert Emmett 1915- *WhoAm 90, WhoWor 91*
McDonald, Robert Herwick *WhoAmA 91*
McDonald, Robert L. *NewYTBS 90*
Mc Donald, Roger Koefod *BiDrAPA 89*
McDonald, Rosa Nell 1953- *WhoAmW 91*
McDonald, Roy Ketner *NewYTBS 90*
Mc Donald, Stephen Lee 1924- *WhoAm 90*
McDonald, Sterling 1949- *St&PR 91*
McDonald, Steven *BioIn 16*
McDonald, Susan Marshall 1918- *WhoAm 90*
McDonald, Susan Schwartz 1949- *St&PR 91*
McDonald, Susan Strong 1943- *WhoAmA 91*
McDonald, T. J. 1949- *St&PR 91*
McDonald, Tex 1891-1943 *Ballpl 90*
McDonald, Thomas F. *ODwPR 91*
McDonald, Tom 1955- *WhoEmL 91*
McDonald, Vickie Christian 1961- *WhoSSW 91*
McDonald, W. Wesley 1946- *WhoE 91*
McDonald, Walter 1934- *ConAu 31NR, DcLB 105 [port]*
Mc Donald, Walter Robert 1934- *WhoWrEP 89*
McDonald, Wanda Jamerson 1961- *WhoAmW 91*
McDonald, Warren A. *EarBlAP*
McDonald, Warren George 1939- *WhoAm 90*
McDonald, Webster 1900-1982 *Ballpl 90*
McDonald, William Andrew 1913- *WhoAm 90*
McDonald, William E. 1942- *St&PR 91*
McDonald, William Henry 1924- *WhoAm 90*
McDonald, William Henry 1946- *WhoEmL 91*
McDonald, William J. *NewYTBS 90*
McDonald, William J. 1904-1989 *BioIn 16*
McDonald, William J. 1927-1990 *BioIn 16*
McDonald, William M. 1953- *BiDrAPA 89*
McDonald, William N., III 1913- *ODwPR 91*
McDonald, William R. 1928- *St&PR 91*
McDonald, Willis, IV 1926- *WhoAm 90, WhoWor 91*
McDonald, Wylene Booth 1956- *WhoAmW 91*
McDonald Rasmussen, Margaret Jean 1960- *WhoAmW 91*
McDonall, Lois 1939- *IntWWM 90*
McDonell, David G. *ODwPR 91*
McDonell, Horace George, Jr. 1928- *St&PR 91, WhoAm 90, WhoE 91*
Mc Donell, Marcella Ann 1945- *WhoWrEP 89*
McDonell, Robert Terry 1944- *WhoAm 90*
Mc Donell, Robert Terry 1944- *WhoWrEP 89*
McDonie, Karen W. 1954- *St&PR 91*
McDoniel, James William 1932- *WhoSSW 91*
McDonnell, Archibald J. 1843- *AmLegL*
McDonnell, Catherine Marie 1958- *WhoAmW 91*
McDonnell, Charles E. *BioIn 16*
McDonnell, Christine 1949- *AuBYP 90, BioIn 16*
McDonnell, Corinne Ann 1947- *WhoE 91*
McDonnell, Eileen *ODwPR 91*
McDonnell, James S. 1899-1980 *EncPaPR 91*
McDonnell, James Smith, III 1936- *St&PR 91*
McDonnell, Jinny *AuBYP 90*
McDonnell, John Beresford William 1940- *WhoWor 91*
McDonnell, John Finney 1938- *WhoAm 90, WhoWor 91*
Mc Donnell, John Thomas 1926- *WhoAm 90*
McDonnell, Joseph Anthony 1936- *WhoAmA 91*
McDonnell, Kevin R. 1952- *St&PR 91*
McDonnell, Lawrence R. 1915- *ODwPR 91*
Mc Donnell, Loretta Wade 1940- *WhoAmW 91*
McDonnell, Lynne M. 1961- *St&PR 91*
McDonnell, Martin J. 1939- *St&PR 91*
McDonnell, Mary Jean 1960- *WhoAmW 91*
McDonnell, Mary Theresa 1949- *WhoAmW 91*
McDonnell, MaryAnn Margaret 1947- *WhoAmW 91*
Mc Donnell, Nancy Jean *BiDrAPA 89*
McDonnell, Pegeen Elizabeth 1966- *WhoAmW 91*
McDonnell, Robert F. *St&PR 91*
McDonnell, Sanford Noyes 1922- *WhoAm 90*
McDonnell, Thomas Anthony 1940- *IntWWM 90*
McDonnell, Thomas E. 1942- *ODwPR 91*
McDonnell, Virginia 1917- *AuBYP 90*
McDonough, Bernard P. 1903-1985 *BioIn 16*
McDonough, Brian Patrick 1958- *WhoE 91*
McDonough, Don *ODwPR 91*
McDonough, Douglas J. 1939- *ODwPR 91*
Mc Donough, George Francis, Jr. 1928- *WhoAm 90*
McDonough, Gerald C. 1928- *St&PR 91*
McDonough, James Francis 1939- *WhoAm 90*
McDonough, James Michael 1945- *WhoEmL 91*
McDonough, John J. 1941- *WhoAm 90*
McDonough, John Michael 1944- *WhoAm 90*

Mc Donough, John Richard 1919- *WhoAm 90*
McDonough, John Thomas 1924- *OxCCanT*
McDonough, Joseph Corbett 1924- *WhoAm 90*
McDonough, Joseph Edward 1937- *WhoAm 90*
McDonough, Katherine A. 1950- *ODwPR 91*
McDonough, Mamie 1952- *WhoAmW 91*
McDonough, Mark Raymond 1950- *St&PR 91*
McDonough, Mary *BioIn 16*
McDonough, Mary Joan 1957- *WhoAmW 91*
McDonough, Michael Charles 1938- *St&PR 91*
McDonough, Michael Richard 1951- *WhoE 91, WhoEmL 91*
McDonough, Patrick Dennis 1942- *WhoAm 90*
Mc Donough, Patrick J 1925- *BiDrAPA 89*
McDonough, Patrick Joseph, Jr. 1941- *WhoE 91*
McDonough, Reginald Milton 1936- *WhoAm 90*
Mc Donough, Richard Doyle 1931- *WhoAm 90, WhoE 91*
McDonough, Russell Charles 1924- *WhoAm 90*
McDonough, Thomas Francis 1947- *St&PR 91*
McDonough, Thomas J. 1911- *WhoAm 90*
McDonough, William J. 1934- *WhoAm 90*
McDonough, William Lee 1935- *St&PR 91*
McDonough, William R. 1944- *St&PR 91*
Mc Donough, William W 1928- *BiDrAPA 89*
McDormand, Thomas B. 1904-1988 *BioIn 16*
McDougal, Alfred Leroy 1931- *WhoAm 90*
McDougal, Bruce Edward 1947- *St&PR 91*
McDougal, Bruce William 1941- *St&PR 91*
McDougal, Bryan L. 1953- *St&PR 91*
McDougal, Edgar P. *ODwPR 91*
McDougal, Ivan Ellis 1927- *WhoAmA 91*
McDougal, Jerome R. 1928- *St&PR 91*
McDougal, Jerome R., Jr. *WhoAm 90*
Mc Dougal, John S *BiDrAPA 89*
McDougal, Luther Love, III 1938- *WhoAm 90*
McDougal, Michele Rogers *WhoAmW 91*
McDougal, Owen J., Jr. 1919- *St&PR 91*
Mc Dougal, Robert C 1930- *BiDrAPA 89*
McDougal, Stuart Yeatman 1942- *WhoAm 90*
McDougal, William Scott 1942- *WhoAm 90*
McDougald, Dana Lovell 1942- *WhoAmW 91*
McDougald, Frank A. 1938- *St&PR 91*
McDougald, Gertrude Elise Johnson 1885-1971 *HarlReB*
McDougald, Gil 1928- *Ballpl 90 [port]*
McDougald Ayer, Gertrude Elise Johnson 1885-1971 *HarlReB*
McDougall, Barbara *BioIn 16*
McDougall, Barbara Jean 1937- *WhoAm 90, WhoAmW 91, WhoE 91*
McDougall, Derek John 1945- *WhoWor 91*
Mc Dougall, Dugald Stewart 1916- *WhoAm 90*
McDougall, Duncan C. 1943- *St&PR 91*
McDougall, I. Ross 1943- *WhoAm 90*
McDougall, Ian 1930- *St&PR 91, WhoAm 90*
McDougall, J. K. 1867-1957 *BioIn 16*
McDougall, Jo Garot 1935- *WhoWrEP 89*
McDougall, John 1825?-1892 *DcCanB 12*
Mc Dougall, John 1916- *WhoAm 90*
McDougall, John Keith 1867-1957 *BioIn 16*
McDougall, Ronald A. 1942- *St&PR 91*
McDougall, Ronald Alexander 1942- *WhoAm 90*
McDougall, Susan 1961- *WhoAmW 91*
McDougall, W. T. *St&PR 91*
McDougall, Walter Allan 1946- *WhoAm 90*
McDougall, William 1871-1931 *EncPaPR 91*
McDougall, William 1871-1938 *EncO&P 3*
McDougall, William Alexander 1951- *WhoE 91*
Mc Dougall-Goodwin, Sharon Lee 1943- *WhoAmW 91*
McDougle, Christopher John *BiDrAPA 89*
McDoulett, C. D., Jr. 1944- *St&PR 91*
Mc Dow, John Jett 1925- *WhoAm 90*
McDow, Lucy London 1950- *St&PR 91*
McDow, Thomas, III 1947- *St&PR 91*
McDowall, John H. 1924- *St&PR 91*
McDowall, Roddy 1928- *BioIn 16, ConTFT 8 [port]*
Mc Dowall, Roddy 1928- *WhoAm 90, WhoWor 91*
McDowall, Roddy 1928- *WorAlBi*
McDowd, Joan Marie 1958- *WhoAmW 91*
McDowell, Ann Bady 1949- *BiDrAPA 89*
McDowell, Boyd, II 1926- *St&PR 91*
McDowell, Cecelia Marie 1952- *WhoAmW 91*
Mc Dowell, Charles Eager 1923- *WhoAm 90*
McDowell, Charles Patrick 1950- *WhoSSW 91*
McDowell, Charles Richard 1936- *St&PR 91*
McDowell, Daniel Quince, Jr. 1949- *WhoWor 91*
McDowell, David Jamison 1947- *WhoE 91*
McDowell, Edward R. H. 1932- *WhoAm 90*
McDowell, Electra B. *BioIn 16*
McDowell, Elizabeth Mary 1940- *WhoAmW 91, WhoE 91*
McDowell, Ellen Gunter 1952- *WhoEmL 91*
McDowell, Eugene A 1845-1893 *OxCCanT [port]*
McDowell, Eugene Addison 1845-1893 *DcCanB 12*
McDowell, Fletcher Hughes 1923- *WhoAm 90*
McDowell, Frederick Glen 1929- *St&PR 91*
McDowell, George Edward 1944- *St&PR 91*
McDowell, Homai Madon 1952- *WhoSSW 91*
McDowell, J. Michael 1958- *WhoSSW 91*
McDowell, Jack 1966- *Ballpl 90*
Mc Dowell, Jack Sherman 1914- *WhoAm 90*
McDowell, James W., Jr. 1942- *WhoAm 90*
McDowell, Janet Lee 1954- *WhoAmW 91*
McDowell, Jean Laramie 1942- *WhoSSW 91*
McDowell, Jeffrey S. 1954- *St&PR 91*
McDowell, Jennifer 1936- *WhoAm 90, WhoAmW 91, WhoWor 91*
McDowell, Joe *St&PR 91*
Mc Dowell, John B. 1921- *WhoAm 90*
McDowell, John Russell 1939- *St&PR 91*
Mc Dowell, Joseph Hampton 1907- *WhoAm 90*
McDowell, Jospehine Sargent 1912- *WhoAmW 91*
McDowell, Joyce Patricia 1935- *WhoAmW 91*
McDowell, Karen Ann 1945- *WhoAmW 91, WhoEmL 91*
McDowell, Lester 1951- *WhoSSW 91*
McDowell, Malcolm 1943- *WorAlBi*
Mc Dowell, Martha Shea 1925- *WhoWrEP 89*
McDowell, Mary E. 1854-1936 *BioAmW*
McDowell, Mary Jane 1953- *WhoAmW 91*
Mc Dowell, Mehl *BiDrAPA 89*
McDowell, Michael David 1948- *WhoAm 90, WhoE 91*
Mc Dowell, Michael Gerald 1953- *WhoWrEP 89*
McDowell, Oddibe 1962- *Ballpl 90*
McDowell, Putnam B. 1924- *St&PR 91*
McDowell, Putnam Ballou 1924- *WhoAm 90*
McDowell, Ralph D. 1924- *St&PR 91*
McDowell, Renfrew Brighton *St&PR 91*
McDowell, Richard Louis 1938- *WhoE 91*
McDowell, Robert A. 1953- *WhoWrEP 89*
McDowell, Robert Alan 1945- *WhoEmL 91*
McDowell, Robert Emmett 1914-1975 *LiHiK*
Mc Dowell, Robert Hull 1927- *WhoAm 90*
McDowell, Robert L. 1941- *St&PR 91*
McDowell, Robert Michael 1961- *WhoEmL 91*
McDowell, Roger 1960- *Ballpl 90*
McDowell, Sam 1942- *Ballpl 90 [port]*
McDowell, Stephen Geoffrey 1943- *St&PR 91*
McDowell, Susan Graham 1952- *WhoAmW 91*
McDowell, Thomas Farrow 1941- *WhoSSW 91*
McDowell, Valerie Elizabeth 1944- *WhoAmW 91*
McDowell, W. Wallace, Jr. *WhoAm 90*
McDowell, William Jackson 1925- *WhoSSW 91*
McDowell, William Wallace 1867-1934 *AmLegL*
Mc Dowell, Yvonne Carrol *BiDrAPA 89*
Mc Duff, David R *BiDrAPA 89*
McDuff, Dusa 1945- *WhoE 91*
McDuff, Judith Diane 1945- *WhoAmW 91*
McDuffee, Renee Renaud 1951- *WhoEmL 91*
McDuffie, Camille *ODwPR 91*
McDuffie, David Wayne 1960- *WhoE 91, WhoEmL 91*
McDuffie, Frederic Clement 1924- *WhoAm 90*
Mc Duffie, Malcolm 1915- *WhoAm 90*
McDuffie, Michael Anthony 1954- *WhoE 91, WhoEmL 91*
McDuffie, Robert 1958- *News 90 [port]*
McDuffie, Terris 1910- *Ballpl 90*
McDunn, William Kevin 1957- *WhoEmL 91*
McEachen, Richard Edward 1933- *WhoAm 90*
McEachern, Allan 1926- *WhoAm 90*
McEachern, James Sterling, III 1960- *WhoSSW 91*
McEachern, John Edward *BiDrAPA 89*
McEachern, Warren Shanks 1954- *WhoSSW 91*
McEachern, Wilbur W. 1904-1989 *BioIn 16*
McEachin, James 1930- *DrBlPA 90*
McEachran, Angus 1939- *WhoE 91*
McEachran, Don 1906- *St&PR 91*
McEachron, Donald Lynn 1953- *WhoE 91*
Mc Eathron, Margaret 1899- *WhoWrEP 89*
McEckron, Boyd H. 1834- *AmLegL*
McElaney, Daniel W. 1932- *St&PR 91*
McEldoon, Susan Ann 1952- *WhoAmW 91*
McEldoon, Wesley Alan *BiDrAPA 89*
McEldowney, Henry Clay 1946- *WhoE 91*
McEleney, Brenda Jean 1956- *WhoAmW 91*
Mc Elfresh, Charles Warner 1932- *BiDrAPA 89*
McElfresh, Newland S. 1934- *St&PR 91*
McElhaney, Jack Beattie 1940- *St&PR 91, WhoAm 90*
McElhaney, James Harry 1933- *WhoAm 90*
Mc Elhaney, James Willson 1937- *WhoAm 90*
Mc Elhaney, John Hess 1934- *WhoAm 90*
Mc Elhaney, Robert Dean *BiDrAPA 89*
McElhaney, Ronald *St&PR 91*
Mc Elheney, Mary Diane *BiDrAPA 89*
Mc Elheny, John Daniel 1914- *WhoAm 90*
McElheny, Richard L. 1936- *ODwPR 91*
McElhinney, Susan Kay 1947- *WhoAmW 91*
McElhinny, Wilson D. 1929- *St&PR 91*
McElhinny, Wilson Dunbar 1929- *WhoAm 90*
McEliece, Robert James 1942- *WhoAm 90*
McElligott, James Patrick, Jr. 1948- *WhoSSW 91*
McElligott, Thomas James 1943- *WhoAm 90*
McElligott, Tom *BioIn 16*
McElliott, Lawrence A. 1937- *St&PR 91*
McElrath, Joseph Richard, Jr. 1945- *WhoEmL 91*
McElrath, Richard Elsworth 1932- *St&PR 91*
Mc Elrath, Richard Elsworth 1932- *WhoAm 90*
McElree, James Mitchell 1960 *WhoEmL 91*
McElroy, Abby Lucille Wolman 1957- *WhoAmW 91*
McElroy, Ann 1922- *WhoAmW 91*
Mc Elroy, Betty Howell *BiDrAPA 89*
McElroy, Charles Joseph 1954- *St&PR 91*
McElroy, Christine Mary 1952- *WhoAmW 91*
McElroy, Clifford D. *AuBYP 90*
McElroy, Clinton Eugene 1938- *St&PR 91*
McElroy, Colleen 1935- *FemiCLE*
Mc Elroy, Colleen Johnson 1935- *WhoWrEP 89*
McElroy, David Michael 1945- *WhoSSW 91*
McElroy, Emilie Lin 1954- *WhoAmW 91*
McElroy, Evan T. 1952- *ODwPR 91*
McElroy, Frances Merle 1938- *WhoSSW 91*
McElroy, Frederick William 1939- *WhoE 91*
McElroy, Gary A. 1943- *St&PR 91*
McElroy, Guy C. *BioIn 16, NewYTBS 90 [port]*
Mc Elroy, Harmon Bruce 1949- *WhoSSW 91*
McElroy, Jacquelyn Ann 1942- *WhoAmA 91*
McElroy, James *NewAgMG*
McElroy, James A. 1932- *St&PR 91*
McElroy, Janice Helen 1937- *WhoAmW 91*
McElroy, John D. 1922-1990 *BioIn 16*
Mc Elroy, John Harley 1936- *WhoAm 90*
McElroy, John Joseph 1940- *WhoE 91*
McElroy, John Lee, Jr. 1931- *WhoAm 90*
McElroy, Joseph L. 1929- *St&PR 91*
Mc Elroy, Joseph Prince 1930- *WhoAm 90*
McElroy, June Patricia 1929- *WhoAmW 91*
McElroy, Ken Rex *BioIn 16*
McElroy, Lee 1926- *BioIn 16*
McElroy, Marla Marie 1968- *WhoEmL 91*
McElroy, Mary Arthur 1841-1917 *BioIn 16*
McElroy, Michael 1939- *WhoAm 90*
McElroy, Neil H. 1904-1972 *WorAlBi*
McElroy, Neil Hosler 1904-1972 *BiDrUSE 89*
McElroy, Paul E. 1952- *St&PR 91*
McElroy, Randolph Williams 1935- *St&PR 91, WhoAm 90*
McElroy, Richard Allen 1946- *WhoE 91*
McElroy, Rosemary 1931- *WhoAmW 91*
Mc Elroy, Ross A, Jr. *BiDrAPA 89*
McElroy, Sandra Neskorik *BiDrAPA 89*
McElroy, Susan Lynn *BiDrAPA 89*
Mc Elroy, William David 1917- *WhoAm 90*
McElroy, William Kilmer 1933- *St&PR 91*
McElroy, William M., Jr. 1929- *St&PR 91*
Mc Elroy, William Theodore 1925- *WhoAm 90*
McElroy-Edwards, Jacquelyn Ann 1942- *WhoAmA 91*
McElroy-Lindell, Lois Ann 1958- *WhoAmW 91*
McElvain, David Plowman 1937- *WhoAm 90*
McElvany, Karen Diane 1954- *WhoAmW 91*
McElveen, Joseph James, Jr. 1939- *WhoE 91, WhoWor 91*
McElveen, Junius Carlisle, Jr. 1947- *WhoAm 90*
McElvenny, Ralph T. 1906- *St&PR 91*
McElwain, David Leroy 1952- *BiDrAPA 89*
McElwain, James E. *BioIn 16*
Mc Elwain, Joseph Arthur 1919- *WhoAm 90*
McElwain, Juanita Muriel 1928- *IntWWM 90*
McElwain, Maxine 1941- *WhoSSW 91*
McElwain, William E. 1921- *WhoAm 90*
McElwee, Dennis John 1947- *WhoWor 91*
McElwee, Frank Dixon, Jr. 1947- *WhoAm 90*
McElwee, John Gerard 1921- *St&PR 91*
Mc Elwee, John Gerard 1921- *WhoAm 90, WhoWor 91*
McElwee, Joseph Monroe 1933- *St&PR 91*
McElwee, Ross *BioIn 16*
McElynn, Philip J. 1931- *St&PR 91*
McEnaney, Will 1952- *Ballpl 90*
Mc Enany, Mary Therese 1950- *BiDrAPA 89*
McEneaney, James F. 1938- *St&PR 91*
McEneely, Kevin *BioIn 16*
McEnelly, Minerva Perez 1955- *WhoHisp 91*
Mc Enery, John Winn 1925- *WhoAm 90*
McEnery, Thomas 1945- *WhoAm 90*
McEniry, Joan Lois 1930- *WhoE 91*
McEnroe, Harry Damian 1960- *WhoE 91*
McEnroe, Jack Allyn 1926- *WhoAm 90*
McEnroe, John *BioIn 16*
McEnroe, John 1959- *WorAlBi*
Mc Enroe, John Patrick, Jr. 1959- *WhoAm 90, WhoWor 91*
McEnroe, Timothy D. 1933- *ODwPR 91*
McEntee, Ducat, II 1939- *WhoSSW 91*
McEntee, Gerald *BioIn 16*
McEntee, Gerald W. 1935- *WhoE 91*
Mc Entee, Grace Hall 1940- *WhoWrEP 89*
McEntee, Howard Garrett 1905- *AuBYP 90*
McEntee, R. Michael 1953- *St&PR 91*
McEntee, Richard J. 1935- *St&PR 91*
McEntee, Robert Edward 1932- *WhoAm 90*
Mc Entee, William J, III *BiDrAPA 89*
McEntee, William John 1917- *St&PR 91*
McEntee, William Joseph, Jr. 1952- *WhoE 91, WhoEmL 91, WhoWor 91*
McEntire, James Edward 1944- *St&PR 91*
McEntire, Maleta Mae 1957- *WhoAmW 91*
McEntire, Reba *BioIn 16*
McEntire, Reba 1954- *WhoNeCM [port]*
McEntire, Reba 1955- *WorAlBi*
McEntire, Reba N. 1955- *WhoAm 90, WhoAmW 91*
Mc Entire, Wesley Edward *BiDrAPA 89*
McErlane, Joseph James 1948- *WhoAm 90*
McEver, Earl Lawson 1926- *WhoSSW 91*
Mc Evers, Robert Darwin 1930- *WhoAm 90*
McEvilley, Thomas 1939- *WhoAmA 91, WhoE 91*
Mc Evilly, Thomas Vincent 1934- *WhoAm 90*
McEvily, John Vincent, Jr. 1949- *WhoSSW 91*
McEvoy, A. H. 1947- *St&PR 91*
McEvoy, Charles Lucien 1917- *WhoAm 90*
McEvoy, Daniel Joseph *WhoE 91*
McEvoy, Gerald William 1948- *St&PR 91*
McEvoy, Gerard Peter 1928- *St&PR 91*
McEvoy, Harry 1902-1984 *DcNaB 1981*

McEvoy, J. P. *EncACom*
McEvoy, Joseph Edward 1942- *WhoAm 90*
McEvoy, Joseph Patrick 1948- *BiDrAPA 89*
McEvoy, Mary Spencer 1870-1941 *BiDWomA*
McEvoy, Ronald James 1947- *WhoSSW 91*
McEvoy, Thomas 1942- *St&PR 91*
McEvoy Johnston, Pamela 1937- *WhoAmW 91, WhoWor 91*
McEwan, Ian 1948- *BestSel 90-4 [port], MajTwCW*
Mc Ewan, Leonard 1925- *WhoAm 90*
McEwan, Neil 1946- *ConAu 130*
McEwen, Aila Erman 1941- *WhoAmW 91*
McEwen, Alexander Campbell 1926- *WhoAm 90*
McEwen, Bob 1950- *WhoAm 90*
McEwen, Curier *BioIn 16*
Mc Ewen, Diane Marylin 1942- *BiDrAPA 89*
McEwen, Gerald Kent 1944- *WhoSSW 91*
McEwen, Jean 1923- *WhoAm 90, WhoAmA 91*
McEwen, John Duncan *BiDrAPA 89*
McEwen, Joyce Lynae 1965- *WhoSSW 91*
McEwen, Mark *BioIn 16*
McEwen, Mary Louise 1960- *WhoAmW 91, WhoE 91*
McEwen, Robert C. *ODwPR 91*
Mc Ewen, Robert Cameron 1920- *WhoAm 90*
McEwen, Robert Joseph 1916- *WhoE 91, WhoWor 91*
McEwen, Robert R. 1950- *St&PR 91*
McEwen, Thomas Ray 1931- *St&PR 91*
McEwen, William Peter *BioIn 16, NewYTBS 90*
McFadden, Alexander Bratton 1929- *WhoSSW 91*
McFadden, Bernard John 1930- *WhoSSW 91*
McFadden, Bernard Joseph 1933- *St&PR 91*
McFadden, Bradford, Jr. 1940- *St&PR 91*
McFadden, Brian Patrick 1950- *WhoE 91*
McFadden, Cheryl *ConTFT 8 [port]*
McFadden, Dan 1950- *ODwPR 91*
McFadden, David 1940- *BioIn 16*
McFadden, David Revere *WhoAmA 91*
McFadden, David Wayne 1942- *WhoE 91*
McFadden, Dennis 1940 *WhoSSW 91*
McFadden, Dennis 1949- *WhoAm 90*
McFadden, Dennis J. 1952- *St&PR 91*
McFadden, Dorothy Loa 1902- *AuBYP 90*
Mc Fadden, Earl B *BiDrAPA 89*
McFadden, Edward H. 1942- *St&PR 91*
McFadden, Frank Hampton 1925- *St&PR 91, WhoAm 90*
Mc Fadden, Frank William 1914- *WhoAm 90*
Mc Fadden, G. Bruce 1934- *WhoAm 90*
McFadden, Gates *ConTFT 8 [port]*
Mc Fadden, George Linus 1927- *WhoAm 90*
McFadden, Glynn Calvin 1925- *WhoSSW 91*
McFadden, Gregory Smith 1948- *BiDrAPA 89*
Mc Fadden, I Joseph 1940- *BiDrAPA 89*
McFadden, James Frederick, Jr. 1920- *WhoAm 90, WhoWor 91*
Mc Fadden, James Patrick 1930- *WhoAm 90, WhoE 91*
McFadden, John 1934- *WhoAm 90, WhoSSW 91*
McFadden, John J. 1937- *St&PR 91*
Mc Fadden, John Volney 1931- *WhoAm 90*
Mc Fadden, Joseph Michael 1932- *WhoAm 90, WhoSSW 91*
McFadden, Joseph Patrick 1939- *St&PR 91, WhoAm 90*
McFadden, Louis Thomas 1876-1936 *EncABHB 7 [port]*
McFadden, Mary *BioIn 16*
McFadden, Mary 1938- *ConDes 90, WhoAmA 91*
McFadden, Mary 1950- *WhoAmW 91*
McFadden, Mary Josephine 1938- *St&PR 91*
Mc Fadden, Mary Josephine 1938- *WhoAm 90, WhoAmW 91*
McFadden, Patrick Joseph James 1952- *WhoE 91, WhoEmL 91, WhoWor 91*
McFadden, Peter William 1932- *WhoAm 90*
McFadden, Polly Lee 1949- *St&PR 91*
McFadden, Robert Barker 1929- *St&PR 91*
McFadden, Rosemary Theresa 1948- *WhoAm 90, WhoAmW 91, WhoWor 91*
Mc Fadden, Sybill Martin 1918- *WhoAmW 91*
McFadden, Thomas 1935- *WhoAm 90*
Mc Fadden, Thomas Bernard 1917- *WhoAm 90*
McFadden, Veronica Sandra 1967- *WhoAmW 91*
McFadin, Robert L. 1921- *St&PR 91*
McFadin, Robert Lee 1921- *WhoAm 90*
McFadzean, Bruce William 1945- *WhoAm 90*
McFall, Catherine Gardner 1952- *WhoAm 90*
McFall, Dan Frank 1945- *St&PR 91*
McFall, Daniel John 1961- *WhoEmL 91*
McFall, Donna Sullivan 1950- *WhoAmW 91*
McFall, John H. 1924- *St&PR 91*
McFall, Kenneth Helicer 1906- *WhoAm 90*
Mc Falls, Frederick D *BiDrAPA 89*
McFalls, Robert Alan 1945- *St&PR 91*
McFarlan, Donald M. 1915- *BioIn 16*
McFarlan, Douglas Robert 1954- *WhoEmL 91*
McFarlan, Franklin Warren 1937- *WhoAm 90*
McFarland, Alan Roberts 1942- *St&PR 91*
Mc Farland, Anne S. 1940- *WhoWrEP 89*
McFarland, Bentson Hayes 1949- *BiDrAPA 89*
McFarland, Chappie 1875-1924 *Ballpl 90*
McFarland, David E. 1938- *WhoAm 90*
McFarland, David Joseph 1916- *St&PR 91*
McFarland, Donna Reyne 1948- *WhoWor 91*
McFarland, Douglas Dale, Jr. 1946- *WhoEmL 91*
McFarland, Ed 1874-1959 *Ballpl 90*
McFarland, Francis Edmund 1947- *St&PR 91*
Mc Farland, Frank Eugene 1918- *WhoAm 90*
McFarland, G. Richmond, Jr. 1934- *St&PR 91*
McFarland, Galen David 1951- *WhoEmL 91*
McFarland, George Emmett 1928- *BioIn 16*
Mc Farland, H. Richard 1930- *WhoAm 90*
McFarland, Herm 1870-1935 *Ballpl 90*
McFarland, James, Jr. 1946- *WhoE 91*
McFarland, James Howard 1937- *St&PR 91, WhoAm 90*
McFarland, James P. 1912- *St&PR 91*
McFarland, James Thomas 1937- *St&PR 91*
McFarland, James W. *WhoAm 90*
McFarland, Jane Elizabeth 1937- *WhoSSW 91*
McFarland, Jim 1949- *ODwPR 91*
McFarland, John A. 1920- *St&PR 91*
Mc Farland, John Bernard 1943- *WhoWrEP 89*
McFarland, Kay Eleanor 1935- *WhoAmW 91*
McFarland, Kay Flowers 1942- *WhoAmW 91*
Mc Farland, Keith Nielson 1921- *WhoAm 90*
McFarland, Kenton D. 1920- *AuBYP 90*
McFarland, Kevin John 1958- *WhoEmL 91, WhoWor 91*
McFarland, Lee Craig 1920- *St&PR 91*
McFarland, Lellan Lee 1937- *St&PR 91*
McFarland, Lynne Vernice 1953- *WhoAmW 91*
McFarland, Margaret B. 1904-1988 *BioIn 16*
McFarland, Maria J. E. 1943- *St&PR 91*
McFarland, Mary Brambilla *BioIn 16*
Mc Farland, Norman Francis 1922- *WhoAm 90*
McFarland, Queenie A. *BioIn 16*
McFarland, Richard D. 1930- *St&PR 91*
McFarland, Richard M. 1923- *St&PR 91*
McFarland, Richard Macklin 1922- *WhoAm 90, WhoWor 91*
Mc Farland, Robert Harold 1918- *WhoAm 90*
McFarland, Ron 1942- *ConAu 32NR*
McFarland, Ronald George 1928- *IntWWM 90*
McFarland, Samuel 1814-1862 *AmLegL*
McFarland, Sharon Jeannette 1938- *WhoAmW 91*
McFarland, Spanky 1928- *BioIn 16*
McFarland, Steven M. *St&PR 91*
McFarland, Susan Louise 1958- *WhoAmW 91*
Mc Farland, Terry Lynn 1947- *WhoSSW 91*
McFarland, Thomas 1926- *BioIn 16*
McFarland, Tom *NewAgMG*
McFarland, Veda Dianne 1958- *WhoAmW 91*
McFarland, Violet Sweet 1908- *WhoAmW 91, WhoWor 91*
McFarland, Waneta Joan 1936- *St&PR 91*
McFarland, William Joseph 1929- *WhoAm 90*
McFarland, Wilma *AuBYP 90*
McFarland-Johnson, Jeffrey Curtis 1955- *IntWWM 90*
McFarlane, Beth Lucetta Troester 1918- *WhoAmW 91*
McFarlane, Clare 1963- *IntWWM 90*
McFarlane, Gregory Alan 1956- *WhoEmL 91*
McFarlane, Harry William 1929- *WhoWor 91*
Mc Farlane, Karen Elizabeth 1942- *WhoAm 90*
McFarlane, Robert C. *BioIn 16*
McFarlane, William F. *WhoAm 90*
McFarlane, William R. 1943- *BiDrAPA 89*
McFarley, Kevin Michael 1951- *WhoSSW 91*
McFarlin, Max M. 1942- *St&PR 91*
Mc Farlin, Robert L *BiDrAPA 89*
McFarlin, Whitney Allyn 1940- *WhoAm 90*
McFarling, Donald Partlow 1922- *St&PR 91*
McFarren, Grace 1914- *WhoAmA 91*
Mc Fate, Patricia Ann 1936- *WhoAm 90*
McFather, Jon Clifford 1934- *WhoSSW 91*
McFatridge, Keith William, Jr. 1946- *St&PR 91*
McFaul, Patricia Louise 1947- *WhoAmW 91*
McFayden, Mike *BioIn 16*
Mc Featters, Dale Stitt 1911- *WhoAm 90, WhoWor 91*
McFedries, Robert, Jr. *St&PR 91*
Mc Fedries, Robert, Jr. 1930- *WhoAm 90*
Mc Fee, Arthur Storer 1932- *WhoAm 90*
McFee, Henry Lee 1886-1953 *WhoAmA 91N*
McFee, John R. 1816- *AmLegL*
McFee, June King 1917- *WhoAmA 91*
McFee, Michael 1954- *ConAu 30NR*
Mc Fee, Michael Alan 1954- *WhoWrEP 89*
McFee, Richard 1925- *WhoAm 90*
Mc Fee, Thomas Stuart 1930- *WhoAm 90*
McFee, William Warren 1935- *WhoAm 90*
Mc Feeley, John Jay 1945- *WhoE 91*
Mc Feely, Laramie J. 1933- *WhoWrEP 89*
Mc Feely, William Shield 1930- *WhoAm 90, WhoSSW 91, WhoWrEP 89*
McFeetors, R. L. 1944- *St&PR 91*
Mc Feron, Dean Earl 1923- *WhoAm 90*
McFerran, Richard Wallace 1937- *St&PR 91*
Mc Ferren, Glen Michael 1955- *BiDrAPA 89*
Mc Ferren, Martha Dean 1947- *WhoWrEP 89*
McFerrin, Bobby *BioIn 16*
McFerrin, Bobby 1950- *DrBlPA 90, WorAlBi*
Mc Ferrin, James Reed 1949- *BiDrAPA 89*
McFerrin, Robert 1921- *DrBlPA 90*
McFerrin, Sam Cox 1945- *WhoSSW 91*
McFerron, Kathryn L. 1951- *St&PR 91*
McFerson, D. Richard 1937- *St&PR 91*
McFillin, Paul Lee 1952- *WhoSSW 91*
Mc Gaffey, Jere D. 1935- *WhoAm 90*
McGaffigan, Andy 1956- *Ballpl 90*
McGaffigan, Edward, Jr. 1948- *WhoE 91*
McGagh, William G. 1929- *St&PR 91*
McGagh, William Gilbert 1929- *WhoAm 90, WhoWor 91*
McGaha, Barbara Joyce 1936- *WhoAmW 91*
McGahan, David Patrick 1960- *WhoSSW 91*
Mc Gahee, Carl Leon 1931- *BiDrAPA 89*
McGahee, Dorothy Braudy *WhoAmA 91*
McGahern, John 1934- *MajTwCW*
McGanity, Brian David 1954- *St&PR 91*
McGann, Dan 1871-1910 *Ballpl 90*
Mc Gann, Geraldine 1937- *WhoAmW 91*
McGann, James Joseph 1949- *WhoE 91*
McGann, Jerome John 1937- *WhoAm 90*
McGann, John M. 1948- *St&PR 91*
McGann, John Milton 1948- *WhoEmL 91*
McGann, John Raymond 1924- *WhoAm 90, WhoE 91*
McGann, Robert George 1947- *St&PR 91*
McGannon, Patrick James 1956- *WhoSSW 91*
McGarey, Charles O'Brien 1929- *WhoE 91*
McGarey, Gladys Taylor 1920- *NewAgE 90*
McGarey, William A. 1919- *NewAgE 90*
Mc Garity, Edmund Cody, Jr. 1928- *WhoAm 90*
Mc Garity, Seaborn S, Jr. *BiDrAPA 89*
McGarr, Anita 1951- *WhoAmW 91*
McGarr, Charles Taylor 1956- *WhoSSW 91*
McGarr, Evelyn Franz 1910- *WhoAmW 91*
McGarr, Frank J. 1921- *WhoAm 90*
McGarr, Paul Rowland 1933- *St&PR 91*
Mc Garr, Paul Rowland 1933- *WhoAm 90*
Mc Garrah, Robert Eynon 1921- *WhoAm 90*
McGarrell, James 1930- *WhoAm 90, WhoAmA 91*
McGarrity, Richard Allen 1948- *WhoSSW 91*
McGarry, Arthur Daniel 1948- *WhoEmL 91*
McGarry, Charles William 1957- *WhoSSW 91*
McGarry, Eugene L. 1930- *WhoAm 90*
McGarry, Frederick Jerome 1927- *WhoAm 90*
McGarry, H. M. 1852- *BioIn 16*
McGarry, John Patrick, Jr. 1939- *WhoAm 90*
McGarry, John Warren *WhoAm 90*
McGarry, Marlane Weber *ODwPR 91*
McGarry, Marlane Weber 1938- *WhoAm 90*
McGarry, Patricia Josephine 1947- *WhoAmA 91*
McGarry, Susan Hallsten 1948- *WhoAmA 91, WhoAmW 91*
McGarry, Thomas F. 1929- *ODwPR 91, St&PR 91*
McGarry, William Andrew, Jr. 1954- *WhoAm 90, WhoSSW 91*
McGarry, William C. 1951- *St&PR 91*
McGarry, William G. 1926- *St&PR 91*
McGartland, Grace 1951- *WhoE 91*
McGarty, John Francis 1947- *WhoE 91*
McGarvey, Annamaria Jude 1964- *WhoAmW 91, WhoE 91*
McGarvey, Mary Hewitt *WhoE 91*
McGarvey, Owen 1821?-1897 *DcCanB 12*
McGarvey, Robert Mattock 1929- *St&PR 91*
McGarvey, Wayne Carlton 1939- *St&PR 91*
McGary, Betty Winstead 1936- *WhoAmW 91*
McGary, Dave *BioIn 16*
McGary, Johnny Sylvester 1948- *WhoSSW 91*
Mc Gaugh, James Lafayette 1931- *WhoAm 90*
Mc Gaughan, Alexander Stanley 1912- *WhoAm 90, WhoE 91*
McGaughey, Claude R. 1951- *BioIn 16*
McGaughey, Emmett Connell 1911- *WhoAm 90*
McGaughey, Frank S. 1923- *St&PR 91*
McGaughey, John Cameron, Jr. 1963- *WhoSSW 91, WhoWor 91*
Mc Gaughey, Kathryn Elizabeth 1918- *WhoWrEP 89*
McGaughey, Miriam *IntWWM 90*
Mc Gaughy, John Bell 1914- *WhoAm 90*
McGaughy, Tim Whittus 1946- *BiDrAPA 89*
McGauley, Jacquelyne Sue 1951- *WhoAmW 91*
McGauley, Lawrence Paul 1926- *St&PR 91*
Mc Gauly, Monica A *BiDrAPA 89*
McGauran, John Charles 1924- *WhoWor 91*
McGavern, John Howard 1926- *WhoAm 90*
McGavin, Darren 1922- *WhoAm 90, WorAlBi*
McGavin, John David 1957- *WhoEmL 91*
McGavran, Brenda Joyce 1946- *WhoAmW 91*
McGavran, Donald 1897-1990? *ConAu 132*
McGavran, Grace Winifred *AuBYP 90*
Mc Gaw, Jessie Brewer 1913- *WhoAmW 91*
McGaw, Kenneth Roy 1926- *WhoAm 90*
McGaw, Sidney Edwin 1908- *WhoWor 91*
McGeachy, Mary C. *ODwPR 91*
McGeady, Kathleen Birmingham 1949- *WhoAmW 91*
McGeady, Leon Joseph 1921- *WhoAm 90*
McGeady, Paul Joseph 1920- *WhoE 91*
McGee, Anita Newcomb 1864-1940 *BioIn 16*
McGee, Ava Lounetta 1949- *WhoSSW 91*
McGee, Barbara 1949- *WhoAmW 91*
McGee, Bill 1909-1987 *Ballpl 90*
McGee, Carla Creighton 1936- *WhoAmW 91*
McGee, David *BioIn 16*
McGee, David 1957- *St&PR 91*
McGee, Dean A. *St&PR 91N*
McGee, Dean Anderson 1904- *ConAmBL*
McGee, Dennis *BioIn 16*
McGee, Dorothy Horton *AuBYP 90*
McGee, Dorothy Horton 1913- *WhoAmW 91, WhoE 91, WhoWor 91*
McGee, Effie Mary 1928- *WhoAmW 91*
McGee, Fibber *BioIn 16*
McGee, Francis David 1934- *St&PR 91*
McGee, Frank 1921-1974 *BioIn 16*
Mc Gee, Gale 1915- *WhoAm 90*
McGee, Gary L. 1949- *St&PR 91*
McGee, Hall Thomas, Jr. 1913- *WhoAm 90, WhoWor 91*
McGee, Harold Johnston 1937- *WhoAm 90, WhoSSW 91*

McGee, Henry Alexander, Jr. 1929- *WhoAm 90*
McGee, Humphrey Glenn 1937- *WhoSSW 91*
McGee, James G., Jr. 1929- *St&PR 91*
McGee, James Lee 1946- *St&PR 91*
McGee, James Patrick 1941- *WhoE 91*
McGee, James Sears 1942- *WhoAm 90*
McGee, Jane Marie 1926- *WhoAmW 91*
McGee, Janet 1958- *WhoSSW 91*
McGee, Janet D. *St&PR 91*
McGee, Jerry V. 1930- *St&PR 91*
McGee, John Frampton 1923- *St&PR 91*
Mc Gee, John Frampton 1923- *WhoAm 90, WhoSSW 91*
Mc Gee, Joseph John, Jr. 1919- *WhoAm 90*
McGee, Joy Ann 1946- *WhoAmW 91*
McGee, Joyce Fantino 1947- *WhoAmW 91*
McGee, Kathleen Agnes 1944- *WhoAmW 91*
McGee, Lynne Kalavsky 1949- *WhoAmW 91*
McGee, Marion Dewitt 1925- *St&PR 91*
McGee, Martha 1933- *WhoSSW 91*
McGee, Mary Alice 1950- *WhoAmW 91*
McGee, Mary S. 1960- *St&PR 91*
McGee, Michael David 1958- *BiDrAPA 89*
McGee, Michael Jay 1952- *WhoEmL 91, WhoWor 91*
McGee, Nancy Rasco 1938- *WhoSSW 91*
McGee, Olivia Jackson 1915-1987 *WhoAmA 91N*
McGee, Patricia Sabyna 1921- *WhoAmW 91, WhoSSW 91*
McGee, Patrick A. *ODwPR 91*
Mc Gee, Patrick Edgar 1944- *WhoWrEP 89*
McGee, Pattie Lee Biggers 1906- *WhoAmW 91*
McGee, Ralph E. 1937- *St&PR 91*
McGee, Reece Jerome 1929- *WhoAm 90*
McGee, Robert Walter 1922- *St&PR 91*
McGee, Suzanne Irene 1949- *WhoE 91*
McGee, Thomas D'Arcy 1825-1868 *DcLB 99 [port]*
McGee, Vonetta *BioIn 16, DrBlPA 90*
McGee, William G. *WhoSSW 91*
McGee, Willie 1958- *Ballpl 90*
McGee, Winston Eugene 1924- *WhoAmA 91*
McGeehan, Daniel P. 1929- *St&PR 91*
McGeehan, Marie L. *ODwPR 91*
McGeehon, Carol Louise 1955- *WhoEmL 91*
McGeer, Edith Graef 1923- *WhoAm 90*
Mc Gehee, Benjamin Harris 1918- *WhoAm 90*
McGehee, C. Coleman 1924- *St&PR 91*
Mc Gehee, Carden Coleman 1924- *WhoAm 90*
Mc Gehee, Claude Smith, Jr. 1944- *WhoSSW 91*
McGehee, Frank S. 1928- *St&PR 91*
Mc Gehee, H. Coleman, Jr. 1923- *WhoAm 90*
Mc Gehee, James Bartley 1939- *BiDrAPA 89*
Mc Gehee, Larry Thomas 1936- *WhoAm 90*
McGehee, Rex Hammond *BiDrAPA 89*
McGehee, Richard Paul 1943- *WhoAm 90*
McGehee, Richard Vernon 1934- *WhoSSW 91*
McGehee, Susan Terrell 1954- *WhoSSW 91*
McGehee, Thomas Ford, Jr. 1928- *WhoSSW 91*
McGehee, Thomas Rives 1924- *St&PR 91, WhoSSW 91*
McGehee, William 1908-1987 *BioIn 16*
McGeorge, Ronald Kenneth 1944- *WhoAm 90*
McGerity, Margaret Ann 1949- *WhoAmW 91*
McGerr, Patricia 1917-1985 *SpyFic, TwCCr&M 91*
McGervey, John Donald 1931- *WhoAm 90*
McGervey, Paul John, III 1947- *WhoWor 91*
McGettigan, Charles Carroll, Jr. 1945- *WhoAm 90*
McGhan, Donald K. 1934- *St&PR 91*
McGhee, Brownie 1915- *OxCPMus*
McGhee, David Wesson 1945- *WhoWor 91*
McGhee, Donald Lorin 1941- *St&PR 91*
McGhee, Donna Susan 1957- *WhoAmW 91*
McGhee, Ed 1924-1986 *Ballpl 90*
McGhee, George Crews 1912- *BioIn 16, WhoAm 90*
Mc Ghee, James Olen 1951- *WhoSSW 91*
McGhee, Wes *WhoNeCM B [port]*
Mc Ghee, William H 1947- *BiDrAPA 89*
McGhehey, John Howard 1943- *St&PR 91*
McGibbon, Donald B. 1935- *ODwPR 91*
McGibbon, J. Ian 1927- *St&PR 91*
Mc Gibbon, Pauline Mills 1910- *WhoAm 90*
McGibney, Frederick Richards 1936- *St&PR 91*
McGiehan, Donna Alene 1957- *WhoAmW 91, WhoSSW 91*
McGiff, John Charles 1927- *WhoAm 90*
Mc Giffert, David Eliot 1926- *WhoAm 90*
Mc Giffert, John Rutherford 1926- *WhoAm 90*
McGiffert, Michael 1928- *WhoAm 90*
Mc Giffert, Michael 1928- *WhoWrEP 89*
McGiffin, Lee 1908- *AuBYP 90*
McGilberry, Velma Gwen 1954- *WhoAmW 91*
McGilchrist, Iain 1953- *ConAu 132*
Mc Gill, Archie Joseph 1931- *WhoAm 90, WhoE 91*
McGill, Bill A. 1925- *St&PR 91*
McGill, Charles B. 1922- *St&PR 91*
McGill, Charles Harry, III 1942- *St&PR 91*
McGill, D. G. 1918- *St&PR 91*
McGill, Dan Mays 1919- *WhoAm 90, WhoWor 91*
Mc Gill, Esby Clifton 1914- *WhoAm 90*
McGill, Evelyn 1952- *WhoAmW 91*
McGill, Forrest 1947- *WhoAm 90, WhoAmA 91*
McGill, Grace Anita 1943- *WhoAmW 91*
McGill, Harold A *WhoAmA 91N*
McGill, J. C. 1928- *St&PR 91*
McGill, James 1744-1813 *WorAlBi*
McGill, James C. 1928- *WhoAm 90*
McGill, John Knox 1956- *WhoSSW 91*
McGill, John Rudolph 1936- *St&PR 91*
McGill, Kenneth Eugene 1941- *WhoSSW 91*
McGill, Kenneth James 1942- *St&PR 91*
McGill, Loy B. 1954- *St&PR 91*
McGill, Maurice Leon 1936- *WhoAm 90*
McGill, Michael Vincent 1943- *WhoE 91*
McGill, Ralph 1898-1969 *BioIn 16*
McGill, Ray 1892-1963 *EncACom*
McGill, Robert Ernest, III 1931- *St&PR 91*
Mc Gill, Robert Ernest, III 1931- *WhoAm 90, WhoWor 91*
McGill, Ross Kim 1955- *WhoWor 91*
McGill, Scott A. 1951- *WhoEmL 91*
McGill, Stephen Andrew 1957- *WhoSSW 91*
McGill, Thomas Emerson 1930- *WhoAm 90*
McGill, Thomas Joseph 1937- *St&PR 91, WhoAm 90*
McGill, Warren Everett 1923- *WhoAm 90*
McGill, William A. 1925- *St&PR 91*
Mc Gill, William Howard 1955- *BiDrAPA 89*
McGill, William J. 1922- *St&PR 91*
McGill, William James, Jr. 1936- *WhoAm 90*
McGilley, Mary Janet 1924- *WhoAm 90, WhoAmW 91*
McGillicuddy, Mr. *AuBYP 90*
McGillicuddy, Charles C. 1932- *ODwPR 91*
McGillicuddy, Cornelius 1862-1956 *BioIn 16*
McGillicuddy, Cornelius 1940- *BioIn 16*
McGillicuddy, Helen F. *BioIn 16*
McGillicuddy, John F. 1930- *St&PR 91*
McGillicuddy, John Francis 1930- *BioIn 16*
Mc Gillicuddy, John Francis 1930- *WhoAm 90, WhoE 91*
McGillicuddy, Trant Valentine O'Connell 1849-1896 *WhNaAH*
McGillis, Eugene Guinane 1934- *St&PR 91*
McGillis, Kelly *BioIn 16*
McGillis, Kelly 1957- *WorAlBi*
McGillis, Kevin Donald H 1951- *WhoWor 91*
McGillivary, Christopher John 1947- *St&PR 91*
McGillivray, Alexander 1759?-1793 *EncCRAm, WhNaAH*
McGillivray, Donald 1857-1900 *DcCanB 12*
McGillivray, Donald Dean 1928- *WhoAm 90*
McGilvery, Laurence 1932- *WhoAmA 91*
McGilvirray, William J. 1943- *St&PR 91*
McGilvrey, Sakura Lee 1949- *WhoAmW 91*
McGimpsey, Ronald A. 1944- *St&PR 91*
Mc Gimpsey, Ronald Alan 1944- *WhoAm 90*
Mc Gimsey, Charles Robert, III 1925- *WhoAm 90*
McGimsey, Edward C. 1921- *St&PR 91*
McGimsey, Edward C., Jr. 1949- *St&PR 91*
McGinity, Gregory Francis 1965- *WhoE 91*
McGinity, James W. *WhoAm 90*
McGinley, John Francis 1928- *St&PR 91*
McGinley, Joseph Patrick 1947- *WhoE 91*
McGinley, Nancy Elizabeth 1952- *WhoAmW 91, WhoSSW 91, WhoWor 91*
McGinley, Patrick 1937- *WorAu 1980 [port]*
McGinley, Patrick John 1938- *St&PR 91*
McGinley, Phyllis 1905-1978 *BioAmW, FemiCLE, WorAlBi*
McGinley, Phyllis Louise 1905-1978 *AuBYP 90*
McGinn, Dan 1943- *Ballpl 90*
McGinn, Eileen 1947- *WhoAmW 91*
McGinn, Frank L. 1929- *St&PR 91*
McGinn, Joseph 1861-1922 *Ballpl 90*
Mc Ginn, Joseph Reginald 1955- *BiDrAPA 89*
McGinn, Mary Lyn 1949- *WhoAmW 91*
McGinn, Robert F. 1951- *St&PR 91*
Mc Ginnes, Edgar Allen, Jr. 1926- *WhoAm 90*
Mc Ginness, William George, III 1948- *WhoAm 90, WhoSSW 91*
McGinnies, Elliott Morse 1921- *WhoAm 90*
McGinnis, Andrew Mosher 1946- *WhoEmL 91*
McGinnis, Arthur J. 1911- *St&PR 91*
Mc Ginnis, Arthur Joseph 1911- *WhoAm 90*
McGinnis, Arthur Joseph, Jr. 1952- *St&PR 91, WhoE 91*
McGinnis, Bernard C., III 1942- *St&PR 91*
McGinnis, Charles Irving 1928- *WhoAm 90*
McGinnis, Christine *WhoAmA 91*
McGinnis, Conrad D. 1938- *St&PR 91*
McGinnis, Daniel L. 1939- *St&PR 91*
McGinnis, Elizabeth A. 1955- *St&PR 91*
McGinnis, James Arthur 1947- *St&PR 91*
Mc Ginnis, James E *BiDrAPA 89*
McGinnis, James Earl, Jr. 1928- *St&PR 91*
Mc Ginnis, James Michael 1944- *WhoAm 90*
McGinnis, Jane Ann Berndt 1954- *WhoEmL 91*
McGinnis, John Oldham 1957- *WhoAm 90*
McGinnis, Larry Micheal 1956- *St&PR 91*
McGinnis, Lyle David 1931- *WhoAm 90*
McGinnis, Marcy Ann 1950- *WhoAmW 91*
Mc Ginnis, Robert Cameron 1925- *WhoAm 90*
McGinnis, Robert William 1930- *St&PR 91*
McGinnis, Sean William 1955- *WhoE 91*
McGinnis, Sid *BioIn 16*
McGinnis, Thomas Michael 1954- *WhoEmL 91*
McGinnis, Timothy 1940- *St&PR 91, WhoAm 90*
McGinnis, Timothy F. *BioIn 16*
McGinnis, William W. 1935- *St&PR 91*
McGinnis-Swiger, Dorothy Kay 1947- *WhoAmW 91*
McGinniss, Edward J. 1929- *St&PR 91*
McGinniss, Joe *BioIn 16*
Mc Ginniss, Joe 1942- *WhoAm 90, WhoWrEP 89*
McGinnity, James M. 1942- *St&PR 91*
McGinnity, Joe 1871-1929 *Ballpl 90 [port], BioIn 16*
McGinnity, Ronald James 1940- *St&PR 91*
McGinty, Anne 1945- *IntWWM 90, WhoAmW 91*
McGinty, Doris Evans 1925- *IntWWM 90*
McGinty, John 1911- *WhoAm 90*
McGinty, John Edward 1946- *St&PR 91*
Mc Ginty, John Milton 1935- *WhoAm 90*
McGinty, Kevin J. 1949- *St&PR 91*
McGinty, Maribeth 1957- *WhoEmL 91*
McGinty, Milton Bradford 1946- *WhoAm 90*
McGinty, Thomas Edward 1929- *WhoAm 90*
McGirr, Edmund 1922-1972 *TwCCr&M 91*
McGirr, Jackelen Richardson 1941- *WhoAmW 91*
McGirr, Sarah Elizabeth 1938- *WhoAmW 91*
McGiverin, Donald Scott 1924- *St&PR 91, WhoAm 90, WhoWor 91*
McGivern, Arthur J. 1947- *St&PR 91*
McGivern, Maureen Daly *AuBYP 90*
McGivern, William P 1922-1982 *TwCCr&M 91*
McGivney, James 1948- *WhoEmL 91*
McGivney, Maria Frances 1963- *WhoAmW 91*
McGivney, William D. 1931- *St&PR 91*
McGivney, William David 1934- *WhoE 91*
McGladdery, Joseph Raymond 1927- *WhoWor 91*
McGlamery, Barbara Coggins 1939- *WhoAmW 91*
Mc Glamery, Marshal Dean 1932- *WhoAm 90*
Mc Glashan, Thomas Hamel 1941- *BiDrAPA 89*
McGlauchlin, Tom 1934- *WhoAmA 91*
McGlaughlin, William 1943- *IntWWM 90*
McGlaun, Bill 1948- *BioIn 16*
McGlennon, Felix 1856-1943 *OxCPMus*
McGlinchey, Dianne Watkins 1949- *WhoAmW 91*
McGlinchey, Joseph D. 1938- *St&PR 91*
McGlinchey, Joseph Dennis 1938- *WhoAm 90*
McGlohon, Loonis Reeves 1921- *WhoAm 90*
McGlone, John Francis 1936- *St&PR 91*
McGlothen, Lynn 1950-1984 *Ballpl 90*
McGlothin, Jim 1943-1975 *Ballpl 90*
McGlothlin, David Edward 1950- *St&PR 91*
McGlothlin, Donald Ernest 1941- *IntWWM 90*
McGlothlin, James Edwin 1935- *St&PR 91*
Mc Glothlin, James Harrison 1910- *WhoAm 90*
McGlothlin, Ray, Jr. *WhoAm 90*
Mc Glothlin, Regina Dwyer 1952- *BiDrAPA 89*
McGlotten, Robert Miller 1938- *WhoAm 90*
McGlown, Kathlyn Joanne 1954- *WhoSSW 91*
Mc Glynn, Brian James 1952- *WhoWrEP 89*
McGlynn, Charles Thomas *BiDrAPA 89*
McGlynn, John Lawrence 1957- *WhoE 91*
McGlynn, Joseph Leo, Jr. 1925- *WhoAm 90*
McGlynn, Richard Bruce 1938- *WhoE 91*
McGlynn, Richard D. 1929- *St&PR 91*
Mc Glynn, Sean Patrick 1931- *WhoAm 90*
McGlynn, Stoney 1872-1941 *Ballpl 90*
McGlynn, Thomas 1906- *WhoAmA 91N*
McGoldrick, John F. 1927- *ODwPR 91*
Mc Goldrick, John Gardiner 1932- *WhoAm 90*
McGoldrick, John Lewis 1941- *WhoE 91*
McGoldrick, Mary A. 1958- *WhoSSW 91*
McGoldrick, Thomas John 1941- *St&PR 91*
McGoldrick, William Patrick 1946- *WhoE 91*
Mc Gonagle, Laurence C *BiDrAPA 89*
McGonegle, Timothy Joseph 1952- *WhoEmL 91*
McGonigal, Pearl 1929- *WhoAm 90*
McGonigle, James Gregory 1945- *WhoE 91, WhoEmL 91, WhoWor 91*
McGonigle, John William 1938- *St&PR 91, WhoAm 90*
Mc Gonigle, Paul John 1942- *WhoAm 90*
Mc Gonigle, Thomas *WhoWrEP 89*
McGonigle, Thomas Patrick 1960- *WhoWor 91*
McGoogan, Judith Dianne 1946- *WhoEmL 91*
McGoohan, Patrick 1928- *WorAlBi*
McGoohan, Patrick Joseph 1928- *WhoAm 90*
McGookey, James E. 1935- *St&PR 91*
McGoon, Cliff 1939- *ODwPR 91*
Mc Goon, Clifford 1939- *WhoWrEP 89*
Mc Goon, Dwight Charles 1925- *WhoAm 90*
McGorrian, Grace Maureen *BiDrAPA 89*
McGorrill, Bruce Courtney 1931- *WhoAm 90, WhoE 91*
McGorty, Frank P. 1930- *St&PR 91*
Mc Gouey, Robert 1928- *WhoWrEP 89*
McGough, Catherine Caya 1933- *WhoE 91*
McGough, Charles E 1927- *WhoAmA 91*
McGough, Duane Theodore 1932- *WhoAm 90, WhoE 91*
McGough, George Vincent 1940- *St&PR 91*
McGough, James John *BiDrAPA 89*
Mc Gough, James W *BiDrAPA 89*
McGough, Jeannne B. 1948- *WhoAmW 91*
McGough, John Paul 1935- *WhoE 91*
McGough, Kelly Lynn 1963- *WhoSSW 91*
McGough, Stephen C 1949- *WhoAmA 91*
Mc Gough, W Edward *BiDrAPA 89*
Mc Gough, Walter Thomas 1919- *WhoAm 90*
McGourty, Kassy J. *ODwPR 91*
McGovern, Ann *AuBYP 90*
McGovern, Catherine Bigley 1939- *WhoAmW 91*
McGovern, David Talmage 1928- *WhoAm 90*
McGovern, Elizabeth *BioIn 16*
McGovern, Elizabeth 1961- *WhoAm 90, WorAlBi*
McGovern, Eugene J. 1932- *St&PR 91*
McGovern, Frances 1927- *WhoAmW 91*
McGovern, George S. 1922- *WorAlBi*
Mc Govern, George Stanley 1922- *WhoAm 90*

McGovern, Glenn Charles 1952- *WhoEmL 91*
McGovern, James 1923-1989 *BioIn 16, ConAu 129*
McGovern, John Francis 1946- *St&PR 91*
McGovern, John Hugh 1924- *WhoE 91, WhoWor 91*
McGovern, John Joseph 1920- *WhoAm 90*
McGovern, John Phillip 1921- *WhoAm 90, WhoWor 91*
McGovern, Joseph James 1925- *WhoAm 90*
Mc Govern, Joseph W. 1909- *WhoAm 90*
McGovern, Lauren MaryAnne 1940- *WhoAmW 91*
Mc Govern, Margaret Mary *BiDrAPA 89*
McGovern, Maureen 1949- *BioIn 16, CurBio 90 [port], WorAlBi*
Mc Govern, Maureen Therese 1949- *WhoAmW 91*
McGovern, Michael 1951- *St&PR 91*
McGovern, Michael Patrick 1955- *WhoSSW 91*
McGovern, Michael Trevor 1955- *WhoEmL 91*
McGovern, Patricia *WhoAmW 91*
McGovern, Patrick *BioIn 16*
McGovern, Patrick Joseph 1938?- *ConAmBL*
McGovern, R. Gordon 1926- *St&PR 91*
McGovern, Raymond E. 1928- *St&PR 91*
McGovern, Richard Gordon 1926- *WhoAm 90, WhoE 91, WhoWor 91*
McGovern, Robert F 1933- *WhoAmA 91*
McGovern, Stan *EncACom*
Mc Govern, Walter T. 1922- *WhoAm 90*
Mc Govern, William Montgomery, Jr. 1934- *WhoAm 90*
McGowan, Andrew 1939- *ODwPR 91*
McGowan, Andrew John 1939- *WhoE 91*
McGowan, Bill 1896-1954 *Ballpl 90*
McGowan, Claire Miller 1936- *WhoE 91*
McGowan, D. W. 1924- *St&PR 91*
McGowan, David Allen 1952- *WhoEmL 91*
McGowan, Diane Lynne 1959- *WhoAmW 91*
McGowan, Dianna Hester 1951- *WhoSSW 91*
McGowan, Donald Edwin 1947- *WhoSSW 91*
McGowan, Frank 1901-1982 *Ballpl 90*
McGowan, Gary V. 1948- *WhoEmL 91*
McGowan, George V. 1928- *St&PR 91*
McGowan, George Vincent 1928- *WhoAm 90, WhoE 91*
McGowan, Harold 1909- *WhoAm 90*
Mc Gowan, Harold 1909- *WhoWrEP 89*
McGowan, J. C. 1937- *St&PR 91*
Mc Gowan, James Atkinson 1914- *WhoAm 90*
Mc Gowan, James Michael 1937- *BiDrAPA 89*
McGowan, Joan Yuhas 1955- *WhoE 91*
McGowan, Joanne Suweyn 1955- *WhoAmW 91*
McGowan, John Edward, Jr. 1942- *WhoSSW 91*
McGowan, John T. 1928- *St&PR 91*
McGowan, Joseph Anthony, Jr. 1931- *WhoAm 90*
McGowan, Joseph Lamar, Jr. 1930- *St&PR 91, WhoAm 90*
McGowan, Kathleen Ann 1955- *WhoEmL 91*
McGowan, Kathleen Joan 1946- *WhoEmL 91*
Mc Gowan, Kathleen Keer 1918- *WhoWrEP 89*
Mc Gowan, Lillian E 1909- *BiDrAPA 89*
McGowan, Michael J. 1952- *ODwPR 91*
McGowan, Michael W. 1948- *St&PR 91*
McGowan, Patrick Francis 1940- *WhoAm 90*
McGowan, Patrick Jude 1939- *WhoAm 90*
McGowan, Peter *ODwPR 91*
McGowan, Stephen W. 1953- *St&PR 91*
McGowan, Steve *BioIn 16*
McGowan, Terrence Patrick 1950- *St&PR 91*
McGowan, William *BioIn 16*
McGowan, William 1931- *WhoAm 90*
McGowan, William G. 1927- *St&PR 91*
McGowan, William George 1927- *ConAmBL*
McGowen, Leon William 1929- *St&PR 91*
McGowen, Reyna Lander *BioIn 16*
McGowen, Roscoe 1886-1966 *Ballpl 90*
McGowen, Thomas 1927- *AuBYP 90*
McGowen, Thomas N., Jr. *St&PR 91*
McGowin, Ed 1938- *WhoAmA 91*
McGowin, Essie Stallworth *BioIn 16*
Mc Gowin, William Edward 1938- *WhoAm 90*
McGown, Jill 1947- *TwCCr&M 91*
McGrady, Corinne Young 1938- *WhoAmW 91*
McGrady, Lisa S. 1959- *ODwPR 91*
McGrady, Mike *AuBYP 90*
McGrail, Albert James 1948- *WhoEmL 91*
McGrail, Jerome Kathryn 1947- *WhoAmA 91*
Mc Grail, John F 1935- *BiDrAPA 89*
Mc Grail, Michael Lance *BiDrAPA 89*
McGranaghan, Joseph Anthony 1943- *WhoE 91*
McGranaghan, Joseph Thomas 1930- *St&PR 91*
McGranery, James Patrick 1895-1962 *BiDrUSE 89*
McGrath, Abigail Hubbell Rosen 1941- *WhoAmW 91*
McGrath, Anthony Charles Ormond *WhoWor 91*
McGrath, Bernard Dennin 1925- *St&PR 91*
McGrath, Brendan 1914-1988 *BioIn 16*
McGrath, Brian 1941- *St&PR 91*
McGrath, Craig James 1948- *WhoEmL 91*
McGrath, Daniele Cushing 1954- *ODwPR 91*
McGrath, David Paul *BiDrAPA 89*
McGrath, Deann *BioIn 16*
McGrath, Dennis B. 1937- *ODwPR 91*
McGrath, Dennis Britton 1937- *WhoAm 90*
McGrath, Don John 1948- *St&PR 91, WhoAm 90*
McGrath, Donald E. 1932- *St&PR 91*
McGrath, Dorn Charles, Jr. 1930- *WhoE 91, WhoWor 91*
McGrath, Earl James 1902- *WhoAm 90, WhoWor 91*
McGrath, Eugene Robert 1942- *St&PR 91*
Mc Grath, Francis Joseph 1908- *WhoAm 90*
McGrath, Frank J. 1900-1989 *BioIn 16*
McGrath, George *BioIn 16*
McGrath, George 1956- *ODwPR 91*
McGrath, Gerald Thomas 1935- *St&PR 91*
McGrath, Gordon J. 1919- *St&PR 91*
Mc Grath, Harold F *BiDrAPA 89*
McGrath, J. Brian 1942- *WhoAm 90*
McGrath, J. David A. 1936- *St&PR 91*
McGrath, James Aloysius 1932- *WhoE 91*
McGrath, James Charles, III 1942- *WhoAm 90*
McGrath, James Edward 1951- *St&PR 91*
McGrath, James Howard 1903-1966 *BiDrUSE 89*
McGrath, James Thomas 1942- *WhoAm 90*
McGrath, Janet Lynne 1955- *St&PR 91*
McGrath, Joan M. 1936- *St&PR 91*
McGrath, John 1920-1987 *BioIn 16*
McGrath, John C. *St&PR 91*
McGrath, John Edward 1938- *St&PR 91*
Mc Grath, John F *BiDrAPA 89*
McGrath, John Francis 1925- *WhoAm 90*
Mc Grath, John J 1937- *BiDrAPA 89*
McGrath, John J. 1944- *ODwPR 91*
Mc Grath, John Joseph 1910- *WhoAm 90*
McGrath, John Patrick 1907-1989 *BioIn 16*
McGrath, Joseph Edward 1927- *WhoAm 90*
Mc Grath, Joseph Michael 1932- *BiDrAPA 89*
McGrath, Kathryn Bradley 1944- *WhoAm 90*
McGrath, Kenneth W. 1949- *St&PR 91*
McGrath, Kevin Charles 1955- *WhoE 91, WhoWor 91*
McGrath, Lawrence A. 1943- *St&PR 91*
Mc Grath, Lee Parr *WhoAm 90, WhoWrEP 89*
McGrath, Marianne Smith 1941- *BiDrAPA 89*
McGrath, Martin Francis 1951- *WhoAm 90*
McGrath, Martin Joseph 1934- *St&PR 91*
McGrath, MartinaMaria Gonetti 1950- *WhoWor 91*
McGrath, Michael Alan 1942- *WhoAm 90*
McGrath, Michael Gerard *BiDrAPA 89*
McGrath, Patrick J 1949- *BiDrAPA 89*
McGrath, Paul K. 1946- *St&PR 91*
Mcgrath, Peter Charles 1943- *BiDrAPA 89*
McGrath, Raymond J. 1942- *WhoAm 90, WhoE 91*
McGrath, Richard William 1943- *WhoWor 91*
McGrath, Robert A. 1916- *St&PR 91*
McGrath, Robert Edward 1947- *WhoWor 91*
McGrath, Robert W. *ODwPR 91*
McGrath, Thomas *NewYTBS 90*
McGrath, Thomas 1916- *ConLC 59 [port], MajTwCW*
Mc Grath, Thomas 1916- *WhoAm 90, WhoWrEP 89*
McGrath, Thomas 1916-1990 *ConAu 132, -33NR*
McGrath, Thomas J. 1932- *WhoAm 90, WhoWor 91*
McGrath, Tom 1916- *EncAL*
McGrath, Tom 1940- *ConAu 130*
Mc Grath, William B 1914- *BiDrAPA 89*
Mc Grath, William Restore 1922- *WhoAm 90, WhoSSW 91*
McGrath Sangston, Susan Elizabeth 1951- *WhoAmW 91*
McGraw, Alice *BioIn 16*
McGraw, Anne Harman 1951- *St&PR 91*
McGraw, B. B. 1832- *AmLegL*
McGraw, Benjamin F. 1949- *St&PR 91*
McGraw, Bob 1895-1978 *Ballpl 90*
McGraw, David Keith 1962- *WhoSSW 91*
McGraw, Donald Jesse 1943- *WhoAm 90*
McGraw, Eloise Jarvis 1915- *AuBYP 90*
Mc Graw, Erin 1957- *WhoWrEP 89*
McGraw, Harold W., III *BioIn 16*
McGraw, Harold W., Jr. 1918- *St&PR 91*
McGraw, Harold Whittlesey, III 1948- *St&PR 91, WhoAm 90*
McGraw, Harold Whittlesey, Jr. 1918- *WhoAm 90*
Mc Graw, Harold Whittlesey, Jr. 1918- *WhoE 91*
McGraw, Jack Wilson 1943- *WhoAm 90*
McGraw, James 1945- *St&PR 91*
McGraw, James E. 1931- *WhoAm 90*
McGraw, James H. 1860-1948 *WorAlBi*
McGraw, James L. 1917- *WhoAm 90*
McGraw, James Michael 1945- *WhoAm 90*
McGraw, John 1873-1934 *Ballpl 90 [port], BioIn 16, WorAlBi*
McGraw, John Melbourne *BiDrAPA 89*
McGraw, John Patrick 1947- *WhoWor 91*
Mc Graw, Karen Kay 1938- *WhoWrEP 89*
McGraw, Lavinia Morgan 1924- *WhoAmW 91, WhoE 91, WhoWor 91*
McGraw, Leland Chester 1924- *WhoAm 90*
McGraw, Myrtle B. 1899-1988 *BioIn 16*
McGraw, Richard L. 1936- *ODwPR 91, St&PR 91*
McGraw, Robert James 1947- *St&PR 91*
McGraw, Robert P. 1954- *St&PR 91*
McGraw, Robert Pierce 1954- *WhoAm 90*
McGraw, Tug 1944- *Ballpl 90 [port]*
McGraw, Walter J. 1928- *St&PR 91*
McGraw, William Corbin 1916- *AuBYP 90*
McGraw-Lewicki, Marjorie Lee 1957- *WhoE 91*
McGreal, Joseph A., Jr. 1935- *WhoAm 90*
McGreevy, Terrence Gerard 1932- *WhoAm 90*
McGreevy, Thomas 1825-1897 *DcCanB 12*
McGreevy, Thomas James 1932- *St&PR 91*
McGregor, Alice M. H. *BioIn 16*
McGregor, Barbara R. 1939- *WhoSSW 91*
McGregor, Charles *DrBIPA 90*
Mc Gregor, Donald Thornton 1924- *WhoAm 90*
Mc Gregor, Douglas Hugh 1939- *WhoWor 91*
McGregor, Duncan Douglass 1930- *WhoE 91*
Mc Gregor, Frank Hamilton, Jr. 1938- *WhoSSW 91*
McGregor, G. Mark 1950- *St&PR 91*
McGregor, Gerald Lee 1935- *St&PR 91*
McGregor, Howard Hill 1919- *St&PR 91*
McGregor, Ian 1947- *St&PR 91*
McGregor, Ian Alexander 1922- *WhoWor 91*
McGregor, Jack E. 1934- *St&PR 91*
McGregor, M. H. 1936- *St&PR 91*
Mc Gregor, Malcolm Francis 1910- *WhoAm 90*
Mc Gregor, Maurice 1920- *WhoAm 90*
McGregor, Patrick Vance 1946- *St&PR 91*
McGregor, Rayanne 1962- *WhoAmW 91*
McGregor, Richard Ewan 1953- *IntWWM 90*
McGregor, Robert G. *WhoAm 90*
McGregor, Robert G. 1947- *St&PR 91*
McGregor, Scott 1954- *Ballpl 90*
McGregor, Simon Craig 1961- *IntWWM 90*
McGregor, Stewart D. 1945- *St&PR 91*
McGregor, Theodore Anthony 1944- *WhoWor 91*
McGregor, Wallace 1928- *St&PR 91*
McGregor, William S. *St&PR 91*
McGrew, Bruce Elwin 1937- *WhoAmA 91*
McGrew, Clinton Jackson, Jr. 1930- *WhoSSW 91*
McGrew, David Rollin 1936- *WhoWor 91*
McGrew, Harry *Ballpl 90*
McGrew, Kenneth Louis 1952- *St&PR 91*
McGrew, R Brownell 1916- *WhoAmA 91*
McGrew, Raymond Daniel 1943- *St&PR 91*
McGrew, Susan Marie 1962- *WhoAmW 91*
McGrew, Thomas James 1942- *WhoAm 90*
McGrew, Wallace Raymond 1929- *St&PR 91*
McGriff, Fred *BioIn 16*
McGriff, Fred 1963- *Ballpl 90*
McGriff, George Emmett, Jr. 1938- *WhoSSW 91*
McGriff, Heywood 1957- *WhoSSW 91*
McGriff, Lulann *BioIn 16*
McGroarty, B. J. 1942- *St&PR 91*
McGroarty, Eleanore Lucille King *BioIn 16*
McGrory, Mary Kathleen 1933- *WhoAmW 91*
McGrotha, Rosemary *BioIn 16*
Mc Gruder, Stephen Jones 1943- *WhoAm 90*
McGuane, Thomas 1939- *BioIn 16, ConTFT 8, MajTwCW*
Mc Guane, Thomas Francis, III 1939- *WhoAm 90, WhoWrEP 89*
McGuckian, Medbh 1950- *FemiCLE*
McGuckin, Barton 1852-1913 *PenDiMP*
McGuckin, James F. *St&PR 91*
Mc Guckin, James Frederick 1930- *WhoAm 90*
McGuckin, John Hugh, Jr. 1946- *St&PR 91*
McGue, Stephen Craig 1947- *St&PR 91*
McGuffey, Alexander Hamilton 1816-1896 *SmATA 60 [port]*
McGuffey, Carroll Wade, Sr. 1922- *WhoAm 90*
McGuffey, William Holmes 1800-1873 *SmATA 60 [port], WorAlBi*
McGuffin, Mary Neta 1939- *WhoAmW 91*
Mc Guigan, Frank Joseph 1924- *WhoAm 90*
Mc Guigan, James Edward 1931- *WhoAm 90*
McGuigan, Kathleen Bailey 1966- *WhoWrEP 89*
McGuigan, Thomas J. 1935- *St&PR 91*
McGuigan, William Patrick 1948- *St&PR 91*
McGuiness, Nancy Fantom 1961- *WhoE 91*
McGuiness, Norah 1903-1980 *BiDWomA*
Mc Guinn, Martin Gregory 1942- *WhoAm 90*
McGuinness, Deborah Louise 1958- *WhoAmW 91*
Mc Guinness, Frank Joseph 1928- *WhoE 91*
McGuinness, George J. 1950- *St&PR 91*
McGuinness, John Seward 1922- *WhoE 91, WhoWor 91*
McGuinness, Rosamond Cohan 1929- *IntWWM 90*
McGuinness, Sheila V. 1961- *WhoAmW 91*
McGuire, Al 1931- *WorAlBi*
McGuire, Amos W. 1930- *St&PR 91*
McGuire, Arthur H. *St&PR 91*
McGuire, Brian Lyle 1959- *WhoSSW 91*
McGuire, Carol Ann 1950- *WhoAmW 91*
McGuire, Charles Carroll 1932- *St&PR 91*
McGuire, Charles Carroll, Jr. 1932- *WhoAm 90*
McGuire, Charles Gerald 1954- *St&PR 91*
Mc Guire, Charles William 1935- *BiDrAPA 89*
McGuire, Deacon 1865-1936 *Ballpl 90 [port]*
McGuire, Delbert 1917- *WhoAm 90*
McGuire, Dianne M. 1950- *WhoAmW 91*
McGuire, Donald F. *ODwPR 91*
McGuire, Dorothy 1919- *WorAlBi*
Mc Guire, Dorothy Hackett 1916- *WhoAm 90*
McGuire, E. James 1914- *WhoWor 91*
McGuire, Earl Eugene, Jr. 1934- *St&PR 91*
McGuire, Edna 1899- *AuBYP 90*
McGuire, Edward 1948- *IntWWM 90*
McGuire, Edward David, Jr. 1948- *WhoE 91*
McGuire, Elinor *BioIn 16*
McGuire, Frances *AuBYP 90*
McGuire, Glenn O. 1911- *St&PR 91*
McGuire, Gregory Michael 1961- *WhoSSW 91*
McGuire, James Bert 1939- *St&PR 91*
McGuire, James Charles 1934- *St&PR 91*
McGuire, James J. *BioIn 16*
Mc Guire, James P D 1941- *BiDrAPA 89*
Mc Guire, James Richard 1949- *BiDrAPA 89*
McGuire, James Vincent 1944- *St&PR 91*
McGuire, Jeremiah 1823-1889 *AmLegL*
McGuire, Jessie G. 1946- *WhoE 91*
McGuire, Joel Frederick 1954- *WhoSSW 91*
McGuire, John *BioIn 16*
McGuire, John E. 1942- *BioIn 16*
McGuire, John Francis, Jr. 1941- *WhoE 91*
McGuire, John J. 1948- *St&PR 91*
McGuire, John Murray 1929- *WhoSSW 91*
McGuire, John T. 1939- *WhoSSW 91*
Mc Guire, Joseph William 1925- *WhoAm 90*
McGuire, Julie Thordarson 1940- *ODwPR 91*
McGuire, Karen Lee 1946- *WhoAmW 91*
McGuire, Larry G. 1947- *St&PR 91*

McGuire, Leslie 1945- *BioIn 16*
McGuire, Lockhart B. 1934-1990 *BioIn 16*
Mc Guire, Marie C. *WhoAm 90*
McGuire, Marie Josephine 1933- *WhoAmW 91*
McGuire, Marsden Hamilton 1956- *BiDrAPA 89*
McGuire, Maureen 1941- *WhoAmA 91*
McGuire, Michael Francis 1946- *WhoAm 90*
McGuire, Michael George 1944- *St&PR 91*
McGuire, Michael William 1960- *WhoWor 91*
McGuire, Nancy L. 1951- *WhoAmW 91*
McGuire, Patricia A. 1952- *WhoAm 90*
McGuire, Patricia Lee *BiDrAPA 89*
Mc Guire, Patricia M *BiDrAPA 89*
McGuire, Patrick Thomas 1944- *St&PR 91*
McGuire, Paul 1903-1978 *TwCCr&M 91*
McGuire, Paul R. 1936- *St&PR 91*
McGuire, Peter J. 1954- *St&PR 91*
McGuire, Peter Joseph 1943- *WhoSSW 91*
Mc Guire, Philip R, Jr. 1934- *BiDrAPA 89*
McGuire, Raymond L. *WhoSSW 91*
McGuire, Richard O. 1936- *St&PR 91*
McGuire, Robert J. 1936- *St&PR 91*
McGuire, Sandra Lynn 1947- *WhoAmW 91*
McGuire, Sondra Lee 1941- *WhoAmW 91*
McGuire, Stephen Craig 1948- *WhoE 91*
Mc Guire, Susan Kay 1951- *BiDrAPA 89*
McGuire, Thomas A. 1932- *St&PR 91*
McGuire, Thomas Peter 1945- *WhoWor 91*
McGuire, Thomas Roger 1943- *WhoAm 90*
McGuire, Timothy J. 1949- *WhoAm 90*
McGuire, Timothy William 1938- *WhoAm 90*
McGuire, Virginia Marie 1955- *St&PR 91*
McGuire, Walter R. 1913- *St&PR 91*
Mc Guire, William 1917- *WhoAm 90, WhoWrEP 89*
Mc Guire, William 1920- *WhoAm 90*
McGuire, William Dennis 1943- *WhoAm 90*
McGuire, William James 1925- *BioIn 16*
Mc Guire, William James 1925- *WhoAm 90*
Mc Guire, William Lawrence 1926- *WhoAm 90*
McGuirk, Bernard 1949- *ConAu 129*
McGuirk, Ronald Charles 1938- *St&PR 91, WhoAm 90*
McGuirk, Terrence 1925- *WhoAm 90*
McGuirl, Janice Iamonaco 1948- *WhoEmL 91*
McGuirl, Marlene Dana Callis 1938- *WhoAmW 91*
McGulpin, Elizabeth Jane 1932- *WhoAmW 91*
McGunnigle, Bill 1855-1899 *Ballpl 90*
Mc Gurk, Charles Ralph 1942- *BiDrAPA 89*
McGurk, Heather 1966- *WhoAmW 91*
McGurk, Joseph E. 1930- *St&PR 91*
McGurk, Laureen Ellen 1961- *WhoSSW 91*
McGurk, Nancy J. 1955- *St&PR 91*
McGurk, Slater *AuBYP 90*
McGurl, Maureen Kathleen 1948- *St&PR 91, WhoE 91*
Mc Gurn, Barrett 1914- *WhoAm 90*
McGurn, Thomas O. 1946- *ODwPR 91*
McGushin, Mary Eileen 1946- *St&PR 91*
McGwier, Robert Westmoreland 1954- *WhoE 91*
McGwire, Mark *BioIn 16*
McGwire, Mark 1963- *Ballpl 90, WorAlBi*
McHale, Edward Robertson 1921- *WhoAm 90*
Mc Hale, Inez Pecore 1908- *WhoAm 90*
Mc Hale, John Joseph 1921- *WhoE 91*
McHale, John Lawrence, III 1942- *WhoSSW 91*
McHale, John M. 1943- *St&PR 91*
McHale, Kevin 1957- *WhoAm 90, WorAlBi*
McHale, Marty 1888-1979 *Ballpl 90*
McHale, Thomas Anthony 1914- *WhoAm 90*
McHale, Thomas J. *St&PR 91*
McHale, Vincent Edward 1939- *WhoAm 90*
McHam, David Oliver 1933- *WhoSSW 91*
McHam, Sarah Blake Wilk *WhoAmA 91, WhoE 91*
McHan, Eva Jane 1941- *WhoWor 91*
McHardy, Louis William 1930- *WhoAm 90*
McHardy, Peter Michael 1941- *St&PR 91*
McHarg, Ian Lennox 1920- *WhoAm 90*
McHarg, James F. 1917- *EncPaPR 91*
McHargue, Charles E. 1952- *St&PR 91*
McHargue, Georgess *AuBYP 90, BioIn 16*
McHarris, William Charles 1937- *WhoAm 90, WhoWor 91*
McHarry, Mark 1951- *ODwPR 91*
Mc Hendrie, Douglas 1906- *WhoAm 90*
McHenry, Austin 1895-1922 *Ballpl 90*
McHenry, Barnabas 1929- *WhoAm 90, WhoWor 91*
McHenry, Charles Steven 1948- *WhoEmL 91*
Mc Henry, Dean Eugene 1910- *WhoAm 90*
McHenry, Debra Anne 1953- *WhoAmW 91*
McHenry, Henry Malcolm 1944- *WhoAm 90*
McHenry, James 1753-1816 *BiDrUSE 89, BioIn 16*
McHenry, Keith Welles, Jr. 1928- *WhoAm 90*
McHenry, Louisa Beth 1961- *WhoAmW 91*
McHenry, Onis Franklin, III 1959- *WhoSSW 91*
McHenry, Powell 1926- *St&PR 91*
Mc Henry, Powell 1926- *WhoAm 90*
McHenry, William James 1937- *WhoE 91*
McHorris, William Henry 1939- *WhoSSW 91*
McHorse, Christine 1948- *MusmAFA*
McHose, James H. 1937- *WhoAm 90*
McHugh, Adeliza Sorenson 1912- *WhoAmA 91*
McHugh, Betsy Baldwin *WhoAmW 91*
McHugh, Brian Joseph 1959- *WhoE 91*
McHugh, Edward Francis, Jr. 1932- *WhoAm 90*
McHugh, Edward J. 1930- *St&PR 91*
McHugh, Elisabet 1941- *BioIn 16, ConAu 32NR*
McHugh, Erin 1952- *WhoAmW 91*
McHugh, Francis Xavier 1955- *WhoE 91*
McHugh, Frank Michael 1935- *WhoSSW 91*
McHugh, H. Bart, III 1933- *St&PR 91*
Mc Hugh, Heather 1948- *WhoWrEP 89*
Mc Hugh, Hugh *BiDrAPA 89*
McHugh, James Bernard 1950- *WhoEmL 91*
McHugh, James C. 1940- *St&PR 91*
McHugh, James Francis *WhoAmA 91N*
McHugh, James Joseph 1930- *WhoAm 90*
McHugh, James Lenahan, Jr. 1937- *WhoAm 90*
McHugh, Jimmy 1894-1969 *BioIn 16, OxCPMus, WorAlBi*
McHugh, John J. *ODwPR 91*
McHugh, John James 1931- *St&PR 91, WhoAm 90*
Mc Hugh, John Laurence 1911- *WhoAm 90*
McHugh, John M. 1948- *WhoE 91*
McHugh, Joseph William *St&PR 91*
McHugh, Josephine Flaherty 1947- *WhoEmL 91, WhoWor 91*
McHugh, Kevin James 1940- *St&PR 91*
McHugh, Larry F. 1949- *St&PR 91*
McHugh, Matthew 1938- *WhoAm 90, WhoE 91*
McHugh, Maureen Carroll 1952- *WhoAmW 91*
McHugh, Michael Joseph 1937 *St&PR 91*
Mc Hugh, Paul R. 1931- *WhoAm 90*
Mc Hugh, Paul Rodney *BiDrAPA 89*
Mc Hugh, Richard B. 1923- *WhoAm 90*
McHugh, Robert C. 1928- *St&PR 91*
Mc Hugh, Robert Clayton 1928- *WhoAm 90*
McHugh, Simon Francis, Jr. 1938- *WhoAm 90*
McHugh, Stuart Lawrence 1949- *WhoEmL 91*
McHugh, Thomas J. 1931- *St&PR 91*
McHugh, Thomas Joseph 1935- *St&PR 91*
McHugh, Toni Walter 1946- *WhoAmW 91*
McHugh, William Dennis 1929- *WhoAm 90*
McHugh-Turner, Karen Lynne 1960- *WhoAmW 91*
McHuron, Greg 1946- *BioIn 16*
McIlhaney, Mortimer G. 1833- *AmLegL*
McIlhaney, Sam Carl 1939- *WhoWrEP 89*
McIlhany, Sterling *AuBYP 90*
Mc Ilhany, Sterling Fisher 1930- *WhoWor 91*
McIlhenny, Henry Plumer 1910-1986 *BioIn 16*
Mc Ilhenny, James Harrison 1927- *WhoAm 90, WhoSSW 91*
Mc Ilhenny, Paul Robert 1934- *BiDrAPA 89*
McIlhnenny, Edmund 1945- *St&PR 91*
McIlhone, John Thomas 1911- *WhoE 91*
Mc Illece, Patricia E *BiDrAPA 89*
McIllmurray, Daniel Bernard 1929- *WhoE 91*
McIlrath, Donald Christner 1929- *WhoAm 90*
McIlrath, Patricia 1917- *BioIn 16*
McIlrath, Patricia Anne 1917- *NotWoAT*
McIlreath, Fred J. 1929- *St&PR 91*
McIlreath, Fred James 1929- *WhoAm 90*
McIlroy, Carol J 1924- *WhoAmA 91*
McIlroy, Harry Alexander 1940- *WhoWor 91*
McIlroy, James R. 1912- *St&PR 91*
McIlroy, Robert Stewart 1935- *WhoAm 90*
McIlroy, William Dawson 1947- *St&PR 91*
McIlvain, Alan 1922- *St&PR 91*
McIlvain, Douglas Lee 1923- *WhoAmA 91*
McIlvain, Frances H 1925- *WhoAmA 91*
McIlvain, Gordon *St&PR 91*
McIlvain, J. Gibson, II 1911- *St&PR 91*
McIlvain, John Gibson, III 1948- *St&PR 91*
McIlvaine, Alice Nicolson 1924- *WhoE 91*
McIlvaine, Herbert R., Jr. 1942- *ODwPR 91*
McIlvaine, Jane *ConAu 130*
McIlvaine, Jane 1919- *AuBYP 90*
McIlvaine, Jane 1919-1990 *SmATA X*
McIlvaine, Joe *BioIn 16*
McIlvaine, John Harmon, Jr. 1936- *St&PR 91*
McIlvaine, John Jamison, III 1962- *WhoSSW 91*
McIlvaine, Stephen Brownlee 1953- *WhoEmL 91*
McIlvane, Edward James 1947- *WhoAmA 91*
McIlvanney, William 1936- *TwCCr&M 91*
McIlveen, Edward E. 1911- *WhoAm 90*
McIlveen, Marion 1911-1989 *BioIn 16*
Mc Ilveen, Walter 1927- *WhoE 91, WhoWor 91*
McIlvoy, Doug Graham 1939- *St&PR 91*
McIlwain, Carl Edwin 1931- *WhoAm 90*
McIlwain, Clara Evans 1919- *WhoAmW 91*
McIlwain, Don Curtis 1938- *St&PR 91*
McIlwain, John Frederick 1938- *St&PR 91*
Mc Ilwain, John Frederick 1938- *WhoAm 90*
McIlwain, John Knox 1943- *WhoE 91*
Mc Ilwain, Thomas P *BiDrAPA 89*
McIlwain, William C. 1926- *St&PR 91*
Mc Ilwain, William Franklin 1925- *WhoAm 90, WhoWrEP 89*
McIlwraith, Cyril Wayne 1947- *WhoAm 90, WhoWor 91*
McIlwraith, Jean Newton 1859-1938 *DcLB 92 [port], FemiCLE*
McIlwraith, Maureen *BioIn 16*
McIlwraith, Maureen Mollie Hunter *AuBYP 90*
Mc Indoe, Darrell Winfred 1930- *WhoAm 90*
McInerney, Gene Joseph 1930- *WhoAmA 91*
McInerney, J. Barrett 1925- *St&PR 91*
McInerney, James 1942- *St&PR 91*
McInerney, James Eugene, Jr. 1930- *WhoAm 90*
McInerney, Jay *BioIn 16*
McInerney, Jay 1955- *WorAlBi*
McInerney, Joseph Aloysius 1939- *WhoAm 90*
McInerney, Joseph John 1932- *WhoAm 90*
McInerney, Judith Whitelock 1945- *AuBYP 90, BioIn 16*
McInerney, Margie Lynn 1953- *WhoAmW 91*
McInerney, Michael Joseph, III 1941- *St&PR 91*
McInerney, Michael Patrick 1941- *St&PR 91*
McInerney, Robert J. 1945- *St&PR 91*
McInerney, Rosemarie Patricia 1929- *WhoAmW 91*
McInerney, Russell Arthur 1943- *WhoSSW 91*
McInerney, Thomas Edward 1960- *WhoWor 91*
McInerney, Thomas F., Jr. 1937- *St&PR 91*
McInerney, Thomas K. *ODwPR 91*
McInerny, Ralph 1929- *TwCCr&M 91*
McInerny, Ralph Matthew 1929- *WhoAm 90*
Mc Ingvale, James Wesley 1954- *WhoWrEP 89*
Mc Ininch, Ralph Aubrey 1912- *WhoAm 90*
McInnes, Allen T. 1937- *WhoAm 90, WhoSSW 91*
McInnes, Donald 1824?-1900 *DcCanB 12*
McInnes, Harold A. 1927- *St&PR 91, WhoAm 90*
McInnes, Robert Malcolm 1930- *St&PR 91*
Mc Innes, Robert Malcolm 1930- *WhoAm 90*
Mc Innes, William Charles 1923- *WhoAm 90*
McInnes, William Wright 1948- *WhoAm 90*
McInnis, James Milton 1934- *WhoE 91*
McInnis, Stuffy 1890-1960 *Ballpl 90 [port]*
McInnis, Thomas Michael 1937- *St&PR 91*
McInroe, Harold Alvis 1930- *St&PR 91*
McInroy, James William 1936- *St&PR 91*
McInteer, Jim Bill 1921- *WhoSSW 91*
McIntire, C T 1939- *ConAu 130*
McIntire, Dennis Keith 1944- *IntWWM 90*
McIntire, Jerald Gene 1938- *WhoAm 90*
McIntire, Kenneth M. 1937- *St&PR 91*
McIntire, Larry Vern 1943- *WhoAm 90*
McIntire, Mary Beth 1943- *WhoSSW 91*
McIntire, Melinda I. *ODwPR 91*
McIntire, Paul Goodloe 1860-1952 *BioIn 16*
Mc Intire, Richard Lee 1934- *WhoAm 90*
McIntire, Samuel 1757-1811 *PenDiDA 89*
McIntire, Thomas J. 1943- *St&PR 91*
McIntosh, Chilly *WhNaAH*
McIntosh, Christine Marie 1961- *WhoAmW 91*
McIntosh, Clifton *AuBYP 90*
McIntosh, Donald Harry 1919- *WhoAm 90*
McIntosh, Donald Keith 1934- *St&PR 91*
McIntosh, Elaine Virginia 1924- *WhoAmW 91*
McIntosh, Frankie L. 1949- *WhoSSW 91*
McIntosh, Grahame John 1956- *WhoWor 91*
McIntosh, Harold 1916- *WhoAmA 91*
McIntosh, J Michael *BiDrAPA 89*
McIntosh, James Arthur 1948- *WhoEmL 91*
Mc Intosh, James Eugene, Jr. 1938- *WhoAm 90*
McIntosh, Jenny Clare 1948- *WhoSSW 91*
McIntosh, Jerry Don 1945- *WhoSSW 91*
McIntosh, Joe 1951- *Ballpl 90*
Mc Intosh, John Richard 1939- *WhoAm 90*
McIntosh, Kara Ann 1962- *WhoAmW 91*
McIntosh, Karen Holt 1965- *WhoAmW 91*
McIntosh, Lawrence White 1934- *St&PR 91, WhoAm 90*
McIntosh, Lorne William 1945- *St&PR 91, WhoAm 90*
McIntosh, Maria 1803-1878 *FemiCLE*
McIntosh, Mary Ann 1955- *WhoSSW 91*
McIntosh, Rhodina Covington 1947- *WhoAm 90, WhoAmW 91, WhoE 91*
McIntosh, Robert Edward, Jr. 1940- *WhoAm 90*
McIntosh, Theresa Schultz 1963- *WhoSSW 91*
McIntosh, Thomas Lee 1938- *IntWWM 90*
McIntosh, Thomas S. 1937- *WhoAm 90*
McIntosh, William 1775-1825 *WhNaAH*
McIntosh, William Andrew 1944- *WhoWor 91*
McIntosh, William E. *BioIn 16*
McIntosh, Winston Hubert *BioIn 16*
McIntyre, Alexander 1841-1892 *DcCanB 12*
McIntyre, Barbara M. 1916- *BioIn 16, NotWoAT*
McIntyre, Brian 1948- *ODwPR 91*
McIntyre, Bruce H. 1959- *WhoSSW 91*
McIntyre, Bruce Herbert 1930- *WhoAm 90*
McIntyre, Bruce Martin 1927- *WhoSSW 91*
McIntyre, Carl Henry, Jr. 1958- *WhoE 91*
McIntyre, Charles John 1921- *WhoAm 90*
McIntyre, Colin 1944- *WhoAm 90, WhoE 91*
McIntyre, Darel Dee 1939- *St&PR 91*
McIntyre, Deborah 1955- *WhoSSW 91*
McIntyre, Dennis *BioIn 16, NewYTBS 90*
McIntyre, Dennis 1943?-1990 *ConAu 130*
McIntyre, Dianne 1946- *DrBlPA 90*
McIntyre, Donald 1934- *PenDiMP*
McIntyre, Donald Conroy 1934- *IntWWM 90, WhoAm 90, WhoWor 91*
McIntyre, Donald F. *BioIn 16*
McIntyre, Douglas Alexander 1955- *St&PR 91, WhoAm 90, WhoE 91*
McIntyre, Douglas Carmichael, II 1956- *WhoEmL 91, WhoSSW 91, WhoWor 91*
McIntyre, Duncan 1834-1894 *DcCanB 12*
McIntyre, Glenn A. *St&PR 91*
McIntyre, Glenn H., Jr. 1927- *St&PR 91*
McIntyre, Hal 1914-1959 *BioIn 16*
McIntyre, Harry 1879-1949 *Ballpl 90*
Mc Intyre, Henry Langenberg 1912- *WhoAm 90*
Mc Intyre, Jack B 1920- *BiDrAPA 89*
McIntyre, James 1827-1906 *DcLB 99 [port]*
McIntyre, James Charles 1922- *WhoAm 90*
McIntyre, James Russel, Jr. 1941- *WhoE 91*
McIntyre, John 1930- *St&PR 91*
McIntyre, John Armin 1920- *WhoAm 90*
McIntyre, John E. 1910- *St&PR 91*
McIntyre, John Finlay 1939- *St&PR 91*
McIntyre, John George Wallace 1920- *WhoAm 90*
McIntyre, John L. 1947- *St&PR 91*

Mc Intyre, John S 1942- *BiDrAPA 89*
McIntyre, John W. 1925- *St&PR 91*
McIntyre, John William 1930- *WhoAm 90*
McIntyre, Joseph Charles 1926- *WhoE 91*
McIntyre, Judith Watland 1930- *WhoAmW 91*
McIntyre, Kathleen A. 1952- *St&PR 91*
Mc Intyre, Kathryn Irene *BiDrAPA 89*
McIntyre, Kaye 1950- *WhoAmW 91, WhoE 91, WhoEmL 91, WhoWor 91*
McIntyre, Kenneth E. 1926- *St&PR 91*
McIntyre, L. Jay 1941- *BiDrAPA 89*
McIntyre, Lamar Calvert 1938- *St&PR 91*
McIntyre, Lee E. 1906- *St&PR 91*
Mc Intyre, Lee Emerson 1906- *WhoAm 90*
McIntyre, Loretta Miller 1944- *WhoAmW 91*
McIntyre, Lorna Aileen 1956- *WhoE 91*
McIntyre, Matty 1880-1920 *Ballpl 90*
Mc Intyre, Maureen Anne 1949- *WhoWrEP 89*
McIntyre, Michael John 1946- *St&PR 91*
McIntyre, O. O. 1884-1938 *BioIn 16*
McIntyre, Oscar Odd 1884-1938 *BioIn 16*
McIntyre, Oswald Ross 1932- *WhoAm 90*
McIntyre, Peter 1818-1891 *DcCanB 12*
McIntyre, Ray 1926- *IntWWM 90*
McIntyre, Richard A. 1943- *St&PR 91*
McIntyre, Richard Rawlings, II 1946- *WhoSSW 91*
Mc Intyre, Robert Allen, Jr. 1940- *WhoAm 90*
McIntyre, Robert Malcolm 1923- *St&PR 91, WhoAm 90*
Mc Intyre, Robert Walter 1922- *WhoAm 90*
McIntyre, Valene Smith 1926- *WhoAmW 91*
McIntyre, Victoria Jean 1966- *WhoE 91*
McIntyre, Vonda N 1948- *MajTwCW, RGTwCSF*
Mc Intyre, Vonda Neel 1948- *WhoAm 90, WhoWrEP 89*
McIntyre, W. D., Jr. 1935- *St&PR 91*
McIntyre, Wilbur Eugene 1925- *St&PR 91*
McIntyre, William David 1932- *WhoWor 91*
McIntyre, William H. 1945- *St&PR 91*
Mc Intyre, William Rogers 1918- *WhoAm 90*
McIntyre-Ivy, Joan Carol 1939- *WhoAmW 91, WhoWor 91*
Mc Isaac, George Scott 1930- *WhoAm 90*
McIsaac, Isabel 1858-1914 *BioIn 16*
McIsaac, John L. 1929- *St&PR 91, WhoAm 90*
McIsaac, Kenneth James 1940- *St&PR 91*
McIsaac, Paul Rowley 1926- *WhoAm 90*
McIsaac, Peter Jon 1941- *St&PR 91*
McIver, Bruce Cooley 1940- *WhoAm 90*
McIver, Jes David 1929- *St&PR 91*
McIver, John F. 1947- *St&PR 91*
McIver, Pearl L. 1893-1976 *BioIn 16*
McIver, Randolph D. 1930- *St&PR 91*
McIver, Ray 1912?-1985 *DrBIPA 90*
McIvor, John Wilfred 1931- *WhoAmA 91*
McIvor, K. M. 1944- *St&PR 91*
McIvor, William Charles 1920- *St&PR 91*
McJames, Doc 1873-1901 *Ballpl 90*
McJoyner, Ernest McClauley, Jr. 1930- *WhoSSW 91*
McJunkin, James D. 1931- *WhoWor 91*
McKague, Lee 1936- *WhoSSW 91*
Mc Kaig, Brady P 1935- *BiDrAPA 89*
McKaig, Dianne L. 1930- *St&PR 91*
McKaig, Robert Lee 1950- *WhoSSW 91*
McKaigney, Eimear P *BiDrAPA 89*
McKain, Archie 1911-1985 *Ballpl 90*
McKain, David *BioIn 16*
Mc Kain, David W. 1937- *WhoWrEP 89*
McKain, Hal 1906-1970 *Ballpl 90*
McKain, Mary Margaret 1940- *WhoAmW 91, WhoWor 91*
McKamie, Reginald Edmund 1953- *WhoSSW 91*
McKamy, Kent 1935- *ODwPR 91*
McKandes, Dorothy Dell 1937- *WhoAmW 91*
McKane, David Bennett 1945- *WhoAm 90*
McKane, Terry John 1941- *WhoAm 90*
McKann, Michael Raysor 1941- *WhoSSW 91*
McKanna, Candace Kay 1948- *BiDrAPA 89*
McKarns, John Charles 1934- *St&PR 91*
McKasson, Robert Edward, Jr. 1945- *WhoWor 91*
Mc Kaughan, Howard Paul 1922- *WhoWor 91*
Mc Kay, Alexander Gordon 1924- *WhoAm 90*
McKay, Alice Maxine 1954- *WhoE 91*
McKay, Alice Vitalich 1947- *WhoAmW 91*
McKay, Angus 1836-1897? *DcCanB 12*
McKay, Arthur Fortescue 1926- *WhoAmA 91*
McKay, Arthur Robinson 1943- *St&PR 91*
McKay, Carol Ruth 1948- *WhoAm 90*
Mc Kay, Charles Alan 1931- *WhoAm 90*
McKay, Claude *BioIn 16, MajTwCW*
McKay, Claude 1889-1948 *PoeCrit 2 [port]*
McKay, Claude 1890-1948 *EncAL*
McKay, Constance Gadow 1928- *WhoAmW 91*
McKay, Constance Marie Farmer 1955- *WhoSSW 91*
McKay, D. Brian 1945- *WhoAm 90*
McKay, Dan Boies, Jr. 1948- *WhoEmL 91*
McKay, Daniel Clifford, Jr. 1926- *WhoE 91*
McKay, Dave 1950- *Ballpl 90*
McKay, David M 1949- *BiDrAPA 89*
McKay, Dean R. 1921- *St&PR 91*
Mc Kay, Dean Raymond 1921- *WhoAm 90, WhoE 91*
McKay, Donald A. 1945- *WhoSSW 91*
McKay, Donald Arthur 1931- *St&PR 91, WhoE 91, WhoWor 91*
McKay, Douglas James 1893-1959 *BiDrUSE 89*
McKay, Elizabeth Norman 1931- *IntWWM 90*
Mc Kay, Emily Gantz 1945- *WhoAm 90, WhoAmW 91, WhoWor 91*
McKay, Esther S. 1941- *St&PR 91*
McKay, Eugene 1941- *WhoSSW 91*
Mc Kay, Evelyn Mc Daniel 1924- *WhoWrEP 89*
McKay, Festus Claudius 1889-1948 *MajTwCW*
McKay, Gene 1934- *St&PR 91*
McKay, Gordon Thomas 1931- *WhoAm 90*
McKay, H. George 1944- *St&PR 91*
McKay, James D. 1924- *St&PR 91*
McKay, James Edgar 1939- *St&PR 91*
McKay, James Rae 1944- *IntWWM 90*
McKay, Jerry Bruce 1935- *WhoSSW 91*
Mc Kay, Jim 1921- *WhoAm 90*
McKay, Jim 1921- *WorAlBi*
McKay, John A. 1933- *St&PR 91, WhoAm 90*
McKay, John D. 1928- *St&PR 91*
McKay, John Edward 1951- *WhoEmL 91*
McKay, John Joseph 1955- *WhoSSW 91*
McKay, John Patrick 1931- *WhoAm 90*
McKay, John Sangster 1921- *WhoAmA 91*
McKay, Joseph Gardiner, Sr. 1932- *St&PR 91*
McKay, Joseph William 1829-1900 *DcCanB 12*
McKay, Kathleen Ann *WhoAmW 91*
McKay, Ken Carroll 1932- *WhoSSW 91*
McKay, Kenneth G. 1917- *St&PR 91*
McKay, Kenneth Gardiner 1917- *WhoAm 90*
McKay, Kenneth R. *TwCCr&M 91*
McKay, Laura L. 1947- *WhoAmW 91*
McKay, Marjory Grieve 1951- *IntWWM 90*
McKay, Michael Dennis 1951- *WhoEmL 91*
McKay, Neil 1917- *St&PR 91*
Mc Kay, Neil 1917- *WhoAm 90*
McKay, Neil 1924- *IntWWM 90*
McKay, Pia *BioIn 16*
McKay, Renee *WhoAmA 91, WhoAmW 91*
McKay, Robert 1921- *AuBYP 90*
McKay, Robert B 1919-1990 *ConAu 132, NewYTBS 90 [port]*
Mc Kay, Robert Budge 1919-1990 *WhoE 91*
McKay, Robert G. 1936- *St&PR 91*
Mc Kay, Robert James, Jr. 1917- *WhoAm 90*
Mc Kay, Samuel Leroy 1913- *WhoSSW 91, WhoWor 91*
McKay, Steve *BioIn 16*
Mc Kay, Thomas, Jr. 1920- *WhoAm 90*
McKayle, Donald 1930- *DrBIPA 90*
McKeachie, Wilbert James 1921- *BioIn 16*
Mc Keachie, Wilbert James 1921- *WhoAm 90*
McKeague, Gordon C. 1926- *St&PR 91*
Mckeague, Ian Wray 1953- *WhoSSW 91*
McKeague, Nancy Palmer 1955- *WhoAmW 91*
McKean, Ed 1864-1919 *Ballpl 90 [port]*
McKean, Frank Newton 1940- *St&PR 91*
McKean, George Albert 1936- *St&PR 91*
McKean, Henry P. *WhoAm 90*
Mc Kean, Hugh Ferguson 1908- *WhoAm 90*
McKean, Hugh Ferguson 1908- *WhoAmA 91*
McKean, Jim 1945- *Ballpl 90*
McKean, John Paul 1952- *WhoE 91*
McKean, John R. 1930- *St&PR 91*
Mc Kean, John Rosseel Overton 1928- *WhoAm 90*
McKean, John Scribner 1925- *St&PR 91*
Mckean, John Wallis 1928- *BiDrAPA 89*
Mc Kean, Keith Ferguson 1915- *WhoAm 90*
Mc Kean, Michael *WhoAm 90*
McKean, Paul A. 1941- *St&PR 91*
McKean, Quincy A. Shaw, Jr. 1924- *St&PR 91*
McKean, Robert Jackson, Jr. 1925- *WhoAm 90*
Mc Kean, Roland Neely 1917- *WhoAm 90*
McKean, Thomas 1734-1817 *BiDrUSE 89, EncCRAm*
McKean, Thomas Wayne 1928- *WhoAm 90*
McKearin, Helen 1898-1988 *BioIn 16*
McKearn, Thomas Joseph 1948- *WhoAm 90*
McKechnie, Bill 1886-1965 *Ballpl 90 [port]*
McKechnie, Donna 1942- *WorAlBi*
McKechnie, Ian D. G. 1937- *St&PR 91*
McKechnie, Timothy Neal 1962- *WhoSSW 91*
McKee, Alasdair 1963- *ConAu 132*
McKee, Alexander 1735?-1799 *WhNaAH*
McKee, Allan Whitney 1947- *St&PR 91*
McKee, Barbara Jeffcott 1948- *WhoAmW 91*
McKee, Barbara Joan 1942- *WhoAmW 91*
McKee, Bill Earl 1916- *WhoWor 91*
McKee, Bob *BioIn 16*
McKee, Christopher Fulton 1935- *WhoAm 90*
McKee, Clark Watson 1940- *St&PR 91*
Mckee, Constance Jean *BiDrAPA 89*
McKee, Craig Lloyd 1960- *WhoE 91*
McKee, David *AuBYP 90*
McKee, David John 1947- *WhoSSW 91*
McKee, David Malcolm 1937- *WhoAmA 91*
McKee, Ed. F. 1930- *St&PR 91*
McKee, Edith Merritt 1918- *WhoAmW 91*
McKee, Ellen Gwendolyn 1953- *WhoSSW 91*
McKee, Ellsworth 1932- *St&PR 91*
Mc Kee, Fran 1926- *WhoAm 90*
McKee, Frances Barrett 1909-1975 *WhoAmA 91N*
McKee, Francis John 1943- *WhoE 91, WhoWor 91*
McKee, Frederick J. 1934- *St&PR 91*
Mc Kee, George Moffitt, Jr. 1924- *WhoWor 91*
Mc Kee, Gerald 1930- *WhoWrEP 89*
McKee, Harold Earl 1937- *WhoAm 90*
McKee, James 1931- *St&PR 91*
Mc Kee, James, Jr. 1918- *WhoAm 90*
McKee, James E., Jr. 1916- *ODwPR 91*
McKee, James W., Jr. 1922- *St&PR 91*
Mc Kee, Jewel Chester, Jr. 1923- *WhoAm 90*
Mc Kee, John Angus 1935- *WhoAm 90*
Mc Kee, John Braxton, Jr. 1933- *BiDrAPA 89*
McKee, John Carothers 1912- *WhoWor 91*
Mc Kee, John De Witt 1919- *WhoWrEP 89*
McKee, John L. 1917- *St&PR 91*
McKee, John Sasser, III 1936- *WhoSSW 91*
McKee, Joseph Fulton 1921- *WhoAm 90*
McKee, Joseph V. 1921-1988 *BioIn 16*
McKee, Karen Lynette 1956- *WhoAmW 91*
McKee, Kathryn Dian 1937- *St&PR 91*
McKee, Kathryn Dian Grant 1937- *WhoAm 90*
McKee, Keith Earl 1928- *WhoAm 90*
Mc Kee, Kinnaird Rowe 1929- *WhoAm 90*
McKee, Laurel J. 1940- *WhoE 91*
McKee, Leo *BioIn 16*
McKee, Lonette 1955- *DrBIPA 90*
Mc Kee, Louis 1951- *WhoWrEP 89*
Mc Kee, Margaret Jean 1929- *WhoAmW 91, WhoE 91*
McKee, Mary Elizabeth 1949- *WhoAmW 91*
McKee, Michael *ODwPR 91*
McKee, Mike B. 1942- *St&PR 91*
McKee, Oather Dorris 1905- *St&PR 91, WhoAm 90, WhoSSW 91*
McKee, Patricia Lynn 1964- *WhoAmW 91*
McKee, Patrick Allen 1937- *WhoAm 90*
McKee, Russell *BioIn 16*
McKee, Russell Ellsworth 1932- *WhoAm 90, WhoWor 91*
McKee, Thomas J. 1930- *WhoAm 90*
McKee, Timothy Carlton 1944- *WhoSSW 91, WhoWor 91*
McKee, William David 1926- *WhoAm 90*
McKee, William Finley 1929- *WhoSSW 91*
McKee, William Paul 1946- *St&PR 91*
McKee-Hammad, Mary Ellen 1950- *WhoAmW 91*
McKeeby, Byron Gordon 1936-1984 *WhoAmA 91N*
McKeel, Sam S. 1926- *BioIn 16*
Mc Keel, Sam Stewart 1926- *WhoAm 90*
McKeen, Chester M., Jr. 1923- *St&PR 91*
Mc Keen, Chester M., Jr. 1923- *WhoAm 90*
McKeen, George B. 1924- *St&PR 91*
McKeen, Lynn Marie 1951- *WhoAmW 91*
McKeen Ramsey Meachem, Margaret 1922- *IntWWM 90*
McKeever, Brian Evans 1949- *WhoE 91*
McKeever, Jeffrey D. 1942- *St&PR 91*
McKeever, John Eugene 1947- *WhoE 91*
Mc Keever, Lewis Goodell *BiDrAPA 89*
McKeever, Porter 1915- *WhoAm 90*
McKeever, Thomas A. 1943- *WhoAm 90*
Mc Kegney, Frank Patrick 1932- *BiDrAPA 89*
McKegney, Tony *BioIn 16*
McKeithen, Walter Fox 1946- *WhoAm 90, WhoSSW 91*
McKeldin, William Evans 1927- *WhoE 91, WhoWor 91*
McKell, Cyrus M. 1926- *WhoAm 90*
McKell, Robert 1923- *St&PR 91*
McKell, Thomas 1935- *St&PR 91*
Mc Kellar, Aida 1923- *BiDrAPA 89*
McKellar, Archibald 1816-1894 *DcCanB 12*
McKellar, C. H. 1937- *WhoAm 90, WhoSSW 91*
McKellar, Danica *BioIn 16*
McKellar, John 1833-1900 *DcCanB 12*
McKellar, Kenneth 1927- *PenDiMP*
McKellen, Ian *BioIn 16*
McKellen, Ian Murray 1939- *WhoWor 91*
McKelvey, Belva Kathleen 1958- *WhoAmW 91*
McKelvey, Gertrude Della *AuBYP 90*
McKelvey, Gregory Alan 1958- *WhoE 91*
McKelvey, James Morgan 1925- *WhoAm 90*
Mc Kelvey, Jean Trepp 1908- *WhoAm 90*
McKelvey, John A. 1951- *St&PR 91*
McKelvey, John Clifford 1934- *St&PR 91*
Mc Kelvey, John Clifford 1934- *WhoAm 90*
Mc Kelvey, John Jay, Jr. 1917- *WhoAm 90*
McKelvey, Judith Grant 1935- *WhoAm 90*
McKelvey, Robert Smith 1944- *BiDrAPA 89*
McKelvie, Donald 1913- *St&PR 91*
McKelvy, Charles Lockhart 1930- *St&PR 91*
Mc Kelvy, Charles Lockhart, Jr. 1930- *WhoAm 90*
McKelway, Russell Brick 1957- *BiDrAPA 89*
McKemmish, Jan 1950- *FemiCLE*
McKemy, Harold D. 1929- *St&PR 91*
Mc Kendrick, Joseph Edward, Jr. 1956- *WhoWrEP 89*
McKendrick, Melveena 1941- *BioIn 16*
McKendry, Donald J. 1927- *St&PR 91*
McKendry, Erwin W. 1929- *St&PR 91*
McKendry, Eugene *BioIn 16*
McKendry, Francis James 1957- *St&PR 91*
McKendry, John 1933-1975 *WhoAmA 91N*
McKendry, John H., Jr. 1950- *WhoEmL 91*
Mc Kenna, Alex George 1914- *WhoAm 90*
McKenna, Andrew James 1929- *St&PR 91, WhoAm 90*
McKenna, Ann Ruth 1933- *WhoE 91*
McKenna, Arthur Lawrence 1941- *WhoE 91*
McKenna, Bernard James 1933- *WhoWor 91*
McKenna, Bruce Alan 1943- *St&PR 91*
McKenna, David Anthony 1962- *WhoE 91*
Mc Kenna, David Loren 1929- *WhoAm 90*
McKenna, David William 1945- *WhoEmL 91*
McKenna, Edward James, Jr. 1950- *WhoEmL 91*
McKenna, Fay Ann 1944- *WhoAmW 91, WhoE 91, WhoWor 91*
McKenna, Frank Joseph 1948- *WhoAm 90, WhoE 91*
McKenna, Frederick Gregory 1952- *WhoEmL 91*
McKenna, George *BioIn 16*
McKenna, George A. *BioIn 16*
McKenna, George Laverne 1924- *WhoAmA 91*
Mc Kenna, Gerald James *BiDrAPA 89*
McKenna, Gwendeline M. 1920- *WhoAmW 91*
McKenna, J. Frank, III 1948- *WhoEmL 91*
Mc Kenna, James A., III 1945- *WhoWrEP 89*
Mc Kenna, James Aloysius 1918- *WhoAm 90*
McKenna, James Michael 1945- *St&PR 91*
McKenna, John Dennis 1940- *WhoSSW 91*
McKenna, John Thomas 1927- *St&PR 91*
McKenna, Joseph 1843-1926 *BiDrUSE 89*
McKenna, Judi Ann 1958- *WhoAmW 91*
McKenna, Kathleen Marie *BiDrAPA 89*
Mc Kenna, Malcolm Carnegie 1930- *WhoAm 90*
McKenna, Margaret Anne 1945- *WhoAm 90, WhoAmW 91, WhoE 91*
McKenna, Margaret S 1948- *BiDrAPA 89*
Mc Kenna, Marian Cecilia 1926- *WhoAm 90*

McKenna, Marian Cecilia 1926- *WhoWrEP 89*
McKenna, Mary Patricia *WhoAmW 91*
McKenna, Michael Francis 1951- *WhoEmL 91*
McKenna, Michael Joseph 1935- *WhoAm 90*
Mc Kenna, Peter *BiDrAPA 89*
McKenna, Peter 1932- *WhoWor 91*
McKenna, Quentin Carnegie 1926- *St&PR 91, WhoAm 90*
McKenna, R Craig 1955- *BiDrAPA 89*
McKenna, Regis 1939- *ODwPR 91, WhoAm 90*
McKenna, Robert J. *WhoAm 90*
McKenna, Robert Patrick 1928- *St&PR 91*
McKenna, Shirley Lee 1935- *WhoAmW 91*
Mc Kenna, Sidney F. 1922- *WhoAm 90*
McKenna, Sidney Francis 1922- *St&PR 91*
McKenna, Terence Joseph 1942- *WhoWor 91*
McKenna, Terence Patrick 1928- *WhoAm 90*
Mc Kenna, Thomas Joseph 1929- *WhoAm 90*
McKenna, Thomas Morrison, Jr. 1937- *WhoAm 90*
McKenna, Timothy 1948- *ODwPR 91*
McKenna, Virgil Vincent 1935- *WhoAm 90*
Mc Kenna, William A., Jr. *WhoAm 90*
McKenna, William A., Jr. 1936- *St&PR 91*
McKenna, William E. 1919- *St&PR 91*
Mc Kenna, William Edward 1919- *WhoAm 90*
McKenna, William J. 1926- *St&PR 91*
McKenna, William John 1926- *WhoAm 90*
McKennan, John T. 1918- *WhoE 91*
McKennan, Thomas McKean Thompson 1794-1852 *BiDrUSE 89*
Mc Kenney, Joel Ray 1934- *BiDrAPA 89*
McKenney, Ruth 1911-1972 *EncAL*
McKenney, Scott Alan 1955- *WhoSSW 91*
McKenney, Thomas Loraine 1785-1859 *WhNaAH [port]*
Mc Kenney, Walter Gibbs, Jr. 1913- *WhoAm 90, WhoWor 91*
McKennon, Keith Robert 1933- *St&PR 91, WhoAm 90*
McKenny, Collin Grad 1944- *WhoAmW 91*
McKenny, Jere W. 1929- *St&PR 91*
McKenny, Jere Wesley 1929- *WhoAm 90, WhoSSW 91*
McKenny, John F. 1950- *St&PR 91*
McKenny, Margaret *AuBYP 90*
McKenry, Robyn Paradice 1954- *WhoAmW 91*
McKenzie, Allan Dean 1930- *WhoAmA 91*
McKenzie, Carl 1905- *MusmAFA*
McKenzie, Catherine L. 1941- *WhoAmW 91*
McKenzie, Charles Hayden 1953- *St&PR 91*
McKenzie, Clyde Ellis 1947- *St&PR 91*
McKenzie, Dan Peter 1942- *WhoWor 91*
McKenzie, Donald J. 1938- *St&PR 91*
McKenzie, Douglas G. 1934- *St&PR 91*
McKenzie, Elizabeth Bobo 1928- *WhoAmW 91*
McKenzie, Ernest L. 1922- *St&PR 91*
McKenzie, Gerald C. 1926- *St&PR 91*
Mc Kenzie, Harold Cantrell, Jr. 1931- *WhoAm 90*
McKenzie, Harold J. 1904- *St&PR 91*
Mc Kenzie, Harold Jackson 1904- *WhoAm 90*
McKenzie, Herbert A. 1934- *St&PR 91*
McKenzie, Herbert Alonzo 1934- *WhoAm 90*
Mc Kenzie, Hilton Eugene 1921- *WhoSSW 91, WhoWor 91*
McKenzie, Ian Farquhar Campbell 1937- *WhoWor 91*
McKenzie, Jack Harris 1930- *IntWWM 90, WhoAm 90*
McKenzie, James D. 1944- *St&PR 91*
McKenzie, James Franklin 1948- *WhoWor 91*
McKenzie, James Henry 1950- *WhoEmL 91*
McKenzie, James Hewat 1869-1929 *EncO&P 3*
McKenzie, James Hewat 1870-1929 *EncPaPR 91*
Mc Kenzie, Jeremy Alec 1941- *WhoAm 90*
Mc Kenzie, John Maxwell 1927- *WhoAm 90*
McKenzie, John Robertson 1936- *St&PR 91*
McKenzie, John Stuart 1922- *St&PR 91*
McKenzie, Kay Branch *ODwPR 91*
McKenzie, Kenneth *WhoAm 90*
Mc Kenzie, Lionel Wilfred 1919- *WhoAm 90*
Mc Kenzie, Malroy Bernard 1951- *WhoWrEP 89*
McKenzie, Mary Beth *WhoE 91*
McKenzie, Mary Beth 1946- *WhoAmA 91*
McKenzie, Merle 1954- *WhoEmL 91*
McKenzie, Michael K. *WhoAm 90*
McKenzie, Michael K. 1943- *St&PR 91*
McKenzie, Miriam Annette 1959- *WhoE 91*
Mc Kenzie, Norma DeeAnn *BiDrAPA 89*
Mc Kenzie, Ray 1927- *WhoAm 90*
McKenzie, Red 1899-1948 *OxCPMus*
McKenzie, Richard Douglas 1950- *WhoSSW 91*
McKenzie, Robert Franklin 1934- *WhoSSW 91*
McKenzie, Robert Gene 1938- *St&PR 91*
McKenzie, Robert Trelford 1917-1981 *DcNaB 1981*
McKenzie, Sherrie Lynn Werndle 1966- *WhoAmW 91*
McKenzie, Susan Helen 1964- *WhoAmW 91*
McKenzie, Vinnorma Shaw 1890-1952 *WhoAmA 91N*
McKenzie, Wallace Chessley 1928- *IntWWM 90*
McKenzie, William P. 1954- *ConAu 130*
McKenzie, William Philip 1954- *WhoE 91*
McKenzie-Hebert, Mary Elizabeth 1955- *WhoAmW 91, WhoE 91*
McKeogh, Aileen 1952- *BiDWomA*
McKeon, Barry J. 1954- *St&PR 91*
McKeon, Brian Kenneth 1935- *WhoWor 91*
Mc Keon, Clementine C *BiDrAPA 89*
McKeon, Donna Forill 1927- *WhoAmW 91, WhoWor 91*
McKeon, Elizabeth F. 1931- *St&PR 91*
McKeon, George A. 1937- *St&PR 91*
McKeon, Jack *BioIn 16*
McKeon, Jack 1930- *Ballpl 90*
McKeon, John Francis 1925- *St&PR 91*
McKeon, Nancy 1966- *ConTFT 8*
McKeon, Paul Valentine 1955- *WhoSSW 91*
McKeon, William Joseph *BioIn 16*
McKeone, David J. 1948- *WhoSSW 91*
Mc Keough, Richard Blair 1927- *WhoAm 90*
McKeough, William Darcy 1933- *WhoAm 90*
McKeown, Anne Willemssen 1952- *WhoAmW 91*
McKeown, Edward N. *BioIn 16*
McKeown, Frank James 1931- *WhoSSW 91*
McKeown, Gerrie Margaret 1955- *WhoE 91*
McKeown, James Charles 1945- *WhoAm 90*
McKeown, James John 1930- *WhoAm 90*
McKeown, Joseph 1959- *WhoE 91*
McKeown, M. Margaret 1951- *St&PR 91, WhoAmW 91*
McKeown, Martin 1943- *WhoE 91*
McKeown, Mary Elizabeth *WhoAmW 91*
Mc Keown, Raymond Meril 1902- *WhoAm 90*
McKeown, Stephan Grue 1947- *WhoE 91*
McKeown, Thomas W. *WhoAm 90*
McKeown, Thomas W. 1929- *St&PR 91*
Mc Keown, Tom 1937- *WhoAm 90, WhoWrEP 89*
Mc Keown, William Taylor 1921- *WhoAm 90, WhoWrEP 89*
McKeracher, Robert Duncan 1943- *WhoAm 90*
McKern, Leo 1920- *ConTFT 8 [port]*
Mc Kernan, John Joseph 1942- *WhoWrEP 89*
McKernan, John Rettie, Jr. 1948- *WhoAm 90, WhoE 91, WhoWor 91*
McKernan, Leo Joseph 1938- *St&PR 91, WhoAm 90*
Mc Kernan, Llewellyn Teresa 1941- *WhoWrEP 89*
McKerns, Charles Joseph 1935- *WhoAm 90*
McKerrow, Amanda *WhoAm 90*
McKerrow, Mary 1915- *ConAu 132*
McKesson, Malcolm Forbes 1909- *WhoAmA 91*
McKessy, Stephen W. *WhoAm 90*
Mc Ketta, John J., Jr. 1915- *WhoAm 90*
McKhann, Charles F. 1898-1988 *BioIn 16*
McKhann, Guy Mead 1932- *WhoAm 90*
McKibben, Bernice Colleen 1926- *WhoAm 90*
McKibben, Bill *ConAu 130*
McKibben, Glen M. 1911- *St&PR 91*
McKibben, Gordon Charles 1930- *WhoAm 90*
McKibben, Howard D. 1940- *WhoAm 90*
McKibben, James Denis 1951- *WhoE 91*
McKibben, John E. 1940- *St&PR 91*
McKibben, Jon S. 1938- *St&PR 91*
McKibben, Michael Steward 1947- *WhoSSW 91*
McKibben, Ryan Timothy 1958- *WhoAm 90*
McKibben, William 1960- *ConAu 130*
McKibbin, John Mead 1915- *WhoAm 90*
McKibbin, John Meek, III 1931- *WhoAm 90*
McKibbin, Robert 1951- *BioIn 16*
McKibbin, Warwick James 1957- *WhoWor 91*
McKie, David K. 1920- *St&PR 91*
Mc Kie, James Warren 1922- *WhoAm 90*
McKie, Ronald Cecil Hamlyn 1909- *WhoWor 91*
Mc Kie, Todd Stoddard 1944- *WhoAm 90*
McKie, Todd Stoddard 1944- *WhoAmA 91*
McKie, William 1901-1984 *PenDiMP*
McKie, William C., Jr. 1949- *St&PR 91*
McKie, William Neil 1901-1984 *DcNaB 1981*
McKiel, Robin Carol 1951- *WhoAmW 91*
McKiernan, John William 1923- *WhoAm 90*
McKiernan, Susan Paolano 1947- *WhoEmL 91*
McKiernan, Thomas Joseph 1938- *St&PR 91*
McKillip, Patricia A. 1948- *AuBYP 90, MajTwCW*
McKillip, Patricia Claire *WhoAmW 91*
McKillip Gage, Donna LuAnn 1953- *WhoAmW 91*
McKillop, Allan A. 1925- *WhoAm 90*
McKillop, Edgar Alexander 1879-1950 *MusmAFA*
McKillop, Lucille 1924- *WhoAmW 91*
McKillop, Peter Dudley 1957- *WhoE 91*
McKim, Audrey Margaret 1909- *BioIn 16*
McKim, Charles F. 1847-1909 *WorAlBi*
McKim, Charles Follen 1847-1909 *BioIn 16*
McKim, Paul Arthur 1923- *WhoAm 90*
McKim, Phyllis R. 1943- *WhoSSW 91*
McKim, Samuel John, III 1938- *WhoAm 90, WhoWor 91*
McKim, William Wind 1916- *WhoAmA 91*
McKimmey, James 1923- *WhoWrEP 89*
McKimmey, Vickie Lynn 1959- *WhoSSW 91*
McKinin, Lawrence 1917- *WhoAmA 91N*
McKinlay, Donald Carl 1916- *WhoAm 90*
Mc Kinlay, Eleanor Grantham 1921- *WhoWrEP 89*
McKinlay, Glenn P. 1878- *AmLegL*
McKinlay, Ronald Archibald 1924- *WhoAm 90*
McKinley, Bill 1910- *Ballpl 90*
McKinley, Brunson 1943- *WhoAm 90, WhoWor 91*
McKinley, Douglas Webster 1917- *WhoAm 90*
McKinley, Edmon Howard 1949- *WhoSSW 91*
McKinley, Ellen Bacon 1929- *WhoAmW 91*
McKinley, Glenn P. 1878- *AmLegL*
Mc Kinley, Gordon Wells 1915- *WhoAm 90*
McKinley, Ida Saxton 1847-1907 *BioAmW, BioIn 16*
McKinley, James Frank 1943- *St&PR 91*
McKinley, James P. *ODwPR 91*
McKinley, James T. 1947- *St&PR 91*
Mc Kinley, Jimmie Joe 1934- *WhoSSW 91*
McKinley, John K. 1920- *St&PR 91*
Mc Kinley, John Key 1920- *WhoAm 90*
McKinley, Karen Lane 1949- *WhoSSW 91*
McKinley, Loren Dhue 1920- *WhoAm 90*
McKinley, Malcolm R. 1928- *St&PR 91*
McKinley, Margaret Ann 1956- *WhoEmL 91*
McKinley, Marjorie M. 1918-1988 *BioIn 16*
McKinley, Martha A. 1954- *ODwPR 91*
McKinley, Marvin Dyal 1937- *WhoAm 90*
McKinley, Paul S. 1947- *St&PR 91*
McKinley, Peggi Zilvitis 1946- *WhoSSW 91*
McKinley, Ray 1910- *BioIn 16, OxCPMus*
McKinley, Rheta Chipman 1926- *WhoE 91*
McKinley, Richard S. 1952- *St&PR 91*
Mc Kinley, Robert A 1923- *BiDrAPA 89*
Mc Kinley, Robert L 1924- *BiDrAPA 89*
Mc Kinley, Robert Louie, Jr. 1929- *BiDrAPA 89*
McKinley, Robin *BioIn 16*
McKinley, Robin 1952- *ConAu 31NR*
McKinley, Royce B. 1921- *St&PR 91*
Mc Kinley, Royce Baldwin 1921- *WhoAm 90*
McKinley, Ruth Gowdy 1931-1981 *WhoAmA 91N*
McKinley, Ruth JoAnn 1933- *WhoAmW 91*
McKinley, William 1843-1901 *BioIn 16, WorAlBi*
McKinley, William, Jr. 1843-1901 *BiDrUSE 89*
McKinley, William A. 1917- *WhoAm 90*
McKinley, William L. 1924- *St&PR 91*
McKinley, William Thomas 1938- *WhoAm 90*
McKinley-Haas, Mary *WhoAmA 91, WhoE 91*
McKinne, Michael Gene 1946- *St&PR 91*
McKinnell, Noel Michael 1935- *WhoAm 90*
Mc Kinnell, Robert Gilmore 1926- *WhoAm 90*
McKinnell, Sue Ellen 1950- *St&PR 91*
Mc Kinney, Alexis 1907- *WhoAm 90*
McKinney, Beverly Garrett 1949- *WhoSSW 91*
McKinney, Bill *ConTFT 8*
McKinney, Carie Goodman 1956- *WhoAmW 91*
McKinney, Caryn *BioIn 16*
McKinney, Ceil Catherine 1956- *WhoAmW 91*
McKinney, Charles Cecil 1931- *WhoAm 90, WhoSSW 91*
McKinney, Clark Elwood 1937- *WhoSSW 91*
Mc Kinney, David Ewing 1934- *WhoAm 90, WhoE 91*
McKinney, Donald 1931- *WhoAmA 91*
McKinney, Donald Eugene 1946- *St&PR 91*
McKinney, Donald Lee 1923- *WhoAm 90*
Mc Kinney, Donald Lee 1923- *WhoWrEP 89*
McKinney, Dwight Cleveland 1945- *WhoSSW 91*
McKinney, E. Kirk, Jr. 1923- *St&PR 91, WhoAm 90*
McKinney, E. Melville 1939- *WhoAm 90*
McKinney, Edward Britt 19--?-194-? *EncAL*
McKinney, Eva Y. 1966- *WhoEmL 91*
McKinney, Frank Edward, Jr. 1938- *St&PR 91*
McKinney, Gene 1935- *ODwPR 91*
Mc Kinney, George Wesley, Jr. 1922- *WhoAm 90*
McKinney, Henry Daniel 1936- *WhoE 91*
McKinney, Hiram Yancey 1928- *St&PR 91*
Mc Kinney, Irene 1939- *WhoWrEP 89*
McKinney, J. Bruce 1937- *St&PR 91*
McKinney, James *IntWWM 90*
McKinney, James Bernard, Jr. 1950- *WhoEmL 91*
Mc Kinney, James Carroll 1921- *WhoAm 90*
McKinney, James Clayton 1940- *WhoAm 90*
McKinney, James I. 1933- *St&PR 91*
McKinney, Jim 1860-1903 *BioIn 16*
McKinney, Joe Clayton 1946- *St&PR 91*
McKinney, John Adams, Jr. 1948- *WhoEmL 91*
McKinney, John Benjamin 1932- *WhoAm 90*
McKinney, Joseph E. 1945- *St&PR 91*
McKinney, Joseph F. 1931- *St&PR 91, WhoAm 90, WhoSSW 91*
Mc Kinney, Joseph K 1932- *BiDrAPA 89*
McKinney, Judson Thad 1941- *WhoAm 90*
McKinney, Kenneth A. 1956- *St&PR 91*
Mc Kinney, Leon R *BiDrAPA 89*
McKinney, Luther C. 1931- *St&PR 91*
McKinney, Margaret Kay 1948- *St&PR 91*
McKinney, Margaret M. 1953- *St&PR 91*
McKinney, Michael Roy 1949- *WhoAm 90*
Mc Kinney, Michael Whitney 1946- *WhoSSW 91*
Mc Kinney, Montgomery Nelson 1910- *WhoAm 90*
McKinney, Nina Mae 1913-1967 *DrBlPA 90*
McKinney, Owen Dwight 1943- *St&PR 91*
McKinney, Owen S. 1849- *AmLegL*
McKinney, Pamela Anne 1947- *WhoAmW 91*
McKinney, Phyllis Louise Kellogg Henry 1932- *WhoAmW 91*
McKinney, Rich 1946- *Ballpl 90*
McKinney, Richard W. *St&PR 91N*
McKinney, Robert H. 1925- *St&PR 91*
Mc Kinney, Robert Hurley 1925- *WhoAm 90*
McKinney, Robert L. 1926- *St&PR 91*
Mc Kinney, Robert Moody 1910- *WhoAm 90*
Mc Kinney, Robert Salter 1941- *WhoAm 90*
McKinney, Roland Joseph 1898- *AuBYP 90*
Mc Kinney, Ross Erwin 1926- *WhoAm 90*
McKinney, Rufus William 1930- *St&PR 91*
McKinney, Sally *St&PR 91*
McKinney, San 1946- *WhoAmW 91*
McKinney, Stewart B. 1931-1987 *BioIn 16*
McKinney, Stuart Bontecou 1919- *St&PR 91*
McKinney, Tatiana Ladygina *WhoAmA 91*

McKinney, Terry Loyd 1954- *WhoE 91*
McKinney, Venora Ware 1937- *WhoAm 90*
McKinney, William 1895-1969 *BioIn 16, OxCPMus*
Mc Kinney, William C 1925- *BiDrAPA 89*
McKinney, William Douthitt, Jr. 1955- *WhoSSW 91*
Mc Kinney, William T, Jr. 1937- *BiDrAPA 89*
McKinnickinnick, Margaret I 1924- *WhoAmA 91, WhoE 91*
McKinnie, Donna Louise Fones 1934- *WhoAmW 91*
McKinnies, Mark H. 1952- *St&PR 91*
McKinnis, Archie Price 1942- *St&PR 91*
McKinnis, Lee Vern 1948- *WhoSSW 91*
McKinnis, Steven Ray 1952- *WhoWor 91*
McKinnish, Richmond Dee 1949- *St&PR 91*
McKinnon, Alexander 1943- *St&PR 91*
McKinnon, Arnold Borden 1927- *St&PR 91, WhoAm 90, WhoSSW 91*
McKinnon, B. E. 1940- *St&PR 91*
Mc Kinnon, Clinton D. 1906- *WhoAm 90*
Mc Kinnon, Clinton Dan 1934- *WhoAm 90*
McKinnon, Daniel Harold 1933- *St&PR 91*
McKinnon, David C. 1916- *St&PR 91*
McKinnon, Floyd Wingfield 1942- *WhoE 91*
Mc Kinnon, Francis Arthur Richard 1933- *WhoAm 90*
McKinnon, James Buckner 1916- *WhoWor 91*
McKinnon, James Douglas 1948- *St&PR 91*
McKinnon, James William 1932- *WhoAm 90*
McKinnon, John Alson 1946- *BiDrAPA 89*
McKinnon, John Borden 1934- *St&PR 91*
McKinnon, Neil 1909-1988 *AnObit 1988*
McKinnon, Perry *BioIn 16*
McKinnon, Roger Hugh 1950- *WhoE 91*
McKinnon, Ronald I 1935- *ConAu 131*
McKinnon, Thomas K. 1945- *St&PR 91*
McKinnon, William S. 1852-1908 *AmLegL*
McKinsey, Linda Schaefer 1947- *St&PR 91*
McKinsey, Marie *ODwPR 91*
McKinstry, Gregory John Duncan 1947- *WhoAm 90*
McKinstry, Ronald Eugene 1926- *WhoAm 90*
McKinzie, Beverly Oma 1927- *WhoAmW 91*
McKirahan, Richard Duncan, Jr. 1945- *WhoAm 90*
McKisack, May 1900-1981 *BioIn 16*
McKissack, Fredrick 1939- *BioIn 16*
McKissack, Leatrice Buchanan 1930- *WhoSSW 91*
McKissack, Pat 1944- *BioIn 16*
McKissack, Patricia C. 1944- *AuBYP 90, BioIn 16, ChILR 23 [port]*
McKissack, Perri *BioIn 16*
McKissick, James Harold 1932- *St&PR 91*
McKissick, Michael Landon 1950- *WhoE 91*
McKissick, Ronald L. 1948- *St&PR 91*
McKissock, David Lee 1933- *St&PR 91*
McKissock, Paul Kendrick 1925- *WhoAm 90*
McKitrick, James T. 1945- *St&PR 91*
McKitrick, James Thomas 1945- *WhoAm 90*
McKitrick, Ron Bruce 1932- *St&PR 91*
McKitterick, Nathaniel M. *BioIn 16*
McKittrick, Brian Letham 1936- *WhoWor 91*
McKittrick, David Jay 1945- *St&PR 91*
McKittrick, William Wood 1915- *WhoAm 90*
McKlveen, Joseph L. 1913- *St&PR 91*
McKlveen, Thomas Goodwin 1947- *St&PR 91*
Mc Knelly, William Von, Jr. 1929- *BiDrAPA 89*
Mc Knew, Donald H, Jr. 1933- *BiDrAPA 89*
McKnew, Thomas W. 1896- *St&PR 91*
McKnew, Thomas Willson *NewYTBS 90*
McKnight, Alexander 1826-1894 *DcCanB 12*
McKnight, Andrew Dennis 1936- *St&PR 91*
McKnight, Barbara Ann Ferrell 1938- *WhoAmW 91*
McKnight, Douglas Garth 1949- *St&PR 91*
McKnight, Elizabeth Conway 1945- *WhoAmW 91*
McKnight, Harriet Mangus 1950- *WhoAmW 91*
Mc Knight, James Moody *BiDrAPA 89*
Mc Knight, Joe Nip 1933- *WhoSSW 91*
Mc Knight, John Lacy 1931- *WhoAm 90*
McKnight, Joseph Webb 1925- *WhoAm 90*
McKnight, Joyce Sheldon 1949- *WhoAmW 91, WhoE 91*
McKnight, Karen Therese 1947- *WhoAmW 91*
Mcknight, Kathleen Kerr *BiDrAPA 89*
McKnight, Lee Warren 1956- *WhoE 91*
Mc Knight, Lenore Ravin 1943- *BiDrAPA 89*
McKnight, Louis Warren, Jr. 1947- *St&PR 91*
Mc Knight, Martha Anne 1955- *BiDrAPA 89*
McKnight, Mary Louise 1954- *WhoE 91*
McKnight, Michael Lance 1939- *WhoWor 91*
Mc Knight, Patricia Ann 1948- *BiDrAPA 89*
Mc Knight, Paul James, Jr. 1935- *WhoAm 90, WhoSSW 91*
McKnight, Paul Sheldon 1947- *WhoE 91*
McKnight, Reginald *ConAu 129*
Mc Knight, Robert Kellogg 1924- *WhoAm 90*
Mc Knight, Robert S 1921- *BiDrAPA 89*
Mcknight, Russell Delbert 1932- *BiDrAPA 89*
McKnight, Thomas Frederick 1941- *WhoAmA 91*
McKnight, William Baldwin 1923- *WhoAm 90*
McKnight, William Edwin 1938- *WhoSSW 91*
McKnight, William Hunter 1940- *WhoAm 90, WhoE 91, WhoWor 91*
McKnight, William J. 1939- *St&PR 91*
Mc Knight, William K 1911- *BiDrAPA 89*
McKnight, William Lester 1887-1978 *ConAmBL*
Mc Knight, William Warren, Jr. 1913- *WhoAm 90*
McKoin, Hazel McKinney 1942- *WhoSSW 91*
McKone, Don T. 1921- *St&PR 91*
Mc Kone, Don T. 1921- *WhoAm 90*
McKone, Francis L. 1934- *St&PR 91*
McKosky, Theodore Stanley 1921- *WhoSSW 91*
McKowen, Dorothy Keeton 1948- *WhoAmW 91, WhoEmL 91*
McKowen, Gary R. 1945- *St&PR 91*
McKowen, Robert H. 1927- *St&PR 91*
McKown, Richard 1947- *St&PR 91*
McKown, Robert Freeman 1936- *WhoE 91*
McKown, Robin *AuBYP 90*
Mc Koy, Basil Vincent Charles 1938- *WhoAm 90*
McKoy, Ellen Molly 1944- *WhoAmW 91*
McKoy, June Marcia 1953- *BiDrAPA 89*
McKoy, Victor Grainger 1947- *WhoAmA 91*
Mc Kuen, Pamela Dittmer 1951- *WhoWrEP 89*
McKuen, Rod 1933- *IntWWM 90, OxCPMus*
Mc Kuen, Rod 1933- *WhoWrEP 89*
McKuen, Rod 1933- *WorAlBi*
Mc Kusick, Victor Almon 1921- *WhoAm 90*
Mc Kusick, Vincent Lee 1921- *WhoAm 90, WhoE 91*
McLachlan, Alexander 1817-1896 *DcCanB 12*
McLachlan, Alexander 1818-1896 *DcLB 99 [port]*
McLachlan, Andrew David 1935- *WhoWor 91*
McLachlan, Iva Wolf 1956- *WhoAmW 91*
McLachlin, Beverley 1943- *WhoAmW 91*
McLaglen, Victor 1883-1959 *WorAlBi*
McLain, Christopher 1943- *WhoAm 90*
McLain, Clifford E. 1931- *St&PR 91*
McLain, Denny 1944- *Ballpl 90 [port], BioIn 16*
McLain, Douglas Walker 1962- *St&PR 91*
McLain, Gerald Grady 1953- *WhoSSW 91*
McLain, H. Jack 1940- *St&PR 91*
McLain, James P. 1923- *WhoSSW 91*
McLain, Janice Darlene 1943- *WhoAmW 91*
McLain, Kathy Hart 1960- *WhoEmL 91*
McLain, Maurice Clayton 1929- *WhoAm 90*
McLain, Merline Plunkett *BiDrAPA 89*
McLain, Patrick M. *ODwPR 91*
McLain, Paul King 1960- *St&PR 91*
McLain, Paul X. 1940- *St&PR 91*
McLain, Philip Michael 1954- *WhoSSW 91*
McLain, Robert K. 1926- *St&PR 91*
McLain, Robert Malcolm 1931- *IntWWM 90*
McLaine, Alice Jeanette 1958- *WhoAmW 91*
McLaine, James Murray 1938- *St&PR 91*
McLallen, John Addison 1905- *St&PR 91*
McLallen, Scott Jay 1948- *St&PR 91*
McLamb, Charles Harold 1951- *WhoSSW 91*
McLanahan, Michael Ward 1938- *St&PR 91*
McLanathan, Richard 1916- *AuBYP 90*
Mc Lanathan, Richard 1916- *WhoAm 90, WhoWrEP 89*
McLane, Austin *WhoSSW 91*
McLane, Bobbie Jones 1927- *WhoAmW 91*
McLane, David Glenn 1943- *WhoAm 90*
McLane, Donald Joseph 1943- *St&PR 91*
McLane, Henry Earl, Jr. 1932- *WhoAm 90*
Mc Lane, John Roy, Jr. 1916- *WhoAm 90*
McLane, John Thomas 1948- *WhoEmL 91*
McLane, L. Thomas 1923- *St&PR 91*
McLane, Louis 1786-1857 *BiDrUSE 89, BioIn 16*
McLane, Robert Drayton, Jr. 1936- *St&PR 91, WhoAm 90*
McLane, Robert Drayton, Sr. 1901- *WhoAm 90*
McLane, Robert Milligan 1815-1898 *BioIn 16*
McLane, Stephen B. *St&PR 91*
McLane, Susan Neidlinger 1929- *WhoAmW 91, WhoE 91*
McLane, Thomas Lawrence 1932- *WhoE 91*
McLane, Timothy E. 1955- *St&PR 91*
McLaren, Archie Campbell, Jr 1942- *WhoWor 91*
McLaren, Digby Johns 1919- *WhoAm 90, WhoWor 91*
McLaren, Felicia Dible 1924- *WhoE 91*
McLaren, James Clark 1925- *WhoAm 90*
McLaren, John *BioIn 16*
Mc Laren, John Alexander 1919- *WhoAm 90*
McLaren, Karen Lynn 1955- *WhoAmW 91*
McLaren, Malcolm *BioIn 16*
Mc Laren, Malcolm Grant, IV 1928- *WhoAm 90*
McLaren, Marilyn Patricia 1942- *WhoAmW 91, WhoE 91*
McLaren, Norman 1914-1987 *BioIn 16*
McLaren, Ruth S. 1955- *St&PR 91*
McLarey, Sandra Roberts 1940- *WhoAmW 91*
McLarey, Tracy Ann 1959- *WhoAmW 91*
McLarnan, Donald Edward 1906- *WhoAm 90*
McLarnon, Mary Frances 1944- *WhoE 91*
McLarnon, Michael Charles 1955- *BiDrAPA 89*
McLarty, Thomas F., III 1946- *WhoAm 90, WhoSSW 91*
McLarty, William T, Jr. 1942- *BiDrAPA 89*
McLauchlan, Russell Walter 1924- *St&PR 91*
McLaughin, John P. 1951- *St&PR 91*
McLaughin, Patricia *ODwPR 91*
McLaughlin, Albert Howard 1924- *WhoE 91*
McLaughlin, Alexander Charles John 1925- *WhoSSW 91, WhoWor 91*
Mc Laughlin, Allan Evert *BiDrAPA 89*
McLaughlin, Ann 1941- *WhoAm 90, WhoAmW 91*
McLaughlin, Ann Dore *BioIn 16*
McLaughlin, Ann Dore 1941- *BiDrUSE 89*
McLaughlin, Audrey *BioIn 16*
McLaughlin, Audrey 1936- *CurBio 90 [port], News 90 [port], -90-3 [port], WhoAmW 91*
McLaughlin, Bette H. 1933- *St&PR 91*
Mc Laughlin, Blaine Edmund *BiDrAPA 89*
McLaughlin, Bo 1953- *Ballpl 90*
McLaughlin, Brian Anthony 1960- *WhoWor 91*
McLaughlin, Brian D. 1942- *St&PR 91*
McLaughlin, Byron 1955- *Ballpl 90*
McLaughlin, Calvin Sturgis 1936- *WhoAm 90*
McLaughlin, Charles Michael 1938- *St&PR 91*
McLaughlin, Cyrus H. 1827- *AmLegL*
McLaughlin, David Jordan 1940- *WhoAm 90*
McLaughlin, David T. 1932- *St&PR 91*
Mc Laughlin, David Thomas 1932- *WhoAm 90*
McLaughlin, Deborah Ann 1952- *WhoAmW 91*
McLaughlin, Denise K. 1947- *St&PR 91*
McLaughlin, Donal 1875-1978 *WhoAmA 91N*
McLaughlin, Edward 1928- *WhoAm 90*
McLaughlin, Elaine M. 1956- *ODwPR 91*
McLaughlin, Ellie Anderson 1944- *WhoSSW 91*
McLaughlin, Evelyn *BioIn 16*
McLaughlin, Foil William 1923- *WhoSSW 91*
McLaughlin, George B. 1922- *St&PR 91*
McLaughlin, Glen 1934- *WhoAm 90*
Mc Laughlin, Harry Roll 1922- *WhoAm 90*
McLaughlin, Harry Y. 1934- *St&PR 91*
McLaughlin, Henry Elwood, Jr. 1946- *WhoSSW 91*
McLaughlin, Ian M. Watson 1945- *St&PR 91*
Mc Laughlin, J. Richard 1939- *WhoWrEP 89*
McLaughlin, Jack *ConAu 129*
McLaughlin, James 1842-1923 *WhNaAH*
McLaughlin, James, Jr. 1944- *WhoSSW 91*
McLaughlin, James Daniel 1947- *WhoWor 91*
McLaughlin, James Higgins 1946- *St&PR 91*
Mc Laughlin, James T 1918- *BiDrAPA 89*
McLaughlin, James W. 1923- *St&PR 91*
McLaughlin, Jean Wallace 1950- *WhoAmA 91*
Mc Laughlin, Jerome Michael 1929- *WhoAm 90*
Mc Laughlin, Jerry Loren 1939- *WhoAm 90*
McLaughlin, Joey 1956- *Ballpl 90*
McLaughlin, John *BioIn 16*
McLaughlin, John 1898-1976 *WhoAmA 91N*
McLaughlin, John 1942- *OxCPMus*
McLaughlin, John A. 1924-1989 *BioIn 16*
McLaughlin, John D. 1917- *WhoAm 90, WhoWor 91*
Mc Laughlin, John Francis 1927- *WhoAm 90*
Mc Laughlin, John J *BiDrAPA 89*
McLaughlin, John Joseph 1926- *ConAu 129*
McLaughlin, John Joseph 1927- *WhoAm 90*
McLaughlin, John Richardson 1929- *St&PR 91*
McLaughlin, John Sherman 1932- *WhoAm 90*
McLaughlin, Jon A. 1955- *St&PR 91*
Mc Laughlin, Joseph Mailey 1928- *WhoAm 90*
McLaughlin, Joseph Michael 1943- *WhoE 91*
McLaughlin, Joseph W. 1940- *St&PR 91*
Mc Laughlin, June *WhoWrEP 89*
McLaughlin, Kathleen *NewYTBS 90*
McLaughlin, Kathleen 1898-1990 *BioIn 16, ConAu 132*
McLaughlin, Kenneth S. 1926- *St&PR 91*
McLaughlin, Kevin Michael 1952- *WhoE 91*
Mc Laughlin, Leighton Bates, II 1930- *WhoAm 90*
McLaughlin, Marguerite P. *WhoAmW 91*
McLaughlin, Marie 1954- *IntWWM 90*
Mc Laughlin, Martha Day *BiDrAPA 89*
McLaughlin, Martin Michael 1918- *WhoSSW 91*
McLaughlin, Mary F. *St&PR 91*
McLaughlin, Mary Louise 1847-1939 *PenDiDA 89*
McLaughlin, Mary Rittling *WhoAm 90*
McLaughlin, Maryellen 1958- *WhoAmW 91*
McLaughlin, Matthew Aloysius 1936- *St&PR 91*
McLaughlin, Michael A. 1946- *St&PR 91*
McLaughlin, Michael Angelo 1950- *WhoEmL 91, WhoWor 91*
McLaughlin, Michael John 1944- *St&PR 91, WhoAm 90*
McLaughlin, Michael John 1951- *WhoAm 90*
McLaughlin, Michael Weston 1954- *St&PR 91*
McLaughlin, Miriam Westerman 1920- *WhoAmW 91*
McLaughlin, Nancy Esther 1947- *WhoAmW 91*
McLaughlin, Patrick Michael 1946- *WhoAm 90*
McLaughlin, Paul Francis 1945- *St&PR 91*
McLaughlin, Philip H. 1935- *St&PR 91*
McLaughlin, Randolph William 1938- *St&PR 91*
McLaughlin, Richard Warren 1930- *WhoAm 90, WhoE 91*
McLaughlin, Robert *BioIn 16*
McLaughlin, Robert Francis 1920- *WhoWor 91*
McLaughlin, Robert William 1900-1989 *BioIn 16*
McLaughlin, Ronald Malcolm 1941- *WhoAm 90*
McLaughlin, Sandra Lee 1942- *WhoAmW 91*
McLaughlin, Sharon Gail 1946- *WhoAmW 91*
McLaughlin, Suzanne Gilmore 1945- *WhoAmW 91*
McLaughlin, T. Mark 1953- *WhoEmL 91*
McLaughlin, Ted John 1921- *WhoAm 90*
McLaughlin, Thomas A., III 1941- *St&PR 91*
McLaughlin, Wallace Alvin 1927- *WhoAm 90*

McLaughlin, Walter Joseph 1931- *WhoE 91*
McLaughlin, Walter T. *BioIn 16*
McLaughlin, Ward W. 1954- *St&PR 91*
Mc Laughlin, William De Witt 1918- *WhoWrEP 89*
Mc Laughlin, William F 1915- *BiDrAPA 89*
McLaughlin, William Thomas, II 1937- *St&PR 91*
McLaulin, John Bryce *BiDrAPA 89*
McLaurin, Benjamin F. 1906-1989 *BioIn 16*
McLaurin, Eugene Bertram, II 1956- *WhoSSW 91*
Mc Laurin, Francis Wallin 1923- *WhoWor 91*
McLaurin, James Evon 1936- *WhoSSW 91*
McLaurin, Martha Regina 1948- *WhoAmW 91*
McLaurin, Monty Earl 1951- *WhoSSW 91*
McLaurin, Neil H. 1944- *St&PR 91*
McLaurin, Robert Thornton 1930- *St&PR 91*
McLaurin, Ronald De 1944- *WhoAm 90, WhoWor 91*
McLaurin, William 1939- *St&PR 91*
McLay, James Kenneth 1945- *WhoWor 91*
McLay, Margaret Purcell 1949- *IntWWM 90*
McLean, Alan A 1925- *BiDrAPA 89*
McLean, Alexander Francis 1917- *St&PR 91*
McLean, Antonia 1919- *ConAu 130*
Mc Lean, Arthur Frederick 1929- *WhoWor 91*
McLean, Barton Keith 1938- *IntWWM 90*
McLean, Bruce A. J. 1943- *St&PR 91*
McLean, Bruce Charles 1924- *WhoE 91*
McLean, Christopher Anthony 1958- *WhoEmL 91*
McLean, Culbert M., Jr. 1952- *St&PR 91*
McLean, Don 1945- *EncPR&S 89*
Mc Lean, Don 1945- *WhoAm 90, WhoE 91*
McLean, Don 1945- *WorAlBi*
McLean, Donald 1945- *IntWWM 90*
Mc Lean, Donald Millis 1926- *WhoAm 90*
McLean, Edward Beale 1886-1941 *BioIn 16*
McLean, Edward Burns 1937- *WhoSSW 91*
McLean, Edward Cochrane, Jr. 1935- *WhoAm 90*
McLean, Edward Peter 1941- *WhoE 91*
McLean, Elaine 1947- *WhoE 91*
McLean, Emily Justine 1953- *BiDrAPA 89*
McLean, Francis P. 1929- *St&PR 91*
Mc Lean, George Francis 1929- *WhoAm 90*
McLean, Heather *ODwPR 91*
McLean, J Sloan *SmATA X [port]*
McLean, J. W. 1922- *St&PR 91*
McLean, Jackie *BioIn 16*
McLean, James A. 1922- *St&PR 91*
McLean, James Albert 1928- *WhoAmA 91*
McLean, James Frederick 1939- *St&PR 91*
McLean, James Ivan 1946- *WhoSSW 91*
McLean, Janet K. 1953- *WhoAmW 91*
McLean, John 1785-1861 *BiDrUSE 89*
McLean, John Roll 1848-1916 *BioIn 16*
Mc Lean, John William 1922- *WhoAm 90*
McLean, John William, Jr. 1936- *WhoSSW 91, WhoWor 91*
McLean, Joyce *IntWWM 90*
McLean, Larry 1881-1921 *Ballpl 90*
McLean, Lauchlin Huiet 1921- *St&PR 91*
McLean, Lee, Jr. 1924- *St&PR 91*
McLean, Leslie C. 1941- *St&PR 91*
McLean, Lionel Deckle 1900-1988 *BioIn 16*
McLean, Lois G 1947- *BiDrAPA 89*
Mc Lean, Malcolm 1927- *WhoAm 90*
McLean, Mark Lyles 1951- *WhoSSW 91*
McLean, Mary S 1954- *BiDrAPA 89*
McLean, Mervyn Evan 1930- *IntWWM 90*
Mc Lean, Paul Edward 1933- *BiDrAPA 89*
McLean, Philip R. 1957- *St&PR 91*
McLean, Porter 1946- *St&PR 91*
McLean, Priscilla Taylor 1942- *IntWWM 90*
McLean, Raymond A. 1923- *St&PR 91*
McLean, Richard 1953- *St&PR 91*
McLean, Richard Arnold 1945- *WhoSSW 91*
McLean, Richard Thorpe 1934- *WhoAmA 91*
Mc Lean, Robert T. 1922- *WhoAm 90*
McLean, Robert William 1940- *St&PR 91*
McLean, Sam Hays, Jr. 1951- *WhoSSW 91*
McLean, Thomas Bruce 1939- *WhoSSW 91*
Mc Lean, Thomas Edwin 1925- *WhoAm 90*
McLean, Thomas Irvin 1943- *St&PR 91*
McLean, Vincent Ronald 1931- *St&PR 91, WhoAm 90*
McLean, Walter Franklin 1936- *WhoAm 90*
McLean, Warner Hugh 1936- *St&PR 91*
McLean, William *Ballpl 90*
McLean, William George 1910- *WhoE 91*
McLean, William Hugh 1916- *St&PR 91*
Mc Lean, William L., III 1927- *WhoAm 90*
McLean, William Ronald 1921- *WhoE 91, WhoWor 91*
McLean, William Youmans 1927- *WhoSSW 91*
McLean, Wilson 1937- *BioIn 16*
McLean-Wainwright, Pamela Lynne 1948- *WhoWor 91*
McLear, William Z. 1903- *St&PR 91*
McLearn, Michael B. 1936- *St&PR 91*
McLearn, Michael Baylis 1936- *WhoAm 90*
McLeary, Benjamin Ward 1944- *WhoE 91*
McLeay, Franklin 1864-1900 *OxCCanT*
McLeay, James Franklin 1864-1900 *DcCanB 12*
McLeer, Laureen Dorothy 1955- *WhoAmW 91*
Mc Leer, Susan V *BiDrAPA 89*
McLees, William Anderson 1925- *WhoAm 90*
McLeese, Donald George 1950- *WhoAm 90*
McLeish, David James Dow 1936- *WhoAm 90*
McLeish, Ernest D. 1939- *St&PR 91*
Mc Leish, John C *BiDrAPA 89*
McLeister, Thomas Millar 1937- *WhoWor 91*
McLeland, Kim Allen 1949- *WhoSSW 91*
McLellan, Catharine *DcCanB 12*
McLellan, Connie Rae 1950- *WhoAmW 91*
McLellan, David 1940- *ConAu 33NR*
McLellan, Donn Scott 1940- *WhoAm 90*
McLellan, H. Linden 1937- *St&PR 91*
McLellan, Joseph Duncan 1929- *WhoAm 90*
McLellan, Kenneth Hugh, Jr. 1931- *St&PR 91*
McLellan, Kristin Lynn 1966- *WhoAmW 91*
McLellan, Michael J. 1941- *IntWWM 90*
McLellan, Richard Douglas 1942- *WhoAm 90*
McLelland, Douglas Charner 1946- *St&PR 91*
McLelland, Joseph Cumming 1925- *WhoAm 90*
McLelland, Robert 1921- *WhoSSW 91*
McLelland, Stan L. 1945- *St&PR 91*
McLemore, A. Keith *St&PR 91*
Mc Lemore, Colleen Owen 1952- *BiDrAPA 89*
McLemore, David Byron 1951- *WhoSSW 91*
McLemore, Lamonte *BioIn 16*
McLemore, Mark 1964- *Ballpl 90*
McLemore, Michael Kerr 1949- *WhoEmL 91, WhoSSW 91, WhoWor 91*
Mc Lemore, Robert Henry 1910- *WhoAm 90*
McLemore, Teresa Sue 1962- *WhoAmW 91*
McLenaghen, T. Newman 1923- *St&PR 91*
McLendon, George Leland 1952- *WhoAm 90*
McLendon, Heath B. 1933- *St&PR 91*
Mc Lendon, Heath Brian 1933- *WhoAm 90*
McLendon, John Aycock 1933- *St&PR 91*
McLendon, Maureen Carter *WhoSSW 91*
McLendon, William 1951- *St&PR 91*
McLendon, William Woodard 1930- *WhoAm 90*
McLenithan, Gordon John 1940- *St&PR 91*
Mc Lennan, Bill 1944- *WhoWrEP 89*
McLennan, Hugh 1825-1899 *DcCanB 12*
McLennan, James Alan, Jr. 1924- *WhoAm 90*
McLennan, John Cunningham 1867-1935 *DcScB S2*
McLennan, Michael 1945- *St&PR 91*
McLennan, Robert Bruce 1948- *WhoEmL 91*
McLennan, Will *ConAu 129*
McLennan, William 1821-1903 *AmLegL*
McLennan, William 1856-1904 *DcLB 92 [port]*
McLeod, Alexander Canaday 1935- *WhoSSW 91*
McLeod, Allan L., Jr. *WhoSSW 91*
McLeod, Allan L., Jr. 1944- *St&PR 91*
McLeod, Angus Jonas 1861-1900 *DcCanB 12*
McLeod, Angus M. 1910- *St&PR 91*
McLeod, Cheryl O'Halloran 1944- *WhoAmW 91*
McLeod, Christopher Kevin 1955- *WhoAm 90*
McLeod, Deborah Jackson 1915- *WhoAm 90, WhoAmW 91*
McLeod, Denny A. 1926- *St&PR 91*
McLeod, Donald 1846-1894 *DcCanB 12*
McLeod, Donald Neil 1934- *St&PR 91*
McLeod, Edwin A. 1927- *St&PR 91*
McLeod, H. D. 1942- *St&PR 91*
McLeod, Harry O'Neal, Jr. 1932- *WhoSSW 91*
McLeod, Henry Murrell 1940- *WhoE 91*
McLeod, Ian B. 1946- *St&PR 91*
McLeod, Jack 1932- *ConAu 129*
Mc Leod, James Richard 1942- *WhoWrEP 89*
McLeod, James S. 1926- *St&PR 91*
McLeod, John T. 1934- *St&PR 91*
McLeod, Kate 1944- *WhoAmW 91, WhoE 91*
McLeod, Laura Lynn 1959- *WhoAmW 91*
Mc Leod, Malcolm Noell *BiDrAPA 89*
McLeod, Marshall Watson 1941- *WhoSSW 91*
McLeod, Morris M. 1939- *St&PR 91*
McLeod, Neil A., Jr. 1938- *St&PR 91*
Mc Leod, Norman William 1904- *WhoAm 90*
McLeod, Rima L. 1945- *WhoAmW 91*
McLeod, Robert Macfarlan 1925- *WhoAm 90*
Mc Leod, Roderick R 1918- *BiDrAPA 89*
McLeod, Wallace 1931- *ConAu 31NR*
McLeod, Walton James, Jr. 1906- *WhoWor 91*
McLeod, William Lasater, Jr. 1931- *WhoSSW 91*
McLeod, William Richard 1933- *WhoWor 91*
McLeod-Bryant, Stephen A. *BiDrAPA 89*
Mc Leran, James Herbert 1931- *WhoAm 90*
McLeroy, Barbre Stringfellow 1953- *WhoAmW 91*
McLeroy, Frederick Grayson 1951- *WhoSSW 91*
McLerran, Alice Enderton 1933- *WhoAmW 91*
McLester, Keith Price 1943- *St&PR 91*
McLester, Keith Robert 1937- *St&PR 91*
McLevy, Jasper *EncAL*
McLewee, Joseph Monroe 1933- *St&PR 91*
McLewin, Philip James 1939- *WhoE 91*
McLin, Clarence Josef 1921-1989 *BioIn 16*
McLin, Nathaniel, Jr. 1928- *WhoWor 91*
McLin, Stephen T. 1946- *WhoAm 90*
McLin, William Merriman 1945- *WhoAm 90*
Mc Linden, Stephen Kerry 1955- *WhoWrEP 89*
McLindon, Gerald Joseph 1923- *WhoAm 90*
McLinn, George 1884- *Ballpl 90*
McLinn, William L. *BioIn 16*
McLintock, Gordon *NewYTBS 90 [port]*
McLintock, Gordon 1903-1990 *BioIn 16, CurBio 90N*
McLish, Cal 1925- *Ballpl 90*
McLish, Rachel Elizondo 1958- *WhoHisp 91*
McLogan, Edward Austin 1920- *St&PR 91*
Mc Loone, James Brian 1950- *BiDrAPA 89*
McLoone, Jeanne Howe 1950- *WhoAmW 91*
McLorg, Terence Wyndham 1922- *WhoSSW 91*
McLoughlin, Donald Craig 1928- *St&PR 91*
McLoughlin, James G. 1938- *ODwPR 91*
McLoughlin, John 1784-1857 *BioIn 16*
McLoughlin, John C. *BioIn 16*
McLoughlin, Joseph M. 1925- *St&PR 91*
McLoughlin, Michael 1947- *St&PR 91*
McLoughlin, Philip Robert 1946- *St&PR 91, WhoAm 90*
McLoughlin, R. B. *MajTwCW*
McLoughlin, Richard F. 1929- *WhoAm 90*
McLoughlin, Susan Emily 1963- *WhoE 91*
Mc Lucas, John Luther 1920- *WhoAm 90*
McLuckey, John Alexander, Jr. 1940- *WhoAm 90*
McLuhan, Eric 1942- *ConAu 130*
McLuhan, Herbert Marshall 1911-1980 *WorAlBi*
McLuhan, Marshall 1911-1980 *BioIn 16, MajTwCW*
Mc Lure, Charles E., Jr. 1940- *WhoAm 90*
McLurkin, Thomas Cornelius, Jr. 1954- *WhoEmL 91, WhoWor 91*
McLuskie, William Grindlay 1931- *WhoWor 91*
McMachen, Kay Ann 1952- *WhoAmW 91*
McMackin, John J. 1925- *St&PR 91*
McMackin, John James 1925- *WhoSSW 91*
McMackin, Lillian Francis 1915- *WhoAmW 91*
McMahan, Calvin L. *St&PR 91*
McMahan, Charles Brown 1946- *St&PR 91*
McMahan, Elizabeth Anne 1924- *EncO&P 3, EncPaPR 91*
McMahan, Gary Lynn 1948- *WhoWor 91*
McMahan, Robert Chandler 1940- *St&PR 91*
McMahan, Robert Tillman 1936- *St&PR 91*
McMahan, Sue Evon 1962- *WhoAmW 91*
McMahand, Willie Bee 1932- *WhoSSW 91*
McMahen, Charles E. 1939- *St&PR 91*
McMahen, P. A. 1925- *St&PR 91*
McMahon, A Philip 1890- *WhoAmA 91N*
McMahon, Ann Marie 1950- *WhoAmW 91*
McMahon, Bernice Georgia 1917- *WhoAmW 91*
McMahon, Brian Thomas 1961- *St&PR 91*
McMahon, Brien 1903-1952 *WorAlBi*
McMahon, Carroll Francis 1923- *St&PR 91*
McMahon, Charles James 1930- *St&PR 91*
Mc Mahon, Charles Joseph, Jr. 1933- *WhoAm 90*
McMahon, Colleen 1951- *WhoEmL 91*
McMahon, David Freyvogel 1949- *BiDrAPA 89, WhoE 91*
McMahon, Don 1930-1987 *Ballpl 90*
McMahon, Donald Aylward 1931- *St&PR 91*
Mc Mahon, Donald Aylward 1931- *WhoAm 90*
McMahon, Ed *BioIn 16*
Mc Mahon, Ed *WhoAm 90*
McMahon, Ed 1923- *WorAlBi*
McMahon, Edward Joseph 1935- *St&PR 91*
McMahon, Edward Joseph 1937- *WhoSSW 91*
McMahon, Edward Peter 1940- *WhoE 91*
McMahon, Eileen Marie 1953- *WhoE 91*
McMahon, Eleanor Marie 1929- *WhoAm 90*
McMahon, Elizabeth R. 1960- *St&PR 91*
McMahon, Ernest E. *BioIn 16, NewYTBS 90*
McMahon, Francis Joseph 1960- *BiDrAPA 89*
McMahon, Frank Albert 1920- *WhoE 91*
McMahon, Gary Francis 1937- *WhoAm 90*
Mc Mahon, George J *BiDrAPA 89*
Mc Mahon, George Joseph 1923- *WhoAm 90*
McMahon, Gregory 1915-1989 *BioIn 16*
McMahon, Howard O. *NewYTBS 90 [port]*
McMahon, Howard Oldford 1914- *St&PR 91*
McMahon, Jack 1928-1989 *BioIn 16*
McMahon, James Charles, Jr. 1951- *WhoE 91*
McMahon, James Edward 1937- *WhoAmA 91*
McMahon, James Patrick 1939- *WhoE 91*
McMahon, Janice C. 1941- *St&PR 91*
McMahon, Jerome F. 1932- *St&PR 91*
McMahon, Jesse D. 1913- *St&PR 91*
McMahon, Jim 1959- *WhoAm 90*
McMahon, John Alexander 1921- *WhoAm 90*
McMahon, John Francis 1910- *WhoAm 90, WhoWor 91*
McMahon, John J., Jr. *WhoSSW 91*
McMahon, John Joseph 1960- *WhoWor 91*
McMahon, John Patrick 1919- *WhoAm 90*
McMahon, John Stevens, Jr. 1943- *WhoE 91*
McMahon, Joseph Einar 1940- *WhoAm 90*
McMahon, Kathleen A *BiDrAPA 89*
McMahon, Kendall Harold 1957- *WhoSSW 91*
McMahon, Kevin John 1956- *St&PR 91*
McMahon, Marghe May 1954- *WhoAmW 91*
McMahon, Maribeth Lovette 1949- *WhoAm 90*
McMahon, Martin James, Jr. 1949- *WhoEmL 91*
McMahon, Mary Frances 1955- *WhoAmW 91*
McMahon, Michael Christopher 1947- *St&PR 91*
McMahon, Michael James 1959- *WhoWor 91*
McMahon, Michael Joseph 1951- *WhoEmL 91*
McMahon, Neil Michael 1953- *WhoE 91*
McMahon, Pat *TwCCr&M 91*
McMahon, Patricia 1959- *WhoAmW 91*
McMahon, Patrick Henry *BioIn 16, NewYTBS 90*
McMahon, Paul Edward 1931- *WhoE 91*
McMahon, Paul Francis 1945- *WhoAm 90, WhoEmL 91*

McMahon, Raymond Dennis 1947- *St&PR 91*
McMahon, Robert Lee, Jr. 1944- *WhoSSW 91*
McMahon, Robert Tyler 1945- *St&PR 91*
McMahon, Ronald E. 1936- *St&PR 91*
McMahon, Russell E. 1946- *St&PR 91*
McMahon, Shirley Anne 1934- *BiDrAPA 89*
McMahon, Terry Calvin 1950- *BiDrAPA 89*
McMahon, Thomas Arthur 1943- *WhoAm 90*
Mc Mahon, Thomas Arthur 1943- *WhoWrEP 89*
McMahon, Thomas Michael 1941- *WhoAm 90*
McMahon, Victoria *BioIn 16*
McMahon, Vince, Jr. *BioIn 16*
McMahon, William 1908-1988 *AnObit 1988, BioIn 16*
Mc Mahon, William M *BiDrAPA 89*
McMain, Eleanor L. 1866-1934 *BioAmW*
McMains, Melvin L. 1941- *St&PR 91*
McMains, Melvin Lee 1941- *WhoAm 90*
Mc Mains, William D 1944- *BiDrAPA 89*
McMakin, Mimi Maddock 1947- *WhoEmL 91*
McManama, Trudy E. 1945- *WhoAmW 91*
McManaman, William Robert 1947- *St&PR 91, WhoAm 90*
Mc Manamy, Margaret C *BiDrAPA 89*
McManes, Alison Ann 1960- *WhoSSW 91*
McManigal, Robert M. 1901- *St&PR 91*
McManigal, Shirley Ann 1938- *WhoAmW 91*
McManis, Robert Bruce 1937- *WhoSSW 91*
McManis, Susan Elizabeth *BiDrAPA 89*
Mc Mann, Renville Hupfel, Jr. 1927- *WhoAm 90*
McMann, Robert William James 1961- *WhoE 91*
McManners, Hugh 1952- *ConAu 132*
McManus, Arthur Terrence 1937- *St&PR 91*
McManus, Arthur Terrence, Jr. 1937- *WhoE 91*
McManus, Brian Edward 1939- *WhoSSW 91*
Mc Manus, Charles Anthony, Jr. 1927- *WhoAm 90*
McManus, Charles Kent 1942- *St&PR 91*
McManus, Doyle *BioIn 16*
Mc Manus, Edward Joseph 1920- *WhoAm 90*
McManus, George 1884-1954 *EncACom*
McManus, Harold Lynn 1919- *WhoAm 90*
McManus, Hugh Leslie Nicholas 1958- *WhoEmL 91*
McManus, James *WhoE 91*
McManus, James 1882-1958 *WhoAmA 91N*
Mc Manus, James 1951- *WhoWrEP 89*
McManus, James F. 1930- *St&PR 91*
McManus, James P. 1937- *St&PR 91*
McManus, James William 1942- *WhoAmA 91*
McManus, Jason Donald 1934- *St&PR 91, WhoAm 90, WhoE 91*
McManus, Lewis Nichols 1929- *WhoAm 90*
McManus, Margaret Mary 1932- *WhoAmW 91*
McManus, Martin Joseph 1919- *WhoWor 91*
McManus, Marty 1900-1966 *Ballpl 90*
McManus, Mary Christine 1962- *WhoAmW 91*
McManus, Michael A., Jr. 1943- *WhoAm 90, WhoE 91*
Mc Manus, Michael Edwin *BiDrAPA 89*
McManus, Michael Francis 1928- *WhoAm 90*
McManus, Patrick F. *BioIn 16*
McManus, Patrick Francis 1947- *WhoE 91*
Mc Manus, Philip Daniel 1916- *WhoAm 90*
McManus, Philip E. 1941- *St&PR 91*
McManus, Richard P. 1929- *St&PR 91*
McManus, Richard Philip 1929- *WhoAm 90*
Mc Manus, Samuel Plyler 1938- *WhoAm 90*
Mc Manus, Terence B 1918- *BiDrAPA 89*
McManus, Timothy 1937- *St&PR 91*
McManus, Walter Leonard 1918- *WhoAm 90*
McManus, William Jay 1900- *WhoAm 90*
McManus, William Raymond, Jr. 1967- *WhoE 91*
Mc Martin, Paula J. 1955- *WhoWrEP 89*
McMaster, Beth 1935- *ConAu 30NR*
McMaster, Brian John 1943- *IntWWM 90, WhoAm 90*
McMaster, David Samuel 1938- *St&PR 91*
McMaster, Jessie Foy, Jr. 1926- *St&PR 91*
McMaster, Juliet Sylvia 1937- *WhoAmW 91, WhoWrEP 89*
McMaster, Majorie 1949- *BiDrAPA 89*
McMaster, Michael David 1943- *WhoAm 90*
McMaster, Philip R B *BiDrAPA 89*
McMaster, Robert Raymond 1948- *WhoAm 90*
McMaster, William D. 1938- *ODwPR 91*
McMasters, R. G. 1940- *WhoAm 90*
McMath, Elizabeth Moore 1930- *WhoAmW 91*
McMath, Jonathan C *BiDrAPA 89*
Mc Math, Phillip H. 1945- *WhoWrEP 89*
McMath, Robert, Jr. 1944- *WhoAm 90*
McMath, Robert C, Jr. 1944- *ConAu 129*
McMath, Sidney Sanders 1912- *BioIn 16*
McMath, Virginia Katherine *WhoAmW 91*
McMeekin, Clark *AuBYP 90, LiHiK*
McMeekin, Dorothy 1932- *WhoAm 90, WhoAmW 91*
McMeekin, Hayne Douglas *BiDrAPA 89*
McMeekin, Isabel 1895-1975 *LiHiK*
McMeekin, Isabel McLennan 1895- *AuBYP 90*
Mc Meel, John Paul 1936- *WhoAm 90*
McMeen, Albert Ralph, III 1942- *WhoE 91*
McMein, Neysa 1888-1949 *BioAmW*
McMein, Neysa 1890- *WhoAmA 91N*
McMenamin, John Robert 1946- *WhoEmL 91*
McMenamin, Joseph E. 1932- *St&PR 91*
McMenamin, Michael Terrence 1943- *WhoWor 91*
McMenamin, Peter David 1948- *WhoE 91*
McMennamin, George Barry 1922- *St&PR 91*
Mc Mennamin, George Barry 1922- *WhoAm 90*
McMennamin, Michael J. 1945- *WhoAm 90*
McMennamin, Michael John 1945- *St&PR 91*
Mc Michael, Alice Olivia *BiDrAPA 89*
McMichael, Allen Edgar 1923- *WhoSSW 91*
McMichael, Francis Clay 1937- *WhoAm 90*
McMichael, Jeane Casey 1938- *WhoWor 91*
McMichael, Jerry L. 1946- *St&PR 91*
McMichael, Kelly Lee 1964- *WhoAmW 91*
Mc Michael, Morton *BiDrAPA 89*
McMichael, Reb *BiDrAPA 89*
McMichen, Robert Sidney 1925- *WhoAm 90*
McMicken, Gilbert 1813-1891 *DcCanB 12*
McMilin, Edward Mulin 1947- *WhoEmL 91*
McMillan, Adell 1933- *WhoAmW 91*
McMillan, Alan Campbell 1942- *WhoAm 90*
McMillan, Alan D. 1945- *ConAu 130*
McMillan, Andrew Pickens, Jr. 1950- *WhoSSW 91*
Mcmillan, Berit Holen 1954- *BiDrAPA 89*
Mc Millan, Brockway 1915- *WhoAm 90*
McMillan, Bruce *BioIn 16*
McMillan, Bruce 1947- *AuBYP 90*
McMillan, C. Steven 1945- *WhoAm 90*
McMillan, Campbell White 1927- *WhoAm 90*
McMillan, Charles H., Jr. 1927- *St&PR 91*
McMillan, Charles William 1926- *WhoAm 90*
McMillan, Constance *WhoAmA 91*
McMillan, David 1927- *St&PR 91*
McMillan, Donald Edgar 1937- *WhoAm 90*
McMillan, Donald Ernest 1931- *WhoSSW 91*
McMillan, Edward L. 1935- *St&PR 91*
McMillan, Edward Neil 1947- *St&PR 91*
McMillan, Edwin M. 1907- *WorAlBi*
McMillan, Edwin Mattison 1907- *WhoAm 90, WhoWor 91*
McMillan, Ellis Earl 1929- *St&PR 91*
Mc Millan, Elma Joyce 1934- *WhoWrEP 89*
Mc Millan, George Duncan Hastie, Jr. 1943- *WhoAm 90*
McMillan, Howard Lamar, Jr. 1938- *WhoAm 90, WhoSSW 91*
McMillan, Ian 1956- *ConAu 132*
Mc Millan, James *WhoAm 90*
McMillan, James Albert 1926- *WhoWor 91*
McMillan, James Bryan 1916- *WhoAm 90, WhoSSW 91*
Mc Millan, James F *BiDrAPA 89*
McMillan, James Gordon 1931- *St&PR 91*
McMillan, James T. 1925- *St&PR 91*
McMillan, James Thomas 1925- *WhoAm 90*
McMillan, Janette *BiDrAPA 89*
McMillan, John A. 1931- *WhoAm 90*
McMillan, John Alexander, III 1932- *WhoAm 90, WhoSSW 91*
Mc Millan, John Clark 1920- *WhoAm 90*
Mc Millan, John Robertson 1909- *WhoAm 90*
Mc Millan, Karen Alice 1961- *WhoWrEP 89*
McMillan, Kenneth *BioIn 16*
McMillan, Lee Richards, II 1947- *WhoEmL 91, WhoSSW 91*
Mc Millan, Leona Pearl 1913- *WhoWrEP 89*
McMillan, M. Helena 1869-1970 *BioIn 16*
McMillan, Mae Frances *BiDrAPA 89*
McMillan, Manuel, Sr. 1957- *WhoSSW 91*
McMillan, Margaret 1860-1931 *BioIn 16*
McMillan, Martin Leslie 1955- *WhoWor 91*
McMillan, Mary 1895- *WhoAmA 91N*
McMillan, Michael Reid 1941- *WhoWor 91*
McMillan, Norm 1895-1969 *Ballpl 90*
Mc Millan, Patricia Ann 1946- *WhoWrEP 89*
McMillan, Peter Aidan 1959- *WhoWrEP 89*
McMillan, Robert A. *ODwPR 91*
McMillan, Robert Allan 1942- *St&PR 91, WhoAm 90*
Mc Millan, Robert Bruce 1937- *WhoAm 90*
McMillan, Robert Ralph 1932- *St&PR 91, WhoAm 90, WhoWor 91*
McMillan, Robert W 1915- *WhoAmA 91*
Mc Millan, Ronald *BiDrAPA 89*
McMillan, Roy 1930- *Ballpl 90 [port]*
Mc Millan, Sally Hill 1949- *WhoWrEP 89*
McMillan, Samuel Sterling, III 1938- *St&PR 91, WhoAm 90*
McMillan, Stephen Walker 1949- *WhoAmA 91*
McMillan, Terry 1951- *ConLC 61 [port]*
Mc Millan, Thomas M *BiDrAPA 89*
McMillen, Bruce Charles 1943- *St&PR 91*
McMillen, Harvey G. 1936- *St&PR 91*
McMillen, James E. 1941- *St&PR 91*
McMillen, John T. 1953- *St&PR 91*
McMillen, Larry *WhoAm 90, WhoSSW 91*
McMillen, Michael C 1946- *WhoAmA 91*
McMillen, Robert Doane 1916- *WhoSSW 91*
McMillen, Russell Gross 1918- *St&PR 91, WhoAm 90*
McMillen, Thomas 1952- *WhoAm 90, WhoE 91*
Mc Millen, Thomas Roberts 1916- *WhoAm 90*
McMillen, Wheeler 1893- *AuBYP 90*
Mc Millen, Wheeler 1893- *WhoAm 90*
Mc Millen, William Earl 1947- *WhoWrEP 89*
McMiller, Anita Williams 1946- *WhoAmW 91, WhoE 91, WhoEmL 91, WhoWor 91*
McMillian, James *WhoSSW 91*
McMillian, Theodore 1919- *WhoAm 90*
McMillin, Alan Edward 1953- *WhoSSW 91*
McMillin, Bo 1895-1952 *BioIn 16*
McMillin, Glenn R. 1930- *St&PR 91*
McMillin, Harvey Scott 1934- *WhoE 91*
McMillin, Jeanie Byrd 1939- *WhoAm 90*
McMillin, John Michael 1940- *WhoAm 90*
McMillin, John P. 1936- *St&PR 91*
McMillin, Lawrence Eugene 1948- *St&PR 91*
McMillin, Timothy David 1943- *St&PR 91*
Mc Million, John Macon 1929- *WhoAm 90*
McMillion, S. Argyle 1936- *St&PR 91*
McMillon, Doris 1951- *DrBlPA 90*
McMindes, Lee P. 1931- *St&PR 91*
McMindes, Roy J. 1923- *St&PR 91*
McMindes, Roy James 1923- *WhoAm 90*
McMinn, B. C. 1921- *WhoAm 90, WhoSSW 91*
McMinn, Douglas W. 1947- *WhoAm 90*
McMinn, James Stephen 1949- *WhoE 91*
McMinn, John Albert 1933- *St&PR 91*
Mc Minn, Monty Ruey *BiDrAPA 89*
McMinn, Richard Lynn 1957- *WhoSSW 91*
McMinn, William Gene 1931- *WhoAm 90*
McMonagle, E. J. 1922- *St&PR 91*
McMonagle, Keith Duane 1947- *WhoE 91*
McMoran, George A. 1934- *ODwPR 91*
McMoran, George Andrew 1934- *St&PR 91*
McMorran, Sydney R. 1939- *St&PR 91*
McMorrin, Maureen Petersen 1955- *WhoAmW 91*
McMorris, Grace Elizabeth 1922- *WhoAmW 91*
McMorrow, Barbara Jean 1947- *WhoAmW 91*
McMorrow, Julie 1960- *WhoAmW 91*
McMorrow, Margaret Mary 1924- *WhoAmW 91*
McMorrow, Ralph J. 1921- *St&PR 91*
McMorrow, Richard M. 1941- *St&PR 91*
Mc Morrow, Richard Mark 1941- *WhoAm 90*
McMorrow, William J. 1931- *St&PR 91*
Mc Moy, John H. 1953- *WhoWrEP 89*
McMulkin, Francis John 1915- *WhoAm 90*
McMullan, Andrew 1923- *St&PR 91*
McMullan, Cornelius P. *St&PR 91*
Mc Mullan, Dorothy 1911- *WhoAm 90*
McMullan, James 1934- *BioIn 16*
McMullan, James Burroughs 1934- *WhoAmA 91*
McMullan, James Franklin 1928- *WhoWor 91*
McMullan, Kate 1947- *BioIn 16*
McMullan, William Patrick, Jr. 1925- *WhoAm 90*
McMullen, Archie Robert 1938- *WhoSSW 91*
McMullen, Barbara Elizabeth 1942- *WhoAmW 91*
Mc Mullen, Betty A. 1936- *WhoWrEP 89*
McMullen, C. C. 1933- *St&PR 91*
McMullen, Charles Haynes 1915- *WhoAm 90*
McMullen, Cynthia Diane 1954- *WhoAmW 91, WhoEmL 91, WhoSSW 91, WhoWor 91*
McMullen, Dana Allyn 1941- *WhoAmW 91*
McMullen, David L. 1946- *ODwPR 91*
McMullen, E Ormond 1888- *WhoAmA 91N*
Mc Mullen, Edwin Wallace, Jr. 1915- *WhoAm 90, WhoWrEP 89*
McMullen, Francis Lee 1926- *WhoWor 91*
McMullen, George Andrew 1926- *St&PR 91*
McMullen, Jack O., Jr. 1953- *St&PR 91*
McMullen, Jeanine *BioIn 16*
McMullen, John 1849-1881 *Ballpl 90*
McMullen, John Henry, Jr. 1944- *WhoE 91*
McMullen, John J. *WhoAm 90, WhoE 91, WhoSSW 91*
McMullen, John J. 1918- *St&PR 91*
McMullen, John Joseph 1933- *St&PR 91*
McMullen, John Roderick 1947- *WhoWor 91*
McMullen, Ken 1942- *Ballpl 90*
Mc Mullen, Leon F. 1930- *WhoWrEP 89*
McMullen, Lowell W. 1960- *St&PR 91*
McMullen, Mary 1920-1986 *TwCCr&M 91*
McMullen, Melinda Kae 1957- *WhoAmW 91*
Mc Mullen, Robert Duncan 1946- *BiDrAPA 89*
Mc Mullen, Thomas Henry 1929- *WhoAm 90*
McMullen, Virginia Elise 1943- *St&PR 91*
McMullen, William 1824-1901 *BioIn 16*
McMullian, Amos Ryals 1937- *St&PR 91*
Mc Mullian, Amos Ryals 1937- *WhoAm 90, WhoSSW 91*
McMullin, Carleton Eugene 1932- *WhoAm 90*
McMullin, Diane M. 1947- *St&PR 91*
Mc Mullin, Ernan Vincent 1924- *WhoAm 90*
McMullin, Fred 1891-1952 *Ballpl 90*
McMullin, Henry H. 1831- *AmLegL*
McMullin, Jeffrey Scott 1947- *WhoEmL 91*
McMullin, Joyce Anne 1952- *WhoAmW 91*
McMullin, Ruth R. 1942- *St&PR 91*
McMullin, Ruth Roney 1942- *WhoAm 90, WhoAmW 91*
Mc Munn, Earl William 1910- *WhoAm 90*
McMunn, John Charles 1951- *WhoE 91*
McMurdo, Mary-Jane 1924- *WhoAmW 91*
McMurphy, Clifford Vaston, III 1949- *WhoSSW 91*
McMurphy, Michael Allen 1947- *WhoE 91*
McMurphy, Michael Henry 1954- *WhoSSW 91*
McMurray, Barbara Alisa 1953- *WhoAmW 91*
McMurray, John *BioIn 16*
Mc Murray, John Harvey 1950- *BiDrAPA 89*
McMurray, Jose Daniel 1949- *WhoHisp 91*
McMurray, Joseph Patrick Brendan 1912- *WhoAm 90*
McMurray, Kay 1918- *WhoAm 90*
McMurray, Lolla Jean 1939- *WhoAmW 91*
McMurray, William 1810-1894 *DcCanB 12*
McMurray, William 1929- *WhoAm 90*
Mc Murrer, James Peter 1941- *BiDrAPA 89*
Mc Murrin, Lee Ray 1930- *WhoAm 90*
Mc Murrin, Sterling Moss 1914- *WhoAm 90*

McMurrin, Trudy Ann 1944- *WhoAmW 91*
Mc Murry, Bryce Elliot 1916- *BiDrAPA 89*
Mc Murry, Idanelle Sam 1924- *WhoAm 90*
McMurry, Lillian *BioIn 16*
McMurry, Norman Edmund 1924- *WhoSSW 91*
McMurry, Richard M. 1939- *ConAu 132*
McMurry, Robert I. 1947- *WhoEmL 91*
McMurry, Timothy D. 1948- *WhoSSW 91*
McMurtrie, Edith 1883- *WhoAmA 91N*
McMurtry, Arthur William 1910- *WhoE 91*
McMurtry, Burton John 1935- *WhoAm 90*
McMurtry, Craig 1959- *Ballpl 90*
McMurtry, Gary Michael 1950- *WhoEmL 91*
McMurtry, George James 1932- *WhoAm 90*
McMurtry, James 1962- *News 90 [port]*
Mc Murtry, James Gilmer, III 1932- *WhoAm 90*
McMurtry, Larry *BioIn 16*
McMurtry, Larry 1936- *MajTwCW, WhoAm 90, WorAlBi*
McMurtry, R. Gerald 1906-1988 *BioIn 16*
McMurtry, R. Roy 1932- *WhoAm 90*
McMurtry, Robert Gerald 1906-1988 *BioIn 16*
McNab, Alexander 1952- *WhoAm 90*
Mc Nab, Brian Robert *BiDrAPA 89*
McNab, Clarissa O. *St&PR 91*
McNab, Gregory R. *BioIn 16*
McNab, Oliver *ConAu 32NR*
McNabb, Darcy LaFountain 1955- *WhoAmW 91*
McNabb, Edward Joseph 1930- *St&PR 91*
McNabb, Frances Perle Cody 1913- *WhoSSW 91*
McNabb, Frank W. 1936- *St&PR 91*
McNabb, Frederick William, Jr. 1932- *St&PR 91, WhoAm 90*
McNabb, James Francis 1931- *St&PR 91*
McNabb, Joanne B. *ODwPR 91*
Mc Nabb, Winfred Lee *BiDrAPA 89*
McNabb-Beardsley, Sue Ellen 1948- *WhoAmW 91*
McNaboe, James Francis 1945- *WhoE 91*
McNagny, William F. 1922- *St&PR 91*
McNair, Barbara 1938- *DrBIPA 90*
McNair, Carl Herbert, Jr. 1933- *WhoAm 90, WhoE 91*
McNair, Clement John 1915-1989 *ConAu 129*
McNair, Eric 1909-1949 *Ballpl 90*
Mc Nair, Francis E 1918- *BiDrAPA 89*
McNair, Frank Cornelious 1946- *WhoE 91*
McNair, Fred Louis 1945- *St&PR 91*
McNair, George N. 1931- *St&PR 91*
McNair, Harry E. 1924- *St&PR 91*
McNair, Hurley 1888-1948 *Ballpl 90*
McNair, John Caldwell 1923- *WhoE 91*
McNair, John Franklin, III 1927- *St&PR 91, WhoAm 90, WhoSSW 91*
McNair, Kate *AuBYP 90*
McNair, Loomis Lindberg 1929- *St&PR 91*
McNair, Marie 1900?-1989 *ConAu 130*
McNair, Nimrod, Jr. 1923- *WhoSSW 91*
McNair, Pamela Hansen 1963- *WhoAmW 91*
Mc Nair, Rogers Mac Gowan *WhoWrEP 89*
McNair, Ronald E. *BioIn 16*
McNair, Russell Arthur, Jr. 1934- *WhoAm 90*
McNair, Sybil Alicia *ODwPR 91*
Mc Nair, Sylvia *WhoAm 90*
McNairy, Charles Banks, III 1928- *St&PR 91*
McNairy, Richard W. 1940- *St&PR 91*
Mcnairy, Scott L *BiDrAPA 89*
McNall, Bruce *WhoAm 90*
McNall, Bruce P. *BioIn 16*
McNall, Scott Grant 1941- *WhoAm 90*
Mc Nallen, James Berl 1930- *WhoAm 90*
McNalley, Janet Marilyn 1960- *WhoAmW 91*
McNally, Andrew, III 1909- *St&PR 91, WhoAm 90*
McNally, Andrew, IV 1939- *St&PR 91, WhoAm 90*
McNally, Andrew, Jr. *AuBYP 90*
McNally, Brian *BioIn 16*
McNally, Dave 1942- *Ballpl 90 [port]*
McNally, E. Evalyn Grumbine *AuBYP 90*
McNally, E. T. 1914- *St&PR 91*
McNally, Edward C. 1942- *St&PR 91*
McNally, Eugene M. 1940- *St&PR 91*
McNally, Frank J. 1943- *ODwPR 91*
McNally, Frank Thomas 1936- *WhoE 91*
McNally, George J. *WhoSSW 91*
McNally, Gloria White 1926- *WhoE 91*
McNally, James F. 1932- *St&PR 91, WhoAm 90*
McNally, James Randy 1944- *WhoSSW 91*
McNally, Jane Dorothy 1947- *WhoE 91*
McNally, John Joseph 1927- *WhoAm 90*
McNally, Lloyd C. 1920- *St&PR 91*
McNally, Mike 1893-1965 *Ballpl 90*
McNally, Patricia Mary 1954- *WhoE 91*
McNally, Regina Marie 1965- *WhoAmW 91*
McNally, Richard Donald 1929- *WhoSSW 91*
McNally, Sheila John 1932- *WhoAmA 91*
McNally, Susan Fowler 1957- *WhoEmL 91*
McNally, Terrence 1939- *BioIn 16, WhoAm 90*
McNally, Thomas Charles, III 1938- *WhoAm 90*
McNally, Thomas W. 1948- *St&PR 91*
McNally, Thomas William 1948- *WhoSSW 91*
McNally, Timothy F. 1952- *St&PR 91*
Mc Namar, Richard Timothy 1939- *WhoAm 90*
McNamara, Ann Dowd 1924- *WhoAmW 91*
McNamara, David G. 1937- *St&PR 91*
McNamara, Denise Ann *BiDrAPA 89*
McNamara, Diane Louise 1949- *St&PR 91*
McNamara, Ed 1921-1986 *OxCCanT*
McNamara, Elsa Mae Broesamle 1958- *WhoAmW 91*
McNamara, Francis John 1915- *WhoE 91*
Mc Namara, Francis Joseph, Jr. 1927- *WhoAm 90, WhoE 91*
McNamara, Francis T. 1927- *WhoWor 91*
McNamara, James B. *EncAL*
McNamara, Jo Anne 1932- *WhoAmW 91*
McNamara, John *WhoAm 90*
McNamara, John 1932- *Ballpl 90, WhoAm 90*
McNamara, John 1950- *WhoAmA 91*
Mc Namara, John Donald 1924- *WhoAm 90, WhoE 91, WhoWor 91*
McNamara, John F. 1935- *WhoAm 90, WhoE 91*
McNamara, John J. *EncAL*
McNamara, John J. *BioIn 16*
McNamara, John J. *BioIn 16*
McNamara, John J. 1934- *St&PR 91*
Mc Namara, John Joseph 1934- *WhoAm 90*
McNamara, John Michael 1946- *St&PR 91, WhoAm 90*
Mc Namara, John P *BiDrAPA 89*
Mc Namara, Joseph Donald 1934- *WhoAm 90*
McNamara, Joseph P. 1906- *St&PR 91*
Mc Namara, Joseph Patrick 1906- *WhoWor 91*
McNamara, Joseph T. 1938- *St&PR 91*
McNamara, Julia Mary 1941- *WhoAmW 91*
McNamara, Julie Smith 1939- *St&PR 91*
McNamara, Kathleen Michele 1957- *WhoAmW 91*
McNamara, Kevin *BioIn 16*
McNamara, Kevin J. 1953- *St&PR 91*
McNamara, Louise *AuBYP 90*
McNamara, Martin Burr 1947- *St&PR 91, WhoAm 90, WhoEmL 91*
McNamara, Martin D. 1949- *St&PR 91*
McNamara, Mary Eileen *BiDrAPA 89, WhoE 91*
Mc Namara, Mary Ellen 1942- *WhoAmW 91*
McNamara, Mary Ellen 1943- *WhoAmW 91*
McNamara, Mary Jo 1950- *WhoAmA 91*
McNamara, Michael *BioIn 16*
McNamara, Michael John 1948- *WhoWor 91*
McNamara, Michael John 1954- *WhoEmL 91*
McNamara, Michael William 1945- *St&PR 91*
Mc Namara, Norbert J *BiDrAPA 89*
McNamara, Patricia Rae 1936- *WhoSSW 91*
McNamara, Patrick Lewis 1959- *WhoE 91, WhoEmL 91, WhoWor 91*
McNamara, Paul 1921- *WhoAm 90, WhoE 91*
McNamara, Paul Gerard 1927- *St&PR 91*
McNamara, Richard Bedle 1950- *WhoEmL 91*
McNamara, Rieman, Jr. 1928- *St&PR 91*
Mc Namara, Rieman, Jr. 1928- *WhoAm 90*
McNamara, Robert B. *WhoAm 90*
McNamara, Robert James 1950- *WhoWrEP 89*
McNamara, Robert S 1916- *ConAu 129, EncABHB 7 [port], WorAlBi*
McNamara, Robert Strange 1916- *BiDrUSE 89, EncABHB 5 [port]*
Mc Namara, Robert Strange 1916- *WhoAm 90, WhoWor 91, WhoWrEP 89*
McNamara, Susan Louise 1952- *WhoAmW 91*
McNamara, Thomas Edmund 1940- *WhoAm 90, WhoWor 91*
McNamara, Thomas Neal 1930- *WhoAm 90*
McNamara, Tim 1898- *Ballpl 90*
McNamara, Timothy James 1952- *WhoE 91*
McNamara, Tom 1886-1964 *EncACom*
McNamara, Tom 1944- *WhoWor 91*
McNamara, William *BioIn 16*
McNamara, William A. 1909- *St&PR 91*
McNamara, William Albinus 1909- *WhoAm 90, WhoWor 91*
McNamara, William Patrick, Jr 1946- *WhoAmA 91*
McNamee, Catherine 1931- *WhoAm 90*
Mc Namee, Dardis 1948- *WhoWrEP 89*
McNamee, Evelyn Haynes 1947- *WhoAmW 91*
McNamee, Frances Cox 1935- *WhoAmW 91*
McNamee, Graham *Ballpl 90*
McNamee, Graham 1888-1942 *BioIn 16*
McNamee, James 1904- *AuBYP 90*
McNamee, James M. 1945- *St&PR 91*
McNamee, James P. *BioIn 16*
McNamee, John Stephen 1946- *St&PR 91*
McNamee, Louise *WhoAm 90, WhoAmW 91*
McNamee, Louise R. *BioIn 16*
Mc Namee, Maurice Basil 1909- *WhoAm 90*
McNamee, Robert 1862- *AmLegL*
McNaney, Heidi Marie 1956- *WhoAmW 91*
McNaney, Robert T. 1934- *St&PR 91*
McNaney, Robert Trainor 1934- *WhoAm 90*
McNarny, Patrick E. 1936- *St&PR 91*
McNary, Oscar L 1944- *WhoAmA 91*
McNatt, Markeeta L. *ODwPR 91*
McNaught, Judith 1944- *WhoAmW 91*
McNaughton, Gary Michael 1948- *St&PR 91*
McNaughton, John H. *WhoAm 90*
McNaughton, John William 1950- *St&PR 91*
McNaughton, Robert Forbes, Jr. 1924- *WhoAm 90*
McNaughton, Robert L. 1935- *St&PR 91*
McNaughton, Samuel Joseph 1939- *WhoAm 90*
McNaull, Thomas E. 1950- *St&PR 91*
McNay, Donald Joseph 1959- *WhoSSW 91*
McNay, Mark L. 1955- *WhoEmL 91*
McNeal, Ann P. Woodhull 1942- *WhoAmW 91*
McNeal, Aquilla Osborne 1948- *WhoAmW 91*
McNeal, Dale William, Jr. 1939- *WhoAm 90*
McNeal, H. P. 1919- *St&PR 91*
Mc Neal, Harley John *WhoAm 90*
McNeal, Jacqueline Frost 1930- *WhoE 91*
McNeal, Jeffery Dean 1961- *WhoE 91*
Mc Neal, Martha von Oesen 1952- *WhoSSW 91*
Mc Neal, Ralph Richard 1925- *WhoWor 91*
McNeal, Robert Hatch 1930-1988 *BioIn 16*
McNeal, Shay 1946- *WhoAmW 91, WhoSSW 91*
McNealy, Robert *WhoAmA 91*
McNealy, Scott *BioIn 16*
Mc Nealy, Scott *WhoAm 90*
McNear, Barbara B. 1939- *ODwPR 91*
McNear, Barbara Baxter 1939- *WhoAm 90, WhoAmW 91, WhoE 91*
McNear, Denman K. 1925- *St&PR 91*
Mc Near, Denman Kittredge 1925- *WhoAm 90*
McNear, Everett C 1904-1984 *WhoAmA 91N*
McNear, Miller Bradley 1930- *St&PR 91*
McNeary, Joseph Allen 1948- *WhoAm 90*
McNee, John William 1887-1984 *DcNaB 1981*
Mc Nee, Robert Bruce 1922- *WhoAm 90*
Mc Nee, Zeida *WhoWrEP 89*
Mc Neel, Burdett H 1909- *BiDrAPA 89*
McNeel, Synott Lance 1923- *St&PR 91*
Mc Neel, Synott Lance 1923- *WhoAm 90*
Mc Neel, Tynus William 1934- *BiDrAPA 89*
McNeel, Van Louis 1925- *St&PR 91*
McNeeley, Donald Robert 1954- *WhoAm 90*
McNeely, Alma Gretchen 1941- *WhoAmW 91*
McNeely, Beverly Ann 1955- *WhoAmW 91*
McNeely, D. Dean 1944- *WhoAm 90*
McNeely, Donald Gregory 1914- *St&PR 91*
McNeely, E. L. 1918- *St&PR 91*
Mc Neely, E. L. 1918- *WhoAm 90*
McNeely, Earl 1898-1971 *Ballpl 90*
McNeely, Eugene J. 1900-1973 *WorAlBi*
McNeely, Harry Gregory, Jr. 1923- *St&PR 91*
McNeely, Herbert Thomas 1955- *WhoSSW 91*
Mc Neely, J David 1939- *BiDrAPA 89*
McNeely, Marilyn DeLong 1940- *WhoSSW 91*
McNeely, Sharon Lynn 1955- *WhoAmW 91*
McNeer, C. S. 1926- *St&PR 91*
McNeer, John Daniel 1934- *St&PR 91*
McNeer, May Yonge 1902- *AuBYP 90*
Mc Neer, Michael D *BiDrAPA 89*
Mc Nees, Patricia Ann 1940- *WhoWrEP 89*
McNees, Stephen Kent 1942- *St&PR 91*
Mc Neese, Aylmer Green, Jr. 1911- *WhoAm 90*
Mc Neese, Wilma Wallace 1946- *WhoWor 91*
McNeff, John Charles 1926- *St&PR 91*
McNeice, John A., Jr. 1932- *St&PR 91*
Mc Neice, John Ambrose, Jr. 1932- *WhoAm 90*
McNeil, Ann Rhoads 1944- *WhoE 91*
McNeil, Barbara Joyce 1941- *WhoAm 90*
McNeil, Bruce W. 1916- *St&PR 91*
McNeil, Chris E., Jr. 1948- *WhoAm 90*
McNeil, Claudia 1917- *DrBIPA 90*
McNeil, David Lang 1950- *BiDrAPA 89*
McNeil, Dean S 1957- *WhoAmA 91*
McNeil, Deanna Simmons *BiDrAPA 89*
Mc Neil, Donald Lewis 1926- *WhoAm 90*
McNeil, Edward Warren 1942- *WhoE 91*
McNeil, Evelyn Virginia Sims 1913- *WhoSSW 91*
McNeil, Florence 1937- *BioIn 16*
McNeil, Frederick Harold 1916- *St&PR 91*
McNeil, George J 1908- *WhoAmA 91*
McNeil, George Joseph 1908- *WhoAm 90, WhoE 91*
McNeil, George Neal 1945- *BiDrAPA 89*
McNeil, Heidi Loretta 1959- *WhoAmW 91*
McNeil, Howard Marvin 1927- *WhoSSW 91*
McNeil, Hoyle Graham, Jr. 1950- *WhoSSW 91*
McNeil, John 1939- *ConAu 131*
McNeil, John D. 1934- *St&PR 91*
McNeil, John R., III 1937- *St&PR 91*
McNeil, Joseph M. 1937- *St&PR 91*
McNeil, Joseph Malcolm 1937- *WhoAm 90*
McNeil, Lawrence Patrick 1933- *St&PR 91*
McNeil, Lori *BioIn 16*
McNeil, Manford Russell 1927- *St&PR 91*
McNeil, Maurice Dale 1929- *St&PR 91*
McNeil, Millard Rock 1927- *WhoSSW 91*
McNeil, Mona Margaret 1947- *WhoAmW 91*
McNeil, Murray Charles 1929- *WhoAm 90*
McNeil, Robert D. 1950- *St&PR 91*
McNeil, Robert Stephen 1944- *St&PR 91*
McNeil, Stephen L *BiDrAPA 89*
McNeil, Steven Arthur 1942- *WhoAm 90*
McNeil, Sue 1955- *WhoAmW 91*
McNeil, William Kinneth 1940- *IntWWM 90*
McNeile, H. C. *TwCCr&M 91*
McNeile, Herman Cyril 1888-1937 *SpyFic, WorAlBi*
McNeill, Alfred Thomas, Jr. 1936- *WhoAm 90, WhoE 91*
McNeill, Blair E. 1944- *St&PR 91*
McNeill, Brandy Rachele 1956- *WhoSSW 91*
Mc Neill, Carmen Mary *WhoWor 91*
Mc Neill, Charles James 1912- *WhoAm 90*
McNeill, Corbin Asahel, Jr. 1939- *St&PR 91, WhoAm 90*
Mc Neill, David 1931- *WhoAm 90*
McNeill, Frederick Wallace 1932- *WhoSSW 91, WhoWor 91*
McNeill, Harry J. *WhoE 91*
McNeill, Ian 1947- *St&PR 91*
McNeill, James W. 1941- *St&PR 91*
McNeill, Janet 1907- *AuBYP 90, FemiCLE*
McNeill, Joan Reagin 1936- *WhoAmW 91*
McNeill, John Henderson 1941- *WhoAm 90*
McNeill, John Hugh 1938- *WhoAm 90*
McNeill, John Ridgway 1947- *St&PR 91*
McNeill, Kenneth Gordon 1926- *WhoAm 90*
McNeill, Larry Richard 1941- *St&PR 91*
McNeill, Louise 1911- *BioIn 16*
McNeill, Paul Spurgeon, Jr. 1948- *WhoEmL 91*
McNeill, Pauline 1960- *WhoSSW 91*
McNeill, Richard William 1945- *St&PR 91*
Mc Neill, Robert Eugene 1921- *WhoAm 90*
McNeill, Robert L. 1924- *WhoAm 90*
McNeill, Robert Patrick 1941- *WhoAm 90*
McNeill, Russell B., Jr. 1941- *St&PR 91*

McNeill, Thomas B. 1934- *WhoAm 90*
McNeill, William Allan 1942- *St&PR 91*
Mc Neill, William Hardy 1917- *WhoAm 90, WhoWor 91, WhoWrEP 89*
McNeilly, Jean Craig 1937- *WhoAm 90, WhoAmW 91*
McNeily, Curtlan Roger 1951- *WhoEmL 91*
McNeily, Mary Zora 1952- *WhoAmW 91*
McNeish, Donald M. 1933- *St&PR 91*
McNeish, Stanlee 1939- *St&PR 91*
Mc Nelis, Desmond P 1922- *BiDrAPA 89*
McNelis, Peter James 1940- *WhoE 91*
McNelley, Donald O. 1944- *St&PR 91*
McNellis, Maggi 1917-1989 *BioIn 16*
McNelly, John Taylor 1923- *WhoAm 90*
Mc Nelly, Theodore Hart 1919- *WhoE 91*
McNemar, Donald William 1943- *WhoAm 90*
McNemar, Quinn *BioIn 16*
Mc Nerney, Joan 1945- *WhoWrEP 89*
McNerney, Patrick E. 1951- *St&PR 91*
McNerney, Walter J. 1925- *St&PR 91*
McNertney, Jerry 1936- *Ballpl 90*
McNett, William Brown 1896-1968 *WhoAmA 91N*
McNeur, John Clarke 1950- *WhoE 91*
Mc New, Bennie Banks 1931- *WhoAm 90*
McNew, Lee Margaret Hayes 1945- *WhoEmL 91*
McNichol, Kristy *BioIn 16*
Mc Nichol, Kristy 1962- *WhoAm 90*
Mc Nichol, Ronald W 1919- *BiDrAPA 89*
McNicholas, David P. 1941- *St&PR 91*
McNicholas, David Paul 1941- *WhoAm 90*
McNicholas, John T. 1877-1950 *WorAlBi*
McNichols, Eugene H. 1947- *St&PR 91*
McNichols, John P., Jr. 1936- *St&PR 91*
McNichols, Robert J. 1922- *WhoAm 90*
Mc Nichols, William Arthur 1951- *WhoWrEP 89*
McNickle, Thomas Glen 1944- *WhoAmA 91*
McNicol, David Leon 1944- *WhoAm 90*
McNicol, Donald E. 1921- *St&PR 91*
Mc Nicol, Donald Edward 1921- *WhoAm 90*
McNicol, George Paul 1929- *WhoWor 91*
McNicol, Gilbert H. 1948- *WhoE 91*
McNicol, Paul Briggs 1918- *St&PR 91*
McNicol, Stanley Page 1947- *BiDrAPA 89*
McNicoll, Anthony Walter 1943-1985 *BioIn 16*
McNicoll, Carol *BioIn 16*
Mc Niece, Dawn Marie *BiDrAPA 89*
McNiel, Bruce Allen 1948- *St&PR 91*
McNiel, James Samuel, Jr. 1921- *St&PR 91*
Mc Niel, Jesse Neal 1935- *BiDrAPA 89*
McNiel, Marianne Marie 1957- *WhoE 91*
McNiel, Norbert Arthur 1914- *WhoSSW 91*
McNiel, Susan Marie 1952- *WhoEmL 91*
McNiesh, Lawrence Melvin 1949- *WhoE 91*
McNiff, Martha Ann *WhoE 91*
McNiff, Philip A. 1926- *St&PR 91*
Mc Niff, Thomas Alfred, Jr. 1940- *WhoWrEP 89*
McNish, James L. 1946- *St&PR 91, WhoWor 91*
McNish, T. A. *St&PR 91*
McNitt, Joseph Edward 1929- *WhoAm 90*
Mc Nitt, Willard Charles 1920- *WhoAm 90*
McNitt, Willard Charles, III 1948- *WhoAm 90*
Mc Niven, Hugh Donald 1922- *WhoAm 90*
McNown, John Stephenson 1916- *WhoWor 91*
McNulty, Brenda Kwee Poey-Ling 1949- *WhoWor 91*
McNulty, C. Howard 1935- *St&PR 91*
McNulty, Chester Howard 1935- *WhoAm 90*
McNulty, Daniel F. 1936- *St&PR 91*
McNulty, David P. 1935- *St&PR 91*
McNulty, Earl Walker 1936- *St&PR 91*
McNulty, Geraldine Myers 1939- *St&PR 91*
McNulty, Henry *BioIn 16*
McNulty, Henry Bryant 1947- *WhoAm 90, WhoE 91*
Mc Nulty, John Bard 1916- *WhoWrEP 89*
McNulty, John Kent 1934- *WhoAm 90*
McNulty, John W. 1927- *ODwPR 91*
McNulty, John William 1927- *WhoAm 90*
McNulty, Karol *ODwPR 91*
McNulty, Karoljean 1961- *WhoE 91*
McNulty, Kathleen Anne 1958- *WhoE 91*
Mc Nulty, Kneeland 1921- *WhoAm 90*
McNulty, Kneeland 1921- *WhoAmA 91*
McNulty, Kristy Lee Ann 1958- *WhoAmW 91*
McNulty, Mary Joy 1938- *WhoAmW 91*
McNulty, Matthew Francis, Jr. 1914- *WhoAm 90, WhoSSW 91, WhoWor 91*
McNulty, Michael R. *BioIn 16*
McNulty, Michael Robert 1947- *WhoAm 90, WhoE 91*
McNulty, Nancy Gillespie 1919- *WhoAmW 91, WhoE 91*
McNulty, Pat 1889-1963 *Ballpl 90*
McNulty, Raymond F. *ODwPR 91*
McNulty, Raymond F. 1946- *St&PR 91*
McNulty, Robert Holmes 1940- *WhoAm 90*
McNulty, Terence Patrick 1938- *WhoAm 90*
McNulty, Thomas A. 1933- *St&PR 91*
McNulty, William Charles 1884-1963 *WhoAmA 91N*
McNurlan, Donald Glen 1949- *WhoE 91*
McNutt, Charlie Fuller, Jr. 1931- *WhoAm 90, WhoE 91*
McNutt, Darrell L. 1945- *St&PR 91*
McNutt, Diane 1948- *ODwPR 91*
Mc Nutt, Edith 1942- *BiDrAPA 89*
McNutt, Gloria C. 1936- *ODwPR 91*
McNutt, Jack W. 1934- *St&PR 91*
McNutt, Jack Wray 1934- *WhoAm 90, WhoSSW 91*
McNutt, John Glenn 1951- *WhoSSW 91*
McNutt, Kathryn Outland 1962- *WhoSSW 91*
McNutt, Kristen Wallwork 1941- *WhoAm 90*
McNutt, Lee William, Jr. 1925- *St&PR 91*
McNutt, Merle Vernon 1928- *St&PR 91*
McNutt, Richard Hunt 1943- *WhoWor 91*
McNutt, Sandra Kay 1949- *WhoEmL 91*
McNutt, Suzzanne Marie 1962- *WhoAmW 91*
McNutt, Theodore Leon 1929- *BiDrAPA 89*
McNutt, Valeria Yvonne 1956- *WhoSSW 91*
McNutt, William James 1927- *WhoAm 90*
McOmber, Warren K. 1935- *St&PR 91*
M'Connel *EncPaPR 91*
McOwen, C Lynn 1953- *WhoAmA 91*
McOwen, Carol M 1927- *WhoAmA 91*
McOwen, Carol Marie 1927- *WhoAmW 91*
McPartland, Jimmy 1907- *BioIn 16, OxCPMus, WorAlBi*
McPartland, Marian *BioIn 16*
McPartland, Marian 1920- *OxCPMus, WorAlBi*
McPartland, Thomas Joseph 1945- *WhoSSW 91*
Mc Partlin, John 1918- *WhoWrEP 89*
McPeak, Allan 1938- *WhoSSW 91*
McPeak, Merrill Anthony 1936- *WhoAm 90*
McPeake, James Mason 1933- *WhoSSW 91*
Mc Peters, Sharon Janese 1951- *WhoWrEP 89*
Mc Phail, Andrew Tennent 1937- *WhoAm 90*
McPhail, David 1940- *AuBYP 90*
McPhail, David M. *BioIn 16*
McPhail, Doreen *ODwPR 91*
McPhail, Neil 1928- *St&PR 91*
McPharlin, Paul 1903-1948 *WhoAmA 91N*
McPhatter, Clyde 1931-1972 *DrBlPA 90*
McPhatter, Clyde 1932-1972 *EncPR&S 89*
McPhatter, Clyde 1933-1972 *OxCPMus*
McPhedran, Marie 1904- *AuBYP 90*
McPhedran, Norman Tait 1924- *WhoAm 90*
McPhee, Alexander Hector 1911- *WhoE 91, WhoWor 91*
McPhee, Bid 1859-1943 *Ballpl 90*
McPhee, Bruce Gordon 1934- *St&PR 91, WhoAm 90*
McPhee, Douglas Michael 1944- *St&PR 91*
McPhee, George McBeth 1937- *IntWWM 90*
Mc Phee, Henry Roemer 1925- *WhoAm 90*
McPhee, John 1931- *MajTwCW*
McPhee, John A. *BioIn 16*
Mc Phee, John Angus 1931- *WhoAm 90*
McPhee, John C. 1921- *St&PR 91*
McPhee, John Rae 1957- *WhoEmL 91*
McPhee, John Roy 1930- *WhoWor 91*
McPhee, Patricia Ann 1945- *St&PR 91*
McPhee, Ronald P. *St&PR 91*
McPhee, Ronald Paul 1933- *WhoAm 90*
McPheeters, Annie L. *BioIn 16*
Mc Pheeters, Edwin Keith 1924- *WhoAm 90*
Mc Pheeters, Harold L 1923- *BiDrAPA 89*
McPherron, Thomas Ralph 1936- *St&PR 91*
Mc Pherson, A. J. *WhoWrEP 89*
McPherson, Aimee Semple 1890-1944 *BioIn 16, WorAlBi*
Mc Pherson, Alice Ruth 1926- *WhoAm 90*
McPherson, Andrew P. 1943- *St&PR 91*
McPherson, Bruce Rice 1951- *WhoAmA 91*
Mc Pherson, Bruce Rice 1951- *WhoWrEP 89*
McPherson, Daniel Lee 1941- *WhoSSW 91*
Mc Pherson, David Ernest *BiDrAPA 89*
McPherson, Donald J. *WhoAm 90*
McPherson, Donald Paxton, III 1941- *WhoAm 90*
McPherson, Edward R. 1945- *ODwPR 91*
McPherson, Edward Russell 1945- *St&PR 91*
McPherson, Eugene Virgil 1927- *WhoWor 91*
McPherson, Ewing W. 1922- *St&PR 91*
McPherson, Frank A. 1933- *St&PR 91*
Mc Pherson, Frank Alfred 1933- *WhoAm 90, WhoSSW 91, WhoWor 91*
McPherson, Gail *WhoAmW 91, WhoSSW 91, WhoWor 91*
McPherson, George Ray 1949- *WhoSSW 91*
Mc Pherson, Harry Cummings, Jr. 1929- *WhoAm 90*
McPherson, Heather 1942- *FemiCLE*
Mc Pherson, Irene Wilson 1919- *WhoWrEP 89*
McPherson, James Alan 1943- *MajTwCW, WhoAm 90*
Mc Pherson, James Allen 1943- *WhoWrEP 89*
McPherson, James M 1936- *ConAu 31NR, MajTwCW*
Mc Pherson, James Munro 1936- *WhoAm 90*
McPherson, Jessamyn West *BioIn 16*
Mc Pherson, John Barkley 1917- *WhoAm 90*
McPherson, Larry E 1943- *WhoAmA 91*
McPherson, Larry Eugene 1943- *WhoAm 90*
McPherson, Mary Patterson 1935- *WhoAm 90, WhoAmW 91, WhoE 91*
McPherson, Melville Peter 1940- *WhoAm 90*
Mc Pherson, Michael C. 1949- *WhoWrEP 89*
Mc Pherson, Michael MacKenzie 1947- *WhoWrEP 89*
McPherson, Michael S. 1947- *WhoE 91*
McPherson, Michelle Marie 1959- *WhoAmW 91*
McPherson, Natalie Jean 1944- *WhoE 91*
McPherson, Pamela Kay 1960- *BiDrAPA 89*
McPherson, Paul Eugene 1953- *WhoSSW 91*
McPherson, Paul F. 1931- *BioIn 16*
Mc Pherson, Paul Francis 1931- *WhoAm 90*
McPherson, Rex Vanburt, II 1952- *WhoSSW 91*
Mc Pherson, Robert Donald 1936- *WhoAm 90*
McPherson, Robert L. 1944- *St&PR 91*
Mc Pherson, Rolf Kennedy *WhoAm 90*
Mc Pherson, Sandra Jean 1943- *WhoWrEP 89*
McPherson, Stephen Mather 1937- *St&PR 91*
McPhilliamy, Fred W. 1931- *St&PR 91*
McPhillips, George Franklin 1925- *St&PR 91*
McPhillips, Hugh *NewYTBS 90*
McPhillips, Joseph William 1951- *WhoEmL 91*
Mc Phillips, Susan Jane *BiDrAPA 89*
McPike, Frank H. 1929- *St&PR 91*
McPike, Frank R., Jr. 1949- *St&PR 91*
Mc Quade, Henry Ford 1915- *WhoAm 90*
McQuade, James Bigelow 1957- *BiDrAPA 89*
McQuade, Joseph J. 1952- *St&PR 91*
McQuade, Lawrence Carroll 1927- *St&PR 91*
Mc Quade, Lawrence Carroll 1927- *WhoAm 90*
McQuade, Mary Virginia *BiDrAPA 89*
Mc Quade, Walter 1922- *WhoAm 90, WhoWrEP 89*
McQuaid, Brian P. 1954- *St&PR 91*
McQuaid, Frank J. 1929- *St&PR 91*
Mc Quaid, Frank John 1929- *WhoAm 90*
McQuaid, J. G. 1918- *St&PR 91*
McQuaid, J. W. 1949- *St&PR 91*
McQuaid, John Stephen 1909- *IntWWM 90*
McQuaid, Joseph Woodbury 1949- *WhoAm 90, WhoE 91*
McQuaid, Phyllis W. 1928- *WhoAmW 91*
McQuaide, Stan R. 1940- *St&PR 91*
McQuaide, William Frederick 1934- *St&PR 91*
McQuarrie, Bruce Cale 1929- *WhoAm 90*
McQuarrie, Donald Gray 1931- *WhoAm 90*
McQuarrie, Gerald H. 1921- *WhoAm 90*
McQueen, Armelia 1952- *DrBlPA 90*
McQueen, Butterfly 1911- *DrBlPA 90, WorAlBi*
McQueen, Cilla 1949- *FemiCLE*
McQueen, Jennifer Robertson 1930- *WhoAm 90*
McQueen, John 1943- *WhoAmA 91*
McQueen, Judith Dorothy 1946- *WhoE 91*
McQueen, Justice Ellis 1927- *WhoAm 90*
McQueen, Kathryn Lynn 1952- *WhoAmW 91*
McQueen, Kenneth J. *St&PR 91*
McQueen, Lorraine Mary 1938- *WhoE 91*
McQueen, Lucinda 1950- *BioIn 16*
Mc Queen, Marjorie 1927- *WhoWrEP 89*
McQueen, Mike 1950- *Ballpl 90*
McQueen, Patrick M. 1946- *St&PR 91*
McQueen, Paula F. 1946- *St&PR 91*
McQueen, Peter *WhNaAH*
McQueen, Rebecca Hodges 1954- *WhoAmW 91, WhoSSW 91*
Mc Queen, Robert Charles 1921- *WhoAm 90*
McQueen, Roberta Jean 1922- *BiDrAPA 89*
McQueen, Samuel C. *St&PR 91N*
McQueen, Sandra Marilyn 1948- *WhoAmW 91*
McQueen, Scott Robert 1946- *WhoAm 90*
McQueen, Steve 1930-1980 *WorAlBi*
McQueen, Thomas Joseph 1947- *WhoSSW 91*
Mc Queeney, Henry Martin, Sr. 1938- *WhoAm 90*
McQueeney, Robert Thomas *BiDrAPA 89*
McQueeney, Thomas A. 1937- *St&PR 91*
McQuern, Marcia Alice 1942- *St&PR 91, WhoAmW 91*
McQuiddy, David L., Jr. 1929- *St&PR 91*
McQuiddy, David Newton, Jr. 1938- *WhoAm 90*
McQuide, Pamela Ann 1951- *WhoAmW 91*
McQuigg, John Dolph 1931- *WhoSSW 91*
McQuiggan, Robert Francis 1938- *St&PR 91*
McQuilkin, John Robertson 1927- *WhoAm 90*
Mc Quilkin, Robert Rennie 1936- *WhoWrEP 89*
McQuillan, Charles Edward 1937- *WhoE 91*
McQuillan, Frances *WhoAmA 91*
McQuillan, George 1885-1940 *Ballpl 90*
McQuillan, Hugh 1897-1947 *Ballpl 90*
McQuillan, Joseph Michael 1931- *St&PR 91*
Mc Quillan, Joseph Michael 1931- *WhoAm 90*
Mc Quillan, Margaret Mary *WhoAmW 91*
McQuillan, Wendy Newfield 1939- *WhoAmW 91*
McQuillan, William Hugh 1935- *St&PR 91, WhoAm 90*
McQuillen, Albert Lawrence, Jr. 1925- *WhoE 91*
McQuillen, Glenn 1915-1989 *BioIn 16*
McQuillen, Harry A. *WhoAm 90, WhoE 91, WhoWor 91*
McQuillen, Jeremiah Joseph 1941- *WhoE 91, WhoWor 91*
Mc Quillen, Michael Paul 1932- *WhoAm 90*
McQuinn, Alvin E. 1931- *St&PR 91*
McQuinn, George 1910-1978 *Ballpl 90*
Mc Quinn, William C 1927- *BiDrAPA 89*
Mc Quinn, William P. 1936- *WhoAm 90*
McQuirk, Rosemary Pummill 1933- *WhoAmW 91*
McQuistion, Hunter L. 1952- *BiDrAPA 89*
McQuiston, Liz 1952- *WhoWor 91*
McQuiston, Robert Earl 1936- *WhoAm 90*
McQuiston, William Calvin 1924- *WhoSSW 91*
McQuitty, Louis L. 1910-1986 *BioIn 16*
Mc Rae, Bettye Martin 1933- *WhoWrEP 89*
McRae, Branson Jackson 1920- *St&PR 91*
McRae, Carmen *BioIn 16*
McRae, Carmen 1922- *DrBlPA 90, OxCPMus*
McRae, Colin D. 1946- *St&PR 91*
McRae, Edna *BioIn 16, NewYTBS 90*
Mc Rae, Garfield 1938- *WhoWrEP 89*
McRae, Glenn 1956- *WhoE 91*
McRae, Gordon 1921-1986 *OxCPMus*
McRae, Gregory J. *BioIn 16*
McRae, Hal 1945- *Ballpl 90 [port]*
McRae, Hamilton Eugene, III 1937- *WhoAm 90, WhoWor 91*
McRae, Hamilton Eugene, Jr. 1905- *WhoAm 90*
McRae, James C. 1950- *St&PR 91*
McRae, John Jones 1815-1868 *AmLegL*
McRae, John M. 1942- *WhoAm 90*
Mc Rae, Kenneth Douglas 1925- *WhoAm 90*
McRae, Nancy Elizabeth 1943- *WhoAmW 91*
McRae, Paul Anthony 1945- *WhoAm 90*

McRae, Robert Malcolm, Jr. 1921- *WhoAm 90, WhoSSW 91*
McRae, Robin S. 1939- *St&PR 91*
McRae, Russell 1934- *ConAu 129, SmATA 63 [port]*
McRae, Thomas Chipman 1851-1929 *BioIn 16*
McRae, Thomas Kenneth 1906- *WhoAm 90*
McRaith, John Jeremiah 1934- *WhoAm 90, WhoSSW 91*
McRaney, Gerald *BioIn 16*
McRaney, Gerald 1947- *WorAlBi*
McRaney, Gerald 1948- *ConTFT 8*
McRaney, Michael P. 1937- *ODwPR 91*
McRary, John Walter, III 1939- *WhoAm 90*
McRea, Joseph 1946- *St&PR 91*
Mc Ree, J Douglas *BiDrAPA 89*
McRee, John Browning, Jr. 1950- *WhoSSW 91*
McRee, Michael Thomason 1943- *St&PR 91*
McReynolds, Cliff 1933- *WhoAmA 91*
McReynolds, David Hobert 1953- *WhoSSW 91*
Mc Reynolds, Edwards U *BiDrAPA 89*
McReynolds, James Clark 1862-1946 *BiDrUSE 89*
McReynolds, Kevin 1959- *Ballpl 90*
McReynolds, Kirk *WhoAmA 91*
McReynolds, Laura Magnus 1959- *WhoAmW 91*
McReynolds, Mary Maureen 1940- *WhoAmW 91*
McReynolds, Neil Lawrence 1934- *St&PR 91, WhoAm 90*
McReynolds, Stephen Ralph 1939- *WhoE 91*
McReynolds, W. Sam 1937- *St&PR 91*
McReynolds, William Thomas 1943- *WhoAm 90*
McRitchie, Bruce D. 1938- *St&PR 91*
McRobbie, Michael Alexander 1950- *WhoWor 91*
McRoberts, James Gordon 1942- *St&PR 91*
McRoberts, Joyce 1941- *WhoAmW 91*
McRoberts, June Hattie 1931- *WhoAmW 91*
McRoberts, Robert Arthur 1928- *St&PR 91*
McRorie, Alice Rhyne 1946- *WhoAmW 91*
McRorie, Wiliam Edward 1940- *WhoAm 90*
McRorie, William Edward 1940- *St&PR 91*
Mc Rostie, Clair Neil 1930- *WhoAm 90*
McRoy, Robert B. 1882-1917 *Ballpl 90*
McRuer, Duane Torrance 1925- *WhoAm 90*
Mc Say, Robert Allan 1947- *BiDrAPA 89*
McShain, John 1898-1989 *BioIn 16*
McShain, John 1899-1989 *AnObit 1989*
McShan, John Tyler 1926- *St&PR 91*
Mc Shane, Claudette *WhoWrEP 89*
McShane, David R. 1941- *St&PR 91*
McShane, Edward J. 1904-1989 *BioIn 16*
Mcshane, Edward Joseph, Jr. 1932- *St&PR 91*
McShane, Harry 1891-1988 *AnObit 1988, BioIn 16*
McShane, John Francis 1928- *St&PR 91*
McShane, Mark 1929- *TwCCr&M 91*
McShane, Michael 1952- *St&PR 91*
McShane, Patricia Mary 1949- *WhoE 91*
McShane, Stephen J. 1943- *St&PR 91*
McShann, Jay *BioIn 16*
McShann, Jay 1909- *OxCPMus*
McShea, Joseph 1907- *WhoAm 90*
McShea, Robert Joseph, Jr. 1940- *WhoE 91*
McSheehy, Cornelia Marie 1947- *WhoAmA 91, WhoE 91*
McShefferty, John 1929- *WhoAm 90*
Mc Sheffrey, Gerald Rainey 1931- *WhoAm 90*
McSherry, Bernard P. 1921-1989 *BioIn 16*
McSherry, Dennis Joseph 1950- *WhoE 91*
McSherry, John 1944- *Ballpl 90*
McShine, Kynaston Leigh 1935- *WhoAmA 91*
McShirley, Susan Ruth 1945- *WhoAmW 91*
McSorley, Arthur 1928- *St&PR 91*
McSorley, Marion Joseph 1933- *St&PR 91*
Mc Spadden, Peter Ford 1930- *WhoAm 90*
McSpiritt, Francis 1836-1895 *DcCanB 12*
McSporran, Seumas *BioIn 16*
McSwain, Lon Arild 1953- *WhoSSW 91*
McSwain, Richard Horace 1949- *WhoSSW 91*
Mc Swain, Ross Francis, Jr. 1929- *WhoSSW 91*
McSwain, Ruth Crowder 1925- *WhoSSW 91*
McSweeney, Declan 1956- *WhoWor 91*
McSweeney, Frances Kaye 1948- *WhoAm 90, WhoAmW 91*
McSweeney, June Elizabeth 1932- *WhoAmW 91*
McSweeney, Maurice J. 1938- *WhoAm 90*
McSweeney, Michael T. 1937- *St&PR 91*
McSweeney, Michael Terrence 1937- *WhoAm 90*
McSweeney, William Francis 1929- *St&PR 91*
Mcsweeny, Austin John *BiDrAPA 89*
McSweeny, John Edward 1936- *WhoAm 90*
McSweeny, William Francis 1929- *WhoAm 90, WhoE 91*
McSwigan, Marie 1907-1962 *AuBYP 90*
McSwiggan, Jacqueline N. 1953- *St&PR 91*
McSwiggan, Robert David 1931- *WhoSSW 91*
McSwiney, C. Ronald 1943- *St&PR 91*
McSwiney, Charles Ronald 1943- *WhoAm 90*
Mc Swiney, James Wilmer 1915- *WhoAm 90*
McTaggart-Cowan, Ian 1910- *WhoAm 90*
McTague, Jerome J. 1920- *St&PR 91*
McTague, John Paul 1938- *St&PR 91, WhoAm 90*
McTague, Shirley Fauber 1924- *St&PR 91*
McTarnaghan, Roy E. *WhoAm 90*
Mc Tavish, John Elser 1926- *WhoAm 90*
McTavish, Simon 1750?-1804 *WhNaAH*
McTeague, Bertrand L. 1935- *St&PR 91*
McTeague, Linda Bragdon *WhoAmW 91, WhoE 91*
McTee, Cindy Karen 1953- *IntWWM 90*
McTier, Duncan Paul 1954- *IntWWM 90*
McTiernan, Timothy Patrick 1952- *WhoWor 91*
McTighe, Robert Michael 1955- *St&PR 91*
McTigue, Bernard Francis 1946- *WhoAm 90*
McTigue, Nancy V *BiDrAPA 89*
McTwigan, Michael 1948- *WhoAmA 91*
McTyeire, Holland Nimmons, IV 1930- *St&PR 91*
McTyeire, Rex Holland 1949- *WhoSSW 91*
McTyre, H. Edward 1944- *St&PR 91*
Mc Umber, Keith Darren 1942- *WhoWrEP 89*
Mc Vaugh, Rogers 1909- *WhoAm 90*
Mc Vay, Barry Lee 1951- *WhoWrEP 89*
McVay, Doris Elaine 1955- *WhoAmW 91*
McVay, Ruth Louise 1942- *WhoAmW 91*
McVea, Warren 1946- *BioIn 16*
McVeagh, Diana Mary 1926- *IntWWM 90*
McVean, Duncan Edward 1936- *St&PR 91*
McVean, James *TwCCr&M 91*
McVeigh, John Newburne, III 1947- *St&PR 91*
McVeigh, Miriam Lenig *WhoAmA 91*
McVerry, Thomas Leo 1938- *St&PR 91, WhoAm 90*
McVetta, Roger Frank 1939- *St&PR 91*
McVety, James Robert 1941- *St&PR 91*
McVey, Cal 1850-1926 *Ballpl 90*
McVey, Devon Palmquist 1961- *WhoAmW 91*
McVey, Diane Elaine 1953- *WhoAmW 91*
McVey, Eugene Steven 1927- *WhoAm 90*
McVey, Henry Hanna, III 1935- *WhoAm 90*
McVey, James William 1931- *WhoAm 90*
McVey, Kenneth 1939- *St&PR 91*
McVey, Kenneth Kent 1923- *St&PR 91*
McVey, Leza 1907-1984 *WhoAmA 91N*
McVey, Marcia Alice 1934- *WhoAmW 91*
McVey, William M 1905- *WhoAmA 91*
McVicar, George Christie 1919- *IntWWM 90*
McVicar, Ronald C. 1946- *St&PR 91*
McVicar, Sherry Fisher 1952- *WhoAmW 91*
McVicar, Victoria 183-?-1899 *DcCanB 12*
Mc Vicker, Charles Taggart 1930- *WhoAm 90*
McVicker, Charles Taggart 1930- *WhoAmA 91*
McVicker, Dana *WhoNeCM [port]*
McVicker, Dawson Scott 1952- *WhoSSW 91*
McVicker, J Jay 1911- *WhoAmA 91*
McVicker, Jesse Jay 1911- *WhoAm 90*
McVicker, Jim *BioIn 16*
McVicker, Mary Ellen Harshbarger 1951- *WhoAmW 91*
Mc Vie, Christine Perfect 1943- *WhoAm 90*
McVisk, William Kilburn 1953- *WhoEmL 91*
McVittie, George C. 1904-1988 *BioIn 16*
McVoy, Helen Couch 1920- *WhoSSW 91*
McVoy, James Earl 1946- *IntWWM 90*
McVoy, Kirk Warren 1928- *WhoAm 90*
McWade, Charles P. 1944- *St&PR 91*
McWalter, Stuart Keith *WhoAm 90*
McWane, James R. *WhoSSW 91*
McWeeny, Doug 1896-1953 *Ballpl 90*
McWethy, John Fleetwood 1947- *WhoAm 90*
McWethy, Patricia Joan 1946- *WhoAm 90*
Mc Wey, Michael 1953- *WhoWrEP 89*
McWherter, Ned Ray 1930- *WhoAm 90, WhoSSW 91, WhoWor 91*
McWhiney, Grady 1928- *WhoAm 90*
Mc Whinney, Edward Watson 1924- *WhoAm 90*
McWhinney, Ian Renwick 1926- *WhoAm 90*
McWhinney, Madeline H. 1922- *St&PR 91, WhoAm 90*
McWhinney, Rodney O. 1933- *St&PR 91*
McWhinney, Will *BioIn 16*
McWhinnie, David E. 1944- *St&PR 91*
McWhinnie, Harold James 1929- *WhoAmA 91*
Mc Whirter, David Parr 1932- *BiDrAPA 89*
McWhirter, Don Ray 1926- *St&PR 91*
McWhirter, George 1939- *BioIn 16*
McWhirter, Glenna Suzanne 1929- *WhoAm 90*
McWhirter, James Herman 1924- *WhoAm 90*
McWhirter, Norris 1925- *WorAlBi*
McWhirter, Norris Dewar 1925- *WhoWor 91*
McWhirter, Richard A. 1934- *St&PR 91*
McWhirter, Ross 1925-1975 *WorAlBi*
McWhorter, Alan Louis 1930- *WhoAm 90*
McWhorter, Anthony L. 1949- *St&PR 91*
McWhorter, Elsie Jean 1932- *WhoAmA 91*
McWhorter, George G. 1833-1891 *AmLegL*
McWhorter, Henry Clay 1836-1913 *AmLegL*
Mc Whorter, Hezzie Boyd 1923- *WhoAm 90*
McWhorter, Jerry Pharr 1943- *St&PR 91*
McWhorter, Ralph Clayton 1933- *St&PR 91, WhoAm 90*
McWhorter, Robert Ligon 1819- *AmLegL*
McWhorter, Susan Malinda 1963- *WhoSSW 91*
McWilliam, Colin 1928-1989 *AnObit 1989*
McWilliam, F. E. 1909- *BioIn 16*
McWilliam, James L. 1928- *St&PR 91*
McWilliam, Robert Sherman 1951- *BiDrAPA 89*
McWilliams, Alden 1916- *EncACom*
McWilliams, Betty Jane *WhoAm 90*
McWilliams, Brent Nelson 1957- *St&PR 91*
McWilliams, Bruce W. 1932- *ODwPR 91*
McWilliams, Bruce Wayne 1932- *WhoAm 90*
McWilliams, Carey 1905-1980 *BioIn 16*
McWilliams, Constance Florence 1945- *WhoAmW 91*
McWilliams, David Charles 1942- *St&PR 91*
McWilliams, Edwin Joseph 1919- *WhoAm 90*
McWilliams, Harry Kenneth 1907- *WhoE 91*
McWilliams, John B. 1947- *St&PR 91*
McWilliams, John Michael 1939- *WhoAm 90*
McWilliams, Larry 1954- *Ballpl 90*
McWilliams, Margaret Ann 1929- *WhoAm 90, WhoAmW 91*
McWilliams, Marianne Birch *ODwPR 91*
McWilliams, Michael G. 1952- *WhoAm 90*
McWilliams, Ralph David 1930- *WhoAm 90*
McWilliams, Robert Hugh 1916- *WhoAm 90*
McWilliams, Sonja Lee 1947- *WhoAmW 91*
McWilliams, Spencer Albert 1944- *WhoSSW 91*
McWilliams, Terry 1954- *ODwPR 91*
Meacci, Sergio 1944- *WhoWor 91*
Meacham, Alfred B 1826-1882 *WhNaAH*
Meacham, Arthur Paul 1946- *WhoWrEP 89*
Meacham, Bobby 1960- *Ballpl 90*
Meacham, Carolyn Lee 1946- *WhoSSW 91*
Meacham, Charles Harding 1925- *WhoAm 90*
Meacham, Daniel Weedon 1954- *WhoSSW 91*
Meacham, Ellis Kirby 1913- *WhoWrEP 89*
Meacham, Harold Scott 1949- *WhoSSW 91*
Meacham, Heather Muir 1941- *WhoAmW 91*
Meacham, Howard Dennis 1950- *WhoEmL 91*
Meacham, Louis *Ballpl 90*
Meacham, Milo Louis, Jr. 1946- *WhoSSW 91*
Meacham, Niles Corley 1932- *St&PR 91*
Meacham, Standish, Jr. 1932- *WhoAm 90*
Meacham, Thomas Downing *BiDrAPA 89*
Meacham, William Feland 1913- *WhoAm 90*
Meachem, Margaret McKeen Ramsey 1922- *IntWWM 90*
Meachin, David James Percy 1941- *WhoAm 90, WhoE 91*
Mead, Abraham 1742-1827 *BioIn 16*
Mead, Beverley T 1923- *BiDrAPA 89*
Mead, Beverley Tupper 1923- *WhoAm 90*
Mead, Carl David 1913- *WhoAm 90*
Mead, Carver *BioIn 16*
Mead, Charles W. *St&PR 91*
Mead, Dana George 1936- *St&PR 91, WhoAm 90*
Mead, David Edmund 1950- *WhoAm 90, WhoE 91*
Mead, David Paul 1949- *St&PR 91*
Mead, Edward M. 1926- *St&PR 91*
Mead, Edward Mathews 1926- *WhoAm 90*
Mead, Elizabeth Vaila 1948- *IntWWM 90*
Mead, Frank F. 1929- *St&PR 91*
Mead, G R S 1863-1933 *EncO&P 3*
Mead, George Herbert 1863-1931 *BioIn 16*
Mead, George Robert Stowe 1863-1933 *EncPaPR 91*
Mead, George W., II 1927- *St&PR 91*
Mead, George Wilson, II 1927- *WhoAm 90*
Mead, Gilbert Dunbar 1930- *WhoAm 90*
Mead, Gordon V. 1906- *WhoAm 90*
Mead, Harriet Council *WhoAmW 91*
Mead, Harriet Councill *WhoWrEP 89*
Mead, Hyrum Anderson 1947- *St&PR 91*
Mead, James M., Jr. 1918- *St&PR 91*
Mead, John M 1930- *BiDrAPA 89*
Mead, John Milton 1924- *WhoAm 90*
Mead, Katherine Harper 1929- *WhoAmA 91N*
Mead, Lawrence Myers, Jr. 1918- *WhoAm 90*
Mead, Margaret 1901-1978 *AuBYP 90, BioAmW, BioIn 16, EncPaPR 91, FemiCLE, MajTwCW, WorAlBi*
Mead, Mark Nathaniel 1961- *WhoWrEP 89*
Mead, Matthew 1924- *ConAu 13AS [port]*
Mead, Philip Bartlett 1937- *WhoAm 90*
Mead, Philip John 1947- *IntWWM 90*
Mead, Randy *NewAgMG*
Mead, Richard Joseph 1943- *BiDrAPA 89*
Mead, Robert 1940-1988 *AnObit 1988*
Mead, Robert E. 1938- *WhoAm 90, WhoSSW 91*
Mead, Robert L. *ODwPR 91, WhoAm 90*
Mead, Robert Norman 1948- *WhoSSW 91*
Mead, Ronald H. 1939- *St&PR 91, WhoAm 90*
Mead, Rosemary Antoinette 1939- *WhoAmW 91*
Mead, Russell *ConAu 30NR*
Mead, Susan W. A. 1950- *St&PR 91*
Mead, Wayland M. 1931- *St&PR 91*
Mead, Wayland McCon 1931- *WhoAm 90*
Mead, William Allen 1943- *St&PR 91*
Mead, William B 1934- *ConAu 32NR*
Mead, William J. 1927- *St&PR 91*
Meade, Donna *WhoNeCM [port]*
Meade, Dorothy Winifred 1935- *WhoAmW 91*
Meade, Edwin Baylies 1896- *WhoAm 90*
Meade, Everard Kidder, Jr. 1919- *WhoAm 90*
Meade, Gary Scott 1946- *St&PR 91*
Meade, George 1815-1872 *WorAlBi*
Meade, James Edward 1907- *WhoAm 90, WhoWor 91*
Meade, Joe Neal 1939- *St&PR 91*
Meade, John 1775-1849 *BioIn 16*
Meade, Joseph F., Jr. 1921- *St&PR 91*
Meade, L. T. 1854-1914 *FemiCLE, TwCCr&M 91*
Meade, Mary Henselman 1963- *WhoAmW 91*
Meade, Patricia Sue 1960- *WhoAmW 91*
Meade, Richard Alan 1952- *St&PR 91*
Meade, Robert J. 1918-1989 *BioIn 16*
Meade, Walter Walthen 1930- *WhoWrEP 89*
Meade, William Young 1934- *WhoAm 90*
Meader, Bruce Ian 1955- *WhoAm 90*
Meader, Cortland J. 1935- *St&PR 91*
Meader, Darrell Lee 1941- *WhoSSW 91*
Meader, John Daniel 1931- *WhoE 91, WhoWor 91*
Meader, Jonathan Grant *WhoAmA 91*
Meader, Jonathan Grant 1943- *WhoAm 90*
Meader, Ralph Gibson 1904- *WhoAm 90*
Meader, Stephen Warren 1892- *AuBYP 90*
Meaders, Otis Donald *BioIn 16*
Meaders, Paul Le Sourd 1930- *WhoAm 90*
Meaders, Quillian Lanier 1917- *MusmAFA*
Meades, Anna *FemiCLE*
Meades, Jonathan 1947- *ConAu 130*
Meadley, Walter E. 1932- *St&PR 91*
Meadlock, James W. 1933- *WhoAm 90, WhoSSW 91*
Meadlock, Nancy B. 1938- *WhoAm 90*

Meadmore, Clement L 1929- WhoAmA 91
Meador, Anna Lee 1934- WhoSSW 91
Meador, Charles Lawrence 1946- WhoE 91, WhoEmL 91, WhoWor 91
Meador, Daniel John 1926- WhoAm 90
Meador, Donald J. 1937- St&PR 91
Meador, Ilean Prater 1934- WhoAmW 91
Meador, Joe BioIn 16
Meador, John Milward, Jr. 1946- WhoAm 90
Meador, Keith Glenn 1956- BiDrAPA 89
Meador, Patricia Lane 1943- WhoAmW 91
Meador, Prentice Avery, Jr. 1938- WhoSSW 91
Meador, Wilma Jean 1932- WhoAmW 91
Meador-Woodruff, James Henry BiDrAPA 89
Meadors, Allen Coats 1947- WhoEmL 91
Meadors, Elizabeth A. 1945- ODwPR 91
Meadors, Howard Clarence, Jr. 1938- WhoAm 90
Meadors, Joe Richard 1931- St&PR 91
Meadow, Charles T. 1929- AuBYP 90
Meadow, Dena Currie BiDrAPA 89
Meadow, Elizabeth Ann 1944- BiDrAPA 89
Meadow, Lynne BioIn 16
Meadow, Lynne 1946- NotWoAT, WhoAm 90
Meadowcroft, Enid 1898-1966 AuBYP 90
Meadowcroft, Robert Stanley 1937- WhoAm 90
Meadowcroft, T. Raymond 1936- St&PR 91
Meadows, Algur H 1899-1980 WhoAmA 91N
Meadows, Audrey 1924- WorAlBi
Meadows, Bernard 1915- BioIn 16
Meadows, Charles Henson 1860-1932 BioIn 16
Meadows, Daniel T, Jr BiDrAPA 89
Meadows, David Edgar 1949- WhoSSW 91
Meadows, Donald Frederick 1937- WhoAm 90
Meadows, George Lee 1938- St&PR 91
Meadows, Glenn Hargus 1929- St&PR 91
Meadows, Gregory Paul 1962- WhoE 91
Meadows, Harry 1937- St&PR 91
Meadows, James Dartlin 1957- WhoSSW 91
Meadows, Jayne 1920- WorAlBi
Meadows, John Thomas 1954- WhoSSW 91
Meadows, John W BiDrAPA 89
Meadows, Jolly Ann Henderson 1952- WhoSSW 91
Meadows, Joseph Marion, Jr. 1928- BiDrAPA 89
Meadows, Lee 1894-1963 Ballpl 90
Meadows, Lynn W. 1943- St&PR 91
Meadows, P B 1938- WhoAmA 91
Meadows, Paul D. 1926- St&PR 91
Meadows, Paul Dwain 1926- WhoAm 90
Meadows, Peter ConAu 131
Meadows, Richard L 1927- BiDrAPA 89
Meadows, Richards D. 1953- St&PR 91
Meadows, Robert E. 1961- St&PR 91
Meadows, Sharon Marie 1950- WhoAm 90
Meadows, Tamara Lynn 1956- WhoSSW 91
Meadows, Tommy C. 1940- WhoSSW 91
Meads, Dave 1964- Ballpl 90
Meads, Donald Edward 1920- St&PR 91, WhoE 91
Meads, Walter Frederick 1923- WhoAm 90, WhoWor 91
Me'aduja, Zane EncCoWW
Meagher, Ann Marie BiDrAPA 89
Meagher, Douglas Raymond 1941- WhoWor 91
Meagher, George Vincent 1919- WhoAm 90
Meagher, H. Michael BiDrAPA 89
Meagher, James Francis 1946- WhoSSW 91
Meagher, James Proctor 1935- WhoE 91
Meagher, John B. 1936- St&PR 91
Meagher, Joseph B. 1945- St&PR 91
Meagher, Joyce Marie 1949- WhoE 91
Meagher, Kevin Charles 1954- St&PR 91
Meagher, Mark Joseph 1932- St&PR 91, WhoAm 90
Meagher, Mary T. BioIn 16
Meagher, Michael J. 1942- St&PR 91
Meagher, Sylvia BioIn 16
Meagher, Thomas F. 1930- St&PR 91
Meaker, M. J. MajTwCW
Meaker, M J 1927- SmATA X [port]
Meaker, Marijane AuBYP 90
Meaker, Marijane 1927- MajTwCW, SmATA 61 [port]
Meaker, Marijane Agnes 1927- WhoAm 90
Meakin, Faith Anne 1943- WhoAmW 91
Meakin, John David 1934- WhoAm 90
Meakins, Gene 1927- ODwPR 91, St&PR 91
Meal, Larie 1939- WhoAmW 91
Meale, Richard 1932- IntWWM 90
Mealia, Joanne Schram 1957- WhoAmW 91
Mealman, Glenn Edward 1934- WhoAm 90
Mealor, William Theodore, Jr. 1940- WhoAm 90
Mealy, Mark Williams 1957- WhoSSW 91
Meana, Mitchell A. 1958- WhoHisp 91
Meaney, Colm ConTFT 8
Meaney, Joseph 1919- BiDrAPA 89
Meaney, Patrick 1925- St&PR 91
Meaney, Patrick Michael 1925- WhoWor 91
Meaney, Thomas Francis 1927- WhoAm 90
Meaney, William Martin 1948- BiDrAPA 89
Means, Cyril Chesnut, Jr. 1918- WhoAm 90
Means, David Hammond 1928- WhoAm 90
Means, Elliott 1905-1962 WhoAmA 91N
Means, Florence Crannell 1891-1980 AuBYP 90
Means, George Robert 1907- WhoAm 90, WhoWor 91
Means, Gordon Paul 1927- WhoWor 91
Means, Jack L. 1935- St&PR 91
Means, John Barkley 1939- WhoAm 90, WhoE 91, WhoWor 91
Means, Lane Lewis 1951- WhoEmL 91
Means, Marianne 1934- WhoAm 90
Means, Raymond B. 1930- WhoAm 90
Means, Richard K., Jr. 1945- St&PR 91
Means, Richard Lawrence 1945- WhoSSW 91
Means, Royce Bryan 1924- BiDrAPA 89
Means, Russell BioIn 16
Means, Thomas Cornell 1947- WhoE 91, WhoEmL 91
Means, Toney Earl 1959- WhoSSW 91
Meany, Daniel 1930- St&PR 91
Meany, George 1894-1980 WorAlBi
Meany, H. Jack 1923- St&PR 91
Meany, John Stewart, Jr. 1945- St&PR 91
Meany, Mary-Liz ODwPR 91
Meany, Sarah Ann 1928- WhoAmW 91
Meany, Tom 1903-1964 Ballpl 90
Meany, William F. St&PR 91
Meara, Anne WhoAm 90, WhoAmW 91
Meara, Anne 1929- WorAlBi
Meara, Charlie 1891-1962 Ballpl 90
Meara, Michael T. 1958- St&PR 91
Meares, Edward F BiDrAPA 89
Mearian, Judy Frank 1936- BioIn 16
Mearin, Robert J 1907- BiDrAPA 89
Mearne, Samuel PenDiDA 89
Mearns, Barbara 1955- ConAu 132
Mearns, Richard 1950- ConAu 132
Mears, A. W. Downing 1953- St&PR 91
Mears, Helen Farnsworth 1872-1916 BiDWomA
Mears, Henrietta C. 1890- BioIn 16
Mears, Madge 1886-1930 FemiCLE
Mears, Otto 1840-1931 WhNaAH
Mears, Patrick Edward 1951- WhoWor 91
Mears, Rick Ravon 1951- WhoAm 90
Mears, Steve Clifford 1953- WhoSSW 91
Mears, Virginia G 1919- BiDrAPA 89
Mears, Walter Robert 1935- St&PR 91, WhoAm 90
Mease, Cecil W. 1933- St&PR 91
Mease, Ronald Franklin 1929- WhoE 91
Measer, George John 1925- St&PR 91, WhoE 91
Measey, Michael PenDiDA 89
Measham, Terence Leonard 1939- WhoWor 91
Meason, Robert D. 1947- St&PR 91
Meath, Brian Patrick 1957- WhoEmL 91
Meathe, Philip J. 1926- St&PR 91
Meathe, Philip James 1926- WhoAm 90
Meats, Stephen 1944- WhoWrEP 89
Meatte, Luke L. 1923- St&PR 91
Meattle, Kamal 1944- WhoWor 91
Meau, Francois Marie Leon 1948- WhoWor 91
Mebane, Andrew Hill 1949- BiDrAPA 89
Mebane, Barbara Margot 1947- WhoAmW 91, WhoEmL 91
Mebane, David Cummins 1933- St&PR 91, WhoAm 90
Mebane, George Allen 1929- WhoAm 90
Mebane, John C 1922- BiDrAPA 89
Mebane, Mary E 1933- ConAu 30NR
Mebane, William Black 1927- WhoAm 90
Mebane, William deBerniere 1949- WhoAm 90
Mebaugh, R. Alan St&PR 91
Mebiame, Leon 1934- WhoWor 91
Meboutou, Michel Mev'aa WhoWor 91
Mebus, Robert Joseph 1943- St&PR 91
Mebust, Winston Keith 1933- WhoAm 90
Mecca, Donato Anthony 1904- WhoWrEP 89
Mecca, Joseph Nicholas 1947- WhoE 91
Mech, Arnold W BiDrAPA 89
Mecham, Evan BioIn 16
Mecham, Evan 1924- WhoAm 90
Mecham, Kenneth Dale 1943- St&PR 91
Mechanic, David 1936- WhoAm 90
Mechanic, Gene Barry 1947- WhoEmL 91
Mechanick, Philip Gerald 1927- BiDrAPA 89
Mechanick, Stephen M 1957- BiDrAPA 89
Mechem, Charles S., Jr. 1930- St&PR 91
Mechem, Charles Stanley, Jr. 1930- WhoAm 90
Mechem, James Harlan 1923- WhoWrEP 89
Mechem, John Edgar 1928- St&PR 91
Mechem, Kirke Lewis 1925- IntWWM 90
Mecheri-Saada, Nadia 1955- IntWWM 90
Mecherikunnel, Ann Pottanat 1934- WhoAmW 91
Mechetti, Fabio 1957- WhoAm 90
Mechigian, Nancy Lee 1941- WhoAmW 91
Mechlin, George Francis 1923- WhoAm 90
Mechlin, Leila 1874-1949 WhoAmA 91N
Mechner, Adolph 1897-1988 BioIn 16
Mechoso, Carlos Roberto 1942- WhoHisp 91
Mechoulam, Raphael 1930- WhoWor 91
Mechutan, Henry BioIn 16
Mecimore, Charles Douglas 1934- WhoAm 90
Mecina WhNaAH
Meck, Walter Charles 1951- WhoAm 90
Mecke, Theodore H., Jr. 1923- ODwPR 91
Mecke, Theodore Hart McCalla, Jr. 1923- WhoAm 90
Meckel, Markus WhoWor 91
Mecking, J. Garvin BioIn 16
Mecklem, Austin Merrill 1894-1951 WhoAmA 91N
Mecklenburg, Gary A. WhoAm 90
Mecklenburg, Virginia McCord 1946- WhoAmA 91
Meckler, Karen Frances 1956- BiDrAPA 89
Meckler, Marcia A BiDrAPA 89
Meckley, Daniel G., III 1923- St&PR 91
Meckley, Daniel Grant, III 1923- WhoE 91
Meckley, Thomas A. 1943- St&PR 91
Meckna, Robert Michael 1945- IntWWM 90
Mecom, Jane Franklin 1712-1794 BioAmW, EncCRAm
Meconis, Claude V. 1918- ODwPR 91
Mecum, Dudley Clarke, II 1934- St&PR 91
Medaglia, Mary-Elizabeth 1947- WhoEmL 91
Medal, Eduardo Antonio 1950- WhoHisp 91
Medalie, Richard James 1929- WhoAm 90
Medalie, Sherman George 1929- St&PR 91
Medalla, David 1942- BioIn 16
Medani, Charles Richard 1949- WhoAm 90
Medanich, David K. 1956- St&PR 91
Medaris, Florence Isabel WhoAmW 91
Medaris, John Bruce 1902- WhoAm 90
Medavoy, Mike 1941- St&PR 91, WhoAm 90
Medavoy, Patricia Duff BioIn 16
Medawar, Peter B. 1915-1987 WorAlBi
Medberry, Chauncey Joseph, III 1917- WhoAm 90
Medbery, Arnold Bunker, Jr. 1955- WhoSSW 91
Medcalf, Robert Randolph, Jr. 1949- WhoWrEP 89
Medcalf-Davenport, Neva Ann 1941- WhoAmW 91
Medd, Charles Leighton 1928-1989 ConAu 130
Meddaugh, R. Jay 1942- St&PR 91
Medders, Clifton Mark 1955- WhoSSW 91
Meddock, Larry Joseph 1946- St&PR 91
Mede, Gary E. 1936- St&PR 91
Medearis, Donald Norman, Jr. 1927- WhoAm 90
Medearis, Kenneth R. 1939- St&PR 91
Medearis, Kenneth Robert 1939- WhoWor 91
Medearis, Roger 1920- WhoAmA 91
Medearis, Roger Norman 1920- WhoAm 90
Medecin, Jacques Francois Xavier Paul 1928- BiDFrPL
Medeiros, Alfonso J 1924- BiDrAPA 89
Medeiros, Barbara Denis Jean 1934- WhoAmW 91
Medeiros, Daniel 1959- WhoEmL 91
Medeiros, Daniel M. 1959- BiDrAPA 89
Medeiros, Peter William 1946- WhoE 91
Medeiros, Prisca D. Bicoy 1928- WhoWrEP 89
Medel, Rebecca Rosalie 1947- WhoAmA 91
Medellin, Jose H. WhoHisp 91
Medellin, Octavio 1907- BioIn 16
Medelman, James Kyle 1937- BiDrAPA 89
Meden, Harold S. 1928- St&PR 91
Meden, Robert Paul 1950- WhoE 91
Medenica, Branislav BiDrAPA 89
Medenwald, Janet Ruth 1955- BiDrAPA 89
Meder, Bennett J. 1949- St&PR 91
Meder, Cornel 1938- WhoWor 91
Mederos, Carolina Luisa 1947- WhoAm 90, WhoAmW 91
Mederos, Julio WhoHisp 91
Medeubekov, Kilybai Usen 1929- WhoWor 91
Medford, Dale L. 1950- St&PR 91
Medford, Dale Leon 1950- WhoAm 90
Medford, William Leroy, Jr. 1942- WhoE 91
Medgyessy, Peter 1942- WhoWor 91
Medgyesy, John P. 1932- St&PR 91
Medhurst, R. G. EncO&P 3
Medhurst, Richard George 1920-1971 EncPaPR 91
Medhus, Sigurd Duane 1929- WhoAm 90
Mediavilla, Angel 1955- WhoWor 91
Medich, Doc 1948- Ballpl 90
Medich, George 1948- BioIn 16
Medici Quartet PenDiMP
Medici, Cosimo I De 1519-1574 WorAlBi
Medici, Emilio Garrastazu 1905-1985 BioIn 16
Medici, Lorenzo Di 1449-1492 WorAlBi
Medici, Stephen Francis 1952- St&PR 91
Medicine Snake Woman DcCanB 12
Medicis, Catherine de 1519-1589 BioIn 16, EncCoWW
Medick, James Thomas 1946- WhoSSW 91
Medicus, Heinrich Adolf 1918- WhoAm 90
Medikonduru, Ravindra 1960- BiDrAPA 89
Medill, Joseph 1823-1899 BioIn 16
Medill, Mary 1936- WhoWrEP 89
Medill, Mary Lawson WhoAmW 91
Medin, A. Louis 1925- WhoAm 90, WhoSSW 91
Medin, Donna Mae 1932- WhoWrEP 89
Medin, Julia Adele 1929- WhoSSW 91
Medin, Lowell Ansgard 1932- WhoWor 91
Medin, Myron James, Jr. 1931- WhoAm 90
Medina, Ada 1948- WhoAmA 91
Medina, Agustin 1946- WhoWor 91
Medina, Alan 1949- BiDrAPA 89, WhoEmL 91
Medina, Azucena 1936- WhoE 91
Medina, Cris WhoHisp 91
Medina, David 1948- WhoE 91
Medina, David Jonathan 1951- WhoHisp 91
Medina, Eleanor Mateo BiDrAPA 89
Medina, Enrique 1953- WhoHisp 91
Medina, Everard Joseph 1930- WhoWor 91
Medina, Gilbert M. WhoHisp 91
Medina, Harold R. BioIn 16
Medina, Harold R 1888-1990 CurBio 90N, NewYTBS 90 [port], WhoHisp 91N
Medina, Harold Raymond, III 1938- WhoE 91
Medina, Jim 1940- WhoHisp 91
Medina, John A. 1942- WhoHisp 91
Medina, Jorge 1951- WhoHisp 91
Medina, Jorge F BiDrAPA 89
Medina, Jose Collado 1952- WhoWor 91
Medina, Jose Enrique 1926- WhoAm 90, WhoHisp 91
Medina, Juan Manuel BiDrAPA 89
Medina, Julian Phillip 1949- WhoHisp 91
Medina, Kathryn Bach WhoAm 90, WhoWrEP 89
Medina, Louis M. 1957- St&PR 91
Medina, Louisa Honor de 1813?-1838 BioIn 16, NotWoAT
Medina, Manuel 1940- WhoHisp 91
Medina, Manuel O. BioIn 16
Medina, Maria Caminos 1941- WhoHisp 91
Medina, Miguel A., Jr. 1946- WhoHisp 91
Medina, Olga Dora BiDrAPA 89
Medina, Robert C. 1924- HispWr 90, WhoHisp 91
Medina, Rodolfo M BiDrAPA 89
Medina, Rubens WhoHisp 91
Medina, Standish Forde, Jr. 1940- WhoAm 90
Medina, Tina Marie 1965- WhoHisp 91
Medina, Vicente 1955- WhoHisp 91
Medina Angarita, Isaias 1897-1953 BioIn 16
Medina Ferrer, Hugo Martin 1929- WhoWor 91
Medina-Juarbe, Arturo 1951- WhoHisp 91
Medina-Mora, Raul Maritn del Campo 1919- WhoWor 91
Medina-Ruiz, Arturo 1941- WhoHisp 91
Medina-Sidonia, Duque De 1550?-1619? WorAlBi
Medinger, Ann Elizabeth 1945- WhoAmW 91
Medinger, Gregor W. 1943- St&PR 91
Medio, Dolores 1914- EncCoWW

Mediratta, Ravinder Pal *BiDrAPA 89*
Medis, Lynn Rebis 1961- *WhoSSW 91*
Meditch, James Stephen 1934- *WhoAm 90*
Meditz, Walter Joseph 1917- *WhoAm 90*
Medland, William James 1944- *WhoAm 90*
Medler, Albert 1913- *St&PR 91*
Medler, Rodney A. 1936- *St&PR 91*
Medley, Bill *EncPR&S 89*
Medley, Diane Bennett 1955- *WhoSSW 91*
Medley, Donald Matthias 1917- *WhoAm 90*
Medley, John 1804-1892 *DcCanB 12*
Medley, Marc Allen 1962- *WhoE 91*
Medley, Mark J. 1953- *St&PR 91*
Medley, Mary Dee 1943- *WhoAmW 91*
Medley, Richard C. *St&PR 91*
Medley, Ronald D. 1934- *St&PR 91*
Medley, Sherrilyn 1946- *WhoAmW 91, WhoEmL 91*
Medley, William J. 1930- *St&PR 91*
Medlin, John Grimes, Jr. 1933- *St&PR 91, WhoAm 90, WhoSSW 91*
Medlock, Ann *BioIn 16*
Medlock, Donald Larson 1927- *WhoAm 90*
Medlock, Richard Kenneth 1960- *WhoE 91*
Medlock, Thomas Travis 1934- *WhoAm 90, WhoSSW 91*
Mednick, Glenn Myles 1953- *WhoEmL 91*
Mednick, Murray 1939- *WhoAm 90*
Mednick, Robert 1940- *WhoAm 90*
Mednis, Edmar John 1937- *WhoAm 90*
Medoff, Eve *WhoAmA 91*
Medoff, James Lawrence 1947- *WhoAm 90*
Medoff, Mark Howard 1940- *WhoAm 90*
Medow, Miriam Lucas 1949- *BiDrAPA 89*
Medowar, Debra B. 1960- *ODwPR 91*
Medowar, Debra Beth 1960- *WhoAmW 91*
Medrano, Ambrosio 1953- *WhoHisp 91*
Medrano, Evangeline M. 1944- *WhoHisp 91*
Medrano, Luisa 1953- *WhoAmW 91*
Medrano, Martha Alicia *BiDrAPA 89*
Medrano, Peter P 1931- *BiDrAPA 89*
Medrich, Libby E *WhoAmA 91*
Medtner, Nikolay *PenDiMP A*
Medvecky, Robert Stephen 1931- *WhoAm 90*
Medveczky, Adam 1941- *IntWWM 90*
Medved, Albert 1934- *WhoE 91*
Medved, Alphonse Anthony 1910- *WhoWrEP 89*
Medved, Diane 1951- *ConAu 132*
Medved, Jon Joseph 1947- *St&PR 91*
Medvedev, Roy Aleksandrovich 1925- *BioIn 16*
Medvedev, Vadim *BioIn 16*
Medvedev, Vadim Andreyevich 1929- *WhoWor 91*
Medvedkin, Alexander Ivanovich 1900-1989 *BioIn 16*
Medvedow, Phyllis Kronick 1931- *WhoAmW 91*
Medvin, Harvey N. 1936- *St&PR 91*
Medwadowski, Stefan J. 1924- *WhoAm 90*
Medwedeff, Fred Marshall 1926- *WhoSSW 91, WhoWor 91*
Medwick, Joe 1911-1975 *Ballpl 90 [port], WorAlBi*
Medwick, Maury P. 1910- *St&PR 91*
Medwid, Stephen 1958- *WhoWrEP 89*
Medzerian, Barbara Lewis 1953- *WhoAmW 91*
Medzihradsky, Fedor 1932- *WhoAm 90*
Medzorian, Jack M. 1926- *St&PR 91*
Mee, Charles L., Jr. 1938- *WhoAm 90*
Mee, Derrick Newton 1937- *St&PR 91*
Mee, Edward William 1951- *WhoWor 91*
Mee, Heidi Baumeister 1955- *WhoAmW 91*
Mee, Herb, Jr. 1928- *St&PR 91, WhoAm 90*
Mee, Janice Kay 1939- *WhoAmW 91*
Mee, John Lawrence 1950- *WhoEmL 91*
Mee, Margaret 1909-1988 *AnObit 1988, BioIn 16*
Mee, Michael Francis 1942- *St&PR 91*
Mee, Tom *BioIn 16*
Mee-Lee, David *BiDrAPA 89*
Mee-Lee, David 1949- *WhoE 91*
Mee-Lee, Denis 1941- *BiDrAPA 89*
Meece, Bernard Clayton 1927- *WhoSSW 91*
Meece, Gregory Robert 1957- *WhoE 91*
Meece, Richard Durward 1942- *WhoSSW 91*
Meech, Richard Campbell 1921- *WhoAm 90*
Meecham, William Coryell 1928- *WhoAm 90*
Meedel, Virgil Gene 1927- *St&PR 91*
Meeder, Donnis Lea 1929- *WhoAmW 91*
Meeder, Jeanne Elizabeth 1950- *WhoSSW 91*
Meeder, Lorin S. 1936- *St&PR 91*
Meegan, George *BioIn 16*
Meehan, Andrew E. 1957- *St&PR 91*
Meehan, Anthony Edward 1943- *WhoWor 91*
Meehan, David Howard 1928- *St&PR 91*
Meehan, David J. 1925- *St&PR 91*
Meehan, David Kevin 1947- *St&PR 91*
Meehan, Fanitsa Frantzis 1944- *WhoAmW 91*
Meehan, Gerry *WhoAm 90, WhoE 91*
Meehan, Joan B. 1959- *ODwPR 91*
Meehan, Joan Barbara 1959- *WhoAmW 91*
Meehan, John E. 1927- *St&PR 91*
Meehan, John J. 1945- *St&PR 91*
Meehan, John Joseph 1945- *WhoAm 90*
Meehan, John Joseph, Jr. 1946- *WhoAm 90*
Meehan, John Patrick *BiDrAPA 89*
Meehan, Joseph Gerard 1931- *St&PR 91, WhoAm 90*
Meehan, Kandy Lee 1951- *WhoAmW 91*
Meehan, Marjorie C 1905- *BiDrAPA 89*
Meehan, Marjorie Mae 1935- *WhoAmW 91*
Meehan, Mary *BioIn 16*
Meehan, Paula Kent 1931- *St&PR 91, WhoAm 90*
Meehan, Richard Thomas, Jr. 1949- *WhoEmL 91*
Meehan, Robert Henry 1946- *WhoE 91*
Meehan, Robert Michael 1936- *WhoSSW 91*
Meehan, Thomas Charles *BiDrAPA 89*
Meehan, Vincent E. 1949- *WhoE 91*
Meehan, William Austin 1946- *St&PR 91*
Meehan, William Dale 1930- *WhoAmA 91*
Meehl, James Robert 1926- *St&PR 91*
Meehl, Paul E 1920- *EncO&P 3*
Meehl, Paul Everett 1920- *WhoAm 90*
Meek, A J 1941- *WhoAmA 91*
Meek, Alexander Beaufort 1814-1865 *AmLegL*
Meek, Amy Gertrude 1928- *WhoAmW 91*
Meek, Bob *BioIn 16*
Meek, Carrie P. 1926- *WhoAmW 91*
Meek, Carroll Lee Larson 1942- *WhoAmW 91*
Meek, Charles Richard 1941- *WhoSSW 91*
Meek, Edward Stanley 1919- *WhoAm 90, WhoWor 91*
Meek, George 1910- *EncPaPR 91*
Meek, H A 1922- *ConAu 129*
Meek, J William, III 1950- *WhoAmA 91*
Meek, Jacklyn O'Hanlon 1933- *BioIn 16*
Meek, Jay 1937- *WhoWrEP 89*
Meek, John B. 1951- *St&PR 91*
Meek, John H. *WhoAm 90*
Meek, Joseph L 1810-1875 *WhNaAH*
Meek, Leslie Applegate 1913- *WhoWor 91*
Meek, M R D 1918- *TwCCr&M 91*
Meek, Max A. 1944- *St&PR 91*
Meek, Michael E 1941- *BiDrAPA 89*
Meek, Paul Derald 1930- *St&PR 91, WhoAm 90, WhoSSW 91*
Meek, Phillip Joseph 1937- *WhoAm 90*
Meek, Ruth Ann 1955- *WhoSSW 91*
Meek, Shelba Diana 1949- *WhoAmW 91*
Meek, Stephen R. 1956- *St&PR 91*
Meek, Violet Imhof 1939- *WhoAmW 91*
Meek, William James 1953- *BiDrAPA 89*
Meeke, Mary *BioIn 16*
Meeke, Mary *FemiCLE*
Meeker, Alvin D. 1937- *St&PR 91*
Meeker, Anthony 1939- *WhoAm 90*
Meeker, Arlene Dorothy 1935- *St&PR 91*
Meeker, Barbara Miller 1930- *WhoAmA 91*
Meeker, Darcy Sue 1946- *WhoWrEP 89*
Meeker, David A. 1939- *ODwPR 91*
Meeker, David Olan 1924-1987 *BioIn 16*
Meeker, Dean Jackson 1920- *WhoAmA 91*
Meeker, Guy Bentley 1945- *WhoE 91, WhoEmL 91, WhoWor 91*
Meeker, Julie Lynn *BiDrAPA 89*
Meeker, Kenneth H. 1938- *St&PR 91*
Meeker, Lavern D. 1947- *St&PR 91*
Meeker, Leonard Carpenter 1916- *WhoAm 90*
Meeker, Lorelei 1952- *WhoEmL 91*
Meeker, Merton David, Jr. 1931- *WhoE 91*
Meeker, Merton L. 1929- *St&PR 91*
Meeker, Nathan Cook 1817-1879 *WhNaAH*
Meeker, Oden 1919?-1976 *AuBYP 90*
Meeker, Ralph 1920-1988 *BioIn 16*
Meeker, Robert Eldon 1930- *WhoAm 90*
Meeker, Thomas Howard 1943- *St&PR 91*
Meeker, William M. 1915- *St&PR 91*
Meekhof, Frances Eleanor 1925- *St&PR 91*
Meekin, Jouett 1867-1944 *Ballpl 90*
Meekings, Margaret 1622-1692 *BiDEWW*
Meekison, MaryFran 1919- *WhoAmW 91, WhoWor 91*
Meeks, Carol Jean 1946- *WhoAmW 91, WhoEmL 91*
Meeks, Curtis Leo 1913- *WhoAm 90*
Meeks, D. Michael 1943- *St&PR 91, WhoAm 90*
Meeks, Donald Eugene 1930- *WhoAm 90*
Meeks, Esther K. *AuBYP 90*
Meeks, Gary A. 1945- *St&PR 91*
Meeks, Herbert Lessig, III 1946- *WhoSSW 91*
Meeks, Howard Samuel *WhoAm 90*
Meeks, John E 1934- *BiDrAPA 89*
Meeks, Reginald Kline 1954- *WhoSSW 91*
Meeks, Warren Leonard 1926- *St&PR 91*
Meeks, Wilkison Winfield 1915- *WhoAm 90*
Meeks, Yvonne Joyce 1955- *WhoAmW 91*
Meelheim, Helen Diane 1952- *WhoAmW 91, WhoSSW 91*
Meem, James Lawrence, Jr. 1915- *WhoAm 90, WhoWor 91*
Meeman, Edward John 1889-1966 *BioIn 16*
Meems, Robert Kevin 1937- *WhoSSW 91*
Meenakshi, Vallabhanemi *BiDrAPA 89*
Meenan, Alan John 1946- *WhoWor 91*
Meenan, James Ronald 1941- *WhoE 91*
Meenan, Patrick Henry 1927- *WhoAm 90*
Meenan, Peter 1942- *St&PR 91*
Meendsen, Fred Charles 1933- *St&PR 91, WhoAm 90*
Meengs, William Lloyd 1942- *WhoWor 91*
Meepagala, Gaminie 1955- *WhoE 91*
Meer, E. Harvey 1942- *St&PR 91*
Meer, Rud Van Der 1936- *IntWWM 90*
Meerbaum, Samuel 1919- *WhoAm 90*
Meerdink, A. Glenn 1927- *St&PR 91*
Meerkamper, Meinrad *St&PR 91*
Meerloo, Joost A M 1903-1976 *EncO&P 3*
Meerman, Peter Marcus 1941- *IntWWM 90*
Meers, Henry W. 1908- *St&PR 91, WhoAm 90*
Meersman, John F. 1937- *St&PR 91*
Meert, Roland Julien 1933- *WhoWor 91*
Meertens, Roelant Willem 1943- *WhoWor 91*
Mees, Barry J. 1947- *St&PR 91*
Meese, Ann Marie 1959- *WhoAmW 91*
Meese, Celia Edwards *WhoAmW 91, WhoWor 91*
Meese, Daniel U. 1947- *St&PR 91*
Meese, Edwin, III *BioIn 16*
Meese, Edwin, III 1931- *BiDrUSE 89, WhoE 91, WhoWor 91, WorAlBi*
Meese, George C. 1932- *St&PR 91*
Meese, Robert Allen 1956- *WhoEmL 91*
Meese, Ursula *BioIn 16*
Meeske, John Frederick 1941- *WhoAm 90*
Meeter, Stephen H. *ODwPR 91*
Meetz, John Eugene 1944- *WhoAm 90*
Meeuse, Adrianus Dirk Jacob 1914- *WhoWor 91*
Meezan, Elias 1942- *WhoAm 90*
Mefferd, Thomas Arthur 1941- *St&PR 91*
Meffert, Amelia A. 1938- *St&PR 91*
Meffert, Marcella Ann 1934- *WhoAmW 91*
Meffert, Robert Forster *BioIn 16*
Meffert-Stewart, Sarah 1962- *WhoAmW 91*
Mega, Lesly Tamarin *BiDrAPA 89*
Megabyte *NewAgMG*
Megan, Thomas Ignatius 1913- *WhoAm 90*
Megapolensis, Johannes 1603-1670 *WhNaAH*
Megarbane, Theodore Antoine 1951- *WhoWor 91*
Megargel, Burton Jonathan 1954- *WhoAm 90*
Megarry, Robert 1910- *WhoWor 91*
Megaw, Robert Neill Ellison 1920- *WhoAm 90*
Megdal, Martin L *BiDrAPA 89*
Mege, Antoine *PenDiDA 89*
Megeath, James Gabriel 1824-1906 *AmLegL*
Megged, Aharon 1920- *ConAu 13AS [port]*
Meggers, Betty Jane 1921- *WhoAm 90*
Meggitt, Mervyn John 1924- *WhoAm 90*
Meggs, Margaret L. 1953- *WhoAmW 91*
Meggs, Philip B 1942- *WhoAmA 91*
Meghelli, Fethi M 1945- *WhoAmA 91*
Meghreblian, Robert Vartan 1922- *WhoAm 90*
Megilligan, John Paul, Jr. 1952- *WhoSSW 91*
Meginniss, Donna Sherwood 1956- *WhoSSW 91*
Megler, Joseph G. 1838-1915 *AmLegL*
Megley, Sheila 1938- *WhoAm 90*
Meglin, Nick 1935- *WhoWrEP 89*
Meglino, Josephine 1928- *St&PR 91*
Megna, Diana Tanina 1963- *WhoAmW 91*
Megna, John Cosimo 1927- *St&PR 91*
Megna, Stephanie Lee 1957- *BiDrAPA 89*
Megofna, Christine Gail 1949- *WhoAmW 91*
Megowen, Gretchen Lee 1954- *BiDrAPA 89*
Megown, John William 1931- *WhoAm 90*
Megson, Ann *BiDEWW*
Mehaffey, John Allen *WhoWor 91*
Mehaffey, Joseph H. 1938- *St&PR 91*
Mehaffey, Paul Wilson 1922- *St&PR 91*
Mehaffy, Thomas N. 1932- *WhoAm 90*
Mehaignerie, Pierre 1939- *BiDFrPL*
Mehal, Steven Robert 1964- *WhoSSW 91*
Mehalchin, John Joseph 1937- *WhoWor 91*
Mehalick, Gerald Thomas 1955- *BiDrAPA 89*
Mehall, J. Robert 1942- *St&PR 91*
Mehall, Margaret Elizabeth 1940- *WhoAmW 91*
Mehan, Arun K. 1949- *St&PR 91*
Mehandru, Sushil Kumar 1947- *WhoE 91*
Meharsham 1838-1911? *BioIn 16*
Mehdevi, Anne Sinclair 1947- *AuBYP 90*
Mehdi, Mohammad Taki 1928- *WhoWor 91*
Mehearg, Clifford Wayne 1937- *WhoSSW 91*
Meher Baba 1894-1969 *EncO&P 3*
Mehl, Cathy Ann 1952- *WhoE 91*
Mehl, Ernest 1900-1986 *Ballpl 90*
Mehl, Lawrence Richard 1946- *St&PR 91*
Mehl, Leo *BioIn 16*
Mehl, Robert Carl 1948- *St&PR 91*
Mehl, Robert Franklin 1898-1976 *DcScB S2*
Mehle, Aileen *BioIn 16*
Mehlenbacher, Dohn Harlow 1931- *WhoWor 91*
Mehler, Conrad 1915- *BiDrAPA 89*
Mehler, David 1919- *St&PR 91*
Mehler, Jeffrey 1949- *St&PR 91*
Mehler, Marianne Dortea Szauer 1952- *WhoAmW 91*
Mehlinger, Howard Dean 1931- *WhoAm 90*
Mehlinger-Mitchell, Renee D. 1952- *BiDrAPA 89*
Mehlis, David L. 1943- *St&PR 91*
Mehlman, Edwin Stephen 1935- *WhoE 91*
Mehlman, Julia S *BiDrAPA 89*
Mehlman, Lon Douglas 1959- *WhoWor 91*
Mehlman, Robert David *BiDrAPA 89*
Mehlman, Samuel J. 1922- *St&PR 91*
Mehlman, Steven 1942- *WhoE 91*
Mehn, Jan 1953- *WhoAmA 91*
Mehn, W. Harrison 1918- *WhoAm 90*
Mehne, Paul Randolph 1948- *WhoSSW 91*
Mehne, Richard G, Jr. *BiDrAPA 89*
Mehos, Nancy Asimo 1946- *WhoE 91*
Mehr, Helen Margulies *WhoAmW 91*
Mehr, Lara J. 1958- *WhoEmL 91*
Mehr, Morton H. 1927- *St&PR 91*
Mehr, Robert I. *BioIn 16*
Mehr-on-Nesa *WomWR*
Mehra, Brij Mohan 1937- *St&PR 91*
Mehra, Manjul R *BiDrAPA 89*
Mehra, Rahul Nandan *BiDrAPA 89*
Mehra, Rajnish 1950- *WhoAm 90, WhoE 91*
Mehra, Raman K. 1943- *St&PR 91*
Mehra, Raman Kumar 1943- *WhoAm 90*
Mehra, Ravinder C. 1942- *St&PR 91*
Mehra, Sanjeev K. 1959- *WhoE 91*
Mehrabian, Robert *WhoAm 90, WhoWor 91*
Mehren, George Louis 1913- *WhoAm 90*
Mehren, Stein 1935- *DcScanL*
Mehreteab, Ghebre Selassie 1949- *St&PR 91*
Mehrguth, Terri *ODwPR 91*
Mehrhof, Edward Gates 1932- *BiDrAPA 89*
Mehring, Clinton Warren 1924- *WhoAm 90*
Mehring, Howard William 1931-1978 *WhoAmA 91N*
Mehringer, Barbara Crooks 1943- *St&PR 91*
Mehrjui, Darius *BioIn 16*
Mehrkam, Q. D. 1921- *St&PR 91*
Mehrotra, Pushpa Lata 1940- *BiDrAPA 89*
Mehrtens, Paul H. 1919- *St&PR 91*
Mehrunissa *WomWR*
Mehta, Amolak Ram 1894-1986 *BioIn 16*
Mehta, Anjalj J *BiDrAPA 89*
Mehta, Darshan 1944- *St&PR 91*
Mehta, Dhirendra 1953- *WhoSSW 91*
Mehta, Dinesh B 1939- *BiDrAPA 89*
Mehta, Eileen Rose 1953- *WhoAmW 91*
Mehta, Gita *BioIn 16, FemiCLE*
Mehta, Haresh S 1951- *BiDrAPA 89*
Mehta, Harish C. 1940- *WhoSSW 91*
Mehta, Harshad M 1947- *BiDrAPA 89*
Mehta, Hiten 1956- *St&PR 91*
Mehta, Homi K. 1938- *St&PR 91*
Mehta, Jarava Lal 1912-1988 *BioIn 16*
Mehta, Kirit T. 1943- *St&PR 91*
Mehta, Malti Praful 1949- *BiDrAPA 89*
Mehta, Mehli 1908- *PenDiMP*
Mehta, Mukesh Harilal 1949- *WhoE 91*
Mehta, Muktiraj B *BiDrAPA 89*
Mehta, Narinder Kumar 1938- *St&PR 91, WhoE 91, WhoWor 91*
Mehta, Nilima Nikhil *BiDrAPA 89*

Mehta, Praful C BiDrAPA 89
Mehta, Pratap N 1929- BiDrAPA 89
Mehta, Purnima M 1956- BiDrAPA 89
Mehta, Raghunath Mal 1937- BiDrAPA 89
Mehta, Rahul 1949- WhoSSW 91
Mehta, Ramanlal C. 1918- IntWWM 90
Mehta, Rashmi Navin BiDrAPA 89
Mehta, Shailesh J. 1949- St&PR 91, WhoAm 90
Mehta, Shanti Devi 1908- BioIn 16
Mehta, Shobhana D BiDrAPA 89
Mehta, Surjit 1948- St&PR 91
Mehta, Tuahar J. BiDrAPA 89
Mehta, Varsha B 1958- BiDrAPA 89
Mehta, Ved 1934- BioIn 16, MajTwCW, WhoWrEP 89
Mehta, Vineet 1952- BiDrAPA 89
Mehta, Zubin 1936- IntWWM 90, PenDiMP, WhoAm 90, WhoE 91, WhoWor 91, WorAlBi
Mehtani, Janak K BiDrAPA 89
Mehuron, William Otto 1937- St&PR 91, WhoAm 90
Mei WomWR
Mei, Dolores M. 1955- WhoAmW 91
Mei, Joseph P. C. BioIn 16
Meibach, Judith Karen IntWWM 90
Meiburg, Charles Owen 1931- WhoAm 90
Meidan, Abraham 1949- WhoWor 91
Meider, Elmer Charles, Jr. 1946- St&PR 91, WhoAm 90
Meidlinger, Richard William 1954- WhoSSW 91
Meier, A. Jay, Jr. 1928- St&PR 91
Meier, August 1923- WhoAm 90, WhoWrEP 89
Meier, Barbara Jane 1961- WhoAmW 91
Meier, C A 1905- ConAu 130, EncO&P 3
Meier, Carl Alfred 1905- EncPaPR 91
Meier, Deborah BioIn 16
Meier, Donald M. 1941- St&PR 91
Meier, Edward Kindt 1914- WhoAm 90
Meier, Enge WhoAmW 91
Meier, Everett 1934- St&PR 91
Meier, Frederick Richard 1934- St&PR 91
Meier, Fritz 1912- WhoWor 91
Meier, George Karl, III 1944- WhoAm 90
Meier, Gerald M 1923- ConAu 30NR
Meier, Heinrich 1953- WhoWor 91
Meier, Helen M R 1943- BiDrAPA 89
Meier, Henry George 1929- WhoAm 90
Meier, James F. 1928- St&PR 91
Meier, Jaroslav 1923- IntWWM 90
Meier, Jeannette 1947- St&PR 91
Meier, Johanna 1938- IntWWM 90
Meier, Judy Ann 1943- WhoAmW 91
Meier, Karen Lorene 1942- WhoAmW 91
Meier, Kay 1933- WhoWrEP 89
Meier, Louis Leonard, Jr. 1918- WhoAm 90
Meier, Margaret 1936- IntWWM 90
Meier, Mary Lou 1947- WhoAmW 91
Meier, Matthias Sebastian 1917- WhoAm 90
Meier, Minta 1906- BioIn 16
Meier, Nancy Jo 1951- WhoAmW 91
Meier, Patricia Ann BiDrAPA 89
Meier, Paul Daniel 1945- BiDrAPA 89
Meier, Paul John 1936- WhoAm 90
Meier, Raymond 1957- BioIn 16
Meier, Richard 1934- BioIn 16
Meier, Richard Alan 1934- WhoAm 90, WhoAmA 91
Meier, Richard Louis 1920- WhoAm 90
Meier, Robert Henry, III 1940- WhoAm 90
Meier, Ronald Richard 1932- St&PR 91
Meier, Thomas Keith 1940- WhoAm 90, WhoE 91
Meier, Timothy Eugene 1952- St&PR 91
Meier, Waltraud BioIn 16
Meier, Waltraud 1956- IntWWM 90
Meier, Wilbur Leroy, Jr. 1939- WhoAm 90, WhoSSW 91, WhoWor 91
Meier, William W. 1929- St&PR 91
Meier-Ruge, William Alfred 1930- WhoWor 91
Meiere, Hildreth WhoAmA 91N
Meierer, Robert E. 1943- St&PR 91
Meiergerd, Donald Clement 1941- St&PR 91
Meierhenry, Roy A. 1938- St&PR 91
Meierhenry, Wesley Carl 1915- WhoAm 90
Meiers, David Evan 1947- WhoWor 91
Meiggs, Henry 1811-1877 BioIn 16
Meiggs, Russell 1902-1989 ConAu 129
Meigh, Job PenDiDA 89
Meighen, Karen Gay BiDrAPA 89
Meighen, Maxwell Charles Gordon 1908- St&PR 91
Meigher, S. Christopher, III 1946- St&PR 91, WhoAm 90
Meigs, Cornelia Lynde 1884-1973 AuBYP 90
Meigs, Elizabeth Bleecker 1923- AuBYP 90
Meigs, John Liggett 1916- WhoAmA 91
Meigs, John Wister 1915- WhoE 91
Meigs, Leo O. 1879- AmLegL
Meigs, Mary 1917- ConAu 132
Meigs, Melinda Moore 1953- IntWWM 90
Meigs, Return Jonathan, Jr. 1764-1824 BiDrUSE 89
Meigs, Walter 1918-1988 WhoAmA 91N
Meigs, Walter Berkeley 1912- WhoAm 90
Meigs, Walter R. 1948- St&PR 91
Meigs, Walter Ralph 1948- WhoEmL 91
Meihaus, George Arthur 1918- WhoAm 90
Meihaus, James D. 1942- St&PR 91
Meij, Johan De 1953- IntWWM 90
Meijer, Frederik 1919- WhoAm 90
Meijer, Paul Herman Ernst 1921- WhoAm 90
Meiji, Emperor 1852-1912 EncJap
Meijler, Frits Louis 1925- WhoWor 91
Meijsing, Doeschka 1947- EncCoWW
Meikle, Fred C. 1931- St&PR 91
Meikle, James Robert 1941- St&PR 91
Meikle, Philip G. 1937- WhoAm 90
Meikle, R. James 1936- St&PR 91
Meikle, Steve M. 1923- St&PR 91
Meikle, Thomas Harry, Jr. 1929- WhoAm 90, WhoWor 91
Meiklejohn, David Shirra 1908-1989 BioIn 16
Meiklejohn, Donald 1909- WhoAm 90
Meiklejohn, Mindy June 1929- WhoAmW 91
Meil, Kate 1925- WhoAmW 91
Meilach, Dona Z 1926- WhoWrEP 89
Meilach, Dona Zweigoron 1926- AuBYP 90
Meilach, Germaine C. 1937- WhoAmW 91
Meilan, Celia 1920- St&PR 91
Meiland, Jack W. WhoAm 90
Meiland, Nicolaas Johannes 1938- St&PR 91
Meile, Jeffrey 1961- St&PR 91
Meilgaard, Morten Christian 1928- St&PR 91, WhoAm 90
Meiling, George Robert Lucas 1942- St&PR 91, WhoAm 90
Meiling, Gerald S. 1936- St&PR 91
Meiling, Gerald Stewart 1936- WhoAm 90
Meiller, Joan 1927- BiDrAPA 89
Meillier, Raymond A. 1934- St&PR 91
Meillon, Alfonso 1926- WhoHisp 91
Meilman, Edward 1915- WhoAm 90
Meily, William Davis 1949- WhoEmL 91
Meima, Ralph Chester, Jr. 1927- WhoAm 90
Mein, John Gordon 1913-1968 BioIn 16
Meinardi, Harry 1932- WhoWor 91
Meincke, Jens Eduard 1941- WhoWor 91
Meincke, Peter Paul Max 1936- WhoE 91
Meindl, James Donald 1933- WhoAm 90, WhoE 91
Meine, Heinie 1896-1968 Ballpl 90
Meineke, John P. 1957- St&PR 91
Meineker, Robert L 1922- BiDrAPA 89
Meinel, Marjorie Pettit 1922- WhoAmW 91
Meinelt, Ellen Marie 1956- WhoAmW 91
Meiner, Sue Ellen Thompson 1943- WhoAmW 91
Meinerding, Paul L. 1948- St&PR 91
Meiners, Donald Edwin 1935- St&PR 91
Meiners, Phyllis A. 1940- WhoWor 91
Meinert, John Raymond 1927- St&PR 91, WhoAm 90
Meinhardt, Carolyn Loris 1949- WhoAmW 91
Meinhardt, John Edward 1931- St&PR 91
Meinhardt, Kenneth BiDrAPA 89
Meinhardt, Myron Keith BiDrAPA 89
Meinhardt, Sharon Kay 1951- WhoSSW 91
Meinhardt, Wilhelm August Ernst 1943- WhoWor 91
Meinhardt, William 1939- St&PR 91
Meinhart, Elaine Mary Knaub 1950- WhoAmW 91
Meinhof, Ulrike 1934-1976 BioIn 16
Meinhof, Ulrike Marie 1934-1976 EncCoWW
Meinhold, Gail Arlene 1962- WhoAmW 91
Meinig, Donald William 1924- WhoAm 90
Meininger, John Alexander 1948- WhoEmL 91
Meinke, Alan Kurt 1952- WhoE 91
Meinke, Peter 1932- WhoSSW 91, WhoWrEP 89
Meinke, Roy Walter 1929- WhoAm 90
Meinkema, Hannes 1943- EncCoWW
Meinschein, Warren G. 1920- WhoAm 90
Meinsen, Phyllis Arlene 1944- WhoAmW 91
Meinsen, Raymond J. 1906- St&PR 91
Meinstein, Crystal Ann 1955- WhoWrEP 89
Meinwald, Jerrold 1927- WhoAm 90
Meir, Golda 1898-1978 BioIn 16, PolLCME, WomWR [port], WorAlBi
Meireles, Cecilia 1901-1964 BioIn 16
Meiri, Pamela Joy 1954- BiDrAPA 89
Meirovitch, Leonard 1928- WhoAm 90
Meirowitz, Claire Cecile 1934- WhoAm 90
Meis, Charles H. 1946- St&PR 91
Meis, Nancy Ruth 1952- WhoAmW 91
Meisburg, John Marshall, Jr. 1946- WhoE 91
Meisch, Jean-Jacques 1932- BiDrAPA 89
Meisch, Richard Alden 1943- BiDrAPA 89
Meisel, Alan 1946- WhoAm 90
Meisel, Alan Nathan 1949- BiDrAPA 89
Meisel, Arthur M 1923- BiDrAPA 89
Meisel, Carl R. 1940- St&PR 91
Meisel, Frederick L 1941- BiDrAPA 89
Meisel, Gail Lutz 1944- BiDrAPA 89
Meisel, George Ira 1920- WhoAm 90
Meisel, George Vincent 1933- WhoAm 90
Meisel, Harald Wolfgang 1943- St&PR 91
Meisel, Jerome 1934- WhoAm 90
Meisel, John 1923- WhoAm 90
Meisel, Julius J. 1914- St&PR 91
Meisel, Louis Koenig 1942- WhoAm 90, WhoAmA 91
Meisel, Martin 1931- WhoAm 90
Meisel, Perry 1949- WhoE 91
Meisel, Philip L. 1928- St&PR 91
Meisel, Sidney 1917- St&PR 91
Meiselas, Harold BiDrAPA 89
Meiselas, Karen Debra 1955- BiDrAPA 89
Meiselas, Susan Clay 1948- WhoAm 90
Meiselman, David Israel 1924- WhoAm 90, WhoSSW 91
Meiselman, Marilyn Newmark WhoAmA 91
Meisels, Gerhard George 1931- WhoAm 90
Meisen, Axel 1943- WhoAm 90
Meisen, Walter August 1934- St&PR 91
Meisenheimer, R. E. 1930- St&PR 91
Meisinger, Peter R. 1955- St&PR 91
Meislahn, Harry Post 1938- WhoAm 90
Meislich, Herbert 1920- WhoAm 90
Meislik, Ira 1944- WhoE 91
Meislin, Bernard J. 1927-1988 BioIn 16
Meisner, Dee Dolores Annette 1936- WhoAmW 91, WhoWor 91
Meisner, Joachim 1933- WhoWor 91
Meisner, Lorentz EncO&P 3
Meiss, Leon 1896-1966 BioIn 16
Meiss, Millard 1904-1975 WhoAmA 91N
Meiss, Norma Dugan BiDrAPA 89
Meiss, Richard Dean 1950- WhoEmL 91
Meissner, Edwin Benjamin, Jr. 1918- WhoAm 90
Meissner, Franklin Newton 1933- St&PR 91
Meissner, Harold C. 1917- WhoAm 90
Meissner, Hartwig 1938- WhoWor 91
Meissner, Leo J 1895-1977 WhoAmA 91N
Meissner, Leonard Arthur, Jr. 1950- WhoEmL 91
Meissner, Walther 1882-1974 DcScB S2
Meissner, Werner 1937- WhoWor 91
Meissner, William Joseph 1948- WhoWrEP 89
Meissner, William W 1931- BiDrAPA 89
Meissner, William Walter 1931- WhoAm 90
Meissonnier, Juste-Aurele 1695-1750 PenDiDA 89
Meistas, Mary Therese 1949- WhoAmW 91, WhoE 91, WhoWor 91
Meister, Alton 1922- WhoAm 90
Meister, Bernard John 1941- WhoAm 90
Meister, Charles Walter 1917- WhoAm 90
Meister, Ernest M. 1923- St&PR 91
Meister, John Edward, Jr. 1956- WhoEmL 91
Meister, Mark J 1953- WhoAmA 91
Meister, Mark Jay 1953- WhoAm 90, WhoE 91
Meister, Michael William 1942- WhoAmA 91, WhoE 91
Meister, Richard J. 1938- WhoAm 90
Meister, Shirley Vogler 1936- WhoWrEP 89
Meister, Steven Gerard 1937- WhoAm 90
Meistrich, Sydney 1927- St&PR 91
Meiszer, Nicholas Michael 1934- WhoSSW 91
Meiszner, John Wolfgang BiDrAPA 89
Meites, Louis 1926- WhoAm 90
Meitin, Deborah Dorsky 1951- WhoAmW 91
Meitner, Lise 1878-1968 BioIn 16, WorAlBi
Meitus, Juli Sergeyevich 1903- IntWWM 90
Meitus, Robert Joseph BiDrAPA 89
Meitus, Stephen Hugh 1942- BiDrAPA 89
Meitzen, Manfred Otto 1930- WhoAm 90
Meitzler, Allen Henry 1928- WhoAm 90
Meitzler, Larry Clair 1946- WhoE 91
Meitzler, Neil 1930- WhoAmA 91
Meives, Joseph Richard 1947- WhoEmL 91
Meixell, David Kevin 1955- WhoE 91
Meixner, Josef 1908- WhoWor 91
Meixner, Mary Louise 1916- WhoAmA 91
Meixner, Susan Turnquist BiDrAPA 89
Meizell, Alvin 1932- St&PR 91
Meizner, Paula WhoAmA 91
Mejer, Robert Lee 1944- WhoAmA 91
Mejeur, Gail 1946- St&PR 91
Mejia, Cecilia 1945- WhoWor 91
Mejia, Ignacia WhoHisp 91
Mejia, Joaquin 1951- WhoHisp 91
Mejia, Paul WhoHisp 91
Mejia, Sergio BiDrAPA 89
Mejia Velilla, David 1935- WhoWor 91
Mejias, Roman 1930- Ballpl 90
Mejillano, Milagros P BiDrAPA 89
Mejo, Robert Walter BiDrAPA 89
Mejta, Cheryl Lee 1952- WhoEmL 91
Mekaisto 1830?-1900 DcCanB 12
Mekeel, Edward R., Jr. 1946- St&PR 91
Mekeel, Joyce Haviland 1931- IntWWM 90
Mekeren, Jan van 1690?-1735? PenDiDA 89
Mekler, Adam 1941- WhoAmA 91
Mekler, Arlen B. 1943- WhoAm 90
Mekler, Jerome ODwPR 91
Mekonnen, Abebe BioIn 16
Mel, Howard Charles WhoAm 90
Melachrino, George 1909-1965 OxCPMus, PenDiMP
Melady, John BioIn 16
Melady, Thomas Patrick 1927- WhoAm 90
Melamed, Abraham 1914- WhoAmA 91
Melamed, Arthur Douglas 1945- WhoAm 90
Melamed, Hope WhoAmA 91
Melamed, Leo BioIn 16
Melamed, Leo 1937- WhoAm 90
Melamed, Michael L 1949- BiDrAPA 89
Melamed, Richard 1952- WhoEmL 91
Melamede, Amos 1933- St&PR 91
Melamid, Alexander WhoAmA 91
Melampy, Donald Francis 1932- St&PR 91
Melancia, Carlos 1927- WhoWor 91
Melancon, Robert 1947- BioIn 16
Melancon, Vick J. 1948- St&PR 91
Meland, Bernard Eugene 1899- WhoAm 90
Melander, Harlan Paul, Jr. 1956- WhoSSW 91
Melandri, Pierre Christian 1946- WhoWor 91
Melandri, Pietro PenDiDA 89
Melangton, John Cleveland 1930- St&PR 91
Melani, Betty Lou 1932- WhoAmW 91
Melanie 1947- WorAlBi
Melanson, Anne M. WhoAmW 91
Melanson, James 1946- WhoAm 90
Melanson, Richard Stephen 1953- St&PR 91
Melantzon, Ricardo Aguilar HispWr 90
Melara, Ana Laura Martinez 1936- WhoAmW 91
Melara, Garrett Philip 1945- St&PR 91
Melba, Nellie BioIn 16
Melba, Nellie 1861-1931 PenDiMP, WorAlBi
Melba, Paul T. St&PR 91
Melberg, Gordon Conrad 1926- St&PR 91
Melberg, Jerald Leigh 1948- WhoAmA 91
Melbin, Murray 1927- WhoAm 90
Melbo, Irving Robert 1908- AuBYP 90, WhoAm 90, WhoWor 91
Melbourne, William Lamb, Viscount 1779-1848 BioIn 16
Melby, Alan Kenneth 1948- WhoWor 91
Melby, Claire Arlene 1931- St&PR 91
Melby, David A 1942- WhoAmA 91
Melby, Edward Carlos, Jr. 1929- WhoAm 90
Melby, James Christian 1928- WhoAm 90
Melby, John B. 1941- IntWWM 90
Melby, John F. 1913- BioIn 16
Melby, Orville Erling 1921- WhoAm 90
Melbye, Mikael 1955- IntWWM 90
Melcarth, Edward WhoAmA 91N
Melcher, Betsy Flagg 1900- WhoAmA 91
Melcher, James Russell 1936- WhoAm 90
Melcher, John 1924- WhoAm 90
Melcher, Katherine Jeannette 1946- WhoAmW 91
Melcher, Raymond H., Jr. 1952- WhoAm 90
Melcher, Stephen Alan 1943- St&PR 91, WhoAm 90
Melcher, Trini Urtuzuastegui 1931- WhoAm 90
Melcher, Wilhelm PenDiMP
Melchert, Helmut 1910- IntWWM 90
Melchert, James Frederick 1930- WhoAm 90, WhoAmA 91
Melchin, Uwe Rudolf 1939- WhoWor 91
Melchiode, Gerald A 1941- BiDrAPA 89
Melchionna, John A 1927- BiDrAPA 89
Melchior, Bonnie Lee 1940- WhoSSW 91
Melchior, Ib 1917- BioIn 16, WhoWrEP 89
Melchior, Ib Jorgen 1917- SpyFic

Melchior, Jacklyn Butler 1918- *WhoAmW 91*
Melchior, Johann Peter 1742-1825 *PenDiDA 89*
Melchior, Lauritz 1890-1973 *BioIn 16, PenDiMP, WorAlBi*
Melchior, Richard William 1947- *St&PR 91*
Melchior, Timothy Miller 1940- *WhoE 91*
Melcon, Maria Luz 1946- *EncCoWW*
Melconian, Jerry Ohanes 1934- *WhoE 91*
Melconian, Linda Jean *WhoAmW 91, WhoE 91*
Melczek, Dale J. 1938- *WhoAm 90*
Melczer, Andrew Henry 1954- *WhoEmL 91*
Melczer, Joseph Treuhaft, Jr. 1912- *WhoAm 90*
Meldahl, Edward Neill 1925- *WhoSSW 91*
Meldahl, Roger G. 1931- *St&PR 91*
Meldman, Monte J 1927- *BiDrAPA 89*
Meldman, Robert Edward *WhoAm 90*
Meldola, Raphael 1849-1915 *DcScB S2*
Meldrum, Alan Hayward 1913- *WhoAm 90*
Meldrum, Don C. 1937- *St&PR 91*
Meldrum, James *ConAu 31NR, TwCCr&M 91*
Meldrum, Peter D. 1947- *St&PR 91*
Meldrum, Peter Durkee 1947- *WhoAm 90*
Meldrum, Tamara *BioIn 16*
Mele, Dennis Anthony 1950- *St&PR 91*
Mele, Frank M. 1935- *AuBYP 90*
Mele, Gregg Charles 1965- *WhoE 91*
Mele, Howard S 1927- *BiDrAPA 89*
Mele, John J. *St&PR 91*
Mele, Joseph C. *St&PR 91*
Mele, Juan 1923- *ArtLatA*
Mele, Robert D. *St&PR 91*
Mele, Sam 1923- *Ballpl 90 [port]*
Mele, Sue A. *St&PR 91*
Melear, Talley Murrell 1938- *WhoAmW 91*
Meleis, Afaf Ibrahim 1942- *WhoAm 90*
Melen, Ferit 1906-1988 *BioIn 16*
Melendez, Al, Jr. 1932- *WhoHisp 91*
Melendez, Bill *WhoHisp 91*
Melendez, Concha 1892- *HispWr 90*
Melendez, Conchita *HispWr 90*
Melendez, Gerardo Javier, Sr. 1959- *WhoHisp 91*
Melendez, Joseph R *BiDrAPA 89*
Melendez, Luis 1716-1780 *IntDcAA 90 [port]*
Melendez, Luis 1949- *Ballpl 90*
Melendez, Manuel J. 1942- *WhoHisp 91*
Melendez, Nicholas Efrain 1932- *WhoWor 91*
Melendez, Richard 1954- *WhoHisp 91*
Melendez, Tony *BioIn 16*
Melendrez, Sonny *WhoHisp 91*
Melendy, Earle R. 1927- *IntWWM 90*
Melendy, Howard Brett 1924- *WhoAm 90*
Melendy, Peter S. 1950- *St&PR 91*
Melervey, Arthur Charles 1923- *WhoAm 90*
Meletio, Jack E. 1915- *St&PR 91*
Melezinek, Adolf 1932- *WhoWor 91*
Melfi, Frank C. 1936- *St&PR 91*
Melfi, James Joseph 1928- *St&PR 91*
Melfi, Mary 1951- *ConAu 32NR*
Melfi, William J. 1942- *St&PR 91*
Melgaard, Hans Leland 1940- *St&PR 91*
Melgaard, Maureen Elizabeth 1944- *WhoAmW 91*
Melgar, Julio 1922- *WhoSSW 91*
Melgar, Myriam Del C. *WhoHisp 91*
Melgarejo, Juan Arturo 1957- *WhoWor 91*
Melgarejo, Mariano 1820-1871 *BioIn 16*
Melgarejo, Matilde M. 1958- *WhoWor 91*
Melges, Buddy *ConAu 130*
Melges, David Louis 1943- *St&PR 91*
Melges, Harry C., Jr. 1930- *ConAu 130*
Melhem, D. H. *WhoWrEP 89*
Melhorn, Wilton Newton 1921- *WhoAm 90*
Meli, Anthony P. 1944- *St&PR 91*
Meli, Joseph John 1940- *WhoWor 91*
Meli, Joseph M. 1957- *WhoWor 91*
Meli, Martha Maria 1964- *WhoAmW 91*
Melia, Daniel Frederick 1944- *WhoWor 91*
Melia, James Patrick 1955- *WhoEmL 91*
Melia, Tamara Moser 1955- *WhoAmW 91*
Melican, James Patrick 1940- *St&PR 91*
Melican, James Patrick, Jr. 1940- *WhoAm 90*
Melich, Doris S. 1913- *WhoAmW 91*
Melich, Mitchell 1912- *WhoAm 90, WhoWor 91*
Melichar, Paul Jan *BiDrAPA 89*
Melicher, Ronald William 1941- *WhoAm 90, WhoWor 91*
Melick, Arden Davis 1940- *WhoE 91, WhoWrEP 89*
Melick, Katherine 1924- *WhoAmW 91*
Melickian, Gary Edward 1935- *WhoE 91*
Melidosian, Mark Wm. 1947- *St&PR 91*
Melieste, Gregory William 1947- *BiDrAPA 89*
Melignano, Carmine 1936- *WhoE 91*
Melikian, Mary *WhoAmA 91*
Melillo, Oscar 1899-1963 *Ballpl 90*
Melillo, Robin Marie Bohacs 1961- *WhoEmL 91*
Melin, David Ellis 1926- *St&PR 91*
Melin, Elias 1889-1979 *BioIn 16*
Meline, Jules Felix 1838-1925 *BiDFrPL*
Melingagio, John *ODwPR 91*
Melinno 1--?BC- *EncCoWW*
Melis, Gyorgy 1923- *IntWWM 90*
Melisende *WomWR*
Melish, Diane Carol 1952- *WhoAmW 91*
Melissande *WomWR*
Melissanthe 1910- *EncCoWW*
Melissanthi *EncCoWW*
Melissaropoulos, Nicos 1926- *WhoWor 91*
Melissinos, Adrian Constantin 1929- *WhoAm 90*
Meljon, Alina 1931- *WhoWor 91*
Melkerson, Alan Conrad 1933- *St&PR 91*
Melkus, Eduard 1928- *IntWWM 90, PenDiMP*
Mell, Betty Lou 1935- *WhoWrEP 89*
Mell, Ed 1942- *WhoAmA 91*
Mell, Gertrud Maria 1947- *IntWWM 90*
Mell, John F., Jr. 1932- *St&PR 91*
Mell, Patricia 1953- *WhoEmL 91*
Mella, Arthur John 1937- *WhoE 91*
Mella, Diego L. 1949- *WhoHisp 91*
Mellado, Raymond G. 1948- *WhoHisp 91*
Mellander, Gustavo A. 1935- *WhoHisp 91*
Mellard, Joan McGuire 1933- *WhoSSW 91*
Melleck, Lydia 1950- *IntWWM 90*
Mellecker, John 1934- *WhoE 91*
Mellen, Arthur W., III 1930- *St&PR 91*
Mellen, Arthur William, III 1930- *WhoAm 90*
Mellen, Charles S. 1929- *St&PR 91*
Mellen, Donald Boyd 1939- *St&PR 91*
Mellen, Evelyn A. 1932- *St&PR 91*
Mellen, Kirk A. 1939- *St&PR 91*
Mellen, Timothy J. 1948- *St&PR 91*
Mellencamp, John Cougar *BioIn 16*
Mellencamp, John Cougar 1951- *EncPR&S 89, WhoAm 90, WorAlBi*
Mellendorf, Loren Dale 1925- *St&PR 91, WhoAm 90*
Meller, George Mieczyslaw Jerzy 1935- *WhoE 91*
Meller, Heikki Juhani 1947- *WhoWor 91*
Meller, Julius 1936- *BiDrAPA 89*
Meller, Robert L *BiDrAPA 89*
Meller, William Henry *BiDrAPA 89*
Mellers, Wilfred Howard 1914- *WorAu 1980*
Mellers, Wilfrid Howard 1914- *IntWWM 90*
Mellersh, Jeanie 1936- *IntWWM 90*
Melles, Carl 1926- *IntWWM 90*
Melles, Warren H. 1935- *St&PR 91*
Mellett, Donald Ring 1891-1926 *BioIn 16*
Mellette, Connie Owen *BiDrAPA 89*
Mellette, Henry C *BiDrAPA 89*
Mellette, M. Susan Jackson 1922- *WhoAm 90*
Mellette, R Ramsey, Jr. 1927- *BiDrAPA 89*
Mellevold, George A. 1938- *St&PR 91*
Melley, William Paul 1931- *St&PR 91*
Melli, Marygold Shire 1926- *WhoAmW 91*
Melli, Roberto 1885-1958 *BioIn 16*
Mellin, Gilbert Myer 1915- *St&PR 91*
Mellin, Jeanne 1929- *AuBYP 90*
Mellin, Stephen David 1941- *St&PR 91*
Melling, Antoine Ignace 1763-1831 *BioIn 16*
Melling, O. R. *BioIn 16*
Mellinger, Frederick *BioIn 16, NewYTBS 90*
Mellinger, Frederick 1914?-1990 *News 90*
Mellinger, Peter J. 1957- *St&PR 91*
Mellink, Machteld Johanna 1917- *WhoAm 90*
Mellinkoff, David 1914- *WhoAm 90*
Mellins, Harry Zachary 1921- *WhoAm 90*
Mellins, Robert B. 1928- *WhoAm 90*
Mellis, Allan *BioIn 16*
Mellis, Joel Paul 1934- *St&PR 91, WhoAm 90*
Mellis, Margaret 1914- *BiDWomA*
Mellis, Robert Scott 1940- *St&PR 91*
Mellish, Timothy Charles 1955- *St&PR 91*
Mellizo, Carlos 1942- *ConAu 130, HispWr 90, WhoHisp 91*
Mellman, Lisa Ann *BiDrAPA 89*
Mellman, Martin L. *BioIn 16*
Mellman, Myer W. 1917- *St&PR 91*
Mellman, Thomas Alan 1956- *BiDrAPA 89*
Mellnik, David Carl 1955- *IntWWM 90*
Mello, Fernando Collor de *BioIn 16*
Mello, Milton Thiago de 1916- *WhoWor 91*
Mellon, Andrew 1855-1937 *EncABHB 7 [port]*
Mellon, Andrew W. 1855-1937 *WorAlBi*
Mellon, Andrew William 1855-1937 *BiDrUSE 89, BioIn 16*
Mellon, Annie Fairlamb 1850?-1935? *EncPaPR 91*
Mellon, Charles David *BiDrAPA 89*
Mellon, J. B., Mrs. *EncO&P 3*
Mellon, Joan Ann 1932- *WhoAmW 91*
Mellon, Paul *BioIn 16*
Mellon, Paul 1907- *WhoAm 90, WhoAmA 91, WorAlBi*
Mellon, Robert *BiDrAPA 89*
Mellon, Seward Prosser 1942- *St&PR 91, WhoAm 90*
Mellon, William D. *ODwPR 91*
Mellon, William Larimer 1910-1989 *BioIn 16*
Mellor, Arthur M. 1942- *WhoAm 90*
Mellor, David 1930- *ConDes 90*
Mellor, Gail McGowan 1942- *WhoAmW 91, WhoSSW 91*
Mellor, George Edward 1928-1987 *WhoAmA 91N*
Mellor, George Lincoln 1929- *WhoAm 90*
Mellor, James Robb 1930- *St&PR 91, WhoAm 90*
Mellor, John Anthony 1935- *St&PR 91*
Mellor, Mark Adams 1951- *WhoAmA 91*
Mellor, Michael Lawton 1922- *WhoAm 90*
Mellor, Rob C. 1934- *St&PR 91*
Mellor, Robert E. 1943- *WhoAm 90*
Mellor, Robert Edward 1943- *St&PR 91*
Mellor, Ulana 1952- *WhoAmW 91*
Mellor, William Bancroft 1906- *AuBYP 90*
Mellors, Robert Charles 1916- *WhoAm 90*
Mellors, Samantha *ConAu 30NR*
Mellos, George Evan *BiDrAPA 89*
Mellott, Cloyd Rowe 1923- *WhoAm 90, WhoE 91, WhoWor 91*
Mellott, John D. 1938- *St&PR 91*
Mellott, Karen Elizabeth 1956- *WhoAmW 91*
Mellott, Paul C. 1926- *St&PR 91*
Mellott, Robert H. 1946- *St&PR 91*
Mellott, Robert Vernon 1928- *WhoAm 90, WhoWor 91*
Mellow, Alan Morris 1952- *BiDrAPA 89*
Mellow, James K. 1927- *St&PR 91*
Mellow, James Robert 1926- *WhoAm 90, WhoWrEP 89*
Mellow, Robert James 1942- *WhoAm 90*
Mellsop, Graham Wilfred 1942- *WhoWor 91*
Melly, Diana 1937- *ConAu 130*
Melly, George 1926- *IntWWM 90*
Melman, David A. 1942- *St&PR 91*
Melman, Israel J. 1920- *WhoE 91*
Melman, Kenneth Newport 1953- *BiDrAPA 89*
Melman, Rich *BioIn 16*
Melman, Seymour *WhoAm 90, WhoWrEP 89*
Melmed, Allan S 1946- *BiDrAPA 89*
Melmed, Ronald M 1930- *BiDrAPA 89*
Melmon, Kenneth Lloyd 1934- *WhoAm 90*
Melneck, Michael Theodore, Jr. 1961- *WhoSSW 91*
Melner, Sinclair Lewis 1928- *WhoAm 90*
Melnick, Daniel 1932- *WhoAm 90*
Melnick, Gilbert Stanley 1930- *WhoAm 90*
Melnick, J. A. 1902- *St&PR 91*
Melnick, Joseph L. 1914- *WhoAm 90, WhoSSW 91*
Melnick, Melvin Philip *BiDrAPA 89*
Melnick, Sandy Dean 1951- *BiDrAPA 89*
Melnick, Sharon Kay 1956- *BiDrAPA 89*
Melnik, Robert Edward 1933- *WhoAm 90*
Melnikoff, Meyer 1918- *WhoAm 90*
Melnikoff, Sarah Ann 1936- *WhoAmW 91*
Melnikov, Ivan 1832-1906 *PenDiMP*
Mel'nikov, Konstantin Stepanovich 1890-1974 *BioIn 16*
Melnizky, Walter 1928- *WhoWor 91*
Melny, Richard Alan *BiDrAPA 89*
Melnyk, Andrej *BioIn 16*
Melnyk, George John 1956- *BiDrAPA 89*
Melnyk, Lubomyr Eugene 1948- *IntWWM 90*
Melnykovych, Andrew O. 1952- *WhoAm 90*
Melo, Denise Marie 1955- *WhoAmW 91*
Melo, Roberto J 1943- *BiDrAPA 89*
Melo Neto, Joao Cabral de 1920- *BioIn 16*
Meloan, Taylor Wells 1919- *WhoAm 90*
Melody, Jay *St&PR 91*
Melody, Michael Edward 1943- *WhoAm 90*
Melone, James T. *St&PR 91*
Melone, Joseph James 1931- *St&PR 91, WhoAm 90*
Melone, Nancy Paule 1948- *WhoAmW 91, WhoE 91*
Melone, Nicholas 1917- *St&PR 91*
Meloni, Loretta Florence 1942- *WhoAmW 91, WhoE 91*
Meloon, Robert A. 1928- *WhoWor 91*
Meloon, Walter O. 1915- *St&PR 91*
Melore, Daniel G. 1959- *St&PR 91*
Melort, A. *PenDiDA 89*
Melos Quartet *PenDiMP*
Melosh, Barbara 1950- *ConAu 130*
Melot, Michel 1943- *ConAu 132*
Meloy, Francis Edward 1917-1976 *BioIn 16*
Meloy, Francis John 1946- *WhoE 91*
Meloy, Gisela Mi 1921- *BiDrAPA 89*
Meloy, Linda Dianne 1955- *WhoAmW 91*
Meloy, Thomas James 1949- *WhoE 91*
Melozzo Da Forli 1438-1494 *IntDcAA 90*
Melrose, Kendrick B. 1940- *St&PR 91*
Melrose, Kendrick Bascom 1940- *WhoAm 90*
Melrose, Patricia Ann 1955- *WhoAmW 91*
Melroy, Jane Ruth 1957- *WhoAmW 91*
Melroy, Robert H. 1930- *St&PR 91*
Melsa, James Louis 1938- *WhoAm 90*
Melsheimer, Mel Powell 1939- *St&PR 91, WhoAm 90*
Melson, Bob *BioIn 16*
Melson, Charlene C. 1943- *St&PR 91*
Melson, Joyce King 1938- *WhoSSW 91*
Melson, Stephen John 1943- *BiDrAPA 89*
Melsop, James William 1939- *St&PR 91*
Melter, Robert Alan 1935- *WhoE 91*
Melton, Andrew Joseph, Jr. 1920- *St&PR 91, WhoAm 90, WhoE 91*
Melton, Arthur Burton 1944- *St&PR 91*
Melton, Augustus Allen, Jr. 1942- *WhoAm 90*
Melton, Barry 1947- *WhoEmL 91*
Melton, Bill 1945- *Ballpl 90*
Melton, Catherine Lynn 1958- *WhoAmW 91*
Melton, Charles Estel 1924- *WhoAm 90*
Melton, Cliff 1912-1986 *Ballpl 90*
Melton, David 1934- *AuBYP 90*
Melton, H. Burt 1942- *St&PR 91*
Melton, Howard Eugene 1915- *St&PR 91, WhoSSW 91*
Melton, Howell Webster 1923- *WhoAm 90, WhoSSW 91*
Melton, J Gordon 1942- *EncO&P 3*
Melton, James Frederick, II 1946- *WhoSSW 91*
Melton, John Wesley 1941- *WhoE 91*
Melton, Joseph Carl 1945- *St&PR 91*
Melton, Joy Regina 1960- *WhoSSW 91*
Melton, Karen Dale 1952- *WhoAmW 91*
Melton, Laurie Alison 1964- *WhoWor 91*
Melton, Loyce Nell 1938- *WhoAmW 91*
Melton, Martha A. 1934- *St&PR 91*
Melton, Michael Eric 1958- *WhoSSW 91, WhoWor 91*
Melton, Nancy Jean 1943- *WhoAmW 91*
Melton, Owen B., Jr. 1946- *St&PR 91*
Melton, Richard H. 1935- *WhoWor 91*
Melton, Robert Graham 1954- *WhoE 91*
Melton, Rube 1917-1971 *Ballpl 90*
Melton, Thomas Ronald 1948- *WhoSSW 91*
Melton, Vera Sophia 1922- *WhoAmW 91*
Melton, Wayne Charles 1954- *WhoEmL 91*
Melton, William Couch 1947- *St&PR 91*
Melton-Scott, Mary Meuli 1943- *WhoAmW 91*
Meltsner, Michael Charles 1937- *WhoAm 90*
Meltzer, Allan *BioIn 16*
Meltzer, Allan H. 1928- *WhoAm 90*
Meltzer, Bernard David 1914- *WhoAm 90*
Meltzer, Bernard Nathan 1916- *WhoAm 90*
Meltzer, Bonnie Rosenberg 1943- *WhoAmW 91*
Meltzer, Bruce G. 1948- *St&PR 91*
Meltzer, D. B. 1929- *St&PR 91*
Meltzer, David *BiDrAPA 89*
Meltzer, David 1937- *WhoAm 90, WhoWrEP 89*
Meltzer, David Brian 1929- *WhoAm 90*
Meltzer, Debra Marie 1954- *St&PR 91, WhoAmW 91*
Meltzer, Donald R. 1932- *St&PR 91*
Meltzer, Donald Richard 1932- *WhoAm 90*
Meltzer, E. Alyne 1934- *WhoAmW 91*
Meltzer, Gerald F. *BioIn 16*
Meltzer, Herbert Y 1937- *BiDrAPA 89*
Meltzer, Herbert Yale 1937- *WhoAm 90*
Meltzer, Jack 1921- *WhoAm 90*
Meltzer, Jay H. 1944- *WhoAm 90*
Meltzer, Jay Howard 1944- *St&PR 91*
Meltzer, Kim I. 1956- *St&PR 91*
Meltzer, Larry A. 1959- *ODwPR 91*
Meltzer, Manny 1930- *St&PR 91*
Meltzer, Milton 1915- *AuBYP 90, BioIn 16, WhoAm 90, WhoWrEP 89*
Meltzer, Milton 1923- *BiDrAPA 89*
Meltzer, Morton 1935- *BiDrAPA 89*
Meltzer, Richard Bernard 1943- *WhoE 91*
Meltzer, Zachary 1935- *St&PR 91*
Melucci, Alberto 1943- *WhoWor 91*
Melucci, Richard Charles 1946- *WhoE 91*
Meluch, Rebecca M. 1956- *WhoWrEP 89*
Melvill, Elizabeth *FemiCLE*

Melvill, Elizabeth *BiDEWW*
Melvill-Jones, Geoffrey 1923- *WhoAm 90*
Melville, Alan 1910-1983 *OxCPMus*
Melville, Alan George 1911- *IntWWM 90*
Melville, Arabella 1948- *ConAu 130*
Melville, Clarissa Brayton 1941- *IntWWM 90*
Melville, Donald Burton 1914- *WhoAm 90*
Melville, Donald Robert 1926- *St&PR 91, WhoAm 90*
Melville, Dorothy Bigelow *BioIn 16*
Melville, Enid L 1934- *BiDrAPA 89*
Melville, Grevis Whitaker 1904- *WhoAmA 91*
Melville, Herman 1819-1891 *BioIn 16, NinCLC 29 [port], WorAlBi, WrPh*
Melville, James 1931- *TwCCr&M 91*
Melville, James Thomas 1951- *St&PR 91, WhoAm 90*
Melville, Jean-Pierre 1917-1973 *BioIn 16*
Melville, Jennie *TwCCr&M 91*
Melville, Mary Lou *BiDrAPA 89*
Melville, Robert Seaman 1913- *WhoAm 90, WhoE 91*
Melville, William Gordon 1928- *St&PR 91*
Melville-Ross, Timothy David 1944- *WhoWor 91*
Melvin, Ben Watson, Jr. 1926- *WhoAm 90*
Melvin, Billy Alfred 1929- *WhoAm 90*
Melvin, Bob 1961- *Ballpl 90*
Melvin, Grace Wilson *WhoAmA 91N*
Melvin, Harold *EncPR&S 89*
Melvin, Harold 1939- *DrBlPA 90*
Melvin, Harold, and the Blue Notes *EncPR&S 89*
Melvin, Harry A 1915- *BiDrAPA 89*
Melvin, Jean Allen 1956- *BiDrAPA 89*
Melvin, John Lewis 1935- *WhoAm 90*
Melvin, Johnny Darrell 1950- *WhoSSW 91*
Melvin, Margaret 1927- *WhoAmW 91, WhoSSW 91, WhoWor 91*
Melvin, Norman Cecil 1916- *WhoAm 90*
Melvin, Peter Joseph 1944- *WhoE 91*
Melvin, Ronald McKnight 1927- *WhoAmA 91*
Melvin, Russell Johnston 1925- *St&PR 91, WhoAm 90, WhoWor 91*
Melvin, T. Stephen 1938- *WhoAm 90, WhoE 91, WhoWor 91*
Melvin, Thomas Robert 1932- *St&PR 91*
Melvold, David J. *BioIn 16*
Melzack, Ronald *BioIn 16*
Melzack, Ronald 1929- *WhoAm 90*
Melzer, Dorothy Garrett *WhoWrEP 89*
Melzer, Heinrich 1873- *EncO&P 3*
Melzer, Helene Licht 1924- *WhoE 91*
Melzer, John T.S. 1938- *WhoWrEP 89*
Melzer, Robert Max 1941- *St&PR 91*
Melzer, Thomas C. 1944- *St&PR 91*
Melzer, Wilhelm Friedrich 1941- *WhoWor 91*
Melzer, William George 1934- *St&PR 91*
Membery, Joan Hathaway 1931- *WhoAmW 91*
Memlinc, Hans 1440?-1494 *IntDcAA 90*
Memling, Carl 1918-1969 *AuBYP 90*
Memling, Hans 1430?-1494 *WorAlBi*
Memling, Hans 1440?-1494 *IntDcAA 90*
Memmer, Russell M. 1931- *St&PR 91*
Memmer, Sandra Kaye 1959- *WhoAmW 91*
Memmert, Guenter 1944- *St&PR 91*
Memmi, Albert 1920- *ConAu 32NR*
Memminger, Christopher G. 1803-1888 *EncABHB 6 [port]*
Memolo, Mary Jane 1937- *WhoAmW 91*
Memory, Jasper Durham 1936- *WhoAm 90*
Memphis Slim 1915-1988 *BioIn 16, OxCPMus*
Mempin, Manolo V 1950- *BiDrAPA 89*
Men At Work *EncPR&S 89*
Mena, Benito *BiDrAPA 89*
Mena, Danilo J. 1937- *WhoE 91*
Mena, David L. 1945- *WhoHisp 91*
Mena, Eva Collier 1932- *BiDrAPA 89*
Mena, Felicitas Marty *BiDrAPA 89*
Mena, J. Joe 1940- *St&PR 91*
Mena, Lilia D *BiDrAPA 89*
Mena, Pablo 1931- *BiDrAPA 89*
Mena, Xavier *WhoHisp 91*
Menachem, Arlene Meryl 1952- *WhoE 91*
Menachery, Jose D 1940- *BiDrAPA 89*
Menack, Max 1915- *BiDrAPA 89*
Menagias, Elias Dennis 1949- *WhoE 91*
Menaker, Esther *BioIn 16*
Menaker, Frank H., Jr. 1940- *St&PR 91, WhoAm 90*
Menaker, Howard Bruce 1936- *St&PR 91*
Menaker, J. Thomas 1938- *WhoAm 90*
Menaker, Michael 1934- *WhoAm 90*
Menaker, Shirley Ann Lasch 1935- *WhoAm 90*
Menaldino, Sharon Rose 1951- *WhoAmW 91*
Menander 342BC-292BC *WorAlBi*
Menapace, John J. 1944- *St&PR 91*
Menard, Antoine Pierre 1766-1844 *WhNaAH*
Menard, Charles Walter 1929- *St&PR 91*
Menard, Edith 1919- *WhoE 91*
Menard, George Francis *St&PR 91N*
Menard, Jacques Edouard 1923- *WhoWor 91*
Menard, Louis Jacques 1946- *WhoAm 90*
Menard, Michael Joseph 1948- *WhoE 91*
Menard, Stanley Clayton 1925- *St&PR 91*
Menard-Buteau, Carole 1957- *BiDrAPA 89*
Menasco, Albert S. *BioIn 16*
Menashe, Samuel 1925- *WhoWrEP 89*
Menashe, Solomon D. 1925- *St&PR 91*
Menassa, Maximilien 1930- *BiDrAPA 89*
Menaster, Michael John 1964- *BiDrAPA 89*
Menatonon *WhNaAH*
Menaugh, Steven A. 1955- *ODwPR 91*
Mencer, Charles David 1944- *St&PR 91, WhoAm 90*
Mencer, Glenn Everell 1925- *WhoAm 90*
Mencer, Jetta 1959- *WhoEmL 91*
Mencey, Helen V. L. 1960- *WhoAmW 91*
Mench, John William 1943- *WhoAm 90*
Menchaca, Peggy B. 1938- *St&PR 91*
Menchaca, Peggy Beard 1938- *WhoAm 90*
Menchel, Donald 1932- *WhoAm 90*
Mencher, Bruce Stephan 1935- *WhoAm 90*
Mencher, Melvin 1927- *WhoAm 90*
Mencher, Peter Milton 1946- *BiDrAPA 89, WhoE 91*
Mencher, Robert B 1935- *BiDrAPA 89*
Mencher, Stuart A. 1939- *St&PR 91*
Mencher, Stuart Alan 1939- *WhoE 91*
Menchhofer, Donald L. 1937- *St&PR 91*
Menchin, Robert Stanley 1923- *WhoAm 90*
Menchinger, Steven R. 1959- *St&PR 91*
Mencini, Jack E. 1943- *St&PR 91*
Mencius 371?BC-289?BC *WorAlBi*
Mencken, H. L. 1880-1956 *BioIn 16*
Mencken, H L 1880-1956 *MajTwCW*
Mencken, H. L. 1880-1956 *WorAlBi*
Mencken, Henry Louis 1880-1956 *BioIn 16*
Menconi, Ralph Joseph 1915-1972 *WhoAmA 91N*
Menconi Blakely, Debra Ellen 1959- *WhoSSW 91*
Menczer, Aron 1917-1943 *BioIn 16*
Mende, Robert Graham 1926- *WhoAm 90*
Mendel, Arthur P. *BioIn 16*
Mendel, Gregor 1822-1884 *BioIn 16*
Mendel, Gregor Johann 1822-1884 *WorAlBi*
Mendel, Herbert D. 1922- *St&PR 91*
Mendel, Jerry Marc 1938- *WhoAm 90*
Mendel, Johann Gregor *BioIn 16*
Mendel, Julius G 1931- *BiDrAPA 89*
Mendel, Kurt 1908- *BiDrAPA 89*
Mendel, Perry 1922- *WhoAm 90*
Mendel, Roberta Joan 1935- *WhoWrEP 89*
Mendel, Samuel Leroy *BioIn 16*
Mendel, Stephen Frank 1947- *WhoEmL 91*
Mendel, Verne Edward 1923- *WhoAm 90*
Mendel, Werner Max 1927- *WhoAm 90*
Mendelberg, Hava Eva 1942- *WhoAmW 91*
Mendeleev, Dmitri 1834-1907 *WorAlBi*
Mendell, Allan Emanuel *BiDrAPA 89*
Mendell, David 1909- *BiDrAPA 89*
Mendell, Jeffrey Varyck 1949- *BiDrAPA 89*
Mendell, Oliver M. 1925- *WhoAm 90*
Mendell, Phyllis 1949- *WhoAmW 91*
Mendell, Rosalind Bremmer 1920- *WhoAmW 91*
Mendeloff, Albert Irwin 1918- *WhoAm 90*
Mendelow, Alexander David 1946- *WhoWor 91*
Mendelowitz, Daniel Marcus 1905-1980 *WhoAmA 91N*
Mendels, Dudley N. 1909- *St&PR 91*
Mendels, Joe *BiDrAPA 89*
Mendels, Joseph 1937- *WhoAm 90, WhoE 91*
Mendels, Josepha 1902- *EncCoWW*
Mendels, Kate *BioIn 16*
Mendelsohn, Barry Loeb *BiDrAPA 89*
Mendelsohn, Erich 1887-1953 *BioIn 16*
Mendelsohn, Everett Irwin 1931- *WhoAm 90*
Mendelsohn, Ezra 1940- *ConAu 130*
Mendelsohn, Frederick S 1932- *BiDrAPA 89*
Mendelsohn, Harold 1923- *WhoAm 90, WhoWrEP 89*
Mendelsohn, Harry A 1928- *BiDrAPA 89*
Mendelsohn, Hindley 1920- *St&PR 91*
Mendelsohn, Irwin 1928- *St&PR 91*
Mendelsohn, Irwin E 1931- *BiDrAPA 89*
Mendelsohn, Jack 1918- *WhoAm 90, WhoWrEP 89*
Mendelsohn, Jack Wolf 1934- *WhoE 91*
Mendelsohn, John 1936- *WhoAm 90*
Mendelsohn, John 1949- *WhoAmA 91*
Mendelsohn, King M 1932- *BiDrAPA 89*
Mendelsohn, Paul Alfred *BiDrAPA 89*
Mendelsohn, Robert V. 1946- *St&PR 91*
Mendelsohn, Robert Victor 1946- *WhoAm 90*
Mendelsohn, Roy M 1927- *BiDrAPA 89*
Mendelsohn, Stuart 1952- *WhoSSW 91*
Mendelsohn, Sylvia R 1952- *BiDrAPA 89*
Mendelsohn, Thomas Charles 1944- *St&PR 91*
Mendelson, Alan Charles 1948- *WhoEmL 91*
Mendelson, Alexander 1922- *WhoAm 90*
Mendelson, Charles L. *BioIn 16*
Mendelson, David Dale 1940- *WhoSSW 91*
Mendelson, Edward James 1946- *WhoAm 90*
Mendelson, Elliott 1931- *WhoAm 90, WhoE 91*
Mendelson, George Jay 1945- *WhoE 91*
Mendelson, Haim 1923- *WhoAm 90, WhoAmA 91*
Mendelson, Harold L 1935- *BiDrAPA 89*
Mendelson, Ira Eliot 1952- *St&PR 91*
Mendelson, Irving 1920- *St&PR 91*
Mendelson, Jack H 1929- *BiDrAPA 89*
Mendelson, Kenneth Earl 1950- *WhoEmL 91*
Mendelson, Kenneth Samuel 1933- *WhoAm 90*
Mendelson, Lee M. 1933- *WhoAm 90*
Mendelson, Leonard 1923- *WhoE 91, WhoWor 91*
Mendelson, Linda *BioIn 16*
Mendelson, Max M *BiDrAPA 89*
Mendelson, Michael 1909- *BiDrAPA 89, WhoE 91*
Mendelson, Morris 1922- *WhoE 91*
Mendelson, Myer *BiDrAPA 89*
Mendelson, Myer D 1924- *BiDrAPA 89*
Mendelson, Peter Michael 1942- *St&PR 91*
Mendelson, Richard Donald 1933- *BioIn 16, WhoAm 90, WhoE 91*
Mendelson, Robert 1933- *St&PR 91*
Mendelson, Roger Bruce 1941- *BiDrAPA 89*
Mendelson, Samuel 1937- *St&PR 91*
Mendelson, Sherry Karen 1951- *BiDrAPA 89*
Mendelson, Wallace 1911- *WhoAm 90*
Mendelson, Wallace Brand 1945- *BiDrAPA 89*
Mendelssohn, Fanny Cecile *BioIn 16*
Mendelssohn, Felix *PenDiMP*
Mendelssohn, Felix 1809-1847 *BioIn 16, PenDiMP A, WorAlBi*
Mendelssohn, George H. de *BioIn 16*
Mendelssohn, Moses 1729-1786 *BioIn 16, DcLB 97 [port]*
Mendelssohn-Bartholdy, George H. de *BioIn 16*
Mendelssohn-Bartholdy, Jacob Ludwig F. 1809-1847 *BioIn 16*
Mendelssohn-Veit-Schlegel, Dorothea 1763-1839 *EncCoWW*
Mendenhall, Dorothy Reed 1874-1964 *BioIn 16*
Mendenhall, Jack 1937- *WhoAmA 91*
Mendenhall, Jeff Ralph 1955- *WhoSSW 91*
Mendenhall, John Miles *BiDrAPA 89*
Mendenhall, John Ryan 1928- *St&PR 91, WhoAm 90*
Mendenhall, Robert Vernon 1920- *WhoAm 90*
Mendenhall, Robert W. 1954- *St&PR 91*
Mendenhall, Rodger Eugene 1928- *WhoAm 90*
Mendenhall, Roy Eugene 1942- *WhoSSW 91*
Mendenhall, Terril Ray 1948- *WhoAm 90*
Mendenhall, Thomas C. 1841-1924 *BioIn 16*
Mendenhall, Walter Dunlap 1948- *WhoSSW 91*
Mendenhall, Wilma Rose 1932- *WhoAmW 91*
Mender, Donald Matthew 1949- *BiDrAPA 89*
Mender, Mona Siegler 1926- *WhoAmW 91, WhoE 91, WhoWor 91*
Menderes, Adnan 1899-1961 *PolLCME*
Menders, Claude Emanuel 1944- *WhoE 91*
Mendes, Alix E. 1953- *ODwPR 91*
Mendes, Aristides de Sousa 1885-1954 *BioIn 16*
Mendes, Avelino 1935- *St&PR 91*
Mendes, Barbara 1948- *WhoAmA 91*
Mendes, Chico *BioIn 16*
Mendes, Chico 1944-1988 *AnObit 1988*
Mendes, Jonathan de Sola *BioIn 16*
Mendes, Sergio 1941- *WorAlBi*
Mendes-France, Pierre 1907-1982 *WorAlBi*
Mendes France, Pierre Isaac Isidore 1907-1982 *BiDFrPL*
Mendes Neto, Arthur Teixeira 1952- *WhoWor 91*
Mendez, Albert Orlando 1935- *WhoE 91*
Mendez, Alfred *WhoHisp 91*
Mendez, Aparicio 1904-1988 *BioIn 16*
Mendez, Carlos Jesus 1956- *WhoSSW 91*
Mendez, Celestino Galo 1944- *WhoWor 91*
Mendez, David B. 1960- *WhoHisp 91*
Mendez, Eugenio Fernandez *HispWr 90*
Mendez, Fredeswinda *BiDrAPA 89*
Mendez, Ileana Maria 1952- *WhoAmW 91, WhoHisp 91*
Mendez, Jana Lynn 1944- *WhoAmW 91*
Mendez, Jesus 1951- *WhoHisp 91*
Mendez, Jorge 1922- *WhoWor 91*
Mendez, Jose 1888?-1928 *Ballpl 90*
Mendez, Julio Enrique 1948- *WhoHisp 91*
Mendez, Julio F. 1960- *WhoHisp 91*
Mendez, Larry Wayne 1956- *WhoSSW 91*
Mendez, Leopoldo 1902-1969 *ArtLatA*
Mendez, Maria Araceli *BiDrAPA 89*
Mendez, Mauricio David 1944- *WhoHisp 91*
Mendez, Miguel M. 1930- *BioIn 16*
Mendez, Miguel Morales 1930- *WhoHisp 91*
Mendez, Olga *WhoHisp 91*
Mendez, Olga A. *WhoAmW 91*
Mendez, Pedro *BiDrAPA 89*
Mendez, Rafael *WhoHisp 91*
Mendez, Rafael 1906-1981 *BioIn 16*
Mendez, Raul H. *WhoHisp 91*
Mendez, Salvador A 1920- *BiDrAPA 89*
Mendez, William, Jr. 1948- *WhoEmL 91, WhoHisp 91*
Mendez, Yasmine M. 1960- *WhoHisp 91*
Mendez-Billington, Susana Elena 1956- *WhoAmW 91*
Mendez Cuesta, Concha 1898-1986 *EncCoWW*
Mendez-Edelson, Nelda *BiDrAPA 89*
Mendez M., Miguel 1930- *ConAu 131, HispWr 90*
Mendez-Perez, Maria Elda 1934- *BiDrAPA 89*
Mendez Santiago, Edwin 1954- *WhoHisp 91*
Mendez-Smith, Freda Ann 1939- *WhoHisp 91*
Mendez Urrutia, F. Vinicio 1957- *WhoHisp 91*
Mendia, Enrique *BiDrAPA 89*
Mendicino, Beverly Roth *BiDrAPA 89*
Mendicino, V. Frank 1939- *WhoAm 90*
Mendieta, Ana 1948-1985 *BioIn 16*
Mendieta, Carlos 1873-1960 *BioIn 16*
Mendini, Alessandro *PenDiDA 89*
Mendini, Douglas A. 1953- *WhoWrEP 89*
Mendini, Gaylen A. 1935- *St&PR 91*
Mendiola, Anna Maria G. 1948- *WhoAmW 91*
Mendiola-McLain, Emma Lilia 1956- *WhoHisp 91*
Mendiratta, Madhu 1951- *BiDrAPA 89*
Mendis, Nalaka 1946- *BiDrAPA 89*
Mendius, Patricia Dodd Winter 1924- *WhoAmW 91*
Mendive, Manuel 1944- *ArtLatA*
Mendivil, Fernando Quihuiz 1937- *WhoHisp 91*
Mendizabal, Juan Alvarez y 1790?-1853 *BioIn 16*
Mendizabal, Maritza S. 1941- *WhoHisp 91*
Mendl, Elsie D. *BioAmW*
Mendler, Edward Charles 1926- *WhoAm 90*
Mendler, Richard L. 1931- *St&PR 91*
Mendlewicz, Julien 1942- *BiDrAPA 89*
Mendlovitz, Sharon Dorothy 1951- *WhoSSW 91*
Mendlowitz, Harold 1935- *St&PR 91*
Mendoker, Anne *BioIn 16*
Mendoker, Richard *BioIn 16*
Mendonca, Susan 1950- *BioIn 16*
Mendonsa, Arthur Adonel 1928- *WhoAm 90, WhoSSW 91*
Mendoza, Agapito 1946- *WhoHisp 91*
Mendoza, Al, Jr. 1943- *WhoHisp 91*
Mendoza, Antonio G 1941- *WhoAmA 91*
Mendoza, Arturo 1948- *BiDrAPA 89*
Mendoza, Candelaria C *BiDrAPA 89*
Mendoza, Candelario Jose 1919- *WhoHisp 91*
Mendoza, Carlos *BiDrAPA 89*
Mendoza, Carmen Sia Gomez 1950- *WhoAmW 91*
Mendoza, Carol Rice 1957- *BiDrAPA 89*
Mendoza, Ecce Iei, II 1963- *WhoHisp 91*
Mendoza, Eduardo 1943- *IntvSpW [port]*
Mendoza, Eva 1950- *WhoHisp 91*
Mendoza, Fernando Sanchez 1948- *WhoHisp 91*
Mendoza, George 1934- *AuBYP 90, WhoAm 90, WhoHisp 91*
Mendoza, George 1955- *WhoHisp 91*
Mendoza, Henry C. *WhoHisp 91*
Mendoza, Joann Audilet 1943- *WhoAmW 91*
Mendoza, Juan Dominguez De *EncCRAm*
Mendoza, Julian Nava 1934- *WhoHisp 91*

Mendoza, Leticia Sanchez 1951- *WhoHisp 91*
Mendoza, Lisa 1958- *WhoHisp 91*
Mendoza, Lydia 1916- *BioIn 16, WhoHisp 91*
Mendoza, Mario *BiDrAPA 89*
Mendoza, Mario 1950- *Ballpl 90*
Mendoza, Mario Valentin 1952- *BiDrAPA 89*
Mendoza, Michael Dennis 1944- *WhoHisp 91*
Mendoza, Pablo, Jr. *WhoHisp 91*
Mendoza, Pedro De 1487?-1537 *WorAlBi*
Mendoza, Raul Yambing *BiDrAPA 89*
Mendoza, Roberto G., Jr. 1945- *WhoAm 90*
Mendoza, Sally Patricia 1951- *WhoEmL 91*
Mendoza, Stanley Atran 1940- *WhoAm 90*
Mendoza, Sylvia D. 1954- *WhoHisp 91*
Mendoza-Cordero, Marlene A 1952- *BiDrAPA 89*
Mendoza De Arce, Daniel Leonel 1940- *IntWWM 90*
Mendozza, Joseph B *BiDrAPA 89*
Mendrey, Kathleen Louise 1946- *WhoAmW 91*
Mendrinas, Konstantine 1943- *WhoE 91*
Mendro, Donna C. 1931- *IntWWM 90*
Mendros, Harry George *BiDrAPA 89*
Meneeley, Edward 1927- *WhoAmA 91*
Meneeley, Edward Sterling 1927- *WhoAm 90*
Menefee, Bruce Tandy 1949- *St&PR 91*
Menefee, Jock 1868-1953 *Ballpl 90*
Menefee, Laura S. 1953- *WhoAmW 91*
Menefee, Samuel Pyeatt 1950- *WhoEmL 91, WhoSSW 91, WhoWor 91*
Menegos, James Menelaos 1941- *WhoSSW 91*
Menelaou, Menelaos Costa 1954- *WhoWor 91*
Menell, Norman J. 1931- *St&PR 91*
Menem, Carlos Saul *BioIn 16*
Menem, Carlos Saul 1932- *WhoWor 91*
Menen, Aubrey 1912-1989 *AnObit 1989, BioIn 16*
Menendez, Albert John 1942- *WhoHisp 91*
Menendez, Ana Maria 1970- *WhoHisp 91*
Menendez, Carlos 1938- *St&PR 91, WhoAm 90, WhoHisp 91*
Menendez, Julio Humberto 1942- *St&PR 91*
Menendez, Kenneth Gary 1954- *WhoEmL 91*
Menendez, Manuel, Jr. 1947- *WhoEmL 91, WhoSSW 91*
Menendez, Manuel Gaspar 1935- *WhoAm 90*
Menendez, Michael Joseph 1949- *WhoHisp 91*
Menendez, Robert 1954- *WhoHisp 91*
Menendez, Silvana Y *BiDrAPA 89*
Menendez, Victor 1944- *St&PR 91*
Menendez De Aviles, Pedro 1519-1574 *EncCRAm, WhNaAH*
Menendez Pidal, Ramon 1869-1968 *BioIn 16, HispWr 90*
Menendez y Pelayo, Marcelino 1856-1912 *BioIn 16*
Menes *WorAlBi*
Menes, Pauline H. 1924- *WhoAmW 91*
Meneses, Antonio 1957- *IntWWM 90*
Menetrez, Jean H *BiDrAPA 89*
Menewa 1765?-1865 *WhNaAH*
Meney, George Harlow 1947- *WhoE 91*
Menez, Cesar V *BiDrAPA 89*
Menezes, Maria Vera Z *BiDrAPA 89*
Menezes, Ralph Charles 1946- *BiDrAPA 89*
Meng, John J. 1906-1988 *BioIn 16*
Meng, Paul Chih *BioIn 16, NewYTBS 90*
Meng, Ralph H 1918- *BiDrAPA 89*
Meng-Koehler, Heinrich Otto 1887- *EncO&P 3*
Mengaroni, Ferruccio *PenDiDA 89*
Mengden, Joseph Michael 1924- *St&PR 91, WhoAm 90*
Menge, Dannette Marie 1958- *WhoAmW 91*
Menge, Richard Cramer 1935- *St&PR 91, WhoAm 90*
Mengedoht, Daniel Edward 1932- *WhoSSW 91*
Mengedoht, Lanville Henry *St&PR 91N*
Mengedoht, Lanville Henry 1926- *WhoAm 90*
Mengedoth, Donald Roy 1944- *WhoAm 90*
Mengel, Charles Edmund 1931- *WhoAm 90*
Mengel, Christopher Emile 1952- *WhoEmL 91*
Mengel, Lynn Irene Sheets 1955- *WhoAmW 91*
Mengel, Philip Richard 1944- *WhoE 91*
Mengelberg, Willem 1871-1951 *PenDiMP*
Mengele, Josef *BioIn 16*
Mengeling, William Lloyd 1933- *WhoAm 90*
Menger, Carl 1840-1921 *BioIn 16*
Menger, Joe L. 1947- *St&PR 91*
Menges, Carl Braun 1930- *WhoAm 90*
Menges, Chris *BioIn 16*
Menges, Chris 1940- *WhoAm 90, WhoWor 91*
Menges, Constantine Christopher *BioIn 16*
Mengistu Haile Mariam 1937- *WhoWor 91*
Mengjia, Yu *WhoE 91*
Mengs, Anton Raphael 1728-1779 *IntDcAA 90*
Menguc, M. Pinar 1955- *WhoSSW 91*
Menguy, Marc 1928- *WhoWor 91*
Menguy, Rene 1926- *WhoAm 90*
Menhall, Dalton Winn 1939- *WhoAm 90*
Menhennett, Alan E. 1929- *St&PR 91*
Menhusen, Monty Jay 1948- *WhoEmL 91*
Menichini, Frank A. 1942- *St&PR 91*
Menihan, John Conway 1908- *WhoAm 90, WhoAmA 91*
Menik, Mitchell G. *St&PR 91*
Menin, Lisa Sara 1958- *WhoAmW 91*
Menitoff, Paul Alan 1946- *BiDrAPA 89, WhoE 91*
Menius, Arthur Clayton, III 1955- *WhoSSW 91*
Menius, Arthur Clayton, Jr. 1916- *WhoAm 90*
Menius, Espie Flynn, Jr. 1923- *WhoSSW 91*
Menjou, Adolphe 1890-1963 *WorAlBi*
Menk, Carl William 1921- *St&PR 91, WhoAm 90, WhoE 91*
Menk, Louis W. 1918- *St&PR 91*
Menk, Louis Wilson 1918- *WhoAm 90*
Menk, Robert L. 1922- *St&PR 91*
Menkart, John 1922- *WhoAm 90*
Menke, Allen Carl 1922- *WhoAm 90*
Menke, Andrea G. *ODwPR 91*
Menke, Andrew G. 1944- *St&PR 91*
Menke, Denis 1940- *Ballpl 90*
Menke, James F. 1931- *St&PR 91*
Menke, John Roger 1919- *St&PR 91*
Menke, Kristina Kay 1956- *WhoAmW 91*
Menke, Terri Jean 1956- *WhoE 91*
Menken, Adah Isaacs 1835-1868 *BioAmW, BioIn 16, NotWoAT*
Menken, Adah Isaacs 1839?-1868 *FemiCLE*
Menken, Jane Ava 1939- *WhoAm 90, WhoAmW 91*
Menkes, Aliana Brodmann 1949- *WhoAmW 91*
Menkes, Ernie J. 1926- *St&PR 91*
Menkes, John Hans 1928- *WhoAm 90*
Menkes, Sigmund J 1896-1986 *WhoAmA 91N*
Menkus, Belden 1931- *ConAu 31NR, WhoWrEP 89*
Menna, Christine A. *ODwPR 91*
Mennel, Donald McKisson 1918- *St&PR 91*
Mennella, Mark A. 1950- *St&PR 91*
Mennen, Herbert 1927- *St&PR 91*
Mennen, William G., Jr. 1913- *St&PR 91*
Mennesson, Michel Claude *BiDrAPA 89*
Mennicken, Baldem *PenDiDA 89*
Mennicken, Jan Baldems *PenDiDA 89*
Mennicken, Jan Emens *PenDiDA 89*
Mennicken, Johann *PenDiDA 89*
Mennicken, Leonhard *PenDiDA 89*
Mennicken, Peter *PenDiDA 89*
Mennicken, Wilhelm *PenDiDA 89*
Mennin, Peter 1923-1983 *PenDiMP A*
Menning, Edward Lee 1931- *WhoE 91*
Menninger, Edward J. *ODwPR 91*
Menninger, Edward Joseph 1931- *WhoE 91*
Menninger, Eliza Wright *BiDrAPA 89*
Menninger, John A *BiDrAPA 89*
Menninger, Karl 1893-1990 *ConAu 132, CurBio 90N, MajTwCW, News 91-1*
Menninger, Karl A 1893- *BiDrAPA 89*
Menninger, Karl A. 1893-1990 *BioIn 16, WorAlBi*
Menninger, Karl Augustus 1893-1990 *NewYTBS 90 [port]*
Menninger, Robert G *BiDrAPA 89*
Menninger, Roy W 1926- *BiDrAPA 89*
Menninger, Roy Wright 1926- *WhoAm 90*
Menninger, W Walter 1931- *BiDrAPA 89*
Menninger, William Walter 1931- *WhoAm 90*
Mennini, Louis Alfred 1920- *IntWWM 90*
Mennis, Edmund Addi 1919- *WhoAm 90*
Menocal, Aniceto Garcia 1836-1908 *BioIn 16*
Menocal, Armando M., III *WhoHisp 91*
Menocal, Mario Garcia 1866-1941 *BioIn 16*
Menolascino, Frank J 1930- *BiDrAPA 89*
Menon, Anandavalli *BiDrAPA 89*
Menon, Gopakumar Rabindranath 1953- *WhoSSW 91*
Menon, K. P. S. 1898-1982 *BioIn 16*
Menon, M Sarada 1923- *BiDrAPA 89*
Menon, Mambillikalathil Govind Kumar 1928- *WhoWor 91*
Menon, Mani *WhoAm 90*
Menon, Prasad 1949- *WhoSSW 91*
Menon, Vijaya Bhaskar 1934- *St&PR 91, WhoAm 90*
Menosky, Mike 1894-1983 *Ballpl 90*
Menotti, Gian-Carlo 1911- *AuBYP 90, BioIn 16, IntWWM 90, PenDiMP A, WhoWor 91, WorAlBi*
Menown, Donald E. 1919- *St&PR 91*
Menoyo, Eric Felix 1944- *WhoAm 90*
Mensah, Albert Addo 1959- *WhoSSW 91, WhoWor 91*
Mensator, Johannes *PenDiDA 89*
Menscer, Darrell Vance 1934- *St&PR 91*
Menschel, Richard Lee 1934- *WhoAm 90*
Menschel, Robert Benjamin 1929- *WhoAm 90*
Menscher, Barnet Gary 1940- *WhoSSW 91*
Mense, Allan Tate 1945- *WhoAm 90*
Menses, Jan 1933- *WhoAm 90, WhoAmA 91, WhoWor 91*
Mensinger, John Boothe 1954- *St&PR 91*
Mensinger, Merle 1930- *St&PR 91*
Mensinger, Peggy Boothe 1923- *WhoAm 90*
Mensinger, Robert Michael 1932- *St&PR 91*
Menson, John Lewis, II 1940- *St&PR 91*
Menson, Richard L. 1943- *WhoAm 90*
Mente, Lawrence John 1929- *St&PR 91*
Menter, Martin 1915- *WhoE 91*
Menter, Sophie 1846-1918 *BioIn 16*
Menter, Sophie 1848-1918 *PenDiMP*
Mentewab *WomWR*
Mentha, Gerald 1921- *WhoWor 91*
Menthe, Melissa 1948- *WhoAmA 91*
Menthon, Francois de 1900- *BiDFrPL*
Mentis, Marc Julius *BiDrAPA 89*
Menton, John Dennis 1932- *St&PR 91*
Menton, Seymour 1927- *ConAu 31NR*
Mentula, Perttu 1936- *ConDes 90*
Mentz, Henry Alvan, Jr. 1920- *WhoAm 90, WhoSSW 91*
Mentz, Lawrence 1946- *WhoE 91*
Mentz, Philip Sherwood 1930- *WhoWor 91*
Mentzer, Carl F. 1945- *St&PR 91*
Mentzer, James S. 1911- *St&PR 91*
Mentzer, John Mahlon, Sr. 1938- *St&PR 91*
Mentzer, John Raymond 1916- *WhoAm 90*
Mentzer, Merleen Mae 1920- *WhoAmW 91*
Mentzer, Robert D. *BioIn 16*
Mentzer, Roslyn 1935- *WhoAmW 91*
Mentzer, Susanne 1957- *IntWWM 90*
Mentzer, Terri Lynne 1962- *WhoAmW 91*
Menuck, Morton Norman 1942- *BiDrAPA 89*
Menuhin, Hephzibah 1920-1981 *PenDiMP*
Menuhin, Jeremy 1951- *IntWWM 90, PenDiMP*
Menuhin, Yalta 1921- *IntWWM 90*
Menuhin, Yaltah 1922- *PenDiMP*
Menuhin, Yehudi 1916- *IntWWM 90, PenDiMP, WhoWor 91, WorAlBi*
Menut, D. Charles 1933- *WhoSSW 91*
Menvielle, Edgardo Jorge 1955- *BiDrAPA 89*
Menville, Douglas 1935- *SmATA 64*
Menyhart, Laszlo 1949- *WhoWor 91*
Menyuk, Paula 1929- *WhoAm 90*
Menz, Craig Alan 1951- *St&PR 91*
Menze, Clemens 1928- *WhoWor 91*
Menzel, Adolph von 1815-1905 *IntDcAA 90*
Menzel, Barbara J 1946- *SmATA 63*
Menzel, Charles Henry 1945- *BiDrAPA 89*
Menzel, Dieter Klaus 1935- *WhoWor 91*
Menzel, Dietrich Hans Lorenz 1935- *WhoWor 91*
Menzel, Jiri *BioIn 16*
Menzel, Pat *BioIn 16*
Menzer, John B. 1951- *St&PR 91*
Menzer, John Bruce 1951- *WhoAm 90*
Menzer, Kim *NewAgMG*
Menzer, Robert Everett 1938- *WhoAm 90, WhoSSW 91*
Menzer-Benaron, Doris *BiDrAPA 89*
Menzie, Donald E. 1922- *WhoAm 90, WhoWrEP 89*
Menzies, Ian Stuart 1920- *WhoAm 90*
Menzies, James Peter 1948- *St&PR 91*
Menzies, Paul T *BiDrAPA 89*
Menzies, Thomas Neal 1945- *WhoEmL 91, WhoWor 91*
Meola, Ralph Anthony, Jr. 1922- *St&PR 91*
Meola, Tony *BioIn 16*
Meola-LiBrizzi, RoseMarie M. *WhoAmW 91*
Meoli, Frank D. *St&PR 91*
Meoli, George 1936- *St&PR 91*
Meoli, Luco F. 1920- *St&PR 91*
Meoli, Rudi 1951- *Ballpl 90*
Meotti, Michael Patrick 1953- *WhoE 91*
Meouchy, Samir A. 1950- *St&PR 91*
Mepham, Derek John Amoore 1954- *WhoWor 91*
Meradith, Dianne Elaine *BiDrAPA 89*
Merahn, Roger N. *ODwPR 91*
Merai, Prakash 1955- *BiDrAPA 89*
Merali, Pandju 1929- *WhoSSW 91*
Meran, Harry Bruce 1948- *WhoEmL 91*
Merani, Peter Pritam Tarachand 1933- *WhoE 91*
Merante, Joseph A. 1941- *WhoAm 90*
Meranus, Arthur R. 1934- *St&PR 91*
Meranus, Arthur Richard 1934- *WhoAm 90*
Meras, Phyllis Leslie 1931- *WhoAm 90, WhoAmW 91, WhoE 91*
Merayo, Huberto Esteban 1951- *BiDrAPA 89*
Mercadante, Saverio 1795-1870 *PenDiMP A*
Mercader, Trina 1919- *EncCoWW*
Mercado, Aurelio 1948- *WhoSSW 91*
Mercado, Carlos 1949- *WhoHisp 91*
Mercado, Edward 1937- *WhoAm 90, WhoHisp 91*
Mercado, Joseph Zacarias 1948- *WhoEmL 91*
Mercado, Medwin Ariano 1949- *WhoWor 91*
Mercado, Orlando 1961- *Ballpl 90*
Mercado, Peter Nelson 1947- *WhoEmL 91, WhoWor 91*
Mercado, Rogaciano *BioIn 16*
Mercado, Roger 1967- *WhoHisp 91*
Mercado-Almodovar, Juan Antonio 1929- *WhoSSW 91*
Mercaldo, Daniel 1939- *WhoE 91*
Mercandino, Sharon Ann 1963- *WhoAmW 91*
Mercardante, Patrick Christopher 1945- *WhoSSW 91*
Mercator, Gerardus 1512-1594 *WorAlBi*
Merced, Nelson 1948- *WhoHisp 91*
Merced, Orlando Luis 1966- *WhoHisp 91*
Merced, Victor 1956- *WhoHisp 91*
Merced-Reyes, Josue 1950- *WhoHisp 91*
Mercer, Alexander John *BiDrAPA 89*
Mercer, Allan Martin 1929- *St&PR 91*
Mercer, Betty Deborah 1926- *WhoAmW 91*
Mercer, Cathie Linn 1952- *WhoWrEP 89*
Mercer, Charles 1917- *WhoWrEP 89*
Mercer, Charles 1917-1988 *SmATA 61*
Mercer, Charles E. 1917-1988 *BioIn 16*
Mercer, Charles Edward 1917- *AuBYP 90*
Mercer, Charles Fenton 1778-1858 *BioIn 16*
Mercer, David 1928-1980 *MajTwCW*
Mercer, Derrik 1944- *ConAu 130*
Mercer, Dorothy L. *WhoSSW 91*
Mercer, Douglas 1918- *WhoAm 90*
Mercer, E. Wayne 1940- *St&PR 91*
Mercer, Edwin Wayne 1940- *WhoAm 90*
Mercer, Elwyn Jarvis 1911- *WhoAm 90*
Mercer, Ethel Viola 1947- *WhoWrEP 89*
Mercer, Frank Woodward 1953- *WhoEmL 91*
Mercer, George *BioIn 16*
Mercer, Greg Ernest 1966- *WhoSSW 91*
Mercer, Gregory Scott 1956- *WhoSSW 91*
Mercer, H. Dwight 1939- *WhoAm 90*
Mercer, Henry Chapman 1856-1930 *BioIn 16, PenDiDA 89*
Mercer, Hugh 1725?-1777 *EncCRAm*
Mercer, James L 1936- *ConAu 30NR*
Mercer, Jesse 1769-1841 *BioIn 16*
Mercer, Jessie *AuBYP 90*
Mercer, Jo 1936- *St&PR 91*
Mercer, John Boyd 1939- *WhoWor 91*
Mercer, John Francis 1759-1821 *BioIn 16*
Mercer, John Moore 1952- *WhoSSW 91*
Mercer, Johnny 1909-1976 *BioIn 16, OxCPMus, WorAlBi*
Mercer, June Greer 1953- *WhoAmW 91*
Mercer, Laura 1959- *ODwPR 91*
Mercer, Lee William 1943- *WhoAm 90*
Mercer, Leonard Preston, II 1941- *WhoAm 90*
Mercer, Linda Lou 1945- *WhoWrEP 89*
Mercer, Mabel 1900-1984 *BioAmW, DrBlPA 90, OxCPMus*
Mercer, Mae *DrBlPA 90*
Mercer, Marian 1935- *WorAlBi*
Mercer, Martyn Clarke, Jr. 1934- *St&PR 91*
Mercer, Mary E 1911- *BiDrAPA 89*
Mercer, Melvin Ray 1946- *WhoEmL 91, WhoSSW 91, WhoWor 91*
Mercer, Michael Wayne 1947- *St&PR 91*
Mercer, Rae Irene 1936- *St&PR 91*
Mercer, Raymond Teegardin 1951- *WhoSSW 91*
Mercer, Richard Joseph 1924- *WhoAm 90*
Mercer, Robert, Jr. *WhoSSW 91*
Mercer, Robert Edward 1924- *St&PR 91*
Mercer, Ruth Seinkiewicz- *BioIn 16*
Mercer, Sid *Ballpl 90*

Mercer, Wayne C *BiDrAPA 89*
Mercer, William Edgar 1941- *St&PR 91*
Mercer, William Edward, II 1956- *WhoSSW 91, WhoWor 91*
Mercer, Win 1874-1903 *Ballpl 90*
Mercer, Zonda 1943- *BiDrAPA 89*
Merchand, Hernando 1942- *WhoHisp 91*
Merchant, Carl William, II 1949- *WhoAm 90*
Merchant, David M. 1937- *St&PR 91*
Merchant, Donald Joseph 1921- *WhoAm 90*
Merchant, Donna Rae 1948- *WhoAmW 91*
Merchant, Edward P. 1953- *St&PR 91*
Merchant, Ismail *BioIn 16*
Merchant, Ismail Noormohamed 1936- *WhoWor 91*
Merchant, Linda Jean Moreno 1955- *BiDrAPA 89*
Merchant, Mylon Eugene 1913- *WhoAm 90*
Merchant, Natalie *BioIn 16*
Merchant, Paul *MajTwCW*
Merchant, Roland Samuel, Sr. 1929- *WhoAm 90, WhoWor 91*
Merchant, Ward J. *St&PR 91*
Mercieca, Charles 1933- *WhoSSW 91*
Mercier, Adrian G. 1931- *St&PR 91*
Mercier, Cheryl Grady 1945- *WhoAmW 91*
Mercier, Denis 1934- *St&PR 91*
Mercier, E. Burton 1927- *St&PR 91*
Mercier, Ernest 1878-1955 *BiDFrPL*
Mercier, Ernest C. 1933- *St&PR 91*
Mercier, Francois 1923- *WhoAm 90*
Mercier, Honore 1840-1894 *DcCanB 12*
Mercier, Jacques Louis 1933- *WhoWor 91*
Mercier, Jean Robert 1918- *WhoWor 91*
Mercier, Jeannette Lorraine 1957- *WhoAmW 91*
Mercier, Marie *EncCoWW*
Mercier, Philippe Jean 1948- *WhoWor 91*
Mercier, Raymond G 1940- *BiDrAPA 89*
Mercier, Ronald H. 1947- *St&PR 91*
Mercier, Tyler Reed 1957- *WhoSSW 91*
Mercier, Vivian 1919-1989 *AnObit 1989, BioIn 16, ConAu 130*
Mercier-Gouin, Yvette 1895-1984 *OxCCanT*
Mercier-Nizet, Marie *EncCoWW*
Merck, Albert W. 1920- *St&PR 91*
Merck, Thomas Charles *BiDrAPA 89*
Mercke, Charles D. 1907- *St&PR 91*
Merckx, Eddy 1945- *BioIn 16*
Mercoeur, Elisa 1809-1835 *EncCoWW*
Mercolino, Veronica Florence *WhoAmA 91*
Mercorella, Anthony Joseph 1927- *WhoAm 90*
Mercorelli, Eugene 1947- *St&PR 91*
Mercoun, Dawn Denise 1950- *WhoAmW 91, WhoE 91*
Mercouri, Melina *BioIn 16*
Mercouri, Melina 1925- *WhoWor 91, WorAlBi*
Mercure, Gilbert Thomas 1934- *St&PR 91*
Mercure, Gilles 1926- *WhoAm 90*
Mercurio, Antonio Marco 1930- *WhoWor 91*
Mercurio, C. W. 1940- *St&PR 91*
Mercurio, Frank 1912- *BiDrAPA 89*
Mercurio, Laura Deubler 1953- *WhoE 91*
Mercurio, Nancy Anne 1953- *WhoAmW 91*
Mercurio, Peter Amedeo 1913- *IntWWM 90*
Mercurio, Renard Michael 1947- *WhoAm 90*
Mercuro, Tobia G. 1933- *St&PR 91*
Merdek, Andrew Austin 1950- *WhoEmL 91*
Merdinger, Charles John 1918- *WhoAm 90*
Merdinger, Susan 1943- *WhoAmW 91, WhoWor 91*
Mere, Manuel H. 1945- *St&PR 91*
Mereau, Sophie 1770-1806 *EncCoWW*
Meredith, Anne *TwCCr&M 91*
Meredith, Burgess 1908- *WorAlBi*
Meredith, Burgess 1909- *WhoAm 90*
Meredith, Catherine Cirillo 1942- *WhoAmW 91*
Meredith, Dale Dean 1940- *WhoAm 90*
Meredith, David Robert 1940- *WhoAm 90*
Meredith, David William *AuBYP 90*
Meredith, Don 1938- *WorAlBi*
Meredith, Dorothy Laverne 1906-1986 *WhoAmA 91N*
Meredith, Edmund Allen 1817-1899 *DcCanB 12*
Meredith, Edwin Thomas 1876-1928 *BiDrUSE 89*
Meredith, Edwin Thomas, III 1933- *St&PR 91, WhoAm 90*
Meredith, Ellis Edson 1927- *WhoAm 90, WhoWor 91*
Meredith, Frank H. 1953- *IntWWM 90*
Meredith, Gary E. 1934- *St&PR 91*
Meredith, George 1828-1909 *BioIn 16, WorAlBi*
Meredith, George 1923- *ODwPR 91, WhoAm 90, WhoE 91*
Meredith, George Davis 1940- *WhoAm 90*
Meredith, Gertrude 1777-1828 *FemiCLE*
Meredith, Gwen 1907- *FemiCLE*
Meredith, Isabel 1875-1960 *FemiCLE*
Meredith, J Stephen 1937- *BiDrAPA 89*
Meredith, James *BioIn 16*
Meredith, James H. 1914-1988 *BioIn 16*
Meredith, John 1933- *WhoAmA 91*
Meredith, John Lee, Jr. 1932- *WhoE 91*
Meredith, John Wylie 1943- *St&PR 91*
Meredith, Lewis Douglas 1905- *WhoAm 90*
Meredith, Louisa Anne 1812-1895 *FemiCLE*
Meredith, Marilyn 1933- *WhoWrEP 89*
Meredith, Morley 1933- *IntWWM 90*
Meredith, Morris *WhoWrEP 89*
Meredith, Nevin W. 1935- *St&PR 91*
Meredith, Nicolete 1896- *AuBYP 90*
Meredith, Orsell Montgomery 1923- *WhoE 91*
Meredith, Owen Nichols 1924- *WhoSSW 91*
Meredith, Pamela Louise 1956- *WhoE 91*
Meredith, Ronald Edward 1946- *WhoAm 90, WhoSSW 91*
Meredith, Scott 1923- *WhoWrEP 89*
Meredith, Spencer B., Jr. 1931- *St&PR 91*
Meredith, Ted Jordan 1950- *WhoWrEP 89*
Meredith, Thomas C. *WhoAm 90, WhoSSW 91*
Meredith, William 1919- *WhoWrEP 89*
Meredith, William Morris 1799-1873 *BiDrUSE 89*
Merel, Richard Wayne 1945- *BiDrAPA 89*
Merenbloom, Paul Elliot 1956- *BiDrAPA 89*
Merenbloom, Robert Barry 1947- *WhoE 91, WhoSSW 91, WhoWor 91*
Merenda, Basil Louis, Jr. 1957- *WhoE 91*
Merenkov, Kimberly E *BiDrAPA 89*
Merenyi, Ferenc 1923- *WhoWor 91*
Meresman, Leila *ODwPR 91*
Meretta, James Leonard 1941- *St&PR 91*
Merewether, David Evan 1936- *WhoWor 91*
Merewether, Torksey Ann 1936- *WhoAmW 91*
Merfeld, Gerald Lydon 1936- *WhoAmA 91*
Mergen, Francois 1925-1989 *BioIn 16*
Mergen, Joseph Michael 1916- *WhoAm 90*
Mergen, Steven J. 1958- *WhoEmL 91*
Mergener, John C *BiDrAPA 89*
Mergener, Peter, and Michael Weisser *NewAgMG*
Mergens, Thomas Robert 1963- *WhoSSW 91*
Mergenthaler, Ottmar *BioIn 16*
Mergenthaler, Ottmar 1854-1899 *WorAlBi*
Mergentime, Charles E. 1931- *St&PR 91*
Mergentime, Charles Eric 1931- *WhoAm 90*
Mergler, H. Kent 1940- *WhoAm 90*
Mergler, Harry Winston 1924- *WhoAm 90*
Mergler, Neil R. 1948- *St&PR 91*
Mergler, Susan Ashby 1963- *WhoAmW 91*
Mergler, William P. *ODwPR 91*
Mergner, Hans Konrad 1917- *WhoWor 91*
Merguerian, Anna 1955- *St&PR 91*
Merguerian, Barbara Joyce *WhoE 91*
Merhige, Phyllis *BioIn 16*
Merhige, Robert R., Jr. *BioIn 16*
Merhige, Robert Reynold, Jr. 1919- *WhoAm 90, WhoSSW 91*
Merholtz, William R. 1948- *St&PR 91*
Meri, Veijo 1928- *DcScanL*
Meriam, James Lathrop 1917- *WhoAm 90*
Merian, Maria Sibylla 1647-1717 *BioIn 16*
Meric, Rene Pierre, Jr. 1925- *St&PR 91*
Merici, Angela 1470?-1540 *EncCoWW*
Mericourt, Theroigne de 1762-1817 *EncCoWW*
Merida, Carlos 1891-1984 *ArtLatA*
Merida, Frederick A 1936- *WhoAmA 91*
Merideth, Charles H 1939- *BiDrAPA 89*
Meridith, Denise Patricia 1952- *WhoEmL 91*
Merigan, Thomas Charles, Jr. 1934- *WhoAm 90*
Merighi, Giorgio 1939- *IntWWM 90*
Merijanian, Jeanette Lewis 1932- *WhoAmW 91, WhoSSW 91*
Merikangas, James Ray 1939- *BiDrAPA 89*
Merilainen, Usko 1930- *IntWWM 90*
Merilan, Charles Preston 1926- *WhoAm 90, WhoWor 91*
Merilan, Michael Preston 1956- *WhoEmL 91*
Merillat, Jeffery Stephen 1951- *St&PR 91*
Meriluoto, Aila 1924- *DcScanL, EncCoWW*
Merimee, Prosper 1803-1870 *ShSCr 7 [port], WorAlBi*
Merimee, Thomas Joseph 1931- *WhoAm 90*
Merims, Arthur M. 1930- *ODwPR 91*
Merin, Andrew Jeffrey 1948- *St&PR 91*
Merin, Moshe 1906-1943 *BioIn 16*
Merino, Francisco F 1910- *BiDrAPA 89*
Merino, Gustavo Gutierrez *ConAu 130, HispWr 90*
Merino Castro, Jose Toribio 1915- *WhoWor 91*
Merion, Richard Donald 1936- *WhoE 91*
Merisalo, Carl B. 1924- *WhoWor 91*
Meritens, Hortense Allart de 1807-1879 *EncCoWW*
Meritt, Lucy Taxis Shoe 1906- *WhoSSW 91*
Meritt, Paul Bruce 1945- *St&PR 91*
Merivale, John *NewYTBS 90*
Merivale, John 1917-1990 *BioIn 16*
Merivale, John Herman 1779-1844 *DcLB 96 [port]*
Meriwether, Charles Minor 1911- *WhoAm 90*
Meriwether, David 1800-1893 *AmLegL*
Meriwether, Elizabeth 1824-1917 *FemiCLE*
Meriwether, Heath J. 1944- *St&PR 91, WhoAm 90*
Meriwether, James A. 1806-1852 *AmLegL*
Meriwether, James Babcock 1928- *WhoAm 90, WhoWrEP 89*
Meriwether, John Samuel, Jr. 1949- *St&PR 91*
Meriwether, John W. *St&PR 91, WhoAm 90*
Meriwether, Louise 1923- *BioIn 16*
Meriwether, Nell W. 1931- *WhoWrEP 89*
Merizalde, Bernardo A *BiDrAPA 89*
Merjanian, Antipas 1916- *BiDrAPA 89*
Merkel, Alfred William 1929- *St&PR 91*
Merkel, Jayne 1942- *WhoAmA 91*
Merkel, Joelen Kilbas 1951- *St&PR 91*
Merkel, Judi Kay 1946- *WhoAmW 91*
Merkel, Neal 1942- *WhoAm 90*
Merkel, Pete 1933- *St&PR 91*
Merkel, Richard L, Jr. *BiDrAPA 89*
Merkel, Roland Peter 1954- *WhoEmL 91*
Merkel-Hart, Angeline Mary 1960- *WhoAmW 91*
Merkelo, Henri 1939- *WhoAm 90*
Merken, Lucretia Wilhelmina van 1721-1789 *EncCoWW*
Merker, Amy Tobin *BiDrAPA 89*
Merker, Frank F *BiDrAPA 89*
Merker, Frank Ferdinand 1909- *WhoAm 90*
Merkes, Edward Peter 1929- *WhoAm 90*
Merkin, A. Barry 1935- *St&PR 91*
Merkin, Daphne *BioIn 16*
Merkin, Michael Edward 1954- *WhoSSW 91*
Merkin, Michael Nutes 1940- *BiDrAPA 89*
Merkin, Richard Marshall 1938- *WhoAmA 91*
Merkin, William Charles 1938- *St&PR 91*
Merkin, William Leslie 1929- *WhoAm 90*
Merkl, Neil Matthew 1931- *WhoAm 90*
Merkle, Fred 1888-1956 *Ballpl 90 [port], BioIn 16*
Merkle, Helen Louise 1950- *WhoAmW 91*
Merkle, Sharon Ann 1946- *WhoAmW 91*
Merklein, Helmut A. 1935- *WhoAm 90*
Merklein, Helmut Martin 1940- *WhoWor 91*
Merklin, David V. 1942- *St&PR 91*
Merklin, Lewis 1938- *WhoE 91*
Merklin, Lewis, Jr. *BiDrAPA 89*
Merkling, Frank 1924- *WhoAm 90, WhoWrEP 89*
Merks, Nicolaas Antonius 1945- *St&PR 91*
Merle, H. Etienne 1944- *WhoE 91*
Merli, Alessandro 1956- *WhoWor 91*
Merlin, Arthur *MajTwCW*
Merlin, James 1906- *WhoSSW 91*
Merlin, Keith Stone 1957- *WhoE 91*
Merlin, Peter Helmuth 1928- *WhoAm 90*
Merlini, The Great *TwCCr&M 91*
Merlini, Giovanni 1929- *WhoWor 91*
Merlino, Andres *WhoWor 91*
Merlino, Anthony Frank 1930- *WhoE 91*
Merlino, Joseph P. *BiDrAPA 89*
Merlino, Massimo 1940- *WhoWor 91*
Merlis, George 1940- *WhoAm 90*
Merlis, Sidney 1925- *BiDrAPA 89*
Merliss, William Sidney 1922- *WhoSSW 91, WhoWor 91*
Merlo, Harry A. 1925- *St&PR 91*
Merlo, Harry Angelo 1925- *WhoAm 90*
Merlo, Larry J. 1955- *St&PR 91*
Merlo, Pier Antonio 1935- *WhoWor 91*
Merlotti, Frank Henry 1926- *St&PR 91, WhoAm 90*
Merlotti, Mark Louis 1956- *WhoEmL 91*
Merman, Ethel *ConAu 129*
Merman, Ethel 1908?-1984 *BioIn 16*
Merman, Ethel 1909-1984 *NotWoAT, OxCPMus, WorAlBi*
Mermaz, Louis 1931- *BiDFrPL*
Mermel, Thaddeus Walter 1907- *WhoAm 90*
Mermelstein, Ann Adams 1961- *WhoAmW 91*
Mermelstein, Hindi T *BiDrAPA 89*
Mermelstein, Isabel Mae Rosenberg 1934- *WhoAmW 91*
Mermelstein, Jules Joshua 1955- *WhoEmL 91*
Mermelstein, Paula 1947- *WhoAm 90*
Mermer, Ira 1924- *WhoE 91*
Mermin, Dorothy Milman 1936- *WhoAm 90*
Mermin, Mildred *WhoAmA 91N*
Mermin, N. David 1935- *WhoAm 90*
Mermin, Rob *BioIn 16*
MernaLyn *WhoAmW 91, WhoE 91*
Mernan, David W. 1928- *St&PR 91*
Mernin, George P 1935- *BiDrAPA 89*
Mernit, Susan 1953- *WhoE 91, WhoWrEP 89*
Mernitz, Joan Moore 1935- *St&PR 91*
Merola, John Joseph 1945- *St&PR 91*
Merola, Mario *BioIn 16*
Merola, Mario 1931- *WhoAmA 91*
Merola, Vincent A. 1938- *St&PR 91*
Merolla, Carmine Ralph 1931- *WhoAm 90*
Merolla, Michele Edward 1940- *WhoE 91*
Merolli, Roy H. 1943- *WhoE 91*
Meron, Nathan David 1933- *WhoWor 91*
Meron, Theodor 1930- *WhoAm 90, WhoE 91*
Meroney, Fern Allen 1921- *WhoAm 90*
Meroney, James Perry 1938- *St&PR 91*
Meroni, Paul Damian 1956- *St&PR 91*
Merow, James F. 1932- *WhoAm 90*
Merow, John Edward 1929- *WhoE 91*
Merowitz, Martin 1940- *BiDrAPA 89*
Merrell, Arnold B. 1937- *St&PR 91*
Merrell, Arthur Nelson 1943- *BiDrAPA 89*
Merrell, James Lee 1930- *St&PR 91, WhoAm 90, WhoWrEP 89*
Merrell, Robert Donald 1933- *St&PR 91*
Merrell, Stanley Wilson 1929- *WhoAm 90*
Merrell, William John, Jr. 1943- *WhoAm 90*
Merrell-Wolf, Franklin 1887?- *EncO&P 3*
Merrheim, Alphonse Adolphe 1871-1925 *BiDFrPL*
Merriam, Eve *WhoAm 90*
Merriam, Eve 1916- *AuBYP 90, BioIn 16, WhoWrEP 89*
Merriam, John LaFaette 1825-1895 *AmLegL*
Merriam, Joseph P. 1911- *St&PR 91*
Merriam, Layton Carl 1934- *St&PR 91*
Merriam, Mary-Linda Sorber 1943- *WhoAm 90, WhoAmW 91, WhoE 91*
Merriam, Richard E. *BioIn 16*
Merriam, Robert Loring 1924- *WhoWrEP 89*
Merriam, William Rush 1849-1931 *AmLegL*
Merrick, Arthur P. 1947- *ODwPR 91*
Merrick, Carol *BioIn 16*
Merrick, David 1912- *WhoE 91, WorAlBi*
Merrick, Frank 1886-1981 *PenDiMP*
Merrick, George Boesch 1928- *WhoAm 90*
Merrick, George Jeffrey 1949- *St&PR 91*
Merrick, Glenn Warren 1954- *WhoEmL 91*
Merrick, Gordon 1916-1988 *BioIn 16*
Merrick, J. Harold 1899-1989 *BioIn 16*
Merrick, James Kirk 1905-1985 *WhoAmA 91N*
Merrick, Lew 1953- *WhoEmL 91*
Merrick, Linda C. 1948- *ODwPR 91*
Merrick, Max Milton 1907- *St&PR 91*
Merrick, R. S. 1914- *St&PR 91*
Merrick, Ronald Caswell 1951- *WhoSSW 91*
Merrick, Roswell Davenport 1922- *WhoAm 90*
Merrick, Thomas William 1939- *WhoAm 90*
Merrick-Mack, Jean Ann 1953- *WhoAmW 91*
Merridew, Reginald P. 1916- *WhoAm 90*
Merrier, Helen 1932- *WhoWor 91*
Merrifield, Donald Paul 1928- *WhoAm 90*
Merrifield, Dudley Bruce 1921- *WhoAm 90*
Merrifield, Gail *WhoE 91*
Merrifield, Heyoehkah *BioIn 16*
Merrifield, John F 1935- *BiDrAPA 89*
Merrifield, John Hastings 1847-1906 *AmLegL*
Merrifield, Lewis Biehl, III 1939- *WhoAm 90*
Merrifield, R. Bruce 1921- *WorAlBi*
Merrifield, Robert Bruce 1921- *WhoAm 90, WhoE 91, WhoWor 91*
Merrigan, Eugene T. 1933- *St&PR 91*
Merrigan, Mary Ellen 1951- *WhoEmL 91*
Merril, Judith 1923- *FemiCLE, MajTwCW, RGTwCSF*
Merrill, Ambrose Pond, Jr. 1909- *WhoAm 90*

Merrill, Arthur Alexander 1906- *WhoAm 90*
Merrill, Augustus Lee 1946- *WhoWrEP 89*
Merrill, Bob 1921- *OxCPMus*
Merrill, Carl 1944- *WhoAm 90, WhoE 91*
Merrill, Carol Roberta 1948- *WhoE 91*
Merrill, Celia Dale 1951- *WhoAmW 91*
Merrill, Charles E. 1885-1956 *EncABHB 7 [port], WorAlBi*
Merrill, Charles F. 1933- *St&PR 91*
Merrill, Charles Merton 1907- *WhoAm 90*
Merrill, Charles Washington 1869-1956 *BioIn 16*
Merrill, Christopher 1957- *ConAu 130*
Merrill, Connie Rae 1947- *WhoAmW 91*
Merrill, Cynthia Ruth 1926- *IntWWM 90*
Merrill, Dale Marie 1954- *WhoAmW 91, WhoE 91, WhoEmL 91*
Merrill, David Kenneth 1935- *WhoAmA 91*
Merrill, Dina 1925- *ConTFT 8 [port]*
Merrill, Durwood 1938- *Ballpl 90*
Merrill, Edward Clifton, Jr. 1920- *WhoAm 90*
Merrill, Evan 1931- *St&PR 91*
Merrill, Evangeline Johnson 1897-1990 *NewYTBS 90 [port]*
Merrill, F Bruce 1927- *BiDrAPA 89*
Merrill, Frank Harrison 1953- *WhoEmL 91*
Merrill, Frank J. 1920- *St&PR 91*
Merrill, Gary 1915-1990 *BioIn 16, ConAu 131, NewYTBS 90 [port], WorAlBi*
Merrill, George *BioIn 16*
Merrill, George G *BiDrAPA 89*
Merrill, George Grenville 1909- *WhoWrEP 89*
Merrill, George Vanderneth 1947- *WhoE 91, WhoEmL 91, WhoWor 91*
Merrill, George W 1837- *AmLegL*
Merrill, Hardy Fairbanks 1943- *St&PR 91*
Merrill, Harvie Martin 1921- *WhoAm 90*
Merrill, Irma Waddell 1960- *WhoAmW 91*
Merrill, James 1926- *MajTwCW, WhoWrEP 89*
Merrill, James Allen 1925- *WhoAm 90*
Merrill, James Campbell, Jr. 1917- *St&PR 91*
Merrill, James Mercer 1920- *WhoAm 90*
Merrill, Jean Fairbanks 1923- *AuBYP 90, WhoAm 90*
Merrill, Joan Carolyn 1941- *WhoWrEP 89*
Merrill, John Calhoun 1924- *WhoAm 90*
Merrill, John Putnam, Jr. 1944- *St&PR 91*
Merrill, Joseph Hartwell 1903- *WhoAm 90*
Merrill, Judith Allyn 1944- *WhoAmW 91*
Merrill, Kenneth Coleman 1930- *St&PR 91, WhoAm 90*
Merrill, Leland Gilbert, Jr. 1920- *WhoAm 90, WhoE 91*
Merrill, Lindsey 1925- *WhoAm 90*
Merrill, Lynne Bartlett 1953- *WhoAmW 91*
Merrill, Mimi 1926- *WhoWrEP 89*
Merrill, Newton Phelps Stokes 1939- *St&PR 91, WhoAm 90*
Merrill, P. J. *TwCCr&M 91*
Merrill, Peter Gray 1952- *WhoE 91*
Merrill, Peter Ross 1954- *WhoE 91*
Merrill, Philip 1934- *St&PR 91*
Merrill, Richard Austin 1937- *WhoAm 90*
Merrill, Richard Glen 1931- *St&PR 91, WhoAm 90*
Merrill, Richard James 1931- *WhoAm 90*
Merrill, Richard T. 1928- *St&PR 91*
Merrill, Richard Thomas 1928- *WhoAm 90, WhoWor 91*
Merrill, Robert 1917- *PenDiMP*
Merrill, Robert 1919- *IntWWM 90, WhoAm 90, WorAlBi*
Merrill, Ronald Thomas 1938- *WhoAm 90*
Merrill, Ross M 1943- *WhoAmA 91*
Merrill, Roy Dewitt 1933- *St&PR 91*
Merrill, Sharon Fitzpatrick *ODwPR 91*
Merrill, Sharon Fitzpatrick 1948- *WhoE 91*
Merrill, Stephen Alan 1941- *BiDrAPA 89*
Merrill, Susan Lee 1942- *WhoWrEP 89*
Merrill, Teryl Toevs 1949- *WhoAmW 91*
Merrill, Thomas Selfridge 1940- *WhoWor 91*
Merrill, Thomas Wendell 1949- *WhoEmL 91*
Merrill, Tom *WhoWrEP 89*
Merrill, Vincent Nichols 1912- *WhoAm 90*
Merrill, Wendy Jane 1961- *WhoAmW 91, WhoE 91*
Merrill, Whitney 1943- *St&PR 91*
Merrill, William Dean 1915- *WhoAm 90*
Merrill, William Dickey 1909- *WhoAm 90*
Merrill, William H., Jr. 1942- *WhoAm 90, WhoWor 91*
Merrills, Roy *WhoAm 90*
Merriman, Alex *MajTwCW*
Merriman, Ilah Coffee 1935- *WhoAmW 91, WhoSSW 91*
Merriman, Jack Childs 1922- *WhoAm 90*
Merriman, James M. 1928- *St&PR 91*
Merriman, Joe Jack 1926- *WhoAm 90*
Merriman, Leslie E. 1926- *St&PR 91*
Merriman, Lloyd 1924- *Ballpl 90*
Merriman, Margarita Leonor 1927- *IntWWM 90*
Merriman, Michael L. 1957- *St&PR 91*
Merriman, Nan 1920- *IntWWM 90*
Merriman, Paul A. 1943- *St&PR 91*
Merriman, Paul Joseph 1948- *WhoSSW 91*
Merriman-Clarke, Kristin Dey 1963- *WhoAmW 91*
Merrin, Edward H 1928- *WhoAmA 91*
Merrin, Edward Louis 1946- *BiDrAPA 89*
Merrin, Seymour 1931- *WhoAm 90*
Merring, Robert Alan 1951- *WhoEmL 91*
Merrion, James Michael 1944- *WhoAm 90*
Merrison, Alec 1924-1989 *AnObit 1989*
Merriss, Philip Ramsay, Jr. 1948- *WhoE 91*
Merrithew, Gerald S. 1931- *WhoE 91*
Merritt, Abraham 1882-1943 *BioIn 16*
Merritt, Allen Charles 1945- *St&PR 91*
Merritt, Anna 1844-1930 *BiDWomA*
Merritt, Benjamin Dean 1899-1989 *BioIn 16*
Merritt, Brenda Tritschler 1963- *WhoAmW 91*
Merritt, Charles W. 1915- *St&PR 91*
Merritt, Chris *BioIn 16*
Merritt, Chris 1952- *IntWWM 90*
Merritt, David Donovan 1953- *WhoSSW 91*
Merritt, Doris Honig 1923- *WhoAm 90*
Merritt, E B *ConAu 30NR*
Merritt, Edward G. 1902- *St&PR 91*
Merritt, Evelyn Caroline 1932- *WhoAm 90*
Merritt, Francis Sumner 1913- *WhoAmA 91*
Merritt, Gilbert Stroud 1936- *WhoAm 90, WhoSSW 91*
Merritt, Harold Kenneth, Jr. 1950- *WhoE 91*
Merritt, Harry Whiting 1952- *WhoSSW 91*
Merritt, Haywood, Jr. 1928- *St&PR 91*
Merritt, Henry Neyron, Sr. 1919- *WhoSSW 91*
Merritt, Howard Sutermeister 1915- *WhoAm 90*
Merritt, Jack Neil 1930- *WhoAm 90*
Merritt, James Edward 1938- *WhoAm 90*
Merritt, Jean 1952- *WhoE 91*
Merritt, Jim 1943- *Ballpl 90*
Merritt, John C. 1940- *WhoAm 90*
Merritt, Joshua Levering, Jr. 1931- *WhoAm 90*
Merritt, Julie Alyson 1963- *WhoAmW 91*
Merritt, LaVere Barrus 1936- *WhoAm 90*
Merritt, Lynn Garnard 1930- *WhoAm 90*
Merritt, Marytherese 1933- *WhoSSW 91*
Merritt, Pamela Kay 1951- *WhoAmW 91*
Merritt, Patricia Anne 1945- *WhoAmW 91*
Merritt, Paul Eugene 1920- *WhoAm 90*
Merritt, Paul J. 1925- *St&PR 91*
Merritt, Ralph L. 1941- *St&PR 91*
Merritt, Richard Lawrence 1933- *WhoAm 90*
Merritt, Robert Edward 1941- *WhoAm 90*
Merritt, Roger 1934- *St&PR 91*
Merritt, Ronald Maurice 1938- *WhoAm 90*
Merritt, Shirley Ann 1936- *WhoAmW 91*
Merritt, Shirley Gay *BiDrAPA 89*
Merritt, Stanley S. 1929- *WhoAm 90*
Merritt, Susan Mary 1946- *WhoAmW 91*
Merritt, Tammy Lynn 1961- *WhoAmW 91*
Merritt, Theresa 1922- *ConTFT 8, DrBlPA 90*
Merritt, Thomas B 1934- *BiDrAPA 89*
Merritt, Thomas Butler 1939- *WhoAm 90*
Merritt, Thomas Carey 1953- *BiDrAPA 89*
Merritt, Virginia Emily *BiDrAPA 89*
Merritt, Walter Davis, Jr. 1936- *WhoAm 90*
Merritt, Wesley 1834-1910 *WhNaAH*
Merritt, William 1939- *St&PR 91*
Merritt, William Alfred, Jr. 1936- *WhoAm 90*
Merritt, William E. 1945- *ConAu 132*
Merritt, Winifred Ann 1953- *BiDrAPA 89*
Merritt, Zenith Samuel 1927- *St&PR 91*
Merritts, Glenn P. 1945- *St&PR 91*
Merriweather-Brown, Ondria 1952- *WhoAmW 91*
Merriwether, Duncan 1903- *WhoWor 91*
Merron, Jules Leonard 1928- *WhoAm 90, WhoE 91*
Merrow, Adin R 1923- *BiDrAPA 89*
Merry Macs, The *OxCPMus*
Merry, Ann Brunton 1769-1808 *BioIn 16*
Merry, Anne Brunton 1769-1808 *NotWoAT*
Merry, Eugene Webster 1912- *St&PR 91*
Merry, Jean Louise Wagner 1949- *WhoEmL 91*
Merry, Marilyn Diana Hoover 1946- *WhoAmW 91, WhoE 91, WhoWor 91*
Merry, Pierce, Jr. 1924- *St&PR 91*
Merry, William E *BiDrAPA 89*
Merry, William Lawrence 1842-1911 *BioIn 16*
Merryman, Emory Hughes 1946- *St&PR 91*
Merryman, Holt Wallace 1927- *St&PR 91*
Merryman, John Henry 1920- *WhoAm 90*
Merryman, Walker 1948- *ODwPR 91*
Mersand, Steve N. 1949- *St&PR 91*
Mersel, Marjorie Kathryn Pedersen 1923- *WhoWor 91*
Merser, Francis Gerard 1930- *St&PR 91, WhoAm 90*
Mersereau, Bertram S 1928- *BiDrAPA 89*
Mersereau, Hiram Stipe 1917- *WhoAm 90*
Mersereau, Joanna Hayes 1928- *WhoAmW 91*
Mersereau, John, Jr. 1925- *WhoAm 90*
Mersereau, Russell Manning 1946- *WhoAm 90*
Mershon, James Harry 1950- *WhoSSW 91*
Mershon, Kathryn M. 1942- *St&PR 91*
Mershon, Ronald B *BiDrAPA 89*
Mershon, Steven Richard *BiDrAPA 89*
Mersiovsky, Billy Ray 1939- *WhoSSW 91*
Merskey, Harold 1929- *BiDrAPA 89*
Merskey-Zeger, Marie Gertrude Fine 1914- *WhoAmW 91*
Mersky, Howard W. *St&PR 91*
Mersky, Roy Martin 1925- *WhoAm 90*
Merson, Billy 1881-1947 *OxCPMus*
Merson, Michael Howard 1945- *WhoWor 91*
Merta, Paul James 1939- *WhoWor 91*
Merta De Velehrad, Jan 1944- *WhoWor 91*
Mertano, Sinikka 1940- *WhoWor 91*
Merte, Herman, Jr. 1929- *WhoAm 90*
Merten, Alan Gilbert 1941- *WhoAm 90*
Merten, Harold A. 1927- *St&PR 91*
Merten, Harold Adams, III 1952- *St&PR 91*
Mertens, David Gerhard 1960- *WhoSSW 91*
Mertens, Hans Eberhard 1949- *WhoE 91*
Mertens, Jane Ursula *BiDrAPA 89*
Mertens, Joan R. 1946- *WhoAm 90*
Mertens, MaryJo Ann *WhoAmW 91*
Mertens, Thomas Robert 1930- *WhoAm 90*
Mertens-Fonck, Paule Anne-Marie 1925- *WhoWor 91*
Mertensotto, Wallace H. 1933- *St&PR 91*
Mertes, Kate 1955- *ConAu 129*
Mertes, Louis H. 1938- *WhoAm 90*
Mertes, Sam 1872-1945 *Ballpl 90*
Mertes, Wayne M. 1936- *St&PR 91*
Mertin, Roger 1942- *WhoAm 90, WhoAmA 91*
Merting, John Webster 1943- *WhoSSW 91*
Mertins, Esther Nicolene 1904- *WhoAmW 91*
Mertins, Marilee Eloise Joeckel Crawley 1942- *IntWWM 90*
Mertl, Duane G. 1945- *St&PR 91*
Mertol, Atila 1953- *WhoEmL 91*
Merton, Louis Thomas 1915-1968 *BioIn 16*
Merton, Robert Cox 1944- *WhoAm 90*
Merton, Robert K 1910- *ConAu 31NR, WhoAm 90, WhoWrEP 89*
Merton, Robert King 1910- *BioIn 16*
Merton, Thomas *LiHiK*
Merton, Thomas 1915-1968 *BioIn 16, MajTwCW, WrPh*
Mertz, Allegra Knapp *BioIn 16*
Mertz, Audrey W 1928- *BiDrAPA 89*
Mertz, Barbara 1927- *BioIn 16*
Mertz, Barbara G. *TwCCr&M 91*
Mertz, Dolores Mary 1928- *WhoAmW 91*
Mertz, Don A. 1926- *St&PR 91*
Mertz, Edgar Theodore 1927- *St&PR 91, WhoAm 90*
Mertz, Edward H. 1937- *St&PR 91*
Mertz, Edwin Theodore 1909- *WhoAm 90*
Mertz, Fred J. 1938- *St&PR 91*
Mertz, Janet Elaine 1949- *WhoAmW 91*
Mertz, Janet S. 1950- *WhoEmL 91*
Mertz, Keith Dale 1953- *WhoE 91*
Mertz, Martin F. 1925- *St&PR 91*
Mertz, Orville R. 1918- *St&PR 91*
Mertz, Stuart Moulton 1915- *WhoAm 90*
Mertz, Walter 1923- *WhoAm 90*
Meruelo, Alex 1962- *WhoHisp 91*
Merullo, Lennie 1917- *Ballpl 90*
Mervielle, Edgardo Jorge 1955- *WhoHisp 91*
Mervis, James Randy 1953- *BiDrAPA 89*
Merwin, Betty Moreland 1914- *St&PR 91*
Merwin, Charles Lewis 1912- *WhoAm 90*
Merwin, Davis Underwood 1928- *WhoAm 90*
Merwin, Jack Clifford 1925- *WhoAm 90*
Merwin, John *BioIn 16*
Merwin, John David 1921- *BioIn 16, WhoAm 90, WhoWor 91*
Merwin, Robert Freeman 1913- *St&PR 91, WhoAm 90*
Merwin, Sam, Jr. 1910- *ConAu 131*
Merwin, Susan L 1950- *BiDrAPA 89*
Merwin, W. S. 1927- *BioIn 16*
Merwin, W S 1927- *MajTwCW*
Merwin, William Charles 1939- *WhoAm 90*
Merwin, William Stanley 1927- *BioIn 16*
Mery, Hubert Beuve- 1902-1989 *BioIn 16*
Mery, Jean 1930- *WhoWor 91*
Meryet-Nit *WomWR*
Meryman, Hope *WhoAmA 91N*
Meryon, Charles 1821-1868 *BioIn 16*
Merz, Albert Joseph *BioIn 16*
Merz, Albert Joseph, Jr. *St&PR 91N*
Merz, Charles 1893-1977 *WorAlBi*
Merz, Edward John 1932- *St&PR 91*
Merz, J. Frederick, Jr. *St&PR 91*
Merz, Josef *PenDiMP*
Merz, Louis Robert 1939- *St&PR 91*
Merz, Richard Alan 1948- *WhoE 91*
Merz, Rollande 1941- *WhoWrEP 89*
Merz, Stuart Oscar Harold 1930- *WhoAm 90*
Merzbacher, Eugen 1921- *WhoAm 90*
Merzkirch, Wolfgang F. 1935- *WhoWor 91*
Mesa, Gonzalo 1939- *BiDrAPA 89*
Mesa, Reynaldo Rene 1959- *WhoHisp 91*
Mesa-Bains, Amalia *WhoAmA 91*
Mesa-Lago, Carmelo 1934- *WhoAm 90, WhoHisp 91*
Mescavage, Alexander Anthony, Jr. 1946- *WhoSSW 91*
Meschan, Isadore 1914- *WhoAm 90*
Mescher, Larry Charles 1947- *WhoSSW 91*
Meschery, Ann *BioIn 16*
Mesches, Arnold 1923- *WhoAmA 91*
Meschke, Debra JoAnn 1952- *WhoAmW 91, WhoSSW 91*
Meschke, Herbert Leonard 1928- *WhoAm 90*
Mesco, Richard Harold T *BiDrAPA 89*
Mesec, Donald F *BiDrAPA 89*
Mesec, Donald Francis 1936- *WhoWor 91*
Mesecher, William Dale 1937- *St&PR 91*
Meseck, Holger 1952- *WhoWor 91*
Mesel, Robert Richard 1936- *St&PR 91*
Meselson, Matthew Stanley 1930- *WhoAm 90*
Mesenbrink, Craig Edward 1962- *WhoSSW 91*
Meserole, Clinton V., III 1943- *St&PR 91*
Meserve, Robert William 1909- *WhoAm 90*
Meserve, Walter Joseph 1923- *WhoAm 90, WhoE 91*
Mesghali, Farid 1952- *WhoEmL 91*
Mesh, Alan Michael 1950- *WhoSSW 91*
Meshbesher, Ronald I. 1933- *BioIn 16*
Meshcherskaya, Ekaterina 1904- *BioIn 16*
Meshibovsky, Alexander 1949- *IntWWM 90*
Meshorer, Edward 1911- *BiDrAPA 89*
Meshowski, Frank Robert 1930- *WhoE 91*
Mesibov, Hugh 1916- *WhoAmA 91, WhoE 91*
Mesic, Michael 1948- *WhoAm 90*
Mesick, Susan *ODwPR 91*
Mesirov, Leon Isaac 1912- *WhoAm 90*
Mesker, David Warren 1931- *St&PR 91*
Meskill, Thomas J. 1928- *WhoAm 90*
Meskill, Victor Peter 1935- *WhoAm 90, WhoE 91*
Meskin, Mort 1916- *EncACom*
Meslin, Philippe Luc Marie 1947- *WhoWor 91*
Meslow, Douglas Bredesen 1959- *WhoEmL 91*
Mesmer, Franz Anton 1733-1815 *EncO&P 3, NewAgE 90*
Mesmer, Franz Anton 1734-1815 *WorAlBi*
Mesmer, Roger 1932- *BiDrAPA 89*
Mesner, Steve 1918-1981 *Ballpl 90*
Mesney, Dorothy Taylor 1916- *WhoAmW 91*
Mesnick, Wendy A. 1962- *WhoAmW 91*
Mesnikoff, Alvin Murray 1925- *BiDrAPA 89, WhoAm 90*
Mesnooh, Christopher Joseph 1958- *WhoWor 91*
Mesple, Mady 1931- *IntWWM 90, PenDiMP*
Mesrobian, Arpena Sachaklian *WhoAm 90, WhoAmW 91*
Mess, George Jo 1898-1962 *WhoAmA 91N*
Mess, Gordon Benjamin 1900-1959 *WhoAmA 91N*
Mess, Suzanne 1928- *OxCCanT*
Messager, Andre *PenDiMP*
Messager, Andre 1853-1929 *OxCPMus, PenDiMP A*
Messam, Leroy Anthony 1923- *WhoE 91*
Messana, Thomas M. 1958- *WhoE 91*

Messano, Edward Anthony 1936- St&PR 91
Messeguer, Villoro Benito 1930-1982 WhoAmA 91N
Messelt, Eric Spencer 1956- WhoEmL 91
Messemer, Glenn Matthew 1947- WhoAm 90
Messemer, Sigrid Vignonne 1940- WhoSSW 91
Messenbaugh, Hildegard W 1940- BiDrAPA 89
Messenger, Charles 1941- BioIn 16
Messenger, Charles 1942- ConAu 31NR
Messenger, Christian K 1943- ConAu 132
Messenger, George Clement 1930- WhoAm 90
Messenger, George Louis 1932- St&PR 91
Messenger, Phyllis Mauch 1950- ConAu 132
Messenger, Thomas 1938- IntWWM 90
Messenheimer, Myron Gifford BiDrAPA 89
Messenkopf, Eugene John 1928- WhoAm 90
Messer, Donald Edward 1941- WhoAm 90
Messer, Edythe Barbara 1941- WhoAmW 91
Messer, James BioIn 16
Messer, James 1934- St&PR 91
Messer, Janice Grabowski 1939- WhoAmW 91
Messer, Kenny L. 1949- St&PR 91
Messer, Michael Maurice BiDrAPA 89
Messer, Mona TwCCr&M 91
Messer, Phillip Lee 1927- St&PR 91
Messer, Richard E. 1938- WhoWrEP 89
Messer, Thomas M. 1920- BioIn 16, WhoAmA 91
Messer, Thomas Maria 1920- WhoAm 90, WhoWor 91
Messer-Rehak, Dabney Lee 1951- WhoAmW 91
Messerli, Douglas 1947- WhoWrEP 89
Messerli, Franz Hannes 1942- WhoAm 90
Messerli, Jonathan Carl 1926- WhoAm 90
Messerschmitt, David Gavin 1945- WhoAm 90
Messerschmitt, John Carl 1922- St&PR 91
Messerschmitt, Norma Florine 1928- WhoAmW 91
Messerschmitt, Wilhelm 1898-1978 WorAlBi
Messersmith, Andy 1945- Ballpl 90
Messersmith, Fred Lawrence 1924- WhoAmA 91
Messersmith, George S. 1883-1960 BioIn 16
Messersmith, Harry Lee 1958- WhoAmA 91
Messersmith, Lanny Dee 1942- WhoWor 91
Messervy, Thomas Walker 1941- BiDrAPA 89
Messiaen, Olivier 1908- IntWWM 90, PenDiMP A, WhoWor 91
Messick, Ben 1901- WhoAmA 91N
Messick, Bill W. 1947- St&PR 91
Messick, Burton L. 1948- St&PR 91
Messick, Dale EncACom
Messick, Dale 1906- BioIn 16, SmATA 64 [port], WhoAmA 91
Messick, Joseph W., Jr. 1939- St&PR 91
Messick, Wiley Sanders 1929- WhoSSW 91
Messier, Charles Joseph 1730-1817 WorAlBi
Messier, David Charles 1946- WhoE 91
Messier, Mark BioIn 16
Messier, Mark 1961- WhoAm 90
Messier, Pierre 1945- WhoAm 90
Messin, Frank E. 1932- St&PR 91
Messin, Marlene Ann 1935- St&PR 91, WhoAmW 91
Messina, Antoinette Josephine 1932- WhoAmW 91
Messina, Charles Francis 1943- St&PR 91
Messina, Dana E. 1956- St&PR 91
Messina, James Vincent 1957- St&PR 91
Messina, Jim BioIn 16
Messina, Jim 1947- WorAlBi
Messina, JoAnn Lorraine 1956- WhoE 91
Messina, Joseph A 1939- BiDrAPA 89
Messina, Joseph F., Jr. 1954- WhoEmL 91
Messina, Joseph Paul 1930- IntWWM 90
Messina, Joseph R 1904- WhoAmA 91
Messina, Joseph R., Jr. 1904- WhoE 91
Messina, Leonard John 1947- WhoE 91
Messina, Maria 1887-1944 EncCoWW
Messina, Raymond Joseph 1938- WhoE 91
Messineo, Leonard E. 1925- St&PR 91
Messing, Carol Sue WhoAmW 91
Messing, Fred M. 1947- WhoSSW 91
Messing, Frederick Andrew, Jr. 1946- WhoAm 90
Messing, Gordon Myron 1917- WhoAm 90
Messing, Janet Agnes Kapelsohn 1918- WhoAm 90
Messing, Paul R. St&PR 91
Messing, Rita Bailey 1945- WhoAmW 91
Messing, Robert H. BioIn 16
Messing, Robin 1953- WhoWrEP 89
Messing, Scott 1953- IntWWM 90
Messing, Vol'f 1899-1974 BioIn 16
Messing, Wolf 1899-1974 EncPaPR 91
Messinger, Charles G. 1933- St&PR 91
Messinger, Clifford F. NewYTBS 90
Messinger, Donald Hathaway 1943- St&PR 91, WhoAm 90
Messinger, Richard C. 1930- St&PR 91
Messinger, Ruth BioIn 16
Messinger, Sheldon Leopold 1925- WhoAm 90
Messinger Jackson, Shirley May 1951- WhoAmW 91
Messiter, Malcolm IntWWM 90
Messman, Bill Ballpl 90
Messman, Jack L. 1940- St&PR 91
Messmer, Donald Davis, Jr. 1926- St&PR 91
Messmer, Donald Joseph 1936- WhoAm 90, WhoSSW 91
Messmer, Harold Maximilian, Jr. 1946- WhoAm 90
Messmer, Harold Maxmilian, Jr. 1946- St&PR 91
Messmer, Michaeline 1954- WhoAmW 91
Messmer, Otto 1892-1983 EncACom
Messmer, Pierre-Auguste Joseph 1916- BiDFrPL
Messmore, David William WhoSSW 91
Messmore, Leonora BioIn 16
Messmore, Scott L. 1947- St&PR 91
Messmore, Thomas E. 1945- St&PR 91
Messner, Edward BiDrAPA 89
Messner, Fredrick Richard 1926- St&PR 91
Messner, Gary R. 1933- St&PR 91
Messner, Howard Myron 1937- WhoAm 90
Messner, Kathryn Hertzog 1915- WhoAmW 91, WhoWor 91
Messner, Nathan BioIn 16
Messner, Robert Thomas 1938- St&PR 91, WhoWor 91
Messner, Ronald Pierce 1935- WhoAm 90
Messner, Zbigniew 1929- WhoWor 91
Messud, Francois Michel 1931- St&PR 91
Mesta, Perle 1889-1975 WorAlBi
Mesta, Perle 1891-1975 BioIn 16
Mestad, Orville Laverne 1923- WhoWor 91
Mestel, Mariella 1948- WhoAmW 91
Mestel, Mark David 1951- WhoEmL 91
Mestepey, John Thomas 1943- WhoSSW 91
Mester, Jorge BioIn 16
Mester, Jorge 1935- IntWWM 90, PenDiMP, WhoHisp 91
Mesterton-Gibbons, Michael Patrick 1954- WhoSSW 91
Mesthene, Emmanuel George 1920-1990 BioIn 16
Mestre, Mercedes A. 1947- WhoHisp 91
Mestres, Ricardo Angelo, Jr. 1933- WhoAm 90
Mestrovic, Ivan 1884-1962 WhoAmA 91N
Meszar, Frank 1915- WhoAm 90
Meszaros, Erno 1935- WhoWor 91
Meszaros, Marta BioIn 16
Mesznik, Joel R. 1945- WhoAm 90
Meszoly, Katalin IntWWM 90
Met, Leon 1942- WhoE 91
Metacom WhNaAH
Metacomet 1642?-1676 EncCRAm [port]
Metal, Jeannine 1956- WhoE 91
Metalious, Grace 1924-1964 BioAmW
Metallo, Laura Jeanne 1946- WhoAmW 91
Metaxas, Ioannis 1871-1941 WorAlBi
Metaxas, John C. 1958- WhoE 91
Metaxas, Pamela H. 1945- WhoAmW 91
Metaxatos, Takis Harry 1953- WhoWor 91
Metaxopoulos, Fotis 1935- WhoWor 91
Metcalf, Arthur George Bradford 1908- WhoAm 90
Metcalf, Aubrey W 1931- BiDrAPA 89
Metcalf, Charles David 1933- WhoAm 90
Metcalf, Conger A 1914- WhoAmA 91
Metcalf, David BioIn 16, St&PR 91
Metcalf, David R 1920- BiDrAPA 89
Metcalf, Douglas Reed 1949- WhoAm 90
Metcalf, Edwin 1823-1894 AmLegL
Metcalf, Frederic Thomas 1935- WhoAm 90
Metcalf, Frederick Thomas 1921- St&PR 91
Metcalf, George Rich 1914- St&PR 91
Metcalf, George W 1921- BiDrAPA 89
Metcalf, Harry Leonard 1934- WhoE 91
Metcalf, James Alfred, Jr. 1962- WhoSSW 91
Metcalf, James Marcus 1927-1977 BioIn 16
Metcalf, James Richard 1950- WhoE 91
Metcalf, Jerry D. 1938- WhoSSW 91
Metcalf, Joel Hastings 1866-1925 BioIn 16
Metcalf, John 1938- BioIn 16
Metcalf, John Philip 1946- IntWWM 90
Metcalf, Keyes DeWitt 1889-1983 BioIn 16
Metcalf, Laura Jane 1964- WhoAmW 91
Metcalf, Laurie 1955?- BioIn 16
Metcalf, Lawrence Vincent 1919- WhoAm 90
Metcalf, Linda Jo 1948- WhoAmW 91
Metcalf, Lynnette Carol 1955- WhoAmW 91, WhoEmL 91, WhoWor 91
Metcalf, Margaret Louise Faber 1943- WhoAmW 91
Metcalf, Mark ConTFT 8
Metcalf, Michael Pierce 1933- St&PR 91
Metcalf, Michael W. 1946- WhoE 91
Metcalf, Paul C. 1917- WhoWrEP 89
Metcalf, Priscilla 1915-1989 AnObit 1989
Metcalf, Robert Clarence 1923- WhoAm 90
Metcalf, Robert Lee 1916- WhoAm 90
Metcalf, Steven Prescott 1948- WhoE 91
Metcalf, Susan Stimmel 1926- WhoAm 90
Metcalf, Suzanne MajTwCW
Metcalf, Victor Howard 1853-1936 BiDrUSE 89
Metcalf, Willard Leroy 1858-1925 BioIn 16
Metcalf, William Edwards 1947- WhoAm 90
Metcalf, William Henry, Jr. 1928- WhoAm 90
Metcalf, William Kenneth 1921- WhoAm 90
Metcalfe, Clifford A., Jr. St&PR 91
Metcalfe, Darrel Seymour 1913- WhoAm 90
Metcalfe, David D. 1922- St&PR 91
Metcalfe, Eric William WhoAmA 91
Metcalfe, Jane M. AuBYP 90
Metcalfe, John Francis 1937- WhoE 91
Metcalfe, Murray Robert 1954- WhoE 91
Metcalfe, Norman J. 1942- St&PR 91
Metcalfe, Ralph Harold 1910-1978 BlkAmsC [port]
Metcalfe, Susan PenDiMP
Metcalfe, Thomas Oren, Jr. 1957- WhoSSW 91
Metcalfe, Tom Brooks 1920- WhoAm 90
Metcalfe, Walter Lee, Jr. 1938- WhoAm 90
Metchnikoff, Elie 1845-1916 WorAlBi
Metdepenninghen, Carlos Maurits W. 1935- WhoWor 91
Metea 1775?-1827 WhNaAH
Metelli, Fabio BioIn 16
Metelli, Joan 1953- IntWWM 90
Meter, Jan Van 1941- ODwPR 91
Meters, The EncPR&S 89
Metesky, George MajTwCW
Metevelis, Peter Joel 1943- WhoWor 91
Meteyard, Eliza 1816-1879 FemiCLE
Meth, Harriet ODwPR 91
Meth, Johannes M 1915- BiDrAPA 89
Meth, Joseph 1943- St&PR 91
Metheney, Bud 1915- Ballpl 90
Metheny, Pat BioIn 16, NewAgMG
Metheny, Patrick Bruce 1954- WhoAm 90
Methey, Andre 1871-1920 PenDiDA 89
Methold, Kenneth 1931- ConAu 32NR
Methot, Michel-Edouard 1826-1892 DcCanB 12
Methven, Jean C. IntWWM 90
Methvin, David BioIn 16
Methvin, John Jasper 1846-1941 WhNaAH
Methvin, Judy Ann WhoSSW 91
MeTivier, Donald Anthony 1936- WhoE 91
Metkovich, Catfish 1921- Ballpl 90
Metlitzki, Dorothee 1914- WhoWrEP 89
Metnedjenet WomWR
Metner, Nikolay 1880-1951 PenDiMP A
Metoyer, Maria Theresa Coincoin BioIn 16
Metoyer, Marie 1925- BiDrAPA 89
Metra, Marco 1957- WhoWor 91
Metras, Gary 1947- WhoWrEP 89
Metraux, Rhoda Anna Elizabeth 1914- WhoAmW 91
Metress, Seamus P. 1933- WhoWrEP 89
Metrey, George David 1939- WhoAm 90, WhoE 91
Metrick, Richard Lawrence 1941- St&PR 91
Metropolis, Nicholas Constantine 1915- WhoAm 90
Metropoulou, Kostoula 1920- EncCoWW
Metros, Mary Teresa 1951- WhoAmW 91
Metros, Nicholas C. 1931- St&PR 91
Mets, Lisa Ann 1954- WhoAmW 91
Metsala, Juha Einari 1925- IntWWM 90
Metsch, Johann Friedrich PenDiDA 89
Metsger, Robert William 1920- WhoE 91
Metsovaara, Marjatta 1927- ConDes 90
Metsu, Gabriel 1629-1667? IntDcAA 90
Mettam, Nancy Elizabeth Widdis 1935- WhoAmW 91
Mettee-McCutchon, Ila 1945- WhoAmW 91
Metten, William M., Jr. 1940- ODwPR 91
Metter, Bert BioIn 16
Metter, Bertram Milton 1927- WhoAm 90
Metternich, Clemens Wenzel L, Furst von 1773-1859 BioIn 16
Metternich, Klemens W. N. L. 1773-1859 WorAlBi
Metters, Colin Raynor 1948- IntWWM 90
Mettey, Joan E. 1931- St&PR 91
Mettinger, Tryggve N. D. 1940- WhoWor 91
Mettler, Mary A. 1937- St&PR 91
Mettler, Ruben Frederick 1924- St&PR 91, WhoAm 90
Metts, Lewis L. 1942- St&PR 91
Metts, Vergil L, III BiDrAPA 89
Metviner, Marion 1939- WhoE 91
Metyko, Michael Joseph 1945- WhoAmA 91
Metz, Alan 1954- BiDrAPA 89
Metz, Arthur 1927- St&PR 91
Metz, Carl Edward 1946- St&PR 91
Metz, Charles Edgar 1942- WhoAm 90
Metz, Charles Herman EncABHB 4
Metz, Claudia BiDrAPA 89
Metz, Clyde Raymond 1940- WhoSSW 91
Metz, Craig Huseman 1955- WhoAm 90, WhoEmL 91, WhoSSW 91
Metz, Dale BioIn 16
Metz, David J. 1933- ODwPR 91, St&PR 91
Metz, Diana Lyn 1957- St&PR 91
Metz, Donald Edward 1962- WhoE 91
Metz, Douglas Wilber 1934- WhoAm 90
Metz, Ed BioIn 16
Metz, Emmanuel Michael 1928- WhoAm 90
Metz, Ernest St. John BioIn 16
Metz, Frank Andrew, Jr. 1934- WhoAm 90
Metz, Frank Robert 1925- WhoAmA 91
Metz, G. Harold 1917- WhoAm 90
Metz, George William 1916- WhoAm 90
Metz, Gerry Michael 1943- WhoAmA 91
Metz, Helen Chapin 1928- WhoE 91
Metz, Helen Morningstar 1933- WhoE 91
Metz, Jerome Joseph, Jr. 1950- WhoEmL 91
Metz, Jerred 1943- WhoWrEP 89
Metz, Lawrence Anthony 1941- WhoAm 90
Metz, Mary Clare 1907- WhoAm 90
Metz, Mary Seawell 1937- WhoAm 90, WhoAmW 91
Metz, Michael Allen 1957- WhoSSW 91
Metz, Michael Miller 1953- St&PR 91, WhoAm 90
Metz, Norman Carl 1948- St&PR 91
Metz, Philip Orin 1941- WhoSSW 91
Metz, Philip Steven 1945- WhoEmL 91
Metz, Richard A. 1946- WhoSSW 91
Metz, Robert Edward 1945- WhoSSW 91
Metz, Robert John 1929- WhoAm 90
Metz, Robert Roy 1929- St&PR 91, WhoAm 90, WhoWrEP 89
Metz, Ronald George, Jr. 1957- WhoSSW 91
Metz, Ronald Irwin 1921- WhoE 91, WhoWor 91
Metz, Shirley BioIn 16
Metz, Theodore John 1932- WhoAm 90
Metz, Thomas Edward 1928- St&PR 91
Metz, Vernon Wahl 1917- WhoE 91
Metz, William Conrad 1921- St&PR 91
Metzbower, John Edgar, III 1949- St&PR 91
Metzenbaum, Howard Morton 1917- WhoAm 90, WhoWor 91
Metzgar, D. Robert 1943- St&PR 91
Metzgar, Margaret Maxine 1953- WhoAmW 91
Metzgar, Patricia C. 1912- St&PR 91
Metzger, Alan W. 1936- St&PR 91
Metzger, Bernard A. 1954- WhoWor 91
Metzger, Bruce Manning 1914- WhoAm 90
Metzger, Burton F. 1940- St&PR 91
Metzger, Butch 1952- Ballpl 90
Metzger, Carina Y. Stafford Smith 1933- WhoAmW 91
Metzger, Carl D 1942- BiDrAPA 89
Metzger, Darryl Eugene 1937- WhoAm 90, WhoWor 91
Metzger, Deena P. 1936- ConAu 130
Metzger, Deena Posy 1936- WhoWrEP 89
Metzger, Diane Hamill 1949- WhoAmW 91, WhoE 91, WhoEmL 91, WhoWor 91, WhoWrEP 89
Metzger, Donald L. 1938- St&PR 91
Metzger, Edward J., Jr. 1935- St&PR 91
Metzger, Eran Daniel 1959- BiDrAPA 89
Metzger, Erich 1921- St&PR 91
Metzger, Ernest Hugh 1923- WhoAm 90
Metzger, Evelyn Borchard 1911- WhoAmA 91, WhoE 91

Metzger, Frank 1929- *St&PR 91, WhoAm 90*
Metzger, H. A. 1933- *St&PR 91*
Metzger, Helen L *BiDrAPA 89*
Metzger, Hermann Philipp 1934- *WhoWor 91*
Metzger, Howell Peter 1931- *WhoAm 90*
Metzger, Imek R. 1925- *St&PR 91*
Metzger, John Mackay 1948- *WhoEmL 91*
Metzger, John U. 1935- *St&PR 91*
Metzger, John V. *St&PR 91*
Metzger, Kathleen Ann 1949- *WhoAmW 91*
Metzger, Marian 1931- *WhoAmW 91*
Metzger, Mark K. *ODwPR 91*
Metzger, Michael Dennis 1947- *St&PR 91*
Metzger, Patricia Louise 1950- *WhoAmW 91*
Metzger, Paul S. 1925- *St&PR 91*
Metzger, Peter M. 1934- *St&PR 91*
Metzger, Pola P. 1928- *St&PR 91*
Metzger, R. William 1930- *St&PR 91*
Metzger, Robert Andrews 1921- *St&PR 91*
Metzger, Robert Paul *WhoAmA 91*
Metzger, Robert Streicher 1950- *WhoEmL 91*
Metzger, Roger 1947- *Ballpl 90*
Metzger, Shirley Jean 1938- *WhoAmW 91*
Metzger, Sidney 1917- *WhoAm 90*
Metzger, Susan *BioIn 16*
Metzger, Thomas Michael 1952- *St&PR 91, WhoAm 90*
Metzger, William E *EncABHB 4*
Metzger-Campbell, Linda Arlene 1957- *WhoWor 91*
Metzheiser, Gerald F. 1932- *St&PR 91*
Metzinger, Raynard Robert 1930- *St&PR 91*
Metzke, Linda Kuzan 1944- *WhoE 91*
Metzker, Ray K. 1931- *WhoAm 90, WhoAmA 91*
Metzler, Alex 1903-1973 *Ballpl 90*
Metzler, David Walter *BiDrAPA 89*
Metzler, Dwight Fox 1916- *WhoAm 90*
Metzler, Edward 1932- *St&PR 91*
Metzler, Eric Harold 1945- *WhoWor 91*
Metzler, Lewis L. 1934- *St&PR 91*
Metzler, Paul Raymond 1949- *WhoEmL 91*
Metzler, William Andrew 1942- *WhoSSW 91*
Metzner, Arthur Berthold 1927- *WhoAm 90*
Metzner, Barbara Stone 1940- *WhoAmW 91*
Metzner, Charles Miller 1912- *WhoAm 90*
Metzner, George F. 1948- *St&PR 91*
Metzner, Jeffrey L 1950- *BiDrAPA 89*
Metzner, Jerome 1911-1990 *BioIn 16*
Metzner, Richard Joel 1942- *BiDrAPA 89, WhoAm 90*
Metzner, Sheila *BioIn 16*
Metzroth, Jane Porvancher 1951- *WhoWrEP 89*
Metzsch, Johann Friedrich *PenDiDA 89*
Meucci, Antonio 1808-1889 *BioIn 16*
Meucci, Renato 1958- *IntWWM 90*
Meudt, Edna Kritz 1906- *WhoWrEP 89*
Meulan, Waleran de Beaumont, Comte de 1104-1166 *BioIn 16*
Meuleman, Gezinus Evert 1925- *WhoWor 91*
Meuleman, Robert Joseph 1939- *St&PR 91, WhoAm 90*
Meulenbelt, Anja *BioIn 16*
Meulenbelt, Anja 1945- *EncCoWW*
Meuli, Judith K. 1938- *WhoAm 90*
Meunier, Paul D. 1950- *St&PR 91*
Meunier, Paul Dennis 1950- *WhoAm 90*
Meurdrac, Marie *BioIn 16*
Meure, Peter *PenDiDA 89*
Meurice, Julianne Kepler 1954- *WhoAmW 91*
Meury, Veronica Kmec 1946- *WhoAmW 91*
Meusburger, Charles Eugene 1954- *BiDrAPA 89*
Meusburger, Jolene Ann 1960- *WhoAmW 91*
Meusel, Bob 1896-1977 *Ballpl 90 [port]*
Meusel, Irish 1893-1963 *Ballpl 90 [port]*
Meusel, Janis Lynn 1956- *WhoAmW 91*
Meuser, Fredrick William 1923- *WhoAm 90*
Meuser, John Francis 1935- *WhoE 91*
Meuwissen, Kenneth H. 1933- *St&PR 91*
Meuwissen, Lawrence Eugene 1947- *WhoEmL 91*
Meven, Peter 1929- *IntWWM 90*
Mevissen, Hein Michael 1939- *WhoWor 91*
Mew, Charlotte 1869-1928 *FemiCLE*
Mew, Charlotte Mary 1869-1928 *BioIn 16*
Mew, Thomas Joseph, III 1942- *WhoAm 90*
Mew, Tommy 1942- *WhoAmA 91*
Mewborne, G. E. 1933- *St&PR 91*
Mewes, Dieter 1940- *WhoWor 91*
Mewshaw, Michael 1943- *BioIn 16, WorAu 1980 [port]*
Mexanno *WhNaAH*
Mexia, Ynes 1870-1938 *WomFie [port]*
Meyaart, Paul Jan 1943- *WhoAm 90*
Meyberg, Bernhard Ulrich 1917- *WhoWor 91*
Meyberg, Joerg-Dietrich Johannes 1951- *WhoWor 91*
Meyburg, Arnim Hans 1939- *WhoAm 90*
Meye, Robert Paul 1929- *WhoAm 90*
Meyen, William M 1905- *BiDrAPA 89*
Meyenburg, Bernd 1949- *BiDrAPA 89*
Meyer, Adele Rosenfeld *BioIn 16*
Meyer, Adolf F. *BioIn 16*
Meyer, Adolph E. 1897-1988 *BioIn 16*
Meyer, Agnes Ernst 1887-1970 *BiDWomA*
Meyer, Alan E. 1950- *St&PR 91*
Meyer, Albert B. *St&PR 91*
Meyer, Albert H. 1935- *St&PR 91*
Meyer, Alden Merrill 1952- *WhoAm 90*
Meyer, Alex 1918- *BiDrAPA 89*
Meyer, Alfred George 1920- *WhoAm 90*
Meyer, Alfred H. 1893-1988 *BioIn 16*
Meyer, Alice Virginia 1921- *WhoE 91*
Meyer, Allen A. 1945- *St&PR 91*
Meyer, Andrea Peroutka 1963- *WhoAmW 91*
Meyer, Andrew C., Jr. 1949- *WhoE 91*
Meyer, Andrew Paul *BiDrAPA 89*
Meyer, Angela 1933- *WhoAmW 91*
Meyer, Ann Jane 1942- *WhoAmW 91*
Meyer, Anne Stringer 1930- *WhoAmW 91*
Meyer, Annie 1867-1951 *FemiCLE*
Meyer, Annie Nathan *EarBlAP*
Meyer, Anthony Edward 1961- *WhoSSW 91*
Meyer, Arden Roger 1926- *St&PR 91*
Meyer, Armin Henry 1914- *BioIn 16, WhoAm 90, WhoWor 91*
Meyer, August C. 1900- *St&PR 91*
Meyer, August Christopher, Jr. 1937- *St&PR 91, WhoAm 90*
Meyer, Axel 1926- *WhoAm 90*
Meyer, Ben Franklin 1903- *WhoAm 90*
Meyer, Benny 1888-1974 *Ballpl 90*
Meyer, Bernard C. 1910-1988 *BioIn 16*
Meyer, Bernard F. 1931- *St&PR 91, WhoAm 90*
Meyer, Bernard Mathew 1933- *St&PR 91*
Meyer, Bernard Stern 1916- *WhoAm 90*
Meyer, Betty Jane 1918- *WhoAmW 91*
Meyer, Bill 1892-1957 *Ballpl 90*
Meyer, Bob 1939- *Ballpl 90*
Meyer, Brian Alan 1961- *WhoSSW 91*
Meyer, Bruce 1941- *BioIn 16*
Meyer, Bruce R. 1941- *St&PR 91*
Meyer, Bruce Russell 1948- *St&PR 91*
Meyer, Brud Richard 1926- *WhoAm 90*
Meyer, Burnett Chandler 1921- *WhoAm 90*
Meyer, C.M., Mrs. *WhoAmW 91*
Meyer, C. Victor 1934- *St&PR 91*
Meyer, Calvin H. 1944- *St&PR 91*
Meyer, Carl Dean 1942- *WhoSSW 91*
Meyer, Carl E. 1947- *St&PR 91*
Meyer, Carl Lincoln 1926- *St&PR 91*
Meyer, Carolyn *BioIn 16*
Meyer, Carolyn 1935- *AuBYP 90*
Meyer, Charles A, Jr. *BiDrAPA 89*
Meyer, Charles Appleton 1918- *St&PR 91, WhoAm 90*
Meyer, Charles Edward 1928- *WhoAm 90, WhoAmA 91*
Meyer, Charles Hilliard 1926- *WhoAm 90*
Meyer, Charles Mulvihill 1951- *WhoEmL 91*
Meyer, Charles Ted 1944- *BiDrAPA 89*
Meyer, Christian *PenDiDA 89*
Meyer, Christoffel Jansz *PenDiDA 89*
Meyer, Christopher Hawkins 1952- *WhoEmL 91*
Meyer, Clarence 1903- *WhoWrEP 89*
Meyer, Claudia Margaret 1957- *St&PR 91*
Meyer, Cynthia Kay 1952- *WhoAmW 91*
Meyer, Dale *ODwPR 91*
Meyer, Dan 1952- *Ballpl 90*
Meyer, Dan Wesley 1956- *WhoEmL 91*
Meyer, Daniel F. 1944- *St&PR 91*
Meyer, Daniel Joseph 1936- *St&PR 91, WhoAm 90*
Meyer, Daniel P. 1927- *ODwPR 91*
Meyer, Daniel Patrick 1927- *St&PR 91*
Meyer, Darren Eric *BiDrAPA 89*
Meyer, Daryl James 1949- *St&PR 91*
Meyer, David *BioIn 16*
Meyer, David Andrew 1949- *BiDrAPA 89*
Meyer, David C. 1955- *St&PR 91*
Meyer, Deanna Sipsma 1937- *WhoAmW 91*
Meyer, Debbie 1952- *WorAlBi*
Meyer, Deborah Lynn 1948- *WhoAmW 91*
Meyer, Dennis Irwin 1935- *WhoAm 90*
Meyer, Don Allan 1929- *St&PR 91*
Meyer, Donald Allen 1946- *WhoSSW 91*
Meyer, Donald Gordon 1934- *WhoAm 90*
Meyer, Donald Jay *BiDrAPA 89*
Meyer, Donald R. 1935- *St&PR 91*
Meyer, Donald Ray 1924- *WhoAm 90*
Meyer, Donald Robert 1942- *WhoAm 90*
Meyer, Donna Maria 1950- *WhoAmW 91*
Meyer, Doris 1942- *ConAu 32NR, -33NR, HispWr 90*
Meyer, Doris A. 1952- *St&PR 91*
Meyer, Dorothy Virginia 1930- *WhoE 91*
Meyer, Dorsey Ray, Sr. 1928- *St&PR 91*
Meyer, Dutch 1915- *Ballpl 90*
Meyer, Edith Patterson 1895- *AuBYP 90*
Meyer, Edmond Gerald 1919- *WhoAm 90, WhoWor 91*
Meyer, Edward David 1919- *BiDrAPA 89*
Meyer, Edward H. 1927- *St&PR 91*
Meyer, Edward Henry 1927- *WhoAm 90, WhoE 91*
Meyer, Edward P. 1949- *ODwPR 91*
Meyer, Edward Paul 1949- *WhoEmL 91*
Meyer, Edwin A., Jr. 1927- *St&PR 91*
Meyer, El 1910- *WhoAmA 91*
Meyer, Elizabeth Anne 1952- *WhoE 91*
Meyer, Ernst 1905-1988 *AnObit 1988*
Meyer, Eugene 1875-1959 *BioIn 16*
Meyer, Eugene Carlton 1923- *WhoAm 90*
Meyer, F. R. 1927- *St&PR 91*
Meyer, F. Weller 1942- *WhoE 91*
Meyer, Francis G. 1952- *St&PR 91*
Meyer, Frank 1936- *WhoE 91*
Meyer, Frank Hildbridge 1923- *WhoAmA 91, WhoSSW 91*
Meyer, Franklyn Edward 1932- *AuBYP 90*
Meyer, Franz Hermann 1928- *WhoWor 91*
Meyer, Fred *WhoAmA 91N*
Meyer, Fred J. 1931- *St&PR 91*
Meyer, Fred Josef 1931- *WhoAm 90*
Meyer, Fred M *BiDrAPA 89*
Meyer, Fred Richard 1939- *St&PR 91*
Meyer, Frederick H 1873-1961 *WhoAmA 91N*
Meyer, Friedrich Elias 1723-1785 *PenDiDA 89*
Meyer, G. Edward 1923- *St&PR 91*
Meyer, George D 1928- *BiDrAPA 89*
Meyer, George G 1931- *BiDrAPA 89*
Meyer, George Gotthold 1931- *WhoAm 90*
Meyer, George Herbert 1928- *WhoAm 90*
Meyer, George Ira 1958- *WhoWrEP 89*
Meyer, George Rex 1928- *WhoWor 91*
Meyer, George Von Lengerke 1858-1918 *AmLegL, BiDrUSE 89*
Meyer, George von Lengerke W. 1858-1918 *BioIn 16*
Meyer, George W. 1884-1959 *BioIn 16, OxCPMus*
Meyer, George William 1941- *St&PR 91*
Meyer, Gerald J. 1940- *St&PR 91*
Meyer, Gerald Justin 1940- *ODwPR 91, WhoAm 90*
Meyer, Gerard Charles 1931- *St&PR 91, WhoAm 90*
Meyer, Gerard Previn *AuBYP 90*
Meyer, Grace Alice 1957- *WhoEmL 91*
Meyer, Greg Charles *BiDrAPA 89*
Meyer, Gregor F. 1926- *St&PR 91*
Meyer, Gregory K. 1959- *St&PR 91*
Meyer, Gregory Torrey 1941- *St&PR 91*
Meyer, Grethe 1918- *ConDes 90*
Meyer, Gustav 1868-1932 *EncO&P 3*
Meyer, H. Theodore 1935- *WhoAm 90*
Meyer, Hank 1920- *ODwPR 91, WhoAm 90*
Meyer, Hans 1950- *WhoWor 91*
Meyer, Harding 1928- *ConAu 130*
Meyer, Harold J. 1923- *St&PR 91*
Meyer, Harold Louis 1916- *WhoWor 91*
Meyer, Harry Edward 1949- *BiDrAPA 89*
Meyer, Harry Martin, Jr. 1928- *WhoAm 90*
Meyer, Harvey Kessler, II 1914- *WhoSSW 91*
Meyer, Helen 1907- *WhoAm 90*
Meyer, Henry *PenDiMP*
Meyer, Henry Hunter 1936- *WhoSSW 91*
Meyer, Henry J. 1927- *St&PR 91*
Meyer, Henry John 1927- *WhoAm 90*
Meyer, Henry L., III 1949- *St&PR 91*
Meyer, Henry Lewis, III 1949- *WhoAm 90*
Meyer, Herbert 1882-1960 *WhoAmA 91N*
Meyer, Hermann F. 1938- *St&PR 91*
Meyer, Horst D. 1926- *WhoAm 90*
Meyer, Howard Robert, Jr. 1955- *WhoEmL 91*
Meyer, Irwin Stephan 1941- *WhoE 91, WhoWor 91*
Meyer, Ivah Gene 1935- *WhoAmW 91*
Meyer, J Allan *BiDrAPA 89*
Meyer, J. Theodore 1936- *WhoWor 91*
Meyer, Jack 1932-1967 *Ballpl 90*
Meyer, Jack 1947- *WhoE 91*
Meyer, Jackie Merri 1954- *WhoAm 90, WhoAmW 91*
Meyer, James J. 1963- *St&PR 91*
Meyer, James M. 1957- *St&PR 91*
Meyer, James R. 1947- *St&PR 91*
Meyer, Jarold Alan 1938- *WhoAm 90*
Meyer, Jay *BiDrAPA 89*
Meyer, Jay 1948- *WhoE 91*
Meyer, Jean *EncO&P 3*
Meyer, Jean 1934- *WhoAmW 91*
Meyer, Jean-Pierre 1949- *WhoWor 91*
Meyer, Jean-Pierre Gustave 1929- *WhoAm 90*
Meyer, Jeanette Marjorie 1961- *WhoAmW 91*
Meyer, Jeffery Wilson 1923- *St&PR 91, WhoAm 90*
Meyer, Jerome Harris 1946- *BiDrAPA 89*
Meyer, Jerome Jurgen *BioIn 16*
Meyer, Jerome Sydney 1895-1975 *AuBYP 90*
Meyer, Jerry Don 1939- *WhoAmA 91*
Meyer, Jill Susan *BiDrAPA 89*
Meyer, Joachim Ernst 1917- *WhoWor 91*
Meyer, Joan Kathryn 1956- *WhoE 91*
Meyer, Joey 1962- *Ballpl 90*
Meyer, Johannes 1929- *St&PR 91*
Meyer, John 1852-1895 *AmLegL*
Meyer, John Austin 1919- *WhoE 91*
Meyer, John Edward *BiDrAPA 89*
Meyer, John Edward 1931- *WhoAm 90*
Meyer, John Frederick 1934- *WhoAm 90*
Meyer, John George 1949- *WhoE 91*
Meyer, John Matthew 1937- *St&PR 91*
Meyer, John Robert 1927- *WhoAm 90, WhoE 91*
Meyer, John Robert 1946- *St&PR 91*
Meyer, John Sigmund 1937- *WhoE 91*
Meyer, Jon Keith 1938- *BiDrAPA 89*
Meyer, Joseph 1894- *OxCPMus*
Meyer, Joseph 1894-1987 *BioIn 16*
Meyer, Joseph B. 1941- *WhoAm 90*
Meyer, Joseph Leo 1943- *St&PR 91*
Meyer, Judith Louise 1933- *WhoAmW 91*
Meyer, Julie Ann 1960- *WhoAmW 91*
Meyer, June *AuBYP 90, MajTwCW*
Meyer, Karen Ann Gritzan 1947- *WhoAmW 91*
Meyer, Karl 1899-1990 *BioIn 16*
Meyer, Karl Ernest 1928- *WhoAm 90*
Meyer, Karl L. 1937- *St&PR 91*
Meyer, Karl William 1925- *WhoAm 90*
Meyer, Kathleen Allan 1918- *BioIn 16*
Meyer, Ken S. 1947- *WhoE 91*
Meyer, Kenneth 1942- *St&PR 91*
Meyer, Kenneth Marven 1932- *WhoAm 90*
Meyer, Kent L. 1943- *St&PR 91*
Meyer, Kerstin 1928- *IntWWM 90, PenDiMP, WhoAm 90*
Meyer, Klaus 1928- *WhoWor 91*
Meyer, Kristi J. 1956- *St&PR 91*
Meyer, Krzysztof 1943- *IntWWM 90*
Meyer, Larry L. 1933- *BioIn 16*
Meyer, Lasker Marcel 1926- *WhoAm 90*
Meyer, Lawrence George 1940- *WhoAm 90, WhoE 91, WhoWor 91*
Meyer, Leonard A. 1925- *St&PR 91*
Meyer, Leonard B. 1918- *WhoAm 90*
Meyer, Leopold de 1816-1883 *BioIn 16*
Meyer, Lester Allen 1923- *WhoSSW 91*
Meyer, Lhary 1947- *WhoEmL 91*
Meyer, Linda Doreen 1948- *WhoWrEP 89*
Meyer, Linda S. 1950- *WhoAmW 91, WhoE 91*
Meyer, Louis B. 1933- *WhoAm 90*
Meyer, Lucero *BioIn 16*
Meyer, Lucy Rider 1849-1922 *BioAmW*
Meyer, Lyle E. 1945- *St&PR 91*
Meyer, M. E. Joseph, III *WhoWor 91*
Meyer, M. Yvonne *WhoWrEP 89*
Meyer, Madeleine C 1952- *BiDrAPA 89*
Meyer, Malcolm Holt 1930- *WhoE 91*
Meyer, Margaret Eleanor 1923- *WhoAm 90*
Meyer, Margaret H. 1916- *WhoWrEP 89*
Meyer, Margaret S *BiDrAPA 89*
Meyer, Marilyn Clarita 1942- *WhoAmW 91*
Meyer, Marion M. 1923- *WhoAmW 91, WhoE 91, WhoWor 91*
Meyer, Mark Alan 1946- *WhoE 91*
Meyer, Marshall Theodore 1930- *BioIn 16*
Meyer, Mary-Beth 1950- *WhoAmW 91*
Meyer, Mary Kay 1963- *WhoE 91*
Meyer, Mary-Louise 1922- *WhoAmW 91, WhoE 91, WhoWor 91*
Meyer, Maurice, Jr. 1911- *St&PR 91*
Meyer, Maurice Wesley 1925- *WhoAm 90*
Meyer, Max Earl 1918- *WhoAm 90*
Meyer, Michael 1958- *WhoE 91*
Meyer, Michael Edwin 1942- *WhoAm 90*
Meyer, Michael Lee 1960- *BiDrAPA 89*
Meyer, Michael Louis 1940- *WhoAm 90*
Meyer, Milton Edward, Jr. 1922- *WhoAm 90*
Meyer, Morton G. 1905- *St&PR 91*
Meyer, Natalie 1930- *WhoAm 90, WhoAmW 91*
Meyer, Nicholas 1945- *TwCCr&M 91*
Meyer, Nicholas Joseph 1953- *WhoEmL 91*
Meyer, Norman J. 1930- *WhoAm 90*
Meyer, Olga Melchior *BioIn 16*
Meyer, Patricia Hanes 1947- *WhoAmW 91*
Meyer, Patricia Morgan 1934- *WhoAm 90*
Meyer, Paul Anthony 1940- *WhoE 91*

Meyer, Paul Joseph 1942- *WhoAm 90*
Meyer, Paul Norman 1940- *WhoAm 90*
Meyer, Paul Reims *WhoAm 90, WhoWor 91*
Meyer, Paul Richard 1930- *WhoE 91*
Meyer, Paul William 1924- *WhoAm 90*
Meyer, Pearl *St&PR 91*
Meyer, Peter 1920- *WhoAm 90*
Meyer, Peter Arnold 1944- *St&PR 91*
Meyer, Philip Edward 1930- *WhoAm 90, WhoSSW 91, WhoWor 91*
Meyer, Philippe Jean Marc 1954- *WhoWor 91*
Meyer, Pucci 1944- *WhoAm 90, WhoWrEP 89*
Meyer, Rabban 1918- *WhoAm 90*
Meyer, Ralph P. 1943- *St&PR 91*
Meyer, Randall 1923- *WhoAm 90*
Meyer, Rasmus Wold 1858-1916 *BioIn 16*
Meyer, Ray *BioIn 16*
Meyer, Raymond Joseph 1913- *WhoAm 90*
Meyer, Richard 1942- *WhoWor 91*
Meyer, Richard B *BiDrAPA 89*
Meyer, Richard Charles 1930- *WhoAm 90*
Meyer, Richard David 1943- *WhoAm 90*
Meyer, Richard Edward 1939- *WhoAm 90, WhoWor 91*
Meyer, Richard Jonah 1933- *WhoAm 90*
Meyer, Richard S *BiDrAPA 89*
Meyer, Richard Schlomer 1945- *St&PR 91, WhoEmL 91*
Meyer, Richart Townsend 1925- *WhoE 91*
Meyer, Rick *BioIn 16*
Meyer, Robert *WhoAm 90*
Meyer, Robert Eugene 1957- *WhoEmL 91*
Meyer, Robert F 1937- *BiDrAPA 89*
Meyer, Robert L. 1949- *St&PR 91*
Meyer, Robert Lewis 1949- *WhoWor 91*
Meyer, Robert Lynn 1949- *WhoEmL 91*
Meyer, Robert Norfleet 1957- *WhoSSW 91*
Meyer, Robert William 1939- *St&PR 91*
Meyer, Robert William 1945- *WhoSSW 91*
Meyer, Roger Emil 1938- *BiDrAPA 89*
Meyer, Roland Harry 1927- *St&PR 91, WhoAm 90*
Meyer, Rolf Arthur 1943- *WhoAm 90*
Meyer, Ron *BioIn 16*
Meyer, Ronald A. 1951- *St&PR 91*
Meyer, Ronald Frederick 1935- *St&PR 91*
Meyer, Ronald L. 1944- *St&PR 91*
Meyer, Russ 1923- *Ballpl 90, BioIn 16*
Meyer, Russell William, Jr. 1932- *St&PR 91, WhoAm 90*
Meyer, Ruth Krueger 1940- *WhoAmA 91*
Meyer, S. Lewis 1944- *St&PR 91*
Meyer, Sally Cave 1937- *WhoAmW 91*
Meyer, Sandra Wasserstein 1937- *WhoAm 90, WhoAmW 91*
Meyer, Scott D. 1949- *ODwPR 91, WhoAm 90*
Meyer, Scott Richard 1953- *WhoE 91*
Meyer, Seymour W *WhoAmA 91*
Meyer, Seymour William 1914- *WhoE 91*
Meyer, Sheldon 1926- *WhoAm 90*
Meyer, Stephan Schutzmeister 1953- *WhoE 91*
Meyer, Stephen Alan 1949- *St&PR 91, WhoE 91*
Meyer, Stephen John 1946- *St&PR 91*
Meyer, Stephen Leonard 1948- *WhoEmL 91*
Meyer, Stephen Norman 1945- *WhoAm 90*
Meyer, Suellen Jackson 1944- *WhoAmW 91*
Meyer, Susan E. 1940- *SmATA 64, WhoAm 90, WhoAmA 91, WhoWrEP 89*
Meyer, Susan Theresa 1950- *WhoAmW 91*
Meyer, Sylvan Hugh 1921- *WhoAm 90*
Meyer, Sylvia Adey 1936- *WhoAmW 91*
Meyer, Taro *BioIn 16*
Meyer, Theodore E. 1931- *WhoWrEP 89*
Meyer, Theresa T. 1944- *St&PR 91*
Meyer, Theresa Tuck 1944- *WhoAmW 91*
Meyer, Thomas Aloysius 1942- *St&PR 91*
Meyer, Thomas Arthur 1947- *WhoEmL 91*
Meyer, Thomas J. 1941- *WhoAm 90*
Meyer, Thomas James 1955- *WhoAm 90*
Meyer, Thomas Louis 1940- *BiDrAPA 89*
Meyer, Thomas R. 1936- *St&PR 91*
Meyer, Thomas Robert 1936- *WhoWor 91*
Meyer, Timothy H. 1943- *St&PR 91*
Meyer, Ursula *WhoAmA 91*
Meyer, Vaughan Benjamin 1920- *WhoSSW 91*
Meyer, Viveca Ann *BiDrAPA 89*
Meyer, Walter 1932- *WhoAm 90*
Meyer, Walter J., III 1916- *WhoAm 90*
Meyer, Wayne C. 1923- *St&PR 91*
Meyer, Wilhelm 1932- *WhoWor 91*
Meyer, Wilhelm Christian 1726-1786 *PenDiDA 89*
Meyer, Willa Dean 1932- *WhoAmW 91*
Meyer, William A. 1932- *St&PR 91*
Meyer, William Andrew 1949- *WhoSSW 91*
Meyer, William Danielson 1923- *WhoAm 90*
Meyer, William E. *ODwPR 91*
Meyer, William Frederick 1933- *St&PR 91*
Meyer, William S. 1946- *St&PR 91*
Meyer, Winifred Jane 1940- *BiDrAPA 89*
Meyer-Abich, Klaus Michael 1936- *WhoWor 91*
Meyer-Bahlburg, Heino F. L. 1940- *WhoAm 90*
Meyer-Christian, Wolf Joachim 1933- *WhoWor 91*
Meyer-Strom, Paul Martin 1957- *BiDrAPA 89*
Meyer Tracy, Catherine Marie 1952- *WhoAmW 91*
Meyer zu Selhausen, Hermann 1940- *WhoWor 91*
Meyerand, Russell Gilbert, Jr. 1933- *St&PR 91*
Meyerbeer, Giacomo 1791-1864 *BioIn 16, PenDiMP A, WorAlBi*
Meyerding, Eugene Villaume 1924- *St&PR 91*
Meyerdirk, Carl F. 1927- *ODwPR 91*
Meyerer, Margaret Christine 1924- *WhoWrEP 89*
Meyerhans, Stuart 1916- *St&PR 91*
Meyerhoff, Erich 1919- *WhoAm 90*
Meyerhoff, Gordon R *BiDrAPA 89*
Meyerhoff, Jack Fulton 1926- *WhoAm 90, WhoSSW 91*
Meyerholz, John Philip 1941- *St&PR 91, WhoAm 90*
Meyerhuber, Lisa Elisabeth 1940- *WhoE 91*
Meyerle, Levi 1845-1921 *Ballpl 90*
Meyerman, Harold John 1938- *St&PR 91*
Meyerowitz, Aaron David 1957- *WhoSSW 91*
Meyerowitz, Jacob 1928- *WhoE 91*
Meyerowitz, Joel *BioIn 16*
Meyerowitz, Joel 1938- *WhoAmA 91, WhoWor 91*
Meyerowitz, Steven A. 1955- *WhoWrEP 89*
Meyerowitz, William 1886-1981 *WhoAmA 91N*
Meyerrose, Sarah L. 1955- *St&PR 91*
Meyers, Abbey S. 1944- *WhoE 91*
Meyers, Albert Irving 1932- *WhoAm 90*
Meyers, Ann Elizabeth 1955- *WhoAmW 91*
Meyers, Anne Akiko 1970- *IntWWM 90*
Meyers, Annette 1934- *ConAu 132*
Meyers, Ari *BioIn 16*
Meyers, Arthur Christian, Jr. 1914- *WhoAm 90*
Meyers, Barbara Florence *WhoE 91*
Meyers, Barnett S 1940- *BiDrAPA 89*
Meyers, Beatrice Nurmi 1929- *WhoSSW 91*
Meyers, Beverly Jean 1949- *WhoAmW 91*
Meyers, Carol L 1942- *ConAu 32NR*
Meyers, Carole Terwilliger 1945- *WhoWrEP 89*
Meyers, Carolyn Winstead 1946- *WhoSSW 91*
Meyers, Charles D 1922- *BiDrAPA 89*
Meyers, Charles J. *BioIn 16*
Meyers, Chief 1880-1971 *Ballpl 90*
Meyers, Christine Laine 1946- *WhoAmW 91, WhoWor 91*
Meyers, Christopher D 1941- *BiDrAPA 89*
Meyers, Dale *WhoAm 90, WhoAmA 91*
Meyers, David Victor 1949- *St&PR 91*
Meyers, Donald I 1926- *BiDrAPA 89*
Meyers, Dorothy 1927- *WhoAmW 91*
Meyers, Ed 1912-1989 *BioIn 16*
Meyers, Edward 1934- *WhoAm 90, WhoE 91*
Meyers, Edwin W. 1927- *St&PR 91*
Meyers, Elizabeth *BioIn 16*
Meyers, Emerson 1910- *IntWWM 90*
Meyers, Eric Barton *NewYTBS 90*
Meyers, Eric Barton 1942-1990 *BioIn 16*
Meyers, Erik Jon 1949- *WhoEmL 91*
Meyers, Eugene 1935- *St&PR 91*
Meyers, Francis Joseph 1921- *WhoAmA 91*
Meyers, Frederick M. *WhoAm 90*
Meyers, George Edward 1928- *WhoWor 91*
Meyers, Gerald 1928- *BioIn 16*
Meyers, Gerald Carl 1928- *WhoAm 90*
Meyers, Glenn Scott 1961- *WhoE 91*
Meyers, Harold A. 1912- *St&PR 91*
Meyers, Helen Carol *BiDrAPA 89*
Meyers, Helen Renich 1916- *WhoWrEP 89*
Meyers, Hyman 1911- *St&PR 91*
Meyers, James Frank 1946- *WhoSSW 91*
Meyers, James M. 1946- *St&PR 91*
Meyers, Jan *WhoAm 90, WhoAmW 91*
Meyers, Jane Kinney 1953- *WhoAmW 91*
Meyers, Jeanne F 1944- *WhoAmA 91*
Meyers, Joan 1927- *AuBYP 90*
Meyers, Jodie Ann 1954- *WhoAmW 91*
Meyers, John Allen 1929- *St&PR 91, WhoAm 90*
Meyers, John Frederick *BiDrAPA 89*
Meyers, John Robert 1947- *St&PR 91*
Meyers, Joyce Selber 1942- *WhoAmW 91*
Meyers, Karen Diane 1950- *WhoAmW 91*
Meyers, Karen Lorayne Donnell 1952- *WhoAmW 91*
Meyers, Kenneth D. 1952- *St&PR 91*
Meyers, Kenneth R. 1954- *St&PR 91*
Meyers, Klara 1924- *IntWWM 90*
Meyers, Laura *BioIn 16*
Meyers, Leonard H 1932-1979 *WhoAmA 91N*
Meyers, Lynn Betty 1952- *WhoAmW 91, WhoWor 91*
Meyers, Maurice 1932- *WhoSSW 91*
Meyers, May Lou 1930- *WhoAmW 91*
Meyers, Michael K 1939- *WhoAmA 91*
Meyers, Morton Allen 1933- *WhoAm 90*
Meyers, Nancy *BioIn 16*
Meyers, Norman O. 1929- *St&PR 91*
Meyers, Otto O'Neil, III 1958- *WhoE 91*
Meyers, Peter A. 1954- *St&PR 91*
Meyers, Peter L. 1939- *St&PR 91*
Meyers, Raymond N. 1938- *St&PR 91*
Meyers, Red *Ballpl 90*
Meyers, Reinhard 1947- *WhoWor 91*
Meyers, Richard James 1940- *WhoAm 90*
Meyers, Richard Stuart 1938- *WhoAm 90*
Meyers, Robert A. 1934- *WhoE 91*
Meyers, Robert S. *St&PR 91*
Meyers, Robert S. 1939- *ODwPR 91*
Meyers, Robert W 1927- *BiDrAPA 89*
Meyers, Robert William 1919-1970 *WhoAmA 91N*
Meyers, Ronald G 1934- *WhoAmA 91*
Meyers, Sanford H *BiDrAPA 89*
Meyers, Sharon Dean 1953- *WhoAmW 91*
Meyers, Sharon May 1946- *WhoAmW 91, WhoEmL 91*
Meyers, Sheldon 1929- *WhoAm 90*
Meyers, Sheldon J 1935- *BiDrAPA 89*
Meyers, Susan 1942- *AuBYP 90*
Meyers, Susan Morand 1957- *WhoAmW 91*
Meyers, Sylvia Robles *BiDrAPA 89*
Meyers, Tedson Jay 1928- *WhoAm 90*
Meyers, Theodore Richard 1950- *WhoEmL 91*
Meyers, Thomas P. 1932- *St&PR 91*
Meyers, Timothy *BioIn 16*
Meyers, Wade Norbert 1929- *St&PR 91*
Meyers, Wayne Marvin 1924- *WhoAm 90*
Meyers, William Francis 1947- *WhoE 91, WhoWor 91*
Meyers, William John 1931- *St&PR 91*
Meyers-Day, Linda Lee 1939- *WhoAmW 91*
Meyersburg, Herman Arnold 1913- *BiDrAPA 89*
Meyersohn, Jonathan *BioIn 16, NewYTBS 90 [port]*
Meyerson, Arthur T *BiDrAPA 89*
Meyerson, George O. 1940- *St&PR 91*
Meyerson, Harvey Eugene 1937- *WhoE 91*
Meyerson, Janice *IntWWM 90*
Meyerson, Joelle A. *St&PR 91*
Meyerson, Martin 1922- *St&PR 91, WhoAm 90*
Meyerson, Martin 1927- *WhoE 91*
Meyerson, Martin Henry 1931- *St&PR 91*
Meyerson, Morton H. *BioIn 16*
Meyerson, Morton Herbert 1938- *WhoAm 90*
Meyerson, Richard 1927- *St&PR 91*
Meyerson, Stan 1925- *St&PR 91*
Meyerson, Stanley Phillip 1916- *WhoWor 91*
Meyfarth, Jutta 1933- *IntWWM 90*
Meylan, Daniel 1953- *IntWWM 90*
Meylan, Jean 1915- *IntWWM 90*
Meyler, William Anthony 1944- *WhoWor 91*
Meymandi, Assad *BiDrAPA 89*
Meyn, John H. 1920- *St&PR 91*
Meynell, Alice 1847-1922 *DcLB 98 [port], FemiCLE*
Meynell, Alice Christiana Thompson 1847-1922 *BioIn 16*
Meynell, Francis 1891-1975 *ConDes 90*
Meynell, Hugo A. 1936- *ConAu 130*
Meynell, Laurence 1899-1989 *AnObit 1989, TwCCr&M 91*
Meynell, Laurence Walter 1899-1989 *SmATA 61*
Meynell, Viola 1886-1956 *FemiCLE*
Meynell, Wilfrid 1852-1948 *BioIn 16*
Meyner, Robert B 1908-1990 *CurBio 90N, NewYTBS 90*
Meyner, Robert Baumle 1908-1990 *BioIn 16*
Meynier, Yvonne 1908- *AuBYP 90*
Meyninger, Rita 1935- *WhoWor 91*
Meyo, Raymond D. 1943- *St&PR 91, WhoAm 90*
Meyocks, Richard D. 1931- *St&PR 91*
Meyrink, Gustav 1868-1932 *EncO&P 3*
Meyrowitz, Paul 1915- *St&PR 91*
Meysenbug, Malwida von 1816-1903 *EncCoWW*
Meyst, Amelia Sue 1946- *WhoAmW 91*
Meystel, Alexander Michael 1935- *WhoE 91*
Meytina, Anna *BioIn 16*
Meyvaert, Paul Jeffrey 1921- *WhoAm 90*
Meza, Carlos J. 1958- *WhoHisp 91*
Meza, Cesar *BiDrAPA 89*
Meza, Guillermo 1917- *ArtLatA*
Meza, Richard Albert 1957- *St&PR 91*
Meza-Overstreet, Mark Lee 1950- *WhoHisp 91*
Mezack, Gary A. 1952- *St&PR 91*
Mezak, Daniel Stephen 1922- *St&PR 91*
Mezei, Gabor 1935- *St&PR 91*
Mezei, Noemi Judit 1938- *BiDrAPA 89*
Mezer, Robert Ross *BiDrAPA 89*
Mezera, James Allen 1930- *WhoAm 90*
Mezerova, Julie W. 1893- *BiDWomA*
Mezey, Peter 1931- *St&PR 91*
Mezie-Okoye, John-Joe Odili 1946- *WhoWor 91*
Mezieres, Marie-Jeanne Laboras de *EncCoWW*
Meznaric, Silva 1939- *WhoWor 91*
Mezo, Laszlo *PenDiMP*
Mezquita, Elva Ruth *BiDrAPA 89*
Mezzanzanica, Cherubino *PenDiDA 89*
Mezzarisa, Francesco di Antonio *PenDiDA 89*
Mezzich, Juan Enrique 1945- *BiDrAPA 89, WhoHisp 91*
Mezzrow, Mezz 1899-1972 *OxCPMus*
Mfume, Kweisi 1948- *BlkAmsC [port], WhoAm 90, WhoE 91*
Mgbako, Ambrose O *BiDrAPA 89*
Mgemane, Isaac Lizo Sheperd 1934- *IntWWM 90*
M'Guckin, Barton 1852-1913 *PenDiMP*
Mhatre, Jyotsna Anil *BiDrAPA 89*
Mhatre, Nagesh S. 1932- *St&PR 91*
Mhire, Herman P 1947- *WhoAmA 91*
Mhley, Rita Rammrath 1946- *WhoE 91*
Miamis, James D. 1927- *WhoAm 90*
Mian, Abid Rashid *BiDrAPA 89*
Mian, Ahmad Zia 1942- *WhoE 91*
Mian, Maqbul Ahmad 1931- *BiDrAPA 89*
Mian, Mary 1902- *BioIn 16*
Miano, Louis Stephen 1934- *St&PR 91, WhoAm 90*
Miantinomo 1600?-1643 *WhNaAH*
Miantonomi 1600?-1643 *WhNaAH*
Miantonomo 1600?-1643 *EncCRAm, WhNaAH*
Miantunnomoh 1600?-1643 *WhNaAH*
Miao, Chi Hsien *BiDrAPA 89*
Miars, Mark J. 1953- *St&PR 91*
Miazzo, Pietro 1959- *BiDrAPA 89*
Mica, David Raymond 1955- *WhoSSW 91*
Micale, Albert *WhoAmA 91*
Micale, Frank Jude 1949- *WhoEmL 91*
Micale, Vincent Joseph 1943- *St&PR 91*
Micales, David E. 1953- *St&PR 91*
Micallef, Joseph C. 1947- *St&PR 91*
Micanopy 1780?-1849 *WhNaAH*
Micci, Alfio *BioIn 16*
Micciche, Romano Joseph 1938- *St&PR 91*
Micciche, Salvatore Joseph 1928- *WhoAm 90*
Miccio, Joseph V. 1915- *WhoAm 90*
Micco-Nuppe 1780?-1849 *WhNaAH*
Miccoli, Arnaldo *WhoAmA 91*
Micconopy 1780?-1849 *WhNaAH*
Micele, Billie Jean 1947- *WhoSSW 91*
Miceli, Anthony J. 1962- *St&PR 91*
Miceli, Ignatius 1918- *WhoAmW 91*
Miceli, Robert V 1952- *WhoE 91*
Michael, Alfred Frederick, Jr. 1928- *WhoAm 90*
Michael, Carola 1921- *WhoAm 90*
Michael, Charles Louis, Jr. 1944- *St&PR 91*
Michael, Chester A., III 1947- *St&PR 91*
Michael, Cleon Mason *BiDrAPA 89*
Michael, Connie Elizabeth Trexler 1945- *WhoAmW 91*
Michael, David *NewAgMG*
Michael, Dennis Mark 1951- *St&PR 91*
Michael, Donald Joseph *BiDrAPA 89*
Michael, Donald Nelson 1923- *WhoAm 90*
Michael, Dorothy Ann 1950- *WhoAmW 91*
Michael, Ellen Violet *BiDrAPA 89*
Michael, Frederick William 1943- *WhoWor 91*
Michael, Gary 1937- *WhoAmA 91*
Michael, Gary G. 1940- *WhoAm 90*
Michael, Gary Glenn 1940- *St&PR 91*
Michael, Gary Linn 1934- *WhoAm 90*
Michael, Gene 1938- *Ballpl 90*
Michael, George *BioIn 16, EncPR&S 89*
Michael, George 1963- *OxCPMus, WorAlBi*
Michael, Gregory Charles 1946- *St&PR 91*
Michael, Harold Louis 1920- *WhoAm 90*
Michael, Henry N. 1913- *WhoAm 90*

Michael, J. Christopher 1951- St&PR 91
Michael, James Eugene 1927- St&PR 91
Michael, James Harry, Jr. 1918- WhoAm 90, WhoSSW 91
Michael, Jeffrey J. 1956- St&PR 91
Michael, Jerrold Mark 1927- WhoAm 90
Michael, Jerry Dean BioIn 16
Michael, Jonathan Edward 1954- St&PR 91
Michael, Julia Warner 1879- FemiCLE
Michael, Kenneth D BiDrAPA 89
Michael, Kurt David 1965- WhoSSW 91
Michael, Lanny H. 1951- St&PR 91
Michael, Mark A. 1948- WhoEmL 91
Michael, Mary Amelia WhoAmW 91
Michael, Max, Jr. 1916- WhoAm 90
Michael, Nancy Barrington BiDrAPA 89
Michael, Patricia Ann 1953- WhoSSW 91
Michael, Patricia Gordon 1940- WhoAmA 91
Michael, Patrick William 1954- WhoSSW 91
Michael, Phyllis Callender 1908- WhoAmW 91
Michael, Richard P 1924- BiDrAPA 89
Michael, Sami I BiDrAPA 89
Michael, Sandra Dale 1945- WhoAmW 91
Michael, Suzanne 1951- WhoAmW 91
Michael, Thomas Hugh Glynn 1918- WhoAm 90
Michael, Toni 1941- WhoAmW 91
Michael, William Burton 1922- WhoAm 90
Michael-Kenney, Shari A. 1957- St&PR 91
Michaeli, Fred C. 1935- St&PR 91
Michaelides, Constantine Evangelos 1930- WhoAm 90
Michaelides, Richard John 1934- St&PR 91
Michaelis, Arthur F. 1941- St&PR 91
Michaelis, Arthur Frederick 1941- WhoE 91
Michaelis, Donald R. 1928- St&PR 91
Michaelis, George H. BioIn 16
Michaelis, George H. 1937- St&PR 91
Michaelis, Hanny 1922- EncCoWW
Michaelis, Karin 1872-1950 EncCoWW
Michaelis, Leonor 1875-1949 DcScB S2
Michaelis, Margaret Helmly 1961- WhoAmW 91
Michaelis, Marty Dean 1964- WhoEmL 91
Michaelis, Michael 1919- WhoAm 90
Michaelis, Paul Charles 1935- WhoAm 90
Michaelis, Peter 1900-1975 DcScB S2
Michaelis-Jena, Ruth 1905- BioIn 16
Michaels, Al BioIn 16
Michaels, Al 1944- Ballpl 90
Michaels, Alan Richard 1944- WhoAm 90
Michaels, Alan Stuart 1954- WhoE 91
Michaels, Alvin B 1935- BiDrAPA 89
Michaels, Anthony Bruce BiDrAPA 89
Michaels, Anthony Bruce 1948- WhoEmL 91
Michaels, Barbara TwCCr&M 91
Michaels, Barbara 1927- BestSel 90-4 [port], BioIn 16
Michaels, Brian Edwin 1939- WhoSSW 91
Michaels, Carol Ann 1948- WhoWrEP 89
Michaels, Cass 1926-1982 Ballpl 90
Michaels, Charles B. St&PR 91
Michaels, Courtland Rand 1937- St&PR 91
Michaels, Craig Adam 1954- WhoE 91
Michaels, David Seth 1946- WhoEmL 91
Michaels, Dennis Joseph 1954- WhoE 91
Michaels, Elizabeth WhoWrEP 89
Michaels, Eric 1948- BioIn 16
Michaels, Gary David 1955- WhoEmL 91
Michaels, George 1923- St&PR 91
Michaels, Glen 1927- WhoAmA 91
Michaels, Gordon Joseph 1930- WhoWor 91
Michaels, Henry H., Jr. 1909- St&PR 91
Michaels, Hollis Lynne 1948- BiDrAPA 89
Michaels, Irene WhoWrEP 89
Michaels, James Walker 1921- WhoAm 90, WhoWrEP 89
Michaels, Jamie NewAgMG
Michaels, Joanne 1950- WhoWrEP 89
Michaels, John A. BioIn 16
Michaels, John Francis, Jr. 1941- BiDrAPA 89
Michaels, John Patrick, Jr. BioIn 16
Michaels, Leonard 1933- BioIn 16, MajTwCW, WhoAm 90, WhoWrEP 89
Michaels, Lorne BioIn 16, WhoAm 90
Michaels, Marilyn 1943- ConTFT 8
Michaels, Molly ConAu 31NR
Michaels, Patrick Francis 1925- WhoWor 91
Michaels, Richard Edward 1952- WhoEmL 91, WhoWor 91
Michaels, Richard Houghton 1928- WhoAm 90
Michaels, Robert H. 1954- St&PR 91
Michaels, Ski BioIn 16
Michaels, Steve TwCCr&M 91
Michaels, Willard A. 1917- WhoAm 90
Michaels, William R. 1936- St&PR 91
Michaels-Paque, J WhoAmA 91
Michaelsen, Alfred L. 1940- St&PR 91
Michaelsen, Edward Hugo 1917-1989 BioIn 16
Michaelsen, Howard K. 1927- St&PR 91
Michaelsen, Mark G. BioIn 16
Michaelson, Arthur M. 1927- WhoAm 90
Michaelson, Benjamin, Jr. 1936- WhoE 91
Michaelson, Brad C. ODwPR 91
Michaelson, Jeffrey Elon 1952- WhoEmL 91
Michaelson, Jerrold Max 1946- WhoSSW 91
Michaelson, John Charles 1953- WhoEmL 91
Michaelson, Lori BioIn 16
Michaelson, Melvin 1928- WhoAm 90
Michaelson, Mike BioIn 16
Michaelson, Peter Lee 1952- WhoWor 91
Michaelson, Richard Aaron 1952- St&PR 91
Michaelson, Richard Delmore, Jr. 1956- WhoSSW 91
Michaelson, Ruth Lenore 1961- WhoAmW 91
Michaesco, Eugene 1937- WhoAmA 91
Michak, Helen Barbara 1926- WhoAmW 91
Michal, Audrey Eubanks 1955- BiDrAPA 89
Michalak, Charles Paul 1946- St&PR 91
Michalak, Edward Francis 1937- WhoAm 90
Michalak, Thomas 1940- IntWWM 90
Michalak, William Steven 1947- WhoEmL 91
Michalczyk, Linda F. 1954- St&PR 91
Michalec, Stephen 1954- St&PR 91
Michalek, Bernard Joseph 1934- St&PR 91
Michalek, Margaret M. 1926- St&PR 91
Michalek, Richard C. 1923- St&PR 91
Michalek, Terry O'Dea 1954- WhoE 91
Michalesko, Paul F. 1950- St&PR 91
Michalik, Andrzej Maria 1944- BiDrAPA 89
Michalik, Edward Francis 1946- WhoAm 90, WhoE 91, WhoWor 91
Michalik, Matthew Peter 1960- WhoEmL 91
Michalik, Richard Edmund 1947- WhoSSW 91
Michalis, Clarence F. 1922- St&PR 91
Michalko, James Paul 1950- WhoAm 90
Michalko, Jan Vladimir 1951- IntWWM 90
Michalos, James 1912- WhoAm 90
Michalowski, Daniel Richard 1938- WhoE 91
Michalowski, Kornel 1923- IntWWM 90
Michalowski, Piotr A. WhoAm 90
Michals, Duane 1932- BioIn 16, WhoAmA 91
Michals, Duane Steven 1932- WhoAm 90
Michals, George Francis 1935- WhoAm 90
Michals, Kathy BioIn 16
Michals, Lee Marie 1939- WhoAmW 91
Michals, Timothy John 1941- BiDrAPA 89
Michalsen, Jan Bjorn 1951- WhoSSW 91
Michalski, Celeste C. 1942- WhoAmW 91
Michalski, Christopher Mark 1954- WhoWor 91
Michalski, Donna Kaye 1946- St&PR 91
Michalski, Edward Charles 1952- WhoEmL 91
Michalski, Joseph Walter 1943- St&PR 91
Michalski, Karen Marie 1960- WhoAmW 91
Michalski, Kenneth J. 1944- St&PR 91
Michalski, Stanley Franklin 1934- IntWWM 90
Michalski, Thomas James 1950- St&PR 91
Michalski, Thomas Joseph 1933- WhoAm 90
Micham, Nancy Sue 1956- WhoAmW 91
Michanowsky, George 1920- WhoAm 90, WhoWor 91
Michas, Athanassios N. 1944- WhoAm 90, WhoE 91
Michas, George 1943- St&PR 91
Michas, George A 1939- BiDrAPA 89
Michaud, Alphee Martial 1938- WhoE 91
Michaud, Ernest C. 1930- St&PR 91
Michaud, Howard Henry 1902- WhoAm 90
Michaud, Jean Fernand 1932- WhoWor 91
Michaud, Michael Alan George 1938- WhoAm 90, WhoE 91, WhoWrEP 89
Michaud, Neil J. 1927- IntWWM 90
Michaud, Norma Alice 1946- WhoAmW 91
Michaut, Gerald Lucien 1944- WhoWor 91
Michaux, Henri 1899-1984 WorAlBi
Michaux, Henry Gaston 1934- WhoSSW 91
Michaux, Ronald Robert 1944- WhoAmA 91
Micheau, Christian 1932- WhoWor 91
Micheaux, Oscar 1884-1951 BioIn 16, DrBlPA 90
Micheaux, Oscar Devereaux 1884-1951 EarBlAP
Micheel, Richard Arthur 1920- WhoE 91
Micheels, Louis J 1917- BiDrAPA 89, BioIn 16
Micheels, Peter A. 1945- ConAu 132
Michel, Anna 1943- BioIn 16
Michel, Anthony Nikolaus 1935- WhoAm 90
Michel, Anthony R. 1937- WhoAm 90
Michel, Barbara Rule 1957- WhoAmW 91
Michel, Benoit 1940- St&PR 91, WhoAm 90
Michel, Bernard 1930- WhoAm 90
Michel, C. Ray 1928- St&PR 91
Michel, Christopher S 1947- BiDrAPA 89
Michel, Claude 1926- WhoWor 91
Michel, Clemence Louise 1830?-1905 BiDFrPL
Michel, Clifford Lloyd 1939- WhoAm 90
Michel, Daniel John 1949- WhoEmL 91, WhoSSW 91, WhoWor 91
Michel, Donald Charles 1935- WhoAm 90
Michel, Francois Claude 1928- WhoWor 91
Michel, Fred Henri BiDrAPA 89
Michel, George J., Jr. 1931- St&PR 91
Michel, George Joseph, Jr. 1931- WhoAm 90
Michel, Georges 1926- ConAu 31NR
Michel, Harding Boehme 1924- WhoAmW 91
Michel, Harmut 1948- WorAlBi
Michel, Harriet Richardson BioIn 16
Michel, Hartmut 1948- BioIn 16, WhoWor 91
Michel, Henri 1907-1986 BioIn 16
Michel, Henry Ludwig 1924- St&PR 91, WhoAm 90, WhoWor 91
Michel, James 1944- WhoWor 91
Michel, James H. 1939- WhoAm 90, WhoWor 91
Michel, Lester Allen 1919- WhoAm 90
Michel, Louise 1830-1905 EncCoWW
Michel, Mable Soudelier 1951- WhoAmW 91, WhoSSW 91
Michel, Madelon 1939- IntWWM 90
Michel, Mary Ann Kedzuf 1939- WhoAm 90
Michel, Mary Lynn 1962- WhoAmW 91
Michel, Paul Redmond 1941- WhoAm 90
Michel, Peter Alexander 1943- St&PR 91, WhoSSW 91
Michel, Philip Martin 1939- St&PR 91
Michel, Richard C. 1953- St&PR 91
Michel, Richard Chris 1945- WhoE 91
Michel, Robert C. 1927- St&PR 91
Michel, Robert Charles 1927- WhoE 91
Michel, Robert Emory 1911- St&PR 91
Michel, Robert F. 1921- St&PR 91
Michel, Robert H. 1923- BioIn 16
Michel, Robert Henry 1923- WhoAm 90
Michel, Sally BioIn 16
Michel, Scott 1916- WhoWrEP 89
Michel, Sharon Lee 1946- WhoAmW 91
Michel, Virgil BioIn 16
Michel-Trapaga, Rene David 1942- BioIn 16
Michelangeli PenDiMP
Michelangeli, Arturo Benedetti 1920- IntWWM 90
Michelangelo 1475-1564 IntDcAA 90, WorAlBi
Michelangelo Buonarroti 1475-1564 BioIn 16
Michele, Michael BioIn 16
Michelena, Juan A. 1939- WhoHisp 91
Michelet, Edmond 1899-1970 BiDFrPL
Michelet, Jules 1798-1874 WorAlBi
Micheletti, Carl Aldo 1936- St&PR 91
Micheletti, Raymond Earl 1926- St&PR 91
Micheletti, Tony N. 1948- St&PR 91
Micheletto, Joe Raymond 1936- St&PR 91, WhoAm 90
Micheli, Frank James 1930- WhoAm 90
Micheli, Gene Saul 1928- WhoSSW 91
Michelini, Sylvia Hamilton 1946- WhoAmW 91
Michelis, Michael Frank 1938- WhoWor 91
Michell, John 1724-1793 WorAlBi
Michell, Keith 1928- ConTFT 8
Michell, Monica Y BiDrAPA 89
Michelle, Simone 1917- WhoWor 91
Michelman, Peggy Crystal 1932- WhoAmW 91
Michelotti, John Richard 1948- St&PR 91
Michelow, Sybil 1925- IntWWM 90
Michelozzo 1396-1472? IntDcAA 90
Michels, Agnes Kirsopp Lake 1909- WhoAm 90
Michels, Allen H. BioIn 16
Michels, Caroll Chesy 1943- WhoAmW 91
Michels, Daniel Lester 1941- WhoAm 90
Michels, David Barry 1942- WhoWor 91
Michels, Eileen Manning 1926- WhoAmA 91
Michels, Eugene 1926- WhoAm 90
Michels, F. Thomas St&PR 91
Michels, Jeff BioIn 16
Michels, Joseph William 1936- WhoAm 90
Michels, Michael E. 1951- WhoWrEP 89
Michels, Robert 1936- BiDrAPA 89, WhoAm 90
Michels, Roy Samuel 1932- WhoSSW 91
Michels, William Charles 1948- St&PR 91
Michelsen, Alfonso Lopez BioIn 16
Michelsen, Christopher Bruce Hermann 1940- WhoE 91
Michelsen, John Lewis 1945- WhoE 91
Michelsen, Neil Raymond 1943- WhoE 91
Michelsen, Per 1954- WhoWor 91
Michelson, Alan 1934- St&PR 91
Michelson, Albert Abraham 1852-1931 BioIn 16, WorAlBi
Michelson, Charles 1869-1948 BioIn 16
Michelson, David BiDrAPA 89
Michelson, Edward Harlan 1926- WhoE 91
Michelson, Edward J. 1915- WhoAm 90
Michelson, Gertrude Geraldine 1925- St&PR 91, WhoAm 90
Michelson, Harley M. 1949- St&PR 91
Michelson, Harry H BiDrAPA 89
Michelson, Irving 1922- WhoAm 90
Michelson, Joan Elaine 1943- WhoWor 91
Michelson, Mark A. 1935- WhoAm 90
Michelson, Max, Jr. 1921- WhoAm 90
Michelson, Pamula Kay 1953- WhoAmW 91
Michelson, Peter F. 1935- WhoWrEP 89
Michelson, Philip L 1948- WhoAmA 91
Michelson, Richard 1953- WhoWrEP 89
Michelson, William BioIn 16
Michelucci, Roberto PenDiMP
Michener, Charles Duncan 1918- WhoAm 90
Michener, David P 1923- BiDrAPA 89
Michener, James 1907- WorAlBi
Michener, James A 1907- ConLC 60 [port], MajTwCW
Michener, James Albert 1907- WhoAm 90, WhoWrEP 89
Michener, John 1942- St&PR 91
Michener, Roland 1900- St&PR 91, WhoAm 90
Michenfelder, Joseph Francis 1929- WhoE 91
Michenopah 1780?-1849 WhNaAH
Michero, William Henderson 1925- St&PR 91, WhoAm 90
Michetschlager, Helen Theresa 1959- IntWWM 90
Michetti, Susan Jane 1948- WhoAmW 91, WhoEmL 91, WhoWor 91
Michich, Velizar WhoAmA 91
Michie, Allan Andrew 1915-1973 AuBYP 90
Michie, Charles Martin, III 1954- WhoSSW 91
Michie, Clarence Richard 1937- St&PR 91
Michie, Donald BioIn 16
Michie, James Charles, Sr. 1928- St&PR 91
Michie, Jonathan 1957- ConAu 132, WhoWor 91
Michie, Mary 1922- WhoAmW 91
Michie, Robin Morris 1965- WhoSSW 91
Michielsen, Jean-Pierre 1933- WhoWor 91
Michiko, Empress EncJap
Michinard, George S. 1935- St&PR 91
Michiru, Imai 1931- WhoWor 91
Michl, Josef 1939- WhoAm 90
Michl, Lynn R. 1959- St&PR 91
Michlin, Irving R. 1936- St&PR 91
Michlin, Norman 1922- St&PR 91
Michlin, Rose Ann 1952- WhoAmW 91
Michlink, Fred P. 1946- St&PR 91
Michlowski, Thomas John 1947- BiDrAPA 89
Michniewski, Wojciech 1947- IntWWM 90
Michnik, Adam BioIn 16
Michnik, Adam 1946- CurBio 90 [port]
Michnik, Ellena B BiDrAPA 89
Michod, Susan A 1945- WhoAmA 91
Michon, John Albertus 1935- WhoWor 91
Michon, Marie EncCoWW
Michuda, Nancy Marie 1956- WhoAmW 91
Michulka, Robert F. 1947- St&PR 91
Mick, Charles Lee 1946- St&PR 91
Mick, Colin Kennedy 1941- WhoWrEP 89
Mick, Diane Joan 1955- WhoAmW 91
Mick, Howard Harold 1934- WhoAm 90
Mick, Margaret Anne 1947- WhoAmW 91
Mick, Robert Lee 1949- BiDrAPA 89
Mick, Thomas S. 1933- ODwPR 91
Micka, Salomea Sophie 1940- WhoAmW 91
Micka, Thomas F 1949- BiDrAPA 89
Mickaelian, Fred, Jr. 1933- ODwPR 91

Mickal, Abe 1913- *WhoAm 90*
Mickans, Viktorija *BiDrAPA 89*
Mickel, Buck 1925- *St&PR 91, WhoAm 90, WhoSSW 91*
Mickel, Ronald J. 1933- *St&PR 91*
Mickells, Edward F. 1952- *St&PR 91*
Mickelson, Alan Rolf 1950- *WhoEmL 91*
Mickelson, Arnold Rust 1922- *WhoAm 90*
Mickelson, Carolyn *BioIn 16*
Mickelson, Cecil Howard *BiDrAPA 89*
Mickelson, George S. 1941- *WhoAm 90, WhoWor 91*
Mickelson, Nadine Rosena 1934- *WhoWrEP 89*
Mickelson, Sig 1913- *BioIn 16, WhoAm 90*
Mickelson, Terry R. 1943- *St&PR 91*
Mickelwait, Lowell Pitzer 1905- *WhoAm 90*
Mickenberg, David 1954- *WhoAm 90, WhoAmA 91*
Mickens, Ronald Elbert 1943- *WhoWrEP 89*
Mickey and Sylvia *DrBIPA 90*
Mickey, John B., Jr. 1949- *St&PR 91*
Mickey, Kevin Michael 1958- *WhoE 91*
Mickey, Paul Albert 1937- *WhoSSW 91*
Mickey, Paul Fogle, Jr. 1949- *WhoAm 90*
Mickey, Roger David 1945- *St&PR 91*
Mickiewicz, Adam 1798-1855 *WorAlBi*
Mickiewicz, Ellen Propper 1938- *WhoAm 90*
Mickish, Verle L 1928- *WhoAmA 91*
Mickle, James C 1933- *BiDrAPA 89*
Mickle, Kathryn Alma 1946- *WhoAmW 91*
Mickle, Shelley Fraser 1944- *ConAu 132*
Micklem, Gerald 1911-1988 *AnObit 1988*
Mickler, Ernest *BioIn 16*
Micklewright, Jerrold J. 1934- *St&PR 91*
Mickley, G. Andrew 1948- *WhoSSW 91*
Mickley, Harold Somers 1918- *WhoAm 90*
Micklin, Harvey G 1936- *BiDrAPA 89*
Micklos, John Joseph, Jr. 1956- *WhoWrEP 89*
Micklos-Maisey, Janet M. 1947- *WhoAmW 91*
Micklow, Craig Woodward 1947- *WhoSSW 91*
Micko, Alexander S. 1947- *St&PR 91, WhoAm 90*
Micks, Don Wilfred 1918- *WhoAm 90*
Micksch, Jurgen 1941- *WhoWor 91*
Mickus, Carolyn *BiDrAPA 89*
Mickus, Donald Vincent 1946- *St&PR 91*
Micle, Veronica 1850-1889 *EncCoWW*
Micoli, Richard Andrew 1949- *WhoE 91*
Micolo, Anthony Michael 1949- *WhoE 91*
Micon, Leonard 1911- *BiDrAPA 89*
Micozzi, Marc Stephen 1953- *WhoE 91*
Micsko, Rudolph J., Jr. 1946- *St&PR 91*
Micucci, Patricia 1934- *WhoAmW 91*
Micus, Stephan *NewAgMG*
Miczek, Klaus Alexander 1944- *WhoAm 90*
Miczulski, Ann M. 1946- *St&PR 91*
Miday, Karen Kallberg *BiDrAPA 89*
Middaugh, Jack Kendall, II 1949- *WhoSSW 91, WhoWor 91*
Middaugh, Robert Burton 1935- *WhoAm 90, WhoAmA 91*
Middelkamp, Deborah S. 1953- *WhoEmL 91*
Middelkamp, John Neal 1925- *WhoAm 90*
Middendorf, Alice Carter 1940- *WhoE 91*
Middendorf, Heidi Elise 1961- *BiDrAPA 89*
Middendorf, J. William 1924- *WhoAm 90*
Middendorf, John Harlan 1922- *WhoAm 90, WhoWrEP 89*
Middendorf, William Henry 1921- *WhoAm 90*
Middleberg, Don 1945- *ODwPR 91*
Middlebrook, David *WhoWrEP 89*
Middlebrook, David A 1944- *WhoAmA 91*
Middlebrook, Diane Wood 1939- *WhoWrEP 89*
Middlebrook, John G. *BioIn 16*
Middlebrook, Martin 1932- *ConAu 31NR*
Middlebrook, Robert W. 1916-1989 *BioIn 16*
Middlebrook, Stephen Beach 1937- *St&PR 91*
Middlebrook, Tom Anderson *BiDrAPA 89*
Middlebrooks, Eddie Joe 1932- *WhoAm 90, WhoSSW 91, WhoWor 91*
Middleditch, Brian Stanley 1945- *WhoWor 91*
Middleditch, Leigh Benjamin, Jr. 1929- *WhoAm 90*
Middlekauff, George Wiles *BiDrAPA 89*
Middlekauff, James Holan 1938- *WhoE 91*
Middlekauff, Robert 1929- *ConAu 130*
Middlekauff, Robert Lawrence 1929- *WhoAm 90, WhoWrEP 89*
Middlekauff, Roger David 1935- *WhoAm 90, WhoE 91*
Middleman, Raoul F 1935- *WhoAmA 91*
Middleman, Sylvia Smith 1939- *WhoE 91*
Middlemass, Frank 1919- *ConTFT 8*
Middlemass, Jean 1834-1919 *FemiCLE*
Middlesworth, Chester Paul 1929- *St&PR 91*
Middleton, Alan Charles 1946- *WhoAm 90*
Middleton, Anthony Wayne, Jr. 1939- *WhoWor 91*
Middleton, Arthur 1742-1787 *EncCRAm*
Middleton, Arthur Everett *BiDrAPA 89*
Middleton, Arthur Wesley 1936- *WhoSSW 91*
Middleton, Carole Foster 1946- *WhoAmW 91, WhoWor 91*
Middleton, Charles Kirkland 1962- *WhoSSW 91*
Middleton, Charles Ronald 1937- *BiDrAPA 89*
Middleton, Christopher *EncCRAm*
Middleton, Christopher 1926- *WhoAm 90*
Middleton, David 1920- *WhoAm 90*
Middleton, David Andrew 1966- *WhoSSW 91*
Middleton, Dironda Lynn 1950- *WhoAmW 91*
Middleton, Donald Earl 1930- *St&PR 91, WhoAm 90*
Middleton, Drew 1913- *WhoWrEP 89*
Middleton, Drew 1913-1990 *BioIn 16, CurBio 90N, NewYTBS 90 [port]*
Middleton, Drew 1914?-1990 *ConAu 130*
Middleton, Elizabeth *BiDEWW, FemiCLE*
Middleton, Elliott, Jr. 1925- *WhoAm 90*
Middleton, Elwyn Linton 1914- *WhoSSW 91, WhoWor 91*
Middleton, Francis Gaillard 1940- *WhoSSW 91*
Middleton, Frank Walters, Jr. 1919- *WhoAm 90*
Middleton, Franklin H. *BioIn 16*
Middleton, Frederick Dobson 1825-1898 *DcCanB 12*
Middleton, Gerard Viner 1931- *WhoAm 90*
Middleton, Harry Joseph 1921- *WhoAm 90, WhoSSW 91*
Middleton, Haydn 1955- *ConAu 132*
Middleton, Henry 1717-1784 *BiDrUSE 89, EncCRAm*
Middleton, Henry 1770-1846 *BioIn 16*
Middleton, Herman David, Sr. 1925- *WhoAm 90*
Middleton, Jack Baer 1929- *WhoAm 90*
Middleton, Jack L. 1930- *St&PR 91*
Middleton, James Arthur 1936- *WhoAm 90, WhoSSW 91*
Middleton, James Franklin 1946- *WhoWrEP 89*
Middleton, John Francis Marchment 1921- *WhoAm 90*
Middleton, Lee 1940- *WhoAmW 91*
Middleton, Linda Greathouse 1950- *St&PR 91*
Middleton, Linda Jean Greathouse 1950- *WhoAm 90, WhoEmL 91*
Middleton, Lowell Glenn 1948- *St&PR 91*
Middleton, Marc Stephen 1950- *WhoEmL 91*
Middleton, Marilyn Wagner 1925- *WhoAmW 91*
Middleton, Milton Green *BiDrAPA 89*
Middleton, Nancy Laura 1949- *BiDrAPA 89*
Middleton, Norman G. 1935- *WhoWrEP 89*
Middleton, Norman Graham 1935- *WhoSSW 91, WhoWor 91*
Middleton, Patricia Jean 1937- *BiDrAPA 89*
Middleton, Paul F. 1902- *St&PR 91*
Middleton, Ray 1907- *OxCPMus*
Middleton, Richard L. 1939- *ODwPR 91, St&PR 91*
Middleton, Robert 1920- *WhoAm 90*
Middleton, Silvia Gilbert 1953- *WhoSSW 91*
Middleton, Stephen 1954- *WhoSSW 91*
Middleton, Susan R *BiDrAPA 89*
Middleton, Thomas *BioIn 16*
Middleton, Thomas Joseph 1942- *St&PR 91*
Middleton, Vincent Francis 1951- *WhoEmL 91*
Middleton, Wallace Pierpont 1946- *St&PR 91*
Middlewood, Martin Eugene 1947- *WhoEmL 91*
Midelfort, Christian F *BiDrAPA 89*
Midelfort, H Berit *BiDrAPA 89*
Midener, Walter 1912- *WhoAmA 91*
Midgett, James Clayton, Jr. 1950- *WhoEmL 91*
Midgett, John Thomas 1952- *WhoSSW 91*
Midgette, Willard Franklin 1937-1978 *WhoAmA 91N*
Midgley, Alvin Rees, Jr. 1933- *WhoAm 90*
Midgley, C. Edward 1937- *St&PR 91*
Midgley, Charles Edward 1937- *WhoAm 90*
Midili, Arthur R. 1931- *St&PR 91*
Midjumdal, Joreidr Hermundardottir i 1239?- *EncCoWW*
Midkiff, Dale *BioIn 16*
Midkiff, Morris E., III 1945- *WhoEmL 91*
Midkiff, Robert R. 1920- *St&PR 91*
Midkiff, Robert Richards 1920- *WhoAm 90*
Midlarsky, Elizabeth *WhoAmW 91*
Midlarsky, Manus Issachar 1937- *WhoAm 90*
Midler, Bette *BioIn 16*
Midler, Bette 1945- *EncPR&S 89, OxCPMus, WhoAm 90, WhoAmW 91, WorAlBi*
Midori 1971- *BioIn 16, CurBio 90 [port]*
Midura, Peter 1918- *BiDrAPA 89*
Midwinter, Thomas Richard 1938- *WhoE 91*
Midwood, Faith Bustard *BiDrAPA 89*
Midwood, George A. 1934- *WhoAm 90*
Midyett, Charles L. 1939- *St&PR 91*
Midzunoe, Yuichi 1941- *WhoWor 91*
Miears, Barbara Ann *BiDrAPA 89*
Mieczkowski, Edwin 1929- *WhoAmA 91*
Miedema, Sylvia Ann 1904- *St&PR 91*
Miegel, Agnes 1879-1964 *BioIn 16*
Miel, Alice *BioIn 16*
Miel, Vicky Ann 1951- *WhoAmW 91*
Mielcuszny, Albert John 1941- *WhoAm 90*
Mielczarski, Jerzy Andrzej 1947- *WhoSSW 91*
Miele, Alfonse Ralph 1922- *WhoAm 90*
Miele, Angelo 1922- *WhoAm 90, WhoWrEP 89*
Miele, Anthony William 1926- *WhoAm 90*
Miele, Frank *BioIn 16*
Miele, Hazel Donnelly 1936- *WhoAmW 91*
Miele, Joel Arthur, Sr. 1934- *WhoE 91, WhoWor 91*
Mielecki, Max C. 1931- *St&PR 91*
Mielke, Clarence Harold, Jr. 1936- *WhoAm 90, WhoWor 91*
Mielke, David Harry 1938- *BiDrAPA 89*
Mielke, Donald Craig 1943- *St&PR 91, WhoAm 90, WhoSSW 91*
Mielke, Frederick William, Jr. 1921- *St&PR 91, WhoAm 90*
Mielke, Lynne Renee 1959- *BiDrAPA 89*
Mielke, Mary Margaret 1947- *WhoAmW 91*
Mielke, Wayne 1954- *ODwPR 91*
Mielke, Wayne Joseph 1954- *WhoWrEP 89*
Mielke, William John 1947- *WhoEmL 91*
Mielziner, Jo 1901-1976 *ConDes 90, WhoAmA 91N, WorAlBi*
Mier, Phyllis Jean 1949- *WhoAmW 91*
Miera, Epimenio A 1865- *AmLegL*
Miercort, Clifford R. 1940- *St&PR 91*
Miercort, Clifford Roy 1940- *WhoAm 90*
Miers, Anthony Cecil Capel 1906-1985 *DcNaB 1981*
Miers, Earl Schenck 1910-1972 *AuBYP 90*
Mierzejewski, Mieczyslaw 1905- *IntWWM 90*
Mies Van Der Rohe 1886-1969 *WorAlBi*
Mies van der Rohe, Ludwig 1886-1969 *BioIn 16, PenDiDA 89, WhoAmA 91N, WorAlBi*
Miesch, Margaret Louise *BiDrAPA 89*
Miesel, Rochelle Kristal 1941- *WhoAmW 91*
Miesner, Terry Ann 1961- *WhoAmW 91*
Miesse, Mary Elizabeth *WhoAmW 91, WhoSSW 91, WhoWor 91*
Miessner, William Otto 1880-1967 *BioIn 16*
Mietens, Carl 1933- *WhoWor 91*
Mietzel, Dennis Oliver 1940- *St&PR 91*
Miewald, Bruce Keith 1956- *BiDrAPA 89*
Miezajs, Dainis 1929- *WhoAmA 91*
Miezio, Stanley *BiDrAPA 89*
Mifflin, Eddie 1923-1971 *Ballpl 90*
Mifflin, Theodore Edward 1946- *WhoSSW 91*
Mifflin, Thomas 1744-1800 *BiDrUSE 89, BioIn 16, EncCRAm*
Mifune Toshiro 1920- *EncJap*
Mifune, Chizuko 1886-1911 *EncPaPR 91*
Mifune, Toshiro 1920- *WhoWor 91*
Miga, George P. *ODwPR 91*
Migala, Lucyna Jozefa 1944- *WhoAmW 91, WhoWor 91*
Migdal, Sheldon Paul 1936- *WhoAm 90*
Migden, Chester L. 1921- *WhoAm 90*
Migden, William 1920- *BiDrAPA 89*
Migel, Parmenia *ConAu 130*
Migel, Richard *BiDrAPA 89*
Migell, Bruce Arthur 1933- *St&PR 91*
Migenes, Julia 1945- *IntWWM 90*
Migeon, Claude Jean 1923- *WhoAm 90*
Migeon, Pierre, II 1701-1758 *PenDiDA 89*
Mighell, Kenneth John 1931- *WhoAm 90, WhoSSW 91*
Mighell, Robert L 1927- *BiDrAPA 89*
Mighels, Henry R. 1830-1879 *AmLegL*
Might, Charles F. *BioIn 16*
Might, Thomas Owen 1951- *WhoAm 90*
Migl, Donald Raymond 1947- *WhoEmL 91, WhoSSW 91*
Migliacci, Steven 1959- *St&PR 91*
Miglietta, Angelo Louis 1928- *St&PR 91*
Miglietti, Mario 1946- *WhoWor 91*
Miglio, Daniel J. 1940- *St&PR 91*
Miglio, Daniel Joseph 1940- *WhoAm 90*
Migliori, A. Tee 1936- *St&PR 91*
Migliozzi, Joseph J. 1950- *St&PR 91*
Migliozzi, Joseph John 1950- *WhoE 91*
Migliuolo, Giovanni 1927-1989 *BioIn 16*
Miglore, Joseph J. 1945- *St&PR 91*
Miglore, Joseph James 1945- *WhoAm 90*
Mignanelli, James R. 1932- *St&PR 91*
Mignanelli, James Robert 1932- *WhoAm 90*
Mignanelli, Thomas D. *WhoAm 90*
Mignanelli, Thomas E. 1948- *St&PR 91*
Mignani, Roberto 1946- *WhoWor 91*
Mignerey, Lester L., Jr. 1944- *St&PR 91*
Mignery, Herb *BioIn 16*
Mignogna, Marie Jean *BiDrAPA 89*
Mignogna, Thomas S. 1933- *St&PR 91*
Mignone, Albert Ernest 1943- *WhoE 91*
Mignone, Mario B. 1940- *WhoAm 90*
Mignone, Robert Joseph *BiDrAPA 89*
Mignosa, Santo 1934- *WhoAmA 91*
Mignucci-Giannoni, Antonio Armando 1964- *WhoSSW 91*
Migone, Paolo 1950- *BiDrAPA 89*
Migue, Jean Luc 1933- *WhoAm 90*
Miguez, Rafael H 1950- *BiDrAPA 89*
Migura, Wallace William 1943- *WhoSSW 91*
Mihaileanu, Andrei Calin 1923- *WhoWor 91*
Mihailescu, Manuela 1950- *WhoE 91*
Mihailoff, Ivan *NewYTBS 90*
Mihajlov, Mihajlo 1934- *ConAu 130*
Mihajlov, Mihajlo N. 1934- *WhoWor 91*
Mihalas, Dimitri Manuel 1939- *WhoAm 90*
Mihalas, Nicholas Michael 1937- *WhoAm 90*
Mihalchik, Larry L. 1947- *St&PR 91*
Mihalik, Betty L. 1933- *St&PR 91*
Mihalik, Gary Joseph *BiDrAPA 89*
Mihalik, Joseph Louis *BiDrAPA 89*
Mihalik, Phyllis Ann 1952- *WhoAmW 91*
Mihalko, Patricia Joyce 1940- *WhoAmW 91*
Mihalovich, Tony L. 1948- *St&PR 91*
Mihalovits, Karl S 1937- *BiDrAPA 89*
Mihaly, Andras 1917- *IntWWM 90, WhoWor 91*
Mihaly, Eugene Bramer 1934- *WhoAm 90, WhoWrEP 89*
Mihaly, Orestes J. 1932- *St&PR 91*
Mihalyi, Louis Leonard 1921- *WhoWrEP 89*
Mihanovich, Clement Simon 1913- *WhoAm 90*
Mihaylo, Steven G. 1943- *St&PR 91*
Mihelcic, Pavel 1937- *IntWWM 90*
Mihelic, Drassko 1950- *WhoWor 91*
Mihelich, Jeanette Amelia 1921- *WhoAmW 91*
Mihelich, John L. 1937- *WhoSSW 91*
Mihelick, Stanley Joseph 1929- *St&PR 91, WhoAm 90*
Miheyev, Yaropolk Leonid 1930- *WhoE 91*
Mihich, Enrico 1928- *WhoAm 90*
Mihills, Joan L. 1929- *St&PR 91*
Mihlik, J. John 1942- *St&PR 91*
Mihlon, Lawrence F. 1935- *ODwPR 91*
Mihm, Martin Charles, Jr. *WhoAm 90, WhoE 91*
Mihm, Michael Martin 1943- *WhoAm 90*
Mihnak, Deborah Ann 1959- *WhoAmW 91*
Miho, James 1933- *ConDes 90*
Miho, Tomoko 1933- *ConDes 90*
Mihok, Andrew Francis, Jr. 1934- *WhoAm 90*
Mihoover, Janis Darlene 1951- *WhoAmW 91*
Mihova, Jodi Laski 1940- *IntWWM 90*
Mihovich, Matthew Fedele 1947- *WhoE 91*
Mihram, George Arthur 1939- *WhoE 91*
Mihran, Theodore Gregory 1924- *WhoAm 90*
Mihu, Basil V *BiDrAPA 89*
Mii, Nobuo 1934- *WhoWor 91*
Miido, Endel 1922- *St&PR 91*
Miimura, Hiroshi 1930- *WhoWor 91*
Mijalis, Elaine Jean 1955- *WhoAmW 91*
Mijalkov, Nikita *BioIn 16*
Mijuskovic, Ben Lazare 1937- *ConAu 132*
Mika, David Bedrick 1957- *BiDrAPA 89*
Mika, John Joseph 1938- *St&PR 91*
Mika, William J. 1931- *St&PR 91*
Mikaelian, Tamar 1962- *St&PR 91*
Mikahestow, John *DcCanB 12*
Mikalac, Cecilia *BiDrAPA 89*
Mikalchus, Eleanor Smolkis 1939- *WhoAmW 91*
Mikalow, Alfred Alexander, II 1921- *WhoWor 91*

Mikalson, Jon Dennis 1943- *WhoAm 90*
Mikalson, Roy Gale 1921- *WhoAm 90*
Mikan, George *BioIn 16*
Mikan, George 1924- *WorAlBi*
Mikanopy 1780?-1849 *WhNaAH*
Mikardo, Ian 1908- *BioIn 16*
Mike, Deborah Denise 1959- *WhoAmW 91*
Mike, Marjoree D. 1963- *WhoAmW 91*
Mike-Nard, Beverly Jean 1957- *WhoAmW 91*
Mikel, Charlene Ann 1938- *WhoAmW 91*
Mikel, Mary Eberlein 1959- *WhoAmW 91*
Mikel, Sarah Ann 1947- *WhoAm 90*
Mikelberg, Arnold S. 1937- *St&PR 91*
Mikelberg, Martin 1938- *St&PR 91*
Mikell, Alan Glen 1951- *WhoSSW 91*
Mikell, Vernon Terry 1937- *WhoE 91, WhoWor 91*
Mikelonis, David A. 1948- *WhoAm 90*
Mikels, James Ronald 1937- *WhoSSW 91*
Mikelsons, Velta H 1925- *BiDrAPA 89*
Mikes, John Andrew 1922- *WhoE 91*
Mikesell, A. David 1937- *WhoAm 90*
Mikesell, Marvin Wray 1929- *WhoAm 90*
Mikesell, Mary 1943- *WhoWor 91*
Mikesell, Raymond Frech 1913- *WhoAm 90*
Mikeska, Rudy *BioIn 16*
Mikhael, Nagib T 1952- *BiDrAPA 89*
Mikhail, Adib R 1941- *BiDrAPA 89*
Mikhail, E H 1926- *ConAu 31NR*
Mikhail, Mary Attalla 1945- *WhoEmL 91*
Mikhail, William Mesiha 1935- *WhoWor 91*
Mikhailov, A. I. 1905-1988 *BioIn 16*
Mikhailov, Aleksandr Ivanovich 1905-1988 *BioIn 16*
Mikhailov, M. *ConAu 130*
Mikhailova, Tamara M 1941- *BiDrAPA 89*
Mikhalkov, Nikita *BioIn 16*
Mikhalkov, Sergey Vladimirovich 1913- *WhoWor 91*
Mikheyev, Yuriy Yakhovlevich 1930- *WhoWor 91*
Miki Takeo 1907-1988 *EncJap*
Miki, Takeo 1907-1988 *AnObit 1988, BioIn 16*
Mikic, Diane *BioIn 16*
Mikiewicz, Anna Daniella 1960- *WhoAmW 91*
Mikita, Joseph Karl 1918- *WhoAm 90*
Mikita, Stan 1940- *WorAlBi*
Mikitka, Gerald Peter 1943- *WhoAm 90*
Mikkelborg, Palle 1941- *IntWWM 90*
Mikkelsen, Charles R. 1954- *WhoEmL 91*
Mikkelsen, Edwin Jens 1948- *BiDrAPA 89*
Mikkelsen, Harold W *BiDrAPA 89*
Mikkelsen, Jerry Conrad 1936- *St&PR 91*
Mikkelsen, Pete 1939- *Ballpl 90*
Mikkelsen, Richard 1920- *WhoWor 91*
Mikkelsen, Robert L. 1957- *WhoSSW 91*
Mikkelson, M. D. 1933- *St&PR 91*
Mikkilineni, Jhansi V *BiDrAPA 89*
Mikkilineni, Prasad Sreerama 1950- *BiDrAPA 89*
Mikkola, Krista Eirene 1956- *WhoWor 91*
Miklas, Kestutis Kostas 1922- *St&PR 91*
Miklaucic, Michael J. 1954- *WhoE 91*
Miklich, Thomas Robert 1947- *St&PR 91, WhoAm 90*
Miklowitz, Gloria 1927- *Au&Arts 6 [port], AuBYP 90*
Miklowitz, Gloria D. *BioIn 16*
Miklowitz, Julius 1919- *WhoAm 90*
Miklusak, Thomas Alan 1946- *BiDrAPA 89*
Miko, Joseph James 1964- *WhoE 91*
Mikoian, A. I. 1895-1978 *BioIn 16*
Mikoian, Anastas Ivanovich 1895-1978 *BioIn 16*
Mikolajczak, Boleslaw 1946- *WhoE 91*
Mikolajczak, James Robert 1947- *BiDrAPA 89, WhoEmL 91*
Mikolajczyk, Stanisiaw 1901-1966 *BioIn 16*
Mikolaycak, Charles 1937- *WhoWor 91*
Mikolji, Boris Hrvoje 1926- *WhoAm 90*
Mikoryak, David Wayne 1950- *St&PR 91*
Mikosz, Mark William 1948- *St&PR 91*
Mikovlich, V *EncCoWW*
Mikovsky, Anthony A. 1966- *WhoEmL 91*
Mikropoulos, Harilaos E 1928- *BiDrAPA 89*
Mikrut, Joseph Louis 1954- *St&PR 91*
Mikrut, Thomas John 1948- *St&PR 91*
Miksanek, Arlene Eloise *BiDrAPA 89*
Miksch, John Hohl 1947- *St&PR 91*
Miksis, Eddie 1926- *Ballpl 90*
Mikula, Andrew Michael 1945- *WhoE 91*
Mikula, Bernard James 1936- *St&PR 91*
Mikulas, Joseph Frank 1926- *WhoAm 90*
Mikulay, Robert Lane 1951- *WhoE 91*
Mikulic, Branko 1928- *WhoWor 91*
Mikuliza, William Edward 1934- *St&PR 91*
Mikulski, Barbara A. *BioIn 16*
Mikulski, Barbara Ann 1936- *WhoAm 90, WhoAmW 91, WhoE 91, WhoWor 91*
Mikulski, James Joseph 1934- *WhoAm 90*
Mikulski, Piotr Witold 1925- *WhoAm 90*
Mikulsky, Joan Marilyn 1932- *WhoAm 90*
Mikuriya, Hisao 1929- *WhoWor 91*
Mikuriya, Tod H 1933- *BiDrAPA 89*
Mikus, Eleanore 1927- *WhoAmA 91*
Mikus, Eleanore Ann 1927- *WhoAm 90*
Mikva, Abner Joseph 1926- *WhoAm 90, WhoE 91*
Mila *NewAgMG*
Mila, Massimo 1910-1988 *BioIn 16*
Milach, Peter Christian 1949- *St&PR 91*
Milack, Gary Paul 1949- *WhoE 91*
Milacki, Bob 1964- *Ballpl 90*
Milad, Emad Ramses 1957- *BiDrAPA 89*
Milakovich, D. V. 1946- *St&PR 91*
Milakovich, F. S. 1937- *St&PR 91*
Milam, Anamari Camis 1955- *BiDrAPA 89*
Milam, Cheryl Perilloux 1947- *WhoSSW 91*
Milam, David Kelton, Sr. 1932- *WhoHisp 91*
Milan, Clyde 1887-1953 *Ballpl 90 [port]*
Milan, Edgar J. 1934- *St&PR 91, WhoHisp 91*
Milan, Edwin Ramon 1950- *WhoE 91*
Milan, Ellen Judith 1937- *WhoE 91*
Milan, Luis 1500?-1561? *PenDiMP*
Milan, Mark J. 1951- *St&PR 91*
Milan, Susan *IntWWM 90*
Milan, Thomas Lawrence 1941- *WhoE 91*
Milan-Padro, Teodoro 1924- *BiDrAPA 89*
Milan-Ponce, Ramon Arturo *BiDrAPA 89*
Milander, Henry Martin 1939- *WhoAm 90*
Milane, M. P. 1943- *WhoAm 90*
Milanes, Fernando Jose 1936- *BiDrAPA 89*
Milanes, Lila Du-Breuil 1925- *WhoAmW 91*
Milanese, Paul Charles *BiDrAPA 89*
Milanesi, David Laurence 1947- *St&PR 91*
Milanesi, Maurizio 1938- *WhoWor 91*
Milani, Diva 1958- *WhoAmW 91*
Milani, Ernest John 1929- *WhoAm 90*
Milani, Milena 1922- *EncCoWW*
Milani-Comparetti, Marco Severo 1926- *WhoWor 91*
Milano, Alyssa *BioIn 16*
Milano, Carol Ellen 1946- *WhoAmW 91*
Milano, Eugene John 1927- *St&PR 91*
Milano, Frank 1911- *St&PR 91*
Milano, Joseph A. 1944- *WhoE 91*
Milano, Michael R 1939- *BiDrAPA 89*
Milano, Nicholas P. 1922- *St&PR 91*
Milano, Robert J. 1912- *St&PR 91*
Milano, Robert L. 1960- *WhoEmL 91*
Milano, Vincent Anthony 1927- *St&PR 91*
Milanov, Zinka 1906-1989 *AnObit 1989, BioIn 16, PenDiMP*
Milanova, Stoika 1945- *IntWWM 90, PenDiMP*
Milant, Jean Robert 1943- *WhoAmA 91*
Milardo, Terrence John 1941- *WhoE 91*
Milas, Lawrence William 1935- *WhoE 91*
Milashkina, Tamara 1934- *PenDiMP*
Milasi, Tony *BioIn 16*
Milaski, John Joseph 1959- *WhoE 91, WhoEmL 91, WhoWor 91*
Milauskas, Steven Joseph 1953- *WhoSSW 91*
Milavic, Jack Antone 1940- *WhoSSW 91*
Milavsky, Harold Phillip 1931- *St&PR 91, WhoAm 90*
Milavsky, J. Ronald 1933- *WhoE 91*
Milazzo, Richard *BioIn 16, WhoAmA 91*
Milbank, Helen Kirkpatrick 1909- *BioIn 16*
Milbank, Jeremiah 1920- *St&PR 91, WhoAm 90*
Milberg, Lawrence 1913-1989 *BioIn 16*
Milberg, Susan Bodner 1949- *WhoAmW 91*
Milborne, Hunter *BioIn 16*
Milbourn, Frank William *St&PR 91N*
Milbourne, Joseph C. 1951- *St&PR 91*
Milbourne, Larry 1951- *Ballpl 90*
Milbourne, Thomas Elwood 1946- *WhoE 91*
Milbrath, Earlon Leroy 1941- *St&PR 91, WhoAm 90*
Milbrath, Jeanne L. *ODwPR 91*
Milbrath, Lester Walter 1925- *WhoE 91*
Milbrath, Mary Merrill Lemke 1940- *WhoAmW 91*
Milbrath, Robert Henry *WhoAm 90*
Milburn, Herbert Theodore 1931- *WhoAm 90, WhoSSW 91*
Milburn, Jackie 1924-1988 *AnObit 1988*
Milburn, Jeffrey Gerald 1935- *St&PR 91, WhoAm 90*
Milburn, Lewis H *BiDrAPA 89*
Milburn, Richard D. 1943- *St&PR 91*
Milburn, Richard Henry 1928- *WhoAm 90*
Milburn, Robert 1907- *ConAu 130*
Milbury, K. David 1939- *St&PR 91*
Milbury, Mike 1953- *WhoAm 90, WhoE 91*
Milby, James Dean, Sr. 1950- *WhoWor 91*
Milch, Erhard 1892-1972 *BioIn 16*
Milch, Harold Carlton 1908- *WhoAmA 91N*
Milch, Neal Bruce 1958- *St&PR 91*
Milch, Pamela H. 1960- *WhoAmW 91*
Milch, Robert Austin 1929- *WhoE 91*
Milcich, Timothy Paul 1952- *WhoSSW 91*
Milcinski, Janez Fran 1913- *WhoWor 91*
Milde, Arij de 1634-1708 *PenDiDA 89*
Milde, Helmut Ingo 1934- *St&PR 91*
Mildenhall, Glen Thomas 1951- *WhoSSW 91*
Mildenstein, Robert Thomas 1947- *St&PR 91*
Milder, Alvin Sherman 1932- *St&PR 91*
Milder, Jay 1934- *WhoAmA 91*
Milder-Hauptmann, Anna 1785-1838 *PenDiMP*
Mildmay, Grace 1522-1620 *BiDEWW*
Mildmay, Grace 1552?-1620 *FemiCLE*
Mildmay, Grace Sherrington 1553-1620 *BioIn 16*
Mildner, Johann Joseph 1764-1808 *PenDiDA 89*
Mildon, James Lee 1936- *WhoWor 91*
Mildon, Marie Roberta 1935- *WhoAmW 91, WhoWor 91*
Mildren, Margaret Joyce 1936- *IntWWM 90*
Mildvan, Donna 1942- *WhoAm 90, WhoAmW 91*
Mileaf, Howard A. 1937- *St&PR 91*
Miledi, Ricardo 1927- *WhoAm 90*
Mileham, William Dunning 1946- *St&PR 91*
Milena 1896-1944 *BioIn 16*
Miler, Martin C. *WhoAm 90, WhoSSW 91*
Miles *PenDiDA 89*
Miles, A. L. *WhoSSW 91*
Miles, A. Stevens 1929- *WhoAm 90*
Miles, Alexander Charles 1958- *WhoWor 91*
Miles, Alfred Lee 1913- *WhoWor 91*
Miles, Algene Stevens 1929- *St&PR 91*
Miles, Arthur J. 1920- *WhoAm 90*
Miles, Ashley 1904-1988 *AnObit 1988*
Miles, Barbara Ann 1940- *WhoAmW 91*
Miles, Betty 1928- *AuBYP 90*
Miles, Bonnie Stroud 1935- *WhoSSW 91*
Miles, Brian John 1961- *St&PR 91*
Miles, Candice St. Jacques 1951- *WhoWrEP 89*
Miles, Carlotta G *BiDrAPA 89*
Miles, Charlene *BioIn 16*
Miles, Charlene 1928- *WhoAmW 91*
Miles, Christine M 1951- *WhoAmA 91*
Miles, Christine Marie 1951- *WhoAm 90, WhoAmW 91, WhoE 91*
Miles, Clifford Arthur 1954- *WhoSSW 91*
Miles, Cyril 1918- *WhoAmA 91*
Miles, Dee 1909-1976 *Ballpl 90*
Miles, Derek Van 1951- *WhoSSW 91*
Miles, Donald Geoffrey 1952- *WhoWor 91*
Miles, Donna Jean 1944- *WhoAmW 91*
Miles, Dorothy Marvin 1940- *WhoE 91*
Miles, Douglas Irving 1949- *WhoSSW 91*
Miles, Dudley 1947- *ConAu 131*
Miles, Ellen Gross 1941- *WhoAmA 91*
Miles, Emma Bell 1879-1919 *BioAmW*
Miles, Frank Charles 1926- *St&PR 91, WhoAm 90*
Miles, Frederick A 1928- *BiDrAPA 89*
Miles, Hampton Michael 1931- *WhoSSW 91*
Miles, Henry 1824-1890 *AmLegL*
Miles, Henry H W 1915- *BiDrAPA 89*
Miles, Henry Hopper 1818-1895 *DcCanB 12*
Miles, Herman Wilbur 1924- *WhoE 91*
Miles, Howard Douglass 1954- *St&PR 91*
Miles, Jack *WhoWrEP 89*
Miles, Jack 1942- *WhoAm 90*
Miles, James Larry, Jr. 1958- *WhoSSW 91*
Miles, Janice Ann 1949- *WhoAmW 91*
Miles, Jeanne Patterson *WhoAm 90*
Miles, Jeanne Patterson 1908- *WhoAmA 91*
Miles, Jeremy John 1933- *WhoWor 91*
Miles, Jesse Mc Lane 1932- *WhoAm 90*
Miles, Joanna 1940- *WhoAm 90, WhoAmW 91*
Miles, John *BioIn 16*
Miles, John C., II 1942- *St&PR 91*
Miles, John J., III 1943- *St&PR 91*
Miles, John Karl 1937- *WhoAm 90*
Miles, John R. 1941- *St&PR 91*
Miles, John Russiano 1942- *WhoWrEP 89*
Miles, John Wilder 1920- *WhoAm 90*
Miles, Josephine 1911-1985 *FemiCLE*
Miles, Julia *BioIn 16*
Miles, Julia 1930?- *NotWoAT*
Miles, L. W. 1933- *St&PR 91*
Miles, Laveda Ann 1945- *WhoAmW 91*
Miles, Lawrence E. 1938- *St&PR 91*
Miles, Leland 1924- *St&PR 91*
Miles, Leland Weber 1924- *WhoAm 90*
Miles, Leo W. 1927- *St&PR 91*
Miles, Lizzie 1895-1963 *BioIn 16*
Miles, M Marianne *WhoAmA 91*
Miles, Marc Adam 1948- *WhoE 91*
Miles, Margaret 1963- *WhoAmW 91*
Miles, Margaret Ruth 1937- *WhoAm 90*
Miles, Michael A. *BioIn 16*
Miles, Michael Arnold 1939- *St&PR 91, WhoAm 90*
Miles, Michael Edward 1954- *WhoE 91*
Miles, Miska *AuBYP 90*
Miles, Miska 1899-1986 *BioIn 16*
Miles, Mitchell 1951- *WhoE 91*
Miles, Nelson Appleton 1839-1925 *BioIn 16, WhNaAH [port], WorAlBi*
Miles, Patricia 1930- *AuBYP 90*
Miles, Raymond Edward 1932- *WhoAm 90*
Miles, Richard Donald 1942- *St&PR 91*
Miles, Richard Ernest 1939- *WhoE 91*
Miles, Richard Jones 1932- *St&PR 91*
Miles, Robert Henry 1944- *WhoSSW 91*
Miles, Robert W *BiDrAPA 89*
Miles, Samuel Israel *BiDrAPA 89*
Miles, Samuel Israel 1949- *WhoAm 90, WhoEmL 91*
Miles, Sarah *BioIn 16*
Miles, Sarah 1941- *WorAlBi*
Miles, Sheila Lee 1952- *WhoAmA 91*
Miles, Sonia Rosemarie *BiDrAPA 89*
Miles, Sonia Rosemarie 1944- *WhoAmW 91*
Miles, Stephen H. 1946- *St&PR 91*
Miles, Susan 1887-1970 *FemiCLE*
Miles, Sylvia *BioIn 16*
Miles, Toni L. 1953- *WhoAmW 91*
Miles, Vera 1930- *WhoAm 90*
Miles, Vic 1937?- *DrBlPA 90*
Miles, Virginia 1916- *WhoAm 90*
Miles, William *BiDrAPA 89*
Miles, William 1931- *DrBlPA 90*
Miles-LaGrange, Vicki 1953- *WhoAmW 91*
Milestone, Ronald *BiDrAPA 89*
Miletic, Michael Joseph 1958- *BiDrAPA 89*
Milewski, Frank R. 1932- *St&PR 91*
Milewski, Michael Gregory 1958- *WhoEmL 91*
Milewski, Miroslaw 1950- *WhoWor 91*
Milewski, Ronald L. 1951- *St&PR 91*
Miley, Bubber 1903-1932 *OxCPMus*
Miley, Chuck 1943- *WhoE 91*
Miley, Chuck E 1943- *WhoAmA 91*
Miley, Deborah Karlene 1949- *WhoAmW 91*
Miley, Dennis P 1950- *BiDrAPA 89*
Miley, Fred 1937- *BiDrAPA 89*
Miley, George Hunter 1933- *WhoAm 90*
Miley, Les 1934- *WhoAmA 91*
Miley, Marion *BioIn 16*
Miley, Mimi Conneen 1946- *WhoAmA 91*
Miley, Samuel A. 1957- *St&PR 91*
Milford, David Sumner 1905-1984 *DcNaB 1981*
Milford, Frederick John 1926- *WhoAm 90*
Milford, Patricia Polino 1940- *WhoAmW 91*
Milfort, Louis Le Clerc *WhNaAH*
Milgate, Murray 1950- *WhoAm 90, WhoE 91*
Milgram, Jerome H. 1938- *WhoAm 90*
Milgram, Joseph E. 1900-1989 *BioIn 16*
Milgram, Morris 1916- *WhoE 91*
Milgram, Richard Myron 1943- *WhoE 91*
Milgrim, Franklin C *BiDrAPA 89*
Milgrim, Franklin Marshall 1925- *WhoAm 90*
Milgrom, Harry 1912- *AuBYP 90*
Milhaud, Darius 1892-1974 *PenDiMP A*
Milhaven, John Giles 1927- *WhoAm 90*
Milhelick, Stanley Joseph 1929- *St&PR 91*
Milhoan, Randall Bell 1944- *WhoAmA 91*
Milholm, Dale Milton 1926- *St&PR 91*
Milhorat, Thomas Herrick 1936- *WhoAm 90, WhoWor 91*
Milhous, Judith 1946- *ConAu 129*
Milhous, Katherine 1894-1977 *AuBYP 90, WhoAmA 91N*
Milhouse, Paul William 1910- *WhoAm 90*
Mili, Fatma 1956- *WhoEmL 91*
Miliacca, John Michael 1959- *WhoEmL 91*
Milian, Arsenio 1945- *St&PR 91*
Milian, Nestor E. *BiDrAPA 89*
Milian, Rudolph Enrique 1950- *WhoSSW 91*
Milic, Louis Tonko 1922- *WhoAm 90*
Milic-Emili, Joseph 1931- *WhoAm 90*
Milich, S. Herb 1955- *St&PR 91*
Milici, John A 1924- *BiDrAPA 89*
Milillo, L. 1946- *St&PR 91*
Miliman, David Jay 1957- *WhoEmL 91*
Milin, Robert Paul *BiDrAPA 89*
Milione, Jeanette Margaret 1947- *WhoAmW 91*
Miliora, Maria Teresa 1938- *WhoAm 90*
Militano, Salvatore *BiDrAPA 89*
Militant *MajTwCW*

Miliukov, Pavel Nikolaevich 1859-1943 *BioIn 16*
Milius, John *BioIn 16*
Milius, John 1944- *ConTFT 8*
Milius, John Frederick 1944- *WhoAm 90*
Milius, Lu Ann 1952- *WhoEmL 91*
Milivojevic, Marko 1957- *WhoWor 91*
Miljevic, Vujo Ilija 1931- *WhoWor 91*
Miljus, Johnny 1895-1976 *Ballpl 90*
Milk, Harvey *BioIn 16*
Milk, Leslie Berg 1943- *WhoAmW 91*
Milk, Robert W. 1926- *WhoAm 90*
Milk, Robert William 1926- *St&PR 91*
Milke, Denis Jerome 1938- *BiDrAPA 89*
Milken, Michael R. *BioIn 16*
Milken, Michael R. 1946- *ConAmBL, EncABHB 7 [port]*
Milkina, Nina 1919- *IntWWM 90*
Milkman, Roger Dawson 1930- *WhoAm 90*
Milkowski, Forrest 1951- *St&PR 91*
Milks, Sally Ann 1949- *WhoAmW 91*
Mill, Andy *BioIn 16*
Mill, Arnold Van 1921- *IntWWM 90*
Mill, Harriet Hardy Taylor 1807-1858 *BioIn 16*
Mill, John Stuart 1806-1873 *BioIn 16, WorAlBi, WrPh P*
Mill, Victor J. 1943- *St&PR 91*
Mill, Victor J., Jr. 1915- *St&PR 91*
Mill, William Robert 1929- *WhoE 91*
Millais, John Everett 1829-1896 *BioIn 16, IntDcAA 90, WorAlBi*
Millan, Angel, Jr. 1945- *WhoHisp 91*
Millan, Carlos Arturo 1937- *BiDrAPA 89*
Millan, Felix 1943- *Ballpl 90*
Millan Astray, Pilar 1879-1949 *EncCoWW*
Millan-Benitez, Ruben 1953- *BiDrAPA 89*
Millan De La O, Juan Carlos 1960- *WhoWor 91*
Milland, Antonio A *BiDrAPA 89*
Milland, Ray 1905-1986 *WorAlBi*
Millane, Arthur Jerome 1925- *St&PR 91*
Millane, Lynn 1928- *WhoAm 90, WhoAmW 91*
Millar, Brian 1947- *EncPaPR 91*
Millar, Edwin N. 1937- *St&PR 91*
Millar, George Robert 1923- *St&PR 91*
Millar, Gertie 1879-1952 *OxCPMus*
Millar, Gordon Halstead 1923- *WhoAm 90*
Millar, Ian *BioIn 16*
Millar, Jack William 1922- *WhoAm 90*
Millar, James Robert 1936- *WhoAm 90*
Millar, Jeffery Lynn 1942- *WhoAm 90*
Millar, John Donald 1934- *WhoAm 90*
Millar, John F. 1936- *St&PR 91*
Millar, Kenneth *TwCCr&M 91*
Millar, Kenneth 1915-1983 *MajTwCW*
Millar, Kenneth Harvey, Jr. 1957- *WhoSSW 91*
Millar, Kenneth Irwin 1947- *WhoAm 90*
Millar, Laurie Sue 1961- *WhoAmW 91*
Millar, Margaret 1915- *FemiCLE, SmATA 61, TwCCr&M 91*
Millar, Margaret Ellis 1915- *WhoAm 90, WhoAmW 91*
Millar, Marian M. 1926- *WhoAmW 91*
Millar, Oliver 1923- *BioIn 16*
Millar, R Gordon T 1919- *BiDrAPA 89*
Millar, Richard W. 1899-1990 *BioIn 16, NewYTBS 90*
Millar, Robert *BioIn 16*
Millar, Robert James 1951- *WhoE 91*
Millar, Sally Gray 1946- *WhoAm 90*
Millar, Stephen Kelly 1948- *St&PR 91*
Millar, Victor Eugene 1935- *WhoAm 90*
Millar, William M *BiDrAPA 89*
Millard, Alice Parsons 1873-1938 *BioIn 16*
Millard, Bryan *BioIn 16*
Millard, Charles E. F. 1932- *WhoAm 90*
Millard, Charles Edward Francis, Jr. 1957- *WhoE 91*
Millard, Charles W. 1904-1988 *BioIn 16*
Millard, Charles Warren, III 1932- *WhoAm 90, WhoAmA 91, WhoSSW 91*
Millard, David B. 1955- *WhoEmL 91*
Millard, David Ralph, Jr. 1919- *WhoAm 90*
Millard, Donald R. 1947- *St&PR 91*
Millard, Edward Howard 1933- *St&PR 91*
Millard, Frank Whittemore 1931- *St&PR 91*
Millard, James Kemper 1948- *WhoE 91*
Millard, Lavergne Harriet 1925- *WhoAmW 91, WhoWor 91*
Millard, Neal Steven 1947- *WhoEmL 91, WhoWor 91*
Millard, Peter Tudor 1932- *WhoAm 90*
Millard, Reed *AuBYP 90*
Millard, Robert Glenn 1931- *St&PR 91*
Millard, Suzanne T. 1936- *St&PR 91*
Millard, William H. 1932- *ConAmBL*
Millares, Joe M. 1953- *St&PR 91*
Millares, Sylma Maria *BiDrAPA 89*
Millasich, Hazel Ashton 1902- *WhoWrEP 89*
Millay, E. Vincent *ConAu 130, MajTwCW*
Millay, Edna St. Vincent 1892-1950 *BioAmW, BioIn 16, ConAu 130*
Millay, Edna St Vincent 1892-1950 *FemiCLE*
Millay, Edna St. Vincent 1892-1950 *MajTwCW, NotWoAT, WorAlBi*
Millay, M.J. *WhoWrEP 89*
Millburn, George P. 1925- *WhoE 91*
Millea, Tom 1944- *WhoAmA 91*
Millen, Robert Andrew 1949- *WhoEmL 91*
Millen, Robert G. 1947- *St&PR 91*
Millen, Robert Gregg 1947- *WhoAm 90*
Millenbach, Lew A. 1942- *WhoE 91*
Millenbruch, Gary Lee 1937- *St&PR 91*
Millender, Dharathula H. 1920- *BioIn 16*
Millender-McDonald, Juanita 1938- *WhoAmW 91*
Millenson, Debra Ann 1947- *WhoAmW 91*
Millenson, Elliott J. 1955- *WhoE 91*
Miller, A. Edward 1918- *WhoAm 90*
Miller, A. Ronald 1934- *St&PR 91*
Miller, Abraham 1910- *BiDrAPA 89*
Miller, Adele Engelbrecht 1946- *WhoAmW 91*
Miller, Adrienne Nyman 1954- *WhoAmW 91*
Miller, Aileen Etta Martha 1924- *WhoAmW 91*
Miller, Ak *BioIn 16*
Miller, Alan B. 1937- *St&PR 91, WhoE 91*
Miller, Alan D 1922- *BiDrAPA 89*
Miller, Alan G 1931- *BiDrAPA 89*
Miller, Alan J. 1949- *St&PR 91*
Miller, Alan Jay 1936- *WhoAm 90*
Miller, Alan N *BiDrAPA 89*
Miller, Alan Nathan 1958- *BiDrAPA 89*
Miller, Alan Scott 1957- *WhoE 91*
Miller, Albert Jay 1927- *WhoAm 90*
Miller, Albert Leon 1953- *WhoSSW 91*
Miller, Albert R. 1947- *St&PR 91*
Miller, Alexander B. 1944- *ODwPR 91*
Miller, Alexander L 1943- *BiDrAPA 89*
Miller, Alfred Jacob 1810-1874 *WhNaAH*
Miller, Alice 1874-1942 *FemiCLE*
Miller, Alice D. 1874-1942 *BioAmW*
Miller, Allan *AuBYP 90, BioIn 16*
Miller, Allan John 1921- *WhoAm 90*
Miller, Allan L. 1932- *St&PR 91*
Miller, Allen B. 1953- *ODwPR 91*
Miller, Allen C. *EarBlAP*
Miller, Allen Cook *BiDrAPA 89*
Miller, Allen Irwin 1938- *St&PR 91*
Miller, Alma E *BiDrAPA 89*
Miller, Andrea Kay 1961- *WhoSSW 91*
Miller, Andrew D. 1930- *St&PR 91*
Miller, Andrew H 1955- *BiDrAPA 89*
Miller, Andrew Pickens 1932- *WhoAm 90*
Miller, Andrew Stewart 1923- *WhoAm 90*
Miller, Andrew Woodfin *St&PR 91*
Miller, Angela Lays *BiDrAPA 89*
Miller, Anita 1926- *WhoWrEP 89*
Miller, Ann *WhoAm 90*
Miller, Ann 1923- *BioIn 16, NotWoAT, WorAlBi*
Miller, Anna 1906- *MusmAFA*
Miller, Anna Catherine *BiDrAPA 89*
Miller, Anne 1741-1781 *FemiCLE*
Miller, Anne Small 1907- *WhoAmW 91, WhoE 91, WhoWor 91*
Miller, Anthony Bernard 1931- *WhoAm 90*
Miller, Arjay 1916- *EncABHB 5 [port], WhoAm 90*
Miller, Arlyn James 1940- *WhoAm 90*
Miller, Arnold 1928- *WhoAm 90*
Miller, Arthur 1915- *BioIn 16, ConAu 30NR, MajTwCW, WhoAm 90, WhoE 91, WhoWrEP 89, WorAlBi, WrPh*
Miller, Arthur Green 1942- *WhoAmA 91*
Miller, Arthur L. *BioIn 16*
Miller, Arthur Leonard 1907- *WhoAm 90*
Miller, Arthur Madden 1953- *WhoEmL 91*
Miller, Arthur Maher 1934- *St&PR 91*
Miller, Arthur Raphael 1934- *WhoAm 90*
Miller, Arthur Selwyn 1917-1988 *BioIn 16*
Miller, Arthur W. 1945- *ODwPR 91*
Miller, Augustus Samuel 1847-1905 *AmLegL*
Miller, Avarina Frances 1957- *WhoWor 91*
Miller, Barbara Ann 1955- *WhoWrEP 89*
Miller, Barbara Darlene *WhoAmA 91*
Miller, Barbara E. *St&PR 91*
Miller, Barbara J 1941- *BiDrAPA 89*
Miller, Barbara Jean 1933- *St&PR 91*
Miller, Barbara Jean 1952- *WhoAmW 91*
Miller, Barbara Lynn *BiDrAPA 89*
Miller, Barbara Stallcup 1919- *WhoAmW 91*
Miller, Barbara Stephenson 1950- *WhoAmW 91*
Miller, Barbara Stoler *WhoAm 90*
Miller, Barry 1942- *WhoAm 90*
Miller, Barry Alan 1954- *WhoEmL 91*
Miller, Barry H. 1957- *WhoE 91*
Miller, Barry M. 1932- *St&PR 91*
Miller, Barry M. 1952- *WhoSSW 91*
Miller, Barry Mark *BiDrAPA 89*
Miller, Barry William 1939- *WhoE 91*
Miller, Barse 1924-1973 *WhoAmA 91N*
Miller, Bebe *BioIn 16*
Miller, Ben 1936- *WhoAm 90*
Miller, Ben Neely 1910- *WhoAm 90*
Miller, Benjamin Louis 1955- *WhoE 91*
Miller, Bennett 1938- *WhoAm 90*
Miller, Bernard *BioIn 16*
Miller, Bernard J. *NewYTBS 90*
Miller, Bernard J., Jr. 1925- *St&PR 91*
Miller, Bernard Paul 1929- *WhoE 91*
Miller, Bertha Mahoney 1882-1969 *BioAmW*
Miller, Berton 1941- *St&PR 91*
Miller, Beth 1941- *WhoAmW 91*
Miller, Beth Andrea *WhoSSW 91*
Miller, Betty 1910-1965 *FemiCLE*
Miller, Betty Brown 1926- *WhoAmW 91*
Miller, Betty Carol 1945- *WhoAmW 91*
Miller, Betty Jean 1958- *WhoAmW 91*
Miller, Betty Jo 1924- *WhoAmW 91*
Miller, Beverly B. 1933- *WhoAmW 91*
Miller, Beverly M. 1949- *WhoAmW 91*
Miller, Beverly White *WhoAm 90, WhoAmW 91, WhoE 91*
Miller, Bill *BioIn 16*
Miller, Bill 1920-1961 *TwCCr&M 91*
Miller, Bill 1926- *Ballpl 90*
Miller, Bill 1933- *WhoWor 91*
Miller, Billie Ruth 1924- *WhoAmW 91*
Miller, Billy *NewAgMG*
Miller, Bing 1894-1966 *Ballpl 90*
Miller, Bob 1926- *Ballpl 90*
Miller, Bob 1935- *Ballpl 90*
Miller, Bob 1939- *Ballpl 90*
Miller, Bonnie K. 1938- *St&PR 91*
Miller, Bonnie Mary 1956- *WhoWrEP 89*
Miller, Bonnie Sewell 1932- *WhoAmW 91*
Miller, Bradley Adam 1959- *WhoE 91*
Miller, Brenda *WhoAmA 91*
Miller, Brenda 1941- *WhoE 91*
Miller, Brent Carlton 1947- *WhoEmL 91*
Miller, Brian Keith 1958- *St&PR 91*
Miller, Bruce 1949- *Ballpl 90*
Miller, Bruce David 1946- *WhoAm 90*
Miller, Bruce I. 1947- *IntWWM 90*
Miller, Bruce Louis 1942- *St&PR 91, WhoAm 90*
Miller, Bruce Richard 1944- *WhoSSW 91, WhoWor 91*
Miller, Bruce Winsterd, III 1951- *WhoWrEP 89*
Miller, Bryan C. 1927- *St&PR 91*
Miller, Burr 1904-1958 *WhoAmA 91N*
Miller, C. Arden 1924- *WhoAm 90*
Miller, C. Leonard *BioIn 16*
Miller, Calvin Pierce 1930- *St&PR 91*
Miller, Carey Brent 1949- *WhoEmL 91, WhoSSW 91, WhoWor 91*
Miller, Carl *BiDrAPA 89*
Miller, Carl George 1942- *St&PR 91, WhoAm 90*
Miller, Carol *St&PR 91*
Miller, Carol A. 1939- *WhoAmW 91*
Miller, Carol Elaine 1961- *WhoAmW 91*
Miller, Caroline 1903- *FemiCLE*
Miller, Carroll Lee Liverpool 1909- *WhoAm 90, WhoWor 91*
Miller, Catherine Diane 1952- *WhoWrEP 89*
Miller, Chapin Bemis 1946- *St&PR 91*
Miller, Charles 1906- *St&PR 91*
Miller, Charles A. 1935- *WhoAm 90*
Miller, Charles Alfred 1945- *WhoSSW 91*
Miller, Charles D. 1928- *St&PR 91*
Miller, Charles D 1942- *ConAu 32NR*
Miller, Charles Daly 1928- *WhoAm 90*
Miller, Charles E. 1944- *WhoSSW 91*
Miller, Charles E. 1950- *St&PR 91*
Miller, Charles Edmond 1938- *WhoAm 90*
Miller, Charles Edward, Jr. 1950- *WhoAm 90*
Miller, Charles Erick 1941- *WhoAm 90*
Miller, Charles Freeman 1948- *St&PR 91*
Miller, Charles Gary 1957- *WhoWor 91*
Miller, Charles Henry 1937- *WhoSSW 91*
Miller, Charles Henry, Jr. 1932- *WhoSSW 91*
Miller, Charles Henry, Jr. 1933- *WhoSSW 91*
Miller, Charles Jay 1924- *WhoE 91, WhoWor 91*
Miller, Charles Leroy 1927- *WhoAm 90*
Miller, Charles Leslie 1929- *WhoAm 90, WhoWor 91*
Miller, Charles O. 1924- *WhoAm 90*
Miller, Charles Thomas 1955- *WhoEmL 91*
Miller, Charles Victor *EncO&P 3*
Miller, Charles W. *St&PR 91*
Miller, Charles W. 1935- *WhoAm 90*
Miller, Charles William 1922- *WhoAm 90*
Miller, Charles Williams 1908- *WhoAm 90*
Miller, Cheryl Denise 1952- *WhoAmW 91*
Miller, Cheryl Lea 1964- *WhoAmW 91*
Miller, Cheryl Waage 1949- *WhoAmW 91*
Miller, Chester Ovid 1940- *BiDrAPA 89*
Miller, Chester Robert 1936- *St&PR 91*
Miller, Christine Marie 1950- *WhoAmW 91*
Miller, Christopher Matthew 1953- *St&PR 91*
Miller, Christy Lynn 1955- *WhoAmW 91*
Miller, Clare Shamer 1944- *WhoSSW 91*
Miller, Clarence E. 1917- *WhoAm 90*
Miller, Clarence S *BiDrAPA 89*
Miller, Clark W. 1930- *St&PR 91*
Miller, Cleaveland 1938- *WhoAm 90*
Miller, Clement A. 1915- *IntWWM 90*
Miller, Clifford A. *ODwPR 91*
Miller, Clyde G *BiDrAPA 89*
Miller, Colin John 1950- *WhoWor 91*
Miller, Connie *WhoWrEP 89*
Miller, Connie Raschke 1943- *WhoAmW 91*
Miller, Corbin R. 1948- *St&PR 91*
Miller, Craig Johnson 1950- *WhoAm 90*
Miller, Craig Russell 1949- *WhoEmL 91*
Miller, Craig S. 1949- *St&PR 91*
Miller, Croix Tompkins 1947- *WhoSSW 91*
Miller, Cynthia Lynne 1952- *WhoAmW 91*
Miller, Dale Merrily 1943- *WhoAmW 91, WhoE 91, WhoWor 91*
Miller, Damon Craddock 1947- *WhoEmL 91*
Miller, Dan S. 1943- *St&PR 91*
Miller, Dane Alan 1946- *St&PR 91*
Miller, Daniel *BiDrAPA 89*
Miller, Daniel 1918- *WhoE 91*
Miller, Daniel D. 1928- *WhoE 91*
Miller, Daniel Dawson 1928- *WhoAmA 91*
Miller, Daniel G. 1925- *St&PR 91*
Miller, Daniel Newton, Jr. 1924- *WhoAm 90*
Miller, Daniel Weber 1926- *WhoAm 90*
Miller, David *BioIn 16*
Miller, David 1905- *WhoAm 90*
Miller, David 1906- *WhoAm 90*
Miller, David 1946- *ConAu 130*
Miller, David 1948- *WhoAmA 91*
Miller, David Allen 1954- *WhoSSW 91*
Miller, David Andrew Barclay 1954- *WhoAm 90*
Miller, David Anthony 1946- *WhoEmL 91*
Miller, David Arthur 1943- *WhoE 91*
Miller, David Charles 1950- *WhoE 91*
Miller, David Charles, Jr. 1942- *WhoAm 90*
Miller, David Danen 1949- *St&PR 91*
Miller, David Earl 1950- *WhoSSW 91*
Miller, David Edmond 1930- *WhoWor 91*
Miller, David Emanuel 1943- *WhoE 91*
Miller, David Eugene 1926- *WhoAm 90*
Miller, David F., III 1948- *St&PR 91*
Miller, David Francis 1929- *St&PR 91, WhoAm 90*
Miller, David Geoffrey *BiDrAPA 89*
Miller, David Hewitt 1918- *WhoAm 90*
Miller, David Jergen 1933- *WhoE 91*
Miller, David L 1928- *BiDrAPA 89*
Miller, David P. 1932- *St&PR 91*
Miller, David Philip 1921- *WhoAm 90*
Miller, David Powell 1942- *WhoAm 90*
Miller, David Randolph 1953- *WhoSSW 91*
Miller, David S. 1916- *St&PR 91*
Miller, David Samuel 1937- *WhoSSW 91*
Miller, David Stuart 1947- *WhoSSW 91*
Miller, David Truxton 1843-1924 *AmLegL*
Miller, David Walter 1957- *WhoEmL 91*
Miller, David William 1940- *WhoAm 90*
Miller, Dawn Marie 1963- *WhoAmW 91*
Miller, Dawn Marie 1964- *WhoAmW 91*
Miller, Dean Arthur 1931- *WhoAm 90*
Miller, Dean Harold 1940- *WhoAm 90*
Miller, Deane Guynes 1927- *WhoAmW 91, WhoWor 91*
Miller, Deborah Ann 1949- *WhoAmW 91*
Miller, Deborah Diane 1944- *WhoE 91*
Miller, Deborah Jean 1951- *WhoAmW 91, WhoEmL 91, WhoWor 91*
Miller, Deborah Uchill 1944- *SmATA 61 [port]*
Miller, Debra Ann 1955- *WhoAmW 91*
Miller, Decatur Howard 1932- *WhoAm 90*
Miller, Dee E. 1908- *St&PR 91*
Miller, Delbert Dwight 1943- *WhoAm 90*
Miller, Demetra Fay Pelat 1933- *WhoAmW 91*
Miller, Denise Mary 1959- *WhoAmW 91*
Miller, Dennis *BioIn 16*
Miller, Dennis James 1943- *WhoAm 90*
Miller, Dennis Maurer 1941- *St&PR 91*
Miller, Derek H *BiDrAPA 89*
Miller, Diana C 1944- *BiDrAPA 89*
Miller, Diane Doris 1954- *WhoAmW 91*
Miller, Diane Dropsey 1929- *WhoAmW 91*
Miller, Dick 1928- *ConTFT 8*
Miller, Dirk J. 1951- *St&PR 91*
Miller, Doc 1883-1938 *Ballpl 90*
Miller, Dodd *WhoSSW 91*

Miller, Dolly 1927- *WhoAmA 91*
Miller, Dolores Ann 1929- *WhoAmW 91*
Miller, Don 1923- *BioIn 16*
Miller, Don Robert 1925- *WhoAm 90*
Miller, Don W. 1952- *St&PR 91*
Miller, Don Wilson 1942- *WhoAm 90*
Miller, Donald 1934- *WhoAmA 91*
Miller, Donald Baldwin 1926- *WhoAm 90*
Miller, Donald Burr 1945- *WhoE 91*
Miller, Donald Charles 1931- *IntWWM 90*
Miller, Donald Dale 1928- *St&PR 91*
Miller, Donald E. 1930- *WhoAm 90*
Miller, Donald E. 1931- *St&PR 91*
Miller, Donald Edwin 1933- *WhoE 91*
Miller, Donald Edwin 1945- *WhoE 91*
Miller, Donald Frederick 1961- *WhoSSW 91*
Miller, Donald George 1909- *AuBYP 90*
Miller, Donald Herbert, Jr. 1914- *WhoAm 90*
Miller, Donald Hope 1907- *WhoSSW 91*
Miller, Donald J. 1943- *St&PR 91*
Miller, Donald Kay 1935- *St&PR 91*
Miller, Donald Lane 1918- *WhoWor 91*
Miller, Donald Larry 1964- *WhoWrEP 89*
Miller, Donald Lee 1934- *BiDrAPA 89*
Miller, Donald Lesessne 1932- *St&PR 91*, *WhoAm 90*
Miller, Donald Lloyd 1923- *WhoAmA 91*
Miller, Donald Morton 1930- *WhoAm 90*
Miller, Donald Paul 1936- *St&PR 91*
Miller, Donald R. 1925-1989 *BioIn 16*
Miller, Donald R. 1931- *St&PR 91*
Miller, Donald Ray 1940- *WhoSSW 91*
Miller, Donald Richard 1925-1989 *WhoAmA 91N*
Miller, Donald Spencer 1932- *WhoAm 90*
Miller, Donald V. 1937- *St&PR 91*
Miller, Donn Biddle 1929- *WhoAm 90*
Miller, Donna Jean 1948- *WhoAmW 91*
Miller, Donna Marie *BiDrAPA 89*
Miller, Donnally James 1951- *WhoE 91*
Miller, Dorothy Anne Smith 1931- *WhoAmW 91*
Miller, Dots 1886-1923 *Ballpl 90*
Miller, Douglas Edward 1951- *WhoE 91*
Miller, Douglas Jerome 1944- *St&PR 91*
Miller, Duane Francis 1931- *St&PR 91*
Miller, Duane King 1931- *WhoAm 90*, *WhoE 91*, *WhoWor 91*
Miller, Duane Leon 1937- *St&PR 91*, *WhoAm 90*
Miller, Dyar 1946- *Ballpl 90*
Miller, E. Barger, III 1938- *St&PR 91*
Miller, E. Willard 1915- *WhoAm 90*
Miller, Earnest Lee *BioIn 16*
Miller, Eddie 1916- *Ballpl 90*
Miller, Edmond Trowbridge 1933- *WhoAm 90*
Miller, Edmund Kenneth 1935- *WhoAm 90*
Miller, Edna *BioIn 16*
Miller, Edna Anita 1920- *AuBYP 90*
Miller, Edna Rae Atkins 1915- *WhoAmW 91*
Miller, Edward Albert 1931- *WhoAm 90*
Miller, Edward B. 1922- *WhoAm 90*
Miller, Edward Daniel 1940- *WhoAm 90*
Miller, Edward Doring, Jr. 1943- *WhoAm 90*
Miller, Edward Douglas 1954- *WhoEmL 91*
Miller, Edward F. 1942- *St&PR 91*
Miller, Edward Henry, Jr. 1925- *St&PR 91*
Miller, Edward J. 1933- *St&PR 91*
Miller, Edward John 1922- *WhoAm 90*
Miller, Edward Percival 1924- *WhoAm 90*
Miller, Edward Robert 1947- *WhoEmL 91*
Miller, Edward Wardlow, Jr. 1935- *St&PR 91*
Miller, Edward William Werner 1930- *WhoWor 91*
Miller, Edwin Louis 1955- *WhoSSW 91*
Miller, Edwin O. 1920- *St&PR 91*
Miller, Eileen Janet 1935- *WhoSSW 91*
Miller, Elaine *BiDrAPA 89*
Miller, Elaine Sandra *WhoAmA 91*
Miller, Eldon Earl 1919- *WhoAm 90*
Miller, Eli Jerry 1946- *BiDrAPA 89*
Miller, Elizabeth *BioIn 16*
Miller, Elizabeth Ann 1962- *WhoAmW 91*
Miller, Elizabeth Jane 1953- *WhoAm 90*, *WhoAmW 91*, *WhoE 91*
Miller, Elizabeth Rodriguez 1954- *WhoHisp 91*
Miller, Elliott *St&PR 91*
Miller, Elliott Cairns 1934- *WhoAm 90*
Miller, Ellora Fogle 1913- *EncO&P 3*
Miller, Elmer 1890-1944 *Ballpl 90*
Miller, Elouise Darlene 1930- *WhoAmW 91*
Miller, Elva Ruby Connes *WhoAmW 91*
Miller, Emanuel 1917- *WhoAm 90*, *WhoSSW 91*
Miller, Emerson Waldo 1920- *WhoWor 91*
Miller, Emilie F. 1936- *WhoAmW 91*
Miller, Emmanuel G. 1913- *St&PR 91*
Miller, Eric Booth 1950- *WhoE 91*
Miller, Eric J. 1953- *St&PR 91*
Miller, Eric Raymond 1943- *WhoAm 90*
Miller, Erica Tillinghast 1950- *WhoAmW 91*
Miller, Ernest Arthur 1925- *WhoE 91*
Miller, Ernest C 1927- *BiDrAPA 89*
Miller, Ernest Charles 1925- *WhoAm 90*
Miller, Ernest Joseph, Jr. 1928- *St&PR 91*
Miller, Estelle Lee 1929- *WhoAmW 91*, *WhoSSW 91*
Miller, Esther Jean 1947- *WhoAmW 91*
Miller, Eugene 1925- *ODwPR 91*, *WhoAm 90*
Miller, Eugene Albert *WhoAm 90*
Miller, Eugene Albert 1937- *St&PR 91*
Miller, Eugene H. 1927- *St&PR 91*
Miller, Eugenia 1916- *AuBYP 90*
Miller, Ewing Harry 1923- *WhoAm 90*
Miller, F John 1929- *WhoAmA 91*
Miller, Fish Bait 1909-1989 *BioIn 16*
Miller, Flora Whitney *BioIn 16*
Miller, Flournoy E. *EarBlAP*
Miller, Flournoy E 1887-1971 *DrBlPA 90*
Miller, Floyd H. *WhoAm 90*
Miller, Foil Allan 1916- *WhoAm 90*
Miller, Frances A. 1937- *BioIn 16*
Miller, Francis Charles *BioIn 16*
Miller, Francis Marion 1925- *WhoAm 90*
Miller, Francis Roy 1926- *St&PR 91*
Miller, Frank 1886-1974 *Ballpl 90*
Miller, Frank 1925-1983 *BioIn 16*
Miller, Frank Albert *BiDrAPA 89*
Miller, Frank Black 1947- *BiDrAPA 89*
Miller, Frank Carl 1936- *WhoAm 90*
Miller, Frank E., Jr. 1914- *St&PR 91*
Miller, Frank George 1930- *WhoSSW 91*
Miller, Frank William 1921- *WhoAm 90*
Miller, Fred D., Jr. 1944- *ConAu 129*
Miller, Fred L. 1907- *St&PR 91*
Miller, Fred L. 1949- *WhoSSW 91*
Miller, Freddie R. 1927- *St&PR 91*
Miller, Frederick 1930- *IntWWM 90*
Miller, Frederick 1937- *WhoAm 90*
Miller, Frederick C *BiDrAPA 89*
Miller, Frederick Eugene 1954- *BiDrAPA 89*
Miller, Frederick M 1941- *BiDrAPA 89*
Miller, Frederick Powell 1936- *WhoAm 90*
Miller, Frederick Robeson 1927- *WhoAm 90*
Miller, Frederick Staten 1930- *WhoAm 90*
Miller, Frederick William 1912- *WhoAm 90*
Miller, Freeman *ODwPR 91*
Miller, G Robert 1946- *BiDrAPA 89*
Miller, G. William 1925- *BiDrUSE 89*, *EncABHB 7 [port]*, *St&PR 91*, *WorAlBi*
Miller, Gabriel Lorimer 1928- *WhoAm 90*
Miller, Garfield Lankard, III 1950- *WhoAm 90*, *WhoE 91*
Miller, Gary E 1935- *BiDrAPA 89*
Miller, Gary Evan 1935- *WhoAm 90*
Miller, Gary Glenn 1950- *St&PR 91*, *WhoAm 90*
Miller, Gary J. 1949- *WhoAm 90*
Miller, Gary W. 1940- *St&PR 91*
Miller, Gavin 1926- *St&PR 91*, *WhoAm 90*
Miller, Gene Edward 1928- *WhoAm 90*
Miller, Genevieve 1914- *WhoAm 90*, *WhoAmW 91*, *WhoWor 91*
Miller, George 1945- *WhoAm 90*
Miller, George Allen 1936- *St&PR 91*
Miller, George Armitage 1920- *WhoAm 90*
Miller, George David 1930- *WhoAm 90*
Miller, George Paul 1950- *WhoE 91*
Miller, George Thomas 1915- *St&PR 91*
Miller, George W. 1833- *AmLegL*
Miller, George Walter 1933- *St&PR 91*
Miller, George Wells 1930- *WhoE 91*
Miller, George William 1925- *WhoAm 90*
Miller, Georgia Blair 1946- *WhoEmL 91*
Miller, Gerald 1927- *WhoE 91*
Miller, Gerald A. 1941- *St&PR 91*
Miller, Gerald D 1939- *WhoAm 90*
Miller, Gerald Lewis 1936- *WhoSSW 91*
Miller, Gerald Raymond 1931- *WhoAm 90*
Miller, Geraldine Blanche 1917- *IntWWM 90*
Miller, Gerard C. 1928- *St&PR 91*
Miller, Gilbert N. 1941- *St&PR 91*
Miller, Glenn *BioIn 16*
Miller, Glenn 1904-1944 *OxCPMus*, *WorAlBi*
Miller, Glenn 1937- *WhoAm 90*, *WhoSSW 91*
Miller, Glenn Alan 1944- *WhoAm 90*
Miller, Glenn D. 1944- *St&PR 91*
Miller, Glenn Elliott *BiDrAPA 89*
Miller, Glenn Howard 1942- *BiDrAPA 89*, *WhoE 91*
Miller, Gordon F. *BioIn 16*
Miller, Gordon R. 1936- *St&PR 91*
Miller, Grant Bruce 1936- *WhoAm 90*
Miller, Grant Durward 1942- *BiDrAPA 89*
Miller, Gregory Alan 1945- *BiDrAPA 89*
Miller, Gregory Allen *BiDrAPA 89*
Miller, Gregory Keith 1957- *WhoSSW 91*
Miller, Gregory Paul *BiDrAPA 89*
Miller, Guy *WhoAmA 91*
Miller, Guy Elmer, Jr. 1932- *WhoAm 90*
Miller, H. Barry 1950- *BiDrAPA 89*
Miller, Hack 1894-1971 *Ballpl 90*
Miller, Halbert B 1940- *BiDrAPA 89*
Miller, Harbaugh 1902- *WhoAm 90*, *WhoE 91*
Miller, Harmon Baker, III 1935- *St&PR 91*
Miller, Harold E. 1926- *St&PR 91*
Miller, Harold Edward 1926- *WhoAm 90*
Miller, Harold Eugene 1952- *WhoE 91*
Miller, Harold Joseph 1923- *WhoAm 90*
Miller, Harold T. 1923- *WhoAm 90*
Miller, Harold Taylor 1923- *St&PR 91*
Miller, Harriet Evelyn 1919- *WhoAm 90*
Miller, Harriet Sanders 1926- *WhoAmW 91*
Miller, Harriett Puffer 1919- *WhoWrEP 89*
Miller, Harry Charles, Jr. 1928- *WhoAm 90*
Miller, Harry George 1941- *WhoAm 90*
Miller, Harvey 1942- *WhoAm 90*
Miller, Harvey Alfred 1928- *WhoAm 90*, *WhoWor 91*
Miller, Harvey Crane 1935- *WhoWor 91*
Miller, Harvey S. Shipley 1948- *St&PR 91*
Miller, Harvey Stokes Shipley 1948- *WhoAm 90*, *WhoE 91*, *WhoEmL 91*, *WhoWor 91*
Miller, Hasbrouck Bailey 1923- *WhoAm 90*
Miller, Helen Elizabeth 1950- *WhoE 91*
Miller, Helen Knapp *AuBYP 90*
Miller, Helen Lewis *BiDrAPA 89*
Miller, Helen Louise *AuBYP 90*
Miller, Helen Marie Dillen *WhoAmW 91*
Miller, Helen Markley *AuBYP 90*
Miller, Helen P. 1936- *St&PR 91*
Miller, Helen Pendleton 1888-1957 *WhoAmA 91N*
Miller, Helen Topping 1884-1960 *AuBYP 90*
Miller, Henry 1891-1980 *BioIn 16*, *ConAu 33NR*, *MajTwCW*, *WorAlBi*, *WrPh*
Miller, Henry E. 1926- *St&PR 91*
Miller, Henry Eugene, Jr. 1937- *St&PR 91*
Miller, Henry F. 1935- *ODwPR 91*
Miller, Henry George 1924- *WhoE 91*
Miller, Henry Sam, Jr. 1914- *St&PR 91*
Miller, Herbert Allan, Jr. 1951- *St&PR 91*
Miller, Herbert D 1926- *BiDrAPA 89*
Miller, Herbert David 1930- *St&PR 91*
Miller, Herbert Dell 1919- *WhoSSW 91*, *WhoWor 91*
Miller, Herbert Elmer 1914- *WhoAm 90*
Miller, Herbert John, Jr. 1924- *WhoAm 90*
Miller, Herman 1919- *WhoAm 90*
Miller, Hope Ridings *WhoAm 90*, *WhoWrEP 89*
Miller, Howard 1944- *WhoWor 91*
Miller, Howard Brian 1947- *BiDrAPA 89*
Miller, Howard C. 1926- *St&PR 91*
Miller, Howard Ross 1949- *WhoEmL 91*
Miller, Hubert *BiDrAPA 89*
Miller, Hubert John 1927- *WhoSSW 91*
Miller, Hugh 1818-1898 *DcCanB 12*
Miller, Hugh Craig 1942- *WhoWor 91*
Miller, Hugh Edward 1935- *WhoE 91*
Miller, Hugh Thomas 1951- *WhoEmL 91*
Miller, I. George 1937- *WhoAm 90*
Miller, Ian C. 1919- *St&PR 91*
Miller, Inge Morath *WhoAmA 91*
Miller, Ira 1955- *WhoWrEP 89*
Miller, Iris Ann 1938- *WhoAmW 91*, *WhoE 91*
Miller, Irvin C. *EarBlAP*
Miller, Irving Franklin 1934- *WhoAm 90*
Miller, Isadore *WhoE 91*
Miller, Israel 1918- *WhoAm 90*
Miller, Ivan Lawrence 1914- *WhoAm 90*
Miller, J David 1940- *BiDrAPA 89*
Miller, J. Duane 1899- *WhoAm 90*
Miller, J. F. *WhoAm 90*
Miller, J. Hillis 1928- *BioIn 16*
Miller, J Hillis 1928- *WorAu 1980*
Miller, J. P. 1919- *BioIn 16*, *WhoWor 91*
Miller, J. Philip 1937- *WhoAm 90*
Miller, Jack Avery 1956- *BiDrAPA 89*
Miller, Jack David R. 1930- *WhoAm 90*
Miller, Jack Richard 1916- *WhoAm 90*, *WhoE 91*
Miller, Jacob Allen 1946- *BiDrAPA 89*
Miller, Jacob J *BiDrAPA 89*
Miller, Jacob M. *BioIn 16*
Miller, Jacqueline Ann *BiDrAPA 89*
Miller, Jacqueline Winslow 1935- *WhoAm 90*, *WhoE 91*
Miller, Jacques Francis 1931- *WhoWor 91*
Miller, Jake 1897-1975 *Ballpl 90*
Miller, Jake Charles 1929- *WhoSSW 91*
Miller, James 1934- *WhoWor 91*
Miller, James 1944-1982 *BioIn 16*
Miller, James Albert, Jr. 1907- *WhoE 91*
Miller, James Alexander 1915- *WhoAm 90*
Miller, James Arthur 1950- *WhoSSW 91*
Miller, James Bernard 1930- *St&PR 91*
Miller, James C. 1929- *St&PR 91*
Miller, James Clarence 1946- *WhoEmL 91*
Miller, James Clifford, III 1942- *WhoAm 90*
Miller, James David 1928- *WhoSSW 91*
Miller, James Duane 1939- *St&PR 91*
Miller, James E. 1936- *St&PR 91*
Miller, James Edward 1940- *WhoWor 91*
Miller, James Edwin, Jr. 1920- *WhoAm 90*, *WhoWrEP 89*
Miller, James G. 1948- *St&PR 91*
Miller, James Gegan 1942- *WhoAm 90*
Miller, James Gormly 1914- *WhoAm 90*
Miller, James Grier *BiDrAPA 89*
Miller, James Grier 1916- *WhoAm 90*, *WhoWor 91*
Miller, James H. 1843-1890 *AmLegL*
Miller, James Halyburton 1940- *St&PR 91*
Miller, James Howard 1934- *WhoSSW 91*
Miller, James Hugh, Jr. 1922- *WhoAm 90*
Miller, James I. 1956- *St&PR 91*
Miller, James I., Jr. 1908- *St&PR 91*
Miller, James Kevin 1957- *St&PR 91*
Miller, James L. 1924- *St&PR 91*
Miller, James Monroe 1933- *WhoAm 90*
Miller, James Pinckney 1919- *BioIn 16*
Miller, James Presley 1938- *WhoSSW 91*
Miller, James R. 1947- *St&PR 91*
Miller, James R., II 1946- *St&PR 91*
Miller, James Ralph 1938- *WhoSSW 91*
Miller, James Roland 1929- *WhoAm 90*
Miller, James Rumrill, III 1937- *WhoAm 90*
Miller, James Victor *BiDrAPA 89*
Miller, James Vince 1920- *WhoAm 90*
Miller, Jane 1925-1989 *BioIn 16*
Miller, Jane Andrews 1952- *WhoAmW 91*, *WhoEmL 91*
Miller, Jane Ruth 1949- *WhoWrEP 89*
Miller, Janel Howell 1947- *WhoAmW 91*, *WhoSSW 91*
Miller, Janet 1954- *WhoAmA 91*
Miller, Janet Ruth 1946- *WhoAmW 91*
Miller, Janice 1925- *WhoAmW 91*
Miller, Janice Ann 1949- *WhoAmW 91*
Miller, Janice L *BiDrAPA 89*
Miller, Jarrell Etson 1913- *WhoAm 90*
Miller, Jason *BiDrAPA 89*
Miller, Jay Earl *WhoWrEP 89*
Miller, Jay F *BiDrAPA 89*
Miller, Jean Baker *BiDrAPA 89*
Miller, Jean H. 1923- *St&PR 91*
Miller, Jean Johnston 1918- *WhoAmA 91*, *WhoE 91*
Miller, Jean Keller 1933- *BiDrAPA 89*
Miller, Jean Marie 1951- *WhoE 91*
Miller, Jean Roger 1927- *WhoAm 90*
Miller, Jeanne Marie 1956- *St&PR 91*
Miller, Jeanne-Marie Anderson 1937- *WhoAmW 91*, *WhoE 91*, *WhoWor 91*
Miller, Jeannette Leah 1941- *WhoAmW 91*
Miller, Jeff *ODwPR 91*
Miller, Jeffrey D. 1949- *WhoE 91*
Miller, Jeffrey Harold 1942- *WhoSSW 91*
Miller, Jeffrey J. *St&PR 91*
Miller, Jeffrey L. 1951- *IntWWM 90*
Miller, Jeffrey M. 1955- *St&PR 91*
Miller, Jeffrey N. 1952- *St&PR 91*
Miller, Jeffrey Robert 1941- *WhoAm 90*
Miller, Jeffrey Veach 1955- *WhoEmL 91*
Miller, Jennifer Ann *BiDrAPA 89*
Miller, Jeremy Matthew 1954- *WhoEmL 91*
Miller, Jerome H. 1938- *WhoAm 90*
Miller, Jerome M. 1917- *WhoSSW 91*
Miller, Jerrold T. 1929- *St&PR 91*
Miller, Jerry *ODwPR 91*
Miller, Jerry B. 1946- *St&PR 91*
Miller, Jerry Darr 1945- *WhoSSW 91*
Miller, Jerry Dwayne 1936- *St&PR 91*
Miller, Jerry Huber 1931- *WhoAm 90*
Miller, Jess Andrews *BiDrAPA 89*
Miller, Jim Wayne 1936- *LiHiK*, *WhoWrEP 89*
Miller, Jo Carolyn 1942- *WhoAmW 91*
Miller, Joan 1910-1988 *AnObit 1988*
Miller, Joan L 1930- *WhoAmA 91*
Miller, Joan L. 1931- *St&PR 91*
Miller, Joan Marie Nonnenmocher 1935- *WhoAmW 91*
Miller, Joan Vita 1946- *WhoAmA 91*
Miller, JoAnn Marie 1954- *WhoSSW 91*
Miller, Joaquin 1837-1913 *WorAlBi*
Miller, Joe Leon 1931- *WhoAm 90*
Miller, Joel B. 1945- *St&PR 91*
Miller, Joel F 1937- *BiDrAPA 89*
Miller, Joel Lawrence 1935- *WhoAm 90*
Miller, John *BioIn 16*, *WhoAmA 91*
Miller, John 1941- *Ballpl 90*
Miller, John A. 1927- *St&PR 91*
Miller, John Adalbert 1927- *WhoAm 90*
Miller, John Albert 1939- *WhoAm 90*
Miller, John Andrew 1942- *WhoSSW 91*
Miller, John Charles 1942- *St&PR 91*
Miller, John Clifford, II 1935- *St&PR 91*
Miller, John Clifford, Jr. 1908- *St&PR 91*
Miller, John D. 1943- *St&PR 91*
Miller, John David 1923- *WhoAm 90*

Miller, John David 1945- WhoAm 90
Miller, John David 1957- WhoE 91
Miller, John Davidson, III 1945- WhoAm 90
Miller, John Dewey 1943- WhoAm 90
Miller, John Douglas BioIn 16
Miller, John Evans 1909- WhoAm 90
Miller, John F. 1927- St&PR 91
Miller, John Francis 1908- WhoAm 90, WhoE 91
Miller, John Franklin 1940- WhoAmA 91
Miller, John Henry 1848-1907 AmLegL
Miller, John Henry 1917- WhoSSW 91
Miller, John Keith 1927- WhoWrEP 89
Miller, John Laurence 1947- WhoAm 90
Miller, John Leslie BiDrAPA 89
Miller, John Michael 1941- WhoSSW 91
Miller, John Paul 1918- WhoAmA 91
Miller, John Paul 1948- WhoE 91
Miller, John Pearse 1914- WhoAm 90
Miller, John Pendleton 1931- WhoSSW 91
Miller, John Perry 1911- WhoE 91
Miller, John R. 1938- WhoAm 90
Miller, John Richard 1927- WhoAm 90
Miller, John Richard, Jr. 1920- St&PR 91
Miller, John Robert 1937- St&PR 91, WhoAm 90
Miller, John T., Jr. 1922- WhoE 91, WhoWor 91
Miller, John Ulman 1914- WhoAm 90
Miller, John W. BioIn 16
Miller, John William, Jr. 1942- WhoAm 90
Miller, Jon Hamilton 1938- St&PR 91, WhoAm 90
Miller, Jonathan 1934- BioIn 16, IntWWM 90, WorAlBi
Miller, Jonathan Wolfe 1934- WhoAm 90, WhoWor 91
Miller, Jordan Yale 1919- WhoAm 90
Miller, Joseph Alfred 1907- WhoSSW 91
Miller, Joseph Dirk 1965- WhoSSW 91
Miller, Joseph Edward, Jr. 1945- WhoEmL 91
Miller, Joseph Herman 1944- WhoSSW 91
Miller, Joseph Hillis 1928- BioIn 16, WhoAm 90, WhoWrEP 89
Miller, Joseph Irwin 1909- St&PR 91, WhoAm 90, WhoWor 91
Miller, Joseph James 1912- St&PR 91
Miller, Joseph K. BioIn 16
Miller, Joseph Keith 1957- WhoSSW 91
Miller, Joseph S. 1921- St&PR 91
Miller, Joseph S A BiDrAPA 89
Miller, Joy 1966- WhoE 91
Miller, Joyce Regina BiDrAPA 89
Miller, Juan BiDrAPA 89
Miller, Judith Ann 1941- WhoAmW 91
Miller, Judith Marie 1942- WhoAmW 91
Miller, Judson Frederick 1924- WhoAm 90
Miller, Judy Anne 1957- St&PR 91
Miller, Judy Statman 1938- WhoAmW 91
Miller, Julian BioIn 16
Miller, Julie Ann 1955- WhoAmW 91
Miller, Karen-Ann 1949- WhoAmW 91
Miller, Karen Jean 1951- WhoAmW 91, WhoSSW 91
Miller, Karen Leslie 1949- BiDrAPA 89
Miller, Karen Lewis 1942- WhoAmW 91
Miller, Karl A. 1931- WhoE 91
Miller, Katherine AuBYP 90
Miller, Kathleen Elizabeth 1942- WhoAm 90
Miller, Kathleen Helfrich- BioIn 16
Miller, Kathleen Marie 1957- BiDrAPA 89
Miller, Kathryn 1935- WhoAmA 91
Miller, Kathryn Kinard 1954- WhoSSW 91
Miller, Kathryn Schultz 1954- WhoWrEP 89
Miller, Kathy Collard 1949- WhoWrEP 89
Miller, Keith Wyatt 1941- WhoAm 90
Miller, Ken Leroy 1933- WhoSSW 91
Miller, Kenneth E. 1926- IntWWM 90
Miller, Kenneth E. 1928- St&PR 91
Miller, Kenneth Edward 1929- WhoAm 90
Miller, Kenneth Edward 1951- WhoWor 91
Miller, Kenneth Hayes 1876-1952 WhoAmA 91N
Miller, Kenneth Hull 1946- WhoE 91
Miller, Kenneth I. 1956- St&PR 91
Miller, Kenneth Joseph 1955- BiDrAPA 89
Miller, Kenneth L. 1927- St&PR 91
Miller, Kenneth Lyall 1927- WhoAm 90
Miller, Kenneth Merrill 1930- WhoE 91
Miller, Kenneth Michael 1921- WhoAm 90
Miller, Kenneth Mount 1947- WhoAm 90, WhoWor 91
Miller, Kenneth Roy 1902- WhoAm 90
Miller, Kenneth Ward 1927- WhoSSW 91
Miller, Kenneth William 1947- WhoSSW 91, WhoWor 91
Miller, Kenneth William, II 1951- WhoEmL 91
Miller, Kerby A. 1944- ConAu 132
Miller, Kevin Bryan 1956- BiDrAPA 89
Miller, Kevin John 1955- WhoSSW 91
Miller, Kim Elizabeth 1956- WhoAmW 91
Miller, L. A. 1925- St&PR 91
Miller, L. Martin 1939- WhoE 91
Miller, Laird O'Neil, Jr. 1915- WhoE 91
Miller, Lajos 1940- IntWWM 90
Miller, Lamar John 1942- St&PR 91
Miller, Larry 1944- St&PR 91, WhoAmA 91
Miller, Larry D. 1934- ODwPR 91
Miller, Larry F. 1938- St&PR 91
Miller, Larry H. WhoAm 90
Miller, Larry James 1939- St&PR 91
Miller, Larry Joseph 1932- WhoAm 90
Miller, Larry S. 1952- St&PR 91
Miller, Laura Jo 1956- BiDrAPA 89
Miller, Laurence Brent 1942- BiDrAPA 89
Miller, Laurence Glenn 1948- WhoAmA 91
Miller, Laurence H 1944- BiDrAPA 89
Miller, Lawrence 1948- St&PR 91
Miller, Lawrence Albert 1932- St&PR 91
Miller, Lawrence C 1925- BiDrAPA 89
Miller, Lawrence Edward 1944- WhoAm 90
Miller, Lee 1907-1977 BioIn 16
Miller, Lee A. 1931- St&PR 91
Miller, Lee Anne WhoAm 90
Miller, Lee C 1943- BiDrAPA 89
Miller, Lee Clyde 1943- WhoE 91
Miller, Lee Denmar 1935- WhoAm 90
Miller, Lee Edward 1951- WhoEmL 91
Miller, Lee Hanford 1926- St&PR 91
Miller, Leland Bishop, Jr. 1931- WhoAm 90
Miller, Lenore 1932- WhoAm 90
Miller, Leon Gordon 1917- WhoAmA 91
Miller, Leonard 1932- St&PR 91
Miller, Leonard David 1930- WhoAm 90
Miller, Leonard Martin 1941- WhoE 91
Miller, Leonard W. 1951- St&PR 91
Miller, Leroy Benjamin 1931- WhoAm 90
Miller, Leslie Adrienne 1956- WhoWrEP 89
Miller, Leta Ellen 1947- IntWWM 90
Miller, Lew WhoWrEP 89
Miller, Lewis N., Jr. 1944- WhoAm 90, WhoSSW 91
Miller, Lillian A. 1936- WhoAmW 91
Miller, Lilyan BioIn 16
Miller, Linda 1952- St&PR 91
Miller, Linda B. 1937- WhoAm 90
Miller, Linda Dianne 1947- WhoWrEP 89
Miller, Linda Lael 1949- ConAu 30NR, WhoAmW 91
Miller, Linda Lou 1955- WhoAmW 91
Miller, Lisa AuBYP 90
Miller, Lloyd Daniel 1916- WhoAm 90
Miller, Lloyd I. St&PR 91N
Miller, Lloyd I. 1924-1990 BioIn 16
Miller, Lloyd Ivan 1924-1990 WhoAm 90
Miller, Lloyd Richard 1947- BiDrAPA 89
Miller, Lois Kathryn 1945- WhoAmW 91
Miller, Lois Lea 1929- WhoAmW 91
Miller, Loren Jay 1945- St&PR 91
Miller, Loring Erik 1951- WhoE 91
Miller, Louis BiDrAPA 89
Miller, Louis Adam 1917- WhoWrEP 89
Miller, Louis Rice 1914- WhoAm 90
Miller, Louise Anne 1963- WhoAmW 91
Miller, Louise M. 1939- St&PR 91
Miller, Louise Moore 1939- WhoAm 90
Miller, Lowell D. 1933- St&PR 91
Miller, Lowell Donald 1933- WhoAm 90
Miller, Loye W. ODwPR 91
Miller, Loye Wheat, Jr. 1930- WhoAm 90
Miller, Lucy Carol BiDrAPA 89
Miller, Lunelle Young 1941- WhoSSW 91
Miller, Lynn E 1943- BiDrAPA 89
Miller, Lynn Hellwarth 1937- WhoE 91
Miller, Lynn Marie 1958- WhoAmW 91
Miller, Lynn Ruth 1933- WhoWrEP 89
Miller, Lynne Marie 1951- WhoAmW 91, WhoWor 91
Miller, M. Hughes 1913- WhoWrEP 89
Miller, M. Hughes 1913-1989 BioIn 16
Miller, M Hughes 1913-1989 ConAu 130
Miller, M. Willard 1914- WhoAm 90
Miller, Mabry Batson WhoSSW 91
Miller, Madelyn Sue 1947- WhoAmW 91
Miller, Madge 1918- SmATA 63
Miller, Malcolm K., Jr. 1927- St&PR 91
Miller, Malcolm Lee 1923- WhoAm 90
Miller, Mara Jayne 1944- WhoE 91
Miller, Marc H 1946- WhoAmA 91
Miller, Marc S 1947- ConAu 31NR
Miller, Marcy Jennifer 1963- WhoAmW 91
Miller, Margaret Ann 1952- BiDrAPA 89, WhoE 91
Miller, Margaret Carnegie 1897-1990 BioIn 16
Miller, Margaret Haigh 1915- WhoAm 90
Miller, Margaret Jean 1943- WhoAmW 91
Miller, Margaret Mary BiDrAPA 89
Miller, Margaret Williams 1933- St&PR 91
Miller, Margery Silberman 1951- WhoAmW 91
Miller, Margery Staman 1945- WhoE 91
Miller, Marguerite Elizabeth 1917- WhoWrEP 89
Miller, Maria B. 1931- WhoSSW 91
Miller, Marian Kathryn 1942- WhoAmW 91
Miller, Marilee Lois 1937- WhoWrEP 89
Miller, Marilyn 1898-1936 BioAmW, BioIn 16, NotWoAT, OxCPMus, WorAlBi
Miller, Mark AuBYP 90
Miller, Mark Allen 1952- WhoWor 91
Miller, Mark Dana 1955- BiDrAPA 89
Miller, Mark David 1955- BiDrAPA 89, WhoE 91
Miller, Mark Dawson 1919- WhoWrEP 89
Miller, Mark Elliott 1960- WhoWrEP 89
Miller, Mark L. 1943- St&PR 91
Miller, Mark S. St&PR 91
Miller, Marlow L. 1930- St&PR 91
Miller, Marsden, Jr. 1941- St&PR 91
Miller, Marsha Tyson 1950- WhoSSW 91
Miller, Marshall V. 1945- WhoAm 90
Miller, Martha AuBYP 90
Miller, Martha 1947- WhoWrEP 89
Miller, Martin 1939- BiDrAPA 89
Miller, Martin A 1934- BiDrAPA 89
Miller, Martin Eugene 1945- WhoSSW 91
Miller, Martin Jessee 1950- WhoWrEP 89
Miller, Martin John 1943- WhoAm 90
Miller, Marvin BioIn 16
Miller, Marvin 1917- Ballpl 90
Miller, Marvin Edward 1929- WhoE 91
Miller, Marvin F 1924- BiDrAPA 89
Miller, Marvin Jay 1946- BiDrAPA 89
Miller, Marvin M. 1916- St&PR 91
Miller, Mary BiDrAPA 89
Miller, Mary Ann 1956- ODwPR 91
Miller, Mary Britton 1883-1975 AuBYP 90, FemiCLE
Miller, Mary Elizabeth 1947- WhoAmW 91
Miller, Mary Emily 1934- WhoAm 90, WhoE 91
Miller, Mary Jane 1953- WhoEmL 91
Miller, Mary Louise 1946- BiDrAPA 89
Miller, Mary M. St&PR 91
Miller, Mary Stephanie 1940- WhoAmW 91
Miller, Matthew Jeffrey 1940- St&PR 91
Miller, Maureen 1922- WhoWrEP 89
Miller, Maurice Hugh, Jr. 1950- WhoSSW 91
Miller, Maurice James 1926- WhoAm 90
Miller, Max Dunham, Jr. 1946- WhoEmL 91, WhoWor 91
Miller, May 1899- EarBlAP, FemiCLE, HarlReB [port]
Miller, Maynard Malcolm 1921- WhoAm 90, WhoWor 91
Miller, Meier 1947- St&PR 91
Miller, Melanie Lee 1952- WhoAmW 91
Miller, Melissa Wren 1951- WhoAmA 91
Miller, Melvin Howard 1939- WhoE 91
Miller, Melvin Orville, Jr 1937- WhoAmA 91, WhoE 91
Miller, Merry Noel 1953- BiDrAPA 89
Miller, Michael Barbree 1938- WhoE 91
Miller, Michael C d'E 1929- St&PR 91
Miller, Michael Craig 1952- BiDrAPA 89
Miller, Michael David 1959- BiDrAPA 89
Miller, Michael E. 1941- St&PR 91
Miller, Michael Edward 1958- BiDrAPA 89
Miller, Michael Eugene 1953- WhoSSW 91
Miller, Michael George 1955- WhoEmL 91
Miller, Michael Michel 1952- BiDrAPA 89
Miller, Michael Paul 1938- St&PR 91, WhoAm 90, WhoE 91
Miller, Michael Stephen 1938- WhoAmA 91
Miller, Michael Wolf 1945- BiDrAPA 89
Miller, Mildred WhoAm 90
Miller, Mildred 1924- IntWWM 90
Miller, Millicent BioIn 16
Miller, Milton 1921- St&PR 91
Miller, Milton H BiDrAPA 89
Miller, Milton H. 1931- St&PR 91
Miller, Milton Howard 1927- WhoAm 90
Miller, Milton L 1904- BiDrAPA 89
Miller, Miranda 1950- ConAu 132
Miller, Mitch 1911- OxCPMus, WorAlBi
Miller, Mona Joy Deutsch 1953- WhoEmL 91
Miller, Monica Lee 1963- WhoEmL 91
Miller, Morgan L. 1924- St&PR 91
Miller, Morgan Lincoln 1924- WhoAm 90
Miller, Morris Folsom 1919- WhoAm 90
Miller, Morton G 1935- BiDrAPA 89, WhoE 91
Miller, Mulgrew BioIn 16
Miller, Nairn L. 1922- St&PR 91
Miller, Nancy Ellen 1947- WhoEmL 91
Miller, Nancy Gannon 1957- WhoSSW 91
Miller, Nancy Janet 1954- WhoE 91
Miller, Nancy Smith 1951- WhoAmW 91
Miller, Nancy Tokar 1941- WhoAmA 91
Miller, Naomi 1928- WhoAm 90
Miller, Nathan 1927- WhoAm 90, WhoWrEP 89
Miller, Nathan Robert 1919- St&PR 91
Miller, Neal Elgar 1909- WhoAm 90
Miller, Neal Robert 1956- WhoSSW 91
Miller, Neil Austin 1932- WhoSSW 91
Miller, Neil S. 1958- WhoE 91
Miller, Newton Edd, Jr. 1920- WhoAm 90
Miller, Nina Beth 1956- WhoEmL 91
Miller, Nolan 1935- ConTFT 8
Miller, Norm 1946- Ballpl 90
Miller, Norma St&PR 91
Miller, Norman 1933- WhoAm 90
Miller, Norman C., Jr. 1925- WhoSSW 91
Miller, Norman Charles, Jr. 1934- WhoAm 90
Miller, Norman Richard 1922- WhoAm 90
Miller, Norman Stanley BiDrAPA 89
Miller, Norman Stanley 1943- WhoE 91
Miller, Norton George 1942- WhoE 91
Miller, Oliver 1824-1892 AmLegL
Miller, Orlando Jack 1927- WhoAm 90
Miller, Oscar Victor, Jr. 1942- WhoSSW 91
Miller, Otto 1889-1962 Ballpl 90
Miller, Pamela 1958- WhoAmW 91
Miller, Pamela B. 1952- WhoWrEP 89
Miller, Pamelia Elizabeth 1948- WhoWrEP 89
Miller, Pat BioIn 16
Miller, Patricia L. G. 1940- WhoAmW 91
Miller, Patricia Louise 1936- WhoAmW 91
Miller, Patricia Lynn 1938- WhoWor 91
Miller, Patrick Dwight, Jr. 1935- WhoAm 90
Miller, Patrick M. 1942- St&PR 91
Miller, Patsy Ruth BioIn 16
Miller, Paul 1906- WhoAm 90
Miller, Paul 1951- BiDrAPA 89
Miller, Paul A. 1924- St&PR 91
Miller, Paul Albert 1924- WhoAm 90
Miller, Paul Ausborn 1917- WhoAm 90
Miller, Paul Charles 1914- St&PR 91
Miller, Paul F., Jr. 1927- St&PR 91
Miller, Paul Fetterolf, Jr. 1927- WhoAm 90
Miller, Paul Henderson 1928- WhoWor 91
Miller, Paul J. 1929- WhoAm 90
Miller, Paul James 1939- WhoAm 90, WhoWor 91
Miller, Paul Kevin 1954- WhoEmL 91
Miller, Paul L. 1919- St&PR 91
Miller, Paul Lukens 1919- WhoAm 90
Miller, Paul M. 1946- St&PR 91
Miller, Paul S. 1939- St&PR 91
Miller, Paul Samuel 1939- WhoAm 90
Miller, Paula Ann 1958- WhoE 91
Miller, Paula Belinda 1957- WhoAmW 91, WhoSSW 91
Miller, Paulette Marie 1948- WhoAmW 91
Miller, Pauline BioIn 16
Miller, Penelope Ann BioIn 16
Miller, Perry 1905-1963 BioIn 16
Miller, Perry Gilbert 1905-1963 WorAlBi
Miller, Peter D. 1946- St&PR 91
Miller, Peter G. 1945- ConAu 129
Miller, Peter John 1960- WhoWor 91
Miller, Peter Putnam 1938- WhoE 91
Miller, Peter S BiDrAPA 89
Miller, Peter Swift 1940- St&PR 91
Miller, Phebe Condict 1949- St&PR 91, WhoAm 90
Miller, Philip Boyd 1938- WhoAm 90
Miller, Philip Francis 1927- St&PR 91
Miller, Philip G. 1946- St&PR 91
Miller, Philip S. 1937- St&PR 91
Miller, Phillip Edward 1935- WhoWrEP 89
Miller, Phyllis 1920- ConAu 131
Miller, Phyllis Yvonne 1951- WhoAmW 91
Miller, Pleasant Voorhees 1922- St&PR 91
Miller, Preston Joel 1944- St&PR 91
Miller, R DeWitt 1910-1958 EncO&P 3
Miller, Rachelle Hasson 1958- BiDrAPA 89
Miller, Radhika NewAgMG
Miller, Raimund Josef 1944- WhoE 91
Miller, Ralph Alexander 1935- WhoSSW 91
Miller, Randal Howard 1947- WhoEmL 91
Miller, Randolph Crump 1910- WhoAm 90
Miller, Randy A. 1954- WhoE 91
Miller, Randy E. 1953- WhoE 91
Miller, Raymond F. 1941- WhoAm 90
Miller, Raymond Francis 1941- St&PR 91
Miller, Raymond Jarvis 1934- WhoAm 90
Miller, Raymond John 1951- St&PR 91
Miller, Raymond K. 1956- St&PR 91
Miller, Raymond L. 1934- St&PR 91
Miller, Raymond N 1927- BiDrAPA 89
Miller, Raymond P. 1930- St&PR 91

Miller, Raymond Russell, Jr. 1944- *WhoWrEP 89*
Miller, Raymond Vincent, Jr. 1954- *WhoEmL 91*
Miller, Rebecca *BioIn 16*
Miller, Rebecca Harvey 1952- *WhoAmW 91*
Miller, Reed 1918- *WhoAm 90*
Miller, Remy 1958- *WhoSSW 91*
Miller, Rene Harcourt 1916- *WhoAm 90, WhoWor 91*
Miller, Reuben George 1930- *WhoAm 90*
Miller, Rex 1929- *ConAu 30NR*
Miller, Richard 1930- *BioIn 16*
Miller, Richard Alan 1931- *WhoAm 90, WhoE 91*
Miller, Richard Alan 1939- *WhoAm 90*
Miller, Richard Alan 1942- *BiDrAPA 89*
Miller, Richard Alan 1943- *BiDrAPA 89*
Miller, Richard Allan 1947- *WhoEmL 91*
Miller, Richard Allen 1934- *BiDrAPA 89*
Miller, Richard Archibald 1927- *WhoAm 90*
Miller, Richard Arthur 1927- *WhoAm 90*
Miller, Richard B. 1926- *WhoAm 90*
Miller, Richard Bruce 1947- *WhoE 91*
Miller, Richard Clark, Jr. 1953- *WhoEmL 91*
Miller, Richard Dwight 1929- *WhoAm 90*
Miller, Richard Elroy 1931- *WhoSSW 91*
Miller, Richard F 1929- *BiDrAPA 89*
Miller, Richard G., Jr. 1918- *St&PR 91*
Miller, Richard Gary 1945- *BiDrAPA 89*
Miller, Richard Graham *WhoAm 90*
Miller, Richard Hamilton 1931- *WhoAm 90*
Miller, Richard Herman 1954- *WhoSSW 91*
Miller, Richard Irwin 1924- *WhoAm 90*
Miller, Richard Jackson 1946- *WhoSSW 91*
Miller, Richard Jerome 1939- *WhoE 91, WhoWor 91*
Miller, Richard Joseph 1941- *WhoSSW 91*
Miller, Richard Judd 1954- *BiDrAPA 89*
Miller, Richard Kidwell 1930- *WhoAm 90, WhoAmA 91*
Miller, Richard L. *ODwPR 91*
Miller, Richard L. 1941- *WhoSSW 91*
Miller, Richard Lee 1925- *St&PR 91*
Miller, Richard Leroy, Jr. 1951- *WhoE 91*
Miller, Richard M. 1931- *St&PR 91*
Miller, Richard Mark 1952- *WhoE 91*
Miller, Richard McDermott 1922- *WhoAm 90, WhoAmA 91*
Miller, Richard Morgan 1931- *WhoAm 90*
Miller, Richard R. *ODwPR 91*
Miller, Richard Sherwin 1930- *WhoAm 90*
Miller, Richard W. *St&PR 91*
Miller, Richard Wesley 1940- *St&PR 91, WhoAm 90*
Miller, Richards Thorn 1918- *WhoE 91*
Miller, Rick *ODwPR 91*
Miller, Rick 1948- *Ballpl 90*
Miller, Rita 1925- *WhoE 91*
Miller, Robert 1915- *St&PR 91*
Miller, Robert 1923- *WhoAm 90, WhoE 91*
Miller, Robert A. *BioIn 16, NewYTBS 90*
Miller, Robert A. 1931- *WhoAm 90*
Miller, Robert Alan 1942- *WhoSSW 91*
Miller, Robert Alan 1945- *WhoE 91*
Miller, Robert Allen 1931- *St&PR 91*
Miller, Robert Arthur 1939- *WhoAm 90*
Miller, Robert B *BiDrAPA 89*
Miller, Robert Bernard 1956- *WhoSSW 91*
Miller, Robert Branson, Jr. 1935- *WhoAm 90*
Miller, Robert Branson, Sr. 1906- *WhoAm 90*
Miller, Robert C. 1930- *WhoAm 90*
Miller, Robert C.J. 1941- *St&PR 91*
Miller, Robert Carmi, Jr. 1942- *WhoAm 90*
Miller, Robert Charles 1925- *WhoAm 90*
Miller, Robert Clinton 1954- *WhoSSW 91*
Miller, Robert Dale 1950- *WhoSSW 91*
Miller, Robert Daniel 1960- *WhoSSW 91*
Miller, Robert David 1932- *St&PR 91*
Miller, Robert David 1941- *BiDrAPA 89*
Miller, Robert E. 1939- *St&PR 91*
Miller, Robert Earl 1932- *WhoAm 90*
Miller, Robert Edvin 1935- *WhoE 91*
Miller, Robert Elmer 1920- *WhoSSW 91*
Miller, Robert F. 1929- *St&PR 91*
Miller, Robert Franklin 1935- *WhoAm 90*
Miller, Robert H. 1930- *St&PR 91*
Miller, Robert H 1935- *BiDrAPA 89*
Miller, Robert Haskins 1919- *WhoAm 90*
Miller, Robert Henry 1938- *WhoAm 90*
Miller, Robert Hopkins 1927- *WhoAm 90*
Miller, Robert Hyland 1937- *WhoWor 91*
Miller, Robert James 1923- *WhoAm 90, WhoWrEP 89*
Miller, Robert James 1933- *WhoAm 90, WhoWrEP 89*
Miller, Robert Joseph 1945- *WhoAm 90*
Miller, Robert L. 1945- *ODwPR 91*
Miller, Robert Lang 1927- *St&PR 91*
Miller, Robert Lee *BiDrAPA 89*
Miller, Robert Leo 1932- *WhoE 91*
Miller, Robert Lindsey 1933- *WhoAm 90*
Miller, Robert Louis 1926- *WhoAm 90*
Miller, Robert Nolen 1940- *WhoAm 90*
Miller, Robert Peter 1939- *BioIn 16, WhoAmA 91*
Miller, Robert R.C. 1925- *St&PR 91*
Miller, Robert Richey Conklin 1925- *WhoAm 90*
Miller, Robert S. 1941- *St&PR 91*
Miller, Robert Scott 1947- *WhoEmL 91, WhoWor 91*
Miller, Robert Sterling 1926- *St&PR 91*
Miller, Robert Stevens, Jr. 1941- *WhoAm 90*
Miller, Robert T *BiDrAPA 89*
Miller, Robert T. 1920- *WhoAm 90*
Miller, Robert Watt, Mrs 1898- *WhoAmA 91*
Miller, Robert Wayne 1941- *WhoAm 90*
Miller, Robert Wayne 1943- *BiDrAPA 89*
Miller, Robert Wesley 1928- *St&PR 91*
Miller, Robert Wiley 1928- *WhoAm 90*
Miller, Robert William 1922- *WhoSSW 91*
Miller, Roberta Davis 1931- *WhoAm 90, WhoWrEP 89*
Miller, Robin Feuer 1947- *ConAu 130*
Miller, Roger 1936- *ConMus 4 [port], OxCPMus, WorAlBi*
Miller, Roger Dean 1936- *WhoAm 90*
Miller, Roger James 1947- *WhoEmL 91*
Miller, Roger William 1946- *WhoE 91*
Miller, Roland Drew 1922- *WhoAm 90*
Miller, Ron M. 1944- *St&PR 91*
Miller, Ronald Alan 1951- *WhoWor 91*
Miller, Ronald Alfred 1943- *WhoAm 90*
Miller, Ronald Eugene 1933- *WhoAm 90*
Miller, Ronald G. 1928- *St&PR 91*
Miller, Ronald Howard 1946- *IntWWM 90*
Miller, Ronald M. 1944- *St&PR 91*
Miller, Ronald R. 1933- *WhoWrEP 89*
Miller, Ronald Thomas 1919- *St&PR 91, WhoAm 90*
Miller, Ronda Gelene 1955- *IntWWM 90*
Miller, Roscoe 1876-1913 *Ballpl 90*
Miller, Rosemary Margaret 1935- *WhoAmW 91, WhoE 91*
Miller, Ross Hays 1923- *WhoAm 90*
Miller, Roy 1883-1938 *Ballpl 90*
Miller, Ruby Sills 1919- *WhoAm 90*
Miller, Rudy R. 1947- *St&PR 91*
Miller, Russell Bryan 1940- *WhoAm 90*
Miller, Russell Loyd, Jr. 1939- *WhoAm 90*
Miller, Russell Ray 1928- *St&PR 91*
Miller, Ruth *ConAu 33NR*
Miller, Sally 1925- *WhoE 91*
Miller, Sam M. 1954- *St&PR 91*
Miller, Sam Scott 1938- *WhoAm 90*
Miller, Samuel Aaron 1952- *WhoAm 90*
Miller, Samuel Aaron 1955- *WhoEmL 91*
Miller, Samuel Clifford 1930- *WhoAm 90, WhoAmA 91*
Miller, Samuel Martin 1938- *WhoAm 90*
Miller, Sandra Long 1955- *St&PR 91*
Miller, Sanford Arthur 1931- *WhoAm 90, WhoSSW 91*
Miller, Sara B 1926- *BiDrAPA 89*
Miller, Sarabeth 1927- *WhoWor 91*
Miller, Scott Allan, III 1955- *WhoEmL 91*
Miller, Scott Andrew 1961- *WhoEmL 91*
Miller, Seymour A *BiDrAPA 89*
Miller, Seymour Michael 1922- *WhoAm 90*
Miller, Sharon Bernard 1943- *St&PR 91*
Miller, Sharon Charlotte 1949- *WhoWrEP 89*
Miller, Sharyl Kay 1945- *WhoAmW 91*
Miller, Shelby Alexander 1914- *WhoWor 91*
Miller, Sheldon Irvin *BiDrAPA 89*
Miller, Sherman *St&PR 91*
Miller, Sherry Ann 1948- *WhoWrEP 89*
Miller, Sherry L. 1962- *WhoAmW 91*
Miller, Shirley Casey 1932- *WhoWrEP 89*
Miller, Shirley Marie 1957- *WhoAmW 91*
Miller, Sidney 1926- *St&PR 91, WhoAm 90, WhoE 91*
Miller, Sieglinde F. 1941- *WhoAmW 91*
Miller, Spencer H., II 1956- *St&PR 91*
Miller, Stanford 1913- *St&PR 91, WhoAm 90*
Miller, Stanley Custer, Jr. 1926- *WhoAm 90*
Miller, Stanley J, Jr. 1931- *BiDrAPA 89*
Miller, Stanley Lloyd 1930- *BioIn 16*
Miller, Stephanie Ann 1964- *WhoAmW 91*
Miller, Stephanie Lee 1950- *WhoAm 90*
Miller, Stephen 1941- *WhoE 91*
Miller, Stephen A. 1940- *St&PR 91*
Miller, Stephen Charles 1944- *St&PR 91*
Miller, Stephen Grant Ross 1959- *WhoSSW 91*
Miller, Stephen Joseph 1945- *WhoEmL 91*
Miller, Stephen M. 1939- *WhoWrEP 89*
Miller, Stephen Marcelles 1952- *WhoWrEP 89*
Miller, Stephen P. 1954- *St&PR 91*
Miller, Stephen Raben 1928- *WhoAm 90*
Miller, Steve *WhoAm 90, WhoAmA 91*
Miller, Steve 1943- *BioIn 16, EncPR&S 89*
Miller, Steven L. 1945- *St&PR 91*
Miller, Steven Peter *BiDrAPA 89*
Miller, Steven Richard 1953- *WhoSSW 91*
Miller, Steven Scott 1947- *WhoEmL 91*
Miller, Stewart Edward 1918- *WhoAm 90*
Miller, Stewart Ransom 1945- *WhoEmL 91*
Miller, Stu 1927- *Ballpl 90*
Miller, Stuart Carl *BiDrAPA 89*
Miller, Stuart J. 1939- *St&PR 91*
Miller, Sue 194-?- *BestSel 90-3 [port]*
Miller, Susan Anne 1946- *WhoE 91*
Miller, Susan Buchanan 1947- *WhoE 91*
Miller, Susan D. *ODwPR 91*
Miller, Susan Leigh 1961- *WhoAmW 91*
Miller, Sybil Ann 1956- *WhoSSW 91*
Miller, Sydell Lois 1937- *WhoWor 91*
Miller, T. Meredith *St&PR 91*
Miller, Tanfield Charles 1947- *WhoAm 90*
Miller, Teresa N. 1955- *St&PR 91*
Miller, Teresa R 1954- *BiDrAPA 89*
Miller, Teresa Welch 1963- *WhoAmW 91*
Miller, Terry Ellis 1945- *IntWWM 90*
Miller, Terry Lynn 1945- *WhoAmW 91*
Miller, Tevie 1928- *WhoAm 90*
Miller, Theodore K. 1932- *WhoSSW 91*
Miller, Theodore Max 1956- *BiDrAPA 89*
Miller, Theodore Robert 1907- *WhoAm 90*
Miller, Theresa Ann 1945- *WhoEmL 91*
Miller, Theresa Ann Wendling 1965- *WhoAmW 91*
Miller, Thomas A. 1960- *St&PR 91*
Miller, Thomas Allen 1944- *WhoWor 91*
Miller, Thomas Bentley 1950- *WhoWrEP 89*
Miller, Thomas Burk 1929- *WhoAm 90*
Miller, Thomas Davis 1913- *St&PR 91*
Miller, Thomas E 1931- *BiDrAPA 89*
Miller, Thomas Earl, Jr. 1936- *WhoSSW 91*
Miller, Thomas Eugene 1929- *WhoWor 91, WhoWrEP 89*
Miller, Thomas Ezekiel 1849-1938 *BlkAmsC [port]*
Miller, Thomas Friday 1922- *St&PR 91*
Miller, Thomas H. 1955- *St&PR 91*
Miller, Thomas Hulbert, Jr. 1923- *WhoAm 90*
Miller, Thomas J. 1944- *WhoAm 90*
Miller, Thomas Marshall 1910- *St&PR 91, WhoAm 90*
Miller, Thomas Milton 1930- *WhoAm 90*
Miller, Thomas R. 1942- *St&PR 91*
Miller, Thomas R. 1949- *WhoAm 90*
Miller, Thomas Raymond 1949- *WhoEmL 91*
Miller, Thomas Robbins 1938- *WhoAm 90*
Miller, Thomas Roy 1957- *WhoEmL 91*
Miller, Thomas W., Jr. 1910- *St&PR 91*
Miller, Thomas W. C. 1938- *WhoWor 91*
Miller, Thomas Wainwright, Jr. 1927- *WhoSSW 91*
Miller, Thomas Williams 1930- *WhoAm 90*
Miller, Thormund Aubrey 1919- *WhoAm 90*
Miller, Timothy 1957- *IntWWM 90*
Miller, Timothy Alan 1956- *WhoE 91*
Miller, Timothy Burke 1952- *WhoSSW 91*
Miller, Timothy Earl 1952- *WhoE 91*
Miller, Toby *BioIn 16*
Miller, Todd 1961- *ODwPR 91*
Miller, Tom 1945- *BioIn 16*
Miller, Tom Polk 1914- *WhoAm 90*
Miller, Tracey Lee 1959- *WhoAmW 91*
Miller, Trudy Joyce *WhoAmW 91*
Miller, Tyree B. *WhoAm 90*
Miller, Vassar 1924- *DcLB 105 [port]*
Miller, Victoria Wood 1949- *WhoAm 90*
Miller, Vincent Eugene 1935- *WhoWor 91*
Miller, Virgil V. 1939- *St&PR 91*
Miller, W. Howard *BioIn 16*
Miller, Wade *TwCCr&M 91*
Miller, Wallace B. 1939- *St&PR 91*
Miller, Walter A. 1904- *St&PR 91*
Miller, Walter Durward 1935- *WhoE 91*
Miller, Walter James 1918- *WhoWrEP 89*
Miller, Walter M., Jr. 1923- *RGTwCSF*
Miller, Walter Neal 1929- *WhoAm 90*
Miller, Walter R., Jr. 1934- *St&PR 91*
Miller, Walter Richard, Jr. 1934- *WhoAm 90, WhoE 91, WhoWor 91*
Miller, Ward 1884-1958 *Ballpl 90*
Miller, Ward MacLaughlin 1933- *St&PR 91*
Miller, Warren E. 1945- *St&PR 91*
Miller, Warren Edward 1924- *WhoAm 90*
Miller, Wayne Dunbar 1934- *WhoE 91*
Miller, Webb 1892-1940 *BioIn 16*
Miller, Wendell Smith 1925- *WhoWor 91*
Miller, Wendy E. 1943- *ODwPR 91*
Miller, Whitney Dillon 1938- *St&PR 91*
Miller, Wilbur Hobart 1915- *WhoAm 90, WhoE 91, WhoWor 91*
Miller, Wilbur Randolph 1932- *WhoAm 90*
Miller, Willard, Jr. 1937- *WhoAm 90*
Miller, William 1906-1988 *BioIn 16*
Miller, William 1909-1989 *ConAu 129*
Miller, William 1947- *WhoSSW 91*
Miller, William A. 1939- *St&PR 91*
Miller, William Albert, Jr. 1932- *WhoE 91*
Miller, William Bayard 1924- *WhoE 91*
Miller, William Bayard, Jr. 1951- *WhoEmL 91*
Miller, William C. 1955- *ODwPR 91*
Miller, William C, Jr. 1925- *BiDrAPA 89*
Miller, William Charles 1937- *WhoAm 90*
Miller, William Charles 1945- *WhoEmL 91*
Miller, William Dawes 1919- *WhoWor 91*
Miller, William E. 1919- *St&PR 91*
Miller, William Elwood 1919- *WhoWor 91*
Miller, William Evans, Jr. 1923- *WhoAm 90*
Miller, William Franklin 1920- *WhoSSW 91*
Miller, William Frederick 1925- *WhoAm 90*
Miller, William Frederick 1937- *St&PR 91*
Miller, William Frederick 1946- *WhoEmL 91, WhoSSW 91*
Miller, William Grady 1956- *WhoE 91*
Miller, William H. 1941- *ODwPR 91*
Miller, William Harlow 1951- *BiDrAPA 89*
Miller, William Henry Harrison 1840-1917 *BiDrUSE 89*
Miller, William Hughes 1941- *WhoAm 90*
Miller, William J. *BioIn 16*
Miller, William Jack 1927- *WhoAm 90*
Miller, William Jacob 1952- *WhoE 91*
Miller, William Jones 1938- *WhoAm 90*
Miller, William L 1943- *ConAu 130*
Miller, William Lawrence 1937- *WhoAm 90*
Miller, William Lee 1926- *WhoAm 90*
Miller, William Marshall, Jr. 1943- *WhoE 91*
Miller, William Michael 1952- *WhoE 91*
Miller, William Mosley 1909-1989 *BioIn 16*
Miller, William Napier Cripps 1930- *WhoAm 90*
Miller, William Read 1823-1887 *BioIn 16*
Miller, William Robert 1928- *St&PR 91, WhoAm 90*
Miller, William S. 1932- *St&PR 91*
Miller, William Talbot 1943- *WhoAm 90*
Miller, William Taylor 1911- *WhoAm 90*
Miller, William W. 1836-1881 *AmLegL*
Miller, Wilma H 1936- *ConAu 30NR*
Miller, Wilmer Glenn 1932- *WhoAm 90*
Miller, Wilton Evans 1937- *St&PR 91*
Miller, Yvonne Bond *WhoAmW 91, WhoSSW 91*
Miller, Zell Bryan 1932- *WhoAm 90, WhoSSW 91*
Miller, Zesta Fayedene 1938- *WhoAmW 91*
Miller, Zoya Dickins 1923- *WhoAmW 91, WhoWor 91*
Miller-Blazak, Kristine Ann 1949- *WhoAmW 91*
Miller-Clark, Denise *WhoAmA 91*
Miller-Jacobson, Jan Barbara 1952- *WhoWrEP 89*
Miller-Lane, Barbara 1934- *WhoAm 90*
Miller-Verghi, Margareta 1864-1951 *EncCoWW*
Miller-Verghy, Margarita *EncCoWW*
Millerand, Etienne-Alexandre 1859-1943 *BiDFrPL*
Millers, Edie 1938- *WhoAmW 91, WhoE 91*
Milles, Carl 1875-1955 *BioIn 16*
Milles, Mary *BiDEWW*
Millet, Blaine William 1954- *WhoEmL 91*
Millet, Clarence 1897-1959 *WhoAmA 91N*
Millet, Francis Davis 1846-1912 *BioIn 16*
Millet, Frank D. *BioIn 16*
Millet, Jean Francois 1814-1875 *BioIn 16, IntDcAA 90, WorAlBi*
Millet, John Bradford 1916- *WhoE 91, WhoWor 91*
Millet, Naomi Cassell 1923- *WhoWor 91*
Millett, Caroline Dunlop 1939- *WhoAmA 91*
Millett, Jeremy J. 1938- *WhoSSW 91*
Millett, Kate *BioIn 16*
Millett, Kate 1934- *ConAu 32NR, FemiCLE, MajTwCW, WorAlBi*
Millett, Katherine Murray 1934- *WhoAm 90, WhoAmW 91, WhoWrEP 89*
Millett, Ralph Linwood, Jr. 1919- *WhoAm 90*
Millett, Robert Eugene 1951- *WhoE 91*
Milley, David Clark 1941- *WhoE 91*
Milley, Jane Elizabeth 1940- *WhoAmW 91*
Millgate, Henry *WhoAm 90*

Milne, Margaret Joan 1914- AuBYP 90
Milne, Margery J 19--?- ChILR 22 [port]
Milne, Margery Joan 1922- WhoAmW 91
Milne, Robert Scott 1917- WhoWrEP 89
Milne, Susan Belisle 1948- WhoE 91
Milne, Teddy 1930- WhoWrEP 89
Milner, Alfred 1854-1919 BioIn 16
Milner, Anthony Francis Dominic 1925- IntWWM 90
Milner, Brenda Atkinson Langford 1918- WhoAm 90, WhoAmW 91
Milner, Curtis Dean 1947- St&PR 91
Milner, David R. 1945- St&PR 91
Milner, Eddie 1955- Ballpl 90
Milner, Gilbert Cecil, III BiDrAPA 89
Milner, Harold William 1934- St&PR 91, WhoAm 90
Milner, Howard Marvin 1937- WhoAm 90, WhoWor 91
Milner, Irvin Myron 1916- WhoAm 90
Milner, Jack Edward, Jr. 1937- WhoSSW 91
Milner, John 1949- Ballpl 90
Milner, Judith R. BiDrAPA 89
Milner, Judith R. 1950- WhoE 91
Milner, Karen Kay BiDrAPA 89
Milner, Max 1914- WhoAm 90
Milner, Moses Embree 1829-1876 WhNaAH
Milner, Neil BioIn 16
Milner, Paul 1941- WhoE 91
Milner, Peter Alan 1951- WhoSSW 91
Milner, Peter Marshall 1919- WhoAm 90
Milner, Richard Coulson 1940- WhoWor 91
Milner, Richard Forbes 1930- St&PR 91
Milner, Robert Teague 1851-1923 AmLegL
Milner, Ron 1938- MajTwCW
Milner, Ronald 1938- DrBIPA 90
Milner, Stanley A. 1938- St&PR 91
Milnes, Arthur George 1922- WhoAm 90
Milnes, Ian 1943- IntWWM 90
Milnes, John Herbert 1912- St&PR 91
Milnes, Richard Monckton 1809-1885 BioIn 16
Milnes, Robert Antrim 1925- St&PR 91
Milnes, Robert Winston 1948- WhoAmA 91
Milnes, Sherill 1935- IntWWM 90
Milnes, Sherrill 1935- PenDiMP, WorAlBi
Milnes, Sherrill Eustace 1935- WhoAm 90
Milnes, William Robert, Jr. 1946- St&PR 91
Milnikel, Robert Saxon 1926- WhoAm 90
Milnor, George Sparks, II 1950- St&PR 91
Milnor, William Robert 1920- WhoAm 90
Milo, Frank Anthony 1946- WhoWor 91
Milo, Henry Louis, Jr. 1920- St&PR 91
Milo, Hjalmar Taeke 1945- WhoWor 91
Milo, Robert C. 1935- St&PR 91
Milo, William P. 1947- St&PR 91
Milobedzki, Jerzy Adam 1924- WhoWor 91
Milock, Richard Lee 1939- St&PR 91
Milofsky, David 1946- WhoWrEP 89
Milojkovic-Djuric, Jelena 1931- IntWWM 90
Milon, Ella Mae 1926- WhoWrEP 89
Milonas, Herodotos WhoAmA 91
Milonas, Minos 1936- WhoAmA 91, WhoE 91
Milone, Anthony M. 1932- WhoAm 90
Milone, Arthur F 1956- BiDrAPA 89
Milone, Charles Louis 1920- WhoSSW 91
Milone, Richard D 1938- BiDrAPA 89
Milosavljevic, Alexander M. 1955- WhoE 91
Milosevic, M. 1955- St&PR 91
Milosevic, Slobodan BioIn 16
Milosevic, Slobodan 1941- CurBio 90 [port], WhoWor 91
Milosi, Rodrigue 1935- IntWWM 90
Milosz, Czcslaw BioIn 16, NewYTBS 90 [port]
Milosz, Czeslaw 1911- EuWr 13, MajTwCW, WhoAm 90, WhoWor 91, WhoWrEP 89, WorAlBi
Milot, Michel 1934- WhoWor 91
Milotte, Alfred G 1904-1989 SmATA 62
Milotte, Alfred George 1904-1989 BioIn 16
Milotte, Elma BioIn 16
Milowe, George BiDrAPA 89
Milowe, Irvin D BiDrAPA 89
Milowe, Irvin D. 1931- WhoE 91
Milrad, Aaron M 1935- WhoAmA 91
Milrod, David 1924- BiDrAPA 89
Milrod, Linda Jane 1953- WhoAm 90
Milroy, Lisa 1959- BiDWomA
Milroy, Thomas Miller 1948- BiDrAPA 89
Milsap, Rebecca Lynn 1952- WhoAmW 91
Milsap, Ronnie WhoAm 90
Milsap, Ronnie 1943- WorAlBi
Mil'Shtein, Samson Khaim 1940- WhoE 91
Milsom, Robert Cortlandt 1924- WhoAm 90
Milstead, Glenn BioIn 16
Milstead, Kathryn Funderburk 1962- WhoAmW 91
Milstead, Neldon W. 1936- St&PR 91
Milstead, William Elmer 1919- St&PR 91
Milstead, Wm. C. 1926- St&PR 91
Milsted, David 1954- ConAu 132
Milstein, Alan Carl 1953- WhoEmL 91
Milstein, Alex BiDrAPA 89
Milstein, Bernard Allen 1941- WhoSSW 91
Milstein, Cesar 1927- WhoAm 90, WhoWor 91, WorAlBi
Milstein, Harold Jacob 1949- WhoAm 90
Milstein, Howard Roy 1944- St&PR 91
Milstein, Laurence Bennett 1942- WhoAm 90
Milstein, Nathan 1904- IntWWM 90, PenDiMP, WhoWor 91
Milstein, Philip S BiDrAPA 89
Milstein, Richard Craig 1946- WhoWor 91
Milstein, Richard Sherman 1926- WhoAm 90, WhoE 91
Milstein, Robert I 1931- BiDrAPA 89
Milstein, Robert Michael BiDrAPA 89
Milstein, Stephen Eric 1956- St&PR 91
Milstein, Vladimir A BiDrAPA 89
Milsten, David Randolph 1903- WhoAm 90
Milsten, Robert B. 1932- WhoAm 90
Miltenberger, Robert Henry, II 1934- WhoSSW 91
Miltenberger, Steven Edward 1946- St&PR 91
Miltner, Emily R. 1908- WhoWrEP 89
Miltner, John Robert 1946- WhoEmL 91
Miltner, Robert Francis 1949- WhoWrEP 89
Milton, Albert Fenner 1940- WhoE 91
Milton, Barbara 1947- WhoWrEP 89
Milton, Benjamin F. 1855-1915 BioIn 16
Milton, Billy 1905-1989 AnObit 1989
Milton, Christian Michel 1947- St&PR 91
Milton, Christopher Wood 1955- WhoSSW 91
Milton, Edith 1931- WhoWrEP 89
Milton, Hilary 1920- WhoWrEP 89
Milton, James 1945- WhoWor 91
Milton, John 1608-1674 WorAlBi, WrPh
Milton, John Charles Douglas 1924- WhoAm 90
Milton, John Ronald 1924- WhoAm 90, WhoWrEP 89
Milton, Joyce BioIn 16
Milton, Joyce Lynne 1946- WhoAmW 91
Milton, Lana L 1948- BiDrAPA 89
Milton, Nancy Melissa 1942- WhoAmW 91
Milton, Peter Winslow 1930- WhoAm 90, WhoAmA 91
Milton, Richard Henry 1938- WhoAm 90
Milton, Robert Mitchell 1920- WhoAm 90
Milton, Wilhelm WhoWrEP 89
Milton, William Hammond, III 1925- St&PR 91
Milton-Thompson, Godfrey James 1930- WhoWor 91
Milutin, Slavenka BiDrAPA 89
Miluwi, John Omirah BioIn 16
Milveden, J. Ingmar G. 1920- IntWWM 90
Milvy, Paul 1931-1989 BioIn 16, ConAu 129
Milwid, Alben Joseph 1924- St&PR 91
Mim, Adrienne C 1931- WhoAmA 91
Mimieux, Yvette 1942?- BioIn 16
Mimless, Lorin Howard BiDrAPA 89
Mimmack, Frederick W 1933- BiDrAPA 89
Mimna, Curtis John 1943- WhoE 91, WhoWor 91
Mims, Dewey Jeffrey 1954- WhoSSW 91
Mims, George BioIn 16
Mims, George L. 1934- ConAu 129
Mims, Inka Fredotovich 1937- WhoAmW 91
Mims, Judy F. 1950- WhoAmW 91
Mims, Madeline Manning- BioIn 16
Mims, Robert Lewis BiDrAPA 89
Mims, Sam 1887- AuBYP 90
Mims, Thomas J. 1899- St&PR 91
Mims, Thomas Jerome 1899- WhoAm 90, WhoSSW 91, WhoWor 91
Min WomWR
Min, Chang Hyun 1937- BiDrAPA 89
Min, Elizabeth 1954- IntWWM 90
Min, Kun Ki 1942- BiDrAPA 89
Min, Laura J. ODwPR 91
Min, Yong Soon 1953- WhoAmA 91
Mina-Mora, Dorise Olson 1932- WhoAmA 91
Mina-Mora, Paul J., Mrs. 1932- WhoAmW 91
Mina-Mora, Raul Jose 1914- WhoAmA 91
Minadakis, Nicholas John 1924- WhoE 91, WhoWor 91
Minagawa, Masa 1917- ConDes 90
Minaguchi, Hiroshi 1933- WhoWor 91
Minahan, Daniel F. 1929- St&PR 91, WhoAm 90, WhoWor 91
Minahan, John English 1933- WhoAm 90, WhoWrEP 89
Minahan, Martha Connors 1945- WhoSSW 91
Minahan, Roger C. 1910- St&PR 91
Minahan, Roger Copp 1910- WhoAm 90
Minakowski, Frances M. 1948- ODwPR 91
Minaldi, Thad David 1957- St&PR 91
Minale, Marcello 1938- ConDes 90
Minami, Satoshi 1955- IntWWM 90
Minamino, Hiroyuki 1951- IntWWM 90
Minamoto Clan EncJap
Minamoto no Yoritomo 1147-1199 EncJap
Minamoto no Yoshitsune 1159-1189 EncJap
Minamyer, William Eric 1953- WhoEmL 91
Minarcin, Rudy 1930- Ballpl 90
Minard, Eugene W 1924- BiDrAPA 89
Minard, Everett Lawrence, III 1949- WhoAm 90
Minard, Frank Pell Lawrence 1945- WhoE 91
Minard, John D. 1951- St&PR 91
Minard, John Lawrence BiDrAPA 89
Minard, Rosemary AuBYP 90
Minard, Rosemary 1939- SmATA 63 [port]
Minarich, Madonna 1949- St&PR 91
Minarik, Else Holmelund 1920- AuBYP 90, WhoAmW 91
Minarik, James Edward 1953- St&PR 91
Minarik, Joseph John 1949- WhoAm 90
Minassian, Jeffery H 1954- BiDrAPA 89
Minasy, Arthur John 1925- St&PR 91, WhoE 91, WhoWor 91
Minatelli, John A. 1948- St&PR 91
Minc, Henryk 1919- WhoAm 90
Mincer, Jacob 1922- WhoAm 90
Mincey, Ethel Louise Berry 1931- WhoE 91
Minch, Gordon Charles 1923- St&PR 91
Minch, Jeffrey Leonard Stephen 1951- WhoSSW 91
Minch, Michael Jon 1941- St&PR 91
Minch, Roger James 1952- WhoEmL 91
Minch, Virgil Adelbert 1924- WhoSSW 91, WhoWor 91
Mincheff, Edison Elaine 1920- WhoSSW 91
Minchell, Peter 1889- MusmAFA
Minchen, Steven Lloyd 1961- WhoSSW 91
Minchener, Vicki Paulson 1946- WhoAmW 91
Mincher, Don 1938- Ballpl 90
Minchew, Edward Leon 1946- WhoE 91
Minchew, Harold R. 1932- St&PR 91
Minchin, Michael M., Jr. 1926- St&PR 91, WhoAm 90
Minchin, William J. 1937- St&PR 91
Minco, Marga 1920- EncCoWW
Minczeski, John WhoWrEP 89
Mind over Matter NewAgMG
Minde, Klaus K 1933- BiDrAPA 89
Minde, Stefan P. 1936- IntWWM 90
Mindel, Eugene D 1934- BiDrAPA 89
Mindel, Laurence Brisker 1937- WhoWor 91
Mindel, Meir 1946- IntWWM 90
Mindel, Seymour Stewart 1911- St&PR 91
Mindell, Carl Eli BiDrAPA 89
Mindell, Eugene Robert 1922- WhoAm 90
Mindell, Sara Marie 1958- WhoAmW 91
Minden, Sarah Lynne 1946- BiDrAPA 89
Minder, Gabriel George 1936- WhoWor 91
Mindes, Gayle Dean 1942- WhoAmW 91
Mindich, Holly Jane 1961- WhoEmL 91
Mindich, Stephen M. 1943- St&PR 91
Mindlin, Helen Mather-Smith AuBYP 90
Mindlin, Paula Rosalie 1944- WhoE 91
Mindlin, Richard Barnett 1926- WhoAm 90
M'Indoe, John B. EncO&P 3
Mindszenty, Jozsef 1892-1975 WorAlBi
Mindt, Dieter 1939- WhoWor 91
Mindt Long, W. Kaye 1953- WhoAmW 91
Minear, Beth 1939- WhoAmA 91
Minear, Leon Pierson 1915- WhoAm 90
Minear, Paul Sevier 1906- WhoAm 90
Minegawa, Mutsuo 1935- Ballpl 90
Minehan, Cathy E. 1947- St&PR 91
Minehart, Margaret Ann 1941- BiDrAPA 89
Minehart, Ralph Conrad 1935- WhoSSW 91
Mineka, Susan 1948- WhoEmL 91
Minellono, George John 1928- St&PR 91
Mineo, Michael Joseph 1950- WhoSSW 91
Mineo, Robert Anthony 1948- WhoEmL 91
Miner, A. Bradford 1947- WhoAm 90
Miner, Bill 1847-1913 BioIn 16
Miner, Charles B. 1942- St&PR 91
Miner, Charles H., Jr. 1907- St&PR 91
Miner, Christopher M. 1951- St&PR 91
Miner, Doris P. WhoAmW 91
Miner, Dorothy Eugenia 1906-1973 WhoAmA 91N
Miner, Earl Howard 1923- WhoAm 90
Miner, Earl Roy 1927- WhoAm 90
Miner, Erica Brown 1946- WhoE 91
Miner, Francis Wayland 1831-1902 AmLegL
Miner, Harlow James, Jr. 1931- WhoE 91
Miner, Henry C., III 1936- St&PR 91
Miner, Horace Mitchell 1912- WhoAm 90
Miner, Irvin V. 1923- St&PR 91
Miner, Jacqueline 1936- WhoAmW 91
Miner, James B, Jr. 1933- BiDrAPA 89
Miner, James Joshua 1928- St&PR 91
Miner, James Monroe BiDrAPA 89
Miner, Jan 1917- WhoWor 91
Miner, John 1947- WhoAm 90
Miner, John Allen 1950- BiDrAPA 89
Miner, John Burnham 1926- WhoE 91, WhoWor 91
Miner, John Ronald 1938- WhoAm 90
Miner, Juanita H. BioIn 16
Miner, Opal Irene Sevrey 1906- AuBYP 90
Miner, Richard Allen 1946- BiDrAPA 89
Miner, Robert Gordon 1923- WhoAm 90, WhoWrEP 89
Miner, Robert W BiDrAPA 89
Miner, Roger Jeffrey 1934- WhoAm 90
Miner, Sydny Weinberg 1951- WhoAm 90
Miner, Thomas Hawley 1927- WhoAm 90, WhoWor 91
Miner, Valerie 1947- FemiCLE, WhoWrEP 89
Minero, Frank Vincent 1942- BiDrAPA 89
Minervini, Francesco 1929- WhoWor 91
Minervino, Louise 1947- WhoE 91
Mines, Jeanette 1948- SmATA 61 [port]
Mines, Jeanette Marie 1948- WhoWrEP 89
Mines, John Erickson 1963- WhoSSW 91
Minet, Paul Piers Brissault 1937- WhoWor 91
Mineta, Norman Y. BioIn 16
Mineta, Norman Yoshio 1931- WhoAm 90
Minette, Dennis Jerome 1937- WhoSSW 91, WhoWor 91
Minetti, Patrick WhoSSW 91
Minetto, Craig 1954- Ballpl 90
Minevich, Eduard 1943- IntWWM 90
Minewski, Alex 1917-1979 WhoAmA 91N
Minford, John 1946- ConAu 130
Ming PenDiDA 89
Ming, Si-Chun 1922- WhoAm 90
Mingay, Arthur Hammond 1919- St&PR 91, WhoAm 90
Minger, Terrell John 1942- WhoWor 91
Minges, Robert James 1923- WhoAm 90
Minghetti, Angelo 1821?-1885 PenDiDA 89
Mingi, Akili ConAu 130
Mingione, Donald L 1933- BiDrAPA 89
Mingle, John Orville 1931- WhoAm 90
Mingo, Frank BioIn 16
Mingo, James William Edgar 1926- WhoAm 90
Mingoia, Michele Ann 1954- WhoAmW 91
Mingori, Steve 1944- Ballpl 90
Mingous, Louada Frances 1947- WhoAmW 91
Mingus, Charles 1922-1979 BioIn 16, DrBIPA 90, OxCPMus, WorAlBi
Minguzzi, Romualdo Carlo 1931- WhoWor 91
Minh, Ho Quang BioIn 16
Mini, Louis James 1962- BiDrAPA 89
Minice, Richard Lee 1937- St&PR 91
Minick, David Gilbert 1923- St&PR 91
Minick, Joseph 1956- BiDrAPA 89
Minick, Michael 1945- WhoAm 90
Minick, Roger 1944- WhoAmA 91
Minick, Steven Alex 1954- WhoSSW 91
Minicucci, Anerico Joseph 1925- WhoSSW 91
Minifie, Benjamin BioIn 16
Minifie, Margaret FemiCLE
Minikes, Stephan Michael 1938- WhoAm 90
Minimic WhNaAH
Minio, Joseph C. 1943- St&PR 91
Minirth, Franklin B 1946- BiDrAPA 89
Minisci, Brenda 1939- WhoAmA 91
Minish, Robert Arthur 1938- St&PR 91
Minisi, Anthony S. 1926- WhoAm 90
Minister, Kristina 1934- WhoAmW 91
Minium, Faye E. 1935- St&PR 91
Mink DeVille EncPR&S 89
Mink, Ernest Frederick, III 1953- WhoEmL 91
Mink, Gary Stuart 1953- WhoE 91, WhoWor 91
Mink, John Robert 1927- WhoAm 90
Mink, John W. 1940- St&PR 91
Mink, Lawrence Albright 1936- WhoSSW 91
Mink, Maxine Mock 1938- WhoAmW 91
Mink, Patsy Takemoto 1927- WhoAmW 91
Mink, Robert Lee 1935- St&PR 91

Mink, Roberta 1941- St&PR 91
Minkel, Edward Joseph 1921- WhoAm 90
Minkenberg, Ilse A. 1938- ODwPR 91
Minker, Jack 1927- WhoAm 90
Minker, Marion J., Jr. 1932- St&PR 91
Minkin, Jacob Samuel 1885-1962 BioIn 16
Minkin, Jean Albert 1925- WhoAmW 91
Minkler, John Archer 1938- WhoWor 91
Minko, Philip Peter 1929- St&PR 91
Minkoff, Andrea Ehrlich 1941- WhoAmW 91
Minkoff, Jack 1925- WhoAm 90
Minkoff, Kenneth 1948- BiDrAPA 89
Minkoff, Kenneth M. 1948- WhoE 91
Minkoff, Sandra Rita 1936- WhoAmW 91
Minkofski-Garrigues, Horst 1925- IntWWM 90
Minkow, Barry BioIn 16
Minkowitz, Norma 1937- WhoAmA 91
Minkowski, Oskar 1858-1931 DcScB S2
Minkowycz, W. J. 1937- WhoAm 90
Minks, Pamela Alsworth 1944- WhoAmW 91
Minks, Wilfried 1930- ConDes 90
Minkus, Raymond 1953- ODwPR 91
Minn, Carol Emiko BiDrAPA 89
Minn, Kyungtak 1941- BiDrAPA 89
Minn-Jinn, Byung Hyun BiDrAPA 89
Minna EncCoWW
Minnegerode, Cuthbert Powell 1876-1951 WhoAmA 91N
Minnella, Corrado 1943- WhoWor 91
Minnelli, Liza BioIn 16
Minnelli, Liza 1946- BioAmW, ConTFT 8 [port], OxCPMus, WhoAm 90, WhoAmW 91, WorAlBi
Minnelli, Vincente 1909-1986 OxCPMus
Minnelli, Vincente 1910-1986 BioIn 16, WorAlBi
Minnema, John Allen 1932- St&PR 91
Minneman, Jill Barbara 1961- WhoE 91
Minnemann, Helmuth Marques 1924- WhoWor 91
Minner, Paul 1923- Ballpl 90
Minner, Robert 1927- St&PR 91
Minner, Ruth Ann 1935- WhoAmW 91
Minner, Thomas Oliran 1956- WhoEmL 91
Minnerop, Henry 1937- WhoAm 90
Minners, Howard Alyn 1931- WhoE 91
Minnette, Rhonda Williams 1952- WhoAmW 91
Minnewit, Peter 1580?-1638 WhNaAH
Minney, Michael Jay 1948- WhoEmL 91
Minnice, Karen Ann 1947- WhoAmW 91
Minnich, Marie Elaine 1955- WhoE 91
Minnich, Virginia 1910- WhoAm 90
Minnick, Carlton Printess, Jr. 1927- WhoAm 90
Minnick, Chris Lawrence BiDrAPA 89
Minnick, Craig Alan 1951- WhoEmL 91
Minnick, Esther Tress WhoAmA 91
Minnick, John B. ODwPR 91
Minnick, Malcolm David 1946- WhoEmL 91
Minnick, Molly BioIn 16
Minnick, Robert P. 1949- St&PR 91
Minnick, Stephen Tate 1948- WhoSSW 91
Minnick, Terry J. 1951- St&PR 91
Minnick, Walter C. 1942- St&PR 91
Minnick, Walter Clifford 1942- WhoAm 90
Minnie, Mary Virginia 1922- WhoAmW 91, WhoWor 91
Minnifield, Wallace Ruso 1948- WhoEmL 91
Minnig, Gary M. 1946- St&PR 91
Minnigerode, Lucy 1871-1935 BioIn 16
Minnihan, John K. 1936- St&PR 91
Minnihan, Richard L. BiDrAPA 89
Minnion, John 1939- ConAu 130
Minnix, Bruce Milton 1923- WhoAm 90
Minnock, Edward William, Jr. 1948- WhoEmL 91
Mino, Carlos Felix 1932- WhoHisp 91
Mino, Debbie W. St&PR 91
Mino, Joseph Sande 1941- St&PR 91
Mino, Shigekazu 1923- St&PR 91
Mino, Yutaka 1941- WhoAm 90
Minogue, John T. 1934- St&PR 91
Minogue, Kylie BioIn 16
Minogue, Kylie 1968- OxCPMus
Minogue, Robert Brophy 1928- WhoAm 90
Minogue, Thomas John 1954- WhoEmL 91
Minogue, Thomas Leo BiDrAPA 89
Minogue, Valerie Pearson 1931- ConAu 132
Minoletti, Alberto H 1944- BiDrAPA 89
Minor, Andrew C. 1918- IntWWM 90
Minor, Charles Daniel 1927- WhoAm 90
Minor, David L. 1943- St&PR 91
Minor, Doug Ballpl 90
Minor, Edward Colquitt 1942- WhoSSW 91
Minor, George Gilmer, III 1940- WhoSSW 91
Minor, George Gilmer, Jr. 1912- St&PR 91, WhoAm 90, WhoSSW 91
Minor, Henry H. 1921- St&PR 91
Minor, Jackson William 1927- St&PR 91
Minor, James Beryll 1919- WhoAm 90
Minor, John Billy 1951- WhoAm 90
Minor, Joseph Edward 1938- WhoAm 90
Minor, Linda Barsom 1950- WhoAmW 91
Minor, Philip Morrison 1915- St&PR 91
Minor, Robert 1884-1952 EncAL
Minor, Robert W. 1919- St&PR 91
Minor, Robert Walter 1919- WhoAm 90
Minor, Rudiger Rainer 1939- WhoWor 91
Minoru, Yakata 1925- WhoWor 91
Minoso, Minnie 1922- Ballpl 90 [port], WhoHisp 91
Minot, George Marshall 1933- St&PR 91
Minot, Otis Northrop 1916- WhoE 91
Minot, Paul Leslie 1955- BiDrAPA 89
Minot, Stephen 1927- WhoWrEP 89
Minot, Susan BioIn 16
Minot, Winthrop Gardner 1951- WhoEmL 91
Minotis, Alexis 1900-1990 NewYTBS 90
Minow, Josephine Baskin 1926- WhoAm 90
Minow, Newton N. 1926- St&PR 91
Minow, Newton Norman 1926- WhoAm 90
Minow-Pinkney, Makiko 1947- WhoWor 91
Minowitz, Abraham A. 1920- St&PR 91
Minoza, Aurora 1923- EncO&P 3
Minsek, Robert C 1930- BiDrAPA 89
Minshall, Brinton Paynter 1943- WhoSSW 91
Minshall, William E. NewYTBS 90
Minshew, Hugh Franklin 1932- St&PR 91
Minshew, Lisa Michelle 1966- WhoEmL 91
Minshull, Ruth Ellen 1926- WhoWrEP 89
Minsker, Robert Stanley 1911- WhoWor 91
Minsky, Gerald L. 1945- St&PR 91
Minsky, Marvin Lee 1927- BioIn 16, WhoAm 90
Minsky, Merton D. 1928- St&PR 91
Minsky, Richard 1947- WhoAmA 91, WhoE 91
Minsky, Stuart A. 1936- St&PR 91
Minster, Kathryn M. ODwPR 91
Minsuk, Lester M. 1934- WhoE 91
Minta, Stephen 1947- ConAu 132
Mintek, Victor J BiDrAPA 89
Minter, David Lee 1935- WhoAm 90
Minter, Edgar Frederick 1935- WhoAm 90
Minter, James Gideon, Jr. 1930- WhoAm 90
Minter, Jerry Burnett 1913- WhoAm 90, WhoWor 91
Minter, Jimmie Ruth 1941- WhoAmW 91
Minter, Marilyn A 1948- WhoAmA 91
Minter, Michael Kent 1950- WhoE 91
Minter, Philip Clayton 1928- WhoAm 90
Minter, R. O., Jr. 1926- St&PR 91
Minter, Richard Eugene BiDrAPA 89
Minter, Steven Alan 1938- WhoAm 90
Minter, William Bethel 1932- St&PR 91
Minthorn, Crista Nel 1954- WhoE 91
Mintich, Mary Ringelberg WhoAmA 91
Mintie, Nancy BioIn 16
Minto, Barbara Lee WhoWor 91
Minto, Clive 1945- St&PR 91, WhoAm 90
Minto, Karl Dean 1958- WhoE 91
Minton, Avalon Nichols 1941- WhoE 91
Minton, Carl 1928- St&PR 91
Minton, Daniel C BiDrAPA 89
Minton, Dwight Church 1934- St&PR 91, WhoAm 90
Minton, Greg 1951- Ballpl 90
Minton, Gwendolyn Louise 1954- St&PR 91
Minton, Jerry Davis 1928- WhoAm 90
Minton, John D. St&PR 91
Minton, John D. 1925- WhoAm 90
Minton, John Dean 1921- WhoAm 90, WhoWrEP 89
Minton, Joseph Paul 1924- WhoAm 90
Minton, Keith G. 1947- St&PR 91
Minton, Paul Dixon 1918- WhoAm 90
Minton, Thomas 1765-1836 PenDiDA 89
Minton, William James 1937- St&PR 91
Minton, Yvonne 1938- PenDiMP
Minton, Yvonne Fay WhoAm 90
Minton, Yvonne Fay 1938- IntWWM 90
Mintonye, Grace AuBYP 90
Mintun, James Harold, Jr. 1937- St&PR 91
Minturn, Darby 1947- WhoAmW 91
Minturn, Robert Bowne, Jr. 1939- St&PR 91
Minty, Judith 1937- WhoWrEP 89
Mintz, Albert 1929- WhoAm 90
Mintz, Anne P. BioIn 16
Mintz, Arthur A 1915- BiDrAPA 89
Mintz, Baron WhoAmA 91
Mintz, Benjamin BioIn 16
Mintz, Carol Sue 1940- WhoAmW 91
Mintz, David Leon 1956- WhoWor 91
Mintz, Donald Edward 1932- WhoAm 90
Mintz, Eli 1904-1988 BioIn 16
Mintz, Ellis 1923- St&PR 91
Mintz, Gilda Yolles ODwPR 91
Mintz, Harry 1909- WhoAm 90, WhoAmA 91
Mintz, Ira L 1926- BiDrAPA 89
Mintz, Jeanne Shirley 1922- WhoAm 90
Mintz, Joel Alan 1949- WhoEmL 91
Mintz, Lenore Chaice 1925- WhoAmW 91
Mintz, Lorelie Miller AuBYP 90
Mintz, M. J. 1940- WhoE 91, WhoWor 91
Mintz, Mitchell Lloyd 1951- St&PR 91
Mintz, Morris M. 1908-1990 BioIn 16
Mintz, Morton Abner 1922- WhoAm 90
Mintz, Nelson K. BioIn 16
Mintz, Norman Nelson 1934- WhoAm 90
Mintz, Patricia Pomboy 1934- WhoE 91
Mintz, Ronald S 1927- BiDrAPA 89
Mintz, Ronald Stephen 1947- St&PR 91
Mintz, Seymour Stanley 1912- WhoAm 90
Mintz, Sharon P. BiDrAPA 89
Mintz, Shlomo 1957- IntWWM 90, PenDiMP, WhoAm 90
Mintz, Sidney Wilfred 1922- WhoAm 90
Mintz, Stephen Allan 1943- St&PR 91, WhoAm 90, WhoE 91, WhoWor 91
Mintz, Thomas 1931- BiDrAPA 89
Mintz, Walter 1929- WhoAm 90
Mintzberg, Henry 1939- WhoAm 90
Mintzer, Bob BioIn 16
Mintzer, David 1926- WhoAm 90
Mintzer, Edward Carl, Jr. 1949- WhoWor 91
Mintzer, Fredric M 1952- BiDrAPA 89
Mintzer, Fredric Maxwell 1952- WhoE 91
Mintzer, Harvey 1936- St&PR 91
Mintzer, Rose Ann Marie 1961- WhoE 91
Mintzis, Nancy Coleman 1948- WhoE 91
Minuchin, Salvador 1921- BiDrAPA 89
Minudri, Regina Ursula 1937- WhoAm 90
Minui, Morteza BiDrAPA 89
Minuit, Peter 1580-1638 EncCRAm, WhNaAH, WorAlBi
Minutilla, Rosemarie Joan 1943- WhoAmW 91
Minutolo, Frank Paul 1935- WhoE 91
Minyard, James Patrick, Jr. 1929- WhoAm 90, WhoSSW 91
Minz, Alexander WhoAm 90
Miodovnik, Menachem 1946- WhoEmL 91
Miola, Robert S 1951- ConAu 129
Miolan, Marie PenDiMP
Miolla, Raymond Louis 1934- St&PR 91
Mion, Pierre Riccardo 1931- WhoAmA 91
Mioni, Jacques 1915- BiDrAPA 89
Miotke, Anne E 1943- WhoAmA 91
Miotke, Thomas Oliver 1946- St&PR 91
Miotte, Jean 1926- WhoAmA 91
Miotti, Vincenzo PenDiDA 89
Miou Miou BioIn 16
Miou-Miou 1950- ConTFT 8
Miquel, Bertrand Edouard 1940- WhoWor 91
Miquel, Jean-Pierre 1939- St&PR 91
Miquelon, Richard R. 1933- St&PR 91
Mir, Carl J. 1956- WhoHisp 91
Mir, Gasper, III 1946- WhoHisp 91
Mira Bai BioIn 16
Mira Bai 1498?- FemiCLE
Mira, John Francis 1945- BiDrAPA 89
Mira Galiana, Jaime Jose Juan 1950- WhoWor 91
Mirabai BioIn 16
Mirabeau, Honore G Riqueti, comte de 1749-1791 BioIn 16
Mirabelk, Alan P. 1943- St&PR 91
Mirabella, Grace BioIn 16
Mirabella, Grace 1930- WhoAm 90, WhoAmW 91, WhoWrEP 89
Mirabella, Paul 1954- Ballpl 90
Mirabella, Stephen W. 1932- St&PR 91
Mirabelle, Alan P. 1943- St&PR 91
Mirabelli, Carlos 1889-1951 EncO&P 3, EncPaPR 91
Mirabi, Mohsen 1941- BiDrAPA 89
Mirabile, Charles S, Jr. 1937- BiDrAPA 89
Mirabile, Mary Ann 1944- St&PR 91
Mirabito, Paul S. 1915- WhoAm 90
Mirabito, Teresa Anne 1941- WhoE 91
Miracle, Gordon Eldon 1930- WhoAm 90, WhoWor 91
Miracle, James Franklin 1938- WhoSSW 91
Miracle, Robert Warren WhoAm 90
Miracle, Robert Warren 1928- St&PR 91
Miracles, The EncPR&S 89
Mirage NewAgMG
Miraglia, Janet 1956- WhoAmW 91
Miraglio, Angela Maria 1944- WhoAmW 91
Miralda, Antoni 1942- WhoAmA 91
Miralles, Royle R BiDrAPA 89
Mirand, Christopher Alexander 1963- WhoE 91
Mirand, Edwin Albert 1926- WhoAm 90
Miranda, Andres, Jr. 1940- WhoHisp 91
Miranda, Anthony Roy 1956- WhoSSW 91
Miranda, Bonny Louise 1941- WhoAmW 91
Miranda, Carmen 1909-1955 BioIn 16, OxCPMus
Miranda, Carmen 1913-1955 WorAlBi
Miranda, Cesar 1941- St&PR 91
Miranda, Charles Robert 1923- St&PR 91
Miranda, Constancio Fernandes 1926- WhoAm 90
Miranda, Estela S BiDrAPA 89
Miranda, Francisco 1750-1816 WorAlBi
Miranda, Francisco de 1750-1816 BioIn 16
Miranda, George 1947- St&PR 91
Miranda, Guillermo, Jr. WhoHisp 91
Miranda, Hector, Sr. 1960- WhoHisp 91
Miranda, Hector Felix BioIn 16
Miranda, Javier HispWr 90, MajTwCW
Miranda, Joseph Charles 1930- WhoE 91
Miranda, Lourdes WhoHisp 91
Miranda, Manuel Robert 1939- WhoHisp 91
Miranda, Maria T. 1936- WhoHisp 91
Miranda, Michael Patrick 1941- WhoE 91
Miranda, Robert Julian 1952- WhoHisp 91
Miranda, Robert N. 1934- St&PR 91
Miranda, Robert Nicholas 1934- WhoAm 90, WhoE 91, WhoWor 91
Miranda, Roger BioIn 16
Miranda, Sonny M BiDrAPA 89
Miranda, Thom Bernard 1953- WhoEmL 91
Miranda, Willie 1926- Ballpl 90
Miranda-Swain, Nubia Jazmina 1956- BiDrAPA 89
Miranda Vargas, Jorge Alberto 1917- BiDrAPA 89
Mirando, Louis 1932- St&PR 91
Mirando, Louis Patrick 1927- WhoE 91
Mirandon, J. Wilmer BioIn 16
Mirante, Arthur J., II 1943- WhoAm 90
Mirante, Rand A. St&PR 91
Mirapaul, Walter Neil 1922- St&PR 91
Mirassou, Marlene Marie 1948- BiDrAPA 89
Miratti, Richard IntWWM 90
Mirbt, Felix 1931- OxCCanT
Mirchandani, Indu C. BiDrAPA 89
Mirczak, John Arnold 1944- BiDrAPA 89
Miree, Aubrey S BiDrAPA 89
Miree, Benjamin Kyser 1955- WhoSSW 91
Miree, David Carrington, II 1963- WhoSSW 91
Miree, Mallory F 1934- BiDrAPA 89
Miree, Wimberly, Jr. 1941- St&PR 91
Mirel, Emanuel 1928- BiDrAPA 89
Mireles, Andy 1950- WhoHisp 91
Mireles, Jovita Gonzalez 1904- BioIn 16
Mireles, R. Christina 1961- WhoHisp 91
Mireles, Sandra 1964- WhoAmW 91
Mirels, Harold 1924- WhoAm 90
Mirenburg, Barry Leonard Staffan 1952- WhoE 91
Mires, Ronald E. 1930- St&PR 91
Mirghani, Ahmad Ali Al- WhoWor 91
Mirick, Henry Dustin 1905- WhoAm 90
Mirin, Steven Martin 1942- BiDrAPA 89
Miripol, Jerilyn Elise WhoAmW 91
Mirisch, Marvin Elliot 1918- WhoAm 90
Mirisch, Walter 1921- ConTFT 8
Mirisch, Walter Mortimer 1921- WhoAm 90
Mirk, Judy Ann 1944- WhoAmW 91
Mirken, Alan WhoAm 90
Mirkin, Abraham Jonathan 1910- WhoAm 90
Mirkin, Bernard Leo 1928- WhoAm 90
Mirkin, Gabe 1935- ConAu 129
Mirkin, Peter M BiDrAPA 89
Mirkin, Ralph William 1932- St&PR 91
Mirkin, Sherril Ann 1932- WhoAmW 91
Mirman, Irving R. 1915- WhoAm 90
Mirmirani, Nooreddin 1945- BiDrAPA 89
Miro, Carlos I. BioIn 16
Miro, Joan 1893-1983 BioIn 16, IntDcAA 90
Miroffsky, Wenzelaus PenDiDA 89
Miroglio, Thierry Jean-Michel 1963- IntWWM 90
Mirojnick, Ellen BioIn 16
Mirolybov, Peter 1918- IntWWM 90
Miron, Gaston 1928- BioIn 16
Miron, Jerry 1936- St&PR 91
Miron, Salvador Diaz HispWr 90
Mirones, Pedro Jacobo 1939- St&PR 91
Miroshkhine, Oleg Semenovich 1928- WhoWor 91
Mirow, Arvin 1952- BiDrAPA 89
Mirow, Kurt Rudolf 1936- ConAu 130
Mirow, Roland S. 1948- St&PR 91
Mirow, Susan BiDrAPA 89
Mirowitz, Leo I. 1923- St&PR 91
Mirowitz, Stuart Ray 1948- WhoE 91
Mirowski, Michel 1924-1990 BioIn 16, NewYTBS 90
Mirra WhoAmA 91
Mirre, Federico 1938- WhoWor 91
Mirren, Helen 1946- WhoWor 91
Mirrielees, James Fay, III 1939- WhoAm 90
Mirrlees, Hope 1887-1978 FemiCLE

Mirrlees, James Alexander 1936- WhoWor 91
Mirro, Daniel Peter 1940- BiDrAPA 89
Mirro, Richard Allen 1951- WhoAm 90
Mirsajadi, Abdol-Amir BiDrAPA 89
Mirsberger, Ralph A. 1933- St&PR 91
Mirse, Ralph Thomas 1924- WhoAm 90
Mirsheidaie, Fatima BiDrAPA 89
Mirski, Michael D. Sviatopolk 1904- WhoE 91
Mirsky, Alfred Ezra 1900-1974 DcScB S2
Mirsky, Arthur 1927- WhoAm 90
Mirsky, Jan S. 1941- St&PR 91
Mirsky, Jeannette 1903-1987 BioIn 16
Mirsky, Mark 1939- BioIn 16
Mirsky, Mark Jay 1939- WhoWrEP 89
Mirsky, Moshe Z. 1955- WhoEmL 91
Mirsky, Reva Paeff 1902-1966 AuBYP 90
Mirsky, Sonya Wohl 1925- WhoAm 90, WhoAmW 91
Mirsky, Susan 1939- WhoAm 90, WhoAmW 91
Mirtala 1929- WhoAmA 91
Mirtallo, Jay Matthew 1953- WhoEmL 91
Mirtsopoulos, Christos 1947- WhoWrEP 89
Mirucki, Jean 1943- WhoWor 91
Mirvis, David Marc 1945- WhoSSW 91
Mirvis, Theodore Neal 1951- WhoE 91
Mirvish, David BioIn 16
Mirvish, Edwin BioIn 16
Mirvish, Edwin 1914- OxCCanT
Mirvish, Robert Franklin 1921- WhoAm 90, WhoWrEP 89
Mirza, Fazal-Ur-Rahman BiDrAPA 89
Mirza, Hafiz Rohman 1955- WhoWor 91
Mirza, Humayun 1928- WhoE 91
Mirza, Leona Lousin 1944- WhoAmW 91
Mirza, Madiha Akhtar BiDrAPA 89
Mirza, Mahmud 1943- BiDrAPA 89
Mirza, Mohammed Nasimuddin 1940- WhoWor 91
Mirza, Nighat BiDrAPA 89
Mirza, Shahina BiDrAPA 89
Mirza, Shaukat 1936- WhoAm 90
Mirzai, Mohammed 1945- WhoWor 91
Mirzai, Pirooz 1953- WhoSSW 91
Mirzatuny, Ardashes 1948- BiDrAPA 89
Mirzoyan, Edward 1921- IntWWM 90
Misa, Kenneth Franklin 1939- WhoAm 90
Misasi, Anthony P. 1943- St&PR 91
Misawa, Giichi 1929- WhoWor 91
Misbach, Grant Lemmon 1929- St&PR 91
Misch, Allene K 1928- WhoAmA 91
Misch, Donald Arthur 1951- BiDrAPA 89
Misch, Robert Jay NewYTBS 90
Misch, Robert Jay 1905- WhoAm 90
Misch, William B. 1923- St&PR 91
Mische, Louis W. 1925- St&PR 91
Mischel, Ellis BiDrAPA 89
Mischenko, G. 1946- St&PR 91
Mischer, Donald Leo 1940- WhoAm 90
Mischer, Walter M. 1923- WhoSSW 91
Mischke, Carl Herbert 1922- WhoAm 90
Mischke, Frederick Charles 1930- St&PR 91, WhoAm 90
Mischler, Harland Louis WhoAm 90
Miscoll, Jim BioIn 16
Misener, Austin Donald 1911- WhoAm 90
Miser, Hugh Jordan 1917- WhoE 91
Miseroni family PenDiDA 89
Miseroni, Dionysio PenDiDA 89
Miseroni, Ferdinand Eusebius PenDiDA 89
Miseroni, Gasparo PenDiDA 89
Miseroni, Giovanni Ambrogio PenDiDA 89
Miseroni, Girolamo 1520?- PenDiDA 89
Miseroni, Giulio 1559-1593 PenDiDA 89
Miseroni, Ottavio PenDiDA 89
Misevic, Gabriel 1921- BiDrAPA 89
Misfeldt, Terry C. 1950- WhoWrEP 89
Mish, Frederick Crittenden 1938- WhoAm 90
Mishalanie, Phillip G., Jr. 1933- St&PR 91
Mishalow, Victor Andrew Steven 1960- IntWWM 90
Mishan, E J 1917- ConAu 30NR
Mishan, Ezra Joshua 1917- WhoWor 91
Mishell, Daniel R., Jr. 1931- WhoAm 90
Misher, Allen 1933- WhoAm 90, WhoE 91
Misher, Robert 1957- WhoE 91
Mishima Yukio 1925-1970 EncJap
Mishima, Yukio MajTwCW
Mishima, Yukio 1925-1970 WorAlBi
Mishkhas, Nawal Ahameed BiDrAPA 89
Mishkin, Arthur I. 1935- St&PR 91
Mishkin, Edwin B. 1937- WhoAm 90
Mishkin, Paul 1923- St&PR 91
Mishkin, Paul J. 1927- WhoAm 90
Mishler, Clifford Leslie 1939- WhoAm 90, WhoWor 91, WhoWrEP 89
Mishler, John Milton, IV 1946- WhoAm 90, WhoE 91, WhoEmL 91
Mishler, William, II 1947- WhoAm 90
Mishoe, Rainelle Dixon 1950- WhoAmW 91
Mishovsky, Zelda 1914- EncCoWW
Mishra, Arun Kumar 1945- WhoWor 91
Mishra, Asha S 1954- BiDrAPA 89
Mishra, Karen Elizabeth 1963- WhoAmW 91
Mishra, Sanjoy BiDrAPA 89
Mishur, Dave ODwPR 91
Misiano, Frank 1949- WhoE 91
Misiaszek, John J 1948- BiDrAPA 89
Misiek, Dale Joseph 1952- WhoSSW 91
Misiewicz, Jerzy Jacek 1930- WhoWor 91
Misisco, Emil Joseph 1928- St&PR 91
Misita, John Mauro 1929- St&PR 91
Misitigh, John 1948- St&PR 91
Miskel, Caroline DcCanB 12
Miskel, Cecil G. WhoAm 90
Miskel-Hoyt, Caroline DcCanB 12
Miskell, Austin 1925- IntWWM 90
Miskell, William Gene 1952- WhoE 91
Miskimen, George William 1930- WhoAm 90
Miskimin, Harry Alvin 1932- WhoAm 90
Miskin, Solomon 1946- BiDrAPA 89
Miskinis, Peter Michael 1923- St&PR 91
Miskoe, William Isaac 1912- St&PR 91
Miskovsky, George, Sr. 1910- WhoAm 90, WhoWor 91
Miskus, Michael Anthony 1950- WhoWor 91
Mislow, Kurt Martin 1923- WhoAm 90
Misner, Charles William 1932- WhoAm 90
Misner, Lorraine 1948- WhoAmW 91
Misner, Robert David 1920- WhoWor 91
Misora, Hibari BioIn 16
Misra, Jayadev 1947- WhoAm 90
Misra, Jogesh 1934- WhoWor 91
Misra, Prem Chandra BiDrAPA 89
Misra, Raghunath P. 1928- WhoSSW 91
Misra, Shekhar 1953- WhoWor 91
Misrach, Richard 1949- News 91-2 [port]
Misrach, Richard Laurence 1949- WhoAm 90, WhoAmA 91
Misri, Shaila BiDrAPA 89
Miss X EncO&P 3
Miss, Mary 1944- BiDWomA, BioIn 16, WhoAm 90, WhoAmA 91
Missal, Joshua M 1915- WhoAmA 91
Missal, Pegge 1923- WhoAmA 91
Missal, Stephen J 1948- WhoAmA 91
Missan, Richard Sherman 1933- WhoAm 90
Missana, Linda Marie 1948- WhoAmW 91
Missar, Charles Donald 1925- WhoAm 90
Missar, Richard Rudolph 1930- St&PR 91
Missavage, Anne Evelyn 1955- WhoAmW 91
Missavage, Edward, Jr. 1924- BiDrAPA 89
Missel, Jerome Lee 1940- BiDrAPA 89
Misseldine, Carol Kay 1959- WhoAmW 91
Missen, Clare NewAgMG
Missett, James Robert 1941- BiDrAPA 89
Missett, Judi Sheppard BioIn 16
Missey, James Lawrence 1935- WhoWrEP 89
Missick, Patricia Ann 1952- WhoE 91
Missie EncPaPR 91
Missimer, William C. WhoSSW 91
Missler, Clinton E. 1931- St&PR 91
Missman, Jeffrey Stephan 1944- St&PR 91
Missoni, Ottavio 1921- ConDes 90
Missoni, Rosita 1931- ConDes 90
Mister T 1952- DrBlPA 90
Mister, Coleen Warren 1934- WhoAmW 91
Mistinguett 1873-1956 OxCPMus
Mistral, Frederic 1830-1914 WorAlBi
Mistral, Gabriela ConAu 131, HispWr 90, MajTwCW
Mistral, Gabriela 1889-1957 BioIn 16, WorAlBi
Mistral, Jacques 1947- WhoWor 91
Mistretta, Nathan Joseph 1937- St&PR 91
Mistric, Mary Ann 1932- WhoWrEP 89
Mistry, Prabhudas Narandas BiDrAPA 89
Mistry, Suhasini S BiDrAPA 89
Misurelly, Frank 1945- WhoE 91
Miswald, R. Scott 1955- St&PR 91
Mita, Katsushige 1924- WhoWor 91
Mitama, Masataka 1944- WhoWor 91
Mitarai, Fujio BioIn 16
Mitaud, Janine 1921- EncCoWW
Mitby, Norman Peter 1916- WhoAm 90
Mitch, David Franklin 1951- WhoE 91
Mitch, Paul Stephen 1945- BiDrAPA 89
Mitcham, Julius Jerome 1941- WhoSSW 91, WhoWor 91
Mitcham, Marylee BioIn 16
Mitchel, Frederick Kent 1927- WhoAm 90
Mitchel, Michael M. 1929- St&PR 91
Mitchelhill, James Moffat 1912- WhoSSW 91
Mitchell, Abbie EarBlAP
Mitchell, Abbie 1884-1960 BioIn 16, DrBlPA 90
Mitchell, Ada Mae Boyd 1927- WhoAmW 91
Mitchell, Agnes E. LiHiK
Mitchell, Alfred Henry 1948- WhoAm 90
Mitchell, Alfred R 1888-1972 WhoAmA 91N
Mitchell, Alison 1947- WhoWor 91
Mitchell, Andrea 1946- WhoAm 90, WhoAmW 91, WhoE 91
Mitchell, Ann Buford 1925- WhoAmW 91
Mitchell, Antoine Philip 1954- IntWWM 90
Mitchell, Arnold 1918- ConAu 131
Mitchell, Arthur 1934- BioIn 16, DrBlPA 90, WhoAm 90, WhoE 91
Mitchell, Arthur Wergs 1883-1968 BlkAmsC [port]
Mitchell, Barbara Joanne 1940- WhoWrEP 89
Mitchell, Bert Breon 1942- WhoAm 90
Mitchell, Bert Norman 1938- WhoAm 90
Mitchell, Betty 1896-1976 OxCCanT
Mitchell, Betty Jo 1931- WhoAmW 91, WhoWrEP 89
Mitchell, Bill L. 1938- WhoSSW 91
Mitchell, Bobby 1943- Ballpl 90
Mitchell, Bobby 1955- Ballpl 90
Mitchell, Bradford William 1927- St&PR 91, WhoAm 90
Mitchell, Brent Olson 1949- St&PR 91
Mitchell, Brian 1957?- DrBlPA 90
Mitchell, Broadus 1892-1988 BioIn 16
Mitchell, Bruce NewAgMG
Mitchell, Bruce Handiside 1908-1963 WhoAmA 91N
Mitchell, Bruce Logan 1947- WhoEmL 91, WhoSSW 91
Mitchell, Bruce Tyson 1928- WhoAm 90
Mitchell, Burley Bayard, Jr. 1940- WhoAm 90
Mitchell, Burroughs 1914?-1979 ConAu 129
Mitchell, Cameron BioIn 16
Mitchell, Carlton S. 1950- St&PR 91
Mitchell, Carol Ann 1957- WhoE 91
Mitchell, CarolAnn 1942- WhoAmW 91
Mitchell, Cassandra Walton 1946- WhoAmW 91
Mitchell, Catherine Sue 1941- WhoAmW 91
Mitchell, Chad L. 1944- St&PR 91
Mitchell, Charles 1929- St&PR 91
Mitchell, Charles Burton 1841-1898 AmLegL
Mitchell, Charles E. 1877-1955 EncABHB 7 [port]
Mitchell, Charles H BiDrAPA 89
Mitchell, Charles James 1946- WhoWor 91
Mitchell, Charles William 1928- St&PR 91
Mitchell, Cherry Anne 1950- WhoAmW 91
Mitchell, Cheryl Denise Talbot 1964- WhoSSW 91
Mitchell, Cheryl Elaine 1951- WhoAmW 91
Mitchell, Chuck Raymond 1947- WhoSSW 91
Mitchell, Clarence 1891-1963 Ballpl 90
Mitchell, Clarence, III BioIn 16
Mitchell, Claybourne, Jr. 1923- WhoAm 90
Mitchell, Clifford 1925- WhoAmA 91
Mitchell, Clyde ConAu 130, MajTwCW
Mitchell, Clyde, III 1954- WhoE 91
Mitchell, Constance Ayer 1952- WhoAmW 91
Mitchell, Cynthia Mary 1946- St&PR 91
Mitchell, Dale 1921-1987 Ballpl 90
Mitchell, Dana Covington, Jr 1918- WhoAmA 91
Mitchell, Daniel Roy 1942- WhoSSW 91
Mitchell, Daniel Wertz 1928- St&PR 91, WhoAm 90
Mitchell, David BioIn 16
Mitchell, David C. 1941- WhoAm 90
Mitchell, David E. WhoAm 90
Mitchell, David J 1928- BiDrAPA 89
Mitchell, David Lee 1951- IntWWM 90
Mitchell, David Ray BiDrAPA 89
Mitchell, David T. 1942- WhoAm 90
Mitchell, David Walker 1935- WhoAm 90
Mitchell, Dean 1957- BioIn 16
Mitchell, Deborah E. 1955- WhoSSW 91
Mitchell, Debra Joy 1949- WhoWrEP 89
Mitchell, Dee A. 1946- WhoAmW 91
Mitchell, Don 1943- DrBlPA 90
Mitchell, Don 1947- ConAu 31NR
Mitchell, Donald A. 1927- St&PR 91
Mitchell, Donald Adelbert 1927- WhoAm 90, WhoE 91
Mitchell, Donald Charles Peter 1925- IntWWM 90
Mitchell, Donald J. 1923- WhoAm 90
Mitchell, Donald R. WhoAm 90
Mitchell, Dora Stryzak BiDrAPA 89
Mitchell, Douglas Donnell 1948- St&PR 91
Mitchell, Douglas F. 1940- St&PR 91
Mitchell, Douglas Farrell 1940- WhoAm 90
Mitchell, E. R., Jr. BioIn 16
Mitchell, Earl Dean 1939- WhoWor 91
Mitchell, Earl Lamonte 1912- St&PR 91
Mitchell, Earl Nelson 1926- WhoAm 90
Mitchell, Edgar D. 1930- EncO&P 3, EncPaPR 91, NewAgE 90
Mitchell, Edward F. 1931- St&PR 91
Mitchell, Edward Franklin 1931- WhoAm 90, WhoE 91
Mitchell, Edward John 1936- St&PR 91
Mitchell, Edward John 1937- WhoAm 90
Mitchell, Edward John 1942- WhoAm 90
Mitchell, Ehrman Burkman, Jr. 1924- WhoAm 90, WhoE 91
Mitchell, Eleanor 1907- WhoAmA 91N
Mitchell, Elizabeth Irwin 1957- WhoAmW 91
Mitchell, Elizabeth L 1950- BiDrAPA 89
Mitchell, Elizabeth Marie 1963- WhoE 91
Mitchell, Ellen Clabaugh 1942- WhoE 91
Mitchell, Elma 1919- FemiCLE
Mitchell, Enid 1919- WhoWrEP 89
Mitchell, Eric Ignatius 1948- WhoE 91
Mitchell, F. Stuart St&PR 91
Mitchell, Flora Eva 1929- WhoAm 90
Mitchell, Francis Douglas 1913- St&PR 91
Mitchell, Frank Warren 1954- WhoEmL 91
Mitchell, Fred 1878-1970 Ballpl 90
Mitchell, Fred 1923- WhoAmA 91
Mitchell, G. B. 1927- St&PR 91
Mitchell, Gary G. 1956- St&PR 91
Mitchell, Geoffrey P. 1916- St&PR 91
Mitchell, Geoffrey Roger 1936- IntWWM 90
Mitchell, Geoffrey Sewell 1940- WhoAm 90
Mitchell, George Charles 1920- WhoWor 91
Mitchell, George Ernest, Jr. 1930- WhoAm 90
Mitchell, George J. BioIn 16
Mitchell, George J. 1933- WorAlBi
Mitchell, George John 1933- WhoAm 90, WhoE 91, WhoWor 91
Mitchell, George Mutch 1919- WhoWor 91
Mitchell, George P. 1919- St&PR 91, WhoAm 90, WhoSSW 91
Mitchell, George Trice 1914- WhoWor 91
Mitchell, George W. 1950- St&PR 91
Mitchell, George Washington, Jr. 1917- WhoAm 90
Mitchell, Gerald R. 1939- St&PR 91
Mitchell, Gladys 1901-1983 BioIn 16, TwCCr&M 91
Mitchell, Glen 1894-1972 WhoAmA 91N
Mitchell, Godfrey Way 1891-1982 DcNaB 1981
Mitchell, Graham Russell 1905-1984 DcNaB 1981
Mitchell, Grant BiDrAPA 89
Mitchell, Grant Edward 1960- WhoEmL 91
Mitchell, Gregory 1951- ConTFT 8 [port]
Mitchell, Gregory Roderick 1960- WhoWor 91
Mitchell, Guy 1927- OxCPMus
Mitchell, Guy Patrick 1937- WhoSSW 91
Mitchell, Gwendolyn Van Derbur 1931- WhoAmW 91
Mitchell, Gwenn DrBlPA 90
Mitchell, H. L. 1906-1989 EncAL
Mitchell, H. Thomas 1957- St&PR 91
Mitchell, Hamilton Barnes 1916- WhoAm 90
Mitchell, Harold L BiDrAPA 89
Mitchell, Harvey R. WhoAm 90
Mitchell, Harvey R. 1935- St&PR 91
Mitchell, Helen Buss 1941- WhoAmW 91
Mitchell, Henry 1915-1980 WhoAmA 91N
Mitchell, Henry 1923- ConAu 130
Mitchell, Henry Clay 1923- WhoAm 90
Mitchell, Herbert Hall 1916- WhoAm 90
Mitchell, Holland C BiDrAPA 89
Mitchell, Homer 1941- WhoE 91
Mitchell, Howard 1911-1988 BioIn 16
Mitchell, Howard Estill 1921- WhoAm 90
Mitchell, Howard R., III 1951- ODwPR 91
Mitchell, Ian 1948- IntWWM 90
Mitchell, Isla AuBYP 90
Mitchell, J. Murray, Jr. 1928-1990 NewYTBS 90 [port]
Mitchell, James 1843-1897 DcCanB 12
Mitchell, James 1926- TwCCr&M 91
Mitchell, James Alan 1945- WhoEmL 91
Mitchell, James Alexander Hugh 1939-1985 DcNaB 1981
Mitchell, James Austin 1941- WhoAm 90
Mitchell, James B. 1954- St&PR 91
Mitchell, James E., Jr. 1950- St&PR 91
Mitchell, James Edward 1939- WhoSSW 91
Mitchell, James Edward, III 1947- BiDrAPA 89
Mitchell, James Fitzallen 1931- BioIn 16, WhoWor 91
Mitchell, James G. 1917- St&PR 91
Mitchell, James H. ODwPR 91
Mitchell, James Kenneth 1930- WhoAm 90

Mitchell, James Lowry 1937- *WhoAm 90, WhoE 91*
Mitchell, James Nicola 1931- *St&PR 91*
Mitchell, James Orville 1938- *WhoSSW 91*
Mitchell, James Paul 1900-1964 *BiDrUSE 89*
Mitchell, James William 1926- *SpyFic*
Mitchell, James Winfield 1943- *WhoAm 90*
Mitchell, Jane Theresa 1957- *WhoAmW 91*
Mitchell, Janet Aldrich 1928- *WhoAmW 91*
Mitchell, Jeanne Olson 1959- *ODwPR 91, WhoAmW 91*
Mitchell, Jeffrey David 1962- *WhoE 91*
Mitchell, Jeffrey L. 1946- *St&PR 91*
Mitchell, Jeffrey R *BiDrAPA 89*
Mitchell, Jennie Clay 1885-1978 *BioIn 16*
Mitchell, Jere Holloway 1928- *WhoWor 91*
Mitchell, Jerry Calvin 1938- *WhoSSW 91*
Mitchell, Jo Ann 1935- *WhoAmW 91*
Mitchell, Jo Kathryn 1934- *WhoAmW 91*
Mitchell, Joan 1926- *BiDWomA, WhoAm 90, WhoAmA 91*
Mitchell, Joan Elizabeth *WhoAmA 91*
Mitchell, Joel Stephenson 1898-1989 *BioIn 16*
Mitchell, John *BioIn 16, EncCRAm*
Mitchell, John 1863-1929 *BioIn 16*
Mitchell, John 1870-1919 *WorAlBi*
Mitchell, John 1913-1988 *AnObit 1988*
Mitchell, John 1965- *Ballpl 90*
Mitchell, John A *BiDrAPA 89*
Mitchell, John Adam, III 1944- *St&PR 91, WhoAm 90*
Mitchell, John Blair 1921- *WhoAmA 91*
Mitchell, John Clark, II 1917- *St&PR 91, WhoAm 90*
Mitchell, John Daniel 1957- *WhoE 91*
Mitchell, John F. 1946- *St&PR 91*
Mitchell, John Francis 1928- *WhoAm 90*
Mitchell, John Francis 1951- *BiDrAPA 89*
Mitchell, John H. 1918- *WhoAm 90*
Mitchell, John Henderson 1933- *WhoAm 90*
Mitchell, John Irby 1939- *St&PR 91*
Mitchell, John James 1934- *WhoE 91*
Mitchell, John Murray, Jr. 1928- *WhoAm 90*
Mitchell, John N. 1913-1988 *WorAlBi*
Mitchell, John Newton 1913-1988 *BiDrUSE 89, BioIn 16*
Mitchell, John R. 1930- *St&PR 91*
Mitchell, John William 1944- *St&PR 91*
Mitchell, Johnny 1894-1965 *Ballpl 90*
Mitchell, Joni *BioIn 16*
Mitchell, Joni 1943- *EncPR&S 89, OxCPMus, WhoAm 90, WhoAmW 91, WorAlBi*
Mitchell, Joseph 1908- *WhoAm 90*
Mitchell, Joseph Brady 1915- *WhoAm 90, WhoSSW 91*
Mitchell, Joseph Cheatham 1929- *WhoSSW 91*
Mitchell, Joseph David *BiDrAPA 89*
Mitchell, Joseph David 1958- *WhoE 91*
Mitchell, Joseph Nathan 1922- *WhoAm 90*
Mitchell, Joseph Patrick 1939- *WhoWor 91*
Mitchell, Joseph Quincy 1908- *WhoWor 91*
Mitchell, Joseph S. 1891- *EarBlAP*
Mitchell, Josephine Gray *IntWWM 90*
Mitchell, Juanita *BioIn 16*
Mitchell, Judith Ann 1941- *WhoSSW 91*
Mitchell, Judith Marie 1950- *WhoAmW 91*
Mitchell, Julia L. 1933- *St&PR 91, WhoAm 90, WhoSSW 91*
Mitchell, Julie Muller *ODwPR 91*
Mitchell, Katherine 1944- *WhoAmA 91*
Mitchell, Kathy 1948- *BioIn 16*
Mitchell, Keith Phillip 1944- *WhoE 91*
Mitchell, Ken *BioIn 16*
Mitchell, Ken 1940- *OxCCanT*
Mitchell, Kenneth J. 1949- *St&PR 91*
Mitchell, Kenneth P. *St&PR 91*
Mitchell, Kenneth Paul *BiDrAPA 89*
Mitchell, Kenneth Stephen 1953- *IntWWM 90*
Mitchell, Kevin *BioIn 16*
Mitchell, Kevin 1962- *Ballpl 90, WorAlBi*
Mitchell, Kevin Robert 1948- *WhoAm 90*
Mitchell, Kurk 1931- *WhoE 91*
Mitchell, Lansing Leroy 1914- *WhoAm 90*
Mitchell, Larry Kenneth 1944- *St&PR 91*
Mitchell, Lee 1951- *IntWWM 90*
Mitchell, Lee M. 1943- *St&PR 91*
Mitchell, Lee Mark 1943- *WhoAm 90*
Mitchell, Leona *BioIn 16*
Mitchell, Leona 1949- *IntWWM 90*
Mitchell, Leona Pearl 1949- *WhoAm 90*
Mitchell, Leslie Scott Falconer 1905-1985 *DcNaB 1981*
Mitchell, Lewis E. 1924- *St&PR 91*
Mitchell, Loften *EarBlAP*
Mitchell, Loften 1919- *DrBlPA 90*
Mitchell, Lucius Quinn 1959- *WhoEmL 91*
Mitchell, Lucy Sprague 1878-1967 *BioAmW*
Mitchell, Madeleine Louise 1957- *IntWWM 90*
Mitchell, Maggie 1832-1918 *BioIn 16, NotWoAT*
Mitchell, Malcolm Stuart 1937- *WhoAm 90*
Mitchell, Margaret 1900-1949 *BioAmW, BioIn 16, FemiCLE, MajTwCW, WorAlBi*
Mitchell, Margaret Anne 1925- *WhoAmW 91*
Mitchell, Margaret Julia 1832-1918 *BioIn 16*
Mitchell, Margaretta K 1935- *WhoAmA 91*
Mitchell, Maria *WhoWrEP 89*
Mitchell, Maria 1818-1889 *BioAmW*
Mitchell, Marilyn R. 1957- *St&PR 91*
Mitchell, Martha Beall 1918-1976 *BioAmW*
Mitchell, Martha M. *ODwPR 91*
Mitchell, Martin Morgan, Jr. 1937- *WhoAm 90*
Mitchell, Mary *BiDEWW*
Mitchell, Mary Monica 1949- *ODwPR 91*
Mitchell, Matthew W. 1942- *St&PR 91*
Mitchell, Maurice B. 1915- *WhoAm 90, WhoWor 91*
Mitchell, Max O. 1928- *WhoAm 90*
Mitchell, Melinda Ann 1950- *WhoEmL 91*
Mitchell, Michael *BioIn 16*
Mitchell, Michael Thomas 1951- *WhoSSW 91*
Mitchell, Michael W. 1939- *St&PR 91*
Mitchell, Mike 1879-1961 *Ballpl 90*
Mitchell, Miles N. 1819- *AmLegL*
Mitchell, Milton 1916- *WhoAm 90*
Mitchell, Mitch 1940- *WhoSSW 91*
Mitchell, Mozella Gordon 1936- *WhoAmW 91, WhoSSW 91*
Mitchell, N Donald 1922- *WhoAmA 91*
Mitchell, Nancy Stack Hanlon 1931- *WhoAmW 91*
Mitchell, Nelli L *BiDrAPA 89*
Mitchell, Nelli Louise 1926- *WhoE 91*
Mitchell, Noble L. 1855-1932 *AmLegL*
Mitchell, Orlan E. 1933- *WhoAm 90*
Mitchell, Otis Clinton, Jr. 1935- *WhoAm 90*
Mitchell, Parren James 1922- *BlkAmsC [port]*
Mitchell, Paul 1950- *Ballpl 90*
Mitchell, Paul Alexander 1948- *WhoE 91*
Mitchell, Paul David 1959- *WhoWrEP 89*
Mitchell, Paul F. *ODwPR 91*
Mitchell, Paula Rae 1951- *WhoAmW 91, WhoEmL 91*
Mitchell, Peggy *MajTwCW*
Mitchell, Penelope 1959- *ODwPR 91*
Mitchell, Percy David, Jr. *BiDrAPA 89*
Mitchell, Peter 1824-1899 *DcCanB 12*
Mitchell, Peter Dennis 1920- *WhoAm 90, WhoWor 91*
Mitchell, Peter McQuilkin 1934- *WhoAm 90*
Mitchell, Peter T. 1945- *WhoAm 90*
Mitchell, Peter Todd 1929- *WhoAmA 91*
Mitchell, R. Clayton, Jr. 1936- *WhoE 91*
Mitchell, Ralph C., III 1935- *St&PR 91*
Mitchell, Ralph Gilbert 1922- *WhoSSW 91*
Mitchell, Raymond Lewis 1915- *St&PR 91*
Mitchell, Richard 1929- *WhoAm 90*
Mitchell, Richard A. 1939- *St&PR 91*
Mitchell, Richard Austin 1949- *WhoEmL 91*
Mitchell, Richard F. 1931- *St&PR 91*
Mitchell, Richard Scott 1929-1988 *BioIn 16*
Mitchell, Richard W. 1937- *St&PR 91*
Mitchell, Robert A 1928- *BiDrAPA 89*
Mitchell, Robert Arthur 1926- *WhoAm 90*
Mitchell, Robert Bertelson, Jr. 1952- *WhoEmL 91*
Mitchell, Robert Charles 1958- *WhoSSW 91*
Mitchell, Robert Dale 1910- *WhoAm 90*
Mitchell, Robert Edward 1930- *WhoAm 90*
Mitchell, Robert Everitt 1929- *WhoAm 90*
Mitchell, Robert Greene 1925- *WhoAm 90*
Mitchell, Robert Irvin 1950- *St&PR 91*
Mitchell, Robert James *BiDrAPA 89*
Mitchell, Robert James 1925- *WhoWor 91*
Mitchell, Robert James 1926- *St&PR 91*
Mitchell, Robert Joseph 1947- *WhoSSW 91*
Mitchell, Robert Judd 1958- *WhoEmL 91*
Mitchell, Robert L. 1932- *St&PR 91, WhoAm 90*
Mitchell, Robert L. 1923- *St&PR 91*
Mitchell, Robert Lynn 1933- *St&PR 91*
Mitchell, Robert Madison 1901- *BioIn 16*
Mitchell, Robert Watson 1910- *WhoAm 90*
Mitchell, Robert Wayne 1950- *WhoWrEP 89*
Mitchell, Robin 1951- *WhoAmA 91*
Mitchell, Roger 1935- *WhoWrEP 89*
Mitchell, Roger Lowry 1932- *WhoAm 90*
Mitchell, Ronald Wayne 1933- *St&PR 91*
Mitchell, Ross *BiDrAPA 89*
Mitchell, Roy 1884-1944 *OxCCanT*
Mitchell, Roy 1885-1959 *Ballpl 90*
Mitchell, Roy Truslow 1945- *St&PR 91*
Mitchell, Russell Harry 1925- *WhoAm 90*
Mitchell, Ruth Ellen 1940- *WhoAmW 91*
Mitchell, Sally Jean 1934- *WhoAmW 91*
Mitchell, Samuel 1798-186-? *AmLegL*
Mitchell, Samuel P. 1932- *St&PR 91*
Mitchell, Samuel U. 1931- *St&PR 91*
Mitchell, Sasha *BioIn 16*
Mitchell, Scott *BioIn 16*
Mitchell, Serette Elizabeth 1953- *WhoAmW 91*
Mitchell, Shannon *BioIn 16*
Mitchell, Sharon Ann 1954- *WhoWrEP 89*
Mitchell, Shawn *BioIn 16*
Mitchell, Shirley Ann 1939- *WhoAmW 91*
Mitchell, Shirley Marie 1953- *WhoAmW 91*
Mitchell, Stan *St&PR 91*
Mitchell, Stephanie J. 1957- *WhoAmW 91*
Mitchell, Stephen Connally 1943- *St&PR 91*
Mitchell, Stephen Craig *BiDrAPA 89*
Mitchell, Stephen Milton 1943- *WhoSSW 91*
Mitchell, Steven Randall 1950- *BiDrAPA 89*
Mitchell, Stuart 1908- *St&PR 91*
Mitchell, Susan Evelyn 1953- *WhoAmW 91*
Mitchell, T W 1869-1944 *EncO&P 3*
Mitchell, Tandie Vera 1942- *WhoAmW 91*
Mitchell, Terence Edward 1937- *WhoAm 90*
Mitchell, Terrell Keith 1955- *St&PR 91*
Mitchell, Theo Walker 1938- *WhoSSW 91*
Mitchell, Thomas 1892-1962 *WorAlBi*
Mitchell, Thomas James 1922- *WhoAm 90*
Mitchell, Thomas Robert 1937- *St&PR 91, WhoAm 90*
Mitchell, Thomas W *WhoAmA 91N*
Mitchell, Thomas Walker 1869-1944 *EncPaPR 91*
Mitchell, Timothy Alan 1957- *BiDrAPA 89*
Mitchell, Timothy Anthony 1927- *WhoE 91*
Mitchell, Timothy Papin 1949- *WhoE 91*
Mitchell, Tom Herron 1924- *WhoSSW 91*
Mitchell, Valerie *BioIn 16*
Mitchell, Velda Jean 1937- *WhoAmW 91*
Mitchell, Vernice Virginia 1921- *WhoAmW 91, WhoWor 91*
Mitchell, Virgil Allen 1914- *WhoAm 90*
Mitchell, W. J. T. 1942- *WhoAm 90*
Mitchell, W.J.T. 1942- *WhoWrEP 89*
Mitchell, W O 1914- *OxCCanT*
Mitchell, W. Randle, Jr. 1934- *WhoAm 90*
Mitchell, Wallace 1911-1977 *WhoAmA 91N*
Mitchell, Warren I. 1937- *St&PR 91*
Mitchell, Wayland J. 1926- *St&PR 91*
Mitchell, Wesley Clair 1874-1948 *BioIn 16*
Mitchell, Wiley Francis, Jr. 1932- *WhoSSW 91*
Mitchell, William 1879-1936 *WorAlBi*
Mitchell, William A 1945- *BiDrAPA 89*
Mitchell, William Avery, Jr. 1933- *WhoSSW 91*
Mitchell, William B. 1936- *WhoSSW 91*
Mitchell, William DeWitt 1874-1955 *BiDrUSE 89*
Mitchell, William E. 1944- *St&PR 91*
Mitchell, William Frank 1925- *St&PR 91*
Mitchell, William George 1931- *St&PR 91*
Mitchell, William Grant 1921- *WhoAm 90*
Mitchell, William Hall 1943- *WhoSSW 91*
Mitchell, William Kenneth 1948- *St&PR 91*
Mitchell, William L. 1912-1988 *BioIn 16*
Mitchell, William O. 1846- *AmLegL*
Mitchell, William Richard 1930- *WhoWrEP 89*
Mitchell, Willie 1889-1973 *Ballpl 90*
Mitchell, Winalee G. 1921- *St&PR 91*
Mitchell, Wylie Hopkins 1946- *St&PR 91*
Mitchell-Bateman, Mildred *BiDrAPA 89*
Mitchelson, Bonnie Elizabeth 1947- *WhoAmW 91*
Mitchelson, Marvin M. 1928- *BioIn 16*
Mitchelson, Marvin Morris 1928- *WhoAm 90*
Mitchelson, Theo Kay 1925- *WhoAm 90*
Mitchelson, William Harry 1942- *St&PR 91*
Mitchill, Samuel Latham 1764-1831 *BioIn 16*
Mitchill, Scoey 1930- *DrBlPA 90*
Mitchinson, John 1932- *PenDiMP*
Mitchinson, John Leslie 1932- *IntWWM 90*
Mitchison, John Murdoch 1922- *WhoWor 91*
Mitchison, Naomi 1897- *BioIn 16, FemiCLE*
Mitchner, Gary L. 1946- *WhoWrEP 89*
Mitchnick, Nancy 1947- *WhoAmA 91*
Mitchum, Donald Chaney 1937- *St&PR 91*
Mitchum, John 1919- *BioIn 16*
Mitchum, Robert *BioIn 16*
Mitchum, Robert 1917- *WorAlBi*
Mitchum, Robert Charles Duran 1917- *WhoAm 90*
Mitchusson, Robert Lee 1932- *St&PR 91*
Mitelman, Bonnie Cossman 1941- *WhoAmW 91*
Mitenieks, Alfred *BiDrAPA 89*
Mitford, Jessica 1917- *WhoAm 90, WhoWrEP 89*
Mitford, Mary Russell 1786-1855 *FemiCLE*
Mitford, Mary Russell 1787-1855 *BioIn 16*
Mitford, Nancy 1904-1973 *BioIn 16, FemiCLE, WorAlBi*
Mitgang, Herbert 1920- *WhoAm 90, WhoWrEP 89*
Mitgutsch, Waltraud Anna 1948- *EncCoWW*
Mithani, Umedlal A 1932- *BiDrAPA 89*
Mithun, Marianne 1946- *WhoEmL 91*
Mithun, Raymond O. 1909- *St&PR 91, WhoAm 90*
Mithun, Raymond Otis *BioIn 16*
Mitiguy, Michael John 1944- *St&PR 91*
Mitis, Charles Z K *BiDrAPA 89*
Mitler, Merrill Morris 1945- *WhoEmL 91*
Mitlyng, Errol Paul 1936- *St&PR 91*
Mitnick, Harold 1923- *WhoE 91*
Mitnick, J. G. 1917- *St&PR 91*
Mitnick, Kevin *BioIn 16*
Mito, Motoko 1957- *IntWWM 90*
Mitos, James Walter 1956- *St&PR 91*
Mitovich, John 1927- *WhoAm 90*
Mitra, Devi 1928- *WhoSSW 91*
Mitra, Dilip Kumar 1923- *WhoWor 91*
Mitra, Gopal C 1928- *WhoAmA 91*
Mitra, Himal 1957- *BiDrAPA 89, WhoE 91*
Mitrani, Anne *BioIn 16*
Mitrano, Daniel Francis 1940- *St&PR 91*
Mitrano, John Prospero 1959- *WhoE 91*
Mitrano, Michael 1956- *St&PR 91*
Mitrany, Devora Lang 1947- *WhoAmW 91, WhoEmL 91*
Mitre, Bartolome 1821-1906 *BioIn 16*
Mitrione, Robert Thomas *BiDrAPA 89*
Mitrisin, Douglas Michael 1942- *St&PR 91*
Mitropoulos, Dimitri 1896-1960 *PenDiMP*
Mitropoulos, Dmitri 1896-1960 *WorAlBi*
Mitrovic, Michael 1952- *St&PR 91*
Mitry, Halim *BiDrAPA 89*
Mitry, Jean 1907-1988 *BioIn 16*
Mitsak, Richard Andrew 1945- *BiDrAPA 89*
Mitsch, Ronald Allen 1934- *WhoAm 90*
Mitschele, H. J. 1929- *St&PR 91*
Mitschele, Michael Douglas 1956- *WhoE 91*
Mitscher, Lester Allen 1931- *WhoAm 90*
Mitscher, Marc A. 1887-1947 *WorAlBi*
Mitscherlich, Margarete 1917- *EncCoWW*
Mitschrich, William Charles 1937- *WhoSSW 91*
Mitseff, Carl 1928- *WhoAm 90*
Mitsis, Fotis John 1926- *WhoWor 91*
Mitsotakis, Constantin 1918- *WhoWor 91*
Mitsotakis, Constantine *BioIn 16*
Mitsotakis, Constantine 1918- *CurBio 90 [port]*
Mitta, Srinivas Rao *BiDrAPA 89*
Mittal, Dinesh *BiDrAPA 89*
Mittel, John J. *WhoE 91, WhoSSW 91, WhoWor 91*
Mittel, Neuman S 1930- *BiDrAPA 89*
Mittell, Larry C. 1941- *St&PR 91*
Mittelman, David L. 1930- *St&PR 91*
Mittelman, Eugene 1912- *BiDrAPA 89*
Mittelman, Gary Lee 1960- *St&PR 91*
Mittelman, Peter 1938- *St&PR 91*
Mittelman, Robert Hirsch 1949- *WhoEmL 91*
Mittelmann, Norman 1932- *IntWWM 90*
Mittelmark, Abraham 1926- *WhoWrEP 89*
Mittelstadt, Charles Anthony 1918- *St&PR 91, WhoAm 90, WhoWor 91*
Mittelstadt, Charles Anthony, Jr. 1959- *WhoE 91*
Mittelstadt, Eric *BioIn 16*
Mittemeyer, Bernhard Theodore 1930- *WhoAm 90*
Mitten, David Gordon 1935- *WhoAm 90*
Mitten, George Thomas 1952- *St&PR 91*
Mittendorf, Theodor Henry 1895- *WhoSSW 91, WhoWor 91*
Mittenthal, Freeman Lee 1917- *WhoAm 90*

Mittenthal, Marilyn 1955- *BiDrAPA 89*
Mitter, Robert Georg 1939- *WhoWor 91*
Mitterer, Erika 1906- *EncCoWW*
Mitterhofer, Ferdinand 1939- *WhoWor 91*
Mitterlehner, Mark Edward 1961- *WhoSSW 91*
Mittermaier, Armin Eugene 1932- *St&PR 91*
Mitterrand, Francois 1916- *BioIn 16, WorAlBi*
Mitterrand, Francois Maurice 1916- *BiDFrPL*
Mitterrand, Francois Maurice Marie 1916- *WhoWor 91*
Mitterwald, George 1945- *Ballpl 90*
Mittleman, Aaron N. 1925- *St&PR 91*
Mittleman, Frederick S 1945- *BiDrAPA 89*
Mittleman, Frederick Stuart 1945- *WhoEmL 91*
Mittlemann, David 1913- *St&PR 91*
Mittler, Diana 1941- *IntWWM 90, WhoAmW 91*
Mittler Battipaglia, Diana 1941- *IntWWM 90*
Mittler-Gasser, Cindy J. 1954- *St&PR 91*
Mittman, Alan Lee 1949- *WhoE 91*
Mittman, Betty *St&PR 91*
Mittman, Ilene Lois 1935- *WhoAmW 91*
Mitton, Michael Anthony 1947- *St&PR 91*
Mitts, Billy Erman 1954- *WhoSSW 91*
Mitty, Lizbeth J 1952- *WhoAmA 91*
Mitty, Virginia Connolly 1919-1989 *BioIn 16*
Mitty, William F. 1922-1989 *BioIn 16*
Mitz, Vladimir 1943- *WhoWor 91*
Mitzel, Donald H. 1925- *WhoAm 90*
Mitzel, Timothy Steven *BiDrAPA 89*
Mitzman, Sharon Lee 1953- *WhoAmW 91*
Mitzner, Kenneth Martin 1938- *WhoAm 90*
Mitzner, Sandra Beth 1953- *BiDrAPA 89*
Miullo, Nathaniel Jerome 1957- *WhoWrEP 89*
Miura, Hajime 1927- *WhoWor 91*
Miura, Karen K. *BiDrAPA 89*
Miura, Katanobu 1939- *St&PR 91*
Miura, Robert Mitsuru 1938- *WhoAm 90*
Miura, Shiroe 1926- *BiDrAPA 89*
Miura, Taiei *BiDrAPA 89*
Miura, Tokuhiro 1928- *WhoWor 91*
Miwa, Hisao Sal 1956- *WhoE 91*
Miwa, Ralph Makoto 1925- *WhoAm 90*
Mix, Terry Platt 1940- *WhoAm 90*
Mix, Tom 1880-1940 *BioIn 16, EncACom, WorAlBi*
Mix, Walter Joseph 1928- *WhoAmA 91*
Mixer, Elizabeth *FemiCLE*
Mixer, Michael Jay 1964- *WhoEmL 91*
Mixon, Aaron Malachi, III 1940- *St&PR 91*
Mixon, Alan 1933- *WhoAm 90*
Mixon, E. P. 1926- *St&PR 91*
Mixon, Forest O. 1931- *St&PR 91*
Mixon, Hayward E. 1928- *St&PR 91*
Mixon, James C., Jr. 1927- *St&PR 91*
Mixon, John 1933- *WhoAm 90*
Mixon, John A. *St&PR 91*
Mixon, Myron Glenn 1950- *St&PR 91*
Mixon, Peggy Dorsey 1935- *WhoSSW 91*
Mixon, Roy Darvin 1922- *WhoSSW 91*
Mixon, William H. 1936- *St&PR 91*
Mixtacki, Steven Bernard 1954- *WhoEmL 91*
Mixter, David Mason 1922- *WhoAm 90*
Mixter, Keith Eugene 1922- *IntWWM 90*
Miya, Tom Saburo 1923- *WhoAm 90*
Miyachi, Iwao 1916- *WhoWor 91*
Miyagawa, Ichiro 1922- *WhoAm 90, WhoSSW 91, WhoWor 91*
Miyagi, Hiroo W. 1917- *St&PR 91*
Miyahara, Yoshihiko 1937- *WhoAm 90*
Miyahira, Dixie Arakaki 1932- *BiDrAPA 89*
Miyahira, Harrison Y. 1935- *St&PR 91*
Miyakado, Masakazu 1947- *WhoWor 91*
Miyakawa, Taihei 1935- *WhoWor 91*
Miyakawa, Toru 1931- *WhoWor 91*
Miyake Issei *EncJap*
Miyake, Akio 1931- *WhoWor 91*
Miyake, Issey 1938- *WhoAm 90, WhoWor 91*
Miyake, Issey 1939- *ConDes 90*
Miyake, Toshinobu 1944- *St&PR 91*
Miyamoto Yuriko 1899-1951 *TwCLC 37*
Miyamoto, Richard Takashi 1944- *WhoAm 90, WhoWor 91*
Miyamoto, Wayne Akira 1947- *WhoAmA 91*
Miyao, Stanley Kenji 1946- *St&PR 91*
Miyares, Benjamin David 1940- *WhoAm 90*
Miyares, Marcelino 1937- *WhoHisp 91*
Miyasaki, Gail Yotsue 1949- *WhoE 91*
Miyasaki, George Joji 1935- *WhoAm 90, WhoAmA 91*
Miyasaki, Nola Nobuyo 1958- *WhoAmW 91*
Miyasaki, Shuichi 1928- *WhoWor 91*
Miyashiro, Akiho 1920- *WhoAm 90*
Miyashiro, Yoshito 1931- *St&PR 91*
Miyashita, Tad 1922-1979 *WhoAmA 91N*
Miyata, Gen 1933- *WhoWor 91*
Miyauchi, Tsutomu 1910- *EncPaPR 91*
Miyawaki, Edison Kazumi *BiDrAPA 89*
Miyazaki, Jim J. 1929- *St&PR 91*
Miyazaki, Nagao 1931- *WhoWor 91*
Miyazaki, Shigeru 1950- *IntWWM 90*
Miyazawa, Akira 1932- *WhoWor 91*
Miyazawa, Kiichi 1919- *WhoWor 91*
Miyazawa, Tatsuo 1927- *WhoWor 91*
Miyori, Kim *ConTFT 8*
Mize, Claiborne Jackson 1958- *WhoSSW 91*
Mize, E. Jack, Jr. 1946- *St&PR 91*
Mize, Franklin H. 1929- *St&PR 91*
Mize, George Michael 1948- *St&PR 91, WhoAm 90*
Mize, Joe Henry 1934- *WhoAm 90, WhoWrEP 89*
Mize, Johnny 1913- *Ballpl 90 [port]*
Mize, Shirley J. *WhoWrEP 89*
Mizel, Ken 1951- *St&PR 91*
Mizel, Larry A. 1942- *WhoAm 90*
Mizel, Mark Stuart 1945- *WhoEmL 91*
Mizel, Steven M. *WhoAm 90*
Mizell, Al Philip 1934- *WhoWor 91*
Mizell, Andrew Hooper, III 1926- *St&PR 91*
Mizell, John E. 1925- *IntWWM 90*
Mizell, Merle 1927- *WhoAm 90*
Mizell, Philip Lewis 1953- *BiDrAPA 89*
Mizell, Vinegar Bend 1930- *Ballpl 90*
Mizell, Walter S 1915- *BiDrAPA 89*
Mizell, William A. 1928- *St&PR 91*
Mizener, Arthur 1907-1988 *AnObit 1988, DcLB 103 [port]*
Mizenko, Michael Raymond 1959- *BiDrAPA 89*
Mizer, Karen Mary 1954- *WhoAmW 91*
Mizer, Richard Anthony 1952- *WhoWor 91*
Mizerek, Diane Marie 1963- *WhoAmW 91*
Mizgala, Henry F. 1932- *WhoAm 90*
Miziolek, Andrzej Wladyslaw 1950- *WhoE 91*
Mizner, Elizabeth Howard *AuBYP 90*
Mizner, George L 1930- *BiDrAPA 89*
Mizobuchi, Masaya 1943- *WhoWor 91*
Mizoguchi Kenji 1898-1956 *EncJap*
Mizrach, Larry Melvin 1932- *St&PR 91*
Mizrahi, Abraham Mordechay 1929- *WhoAm 90*
Mizrahi, Aslan Marco *BiDrAPA 89*
Mizrahi, David *NewYTBS 90*
Mizrahi, Isaac *BioIn 16*
Mizrahi, Isaac 1961- *News 91-1 [port]*
Mizrahi, Jack David 1948- *St&PR 91*
Mizrahi, Joseph Martin 1919- *St&PR 91*
Mizroch, John F. 1948- *WhoAm 90, WhoWor 91*
Mizruchi, Mark S 1953- *ConAu 30NR*
Mizuguchi, Yasuo 1935- *WhoWor 91*
Mizuno, Atsushi 1959- *WhoE 91*
Mizuno, Ryozo 1910- *WhoWor 91*
Mizuno, Ryuichi Jerome 1962- *WhoWor 91*
Mizushima, Keiichi 1928- *WhoWor 91*
Mizushima, Shoji 1932- *WhoWor 91*
Mizushima, Yoshihiko 1925- *WhoWor 91*
Mizuta, Mary Ellen 1949- *WhoWrEP 89*
Mizuta, Takashi 1938- *WhoWor 91*
Mizutani, Diane Lisa 1963- *WhoAmW 91*
Mizuuchi, Kiyoshi 1944- *WhoAm 90*
Mizwa, Mary Jane House 1936- *WhoSSW 91*
Mizzaro, Franco 1935- *WhoWor 91*
Mizzau, Marina 1936- *EncCoWW*
Mizzell, David Allan 1961- *WhoSSW 91*
Mizzi, Alfred Paul 1934- *IntWWM 90*
Mkapa, Benjamin William 1938- *WhoWor 91*
Mladek, Jan Viktor 1911-1989 *BioIn 16*
Mladenov, Peter Toshev 1936- *WhoWor 91*
Mladick, Richard Anthony 1934- *WhoSSW 91*
Mladota, John 1917- *St&PR 91*
Mlakar, Charles L., Jr. 1946- *St&PR 91*
Mlakar, Roy A. 1953- *WhoAm 90*
Mlay, Marian 1935- *WhoAm 90*
M'Lehose, Agnes 1759-1841 *FemiCLE*
M'Leod, E. H. *FemiCLE*
Mlinaric, David *BioIn 16*
Mlodozeniec, Jan 1929- *ConDes 90*
Mlot, Eugene 1954- *WhoEmL 91*
Mlynarski, Emil 1870-1935 *PenDiMP*
Mlyniec, Wallace John 1945- *WhoEmL 91*
Mmahat, Arlene Cecile 1943- *WhoAmW 91*
Mme de Maintenon *EncCoWW*
Mmusi, Peter *WhoWor 91*
Mnacko, Ladislav 1919- *ConAu 31NR*
Mnookin, Robert Harris 1942- *WhoAm 90*
Mo, Luke Wei 1934- *WhoAm 90*
Mo, Timothy 1950?- *MajTwCW*
Mo, Y. Joseph 1948- *St&PR 91*
Mo-ki-lien *WomWR*
Moadel, Yahya 1936- *BiDrAPA 89*
Moak, Darlene Harriet *BiDrAPA 89*
Moak, E. H. 1904- *St&PR 91*
Moak, Gary Stuart *BiDrAPA 89*
Moak, Robert E. 1939- *St&PR 91*
Moak-Mazur, Connie J. 1947- *WhoE 91*
Moake, Brenda Joy 1959- *St&PR 91*
Moakley, Joe 1927- *NewYTBS 90 [port]*
Moakley, John J. *BioIn 16*
Moakley, John Joseph 1927- *WhoAm 90, WhoE 91*
Moanahonga *WhNaAH*
Moaney, Gail L. *ODwPR 91*
Moar, Peter J. 1936- *St&PR 91*
Moats, Alice-Leone *BioIn 16*
Moats, Edwin W., Jr. 1947- *WhoAm 90*
Moats, Francis Pierpont 1869- *AmLegL*
Moats, Harold 1939- *WhoWor 91*
Moats, Murray Blaine 1954- *IntWWM 90*
Moats, Pamela Helene 1949- *WhoEmL 91*
Moawad, Atef 1935- *WhoAm 90*
Moawad, Rene *BioIn 16*
Moawad, Rene 1925-1989 *AnObit 1989*
Moazzami, Dara 1949- *WhoE 91*
Mobarak, Ahmed M *BiDrAPA 89*
Mobberley, James C. 1954- *IntWWM 90*
Mobbs, Kenneth William 1925- *IntWWM 90*
Moberg, Carl Artur Vilhelm 1898-1973 *DcScanL*
Moberg, David Oscar 1922- *WhoAm 90*
Moberg, Vilhelm 1898-1973 *WorAlBi*
Moberly, David Lindsey 1929- *WhoAm 90*
Moberly, Linden Emery 1923- *WhoWor 91*
Moberly, Robert *BioIn 16*
Moberly, Robert Blakely 1941- *WhoAm 90*
Mobile, David C. 1946- *St&PR 91*
Mobilia, Louis 1932- *St&PR 91*
Mobilio, Joseph Nicholas 1953- *BiDrAPA 89*
Mobius, August Ferdinand 1790-1868 *WorAlBi*
Mobley, Andrew Hundley 1953- *WhoSSW 91*
Mobley, Forrest Causey, Jr. 1941- *WhoSSW 91*
Mobley, G. N. *ODwPR 91*
Mobley, John Homer, II 1930- *WhoAm 90, WhoWor 91*
Mobley, Karen R *WhoAmA 91*
Mobley, Karen Ruth 1961- *WhoAmW 91*
Mobley, Lawrence Edward, III 1952- *BiDrAPA 89*
Mobley, Mary Ann *BioIn 16*
Mobley, Michael C 1950- *BiDrAPA 89*
Mobley, Michael Howard 1945- *WhoAm 90*
Mobley, Mona Lejeune 1933- *WhoAmW 91*
Mobley, Norma Mason Garland 1923- *WhoAmW 91*
Mobley, Paul W. 1940- *St&PR 91*
Mobley, Robert 1953- *WhoE 91*
Mobley, Stacey J. 1945- *St&PR 91*
Mobley, Steven Clark 1948- *WhoSSW 91*
Mobley, Tammy Ann 1963- *WhoSSW 91*
Mobley, Tony Allen 1938- *WhoAm 90*
Mobley, William H. 1941- *WhoAm 90, WhoSSW 91*
Mobraaten, William Lawrence 1929- *St&PR 91, WhoAm 90*
Mobutu Sese Seko 1930- *WhoWor 91*
Mocarski, Cara Schmid 1958- *WhoAmW 91*
Moccia, Alfred J. 1917- *St&PR 91*
Moceri, William Thomas 1936- *St&PR 91*
Moch, Jules-Salvator 1893-1985 *BiDFrPL*
Moch, Mary Inez 1943- *WhoAmW 91*
Moch, Robert Gaston 1914- *WhoAm 90*
Mocharla, Raman 1953- *WhoWor 91*
Mochary, Mary Veronica 1942- *WhoAmW 91*
Mochi, Ugo 1894-1977 *WhoAmA 91N*
Mochida, Isao 1940- *WhoWor 91*
Mochida, Yoshihiro 1931- *WhoWor 91*
Mochizuki, Shigeru 1931- *WhoWor 91*
Mochon, Donald 1916- *WhoAmA 91N*
Mochrie, Richard Douglas 1928- *WhoAm 90*
Mock, Alois 1934- *WhoWor 91*
Mock, Bette Marie 1937- *WhoAmW 91*
Mock, Bruno Paul 1937- *WhoWor 91*
Mock, Charles A. 1945- *WhoE 91*
Mock, Charles Newman 1927- *St&PR 91, WhoAm 90*
Mock, Clyde A. 1948- *St&PR 91*
Mock, Clyde Alan 1948- *WhoE 91*
Mock, David Clinton, Jr. 1922- *WhoAm 90, WhoWor 91*
Mock, David George 1925- *St&PR 91*
Mock, Douglas F. 1955- *St&PR 91*
Mock, George Andrew 1886- *WhoAmA 91N*
Mock, Harmon Roy 1938- *WhoE 91*
Mock, Henry Byron 1911- *WhoAm 90*
Mock, Jesse Alexander, Jr. 1920- *WhoAm 90, WhoWrEP 89*
Mock, John E 1923- *BiDrAPA 89*
Mock, John L. 1927- *St&PR 91*
Mock, Lawrence Edward 1917- *WhoAm 90*
Mock, Lawrence Edward, Jr. 1946- *WhoEmL 91*
Mock, Linda Colangelo 1948- *WhoAmW 91*
Mock, Melinda Smith 1947- *WhoWor 91*
Mock, Richard Basil 1944- *WhoAmA 91*
Mock, Robert Claude 1928- *WhoAm 90, WhoE 91, WhoWor 91*
Mock, Sandra Ford 1944- *WhoAmW 91*
Mock, Theodore Jaye 1941- *WhoAm 90*
Mockbee, Charles W *BiDrAPA 89*
Mockbee, Samuel *BioIn 16*
Mockbee, William Clyde 1926- *St&PR 91*
Mockett, Alfred T. 1949- *St&PR 91, WhoAm 90*
Mockett, John H., Jr. 1860-1944 *AmLegL*
Mockler, Colman Michael, Jr. 1929- *St&PR 91, WhoAm 90, WhoE 91*
Mockler, Edward Joseph 1954- *WhoE 91*
Mockoviak, John Wade 1944- *WhoE 91*
Mockridge, Norton 1915- *WhoAm 90*
Mocnik, Joseph 1939- *St&PR 91*
Mocny, R. C. 1929- *St&PR 91*
Mocquot, Germain Pierre Charles Edouard *BioIn 16*
Mocsary, Attila Laszlo 1931- *St&PR 91*
Mocumbi, Pascoal Manuel 1941- *WhoWor 91*
Moczula, Boris 1956- *WhoEmL 91*
Modali, Yasoda 1948- *BiDrAPA 89*
Modan, Baruch 1932- *WhoWor 91*
Modansky, Aaron 1923- *St&PR 91*
Modarress Sadeghi, Jaafar 1954- *WhoWor 91*
Modarressi, Hossein 1942- *WhoAm 90*
Modarressi, Taghi M 1931- *BiDrAPA 89*
Modarressi, Taghi M., Mrs. *WhoAmW 91*
Modderman, Melvin Earl 1940- *WhoSSW 91*
Mode, Arthur Sander *BiDrAPA 89*
Mode, Carol A 1943- *WhoAmA 91*
Mode, Charles J. 1927- *WhoAm 90*
Mode, Paul J., Jr. 1938- *WhoAm 90*
Model, Elisabeth D *WhoAmA 91*
Model, Elisabeth Dittman *WhoAm 90, WhoE 91*
Model, Evsa 1901-1976 *WhoAmA 91N*
Model, Hanns 1908- *PenDiDA 89*
Model, Peter 1933- *WhoAm 90*
Model, Philippe 1957- *BioIn 16*
Model, Reiner 1941- *PenDiDA 89*
Modell, Arnold H 1924- *BiDrAPA 89, WhoE 91*
Modell, Franklyn B. *WhoAm 90*
Modell, Jack Gary 1956- *BiDrAPA 89*
Modell, Jerome Herbert 1932- *WhoAm 90*
Modell, John 1941- *WhoAm 90*
Modell, Michael S. 1953- *St&PR 91*
Modell, William 1921- *St&PR 91*
Modena, Leone da 1571-1648 *BioIn 16*
Moder, John Joseph 1948- *WhoAm 90*
Moderacki, Edmund Anthony 1946- *WhoE 91*
Modern Jazz Quartet *OxCPMus*
Modernaires, The *OxCPMus*
Moderow, Joseph Robert 1948- *St&PR 91*
Modershohn-Becker, Paula 1876-1907 *EncCoWW*
Modersohn-Becker, Paula 1876-1907 *BiDWomA, BioIn 16, IntDcAA 90, ModArCr 1 [port]*
Moderson, Christopher Paul 1959- *WhoEmL 91*
Modert, Jo 1921- *ConAu 132*
Modery, Richard G. 1941- *St&PR 91*
Modery, Richard Gillman 1941- *WhoWor 91*
Modesitt, Jeanne *AuBYP 90*
Modestini, Mario 1907- *BioIn 16*
Modglin, Dara Sue 1964- *WhoEmL 91*
Modha, Vithalji *BiDrAPA 89*
Modi, Jagdish Jamnadas 1956- *WhoWor 91*
Modi, Suresh R 1934- *BiDrAPA 89*
Modi-Vitale, Lydia *WhoAmA 91*
Modiano, Marko 1953- *WhoWor 91*
Modiano, Patrick Jean 1945- *WhoWor 91*
Modic, Frank A. 1929- *St&PR 91*
Modic, Stanley John 1936- *WhoAm 90, WhoWrEP 89*
Modica, Frank A. 1928- *St&PR 91*
Modica, Roy H. *St&PR 91*
Modica, Terry Ann 1955- *WhoWrEP 89*
Modigliani, Amedeo 1884-1920 *BioIn 16, IntDcAA 90, WorAlBi*
Modigliani, Franco 1918- *WhoAm 90, WhoE 91, WhoWor 91, WorAlBi*
Modigliani, Lazzaro 1932- *St&PR 91*
Modine, Matthew *BioIn 16*
Modir, Kamal K 1937- *BiDrAPA 89*
Modjeska, Helena 1840-1909 *BioIn 16, NotWoAT*
Modl, Martha 1912- *IntWWM 90, PenDiMP*
Modlin, Elihu H. 1928- *St&PR 91*

Modlin, George Matthews 1903- *WhoAm 90*
Modlin, Herbert C 1913- *BiDrAPA 89*
Modlin, Howard S. 1931- *St&PR 91, WhoAm 90, WhoE 91, WhoWor 91*
Modlin, Philip Hodgin 1926- *WhoAm 90*
Modlowski, Paul Barry 1948- *St&PR 91*
Modrall, James R. 1932- *St&PR 91*
Modrell, Jim B. 1935- *St&PR 91*
Modresky, Michael John 1946- *WhoE 91*
Modrow, Hans 1928- *WhoWor 91*
Modzelewski, Jack 1954- *ODwPR 91*
Moe, Bjorn Kare 1946- *IntWWM 90*
Moe, Chesney Rudolph 1908- *WhoAm 90*
Moe, Doug *BioIn 16*
Moe, Douglas Edwin 1938- *WhoAm 90*
Moe, Frank Harrison 1941- *St&PR 91*
Moe, Gordon K. 1915-1989 *BioIn 16*
Moe, Henrik 1940- *St&PR 91*
Moe, Henry Allen 1894-1975 *WhoAmA 91N*
Moe, Karin 1945- *EncCoWW*
Moe, Lawrence Henry 1917- *WhoAm 90*
Moe, Marxianna M. 1953- *St&PR 91*
Moe, Maynard L. 1935- *St&PR 91*
Moe, Palmer 1944- *St&PR 91*
Moe, Palmer L. 1944- *WhoAm 90, WhoSSW 91*
Moe, Richard D 1928- *WhoAmA 91*
Moe, Richard Palmer 1936- *WhoAm 90*
Moe, Vida Delores 1928- *WhoAmW 91*
Moe, W Wyatt 1929- *BiDrAPA 89*
Moe-Fishback, Barbara Ann 1955- *WhoAmW 91*
Moebius, Dieter *NewAgMG*
Moebius, Mary Margaret 1957- *BiDrAPA 89*
Moebius, Robert Edward 1925- *BiDrAPA 89*
Moebius, William 1941- *WhoWrEP 89*
Moebus, Jo Vance 1945- *WhoSSW 91*
Moeck, Hermann 1922- *IntWWM 90*
Moeck, Walter Francis 1922- *IntWWM 90*
Moeckel, Bill Reid 1925- *WhoAm 90*
Moeckel, Henry Theodore 1918- *WhoE 91*
Moede, Austin Lyn 1934- *WhoAm 90*
Moede, Gustave Herman 1916- *St&PR 91*
Moehl, Karl J 1925- *WhoAmA 91*
Moehlig, Jozef Karel 1929- *WhoWor 91*
Moehlman, Michael Scott 1938- *WhoAm 90*
Moehring, Karl-Heinz 1922- *St&PR 91*
Moeling, Walter Goos, IV 1943- *WhoAm 90, WhoSSW 91*
Moelis, Herbert 1931- *St&PR 91*
Moelleken, Wolfgang Wilfried 1934- *WhoAm 90*
Moeller, Achim Ferdinand Gerd 1942- *WhoWor 91*
Moeller, Audrey Carolyn 1935- *St&PR 91, WhoAm 90*
Moeller, Dade William 1927- *WhoAm 90*
Moeller, Danny 1885-1951 *Ballpl 90*
Moeller, Donald Joseph 1933- *WhoAm 90*
Moeller, Donna Jeanne 1950- *WhoE 91*
Moeller, Frederick G. 1959- *BiDrAPA 89*
Moeller, Helen Hergenroder 1954- *WhoAmW 91*
Moeller, Henry G., Jr. *BiDrAPA 89*
Moeller, James 1933- *WhoAm 90*
Moeller, Jerome Frederick 1939- *WhoSSW 91*
Moeller, Joe 1943- *Ballpl 90*
Moeller, John A. 1936- *WhoAm 90*
Moeller, John Roger 1940- *BiDrAPA 89*
Moeller, Laura Lee 1927- *WhoAmW 91*
Moeller, Lynn H. 1942- *St&PR 91*
Moeller, Mark Stephen *BiDrAPA 89*
Moeller, Mary Ella 1938- *WhoAmW 91, WhoE 91*
Moeller, Raymond M. 1927- *St&PR 91*
Moeller, Richard 1939- *St&PR 91*
Moeller, Richard Jon 1939- *WhoAm 90*
Moeller, Robert C. *BioIn 16*
Moeller, Robert Charles 1954- *WhoEmL 91, WhoWor 91*
Moeller, Robert Charles, III 1938- *WhoAm 90, WhoAmA 91*
Moeller, Robert John 1938- *WhoAm 90*
Moeller, Ron 1938- *Ballpl 90*
Moeller, Therald 1913- *WhoAm 90*
Moeller, Warren Elbert 1926- *WhoSSW 91*
Moeller, Wayne Eldon 1926- *WhoSSW 91*
Moeller, William E. 1942- *WhoSSW 91*
Moellering, Alfred William 1926- *WhoAm 90*
Moellering, John H. 1938- *St&PR 91*
Moellering, John Henry 1938- *WhoAm 90*
Moellering, Richard Edwin 1929- *St&PR 91*
Moellering, Robert Charles, Jr. 1936- *WhoAm 90, WhoWor 91*
Moely, Barbara E. 1940- *WhoAmW 91*
Moen, Donald Philip 1921- *WhoAm 90*
Moench, Louis Alan *BiDrAPA 89*
Moench, Louis G *BiDrAPA 89*
Moench, Priscilla Waters 1957- *WhoAmW 91*
Moench, Robert W. 1927- *St&PR 91*
Moench, Robert William 1927- *WhoAm 90*
Moenjak, Thamrongsak 1945- *WhoWor 91*
Moenne-Loccoz, Philippe 1953- *IntWWM 90*
Moens, Peter B. 1931- *WhoAm 90*
Moentmann, Melanie Ruth 1960- *WhoAmW 91*
Moeran, E J 1894-1950 *PenDiMPA*
Moerdani, Leonardus Benny *WhoWor 91*
Moerdler, Charles Gerard 1934- *WhoAm 90, WhoE 91, WhoWor 91*
Moerer, Gary 1938- *St&PR 91*
Moerings, Bert Joseph 1945- *WhoWor 91*
Moerk, Edward Stabel 1944- *WhoE 91*
Moerner, Magnus 1924- *ConAu 132*
Moero 320?BC- *EncCoWW*
Moers, William Otto 1926- *St&PR 91*
Moerschel, Chiara *WhoAmA 91*
Moershel, William J *BiDrAPA 89*
Moertel, Charles George 1927- *WhoAm 90*
Moes, Charles E., Jr. 1953- *St&PR 91*
Moeschel, Wernhard 1941- *WhoWor 91*
Moeslein, Frank A. 1943- *St&PR 91, WhoAm 90*
Moevs, Robert Walter 1920- *IntWWM 90*
Mofenson, Lynne Meryl 1950- *WhoAmW 91*
Moffat, Abbot Low 1901- *WhoE 91*
Moffat, Alan Lyndon 1949- *IntWWM 90*
Moffat, Alec W. 1947- *St&PR 91*
Moffat, Daniel *BioIn 16*
Moffat, David Halliday 1839-1911 *BioIn 16*
Moffat, David Halliday, Jr. 1839-1911 *EncABHB 6 [port]*
Moffat, Donald 1930- *WhoAm 90*
Moffat, Gwen 1924- *FemiCLE, TwCCr&M 91*
Moffat, James N. C., III 1941- *St&PR 91*
Moffat, Jay Pierrepont 1896-1943 *BioIn 16*
Moffat, John P *BiDrAPA 89*
Moffat, John William 1932- *WhoAm 90*
Moffat, Kenneth M. 1932- *St&PR 91*
Moffat, MaryBeth 1951- *WhoAmW 91*
Moffat, Robert John 1927- *WhoAm 90*
Moffatt, Alan William 1952- *WhoSSW 91*
Moffatt, David John 1939- *WhoAm 90*
Moffatt, Hugh McCulloch, Jr. 1933- *WhoWor 91*
Moffatt, Joyce Anne 1936- *WhoAm 90*
Moffatt, Katy 1950- *WhoAm 90*
Moffatt, Leslie Mack 1928- *St&PR 91*
Moffatt, Lewis 1809?-1892 *DcCanB 12*
Moffatt, Mindy Ann 1951- *WhoAmW 91*
Moffatt, Seth Crittenden 1841-1887 *AmLegL*
Moffet, Donald Pratt 1932- *WhoAm 90*
Moffet, Eric David *BiDrAPA 89*
Moffet, John *BioIn 16*
Moffet, Mark Alan *BiDrAPA 89*
Moffett, Barry A. 1945- *WhoE 91*
Moffett, Charnett *BioIn 16*
Moffett, Dawn Schulten 1946- *WhoAmW 91*
Moffett, Frank Cardwell 1931- *WhoWor 91*
Moffett, George H. 1845-189-? *AmLegL*
Moffett, Jack Edward 1944- *St&PR 91*
Moffett, James Robert 1938- *WhoAm 90, WhoSSW 91*
Moffett, Jane Daniels 1949- *WhoE 91, WhoEmL 91*
Moffett, Jonathan Phillip 1954- *WhoWor 91*
Moffett, Karma *NewAgMG*
Moffett, Kenworth William 1934- *WhoAmA 91*
Moffett, Lawrence Rector 1927- *St&PR 91*
Moffett, Pamela Amy 1954- *WhoAmW 91*
Moffett, Paul Michael 1947- *BiDrAPA 89*
Moffett, Robert K. *AuBYP 90*
Moffett, Ross E 1888-1971 *WhoAmA 91N*
Moffett, Roy James 1947- *WhoE 91*
Moffett, Terrill Kay 1949- *WhoSSW 91*
Moffett, William Andrew 1933- *WhoAm 90*
Moffic, H. Steven 1946- *BiDrAPA 89*
Moffit, George Seth 1947- *WhoAm 90*
Moffit, William C. 1925- *WhoAm 90, WhoWor 91*
Moffitt, Charles William 1932- *WhoAm 90*
Moffitt, Dale *BioIn 16*
Moffitt, Dale Edwin 1934- *WhoSSW 91*
Moffitt, David A. 1927- *ODwPR 91*
Moffitt, Donald Eugene 1932- *St&PR 91, WhoAm 90*
Moffitt, George, Jr. 1918- *WhoAm 90, WhoWor 91*
Moffitt, George James 1915- *WhoWor 91*
Moffitt, Harry Joseph *BiDrAPA 89*
Moffitt, John Francis 1940- *WhoAmA 91*
Moffitt, Joseph V., Jr. 1908- *St&PR 91*
Moffitt, Peter M. 1926- *St&PR 91*
Moffitt, Phillip William 1946- *WhoAm 90*
Moffitt, Randy 1948- *Ballpl 90*
Moffitt, Richard L. 1947- *WhoE 91*
Moffitt, William C. 1944- *St&PR 91*
Moffitt, William F. 1949- *St&PR 91*
Moffo, Anna 1932- *IntWWM 90, PenDiMP, WorAlBi*
Moffo, Doreen Ann 1962- *WhoAmW 91*
Mofford, Rose *BioIn 16*
Mofford, Rose 1922- *WhoAm 90, WhoAmW 91, WhoWor 91*
Mofield, William Ray 1921- *WhoSSW 91, WhoWor 91*
Mofokeng, Connie *BioIn 16*
Moford, Herb 1928- *Ballpl 90*
Mofran, John R. *St&PR 91*
Mofsen, Ricky S 1952- *BiDrAPA 89*
Mofsky, James Steffan 1935- *WhoAm 90*
Mogabgab, William Joseph 1921- *WhoAm 90*
Mogador, Celeste 1824-1909 *EncCoWW*
Mogal, Sol *BioIn 16*
Mogali, Sreenivasa R *BiDrAPA 89*
Mogami, Takeo 1943- *WhoWor 91*
Mogan, John Joseph *BiDrAPA 89*
Mogar, Joseph 1934- *St&PR 91*
Mogas, Vincent Louis 1939- *WhoSSW 91*
Mogavero, Michael James 1950- *WhoAmA 91*
Mogavero, Samuel 1936- *St&PR 91*
Mogel, Marcia G. 1950- *St&PR 91*
Mogelever, Bernard *ODwPR 91*
Mogelever, Bernard 1940- *WhoE 91*
Mogen, James August, Sr. 1946- *St&PR 91*
Mogensen, Borge 1914-1972 *ConDes 90, PenDiDA 89*
Mogensen, Finn 1934- *WhoWor 91*
Mogensen, Paul 1941- *WhoAmA 91*
Mogensen, Paul Robert 1941- *WhoE 91*
Mogerman, John Steven *BiDrAPA 89*
Mogerman, Michael Scott *BiDrAPA 89*
Mogerman, Veronica Linda 1954- *WhoAmW 91, WhoE 91, WhoEmL 91, WhoWor 91*
Mogford, Sharon Marie 1959- *WhoAmW 91*
Mogg, Donald Whitehead 1924- *WhoWor 91*
Moggach, Deborah 1948- *FemiCLE*
Mogge, Harriet Morgan *WhoAmW 91, WhoSSW 91*
Moghaddasi, Mohammad Reza 1941- *WhoWor 91*
Moghissi, Kamran S. 1925- *WhoWor 91*
Moghtader, Linda Diane 1958- *BiDrAPA 89*
Mogi, Yuzaburo 1935- *BioIn 16*
Mogil, Bernard Marc 1949- *WhoE 91, WhoWor 91*
Mogilner, Alan J. 1941- *St&PR 91*
Mogk, John Edward 1939- *WhoAm 90*
Mogolov, Cynthia Jo 1950- *WhoEmL 91*
Mogor, John Richard *BiDrAPA 89*
Mogore, Dorota Tlalka *BioIn 16*
Mogore, Malgorzata Tlalka *BioIn 16*
Mogren, William John 1948- *St&PR 91*
Mogridge, Christopher Alan 1949- *WhoE 91*
Mogridge, George 1889-1962 *Ballpl 90*
Mogstad, Rolf 1932- *St&PR 91*
Mogubgub, Fred *BioIn 16*
Moguel, Kathleen Doris 1957- *WhoSSW 91*
Mogul, Harve Alan 1942- *WhoSSW 91*
Mogul, Kathleen M *BiDrAPA 89*
Mogul, Leslie Anne *ODwPR 91*
Mogul, Malcolm Daniel 1930- *St&PR 91*
Mogul, S Louis 1926- *BiDrAPA 89*
Mohabbat, Mohammad Omar *BiDrAPA 89*
Mohacsy, Ildiko *BiDrAPA 89*
Mohagen, Jane Renee 1952- *WhoEmL 91*
Mohair, John P *BiDrAPA 89*
Mohajer, Morteza 1944- *BiDrAPA 89*
Mohamed Ali Jinnah 1876-1948 *BioIn 16*
Mohamed, Elaine *BioIn 16*
Mohamed, Ethel Wright 1906- *MusmAFA*
Mohamed, Hussain Sadiq 1919- *IntWWM 90*
Mohamed, Ibrahim Refaat *BiDrAPA 89*
Mohamed, Zoser Zakaria *BiDrAPA 89*
Mohammad Reza Pahlavi 1919-1980 *PolLCME*
Mohammad Zahir Shah *NewYTBS 90 [port]*
Mohammad, Ali Nasser 1939- *PolLCME*
Mohammad, Wali 1949- *BiDrAPA 89*
Mohammad, Yar 1939- *BiDrAPA 89*
Mohammadioun, Said 1947- *St&PR 91*
Mohammed *BioIn 16*
Mohammed 570-632 *WorAlBi*
Mohammed V 1909?-1961 *PolLCME*
Mohammed Ibn Abdel-Aziz 1910-1988 *BioIn 16*
Mohammed Reza Pahlavi, Shah of Iran 1919-1980 *BioIn 16*
Mohammed Zahir Shah, King of Afghanistan 1914- *BioIn 16*
Mohammed, Shakil 1933- *BiDrAPA 89*
Mohan, Anil 1951- *WhoWor 91*
Mohan, Arni Natesan 1937- *BiDrAPA 89*
Mohan, Beverly 1918- *AuBYP 90*
Mohan, Brij 1939- *WhoSSW 91*
Mohan, Chander *BiDrAPA 89*
Mohan, Chandra 1950- *WhoEmL 91*
Mohan, D. Mike 1945- *WhoAm 90*
Mohan, Geetha *BiDrAPA 89*
Mohan, J. Patrick 1948- *WhoAm 90*
Mohan, John T., Jr., Mrs. 1944- *WhoE 91*
Mohan, Rakesh 1948- *WhoWor 91*
Mohan, Ramanujam 1949- *BiDrAPA 89*
Mohan, S *BiDrAPA 89*
Mohan, S C *BiDrAPA 89*
Mohan, Sal 1941- *St&PR 91*
Mohan, Sushila Nagnur 1946- *BiDrAPA 89*
Mohan, Suvarna *BiDrAPA 89*
Mohan, Tungesh Nath 1949- *WhoSSW 91, WhoWor 91*
Mohanarangan, S. 1950- *WhoWor 91*
Mohankumar, H. Thamiah 1952- *BiDrAPA 89*
Mohassess, Ardeshir 1938- *BioIn 16*
Mohel, Selma Zippert 1911- *WhoAmW 91*
Moheno, Phillip Bertrand Berkey 1952- *WhoEmL 91*
Mohide, Thomas Patrick 1921- *WhoE 91*
Mohini, Radha 1946- *WhoEmL 91*
Mohiuddin, Aziz 1954- *BiDrAPA 89*
Mohiuddin, Syed Maqdoom 1934- *WhoAm 90*
Mohl, Paul Cecil 1944- *BiDrAPA 89*
Mohl, Raymond A 1939- *ConAu 30NR*
Mohle, Brenda Simonson 1959- *WhoAmA 91*
Mohleji, Satish Chandra 1940- *WhoSSW 91*
Mohlenbrock, Robert Herman, Jr. 1931- *WhoAm 90, WhoWrEP 89*
Mohlenbrok, Karen Marie 1963- *WhoE 91*
Mohler, Delmar Ray 1950- *WhoEmL 91*
Mohler, Harold Sheaffer 1919-1988 *BioIn 16*
Mohler, Irvin Charles, Jr. 1925- *WhoE 91*
Mohler, James Dawson 1926- *WhoAm 90*
Mohler, Kid 1874-1961 *Ballpl 90*
Mohler, Linda S. 1949- *WhoAmW 91*
Mohler, Mary Gail 1948- *WhoAm 90*
Mohler, Randall Lynn 1958- *WhoWrEP 89*
Mohler, Richard Edmond 1950- *St&PR 91*
Mohler, Ronald Rutt 1931- *WhoAm 90*
Mohler, Stanley Ross 1927- *WhoAm 90*
Mohler, Terence John 1929- *WhoWor 91*
Mohlie, Raymond Eugene 1928- *WhoAm 90*
Mohlman, Robert Henry 1918- *St&PR 91*
Mohlman, Robert Peter 1945- *BiDrAPA 89*
Mohlmann, Neal Mitchell 1958- *WhoE 91*
Mohn, Blair B. 1959- *St&PR 91*
Mohn, Cheri 1936- *WhoAmA 91*
Mohn, Elaine Louise 1948- *WhoAmW 91*
Mohn, Gottlob Samuel 1789-1825 *PenDiDA 89*
Mohn, Melvin Paul 1926- *WhoAm 90*
Mohn, Patrice *BioIn 16*
Mohn, Reinhard 1921- *BioIn 16, WhoWor 91*
Mohn, Samuel 1761-1815 *PenDiDA 89*
Mohn, Walter Rosing 1948- *WhoSSW 91*
Mohner Langhamer, Wilma Maria 1942- *WhoSSW 91*
Mohney, Franklin Walter 1927- *WhoAm 90*
Mohney, Ralph Wilson 1918- *WhoAm 90*
Mohney, Reed A. 1924- *St&PR 91*
Mohney, Sharon Eileen 1944- *WhoAmW 91*
Mohns, Edward Bergen 1940- *BiDrAPA 89*
Moholy, Noel Francis 1916- *WhoWor 91*
Moholy-Nagy, Laszlo *PenDiDA 89*
Mohon, Earlene Mann 1939- *WhoSSW 91*
Mohongo *WhNaAH*
Mohorc, Daniel C. 1952- *St&PR 91*
Mohorcic, Dale 1956- *Ballpl 90*
Mohoreanu, Corneliu Dumitru 1950- *WhoE 91*
Mohorovic, Jesse Roper 1942- *St&PR 91*
Mohr, Barbara Jeanne 1953- *WhoAmW 91*
Mohr, Carolyn Stevens 1935- *BiDrAPA 89*
Mohr, Charles 1929-1989 *BioIn 16*
Mohr, Charles Donald 1930- *St&PR 91*
Mohr, Charles Jeffrey 1947- *St&PR 91, WhoAm 90*
Mohr, Donald F. 1932- *WhoAm 90*
Mohr, Frederick W., III 1927- *St&PR 91*
Mohr, Hans 1930- *WhoWor 91*
Mohr, Jane *BioIn 16*
Mohr, Jay Preston 1937- *WhoAm 90*
Mohr, Jeffrey Michael 1960- *WhoSSW 91*
Mohr, John Joseph 1946- *St&PR 91*
Mohr, John Luther 1911- *WhoAm 90, WhoWor 91*
Mohr, John Thomas 1953- *WhoSSW 91*
Mohr, Julian Boehm 1930- *WhoWor 91*
Mohr, Kent Wood *St&PR 91*
Mohr, Konrad 1942- *WhoWor 91*
Mohr, Larry 1950- *St&PR 91*

Mohr, Lawrence Charles 1947- WhoAm 90
Mohr, Lillian Holmen 1926- WhoSSW 91
Mohr, Matthew D. 1960- St&PR 91
Mohr, Michaela Siemes 1941- BiDrAPA 89
Mohr, Nicholasa 1935- AuBYP 90, BioIn 16, ChlLR 22 [port], ConAu 32NR, HispWr 90, WhoHisp 91
Mohr, Pauline Catherine 1948- WhoAmA 91
Mohr, Robert C 1929- BiDrAPA 89
Mohr, Robert Roy 1950- WhoAm 90
Mohr, Roger John 1931- St&PR 91, WhoAm 90
Mohr, Sigismund 1827-1893 DcCanB 12
Mohr, William G. 1936- St&PR 91
Mohrdick, Eunice Marie WhoAmW 91
Mohrer, Peter Laurence 1956- BiDrAPA 89
Mohrfeld, Richard Gentel 1945- WhoE 91
Mohrhardt, Foster Edward 1907- WhoAm 90, WhoWor 91
Mohrhauser, James Edward 1922- St&PR 91
Mohri, Hideo 1930- WhoWor 91
Mohri, Jiro 1929- WhoWor 91
Mohringer, Karel Johannes Frederick 1930- IntWWM 90
Mohrmann, Robert E. WhoAm 90
Mohrmann, Sue Ross 1940- WhoAmW 91
Mohrnheim, Johanna E BiDrAPA 89
Mohs, Frederic Edward 1910- WhoAm 90
Mohs, Friedrich 1773-1839 WorAlBi
Mohsen, Mohamed Yosry Abdel BiDrAPA 89
Mohsenian, Javad BiDrAPA 89
Mohsenin, Shahla 1950- BiDrAPA 89
Mohtadi, Shahruz 1955- WhoE 91
Moi, Daniel arap 1924- WhoWor 91
Moilanen, Thomas Alfred 1944- WhoWor 91
Moilanen, William Robert 1950- WhoEmL 91
Moily, Jaya Padubidri 1951- WhoE 91
Moinet, Eric Emil 1952- WhoEmL 91, WhoSSW 91, WhoWor 91
Moir, Alfred 1924- WhoAmA 91
Moir, Alfred Kummer 1924- WhoAm 90, WhoWrEP 89
Moir, David 1933- WhoAm 90
Moir, Duncan MacDonald 1938- St&PR 91
Moir, Edward 1932- WhoAm 90
Moir, Judy 1957- WhoWor 91
Moir, Robert Jesse 1942- St&PR 91
Moir, Robin Noel 1941- BiDrAPA 89
Moir, Virgil Peter, III 1932- St&PR 91
Moir, William Church 1822-1896 DcCanB 12
Moisan, Anne Sherman 1936- WhoAmW 91
Moise, Edward Warren 1811-1868 AmLegL
Moise, Edwin E 1946- ConAu 130
Moise, Edwin Evariste 1918- WhoAm 90, WhoE 91, WhoWrEP 89
Moise, Edwin Evariste 1946- WhoSSW 91
Moise, Penina 1797-1880 FemiCLE
Moise, Rebecca Zerby 1944- WhoAmW 91
Moiseivich, Benno 1890-1963 PenDiMP
Moiseiwitsch, Benno 1890-1963 PenDiMP
Moiseiwitsch, Tanya 1914- BioIn 16, ConDes 90, NotWoAT, OxCCanT
Moisen, Chandler Jon 1935- St&PR 91
Moises, David 1946- BiDrAPA 89
Moises, Massaud 1928- WhoWor 91
Moiseyev, Igor 1906- WorAlBi
Moisse, Gaston Jules 1928- WhoWor 91
Moix Meseguer, Ana Maria 1947- EncCoWW
Mojden, Wallace William 1922- St&PR 91
Mojica, Aurora 1939- WhoAmW 91
Mojo, Melissa A. 1953- ODwPR 91
Mojsilov, Ilene Krug 1952- WhoAmA 91
Mojsov, Lazar 1920- WhoWor 91
Mojtabai, Ann Grace 1937- WhoAm 90, WhoWrEP 89
Mojumder, Abu Taher 1940- WhoWor 91
Mok, Carson Kwok-Chi 1932- WhoE 91, WhoWor 91
Mok, Michael BioIn 16
Mok, Peter Pui Kwan 1938- WhoE 91
Mokae, Zakes DrBlPA 90
Mokan, John 1895-1985 Ballpl 90
Mokcsa, Agoston Haraszthy de 1812-1869 BioIn 16
Moke, Anne Marie 1955- WhoAmW 91
Moke, Marilie 1941- St&PR 91
Mokhtari, Faramarz L 1949- BiDrAPA 89
Mokodean, George David 1955- St&PR 91
Mokodean, Michael John 1923- WhoAm 90
Mokrasch, Lewis Carl 1930- WhoAm 90
Mokray, Joan Pallay 1947- WhoE 91
Mokrosch, Reinhold Erich 1940- WhoWor 91
Mokrzycki, Andrew Gustav 1899- WhoAm 90
Mokubei, Aoki 1767-1833 PenDiDA 89
Mokulis, Paula 1947- WhoAmW 91
Mola, Emilio 1887-1937 BioIn 16
Mola, Gaspare 1567-1640 PenDiDA 89
Molaison, Robert Mark 1930- St&PR 91
Molan, Herbert D. 1936- St&PR 91
Molan, John Edward 1927- WhoE 91
Molander, Roger Carl 1940- WhoAm 90
Molaroni, Eliseo PenDiDA 89
Molaroni, Telesforo PenDiDA 89
Molaroni, Vincenzo PenDiDA 89
Molarsky, Maurice 1885-1950 WhoAmA 91N
Molava, Pamela May 1924- IntWWM 90
Molchan, Donald Norman 1924- St&PR 91
Molchan, Thomas Michael 1955- St&PR 91
Molchanoff, Robert Michael 1932- St&PR 91
Molchon, Andrew B 1941- BiDrAPA 89
Mold, Herman WhoWrEP 89
Moldan, Bedrich 1935- WhoWor 91
Moldauer, Leslie P 1947- BiDrAPA 89
Moldavan, N PenDiMP
Moldaw, Stuart G. WhoAm 90
Moldawsky, Stanley BioIn 16
Molde, Donald Allen 1937- BiDrAPA 89
Molde, Kent Douglas 1945- WhoEmL 91
Molden, Herbert George 1912- WhoAm 90
Moldenhauer, Howard Herman 1929- St&PR 91, WhoAm 90
Moldenhauer, Judith A. 1951- WhoAm 90
Moldenhauer, William Calvin 1923- WhoAm 90
Molder, Michael Jay 1963- WhoE 91
Molders, Werner 1913-1941 BioIn 16
Moldofsky, Harvey BiDrAPA 89
Moldofsky, Jack 1925- BiDrAPA 89
Moldon, Peter L. 1937- BioIn 16
Moldovan, Stanton I 1941- BiDrAPA 89
Moldoveanu, Eugenia 1944- IntWWM 90
Moldoveanu, Vasile 1935- IntWWM 90
Moldowan, John Michael 1946- WhoEmL 91
Moldroski, Al R 1928- WhoAmA 91
Mole, Harvey E. 1908- St&PR 91
Mole, Miff 1898-1961 OxCPMus
Molenaar, Nicolaas 1949- WhoWor 91
Moler, Elizabeth Anne 1949- WhoAmW 91
Moler, Spencer C. 1947- St&PR 91
Molero, Wilson Joseph 1909- WhoWrEP 89
Moles, Robert Lee 1941- St&PR 91
Molese, Michele BioIn 16
Molese, Michele 1936- IntWWM 90
Moleski, Desmond D BiDrAPA 89
Molesworth, Mary Louisa 1839-1921 BioIn 16, FemiCLE
Moley, Kevin E. WhoAm 90
Molfino, Alessandra Mottola 1939- WhoWor 91
Molho, Anthony 1939- WhoAm 90
Molho, Emanuel 1936- St&PR 91, WhoAm 90
Molho, Isaac E. BioIn 16
Molholm, Kurt Nelson 1937- WhoSSW 91
Molholt, Pat 1943- WhoAm 90
Moliere 1622?-1673 WorAlBi
Moliere, Donna Renee 1958- WhoEmL 91
Moliken, Louis Lee 1949- WhoE 91
Molin, Edward G. 1919- St&PR 91
Molin, Stanley 1941- St&PR 91
Molina, Alfonso Rafael 1949- WhoWor 91
Molina, Alfred 1953?- ConTFT 8 [port]
Molina, Enrique 1910- HispWr 90
Molina, Gloria BioIn 16
Molina, Gloria 1948- WhoHisp 91
Molina, Jose A BiDrAPA 89
Molina, Jose Efren 1929- WhoHisp 91
Molina, Juan Ramon 1875-1908 BioIn 16
Molina, Julio Alfredo 1948- BiDrAPA 89, WhoHisp 91
Molina, Magdalena T. 1928- WhoHisp 91
Molina, Mario Jose 1943- WhoAm 90
Molina, Rafael Leonidas Trujillo 1891-1961 BioIn 16
Molina, Steve 1957- WhoHisp 91
Molinari, Bernardino 1880-1952 PenDiMP
Molinari, Delmo Charles 1926- St&PR 91
Molinari, Guido 1933- WhoAmA 91
Molinari, Guy Victor 1928- WhoE 91
Molinari, Joseph Francis WhoWor 91
Molinari, Ricardo E. 1898- BioIn 16
Molinari, Susan K. 1958- WhoAm 90, WhoAmW 91, WhoE 91
Molinari-Pradelli, Francesco 1911- IntWWM 90, PenDiMP
Molinaro, Al 1919- ConTFT 8
Molinaro, Albert Philip, Jr. 1928- WhoAm 90
Molinaro, Bob 1950- Ballpl 90
Molinaro, Edouard 1928- ConTFT 8
Molinaro, Robert 1949- St&PR 91
Molinaro, Ursule FemiCLE
Molinaro, Valerie Ann 1956- WhoAmW 91
Molinder, John Irving 1941- WhoAm 90
Moline, Gary L. 1952- WhoEmL 91
Moline, Jon Nelson 1937- WhoAm 90
Moline, Judith Ann 1941- WhoWrEP 89
Moline, Michael Edward 1953- WhoSSW 91
Moline, Ronald Alfred 1937- BiDrAPA 89
Molineaux, Charles Borromeo 1930- WhoAm 90
Molinero, Donald Peter BiDrAPA 89
Molines, Joseph S. WhoHisp 91
Molino, Patricia ODwPR 91
Molinski, Frank David 1944- St&PR 91
Molique, Bernard 1802-1869 PenDiMP
Molisa, Grace Mera 1946?- FemiCLE
Molitch, Matthew BiDrAPA 89
Moliteus, Magnus 1939- St&PR 91, WhoAm 90
Molitor, Bernard PenDiDA 89
Molitor, Doris Jean 1957- WhoAmW 91
Molitor, Gary William 1940- WhoWor 91
Molitor, Graham Thomas Tate 1934- WhoAm 90, WhoWrEP 89
Molitor, Margaret Anne 1920- WhoAm 90
Molitor, Michel 1734-1810 PenDiDA 89
Molitor, Paul 1956- Ballpl 90
Molitor, Raymond B. 1930- ODwPR 91
Molitor, Robert P. 1921- St&PR 91
Molitoris, Joseph John 1961- WhoE 91
Molitorisz, Marilyn Parrott 1947- ODwPR 91
Molkenbuhr, M. Edward 1947- St&PR 91
Molkner, Kenneth C 1936- BiDrAPA 89
Moll, Albert E BiDrAPA 89
Moll, Bertram Daniel 1926- St&PR 91
Moll, Clarence Russel 1913- St&PR 91, WhoAm 90, WhoE 91, WhoWor 91
Moll, Curtis E. 1933- St&PR 91
Moll, David Carter 1948- WhoSSW 91
Moll, Don L. 1949- WhoWor 91
Moll, Edwin Allan 1934- WhoWor 91
Moll, Gary Daniel 1950- WhoEmL 91
Moll, Jack Auldin 1922- St&PR 91
Moll, John Edgar 1934- St&PR 91, WhoAm 90
Moll, John Lewis 1921- WhoAm 90
Moll, Kenneth Leon 1932- WhoAm 90
Moll, Kevin Norman 1954- IntWWM 90
Moll, Kurt 1938- IntWWM 90, PenDiMP
Moll, Lloyd Henry 1925- St&PR 91, WhoAm 90
Moll, Louis Jean BiDrAPA 89
Moll, Marg 1884-1977 BiDWomA
Moll, Otto E. 1929- St&PR 91
Moll, Pamela Jean 1958- WhoE 91
Moll, Richard 1943- BioIn 16
Moll, Richard L. 1938- St&PR 91
Moll, Robert C. 1933- St&PR 91
Moll, William Gene 1937- St&PR 91
Mollah, Mohammed S BiDrAPA 89
Mollard, John Douglas 1924- WhoAm 90, WhoWor 91
Mollegen, Albert Theodore, Jr. 1937- St&PR 91, WhoAm 90
Mollehave, Herdis 1945?- EncCoWW
Mollel, Paul Lucas 1947- WhoEmL 91, WhoWor 91
Mollenberg, Richard Henry 1906- St&PR 91
Mollenhauer, Klaus Wilhelm Karl 1931- WhoWor 91
Mollenhoff, Clark Raymond 1921- WhoAm 90, WhoWrEP 89
Mollenkamp, Jane 1946- ODwPR 91
Mollenstedt, Gottfried Heinrich 1912- WhoWor 91
Moller, Aage Richard Moller 1932- WhoWor 91
Moller, Anthea Mary 1939- IntWWM 90
Moller, Barbara BioIn 16
Moller, George 1903- St&PR 91
Moller, Hans 1905- WhoAm 90, WhoAmA 91
Moller, Hans-Jurgen 1945- WhoWor 91
Moller, Lis Birgit 1955- WhoWor 91
Moller, Maersk McKinney 1913- WhoWor 91
Moller, Mats 1954- IntWWM 90
Moller, Paul BioIn 16
Moller, Peter 1947- IntWWM 90
Moller, Poul Martin 1794-1838 DcScanL
Moller, Regina Mary BiDrAPA 89
Moller, Wilhelmus J. 1930- WhoWor 91
Moller, William Richard, Jr. 1941- St&PR 91, WhoAm 90, WhoWor 91
Moller, William Thomas 1954- WhoWor 91
Mollerick, Jeffrey D. 1958- St&PR 91
Mollet, Guy Alcide 1905-1975 BiDFrPL
Molleur, E. Claude 1941- St&PR 91
Molleur, Kermit Joseph 1936- St&PR 91
Mollica, Richard F 1946- BiDrAPA 89
Mollica, Rosario 1963- WhoE 91
Mollichelli, Edward Vincent 1930- St&PR 91
Mollick, Ira Franklin 1952- BiDrAPA 89
Mollineux, Mary 1651?-1695 FemiCLE
Mollineux, Mary 1652?-1695 BiDEWW
Mollinger, Judith Ellen 1943- WhoAmW 91
Mollino, Carlo 1905-1973 ConDes 90, PenDiDA 89
Mollins, Herman 1926- St&PR 91
Mollison, Richard Devol 1916- WhoAm 90
Mollman, John Peter 1931- WhoAm 90
Mollner, Terry Jerome 1944- WhoE 91
Mollo-Christensen, Erik Leonard 1923- WhoAm 90
Mollohan, Alan B. 1943- WhoAm 90, WhoSSW 91
Mollohan, Helen Gail 1946- WhoWrEP 89
Molloy, Anne Stearns 1907- AuBYP 90
Molloy, Brian Joseph 1953- WhoEmL 91
Molloy, Elizabeth Ann 1964- WhoAmW 91
Molloy, James Lyman 1837-1900 OxCPMus
Molloy, Kenneth H. 1938- St&PR 91
Molloy, Marshall E. ODwPR 91
Molloy, Michael John 1940- SpyFic
Molloy, Michael S. 1958- WhoWor 91
Molloy, Robert 1936- WhoWor 91
Molloy, Robert Edwin WhoE 91
Molloy, Spencer George 1927- St&PR 91
Molloy, Susanne Prattson 1952- St&PR 91
Molloy, William Dennis, Jr. 1952- WhoE 91
Mollura, Carlos A. 1934- St&PR 91, WhoHisp 91
Mollwitz, Fritz 1890-1967 Ballpl 90
Mollycheck, Ralph BiDrAPA 89
Molnar, Andras 1948- IntWWM 90
Molnar, Anthony William 1938- WhoAm 90
Molnar, Bela 1951- WhoEmL 91
Molnar, Ferenc 1878-1952 WorAlBi
Molnar, Harriet L. 1938- WhoAmW 91
Molnar, Jeep BioIn 16
Molnar, Joseph George 1931- BiDrAPA 89
Molnar, Julius V BiDrAPA 89
Molnar, Laura Anne BiDrAPA 89
Molnar, Laurie Dennery 1958- WhoAmW 91
Molnar, Michael R. 1945- St&PR 91
Molnar, Thomas 1921- WhoAm 90, WhoWrEP 89
Molnar, Thomas J. 1944- St&PR 91
Molny, Erika 1932- EncCoWW
Molomjamts, Luvsangombyn WhoWor 91
Moloney, John Michael BiDrAPA 89
Moloney, Terrence Patrick 1960- WhoWrEP 89
Moloney, Thomas E. 1943- St&PR 91
Moloney, Thomas Joseph 1952- WhoEmL 91
Moloney, Thomas Walter 1946- WhoAm 90
Moloney, William Brendan 1943- WhoE 91
Molony, Brian BioIn 16
Molony, Gretchen St&PR 91
Molony, Michael Janssens, Jr. 1922- WhoAm 90, WhoSSW 91, WhoWor 91
Molotov, Vyacheslav 1890-1986 BioIn 16, WorAlBi
Molotsky, Barbara ODwPR 91
Molpus, C. Manly 1941- WhoSSW 91
Molpus, Dick 1949- WhoAm 90, WhoSSW 91
Mols, Jean Marie 1941- BiDrAPA 89
Mols, Manfred 1935- WhoWor 91
Molski, Frank Wlodzimierz 1942- WhoSSW 91
Molson, Anne 1824-1899 DcCanB 12
Molson, Eric H. 1937- WhoAm 90
Molstad, Runar 1964- WhoWor 91
Molster, Charles B., Jr. 1928- St&PR 91
Molster, Charles Bennett, Jr. 1928- WhoAm 90
Molt, Cynthia Marylee 1957- WhoAmW 91
Molteni, George James, Jr. 1943- WhoE 91
Moltke, Helmuth J. L., Graf Von 1848-1916 WorAlBi
Moltke, Helmuth K. B., Graf Von 1800-1891 WorAlBi
Moltmann, Gunter Ernst 1926- WhoWor 91
Moltz, David Albert BiDrAPA 89
Moltz, Howard 1927- WhoAm 90
Moltz, James Edward 1932- St&PR 91, WhoAm 90
Moltzau, Hughitt Gregory 1914- WhoSSW 91
Molyneax, Lyle Gordon 1934- St&PR 91
Molyneuy, Larry Earl 1954- St&PR 91
Molz, Emmet George 1922- St&PR 91
Molz, Fred John, III 1943- WhoAm 90
Molz, Redmond Kathleen 1928- WhoAm 90
Molz, Robert Joseph 1937- WhoAm 90
Molzahn, Ilse 1895-1981 EncCoWW
Molzahn, Martin 1938- WhoWor 91
Molzen, Dayton Frank 1926- WhoAm 90
Momaday, N. Scott BioIn 16
Momaday, N Scott 1934- MajTwCW

Momaday, Navarre Scott 1934- *WhoWrEP 89*
Momand, Pop 1886-1987 *EncACom*
Mombaers, Corneille *PenDiDA 89*
Moment, Gairdner B 1905- *WhoAm 90*
Moment, Gairdner Bostwick 1905- *WhoE 91*
Moment, Joan 1938- *WhoAmA 91*
Momigliano, Arnaldo *BioIn 16*
Momirovicc, Konstantin 1932- *WhoWor 91*
Momiyama, Nanae *WhoAmA 91*
Momjian, Set Charles 1930- *WhoAm 90*
Mommsen, Katharina 1925- *WhoAm 90*
Momoh, Joseph Saidu 1937- *WhoWor 91*
Momozawa, Chikara 1918- *WhoWor 91*
Mompati, Ruth *BioIn 16*
Mompesson, John *EncO&P 3*
Momsen, Wiliam Laurence 1932- *WhoWrEP 89*
Mona, David L. 1943- *ODwPR 91, WhoAm 90*
Mona, David Luther 1943- *St&PR 91*
Mona, Stephen Francis 1957- *WhoSSW 91*
Monacella, Suzana *BioIn 16*
Monacelli, Amleto Andres 1961- *WhoHisp 91*
Monacelli, Andrea 1958- *St&PR 91*
Monacelli, Gianfranco 1939- *WhoAm 90*
Monachino, Francis Leonard *WhoAm 90*
Monack, Ronald Albert 1929- *St&PR 91*
Monaco, Anthony Peter 1932- *WhoAm 90*
Monaco, Eugene A. *St&PR 91*
Monaco, Fabrizio 1942- *WhoWor 91*
Monaco, James 1942- *ConAu 33NR, WhoWrEP 89*
Monaco, James V 1885-1945 *OxCPMus*
Monaco, John 1932- *BiDrAPA 89*
Monaco, Joseph R. 1945- *WhoAm 90*
Monaco, Lenora Mae 1942- *WhoAmW 91*
Monaco, Mario del *PenDiMP*
Monaco, Michael Peter 1944- *WhoAm 90*
Monaco, Renato P *BiDrAPA 89*
Monaco, Richard 1940- *ConAu 33NR*
Monagan, Marilee 1947- *WhoAmW 91*
Monagas, Jose Gregorio 1795-1858 *BioIn 16*
Monagas, Jose Tadeo 1784-1868 *BioIn 16*
Monaghan, Dennis Michael 1943- *St&PR 91*
Monaghan, Gerard Joseph 1945- *WhoE 91*
Monaghan, James Peter 1927- *St&PR 91*
Monaghan, Keith 1921- *WhoAm 90, WhoAmA 91*
Monaghan, Leo Kenneth 1952- *WhoEmL 91*
Monaghan, Mary Patricia 1946- *WhoWrEP 89*
Monaghan, Nancy C. 1945- *WhoAm 90, WhoAmW 91*
Monaghan, Robert Emmet 1931- *St&PR 91*
Monaghan, Thomas *BioIn 16*
Monaghan, Thomas S. 1937- *ConAmBL*
Monaghan, Thomas Stephen 1937- *WhoAm 90*
Monaghan, Tom 1937- *CurBio 90 [port]*
Monaghan, William Henry 1928- *St&PR 91, WhoAm 90*
Monaghan, William Patrick 1944- *WhoE 91*
Monaghan, William Scott 1944- *WhoAmA 91*
Monago, Frank Anthony 1941- *St&PR 91*
Monahan, Bernard Dale 1931- *St&PR 91*
Monahan, Bernard Patrick 1936- *St&PR 91*
Monahan, Boyce Roderick 1947- *WhoSSW 91*
Monahan, David Emory 1937- *WhoAm 90*
Monahan, Edward F. 1928- *St&PR 91*
Monahan, Edward Francis 1928- *WhoAm 90*
Monahan, Gene Ritchie 1908- *WhoAmA 91*
Monahan, George Lennox, Jr. 1933- *WhoAm 90*
Monahan, Joe 1918-1973 *Ballpl 90*
Monahan, John *TwCCr&M 91*
Monahan, John E. 1940- *St&PR 91*
Monahan, John Franklin 1945- *WhoE 91*
Monahan, Kathleen Marie 1947- *WhoAmW 91*
Monahan, Kathleen Mary 1938- *WhoAmW 91*
Monahan, Len Francis 1948- *IntWWM 90*
Monahan, Marie Terry 1927- *WhoAmW 91*
Monahan, Marilyn Grace 1948- *WhoAmW 91*
Monahan, Thomas Andrew, Jr. 1920- *WhoE 91*
Monahan, Thomas F., Jr. 1939- *St&PR 91*
Monahan, Thomas Paul 1951- *WhoSSW 91*
Monahan, William G 1927?- *ConAu 132*
Monahan, William Louis 1940- *St&PR 91*
Monajem, Fred 1931- *St&PR 91*
Monan, James Donald 1924- *WhoAm 90, WhoE 91*
Monarrez, Alicia 1964- *WhoHisp 91*
Monas, Sidney 1924- *WhoAm 90, WhoSSW 91*
Monasee, Charles Arthur 1924- *WhoAm 90*
Monash, Curt Alfred 1960- *WhoE 91*
Monaster, Nathan *BioIn 16*
Monaster, Nathan 1916?-1990 *ConAu 131*
Monat, William Robert 1924- *WhoAm 90*
Monat-Haller, Rosalyn Kramer 1945- *WhoAmW 91, WhoSSW 91*
Monath, Norman *WhoAm 90*
Monath, Thomas Patrick 1940- *WhoE 91*
Monberg, Torben Axel 1929- *WhoWor 91*
Monbiot, George 1963- *ConAu 132*
Monboquette, Bill 1936- *Ballpl 90*
Moncachtape *WhNaAH*
Moncalvo, Franco Domenico 1928- *WhoWor 91*
Monchek, Lana Teri *WhoAmW 91*
Monchek, Meyer 1909- *BiDrAPA 89*
Moncher, Daniel Joseph 1960- *WhoEmL 91*
Moncivais, Emil Ray 1942- *WhoHisp 91*
Monck, Charles Stanley 1819-1894 *DcCanB 12*
Monck, Francis Ward *EncO&P 3*
Monck, Mary *BioIn 16*
Monck, Mary 1677?-1715 *BiDEWW*
Monck, Mary 1680?-1715 *FemiCLE*
Monckton, Lionel 1861-1924 *OxCPMus*
Monckton, Robert 1726-1782 *EncCRAm*
Monclova, Lidio Cruz *HispWr 90*
Moncreiff, Robert P. 1930- *St&PR 91, WhoAm 90*
Moncreiffe of that Ilk, Iain 1919-1985 *DcNaB 1981*
Moncure, Anne Marie 1956- *WhoSSW 91*
Moncure, Ashby Carter 1934- *WhoE 91, WhoWor 91*
Moncure, James Ashby 1926- *WhoAm 90*
Moncure, John Conway 1827- *AmLegL*
Moncure, John Lewis 1930- *WhoAm 90*
Moncys, Maria Teresa 1931- *WhoAmW 91*
Mond, Keith 1935- *St&PR 91*
Mond, Ludwig 1839-1909 *BioIn 16*
Mondabaugh, Susan May 1951- *WhoEmL 91*
Mondal, Wali Islam 1949- *WhoSSW 91*
Mondale, Eleanor *BioIn 16*
Mondale, Jason Edward 1941- *BiDrAPA 89*
Mondale, Joan Adams 1930- *WhoAm 90, WhoAmA 91*
Mondale, Walter F. 1928- *WorAlBi*
Mondale, Walter Frederick 1928- *BiDrUSE 89, WhoAm 90, WhoWor 91*
Mondani, Carol Frances 1964- *WhoE 91*
Mondavi, Margrit Biever- *BioIn 16*
Mondavi, Robert *BioIn 16*
Mondavi, Robert Gerald *WhoAm 90*
Mondavi, Rosa 1890?-1976 *BioIn 16*
Monday, John C. 1925- *St&PR 91*
Monday, John Christian 1925- *WhoAm 90*
Monday, Rick 1945- *Ballpl 90*
Mondecar, Mercedes Consuelo 1951- *WhoAmW 91*
Mondello, Joseph N. 1938- *WhoHisp 91*
Monder, Carl 1928- *WhoE 91*
Monder, Steven I. 1945- *WhoAm 90*
Monderer, Howard *BioIn 16*
Mondimore, Francis Mark 1953- *BiDrAPA 89*
Mondlin, Marvin 1927- *WhoE 91*
Mondon, Francois-Thomas 1709-1755 *PenDiDA 89*
Mondor, Kenneth James 1949- *St&PR 91, WhoAm 90*
Mondragon, Delfi 1941- *WhoHisp 91*
Mondragon, James I. *WhoHisp 91*
Mondragon, Jovencio Descarte 1946- *WhoSSW 91*
Mondragon, Roberto A. 1940- *BioIn 16, WhoHisp 91*
Mondrian, Piet 1872-1944 *BioIn 16, IntDcAA 90, WorAlBi*
Mondry, Ira *WhoAm 90*
Mondry, Ira 1953- *St&PR 91*
Mondshine, Clara *NewAgMG*
Mondy, Nell Irene 1921- *WhoAm 90*
Mone, Deborah Leigh-Wood 1959- *WhoE 91*
Mone, Robert Paul 1934- *WhoAm 90*
Moneda, Josefina M *BiDrAPA 89*
Monegal, Emir Rodriguez *ConAu 131, HispWr 90*
Monek, Donna Marie 1947- *WhoAmW 91*
Monek, Francis Herman 1913- *WhoAm 90*
Monelle, Raymond John 1937- *IntWWM 90*
Monello, Joseph D. 1945- *St&PR 91*
Moneo, Jose Rafael 1937- *BioIn 16, WhoAm 90*
Mones, Arthur 1919- *WhoAmA 91*
Monet, Claude 1840-1926 *BioIn 16, IntDcAA 90, WorAlBi*
Monet, Maria Pereira 1949- *WhoAm 90, WhoWor 91*
Moneti, Giancarlo 1931- *WhoE 91*
Monette, Donald J. 1934- *St&PR 91*
Monette, Francis Charles 1941- *WhoE 91*
Monette, Paul *BioIn 16*
Monette, Richard 1944- *OxCCanT*
Monette, Yvan *BiDrAPA 89*
Money, Charles Stewart 1941- *St&PR 91*
Money, David 1912- *IntWWM 90*
Money, Don 1947- *Ballpl 90*
Money, Jack W. 1929- *St&PR 91*
Money, James E. 1942- *St&PR 91*
Money, John 1921- *BioIn 16*
Money, John Marshall 1900- *St&PR 91*
Money, John William 1921- *WhoAm 90*
Moneypenny, Edward William 1942- *St&PR 91, WhoAm 90*
Moneypenny, Patricia M. 1963- *St&PR 91*
Monferrato, Angela Maria Poole 1948- *WhoAmW 91*
Monfils, Daryl Kenneth 1955- *WhoWor 91*
Monfort, Elias Riggs, III 1929- *WhoWor 91*
Monfort, Fernando Alberto 1954- *WhoSSW 91*
Monfort, Kenneth 1928- *St&PR 91*
Monfort, Myra Harriet 1938- *St&PR 91, WhoAm 90*
Monfried, David M. *ODwPR 91*
Monfried, Thomas S. 1932- *St&PR 91*
Mongan, Agnes 1905- *WhoAm 90, WhoAmA 91*
Mongan, Edwin Lawrence, Jr. 1919- *WhoE 91*
Mongan, James J. *BioIn 16*
Mongan, James John 1942- *WhoAm 90*
Mongan, Janet 1931- *WhoAm 90*
Mongan, Susan Annette 1965- *WhoE 91*
Mongan, Thomas R. *St&PR 91*
Mongan, Tod Vernon 1950- *St&PR 91*
Mongarella, Georgene Hughes 1951- *WhoAmW 91*
Monge, Carl Albert, Jr. 1930- *St&PR 91*
Monge, Gaspard 1746-1818 *BioIn 16*
Monge, Luis *BiDrAPA 89*
Monge, Luis Alberto *BioIn 16*
Monge, Pedro R. 1943- *WhoHisp 91*
Monge, Sid 1951- *Ballpl 90*
Mongeau, David C. 1956- *St&PR 91*
Mongeau, John Cecil 1946- *WhoE 91*
Mongelli, Thomas Guy 1952- *WhoE 91, WhoWor 91*
Mongeon, Marcel Dydzak 1956- *WhoWor 91*
Monger, Albert Jackson 1926- *WhoAm 90*
Monger, Harold Joseph 1910- *St&PR 91*
Mongiello, Frank P. 1928- *WhoE 91*
Mongilardi, Erman Piero 1932- *WhoWor 91*
Mongillo, Romolo T. 1939- *St&PR 91*
Mongno, Adele Grace 1947- *WhoE 91*
Mongold, Sandra K. 1947- *WhoAmW 91*
Mongoven, John O. 1938- *ODwPR 91*
Mongrain, Claude 1948- *WhoAmA 91*
Monguzzi, Bruno 1941- *ConDes 90*
Monheit, David *BiDrAPA 89*
Monhollon, Jimmie R. 1933- *St&PR 91*
Moniba, Harry Fumba 1937- *WhoWor 91*
Monica, Saint 332-387 *BioIn 16*
Monica, Laura L. 1957- *St&PR 91*
Monical, Mary Christine 1950- *WhoAmW 91*
Monical, Robert Duane 1925- *WhoAm 90*
Monical, Stuart Dean 1951- *WhoEmL 91*
Monicelli, Mario *BioIn 16*
Monier, J.-B. *PenDiDA 89*
Monig, Christopher *TwCCr&M 91*
Monillas, Albert Aloysius 1948- *WhoE 91*
Monios, Thomas 1938- *St&PR 91*
Monis, Ernest Antoine Emmanuel 1846-1929 *BiDFrPL*
Monismith, Carl Leroy 1926- *WhoAm 90*
Monita, Alfonso 1942- *St&PR 91*
Moniz, Antonio 1874-1955 *WorAlBi*
Moniz, Antonio Brandao 1956- *WhoWor 91*
Moniz, Ernest Jeffrey 1944- *WhoAm 90*
Monjo, F. N. 1924-1978 *AuBYP 90*
Monjo, John Cameron 1931- *WhoAm 90, WhoWor 91*
Monjoie, Alberic Marie Julien 1937- *WhoWor 91*
Monk, Allan 1942- *IntWWM 90*
Monk, Allan James 1942- *WhoAm 90*
Monk, Darilyn Anita 1951- *WhoAmW 91*
Monk, Douglas R. 1945- *St&PR 91*
Monk, Henry Wentworth 1827-1896 *DcCanB 12*
Monk, Janice Jones 1937- *WhoAmW 91*
Monk, Kathleen 1954- *WhoE 91*
Monk, Keith Victor 1926- *WhoWor 91*
Monk, Meredith *WhoAmA 91*
Monk, Meredith 1942- *BioIn 16*
Monk, Meredith 1943- *NotWoAT*
Monk, Meredith Jane 1942- *IntWWM 90, WhoAm 90, WhoE 91*
Monk, Nancy 1951- *WhoAmA 91*
Monk, Peter Anthony 1946- *IntWWM 90*
Monk, Robert Clarence 1930- *WhoSSW 91*
Monk, Robert Evan, Jr 1950- *WhoAmA 91*
Monk, Samuel Holt, II 1946- *WhoSSW 91*
Monk, Sean Charles 1916- *WhoWrEP 89*
Monk, Thelonious 1917-1982 *BioIn 16, WorAlBi*
Monk, Thelonious 1918-1982 *DrBlPA 90*
Monk, Thelonious Sphere 1917-1982 *OxCPMus*
Monk, Thymol *FemiCLE*
Monk, Wiley Philip 1950- *WhoSSW 91*
Monke, Edwin John 1925- *WhoAm 90*
Monke, J Victor *BiDrAPA 89*
Monkees, The *EncPR&S 89, OxCPMus, WhoNeCM A [port], WorAlBi*
Monkemeier, Edward Norbert 1926- *St&PR 91*
Monkman, Phyllis 1892-1976 *OxCPMus*
Monks, Robert Augustus Gardner 1933- *WhoAm 90*
Monkswell, Mary J H Collier, Baroness 1849-1930 *BioIn 16*
Monllor, Eduardo 1957- *WhoSSW 91*
Monlux, Andrew W. 1920- *WhoAm 90*
Monmonier, Mark 1943- *WhoAm 90*
Monmouth, James Scott, Duke of 1649-1685 *BioIn 16*
Monn, Gordon R. *St&PR 91*
Monnar, Marlene Mercedez 1953- *WhoHisp 91*
Monnard, Jean-Francois 1941- *IntWWM 90*
Monne, Noelia 1948- *WhoHisp 91*
Monnerville, Gaston 1897- *BiDFrPL*
Monnet, Jean 1888-1979 *BioIn 16, WorAlBi*
Monnet, Jean-Marie Omer Gabriel 1888-1979 *BiDFrPL*
Monnett, John Hamilton 1944- *WhoWrEP 89*
Monnett, Kenneth Eugene 1936- *St&PR 91*
Monnett, Victor Brown 1915- *WhoAm 90*
Monnier, Adrienne *BioIn 16*
Monnier, Jackie 1931- *WhoAmA 91*
Monnier, Mathilde 1887- *EncCoWW*
Monnier, Sophie de *EncCoWW*
Monnier, Sophie de Ruffey, Marquise de 1754-1789 *EncCoWW*
Monnier, Thyde *EncCoWW*
Monnig, John J. 1951- *St&PR 91*
Monnin, Michael J. 1951- *St&PR 91*
Monning, Richard Frank 1946- *WhoE 91*
Monninger, Joseph *BioIn 16*
Monninger, Robert Harold George 1918- *WhoAm 90, WhoWor 91*
Monnington, W. *BiDWomA*
Monnot, Gail Echols 1941- *WhoAmW 91*
Monnot, Marguerite 1903-1961 *OxCPMus*
Monnoyer, Jean-Baptiste 1635-1692 *PenDiDA 89*
Mono, Rune 1920- *ConDes 90*
Monod, Jacques 1910-1976 *WorAlBi*
Monod, Jacques-Louis 1927- *IntWWM 90*
Monod, Jacques Lucien 1910-1976 *DcScB S2*
Monongye, Preston Lee 1927-1988 *WhoAmA 91N*
Monopolis, Spyros John *BiDrAPA 89*
Monosiet, Frederic Louis 1953- *BiDrAPA 89*
Monosoff, Sonya 1927- *IntWWM 90*
Monosson, Adolf F. 1926- *St&PR 91*
Monoszon, Boris 1955- *IntWWM 90*
Monot, Pierre-Alain 1961- *IntWWM 90*
Monplaisir, Sharon *BioIn 16*
Monrad, Ditlev Gothard 1811-1887 *BioIn 16*
Monrad, Ernest E. 1930- *St&PR 91*
Monrad, Ernest Ejner 1930- *WhoE 91*
Monreal, Gerhard 1928- *WhoWor 91*
Monro, Alexander 1813-1896 *DcCanB 12*
Monro, David Hector 1911- *WhoWor 91*
Monro, Frances Berniece 1922- *WhoAmW 91*
Monro, James Alexander, Jr. 1949- *WhoAm 90*
Monro, Matt 1930-1985 *DcNaB 1981, OxCPMus*
Monro-Borton, Marsha *ODwPR 91*
Monroche, Andre Victor Jacques 1941- *WhoWor 91*
Monroe Brothers *WhoNeCM C*
Monroe, Alexander 1817-1905 *AmLegL*
Monroe, Barbara 1913- *St&PR 91*
Monroe, Betty Iverson 1922- *WhoAmA 91*
Monroe, Bill *WhoNeCM C [port]*
Monroe, Bill 1877-1915 *Ballpl 90*
Monroe, Bill 1911- *BioIn 16, OxCPMus*
Monroe, Brooks 1925- *St&PR 91, WhoAm 90*
Monroe, Burt Leavelle, Jr. 1930- *WhoAm 90*
Monroe, C. Conrad 1928- *St&PR 91*
Monroe, Carl Dean, III 1960- *WhoSSW 91*
Monroe, Carroll Dean *BiDrAPA 89*
Monroe, Charles L., III 1943- *St&PR 91*

Monroe, Christopher John 1951- *WhoE 91*
Monroe, Diana Lynn 1948- *WhoSSW 91*
Monroe, Donald Oran 1930- *St&PR 91*
Monroe, Earl 1944- *WorAlBi*
Monroe, Edwin Wall 1927- *WhoAm 90*
Monroe, Elizabeth Kortright 1768-1830 *BioIn 16*
Monroe, Gerald 1926- *WhoAmA 91*
Monroe, Harriet 1860-1936 *BioAmW, FemiCLE*
Monroe, Haskell M., Jr. 1931- *WhoAm 90, WhoWor 91*
Monroe, Herman Eugene, Jr. 1930- *St&PR 91*
Monroe, Hunter Kelly 1962- *WhoE 91*
Monroe, James 1758-1831 *BiDrUSE 89, BioIn 16, WorAlBi*
Monroe, James Ivan 1945- *St&PR 91*
Monroe, James Walter 1936- *WhoAm 90*
Monroe, Joan Kiddell- 1908-1972 *BioIn 16*
Monroe, John Thaddeus, Jr. 1929- *BiDrAPA 89*
Monroe, Julia Kathryn 1961- *WhoAmW 91*
Monroe, Karen Marie 1962- *WhoAmW 91*
Monroe, Kendyl Kurth 1936- *WhoAm 90*
Monroe, L. A. J. 1919- *WhoAm 90*
Monroe, Leanne E. 1960- *ODwPR 91*
Monroe, Lee Alexander 1932- *WhoAm 90*
Monroe, Linda Roach 1952- *WhoHisp 91*
Monroe, Lyle *AuBYP 90, MajTwCW*
Monroe, Malcolm *BioIn 16*
Monroe, Margaret Ellen 1914- *WhoAmW 91*
Monroe, Marilyn *ConAu 129*
Monroe, Marilyn 1926-1962 *BioAmW, BioIn 16, WorAlBi*
Monroe, Mark Eden 1954- *St&PR 91*
Monroe, Mary Beth 1947- *WhoSSW 91*
Monroe, Max 1956- *WhoSSW 91*
Monroe, Melrose 1919- *WhoSSW 91*
Monroe, Michael J. 1948- *ODwPR 91, St&PR 91*
Monroe, Moses 1842-1895 *DcCanB 12*
Monroe, Murray Shipley 1925- *WhoAm 90, WhoWor 91*
Monroe, N. Carl 1921- *St&PR 91*
Monroe, Robert A. 1915- *EncPaPR 91*
Monroe, Robert Rawson 1927- *WhoAm 90*
Monroe, Ronald *BioIn 16*
Monroe, Ronald B. *BioIn 16*
Monroe, Rose Maria Mask 1955- *WhoE 91*
Monroe, Russell R 1920- *BiDrAPA 89*
Monroe, Russell Ronald 1920- *WhoAm 90*
Monroe, Russell Ronald, Jr. 1954- *BiDrAPA 89*
Monroe, Stanley Edwin 1902- *WhoWor 91*
Monroe, Thomas Edward 1947- *WhoAm 90*
Monroe, Thomas Frank 1944- *WhoAm 90*
Monroe, Vaughn 1911-1973 *OxCPMus, WorAlBi*
Monroe, William Eugene 1930- *St&PR 91, WhoSSW 91*
Monroe, William R. 1921- *St&PR 91*
Monroe, Willys H. 1924- *St&PR 91*
Monroe, Yvonne Lee *BiDrAPA 89*
Monroy, Gladys H. 1937- *WhoAmW 91*
Monsees, Gregg Peters 1949- *WhoEmL 91*
Monsees, Gregg Peters, Sr. 1949- *St&PR 91*
Monsees, Warren R. 1922- *St&PR 91*
Monsell, Elizabeth G. 1955- *St&PR 91*
Monsell, Elizabeth Gay 1955- *WhoEmL 91*
Monsen, Elaine Ranker 1935- *WhoAm 90, WhoWor 91*
Monsen, Raymond Joseph, Jr. 1931- *WhoAm 90*
Monserda de Macia, Dolors 1845-1919 *EncCoWW*
Monshaw, Valdemar Russell 1926- *WhoAm 90*
Monsky, John Bertrand 1930- *WhoAm 90*
Monsky, Michael David Wolf Von Sommer 1947- *WhoEmL 91*
Monsky, Sharon *BioIn 16*
Monson, Ann Marie 1951- *WhoAmW 91*
Monson, Arch, Jr. 1913- *WhoAm 90*
Monson, Carol Lynn 1946- *WhoAmW 91, WhoWor 91*
Monson, David Smith 1945- *WhoAm 90*
Monson, Dianne Lynn 1934- *WhoAmW 91*
Monson, Forrest Truman 1915- *WhoAm 90*
Monson, James Edward 1932- *WhoAm 90*
Monson, Nancy Eleanor 1942- *WhoAmW 91*
Monson, Nancy Peckel 1959- *WhoAmW 91*
Monson, Nicholas *BioIn 16*
Monson, Robert Joseph 1947- *WhoE 91*
Monson, Terry Lewis 1947- *WhoEmL 91*
Monson, Thomas Lee 1951- *WhoEmL 91*
Monson, Thomas Spencer 1927- *St&PR 91, WhoAm 90*
Monsour, Roy Christopher *BiDrAPA 89*
Mont, Hallie Buchanan 1922- *WhoAmW 91*
Mont, Willem de *PenDiMP*
Mont, William G. 1929- *St&PR 91*
Montag, Anthony 1934- *St&PR 91*
Montag, David 1954- *St&PR 91*
Montag, John Joseph, II 1948- *WhoAm 90*
Montag, Rudolf Curt 1942- *WhoWor 91*
Montaggioni, Francois 1931- *St&PR 91*
Montagna, Richard A. 1948- *St&PR 91*
Montagna, William 1913- *WhoAm 90*
Montagnier, Francois Paul 1931- *WhoWor 91*
Montagnier, Luc *BioIn 16*
Montagnier, Luc Antoine 1932- *WhoWor 91*
Montagu, Ashley 1905- *WhoAm 90, WorAlBi*
Montagu, Elizabeth 1720-1800 *FemiCLE*
Montagu, Elizabeth Robinson 1720-1800 *BioIn 16*
Montagu, Ewen Edward Samuel 1901-1985 *DcNaB 1981*
Montagu, Ivor Goldsmid Samuel 1904-1984 *DcNaB 1981*
Montagu, Mary Pierrepont Wortley 1689-1762 *BioIn 16*
Montagu, Mary Wortley 1689-1762 *BiDEWW, DcLB 101 [port], -95 [port], FemiCLE*
Montague, Barbara Ann 1929- *WhoAmW 91*
Montague, Bert Larry 1943- *St&PR 91*
Montague, Brian John 1951- *WhoAm 90*
Montague, David Ririe 1944- *WhoWrEP 89*
Montague, Diana 1954- *IntWWM 90*
Montague, Ed 1948- *Ballpl 90*
Montague, Eddie 1905-1988 *Ballpl 90*
Montague, Eugene Bryan 1928- *WhoAm 90*
Montague, Gary Leslie 1939- *WhoWor 91*
Montague, James L 1906- *WhoAmA 91, WhoE 91*
Montague, John *BioIn 16*
Montague, John 1929- *MajTwCW*
Montague, John 1947- *Ballpl 90*
Montague, Mary Seymour *FemiCLE*
Montague, Owen Douglas 1962- *WhoAm 90*
Montague, Rene Ann 1960- *WhoAmW 91*
Montague, Robert Joseph 1946- *St&PR 91*
Montague, Ruth Dubarry *WhoAmA 91*
Montague, Stephen Rowley 1943- *IntWWM 90*
Montague, Thersey Roshaiy 1955- *WhoE 91*
Montague, William Patrick 1946- *St&PR 91*
Montaigne, La Fille d'Alliance de M. de *EncCoWW*
Montaigne, Michel De 1533-1592 *WorAlBi*
Montalba, Clara 1840?-1929 *BiDWomA*
Montalba, Ellen 1846?-1902? *BiDWomA*
Montalba, Henrietta Skerret 1856-1893 *BiDWomA*
Montalba, Hilda 1844?-1919 *BiDWomA*
Montalban, Ricardo 1920?- *BioIn 16, WhoAm 90, WhoHisp 91, WorAlBi*
Montalbano, Carmelo 1950- *St&PR 91*
Montalbano, Joseph A. 1954- *WhoE 91*
Montalbano, Joseph Edward 1927- *WhoAm 90*
Montalbano, Salvatore Aurelio 1938- *WhoSSW 91*
Montalbetti, David Joseph *BiDrAPA 89*
Montalcini, Paola Levi- 1909- *BioIn 16*
Montalcini, Rita Levi- 1909- *BioIn 16*
Montale, Eugenio 1896-1981 *ConAu 30NR, MajTwCW, WorAlBi*
Montalenti, Giuseppe 1904- *WhoWor 91*
Montalto, Richard Michael 1951- *WhoSSW 91*
Montalva, Eduardo Frei 1911-1982 *BioIn 16*
Montalvo, Francisco E 1942- *BiDrAPA 89*
Montalvo, Frank A. 1950- *WhoHisp 91*
Montalvo, Jose Luis 1946- *WhoHisp 91, WhoWrEP 89*
Montalvo, Juan 1832-1889 *BioIn 16*
Montalvo, Maria Antonia 1951- *WhoHisp 91*
Montalvo, Sergio 1945- *WhoWor 91*
Montalvo-Carbia, Andres *BiDrAPA 89*
Montambault, Leonce 1932- *WhoAm 90*
Montana, Arthur 1935- *WhoAm 90*
Montana, Bob 1920-1975 *EncACom, WhoAmA 91N*
Montana, Claude *BioIn 16*
Montana, Claude 1949- *ConDes 90*
Montana, Janice 1954- *WhoEmL 91*
Montana, Joe *BioIn 16*
Montana, Joe 1956- *WorAlBi*
Montana, Jordi 1949- *WhoWor 91*
Montana, Joseph C., Jr. 1956- *WhoAm 90*
Montana, Patrick Joseph 1937- *WhoAm 90*
Montana, Patsy *WhoNeCM C*
Montana, Paul Bernard 1947- *WhoE 91*
Montana, Pietro 1890-1978 *WhoAmA 91N*
Montanari, Fred W. 1935- *St&PR 91*
Montanari, Mauro 1955- *WhoWor 91*
Montanaro, Robert Joseph 1961- *St&PR 91*
Montanaro-McMullen, Linda 1945- *WhoAmW 91*
Montand, Yves *BioIn 16*
Montand, Yves 1921- *OxCPMus, WhoWor 91, WorAlBi*
Montandon, Denys 1938- *WhoWor 91*
Montane, Olga Gonzalez 1927- *WhoHisp 91*
Montaner, Jose L 1958- *BiDrAPA 89*
Montanez, Marta *PenDiMP*
Montanez, Pablo I. 1958- *WhoHisp 91*
Montanez, William Joseph 1952- *WhoHisp 91*
Montanez, Willie 1948- *Ballpl 90*
Montani, Anthony Albert 1939- *St&PR 91*
Montano, Carlos Xavier 1955- *WhoHisp 91*
Montano, David Ricardo 1951- *IntWWM 90*
Montano, Linda 1942- *WhoAmA 91*
Montano, Mary L. *WhoHisp 91*
Montanus, Lawrence W. 1945- *WhoAm 90, WhoSSW 91*
Montarsolo, Paolo 1925- *IntWWM 90*
Montasser, Hany Mohamed *BiDrAPA 89*
Montavon, Dennis R. 1948- *St&PR 91*
Montblanc, Robert Gene 1926- *St&PR 91*
Montcalm, Louis-Joseph De 1712-1759 *EncCRAm*
Montcalm, Norman Joseph 1945- *WhoAm 90*
Montcalm-Gozon, Louis Joseph De 1712-1759 *WhNaAH*
Montcalm-Grozon, Louis Joseph De 1712-1759 *WorAlBi*
Monte, Bryan Robert 1957- *WhoWrEP 89*
Monte, Nick 1916- *St&PR 91*
Monte, Salvatore Joseph 1939- *St&PR 91*
Monte, Toti dal *PenDiMP*
Monteagudo, Aurelio 1943- *Ballpl 90*
Monteagudo, Eduardo 1953- *WhoHisp 91*
Monteagudo, Lourdes Maria 1955- *WhoHisp 91*
Monteagudo, Rene 1916-1973 *Ballpl 90*
Montealegre, Jose Ramiro 1959- *WhoWor 91*
Montealegre, Lily Bendana 1961- *WhoHisp 91*
Montean, John Joseph 1916- *WhoAm 90*
Montebello, Angelina 1922- *St&PR 91*
Montecalvo, Anthony Louis *BiDrAPA 89*
Montecino, Marcel *ConAu 131*
Monteferrante, Judith Catherine 1949- *WhoAmW 91*
Montefiore, Moses 1784-1885 *BioIn 16*
Montefusco, John 1950- *Ballpl 90*
Monteilhet, Hubert 1928- *TwCCr&M 91B*
Monteiro, Edward Joseph *BiDrAPA 89*
Monteiro, Isaac 1938- *WhoAmA 91*
Monteiro, Manuel James 1926- *St&PR 91, WhoAm 90*
Monteith, David Yates, III 1935- *WhoSSW 91*
Monteith, Diana Lynne 1957- *St&PR 91*
Monteith, Dianne Souther 1935- *WhoAmW 91*
Monteith, Don 1942- *St&PR 91*
Monteith, Edward Everett, Jr. 1922- *St&PR 91*
Monteith, Linda Gail 1955- *BiDrAPA 89*
Monteith, Walter H., Jr. 1930- *St&PR 91*
Monteith, Walter Henry, Jr. 1930- *WhoAm 90, WhoE 91*
Montejano, Rodolfo 1938- *WhoHisp 91*
Montel, Janet Marie 1954- *WhoAmW 91*
Montel, Paul 1876-1975 *DcScB S2*
Monteleone, Constantine *BiDrAPA 89*
Monteleone, Iona *St&PR 91*
Monteleone, Luigi *BiDrAPA 89*
Monteleone, Rich 1963- *Ballpl 90*
Montelione, Louis *BioIn 16*
Montelius, Susan Ann 1956- *WhoWrEP 89*
Montellaro, Lee R. 1945- *St&PR 91*
Montemarano, Anthony 1946- *St&PR 91*
Montemayor, Carlos R. 1945- *WhoSSW 91*
Montemayor, Carlos Rene 1945- *WhoHisp 91*
Montemayor, Fernando R. *St&PR 91*
Montemurro, G. A. 1933- *St&PR 91*
Montenay, Georgette de 1540-1581 *EncCoWW*
Montenecourt, Bland Symington 1942-1987 *BioIn 16*
Montenegro, Benito Jeronimo Feijoo y 1676-1764 *BioIn 16*
Montenegro, Milton 1934- *BioIn 16*
Montenegro, Roberto 1887-1968 *ArtLatA, BioIn 16*
Montenegro, Roger Maximiliano 1936- *BiDrAPA 89*
Monteneri, Alessandro *PenDiDA 89*
Montenes, Francis Anthony 1930- *St&PR 91*
Monterey, Honey *WhoWrEP 89*
Montero, Darrel Martin 1946- *WhoEmL 91, WhoWor 91*
Montero, Edmundo 1945- *WhoWor 91*
Montero, Emilio F 1932- *BiDrAPA 89*
Montero, Gerardo M 1947- *BiDrAPA 89*
Montero, J A 1937- *BiDrAPA 89*
Montero, Rosa 1951- *EncCoWW, IntvSpW [port]*
Montero-Decock, Francisco *BiDrAPA 89*
Montero Rodriguez, Juan Esteban 1879?-1948 *BioIn 16*
Monterrey, Maximo R *BiDrAPA 89*
Monterroso, Amalia *WhoHisp 91*
Monterroso, Augusto 1921- *HispWr 90*
Montes, Alberto L 1928- *BiDrAPA 89*
Montes, Fidel Eugenio *BiDrAPA 89*
Montes, Francisco 1932- *BiDrAPA 89*
Montes, Ismael 1861-1933 *BioIn 16*
Montes, Jesus Enrique 1944- *WhoHisp 91*
Montes, Jose Cortez *BiDrAPA 89*
Montes, Jose M. 1931- *WhoWor 91*
Montes, Mary *WhoHisp 91*
Montes, Segundo *BioIn 16*
Montes, Virginia E. 1943- *WhoHisp 91*
Montes de Oca, Marco Antonio 1932- *HispWr 90*
Montes-Gallo, Delia M Clara 1932- *BiDrAPA 89*
Montes Huidobro, Matias 1931- *BioIn 16*
Montesano, Aldo Mazia 1939- *WhoWor 91*
Montesano, Frank Anthony 1939- *St&PR 91*
Montesano, Gail Jean 1948- *WhoE 91*
Montesi, John W. 1920- *St&PR 91*
Montesino, Orlando C. 1950- *St&PR 91*
Montesino, Paul V. 1937- *St&PR 91, WhoHisp 91*
Montesinos Santalucia, Vicente 1951- *WhoWor 91*
Montesquieu, Baron de 1689-1755 *BioIn 16*
Montesquieu, Baron De La Brede Et De 1689-1755 *WorAlBi*
Montessori, Maria 1870-1952 *BioIn 16, WorAlBi*
Monteux, Claude 1920- *IntWWM 90, PenDiMP*
Monteux, Pierre 1875-1964 *PenDiMP, WorAlBi*
Montevecchi, Liliane *BioIn 16*
Monteverde, Ronald Peter 1947- *BiDrAPA 89*
Monteverdi, Claudio 1567-1643 *BioIn 16, PenDiMP A, WorAlBi*
Montezon, Lourdes L *BiDrAPA 89*
Montezuma 1466-1520 *EncCRAm*
Montezuma, Carlos 1867?-1923 *WhNaAH*
Montford, John Thomas 1943- *WhoSSW 91*
Montforts, Franz-Peter 1948- *WhoWor 91*
Montgelas, Rudolph Maximilian 1913-1988 *BioIn 16*
Montgolfier, Jacques Etienne 1745-1799 *WorAlBi*
Montgolfier, Joseph Michel 1740-1810 *WorAlBi*
Montgomerie, Norah 1913- *AuBYP 90*
Montgomery, Alexandra E. 1957- *St&PR 91*
Montgomery, Andrew Stuart 1960- *WhoEmL 91, WhoWor 91*
Montgomery, Barbara 1939- *DrBlPA 90*
Montgomery, Benjamin F. 1835?- *AmLegL*
Montgomery, Bernard Law 1887-1976 *WorAlBi*
Montgomery, Betty D. *WhoAmW 91*
Montgomery, Billie Lee 1953- *WhoAmW 91*
Montgomery, Bob 1944- *Ballpl 90*
Montgomery, Bruce 1927- *IntWWM 90*
Montgomery, C. Lew 1930- *St&PR 91*
Montgomery, C. Lewis 1930- *WhoAm 90*
Montgomery, Carl Robert 1939- *WhoSSW 91*
Montgomery, Catherine Ann 1928- *WhoWrEP 89*
Montgomery, Charles Franklin 1910-1978 *WhoAmA 91N*
Montgomery, Charles Howard 1930- *WhoAm 90*
Montgomery, Charlotte A. *WhoAmW 91*
Montgomery, Chester Craig 1937- *St&PR 91*
Montgomery, Clark Taylor 1941- *St&PR 91, WhoAm 90*
Montgomery, Claude 1912- *WhoE 91*
Montgomery, Claude 1912-1990 *WhoAmA 91N*
Montgomery, Clinton 1938- *BiDrAPA 89*
Montgomery, David Bruce 1938- *WhoAm 90, WhoWrEP 89*
Montgomery, David Campbell 1936- *WhoAm 90*
Montgomery, David Paul *WhoAm 90*
Montgomery, De Witt H, Jr. *BiDrAPA 89*

Montgomery, Deane 1909- *WhoAm 90, WhoSSW 91*
Montgomery, Denise Karen 1951- *WhoAmW 91*
Montgomery, Don W. 1925- *St&PR 91*
Montgomery, Donald Joseph 1917- *WhoAm 90*
Montgomery, Donald Russell 1920- *WhoAm 90*
Montgomery, Edward Alembert, Jr. 1934- *St&PR 91, WhoAm 90*
Montgomery, Edward Benjamin 1915- *WhoAm 90*
Montgomery, Elizabeth 1902-1985 *AuBYP 90*
Montgomery, Elizabeth 1933- *WhoAm 90, WorAlBi*
Montgomery, Florence 1843-1923 *FemiCLE*
Montgomery, Frank *EarBlAP*
Montgomery, Frederick A 1939- *BiDrAPA 89*
Montgomery, George 1938- *WhoWrEP 89*
Montgomery, George Cranwell 1944- *WhoAm 90, WhoE 91, WhoWor 91*
Montgomery, George Franklin 1921- *WhoAm 90*
Montgomery, Gillespie V. *BioIn 16, WhoAm 90, WhoSSW 91*
Montgomery, Gladys *WhoAmW 91*
Montgomery, Harold Hench 1959- *WhoSSW 91*
Montgomery, Helen 1861-1934 *BioIn 16*
Montgomery, Henry Irving 1924- *WhoWor 91*
Montgomery, Herbert D. 1942- *St&PR 91*
Montgomery, Howard Kent 1943- *WhoSSW 91*
Montgomery, Hubert Theron, Jr. 1935- *WhoSSW 91*
Montgomery, Jack *NewAgMG*
Montgomery, James 1771-1854 *DcLB 93 [port]*
Montgomery, James 1943- *IntWWM 90*
Montgomery, James E. 1929- *St&PR 91*
Montgomery, James F. 1934- *St&PR 91*
Montgomery, James Fischer 1934- *WhoAm 90*
Montgomery, James Loyd 1924- *St&PR 91*
Montgomery, James Morton 1931- *WhoAm 90*
Montgomery, Janet Ann 1946- *WhoAmW 91*
Montgomery, Jeff 1962- *Ballpl 90*
Montgomery, Jerry E. 1946- *WhoSSW 91*
Montgomery, Jim 1927- *WhoAm 90*
Montgomery, Joel E. 1942- *St&PR 91*
Montgomery, John *WhoWrEP 89*
Montgomery, John Atterbury 1924- *WhoAm 90*
Montgomery, John Dickey 1920- *WhoAm 90, WhoWrEP 89*
Montgomery, John Joseph 1858-1911 *BioIn 16*
Montgomery, John McVey 1919- *WhoWrEP 89*
Montgomery, John Sloan 1933- *BiDrAPA 89*
Montgomery, John Vincent 1947- *WhoEmL 91*
Montgomery, John Warwick 1931- *WhoAm 90, WhoWor 91*
Montgomery, Johnny Lester 1934- *WhoAm 90*
Montgomery, Joseph William 1951- *WhoEmL 91*
Montgomery, Judy Glass 1945- *WhoAmW 91*
Montgomery, K. L. *FemiCLE*
Montgomery, Kenneth 1943- *IntWWM 90, PenDiMP*
Montgomery, L. M. 1874-1942 *BioIn 16, FemiCLE*
Montgomery, Larry H. 1945- *St&PR 91*
Montgomery, Laurie Chase *ODwPR 91*
Montgomery, Leslie David 1939- *WhoAm 90*
Montgomery, Lewis Hipple 1928- *WhoWor 91*
Montgomery, Lloyd Dan *BiDrAPA 89*
Montgomery, Lola June 1917- *WhoAmW 91*
Montgomery, Lucy Maud 1874-1942 *BioIn 16, DcLB 92 [port]*
Montgomery, Lyle Barnes *BiDrAPA 89*
Montgomery, Lynn Cobb 1949- *BiDrAPA 89, WhoE 91*
Montgomery, M. Ann 1945- *BiDrAPA 89*
Montgomery, Marianne Beatty 1931- *WhoSSW 91*
Montgomery, Marion 1925- *WhoWrEP 89*
Montgomery, Maurice R. *BioIn 16*
Montgomery, Melvin Boyce 1925- *IntWWM 90*
Montgomery, Michael Davis 1936- *St&PR 91*
Montgomery, Parker G. 1928- *St&PR 91*
Montgomery, Parker Gilbert 1928- *WhoAm 90*
Montgomery, Patricia Aline 1954- *WhoE 91*
Montgomery, Patrick 1949- *St&PR 91*
Montgomery, R. L. 1922- *St&PR 91*
Montgomery, Rex 1923- *WhoAm 90*
Montgomery, Richard 1738-1775 *EncCRAm, WorAlBi*
Montgomery, Richard Harlan 1923- *St&PR 91*
Montgomery, Robert 1904-1981 *WorAlBi*
Montgomery, Robert 1924-1988 *BioIn 16*
Montgomery, Robert Alexander Gaw, Jr. 1936- *WhoE 91*
Montgomery, Robert H., Jr. 1953- *WhoEmL 91*
Montgomery, Robert Humphrey, Jr. 1923- *WhoAm 90*
Montgomery, Robert Morel, Jr. 1930- *WhoAm 90*
Montgomery, Robert Raynor 1943- *St&PR 91*
Montgomery, Robert William 1933- *IntWWM 90*
Montgomery, Roger 1925- *WhoAm 90*
Montgomery, Roy Delbert 1926- *WhoAm 90*
Montgomery, Royce W. 1945- *St&PR 91*
Montgomery, Ruth *EncO&P 3, EncPaPR 91*
Montgomery, Ruth C. *WhoAmW 91*
Montgomery, Ruth Shick *NewAgE 90, WhoAm 90, WhoWrEP 89*
Montgomery, Rutherford George 1894- *AuBYP 90*
Montgomery, Sheryl Elizabeth 1958- *WhoSSW 91*
Montgomery, Spencer W. *St&PR 91*
Montgomery, Steven J. 1946- *St&PR 91*
Montgomery, Susan Jane 1944- *St&PR 91*
Montgomery, Susan Renee 1954- *WhoAmW 91*
Montgomery, Suzanne Howard 1949- *WhoAmW 91*
Montgomery, Theodore Ashton 1923- *WhoAm 90*
Montgomery, Thomas Charles 1955- *St&PR 91, WhoEmL 91*
Montgomery, Thomas Larry 1939- *WhoE 91*
Montgomery, Velmanette *BioIn 16, WhoAmW 91*
Montgomery, Walter G. *ODwPR 91*
Montgomery, Walter George 1945- *WhoAm 90*
Montgomery, Walter S. *BioIn 16*
Montgomery, Walter S. 1900- *St&PR 91*
Montgomery, Wes 1925-1968 *BioIn 16, OxCPMus, WorAlBi*
Montgomery, William Adam 1933- *WhoAm 90*
Montgomery, William David 1944- *WhoE 91*
Montgomery, William J. 1930- *WhoAm 90*
Montgomery, William Jackson 1929- *WhoAm 90*
Montgomery, William Jester 1930- *St&PR 91*
Montgomery, William L. 1934- *IntWWM 90*
Montgomery, William Wayne 1923- *WhoAm 90*
Montgomery, Yolonda Denese 1958- *WhoAmW 91, WhoE 91*
Montgoris, William J. *St&PR 91*
Montgrain, Noel 1933- *BiDrAPA 89, WhoAm 90*
Monthan, Guy 1925- *WhoAmA 91*
Montherlant, Henry de 1896-1972 *MajTwCW*
Monti, Dennis Joseph 1948- *WhoE 91*
Monti, Donald Peter 1941- *WhoSSW 91*
Monti, John 1957- *WhoAmA 91*
Monti, John Louis 1933- *WhoSSW 91*
Monti, Laura Anne 1959- *WhoAmW 91*
Monti, Renard George 1950- *WhoEmL 91*
Monti, Stephen Arion 1939- *WhoAm 90*
Monti, Vincent Morris 1926- *St&PR 91*
Monticciolo, Joseph Domenick 1937- *WhoAm 90*
Monticelli, Adolphe Joseph Thomas 1824-1886 *BioIn 16*
Monticue, William Edward 1953- *WhoE 91*
Montidoro, Emy B. 1957- *St&PR 91*
Montiel, Eduardo Luis 1949- *WhoWor 91*
Montiel, Jose *WhoHisp 91*
Montiel, Sue 1960- *WhoAmW 91*
Montigny, Jenny 1875-1937 *BiDWomA*
Montigny, Louvigny de 1876-1955 *DcLB 92 [port]*
Montijn, Ida Helena 1952- *WhoWor 91*
Montijn, Justus Adriaan Pieter 1922- *WhoWor 91*
Montijo, Ben 1940- *WhoHisp 91*
Montijo, Ralph Elias, Jr. 1928- *WhoAm 90, WhoHisp 91, WhoSSW 91, WhoWor 91*
Montileone, Dominic Anthony 1943- *WhoE 91*
Montilla, Cesar A., Jr. 1942- *St&PR 91*
Montini, Giovanni Battista 1897-1978 *BioIn 16*
Montinola, Antonio B 1938- *BiDrAPA 89*
Montjoy, Richard Wilson, II 1953- *WhoEmL 91*
Montlack, Edith *WhoAmA 91*
Montlack, Edith 1921- *WhoE 91*
Montle, Janice E. 1951- *WhoAmW 91*
Montle, Paul J. 1947- *St&PR 91*
Montle, Paul Joseph 1947- *WhoAm 90*
Montmerle, Bruno Didier 1949- *St&PR 91*
Montminy, Theophile 1842-1899 *DcCanB 12*
Montminy, Tracy 1911- *WhoAmA 91*
Monto, Alexander V *BiDrAPA 89*
Monto, Pertti Ilmari 1936- *WhoWor 91*
Montolieu, baronne de 1751-1832 *EncCoWW*
Montonen, Michael Kari 1957- *WhoSSW 91*
Montooth, Sheila Christine 1952- *WhoAmW 91*
Montopoli, Duane Carmen 1948- *St&PR 91*
Montori, Rosa Tudela Bentin de 1941- *WhoWor 91*
Montorsi, Sergio 1925- *ODwPR 91*
Montoto, Manuel 1942- *St&PR 91*
Montour, Madame 1684?-1752? *EncCRAm*
Montouri, Claudia B. 1951- *St&PR 91*
Montoya, A. R. *WhoHisp 91*
Montoya, Abran Felipe, Jr. 1948- *WhoHisp 91*
Montoya, Alfredo C. 1921- *WhoHisp 91*
Montoya, Alvaro 1942- *WhoHisp 91*
Montoya, Benjamin F. *WhoHisp 91*
Montoya, Carlos Garcia 1903- *WhoAm 90, WhoE 91*
Montoya, Charles William 1937- *WhoHisp 91*
Montoya, Demetrio H. 1937- *WhoHisp 91*
Montoya, Florentino 1858-1918 *BioIn 16*
Montoya, Frieda M. 1923- *WhoHisp 91*
Montoya, Gregory R 1948- *BiDrAPA 89*
Montoya, John J. 1945- *WhoHisp 91*
Montoya, Jorge P. 1946- *St&PR 91, WhoAm 90, WhoHisp 91*
Montoya, Jose 1932- *BioIn 16, ConAu 131, HispWr 90*
Montoya, Joseph M. 1915-1978 *BioIn 16*
Montoya, Joseph O. 1945- *WhoHisp 91*
Montoya, Juan *BioIn 16*
Montoya, Julio Cesar 1948- *WhoHisp 91*
Montoya, Malaquias 1938- *BioIn 16, WhoHisp 91*
Montoya, Max *WhoHisp 91*
Montoya, Nancy Lucero 1954- *WhoHisp 91*
Montoya, Nestor 1862-1923 *AmLegL, BioIn 16*
Montoya, Regina T. 1953- *WhoHisp 91*
Montoya, Richard 1960- *WhoHisp 91*
Montoya, Steve Leo 1949- *WhoEmL 91*
Montoya, Thomas Paul 1953- *WhoHisp 91*
Montpensier, Duchesse de 1627-1693 *EncCoWW*
Montresor, Beni 1926- *AuBYP 90, IntWWM 90*
Montresor, F. F. 1843-1923 *FemiCLE*
Montrone, Paul M. 1941- *St&PR 91*
Montrone, Paul Michael 1941- *WhoAm 90*
Montrone, Thomas L. 1948- *St&PR 91*
Mont'Ros-Mendoza, Theresa 1952- *WhoHisp 91*
Montrose, Donald W. 1923- *WhoAm 90*
Montrose, Maynard Ellsworth 1903- *WhoAm 90*
Montross, Franklin, IV 1956- *St&PR 91*
Montry, Gerald F. 1938- *St&PR 91*
Monts, Pierre Du Guast, Sieur De 1560?-1628 *EncCRAm*
Monts De Oca, Clinton H., Jr. 1946- *St&PR 91*
Montsalvatge, Xavier 1912- *PenDiMP A*
Montseny, Federica 1905- *BioIn 16*
Montt, Manuel 1809-1880 *BioIn 16*
Montt, Pedro 1846-1910 *BioIn 16*
Montt Alvarez, Jorge 1846?-1922 *BioIn 16*
Montupet, Jean-Paul Leon 1947- *WhoAm 90*
Montville, Leigh *BioIn 16*
Monty Python *ConAu 129*
Monty, Barbara Helen 1931- *WhoSSW 91*
Monty, Charles Embert 1927- *WhoAm 90*
Monty, Gloria *WhoAm 90, WhoAmW 91*
Monty, Jean Claude 1947- *St&PR 91, WhoAm 90*
Monty, Kenneth James 1930- *WhoAm 90, WhoSSW 91*
Monty, Louis H. 1958- *BiDrAPA 89*
Montz, Sidney J, Jr. *BiDrAPA 89*
Monville, Francois-N-H Racine, Baron de 1737-1794 *BioIn 16*
Mony, Daniel 1940- *WhoWor 91*
Monyak, Wendell Peter 1931- *WhoWor 91*
Monyake, Lengolo Bureng 1930- *WhoWor 91*
Monyek, Marcia *ODwPR 91*
Monyek, Marcia Edith 1959- *WhoAmW 91, WhoEmL 91*
Monypenny, Edwin Richard 1917- *WhoWor 91*
Monza, Louis 1897-1984 *MusmAFA*
Monzant, Ray 1933- *Ballpl 90*
Monzie, Pierre Armand Anatole de 1876-1947 *BiDFrPL*
Monzingo, Agnes Yvonne 1942- *WhoAmW 91*
Monzon-Aguirre, Victor J. 1949- *WhoHisp 91*
Moo, Paul Edward 1949- *WhoSSW 91*
Moodey, James Collins 1941- *St&PR 91*
Moodey, James R. 1932- *WhoAm 90*
Moodie, James Lawrence *BiDrAPA 89*
Moodie, John Wedderburn Dunbar 1797-1869 *DcLB 99 [port]*
Moodie, Susanna 1803-1885 *DcLB 99 [port], FemiCLE*
Moody Blues *EncPR&S 89, OxCPMus*
Moody, Christina 1896?- *HarlReB*
Moody, Dale George 1944- *St&PR 91*
Moody, Dan T. 1950- *St&PR 91*
Moody, David Tipton *BiDrAPA 89*
Moody, Deborah *EncCRAm*
Moody, Denman, Jr. 1942- *WhoSSW 91*
Moody, Dwight 1837-1899 *WorAlBi*
Moody, Dwight Lyman 1837-1899 *BioIn 16*
Moody, Elizabeth *FemiCLE*
Moody, Elizabeth C 1944- *WhoAmA 91*
Moody, Fanny 1866-1945 *PenDiMP*
Moody, Florence Elizabeth 1932- *WhoAm 90*
Moody, Frances *BioIn 16*
Moody, Frank M. 1915- *St&PR 91*
Moody, Frederick Jerome 1935- *WhoAm 90*
Moody, G. W. 1928- *St&PR 91*
Moody, G. William 1928- *WhoAm 90*
Moody, George Ernest 1938- *WhoE 91, WhoSSW 91*
Moody, George F. 1930- *St&PR 91*
Moody, George Franklin 1930- *WhoAm 90*
Moody, George Walter 1943- *WhoSSW 91, WhoWor 91*
Moody, Gideon Curtis 1832-1904 *AmLegL*
Moody, Graham Blair 1925- *WhoAm 90*
Moody, Harriet C. T. 1857-1932 *BioAmW*
Moody, Harry Richardson 1945- *WhoE 91*
Moody, Helen Wills 1905- *BioIn 16*
Moody, Hiram F., Jr. 1935- *St&PR 91*
Moody, Hiram Frederick, Jr. 1935- *WhoAm 90*
Moody, J. Roger 1932- *WhoAm 90*
Moody, James Carol 1937- *St&PR 91*
Moody, James L., Jr. 1931- *WhoAm 90*
Moody, James Leander, Jr. *BioIn 16*
Moody, James Leander, Jr. 1931- *St&PR 91*
Moody, James Michael 1954- *WhoWrEP 89*
Moody, James Shelton, Jr. 1947- *WhoEmL 91*
Moody, James Tyne 1938- *WhoAm 90*
Moody, Jay M. 1936- *ODwPR 91*
Moody, Jim 1935- *WhoAm 90*
Moody, Joan Elizabeth 1954- *WhoSSW 91*
Moody, Joanne Barker 1950- *WhoSSW 91*
Moody, John Michael 1939- *St&PR 91*
Moody, John Stephen 1948- *WhoEmL 91*
Moody, John W. 1949- *St&PR 91*
Moody, Judith Barbara 1942- *WhoAmW 91*
Moody, Kenton James 1954- *WhoEmL 91*
Moody, Lamon Lamar, Jr. 1924- *WhoSSW 91, WhoWor 91*
Moody, Laura Bettye 1944- *St&PR 91*
Moody, Lawrence C. 1929- *St&PR 91*
Moody, Linda A. 1954- *WhoAmW 91*
Moody, Lynne *DrBlPA 90*
Moody, Michael *BioIn 16*
Moody, Peter R 1943- *ConAu 130*
Moody, R. Bruce 1933- *WhoWrEP 89*
Moody, Ralph Owen 1898- *AuBYP 90*
Moody, Raymond A, Jr. 1944- *EncPaPR 91*
Moody, Rex Jason 1961- *BiDrAPA 89*
Moody, Rhea Phenon 1930- *WhoAmW 91*
Moody, Richard 1911- *WhoAm 90*
Moody, Richard Steven 1948- *St&PR 91*
Moody, Robert Adams 1934- *WhoAm 90*
Moody, Robert Elbridge 1897- *WhoE 91*
Moody, Robert L. *WhoAm 90, WhoSSW 91*
Moody, Robert Vaughan 1941- *WhoAm 90*
Moody, Rodger 1950- *WhoWrEP 89*
Moody, Roland Herbert 1916- *WhoAm 90*
Moody, Ron 1924- *ConTFT 8 [port], WhoWor 91*
Moody, Ruth T. 1917- *St&PR 91*
Moody, Sarah Tuttle 1948- *WhoSSW 91*
Moody, Stephen Kreigh 1942- *St&PR 91*
Moody, Susan *TwCCr&M 91*
Moody, Susan Anne 1956- *St&PR 91*

Moody, Tom Rush, Jr. 1930- WhoAm 90
Moody, Vicky L 1947- BiDrAPA 89
Moody, Virginia Jane 1953- BiDrAPA 89
Moody, W. B., Sr. 1933- St&PR 91
Moody, William Henry 1853-1917 BiDrUSE 89
Moody, William Terry 1939- St&PR 91
Moody, Zenas Ferry 1832-1917 AmLegL
Moody-Manners, Fanny 1866-1945 PenDiMP
Mooers, Christopher Northrup Kennard 1935- WhoAm 90, WhoWor 91
Moog, Helmut 1927- WhoWor 91
Moog, Hubert C. 1912- St&PR 91
Moog, Robert BioIn 16
Moogk, Donald H 1925- BiDrAPA 89
Mooibroek, Joseph 1942- St&PR 91, WhoSSW 91
Mook, James 1939- WhoWrEP 89
Mook, Sarah 1929- WhoAmW 91
Mookerjee, Rajen 1956- WhoE 91
Moola, Jagadeesh K BiDrAPA 89
Mooleyser, Willem PenDiDA 89
Moolick, Richard Terrence 1920- St&PR 91
Moollan, Cassam Ismael 1927- WhoWor 91
Mooller, Bengt Olof 1949- WhoWor 91
Moomaw, Ronald Clifford BiDrAPA 89
Moomaw, Ronald Lee 1943- WhoSSW 91
Moomjian, Cary Avedis, Jr. 1947- St&PR 91, WhoEmL 91
Moomjian, Gary Thomas 1952- WhoEmL 91
Moon, Anna M. 1956- St&PR 91
Moon, Carl 1879-1948 AuBYP 90, WhoAmA 91N
Moon, Charlotte 1840-1912 BioIn 16
Moon, Cheung Oh BiDrAPA 89
Moon, David 1941- St&PR 91
Moon, Dong Soo 1944- BiDrAPA 89
Moon, Franklin Boyd 1922- St&PR 91
Moon, Grace Purdie 1877?-1946 AuBYP 90
Moon, Ilse 1932- WhoAm 90
Moon, James E. 1929- WhoAm 90, WhoSSW 91
Moon, Jerome Firmin 1947- WhoEmL 91
Moon, Jim 1928- WhoAmA 91
Moon, John Henry, Sr. 1937- WhoSSW 91
Moon, Joseph 1912-1988 BioIn 16
Moon, Joseph W EncABHB 4
Moon, Lottie D. 1840-1912 BioAmW
Moon, Marc 1923- WhoAmA 91
Moon, Marcia A. 1945- WhoAmW 91
Moon, Maria Elena 1945- WhoHisp 91
Moon, Marjorie Ruth 1926- WhoAm 90, WhoAmW 91
Moon, Marla Lynn 1956- WhoAmW 91
Moon, Michael J. 1944- WhoE 91
Moon, Mollie NewYTBS 90 [port]
Moon, Mona McTaggart 1934- WhoAmW 91
Moon, Richard L 1935- BiDrAPA 89
Moon, Rodger A BiDrAPA 89
Moon, Sheila 1910- AuBYP 90
Moon, Steven Todd 1959- WhoSSW 91
Moon, Sucmyun 1934- BiDrAPA 89
Moon, Sun Myung BioIn 16
Moon, Sun Myung 1920- EncO&P 3, WorAlBi
Moon, Theresa K BiDrAPA 89
Moon, Thomas Young-Jun 1934- St&PR 91
Moon, Wally 1930- Ballpl 90
Moon, Warren G. 1945- WhoAm 90, WhoWrEP 89
Moon, Willard Bailey 1938- St&PR 91
Moon, Wilson L. 1916- St&PR 91
Moon-Meier, Delia Ann 1965- WhoAmW 91
Moonan, Jeffrey Patrick 1956- St&PR 91
Moonan, Robert John 1930- St&PR 91
Moonblood, Q. ConTFT 8
Moondog BioIn 16
Moonelis, Judith C 1953- WhoAmA 91
Mooney, Cathi BioIn 16
Mooney, Charles P. J. 1938- St&PR 91
Mooney, Clifford Eugene 1918- St&PR 91
Mooney, David Walton 1955- WhoAm 90
Mooney, Donald J. 1926- St&PR 91
Mooney, Donna Hancock 1951- WhoAmW 91
Mooney, Edward 1951- ConAu 130
Mooney, Edward Joseph, Jr. 1941- St&PR 91, WhoAm 90
Mooney, Elizabeth Comstock 1918-1986 BioIn 16
Mooney, Francis B. BioIn 16
Mooney, Granville W. AmLegL
Mooney, Harold Alfred 1932- WhoAm 90
Mooney, Horace B 1923- BiDrAPA 89
Mooney, James 1861-1921 WhNaAH
Mooney, James Eugene 1932- WhoE 91
Mooney, James Hugh 1929- WhoAm 90, WhoSSW 91, WhoWrEP 89
Mooney, James Patrick 1931- St&PR 91
Mooney, James Pierce BioIn 16
Mooney, James Pierce 1943- WhoAm 90, WhoWor 91
Mooney, Jim 1906-1979 Ballpl 90
Mooney, Joe BioIn 16
Mooney, Joe 1911-1975 BioIn 16
Mooney, John Allen 1918- WhoAm 90, WhoWor 91
Mooney, John Fred 1934- St&PR 91, WhoAm 90
Mooney, John James 1924- St&PR 91
Mooney, Joseph 1935- BiDrAPA 89
Mooney, Joyce E. 1930- St&PR 91
Mooney, Lori 1929- WhoE 91
Mooney, Michael Edward 1945- WhoAm 90
Mooney, Michael J WhoAmA 91
Mooney, Michael Joseph 1942- WhoAm 90
Mooney, Michael Morse 1939- WhoWrEP 89
Mooney, Nancy 1959- WhoAmW 91
Mooney, Patricia Anne 1948- WhoAmW 91
Mooney, Raymond 1951- St&PR 91
Mooney, Richard E. 1927- WhoAm 90
Mooney, Richard J. 1942- St&PR 91
Mooney, Robert Emmet, Jr. 1935- WhoE 91
Mooney, Robert Knapp 1930- WhoAm 90
Mooney, Robert Michael 1945- WhoE 91
Mooney, Robert W. 1949- St&PR 91
Mooney, Silvester 1886-1988 BioIn 16
Mooney, Stephen Eugene 1944- St&PR 91
Mooney, Ted ConAu 130
Mooney, Thomas J. 1892-1942 EncAL
Mooney, Thomas T. WhoE 91
Mooney, Vita Maria Elena 1941- WhoAmW 91
Mooney, William E 1929- BiDrAPA 89
Mooney, William Piatt 1936- WhoAm 90
Mooney, William Q. BioIn 16
Mooneyham, Walter Stanley 1926- WhoAm 90
Mooneyhan, Esther Louise 1920- WhoAm 90, WhoWor 91
Moonglows, The EncPR&S 89
Moonie, Clyde Wickliffe 1918- WhoAm 90
Moonie, Liana WhoAmA 91
Moons, Karla R. 1946- WhoAmW 91
Moons, Molly 1957- ODwPR 91
Moonwalker, Tu BioIn 16
Moor, Dina Mavis 1943- WhoAmW 91
Moor, Edward BioIn 16
Moor, Emanuel 1863-1931 PenDiMP
Moor, Emily TwCCr&M 91
Moor, Manly Eugene, Jr. 1923- St&PR 91, WhoAm 90
Moor, Roy Edward 1924- WhoAm 90
Moor, William Louis 1927- WhoSSW 91
Moorad, Philip J 1904- BiDrAPA 89
Moorad, Philip J, Jr. BiDrAPA 89
Mooradian, Leo 1909- WhoSSW 91
Moorcock, Michael 1939- BioIn 16, MajTwCW, RGTwCSF
Moorcock, Michael John 1939- WhoWor 91
Moorcroft, William 1872-1945 BioIn 16
Moore, A. Ronald 1937- St&PR 91
Moore, Acel 1940- WhoAm 90
Moore, Alan BioIn 16
Moore, Alan Geoffrey 1924- WhoAm 90
Moore, Albert Cunningham 1931- WhoAm 90
Moore, Albert Preston 1919- WhoE 91
Moore, Albert Wendell 1934- St&PR 91
Moore, Alderine Bernice Jennings 1915- WhoAmW 91
Moore, Aleda Major 1927- WhoAmW 91
Moore, Alexander 1937- WhoAm 90
Moore, Alfred Anson 1925- WhoAm 90
Moore, Alice Ruth MajTwCW
Moore, Alison Tetenman 1964- WhoAmW 91
Moore, Alma C. WhoWor 91
Moore, Alvin Crawford, Jr. 1943- WhoWor 91
Moore, Amy Girdler BiDrAPA 89
Moore, Andrew G. T., II BioIn 16
Moore, Andrew Given Tobias, II 1935- WhoAm 90, WhoE 91
Moore, Andrew T., Jr. 1940- St&PR 91
Moore, Andrew Taylor, Jr. 1940- WhoAm 90
Moore, Anne BioIn 16
Moore, Anne Carroll 1871-1961 AuBYP 90, BioAmW
Moore, Anthony Roger 1945- WhoWor 91
Moore, Arch A., Jr. 1923- WhoWor 91
Moore, Archie 1913- BioIn 16, WorAlBi
Moore, Archie 1916- DrBIPA 90
Moore, Ardean Carol 1944- BiDrAPA 89
Moore, Arthur Cotton 1935- WhoAm 90
Moore, Arthur James 1922- WhoAm 90
Moore, Austin BiDrAPA 89
Moore, B. H. Rutledge 1937- St&PR 91
Moore, Balor 1951- Ballpl 90
Moore, Barbara DeMont 1944- WhoAmW 91
Moore, Barbara Jeanne 1961- WhoEmL 91, WhoWor 91
Moore, Barbara Patricia Hill 1942- IntWWM 90
Moore, Barney M., Jr. 1937- St&PR 91
Moore, Barry 1943- Ballpl 90
Moore, Barry Allen BiDrAPA 89
Moore, Basil John 1933- WhoAm 90
Moore, Becky Sue 1955- WhoE 91
Moore, Benjamin Cheney 1935- WhoE 91
Moore, Benjamin E BiDrAPA 89
Moore, Benjamin Powell 1952- WhoAmA 91
Moore, Bernard 1850-1935 PenDiDA 89
Moore, Beth Anne 1961- WhoSSW 91
Moore, Betty Jean 1927- WhoSSW 91
Moore, Beveridge 1915- WhoAmA 91
Moore, Beverly Cooper 1909- WhoAm 90
Moore, Billie Lee 1931- WhoWor 91
Moore, Blanche Kiser Taylor BioIn 16
Moore, Bob Stahly 1936- WhoAm 90, WhoE 91, WhoWor 91
Moore, Brad R. BioIn 16
Moore, Brian 1921- MajTwCW, WhoAm 90, WhoWor 91, WhoWrEP 89
Moore, Brian C. 1945- St&PR 91
Moore, Brian Clive 1945- WhoE 91
Moore, Bridget Liane 1957- WhoAmA 91
Moore, Brooke Noel 1943- WhoAm 90
Moore, Burness E BiDrAPA 89
Moore, Burton Eberle 1914- St&PR 91
Moore, C. Bradley 1939- WhoAm 90
Moore, C E McDaniel 1934- BiDrAPA 89
Moore, C. Eugene 1931- ODwPR 91
Moore, C. L. 1911-1987 RGTwCSF
Moore, Calvin C. 1936- WhoAm 90
Moore, Candace Rae 1952- WhoAmW 91
Moore, Carleton Bryant 1932- WhoAm 90
Moore, Carman 1936- BioIn 16
Moore, Carman Leroy 1936- DrBIPA 90, IntWWM 90
Moore, Carol Ann 1947- WhoAmW 91
Moore, Carol Lynn 1960- WhoAmW 91
Moore, Carol Millinghausen 1953- WhoAmW 91
Moore, Carolyn Calista 1953- WhoAmW 91
Moore, Catherine D BiDrAPA 89
Moore, Ceil Williams 1917- WhoSSW 91
Moore, Celesta Rose 1944- WhoAmW 91
Moore, Charles BioIn 16
Moore, Charles 1928- DrBIPA 90
Moore, Charles Brown 1941- WhoSSW 91
Moore, Charles F. BioIn 16
Moore, Charles Hewes, Jr. 1929- St&PR 91, WhoAm 90
Moore, Charles Julian 1931- WhoAm 90
Moore, Charles Neil IntWWM 90
Moore, Charles Willard BioIn 16
Moore, Charles Willard 1925- WhoAm 90
Moore, Charles Willard 1930- WhoSSW 91
Moore, Charlie 1953- Ballpl 90
Moore, Charlotte Eleanor 1923- WhoAmW 91
Moore, Cheryl Hannert 1958- WhoSSW 91
Moore, Claire 1912?-1988 BioIn 16
Moore, Clarence H. 1909-1988 BioIn 16
Moore, Clark D'Arcy 1932- WhoSSW 91
Moore, Claude N. BioIn 16
Moore, Claude N. 1929- St&PR 91
Moore, Clement 1779-1863 WorAlBi
Moore, Cleon 1928- St&PR 91
Moore, Cleon Emerson 1928- WhoSSW 91
Moore, Clyde B. 1886-1973 AuBYP 90
Moore, Colleen 1902-1988 AnObit 1988
Moore, Constance BiDrAPA 89
Moore, Cornell Leverette 1939- St&PR 91
Moore, Cy 1905-1972 Ballpl 90
Moore, Daisy Seale 1933- WhoWrEP 89
Moore, Dale 1932- IntWWM 90
Moore, Dalton, Jr. 1918- WhoSSW 91, WhoWor 91
Moore, Dan Tyler 1908- WhoAm 90, WhoWor 91
Moore, Dana L. 1933- WhoAmW 91
Moore, Daniel B. 1944- St&PR 91
Moore, Daniel Carl 1947- BiDrAPA 89
Moore, Daniel Charles 1918- WhoAm 90
Moore, Daniel E. 1931- St&PR 91
Moore, Daniel Edmund 1926- WhoE 91, WhoWor 91
Moore, Daniel Horatio 1959- WhoEmL 91
Moore, Daniel Michael 1954- WhoEmL 91
Moore, Daniel Thomas 1953- WhoSSW 91
Moore, Daryl Duane 1957- St&PR 91
Moore, Davey BioIn 16
Moore, David Austin 1935- WhoWor 91
Moore, David Brian 1957- WhoSSW 91
Moore, David Bruce 1956- WhoSSW 91, WhoWor 91
Moore, David F 1920- BiDrAPA 89
Moore, David Graham 1918- WhoAm 90
Moore, David Lloyd 1948- WhoE 91, WhoWor 91
Moore, David Lowell 1930- WhoAm 90
Moore, David Pringle BiDrAPA 89
Moore, David William AuBYP 90
Moore, Demi BioIn 16
Moore, Demi 1962- WorAlBi
Moore, Denis A. 1938- St&PR 91
Moore, Detlef Basil 1950- WhoSSW 91
Moore, Diana Sue 1958- WhoEmL 91
Moore, Dick 1925- WhoE 91
Moore, Dobie 1893- Ballpl 90
Moore, Don 1942- WhoSSW 91
Moore, Don W. BioIn 16
Moore, Donald Emerson, III 1954- WhoE 91
Moore, Donald Eugene 1928- WhoAm 90
Moore, Donald Floyd BiDrAPA 89
Moore, Donald Francis 1937- WhoAm 90
Moore, Donald John 1959- WhoWrEP 89
Moore, Donald Roland 1933- WhoSSW 91
Moore, Donald William 1941- WhoWor 91
Moore, Donna Jean 1955- St&PR 91
Moore, Donnica Lauren 1961- WhoE 91
Moore, Donnie 1954-1989 Ballpl 90, BioIn 16
Moore, Dora Mavor 1888-1979 DcLB 92, OxCCanT
Moore, Dora Viola 1948- WhoAmW 91
Moore, Doris Langley 1903-1989 AnObit 1989
Moore, Dorothy Marie 1928- WhoAm 90
Moore, Dorothy Marie 1949- WhoSSW 91
Moore, Dorothy N 1915- WhoWrEP 89
Moore, Dorsey Jerome 1935- WhoAm 90
Moore, Douglas 1893-1969 PenDiMP A
Moore, Douglas Bryant 1946- IntWWM 90
Moore, Douglas R BiDrAPA 89
Moore, Douglas Raymond 1957- St&PR 91
Moore, Dudley BioIn 16
Moore, Dudley 1935- ConTFT 8 [port], OxCPMus, WorAlBi
Moore, Dudley Donald 1928- St&PR 91
Moore, Dudley Lester, Jr. 1936- WhoSSW 91
Moore, Dudley Stuart John 1935- WhoAm 90, WhoWor 91
Moore, Dwight McClintock 1956- WhoEmL 91, WhoSSW 91
Moore, E. Joseph 1916- St&PR 91
Moore, E. Keith 1922- St&PR 91
Moore, Earl 1878-1961 Ballpl 90
Moore, Earl S., Jr. 1930- St&PR 91
Moore, Earle Kennedy 1921- WhoAm 90
Moore, Eddie 1899-1976 Ballpl 90
Moore, Eddie N. WhoSSW 91
Moore, Edgar M. 1940- St&PR 91
Moore, Edith Mary 1909-1935 FemiCLE
Moore, Edward PenDiDA 89
Moore, Edward B. 1922- St&PR 91
Moore, Edward Carter 1917- WhoAm 90
Moore, Edward F., Jr. 1920- St&PR 91
Moore, Edward Forrest 1925- WhoAm 90
Moore, Edward P. BioIn 16
Moore, Edwina Vesta WhoAmW 91
Moore, Eleanor Marchman 1913- WhoAmW 91
Moore, Elizabeth BiDEWW, FemiCLE
Moore, Elizabeth Doreen 1954- WhoAmW 91
Moore, Elizabeth Elkins 1946- WhoAmW 91
Moore, Elizabeth J. St&PR 91
Moore, Elizabeth Kimberly 1954- WhoSSW 91
Moore, Ellen Ann 1936- WhoAmW 91
Moore, Ellis 1924- ODwPR 91
Moore, Ellis Oglesby 1924- WhoAm 90
Moore, Emerson John 1938- WhoAm 90
Moore, Emily 1948- BioIn 16
Moore, Emma Sims 1937- WhoAmW 91
Moore, Emmett Burris, Jr. 1929- WhoAm 90
Moore, Eric Brian 1955- WhoSSW 91
Moore, Ernest Eugene, Jr. 1946- WhoAm 90
Moore, Ernest Jerome 1937- WhoAm 90
Moore, Euel 1908- Ballpl 90
Moore, Eva 1942- AuBYP 90
Moore, Evan G 1923- BiDrAPA 89
Moore, Everett T. BioIn 16
Moore, Evie B. 1945- WhoAmW 91
Moore, Fay WhoAmA 91
Moore, Fay Linda 1942- WhoAmW 91
Moore, Faye Halford 1941- WhoAmW 91
Moore, Fletcher Brooks 1926- WhoAm 90
Moore, Forrest W. 1931- ODwPR 91
Moore, Forrest Weatherford 1931- WhoSSW 91
Moore, Frances 1789?-1881 FemiCLE
Moore, Francis Daniels 1913- WhoAm 90
Moore, Frank 1915-1990 BioIn 16
Moore, Franklin Hall, Jr. 1937- WhoAm 90
Moore, Frederick C. 1933- WhoAm 90
Moore, Frederick Salling 1938- St&PR 91
Moore, Garry 1915- WorAlBi
Moore, Gary Richard 1945- St&PR 91
Moore, Gary Vern 1951- St&PR 91
Moore, Gene 1909-1978 Ballpl 90
Moore, Gene 1910- ConDes 90
Moore, Geoffrey Hoyt 1914- WhoAm 90, WhoE 91, WhoWrEP 89

Moore, George 1852-1933 *BioIn 16, WorAlBi*
Moore, George Andrew, Jr. 1927- *WhoAm 90*
Moore, George Campp 1935- *St&PR 91*
Moore, George E 1912- *BiDrAPA 89*
Moore, George Emerson, Jr. 1914- *WhoAm 90*
Moore, George Eugene 1920- *WhoAm 90*
Moore, George Jackson 1930- *WhoSSW 91*
Moore, George John 1943- *BiDrAPA 89*
Moore, George Kenneth 1927- *St&PR 91*
Moore, George Patterson 1932- *WhoAm 90*
Moore, George Paul 1907- *WhoWor 91*
Moore, George S. 1905- *St&PR 91*
Moore, Gerald 1899-1987 *PenDiMP*
Moore, Gerald Lee *BiDrAPA 89*
Moore, Gerald Louis 1946- *WhoEmL 91*
Moore, Gerald Thomas 1932- *St&PR 91*
Moore, Gerald Wayne 1940- *WhoAm 90*
Moore, Gilbert Deering *BioIn 16*
Moore, Glenn Ray 1937- *St&PR 91*
Moore, Gordon E. 1929- *ConAmBL, St&PR 91, WhoAm 90*
Moore, Grace 1898-1947 *PenDiMP*
Moore, Grace 1901-1947 *BioAmW, OxCPMus*
Moore, Gregory Clayton 1954- *St&PR 91*
Moore, H. Brian 1948- *St&PR 91*
Moore, Hal G. 1929- *WhoAm 90*
Moore, Hallie E *BiDrAPA 89*
Moore, Harold E. 1928- *WhoSSW 91*
Moore, Harriett *BioIn 16*
Moore, Harrison Lyman 1946- *WhoWrEP 89*
Moore, Harry E., Jr. 1918- *WhoWrEP 89*
Moore, Harry Russell 1921- *WhoSSW 91, WhoWor 91*
Moore, Harvielee Ann Offutt 1948- *WhoWrEP 89*
Moore, Harvin Cooper 1905- *WhoAm 90*
Moore, Hayden Albert 1929- *WhoAm 90*
Moore, Hazel Goodall 1939- *WhoAmW 91*
Moore, Helen Elizabeth 1920- *WhoAmW 91, WhoWor 91*
Moore, Henderson Alfred, Jr. 1912- *WhoWor 91*
Moore, Henry 1713-1769 *EncCRAm*
Moore, Henry 1898-1986 *BioIn 16, IntDcAA 90, ModArCr 1 [port], WorAlBi*
Moore, Henry Ludwell 1869-1958 *BioIn 16*
Moore, Henry R. 1916- *St&PR 91*
Moore, Henry Rogers 1916- *WhoAm 90*
Moore, Herbert Bell 1926- *WhoAm 90*
Moore, Herff Leo, Jr. 1937- *WhoSSW 91*
Moore, Honor 1945- *FemiCLE, WhoWrEP 89*
Moore, Howard Earl 1932- *WhoSSW 91*
Moore, Howard Ellison, Jr. 1936- *St&PR 91*
Moore, Howard Roswald, Jr. 1932- *WhoAm 90*
Moore, Howard Wolfe 1930- *St&PR 91*
Moore, Hugh M., Jr. 1931- *St&PR 91*
Moore, Hugh P. 1912- *St&PR 91*
Moore, Ina May 1920- *WhoAmA 91*
Moore, J. T. 1939- *WhoSSW 91*
Moore, Jack 1926-1988 *BioIn 16*
Moore, Jack Lynne 1920- *WhoSSW 91*
Moore, Jack Zebulon 1933- *St&PR 91*
Moore, Jackson Bernice 1931- *WhoWor 91*
Moore, Jackson Watts 1948- *WhoAm 90*
Moore, Jacqueline 1937- *WhoAmW 91*
Moore, Jamel L., Jr. 1942- *St&PR 91*
Moore, James *EncCRAm*
Moore, James *PenDiDA 89*
Moore, James, III 1940- *IntWWM 90*
Moore, James A. 1915- *St&PR 91*
Moore, James Alfred 1915- *WhoAm 90*
Moore, James Collins 1941- *WhoAm 90*
Moore, James Dalton 1952- *WhoEmL 91*
Moore, James E., III 1950- *St&PR 91*
Moore, James Edward 1948- *BiDrAPA 89*
Moore, James Howard 1928- *St&PR 91*
Moore, James L., Jr. 1942- *WhoSSW 91*
Moore, James Layne *BiDrAPA 89*
Moore, James Mack, Jr. 1945- *WhoEmL 91*
Moore, James Mendon 1925- *WhoAm 90*
Moore, James Patrick, Jr. 1953- *WhoAm 90, WhoE 91*
Moore, James Robert 1925- *WhoAm 90*
Moore, James T, III 1939- *ConAu 31NR*
Moore, James Timothy 1950- *WhoSSW 91*
Moore, James Tracy 1945- *BiDrAPA 89*
Moore, James W. *BioIn 16*
Moore, James Warren 1942- *St&PR 91*
Moore, James Young 1913- *WhoWor 91*
Moore, Jane Elizabeth 1738- *FemiCLE*
Moore, Jane Ross 1929- *WhoAm 90*
Moore, Janet Marie 1947- *WhoAmW 91*
Moore, Janet Ruth 1949- *WhoAmW 91, WhoE 91*
Moore, Janet S. *ODwPR 91*
Moore, Janice Townley 1939- *WhoWrEP 89*
Moore, Jean Oliver 1925- *St&PR 91, WhoWor 91*
Moore, Jean S. *ConAu 130*
Moore, Jean Sutherland 1924- *WhoAmW 91*
Moore, Jeanne Crewes 1939- *WhoE 91*
Moore, Jeffrey Lee 1956- *BiDrAPA 89*
Moore, Jeri 1953- *WhoAmW 91*
Moore, Jerry J. *BioIn 16*
Moore, Jerry Lamar 1942- *WhoAm 90*
Moore, Jesse A. 1951- *St&PR 91*
Moore, Jimmy *ConAu 31NR*
Moore, Joan Elizabeth 1951- *WhoAmW 91, WhoEmL 91*
Moore, Joanna Elizabeth 1937- *WhoSSW 91*
Moore, Joanna Patterson 1832-1916 *BioIn 16*
Moore, Joanne *BiDrAPA 89*
Moore, Joanne Iweita 1928- *WhoAm 90, WhoAmW 91*
Moore, Joe 1908- *Ballpl 90*
Moore, Joe Stelzer 1912- *WhoSSW 91*
Moore, John *PenDiMP*
Moore, John 1659-1732 *EncCRAm*
Moore, John, Jr. 1945- *IntWWM 90*
Moore, John Allen 1912- *WhoWrEP 89*
Moore, John Arthur 1939- *WhoAm 90*
Moore, John Atkin 1931- *St&PR 91, WhoAm 90*
Moore, John B. *ODwPR 91*
Moore, John Bassett 1860-1947 *BioIn 16*
Moore, John Chandler 1832-1851 *PenDiDA 89*
Moore, John Coleman 1923- *WhoAm 90, WhoE 91*
Moore, John Cordell 1912- *WhoAm 90, WhoWor 91*
Moore, John D. J. 1910-1988 *BioIn 16*
Moore, John Dennis 1931- *WhoAm 90*
Moore, John Duain 1913- *WhoAm 90*
Moore, John Edward 1920- *WhoWor 91*
Moore, John Edwin, Jr. 1942- *WhoAm 90*
Moore, John George, Jr. 1917- *WhoAm 90*
Moore, John H. 1926- *St&PR 91*
Moore, John Hampton 1935- *WhoAm 90, WhoE 91*
Moore, John Hebron 1920- *WhoSSW 91*
Moore, John Isaac 1856-1937 *AmLegL*
Moore, John Ivan 1954- *St&PR 91*
Moore, John J 1941- *WhoAmA 91*
Moore, John Joseph 1933- *WhoAm 90*
Moore, John Joseph 1941- *WhoE 91*
Moore, John L. *BioIn 16*
Moore, John Lovell, Jr. 1929- *WhoAm 90*
Moore, John Newton 1920- *WhoAm 90*
Moore, John Norton 1937- *WhoAm 90, WhoWrEP 89*
Moore, John Parker 1942- *IntWWM 90*
Moore, John Porfilio 1934- *WhoAm 90*
Moore, John Rees 1918- *WhoWrEP 89*
Moore, John Robert 1916- *WhoAm 90*
Moore, John Robert 1934- *WhoE 91*
Moore, John Robert 1947- *WhoSSW 91*
Moore, John Ronald 1935- *WhoAm 90*
Moore, John Runyan 1929- *WhoE 91*
Moore, John Scott 1951- *St&PR 91*
Moore, John T. 1915- *St&PR 91*
Moore, John Thomas 1950- *WhoEmL 91*
Moore, John Thomas 1954- *BiDrAPA 89, WhoE 91*
Moore, John Travers 1908- *WhoAm 90*
Moore, John Warren 1812-1893 *DcCanB 12*
Moore, John William 1939- *WhoAm 90*
Moore, John Wilson 1920- *WhoAm 90*
Moore, Johnny 1902- *Ballpl 90*
Moore, Jonathan 1932- *WhoAm 90*
Moore, Joseph 1920- *WhoWor 91*
Moore, Joseph Burton 1926- *WhoAm 90*
Moore, Joseph William 1954- *BiDrAPA 89*
Moore, Josephine Carroll 1925- *WhoAmW 91*
Moore, Joyce Kristina 1955- *WhoAmW 91, WhoE 91, WhoWor 91*
Moore, Juanita 1922- *DrBIPA 90*
Moore, Judith Sullivan 1946- *WhoSSW 91*
Moore, Julia Frances Tybor 1943- *BiDrAPA 89*
Moore, Julie E. 1957- *WhoEmL 91*
Moore, Julius David, Jr. 1946- *BiDrAPA 89*
Moore, Junior 1953- *Ballpl 90*
Moore, Junius T., Jr. 1922- *St&PR 91*
Moore, Justin Edward 1952- *WhoEmL 91*
Moore, Karen Lindsay 1946- *WhoAmW 91*
Moore, Karen Nelson 1948- *WhoEmL 91*
Moore, Kate *WhoAm 90*
Moore, Katherine B. 1941- *WhoAmW 91*
Moore, Kathleen Ann 1958- *WhoEmL 91*
Moore, Kay 1948- *ConAu 130*
Moore, Kenneth B *BiDrAPA 89*
Moore, Kenneth Creyton 1932- *St&PR 91*
Moore, Kenneth Edwin 1933- *WhoAm 90*
Moore, Kenneth Ray 1937- *WhoAm 90*
Moore, Kermit 1929- *IntWWM 90*
Moore, Kevin Dale 1961- *BiDrAPA 89*
Moore, Kim Alan 1951- *WhoSSW 91*
Moore, Kurt Richard 1955- *WhoEmL 91*
Moore, L. Franklin, Jr. 1922- *St&PR 91*
Moore, Lahman D. 1946- *St&PR 91*
Moore, Lamont 1909- *AuBYP 90*
Moore, Larry Vernon 1940- *WhoAm 90*
Moore, Larry Wayne 1947- *WhoSSW 91*
Moore, Laurence 1919- *WhoAm 90*
Moore, Laurence John 1938- *WhoAm 90*
Moore, Laurie Jo 1947- *BiDrAPA 89*
Moore, Lee Llewellyn 1939- *BioIn 16*
Moore, Lee Permenter 1923- *St&PR 91*
Moore, Lenard Duane 1958- *WhoWrEP 89*
Moore, Leonard W. 1933- *St&PR 91*
Moore, Leroy Everett 1930- *BiDrAPA 89*
Moore, Leslie David 1931- *WhoSSW 91*
Moore, Lewis Edward, Jr. 1932- *WhoSSW 91*
Moore, Libbie Ann 1960- *WhoAmW 91, WhoWor 91*
Moore, Lilian *AuBYP 90*
Moore, Lilian 1909- *BioIn 16*
Moore, Linda B. *St&PR 91*
Moore, Linda Ely 1942- *WhoAmW 91*
Moore, Linda Jean 1954- *WhoAmW 91*
Moore, Linda Kathleen 1944- *WhoAmW 91*
Moore, Linda Marie Zajicek 1943- *WhoAmW 91, WhoSSW 91*
Moore, Linda Perigo 1946- *WhoAmW 91, WhoWor 91*
Moore, Linda Picarelli 1943- *WhoAmW 91*
Moore, Lisbeth A. 1960- *WhoAmW 91*
Moore, Lori Lynn 1967- *WhoAmW 91*
Moore, Lorrie *BioIn 16*
Moore, Lorrie 1957- *WhoWrEP 89*
Moore, Louis 1946- *ConAu 130*
Moore, Louis de B., II 1941- *ODwPR 91*
Moore, Louis P *BiDrAPA 89*
Moore, Louis Robert, III 1948- *WhoEmL 91*
Moore, Loy Beene 1937- *WhoSSW 91*
Moore, Luana Regina C. 1955- *WhoE 91*
Moore, Lucile 1910- *WhoAmW 91*
Moore, M. Thomas 1934- *St&PR 91*
Moore, Maggie L. 1965- *WhoAmW 91*
Moore, Malcolm A. S. 1944- *WhoAm 90*
Moore, Malcolm Arthur 1937- *WhoAm 90*
Moore, Marc Anthony 1928- *WhoAm 90*
Moore, Marcia Williams 1939- *WhoAmW 91*
Moore, Margaret Anne Fort 1933- *WhoAmW 91*
Moore, Margaret Carrington 1896- *WhoSSW 91*
Moore, Margaret D. 1948- *St&PR 91*
Moore, Margaret Perlin 1935- *WhoAmW 91*
Moore, Marianne 1887-1972 *BioIn 16, FemiCLE, MajTwCW, WorAlBi*
Moore, Marianne 1888-1972 *Ballpl 90*
Moore, Marianne C. 1887-1972 *BioAmW*
Moore, Marie 1933- *WhoAm 90*
Moore, Marilyn Doris *BiDrAPA 89*
Moore, Marilyn M. 1932- *WhoWrEP 89*
Moore, Marion R 1923- *BiDrAPA 89*
Moore, Marjorie 1944- *WhoAmA 91*
Moore, Marjorie Silcox 1935- *WhoAmW 91*
Moore, Marjorie W. 1944- *WhoE 91*
Moore, Mark Harrison 1947- *WhoAm 90, WhoWrEP 89*
Moore, Marlin Charles 1911- *BiDrAPA 89*
Moore, Marnie *BioIn 16*
Moore, Mary *BiDEWW, WhoAm 90, WhoAmW 91*
Moore, Mary Carr 1873-1957 *BioIn 16*
Moore, Mary Charlotte 1945- *WhoAm 90*
Moore, Mary French 1938- *WhoWor 91*
Moore, Mary Needham 1934- *WhoAmW 91*
Moore, Mary Susan 1945- *WhoAmW 91*
Moore, Mary Tyler *BioIn 16*
Moore, Mary Tyler 1936- *WhoAm 90, WhoAmW 91*
Moore, Mary Tyler 1937- *WorAlBi*
Moore, Mary Warner *BioIn 16*
Moore, Matthew T *BiDrAPA 89*
Moore, Maurice Malcolm 1920- *WhoWor 91*
Moore, Maurine 1932- *WhoWrEP 89*
Moore, Mavor 1919- *ConAu 132, OxCCanT, WhoAm 90*
Moore, Mechlin D. 1930- *ODwPR 91*
Moore, Mechlin Dongan 1930- *St&PR 91, WhoAm 90*
Moore, Mehri Damavandi *BiDrAPA 89*
Moore, Melanie Ethel 1952- *WhoAmW 91, WhoE 91, WhoWor 91*
Moore, Melba 1945- *DrBIPA 90, WorAlBi*
Moore, Melba 1947- *WhoAm 90*
Moore, Merijeanne Anne 1958- *BiDrAPA 89*
Moore, Mervyn *BioIn 16*
Moore, Michael *BioIn 16*
Moore, Michael 1954?- *News 90 [port], -90-3 [port]*
Moore, Michael Dwaine 1961- *WhoSSW 91*
Moore, Michael Frederick 1957- *St&PR 91*
Moore, Michael Harve 1944- *St&PR 91*
Moore, Michael Henry 1943- *St&PR 91*
Moore, Michael Kenneth *WhoWor 91*
Moore, Michael Scott 1943- *WhoAm 90*
Moore, Michael Thomas 1934- *WhoAm 90*
Moore, Michael Timothy 1950- *WhoSSW 91*
Moore, Mike *WhoAm 90, WhoSSW 91*
Moore, Mike 1959- *Ballpl 90*
Moore, Milcah Martha 1740-1829 *FemiCLE*
Moore, Mildred Thorpe 1924- *WhoSSW 91*
Moore, Milo Anderson 1942- *WhoAm 90*
Moore, Mitchell Jay 1954- *WhoEmL 91*
Moore, Mollie 1950- *WhoAmW 91*
Moore, Mona 1952- *WhoWrEP 89*
Moore, Morgan F, Jr. 1928- *BiDrAPA 89*
Moore, Myreen 1940- *WhoAmA 91*
Moore, Myron L., Jr. 1924- *St&PR 91*
Moore, Nancy *AuBYP 90*
Moore, Nancy Lorene 1938- *WhoWrEP 89*
Moore, Norman Charles *BiDrAPA 89*
Moore, Norman Slawson 1901- *WhoAm 90*
Moore, Olga *WhoAmA 91*
Moore, Olga Bunta *WhoE 91*
Moore, Omar Khayyam 1920- *WhoE 91*
Moore, Pat Howard 1930- *St&PR 91, WhoAm 90*
Moore, Patricia A. 1944- *WhoAmW 91*
Moore, Patricia Ann 1954- *WhoAmW 91*
Moore, Patricia Kay 1947- *WhoAmW 91*
Moore, Patrick *BioIn 16*
Moore, Patrick Alfred 1923- *AuBYP 90*
Moore, Patrick J *BiDrAPA 89*
Moore, Paul 1919- *BioIn 16*
Moore, Paul, Jr. 1919- *WhoAm 90*
Moore, Paula Jane 1960- *WhoSSW 91*
Moore, Paula R. 1953- *WhoSSW 91*
Moore, Peggy Sue 1942- *WhoAmW 91, WhoWor 91*
Moore, Penny Lynn 1961- *WhoSSW 91*
Moore, Perry Glen 1959- *WhoEmL 91*
Moore, Peter 1932- *WhoAmA 91*
Moore, Peter Bartlett 1939- *WhoAm 90*
Moore, Peter D. 1943- *ODwPR 91*
Moore, Peter Innisfree 1932- *WhoAm 90*
Moore, Peter V C *BiDrAPA 89*
Moore, Phil 1918-1987 *DrBIPA 90*
Moore, Philip *AmLegL*
Moore, Philip Hubert Hamond 1940- *IntWWM 90*
Moore, Philip John 1943- *IntWWM 90*
Moore, Philip Walsh 1920- *WhoE 91, WhoSSW 91*
Moore, Phyllis Lee 1953- *WhoWrEP 89*
Moore, Powell Allen 1938- *WhoAm 90, WhoSSW 91*
Moore, Preston 1931- *St&PR 91*
Moore, Queen Mother 1898- *EncAL*
Moore, R. Keith 1943- *ODwPR 91*
Moore, R. Stuart 1924- *St&PR 91*
Moore, Ralph W 1943- *BiDrAPA 89*
Moore, Randolph Graves 1939- *St&PR 91*
Moore, Randy 1905- *Ballpl 90*
Moore, Rasheeda *BioIn 16*
Moore, Ray *EncACom*
Moore, Ray 1926- *Ballpl 90*
Moore, Ray 1942-1989 *AnObit 1989*
Moore, Rayburn Sabatzky 1920- *WhoAm 90*
Moore, Raymond 1920-1987 *BioIn 16*
Moore, Raymond Cecil 1892-1974 *DcScB S2*
Moore, Raymond S. 1915- *WhoWrEP 89*
Moore, Raymond Thomas 1926- *St&PR 91*
Moore, ReBecca *BioIn 16*
Moore, Regina *AuBYP 90*
Moore, Richard *ODwPR 91*
Moore, Richard 1927- *DcLB 105 [port], WhoWrEP 89*
Moore, Richard Alan 1930- *WhoAm 90*
Moore, Richard Alan 1948- *WhoEmL 91, WhoWor 91*
Moore, Richard Albert 1915- *WhoAm 90*
Moore, Richard Allan 1924- *WhoAm 90*
Moore, Richard Anthony 1914- *WhoAm 90*
Moore, Richard Cone 1936- *St&PR 91*
Moore, Richard Donald 1924- *WhoAm 90*
Moore, Richard Earl 1940- *WhoAm 90*
Moore, Richard F. 1944- *IntWWM 90*
Moore, Richard H., Jr. 1931- *St&PR 91*
Moore, Richard Harlan 1945- *WhoSSW 91*
Moore, Richard Ilsley 1943- *St&PR 91*
Moore, Richard John *BiDrAPA 89*
Moore, Richard K. 1923- *ODwPR 91*
Moore, Richard Kerr 1923- *WhoAm 90*
Moore, Richard L. 1923- *ODwPR 91*
Moore, Richard Leroy, II 1948- *WhoE 91*
Moore, Richard P. 1949- *St&PR 91*
Moore, Richard W. 1927- *St&PR 91*
Moore, Richard Wraxall 1949- *WhoE 91*
Moore, Ricki John 1952- *WhoSSW 91*
Moore, Robert A *BiDrAPA 89*

Moore, Robert A. 1920- *St&PR 91*
Moore, Robert A 1925- *BiDrAPA 89*
Moore, Robert Anthony 1947- *WhoE 91*
Moore, Robert B. 1949- *St&PR 91*
Moore, Robert Byron, Jr. 1957- *WhoEmL 91*
Moore, Robert Charles 1921- *WhoE 91*
Moore, Robert Clay 1934- *St&PR 91, WhoAm 90*
Moore, Robert Clyde, Jr. 1947- *St&PR 91*
Moore, Robert Condit 1921- *WhoAm 90*
Moore, Robert E. 1925- *St&PR 91*
Moore, Robert E. 1940- *ODwPR 91*
Moore, Robert Edmund 1925- *WhoE 91*
Moore, Robert Edward 1923- *WhoAm 90*
Moore, Robert Eric 1927- *WhoAmA 91*
Moore, Robert F 1920- *BiDrAPA 89*
Moore, Robert Forrest 1931- *WhoSSW 91*
Moore, Robert Francis 1920- *WhoE 91*
Moore, Robert Franklin 1945- *WhoSSW 91*
Moore, Robert H. 1940- *ODwPR 91*
Moore, Robert Henry 1940- *WhoAm 90, WhoWor 91*
Moore, Robert Henry, Jr. 1923- *WhoSSW 91*
Moore, Robert Howard 1940- *St&PR 91*
Moore, Robert J. 1928- *St&PR 91*
Moore, Robert J. 1930- *ODwPR 91*
Moore, Robert James 1922- *WhoAmA 91*
Moore, Robert James 1923- *WhoAm 90*
Moore, Robert Laurence 1940- *WhoAm 90, WhoWrEP 89*
Moore, Robert Lee 1882-1974 *DcScB S2*
Moore, Robert Lowell, Jr. 1925- *WhoAm 90, WhoWrEP 89*
Moore, Robert Madison 1925- *WhoAm 90*
Moore, Robert Morrell 1935- *St&PR 91*
Moore, Robert Russell 1937- *WhoAm 90*
Moore, Robert Scott 1958- *WhoSSW 91*
Moore, Robert Shelton 1926- *St&PR 91*
Moore, Robert Stuart 1924- *WhoAm 90, WhoSSW 91*
Moore, Robert W. 1929- *St&PR 91*
Moore, Robert William 1924- *WhoAm 90*
Moore, Robert Yates 1931- *WhoAm 90*
Moore, Roberta Lynn 1952- *WhoWrEP 89*
Moore, Robin 1925- *WhoAm 90*
Moore, Robin James 1934- *WhoWor 91*
Moore, Rod Alan 1930- *St&PR 91*
Moore, Roger 1927- *WorAlBi*
Moore, Roger A. 1931-1990 *BioIn 16*
Moore, Roger Allan *St&PR 91N*
Moore, Roger George 1927- *WhoAm 90*
Moore, Ronald Gresham 1926- *IntWWM 90*
Moore, Ronald L. *WhoAm 90*
Moore, Ronald Lester 1924- *St&PR 91*
Moore, Rosalie 1910- *WhoWrEP 89*
Moore, Rosemary *ODwPR 91*
Moore, Roy 1898-1951 *Ballpl 90*
Moore, Roy Dean 1940- *WhoAm 90*
Moore, Roy L. 1932- *St&PR 91*
Moore, Russell James 1947- *WhoAmA 91*
Moore, Ruth E. 1908-1989 *BioIn 16*
Moore, S. Donald *St&PR 91*
Moore, Sabra 1943- *WhoAmA 91*
Moore, Sally Falk 1924- *WhoAm 90*
Moore, Sally Jane 1936- *WhoAmW 91*
Moore, Sally Joy Dondroe 1943- *WhoAmW 91*
Moore, Sam *BioIn 16*
Moore, Sanders Harrison 1944- *WhoSSW 91*
Moore, Sandra 1945- *WhoE 91*
Moore, Sandra Kay 1957- *WhoAmW 91*
Moore, Sara Jane 1930- *WorAlBi*
Moore, Sarah Copeland 1939- *WhoAmW 91*
Moore, Scott Jamieson 1957- *WhoSSW 91*
Moore, Scott Martin 1949- *WhoAmA 91*
Moore, Sean 1926- *WhoAm 90*
Moore, Sheror Caton 1943- *WhoWrEP 89*
Moore, Shirley Beaham 1934- *WhoAmW 91*
Moore, Shirley Throckmorton 1918- *WhoAmW 91, WhoWor 91*
Moore, Simon *BioIn 16*
Moore, Sonia 1902- *WhoAm 90, WhoWor 91*
Moore, Stan Lee 1950- *BiDrAPA 89*
Moore, Stanford 1913-1982 *WorAlBi*
Moore, Stephen Arthur 1931- *WhoAm 90*
Moore, Stephen Jefferson 1948- *St&PR 91*
Moore, Stephen Thomson 1956- *IntWWM 90*
Moore, Susan *WhoAmA 91*
Moore, Susan Evelyn 1954- *WhoAmW 91, WhoEmL 91*
Moore, Susan Lynn 1949- *WhoAmW 91*
Moore, T. Justin, Jr. 1925- *St&PR 91*
Moore, Tanna Lynn 1954- *WhoAmW 91*
Moore, Tara 1950- *SmATA 61 [port]*
Moore, Ted Benjamin *BiDrAPA 89*
Moore, Terence 1931- *WhoWor 91*
Moore, Teresa *WhoWrEP 89*
Moore, Terri Board 1955- *WhoSSW 91*
Moore, Terrill Mackenzie 1955- *St&PR 91*
Moore, Terris 1908- *WhoAm 90, WhoWor 91*
Moore, Terry 1912- *Ballpl 90*
Moore, Terry 1949- *ODwPR 91*
Moore, Theodore *St&PR 91*
Moore, Thomas *PenDiDA 89*
Moore, Thomas 1779-1852 *BioIn 16, DcLB 96 [port], OxCPMus*
Moore, Thomas 1940- *ConAu 132*
Moore, Thomas Carrol 1936- *WhoAm 90*
Moore, Thomas David 1937- *WhoAm 90*
Moore, Thomas Dickson 1930- *St&PR 91*
Moore, Thomas Gale 1930- *WhoAm 90*
Moore, Thomas Holmes 1920- *WhoAm 90*
Moore, Thomas J. 1944- *BioIn 16*
Moore, Thomas James 1928- *St&PR 91*
Moore, Thomas LeVal *NewYTBS 90 [port]*
Moore, Thomas Lloyd 1942- *WhoAm 90*
Moore, Thomas Nash 1927- *WhoAm 90*
Moore, Thomas Paul 1928- *WhoAm 90*
Moore, Thomas R. 1932- *WhoAm 90, WhoE 91*
Moore, Thomas W. 1939- *St&PR 91*
Moore, Tim 1888-1958 *DrBIPA 90*
Moore, Timothy 1922- *IntWWM 90*
Moore, Todd Somers 1952- *WhoAmA 91*
Moore, Tom *NewAgMG*
Moore, Tom 1943- *WhoAm 90*
Moore, Tom Richard 1935- *WhoE 91*
Moore, Truman Ellinwood 1935- *WhoE 91*
Moore, Undine Smith 1904-1989 *DrBIPA 90*
Moore, VanAnn Erion 1949- *IntWWM 90*
Moore, Vardine 1906- *AuBYP 90*
Moore, Vernon Lee 1928- *WhoAm 90*
Moore, Victor 1876-1962 *OxCPMus*
Moore, Virginia *AuBYP 90*
Moore, Virginia Blanck 1915- *WhoWrEP 89*
Moore, Virginia Bradley 1932- *WhoAmW 91, WhoE 91, WhoWor 91*
Moore, W. Clark 1922- *St&PR 91*
Moore, W. Henson, III 1939- *WhoAm 90*
Moore, W. James 1916- *St&PR 91*
Moore, W. Thomas 1933- *IntWWM 90*
Moore, Walter 1918- *ConAu 131*
Moore, Walter D., Jr. 1924- *WhoSSW 91*
Moore, Walter E. 1856-1933 *AmLegL*
Moore, Walter Edward Cladek 1927- *WhoAm 90*
Moore, Walter L *BiDrAPA 89*
Moore, Walter Leon 1916- *WhoAm 90*
Moore, Ward F. *St&PR 91N*
Moore, Ward Wilfred 1924- *WhoAm 90*
Moore, Wayland D 1935- *WhoAmA 91*
Moore, Wesley Craig 1946- *WhoAm 90*
Moore, Wesley Sanford 1935- *WhoAm 90*
Moore, Whitey 1912- *Ballpl 90*
Moore, Wilcy 1897-1963 *Ballpl 90*
Moore, William Armstead 1831-1884 *AmLegL*
Moore, William B. 1942- *St&PR 91*
Moore, William B. 1952- *St&PR 91*
Moore, William Black, Jr. 1924- *WhoSSW 91, WhoWor 91*
Moore, William E *BiDrAPA 89*
Moore, William E., Jr. *St&PR 91N*
Moore, William Evan, II 1925- *St&PR 91*
Moore, William Grover, Jr. *WhoAm 90*
Moore, William H. 1848-1923 *WorAlBi*
Moore, William H., III 1940- *St&PR 91*
Moore, William J. 1934- *St&PR 91*
Moore, William Jason 1938- *WhoAm 90, WhoSSW 91*
Moore, William John Myles 1924- *WhoAm 90*
Moore, William M. 1837- *AmLegL*
Moore, William Patrick 1928- *BiDrAPA 89*
Moore, William T 1925- *BiDrAPA 89*
Moore, William Taft *BiDrAPA 89*
Moore, William Thomas *BiDrAPA 89*
Moore, William Whitney 1918- *WhoWrEP 89*
Moore, William Wilson 1937- *WhoAm 90*
Moore, William Wyatt 1832?- *AmLegL*
Moore, Woodrow L. 1945- *St&PR 91*
Moore, Woodvall Ray 1942- *WhoWor 91*
Moore, Yancey Scott 1932- *BiDrAPA 89*
Moore, Yvonne L.H.R. 1943- *WhoAmW 91*
Moore-Betty, Maurice *BioIn 16*
Moore-Carroll, Patricia Susan 1957- *WhoAmW 91*
Moore-Day, Bonnie Lou 1956- *WhoAmW 91*
Moore-Ede, Martin Christopher 1945- *WhoE 91*
Moore-Sanders, Bethanne L *BiDrAPA 89*
Moore-Westbrook, Elizabeth H 1953- *BiDrAPA 89*
Moorefield, James Lee 1922- *WhoAm 90*
Moorehead, Agnes 1900?-1974 *BioIn 16, NotWoAT*
Moorehead, Agnes 1906-1974 *BioAmW, WorAlBi*
Moorehead, Alan McCrae 1910-1983 *DcNaB 1981*
Moorehead, Finola 1947- *FemiCLE*
Moorehead, Victoria Rose 1951- *WhoAmW 91*
Moorer, Thomas H. 1912- *WorAlBi*
Moorer, Thomas Hinman 1912- *St&PR 91, WhoAm 90*
Moores, Charles Bruce 1849-1930 *AmLegL*
Moores, Dick 1909-1986 *BioIn 16, EncACom*
Moores, Donna M 1948- *BiDrAPA 89*
Moores, Edward Harrison 1926- *St&PR 91*
Moores, Isaac R., Jr. *AmLegL*
Moores, R. John 1928- *WhoAm 90*
Moorey, P R S 1937- *ConAu 132*
Moorey, Roger *ConAu 132*
Moorfoot, Mark V. 1945- *St&PR 91*
Moorhead, Bob 1938- *Ballpl 90*
Moorhead, Carlos J. 1922- *WhoAm 90*
Moorhead, David Farrell 1932- *St&PR 91*
Moorhead, Gerald Lee 1947- *WhoSSW 91*
Moorhead, Horace Reynolds *BioIn 16*
Moorhead, Hugh S. 1922- *ConAu 130*
Moorhead, Jennelle Vandevort 1903- *WhoAm 90*
Moorhead, John *BioIn 16*
Moorhead, Lee C. 1937- *WhoE 91*
Moorhead, Lucy Galpin 1926- *WhoE 91*
Moorhead, Paul Sidney 1924- *WhoAm 90*
Moorhead, Robert G. 1921- *St&PR 91*
Moorhead, Rodman W., III *WhoE 91*
Moorhead, Sarah *FemiCLE*
Moorhead, Sylvester Andrew 1920- *WhoAm 90*
Moorhead, Thomas Burch 1934- *WhoE 91*
Moorhead, Thomas Leib 1936- *St&PR 91*
Moorhouse, Douglas Cecil 1926- *WhoAm 90*
Moorhouse, Herbert C 1907- *BiDrAPA 89*
Moorhouse, Linda Virginia 1945- *WhoAmW 91*
Moorhouse, Robert E. 1943- *St&PR 91*
Mooring, Robert Franklin 1946- *St&PR 91*
Moorman, Billie R. *ODwPR 91*
Moorman, Charles Wickliffe 1925- *WhoAm 90*
Moorman, Gilbert Wayne 1943- *St&PR 91*
Moorman, Kay 1922- *WhoAm 90*
Moorman, Lilot S. 1937- *ODwPR 91*
Moorman, Michael Field 1942- *St&PR 91*
Moorman, Robert Boyd 1943- *WhoSSW 91*
Moorman, Rosemary Lucille 1957- *WhoWrEP 89*
Moorshead, John Earl 1939- *St&PR 91*
Moorsom, Sasha 1931- *AuBYP 90*
Moorstein, Benjamin *BiDrAPA 89*
Moorthi, Kris Sankar 1941- *WhoE 91*
Moorthy, Subramania Lakshmi Varaha 1945- *WhoWor 91*
Moorwessel, George H. 1929- *St&PR 91*
Moos, Anthony Manuel 1913-1988 *BioIn 16*
Moos, Edward A. 1937- *St&PR 91, WhoE 91, WhoWor 91*
Moos, Julian Clifford 1923- *St&PR 91*
Moos, Rudolf H. 1934- *WhoAm 90*
Moos, Walter A 1926- *WhoAmA 91*
Moosbrugger, Mary Coultrip 1947- *WhoAmW 91*
Moosdorf, Johanna 1911- *EncCoWW*
Moose, Bob 1947-1976 *Ballpl 90*
Moose, George E. 1944- *WhoAm 90, WhoWor 91*
Moose, Lynne Suzanne 1966- *WhoAmW 91*
Moose, Nicole Stroman 1946- *WhoSSW 91*
Moose, Philip Anthony 1921- *WhoAmA 91*
Moose, Ruth Morris 1938- *WhoWrEP 89*
Moose, Talmadge Bowers 1933- *WhoAmA 91*
Mooshei, Bruno *BioIn 16*
Moosman, George L. 1941- *St&PR 91*
Moosnick, Sidney Calman 1939- *St&PR 91*
Moossa, A. R. 1939- *WhoAm 90*
Moossavi, Homayoon *BioIn 16*
Moossy, Yvonne Reese 1927- *WhoE 91*
Moote, A. Lloyd 1931- *WhoAm 90*
Mooty, David Nelson 1953- *WhoEmL 91*
Mooty, Jake 1913-1970 *Ballpl 90*
Mooty, John W. 1922- *St&PR 91*
Mooty, John William 1922- *WhoAm 90*
Mooz, R Peter 1940- *WhoAmA 91*
Mooz, Ralph Peter 1940- *WhoAm 90*
Moquin, Richard Attilio 1934- *WhoAmA 91*
Mor, Anthonis 1520?-1576 *IntDcAA 90*
Mora, Andres 1955- *Ballpl 90*
Mora, Charles John 1946- *BiDrAPA 89*
Mora, David Richard 1945- *WhoHisp 91*
Mora, Ernest J. *St&PR 91*
Mora, Francisco 1922- *WhoAm 90*
Mora, George 1923- *BiDrAPA 89*
Mora, James Ernest 1935- *WhoAm 90, WhoSSW 91*
Mora, Juan Rafael 1814-1860 *BioIn 16*
Mora, Lourdes 1956- *WhoSSW 91*
Mora, Maria-Alicia 1959- *WhoHisp 91*
Mora, Miguel A *BiDrAPA 89*
Mora, Narciso Andres 1934- *WhoHisp 91*
Mora, Pat 1942- *ConAu 129, HispWr 90, WhoHisp 91*
Mora, Rafael A 1917- *BiDrAPA 89*
Mora, Virgilio A *BiDrAPA 89*
Mora Valverde, Manuel 1908- *BioIn 16*
Mora y Aragon, Fabiola de 1928- *EncCoWW*
Morabe, Jeannette L *BiDrAPA 89*
Morabito, Bruno Paul 1922- *WhoAm 90*
Morabito, David Robertson, Sr. 1954- *WhoEmL 91*
Morabito, John R. 1924- *WhoE 91*
Morack, Albert John, Jr. 1948- *St&PR 91*
Moraczewski, Robert Leo 1942- *WhoAm 90*
Moradeyo, Israel Olufemi 1941- *WhoWor 91*
Moradi, Ahmad E. 1955- *WhoSSW 91*
Moradi, Robert 1948- *BiDrAPA 89*
Moradi-Araghi, Ahmad 1943- *WhoWor 91*
Moraes, Claude Louis *BiDrAPA 89*
Moraff, Barbara 1939- *WhoWrEP 89*
Moraga, Cherrie 1952- *ConAu 131, HispWr 90, WhoHisp 91*
Moragn e Silva, Michele Lowe 1955- *WhoAmW 91*
Moragne, Lenora *WhoE 91*
Moragne, Sidney 1958- *BiDrAPA 89*
Morahan, Daniel Michael 1940- *WhoE 91*
Morahan, Matthew Joseph 1949- *WhoAm 90*
Morahan, Page S. 1940- *WhoAmW 91*
Morain, Lloyd L. 1917- *St&PR 91*
Morain, Mary Stone Dewing 1911- *WhoWor 91*
Morain, Stephen Michael 1945- *St&PR 91*
Morais, Sabato 1823-1897 *BioIn 16*
Moraitis, George 1926- *BiDrAPA 89*
Moraitis, Karen Karl 1943- *WhoAmW 91, WhoSSW 91*
Moraitis, Nicoclis George 1924- *IntWWM 90*
Morakis, James A. 1934- *ODwPR 91*
Moral, Jose Luis *BiDrAPA 89*
Morales *WhoWrEP 89*
Morales, Abram 1939- *IntWWM 90*
Morales, Adela 1942- *WhoAmW 91*
Morales, Albert 1966- *WhoE 91*
Morales, Aldo, Jr. *BiDrAPA 89*
Morales, Alejandro 1944- *ConAu 131, HispWr 90*
Morales, Alice *BiDrAPA 89*
Morales, Alvino 1950- *WhoHisp 91*
Morales, Angel E. 1953- *WhoHisp 91*
Morales, Angel L. 1952- *WhoHisp 91*
Morales, Angel Luis 1919- *HispWr 90*
Morales, Anthony Russell 1960- *WhoHisp 91*
Morales, Antonio 1937- *WhoHisp 91*
Morales, Armando 1927- *WhoAmA 91*
Morales, Armando 1932- *WhoWor 91*
Morales, Arturo Esteben *BiDrAPA 89*
Morales, Carlota Eloisa 1946- *WhoSSW 91*
Morales, Charles S. 1946- *WhoHisp 91*
Morales, Claudio H. 1945- *WhoHisp 91*
Morales, Dan 1956- *WhoHisp 91*
Morales, David *WhoHisp 91*
Morales, Dionicio *WhoHisp 91*
Morales, Enrique C. Miguel 1949- *WhoWor 91*
Morales, Enrique David 1927- *BiDrAPA 89*
Morales, Esai *BioIn 16*
Morales, Esai 1963- *WhoHisp 91*
Morales, Evelyn C 1945- *BiDrAPA 89*
Morales, Felicita 1951- *WhoHisp 91*
Morales, Fred 1924- *WhoHisp 91*
Morales, Gerardo Machado y 1871-1939 *BioIn 16*
Morales, Gertrude *BiDrAPA 89*
Morales, Gilbert 1965- *WhoHisp 91*
Morales, Hernan 1950- *IntWWM 90*
Morales, Hortensia Maria 1944- *WhoAmW 91*
Morales, Hugo *BioIn 16*
Morales, Hugo M 1933- *BiDrAPA 89*
Morales, Ibra 1945- *WhoHisp 91*
Morales, Jeanette *BiDrAPA 89*
Morales, Jeanette 1956- *WhoE 91*
Morales, Jenny 1949- *WhoHisp 91*
Morales, Jerry 1949- *Ballpl 90*
Morales, Jorge Juan 1945- *WhoHisp 91*
Morales, Jorge Luis 1930- *HispWr 90*
Morales, Jose 1944- *Ballpl 90*
Morales, Jose 1945- *WhoHisp 91*
Morales, Jose 1952- *WhoHisp 91*
Morales, Joselito B *BiDrAPA 89*
Morales, Joseph M. 1955- *WhoHisp 91*
Morales, Juan E 1921- *BiDrAPA 89*
Morales, Judy 1941- *WhoHisp 91*
Morales, Julio, Jr. 1942- *WhoHisp 91*
Morales, Julio K. 1948- *WhoEmL 91*

Morales, Magda Hernandez 1943- *WhoHisp 91*
Morales, Manuel, Jr. 1945- *WhoAm 90*
Morales, Manuel Francisco 1919- *WhoHisp 91*
Morales, Marco Aurelio Guillen 1955- *WhoWor 91*
Morales, Michael 1963- *WhoHisp 91*
Morales, Milsa 1952- *WhoHisp 91*
Morales, Nancy Barbara 1950- *WhoHisp 91*
Morales, Naomi M. 1954- *WhoAmW 91*
Morales, Nora 1911-1964 *OxCPMus*
Morales, Ophelia C. 1928- *WhoHisp 91*
Morales, Ralph, Jr. 1940- *WhoHisp 91*
Morales, Ramon Villeda *BioIn 16*
Morales, Raul 1935- *WhoHisp 91*
Morales, Raymond C. *WhoHisp 91*
Morales, Raymond Chacon 1946- *WhoHisp 91*
Morales, Raymond Peter *WhoE 91*
Morales, Rich 1943- *Ballpl 90*
Morales, Richard *BiDrAPA 89*
Morales, Richard 1938- *WhoHisp 91*
Morales, Richard 1949- *WhoHisp 91*
Morales, Robert A. 1956- *ODwPR 91*
Morales, Rodolfo 1925- *WhoAmA 91*
Morales, Thomas Frime, Jr. 1947- *WhoHisp 91*
Morales Bermudez, Francisco 1921- *BioIn 16*
Morales Carrion, Arturo *BioIn 16*
Morales Carrion, Arturo 1913-1989 *ConAu 131, HispWr 90, WhoHisp 91N*
Morales Carrion, Arturo 1914?-1989 *ConAu 129*
Morales-Counertier, Angel Luis 1919- *WhoHisp 91*
Morales-Galarreta, Julio 1936- *BiDrAPA 89, WhoWor 91*
Morales-Lebron, Mariano 1935- *WhoHisp 91*
Morales-Loebl, Maria 1953- *WhoHisp 91*
Morales-Nieves, Alfredo 1956- *WhoHisp 91*
Morales-Padro, Jose M 1960- *BiDrAPA 89*
Morales-Ramos, Ubaldo *BiDrAPA 89*
Morales Reyes, Luis 1936- *WhoAm 90*
Morales-Rivas, Alice 1961- *WhoHisp 91*
Morales Troncoso, Carlos A. 1940- *WhoWor 91*
Moralez, Joselyn Hope 1966- *WhoAmW 91, WhoHisp 91*
Moran, Barbara Burns 1944- *WhoAmW 91, WhoSSW 91*
Moran, Benjamin 1820-1886 *BioIn 16*
Moran, Billy 1933- *Ballpl 90*
Moran, Byron L. 1942- *St&PR 91*
Moran, Charles A. 1943- *WhoAm 90*
Moran, Charley 1878-1949 *Ballpl 90*
Moran, Christa Ilse Merkel 1946- *WhoWor 91*
Moran, Daniel Austin 1936- *WhoAm 90*
Moran, Daniel Edward 1941- *St&PR 91*
Moran, Deborah *BioIn 16*
Moran, Deborah Mary *BiDrAPA 89*
Moran, Donald J. 1951- *WhoEmL 91*
Moran, Douglas E. *BioIn 16*
Moran, Edward Martin 1956- *St&PR 91*
Moran, Ellen O'Kelley 1963- *WhoEmL 91*
Moran, Ellen Rose 1951- *WhoSSW 91*
Moran, Emilio Federico 1946- *WhoEmL 91*
Moran, Eugene Francis 1872- *AuBYP 90*
Moran, Frank E., Jr. 1919- *WhoSSW 91*
Moran, Gary M. 1941- *St&PR 91*
Moran, George William 1964- *WhoE 91*
Moran, Gerald Joseph 1939- *St&PR 91*
Moran, Glenn J. 1947- *St&PR 91*
Moran, Gordon William 1938- *WhoAm 90*
Moran, Gregory J. 1954- *St&PR 91*
Moran, Harold Joseph 1907- *WhoSSW 91, WhoWor 91*
Moran, Harry 1889-1962 *Ballpl 90*
Moran, Herbie 1884-1954 *Ballpl 90*
Moran, J. A. 1932- *St&PR 91*
Moran, James *ODwPR 91*
Moran, James B. 1924- *WhoAm 90, WhoWor 91*
Moran, James Byron 1930- *WhoAm 90*
Moran, James D., III 1951- *WhoEmL 91, WhoSSW 91*
Moran, James H. 1939- *ODwPR 91*
Moran, James Joseph 1925- *St&PR 91*
Moran, James M. 1916- *St&PR 91*
Moran, James Patrick, Jr. 1945- *WhoSSW 91*
Moran, Jeffrey 1947- *BiDrAPA 89*
Moran, Jeffrey William 1954- *WhoE 91*
Moran, Jennifer 1949- *St&PR 91*
Moran, Jim *BioIn 16*
Moran, John A. 1932- *WhoAm 90*
Moran, John Bernard 1936- *WhoAm 90*
Moran, John Charles 1942- *WhoWrEP 89*
Moran, John F. 1936- *WhoE 91*
Moran, John Henry, Jr. 1923- *WhoAm 90*
Moran, John J. 1929- *St&PR 91*
Moran, John Joseph 1916- *WhoAm 90*
Moran, John Patrick, Jr. 1943- *WhoE 91*
Moran, John Richard 1926- *St&PR 91*
Moran, John Sullivan *BiDrAPA 89*
Moran, John Vincent 1913- *WhoAm 90*
Moran, Joseph M. 1921- *ODwPR 91*
Moran, Joseph Milbert 1929- *St&PR 91, WhoAm 90*
Moran, Joseph Richard 1942- *St&PR 91*
Moran, Joseph William 1927- *St&PR 91*
Moran, Juliette M. 1917- *WhoAm 90, WhoAmW 91*
Moran, Katherine Jean 1958- *WhoAmW 91*
Moran, Kevin P. 1952- *St&PR 91*
Moran, Lawrence Joseph 1935- *WhoE 91*
Moran, M. Marcus, Jr. 1943- *St&PR 91*
Moran, Malcolm C. *St&PR 91*
Moran, Martin Joseph 1930- *WhoAm 90, WhoE 91, WhoWor 91*
Moran, Mary 1842-1899 *BiDWomA*
Moran, Mary Chapar *WhoAmW 91*
Moran, Melvin Robert 1930- *St&PR 91*
Moran, Michael 1948- *IntWWM 90*
Moran, Michael Gordon 1949- *BiDrAPA 89*
Moran, Michael Joseph 1947- *BiDrAPA 89*
Moran, Michael R. 1946- *St&PR 91*
Moran, Mike *ODwPR 91, TwCCr&M 91*
Moran, Mike 1942- *ODwPR 91*
Moran, Noel F. 1936- *St&PR 91*
Moran, Pat 1876-1924 *Ballpl 90*
Moran, Patricia Rose 1930- *WhoAmW 91*
Moran, Peter 1842-1914 *WhNaAH*
Moran, Philip David 1937- *WhoE 91, WhoWor 91*
Moran, Richard Adrian 1931- *St&PR 91*
Moran, Richard Edward 1957- *WhoWor 91*
Moran, Robert 1857- *BioIn 16*
Moran, Robert Daniel 1929- *WhoAm 90*
Moran, Robert Earl 1936- *St&PR 91*
Moran, Robert J. 1941- *St&PR 91*
Moran, Rosemary Theresa 1959- *WhoE 91*
Moran, S. Joseph *ODwPR 91*
Moran, Sean Farrell 1951- *WhoE 91*
Moran, Stephen R. 1931- *ODwPR 91*
Moran, Teresita Chavez 1948- *WhoWor 91*
Moran, Terrence R. 1941- *St&PR 91*
Moran, Terrence Raymond 1941- *WhoAm 90*
Moran, Thomas 1837-1926 *WhNaAH*
Moran, Thomas 1918- *St&PR 91*
Moran, Thomas E. *St&PR 91*
Moran, Thomas Francis 1936- *WhoSSW 91*
Moran, Thomas Henry Edward 1940- *WhoAm 90*
Moran, Thomas Joseph 1920- *WhoAm 90*
Moran, Thomas M 1940- *BiDrAPA 89*
Moran, Tom 1943- *SmATA 60*
Moran, W. Dennis 1940- *St&PR 91, WhoAm 90, WhoWor 91*
Moran, Wilfred F. 1928- *St&PR 91*
Moran, William Dermott *BioIn 16*
Moran, William Edward 1932- *WhoAm 90, WhoSSW 91*
Moran, William J 1930- *BiDrAPA 89*
Moran, William Madison 1948- *WhoSSW 91*
Morana, Jacqueline Letitia 1939- *WhoE 91*
Morand, Paul 1888-1976 *BioIn 16*
Moranda, Nancy Leigh 1957- *WhoAmW 91*
Morandi, Giorgio 1890-1964 *BioIn 16, IntDcAA 90*
Morandini, Giuliana 1926- *EncCoWW*
Morang, Alfred Gwynne 1901-1958 *WhoAmA 91N*
Morani, Alma Dea 1907- *WhoAm 90*
Morano, Albert P. 1908-1987 *BioIn 16*
Morano, Kevin R. *St&PR 91*
Morano, Michael Robert 1918- *St&PR 91*
Morant, Mack Bernard 1946- *WhoWrEP 89*
Morant, Peter Josef 1952- *WhoE 91*
Morant, Ricardo Bernardino 1926- *WhoAm 90*
Morante, Elsa 1912-1986 *EncCoWW*
Morante, Elsa 1918-1985 *MajTwCW*
Moranville, Gary Lee *BiDrAPA 89*
Moranville, John Thomas 1958- *BiDrAPA 89*
Moranz, Gary A. 1950- *St&PR 91*
Morari, Manfred 1951- *WhoAm 90, WhoEmL 91*
Morash, Frederick Douglas 1947- *St&PR 91*
Morash, Kenneth R. 1943- *St&PR 91*
Morash, Stanley Angus 1920- *St&PR 91*
Morath, Inge 1923- *WhoAm 90, WhoAmA 91*
Morath, Max 1926- *OxCPMus*
Morath, Max Edward 1926- *WhoAm 90*
Moratz, Hermann 1921- *St&PR 91*
Moravcik, Gary Joseph 1959- *St&PR 91*
Moravcova, Jana 1937- *EncCoWW*
Moravec, Hans P. *BioIn 16*
Moravec, Lisa Kay 1962- *WhoAmW 91*
Moravec, Paul 1957- *IntWWM 90*
Moravia, Alberto *ConAu 132, -33NR, MajTwCW*
Moravia, Alberto 1907- *EuWr 12, WhoWor 91, WorAlBi*
Moravia, Alberto 1907-1990 *BioIn 16, CurBio 90N, NewYTBS 90 [port]*
Moravitz, Francis Edward 1933- *WhoAm 90*
Moravy, L. Joe 1950- *WhoAm 90, WhoEmL 91*
Morawetz, Cathleen Synge 1923- *WhoAm 90*
Morawetz, Herbert 1915- *WhoAm 90*
Morawetz, Oskar 1917- *IntWWM 90, PenDiMP A*
Morawiec, Alicja 1946- *WhoE 91*
Morawski, Jerzy 1932- *IntWWM 90*
Moray, Sherry 1963- *WhoAmW 91, WhoEmL 91, WhoWor 91*
Morayati, Shamil Jassim 1953- *WhoWor 91*
Moraz, Patrick *NewAgMG*
Morazan, Francisco 1792-1842 *BioIn 16*
Morbach, John P. 1943- *St&PR 91*
Morbidi, Mario 1953- *WhoWor 91*
Morbitzer, Kurt M 1919- *BiDrAPA 89*
Morby, Jacqueline 1937- *WhoAm 90*
Morcerf, Lester Anthony, Jr. 1928- *WhoE 91*
Morch, Dea Trier *DcScanL*
Morch, Dea Trier 1941- *EncCoWW*
Morcheles, Bernard 1939- *St&PR 91*
Morchower, Scott Irwin 1957- *WhoSSW 91*
Morck, Paal *DcScanL*
Morcos, John Elias 1943- *BiDrAPA 89*
Morcos, Maher N 1946- *WhoAmA 91*
Morcos, Victor Hanna 1940- *BiDrAPA 89*
Morcott, Anne *BiDEWW*
Morcott, Southwood J. 1938- *St&PR 91*
Morcott, Southwood J. 1939- *WhoAm 90*
Mordaunt, Elinor 1877-1942 *FemiCLE*
Mordaunt, Elizabeth 1632?-1679 *BiDEWW, FemiCLE*
Mordaunt, Penelope *BiDEWW*
Mordecai, Pamela 1942- *FemiCLE*
Mordek, Hubert Klaus Wolfgang 1939- *WhoWor 91*
Mordell, Louis Joel 1888-1972 *DcScB S2*
Morden, John Reid 1941- *WhoAm 90*
Mordenti, Joyce Jenney 1952- *WhoEmL 91*
Mordler, John Michael 1938- *WhoWor 91*
Mordo, Jean Henri 1945- *St&PR 91, WhoAm 90*
Mordue, Howard Wilbur 1930- *WhoSSW 91*
Mordvinoff, Nicolas 1911-1973 *AuBYP 90, WhoAmA 91N*
Mordwin, John Rickford 1947- *WhoE 91*
Mordy, C. Edward 1943- *St&PR 91*
Mordy, James Calvin 1927- *WhoAm 90*
More, Agnes 1563?- *FemiCLE*
More, Agnes 1591-1655? *BiDEWW*
More, Brian 1921- *WorAlBi*
More, Carey Elizabeth 1957- *WhoWor 91*
More, Caroline *AuBYP 90*
More, Douglas McLochlan 1926- *WhoAm 90*
More, Eduardo A. 1929- *WhoHisp 91*
More, Gertrude 1606-1633 *BiDEWW, FemiCLE*
More, Gregory Paul 1953- *WhoEmL 91*
More, Hannah 1745-1833 *BioIn 16, FemiCLE, NinCLC 27 [port]*
More, Hermon 1887-1968 *WhoAmA 91N*
More, Joseph 1935- *BiDrAPA 89*
More, Mary *FemiCLE*
More, Philip Jerome 1911- *WhoAm 90, WhoSSW 91, WhoWor 91*
More, Rebecca Sherrill 1947- *WhoE 91*
More, Richard W. 1924- *St&PR 91*
More, Syver Wakeman 1950- *WhoWor 91*
More, Thomas 1477-1535 *WorAlBi*
Moreano, Augusto G 1929- *BiDrAPA 89*
Moreau Defarges 1948- *WhoWor 91*
Moreau, Donna *BiDrAPA 89*
Moreau, Gustave 1826-1878 *BioIn 16*
Moreau, Gustave 1826-1889 *IntDcAA 90*
Moreau, Hugues Andre 1948- *WhoWor 91*
Moreau, Jay Michael 1965- *WhoSSW 91*
Moreau, Jean 1763-1813 *WorAlBi*
Moreau, Jeanne *BioIn 16*
Moreau, Jeanne 1928- *ConTFT 8, WhoWor 91, WorAlBi*
Moreau, John Adam *ODwPR 91*
Moreau, Robert 1939- *St&PR 91*
Moreau, Ronald A. 1947- *St&PR 91*
Moreau-Nelaton, Camille 1840-1897 *PenDiDA 89*
Moreau-Nelaton, Etienne 1859-1927 *PenDiDA 89*
Morecambe, Eric 1926-1984 *DcNaB 1981*
Morecroft, Mike John 1942- *St&PR 91*
Morehart, Donald Hadley 1938- *St&PR 91, WhoAm 90*
Morehart, Ray 1899-1989 *BioIn 16*
Morehead, Charles Richard 1947- *St&PR 91, WhoAm 90*
Morehead, Dave 1943- *Ballpl 90*
Morehead, James Caddall, Jr. 1913- *WhoAm 90*
Morehead, John 1946- *St&PR 91*
Morehead, Martha Hines 1923- *WhoSSW 91*
Morehead, Mildred Ada 1919- *WhoAmW 91*
Morehead, Russel R. 1947- *St&PR 91*
Morehead, Seth 1934- *Ballpl 90*
Morehead, Simon Eber 1941- *St&PR 91*
Morehead-Morris, Patricia S. 1936- *WhoAmW 91*
Morehen, John Manley 1941- *IntWWM 90*
Morehouse College Quartet *DcAfAmP*
Morehouse, Dale H. 1933- *St&PR 91*
Morehouse, Henry Lyman 1834-1917 *BioIn 16*
Morehouse, James Ernest 1944- *St&PR 91*
Morehouse, M. Dutton, Jr. 1936- *ODwPR 91*
Morehouse, Sherri K. 1955- *WhoAmW 91*
Morehouse, William Paul 1929- *WhoAmA 91*
Moreillon, Jacques Pierre 1939- *WhoWor 91*
Moreillon, Robert E. 1930- *ODwPR 91*
Moreines, Robert Neil *BiDrAPA 89*
Moreira, Airto Guimorva 1941- *BioIn 16*
Moreira, Alvaro F 1930- *BiDrAPA 89*
Moreira, Gerald M. 1941- *St&PR 91*
Moreira, Marcio Martins 1947- *WhoAm 90, WhoEmL 91, WhoWor 91*
Moreira, Ruben 1922?- *EncACom*
Moreira Neves, Lucas 1925- *WhoWor 91*
Morel, Benoit Ferdinand 1949- *WhoE 91*
Morel, Francois 1926- *IntWWM 90*
Morel-Ladeuil, Leonard *PenDiDA 89*
Morelan, Paula Kay 1949- *WhoAm 90, WhoSSW 91*
Moreland, Alvin Franklin 1931- *WhoAm 90*
Moreland, Brendan Francis 1933- *St&PR 91*
Moreland, Keith 1954- *Ballpl 90, BioIn 16*
Moreland, Mantan 1902-1973 *DrBlPA 90*
Moreland, Richard James 1947- *St&PR 91, WhoAm 90*
Moreland, Suzanne 1951- *WhoAmW 91, WhoE 91*
Morelewicz, R. H. 1943- *St&PR 91*
Morell, Frank P. 1947- *St&PR 91*
Morell, James Livingston 1933- *St&PR 91*
Morell, Theodor Gilbert 1886-1948 *BioIn 16*
Morell, William Nelson, Jr. 1920- *WhoWor 91*
Morella, Constance Albanese 1931- *WhoAm 90, WhoAmW 91, WhoE 91*
Morellet, Francois Charles 1926- *WhoWor 91*
Morelli, Al 1953- *WhoEmL 91*
Morelli, Alessio *PenDiDA 89*
Morelli, Anthony Frank 1956- *WhoEmL 91, WhoWor 91*
Morelli, Domenico 1826-1901 *BioIn 16*
Morelli, Joseph 1947- *St&PR 91*
Morelli, Luigi 1943- *WhoWor 91*
Morelli, Maria Maddelena 1727-1800 *EncCoWW*
Morelli, Richard Joseph 1952- *St&PR 91, WhoE 91*
Morelli, Robert Michael 1938- *BiDrAPA 89*
Morelli, Roger H. 1944- *St&PR 91*
Morelli, William Annibale, Sr. 1938- *WhoAm 90*
Morello, Carol Jean 1957- *WhoAmW 91*
Morello, Joe *BioIn 16*
Morello, John Patrick 1952- *St&PR 91*
Morello, Joseph Louis 1950- *BiDrAPA 89*
Morelock, James Crutchfield 1920- *WhoSSW 91, WhoWor 91*
Morelos, Alfredo, Jr. 1952- *WhoHisp 91*
Moren, Halldis Vesaas *DcScanL*
Moren, Lew 1883-1966 *Ballpl 90*
Moren, Nicholas Charles 1946- *St&PR 91*
Moren, Robert Alan 1937- *St&PR 91*
Morena *EncCoWW*
Morena, Ol'ga *EncCoWW*
Morency, Pierre *BioIn 16*
Moreno, Alejandro 1947- *WhoHisp 91*
Moreno, Alfredo A., Jr. 1919- *WhoHisp 91*
Moreno, Antonio Elosegui 1918- *WhoHisp 91*
Moreno, Arnaldo Nobleza *BiDrAPA 89*
Moreno, Arturo 1934- *WhoHisp 91*
Moreno, Arturo 1954- *St&PR 91*
Moreno, Baldomero Fernandez *HispWr 90*
Moreno, Carlos Americo 1951- *WhoSSW 91*
Moreno, Carlos Martinez *ConAu 131, HispWr 90*
Moreno, Carlos W. 1936- *WhoHisp 91*
Moreno, Catherine Hartmus 1935- *WhoWrEP 89*
Moreno, Celia M *BiDrAPA 89*

Moreno, Cesar Fernandez *ConAu 131, HispWr 90*
Moreno, Dario Vincent 1958- *WhoHisp 91*
Moreno, Elida 1944- *WhoHisp 91*
Moreno, Enrique Garrido 1952- *WhoWor 91*
Moreno, Eusebio Carlos 1960- *WhoWrEP 89*
Moreno, Federico Antonio 1952- *WhoEmL 91*
Moreno, Federico Antonio, Sr. 1952- *WhoHisp 91*
Moreno, Fernando 1946- *WhoHisp 91*
Moreno, Gabriel Garcia 1821-1875 *BioIn 16*
Moreno, Gilberto 1936- *WhoHisp 91*
Moreno, Glen Richard 1943- *WhoAm 90*
Moreno, Jose Codina 1949- *WhoWor 91*
Moreno, Jose Guillermo *BiDrAPA 89*
Moreno, Jose Guillermo 1951- *WhoE 91, WhoHisp 91*
Moreno, Joseph Florencio 1964- *WhoEmL 91, WhoSSW 91*
Moreno, Juan Ramon *BioIn 16*
Moreno, Julio 1921-1987 *Ballpl 90*
Moreno, Luis Fernando 1951- *WhoHisp 91*
Moreno, Luisa 1907- *BioIn 16*
Moreno, Luz Maria 1955- *St&PR 91*
Moreno, M. Cristina 1952- *WhoEmL 91*
Moreno, Manuel 1945- *WhoHisp 91*
Moreno, Manuel D. 1930- *WhoAm 90*
Moreno, Marcelino, Jr. 1961- *WhoHisp 91*
Moreno, Maria 1933- *BiDWomA*
Moreno, Mary A. *WhoHisp 91*
Moreno, Michael Rafael 1954- *WhoHisp 91*
Moreno, Michelle Adrienne 1959- *WhoAmW 91*
Moreno, Omar 1953- *Ballpl 90*
Moreno, Orlando Julio 1944- *WhoHisp 91*
Moreno, Oscar *WhoHisp 91*
Moreno, Paul 1931- *WhoHisp 91*
Moreno, Richard D. 1940- *WhoHisp 91*
Moreno, Rita 1931- *WhoAm 90, WhoHisp 91, WorAlBi*
Moreno, Susan Ingalls 1959- *WhoAmW 91*
Moreno, Susan Scholey 1934- *BiDrAPA 89*
Moreno, Valerie Lucille 1939- *WhoE 91*
Moreno, Victor John 1955- *WhoHisp 91*
Moreno Barbera, Fernando 1913- *WhoWor 91*
Moreno Uriegas, Maria De Los Angeles 1945- *WhoWor 91*
Morenon, Elise 1939- *WhoAmA 91*
Morente, Flora Fesalbon *BiDrAPA 89*
Morenus, Richard 1897- *AuBYP 90*
Morenz, Bernard Martin 1953- *BiDrAPA 89*
Morenz, Howie 1902-1937 *WorAlBi*
Morenzi, Vanessa Ann 1958- *WhoAmW 91*
Morera, Osvaldo Francisco 1966- *WhoHisp 91*
Mores, Jacob 1578-1609? *PenDiDA 89*
Moreschi, Alessandro 1858-1922 *PenDiMP*
Moreschi, Patricia R 1927- *BiDrAPA 89*
Moreschi, Patricia Reed 1927- *WhoE 91*
Moreschi, Roger P. 1938- *St&PR 91*
Moreshead, Joseph A. 1957- *St&PR 91*
Moress, Ralph 1934- *BiDrAPA 89*
Moret, Leon 1890-1972 *DcScB S2*
Moret, Louis F. 1944- *WhoHisp 91*
Moret, Michael R *BiDrAPA 89*
Moret, Neil 1878-1943 *BioIn 16*
Moret, Roger 1949- *Ballpl 90*
Moret, Vernon H. 1925- *St&PR 91*
Moreto, Jorge Luiz 1961- *WhoWor 91*
Moreton, Charles P. 1927- *St&PR 91*
Moreton, Edward Burton 1932- *St&PR 91*
Moreton, Frederick A., Jr. 1939- *St&PR 91*
Moreton, John *AuBYP 90*
Moreton, Julian 1825-1900 *DcCanB 12*
Morett, Angela Marie 1952- *WhoHisp 91*
Morett, Margaret 1938- *WhoWrEP 89*
Moretti, Frank Fred 1928- *WhoSSW 91*
Moretti, Hans 1928- *BioIn 16*
Moretti, Nanni *BioIn 16*
Moretti, Peter M. A. 1935- *WhoSSW 91*
Moretz, Cheryl Ann 1950- *WhoAmW 91, WhoE 91*
Moretz, George A. 1942- *St&PR 91*
Moretz, Lori Susan *WhoAmW 91*
Morewitz, Jerry Howard *BiDrAPA 89*
Morey, Carl Reginald 1934- *IntWWM 90, WhoAm 90*
Morey, David Edward 1956- *WhoE 91*
Morey, Dewans 1644?-1684 *BiDEWW, FemiCLE*
Morey, Frederick Arnold 1925- *WhoE 91*
Morey, Helen Jean 1940- *WhoAmW 91*
Morey, James Newman 1933- *WhoAm 90*
Morey, John W. 1943- *St&PR 91*
Morey, Kathleen Johnson 1946- *WhoWrEP 89*
Morey, Larry Wayne 1949- *WhoEmL 91, WhoWor 91*
Morey, Lloyd William, Jr. 1930- *WhoWor 91*
Morey, Marion Louise 1926- *WhoAmW 91*
Morey, Melinda Louise 1955- *WhoAmW 91*
Morey, Robert A 1946- *ConAu 32NR*
Morey, Robert Hardy 1956- *WhoWor 91*
Morey, Robert M. 1947- *St&PR 91*
Morey, Robert Thomas 1933- *WhoE 91*
Morey, Walt 1907- *AuBYP 90, BioIn 16, ConAu 31NR*
Morfopoulos, Vassilis C. P. 1937- *St&PR 91*
Morforpoulos, Vassilis Constantinos P. 1937- *WhoAm 90*
Morga, George B 1949- *BiDrAPA 89*
Morga Bellizzi, Celeste 1921- *WhoAmW 91*
Morgado, Ernest F. 1917- *St&PR 91*
Morgado, Richard Joseph 1946- *WhoE 91*
Morgagni, Giovanni Battista 1682-1771 *BioIn 16, WorAlBi*
Morgan, Lady 1776?-1859 *NinCLC 29 [port]*
Morgan, A James 1930- *BiDrAPA 89*
Morgan, A Michelle *BiDrAPA 89*
Morgan, Agnes 1879-1976 *BioIn 16, NotWoAT*
Morgan, Alan Vivian 1943- *WhoAm 90*
Morgan, Alexander C 1941- *BiDrAPA 89*
Morgan, Alexander Charles 1941- *WhoE 91*
Morgan, Alfred Powell 1889-1972 *AuBYP 90*
Morgan, Alfred Y., Jr. 1939- *St&PR 91*
Morgan, Allen *AuBYP 90*
Morgan, Allen Benners, Jr. 1942- *St&PR 91*
Morgan, Allen H. *BioIn 16, NewYTBS 90*
Morgan, Andrew Wesley 1922- *WhoAm 90*
Morgan, Angela *ConAu 31NR*
Morgan, Ann Haven 1882-1966 *WomFie [port]*
Morgan, Anna 1851-1936 *BioAmW*
Morgan, Anne Tracy 1873-1952 *BioIn 16*
Morgan, Arlene *ConAu 31NR*
Morgan, Arlene Notoro 1945- *WhoAm 90*
Morgan, Arthur Anthony 1938- *St&PR 91*
Morgan, Arthur C 1904- *WhoAmA 91*
Morgan, Arthur Edward 1929- *St&PR 91, WhoAm 90*
Morgan, Arthur Ivason, Jr. 1923- *WhoAm 90*
Morgan, Audrey 1931- *WhoWor 91*
Morgan, Austen 1949- *ConAu 130*
Morgan, Bailey *TwCCr&M 91*
Morgan, Barbara Brooks 1900- *WhoAmA 91*
Morgan, Barbara Joan 1940- *WhoAmW 91*
Morgan, Betty Lou 1931- *WhoAmW 91*
Morgan, Beverly 1952- *IntWWM 90*
Morgan, Beverly Carver 1927- *WhoAm 90*
Morgan, Bill 1949- *ConAu 30NR*
Morgan, Bobby 1926- *Ballpl 90*
Morgan, Brian S. 1942- *St&PR 91*
Morgan, Bruce Douglas 1947- *WhoE 91*
Morgan, Bruce Ray 1932- *WhoAm 90*
Morgan, Bryan Stanford 1923-1976 *AuBYP 90*
Morgan, Burton D. 1916- *St&PR 91*
Morgan, Calvert A., Jr. 1948- *St&PR 91*
Morgan, Carol M. 1944- *ODwPR 91*
Morgan, Catherine Marie 1947- *WhoSSW 91*
Morgan, Cathy Lynn 1959- *WhoAmW 91*
Morgan, Charles 1894-1958 *DcLB 100 [port]*
Morgan, Charles Alexander, III 1960- *BiDrAPA 89*
Morgan, Charles Hermann, Jr. 1949- *WhoSSW 91*
Morgan, Charles James *BiDrAPA 89*
Morgan, Charles Russell 1946- *WhoAm 90, WhoWor 91*
Morgan, Charles Sumner 1915- *WhoAm 90*
Morgan, Charles Thomas 1933- *St&PR 91*
Morgan, Charles Wesley 1951- *WhoSSW 91*
Morgan, Claire *MajTwCW*
Morgan, Clarence 1950- *WhoAmA 91*
Morgan, Colin J. 1935- *St&PR 91*
Morgan, Colin John 1935- *WhoAm 90*
Morgan, Constance Louise 1941- *WhoAmW 91, WhoSSW 91*
Morgan, Craig McDonald 1950- *WhoEmL 91*
Morgan, Cy 1878-1962 *Ballpl 90*
Morgan, Dale Lowell 1914-1971 *BioIn 16*
Morgan, Daniel 1736-1802 *EncCRAm, WorAlBi*
Morgan, Danny Ray 1951- *WhoSSW 91*
Morgan, Daryle Whitney 1929- *WhoSSW 91*
Morgan, David 1932- *IntWWM 90*
Morgan, David Allen 1962- *WhoWor 91*
Morgan, David George 1943- *WhoWor 91*
Morgan, David Griffith 1952- *WhoEmL 91*
Morgan, David Lewis 1936- *St&PR 91*
Morgan, David Page 1927- *WhoWrEP 89*
Morgan, David S. 1927- *St&PR 91*
Morgan, Debbi *BioIn 16, DrBlPA 90*
Morgan, Deloris Jackson 1947- *WhoAmW 91*
Morgan, Dennis Alan 1947- *WhoE 91*
Morgan, Dennis Del 1949- *WhoSSW 91*
Morgan, Diane M. *WhoAmW 91*
Morgan, Diane Pope 1949- *WhoAmW 91*
Morgan, Dodge D. *BioIn 16*
Morgan, Donald Farrell 1938- *St&PR 91*
Morgan, Donald W 1934- *BiDrAPA 89*
Morgan, Donna *BioIn 16*
Morgan, Donna J. 1955- *WhoAmW 91*
Morgan, Douglas P *BiDrAPA 89*
Morgan, E. Louise 1929- *St&PR 91*
Morgan, Eben Cornelius 1934- *St&PR 91*
Morgan, Ed 1904-1980 *Ballpl 90*
Morgan, Edmund Sears 1916- *WhoAm 90*
Morgan, Edward Charles 1933- *St&PR 91*
Morgan, Edward L., Jr. *ODwPR 91*
Morgan, Edward Paddock 1910- *BioIn 16*
Morgan, Edwin J. *EarBlAP*
Morgan, Edwin Vernon 1865-1934 *BioIn 16*
Morgan, Elaine 1920- *FemiCLE*
Morgan, Elizabeth 1947- *BioIn 16, WhoAm 90*
Morgan, Elizabeth Anne 1947- *WhoAmW 91*
Morgan, Ellen 1918-1987 *BioIn 16*
Morgan, Ellen Nannie 1935- *WhoAmW 91*
Morgan, Elmo Rich 1913- *WhoAm 90*
Morgan, Eric Lee 1940- *WhoWor 91*
Morgan, Ernest 1905- *WhoWrEP 89*
Morgan, Eunice V *BiDrAPA 89*
Morgan, Evan 1930- *WhoSSW 91*
Morgan, Evelyn Buck 1931- *WhoAmW 91, WhoSSW 91, WhoWor 91*
Morgan, Evelyn Mary de 1855-1919 *BiDWomA*
Morgan, Frances Tracy *BioIn 16*
Morgan, Frank *BioIn 16, ConAu 31NR*
Morgan, Frank 1890-1949 *WorAlBi*
Morgan, Frank 1935- *ODwPR 91*
Morgan, Frank Brown Webb, Jr. 1935- *WhoAm 90*
Morgan, Frank Edward, II 1952- *St&PR 91, WhoAm 90, WhoEmL 91*
Morgan, Frank J. 1925- *WhoAm 90*
Morgan, Frederick 1922- *WhoAm 90, WhoWrEP 89, WorAu 1980 [port]*
Morgan, Garrett A. 1877-1963 *BioIn 16*
Morgan, Gary 1955- *WhoE 91*
Morgan, Gay Hattaway 1952- *WhoSSW 91*
Morgan, Gayle Bankes 1957- *WhoE 91*
Morgan, Geoffrey 1916- *AuBYP 90*
Morgan, Geoffrey David 1945- *IntWWM 90*
Morgan, George Carl 1931- *WhoAm 90*
Morgan, George Dennis 1935- *St&PR 91*
Morgan, George H. 1936- *St&PR 91*
Morgan, George Jefferson 1908- *WhoAm 90*
Morgan, George Tad 1933- *St&PR 91, WhoAm 90*
Morgan, George Walter 1924- *WhoE 91*
Morgan, George Williams 1935- *WhoSSW 91*
Morgan, Georgia Bazacos 1926- *WhoAmW 91*
Morgan, Gerthon Laird 1953- *WhoSSW 91*
Morgan, Gertrude 1900-1980 *MusmAFA*
Morgan, Gladys B 1899-1981 *WhoAmA 91N*
Morgan, Glenn R. 1947- *St&PR 91*
Morgan, Gordon K. 1939- *St&PR 91*
Morgan, Graham James 1917- *St&PR 91*
Morgan, Gregory Paul 1958- *WhoSSW 91*
Morgan, Gretna Faye 1927- *WhoAmW 91*
Morgan, Gwen Cartee 1927- *WhoSSW 91*
Morgan, Gwen Vickery *BiDrAPA 89*
Morgan, Harold C 1936- *BiDrAPA 89*
Morgan, Harold Thomas 1954- *WhoSSW 91*
Morgan, Harriet *MajTwCW*
Morgan, Harry 1915- *WorAlBi*
Morgan, Harry Casswallon 1928- *St&PR 91*
Morgan, Harry E 1948- *BiDrAPA 89*
Morgan, Helen 1900-1941 *OxCPMus, WorAlBi*
Morgan, Helen Fairley 1931- *St&PR 91*
Morgan, Henry 1819-1893 *DcCanB 12*
Morgan, Henry 1915- *WorAlBi*
Morgan, Henry Sturgis 1901-1982 *BioIn 16*
Morgan, Herbert Roy 1914- *WhoAm 90*
Morgan, Hillary A. 1958- *St&PR 91*
Morgan, Holly Ann Herrick 1958- *WhoAmW 91*
Morgan, Howard Campbell 1935- *WhoAm 90*
Morgan, Howard Edwin 1927- *WhoAm 90*
Morgan, Howard K. 1917- *St&PR 91*
Morgan, Hugh Jackson, Jr. 1928- *St&PR 91, WhoAm 90*
Morgan, Ike 1958- *MusmAFA*
Morgan, Inga Borgstrom *WhoAmW 91*
Morgan, J. P. 1867-1943 *BioIn 16*
Morgan, J. Ronald 1938- *WhoAm 90*
Morgan, Jack Colbert *BiDrAPA 89*
Morgan, Jack Collins 1937- *WhoSSW 91*
Morgan, Jacqui 1939- *WhoAm 90, WhoWor 91*
Morgan, James 1944- *WhoWrEP 89*
Morgan, James Alvin 1935- *St&PR 91*
Morgan, James Andrew 1948- *WhoSSW 91*
Morgan, James Chandler 1938- *St&PR 91*
Morgan, James Durward 1936- *WhoE 91, WhoWor 91*
Morgan, James J. 1942- *St&PR 91*
Morgan, James Jay 1942- *WhoAm 90*
Morgan, James John 1932- *WhoAm 90*
Morgan, James L *WhoAmA 91*
Morgan, James Orval 1933- *WhoE 91*
Morgan, James Richard 1938- *WhoAm 90*
Morgan, James Sill 1917- *St&PR 91*
Morgan, Jane Brennan 1955- *WhoE 91*
Morgan, Jane Hale 1926- *WhoAm 90*
Morgan, Jane Norton Grew *BioIn 16*
Morgan, Janet F. *WhoWrEP 89*
Morgan, Janet Marie Fain 1956- *WhoWrEP 89*
Morgan, Jasper William, Jr. 1936- *St&PR 91*
Morgan, Jo Valentine, Jr. 1920- *WhoE 91*
Morgan, Joe *BioIn 16*
Morgan, Joe 1930- *Ballpl 90*
Morgan, Joe 1943- *Ballpl 90 [port], WorAlBi*
Morgan, Joe Leonard 1943- *WhoAm 90*
Morgan, John *ConAu 31NR*
Morgan, John A. 1930- *WhoAm 90*
Morgan, John Adams, Jr. 1954- *WhoE 91*
Morgan, John Albert Leigh 1929- *WhoWor 91*
Morgan, John Augustine 1934- *WhoSSW 91, WhoWor 91*
Morgan, John Black 1938- *WhoE 91*
Morgan, John Bruce 1919- *WhoAm 90*
Morgan, John D 1904- *BiDrAPA 89*
Morgan, John Davis 1921- *WhoAm 90*
Morgan, John Derald 1939- *WhoAm 90*
Morgan, John F. *BioIn 16*
Morgan, John L. *St&PR 91*
Morgan, John Peter 1952- *WhoE 91*
Morgan, John Pierpont 1837-1913 *BioIn 16, EncABHB 6 [port], WorAlBi*
Morgan, John Pierpont 1867-1943 *BioIn 16*
Morgan, John Pierpont, Jr. 1867-1943 *EncABHB 7 [port]*
Morgan, John Smith 1921- *WhoWrEP 89*
Morgan, John Thomas 1929- *St&PR 91, WhoAm 90*
Morgan, John Tyler 1824-1907 *BioIn 16*
Morgan, Jonathan G. 1954- *St&PR 91*
Morgan, Joseph L. 1927- *St&PR 91*
Morgan, Joseph Michael 1930- *WhoAm 90, WhoE 91*
Morgan, Julia *BioIn 16*
Morgan, Julia 1872-1957 *BioAmW*
Morgan, Julian Earl, III 1950- *WhoSSW 91*
Morgan, Junius S. 1813-1890 *EncABHB 6 [port]*
Morgan, Junius S. 1947- *St&PR 91*
Morgan, Junius Spencer 1813-1890 *BioIn 16*
Morgan, Junius Spencer 1892-1960 *BioIn 16*
Morgan, Karen Ann 1948- *WhoEmL 91*
Morgan, Keith Alan 1961- *WhoE 91, WhoWor 91*
Morgan, Kimberly Ann 1963- *WhoAmW 91*
Morgan, Lanier Vernon *WhoWrEP 89*
Morgan, Larry Don 1944- *WhoSSW 91*
Morgan, Larry Ronald 1936- *WhoAm 90, WhoSSW 91*
Morgan, Lee 1938-1972 *BioIn 16*
Morgan, Lee Anne 1943- *WhoAmW 91*
Morgan, Lee L. 1920- *St&PR 91*
Morgan, Lee Laverne 1920- *ConAmBL*
Morgan, Leigh *WhoWrEP 89*
Morgan, Leon 1897- *St&PR 91*
Morgan, Leon Alford 1934- *St&PR 91*
Morgan, Leonard Eugene 1946- *WhoSSW 91*
Morgan, Lewis Henry 1818-1881 *EncAL, WhNaAH*
Morgan, Lewis Render 1913- *WhoAm 90*
Morgan, Linda C. 1958- *WhoAmW 91*
Morgan, Linda Rice 1949- *WhoSSW 91*
Morgan, Linda Rogers 1950- *WhoAmW 91*
Morgan, Lisa *ODwPR 91*
Morgan, Louis S, Jr. 1922- *BiDrAPA 89*

Morgan, Lucy W. 1940- *WhoAm 90*
Morgan, Lynn Patrice 1953- *WhoSSW 91*
Morgan, M. Jane 1945- *WhoAmW 91, WhoSSW 91, WhoWor 91*
Morgan, Madel Jacobs 1918- *WhoAm 90, WhoAmW 91*
Morgan, Malcolm Bruce 1938- *WhoSSW 91*
Morgan, Marabel 1937- *WhoAm 90, WhoWrEP 89*
Morgan, Margaret E *BiDrAPA 89*
Morgan, Marianne 1940- *WhoSSW 91*
Morgan, Marion K. *BioIn 16*
Morgan, Maritza Leskovar 1920- *WhoAmW 91*
Morgan, Maritza Leskovar 1921- *WhoAmA 91*
Morgan, Mark Quenten 1950- *WhoEmL 91*
Morgan, Mary 1943- *ConAu 132*
Morgan, Mary Louise Fitzsimmons 1941- *WhoAmW 91*
Morgan, Melinda 1956- *ODwPR 91*
Morgan, Meli'sa *BioIn 16*
Morgan, Melvin Dailey *BiDrAPA 89*
Morgan, Merrill Elmer 1912- *St&PR 91*
Morgan, Michael *BioIn 16*
Morgan, Michael DeVard 1957- *IntWWM 90*
Morgan, Michael Gavin 1946- *WhoE 91*
Morgan, Michael Leon 1954- *WhoSSW 91*
Morgan, Mike *BioIn 16*
Morgan, Mike 1959- *Ballpl 90*
Morgan, Millett Granger 1941- *WhoAm 90*
Morgan, Monroe 1921- *WhoAm 90*
Morgan, Myfanwy Irene 1951- *WhoAmW 91*
Morgan, Myra Jean 1938- *WhoAmA 91*
Morgan, Nancy *BioIn 16*
Morgan, Neil 1924- *WhoAm 90, WhoWrEP 89*
Morgan, Nicholas Heath 1953- *WhoE 91*
Morgan, Niel C. *St&PR 91*
Morgan, Norma 1928- *BiDWomA*
Morgan, Norma Gloria *WhoAmA 91, WhoE 91*
Morgan, Pamela Antoinette 1947- *WhoE 91*
Morgan, Patrick Michael 1944- *WhoSSW 91*
Morgan, Paul 1928- *IntWWM 90*
Morgan, Paul E. 1917- *ODwPR 91*
Morgan, Paul Evan 1961- *WhoEmL 91*
Morgan, Paul William 1952- *WhoEmL 91*
Morgan, Paul Winthrop 1911- *WhoAm 90*
Morgan, Raleigh, Jr. 1916- *WhoAm 90*
Morgan, Randall H. 1948- *St&PR 91*
Morgan, Ray 1889-1940 *Ballpl 90*
Morgan, Ray Ellingwood, Jr. 1922- *WhoAm 90, WhoWor 91*
Morgan, Raymond F. 1948- *WhoAm 90*
Morgan, Rebecca Quinn 1938- *WhoAmW 91*
Morgan, Rhea Volk 1952- *WhoAmW 91*
Morgan, Richard 1951- *IntWWM 90*
Morgan, Richard Ernest 1937- *WhoAm 90*
Morgan, Richard Hugh 1938- *WhoSSW 91*
Morgan, Richard Thomas 1937- *WhoAm 90, WhoWor 91*
Morgan, Robert 1917- *WhoAm 90*
Morgan, Robert B. 1931- *WhoWrEP 89*
Morgan, Robert Bruce 1934- *St&PR 91*
Morgan, Robert Churchman, II 1940- *St&PR 91*
Morgan, Robert Coolidge 1943- *WhoAmA 91, WhoE 91*
Morgan, Robert Crawley 1933- *WhoAm 90*
Morgan, Robert Dale 1912- *WhoAm 90*
Morgan, Robert Edward 1924- *WhoAm 90*
Morgan, Robert F. 1929- *BioIn 16*
Morgan, Robert George 1941- *WhoWor 91*
Morgan, Robert H. 1944- *St&PR 91*
Morgan, Robert M. *BioIn 16*
Morgan, Robert Marion 1930- *WhoAm 90*
Morgan, Robert P. 1934- *IntWWM 90, WhoAm 90*
Morgan, Robert Peter 1934- *WhoAm 90*
Morgan, Robert Ray 1944- *WhoWrEP 89*
Morgan, Robert S. 1934- *ODwPR 91*
Morgan, Robin 1941- *FemiCLE, MajTwCW, News 91-1 [port]*
Morgan, Robin Evonne 1941- *WhoAm 90, WhoAmW 91*
Morgan, Roger Hugh Vaughan Charles 1926- *WhoWor 91*
Morgan, Roger L. 1942- *St&PR 91*
Morgan, Rosemarie *ConAu 131*
Morgan, Roy Edward 1908- *WhoAm 90*
Morgan, Russ 1904-1969 *OxCPMus*
Morgan, Russell E. 1956- *St&PR 91*
Morgan, Ruth 1938- *WhoE 91*
Morgan, Ruth Prouse 1934- *WhoAm 90*
Morgan, Sally 1951- *BioIn 16*
Morgan, Samuel Pope 1923- *WhoAm 90*
Morgan, Sandra Parowski *ODwPR 91*
Morgan, Sarah Taylor Wilson 1956- *WhoSSW 91*
Morgan, Scott *BioIn 16*
Morgan, Seth *NewYTBS 90 [port]*
Morgan, Seth 1949?-1990 *ConAu 132*
Morgan, Sharon Denise 1964- *WhoAmW 91*
Morgan, Sheldon LeGrande 1929- *St&PR 91*
Morgan, Sherry Rita Guy 1949- *WhoSSW 91*
Morgan, Sidney L. 1948- *WhoSSW 91, WhoWor 91*
Morgan, Silver *WhoWrEP 89*
Morgan, Speer 1946- *WhoWrEP 89*
Morgan, Stacy *ODwPR 91*
Morgan, Stanley Leins 1918- *St&PR 91, WhoAm 90*
Morgan, Stephen Charles 1946- *WhoAm 90*
Morgan, Sterling William 1922- *WhoAm 90*
Morgan, Steven Wesley 1947- *BiDrAPA 89*
Morgan, Susan 1953- *WhoAmA 91*
Morgan, Sybil Andrews *WhoAmA 91*
Morgan, Sybil Florine 1934- *St&PR 91*
Morgan, Sydney 1776-1859 *FemiCLE*
Morgan, Sydney Owenson, Lady 1783?-1859 *BioIn 16*
Morgan, Theodora *WhoAmA 91*
Morgan, Theodore N. 1940- *St&PR 91*
Morgan, Thomas E. 1925- *ODwPR 91*
Morgan, Thomas H. 1866-1945 *WorAlBi*
Morgan, Thomas Jefferson 1839-1902 *BioIn 16*
Morgan, Thomas Logan, III 1953- *WhoEmL 91*
Morgan, Thomas Rowland 1930- *WhoAm 90*
Morgan, Thomas Sellers 1934- *WhoSSW 91*
Morgan, Timothy James *BiDrAPA 89*
Morgan, Timothy Joe 1953- *WhoEmL 91*
Morgan, Todd Byers 1956- *WhoE 91*
Morgan, Todd Michael 1947- *WhoAm 90*
Morgan, Tom 1930-1987 *Ballpl 90*
Morgan, Travis Crue 1929- *St&PR 91*
Morgan, Valerie *ConAu 31NR*
Morgan, Vicki 1953?-1983 *BioAmW*
Morgan, W. Robert 1924- *WhoWrEP 89*
Morgan, Wallace 1873-1948 *WhoAmA 91N*
Morgan, Walter Leroy 1930- *WhoE 91*
Morgan, Wanda Busby 1930- *WhoAmW 91, WhoE 91*
Morgan, Wayne Philip 1942- *WhoAm 90*
Morgan, Wesley K. 1918- *WhoAm 90*
Morgan, William 1545-1604 *BioIn 16*
Morgan, William 1944- *WhoAmA 91*
Morgan, William Bruce 1926- *WhoAm 90*
Morgan, William De *PenDiDA 89*
Morgan, William Douglass 1925- *WhoAm 90*
Morgan, William J. 1947- *WhoAm 90*
Morgan, William Jason 1935- *WhoAm 90*
Morgan, William Lionel, Jr. 1927- *WhoAm 90*
Morgan, William Robert 1924- *WhoAm 90*
Morgan, William T. 1928- *WhoAm 90*
Morgan, William Travis 1928- *St&PR 91*
Morgan, William Wilson 1906- *WhoAm 90*
Morgan, Wilson Wright 1926- *St&PR 91*
Morgan, Winfield Scott, III 1921- *WhoAm 90*
Morgan, Winthrop Brewster 1956- *WhoE 91*
Morgan-Minott, Melodie 1943- *BiDrAPA 89*
Morgan-O'Connor, Richard Leon 1948- *WhoE 91*
Morgan-Pond, Caroline Gail *WhoAmW 91*
Morgan-Powell, Samuel 1867-1962 *OxCCanT*
Morganfield, Mercy Della 1960- *WhoAmW 91*
MorganJones, Karen Irene 1956- *WhoAmW 91*
Morgano, Anthony Frank 1939- *St&PR 91*
Morganroth, Mayer 1931- *WhoWor 91*
Morgans, David Bryan 1933- *St&PR 91*
Morgans, James Patrick 1946- *WhoWrEP 89*
Morganstern, Anne McGee 1936- *WhoAmA 91*
Morganstern, Daniel Robert 1940- *WhoAm 90*
Morganstern, Ira Richard 1942- *BiDrAPA 89*
Morganstern, James 1936- *WhoAmA 91*
Morganstern, Kennard Harold 1924- *St&PR 91*
Morganstern, Monroe Jay 1931- *St&PR 91*
Morganti, Franco 1931- *WhoWor 91*
Morgart, Michele 1947- *WhoAmW 91*
Morgart, Richard Eugene 1928- *St&PR 91*
Morgen, Lynn *ODwPR 91*
Morgenbesser, Sidney *WhoAm 90*
Morgenlander, Ella Kramer 1931- *WhoAmA 91*
Morgenlander, Stanley B *BiDrAPA 89*
Morgenroth, Earl Eugene 1936- *WhoWor 91*
Morgens, Virginia Dare Davis 1934- *WhoWrEP 89*
Morgens, Warren Kendall 1940- *WhoE 91*
Morgensen, Jerry L. 1942- *St&PR 91*
Morgensen, Jerry Lynn 1942- *WhoAm 90*
Morgenstein, William 1933- *WhoE 91, WhoWor 91*
Morgenstern, Alan L 1933- *BiDrAPA 89*
Morgenstern, Barbara Weisman 1936- *St&PR 91*
Morgenstern, Beate 1946- *EncCoWW*
Morgenstern, Dan Michael 1929- *WhoAm 90, WhoWrEP 89*
Morgenstern, Daniel 1947- *St&PR 91*
Morgenstern, Fredric V 1915- *BiDrAPA 89*
Morgenstern, Frieda Homnick 1917- *WhoWrEP 89*
Morgenstern, Jack A 1934- *BiDrAPA 89*
Morgenstern, Jacob 1897- *BiDrAPA 89*
Morgenstern, Jonathan David 1954- *WhoEmL 91*
Morgenstern, Leon 1919- *WhoAm 90*
Morgenstern, Mark 1949- *BiDrAPA 89*
Morgenstern, Matthew *WhoWor 91*
Morgenstern, Norbert Rubin 1935- *WhoAm 90*
Morgenstern, Sam *BioIn 16*
Morgenstern, Stephen 1940- *WhoE 91*
Morgenstern, Stephen Allen *BiDrAPA 89*
Morgenstern, Walter J. 1948- *St&PR 91*
Morgenthal, Becky Holz 1947- *WhoAmW 91, WhoE 91*
Morgenthaler, Frederic Richard 1933- *WhoAm 90*
Morgenthaler, George Jefferson 1949- *St&PR 91*
Morgenthaler, Larry Carl 1944- *St&PR 91*
Morgenthau, Henry 1891-1967 *BioIn 16*
Morgenthau, Henry, Jr. 1891-1967 *BiDrUSE 89, EncABHB 7 [port], WorAlBi*
Morgenthau, Rita 1880-1964 *BioIn 16*
Morgenthau, Rita Wallach 1880-1964 *NotWoAT*
Morgenthau, Robert Morris 1919- *WhoAm 90*
Morgner, Aurelius 1917- *WhoAm 90*
Morgner, Evelyn 1955- *WhoAmW 91*
Morgner, Irmtraud 1933-1990 *EncCoWW*
Morgner, Ronald H. 1943- *St&PR 91*
Morgo, Charles F. *St&PR 91*
Morgridge, Howard Henry 1919- *WhoAm 90*
Morhauser, Edward George *BiDrAPA 89*
Mori Hanae 1926- *EncJap*
Mori, Hanae *BioIn 16*
Mori, Hanae 1926- *ConDes 90, WhoAm 90, WhoAmW 91*
Mori, Junko 1948- *IntWWM 90*
Mori, Marisa 1900- *BiDWomA*
Mori, Masataka 1940- *WhoWor 91*
Mori, Nobuo 1932- *WhoWor 91*
Mori, Ogai 1862-1922 *BioIn 16*
Mori, Taikichiro 1904- *WhoWor 91*
Mori, Toshio 1933- *St&PR 91*
Mori, Toshio 1946- *WhoWor 91*
Moriah, Sonja-Jacqueline 1944- *WhoWor 91*
Morial, Ernest 1929-1989 *AnObit 1989*
Morial, Ernest Nathan *BioIn 16*
Morial, Marc Haydel 1958- *WhoSSW 91, WhoWor 91*
Moriarty, Anna Marie 1945- *WhoAmW 91*
Moriarty, Brian David 1942- *St&PR 91*
Moriarty, Daniel J. 1941- *ODwPR 91*
Moriarty, Donald W. 1939- *St&PR 91*
Moriarty, Donald William, Jr. 1939- *WhoAm 90*
Moriarty, Frederic Barstow 1940- *WhoAm 90, WhoE 91, WhoWor 91*
Moriarty, George 1884-1964 *Ballpl 90*
Moriarty, James Paul 1955- *WhoEmL 91*
Moriarty, John 1930- *IntWWM 90, WhoAm 90*
Moriarty, John D 1915- *BiDrAPA 89*
Moriarty, John W. 1930- *St&PR 91*
Moriarty, Laura Jean 1961- *WhoSSW 91*
Moriarty, Mary Elizabeth 1962- *WhoE 91*
Moriarty, Maryanne 1961- *WhoE 91*
Moriarty, Michael 1941- *WhoAm 90, WorAlBi*
Moriarty, Michael John 1961- *WhoE 91*
Moriarty, Morgan Johanna 1955- *WhoWrEP 89*
Moriarty, Patricia J. 1953- *St&PR 91*
Moriarty, Philip S. J. 1940- *St&PR 91*
Moriarty, Richard Patrick 1933- *St&PR 91*
Moriarty, Richard William 1939- *WhoAm 90*
Moriarty, Robert Brian 1940- *WhoE 91*
Moriarty, Thomas Vincent, II 1943- *St&PR 91*
Moriarty, William Edward 1926- *St&PR 91*
Moribondo, Thomas Peter 1954- *WhoEmL 91*
Morice, Anne 1918- *TwCCr&M 91*
Morice, David Jennings 1946- *WhoWrEP 89*
Morice, James L. 1948- *ODwPR 91*
Morice, James Lowry 1937- *WhoWor 91*
Morice, Joseph Richard 1923- *WhoAm 90*
Morich, Joyce Pigeon 1954- *WhoAmW 91*
Morici, Peter George, Jr. 1948- *WhoE 91*
Moricle, Lea Ann 1958- *BiDrAPA 89*
Moriconi, Italo 1953- *WhoWor 91*
Morie, G. Glen 1942- *St&PR 91*
Morien *EncO&P 3*
Morienus *EncO&P 3*
Morier, Gisele Suzanne *BiDrAPA 89*
Morihisa, John Masao 1951- *BiDrAPA 89*
Morike, Eduard 1804-1875 *WorAlBi*
Morimanno, Paul 1939- *St&PR 91*
Morimoto, Akiko Charlene 1948- *WhoAmW 91*
Morimoto, Carl Noboru 1942- *WhoAm 90*
Morimoto, Gary S. 1941- *St&PR 91*
Morimoto, Iwataro 1928- *WhoWor 91*
Morin, Achille 1815-1898 *DcCanB 12*
Morin, Carlton Paul 1932- *WhoAm 90*
Morin, Charles *PenDiMP*
Morin, Craig Richard *BiDrAPA 89*
Morin, Curtis L. 1952- *St&PR 91*
Morin, David Joseph 1952- *WhoE 91*
Morin, Earl U. 1935- *St&PR 91*
Morin, France *WhoAmA 91*
Morin, Gaston Jean Francois 1938- *WhoE 91*
Morin, Gilles R *BiDrAPA 89*
Morin, James Corcoran 1953- *WhoAmA 91*
Morin, Johanne *BiDrAPA 89*
Morin, Luc M 1940- *BiDrAPA 89*
Morin, Michael 1934-1990 *BioIn 16*
Morin, Nancy Ruth 1948- *WhoAmW 91*
Morin, Patrick Joyce 1938- *WhoAm 90*
Morin, Paul 1889-1963 *DcLB 92*
Morin, Penny B. *WhoHisp 91*
Morin, Pierre Jean 1931- *WhoAm 90*
Morin, Raul R. 1913-1967 *BioIn 16*
Morin, Richard Arthur 1928- *BiDrAPA 89*
Morin, Richard Wedge 1902-1988 *BioIn 16*
Morin, Rudolph G. 1937- *St&PR 91*
Morin, Stephen F. 1945- *BioIn 16*
Morin, Theodore J. 1931- *St&PR 91*
Morin, Thomas Edward 1934- *WhoAmA 91*
Morin, William Raymond 1949- *WhoEmL 91*
Morin, Wm. J. 1940- *St&PR 91*
Morin, Wollaston G. 1936- *St&PR 91*
Morin, Wollaston Gerald 1936- *WhoAm 90*
Morin, Yves-Charles 1944- *WhoAm 90*
Morin-Miller, Carmen A *WhoAmA 91*
Morina, Sam Frank, Jr. 1957- *WhoSSW 91*
Morine, Bruce Phillip 1947- *St&PR 91*
Morine, Hoder *ConAu 131*
Moring, James D. 1936- *St&PR 91*
Moring, John Frederick 1935- *WhoAm 90*
Moring, John Madison 1841-1891 *AmLegL*
Moring, Sylvia Arlene *BiDrAPA 89*
Morini, Christopher E. 1955- *St&PR 91*
Morini, Erica 1910- *IntWWM 90*
Morinigo, Higinio 1897- *BioIn 16*
Morios, Armando *WhoHisp 91*
Morisaki Page, Karen G *BiDrAPA 89*
Morisato, Susan Cay 1955- *WhoAmW 91*
Morishita, Joyce Chizuko 1944- *WhoAmA 91*
Morison, Elsie *PenDiMP*
Morison, Elsie 1924- *IntWWM 90*
Morison, Elting Elmore 1909- *WhoAm 90*
Morison, Frank Harold 1925- *WhoAm 90*
Morison, John H. 1913- *St&PR 91*
Morison, John Hopkins 1913- *WhoE 91*
Morison, Julia Mary 1952- *WhoWor 91*
Morison, Robert David 1930- *St&PR 91*
Morison, Samuel Eliot 1887-1976 *AuBYP 90, BioIn 16, WorAlBi*
Morisot, Berthe 1841-1895 *BiDWomA, BioIn 16, IntDcAA 90, WorAlBi*
Morisseau, Dolores Schanne 1936- *WhoE 91*
Morisset, Gerard 1898-1970 *WhoAmA 91N*
Morissette, Raymond *BiDrAPA 89*
Morita Akio 1921- *EncJap*
Morita, Akio *BioIn 16*
Morita, Akio 1921- *WhoAm 90, WhoWor 91*
Morita, James Masami 1913- *WhoAm 90, WhoWor 91*
Morita, John Takami 1943- *WhoAmA 91*
Morita, Katsura 1925- *WhoWor 91*
Morita, Masami 1927- *WhoWor 91*
Morita, Masayoshi Teddy 1947- *WhoWor 91*
Morita, Noriyuki 1930- *WorAlBi*

Morita, Pat *BioIn 16*
Morita, Richard Yukio 1923- *WhoAm 90*
Morita, Tetsuro 1914- *WhoWor 91*
Morits, Yunna Pinkhusovna 1937- *EncCoWW*
Moritsugu, Kenneth Paul 1945- *WhoAm 90*
Moritz, Amy 1959- *WhoEmL 91*
Moritz, Carl A. 1906- *WhoE 91*
Moritz, Charles Fredric 1917- *WhoAm 90, WhoWrEP 89*
Moritz, Charles Worthington 1936- *St&PR 91, WhoAm 90, WhoE 91*
Moritz, Donald B. 1927- *St&PR 91*
Moritz, Donald Brooks 1927- *WhoAm 90*
Moritz, Donald I. 1927- *St&PR 91*
Moritz, Donald Irwin 1927- *WhoAm 90*
Moritz, Edward 1920- *WhoAm 90*
Moritz, James R. 1945- *WhoE 91*
Moritz, Jane Andrews *WhoAmW 91*
Moritz, John Matthew, Jr. 1962- *WhoEmL 91, WhoSSW 91*
Moritz, Karen Lynne 1940- *BiDrAPA 89*
Moritz, Karl Philipp 1756-1793 *DcLB 94 [port]*
Moritz, Michael Everett 1933- *St&PR 91, WhoAm 90*
Moritz, Milton Edward 1931- *WhoE 91, WhoWor 91*
Moritz, Milton Irving 1933- *St&PR 91*
Moritz, Richard T. *ODwPR 91*
Moritz, Timothy B 1936- *BiDrAPA 89*
Moriyama, Raymond 1929- *WhoAm 90*
Mork, Gordon Robert 1938- *WhoWor 91*
Mork, Phillip W. 1939- *St&PR 91*
Mork, William John 1942- *St&PR 91*
Morkan, John Francis 1932- *St&PR 91*
Morken, Carol Linn 1952- *WhoEmL 91*
Morkovsky, John L. 1909-1990 *BioIn 16*
Morkwed, Richard Arlan 1930- *St&PR 91*
Morlan, John 1947- *Ballpl 90*
Morland, Berit Sofie 1942- *WhoWor 91*
Morland, Dick *ConAu 32NR*
Morland, Jessie Parrish 1924- *WhoSSW 91*
Morland, John Kenneth 1916- *WhoAm 90*
Morland, Nigel 1905-1986 *TwCCr&M 91*
Morland, Richard Boyd 1919- *WhoSSW 91*
Morley, Alfred Charles, Jr. 1927- *WhoAm 90*
Morley, David Clark *BiDrAPA 89*
Morley, Deborah Jean 1954- *WhoE 91*
Morley, Edward Francis, Jr. 1940- *WhoE 91*
Morley, Edward Williams 1838-1923 *WorAlBi*
Morley, George William 1923- *WhoAm 90*
Morley, Harry Thomas, Jr. 1930- *WhoAm 90*
Morley, James *PenDiDA 89*
Morley, John 1838-1923 *BioIn 16*
Morley, John 1931?- *BioIn 16*
Morley, John C. 1931- *St&PR 91, WhoAm 90*
Morley, John F 1936- *ConAu 132*
Morley, Jonathan 1948- *BiDrAPA 89*
Morley, Lawrence Whitaker 1920- *WhoAm 90*
Morley, Malcolm 1931- *WhoAmA 91*
Morley, Malcolm A. 1931- *WhoAm 90*
Morley, R. *ConAu 130*
Morley, Raymond Albert 1922- *St&PR 91*
Morley, Robert 1908- *ConAu 130, WorAlBi*
Morley, Steve 1953- *ConAu 132*
Morley, Susan 1836-1921 *FemiCLE*
Morley, Thomas Sumner 1935- *St&PR 91*
Morlock, Carl Grismore 1906- *WhoAm 90*
Morlock, Dieter Bruno 1938- *St&PR 91*
Morlock, Jill Elizabeth 1963- *WhoAmW 91*
Morlock, Ronald J. 1929- *St&PR 91*
Morlotti, Dominique 1955- *WhoWor 91*
Mormol, Leslie Ruth 1962- *BiDrAPA 89*
Morne, Arvid 1876-1946 *DcScanL*
Mornell, Pierre 1935- *ConAu 131*
Mornell, Pierre W 1935- *BiDrAPA 89*
Morner, Magnus *ConAu 132*
Mornex, Jean-Francois 1955- *WhoWor 91*
Morningstar, Mildred 1912- *SmATA 61 [port]*
Morningstar, Richard Louis 1945- *St&PR 91*
Morningstar, Robert David 1948- *WhoE 91*
Moro, Aldo 1916-1978 *WorAlBi*
Moro, Cesar 1903-1956 *ConAu 131, HispWr 90*
Moro, Richard Joseph 1951- *WhoSSW 91*
Moro, Vincenzo Angelo 1922- *WhoWor 91*
Morokuma, Shinji *ODwPR 91*
Moroles, Jesus Bautista 1950- *WhoAmA 91, WhoHisp 91*
Morone, John Henry Joseph 1941- *WhoE 91*
Moroney, Dennis Charles 1947- *WhoE 91*
Moroney, Edward Francis Pius 1949- *IntWWM 90*
Moroney, James M., Jr. 1921- *St&PR 91*
Moroney, Linda L. S. 1943- *WhoAmW 91, WhoSSW 91*
Moroney, Robert Emmet 1903- *WhoWor 91*
Morong, C. Oscar, Jr. 1935- *St&PR 91*
Moroni, Aldo Leonard, Jr 1953- *WhoAmA 91*
Moronobu *EncJap*
Moros, David 1936- *St&PR 91*
Moros, Nicholas P. 1947- *St&PR 91*
Morosan, Ron 1947- *WhoAmA 91*
Morosani, George Warrington 1941- *WhoSSW 91, WhoWor 91*
Morosani, John Warrington 1953- *WhoAm 90*
Morosky, Robert Harry 1941- *WhoAm 90*
Morosky, Thomas 1925- *St&PR 91*
Moroso, Michael Joseph 1923- *WhoWor 91*
Morosoli, Eugene Baptista, Jr. 1930- *St&PR 91*
Moross, Jerome 1913-1983 *OxCPMus*
Morot-Sir, Edouard Barthelemy 1910- *WhoAm 90*
Moroux, Anthony Drexel, Sr. 1948- *WhoEmL 91, WhoSSW 91, WhoWor 91*
Morowitz, Harold Joseph 1927- *WhoAm 90*
Morowitz, Murray 1924- *St&PR 91*
Moroz, Georges *BiDrAPA 89*
Moroz, Georges 1949- *WhoWor 91*
Moroz, Mychajlo 1904- *WhoAmA 91*
Morozov, Vladimir Mikhailovich 1933- *IntWWM 90*
Morpeth, Mary *BiDEWW*
Morphesis, Jim 1948- *WhoAmA 91*
Morphew, Dorothy Richards-Bassett 1918- *WhoAmW 91*
Morphis, Gene Sanders 1948- *St&PR 91*
Morphonios, Dale James 1954- *WhoSSW 91*
Morphonios, Ellen *BioIn 16*
Morphy, John 1947- *St&PR 91, WhoAm 90*
Morphy, Michael A. 1932- *St&PR 91*
Morphy, Murray A 1947- *BiDrAPA 89*
Morphy, Paul 1837-1884 *WorAlBi*
Morphy, William N. *BioIn 16*
Morr, Darlene Carter 1957- *WhoAmW 91*
Morr, Helen Yvonne 1938- *WhoAmW 91*
Morr, Theresa Helen 1939- *WhoAmW 91*
Morra, Isabella di 1520?-1545? *EncCoWW*
Morra, Robert G. 1935- *St&PR 91*
Morrall, John F 1919- *BiDrAPA 89*
Morrar, Atef Ismail 1950- *WhoEmL 91, WhoWor 91*
Morre, D. James 1935- *WhoAm 90*
Morreau, Annette Scawen 1943- *IntWWM 90*
Morreau, Jacqueline 1929- *BiDWomA, WhoWor 91*
Morrel, William Griffin, Jr. 1933- *St&PR 91, WhoE 91, WhoWor 91*
Morrell, Charles Raynor 1928- *St&PR 91*
Morrell, Charles Vincent 1955- *WhoEmL 91*
Morrell, David 1943- *BioIn 16*
Morrell, Gene Paul 1932- *St&PR 91, WhoAm 90*
Morrell, Herbert Ketcham 1927- *WhoAm 90*
Morrell, James Kirby 1943- *WhoE 91*
Morrell, James Lloyd 1953- *St&PR 91*
Morrell, James Wilson 1931- *WhoAm 90*
Morrell, Michael Preston 1948- *WhoAm 90*
Morrell, Ottoline 1873-1938 *FemiCLE*
Morrell, Samuel *BioIn 16*
Morrell, Wayne 1923- *WhoAmA 91*
Morrer, Lizelia Augusta *FemiCLE*
Morressy, John 1930- *AuBYP 90, WhoWrEP 89*
Morretta, Carol Anne *BiDrAPA 89*
Morrice, Norman Alexander 1931- *WhoWor 91*
Morril, Mark C. 1947- *St&PR 91*
Morrill, David Earl 1932- *WhoAm 90*
Morrill, DeWitt C. 1922- *ODwPR 91*
Morrill, Dexter 1938- *IntWWM 90*
Morrill, Edgar Miner, Jr. 1940- *WhoAm 90*
Morrill, James Frederick 1930- *WhoAm 90*
Morrill, John Rhodes 1916- *WhoAm 90*
Morrill, John S. 1946- *ConAu 130*
Morrill, Justin Smith 1810-1898 *BioIn 16*
Morrill, Leslie H. *BioIn 16*
Morrill, Lot Myrick 1812-1883 *BiDrUSE 89*
Morrill, Richard G *BiDrAPA 89*
Morrill, Richard Leland 1934- *WhoAm 90*
Morrill, Richard Leslie 1939- *WhoAm 90*
Morrill, Rowena 1944- *BioIn 16*
Morrill, Thomas C. 1909- *St&PR 91*
Morrill, Thomas Clyde 1909- *WhoAm 90*
Morrill, William Ashley 1930- *St&PR 91, WhoAm 90*
Morrin, Peter Patrick 1945- *WhoAmA 91*
Morrin, Thomas Harvey 1914- *WhoAm 90*
Morrin, Virginia White 1913- *WhoAmW 91, WhoWor 91*
Morring, Don 1936- *St&PR 91*
Morrione, Paolo *WhoAm 90*
Morris Pratt *EncO&P 3*
Morris, Adrian Anthony 1956- *BiDrAPA 89, WhoE 91*
Morris, Alan R. *St&PR 91*
Morris, Albert Jerome 1919- *WhoAm 90*
Morris, Allen Ray 1932- *St&PR 91*
Morris, Alpha Lockhart 1932- *WhoWor 91*
Morris, Alvin Lee 1920- *WhoWor 91*
Morris, Alvin Leonard 1927- *WhoAm 90*
Morris, Andrew Bryson 1946- *IntWWM 90*
Morris, Andrew W *BiDrAPA 89*
Morris, Andrew William 1948- *IntWWM 90*
Morris, Anita *ConTFT 8*
Morris, Ann *AuBYP 90*
Morris, Ann G. *ODwPR 91*
Morris, Arlene Myers 1951- *WhoAmW 91, WhoE 91*
Morris, Barbara Albers 1956- *WhoAmW 91*
Morris, Barbara-Allen Wilkey 1945- *WhoAmW 91*
Morris, Barbara Young 1945- *St&PR 91*
Morris, Barry A. 1954- *St&PR 91*
Morris, Barry Livingston 1947- *WhoE 91*
Morris, Ben 1910-1990 *ConAu 132*
Morris, Ben Rankin 1922- *St&PR 91, WhoAm 90*
Morris, Berenice Robinson *NewYTBS 90*
Morris, Berenice Robinson 1909?-1990 *ConAu 132*
Morris, Brewster H. *NewYTBS 90*
Morris, Brock Allen *BiDrAPA 89*
Morris, C. Eugene *BioIn 16*
Morris, C R 1898-1990 *ConAu 131*
Morris, Carl 1911- *WhoAm 90, WhoAmA 91*
Morris, Carloss 1915- *WhoAm 90*
Morris, Carlton Earl 1952- *WhoSSW 91*
Morris, Carol J. 1953- *WhoAmW 91*
Morris, Caroline Jane McMasters Stewart 1923- *WhoAmW 91*
Morris, Carolyn A. 1948- *WhoSSW 91*
Morris, Cecelia Maltby 1916- *WhoWrEP 89*
Morris, Charles A. 1936- *WhoAm 90*
Morris, Charles Elliot 1929- *WhoAm 90*
Morris, Charles Howard 1937- *WhoSSW 91*
Morris, Christine Coalson 1952- *WhoAmW 91*
Morris, Christopher Dana 1955- *WhoSSW 91*
Morris, Christopher John 1922- *IntWWM 90*
Morris, Cindy Lynn 1959- *WhoEmL 91*
Morris, Clara 1847?-1925 *NotWoAT*
Morris, Clara 1848?-1925 *BioIn 16, OxCCanT*
Morris, Colin 1952- *IntWWM 90*
Morris, Cooper H. 1953- *St&PR 91*
Morris, Cordell Yvonne 1944- *WhoE 91*
Morris, Craig Madden 1945- *BiDrAPA 89, WhoE 91*
Morris, Daniel Kearns 1954- *WhoAm 90*
Morris, Daniel T. 1950- *WhoEmL 91*
Morris, David *BioIn 16*
Morris, David Brown 1942- *WhoWrEP 89*
Morris, David H. 1941- *St&PR 91*
Morris, David Hugh 1941- *WhoAm 90*
Morris, David James 1945- *WhoE 91*
Morris, David Michael 1948- *WhoE 91, WhoEmL 91*
Morris, David Woollard 1935- *WhoE 91*
Morris, Delyte Wesley 1906-1982 *BioIn 16*
Morris, Desmond *WhoAm 90*
Morris, Desmond 1928- *MajTwCW*
Morris, Dexter L. 1952- *WhoSSW 91*
Morris, Diana Ethelreda 1940- *WhoAmW 91*
Morris, Diane Carol 1964- *WhoAmW 91*
Morris, Donal Franklin 1932- *St&PR 91*
Morris, Donald 1945- *WhoEmL 91*
Morris, Donald Arthur Adams 1934- *WhoAm 90*
Morris, Donald Charles 1925- *St&PR 91, WhoAm 90*
Morris, Donald E. 1946- *St&PR 91*
Morris, Donald Fischer 1925- *WhoAmA 91*
Morris, Doris Mullins 1938- *St&PR 91*
Morris, Dorothy Edith 1931- *WhoAmW 91*
Morris, Dorothy Mathews 1918- *St&PR 91*
Morris, Douglas Peter 1938- *WhoAm 90*
Morris, Dudley E. 1937- *WhoAm 90*
Morris, Dudley H, Jr 1912-1966 *WhoAmA 91N*
Morris, Earl Franklin 1909- *WhoAm 90*
Morris, Earl L. 1913- *St&PR 91*
Morris, Earle Elias, Jr. 1928- *WhoAm 90, WhoSSW 91*
Morris, Ed 1899-1932 *Ballpl 90*
Morris, Edmund *BioIn 16*
Morris, Edmund 1940- *WhoWrEP 89*
Morris, Edward 1935- *ConAu 31NR*
Morris, Edward Austin 1951- *St&PR 91*
Morris, Edward L. 1942- *St&PR 91*
Morris, Edward S *BiDrAPA 89*
Morris, Edwin Alexander 1903- *WhoAm 90*
Morris, Edwin Bateman, III 1939- *St&PR 91, WhoAm 90*
Morris, Edwin Thaddeus 1912- *WhoAm 90*
Morris, Elias Camp 1855-1922 *BioIn 16*
Morris, Elizabeth J. 1934- *WhoWrEP 89*
Morris, Elizabeth Treat 1936- *WhoAmW 91, WhoWor 91*
Morris, Elliott J. 1933- *St&PR 91*
Morris, Emma Ward 1952- *St&PR 91*
Morris, Eric 1931- *BioIn 16*
Morris, Errol *BioIn 16*
Morris, Esther 1814-1902 *WorAlBi*
Morris, Eugene *BioIn 16*
Morris, Eugene Jerome 1910- *WhoAm 90*
Morris, Everett Lee 1928- *St&PR 91*
Morris, Florence Marie 1928- *WhoAmA 91*
Morris, Francis Edward 1942- *WhoE 91*
Morris, Frank Charles, Jr. 1948- *WhoWor 91*
Morris, Frank Eugene 1923- *St&PR 91, WhoAm 90*
Morris, G. L. 1941- *St&PR 91*
Morris, G. Ronald 1936- *WhoAm 90*
Morris, Gareth Charles Walter 1920- *IntWWM 90*
Morris, Garrett *WhoAm 90*
Morris, Garrett 1937- *DrBlPA 90*
Morris, Garrett 1944- *ConTFT 8*
Morris, George Anthony *PenDiDA 89*
Morris, George B. *BioIn 16*
Morris, George Berrien 1937- *WhoAm 90*
Morris, George Cooper, Jr. 1924- *WhoAm 90*
Morris, George Ford *WhoAmA 91N*
Morris, George L K 1905-1975 *WhoAmA 91N*
Morris, George N. 1930- *St&PR 91*
Morris, George Ronald 1943- *St&PR 91*
Morris, Gouverneur 1752-1816 *BioIn 16, EncCRAm [port], WorAlBi*
Morris, Grant Harold 1940- *WhoAm 90*
Morris, Greg 1934- *DrBlPA 90*
Morris, Greg Arthur 1953- *WhoEmL 91*
Morris, Gregg 1951- *WhoAmA 91*
Morris, Greggory *AuBYP 90*
Morris, Gregory Bernard, Sr. 1950- *WhoSSW 91*
Morris, Gretchen Suzanne 1963- *WhoAmW 91*
Morris, Griffith Ross 1938- *St&PR 91*
Morris, Harold G. 1948- *St&PR 91*
Morris, Harry Leland 1928- *WhoAm 90*
Morris, Harry T. *BioIn 16*
Morris, Heather Mae *BiDrAPA 89*
Morris, Henry A. 1928- *St&PR 91*
Morris, Henry Allen, Jr. 1940- *WhoSSW 91*
Morris, Henry Madison, III 1942- *WhoWor 91*
Morris, Henry Madison, Jr. 1918- *WhoAm 90*
Morris, Herbert 1928- *WhoAm 90*
Morris, Herman 1951- *St&PR 91*
Morris, Hilda *WhoAmA 91*
Morris, Hildred Ann 1955- *WhoAmW 91*
Morris, Horton Harold 1922- *WhoE 91*
Morris, Howard Eugene 1934- *WhoSSW 91*
Morris, Hugh C. 1932- *St&PR 91*
Morris, Humphrey *BiDrAPA 89*
Morris, J. Roy 1938- *St&PR 91*
Morris, Jack 1955- *Ballpl 90 [port], WorAlBi*
Morris, Jack Austin, Jr 1939- *WhoAmA 91*
Morris, Jack Pershing 1918- *WhoAm 90*
Morris, Jacqueline Kim *BiDrAPA 89*
Morris, James *MajTwCW, NewYTBS 90 [port]*
Morris, James 1926- *BioIn 16*
Morris, James 1947- *BioIn 16, IntWWM 90*
Morris, James Allen 1929- *WhoSSW 91*
Morris, James Aloysius 1918- *WhoAm 90, WhoWor 91*
Morris, James Bruce 1943- *WhoSSW 91*
Morris, James E. 1937- *St&PR 91*
Morris, James Francis 1943- *WhoSSW 91*
Morris, James G. 1951- *St&PR 91*
Morris, James Griffith 1957- *WhoAm 90*
Morris, James LaRoy 1945- *BiDrAPA 89*
Morris, James Leo 1963- *WhoE 91*
Morris, James M 1928- *BiDrAPA 89*
Morris, James Malachy 1952- *WhoE 91, WhoEmL 91, WhoWor 91*
Morris, James Matthew 1935- *WhoSSW 91*

Morris, James Peppler 1947- *WhoAm 90*
Morris, James Phillip 1942- *St&PR 91*
Morris, James Thomas 1943- *WhoAm 90*
Morris, James W., III *BioIn 16*
Morris, Jan 1926- *BioIn 16, MajTwCW, WhoWor 91*
Morris, Jane Elizabeth 1940- *WhoWor 91*
Morris, Janet Lee *BioIn 16*
Morris, Janine Inez 1956- *WhoAmW 91*
Morris, Jean Crittenden 1930- *WhoSSW 91*
Morris, Jeff 1927- *IntWWM 90*
Morris, Jefferson E *BiDrAPA 89*
Morris, Jeffrey Bryant 1959- *WhoSSW 91*
Morris, Jeffrey Lee 1959- *WhoEmL 91*
Morris, Jerry Dean 1935- *WhoAm 90, WhoSSW 91*
Morris, Jerry O'S 1937- *St&PR 91*
Morris, Jim *BioIn 16*
Morris, Joan Clair 1943- *IntWWM 90*
Morris, Joe *BioIn 16*
Morris, Joe A 1904-1990 *ConAu 130*
Morris, Joe Alex *NewYTBS 90*
Morris, Joe Alex 1904-1990 *BioIn 16*
Morris, John *MajTwCW*
Morris, John 1941- *Ballpl 90*
Morris, John B. 1910- *St&PR 91*
Morris, John Barton 1910- *WhoE 91*
Morris, John E. 1916- *WhoE 91, WhoWor 91*
Morris, John E 1945- *BiDrAPA 89*
Morris, John H. 1942- *St&PR 91*
Morris, John Holmes, III 1931- *WhoAm 90*
Morris, John Humphrey Carlile 1910-1984 *DcNaB 1981*
Morris, John M. 1931- *ODwPR 91*
Morris, John McLean 1914- *WhoAm 90, WhoE 91*
Morris, John Milton 1906- *WhoAm 90*
Morris, John N. 1931- *ConAu 13AS [port]*
Morris, John R. 1909- *St&PR 91*
Morris, John Ryland 1955- *WhoSSW 91*
Morris, John Scott 1955- *WhoSSW 91*
Morris, John Selwyn 1925- *WhoAm 90, WhoE 91*
Morris, John William, Jr. 1943- *WhoAm 90*
Morris, John Woodland 1921- *WhoAm 90*
Morris, Jonathan Edward *BiDrAPA 89*
Morris, Jonathan Edward 1956- *WhoE 91*
Morris, Joseph Anthony 1918- *WhoE 91, WhoWor 91*
Morris, Joseph Dean 1948 *WhoEmL 91*
Morris, Joseph Erwin, III 1959- *WhoSSW 91*
Morris, Joseph Getehmnah 1929- *WhoWor 91*
Morris, Joseph Michael 1957- *WhoSSW 91*
Morris, Joshua *PenDiDA 89*
Morris, Joyce Darlene 1937- *WhoAmW 91*
Morris, Judy K 1936- *SmATA 61*
Morris, Julian *MajTwCW*
Morris, Kathleen Elizabeth 1949- *WhoAmW 91*
Morris, Kenneth Baker 1922- *WhoAm 90*
Morris, Kenneth Donald 1946- *WhoE 91, WhoEmL 91*
Morris, Kenneth Paul 1948- *WhoWor 91*
Morris, Kevin L. 1954- *ConAu 129*
Morris, Kyle Randolph 1918-1979 *WhoAmA 91N*
Morris, L A Meurig, Mrs. 1899- *EncO&P 3*
Morris, Larry Garner 1938- *St&PR 91, WhoAm 90*
Morris, Lee B. 1944- *WhoAm 90*
Morris, Lee Butler 1944- *St&PR 91*
Morris, Lester A. 1938- *St&PR 91*
Morris, Lester Joseph 1915- *St&PR 91*
Morris, Lewis 1726-1798 *EncCRAm*
Morris, Linda Marie 1950- *WhoSSW 91*
Morris, Lois Lawson 1914- *WhoAmW 91, WhoWor 91*
Morris, Lynda Mitchum 1950- *WhoSSW 91*
Morris, Lyndon H. 1945- *St&PR 91*
Morris, Lynne Louise 1946- *WhoAmW 91*
Morris, Mac Glenn 1922- *WhoAm 90*
Morris, Malcolm S. 1946- *St&PR 91*
Morris, Marcus 1915-1989 *AnObit 1989*
Morris, Margaret *BioIn 16*
Morris, Margaret 1737-1816 *FemiCLE*
Morris, Margaret Elizabeth 1962- *WhoAmW 91*
Morris, Margaret Marco *BioIn 16*
Morris, Mark *BioIn 16, WhoWor 91*
Morris, Mark 1956- *News 91-1 [port]*
Morris, Marna Jay 1949- *WhoWrEP 89*
Morris, Mary *BiDEWW*
Morris, Mary 1895?-1970 *BioIn 16, NotWoAT*
Morris, Mary 1915-1988 *AnObit 1988, ConTFT 8*
Morris, Mary 1947- *BioIn 16, ConAu 132, WhoWrEP 89*
Morris, Mary Ann 1946- *WhoAmW 91*
Morris, Mary Elizabeth 1913- *WhoWrEP 89*
Morris, Mary Rosalind 1920- *WhoAmW 91*
Morris, Mary White 1749-1827 *BioIn 16*
Morris, Mercury *BioIn 16*
Morris, Michael 1914- *WhoWor 91*
Morris, Michael 1938- *ODwPR 91*
Morris, Michael Boris 1920- *St&PR 91*
Morris, Michael G. *St&PR 91*
Morris, Michael Henry 1950- *WhoEmL 91*
Morris, Michael Lee 1948- *WhoWrEP 89*
Morris, Monica Kathleen 1955- *BiDrAPA 89*
Morris, Muriel Gold *BiDrAPA 89*
Morris, Myra 1873-1966 *FemiCLE*
Morris, Neil Eugene 1937- *St&PR 91*
Morris, Newton Augustus 1867- *AmLegL*
Morris, Nicholas Benjamin 1965- *WhoSSW 91*
Morris, Nila-Vae Lanier 1933- *St&PR 91*
Morris, Norval 1923- *WhoAm 90*
Morris, Olin Franklin 1935- *WhoSSW 91*
Morris, Owen Glenn 1927- *WhoAm 90*
Morris, Patricia Alpha 1962- *WhoAmW 91*
Morris, Patricia Armstrong 1957- *WhoAmW 91*
Morris, Patrick Francis 1925- *WhoAm 90*
Morris, Patrick John 1948- *IntWWM 90*
Morris, Paul F. *St&PR 91*
Morris, Peter *WhoAm 90*
Morris, Peter R. *St&PR 91*
Morris, Phil *BioIn 16*
Morris, Philip Edward 1934- *St&PR 91*
Morris, Philip John 1946- *WhoE 91*
Morris, R. E. 1921- *St&PR 91*
Morris, Ralph William 1928- *WhoAm 90*
Morris, Raymond Philip *NewYTBS 90*
Morris, Rebecca Elizabeth 1958- *WhoSSW 91*
Morris, Rebecca Robinson 1945- *WhoEmL 91*
Morris, Richard Alan 1944- *St&PR 91*
Morris, Richard B 1904-1989 *WorAu 1980 [port]*
Morris, Richard Brandon 1904- *AuBYP 90*
Morris, Richard Brandon 1904-1989 *BioIn 16*
Morris, Richard E. 1918- *St&PR 91*
Morris, Richard Herbert 1928- *WhoAm 90*
Morris, Richard Joel 1945- *St&PR 91*
Morris, Richard Scott 1932- *St&PR 91, WhoAm 90*
Morris, Richard Valentine 1768-1815 *BioIn 16*
Morris, Richard W. 1939- *WhoWrEP 89*
Morris, Robert 1734-1806 *BioIn 16, EncABHB 6 [port], EncCRAm, WorAlBi*
Morris, Robert 1910- *WhoE 91*
Morris, Robert 1915- *WhoAm 90*
Morris, Robert 1923- *WhoE 91*
Morris, Robert 1931- *BioIn 16, WhoAm 90, WhoAmA 91*
Morris, Robert A. 1934- *ODwPR 91*
Morris, Robert Alan 1934- *WhoAm 90*
Morris, Robert Albert 1913- *WhoWor 91*
Morris, Robert Arthur 1942- *St&PR 91*
Morris, Robert Booton 1931- *St&PR 91*
Morris, Robert C. 1942- *WhoAm 90*
Morris, Robert Christian 1948- *WhoEmL 91, WhoSSW 91*
Morris, Robert Clarke 1931- *WhoAmA 91*
Morris, Robert Crawford 1916- *WhoAm 90*
Morris, Robert Daniel 1943- *IntWWM 90*
Morris, Robert Darrell 1914- *WhoSSW 91*
Morris, Robert Gemmill 1929- *WhoAm 90*
Morris, Robert John 1934- *WhoWor 91*
Morris, Robert Julian, Jr. 1932- *WhoAm 90*
Morris, Robert L. 1942- *EncO&P 3*
Morris, Robert Louis 1932- *St&PR 91, WhoAm 90*
Morris, Robert Lyle 1942- *EncPaPR 91*
Morris, Robert McQuary 1933- *WhoWrEP 89*
Morris, Robert Preston, Jr. 1945- *WhoSSW 91*
Morris, Robert R *BiDrAPA 89*
Morris, Robert Smith 1952- *WhoEmL 91*
Morris, Robert Steven *BioIn 16*
Morris, Roger Dale 1947- *WhoAmA 91*
Morris, Roland 1933- *WhoAm 90*
Morris, Roland Sletor 1874-1945 *BioIn 16*
Morris, Ronald Lee 1947- *St&PR 91*
Morris, Ruth Ann 1947- *WhoAmW 91*
Morris, Samuel Solomon *BioIn 16*
Morris, Sandra Chass 1936- *WhoAmW 91*
Morris, Seth Irwin 1914- *WhoAm 90*
Morris, Sharon Louise 1956- *WhoAmW 91*
Morris, Stanley E. 1942- *WhoAm 90*
Morris, Stanley M. 1942- *WhoAm 90*
Morris, Stephanie Anne 1950- *WhoAmW 91*
Morris, Stephen Alan 1950- *St&PR 91*
Morris, Stephen Brent 1950- *WhoE 91*
Morris, Stephen Burritt 1943- *WhoAm 90*
Morris, Stephen James Michael 1934- *WhoAm 90*
Morris, Stephen Jay 1956- *IntWWM 90*
Morris, Steveland *BioIn 16*
Morris, Steven Barry 1944- *WhoSSW 91*
Morris, Steven C. 1949- *St&PR 91*
Morris, Stevland *WhoWor 91*
Morris, Susan C. 1962- *ODwPR 91*
Morris, Susan Elizabeth 1952- *WhoAmW 91*
Morris, Susan Marie 1955- *WhoAmW 91*
Morris, Susan McDonald 1946- *WhoAmW 91*
Morris, Sylvia Marie *BiDrAPA 89*
Morris, Sylvia Marie 1952- *WhoAmW 91*
Morris, T. J. 1929- *St&PR 91*
Morris, Tamara 1962- *WhoSSW 91*
Morris, Tammy Mynetta 1959- *WhoAmW 91*
Morris, Teresa Ann 1960- *WhoAmW 91*
Morris, Thad James, Jr. 1929- *St&PR 91*
Morris, Thelma Lovette 1948- *WhoAmW 91*
Morris, Thomas A, Jr. 1916- *BiDrAPA 89*
Morris, Thomas Bateman, Jr. 1936- *WhoAm 90*
Morris, Thomas Edward 1942- *WhoSSW 91*
Morris, Thomas F. 1932- *St&PR 91*
Morris, Thomas Quinlan 1933- *WhoAm 90*
Morris, Thomas William 1944- *WhoAm 90*
Morris, Tracy Lee 1960- *BiDrAPA 89*
Morris, Victor Franklin, Jr. 1947- *WhoSSW 91*
Morris, W. S., III 1934- *St&PR 91*
Morris, Walter Kenneth 1930- *St&PR 91*
Morris, Walter Scott 1912- *WhoAm 90*
Morris, Wendy Valerie Anne 1952- *WhoWor 91*
Morris, William 1834-1896 *BioIn 16, PenDiDA 89, WorAlBi*
Morris, William 1899-1989 *BioIn 16*
Morris, William 1913- *WhoAm 90, WhoWrEP 89*
Morris, William Charles 1938- *WhoAm 90*
Morris, William Harrell, Jr. 1929- *WhoAm 90*
Morris, William Joseph 1923- *WhoAm 90*
Morris, William L. 1908- *St&PR 91*
Morris, William Noel, Jr. 1932- *WhoAm 90, WhoSSW 91*
Morris, William Otis, Jr. 1922- *WhoAm 90*
Morris, William Samuel, IV 1955- *WhoWor 91*
Morris, William Shivers, III 1934- *WhoAm 90*
Morris, William T. 1937- *St&PR 91*
Morris, Willie 1934- *AuBYP 90, WhoAm 90, WorAlBi*
Morris, Willie Herman, III 1953- *WhoSSW 91*
Morris, Wm. David 1947- *St&PR 91*
Morris, Wright 1910- *MajTwCW, WhoAm 90, WhoAmA 91, WhoWrEP 89, WorAlBi*
Morris, Wyn 1929- *IntWWM 90*
Morris, Yvonne Marie 1949- *WhoSSW 91*
Morris-Sweetland, Gayle D. 1943- *St&PR 91*
Morris-Yamba, Trish *WhoE 91*
Morrisett, H. Dallas 1937- *St&PR 91*
Morrisett, Lloyd N. 1929- *WhoAm 90*
Morrisey, Donald C. 1931- *St&PR 91*
Morrisey, Michael A. 1952- *WhoSSW 91*
Morrisey, P. D. 1939- *St&PR 91*
Morrisey, Thomas 1952- *WhoWrEP 89*
Morrish, Allan Henry 1924- *WhoAm 90*
Morrish, Kathleen Anne 1956- *WhoE 91*
Morrison, Alec P. 1943- *St&PR 91*
Morrison, Alexander Damien *WhoWrEP 89*
Morrison, Andrew Lewis 1945- *BiDrAPA 89*
Morrison, Andrew Philip 1937- *BiDrAPA 89*
Morrison, Angus Curran 1919- *WhoAm 90*
Morrison, Ann Kerr *BiDrAPA 89*
Morrison, April Dawn 1971- *WhoWrEP 89*
Morrison, Arthur 1863-1945 *BioIn 16, TwCCr&M 91*
Morrison, Ashton Byrom 1922- *WhoAm 90, WhoE 91*
Morrison, Audrey A. Lesiak 1941- *St&PR 91*
Morrison, Bee 1908- *WhoAmA 91*
Morrison, Benjamin Yoe 1891-1966 *BioIn 16*
Morrison, Bernard Jerome 1936- *WhoE 91*
Morrison, Betty Lee Yarborough 1946- *WhoAmW 91*
Morrison, Boone M 1941- *WhoAmA 91*
Morrison, Bruce Andrew 1944- *WhoAm 90, WhoE 91*
Morrison, Bruce William 1926- *St&PR 91*
Morrison, Bryce 1938- *IntWWM 90*
Morrison, Carberta Ann 1957- *WhoAmW 91*
Morrison, Carol Weiss *WhoAmW 91*
Morrison, Charles Edgar 1947- *WhoSSW 91*
Morrison, Charles H. *AmLegL*
Morrison, Charlotte 1832-1910 *OxCCanT*
Morrison, Chase Pamela 1955- *IntWWM 90*
Morrison, Cheryl Lynn 1953- *WhoAmW 91*
Morrison, Chloe Anthony *WhoAm 90*
Morrison, Clinton 1915- *WhoAm 90*
Morrison, Connie Faith *WhoAmW 91*
Morrison, Darrel Gene 1937- *WhoAm 90*
Morrison, Daryl 1929- *St&PR 91*
Morrison, Daryl 1931- *St&PR 91*
Morrison, David 1940- *ConAu 30NR*
Morrison, David A. 1960- *St&PR 91*
Morrison, David Campbell 1941- *WhoAm 90*
Morrison, David Evan *BiDrAPA 89*
Morrison, David Lee 1933- *St&PR 91, WhoAm 90*
Morrison, Debra Lynn 1956- *WhoAmW 91*
Morrison, Delcy Schram 1935- *WhoAmW 91, WhoWor 91*
Morrison, Denis *BiDrAPA 89*
Morrison, Denise Annette *WhoWrEP 89*
Morrison, Dennis Brian 1946- *St&PR 91*
Morrison, Dolphus Compton 1934- *St&PR 91*
Morrison, Donald A. 1931- *St&PR 91*
Morrison, Donald Bruce 1929- *St&PR 91*
Morrison, Donald Franklin 1931- *WhoAm 90*
Morrison, Donald Graham 1939- *WhoAm 90*
Morrison, Donald William 1926- *WhoAm 90*
Morrison, Doris *WhoAmA 91*
Morrison, Doris 1906- *WhoAmW 91*
Morrison, Edward W., Jr. 1921- *St&PR 91*
Morrison, Edward Walter, Jr. 1921- *WhoSSW 91*
Morrison, Elizabeth Ann 1950- *BiDrAPA 89*
Morrison, Elliot I *BiDrAPA 89*
Morrison, Ellis 1850- *AmLegL*
Morrison, Francis Secrest 1931- *WhoAm 90*
Morrison, Frank 1918- *WhoWrEP 89*
Morrison, Frank Barron 1887-1958 *BioIn 16*
Morrison, Fred Beverly 1927- *WhoAm 90*
Morrison, Frederic *BioIn 16*
Morrison, Fritzi Mohrenstecher *WhoAmA 91*
Morrison, Gayle V. 1921- *St&PR 91*
Morrison, Geoffrey Keith 1946- *St&PR 91*
Morrison, George 1919- *WhoAm 90, WhoAmA 91*
Morrison, George Harold 1921- *WhoAm 90*
Morrison, Gilbert C 1931- *BiDrAPA 89*
Morrison, Gilbert Caffall 1931- *WhoAm 90*
Morrison, Glen Warren 1934- *WhoWor 91*
Morrison, Glenn Scott *BiDrAPA 89*
Morrison, Gloria Jean 1948- *WhoAmW 91*
Morrison, Gordon Mackay, Jr. 1930- *WhoE 91*
Morrison, Grace *WhoWrEP 89*
Morrison, Grace Blanch Simpson 1933- *WhoAmW 91*
Morrison, Gregg Scott 1964- *WhoSSW 91*
Morrison, Gus 1935- *WhoAm 90*
Morrison, Gwendolynn Sue Slover 1945- *WhoAmW 91*
Morrison, H. D., Jr. 1926- *St&PR 91*
Morrison, H. Robert 1938- *WhoE 91*
Morrison, H. Russell, Jr. 1929- *St&PR 91*
Morrison, Harry 1937- *WhoAm 90*
Morrison, Harvey Lee, Jr. 1947- *WhoEmL 91*
Morrison, Helen 1928- *WhoAmW 91*
Morrison, Helen Louise 1942- *BiDrAPA 89*
Morrison, Herbert *BioIn 16*
Morrison, Howard Irwin 1929- *WhoSSW 91*
Morrison, Ian Alastair 1924- *WhoE 91*
Morrison, J. Ken 1950- *WhoWrEP 89*
Morrison, James *BioIn 16*
Morrison, James 1940- *BiDrAPA 89*
Morrison, James Harris 1918- *St&PR 91*
Morrison, James R. 1924- *WhoAm 90*
Morrison, James S. 1929- *WhoAm 90*
Morrison, James Wayne 1957- *WhoSSW 91*
Morrison, Jane Thornton 1949- *WhoSSW 91*
Morrison, Jeannine R. 1930- *IntWWM 90*
Morrison, Jim 1943-1971 *BioIn 16, WorAlBi*
Morrison, Jim 1952- *Ballpl 90*

Morrison, Joan 1922- *WhoAmW 91*
Morrison, Joe *BioIn 16*
Morrison, John Haddow, Jr. 1933- *St&PR 91*
Morrison, John Horton 1933- *WhoAm 90*
Morrison, John Lance 1953- *WhoE 91*
Morrison, John Lewis 1945- *WhoAm 90*
Morrison, John Michael 1957- *WhoE 91*
Morrison, John R. 1928- *St&PR 91*
Morrison, John Washburn 1922- *WhoAm 90*
Morrison, Johnny 1895-1966 *Ballpl 90*
Morrison, Joseph Francis, Jr. 1943- *WhoAm 90*
Morrison, Joseph Louis 1936- *WhoE 91*
Morrison, Joseph Young 1951- *WhoSSW 91*
Morrison, Joshua 1900- *St&PR 91*
Morrison, K. Jaydene 1933- *WhoSSW 91*
Morrison, Karl Frederick 1936- *WhoAm 90*
Morrison, Kay Ellen 1961- *WhoAmW 91*
Morrison, Keith Anthony 1942- *WhoAmA 91, WhoE 91*
Morrison, Kenneth 1921- *St&PR 91*
Morrison, Kenneth Allen 1940- *WhoE 91*
Morrison, Kenneth Douglas 1918- *WhoAm 90*
Morrison, Kenneth Ray 1948- *St&PR 91*
Morrison, L Jed *BiDrAPA 89*
Morrison, Laura Mary 1927- *WhoWrEP 89*
Morrison, Laurance Stephan 1940- *WhoE 91*
Morrison, Lea *ODwPR 91*
Morrison, Leonette S *BiDrAPA 89*
Morrison, Lillian 1917- *BioIn 16, WhoWrEP 89*
Morrison, Mabel Jean 1927- *WhoSSW 91*
Morrison, Madison 1940- *WhoWrEP 89*
Morrison, Majorie G E *BiDrAPA 89*
Morrison, Manley Glenn 1915- *WhoAm 90*
Morrison, Marion Michael 1907-1979 *BioIn 16*
Morrison, Mark Bryant *BiDrAPA 89*
Morrison, Martin Earl 1947- *WhoAm 90*
Morrison, Marvin 1964- *WhoSSW 91*
Morrison, Marvin L. 1940- *WhoWrEP 89*
Morrison, Meredith 1921- *St&PR 91*
Morrison, Michael Frank 1951- *WhoWor 91*
Morrison, Michael Gordon 1937- *WhoAm 90*
Morrison, Michael Ian Donald 1929- *St&PR 91, WhoAm 90*
Morrison, Morris Robert 1908- *WhoAm 90*
Morrison, Nan Jody 1962- *WhoAmW 91*
Morrison, Nancy Kay 1946- *BiDrAPA 89*
Morrison, Pat *BioIn 16*
Morrison, Perry David 1919- *WhoAm 90*
Morrison, Perry Erwin 1929- *St&PR 91*
Morrison, Peter Daniel 1943- *St&PR 91*
Morrison, Peter H. 1935-1988 *BioIn 16*
Morrison, Philip 1915- *WhoAm 90*
Morrison, Porter, Jr. 1938- *WhoE 91*
Morrison, R. F. *WhoAm 90*
Morrison, R. M. *St&PR 91*
Morrison, Ray 1942- *IntWWM 90*
Morrison, Richard Charles 1938- *WhoE 91*
Morrison, Richard N. 1958- *St&PR 91*
Morrison, Richard Scott 1944- *St&PR 91*
Morrison, Robert 1921- *St&PR 91*
Morrison, Robert Clifton 1924- *WhoAmA 91*
Morrison, Robert Irwin 1938- *St&PR 91*
Morrison, Robert R. 1935- *St&PR 91*
Morrison, Robert S. 1909- *St&PR 91*
Morrison, Robert Scheck 1942- *WhoAm 90*
Morrison, Roger Barron 1914- *WhoWor 91*
Morrison, Roger F. 1937- *St&PR 91*
Morrison, S Bergen 1925- *BiDrAPA 89*
Morrison, Samuel F. 1936- *WhoAm 90*
Morrison, Shelley 1936- *WhoAm 90*
Morrison, Sid 1933- *WhoAm 90*
Morrison, Stan *St&PR 91*
Morrison, Steven Howard 1945- *WhoEmL 91*
Morrison, Susan M. *WhoAm 90, WhoAmW 91*
Morrison, Susan Orinda 1948- *WhoWrEP 89*
Morrison, T. H. *PenDiMP*
Morrison, T. Truxtun *WhoAm 90*
Morrison, Tamara Kyle 1949- *WhoAmW 91*
Morrison, Theodore 1901-1988 *BioIn 16*
Morrison, Tim *BioIn 16*
Morrison, Toni 1931- *BioIn 16, FemiCLE, MajTwCW, WhoAm 90, WhoAmW 91, WhoWrEP 89, WorAlBi*
Morrison, Van 1945- *EncPR&S 89, OxCPMus, WhoAm 90*
Morrison, Virden H. 1927- *St&PR 91*
Morrison, W. Rodney 1946- *WhoSSW 91*
Morrison, Walton Stephen 1907- *WhoSSW 91, WhoWor 91*
Morrison, Wilbur Howard 1915- *SmATA 64*
Morrison, Wilbur J. 1931- *St&PR 91*
Morrison, William E. 1930- *St&PR 91*
Morrison, William Fowler, Jr. 1928- *WhoAm 90, WhoSSW 91*
Morrison, William Leo 1931- *WhoAm 90*
Morrison, William McCutchan 1867-1918 *BioIn 16*
Morrison, William Ralls 1825-1909 *AmLegL*
Morrison, Winifred Elaine Haas 1925- *WhoAmW 91*
Morrison-Rose, Mary Etta 1917- *IntWWM 90*
Morrisroe, Edward L. 1948- *St&PR 91*
Morriss, Frank Howard, Jr. 1940- *WhoAm 90*
Morriss, George Wyman 1947- *St&PR 91*
Morriss, James A. 1930- *St&PR 91*
Morriss, James E. 1932- *AuBYP 90*
Morriss, Mary Rachel *WhoAmA 91, WhoAmW 91, WhoWor 91*
Morriss, Randy *NewAgMG*
Morrissette, Bruce Archer 1911- *WhoAm 90*
Morrissette, Sheryln Berg 1943- *WhoE 91*
Morrissey, Andrea 1962- *WhoAmW 91*
Morrissey, Charles D. 1926-1989 *BioIn 16*
Morrissey, Charles Thomas 1933- *WhoAm 90, WhoE 91*
Morrissey, Dolores Josephine *WhoAm 90*
Morrissey, Edmond Joseph 1943- *WhoAm 90*
Morrissey, James Joseph, Jr. 1938- *WhoE 91*
Morrissey, Jo-Jo 1904-1950 *Ballpl 90*
Morrissey, John Carroll 1914- *WhoAm 90*
Morrissey, John Daniel 1929- *St&PR 91, WhoAm 90*
Morrissey, John Edward 1930- *St&PR 91, WhoAm 90*
Morrissey, Leo 1958- *WhoAmA 91*
Morrissey, Martin G. 1952- *St&PR 91*
Morrissey, Paul 1939- *ConTFT 8*
Morrissey, Peter 1953- *ODwPR 91, WhoAm 90*
Morrissey, Robert J. 1944- *ODwPR 91, St&PR 91*
Morrissey, Thomas Francis 1932- *St&PR 91*
Morrissey, Thomas J. 1936- *St&PR 91*
Morrissey, William Paul 1927- *St&PR 91*
Morrissy, Mary Jule 1952- *WhoEmL 91*
Morriston, Donald Robert 1941- *St&PR 91*
Morritt, Graham Nathaniel 1942- *WhoWor 91*
Morros, Linda 1958- *BiDrAPA 89*
Morros, Linda Joy 1958- *WhoE 91*
Morros, Lucy Schmitz *WhoAm 90, WhoAmW 91*
Morrow, Allen Roy 1949- *St&PR 91*
Morrow, Andrew Nesbit 1929- *WhoAm 90*
Morrow, Ann Bolton 1952- *St&PR 91*
Morrow, Ann Patricia *ConAu 130*
Morrow, Barry Nelson 1948- *WhoAm 90*
Morrow, Benjamin Francis 1891-1958 *WhoAmA 91N*
Morrow, Bradford 1951- *ConAu 32NR*
Morrow, Bruce W. 1946- *WhoSSW 91*
Morrow, C Lynn D 1951- *BiDrAPA 89*
Morrow, Cherylle Ann 1950- *WhoAmW 91*
Morrow, David Austin, III 1935- *WhoAm 90*
Morrow, David G. 1946- *St&PR 91*
Morrow, Dennis 1952- *ConAu 132*
Morrow, Dwight Graydon 1934- *WhoE 91*
Morrow, Dwight W. 1873-1931 *EncABHB 7 [port]*
Morrow, Dwight Whitney 1873-1931 *BioIn 16*
Morrow, E. Frederic 1909- *WhoAm 90*
Morrow, Elizabeth 1947- *WhoAmW 91, WhoWor 91*
Morrow, Emily May 1959- *WhoE 91*
Morrow, Emily Rubenstein 1952- *WhoAmW 91, WhoEmL 91*
Morrow, Felix 1906-1988 *EncO&P 3*
Morrow, Fred C. 1926- *St&PR 91*
Morrow, Gay *BiDrAPA 89*
Morrow, George Lester 1922- *WhoAm 90*
Morrow, George Telford, II 1943- *WhoWrEP 89*
Morrow, Gerald L. 1932- *St&PR 91*
Morrow, Giles 1908- *WhoAm 90*
Morrow, Hilda Howard 1942- *WhoSSW 91*
Morrow, Hugh 1915- *WhoAm 90*
Morrow, James B. 1926- *St&PR 91, WhoAm 90*
Morrow, James Coles 1931- *St&PR 91*
Morrow, Jane Bates 1947- *WhoSSW 91*
Morrow, Janet Ebba 1953- *IntWWM 90*
Morrow, Jeanne Chadwick *BiDrAPA 89*
Morrow, Jennifer Lee 1955- *WhoAmW 91*
Morrow, Jerry F 1938- *BiDrAPA 89*
Morrow, John D. 1923- *St&PR 91*
Morrow, John Howard 1910- *WhoAm 90*
Morrow, Joseph T. 1930- *St&PR 91*
Morrow, Joyce L. 1964- *WhoAmW 91*
Morrow, Larry Gaither, Sr. 1946- *WhoSSW 91*
Morrow, Laura Annette 1958- *WhoAmW 91*
Morrow, Laura E 1913- *BiDrAPA 89*
Morrow, Mary Jane 1952- *St&PR 91*
Morrow, Mary Katherine 1957- *WhoAmW 91*
Morrow, Mary Louise Stirewalt 1935- *WhoAmW 91*
Morrow, Merlin E. 1936- *WhoSSW 91*
Morrow, Nancy Ann 1958- *WhoAmW 91*
Morrow, Pat *BioIn 16*
Morrow, Patricia A. 1959- *ODwPR 91*
Morrow, Patricia Ann 1959- *WhoAmW 91*
Morrow, Paul Edward 1922- *WhoAm 90*
Morrow, Ralph Ernest 1920- *WhoAm 90*
Morrow, Regina Davis 1961- *WhoSSW 91*
Morrow, Richard C. 1923- *St&PR 91*
Morrow, Richard Forrest 1935- *St&PR 91*
Morrow, Richard Martin 1926- *St&PR 91, WhoAm 90, WhoWor 91*
Morrow, Richard Towson 1926- *WhoAm 90*
Morrow, Robert 1930- *St&PR 91*
Morrow, Robert Earl 1917- *WhoAmA 91*
Morrow, Robert Edward *BiDrAPA 89*
Morrow, Robert Maxwell 1946- *WhoE 91*
Morrow, Robert Sproul 1928- *St&PR 91*
Morrow, Sam R. 1949- *St&PR 91*
Morrow, Samuel Roy, III 1949- *WhoAm 90*
Morrow, Scott Douglas 1954- *WhoE 91, WhoWor 91*
Morrow, Sheila Ann 1936- *WhoWrEP 89*
Morrow, Skip *ConAu 132*
Morrow, Stanley 1843-1921 *WhNaAH*
Morrow, Susan Dagmar 1932- *WhoAmW 91*
Morrow, Susan H. 1943- *WhoAmW 91*
Morrow, Suzanne Stark *AuBYP 90*
Morrow, Terry 1939- *WhoAmA 91*
Morrow, Thomas Allen 1956- *WhoEmL 91*
Morrow, Thomas F 1921- *BiDrAPA 89*
Morrow, Thomas H. 1941- *St&PR 91*
Morrow, Timothy Titus 1911- *WhoWor 91*
Morrow, Victoria R 1954- *BiDrAPA 89*
Morrow, Walter Edwin, Jr. 1928- *WhoAm 90*
Morrow, William Clarence 1935- *WhoAm 90*
Morrow, William L 1943- *WhoWrEP 89*
Morrow, William Owen 1927- *St&PR 91, WhoAm 90*
Morrow, William Penn, Jr. 1933- *St&PR 91*
Morrow, Winston Vaughan 1924- *St&PR 91, WhoAm 90, WhoWor 91*
Morrow-Jones, Hazel Ann 1952- *WhoAmW 91*
Morsch, Thomas Harvey 1931- *WhoAm 90*
Morsching, Germaine Ann 1934- *WhoAmW 91*
Morse, Alan R., Jr. 1938- *St&PR 91*
Morse, Alfred L. *BioIn 16*
Morse, Andrew Richard 1946- *WhoAm 90*
Morse, Anne Elizabeth 1947- *WhoWor 91*
Morse, Bart J 1938- *WhoAmA 91*
Morse, Bradford 1921- *WhoAm 90*
Morse, Brenton Tupper, Jr. 1925- *WhoSSW 91*
Morse, Carl A. *BioIn 16*
Morse, Carlton E. 1901- *WhoAm 90*
Morse, Carmel Lei 1953- *WhoWrEP 89*
Morse, Carol *AuBYP 90*
Morse, Carol Lynn 1945- *WhoSSW 91*
Morse, Carole E. *ODwPR 91*
Morse, Charles William, Jr. 1934- *WhoAm 90*
Morse, Charlotte Cook 1942- *WhoSSW 91*
Morse, Charlotte Elaine *BiDrAPA 89*
Morse, Christopher Jeremy *BioIn 16*
Morse, David A. 1907- *WhoAm 90*
Morse, David A. 1907-1990 *NewYTBS 90*
Morse, David Bradford 1943- *St&PR 91*
Morse, David Rockwell 1954- *St&PR 91*
Morse, Donald R 1931- *WhoWrEP 89*
Morse, Dorothy B 1906-1979 *WhoAmA 91N*
Morse, Duane Dale 1950- *WhoEmL 91*
Morse, Edmond N. 1922- *St&PR 91*
Morse, Edmond Northrop 1922- *WhoAm 90*
Morse, Edward Sylvester 1838-1925 *BioIn 16, EncJap*
Morse, Ella Mae 1924- *OxCPMus*
Morse, Elwood *NewAgE 90*
Morse, Emily Bomberger 1899- *WhoAmW 91*
Morse, Ephraim *BioIn 16*
Morse, Erskine Vance 1921- *WhoAm 90*
Morse, F. D., Jr. 1928- *WhoWor 91*
Morse, Frank Alan 1938- *St&PR 91*
Morse, Garlan, Jr. 1947- *WhoAm 90*
Morse, George Wray, II 1942- *WhoSSW 91*
Morse, Glenn Tilley 1870-1950 *WhoAmA 91N*
Morse, Grant Wesley 1926- *WhoAm 90*
Morse, Hazel Red 1937- *WhoAmW 91*
Morse, Herbert R. 1929- *St&PR 91*
Morse, J.J. 1848-1919 *EncO&P 3*
Morse, Jack Hatton 1923- *WhoAm 90*
Morse, Jacob C. 1860-1937 *Ballpl 90*
Morse, James Buckner 1930- *WhoAm 90*
Morse, James K. 1937- *St&PR 91*
Morse, James L. 1940- *WhoE 91*
Morse, Jedediah 1761-1826 *WhNaAH*
Morse, Jeffrey Andrews 1938- *WhoE 91*
Morse, Joan Hollis 1951- *WhoE 91*
Morse, John Flavel 1801-1884 *AmLegL*
Morse, John H. 1910- *St&PR 91*
Morse, John Harleigh 1910- *WhoAm 90*
Morse, John L. 1932- *St&PR 91*
Morse, John Lougee 1932- *WhoAm 90, WhoE 91*
Morse, John Moore 1911- *WhoAm 90*
Morse, Joseph 1920- *St&PR 91, WhoAm 90*
Morse, Karen Williams 1940- *WhoAm 90*
Morse, Kenneth Pratt 1905- *WhoAm 90*
Morse, L A 1945- *TwCCr&M 91*
Morse, Leon William 1912- *WhoWor 91*
Morse, Louise *NewAgE 90*
Morse, Lucius B., III 1938- *St&PR 91*
Morse, Luis C. 1940- *WhoHisp 91*
Morse, Marcia Roberts 1944- *WhoAmA 91*
Morse, Margaret Patricia 1912- *WhoWrEP 89*
Morse, Marian Margaret 1945- *WhoE 91*
Morse, Marvin Henry 1929- *WhoAm 90, WhoE 91*
Morse, Michael Stephen 1960- *WhoSSW 91*
Morse, Mitchell Ian 1926- *WhoAmA 91*
Morse, Nancy Wood 1930- *St&PR 91*
Morse, Peggy Mansfield *WhoWrEP 89*
Morse, Peter 1935- *WhoAmA 91*
Morse, Peter Hodges 1935- *WhoAm 90*
Morse, Rebecca Lynne 1956- *WhoSSW 91*
Morse, Richard 1922- *WhoAm 90*
Morse, Richard McGee 1922- *WhoAm 90*
Morse, Richard Stetson 1911-1988 *BioIn 16*
Morse, Richard Stetson, Jr. 1941- *St&PR 91*
Morse, Robert *BioIn 16*
Morse, Robert Alan 1931- *WhoAm 90, WhoE 91*
Morse, Robert Harry 1941- *WhoAm 90*
Morse, Robert Mark 1934- *BiDrAPA 89*
Morse, Robert Moreton 1937- *St&PR 91*
Morse, Robert Parker 1945- *St&PR 91*
Morse, Robert Warren 1921- *WhoAm 90*
Morse, Samuel 1906- *St&PR 91*
Morse, Samuel F. 1791-1872 *WorAlBi*
Morse, Samuel Finley Breese 1791-1872 *BioIn 16*
Morse, Saul Julian 1948- *WhoEmL 91*
Morse, Scott David 1950- *WhoEmL 91*
Morse, Theodore F. 1873-1924 *BioIn 16, OxCPMus*
Morse, True Delbert 1896- *WhoAm 90*
Morse, Wayne 1900-1974 *WorAlBi*
Morse, William R 1920- *BiDrAPA 89*
Morselli, Enrico 1852-1929 *EncO&P 3, EncPaPR 91*
Morselli, Paolo Lucio 1937- *WhoWor 91*
Morshead, Richard Williams 1931- *WhoAm 90*
Morson, A. E. 1934- *St&PR 91*
Morson, Alan Ernest 1934- *WhoAm 90*
Morss, Charles Anthony, Jr. 1931- *St&PR 91, WhoAm 90*
Morss, Esther Proctor 1964- *WhoAmW 91*
Morstyn, Ron *BiDrAPA 89*
Morsy, Magali 1933- *ConAu 132*
Mort, Charles Edwin 1946- *WhoSSW 91*
Mortarelli, Robert J. 1941- *St&PR 91*
Mortati, Saverio G *BiDrAPA 89*
Morte, Armand E. 1929- *St&PR 91*
Mortell, Edward J 1918- *BiDrAPA 89*
Mortellito, Domenico 1906- *WhoAmA 91, WhoE 91*
Mortemore, Lenore Mary 1927- *WhoWrEP 89*
Morten, Spencer W., Jr. 1922- *St&PR 91*
Morten, Stanley W. 1943- *St&PR 91*
Mortensen, Arvid LeGrande 1941- *WhoAm 90*
Mortensen, C. A. 1935- *St&PR 91*
Mortensen, Davis K. *WhoSSW 91*
Mortensen, Diane *BioIn 16*
Mortensen, Ellen L. 1943- *WhoAmW 91*
Mortensen, Enok 1902-1984 *DcScanL*
Mortensen, Eugene Phillips 1941- *WhoE 91*
Mortensen, Gordon 1938- *BioIn 16*
Mortensen, Gordon Louis 1938- *WhoAm 90, WhoAmA 91*

Mortensen, James E. 1925- *WhoAm 90*
Mortensen, Morris D. 1929- *St&PR 91*
Mortensen, Peter 1935- *WhoAm 90*
Mortensen, Robert Henry 1939- *WhoAm 90*
Mortensen, Robert Monrad 1946- *WhoSSW 91*
Mortensen, Roberta *WhoWrEP 89*
Mortensen, Stanley John 1949- *WhoEmL 91, WhoWor 91*
Mortensen, Susan Marie 1950- *WhoAmW 91*
Mortensen, William H. 1903-1990 *NewYTBS 90*
Mortensen, William Henry 1903- *WhoAm 90*
Mortenson, Carl Norman 1919- *St&PR 91*
Mortenson, Cheryl Darlene 1959- *WhoSSW 91*
Mortenson, Thomas Theodore 1934- *St&PR 91*
Morter, Raymond Lione 1920- *WhoAm 90*
Mortera, Marianne Hidalgo 1961- *WhoAmW 91*
Mortham, Sandra Barringer 1951- *WhoAmW 91*
Morthland, Constance Amelia Grant 1915- *WhoAmW 91*
Morthland, John 1947- *ConAu 129*
Mortier, Gerard 1943- *IntWWM 90, WhoWor 91*
Mortimer *OxCPMus*
Mortimer, Alan John 1950- *WhoAm 90*
Mortimer, Alex *OxCPMus*
Mortimer, Anita Louise 1950- *WhoAmW 91, WhoEmL 91, WhoWor 91*
Mortimer, Dale Burton *BiDrAPA 89*
Mortimer, Edward Albert, Jr. 1922- *WhoAm 90*
Mortimer, Fred 1880-1953 *OxCPMus*
Mortimer, Gigi *BioIn 16*
Mortimer, Harold E. 1928- *St&PR 91*
Mortimer, Harold Edward 1928- *WhoAm 90*
Mortimer, Harry 1902- *OxCPMus, PenDiMP*
Mortimer, Henry T. 1916- *St&PR 91*
Mortimer, Henry Tilford 1942- *WhoAm 90*
Mortimer, Henry Tilford, Jr. 1942- *St&PR 91*
Mortimer, J. Thomas 1939- *WhoAm 90*
Mortimer, Jay C *BiDrAPA 89*
Mortimer, John 1923- *MajTwCW, TwCCr&M 91*
Mortimer, John Clifford 1923- *BioIn 16*
Mortimer, Kenneth P. *BioIn 16*
Mortimer, Mary 1816-1877 *BioAmW*
Mortimer, Penelope 1918- *BioIn 16, FemiCLE*
Mortimer, Peter *ConAu 131*
Mortimer, Raymond E *BiDrAPA 89*
Mortimer, Rex *OxCPMus*
Mortimer, Robert Thomas, Jr. 1954- *St&PR 91*
Mortimer, William James 1932- *WhoAm 90*
Mortimer, William John 1934- *WhoWrEP 89*
Mortimer, Wm. James 1932- *St&PR 91*
Mortlock, Robert Paul 1931- *WhoAm 90*
Mortman, Doris *ConAu 129*
Mortmane, J. D. *ConAu 131*
Mortola, Edward Joseph 1917- *WhoAm 90, WhoE 91*
Morton, Alan Whitman 1938- *St&PR 91*
Morton, Anne Douglas, Countess of *BiDEWW*
Morton, Anne Marie Judith 1965- *WhoWrEP 89*
Morton, Anthony *MajTwCW, TwCCr&M 91*
Morton, Beecher Edward 1922- *WhoSSW 91*
Morton, Benny 1907- *DrBIPA 90*
Morton, Bernice Finley 1923- *WhoAmW 91*
Morton, Bubba 1931- *Ballpl 90*
Morton, Carl 1944-1983 *Ballpl 90*
Morton, Carlos 1947- *BioIn 16, ConAu 32NR, HispWr 90, WhoHisp 91*
Morton, Caroline Joy French *BioIn 16*
Morton, Caroline Julia *WhoAmW 91*
Morton, Carolyn K. 1951- *St&PR 91*
Morton, Catharine 1837-1892 *DcCanB 12*
Morton, Charles Brinkley 1926- *WhoAm 90*
Morton, Charles F. 1945- *St&PR 91*
Morton, Charles Harrison 1960- *WhoSSW 91*
Morton, Charles M. 1908- *St&PR 91*
Morton, Charlotte Ann 1958- *WhoWrEP 89*
Morton, Claude Cammack 1951- *WhoE 91*
Morton, David *LiHiK*
Morton, David 1886-1957 *LiHiK*
Morton, David 1929- *WhoAm 90, WhoWor 91*
Morton, Dean O. 1932- *WhoAm 90*
Morton, Desmond 1937- *ConAu 32NR*
Morton, Don Ray 1944- *WhoSSW 91*
Morton, Donald Charles 1933- *WhoAm 90*
Morton, Donald John 1931- *WhoAm 90*
Morton, Donald Lee 1934- *WhoAm 90, WhoWor 91*
Morton, Edward Francis 1951- *WhoSSW 91*
Morton, Edward James 1926- *St&PR 91, WhoAm 90, WhoE 91*
Morton, Effie-May *BioIn 16*
Morton, Florrinell 1905-1990 *BioIn 16*
Morton, Frederic 1924- *WhoAm 90, WhoWrEP 89*
Morton, Gary Dale 1956- *BiDrAPA 89*
Morton, George 1585-1624 *EncCRAm*
Morton, George Elkana 1811-1892 *DcCanB 12*
Morton, Gregory Keith, III 1948- *WhoSSW 91*
Morton, Guy 1893-1934 *Ballpl 90*
Morton, Henry Royal 1935- *St&PR 91*
Morton, Herbert Charles 1921- *WhoAm 90*
Morton, Herwald Hutchins 1931- *WhoAm 90*
Morton, J. 1927- *St&PR 91*
Morton, James Alexander 1940- *WhoSSW 91*
Morton, Jane 1908- *LiHiK*
Morton, Jane 1931- *BioIn 16*
Morton, Jelly Roll *BioIn 16*
Morton, Jelly Roll 1885-1941 *DrBIPA 90, WorAlBi*
Morton, Jelly Roll 1890-1941 *OxCPMus*
Morton, Jerome Holdren 1942- *WhoSSW 91, WhoWor 91*
Morton, Joanne McKean 1953- *WhoAmW 91*
Morton, Joe *BioIn 16*
Morton, Joe 1947- *DrBIPA 90*
Morton, John 1724?-1777 *EncCRAm*
Morton, John, III 1943- *WhoAm 90*
Morton, Joseph Neil 1902- *WhoAm 90*
Morton, Joy 1855-1934 *WorAlBi*
Morton, Julius Sterling 1832-1902 *BiDrUSE 89*
Morton, Leslie Thomas 1907- *BioIn 16*
Morton, Levi P 1824-1920 *EncABHB 6 [port]*
Morton, Levi Parsons 1824-1920 *BiDrUSE 89, BioIn 16*
Morton, Lois Ann *BiDrAPA 89*
Morton, Margaret E. 1924- *WhoAmW 91*
Morton, Margaret Louise 1932- *WhoAm 90*
Morton, Marilyn Miller 1929- *WhoAmW 91, WhoSSW 91*
Morton, Mark 1913- *WhoE 91*
Morton, Mark Edward 1956- *St&PR 91, WhoSSW 91*
Morton, Marshall Nay 1945- *St&PR 91*
Morton, Martha 1865?-1925 *BioIn 16, FemiCLE, NotWoAT*
Morton, Michael Dale 1957- *St&PR 91*
Morton, Michael Ray 1952- *WhoSSW 91*
Morton, Miriam 1918-1985 *AuBYP 90*
Morton, Paul 1857-1911 *BiDrUSE 89*
Morton, Perry Williams 1939- *St&PR 91*
Morton, Philip M 1930- *BiDrAPA 89*
Morton, Randall Eugene 1950- *WhoEmL 91*
Morton, Ree 1936-1977 *WhoAmA 91N*
Morton, Richard H 1921- *WhoAmA 91*
Morton, Richard Hardwick 1921- *WhoE 91*
Morton, Robert Alan 1934- *WhoAmA 91*
Morton, Robert Dallas 1940- *St&PR 91*
Morton, Robert John 1949- *WhoE 91*
Morton, Rogers C. B. 1914-1979 *WorAlBi*
Morton, Rogers Clark Ballard 1914-1979 *BiDrUSE 89*
Morton, Sarah W. 1759-1846 *BioAmW*
Morton, Sarah Wentworth 1759-1846 *FemiCLE*
Morton, Susan Diane 1959- *WhoEmL 91*
Morton, Tamara Turner 1960- *WhoAmW 91*
Morton, Thomas 1590?-1647? *EncCRAm, WhNaAH*
Morton, Thomas John 1958- *St&PR 91*
Morton, Thomas Judson 1949- *WhoE 91*
Morton, Thruston B. 1907-1982 *WorAlBi*
Morton, Victoria C. 1952- *St&PR 91*
Morton, William G. 1937- *St&PR 91*
Morton, William Gilbert 1906- *WhoAm 90*
Morton, William Gilbert, Jr. 1937- *WhoAm 90*
Morton, William T. 1819-1868 *WorAlBi*
Mortvedt, John Jacob 1932- *WhoAm 90, WhoSSW 91*
Mortyn, Mollie C. 1937- *St&PR 91*
Mortz, Betty Jane 1924- *WhoAmW 91*
Morvan, Alain Yves 1939- *St&PR 91*
Morvay, Steven Elliot 1954- *WhoAm 90*
Morvilius, Richard Charles *St&PR 91N*
Morwood, Betty Jo 1948- *BiDrAPA 89*
Mory, Douglas C. 1943- *St&PR 91*
Mory, Nancy L. 1956- *St&PR 91*
Moryck, Brenda Ray 1894-1949 *HarlReB [port]*
Moryck Francke, Brenda Ray 1894-1949 *HarlReB [port]*
Moryl, Walter John 1931- *St&PR 91*
Moryl, Walter John 1937- *WhoAm 90*
Moryn, Walt 1926- *Ballpl 90*
Morzik, Fritz *BioIn 16*
Mosack, Carl Lewis 1931- *St&PR 91*
Mosaddeq, Mohammad 1880-1967 *BioIn 16*
Mosaic *NewAgMG*
Mosak, Barbara Marcia 1950- *WhoAmW 91*
Mosatche, Harriet Sandra 1949- *WhoE 91*
Mosbacher, Diane *BiDrAPA 89*
Mosbacher, Emil, Jr. 1922- *WhoAm 90*
Mosbacher, Georgette *BioIn 16*
Mosbacher, Georgette Paulsin 1947- *WhoE 91*
Mosbacher, Heidi *BioIn 16*
Mosbacher, Martin Bruce 1951- *ODwPR 91*
Mosbacher, Robert *BioIn 16*
Mosbacher, Robert 1927- *St&PR 91*
Mosbacher, Robert Adam 1927- *BiDrUSE 89, WhoAm 90, WhoE 91, WhoWor 91*
Mosbakk, Kurt Malvin 1934- *WhoWor 91*
Mosby, Aline *BioIn 16*
Mosby, Aline 1922- *ConAu 130*
Mosby, David Gregory 1957- *WhoSSW 91*
Mosby, Dewey Franklin 1942- *WhoAmA 91*
Mosby, Dorothea Susan 1948- *WhoEmL 91*
Mosby, John Oliver 1917- *WhoSSW 91*
Mosby, John Singleton, Jr. 1950- *WhoWor 91*
Mosby, Randall Lee 1953- *WhoSSW 91*
Mosby, William Harry 1898-1964 *WhoAmA 91N*
Mosca, August 1907- *WhoAmA 91*
Moscardi, Nino 1951- *St&PR 91*
Moscarillo, Frank M *BiDrAPA 89*
Moscatelli, John J. *ODwPR 91*
Moscati, Anthony F. 1947- *St&PR 91*
Moscati, Maree 1952- *WhoAmW 91*
Moscato, Deborah Fett 1952- *WhoSSW 91*
Moscato, Jacques *IntWWM 90*
Moscato, Joseph Anthony 1925- *St&PR 91*
Moscato, Nicholas, Jr. 1942- *WhoE 91*
Moscatt, Paul N 1931- *WhoAmA 91*
Mosch, Ernst 1925- *OxCPMus*
Moscheles, Ignaz 1794-1870 *BioIn 16, PenDiMP, -A*
Moschella, Samuel L. 1921- *WhoAm 90*
Mosches, Julio Cesar 1912- *WhoHisp 91*
Moschino, Franco *BioIn 16*
Moscicki, John Martin 1951- *WhoEmL 91*
Moscinski, David Joseph 1948- *WhoEmL 91*
Mosco, Marlene D. 1946- *St&PR 91*
Moscona, Aron Arthur 1922- *WhoAm 90*
Mosconi, Willie 1913- *WorAlBi*
Moscotti, Richard W 1929- *BiDrAPA 89*
Moscotti, Richard William 1929- *WhoE 91*
Moscovit, Andrei *WhoWrEP 89*
Moscovitch, Adam 1954- *BiDrAPA 89*
Moscow Philharmonic Quartet *PenDiMP*
Moscow, Alvin 1925- *AuBYP 90*
Moscow, David Hirsh 1937- *St&PR 91*
Moscow, Warren 1908- *WhoAm 90*
Moscowitz, Albert Joseph 1929- *WhoAm 90, WhoWor 91*
Mose, Carl C 1903-1973 *WhoAmA 91N*
Moseby, Earl 1884-1963 *Ballpl 90*
Moseby, Lloyd 1959- *Ballpl 90*
Mosel, Arlene 1921- *AuBYP 90*
Mosel, Edward Frank 1949- *St&PR 91*
Moseley, Aubrey Howard 1936- *WhoSSW 91*
Moseley, Carlos DuPre 1914- *WhoAm 90*
Moseley, Carolyn Oare 1962- *WhoSSW 91*
Moseley, Chris Rosser 1950- *WhoE 91*
Moseley, Edward H 1931- *ConAu 132*
Moseley, Frederick R. *BioIn 16*
Moseley, Frederick Strong, III 1928- *St&PR 91, WhoAm 90*
Moseley, George Edward 1939- *St&PR 91*
Moseley, Henry G. J. 1887-1915 *WorAlBi*
Moseley, Jack 1931- *St&PR 91, WhoAm 90, WhoE 91*
Moseley, James B 1952- *BiDrAPA 89*
Moseley, James Francis 1936- *WhoAm 90, WhoSSW 91, WhoWor 91*
Moseley, John Carter 1951- *WhoSSW 91*
Moseley, M. Lewis 1937- *St&PR 91*
Moseley, Mark DeWayne 1948- *WhoAm 90*
Moseley, Norman Byron 1929- *St&PR 91*
Moseley, Patricia Ann 1946- *WhoEmL 91*
Moseley, S. Kelley 1946- *WhoSSW 91*
Moseley, Samuel G. 1952- *St&PR 91*
Moseley, Setil Hamilton, III 1933- *St&PR 91*
Moseley, Smith *BioIn 16*
Moseley, Thomas James 1913- *St&PR 91*
Moseley, Virginia Douglas 1917- *WhoAmW 91*
Moseley, William 1935- *WhoWrEP 89*
Moseley, William Latimer Tim 1936- *WhoSSW 91*
Moseley, William R. *NewYTBS 90 [port]*
Moseley, William Ward 1930- *WhoAm 90*
Moseley, Willie B 1942- *BiDrAPA 89*
Moselsio, Simon 1890- *WhoAmA 91N*
Mosely, Linda Hays 1941- *WhoAm 90*
Mosely, Oswald 1896-1980 *WorAlBi*
Mosemann, Lloyd Kenneth, II 1936- *WhoAm 90*
Mosen, Peter *BioIn 16*
Mosenfelder, Donn Merrill 1928- *St&PR 91*
Mosenthal, Charlotte Dembo *WhoAmA 91*
Mosenthine, Amy Manuel 1963- *WhoSSW 91*
Moser, Anton Alfred Richard 1939- *WhoWor 91*
Moser, Barry *BioIn 16*
Moser, Barry 1940- *WhoAmA 91*
Moser, Byron, Jr. 1915- *St&PR 91*
Moser, Clarence John 1928- *St&PR 91*
Moser, Claus Adolf 1922- *WhoWor 91*
Moser, D. J. 1942- *St&PR 91*
Moser, Deborah *WhoE 91*
Moser, Dietz-Rudiger 1939- *WhoWor 91*
Moser, Donald Bruce 1932- *WhoAm 90, WhoWrEP 89*
Moser, Edda 1938- *IntWWM 90*
Moser, Edgar A *BiDrAPA 89*
Moser, Edmund W. 1944- *ODwPR 91*
Moser, Fanny Hoppe 1872-1953 *EncPaPR 91*
Moser, Francesco *BioIn 16*
Moser, Frank H 1886-1964 *WhoAmA 91N*
Moser, George M. 1945- *St&PR 91*
Moser, George Michael 1706-1783 *PenDiDA 89*
Moser, Hanna M *BiDrAPA 89*
Moser, Harold Dean 1938- *WhoAm 90, WhoWrEP 89*
Moser, Harry Crane 1944- *St&PR 91*
Moser, Heribert Markus 1922- *WhoWor 91*
Moser, Hugo Wolfgang 1924- *WhoAm 90*
Moser, Jack L. 1943- *St&PR 91*
Moser, Jean Hudgens 1934- *WhoSSW 91*
Moser, Jeanette Barber 1952- *WhoAmW 91*
Moser, Joann *WhoAmA 91*
Moser, Joann Gail 1948- *WhoAm 90*
Moser, Justus 1720-1794 *DcLB 97 [port]*
Moser, Kenneth Miles 1929- *WhoAm 90*
Moser, Kolo 1868-1918 *PenDiDA 89*
Moser, Kurt George 1944- *St&PR 91*
Moser, Leo John 1929- *WhoWrEP 89*
Moser, Ludwig 1833-1916 *PenDiDA 89*
Moser, Lukas *IntDcAA 90*
Moser, Martin F. 1938- *WhoAm 90*
Moser, Martin Peter 1928- *WhoAm 90*
Moser, Marvin 1924- *WhoAm 90, WhoE 91*
Moser, Michael Joseph 1950- *WhoWor 91*
Moser, Norman Calvin 1931- *WhoAm 90, WhoWrEP 89*
Moser, Penny Ward *BioIn 16*
Moser, Robert Gary 1945- *WhoSSW 91*
Moser, Robert Harlan 1923- *WhoAm 90, WhoWor 91*
Moser, Robert W. 1938- *St&PR 91*
Moser, Roger Alden 1929- *St&PR 91, WhoAm 90*
Moser, Royce, Jr. 1935- *WhoAm 90*
Moser, Sarah Gunning 1953- *WhoAmW 91*
Moser, Thomas *BioIn 16*
Moser, Thomas 1950- *IntWWM 90*
Moser, Thomas Michael 1948- *WhoE 91*
Moser, William Oscar Jules 1927- *WhoAm 90*
Moses *BioIn 16*
Moses 1350?BC-1250?BC *WorAlBi*
Moses 1571?BC-1451BC *EncPaPR 91*
Moses 1829?-1899 *WhNaAH*
Moses, Abe Joseph 1931- *WhoAm 90*
Moses, Alan Alcott 1931- *St&PR 91*
Moses, Alfred 1914- *St&PR 91*
Moses, Alfred Henry 1929- *WhoAm 90*
Moses, Anna Mary 1860-1961 *AuBYP 90, BiDWomA*
Moses, Anna Mary Robertson 1860-1961 *BioIn 16, MusmAFA, WhoAmA 91N*
Moses, Bernhard Charles 1920- *WhoSSW 91*
Moses, Bette J *WhoAmA 91*
Moses, Billy *BioIn 16*
Moses, Bonnie Smith 1955- *WhoEmL 91*
Moses, Bradley Lynn 1947- *WhoE 91*
Moses, Bruce Hadley 1933- *WhoAm 90*
Moses, Claire Goldberg 1941- *WhoWrEP 89*

Moses, David P. 1924- *St&PR 91*
Moses, Deborah Watson 1951- *WhoAmW 91*
Moses, Don V. 1936- *IntWWM 90*
Moses, Donald Allen 1938- *BiDrAPA 89, WhoE 91*
Moses, Dorothy Norris 1932- *BioIn 16*
Moses, Ed 1926- *WhoAmA 91*
Moses, Edward *BiDrAPA 89*
Moses, Edward 1926- *ModArCr 1 [port]*
Moses, Edward Crosby *WhoAm 90*
Moses, Edwin *BioIn 16*
Moses, Edwin 1953- *WorAlBi*
Moses, Edwin 1955- *WhoAm 90*
Moses, Elbert Raymond, Jr. 1908- *WhoWor 91, WhoWrEP 89*
Moses, Ethel *DrBlPA 90*
Moses, Forrest 1934- *WhoAm 90*
Moses, Forrest, Jr 1934- *WhoAmA 91*
Moses, Forrest King 1893-1974 *WhoAmA 91N*
Moses, Franklin J., Jr. 1838-1906 *AmLegL*
Moses, Franklin Maxwell 1918- *WhoAm 90*
Moses, Geoffrey 1952- *IntWWM 90*
Moses, Gerry 1946- *Ballpl 90*
Moses, Gilbert 1942- *DrBlPA 90, WhoAm 90*
Moses, Grandma 1860-1961 *BioAmW, BioIn 16, WorAlBi*
Moses, Gregory Hayes, Jr. 1933- *WhoAm 90*
Moses, Hamilton, III 1950- *WhoE 91*
Moses, Harold Konan 1943- *WhoE 91*
Moses, Irving Byron 1925- *WhoAm 90*
Moses, Irving M. 1939- *St&PR 91*
Moses, Janet Estelle 1946- *WhoAmW 91*
Moses, Jennifer *BioIn 16*
Moses, Jerome J. 1912- *St&PR 91*
Moses, Joel 1941- *WhoAm 90*
Moses, John 1957- *Ballpl 90*
Moses, Kathy Sue 1948- *WhoAmW 91*
Moses, Leonard 1932- *IntWWM 90*
Moses, Lincoln E. 1921- *WhoAm 90*
Moses, Lucy Goldschmidt *NewYTBS 90 [port]*
Moses, Mark *BioIn 16*
Moses, Marvin C. 1944- *St&PR 91*
Moses, Marvin Charles 1944- *WhoAm 90*
Moses, Mary Jane 1928- *WhoAmW 91*
Moses, Michael Howard 1940- *St&PR 91*
Moses, Michael W. 1945- *St&PR 91*
Moses, Nancy Lee Heise 1947- *WhoEmL 91, WhoWor 91*
Moses, Rafael 1924- *BiDrAPA 89*
Moses, Raphael Jacob 1913- *WhoAm 90*
Moses, Rebecca *BioIn 16*
Moses, Robert 1888-1981 *BioIn 16, WorAlBi*
Moses, Robert Davis 1919- *WhoAm 90*
Moses, Robert K., Jr. 1940- *St&PR 91*
Moses, Robert Wilkins 1945- *St&PR 91*
Moses, Ronald Elliot 1930- *St&PR 91, WhoE 91*
Moses, Stephen A. 1943- *WhoSSW 91*
Moses, Stephen Arthur 1943- *St&PR 91*
Moses, Susan Colleen 1953- *WhoAmW 91*
Moses, Wally 1910- *Ballpl 90 [port]*
Moses, William Daniel 1936- *St&PR 91*
Moses, William Robert 1911- *WhoWrEP 89*
Moses, William Stainton 1839-1892 *EncO&P 3, EncPaPR 91*
Mosettig, Michael David 1942- *WhoAm 90, WhoE 91*
Mosey, Caron Lee 1956- *WhoWrEP 89*
Mosey, Edward F. *ODwPR 91*
Mosgard, Jens 1925- *WhoWor 91*
Mosgovoy, Paul Vadim 1960- *WhoEmL 91*
Mosher, Albert Frederick, Jr. 1936- *St&PR 91*
Mosher, Arthur A. 1942- *St&PR 91*
Mosher, Burr J., Jr. 1928- *St&PR 91*
Mosher, Don T 1931- *BiDrAPA 89*
Mosher, Frederic D. 1937- *St&PR 91*
Mosher, Frederick C. *BioIn 16*
Mosher, Frederick C. *NewYTBS 90*
Mosher, Frederick C 1913-1990 *ConAu 131*
Mosher, Frederick Kenneth 1943- *WhoE 91, WhoWor 91*
Mosher, Gary S. *BiDrAPA 89*
Mosher, George Allan 1939- *WhoAm 90*
Mosher, Giles E., Jr. 1933- *St&PR 91*
Mosher, Giles Edmund, Jr. 1933- *WhoAm 90*
Mosher, Gregory Dean 1949- *WhoAm 90, WhoE 91*
Mosher, Howard Frank 19--?- *ConLC 62*
Mosher, Lawrence Forsyth 1929- *WhoE 91*
Mosher, Loren R 1933- *BiDrAPA 89*
Mosher, Martin L, Jr. *BiDrAPA 89*
Mosher, Michael Mark 1950- *WhoWor 91*
Mosher, Paul H. 1936- *WhoAm 90*
Mosher, Paul W 1936- *BiDrAPA 89*
Mosher, Ronald Francis 1943- *St&PR 91*
Mosher, Sally Ekenberg 1934- *WhoAmW 91, WhoWor 91*
Mosher, Walter W., Jr. 1934- *St&PR 91*
Moshier, Katherine Marie 1966- *WhoEmL 91*
Moshinsky, Elijah 1946- *IntWWM 90*
Moshir Fatemi, Roya 1956- *WhoWor 91*
Moshiri, Ali *BiDrAPA 89*
Moshman, Jack 1924- *WhoAm 90, WhoE 91*
Moshoeshoe II 1938- *WhoWor 91*
Mosholder, Andrew Donald *BiDrAPA 89*
Moshy, Diana Boutross 1953- *WhoAmW 91*
Mosich, Anelis Nick 1928- *WhoAm 90*
Mosienko, Peter 1935- *WhoSSW 91*
Mosier, Arvin Ray 1945- *WhoEmL 91*
Mosier, Eugene Bruce 1939- *St&PR 91*
Mosier, Frank Eugene 1930- *St&PR 91, WhoAm 90*
Mosier, Gregory C. 1956- *WhoSSW 91*
Mosier, Harry David, Jr. 1925- *WhoAm 90*
Mosier, Joan Marie 1953- *WhoAmW 91, WhoE 91*
Mosier, John 1944- *WhoWrEP 89*
Mosier, Kenneth Cope, II 1944- *St&PR 91*
Mosier, Olive 1952- *WhoAm 90, WhoWor 91*
Mosier, Virginia Lou 1951- *WhoAmW 91*
Mosiman, William Edward 1958- *BiDrAPA 89*
Mosimann, Anton *BioIn 16*
Mosk, Richard Mitchell 1939- *WhoAm 90*
Mosk, Stanley 1912- *WhoAm 90, WhoWor 91*
Moskal, Anthony John 1946- *WhoE 91*
Moskal, Harry Matthew 1937- *St&PR 91*
Moskal, Janina 1944- *WhoAmW 91*
Moskal, Robert M. 1937- *WhoAm 90*
Moskalski, E. A. 1939- *St&PR 91*
Moskatel, Ira Dennis 1950- *WhoEmL 91*
Moskau, Paul 1953- *Ballpl 90*
Moskin, John Robert 1923- *WhoAm 90, WhoWor 91*
Moskin, Morton 1927- *St&PR 91, WhoAm 90*
Mosko, John Edward 1928- *St&PR 91*
Moskos, Charles C. 1934- *WhoAm 90*
Moskovic, Jacob L 1933- *BiDrAPA 89*
Moskovitz, Charlene *BiDrAPA 89*
Moskovitz, David Allen 1944- *BiDrAPA 89*
Moskovitz, Gary S. *St&PR 91*
Moskovitz, I. L. 1904- *St&PR 91*
Moskovitz, Irving 1912- *WhoAm 90*
Moskovitz, Randall J 1949- *BiDrAPA 89*
Moskovitz, Richard Alan 1947- *BiDrAPA 89*
Moskoviz, Marc B. 1953- *St&PR 91*
Moskovsky, Alexander *PenDiMP*
Moskow, Bernard 1937- *St&PR 91*
Moskow, Michael H. 1938- *St&PR 91, WhoAm 90*
Moskow, Shirley Blotnick 1935- *WhoWrEP 89*
Moskowitz, Arnold X. 1944- *WhoAm 90*
Moskowitz, Belle 1877-1933 *BioAmW*
Moskowitz, Carl 1935- *ODwPR 91*
Moskowitz, David L 1938- *BiDrAPA 89*
Moskowitz, Harry *BiDrAPA 89*
Moskowitz, Ira 1912- *WhoAmA 91, WhoE 91*
Moskowitz, Jay 1943- *WhoAm 90*
Moskowitz, Joel A 1932- *BiDrAPA 89*
Moskowitz, Joel P. 1939- *St&PR 91*
Moskowitz, Karl 1948- *WhoE 91*
Moskowitz, Louis *WhoAm 90*
Moskowitz, Maurice Lee 1939- *BiDrAPA 89*
Moskowitz, Miriam Sherri 1953- *WhoAmW 91*
Moskowitz, Moses *NewYTBS 90*
Moskowitz, Moses 1911-1990 *BioIn 16, ConAu 131*
Moskowitz, Randi Zucker 1948- *WhoAmW 91*
Moskowitz, Reed Craig 1946- *BiDrAPA 89*
Moskowitz, Robert S 1935- *WhoAmA 91*
Moskowitz, Ronald 1939- *St&PR 91, WhoAm 90*
Moskowitz, Sam 1920- *WhoAm 90*
Moskowitz, Samuel J. 1905-1989 *BioIn 16*
Moskowitz, Samuel Zouri 1905- *WhoAm 90*
Moskowitz, Shirley 1920- *WhoAmA 91*
Moskowitz, Stanley Alan 1956- *WhoWor 91*
Moskowitz, Stephen Eric *BiDrAPA 89*
Moslehi, Behzad Mohamad Reza 1956- *WhoEmL 91*
Mosler, John *St&PR 91*
Mosler, John 1922- *WhoAm 90*
Mosley, David Lee 1958- *IntWWM 90*
Mosley, Donald Crumpton 1932- *WhoAm 90*
Mosley, Elizabeth Robards *AuBYP 90*
Mosley, Elwood A. 1943- *St&PR 91*
Mosley, Francis 1957- *BioIn 16*
Mosley, Ivan Sigmund, Jr. 1946- *St&PR 91, WhoSSW 91*
Mosley, J. Brooke 1915-1988 *BioIn 16*
Mosley, Oswald 1896-1980 *BioIn 16*
Mosley, Philip 1947- *ConAu 130*
Mosley, Roger E. *BioIn 16, DrBlPA 90*
Mosley, Samuel Adolphus 1923- *WhoSSW 91*
Mosley, Sandra Sherrill 1946- *WhoWrEP 89*
Mosley, Snub 1909-1981 *DrBlPA 90*
Mosley, Zack 1906- *EncACom*
Mosley, Zack T 1906- *WhoAmA 91*
Mosley, Zack Terrell 1906- *WhoAm 90*
Mosoff, Serle Ian 1942- *St&PR 91*
Mosovich, Abraham 1914- *BiDrAPA 89*
Mosovich, Serge Alexander 1944- *BiDrAPA 89*
Mosquera, T. C. de 1798-1878 *BioIn 16*
Mosquera, Tomas Cipriano de 1798-1878 *BioIn 16*
Moss, Adam Wender 1957- *WhoE 91*
Moss, Albert M 1922- *BiDrAPA 89*
Moss, Alison Leslie 1959- *WhoAmW 91*
Moss, Ambler Holmes, Jr. 1937- *WhoAm 90, WhoWor 91*
Moss, Andrea 1943- *WhoAmW 91*
Moss, Anthony Leslie Hugh 1946- *WhoWor 91*
Moss, Arnold *BioIn 16*
Moss, Arthur Henshey 1930- *WhoE 91*
Moss, Bernard 1937- *WhoAm 90*
Moss, Bill Ralph 1950- *WhoEmL 91, WhoSSW 91, WhoWor 91*
Moss, Brian 1933- *WhoWor 91*
Moss, Carlton 1910- *EarBlAP*
Moss, Charles 1938- *St&PR 91, WhoAm 90*
Moss, Charles Leland 1946- *St&PR 91*
Moss, Charles Norman 1914- *WhoWor 91*
Moss, Claude Scott 1924- *WhoAm 90*
Moss, Clement Murphy, Jr. 1926- *WhoAm 90*
Moss, Cruse Watson 1926- *St&PR 91, WhoAm 90*
Moss, Dan, Jr. 1948- *WhoSSW 91*
Moss, David Michael 1949- *IntWWM 90*
Moss, David R 1954- *BiDrAPA 89*
Moss, Debra Ann 1953- *WhoAmW 91*
Moss, Donald Jack *BiDrAPA 89*
Moss, Duane W. 1948- *St&PR 91*
Moss, Edgar G. E. *BioIn 16*
Moss, Elaine 1924- *BioIn 16*
Moss, Elizabeth 1663?-1702 *BiDEWW*
Moss, Elizabeth Lucille 1939- *WhoAmW 91*
Moss, Gayla Louise 1960- *WhoAmW 91*
Moss, Gene Richard 1938- *BiDrAPA 89*
Moss, Geoffrey 1938- *WhoAm 90*
Moss, George *EncPaPR 91*
Moss, George F. 1936- *St&PR 91*
Moss, Grave Yard 1946- *WhoWrEP 89*
Moss, Harold 1932- *St&PR 91*
Moss, Howard 1922-1987 *BioIn 16*
Moss, Howard Barry 1950- *BiDrAPA 89*
Moss, Irene *WhoAmA 91*
Moss, Jack 1928- *WhoE 91*
Moss, Jacqueline *WhoAmA 91*
Moss, Jaime Ruth 1948- *WhoAmW 91*
Moss, James H. 1953- *St&PR 91*
Moss, Jean *WhoAmW 91*
Moss, Joe 1933- *WhoAmA 91*
Moss, Joe A. 1925- *St&PR 91*
Moss, Joe Albaugh 1925- *WhoAm 90*
Moss, Joe Francis 1933- *WhoAm 90*
Moss, John Emerson 1915- *WhoAm 90*
Moss, John F. *WhoAm 90*
Moss, Joseph H., Jr. 1950- *St&PR 91*
Moss, Karen Canner 1944- *WhoAmA 91*
Moss, Kenneth Larry 1957- *BiDrAPA 89*
Moss, Lawrence Craig 1952- *WhoE 91*
Moss, Lawrence Kenneth 1927- *WhoAm 90*
Moss, Lawrence R 1955- *BiDrAPA 89*
Moss, Leland *BioIn 16, NewYTBS 90*
Moss, Leonard M *BiDrAPA 89*
Moss, Les 1925- *Ballpl 90*
Moss, Leslie Otha 1952- *WhoAmW 91*
Moss, Leslie W. 1932- *St&PR 91*
Moss, Louis B. 1917- *St&PR 91*
Moss, Lynda Bourque 1950- *WhoAmW 91*
Moss, Malcolm Howard 1931- *WhoE 91*
Moss, Marlow 1890-1958 *BiDWomA*
Moss, Mary *BiDEWW*
Moss, Melvin Lionel 1923- *WhoAm 90*
Moss, Mitchell Lawrence 1948- *WhoE 91*
Moss, Monika 1961- *WhoAmW 91*
Moss, Morrie A. *BioIn 16*
Moss, Morrie Alfred 1907- *St&PR 91*
Moss, Norman Bernard 1928- *WhoAm 90*
Moss, Norman I 1935- *BiDrAPA 89*
Moss, Pamela Florence 1955- *BiDrAPA 89*
Moss, Pat *St&PR 91*
Moss, Patricia Diane 1960- *WhoAmW 91*
Moss, Ray 1901- *Ballpl 90*
Moss, Richard *BioIn 16*
Moss, Richard Spencer 1949- *WhoWor 91*
Moss, Robert Drexler 1909- *WhoAm 90*
Moss, Robert S. *BioIn 16*
Moss, Roger William, Jr. 1940- *WhoAm 90, WhoE 91*
Moss, Ronald Eugene 1932- *St&PR 91*
Moss, Ronald Jay 1930- *WhoAm 90*
Moss, Rosalind 1890-1990 *ConAu 131*
Moss, Rose 1937- *WhoWrEP 89*
Moss, Sandra Hughes 1945- *WhoSSW 91*
Moss, Stanley 1935- *WhoAm 90*
Moss, Stephen Edward 1940- *WhoE 91, WhoWor 91*
Moss, Stirling 1929- *BioIn 16*
Moss, Thelma *EncO&P 3*
Moss, Thelma S. *EncPaPR 91*
Moss, Thomas Henry 1939- *WhoAm 90*
Moss, Tobey C 1928- *WhoAmA 91*
Moss, Victor I *BiDrAPA 89*
Moss, William John 1921- *WhoAm 90*
Moss, William W. 1935- *St&PR 91*
Moss, William Wallace 1948- *WhoSSW 91*
Moss, William Warner, III 1935- *WhoAm 90*
Moss-Vreeland, Patricia 1951- *WhoAmA 91*
Mossadegh, Mohammad 1882-1967 *PolLCME*
Mossaides, Paula Xenis 1954- *WhoAmW 91*
Mossbauer, Rudolf L. 1929- *WorAlBi*
Mossbauer, Rudolf Ludwig 1929- *WhoAm 90, WhoWor 91*
Mossberg, Howard 1932- *WhoAm 90*
Mossblad, Sandra Ann 1957- *WhoAmW 91*
Mosse, George L. 1918- *WhoAm 90, WhoWrEP 89*
Mosse, Henrietta *FemiCLE*
Mosse, Peter John Charles 1947- *St&PR 91, WhoE 91, WhoEmL 91, WhoWor 91*
Mosseen, Annalena 1952- *WomArch [port]*
Mossell, Gertrude E. H. Bustill 1855-1948 *BioIn 16*
Mossell, N. F., Mrs. 1855-1948 *BioIn 16*
Mossell, Nathan Francis, Mrs. 1855-1948 *BioIn 16*
Mosser, Amy Aletha 1963- *WhoAmW 91*
Mosser, Benjamin D., II 1927- *St&PR 91*
Mosser, Thomas J. *ODwPR 91*
Mosser, Thomas Joseph 1944- *WhoAm 90*
Mossholder, Stephen B. 1942- *St&PR 91*
Mossi, Don 1929- *Ballpl 90*
Mossinghoff, Gerald Joseph 1935- *WhoAm 90, WhoE 91, WhoWor 91*
Mossman, Deborah Jean 1956- *WhoAmW 91*
Mossman, Douglas 1954- *BiDrAPA 89*
Mossman, Nancy Elizabeth *BiDrAPA 89*
Mossman, Thomas Mellish, Jr. 1938- *WhoAm 90*
Mosso, Claudia Gruenwald 1952- *WhoAmW 91*
Mosso, David Lyle 1926- *WhoAm 90*
Most, Bernard 1937- *BioIn 16*
Most, Harry 1907- *WhoAm 90*
Most, Jack Lawrence 1935- *St&PR 91, WhoE 91*
Most, Johann 1846-1906 *EncAL*
Most, Mel *BioIn 16*
Most, Nathan 1914- *St&PR 91, WhoAm 90*
Most, Robert Elmer *BiDrAPA 89*
Most, Woodrow Lloyd 1917- *WhoAm 90*
Mostad, Jon 1942- *IntWWM 90*
Mostarda, Mario Steven 1944- *St&PR 91*
Mostart, August Egbert Laurent Marie 1951- *WhoAm 90*
Mostehy, Randa 1962- *WhoAmW 91*
Mostel, Josh *BioIn 16*
Mostel, Josh 1946- *ConTFT 8 [port]*
Mostel, Marcy E *BiDrAPA 89*
Mostel, Marcy Ellen 1956- *WhoE 91*
Mostel, Zero 1915-1977 *BioIn 16, OxCPMus, WorAlBi*
Mosteller, David Elias 1944- *St&PR 91*
Mosteller, Frederick 1916- *WhoAm 90*
Mosteller, J. R. *WhoSSW 91*
Mosteller, Robert Edward 1931- *BiDrAPA 89*
Moster, Mary C. 1950- *ODwPR 91*
Mostert, Marcelle Ann 1954- *BiDrAPA 89*
Mostert, Paul Stallings 1927- *WhoAm 90*
Mosti, Ellen Louise 1961- *WhoAmW 91*
Mostil, Johnny 1896-1970 *Ballpl 90*
Mostoff, Allan Samuel 1932- *WhoAm 90*
Mostofi, Fathollah Keshvar 1911- *WhoE 91*
Mostofi, Khosrow 1921- *WhoAm 90, WhoWor 91*
Mostovoy, Marc Sanders 1942- *IntWWM 90*
Mostow, George Daniel 1923- *St&PR 91, WhoAm 90, WhoE 91*
Mostowska, Anna 1762?-1833? *EncCoWW*
Mostowski, Andrzej 1913-1975 *DcScB S2*
Mostyn, Margaret 1625-1679 *BiDEWW*
Mostyn, Trevor 1946- *ConAu 129*
Mosunic, John Ignatius 1928- *St&PR 91*
Moszkowski, David 1946- *St&PR 91*
Moszkowski, Lena Iggers 1930- *WhoAmW 91*

Moszkowski, Steven Alexander 1927- WhoAm 90
Moszynski, Andrew WhoAmA 91
Mota, Agostihno Jose da 1821-1878 ArtLatA
Mota, Carlos Guilherme 1941- WhoWor 91
Mota, Manny 1938- Ballpl 90, BioIn 16, WhoHisp 91
Mota, Rosa BioIn 16
Mote, Clayton Daniel, Jr. 1937- WhoAm 90
Mote, Harry J. ODwPR 91
Mote, Karl William 1927- St&PR 91
Mote, Larry Roger 1937- St&PR 91
Mote, Nancy Stammelbach 1940- WhoE 91
Motelet, Kathleen P BiDrAPA 89
Motels, The EncPR&S 89
Moten, Bennie 1894-1935 DrBlPA 90, OxCPMus
Moten, Etta 1901- DrBlPA 90
Motes, Carl Dalton 1949- WhoWor 91
Mother Ann 1736-1784 EncPaPR 91
Mother Jones 1830-1930 BioIn 16
Mother York BioIn 16
Motheral, M. Susan 1952- WhoAmW 91
Mothers of Invention, The EncPR&S 89
Mothershead, Wilson 1905-1990 BioIn 16
Motherway, Joseph Edward 1930- WhoAm 90
Motherwell, Cathryn 1957- ConAu 132
Motherwell, Robert 1915- IntDcAA 90, WhoAm 90, WhoAmA 91, WorAlBi
Mothes, Joan M. 1934- St&PR 91
Mothkur, Sridhar Rao 1950- WhoEmL 91
Mothon, Philip 1949- WhoE 91
Mothopeng, Zephania Lakonane BioIn 16
Mothopeng, Zephania Lekoane 1913-1990 NewYTBS 90
Motier, Donald 1943- WhoWrEP 89
Motihar, Kamla 1933- WhoE 91
Motion, Andrew 1952- WorAu 1980 [port]
Motiram, Veronica R BiDrAPA 89
Motiwalla, Dadi Noshir 1954- WhoWor 91
Motl, Daniel Francis 1946- St&PR 91
Motley Crue EncPR&S 89
Motley, Andrea Yvette 1958- WhoAmW 91
Motley, Constance Baker 1921- WhoAm 90, WhoE 91
Motley, Darryl 1960- Ballpl 90
Motley, James A. 1928- St&PR 91
Motley, John Lothrop 1814-1877 BioIn 16
Motley, John P 1927- BiDrAPA 89
Motley, John Paul 1927- WhoAm 90
Motley, Lyle Carter, Jr. 1941- St&PR 91
Motlik, Jaroslav PenDiMP
Motoki, Hisashi 1942- WhoWor 91
Motoki, Ken 1930- WhoWor 91
Motola, Nancy Carmen 1952- WhoAmW 91
Motolo, Paul Leon 1964- WhoE 91
Motono, Moriyuki 1924- WhoWor 91
Motoyama, Hiroshi 1925- EncPaPR 91
Motozuna, Kazumichi 1932- WhoWor 91
Motsch, John Vincent 1928- WhoSSW 91
Motschwiller, Kenneth W. 1956- St&PR 91
Motsinger, Kenneth L. 1953- St&PR 91
Motsko, Donald Russell 1935- St&PR 91
Mott the Hoople EncPR&S 89
Mott, Alyce Evelyn 1946- WhoAmW 91
Mott, Charles Stewart 1875-1973 EncABHB 4 [port]
Mott, Charles Stewart 1906-1989 BioIn 16
Mott, Edward David Kynaston 1942- WhoWor 91
Mott, Fay F 1943- BiDrAPA 89
Mott, George Edward 1935- EncO&P 3
Mott, Gilbert Stewart, Jr. 1951- WhoSSW 91
Mott, James C. 1928- St&PR 91
Mott, John Raleigh 1865-1955 WorAlBi
Mott, June Marjorie 1920- WhoWor 91
Mott, Karen Rae 1942- WhoAmW 91
Mott, Lucretia 1793-1880 FemiCLE, WorAlBi
Mott, Lucretia Coffin 1793-1880 BioAmW
Mott, Mary Elizabeth 1931- WhoAmW 91
Mott, Michael Charles Alston 1930- WhoWrEP 89
Mott, N F 1905- ConAu 129
Mott, Nevill ConAu 129
Mott, Nevill 1905- WhoAm 90, WhoWor 91
Mott, Nevill F. 1905- WorAlBi
Mott, Raymond E. St&PR 91
Mott, Stephen Craig 1949- St&PR 91
Mott, Stewart Rawlings 1937- WhoAm 90
Mott, Thomas H. 1924-1989 BioIn 16
Mott, Thurman 1927- WhoE 91
Mott, Thurman, Jr. BiDrAPA 89
Mott, Vincent Valmon 1916- WhoAm 90
Mott, Wanda Laurie Thornton 1952- WhoAmW 91
Mott, William Chamberlain 1911- WhoAm 90, WhoWor 91
Mott, William Chamberlain, Jr. 1960- WhoSSW 91
Mott, William Penn, Jr. BioIn 16
Mott-Smith, May 1879-1952 WhoAmA 91N
Motta, John J. 1949- St&PR 91
Motta, John Richard 1931- WhoAm 90
Motta, Richard B. 1931- St&PR 91
Motta, Richard P. 1943- St&PR 91
Mottahedeh, Mildred BioIn 16
Mottahedeh, Roy Parviz 1940- WhoWrEP 89
Motte, Calvin Earl 1934- WhoE 91
Motte, Daryl 1922- St&PR 91
Mottek, Carl T. BioIn 16
Mottek, Carl T. 1928- WhoAm 90
Mottelson, Ben R. 1926- WhoAm 90, WhoWor 91
Mottelson, Ben Roy 1926- WorAlBi
Motter, David Calvin 1926- WhoAm 90
Motter, Diane Allyn 1950- St&PR 91
Motter, Frank 1927- St&PR 91
Motter, Gene R. 1935- St&PR 91
Motter, John C., Sr. St&PR 91
Motter, William D. 1957- St&PR 91
Mottet, Norman Karle 1924- WhoAm 90
Motteville, Dame Langlois de 1615?-1689 EncCoWW
Mottl, Felix 1856-1911 PenDiMP
Motto, Anna Lydia WhoAm 90
Motto, Jerome A 1921- BiDrAPA 89, WhoAm 90
Motto, Rocco L 1917- BiDrAPA 89
Mottola, Joseph James 1928- St&PR 91
Motton, Curt 1940- Ballpl 90
Motton, Robert 1832?-1898 DcCanB 12
Mottram, Patricia B. 1952- ODwPR 91
Mottram-Doss, Renee 1939- WhoAm 90
Motts, David 1952- St&PR 91
Motulsky, Arno Gunther 1923- WhoAm 90
Motush, James 1954- St&PR 91
Moty, Eleanor H WhoAmA 91
Motz, John Frederick 1942- WhoAm 90, WhoE 91
Motz, Kenneth Lee 1922- WhoAm 90
Motz, Paul John 1950- WhoAm 90
Motz, Robin Owen 1939- WhoE 91
Motzenbecker, Helen Kenny 1929- WhoAmW 91
Motzer, William Raymond 1947- St&PR 91
Motzfeldt, Jonathan 1938- WhoWor 91
Motzkin, Evelyn 1933- BiDrAPA 89
Motzkin, Evelyn Herszkorn 1933- WhoAmW 91
Moucha, Nancy S 1960- ODwPR 91
Moucha, Nicolette BiDrAPA 89
Moucharafieh, Sana Chamel 1946- BiDrAPA 89
Mouchet, Marc 1955- IntWWM 90
Mouchly-Weiss, Harriet ODwPR 91
Mouchly-Weiss, Harriet 1942- WhoAm 90, WhoAmW 91
Mouchy, Duchesse de 1935- WhoAmW 91, WhoWor 91
Moucka, Viktor PenDiMP
Moufang, Ruth 1905-1977 DcScB S2
Moufarrege, Nicholas A 1947- WhoAmA 91N
Moufti, Fouad Sadik 1938- WhoWor 91
Mougeot, Robert F. 1943- St&PR 91
Mougharbel, Anneliese 1960- WhoE 91
Mouille, Serge 1922-1988 BioIn 16
Mouis, Marie-Christine BioIn 16, WhoAm 90
Moul, Douglas Edward 1952- BiDrAPA 89
Moul, Francis D. 1940- St&PR 91
Moul, Maxine Burnett 1947- St&PR 91
Moul, William Charles 1940- WhoAm 90
Mould, Bob BioIn 16
Mould, Thomas M 1929- BiDrAPA 89
Moulder, James Edwin 1926- WhoAm 90
Mouldey, R Gordon BiDrAPA 89
Moulding, Mary Baker 1907- WhoAmW 91
Moulds, JoAnn Mary 1949- WhoAmW 91
Moulds, Ronald Gary 1940- St&PR 91
Moule-Evans, David 1905- IntWWM 90
Moulier, Jose Emmanuel 1946- BiDrAPA 89
Moulin, Cesar PenDiDA 89
Moulin, Jane Ann Freeman 1946- IntWWM 90
Moulin, Jean 1899-1943 BiDFrPL
Moulin, Jeanine 1912- EncCoWW
Moulthrop, Edward Allen 1916- WhoAm 90
Moulthrop, Robert W. 1940- ODwPR 91
Moulton, Alex 1920- ConDes 90
Moulton, Anna Lee 1954- WhoE 91
Moulton, Charles H. 1843-1866 BioIn 16
Moulton, Claude Robert 1946- St&PR 91
Moulton, E. Curtis, III 1959- St&PR 91
Moulton, Edward Quentin 1926- WhoAm 90
Moulton, Grace Charbonnet 1923- WhoAmW 91
Moulton, Henry H. 1924- St&PR 91
Moulton, Hugh Geoffrey 1933- WhoAm 90
Moulton, James Roger 1950- WhoSSW 91
Moulton, John Harmon 1956- WhoSSW 91
Moulton, John Porter 1944- BiDrAPA 89
Moulton, Joy Wade 1928- WhoAmW 91
Moulton, Katherine Klauber 1956- WhoAmW 91
Moulton, Lillian G BiDrAPA 89
Moulton, Louise 1835-1908 FemiCLE
Moulton, Louise C. 1835-1908 BioAmW
Moulton, Michael J. 1957- St&PR 91
Moulton, Patricia Jean 1948- WhoAmW 91
Moulton, Patti Gayle BiDrAPA 89
Moulton, Paul Douglas 1944- WhoE 91
Moulton, Phillips Prentice 1909- WhoAm 90
Moulton, Richard Way 1948- WhoSSW 91
Moulton, Robert Alan 1949- St&PR 91
Moulton, Robert Henry 1925- WhoAm 90
Moulton, Rosalind Kimball 1941- WhoAmA 91
Moulton, Ruth 1915- BiDrAPA 89
Moulton, Sara Jonene 1958- WhoAmW 91
Moulton, Susan Gene 1944- WhoAmA 91
Moulton, Suzanne Carey LeRoy 1950- IntWWM 90
Moulton, Virginia Nodine 1925- WhoWrEP 89
Moulton, Wilbur Wright, Jr. 1935- WhoAm 90
Moulton, William Gamwell 1914- WhoAm 90
Moulton-Barrett, Maria L BiDrAPA 89
Moulton-Patterson, Linda 1943- WhoAmW 91
Moultrie, Fred 1923- WhoAm 90
Moultrie, John Wesley, Jr. 1904- WhoWor 91
Moultrie, William 1730-1805 EncCRAm, WorAlBi
Moulun, Roberto D BiDrAPA 89
Mouly, Eileen Louise 1955- WhoWor 91
Moulyn, Adrian C BiDrAPA 89
Moumin, Amini Ali 1944- WhoWor 91
Mounce, Irene 1894-1987 BioIn 16
Mound, Lois Renee BiDrAPA 89
Mounds, Leona Mae Reed 1945- WhoAmW 91, WhoWor 91
Mounier, Emmanuel 1905-1950 BiDFrPL
Mounsey, Joseph Backhouse 1949- St&PR 91
Mount, Alan Richard 1936- ODwPR 91
Mount, George Ray 1941- WhoSSW 91
Mount, James Webster 1937- WhoSSW 91
Mount, John Meredith 1942- St&PR 91, WhoAm 90
Mount, John Wallace 1946- IntWWM 90
Mount, Karen 1953- WhoAmW 91
Mount, Karl A. 1945- St&PR 91
Mount, Lloyd Gordon 1916- St&PR 91
Mount, Marshall Ward 1927- WhoAmA 91
Mount, Richard Edward 1947- WhoE 91
Mount, Stephen Joseph John 1968- WhoWrEP 89
Mount, Thomas Henderson 1948- WhoAm 90
Mount, Ward WhoAmA 91
Mount, Ward 1898- WhoAm 90, WhoAmW 91, WhoE 91, WhoWor 91
Mount, Wendy Elizabeth 1954- WhoAmW 91
Mountain Chief 1848-1942 WhNaAH
Mountain Wolf Woman 1884- FemiCLE
Mountain, Clifton Fletcher 1924- WhoAm 90, WhoWor 91
Mountain, Evelyn Marie 1917- WhoAmW 91
Mountain, Peter 1923- IntWWM 90
Mountain, Robert E. 1929- St&PR 91
Mountain, Steven R. 1957- WhoSSW 91
Mountain, Thomas Raymond 1916- St&PR 91
Mountain, Worrall Frederick 1909- WhoAm 90
Mountbatten of Burma, Earl 1900-1979 BioIn 16
Mountcastle, Katharine Babcock 1931- WhoAm 90
Mountcastle, Kenneth F. 1928- St&PR 91
Mountcastle, Kenneth Franklin, Jr. 1928- WhoE 91, WhoWor 91
Mountcastle, Thomas Lamar 1953- WhoEmL 91
Mountcastle, Vernon Benjamin, Jr. 1918- WhoAm 90
Mounter, Julian 1944- WhoWor 91
Mountjoy, Donald A. St&PR 91
Mountjoy, Paul Tomb 1924- WhoAm 90
Mountjoy, Roberta Jean WhoWrEP 89
Mounty, Elizabeth Jane 1955- BiDrAPA 89
Mountz, Louise Carson Smith 1911- WhoAmW 91, WhoWor 91
Mountz, Wade 1924- WhoAm 90, WhoSSW 91
Mouquin, Charles H. St&PR 91
Moura, Jose Manuel Fonseca 1946- WhoE 91
Moura, Venancio de BioIn 16
Mourat, Stephen 1918- BiDrAPA 89
Mouravieff-Apostol, Andrew 1913- WhoWor 91
Moure, Erin 1953- FemiCLE
Moure, Erin 1955- BioIn 16
Moureaux, Philippe 1939- WhoWor 91
Mourek, Joseph Edward 1910- WhoAm 90
Mourelatos, Alexander Phoebus Dionysiou 1936- WhoAm 90
Mouren, Herve 1948- WhoWor 91
Mourge, Olivier PenDiDA 89
Mourgue, Olivier 1939- ConDes 90
Mourgues, Odette de BioIn 16
Mourgues, Odette de 1914-1988 AnObit 1988
Mourier de Neergaard, Pierre Paul F. 1907-1987 BioIn 16
Mourning Dove 1888-1936 FemiCLE
Mouro, Mark Anthony 1959- WhoSSW 91
Moursund, Albert Wadel, III 1919- WhoSSW 91
Moursund, David G 1936- ConAu 30NR
Moursund, Janet 1936- ConAu 30NR
Moursund, Kenneth Carroll 1937- WhoSSW 91
Moursund, M. Waddell 1919- WhoAm 90
Mousa, John J. 1948- St&PR 91
Mousa, Moustafa Wafey 1947- WhoWor 91
Moushey, Lois Ann 1953- WhoAmW 91
Moushoutas, Constantine Michael WhoWor 91
Mouskouri, Nana 1936- OxCPMus
Mousourakis, Ioannis Nikolaos 1944- WhoSSW 91
Moussa, Farid George St&PR 91
Moussa, Pierre Louis 1922- St&PR 91, WhoWor 91
Moussab, Albert N. 1953- St&PR 91
Moussavi, Hussein 1942- WhoWor 91
Moussavian, Hamid BiDrAPA 89
Mousseau, Doris Naomi Barton 1934- WhoAmW 91, WhoWor 91
Moussorgsky, Modest 1839-1881 WorAlBi
Moutal, Patrick 1951- IntWWM 90
Moute, Francois Claude 1944- WhoWor 91
Moutet, Anne-Elisabeth 1959- WhoWor 91
Moutet, Marius 1876-1968 BiDFrPL
Mouton, Jane Srygley BioIn 16
Mouton, Sylvia Craig 1951- WhoAmW 91
Moutoussamy, John Warren 1922- WhoAm 90
Moutrie, Chester L. 1946- St&PR 91
Moutsa-Martinengou, Elisavet EncCoWW
Moutsoploulos, Evanghelos A. 1930- IntWWM 90
Moutza-Martinengou, Elisavet EncCoWW
Moutzan-Martinengou, Elisavet 1801-1832 EncCoWW
Mouzakes-Siler, Helen Harriet 1929- WhoAmW 91
Mouzon, Alphonse NewAgMG
Mouzon, Margaret Walker 1940- WhoAmW 91
Movalli, Charles Joseph 1945- WhoAmA 91, WhoE 91
Movila, Sanda 1900-1970 EncCoWW
Movitz, Edward Michael 1959- WhoSSW 91
Movsesian, Viguen 1953- BiDrAPA 89
Movshon, Joseph Anthony 1950- WhoE 91
Movva, Usha Rani BiDrAPA 89
Mow, Douglas Farris 1928- WhoAm 90
Mow, Van C. 1939- WhoAm 90
Mowafy, Abdou Mohamed 1949- WhoWor 91
Mowat, Claire 1933- ConAu 131
Mowat, Farley BioIn 16
Mowat, Farley 1921- AuBYP 90, MajTwCW
Mowat, Farley McGill 1921- WhoAm 90, WhoWor 91, WhoWrEP 89
Mowat, John Bower 1825-1900 DcCanB 12
Mowat, Thomas 1859-1891 DcCanB 12
Mowatt, Anna 1819-1870 FemiCLE
Mowatt, Anna Cora 1819-1870 BioAmW
Mowatt, Anna Cora Ogden 1819-1870 BioIn 16, NotWoAT
Mowatt, Mary Lucinda 1961- WhoAmW 91
Mowatt, Paul BioIn 16
Mowatt, Robert Henderson, III 1950- WhoE 91
Mowbray, C. W. BioIn 16
Mowbray, Charles Wilfred BioIn 16
Mowbray, Joanna 1955- BiDWomA
Mowbray, John Code 1918- WhoAm 90
Mowbray, Robert Norman 1935- WhoE 91
Mowday, Richard Thomas 1947- WhoAm 90
Mowder, Gary Leroy 1940- WhoAm 90
Mowell, George Mitchell 1951- WhoEmL 91

Mowell, John 1934- St&PR 91
Mower, Eric Andrew 1944- WhoAm 90
Mower, Henry William 1943- St&PR 91
Mower, Lyman 1927- WhoAm 90
Mowerman, Samuel 1942- BiDrAPA 89
Mowers, Thomas John 1943- St&PR 91
Mowery, Bob Lee 1920- WhoAm 90
Mowrer, Edgar Ansel 1892-1977 BioIn 16
Mowrer, Lilian Thomson NewYTBS 90
Mowrer, Lilian Thomson 1889?-1990 ConAu 132
Mowrer, Paul Scott 1887-1971 BioIn 16
Mowrey, Eric Ryan 1955- WhoSSW 91
Mowrey, John William 1940- St&PR 91
Mowrey, Mike 1884-1947 Ballpl 90
Mowry, Greg Stephen 1954- WhoEmL 91
Mowry, Oliver Warren, Jr. 1956- WhoSSW 91
Mowry, Philip Stephen 1953- WhoSSW 91
Mowry, Robert Dean 1945- WhoAm 90
Mowry, Robert Wilbur 1923- WhoAm 90
Moxey, Keith Patricio Fleming 1943- WhoAmA 91
Moxley, David BioIn 16
Moxley, John Howard, III 1935- WhoAm 90
Moxnees, Bennie A 1899- BiDrAPA 89
Moxness, Margaret Anne BiDrAPA 89
Moxon, Gaylord E. 1922- St&PR 91
Moxus WhNaAH
Moy, Audrey 1942- WhoAmW 91
Moy, Cara L. 1964- WhoAmW 91
Moy, Clifford Keith BiDrAPA 89
Moy, Curt Wayne 1961- WhoWor 91
Moy, James S. 1948- WhoWrEP 89
Moy, May 1913- WhoAmA 91
Moy, Richard Henry 1931- WhoAm 90
Moy, Robert Clifford 1938- WhoSSW 91
Moy, Seong 1921- WhoAmA 91
Moy, Willie 1942- BioIn 16
Moya, Hidalgo 1920- WhoWor 91
Moya, Sara Dreier 1945- WhoAmW 91
Moya Soto, Roberto 1935- WhoAmA 91
Moya Valganon, Jose Gabriel 1939- WhoWor 91
Moyal, A. Henri 1936- BiDrAPA 89
Moyano, Daniel 1930- ConAu 131, HispWr 90
Moyar, David Cunningham 1928- St&PR 91
Moyars-Johnson, Mary A. 1938- WhoAmW 91
Moyce, Paul Robert BiDrAPA 89
Moye, Charles Allen, Jr. 1918- WhoAm 90
Moye, Eric Vaughn 1954- WhoEmL 91
Moye, John Edward 1944- WhoAm 90
Moyed, Ralph Sam 1930- WhoE 91
Moyen, Jean 1828-1899 DcCanB 12
Moyenda, Kamau BiDrAPA 89
Moyer, Alan Dean 1928- WhoAm 90
Moyer, Anna Blackburn 1938- WhoE 91
Moyer, Birgitte Plesner 1938- IntWWM 90
Moyer, Craig Alan 1955- WhoWor 91
Moyer, David S. 1952- WhoEmL 91
Moyer, Eugene E. 1928- St&PR 91
Moyer, F. Stanton 1929- WhoAm 90
Moyer, Geralyn Marie 1959- WhoAmW 91
Moyer, Gordon Van Zandt 1921- WhoAm 90
Moyer, Homer Edward, Jr. 1942- WhoE 91
Moyer, J. Harold 1927- IntWWM 90
Moyer, James Wallace 1919- WhoE 91
Moyer, Jamie 1962- Ballpl 90
Moyer, Jay B. 1937- St&PR 91
Moyer, John Henry, IV 1950- WhoE 91
Moyer, Karl Eby 1937- IntWWM 90
Moyer, Kenneth Evan 1919- WhoAm 90
Moyer, Kerri Salls 1954- WhoAmW 91
Moyer, Lynne Denise 1963- WhoAmW 91
Moyer, Marina Pavlov 1952- WhoSSW 91
Moyer, Marina Pavlova 1952- WhoAmA 91
Moyer, Marlene Cynthia 1949- WhoAmW 91
Moyer, Merrill S. 1934- St&PR 91
Moyer, R. Charles 1945- WhoEmL 91
Moyer, Ray Allen 1946- WhoE 91
Moyer, Robert Howard 1928- St&PR 91
Moyer, Roy 1921- WhoAmA 91
Moyer, Sandra Jean 1943- WhoAmW 91
Moyer, Steven G. 1952- St&PR 91
Moyer, Sylvia Dianne 1954- WhoEmL 91
Moyer, Thomas J. 1939- WhoAm 90
Moyer, William C. 1937- St&PR 91
Moyer, William L. 1939- St&PR 91
Moyers, Bill BioIn 16
Moyers, Bill 1934- ConAu 31NR
Moyers, Bill D. 1934- WhoAm 90, WorAlBi
Moyers, Ernest Everett S. 1933- WhoSSW 91
Moyers, Gary W. St&PR 91
Moyers, Robert Charles 1951- WhoSSW 91
Moyers, Sylvia Dean 1936- WhoSSW 91
Moyers, William 1916- WhoAmA 91
Moyes, Patricia 1923- FemiCLE, SmATA 63 [port], TwCCr&M 91
Moyes, Winifred EncO&P 3
Moylan, David John, III 1951- WhoE 91
Moylan, James E., Jr. 1951- WhoAm 90
Moylan, James Emmett, Jr. 1951- St&PR 91
Moylan, James Joseph 1948- WhoWor 91
Moylan, John Edward, Sr. 1933- St&PR 91
Moylan, Michael Thomas 1948- St&PR 91
Moylan, Oliver Joseph 1935- WhoWor 91
Moylan, Stephen Craig 1952- WhoEmL 91
Moylan, Susan Nelis 1941- WhoAmW 91
Moylan, William David 1956- IntWWM 90
Moyle, Katherine McKinney 1934- WhoSSW 91
Moyle, Larry Wayne 1941- St&PR 91
Moyle, Peter Briggs 1942- WhoAm 90
Moyle, Richard Michael 1944- IntWWM 90
Moyles, William Philip 1930- St&PR 91
Moyls, Benjamin Nelson 1919- WhoAm 90
Moynaham, John F. 1957- St&PR 91
Moynahan, John Daniel, Jr. 1935- St&PR 91, WhoAm 90
Moynahan, Julian Lane 1925- WhoAm 90, WhoWrEP 89
Moyne, John Abel 1920- WhoAm 90
Moynihan, Daniel P. 1927- BioIn 16
Moynihan, Daniel Patrick 1927- NewYTBS 90 [port], WhoAm 90, WhoE 91, WhoWor 91, WorAlBi
Moynihan, Daniel Patrick 1948- WhoE 91
Moynihan, James J. 1944- St&PR 91
Moynihan, John Jeremiah 1942- WhoE 91
Moynihan, Jonathan Patrick 1948- WhoEmL 91
Moynihan, Margaret Phipps BioIn 16
Moynihan, Rodrigo 1910-1990 NewYTBS 90 [port]
Moynihan, T. P. BioIn 16
Moynihan, Walter R. 1923- St&PR 91
Moynihan, William Trumbull 1926- WhoAm 90
Moyse, Hermann, III 1948- St&PR 91, WhoEmL 91
Moyse, Hermann, Jr. 1921- WhoAm 90, WhoSSW 91
Moyse, Hollis Weaver 1930- St&PR 91
Moyse, Marcel 1889-1984 PenDiMP
Moyseowicz, Gabriela Maria 1944- IntWWM 90
Moysey, A. Warren BioIn 16
Moysey, A. Warren 1939- WhoAm 90
Moytoy WhNaAH
Mozart, Johann Chrysostom Wolfgang A. 1756-1791 BioIn 16
Mozart, Leopold 1719-1787 BioIn 16
Mozart, Wolfgang Amadeus 1756-1791 BioIn 16, EncPaPR 91, PenDiMP A, WorAlBi
Mozdzierz, Richard Lawrence 1943- St&PR 91
Mozeley, Thomas Edwin 1944- WhoSSW 91
Mozer, Doris Ann 1929- WhoAmW 91, WhoWor 91
Mozer, Edwin Lee 1944- BiDrAPA 89
Mozer, Patricia BioIn 16
Mozes, Samuel R. NewYTBS 90
Mozes, Samuel R. 1923-1990 BioIn 16
Mozeson, Isaac Elchanan 1951- WhoWrEP 89
Mozetich, Marjan 1948- IntWWM 90
Mozian, Gerard P. 1945- St&PR 91
Mozian, Gerard Paul 1945- WhoAm 90
Mozilo, Angelo Robert BioIn 16
Mozingo, George William, III 1950- WhoSSW 91
Mozinski, Cathlee Rae 1940- WhoWrEP 89
Mozley, Anita Ventura 1928- WhoAmA 91
Mozley, Anne 1809-1891 FemiCLE
Mozley, Harriet 1803-1852 FemiCLE
Mozley, Harriet Newman 1803-1852 BioIn 16
Mozley, P David, Jr. 1957- BiDrAPA 89
Mozley, Paul David 1928- BiDrAPA 89, WhoAm 90
Mozo, Ann Elizabeth 1958- WhoAmW 91
Mozzer, Alanna 1752- WhoAmW 91
Mozzer, Alanna Jean 1952- WhoWrEP 89
Mozzicato, Sebastian 1942- BiDrAPA 89
Mpelkas, Christos Charles 1920- WhoWor 91
Mpho, Motsamai Keyecwe 1921- WhoWor 91
Mpouho-Epigat, Julien WhoWor 91
Mr. Jacobs of Simla EncO&P 3
Mr. T BioIn 16
Mr. Wizard ConAu 30NR
Mracek, Jaroslav John Stephen 1928- IntWWM 90
Mrak, Ralph Joseph 1931- St&PR 91
Mrak, Robert Emil 1948- WhoSSW 91
Mravinsky, Yevgeny 1903-1988 PenDiMP
Mravinsky, Yevgeny 1906-1988 AnObit 1988
Mrazek, David Allen 1947- BiDrAPA 89, WhoAm 90, WhoEmL 91
Mrazek, Frank BioIn 16
Mrazek, Hazel Schayes 1920- BiDrAPA 89
Mrazek, Robert J. 1945- WhoAm 90, WhoE 91
Mrazek, Robert Vernon 1936- WhoAm 90
Mricksah WhNaAH
Mriksah WhNaAH
Mroczek, James Gordan 1942- WhoE 91
Mroczek, William Joseph 1940- WhoWor 91
Mroczkowski, Casimir BiDrAPA 89
Mroczkowski, James V. 1945- St&PR 91
Mroczkowski, Mark Lee 1953- WhoSSW 91
Mroszczak, Jozef 1910-1975 ConDes 90
Mroszczak, Marcin 1950- ConDes 90
Mroz, Chester Joseph 1944- WhoE 91
Mroz, John Edwin 1948- WhoE 91, WhoWor 91
Mroz, John Martin 1957- WhoEmL 91
Mroz, Mitchell D. 1944- St&PR 91
Mroz, Sue 1943- WhoWrEP 89
Mrozek, Colette Ann 1950- WhoAmW 91
Mrozek, Slawomir 1930- MajTwCW
Mruk, Charles Karzimer 1926- WhoE 91
Mruk, Eugene Robert 1927- St&PR 91, WhoE 91, WhoWor 91
Mryc, Bohdan M BiDrAPA 89
Msarsa, Johnnie BioIn 16
Mstislavskii, Sergei 1876-1943 BioIn 16
Mswati III 1968- WhoWor 91
Mt. Pleasant, Edison P. BioIn 16
M'Taggart, Ann 1753?-1834 FemiCLE
Mtewa, Mekki 1946- WhoAm 90, WhoE 91, WhoWor 91
Muan, Arnulf 1923- WhoAm 90
Muawiyah I 602?-680 WorAlBi
Mubarak, Hosni 1928- NewYTBS 90 [port], PolLCME
Mubarak, Muhammad Hosni 1928- WhoWor 91
Mubbashar, Malik Hussain BiDrAPA 89
Muca, Mirvet Sinan 1939- WhoE 91
Mucchi-Wiegmann, J. BiDWomA
Mucci, Catherine Leola 1957- WhoAmW 91
Mucci, Donald Robert 1942- St&PR 91
Mucci, Patrick John 1947- St&PR 91, WhoE 91
Mucci, Paul Leonard 1952- St&PR 91
Muccia, Joseph William 1948- WhoE 91
Muccino, Robert D. 1930- St&PR 91
Muccio, John Joseph 1900-1989 BioIn 16
Muccioli, Anna Maria 1922- WhoAmA 91
Muccioli, Nathan Thomas 1951- WhoEmL 91
Muccioli, Vincenzo BioIn 16
Mucciolo, Michael Russell 1942- St&PR 91
Muccione, Gary J. 1943- St&PR 91
Muccione, Irene T. St&PR 91
Muccione, Vincent J. 1937- St&PR 91
Muccitelli, John Anthony 1953- WhoE 91
Muce, Paul Maximilian 1940- WhoWor 91
Much, Kathleen 1942- WhoAmW 91
Much, R. Donald 1926- St&PR 91
Mucha, Alfons Maria 1860-1939 PenDiDA 89
Mucha, Alphonse 1860-1939 BioIn 16
Mucha, Frank A. 1927- St&PR 91
Mucha, Jiri BioIn 16
Mucha, Robert John 1939- St&PR 91
Mucha, Theodore F 1939- BiDrAPA 89
Muchmore, Carolin M. 1944- WhoAmW 91
Muchmore, Don Moncrief 1922- WhoAm 90
Muchmore, Maggie 1946- BioIn 16
Muchmore, Robert Boyer 1917- WhoAm 90
Muchmore, William Breuleux 1920- WhoAm 90
Muchnic, Suzanne WhoAmA 91
Muchnick, Richard Stuart 1942- WhoE 91, WhoWor 91
Muchow, Arthur Paul, Jr. 1953- WhoSSW 91
Muchow, William Charles 1922- WhoAm 90
Muchowski, Patrice Maureen 1951- WhoAmW 91
Muck, Carl 1895-1940 PenDiMP
Muck, George Arthur 1937- St&PR 91
Muck, Kin Choong 1954- WhoE 91
Muck, Otto 1928- WhoWor 91
Muck, Philip Francis 1938- St&PR 91
Muck, Terry Charles 1947- WhoWrEP 89
Muckenhoupt, Benjamin 1933- WhoAm 90, WhoE 91
Muckerman, Norman James 1917- WhoAm 90
Muckle, David Sutherland 1939- WhoWor 91
Muckler, John WhoAm 90
Muckleroy, Jon Michael 1930- WhoAm 90
Muckleroy, Merle Clint 1935- WhoAm 90
Mucklin, Annette BioIn 16
Muczynski, Robert 1929- IntWWM 90
Muda Hassanal Bolkiah 1946- BioIn 16
Mudano, Frank Robert 1928- WhoAm 90
Mudarra, Alonso 1510?-1580 PenDiMP
Mudbone, Butch R. WhoWrEP 89
Mudbone, Vivian Esmeralda WhoWrEP 89
Mudd, Ann BiDEWW
Mudd, Ann 1613?- FemiCLE
Mudd, Anne Chestney 1944- WhoAmW 91
Mudd, Anthony John 1939- WhoE 91
Mudd, Emily Hartshorne 1898- WhoAm 90
Mudd, Harvey 1940- ConAu 130
Mudd, John Philip 1932- WhoAm 90
Mudd, John W 1942- BiDrAPA 89
Mudd, Lawrence R BiDrAPA 89
Mudd, Reginald M. 1953- St&PR 91
Mudd, Richard Alan 1952- St&PR 91
Mudd, Roger 1928- WorAlBi
Mudd, Roger Harrison 1928- WhoAm 90
Mudd, Sidney Emanuel 1858-1911 AmLegL
Mudd, Sidney Peter 1917- WhoAm 90, WhoE 91
Mudd, Stephen B. 1932- St&PR 91
Mudd, Susan Elizabeth 1955- WhoAmW 91
Mudd, William R. 1943- St&PR 91
Muddasani, Narsimha R 1961- BiDrAPA 89
Mude, Malini Avinash BiDrAPA 89
Mude, O ConAu 30NR
Mudford, Anthony L. 1939- St&PR 91
Mudford, Grant Leighton 1944- WhoAmA 91
Mudge, Edmond Webster, Jr 1904-1984 WhoAmA 91N
Mudge, Isadore G. 1875-1957 BioAmW
Mudge, Lewis Seymour 1929- WhoAm 90
Mudge, Shaw, Jr. 1953- St&PR 91
Mudge, Stephen Holmes 1953- WhoSSW 91
Mudge, William O'Brien 1930- St&PR 91
Mudget, Vicky Elaine 1955- WhoAmW 91
Mudgett, Fred Austin 1920- St&PR 91
Mudgett, John Scott BiDrAPA 89
Mudholkar, Govind Shrikrishna 1934- WhoWor 91
Mudholkar, Shivdas Shivling elias Rajas 1946- WhoWor 91
Mudie, Charles Edward 1818-1890 BioIn 16
Mudigonda, Krishna Moorthy D BiDrAPA 89
Mudragada, Suryarao 1946- BiDrAPA 89
Mudrick, David Phillip 1951- WhoEmL 91
Mudrick, Lucy J. 1928- St&PR 91
Muecke, Manfred K. 1942- St&PR 91
Muedeking, George Herbert 1915- WhoAm 90
Muegel, Glenn Allen 1934- WhoSSW 91
Muehl, Lois Baker 1920- AuBYP 90
Muehlbauer, James H. 1940- St&PR 91
Muehlbauer, James Herman 1940- WhoAm 90
Muehlbauer, Renice Ann 1947- WhoAmW 91, WhoEmL 91, WhoWor 91
Muehlberg, Robert Steven 1954- St&PR 91
Muehleib, William Henry 1922- St&PR 91
Muehleis, Mary Lou 1937- St&PR 91
Muehleis, Victor Emanuel 1926- St&PR 91
Muehleisen, Gene Sylvester 1915- WhoAm 90
Muehlemann, Kathy WhoAmA 91
Muehlenbeck, Thomas Howard 1941- WhoAm 90
Muehlenberg, Ekkehard Friedrich Wilhelm 1938- WhoWor 91
Muehlhausen, Richard W. 1938- St&PR 91
Muehlig, G Kenneth BiDrAPA 89
Muehlstein, Sophia E. 1910- St&PR 91
Muehrcke, Juliana Obright 1945- WhoAmW 91
Muehrcke, Robert Carl 1921- WhoAm 90
Muehsam, Gerd 1913-1979 WhoAmA 91N
Muelas Medrano, Santiago 1943- WhoWor 91
Mueller, Anne 1929- WhoAmW 91
Mueller, Anton Peter 1948- WhoWor 91
Mueller, Barbara Ruth 1925- WhoAm 90, WhoAmW 91
Mueller, Berndt 1950- WhoWor 91
Mueller, Betty Jeanne 1925- WhoAm 90, WhoAmW 91
Mueller, C. J. BioIn 16
Mueller, Carl Gustav, Jr. 1929- WhoAm 90
Mueller, Carl Richard 1931- WhoAm 90
Mueller, Charles Barber 1917- WhoAm 90, WhoWor 91

Mueller, Charles William 1938- *St&PR 91, WhoAm 90*
Mueller, Claus 1941- *ConAu 31NR*
Mueller, Cookie *BioIn 16*
Mueller, D. D. 1937- *St&PR 91*
Mueller, David Brian 1953- *WhoEmL 91*
Mueller, David John 1950- *St&PR 91*
Mueller, David R. 1952- *St&PR 91*
Mueller, Dennis Cary 1940- *WhoE 91*
Mueller, Don 1948- *Ballpl 90*
Mueller, Donald Dean 1937- *WhoAm 90*
Mueller, Dorothy 1949?-1989 *ConAu 130*
Mueller, Edward Albert 1923- *WhoAm 90*
Mueller, Edward Eugene 1924- *WhoE 91*
Mueller, Egbert H J 1928- *BiDrAPA 89*
Mueller, Emmett 1912-1986 *Ballpl 90*
Mueller, Ernest 1925- *St&PR 91*
Mueller, F Carl *BiDrAPA 89*
Mueller, Frederic Bernhardt *BioIn 16*
Mueller, Frederick A. 1921- *IntWWM 90*
Mueller, Frederick Henry 1893-1976 *BiDrUSE 89*
Mueller, George E. 1918- *WhoAm 90*
Mueller, Gerhard Gottlob 1930- *WhoAm 90*
Mueller, Gerhard Joseph 1936- *St&PR 91*
Mueller, Gerhard O.W. 1926- *WhoE 91*
Mueller, Gerhard Otto 1930- *St&PR 91*
Mueller, Hans Gerhard 1944- *WhoWor 91*
Mueller, Hans P. 1942- *St&PR 91*
Mueller, Hans Robert 1911- *WhoWor 91*
Mueller, Hans-Wolfgang 1907- *WhoWor 91*
Mueller, Harold 1920- *WhoAm 90*
Mueller, Heinie 1899-1975 *Ballpl 90*
Mueller, Helga L *BiDrAPA 89*
Mueller, Helmut Charles 1931- *WhoAm 90*
Mueller, Henrietta Waters 1915- *WhoAmA 91*
Mueller, Herbert Adolph 1914- *WhoAm 90*
Mueller, Jack William 1921- *WhoAm 90*
Mueller, James Edward 1931- *St&PR 91*
Mueller, Janel M 1938- *ConAu 132*
Mueller, Janie Schieffelin 1960- *WhoEmL 91*
Mueller, John Alfred 1906- *WhoAm 90*
Mueller, John David 1934- *St&PR 91*
Mueller, John E. *BioIn 16*
Mueller, John E. 1937- *WhoAm 90, WhoE 91*
Mueller, John Kenton 1935- *BiDrAPA 89*
Mueller, John S. 1930- *St&PR 91*
Mueller, John Storm 1927- *IntWWM 90*
Mueller, Keith Richard 1957- *WhoEmL 91*
Mueller, Lisel 1924- *DcLB 105 [port]*
Mueller, Loraine Dorothy 1920- *WhoWrEP 89*
Mueller, M Gerardine Op *WhoAmA 91*
Mueller, Margaret Reid 1929- *WhoAmW 91*
Mueller, Margaret Snodgrass 1924- *IntWWM 90*
Mueller, Marilyn Jean 1946- *WhoAmW 91*
Mueller, Mark Christopher 1945- *WhoEmL 91, WhoSSW 91, WhoWor 91*
Mueller, Marnie *BioIn 16*
Mueller, Marnie Wagstaff 1937- *St&PR 91, WhoAm 90*
Mueller, Mary Kathryn 1961- *WhoAmW 91*
Mueller, Michael J. 1948- *St&PR 91*
Mueller, Nancy Schneider 1933- *WhoAmW 91*
Mueller, Neal R. 1954- *St&PR 91*
Mueller, P. S. *BioIn 16*
Mueller, Patricia Ann 1940- *BiDrAPA 89*
Mueller, Paul Henry 1917- *WhoAm 90, WhoE 91, WhoWor 91*
Mueller, Peggy Jean 1952- *WhoAmW 91, WhoEmL 91, WhoSSW 91, WhoWor 91*
Mueller, Peter S 1930- *BiDrAPA 89*
Mueller, Peter Sterling 1930- *WhoAm 90, WhoWor 91*
Mueller, Ray 1912- *Ballpl 90*
Mueller, Raymond A. 1922- *St&PR 91*
Mueller, Richard Edward 1927- *WhoAm 90*
Mueller, Richard Walter 1944- *WhoAm 90*
Mueller, Robert Clemens 1923- *St&PR 91*
Mueller, Robert J 1912- *BiDrAPA 89*
Mueller, Robert J. 1929- *St&PR 91*
Mueller, Robert J. 1930- *WhoAm 90*
Mueller, Robert Kirk 1913- *St&PR 91, WhoAm 90, WhoE 91*
Mueller, Robert L. 1927- *St&PR 91*
Mueller, Robert Louis 1927- *WhoAm 90*
Mueller, Ronald James 1935- *St&PR 91*
Mueller, Ronald R. 1947- *ODwPR 91*
Mueller, Ronald Raymond 1947- *WhoAm 90*
Mueller, Sandra Renee 1962- *WhoAmW 91*
Mueller, Scott Allen 1942- *St&PR 91*
Mueller, Shannon Marie 1963- *WhoAmW 91*
Mueller, Sharon 1956- *WhoEmL 91*
Mueller, Stephan 1930- *WhoWor 91*
Mueller, Stephen *BioIn 16*
Mueller, Stephen Otto 1948- *BiDrAPA 89*
Mueller, Steve Carl 1945- *WhoEmL 91*
Mueller, Timothy Ian *BiDrAPA 89*
Mueller, Trude *WhoAmA 91*
Mueller, Ulrich 1940- *WhoWor 91*
Mueller, Virginia Rumely 1949- *WhoEmL 91*
Mueller, Warren Arthur 1932- *St&PR 91*
Mueller, Werner August 1947- *WhoWor 91*
Mueller, Willard Fritz 1925- *WhoAm 90*
Mueller, William Alan 1947- *WhoEmL 91*
Mueller, William Martin 1917- *WhoAm 90*
Mueller, William R. 1921- *St&PR 91*
Mueller, William Randolph 1916- *WhoAm 90*
Mueller, Wolfgang Siegfried 1937- *St&PR 91*
Mueller-Heubach, Eberhard August 1942- *WhoAm 90, WhoWor 91*
Muelling, Anna E 1952- *BiDrAPA 89*
Muellner, Ralph Anton 1936- *WhoSSW 91*
Muellner, Robert L 1938- *BiDrAPA 89*
Muench, David *BioIn 16*
Muench, Donald P. 1931- *St&PR 91*
Muench, John 1914- *WhoAm 90, WhoAmA 91*
Muench, Kristian 1964- *WhoE 91*
Muender, Peter Rudolph 1941- *WhoWor 91*
Muenster, Karen *WhoAmW 91*
Muenster, Rudolf Walter Theodor 1934- *WhoWor 91*
Muensterman, Vivian Darlene 1942- *WhoAmW 91*
Muenzberg, Wolfgang 1928- *WhoWor 91*
Muenzen, Lee J. 1942- *St&PR 91*
Muenzen, Lee John 1942- *WhoAm 90, WhoE 91*
Muenzer, Daniel R. 1929- *WhoE 91*
Muesing Ellwood, Edith Elizabeth 1947- *WhoAm 90, WhoE 91, WhoWrEP 89*
Muessen, Joan Lillian *St&PR 91N*
Muessig, Raymond Henry 1928- *WhoAm 90*
Mueth, Dale 1947- *St&PR 91*
Mueth, Jane Ellen 1946- *WhoAmW 91*
Mueth, Joseph Edward 1935- *WhoAm 90*
Muetzel, Janice *BioIn 16*
Muff, Alfred 1949- *IntWWM 90*
Muffett, Billy 1930- *Ballpl 90*
Muffly, Robert B *BiDrAPA 89*
Muffolett, Joseph Robert 1934- *WhoE 91*
Muffoletto, Mary Lu 1932- *WhoAmW 91*
Mufson, Maurice Albert 1932- *WhoAm 90*
Mufson, Michael J. 1954- *St&PR 91*
Mufson, Michael Jon *BiDrAPA 89*
Mufti, Said El- 1898-1989 *BioIn 16*
Mugabe, Robert Gabriel 1924- *BioIn 16, WhoWor 91*
Mugalian, Ruth *ODwPR 91*
Mugavero, Francis J. 1914- *WhoAm 90, WhoE 91*
Mugemana, Jean Marie Vianney 1951- *WhoWor 91*
Mugford, Alfred George 1928- *WhoAm 90*
Mugford, Roger *BioIn 16*
Muggeridge, Malcolm 1903- *BioIn 16, MajTwCW, WhoWor 91*
Muggeridge, Malcolm 1903-1990 *ConAu 33NR, NewYTBS 90 [port]*
Muggia, Judith Palmer 1938- *WhoAmW 91*
Muggli, Clara Barbara 1927- *WhoAmW 91*
Muggli, Robert Zeno 1929- *WhoAm 90*
Mughniyah, Imad *BioIn 16*
Mugits, Michael James 1953- *WhoWor 91*
Mugler, Larry George 1946- *WhoEmL 91*
Mugler, Molly Scott 1951- *WhoEmL 91*
Mugler, Thierry 1946- *ConDes 90*
Mugnaini, Enrico 1937- *WhoE 91*
Mugnaini, Erna Haanaes 1936- *BiDrAPA 89*
Mugo, Micere 1942- *FemiCLE*
Mugot, Hazel 1947?- *FemiCLE*
Muguruza, Francisco J. *WhoHisp 91*
Muha, Andrew Thomas 1929- *St&PR 91*
Muhammad *BioIn 16*
Muhammad Adh-Dhib *BioIn 16*
Muhammad bin Khalifa Hamid Al-Khalifa 1937- *WhoWor 91*
Muhammad Bin Mubarak Al-Khalifa, Sheikh 1935- *WhoWor 91*
Muhammad ibn 'Abd Allah ibn Batutah 1304-1377 *BioIn 16*
Muhammad ibn Rashid Al-Maktum, Sheikh 1946- *WhoWor 91*
Muhammad, Prince of Saudi Arabia 1910-1988 *BioIn 16*
Muhammad Rashid Rida 1865-1935 *BioIn 16*
Muhammad, Alberta 1937- *WhoAmW 91*
Muhammad, Elijah 1897-1975 *WorAlBi*
Muhammad, Fareeda Saahir 1936- *WhoAmW 91*
Muhammad, Ozier 1950- *WhoAm 90*
Muhani, Ahmad Ali *WhoWor 91*
Muhassis, Ardashir 1938- *BioIn 16*
Muhe, Erich 1938- *WhoWor 91*
Muhich, Lisa *BioIn 16*
Muhich, Ralph A 1926- *BiDrAPA 89*
Muhl, Edward L. 1945- *St&PR 91*
Muhlanger, Erich 1941- *WhoWor 91*
Muhlbauer, Helen Gertrude *BiDrAPA 89*
Muhlberger, Richard Charles 1938- *WhoAm 90, WhoAmA 91*
Muhleman, Janet Christie 1951- *WhoAm 90, WhoAmW 91*
Muhlen, Raimund von zur *PenDiMP*
Muhlenberg, Frederick Augustus Conrad 1750-1801 *BioIn 16, WorAlBi*
Muhlenberg, Heinrich M. 1711-1787 *WorAlBi*
Muhlenberg, Henry Augustus Philip 1782-1844 *BioIn 16*
Muhlenberg, Henry Melchior 1711-1787 *EncCRAm*
Muhlenberg, John 1746-1807 *WorAlBi*
Muhlenbrock, Susanne 1964- *BioIn 16*
Muhlenbruch, Carl W. 1915- *WhoAm 90, WhoWor 91*
Muhlendyck, Wim *PenDiDA 89*
Muhlenkamp, Bernard Joseph 1945- *St&PR 91*
Muhlenweg, Fritz *AuBYP 90*
Muhlert, Christopher Layton 1933- *WhoAmA 91*
Muhlert, Jan Keene 1942- *WhoAm 90, WhoAmA 91, WhoAmW 91*
Muhlfeld, Edward Dixon 1928- *WhoE 91*
Muhlfeld, Richard 1856-1907 *PenDiMP*
Muhlfelder, Warren J 1910- *BiDrAPA 89*
Muhlke, William E. 1941- *St&PR 91*
Muhlsteff, Herman A. *St&PR 91N*
Muhly, Paul Scott 1944- *WhoAm 90*
Muhn, Judy Ann 1952- *WhoSSW 91*
Muhrcke, Gary *BioIn 16*
Muhri, Franz 1924- *WhoWor 91*
Muhringer, Doris 1920- *EncCoWW*
Mui, Frank Kwong-fun 1953- *IntWWM 90*
Mui, Jimmy 1958- *WhoE 91*
Mui, Kan Chi 1917- *WhoSSW 91*
Muilenburg, Robert Henry 1941- *WhoAm 90*
Muilenburg, Robert W. 1933- *ODwPR 91*
Muilenburg, Robert William 1933- *St&PR 91*
Muir, Brockett 1905- *WhoE 91*
Muir, D. Stephen 1951- *St&PR 91*
Muir, David Edward 1962- *WhoSSW 91*
Muir, Dexter *TwCCr&M 91*
Muir, Douglas Farrington 1948- *WhoE 91*
Muir, Edwin 1887-1959 *DcLB 100 [port]*
Muir, Emily Lansingh *WhoAmA 91*
Muir, Emily Lansingh 1904- *WhoE 91*
Muir, Glenn Patrick 1959- *WhoE 91*
Muir, Helen 1911- *WhoAmW 91, WhoSSW 91*
Muir, Helen 1937- *ConAu 130*
Muir, J. Dapray 1936- *WhoAm 90*
Muir, J. Duncan 1938- *ODwPR 91*
Muir, James Dyer 1932- *St&PR 91*
Muir, Jean *BioIn 16*
Muir, Jean 1933- *ConDes 90*
Muir, Jean Elizabeth *WhoWor 91*
Muir, Jeffrey Shepardd 1949- *St&PR 91*
Muir, John 1838-1914 *BioIn 16, EncPaPR 91, WorAlBi*
Muir, John Carl 1954- *WhoSSW 91*
Muir, John Robert 1936- *WhoWor 91*
Muir, Keith Mervyn 1944- *BiDrAPA 89*
Muir, Lewis F 1884-1950 *OxCPMus*
Muir, Lewis Frank 1883-1915 *BioIn 16*
Muir, Malcolm 1885-1979 *WorAlBi*
Muir, Malcolm 1914- *WhoAm 90*
Muir, Michael Bill 1941- *St&PR 91*
Muir, Nigel D. 1944- *ODwPR 91*
Muir, Richard 1955- *St&PR 91*
Muir, Richard Myles 1963- *WhoE 91*
Muir, Robert F. 1924- *St&PR 91*
Muir, Robert F. 1945- *St&PR 91*
Muir, Sandra May 1956- *WhoAmW 91*
Muir, Warren R. 1945- *WhoAm 90*
Muir, Willa 1890-1970 *BioIn 16, FemiCLE*
Muir, William Horace 1902-1965 *WhoAmA 91N*
Muir, William Ker, Jr. 1931- *WhoAm 90*
Muir, William W., Jr. 1936- *St&PR 91*
Muir-Broaddus, Jacqueline Elizabeth 1961- *WhoAmW 91*
Muirhead, John *BioIn 16*
Muirhead, Robert Lloyd 1924- *St&PR 91*
Muirhead, Vincent Uriel 1919- *WhoAm 90*
Muirhead, William, III 1932- *St&PR 91*
Muis, Patrice Raia 1953- *WhoWrEP 89*
Muittari, Antero 1933- *WhoWor 91*
Mujagic, Christophe Alexandre 1940- *WhoWor 91*
Mujica, Barbara Louise 1943- *WhoWrEP 89*
Mujica, Mauro E. 1941- *WhoE 91, WhoWor 91*
Mujica, Raul 1926- *BiDrAPA 89*
Mujica Lainez, Manuel 1910-1984 *ConAu 32NR, HispWr 90*
Mukaidono, Masao 1942- *WhoWor 91*
Mukamal, Steven Sasoon 1940- *WhoE 91*
Mukasa, Hidehiko 1939- *WhoWor 91*
Mukawa, Akio 1928- *WhoWor 91*
Mukerjee, Pasupati 1932- *WhoAm 90*
Mukerjee, Venu *BiDrAPA 89*
Mukerji, Dhan Gopal 1890-1936 *AuBYP 90*
Mukerji, Milan M *BiDrAPA 89*
Mukherjea, Swapna Banerjee *BiDrAPA 89*
Mukherjee, Bharati *BioIn 16*
Mukherjee, Bharati 1940- *FemiCLE, MajTwCW, WhoAm 90, WhoAmW 91*
Mukherjee, Kalinath 1932- *WhoAm 90*
Mukherjee, Nalini 1947- *WhoWor 91*
Mukherjee, Sukdeb *BiDrAPA 89*
Mukhina, Vera Ignat'evna 1889-1953 *BiDWomA*
Mukhopadhyay, Nikhiles 1944- *WhoE 91*
Mukhoti, Bela Banerjee 1932- *WhoE 91*
Mukle, Nora Janne 1911- *IntWWM 90*
Mukoyama, Helen Kiyoko 1914- *WhoAmW 91*
Muktanada, Swami 1908-1982 *EncO&P 3*
Mulach, J.F., Jr. 1907- *St&PR 91*
Mulaik, Stanley Allen 1935- *WhoSSW 91*
Mularczyk, Margaret J. 1956- *St&PR 91*
Mulari, Mary Elizabeth 1947- *WhoAmW 91, WhoWrEP 89*
Mularski, Victoria A. *WhoAmW 91*
Mularz, Theodore Leonard 1933- *WhoAm 90*
Mulcahy, Hugh 1913- *Ballpl 90*
Mulcahy, James Frederick 1926- *St&PR 91*
Mulcahy, John 1950- *WhoE 91*
Mulcahy, John J. 1922- *WhoAm 90, WhoE 91*
Mulcahy, John J. 1947- *St&PR 91*
Mulcahy, Joseph L. 1938- *St&PR 91*
Mulcahy, Kathleen 1950- *WhoAmA 91*
Mulcahy, Kathleen Ann 1950- *WhoE 91*
Mulcahy, Lucille Burnett *AuBYP 90*
Mulcahy, Paul N. 1930- *St&PR 91*
Mulcahy, Richard T. 1938- *St&PR 91*
Mulcahy, Robert Edward 1932- *WhoAm 90, WhoE 91*
Mulcahy, Sean 1930- *OxCCanT*
Mulcahy, Thomas F. 1921- *St&PR 91*
Mulch, Robert F., Jr. 1951- *WhoEmL 91*
Mulchuyse, S. *EncO&P 3*
Muldaur, Diana 1938- *ConTFT 8*
Muldaur, Diana Charlton 1938- *WhoAm 90, WhoAmW 91*
Muldaur, Maria 1942- *BioIn 16*
Muldawer, Michael David *BiDrAPA 89*
Mulder, Connie 1925-1988 *AnObit 1988*
Mulder, David S. 1938- *WhoAm 90*
Mulder, Donald Gerrit 1924- *WhoAm 90*
Mulder, Donald Ray 1944- *St&PR 91*
Mulder, Donald William 1917- *WhoAm 90*
Mulder, Hendrik, IV 1934- *WhoWor 91*
Mulder, Henry John *BiDrAPA 89*
Mulder, John Mark 1946- *WhoEmL 91*
Mulder, Martin Jan 1923- *WhoWor 91*
Mulder, Tiny 1921- *EncCoWW*
Mulder, Willem Gerard 1921- *St&PR 91*
Mulder de Daumer, Elisabeth 1904- *EncCoWW*
Mulderig, James Kevin 1959- *BiDrAPA 89*
Muldoon, Catherine *WhoHisp 91*
Muldoon, Edward Gerard *BioIn 16*
Muldoon, Francis Creighton 1930- *WhoE 91*
Muldoon, Michael Dennis 1941- *WhoSSW 91*
Muldoon, Nancy Louise 1946- *St&PR 91*
Muldoon, Paul 1951- *ConAu 129*
Muldoon, Robert Joseph, Jr. 1936- *WhoAm 90*
Muldoon, Sylvan J 1903?-1971 *EncO&P 3*
Muldoon, Sylvan Joseph 1903-1971 *EncPaPR 91*
Muldowney, Dominic 1952- *PenDiMP A*
Muldowney, Dominic John 1952- *IntWWM 90*
Muldowney, Tyrone F. 1957- *St&PR 91*
Muldrow, Clifford Lundale 1939- *WhoSSW 91*
Muldrow, Tressie Wright 1941- *WhoAmW 91*
Mule, Anthony V. 1943- *St&PR 91*
Mule, Guy R. 1946- *St&PR 91*
Mule, Marcel 1901- *PenDiMP*
Mule, Nat Thomas 1942- *St&PR 91*
Muleh, Salvatore 1946- *BiDrAPA 89*
Mules, Janet E. *BiDrAPA 89*
Mules, Norman A. 1930- *St&PR 91*
Mulford, Arthur *St&PR 91*
Mulford, Donald L. *BioIn 16*
Mulford, Donald Lewis 1918- *WhoWor 91*
Mulford, James Frank 1963- *WhoE 91*

Mulford, Philippa Greene 1948- *WhoAmW 91, WhoWrEP 89*
Mulford, Prentice 1834-1891 *EncO&P 3*
Mulford, Rand P. 1943- *St&PR 91*
Mulford, Ren 1859-1932 *Ballpl 90*
Mulford, Robert D. 1942- *St&PR 91*
Mulford, Wendy 1941- *FemiCLE*
Mulgaonkar, Shamkant P. 1952- *WhoE 91*
Mulgrew, Katherine Kiernan 1955- *WhoAm 90*
Mulhall, Robert Lee 1920- *WhoWrEP 89*
Mulhall, Walter R. *ODwPR 91*
Mulhare, Edward 1923- *WorAlBi*
Mulhaupt, Laurinda *BioIn 16*
Mulheren, John *BioIn 16*
Mulherin, Lori Gene M 1956- *WhoSSW 91*
Mulhern, John David 1928- *WhoAm 90*
Mulhern, Joseph Patrick 1921- *WhoAm 90*
Mulhern, Laurence F. 1954- *St&PR 91*
Mulhern, Michael *WhoAmA 91*
Mulhollan, Paige Elliott 1934- *WhoAm 90*
Mulholland, Angela Broadway 1957- *WhoSSW 91*
Mulholland, Charles Bradley 1941- *WhoAm 90*
Mulholland, David Baker 1932- *WhoE 91*
Mulholland, Jack Russell 1929- *St&PR 91*
Mulholland, Kenneth D. 1946- *St&PR 91*
Mulholland, Kenneth Leo, Jr. 1943- *WhoAm 90*
Mulholland, Robert Edge 1933- *WhoAm 90*
Mulholland, Rosa 1841-1921 *FemiCLE*
Mulholland, S. Grant 1936- *WhoAm 90*
Mulholland, Terry 1963- *Ballpl 90*
Mulholland, William David 1926- *St&PR 91*
Mulholland, William David, Jr. 1926- *WhoAm 90, WhoWor 91*
Mulianto, Haji Sindhu 1940- *WhoWor 91*
Mulikita, Fwanyanga Matale 1928- *WhoWor 91*
Mulinari, Acir 1934- *WhoWor 91*
Mulinix, Douglas M *BiDrAPA 89*
Mulitz, Lewis 1926- *St&PR 91*
Mulitz, Milton M. 1918- *St&PR 91*
Muljacic, Zarko 1922- *WhoWor 91*
Muljono, Winar Hartono 1943- *WhoWor 91*
Mulkerin, John Patrick 1937- *St&PR 91*
Mulkern, Anne Marie *BiDrAPA 89*
Mulkey, Jack Clarendon 1939- *WhoAm 90*
Mulkey, Terry Douglas 1946- *St&PR 91*
Mull, Charles Leroy, II 1927- *WhoE 91*
Mull, Gale W. 1945- *WhoEmL 91*
Mull, Gary William 1947- *St&PR 91*
Mull, Kayla *BioIn 16*
Mull, Martin 1943- *WhoAm 90, WorAlBi*
Mull, Om Chand 1929- *WhoWor 91*
Mulla, Dawood Adem *BiDrAPA 89*
Mullaley, Robert Charles 1926- *WhoAm 90*
Mullally, Henry 1949-1988 *BioIn 16*
Mullally, Robert E. 1933- *St&PR 91*
Mullaly, Marjorie *BioIn 16*
Mullan, David George 1951- *ConAu 130*
Mullan, Hugh 1911- *BiDrAPA 89*
Mullan, James Boyd 1903- *WhoAm 90*
Mullan, James F. 1939- *St&PR 91*
Mullan, John Francis 1925- *WhoAm 90*
Mullane, Denis Francis 1930- *St&PR 91, WhoAm 90, WhoE 91*
Mullane, Donald A. 1938- *WhoAm 90*
Mullane, John Francis 1937- *WhoAm 90*
Mullane, Richard M. *BioIn 16*
Mullane, Robert E. 1932- *St&PR 91, WhoAm 90*
Mullane, Tim *BioIn 16*
Mullane, Tony 1859-1944 *Ballpl 90 [port]*
Mullaney, Dora Aileen 1943- *WhoAmW 91*
Mullaney, Edward John 1937- *St&PR 91*
Mullaney, Elizabeth Mary 1952- *WhoE 91*
Mullaney, Frank C. 1923- *St&PR 91*
Mullaney, John *BiDrAPA 89*
Mullaney, Joseph E. 1933- *St&PR 91, WhoAm 90*
Mullaney, Thomas F., Jr. 1939- *St&PR 91*
Mullaney, Thomas H. 1932- *St&PR 91*
Mullani, Nizar Abdul 1942- *WhoWor 91*
Mullany, Brian Robert 1945- *St&PR 91*
Mullany, David John 1965- *St&PR 91*
Mullany, Jack *BioIn 16*
Mullany, Martin *BioIn 16*
Mullany, Stephanie Hathaway 1948- *BiDrAPA 89*
Mullare, T. Kenwood, Jr. 1939- *St&PR 91*
Mullare, Thomas Kenwood, Jr. 1939- *WhoAm 90*
Mullarkey, Mary J. 1943- *WhoAm 90, WhoAmW 91*
Mullarkey, Maureen 1942- *WhoAmA 91*
Mullarky, Kevin H *BiDrAPA 89*
Mulle, George Ernest 1919- *WhoSSW 91*
Mulle, Robert J. 1922- *St&PR 91*
Mulleedy, Joyce Elaine 1948- *WhoAmW 91*
Mullen, Andrew J 1923- *BiDrAPA 89*
Mullen, Andrew Judson 1923- *WhoSSW 91, WhoWor 91*
Mullen, Brian *BioIn 16*
Mullen, Bruce Diedrich 1962- *WhoSSW 91*
Mullen, C. Richard 1937- *St&PR 91*
Mullen, Charles H. *St&PR 91*
Mullen, Daniel Robert 1941- *St&PR 91, WhoAm 90*
Mullen, David Bruce 1950- *St&PR 91*
Mullen, David James 1961- *BiDrAPA 89*
Mullen, David P. *St&PR 91*
Mullen, Diane Chlebo 1961- *WhoSSW 91*
Mullen, Dorothy Mae Huffman 1936- *WhoAmW 91*
Mullen, Douglas B. 1940- *St&PR 91*
Mullen, Douglas T. 1940- *St&PR 91*
Mullen, Edward John, Jr. 1942- *WhoAm 90*
Mullen, Eileen Anne 1943- *WhoE 91*
Mullen, Frank *BioIn 16*
Mullen, Frank Ernest 1896-1977 *BioIn 16*
Mullen, Gary L. 1947- *WhoE 91*
Mullen, George J. *St&PR 91*
Mullen, James Gentry 1933- *WhoAm 90*
Mullen, James Martin 1935- *WhoAmA 91*
Mullen, Jamie A. 1957- *BiDrAPA 89*
Mullen, Januarius Arthur 1905- *WhoAm 90*
Mullen, Jo Stauffer 1908- *WhoAmA 91*
Mullen, Joey *BioIn 16*
Mullen, John Harold, III 1951- *WhoAm 90*
Mullen, John Wilfred 1924- *WhoAm 90*
Mullen, Joseph J 1927- *BiDrAPA 89*
Mullen, Julia Elizabeth 1930- *WhoAmW 91*
Mullen, Kevin Edward 1955- *St&PR 91*
Mullen, Patrick B 1948- *BiDrAPA 89*
Mullen, Perry W. 1922- *St&PR 91*
Mullen, Philip Edward 1942- *WhoAmA 91*
Mullen, Regina Marie 1948- *WhoAmW 91*
Mullen, Ron 1939- *WhoAm 90*
Mullen, Ronald E *BiDrAPA 89*
Mullen, Roy C. *St&PR 91*
Mullen, Samuel, Jr. 1950- *WhoE 91*
Mullen, Sanford Allen 1925- *WhoAm 90, WhoSSW 91, WhoWor 91*
Mullen, Sarah C. 1957- *ODwPR 91*
Mullen, T. David 1927- *St&PR 91*
Mullen, Thomas Edgar 1936- *WhoWor 91*
Mullen, Thomas Moore 1915- *WhoAm 90*
Mullen, William 1940- *St&PR 91*
Mullen, William David 1949- *WhoEmL 91*
Mullen, William Thomas 1931- *WhoSSW 91*
Mullenbach, Linda Herman 1948- *WhoEmL 91*
Mullendore, Edward Clinton 1927- *St&PR 91*
Mullendore, John W. 1934- *St&PR 91*
Mullendore, Walter Edward 1940- *WhoAm 90, WhoSSW 91*
Mullenix, Kenneth Eugene 1947- *WhoSSW 91*
Mullenix, Martha Bode 1940- *WhoAmW 91*
Mullenix, Paul Douglas 1957- *WhoSSW 91*
Mullens, Priscilla *BioIn 16, WorAlBi*
Mullens, Robert J. *BioIn 16*
Mullens, William Reese 1921- *WhoAm 90*
Muller, Albin 1871-1941 *PenDiDA 89*
Muller, Andre 1925- *WhoWor 91*
Muller, Auguste *EncO&P 3*
Muller, Bart 1943- *BiDrAPA 89*
Muller, Betty Ann J *BiDrAPA 89*
Muller, Brigitte Denise 1921- *WhoAmW 91*
Muller, Bruce M. 1942- *St&PR 91*
Muller, Burton Harlowe 1924- *WhoAm 90*
Muller, Carl Anton 1938- *St&PR 91*
Muller, Charlotte Feldman 1921- *WhoAm 90*
Muller, Christa 1936- *EncCoWW*
Muller, Christopher Orin 1956- *WhoSSW 91*
Muller, Clara 1861-1905 *EncCoWW*
Muller, Claudya Barbara 1946- *WhoAm 90*
Muller, Daniel Ernst *PenDiDA 89*
Muller, Daniel Victor 1943- *St&PR 91*
Muller, David F. 1948- *St&PR 91*
Muller, David John 1935- *BiDrAPA 89*
Muller, Dietrich Alfred Helmut 1936- *WhoAm 90*
Muller, Edward Robert 1952- *St&PR 91, WhoAm 90*
Muller, Elsie Ferrar 1913- *WhoAmW 91*
Muller, Emile 1915-1988 *BiDFrPL*
Muller, Ernest H. 1923- *WhoAm 90*
Muller, Eva 1928- *BiDrAPA 89*
Muller, Ferdinand *PenDiDA 89*
Muller, Francis J, Jr. 1940- *BiDrAPA 89*
Muller, Frank B. 1926- *WhoAm 90*
Muller, Frantz Heinrich *PenDiDA 89*
Muller, Fred Paul 1926- *WhoWor 91*
Muller, Gene Alan 1943- *WhoSSW 91*
Muller, George Ann 1954- *WhoE 91*
Muller, George F 1866-1958 *WhoAmA 91N*
Muller, George T. 1949- *St&PR 91*
Muller, Georgene K. 1950- *WhoWrEP 89*
Muller, Gert Heinz 1923- *WhoWor 91*
Muller, Heinrich *BioIn 16*
Muller, Henry John 1919- *WhoAm 90*
Muller, Henry Nicholas, III 1938- *WhoAm 90*
Muller, Herbert F *BiDrAPA 89*
Muller, Herman N. J. 1890-1967 *WorAlBi*
Muller, Herta 1953- *EncCoWW*
Muller, Ingo 1936- *WhoWor 91*
Muller, Iwan 1786-1854 *PenDiMP*
Muller, James Lawrence, II 1964- *WhoSSW 91*
Muller, James W 1953- *ConAu 132*
Muller, Jan 1922-1958 *WhoAmA 91N*
Muller, Jans 1930- *WhoAm 90*
Muller, Jennifer 1944- *WhoAm 90*
Muller, Jenny H 1953- *BiDrAPA 89*
Muller, Jerome Kenneth 1934- *WhoAmA 91, WhoWor 91*
Muller, John Bartlett 1940- *WhoAm 90*
Muller, John E. *ConAu 32NR*
Muller, John Henry, Jr. 1924- *St&PR 91*
Muller, Jorg *BioIn 16*
Muller, Jorge Ernesto 1943- *WhoWor 91*
Muller, K. Alex 1927- *WhoAm 90, WhoWor 91, WorAlBi*
Muller, Karl *PenDiDA 89*
Muller, Karl E 1893- *EncO&P 3*
Muller, Karl E. 1893-1969 *EncPaPR 91*
Muller, Kurt Alexander 1955- *WhoEmL 91*
Muller, Linda Lee 1939- *WhoAmW 91*
Muller, Maler 1749-1825 *DcLB 94 [port]*
Muller, Marcia 1944- *FemiCLE, TwCCr&M 91*
Muller, Margie H. 1927- *WhoAmW 91*
Muller, Mary Ann 1820-1900 *FemiCLE*
Muller, Max Paul 1935- *WhoAmA 91*
Muller, Mervin Edgar 1928- *WhoAm 90*
Muller, Mette Vibeke 1930- *IntWWM 90*
Muller, Michael *PenDiDA 89*
Muller, Nicholas Guthrie 1942- *WhoAm 90*
Muller, Patricia Ann 1943- *WhoAmW 91, WhoSSW 91*
Muller, Paul 1899-1965 *WorAlBi*
Muller, Paul F. 1915- *St&PR 91*
Muller, Peter *BioIn 16*
Muller, Peter 1920- *St&PR 91*
Muller, Peter 1947- *St&PR 91, WhoAm 90*
Muller, Peter Paul *BioIn 16*
Muller, Priscilla Elkow 1930- *WhoAmA 91, WhoE 91*
Muller, R.G. *St&PR 91*
Muller, Reinhard 1948- *WhoWor 91*
Muller, Richard Matthias 1926- *WhoWor 91*
Muller, Robert J. 1946- *St&PR 91*
Muller, Robert Joseph, Jr. 1946- *WhoAm 90*
Muller, Roland F *BiDrAPA 89*
Muller, Rolf Felix 1932- *ConDes 90*
Muller, Rolf Hugo 1929- *WhoWor 91*
Muller, Ronald Ernst 1939- *WhoAm 90*
Muller, Ronald H. 1946- *St&PR 91*
Muller, Sigfrid Augustine 1930- *WhoAm 90*
Muller, Stephen Anthony 1933- *St&PR 91*
Muller, Steven 1927- *WhoAm 90, WhoE 91, WhoWor 91*
Muller, Sylvia Ruth Barbush 1935- *IntWWM 90*
Muller, Thomas Walter *BiDrAPA 89*
Muller, Walter J. *BioIn 16*
Muller, Walter Joseph, III 1934- *BiDrAPA 89*
Muller, Warren *St&PR 91*
Muller, Werner E.G. 1942- *WhoWor 91*
Muller, Wilhelm *PenDiMP*
Muller, Willard Chester 1916- *WhoAm 90*
Muller, William Henry, Jr. 1919- *WhoAm 90*
Muller-Brockmann, Josef 1914- *ConDes 90*
Muller-Brunotte, Robert 1959- *WhoWor 91*
Muller-Eberhard, Hans Joachim 1927- *WhoAm 90*
Muller-Graff, Peter Christian 1945- *WhoWor 91*
Muller-Groeling, Hubertus 1929- *WhoWor 91*
Muller-Hill, Benno Andreas 1933- *WhoWor 91*
Muller-Ruchholtz, Wolfgang 1928- *WhoWor 91*
Muller-Schwefe, Gerhard Matthew 1914- *WhoWor 91*
Muller-Warmuth, Werner 1929- *WhoWor 91*
Muller-Zimmermann, Klaus 1927- *St&PR 91*
Mullett, Charles Samuel 1931- *St&PR 91*
Mullette, Julienne Patricia 1940- *WhoAmW 91, WhoE 91, WhoWor 91*
Mullican, Billy Akers, Sr. 1920- *St&PR 91*
Mullican, Lee 1919- *WhoAmA 91*
Mullican, Matt 1951- *BioIn 16*
Mullick, Prabir K *BiDrAPA 89*
Mulligan, Eddie 1894-1982 *Ballpl 90*
Mulligan, Edward E. 1930- *St&PR 91, WhoAm 90*
Mulligan, Edward W. 1925- *St&PR 91*
Mulligan, Elinor Patterson 1929- *WhoWor 91*
Mulligan, Gerald Joseph 1927- *WhoAm 90*
Mulligan, Gerald T. 1945- *St&PR 91*
Mulligan, Gerry *BioIn 16*
Mulligan, Gerry 1927- *OxCPMus, WorAlBi*
Mulligan, Hugh Augustine 1925- *WhoAm 90*
Mulligan, James Francis 1925- *WhoAm 90*
Mulligan, James Hilary 1844-1915 *LiHiK*
Mulligan, James J. 1921- *St&PR 91*
Mulligan, James Joseph 1921- *WhoAm 90*
Mulligan, James Kenneth 1911- *WhoAm 90*
Mulligan, Joseph Francis 1920- *WhoAm 90*
Mulligan, Martin Frederick 1940- *WhoAm 90*
Mulligan, Richard *BioIn 16*
Mulligan, Richard 1932- *WorAlBi*
Mulligan, Richard F. 1933- *St&PR 91*
Mulligan, Robert 1925- *BioIn 16*
Mulligan, Robert J. 1938- *St&PR 91, WhoAm 90*
Mulligan, Robert Patrick *WhoAm 90*
Mulligan, Robert Peter 1924- *St&PR 91*
Mulligan, Robert William 1916- *WhoAm 90*
Mulligan, Susan Amrhein 1943- *St&PR 91*
Mulligan, Thomas J. 1933- *St&PR 91*
Mulligan, Thomas James 1935- *WhoAm 90*
Mulligan, William G. 1930- *St&PR 91*
Mulligan, William George 1906- *WhoAm 90, WhoE 91*
Mulligan, William Goeckel 1930- *WhoAm 90*
Mulligan, William Hughes 1918- *WhoAm 90*
Mulliken, Robert Sanderson 1896-1986 *BioIn 16*
Mulliken, William D. 1939- *St&PR 91*
Mullikin, Harry Copeland 1940- *WhoAm 90*
Mullikin, Morgan James 1953- *St&PR 91*
Mullikin, Thomas Wilson 1928- *WhoAm 90*
Mullikin, Vernon Eugene 1935- *WhoAm 90*
Mullin, Albert Alkins 1933- *EncO&P 3*
Mullin, Albert Edward, Jr. 1933- *St&PR 91, WhoAm 90, WhoE 91*
Mullin, Charles Samuel *BiDrAPA 89*
Mullin, Chris 1947- *ConAu 132*
Mullin, Christopher John 1947- *SpyFic*
Mullin, Constance 1939- *IntWWM 90, WhoAmW 91*
Mullin, Cynthia Marie 1956- *WhoAmW 91*
Mullin, Delcie Ann 1955- *WhoAmW 91*
Mullin, George 1880-1944 *Ballpl 90*
Mullin, J. Shan 1934- *WhoAm 90*
Mullin, Jerome Patrick 1933- *WhoAm 90*
Mullin, Joe 1957- *WorAlBi*
Mullin, John Frederick 1940- *St&PR 91*
Mullin, John Hatchman, III 1941- *St&PR 91, WhoAm 90*
Mullin, John Stanley 1907- *St&PR 91*
Mullin, Lawrence J. *ODwPR 91*
Mullin, Leo F. 1943- *St&PR 91*
Mullin, Leo Francis 1943- *WhoAm 90*
Mullin, Mark Hill 1940- *WhoE 91*
Mullin, Maurice L. 1928- *St&PR 91*
Mullin, Pat 1917- *Ballpl 90*
Mullin, Patricia Evelyn *St&PR 91*
Mullin, Richard J. 1951- *St&PR 91*
Mullin, Roger William, Jr. 1914- *WhoAm 90*
Mullin, Willard 1902-1978 *Ballpl 90, WhoAmA 91N*
Mullin, William Edward 1902- *St&PR 91*
Mullin, William Francis 1921- *WhoSSW 91*
Mullinax, Carl Robert 1950- *WhoSSW 91*
Mullinax, D. Richard *ODwPR 91*
Mullinax, Harvey Owen 1913- *St&PR 91*
Mullinax, James Parker 1945- *WhoSSW 91*
Mullinax, Otto B. 1912- *WhoAm 90*
Mullineaux, Donal Ray 1925- *WhoAm 90*
Mullineaux, Jewel E. 1917- *WhoAmW 91*
Mullings, Frank 1881-1953 *PenDiMP*
Mullington, Hugh J. 1935- *WhoAm 90*
Mulliniks, Rance 1956- *Ballpl 90*
Mullinix, Edward W., Jr. 1953- *St&PR 91*
Mullinix, Edward Wingate 1924- *WhoAm 90, WhoE 91*

Mullinix, Steve 1949- *WhoSSW 91*
Mullins, Anna Crabtree 1946- *WhoAmW 91*
Mullins, Betty Kaye 1942- *WhoE 91*
Mullins, Brian C. 1941- *St&PR 91*
Mullins, Carolyn Johns 1940- *WhoWrEP 89*
Mullins, Claude Andrew 1954- *WhoEmL 91*
Mullins, David W., Jr. 1946- *WhoAm 90*
Mullins, Edgar Young 1860-1928 *BioIn 16*
Mullins, Elizabeth Ione 1928- *WhoAmW 91*
Mullins, Helene 1899- *WhoWrEP 89*
Mullins, Homer Stewart 1946- *St&PR 91*
Mullins, James Boll 1934- *St&PR 91*
Mullins, Janet G. *WhoAm 90*
Mullins, Jeremiah Andrew 1936- *WhoAm 90*
Mullins, Jim Austin 1942- *St&PR 91*
Mullins, John 1838-1894 *EncO&P 3*
Mullins, John Madison 1919- *WhoAm 90, WhoE 91*
Mullins, Kenneth Delbert 1957- *WhoSSW 91*
Mullins, Lorin John 1917- *WhoAm 90*
Mullins, Margaret Ann Frances 1953- *WhoEmL 91*
Mullins, Melinda C 1954- *BiDrAPA 89*
Mullins, Michael Gordon 1937- *WhoAm 90*
Mullins, Nancy Ruth 1959- *WhoSSW 91*
Mullins, Obera 1927- *WhoAmW 91*
Mullins, Philip Aldon, III 1940- *St&PR 91*
Mullins, Richard Austin 1918- *WhoWor 91*
Mullins, Richard Edward 1951- *WhoSSW 91*
Mullins, Robin Hassler 1953- *WhoAmW 91*
Mullins, Ronald Gift 1938- *WhoWrEP 89*
Mullins, Terry *BioIn 16*
Mullins, Theodore C. 1932- *St&PR 91*
Mullins, Thomas Darragh, II 1935- *WhoWor 91*
Mullins, Wayman C. 1951- *WhoSSW 91*
Mullins, William B. *BioIn 16, NewYTBS 90*
Mullins, William Harvey Lowe 1935- *WhoAm 90*
Mullins, William Wilson 1927- *WhoAm 90*
Mullis, Brent Barker 1942- *St&PR 91*
Mullis, Perry E. 1933- *St&PR 91*
Mullis, Ronald Lynn 1942- *WhoSSW 91*
Mulloney, Peter Black 1932- *St&PR 91, WhoAm 90*
Mullova, Viktoria 1959- *IntWWM 90, PenDiMP*
Mulqueen, Ellen 1941- *WhoAm 90*
Mulready, William 1786-1863 *BioIn 16*
Mulreany, Robert Henry 1915- *St&PR 91, WhoAm 90*
Mulrennan, Sheila 1950- *WhoAmW 91*
Mulroney, Brian *BioIn 16*
Mulroney, Brian 1939- *WhoAm 90, WhoE 91, WhoWor 91, WorAlBi*
Mulroney, Graham William 1946- *WhoWor 91*
Mulroney, John Patrick 1935- *St&PR 91, WhoAm 90, WhoE 91*
Mulroney, Mila 1953- *WhoAm 90, WhoAmW 91*
Mulrooney, Charles R. 1906-1989 *BioIn 16*
Mulrooney, Jacqueline Downing 1957- *WhoAmW 91*
Mulrooney, Virginia Frances 1939- *WhoAmW 91*
Mulrow, Patrick Joseph *WhoAm 90*
Mulroy, Barry Michael 1946- *St&PR 91*
Mulroy, George Alan 1934- *St&PR 91*
Mulroy, Thomas R. 1905-1989 *BioIn 16*
Mulroy, Thomas Robert, Sr. 1905- *WhoAm 90*
Mulryan, Henry Trist 1927- *WhoAm 90*
Mulryan, Lawrence E. 1937- *St&PR 91*
Mulryan, Thomas Stephen 1942- *St&PR 91*
Mulsant, Benoit Henri 1960- *BiDrAPA 89*
Mulshine, Michael A. 1939- *St&PR 91*
Multani, Gurmeet Singh 1955- *BiDrAPA 89*
Multani, Harbans Singh *BiDrAPA 89*
Multer, Gerald Jay 1929- *ODwPR 91*
Multscher, Hans 1400?-1467? *IntDcAA 90*
Mulva, J. J. 1946- *St&PR 91*
Mulva, James Joseph 1946- *WhoAm 90*
Mulvahill, John E 1924- *BiDrAPA 89*
Mulvaney, James Edward, Jr. 1954- *WhoE 91*
Mulvaney, James Norbert 1937- *St&PR 91*
Mulvaney, John J *BiDrAPA 89*
Mulvaney, John Quincy 1940- *St&PR 91*
Mulvaney, Mary Frederica 1945- *WhoAmW 91*
Mulvaney, Mary Jean 1927- *WhoAm 90*
Mulvaney, Maureen Gail 1950- *WhoAmW 91*
Mulvaney, Thomas F. 1950- *St&PR 91*
Mulvaney, Thomas Joseph 1937- *St&PR 91*
Mulvany, John 1844-1906 *WhNaAH*
Mulvee, Robert Edward 1930- *WhoAm 90, WhoE 91*
Mulveney, William Harold 1936- *St&PR 91*
Mulvenna, Jerry *BioIn 16*
Mulvey, John Thomas, Jr. 1941- *WhoSSW 91*
Mulvey, Margaret Ellen 1952- *WhoAmW 91*
Mulvey, Robert Joseph *BiDrAPA 89*
Mulvihill, David Brian 1956- *WhoEmL 91*
Mulvihill, Edward Robert 1917- *WhoAm 90*
Mulvihill, Francis J, Jr. 1940- *BiDrAPA 89*
Mulvihill, James Edward 1940- *WhoAm 90*
Mulvihill, John Timothy 1931- *WhoAm 90*
Mulvihill, Peter James 1956- *WhoWor 91*
Mulvihill, Terence Joseph 1931- *WhoAm 90*
Mulvihill, Thomas C. 1946- *St&PR 91*
Mulvihill-Byers, Teresa Gayle *BiDrAPA 89*
Mulvin, Noel Southwell 1922- *WhoWor 91*
Mulvoy, Thomas F., Jr. 1943- *WhoAm 90, WhoE 91*
Mulzer, Johann Hermann 1944- *WhoWor 91*
Mumaw, James Webster 1920- *WhoAm 90*
Mumford, Amanda Melvina 1955- *BiDrAPA 89*
Mumford, Christopher G. 1945- *St&PR 91*
Mumford, Christopher Greene 1945- *WhoAm 90*
Mumford, David Bryant 1937- *WhoAm 90*
Mumford, Erika *BioIn 16*
Mumford, George Saltonstall, Jr. 1928- *WhoAm 90*
Mumford, Lewis 1895-1990 *BioIn 16, ConAu 130, CurBio 90N, NewYTBS 90 [port], News 90, WorAlBi*
Mumford, Manly Whitman 1925- *WhoAm 90*
Mumford, Robert S *BiDrAPA 89*
Mumford, Robert Sutton 1918- *WhoE 91*
Mumford, Ronald W. 1946- *St&PR 91*
Mumford, Sherwood Dean 1952- *WhoSSW 91*
Mumford, William Porter, II 1920- *WhoAm 90*
Mumler, Wiliam *EncPaPR 91*
Mumler, William H. *EncO&P 3*
Mumma, Albert G. 1906- *WhoAm 90, WhoWor 91*
Mumma, Albert Girard, Jr. 1928- *WhoAm 90*
Mumma, Ed 1908-1986 *MusmAFA*
Mumma, Gordon 1935- *IntWWM 90, WhoAm 90*
Mumma, Karolyn *WhoAmW 91*
Mumma, Michael Jon 1941- *WhoAm 90*
Mummert, Gregory J. 1950- *St&PR 91*
Mumola, Peter Benedict 1944- *WhoAm 90*
Mumphrey, Jerry 1952- *Ballpl 90*
Mumtaz Mahal 1592-1631 *WorAlBi*
Mumtaz, Syed Shahid *BiDrAPA 89*
Mumy, Bill 1954- *ConTFT 8*
Mun, Adrien Albert-Marie de 1841-1914 *BiDFrPL*
Mun, Thomas 1571-1641 *BioIn 16*
Munafo, Joseph Charles, III 1959- *BiDrAPA 89*
Munakata Shiko 1903-1975 *EncJap*
Munari, Bruno 1907- *AuBYP 90, ConDes 90*
Munari, Franco 1920- *WhoWor 91*
Munas, Falies A 1946- *BiDrAPA 89*
Munasifi, Faisal Ahmad 1945- *BiDrAPA 89*
Munbach, G. Peter 1938- *St&PR 91*
Munby, Arthur Joseph 1828-1910 *BioIn 16*
Muncaster, Clive 1936- *IntWWM 90*
Muncaster, J.D. 1933- *St&PR 91*
Munce, James Charles 1938- *WhoAmA 91*
Muncey, Barbara Deane 1952- *WhoAmW 91*
Muncey, James Arthur, Jr. 1933- *WhoSSW 91*
Munch, Charles *ODwPR 91*
Munch, Charles 1891-1968 *PenDiMP, WorAlBi*
Munch, Douglas Francis 1947- *WhoAm 90*
Munch, Edvard 1863-1944 *BioIn 16, IntDcAA 90 [port], WorAlBi*
Munch, Jean 1932- *WhoAmW 91*
Munch, William, Jr. 1927- *St&PR 91*
Munch-Petersen, Gustaf 1912-1938 *DcScanL*
Munchhausen, Karl Friedrich H, Baron Von 1720-1797 *WorAlBi*
Munchinger, Karl 1915- *IntWWM 90, PenDiMP*
Muncie, Aletha McCroskey 1920- *WhoAmW 91*
Munck, Allan Ulf 1925- *WhoAm 90*
Muncrief, Bob 1916- *Ballpl 90*
Muncy, James Alonzo, Sr. 1955- *WhoSSW 91*
Muncy, Martha Elizabeth 1919- *WhoAmW 91*
Muncy, Raymond Lee 1928- *WhoSSW 91*
Mund, Geraldine 1943- *WhoAmW 91*
Mund, Richard Gordon 1942- *WhoAm 90*
Munda, Constantia *FemiCLE*
Mundadan, Anthony Mathias 1923- *WhoWor 91*
Mundale, Susan M. *ODwPR 91*
Mundassery, Sarala C 1940- *BiDrAPA 89*
Munday, Anthony 1553-1633 *BioIn 16*
Munday, Howard E. 1946- *St&PR 91*
Mundel, Marvin Everett 1916- *WhoAm 90*
Mundell, D.E. 1931- *St&PR 91*
Mundell, David Edward 1931- *WhoAm 90*
Mundell, Robert Alexander 1932- *WhoAm 90*
Mundell, Robert David 1936- *WhoAm 90*
Mundell, W. Jed 1950- *St&PR 91*
Munden, Elisabeth von *EncCoWW*
Munden, Robin Ghezzi 1947- *St&PR 91*
Munder, Barbara Ann 1945- *St&PR 91*
Munder, Fred *St&PR 91N*
Munder, Terrie Hollowed 1930- *WhoAmW 91*
Munderloh, Royce M. 1935- *St&PR 91*
Mundheim, Robert Harry 1933- *WhoAm 90*
Mundia, Nalumino 1927-1988 *BioIn 16*
Mundinger, Donald Charles 1929- *WhoAm 90*
Mundinger, William David 1941- *St&PR 91*
Mundlak, Yair 1927- *WhoAm 90*
Mundle, Clement Williams Kennedy 1916-1989 *EncO&P 3, EncPaPR 91*
Mundle, Linda Bick *BiDrAPA 89*
Mundorf, George 1921- *BiDrAPA 89*
Mundorff Shrestha, Sheila Ann 1945- *WhoAmW 91*
Mundra, Anand Damodardas 1946- *WhoE 91*
Mundschau, Walter 1935- *St&PR 91*
Mundt, Barry Maynard 1936- *WhoAm 90*
Mundt, Ernest Karl 1905- *WhoAmA 91*
Mundt, Gerald D. 1936- *St&PR 91*
Mundt, Randolph P. 1950- *St&PR 91*
Mundt, Ray B. 1928- *WhoAm 90, WhoE 91*
Mundus, Frank *BioIn 16*
Mundy, Christopher Thoresen 1953- *WhoSSW 91*
Mundy, Ethel Frances *WhoAmA 91N*
Mundy, Gardner M. 1941- *St&PR 91*
Mundy, Jimmy 1907- *OxCPMus*
Mundy, John Francis 1946- *St&PR 91, WhoEmL 91*
Mundy, John Hine 1917- *WhoAm 90*
Mundy, Laurence R *BiDrAPA 89*
Mundy, Louise Easterday 1870-1952 *WhoAmA 91N*
Mundy, Simon 1954- *SmATA 64*
Mundy, William G. 1950- *St&PR 91*
Mundy, William Greg 1950- *WhoAm 90*
Munera, Gerard Emmanuel 1935- *WhoAm 90, WhoWor 91*
Muneses, Todd I. 1961- *BiDrAPA 89*
Munetz, Mark Richard 1950- *BiDrAPA 89*
Munford, Dillard 1918- *St&PR 91, WhoSSW 91*
Munford, Gordon E. 1929- *IntWWM 90*
Munford, Joan Hardie 1933- *WhoAmW 91*
Munford, JoAnn 1955- *WhoSSW 91*
Munford, John Durburrow 1928- *St&PR 91, WhoAm 90*
Munford, Mary Cooke 1865-1938 *BioAmW*
Munford, Robert Watson 1925- *WhoAmA 91*
Mungai, Evelyn Karungari *BioIn 16*
Mungall, Thomas Gordon, III 1954- *WhoSSW 91*
Munger, Benson Scott 1942- *WhoAm 90*
Munger, Bryce L. 1933- *WhoAm 90*
Munger, Charles T. *BioIn 16*
Munger, Charles T. 1924- *WhoAm 90*
Munger, Charles Thomas 1924- *St&PR 91*
Munger, Edwin Stanton 1921- *WhoAm 90*
Munger, Elmer Lewis 1915- *WhoAm 90, WhoWor 91*
Munger, George 1918- *Ballpl 90*
Munger, Harold Charles 1929- *WhoAm 90, WhoWor 91*
Munger, James Elliott 1929- *St&PR 91*
Munger, James Guy 1951- *WhoSSW 91*
Munger, Judy Powell 1943- *WhoSSW 91*
Munger, Nicholas E. 1949- *St&PR 91*
Munger, Nicholas Edward 1949- *WhoSSW 91*
Munger, Sharon *WhoAmW 91*
Munger, Sharon M. 1946- *St&PR 91*
Mungin, Horace L. 1941- *WhoWrEP 89*
Mungo Jerry *OxCPMus*
Mungo, Van Lingle 1911-1985 *Ballpl 90 [port]*
Munguia, Gus *WhoHisp 91*
Munhollon, Samuel Clifford 1948- *WhoSSW 91*
Muni, Paul 1895-1967 *WorAlBi*
Munich, Richard Lee 1939- *BiDrAPA 89*
Munier, Bertrand Rene 1943- *WhoWor 91*
Munier, Robert S.C. 1953- *St&PR 91*
Munier, Ronald Alan 1933- *St&PR 91*
Munier, William Boss 1942- *WhoE 91*
Munim, Fazle Kaderi Muhammad A. 1924- *WhoWor 91*
Muniot, Barbara King *WhoAmA 91*
Munir, Kerim Mehmet *BiDrAPA 89*
Munir, Mazhar 1948- *BiDrAPA 89*
Munisteri, Joseph George 1930- *WhoAm 90*
Munitz, Barry Allen 1941- *WhoAm 90*
Munive Escobar, Luis 1920- *WhoAm 90*
Muniz, Amado Luis *BiDrAPA 89*
Muniz, Angelina 1936- *ConAu 131, HispWr 90*
Muniz, Carlos E 1924- *BiDrAPA 89*
Muniz Arrambide, Isabel 1960- *WhoHisp 91*
Munjack, Dennis Joseph *BiDrAPA 89*
Munjal, Yogesh Chander 1940- *WhoWor 91*
Munk, Andrzej 1921-1961 *BioIn 16*
Munk, Barbara D *BiDrAPA 89*
Munk, Kaj 1898-1944 *DcScanL*
Munk, Max Nosson 1942- *St&PR 91*
Munk, Vladimir 1925- *WhoE 91*
Munk, Walter Heinrich 1917- *WhoAm 90*
Munk, Zev Moshe 1950- *WhoSSW 91*
Munn, Cecil E. 1923- *St&PR 91*
Munn, Cecil Edwin 1923- *WhoAm 90*
Munn, Debra Dee 1953- *WhoWrEP 89*
Munn, Edward Thomas 1933- *St&PR 91*
Munn, Harold Glynn 1925- *St&PR 91*
Munn, Jacob 1951- *St&PR 91*
Munn, James T. *St&PR 91*
Munn, John S. 1933- *St&PR 91*
Munn, John Symonds 1933- *WhoAm 90*
Munn, Kelly Ann 1956- *WhoAmW 91*
Munn, Nathan Allen *BiDrAPA 89*
Munn, Robert Stewart 1829-1894 *DcCanB 12*
Munn, Roza 1919- *St&PR 91*
Munn, Stephen P. *WhoAm 90*
Munn, Stephen P. 1942- *St&PR 91*
Munn, Susan Ann 1961- *WhoAmW 91*
Munn, William C, II 1938- *BiDrAPA 89*
Munna, John Charles 1934- *WhoSSW 91*
Munnecke, Donald Edwin 1920- *WhoAm 90*
Munnell, Alicia H 1942- *ConAu 30NR*
Munnell, Alicia Haydock 1942- *WhoAm 90, WhoAmW 91, WhoE 91*
Munnell, Douglas Martin 1959- *WhoSSW 91*
Munnell, Rebecca Howard *ODwPR 91*
Munnichs, Joep Mathieu Andre 1927- *WhoWor 91*
Munnikhuis, Bert H. 1952- *St&PR 91*
Munnings, Frederick T *EncO&P 3*
Munnings, Frederick Tansley *EncPaPR 91*
Muno, Richard Carl 1939- *WhoAmA 91*
Munowitz, Ken 1936-1978 *WhoAmA 91N*
Munoz, Adan, Jr. 1948- *WhoHisp 91*
Munoz, Anthony 1958- *WhoHisp 91, WorAlBi*
Munoz, Braulio 1946- *WhoHisp 91*
Munoz, Carlos, Jr. 1939- *WhoHisp 91, WhoWrEP 89*
Munoz, Carlos Ramon *WhoHisp 91*
Munoz, Carlos Ramon 1935- *St&PR 91, WhoE 91*
Munoz, Carmen 1936- *WhoHisp 91*
Munoz, Edward H. 1944- *WhoHisp 91*
Munoz, Elias Miguel 1954- *WhoHisp 91*
Munoz, George 1951- *WhoHisp 91*
Munoz, Hector M *BiDrAPA 89*
Munoz, Joanne Maura *WhoHisp 91*
Munoz, John Anthony *WhoHisp 91*
Munoz, John Joaquin 1918- *WhoAm 90, WhoHisp 91*
Munoz, John Richard 1948- *WhoHisp 91*
Munoz, Jose E., Jr. 1946- *St&PR 91*
Munoz, Jose Luis 1945- *WhoHisp 91*
Munoz, Manuel Anthony 1945- *WhoHisp 91*
Munoz, Mario Alejandro 1928- *WhoWor 91*
Munoz, Memo 1955- *WhoHisp 91*
Munoz, Michael Anthony 1958- *WhoAm 90*
Munoz, Michael John 1963- *WhoHisp 91*
Munoz, Moises Garcia 1922- *WhoHisp 91*
Munoz, Paul Anthony 1948- *WhoE 91*
Munoz, Raul 1932- *WhoHisp 91*
Munoz, Raymond Anibal 1933- *WhoSSW 91*
Munoz, Rie *WhoAmA 91*
Munoz, Robert Francis 1953- *WhoEmL 91*
Munoz, Robinson J *BiDrAPA 89*
Munoz, Rodrigo A 1939- *BiDrAPA 89*
Munoz, Rodrigo Jose *BiDrAPA 89*
Munoz, Steven Michael 1952- *WhoSSW 91*

Munoz, Victor Ballpl 90
Munoz, Victoria WhoHisp 91
Munoz, Willy Oscar 1949- WhoHisp 91
Munoz-Andrade, Oscar Eduardo BiDrAPA 89
Munoz-Blanco, Maria M. 1963- WhoHisp 91
Munoz de Bustillo, Rafael 1957- WhoWor 91
Munoz Marin, Luis 1898-1980 BioIn 16, HispWr 90, WorAlBi
Munoz-Mellowes, Carlos Rafael BiDrAPA 89
Munoz-Millan, Robinson Jorge WhoE 91
Munoz Molina, Antonio 1956- IntvSpW [port]
Munoz Nunez, Rafael 1925- WhoAm 90
Munoz-Perez, Jose Maria 1964- WhoWor 91
Munoz Rivera, Luis 1859-1916 BioIn 16
Munoz-Sandoval, Ana Felicia 1947- WhoHisp 91
Munoz Vega, Pablo 1903- WhoWor 91
Munro, Alice 1931- ConAu 33NR, CurBio 90 [port], FemiCLE, MajTwCW, WhoAm 90, WhoAmW 91, WorAlBi, WorAu 1980 [port]
Munro, C. Lynn 1949- WhoAmW 91
Munro, Charles Robert Orrock 1925- WhoAm 90
Munro, Cristina Stirling 1940- WhoAmW 91
Munro, Dana Gardner NewYTBS 90
Munro, Dana Gardner 1892-1990 ConAu 131
Munro, Donald Jacques 1931- WhoAm 90
Munro, Eleanor 1928- WhoAmA 91
Munro, Eleanor C. 1928- AuBYP 90
Munro, Evelyn Smith 1914- EncAL
Munro, George 1825-1896 DcCanB 12
Munro, Georgina FemiCLE
Munro, H H 1870-1916 ConAu 130, MajTwCW
Munro, Hamish Nisbet 1915- WhoAm 90
Munro, Hector H. ConAu 130
Munro, Hedi 1916- WhoAmW 91
Munro, J. Richard BioIn 16
Munro, J. Richard 1931- WhoAm 90
Munro, James TwCCr&M 91
Munro, Janet 1934-1972 BioIn 16
Munro, Janet Andrea 1949- WhoAmA 91
Munro, John Henry Alexander 1938- WhoAm 90
Munro, John Stuart 1954- BiDrAPA 89
Munro, Joseph Barnes, Jr. 1930- WhoE 91, WhoWor 91
Munro, Meredith Vance 1938- WhoAm 90
Munro, Peter 1930- WhoWor 91
Munro, Ralph Davies 1943- WhoAm 90
Munro, Richard Grant 1935- WhoAm 90
Munro, Robert C. 1932- St&PR 91
Munro, Roxie AuBYP 90
Munro, Roxie 1945- BioIn 16
Munro, Sanford Sterling, Jr. 1932- WhoAm 90
Munro, Thomas 1761-1827 BioIn 16
Munro, Thomas 1897-1974 WhoAmA 91N
Munro, William G. 1926- St&PR 91
Munroe, Donna Scott 1945- WhoAmW 91, WhoEmL 91
Munroe, George B. 1922- St&PR 91
Munroe, George Barber 1922- WhoAm 90
Munroe, James Edward 1923- St&PR 91
Munroe, John MacGregor 1931- WhoSSW 91
Munroe, Maria Lyn 1946- WhoAmW 91
Munroe, Martin J. BioIn 16
Munroe, Mary Lou Schwarz 1927- WhoAmW 91
Munroe, Pat 1916- WhoAm 90
Munroe, Shirley Ann 1924- WhoAmW 91
Munroe, Thomas E. 1937- St&PR 91
Munrow, David 1942-1976 PenDiMP
Muns Albuixech, Joaquim 1935- WhoWor 91
Munsat, Stanley Morris 1939- WhoAm 90, WhoWrEP 89
Munsat, Theodore L. 1930- WhoAm 90
Munsch, Robert N. 1945- BioIn 16
Munschauer, Frederick E., Jr. 1920- St&PR 91
Munsel, Patrice 1925- IntWWM 90
Munsell, Elsie Louise 1939- WhoAm 90
Munsell, Everett William 1925- St&PR 91
Munsell, F Darrell 1934- ConAu 129
Munsell, Susan Grimes 1951- WhoAmW 91
Munsey, Bernice Ann Wilson 1935- WhoE 91
Munsey, Douglas Finley 1955- BiDrAPA 89, WhoE 91
Munsey, Frank A. 1854-1925 BioIn 16
Munsey, Virdell Everard, Jr. 1933- WhoAm 90
Munshaw, Nancy Clare 1947- WhoAmW 91
Munshi, Autar Krishen BiDrAPA 89
Munshi, Sushil Gajendrari 1939- St&PR 91
Munshower, Suzanne ODwPR 91
Munsick, Lee Ronald 1936- WhoE 91
Munsky, Maina Miriam 1943- BiDWomA
Munson, Alex K 1932- BiDrAPA 89
Munson, Alex Robert 1941- WhoAm 90
Munson, Alexander Lee 1931- WhoAm 90
Munson, Alfred D 1923- BiDrAPA 89
Munson, Arvid Washburn 1933- WhoAm 90
Munson, Carrie BioIn 16
Munson, Courtney John 1941- WhoAm 90
Munson, Edwin Palmer 1935- St&PR 91
Munson, Gorham 1896-1969 AuBYP 90
Munson, H. Carl 1930- St&PR 91
Munson, Harold Lewis 1923- WhoAm 90
Munson, Howard G. 1924- WhoAm 90, WhoE 91
Munson, Janis Elizabeth Tremblay 1948- WhoAmW 91
Munson, John Backus 1933- WhoAm 90, WhoWor 91
Munson, John Christian 1926- WhoAm 90
Munson, Julie Ann 1950- WhoAmW 91
Munson, Lawrence Shipley 1920- WhoAm 90
Munson, Lucille Marguerite 1914- WhoAmW 91
Munson, Nancy Kay 1936- WhoAmW 91, WhoE 91, WhoWor 91
Munson, Paul Lewis 1910- WhoAm 90
Munson, Richard Howard 1948- WhoE 91
Munson, Shipley John 1958- WhoAm 90
Munson, Stephen W BiDrAPA 89
Munson, Thurman 1947-1979 Ballpl 90 [port], WorAlBi
Munson, Virginia Aldrich 1932- WhoWor 91
Munson, William Leslie 1941- WhoAm 90
Munster, Anna J 1913- BiDrAPA 89
Munster, Sebastien 1489-1552 BioIn 16
Munsterberg, Hugo 1863-1916 EncPaPR 91
Munsterberg, Hugo 1916- WhoAm 90, WhoAmA 91, WhoWrEP 89
Muntasir, Umar Mustafa al- 1930- WhoWor 91
Munter, Gabriele 1877-1962 BiDWomA, BioIn 16
Munter, Larry Arlan 1945- WhoEmL 91
Munter, Preston K 1920- BiDrAPA 89
Munthe, Nelly 1947- BioIn 16
Munthe-Kaas, Harald 1937- WhoWor 91
Muntz, Andrew John 1952- WhoEmL 91
Muntz, Eric Phillip 1934- WhoAm 90
Muntz, Ernest Gordon 1923- WhoAm 90
Muntz, Richard Karl 1951- WhoEmL 91
Muntzer, Thomas 1490?-1525 BioIn 16
Muntzing, Lewis Manning 1934- WhoAm 90, WhoE 91
Munver, Uttam L BiDrAPA 89
Munves, David W. 1955- St&PR 91
Munves, James Albert 1922- WhoE 91
Munyon, William H 1931- BiDrAPA 89
Munz, Mary BioIn 16
Munzel, Edgar 1907- Ballpl 90
Munzenrider, Robert Emmett 1945- St&PR 91
Munzer, Cynthia Brown 1948- WhoAm 90
Munzer, Eleanor Roe 1921- WhoAmW 91
Munzer, Jean BiDrAPA 89
Munzer, Martha 1899- AuBYP 90
Munzer, Robert A. 1942- St&PR 91
Munzer, Stephen Ira 1939- WhoWor 91
Munzer, Thomas 1490?-1525 BioIn 16
Munzingen, Anna von EncCoWW
Munzner, Aribert 1930- WhoAmA 91
Muorie, Ida Rosemary 1950- WhoAmW 91
Mupo, Angelo 1944- St&PR 91
Muqtadir, Syeda S BiDrAPA 89
Mur, Raphael 1927- WhoAm 90
Mura, Linda A. ODwPR 91
Mura, Marlene BioIn 16
Mura, Peter 1924- IntWWM 90
Mura, Steve 1955- Ballpl 90
Mura, Toshio 1925- WhoAm 90
Muracco, Louis J. 1939- St&PR 91
Murad, Edmond 1934- WhoE 91
Murad, Ferid 1936- WhoAm 90
Murad, John Louis 1932- WhoAm 90
Murad, Tarrunumn 1951- WhoAmW 91
Murad, Thierry Joseph Lee 1960- WhoSSW 91
Muradian, Vazgen 1921- IntWWM 90, WhoAm 90
Murai, Hajime Teri 1953- IntWWM 90
Murai, Norimoto 1944- WhoSSW 91
Murakami, Glenn Hideo 1946- WhoEmL 91
Murakami, Glenn Nobuki 1953- St&PR 91
Murakami, Koji 1931- WhoWor 91
Murakami, Masanori 1944- Ballpl 90
Murakami, Takashi 1937- WhoWor 91
Murakami, Yasusuke 1931- WhoWor 91
Murakhovskiy, Vsevolod Serafimovich 1926- WhoWor 91
Muraliraj, Jhansi BiDrAPA 89
Muralles, Carlos A BiDrAPA 89
Muramatsu, Ichiro 1928- WhoWor 91
Muranaka, Hideo 1946- WhoAmA 91
Murane, William Edward 1933- WhoAm 90
Muranishi, Shozo 1932- WhoWor 91
Murany, Andrew J. 1944- St&PR 91
Muranyi, Gustave 1872-1961 WhoAmA 91N
Murao, Motoaki 1942- WhoWor 91
Murasaki Shikibu 97-?- EncJap
Murasaki, Shikibu 978?-1026? WorAlBi
Murase, Jiro 1928- WhoAm 90, WhoWor 91
Murase, Robert K. BioIn 16
Murashima, Kumiko WhoAmA 91, WhoAmW 91, WhoE 91
Muraski, Anthony Augustus 1946- WhoEmL 91, WhoWor 91
Murasky, Thomas F. 1945- St&PR 91
Murasugi, Kunio 1929- WhoAm 90
Murat, Amelie 1882-1940 EncCoWW
Murat, Ines 1939- ConAu 130
Murat, Joachim 1767-1815 WorAlBi
Murata, Akira 1921- WhoAm 90
Murata, Akira 1935- WhoWor 91
Murata, Hiroshi 1941- WhoAmA 91
Murata, Kaneji BioIn 16
Murata, Kiyoaki 1922- ConAu 130
Murata, Ryohei 1929- BioIn 16, WhoWor 91
Murata, Tadao 1938- WhoAm 90
Muratore, Carmine J. 1934- St&PR 91
Muratore, Lucien PenDiMP
Muratore, Peter Frederick 1932- WhoAm 90
Muratori, Fred 1951- WhoWrEP 89
Muratori, Walter James 1943- St&PR 91
Muratorio, Jose Luis 1918- BiDrAPA 89
Murawinski, Daniel Jude 1949- WhoE 91
Murawski, Juanita Marie BiDrAPA 89
Murawski, Thomas Frank 1945- St&PR 91, WhoAm 90
Murayama, Hiromi 1941- WhoWor 91
Murayama, Makio 1912- WhoAm 90, WhoWor 91
Murayama, Minoru 1936- Ballpl 90
Murbach, David Paul 1952- WhoE 91
Murbach, Jack Wesley BiDrAPA 89
Murbach, Jacob Frederick 1911- WhoE 91
Murburg, M Michele BiDrAPA 89
Murcer, Bobby 1946- Ballpl 90 [port]
Murch, Anna Valentina 1948- WhoAmA 91
Murch, Gary L. St&PR 91
Murch, Karl D. 1954- St&PR 91
Murch, Stephen Dean 1956- St&PR 91
Murch, Walter 1907-1967 WhoAmA 91N
Murchake, John Phillip 1922- St&PR 91
Murcheck, Theodore Robert 1939- WhoE 91
Murchie, Donald John 1943- WhoAmA 91
Murchie, Edward M. 1947- St&PR 91
Murchie, Edward Michael 1947- WhoAm 90
Murchie, Guy 1907- WhoAm 90
Murchie, James 1813-1900 DcCanB 12
Murchie, James Skiffington WhoAm 90
Murchison, Bruce K. St&PR 91
Murchison, David Claudius 1923- WhoAm 90, WhoE 91, WhoWor 91
Murchison, John D 1921-1979 WhoAmA 91N
Murchison, Laura Edwards 1954- WhoAmW 91, WhoSSW 91
Murchison, Nola Faye 1929- WhoAmW 91
Murcia, Andy BioIn 16
Murciano, Marianne 1957- WhoHisp 91
Murden, Jane Patricia 1956- WhoEmL 91
Murdoch, Anna BioIn 16
Murdoch, Bernard Constantine 1917- WhoAm 90
Murdoch, Britton 1957- St&PR 91
Murdoch, David Armor 1942- WhoE 91, WhoWor 91
Murdoch, Helen Hembree 1928- St&PR 91
Murdoch, Iris BioIn 16
Murdoch, Iris 1919- FemiCLE, MajTwCW, WhoAm 90, WhoWor 91, WorAlBi, WrPh
Murdoch, Lawrence Corlies, Jr. 1926- St&PR 91, WhoAm 90
Murdoch, Richard 1907- ConTFT 8 [port]
Murdoch, Robert John 1946- WhoAm 90
Murdoch, Robert W. WhoAm 90
Murdoch, Robert W. 1942- St&PR 91
Murdoch, Robert Whitten 1937- WhoE 91, WhoWor 91
Murdoch, Rupert BioIn 16
Murdoch, Rupert 1931- NewYTBS 90 [port], WhoAm 90, WhoWor 91, WorAlBi
Murdoch, William G C, Jr. BiDrAPA 89
Murdoch, William R. BioIn 16
Murdock, Betsy Boland 1949- WhoAmW 91
Murdock, Chad Lewis BiDrAPA 89
Murdock, Charles William 1935- WhoAm 90
Murdock, David H. BioIn 16
Murdock, David H. 1923- WhoAm 90
Murdock, Douglas William 1950- WhoEmL 91
Murdock, Eugene Converse 1921- WhoAm 90
Murdock, Greg 1954- WhoAmA 91
Murdock, Harold George, Jr. 1935- St&PR 91
Murdock, Jay Walter 1947- WhoSSW 91
Murdock, John Carey 1922- WhoAm 90
Murdock, Joyce Marilyn 1929- WhoAmW 91
Murdock, M S 1947- ConAu 32NR
Murdock, Mary-Elizabeth 1930- WhoAm 90
Murdock, Michele 1942- WhoAmW 91
Murdock, Michelle Marie 1959- WhoAmW 91
Murdock, Mickey Lane 1942- St&PR 91
Murdock, Moni 1938- WhoAmW 91
Murdock, Pamela Ervilla 1940- WhoAmW 91
Murdock, R.B. 1932- St&PR 91
Murdock, Robert Mead 1941- WhoAm 90, WhoAmA 91
Murdock, Robert Miller 1911- St&PR 91
Murdock, Ronald Wayne 1946- WhoSSW 91
Murdock, Stuart Laird 1926- St&PR 91, WhoAm 90
Murdy, Wayne W. 1944- St&PR 91
Murdy, Wayne William 1944- WhoAm 90
Mure, David William Alexander 1912-1986 SpyFic
Mure, Frank Thomas 1927- St&PR 91
Murena, H. A. HispWr 90
Murena, Hector Alberto Alvarez HispWr 90
Murer, Christoph 1558-1614 PenDiDA 89
Murer, Josias 1564-1630 PenDiDA 89
Murfee, Donald Gilbert, Jr. 1944- St&PR 91
Murfee, Elizabeth 1946- ODwPR 91
Murfee, Mary N. 1850-1922 BioAmW
Murff, William Denton 1922- St&PR 91
Murfin, Donald Leon 1943- WhoAm 90
Murfin, Mark 1913- WhoAm 90
Murfin, Ross C 1948- WhoAm 90
Murfree, Mary Noailles 1850-1922 FemiCLE
Murgel, George Anthony 1954- WhoE 91, WhoEmL 91
Murguia, D. Edward 1943- WhoHisp 91
Murguia, Filiberto 1932- WhoHisp 91
Muria i Romani, Anna 1904- EncCoWW
Murias, Alfredo Ortiz- BioIn 16
Murillo, Bartolome 1618?-1682 WorAlBi
Murillo, Bartolome Esteban 1617-1682 IntDcAA 90 [port]
Murillo, Gerardo 1875-1964 ArtLatA
Murillo, Juan Bravo 1803-1873 BioIn 16
Murillo, Luis G BiDrAPA 89
Murillo-Rohde, Ildaura Maria WhoAm 90
Murinde, Victor Mwerinde 1956- WhoWor 91
Murino, Clifford John 1929- WhoAm 90
Muriot, Edward E. 1924- St&PR 91
Muris, Timothy Joseph 1949- WhoAm 90, WhoEmL 91
Murison, Gerald Leonard 1939- WhoSSW 91
Murkett, Philip Tillotson 1931- WhoSSW 91
Murkofsky, Charles A BiDrAPA 89
Murkowski, Frank Hughes 1933- WhoAm 90, WhoWor 91
Murley, F.S. 1934- St&PR 91
Murley, Harris D 1937- BiDrAPA 89
Murlin-Gardner, Michelle 1964- WhoAmW 91
Murlowski, R.L. St&PR 91
Murnaghan, Francis Dominic, Jr. 1920- WhoAm 90, WhoE 91
Murnane, James A. 1933- St&PR 91
Murnane, Thomas William 1936- WhoE 91
Murnane, Tim 1852-1917 Ballpl 90
Murnin, Bette F. 1918- WhoAmW 91
Muro, Amado ConAu 131, HispWr 90
Muro, Michael John 1949- WhoE 91
Muro, Roy Alfred 1942- St&PR 91, WhoAm 90
Muro-Garcia, Linda Christine 1951- WhoAmW 91, WhoWor 91
Murobuse, Fumiro 1925- WhoWor 91
Muroff, Lawrence Ross 1942- WhoAm 90, WhoWor 91
Muroyama, Paul Michihisa 1950- WhoE 91
Murphey, Arthur Gage, Jr. 1927- WhoAm 90
Murphey, Bradford G 1925- BiDrAPA 89
Murphey, Dennis Donn 1949- WhoSSW 91
Murphey, Elwood 1909- WhoAm 90

Murphey, Michael Martin WhoNeCM [port]
Murphey, Murray Griffin 1928- WhoAm 90
Murphey, Rhoads 1919- WhoAm 90
Murphey, Robert J. 1934- St&PR 91
Murphey, Robert Stafford 1921- St&PR 91, WhoAm 90
Murphree, Gwendolyn Cribbs 1921- WhoWor 91
Murphree, Henry Bernard Scott 1927- BiDrAPA 89, WhoE 91
Murphree, Jon Tal 1936- WhoSSW 91
Murphree, Sharon Ann 1949- WhoAmW 91, WhoEmL 91, WhoSSW 91, WhoWor 91
Murphy, Alan Gregory, Jr. 1940- St&PR 91
Murphy, Albert Thomas 1924- WhoAm 90
Murphy, Alfred W 1921- BiDrAPA 89
Murphy, Alvin Leo 1934- WhoSSW 91
Murphy, Andrew Lawrence BioIn 16
Murphy, Ann Pleshette BioIn 16
Murphy, Anne G. 1950- WhoAmW 91
Murphy, Anne M. 1926-1989 BioIn 16
Murphy, Anne St. Germaine 1951- WhoAmW 91
Murphy, Annette C. BioIn 16
Murphy, Arthur Ellery 1948- WhoSSW 91
Murphy, Arthur Lister 1906-1985 OxCCanT
Murphy, Arthur Thomas 1929- WhoAm 90, WhoE 91
Murphy, Arthur William 1922- WhoAm 90
Murphy, Audie BioIn 16
Murphy, Austin de la Salle 1917- WhoAm 90
Murphy, Austin John 1927- WhoAm 90, WhoE 91
Murphy, Austin S. 1917- St&PR 91
Murphy, B William 1921- BiDrAPA 89
Murphy, Barry Ames 1938- WhoAm 90
Murphy, Barry John 1940- WhoAm 90
Murphy, Beatrice Campbell 1908- HarlReB
Murphy, Ben Preston, Jr. 1923- St&PR 91
Murphy, Benjamin Edward 1942- WhoAm 90
Murphy, Bernard Thomas 1932- WhoAm 90
Murphy, Betty Jane Southard WhoAm 90, WhoE 91
Murphy, Beverley Elaine Pearson 1929- WhoAm 90
Murphy, Brenda B. St&PR 91
Murphy, Brian Alfred 1949- BioIn 16
Murphy, C. W. 1875-1913 OxCPMus
Murphy, Calvin 1948- WorAlBi
Murphy, Carl L. 1922- St&PR 91
Murphy, Carol Ann 1942- WhoAmW 91
Murphy, Carole BiDrAPA 89
Murphy, Catherine 1946- BiDWomA, WhoE 91
Murphy, Catherine C. St&PR 91
Murphy, Catherine E 1946- WhoAmA 91
Murphy, Charles Arnold BiDrAPA 89
Murphy, Charles Arnold 1932- WhoAm 90
Murphy, Charles D., III 1944- St&PR 91
Murphy, Charles H. 1945- St&PR 91
Murphy, Charles H., Jr. BioIn 16
Murphy, Charles Haywood, Jr. 1920- St&PR 91, WhoAm 90, WhoSSW 91
Murphy, Charles Joseph 1947- WhoAm 90
Murphy, Charles W. Ballpl 90
Murphy, Chester Glenn 1907- WhoAmA 91
Murphy, Christopher J., III 1946- St&PR 91
Murphy, Christopher Joseph, III 1946- WhoAm 90
Murphy, Colette ODwPR 91
Murphy, Colin T. 1949- St&PR 91
Murphy, Colleen Frances 1960- WhoAmW 91
Murphy, Colleen Patricia 1943- WhoAmW 91
Murphy, Cornelius Joseph 1930- St&PR 91
Murphy, Cyril Daniel 1941- St&PR 91
Murphy, Dale BioIn 16
Murphy, Dale 1956- Ballpl 90 [port], WorAlBi
Murphy, Dale Bryan 1956- WhoAm 90
Murphy, Daniel Hayes, II 1941- WhoAm 90
Murphy, Daniel J. 1922- ODwPR 91
Murphy, Daniel R. St&PR 91
Murphy, Daniel R. 1941- ODwPR 91
Murphy, Daniel T. 1939- St&PR 91
Murphy, Danny 1876-1955 Ballpl 90
Murphy, Danny 1942- Ballpl 90
Murphy, David Frank 1946- WhoSSW 91
Murphy, David McGregor 1917- St&PR 91
Murphy, David Thomas 1929- WhoAm 90
Murphy, Dawn W BiDrAPA 89
Murphy, De Bora Clara BiDrAPA 89
Murphy, Debora Herrmann 1959- WhoE 91
Murphy, Deborah June 1955- WhoAmW 91
Murphy, Denise Ann 1957- WhoAmW 91
Murphy, Dennis F. 1937- St&PR 91, WhoAm 90
Murphy, Dennis Patrick 1958- WhoE 91, WhoEmL 91, WhoWor 91
Murphy, Derek James Murtagh 1946- WhoWor 91
Murphy, Dervla 1931- BioIn 16, FemiCLE
Murphy, Diana E. 1934- WhoAm 90, WhoAmW 91
Murphy, Dominic Ignatius 1847-1930 BioIn 16
Murphy, Donald 1938- St&PR 91
Murphy, Donald B. 1940- St&PR 91
Murphy, Donald Daniel 1946- WhoE 91
Murphy, Donald Gerald 1948- St&PR 91
Murphy, Douglas E. 1926- St&PR 91
Murphy, Dudley C 1940- WhoAmA 91
Murphy, Dwayne 1955- Ballpl 90
Murphy, E. C. 1926- ODwPR 91
Murphy, E. Jefferson 1926- AuBYP 90
Murphy, Ed 1877-1935 Ballpl 90
Murphy, Eddie BioIn 16
Murphy, Eddie 1891-1969 Ballpl 90
Murphy, Eddie 1961- DrBlPA 90, WhoAm 90, WorAlBi
Murphy, Edmond Lawrence 1931- St&PR 91
Murphy, Edmund Michael 1936- WhoAm 90
Murphy, Edrie Lee 1953- WhoAmW 91
Murphy, Edward Arthur 1941- St&PR 91
Murphy, Edward Francis BioIn 16
Murphy, Edward Jerome, Jr 1938- WhoE 91
Murphy, Edward Patrick, Jr. 1943- WhoAm 90
Murphy, Edwin J. 1932- St&PR 91
Murphy, Eileen Margaret 1956- WhoAmW 91
Murphy, Elizabeth D. ODwPR 91
Murphy, Elliott BioIn 16
Murphy, Ellis WhoAm 90
Murphy, Elsie M. BioIn 16
Murphy, Emily 1868-1933 DcLB 99 [port], FemiCLE
Murphy, Ernest Walter 1930- St&PR 91
Murphy, Eugene 1930- St&PR 91
Murphy, Eugene F. 1936- WhoAm 90
Murphy, Eugene Francis 1913- WhoAm 90
Murphy, Eva Thompson 1936- WhoE 91
Murphy, Evelyn Francis 1940- WhoAm 90, WhoAmW 91, WhoE 91
Murphy, Ewell Edward, Jr. 1928- WhoAm 90
Murphy, Frances Louise, II WhoAmW 91
Murphy, Francie 1955- ODwPR 91
Murphy, Francine 1940- WhoAmW 91
Murphy, Francis 1932- WhoAm 90
Murphy, Francis H. 1938- St&PR 91
Murphy, Francis J. 1946- St&PR 91
Murphy, Francis Seward 1914- WhoWor 91
Murphy, Frank 1890-1949 BiDrUSE 89
Murphy, Franklin David 1916- WhoAm 90, WhoWor 91
Murphy, Galvin Charles 1934- WhoE 91
Murphy, Gardner 1895-1979 EncO&P 3, EncPaPR 91
Murphy, Gary Peter 1948- WhoEmL 91
Murphy, George 1902- WorAlBi
Murphy, George E 1922- BiDrAPA 89
Murphy, George Evans, Jr. 1941- St&PR 91
Murphy, George Francis, Jr. 1924- WhoAm 90
Murphy, George William 1935- St&PR 91
Murphy, Gerald BioIn 16
Murphy, Gerald 1938- WhoAm 90
Murphy, Gerald D. 1928- St&PR 91
Murphy, Gerald Patrick 1934- WhoAm 90
Murphy, Geraldine 1920-1990 BioIn 16, ConAu 131
Murphy, Gladys Wilkins 1907-1985 WhoAmA 91N
Murphy, Gordon John 1927- WhoAm 90
Murphy, Gordon Laurence 1935- St&PR 91, WhoAm 90
Murphy, Grace Elizabeth 1949- WhoAmW 91
Murphy, H. Gabriel 1903- St&PR 91
Murphy, Harold Loyd 1927- WhoAm 90, WhoSSW 91
Murphy, Harold Morgan 1925- St&PR 91
Murphy, Harry Aloysius 1940- BiDrAPA 89
Murphy, Hass 1950- WhoAmA 91
Murphy, Haughton ConAu 131
Murphy, Hayes Dewey 1950- WhoSSW 91
Murphy, Henry B. 1925- St&PR 91
Murphy, Herbert A 1911- WhoAmA 91
Murphy, Herman Dudley 1867-1945 BioIn 16
Murphy, Hoyt Campbell 1911- St&PR 91
Murphy, Irene Helen WhoAmW 91
Murphy, Isaac 1802-1882 BioIn 16
Murphy, J. Hugh 1932- St&PR 91
Murphy, J. Kevin 1927- WhoAm 90
Murphy, J. Neil 1934- WhoSSW 91
Murphy, Jacqueline BioIn 16
Murphy, James 1937- St&PR 91, WhoAm 90
Murphy, James Allen 1938- WhoAm 90
Murphy, James B., Jr. 1932- St&PR 91
Murphy, James Bryson, Jr. 1932- WhoAm 90
Murphy, James D. 1930- St&PR 91
Murphy, James E. ODwPR 91
Murphy, James F. 1933- WhoAm 90
Murphy, James F. 1934- St&PR 91
Murphy, James F. 1946- ODwPR 91
Murphy, James J. 1943- St&PR 91
Murphy, James Jean, Jr. 1933- WhoE 91
Murphy, James Joseph 1944- WhoAm 90, WhoWor 91
Murphy, James L. 1939- WhoAm 90
Murphy, James Lawson 1951- IntWWM 90
Murphy, James Milton 1927- BiDrAPA 89
Murphy, James R. 1922- St&PR 91
Murphy, James Richard 1957- WhoSSW 91
Murphy, Janet Gorman 1937- WhoAm 90, WhoAmW 91
Murphy, Jay 1948- WhoSSW 91
Murphy, Jeanette Carol 1931- WhoAmW 91
Murphy, Jeffrey John 1946- St&PR 91
Murphy, Jenny Long 1955- St&PR 91
Murphy, Jerome F. 1951- St&PR 91
Murphy, Jerrold Vaughn 1938- WhoSSW 91
Murphy, Jill 1949- AuBYP 90, BioIn 16
Murphy, Jim BioIn 16
Murphy, Jimmy 1892-1965 EncACom [port]
Murphy, Jo Anne WhoAmW 91
Murphy, Joanne Becker WhoAmW 91
Murphy, Joanne M. 1957- WhoAmW 91
Murphy, Joanne McCormick 1932- WhoAmW 91
Murphy, John A. 1931- St&PR 91
Murphy, John Anthony 1939- WhoAm 90, WhoE 91
Murphy, John Arthur 1929- St&PR 91, WhoAm 90, WhoE 91, WhoWor 91
Murphy, John Benjamin 1857-1916 BioIn 16
Murphy, John C. BioIn 16
Murphy, John Carter 1921- WhoAm 90
Murphy, John Cullen 1919- EncACom, WhoAm 90
Murphy, John F. 1930-1989 BioIn 16
Murphy, John Francis 1923- WhoAm 90
Murphy, John Francis 1937- WhoE 91
Murphy, John George BioIn 16, NewYTBS 90
Murphy, John J., Jr. 1920- St&PR 91
Murphy, John Joseph 1931- St&PR 91, WhoAm 90, WhoSSW 91
Murphy, John Joseph, Jr. 1951- WhoWor 91
Murphy, John Montague BiDrAPA 89
Murphy, John N. 1939- WhoE 91
Murphy, John P. 1945- ODwPR 91
Murphy, John R. 1934- St&PR 91
Murphy, John Thomas 1928- WhoSSW 91
Murphy, John Vincent 1949- St&PR 91
Murphy, John W 1948- ConAu 30NR
Murphy, Johnny 1908-1970 Ballpl 90 [port]
Murphy, Joseph F. 1915- WhoAm 90
Murphy, Joseph F, Jr. 1922- BiDrAPA 89
Murphy, Joseph J. 1939- St&PR 91
Murphy, Joseph S. 1933- WhoAm 90, WhoE 91
Murphy, Joseph T. 1940- St&PR 91
Murphy, Joy Waldron 1942- WhoWrEP 89
Murphy, Judith Chisholm 1942- WhoAmW 91
Murphy, Juneann 1937- WhoAmW 91
Murphy, Kathleen Ann 1950- St&PR 91
Murphy, Kathleen Mary 1945- WhoAmW 91
Murphy, Kathryn Cochrane 1949- WhoE 91
Murphy, Kathryn Marguerite WhoAmW 91
Murphy, Kay Ann 1942- WhoWrEP 89
Murphy, Kenneth Ray 1958- WhoSSW 91
Murphy, Kenneth T. 1937- St&PR 91, WhoAm 90
Murphy, Kevin George 1952- WhoE 91
Murphy, Kevin K. 1962- WhoE 91, WhoEmL 91
Murphy, Kevin La Bran BiDrAPA 89
Murphy, Larry Duane 1942- WhoAm 90
Murphy, Lewis Curtis 1933- WhoAm 90
Murphy, Linda Sue 1948- WhoAmW 91
Murphy, Louise 1943- LiHiK
Murphy, Mabel Ansley 1870- AuBYP 90
Murphy, Margaret H. 1948- WhoAmW 91
Murphy, Margarette Celestine Evans 1926- WhoAmW 91
Murphy, Marie Ann WhoE 91
Murphy, Marilyn L 1950- WhoAmA 91
Murphy, Mark Joseph 1956- St&PR 91
Murphy, Martha Wynne 1951- WhoEmL 91
Murphy, Martin 1934- ConAu 132
Murphy, Martin Charles 1952- WhoE 91
Murphy, Martin James 1951- WhoEmL 91
Murphy, Mary Ann BiDrAPA 89
Murphy, Mary Ann Burnett 1954- WhoAmW 91
Murphy, Mary C. WhoAmW 91
Murphy, Mary Kathleen Connors 1938- WhoAmW 91, WhoSSW 91, WhoWor 91
Murphy, Mary Kathryn 1941- WhoAmW 91
Murphy, Marynell 1954- WhoAmW 91
Murphy, Matthew M. 1956- WhoEmL 91
Murphy, Maureen Ann 1935- WhoAmW 91
Murphy, Melinda Lynn 1944- WhoAmW 91
Murphy, Michael 1930- EncPaPR 91, WhoWrEP 89
Murphy, Michael 1948- BiDrAPA 89
Murphy, Michael Conlon 1937- WhoAm 90, WhoSSW 91
Murphy, Michael D BiDrAPA 89
Murphy, Michael Denis 1956- WhoWor 91
Murphy, Michael E. 1936- St&PR 91
Murphy, Michael Emmett 1936- WhoAm 90
Murphy, Michael F 1946- BiDrAPA 89
Murphy, Michael George 1938- WhoAm 90
Murphy, Michael Joseph 1915- WhoAm 90, WhoE 91
Murphy, Michael R. 1947- WhoEmL 91
Murphy, Michael W. 1891-1990 BioIn 16
Murphy, Michael William 1949- St&PR 91
Murphy, Minnette Black BiDrAPA 89
Murphy, Morg 1867-1938 Ballpl 90
Murphy, Myles Patrick 1962- WhoE 91
Murphy, Myrlin Lee BiDrAPA 89
Murphy, Nancy Ann 1936- WhoAmW 91
Murphy, Nancy L. 1929- WhoAmW 91
Murphy, Nancy Lee 1933- St&PR 91
Murphy, Newton Jerome 1928- WhoAm 90
Murphy, Nora Sharkey 1940- WhoE 91
Murphy, Patrice Ann 1955- WhoWrEP 89
Murphy, Patricia 1959- WhoAmW 91
Murphy, Patricia A WhoAmW 91
Murphy, Patricia Sue 1961- WhoAmW 91
Murphy, Patrick Dennis 1951- WhoWrEP 89
Murphy, Patrick F. 1951- St&PR 91
Murphy, Patrick Francis 1958- WhoSSW 91
Murphy, Patrick Gregory 1947- WhoSSW 91
Murphy, Paul C. 1944- St&PR 91
Murphy, Paul F. 1956- St&PR 91
Murphy, Paul Warren 1949- BiDrAPA 89
Murphy, Peter ODwPR 91
Murphy, Peter Francis 1955- WhoEmL 91
Murphy, Peter Francis, III 1950- WhoEmL 91
Murphy, Philip Francis 1933- WhoE 91
Murphy, R. Anthony 1947- WhoEmL 91
Murphy, Ralph Edgar 1931- WhoE 91, WhoWor 91
Murphy, Randall Kent 1943- WhoSSW 91, WhoWor 91
Murphy, Randolph BiDrAPA 89
Murphy, Regina 1945 WhoE 91
Murphy, Rhonda Foster 1962- WhoAmW 91
Murphy, Richard WhoAm 90
Murphy, Richard William 1929- BioIn 16, WhoAm 90
Murphy, Rob 1960- Ballpl 90
Murphy, Robert Anthony, Jr. 1953- WhoEmL 91
Murphy, Robert Barry 1954- WhoE 91
Murphy, Robert Blair 1931- WhoE 91
Murphy, Robert Brady Lawrence 1905- WhoAm 90
Murphy, Robert C 1915- BiDrAPA 89
Murphy, Robert Charles 1926- WhoAm 90, WhoE 91
Murphy, Robert D. 1894-1978 BioIn 16
Murphy, Robert Earl 1941- WhoAm 90
Murphy, Robert Francis NewYTBS 90
Murphy, Robert Francis 1921- WhoAm 90
Murphy, Robert Harry 1938- St&PR 91, WhoAm 90
Murphy, Robert William 1902-1971 AuBYP 90
Murphy, Robin ODwPR 91
Murphy, Roderick Patrick 1939- WhoE 91
Murphy, Rose 1913- DrBlPA 90
Murphy, Rose 1913-1989 AnObit 1989, BioIn 16, OxCPMus
Murphy, Rosemary WhoAm 90

Murphy, Rowley Walter 1891-1975 *WhoAmA 91N*
Murphy, Roy James 1927- *St&PR 91*
Murphy, Ruth M 1922- *BiDrAPA 89*
Murphy, Ruth Markmann 1922- *WhoE 91*
Murphy, Samuel Wilson, Jr. 1927- *St&PR 91, WhoAm 90*
Murphy, Sandra Jean 1950- *WhoAmW 91*
Murphy, Sara *BioIn 16*
Murphy, Sara W. 1883-1975 *BioAmW*
Murphy, Sean K. *ODwPR 91*
Murphy, Sharon Ann 1947- *BiDrAPA 89*
Murphy, Sharon Funcheon 1954- *WhoEmL 91*
Murphy, Sharon Margaret 1940- *WhoAm 90*
Murphy, Sheila E. 1951- *WhoWrEP 89*
Murphy, Sheila Ellen 1951- *WhoAmW 91*
Murphy, Sheldon Douglas 1933-1990 *BioIn 16*
Murphy, Shirley Rousseau 1928- *BioIn 16*
Murphy, Spencer A. *St&PR 91*
Murphy, Stephen Paul 1926- *St&PR 91*
Murphy, Stephen Vincent 1945- *St&PR 91*
Murphy, Steven John 1958- *St&PR 91*
Murphy, Steven Lee *BioIn 16*
Murphy, Susan 1950- *WhoAmA 91, WhoAmW 91*
Murphy, Suzanne *IntWWM 90*
Murphy, Tanya Kaye *BiDrAPA 89*
Murphy, Terence Donald 1937- *WhoWor 91*
Murphy, Terence Martin 1942- *WhoAm 90*
Murphy, Terence Roche 1937- *WhoE 91*
Murphy, Teresa Hodes 1955- *WhoAmW 91*
Murphy, Terrence John 1920- *WhoAm 90*
Murphy, Terry M. 1948- *St&PR 91*
Murphy, Therrell 1942- *St&PR 91*
Murphy, Thomas 1942- *WhoAm 90*
Murphy, Thomas Aquinas 1915- *EncABHB 5 [port], WhoAm 90*
Murphy, Thomas Austin 1911- *WhoAm 90*
Murphy, Thomas Bailey 1924- *WhoSSW 91*
Murphy, Thomas Bernard 1927- *St&PR 91*
Murphy, Thomas C 1932- *BiDrAPA 89*
Murphy, Thomas F. *BioIn 16*
Murphy, Thomas Francis 1905- *WhoAm 90*
Murphy, Thomas Francis 1942- *WhoE 91, WhoWor 91*
Murphy, Thomas G. 1952- *St&PR 91*
Murphy, Thomas James 1931- *St&PR 91*
Murphy, Thomas James 1956- *WhoEmL 91*
Murphy, Thomas John 1931- *WhoAm 90*
Murphy, Thomas Joseph 1932- *WhoAm 90*
Murphy, Thomas S. *BioIn 16*
Murphy, Thomas S. 1925- *St&PR 91, WhoAm 90, WhoE 91*
Murphy, Thomas W 1933- *BiDrAPA 89*
Murphy, Timothy 1751-1818 *WhNaAH*
Murphy, Timothy Alan 1954- *BiDrAPA 89*
Murphy, Timothy Edward 1947- *St&PR 91*
Murphy, Timothy Patrick 1928- *St&PR 91*
Murphy, Todd Robert 1953- *ODwPR 91*
Murphy, Tom 1945- *Ballpl 90*
Murphy, Turk 1915-1987 *OxCPMus*
Murphy, Vanissa Dawn 1953- *WhoAmW 91*
Murphy, Walter Francis 1929- *WhoAm 90, WhoWrEP 89*
Murphy, Walter James 1943- *WhoE 91*
Murphy, Walter Young 1930- *WhoAm 90*
Murphy, Warren 1933- *TwCCr&M 91*
Murphy, Warren B 1933- *ConAu 31NR*
Murphy, Warren Burton 1933- *WhoAm 90*
Murphy, William Beverly 1907- *WhoAm 90*
Murphy, William C. *BioIn 16*
Murphy, William E. 1918- *St&PR 91*
Murphy, William Holland 1931- *St&PR 91*
Murphy, William James 1927- *WhoAm 90*
Murphy, William K. 1940- *St&PR 91*
Murphy, William Michael 1916- *WhoAm 90*
Murphy, Winifred Lee 1931- *WhoWrEP 89*
Murphy-Kesling, Debra Jean 1954- *WhoEmL 91*
Murphy-Lydy, Mary 1870?- *EncO&P 3*
Murr, Danny Lee 1930- *WhoWrEP 89*
Murra, John Victor 1916- *WhoAm 90*
Murra, Prokop 1921- *WhoWor 91*
Murrah, Judith Ann 1958- *WhoE 91*
Murrah, Peggy Ferguson 1963- *WhoSSW 91*
Murray, A. Brean 1937- *WhoAm 90*
Murray, Albert 1906- *WhoAmA 91*
Murray, Albert L. 1916- *WhoAm 90*
Murray, Alison Jane 1964- *WhoEmL 91*
Murray, Allen Edward 1929- *St&PR 91, WhoAm 90, WhoE 91, WhoWor 91*
Murray, Angie Anna Alice 1949- *WhoAmW 91, WhoEmL 91, WhoSSW 91, WhoWor 91*
Murray, Anita Jean 1943- *WhoAmW 91, WhoE 91*
Murray, Ann 1949- *PenDiMP*
Murray, Ann Pennington 1959- *WhoWrEP 89*
Murray, Anne 1945- *ConMus 4 [port], WhoAm 90, WhoAmW 91, WorAlBi*
Murray, Anne 1947- *BioIn 16*
Murray, Arthur 1895- *WhoAm 90, WorAlBi*
Murray, Arthur A 1921- *BiDrAPA 89*
Murray, Arthur R. 1931- *St&PR 91*
Murray, Barbara J *BiDrAPA 89*
Murray, Betty Jean Kafka 1935- *WhoAmW 91*
Murray, Bill *BioIn 16*
Murray, Bill 1950- *WhoAm 90*
Murray, Bruce C. 1931- *WhoAm 90*
Murray, Bruce C. 1937- *St&PR 91, WhoAm 90*
Murray, Bryan Clarence 1942- *WhoAm 90, WhoE 91*
Murray, C.A., Jr. 1928- *St&PR 91*
Murray, Caroline Fish 1920- *WhoAm 90*
Murray, Cavlin J. 1924- *St&PR 91*
Murray, Charles 1943- *NewYTBS 90 [port]*
Murray, Charles Coursen 1933- *St&PR 91*
Murray, Charles Mansfield 1932- *WhoAm 90*
Murray, Cherry Ann 1952- *WhoAmW 91*
Murray, Cherry Roberts 1921- *WhoAmW 91*
Murray, Christine A *BiDrAPA 89*
Murray, Christopher Charles, III 1950- *WhoWor 91*
Murray, Claude Hollis 1930- *WhoWor 91*
Murray, Claude Robert, Jr. 1947- *WhoSSW 91*
Murray, Constance Ann 1929- *WhoAm 90*
Murray, Cynthia Ann 1956- *WhoAmW 91, WhoSSW 91*
Murray, Cynthia Jo 1959- *WhoAmW 91*
Murray, Dale 1950- *Ballpl 90*
Murray, Dale Norris 1945- *WhoSSW 91, WhoWor 91*
Murray, David 1925- *WhoAm 90*
Murray, David 1955- *BioIn 16*
Murray, David George 1930- *WhoAm 90*
Murray, David Paul 1953- *WhoE 91*
Murray, David Stuart 1953- *St&PR 91*
Murray, Delbert Milton 1941- *WhoWor 91*
Murray, Dennis Joseph 1946- *WhoAm 90, WhoE 91*
Murray, Don 1924- *AuBYP 90*
Murray, Don 1929- *WorAlBi*
Murray, Donald F. 1921- *St&PR 91*
Murray, Donald Patrick 1929- *WhoAm 90*
Murray, Doug 1947- *WhoE 91*
Murray, Douglas Timothy Gordon 1938- *WhoSSW 91*
Murray, E. Howard, Jr. 1959- *WhoSSW 91*
Murray, Eddie *BioIn 16*
Murray, Eddie 1956- *Ballpl 90 [port], WorAlBi*
Murray, Eddie Clarence 1956- *WhoAm 90*
Murray, Edmund P. *ODwPR 91*
Murray, Edward 1928- *WhoSSW 91*
Murray, Edward James 1928- *WhoE 91*
Murray, Edward N. 1921- *St&PR 91*
Murray, Eleanor F. 1916- *WhoAmW 91*
Murray, Elizabeth *BioIn 16*
Murray, Elizabeth 1815-1882 *BiDWomA*
Murray, Elizabeth 1940- *BiDWomA, WhoAm 90, WhoAmA 91*
Murray, Elizabeth Ann 1947- *WhoEmL 91*
Murray, Elizabeth Davis Reid 1925- *WhoAm 90*
Murray, Ernest Don 1930- *WhoAm 90*
Murray, Eunice Guthrie 1878-1960 *FemiCLE*
Murray, Feg *EncACom*
Murray, Florence Kerins 1916- *WhoAm 90, WhoAmW 91, WhoE 91*
Murray, Floretta May *WhoAmA 91*
Murray, Foster S *BiDrAPA 89*
Murray, Francis Eugene 1924- *WhoE 91, WhoWor 91*
Murray, Francis W., III 1928- *St&PR 91*
Murray, Frank Bush 1939- *WhoE 91*
Murray, Frank Waldo 1884-1956 *WhoAmA 91N*
Murray, Frederick Franklin 1950- *WhoEmL 91, WhoSSW 91, WhoWor 91*
Murray, Galen Keith 1950- *WhoEmL 91*
Murray, George 1898-1955 *Ballpl 90*
Murray, George Raymond 1935- *WhoAm 90*
Murray, George Washington 1853-1926 *BlkAmsC [port]*
Murray, Gerald E. 1945- *ODwPR 91*
Murray, Gerald Edward 1945- *WhoWrEP 89*
Murray, Geri D. 1927- *WhoAmW 91*
Murray, Gilbert 1866-1957 *EncO&P 3, EncPaPR 91*
Murray, Gladys Hall *AuBYP 90*
Murray, Glenn Richard, Jr. 1930- *WhoAm 90*
Murray, Graham Christopher 1948- *WhoWor 91*
Murray, Grisell 1692-1759 *FemiCLE*
Murray, Grover Elmer 1916- *WhoAm 90*
Murray, Harlan W. 1933- *St&PR 91*
Murray, Haydn H. *BioIn 16*
Murray, Haydn Herbert 1924- *WhoAm 90*
Murray, Henry A. 1893-1988 *BioIn 16*
Murray, Henry Wilke 1946- *WhoAm 90*
Murray, Herbert Frazier 1923- *WhoAm 90*
Murray, Hugh C 1932- *BiDrAPA 89*
Murray, Hugh T., Jr. 1938- *WhoWrEP 89*
Murray, Ian Stewart 1951- *WhoAmA 91*
Murray, J. Ralph 1916- *WhoAm 90*
Murray, J. Terrence 1939- *St&PR 91*
Murray, J. Thomas 1951- *WhoE 91*
Murray, Jack Dale 1946- *St&PR 91*
Murray, James Calhoun 1939- *St&PR 91*
Murray, James Cunningham, Jr. 1944- *WhoAm 90*
Murray, James Doyle 1938- *WhoAm 90, WhoE 91, WhoWor 91*
Murray, James Edward 1932- *WhoAm 90*
Murray, James Edwin 1946- *WhoEmL 91*
Murray, James G. 1934- *St&PR 91*
Murray, James H. 1928- *St&PR 91*
Murray, James Joseph, III 1933- *WhoAm 90*
Murray, James Lore 1919- *St&PR 91*
Murray, James Michael 1944- *WhoWor 91*
Murray, James P. *St&PR 91*
Murray, James P 1946- *DrBlPA 90*
Murray, James Patrick 1919- *WhoAm 90*
Murray, James W. *WhoAm 90*
Murray, Janet *BiDEWW*
Murray, Jean Carolyn 1927- *WhoAm 90, WhoAmW 91*
Murray, Jeanne *WhoAmW 91*
Murray, Jeanne Evelyn 1932- *WhoAmW 91*
Murray, Jeanne Morris 1925- *WhoSSW 91*
Murray, Jelena Jovanovic 1955- *WhoAmW 91*
Murray, Jesse George 1909- *WhoSSW 91*
Murray, Jo Bumbarger 1945- *WhoEmL 91*
Murray, Joan 1927- *WhoAmA 91*
Murray, Joan 1941- *DrBlPA 90*
Murray, Joan Elizabeth 1941- *WhoAm 90*
Murray, Joan Kathleen 1957- *WhoE 91*
Murray, Jody I. *St&PR 91*
Murray, John *EarBlAP*
Murray, John 1732-1809 *BioIn 16*
Murray, John 1741-1815 *EncCRAm*
Murray, John Arthur 1937- *St&PR 91*
Murray, John E, Jr. 1932- *ConAu 31NR*
Murray, John Edward, Jr. 1932- *WhoAm 90*
Murray, John Einar 1918- *WhoAm 90*
Murray, John F. 1939- *St&PR 91*
Murray, John Frederic 1927- *WhoAm 90*
Murray, John Joseph 1915- *WhoAm 90, WhoWor 91, WhoWrEP 89*
Murray, John L. 1927- *St&PR 91*
Murray, John Michael 1931- *WhoAmA 91*
Murray, John Morton 1933- *St&PR 91*
Murray, John Patrick 1943- *WhoAm 90*
Murray, John S. 1927- *St&PR 91*
Murray, John Thomas, Jr. 1922- *BiDrAPA 89*
Murray, John William, Jr. 1918- *St&PR 91*
Murray, Joseph 1694-1757 *EncCRAm*
Murray, Joseph Edward 1919- *WhoAm 90*
Murray, Joseph James, Jr. 1930- *WhoAm 90*
Murray, Joseph William 1944- *WhoAm 90, WhoE 91*
Murray, Judith 1751-1820 *FemiCLE*
Murray, Judith 1941- *WhoAmA 91, WhoE 91*
Murray, Judith Sargent 1751-1820 *BioAmW, EncCRAm*
Murray, Julia Harby *BiDrAPA 89*
Murray, Julia Kaoru 1934- *WhoAmW 91*
Murray, Kathleen Anne 1946- *WhoEmL 91*
Murray, Kathryn 1906- *WorAlBi*
Murray, Keith 1892-1981 *PenDiDA 89*
Murray, Kelley A. *ODwPR 91*
Murray, Ken 1903-1988 *BioIn 16*
Murray, Kenneth Richard 1938- *St&PR 91*
Murray, Lawrence 1939- *St&PR 91, WhoE 91, WhoWor 91*
Murray, Lawrence M. 1942- *St&PR 91*
Murray, Lee Winslow 1949- *WhoWrEP 89*
Murray, Leonard Hugh 1913- *WhoAm 90*
Murray, Les A 1938- *WorAu 1980 [port]*
Murray, Lillian Anderson 1943- *WhoAmW 91*
Murray, Lois A. Heil 1953- *WhoAmW 91*
Murray, Louisa 1818-1894 *FemiCLE*
Murray, Louisa Annie 1818-1894 *DcCanB 12*
Murray, Lowell *BioIn 16*
Murray, Lowell 1936- *WhoAm 90, WhoE 91*
Murray, Lucille M. 1911- *St&PR 91*
Murray, Lyn 1909-1989 *BioIn 16*
Murray, Margaret A 1863-1963 *EncO&P 3*
Murray, Marguerite 1917- *SmATA 63 [port]*
Murray, Marianne *ODwPR 91*
Murray, Marie Jeannine 1962- *WhoSSW 91*
Murray, Marilyn C. 1946- *WhoAmW 91*
Murray, Mark Andrew 1954- *WhoEmL 91*
Murray, Mark H. 1950- *St&PR 91*
Murray, Martha Jean *BiDrAPA 89*
Murray, Martin J 1945- *ConAu 132*
Murray, Mary *ODwPR 91*
Murray, Mary McFarlane 1947- *WhoAmW 91*
Murray, Mary Raymond 1947- *WhoAmW 91*
Murray, Maureen Theresa 1947- *WhoAmW 91*
Murray, Maurice Avery 1938- *St&PR 91*
Murray, Maurice Sidney 1925- *WhoE 91*
Murray, Max 1901-1956 *TwCCr&M 91*
Murray, Max Davis 1915- *WhoSSW 91*
Murray, Melissa 1954- *FemiCLE*
Murray, Melita Frances 1931- *WhoAmW 91*
Murray, Michael Arthur 1941- *WhoAm 90*
Murray, Michael J. 1939- *St&PR 91*
Murray, Michael Peter 1946- *WhoAm 90, WhoE 91*
Murray, Michele Freedman 1933-1974 *AuBYP 90*
Murray, N. Leight 1951- *St&PR 91*
Murray, Niall 1948- *IntWWM 90*
Murray, Nigel 1943- *IntWWM 90*
Murray, Norman J. 1917- *St&PR 91*
Murray, Patricia Anne 1946- *WhoSSW 91*
Murray, Patty 1950- *WhoAmW 91*
Murray, Paul Brady 1923- *St&PR 91, WhoAm 90*
Murray, Paul Burns 1927- *IntWWM 90*
Murray, Pauli 1910- *FemiCLE*
Murray, Pauli 1910-1985 *BioIn 16, HarlReB*
Murray, Peter 1920- *WhoAm 90, WhoWor 91*
Murray, Peter Bryant 1927- *WhoAm 90*
Murray, Peter John 1951- *St&PR 91*
Murray, Peter Loos 1943- *WhoAm 90*
Murray, Peter Robert 1956- *St&PR 91*
Murray, Philip 1886-1952 *WorAlBi*
Murray, Ralbern H. 1929- *St&PR 91*
Murray, Ralbern Hugh 1929- *WhoAm 90*
Murray, Ralph Day 1944- *St&PR 91*
Murray, Randolph Sutherland 1910- *St&PR 91*
Murray, Ray 1917- *Ballpl 90*
Murray, Raymond Carl 1929- *WhoAm 90*
Murray, Raymond Gorbold 1916- *WhoAm 90*
Murray, Raymond Harold 1925- *WhoAm 90*
Murray, Raymond Le Roy 1920- *WhoAm 90*
Murray, Red 1884-1958 *Ballpl 90*
Murray, Richard Bennett 1928- *WhoAm 90*
Murray, Richard Deibel 1921- *WhoWor 91*
Murray, Richard Maximilian 1922- *WhoAm 90, WhoWor 91*
Murray, Richard Newton 1942- *WhoAm 90, WhoAmA 91*
Murray, Richard W *BiDrAPA 89*
Murray, Robb 1953- *WhoEmL 91*
Murray, Robert 1936- *WhoAmA 91*
Murray, Robert E. 1940- *BioIn 16*
Murray, Robert Edward 1956- *WhoSSW 91*
Murray, Robert F. 1924- *St&PR 91*
Murray, Robert Fulton, Jr. 1931- *WhoAm 90*
Murray, Robert G. 1937- *St&PR 91*
Murray, Robert G. 1945- *St&PR 91*
Murray, Robert Gerald 1937- *WhoAm 90*
Murray, Robert Gray 1936- *WhoAm 90*
Murray, Robert Hale, III 1953- *WhoWor 91*
Murray, Robert John 1947- *WhoSSW 91*
Murray, Robert Keith 1922- *WhoAm 90*
Murray, Robert Nelson 1937- *St&PR 91*
Murray, Robert Wallace 1928- *WhoAm 90*
Murray, Robert William 1936- *WhoAm 90*
Murray, Rochelle Ann 1936- *WhoAmW 91*
Murray, Roger Franklin 1911- *St&PR 91, WhoAm 90, WhoE 91*
Murray, Rona 1924- *FemiCLE*
Murray, Ronald 1931- *WhoE 91*
Murray, Rosalind E Cummings 1908- *BiDrAPA 89*
Murray, Russell, II 1925- *WhoAm 90*

Murray, Samuel E. 1906-1989 BioIn 16
Murray, Sarah 1744-1811 FemiCLE
Murray, Sarah Showalter 1959- WhoAmW 91
Murray, Scott Michael BiDrAPA 89
Murray, Simon 1940- WhoAm 90
Murray, Sims L. 1943- WhoSSW 91
Murray, Sterling Ellis 1944- IntWWM 90
Murray, Steven T. 1943- WhoWrEP 89
Murray, Suzanne Helen 1932- WhoAmW 91
Murray, Terrence 1939- WhoAm 90, WhoE 91
Murray, Terrence Leo 1943- WhoAm 90
Murray, Thomas A BiDrAPA 89
Murray, Thomas B BiDrAPA 89
Murray, Thomas Dwight 1923- WhoAm 90
Murray, Thomas Francis 1910- WhoAm 90
Murray, Thomas John 1938- WhoAm 90
Murray, Thomas Joseph 1924- WhoAm 90
Murray, Tim 1938- WhoAmA 91
Murray, Timothy M. 1952- St&PR 91
Murray, Tracy 1940- WhoSSW 91
Murray, Valerie Ann 1957- BiDrAPA 89
Murray, Verna Hazard 1909- WhoAmW 91
Murray, Veronica F BiDrAPA 89
Murray, Virginia R. 1914- WhoWrEP 89
Murray, Wallace Shordon 1921- WhoAm 90
Murray, Walter Charles 1866-1946 BioIn 16
Murray, Warren James 1936- WhoAm 90
Murray, William Barlow 1941- WhoWor 91
Murray, William Colman 1899-1977 WhoAmA 91N
Murray, William Daniel 1908- WhoAm 90
Murray, William E BiDrAPA 89
Murray, William Franklin 1940- St&PR 91
Murray, William Henry 1869-1956 AmLegL
Murray, William Henry Harrison 1840-1904 BioIn 16
Murray, William J., III BioIn 16
Murray, William James 1933- WhoSSW 91
Murray, William John, III 1947- WhoE 91
Murray, William Joseph 1946- WhoSSW 91
Murray, William Michael 1953- WhoE 91
Murray, William P. 1957- ODwPR 91
Murray, William Peter 1924- WhoWor 91
Murray, William Rickman 1955- WhoSSW 91
Murray, William Staite 1881-1962 PenDiDA 89
Murray, William Vans 1760-1803 BioIn 16
Murray-Keetz, Madelyn Patricia 1959- WhoAmW 91
Murrel, Kathleen Rice 1953- WhoAmW 91
Murrell, Carlton D 1945- WhoAmA 91
Murrell, Castella Burnley 1926- WhoAmW 91
Murrell, Donna Marie 1941- WhoSSW 91
Murrell, Irvin Henry, Jr. 1945- IntWWM 90
Murrell, Ivan 1945- Ballpl 90
Murrell, Janice Marie 1937- IntWWM 90, WhoAmW 91
Murrell, Jeffrey Auby 1945- WhoSSW 91
Murrell, Jim ConAu 132
Murrell, John 1945- OxCCanT
Murrell, John Rals 1954- WhoSSW 91
Murrell, Judith A. 1940- St&PR 91
Murrell, Kenneth E. 1939- St&PR 91
Murrell, Kenneth Lynn 1945- WhoSSW 91
Murrell, Kevin Joseph BiDrAPA 89
Murrell, Leslie A. 1950- St&PR 91
Murrell, Michael David 1951- St&PR 91
Murrell, Michael Fleming 1948- WhoEmL 91
Murrell, Stratton Chadwick 1928- WhoSSW 91
Murrell, T.M. 1923- St&PR 91
Murrell, Vernon James 1934- ConAu 132
Murrell-Fax, Elizabeth V. BioIn 16
Murrie, Michael Howard 1951- WhoWrEP 89
Murrieta, Joaquin 1832?-1853 BioIn 16
Murrill, Gwynn 1942- WhoAmA 91
Murrill, Molly Lee 1930- WhoWrEP 89
Murrill, Paul Whitfield 1934- St&PR 91, WhoAm 90
Murrillo, Kathleen Marie 1958- WhoAmW 91
Murrin, Charles John 1931- St&PR 91
Murrin, Craig Martin 1953- WhoAm 90
Murrin, Regis Doubet 1930- WhoAm 90
Murrin, T.J. 1929- St&PR 91
Murrin, Thomas Edward 1923- WhoAm 90
Murrish, Charles Howard 1940- WhoAm 90, WhoSSW 91
Murrone, Pietro Di 1215-1296 BioIn 16
Murrow, Edward R. BioIn 16
Murrow, Edward R. 1908-1965 WorAlBi
Murrow, Richard Will BiDrAPA 89
Murry, Albert Bard 1940- St&PR 91
Murry, Ann FemiCLE
Murry, Charles Emerson 1924- WhoAm 90
Murry, Dan WhoWrEP 89
Murry, Harold David, Jr. 1943- WhoE 91
Murry, Jay Bradford 1952- WhoSSW 91
Murry, John 1908-1988 MusmAFA
Murry, John Middleton 1889-1957 BioIn 16
Murry, Paul 1911- EncACom
Mursay, Marthe-Marguerite le Valois EncCoWW
Murschel, William C. 1953- ODwPR 91
Murska, Ilma di PenDiMP
Murstein, Bernard Irving 1929- WhoE 91
Murstein, Danielle BiDrAPA 89
Mursten, Michael Richard 1964- WhoSSW 91
Murtagh, Frederick, Jr. 1917- WhoAm 90
Murtagh, James J. 1924- St&PR 91
Murtagh, Katherine ODwPR 91
Murtaugh, Danny 1917-1976 Ballpl 90
Murtaugh, John Patrick 1952- WhoEmL 91
Murtaugh, Robert Jean BiDrAPA 89
Murtaugh, Rodger W. 1938- St&PR 91
Murtfeldt, Robert L. 1952- St&PR 91
Murtha, Gerilynn Quatama 1956- WhoAmW 91
Murtha, John Francis 1930- WhoAm 90
Murtha, John Patrick WhoAm 90, WhoE 91
Murtha, John S. 1913- St&PR 91
Murtha, John Stephen 1913- WhoAm 90
Murtha, Patricia Ann 1947- WhoAmW 91
Murtha, Richard A. 1933- St&PR 91
Murthi, Nagaprasad B BiDrAPA 89
Murthy, Andiappan 1943- WhoE 91
Murthy, Hassan Srinivasamurthy Gopala K 1951- WhoWor 91
Murthy, Jayathi 1958- WhoE 91
Murthy, Kode 1939- BiDrAPA 89
Murthy, Kumbaiah N 1948- BiDrAPA 89
Murthy, Padmanaban Krishna 1937- WhoE 91
Murthy, Sheshakumari 1946- BiDrAPA 89
Murthy, Srinivas H. G. 1918- WhoE 91
Murthy, Srinivasa B. 1944- St&PR 91
Murthy, Srinivasa K. 1949- WhoEmL 91, WhoWor 91
Murthy, Swatantra B BiDrAPA 89
Murto, Matti Yrjo Juhani 1947- IntWWM 90
Murton, Thomas NewYTBS 90 [port]
Murton, Thomas O'Rhelius 1929-1990 ConAu 132
Murton, Tom ConAu 132
Murzanski, Michael J. 1955- St&PR 91
Murzinski, Edward John 1946- St&PR 91
Musa bin Hitam 1934- BioIn 16
Musa, Abu BioIn 16
Musa, John Davis 1933- WhoAm 90
Musa, Mahmoud Nimir 1943- BiDrAPA 89
Musa, Said 1944- WhoWor 91
Musa, Samuel Albert WhoAm 90
Musa Hussain, Ghazala 1953- BiDrAPA 89
Musacchia, Xavier Joseph 1923- WhoAm 90
Musacchio, Marilyn Jean 1938- WhoAmW 91
Musafia, Judith N 1941- WhoWrEP 89
Musal, Edward Alfred 1946- WhoE 91
Musalem, Alberto Roque 1940- WhoE 91
Musallam, L. Sam 1950- WhoSSW 91
Musante, Tony WhoAm 90
Musarurwa, Willie BioIn 16
Musarurwa, Willie 1928?-1990 ConAu 131
Musaus, Johann Karl August 1735-1787 DcLB 97 [port]
Musavi-Khamenei, Mir Hosein 1942- WhoWor 91
Musburger, Brent 1939- WorAlBi
Musburger, Brent Woody 1939- WhoAm 90
Muscarella, Joseph 1946- St&PR 91
Muscarelle, Jos. L. St&PR 91N
Muscarelle, Joseph L. BioIn 16
Muscarnera, Simone A. 1940- St&PR 91
Muscatine, Charles 1920- WhoAm 90
Muscató, Andrew 1953- WhoEmL 91
Muschauer, John Lathrop 1919- WhoE 91
Muschel, Louis Henry 1916- WhoAm 90
Muschenheim, William NewYTBS 90
Muschenheim, William 1902-1990 ConAu 130
Muschg, Adolf 1934- WorAu 1980 [port]
Muschlitz, Larry D. 1948- St&PR 91
Musciano, Walter A. AuBYP 90
Muscosky, Robert A. 1946- St&PR 91
Muse, A.C. 1936- St&PR 91
Muse, Charles Howard, Jr. 1936- St&PR 91
Muse, Clarence 1889-1979 EarBlAP
Muse, Clarence E 1889-1979 DrBlPA 90
Muse, Edward D. 1932- St&PR 91
Muse, Ewell Henderson, III 1938- St&PR 91, WhoAm 90
Muse, Helen Elizabeth 1917- WhoWrEP 89
Muse, Helen Rose 1937- WhoAmW 91
Muse, Martha Twitchell 1926- WhoAm 90
Muse, Maude Blanche 1879-1962 BioIn 16
Muse, McGillivray 1909- WhoAm 90
Muse, Nina Jo 1954- BiDrAPA 89
Muse, Patricia Alice 1923- WhoAmW 91
Muse, Raquel 1962- WhoAmW 91
Muse, Scott Thomas, Jr. 1930- WhoSSW 91
Muse, William Van 1939- WhoAm 90
Musegades, Wally W. 1940- St&PR 91
Musel, Robert J. 1925- St&PR 91
Museler, William J. 1941- St&PR 91
Museles, Melvin 1929- WhoAm 90
Muser, Tony 1947- Ballpl 90
Muses, C A 1919- EncO&P 3
Musetti, Myrtle Jane Holt WhoAmW 91
Musetto, Vincent Albert, Jr. 1941- WhoAm 90
Museveni, Yoweri BioIn 16
Museveni, Yoweri 1944- CurBio 90 [port]
Museveni, Yoweri Kaguta 1944- WhoWor 91
Musgrave, Agnes FemiCLE
Musgrave, Florence 1902- AuBYP 90
Musgrave, Frank Webster 1932- WhoE 91
Musgrave, Jerry Donald 1941- St&PR 91
Musgrave, Mary Elizabeth 1954- WhoSSW 91
Musgrave, Richard Abel 1910- WhoAm 90
Musgrave, Shirley H 1935- WhoAmA 91
Musgrave, Stanley Dean 1919- WhoAm 90
Musgrave, Story 1935- WhoAm 90
Musgrave, Susan 1951- FemiCLE
Musgrave, Thea WhoAm 90, WhoAmW 91
Musgrave, Thea 1928- IntWWM 90, PenDiMP A
Musgrove, A J WhoAmA 91N
Musgrove, David Gregory 1944- St&PR 91
Musgrove, John Conner 1929- WhoSSW 91
Musgrove, Judy Autry 1946- WhoAmW 91
Musgrove, Margaret 1943- AuBYP 90, BioIn 16
Musgrove, Mary WhNaAH
Musgrove, Stephen Ward 1949- WhoAmA 91
Musha, Jacob Roman 1936- WhoAm 90
Mushalatubbee WhNaAH
Mushalla, Mark Steven 1959- WhoE 91
Musham, William C. 1915- St&PR 91
Musham, William Charles 1915- WhoAm 90
Mushatt, Cecil 1913- BiDrAPA 89
Mushegan-Watson, Janet 1955- WhoSSW 91
Mushen, Robert Linton 1943- WhoWor 91
Musher, Jeremy Seth BiDrAPA 89
Musher, Sidney NewYTBS 90 [port]
Musher, Sidney 1905- St&PR 91
Mushik, Corliss WhoAmW 91
Mushin, Alan Spencer 1938- WhoWor 91
Mushinski, Mark Alan 1959- St&PR 91
Mushkat, Miron 1945- WhoWor 91
Mushkin, Albert S. 1935- St&PR 91
Mushkin, Eliyahu BioIn 16
Mushobekwa, Kalimba wa Katana 1943- WhoWor 91
Musholt, Frank H. 1939- St&PR 91
Mushotzky, Richard Fred 1947- WhoE 91
Mushrush, Grace J BiDrAPA 89
Musial, Joe 1905-1977 EncACom
Musial, Stan 1920- Ballpl 90 [port], WorAlBi
Musial, Stanley 1920- WhoAm 90
Music for Progressive Relaxation NewAgMG
Music, John Farris 1921- WhoE 91
Music, Lorenzo 1937- ConTFT 8
Music, Zoran 1909- BioIn 16
Musici, I PenDiMP
Musick, Diana Sue 1940- WhoSSW 91
Musick, Stuart 1934- St&PR 91
Musielak, Victor A. 1929- St&PR 91
Musihin, Konstantin K. 1927- WhoWor 91
Musikant-Weiser, Laura E BiDrAPA 89
Musil, Robert 1880-1942 WrPh
Musilli, Thomas Gordon 1944- St&PR 91
Musinsky, Gerald 1954- WhoWrEP 89
Muska, Nick 1942- WhoWrEP 89
Muska, Thomas Wayne 1957- WhoSSW 91
Muskardin, Anna 1958- WhoWor 91
Muskas, Robert 1938- St&PR 91
Muskat, Carl S. 1938- St&PR 91
Muskat, David I BiDrAPA 89
Muskatt, Philip H. 1950- St&PR 91
Muskau, Hermann Puckler- 1785-1871 BioIn 16
Muske, Carol ConAu 32NR
Muske, Carol Anne 1945- WhoWrEP 89
Muske-Dukes, Carol 1945- ConAu 32NR
Muskett, Doreen Lydia 1931- IntWWM 90
Muskett, Michael Peter 1928- IntWWM 90
Muskie, Edmund S. BioIn 16
Muskie, Edmund S. 1914- WorAlBi
Muskie, Edmund Sixtus 1914- BiDrUSE 89, WhoAm 90, WhoE 91
Muskie, Stephen O. BioIn 16
Muskin, Philip R 1948- BiDrAPA 89, WhoE 91
Musler, Jay 1949- BioIn 16
Muslin, Hyman L 1929- BiDrAPA 89
Muslin, Lawrence Richard 1943- St&PR 91
Musoke, Theresa 1945- BioIn 16
Musokotwane, Kebby Sililo Kambulu 1946- WhoWor 91
Musolf, Lloyd Daryl 1919- WhoAm 90
Musolino, Angelo 1923- IntWWM 90
Musolino, Joseph R. 1937- St&PR 91
Musolino, Joseph Richard 1937- WhoAm 90
Musolino-Alber, Ella Marie 1942- WhoAmW 91
Muson, Howard Henry 1935- WhoAm 90
Musone, Fred James 1944- WhoAm 90
Musonis, Vytautas 1920- BiDrAPA 89
Musorgsky, Modest 1839-1881 PenDiMP A
Musorgsky, Modest Petrovich 1839-1881 BioIn 16
Muss, David BioIn 16
Musscher, Michiel van 1645-1705 BioIn 16
Mussehl, Robert Clarence 1936- WhoAm 90
Mussell, Pamela Greer BiDrAPA 89
Musselman, Bill BioIn 16, WhoAm 90
Musselman, Clifford Allen 1947- St&PR 91
Musselman, Darwin B 1916- WhoAmA 91
Musselman, Deborah Myers 1964- WhoAmW 91
Musselman, Francis Haas 1925- WhoAm 90, WhoE 91
Musselman, Jamie Boothe 1950- St&PR 91, WhoSSW 91
Musselman, Jeff 1963- Ballpl 90
Musselman, John J. 1926- St&PR 91
Musselman, Kathleen J. 1957- WhoAmW 91
Musselman, Kenneth Jack 1947- WhoEmL 91
Musselman, Larry L. 1947- WhoEmL 91
Musselman, Laurence K BiDrAPA 89
Musselman, Lois WhoAmW 91
Musselman, Lois 1946- ODwPR 91
Musselman, Paul Ernest 1950- St&PR 91
Musselman, Peter R. St&PR 91N
Musselman, Robert Metcalfe 1914- WhoSSW 91
Musselman, Robert Phillip 1950- St&PR 91
Musselman, Vernon Armor 1912- WhoAm 90
Musselwhite, Charlie BioIn 16
Musselwhite, Harry 1953- IntWWM 90
Musser, A. Wendell 1930- WhoAm 90
Musser, Amelia E. 1935- St&PR 91
Musser, C. Walton 1909- WhoAm 90
Musser, Ellyn Zunker 1937- WhoSSW 91
Musser, Harry Plaine, Jr. 1922- St&PR 91
Musser, John Shenberger, III 1950- WhoSSW 91
Musser, Robert D. 1932- St&PR 91
Musser, Stanton Richard 1936- WhoAm 90
Musser, Tharon BioIn 16
Musser, Tharon 1925- ConDes 90, WhoAm 90
Musser, Tharon Myrene 1925- NotWoAT
Musser, Warren V. 1926- St&PR 91
Musser, Willard Isaac 1913- IntWWM 90
Musser, William Allen 1924- St&PR 91
Musser, William Wesley, Jr. 1918- WhoAm 90
Mussert, Anton Adriaan 1894-1946 BioIn 16
Musset, Alfred De 1810-1857 WorAlBi
Mussett, Richard Earl 1948- WhoSSW 91
Mussey, Dexter 1811-1890 AmLegL
Mussey, Joseph A. 1948- St&PR 91
Mussey, Joseph Arthur 1948- WhoAm 90
Mussfeldt, Maria Mercedes Gomez 1957- WhoWor 91
Musshoff, Karl Albert 1910- WhoWor 91
Mussini, Mario Paride 1922- WhoWor 91
Mussio, Lesley Ann 1959- BiDrAPA 89
Mussman, Steven 1961- St&PR 91
Mussman, William Edward 1919- WhoWor 91
Mussmann, Linda L 1947- WhoAmA 91, WhoE 91

Musso, Benedetto PenDiDA 89
Musso, Daniel Leo BiDrAPA 89
Musso, Gianni Luca 1958- WhoWor 91
Musso, J Ricardo 1917- EncO&P 3
Musso, Laurie Duston 1919- WhoWrEP 89
Mussolini, Alessandra BioIn 16
Mussolini, Benito 1883-1945 BioIn 16, WorAlBi
Mussorgsky, Modest Petrovich 1839-1881 BioIn 16
Mussulman, Ronald 1943- WhoAm 90
Must, Alan H. 1939- St&PR 91
Must, Meyer Nathan 1915- St&PR 91
Mustacchi, Henry 1930- St&PR 91
Mustacchi, Piero 1920- WhoAm 90, WhoWor 91
Mustafa Kemal 1881-1938 BioIn 16
Mustafa, Ghulam BiDrAPA 89
Mustafa, Rayman St&PR 91
Mustain, Donald, II 1935- St&PR 91
Mustain, William G. 1942- St&PR 91
Mustapaa, P. 1899-1973 DcScanL
Mustard, James Fraser 1927- WhoAm 90
Mustarde, Bonnie Jean 1959- WhoAmW 91
Muste, A. J. 1885-1967 EncAL
Muster, Douglas Frederick 1918- WhoAm 90
Mustiful, June Carolyn Lewis WhoAmW 91
Mustille, Anthony N BiDrAPA 89
Musto, David Franklin 1936- WhoAm 90, WhoWor 91
Musto, Michael 1955- ConAu 132
Mustone, Amelia P. 1928- WhoAmW 91, WhoE 91
Mustonen, Aki Kaarlo 1948- WhoWor 91
Mustonen, Olli 1967- IntWWM 90
Musulin, Melissa 1957- WhoWor 91
Musum, Veny William 1955- WhoEmL 91
Musunuru, Jagadeeswara R BiDrAPA 89
Muszynski, Peter Charles 1928- St&PR 91
Mutafcieva, Vera 1929- EncCoWW
Mutagi, Ramachandra Narayan 1948- WhoWor 91
Mutchler, Thomas Edward 1945- St&PR 91
Muth, Douglas Cameron 1957- St&PR 91
Muth, George Edward 1906- WhoAm 90
Muth, John Francis 1918- WhoAm 90
Muth, John Fraser 1930- WhoAm 90
Muth, Michael Don 1943- St&PR 91
Muth, Richard Ferris 1927- WhoAm 90, WhoSSW 91
Muth, Robert James 1933- St&PR 91, WhoAm 90
Muth, Stephen Anthony, Jr. 1936- St&PR 91
Muther, Ellis F BiDrAPA 89
Muthesius, Hermann 1861-1927 PenDiDA 89
Muthu, Francis Savari 1934- WhoWor 91
Muthuswami, Mullai BiDrAPA 89
Muti, Riccardo BioIn 16
Muti, Riccardo 1941- IntWWM 90, PenDiMP, WhoAm 90, WhoE 91, WhoWor 91, WorAlBi
Mutis, Alvaro 1923- HispWr 90
Mutlu, Ilhan Ahmet BiDrAPA 89
Muto, Gene Thomas 1951- WhoSSW 91
Muto, Nick Francis 1928- WhoE 91
Muto, Susan Annette 1942- WhoAm 90
Muto, Takasuke 1930- WhoWor 91
Mutrie, Annie Feray 1826-1893 BiDWomA
Mutrie, James 1851-1938 BioIn 16
Mutrie, Jim 1851-1938 Ballpl 90
Mutrie, Martha Darley 1824-1885 BiDWomA
Mutschler, Herbert Frederick 1919- WhoAm 90
Mutschler, John Robert 1947- St&PR 91
Mutschler, Louis Henry 1940- BiDrAPA 89
Mutsuhito 1852-1912 WorAlBi
Muttakin, Moinuddin H BiDrAPA 89
Mutter, Anne-Sophie 1963- BioIn 16, CurBio 90 [port], IntWWM 90, News 90 [port], -90-3 [port], PenDiMP
Mutter, Arthur Z 1927- BiDrAPA 89
Mutter, Charles B 1933- BiDrAPA 89
Mutterperl, William Charles 1946- WhoAm 90
Mutters, David Ray 1949- WhoSSW 91
Mutty, Lawrence B 1934- BiDrAPA 89
Mutty, Paul Roland 1939- WhoWor 91
Mutz, Oscar Ulysses 1928- St&PR 91, WhoAm 90
Mutz, Richard 1872-1931 PenDiDA 89
Mutzbauer, Otto Adolf Klaus 1943- WhoWor 91
Mutziger-Beck, Judy Lynn 1947- WhoEmL 91, WhoWor 91
Muul, Illar 1938- WhoSSW 91
Muurinen, Eljas 1936- WhoWor 91
Muuss, Rolf Eduard 1924- WhoAm 90
Muybridge, Eadweard 1830-1904 WorAlBi
Muybridge, Eadweard James 1830-1904 WhNaAH
Muyuela, Roberto 1955- St&PR 91
Muzekari, Louis Harry 1935- WhoSSW 91
Muzenda, Simon Vengai 1922- WhoWor 91
Muzio, Claudia 1889-1936 PenDiMP
Muzorewa, Abel Tendekayi 1925- WhoWor 91
Muzquiz y Goyeneche, Miguel de 1719-1785 BioIn 16
Muzyka, Donald Richard 1938- WhoAm 90
Muzyka-McGuire, Amy ODwPR 91
Muzzall, David Cleveland 1924- St&PR 91
Muzzarelli, Lisa Mary 1961- WhoAmW 91
Muzzatti, Loris D. 1957- St&PR 91
Muzzillo, William Allen 1958- WhoEmL 91
Muzzio, Charles Joseph 1940- WhoE 91
Muzzy, Diana Lee 1949- WhoAmW 91
Muzzy, Richard W. 1923- St&PR 91
Mvungi, Martha FemiCLE
Mwadilifu, Mwalima Imara WhoWrEP 89
Mwai, George Kangonga 1934- WhoWor 91
Mwamwenda, Tuntufye Selemani 1945- WhoWor 91
Mwananshiku, Luke J. WhoWor 91
Mwemba, Mike Hamusonde 1957- WhoWor 91
Mwinyi, Ali Hassan BioIn 16
Mwinyi, Ali Hassan 1925- WhoWor 91
My 1920- SmATA X
Myaskovsky, Nikolay Yakovlevich 1881-1950 PenDiMP A
Myatt, George 1914- Ballpl 90
Myatt, Glenn 1897-1969 Ballpl 90
Myatt, Greely 1952- WhoAmA 91
Myatt, Sue Henshaw 1956- WhoAmW 91
Mybsberge, Richard C. 1934- St&PR 91
Myburgh, Johannes Albertus 1928- WhoWor 91
Mycielski, Jan 1932- WhoAm 90
Mycue, Edward Delehant 1937- WhoWrEP 89
Mydans, Shelley Smith 1915- BioIn 16
Mydlack, Danny BioIn 16
Mydland, Brent 1952-1990 NewYTBS 90
Mydland, Gordon James 1922- WhoAm 90
Myer, Bentley McCloud 1946- St&PR 91
Myer, Buddy 1904-1974 Ballpl 90
Myer, Carole Wendy 1944- WhoAmW 91
Myer, Charles B 1954- WhoWrEP 89
Myer, Charles Randolph 1921- WhoE 91, WhoWor 91
Myer, Elijah Reed 1818-1911 AmLegL
Myer, Elizabeth Gallup WhoAm 90
Myer, Harold K. 1927- St&PR 91
Myer, John Daniel, II 1950- WhoSSW 91
Myer, Mari Lynn 1961- WhoAmW 91
Myer, Peter Livingston 1934- WhoAmA 91
Myerburg, Robert Jerome 1937- WhoAm 90
Myerowitz, P. David 1947- WhoWor 91
Myers, A. Maurice 1940- St&PR 91
Myers, A T 1851-1894 EncO&P 3
Myers, Alan Lawton BiDrAPA 89
Myers, Albert G., Jr. 1917- WhoAm 90
Myers, Alfred Edward 1920- St&PR 91
Myers, Alfred Frantz 1936- WhoE 91
Myers, Allen 1925- WhoAm 90
Myers, Amina Claudine BioIn 16
Myers, Andrew Breen 1920- WhoAm 90, WhoE 91
Myers, Andrew S. 1948- St&PR 91
Myers, Anthony Maurice 1940- WhoAm 90
Myers, Arno R. 1907- St&PR 91
Myers, Arnold D. 1933- St&PR 91
Myers, Arthur B. 1917- WhoAm 90
Myers, Arthur E. 1935- St&PR 91
Myers, Arthur Thomas 1851-1894 EncPaPR 91
Myers, Barnwell Rhett BiDrAPA 89
Myers, Barton 1934- WhoAm 90
Myers, Benjamin John 1943- WhoE 91
Myers, Beverle G 1951- BiDrAPA 89
Myers, Beverly Ann 1935- BiDrAPA 89
Myers, Billy 1910- Ballpl 90
Myers, Bob 1949- WhoWrEP 89
Myers, Bonny E. WhoWrEP 89
Myers, C. Roger 1906- BioIn 16
Myers, C Stowe 1906- WhoAmA 91
Myers, Carole WhoAmA 91
Myers, Carole Ann 1934- WhoAmA 91
Myers, Carole Ann 1938- WhoAmW 91, WhoWor 91
Myers, Catherine R. 1934- WhoAm 90
Myers, Charles Andrew 1913- WhoAm 90
Myers, Charles Arthur 1923- IntWWM 90
Myers, Charles Roger 1906- BioIn 16
Myers, Clark Everett 1915- WhoAm 90
Myers, Clay 1927- WhoAm 90
Myers, Craig Michael 1944- St&PR 91
Myers, Cynthia M. 1950- St&PR 91
Myers, Dale DeHaven 1922- WhoAm 90
Myers, Dale Kamerer 1938- WhoSSW 91
Myers, Dan Allen 1937- BiDrAPA 89
Myers, Darlene Marie 1950- WhoAmW 91, WhoEmL 91
Myers, David Fredric 1936- St&PR 91, WhoAm 90
Myers, David G. 1942- WhoWrEP 89
Myers, David N. 1900- WhoAm 90
Myers, David N. 1910- St&PR 91
Myers, David Richard 1948- WhoE 91
Myers, Dennis M. 1942- WhoSSW 91
Myers, Denys Peter, Jr. 1916- WhoAm 90
Myers, Diana BioIn 16
Myers, Donald Allen 1932- WhoAm 90
Myers, Donald Dean 1937- WhoSSW 91
Myers, Donald S. 1925- St&PR 91
Myers, Donna H. 1938- ODwPR 91
Myers, Dorothy Roatz 1921- WhoAmA 91
Myers, Douglas D. 1945- St&PR 91
Myers, Douglas Stuart 1947- WhoSSW 91
Myers, Douglass Nelson 1953- WhoEmL 91
Myers, Edward Doran 1952- WhoEmL 91
Myers, Eldon Woodrow, Jr. 1953- WhoSSW 91
Myers, Elijah E. BioIn 16
Myers, Elizabeth Perkins 1918- AuBYP 90
Myers, Ellen H. 1948- ODwPR 91
Myers, Elmer 1894-1976 Ballpl 90
Myers, Ethel 1881-1960 BiDWomA
Myers, Ethel K 1881-1960 WhoAmA 91N
Myers, Eugene Ekander 1914- WhoAm 90, WhoWor 91
Myers, Eugene Nicholas 1933- WhoAm 90
Myers, Eugene Wimberly 1921- St&PR 91
Myers, Evelyn Stephenson 1922- WhoAm 90
Myers, Forrest Warden 1941- WhoAmA 91
Myers, Frances 1936- WhoAmA 91
Myers, Frances 1938- WhoAm 90
Myers, Frank Harmon 1899-1956 WhoAmA 91N
Myers, Franklin 1952- WhoAm 90, WhoSSW 91
Myers, Fred A 1937- WhoAmA 91
Myers, Fred Arthur 1937- WhoAm 90, WhoSSW 91
Myers, Frederic William Henry 1843-1901 EncO&P 3, EncPaPR 91
Myers, Gail Eldridge 1923- WhoAm 90
Myers, Gail Elizabeth 1949- WhoWrEP 89
Myers, Garry C., III 1945- St&PR 91
Myers, Gary Lee 1953- St&PR 91
Myers, George, Jr. 1953- WhoWrEP 89
Myers, George Carleton 1931- WhoSSW 91
Myers, George Hewitt 1865-1957 WhoAmA 91N
Myers, Gerald E. 1923- WhoAm 90
Myers, Gregory Edwin 1960- WhoEmL 91, WhoWor 91
Myers, Gretchen Hardy Godar 1958- WhoEmL 91, WhoWor 91
Myers, H. Carter 1941- St&PR 91
Myers, Hank BioIn 16
Myers, Hannah BiDEWW
Myers, Hap 1888-1967 Ballpl 90
Myers, Harold Mathews 1915- WhoAm 90, WhoWor 91
Myers, Harry 1921- St&PR 91
Myers, Harry J., Jr. 1931- WhoAm 90
Myers, Harvey, Jr. 1859- AmLegL
Myers, Helen Loretta 1934- WhoAmW 91
Myers, Helen Priscilla 1946- IntWWM 90
Myers, Henry J 1916- BiDrAPA 89
Myers, Herman Edson, Jr. 1926- St&PR 91
Myers, Howard BiDrAPA 89
Myers, Howard Milton 1923- WhoAm 90
Myers, Hy 1889-1965 Ballpl 90
Myers, Ila May 1921- WhoAmW 91
Myers, Ina Vetra 1916- WhoAmW 91
Myers, Ira Lee 1924- WhoAm 90
Myers, Irving L 1930- BiDrAPA 89
Myers, Israel 1906- WhoAm 90
Myers, J. Jay 1919- WhoWrEP 89
Myers, J Martin BiDrAPA 89
Myers, J William 1919- ConAu 30NR
Myers, Jack Charles 1947- WhoE 91
Myers, Jack Duane 1913- WhoAm 90
Myers, Jack Edgar 1913- WhoAm 90
Myers, Jack Elliott 1941- WhoWrEP 89
Myers, Jack Fredrick 1927- WhoAmA 91
Myers, Jacob Joseph, Jr. 1918- St&PR 91
Myers, Jacob Martin 1904- WhoAm 90
Myers, Jacob Martin 1919- WhoE 91
Myers, James Andrew 1878?-1928 DcAfAmP
Myers, James C. 1941- ODwPR 91
Myers, James Jefferson 1842-1915 AmLegL
Myers, James Nelson 1941- WhoAm 90
Myers, James William 1950- WhoSSW 91
Myers, James Woodrow, III 1954- WhoEmL 91
Myers, Jed Anthony 1952- BiDrAPA 89
Myers, Jeff BioIn 16
Myers, Jeffrey Allen 1959- WhoEmL 91
Myers, Jennifer Lynn 1953- WhoAmW 91
Myers, Jerome Keeley 1921- WhoAm 90
Myers, Jess J. 1940- St&PR 91
Myers, Jesse Jerome 1940- WhoAm 90
Myers, Jo Ann 1928- BiDrAPA 89
Myers, Jo Ann 1946- WhoAmW 91
Myers, Joel Norman 1939- WhoAm 90
Myers, Joel Philip 1934- WhoAmA 91
Myers, John EncO&P 3
Myers, John Dana, Sr. 1944- WhoSSW 91
Myers, John E. 1930- St&PR 91
Myers, John Holt 1923- WhoE 91, WhoWor 91
Myers, John Joseph 1941- WhoAm 90
Myers, John Lytle 1929- WhoAm 90
Myers, John Michael 1942- BiDrAPA 89
Myers, John S. 1945- St&PR 91
Myers, John Thomas 1927- WhoAm 90
Myers, John Wescott 1911- WhoAm 90
Myers, Joseph Allen 1946- WhoSSW 91
Myers, Joyce A. ODwPR 91
Myers, Joyce Elizabeth BiDrAPA 89
Myers, Judy Ann 1957- WhoSSW 91
Myers, Kathleen Mary 1947- BiDrAPA 89
Myers, Kenneth Ellis 1932- WhoAm 90
Myers, Kenneth Melvin 1921- St&PR 91
Myers, Kenneth Raymond 1939- WhoAm 90
Myers, Kent William 1941- St&PR 91
Myers, Kim Lorraine 1957- WhoAmW 91
Myers, Kurt Jacob 1956- St&PR 91
Myers, Larry A. 1947- St&PR 91
Myers, Larry F. 1938- St&PR 91
Myers, Larry H. 1922- St&PR 91
Myers, Larry Stewart 1947- BiDrAPA 89
Myers, Laura Ann 1961- WhoAmW 91
Myers, Legh 1916- WhoAmA 91
Myers, Letitia Sharrits 1929- WhoAm 90
Myers, Lily Elizabeth 1948- WhoAmW 91
Myers, Lonn William 1946- WhoEmL 91
Myers, Lora Belle 1954- WhoAmW 91
Myers, Louis S. 1913- St&PR 91
Myers, Madeline Neuberger 1896- AuBYP 90
Myers, Malcolm Comer 1923- St&PR 91
Myers, Malcolm Haynie 1917- WhoAm 90, WhoAmA 91
Myers, Marcia K. 1938- WhoAmW 91
Myers, Margaret Good 1899-1988 BioIn 16
Myers, Martin 1951- WhoAmA 91
Myers, Martin T. 1953- St&PR 91
Myers, Marvin Scott 1922- WhoSSW 91
Myers, Mary Jo Joyce BiDrAPA 89
Myers, Mary Lynn 1945- WhoAm 90
Myers, Melanie Jean 1955- WhoAmW 91
Myers, Michael Francis 1943- BiDrAPA 89
Myers, Michele Tolela 1941- WhoAm 90
Myers, Mildred 1922- St&PR 91
Myers, Miller Franklin 1929- St&PR 91
Myers, Minor, Jr. 1942- WhoAm 90
Myers, Myer 1723-1795 PenDiDA 89
Myers, Nan ODwPR 91
Myers, Natalie Lapkin 1916- WhoAmW 91
Myers, Norman 1935- St&PR 91
Myers, Norman Allan 1935- WhoAm 90
Myers, Norval F. BioIn 16
Myers, Orie Eugene, Jr. 1920- WhoAm 90
Myers, Paul Ivan 1928- St&PR 91
Myers, Paul John 1945- WhoE 91
Myers, Pauline DrBlPA 90
Myers, Peter C. BioIn 16
Myers, Peter C. 1931- WhoAm 90
Myers, Phillip Fenton 1935- WhoAm 90, WhoWor 91
Myers, Phillip I. ODwPR 91
Myers, Phillip Ward 1939- WhoAm 90
Myers, Ralph Chandler 1933- WhoAm 90
Myers, Randy 1962- Ballpl 90
Myers, Raymond Reever 1920- WhoAm 90
Myers, Rex Charles 1945- WhoAm 90
Myers, Richard Allen 1936- St&PR 91
Myers, Richard C. 1940- St&PR 91
Myers, Richard Dean 1932- St&PR 91
Myers, Richard L. 1936- St&PR 91
Myers, Richard Stein 1953- BiDrAPA 89
Myers, Rita 1947- WhoAmA 91
Myers, Rita Koors 1942- IntWWM 90
Myers, Robert Aeolus NewAgMG
Myers, Robert David 1937- WhoAm 90
Myers, Robert Durant 1931- WhoAm 90
Myers, Robert Eugene 1928- WhoWor 91
Myers, Robert Eugene 1953- WhoWor 91
Myers, Robert Gilbert 1932- WhoAm 90
Myers, Robert Jay 1934- St&PR 91, WhoAm 90, WhoE 91
Myers, Robert John 1924- WhoAm 90
Myers, Robert Julius 1912- WhoAm 90
Myers, Robert L. 1923-1989 BioIn 16
Myers, Robert Manson 1921- WhoAm 90
Myers, Roderick Douglas 1932- St&PR 91
Myers, Roger W. 1946- WhoWrEP 89
Myers, Rolland Graham 1945- WhoE 91
Myers, Ronald Elwood 1929- WhoAm 90
Myers, Ronald Lee 1939- BiDrAPA 89
Myers, Roy W. 1947- St&PR 91

Myers, Russell 1938- *EncACom, WhoAm 90*
Myers, Samuel 1934- *WhoWor 91*
Myers, Samuel Lloyd 1919- *WhoAm 90*
Myers, Sara Snipes 1923- *St&PR 91*
Myers, Stanley Thomas 1936- *St&PR 91*
Myers, Steven Alan 1937- *BiDrAPA 89*
Myers, Steven E. 1949- *St&PR 91*
Myers, Sue Ann 1957- *WhoWrEP 89*
Myers, Susan Gail *BiDrAPA 89*
Myers, Susan Sloat 1944- *WhoSSW 91*
Myers, Theodore A. 1930- *St&PR 91*
Myers, Theodore Ash 1930- *WhoAm 90*
Myers, Thomas Arthur 1945- *WhoWor 91*
Myers, Thomas Henry 1932- *WhoAm 90, WhoE 91*
Myers, Thomas Rawlings 1840-1919 *AmLegL*
Myers, Toby Millicent 1937- *WhoSSW 91*
Myers, Truman M. 1931- *ODwPR 91*
Myers, Vernon C. *NewYTBS 90*
Myers, Vernon C. 1911-1990 *BioIn 16, ConAu 130*
Myers, Virginia Anne 1927- *WhoAmA 91*
Myers, Wade Cooper 1957- *BiDrAPA 89*
Myers, Walter Dean 1937- *AuBYP 90, BioIn 16*
Myers, Warren Powers Laird 1921- *WhoAm 90*
Myers, Wayne Alan 1931- *BiDrAPA 89, WhoE 91*
Myers, William *St&PR 91*
Myers, William 1939- *ConAu 132*
Myers, William A. 1937- *WhoSSW 91*
Myers, William C., Jr. 1946- *St&PR 91*
Myers, William H., III 1949- *WhoSSW 91*
Myers, William Harvey 1923- *St&PR 91*
Myers, William Hershell 1932- *WhoSSW 91*
Myers, William R. *WhoSSW 91*
Myers, Wm. D. 1936- *St&PR 91*
Myers, Woodrow Augustus, Jr. 1954- *WhoAm 90, WhoE 91*
Myers-May, Yvette *WhoAmW 91*
Myers Medeiros, Patricia Jo 1942- *WhoAmW 91*
Myers-Turner, Daraugh Anne 1956- *WhoAmW 91*
Myers-Walls, Judith Ann 1952- *WhoEmL 91*
Myerson, Alan 1936- *WhoAm 90*
Myerson, Albert Leon 1919- *WhoSSW 91*
Myerson, Andrew Abraham 1949- *BiDrAPA 89*
Myerson, Bess *BioIn 16*
Myerson, Bess 1924- *BioAmW*
Myerson, David J 1919- *BiDrAPA 89*
Myerson, David J. 1939- *WhoAm 90*
Myerson, Harvey Daniel 1939- *WhoAm 90*
Myerson, Jacob Myer 1926- *WhoAm 90*
Myerson, Joel Arthur 1945- *WhoAm 90*
Myerson, Paul G 1914- *BiDrAPA 89*
Myerson, Paul Graves 1914- *WhoAm 90*
Myerson, Roger Bruce 1951- *WhoAm 90*
Myford, James C 1940- *WhoAmA 91*
Myhre, Byron Arnold 1928- *WhoAm 90*
Myhre, Jeffrey Dean 1961- *WhoE 91*
Myhre, Lawrence Eugene 1942- *St&PR 91*
Myhre, Terje 1962- *WhoWor 91*
Myhren, Trygve Edward 1937- *WhoAm 90, WhoWor 91*
Myint, Aye *BiDrAPA 89*
Myint, Hla *BiDrAPA 89*
Myint, Tin T 1937- *BiDrAPA 89*
Mykelystar, Tomasco *WhoWrEP 89*
Mykkanen, Martti 1926- *ConDes 90*
Mykkeltveit, Johannes 1941- *WhoWor 91*
Mykle, Agnar 1915- *DcScanL*
Myklebust, Helmer Rudolph 1910- *WhoAm 90*
Myklebust, Rolf 1908- *IntWWM 90*
Mykles, Donald Lee 1950- *WhoEmL 91*
Mykytyn, Nicholas John, Jr. 1952- *WhoE 91*
Mylander, Lisa Anne 1962- *WhoAmW 91*
Myler, Bernard J. 1926- *St&PR 91*
Myler, Harley Ross 1953- *WhoSSW 91*
Myles, Alannah 195-?- *ConMus 4 [port]*
Myles, John 1621?-1683 *BioIn 16*
Myles, Randy A. 1961- *St&PR 91*
Myles, Sandra Christine 1948- *WhoSSW 91*
Myles, Symon *ConAu 33NR, MajTwCW, TwCCr&M 91, WhoWrEP 89*
Myles, Symon 1949- *BioIn 16, WhoAm 90, WhoWor 91*
Myller, Rolf 1926- *AuBYP 90*
Myllyla, Wesley Wilhelm 1911- *St&PR 91*
Myllymaki, Rachel *BioIn 16*
Mylona, Eva 1938- *EncCoWW*
Mylonas, George E. 1898-1988 *BioIn 16*
Mylonas, Theodore P. 1947- *WhoWor 91*
Mylroie, Gerald Richard 1945- *WhoE 91*
Mylroie, Willa Wilcox 1917- *WhoAm 90*
Mynahan, Eugene 1936- *St&PR 91*
Mynard, Charles William 1938- *St&PR 91*
Mynard, Don Allen 1944- *WhoSSW 91*
Mynatt, Cecil Ferrell 1920- *WhoWrEP 89*
Mynatt, Elaine Simpson 1947- *WhoWrEP 89*
Mynatt, James C. 1942- *St&PR 91*
Mynatt, Joe Dennis 1960- *WhoSSW 91*
Mynett, G.E. 1946- *St&PR 91*
Mynors, R. A. B. 1903-1989 *BioIn 16*
Mynors, Roger 1903-1989 *AnObit 1989*
Mynors, Roger A B 1903-1989 *ConAu 129*
Mynors, Roger Aubrey Baskerville 1903-1989 *BioIn 16*
Myojo-tenno 1623-1696 *WomWR*
Myosho *WomWR*
Myra, Harold Lawrence 1939- *WhoAm 90*
Myran, David Douglas *BiDrAPA 89*
Myrberg, Arthur August, Jr. 1933- *WhoAm 90*
Myrdal, Gunnar 1898-1987 *BioIn 16, WorAlBi*
Myrdal, Jan 1927- *ConAu 132, DcScanL, WhoWor 91*
Myrdal, Rosemarie Caryle 1929- *WhoAmW 91*
Myren, Per-Olof 1952- *WhoWor 91*
Myren, Richard Albert 1924- *WhoAm 90*
Myren, Richard Thomas 1936- *St&PR 91*
Myrer, Anton Olmstead 1922- *WhoAm 90*
Myres, J N L 1902-1989 *ConAu 129*
Myres, Nowell 1902-1989 *AnObit 1989*
Myrick, Bob 1952- *Ballpl 90*
Myrick, Debby Jayne 1960- *WhoSSW 91*
Myrick, H. L. 1827-1913 *AmLegL*
Myrick, Henry L. 1946- *St&PR 91*
Myrick, Irma S. Kitchen 1915- *WhoAmW 91*
Myrick, John Southall, II 1933- *WhoSSW 91*
Myrick, Katherine S *WhoAmA 91N*
Myrick, Kimberly Marie 1960- *WhoAmW 91*
Myrick, Marilou Rightley 1947- *WhoAmW 91*
Myrick, Mildred *AuBYP 90*
Myrick, Sue 1941- *WhoAm 90, WhoAmW 91, WhoSSW 91*
Myrick, Vera Mae 1952- *WhoAmW 91*
Myricks, Larry *BioIn 16*
Myrmo, Emil A. 1917- *St&PR 91*
Myrmo, George Arthur 1946- *St&PR 91*
Myro *EncCoWW*
Myron *BioIn 16*
Myron, Kathleen Sarah *BiDrAPA 89*
Myron, Robert 1926- *AuBYP 90*
Myron, Robert 1928- *WhoAmA 91*
Myron, Robert Elias 1926- *WhoE 91*
Myrsiades, Kostas Yannis 1940- *WhoE 91*
Myrtiotissa *EncCoWW*
Myrtis *EncCoWW*
Myrus, Donald Richard 1927- *AuBYP 90*
Mysak, Edward D. 1930-1989 *BioIn 16, ConAu 130*
Mysak, Lawrence Alexander 1940- *WhoAm 90*
Myslinski, Charles Edward 1929- *St&PR 91*
Myslinski, Norbert Raymond 1947- *WhoE 91*
Mysliwiec, Christine Rose 1950- *WhoAmW 91*
Mysorewala, M. Anwer 1949- *WhoWor 91*
Myster, Jay D. 1938- *St&PR 91*
Myung, Ho-Jin 1931- *WhoWor 91*
Mzali, Mohamed 1925- *WhoWor 91*

N

N, M *BiDEWW*
Na-ai-che 1857?-1921 *WhNaAH*
Naar, Alan S. 1951- *WhoEmL 91*
Naar, Harry I 1946- *WhoAmA 91*
Naas, David Hugh 1956- *WhoSSW 91*
Nabavi, Abdollah *BiDrAPA 89*
Nabb, Lowery H. 1941- *St&PR 91*
Nabb, Magdalen 1947- *TwCCr&M 91*
Nabbes, Thomas 1605?-1641 *BioIn 16*
Naber, Cynthia Sheridan 1949- *WhoAmW 91*
Naber, Steven John 1952- *St&PR 91*
Naber, Thomas W. 1951- *St&PR 91*
Naber, Walter Jerome, Jr. 1919- *WhoAm 90*
Nabers, Drayton, Jr. 1940- *St&PR 91, WhoAm 90*
Nabholz, Walter Karl 1918- *WhoWor 91*
Nabi, Stanley A. 1930- *St&PR 91*
Nabi, Stanley Andrew 1930- *WhoAm 90*
Nabial, John Walter 1957- *St&PR 91*
Naboicheck, N. Aaron 1917- *St&PR 91*
Naboicheck, Peter Mark 1952- *St&PR 91*
Naboicheck, Robert Jon 1954- *St&PR 91*
Nabokov, Dmitri 1934- *ConAu 132, WhoWor 91*
Nabokov, Vladimir 1899-1977 *ConLC 64 [port], MajTwCW, WorAlBi*
Nabokov, Vladimir Vladimirovich 1899-1977 *BioIn 16*
Nabonidus, King of Babylonia *BioIn 16*
Nabors, Clair Alson 1912- *St&PR 91*
Nabors, Eddie Owen 1954- *St&PR 91*
Nabors, Jack 1887-1923 *Ballpl 90*
Nabors, James Douglas 1942- *St&PR 91*
Nabors, Jim 1933- *WorAlBi*
Nabuco, Joaquim 1849-1910 *BioIn 16*
Naccarato, Duane Gabriel 1945- *St&PR 91, WhoAm 90*
Naccarato, Vincent A. 1938- *St&PR 91*
Naccarella, Anthony D. 1931- *St&PR 91*
Nace, Edgar Paul 1939- *BiDrAPA 89*
Nace, Harold Russ 1921- *WhoAm 90*
Nace, Thomas C. 1944- *St&PR 91*
Nacey, Michael 1930- *St&PR 91*
Nachamie, Susan Schiffres 1942- *WhoAmW 91*
Nachbar, Randa Roen 1956- *WhoAmW 91*
Nachbar Hapai, Marlene M. 1949- *WhoAmW 91*
Nache 1857?-1921 *WhNaAH*
Nachem, Ira Wolfe 1949- *WhoE 91*
Nachemson, Alf Louis 1931- *WhoWor 91*
Nachez 1857?-1921 *WhNaAH*
Nachi 1857?-1921 *WhNaAH*
Nachise 1857?-1921 *WhNaAH*
Nachite 1857?-1921 *WhNaAH*
Nachman, Gerald 1930- *St&PR 91*
Nachman, Gerald Weil 1938- *WhoAm 90*
Nachman, Merton Roland, Jr. 1923- *WhoAm 90*
Nachman, Ronald James 1954- *WhoEmL 91, WhoWor 91*
Nachmanovitch, Stephen M. 1950- *IntWWM 90*
Nachmansohn, Edith 1903- *BiDrAPA 89*
Nachshon, Aharon 1925- *WhoWor 91*
Nacht, Daniel Joseph 1915- *WhoAm 90*
Nacht, Sacha 1901- *EncO&P 3*
Nacht, Steve Jerry 1948- *WhoEmL 91*
Nachtigal, Beatrice *BiDrAPA 89*
Nachtman, Ronald Gene 1954- *WhoSSW 91*
Nachtrieb, Norman Harry 1916- *WhoAm 90*
Nachtsheim, Edward Ernest 1930- *WhoAm 90*
Nachtwey, James 1948- *BioIn 16*
Nachumi, Gideon 1927- *BiDrAPA 89*
Nack, William *BioIn 16*
Nackenson, Burton L 1928- *BiDrAPA 89, WhoE 91*
Nacknouck, James Dominic 1950- *WhoE 91*
Naclerio, Thomas A 1911- *BiDrAPA 89*
Nacol, Habeeb Mattar 1947- *St&PR 91*
Nacol, Mae 1944- *WhoAmW 91, WhoWor 91*
Nacu-Brandewie, Pilar *BiDrAPA 89*
Nad, Leon Marion 1927- *WhoAm 90*
Nada, Juanita A. *WhoSSW 91*
Nadabrahmananda Saraswati, Swami 1896- *EncO&P 3*
Nadal, Ramon A. 1935- *BioIn 16*
Nadal, Ramon Antonio 1935- *St&PR 91*
Nadalini 1927- *WhoAmA 91*
Nadar 1820-1910 *BioIn 16*
Nadas, Alexander Sandor 1913- *WhoAm 90*
Nadas, John Adalbert 1949- *BiDrAPA 89, WhoEmL 91*
Naddafi, Nancy Lee 1947- *WhoAmW 91*
Naddeo, Alighiero 1930- *EncO&P 3*
Nadeau, Conrad J L *BiDrAPA 89*
Nadeau, John 1934- *ODwPR 91*
Nadeau, Paul Joseph 1953- *St&PR 91*
Nadeau, Robert Earle 1938- *BiDrAPA 89*
Nadeau, Timothy 1940- *St&PR 91*
Nadel, Ann Honig 1940- *WhoAmA 91*
Nadel, Charlotte *BiDrAPA 89*
Nadel, Ignat 1914- *BiDrAPA 89*
Nadel, Jack 1923- *St&PR 91*
Nadel, Jay C. 1957- *St&PR 91*
Nadel, Kay Chaney 1945- *WhoE 91*
Nadel, Marvin 1926- *St&PR 91, WhoAm 90*
Nadel, Milton 1915- *St&PR 91*
Nadel, Norman Allen 1927- *WhoAm 90*
Nadel, Stanley Mark 1942- *BiDrAPA 89*
Nadel, William R 1940- *BiDrAPA 89*
Nadelberg, Eric Paul 1947- *WhoE 91*
Nadelhoffer, Hans *BioIn 16*
Nadell, Andrew Thomas 1946- *BiDrAPA 89, WhoWor 91*
Nadell, Raymond *BiDrAPA 89*
Nadelman, Elie 1882-1946 *BioIn 16*
Nadelman, Maurice S *BiDrAPA 89*
Nadelmann, Ethan Avram 1957- *WhoE 91*
Nadelson, Carol C 1936- *BiDrAPA 89*
Nadelson, Theodore *BiDrAPA 89*
Naden, Constance 1858-1889 *FemiCLE*
Naden, Constance Caroline Woodhill 1858-1889 *BioIn 16*
Nader, Abraham Lee 1941- *St&PR 91*
Nader, Blair 1931- *St&PR 91*
Nader, Francois Emile 1956- *WhoWor 91*
Nader, Julianna Chapman 1935- *WhoAmW 91*
Nader, Michael 1945- *ConTFT 8*
Nader, Ralph *BioIn 16*
Nader, Ralph 1934- *EncABHB 5 [port], NewYTBS 90 [port], WhoAm 90, WhoWrEP 89, WorAlBi*
Nader, Robert Alexander 1928- *WhoAm 90*
Nader, Toni *BioIn 16*
Naderi, Jamie Benedict 1951- *WhoAmW 91*
Nadershahi, Hooshang *BiDrAPA 89*
Nadherny, Ferdinand *WhoAm 90*
Nadich, Judah 1912- *BioIn 16, WhoAm 90, WhoE 91*
Nadig, Gerald George 1945- *WhoAm 90*
Nadin, Peter *BioIn 16*
Nadir, Moshe *EncAL*
Nadiri, M. Ishaq 1936- *WhoAm 90*
Nadjafi, Morteza 1945- *BiDrAPA 89*
Nadkarni, Gajanan Shivarao 1939- *WhoWor 91*
Nadkarni, Girish Vishwanath 1957- *WhoE 91*
Nadkarni, Govind Bhalchandra 1950- *St&PR 91*
Nadler, Dorothy Luria *WhoWrEP 89*
Nadler, Emanuel 1934- *St&PR 91*
Nadler, Eric N. 1943- *St&PR 91*
Nadler, Gerald 1924- *WhoAm 90*
Nadler, Harry 1930- *WhoAmA 91*
Nadler, Henry Louis 1936- *WhoAm 90*
Nadler, Leonard *BioIn 16*
Nadler, Maurice 1908- *WhoSSW 91*
Nadler, Myron Jay 1923- *WhoAm 90*
Nadler, Paul S. 1930- *St&PR 91*
Nadler, Sheila June 1943- *WhoAm 90*
Nadler, Sigmond Harold 1932- *WhoAm 90*
Nadler-Hurvich, Hedda C. 1944- *ODwPR 91*
Nadley, Harris Jerome 1926- *WhoAm 90, WhoE 91*
Nadol, Joseph B., Jr. 1943- *WhoAm 90*
Nadol, Robert 1944- *BiDrAPA 89*
Nadolny, Grace Christine *BiDrAPA 89*
Nadolski, Stephanie Lucille 1945- *WhoAmA 91*
Nadolsky, Richard J. 1940- *St&PR 91*
Nador, Frank *BiDrAPA 89*
Nadrich, Richard Maxwell 1950- *WhoE 91*
Nadzick, Judith Ann 1948- *St&PR 91, WhoAm 90, WhoAmW 91*
Naeem, Ahmad 1946- *WhoWor 91*
Naef, Weston John 1942- *WhoAm 90*
Naeff, Top 1878-1953 *EncCoWW*
Naegele, Carl Joseph 1939- *WhoAm 90*
Naegele, David *NewAgMG*
Naegele, Philipp Otto 1928- *IntWWM 90, WhoAm 90*
Naegle, Montana 1940- *WhoAmA 91*
Naegle, Stephen Howard 1938-1981 *WhoAmA 91N*
Naegli-Osjord, Hans 1909- *EncPaPR 91*
Nael, Siavash 1945- *BiDrAPA 89*
Naeser, Nancy Dearien 1944- *WhoAmW 91*
Naessens, Michael Garrett 1964- *WhoE 91*
Naeve, Milo M 1931- *WhoAmA 91*
Naeve, Milo Merle 1931- *WhoAm 90*
Naeye, Richard L. 1929- *WhoAm 90*
Naf, Anton Beat 1946- *WhoWor 91*
Nafe, Alicia 1947- *IntWWM 90*
Nafe, John Elliott 1914- *WhoAm 90*
Naficy, Mohamad Javad 1942- *BiDrAPA 89*
Nafie, Ibrahim Abdel Fattah 1934- *WhoWor 91*
Nafie, Laurence Allen 1945- *WhoAm 90*
Nafilyan, Guy 1945- *St&PR 91*
Nafis, Robert Allen 1928- *WhoAm 90*
Naftalin, Arthur 1917- *WhoAm 90*
Naftalin, Moses *BiDrAPA 89*
Naftalis, Gary Philip 1941- *WhoAm 90, WhoE 91, WhoWor 91*
Naftel, Albert Jackson 1952- *BiDrAPA 89*
Naftolin, Frederick 1936- *WhoAm 90*
Naftulin, Donald H 1932- *BiDrAPA 89*
Naftulin, Rose *WhoAmA 91*
Naftzger, Dale A. 1945- *St&PR 91*
Naftzger, John E. 1918- *St&PR 91*
Naftzinger, H. Robert 1928- *St&PR 91*
Nafzger, Carl *NewYTBS 90*
Nafziger, Estel Wayne 1938- *WhoAm 90*
Nafziger, George F 1949- *ConAu 132*
Nafziger, J Calvin 1941- *BiDrAPA 89*
Nafziger, Marvin J. 1933- *St&PR 91*
Nag, Tore 1953- *St&PR 91*
Nagae, Yoshio 1928- *WhoWor 91*
Nagai, Hiroshi 1921- *WhoWor 91*
Nagai, Kanegi 1931- *St&PR 91*
Nagai, Kazumasa 1929- *ConDes 90*
Nagai, Kunio 1915- *WhoWor 91*
Nagai, Tsuneji 1933- *WhoWor 91*
Nagako, Empress *EncJap*
Nagakubo, Masahiro 1949- *WhoWor 91*
Nagamatsu, Henry Takeshi 1916- *WhoAm 90*
Nagamoto, Herbert T 1956- *BiDrAPA 89*
Nagamura, Toshio *BioIn 16*
Nagan, Douglas A. 1941- *St&PR 91*
Nagan, Douglas Andrew 1941- *WhoE 91*
Nagan, Peter Seymour 1920- *WhoE 91*
Nagano, Kent 1951- *IntWWM 90*
Nagano, Osami 1880-1947 *WorAlBi*
Nagano, Paul Tatsumi 1938- *WhoAmA 91*
Nagano, Shozo *WhoAmA 91*
Nagar, Shyam Sunder 1935- *WhoWor 91*
Nagaraj, Padmini *BiDrAPA 89*
Nagaraju, Arramraju 1948- *BiDrAPA 89*
Nagarakanti, Nagaswara Rao *BiDrAPA 89*
Nagarkar, Sachin B *BiDrAPA 89*
Nagarkatti, Jai P. 1947- *St&PR 91*
Nagasaki, Hojun 1934- *WhoWor 91*
Nagasawa, Hiroshi 1936- *WhoWor 91*
Nagashima, Shigeo 1937- *Ballpl 90*
Nagasubramanian, Suryanarayanan 1938- *WhoWor 91*
Nagata, Isamu 1930- *WhoWor 91*
Nagata, Jun-Iti 1925- *WhoWor 91*
Nagata, Kenneth Masuhisa 1945- *WhoEmL 91*
Nagata, Ryo 1924- *WhoWor 91*
Nagata, Takao 1943- *WhoWor 91*
Nagatsu, Toshiharu 1930- *WhoWor 91*
Nagawara, Makoto 1927- *WhoWor 91*
Nagaya, Yoshihiko 1941- *St&PR 91*
Nagayama, Akira 1949- *WhoWor 91*
Nagel, Andreas Fisher- 1951- *BioIn 16*
Nagel, Bruce F. 1946- *St&PR 91*
Nagel, Charles 1849-1940 *BiDrUSE 89*
Nagel, Charles L *BiDrAPA 89*
Nagel, Chris B., Jr. 1952- *WhoE 91*
Nagel, Conrad 1896-1970 *WorAlBi*
Nagel, Denise M 1952- *BiDrAPA 89*
Nagel, Edward M. 1926- *St&PR 91*
Nagel, Edward McCaul 1926- *WhoAm 90*
Nagel, Elizabeth Marie *BiDrAPA 89*
Nagel, Enrique G 1928- *BiDrAPA 89*
Nagel, Hans 1930- *WhoWor 91*
Nagel, Heiderose Fischer- 1956- *BioIn 16*
Nagel, Kim Elliot *BiDrAPA 89*

Nagel, Madeline 1939- WhoAmW 91
Nagel, Paul Chester 1926- WhoAm 90
Nagel, Richard 1957- WhoWrEP 89
Nagel, Robert Forder 1947- WhoEmL 91
Nagel, Robert Hamilton 1918- WhoAm 90
Nagel, Robert Harry 1955- WhoE 91
Nagel, Robert W. 1940- St&PR 91
Nagel, Sidney Robert 1948- WhoAm 90
Nagel, Spencer Carlyle 1927- St&PR 91
Nagel, Stephen R. 1950- St&PR 91
Nagel, Stina 1918-1969 WhoAmA 91N
Nagel, Stuart S. 1934- ConAu 33NR
Nagel, Stuart Samuel 1934- WhoAm 90
Nagel, Thomas 1937- WhoAm 90
Nagel, Tracy Lynn 1967- WhoAmW 91
Nagel, Warren 1945- WhoE 91
Nagel Soepenberg, Everhardus 1933- WhoWor 91
Nagele, Emil John 1924- St&PR 91
Nagele, Rainer 1943- WhoAm 90
Nageli, Philip PenDiMP
Nagenda, Musa 1928- BioIn 16
Nagengast, William Joseph 1934- WhoAmA 91
Nageotte, Catherine Ann 1961- BiDrAPA 89
Nager, Rob 1948- St&PR 91
Nager, Steve 1949- WhoWor 91
Nagera, Humberto 1927- BiDrAPA 89, WhoAm 90
Nagesh, Priyamvada BiDrAPA 89
Nagey, David Augustus 1950- WhoEmL 91
Naggar, Jean BioIn 16
Naggs, Karle Frederick 1933- St&PR 91
Nagi, Mostafa Helmey 1934- WhoWor 91
Nagi, Saad Zaghloul 1925- WhoAm 90, WhoWor 91
Nagi, Terry Allen 1939- WhoE 91
Nagiel, Esther-Marie 1956- WhoWrEP 89
Nagin, Lawrence M. ODwPR 91
Nagin, Lawrence M. 1941- St&PR 91
Nagl, Ludwig 1944- WhoWor 91
Naglak, Jeanne Rand 1959- WhoE 91
Nagle, Arlington, Jr. 1943- St&PR 91, WhoAm 90
Nagle, Arthur Joseph 1938- St&PR 91, WhoAm 90
Nagle, Avery AuBYP 90
Nagle, Charles Leo, IV 1955- WhoSSW 91
Nagle, David Patrick, Jr. 1952- WhoSSW 91
Nagle, David R. 1943- WhoAm 90
Nagle, Friend Richard 1930- St&PR 91
Nagle, George, Jr. 1932- WhoE 91
Nagle, George Raymond 1947- WhoE 91
Nagle, Hubert Troy, Jr. 1942- WhoAm 90
Nagle, James Francis 1948- WhoE 91
Nagle, James M. 1946- St&PR 91
Nagle, Justine Teresa 1940- WhoWor 91
Nagle, Richard Kent 1947- WhoEmL 91
Nagle, Robert John 1958- WhoE 91
Nagle, Robert R. ODwPR 91
Nagle, Ron 1939- WhoAmA 91
Naglee, David Ingersoll 1930- WhoWrEP 89
Nagler, Alois Maria 1907- WhoAm 90
Nagler, Barney 1912-1990 ConAu 132
Nagler, David Bruce BiDrAPA 89
Nagler, Edith Kroger 1895-1986 WhoAmA 91N
Nagler, Eric BioIn 16
Nagler, Fred 1891-1983 WhoAmA 91N
Nagler, Leon Gregory 1932- St&PR 91, WhoAm 90
Nagler, Ronald Markland 1931- St&PR 91
Nagler, Simon H 1910- BiDrAPA 89
Nagler, Stewart Gordon 1943- St&PR 91, WhoAm 90
Nagler, William 1951- BiDrAPA 89
Nagler, Yaacov 1947- St&PR 91
Nagley, Winfield Eugene 1918- WhoAm 90
Naglich, Donald Ray 1951- WhoEmL 91
Naglieri, Thomas Joseph 1937- WhoAm 90
Naglin, Nancy 1949- ODwPR 91
Naglo, Olof 1928- WhoWor 91
Nagobads, Ilgvars J 1927- BiDrAPA 89
Nagorniak, John Joseph 1944- WhoE 91
Nagorske, Lynn A. 1956- St&PR 91
Nagorski, Edwin Allan 1926- St&PR 91
Nagoshi, Craig Tetsuo 1956- WhoEmL 91
Nagoshi, Douglas N. 1942- St&PR 91
Nagourney, Herbert 1926- St&PR 91, WhoAm 90
Nagrani, Shyam Kishinchand 1948- WhoEmL 91
Nagucka, Ruta Rafaela 1930- WhoWor 91
Naguib, Mohsen Sobhy 1949- WhoWor 91
Nagulendran, Nirmalam BiDrAPA 89
Nagulendran, Veluppillai BiDrAPA 89
Nagumo, Chuichi 1887?-1944 WorAlBi
Nagurski, Bronislaw 1908-1990 WorAlBi
Nagurski, Bronko 1908-1990 BioIn 16, NewYTBS 90 [port]
Nagus, Edward Leo 1945- WhoE 91
Nagy, Agnes Nemes 1922- EncCoWW
Nagy, Alexander Joseph 1950- IntWWM 90
Nagy, Andrew Francis 1932- WhoAm 90
Nagy, Bartholomew Stephen 1927- WhoAm 90
Nagy, Bela Boszormenyi- 1912-1990 BioIn 16
Nagy, Brian R 1937- BiDrAPA 89
Nagy, Christa Fiedler 1943- WhoAmW 91
Nagy, Clive Michael 1936- St&PR 91
Nagy, Dennis Joseph 1953- WhoE 91
Nagy, Drew Pollander 1961- WhoAmW 91
Nagy, Gerald P. St&PR 91
Nagy, Imre BioIn 16
Nagy, Imre 1896-1958 WorAlBi
Nagy, Ivan WhoWor 91
Nagy, Janos B. 1943- IntWWM 90
Nagy, Jo Anne 1952- WhoEmL 91
Nagy, Joan C BiDrAPA 89
Nagy, Laszlo 1925-1978 ConAu 129
Nagy, Linda Mae 1957- BiDrAPA 89
Nagy, Mike 1948- Ballpl 90
Nagy, Peter 1920- WhoWor 91
Nagy, Robert 1929- IntWWM 90
Nagy, Robert David 1929- WhoAm 90
Nagy, Robert E. 1942- St&PR 91
Nagy, Robert Michael 1960- BiDrAPA 89
Nagy, Shamin Nafees BiDrAPA 89
Nagy, Stephen Felsobuki 1944- WhoAm 90
Nagy, Stephen Sumner 1950- BiDrAPA 89
Nagy, Stephen William 1940- St&PR 91
Nagy, Steven 1936- WhoSSW 91
Nagyte-KatiliSkiene, Zinaida EncCoWW
Nagyvary, Joseph BioIn 16
Naha, Raymond WhoAmA 91N
Naharro, Jose Maria 1912- St&PR 91
Naharro-Calderon, Jose Maria 1953- WhoHisp 91
Nahas, Abbas D BiDrAPA 89
Nahas, Fred 1913- WhoSSW 91
Nahas, Gabriel G. 1920- BioIn 16
Nahas, Gabriel Georges 1920- WhoAm 90, WhoWor 91
Nahat, Dennis F. 1946- WhoAm 90
Nahavandi, Amir Nezameddin 1924- WhoAm 90
Nahay, Paul 1958- IntWWM 90
Nahche 1857?-1921 WhNaAH
Nahem, Sam 1915- Ballpl 90
Nahhas, Mustafa Al- 1879-1965 PolLCME
Nahienaena 1815?-1836 BioAmW
Nahigian, Alma Louise 1936- WhoAmW 91
Nahigian, Robert John 1956- WhoE 91, WhoEmL 91, WhoWor 91
Nahikian, Willaim Orr 1944- St&PR 91
Nahl, Johann August 1710-1785 PenDiDA 89
Nahlen, Dana Gayle 1955- WhoEmL 91
Nahmad, Albert Henry 1940- St&PR 91
Nahman, Murray 1927- St&PR 91
Nahman, Norris Stanley 1925- WhoAm 90
Nahmias, Andre Joseph 1930- WhoAm 90
Nahmias, Larry M BiDrAPA 89
Nahmias, Victor Jay 1951- WhoEmL 91
Nahon, Alice 1896-1933 EncCoWW
Nahon, Gerard 1931 WhoWor 91
Nahon, Marco 1895- BioIn 16
Nahorodny, Bill 1953- Ballpl 90
Nahoun, Martin Joel 1945- St&PR 91
Nahra, Nancy Ann 1947- WhoWrEP 89
Nahrwold, David Lange 1935- WhoAm 90
Nahstoll, Richardson Wadsworth 1918- WhoAm 90
Nahum, Daniel David 1946- BiDrAPA 89
Nahum, Jeremy P BiDrAPA 89
Naiche 1857?-1921 WhNaAH
Naida, Ludmilla BioIn 16
Naides, Philip 1930- St&PR 91
Naidoo, Beverley 1943- SmATA 63 [port]
Naidoo, Beverly AuBYP 90
Naidoo, Stephen BioIn 16
Naidoo, Sury 1961- BiDrAPA 89
Naidorf, Louis Murray 1928- WhoAm 90
Naidu, Jayarama K BiDrAPA 89
Naidu, Manoranjani I 1943- BiDrAPA 89
Naidu, Sarojini 1879-1949 FemiCLE
Naidu, Tummala P 1942- BiDrAPA 89
Naif Ibn Abdulaziz, Prince 1933- WhoWor 91
Naifeh, John Thomas 1958- WhoSSW 91
Naifeh, Sam Charles 1943- BiDrAPA 89
Naik, Nalini D BiDrAPA 89
Nail, B.G. 1923- St&PR 91
Nail, Dawson B. 1928- WhoWrEP 89
Nail, Elizabeth Joana 1937- WhoAmW 91
Nail, Jasper Monroe 1939- WhoSSW 91
Nail, Ronald Albert 1943- IntWWM 90
Nail, Sharon Alexis 1949- WhoAmW 91
Nail, Sonya Kaye 1962- WhoSSW 91
Naille, Richard Allen, II 1945- WhoAm 90
Naillon, Valerine 1960- WhoWrEP 89
Nailor, Gerald Lloyde 1917-1952 WhoAmA 91N
Nailor, Richard Anthony 1935- WhoSSW 91
Naim, Joseph 1955- WhoWor 91
Naiman, James 1926- BiDrAPA 89
Naiman, Lee WhoAmA 91
Naiman, Lilya Borisovna 1951- BiDrAPA 89
Naiman, Robert Morton BiDrAPA 89
Naimark, Arnold 1933- WhoAm 90
Naimark, George Modell 1925- WhoE 91
Naimark, Mark Aronovich 1909-1978 DcScB S2
Naimi, Shapur 1928- WhoAm 90, WhoE 91
Naimoli, Raymond Anthony 1942- WhoE 91
Naimoli, Vincent Joseph 1937- St&PR 91, WhoAm 90
Naimy, Mikhail 1889-1988 BioIn 16
Naini, Bhoopal Reddy 1944- WhoSSW 91
Naipaul, Shiva 1945-1985 ConAu 33NR, MajTwCW, WorAu 1980 [port]
Naipaul, Shivadhar Srinivasa 1945-1985 DcNaB 1981
Naipaul, V. S. 1932- BioIn 16
Naipaul, V.S. 1932- ConAu 33NR, MajTwCW
Naipaul, V. S. 1932- WorAlBi
Naipaul, Vidiadhar Surajprasad 1932- BioIn 16, WhoAm 90, WhoWor 91
Nair, Bala Radhakrishnan 1936- WhoE 91
Nair, D Sreedharan 1936- BiDrAPA 89
Nair, Garyth 1943- IntWWM 90
Nair, K C R 1938- BiDrAPA 89
Nair, Malathy S BiDrAPA 89
Nair, Mira BioIn 16
Nair, Mohan S 1950- BiDrAPA 89
Nair, N P Vasavan BiDrAPA 89
Nair, Nalapat S BiDrAPA 89
Nair, Ramachandran P.K. 1942- WhoSSW 91
Nair, Shanta BiDrAPA 89
Nair, Velayudhan 1928- WhoAm 90, WhoWor 91
Nairn, James Francis 1945- St&PR 91, WhoEmL 91
Nairn, Penny Sue 1949- WhoAmW 91
Nairn, Stephen 1838-1900 DcCanB 12
Nairn, Tom Cunningham 1932- WhoWor 91
Nairne, Carolina 1766-1845 FemiCLE, OxCPMus
Nairne, Carolina Oliphant 1766-1845 BioIn 16
Nairne, Thomas 1715- EncCRAm
Naisbitt, H.A. 1908- St&PR 91
Naisbitt, John, and Patricia Aburdene BestSel 90-3 [port]
Naisbitt, John H. WorAlBi
Naish, J. Carroll 1900-1973 WorAlBi
Naismith, James 1861-1939 BioIn 16, WorAlBi
Naito, Bill BioIn 16
Naito, Kenji 1933- WhoWor 91
Naito, Takeshi 1929- St&PR 91, WhoAm 90, WhoWor 91
Naitove, Matthew Henry 1949- WhoAm 90
Najafi, Hassan 1930- WhoAm 90
Najar, Leo Michael 1953- WhoEmL 91
Najarian, Beverly Elizabeth 1935- St&PR 91
Najarian, John Sarkis 1927- WhoAm 90, WhoWor 91
Najarian, Louis M 1942- BiDrAPA 89
Najarian, Melvin Kenneth 1939- WhoAm 90
Najder, Kenneth John 1960- WhoSSW 91
Najdzin, Jean M. 1932- St&PR 91
Najera, Edmund L. 1936- WhoHisp 91
Najera, Enrique 1934- WhoWor 91
Najera, Gabriel A 1927- BiDrAPA 89, WhoE 91
Najera, Manuel Gutierrez 1859-1895 BioIn 16
Najera, Rafael 1938- WhoWor 91
Najera, Richard Almeraz 1937- WhoHisp 91
Najibullah, Mohammed BioIn 16
Najibullah, S'ayid Mohammad 1947- WhoWor 91
Najimy, Kathy BioIn 16
Najita, Tetsuo 1936- WhoAm 90
Najjar, Edward George 1934- St&PR 91
Najjoum, Linda Lemmon 1946- WhoEmL 91
Najmajer, Marie von 1844-1904 EncCoWW
Naka, Syuzo BiDrAPA 89
Nakadate, Neil Edward 1943- WhoWrEP 89
Nakae, Chomin 1847-1901 BioIn 16
Nakae, Kinichi 1940- St&PR 91
Nakae, Noriko 1940- AuBYP 90, BioIn 16
Nakae, Tokusuke 1847-1901 BioIn 16
Nakagami, Hidetoshi 1945- WhoWor 91
Nakagawa, Jean H. 1943- St&PR 91
Nakagawa, Jean Harue 1943- WhoAm 90
Nakagawa, Roger T. 1947- St&PR 91
Nakagawa, Yasuaki 1929- WhoWor 91
Nakahama, Karl 1935- St&PR 91
Nakahira, Kosuke 1939- BioIn 16
Nakai, Bhupinder Singh 1954- BiDrAPA 89
Nakai, Mitsuru 1933- WhoWor 91
Nakai, R. Carlos NewAgMG
Nakai, Teresa 1960- WhoAmW 91
Nakaidoklini WhNaAH
Nakajima, Hiroshi 1928- WhoWor 91
Nakajima, Toshinari 1930- WhoWor 91
Nakajima, Tsuneo 1937- WhoWor 91
Nakajima, Yasuko 1932- WhoAmW 91
Nakakuki, Masafumi 1930- BiDrAPA 89, WhoWor 91
Nakamine, Wendell Tadao 1948- WhoAm 90
Nakamizo, Fuji 1889- WhoAmA 91N
Nakamoto, Hiroko AuBYP 90
Nakamoto, Kazuo 1922- WhoAm 90
Nakamura, Akira 1934- WhoWor 91
Nakamura, Diane ODwPR 91
Nakamura, Eiko 1931- WhoWor 91
Nakamura, Hiromichi 1942- WhoWor 91
Nakamura, Hiromu 1926- WhoWor 91
Nakamura, Hisao 1923- WhoWor 91
Nakamura, James I. 1919- WhoAm 90
Nakamura, Kazuo 1926- WhoAm 90, WhoAmA 91
Nakamura, Kazuya 1948- WhoWor 91
Nakamura, Kenichi 1933- WhoWor 91
Nakamura, Kenzo 1924- St&PR 91
Nakamura, Kikuko 1931- IntWWM 90
Nakamura, Leonard Isamu 1948- WhoE 91
Nakamura, Makoto 1936- ConDes 90
Nakamura, Masako 1930- WhoWor 91
Nakamura, Melvin Masato 1936- St&PR 91
Nakamura, Mitsuru James 1926- WhoAm 90
Nakamura, Robert Motoharu 1927- WhoAm 90
Nakamura, Shoshiro 1929- WhoWor 91
Nakamura, Toru 1929- WhoWor 91
Nakamura, Yasuo St&PR 91
Nakane, Chie 1926- BioIn 16
Nakane, Keiichi 1918- WhoWor 91
Nakanishi, Futoshi 1931- Ballpl 90
Nakanishi, Koji 1925- WhoAm 90
Nakanishi, Tsutomu 1939- WhoWor 91
Nakano, Dokuohtei 1929- AuBYP 90
Nakano, Raymond T. 1945- St&PR 91
Nakano, Takeo 1926- WhoWor 91
Nakano, Yasuo 1922- WhoWor 91
Nakaoka, John Tatsuya 1952- WhoEmL 91, WhoWor 91
Nakarai, Charles Frederick Toyozo 1936- IntWWM 90
Nakashian, Mary Rose 1947- WhoAmW 91
Nakashima, George 1905- EncJap, PenDiDA 89
Nakashima, George 1905-1990 BioIn 16, NewYTBS 90
Nakashima, Izumi 1940- WhoWor 91
Nakashima, Kunio 1939- WhoWor 91
Nakasone Yasuhiro 1918- EncJap
Nakasone, Yasuhiro BioIn 16
Nakasone, Yasuhiro 1918- WhoWor 91
Nakata, Herbert Minoru 1930- WhoAm 90
Nakata, Ikuo 1935- WhoWor 91
Nakata, Shuji 1937- WhoWor 91
Nakata, Thomas BiDrAPA 89
Nakata, William Jiro 1950- St&PR 91
Nakata, Yoshi-Fumi 1955- WhoWor 91
Nakatani, Chiyoko 1930-1981 BioIn 16
Nakatani, Roy Eiji 1918- WhoAm 90
Nakatomi Clan EncJap
Nakatsuji, Norio 1950- WhoWor 91
Nakatsuji, Teruyuki 1947- WhoWor 91
Nakatsuka, Kazuo 1933- WhoWor 91
Nakatsuka, Lawrence Kaoru 1920- WhoWrEP 89
Nakauchi, Isao BioIn 16
Nakauchi, Shunsaku 1920- WhoWor 91
Nakayama, Akiyoshi 1930- WhoWor 91
Nakayama, Roy M. 1923-1988 BioIn 16
Nakayama, Tadashi 1932- WhoE 91
Nakayama, Taro 1924- WhoWor 91
Nakazato, Hitoshi 1936- WhoAmA 91
Nakazawa, Hiromu 1938- WhoWor 91
Nakazawa, Kazuto 1926- WhoWor 91
Nakazawa, Paul Wesley 1951- WhoEmL 91, WhoSSW 91
Nakdimen, Kenneth Alan 1947- BiDrAPA 89, WhoE 91
Naker, Mary Leslie 1954- WhoAmW 91, WhoEmL 91, WhoWor 91
Nakhjiri, Karen Sue 1955- WhoEmL 91
Nakhla, Fayek Latif 1933- BiDrAPA 89
Nakhleh, Emile A. 1938- WhoAm 90, WhoE 91
Nakhleh, Faraj M. 1945- St&PR 91
Nakhleh, Faraj Mueen 1945- WhoWor 91
Nakhosteen, John Alexander 1937- WhoWor 91
Nakoa, Austin Paakaula 1949- St&PR 91
Nakoneczny, Michael 1952- WhoAmA 91
Nakonek, Michael L. 1951- St&PR 91
Nakou, Lilika 1903-1989 EncCoWW

Nakovich, Frank 1947- *WhoE 91*
Nakra, Bharat Raj S 1943- *BiDrAPA 89*
Nakra, Rashmi Rani 1947- *BiDrAPA 89*
Naktenis, Peter E. 1914- *St&PR 91*
Nakura, Yoshiko *PenDiMP*
Nalbert, Richard Walter 1933- *St&PR 91*
Nalcioglu, Orhan 1944- *WhoAm 90*
Nalder, Eric Christopher 1946- *WhoAm 90*
Naldrett, Anthony James 1933- *WhoAm 90*
Nalebuff, Barry James 1958- *WhoE 91*
Nalecz *EncCoWW*
Nalen, Craig A. *BioIn 16*
Nalen, Craig Anthony 1930- *WhoAm 90*
Nalewaja, Donna *WhoAmW 91*
Nalewako, Mary A. 1934- *St&PR 91*
Nalkowska, Zofia 1884-1954 *EncCoWW*
Nall, J. Rodman 1937- *ODwPR 91, St&PR 91*
Nall, Joseph T. *BioIn 16*
Nall, LaWanda Carol 1964- *WhoAmW 91, WhoEmL 91*
Nall, Sandra Lillian 1943- *WhoSSW 91*
Nall, T. Otto 1900-1989 *BioIn 16*
Nall, Torney Otto 1900-1989 *BioIn 16*
Nalle, George S., III 1945- *St&PR 91*
Nalle, George S., Jr. 1919- *St&PR 91*
Nalle, Horace Disston, Jr. 1956- *WhoEmL 91*
Nalle, Peter Devereux 1947- *WhoAm 90*
Nalley, Blanche Almedia 1939- *WhoAmW 91*
Nalley, George Burdine, Jr. 1938- *St&PR 91*
Nallin, Dick *Ballpl 90*
Nallinmaa, Eero Veikko 1917- *IntWWM 90*
Nalls, C Arthur, III 1945- *BiDrAPA 89*
Nalluri, Anil Choudary 1947- *BiDrAPA 89*
Nally, Thomas John 1949- *WhoE 91*
Nalywajko, Eugene 1926- *St&PR 91*
Nam, Charles Benjamin 1926- *WhoAm 90, WhoWor 91*
Nam, Sang Boo 1936- *WhoAm 90*
Nam, Sang Kyu *BiDrAPA 89*
Nam, Theodore S *BiDrAPA 89*
Nama, George Allen 1939- *WhoAmA 91*
Namaliu, Rabbie *WhoWor 91*
Namath, Joe *BioIn 16*
Namath, Joe 1943- *WorAlBi*
Namath, Joseph William 1943- *WhoAm 90*
Namba, Tatsuji 1927- *WhoAm 90, WhoE 91, WhoWor 91*
Namboodiri, Krishnan 1929- *WhoAm 90*
Nambu, Yasuyuki *BioIn 16*
Nambudiri, Draupathi *BiDrAPA 89*
Namdari, Bahram 1939- *WhoWor 91*
Namekata, Akio 1931- *WhoWor 91*
Nameny, Grace Westberg 1921- *WhoAmW 91*
Namias, Jerome 1910- *WhoAm 90*
Namier, Lewis 1888-1960 *BioIn 16*
Namihira, Isao *WhoWor 91*
Namingha, Dan 1950- *BioIn 16, WhoAmA 91*
Namiot, Milton *St&PR 91*
Namjoshi, Suniti 1941- *FemiCLE*
Namkung, Kang 1958- *WhoWor 91*
Namnum, Alfredo 1919- *BiDrAPA 89*
Namontack *WhNaAH*
Namora, Fernando 1919-1989 *BioIn 16*
Namour, Michel Alexandre 1935- *WhoE 91*
Namovicz, Gene Inyart 1927- *AuBYP 90*
Nampayo 1860?-1942 *WhNaAH [port]*
Nampayu 1860?-1942 *WhNaAH [port]*
Nampeyo 1860?-1942 *MusmAFA, WhNaAH [port]*
Namphy, Henri 1932- *WhoWor 91*
Namphy, Henry 1932- *BioIn 16*
Nampoothiri, Sreedevi 1947- *BiDrAPA 89*
Namuth, Hans 1915- *WhoAm 90*
Namuth, Hans 1915-1990 *NewYTBS 90 [port], WhoAmA 91N*
Nana 1810?-1895 *WhNaAH*
Nanadiego, Maria C S 1952- *BiDrAPA 89*
Nanak, Guru 1469-1538 *BioIn 16*
Nanasi, Leslie 1920- *St&PR 91*
Nanasy, Connie Smith 1932- *WhoAmW 91*
Nanavati, Dinesh M 1935- *BiDrAPA 89*
Nanavati, Mahendra B 1935- *BiDrAPA 89*
Nanawala, Jitendra N *BiDrAPA 89*
Nanay 1810?-1895 *WhNaAH*
Nanay, Julia 1951- *WhoAmW 91*
Nanberg, Leslie J. 1945- *St&PR 91*
Nancarrow, Conlon 1912- *IntWWM 90*
Nancarrow, David Guy 1926- *St&PR 91*
Nance, Albinus *AmLegL*
Nance, Allan Taylor 1933- *WhoAm 90*
Nance, Betty Love 1923- *WhoAm 90, WhoAmW 91, WhoSSW 91, WhoWor 91*
Nance, Cecil Boone, Jr. 1925- *WhoAm 90*
Nance, Earl Charles 1939- *WhoSSW 91*
Nance, Harold W. 1924- *St&PR 91*
Nance, Howard Lynn 1947- *WhoSSW 91*
Nance, Jean Claire 1924- *WhoAmW 91*
Nance, Joel H 1942- *BiDrAPA 89*
Nance, Joseph Milton 1913- *WhoAm 90*
Nance, Marjorie Greenfield 1949- *WhoE 91*
Nance, Mary Joe 1921- *WhoAmW 91, WhoSSW 91, WhoWor 91*
Nance, Mary Judene 1961- *WhoAmW 91*
Nance, Mary L *BiDrAPA 89*
Nance, Peter Maurice 1944- *St&PR 91, WhoAm 90*
Nance, Ray 1913-1976 *OxCPMus*
Nance, Ronald Gene 1957- *WhoSSW 91*
Nance, Thomas K. *St&PR 91*
Nance, Tony Max-Perry 1955- *WhoAm 90*
Nanda, Dave Kumar 1938- *St&PR 91*
Nanda, Kapil Kumar 1945- *St&PR 91*
Nanda, Nandita 1948- *BiDrAPA 89*
Nandakumar, Vellore G 1942- *BiDrAPA 89*
Nandani, Sarla M *BiDrAPA 89*
Nandi, Dhirendra N *BiDrAPA 89*
Nandi, Dipak *BiDrAPA 89*
Nandi, Satyabrata 1931- *WhoAm 90*
Nandoe, Kriesnadath 1935- *WhoWor 91*
Nane 1810?-1895 *WhNaAH*
Nanfria, Linda Jean 1949- *WhoWrEP 89*
Nangeroni, John Arthur 1953- *WhoE 91*
Nangle, John Francis 1922- *WhoAm 90*
Nanjundasamy, Anaimalai V 1935- *BiDrAPA 89*
Nank, Lois Rae *WhoAmW 91, WhoWor 91*
Nannapaneni, Meena Kumari *BiDrAPA 89*
Nannarello, Joseph John 1915- *BiDrAPA 89*
Nannary, William 1839-1887? *OxCCanT*
Nanne, Louis Vincent 1941- *WhoAm 90*
Nanney, David Ledbetter 1925- *WhoAm 90*
Nanney, Herbert Boswell 1918- *IntWWM 90, WhoAm 90*
Nanni di Banco 137-?-1421 *IntDcAA 90*
Nannos, Arthur 1927- *St&PR 91*
Nanogak, Agnes 1925- *SmATA 61*
Nanovic, John P. 1938- *ODwPR 91*
Nanovsky, William T. 1948- *St&PR 91*
Nanpei, Henry *BioIn 16*
Nansen, Fridtjof 1861-1930 *WorAlBi*
Nanson, Deborah Faye 1953- *WhoAmW 91*
Nantell, Timothy James 1945- *WhoAm 90*
Nanto, Dick Kazuyuki 1941- *WhoE 91*
Nanton, Joe 1904-1946 *OxCPMus*
Nantz, William C. 1935- *WhoSSW 91*
Nanuntenoo *WhNaAH*
Nanut Ries, Lucia Neda 1938- *WhoWor 91*
Nanz, Robert Hamilton 1923- *WhoAm 90*
Naone, D. L. *AmLegL*
Naor, Amos 1934- *BiDrAPA 89*
Naoroji, Dadabhai 1825-1917 *BioIn 16*
Naparstek, Arthur J. 1938- *WhoAm 90*
Napello, Dolores Walters 1950- *WhoE 91*
Napier, Alan 1903-1988 *BioIn 16*
Napier, Austin 1947- *WhoE 91, WhoEmL 91*
Napier, Bill 1940- *ConAu 130*
Napier, Douglas William 1951- *WhoSSW 91, WhoWor 91*
Napier, Elizabeth Ryder 1950- *WhoEmL 91*
Napier, Elma 1892-1975? *FemiCLE*
Napier, Ernest D. 1954- *St&PR 91*
Napier, George C. 1945- *St&PR 91*
Napier, Gerald Edward 1927- *WhoAm 90*
Napier, Geraldine *ConAu 131*
Napier, James Voss 1937- *St&PR 91*
Napier, John 1550-1617 *WorAlBi*
Napier, John 1944- *ConDes 90*
Napier, John Hawkins, III 1925- *WhoSSW 91, WhoWor 91*
Napier, John Light 1947- *WhoAm 90*
Napier, Lois Christine 1942- *WhoAmW 91*
Napier, Marita 1939- *IntWWM 90*
Napier, Richard 1559-1634 *EncO&P 3*
Napier, Robert Cornelis 1810-1890 *WorAlBi*
Napier, Robert Jon 1934- *WhoAm 90, WhoWor 91*
Napier, William H. *BioIn 16*
Napierski, Geraldine E. 1949- *WhoAmW 91*
Napiorkowski, Patricia Ann *BiDrAPA 89*
Naples, Ronald James 1945- *St&PR 91*
Naples, Sharon J. 1952- *WhoE 91*
Napley, David 1915- *ConAu 129*
Napley, David, Sir *ConAu 129*
Napodano, Rudolph Joseph 1933- *WhoAm 90*
Napoleon I 1769-1821 *WorAlBi*
Napoleon III 1803-1873 *BiDFrPL*
Napoleon I, Emperor of the French 1769-1821 *BioIn 16*
Napoleon III, Emperor of the French 1808-1873 *BioIn 16*
Napoleon, Donald Paul 1954- *WhoE 91*
Napoles, Veronica 1951- *BioIn 16*
Napoles, Veronica Kleeman 1951- *WhoAm 90, WhoAmA 91*
Napoli, Brian Patrick 1951- *WhoSSW 91*
Napoli, Jacopo 1911- *IntWWM 90*
Napoli, Joseph A. 1946- *St&PR 91*
Napoli, Joseph C P *BiDrAPA 89*
Napoli, Thomas A. 1941- *St&PR 91*
Napoliello, Louis R. 1949- *St&PR 91*
Napoliello, Michael John 1942- *BiDrAPA 89, WhoE 91*
Napolitan, Gene J., Jr. 1935- *St&PR 91*
Napolitan, Gene Joseph, Jr. 1935- *WhoE 91*
Napolitano, Carmel Germaine 1959- *WhoE 91*
Napolitano, Joseph Anthony 1942- *St&PR 91*
Napolitano, Leonard Michael 1930- *WhoAm 90*
Napolitano, Michael J. 1928-1989 *BioIn 16*
Napolitano, Pat 1916- *WhoSSW 91, WhoWor 91*
Napolitano, Rosalba Gina 1961- *WhoAmW 91*
Naponic, Tony 1954- *WhoAmA 91*
Napp, Larry 1919- *Ballpl 90*
Napp-Zinn, Klaus 1927- *WhoWor 91*
Nappe, Neil *NewAgMG*
Napper, Jean Ann 1930- *WhoAmW 91*
Napper, Richard 1559-1634 *EncO&P 3*
Nappi, Anthony 1938- *BiDrAPA 89*
Nappi, Anthony R. 1935- *St&PR 91*
Nappi, Robert A. 1949- *St&PR 91*
Nappo, Elizabeth Hubbell 1959- *WhoAmW 91*
Napravnik, Eduard 1839-1916 *PenDiMP*
Naprstek, Kaya M. 1939- *St&PR 91*
Naqi'a *WomWR*
Naquet, Alfred-Joseph 1834-1916 *BiDFrPL*
Naquin, Linton Joseph, Jr. 1947- *St&PR 91*
Naquin, Oliver F. *BioIn 16*
Naqvi, Rehan Hasan 1933- *St&PR 91*
Nara, Bonnie Ann 1949- *WhoAmW 91*
Nara, Harry Raymond 1921- *WhoAm 90*
Narabayashi, Hirotaro 1922- *WhoWor 91*
Narad, Joan Stern 1943- *BiDrAPA 89, WhoE 91*
Narad, Richard M. 1935- *WhoE 91*
Naragon, Hal 1928- *Ballpl 90*
Narahashi, Keiko *AuBYP 90*
Narahashi, Toshio 1927- *WhoAm 90*
Naramore, George Harold *BiDrAPA 89*
Naramore, Lee Ellen *BiDrAPA 89*
Narang, Ashok Kumar 1939- *WhoAm 90*
Narang, Gopi Chand 1931- *ConAu 31NR*
Narang, Roshan Lal 1941- *BiDrAPA 89*
Naranja, Rogelio D 1939- *BiDrAPA 89*
Naranjo, Emilio *WhoHisp 91*
Naranjo, Filggia 1948- *WhoWor 91*
Naranjo, Jose de J. 1957- *WhoHisp 91*
Naranjo, Louis 1932- *MusmAFA*
Naranjo, Michael Alfred 1944- *BioIn 16, WhoAmA 91*
Narasimhan, Padma Mandyam 1947- *WhoAmW 91*
Narasimhan, Ram 1947- *WhoAm 90*
Narath, Albert 1933- *WhoAm 90*
Narayan, R. K. 1906- *BioIn 16*
Narayan, R.K. 1906- *ConAu 33NR, MajTwCW, SmATA 62 [port]*
Narayana, Gonchigari 1948- *BiDrAPA 89*
Narayana, M. Sankar 1961- *WhoWor 91*
Narayanamurti, Venkatesh 1939- *WhoAm 90*
Narayanan, V. 1955- *St&PR 91*
Narber, Gregg Ross 1946- *St&PR 91, WhoEmL 91*
Narbonne, Albert Joseph, Sr. 1929- *St&PR 91*
Narbutovskih, Paula *BioIn 16*
Narby, Ann Elaine 1941- *WhoE 91*
Narcisi, Calvern Eliot 1947- *BiDrAPA 89*
Nardacci, David Earl *BiDrAPA 89*
Nardi, Dann 1950- *WhoAmA 91*
Nardi, George L. 1923-1989 *BioIn 16*
Nardi, James C. 1943- *St&PR 91*
Nardi-Riddle, Clarine 1949- *WhoAm 90, WhoAmW 91, WhoE 91*
Nardiello, Catherine Cathy 1958- *IntWWM 90*
Nardin, George Frederick 1954- *WhoSSW 91*
Nardin, Mario 1940- *WhoAmA 91*
Nardini, Pietro 1722-1793 *PenDiMPA*
Nardino, Gary 1935- *WhoAm 90*
Nardo, John M *BiDrAPA 89*
Nardo, Sebastian Vincent 1917- *WhoAm 90*
Nardone, Colleen Burke 1940- *WhoAmW 91*
Nardone, Robert Carlo *BiDrAPA 89*
Nardone, Vincent Joseph 1937- *WhoAmA 91*
Nardozzi, Lawrence John *BiDrAPA 89*
Narduzzi, Joann Virginia 1937- *WhoAmW 91*
Narel, Dorothy Alma 1924- *WhoE 91, WhoWor 91*
Narell, Irena Penzik 1923- *WhoWrEP 89*
Narendra, Kumpati Subrahmanya 1933- *WhoAm 90*
Nargi, Janice Mary 1951- *WhoE 91, WhoWrEP 89*
Narhi, Sally Ann 1948- *WhoAmW 91*
Nariboli, Gundo Annacharya 1925- *WhoAm 90*
Narigan, Harold W. 1925- *WhoAm 90*
Narigan, Harold William 1925- *St&PR 91*
Narimanov, Nariman 1870-1925 *BioIn 16*
Narin, Stephen B. 1929- *WhoAm 90*
Narins, Charles Seymour 1909- *WhoWor 91*
Narins, Lyn Ross 1937- *St&PR 91*
Narisi, Stella Maria 1950- *St&PR 91*
Narkis, Robert Joseph 1934- *St&PR 91*
Narleski, Ray 1928- *Ballpl 90*
Narlikar, Jayant Vishnu 1938- *WhoWor 91*
Narodick, Sally G. 1945- *St&PR 91, WhoAm 90, WhoAmW 91*
Narola, Jaisukh Kumar *BiDrAPA 89*
Narolewski, Bernard J. 1933- *St&PR 91*
Narotzky, Norman David 1928- *WhoAmA 91*
Narotzky, Shelly Aberson 1952- *WhoE 91*
Narra, Anjani Devi *BiDrAPA 89*
Narrache, Jean 1893-1970 *DcLB 92 [port]*
Narrett, Zachary M. 1952- *ODwPR 91*
Narrin, Roberta Petronella 1939- *WhoAmW 91*
Narro-DelGiudice, Margaret Maria 1953- *WhoE 91*
Narron, Jerry 1956- *Ballpl 90*
Narrow, William E 1957- *BiDrAPA 89*
Narsavage, David A. 1946- *ODwPR 91*
Naruhito, Crown Prince *EncJap*
Narula, Amarjot Singh 1956- *BiDrAPA 89*
Narum, Buster 1940- *Ballpl 90*
Naruse, Tomonori 1933- *St&PR 91*
Narusis, Regina Gyte Firant 1936- *WhoAmW 91, WhoWor 91*
Narvaez, Panfilo De 1470?-1528 *WhNaAH*
Narvaez, Panfilo De 1478?-1528 *EncCRAm*
Narvaez, Ramon Maria 1800-1868 *BioIn 16*
Narvekar, Prabhakar Ramkrishna 1932- *WhoE 91*
Narver, John Colin 1935- *WhoAm 90*
Narveson, Alan Duane 1945- *St&PR 91*
Narveson, Jan Fredric 1936- *WhoAm 90, WhoWrEP 89*
Narwold, Lewis Lammers 1921- *WhoAm 90*
Nary, Gilbert Roy *WhoAm 90*
Nary, Gilbert Roy 1922- *St&PR 91*
Nasalli Rocca Di Corneliano, Mario 1903-1988 *BioIn 16*
Nasalroad, Kennieth Jean 1950- *WhoAmW 91*
Nasar, Jack Leon 1947- *WhoWrEP 89*
Nasar, Syed Abu 1932- *WhoAm 90*
Nasatir, Abraham Phineas 1904- *BioIn 16*
Nasby, David Asher 1939- *WhoWor 91*
Nasca, Peter *ODwPR 91*
Nascimento, Milton *BioIn 16*
Naseman, David Milford 1948- *St&PR 91*
Nasgaard, Roald 1941- *WhoAm 90, WhoAmA 91*
Nash, Abigail Jones 1950- *St&PR 91*
Nash, Alanna 1950- *ConAu 129*
Nash, Alanna K. 1950- *WhoWrEP 89*
Nash, Alanna Kay 1950- *WhoAmW 91*
Nash, Alice Louise 1915- *WhoAmA 91*
Nash, Billy 1865-1929 *Ballpl 90*
Nash, Bradley DeLamater 1900- *WhoAm 90*
Nash, Carroll B 1914- *EncO&P 3*
Nash, Carroll Blue 1914- *EncPaPR 91*
Nash, Catherine S 1919- *EncO&P 3*
Nash, Catherine Stifler 1919- *EncPaPR 91*
Nash, Charles Crawford *BioIn 16*
Nash, Charles D. 1943- *WhoSSW 91*
Nash, Charles Edmund 1844-1913 *BlkAmsC [port]*
Nash, Charles Presley 1932- *WhoAm 90*
Nash, Charles W. 1864-1948 *EncABHB 4 [port], WorAlBi*
Nash, Clara Mae 1935- *WhoAmW 91*
Nash, David Bret 1955- *WhoE 91*
Nash, David J. 1942- *St&PR 91*
Nash, David John 1942- *WhoAm 90*
Nash, Donald Gene 1945- *WhoAm 90*
Nash, Edward L. 1936- *WhoE 91*
Nash, Elizabeth Hamilton 1934- *IntWWM 90*
Nash, Frank Erwin 1916- *WhoAm 90*
Nash, Frederick Copp 1908- *WhoWor 91*
Nash, Fredric Ogden 1902-1971 *AuBYP 90*
Nash, Garth H. 1949- *St&PR 91*
Nash, Gary Baring 1933- *WhoAm 90*
Nash, Gerald David 1928- *WhoAm 90*
Nash, Gerald Mark 1945- *BiDrAPA 89*

Nash, Gordon Bernard, Jr. 1944- WhoAm 90
Nash, Grace Chapman 1909- WhoWrEP 89
Nash, Graham BioIn 16
Nash, Graham 1942- WorAlBi
Nash, Graham Thomas 1952- IntWWM 90
Nash, Harold Garth 1940- St&PR 91
Nash, Harold Ronald, Jr. 1949- WhoSSW 91
Nash, Heddle 1896-1961 PenDiMP
Nash, Henry Warren 1927- WhoAm 90
Nash, James E. 1950- St&PR 91
Nash, James Loren 1942- BiDrAPA 89
Nash, Jay Robert, III 1934- WhoWrEP 89
Nash, Jay Robert, III 1937- WhoAm 90, WhoWor 91
Nash, Jim 1945- Ballpl 90
Nash, John 1830-1901 OxCPMus
Nash, John Arthur 1938- St&PR 91
Nash, John Heddle 1928- PenDiMP
Nash, John N. 1946- WhoAm 90, WhoE 91
Nash, Johnny 1940- DrBlPA 90, OxCPMus
Nash, Johnny Collin 1949- WhoSSW 91
Nash, Jonathon Michael 1942- WhoAm 90
Nash, Julie Watts 1956- WhoAmW 91
Nash, June Caprice 1927- WhoAmW 91
Nash, Karen Marsteller 1943- WhoE 91
Nash, Karl S. 1908- St&PR 91
Nash, Kenneth NewAgMG
Nash, Kenneth Laverne 1950- WhoEmL 91
Nash, Kenneth M. 1931- St&PR 91
Nash, Kenneth P BiDrAPA 89
Nash, Kenneth Thomas, Jr. 1958- WhoE 91
Nash, Knowlton 1927- WhoWor 91
Nash, Lee J. 1939- WhoAm 90
Nash, Leonard Kollender 1918- WhoAm 90
Nash, Lillian Dorothy 1931- WhoAmW 91
Nash, Manning 1924- WhoAm 90
Nash, Marjorie Ann Moss 1948- WhoAmW 91
Nash, Marlene B. 1948- BiDrAPA 89
Nash, Mary 1925- AuBYP 90
Nash, Mary 1951- WhoAmA 91
Nash, Mary Frances Heddle 1928- IntWWM 90
Nash, Michael O'R BioIn 16
Nash, Michaux, Jr. 1933- WhoAm 90
Nash, Monroe 1912- St&PR 91
Nash, Myrtle Corliss 1915- WhoAmW 91
Nash, N. Frederick 1936- WhoAm 90
Nash, Nicholas David 1939- WhoAm 90
Nash, Ogden 1902-1971 BioIn 16, MajTwCW, WorAlBi
Nash, Paige Eileen 1961- WhoAmW 91
Nash, Pamela Lucille 1959- IntWWM 90
Nash, Paul WhoAm 90
Nash, Peter David 1951- WhoE 91
Nash, Peter Edward 1949- WhoSSW 91
Nash, Peter Hugh John 1921- WhoAm 90
Nash, Peter Paul 1950- IntWWM 90
Nash, Philleo 1909-1987 BioIn 16
Nash, Ray 1905-1982 WhoAmA 91N
Nash, Richard, Jr. 1929- St&PR 91
Nash, Richard Mark 1958- WhoWor 91
Nash, Robert A 1931- BiDrAPA 89
Nash, Robert Fred 1933- St&PR 91, WhoAm 90
Nash, Robert McLean 1925- St&PR 91
Nash, Roderick BioIn 16
Nash, Ronald H. 1936- WhoSSW 91
Nash, Royston Hulbert 1933- IntWWM 90
Nash, Rufus Wilson 1917- St&PR 91
Nash, Ruth Cowan BioIn 16, WhoAmW 91
Nash, Sonja Huddleston 1947- WhoAmW 91
Nash, Spencer James 1938- WhoAm 90, WhoWor 91
Nash, Stephen Michael 1947- WhoEmL 91, WhoWor 91
Nash, Steven Alan 1944- WhoAm 90, WhoAmA 91
Nash, Suzanne Patterson 1944- St&PR 91
Nash, Thomas B. 1953- St&PR 91
Nash, Thomas M. 1948- St&PR 91
Nash, Veronica WhoAmW 91
Nash, Virginia O. 1922- St&PR 91
Nash, Warren Leslie 1955- WhoSSW 91
Nash, William Arthur 1922- WhoAm 90
Nash, William Kelly 1959- WhoEmL 91
Nash, William L. 1943- BioIn 16
Nashan, Joy Ortiz 1948- WhoAmW 91
Nashawaty, Brenda ODwPR 91
Nashe, Carol ODwPR 91, WhoE 91
Nasher, Patsy BioIn 16
Nasher, Raymond BioIn 16
Nashman, Alvin E. 1926- St&PR 91
Nashman, Alvin Eli 1926- WhoAm 90
Nasi, Brian T. 1950- St&PR 91
Nasi, Cynthia Wilberg 1960- WhoAmW 91
Nasielski, Jacques 1929- WhoWor 91
Nasisse, Andy S 1946- WhoAmA 91
Naske, Claus-M 1935- ConAu 31NR
Nasky, H. Gregory 1942- St&PR 91
Naslund, Alan Joseph 1941- WhoWrEP 89
Nasman, David F. 1935- St&PR 91
Nason, Charles T. 1946- St&PR 91
Nason, Charles Tuckey 1946- WhoAm 90
Nason, Charles William 1944- St&PR 91
Nason, Dolores Irene 1934- WhoAmW 91
Nason, Fred, Jr. 1930- St&PR 91
Nason, Gertrude 1890- WhoAmA 91N
Nason, Heather Elizabeth 1959- WhoAmW 91
Nason, Howard King 1913- WhoAm 90
Nason, Jeffrey David 1939- BiDrAPA 89
Nason, John Blaisdell, III 1937- WhoAm 90
Nason, John William 1905- WhoAm 90
Nason, Robert Randolph 1930- WhoSSW 91
Nason, Stephen Howard WhoSSW 91
Nason, Susan BioIn 16
Nason, Thelma Stein WhoAmW 91
Nason, Thomas W 1889-1971 WhoAmA 91N
Nason, Walton Hooker, Jr. 1922- St&PR 91
Nason-Cruz, Sally Aurelia 1946- WhoE 91, WhoEmL 91
Nasr, Amin Marwan 1953- WhoWor 91
Nasr, Faisal Adel 1950- WhoWor 91
Nasr, Mohamed Zaki BiDrAPA 89
Nasr, Salah 1952- WhoE 91
Nasr, Suhayl Joseph 1948- BiDrAPA 89
Nasra, George Yousef 1947- WhoE 91
Nasrallah, Henry A 1947- BiDrAPA 89
Nasrallah, Henry Ata 1947- WhoAm 90
Nasru, Omar 1945- WhoWor 91
Nass, Deanna Rose 1939- WhoAmW 91
Nass, Howard 1940- St&PR 91
Nass, Jack 1948- BiDrAPA 89, WhoE 91
Nassar, George BioIn 16
Nassar, Max Joseph 1950- WhoSSW 91
Nassar, Paul William BiDrAPA 89
Nassau, Elizabeth Sussman 1956- WhoAmW 91, WhoEmL 91
Nassau, Michael Jay 1935- WhoAm 90
Nassau, Robert Hamill 1941- St&PR 91, WhoAm 90
Nassberg, Richard T. 1942- WhoSSW 91, WhoWor 91
Nasse, John Thos, Jr. 1933- BiDrAPA 89
Nasser, Essam 1931- WhoWor 91
Nasser, Gamal Abdel 1918-1970 BioIn 16, WorAlBi
Nasser, Gamal Abdul 1918-1970 PolLCME
Nasser, Moes Roshanali 1956- WhoEmL 91, WhoSSW 91
Nasser, Peter Harold 1957- WhoSSW 91
Nasser, William Edward 1939- St&PR 91
Nasshan, John Kenneth 1957- WhoE 91
Nassi, Isaac Robert 1949- WhoAm 90
Nassif, David 1924- St&PR 91
Nassif, Merph 1928- WhoAmW 91
Nassif, Thomas Anthony 1941- WhoAm 90
Nassif, Walid Michel 1960- BiDrAPA 89
Nassiff, Tonius WhoWrEP 89
Nassikas, John Nicholas 1917- WhoAm 90
Nassof, Russell S. 1955- St&PR 91
Nassr, Donald G BiDrAPA 89
Nassr, Donald Gregory 1932- WhoSSW 91
Nast, Conde 1874-1942 WorAlBi
Nast, Dianne Martha 1944- WhoAm 90
Nast, Thomas 1840-1902 BioIn 16, WorAlBi
Nast, V. Frederick, III 1941- St&PR 91
Nasta, Susheila Mary 1953- WhoWor 91
Nastas, Thomas Dennis 1949- WhoEmL 91
Nastase, Adrian WhoWor 91
Nastase, Cristina BiDrAPA 89
Nastase, Ilie 1946- WorAlBi
Nastich, Milan M. 1926- St&PR 91
Nastiuk, Virginia 1923- WhoAmW 91
Nastro, Charles P. 1942- St&PR 91
Nastro, Charles Paul 1942- WhoAm 90
Nastu, Phil 1955- Ballpl 90
Nasu, Masahiko 1928- WhoWor 91
Nasvytis, K Joseph BiDrAPA 89
Naszinski, Lara BioIn 16
Nata, Theophile WhoWor 91
Nataf, Helene Michele 1939- WhoAmW 91
Natal, Fausto A 1935- BiDrAPA 89
Natale, A. Charles 1931- St&PR 91
Natale, Anthony Gilbert 1952- St&PR 91
Natale, Lynda Lee 1959- WhoAmW 91
Natale, Samuel Michael 1943- WhoAm 90
Natale, Sherry G BiDrAPA 89
Natali, Lorenzo 1922-1989 BioIn 16
Natalicio, Diana S. 1939- WhoAm 90, WhoAmW 91, WhoSSW 91
Natanek, Adam Tadeusz 1933- IntWWM 90
Natanson, Maurice Alexander 1924- WhoAm 90, WhoWrEP 89
Natarajan, Anjula Devi BiDrAPA 89
Natarajan, Ramachandran 1950- WhoSSW 91
Natarajan, Sundaram 1942- WhoSSW 91
Natawista 1824?-1893 DcCanB 12
Natawista 1825?-1895? WhNaAH
Natawista Iksana 1824?-1893 DcCanB 12
Natawista Iksana 1825?-1895? WhNaAH
Natcher, Stephen Darlington 1940- WhoAm 90
Natcher, William Huston BioIn 16
Natcher, William Huston 1909- WhoAm 90, WhoSSW 91
Nate, Thomas Edward 1954- WhoSSW 91
Natelson, Stephen Ellis 1937- WhoAm 90
Nater, James Ronald 1931- St&PR 91
Natesh, N. 1944- WhoWor 91
Nath, Bernard 1899- St&PR 91
Nath, Florine N. St&PR 91
Nath, Joginder 1932- WhoAm 90, WhoSSW 91
Nath, Moitri BiDrAPA 89
Nathan, Swami 1942- WhoE 91
Nathan, Adele 1900?-1986 AuBYP 90
Nathan, Adele Gutman BioIn 16
Nathan, Anthony Wayne 1952- WhoWor 91
Nathan, Arturo 1891-1944 BioIn 16
Nathan, Carl Francis 1946- WhoAm 90
Nathan, Daniel AuBYP 90, MajTwCW
Nathan, David Gordon 1929- WhoAm 90
Nathan, Debra 1954- WhoE 91
Nathan, Emanuel 1916- WhoSSW 91
Nathan, Frederic Solis 1922- WhoAm 90
Nathan, Habib 1935- BiDrAPA 89
Nathan, Helmuth Max 1901-1979 WhoAmA 91N
Nathan, Jean ConAu 132
Nathan, Joseph Anthony 1952- WhoAm 90
Nathan, Keith Harold 1955- WhoSSW 91
Nathan, Leon 1942- BiDrAPA 89
Nathan, Leonard Edward 1924- WhoAm 90, WhoWrEP 89
Nathan, Margaret A. 1956- ODwPR 91
Nathan, Myron L 1936- BiDrAPA 89
Nathan, Norman 1915- WhoWrEP 89
Nathan, Ove 1926- WhoWor 91
Nathan, Paul S. 1913- WhoAm 90
Nathan, Peter E. 1935- WhoAm 90
Nathan, Phyllis Kleinfeld 1947- WhoE 91
Nathan, Pramila Mungara BiDrAPA 89
Nathan, Richard Arnold 1944- St&PR 91, WhoAm 90
Nathan, Richard Perle 1935- WhoAm 90
Nathan, Robert Clark 1924- St&PR 91
Nathan, Robert J 1929- BiDrAPA 89
Nathan, Robert R. 1908- St&PR 91
Nathan, Robert Stuart 1948- WhoWrEP 89
Nathan, Ronald G 1938- BiDrAPA 89
Nathan, Ronald Gene 1951- WhoE 91
Nathan, Shepherd 1928- BiDrAPA 89, WhoAm 90
Nathan, Susan BioIn 16
Nathan, Swami 1942- BiDrAPA 89
Nathan, Theodore Reade 1911- WhoAm 90
Nathan, William Allen 1948- BiDrAPA 89
Nathaniel, Roger Steven BiDrAPA 89
Nathans, Daniel 1928- WhoAm 90, WhoE 91, WhoWor 91, WorAlBi
Nathans, Jeremy Hillel 1958- WhoAm 90
Nathans, Rhoda R 1940- WhoAmA 91
Nathanson, A. Lynn 1955- WhoAmW 91
Nathanson, Carol 1922- ConAu 132
Nathanson, David H. 1960- ODwPR 91
Nathanson, Donald L 1936- BiDrAPA 89
Nathanson, Donald Lawrence 1936- WhoE 91
Nathanson, Gerald WhoAm 90
Nathanson, Harvey Charles 1936- WhoAm 90
Nathanson, Ira ODwPR 91
Nathanson, Joseph 1895-1989 BioIn 16
Nathanson, Laura 1941- BioIn 16
Nathanson, Linda Sue 1946- WhoAmW 91, WhoE 91, WhoEmL 91
Nathanson, Mark Reed 1954- BiDrAPA 89
Nathanson, Melvyn Bernard 1944- WhoAm 90, WhoE 91
Nathanson, Michael WhoAm 90
Nathanson, Neal 1927- WhoAm 90
Nathanson, Wayne R. 1934- St&PR 91
Nathusius, Marie 1817-1857 EncCoWW
Nati, Carol A 1959- BiDrAPA 89
Nation, Bob AuBYP 90
Nation, Carry 1846-1911 BioAmW, WorAlBi
Nation, Carry Amelia Moore 1846-1911 BioIn 16
Nation, Edna Leona 1937- WhoWrEP 89
Nation, James Edward 1933- WhoAm 90
Nation, James Lamar 1936- WhoSSW 91
Nation, Kay AuBYP 90
Nation, Roger John 1941- St&PR 91
National Commission Ballpl 90
Nations, Andrew Hall 1949- St&PR 91
Nations, Chester Bradley, Jr. 1939- St&PR 91
Nations, James Dale 1947- WhoWrEP 89
Nations, John Drewry 1918- St&PR 91
Nations, Robert Lloyd 1960- WhoSSW 91
Natiotish WhNaAH
Natiss, Gary Mitchell 1956- WhoWor 91
Native American Church of North America NewAgMG
Natividad, Rosa Maria Villescas 1947- WhoSSW 91
Natkin, Alvin Martin 1928- WhoAm 90
Natkin, Efrem Norman 1929- St&PR 91
Natkin, Rick 1952- ConAu 129
Natkin, Robert 1930- WhoAmA 91
Natkin, Roger A BiDrAPA 89
Natole, Timothy A. 1948- WhoAm 90
Natoli, John Francis 1948- WhoE 91
Natoli, Joseph ConAu 132
Natoli, Joseph P. 1943- ConAu 132
Natoli, Salvatore J. BioIn 16
Natori, Josie Cruz 1947- WhoAmW 91
Natori, Shunji 1938- WhoWor 91
Natori, Yasuo 1933- WhoWor 91
Natos-Api 1819?-1897 DcCanB 12
Natoyist-siksina 1824?-1893 DcCanB 12
Natra, Sergiu 1924- IntWWM 90
Natsios, Nicholas Andrew 1920- WhoAm 90, WhoWor 91
Natsios, Peter Andrew BiDrAPA 89
Natsoulas, Anthony 1959- WhoAmA 91
Natsuki, Shizuko 1938- TwCCr&M 91B
Natsume Soseki 1867-1916 EncJap
Natt-Jaffe, Helana 1961- WhoE 91
Natta, Alessandro 1918- WhoWor 91
Natta, Giulio 1903-1979 DcScB S2
Natter, Lonny R. 1956- BiDrAPA 89
Natter, Martin Rittenhouse 1936- WhoSSW 91
Natterer, Frank 1941- WhoWor 91
Natterson, Joseph M 1923- BiDrAPA 89
Nattiel, Christine Henry 1939- WhoSSW 91
Nattinger, Christopher Wallis 1942- St&PR 91
Natu, Himani Waman 1949- BiDrAPA 89
Naturman, Louis 1931- St&PR 91
Natwick, Mildred 1908- WorAlBi
Natz, Daryl C. 1934- ODwPR 91
Natzke, Gail Louise 1932- WhoAmW 91
Natzke, Paulette Ann 1943- WhoAmW 91
Natzler, Gertrud PenDiDA 89
Natzler, Gertrud 1908-1971 WhoAmA 91N
Natzler, Otto PenDiDA 89
Natzler, Otto 1908- WhoAm 90, WhoAmA 91
Natzmer, Cheryl Lynn 1947- WhoAmA 91
Nau, Cornelius Hugo, Jr. BiDrAPA 89
Nau, H. Gene WhoAm 90
Nau, Heinz 1943- WhoWor 91
Nau, Henry Richard 1941- WhoE 91
Naubert, Christiane Benedikte Eugenie 1756-1819 EncCoWW
Nauckhoff, Marcia Dawkins BioIn 16
Naudzius, Ruth Winters 1929- WhoAmW 91
Nauert, Roger C. BioIn 16
Nauert, Roger Charles 1943- WhoAm 90, WhoWor 91
Nauful, Ernest Joseph, Jr. 1941- WhoSSW 91
Naughton, Ann Elsie 1942- WhoAmW 91, WhoE 91, WhoWor 91
Naughton, Bill 1910- MajTwCW
Naughton, James Franklin 1957- ConAu 132
Naughton, James Martin 1938- WhoAm 90
Naughton, Jim ConAu 132
Naughton, John M. 1936- St&PR 91
Naughton, John Patrick 1933- WhoAm 90
Naughton, Marie Ann 1954- WhoAmW 91
Naughton, Thomas Noel 1929- St&PR 91
Naughton, William Aloysius 1930- St&PR 91, WhoAm 90, WhoE 91
Naugle, Jonathan Edward 1959- WhoE 91
Naugle, Robert Paul 1951- WhoWor 91
Nauhaus, Gerd Ernst Hermann 1942- IntWWM 90
Naul, Roland Hans-Georg 1948- WhoWor 91
Nault, Fernand 1921- WhoAm 90
Nault, Marc Aurele 1933- WhoE 91
Nault, William Henry 1926- WhoAm 90
Nauman, Bruce 1941- BioIn 16, CurBio 90 [port], WhoAmA 91
Nauman, Frances Irma 1914- WhoWrEP 89
Naumann, Francis M 1948- WhoAmA 91
Naumann, Hans J. 1935- WhoE 91
Naumann, Hans Juergen 1935- St&PR 91
Naumann, Hans Richard Ernst 1936- WhoAm 90
Naumann, Joerg K.H.D. 1941- WhoWor 91
Naumann, Robert Bruno Alexander 1929- WhoAm 90
Naumann, William C. 1938- St&PR 91

Naumann, William Edward 1909- St&PR 91
Naumburg, George W BiDrAPA 89
Naumenko, Ivan Y. WhoWor 91
Naumer, Helmuth 1907- WhoAmA 91
Naumer, Helmuth Jacob 1934- WhoAm 90
Naumoff, Philip 1914- WhoAm 90
Naumov, Boris Nikolaevich BioIn 16
Naumovski, Nikolche Jonce 1949- BiDrAPA 89
Naunas, Thomas Ash 1951- WhoEmL 91
Naunton, Ralph Frederick 1921- WhoAm 90
Nausch, Melissa Beth 1961- WhoAmW 91
Nauser, Debbie Engmark 1952- St&PR 91
Nauss, Richard 1938- St&PR 91
Nauss, Wendolin John 1920-1989 BioIn 16
Nauta, Ronald H. 1935- St&PR 91
Nauts, William Boone BioIn 16
Nava, Eloy Luis 1942- WhoE 91
Nava, Gregory 1949- ConAu 131, HispWr 90
Nava, Julian 1927- BioIn 16, HispWr 90, WhoHisp 91
Nava, Samuel N BiDrAPA 89
Nava-Villarreal, Hector Rolando 1943- WhoHisp 91
Navab, Farhad 1938- WhoAm 90
Navajas-Mogro, Hugo 1923- WhoWor 91
Navakas, Edward Harry BiDrAPA 89
Navales, Ana Maria 1943?- EncCoWW
Navalkar, Ramchandra Govindrao 1924- WhoAm 90
Navar, Luis Gabriel 1941- WhoAm 90
Navaretta, Cynthia WhoAmA 91
Navarra, Andre 1911-1988 AnObit 1988, BioIn 16, PenDiMP
Navarra, John Gabriel 1927- AuBYP 90
Navarre, Marguerite de 1492-1549 EncCoWW, FemiCLE
Navarre, Max BioIn 16
Navarre, Robert 1918- BiDrAPA 89, WhoE 91
Navarre, Robert Ward 1933- St&PR 91, WhoAm 90
Navarre, Tommy R. 1960- St&PR 91
Navarre, Yves Henri Michel 1940- WhoWor 91
Navarro, Andrew Jesus 1946- WhoEmL 91, WhoSSW 91, WhoWor 91
Navarro, Antonio 1922- St&PR 91, WhoAm 90
Navarro, Armando Salovicz 1930- WhoWor 91
Navarro, Artemio Edward 1950- WhoHisp 91
Navarro, Bruce 1954- WhoHisp 91
Navarro, Bruce Charles 1954- WhoAm 90
Navarro, Carlos Arias 1908-1989 BioIn 16
Navarro, Carlos Salvador 1946- WhoHisp 91
Navarro, Fats 1923-1950 BioIn 16, OxCPMus
Navarro, Flor Hernandez 1939- WhoHisp 91
Navarro, Imelda 1958- St&PR 91
Navarro, Janyte Janeen 1935- WhoAmW 91
Navarro, Joaquin R. BiDrAPA 89
Navarro, Jose WhoHisp 91
Navarro, Jose Antonio 1795-1870 BioIn 16
Navarro, Jose Marco 1958- WhoWor 91
Navarro, Joseph Anthony 1927- WhoAm 90
Navarro, Julio 1936- Ballpl 90
Navarro, Karyl Kay 1956- WhoAmW 91, WhoSSW 91, WhoWor 91
Navarro, Luis A. 1958- WhoHisp 91
Navarro, Manuel 1945- WhoWor 91
Navarro, Maria M BiDrAPA 89
Navarro, Mary Louise 1933- WhoHisp 91
Navarro, Miguel 1928- WhoHisp 91
Navarro, Mireya 1957- WhoHisp 91
Navarro, Nestor J., Jr. 1947- WhoHisp 91
Navarro, Octavio R. 1959- WhoHisp 91
Navarro, Rafael A. 1935- St&PR 91, WhoHisp 91
Navarro, Richard A. 1955- WhoHisp 91
Navarro, Richard J. 1952- St&PR 91
Navarro, Robert 1939- WhoHisp 91
Navarro, Robert David 1941- WhoHisp 91
Navarro, Sally Marie 1954- WhoAmW 91
Navarro, Theodore 1923-1950 WorAlBi
Navarro-Alicea, Jorge L. 1937- WhoHisp 91
Navarro-Bermudez, Francisco Jose 1935- WhoHisp 91
Navas, Elizabeth S 1895- WhoAmA 91N
Navas, John Joseph 1962- BiDrAPA 89
Navas, Linda Moore 1949- WhoEmL 91
Navas, Stanley R. 1919- St&PR 91
Navas, William A., Jr. WhoHisp 91
Navas, William Antonio, Jr. 1942- WhoE 91
Navasky, Bernard Seymour 1908- St&PR 91
Navasky, Edward 1933- St&PR 91
Navasky, Victor Saul 1932- WhoAm 90, WhoWrEP 89
Nave, Dennis Wayne 1949- BiDrAPA 89
Navedo, Angel C., Sr. 1941- WhoHisp 91
Naveh, Ben Zion Meir 1938- WhoWor 91
Navia, Juan M. 1927- WhoHisp 91
Navia, Juan Marcelo 1927- WhoSSW 91
Navia, Luis E. 1940- WhoHisp 91
Navin, Frank 1871-1935 Ballpl 90
Navin, Louis E. 1938- St&PR 91
Navin, MaryAnn Elizabeth 1951- WhoAmW 91
Navin, William Henry 1945- WhoAm 90
Navon, Ionel Michael 1940- WhoSSW 91
Navon, Itzhak 1923- WhoWor 91
Navon, Robert 1954- WhoWrEP 89
Navon, Yitzhak 1921- WhoWor 91
Navrat, Den 1942- WhoAmA 91
Navratil, Amy WhoAmA 91
Navratil, Augustin BioIn 16
Navratil, James Dale 1941- WhoWor 91
Navratil, Liz 1960- St&PR 91
Navratilova, Martina 1956- BioIn 16, WhoAm 90, WhoAmW 91, WhoWor 91, WorAlBi
Navuluri, Someswara Naidu BiDrAPA 89
Nawara, Jim 1945- WhoAmA 91
Nawara, Lucille Procter 1941- WhoAmA 91
Nawat WhNaAH
Nawaz, Sara Akhter BiDrAPA 89
Nawkaw 1735-1833 WhNaAH
Nawrocki, Thomas Dennis 1942- WhoAmA 91, WhoSSW 91
Nawrocki, Tom L. 1947- WhoWrEP 89
Nawrot, Richard E. 1947- St&PR 91
Nawroz, Safia BiDrAPA 89
Nawy, Edward George 1926- WhoAm 90
Nay, Harvey Orin 1925- WhoAm 90
Nay, James Allen 1934- WhoSSW 91
Nay, Mary Spencer 1913- WhoAmA 91
Nayak, Bannanje Sunanda BiDrAPA 89
Nayak, Bhaskar C BiDrAPA 89
Nayak, Devdutt V. 1946- BiDrAPA 89
Nayak, P. Narayan 1940- St&PR 91
Nayar, Anju 1956- BiDrAPA 89
Nayar, Baldev Raj 1931- WhoAm 90
Nayeem, Juhi F BiDrAPA 89
Nayer, Louise Bedford 1949- WhoWrEP 89
Nayfa, James E. 1924- WhoSSW 91
Nayfack, Bert 1939- BiDrAPA 89
Nayfeh, Ali Hasan 1933- WhoAm 90
Naygrow, Ritz 1920- St&PR 91
Naygrow, Thomas John 1946- St&PR 91
Nayler, James 1617?-1660 EncO&P 3
Naylon, Betsy Zimmermann 1934- WhoAmA 91
Naylor, Alan Ford 1935- WhoAm 90
Naylor, Aubrey Willard 1915- WhoAm 90, WhoSSW 91
Naylor, Christine ODwPR 91
Naylor, Claudette 1933- WhoE 91
Naylor, Douglas F. 1918- St&PR 91
Naylor, Eleanor R. 1928- St&PR 91
Naylor, Frank Wesley, Jr. 1939- WhoAm 90
Naylor, Genevieve BioIn 16
Naylor, George LeRoy 1915- WhoWor 91
Naylor, Gloria BioIn 16
Naylor, Gloria 1950- Au&Arts 6 [port], FemiCLE, MajTwCW, WorAu 1980 [port]
Naylor, Harry Brooks 1914- WhoAm 90
Naylor, James Charles 1932- WhoAm 90
Naylor, Jean Ann 1948- WhoEmL 91
Naylor, John Geoffrey 1928- WhoAmA 91
Naylor, John Lewis, Jr. 1927- St&PR 91
Naylor, John Thomas 1913- WhoAm 90
Naylor, Lois Anne McCrea 1948- WhoWrEP 89
Naylor, Magdalena Raczkowska BiDrAPA 89
Naylor, Mary 1955- WhoAmW 91
Naylor, Michael Wayne BiDrAPA 89
Naylor, Peter Russell 1933- IntWWM 90
Naylor, Phyllis Reynolds 1933- AuBYP 90, BioIn 16, WhoWrEP 89
Naylor, Ralph A. 1923- St&PR 91
Naylor, Richard N. 1943- St&PR 91
Naylor, Robert Ernest 1932- St&PR 91
Naylor, Robert Ernest, Jr. 1932- WhoAm 90
Naylor, Robert L. 1934- WhoWrEP 89
Naylor, Robert Windsor 1926- St&PR 91
Naylor, Rollie 1892-1966 Ballpl 90
Naylor, Ruth Eileen 1934- WhoWrEP 89
Naylor, Thomas Herbert 1936- WhoAm 90
Naymark, Sherman 1920- WhoAm 90
Nazarbayev, Nursultan Abishevich 1940- WhoWor 91
Nazarenko, Bonnie Coe 1933- WhoAmA 91
Nazareno, Romulo Arenas BiDrAPA 89
Nazareth, Annette La Porte 1956- St&PR 91
Nazareth, Annette LaPorte 1956- WhoAmW 91
Nazareth, Beatrijs van 1200-1268 EncCoWW
Nazareth, George R. 1930- St&PR 91
Nazareth, Ronald V BiDrAPA 89
Nazarewicz, Walter 1927- WhoAm 90
Nazario, Janira BiDrAPA 89
Nazario, Juan B. WhoAm 90
Nazario-Rodriguez, Ruben BiDrAPA 89
Nazaroff, Alexander I. 1898- AuBYP 90
Nazarov, Talbak 1938- WhoWor 91
Nazarowski, James J. 1949- St&PR 91
Nazaruk, Pamela A. 1954- ODwPR 91
Nazem, Fereydoun F. 1940- WhoAm 90
Nazer, Hisham Mohyeddin 1932- WhoWor 91
Nazette, Richard Follett 1919- WhoAm 90
Nazimova, Alla 1878-1945 NotWoAT
Nazimova, Alla 1879-1945 BioIn 16, WorAlBi
Nazimovitz, Roberta Yvonne 1932- WhoE 91
Nazir, Ahmed Khan 1934- BiDrAPA 89
Nazir, Shahnaz BiDrAPA 89
Nazir-Ahmed, Vellore Sherif 1929- WhoWor 91
Nazos, Demetri Eleftherios 1949- WhoEmL 91, WhoWor 91
Nazz EncPR&S 89
Nazzaro, A. John 1927- WhoWor 91
Nazzaro, Joseph J. NewYTBS 90
Nazzaro, Joseph James 1913-1990 BioIn 16
Ndiaye, Babacar WhoWor 91
Ndiaye, Babacar 1936- WhoWor 91
Ndinga-Oba, Antoine 1941- WhoWor 91
N'Dour, Youssou BioIn 16
Ndukwu, Ikeadi Maurice BiDrAPA 89
Ne-Can-Nete DcCanB 12
Ne-Kah-Nea DcCanB 12
Ne-kah-new DcCanB 12
Neafsey, John Patrick 1939- St&PR 91, WhoAm 90
Neagle, Anna 1904-1986 OxCPMus
Neagle, Connie M. 1952- St&PR 91
Neah Emarthla WhNaAH
Neaher, Edward Raymond 1912- WhoAm 90
Neal, A. Curtis 1922- WhoSSW 91
Neal, Ann Parker WhoAmA 91
Neal, Ann Parker 1934- WhoAm 90
Neal, Anthony 1955- WhoE 91
Neal, Archie Eugene 1934- St&PR 91
Neal, Avon 1922- WhoAm 90, WhoAmA 91, WhoWrEP 89
Neal, Bill L. St&PR 91
Neal, Bill Lee 1932- WhoSSW 91
Neal, Bonnie Jean 1930- WhoAmW 91
Neal, Brenda Joyce Chaplin 1946- WhoAmW 91
Neal, Charlie 1931- Ballpl 90
Neal, Constance 1942- WhoAmW 91
Neal, Curtley F., Jr. 1940- WhoSSW 91
Neal, Darwina Lee 1942- WhoAm 90
Neal, David Scott 1952- WhoSSW 91
Neal, Donald L. 1930- St&PR 91
Neal, Douglas Paul 1942- St&PR 91
Neal, Edmond A. 1934- St&PR 91
Neal, Fred Warner 1915- WhoAm 90
Neal, George P. 1926- St&PR 91
Neal, Gib BioIn 16
Neal, Harry Edward 1906- AuBYP 90, WhoAm 90
Neal, Homer Alfred 1942- WhoAm 90
Neal, Irene 1936- WhoAmA 91
Neal, J. Alan WhoSSW 91
Neal, J Gregory BiDrAPA 89
Neal, James Edward, Jr. 1933- WhoWrEP 89
Neal, James Erskine 1846-1908 AmLegL
Neal, James Preston 1935- WhoE 91
Neal, Jasper Taylor, Jr. 1942- St&PR 91
Neal, Jean AuBYP 90
Neal, Jerry Harold 1943- WhoAm 90, WhoSSW 91
Neal, John 1793-1876 BioIn 16
Neal, Joyce Olivia 1943- WhoAmW 91
Neal, Karen Sue 1956- WhoSSW 91
Neal, Kenneth Alton 1953- WhoSSW 91
Neal, Kevin R. 1951- St&PR 91
Neal, Larry 1937-1981 DrBIPA 90
Neal, Leo Cameron, Jr. 1950- WhoSSW 91
Neal, Leonard St&PR 91
Neal, Leora Louise Haskett 1943- WhoAmW 91
Neal, Lewis Grant 1933- St&PR 91
Neal, Louise Kathleen 1951- St&PR 91, WhoAm 90
Neal, Margaret Ruth 1944- WhoAmW 91
Neal, Margaret Sherrill 1950- WhoAmW 91, WhoEmL 91, WhoSSW 91, WhoWor 91
Neal, Marie Augusta 1921- ConAu 32NR
Neal, Michelle Lee 1968- WhoAmW 91
Neal, Mike 1939- WhoWor 91
Neal, Miron Williams, II BiDrAPA 89
Neal, Nelson Douglas 1947- WhoSSW 91
Neal, Patricia BioIn 16
Neal, Patricia 1926- WhoAm 90, WhoWor 91, WorAlBi
Neal, Phil Hudson, Jr. 1926- WhoAm 90
Neal, Philip Mark 1940- St&PR 91
Neal, Ralph A. 1936- St&PR 91
Neal, Randolph Dale BiDrAPA 89
Neal, Rebecca Reetz BiDrAPA 89
Neal, Reginald H 1909- WhoAmA 91
Neal, Richard E. BioIn 16
Neal, Richard Edmund 1949- WhoAm 90, WhoE 91
Neal, Richard Edward 1925- St&PR 91
Neal, Robert A BiDrAPA 89
Neal, Robert Allan 1928- St&PR 91, WhoAm 90
Neal, Robert Bell 1938- St&PR 91
Neal, Roger Lee 1930- St&PR 91
Neal, Russell William 1922- WhoAm 90
Neal, Stephen L. BioIn 16
Neal, Stephen Lybrook 1934- WhoAm 90, WhoSSW 91
Neal, Steven George 1949- WhoAm 90
Neal, Teresa Schreibeis 1956- WhoAmW 91
Neal, Thomas Solomon 1927- St&PR 91
Neal, W Keith 1905-1990 ConAu 131
Neal, Wallace T. 1940- St&PR 91
Neal, William H., Jr. 1930- St&PR 91
Neal, William Weaver 1932- WhoAm 90, WhoWor 91
Neal, Wilmer Lewis 1934- WhoSSW 91
Neal-Smith, Denys John 1915- IntWWM 90
Neale, Allen R. 1951- St&PR 91
Neale, Daniel Christopher 1931- WhoAm 90
Neale, Edward George, Jr. 1926- St&PR 91
Neale, Ernest Richard Ward 1923- WhoAm 90
Neale, Gary L. 1940- St&PR 91
Neale, Greasy 1891-1973 Ballpl 90
Neale, Henrietta FemiCLE
Neale, J. Henry 1904-1989 BioIn 16
Neale, Jack Carlysle, III BiDrAPA 89
Neale, John Hamilton, Jr. 1946- WhoE 91
Neale, Marilyn BioIn 16
Neale, Perry 1931- St&PR 91
Neale, Timothy Arthur 1948- WhoE 91
Neale-May, Donovan A. 1952- ODwPR 91
Nealer, James Keifer 1928- WhoSSW 91
Nealer, Kevin Glenn 1954- WhoEmL 91
Nealley, Edward Bowdoin 1837-1905 AmLegL
Nealon, Meilor Edmond 1935- WhoWor 91
Nealon, William Joseph, Jr. 1923- WhoE 91
Neals, Otto 1930- WhoAmA 91
Nealy, Anthony Leon BiDrAPA 89
Neaman, Yfrah 1923- IntWWM 90, PenDiMP
Neamathla WhNaAH
Neame, Mortimer 1901-1988 AnObit 1988
Neame, Ronald 1911- WhoAm 90
Neander, John Michael BiDrAPA 89
Neandross, Sigurd 1869-1958 WhoAmA 91N
Neapope 1800?- WhNaAH
Near, Earl Wayne 1943- St&PR 91
Near, Holly BioIn 16
Near, James W. BioIn 16
Near, Mary Jane Willis 1915- St&PR 91
Nearburg, Charles Eugene 1950- WhoSSW 91
Nearhood, Gerald Edward BiDrAPA 89
Nearing, Dudley Woodruff, Jr. 1925- WhoAm 90
Nearing, Penny 1916- BioIn 16
Nearing, Scott 1883-1983 EncAL, WorAlBi
Neary, Brian Joseph 1951- WhoEmL 91
Neary, Colleen 1952- WhoAm 90
Neary, Dennis R. 1952- St&PR 91
Neary, Lynn Patricia 1950- WhoAm 90
Neary, Martin 1940- PenDiMP
Neary, Martin Gerard James 1940- IntWWM 90
Neary, Patricia Elinor WhoWor 91
Neary, Robert J. ODwPR 91
Neas, John Theodore 1940- WhoSSW 91, WhoWor 91
Nease, Carl M. 1932- St&PR 91
Nease, Stephen Wesley 1925- WhoAm 90
Nease, Victor Ferris BiDrAPA 89
Neatby, William James 1860-1910 PenDiDA 89
Neate, Charles 1784-1877 PenDiMP
Neate, Ken 1914- IntWWM 90
Neathery, Patricia Sue 1934- WhoSSW 91
Neaves, Carol L. 1926- St&PR 91
Neaves, Noe 1926- BiDrAPA 89
Neaves, William Barlow 1943- WhoAm 90
Nebb, Edward A. ODwPR 91
Nebe, Arthur 1894-1945? BioIn 16
Nebe, Michael 1947- IntWWM 90
Nebeker, Frank Quill 1930- WhoAm 90
Nebeker, Gordon Alston 1945- WhoWor 91
Nebeker, Sidney Jay 1929- St&PR 91
Nebel, Berthold 1889-1964 WhoAmA 91N

Nebel, Carl 1800?-1865 *ArtLatA*
Nebel, Carl 1937- *St&PR 91*
Nebel, Frederick 1903-1967 *TwCCr&M 91*
Nebel, Henry Martin, Jr. 1921- *WhoAm 90*
Nebel, Laurie Jean 1957- *WhoWrEP 89*
Nebel, Reynold 1928- *WhoSSW 91*
Nebel, Richard Andrew, II 1956- *WhoEmL 91*
Nebel, William Arthur 1936- *WhoSSW 91, WhoWor 91*
Nebergall, Roger Ellis 1926- *WhoAm 90*
Nebert, Daniel Walter 1938- *WhoAm 90*
Nebil, Corinne Elizabeth 1918- *WhoAm 90*
Neblett, Boyd Lewis 1926- *WhoSSW 91*
Neblett, Carol 1946- *IntWWM 90*
Neblett, George R. 1943- *St&PR 91*
Neblo, Albert A. 1936- *St&PR 91*
Neborsky, Robert Jay *BiDrAPA 89*
Nebot, Bernard Adrien 1942- *WhoSSW 91*
Nebuchadnezzar II 630BC-562BC *WorAlBi*
Necarsulmer, Henry 1914- *WhoAm 90*
Necciai, Ron 1932- *Ballpl 90*
Nechaev, Sergei Gennadievich 1847-1882 *BioIn 16*
Nechay, Bohdan Roman 1925- *WhoSSW 91*
Neches, Philip M. 1952- *St&PR 91*
Neches, Robert *BioIn 16*
Nechis, Barbara 1937- *WhoAmA 91*
Nechvatal, Joseph James 1951- *WhoAmA 91*
Necio, Therese 1963- *WhoWor 91*
Necker, David C. 1944- *St&PR 91*
Necker, Jacques 1732-1804 *BioIn 16, WorAlBi*
Necker, Suzanne 1737-1794 *EncCoWW*
Neckerman, Peter Josef 1935- *St&PR 91*
Neckermann, Peter Josef 1935- *WhoAm 90*
Necoechea, W.M. 1930- *St&PR 91*
Necula, Nick 1940- *WhoE 91*
Nedbal, Oskar 1874-1930 *PenDiMP*
Nedd, Priscilla Anne 1955- *WhoAmW 91*
Neddeau, Donald Frederick Price 1913- *WhoAmA 91*
Nedderman, Wendell Herman 1921- *WhoAm 90, WhoSSW 91*
Neddermeyer, Seth H. *BioIn 16*
Nedelcovych, Sava Miodrag *WhoAm 90*
Nedelec, Jean-Marie 1834-1896 *DcCanB 12*
Nedelmann, Birgitta Eva Margareta 1941- *WhoWor 91*
Nederlander, James Morton 1922- *WhoAm 90, WhoE 91, WhoWor 91*
Nederlander, Marjorie Smith 1922- *WhoAmW 91*
Nederlander, Robert E. *BioIn 16*
Nederveld, Ruth Elizabeth 1933- *WhoAmW 91*
Nedohon, James Francis 1955- *WhoE 91*
Nedom, H. Arthur 1925- *WhoAm 90*
Nedreaas, Torborg 1906- *DcScanL*
Nedreaas, Torborg 1906-1987 *EncCoWW*
Nedved, Petr *BioIn 16*
Nedwick, James C. 1945- *St&PR 91*
Nedyalkov, Hristo 1932- *IntWWM 90*
Nedza, Sandra Louise 1951- *WhoAmW 91*
Nedzi, Lucien Norbert 1925- *WhoAm 90, WhoE 91*
Nee, Frank W. 1936- *St&PR 91*
Nee, Frank Walter 1936- *WhoAm 90*
Nee, Johnny 1890-1957 *Ballpl 90*
Nee, Kay Bonner *ConAu 31NR, WhoWrEP 89*
Nee, Linda Elizabeth 1938- *WhoE 91*
Nee, Mary Coleman 1917- *WhoAm 90*
Neeb, Judy Ann 1937- *WhoAmW 91*
Neeb, Louis Patrick 1939- *WhoAm 90*
Neece, Marsha Jan 1943- *St&PR 91*
Neece, Olivia Helene 1948- *WhoAmW 91*
Neece, Richard Dale 1945- *St&PR 91*
Neece-Baltaro, Laura Elizabeth 1951- *WhoAmW 91*
Need, James D. 1944- *St&PR 91*
Need, Thomas 1808-1895 *DcCanB 12*
Needell, Elaine F 1926- *BiDrAPA 89*
Needell, Elise Louise 1957- *WhoAmW 91*
Needell, Mary Anne 1830-1922 *FemiCLE*
Needell, Russell Lawrence 1956- *WhoEmL 91*
Needell, Stanley S 1931- *BiDrAPA 89*
Needham, Charles William 1936- *WhoAm 90, WhoWor 91*
Needham, George Austin 1943- *St&PR 91, WhoAm 90*
Needham, Hal 1931- *WhoAm 90*
Needham, Hilary Margaret 1934- *IntWWM 90*
Needham, Horatio 1796-1863 *AmLegL*
Needham, Jack L. 1931- *St&PR 91*
Needham, James *EncCRAm*
Needham, James Joseph 1926- *St&PR 91, WhoAm 90*
Needham, Joseph 1900- *BioIn 16, WhoAm 90*
Needham, Louise 1938- *IntWWM 90*
Needham, Lucien Arthur 1929- *WhoAm 90*
Needham, Richard Lee 1939- *WhoAm 90, WhoWrEP 89*
Needham, Tom 1879-1926 *Ballpl 90*
Needleman, Alan 1944- *WhoAm 90*
Needleman, Elliot 1939- *WhoAm 90*
Needleman, Harry 1949- *St&PR 91*
Needleman, Laurence 1948- *St&PR 91*
Needleman, Max *BiDrAPA 89*
Needleman, Philip 1939- *BioIn 16*
Needleman, Wanda S 1944- *BiDrAPA 89*
Needler, George Treglohan 1935- *WhoAm 90*
Needler, Mabel Glidden *WhoAmA 91*
Needles, William 1919- *OxCCanT*
Neef, Elton T. *ConAu 32NR*
Neefe, Douglas Charles 1944- *St&PR 91, WhoAm 90*
Neel, Alice 1900-1984 *BiDWomA, BioIn 16, WhoAmA 91N*
Neel, Ama Lynn 1957- *WhoSSW 91*
Neel, Boyd 1905-1981 *DcNaB 1981, PenDiMP*
Neel, Curtis Dean 1946- *St&PR 91*
Neel, Curtis Dean, Jr. 1946- *WhoEmL 91*
Neel, Harry Bryan, III 1939- *WhoAm 90*
Neel, Holmes *WhoAm 90*
Neel, James Van Gundia 1915- *WhoAm 90*
Neel, John D. 1923- *St&PR 91*
Neel, John Dodd 1923- *WhoAm 90*
Neel, Judy Murphy 1926- *WhoAm 90*
Neel, Louis 1904- *WorAlBi*
Neel, Louis Eugene Felix 1904- *WhoWor 91*
Neel, Richard Eugene 1932- *WhoAm 90*
Neel, Samuel Ellison 1914- *WhoAm 90*
Neel, Spurgeon Hart, Jr. 1919- *WhoAm 90*
Neel, Thomas Howard 1941- *WhoAm 90*
Neel, Thomas M. 1937- *St&PR 91*
Neel, Timothy Joseph 1952- *WhoE 91*
Neelan, Pillaipakkam Nattu 1932- *WhoWor 91*
Neeld, Jerele Don 1960- *WhoSSW 91*
Neeld, Judith 1928- *WhoWrEP 89*
Neeld, Vaughn DeLeath 1943- *WhoAmW 91*
Neeley, Bruce Carlton *BiDrAPA 89*
Neeley, Charles Henry 1929- *WhoSSW 91*
Neeley, M.J. 1898- *St&PR 91*
Neelly, E.C., III 1939- *St&PR 91*
Neelly, Edwin Clyde, III 1939- *WhoAm 90*
Neelon, Sylvester 1825-1897 *DcCanB 12*
Neely, Bruce A. 1942- *St&PR 91*
Neely, Charles Lea, Jr. 1927- *WhoAm 90*
Neely, Edgar Adams, Jr. 1910- *WhoAm 90*
Neely, Harry A. 1946- *St&PR 91*
Neely, Homer Clifford 1930- *WhoE 91*
Neely, J. Randall 1943- *ODwPR 91*
Neely, Jack Hubert 1924- *WhoSSW 91*
Neely, James R. 1935-1988 *BioIn 16*
Neely, Jerome Charles 1940- *St&PR 91*
Neely, Jerry W. 1936- *St&PR 91*
Neely, Karen S. 1962- *WhoAmW 91*
Neely, Kimberly Dorristene 1964- *WhoAmW 91, WhoEmL 91*
Neely, Larry F. 1938- *St&PR 91*
Neely, Paul 1946- *WhoEmL 91, WhoSSW 91*
Neely, Paul A. 1920- *St&PR 91*
Neely, Richard *TwCCr&M 91*
Neely, Richard 1941- *WhoAm 90, WhoSSW 91*
Neely, Robert Allen 1921- *WhoSSW 91*
Neely, Robert Craig 1953- *St&PR 91, WhoSSW 91*
Neely, Samuel Eugene *BiDrAPA 89*
Neely, Susan 1956- *ODwPR 91*
Neely, Willard Ross 1925- *St&PR 91*
Neeman, Cal 1929- *Ballpl 90*
Ne'Eman, Yuval 1925- *WhoWor 91*
Neenan, William Braunger 1929- *WhoE 91*
Neeper, Leonard A. 1930- *St&PR 91*
Neeper, Ralph Arnold 1940- *WhoSSW 91*
Neer, Charles Sumner, II 1917- *WhoAm 90, WhoWor 91*
Neera 1846-1918 *EncCoWW*
Neergaard, Ole Henry 1952- *WhoWor 91*
Neergaard, Pierre Paul Ferdinand M. de 1907-1987 *BioIn 16*
Neerhout, John 1931- *St&PR 91*
Neermann, Carolyn Grieser *WhoSSW 91*
Nees, Gary Alan 1945- *St&PR 91*
Nees, Harol Hugh, II 1947- *WhoEmL 91*
Nees, Harry F. *BioIn 16*
Nees, Lawrence 1949- *WhoAmA 91*
Nees, Lawrence Paul 1949- *WhoE 91*
Nees, Vic 1936- *IntWWM 90*
Neese, Dwight Vincent 1950- *WhoSSW 91*
Neese, Elbert Haven 1923- *WhoAm 90*
Neese, James Edwin 1938- *St&PR 91*
Neese, Robert Stuart 1938- *St&PR 91*
Neese, Ruby S. 1930- *WhoWrEP 89*
Neesley, William Charles 1935- *St&PR 91*
Neeson, Liam *BioIn 16*
Neeson, Margaret Graham 1918- *WhoAmW 91*
Neeve, Robbert Jan De 1943- *IntWWM 90*
Neevel, Raymond Richard 1922- *St&PR 91*
Nef, Evelyn Stefansson *AuBYP 90*
Nef, Evelyn Stefansson 1913- *WhoAm 90*
Nef, John Ulric 1899-1988 *BioIn 16*
Nef, Walter T. 1882-1960? *EncAL*
Nefedov, Oleg 1931- *WhoWor 91*
Neff, Andrew Love 1878-1936 *BioIn 16*
Neff, Arlene Merle 1946- *WhoAmW 91*
Neff, Barbara Estella 1950- *WhoAmW 91*
Neff, Benjamin Clarence 1934- *WhoAm 90*
Neff, Carole Cukell 1951- *WhoSSW 91*
Neff, Charles Amos *BiDrAPA 89*
Neff, Charles Barton 1932- *WhoE 91*
Neff, Charles Y. 1913- *St&PR 91*
Neff, David E. 1953- *St&PR 91*
Neff, Donald Lloyd 1930- *WhoAm 90*
Neff, Edith 1943- *WhoAmA 91, WhoE 91*
Neff, Edward August 1947- *WhoE 91*
Neff, Francine Irving 1925- *WhoAm 90*
Neff, Fred Leonard 1948- *WhoEmL 91, WhoWor 91*
Neff, Frederick Clifton 1913- *WhoAm 90*
Neff, Gerald David, Jr. 1939- *WhoSSW 91*
Neff, Howard L. *St&PR 91*
Neff, Jack Hillman 1938- *St&PR 91*
Neff, Jack Kenneth 1938- *WhoAm 90*
Neff, James D. 1937- *St&PR 91*
Neff, James Dennis 1937- *WhoAm 90*
Neff, John A 1926- *WhoAmA 91*
Neff, John B. *BioIn 16*
Neff, John Hallmark 1944- *WhoAmA 91*
Neff, Joseph 1900-1969 *WhoAmA 91N*
Neff, Kent Edward *BiDrAPA 89*
Neff, Leonard 1925- *BiDrAPA 89*
Neff, Michele Dubois 1942- *WhoE 91*
Neff, Pamela Jean 1954- *WhoSSW 91*
Neff, Pat Morris 1871-1952 *AmLegL*
Neff, Peter John 1938- *WhoAm 90, WhoE 91*
Neff, Ray Quinn 1928- *WhoSSW 91*
Neff, Richard F. 1948- *WhoE 91*
Neff, Robert Arthur 1931- *WhoAm 90*
Neff, Robert Clark 1921- *WhoWor 91*
Neff, Robert Matthew 1955- *WhoEmL 91*
Neff, Robert Wilbur 1936- *WhoAm 90*
Neff, Scott Richard 1958- *WhoEmL 91*
Neff, Severine 1949- *IntWWM 90*
Neff, Thomas Joseph 1937- *WhoAm 90, WhoE 91, WhoWor 91*
Neff, W. Perry 1927- *St&PR 91*
Neff, William DuWayne 1912- *WhoAm 90*
Neffgen, James Michael 1948- *WhoWor 91*
Neffson, Robert 1949- *WhoAmA 91*
Nefrusobek *WomWR*
Nefsky, William Frank 1947- *WhoSSW 91*
Neft, David Samuel 1937- *WhoE 91*
Negabamet, Noel 1600?-1666 *WhNaAH*
Negele, John William 1944- *WhoAm 90*
Negelow, Elizabeth Pribor *BiDrAPA 89*
Neggers, Carla A 1955- *ConAu 30NR*
Negherbon, Vincent Robert 1920- *WhoAm 90*
Neghme, Jacar *BioIn 16*
Negi, Sharad Singh 1957- *WhoWor 91*
Negoda, Natalya *BioIn 16*
Negovetich, John A. 1945- *St&PR 91*
Negray, Ron 1930- *Ballpl 90*
Negrelli, Mark John, III 1953- *St&PR 91*
Negrelli, Robert Sam 1947- *WhoSSW 91*
Negrepontis, Michael 1928- *WhoAm 90*
Negrete, Louis Richard 1934- *WhoHisp 91*
Negri, Ada 1870-1945 *EncCoWW*
Negri, Ann 1954- *BiDrAPA 89*
Negri, Gerald Louis 1936- *St&PR 91*
Negri, Pola 1899-1987 *WorAlBi*
Negri, Robert Joseph 1926- *St&PR 91, WhoAm 90*
Negri, Rocco Antonio 1932- *WhoAmA 91*
Negri, Rodrigo Rojas de *BioIn 16*
Negri, Steven Joseph 1952- *WhoE 91*
Negri, Susan Debra 1965- *WhoE 91*
Negri, Vittorio 1923- *IntWWM 90*
Negrin, Arnold Fernandez *BiDrAPA 89*
Negrin, I. Allen 1934- *St&PR 91*
Negrin, Juan 1892-1956 *BioIn 16*
Negrin, Robert Bruce 1952- *WhoE 91*
Negron, George Luis *BiDrAPA 89*
Negron, Luis Humberto *BiDrAPA 89*
Negron, Victor H., Jr. 1953- *WhoSSW 91*
Negron-Olivieri, Francisco A. 1933- *WhoHisp 91*
Negroponte, George 1953- *WhoAmA 91*
Negroponte, John *BioIn 16*
Negroponte, John Dimitri 1939- *WhoAm 90, WhoWor 91*
Negroponte, Nicholas P. *BioIn 16*
Negwagon *WhNaAH*
Negyesy, Janos 1938- *IntWWM 90*
Nehamas, Alexander 1946- *WhoAm 90*
Neher, Fred 1903- *WhoAmA 91*
Neher, James Edward 1953- *WhoE 91*
Neher, Leslie Irwin 1906- *WhoWor 91*
Neher, Patrick 1959- *IntWWM 90*
Neher, Ross James 1949- *WhoAmA 91, WhoE 91*
Neher, Timothy Pyper 1947- *WhoAm 90*
Nehf, Art 1892-1960 *Ballpl 90 [port]*
Nehlsen, Kerri Savage 1961- *WhoAmW 91*
Nehmer, Stanley 1920- *WhoAm 90*
Nehou, Louis-Lucas de *PenDiDA 89*
Nehracher, Mathias *PenDiDA 89*
Nehrer, Jonathan Mark 1958- *BiDrAPA 89*
Nehring, Earl Arthur 1920- *WhoAm 90*
Nehrkorn, William Howard 1941- *St&PR 91*
Nehrling, Arno Herbert, Jr. 1928- *WhoE 91, WhoWor 91*
Nehrt, Lee Charles 1926- *WhoAm 90*
Nehru, Jawaharlal 1889-1964 *BioIn 16, MajTwCW, WorAlBi*
Nei, Gary Edward 1944- *WhoAm 90*
Nei-Nei *WhoWrEP 89*
Neibauer, Bonnie Virginia 1951- *WhoAmW 91*
Neibauer, Gary 1944- *Ballpl 90*
Neibauer, Rodney Dean 1937- *WhoE 91*
Neidermyer, James Richard 1945- *St&PR 91*
Neidert, Jamie Bradley 1960- *WhoSSW 91*
Neidert, Kalo Edward 1918- *WhoAm 90*
Neidhardt, Carl Richard 1921- *WhoAmA 91*
Neidhardt, Frederick Carl 1931- *WhoAm 90*
Neidhardt, George Henry 1939- *St&PR 91*
Neidhart, Carol Lynn 1953- *WhoAmW 91*
Neidhart, Christoph 1954- *WhoWor 91*
Neidhart, James Allen 1940- *WhoAm 90*
Neidig, Charles Petersen 1919- *St&PR 91*
Neidigh, Kim Lee 1952- *WhoWrEP 89*
Neidle, Michael 1942- *St&PR 91*
Neidlinger, Buell *BioIn 16*
Neidlinger, Gustav 1910- *IntWWM 90, PenDiMP*
Neidorf, Barry Michael 1942- *St&PR 91*
Neidrick, Darla June 1947- *WhoWrEP 89*
Neier, Aryeh 1937- *BioIn 16, WhoAm 90, WhoWrEP 89*
Neiger, Michael Alan 1953- *WhoWrEP 89*
Neiggemann, Michael F. 1938- *St&PR 91*
Neighbors, Melissa L. 1961- *WhoSSW 91*
Neighbour, Oliver Wray 1923- *IntWWM 90*
Neighmond, Patricia 1949- *WhoAm 90*
Neihardt, John G 1881-1973 *EncO&P 3*
Neihardt, John Gneisenau 1881-1973 *EncPaPR 91*
Neihart, James Everett 1932- *St&PR 91*
Neikirk, Joseph Randolph 1928- *St&PR 91, WhoAm 90, WhoSSW 91*
Neikirk, William Robert 1938- *WhoAm 90*
Neikrug, Marc 1946- *IntWWM 90, PenDiMP A*
Neikrug, Marjorie *WhoAmA 91*
Neil, Fred Applestein 1933- *WhoWrEP 89*
Neil, Garry Thomas 1951- *WhoAm 90*
Neil, Gary Lawrence 1940- *WhoAm 90*
Neil, J M 1937- *WhoAmA 91*
Neil, Jessie Pruitt 1927- *WhoAmW 91*
Neil, Richard H. 1932- *St&PR 91*
Neil, Robert L 1927- *BiDrAPA 89*
Neil, Ronald D. 1937- *St&PR 91*
Neil, William 1954- *WhoAm 90*
Neil-Smith, Christopher *EncO&P 3*
Neilan, Lee Lowry 1938- *BiDrAPA 89*
Neild, Frank R *BiDrAPA 89*
Neild, Robert Ralph 1924- *WhoWor 91*
Neill, Alexander Sutherland 1883-1973 *BioIn 16*
Neill, Ben E 1914- *WhoAmA 91*
Neill, Charles William 1916- *WhoWor 91*
Neill, Denis Michael 1943- *WhoAm 90, WhoE 91, WhoWor 91*
Neill, Dennis Row 1952- *St&PR 91*
Neill, Eldeva M. Wyatt 1925- *St&PR 91*
Neill, George 1944- *St&PR 91*
Neill, Jimmy Dyke 1939- *WhoAm 90*
Neill, Joe 1944- *WhoAmA 91*
Neill, John Dickey 1955- *WhoSSW 91*
Neill, John Randolph 1947- *BiDrAPA 89*
Neill, Patrick 1926- *WhoWor 91*
Neill, Richard Robert 1925- *WhoAm 90*
Neill, Robert 1945- *St&PR 91*
Neill, Roger Graham 1944- *WhoWor 91*
Neill, Rolfe 1932- *WhoAm 90, WhoSSW 91*
Neill, S. Colin 1946- *St&PR 91*
Neill, Stephen Charles 1900-1984 *DcNaB 1981*
Neill, William *BioIn 16*
Neillie, Lynn Sawyer 1957- *ODwPR 91*
Neilly, Andrew Hutchinson, Jr. 1923- *St&PR 91, WhoAm 90*
Neilson, Benjamin Reath 1938- *WhoAm 90*
Neilson, Elizabeth Anastasia 1913- *WhoAm 90*
Neilson, Frances Fullerton 1910- *AuBYP 90*
Neilson, James *PenDiDA 89*
Neilson, John Wilbert Tennant 1944- *WhoWor 91*

Neilson, Katherine B 1902-1977 *WhoAmA 91N*
Neilson, Kenneth T. 1948- *St&PR 91*
Neilson, Lewis 1924- *St&PR 91*
Neilson, Martin Fredrick 1946- *WhoAm 90*
Neilson, Melany 1958- *ConAu 132*
Neilson, Raymond P R 1881-1964 *WhoAmA 91N*
Neilson, Robert McKenzie, Jr. 1949- *WhoAm 90*
Neilson, Roger *WhoAm 90, WhoE 91*
Neilson, William Allen 1869-1946 *WorAlBi*
Neilson, Winthrop C., III 1934- *ODwPR 91*
Neilson, Winthrop Cunningham, III 1934- *WhoAm 90*
Neily, Harry 1884-1948 *Ballpl 90*
Neilz, Jacques *PenDiMP*
Neiman, Allen Robert 1956- *BiDrAPA 89*
Neiman, Donald 1943- *St&PR 91*
Neiman, John Hammond 1917- *WhoAm 90*
Neiman, LeRoy 1927- *WhoAm 90, WhoAmA 91, WhoE 91, WhoWor 91*
Neiman, Lionel Joseph 1921- *WhoAm 90*
Neiman, Morris *BioIn 16*
Neiman, Morris 1910?-1989 *ConAu 130*
Neiman, Norman 1935- *WhoSSW 91*
Neiman, Robert LeRoy 1930- *WhoWor 91*
Neiman, Tanya Marie 1949- *WhoAmW 91, WhoEmL 91, WhoWor 91*
Neiman, William Lee 1929- *St&PR 91*
Neimann, Albert Alexander 1939- *WhoWor 91*
Neimark, Paul G. *AuBYP 90*
Neimark, Philip John 1939- *WhoWor 91*
Neimark, Sheridan 1935- *WhoAm 90*
Neimark, Tanya Lee 1960- *WhoAmW 91*
Neimark, Vassa 1954- *WhoAmW 91, WhoWor 91*
Neimeth, Robert 1935- *St&PR 91*
Neims, Allen Howard 1938- *WhoAm 90, WhoSSW 91*
Nein, Jo *EncCoWW*
Nein, Lawrence Frederick 1936- *St&PR 91*
Neiner, Andrew Joseph 1950- *St&PR 91, WhoAm 90, WhoEmL 91, WhoWor 91*
Neipris, Janet *ConAu 30NR*
Neira, Daniel Alejandro 1955- *WhoHisp 91*
Neira, Gail Elizabeth *WhoHisp 91*
Neira, Teresa *BiDrAPA 89*
Neis, Arnold Hayward 1938- *WhoAm 90, WhoE 91*
Neis, Arthur V. 1940- *St&PR 91*
Neis, Arthur Veral 1940- *WhoWor 91*
Neis, Bernie 1895-1972 *Ballpl 90*
Neisel, Peter 1939- *St&PR 91*
Neiser, Brent Allen 1954- *WhoEmL 91*
Neiser, Richard William 1938- *WhoAm 90, WhoSSW 91*
Neises, John Theodore 1930- *WhoE 91*
Neislar, W. Ronald 1934- *St&PR 91*
Neisler, Charles Andrew 1927- *St&PR 91*
Neisler, David Carl 1959- *St&PR 91*
Neisloss, Melvin 1927- *St&PR 91*
Neisloss, Susan M. *ODwPR 91*
Neisner, Melvin B. 1914- *St&PR 91*
Neisner, Melvin Bauer 1914- *WhoAm 90*
Neiss, Edgar 1939- *WhoSSW 91*
Neisser, Ulric 1928- *WhoAm 90*
Neiswander, Arlyn Claud 1926- *St&PR 91*
Neiter, Gerald Irving 1933- *WhoAm 90*
Neith, Jack David 1952- *WhoE 91*
Neitz, Robert Henry 1929- *WhoSSW 91*
Neitzke, Eric Karl 1955- *WhoWor 91*
Neiwirth, Mark A. 1957- *IntWWM 90*
Neizert, Christoph 1956- *WhoWor 91*
Nejdawi, Bashar 1962- *WhoSSW 91*
Nejelski, Marilyn M. 1934- *WhoAmW 91*
Nejelski, Paul Arthur 1938- *WhoAm 90*
Nejfelt, Henry Victor 1939- *St&PR 91*
Neki, Jaswant S *BiDrAPA 89*
Nekien, Horst G. 1927- *St&PR 91*
Nekola, Bots 1906-1987 *Ballpl 90*
Nekola, Joseph *PenDiDA 89*
Nekola, Karl *PenDiDA 89*
Nekola, Savitri 1954- *WhoWrEP 89*
Nekos, Steve *BioIn 16*
Nekrasov, Nikolai 1821-1878 *WorAlBi*
Nekrosius, W Scott D 1945- *BiDrAPA 89*
Nekvasil, Charles A. 1945- *ODwPR 91*
Nel, Anton *BioIn 16*
Nel, Anton 1961- *IntWWM 90*
Nelder, John Ashworth 1924- *WhoWor 91*
Neligh, Gordon Leigh, III *BiDrAPA 89*
Nelipovich, Sandra Grassi 1939- *WhoAmW 91, WhoWor 91*
Nelken, Margarita 1896-1968 *EncCoWW*
Nelken, Michael Alonzo 1939- *BiDrAPA 89*
Nelken, Sam 1913- *BiDrAPA 89*
Nelker, Bruce Edward 1949- *WhoSSW 91*
Nelkin, Dorothy 1933- *ConAu 31NR, WhoAm 90*
Nelkin, Mark 1931- *WhoAm 90*
Nellbeck, Lennart Bror 1936- *WhoWor 91*
Nellemann, David Oscar 1933- *WhoAm 90*
Nellemose, Knud 1908- *WhoWor 91*
Nellens, Roger 1937- *BioIn 16*
Neller, Gary Keith 1943- *BiDrAPA 89*
Nelles, Maurice 1906- *WhoAm 90*
Nellessen, Robyn Celeste 1956- *WhoAmW 91*
Nelli, Donald James 1917- *WhoE 91, WhoWor 91*
Nelligan, Emile 1879-1941 *DcLB 92 [port]*
Nelligan, Kate 1951- *OxCCanT, WhoAm 90, WhoWor 91, WorAlBi*
Nelligan, Katherine Rosalie 1938- *WhoAmW 91*
Nelligan, Michael Thomas 1939- *St&PR 91*
Nelligan, William David 1926- *WhoAm 90*
Nellis, Jennifred Gene *WhoAmA 91*
Nellis, Kirk Keith 1950- *St&PR 91*
Nellis, Muriel Gollon 1931- *WhoWor 91*
Nellis-Godwin, Corrine Mary *BiDrAPA 89*
Nellius, Lynn 1943- *St&PR 91*
Nelme, Anthony *PenDiDA 89*
Nelme, Francis *PenDiDA 89*
Nelms, Dan E. *WhoAm 90*
Nelms, Jerry Lynn 1930- *St&PR 91*
Nelms, Michael Richard 1954- *St&PR 91*
Nelms, Sheryl Lynne 1944- *WhoWrEP 89*
Nelms, Steven Ben 1954- *WhoSSW 91*
Nelsen, Hart Michael 1938- *WhoAm 90, WhoWrEP 89*
Nelsen, Ibsen Andreas 1919- *WhoAm 90*
Nelsen, William Cameron 1941- *WhoAm 90*
Nelson, A. Foster 1941- *St&PR 91*
Nelson, Agnes Miriam 1951- *WhoAmW 91*
Nelson, Alan *BioIn 16*
Nelson, Alan Arthur 1952- *BiDrAPA 89*
Nelson, Alan Curtis 1933- *WhoAm 90*
Nelson, Alan Ray 1933- *WhoAm 90*
Nelson, Albert Alvin 1949- *WhoEmL 91*
Nelson, Albert H. 1917- *St&PR 91*
Nelson, Albert Louis, III 1938- *WhoWor 91*
Nelson, Alexander Montgomery, III 1938- *St&PR 91*
Nelson, Alfred John 1922- *WhoAm 90*
Nelson, Alice Elizabeth Hill 1921- *WhoAmW 91*
Nelson, Alice Ruth Moore Dunbar 1875-1935 *MajTwCW*
Nelson, Allan D 1936- *BiDrAPA 89*
Nelson, America Elizabeth 1932- *WhoAmW 91, WhoWor 91*
Nelson, Andrew Allen Laing 1963- *WhoE 91*
Nelson, Angela Robinson 1956- *WhoAmW 91*
Nelson, Anita Marie 1946- *WhoEmL 91*
Nelson, Anne Gardner *BioIn 16*
Nelson, April Lynn 1960- *WhoAmW 91*
Nelson, Arlene B. 1925- *WhoAmW 91*
Nelson, Arlene Cassell 1952- *WhoAmW 91*
Nelson, Arnold Bernard 1922- *WhoAm 90*
Nelson, Arnold S. 1928- *St&PR 91*
Nelson, Arthur 1928- *BiDrAPA 89*
Nelson, Arthur Alexander, Jr. 1946- *WhoAm 90*
Nelson, Arthur Christian 1952- *WhoSSW 91*
Nelson, Arthur Hunt 1923- *WhoE 91*
Nelson, Artie Cortez *BiDrAPA 89*
Nelson, Averly Henry *BiDrAPA 89*
Nelson, Barbara Ann 1939- *St&PR 91*
Nelson, Barbara Anne 1951- *WhoAmW 91*
Nelson, Barbara Kay 1947- *WhoAmW 91*
Nelson, Barry 1920- *WorAlBi*
Nelson, Barry Kenneth 1947- *BiDrAPA 89*
Nelson, Basha Ruth *WhoAmA 91*
Nelson, Bernard Edward 1950- *WhoEmL 91*
Nelson, Bill *BioIn 16*
Nelson, Bill 1942- *WhoAm 90, WhoSSW 91*
Nelson, Bobby Jack 1938- *WhoWrEP 89*
Nelson, Bobby Wayne 1941- *BiDrAPA 89*
Nelson, Bonnie Kay 1950- *WhoAmW 91*
Nelson, Bradley Richard 1950- *IntWWM 90*
Nelson, Bruce F. 1927- *St&PR 91*
Nelson, Bruce K. 1954- *St&PR 91*
Nelson, Bruce Sherman 1951- *WhoAm 90*
Nelson, Bruce Warren 1929- *WhoAm 90*
Nelson, Bryan Herbert 1956- *WhoEmL 91*
Nelson, Byron 1912- *WorAlBi*
Nelson, Byron D. 1946- *St&PR 91*
Nelson, C. Emil *BioIn 16*
Nelson, Calvin L. 1927- *St&PR 91*
Nelson, Calvin Richard 1927- *WhoSSW 91*
Nelson, Candace Therase 1961- *WhoAmW 91*
Nelson, Carey Boone *WhoAmA 91, WhoE 91*
Nelson, Carl 1956- *ODwPR 91*
Nelson, Carl Roger 1915- *WhoAm 90*
Nelson, Carol Ann 1952- *WhoAmW 91*
Nelson, Carol J. *BiDrAPA 89*
Nelson, Carol Susag 1947- *WhoEmL 91*
Nelson, Carole Ann 1941- *WhoAmW 91*
Nelson, Carolyn *BiDrAPA 89*
Nelson, Carolyn Berryhill 1933- *St&PR 91*
Nelson, Carolyn Marie 1945- *WhoEmL 91*
Nelson, Charles Abbott 1961- *WhoEmL 91*
Nelson, Charles Arthur 1922- *WhoAm 90*
Nelson, Charles Dale 1939- *St&PR 91*
Nelson, Charles E. *St&PR 91N*
Nelson, Charles F. 1947- *St&PR 91*
Nelson, Charles J. 1920- *WhoAm 90*
Nelson, Charles Lamar 1917- *WhoWrEP 89*
Nelson, Charles Schreiner 1937- *St&PR 91*
Nelson, Charles W. 1947- *St&PR 91*
Nelson, Cholmondeley M. 1903- *AuBYP 90*
Nelson, Clara Singleton 1935- *WhoAmW 91*
Nelson, Clarence C *BiDrAPA 89*
Nelson, Clayton H. 1937- *St&PR 91*
Nelson, Clifford 1950- *St&PR 91*
Nelson, Clifford Arnold 1923- *WhoAm 90*
Nelson, Cordner 1918- *BioIn 16*
Nelson, Craig T. *BioIn 16, WhoAm 90*
Nelson, Craig T. 1946- *WorAlBi*
Nelson, Curtis Norman 1941- *WhoE 91*
Nelson, Curtis Scott 1929- *WhoWrEP 89*
Nelson, Cynthia Kaye 1949- *WhoAmW 91*
Nelson, Cyril I. *BioIn 16*
Nelson, Daniel A 1958- *BiDrAPA 89*
Nelson, Daniel Raymond 1937- *St&PR 91*
Nelson, Darrell Wayne 1939- *WhoAm 90*
Nelson, Darwin Bruce 1942- *WhoSSW 91*
Nelson, Dave 1944- *Ballpl 90*
Nelson, David 1977- *BioIn 16*
Nelson, David Aldrich 1932- *WhoAm 90*
Nelson, David Allan *BiDrAPA 89*
Nelson, David Edward 1930- *WhoAm 90*
Nelson, David F. 1920- *WhoAm 90*
Nelson, David L. 1930- *St&PR 91*
Nelson, David Lee 1942- *WhoAm 90*
Nelson, David Leonard 1930- *WhoAm 90*
Nelson, David Lowell 1957- *WhoSSW 91*
Nelson, David Robert 1951- *WhoAm 90*
Nelson, David Robert 1962- *WhoE 91*
Nelson, David S. 1933- *WhoE 91*
Nelson, David Wayne 1951- *WhoEmL 91*
Nelson, Deborah Jeanne 1952- *WhoAmW 91*
Nelson, Diane 1940- *ODwPR 91*
Nelson, Don F. 1915- *St&PR 91*
Nelson, Dona Rae 1947- *WhoAmA 91*
Nelson, Donald Albert 1922- *WhoWor 91*
Nelson, Donald Arvid 1940- *WhoAm 90*
Nelson, Donald J. 1944- *St&PR 91*
Nelson, Donald K. 1943- *St&PR 91*
Nelson, Donald Lloyd 1923- *WhoAm 90*
Nelson, Donald Martin 1948- *St&PR 91*
Nelson, Donald W. 1933- *ODwPR 91*
Nelson, Donna Gayle 1943- *St&PR 91*
Nelson, Donna Lynn 1967- *WhoSSW 91*
Nelson, Doriska Augustine *BiDrAPA 89*
Nelson, Dorothy Wright 1928- *WhoAmW 91*
Nelson, Dotson McGinnis, Jr. 1915- *WhoAm 90*
Nelson, Douglas A. 1927- *WhoAm 90*
Nelson, Douglas Thomas 1946- *WhoEmL 91*
Nelson, Drew Vernon 1947- *WhoEmL 91*
Nelson, Edward Gage 1931- *St&PR 91, WhoAm 90*
Nelson, Edward Humphrey 1918- *WhoAm 90*
Nelson, Edward Sheffield 1941- *WhoAm 90, WhoWor 91*
Nelson, Edwin Clarence 1922- *WhoAm 90*
Nelson, Edwin Stafford 1928- *WhoAm 90*
Nelson, Elaine Marie 1939- *WhoAmW 91*
Nelson, Elizabeth Alice 1948- *WhoAmW 91*
Nelson, Elizabeth Fairhurst 1949- *WhoEmL 91*
Nelson, Elmer Kingsholm, Jr. 1922- *WhoAm 90*
Nelson, Ethelyn Barnett 1925- *WhoAmW 91*
Nelson, Evelyn J *BiDrAPA 89*
Nelson, Frances Roberson 1945- *WhoAmW 91*
Nelson, Frederick Carl 1932- *WhoAm 90*
Nelson, Frederick Dickson 1958- *WhoAm 90*
Nelson, Frederick N. 1941- *St&PR 91*
Nelson, G. Erick 1942- *St&PR 91*
Nelson, Gail 1946- *DrBlPA 90*
Nelson, Garrett R. *WhoAm 90*
Nelson, Gary D. *St&PR 91*
Nelson, Gary Thomas 1949- *WhoSSW 91*
Nelson, Gaylord A. 1916- *WorAlBi*
Nelson, Gaylord Anton 1916- *WhoAm 90*
Nelson, Gene 1960- *Ballpl 90*
Nelson, Geneva E. 1942- *WhoAmW 91*
Nelson, Genevieve Muriel 1921- *WhoAmW 91*
Nelson, George *ODwPR 91, PenDiDA 89*
Nelson, George 1908-1934 *WorAlBi*
Nelson, George 1908-1986 *ConDes 90*
Nelson, George D. 1950- *BioIn 16*
Nelson, George Laurence 1887-1978 *WhoAmA 91N*
Nelson, George Leonard 1897- *WhoAm 90*
Nelson, George N. 1932- *WhoAm 90, WhoWor 91*
Nelson, Gerald Kenneth 1922- *WhoAm 90*
Nelson, Geraldine Simonson 1932- *ODwPR 91*
Nelson, Ginger K. 1939- *WhoWrEP 89*
Nelson, Gordon Leigh 1943- *WhoAm 90, WhoSSW 91, WhoWor 91*
Nelson, Gordon Leon 1919- *WhoAm 90*
Nelson, Grace Rand 1950- *WhoAmW 91*
Nelson, Grant Steel 1939- *WhoAm 90*
Nelson, Gwendolyn Diane 1950- *WhoAmW 91*
Nelson, Harold B 1947- *WhoAmA 91*
Nelson, Harold H 1917- *BiDrAPA 89*
Nelson, Harriet 1914- *WorAlBi*
Nelson, Harry 1923- *WhoAm 90*
Nelson, Harry Donald 1933- *WhoAm 90*
Nelson, Harry William 1908- *WhoAmA 91, WhoE 91*
Nelson, Harvey Frans, Jr. 1924- *WhoAm 90*
Nelson, Havelock 1917- *IntWWM 90*
Nelson, Haywood 1960?- *DrBlPA 90*
Nelson, Hedwig Potok 1954- *WhoAmW 91*
Nelson, Helaine Q. 1945- *St&PR 91*
Nelson, Henry B, III 1950- *BiDrAPA 89*
Nelson, Herbert *NewYTBS 90*
Nelson, Herbert L *BiDrAPA 89*
Nelson, Herbert Leroy 1922- *WhoAm 90*
Nelson, Horatio 1758-1805 *BioIn 16, WorAlBi*
Nelson, Howard Joseph 1919- *WhoAm 90*
Nelson, Howard L. 1954- *St&PR 91*
Nelson, Hugh 1830-1893 *DcCanB 12*
Nelson, Jack D 1929- *WhoAmA 91*
Nelson, Jack Henry 1930- *St&PR 91*
Nelson, Jack Lee 1932- *WhoAm 90*
Nelson, Jack Russell 1929- *WhoAm 90*
Nelson, James Alan 1946- *St&PR 91*
Nelson, James Albert 1941- *WhoAm 90, WhoSSW 91*
Nelson, James C. 1939- *ODwPR 91*
Nelson, James Carmer, Jr. 1921- *WhoAm 90*
Nelson, James Cecil 1908- *WhoAm 90*
Nelson, James Clifford 1930- *WhoAm 90*
Nelson, James D *BiDrAPA 89*
Nelson, James Dean 1956- *WhoSSW 91*
Nelson, James Delbert 1944- *St&PR 91*
Nelson, James Douglas 1944- *WhoE 91*
Nelson, James E. *BioIn 16*
Nelson, James Harold 1936- *WhoE 91*
Nelson, James P 1949- *WhoAmA 91*
Nelson, James Richard 1955- *WhoEmL 91*
Nelson, James Vincent 1950- *St&PR 91*
Nelson, Jane Byrne 1926- *St&PR 91*
Nelson, Jane Eleanor 1959- *WhoAmW 91*
Nelson, Jane Gray 1928- *WhoAmA 91*
Nelson, Janet Kathryn 1954- *WhoAmW 91, WhoEmL 91*
Nelson, Janice Eileen 1943- *WhoAmW 91, WhoE 91*
Nelson, Janice Marian 1951- *WhoAmW 91*
Nelson, Janie Rish 1941- *WhoAmW 91*
Nelson, Jean Davenport 1931- *St&PR 91*
Nelson, Jean Edward, II 1952- *WhoE 91*
Nelson, Jefferson E 1947- *BiDrAPA 89*
Nelson, Jerry A. 1935- *St&PR 91*
Nelson, Jerry R. *WhoSSW 91*
Nelson, Jim 1947- *Ballpl 90*
Nelson, Jo Ann 1946- *WhoWrEP 89*
Nelson, Joel L. *St&PR 91*
Nelson, Joel Peter 1939- *St&PR 91*
Nelson, John 1794-1860 *BiDrUSE 89*
Nelson, John 1922- *St&PR 91*
Nelson, John 1945- *IntWWM 90*
Nelson, John Allan 1952- *WhoWrEP 89*
Nelson, John H. 1930- *St&PR 91*
Nelson, John Howard 1929- *WhoAm 90*
Nelson, John Howard 1930- *WhoAm 90*
Nelson, John M. 1931- *St&PR 91*
Nelson, John Martin 1931- *WhoAm 90, WhoE 91*
Nelson, John Oliver 1909-1990 *BioIn 16, ConAu 131*
Nelson, John Paul 1940- *BiDrAPA 89*
Nelson, John R. *ODwPR 91*
Nelson, John Ray 1926- *St&PR 91*
Nelson, John Robert 1920- *WhoAm 90*
Nelson, John Robert 1939- *WhoE 91*
Nelson, John Thilgen 1921- *WhoAm 90*
Nelson, John W. 1942- *St&PR 91*
Nelson, John Wilton 1941- *WhoAm 90*
Nelson, John Woolard 1928- *WhoAm 90*
Nelson, Jon 1936- *IntWWM 90*
Nelson, Jon Allen 1936- *WhoAmA 91*

Nelson, Jonathan Brent 1966- *WhoEmL 91*
Nelson, Jonathan Robert 1956- *WhoE 91*
Nelson, Joni Lysett 1938- *WhoAm 90*
Nelson, Joseph Conrad 1926- *WhoAm 90*
Nelson, Joseph H. 1931- *St&PR 91*
Nelson, Joseph J. 1941- *St&PR 91*
Nelson, Judd 1959- *WhoAm 90*
Nelson, Judith 1939- *IntWWM 90*
Nelson, Judy 1954- *WhoAmW 91*
Nelson, Karen Lynnette *BiDrAPA 89*
Nelson, Karin Becker 1933- *WhoAmW 91*
Nelson, Karl 1960- *BioIn 16*
Nelson, Kathleen Ann 1958- *WhoEmL 91*
Nelson, Kathleen Ethel 1947- *WhoAmW 91*
Nelson, Kay LeRoi 1926- *WhoAm 90*
Nelson, Kay Louise 1956- *WhoAmW 91*
Nelson, Keith Alan 1959- *WhoSSW 91*
Nelson, Keith L. 1943- *St&PR 91*
Nelson, Keithe Eugene 1935- *WhoAm 90*
Nelson, Kenneth Edward 1948- *WhoAm 90*
Nelson, Kenneth Eric *BiDrAPA 89*
Nelson, Kenneth Sigurd 1943- *WhoE 91*
Nelson, Kenneth V. 1918- *St&PR 91*
Nelson, Kent *WhoWrEP 89*
Nelson, Kent Charles 1937- *St&PR 91*
Nelson, Kenwyn Gordon 1926- *WhoAm 90*
Nelson, Kirk L 1950- *BiDrAPA 89*
Nelson, L. Clair 1918- *St&PR 91*
Nelson, L. Scott 1938- *St&PR 91*
Nelson, Lance Shaylor 1939- *St&PR 91*
Nelson, Larry 1939- *St&PR 91*
Nelson, Larry Dean 1937- *WhoWor 91*
Nelson, Larry Wayne *BiDrAPA 89*
Nelson, Lars-Erik 1941- *WhoAm 90*
Nelson, Laura *ODwPR 91*
Nelson, Laura Kay 1962- *WhoAmW 91, WhoSSW 91*
Nelson, Laurence Clyde 1947- *WhoSSW 91*
Nelson, Lawrence Barclay 1931- *WhoAm 90*
Nelson, Lawrence Evan 1932- *WhoAm 90*
Nelson, Lawrence Olaf 1926- *WhoAm 90*
Nelson, Layne Meredith 1952- *WhoAmW 91*
Nelson, Leland Carl 1924- *St&PR 91*
Nelson, Leonard 1912- *WhoAmA 91, WhoE 91*
Nelson, Leonard 1920- *WhoAm 90*
Nelson, Leonard Earl 1944- *WhoE 91, WhoWor 91*
Nelson, Leslie Bergen 1925- *St&PR 91*
Nelson, Lester 1928- *WhoE 91*
Nelson, Lewis Clair 1918- *WhoAm 90*
Nelson, Linda Carol 1954- *WhoAmW 91*
Nelson, Linda Jane 1957- *WhoAmW 91*
Nelson, Lindsey 1919- *Ballpl 90*
Nelson, Liza 1950- *WhoWrEP 89*
Nelson, Lloyd Steadman 1922- *St&PR 91, WhoAm 90*
Nelson, Louis 1902-1990 *BioIn 16, NewYTBS 90*
Nelson, Lowry, Jr. 1926- *WhoAm 90*
Nelson, Luella Eline 1952- *WhoEmL 91*
Nelson, Lyle Morgan 1918- *WhoAm 90*
Nelson, Lynn 1905-1955 *Ballpl 90*
Nelson, M.G. 1914- *St&PR 91*
Nelson, Magnus Charles 1938- *WhoAm 90*
Nelson, Marg 1899- *AuBYP 90*
Nelson, Mark Allan 1957- *IntWWM 90*
Nelson, Mark Bruce 1921- *WhoAm 90*
Nelson, Marshall Scott 1954- *WhoEmL 91*
Nelson, Martha Jane 1952- *WhoAm 90, WhoAmW 91*
Nelson, Martin O. 1912- *St&PR 91*
Nelson, Martin Oliver, Jr. 1946- *St&PR 91*
Nelson, Marvin R. 1926- *St&PR 91*
Nelson, Marvin Ray 1926- *WhoAm 90*
Nelson, Mary *BioIn 16*
Nelson, Mary Carroll 1929- *WhoAmA 91, WhoAmW 91*
Nelson, Mary Ellen Dickson 1933- *WhoAmW 91*
Nelson, Mary Pennell 1943- *WhoAmW 91*
Nelson, Mary S. 1943- *WhoAmW 91*
Nelson, Mary Virginia Boles 1938- *WhoAmW 91*
Nelson, Maureen Danette 1960- *WhoAmW 91*
Nelson, Maureen Elizabeth 1939- *WhoAmW 91*
Nelson, Maxine Marie 1932- *WhoAmW 91*
Nelson, Mel 1936- *Ballpl 90*
Nelson, Melissa Haenisch *BiDrAPA 89*
Nelson, Melvin Dennis 1947- *WhoEmL 91*
Nelson, Merle Chandler 1908- *WhoAmW 91, WhoSSW 91*
Nelson, Merle R. 1934- *St&PR 91*
Nelson, Merlin Edward 1922- *WhoAm 90*
Nelson, Michael *BioIn 16*
Nelson, Michael Dean 1956- *WhoEmL 91*
Nelson, Michael Hugh *BiDrAPA 89*
Nelson, Michael James 1951- *WhoSSW 91*
Nelson, Michael Richard 1947- *WhoWor 91*
Nelson, Michael Underhill 1932- *WhoAm 90*
Nelson, Michelle Hoghland 1953- *WhoWrEP 89*
Nelson, Mildred 1915- *WhoWrEP 89*
Nelson, Milo Gabriel 1938- *WhoWrEP 89*
Nelson, Milton Eugene 1925- *WhoAm 90*
Nelson, Monteiro Harris, III 1956- *WhoE 91*
Nelson, Nan Elaine *BiDrAPA 89*
Nelson, Nancy Eleanor 1933- *WhoAm 90, WhoWor 91*
Nelson, Nancy Jane 1956- *WhoAmW 91*
Nelson, Natalie Ann 1962- *WhoAmW 91*
Nelson, Neal Norman 1952- *WhoAm 90*
Nelson, Neill Davenport 1954- *St&PR 91*
Nelson, Nels Robert 1923- *WhoAm 90*
Nelson, Nette Adaline 1939- *WhoAmW 91*
Nelson, Nevin Mary 1941- *WhoAmW 91*
Nelson, Norman Crooks 1929- *WhoAm 90*
Nelson, Norman Roy 1944- *WhoE 91*
Nelson, Norton *NewYTBS 90*
Nelson, Norton 1910-1990 *BioIn 16*
Nelson, Novella 1939- *DrBIPA 90*
Nelson, O Terry 1941- *SmATA 62*
Nelson, Oliver 1932-1975 *DrBIPA 90, OxCPMus*
Nelson, Oliver 1933-1975 *BioIn 16*
Nelson, Oliver Evans, Jr. 1920- *WhoAm 90*
Nelson, Otto Millard 1935- *WhoSSW 91*
Nelson, Ozzie 1907-1975 *WorAlBi*
Nelson, Pamela *WhoAmW 91*
Nelson, Pamela Hudson 1947- *WhoAmA 91*
Nelson, Patricia Sweazey 1927- *WhoAmW 91*
Nelson, Paul Richard 1947- *WhoAm 90*
Nelson, Paula Morrison Bronson 1944- *WhoAmW 91, WhoWor 91*
Nelson, Peter Alan 1932- *St&PR 91, WhoAm 90*
Nelson, Peter Christian 1945- *St&PR 91*
Nelson, Philip Francis 1928- *IntWWM 90, WhoAm 90*
Nelson, Philip G *BiDrAPA 89*
Nelson, Pierce D 1921- *BiDrAPA 89*
Nelson, Prince Rogers *BioIn 16*
Nelson, Ralph Alfred 1927- *WhoAm 90*
Nelson, Ralph Erwin 1946- *WhoSSW 91*
Nelson, Ralph James 1925- *St&PR 91*
Nelson, Ralph Lowell 1926- *WhoAm 90*
Nelson, Ray Faraday 1931- *WhoWrEP 89*
Nelson, Raymond John 1917- *WhoAm 90*
Nelson, Rebecca J. 1845- *BioAmW*
Nelson, Rebecca Jean 1954- *WhoWor 91*
Nelson, Richard 1950- *ConAu 129, ConTFT 8*
Nelson, Richard Alan 1942- *WhoSSW 91*
Nelson, Richard Alan 1954- *WhoEmL 91*
Nelson, Richard Bruce 1952- *WhoSSW 91*
Nelson, Richard Burton 1911- *WhoAm 90*
Nelson, Richard Copeland 1930- *WhoAm 90*
Nelson, Richard D. 1940- *St&PR 91*
Nelson, Richard David 1940- *WhoAm 90*
Nelson, Richard E., Jr. 1905- *St&PR 91*
Nelson, Richard Henry 1939- *WhoE 91, WhoWor 91*
Nelson, Richard K 1941- *ConAu 30NR*
Nelson, Richard L. 1953- *ODwPR 91*
Nelson, Richard W *BiDrAPA 89*
Nelson, Rick 1940-1985 *EncPR&S 89, OxCPMus*
Nelson, Rick 1940-1986 *WorAlBi*
Nelson, Robbin Newel 1948- *WhoAmW 91*
Nelson, Robert A. 1927- *St&PR 91*
Nelson, Robert A. 1939- *St&PR 91*
Nelson, Robert Bruce 1935- *WhoAm 90*
Nelson, Robert Bruce, III 1954- *WhoEmL 91*
Nelson, Robert C. 1956- *St&PR 91*
Nelson, Robert Charles 1924- *WhoAm 90*
Nelson, Robert Charles 1947- *WhoE 91*
Nelson, Robert Dale 1934- *St&PR 91*
Nelson, Robert Earl, Jr. 1938- *WhoSSW 91, WhoWor 91*
Nelson, Robert Eddinger 1928- *WhoWor 91*
Nelson, Robert Gerald 1942- *St&PR 91*
Nelson, Robert Hartley 1921- *WhoAm 90*
Nelson, Robert John 1926- *WhoWor 91*
Nelson, Robert L. 1943- *St&PR 91*
Nelson, Robert Louis 1931- *WhoAm 90*
Nelson, Robert Norton 1941- *WhoSSW 91*
Nelson, Rocky 1924- *Ballpl 90*
Nelson, Rodney 1941- *WhoWrEP 89*
Nelson, Rodney Ellsworth 1934- *WhoAm 90*
Nelson, Roger 1944- *Ballpl 90*
Nelson, Roger F. *BioIn 16*
Nelson, Roger Hugh 1931- *WhoAm 90*
Nelson, Roger K. 1947- *St&PR 91*
Nelson, Roger William 1947- *IntWWM 90*
Nelson, Roland Edward 1927- *St&PR 91*
Nelson, Roland Hill, Jr. 1928- *WhoAm 90*
Nelson, Ron 1929- *IntWWM 90, WhoAm 90*
Nelson, Ronald Axel 1927- *IntWWM 90*
Nelson, Ronald Harvey 1918- *WhoAm 90*
Nelson, Ronald Roy 1941- *WhoSSW 91*
Nelson, Roy Lee 1949- *WhoSSW 91*
Nelson, Roy Paul 1923- *BioIn 16, WhoWrEP 89*
Nelson, Ruben F W 1939- *ConAu 31NR*
Nelson, Russell Andrew 1913- *WhoAm 90*
Nelson, Russell Marion 1924- *WhoAm 90*
Nelson, Ruth Basha 1939- *WhoAmA 91*
Nelson, Sally Genise 1957- *WhoSSW 91*
Nelson, Sally Irene 1941- *WhoAmW 91*
Nelson, Sarah Burton *BiDrAPA 89*
Nelson, Sarah Milledge 1931- *WhoAmW 91*
Nelson, Sarah Suzanne 1942- *WhoAmW 91*
Nelson, Scott H *BiDrAPA 89*
Nelson, Scott Michael 1959- *WhoEmL 91*
Nelson, Scott Russell 1954- *WhoEmL 91*
Nelson, Shannon 1961- *WhoAmW 91*
Nelson, Signe 1937- *WhoAmA 91*
Nelson, Stanley Fitzgerald 1926- *WhoE 91*
Nelson, Stephen M. 1948- *St&PR 91*
Nelson, Steven Lee *BiDrAPA 89*
Nelson, Susan 1936- *WhoAmW 91*
Nelson, Susan Margaret 1960- *WhoAmW 91*
Nelson, Sydney B. 1935- *WhoSSW 91*
Nelson, Ted Long 1927- *WhoSSW 91*
Nelson, Terry Ellan Elisabeth 1954- *WhoAmW 91*
Nelson, Terry L. 1945- *St&PR 91*
Nelson, Terry Lee 1953- *WhoEmL 91*
Nelson, Theophila 1654-1705? *BiDEWW*
Nelson, Theresa *AuBYP 90*
Nelson, Theresa Decker 1926- *WhoAmW 91*
Nelson, Thomas 1738-1789 *BioIn 16*
Nelson, Thomas, Jr. 1738-1789 *EncCRAm*
Nelson, Thomas Adams 1921- *WhoWor 91*
Nelson, Thomas Carl 1943- *WhoAm 90*
Nelson, Thomas Karl 1959- *BiDrAPA 89*
Nelson, Thomas William 1921- *WhoAm 90*
Nelson, Toni Cooke 1949- *WhoAmW 91, WhoSSW 91*
Nelson, Tracy *BioIn 16*
Nelson, Tyka *BioIn 16*
Nelson, Vera Joyce 1903- *WhoWrEP 89*
Nelson, Vi 1944- *ODwPR 91*
Nelson, Victoria C. 1958- *WhoAmW 91*
Nelson, Violet M. 1935- *WhoAmW 91*
Nelson, Virginia L. 1918- *WhoWrEP 89*
Nelson, Vita Joy 1937- *WhoWor 91*
Nelson, Waldemar Stanley 1916- *St&PR 91*
Nelson, Waldo Emerson 1898- *WhoAm 90*
Nelson, Wallace Boyd 1923- *WhoAm 90, WhoSSW 91*
Nelson, Walter Gerald 1930- *WhoAm 90*
Nelson, Wayne A. 1930- *St&PR 91*
Nelson, Wayne P. 1941- *St&PR 91*
Nelson, Wendel Lane 1939- *WhoAm 90*
Nelson, Werner Lind 1914- *WhoAm 90*
Nelson, William 1908-1978 *DcLB 103 [port]*
Nelson, William Bruce 1950- *WhoAm 90*
Nelson, William Bruce 1954- *WhoSSW 91*
Nelson, William Curry 1945- *St&PR 91*
Nelson, William Curtis 1937- *WhoAm 90*
Nelson, William E. 1926- *St&PR 91*
Nelson, William H. *BioIn 16*
Nelson, William H 1947- *BiDrAPA 89*
Nelson, William H., III 1928- *St&PR 91*
Nelson, William James, Jr. 1939- *St&PR 91*
Nelson, William Newell 1945- *WhoSSW 91*
Nelson, William Rankin 1921- *WhoAm 90*
Nelson, William Rockhill 1841-1915 *BioIn 16*
Nelson, William Roy 1952- *WhoEmL 91*
Nelson, Willie *BioIn 16, WhoNeCM A [port]*
Nelson, Willie 1933- *OxCPMus, WhoAm 90, WorAlBi*
Nelson Creskey, Marguerite 1947- *WhoAmW 91*
Nelson-Humphries, Tessa *WhoSSW 91, WhoWrEP 89*
Nelson-Mayson, Linda Ruth 1954- *WhoAm 90*
Nelson-Rees, Walter Anthony 1929- *WhoWor 91*
Nelsova, Zara 1918- *IntWWM 90, PenDiMP*
Nelsson, Woldemar 1938- *IntWWM 90*
Nelton, Sharon Lee 1937- *WhoE 91*
Nemacolin *WhNaAH*
Neman, David 1951- *St&PR 91*
Nemani, Bal Mukund 1938- *BiDrAPA 89*
Nemara, Vanessa Anne 1953- *WhoAmW 91*
Nemazee, Reza 1949- *WhoE 91, WhoEmL 91, WhoWor 91*
Nemcova, Bo'ena 1820-1862 *EncCoWW*
Nemec, Carl Joseph 1940- *St&PR 91*
Nemec, Corky *BioIn 16*
Nemec, Jan 1936- *BioIn 16*
Nemec, Michael Lee 1949- *WhoSSW 91*
Nemec, Nancy 1923- *WhoAmA 91*
Nemec, Nancy Lewis 1923- *WhoE 91*
Nemec, Vernita McClish 1942- *WhoAmA 91*
Nemecek, Albert Duncan, Jr. 1936- *WhoAm 90, WhoWor 91*
Nemecek, John Martin 1930- *St&PR 91*
Nemecek, Joseph George 1918- *BiDrAPA 89*
Nemenoff, Genia 1905-1989 *BioIn 16*
Nemer, Robert G. 1930- *St&PR 91*
Nemere, Ilka Maria 1953- *WhoEmL 91*
Nemerof, Victor Jay 1953- *BiDrAPA 89*
Nemeroff, Bernard G. 1907-1990 *BioIn 16*
Nemeroff, Carol Jill 1960- *WhoAmW 91*
Nemeroff, Charles Barnet 1949- *BiDrAPA 89*
Nemeroff, Michael Alan 1946- *WhoE 91*
Nemerov, David *WhoAmA 91N*
Nemerov, Howard *BioIn 16*
Nemerov, Howard 1920- *MajTwCW, WhoAm 90, WhoWrEP 89, WorAlBi*
Nemery de Bellevaux, Jacques Marie 1926- *WhoWor 91*
Nemes, Arthur J. 1935- *St&PR 91*
Nemes, Zita C 1937- *BiDrAPA 89*
Nemescu, Octavian 1940- *IntWWM 90*
Nemeshegyi, Peter 1923- *ConAu 130*
Nemet, Mary Ann 1936- *IntWWM 90*
Nemeth, Alan Peter 1940- *St&PR 91*
Nemeth, Andrew Martin 1926- *BiDrAPA 89*
Nemeth, Charlan Jeanne 1941- *WhoAm 90*
Nemeth, Charles Paul 1951- *WhoEmL 91*
Nemeth, Eva Maria *BiDrAPA 89*
Nemeth, Geza *PenDiMP*
Nemeth, Gusztav 1927- *IntWWM 90*
Nemeth, Joseph George 1923- *St&PR 91*
Nemeth, Joseph Martin, III 1947- *BiDrAPA 89*
Nemeth, Karoly 1922- *WhoWor 91*
Nemeth, Lane *BioIn 16*
Nemeth, Linda Johanna 1946- *WhoE 91*
Nemeth, Louis Ernest 1923- *WhoE 91*
Nemeth, Maria 1897-1967 *PenDiMP*
Nemeth, Miklos 1948- *WhoWor 91*
Nemeth, Pal 1950- *IntWWM 90*
Nemetz, Christine Arax 1961- *WhoWrEP 89*
Nemetz, Nathaniel Theodore 1913- *WhoAm 90*
Nemetz, Paul Sidney 1935- *BiDrAPA 89*
Nemetz, S Joseph *BiDrAPA 89*
Nemeyer, Frank L. 1927- *St&PR 91*
Nemhauser, George Lann 1937- *WhoAm 90, WhoSSW 91*
Nemia, Frank J. 1948- *St&PR 91*
Nemiah, John C 1918- *BiDrAPA 89*
Nemir, Rosalee 1905- *WhoAmW 91*
Nemir, Stuart S, Jr. 1929- *BiDrAPA 89*
Nemiro, Beverly Mirium Anderson 1925- *WhoAmW 91, WhoWor 91*
Nemiroff, Paul Raphael 1932- *WhoE 91*
Nemiroff, Robert A 1936- *BiDrAPA 89*
Nemirovsky, Natan I *BiDrAPA 89*
Nemirow, Arnold Myles 1943- *St&PR 91, WhoAm 90*
Nemirow, Jill Karin 1961- *WhoWrEP 89*
Nemirow, Joel Alan 1951- *WhoEmL 91*
Nemitz, Kurt 1925- *WhoWor 91*
Nemitz, Sanford C. 1932- *St&PR 91*
Nemko, Barbara Gail 1945- *WhoAmW 91*
Nemmers, Sherry J. 1954- *WhoAmW 91, WhoE 91*
Nemmers, Stephen Jeffrey 1946- *WhoEmL 91*
Nemo, Lawrence 1916- *St&PR 91*
Nemoianu, Virgil 1940- *ConAu 130*
Nemon, Oscar 1906-1985 *DcNaB 1981*
Nemophila *EncCoWW*
Nemser, Cindy 1937- *WhoAmA 91, WhoE 91*
Nemser, Lynn Seavey 1949- *WhoAmW 91*
Nemser, Robert Solomon 1938- *WhoAm 90*
Nemzer, Elaine Davidson 1952- *BiDrAPA 89*
Nemzoff, Sol L *BiDrAPA 89*
Nen, Dick 1939- *Ballpl 90*
Nenart, Judy Mary 1964- *WhoE 91*
Nenashev, Mikhail Fedorovich 1929- *WhoWor 91*
Nendick, Josephine 1931- *PenDiMP*
Nendick, Thomas Bernard 1929- *St&PR 91*
Nenneman, Richard Arthur 1929- *WhoAm 90*
Nenner, Rodney Andrew 1961- *WhoE 91*
Nenner, Victoria Corich 1945- *WhoEmL 91*
Nenno, David J. 1947- *St&PR 91*
Nenno, Robert P 1922- *BiDrAPA 89*
Nenno, Robert Peter 1922- *WhoAm 90*
Nenonen, Tarmo Olavi 1946- *WhoWor 91*

Nenstiel, Susan Kisthart 1951- *WhoAmW 91*
Nentwig, Franz Ferdinand 1929- *IntWWM 90*
Nentwig, James Richard 1936- *St&PR 91*
Neofes, Melissa Patterson 1958- *WhoAmW 91*
Neolin 1725?-1775 *EncCRAm*
Nepela, Ondrej *BioIn 16*
Nephew, Oliver Thomas 1929- *St&PR 91*
Nephew, William *AuBYP 90*
Nepo, Mark Evan 1951- *WhoWrEP 89*
Nepote, Alexander 1913- *WhoAmA 91*
Neppl, Walter J. 1922- *St&PR 91*
Neppl, Walter Joseph 1922- *WhoAm 90*
Neptune, John Addison 1919- *WhoAm 90*
Neptune, John Kaizan *NewAgMG*
Neptune, Richard Allan 1934- *WhoSSW 91*
Neptune, Richard G. 1950- *St&PR 91*
Neptune, Robert Herndon 1913- *WhoAm 90*
Neptune, William Everett 1928- *WhoAm 90*
Nequist, John Leonard 1929- *WhoAm 90*
Nerad, Jerry 1942- *St&PR 91*
Nerad, Richard A. 1927- *WhoAm 90*
Nerburn, Kent Michael 1946- *WhoAmA 91*
Nerdrum, Odd *WhoAmA 91*
Nerdrum, Odd Olaf 1944- *WhoE 91*
Nerem, Tracy Linn 1963- *WhoWrEP 89*
Nerenberg, Aaron 1940- *WhoAm 90*
Neri, Antonio 1576-1614 *PenDiDA 89*
Neri, Manuel 1930- *BioIn 16, WhoAm 90, WhoAmA 91, WhoHisp 91*
Neri, Phillip A. 1956- *St&PR 91*
Neril, Morton Marvin *BiDrAPA 89*
Nerio, Yolanda Paramo 1943- *WhoHisp 91*
Neris, Salomeja *EncCoWW*
Nerken, Albert 1912- *St&PR 91*
Nerlinger, John William 1920- *WhoAm 90*
Nerlove, Marc L. 1933- *WhoAm 90*
Nerlove, Miriam 1959- *BioIn 16*
Nerness, Rebecca J. 1955- *WhoAmW 91*
Nerney, Christopher P. *ODwPR 91*
Nernst, Walther H. 1864-1941 *WorAlBi*
Nero, Emperor of Rome 37-68 *BioIn 16*
Nero, Ann Briscoe 1947- *WhoSSW 91*
Nero, Anthony Vincent, Jr. 1942- *WhoAm 90*
Nero, John *ODwPR 91*
Nero, John Clark 1949- *WhoSSW 91*
Nero, Peter *IntWWM 90*
Nero, Peter 1934- *WhoE 91, WorAlBi*
Nero, Shirley Mae 1936- *WhoSSW 91*
Nero, William Thomas, Sr. 1935- *WhoAm 90, WhoE 91*
Neroccio, di Bartolomeo di Benedetto de' 1447-1500 *BioIn 16*
Nerode, Anil 1932- *WhoAm 90*
Neroni, Peter Joseph 1932- *St&PR 91*
Neroni, Roland 1931- *St&PR 91*
Nerren, Gene H. 1932- *St&PR 91*
Nersesian, G.A. 1935- *St&PR 91*
Nersesian, Robert S. 1950- *WhoWrEP 89*
Nersessian, Edward 1944- *BiDrAPA 89, WhoE 91*
Nerska, Olga *EncCoWW*
Nersoyan, Tiran 1904-1989 *BioIn 16*
Neruda, Francis Donald 1939- *St&PR 91*
Neruda, Pablo 1904-1973 *BioIn 16, ConLC 62 [port], HispWr 90, MajTwCW, WorAlBi*
Neruda, Wilma 1839-1911 *PenDiMP*
Nervi, Pier Luigi 1891-1979 *WorAlBi*
Nervo, Amado 1870-1919 *BioIn 16, ConAu 131, HispWr 90*
Nery, Felipe B. 1920- *BioIn 16*
Nes, David Gulick 1917- *WhoE 91*
Nesbeda, Eugene P. 1954- *St&PR 91*
Nesbert, Vincent *WhoAmA 91N*
Nesbit, Douglas Charles 1926- *WhoE 91, WhoWor 91*
Nesbit, E. *AuBYP 90*
Nesbit, E. 1858-1924 *BioIn 16, FemiCLE*
Nesbit, Edith 1858-1924 *BioIn 16*
Nesbit, Evelyn 1884-1967 *WorAlBi*
Nesbit, Evelyn 1885-1967 *BioAmW*
Nesbit, Frederick 1923- *BiDrAPA 89*
Nesbit, Lynn 1938- *BioIn 16*
Nesbit, Richard Allison 1935- *WhoAm 90*
Nesbit, Robert Carrington 1917- *WhoAm 90, WhoWor 91, WhoWrEP 89*
Nesbit, Robert Grover 1932- *WhoAm 90*
Nesbit, Troy *AuBYP 90*
Nesbit, Wm. J., Jr. 1935- *St&PR 91*
Nesbitt, Alexander John 1901- *WhoAmA 91, WhoE 91*
Nesbitt, Archie J. 1949- *St&PR 91*
Nesbitt, Arthur W. 1927- *St&PR 91*
Nesbitt, Arthur Wallace 1927- *WhoAm 90*
Nesbitt, Charles Rudolph 1921- *WhoAm 90*
Nesbitt, DeEtte DuPree 1941- *WhoSSW 91*
Nesbitt, Dorothy Buckeridge 1922- *BioIn 16*
Nesbitt, Duncan P. 1942- *St&PR 91*
Nesbitt, George Davis 1929- *BiDrAPA 89*
Nesbitt, Gregory Leon 1938- *St&PR 91*
Nesbitt, Harry 1905-1968 *OxCPMus*
Nesbitt, Ilse Buchert 1932- *WhoAmA 91*
Nesbitt, Jeffrey Joseph 1947- *WhoSSW 91*
Nesbitt, John Arthur 1933- *WhoAm 90*
Nesbitt, John Dawson 1951- *WhoSSW 91*
Nesbitt, Lenore Carrero *WhoAmW 91, WhoSSW 91*
Nesbitt, Leroy Edward 1925- *WhoWor 91*
Nesbitt, Lloyd Ivan 1951- *WhoE 91*
Nesbitt, Lowell 1933- *WhoAm 90, WhoAmA 91*
Nesbitt, Margot Lord 1927- *WhoAmW 91*
Nesbitt, Max 1903-1966 *OxCPMus*
Nesbitt, Radian Beth 1945- *WhoAmW 91*
Nesbitt, Robert Edward Lee, Jr. 1924- *WhoAm 90*
Nesbitt, Rosemary Sinnett 1924- *WhoAm 90*
Nesbitt, Sharon Lucille 1956- *WhoE 91*
Nesbitt, Thomas Dean 1938- *St&PR 91*
Nesbitt-Blyden, Thelma Ebethi 1910- *WhoE 91*
Neschis, Ronald Leon 1937- *BiDrAPA 89*
Nesemann, Enno 1861-1949 *WhoAmA 91N*
Neshapanasumin 1817-1894 *BioIn 16*
Nesheim, John Lamson 1942- *St&PR 91*
Nesheim, Robert Olaf 1921- *WhoAm 90*
Nesheim, Robert Scott *BiDrAPA 89*
Nesher, Robert Allen 1946- *St&PR 91*
Neshiem, Roberta Mary 1934- *WhoAmW 91*
Neshkes, Robert Elliott 1950- *BiDrAPA 89*
Neshyba, Victor Peter 1922- *WhoSSW 91*
Nesin, Asher 1918- *St&PR 91*
Nesin, Noah 1929- *St&PR 91*
Nesius, Leo Anthony 1917- *St&PR 91*
Neslage, Oliver John, Jr 1925- *WhoAmA 91*
Nesler, Dennis John 1943- *St&PR 91*
Nesler, Dottie Ann 1962- *WhoSSW 91*
Nesmith, Donald Powell 1945- *WhoSSW 91*
Nesmith, Frances Jane 1926- *WhoAmW 91*
Nesmith, Linda Carol 1950- *WhoAmW 91*
Nesmith, Michael *WhoNeCM A [port]*
Nesmith, Michael 1942- *WhoAm 90*
Nesmith, Mike 1942- *EncPR&S 89*
Nesmith, Richard Duey 1929- *WhoAm 90*
Nesnick, Victoria Gilvary 1945- *WhoE 91*
Nesom, Barbara B. 1939- *St&PR 91*
Nesom, John H. 1936- *St&PR 91*
Nesom, Ruth Evelyn 1916- *WhoWrEP 89*
Nespole, Joseph James 1936- *WhoAm 90*
Ness, Albert Kenneth 1903- *WhoAm 90, WhoSSW 91, WhoWor 91*
Ness, Arthur J. 1936- *IntWWM 90*
Ness, Claire M *BiDrAPA 89*
Ness, David Eli 1946- *BiDrAPA 89*
Ness, Eliot 1903-1957 *BioIn 16, WorAlBi*
Ness, Evaline 1911- *WhoAmA 91N*
Ness, Evaline 1911-1986 *AuBYP 90, BioIn 16*
Ness, Frederic William 1914- *WhoAm 90*
Ness, Gene Charles 1944- *WhoSSW 91*
Ness, Julius B. 1916- *WhoAm 90*
Ness, Kenneth 1903- *WhoAmA 91*
Ness, Norman Frederick 1933- *WhoAm 90*
Ness, Philip W. 1936- *St&PR 91*
Ness, Philip Wahmann, Jr. 1936- *WhoAm 90*
Ness, Richard G 1946- *BiDrAPA 89*
Ness, Ruth *BioIn 16*
Ness, Steven Allyn 1947- *St&PR 91*
Nesse, Randolph Martin 1948- *BiDrAPA 89*
Nessel, Edward Harry 1945- *WhoE 91*
Nessel, Jack Howard 1938- *WhoAm 90*
Nessel, Mark A 1930- *BiDrAPA 89*
Nessen, Maurice Norman 1927- *WhoAm 90*
Nessen, Robert Lewis 1932- *WhoAm 90*
Nessen, Ronald H. 1934- *ODwPR 91*
Nessen, Ronald Harold 1934- *WhoAm 90*
Nessen, Ward Henry 1909- *WhoE 91, WhoWor 91*
Nesset, David George 1937- *BiDrAPA 89*
Nessi, Jose M. *WhoHisp 91*
Nessi, Pio Baroja 1872-1956 *BioIn 16*
Nessim, Barbara 1930- *WhoAmA 91*
Nessim, Barbara 1939- *WhoE 91*
Nessim, David Jacques 1925- *St&PR 91, WhoAm 90*
Nesslin, Robert E. 1936- *ODwPR 91*
Nessmith, Herbert Alva 1935- *WhoSSW 91*
Nesson, Marlene 1956- *WhoAmW 91*
Nesstfell, Johann Georg 1694-1762 *PenDiDA 89*
Nesta, William A. 1951- *St&PR 91*
Nestadt, Gerald 1952- *BiDrAPA 89*
Nestelbaum, Zamir 1953- *BiDrAPA 89*
Nester, Francis J. 1929- *St&PR 91*
Nester, Johleen Denise 1960- *WhoE 91*
Nester, Marian L 1910- *EncO&P 3, EncPaPR 91*
Nester, William Raymond, Jr. 1928- *WhoAm 90*
Nesterenko, Evgeny 1938- *IntWWM 90*
Nesterenko, Yevgeniy Yevgeniyevich 1938- *WhoWor 91*
Nesterenko, Yevgeny 1938- *PenDiMP*
Nestico, Sammy *BioIn 16*
Nestle, Joan 1940- *BioIn 16, WhoWrEP 89*
Nestler, Eric J 1954- *BiDrAPA 89*
Nestler, Kimberly Sharp *BiDrAPA 89*
Nestler, Lloyd L., Jr. 1941- *St&PR 91*
Nestman, Chadwick Henry 1945- *WhoE 91*
Nestor, Byron L 1923- *BiDrAPA 89*
Nestor, Donald Eugene 1962- *St&PR 91*
Nestor, Hubert R *BiDrAPA 89*
Nestor, Jack I. 1933- *St&PR 91*
Nestor, Lula B *WhoAmA 91*
Nestor, William P. 1947- *BioIn 16*
Nestor Castellano, Brenda Diana 1955- *WhoAmW 91, WhoEmL 91*
Nestoros, Joannis N 1948- *BiDrAPA 89*
Nestrick, Dwight L. 1947- *St&PR 91*
Nestroy, Johann 1801-1862 *WorAlBi*
Nesutan *WhNaAH*
Nesvig, Elliot M. 1920- *St&PR 91*
Nesvold, Betty Anne Krambuhl 1922- *WhoAm 90*
Neswald, Barbara Anne 1935- *WhoE 91*
Neta, Beny 1945- *WhoEmL 91*
Netemeyer, Maurice E. 1954- *St&PR 91*
Neter, John 1923- *WhoAm 90*
Nethen, Carol Cecelia 1952- *IntWWM 90*
Nethercott, J.W. 1927- *St&PR 91*
Nethercut, Philip Edwin 1921- *WhoAm 90*
Nethercut, William Robert 1936- *WhoAm 90*
Netherland, Sally N. 1951- *St&PR 91*
Nethers, Jerry Steven 1939- *St&PR 91*
Netherton, Janet L. 1952- *WhoAmW 91*
Netherton, Truman W. 1935- *St&PR 91*
Nethery, John Jay 1941- *WhoAm 90*
Neto, Eugenia 1934- *BioIn 16*
Neto, Joao Cabral de Melo 1920- *BioIn 16*
Neto, Maria Eugenia 1934- *BioIn 16*
Neto, Raul Verner Brangaca *WhoWor 91*
Netolicka, Karel 1929- *IntWWM 90*
Netravali, Arun N. 1946- *WhoAm 90*
Netsch, Dawn Clark 1926- *WhoAmW 91*
Netscher, Ruth Evans 1952- *BiDrAPA 89*
Netsky, Hankus 1955- *WhoAm 90*
Netsky, Richard I 1946- *BiDrAPA 89*
Nett, Ann T. *WhoWrEP 89*
Nett, Carl Nicholas 1960- *WhoSSW 91*
Nettelbeck, Fred Arthur 1950- *WhoWrEP 89*
Nettels, Elsa 1931- *WhoAm 90*
Nettels, George Edward, Jr. 1927- *St&PR 91, WhoAm 90*
Netter, Alfred E. 1950- *St&PR 91*
Netter, Cornelia Ann 1933- *WhoAmW 91, WhoE 91, WhoWor 91*
Netter, Eric Max 1920- *WhoAm 90*
Netter, Jean-Patrice 1940- *WhoWor 91*
Netter, K. Fred 1919- *St&PR 91*
Netter, Kurt Fred 1919- *WhoE 91, WhoWor 91*
Netter, Robert 1927- *WhoWor 91*
Netter, Virginia Thompson 1931- *WhoAmW 91*
Netterville, George Bronson 1929- *WhoSSW 91*
Netterville, John Thomas 1930- *WhoAm 90*
Nettesheim, Christine Cook 1944- *WhoAm 90, WhoAmW 91*
Netting, Florence Ellen 1949- *WhoEmL 91*
Netting, John W.A. 1943- *St&PR 91*
Nettl, Bruno 1930- *IntWWM 90, WhoAm 90*
Nettles, Bert S. 1936- *WhoSSW 91*
Nettles, Graig *BioIn 16*
Nettles, Graig 1944- *Ballpl 90 [port]*
Nettles, Jim 1947- *Ballpl 90*
Nettles, John Barnwell 1922- *WhoAm 90, WhoSSW 91, WhoWor 91*
Nettles, William Carl, Jr. 1934- *WhoSSW 91*
Nettleship, Lois E. 1942- *WhoAmW 91*
Nettleton, Daniel M. 1840- *AmLegL*
Nettleton, David *WhoAm 90*
Nettleton, James Warner 1940- *WhoE 91*
Nettleton, Joyce A. *WhoE 91*
Netupsky-Lang, Lorna Louise 1946- *WhoWor 91*
Netz, Pamela Belport 1954- *WhoEmL 91*
Netzer, Dick 1928- *WhoAm 90*
Netzer, Lanore Agnes 1916- *WhoAm 90*
Netzer, Victoria Marie 1954- *St&PR 91*
Netzley, Terry E. 1936- *St&PR 91*
Netzloff, Michael Lawrence 1942- *WhoAm 90*
Netzly, Vernon Dale 1930- *St&PR 91*
Neu, Carl Herbert, Jr. 1937- *WhoAm 90*
Neu, Carlos A 1942- *BiDrAPA 89*
Neu, Charles Eric 1936- *WhoAm 90*
Neu, Gladys Inez 1908- *WhoSSW 91*
Neu, Harold Conrad 1934- *WhoAm 90*
Neu, Kenneth G. 1955- *St&PR 91*
Neu, Richard W. 1956- *St&PR 91*
Neu, Robert B 1921- *BiDrAPA 89*
Neubarth, Sanford L. 1948- *St&PR 91*
Neubauer, Carlyle E. 1921- *WhoAmW 91*
Neubauer, Charles Frederick 1950- *WhoAm 90*
Neubauer, David N *BiDrAPA 89*
Neubauer, Joseph 1941- *St&PR 91, WhoAm 90, WhoE 91*
Neubauer, Otto 1874-1957 *DcScB S2*
Neubauer, Perry K. 1940- *St&PR 91*
Neubauer, Peter B 1913- *BiDrAPA 89*
Neubauer, Peter Bela 1913- *WhoAm 90*
Neubeck, Greg *WhoSSW 91*
Neuber, Dieter 1937- *St&PR 91*
Neuber, Friedel 1935- *WhoWor 91*
Neuber, Friedericke Caroline 1697-1760 *EncCoWW*
Neuber, Johann Christian 1735-1808 *PenDiDA 89*
Neuberg, William B. 1930- *St&PR 91*
Neuberger, Albert 1908- *WhoWor 91*
Neuberger, Dan 1929- *WhoE 91*
Neuberger, Egon 1925- *ConAu 30NR, WhoAm 90*
Neuberger, Hans *PenDiMP*
Neuberger, Marie S. 1908- *St&PR 91*
Neuberger, Roy R. 1903- *St&PR 91, WhoAm 90, WhoAmA 91*
Neuberger, Sigmund 1871-1911 *BioIn 16*
Neubert, B. David 1953- *IntWWM 90*
Neubert, Gail Schaffer 1945- *WhoE 91*
Neubert, George W. 1942- *WhoAm 90*
Neubert, George Walter 1942- *WhoAmA 91*
Neubert, Robert 1945- *ODwPR 91*
Neubig, Herbert Frederick 1934- *St&PR 91*
Neubohn, Naneen Hunter 1939- *WhoE 91*
Neuburg, Hans 1904-1983 *ConDes 90*
Neuburg, Victor 1883-1940 *EncO&P 3*
Neuburger, Werner 1926- *St&PR 91*
Neudecker, Jerry 1930- *Ballpl 90*
Neuefeind, Wilhelm 1939- *WhoAm 90*
Neuenschwander, Frederick Phillip 1924- *WhoWor 91*
Neuenschwander, Gordon Earle 1927- *St&PR 91*
Neuenschwander, Stanley Wayne 1935- *WhoSSW 91*
Neuer, Hans 1897- *BiDrAPA 89*
Neuer, Paul Frederick 1946- *WhoSSW 91*
Neufeld, Edward Peter 1927- *WhoAm 90*
Neufeld, Elizabeth Fondal 1928- *WhoAm 90, WhoAmW 91*
Neufeld, John 1938- *AuBYP 90*
Neufeld, Karl Melvine *WhoSSW 91*
Neufeld, Mace Alvin 1928- *WhoAm 90, WhoWor 91*
Neufeld, Philip M. *BioIn 16*
Neufeld, Ray *BioIn 16*
Neufforge, Jean-Francois 1714-1791 *PenDiDA 89*
Neugart, Lourdes 1952- *BiDrAPA 89*
Neugarten, Bernice Levin 1916- *BioIn 16, WhoAm 90, WhoAmW 91, WhoWrEP 89*
Neugarten, Jerrold Lee 1948- *WhoE 91*
Neugebauer, Marcia 1932- *WhoAm 90*
Neugeberger, Margot 1929-1986 *WhoAmA 91N*
Neugeboren, Jay 1938- *WhoWrEP 89*
Neugroschl, Jill Paulette 1949- *WhoE 91*
Neuharth, Allen *BioIn 16*
Neuharth, Allen Harold 1924- *ConAmBL, WhoAm 90, WhoSSW 91, WhoWrEP 89*
Neuhaus, Heinrich 1888-1964 *PenDiMP*
Neuhaus, Julius Victor, III 1926- *St&PR 91, WhoAm 90*
Neuhaus, Konstantin 1940- *WhoWor 91*
Neuhaus, Marcia *ODwPR 91*
Neuhaus, Mary Lynn 1953- *WhoEmL 91*
Neuhaus, Max *BioIn 16*
Neuhaus, Max 1939- *WhoAm 90, WhoAmA 91*
Neuhaus, Otto Wilhelm 1922- *WhoAm 90*
Neuhaus, Philip Ross 1919- *WhoAm 90*
Neuhaus, Richard John *BioIn 16*
Neuhaus, Rudolf 1914- *IntWWM 90*
Neuhaus, Sydney *ODwPR 91*
Neuhaus, William Oscar, III 1944- *WhoSSW 91*
Neuhausen, Benjamin Simon 1950- *WhoAm 90*
Neuhauser, Duncan von Briesen 1939- *WhoAm 90*
Neuhauser, Mary Helen 1943- *WhoE 91, WhoWor 91*
Neuhoff, Kathleen Toepp 1953- *WhoAmW 91*
Neuhoff, Robert M. *St&PR 91*
Neuhold, Gunter 1947- *IntWWM 90*
Neukam, Randall Maurice 1951- *WhoE 91*

Neukranz, Donald W. *WhoAm 90*
Neulander, Arthur *BiDrAPA 89*
Neulander, Arthur H. 1896- *BioIn 16*
Neumaier, Gerhard John 1937- *WhoAm 90*
Neumaier, Mark Adam 1958- *WhoSSW 91*
Neuman, Abraham Aaron 1890-1970 *BioIn 16*
Neuman, Charles P. 1940- *WhoAm 90*
Neuman, Cynthia Jean 1943- *WhoAmW 91*
Neuman, Daniel Moses 1944- *IntWWM 90*
Neuman, David A. 1928-1989 *BioIn 16*
Neuman, Donald Bernard 1934- *WhoAm 90, WhoWrEP 89*
Neuman, Fredric Jay 1934- *BiDrAPA 89, WhoE 91*
Neuman, Gail L. 1953- *St&PR 91*
Neuman, Glen H. 1920- *St&PR 91*
Neuman, Irving J. *St&PR 91*
Neuman, K. Sidney 1936- *WhoAm 90, WhoE 91*
Neuman, Leon 1920- *St&PR 91*
Neuman, Linda Kinney *WhoAmW 91*
Neuman, Maxine Darcy 1948- *WhoWor 91*
Neuman, Monroe L 1932- *BiDrAPA 89*
Neuman, Nancy Adams Mosshammer 1936- *WhoAmW 91*
Neuman, Norman R. 1940- *St&PR 91*
Neuman, Philippe 1953- *WhoWor 91*
Neuman, Phillip Jerome 1958- *WhoEmL 91*
Neuman, Richard Frank 1944- *St&PR 91*
Neuman, Robert Henry 1936- *WhoAm 90*
Neuman, Robert S 1926- *WhoAmA 91*
Neuman, Robert Sterling 1926- *WhoAm 90*
Neuman, Stephanie Sellors 1945- *WhoWrEP 89*
Neuman, Susan *ODwPR 91*
Neuman, Victor Allen 1955- *WhoEmL 91*
Neumann, Alfred 1895-1952 *BioIn 16*
Neumann, Alfred 1909- *WhoWor 91*
Neumann, Andrew Conrad 1933- *WhoAm 90*
Neumann, Bernd 1943- *WhoWor 91*
Neumann, Bernhard Hermann 1909- *WhoWor 91*
Neumann, Calvin Lee 1938- *WhoSSW 91*
Neumann, Forrest Karl 1930- *WhoAm 90, WhoWor 91*
Neumann, Fred C. *BioIn 16*
Neumann, Frederick Loomis 1930- *WhoAm 90*
Neumann, Gerald Erwin 1926- *WhoAm 90*
Neumann, Gerhard 1917- *ConAu 132*
Neumann, Harry 1930- *WhoAm 90*
Neumann, Herschel 1930- *WhoAm 90*
Neumann, J B 1887-1961 *WhoAmA 91N*
Neumann, Jeffrey Jay 1948- *WhoEmL 91, WhoWor 91*
Neumann, Johanna *BioIn 16*
Neumann, John Nepomucene 1811-1860 *WorAlBi*
Neumann, John Von 1903-1957 *WorAlBi*
Neumann, Jonathan 1950- *WhoAm 90*
Neumann, Joseph 1930- *WhoWor 91*
Neumann, Leslie Lucas 1941- *WhoSSW 91*
Neumann, Lois Lyon *BiDrAPA 89*
Neumann, Lois Lyon 1928- *WhoE 91*
Neumann, Mark Erwin 1959- *WhoWrEP 89*
Neumann, May Althea 1924- *WhoAmW 91*
Neumann, Michael J. 1951- *St&PR 91*
Neumann, Nancy Ruth 1948- *WhoAmW 91, WhoEmL 91, WhoWor 91*
Neumann, Peter 1946- *St&PR 91*
Neumann, Robert G. 1954- *St&PR 91*
Neumann, Robert Gerhard 1916- *WhoAm 90, WhoWor 91, WhoWrEP 89*
Neumann, Robert William 1952- *WhoE 91*
Neumann, Roy Covert 1921- *WhoAm 90*
Neumann, Sandra Anne 1957- *WhoE 91*
Neumann, Theodore W, Jr. 1922- *BiDrAPA 89*
Neumann, Therese 1898-1962 *EncO&P 3, EncPaPR 91*
Neumann, Thomas Lee 1945- *St&PR 91*
Neumann, Vaclav 1920- *IntWWM 90, PenDiMP, WhoWor 91*
Neumann, Vivian Coralie 1946- *WhoSSW 91*
Neumann, Wayne Newton 1934- *St&PR 91*
Neumann, Wencel A., Jr. 1914- *St&PR 91*
Neumann, Wilhelm Paul 1926- *WhoWor 91*
Neumann, William 1943- *St&PR 91*
Neumann, William A 1924-1985 *WhoAmA 91N*
Neumann, Wolfgang 1945- *IntWWM 90*
Neumann-Mahlkau, Peter Klaus 1934- *WhoWor 91*
Neumark, Gertrude Fanny 1927- *WhoAmW 91*
Neumark, Michael 1946- *St&PR 91*
Neumeier, John 1942- *WhoAm 90, WhoWor 91*
Neumeier, Matthew Michael 1954- *WhoEmL 91, WhoWor 91*
Neumeister, Alexander 1941- *ConDes 90*
Neumeister, Susan Mary 1958- *WhoAmW 91*
Neumeyer, Alfred 1901-1973 *WhoAmA 91N*
Neumeyer, Alvin Edward *BiDrAPA 89*
Neumeyer, John Leopold 1930- *WhoE 91*
Neumeyer, Kathleen 1944- *WhoWrEP 89*
Neumeyer, Peter F 1929- *ConAu 30NR*
Neumiller, Catherine Anne 1964- *WhoAmW 91*
Neumiller, Louis B. 1896-1989 *BioIn 16*
Neumiller, Louis Bontz 1896- *ConAmBL*
Neumuller, Heinz 1920- *WhoWor 91*
Neun, Carl W. *St&PR 91*
Neun, Johnny 1900- *Ballpl 90*
Neun, Johnny 1900-1990 *BioIn 16*
Neuner, Charles Louis 1925- *St&PR 91*
Neunteufel, Michael 1958- *IntWWM 90*
Neurath, Hans 1909- *WhoAm 90*
Neurath, Konstantin H Karl, Freiherr von 1873-1956 *BioIn 16*
Neuren, Alan Peter 1948- *BiDrAPA 89*
Neuren, Michael Scott 1958- *WhoEmL 91*
Neuschel, Robert P. 1919- *St&PR 91*
Neuschel, Robert Percy 1919- *WhoAm 90, WhoWor 91*
Neusner, Jacob 1932- *WhoAm 90*
Neustadt, Barbara Mae 1922- *WhoAm 90*
Neustadt, David Harold 1925- *WhoAm 90*
Neustadt, Elsie S 1898- *BiDrAPA 89*
Neustadt, Karen Anderson 1942- *WhoWrEP 89*
Neustadt, Paul 1931- *St&PR 91*
Neustadt, Walter, Jr. 1919- *St&PR 91*
Neustein, Joshua 1940- *WhoAmA 91*
Neustrom, Patrik William 1951- *WhoEmL 91*
Neutra, Richard 1892-1970 *WhoAmA 91N*
Neutze, Graeme Max 1934- *WhoWor 91*
Neutzler, George Daniel 1945- *St&PR 91*
Neutzling, Virginia Ruth 1942- *WhoAmW 91*
Neuville, Anne-Marguerite-Henriette R. 1749?-1849 *BioIn 16*
Neuville, Charlotte *BioIn 16*
Neuville, Jean-Guillaume Hyde de 1776-1857 *BioIn 16*
Neuwald, Ellen *BioIn 16*
Neuwalder, Teruko S 1935- *BiDrAPA 89*
Neuwirth, Abraham *BioIn 16*
Neuwirth, Alexander 1932- *WhoE 91*
Neuwirth, Bebe *BioIn 16, WhoAmW 91*
Neuwirth, Bernard Ernest 1950- *IntWWM 90*
Neuwirth, Frank J. 1932- *St&PR 91*
Neuwirth, Peyton Sidney *WhoWor 91*
Neuwirth, Robert Samuel 1933- *WhoAm 90*
Neuwirth, Sherri Gay 1953- *WhoAmW 91*
Neuwoehner, Robert F. 1918- *St&PR 91*
Neva, Franklin Allen 1922- *WhoAm 90*
Nevada, Emma 1859-1940 *PenDiMP*
Nevada, Mignon 1886-1971 *PenDiMP*
Nevanlinna, Rolf Herman 1895-1980 *DcScB S2*
Nevans, Roy Norman 1931- *St&PR 91, WhoE 91*
Nevarez, Juan A. 1951- *WhoHisp 91*
Nevarez, Miguel A. *WhoSSW 91*
Nevarez, Miguel A. 1937- *WhoHisp 91*
Nevarez-Tapia, Mariano, Jr. *BiDrAPA 89*
Nevaril, Charles G. 1940- *St&PR 91*
Nevas, Alan Harris 1928- *WhoE 91*
Neve, Kaj A *BiDrAPA 89*
Neve, Paul Lucien 1933- *WhoWor 91*
Neve, Trevor Leonard 1947- *WhoE 91*
Neve, Victoria Rider 1950- *IntWWM 90*
Nevejans, Mark Brian 1951- *St&PR 91*
Nevejean, Yvonne *BioIn 16*
Nevel, Avishai 1953- *St&PR 91*
Neveloff, Jay A. 1950- *WhoEmL 91, WhoWor 91*
Nevels, Charles T 1949- *BiDrAPA 89*
Nevelson, Louise 1899-1988 *BiDWomA, WorAlBi*
Nevelson, Louise 1900-1988 *AnObit 1988, BioIn 16*
Nevelson, Louise B. 1900-1988 *BioAmW*
Nevelson, Mike *BioIn 16*
Nevelson, Mike 1922- *WhoAmA 91*
Nevelson, Myron *BioIn 16*
Nevens, David 1945- *IntWWM 90*
Nevers, Ernie 1903-1976 *Ballpl 90*
Neves, Stella Boudrias 1949- *WhoAmW 91*
Neves, Tancredo *BioIn 16*
Neves-Perman, Maria 1937- *WhoHisp 91*
Nevett, Robert Edmund 1929- *St&PR 91*
Neveu, Ginette 1919-1949 *PenDiMP*
Neveu, Madeleine *EncCoWW*
Neveu, Raymond Philip 1938- *WhoE 91*
Nevia *WhoAmA 91*
Neviaser, Michael Charles 1954- *WhoEmL 91*
Neviaser, Robert Jon 1936- *WhoAm 90*
Nevile, Christopher *BioIn 16*
Nevile, John Warwick 1932- *WhoWor 91*
Nevill, William Albert 1929- *WhoAm 90*
Neville Brothers, The *ConMus 4 [port], EncPR&S 89*
Neville, Aaron *BioIn 16*
Neville, Aaron 1941- *ConMus 5 [port]*
Neville, Alan B. 1947- *St&PR 91*
Neville, Art *BioIn 16*
Neville, Charles *BioIn 16*
Neville, Charles W, Jr. *BiDrAPA 89*
Neville, Cyril *BioIn 16*
Neville, Emily Cheney 1919- *AuBYP 90, WhoAm 90, WhoWrEP 89*
Neville, Fred J. 1936- *St&PR 91*
Neville, George *PenDiDA 89*
Neville, Gerald Worley 1943- *St&PR 91*
Neville, Gwen Kennedy 1938- *WhoSSW 91*
Neville, James Francis 1907- *WhoAm 90*
Neville, James Morton 1939- *St&PR 91, WhoAm 90*
Neville, John 1925- *OxCCanT, WhoAm 90, WhoWor 91*
Neville, Joseph Patrick 1934- *St&PR 91*
Neville, Katherine 1945- *BioIn 16*
Neville, Kris 1925-1980 *ConAu 132*
Neville, Laura White 1922- *BiDrAPA 89*
Neville, Lloyd L. 1929- *St&PR 91*
Neville, Margaret 1939- *IntWWM 90*
Neville, Margaret Brown *BiDrAPA 89*
Neville, Margaret Cobb 1934- *WhoAm 90, WhoAmW 91*
Neville, Margot *TwCCr&M 91*
Neville, Nancy Marie 1937- *WhoE 91*
Neville, Patrick Lyn 1946- *St&PR 91*
Neville, Phoebe 1941- *WhoAm 90*
Neville, R. Geoffrey 1932- *St&PR 91*
Neville, Robert Cummings 1939- *WhoAm 90*
Neville, Roger Jackson 1942- *St&PR 91*
Neville, Roy Gerald 1926- *WhoAm 90*
Neville, Susan Diane 1960- *WhoAmW 91*
Nevin, Crocker 1923- *St&PR 91, WhoAm 90*
Nevin, Ethelbert 1862-1901 *OxCPMus*
Nevin, Jean Shaw 1934- *WhoAmW 91*
Nevin, John Anthony 1933- *WhoAm 90*
Nevin, John J. 1927- *St&PR 91*
Nevin, John Joseph 1927- *WhoAm 90*
Nevin, Robert Charles 1940- *St&PR 91, WhoAm 90*
Nevins, Albert J. 1915- *AuBYP 90, WhoAm 90*
Nevins, Allan 1890-1971 *ConAu 30NR, WorAlBi*
Nevins, Blanche 1841-1925 *BiDWomA*
Nevins, David Howard 1954- *WhoE 91*
Nevins, Donald Bruce 1941- *BiDrAPA 89*
Nevins, Donald H. 1936- *St&PR 91*
Nevins, Francis M, Jr. 1943- *TwCCr&M 91*
Nevins, James 1821-1893 *DcCanB 12*
Nevins, James Lawrence 1934- *St&PR 91*
Nevins, John Edward 1940- *St&PR 91*
Nevins, John J. 1932- *WhoSSW 91*
Nevins, Joseph William 1928- *St&PR 91*
Nevins, Mary Frances 1937- *WhoE 91*
Nevins, Richard, Jr. 1947- *WhoEmL 91*
Nevins, Robert Charles 1933- *St&PR 91*
Nevins, Sheila 1939- *WhoAmW 91*
Nevis, Leonard J *BiDrAPA 89*
Nevitt, Chuck *BioIn 16*
Nevitt, Neal 1946- *St&PR 91*
Nevius, Blake Reynolds 1916- *WhoAm 90, WhoWrEP 89*
Nevling, Harry Reed 1946- *WhoEmL 91*
Nevo, Eviatar 1929- *WhoWor 91*
Nevskii, V. I. 1876-1937 *BioIn 16*
Nevskii, Vladimir Ivanovich 1876-1937 *BioIn 16*
New Grass Revival *WhoNeCM [port]*
New Grass Revival, The *ConMus 4*
New Kids on the Block *News 91-2 [port]*
New London Quartet *PenDiMP*
New Orleans Rhythm Kings *OxCPMus*
New Riders of the Purple Sage, The *WhoNeCM A [port]*
New String Quartet *PenDiMP*
New York Dolls, The *EncPR&S 89*
New, Anne Latrobe 1910- *WhoAmW 91*
New, Bertrand L 1926- *BiDrAPA 89*
New, Bertrand Latimer 1926- *WhoE 91*
New, Bertrand Latimer 1926-1990 *BioIn 16*
New, Erica M *BiDrAPA 89*
New, Harry Stewart 1858-1937 *BiDrUSE 89*
New, James S 1914- *BiDrAPA 89*
New, Karyn Marie 1945- *WhoAmW 91*
New, Laurence Anthony Wallis 1932- *WhoWor 91*
New, Leon John 1933- *IntWWM 90*
New, Lloyd H *WhoAmA 91*
New, Lloyd Kiva *WhoAmA 91*
New, Maria Iandolo *WhoAm 90*
New, Ralph Edward, Jr. 1929- *St&PR 91*
New, Robert Valentine, Jr. 1951- *WhoSSW 91*
New, Samuel 1921- *St&PR 91*
New, William L. 1943- *St&PR 91*
New, William Neil 1908- *WhoAm 90*
Newall, James Edward Malcolm 1935- *St&PR 91, WhoAm 90*
Newall, Sondra Carol Kurtz 1945- *WhoSSW 91*
Newandee, Kimberly Ann 1963- *WhoAmW 91*
Newark, Elizabeth 1929- *SmATA X*
Neway, Patricia 1919- *IntWWM 90*
Newbauer, John Arthur 1928- *WhoAm 90, WhoWrEP 89*
Newberg, Dorothy Beck 1919- *WhoAmW 91*
Newberg, Herbert Barkan 1937- *WhoAm 90*
Newberg, James Henry 1946- *WhoSSW 91*
Newberger, Eli Herbert 1940- *IntWWM 90*
Newberger, Seth A. 1937- *St&PR 91*
Newbern, Gloria J. 1925- *St&PR 91*
Newbern, James Marshall *BiDrAPA 89*
Newbern, William David 1937- *WhoAm 90*
Newberry, Carol Yvonne 1952- *WhoSSW 91*
Newberry, Clare 1903-1970 *AuBYP 90*
Newberry, Clare Turlay 1903-1970 *WhoAmA 91N*
Newberry, Conrad Floyde 1931- *WhoAm 90*
Newberry, Elizabeth Carter 1921- *WhoAmW 91*
Newberry, James Henry, Jr. 1956- *WhoEmL 91*
Newberry, John S *WhoAmA 91N*
Newberry, Michael *BiDrAPA 89*
Newberry, Robert Curtis, Sr. 1945- *WhoSSW 91*
Newberry, Thomas Brent *BiDrAPA 89*
Newberry, Tom 1946- *St&PR 91*
Newberry, Truman Handy 1864-1945 *BiDrUSE 89*
Newberry, William Marcus 1938- *WhoAm 90*
Newbert, Robert L., Jr. 1947- *ODwPR 91*
Newbery, David Michael Garrood 1943- *WhoWor 91*
Newbery, Jessie R. 1864-1919 *PenDiDA 89*
Newbill, Sallie Puller 1940- *WhoAmW 91*
Newbold, Herbert Leon, Jr. 1921- *WhoAm 90, WhoE 91, WhoWor 91*
Newbold, John L. 1935- *St&PR 91*
Newbold, John Lowe 1935- *WhoWor 91*
Newbold, Paul 1945- *WhoAm 90*
Newbold, William Romaine 1865-1926 *EncO&P 3, EncPaPR 91*
Newborg, Barbara Carol 1921- *WhoSSW 91*
Newborn, Alan David 1926- *St&PR 91*
Newborn, Jud 1952- *WhoAm 90*
Newborn, Phineas 1931-1989 *BioIn 16*
Newborn, Samuel Reuben 1954- *WhoEmL 91*
Newbould, A. William 1952- *ODwPR 91*
Newbould, Brian Raby 1936- *IntWWM 90*
Newbound, Betty J. 1928- *WhoWrEP 89*
Newbrand, Charles Michael 1944- *WhoAm 90*
Newbrough, Edgar Truett 1917- *WhoAm 90*
Newbrough, John Ballou 1828-1891 *EncO&P 3*
Newbry, Lyndel Warren 1923- *St&PR 91*
Newburg, Andre W. G. 1928- *WhoAm 90, WhoE 91*
Newburg, Betty A. 1931- *WhoAmW 91*
Newburger, Beth Weinstein 1937- *WhoE 91*
Newburger, Frank L., Jr. 1908- *WhoAm 90*
Newburger, Frank Lieberman, Jr. 1908- *St&PR 91*
Newburger, Howard Martin 1924- *WhoAm 90*
Newbury, George A *BiDrAPA 89*
Newby, Eric *BioIn 16*
Newby, Eric 1919- *WorAu 1980 [port]*
Newby, Howard 1918- *WhoWor 91*
Newby, Idus Atwell 1931- *WhoAm 90, WhoWrEP 89*
Newby, Judith Asel 1941- *ODwPR 91*
Newby, Margaret *BiDEWW*
Newby, P H 1918- *ConAu 32NR, MajTwCW*
Newby, Viola E V 1909- *BiDrAPA 89*
Newby-Frazier, Paula *BioIn 16*
Newcastle, Duchess of 1624?-1674 *BioIn 16*
Newcastle, Margaret, Duchess of *BiDEWW*
Newcastle, Margaret Cavendish 1623-1673 *FemiCLE*
Newcomb, Alan Eugene 1949- *WhoE 91*
Newcomb, Betty Lou Atkinson 1938- *WhoSSW 91*
Newcomb, Boyd Lawrence 1926- *WhoE 91*

Newcomb, Covelle 1908- *AuBYP 90*
Newcomb, David Royal 1923- *St&PR 91*
Newcomb, Eldon Henry 1919- *WhoAm 90*
Newcomb, James M. 1948- *St&PR 91*
Newcomb, James Pearson 1837-1907 *BioIn 16*
Newcomb, James Q. 1961- *St&PR 91*
Newcomb, John Lewis 1947- *BiDrAPA 89*
Newcomb, Jonathan 1946- *WhoAm 90*
Newcomb, Kate Pelham 1885-1956 *BioAmW*
Newcomb, Kelly *ODwPR 91*
Newcomb, Lawrence Howard 1947- *WhoAm 90*
Newcomb, Mary 1922- *BiDWomA*
Newcomb, Robert Carl 1926- *WhoSSW 91*
Newcomb, Robert Wayne 1933- *WhoAm 90*
Newcomb, Simon 1835-1909 *BioIn 16, EncO&P 3, EncPaPR 91*
Newcomb, Wilburn Wendell 1935- *WhoWrEP 89*
Newcomb, William Wilmon, Jr. 1921- *WhoAm 90*
Newcombe, Arthur Rowell, III 1932- *St&PR 91*
Newcombe, Don 1926- *Ballpl 90 [port], BioIn 16*
Newcombe, Eugene A. 1923-1990 *ConAu 130*
Newcombe, Harry S. 1901-1988 *BioIn 16*
Newcombe, Howard Borden 1914- *WhoAm 90*
Newcombe, Jack *AuBYP 90, BioIn 16, ConAu 130*
Newcombe, Jack 1923-1990 *NewYTBS 90*
Newcombe, John 1943- *WorAlBi*
Newcombe, Richard Sumner 1950- *WhoAm 90*
Newcome, Claire L. 1924- *St&PR 91*
Newcome, Susannah 1685-1763 *FemiCLE*
Newcomer, Carr 1922- *St&PR 91*
Newcomer, Clarence Charles 1923- *WhoAm 90*
Newcomer, John Whitney *BiDrAPA 89*
Newcomer, Richard Gary 1934- *ODwPR 91*
Newcorn, Claudia Dana 1958- *WhoAmW 91*
Newcorn, Jeffrey H 1951- *BiDrAPA 89*
Newdick, Mark Mattingsley 1954- *WhoE 91*
Newell, Alma 1936- *WhoAmW 91*
Newell, Arlo F. 1926- *St&PR 91*
Newell, Audrey Riker *BiDrAPA 89*
Newell, Barbara Warne 1929- *WhoAm 90*
Newell, Byron Bruce, Jr. 1932- *WhoAm 90*
Newell, Cam McGillicuddy 1947- *WhoE 91*
Newell, Charldean 1939- *WhoAmW 91*
Newell, Dare 1916-1988 *AnObit 1988*
Newell, David W. 1940- *St&PR 91*
Newell, E. Owen 1929- *St&PR 91*
Newell, Elizabeth Jeanie Broome 1956- *WhoAmW 91*
Newell, Eric James 1930- *WhoAm 90*
Newell, Frank William 1916- *WhoAm 90*
Newell, Gary Layton 1941- *BiDrAPA 89*
Newell, Gladys Elizabeth 1908- *WhoAmW 91*
Newell, Gregory John 1949- *WhoAm 90, WhoWor 91*
Newell, Henry H. 1907- *St&PR 91*
Newell, Homer Edward 1915-1983 *AuBYP 90*
Newell, Hope 1896-1965 *AuBYP 90*
Newell, J. Louis 1936- *St&PR 91*
Newell, Jack C. 1938- *St&PR 91*
Newell, James David 1933- *St&PR 91*
Newell, James R. 1957- *St&PR 91*
Newell, James Robert 1941- *WhoSSW 91*
Newell, Jeanne Ann 1947- *WhoAmW 91*
Newell, John Wallace 1940- *WhoSSW 91*
Newell, Katherine Ann 1947- *WhoAmW 91*
Newell, Mary Etna 1944- *WhoAmW 91*
Newell, Neil K. 1953- *WhoWrEP 89*
Newell, Norman Dennis 1909- *WhoAm 90*
Newell, Oswald, Jr. 1925- *St&PR 91*
Newell, Patrick *ConTFT 8*
Newell, Paul Haynes, Jr. 1933- *WhoAm 90*
Newell, Peter Carroll 1933- *St&PR 91*
Newell, Rebecca Gail 1953- *WhoAmW 91*
Newell, Reginald Edward 1931- *WhoAm 90*
Newell, Richard N. 1932- *St&PR 91*
Newell, Robert L. 1922- *St&PR 91*
Newell, Robert Lincoln 1922- *WhoAm 90*
Newell, Roger D. 1913- *St&PR 91*
Newell, Ronald Allin 1948- *WhoSSW 91*
Newell, Silvia Anna 1953- *WhoSSW 91*
Newell, Sterling, Jr. 1921- *WhoAm 90*
Newell, William Edward 1936- *St&PR 91*
Newell, William Talman, Jr. 1932- *WhoAm 90*
Newer, Thesis *WhoAmA 91*
Newey, Paul Davis 1914- *WhoAm 90, WhoWor 91*
Newey, Vincent 1943- *ConAu 132*
Newfield, Jack *BioIn 16*
Newfield, Mayer Ullman 1905- *WhoAm 90*
Newgaard, Patricia Ann 1944- *WhoWrEP 89*
Newhall, Adelaide May 1884-1960 *WhoAmA 91N*
Newhall, Beaumont 1908- *BioIn 16, WhoAm 90, WhoAmA 91N*
Newhall, Charles Crosby 1928- *St&PR 91*
Newhall, Charles Watson, III 1944- *WhoE 91*
Newhall, David, III 1937- *WhoAm 90*
Newhall, David Sowle 1929- *WhoSSW 91*
Newhall, John Breed 1932- *St&PR 91*
Newhall, John Harrison 1933- *WhoAm 90*
Newhall, Julie S. *ODwPR 91*
Newhall, Patricia 1927- *WhoE 91*
Newhard, Harry Wallace 1930- *St&PR 91*
Newhard, Ronald Arthur 1944- *St&PR 91*
Newhard, Steven B. 1949- *St&PR 91*
Newhart, Bob *BioIn 16*
Newhart, Bob 1929- *WhoAm 90, WorAlBi*
Newhart, Lawrence E., Jr. 1942- *St&PR 91*
Newhauser, Richard Gordan 1947- *WhoWor 91*
Newhoff, Stanley Neal 1944- *WhoWor 91*
Newhouse, Alan Russell 1938- *WhoE 91*
Newhouse, Bertram Maurice 1888-1982 *WhoAmA 91N*
Newhouse, Clyde Mortimer 1920- *WhoAmA 91*
Newhouse, Dave 1938- *Ballpl 90*
Newhouse, Edward, Mrs. *WhoAmW 91*
Newhouse, Hazel R. 1906-1989 *BioIn 16*
Newhouse, Joseph Paul 1942- *WhoAm 90, WhoE 91*
Newhouse, Maggi 1917-1989 *BioIn 16*
Newhouse, Michael Allen 1940- *BiDrAPA 89*
Newhouse, Mitzi E. *BioIn 16*
Newhouse, Nancy R. *WhoAm 90*
Newhouse, Norman 1906-1988 *AnObit 1988*
Newhouse, Norman N. 1906-1988 *BioIn 16*
Newhouse, Paul A 1953- *BiDrAPA 89*
Newhouse, Richard G *BiDrAPA 89*
Newhouse, Robert Louis 1939- *BiDrAPA 89*
Newhouse, Robert M *BiDrAPA 89*
Newhouse, S. I., Jr. 1947- *WorAlBi*
Newhouse, Samuel I. 1895-1979 *BioIn 16, WorAlBi*
Newhouse, Samuel I., Jr. *BioIn 16*
Newhouse, Samuel I., Jr. 1928- *WhoE 91, WhoWor 91*
Newhouser, Hal 1921- *Ballpl 90 [port]*
Newick, Craig D *WhoAmA 91*
Newitt, Ben J. 1924- *St&PR 91*
Newitt, John Garwood, Jr. 1941- *WhoSSW 91, WhoWor 91*
Newitter, Ralph S., Jr. 1943- *St&PR 91*
Newkerk, Deborah *WhoAmW 91*
Newkirk, Cassandra F 1953- *BiDrAPA 89*
Newkirk, Dennis G. 1950- *St&PR 91*
Newkirk, Elizabeth Ann 1935- *WhoSSW 91*
Newkirk, Gerald Edward 1946- *St&PR 91*
Newkirk, Ingrid *BioIn 16*
Newkirk, Isaac L. 1950- *WhoSSW 91*
Newkirk, John Burt 1920- *WhoAm 90*
Newkirk, Raymond Leslie 1944- *WhoWor 91*
Newland, Chester Albert 1930- *WhoAm 90*
Newland, Hillary Reid 1940- *WhoSSW 91*
Newland, James Leroy 1942- *WhoSSW 91*
Newland, Joseph Nelson 1953- *WhoAmA 91*
Newland, Larry 1935- *IntWWM 90*
Newland, Larry J. 1935- *WhoAm 90*
Newland, R. G. 1823- *AmLegL*
Newland, Ruth Laura 1949- *WhoAmW 91, WhoEmL 91, WhoWor 91*
Newland, William 1815-1874 *AmLegL*
Newlands, George 1941- *ConAu 129*
Newlands, Sheila Ann 1953- *WhoAmW 91*
Newler, Jerome Marc 1947- *WhoE 91, WhoEmL 91, WhoWor 91*
Newley, Anthony 1931- *OxCPMus, WhoAm 90, WorAlBi*
Newlin, Beverly Agnew 1947- *WhoAmW 91*
Newlin, Carol McNary 1941- *BiDrAPA 89*
Newlin, Charles Fremont 1953- *WhoEmL 91*
Newlin, Charles William 1924- *WhoAm 90*
Newlin, Dika 1923- *IntWWM 90*
Newlin, G.W. 1917- *St&PR 91*
Newlin, John Wigton, Jr. 1937- *St&PR 91*
Newlin, Kimrey Dayton 1944- *WhoSSW 91*
Newlin, Lyman Wilbur 1910- *WhoWor 91*
Newlin, Margaret Rudd 1925- *WhoWrEP 89*
Newlin, Patricia E. 1950- *ODwPR 91*
Newlin, Patricia Ellen 1950- *WhoE 91*
Newlin, William Rankin 1940- *St&PR 91, WhoAm 90*
Newling, Donald William 1941- *WhoWor 91*
Newlon, Clarke *AuBYP 90*
Newlove, Bobbie 1922-1932 *EncPaPR 91*
Newlove, Donald *BioIn 16*
Newlson, Albert Harold, Jr. 1917- *St&PR 91*
Newlyn, Thomas P 1941- *BiDrAPA 89*
Newman, Aisik 1946- *BiDrAPA 89*
Newman, Al 1960- *Ballpl 90*
Newman, Alan C. 1945- *St&PR 91*
Newman, Alan G. 1950- *St&PR 91*
Newman, Alan Harvey 1946- *WhoE 91, WhoEmL 91*
Newman, Alfred 1900-1970 *OxCPMus*
Newman, Allen I *BiDrAPA 89*
Newman, Andrew Douglas 1960- *WhoEmL 91*
Newman, Andrew Edison 1944- *St&PR 91, WhoAm 90*
Newman, Anita 1927- *St&PR 91*
Newman, Anne *BiDEWW*
Newman, Annette Goerlich 1940- *WhoAmW 91*
Newman, Anthony 1941- *BioIn 16, IntWWM 90*
Newman, Arnold 1918- *BioIn 16, WhoAm 90, WhoAmA 91*
Newman, Barbara *BioIn 16, ConAu 31NR*
Newman, Barbara 1939- *ConAu 132*
Newman, Barbara Pollock 1939- *WhoAmW 91*
Newman, Barnett 1905-1970 *IntDcAA 90, WhoAmA 91N, WorAlBi*
Newman, Barry 1938- *BioIn 16*
Newman, Barry Ingalls 1932- *St&PR 91, WhoAm 90*
Newman, Benny *WhoSSW 91*
Newman, Bernard 1897-1968 *AuBYP 90, TwCCr&M 91*
Newman, Bernard 1941- *St&PR 91*
Newman, Bernard Charles 1897-1968 *SpyFic*
Newman, Bernard I 1933- *BiDrAPA 89*
Newman, Brian Kevin 1961- *WhoSSW 91*
Newman, Bruce *BioIn 16*
Newman, Bruce Lee 1936- *WhoAm 90*
Newman, Bryce Herbert 1931- *St&PR 91*
Newman, C Janet *BiDrAPA 89*
Newman, Cecil E. 1903-1976 *BioIn 16*
Newman, Charles 1900-1989 *ConAu 129*
Newman, Charles 1938- *WhoAm 90, WhoWrEP 89*
Newman, Charles Andrew 1949- *WhoEmL 91, WhoWor 91*
Newman, Charles Forrest 1937- *WhoSSW 91*
Newman, Charles Judson 1950- *WhoSSW 91*
Newman, Charles L. 1926- *WhoSSW 91*
Newman, Charles William 1949- *WhoAm 90*
Newman, Claire Poe 1926- *WhoAmW 91*
Newman, Clinton Harlin, II 1942- *WhoSSW 91*
Newman, Daisy 1904- *AuBYP 90*
Newman, Danny 1919- *IntWWM 90*
Newman, David *BioIn 16, NewYTBS 90*
Newman, David 1933- *BiDrAPA 89*
Newman, David Henry 1951- *WhoE 91*
Newman, Deborah Carol 1952- *BiDrAPA 89*
Newman, Della *WhoAmW 91, WhoWor 91*
Newman, Denis 1930- *St&PR 91, WhoAm 90*
Newman, Don Melvin 1923- *WhoAm 90*
Newman, Donald A. *ODwPR 91*
Newman, Donald E *BiDrAPA 89*
Newman, Donald J. *BioIn 16*
Newman, Donald J. *NewYTBS 90 [port]*
Newman, Donald R. 1913- *St&PR 91*
Newman, Donald Ray 1927- *WhoAm 90*
Newman, Dorothy Anne 1947- *WhoAmW 91, WhoSSW 91, WhoWor 91*
Newman, Dwight Ashley 1932- *St&PR 91*
Newman, E Gustave 1925- *BiDrAPA 89*
Newman, Edith Squire 1938- *WhoAmW 91*
Newman, Edward Harry 1940- *St&PR 91*
Newman, Edwin H. 1919- *WorAlBi*
Newman, Edwin Harold 1919- *WhoAm 90*
Newman, Edwin Stanley 1922- *WhoE 91*
Newman, Eileen Meryl 1961- *WhoAmW 91*
Newman, Elias 1903- *WhoAm 90, WhoAmA 91*
Newman, Elizabeth H *WhoAmA 91*
Newman, Eric P. 1911- *St&PR 91*
Newman, Eric Pfeiffer 1911- *WhoAm 90*
Newman, Ernest W. *WhoAm 90*
Newman, Estelle Ruth 1935- *WhoAmW 91*
Newman, F. Barry 1946- *WhoE 91*
Newman, Floyd R. *NewYTBS 90*
Newman, Frances 1883-1928 *FemiCLE*
Newman, Francine Mason 1944- *St&PR 91*
Newman, Frank Cecil 1917- *WhoAm 90*
Newman, Frank Neil 1942- *St&PR 91, WhoAm 90*
Newman, Frank W *BiDrAPA 89*
Newman, Fred 1942- *Ballpl 90*
Newman, Fred C. 1931- *St&PR 91*
Newman, Fredric Samuel 1945- *WhoAm 90*
Newman, G F 1945- *TwCCr&M 91*
Newman, G. Robert 1946- *St&PR 91*
Newman, George F *BiDrAPA 89*
Newman, George Henry 1949- *WhoEmL 91*
Newman, George S. 1919- *St&PR 91*
Newman, George W., III 1940- *St&PR 91*
Newman, Gerald 1931- *St&PR 91, WhoAm 90*
Newman, Geraldine Anne *WhoAm 90, WhoE 91*
Newman, Gordon Harold 1933- *St&PR 91, WhoAm 90*
Newman, Harold H. 1918- *WhoE 91*
Newman, Harold W., Jr. 1899- *WhoAm 90*
Newman, Harry 1947- *St&PR 91*
Newman, Harry Alexander 1928- *WhoSSW 91*
Newman, Harry Rudolph 1909- *WhoAm 90*
Newman, Harry Samuel 1930- *BiDrAPA 89*
Newman, Harvey 1935- *St&PR 91*
Newman, Horatio Hackett 1875-1957 *DcScB S2*
Newman, Howard Neal 1935- *WhoAm 90*
Newman, Hugh Damian 1911- *St&PR 91*
Newman, Ira Bernard 1950- *WhoE 91*
Newman, Irving *BioIn 16*
Newman, Irwin J. 1948- *St&PR 91*
Newman, Jacqueline M. 1932- *WhoAmW 91*
Newman, James A. 1914- *St&PR 91*
Newman, James B. 1929- *St&PR 91*
Newman, James Blakey 1917- *WhoAm 90*
Newman, James Clair 1930- *BiDrAPA 89*
Newman, James E. 1947- *St&PR 91*
Newman, James Gardner 1920- *St&PR 91*
Newman, James Heflin 1908- *WhoAm 90*
Newman, James Louis 1942- *BiDrAPA 89*
Newman, James Michael 1946- *WhoE 91, WhoEmL 91, WhoWor 91*
Newman, James W., Jr. *ODwPR 91*
Newman, James Wilson 1909- *WhoAm 90*
Newman, Jane *BioIn 16*
Newman, Jane 1947- *WhoAm 90, WhoAmW 91*
Newman, Jane E. 1945- *WhoAm 90, WhoE 91*
Newman, Janice Marie 1951- *WhoAmW 91*
Newman, Jay Hartley 1951- *WhoEmL 91*
Newman, Jeanne Louise 1946- *WhoAmW 91*
Newman, Jeff 1948- *Ballpl 90*
Newman, Jeffrey K. 1951- *WhoEmL 91*
Newman, Jerald Conway 1932- *WhoAm 90*
Newman, Jeremy R. 1933- *St&PR 91*
Newman, Jerrold Mitchell 1954- *WhoEmL 91*
Newman, Jill N *BiDrAPA 89*
Newman, Joel 1942- *WhoAm 90*
Newman, John B. 1917-1989 *BioIn 16*
Newman, John Beatty 1933- *WhoAmA 91*
Newman, John H. 1801-1890 *WorAlBi*
Newman, John H. 1950- *St&PR 91*
Newman, John Henry 1801-1890 *BioIn 16*
Newman, John Kevin 1928- *WhoAm 90*
Newman, John Nicholas 1935- *WhoAm 90*
Newman, John Robert 1932- *WhoAm 90*
Newman, John Scott 1938- *WhoAm 90*
Newman, Jon O. 1932- *WhoAm 90*
Newman, Jon Paul 1940- *St&PR 91*
Newman, Joseph 1929- *St&PR 91*
Newman, Joseph H. 1928- *WhoAm 90*
Newman, Joseph Herbert 1925- *WhoE 91*
Newman, Joseph Westley *BioIn 16*
Newman, Joshua P *BiDrAPA 89*
Newman, Joyce 1942- *ODwPR 91*
Newman, Joyce Kligerman 1927- *WhoAm 90*
Newman, Julian J *BiDrAPA 89*
Newman, Karen Beth 1960- *WhoAmW 91*
Newman, Karen Gwen 1954- *BiDrAPA 89*
Newman, Karen Sachiko 1961- *WhoAmW 91*
Newman, Keith M. 1944- *St&PR 91*
Newman, Kevin P. 1946- *St&PR 91, WhoAm 90*
Newman, Kim Diane 1954- *WhoAmW 91*
Newman, Laura Eager 1928- *WhoSSW 91*
Newman, Lawrence E *BiDrAPA 89*
Newman, Lawrence W. 1939- *St&PR 91*
Newman, Lawrence Walker 1935- *WhoAm 90, WhoWor 91*
Newman, Leonard 1924- *St&PR 91*
Newman, Leslea 1955- *WhoWrEP 89*
Newman, Libby *WhoAmA 91*
Newman, Linda *BioIn 16*
Newman, Linda 1937- *WhoAmW 91, WhoE 91*

Newman, Linnaea Rose 1953- *WhoWor 91*
Newman, Lionel 1916- *OxCPMus*
Newman, Lionel 1916-1989 *AnObit 1989, BioIn 16, ConTFT 8*
Newman, Lloyd N. 1931- *ODwPR 91*
Newman, Louis 1947- *WhoAmA 91*
Newman, Louis Benjamin *WhoAm 90*
Newman, M. W. 1917- *WhoAm 90*
Newman, Marc Alan 1955- *WhoEmL 91, WhoWor 91*
Newman, Margaret Ann 1933- *WhoAmW 91*
Newman, Marjorie Yospin 1945- *BiDrAPA 89*
Newman, Mark D. 1950- *WhoE 91*
Newman, Mark Stuart 1949- *St&PR 91*
Newman, Martin Donald 1938- *St&PR 91*
Newman, Martin H. 1913-1990 *BioIn 16*
Newman, Matthew 1955- *BioIn 16*
Newman, Maurice Barton *St&PR 91*
Newman, Maxine Placker 1922- *WhoAmW 91*
Newman, Maxwell Herman Alexander 1897-1984 *DcNaB 1981*
Newman, Melissa Susan 1957- *WhoSSW 91*
Newman, Melvin D. 1942- *St&PR 91*
Newman, Melvin Spencer 1908- *WhoAm 90*
Newman, Michael 1936- *WhoAm 90*
Newman, Michael Joseph 1936- *St&PR 91*
Newman, Michael M *BiDrAPA 89*
Newman, Michael Rodney 1945- *WhoWor 91*
Newman, Milton 1930- *WhoE 91*
Newman, Mona Alice Jean *ConAu 31NR*
Newman, Monroe 1929- *WhoAm 90*
Newman, Morris 1924- *WhoAm 90*
Newman, Morton B 1930- *BiDrAPA 89*
Newman, Muriel Kallis Steinberg 1914- *WhoAm 90*
Newman, Murray Arthur 1924- *WhoAm 90*
Newman, Nancy Jean 1956- *WhoAmW 91*
Newman, P B 1919- *WhoWrEP 89*
Newman, Patricia Ann 1953- *WhoSSW 91*
Newman, Paul 1925- *BioIn 16, WhoAm 90, WorAlBi*
Newman, Pauline 1927- *WhoAmW 91*
Newman, Pauline M. 1888?-1986 *EncAL*
Newman, Peggy Jo 1926- *WhoAmW 91*
Newman, Peter Charles 1929- *WhoAm 90*
Newman, Peter John 1944- *WhoWor 91*
Newman, Peter Kenneth 1928- *WhoAm 90*
Newman, Phillip Barbour, III 1932- *St&PR 91, WhoAm 90*
Newman, Phyllis *BioIn 16*
Newman, Phyllis 1933- *WhoAmW 91*
Newman, Rachel 1938- *WhoAm 90, WhoWrEP 89*
Newman, Ralph Geoffrey 1911- *WhoAm 90*
Newman, Ralph Howard *BiDrAPA 89*
Newman, Randy *BioIn 16*
Newman, Randy 1943- *ConMus 4 [port], EncPR&S 89, WhoAm 90, WorAlBi*
Newman, Randy 1944- *OxCPMus*
Newman, Randy L 1953- *St&PR 91*
Newman, Richard *BiDrAPA 89*
Newman, Richard A 1931- *BiDrAPA 89*
Newman, Richard Alan 1930- *WhoAm 90, WhoWrEP 89*
Newman, Richard Charles 1938- *WhoAmA 91, WhoE 91*
Newman, Richard Galloway 1934- *St&PR 91*
Newman, Richard M. 1943- *ODwPR 91*
Newman, Richard Oakley 1920- *WhoAm 90*
Newman, Richard Paul 1952- *WhoSSW 91*
Newman, Rita R *BiDrAPA 89*
Newman, Robert 1909- *AuBYP 90*
Newman, Robert 1909-1988 *BioIn 16, SmATA 60*
Newman, Robert A. *ODwPR 91*
Newman, Robert E 1948- *BiDrAPA 89*
Newman, Robert Gabriel 1937- *WhoAm 90*
Newman, Robert J. 1928- *St&PR 91*
Newman, Robert Jacob 1904- *WhoWor 91*
Newman, Robert James 1907-1988 *BioIn 16*
Newman, Robert Joseph 1928- *WhoAm 90*
Newman, Robert L, Jr. 1936- *BiDrAPA 89*
Newman, Rochelle Joyce 1939- *WhoE 91*
Newman, Ronald Peter 1946- *St&PR 91*
Newman, Ruby M. 1909- *WhoWrEP 89*
Newman, Samuel 1938- *St&PR 91, WhoAm 90, WhoWor 91*
Newman, Samuel Mark 1957- *WhoSSW 91*
Newman, Scott David 1947- *WhoAm 90, WhoE 91, WhoWor 91*
Newman, Seraine Deene 1942- *EncPaPR 91*
Newman, Seraine Dianne 1942- *WhoAmW 91*
Newman, Sheldon O. 1923- *St&PR 91*
Newman, Sheldon Oscar 1923- *WhoE 91*
Newman, Shirlee Petkin 1924- *AuBYP 90*
Newman, Slater Edmund 1924- *WhoAm 90*
Newman, Sophie 1925- *WhoAmA 91*
Newman, Stanley *BioIn 16*
Newman, Stanley 1935- *St&PR 91*
Newman, Stanley Ray 1923- *WhoWor 91*
Newman, Stanley Simeon 1925- *WhoE 91*
Newman, Stephen Alexander 1938- *WhoE 91*
Newman, Stephen L. 1952- *ConAu 132*
Newman, Steven H. 1943- *St&PR 91*
Newman, Steven Harvey 1943- *WhoAm 90*
Newman, Susan Langley 1960- *WhoSSW 91*
Newman, Suzanne Dinkes 1949- *WhoAmW 91*
Newman, Terrie Lynne *WhoSSW 91*
Newman, Theodore Roosevelt, Jr. 1934- *WhoAm 90, WhoE 91*
Newman, Thomas Benjamin, Jr. 1942- *WhoE 91*
Newman, Thomas Daniel 1922- *WhoAm 90, WhoWor 91*
Newman, Thomas Patrick 1937- *St&PR 91*
Newman, Thomas Rubin 1933- *WhoAm 90*
Newman, Thomas Walter Goldberg 1955- *WhoSSW 91*
Newman, Tillman Eugene, Jr. 1938- *WhoSSW 91*
Newman, Tim *BioIn 16*
Newman, Victor Emanuel 1930- *WhoAm 90*
Newman, Vincent Charles 1953- *WhoE 91*
Newman, Wade Davis 1936- *WhoAm 90*
Newman, Walter Andrews, Jr 1930- *WhoAmA 91*
Newman, William Bernard, Jr. 1950- *St&PR 91, WhoAm 90*
Newman, William Guy 1952- *WhoE 91*
Newman, William Herman 1829-1894 *DcCanB 12*
Newman, William L. 1931- *St&PR 91*
Newman, William Louis 1920- *WhoAm 90*
Newman, William Richard, III 1939- *St&PR 91*
Newman, William S. 1912- *IntWWM 90*
Newman, William Stein 1912- *WhoAm 90*
Newman, Winifred *BiDEWW*
Newman-Gordon, Pauline 1925- *WhoAm 90*
Newman-Rice, Nancy 1950- *WhoAmA 91*
Newman-Rutstein, Joyce Enith Watkins 1930- *IntWWM 90*
Newmarch, Rosa 1857-1940 *FemiCLE*
Newmark, Brooks Phillip V. 1958- *WhoWor 91*
Newmark, Emanuel 1936- *WhoSSW 91*
Newmark, Harry *St&PR 91*
Newmark, Howard 1944- *WhoSSW 91*
Newmark, Leonard Daniel 1929- *WhoAm 90, WhoWrEP 89*
Newmark, Marilyn 1928- *WhoAmA 91, WhoWor 91*
Newmark, Thomas S 1944- *BiDrAPA 89*
Newmeyer, Frederick Jaret 1944- *WhoAm 90*
Newmyer, Arthur G., III 1949- *ODwPR 91*
Newmyer, Arthur G., Jr. 1915- *ODwPR 91*
Newmyer, James M. 1919- *ODwPR 91*
Newnham, Dennis M. 1940- *St&PR 91*
Newnham, Margaret Lois 1944- *WhoSSW 91*
Newport, Christopher *EncCRAm*
Newport, John Paul 1917- *WhoAm 90*
Newport, Marvin Gene 1935- *WhoAm 90*
Newport, Walter A., Jr. 1917- *St&PR 91*
Newquist, Lester J. *BioIn 16*
Newrick, Henry Patrick 1946- *WhoWor 91*
News, Kathryn Anne 1934- *WhoAm 90*
Newsham, John W. 1932- *St&PR 91*
Newsom, Barbara Ylvisaker 1926- *WhoAmA 91*
Newsom, Barry Douglas 1953- *WhoSSW 91*
Newsom, Bobo 1907-1962 *Ballpl 90 [port]*
Newsom, Carolyn Cardall 1941- *WhoE 91*
Newsom, Carroll V. *NewYTBS 90 [port]*
Newsom, Carroll V 1904-1990 *ConAu 130*
Newsom, Carroll Vincent 1904-1990 *BioIn 16, CurBio 90N*
Newsom, David Dunlop 1918- *WhoAm 90*
Newsom, Douglas Ann Johnson 1934- *WhoAmW 91, WhoSSW 91, WhoWor 91*
Newsom, Francis C 1918- *BiDrAPA 89*
Newsom, Gary Randell *BiDrAPA 89*
Newsom, Gene A. 1936- *St&PR 91*
Newsom, Gerald Higley 1939- *WhoAm 90*
Newsom, Jan Reimann 1947- *St&PR 91*
Newsom, Leo Dale 1915-1987 *BioIn 16*
Newsom, Lionel Hodge 1919- *WhoAm 90*
Newsom, Melvin Max 1931- *WhoAm 90*
Newsom, Ray 1926- *St&PR 91*
Newsom, Will Roy 1912- *WhoAm 90*
Newsome, Alvin C. 1930- *St&PR 91*
Newsome, Arden J. 1932- *AuBYP 90*
Newsome, Dick 1909-1965 *Ballpl 90*
Newsome, Donna Wildening 1951- *BiDrAPA 89*
Newsome, Edward B. 1933- *St&PR 91*
Newsome, George Lane, Jr. 1923- *WhoAm 90*
Newsome, John *St&PR 91*
Newsome, June Beeson 1960- *WhoSSW 91*
Newsome, Larry James, Sr. 1948- *WhoSSW 91*
Newsome, Mark Ronald 1960- *WhoSSW 91*
Newsome, Mary De Sevigne *BiDrAPA 89*
Newsome, Mary Effie Lee 1885-1979 *HarlReB*
Newsome, Roy 1930- *IntWWM 90*
Newsome, Skeeter 1910- *Ballpl 90*
Newsome, William Roy, Jr. 1934- *WhoAm 90*
Newson, Anyalynn *BiDrAPA 89*
Newson, Eula Mae 1931- *WhoWrEP 89*
Newson, Roosevelt 1946- *IntWWM 90*
Newstadt, Geoffrey J 1935- *BiDrAPA 89*
Newstead, Robert Richard 1935- *WhoWor 91*
Newstead, Ronald Arthur 1925- *WhoWor 91*
Newstone, Harry 1921- *IntWWM 90*
Newton, Alan B. 1939- *St&PR 91*
Newton, Alexander Worthy 1930- *WhoAm 90*
Newton, Alice F. 1937- *St&PR 91*
Newton, Alice Faye 1937- *WhoAm 90, WhoWor 91*
Newton, Alice Spohn *BioIn 16*
Newton, Anne 1941- *BiDrAPA 89*
Newton, Antonio *NewAgMG*
Newton, C.M., Jr. 1915- *St&PR 91*
Newton, Carl Davidson, Jr. 1919- *St&PR 91*
Newton, Carl E. 1898-1989 *BioIn 16*
Newton, Charles Chartier 1933- *WhoAm 90*
Newton, Charles G., Jr. 1945- *ODwPR 91*
Newton, Charlotte R. *ODwPR 91*
Newton, Christopher *BioIn 16*
Newton, Christopher 1936- *IntWWM 90, OxCCanT*
Newton, Christopher C. 1945- *ODwPR 91*
Newton, Courtland G., Jr. 1935- *ODwPR 91*
Newton, Debra *ODwPR 91*
Newton, Derek Arnold 1930- *WhoAm 90*
Newton, Doc 1877-1931 *Ballpl 90*
Newton, Don Allen 1934- *WhoSSW 91*
Newton, Donald Michael 1958- *WhoSSW 91*
Newton, Dorothy Ruth Armstrong 1923- *WhoAmW 91*
Newton, Douglas 1920- *WhoAm 90, WhoAmA 91*
Newton, Earle Williams 1917- *WhoAm 90, WhoAmA 91, WhoSSW 91*
Newton, Elizabeth *BiDEWW*
Newton, Elizabeth Anne Caswell 1949- *WhoE 91*
Newton, Francis Lanneau 1928- *WhoAm 90*
Newton, Frank Cota-Robles 1946- *WhoHisp 91*
Newton, Fred Julian 1937- *WhoSSW 91*
Newton, Frederick Carter 1924- *St&PR 91*
Newton, Fredrick 1946- *WhoSSW 91*
Newton, Gale JoAnn 1954- *WhoAmW 91, WhoEmL 91*
Newton, George Addison 1911- *WhoAm 90, WhoWor 91*
Newton, George D., Jr. 1931- *St&PR 91*
Newton, George Durfee, Jr. 1931- *WhoAm 90*
Newton, Grace Hamilton *WhoAmA 91N*
Newton, Hector Carlton, III 1936- *St&PR 91*
Newton, Helmut *BioIn 16*
Newton, Huey *BioIn 16*
Newton, Huey 1942-1989 *AnObit 1989, News 90*
Newton, Huey P 1942-1989 *ConAu 129*
Newton, Isaac 1642-1727 *BioIn 16, WorAlBi*
Newton, Isabel *EncPaPR 91*
Newton, Ivor 1892-1981 *PenDiMP*
Newton, J. R. 1810-1883 *EncO&P 3*
Newton, Jack 1942- *BioIn 16*
Newton, James *NewAgMG*
Newton, James John 1949- *WhoSSW 91, WhoWrEP 89*
Newton, James Quigg, Jr. 1911- *WhoAm 90*
Newton, Jeffrey H 1943- *BiDrAPA 89*
Newton, John 1725-1807 *BioIn 16*
Newton, John Milton 1929- *WhoAm 90*
Newton, John Neil 1933- *WhoAmA 91*
Newton, John Skillman 1908- *WhoAm 90*
Newton, John Thomas 1930- *St&PR 91*
Newton, John Thomas 1936- *WhoAm 90, WhoSSW 91*
Newton, Joseph Emory *BiDrAPA 89*
Newton, Karen Cantey 1959- *WhoAmW 91*
Newton, Karl 1935- *BiDrAPA 89*
Newton, Laura P. *AuBYP 90*
Newton, Leonard Frank 1925- *St&PR 91*
Newton, Lisa Haenlein 1939- *WhoAm 90, WhoE 91*
Newton, Margaret 1893-1960 *WhoAmA 91N*
Newton, Maxwell 1929- *WhoAm 90*
Newton, Michael 1934- *St&PR 91*
Newton, Michael A *BiDrAPA 89*
Newton, Mildred Emily 1901-1972 *BioIn 16*
Newton, Niles Rumely 1923- *WhoAm 90*
Newton, Norman Thomas 1898- *WhoAm 90*
Newton, Patricia Ann *BiDrAPA 89*
Newton, Patricia Ann 1955- *BiDrAPA 89*
Newton, Paul 1931- *ODwPR 91*
Newton, Randolph Harrison 1947- *St&PR 91*
Newton, Rhonwen Leonard 1940- *WhoAmW 91, WhoSSW 91*
Newton, Richard Aaron 1935- *WhoAm 90*
Newton, Richard Edward 1948- *WhoAmA 91*
Newton, Robert Eugene 1917- *WhoAm 90*
Newton, Robert M. 1933- *ODwPR 91*
Newton, Robert R. 1939- *St&PR 91*
Newton, Rodney Stephen 1945- *IntWWM 90*
Newton, Roger Gerhard 1924- *WhoAm 90*
Newton, S. T. 1941- *WhoSSW 91*
Newton, Saul *BioIn 16*
Newton, Scott *BiDrAPA 89*
Newton, Sonya Berk 1942- *WhoSSW 91*
Newton, Stephen Albert *WhoSSW 91*
Newton, Suzanne 1936- *AuBYP 90, BioIn 16*
Newton, T. Eugene 1935- *St&PR 91*
Newton, Thomas 1660-1721 *EncCRAm*
Newton, Thomas Collins 1951- *WhoEmL 91*
Newton, Thomas Monroe 1927- *WhoSSW 91*
Newton, Victor Joseph 1937- *WhoE 91*
Newton, Virginia *BioIn 16*
Newton, Wallace Berkeley 1949- *St&PR 91*
Newton, Walter Logan 1956- *St&PR 91*
Newton, Wayne *BioIn 16*
Newton, Wayne 1942- *CurBio 90 [port], WorAlBi*
Newton, William Allen, Jr. 1923- *WhoAm 90*
Newton, William C. 1930- *St&PR 91*
Newton, William Lee 1945- *BiDrAPA 89*
Newton, William Meese 1907- *BioIn 16*
Newton, William Ritchey 1945- *WhoE 91*
Newton, Willis H., Jr. 1949- *St&PR 91*
Newton-Cerkas, Paula Sue 1951- *WhoAmW 91*
Newton-John, Olivia 1947- *EncPR&S 89*
Newton-John, Olivia 1948- *OxCPMus, WhoAm 90, WorAlBi*
Newtowne, Sylvia M *BiDrAPA 89*
Newyear, Albert Richard 1948- *St&PR 91*
Nexo, Martin Andersen 1869-1954 *DcScanL*
Nexsen, Julian Jacobs 1924- *WhoAm 90*
Ney, Edward N. *BioIn 16*
Ney, Edward Noonan 1925- *WhoAm 90*
Ney, Edward Purdy 1920- *WhoAm 90*
Ney, Elizabet 1833-1907 *BiDWomA*
Ney, Elly 1882-1968 *PenDiMP*
Ney, Genevieve J *BiDrAPA 89*
Ney, James Walter Edward Colby 1932- *WhoAm 90, WhoWrEP 89*
Ney, Jerome M. *St&PR 91N*
Ney, John *AuBYP 90*
Ney, Michel 1769-1815 *WorAlBi*
Ney, Randolph J. 1937- *St&PR 91*
Neyhard, Pamela Ann 1951- *WhoSSW 91*
Neyhart, Amos E. *NewYTBS 90*
Neyhart, Louise Albright *AuBYP 90*
Neylan, Thomas Coogan 1957- *BiDrAPA 89*
Neyland, Randolph Archer 1945- *WhoSSW 91*
Neylon, Jeanne A. *ODwPR 91*
Neylon, Martin Joseph 1920- *WhoAm 90*
Neyman, Jerzy 1894-1981 *DcScB S2*
Neyzi, Ahmet H. 1920- *WhoWor 91*
Nezer, Steven S. 1947- *St&PR 91*
Nezhadian, Fariborz 1963- *BiDrAPA 89*
Nezhdanova, Antonina 1873-1950 *PenDiMP*
Neziroglu, Cevat 1923- *BiDrAPA 89*
Nezworski, M. Teresa 1954- *WhoAmW 91*
Nezzo, Alessandro 1920- *WhoWor 91*
Ng, Albert Poon-On 1957- *WhoWor 91*
Ng, Eugene Kwan Sang 1953- *WhoSSW 91*
Ng, Hak-Kim 1952- *WhoWor 91*
Ng, James C. 1943- *St&PR 91*
Ng, Kok Koon 1948- *IntWWM 90*
Ng, Lawrence Ming-Loy 1940- *WhoWor 91*
Ng, Michael Lee 1957- *WhoE 91*
Ng, Peter Joseph 1949- *WhoEmL 91*
Ng, Yew-Kwang 1942- *WhoWor 91*
Ngai, Shih Hsun 1920- *WhoAm 90*

Ngai, Yin Leung Stephen 1949- *WhoWor 91*
Ngandu, Mudiayi Sylvain 1948- *WhoE 91*
Ngcobo, Lauretta 1931- *FemiCLE*
Ngei, Paul 1923- *WhoWor 91*
Ngo, Brian Trung 1947- *WhoE 91*
Ngo, Khai Doan The 1957- *WhoSSW 91*
Ngor, Haing S. *BioIn 16*
Ngqika 1779?-1829 *BioIn 16*
Ngugi wa Thiong'o 1938- *MajTwCW, WorAlBi*
Ngugi, James T *MajTwCW*
Ngugi, Wa Thiong'o 1938- *WhoWor 91*
Nguyen Co Thach *WhoWor 91*
Nguyen Huu Tho 1910- *WhoWor 91*
Nguyen Quyet *WhoWor 91*
Nguyen Tat Thanh 1890-1969 *BioIn 16*
Nguyen Thi Dinh *WhoWor 91*
Nguyen Van Linh 1915- *WhoWor 91*
Nguyen, Ann Cac Khue *WhoAmW 91, WhoWor 91*
Nguyen, Binh P. 1941- *WhoSSW 91*
Nguyen, Charles Cuong 1956- *WhoEmL 91, WhoWor 91*
Nguyen, Cuong Thuc *BiDrAPA 89*
Nguyen, Duc Qui 1942- *BiDrAPA 89*
Nguyen, Duong Huu *BiDrAPA 89*
Nguyen, Dustin *BioIn 16*
Nguyen, Duyen Ngoc 1927- *BiDrAPA 89*
Nguyen, Dzung *BiDrAPA 89*
Nguyen, Han Tran *BiDrAPA 89*
Nguyen, Huy Han *BioIn 16*
Nguyen, Kim Loan Thi 1953- *WhoE 91*
Nguyen, Kinh Van *BiDrAPA 89*
Nguyen, Long 1958- *WhoAmA 91*
Nguyen, Mary Xinh *BioIn 16*
Nguyen, Nam Ngoc 1930- *WhoE 91*
Nguyen, Nga Anh *BiDrAPA 89*
Nguyen, Nguyen Nhu *BiDrAPA 89*
Nguyen, Nhien Duc 1947- *BiDrAPA 89, WhoE 91*
Nguyen, Paul Dung Quoc 1943- *WhoWor 91*
Nguyen, Phong 1946- *IntWWM 90*
Nguyen, Phung Duc 1949- *BiDrAPA 89*
Nguyen, Quynh Ngoc 1940- *BiDrAPA 89*
Nguyen, Son Van 1956- *WhoWor 91*
Nguyen, Son Vi *BiDrAPA 89*
Nguyen, Tai Quyen 1944- *WhoSSW 91*
Nguyen, Tao Van 1950- *BiDrAPA 89*
Nguyen, Thanh Duc 1941- *WhoSSW 91*
Nguyen, Thoa *BioIn 16*
Nguyen, Tuong Trieu 1948- *BiDrAPA 89*
Nguyen, Viet Tan 1928- *WhoWor 91*
Nguyen, Vong Hy 1932- *BiDrAPA 89*
Nguyen, Vuong Duc *BiDrAPA 89*
Nguyen, Xuan-Ba Thi 1959- *WhoAmW 91*
Nguyen-Dinh, Thanh 1950- *WhoE 91*
Nguyen-Trong, Huang 1936- *WhoWor 91*
Nguz a Karl-i-Bond 1938- *WhoWor 91*
Nhu, Nguyen To 1948- *WhoWor 91*
Ni, Yangchou Michael 1949- *WhoE 91*
Ni, Zhengjian 1930- *WhoWor 91*
Ni Bhraonian, Eithne *BioIn 16*
Ni Bhrolchain, Maire 1948- *WhoWor 91*
Ni Chuilleanain, Eilean 1942- *FemiCLE*
Niachile Pokaraga, Boki Raja *BioIn 16*
Niarchos, Stavros S. 1909- *WorAlBi*
Niarhos, Gus 1920- *Ballpl 90*
Nias, Anthony Hugh Wade 1926- *WhoWor 91*
Niati, Houria 1948- *BiDWomA*
Niatum, Duane 1938- *WhoWrEP 89*
Niazi, Saifullah K 1948- *BiDrAPA 89*
Nibbi, Filippo 1935- *WhoWor 91*
Niblack, Mason Jenks 1857-1926 *AmLegL*
Niblett, Gary 1943- *BioIn 16*
Niblett, Gary Lawrence 1943- *WhoAmA 91*
Nibley, Robert Ricks 1913- *WhoAm 90*
Niblo, Grady, Jr. 1922- *BiDrAPA 89*
Niblo, William 1790-1878 *OxCPMus*
Niblock, Phill 1933- *WhoAmA 91*
Niblock, W. Robert 1928- *St&PR 91*
Niblock, Walter Raymond 1927- *WhoAm 90*
Nibungco, Darfrente Tuason, Jr. 1951- *WhoE 91*
Nic Leodhas, Sorche *AuBYP 90*
Nica, Grigore 1936- *IntWWM 90*
Nicaagat *WhNaAH*
Nicandros, Constantine Stavros 1933- *St&PR 91, WhoAm 90*
Nicastri, Monica 1958- *St&PR 91*
Nicastro, Francis Efisio 1942- *WhoAm 90*
Nicastro, Lawrence William 1953- *WhoE 91*
Niccolai, Giulia 1934- *EncCoWW*
Niccolini, Dianora 1936- *WhoAmW 91, WhoE 91, WhoWor 91*
Niccolini, Julian *BioIn 16*
Niccolini, Robert 1941- *BiDrAPA 89*
Niccolo Dell'Arca 1435?-1494 *IntDcAA 90*
Niccum, Leonard Maines 1928- *St&PR 91*
Niccum, Ronald J. 1932- *St&PR 91*
Nice, Carter 1940- *IntWWM 90, WhoAm 90*
Nice, Charles Monroe, Jr. 1919- *WhoAm 90*
Nice, Don 1932- *WhoAmA 91*
Nice, Durward Gale, Jr. 1939- *WhoWor 91*
Nice, Margaret Morse 1883-1974 *WomFie [port]*
Niceley, Harvey Tarver, Jr. 1935- *WhoSSW 91*
Nicely, C.M. 1911- *St&PR 91*
Nicely, James Richard 1940- *WhoSSW 91*
Nicely, Marian Rose 1933- *WhoWrEP 89*
Nicely, Patricia *BioIn 16*
Nicely, Patricia *NewYTBS 90 [port]*
Nicely, Roy Edward 1927- *St&PR 91*
Nicely, William Abbott 1930- *St&PR 91*
Nicewander, Dan Leon 1941- *WhoAm 90*
Nicewonger, John D. 1943- *WhoSSW 91*
Nichinson, Bradley B *BiDrAPA 89*
Nichiren 1222-1282 *EncJap*
Nicho, Raul A. 1954- *St&PR 91*
Nichol, Betsy *ODwPR 91*
Nichol, Fred Joseph 1912- *WhoAm 90*
Nichol, Henry Ferris 1911- *WhoAm 90*
Nichol, James W 1940- *OxCCanT*
Nichol, Norman J. 1944- *WhoAm 90*
Nichol, Victor E., Jr. 1946- *St&PR 91*
Nichol, William H. 1951- *St&PR 91*
Nicholas Brothers *DrBlPA 90*
Nicholas II, Emperor of Russia 1868-1918 *BioIn 16*
Nicholas of Cusa 1401-1464 *WorAlBi*
Nicholas, Albert 1900-1973 *BioIn 16*
Nicholas, Albert O. 1931- *St&PR 91*
Nicholas, Andrew James, Jr. 1949- *WhoE 91*
Nicholas, Arthur S. 1930- *St&PR 91*
Nicholas, Arthur Soterios 1930- *WhoAm 90*
Nicholas, Bernie 1961- *WorAlBi*
Nicholas, Calvin *BioIn 16*
Nicholas, Cecile Teresa 1958- *WhoAmW 91*
Nicholas, Charles Raymond 1931- *St&PR 91*
Nicholas, Christopher Dale 1952- *WhoSSW 91*
Nicholas, Cindy 1957- *WhoAmW 91*
Nicholas, Colombe *BioIn 16*
Nicholas, Cyndi Bowers 1960- *ODwPR 91*
Nicholas, Denise 1944- *DrBlPA 90*
Nicholas, Dimitri 1914- *St&PR 91*
Nicholas, Donald Y. 1915- *St&PR 91*
Nicholas, Donna Lee 1938- *WhoAmA 91, WhoE 91*
Nicholas, H.D. 1947- *St&PR 91*
Nicholas, James 1957- *IntWWM 90*
Nicholas, James A. 1921- *WhoWor 91*
Nicholas, James R 1929- *BiDrAPA 89*
Nicholas, James William 1954- *BiDrAPA 89*
Nicholas, Lawrence Bruce 1945- *WhoSSW 91, WhoWor 91*
Nicholas, Louis Thurston 1910- *IntWWM 90*
Nicholas, Michael *WhoWrEP 89*
Nicholas, Michael Bernard 1938- *IntWWM 90*
Nicholas, Michael Lee *BiDrAPA 89*
Nicholas, Michael Patrick 1947- *St&PR 91*
Nicholas, Nicholas J., Jr. *BioIn 16*
Nicholas, Nicholas J., Jr. 1939- *St&PR 91*
Nicholas, Nicholas John, Jr. 1939- *WhoAm 90, WhoE 91*
Nicholas, Nickie Lee 1938- *WhoAmW 91*
Nicholas, Ralph Wallace 1934- *WhoAm 90*
Nicholas, Richard A. 1938- *St&PR 91*
Nicholas, Robert Bates 1929- *St&PR 91*
Nicholas, Robert Carter 1728-1780 *EncCRAm*
Nicholas, Robert Jon 1942- *WhoWor 91*
Nicholas, Samuel John, Jr. 1937- *WhoWor 91*
Nicholas, Tammie Lewis 1961- *WhoSSW 91*
Nicholas, Thomas Andrew 1934- *WhoAm 90, WhoAmA 91*
Nicholas, Thomas Peter 1948- *WhoAm 90*
Nicholas, William Richard 1934- *WhoAm 90*
Nicholi, Armand Mayo, Jr. *BiDrAPA 89*
Nicholl, Nobes Finsel, Jr. 1936- *WhoE 91*
Nicholl, Ramon Victor 1931- *St&PR 91*
Nicholls, Agnes 1877-1959 *PenDiMP*
Nicholls, David Roy 1955- *IntWWM 90*
Nicholls, Douglas 1906-1988 *AnObit 1988*
Nicholls, Elizabeth *BiDEWW*
Nicholls, Francis T. 1834-1912 *BioIn 16*
Nicholls, Grant Telfer 1946- *WhoAm 90*
Nicholls, Horatio 1888-1964 *OxCPMus*
Nicholls, Joan Wentzel 1929- *BiDrAPA 89*
Nicholls, Judith 1941- *SmATA 61 [port]*
Nicholls, Julia Mary 1952- *WhoWor 91*
Nicholls, Kathryn Lynn 1947- *WhoE 91*
Nicholls, Ralph William 1926- *WhoAm 90*
Nicholls, Richard Aurelius 1941- *WhoSSW 91, WhoWor 91*
Nicholls, Richard Ernest 1949- *WhoE 91*
Nicholls, Richard H. 1938- *WhoAm 90*
Nicholls, S. Scott, Jr. 1934- *St&PR 91*
Nicholls, Sandra Anne 1944- *WhoAmW 91*
Nicholls, Sidney Oliver 1947- *St&PR 91*
Nicholls, Simon 1882-1911 *Ballpl 90*
Nicholls, Simon 1951- *IntWWM 90*
Nichols, Alan Richard 1949- *WhoSSW 91*
Nichols, Albert L. 1951- *WhoE 91*
Nichols, Allie Jo 1932- *WhoAmW 91*
Nichols, Andrew L. 1936- *St&PR 91*
Nichols, Andrew Livingston 1936- *WhoAm 90*
Nichols, Anne 1891?-1966 *BioIn 16, NotWoAT*
Nichols, Barbara Ann 1947- *WhoAmW 91*
Nichols, Basil Bernard 1927- *WhoSSW 91*
Nichols, Beverley 1898-1983 *DcNaB 1981, TwCCr&M 91*
Nichols, Bill 1918-1988 *BioIn 16*
Nichols, Bridget *BiDEWW*
Nichols, Bruce W. 1930-1990 *BioIn 16, WhoAm 90, WhoE 91*
Nichols, C. Walter, III 1937- *WhoE 91*
Nichols, Caleb Leroy 1947- *WhoE 91, WhoEmL 91*
Nichols, Carl W. 1923- *St&PR 91*
Nichols, Carl Wheeler 1923- *WhoAm 90*
Nichols, Carol Jean 1954- *WhoEmL 91*
Nichols, Charles G *BiDrAPA 89*
Nichols, Charles P. *St&PR 91*
Nichols, Charles Warren 1939- *WhoAm 90*
Nichols, Chet 1897-1982 *Ballpl 90*
Nichols, Chet 1931- *Ballpl 90*
Nichols, Christopher Owen 1939- *WhoE 91*
Nichols, Claude R, Jr. 1921- *BiDrAPA 89*
Nichols, Daniel A. 1940- *St&PR 91*
Nichols, Daniel Lanham 1951- *WhoSSW 91*
Nichols, David 1947- *ODwPR 91*
Nichols, David Arthur 1917- *WhoAm 90, WhoE 91, WhoWor 91*
Nichols, David H. 1828- *AmLegL*
Nichols, David Harry 1925 *WhoAm 90*
Nichols, David Lee 1934- *WhoAm 90*
Nichols, David Monroe *BiDrAPA 89*
Nichols, David R. 1958- *St&PR 91*
Nichols, Dianna Rae 1945- *WhoWor 91*
Nichols, Donald Arthur 1940- *WhoAm 90*
Nichols, Donald Clyde 1939- *St&PR 91*
Nichols, Donald Edward 1922-1987 *WhoAmA 91N*
Nichols, Donald Richardson 1911- *WhoAm 90*
Nichols, Edgar Walker 1923- *St&PR 91*
Nichols, Edie Diane 1939- *WhoAmW 91*
Nichols, Edward Edson 1929- *WhoAmA 91*
Nichols, Elaine C. 1947- *WhoAmW 91*
Nichols, Eleanor Cary 1903-1988 *WhoAmA 91N*
Nichols, Elizabeth Christie 1963- *WhoAmW 91*
Nichols, Elizabeth Grace 1943- *WhoAm 90*
Nichols, Elizabeth L. 1922- *WhoWrEP 89*
Nichols, Eugene Douglas 1923- *WhoAm 90*
Nichols, Fenwick Tattnall, III 1950- *WhoSSW 91*
Nichols, Francis N, II *WhoAmA 91*
Nichols, Frank J. 1929- *St&PR 91*
Nichols, Franklin Allen 1918- *WhoAm 90*
Nichols, Frederick Doveton 1911- *WhoAm 90*
Nichols, Frederick Ralph, Jr. 1936- *St&PR 91*
Nichols, Gene 1933- *ODwPR 91*
Nichols, George Calloway 1943- *WhoE 91*
Nichols, George L 1937- *BiDrAPA 89*
Nichols, George Quincy 1929- *St&PR 91*
Nichols, Gerald Lee 1935- *St&PR 91*
Nichols, Gerard Kendric 1941- *St&PR 91*
Nichols, Grace 1950- *FemiCLE*
Nichols, Guy W. 1925- *St&PR 91, WhoAm 90*
Nichols, H. Gilman 1927- *St&PR 91*
Nichols, Hans Paul Keith 1953- *WhoE 91*
Nichols, Harold G 1930- *BiDrAPA 89*
Nichols, Harold Neil 1937- *WhoAm 90*
Nichols, Henry Eliot 1924- *WhoAm 90*
Nichols, Henry Louis 1916- *WhoAm 90*
Nichols, Hobart 1869-1962 *WhoAmA 91N*
Nichols, Horace Elmo 1912- *WhoAm 90*
Nichols, Irby Coghill, Jr. 1926- *WhoAm 90*
Nichols, Irene Delores 1938- *WhoAmW 91*
Nichols, J. Hugh 1930- *WhoSSW 91*
Nichols, J. Larry 1942- *St&PR 91, WhoSSW 91*
Nichols, Jack Britt 1936- *WhoSSW 91*
Nichols, James J 1931- *BiDrAPA 89*
Nichols, James Phillip 1944- *WhoE 91, WhoWor 91*
Nichols, James Richard 1923- *WhoAm 90*
Nichols, James Richard 1938- *WhoWrEP 89*
Nichols, James Robbs 1926- *WhoAm 90*
Nichols, James William 1928- *WhoAmA 91*
Nichols, John 1940- *WorAu 1980 [port]*
Nichols, John Aben 1939- *WhoE 91*
Nichols, John D. 1930- *WhoAm 90*
Nichols, John David 1947- *WhoSSW 91*
Nichols, John David 1948- *WhoE 91*
Nichols, John Doane 1930- *St&PR 91*
Nichols, John H., Jr. 1928- *St&PR 91*
Nichols, John Treadwell 1940- *BioIn 16*
Nichols, John W. 1914- *St&PR 91*
Nichols, Joseph 1917- *St&PR 91*
Nichols, Joseph A. 1940- *St&PR 91*
Nichols, Kenneth Charles 1923- *St&PR 91, WhoAm 90*
Nichols, Kenneth David 1907- *WhoAm 90*
Nichols, Kid 1869-1953 *Ballpl 90 [port]*
Nichols, Kyra *BioIn 16*
Nichols, Kyra 1959- *WhoAm 90, WhoE 91*
Nichols, Leigh *MajTwCW*
Nichols, Leo Thomas 1935- *St&PR 91*
Nichols, Mack G. 1938- *St&PR 91*
Nichols, Maria *PenDiDA 89*
Nichols, Marian Theresa 1947- *WhoSSW 91*
Nichols, Martha Jean 1941- *WhoAmW 91*
Nichols, Mary 1810-1884 *FemiCLE*
Nichols, Mary Ivancevic 1951- *WhoAmW 91*
Nichols, Mary Perot 1926- *WhoE 91*
Nichols, Maxine McClendon *WhoAmA 91*
Nichols, Michael Cooper 1952- *St&PR 91*
Nichols, Michael Frederick 1948- *WhoEmL 91*
Nichols, Michael K. 1953- *BioIn 16*
Nichols, Mike *BioIn 16*
Nichols, Mike 1931- *ConTFT 8 [port], WhoAm 90, WorAlBi*
Nichols, Nancy 1921- *BiDrAPA 89*
Nichols, Nancy 1939- *WhoAmW 91*
Nichols, Nancy Grayson 1958- *BiDrAPA 89*
Nichols, Nell B. *AuBYP 90*
Nichols, Nichelle *BioIn 16*
Nichols, Nichelle 1936- *ConTFT 8, DrBlPA 90*
Nichols, Owen Harvey 1926- *WhoAm 90*
Nichols, Pamela Amber 1956- *WhoWrEP 89*
Nichols, Paul *BioIn 16, NewYTBS 90*
Nichols, Paul 1948- *ODwPR 91*
Nichols, Peter 1927- *BioIn 16, ConAu 33NR, MajTwCW*
Nichols, Peter 1928-1989 *BioIn 16*
Nichols, Philip 1907-1990 *BioIn 16*
Nichols, Philip, Jr. *NewYTBS 90*
Nichols, Ralph Arthur 1919- *WhoAm 90*
Nichols, Raymond Stanley 1946- *WhoE 91*
Nichols, Red *BioIn 16*
Nichols, Red 1905-1965 *OxCPMus, WorAlBi*
Nichols, Reid 1958- *Ballpl 90*
Nichols, Richard Maurice 1905- *St&PR 91, WhoAm 90*
Nichols, Rip Wood 1915- *WhoSSW 91*
Nichols, Robert David 1935- *BiDrAPA 89*
Nichols, Robert Edmund 1925- *WhoAm 90*
Nichols, Robert Lee 1924- *WhoAm 90*
Nichols, Robert Leighton 1926- *WhoAm 90*
Nichols, Robert W. 1934- *St&PR 91*
Nichols, Rod 1964- *Ballpl 90*
Nichols, Rodney Wayson 1937- *WhoAm 90, WhoE 91*
Nichols, Ronald Lee 1941- *WhoAm 90, WhoWor 91*
Nichols, Russell L. *WhoAm 90*
Nichols, Ruth 1948- *AuBYP 90, BioIn 16*
Nichols, Sarah How-Ree 1933- *WhoWrEP 89*
Nichols, Sharon D. 1936- *WhoWrEP 89*
Nichols, Shuford R. 1909- *St&PR 91*
Nichols, Spencer B 1875-1950 *WhoAmA 91N*
Nichols, Stephen Edward 1930- *WhoE 91*
Nichols, Stephen G 1936- *ConAu 31NR*
Nichols, Stephen George 1936- *WhoAm 90*
Nichols, Stephen George, Jr. 1936- *WhoWrEP 89*
Nichols, Stephen Wayne 1955- *WhoEmL 91*
Nichols, Stuart E, Jr. 1936- *BiDrAPA 89*
Nichols, Susan Leslie *BiDrAPA 89*
Nichols, Terri Dawn Morris 1958- *WhoSSW 91*
Nichols, Thomas *WhoSSW 91*
Nichols, Thomas C., Jr. *WhoSSW 91*
Nichols, Verona Schmidt 1942- *WhoAmW 91*
Nichols, Vicki Anne 1949- *WhoAmW 91*
Nichols, Victoria 1944- *ConAu 132*
Nichols, Virginia V. 1928- *WhoAmW 91*
Nichols, Wade Hampton, III 1942- *WhoAm 90*
Nichols, Wade Hampton, Jr. 1915- *WhoAm 90*
Nichols, Wallace Joseph, Jr. 1939- *St&PR 91*
Nichols, Ward H 1930- *WhoAmA 91*

Nichols, Warren De Forrest 1926- *WhoAm 90*
Nichols, Willard R. 1947- *St&PR 91*
Nichols, William Allyn 1942- *WhoAmA 91*
Nichols, William Curtis, Jr. 1929- *WhoAm 90*
Nichols, William Deming 1924- *WhoAm 90*
Nichols, William Ford, Jr. 1934- *WhoAm 90*
Nichols, William H. 1852-1930 *WorAlBi*
Nicholsen, James Therman 1950- *WhoEmL 91, WhoWor 91*
Nicholson, Arthur Raymond 1935- *St&PR 91*
Nicholson, Barbara Robinson *BioIn 16*
Nicholson, Ben 1894-1982 *IntDcAA 90, WhoAmA 91N*
Nicholson, Benjamin Lauder 1894-1982 *DcNaB 1981*
Nicholson, Bill 1914- *Ballpl 90*
Nicholson, Brent Bentley 1954- *WhoEmL 91*
Nicholson, Cathy Ann 1947- *WhoSSW 91*
Nicholson, Charles D. 1952- *WhoE 91*
Nicholson, Charles Henry 1951- *BiDrAPA 89*
Nicholson, Charles Preston 1934- *WhoSSW 91*
Nicholson, Christine 1930- *SpyFic*
Nicholson, Dave 1939- *Ballpl 90*
Nicholson, David 1919- *IntWWM 90*
Nicholson, Douglas Robert 1921- *WhoAm 90*
Nicholson, Edna Elizabeth 1907- *WhoAmW 91, WhoWor 91*
Nicholson, Edwin Farnham 1938- *St&PR 91*
Nicholson, Eliza 1849-1896 *BioIn 16*
Nicholson, Eliza Jane *BioAmW*
Nicholson, Francis 1655-1728 *EncCRAm*
Nicholson, Francis Joseph 1921- *WhoE 91*
Nicholson, Frank *BioIn 16*
Nicholson, Frank Russell, Jr. 1933- *St&PR 91*
Nicholson, Fred 1894-1972 *Ballpl 90*
Nicholson, Freda Hyams 1934- *WhoAm 90, WhoAmW 91, WhoSSW 91*
Nicholson, G. Randy *WhoAm 90*
Nicholson, Gary Dana 1936- *St&PR 91*
Nicholson, Geoff 1953- *ConAu 130*
Nicholson, George Albert, Jr. 1908- *WhoAm 90*
Nicholson, George Thomas Frederick 1949- *IntWWM 90*
Nicholson, Glen Ira 1925- *WhoAm 90*
Nicholson, Homer Kittrell 1922- *WhoSSW 91*
Nicholson, J.F. 1919- *St&PR 91*
Nicholson, Jack *BioIn 16*
Nicholson, Jack 1937- *WhoAm 90, WorAlBi*
Nicholson, James Evans, III 1952- *WhoSSW 91*
Nicholson, James J. 1926- *St&PR 91*
Nicholson, James Lloyd, Jr. 1928- *St&PR 91*
Nicholson, Lani Jeanne 1956- *BiDrAPA 89*
Nicholson, Leland Ross 1924- *WhoAm 90*
Nicholson, Linda Barton 1949- *WhoAmW 91*
Nicholson, Luther Beal 1921- *WhoSSW 91, WhoWor 91*
Nicholson, Marilyn Dietz 1926- *WhoAmW 91, WhoE 91*
Nicholson, Marion Crawford 1917- *WhoWor 91*
Nicholson, Mary *BioIn 16*
Nicholson, Michelle Renee 1960- *WhoAmW 91*
Nicholson, Morris Emmons, Jr. 1916- *WhoAm 90*
Nicholson, Myreen Moore *WhoAmA 91*
Nicholson, Myreen Moore 1940- *WhoAmW 91, WhoWor 91*
Nicholson, Natasha 1945- *WhoAmA 91*
Nicholson, Patrick James 1920- *WhoAm 90*
Nicholson, Paul Douglas 1938- *WhoWor 91*
Nicholson, Paul E. 1947- *St&PR 91*
Nicholson, Paul M. 1949- *St&PR 91*
Nicholson, R. Stephen 1926- *WhoAm 90, WhoWor 91*
Nicholson, Ralph Ward 1907- *IntWWM 90*
Nicholson, Richard Joseph 1932- *WhoAm 90*
Nicholson, Richard S. 1938- *BioIn 16*
Nicholson, Richard Selindh 1938- *WhoAm 90*
Nicholson, Robert Arthur 1923- *WhoAm 90*
Nicholson, Robert Edward, Sr. 1959- *WhoSSW 91*
Nicholson, Robert J. 1939- *St&PR 91*
Nicholson, Robert W. 1943- *ODwPR 91*
Nicholson, Roy S. 1903- *WhoAm 90*
Nicholson, Roy William 1943- *WhoAmA 91*
Nicholson, Shelia Elaine 1963- *WhoAmW 91*
Nicholson, Susan Jane Brown 1942- *WhoWrEP 89*
Nicholson, Sydney 1875-1947 *PenDiMP*
Nicholson, Thomas D 1922- *WhoAmA 91*
Nicholson, Thomas Dominic 1922- *WhoAm 90*
Nicholson, Thomas Laurence 1923- *WhoAm 90*
Nicholson, Thomas N. 1953- *St&PR 91*
Nicholson, Thomas P. 1954- *ODwPR 91*
Nicholson, Will F., Jr. 1929- *St&PR 91*
Nicholson, Will Faust, Jr. 1929- *WhoAm 90*
Nicholson, William 1753-1815 *WorAlBi*
Nicholson, William Edward 1947- *St&PR 91*
Nicholson, Winifred 1893- *BioIn 16*
Nicholson, Winifred 1893-1981 *BiDWomA*
Nichter, Mark S. 1951- *St&PR 91*
Nichtern, Claire Joseph *WhoAm 90*
Nichtern, Edith *BioIn 16*
Nichtern, Sol 1920-1988 *BioIn 16*
Nick, George 1927- *WhoAmA 91*
Nick, Richard J. 1943- *St&PR 91*
Nickalls, Paul C. 1933- *St&PR 91*
Nickard, Gary Laurence 1954- *WhoAmA 91*
Nickel, Albert George 1943- *WhoE 91, WhoWor 91*
Nickel, Charles Lynn 1946- *WhoEmL 91*
Nickel, Dieter Heinz 1936- *St&PR 91*
Nickel, Donald Lloyd 1933- *WhoAm 90*
Nickel, Gerhard 1928- *WhoWor 91*
Nickel, Hans E. 1928- *St&PR 91*
Nickel, Hans Erich 1928- *WhoAm 90*
Nickel, Helmut 1924- *BioIn 16*
Nickel, Herman Wilhelm 1928- *WhoAm 90, WhoWor 91*
Nickel, Horst Wilhelm 1929- *WhoWor 91*
Nickel, Hubertus 1930- *WhoWor 91*
Nickel, Kathryn Louise 1958- *WhoE 91*
Nickel, Kenneth C 1917- *BiDrAPA 89*
Nickel, Robert J. 1918- *St&PR 91*
Nickel, Rosalie Jean 1939- *WhoAmW 91*
Nickel, Susan Earlene 1951- *WhoAmW 91*
Nickell, Bruce *BioIn 16*
Nickell, Grason Templeton 1923- *St&PR 91*
Nickell, Katherine Mary 1960- *WhoAmW 91*
Nickell, Laurel Kay 1943- *St&PR 91*
Nickell, Patton Van Meter 1956- *BiDrAPA 89*
Nickell, Stella *BioIn 16*
Nickels, Carl E., Jr. 1931- *St&PR 91*
Nickels, Harold F. 1931- *St&PR 91*
Nickels, Mark William *BiDrAPA 89*
Nickels, Robert Edward 1943- *WhoSSW 91*
Nickels, William Carl 1920- *St&PR 91*
Nickelson, Donald Eugene 1932- *St&PR 91, WhoAm 90, WhoE 91*
Nickelson, James Edward 1932- *St&PR 91*
Nickelson, Kim Rene 1956- *WhoAmW 91*
Nickens, Herbert Wallace 1947- *BiDrAPA 89*
Nickerson, Albert Lindsay 1911- *WhoAm 90*
Nickerson, Arthur H *BiDrAPA 89*
Nickerson, Bob *BioIn 16*
Nickerson, Camille Lucie 1888-1982 *DcAfAmP*
Nickerson, Clarke Casey 1951- *St&PR 91*
Nickerson, David Charles 1959- *St&PR 91*
Nickerson, Eileen Tressler 1927- *WhoAm 90*
Nickerson, Eugene H. 1918- *WhoAm 90*
Nickerson, Gary Thomas 1943- *WhoAm 90*
Nickerson, George Fuller 1932- *WhoE 91*
Nickerson, Greg *ODwPR 91*
Nickerson, Guy Robert 1956- *St&PR 91*
Nickerson, James Arnold 1931- *St&PR 91*
Nickerson, James Findley 1910- *WhoAm 90*
Nickerson, Jan *AuBYP 90*
Nickerson, Jerry Edgar Alan 1936- *WhoAm 90*
Nickerson, John Henry 1939- *WhoAmA 91*
Nickerson, John Mitchell 1937- *WhoAm 90, WhoWor 91*
Nickerson, Joseph 1914-1990 *ConAu 131*
Nickerson, Leroy C. 1950- *St&PR 91*
Nickerson, Lucille M. 1947- *St&PR 91*
Nickerson, Raymond Stephen 1931- *St&PR 91*
Nickerson, Ruth 1905- *WhoAm 90, WhoAmA 91*
Nickerson, Sheila B. 1942- *WhoWrEP 89*
Nickerson, Susan Adams 1948- *WhoWor 91*
Nickerson, Terry Muir 1939- *St&PR 91, WhoAm 90*
Nickey, Karyl Kristine 1950- *WhoSSW 91*
Nickford, Juan 1925- *WhoAm 90, WhoAmA 91*
Nickinson, John 1808-1864 *OxCCanT*
Nickisch, Willard Wayne 1939- *WhoWor 91*
Nickl, Barbara 1939- *BioIn 16*
Nicklas, James B. 1949- *St&PR 91*
Nicklas, Robert Bruce 1932- *WhoAm 90*
Nicklaus, Carol *SmATA 62*
Nicklaus, Frederick 1936- *WhoWrEP 89*
Nicklaus, Jack *BioIn 16*
Nicklaus, Jack 1940- *WorAlBi*
Nickle, Dennis Edwin 1936- *WhoSSW 91, WhoWor 91*
Nickle, Robert W 1919-1980 *WhoAmA 91N*
Nickles, Connie Sue 1960- *WhoAmW 91*
Nickles, Don 1948- *WhoAm 90, WhoSSW 91, WhoWor 91*
Nickles, Elizabeth *BioIn 16*
Nickles, Liz *BioIn 16*
Nickles-Murray, Elizabeth 1948- *WhoAm 90, WhoAmW 91*
Nickless, Daniel J. 1955- *St&PR 91*
Nicklin, Emily 1953- *WhoEmL 91*
Nicklin, George L. *BiDrAPA 89*
Nicklin, George Leslie, Jr. 1925- *WhoAm 90*
Nickman, Steven Louis 1939- *BiDrAPA 89, WhoE 91*
Nickodem, Robert J. 1929- *St&PR 91*
Nickodemus, Timothy David 1958- *WhoEmL 91*
Nickolas, George Tom 1933- *WhoWrEP 89*
Nickolaus, Nicholas 1925- *St&PR 91*
Nickolich, Barbara Ellen 1937- *WhoAmW 91*
Nickolls, Charles L *BiDrAPA 89*
Nickoloff, John Elia 1925- *St&PR 91*
Nickoloff, Peter Joseph 1965- *WhoE 91*
Nickoloff, Steven Ernst 1958- *BiDrAPA 89*
Nickolova, Maria K 1951- *BiDrAPA 89*
Nickols, Louise M. 1935- *WhoAmW 91*
Nickon, Alex 1927- *WhoAm 90*
Nickow, Martin Allen 1928- *St&PR 91*
Nicks, Carla Denise *BioIn 16*
Nicks, Larry 1942- *St&PR 91*
Nicks, Stevie 1948- *EncPR&S 89, WhoAm 90*
Nickson, Graham G 1946- *WhoAmA 91*
Nickson, J. Richard 1917- *ConAu 129*
Nickson, M. Scott, Jr. 1934- *St&PR 91*
Nickson, Richard 1917- *WhoWrEP 89*
Nickson, Sheila Joan 1936- *WhoAm 90*
Nickum, Mary Josephine 1945- *WhoAmW 91*
Nico *BioIn 16*
Nico 1944-1988 *AnObit 1988*
Nicodemus, Chester Roland 1901- *WhoAmA 91*
Nicodemus, William Byron 1943- *WhoWor 91*
Nicol, Anne Francis 1940 *BiDrAPA 89*
Nicol, Betty Humphrey 1917- *EncO&P 3, EncPaPR 91*
Nicol, David John 1945- *St&PR 91*
Nicol, Dominik 1930- *WhoE 91, WhoWor 91*
Nicol, Eric 1919- *OxCCanT*
Nicol, J Fraser *EncO&P 3*
Nicol, J. Fraser *EncPaPR 91*
Nicol, James William 1923- *St&PR 91*
Nicol, Marjorie Carmichael 1926- *WhoAmW 91, WhoE 91, WhoWor 91*
Nicol, Michael Frederick 1951- *WhoSSW 91*
Nicol, William James 1943- *St&PR 91, WhoAm 90*
Nicola da Guardiagrele *PenDiDA 89*
Nicola da Urbino *PenDiDA 89*
Nicola, Ben A. 1945- *St&PR 91*
Nicola, Robert 1924- *St&PR 91*
Nicoladis, Michael Frank 1960- *WhoSSW 91*
Nicolaevsky, Boris I. 1887-1966 *BioIn 16*
Nicolai, Christoph Friedrich 1733-1811 *EncO&P 3*
Nicolai, Claudio 1929- *IntWWM 90*
Nicolai, Frank Al 1941- *St&PR 91*
Nicolai, Friedrich 1733-1811 *DcLB 97 [port]*
Nicolai, Judithe 1945- *WhoAmW 91, WhoWor 91*
Nicolai, Otto 1810-1849 *PenDiMP A*
Nicolai, Robert Louis 1940- *St&PR 91, WhoAm 90*
Nicolaides, John Dudley 1923- *WhoAm 90*
Nicolaides, Paris L. 1929- *St&PR 91*
Nicolaidis, Nicholas Anthony C. 1943- *St&PR 91*
Nicolais, Michael A. 1925- *St&PR 91*
Nicolarsen, David Jack 1948- *St&PR 91*
Nicolas *AuBYP 90*
Nicolas of Verdun *PenDiDA 89*
Nicolas, F. R. E. *TwCCr&M 91*
Nicolas, Georges Charles 1932- *WhoWor 91*
Nicolas, Georges Spiridon 1952- *WhoWor 91*
Nicolatos, Dia Helen 1957- *WhoE 91*
Nicolau, Valeriano Weyler 1839-1930 *BioIn 16*
Nicolay, Harry Joseph 1935- *WhoAm 90*
Nicolay, Helen 1866- *AuBYP 90*
Nicolaysen, Peter Smith 1934- *WhoAm 90*
Nicolazzo, Richard E. 1945- *ODwPR 91*
Nicole *WomWR*
Nicole, Christopher *TwCCr&M 91*
Nicole, Christopher Robin 1930- *SpyFic*
Nicolelis, Nancy *ODwPR 91*
Nicolescu, Ada *BiDrAPA 89*
Nicolescu, Marianna 1948- *IntWWM 90*
Nicolet, Aurele 1926- *IntWWM 90, PenDiMP*
Nicolet, Jean 1598-1642 *EncCRAm, WhNaAH, WorAlBi*
Nicolette, Thomas Albert 1950- *St&PR 91*
Nicoletti, Anthony 1928- *St&PR 91*
Nicoletti, Francois-Xavier 1936- *WhoWor 91*
Nicoletti, Myra Diane 1950- *WhoAmW 91*
Nicolini 1673?-1732 *PenDiMP*
Nicolini, Ernest 1834-1898 *PenDiMP*
Nicolini, Giuseppe *BioIn 16*
Nicolis, Gregoire 1939- *WhoWor 91*
Nicolitz, Ernst 1947- *WhoAm 90*
Nicoll, Anne Louise 1962- *WhoAmW 91*
Nicoll, Charles Samuel 1937- *WhoAm 90*
Nicoll, David J.H. 1937- *St&PR 91*
Nicoll, Maurice 1884-1953 *EncO&P 3*
Nicoll, Stephen G. 1931- *WhoAm 90*
Nicoll, Wallace 1931- *ODwPR 91*
Nicolle, Lori Anne 1961- *WhoAmW 91*
Nicollet de Bellesborne, Jean 1598?-1642 *WhNaAH*
Nicolli, Renaldo R. 1923- *St&PR 91*
Nicolopulos, Thania 1924- *WhoWor 91*
Nicolosi, Anthony Salvatore 1930- *WhoE 91*
Nicolosi, Dorothy Emily 1931- *WhoAmW 91, WhoE 91*
Nicolosi, Joseph 1893-1961 *WhoAmA 91N*
Nicolson, Charles White 1931- *St&PR 91, WhoAm 90*
Nicolson, Harold 1886-1968 *DcLB 100 [port]*
Nicolson, Harold George 1886-1968 *BioIn 16*
Nicolson, Robina 1940- *IntWWM 90*
Nicosia, Roberto F. 1952- *WhoE 91*
Nicosia, Steve 1955- *Ballpl 90*
Nicotra, Joseph Charles 1931- *WhoAmA 91*
Nicpon, Norbert F. 1943- *St&PR 91*
Niculescu, Stefan 1927- *IntWWM 90*
Niculoso, Francisco *PenDiDA 89*
Nicusanti, Albert R., Jr. *St&PR 91*
Nicz-Borowiak, Maria 1896-1944 *BiDWomA*
Nida, Eugene Albert 1914- *WhoAm 90*
Nida, Jane Bolster 1918- *WhoAm 90*
Nida, R. Jack 1930- *WhoSSW 91*
Nidal, Abu *BioIn 16*
Nidecker, John E. 1913-1988 *BioIn 16*
Nidetch, Jean *BioIn 16*
Nidetch, Jean 1923- *WorAlBi*
Nidhiry, Thresiamma S *BiDrAPA 89*
Nidiffer, Jana 1957- *WhoAmW 91*
Nie Weiping *BioIn 16*
Nie, Louis W 1916- *BiDrAPA 89*
Nie, Norman H. 1943- *WhoWrEP 89*
Nie, Zenon S. 1950- *St&PR 91*
Nie, Zenon Stanley 1950- *WhoEmL 91*
Niebel, Robert Jack 1938- *St&PR 91*
Niebla, Eduardo *NewAgMG*
Niebla, Jesus Fernando *WhoHisp 91*
Nieboer, James M. 1944- *St&PR 91*
Nieboer, W. 1937- *St&PR 91*
Niebuhr, Reinhold 1892-1971 *BioIn 16, WorAlBi, WrPh P*
Niebuhr, Richard Reinhold 1926- *WhoAm 90*
Niebur, Stanley Louis 1926- *St&PR 91*
Nieburg, Herbert Alan 1946- *WhoE 91*
Niece, Julie Cole 1945- *WhoAmW 91*
Nied, Harriet Therese 1923- *WhoAmW 91*
Nied, Renee Bundi 1962- *WhoE 91*
Nied, Thomas H. 1942- *WhoAm 90*
Niedecken, George Mann *PenDiDA 89*
Niedecker, Lorine 1903-1970 *WorAu 1980*
Niedenfuer, Tom 1959- *Ballpl 90*
Nieder, Joseph M 1941- *BiDrAPA 89*
Niederer, Carl 1927- *WhoAmA 91*
Niederer, Edward, Jr. 1912- *St&PR 91*
Niederer, Roberto 1928- *PenDiDA 89*
Niedergeses, James D. 1917- *WhoSSW 91*
Niederhauser, Tom D. 1945- *St&PR 91*
Niederhofer, Laurence John 1932- *St&PR 91, WhoAm 90*
Niederhut, William Ernest 1957- *BiDrAPA 89*
Niederjohn, Russell James 1944- *WhoAm 90*

Niederlaender, Hubert 1921- *WhoWor 91*
Niederland, William G 1904- *BiDrAPA 89*
Niederland, William Guglielmo 1904- *WhoAm 90*
Niederlehner, Leonard 1914- *WhoAm 90*
Niederman, James Corson 1924- *WhoAm 90*
Niedermayer, Johann Josef *PenDiDA 89*
Niedermayer, Mathias *PenDiDA 89*
Niedermayer, Virginie Soubiran 1961- *WhoE 91*
Niedermeier, Mary B. 1914- *WhoAmW 91*
Niedermeier, Robert P. 1918-1989 *BioIn 16*
Niedermeyer, Gregory Edward 1954- *St&PR 91*
Niedermeyer, Terrence Patrick 1956- *St&PR 91*
Niederquell, Michael O. *ODwPR 91*
Niederweelen, Marianne *EncCoWW*
Nieding, Seth Frank 1948- *WhoEmL 91*
Niedorf, Saul 1931- *BiDrAPA 89*
Niedra, Aida 1899-1972 *EncCoWW*
Niedra, Ida *EncCoWW*
Niedzialek, Terry *BioIn 16*
Niedziela, Ronald L. 1940- *St&PR 91*
Niedzielski, Henri Zygmunt 1931- *WhoAm 90*
Niedzielski, James Peter 1939- *WhoWor 91*
Niedzielski, Margaret Mary 1961- *WhoAmW 91*
Niedzwiecki, Alex *BiDrAPA 89*
Niefeld, Jaye Sutter 1924- *WhoAm 90*
Niefeld, Samuel M. *BioIn 16*
Nieforth, Karl Allen 1936- *WhoAm 90*
Niegelsky, Leon S. 1957- *St&PR 91*
Niegsch, William Charles 1952- *St&PR 91*
Niehans, Michael 1952- *BiDrAPA 89*
Niehaus, Chloe Mae 1929- *WhoAmW 91*
Niehaus, Lorene Mathewson 1959- *WhoAmW 91*
Niehaus, Nancy Ruth 1945- *WhoAmW 91*
Niehaus, Robert Henry 1955- *WhoE 91*
Niehaus, Robert James 1930- *WhoAm 90*
Niehenke, John Joseph 1944- *WhoAm 90*
Niehm, Bernard Frank 1923- *WhoAm 90*
Niehoff, Bert 1884-1974 *Ballpl 90*
Niehoff, K. Richard B. 1943- *WhoAm 90*
Niehoff, Marilee Schultz *WhoWrEP 89*
Niehouse, Oliver Leslie 1920- *WhoWor 91*
Niehuis, Charles C. *AuBYP 90*
Niekamp, Albert 1930- *WhoWor 91*
Niekamp, Ronald Edward 1942- *St&PR 91*
Niekro, Joe 1944- *Ballpl 90 [port], BioIn 16*
Niekro, Phil *BioIn 16*
Niekro, Phil 1939- *Ballpl 90 [port]*
Nield, Darrell Garth 1959- *WhoSSW 91*
Nield, David A. 1938- *St&PR 91*
Nield, Edward Crompton 1938- *St&PR 91*
Nields, Morgan Wesson 1946- *WhoAm 90*
Nielsen, Aksel 1932- *WhoWor 91*
Nielsen, Aldon Dale 1922- *WhoAm 90*
Nielsen, Alvin Herborg 1910- *WhoAm 90*
Nielsen, Andreas 1899-1957 *BioIn 16*
Nielsen, Arthur C. 1897- *WorAlBi*
Nielsen, Arthur C 1945- *BiDrAPA 89*
Nielsen, Arthur C., Jr. 1919- *St&PR 91*
Nielsen, Arthur R. 1942- *St&PR 91*
Nielsen, Bent Christoffer 1923- *IntWWM 90*
Nielsen, Bernard Louis 1937- *St&PR 91*
Nielsen, Brian 1959- *WhoEmL 91*
Nielsen, Brigitte *BioIn 16*
Nielsen, Bruce John 1948- *St&PR 91*
Nielsen, Cantril 1937- *BiDrAPA 89*
Nielsen, Carl 1865-1931 *PenDiMP A*
Nielsen, Carl Fredegod 1918- *St&PR 91*
Nielsen, Charles Lester, Jr. 1938- *St&PR 91*
Nielsen, Christian Tage 1941- *WhoE 91*
Nielsen, David Christopher 1955- *WhoEmL 91*
Nielsen, Dennis Ernest 1937- *St&PR 91*
Nielsen, Diane Tappen 1947- *WhoEmL 91, WhoWor 91*
Nielsen, Douglas E. 1936- *St&PR 91*
Nielsen, Edgar W. 1923- *St&PR 91*
Nielsen, Einer *EncO&P 3, EncPaPR 91*
Nielsen, Emiel Theodore, Jr. 1914- *WhoAm 90*
Nielsen, Eric C. 1920- *St&PR 91*
Nielsen, Gail Ann 1947- *WhoAmW 91*
Nielsen, George Lee 1937- *WhoAm 90*
Nielsen, Hans-Jorgen 1941- *DcScanL*
Nielsen, Harald Christian 1930- *WhoAm 90*
Nielsen, Helen 1918- *TwCCr&M 91*
Nielsen, Inger 1946- *IntWWM 90*
Nielsen, John Phillip 1911-1989 *BioIn 16*
Nielsen, Jorgen 1935- *WhoWor 91*
Nielsen, Jorn 1947- *WhoWor 91*
Nielsen, June M. 1940- *St&PR 91*
Nielsen, Lauge 1947- *WhoWor 91*
Nielsen, Laura Christine 1960- *WhoAmW 91*
Nielsen, Lawrence Ernie 1917- *WhoAm 90*
Nielsen, Les H. 1937- *St&PR 91*
Nielsen, Leslie *BioIn 16*
Nielsen, Leslie 1926- *WhoAm 90*
Nielsen, Lowell Wendell 1910-1988 *BioIn 16*
Nielsen, Mark Joseph 1959- *WhoEmL 91*
Nielsen, Martin Nicolai 1943- *BiDrAPA 89*
Nielsen, Nancy 1950- *ODwPR 91*
Nielsen, Niels Christian, Jr. 1921- *WhoAm 90*
Nielsen, Nina I M 1940- *WhoAmA 91*
Nielsen, Peter L *BiDrAPA 89*
Nielsen, Philip R. 1929- *St&PR 91*
Nielsen, Raymond Eldon 1934- *St&PR 91*
Nielsen, Riccardo 1908- *IntWWM 90*
Nielsen, Richard C. 1945- *St&PR 91*
Nielsen, Robert Louis 1925- *WhoAm 90*
Nielsen, Roberta Deane 1934- *St&PR 91*
Nielsen, Ruth 1952- *WhoEmL 91*
Nielsen, S. Christian *St&PR 91*
Nielsen, Scott 1958- *Ballpl 90*
Nielsen, Susan Eileen 1949- *WhoAmW 91*
Nielsen, Svend 1937- *IntWWM 90*
Nielsen, Svend Aage Damgaard 1935- *WhoWor 91*
Nielsen, Tage 1929- *IntWWM 90*
Nielsen, Tore K 1934- *BiDrAPA 89*
Nielsen, Victor S. 1928- *St&PR 91*
Nielsen, Willard D. 1941- *ODwPR 91*
Nielsen, William E. 1947- *St&PR 91*
Nielsen, William Robert 1954- *WhoEmL 91*
Nielsen, Winnifred Moon 1917- *EncO&P 3*
Nielson, Howard Curtis 1924- *WhoAm 90*
Nielson, James E. 1931- *St&PR 91*
Nielson, James Melvin 1921- *WhoAm 90*
Nielson, John Alexander 1881-1954 *BioIn 16*
Nielson, Niels L. 1934- *St&PR 91*
Nielson, Norma Lee 1953- *WhoAmW 91*
Nielson, Ronald F. 1932- *St&PR 91*
Nielson, Thomas Milton 1933- *St&PR 91*
Nielson, William E. 1947- *St&PR 91*
Nielson, William Paul 1929- *WhoWor 91*
Nielsson, Harald *EncO&P 3*
Nieman, Alfred 1913- *IntWWM 90*
Nieman, Bob 1927-1985 *Ballpl 90*
Nieman, Butch 1918- *Ballpl 90*
Nieman, Cornelis 1924- *WhoWor 91*
Nieman, Lucius W. 1857-1935 *BioIn 16*
Niemann, Albert 1831-1917 *BioIn 16, PenDiMP*
Niemann, Bernard John, Jr. 1937- *WhoAm 90*
Niemann, Christi Cay 1956- *WhoAmW 91*
Niemann, Doyle L. 1947- *ODwPR 91*
Niemann, Doyle Larry 1947- *WhoE 91*
Niemann, Edmund E *WhoAmA 91*
Niemann, Ferd E., Jr. 1928- *St&PR 91*
Niemann, Harry Charles, III 1932- *St&PR 91*
Niemann, Joseph Harold, Jr. 1937- *St&PR 91*
Niemann, Lewis Keith 1930- *WhoAm 90*
Niemann, Linda *BioIn 16*
Niemann, Nicholas Kent 1956- *WhoEmL 91*
Niemann, Randy 1955- *Ballpl 90*
Niemann, Richard Henry 1931- *St&PR 91*
Niemczyk, Julian Martin 1920- *WhoAm 90, WhoWor 91*
Niemczynski, Adam Jozef 1942- *WhoWor 91*
Niemeth, Charles Frederick 1939- *WhoAm 90*
Niemeyer, Arnold Matthew 1913- *WhoAmA 91*
Niemeyer, Gerhart 1907- *ConAu 30NR, WhoAm 90*
Niemeyer, Glenn Alan 1934- *WhoAm 90*
Niemeyer, Irene E. *St&PR 91*
Niemeyer, James Edward 1936- *St&PR 91*
Niemeyer, Lucian Lenzner 1937- *WhoE 91*
Niemeyer, Michael L. 1947- *St&PR 91*
Niemeyer, Oscar 1907- *BioIn 16*
Niemeyer, Paul Victor 1941- *WhoAm 90*
Niemeyer, Robert W. *St&PR 91*
Niemi, Albert William, Jr. 1942- *WhoAm 90, WhoSSW 91*
Niemi, Bruce Alan 1950- *WhoEmL 91*
Niemi, Clarence *ODwPR 91*
Niemi, Edwin Eugene 1950- *WhoEmL 91*
Niemi, Janice 1928- *WhoAmW 91*
Niemi, Nicole 1957- *WhoWrEP 89*
Niemi, Osmo Juhani 1952- *WhoWor 91*
Niemi, Richard Gene 1941- *WhoAm 90*
Niemi, Robert John 1961- *WhoWor 91*
Niemi, Tapio Juhani 1949- *WhoWor 91*
Niemiec, David Wallace 1949- *WhoAm 90*
Niemiec, Edward Walter 1936- *St&PR 91, WhoAm 90*
Niemiec, Eugene W. 1940- *St&PR 91*
Niemiryczowa, Antonina 1702?-1760? *EncCoWW*
Niemitz, Carsten 1945- *WhoWor 91*
Niemoller, Arthur B. 1912- *WhoWor 91*
Niemoller, Martin 1892-1984 *BioIn 16*
Niemotko, Krystyna Anna 1938- *IntWWM 90*
Nienaltow, Daniel 1952- *WhoE 91*
Nienaltow, M. Daniel *BiDrAPA 89*
Nienast, Lamont *St&PR 91*
Nienburg, George Frank 1938- *WhoE 91*
Nienow, Ronald William 1937- *St&PR 91*
Nienstedt, Gerd 1932- *IntWWM 90*
Nieper, Hans A. 1928- *WhoWor 91*
Nieporent, Hans J 1929- *BiDrAPA 89*
Nier, Alfred Otto Carl 1911- *WhoAm 90*
Nierda, Aida *EncCoWW*
Nierenberg, Andrew Alan 1955- *BiDrAPA 89*
Nierenberg, Ivey Lois 1925- *WhoAmW 91*
Nierenberg, Marvin Alfred 1935- *BiDrAPA 89*
Nierenberg, Norman 1919- *WhoWor 91*
Nierenberg, Roger 1947- *WhoSSW 91*
Nierenberg, Sondra 1936- *WhoAmW 91*
Nierenberg, Susan 1955- *WhoAmW 91*
Nierenberg, William Aaron 1919- *WhoAm 90*
Nieriker, M. *BiDWomA*
Nieriker, May Alcott 1840-1879 *BioAmW*
Niering, William Albert 1924- *WhoE 91*
Nierman, Dennis Edward 1942- *St&PR 91*
Nierman, Eliot Hillel 1950- *WhoE 91*
Nierman, Leonardo M 1932- *WhoAmA 91*
Nierman, Leonardo Mendelejis 1932- *WhoAm 90, WhoWor 91*
Nierman, Max *BioIn 16*
Niermeyer, David 1941- *St&PR 91*
Niermeyer, Florence R. 1941- *St&PR 91*
Niermeyer, Richard *BioIn 16*
Nierob, Alan 1957- *ODwPR 91*
Nierste, Joseph Paul 1952- *WhoWor 91*
Nierva, Emmanuel A *BiDrAPA 89*
Nierzwicki, Paul Edward 1951- *St&PR 91*
Nies, Alan Sheffer 1937- *WhoAm 90*
Nies, Alexander 1930- *BiDrAPA 89*
Nies, Cynthia Ann Phillips 1947- *WhoSSW 91*
Nies, Friedrich Heinrich 1934- *WhoWor 91*
Nies, Helen Wilson *WhoAm 90, WhoAmW 91*
Nieschlag, Eberhard 1941- *WhoWor 91*
Niese, Harry Allan 1945- *St&PR 91*
Niese, Henry Ernst 1924- *WhoAmA 91*
Nietfeld, Dick David 1940- *St&PR 91*
Niethammer, Dietrich Gerhard 1939- *WhoWor 91*
Nieto, Ernesto *WhoHisp 91*
Nieto, Eva Margarita *WhoHisp 91*
Nieto, Eva Maria 1922- *WhoHisp 91*
Nieto, J Felipe *BiDrAPA 89*
Nieto, John W 1936- *WhoAmA 91*
Nieto, Juan Manuel 1949- *WhoEmL 91, WhoSSW 91, WhoWor 91*
Nieto, Michael Martin 1940- *WhoHisp 91*
Nieto, Minerva 1948- *WhoHisp 91*
Nieto, Ramon Dante 1957- *WhoHisp 91*
Nieto, Rey J. *WhoHisp 91*
Nieto, Tom 1960- *Ballpl 90*
Nietzsche, Friedrich 1844-1900 *WorAlBi, WrPh P*
Nietzsche, Friedrich Wilhelm 1844-1900 *BioIn 16, EncPaPR 91*
Nieuwdorp, Henricus Marius Joseph 1944- *WhoWor 91*
Nieuwenburg, Cornelis 1937- *WhoWor 91*
Nieuwendyk, Joe *BioIn 16*
Nieuwendyk, Joe 1966- *WorAlBi*
Nieuwenhuis, Theodore 1866-1951 *PenDiDA 89*
Nieuwenhuizen, Johannes Kornelis 1933- *WhoWor 91*
Nieuwenhuizen, Maarten *BiDrAPA 89*
Nieuwenkamp, Willem 1903-1979 *DcScB S2*
Nieuwkerk, Willem F *BiDrAPA 89*
Nieva, Nora M C *BiDrAPA 89*
Nieva, Ricardo R. 1965- *WhoEmL 91*
Nieva-Woodgate, Arthur Edward 1935- *WhoE 91*
Nievergelt, Jurg 1938- *WhoAm 90*
Nieves, Agustin Alberto 1963- *WhoHisp 91*
Nieves, Jose Edwin 1957- *BiDrAPA 89*
Nieves, Juan 1965- *Ballpl 90*
Nieves, Juan Manuel 1965- *WhoHisp 91*
Nieves, Julio Rafael 1936- *St&PR 91*
Nieves, Marcos Rafael *BiDrAPA 89*
Nieves, Theresa 1952- *WhoHisp 91*
Nieves, Walter Leo *BiDrAPA 89*
Nieves, Wilfredo 1949- *WhoHisp 91*
Nieweg, Clinton Fairlamb 1937- *IntWWM 90*
Niezabitowska, Malgorzata *BioIn 16*
Nigaglioni, Guillermo Antonio 1937- *WhoSSW 91*
Nigam, Bishan Perkash 1928- *WhoAm 90*
Nigam, Rajendra Kumar *BiDrAPA 89*
Nigg, Joseph Eugene 1938- *WhoWrEP 89*
Nigg, Serge 1924- *IntWWM 90*
Niggeling, Johnny 1903-1963 *Ballpl 90*
Niggl, Gunter 1934- *WhoWor 91*
Niggli, Josefina 1910- *ConAu 32NR, HispWr 90*
Nigh, George 1927- *WhoAm 90*
Nighbert, David L. 1932- *St&PR 91*
Night Ark *NewAgMG*
Night Ranger *EncPR&S 89*
Nightengale, Robert Webster, Jr. 1936- *WhoE 91*
Nightingale, Barbra 1949- *WhoWrEP 89*
Nightingale, Benedict 1939- *ConAu 132*
Nightingale, Daniel 1950- *IntWWM 90*
Nightingale, Earl 1921-1989 *BioIn 16*
Nightingale, Edmund Joseph 1941- *WhoWor 91*
Nightingale, Elena Ottolenghi 1932- *WhoAm 90, WhoAmW 91*
Nightingale, Florence 1820-1910 *BioIn 16, FemiCLE, WorAlBi*
Nightingale, Geoffrey J. *ODwPR 91*
Nightingale, Geoffrey Joseph 1938- *WhoAm 90, WhoE 91, WhoWor 91*
Nightingale, Luke Mahlon 1955- *WhoE 91*
Nightingale, Maxine *DrBlPA 90*
Nightingale, Myron *BioIn 16*
Nightingale, R. Thomas 1945- *St&PR 91*
Nightingale, Richard *BiDrAPA 89*
Nightingale, William Joslyn 1929- *WhoWor 91*
Nigl, Alfred James 1949- *WhoWor 91*
Nigl, Jeffrey M. 1958- *St&PR 91*
Niglett, John *PenDiDA 89*
Niglio, Richard Anthony 1942- *St&PR 91*
Nigoghossian, Jean-Pierre Daniel 1943- *WhoWor 91*
Nigon, Christopher S. 1953- *St&PR 91*
Nigon, Christopher Scott 1953- *WhoE 91*
Nigra, John D. 1931- *St&PR 91*
Nigrelli, Charles Samuel 1923- *St&PR 91*
Nigrelli, Ross Franco 1903-1989 *BioIn 16*
Nigrin, Raphael *BiDrAPA 89*
Nigro, Bernard A 1934- *BiDrAPA 89*
Nigro, Felix Anthony 1914- *WhoAm 90, WhoWrEP 89*
Nigro, Giovanni 1945- *WhoWor 91*
Nigro, Mario Joseph 1937- *St&PR 91*
Nigro, Robert Allen 1949- *St&PR 91*
Nigro, Samuel Angelo 1937- *BiDrAPA 89*
Nigrosh, Leon Isaac 1940- *WhoAmA 91*
Niguidula, Faustino Nazario 1926- *WhoAm 90*
Nihart, Franklin Brooke 1919- *WhoAm 90, WhoE 91*
Nihart, Ruth Lucille *WhoAmW 91*
Nihell, Elizabeth *FemiCLE*
Nihen, Robert G. 1952- *ODwPR 91*
Nihill, Karen Bailey 1947- *WhoWor 91*
Nihmura, Masazumi 1939- *WhoWor 91*
Niinivirta, Pentti Olavi 1935- *WhoWor 91*
Niino, Mabito 1921- *WhoWor 91*
Niitti, Ilpo Ilari 1946- *WhoWor 91*
Niitu, Yasutaka 1920- *WhoWor 91*
Niizeki, Fumiaki 1935- *St&PR 91*
Niizuma, Minoru 1930- *WhoAmA 91*
Nij-Kwenatc-Anibic *DcCanB 12*
Nijenhuis, Albert 1926- *WhoAm 90*
Nijenhuis, Emmie te 1931- *IntWWM 90*
Nijinska, Bronislava 1891-1972 *BioIn 16*
Nijinska, Irina *BioIn 16*
Nijinsky, Vaslav 1890-1950 *WorAlBi*
Nijinsky, Waslaw 1890-1950 *BioIn 16*
Nikakhtar, Manijeh *BiDrAPA 89*
Nikas, George A. 1933- *St&PR 91*
Nikels, Robert Andrew 1939- *St&PR 91*
Nikiforuk, Peter Nick 1930- *WhoAm 90*
Nikirk, Robert L. *NewYTBS 90*
Nikisch, Arthur 1855-1922 *PenDiMP*
Nikischer, Frank William, Sr. 1931- *WhoE 91*
Nikitin, Vladilen V. *WhoWor 91*
Nikitovitch-Winer, Miroslava B. 1929- *WhoAm 90*
Nikka, David Wayne 1954- *IntWWM 90*
Nikkal, Nancy Egol 1944- *WhoAmA 91*
Nikkanen, Kurt 1965- *IntWWM 90*
Nikkel, John Glen 1935- *St&PR 91*
Nikkhah, Shahrokh *BioIn 16*
Nikkhoo, Alexander Amir Ghassem 1942- *WhoSSW 91*
Niklewski, Edmund V *BiDrAPA 89*
Nikodem, Edward Francis 1949- *WhoEmL 91*
Nikolaev, Viktor Arsenievich 1893-1960 *DcScB S2*
Nikolaev, Vsevolod A 1909- *ConAu 130*
Nikolaeva, Galina Evgenievna *EncCoWW*
Nikolai, James A. *WhoAm 90*
Nikolai, Loren Alfred 1943- *WhoAm 90*
Nikolai Ortlieb, Monica Dagmar 1955- *IntWWM 90*
Nikolayeva, Tatyana 1924- *PenDiMP*
Nikolich, Michael L. *ODwPR 91*
Nikoloff, John Andon 1950- *WhoE 91*
Nikolovski, Oliver T *BiDrAPA 89*
Nikonorow, Andrzej 1942- *BiDrAPA 89, WhoE 91*
Nikonov, Viktor Petrovich 1929- *WhoWor 91*
Nikopoulos, George John *BiDrAPA 89*
Niku, Vaino 1927- *WhoWor 91*

Nikula, Henrik Viking 1942- *WhoWor 91*
Nil, Guven 1944- *WhoWor 91*
Niland, Edward John 1916- *WhoAm 90*
Nile, Dorothea *TwCCr&M 91*
Niles, Amy 1959- *WhoAmW 91*
Niles, Barbara Elliott 1939- *WhoAmW 91*
Niles, Charles Kenneth 1945- *St&PR 91*
Niles, Don William 1955- *IntWWM 90*
Niles, Franklin Elvie 1934- *WhoAm 90*
Niles, Gerald T 1920- *BiDrAPA 89*
Niles, Harry 1880-1953 *Ballpl 90*
Niles, Hezekiah 1777-1839 *BioIn 16*
Niles, John Denison 1934-1990 *BioIn 16*
Niles, John Jacob 1892-1980 *ConAu 33NR, LiHiK, OxCPMus*
Niles, John Lowell 1930- *St&PR 91*
Niles, John Milton 1787-1856 *BiDrUSE 89*
Niles, Judith Ann 1936- *WhoE 91*
Niles, Ken *BioIn 16*
Niles, Nathaniel 1835-1917 *AmLegL*
Niles, Nicholas Hemelright 1938- *St&PR 91, WhoAm 90*
Niles, Rosamond 1881- *WhoAmA 91N*
Niles, Terry L. 1954- *St&PR 91*
Niles, Thomas *BioIn 16*
Niles, Thomas Michael Tolliver 1939- *WhoWor 91*
Nill, C. John 1938- *St&PR 91*
Nill, Heather Anne 1963- *WhoAmW 91*
Nill, William C. 1938- *St&PR 91*
Nilon, Laura Ann 1960- *WhoAmW 91*
Nilsen, Barbara Yvonne 1941- *St&PR 91*
Nilsen, Clifford T. 1932- *St&PR 91*
Nilsen, John *NewAgMG*
Nilsen, Nicholas 1937- *St&PR 91*
Nilsen, Richard Haldor 1948- *WhoWrEP 89*
Nilsen, Thomas Theodore 1963- *WhoEmL 91*
Nilsen, Tove 1952- *EncCoWW*
Nilson, Arne Einar 1920- *WhoWor 91*
Nilson, Christian 1952- *WhoEmL 91*
Nilson, David Albert 1947- *St&PR 91*
Nilson, Larry A. 1946- *St&PR 91*
Nilson, Paul Herman 1927- *WhoE 91*
Nilson, Richard Edwin 1948- *BiDrAPA 89, WhoE 91*
Nilssen, Per Arnljot 1936- *WhoWor 91*
Nilsson 1941- *EncPR&S 89*
Nilsson, A. Kenneth 1933- *St&PR 91*
Nilsson, Barbro 1899-1983 *ConDes 90*
Nilsson, Birgit 1918- *ConAu 129, IntWWM 90, PenDiMP, WhoWor 91, WorAlBi*
Nilsson, Bo 1937- *IntWWM 90*
Nilsson, Bo Ingvar 1947- *WhoWor 91*
Nilsson, Christine 1843-1921 *PenDiMP*
Nilsson, Edward Olof 1947- *WhoE 91*
Nilsson, Gladys 1940- *WhoAmA 91*
Nilsson, Hans Lennart 1943- *WhoWor 91*
Nilsson, Harry 1941- *OxCPMus*
Nilsson, K. Goran 1936- *WhoWor 91*
Nilsson, Larsgunnar Lennart 1947- *WhoWor 91*
Nilsson, Lennart 1941- *WhoWor 91*
Nilsson, Leopoldo Torre 1924-1978 *BioIn 16*
Nilsson, Nic 1933- *WhoWor 91*
Nilsson, Olof Robert 1949- *WhoWor 91*
Nilsson, Roland Alf Ake 1942- *WhoWor 91*
Nilsson, Sam Olaf *WhoWor 91*
Nilsson, Stefan K. 1954- *WhoWor 91*
Nilsson, Sten Ake 1936- *WhoWor 91*
Nilsson, Ulf *AuBYP 90*
Nilsson, Vera 1888-1978 *BiDWomA*
Nim, Naomi Barbara 1948- *WhoAmW 91*
Nimeiri, Jafar Mohammed 1930- *PolLCME*
Nimer, Daniel A. 1921- *St&PR 91*
Nimetz, Matthew 1939- *WhoAm 90*
Nimitz, Chester W. 1885-1966 *WorAlBi*
Nimitz, Chester W., Jr. 1915- *St&PR 91*
Nimitz, Chester William, Jr. 1915- *WhoAm 90*
Nimkin, Bernard William 1923- *WhoAm 90*
Nimkin, Margaret Lee 1955- *WhoAmW 91*
Nimlos, Kenneth Odeen 1922- *BiDrAPA 89*
Nimmagadda, Lokanadha Babu 1947- *BiDrAPA 89*
Nimmo, Ian A. 1941- *St&PR 91*
Nimmo, Robert Allen 1936- *St&PR 91*
Nimmo, Thomas Dewey 1939- *St&PR 91*
Nimmo, William S. *St&PR 91*
Nimmons, Major Stuart, III 1940- *WhoSSW 91*
Nimmons, Phillip Rista 1923- *WhoAm 90*
Nimnicht, Billie Nugent, Jr. 1941- *St&PR 91*
Nimnicht, Edward Aaron, II 1943- *St&PR 91*
Nimnicht, Nona Vonne 1930- *WhoWrEP 89*
Nimoy, Leonard *BioIn 16*
Nimoy, Leonard 1931- *WhoAm 90, WorAlBi*
Nimpoeno, Harjo 1927- *WhoWor 91*
Nims, Arthur Lee, III 1923- *WhoAm 90*
Nims, John Frederick 1913- *WhoAm 90, WhoWrEP 89*
Nims, Judith Christopher 1944- *WhoAm 90*
Nims, Leslie Irving 1940- *WhoWor 91*
Nims, Peter Edward 1939- *BiDrAPA 89*
Nims, Walter Worthington 1949- *WhoEmL 91*
Nimsgern, Siegmund 1940- *IntWWM 90, PenDiMP*
Nin, Anais 1903-1977 *BioAmW, BioIn 16, ConLC 60 [port], FemiCLE, MajTwCW, WorAlBi*
Nin-Culmell, Joaquin Maria 1908- *IntWWM 90*
Ninagawa, Yukio *BioIn 16*
Ninan, Oommen P 1950- *BiDrAPA 89*
Ninan, Philip Mohan *BiDrAPA 89*
Ninan, Philip Thoppil 1951- *BiDrAPA 89*
Ninci, Clemenza 16--?- *EncCoWW*
Nind, Jean 1930- *WhoAmA 91*
Nine, John Edward 1936- *WhoWor 91*
Nineberg, Allan S 1951- *BiDrAPA 89*
Niness, Samuel Francis, Jr. 1935- *St&PR 91*
Ning, Tak Hung 1943- *WhoAm 90*
Ning, Tak-Ling D *BiDrAPA 89*
Ninham 1710?-1778 *WhNaAH*
Ninicraft 1600?-1678 *WhNaAH*
Niniglud 1600?-1678 *WhNaAH*
Ninigret 1600?-1678 *WhNaAH*
Nininger, Engel Scott 1928- *BiDrAPA 89*
Nininger, Eugene V *BiDrAPA 89*
Nininger, James Edward 1948- *BiDrAPA 89*
Nininger, Robert D. *WhoE 91*
Ninivaggi, Frank John *BiDrAPA 89*
Ninkovich, Thomas 1943- *WhoWrEP 89*
Nino, Jose *WhoHisp 91*
Nino de Guzman, Jaime 1934- *WhoWor 91*
Nino-Murcia, German 1948- *BiDrAPA 89*
Ninos, Nicholas Peter 1936- *WhoAm 90, WhoWor 91*
Ninsei *EncJap*
Ninsei, Nonomura Seiemon 1574?-1660? *PenDiDA 89*
Nio, Matthew H B 1934- *BiDrAPA 89*
Niosi, James Peter 1935- *St&PR 91, WhoAm 90*
Niosi, Jorge 1945- *ConAu 129, HispWr 90*
Niosi, Willemina Van Der Veen 1937- *BiDrAPA 89*
Niou, Hideo 1929- *WhoWor 91*
Nipert, Donna Ann 1952- *WhoAmW 91, WhoEmL 91*
Nipitella, Alfio 1913- *WhoWor 91*
Nipon, Albert 1927- *WhoAm 90*
Nipp, Francis Stuart 1914- *WhoWrEP 89*
Nipper, Al 1959- *Ballpl 90*
Nipper, Stephan Lindall 1949- *WhoSSW 91*
Nipperdey, Thomas H. 1927- *WhoWor 91*
Nippert, Alfred Kuno, Jr. 1951- *WhoEmL 91*
Nippert, Russell A. 1937- *St&PR 91*
Nips, Nick L. *WhoWrEP 89*
Nir, Yehuda 1930- *BiDrAPA 89, WhoE 91*
Nirad C. Chaudhuri 1897- *BioIn 16*
Nirenberg, Charles 1923- *WhoAm 90*
Nirenberg, Louis 1925- *WhoAm 90, WhoWor 91*
Nirenberg, Marshall W. 1927- *WorAlBi*
Nirenberg, Marshall Warren 1927- *WhoAm 90, WhoE 91, WhoWor 91*
Nirk, Gunnar 1921- *BiDrAPA 89*
Nirmala Devi Srivastava 1923- *EncO&P 3*
Nirouet, Jean 1958- *IntWWM 90*
Nisbet, Joanne 1931- *WhoAm 90*
Nisbet, John Stirling 1927- *WhoAm 90*
Nisbet, Noel Laura 1887-1956 *BiDWomA*
Nisbet, P. A. 1948- *BioIn 16*
Nisbet, Pauline Randow 1946- *WhoSSW 91*
Nisbet, Robert A. 1913- *WhoAm 90, WhoWrEP 89*
Nisbet, Robert Baxter 1937- *BiDrAPA 89*
Nisbet, Robert H 1879-1961 *WhoAmA 91N*
Nisbet, Shirley J. 1935- *St&PR 91*
Nisbet, W. Robb 1924- *St&PR 91*
Nisbett, Richard Eugene 1941- *WhoAm 90*
Nisbett, Susan Isaacs 1948- *WhoAm 90*
Nischan, Gerda M. 1940- *WhoWrEP 89*
Nischwitz, Ron 1937- *Ballpl 90*
Nise, Michael 1943- *WhoE 91*
Nishi, Yoshio 1940- *WhoAm 90*
Nishida Kitaro 1870-1945 *EncJap*
Nishida, Yoshito 1929- *WhoWor 91*
Nishida-Vela, Chizuru 1958- *WhoSSW 91*
Nishiguchi, Don Jerry 1955- *WhoWor 91*
Nishihara, Haruo 1928- *WhoWor 91*
Nishikata, Masumi 1933- *WhoWor 91*
Nishikawa, Hitoshi 1955- *WhoWor 91*
Nishikawa, Shingo Leonard 1941- *WhoSSW 91*
Nishikawa, Takeji 1940- *WhoWor 91*
Nishimoto, Kichisuke 1932- *WhoWor 91*
Nishimoto, Nobushige 1929- *WhoWor 91*
Nishimura, Joseph Yo 1933- *St&PR 91, WhoAm 90*
Nishimura, Kiyohiko Giichi 1953- *WhoWor 91*
Nishimura, Masaru 1922- *WhoWor 91*
Nishimura, Pete Hideo 1922- *WhoAm 90*
Nishina, Yoshio 1890-1951 *DcScB S2*
Nishino, Katsuhiro 1953- *WhoWor 91*
Nishio, Karen T. *WhoAmW 91*
Nishitani, Martha 1920- *WhoAm 90*
Nishiyama, Chiaki 1924- *WhoWor 91*
Nishiyama, Ken'Ichi *WhoWor 91*
Nishiyama, Toshiyuki 1922- *WhoWor 91*
Nishizawa, Michio 1919- *Ballpl 90*
Nishizono, Masahisa 1928- *BiDrAPA 89*
Nishkian, Byron Levon 1916- *WhoAm 90*
Niska, Maralin 1930- *IntWWM 90*
Niskanen, William Arthur, Jr. 1933- *WhoAm 90, WhoE 91*
Nisker, Amiram Nir *BioIn 16*
Nisonoff, Alfred 1923- *WhoAm 90*
Niss, Robert Sharples 1949- *WhoE 91*
Nissanka, Manage D S 1945- *BiDrAPA 89*
Nissel, Siegmund *PenDiMP*
Nissel, Siegmund 1922- *IntWWM 90*
Nissen, Archie S *BiDrAPA 89*
Nissen, Hans Jorg 1935- *WhoWor 91*
Nissen, Judy Kay 1942- *WhoAmW 91*
Nissen, Thomas Jay 1942- *St&PR 91*
Nissen, William Myron 1944- *BiDrAPA 89*
Nissenfeld, Robert H. 1944- *St&PR 91*
Nissenson, Hugh 1933- *WhoWrEP 89*
Nissinen, Mikko *BioIn 16*
Nissl, Colleen Kaye 1950- *WhoEmL 91*
Nissman, Barbara 1944- *IntWWM 90*
Nissman, Harvey Leonard 1950- *BiDrAPA 89*
Nist, Charles William 1942- *St&PR 91*
Nistico, Giuseppe 1941- *WhoWor 91*
Nistler, James Charles 1931- *WhoAm 90*
Nisula, Larry 1960- *WhoAmA 91*
Niswender, Gordon Dean 1940- *WhoAm 90*
Niswonger, Jeanne Du Chateau *WhoAm 90, WhoAmW 91, WhoSSW 91, WhoWor 91*
Nitcher, Rodney Lee *BiDrAPA 89*
Nitchke, Howard Dean 1949- *WhoAm 90*
Nitecki, Joseph Zbigniew 1922- *WhoAm 90*
Nithsdale, Winifrede, Countess of 1672-1749 *FemiCLE*
Nitkowski, James Walter 1940- *St&PR 91*
Nitowsky, Harold Martin 1925- *WhoAm 90*
Nitrocris *WomWR*
Nitrocris 647BC-547?BC *WomWR*
Nitsch, Manfred 1940- *WhoWor 91*
Nitsch, Robert A. 1928- *St&PR 91*
Nitsche, Johannes Carl Christian 1925- *WhoAm 90*
Nitsche, Peter 1936- *WhoWor 91*
Nitsche, Richard A. 1931- *St&PR 91*
Nitschke, Robert E. 1922- *St&PR 91*
Nitso, Evelyn Agnes 1934- *WhoWrEP 89*
Nitterhouse, Craig J. 1956- *St&PR 91*
Nitterhouse, Denise 1950- *WhoEmL 91*
Nitterhouse, William K. 1932- *St&PR 91*
Nittiskie, Leslie Collin 1957- *WhoAmW 91*
Nittner, Konrad 1921- *WhoWor 91*
Nittolo, Albert P. 1928- *St&PR 91*
Nitty Gritty Dirt Band *OxCPMus, WhoNeCM [port]*
Nituch, Nestor E. 1947- *St&PR 91*
Nitz, Gary L 1936- *BiDrAPA 89*
Nitzberg, Ramon 1929- *WhoAm 90*
Nitzburg, Arthur R. 1944- *WhoE 91*
Nitze, Paul H. *BioIn 16*
Nitze, Paul Henry 1907- *WhoAm 90*
Nitze, William Albert 1942- *WhoE 91*
Nitzsche, Elsa Koenig 1880-1952 *WhoAmA 91N*
Nitzsche, Jack 1937?- *ConTFT 8*
Nitzsche, Jane Chance *WhoWrEP 89*
Nitzschke, Dale F. 1937- *WhoAm 90*
Niu Weiyu *BioIn 16*
Nivat, Georges Michel 1935- *WhoWor 91*
Niven, David 1910-1983 *ConAu 31NR, DcNaB 1981, WorAlBi*
Niven, Frederick John 1878-1944 *DcLB 92 [port]*
Niven, Ivan Morton 1915- *BioIn 16*
Niven, James *BioIn 16*
Niven, Larry *MajTwCW*
Niven, Larry 1938- *ConAu 12AS [port], RGTwCSF*
Niven, Laurence Van Cott 1938- *MajTwCW, WhoAm 90, WhoWrEP 89*
Niven, Laurence Von Cott 1938- *WorAlBi*
Niven, Robert Gordon 1944- *BiDrAPA 89*
Niver, Edwin O *BiDrAPA 89*
Niver, Kemp R. *BioIn 16*
Nivison, David Shepherd 1923- *WhoAm 90*
Nivoche, Christine Nelly 1953- *WhoWor 91*
Nivola, Constantino 1911-1988 *BioIn 16*
Niwano, Nikkyo 1906- *ConAu 130*
Nix, Alice Pearl 1912- *WhoAmW 91*
Nix, Barbara Lois 1929- *WhoAmW 91, WhoWor 91*
Nix, Beverly Ann 1951- *WhoAmW 91*
Nix, Dennis W. 1945- *St&PR 91*
Nix, Edmund Alfred 1929- *WhoAm 90*
Nix, Edward J. 1930- *St&PR 91*
Nix, Edward Oliver 1939- *BiDrAPA 89*
Nix, Howard W., Jr. 1929- *St&PR 91*
Nix, Joseph Hanson, Jr. 1930- *WhoSSW 91*
Nix, Pamela Dianne 1964- *WhoAmW 91*
Nix, Patricia *WhoAmA 91*
Nix, Patricia Lea 1943- *WhoE 91*
Nix, Phyllis L. 1936- *St&PR 91*
Nix, Robert Nelson Cornelius, Jr. 1928- *WhoAm 90, WhoE 91*
Nix, Robert Nelson Cornelius, Sr. 1905-1987 *BlkAmsC [port]*
Nix, Robert Patrick 1955- *WhoEmL 91*
Nix, Stephan Jack 1952- *WhoE 91*
Nix, Susan Mae 1946- *WhoSSW 91*
Nix, William Dale 1936- *WhoAm 90*
Nix, William J. 1940- *St&PR 91*
Nixdorf, Brenda Brauer 1957- *WhoAmW 91*
Nixon, Agnes Eckhardt *WhoAm 90, WhoAmW 91*
Nixon, Al 1886-1960 *Ballpl 90*
Nixon, Alan Charles 1908- *WhoAm 90*
Nixon, Alfred J. 1927- *St&PR 91*
Nixon, Ann Karen 1944- *St&PR 91*
Nixon, Arlie James 1914- *WhoSSW 91*
Nixon, Barbara Elizabeth 1954- *WhoAmW 91*
Nixon, Charles Richard 1940- *St&PR 91*
Nixon, Charlotte Macdonald 1929- *St&PR 91*
Nixon, Clarence H., Jr. 1908?-1990 *ConAu 130*
Nixon, David *WhoAm 90*
Nixon, David Allen 1921- *St&PR 91*
Nixon, David Michael 1945- *WhoWrEP 89*
Nixon, Donald H *BiDrAPA 89*
Nixon, Donnell 1961- *Ballpl 90*
Nixon, E. D. *BioIn 16*
Nixon, E.J., Jr. 1931- *St&PR 91*
Nixon, Eugene Ray 1919- *WhoAm 90*
Nixon, Frances Edna 1937- *BiDrAPA 89*
Nixon, Hollowell Cox 1920- *St&PR 91*
Nixon, Jack Lowell 1926- *WhoAm 90*
Nixon, James Frederick 1947- *WhoSSW 91*
Nixon, Joan 1927- *AuBYP 90*
Nixon, Joan Lowery 1927- *BioIn 16, WhoAm 90*
Nixon, John 1733-1808 *EncCRAm*
Nixon, John Richard 1941- *WhoWor 91*
Nixon, John Thompson 1820-1889 *AmLegL*
Nixon, John Trice 1933- *WhoAm 90, WhoSSW 91*
Nixon, John W. 1926- *St&PR 91*
Nixon, Joyce Elaine 1925- *WhoAmW 91, WhoE 91*
Nixon, K. *AuBYP 90*
Nixon, Kathleen Irene *AuBYP 90*
Nixon, Kathleen Irene 1894- *BioIn 16*
Nixon, Kenneth Long 1960- *WhoSSW 91*
Nixon, Marni 1930- *PenDiMP, WhoAm 90, WhoAmW 91*
Nixon, Nichols 1947- *WhoAmA 91*
Nixon, Norm *BioIn 16*
Nixon, Norman *BiDrAPA 89*
Nixon, Otis 1959- *Ballpl 90*
Nixon, P. Andrews 1938- *St&PR 91*
Nixon, Patricia *BioIn 16*
Nixon, Patricia 1912- *WorAlBi*
Nixon, Patricia Ryan 1912- *BioAmW, WhoAm 90, WhoAmW 91, WhoE 91*
Nixon, Patrick Michael 1944- *WhoWor 91*
Nixon, Peter Marlborough 1929- *St&PR 91, WhoAm 90*
Nixon, Philip Andrews 1938- *WhoAm 90*
Nixon, Queenie 1918?-1989 *EncO&P 3*
Nixon, Ralph Angus 1947- *BiDrAPA 89*
Nixon, Raymond Blalock 1903- *WhoAm 90*
Nixon, Richard *EncAL*
Nixon, Richard 1913- *BestSel 90-3 [port]*
Nixon, Richard M. 1913- *BioIn 16, ConAu 33NR, MajTwCW, WorAlBi*
Nixon, Richard Milhous 1913- *BiDrUSE 89, WhoAm 90, WhoE 91, WhoWor 91*
Nixon, Richard Neal 1942- *WhoAm 90*
Nixon, Robert Eugene 1943- *St&PR 91*
Nixon, Robert H. 1936- *St&PR 91*
Nixon, Robert James 1930- *WhoAm 90*
Nixon, Robert Pleasants 1913- *WhoAm 90, WhoWor 91*
Nixon, Robert W. 1940- *ODwPR 91*
Nixon, Russ 1935- *Ballpl 90*
Nixon, Sallie White 1914- *WhoWrEP 89*
Nixon, Samuel Frederick 1860-1905 *AmLegL*

Nixon, Scott West 1943- *WhoAm 90*
Nixon, Shirnette Marilyn 1947- *WhoAmW 91*
Nixon, Stanley Elkin *St&PR 91N*
Nixon, Stanley Elkin 1912- *WhoAm 90*
Nixon, Suzi 1950- *WhoAmW 91*
Nixon, Tamara Friedman 1938- *WhoAmW 91*
Nixon, Walter L., Jr. *BioIn 16*
Nixon, Willard 1928- *Ballpl 90*
Niza, Marcos De 1495?-1558 *WhNaAH*
Niza, Marcos de 1500?-1558 *EncCRAm*
Nizalowski, Edward Michael 1947- *WhoWrEP 89*
Nizalowski, John Anthony 1956- *WhoWrEP 89*
Nizam, Ihsan J. 1939- *St&PR 91*
Nizami, Tariq Ahmed 1958- *WhoWor 91*
Nizan, Paul 1905-1940 *TwCLC 40 [port]*
Nizan, Paul Yves 1905-1940 *BiDFrPL*
Nizen, Donald *BioIn 16*
Nizer, Louis 1902- *St&PR 91, WorAlBi*
Nizet, Marie 1859-1922 *EncCoWW*
Nizetic, Branko Z. 1925- *WhoWor 91*
Nizetic, Nina Betty *BiDrAPA 89*
Nizio, Frank 1948- *WhoEmL 91*
Niznik, Monica Lynne 1953- *WhoAmW 91*
Nizny, Melvyn M 1937- *BiDrAPA 89*
Nizzoli, Marcello 1887-1969 *PenDiDA 89*
Njaka, Shirley 1954- *WhoAmW 91*
Njao, Njuguna 1927- *BioIn 16*
Njau, Rebeka 1932- *FemiCLE*
Njogu Touray 1959- *BioIn 16*
Nkala, Enos Mzombi 1932- *WhoWor 91*
Nkoane, Joseph Simeon *BioIn 16*
Nkomo, Joshua 1917- *WhoWor 91*
Nkosi, Lewis 1936- *WorAu 1980 [port]*
Nkrumah, Kwame 1909-1972 *BioIn 16, ConAu 132, WorAlBi*
nn *EncCoWW*
No Strings Attached *NewAgMG*
No, Rafael Lorente de 1902-1990 *BioIn 16*
Noa, Florence 1941-1989 *WhoAmA 91N*
Noack, Fritz 1935- *IntWWM 90*
Noack, Ken Everett 1948- *WhoSSW 91*
Noack, William Raymond, Jr. 1952- *St&PR 91*
Noah, Harold J 1925- *ConAu 30NR*
Noah, Hope E. 1943- *WhoWrEP 89*
Noah, Hope Ellen 1943- *WhoAmW 91*
Noah, Julia Jeanine 1932- *WhoAmW 91*
Noah, Lester Victor 1942- *WhoE 91*
Noailles, Anna-Elizabeth de 1876-1933 *EncCoWW*
Noakes, John Ernest 1920- *WhoAm 90*
Noall, Nancy Ann 1957- *WhoAmW 91*
Noall, Roger 1935- *St&PR 91, WhoAm 90*
Noam, Eli M. *BioIn 16*
Noami 1397-1471 *EncJap*
Noback, Charles Robert 1916- *WhoAm 90*
Nobe, Ken 1925- *WhoAm 90*
Nobe, Kenneth Charles 1930- *WhoAm 90*
Nobel, Alfred B. 1833-1896 *WorAlBi*
Nobel, Alfred Bernhard 1833-1896 *BioIn 16*
Nobel, Cecelia V 1935- *BiDrAPA 89*
Nobel, Fred I. 1917- *St&PR 91*
Nobel, Golda R 1906- *BiDrAPA 89*
Nobel, Joel J. 1934- *WhoAm 90*
Nobel, Kenneth *BiDrAPA 89*
Nobel, Peter 1931- *WhoWor 91*
Nobil, James Howard 1930- *St&PR 91*
Nobil, James Howard, Jr. 1955- *WhoE 91, WhoWor 91*
Nobile, Karin A. *ODwPR 91*
Nobile, Karin Ann 1960- *WhoAmW 91*
Nobile, Umberto 1885-1978 *WorAlBi*
Nobiletti, John Douglas 1955- *WhoE 91*
Nobilski-Clancy, Mary S *BiDrAPA 89*
Noble, Bruce Alexander 1945- *WhoWor 91*
Noble, Chester Lehner 1912- *St&PR 91, WhoAm 90*
Noble, Dale Spencer 1958- *IntWWM 90*
Noble, David J. 1931- *St&PR 91*
Noble, David Jeff 1931- *WhoAm 90*
Noble, David Watson 1925- *WhoWrEP 89*
Noble, Denis 1936- *WhoWor 91*
Noble, Dennis 1899-1966 *PenDiMP*
Noble, Douglas G. 1956- *ODwPR 91*
Noble, Douglas Leonard 1943- *WhoAm 90*
Noble, Edward J. 1882-1958 *WorAlBi*
Noble, Ernest Pascal 1929- *WhoAm 90*
Noble, F. Pierce 1943- *St&PR 91*
Noble, George Cochran 1944- *WhoWor 91*
Noble, Gil 1932- *DrBlPA 90*
Noble, Gladwyn Kingsley 1894-1940 *DcScB S2*
Noble, Harold 1903- *IntWWM 90*
Noble, Helen 1922- *WhoAmA 91*
Noble, Iris 1922-1986 *AuBYP 90, BioIn 16*
Noble, James Kendrick, Jr. 1928- *WhoAm 90, WhoE 91, WhoWor 91*
Noble, James Ronald 1935- *WhoE 91*
Noble, James Wilkes 1922- *WhoAm 90*
Noble, Jennifer *BioIn 16*
Noble, Jeremy 1930- *IntWWM 90*
Noble, John 1931- *IntWWM 90*
Noble, John A 1913- *WhoAmA 91*
Noble, John A 1913-1983 *WhoAmA 91N*
Noble, John R. 1921- *St&PR 91*
Noble, John Willock 1831-1912 *BiDrUSE 89*
Noble, Johnny *BioIn 16*
Noble, Johnny 1892-1944 *OxCPMus*
Noble, Joseph Veach 1920- *WhoAm 90, WhoAmA 91*
Noble, Jud 1926- *St&PR 91*
Noble, Marion Ellen 1914- *WhoAmW 91*
Noble, Marty 1947- *BioIn 16*
Noble, Merrill Emmett 1923- *WhoAm 90*
Noble, Morag Jane 1931- *IntWWM 90*
Noble, Nicholas R. *WhoWrEP 89*
Noble, Noel Alfred 1923- *IntWWM 90*
Noble, Ray 1903-1978 *OxCPMus*
Noble, Ray 1919- *Ballpl 90*
Noble, Reuben 1821-1896 *AmLegL*
Noble, Richard Lloyd 1939- *WhoAm 90, WhoWor 91*
Noble, Richard William 1952- *St&PR 91*
Noble, Scott Alan 1951- *WhoAm 90*
Noble, Scott C. 1946- *WhoAm 90*
Noble, Stephanie Margaret Culler 1947- *WhoEmL 91*
Noble, Sunny A. 1940- *WhoAmW 91*
Noble, Trinka Hakes *BioIn 16*
Noble, Ward S. 1930- *St&PR 91*
Noble, Weston H. 1922- *IntWWM 90*
Noble, Yvonne 1935- *WhoWor 91*
Nobleman, Maurice 1927- *IntWWM 90*
Nobles, Charles Norman 1929- *St&PR 91*
Nobles, Gene *BioIn 16*
Nobles, Hinton Folsom, Jr. 1945- *St&PR 91*
Nobles, John E. *St&PR 91*
Nobles, Laurence Hewit 1927- *WhoAm 90*
Nobles, Lewis 1925- *WhoAm 90*
Nobleza, Luzviminda J *BiDrAPA 89*
Noblit, Betty Jean 1948- *WhoAmW 91*
Noblitt, Harding Coolidge 1920- *WhoAm 90*
Noblitt, James Paul 1934- *St&PR 91*
Noblitt, John R. 1936- *St&PR 91*
Noblitt, Nancy Anne 1959- *WhoAmW 91, WhoE 91*
Noblitt, Niles Leonard 1951- *St&PR 91*
Noblitt, William Franklin 1950- *WhoSSW 91*
Noboa-Stanton, Patricia Lynn 1947- *WhoAmW 91*
Nobre, Fernando Jose de la Vieter R 1951- *WhoWor 91*
Nobre, Marlos 1939- *WhoWor 91*
Nobrega, Mailson Da *BioIn 16*
Nobs, Charles Herman 1952- *WhoAm 90*
Nobunaga Oda *EncJap*
Nobuo, Takamiya 1924- *WhoWor 91*
Nobutaro, Hara 1919- *WhoWor 91*
Noce, Robert H *BiDrAPA 89*
Noce, Robert Henry 1914- *WhoAm 90*
Noce, Walter William, Jr. 1945- *WhoAm 90*
Nocek, James Edward 1952- *WhoE 91*
Nocentelli, Leo *BioIn 16*
Nocenti, Mero Raymond 1928- *WhoAm 90*
Nocera, Bruce *St&PR 91*
Nocera, Joseph *BioIn 16*
Nocerino, Kathryn M. 1947- *WhoWrEP 89*
Nochese, Thomas Anthony *BioIn 16*
Nochlin, Linda 1931- *BioIn 16, WhoAmA 91*
Nochman, Lois Wood Kivi 1924- *WhoAmW 91*
Nochur, Kumar Subramaniam 1955- *WhoE 91*
Nociforo, Sal Frank 1941- *St&PR 91*
Nocita, Gerard Ralph 1936- *St&PR 91*
Nock, Gilbert J, Jr. 1931- *BiDrAPA 89*
Nock, William H. 1945- *St&PR 91, WhoAm 90*
Nocke, Henry Herman 1916- *WhoSSW 91*
Nocker, Hans Gunter 1927- *IntWWM 90*
Nocks, James Jay 1943- *BiDrAPA 89, WhoE 91*
Nocton, Francois Gerard 1934- *WhoWor 91*
Noda, Ken 1962- *IntWWM 90*
Noda, Takayo *WhoAmA 91*
Nodal, Guido Francisco, Jr. *BiDrAPA 89*
Noddack, Ida 1896-1978 *BioIn 16*
Noddin, Kevin L. 1955- *St&PR 91*
Noddings, Nel 1929- *WhoAmW 91*
Noddings, Thomas Clayton 1933- *WhoWor 91*
Nodel, Sol 1912-1976 *WhoAmA 91N*
Nodelman, Jared Robert 1937- *St&PR 91*
Nodine, Jane Allen 1954- *WhoAmA 91*
Nodine, Robert C 1928- *BiDrAPA 89*
Nodohara, Shoso 1924- *WhoWor 91*
Nodset, Joan L. *AuBYP 90*
Nodtvedt, Magnus 1924- *St&PR 91*
Nodvin, Joseph J. 1944- *WhoSSW 91*
Noe, Allan A. 1942- *ODwPR 91*
Noe, Clifford Dixon *BioIn 16*
Noe, Elnora 1928- *WhoAmW 91*
Noe, Guy 1934- *WhoAm 90*
Noe, J.T. Cotton 1869-1953 *LiHiK*
Noe, Jerry Lee 1940- *WhoAmA 91*
Noe, Juanita Louise 1947- *WhoAmW 91*
Noe, Judith Ann 1945- *WhoAmW 91*
Noe, Kurt Anthony 1961- *WhoE 91*
Noe, Ralph Henderson, Jr. 1930- *WhoSSW 91*
Noe, Randolph 1939- *WhoSSW 91*
Noecker, Rebecca H. *St&PR 91*
Noehren, Robert 1910- *WhoWor 91*
Noel, Barbara Hughes McMurtry 1929- *WhoAmW 91*
Noel, Cyril Thomas 1924- *St&PR 91*
Noel, Earl F. 1912- *St&PR 91*
Noel, Earl F., Jr. 1946- *St&PR 91*
Noel, Edwin Lawrence 1946- *WhoEmL 91*
Noel, Emile *BioIn 16*
Noel, Emile 1922- *WhoWor 91*
Noel, Georges 1924- *WhoAmA 91*
Noel, Hambleton Bridger *BioIn 16*
Noel, Howard George 1948- *WhoEmL 91*
Noel, James Latane, Jr. 1909- *WhoAm 90*
Noel, Jean 1940- *WhoAmA 91*
Noel, Jeanne Kay 1946- *WhoAmW 91*
Noel, John Baptist Lucius 1890-1989 *BioIn 16*
Noel, John Vavasour N., Mrs. 1815-1873 *FemiCLE*
Noel, Kenly McGee 1953- *WhoSSW 91*
Noel, Kenneth Duane 1932- *St&PR 91*
Noel, L. 1939- *St&PR 91*
Noel, Laurent 1920- *WhoAm 90*
Noel, Leon 1888-1987 *BiDFrPL*
Noel, Lloyd T., Jr. 1935- *WhoSSW 91*
Noel, Louise J 1914- *BiDrAPA 89*
Noel, Marc 1952- *WhoSSW 91*
Noel, Marie 1883-1967 *EncCoWW*
Noel, Michael Lee 1941- *St&PR 91, WhoAm 90*
Noel, Randall Deane 1953- *WhoEmL 91, WhoSSW 91*
Noel, Richard Lane 1947- *WhoWor 91*
Noel, Robert E. 1931- *St&PR 91*
Noel, Ruth *BiDrAPA 89*
Noel, Tallulah Ann 1945- *WhoAmW 91*
Noel, Thomas Elbert 1938- *WhoSSW 91*
Noel, Thurman C. 1934- *WhoAm 90*
Noel, Trevia Griffin 1949- *WhoAmW 91*
Noel, Vanessa *BioIn 16*
Noel-Baker, Philip John 1889-1982 *DcNaB 1981*
Noel Hume, Ivor 1927- *WhoAm 90*
Noelke, Paul 1915- *WhoAm 90*
Noell, Christopher N 1945- *BiDrAPA 89*
Noell, Edward Speed 1927- *St&PR 91*
Noell, Ivana Mae 1936- *WhoAmW 91*
Noell, Nick John 1946- *St&PR 91*
Noelle, Horst Carl 1924- *WhoWor 91*
Noennig, Alan H. 1938- *St&PR 91*
Noer, David Michael 1939- *WhoAm 90*
Noer, Richard J. 1937- *WhoAm 90*
Noering, Thomas William 1941- *WhoWor 91*
Noeske, Nancy R. 1937- *St&PR 91*
Noestheden, John 1945- *WhoAmA 91*
Noestlinger, Christine 1936- *SmATA 64*
Noeth, Carolyn Frances 1924- *WhoAmW 91, WhoWor 91*
Noeth, Cynthia Lou 1958- *WhoE 91*
Noeth, Winfried Maximilian 1944- *WhoWor 91*
Noether, Amalie Emmy 1882-1935 *BioIn 16*
Noether, Emiliana Pasca *WhoAm 90*
Noether, Emmy 1882-1935 *BioIn 16*
Noether, Gottfried Emanuel 1915- *WhoAm 90*
Noetzel, Grover Archibald Joseph 1908- *WhoAm 90, WhoSSW 91*
Noever, Nancy Kay 1961- *WhoSSW 91*
Nofer, Frank 1929- *WhoAmA 91*
Nofer, George Hancock 1926- *WhoAm 90*
Noffke, Maggie L. 1963- *WhoEmL 91*
Noffsinger, Donald Allen 1929- *St&PR 91*
Noffsinger, James Philip 1925- *WhoAm 90*
Noffsinger, Sheree Eader 1957- *WhoEmL 91*
Noffsinger, Stephen George 1962- *BiDrAPA 89*
Nofsinger, William M. 1932- *St&PR 91*
Nofziger, Margaret 1946- *ConAu 30NR*
Nofziger, Sally A. 1936- *St&PR 91*
Nofziger, Sally Alene *WhoAm 90*
Nofzinger, Eric Allen 1959- *BiDrAPA 89*
Noga, J Thomas *BiDrAPA 89*
Noga, John Stephen *St&PR 91N*
Noga, Joseph Peter 1941- *St&PR 91*
Nogal, Richard John 1956- *WhoEmL 91*
Nogales, Luis *BioIn 16*
Nogales, Luis Guerrero 1943- *WhoAm 90*
Nogales, Patti Diane 1961- *WhoAmW 91*
Nogami, Nobuyoshi 1937- *WhoWor 91*
Nogaret, Pierre 1720-1771 *PenDiDA 89*
Nogarola, Isotta 1416?-1466 *EncCoWW*
Nogee, Jeffrey Laurence 1952- *WhoEmL 91*
Nogelo, A. Miles 1943- *St&PR 91*
Nogelo, Anthony Miles 1943- *WhoAm 90*
Nogge, Gunther 1942- *WhoWor 91*
Noggle, Anne 1922- *WhoAmA 91*
Noggle, Dennis Allen 1936- *WhoSSW 91*
Noggle, Lawrence Wesley 1935- *WhoWor 91*
Nogi, Tiaki 1937- *WhoWor 91*
Nogin, Viktor Pavlovich 1878-1924 *BioIn 16*
Nogradi, Peter G. 1927- *St&PR 91*
Noguchi, Hideo 1945- *WhoEmL 91, WhoWor 91*
Noguchi, Hiroshi 1946- *WhoWor 91*
Noguchi, Isamu 1904- *PenDiDA 89*
Noguchi, Isamu 1904-1988 *AnObit 1988, BioIn 16, EncJap, WhoAmA 91N, WorAlBi*
Noguchi, Shun 1930- *WhoWor 91*
Noguchi, Teruo 1917- *WhoWor 91*
Noguchi, Thomas Tsunetomi 1927- *WhoAm 90*
Nogueira, Carlos Alberto Da Silva 1935- *WhoWor 91*
Nogueira, Jose Carlos *BiDrAPA 89*
Nogueres, Henri 1916- *WhoWor 91*
Nogues, Alexander Omar, Sr. 1926- *WhoHisp 91*
Nogues, Juan Francisco 1925- *WhoHisp 91*
Noh, Kyung Sun 1941- *BiDrAPA 89*
Noha, Edward J. 1927- *WhoAm 90*
Nohalty, John P. 1952- *St&PR 91*
Nohl, Jeffrey Joseph 1951- *St&PR 91*
Nohowel, Stephen Rehm 1949- *WhoE 91*
Noia, Alan James 1947- *St&PR 91, WhoAm 90*
Noir, Michel 1944- *BiDFrPL, WhoWor 91*
Noiseux, Robert 1950- *BiDrAPA 89*
Noja, Gian Paolo 1944- *WhoWor 91*
Noka *WhNaAH*
Noke, Cecil Jack *PenDiDA 89*
Noke, Charles John 1858-1941 *PenDiDA 89*
Nokes, John Richard 1915- *WhoAm 90*
Nokes, Matt 1963- *Ballpl 90*
Nolan, Agnes Peters 1908- *WhoWrEP 89*
Nolan, Alan Tucker 1923- *WhoAm 90*
Nolan, Barry Hance 1942- *WhoAm 90*
Nolan, Ben Davis, III 1957- *WhoSSW 91*
Nolan, Betsy 1941- *ODwPR 91*
Nolan, Carol L. 1938- *St&PR 91*
Nolan, Carson Young 1925- *WhoAm 90*
Nolan, Christopher 1965- *BioIn 16*
Nolan, Christopher Aloysius, III 1950- *WhoE 91*
Nolan, Chuck *ConAu 30NR*
Nolan, David 1946- *ConAu 132*
Nolan, David Brian 1951- *WhoEmL 91, WhoWor 91*
Nolan, Denise Susan 1952- *WhoAmW 91*
Nolan, Dennis 1945- *ConAu 32NR*
Nolan, Dennis C. *St&PR 91*
Nolan, Dennis M. *St&PR 91*
Nolan, Diane Agnes 1939- *WhoAm 90, WhoAmW 91*
Nolan, Doris Johnson 1933- *WhoAmW 91*
Nolan, Ernest Isaiah 1948- *WhoEmL 91*
Nolan, Finbarr 1952- *EncO&P 3*
Nolan, Florence Dorothy 1955- *St&PR 91*
Nolan, Francis Thomas 1931- *WhoE 91*
Nolan, Frederick William 1931- *SpyFic*
Nolan, Gary 1948- *Ballpl 90*
Nolan, Gerald 1947- *WhoSSW 91*
Nolan, Howard Charles, Jr. 1932- *WhoE 91*
Nolan, Irene Clare 1946- *WhoAm 90, WhoAmW 91*
Nolan, James Francis, Jr. 1950- *WhoE 91*
Nolan, James Paul 1929- *WhoAm 90*
Nolan, James Robert 1935- *St&PR 91*
Nolan, Jeannette Covert 1897-1974 *AuBYP 90*
Nolan, Joan Parmeter 1934- *WhoE 91*
Nolan, Joan S. 1930- *St&PR 91*
Nolan, Joe 1951- *Ballpl 90*
Nolan, John Blanchard 1943- *WhoAm 90*
Nolan, John Edward 1925- *WhoAm 90*
Nolan, John Edward 1927- *WhoAm 90*
Nolan, John Francis 1940- *St&PR 91*
Nolan, John Patrick 1954- *WhoE 91*
Nolan, Joseph Richard 1925- *WhoAm 90, WhoE 91*
Nolan, Joseph Thomas 1920- *WhoAm 90*
Nolan, Karen L. 1958- *ODwPR 91*
Nolan, Kathleen 1933- *WhoAm 90*
Nolan, Kathleen 1949- *ODwPR 91*
Nolan, Kevin Barry 1952- *St&PR 91*
Nolan, Lawrence Patrick 1948- *WhoEmL 91*
Nolan, Lewis Earle 1943- *WhoSSW 91*
Nolan, Lloyd 1902-1985 *WorAlBi*
Nolan, Lorene Susan 1958- *WhoAmW 91*
Nolan, Louise Mary 1947- *WhoAmW 91, WhoE 91, WhoEmL 91, WhoWor 91*
Nolan, Margaret Maley 1935- *WhoE 91*
Nolan, Margaret Patterson *WhoAmA 91*
Nolan, Mark S. *ODwPR 91*
Nolan, Michael Edward 1949- *WhoEmL 91*
Nolan, Patrick Joseph 1933- *WhoAm 90*
Nolan, Patrick Joseph 1938- *St&PR 91, WhoAm 90*

Nolan, Paul T. *WhoAm 90*
Nolan, Paul T. 1919- *BioIn 16*
Nolan, Paul Thomas 1919- *WhoAm 90, WhoWrEP 89*
Nolan, Peter F. 1943- *St&PR 91*
Nolan, Ralph H. 1912- *St&PR 91*
Nolan, Richard Edward 1928- *WhoAm 90*
Nolan, Richard Thomas 1937- *WhoE 91, WhoWor 91*
Nolan, Robert Dan 1938- *WhoSSW 91*
Nolan, Robert E. *ODwPR 91*
Nolan, Robert Emmett 1933- *WhoAm 90*
Nolan, Robert F. 1927- *St&PR 91*
Nolan, Robert Myles 1945- *St&PR 91*
Nolan, Robert W. 1943- *St&PR 91*
Nolan, Sara *BioIn 16*
Nolan, Sheila Mary *BiDrAPA 89*
Nolan, Stanton Peelle 1933- *WhoAm 90, WhoWor 91*
Nolan, Stuart Walter 1968- *WhoEmL 91*
Nolan, Terence Magie 1941- *WhoAm 90*
Nolan, Terrance Joseph, Jr. 1950- *WhoEmL 91*
Nolan, Thomas J. 1954- *St&PR 91*
Nolan, Thomas Patrick 1933- *St&PR 91*
Nolan, Timothy F. *BiDrAPA 89*
Nolan, Val, Jr. 1920- *WhoAm 90*
Nolan, Victoria Holmes 1952- *WhoAmW 91*
Nolan, Walter Joseph 1924- *St&PR 91*
Nolan, William F. 1928- *BioIn 16, TwCCr&M 91*
Nolan, William Joseph, III 1947- *WhoAm 90*
Noland, Anginette Roberts 1930- *WhoAmW 91, WhoSSW 91*
Noland, Cara Holly 1958- *WhoAmW 91*
Noland, Charles Eugene 1930- *WhoWrEP 89*
Noland, Cookie Katherine 1944- *WhoAmW 91*
Noland, Douglas Eugene 1957- *WhoSSW 91*
Noland, James Ellsworth 1920- *WhoAm 90*
Noland, John W. 1949- *St&PR 91*
Noland, Jon David 1938- *St&PR 91, WhoAm 90*
Noland, Kenneth 1924- *BioIn 16, WhoAmA 91*
Noland, Kenneth Clifton 1924- *WhoAm 90*
Noland, Lloyd U., III 1943- *St&PR 91, WhoSSW 91*
Noland, Lloyd U., Jr. 1917- *St&PR 91*
Noland, Mariam Charl 1947- *WhoAmW 91*
Noland, Patricia Ann 1945- *WhoAmW 91*
Noland, Robert LeRoy 1918- *WhoAm 90*
Noland, Royce Paul 1928- *WhoAm 90*
Noland, Thomas Turley 1918- *St&PR 91*
Noland, Thomas Turley, Jr. 1953- *WhoSSW 91*
Noland, William 1954- *WhoAmA 91*
Nolasco, Antonio Cases *BiDrAPA 89*
Nold, Carl R 1955- *WhoAmA 91*
Nold, Carl Richard 1955- *WhoAm 90, WhoE 91*
Nold, Michael F. 1938- *St&PR 91*
Nolde, Emil 1867-1956 *IntDcAA 90*
Nolder, Craig Allen 1958- *WhoSSW 91*
Nolder, Sharlene J. 1949- *WhoAmW 91*
Nole, Robert James 1933- *St&PR 91*
Nolen, Jerry Aften, Jr. 1940- *WhoAm 90*
Nolen, John 1869-1937 *BioIn 16*
Nolen, Raymond R. *WhoSSW 91*
Nolen, Richard R 1923- *BiDrAPA 89*
Nolen, William Anthony 1928- *WhoWrEP 89*
Nolen, William Giles 1931- *WhoAm 90*
Nolen, William Lawrence, Jr. 1922- *WhoSSW 91*
Noles, Dickie 1956- *Ballpl 90*
Noles, Jackie Lewis 1938- *WhoSSW 91*
Noles, Sharon Rebecca 1946- *WhoAmW 91*
Noles, Tammy Gaye 1965- *WhoAmW 91*
Nolf, David Manstan 1942- *St&PR 91*
Nolfi, Frank Vincent, Jr. 1941- *WhoE 91*
Nolfo, Louis A. *BioIn 16*
Nolin, Lillian Renee 1923- *WhoWrEP 89*
Noling, Lawrence J. 1930- *St&PR 91*
Noll, Andrew F., III 1930- *St&PR 91*
Noll, Bruce Kevin 1954- *BiDrAPA 89*
Noll, Charles Henry 1931- *WhoAm 90, WhoE 91*
Noll, Chris Alan 1952- *St&PR 91*
Noll, Chuck 1931- *WorAlBi*
Noll, Clair W. 1933- *St&PR 91*
Noll, Irwin 1938- *St&PR 91*
Noll, Laureen Judy 1960- *BiDrAPA 89*
Noll, Mary Lou 1954- *WhoAmW 91*
Noll, Peter *BioIn 16*
Noll, Phyllis I. *St&PR 91*
Noll, Rhona Susan 1947- *WhoE 91*
Noll, Roger Gordon 1940- *WhoAm 90*
Noll, S. Darwin 1920- *St&PR 91*
Noll, Sally *AuBYP 90*
Noll, Walter 1925- *WhoAm 90*
Noll, Warren Philip 1938- *St&PR 91*
Nollau, Lee Gordon 1950- *WhoE 91*
Nollekens, Joseph 1737-1823 *BioIn 16, IntDcAA 90*
Nollet, Lois Sophia 1921- *WhoWrEP 89*
Nolley, J. Robert, Jr. 1929- *ODwPR 91*
Nollsch, William E. 1941- *St&PR 91*
Nolt, Douglas Eugene 1957- *WhoEmL 91*
Nolt, Joseph P. 1936- *St&PR 91*
Nolt, Sally Kulp 1946- *WhoAmW 91*
Nolte, Ann E. *BioIn 16*
Nolte, Charles Winfield 1945- *WhoWrEP 89*
Nolte, Eric 1964- *Ballpl 90*
Nolte, Ernst H. 1923- *WhoWor 91*
Nolte, Ewald Valentin 1909- *IntWWM 90*
Nolte, George Washington 1904- *WhoWor 91*
Nolte, Gunter 1938- *WhoAmA 91*
Nolte, Hans-Heinrich 1938- *WhoWor 91*
Nolte, Henry R., Jr. 1924- *WhoAm 90*
Nolte, Judith Ann 1938- *WhoAm 90*
Nolte, Melvin, Jr. 1947- *WhoEmL 91*
Nolte, Nick *BioIn 16*
Nolte, Nick 1940- *WorAlBi*
Nolte, Nick 1942- *WhoAm 90*
Nolte, Richard Henry 1920- *WhoAm 90*
Nolte, Sharon H. *BioIn 16*
Nolte, Thomas Charles 1949- *BiDrAPA 89*
Nolte, Walter Eduard 1911- *WhoAm 90*
Nolte, William Henry 1928- *WhoAm 90*
Nolte, Wolfram 1949- *WhoWor 91*
Noltemeier, Hartmut W. *WhoWor 91*
Nolting, Frederick 1911-1989 *BioIn 16, ConAu 130*
Nolting, Frederick William 1950- *WhoEmL 91*
Nolting, Paul 1939- *St&PR 91*
Nomeland, Leslie C. 1936- *St&PR 91*
Nomeland, Leslie Cornell 1936- *WhoAm 90*
Nomm, Rein 1945- *ODwPR 91*
Nomoto, Otohiko 1912- *WhoWor 91*
Nomura Kichisaburo 1877-1964 *EncJap*
Nomura, Katsuya 1934- *Ballpl 90*
Nomura, Kikuo 1926- *WhoAm 90*
Nomura, Masayasu 1927- *WhoAm 90*
Nomura, Tetsuzo *St&PR 91*
Nomura, Toshio 1929- *St&PR 91*
Nomura, Yosio Francesco 1908- *IntWWM 90*
Nonaka, Taijiro 1936- *WhoWor 91*
Nonas, Richard 1936- *WhoAmA 91*
Nonell, Vicente E 1930- *BiDrAPA 89*
Nonet, Philippe 1939- *WhoAm 90*
Nong 1930- *WhoAm 90, WhoAmA 91*
Nonn, James C. 1953- *St&PR 91*
Nonne, Christian *PenDiDA 89*
Nonni, Francesco *PenDiDA 89*
Nono, Luigi *BioIn 16*
Nono, Luigi 1924- *PenDiMP A*
Nono, Luigi 1924-1990 *NewYTBS 90*
Nonomura Ninsei *EncJap*
Nonoyama, Toru *BioIn 16*
Nonus, Maurice Joseph 1954- *WhoWor 91*
Noodfin, Thomas L. 1948- *St&PR 91*
Noojin, Ray Oscar, Jr. 1945- *WhoEmL 91*
Noon, James H., Jr. 1946- *St&PR 91*
Noon, Maurice Norman 1924- *St&PR 91*
Noon, Walter D. 1930- *St&PR 91*
Noonan, Augustine J P *BiDrAPA 89*
Noonan, Charles A 1949- *BiDrAPA 89*
Noonan, Elmer James 1927- *St&PR 91*
Noonan, Frank R. 1942- *WhoAm 90*
Noonan, Jacqueline Anne 1928- *WhoAmW 91*
Noonan, James Charles 1946- *St&PR 91*
Noonan, John Michael 1933- *St&PR 91*
Noonan, John T., Jr. 1926- *WhoAm 90*
Noonan, Melinda Dunham 1954- *WhoAmW 91*
Noonan, Michael Dennis 1941- *St&PR 91, WhoE 91*
Noonan, Michael John 1947- *WhoEmL 91*
Noonan, Michael Joseph 1935- *WhoWor 91*
Noonan, Nancy Anderson 1940- *WhoSSW 91*
Noonan, Norine Elizabeth 1948- *WhoAm 90*
Noonan, Patrick Francis 1942- *WhoAm 90, WhoWor 91*
Noonan, Patrick Matthew 1952- *WhoEmL 91*
Noonan, Patrick Sutton 1955- *WhoEmL 91*
Noonan, Peggy *BioIn 16*
Noonan, Peggy 1950- *BestSel 90-3 [port], ConAu 132, CurBio 90 [port], News 90 [port], -90-3 [port]*
Noonan, Ray John 1914- *WhoAm 90*
Noonan, Susan A. 1960- *ODwPR 91*
Noonan, Thomas F. 1939- *St&PR 91*
Noonan, Thomas Schaub 1938- *WhoAm 90*
Noonan, Tom 1951- *ConTFT 8*
Noonan, William Ewart 1928- *WhoAm 90, WhoWor 91*
Noonan, William F. 1932- *ODwPR 91*
Noonberg, Lewis Allan 1938- *WhoAm 90*
Noonburg, Joseph Nellis 1935- *St&PR 91*
Noone, Edwina *TwCCr&M 91*
Noone, Jack J. *BioIn 16*
Noone, Jean Abbott 1939- *WhoSSW 91*
Noone, Jimmie 1895-1944 *OxCPMus, WorAlBi*
Noone, Jimmy 1895-1944 *BioIn 16*
Noone, Joseph A *BiDrAPA 89*
Noone, Michael Francis, Jr. 1934- *WhoE 91*
Noone, Peter *BioIn 16*
Noone, Peter 1947- *EncPR&S 89*
Noone, Robert Barrett 1939- *WhoE 91*
Noone, William Francis 1948- *St&PR 91*
Nooney, John J. 1929- *St&PR 91*
Nooney, John J. 1939- *St&PR 91*
Noonkester, James Ralph 1924- *WhoAm 90*
Noonuccal, Oodgeroo 1920- *FemiCLE*
Noor, Ismail 1942- *WhoWor 91*
Noor, Muhammed Aslam 1945- *WhoWor 91*
Noorda, Bob 1927- *ConDes 90*
Noordergraaf, Abraham 1929- *WhoAm 90*
Noordhoek, Harry Cecil 1909- *WhoAmA 91*
Noordsij, A Johan 1927- *BiDrAPA 89*
Noordsij, Arie Johan 1927- *WhoE 91*
Noordsy, Douglas *BiDrAPA 89*
Noordzij, Nel 1923- *EncCoWW*
Noorthey, P. *EncCoWW*
Noot, Donald Scott 1933- *St&PR 91*
Nootbaar, H.V. 1908- *St&PR 91*
Nooteboom, Cees 1933- *ConAu 130*
Nooth, Charlotte *FemiCLE*
Nopar, Alan Scott 1951- *WhoWor 91*
Nops, Jerry 1875-1937 *Ballpl 90*
Nora, Audrey Hart 1936- *WhoAmW 91*
Nora, Hope 1949- *WhoAmW 91*
Nora, James Jackson 1928- *WhoAm 90*
Nora, Rena Magno *BiDrAPA 89*
Norair, Jill S. 1956- *St&PR 91*
Norair, Richard H. 1929- *St&PR 91*
Noran, William Harold 1943- *WhoSSW 91*
Norat, Manuel Eric 1950- *WhoHisp 91*
Norat-Phillips, Sarah L. 1956- *WhoHisp 91*
Norback, Craig Thomas 1943- *WhoAm 90, WhoE 91*
Norbeck, Edward 1915- *WhoWrEP 89*
Norbeck, George P 1937- *BiDrAPA 89*
Norbeck, Timothy Burns 1938- *WhoE 91*
Norberg, Ann Dee Hodak 1944- *WhoAmW 91*
Norberg, Charles Robert 1912- *WhoAm 90*
Norberg, Jaron B. 1937- *WhoAm 90*
Norberg, John Henry 1957- *St&PR 91*
Norberg, Richard Edwin 1922- *WhoAm 90*
Norbitz, Harold 1921- *St&PR 91*
Norbitz, Wayne *St&PR 91*
Norborg, Ake 1943- *IntWWM 90*
Norbury, J. Thom *St&PR 91*
Norbury, Louise H 1878-1952 *WhoAmA 91N*
Norby, Barbara H. 1936- *St&PR 91*
Norby, Erik 1936- *IntWWM 90*
Norby, John K. 1931- *St&PR 91*
Norby, Mark Alan 1955- *WhoEmL 91*
Norby, Rockford Douglas 1935- *WhoAm 90*
Norcel, Jacqueline Joyce Casale 1940- *WhoAmW 91*
Norcott, Alfred A. 1918- *WhoAm 90*
Norcross, David Frank Armstrong 1937- *WhoE 91*
Norcross, John *ConAu 131*
Norcross, Lois Manley *WhoE 91*
Norcross, Marvin Augustus 1931- *WhoAm 90*
Nord, Daniel A. 1953- *St&PR 91*
Nord, Deanna Lynn 1956- *WhoEmL 91*
Nord, Eric *BioIn 16*
Nord, Eric T. 1917- *St&PR 91*
Nord, Eric Thomas 1917- *WhoAm 90*
Nord, Evan Walter 1919- *St&PR 91*
Nord, Henry J. 1917- *WhoAm 90*
Nord, Patricia Fitzgerald 1929- *WhoSSW 91*
Nord, Peter J. 1939- *St&PR 91*
Nord, Walter Robert 1939- *WhoAm 90*
Nordahl, David *BioIn 16*
Nordahl, Norris George 1918- *WhoWor 91*
Nordahl, Thomas Edward 1948- *BiDrAPA 89*
Nordal, Johannes 1924- *WhoWor 91*
Nordal, Jon 1926- *IntWWM 90*
Nordan, Lewis Alonzo 1939- *WhoWrEP 89*
Nordberg, Carl Alfred, Jr. 1935- *WhoAm 90*
Nordberg, E. Wayne 1938- *WhoAm 90*
Nordberg, John Albert 1926- *WhoAm 90*
Nordbrandt, Henrik 1945- *DcScanL*
Nordby, Eugene Jorgen 1918- *WhoAm 90, WhoWor 91*
Nordby, Gene Milo 1926- *WhoAm 90*
Nordby, Reidar Frode 1948- *WhoWor 91*
Nordby, Roger A. 1945- *St&PR 91*
Nordbye, Richard Arthur 1919- *WhoAm 90*
Nordbye, Rodger Lincoln 1918- *WhoAm 90*
Norddahl, Birgir Valson 1947- *WhoWor 91*
Nordeen, William E. 1936-1988 *BioIn 16*
Nordell, Emma Parker *WhoAmA 91N*
Nordell, Hans Roderick 1925- *WhoAm 90*
Norden, Carl William 1935- *WhoAm 90*
Norden, Charles *ConAu 132, MajTwCW*
Norden, Christine *BioIn 16*
Norden, Christine 1924-1988 *AnObit 1988*
Norden, F.A. 1930- *St&PR 91*
Norden, Howard B. 1930- *St&PR 91*
Norden, K. Elis 1921- *WhoWor 91*
Norden, Martin Frank 1951- *WhoWrEP 89*
Norden, Michael James *BiDrAPA 89*
Norden, Peter Christopher 1949- *WhoE 91*
Norden, Roger Craig 1950- *St&PR 91*
Nordenflycht, Hedvig Charlotta 1718-1763 *DcScanL, EncCoWW*
Nordenskiold, A. E. 1832-1901 *BioIn 16*
Nordenskiold, Adolf Erik 1832-1901 *BioIn 16*
Nordenstam, Tore Sigvard 1934- *WhoWor 91*
Nordenstrom, Gladys 1924- *IntWWM 90*
Nordgard, Per 1932- *IntWWM 90*
Nordgren, Anna 1847-1916 *BiDWomA*
Nordgren, Cinda *ODwPR 91*
Nordgren, Pehr Henrik 1944- *IntWWM 90*
Nordgren, Ronald Paul 1936- *WhoAm 90, WhoSSW 91*
Nordgren, Stanford Robert 1928- *St&PR 91*
Nordhagen, Hallie Huerth 1914- *WhoAmW 91*
Nordhagen, Wayne 1948- *Ballpl 90*
Nordhaus, Jean 1939- *WhoWrEP 89*
Nordhaus, John P. 1920- *St&PR 91*
Nordhaus, William Dawbney 1941- *WhoAm 90, WhoE 91*
Nordhausen, A Henry 1901- *WhoAmA 91*
Nordhoff, Charles Bernard 1887-1947 *AuBYP 90, WorAlBi*
Nordhoff, Heinz 1889-1968 *WorAlBi*
Nordica, Lillian 1857-1914 *PenDiMP*
Nordica, Lillian 1859-1914 *BioAmW*
Nordin, Bertil Donald 1934- *St&PR 91*
Nordin, John Algot 1916- *WhoAm 90*
Nordin, Larry F. 1950- *St&PR 91*
Nordin, Phyllis E *WhoAmA 91*
Nordin, Phyllis Eck *WhoAmW 91*
Nordin, Vidar John 1924- *WhoAm 90*
Nordine, Gaylord Carl 1944- *BiDrAPA 89*
Nordland, Gerald John *WhoAm 90*
Nordland, Gerald John 1927- *WhoAmA 91*
Nordlander, Britt Eva Margareta 1947- *WhoWor 91*
Nordlicht, Stephen 1909- *BiDrAPA 89*
Nordlie, Robert Conrad 1930- *WhoAm 90*
Nordling, Klaus 1915-1986 *EncACom*
Nordling, Robert George 1932- *WhoAm 90*
Nordlinger, Douglas Edward 1956- *WhoEmL 91*
Nordlinger, Eric Allen 1939- *WhoAm 90*
Nordlinger, Gerson, Jr. 1916- *WhoWor 91*
Nordlinger, Richard E. 1919- *St&PR 91*
Nordlund, Donald Craig 1949- *WhoAm 90*
Nordlund, Donald Elmer 1922- *WhoAm 90*
Nordlund, William Chalmers 1954- *WhoEmL 91*
Nordman, Christer Eric 1925- *WhoAm 90*
Nordman, Richard D. 1946- *St&PR 91*
Nordmann, Gary Arnold 1942- *WhoAm 90*
Nordmann, Nancy Olivia 1945- *WhoAmW 91*
Nordmeyer, Mary Betsy 1939- *WhoAmW 91*
Nordquist, Myron Harry 1940- *WhoE 91*
Nordquist, Stephen Glos 1936- *WhoE 91, WhoWor 91*
Nordqvist, Erik Askbo 1943- *WhoWor 91*
Nordstrand, Dennis L. 1935- *St&PR 91*
Nordstrand, Nathalie Elizabeth Johnson 1932- *WhoE 91*
Nordstrand, Nathalie Johnson *WhoAmA 91*
Nordstrand, Raymond William 1932- *WhoAm 90*
Nordstroem, Carl Otto 1916- *WhoWor 91*
Nordstrom, Bruce A. 1933- *WhoAm 90*
Nordstrom, Harold 1946- *St&PR 91*
Nordstrom, James F. 1940- *WhoAm 90*
Nordstrom, Jeanette *ODwPR 91*
Nordstrom, John N. 1937- *St&PR 91*
Nordstrom, Mary Susan 1952- *WhoAmW 91*
Nordstrom, Robert John 1924- *WhoAm 90*
Nordstrom, Sven J. *BioIn 16*
Nordstrom, Ursula 1910-1988 *AuBYP 90, BioIn 16*
Nordstrom, Wayne Jerome 1950- *WhoEmL 91*
Nordstrom, Wilber C. 1918- *St&PR 91*

Nordt, Paul W., III 1941- *St&PR 91*
Nordt, Paul W., Jr. 1914- *St&PR 91*
Nordwall, Eva Marie 1944- *IntWWM 90*
Nordyke, Charlotta Fincher 1953- *WhoAmW 91*
Nordyke, Eleanor Cole 1927- *WhoAmW 91, WhoWor 91*
Nordyke, James Walter 1930- *WhoAm 90*
Nordyke, Stephen Keith 1953- *WhoEmL 91*
Norehad, Bedros *BioIn 16*
Noreika, Sofia 1945- *WhoAmW 91, WhoE 91, WhoWor 91*
Norek, Frances Therese 1947- *WhoAmW 91*
Norell, Dagmar I 1917- *BiDrAPA 89*
Norell, Norman 1900-1972 *ConDes 90, WorAlBi*
Norelli, Lisa 1961- *BiDrAPA 89*
Norelli, Martina Roudabush 1942- *WhoAmA 91*
Norelli, Patricia Ann 1941- *WhoAmW 91*
Norem, Bonnie Lou 1936- *WhoAmW 91*
Norem, Richard Frederick 1931- *WhoAm 90*
Noren, Irv 1924- *Ballpl 90*
Noren, Paul Harold Andreas 1910- *WhoWor 91*
Noren, Rees E. 1932- *St&PR 91*
Noren, Robert Alexander 1943- *WhoSSW 91*
Noren, Vern Michael 1948- *WhoSSW 91*
Norena, Eide 1884-1968 *PenDiMP*
Norena, Maria Claudia 1963- *WhoHisp 91*
Norfleet, Barbara Chapman 1943- *WhoAmW 91*
Norfleet, Barbara Pugh *WhoAmA 91*
Norfleet, Barbara Pugh 1926- *WhoE 91*
Norfleet, Edourd K 1924- *BiDrAPA 89*
Norfleet, Francesca Maria 1953- *WhoAmW 91*
Norfleet, George S. 1947- *St&PR 91*
Norfleet, Morris Lee 1930- *WhoAm 90*
Norfleet, Robert F., Jr. 1940- *WhoSSW 91*
Norfleet, Robert Fillmore 1940- *St&PR 91*
Norfleet, Shirley J. 1934- *St&PR 91*
Norfolk, Mary, Duchess of 1659-1705 *BiDEWW*
Norfolk, William Ray 1941- *WhoE 91*
Norford, George 1918- *DrBlPA 90*
Norford, George E. 1918- *EarBlAP*
Norgaard, Bjorn 1947- *WhoWor 91*
Norgaard, Jens *BioIn 16*
Norgan, Anne F *BiDrAPA 89*
Norgay, Tenzing 1914-1986 *BioIn 16*
Norgle, Charles Ronald, Sr. 1937- *WhoAm 90*
Norgren, C. Neil 1923- *WhoAm 90*
Norholm, Ib 1931- *IntWWM 90*
Norian, Roger W. 1943- *St&PR 91, WhoAm 90*
Norick, Ronald 1941- *WhoSSW 91*
Noriega, Lamar Jernigan 1943- *WhoSSW 91*
Noriega, Manuel Antonio *BioIn 16*
Noriega, Richard, Jr. 1950- *WhoHisp 91*
Noriega, Rudy Jorge 1937- *WhoSSW 91*
Noriega, Saturnino N. 1939- *WhoHisp 91*
Noriega Moreno, Manuel 1940- *WorAlBi*
Norins, Arthur Leonard 1928- *WhoAm 90*
Norinsky, Marvin 1927- *ConAu 130*
Norkin, Cynthia Clair 1932- *WhoAmW 91, WhoWor 91*
Norko, Michael A. *BiDrAPA 89*
Norko, Michael Albert 1957- *WhoE 91*
Norkus, Herbert 1916-1932 *BioIn 16*
Norkus, Michael 1946- *WhoE 91*
Norland, Cheryl M. 1950- *WhoAmW 91*
Norland, Donald Richard 1924- *WhoAm 90*
Norlander, John Allen 1930- *WhoAm 90*
Norlander, Lyle E. 1937- *St&PR 91*
Norling, Ernest Ralph 1892- *AuBYP 90*
Norling, James A. *WhoAm 90*
Norling, James Albert 1942- *St&PR 91*
Norling, James F. 1928- *St&PR 91*
Norling, Josephine 1895- *AuBYP 90*
Norman, Albert George, Jr. 1929- *WhoAm 90, WhoSSW 91, WhoWor 91*
Norman, Anthony Westcott 1938- *WhoAm 90*
Norman, Barbara Ann 1928- *WhoSSW 91*
Norman, Charles 1904- *AuBYP 90*
Norman, Colin Arthur 1948- *WhoE 91*
Norman, David A. 1935- *St&PR 91, WhoAm 90*
Norman, David Taylor 1947- *WhoSSW 91*
Norman, Donald Arthur 1935- *WhoAm 90*
Norman, Dora Cole *EarBlAP*
Norman, Dorothy 1905- *WhoAmA 91*
Norman, Dudley Kent 1949- *WhoAm 90*
Norman, Edward C 1913- *BiDrAPA 89*
Norman, Emile 1918- *WhoAmA 91*
Norman, Fred 1942- *Ballpl 90*
Norman, Frederick C. 1909- *St&PR 91*
Norman, Geoffrey *BioIn 16*
Norman, Geoffrey R. 1944- *St&PR 91*
Norman, Geoffrey Robert 1944- *WhoE 91*
Norman, George Buford, Jr. 1945- *WhoSSW 91*
Norman, George C. 1943- *St&PR 91*
Norman, George Emerson, Jr. 1914- *WhoAm 90*
Norman, Greg 1955- *BioIn 16, WhoWor 91, WorAlBi*
Norman, Gurney 1937- *LiHiK*
Norman, Haskell F 1915- *BiDrAPA 89*
Norman, Homer Howard 1933- *WhoSSW 91*
Norman, Howard 1949?- *ConAu 129*
Norman, Jackie Delois 1941- *WhoWrEP 89*
Norman, Jan *ODwPR 91*
Norman, Jeff *BioIn 16*
Norman, Jessye *BioIn 16*
Norman, Jessye 1945- *DrBlPA 90, IntWWM 90, PenDiMP, WhoAm 90, WhoAmW 91, WhoWor 91, WorAlBi*
Norman, Joe G., Jr. 1947- *WhoAm 90, WhoEmL 91*
Norman, John Barstow, Jr. 1940- *WhoAm 90*
Norman, John Edward 1922- *WhoWor 91*
Norman, Julie Anne 1943- *WhoAmW 91*
Norman, LaLander Stadig 1912- *WhoAm 90*
Norman, Lewis Sheppard, Jr. 1923- *WhoAm 90*
Norman, Linda Kay *BiDrAPA 89*
Norman, Maidie 1912- *DrBlPA 90*
Norman, Marc Ellington 1961- *WhoE 91*
Norman, Marsha *BioIn 16*
Norman, Marsha 1947- *FemiCLE, LiHiK, NotWoAT, WhoAm 90, WhoAmW 91, WorAu 1980 [port]*
Norman, Mary Marshall 1937- *WhoAmW 91*
Norman, Max E. 1927- *St&PR 91*
Norman, Michael *BioIn 16*
Norman, Michael 1947- *ConAu 129, WhoWrEP 89*
Norman, Monty 1928- *OxCPMus*
Norman, Neil *NewAgMG*
Norman, Norman B. 1914- *WhoAm 90*
Norman, Patrick A 1951- *BiDrAPA 89*
Norman, Paul Ray 1951- *WhoSSW 91*
Norman, Philip Sidney 1924- *WhoAm 90*
Norman, Philip Thomas 1953- *IntWWM 90*
Norman, Ralph David 1915- *WhoAm 90*
Norman, Ralph Louis 1933- *WhoAm 90*
Norman, Richard Arthur 1915- *WhoAm 90*
Norman, Richard Oswald Chandler 1932- *WhoWor 91*
Norman, Samuel *PenDiDA 89*
Norman, Sharon Anne 1939- *WhoAmW 91*
Norman, Shirley Ann 1940- *WhoAmW 91*
Norman, Stephen Peckham 1942- *WhoAm 90*
Norman, Thomas Hayward 1917- *St&PR 91*
Norman, Trudy 1936- *WhoWor 91*
Norman, Tyler *BioIn 16*
Norman, William E. 1914- *St&PR 91*
Norman, William Stanley 1938- *BioIn 16, St&PR 91, WhoAm 90*
Norman-Neruda, Wilma *PenDiMP*
Normand, Jacques Marie 1936- *WhoWor 91*
Normand, Mabel 1894-1930 *BioAmW*
Normand, Patricia Susan 1952- *BiDrAPA 89*
Normand, Robert 1940- *St&PR 91, WhoAm 90*
Normand, William C 1922- *BiDrAPA 89*
Normandeau, Andre Gabriel 1942- *WhoAm 90*
Normandin, Robert A. 1945- *St&PR 91*
Normann, Regine 1867-1939 *EncCoWW*
Normile, Barbara 1951- *WhoAmW 91*
Normile, Michael T. 1949- *WhoAm 90*
Normile, Michael Timothy 1949- *St&PR 91*
Normington, Norma Shotwell 1924- *WhoAmW 91*
Normington, Richard 1935- *BiDrAPA 89*
Norniella, Jesus, Jr. 1940- *WhoHisp 91*
Norodom Chakrapong *WhoWor 91*
Norodom Sihanouk 1922- *WhoWor 91*
Norodom Sihanouk, Prince 1922- *BioIn 16*
Norodom Sihanouk, Samdech Preah 1922- *ConAu 129*
Norquist, Ellen Johnson 1951- *WhoAmW 91*
Norquist, Galen R. 1926- *St&PR 91*
Norquist, Grayson Swayze *BiDrAPA 89*
Norquist, John Olof 1949- *WhoAm 90*
Norrback, Johan Ole 1941- *WhoWor 91*
Norrby, Johannes E. V. 1904- *IntWWM 90*
Norregaard, Asta Elisa Jakobine 1853-1933 *BiDWomA*
Norrell, J. Elizabeth 1958- *WhoAmW 91*
Norrell, Susan T. 1959- *WhoAmW 91*
Norrgard, Kristin Ann 1957- *WhoAm 90, WhoAmW 91*
Norrie, K. Peter 1939- *St&PR 91*
Norrington, Arthur Lionel Pugh 1899-1982 *DcNaB 1981*
Norrington, Roger 1934- *BioIn 16, CurBio 90 [port], PenDiMP*
Norrington, Roger Arthur Carver 1934- *IntWWM 90, WhoWor 91*
Norris, Alan Eugene 1935- *WhoAm 90*
Norris, Albert S 1926- *BiDrAPA 89*
Norris, Albert Stanley 1926- *WhoAm 90*
Norris, Alfred Lloyd 1938- *WhoSSW 91*
Norris, Andrea Spaulding 1945- *WhoAm 90, WhoAmA 91*
Norris, Annette Crockett 1940- *WhoAmW 91*
Norris, Arthur George 1937- *BiDrAPA 89*
Norris, Ben 1910- *WhoAmA 91*
Norris, Benjamin Franklin 1870-1902 *BioIn 16*
Norris, Carol Ann 1961- *WhoAmW 91*
Norris, Carole Veronica 1948- *WhoWrEP 89*
Norris, Catherine Bowden 1930- *WhoAmW 91*
Norris, Charlene Marie 1958- *WhoAmW 91*
Norris, Charles Head, Jr. 1940- *WhoE 91, WhoWor 91*
Norris, Charles Morgan 1915- *WhoAm 90*
Norris, Charles R, Jr. *BiDrAPA 89*
Norris, Chester Edward 1927- *WhoAm 90, WhoWor 91*
Norris, Chuck *BioIn 16, WhoAm 90*
Norris, Chuck 1939- *WorAlBi*
Norris, Clarence 1912-1989 *AnObit 1989, BioIn 16*
Norris, Clayton 1922- *WhoE 91*
Norris, Curtis Bird 1927- *WhoE 91*
Norris, Darell Forest 1928- *WhoAm 90*
Norris, David C *BiDrAPA 89*
Norris, David Owen 1953- *IntWWM 90*
Norris, David S. 1938- *St&PR 91*
Norris, David Stuart 1938- *WhoAm 90*
Norris, Diane Lee 1941- *WhoWrEP 89*
Norris, Donna Marie 1943- *BiDrAPA 89*
Norris, Edward P. 1940- *St&PR 91*
Norris, Eileen C. 1953- *WhoWrEP 89*
Norris, Elizabeth Downe 1914- *WhoAmW 91*
Norris, Faith Grigsby *AuBYP 90*
Norris, Frances McMurtray 1946- *WhoAm 90, WhoAmW 91*
Norris, Frank 1870-1902 *BioIn 16, WorAlBi*
Norris, Frank William 1920- *St&PR 91*
Norris, Franklin Gray 1923- *WhoAm 90*
Norris, Frederick Walter 1941- *WhoSSW 91*
Norris, Geoffrey 1937- *WhoAm 90*
Norris, Geoffrey 1947- *IntWWM 90*
Norris, George W. 1861-1944 *WorAlBi*
Norris, George William 1861-1944 *BioIn 16*
Norris, George William 1933- *St&PR 91*
Norris, Gunilla B. *AuBYP 90*
Norris, H. Coleman 1931- *St&PR 91*
Norris, H. Jones, Jr. 1943- *St&PR 91*
Norris, H. Thomas 1934- *WhoSSW 91*
Norris, Hunt T., Jr. *St&PR 91*
Norris, James A. 1928- *St&PR 91*
Norris, James Goodrum 1964- *WhoSSW 91*
Norris, James Robert 1947- *WhoEmL 91*
Norris, James S. 1810-1874 *AmLegL*
Norris, Janet Clare 1952- *WhoEmL 91*
Norris, Jim 1948- *Ballpl 90*
Norris, John Anthony 1946- *WhoAm 90, WhoE 91, WhoEmL 91*
Norris, John Franklyn 1877-1952 *BioIn 16*
Norris, John Hart 1942- *WhoAm 90*
Norris, John L. 1904-1989 *BioIn 16*
Norris, John L., Jr. 1914- *St&PR 91*
Norris, John Windsor, Jr. 1936- *WhoAm 90, WhoSSW 91*
Norris, Joseph P *BiDrAPA 89*
Norris, Kathleen 1880-1966 *FemiCLE*
Norris, Kathleen 1947- *WhoWrEP 89*
Norris, Kenneth Edward 1948- *St&PR 91*
Norris, Kenneth Michael 1952- *WhoSSW 91*
Norris, Leo 1908- *Ballpl 90*
Norris, Leonard Matheson 1913- *WhoAmA 91*
Norris, Mackenzie Charles 1925- *St&PR 91*
Norris, Margaret Swann 1925- *BiDrAPA 89, WhoAmW 91*
Norris, Marianna *AuBYP 90*
Norris, Marilyn Ruth 1933- *WhoSSW 91*
Norris, Martin Joseph 1907- *WhoAm 90*
Norris, Melvin 1931- *WhoAm 90*
Norris, Merry *WhoAmA 91*
Norris, Mike *BioIn 16*
Norris, Mike 1955- *Ballpl 90*
Norris, P.E. 1942- *St&PR 91*
Norris, Patrick *BioIn 16*
Norris, Peter Justin 1954- *WhoE 91*
Norris, Reginald M., Jr. *St&PR 91*
Norris, Richard Anthony 1943- *WhoAm 90*
Norris, Richard Paul 1948- *St&PR 91*
Norris, Richard S. 1930- *St&PR 91*
Norris, Robert 1943- *IntWWM 90*
Norris, Robert Benjamin 1910- *WhoE 91*
Norris, Robert Fogg 1905- *WhoAm 90*
Norris, Robert J. 1925- *St&PR 91*
Norris, Robert Matheson 1921- *WhoAm 90*
Norris, Robert Wheeler 1932- *WhoAm 90*
Norris, Roger Henry 1940- *WhoWrEP 89*
Norris, Russell Bradner, Jr. 1942- *WhoSSW 91*
Norris, Sellers Brown, II 1943- *WhoSSW 91*
Norris, Thomas Clayton 1938- *St&PR 91, WhoAm 90*
Norris, Victoria P S *BiDrAPA 89*
Norris, Wayne Bruce 1947- *WhoWrEP 89*
Norris, William A 1927- *WhoAmA 91*
Norris, William A. 1953- *St&PR 91*
Norris, William Albert 1927- *WhoAm 90*
Norris, William C. *BioIn 16*
Norris, William C. 1911- *St&PR 91*
Norris, William Charles 1911- *ConAmBL*
Norris, William Patrick, Jr. 1944- *St&PR 91*
Norrish, Robert M. 1934- *ODwPR 91*
Norrish, Ronald G. W. 1897-1978 *WorAlBi*
Norrod, James Douglas 1948- *WhoE 91*
Norsa, Luigia *BiDrAPA 89*
Norse, Edwin Michael 1945- *St&PR 91*
Norse, Harold 1916- *BioIn 16*
Norsman, Annette Sonja 1941- *WhoAmW 91, WhoWor 91*
Norstad, Lauris 1907-1988 *AnObit 1988, BioIn 16*
Norstrand, Iris Fletcher 1915- *BiDrAPA 89, WhoE 91*
Norstrand, Rolf 1946- *WhoWor 91*
Norstrom, Eugene N. 1943- *St&PR 91*
Norsworthy, John Randolph 1939- *WhoAm 90, WhoE 91, WhoWor 91*
Norsworthy, Naomi 1877-1916 *BioAmW*
North, A. Frederick 1931- *WhoE 91*
North, Alastair Macarthur 1932- *WhoWor 91*
North, Alex 1910- *IntWWM 90, OxCPMus, WhoAm 90*
North, Andrew *ConAu 31NR, MajTwCW*
North, Anne 1614-1681 *BiDEWW*
North, Anthony *MajTwCW, TwCCr&M 91*
North, Billy 1948- *Ballpl 90*
North, Brownlow 1810-1875 *BioIn 16*
North, Carol Sue *BiDrAPA 89*
North, Carol Sue 1954- *WhoAmW 91*
North, Charles Laurence 1941- *WhoWrEP 89*
North, Douglas *WhoAm 90*
North, Douglass Cecil 1920- *WhoAm 90*
North, Dudley 1641-1691 *BioIn 16*
North, Edmund H 1911-1990 *ConAu 132, NewYTBS 90*
North, Edmund Hall 1911- *WhoAm 90*
North, Frances Doub 1895-1987 *BioIn 16*
North, Frank Joshua 1840-1885 *WhNaAH*
North, Frederick 1732-1792 *EncCRAm, WorAlBi*
North, Gil 1916- *TwCCr&M 91*
North, Gladys Buchanan *BioIn 16*
North, Helen Florence *WhoAm 90, WhoWrEP 89*
North, Henry Ringling 1909- *St&PR 91*
North, Howard *TwCCr&M 91*
North, Hugh Davis, Jr. 1921- *St&PR 91, WhoAm 90*
North, James Dennis 1911- *WhoAm 90*
North, Jessica Nelson 1894-1988 *FemiCLE*
North, Joan 1920- *AuBYP 90*
North, John David 1934- *WhoWor 91*
North, John S. 1930- *St&PR 91*
North, Judy 1937- *WhoAmA 91*
North, Kathryn E. Keesey 1916- *WhoAmW 91*
North, Kenneth Earl 1945- *WhoEmL 91, WhoWor 91*
North, Kory Gray 1959- *St&PR 91*
North, Leon L 1920- *BiDrAPA 89*
North, Leon Levi 1920- *WhoE 91*
North, Lex 1931- *WhoE 91*
North, Lou 1891-1974 *Ballpl 90*
North, Luther 1846-1935 *WhNaAH*
North, Marianne 1830-1890 *BiDWomA*
North, Maxine Woodfield *WhoWor 91*
North, Meg *ODwPR 91*
North, Milou *MajTwCW*
North, Oliver L., Jr. *BioIn 16*
North, Phil Record 1918- *WhoAm 90*
North, Richard Ralph 1934- *WhoSSW 91*
North, Robert *ConAu 30NR*
North, Robert Carver 1914- *WhoAm 90*
North, Robert John 1935- *WhoAm 90*
North, Roger Dudley 1926- *IntWWM 90*
North, Sterling 1906-1974 *AuBYP 90*
North, Thomas Brian 1956- *WhoEmL 91*

North, Warren James 1922- *WhoAm 90*
North, Wheeler James 1922- *WhoAm 90*
North, William Charles 1925- *WhoAm 90*
North, William Denson 1930- *WhoAm 90*
North, William Haven 1926- *WhoAm 90*
Northacker, Alfred Austin 1915- *WhoWrEP 89*
Northage Glick, Jennifer Isabella 1953- *WhoAmW 91*
Northam, Robert E. 1930- *St&PR 91*
Northampton, Margaret, Marchioness of 1793-1830 *FemiCLE*
Northart, Leo Joseph 1929- *WhoWrEP 89*
Northchurch, Baroness 1894-1985 *DcNaB 1981*
Northcliffe, Alfred Harmsworth, Viscount 1865-1922 *BioIn 16, WorAlBi*
Northcote, Ann 1932- *WhoAm 90*
Northcott, Bayan Peter 1940- *IntWWM 90*
Northcott, Harlan E. 1927- *St&PR 91*
Northcott, William Cecil 1902-1987 *BioIn 16*
Northcraft, Julian O. 1923- *St&PR 91*
Northcross, Lydia Ann 1955- *WhoAmW 91*
Northcross, Wendy Geradine 1954- *WhoAmW 91*
Northcutt, Barbara 1954- *IntWWM 90*
Northcutt, Clarence Dewey 1916- *WhoAm 90, WhoWor 91*
Northcutt, Ernest O. 1929- *St&PR 91*
Northcutt, James Ervin 1927- *St&PR 91*
Northcutt, Lee Edwin 1964- *IntWWM 90*
Northcutt, Marie Rose 1950- *WhoAmW 91*
Northcutt, Mary Sue 1943- *WhoAmW 91*
Northcutt, Robert Hull 1934- *St&PR 91*
Northcutt, Robert Hull, Jr. 1934- *WhoAm 90*
Northcutt, Travis J., Jr. 1929- *WhoAm 90*
Northen, Charles Swift, III 1937- *St&PR 91, WhoAm 90*
Northen, Helen *WhoWrEP 89*
Northey, Ron 1920-1971 *Ballpl 90*
Northover, Robert R. 1930- *St&PR 91*
Northrop, Cynthia E. *BioIn 16*
Northrop, Edward Skottowe 1911- *WhoAm 90, WhoE 91*
Northrop, Granger Harold 1936- *St&PR 91*
Northrop, Jack 1895-1981 *BioIn 16*
Northrop, James A. 1947- *St&PR 91*
Northrop, James Allen 1947- *WhoE 91*
Northrop, John Howard 1891-1987 *WorAlBi*
Northrop, John K. 1895-1981 *WorAlBi*
Northrop, John L.S. 1930- *St&PR 91*
Northrop, Monroe 1931- *WhoAm 90*
Northrop, Sam, Jr. 1931- *St&PR 91*
Northrop, Stuart Johnston 1925- *St&PR 91, WhoAm 90*
Northrup, Chris K. 1945- *ODwPR 91*
Northrup, David H. 1913- *St&PR 91*
Northrup, Gordon E 1923- *BiDrAPA 89*
Northrup, Herbert Roof 1918- *WhoAm 90*
Northrup, Jim 1939- *Ballpl 90*
Northrup, Joan Cooke 1953- *WhoAmW 91*
Northrup, Kenneth Virgil 1935- *St&PR 91*
Northrup, Malcolm Bruce 1939- *WhoAm 90*
Northrup, Steven Paul 1949- *WhoE 91*
Northumberland, Duchess of 1716-1776 *BioIn 16*
Northumberland, Elizabeth P, Countess of 1666-1722 *BiDEWW*
Northumberland, Hugh A. Percy, Duke of *BioIn 16*
Northup, Anne Meagher 1948- *WhoAmW 91*
Northup, John David 1910- *WhoAm 90*
Northup, Laurel Puck 1952- *BiDrAPA 89*
Northup, Patrick B. *BioIn 16*
Northwall, Karl Walter 1952- *BiDrAPA 89*
Northway, Daniel Page 1942- *BiDrAPA 89*
Northway, Dennis Edward 1958- *IntWWM 90*
Northway, Martin 1947- *WhoWrEP 89*
Northway, Wanda I. 1942- *WhoAmW 91*
Northwood, David Weston 1909- *St&PR 91*
Northwood, John 1836-1902 *PenDiDA 89*
Northwood, John 1870- *PenDiDA 89*
Northwood, Joseph 1839-1915 *PenDiDA 89*
Northwood, William 1858-1937 *PenDiDA 89*
Norton, Alice 1926- *ODwPR 91*
Norton, Alice Mary 1912- *AuBYP 90*
Norton, Andre *AuBYP 90*
Norton, Andre 1912- *ConAu 31NR, MajTwCW, RGTwCSF*
Norton, Andre Alice *WhoAm 90, WhoAmW 91*
Norton, Andrea Meredith *BiDrAPA 89*
Norton, Andrew *AuBYP 90*
Norton, Ann *BioIn 16*
Norton, Ann W *WhoAmA 91N*
Norton, Arthur H 1926- *BiDrAPA 89*
Norton, Augustus Richard 1946- *WhoAm 90, WhoE 91*
Norton, Beverly Joan 1932- *WhoE 91*
Norton, Billie Fostina 1927- *WhoAmW 91*
Norton, Caroline 1808-1877 *FemiCLE*
Norton, Caroline Elizabeth Sarah 1808-1877 *BioIn 16*
Norton, Charles Bryan, Jr. *BiDrAPA 89*
Norton, Charles Eliot 1827-1908 *BioIn 16*
Norton, Charles William, Jr. 1921- *St&PR 91*
Norton, Chris W. 1941- *St&PR 91*
Norton, Clifford Charles 1918- *WhoAm 90*
Norton, Dale Bentsen 1925- *St&PR 91*
Norton, Daniel Thomas 1955- *WhoSSW 91*
Norton, David *BioIn 16*
Norton, David L. 1945- *St&PR 91*
Norton, David Phillip 1950- *WhoSSW 91*
Norton, Deborah Ruth 1958- *WhoSSW 91*
Norton, Delmar Lynn 1944- *WhoAm 90*
Norton, Desmond Anthony 1942- *WhoWor 91*
Norton, Diana Mae 1945- *WhoAmW 91*
Norton, Earl Wardell 1951- *WhoSSW 91*
Norton, Edgar Albert, Jr. 1957- *WhoE 91*
Norton, Edward Leon 1942- *St&PR 91*
Norton, Eleanor Holmes 1937- *WhoAmW 91, WorAlBi*
Norton, Elizabeth Wychgel 1933- *WhoAmW 91*
Norton, Ellen Rae *BiDrAPA 89*
Norton, Eric 1925- *WhoSSW 91*
Norton, Eunice 1908- *IntWWM 90, WhoAm 90*
Norton, Floyd Ligon, IV 1950- *WhoEmL 91*
Norton, Frances 1640-1731 *BiDEWW, BioIn 16, FemiCLE*
Norton, Frederic 1875-1946 *OxCPMus*
Norton, Gale 1954- *WhoAmW 91*
Norton, George Dawson 1930- *WhoAm 90*
Norton, Gerald Patrick 1940- *WhoAm 90*
Norton, Gregory Armstrong 1948- *St&PR 91*
Norton, H. Gaither 1918- *WhoE 91, WhoWor 91*
Norton, H. Steve 1934- *St&PR 91*
Norton, Hamish William Mazur 1959- *WhoE 91*
Norton, Herbert Steven 1934- *WhoAm 90*
Norton, Howard Melvin 1911- *WhoAm 90*
Norton, Hugh Stanton 1921- *WhoAm 90*
Norton, Ilena Marie *BiDrAPA 89*
Norton, J. B. 1861- *AmLegL*
Norton, James Adolphus 1922- *WhoAm 90*
Norton, James Edward 1939- *St&PR 91*
Norton, James Gerald 1933- *St&PR 91*
Norton, James J. 1930- *WhoAm 90*
Norton, James Lonnie, Jr. *WhoWrEP 89*
Norton, Jan *ODwPR 91*
Norton, Jan Auburn 1946- *WhoAm 90*
Norton, Jane Marie 1954- *WhoEmL 91*
Norton, Jane Morton 1908- *LiHiK*
Norton, Jeanna 1952- *WhoAmW 91*
Norton, Jeffrey 1925- *WhoE 91*
Norton, Jeffrey A. 1942- *St&PR 91*
Norton, Jim 1954- *BioIn 16*
Norton, John *PenDiDA 89*
Norton, John 1760?-1826? *WhNaAH*
Norton, John Croft 1948- *WhoSSW 91*
Norton, John F. *St&PR 91*
Norton, John Westbrook *BiDrAPA 89*
Norton, John William 1941- *St&PR 91*
Norton, John William 1954- *WhoEmL 91*
Norton, Joseph Randolph 1915- *WhoAm 90*
Norton, Julius *PenDiDA 89*
Norton, Karen Ann 1950- *WhoAmW 91*
Norton, Kathryn D. *ODwPR 91*
Norton, Kelly E. 1938- *St&PR 91, WhoAm 90*
Norton, Kenneth Edward 1932- *St&PR 91*
Norton, Larry Allan 1947- *WhoSSW 91*
Norton, Leal F. *BioIn 16*
Norton, Leslie Forth 1953- *WhoSSW 91*
Norton, Lewis Franklin 1930- *St&PR 91*
Norton, Louise Charnette 1941- *WhoAmW 91*
Norton, Lucy 1902-1989 *ConAu 129*
Norton, Luman *PenDiDA 89*
Norton, Mary 1903- *AuBYP 90, BioIn 16, SmATA 60 [port]*
Norton, Mary Beth 1943- *WhoAm 90*
Norton, Mary Elizabeth 1965- *WhoEmL 91*
Norton, Mary Joyce *WhoAmA 91*
Norton, Nick *WhoWrEP 89*
Norton, Norman James 1933- *WhoAm 90*
Norton, Oliver W. 1839-1920 *WorAlBi*
Norton, Paul Allen 1913- *WhoAm 90*
Norton, Paul Foote 1917- *WhoAm 90, WhoAmA 91, WhoE 91*
Norton, Paula C. 1945- *ODwPR 91*
Norton, Peter Bowes 1929- *St&PR 91, WhoAm 90*
Norton, Ralph Gage 1932- *St&PR 91*
Norton, Randolph Harrison 1939- *St&PR 91*
Norton, Robert 1946- *St&PR 91*
Norton, Robert Leo, Sr. 1939- *WhoWor 91*
Norton, Robyn Lynn 1963- *WhoAmW 91*
Norton, Roger L. 1937- *St&PR 91*
Norton, Sharon Sue 1942- *WhoAmW 91*
Norton, Stephen Allen 1940- *WhoAm 90*
Norton, Susan Jean 1958- *WhoAmW 91*
Norton, Thomas *EncO&P 3*
Norton, Thomas 1532-1584 *BioIn 16*
Norton, Thomas Edward 1934- *WhoE 91*
Norton, Victor Thane 1904-1989 *BioIn 16*
Norton, Virginia Skeen 1907- *WhoAmW 91*
Norton, William 1944- *WhoAm 90*
Norton, William W. 1934- *St&PR 91*
Norton-Taylor, Judy *WhoAm 90, WhoEmL 91*
Norum, David P. 1931- *WhoAm 90*
Norum, Vance Donald *BiDrAPA 89*
Norup, Bent 1936- *IntWWM 90*
Norvell, Nancy Kathleen 1957- *WhoAmW 91*
Norvell, Patsy 1942- *WhoAmA 91*
Norville, Craig Hubert 1944- *St&PR 91, WhoAm 90*
Norville, Deborah *BioIn 16*
Norville, Deborah 1958- *CurBio 90 [port], News 90 [port], -90-3 [port]*
Norville, Richard Allen *BiDrAPA 89*
Norville, Russell Manley 1938- *St&PR 91*
Norvo, Red 1908- *BioIn 16, OxCPMus, WorAlBi*
Norwalk, Thomas S. 1930- *ODwPR 91*
Norwich, Billy *BioIn 16*
Norwich, William *BioIn 16*
Norwick, Edmund G., Jr. 1919- *St&PR 91*
Norwood, Alice Lynn 1962- *WhoAmW 91*
Norwood, Barbara Kinman 1954- *WhoSSW 91*
Norwood, Barbara Mann 1946- *WhoAmW 91*
Norwood, Bernard 1922- *WhoAm 90*
Norwood, Donald Mason 1952- *St&PR 91*
Norwood, George Joseph 1938- *WhoAm 90*
Norwood, Janet Lippe 1923- *WhoAm 90, WhoAmW 91*
Norwood, Joe *BioIn 16*
Norwood, Joy Janell 1936- *WhoAmW 91*
Norwood, Malcolm Mark 1928- *WhoAmA 91*
Norwood, Richard Harland 1916-1989 *BioIn 16*
Norwood, Robert 1874-1932 *DcLB 92 [port]*
Norwood, Ronald Eugene 1952- *WhoEmL 91*
Norwood, Samuel Wilkins, III 1941- *St&PR 91*
Norwood, Walter Edward 1924- *WhoSSW 91*
Norwood, Willie 1950- *Ballpl 90*
Norworth, Jack 1879-1959 *OxCPMus*
Norz, Charles Henry 1937- *WhoAm 90*
Nosanow, Barbara Shissler *WhoE 91*
Nosari, Raymond John 1931- *St&PR 91*
Noseck, Kenneth A. *BioIn 16*
Nosek, Margaret Ann 1952- *WhoSSW 91*
Noshpitz, Joseph D 1922- *BiDrAPA 89*
Noshpitz, Joseph Dove 1922- *WhoAm 90*
Nosille, Nabrah *MajTwCW*
Nosker, John Louis 1912- *St&PR 91*
Nosnik, Pedro 1952- *WhoSSW 91*
Noss, Harry Joseph, Jr. 1934- *St&PR 91*
Noss, Luther 1907- *IntWWM 90*
Noss, Stanley 1925- *St&PR 91*
Nossek, Joe 1940- *Ballpl 90*
Nosseni, Giovanni Maria 1544-1620 *PenDiDA 89*
Nossig, Alfred 1864-1943 *BioIn 16*
Nossis *EncCoWW*
Nossiter, Bernard Daniel 1926- *WhoAm 90, WhoE 91*
Nost, John van *BioIn 16*
Nostlinger, Christine 1936- *EncCoWW*
Nostradame, Michael de 1503-1566 *EncO&P 3*
Nostradamus 1503-1566 *EncO&P 3, EncPaPR 91*
Nostrand, S. Dudley *BioIn 16*
Nota, Josephus Antonius 1925- *WhoWor 91*
Notarbartolo, Albert *WhoAmA 91*
Notarbartolo, Albert 1934- *WhoAm 90*
Notari, Paul Celestin 1926- *WhoAm 90*
Notarius, Morton S *BiDrAPA 89*
Notaro, Anthony 1915- *WhoAmA 91*
Notaro, Michael R. 1914- *WhoAm 90*
Notaro, Michael R. 1918- *St&PR 91*
Notas, Bernard M. 1950- *St&PR 91*
Notch, James Stephen 1950- *WhoSSW 91, WhoWor 91*
Notebaert, Richard J. 1943- *St&PR 91*
Notenboom, Jacob T.M. 1945- *St&PR 91*
Noterman, Marjorie L. 1946- *WhoAmW 91*
Notes, Richard D 1943- *BiDrAPA 89*
Notestine, Dorothy J 1921- *WhoAmA 91*
Notestine, Tom W 1919- *WhoAmA 91*
Notestine, Wilbur Edmund 1931- *WhoAm 90*
Noteware, James D. 1952- *WhoAm 90*
Noth, Nancy Claire 1950- *WhoAmW 91*
Nothdurft, Hans Jakob 1911- *WhoWor 91*
Nothmann, Gerhard Adolf 1921- *WhoAm 90*
Nothmann, Gerhard S 1912- *BiDrAPA 89*
Nothmann, Rudolf S. 1907- *WhoWor 91*
Nothstine, S. Ellsworth 1907- *WhoWrEP 89*
Nothwang, William L. 1937- *St&PR 91*
Notis-McConarty, Edward *St&PR 91*
Notkin, Leonard Sheldon 1931- *WhoAm 90*
Notkin, Richard T 1948- *WhoAmA 91*
Notkin, Robert Mark 1956- *BiDrAPA 89*
Notko, Terry Joseph 1951- *St&PR 91*
Notley, Alice 1945- *FemiCLE*
Notley, Frances 1820-1912 *FemiCLE*
Notman, Malkah T *BiDrAPA 89*
Notman, William 1826-1891 *DcCanB 12*
Notman, William McFarlane 1826-1891 *BioIn 16*
Noto, Don Joseph 1932- *St&PR 91*
Noto, Frank A. 1934- *St&PR 91*
Noto, Patricia Hoffman 1954- *WhoE 91*
Noto, Samuel John 1958- *WhoE 91*
Notorangelo, Susan *BioIn 16*
Notowidigdo, Musinggih Hartoko 1938- *St&PR 91, WhoWor 91*
Notowitz, Scott Seldon 1957- *WhoSSW 91*
Notsten, Gunborg Britta 1934- *WhoWor 91*
Nott, Kathleen 1909?- *FemiCLE*
Nott, Kathleen 1910- *BioIn 16*
Nottage, Daniel Bruce 1948- *St&PR 91*
Nottberg, Henry, III 1949- *St&PR 91, WhoAm 90*
Notte, Rocco *NewAgMG*
Nottebart, Don 1936- *Ballpl 90*
Notter, Randall P. *ODwPR 91*
Nottingham, Edward Willis, Jr. 1948- *WhoEmL 91*
Nottingham, John David 1938- *BiDrAPA 89*
Nottingham, Robinson Kendall 1938- *WhoE 91*
Nottke, Robert Matthias 1943- *WhoE 91*
Nottle, Diane 1955- *WhoWrEP 89*
Notz, John Kranz, Jr. 1932- *WhoAm 90*
Nouailhetas, Herve Louis Henri 1947- *WhoWor 91*
Noue, Zacharie Robutel De La 1624-1691 *EncCRAm*
Noumair, George J. 1930- *WhoAm 90*
Nouri, Abdul Motey Mohammed 1941- *WhoWor 91*
Nouri-Moghadam, Mohamad Reza 1949- *WhoE 91*
Nourian, Ali Akbar 1937- *BiDrAPA 89*
Nourrit, Adolphe 1802-1839 *PenDiMP*
Nourse, Alan E. 1928- *WhoWrEP 89*
Nourse, Alan Edward 1928- *AuBYP 90, BioIn 16*
Nourse, Elizabeth 1859-1938 *BiDWomA*
Nourse, Hugh Oliver 1933- *WhoSSW 91*
Nourse, Jennifer Jon Williams 1953- *WhoAmW 91*
Nourse, Nancy Elaine 1952- *IntWWM 90*
Nourtier, Claude H. *BioIn 16*
Nousiainen, Jaakko Ilmari 1931- *WhoWor 91*
Nouvel, Jean 1945- *BioIn 16*
Nouvellet, Jean-Pierre 1947- *WhoWor 91*
Nouwen, Jan Johannes 1932- *WhoWor 91*
Nova, Craig 1945- *WhoAm 90*
Nova, Harvey R. 1935-1989 *BioIn 16*
Novac, Andrei 1953- *BiDrAPA 89*
Novacek, John Allen 1964- *IntWWM 90*
Novacek, Ottokar *PenDiMP*
Novack, Alvin John 1925- *WhoAm 90*
Novack, George 1905- *WhoAm 90*
Novack, Gianella Marie 1957- *WhoSSW 91*
Novack, Irwin Mark 1947- *St&PR 91*
Novack, Kenneth Joseph 1941- *WhoAm 90*
Novack, Richard Victor 1945- *WhoWor 91*
Novack, Sheldon 1938- *WhoE 91, WhoWor 91*
Novaes, Guiomar 1895-1979 *BioIn 16, PenDiMP*
Novak, Alan Lee 1928- *WhoSSW 91*
Novak, Alan Richard 1934- *WhoE 91*
Novak, Alfred 1915- *WhoAm 90*
Novak, Alfred J. 1948- *St&PR 91*
Novak, Alfred Joseph 1948- *WhoEmL 91*
Novak, Ann-Nadine 1951- *WhoAmW 91*
Novak, Barbara *WhoAm 90, WhoAmA 91*
Novak, Barbara Jean *BiDrAPA 89*
Novak, Charleen Marie 1929- *St&PR 91*
Novak, Charles Chris 1954- *BiDrAPA 89*
Novak, Daria Irene 1957- *WhoAmW 91*
Novak, Dennis Wayne 1941- *St&PR 91*
Novak, Esther Eve *BiDrAPA 89*
Novak, Eugene Andrew 1950- *St&PR 91*

Novak, Eugene Francis 1925- *WhoAm 90*
Novak, Eva 1899-1988 *BioIn 16*
Novak, Francis Edward 1943- *WhoAm 90*
Novak, Frank Walter 1926- *St&PR 91*
Novak, Franz 1913- *BioIn 16*
Novak, George 1948- *WhoSSW 91*
Novak, Gregory 1949- *WhoE 91*
Novak, Helga 1935- *EncCoWW*
Novak, James Michael 1944- *WhoAm 90*
Novak, Jan 1953- *BioIn 16*
Novak, Jiri *PenDiMP*
Novak, Jo-Ann Stout 1956- *WhoAmW 91*
Novak, John Goodman *BiDrAPA 89*
Novak, John Robert 1944- *St&PR 91, WhoAm 90*
Novak, John William, Jr. 1953- *WhoE 91*
Novak, Joseph *MajTwCW, WhoWrEP 89*
Novak, Joseph Donald 1930- *WhoAm 90*
Novak, Kim 1933- *WhoAm 90, WorAlBi*
Novak, Leon 1945- *WhoSSW 91*
Novak, Linda Moses 1949- *WhoAmW 91*
Novak, Marian Faye *BioIn 16*
Novak, Marian Joyce 1954- *WhoAmW 91*
Novak, Matt *AuBYP 90*
Novak, Matt 1962- *BioIn 16, SmATA 60 [port]*
Novak, Maximillian Erwin 1930- *WhoAm 90*
Novak, Michael 1933- *ConAu 30NR*
Novak, Michael, Jr. 1933- *WhoAm 90, WhoWor 91, WhoWrEP 89, WorAlBi*
Novak, Michael Paul 1935- *WhoWrEP 89*
Novak, Michael Peter 1962- *WhoE 91*
Novak, Milan 1927- *WhoWor 91*
Novak, Milan Vaclav 1907- *WhoAm 90*
Novak, Norman George 1946- *St&PR 91*
Novak, Paul 1946- *WhoE 91*
Novak, Peter John 1939- *WhoAm 90*
Novak, Ralph *BioIn 16*
Novak, Raymond A. 1930- *St&PR 91*
Novak, Richard E. 1944- *WhoWor 91*
Novak, Robert *ConAu 31NR*
Novak, Robert D. *BioIn 16*
Novak, Robert David Sanders 1931- *WhoAm 90*
Novak, Robert Lee 1933- *WhoWrEP 89*
Novak, Roger Wayne 1951- *WhoEmL 91*
Novak, Rose 1940- *WhoWrEP 89*
Novak, Sandra Bernadean 1953- *WhoAmW 91*
Novak, Steven Paul 1957- *WhoWor 91*
Novak, Terry Lee 1940- *WhoAm 90*
Novak, Theresa Anne 1949- *WhoE 91*
Novak, Walter 1932- *WhoE 91*
Novak, William *BioIn 16*
Novak, William Arnold 1948- *WhoAm 90*
Novak, William J 1926- *BiDrAPA 89*
Novak, William Joseph 1926- *St&PR 91*
Novak, Yvette 1946- *WhoSSW 91*
Novakhov, Michael 1952- *BiDrAPA 89*
Novakova, Tereza 1853-1912 *EncCoWW*
Noval, Tara 1969- *IntWWM 90*
Novales, Ronald Richards 1928- *WhoAm 90*
Novalis, Peter Nicholas *BiDrAPA 89*
Novarro, Ramon 1899-1968 *BioIn 16, WorAlBi*
Novas, Alfred Robert 1963- *WhoSSW 91*
Novas, Joseph, Jr. 1921- *WhoAm 90*
Novas Calvo, Lino 1905-1983 *HispWr 90*
Novatny, Donald A. 1935- *St&PR 91, WhoAm 90*
Noveck, Simon 1914- *BioIn 16*
Novell, Philip M. 1938- *St&PR 91*
Novell, Richard S. 1949- *St&PR 91*
Novella, Carmen 1924- *BiDrAPA 89*
Novelli, Luca 1947- *SmATA 61 [port]*
Novelli, Thomas Charles 1942- *St&PR 91*
Novelli, William Dominic 1941- *WhoAm 90*
Novellino, Anthony Ronald 1949- *WhoAm 90*
Novello, Antonia *BioIn 16*
Novello, Antonia 1944- *News 91-2 [port]*
Novello, Antonia Coello 1944- *WhoAm 90, WhoAmW 91, WhoHisp 91*
Novello, Clara 1818-1908 *BioIn 16, PenDiMP*
Novello, Don 1943- *WhoAm 90, WhoWrEP 89*
Novello, Ivor 1893-1951 *OxCPMus, PenDiMP*
Novello, Joseph Robert 1941- *BiDrAPA 89*
Novello, Robert James 1938- *WhoAm 90*
Novello, Vincent 1781-1861 *PenDiMP*
Novello-Davies, Clara 1861-1943 *PenDiMP*
November, Robert 1936- *St&PR 91*
November, Robert Stephen 1936- *WhoAm 90*
Novenstern, Samuel 1926- *WhoAm 90*
Nover, David 1959- *BiDrAPA 89*
Nover, Fred Stuart 1937- *St&PR 91*
Nover, Naomi *WhoAm 90, WhoWor 91*
Nover, Robert Allen 1940- *BiDrAPA 89*
Noveras, Teresita Lorenzo *BiDrAPA 89*
Noverre, Jean-Georges 1727-1810 *WorAlBi*
Noveske, F Gregory 1948- *BiDrAPA 89*
Novetzke, Sally J. 1932- *WhoAmW 91, WhoWor 91*
Novey, Harold Sidney 1926- *WhoWor 91*
Novey, Linda Simmons 1940- *WhoAmW 91*
Novey, Riva 1915- *BiDrAPA 89*
Novgorod, Nancy *WhoAmW 91*
Novick, Andrew Carl 1948- *WhoAm 90*
Novick, David 1926- *WhoAm 90*
Novick, Ivan J. 1927- *St&PR 91*
Novick, Julius Lerner 1939- *WhoAm 90*
Novick, Mark Douglas 1952- *WhoE 91*
Novick, Mark R 1936- *BiDrAPA 89*
Novick, Martin 1936- *St&PR 91*
Novick, Marvin 1931- *WhoAm 90*
Novick, Mary 1959- *St&PR 91*
Novick, Nelson Lee 1949- *WhoAm 90, WhoE 91*
Novick, Paul 1891-1989 *BioIn 16, ConAu 130*
Novick, Robert 1923- *WhoAm 90*
Novick, Rudolph G 1910- *BiDrAPA 89*
Novick, Sheldon M. 1941- *WhoAm 90*
Novick, Wilma Joyce 1938- *WhoAmW 91*
Novicki, Carroll A. 1938- *WhoAm 90*
Novicki, William Alan 1950- *St&PR 91*
Novicky, Genevieve 1919- *WhoSSW 91*
Novicoff, Melvyn Burt 1939- *St&PR 91*
Novik, Jack 1946-1988 *BioIn 16*
Novik, Morris *BioIn 16*
Novik, Sheffield 1918- *St&PR 91*
Novikoff, Alex Benjamin 1913-1987 *BioIn 16*
Novikoff, Eugene Benjamin 1923- *St&PR 91*
Novikoff, Lou 1915-1970 *Ballpl 90*
Novikoff, Phyllis Marie 1936- *WhoAmW 91*
Novikov, Petr Sergeevich 1901-1975 *DcScB S2*
Novillo, Pauli Enrique 1919- *EncPaPR 91*
Novin, Donald 1936- *WhoAm 90*
Novina, Trudi *WhoAmW 91*
Novinger, Cathy Blackburn 1949- *WhoAm 90*
Novins, Douglas Keith 1961- *BiDrAPA 89*
Novins, Jay Robert *BiDrAPA 89*
Novins, Louis A. 1909-1988 *BioIn 16*
Novins, Stuart *BioIn 16*
Novins, Stuart 1914?-1989 *ConAu 130*
Novinski, Lyle Frank 1932- *WhoAmA 91*
Novinskie, Gary John 1950- *St&PR 91*
Novis, Emile *EncCoWW*
Novis, Lawrence *BiDrAPA 89*
Novitch, Mark 1932- *St&PR 91, WhoAm 90*
Novitski, Lois Conrad 1937- *WhoAmW 91*
Novitsky, Mark Anthony 1953- *BiDrAPA 89*
Novitt, Rita Amelia *WhoAmW 91*
Novitz, Charles Richard 1934- *WhoAm 90*
Novkov, David A. 1931- *St&PR 91*
Novo, Salvador 1904-1974 *ConAu 131, HispWr 90*
Novo, Salvatore 1948- *WhoWor 91*
Novoa, John David Bruce *HispWr 90*
Novoa, Jose I. *WhoHisp 91*
Novoa, Juan Bruce *HispWr 90*
Novoa, Salvador 1937- *IntWWM 90*
Novograd, Irwin *BioIn 16*
Novogrod, Nancy Ellen 1949- *WhoAm 90, WhoE 91, WhoWor 91*
Novogrodsky, Abraham 1932- *WhoWor 91*
Novorro, Jane 1961- *WhoAmW 91*
Novosal, Paul Peter 1918- *WhoAm 90*
Novosel, Josip 1932- *IntWWM 90*
Novotna, Jarmila 1907- *BioIn 16, IntWWM 90, PenDiMP*
Novotney, Norbert James 1921- *St&PR 91*
Novotny, Deborah Ann 1964- *WhoAmW 91*
Novotny, Donald Wayne 1934- *WhoAm 90*
Novotny, Edward G. 1938- *ODwPR 91*
Novotny, Elmer Ladislaw 1909- *WhoAmA 91*
Novotny, Harold R 1932- *BiDrAPA 89*
Novotny, Jan 1935- *IntWWM 90*
Novotny, Joyce Ann 1964- *WhoE 91*
Novotny, Milos V. *WhoAm 90*
Novotny, Peter C *BiDrAPA 89*
Novovesky, Michael Paul 1938- *St&PR 91*
Novovich, Serge *St&PR 91*
Novovich, Serge 1932- *WhoAm 90*
Novros, David 1941- *WhoAmA 91*
Nowack, George Paul 1948- *WhoE 91*
Nowack, Wayne Kenyon 1923- *WhoAmA 91*
Nowaczek, Frank Huxley 1930- *WhoE 91*
Nowak, Carol A. 1950- *WhoAmW 91*
Nowak, Colleen M. 1963- *ODwPR 91*
Nowak, Edward, Jr. 1920- *WhoWrEP 89*
Nowak, Emmy 1923- *St&PR 91*
Nowak, Gerald L. 1930- *St&PR 91*
Nowak, Grzegorz 1951- *IntWWM 90*
Nowak, Henry James 1935- *WhoAm 90, WhoE 91*
Nowak, Jacquelyn Louise 1937- *WhoAm 90, WhoAmW 91*
Nowak, James E. 1947- *St&PR 91*
Nowak, James M. 1950- *St&PR 91*
Nowak, Jan Zdzislaw 1913- *WhoAm 90*
Nowak, Jean Ray *WhoE 91*
Nowak, John E. 1947- *WhoWor 91*
Nowak, John W. 1941- *St&PR 91*
Nowak, Judith Ann 1948- *BiDrAPA 89, WhoE 91*
Nowak, Leo 1907- *WhoAmA 91*
Nowak, Leopold 1904- *IntWWM 90*
Nowak, Lionel 1911- *IntWWM 90*
Nowak, Michael Roman 1953- *WhoEmL 91*
Nowak, Raymond M. 1952- *St&PR 91*
Nowak, Robert Joseph 1936- *St&PR 91*
Nowak, Stanley 1903- *BioIn 16, EncAL*
Nowak, Susan Marie *BiDrAPA 89*
Nowakowski, Jack Michal 1955- *WhoAm 90*
Nowakowski, James A. *ODwPR 91*
Nowakowski, James Anthony 1947- *St&PR 91*
Nowakowski, Stanley Francis 1931- *St&PR 91*
Nowalk, Joseph J. *WhoAm 90*
Nowell, Eddie L. 1943- *St&PR 91*
Nowell, Elizabeth Cameron Clemons *WhoAmW 91*
Nowell, Hugh Oliver 1943- *St&PR 91*
Nowell, Linda G. 1949- *WhoAmW 91*
Nowell, Peter Carey 1928- *WhoAm 90*
Nowell, Peter David *BiDrAPA 89*
Nowels, Anthony 1942- *BiDrAPA 89*
Nowers, Walter J 1920- *BiDrAPA 89*
Nowick, Arthur Stanley 1923- *WhoAm 90*
Nowicki, Alicia Leigh 1947- *WhoAmW 91*
Nowicki, George Lucian 1926- *WhoAm 90*
Nowik, Charlyne A *BiDrAPA 89*
Nowik, Dorothy Adam 1944- *WhoAmW 91*
Nowik, Henry Ian 1917- *WhoSSW 91, WhoWor 91*
Nowinski, Thomas Stephen 1946- *WhoEmL 91*
Nowlan, Alden 1933-1983 *OxCCanT*
Nowlan, Hiram Merrill 1929- *St&PR 91, WhoAm 90*
Nowlan, Nora *AuBYP 90*
Nowlan, Philip *EncACom*
Nowlan, Raymond J. 1927- *St&PR 91*
Nowlan, Robert Anthony, Jr. 1934- *ConAu 32NR*
Nowlen, Philip M. *WhoAm 90*
Nowlin, Duane Dale 1937- *St&PR 91*
Nowlin, James Robertson 1937- *WhoAm 90, WhoSSW 91*
Nowlin, Jerry L. *St&PR 91*
Nowlin, Linda Sue 1950- *WhoEmL 91*
Nowlin, William Gerard, Jr. 1945- *WhoE 91*
Nowling, Jack R. 1928- *ODwPR 91*
Nowling, Scott Allen 1952- *St&PR 91*
Nowlis, Helen 1913-1986 *BioIn 16*
Nowotny, Ewald Otto 1944- *WhoWor 91*
Nowotny, Helga 1937- *WhoWor 91*
Nowotny, Mary *ODwPR 91*
Nowotny, Thomas J. 1937- *WhoWor 91*
Nowotny, Thomas John 1957- *BiDrAPA 89*
Nowytski, Sviatoslav 1934- *WhoAmA 91*
Noxon, Deborah H. 1950- *ODwPR 91*
Noxon, Deborah Homzak 1950- *WhoSSW 91*
Noxon, George Bayard 1955- *WhoSSW 91*
Noxon, Jean Kessler *BiDrAPA 89*
Noxon, Margaret Walters 1903- *WhoAmW 91, WhoE 91*
Noyce, Robert 1927-1990 *BioIn 16*
Noyce, Robert N. *NewYTBS 90 [port]*
Noyce, Robert N. 1927- *ConAmBL, St&PR 91*
Noye, Fred C. 1946- *WhoE 91*
Noyes, Alfred 1880-1958 *AuBYP 90*
Noyes, Androus Duane 1936- *WhoE 91*
Noyes, Barbara Moore 1953- *St&PR 91*
Noyes, Charles Johnson 1841- *AmLegL*
Noyes, Charles Robert, Jr. 1953- *WhoE 91*
Noyes, Clara Dutton 1869-1936 *BioIn 16*
Noyes, Crosby S. 1921-1988 *BioIn 16*
Noyes, Edward Follansbee 1832-1890 *BioIn 16*
Noyes, Eliot 1910-1977 *ConDes 90, PenDiDA 89, WhoAmA 91N*
Noyes, Elisabeth J. 1940- *WhoAmW 91*
Noyes, Elisabeth Joyce 1940- *WhoE 91*
Noyes, Frank Brett 1863-1948 *BioIn 16*
Noyes, Henry Pierre 1923- *WhoAm 90*
Noyes, James Elliot 1946- *St&PR 91*
Noyes, Jansen, Jr. 1917- *St&PR 91*
Noyes, Nancy Pope 1964- *WhoAmW 91, WhoE 91*
Noyes, Pamela J. 1959- *ODwPR 91*
Noyes, Pierrepont T. 1914- *St&PR 91*
Noyes, Ralph Richard 1947- *St&PR 91*
Noyes, Richard Francis 1952- *WhoWor 91*
Noyes, Richard Hall 1930- *WhoAm 90*
Noyes, Richard M. 1919- *BioIn 16*
Noyes, Richard Macy 1919- *WhoAm 90*
Noyes, Robert E. 1925- *St&PR 91*
Noyes, Robert Edwin 1925- *WhoAm 90*
Noyes, Robert Slater 1955- *WhoSSW 91*
Noyes, Robert Speir 1921- *St&PR 91*
Noyes, Russell, Jr. *BiDrAPA 89*
Noyes, Sandy 1941- *WhoAmA 91*
Noyes, Stanley 1924- *WhoWrEP 89*
Noyes, Ted L. 1925- *St&PR 91*
Noyes, Thomas 1922-1989 *ConTFT 8*
Noyes, Thomas Ewing 1922-1989 *BioIn 16*
Noyes, Tom Enderby *BiDrAPA 89*
Noyes, Ward David 1927- *WhoAm 90*
Noyes, Wynn 1889-1969 *Ballpl 90*
Noymer, Bernard 1927- *St&PR 91*
Noymer, David S. 1953- *St&PR 91*
Noyons, Bennie 1941- *WhoWor 91*
Nozaki, Masahiko 1927- *WhoWor 91*
Nozato, Ryoichi 1926- *WhoWor 91*
Nozette, Mark Dee 1950- *WhoE 91*
Nozick, Robert 1938- *WhoAm 90*
Nozieres, Philippe Pierre 1932- *WhoWor 91*
Noziglia, Carla Miller 1941- *WhoAmW 91*
Noziska, Charles R *BiDrAPA 89*
Nozko, Henry W., Sr. 1920- *St&PR 91*
Nozko, Henry Walter, Jr. 1947- *St&PR 91*
Nozkowski, Thomas *BioIn 16*
Nsekela, Rodgers Monday 1948- *WhoWor 91*
Nsono Ebendeng, Melanio *WhoWor 91*
Nsouli, Talal Mounir 1952- *WhoEmL 91, WhoWor 91*
Nsubuga, Emmanuel 1914- *WhoWor 91*
Ntube, Dominic Kwang 1950- *WhoWrEP 89*
Nuanes, William E. *WhoHisp 91N*
Nuber, Richard Howard 1943- *WhoAm 90, WhoSSW 91*
Nucci, Leo *BioIn 16*
Nucci, Leo 1942- *IntWWM 90, WhoAm 90*
Nucciarone, A. Patrick 1947- *WhoEmL 91*
Nuccitelli, Michael Robert 1962- *St&PR 91*
Nuccitelli, Saul Arnold 1928- *WhoAm 90, WhoWor 91*
Nucifora, Alfred John 1946- *WhoAm 90*
Nuckels, Jim C. 1938- *St&PR 91*
Nuckolls, John Hopkins 1930- *WhoAm 90*
Nuckolls, Leonard Arnold 1917- *WhoAm 90*
Nuckolls, Robert Theodore 1933- *WhoAm 90*
Nuckols, Frank J 1926- *BiDrAPA 89*
Nuckols, Joe *BioIn 16*
Nuckols, John Thomas 1940- *BiDrAPA 89*
Nuckols, Robert M. 1937- *St&PR 91*
Nuckols, William M. 1939- *St&PR 91*
Nudel, Ida *BioIn 16*
Nudell, Mayer 1949- *WhoE 91*
Nudelman, Melvin D 1920- *BiDrAPA 89*
Nudelman, Shirley Soble 1933- *WhoAmW 91*
Nuderscher, Frank Bernard 1880-1959 *WhoAmA 91N*
Nudo, Alan Frank 1948- *St&PR 91*
Nudo, Samuel 1956- *St&PR 91*
Nudo, Thomas 1951- *St&PR 91*
Nudo, Wanda M. *St&PR 91*
Nuechterlein, Gerald F. 1930- *St&PR 91*
Nuehring, Stanley Paul 1952- *St&PR 91*
Nuernberg, Robert Alan 1940- *St&PR 91*
Nuernberger, Louis Dean 1924- *IntWWM 90*
Nuesse, Celestine Joseph 1913- *WhoAm 90*
Nuessel, Frank H 1943- *ConAu 31NR*
Nuetzel, Eric James 1950- *BiDrAPA 89*
Nuetzel, John Arlington 1947- *WhoEmL 91*
Nuffer, David 1932- *ODwPR 91*
Nuffer, William G. 1931- *St&PR 91*
Nuffield, Edward Joseph *BiDrAPA 89*
Nugel, Bernfried 1940- *WhoWor 91*
Nugen, Brenda Elaine 1957- *WhoSSW 91*
Nugent, Arthur William 1891-1975 *WhoAmA 91N*
Nugent, Barbara Ann 1941- *WhoAmW 91*
Nugent, Bill Allen 1934- *WhoAm 90*
Nugent, Bob L 1947- *WhoAmA 91*
Nugent, Catherine Marie 1966- *WhoAmW 91*
Nugent, Charles Arter 1924- *WhoAm 90*
Nugent, Charles Michael 1938- *St&PR 91*
Nugent, D. Eugene 1927- *St&PR 91*
Nugent, Daniel Eugene 1927- *WhoAm 90*
Nugent, Edgar H., Jr. 1932- *St&PR 91*
Nugent, Edward James 1921- *St&PR 91*
Nugent, Frances Roberts 1904-1964? *AuBYP 90*
Nugent, Gerry *Ballpl 90*
Nugent, Gregory 1911- *WhoAm 90*
Nugent, John O'Connell 1942- *St&PR 91*
Nugent, John W. *St&PR 91*
Nugent, Joseph C. *BioIn 16*
Nugent, Lori S. 1962- *WhoAmW 91*
Nugent, Maria 1771-1834 *FemiCLE*

Nugent, Nelle 1939- *BioIn 16, NotWoAT, WhoAm 90, WhoAmW 91*
Nugent, Richard Bruce 1905- *EarBlAP*
Nugent, Richard L. 1951- *St&PR 91*
Nugent, Robert J., Jr. 1942- *WhoAm 90*
Nugent, Ted 1948- *EncPR&S 89*
Nugent, Thomas D. 1943- *St&PR 91*
Nugent, Walter Terry King 1935- *WhoAm 90, WhoWrEP 89*
Nugent-Crocitto, Margaret Mary 1966- *WhoAmW 91*
Nuggud, Jamshed Ruttons *BiDrAPA 89*
Nugnes, Frank Anthony 1954- *WhoE 91*
Nugteren, Cornelius 1928- *WhoAm 90*
Nuhn, Charles Kelsey 1925- *WhoE 91*
Nuhn, Perry Richard 1933- *WhoSSW 91*
Nuis, Jan 1931- *WhoWor 91*
Nujoma, Sam *BioIn 16*
Nujoma, Sam 1929- *CurBio 90 [port], News 90 [port]*
Nujoma, Sam Daniel 1929- *WhoWor 91*
Nuki 1919-1984 *WhoAmA 91N*
Nukiwa, Toshihiro 1947- *WhoWor 91*
Nulicek, Jiri 1934- *WhoWor 91*
Null, Douglas Peter 1926- *St&PR 91*
Null, Earl Eugene 1936- *St&PR 91, WhoAm 90*
Null, Kathleen 1949- *WhoWrEP 89*
Nulman, Philip Roy 1951- *WhoE 91*
Nulman, Robert Alan 1942- *WhoE 91*
Nulman, Seymour Shlomo 1921- *WhoAm 90, WhoWor 91*
Nultsch, Wilhelm 1927- *WhoWor 91*
Nulty, Bonnie *ODwPR 91*
Nulty, George Patrick 1942- *St&PR 91*
Numaga *WhNaAH*
Numan, Yasin Said 1948- *WhoWor 91*
Numann, Guy William 1932- *St&PR 91*
Numano, Mitsuyoshi 1954- *WhoWor 91*
Numata, Nobuo 1954- *WhoE 91, WhoWor 91*
Numbers, Judy M. 1949- *WhoAmW 91*
Numeriano, Ciudad Javier 1934- *St&PR 91*
Numers, Lorenz Torbjorn Gustaf G. von 1913- *DcScanL*
Nummelin, Bo 1926- *WhoWor 91*
Numminen, Kalevi 1932- *WhoWor 91*
Nunamaker, Les 1889-1938 *Ballpl 90*
Nunchuck, Mary Inez 1948- *BiDrAPA 89*
Nuncio, Pete N. 1942- *WhoHisp 91*
Nundy, Julian 1947- *WhoWor 91*
Nunemaker, Barbara Ann 1956- *St&PR 91*
Nunemaker, Richard A. 1948- *St&PR 91*
Nunemaker, Richard E. 1942- *IntWWM 90*
Nunes, Alan Anthony 1957- *St&PR 91*
Nunes, Anthony A. 1928- *St&PR 91*
Nunes, Edward Vernon 1955- *BiDrAPA 89*
Nunes, Edward Vernon, Jr. 1955- *WhoE 91*
Nunes, Geoffrey 1930- *St&PR 91*
Nunes, Gordon Maxwell 1914- *WhoAm 90*
Nunes, Joao Vieira *BiDrAPA 89*
Nunes, M. Adelaide *St&PR 91*
Nunes, Mary Louise 1960- *WhoE 91*
Nunes Vais, Mario 1856-1932 *BioIn 16*
Nunez, Aida Rodrigo *BiDrAPA 89*
Nunez, Alex 1938- *WhoHisp 91*
Nunez, Ana Rosa 1926- *WhoHisp 91*
Nunez, Antonio 1922- *St&PR 91*
Nunez, Edwin 1963- *Ballpl 90, WhoHisp 91*
Nunez, Elpidio *WhoHisp 91*
Nunez, Jairo Rafael *BiDrAPA 89*
Nunez, Jose 1964- *Ballpl 90*
Nunez, Juan Solomon, Jr. 1945- *WhoHisp 91*
Nunez, Julio V. 1960- *WhoHisp 91*
Nunez, Louis *WhoHisp 91*
Nunez, Matias 1922- *BiDrAPA 89*
Nunez, Nicolas *BiDrAPA 89*
Nunez, Rafael 1825-1894 *BioIn 16*
Nunez, Rene Jose 1941- *WhoHisp 91*
Nunez, Santiago *BiDrAPA 89*
Nunez-del Toro, Orlando 1940- *WhoHisp 91*
Nunez de Villavicencio, Orlando 1940- *WhoHisp 91*
Nunez-Hinestrosa, Julio *BiDrAPA 89*
Nunez-Lawton, Miguel Guillermo 1949- *WhoE 91*
Nunez-Lopez, Jose A 1933- *BiDrAPA 89*
Nunez-Portuondo, Ricardo 1933- *WhoAm 90, WhoWor 91*
Nunez Tellez, Carlos *NewYTBS 90*
Nungesser, Martha Kate 1953- *WhoAmW 91*
Nunis, Doyce Blackman, Jr. 1924- *WhoAm 90*
Nunis, Richard Arlen 1932- *WhoAm 90*
Nunley, Charles Eugene 1928- *WhoE 91*
Nunley, Richard L. 1927- *St&PR 91*
Nunn, Frederic 1879- *WhoAmA 91N*
Nunn, Grady Harrison 1918- *WhoAm 90*
Nunn, Howard S. 1923- *St&PR 91*
Nunn, Janet L *BiDrAPA 89*
Nunn, Jessie Alford *AuBYP 90*
Nunn, Margaret Baker 1912- *WhoAmW 91*
Nunn, Michael *BioIn 16*
Nunn, Paula S. *BiDrAPA 89*
Nunn, Robert R 1926- *BiDrAPA 89*
Nunn, Robert T. 1954- *St&PR 91*
Nunn, Sam *BioIn 16*
Nunn, Sam 1938- *News 90 [port], WhoAm 90, WhoSSW 91, WhoWor 91, WorAlBi*
Nunn, Trevor Robert 1940- *WhoAm 90, WhoWor 91*
Nunn, Wallace H. 1943- *St&PR 91*
Nunn, Wilfred 1926- *WhoWrEP 89*
Nunn, William Curtis 1908- *WhoWrEP 89*
Nunnally, James Thomas, III *BiDrAPA 89*
Nunnally, Marney Thomas 1942- *St&PR 91*
Nunnally, Sue Ann 1959- *WhoAmW 91*
Nunnelley, Douglas Buchanan 1942- *St&PR 91*
Nunnelley, John Thomas 1926- *St&PR 91*
Nunnelley, Robert B 1929- *WhoAmA 91*
Nunnelly, Walter Sandels, III 1943- *WhoAm 90*
Nunnerley, Sandra T. 1953- *WhoAmW 91*
Nuno, Juan Antonio 1927- *WhoWor 91*
Nuno, Olga Maria *BiDrAPA 89*
Nunoi, Keijiro 1930- *WhoWor 91*
Nunz, Gregory Joseph 1934- *WhoWor 91*
Nunz, William Robert, Sr. 1932- *St&PR 91*
Nunziato, Carl A. 1938- *St&PR 91*
Nuotio-Antar, Vappu Sinikka 1940- *WhoAmW 91*
Nuova Quartetto Italiano *PenDiMP*
Nur Jahan 1577-1646 *WomWR [port]*
Nurcombe, Barry 1933- *BiDrAPA 89*
Nuredini, Raymond F 1956- *BiDrAPA 89*
Nuremberg, Michael Robert 1944- *St&PR 91*
Nurenberg, David 1939- *WhoAm 90*
Nurenberg, Jeffry Raul *BiDrAPA 89*
Nurenberg, Thelma 1903-1984 *AuBYP 90*
Nureyev, Rudolf 1938- *WorAlBi*
Nureyev, Rudolf Hametovich 1938- *WhoAm 90, WhoWor 91*
Nurge, Donald Fred 1933- *St&PR 91*
Nurick, Gilbert 1906- *WhoAm 90*
Nurkin, Harry Abraham 1944- *WhoAm 90, WhoSSW 91*
Nurkse, Alan D. 1949- *WhoWrEP 89*
Nurmesniemi, Antti 1927- *ConDes 90*
Nurmi, Paavo 1897-1973 *WorAlBi*
Nurnberg, H George 1942- *BiDrAPA 89*
Nurnberg, Joseph 1913- *St&PR 91*
Nurnberger, David W. *ODwPR 91*
Nurnberger, John I *BiDrAPA 89*
Nurnberger, John Ignatius, Jr. 1946- *BiDrAPA 89*
Nurnberger, Thomas S. 1918- *St&PR 91*
Nurock, Robert Jay 1937- *WhoAm 90, WhoE 91*
Nurse, Rebecca 1621-1692 *EncCRAm*
Nusaybah, Azmi Izzat 1923- *WhoWor 91*
Nusbaum, Charles Joseph 1906-1987 *BioIn 16*
Nusbaum, E Daniel *BiDrAPA 89*
Nusbaum, Jack *BioIn 16*
Nusbaum, Jack H. 1940- *St&PR 91*
Nusbaum, Marlene Ackerman 1949- *WhoAmW 91, WhoE 91*
Nuse, Cathy Cates 1949- *WhoSSW 91*
Nuse, Oliver William 1914- *WhoAmA 91*
Nuse, Thelma Pauline 1934- *WhoAmW 91*
Nushawg, Michael Allan 1944- *WhoAmA 91*
Nusim, Roberta 1943- *WhoAmW 91*
Nuss, Eldon Paul 1933- *WhoAm 90*
Nuss, Robert Conrad 1937- *WhoSSW 91*
Nussbaum, Adolf Edward 1925- *WhoAm 90*
Nussbaum, Alan Charles *BiDrAPA 89*
Nussbaum, Bernard J. 1931- *WhoAm 90*
Nussbaum, Hedda 1942- *BioIn 16*
Nussbaum, Joel Herbert 1940- *St&PR 91*
Nussbaum, Joseph William 1931- *St&PR 91*
Nussbaum, Larry Jay *BiDrAPA 89*
Nussbaum, Leo Lester 1918- *WhoAm 90, WhoWor 91*
Nussbaum, Martha Craven 1947- *WhoAm 90, WhoAmW 91*
Nussbaum, Paul Allan 1947- *WhoE 91, WhoEmL 91*
Nussbaum, Paul Eugene 1952- *WhoAm 90*
Nussbaum, Sheila Ford 1940- *WhoAmA 91, WhoE 91*
Nussbaum, V. M., Jr. 1919- *WhoSSW 91*
Nussbaum, Walter 1926- *St&PR 91*
Nussbaumer, John George, II 1937- *St&PR 91*
Nussbaumer, Josef 1951- *WhoWor 91*
Nussbaumer, Roger 1944- *St&PR 91*
Nussenzveig, Herch Moyses 1933- *WhoWor 91*
Nussman, Donna Sue 1957- *WhoAmW 91, WhoSSW 91*
Nuta, Vladimir 1950- *WhoE 91*
Nutant, John Albert 1935- *St&PR 91, WhoAm 90*
Nute, Grace Lee *NewYTBS 90*
Nute, Grace Lee 1895-1990 *BioIn 16, ConAu 131*
Nute, James Boyce 1935- *St&PR 91*
Nuth, Robert 1927- *WhoAm 90*
Nutt, Charles W., Jr. 1948- *St&PR 91*
Nutt, Craig 1950- *WhoAmA 91*
Nutt, Donald Arthur 1932- *St&PR 91*
Nutt, Fred L., Jr *WhoAm 90*
Nutt, Jim 1938- *WhoAmA 91*
Nutt, Nan 1925- *WhoAmW 91*
Nutt, Niven Robert, Jr. 1929- *WhoSSW 91, WhoWor 91*
Nutt, Paul Charles 1939- *WhoAm 90*
Nutt, Roy *NewYTBS 90*
Nutt, Vinton Snyder 1924- *St&PR 91*
Nutt, William James 1945- *WhoAm 90, WhoE 91*
Nuttall, Charles Edwin 1945- *WhoE 91*
Nutter, Caroline 1958- *ODwPR 91*
Nutter, Charles A. 1903- *St&PR 91*
Nutter, Edward H. 1926- *St&PR 91*
Nutter, Franklin Winston 1946- *WhoAm 90, WhoEmL 91*
Nutter, Harold Lee 1923- *WhoAm 90*
Nutter, June Ann Knight 1947- *WhoAmW 91*
Nutter, Wallace Lee 1944- *WhoAm 90*
Nutting, Cary James 1961- *WhoSSW 91*
Nutting, Charles Bernard 1906- *WhoAm 90*
Nutting, George Ogden 1935- *St&PR 91, WhoAm 90*
Nutting, M. Adelaide 1858-1948 *BioIn 16*
Nutting, Mary A. 1858-1948 *BioAmW*
Nutting, Mary Adelaide 1858-1948 *BioIn 16*
Nutting, Patricia Fink 1926- *ConAu 129*
Nutting, Robert M. 1962- *St&PR 91*
Nutting, Wallace 1861-1941 *BioIn 16*
Nutting, Wallace Hall 1928- *WhoAm 90*
Nuttle, Thomas O. 1929- *St&PR 91*
Nuttle, Thomas Oliver 1929- *WhoAm 90*
Nutzhorn, Carl Robbins 1927- *WhoSSW 91*
Nutzinger, Hans Gottfried 1945- *WhoWor 91*
Nutzle, Futzie *ConAu 132*
Nutzle, Futzie 1942- *WhoAm 90, WhoAmA 91*
Nuuttila, Seppo Juhani 1939- *WhoWor 91*
Nuvolari, Tazio 1892-1953 *BioIn 16*
Nuwer, Marc Roman 1948- *WhoEmL 91*
Nuxhall, Joe 1928- *Ballpl 90*
Nuzio, Alfred Anthony 1933- *St&PR 91*
Nuzum, John M. 1939- *St&PR 91*
Nuzum, John M., Jr. 1939- *WhoAm 90*
Nuzzarello, Angela 1959- *BiDrAPA 89*
Nuzzarello, Salvatore T *BiDrAPA 89*
Nuzzo, Paul L. 1944- *St&PR 91*
Nuzzo, Salvatore Joseph 1931- *St&PR 91, WhoAm 90*
Nwako, M. P. K. 1923- *WhoWor 91*
Nwankpa, Bennett Onyema *BiDrAPA 89*
Nwankwo, Victor Uzoma 1944- *WhoWor 91*
Nwanna, Gladson I. N. 1954- *WhoEmL 91*
Nwaomah, Onyema Aaron *BiDrAPA 89*
Nwapa, Flora 1931- *FemiCLE*
Nwaukwa, Ken Douglas Chinazom 1946- *WhoWor 91*
Nwokeji, Emmanuel Igweze *BiDrAPA 89*
Nwosu, Caroline Chinwe 1960- *WhoAmW 91*
Nyaboya, Isidore 1946- *WhoWor 91*
Nyarady, Elemer 1923- *St&PR 91*
Nybakken, James Willard 1936- *WhoAm 90*
Nyberg, Charles D. 1930- *St&PR 91, WhoAm 90*
Nyberg, Richard John 1963- *WhoWor 91*
Nyberg, Richard Lawrence 1940- *St&PR 91*
Nyberg, William Arthur 1947- *WhoWor 91*
Nyblom, Helena Augusta 1843-1926 *EncCoWW*
Nybo, Dennis O. 1944- *St&PR 91*
Nyborg, Wesley Lemars 1917- *WhoAm 90*
Nyce, H. Edward 1932- *WhoAm 90*
Nychka, Ronda *BioIn 16*
Nycum, Susan Hubbell *WhoAm 90*
Nycz, Edward *St&PR 91N*
Nydam, Darlene 1961- *WhoAmW 91*
Nydick, David 1929- *WhoAm 90, WhoE 91*
Nydick, Robert Lincoln, Jr. 1957- *WhoE 91*
Nydorf, Roy Herman 1952- *WhoAmA 91*
Nye, Bill 1850-1896 *BioIn 16*
Nye, Daniel Alan 1952- *WhoEmL 91*
Nye, Edgar Wilson 1850-1896 *BioIn 16*
Nye, Edwin Packard 1920- *WhoAm 90*
Nye, Elwood L. *BioIn 16*
Nye, Erle 1937- *St&PR 91*
Nye, Erle Allen 1937- *WhoAm 90, WhoSSW 91*
Nye, F. Ivan 1918- *WhoWrEP 89*
Nye, Gary Scott 1939- *BiDrAPA 89*
Nye, George F. 1919- *St&PR 91*
Nye, Hethea *BioIn 16*
Nye, John Robert 1947- *WhoEmL 91, WhoWor 91*
Nye, Joseph Samuel, Jr. 1937- *WhoAm 90*
Nye, Martin Nicholas 1944- *St&PR 91*
Nye, Miriam Maurine Baker 1918- *WhoAmW 91*
Nye, Molly Harding *WhoAmA 91*
Nye, Molly Harding 1939- *WhoE 91*
Nye, Naomi Shihab 1952- *WhoWrEP 89*
Nye, Nelson Coral 1907- *BioIn 16*
Nye, Pat 1951- *BiDrAPA 89*
Nye, Rich 1944- *Ballpl 90*
Nye, Richard S. *BioIn 16*
Nye, Robert 1939- *MajTwCW*
Nye, Robert E. 1931- *St&PR 91*
Nye, Robert W. 1959- *St&PR 91*
Nye, Roger H. *BioIn 16*
Nye, Rollie Clayton, Jr. 1945- *WhoSSW 91*
Nye, Sarah Litsey 1903- *LiHiK*
Nye, Simon 1958- *ConAu 131*
Nye, Thomas Russell 1928- *WhoAm 90*
Nye, W. Marcus W. 1945- *WhoEmL 91, WhoWor 91*
Nye, Warren Kirkeby 1914- *St&PR 91*
Nye, William Allen 1937- *WhoAm 90*
Nye, William Roger 1940- *WhoE 91*
Nye DeHaan, Susan Janet 1945- *WhoAmW 91*
Nye-Sestokas, Sally Lewis 1939- *WhoE 91*
Nyeboe, Sven Jesper *BioIn 16*
Nyemaster, Ray 1914- *WhoAm 90*
Nyenhuis, Jacob Eugene 1935- *WhoAm 90*
Nyer, Samuel 1925- *St&PR 91*
Nyere, Robert Alan 1917- *WhoAm 90*
Nyerges, Alexander Lee 1957- *WhoAm 90, WhoAmA 91, WhoSSW 91*
Nyerges, Christopher John 1955- *WhoWrEP 89*
Nyers, Rezso 1923- *WhoWor 91*
Nyers, Stephen J., III 1935- *St&PR 91*
Nyfenger, Thomas 1936-1990 *NewYTBS 90*
Nygaard, Finn *BioIn 16*
Nygaard, Henry Sigurd 1929- *WhoAm 90*
Nygaard, Kaare K. *BioIn 16*
Nygaard, Marvin Richard 1929- *St&PR 91*
Nygaard, Richard Lowell 1940- *WhoAm 90*
Nygard, Dewayne Dennis 1949- *St&PR 91*
Nygard, Holger Olof 1921- *WhoAm 90*
Nygren, John Fergus 1940- *WhoAmA 91*
Nygren, Karl Francis 1927- *WhoAm 90, WhoWor 91*
Nygren, Lars Johan 1940- *WhoWor 91*
Nygren, Linda LaVerne 1947- *WhoAmW 91*
Nygren, W.D. 1926- *St&PR 91*
Nyhan, William Leo 1926- *WhoAm 90*
Nyhart, Eldon Howard 1927- *WhoAm 90*
Nyhlen, Karen Elizabeth 1960- *WhoAmW 91*
Nyholm, Kurt Rainer 1932- *WhoWor 91*
Nyhus, Lloyd Milton 1923- *WhoAm 90*
Nyikos, Markus Andreas 1948- *IntWWM 90*
Nyiregyhazi, Erwin 1903-1987 *PenDiMP*
Nyiri, Joseph Anton 1937- *WhoWor 91*
Nyirjesy, Istvan 1929- *WhoAm 90*
Nykanen, Matti *BioIn 16*
Nykerk, K.M. 1940- *St&PR 91*
Nykiel, Frank Peter 1917- *WhoAm 90*
Nykiel, Ronald Alan 1945- *St&PR 91, WhoAm 90*
Nykrog, Per 1925- *WhoAm 90*
Nykvist, Sven 1922- *BioIn 16*
Nykvist, Sven Vilhem 1922- *WhoAm 90*
Nyland, James R. 1930- *St&PR 91*
Nylander, Carl R.G. 1932- *WhoWor 91*
Nylander, Jane Louise 1938- *WhoE 91*
Nylander, Mark C. 1952- *ODwPR 91*
Nylander, Suzanne Hilma 1956- *WhoAmW 91*
Nylander, Ulf Magnus Yngve 1931- *WhoWor 91*
Nyman, Carl John, Jr. 1924- *WhoAm 90*
Nyman, Donald Hilding 1934- *St&PR 91*
Nyman, Gary William 1941- *BiDrAPA 89*
Nyman, Georg Nikolaus 1949- *WhoWor 91*
Nyman, Georgianna Beatrice 1930- *WhoAmA 91, WhoE 91*
Nyman, Jerry 1942- *Ballpl 90*
Nyman, Leslie Joel *BiDrAPA 89*
Nyman, Mary Mallon 1935- *WhoWrEP 89*
Nyman, Maud Ingalill 1932- *WhoWor 91*
Nyman, Nancy Ann 1946- *WhoEmL 91*
Nyman, Robert Jay 1948- *WhoE 91*
Nyquist, Arild 1937- *DcScanL*
Nyquist, John Davis 1918- *WhoAm 90*
Nyquist, R. Peter *BioIn 16*
Nyquist, Robert *WhoAm 90*
Nyquist, Robert Earl *BiDrAPA 89*
Nyquist, Steven Richard *BiDrAPA 89*
Nyquist, Thomas Eugene 1931- *WhoAm 90, WhoE 91*
Nyren, Karl 1921-1988 *BioIn 16*
Nyren, Neil Sebastian 1948- *WhoAm 90*

Nyro, Laura 1947- *EncPR&S 89, OxCPMus, WorAlBi*
Nyrop, Donald William 1912- *WhoAm 90*
Nysether, Mark A. 1955- *St&PR 91*
Nysetvold, Wayne E. 1940- *St&PR 91*
Nysmith, Charles Robert 1935- *WhoAm 90*
Nyssen, Gerard Allan 1942- *WhoSSW 91*
Nyssen, Michel Paul 1935- *St&PR 91*
Nystedt, Knut 1915- *IntWWM 90*
Nystrand, Daniel I. 1936- *St&PR 91*
Nystrand, Raphael Owens 1937- *WhoAm 90*
Nystrom, Clair Karl 1947- *WhoWor 91*
Nystrom, Harold Charles 1906- *WhoAm 90*
Nystrom, Harry Gustav 1936- *WhoWor 91*
Nystrom, John Warren 1913- *WhoAm 90*
Nystrom, Karl F *BiDrAPA 89*
Nystrom, Kent Krister 1948- *WhoWor 91*
Nystrom, Lowell D. 1935- *St&PR 91*
Nystrom, Robert I. 1929- *St&PR 91*
Nystrom, Steven George 1941- *St&PR 91*
Nyswander, Marie *BiDrAPA 89*
Nytko, Edward C. 1943- *WhoAm 90*
Nytko, Edward Charles 1943- *St&PR 91*
Nyvlt, Jaroslav 1932- *WhoWor 91*
Nyy, Linda Kathleen 1950- *WhoAmW 91*
Nzeyimana, Noah *WhoAm 90*
Nzinga Mbandi 1580?-1663 *WomWR*
Nzinga, Queen of Matamba 1582-1663 *BioIn 16*

O

Oacpicagigua, Luis *EncCRAm, WhNaAH*
Oak Ridge Boys *ConMus 4 [port]*
Oak, Alan Douglas 1946- *St&PR 91*
Oakander, Margaret Agnes *BiDrAPA 89*
Oakar, Mary Rose *BioIn 16*
Oakar, Mary Rose 1940- *WhoAm 90, WhoAmW 91*
Oakeley, Anne *BiDEWW*
Oakes, Betty *BioIn 16*
Oakes, Catherine Marie 1950- *WhoE 91*
Oakes, Derek W. 1930- *St&PR 91*
Oakes, Ellen Ruth 1919- *WhoAmW 91*
Oakes, Gordon N., Jr. 1941- *WhoAm 90, WhoE 91*
Oakes, Gordon Norman, Jr. 1941- *St&PR 91*
Oakes, Harry Scott 1932- *St&PR 91, WhoAm 90*
Oakes, Helen Miller 1932- *WhoSSW 91*
Oakes, Jack C. 1931- *St&PR 91*
Oakes, James L. 1924- *WhoAm 90, WhoE 91*
Oakes, John Bertram 1913- *BioIn 16, WhoAm 90, WhoWor 91*
Oakes, John Warren 1941- *WhoAmA 91*
Oakes, Kingsland 1928- *ODwPR 91*
Oakes, Lester Cornelius 1923- *WhoAm 90*
Oakes, Marvin Gordon 1945- *St&PR 91*
Oakes, Maud 1903-1990 *BioIn 16*
Oakes, Maud Van Cortlandt *NewYTBS 90*
Oakes, Melvin Ervin Louis 1936- *WhoAm 90*
Oakes, R.L. 1929- *St&PR 91*
Oakes, Rebel 1886-1948 *Ballpl 90*
Oakes, Robert James 1936- *WhoAm 90*
Oakes, Robert Roy 1951- *WhoEmL 91*
Oakes, Timothy Wayne 1938- *St&PR 91, WhoAm 90*
Oakes, Virginia Armstrong *AuBYP 90*
Oakes, Walter Jerry 1946- *WhoAm 90*
Oakes, William Larry 1944- *WhoAmA 91*
Oakes Smith, Elizabeth 1806-1893 *FemiCLE*
Oakeshott, Gordon Blaisdell 1904- *WhoAm 90*
Oakeshott, Michael *NewYTBS 90*
Oakeshott, Walter 1903-1987 *BioIn 16*
Oakey, John Martin, Jr. 1935- *WhoAm 90*
Oakie, Jack 1903-1978 *WorAlBi*
Oakland, Velma LeAne 1939- *WhoAmW 91*
Oakland, William Horace 1939- *WhoAm 90*
Oakley, Ann 1944- *FemiCLE*
Oakley, Annie 1860-1926 *BioAmW, BioIn 16, WorAlBi*
Oakley, Carolyn Cobb 1946- *WhoSSW 91*
Oakley, Carolyn Le 1942- *WhoAmW 91*
Oakley, Claron Louis 1924- *St&PR 91*
Oakley, Deborah Jane 1937- *WhoAmW 91*
Oakley, Francis Christopher 1931- *WhoAm 90, WhoE 91*
Oakley, Harry *ODwPR 91*
Oakley, Jerrold *St&PR 91*
Oakley, Keith LeRoy 1951- *WhoE 91*
Oakley, Kenneth Page 1911-1981 *DcNaB 1981*
Oakley, Leah Fitzgerald 1932- *WhoWrEP 89*
Oakley, Margaret Mary 1929- *WhoAmW 91*
Oakley, Marion Dabney, Jr. 1948- *WhoE 91*
Oakley, Mary Ann Bryant 1940- *WhoAmW 91*
Oakley, Richard B. 1946- *St&PR 91*
Oakley, Richard Embrey, III 1952- *WhoSSW 91*
Oakley, Richard Putney 1920- *WhoAm 90*
Oakley, Robert Alan 1946- *St&PR 91*
Oakley, Robert Bigger 1931- *WhoAm 90, WhoWor 91*
Oakley, Stanley Preston, Jr. 1956- *BiDrAPA 89*
Oakley, Violet 1874-1960 *WhoAmA 91N*
Oakley, Violet 1874-1961 *BiDWomA*
Oakley, Wanda Faye 1950- *WhoAmW 91*
Oakley, William Edwin 1939- *St&PR 91*
Oaks, Dallin Harris 1932- *WhoAm 90*
Oaks, Floyd Lawerence 1943- *WhoSSW 91*
Oaks, James Allan 1928- *St&PR 91*
Oaks, Margaret Marlene 1940- *WhoAmW 91, WhoWor 91*
Oaks, Maurice David 1934- *St&PR 91, WhoE 91*
Oaksey, John Geoffrey T Lawrence, Baron 1929- *BioIn 16*
Oana, Katherine D. 1929- *BioIn 16*
Oancea, Belinda Ann Lentz 1951- *WhoEmL 91*
Oandasan, William 1947- *WhoWrEP 89*
Oasin, Ricardo V *BiDrAPA 89*
Oast, Samuel P 1924- *BiDrAPA 89*
Oaten, Ernest W *EncO&P 3*
Oates, Carl Everette 1931- *WhoAm 90*
Oates, Dennis Matthew 1952- *St&PR 91*
Oates, Edward Rumsey 1953- *WhoSSW 91*
Oates, Frederic W. *BioIn 16*
Oates, Frederick Burnell 1945- *WhoEmL 91*
Oates, James Maclay 1946- *St&PR 91, WhoAm 90*
Oates, James Robert 1958- *WhoEmL 91*
Oates, John 1948- *WorAlBi*
Oates, John Alexander, III 1932- *WhoAm 90*
Oates, John Francis 1934- *WhoAm 90*
Oates, Johnny 1946- *Ballpl 90*
Oates, Joyce Carol 1938- *BioAmW, BioIn 16, FemiCLE, MajTwCW, ShSCr 6 [port], WhoAm 90, WhoAmW 91, WhoWrEP 89, WorAlBi*
Oates, Oliver H. *AmLegL*
Oates, Richard Jordan 1948- *St&PR 91*
Oates, Ronald Kim 1943- *WhoWor 91*
Oates, Stephen B. 1936- *BioIn 16*
Oates, Stephen Baery 1936- *WhoAm 90*
Oates, Wallace Eugene 1937- *WhoE 91*
Oates, Wanda *BioIn 16*
Oates, William Armstrong, Jr. 1942- *WhoAm 90*
Oatess, Frank *ODwPR 91*
Oatman, Eric Furber 1939- *WhoE 91, WhoWrEP 89*
Oatman, James Edward 1949- *St&PR 91*
Oatney, Cecilia Kay 1956- *WhoAmW 91*
Oats, Edwin Olen 1937- *WhoSSW 91*
Oatts, Dick *BioIn 16*
Oatway, Francis Carlyle 1936- *WhoAm 90*
Oaxaca, Jaime 1931- *WhoHisp 91*
Obadia, Andre Isaac 1927- *WhoWor 91*
Obadiah, Victor 1942- *St&PR 91*
Obando, Jose Maria 1795-1861 *BioIn 16*
Obando Bravo, Miguel 1926- *WhoWor 91*
Obando y Bravo, Miguel *BioIn 16*
O'Banion, Nance 1949- *WhoAmA 91*
O'Bannion, Mindy Martha Martin 1953- *WhoAmW 91*
O'Bannion, Tami Helene 1963- *WhoAmW 91*
O'Bannon, Dan 1946- *ConTFT 8*
O'Bannon, Daniel Thomas 1946- *WhoWor 91*
O'Bannon, Evan Patrick 1952- *WhoSSW 91*
O'Bannon, Frank Lewis 1930- *WhoAm 90*
O'Bannon, Helen B. 1939-1988 *BioIn 16*
Obara, Patricia E. 1952- *St&PR 91*
O'Barr, Jean Fox 1942- *WhoWrEP 89*
O'Barr, William McAlston 1942- *WhoAm 90*
Obasanjo, Olusegun 1937- *BioIn 16*
Obata, Gyo 1923- *BioIn 16, WhoAm 90*
Obayashi, Kyoko *BioIn 16*
Obear, Frederick Woods 1935- *WhoAm 90, WhoSSW 91*
Obedencio, Santiago Uyguangco 1940- *St&PR 91*
O'Beil, Hedy *WhoAmA 91, WhoE 91*
O'Beirne, Patrick O *BiDrAPA 89*
Obek, Aydogan 1934- *WhoWor 91*
Obenauf, Henry C. 1930- *St&PR 91*
Obenchain, Eliza Calvert 1856-1936 *LiHiK*
Obendorf, Ralph Louis 1938- *WhoE 91*
Obenhaus, Victor 1903- *WhoAm 90*
Ober, A. Clinton 1944- *St&PR 91*
Ober, Douglas Gary 1946- *St&PR 91*
Ober, Eric Wayne *BioIn 16*
Ober, Ken *BioIn 16*
Ober, Richard Francis, Jr. 1943- *St&PR 91*
Ober, Russell John, Jr. 1948- *WhoAm 90, WhoE 91, WhoWor 91*
Ober, Scott Karl 1964- *BiDrAPA 89*
Ober, Steve *BioIn 16*
Ober, Stuart A. 1946- *WhoWrEP 89*
Ober, Stuart Alan 1946- *WhoAm 90, WhoEmL 91*
Oberbeck, Paul A. 1934- *St&PR 91*
Obercit, Jacques Hermann 1725-1798 *EncO&P 3*
Oberdier, Ronald Ray 1945- *WhoSSW 91*
Oberdoerster, Michael Paul *BiDrAPA 89*
Oberdorfer, Don 1931- *ConAu 129*
Oberdorfer, Louis F. 1919- *WhoAm 90*
Oberdorfer, Paul Ellsworth, III 1950- *WhoSSW 91*
Oberender, Frederick Garrett 1933- *WhoAm 90*
Oberender, Peter Otto Christian 1941- *WhoWor 91*
Oberer, Sarah Lucille *BiDrAPA 89*
Oberfield, Richard Allan 1948- *BiDrAPA 89*
Oberfield, Richard Thomas 1925- *St&PR 91*
Oberfield, William Jay 1945- *BiDrAPA 89*
Oberfranc, Carl Frank 1956- *WhoEmL 91*
Oberg, Carl Albrecht 1897-1965 *BioIn 16*
Oberg, Debra A. 1965- *St&PR 91*
Oberg, Gary David 1955- *BiDrAPA 89*
Oberg, John 1951- *St&PR 91*
Oberg, Ralph E. 1951- *BioIn 16*
Oberg, Roger Winston 1919- *WhoAm 90*
Oberg, Thure *PenDiDA 89*
Obergfell, Richard R. 1934- *St&PR 91*
Oberhardt, William 1882-1958 *WhoAmA 91N*
Oberhausen, Joyce Ann Wynn 1941- *WhoAmW 91, WhoSSW 91, WhoWor 91*
Oberheim, The Baron 1951- *WhoWor 91*
Oberhellman, Theodore Arnold, Jr. 1934- *St&PR 91*
Oberhelman, Harley Dean 1928- *WhoAm 90*
Oberhelman, Harry Alvin, Jr. 1923- *WhoAm 90*
Oberholtzer, Craig S. 1952- *St&PR 91*
Oberhuber, Konrad *BioIn 16*
Oberhuber, Konrad Johannes 1935- *WhoAm 90*
Oberkampf, Christophe-Philippe 1738-1815 *PenDiDA 89*
Oberkfell, Ken 1956- *Ballpl 90*
Oberkirch, Ann Marie 1944- *BiDrAPA 89*
Oberlander, Michael 1931- *St&PR 91*
Oberlander, Ronald Y. *WhoAm 90*
Oberle, Edwin Francis 1941- *St&PR 91*
Oberle, Frank 1932- *WhoAm 90, WhoE 91*
Oberle, Holly Elizabeth 1947- *IntWWM 90*
Oberle, Mark S. 1956- *St&PR 91*
Oberlies, John W. 1939- *St&PR 91*
Oberlies, John William 1939- *WhoAm 90*
Oberlin, Richard Paul 1932- *WhoAm 90*
Oberlin, Robert James 1931- *St&PR 91*
Oberlin, Russell 1928- *IntWWM 90, PenDiMP*
Oberly, Charles Monroe, III 1946- *WhoE 91*
Oberly, Robert Peters 1931- *WhoAm 90*
Obermaier, Otto George 1936- *BioIn 16*
Oberman, Carl Marc 1952- *WhoSSW 91*
Oberman, I Jay *BiDrAPA 89*
Oberman, Lawrence H. 1940- *St&PR 91*
Oberman, Paul E. 1945- *St&PR 91*
Obermann, C. Esco 1904- *WhoAm 90, WhoWor 91*
Obermann, George 1935- *WhoWor 91*
Obermann, Richard Michael 1949- *WhoE 91, WhoEmL 91, WhoWor 91*
Obermayer, Herman Joseph 1924- *WhoWor 91*
Obermayer, Judith Hirschfield 1935- *WhoE 91*
Obermeier, Klaus Karl 1954- *WhoEmL 91*
Obermeier, Otto Robert 1928- *St&PR 91*
Obermeyer, Theresa Nangle 1945- *WhoAmW 91*
Obermeyr, Franz Michael 1954- *WhoWor 91*
Obernauer, Marne 1919- *St&PR 91, WhoAm 90*
Obernauer, Marne, Jr. 1943- *St&PR 91, WhoAm 90*
Oberndorf, Meyera E. *WhoAmW 91*
Oberndorfer, Wolfgang Johannes 1941- *WhoWor 91*
Obernier, Robert Bradley 1937- *St&PR 91, WhoAm 90*
Oberoi, Mohan Singh *BioIn 16*
Oberon, Merle 1911-1979 *BioIn 16, WorAlBi*
Oberpaul, Helmuth 1948- *WhoWor 91*
Oberreit, Walter William 1928- *WhoWor 91*
Oberrieder, John L. 1924- *St&PR 91*
O'Berry, Phillip Aaron 1933- *WhoAm 90*

Oberschlake, Dwight 1925- *St&PR 91*
Oberson, Rene 1945- *IntWWM 90*
Oberst, Paul 1914- *WhoAm 90*
Oberst, Robert Bruce 1931- *St&PR 91*
Oberst, Robert C. 1952- *St&PR 91*
Oberst, Robert John 1929- *WhoE 91*
Oberstar, Helen Elizabeth *WhoAmW 91*
Oberstar, James L. 1934- *WhoAm 90*
Oberstein, Marydale 1942- *WhoAmW 91*
Obert, Charles Frank 1937- *WhoAm 90*
Obert, Edward Fredric 1910- *WhoAm 90*
Obert, Jessie Craig 1911- *WhoAmW 91*
Obert, Kathleen *ODwPR 91*
Obert, Paul R. 1928- *St&PR 91*
Obert, Paul Richard 1928- *WhoAm 90*
Obert, Sherry Jean 1955- *WhoE 91*
Oberth, H 1894-1989 *CurBio 90N*
Oberth, Hermann *BioIn 16*
Obeso Rivera, Sergio 1931- *WhoAm 90*
Obetz, S Wendell 1930- *BiDrAPA 89*
Obey, David Ross 1938- *WhoAm 90*
Obey, Richard Arthur 1945- *WhoSSW 91*
Obi, Keiichiro 1927- *WhoWor 91*
Obiang Nguema Mbasogo, Teodoro 1942- *WhoWor 91*
Obici, Amedeo 1877-1947 *BioIn 16, WorAlBi*
Obieleski, Chester C. 1942- *St&PR 91*
Obin, Philome 1892-1984? *ArtLatA*
Obis, Paul Barrett Luty, Jr. 1951- *WhoAm 90*
O'Biso, Carol *BioIn 16*
Oblad, Alexander Golden 1909- *WhoAm 90*
Oblak, John Byron 1942- *WhoAm 90*
Obledo, Mario *BioIn 16*
Obledo, Mario Guerra 1932- *WhoHisp 91*
Obler, Geri 1942- *WhoAmA 91*
Obleski, Bert Michael 1954- *WhoEmL 91*
Obligado, Lilian 1931- *SmATA 61 [port]*
Oblinger, Josephine Kneidl Harrington 1913- *WhoAmW 91*
Oblinger, Nancy L. 1945- *ODwPR 91*
O'Block, Robert Paul 1943- *WhoE 91, WhoWor 91*
Obloy, Gregory J. 1943- *St&PR 91*
Obo, Takeo 1927- *WhoWor 91*
Obolenskii, Valerian Valerianovich 1887-1938 *BioIn 16*
Obolensky, Aleksei Dmitrievich 1855- *BioIn 16*
Obolensky, Alexander Dmitrievich 1847- *BioIn 16*
Obolensky, Ivan 1925- *WhoAm 90, WhoE 91, WhoWor 91*
Obolensky, Marilyn Wall 1929- *WhoAm 90*
Obolsky, Alexander Eduard 1962- *BiDrAPA 89*
Oborin, Lev 1907-1974 *PenDiMP*
Obourn, Robert Lyle *BiDrAPA 89*
O'Boyle, Edward J. 1923- *St&PR 91*
O'Boyle, James Bernard 1928- *WhoAm 90*
O'Boyle, Michael 1942- *BiDrAPA 89*
O'Boyle, Robert L. 1935- *WhoAm 90*
O'Boyle, Thomas Patrick 1920- *St&PR 91*
Oboyski-Battelene, Joanne Marie 1956- *WhoAmW 91*
Obradovich, Aleksandar 1927- *IntWWM 90*
Obrand, Barry S. 1948- *St&PR 91*
O'Brasky, David M. 1934- *WhoAm 90*
Obraztova, Elena 1937- *WhoWor 91*
Obraztsova, Elena 1937- *PenDiMP*
Obraztsova, Yelena Vasilyevna 1937- *IntWWM 90*
Obre, Barbara Guggenheim 1904-1985 *BioIn 16*
Obrecht, Jacob *BioIn 16*
Obrecht, Kenneth W. 1933- *St&PR 91*
O'Bree, Michael Peter 1949- *St&PR 91*
Obregon, Alejandro 1920- *WhoWor 91*
Obregon, Alvaro 1880-1928 *BioIn 16, EncPaPR 91*
Obregon, Carlos Daniel 1959- *WhoHisp 91*
Obregon, Jose Maria 1832-1902 *ArtLatA*
Obregon, Maning 1939-1989 *BioIn 16*
Obregon, Valentin 1953- *WhoHisp 91*
Obremski, Charles Peter 1946- *WhoEmL 91*
Obrestad, Tor 1938- *DcScanL*
O'Briain, Niall P. *WhoAm 90*
O'Brian, Frank *WhoWrEP 89*
O'Brian, Hugh *BioIn 16*
O'Brian, Hugh 1930- *WorAlBi*
O'Brian, Jack 1921- *WhoAm 90*
O'Briant, Jannis Lynn 1950- *WhoAmW 91*
O'Brien, Al 1923- *ODwPR 91*
O'Brien, Albert J. 1914- *St&PR 91*
O'Brien, Albert James 1914- *WhoAm 90*
O'Brien, Alice Merrill *BioIn 16*
O'Brien, Anna Belle Clement *WhoAmW 91*
O'Brien, Anne Pace 1930- *WhoAmW 91*
O'Brien, Anne Sibley 1952- *BioIn 16*
O'Brien, Arthur J. *NewYTBS 90*
O'Brien, Arthur J. 1910-1990 *BioIn 16*
O'Brien, Barbara Ellen 1936- *BiDrAPA 89*
O'Brien, Barry C. 1927- *WhoAm 90*
O'Brien, Beatrice Marie 1920- *WhoWrEP 89*
O'Brien, Bernard C. 1927- *St&PR 91, WhoAm 90*
O'Brien, Billy Thomas 1936- *St&PR 91*
O'Brien, Brett William 1963- *WhoE 91*
O'Brien, Brian John 1934- *WhoWor 91*
O'Brien, Brighid Maire 1950- *WhoE 91*
O'Brien, Buck 1882-1959 *Ballpl 90*
O'Brien, Carol Jean 1939- *WhoAmW 91, WhoWor 91*
O'Brien, Catharine *BioIn 16*
O'Brien, Catherine Louise 1930- *WhoAmW 91*
O'Brien, Charles G. 1931- *St&PR 91*
O'Brien, Charles H. 1920- *WhoAm 90, WhoSSW 91*
O'Brien, Charles James 1935- *St&PR 91*
O'Brien, Charles Maryon, Jr. 1943- *WhoAm 90*
O'Brien, Charles O. 1929- *WhoAm 90, WhoE 91*
O'Brien, Charles P. 1936- *St&PR 91*
O'Brien, Charles P 1939- *BiDrAPA 89*
O'Brien, Charlotte 1845-1909 *FemiCLE*
O'Brien, Christine R. *ODwPR 91*
O'Brien, Christopher Edward 1955- *WhoEmL 91*
O'Brien, Clarence J. 1942- *St&PR 91*
O'Brien, Claudine Michele Niedzielski 1953- *WhoEmL 91*
O'Brien, Colleen Ann 1967- *WhoE 91*
O'Brien, Conor Cruise 1917- *WhoWor 91*
O'Brien, Cynthia Jason *BiDrAPA 89*
O'Brien, Daniel Louis 1952- *WhoEmL 91*
O'Brien, Daniel R. 1946- *St&PR 91*
O'Brien, Daniel William 1926- *St&PR 91, WhoAm 90*
O'Brien, Darcy 1939- *WhoAm 90, WhoSSW 91, WhoWrEP 89*
O'Brien, David H. 1941- *St&PR 91*
O'Brien, David Joseph 1947- *St&PR 91*
O'Brien, David Peter 1941- *WhoAm 90*
O'Brien, David V. 1932-1989 *BioIn 16*
O'Brien, Dennis Arthur *BiDrAPA 89*
O'Brien, Dennis H. 1951- *St&PR 91*
O'Brien, Donald Eugene 1923- *WhoAm 90*
O'Brien, Donald Gerard 1922- *St&PR 91*
O'Brien, Donough 1923- *WhoAm 90*
O'Brien, Duncan Munroe, Jr. 1959- *WhoEmL 91*
O'Brien, E. G. *AuBYP 90, MajTwCW*
O'Brien, Eddie 1930- *Ballpl 90*
O'Brien, Edmond 1915-1985 *WorAlBi*
O'Brien, Edna *BioIn 16*
O'Brien, Edna 1930- *WhoWor 91, WorAlBi*
O'Brien, Edna 1932- *FemiCLE*
O'Brien, Edna 1936- *MajTwCW*
O'Brien, Edward *BioIn 16*
O'Brien, Edward Ignatius 1928- *WhoAm 90*
O'Brien, Eileen Patricia 1956- *WhoE 91*
O'Brien, Elmer John 1932- *WhoAm 90*
O'Brien, Erin Kathleen 1952- *WhoAmW 91*
O'Brien, Ethel F. Hieronymus *BiDrAPA 89*
O'Brien, Eugene 1927- *WhoAm 90*
O'Brien, Frances *NewYTBS 90*
O'Brien, Francis Anthony 1936- *WhoAm 90*
O'Brien, Francis Joseph, Jr. 1946- *WhoE 91*
O'Brien, Frank B. 1926- *WhoAm 90*
O'Brien, Frank B. 1946- *WhoAm 90*
O'Brien, G. Robert 1936- *St&PR 91*
O'Brien, George 1945- *ConAu 131*
O'Brien, George Aloysius 1944- *WhoAm 90*
O'Brien, George Dennis 1931- *WhoAm 90, WhoE 91, WhoWor 91*
O'Brien, George W *BiDrAPA 89*
O'Brien, Gerald *NewAgMG*
O'Brien, Gerald J *BiDrAPA 89*
O'Brien, Gerald James 1923- *WhoAm 90*
O'Brien, Gregory Francis 1950- *WhoE 91*
O'Brien, Gregory Michael St. Lawrence 1944- *WhoAm 90, WhoSSW 91*
O'Brien, Henry X. 1903-1990 *BioIn 16*
O'Brien, Hubert J., Jr. 1952- *St&PR 91*
O'Brien, J. Willard 1930- *WhoAm 90*
O'Brien, Jack *PenDiMP*
O'Brien, Jack 1873-1933 *Ballpl 90*
O'Brien, Jack 1939- *ConTFT 8*
O'Brien, James Aloysius 1936- *WhoAm 90*
O'Brien, James Edward *BiDrAPA 89*
O'Brien, James Edward 1912- *WhoAm 90*
O'Brien, James Henry, Jr. 1946- *WhoE 91*
O'Brien, James Jerome 1929- *WhoAm 90*
O'Brien, James L. 1926- *WhoE 91*
O'Brien, James Leo 1924- *St&PR 91*
O'Brien, James W. 1935- *St&PR 91*
O'Brien, Joan 1936- *BioIn 16*
O'Brien, Joan Karen 1952- *WhoAmW 91*
O'Brien, Joanne Katherine 1955- *WhoWor 91*
O'Brien, John *WhoAm 90, WhoE 91*
O'Brien, John 1953- *ConAu 132*
O'Brien, John Charles 1966- *WhoEmL 91*
O'Brien, John Conway *WhoAm 90, WhoWor 91*
O'Brien, John Daniel *BiDrAPA 89*
O'Brien, John Daniel 1939- *WhoE 91*
O'Brien, John Daniel O'Connell 1831-1891 *DcCanB 12*
O'Brien, John Feighan 1936- *WhoAm 90*
O'Brien, John Francis 1943- *St&PR 91*
O'Brien, John Gerald 1938- *WhoE 91*
O'Brien, John L. 1911- *BioIn 16*
O'Brien, John M. 1942- *St&PR 91*
O'Brien, John Patrick 1941- *BiDrAPA 89*
O'Brien, John S 1934- *BiDrAPA 89*
O'Brien, John Sebastian, II *BiDrAPA 89*
O'Brien, John Sherman 1898-1938 *AuBYP 90*
O'Brien, John Thomas 1945- *WhoWrEP 89*
O'Brien, John Wilfrid 1931- *WhoAm 90*
O'Brien, John William, Jr. 1937- *WhoWor 91*
O'Brien, Johnny 1930- *Ballpl 90*
O'Brien, Jon Joseph 1926- *BiDrAPA 89*
O'Brien, Joseph E. 1933- *St&PR 91*
O'Brien, Joseph P. 1940- *St&PR 91*
O'Brien, Joseph Patrick, Jr. 1940- *WhoAm 90*
O'Brien, Karen Sue 1964- *WhoSSW 91*
O'Brien, Kate 1897-1974 *BioIn 16, FemiCLE*
O'Brien, Katharine *WhoWrEP 89*
O'Brien, Kenneth Robert 1937- *St&PR 91, WhoAm 90*
O'Brien, Kevin Benjamin 1925- *WhoWor 91*
O'Brien, Kevin J. 1934- *WhoAm 90*
O'Brien, Kevin Patrick 1944- *St&PR 91*
O'Brien, Kevin Patrick 1952- *WhoE 91*
O'Brien, Lawrence 1917- *WorAlBi*
O'Brien, Lawrence Alan 1956- *WhoSSW 91*
O'Brien, Lawrence F 1917-1990 *CurBio 90N*
O'Brien, Lawrence F, Jr. 1917-1990 *NewYTBS 90 [port]*
O'Brien, Lawrence Francis 1917- *BiDrUSE 89, WhoAm 90*
O'Brien, Lawrence John 1949- *WhoSSW 91*
O'Brien, Lawrence William 1924- *St&PR 91*
O'Brien, Lawrence William 1949- *WhoE 91*
O'Brien, Leonard D. 1928- *St&PR 91*
O'Brien, Libby Atkins 1913- *WhoE 91*
O'Brien, Lisa Marie 1969- *WhoHisp 91*
O'Brien, Loretta Sullivan 1930- *WhoAmW 91*
O'Brien, Lucius Richard 1832-1899 *DcCanB 12*
O'Brien, Lucrezia Florence 1940- *WhoAmW 91*
O'Brien, Margaret 1937- *WorAlBi*
O'Brien, Mark Stephen 1933- *WhoAm 90*
O'Brien, Martin James, Jr. 1940- *St&PR 91*
O'Brien, Mary *FemiCLE*
O'Brien, Mary Devon 1944- *WhoAmW 91, WhoE 91, WhoWor 91*
O'Brien, Mary Kaye 1960- *WhoAmW 91*
O'Brien, Maurice James 1925- *WhoAm 90*
O'Brien, Michael 1948- *WhoEmL 91*
O'Brien, Michael John 1930- *WhoAm 90*
O'Brien, Michael Joseph 1947- *WhoE 91*
O'Brien, Michael Wilfrid 1944- *St&PR 91*
O'Brien, Murrough Hall 1945- *WhoE 91*
O'Brien, Neal Ray 1937- *WhoAm 90*
O'Brien, Neil Justin 1932- *St&PR 91*
O'Brien, Pat 1899-1983 *WorAlBi*
Obrien, Patricia Mary 1951- *WhoAmW 91*
O'Brien, Patricia Nevin 1957- *WhoAmW 91*
O'Brien, Patrick Michael 1943- *WhoAm 90*
O'Brien, Patrick W. *BioIn 16, NewYTBS 90*
O'Brien, Paul A. 1956- *St&PR 91*
O'Brien, Paul Charles 1939- *St&PR 91, WhoAm 90, WhoE 91*
O'Brien, Paul Herbert 1930- *WhoAm 90*
O'Brien, Paul Jerry 1925- *St&PR 91, WhoAm 90*
O'Brien, Penny 1928- *WhoWrEP 89*
O'Brien, Pete 1958- *Ballpl 90*
O'Brien, Ralph H. 1929- *St&PR 91*
O'Brien, Raymond F. 1922- *St&PR 91*
O'Brien, Raymond V., Jr. 1927- *St&PR 91*
O'Brien, Raymond Vincent, Jr. 1927- *WhoAm 90*
O'Brien, Richard Desmond 1929- *WhoAm 90*
O'Brien, Richard Francis 1942- *St&PR 91, WhoAm 90*
O'Brien, Richard Lee 1934- *WhoAm 90*
O'Brien, Richard Stephen 1936- *St&PR 91*
O'Brien, Robert 1918- *Au&Arts 6 [port]*
O'Brien, Robert B. 1936- *St&PR 91*
O'Brien, Robert B., Jr. 1934- *St&PR 91*
O'Brien, Robert Brownell, Jr. 1934- *WhoAm 90, WhoE 91*
O'Brien, Robert C. 1918?-1973 *AuBYP 90*
O'Brien, Robert Charles 1957- *WhoSSW 91*
O'Brien, Robert Emmet 1923- *WhoE 91*
O'Brien, Robert Felix 1921- *IntWWM 90*
O'Brien, Robert John, Jr. 1935- *WhoAm 90*
O'Brien, Robert K. 1934- *St&PR 91*
O'Brien, Robert Kenneth 1934- *WhoAm 90*
O'Brien, Robert Lewis 1942- *St&PR 91*
O'Brien, Robert Neville 1921- *WhoAm 90*
O'Brien, Robert S. 1918- *WhoAm 90*
O'Brien, Robert Stephen Cox 1929- *WhoAm 90*
O'Brien, Robert Thomas 1941- *WhoE 91, WhoWor 91*
O'Brien, Robert William 1935- *St&PR 91*
O'Brien, Roger Joseph 1947- *WhoE 91*
O'Brien, Romaine M. 1936- *WhoAmW 91*
O'Brien, Ronald Joseph 1948- *WhoEmL 91*
O'Brien, Rosanne *ODwPR 91*
O'Brien, Rosanne P. 1943- *St&PR 91*
O'Brien, Rosemary Grace 1952- *WhoE 91*
O'Brien, Scott Timothy 1954- *St&PR 91*
O'Brien, Shaun John-Peter 1925- *WhoAm 90*
O'Brien, Sue 1939- *WhoAmW 91*
O'Brien, Susan Barbara 1954- *WhoWrEP 89*
O'Brien, Susan Theresa 1965- *WhoAmW 91*
O'Brien, Syd 1944- *Ballpl 90*
O'Brien, Thomas *BioIn 16*
O'Brien, Thomas E. 1938- *St&PR 91*
O'Brien, Thomas F. 1938- *St&PR 91*
O'Brien, Thomas Francis 1938- *WhoAm 90*
O'Brien, Thomas George, III 1942- *WhoAm 90, WhoSSW 91*
O'Brien, Thomas Henry 1937- *WhoAm 90, WhoE 91*
O'Brien, Thomas James 1842-1933 *BioIn 16*
O'Brien, Thomas James 1946- *WhoWor 91*
O'Brien, Thomas Joseph 1928- *WhoAm 90*
O'Brien, Thomas Joseph 1935- *WhoAm 90*
O'Brien, Thomas M. 1926- *St&PR 91*
O'Brien, Thomas P 1937- *BiDrAPA 89*
O'Brien, Thomas William 1939- *WhoAm 90*
O'Brien, Tim 1946- *BioIn 16, WorAu 1980 [port]*
O'Brien, Timothy 1929- *ConDes 90*
O'Brien, Timothy Andrew 1943- *WhoAm 90*
O'Brien, Timothy Charles 1948- *St&PR 91*
O'Brien, Timothy James 1945- *WhoEmL 91*
O'Brien, Tom 1873-1901 *Ballpl 90*
O'Brien, Tommy 1918-1978 *Ballpl 90*
O'Brien, William 1928- *St&PR 91*
O'Brien, William Francis 1948- *WhoAm 90*
O'Brien, William Howard 1918- *WhoAm 90*
O'Brien, William James 1954- *WhoSSW 91*
O'Brien, William John 1932- *WhoAm 90, WhoE 91*
O'Brien, William M *BiDrAPA 89*
O'Brien, William R *BiDrAPA 89*
O'Brien, William Vincent 1902- *WhoAmA 91N*
O'Brien-Bell, John 1929- *WhoAm 90*
O'Brien-Pennisi, Mary Evelyn 1946- *WhoAmW 91*
O'Brient, David Warren 1927- *WhoSSW 91*
Obringer, Daniel J. 1948- *St&PR 91*
Obrisset, John *PenDiDA 89, -89*
Obrist, Hermann 1863-1927 *PenDiDA 89*
Obrist, Theo. J. 1936- *St&PR 91*
Obrow, D. Irving *St&PR 91*
O'Bryan, Mary Josephine 1952- *WhoAmW 91*
O'Bryan, Thomas W. 1947- *St&PR 91*
O'Bryan, William Hall 1919- *WhoAm 90*
O'Bryan, William Monteith 1912- *WhoAm 90*
O'Bryon, Eleanor Dart 1946- *BioIn 16*
O'Bryon, Linda Elizabeth 1949- *WhoAmW 91*
Obst, Richard C., Sr. 1936- *St&PR 91*
Obstfeld, Raymond *WhoWrEP 89*
Obstfelder, Sigbjorn 1866-1900 *DcScanL*
Obstler, Harold 1925- *St&PR 91, WhoAm 90*
Obuchowski, Janice *WhoAm 90*
Obuchowski, Joseph *ODwPR 91*
Obuck, John Francis 1946- *WhoAmA 91*
Oby, Karen Jean 1946- *WhoEmL 91*

O'Byrne, Brian John 1948- *St&PR 91*
O'Byrne, David Michael *BiDrAPA 89*
O'Byrne, Natalie K 1933- *BiDrAPA 89*
O'Byrne, Paul J. 1922- *WhoAm 90*
O'Byrne, Roger A. 1930- *St&PR 91*
Obzina, Jaromir 1929- *WhoWor 91*
Oca, Marco Antonio Montes de *HispWr 90*
O'Callaghan, Brian Richard 1944- *WhoSSW 91*
O'Callaghan, J. Patrick 1925- *WhoAm 90*
O'Callaghan, James Patrick 1949- *WhoSSW 91*
O'Callaghan, Jerry Alexander 1922- *WhoAm 90*
O'Callaghan, Joseph Edward 1938- *St&PR 91*
O'Callaghan, Mary Lou *ODwPR 91*
O'Callaghan, R.A. 1935- *St&PR 91*
O'Callaghan, Roger E. 1944- *St&PR 91*
Ocampo, Angela Patricia 1946- *WhoSSW 91*
Ocampo, Benjamin Paz *BiDrAPA 89*
Ocampo, Isidoro 1910- *ArtLatA*
Ocampo, Miguel 1922- *WhoAmA 91*
Ocampo, Silvina 1906- *ConAu 131, HispWr 90*
Ocampo, Teresito P 1942- *BiDrAPA 89*
Ocampo, Victoria 1890-1979 *HispWr 90*
Ocampo, Victoria 1891-1979 *BioIn 16*
O'Canainn, Thomas 1930- *IntWWM 90*
Ocanas, Gilberto S. 1953- *WhoHisp 91*
O'Carroll, James *BiDrAPA 89*
O'Carroll, Patrick 1951- *St&PR 91*
Ocasek, Ric 1949?- *ConMus 5 [port]*
O'Casey, Brenda *WorAu 1980*
O'Casey, Eileen *BioIn 16*
O'Casey, Sean 1880-1964 *BioIn 16, MajTwCW, WorAlBi*
Ocasio-Ferrer, Ruben *BiDrAPA 89*
O'Cathasaigh, Donal *WhoWrEP 89*
O'Cathasaigh, Sean *MajTwCW*
Occelli de Salinas de Gortari, Yolanda C *WhoAmW 91*
Occhetto, Achille 1936- *WhoWor 91*
Occhiato, Michael Anthony *WhoAm 90*
Occhicone, Michael J. 1953- *St&PR 91*
Occhiogrosso, Lola *BiDrAPA 89*
Occhiogrosso, Marilyn 1937- *WhoE 91*
Occhiuzzo, Lucia Rajszel 1951- *WhoAmW 91, WhoEmL 91*
Occom 1723-1792 *WhNaAH*
Occom, Samson 1723-1792 *EncCRAm*
Occum, Samson 1723-1792 *WhNaAH*
Ocean, Billy *BioIn 16*
Ocean, Billy 1950- *ConMus 4 [port]*
Ocean, Billy 1952?- *DrBlPA 90, WorAlBi*
Ocepek, Lou 1942- *WhoAmA 91*
Och, Mohamad Rachid 1956- *WhoE 91*
Och, Mohamed R 1956- *BiDrAPA 89*
Ochab, Edward 1906-1989 *BioIn 16*
Ochai, Hiromitsu 1953- *Ballpl 90*
Ochberg, Frank Martin 1940- *WhoAm 90*
Ocheltree, Richard Lawrence 1931- *WhoAm 90*
Ochenkowski, Janice 1948- *WhoAmW 91*
Ochester, Ed 1939- *WhoWrEP 89*
O'Chester, Harold Eugene 1927- *WhoSSW 91*
Ochi, F Denis 1946- *WhoAmA 91*
Ochi, Yasou 1944- *EncPaPR 91*
Ochiai, Hideo 1931- *WhoWor 91*
Ochiai, Shinya 1935- *WhoSSW 91*
Ochikubo, Tetsuo 1923-1975 *WhoAmA 91N*
Ochiltree, Ned A., Jr. 1919- *St&PR 91, WhoAm 90*
Ochiltree, Stuart Anderson 1941- *St&PR 91*
Ochirbat, Punsalmaagiyn 1942- *WhoWor 91*
Ochman, B. L. 1949- *ODwPR 91*
Ochman, Wieslaw 1937- *PenDiMP*
Ochmann, Wieslaw 1937- *IntWWM 90*
Ochoa, Antonio A., Jr. 1930- *WhoHisp 91*
Ochoa, Ellen 1958- *WhoHisp 91*
Ochoa, Esteban 1831-1888 *BioIn 16*
Ochoa, Frank Joseph 1950- *WhoHisp 91*
Ochoa, Jesus Zeferino 1936- *WhoHisp 91*
Ochoa, Ricardo 1945- *WhoHisp 91*
Ochoa, Richard 1955- *WhoHisp 91*
Ochoa, Sandor Rodolfo 1944- *WhoHisp 91*
Ochoa, Severo 1905- *WhoAm 90, WhoWor 91, WorAlBi*
Ochoa, Victor Orozco 1948- *WhoHisp 91*
Ochoa Mejia, Jose 1940- *WhoWor 91*
Ochoa Sanchez, Arnaldo *BioIn 16*
Ochorowicz, Julien 1850-1917 *EncO&P 3*
Ochotnicky, John 1942- *ODwPR 91*
Ochs, Adolph 1858-1935 *WorAlBi*
Ochs, Adolph Simon 1858-1935 *BioIn 16*
Ochs, Ann W. 1955- *St&PR 91*
Ochs, Donald Elias 1936- *St&PR 91*
Ochs, Jennifer Ann 1965- *WhoAmW 91*
Ochs, Joan Paulson 1934- *WhoE 91*
Ochs, Michael 1937- *WhoAm 90*
Ochs, Peter M. *BioIn 16*
Ochs, Phil 1940-1976 *OxCPMus*
Ochs, Robert David 1915- *WhoAm 90, WhoAmA 91*
Ochs, Sidney 1924- *WhoAm 90*
Ochs, Siegfried 1858-1929 *PenDiMP*
Ochse, Orpha C. 1925- *IntWWM 90*
Ochsenreiter, Richard Edward 1953- *WhoE 91*
Ochsenwald, William Leo 1943- *WhoSSW 91*
Ochshorn, Susan 1953- *WhoAm 90*
Ochsner, John Lockwood 1927- *WhoAm 90*
Ochsner, Othon Henry, II 1934- *WhoWor 91*
Ochsner, Robert C. 1940- *St&PR 91*
Ochtman, Dorothy 1892-1971 *WhoAmA 91N*
Ockeghem, Johannes *BioIn 16*
Ockels, Theodore S. 1926- *St&PR 91*
Ockenga, Starr 1938- *WhoAmA 91*
Ockerbloom, Richard C. 1929- *St&PR 91, WhoAm 90*
Ockerman, Edwin Foster, Jr. 1952- *WhoEmL 91*
Ockerse, Thomas 1940- *WhoAm 90, WhoAmA 91*
Ockham, William of 1285?-1349? *WorAlBi*
Ocko, Felix H 1912- *BiDrAPA 89*
Ockrymiek, Douglas A 1945- *BiDrAPA 89*
O'Clair, Robert 1923-1989 *BioIn 16*
O'Clery, Helen 1910- *AuBYP 90*
O'Connell, Agnes Anne Nahmie *WhoAmW 91*
O'Connell, Ann 1934- *WhoAmW 91*
O'Connell, Ann Brown 1931- *WhoAmA 91*
O'Connell, Barbara E 1926- *BiDrAPA 89*
O'Connell, Barbara Eustace 1926- *WhoE 91*
O'Connell, Brian 1930- *WhoAm 90*
O'Connell, Brian James 1940- *WhoAm 90*
O'Connell, Carmela Digristina 1925- *WhoE 91, WhoWor 91*
O'Connell, Catherine Ann 1946- *WhoAmW 91*
O'Connell, Charles Francis 1955- *WhoE 91, WhoEmL 91*
O'Connell, Colman *WhoAm 90, WhoAmW 91*
O'Connell, Daniel *BioIn 16, ODwPR 91*
O'Connell, Daniel 1775-1847 *WorAlBi*
O'Connell, Daniel Craig 1928- *WhoAm 90*
O'Connell, Daniel J *BiDrAPA 89*
O'Connell, Daniel Kevin 1929- *St&PR 91*
O'Connell, Daniel Moylan 1949- *WhoAmA 91, WhoE 91*
O'Connell, Daniel Walter 1946- *WhoWor 91*
O'Connell, Danny 1927-1969 *Ballpl 90*
O'Connell, Desmond Henry, Jr. 1936- *WhoAm 90*
O'Connell, Edward E *WhoAmA 91*
O'Connell, Edward J. 1952- *St&PR 91*
O'Connell, Edward James, Jr. 1932- *WhoAm 90*
O'Connell, Edward Joseph, III 1952- *WhoAm 90*
O'Connell, Erin Maureen *WhoAmW 91*
O'Connell, Francis Joseph 1913- *WhoE 91, WhoWor 91*
O'Connell, Frank Joseph 1943- *WhoAm 90*
O'Connell, George C. 1917- *St&PR 91*
O'Connell, George D 1926- *WhoAmA 91*
O'Connell, George Danthine 1926- *WhoAm 90*
O'Connell, H.E. 1916- *St&PR 91*
O'Connell, Hans James 1947- *WhoEmL 91*
O'Connell, Harold Patrick, Jr. 1933- *WhoAm 90*
O'Connell, Helen 1920- *WorAlBi*
O'Connell, Henry Francis 1922- *WhoE 91, WhoWor 91*
O'Connell, Howard Vincent 1930- *St&PR 91*
O'Connell, Hugh Mellen, Jr. 1929- *WhoAm 90*
O'Connell, Isabelle L. 1963- *WhoEmL 91*
O'Connell, J. Michael *ODwPR 91*
O'Connell, Jane S. 1930- *WhoAmW 91*
O'Connell, Jeanne Marie 1948- *WhoEmL 91*
O'Connell, Jeffrey 1928- *WhoAm 90, WhoSSW 91, WhoWrEP 89*
O'Connell, Jimmy 1901-1976 *Ballpl 90*
O'Connell, Joan 1934- *WhoWor 91*
O'Connell, John E. 1931- *St&PR 91*
O'Connell, John J., Jr. 1944- *ODwPR 91*
O'Connell, John Joseph 1938- *St&PR 91*
O'Connell, John Joseph, Jr. 1947- *WhoAm 90*
O'Connell, Joseph Patrick 1943- *St&PR 91*
O'Connell, Kathleen Ann 1956- *WhoAmW 91*
O'Connell, Kenneth John 1909- *WhoAm 90*
O'Connell, Kenneth Mark 1938- *St&PR 91*
O'Connell, Kenneth Robert 1945- *WhoAmA 91*
O'Connell, Kevin 1933- *WhoAm 90*
O'Connell, Kevin George 1938- *WhoAm 90*
O'Connell, Kevin Michael 1948- *WhoEmL 91*
O'Connell, Leslie Ann *BiDrAPA 89*
O'Connell, Margaret F. 1935-1977 *BioIn 16*
O'Connell, Mark Maurice *BiDrAPA 89*
O'Connell, Mary Ita 1929- *WhoAmW 91*
O'Connell, Maurice Daniel 1929- *WhoAm 90*
O'Connell, Michael P. 1949- *St&PR 91*
O'Connell, Michael William 1943- *WhoAm 90*
O'Connell, Patrick F 1926- *BiDrAPA 89*
O'Connell, Paul Edmund 1924- *WhoAm 90*
O'Connell, Philip R. 1928- *St&PR 91*
O'Connell, Philip Raymond 1928- *WhoAm 90, WhoWor 91*
O'Connell, Quinn 1924- *WhoAm 90*
O'Connell, Ralph A 1938- *BiDrAPA 89*
O'Connell, Ralph Anthony 1938- *WhoE 91*
O'Connell, Richard 1928- *WhoE 91, WhoWor 91, WhoWrEP 89*
O'Connell, Richard Lawrence 1929- *St&PR 91*
O'Connell, Robert Francis 1933- *WhoAm 90*
O'Connell, Robert John 1943- *WhoAm 90*
O'Connell, Robert Thomas 1938- *St&PR 91, WhoAm 90*
O'Connell, Ronald Vincent 1944- *St&PR 91*
O'Connell, Rosann Joy 1946- *WhoAmW 91*
O'Connell, Suzanne 1938- *St&PR 91*
O'Connell, William Butler 1923- *WhoAm 90*
O'Connell, William Edward, Jr. 1937 *WhoSSW 91*
O'Connell, William J. 1920- *St&PR 91*
O'Connell, William Parnell 1939- *St&PR 91*
O'Connell, William Raymond, Jr. 1933- *WhoAm 90, WhoE 91*
O'Conner, Bert *ConAu 31NR*
O'Conner, Clint *ConAu 31NR*
O'Conner, Feather 1942- *WhoE 91*
O'Conner, Joseph Patrick 1933- *St&PR 91*
O'Connor, Alan P. 1943- *St&PR 91*
O'Connor, Allison Carr 1960- *WhoE 91*
O'Connor, Arthur William 1933- *St&PR 91*
O'Connor, Audrey Rita 1954- *WhoEmL 91*
O'Connor, Barbara Blough 1932- *WhoAmW 91*
O'Connor, Bernard James 1953- *WhoEmL 91*
O'Connor, Betty Lou 1927- *WhoAmW 91*
O'Connor, Brendan Michael 1945- *St&PR 91, WhoAm 90, WhoSSW 91*
O'Connor, Bridget Marie 1948- *WhoAmW 91*
O'Connor, Carol Ann 1958- *WhoAmW 91*
O'Connor, Carolyn Riester 1952- *WhoAmW 91*
O'Connor, Carroll *BioIn 16*
O'Connor, Carroll 1924- *WhoAm 90, WorAlBi*
O'Connor, Charles J. 1924- *ODwPR 91*
O'Connor, Charles T 1935- *BiDrAPA 89*
O'Connor, Christian Charles 1923- *St&PR 91*
O'Connor, Clarence D. *NewYTBS 90*
O'Connor, Colleen Mary 1956- *WhoAmW 91*
O'Connor, Daniel Patrick 1941- *St&PR 91*
O'Connor, Daniel William 1925- *WhoAm 90*
O'Connor, D'Arcy *BioIn 16*
O'Connor, David James, Jr. 1926- *St&PR 91*
O'Connor, David Rush 1934- *St&PR 91*
O'Connor, Denise Lynn 1958- *WhoAmW 91*
O'Connor, Dennis L. 1913-1989 *BioIn 16*
O'Connor, Dennis M 1942- *BiDrAPA 89*
O'Connor, Dennis Patrick 1955- *WhoWrEP 89*
O'Connor, Donald 1925- *OxCPMus, WorAlBi*
O'Connor, Donald J. 1922- *WhoAm 90*
O'Connor, Donald John 1932- *WhoAm 90*
O'Connor, Donald Thomas 1935- *WhoAm 90*
O'Connor, Doris Julia 1930- *WhoAmW 91*
O'Connor, Duane Lawrence 1940- *St&PR 91*
O'Connor, Duane T. 1946- *St&PR 91*
O'Connor, Earl Eugene 1922- *WhoAm 90*
O'Connor, Edward Cornelius 1931- *WhoAm 90*
O'Connor, Edward Dennis 1922- *WhoAm 90*
O'Connor, Edward Gearing 1940- *WhoAm 90*
O'Connor, Edward Gerard 1952- *WhoSSW 91*
O'Connor, Edward J. *St&PR 91*
O'Connor, Edward S. 1916- *St&PR 91*
O'Connor, Edward Thomas, Jr. 1942- *WhoE 91*
O'Connor, Edward Vincent, Jr. 1952- *WhoSSW 91*
O'Connor, Edwin 1918-1968 *WorAlBi*
O'Connor, Eileen Mae *BiDrAPA 89*
O'Connor, Eileen Mae 1944- *WhoE 91*
O'Connor, Eleanor M. 1956- *ODwPR 91*
O'Connor, Elizabeth 1921- *ConAu 30NR*
O'Connor, Feargus *BioIn 16*
O'Connor, Flannery *BioIn 16*
O'Connor, Flannery 1925-1964 *BioAmW, FemiCLE, MajTwCW, WorAlBi, WrPh*
O'Connor, Francine Marie 1930- *WhoAm 90, WhoAmW 91, WhoWrEP 89*
O'Connor, Francis Martin 1926- *St&PR 91*
O'Connor, Francis Patrick 1927- *WhoAm 90, WhoE 91*
O'Connor, Francis Valentine 1937- *WhoAmA 91, WhoE 91*
O'Connor, Francis X. 1929- *WhoAm 90*
O'Connor, Frank 1903-1966 *BioIn 16, WorAlBi*
O'Connor, Garrett *BiDrAPA 89*
O'Connor, Geo W 1910- *St&PR 91*
O'Connor, George Aquin 1921- *WhoAm 90, WhoAmW 91*
O'Connor, George Richard 1928- *WhoAm 90*
O'Connor, Harold C. 1929- *St&PR 91*
O'Connor, Hubert Patrick 1928- *WhoAm 90*
O'Connor, Jack 1902-1978 *BioIn 16*
O'Connor, Jack 1958- *Ballpl 90*
O'Connor, James J. 1917-1989 *BioIn 16*
O'Connor, James J. 1937- *St&PR 91*
O'Connor, James J. 1942- *St&PR 91*
O'Connor, James John 1937- *WhoAm 90, WhoWor 91*
O'Connor, James Joseph 1930- *WhoAm 90*
O'Connor, James Patrick Mel 1918- *WhoWor 91*
O'Connor, James V. 1944- *ODwPR 91*
O'Connor, Jane 1947- *BioIn 16*
O'Connor, Janet Ruth 1934- *WhoE 91*
O'Connor, Jean M C 1930- *BiDrAPA 89*
O'Connor, Jeremiah F. 1948- *St&PR 91*
O'Connor, John 1920- *News 90 [port], -90-3 [port], WhoAm 90, WhoE 91, WhoWor 91*
O'Connor, John A., Jr. 1931- *St&PR 91*
O'Connor, John Albert, Jr. 1913- *St&PR 91*
O'Connor, John Arthur 1940- *WhoAmA 91*
O'Connor, John Charles 1949- *WhoEmL 91*
O'Connor, John Edward, Jr. 1942- *WhoAm 90*
O'Connor, John F 1926- *BiDrAPA 89*
O'Connor, John Francis 1926- *WhoE 91*
O'Connor, John J. 1948- *St&PR 91*
O'Connor, John Jay, III 1930- *WhoAm 90*
O'Connor, John Joseph 1920- *BioIn 16, WorAlBi*
O'Connor, John Joseph, Jr. 1913- *WhoAm 90*
O'Connor, John Lanning 1927- *WhoAm 90*
O'Connor, John Martin 1929- *St&PR 91, WhoAm 90*
O'Connor, John Morris, III 1937- *WhoAm 90*
O'Connor, John P., Jr. 1943- *St&PR 91*
O'Connor, Jon Joseph 1931- *WhoAm 90*
O'Connor, Joseph A., Jr. 1937- *WhoAm 90*
O'Connor, Joseph Michael 1914- *St&PR 91*
O'Connor, Joseph William 1942- *WhoAm 90*
O'Connor, Julia Elizabeth 1962- *WhoAmW 91*
O'Connor, June Elizabeth 1941- *WhoAmW 91*
O'Connor, Karl William 1931- *WhoAm 90*
O'Connor, Kathleen Lucille 1944- *WhoAmW 91*
O'Connor, Kevin Arthur *BiDrAPA 89*
O'Connor, Laurence P. 1941- *St&PR 91*
O'Connor, Lawrence Joseph, Jr. 1914- *WhoAm 90*
O'Connor, Leonard A. 1926- *St&PR 91*
O'Connor, Leonard Albert 1926- *WhoAm 90*
O'Connor, Lily 1876-1941 *BioIn 16*
O'Connor, Marge *ODwPR 91*
O'Connor, Marianne *ODwPR 91*
O'Connor, Marianne R. 1954- *St&PR 91*
O'Connor, Mark *NewAgMG, WhoNeCM [port]*
O'Connor, Mark 1945- *ConAu 31NR*

O'Connor, Martha Susan 1941- *WhoAmW 91, WhoSSW 91*
O'Connor, Martin M. *St&PR 91*
O'Connor, Marty 1924?-1990 *ConAu 131*
O'Connor, Mary B. 1940- *WhoAmW 91*
O'Connor, Mary Flannery *BioIn 16*
O'Connor, Mary S. 1942- *ODwPR 91*
O'Connor, Mary Scranton 1942- *WhoAm 90, WhoE 91*
O'Connor, Maureen 1946- *WhoAm 90, WhoAmW 91*
O'Connor, Michael Francis 1938- *WhoSSW 91*
O'Connor, Michael Kevin 1943- *BiDrAPA 89*
O'Connor, Neal William 1925- *WhoAm 90*
O'Connor, Neil Emmett 1944- *WhoE 91*
O'Connor, Patricia Weeks 1961- *WhoAmW 91*
O'Connor, Patrick *AuBYP 90, BioIn 16*
O'Connor, Patrick 1949- *ConAu 130*
O'Connor, Paul Daniel 1936- *WhoAm 90*
O'Connor, Pedro 1864?-1942 *BioIn 16*
O'Connor, Peggy Lee 1953- *WhoAmW 91*
O'Connor, Peter J. 1929-1988 *BioIn 16*
O'Connor, Peter Joseph 1932- *WhoAm 90, WhoE 91*
O'Connor, Philip *BioIn 16*
O'Connor, Philip F. *WhoWrEP 89*
O'Connor, Ralph Sturges 1926- *WhoAm 90*
O'Connor, Richard 1915-1975 *AuBYP 90*
O'Connor, Richard D. 1931- *St&PR 91*
O'Connor, Richard Donald 1931- *WhoAm 90, WhoE 91*
O'Connor, Richard E. 1932- *St&PR 91*
O'Connor, Richard Nugent 1889-1981 *DcNaB 1981*
O'Connor, Richard R. 1918-1989 *BioIn 16*
O'Connor, Robert Benson 1941- *WhoSSW 91*
O'Connor, Robert E 1922- *BiDrAPA 89*
O'Connor, Robert Edward 1931- *St&PR 91*
O'Connor, Robert Emmet 1919- *WhoAm 90*
O'Connor, Robert Francis 1928- *St&PR 91*
O'Connor, Robert James 1939- *WhoAm 90*
O'Connor, Robert Jerome 1927- *WhoAm 90*
O'Connor, Robert R *BiDrAPA 89*
O'Connor, Rod 1934- *WhoAm 90*
O'Connor, Ronald T. 1943- *ODwPR 91*
O'Connor, Ruth Elkinton 1927- *WhoAmW 91, WhoWor 91*
O'Connor, Sandra Day *BioIn 16*
O'Connor, Sandra Day 1930- *News 91-1 [port], WhoAm 90, WhoAmW 91, WhoE 91, WhoWor 91*
O'Connor, Sara Andrews 1932- *BioIn 16, NotWoAT, WhoAmW 91*
O'Connor, Shirley *BioIn 16*
O'Connor, Sinead *BioIn 16*
O'Connor, Sinead 1967- *News 90 [port]*
O'Connor, Stanley James *WhoAmA 91*
O'Connor, Stanley James 1926- *WhoAm 90*
O'Connor, Teresa McCann 1956- *WhoEmL 91*
O'Connor, Terrence John 1936- *St&PR 91*
O'Connor, Thom 1937- *WhoAmA 91*
O'Connor, Thomas 1833-1893? *AmLegL*
O'Connor, Thomas Patrick 1944- *St&PR 91*
O'Connor, Thomas V., Jr. 1930- *St&PR 91*
O'Connor, Timothy Charles 1945- *WhoEmL 91*
O'Connor, Timothy Edmond 1925- *WhoAm 90*
O'Connor, Tom 1942- *WhoE 91, WhoWor 91*
O'Connor, Tracy Allen 1964- *WhoAmW 91*
O'Connor, Vincent Max 1935- *St&PR 91*
O'Connor, William Charles 1927- *St&PR 91*
O'Connor, William Francis 1939- *St&PR 91, WhoAm 90*
O'Connor, William James 1921- *WhoE 91, WhoWor 91*
O'Connor, William John 1931- *WhoE 91*
O'Connor, William Joseph 1862-1892 *DcCanB 12*
O'Connor, William Matthew 1955- *WhoE 91*
O'Connor, William Michael 1947- *WhoEmL 91, WhoWor 91*
O'Connor-Brokaw, Christine 1962- *WhoAmW 91*
O'Conor, Paul Ford 1947- *St&PR 91*
O'Conor, William Cunningham 1956- *St&PR 91*
Oconostota 1710?-1783 *EncCRAm*
Oconostota 1710?-1785 *WhNaAH*
O'Crowley, James Francis, III 1953- *WhoEmL 91*
O'Crowley, James Francis, Jr. 1923- *WhoAm 90*
Octave, James Joseph 1947- *WhoE 91*
Octavian 63BC-14AD *BioIn 16*
Ocvirk, Otto G 1922- *WhoAmA 91*
Ocvirk, Otto George 1922- *WhoAm 90*
Oda Nobunaga 1534-1582 *EncJap*
Oda, George T. 1930- *St&PR 91*
Oda, Margaret Yuriko 1925- *WhoAm 90*
Oda, Masao 1935- *WhoWor 91*
Oda, Masayuki 1950- *WhoAmA 91*
Oda, Mayumi 1941- *WhoAmA 91*
Oda, Nobuo 1924- *WhoWor 91*
Oda, Shigeru 1924- *WhoWor 91*
Oda, Toshitsugu 1922- *WhoWor 91*
Odagescu, Irina 1937- *IntWWM 90*
Odahowski, David Anthony 1956- *WhoEmL 91*
O'Dair, William J. 1929- *St&PR 91*
Odaldi, Annalena 1572-1638 *EncCoWW*
O'Daly, Fergus 1943- *St&PR 91*
Odam, George Neville 1938- *IntWWM 90*
O'Daniel, Jean Elizabeth 1955- *WhoEmL 91*
Odate, Toshio 1930- *WhoAmA 91*
Odato, Richard 1950- *WhoSSW 91*
Odawara, Ken'ichi 1933- *WhoWor 91*
O'Day, Anderson 1928- *St&PR 91*
O'Day, Anita 1919- *BioIn 16, CurBio 90 [port], OxCPMus, WorAlBi*
O'Day, Anita Belle Colton 1919- *WhoAm 90*
O'Day, Digger *BioIn 16*
O'Day, Edwin Robert 1926- *St&PR 91*
O'Day, Hank 1863-1935 *Ballpl 90*
O'Day, Paul Thomas 1935- *WhoAm 90*
O'Day, Royal Lewis 1913- *St&PR 91, WhoAm 90*
O'Day, Sharon 1948- *WhoAmW 91, WhoSSW 91*
Oddi, Phyllis Marie 1931- *WhoAmW 91*
Oddi, Silvio 1910- *WhoWor 91*
Oddi, Vincent J. 1943- *St&PR 91*
Oddis, Joseph Anthony 1928- *WhoAm 90*
Oddis, Ronald Michael, Sr. 1938- *St&PR 91*
Oddleifson, Peter 1932- *St&PR 91*
Oddner, Georg 1923- *ConAu 129*
Oddo, Ross Vincent 1939- *St&PR 91*
Oddo, Thomas 1944-1989 *BioIn 16*
Oddy, John George 1934- *WhoE 91*
Oddy, William Edgar 1936- *St&PR 91*
Ode, Philip Enerson 1935- *WhoE 91*
O'Dea, Ken 1913-1985 *Ballpl 90*
O'Dea, Michael Joseph, Jr. 1914- *WhoWor 91*
O'Dea, Thomas William 1942- *WhoE 91*
O'Dea, William P. 1947- *St&PR 91*
Odean, Kathleen 1953- *WhoWrEP 89*
Odegaard, Bjorn Skar 1946- *WhoWor 91*
Odegaard, Charles Edwin 1911- *WhoAm 90*
Odegard, Richard E. 1940- *St&PR 91*
Odegard, Richard Erwin 1940- *WhoAm 90*
Odeh, Aziz Salim 1925- *WhoAm 90*
Odell, Arthur G. 1913-1988 *BioIn 16*
O'Dell, Billy 1933- *Ballpl 90*
O'Dell, Charles Robert 1937- *WhoAm 90*
Odell, Clinton Brice 1933- *St&PR 91*
O'Dell, Clovis Jay 1940- *WhoE 91*
Odell, Donald Austin 1925- *St&PR 91, WhoAm 90*
O'Dell, Edward Thomas, Jr. 1935- *St&PR 91, WhoAm 90*
O'Dell, Erin 1938- *WhoAmA 91*
Odell, Frank H. 1922- *St&PR 91*
Odell, Frank Harold 1922- *WhoAm 90*
O'Dell, Gail Patricia 1957- *WhoSSW 91*
O'Dell, George Hamley 1942- *WhoSSW 91*
Odell, Herbert 1937- *WhoAm 90, WhoWor 91*
Odell, Jerry A. 1926- *St&PR 91*
O'Dell, Joan Elizabeth 1932- *WhoE 91*
Odell, John Edward 1934- *St&PR 91*
Odell, Jonathan 1737-1818 *DcLB 99 [port]*
O'Dell, Karol Joanne 1936- *WhoAmW 91*
O'Dell, Len *WhoWrEP 89*
Odell, Leonard Eugene 1945- *St&PR 91*
O'Dell, Lynn Marie Luegge 1938- *WhoAmW 91*
O'Dell, Mary Ernestine 1935- *WhoWrEP 89*
Odell, Mary Jane 1923- *WhoAm 90, WhoAmW 91*
O'Dell, Michael James 1949- *WhoE 91*
O'Dell, Michael Ray 1951- *St&PR 91*
Odell, Patrick Lowry 1930- *WhoAm 90*
O'Dell, Scott 1898-1989 *AnObit 1989, ConAu 129, -30NR, SmATA 60 [port]*
O'Dell, Scott 1903-1989 *AuBYP 90, BioIn 16*
O'Dell, Tiny 1899- *Ballpl 90*
O'Dell, Walden Wesley 1945- *St&PR 91*
Odell, William Douglas 1929- *WhoAm 90, WhoWor 91*
O'Dell, William Francis 1909- *WhoAm 90*
Odell, William Hunter 1811-1891 *DcCanB 12*
Oden, Chandra Renee 1968- *WhoAmW 91*
Oden, Gloria Catherine *WhoWrEP 89*
Oden, Jean Phifer 1936- *WhoAmW 91*
Oden, John Tinsley 1936- *WhoAm 90*
Oden, Kenneth 1923- *WhoSSW 91*
Oden, Miles Gregory 1957- *BiDrAPA 89*
Oden, William Bryant 1935- *WhoAm 90, WhoSSW 91*
Odenkirchen, Carl Josef 1921- *WhoAm 90*
Odenwald, Robert Paul 1899-1965 *AuBYP 90*
Odenweller, John A. 1946- *St&PR 91*
Oder, Frederic Carl Emil 1919- *WhoAm 90*
Oder, Frederic Emil 1942- *BiDrAPA 89*
Odermatt, Robert Allen 1938- *WhoAm 90*
Odermatt, Siegfried 1926- *ConDes 90*
Odersky, Walter 1937- *WhoWor 91*
Odescalchi, Edmond Pery 1928- *WhoWor 91*
O'Dess, Mary Abigail 1954- *WhoAmW 91*
Odet D'Orsonnens, Thomas-Edmond D' 1818-1892 *DcCanB 12*
Odets, Clifford 1906-1963 *BioIn 16, EncAL, MajTwCW, WorAlBi*
Odetta 1930- *DrBlPA 90, WorAlBi*
Odgers, Richard William 1936- *WhoAm 90*
Odijk, Theo 1952- *WhoWor 91*
O'Dillon, Richard Hill 1934- *WhoWor 91*
Odim, Usim 1923- *BiDrAPA 89*
Odin, Kyle Abram 1962- *St&PR 91*
Odintz, Alvin Aaron 1924- *St&PR 91*
Odio, Cesar H. *WhoHisp 91*
Odio, Rodrigo Carazo 1926- *BioIn 16*
Odio, Saturnino Portuondo 1928- *MusmAFA*
Odiorne, George Stanley 1920- *WhoAm 90*
Odioso, Raymond C. 1923- *St&PR 91*
Odiot, Charles *PenDiDA 89*
Odiot, Jean-Baptiste 1828-1912 *PenDiDA 89*
Odiot, Jean-Baptiste-Claude 1763-1850 *PenDiDA 89*
Odland, George Fisher 1922- *WhoAm 90*
Odland, Gerald Clark 1946- *WhoAm 90*
Odland, Theodore M 1924- *BiDrAPA 89*
Odle, Robert Charles, Jr. 1944- *WhoAm 90*
Odle, Wesley Paul, Jr. 1933- *WhoSSW 91, WhoWor 91*
Odlevak, Robert John 1933- *St&PR 91*
Odlin, Richard Bingham 1934- *WhoAm 90*
Odling-Smee, John Charles 1943- *WhoWor 91*
Odlum, Karen Laubach 1949- *WhoE 91*
Odmann, Jan-Christer 1920- *WhoWor 91*
Odnoha, Andrew A. 1930- *St&PR 91*
Odnoposoff, Adolfo 1917- *IntWWM 90, PenDiMP*
Odnoposoff, Ricardo 1914- *IntWWM 90, PenDiMP*
Odoevskii, V. F. 1803-1869 *BioIn 16*
Odoevtseva, Irina Vladimirovna *EncCoWW*
O'Doherty, Shane *BioIn 16*
Odom, Beth Helen 1960- *WhoAmW 91*
Odom, Blue Moon 1945- *Ballpl 90*
Odom, Bob 1946- *St&PR 91*
Odom, Edwin Dale 1929- *WhoSSW 91*
Odom, Guy Leary 1911- *WhoAm 90*
Odom, Ira Edgar 1932- *St&PR 91*
Odom, Karen D. *WhoWrEP 89*
Odom, Keith Conrad 1931- *WhoSSW 91*
Odom, Linda Ann 1945- *WhoAmW 91*
Odom, Linda Love 1962- *WhoAmW 91*
Odom, Melissa Kay *WhoSSW 91*
Odom, Oris Leon, II 1946- *WhoSSW 91*
Odom, Robert William 1946- *St&PR 91*
Odom, Susan Ann 1957- *WhoAmW 91, WhoE 91, WhoEmL 91, WhoWor 91*
Odom, Wayne David 1952- *WhoSSW 91*
Odom, William E. 1936- *WhoAm 90*
Odom, William Eldridge 1932- *WhoAm 90, WhoE 91*
O'Domhnaill, Michael *NewAgMG*
O'Donnell, Adrian W. 1932- *St&PR 91*
O'Donnell, Alice Louise *WhoAm 90*
O'Donnell, Arthur Burgess 1924- *St&PR 91*
O'Donnell, Bill *BioIn 16*
O'Donnell, Bryant 1925- *St&PR 91*
O'Donnell, Charles Oliver 1958- *WhoWor 91*
O'Donnell, Charles Patrick 1920- *WhoAm 90*
O'Donnell, Christina Jirak 1961- *WhoE 91*
O'Donnell, Cletus Francis 1917- *WhoAm 90*
O'Donnell, Daniel Gerard 1955- *WhoAm 90*
O'Donnell, David Daniel 1941- *WhoWor 91*
O'Donnell, Dick 1935- *SmATA X*
O'Donnell, Edward Joseph 1931- *WhoAm 90*
O'Donnell, Elliott 1872-1965 *EncO&P 3*
O'Donnell, F. Scott 1940- *St&PR 91, WhoAm 90*
O'Donnell, Guy 1932- *WhoSSW 91*
O'Donnell, James F. *ODwPR 91*
O'Donnell, James F. 1947- *St&PR 91*
O'Donnell, James Francis 1928- *WhoAm 90*
O'Donnell, James Michael 1944- *WhoSSW 91*
O'Donnell, James P. *NewYTBS 90*
O'Donnell, James P 1917-1990 *ConAu 131*
O'Donnell, James P. 1951- *ODwPR 91*
O'Donnell, James Preston 1917-1990 *BioIn 16*
O'Donnell, James Vincent 1941- *WhoAm 90*
O'Donnell, Janet Tomasiello 1943- *WhoE 91*
O'Donnell, John Francis 1928- *St&PR 91*
O'Donnell, John George 1936- *St&PR 91*
O'Donnell, John Howard 1950- *BiDrAPA 89*
O'Donnell, John James 1946- *WhoEmL 91*
O'Donnell, John Logan 1914- *WhoAm 90*
O'Donnell, John M. 1945- *St&PR 91*
O'Donnell, John Thornton *BiDrAPA 89*
O'Donnell, Joseph Michael 1946- *WhoEmL 91*
O'Donnell, K. M. *AuBYP 90*
O'Donnell, Kevin 1925- *St&PR 91, WhoAm 90*
O'Donnell, Kevin Patrick 1951- *WhoSSW 91*
O'Donnell, Laurence Gerard 1935- *WhoAm 90, WhoWrEP 89*
O'Donnell, Lillian 1920- *FemiCLE*
O'Donnell, Lillian 1926- *TwCCr&M 91*
O'Donnell, Linda Fleming 1953- *WhoAmW 91*
O'Donnell, Mark 1954- *WhoWrEP 89*
O'Donnell, Mark Joseph 1954- *WhoEmL 91, WhoWor 91*
O'Donnell, Mary Murphy 1918- *WhoSSW 91*
O'Donnell, Michael James 1952- *WhoEmL 91*
O'Donnell, Michael R. 1957- *St&PR 91*
O'Donnell, Mietta *WhoWor 91*
O'Donnell, Peter 1920- *SpyFic, TwCCr&M 91*
O'Donnell, Richard Michael 1951- *WhoWrEP 89*
O'Donnell, Richard Paul 1935- *St&PR 91*
O'Donnell, Richard W. 1945- *St&PR 91*
O'Donnell, Richard Walter 1945- *WhoAm 90*
O'Donnell, Robert *WhoAm 90*
O'Donnell, Robert D. 1923- *St&PR 91*
O'Donnell, Robert John 1943- *WhoE 91, WhoWor 91*
O'Donnell, Robert Michael 1941- *WhoAm 90*
O'Donnell, Robert W 1942- *BiDrAPA 89*
O'Donnell, Therese M. 1966- *WhoAmW 91*
O'Donnell, Thomas Anthony *BiDrAPA 89*
O'Donnell, Thomas F. 1942- *St&PR 91*
O'Donnell, Thomas Lawrence Patrick 1926- *WhoAm 90*
O'Donnell, Thomas M. 1936- *St&PR 91*
O'Donnell, Thomas Vianney 1926- *WhoWor 91*
O'Donnell, V. Ruth Hensley 1920- *WhoAmW 91*
O'Donnell, Walter Gregory 1903- *WhoAm 90*
O'Donnell, William C. 1938- *St&PR 91*
O'Donnell, William David 1926- *WhoAm 90, WhoWor 91*
O'Donnell, William Hugh 1940- *WhoSSW 91*
O'Donnell, William J. 1935- *St&PR 91*
O'Donnell, William James 1935- *WhoAm 90, WhoWor 91*
O'Donnell, William Robert 1960- *WhoSSW 91*
O'Donnell, Wilson Edward 1952- *WhoAm 90*
O'Donnell y Joris, Leopoldo 1809-1867 *BioIn 16*
O'Donoghue, Brigid 1931- *WhoWrEP 89*
O'Donoghue, John 1939- *Ballpl 90*
O'Donoghue, John J. 1929- *St&PR 91*
O'Donoghue, Nannie Power *FemiCLE*
O'Donoghue, Paul H. 1931- *St&PR 91*
O'Donohoe, John F. 1926- *St&PR 91*
O'Donohoe, Nicholas Benjamin 1952- *WhoWrEP 89*
O'Donohue, Cynthia Helmintoller 1936- *WhoAmW 91*
O'Donohue, Daniel Anthony 1931- *WhoAm 90, WhoWor 91*
O Donohue, Teige Ros 1942- *WhoAmA 91*
O'Donohue, Walter John, Jr. 1934- *WhoAm 90*
O'Donovan, John 1809-1861 *BioIn 16*
O'Donovan, Leo Jeremiah 1934- *WhoAm 90, WhoE 91*
O'Donovan, Thomas Raphael 1931- *WhoAm 90*
O'Donovan, Timothy James 1945- *St&PR 91*
Odor, Garlan 1924- *St&PR 91*

O'Dorisio, Thomas Michael 1943- WhoAm 90
O'Doul, Lefty 1897-1969 Ballpl 90 [port]
O'Dowd, David ODwPR 91
O'Dowd, Edward James 1943- St&PR 91
O'Dowd, George BioIn 16
O'Dowd, Mary Alice 1942- BiDrAPA 89
O'Dowd, Robert WhoAmA 91
O'Dowd-Jana, Patricia Margaret 1949- WhoAmW 91
Odoysvskii, Vladimir Fedorovich 1803-1869 BioIn 16
Odreanu, Mircea 1928- IntWWM 90
Odria, Manuel Arturo 1897-1974 BioIn 16
O'Driscoll, Gerald P. St&PR 91
O'Driscoll, James Edward 1935- WhoE 91
O'Driscoll, Jeremiah Joseph, Jr. 1925- WhoSSW 91
O'Driscoll, Karen M. St&PR 91
O'Driscoll, Michael G. 1954- St&PR 91
O'Driscoll, Sean Joffre 1915- WhoWor 91
O'Driscoll-O'Malley, Mary J. 1944- BiDrAPA 89
Odron, Edward Andrew 1938- WhoAm 90
Odu, Michael 1963- WhoEmL 91
Oduber, Nelson 1947- WhoWor 91
Oduber Quiros, Daniel 1921- BioIn 16
O'Duffy, John Desmond 1934- WhoAm 90
Odum, Eugene Pleasants 1913- BioIn 16, WhoAm 90
Odum, Howard T. 1924- BioIn 16
Odum, Jeffery Neal 1956- WhoSSW 91
Odum, William Eugene 1942- WhoAm 90
Odvarko, Jaroslava 1950- WhoAmW 91
Odwell, Fred 1872-1948 Ballpl 90
O'Dwyer, Brian 1945- WhoE 91
O'Dwyer, Eamonn 1923- St&PR 91
O'Dwyer, John Joseph 1925- WhoAm 90
O'Dwyer, William 1890-1964 BioIn 16
Odyniec, Francis A., Jr. ODwPR 91
Odzinski, Christopher S. 1948- St&PR 91
Oe Kenzaburo 1935- EncJap, WorAu 1980 [port]
Oe, Kenzaburo 1935- MajTwCW
Oeben, Jean-Francois 1721?-1763 PenDiDA 89
Oeben, Simon Francois PenDiDA 89
Oebser, Robert Charles 1939- St&PR 91
Oechsli, Kelly 1918- WhoAmA 91, WhoE 91
Oechsli, Leonard Paul 1922- WhoAm 90
Oechsner, Allen G. 1945- St&PR 91
Oeding, Per 1916- WhoWor 91
Oehl, Kurt 1923- IntWWM 90
Oehlen, Albert BioIn 16
Oehlenschlager, Adam 1779-1850 DcScanL
Oehlenschlager, Adam Gottlob 1779-1850 WorAlBi
Oehler, Christoph 1928- WhoWor 91
Oehler, Gretchen Pauline WhoE 91
Oehler, Hugo 1903-1983 EncAL
Oehler, Richard Dale 1925- WhoSSW 91
Oehlert, Charles F. 1948- St&PR 91
Oehlert, Mark Edward 1965- WhoSSW 91
Oehlschlaeger, Frank J 1910- WhoAmA 91
Oehme, Frederick Wolfgang 1933- WhoAm 90
Oehme, Reinhard 1928- WhoAm 90
Oehmke, Robert Harvey 1927- WhoAm 90
Oehmke, Thomas Harold 1947- WhoEmL 91
Oehmler, George Courtland 1926- WhoAm 90
Oehms, Glenn Edward 1946- WhoSSW 91
Oehrig, Robert J. 1921- St&PR 91
Oehrlein, Mary Lou 1950- WhoAmW 91
Oehser, Paul Henry 1904- WhoAm 90, WhoWrEP 89
Oei, Alexander G BiDrAPA 89
Oei, Tat Hway 1923- WhoWor 91
Oei, Tat Ie 1921- WhoWor 91
Oelbaum, Harold 1931- St&PR 91, WhoAm 90
Oelberg, David George 1952- WhoSSW 91
Oelfken, Tami 1888-1957 EncCoWW
Oelgeschlager, Guenther Karl 1934- WhoAm 90
Oelkers, Bryan 1961- Ballpl 90
Oelkers, Kenneth Henry 1928- St&PR 91
Oellerich, Michael 1944- WhoWor 91
Oellers, Peter Norbert 1936- WhoWor 91
Oelman, Bradford C. 1938- St&PR 91
Oelman, Robert Schantz 1909- WhoAm 90
Oelofse, Jan Harm 1934- WhoWor 91
Oelschlaeger, Renee Louise 1948- WhoWrEP 89
Oelschlager, Jean Kay 1957- BiDrAPA 89
Oelsner, Edward C. BioIn 16, NewYTBS 90
Oelsner, Edward Carl, III 1942- St&PR 91
Oemler, Augustus, Jr. 1945- WhoAm 90
Oenslager, Donald 1902-1975 ConDes 90
Oenslager, Donald Mitchell 1902-1975 WhoAmA 91N
Oerding, James Bryan 1935- WhoE 91
Oeri, Georgine WhoAmA 91N
Oeripan, Soegiharto 1963- WhoWor 91
Oerkfitz, Robin Leigh 1963- WhoAmW 91
Oerlemans, Christian Jan 1937- WhoWor 91
Oersted, Hans Christian 1777-1851 WorAlBi
Oertel, Cindy ODwPR 91
Oertel, Goetz K. H. 1934- WhoAm 90
Oertel, John N. 1943- St&PR 91
Oerter, Al BioIn 16
Oerter, Al 1936- WorAlBi
Oerter, Rolf 1931- WhoWor 91
Oertley, Karen Oberlaender 1952- WhoAmW 91, WhoSSW 91
Oertli, Charles William 1930- St&PR 91
Oertli, Philip A. 1927- St&PR 91
Oertli-Cajacob, Peter 1941- WhoWor 91
Oerum, Poul 1919- ConAu 32NR
Oeschger, Joe 1892-1986 Ballpl 90
Oess, George Peter 1936- St&PR 91
Oester, Ron 1956- Ballpl 90
Oesterheld, Jessica R BiDrAPA 89
Oesterle, John Harry 1931- WhoSSW 91
Oesterle, Leonhard Friedrich 1915- WhoAmA 91
Oesterling, Thomas Ovid 1938- WhoAm 90
Oesterling, Wendy Lee 1949- WhoAmW 91
Oesterreich, Traugott Konstantin 1880-1949 EncO&P 3
Oesterwinter, Horst 1929- WhoE 91
Oesthol, Erik 1916- WhoWor 91
Oestman, Arnold 1939- IntWWM 90
Oestreich, Charles Henry 1932- WhoAm 90
Oestreich, David Arthur 1933- St&PR 91
Oestreich, George H. 1919-1988 BioIn 16
Oestreich, Gerald F., Jr. 1944- St&PR 91
Oestreich, Jeffrey 1947- WhoAmA 91
Oestreich, Martin Roy 1946- St&PR 91
Oestreicher, Anette Muriel 1943- WhoAmW 91, WhoE 91
Oestreicher, Charles 1935- BiDrAPA 89
Oestreicher, Paul ODwPR 91
Oetama, Jakob 1931- WhoWor 91
Oetjen, Robert Adrian 1912- WhoAm 90
Oetjens, Rebecca Elizabeth 1951- WhoAmW 91
Oetken, Stanley Gene 1948- WhoSSW 91
Oettgen, Herbert Friedrich 1923- WhoAm 90
Oettig, Mildred Katherine WhoAmW 91, WhoE 91, WhoWor 91
Oettinger, Anthony Gervin 1929- ConAu 31NR, WhoAm 90
Oettinger, Jack Edgar 1913- St&PR 91
Oettinger, Katherine Brownell 1903- WhoAm 90
Oettle, Karl Wilhelm Gottlob 1926- WhoWor 91
O'Fallon, Benjamin 1793-1842 WhNaAH
O'Fallon, Peter BioIn 16
O'Faolain, Julia 1932- BioIn 16, FemiCLE, MajTwCW, WorAu 1980 [port]
O'Faolain, Sean 1900- BioIn 16, CurBio 90 [port], MajTwCW, WhoWor 91, WorAlBi
O'Farrell, Bob 1896-1988 Ballpl 90
O'Farrell, Patrick James 1933- WhoWor 91
O'Farrell, William 1904-1962 TwCCr&M 91
Ofcharsky, Edward Joseph 1947- St&PR 91
O'Fee, Robert Philip 1954- WhoE 91
Ofelia EncCoWW
O'Ferrall, P.C.K. 1934- St&PR 91
Offen, Matt D. 1921- St&PR 91
Offenbach, Jacques 1819-1880 OxCPMus, PenDiMP A, WorAlBi
Offenberger, Allan Anthony 1938- WhoAm 90
Offenberger, J. Brett 1959- BiDrAPA 89
Offenborn, Hans P. 1936- St&PR 91
Offenhartz, Colin O'Donnell 1943- St&PR 91
Offenhartz, Edward 1928- WhoE 91
Offenkrantz, William C BiDrAPA 89
Offer, Daniel BiDrAPA 89
Offer, Daniel 1930- WhoAm 90
Offerle, Joan Melinda 1945- WhoAmW 91
Offerman, Christiane Toenne 1947- WhoAmW 91
Offerman, Max 1931- St&PR 91
Offerman, Michael 1941- St&PR 91
Offerman, Muriel Kramer 1935- St&PR 91
Offermanns, Ernst Ludwig 1931- WhoWor 91
Offet, Betty Vie 1934- WhoAmW 91
Office, Gerald Simms, Jr. 1941- St&PR 91
Office, Rowland 1952- Ballpl 90
Officer, Marion E. BioIn 16
Officina, Stanley 1944- St&PR 91
Offield, Wrigley 1917- St&PR 91
Offill, David Malcolm 1945- WhoSSW 91
Offin, Charles Z. 1899-1989 BioIn 16, WhoAmA 91N
Offit, Avodah Komito BiDrAPA 89
Offit, Morris Wolf 1937- WhoAm 90, WhoE 91
Offit, Saul B. St&PR 91
Offit, Sidney 1928- AuBYP 90, WhoAm 90, WhoWrEP 89
Offner, Carl David 1943- WhoE 91
Offner, Elliot 1931- WhoAmA 91
Offner, Elliot Melville 1931- WhoAm 90
Offner, Eric Delmonte 1928- WhoAm 90
Offner, Franklin Faller 1911- WhoAm 90
Offord, David R BiDrAPA 89
Offord, Lenore 1905- AuBYP 90, FemiCLE
Offord, Lenore Glen 1905- TwCCr&M 91
Offord, Robin Ewart 1940- WhoWor 91
Offredi, Paul St&PR 91
Offsay, Julian BiDrAPA 89
Offsey, Sol 1922- WhoWrEP 89
Offutt, Charles 1856- AmLegL
Offutt, Donald N 1936- BiDrAPA 89
Offutt, James A. 1934- St&PR 91
Offutt, Warren Bernard 1928- St&PR 91, WhoAm 90
Ofhand, Jack WhoWrEP 89
O Fiaich, Tomas BioIn 16
O Fiaich, Tomas 1923-1990 ConAu 131
Ofiara, Henry George, Jr. 1953- WhoEmL 91
O'Flaherty, John Francis 1944- St&PR 91
O'Flaherty, Joseph S. 1915- St&PR 91
O'Flaherty, Liam 1896- WorAlBi
O'Flaherty, Liam 1896-1984 MajTwCW, ShSCr 6 [port]
O'Flaherty, Michael Gerard 1938- WhoAm 90
O'Flaherty, Paul Benedict 1925- WhoAm 90
O'Flaherty, Terrence 1917- WhoAm 90
O'Flaherty, Thomas Joseph 1940- WhoE 91
O'Flarity, James P. 1923- WhoAm 90, WhoWor 91
O'Flinn, Peter ConAu 32NR
Oflock, Jerry D. 1940- St&PR 91
O'Flynn, Peter ConAu 32NR
Ofner, James Alan 1922- WhoAm 90
Ofner, William Bernard 1929- WhoWor 91
O'Friel, Daniel John 1935- St&PR 91
Ofstedahl, Larry Raymond 1935- St&PR 91
Ofte, Donald 1929- WhoAm 90
Ofte-Gibson, Nancy Carolyn 1957- WhoAmW 91
Oftedal, Ivar Toralf 1928- WhoWor 91
Oftedal, Per 1919- WhoWor 91
Ofverholm, Stefan 1936- WhoWor 91
Ogami, David Noboru BiDrAPA 89
Ogan, George F. AuBYP 90
Ogan, Gerald Stanley 1925- St&PR 91
Ogan, Margaret 1923-1979 AuBYP 90
Ogan, Russell Griffith 1923- WhoAm 90
O'Gara, Barbara Ann 1953- WhoAmW 91
O'Gara, Elaine Janet 1944- WhoWrEP 89
O'Gara, James Vincent 1953- WhoEmL 91
O'Gara, Patrick Thomas 1952- WhoE 91
O'Gara, Robert J. 1943- ODwPR 91
Ogata Korin EncJap
Ogata, Hiromaru 1931- WhoWor 91
Ogata, Katsuhiko 1925- WhoAm 90, WhoWor 91
Ogata, Keith K. 1954- St&PR 91
Ogata, Shoitsu 1927- WhoWor 91
Ogawa, Hisashi 1939- WhoWor 91
Ogawa, Keiji 1927- WhoWor 91
Ogawa, Masaru 1915-1990 BioIn 16, NewYTBS 90
Ogawa, Mathew Seishi BioIn 16
Ogawa, Mizuho 1931- WhoWor 91
Ogawa, Noriko 1962- IntWWM 90
Ogawa, Osamu 1945- WhoWor 91
Ogawa, Takero 1941- WhoWor 91
Ogbonnaya, Chuks Alfred 1953- WhoSSW 91
Ogbu, Osita Michael 1957- WhoE 91
Ogburn, Benjamin R 1931- BiDrAPA 89
Ogburn, Charles Harris 1955- WhoSSW 91
Ogburn, Charlton 1911- WhoAm 90, WhoWrEP 89
Ogburn, Hugh B. 1923- St&PR 91
Ogburn, Hugh Bell 1923- WhoAm 90
Ogburn, James St&PR 91
Ogden, Alfred 1909- WhoAm 90
Ogden, Chester Robert 1923- St&PR 91
Ogden, Curly 1901-1964 Ballpl 90
Ogden, Dayton BioIn 16
Ogden, Henry Warren 1842-1905 AmLegL
Ogden, Howard ConAu 132
Ogden, Jack 1897-1977 Ballpl 90
Ogden, James Russell 1954- WhoEmL 91
Ogden, Joanne 1941- WhoAmW 91, WhoSSW 91
Ogden, Kyle W. 1955- St&PR 91
Ogden, Michael 1931- BiDrAPA 89
Ogden, Myron Waldo 1917- WhoWor 91
Ogden, Peter James 1947- WhoAm 90, WhoEmL 91
Ogden, Peter Skene 1794-1854 WhNaAH
Ogden, Ralph E WhoAmA 91N
Ogden, Ralph Lindsey 1941- WhoAm 90
Ogden, Robert Morris 1877-1959 WorAlBi
Ogden, Robert N. AmLegL
Ogden, Robert Schuyler 1934- WhoAm 90
Ogden, Roger Wayne 1946- WhoSSW 91
Ogden, Rollo 1856-1937 BioIn 16
Ogden, Schubert Miles 1928- WhoAm 90
Ogden, Sylvester O. 1935- WhoAm 90, WhoSSW 91, WhoWor 91
Ogden, Thomas Henry 1946- BiDrAPA 89
Ogden, Tina Louise 1959- WhoSSW 91
Ogden, Valeria Juan 1924- WhoAmW 91
Ogden, William B. 1945- St&PR 91
Ogdon, John 1937-1989 AnObit 1989, BioIn 16, PenDiMP
Ogdon, Thomas Hammer 1935- WhoAm 90
Ogdon, Wilbur 1921- WhoAm 90
Ogdon, Wilbur L. 1921- IntWWM 90
O'Geary, Dennis Traylor 1925- WhoSSW 91
Ogel, Tunc 1953- WhoWor 91
Ogens, Ronald Lee 1942- WhoE 91
Ogesen, Robert Bruce BiDrAPA 89
Ogg, George Wesley 1932- WhoAm 90
Ogg, James Elvis 1924- WhoAm 90
Ogg, Mary Ann 1948- WhoAmW 91
Ogg, Oscar 1908-1971 WhoAmA 91N
Ogg, Robert D. 1918- St&PR 91
Ogg, Robert Danforth 1918- WhoWor 91
Ogg, Robert Kelley 1947- WhoEmL 91
Ogg, Ronald Robert 1938- St&PR 91
Ogg, Thomas Charles 1947- St&PR 91
Ogg, Wilson Reid 1928- WhoWor 91
Oggenfuss, Robert Walter 1933- St&PR 91
Oghul Qamish WomWR
Ogida, Mikio 1938- WhoWor 91
Ogier, Walter Thomas 1925- WhoAm 90
Ogilbee, Michael Francis 1958- WhoSSW 91
Ogilby, Lyman Cunningham 1922- WhoAm 90
Ogilby, Peter Remsen 1955- WhoEmL 91
Ogilvie, Donald Gordon 1943- WhoAm 90
Ogilvie, Elisabeth 1917- AuBYP 90
Ogilvie, Fan S. 1944- WhoWrEP 89
Ogilvie, Frances 1902-1942 LiHiK
Ogilvie, Kelvin BioIn 16
Ogilvie, Kelvin Kenneth 1942- WhoAm 90
Ogilvie, Lloyd John 1930- WhoWrEP 89
Ogilvie, Margaret Pruett 1922- WhoAmW 91
Ogilvie, Orin Howard 1950- BiDrAPA 89
Ogilvie, Richard Buell 1923-1988 BioIn 16
Ogilvie, Richard Ian 1936- WhoAm 90
Ogilvie, Thomas Francis 1929- WhoAm 90
Ogilvie, Victor Nicholas 1942- WhoSSW 91
Ogilvie, Walter W., Jr. 1930- St&PR 91
Ogilvie, Will 1901- WhoAmA 91
Ogilvie, Will 1901-1989 WhoAmA 91N
Ogilvie, William G 1899- ConAu 130
Ogilvie, William Watson 1835-1900 DcCanB 12
Ogilvy, David 1911- BioIn 16
Ogilvy, David John 1958- BioIn 16
Ogilvy, David M. 1911- WorAlBi
Ogilvy, David Mackenzie 1911- ConAmBL, WhoAm 90
Ogilvy, David Wallace 1945- St&PR 91
Ogilvy, Eliza 1822-1912 FemiCLE
Ogilvy, Marina BioIn 16
Ogilvy, Maud FemiCLE
Ogino, Yoshio 1925- WhoWor 91
Oginz, Richard 1944- WhoAmA 91
Ogland, Olaf Johan BiDrAPA 89
Ogle, Anne 1832-1918 FemiCLE
Ogle, Clive William 1933- WhoWor 91
Ogle, Lucille AuBYP 90
Ogle, Lucille 1904-1988 BioIn 16
Ogle, Lynn 1927- St&PR 91
Ogle, Mark Robert 1960- BiDrAPA 89
Ogle, Mary Ellen 1944- WhoAmW 91
Ogle, Peggy Ann 1950- WhoAmW 91
Ogle, Sharon Ruth 1950- WhoSSW 91
Ogle, William A 1917- BiDrAPA 89
Oglesbee, Ronald Martin 1940- WhoSSW 91
Oglesby, Carole A. BioIn 16
Oglesby, Clarkson Hill 1908- WhoAm 90
Oglesby, Daniel Kirkland, Jr. 1930- WhoAm 90
Oglesby, Dwight Hadley 1941- St&PR 91
Oglesby, John Norman 1948- WhoEmL 91
Oglesby, Michael St&PR 91
Oglesby, R. Michael 1954- ODwPR 91
Oglesby, Ray Thurmond 1932- WhoAm 90
Oglesby, Richard James, IV 1947- WhoEmL 91, WhoWor 91
Oglesby, Sabert, Jr. 1921- WhoAm 90
Oglesby, Theodore Nathaniel, Jr. 1932- WhoWrEP 89
Oglesby, Thomas J, Jr. 1945- BiDrAPA 89
Oglesby, Walter R BiDrAPA 89
Oglesby, William Geddy 1955- WhoSSW 91
Oglethorpe, James E. 1696-1785 WorAlBi

Oglethorpe, James Edward 1696-1785 *BioIn 16, EncCRAm [port], WhNaAH*
Oglevee, Jeffrey M. 1941- *St&PR 91*
Ogliaruso, Michael Anthony 1938- *WhoAm 90*
Oglivie, Ben 1949- *Ballpl 90*
Ognibene, Andre John 1931- *WhoAm 90*
Ognyanov, Voislav Filip 1932- *BiDrAPA 89*
O'Gorman, Eugene R. 1939- *St&PR 91*
O'Gorman, Hubert J. 1925-1990 *BioIn 16, ConAu 131*
O'Gorman, James Francis 1933- *WhoAmA 91*
O'Gorman, John Joseph 1933- *WhoAm 90*
O'Gorman, Juan 1905-1982 *ArtLatA*
O'Gorman, Ned 1931- *WhoWrEP 89*
O'Gorman, Pamela Eadith 1935- *IntWWM 90*
O'Gorman, Peter Joseph 1938- *St&PR 91*
O'Gorman, William D *BiDrAPA 89*
Ogot, Grace 1930- *FemiCLE*
Ogra, Pearay L. 1939- *WhoAm 90*
O'Grady, Arthur S 1934- *BiDrAPA 89*
O'Grady, Desmond Patrick 1945- *St&PR 91*
O'Grady, Elinor M. *WhoAmW 91*
O'Grady, George L. 1908-1988 *BioIn 16*
O'Grady, Henry *WhoWrEP 89*
O'Grady, James Mary Early 1863-1928 *AmLegL*
O'Grady, Jean Patricia 1951- *WhoAmW 91*
O'Grady, John Joseph, III 1933- *WhoAm 90*
O'Grady, John L. 1942-1989 *BioIn 16*
O'Grady, Laurence Joseph 1943- *St&PR 91*
O'Grady, Mary J. 1951- *WhoE 91*
O'Grady, Rosemary Elizabeth 1937- *WhoE 91*
O'Grady, Thomas Bernard 1926- *St&PR 91*
O'Grady, Thomas Joseph 1943- *WhoWrEP 89*
O'Grady, Timothy 1951- *ConLC 59 [port]*
O'Grady, William M. 1939- *St&PR 91, WhoAm 90*
Ogram, Gordon F 1921- *BiDrAPA 89*
Ogram, John Donald *BiDrAPA 89*
O'Green, Frederick Wilbert 1921- *St&PR 91, WhoAm 90*
Ogren, Carroll Woodrow 1927- *WhoAm 90*
Ogren, David Carl 1938- *St&PR 91*
Ogren, Robert Edward 1922- *WhoAm 90*
Ogren, William Lewis 1938- *WhoAm 90*
O'Griofa, Fionan Maire *BiDrAPA 89*
Ogris, Werner 1935- *WhoWor 91*
Ogrizovich, Dorothy Ann 1928- *WhoWrEP 89*
Ogrizovich, John Jay 1945- *St&PR 91*
Ogron, Y. *St&PR 91*
Ogston, William D 1930- *BiDrAPA 89*
O'Guinn, Jo 1954- *WhoSSW 91*
Ogul, Morris Samuel 1931- *WhoAm 90*
Oguma, Taranosuke 1888-1978 *EncPaPR 91*
Ogunbambi, Rafiq Olayiwola 1949- *WhoWor 91*
Ogunbiyi, Yemi 1947- *WhoWor 91*
Ogundipe-Leslie, Omolara *FemiCLE*
Oguntoye, Ferdinand Abayomi 1949- *WhoWor 91*
Ogura, Haruo 1928- *WhoWor 91*
Ogura, Isao 1922- *WhoWor 91*
Ogura, Kiyoshi 1932- *BiDrAPA 89*
Ogura, Tadao *BiDrAPA 89*
Ogura, Yoshiaki 1937- *WhoWor 91*
Oguri, Hiroshi 1920- *WhoWor 91*
Oguz, Sadi 1929- *BiDrAPA 89*
Oh Saduharu *EncJap*
Oh, Harry Hak-keun 1935- *WhoWor 91*
Oh, John Kie-Chiang 1930- *WhoAm 90*
Oh, May Buong Yu Lau 1940- *WhoWor 91*
Oh, Sadaharu 1940- *Ballpl 90, WorAlBi*
Oh, Sae Kun *BiDrAPA 89*
Oh, Suk-Whan 1926- *BiDrAPA 89*
Oh, Susan Yunsoo 1936- *BiDrAPA 89*
Oh, Taeho 1958- *WhoSSW 91*
Oh, Tai Keun 1934- *WhoWor 91*
Oh, Tong Yal 1926- *BiDrAPA 89*
Oh, William 1931- *WhoAm 90*
Oh, Yeung-Rock *BiDrAPA 89*
O'Hagan, Desmond 1960- *BioIn 16*
O'Hagan, Harriet *BiDrAPA 89*
O'Hagan, James H. *BioIn 16*
O'Hagan, Joan *TwCCr&M 91*
O'Hagan, Joan 1926- *ConAu 132*
O'Hagan, Malcolm E. 1940- *WhoE 91*
O'Hagan, William D. 1942- *St&PR 91*
O'Hagen, Patricia *WhoE 91*
O'Hagin-Estrada, Isabel Barbara 1954- *WhoHisp 91*
O'Hair, Douglas Rolph 1917- *St&PR 91*
O'Hair, Madalyn Murray 1919- *WorAlBi*
O'Haire, Tony *BioIn 16*
Ohala, John Jerome 1941- *WhoAm 90*
O'Halloran, Colin Michael 1950- *WhoWor 91*
O'Halloran, Harry John 1939- *WhoSSW 91*
O'Halloran, Judy Mackenzie 1946- *WhoWrEP 89*
O'Halloran, Thomas Alphonsus, Jr. 1931- *WhoAm 90*
Ohana, Maurice 1914- *IntWWM 90, PenDiMP A*
O'Handley, Douglas Alexander 1937- *WhoE 91*
O'Handley, Joseph Francis 1926- *WhoAm 90*
Ohanesian, Robert S. 1936- *St&PR 91*
Ohanesian, Susan Marie 1949- *WhoAmW 91*
Ohaneson, Edward M 1915- *BiDrAPA 89*
Ohanian, Mihran Jacob 1933- *WhoAm 90*
O'Hanlon, Alvin Merle 1932- *WhoWrEP 89*
O'Hanlon, Dorothy Etta 1932- *WhoAmW 91*
O'Hanlon, George *BioIn 16*
O'Hanlon, James Barry 1927- *WhoAm 90*
O'Hanlon, James Patrick 1943- *St&PR 91*
O'Hanlon, Redmond *BioIn 16*
O'Hanlon, Richard E 1906-1985 *WhoAmA 91N*
Ohanneson, Joan 1930- *ConAu 130*
O'Hara, Alfred Peck 1919- *WhoAm 90*
O'Hara, David Oakes 1950- *WhoE 91*
O'Hara, Edward Joseph 1957- *St&PR 91*
O'Hara, Eliot 1890-1969 *WhoAmA 91N*
O'Hara, Eugene Michael 1937- *St&PR 91*
O'Hara, Frank 1926-1966 *ConAu 33NR, MajTwCW*
O'Hara, Frederick 1904-1980 *WhoAmA 91N*
O'Hara, J. D. Michael 1936- *ODwPR 91*
O'Hara, James Edward 1844-1905 *BlkAmsC [port]*
O'Hara, James Grant 1925-1989 *BioIn 16*
O'Hara, James Thomas 1936- *WhoAm 90*
O'Hara, Jenny *ConTFT 8*
O'Hara, Jocelyne Cote- *BioIn 16*
O'Hara, John 1905-1970 *ConAu 31NR, MajTwCW, WorAlBi*
O'Hara, John Francis 1917- *WhoAm 90*
O'Hara, John Martin 1955- *WhoE 91*
O'Hara, John Montross 1929- *St&PR 91*
O'Hara, John Paul, III 1946- *WhoEmL 91*
O'Hara, Margaret 1951- *WhoAmW 91*
Ohara, Maricarmen 1945- *WhoHisp 91*
O'Hara, Maureen 1921- *ConTFT 8, WorAlBi*
O'Hara, Maureen 1953- *WhoAmW 91*
O'Hara, Michael *ODwPR 91*
O'Hara, Michael Louis *BiDrAPA 89*
O'Hara, Morgan 1941- *WhoAmA 91*
O'Hara, Paul F. 1934- *St&PR 91*
O'Hara, Ralph L. 1944- *St&PR 91*
O'Hara, Robert Melvin 1926- *St&PR 91*
O'Hara, Sheila Mary 1953- *WhoAmA 91*
O'Hara, Theodore 1820-1867 *LiHiK*
O'Hara, Thomas Edwin 1915- *WhoAm 90*
O'Hara, Thomas J. 1926- *St&PR 91*
O'Hara, William F., Jr. 1953- *WhoWrEP 89*
O'Hara, William James 1930- *St&PR 91, WhoAm 90*
O'Hara, William Thomas 1932- *WhoE 91*
O'Hare, Anne Marie 1960- *WhoE 91*
O'Hare, Carrie Jane 1959- *WhoAmW 91, WhoE 91*
O'Hare, Dean Raymond 1942- *St&PR 91, WhoAm 90, WhoE 91*
O'Hare, Don R. 1922- *St&PR 91, WhoAm 90*
O'Hare, Donald James 1926- *St&PR 91*
O'Hare, Edward H. 1914-1943 *WorAlBi*
O'Hare, James Raymond 1938- *St&PR 91, WhoAm 90*
O'Hare, John A. 1957- *ODwPR 91*
O'Hare, John Joseph 1925- *WhoE 91*
O'Hare, Joseph Aloysius 1931- *WhoAm 90, WhoE 91*
O'Hare, Kate Richards 1876-1948 *EncAL*
O'Hare, Linda P. 1947- *WhoAm 90*
O'Hare, Patrick Joseph 1922- *WhoWor 91*
O'Hare, Robert Joseph Michael, Jr. 1943- *St&PR 91*
O'Hare, Stephen T. 1928- *St&PR 91*
O'Hare, Stephen Thomas 1928- *WhoAm 90*
O'Hare, Terrence William 1952- *WhoEmL 91*
O'Haren, Thomas Joseph 1934- *WhoSSW 91*
Ohashi, Isamu 1924- *WhoWor 91*
Ohashi, Kiyohide 1924- *WhoWor 91*
Ohashi, Kosuke 1943- *WhoAm 90*
Ohashi, Tsutomu 1925- *WhoWor 91*
Ohaus, James G. 1950- *St&PR 91*
O'Hayer, Matthew 1955- *WhoSSW 91*
Ohayon, Michel Y. 1946- *St&PR 91*
Ohba, Yujiro 1926- *WhoWor 91*
Ohe, Katie 1937- *WhoAmA 91*
Ohe, Shuzo 1938- *WhoWor 91*
O'Hea, Timothy E. 1945- *St&PR 91*
O'Heaney, Sheilah Maura 1959- *WhoSSW 91*
O'Hearn, John Howard 1937- *St&PR 91*
O'Hearn, Patrick *NewAgMG*
O'Hearn, Robert Raymond 1921- *WhoAm 90*
O'Hearne, John J 1922- *BiDrAPA 89*
O'Hearne, John Joseph 1922- *WhoAm 90*
Ohebshalom, Ebby 1935- *BiDrAPA 89*
O hEithir, Breandan 1930-1990 *ConAu 132, NewYTBS 90*
O'Henly, W.M. 1954- *St&PR 91*
O'Herin, Timothy Patrick 1955- *WhoWrEP 89*
O'Herlihy, Dan 1919- *WorAlBi*
O'Hern, Daniel Joseph 1930- *WhoAm 90, WhoE 91*
O'Hern, Elizabeth Moot 1913- *WhoAm 90*
O'Hern, Jane Susan 1933- *WhoAm 90*
O'Herron, Jonathan 1929- *St&PR 91, WhoAm 90*
Ohga, Norio *BioIn 16, NewYTBS 90 [port]*
Ohga, Norio 1930- *WhoWor 91*
O'Higgins, Bernardo 1778-1842 *BioIn 16*
O'Higgins, Pablo 1904-1983 *ArtLatA*
O'Higgins, Paul 1927- *ConAu 130*
Ohira Masayoshi 1910-1980 *EncJap*
Ohira, Takahisa *WhoAm 90*
Ohkawa, Hiromichi 1937- *WhoAm 90*
Ohkawa, Hironori 1936- *WhoWor 91*
Ohkawa, Tihiro 1928- *WhoAm 90*
Ohkita, Shuichi 1940- *St&PR 91*
Ohkubo, Masamichi 1940- *WhoWor 91*
Ohl, Glenn Joseph 1954- *St&PR 91*
Ohl, Herbert 1926- *ConDes 90*
Ohl, Ronald Edward 1936- *WhoAm 90*
Ohl, Wolfgang 1931- *WhoWor 91*
Ohlau, Juergen Uwe 1940- *WhoAmA 91*
Ohlemacher, Bradley R. 1963- *St&PR 91*
Ohlendorf, Otto 1908-1951 *BioIn 16*
Ohler, Jason *BioIn 16*
Ohlhausen, Beverly J. 1931- *WhoAmW 91*
Ohlke, Clarence Carl 1916- *WhoAm 90*
Ohlman, Charles Edward 1926- *St&PR 91, WhoAm 90*
Ohlman, Douglas Ronald 1949- *WhoWor 91*
Ohlman, Herbert 1927- *WhoWor 91*
Ohlman, Maxwell 1918- *WhoE 91*
Ohlmann, John Philip 1935- *St&PR 91*
Ohlms, David Lee *BiDrAPA 89*
Ohlmuller, Raymond P. 1939- *St&PR 91*
Ohlson, Douglas Dean 1936- *WhoAm 90, WhoAmA 91*
Ohlson, Robert *BioIn 16*
Ohlson, Robert N. 1946- *St&PR 91*
Ohlson, Sara Faye 1944- *WhoAmW 91*
Ohlson, William J. 1926- *St&PR 91*
Ohlsson, Garrick 1948- *IntWWM 90, PenDiMP*
Ohm, Georg Simon 1789-1854 *WorAlBi*
Ohm, Holly Van Valkenburgh 1936- *WhoAmW 91*
Ohm, Mina Elizabeth *BiDrAPA 89*
Ohm, Mina Elizabeth 1958- *WhoE 91*
Ohm, Robert Lee, II 1953- *WhoEmL 91*
Ohman, Lazzette M. 1919- *BioIn 16*
Ohman, Richard Michael 1946- *WhoEmL 91*
Ohman, Ulf Karl Gustaf 1931- *WhoWor 91*
Ohmann, Carol Burke *BioIn 16*
Ohmann, Carol Burke 1929?-1989 *ConAu 129*
Ohmann, Richard Malin 1931- *WhoWrEP 89*
Ohmstede, John Robert 1957- *St&PR 91*
Ohmstede, Robert Lee 1916- *St&PR 91*
Ohnishi, Shun-ichi 1930- *WhoWor 91*
Ohno, Mitsugi 1926- *WhoAmA 91*
Ohno, Susumu *BioIn 16*
Ohno, Susumu 1928- *WhoAm 90*
Ohno, Taiichi 1912-1990 *BioIn 16, NewYTBS 90 [port]*
Ohno, Tom *BioIn 16*
Ohnsman, David Robert 1943- *WhoSSW 91*
Ohnuma, Masahiko 1932- *WhoWor 91*
O'Hogan, Roger Matthew 1917- *IntWWM 90*
O'Hora, Ronan 1964- *IntWWM 90*
Ohotnicky, Stephen Thaddeus 1943- *WhoSSW 91*
Ohr, George E. 1857-1918 *PenDiDA 89*
Ohrbach, Barbara Milo *BioIn 16*
Ohrbach, Jerome K. *NewYTBS 90 [port]*
Ohrel, Alain Robert 1935- *WhoWor 91*
Ohrenstein, Manfred 1925- *WhoE 91*
Ohrenstein, Roman Abraham 1920- *WhoAm 90*
Ohresser, Phillipe 1936- *WhoWor 91*
Ohrn, James B. 1951- *St&PR 91*
Ohrn, Nils Yngve 1934- *WhoAm 90*
Ohrn, Rolf 1944- *WhoWor 91*
Ohsawa, George 1893-1966 *NewAgE 90*
Ohsol, Ernest Osborne 1916- *WhoAm 90*
Ohta, Hiroshi 1940- *WhoWor 91*
Ohta, Koichi 1951- *Ballpl 90*
Ohta, Minoru 1923- *WhoWor 91*
Ohta, Tomoko 1933- *WhoWor 91*
Ohtaka, Naomasa 1941- *WhoAm 90*
Ohtani, Yasukiyo 1947- *WhoWor 91*
Ohtsu, Masakazu 1937- *St&PR 91*
Ohtsubo, Hideto 1932- *WhoWor 91*
Ohuoha, Donald Chideha *BiDrAPA 89*
Ohuoha, Donald Chideha 1954- *WhoE 91*
Ohwada, Atsushi Andy 1937- *WhoWor 91*
Ohyama, Heiichiro 1947- *IntWWM 90, WhoAm 90*
Oi, Motoi 1910- *WhoAmA 91*
Oide, Kyoji 1940- *WhoWor 91*
Oignies, Hugo d' *PenDiDA 89*
Oihus, Arthur L. 1925- *St&PR 91*
Oikawa, Atsushi 1929- *WhoWor 91*
Oikonomides, Nicholas Constantine 1934- *WhoWrEP 89*
Oimoen, Roger E. 1931- *St&PR 91*
Oinas, Felix Johannes 1911- *WhoAm 90, WhoWor 91*
Oingo Boingo *EncPR&S 89*
Oishi, Gene *BioIn 16*
Oishi, Roy Takashi 1943- *WhoE 91*
Oishi, Satoshi 1927- *St&PR 91, WhoAm 90*
Oisly, Maurice d' *PenDiMP*
Oiso, Toshio 1908- *WhoWor 91*
Oisteanu, Valery 1943- *WhoWrEP 89*
Oistrakh, David 1908-1974 *PenDiMP*
Oistrakh, Igor 1931- *PenDiMP*
Oistrakh, Igor Davidovich 1931- *IntWWM 90*
Oiticica, Helio 1937-1980 *ArtLatA*
Oitto, William A. 1913-1986 *BioIn 16*
Oitzinger, John J. 1939- *St&PR 91*
Oizumi, Hiroshi *St&PR 91*
Ojakli, Sumya 1961- *WhoAmW 91*
Ojala, Kauko Veli J. 1942- *WhoWor 91*
Ojalvo, Irving Ulysses 1936- *WhoE 91*
Ojalvo, Maurice 1939- *St&PR 91*
Ojalvo, Morris 1924- *WhoAm 90*
Ojard, Bruce Allen 1951- *WhoEmL 91, WhoWor 91*
O'Jay, Eddie *BioIn 16*
O'Jays *EncPR&S 89*
Ojeda, Bob 1957- *Ballpl 90, BioIn 16, WhoHisp 91*
Ojeda, Pedro Antonio *BiDrAPA 89*
Ojeda, Pino 1916- *EncCoWW*
Ojeda-Castaneda, Jorge 1949- *WhoWor 91*
Ojemann, Robert Gerdes 1931- *WhoAm 90*
Ojiji *BioIn 16*
Ojika, Masao 1926- *WhoWor 91*
Ojika, Takeo 1939- *WhoWor 91*
Ojil, Helen Shizuko 1950- *WhoAmA 91*
Ojinaga, Raymond B. 1949- *WhoHisp 91*
Oka, Masuichiro 1931- *WhoWor 91*
Oka, Takeshi 1932- *WhoAm 90*
Okabayashi, Ichizo 1926- *WhoWor 91*
Okabayashi, Toyoki 1925- *WhoWor 91*
Okabe, Naosuke 1926- *WhoWor 91*
Okabe, Yoji 1934- *WhoWor 91*
Okada, Fumihiko 1940- *WhoWor 91*
Okada, Kenzo 1902-1982 *WhoAmA 91N*
Okada, Mutsumi 1931- *WhoWor 91*
Okada, Ryozo 1931- *WhoWor 91*
Okada, Sumie 1940- *ConAu 132*
Okada, Tomoji 1936- *ConDes 90*
Okada, Yasuo 1937- *WhoWor 91*
Okada, Yoshihisa 1939- *St&PR 91*
Okahashi, Sumio 1917- *WhoWor 91*
Okajima, Eigoro 1931- *WhoWor 91*
Okakura Kakuzo 1862-1913 *EncJap*
Okamoto, Akio 1945- *WhoWor 91*
Okamoto, D.I. 1943- *St&PR 91*
Okamoto, Jeffrey Akira *BiDrAPA 89*
Okamoto, Jeffrey Akira 1954- *WhoE 91*
Okamoto, Nobuyuki 1941- *WhoWor 91*
Okamoto, Taichi 1941- *WhoWor 91*
Okamoto, Takashi 1933- *WhoWor 91*
Okamoto, Thomas Hiroshi *BiDrAPA 89*
Okamoto, Toshio 1914- *WhoWor 91*
Okamoto, Tsunenori 1939- *IntWWM 90, WhoWor 91*
Okamoto, Yoshihiro 1928- *WhoWor 91*
Okamura, Arthur 1932- *WhoAm 90, WhoAmA 91*
O'Kane, Dick *AuBYP 90*
Okane, Janine Margot *BiDrAPA 89*
O'Kane, Maureen Therese 1957- *St&PR 91*
O'Kane, Robert Emmett 1943- *St&PR 91*
O'Kane, Robert Maxwell 1920- *WhoAm 90*
O'Kanes, The *WhoNeCM [port]*
Okasha, Ahmed Mahmoud 1935- *BiDrAPA 89*
Okasha, Mahmoud S 1943- *BiDrAPA 89*
Okawa, Yoshio *BioIn 16*
Okawara, Yoshio 1919- *WhoWor 91*
Okazaki, Kenji 1934- *WhoSSW 91*
Okazaki, Tuneko 1933- *WhoWor 91*
Oke, Alan 1956- *IntWWM 90*
Oke, John Beverley 1928- *WhoAm 90*
Okebugwu, Andrew Nkasiobi 1937- *WhoWor 91*

Okebukola, Peter Akinsola 1948- *WhoWor 91*
O'Keefe, Arthur F. 1930- *St&PR 91*
O'Keefe, Bernard J. *BioIn 16*
O'Keefe, Bernard J. 1919- *St&PR 91*
O'Keefe, Bernard J 1919-1989 *ConAu 129*
O'Keefe, Beverly Disbrow 1946- *WhoAmW 91, WhoSSW 91*
O'Keefe, Christine Marie 1951- *WhoAmW 91*
O'Keefe, Constance 1948- *WhoE 91*
O'Keefe, Daniel J. 1942- *St&PR 91*
O'Keefe, Dorothy Ann 1957- *BiDrAPA 89*
O'Keefe, Drew J. T. 1915-1989 *BioIn 16*
O'Keefe, Edward Franklin 1937- *WhoAm 90*
O'Keefe, Frank Robert, Jr. 1929- *St&PR 91*
O'Keefe, Fredrick Rea 1944- *WhoSSW 91*
O'Keefe, George W. 1924- *St&PR 91*
O'Keefe, Gerald Francis 1918- *WhoAm 90*
O'Keefe, James William, Jr. 1948- *WhoAm 90*
O'Keefe, John David 1941- *WhoAm 90*
O'Keefe, Joseph Ross 1954- *St&PR 91*
O'Keefe, Joseph Thomas 1919- *WhoE 91*
O'Keefe, Kathleen Mary 1933- *WhoAmW 91*
O'Keefe, Kevin M. *ODwPR 91*
O'Keefe, Lynn Marie 1955- *WhoSSW 91*
O'Keefe, Mellen Patricia 1954- *WhoE 91*
O'Keefe, Michael J. 1952- *St&PR 91*
O'Keefe, Nancy Jean 1926- *WhoAmW 91*
O'Keefe, Patricia Rigg 1926- *WhoAmW 91*
O'Keefe, Patrick E *ConAu 31NR*
O'Keefe, Patrick Francis 1947- *WhoEmL 91*
O'Keefe, Patrick Shaw 1952- *WhoE 91*
O'Keefe, Paul Alexander 1932- *WhoSSW 91*
O'Keefe, Raymond Michael 1925- *St&PR 91*
O'Keefe, Robert James 1926- *WhoAm 90*
O'Keefe, Ronald David 1933- *St&PR 91*
O'Keefe, Thomas Joseph 1935- *WhoAm 90*
O'Keefe, Thomas Michael 1940- *WhoAm 90*
O'Keefe, Tyler R. 1940- *St&PR 91*
O'Keefe, Vincent Thomas 1920- *WhoAm 90*
O'Keefe, William Francis 1938- *WhoE 91*
O'Keeffe, Adelaide 1776-1865 *FemiCLE*
O'Keeffe, Daniel John 1923- *St&PR 91*
O'Keeffe, Georgia 1887-1986 *BioAmW, BioIn 16, IntDcAA 90, ModArCr 1 [port], WhoAmA 91N, WorAlBi*
O'Keeffe, Georgia Totto 1887-1986 *BiDWomA*
O'Keeffe, John Joseph, Jr. 1941- *WhoAm 90*
O'Keeffe, Neil 1893- *EncACom*
O'Keeffe, Peter Laurence 1931- *WhoWor 91*
O'Keeffe, Shan 1945- *St&PR 91*
O'Keeffe, Thomas J. *St&PR 91*
O'Keeffe, William 1939- *St&PR 91*
O'Keeffe, William B. 1939- *St&PR 91*
O'Kehie, Collins Emeka 1952- *WhoSSW 91, WhoWor 91*
Okell, Jobyna Louise 1937- *WhoAmW 91, WhoSSW 91, WhoWor 91*
O'Kelley, Mattie Lou 1908- *MusmAFA*
O'Kelley, Michael L. 1953- *St&PR 91*
O'Kelley, William Clark 1930- *WhoAm 90, WhoSSW 91*
Okello, Basilio Olara *NewYTBS 90*
Okello, Tito *BioIn 16*
O'Kelly, Bernard 1926- *WhoAm 90*
O'Kelly, Peter Bernard John 1961- *WhoE 91*
Oken, Donald 1928- *BiDrAPA 89*
Oken, Donald Edward 1928- *WhoAm 90*
Okenson, Lois Wiley 1919- *WhoWrEP 89*
Oker, Stephen David 1931- *St&PR 91*
Okerlund, Arlene Naylor 1938- *WhoAm 90*
O'Key Sisters *EncO&P 3*
O'Key, Elizabeth *EncO&P 3*
O'Key, Jane *EncO&P 3*
Okey, Ruth 1893-1973 *BioIn 16*
Oki, Masahiro 1921- *EncO&P 3*
Okie, Frederick W., Jr. 1937- *St&PR 91*
Okigbo, Christopher 1905-1967 *WorAlBi*
Okigbo, Christopher 1932-1967 *MajTwCW*
Okiishi, Theodore Hisao 1939- *WhoAm 90*
Okimoto, Joseph T 1938- *BiDrAPA 89*
Okin, Jay Alan 1942- *WhoE 91*
Okin, Robert L 1942- *BiDrAPA 89*
Okins, Elliott Eugene 1915- *WhoWrEP 89*
Okishio, Soichiro 1928- *WhoWor 91*
Okita, George T. 1922- *WhoAm 90*
Okita, Saburo 1914- *WhoWor 91*
Okiyama, Yasuhiko 1932- *St&PR 91*
Okkema, Matthew 1931- *St&PR 91*
Oklan, Edward 1948- *BiDrAPA 89*
Okland, Einar 1940- *DcScanL*
Oko, Andrew Jan 1946- *WhoAm 90*
Oko, Benjamin Kuhn 1937- *BiDrAPA 89*
Okobo, Hiroshi 1929- *WhoWor 91*
Okola, Michael Joseph 1938- *St&PR 91*
O'Kon, James Alexander 1937- *WhoSSW 91, WhoWor 91*
O'Konski, Chester Thomas 1921- *WhoAm 90*
Okoshi, E Sumiye *WhoAmA 91*
Okoshi, Sumiye *WhoAmW 91, WhoWor 91*
Okoshi, Takanori 1932- *WhoWor 91*
Okoso, Yoshinori 1915- *WhoWor 91*
Okovic-Goodman, Johanna Valeria 1945- *WhoE 91*
Okoye, Christian *BioIn 16*
Okoye, Christian 1961- *News 90 [port]*
Okoye, Ifeoma *FemiCLE*
Okpa, Ejike Edward, Jr. 1960- *WhoSSW 91*
Okpaku, Joseph O O 1943- *DrBlPA 90*
Okpaku, Samuel Osifo *BiDrAPA 89*
Okray, Albert P. 1917- *St&PR 91*
Okrent, Daniel 1948- *Ballpl 90, WhoWrEP 89*
Okrent, David 1922- *WhoAm 90*
O'Krent, Ed 1929- *St&PR 91*
Okri, Ben 1959- *ConAu 130*
Okrusch, Martin Alfred 1934- *WhoWor 91*
Oksanen, Heikki 1947- *WhoWor 91*
Oksas, Joan K. 1927- *WhoAm 90*
Okscin, Allan 1951- *St&PR 91*
Oksenberg, Michel Charles 1938- *WhoAm 90*
Oksendahl, Douglas Curtis 1947- *St&PR 91*
Oksner, Bob 1916- *EncACom*
Oktem, Nizamettin 1922- *BiDrAPA 89*
Okubo Toshimichi 1830-1878 *EncJap*
Okubo, Toshiteru 1939- *WhoWor 91*
Okuda, Kunio 1921- *WhoWor 91*
Okuda, Kyuichiro 1927- *WhoWor 91*
Okudzhava, Bulat Shalvovich 1924- *ConAu 129*
Okuhara, Tetsu 1940- *WhoAmA 91*
Okui, Kazumitsu 1933- *WhoWor 91*
Okulick, John A 1947- *WhoAmA 91*
Okulitch, Vladimir Joseph 1906- *WhoAm 90*
Okulski, John Allen 1944- *WhoE 91*
Okuma Shigenobu 1838-1922 *EncJap*
Okuma, Albert Akira, Jr. 1946- *WhoEmL 91*
Okumoto, Clifford Iwao *BiDrAPA 89*
Okumura, Hidemasa 1926- *WhoWor 91*
Okumura, Lydia *WhoAmA 91*
Okun, Barbara Frank 1936- *WhoAm 90*
Okun, Barbara J 1932- *WhoAmA 91*
Okun, Charles 1942- *St&PR 91*
Okun, Daniel Alexander 1917- *WhoAm 90*
Okun, Erwin D. *ODwPR 91*
Okun, Erwin Donald 1934- *St&PR 91*
Okun, Gail Sheila 1943- *WhoAmW 91*
Okun, Herbert Stuart 1930- *WhoAm 90*
Okun, Milton H *BiDrAPA 89*
Okun, Philip *BiDrAPA 89*
Okun, Rob A. 1950- *WhoE 91*
Okundaye, Osazuwa John 1957- *WhoSSW 91*
Okuni *EncJap*
Okuni, Masahiko 1927- *WhoWor 91*
Okuninushi no Mikoto *EncJap*
Okusami, Taiwo *BiDrAPA 89*
Okutsu, Fumio 1935- *WhoWor 91*
Okuyama, Shinichi 1935- *WhoWor 91*
Okwumabua, Benjamin N. 1939- *St&PR 91*
Olaciregui, Andres 1940- *BiDrAPA 89*
Olack, Neil Peter 1956- *WhoEmL 91*
Olaeta, Julia O'Keeffe 1923- *WhoAmW 91*
Olafson, Donald G. 1936- *St&PR 91*
Olafson, Frederick Arlan 1924- *WhoAm 90*
Olafson, Harlan Nestor 1928- *WhoWrEP 89*
Olafson, James W. 1938- *WhoAm 90, WhoSSW 91*
Olafson, Robert M. 1949- *St&PR 91*
Olafsson, Johann Johannsson 1935- *WhoWor 91*
Olafsson, Magnus 1950- *WhoWor 91*
Olafur Johann Sigurdsson *DcScanL*
Olague, Ruben, Jr. 1957- *WhoHisp 91*
Olah, George Andrew 1927- *WhoAm 90*
Olajuwon, Akeem *BioIn 16*
Olajuwon, Akeem 1963- *WorAlBi*
Olajuwon, Akeem Abdul 1963- *WhoAm 90*
Oland, Derek *BioIn 16*
Oland, Mark 1947- *WhoE 91*
Oland, S. M. *WhoAm 90*
Oland, Sidney M. *BioIn 16*
Oland, Warner 1880-1938 *WorAlBi*
Olander, Donald Edgar 1929- *WhoWor 91*
Olander, Joseph D. *WhoAm 90*
Olander, Ray Gunnar 1926- *St&PR 91, WhoAm 90, WhoWor 91*
Olander, William *BioIn 16*
Olanich, Catherine Cecilia 1959- *WhoAmW 91*
Olansky, Ilene Rosen 1930- *WhoAmW 91*
Olar, Terry Thomas 1947- *WhoSSW 91*
Olarte, Silvia Wybert *BiDrAPA 89*
Olasky, Marvin *BioIn 16*
Olatunji, Michael Babatunde *AuBYP 90, DrBlPA 90*
O'Laughlin, Jeanne 1929- *WhoAmW 91, WhoSSW 91*
O'Laughlin, Marjorie Hartley *WhoAmW 91*
Olausson, Ingrid 1934- *WhoWor 91*
Olav 1903- *WhoWor 91*
Olav V 1903- *WorAlBi*
Olaves, Jorge L. 1956- *WhoHisp 91*
Olavus Petri 1493-1552 *DcScanL*
Olaya, Dario Echandia 1897-1989 *BioIn 16*
Olaya Herrera, Enrique 1881-1937 *BioIn 16*
Olayan, Suliman Saleh 1918- *WhoAm 90, WhoWor 91*
Olberding, Elaine Johnson 1955- *WhoAmW 91*
Olberg, F. Forbes 1923- *St&PR 91*
Olbrantz, John Paul 1950- *WhoAm 90*
Olbrich, Josef Maria 1867-1908 *BioIn 16*
Olbrich, Joseph Maria 1867-1908 *PenDiDA 89*
Olbricht, Charles G. 1940- *ODwPR 91*
Olbromska-Mele, Celina *BiDrAPA 89*
Olbrysh, R. Terry 1948- *ODwPR 91*
Olbum, Carolyn 1937- *WhoAmW 91*
Olcer, Nuri Yelman 1932- *St&PR 91*
Olcese, Edward Lewis 1940- *St&PR 91*
Olch, Gerald B *BiDrAPA 89*
Olcott, Alfred van Santvoord *BioIn 16*
Olcott, Anthony 1950- *SpyFic*
Olcott, Ben Wilson 1872-1952 *BioIn 16*
Olcott, Charles *WhoSSW 91*
Olcott, Chauncey 1858-1932 *OxCPMus*
Olcott, Emery G. 1938- *St&PR 91*
Olcott, Frances Jenkins 1872?-1963 *AuBYP 90*
Olcott, Henry Steel *NewAgE 90*
Olcott, Henry Steel 1832-1907 *EncO&P 3, EncPaPR 91, WorAlBi*
Olcott, James Louis 1944- *IntWWM 90*
Olcott, John W. 1936- *St&PR 91*
Olcott, William Alfred 1931- *WhoAm 90*
Olczewska, Maria *PenDiMP*
Old Britain *WhNaAH*
Old Briton *WhNaAH*
Old John *WhNaAH*
Old Jowett *ConAu 129*
Old Moore *EncO&P 3*
Old Moore 1657- *EncO&P 3*
Old Smoke *WhNaAH*
Old Sun *DcCanB 12*
Old, Bruce S. 1913- *St&PR 91*
Old, Bruce Scott 1913- *WhoAm 90, WhoWor 91*
Old, Carl Angelo 1954- *WhoEmL 91*
Old, Hughes Oliphant 1933- *WhoE 91*
Old, John M. *ConTFT 8*
Old, Lloyd John 1933- *WhoAm 90*
Old, Walter G. 1864-1929 *EncO&P 3*
Old-Man-Afraid-of-His-Horses *WhNaAH*
Oldam, Paul Bernard 1934- *St&PR 91*
Oldberg, Carl Malcolm 1947- *WhoAm 90*
Olden, Kevin William *BiDrAPA 89*
Olden, Sam *AuBYP 90*
Oldenbourg, Zoe 1916- *EncCoWW*
Oldenburg, Carl *ConAu 132*
Oldenburg, Claes 1929- *IntDcAA 90*
Oldenburg, Claes Thure 1929- *WhoAm 90, WhoAmA 91, WhoWor 91, WorAlBi*
Oldenburg, Henry 1617?-1677 *BioIn 16*
Oldenburg, Kimberle Marie 1957- *WhoAmW 91*
Oldenburg, Peter *NewYTBS 90*
Oldenburg, Ray 1932- *ConAu 132*
Oldenburg, Richard *BioIn 16*
Oldenburg, Richard Erik 1933- *WhoAm 90, WhoAmA 91, WhoE 91, WhoWor 91*
Oldenburg, William R. 1946- *St&PR 91*
Oldenkott, Bernd Adrian 1925- *WhoWor 91*
Oldenquist, Andrew G. 1932- *WhoAm 90*
Older, Effin 1942- *WhoWrEP 89*
Older, Fremont 1856-1935 *BioIn 16*
Older, Jack Stanley 1934- *WhoAm 90*
Older, Julia D. 1941- *WhoWrEP 89*
Olders, Henry Gerard 1948- *BiDrAPA 89*
Oldershaw, Louis Frederick 1917- *WhoAm 90*
Oldershaw, Paul John 1947- *WhoWor 91*
Oldfather, Charles Eugene 1927- *WhoAm 90*
Oldfather, Grayson W. *St&PR 91*
Oldfield, Ann Sybil 1938- *WhoWor 91*
Oldfield, Anne 1683-1730 *BioIn 16*
Oldfield, Barney 1878-1946 *WorAlBi*
Oldfield, Bruce *BioIn 16*
Oldfield, Bruce 1950- *WhoWor 91*
Oldfield, Edward Charles, Jr. 1919- *WhoAm 90*
Oldfield, Joe *St&PR 91*
Oldfield, Keith D. *WhoAm 90*
Oldfield, Margaret J. 1932- *BioIn 16*
Oldfield, Maurice 1915-1981 *DcNaB 1981*
Oldfield, Michael *NewAgMG*
Oldfield, Michael Gordon 1953- *IntWWM 90*
Oldfield, Mike 1953- *OxCPMus*
Oldfield, Russell Miller 1946- *St&PR 91, WhoEmL 91*
Oldford, William G. 1929- *St&PR 91*
Oldham, Arthur 1926- *IntWWM 90*
Oldham, Betty J. 1927- *St&PR 91*
Oldham, Dale R. 1943- *St&PR 91*
Oldham, Darius Dudley 1941- *WhoAm 90, WhoSSW 91*
Oldham, David Graham *BiDrAPA 89*
Oldham, Elaine Dorothea 1931- *WhoWor 91*
Oldham, Jean Kae 1952- *WhoAmW 91*
Oldham, Joe 1943- *WhoWrEP 89*
Oldham, John Michael 1940- *BiDrAPA 89*
Oldham, Lea Leever 1931- *WhoWor 91*
Oldham, Mark Frank 1948- *WhoEmL 91*
Oldham, Marylyn Tyra 1964- *WhoAmW 91*
Oldham, Maxine Jernigan 1923- *WhoAmW 91, WhoWor 91*
Oldham, Philip Bryan 1958- *WhoSSW 91*
Oldham, Phyllis Virginia Kidd 1926- *WhoAmW 91*
Oldham, Red 1893-1961 *Ballpl 90*
Oldham, Robert Lee 1940- *BiDrAPA 89*
Oldham, William George 1938- *WhoAm 90*
Oldhouser, Kay Adams 1945- *WhoSSW 91*
Oldin, Arthur K. 1931- *St&PR 91*
Oldknow, Antony 1939- *WhoWrEP 89*
Oldknow, William Henry 1924- *St&PR 91*
Oldman, Gary *BioIn 16*
Oldrin, John 1901- *AuBYP 90*
Oldring, Rube 1884-1961 *Ballpl 90*
Olds, David Douglas *BiDrAPA 89*
Olds, David Mark 1920- *WhoAm 90*
Olds, Elizabeth 1896- *AuBYP 90, BiDWomA*
Olds, Helen 1895-1981 *AuBYP 90*
Olds, Jacqueline M 1947- *BiDrAPA 89*
Olds, Jacqueline Nicole 1947- *WhoE 91*
Olds, John Theodore 1943- *WhoAm 90, WhoE 91*
Olds, Ransom E. 1864-1950 *EncABHB 4 [port]*
Olds, Ranson E. 1864-1950 *WorAlBi*
Olds, Robert Willard *BiDrAPA 89*
Olds, Sharon 1942- *FemiCLE, WhoAmW 91, WhoWrEP 89, WorAu 1980 [port]*
Olds, Sharron Lee 1939- *WhoAmW 91*
Olds, Stuart O. *BioIn 16*
Oldshue, James Y. 1925- *St&PR 91, WhoAm 90, WhoWor 91*
Oldshue, Mary Holl 1951- *St&PR 91*
Oldshue, Paul Frederick 1949- *WhoWor 91*
Oldson, William Orville 1940- *WhoSSW 91*
Oldt, Claude R. 1934- *St&PR 91*
Olea, Efren Saucedo *BiDrAPA 89*
Olea, Greg Manuel 1959- *WhoHisp 91*
Olea, Victor Flores 1933- *BioIn 16*
Olearchyk, Andrew S. 1935- *WhoAm 90, WhoWor 91*
O'Leary, Alice 1932- *WhoAmW 91*
O'Leary, Arthur Francis 1924- *WhoAm 90*
O'Leary, Arthur Hugh 1952- *BiDrAPA 89*
O'Leary, Charley 1882-1941 *Ballpl 90*
O'Leary, Daniel Vincent, Jr. 1942- *WhoAm 90*
O'Leary, David W. 1951- *St&PR 91*
O'Leary, Denis Joseph 1924- *WhoAm 90*
O'Leary, Dennis Sophian 1938- *WhoAm 90*
O'Leary, E.M. 1946- *St&PR 91*
O'Leary, Edward Cornelius 1920- *WhoAm 90, WhoE 91*
O'Leary, Edward T. 1938- *St&PR 91*
O'Leary, Ellen 1831-1889 *FemiCLE*
O'Leary, Florence Ann 1954- *WhoAmW 91*
O'Leary, Frank 1922- *AuBYP 90*
O'Leary, Gertrude Eileen 1941- *WhoAmW 91, WhoWor 91*
O'Leary, Gloria Mary *BiDrAPA 89*
O'Leary, Hazel R. 1937- *St&PR 91, WhoAmW 91*
O'Leary, Henry 1832-1897 *DcCanB 12*
O'Leary, Jack Arnold 1931- *WhoE 91*
O'Leary, James John 1914- *St&PR 91, WhoAm 90*
O'Leary, James Patrick 1951- *WhoE 91*
O'Leary, Jane Strong 1946- *IntWWM 90*
O'Leary, Joseph H 1955- *BiDrAPA 89*
O'Leary, Kathleen A. 1946- *WhoE 91*
O'Leary, Marion Hugh 1941- *WhoAm 90*
O'Leary, Neil Joseph 1925- *St&PR 91*
O'Leary, Patrick J. 1951- *WhoAm 90*
O'Leary, Paul A. 1927- *St&PR 91*
O'Leary, Paul Alistair 1942- *WhoWor 91*

O'Leary, Paul Gerard 1935- *WhoAm 90*
O'Leary, R. Donald 1942- *St&PR 91*
O'Leary, Roberta Ann 1962- *WhoAmW 91*
O'Leary, Thomas Howard 1934- *St&PR 91, WhoAm 90*
O'Leary, Thomas Michael 1948- *WhoAm 90*
O'Leary, Timothy H. 1933- *St&PR 91*
O'Leary, Timothy Michael 1946- *WhoEmL 91*
O'Leary, Wilfred Leo 1906- *WhoAm 90*
O'Leary Moore, Donna Marie 1964- *WhoAmW 91*
Olechowski, Tadeusz 1926- *WhoWor 91*
Oleck, Howard L. 1911- *WhoAm 90*
Oledzki, Bogdan 1949- *IntWWM 90*
Oleen, Lana 1949- *WhoAmW 91*
Oleen-Burkey, MerriKay Adelle 1949- *WhoAmW 91*
Oleg, Raphael 1959- *IntWWM 90*
Olejar, Paul Duncan 1906- *WhoSSW 91, WhoWor 91*
O Lejarraga, Maria de la *EncCoWW*
Olejer, Andrew Joseph 1925- *WhoSSW 91*
Olejniczak, Dominic 1908-1989 *BioIn 16*
Oleksa, Michael John 1950- *IntWWM 90*
Oleksey, Vicky Joyce 1952- *WhoAmW 91*
Oleksik, Mark Edward 1952- *St&PR 91*
Oleksiw, Daniel Philip 1921- *WhoAm 90*
Oleksy, Walter G. 1930- *AuBYP 90*
Olen, Arthur Joseph, Jr. 1953- *St&PR 91*
Olen, David J 1941- *BiDrAPA 89*
Olen, Gary 1942- *St&PR 91*
Olenchak, Frank Richard 1950- *WhoSSW 91*
Olender, Allen Mark 1949- *St&PR 91*
Olender, Arnold Bruce 1952- *WhoSSW 91*
Olender, Jack Harvey 1935- *WhoE 91*
Olender, Jeffrey Steven 1954- *St&PR 91*
Olendorf, William Carr 1924- *WhoAmA 91*
Olendorf, William Carr, Jr. 1945- *WhoEmL 91, WhoSSW 91, WhoWor 91*
O'Lenick, Anthony John, Jr. 1953- *WhoSSW 91*
Olenick, David Charles 1947- *WhoAmA 91*
Olenick, Joseph J. 1943- *St&PR 91*
Olenik, David Anthony 1940- *BiDrAPA 89*
Olenina-d'Alheim, Marya 1869-1970 *PenDiMP*
Olenski, Paul Edward *BiDrAPA 89*
Oler, Douglas Blair 1940- *St&PR 91*
Oler, Irwin Aaron 1949- *St&PR 91*
Oler, Wesley Marion, III 1918- *WhoAm 90, WhoWor 91*
Olerys, Joseph 1697-1749 *PenDiDA 89*
Oles, Douglas Stuart 1954- *WhoEmL 91*
Oles, Laura Treadgold 1956- *WhoEmL 91*
Oles, Paul Stevenson 1936- *WhoAm 90*
Olesen, Donald Louis 1952- *WhoE 91*
Olesen, Dorte Marianne 1948- *WhoWor 91*
Olesen, Douglas Eugene *BioIn 16*
Olesen, Douglas Eugene 1939- *St&PR 91, WhoAm 90*
Olesen, Jens 1943- *WhoWor 91*
Olesen, Karsten Marinus 1944- *WhoWor 91*
Olesen, Mark William 1961- *WhoSSW 91*
Olesen, Mogens Norgaard 1948- *WhoWor 91*
Olesen, Per Anders 1947- *WhoWor 91*
Olesen, Preben Byriel 1933- *WhoWor 91*
Olesen, Torben Toftdahl 1952- *WhoWor 91*
Oleshansky, Marvin Alan 1946- *BiDrAPA 89*
Olesiuk, W.W.J. 1950- *St&PR 91*
Oleskiewicz, Francis Stanley 1928- *WhoAm 90*
Oleson, Claire *AuBYP 90*
Oleszko, Patricia *WhoAmA 91*
Oleyar, Rita Balkey *ConAu 30NR*
Olfson, James Oliver 1927- *St&PR 91*
Olga *WomWR*
Olga 890?-969 *WomWR*
Olgaard, Anders 1926- *WhoWor 91*
Olgaard, Mark Kermit 1952- *WhoEmL 91*
Olgiati, Sandro G 1940- *BiDrAPA 89*
Olgin, Moissaye J. 1878-1939 *EncAL*
Olguin, Dolores C. 1939- *WhoHisp 91*
Olguin, M. Michael 1948- *WhoHisp 91*
Olian, JoAnne Constance *WhoAmW 91*
Olian, Robert Martin 1953- *WhoEmL 91*
Oliansky, Joel 1935- *WhoAm 90*
Olichney, John Michael *BiDrAPA 89*
Olick, Arthur Seymour 1931- *WhoAm 90*
Olick, Philip Stewart 1936- *WhoAm 90*
Oliel, Serge George 1929- *WhoE 91*
Olien, Diana Davids 1943- *ConAu 32NR*
Oliensis, Sheldon 1922- *WhoAm 90*
Oligher, Robert Leo 1929- *St&PR 91*
Oligny, Huguette 1922- *OxCCanT*
Oliker, Vladimir 1945- *WhoAm 90*
Olikut 1845?-1877 *WhNaAH*
Olimpica, Corilla *EncCoWW*
Olin, Burton Howard 1925- *St&PR 91*
Olin, Ferris *WhoAmA 91*
Olin, Frank 1860-1951 *Ballpl 90*
Olin, Harry S 1930- *BiDrAPA 89*
Olin, Jacqueline S. 1932- *WhoAmW 91*
Olin, James R. 1920- *WhoAm 90, WhoSSW 91*
Olin, Janet L. 1955- *WhoAmW 91*
Olin, John George 1939- *St&PR 91*
Olin, John M. 1892-1982 *WorAlBi*
Olin, Ken *BioIn 16*
Olin, Kent O. 1930- *St&PR 91*
Olin, Kent Oliver 1930- *WhoAm 90*
Olin, Lena 1956- *News 91-2 [port]*
Olin, Robert Floyd 1948- *WhoSSW 91*
Olin, William Harold 1924- *WhoAm 90*
Olinde, Alfred A 1932- *BiDrAPA 89*
Oline, Gary J. 1940- *St&PR 91*
Oliner, Arthur Aaron 1921- *WhoAm 90*
Oliner, Samuel P. 1930- *ConAu 129*
Olinger, Glenn S. 1929- *St&PR 91*
Olinger, Glenn Slocum 1929- *WhoAm 90, WhoWor 91*
Olinger, Leon *BiDrAPA 89*
Olinger, Leon J. 1940- *St&PR 91*
Olinger, Marc Jean 1954- *WhoWor 91*
Olinick, Stanley L *BiDrAPA 89*
Olinick, Stanley L. 1915- *WhoE 91*
Olins, Robert Abbot 1942- *WhoAm 90*
Olinsky, Ivan G 1878-1962 *WhoAmA 91N*
Oliphant, Betty 1918- *WhoAm 90, WhoAmW 91*
Oliphant, Charles Romig 1917- *WhoWor 91*
Oliphant, Dave 1939- *WhoWrEP 89*
Oliphant, Ernie L. 1934- *WhoAmW 91, WhoWor 91*
Oliphant, Hugh B. 1937- *St&PR 91*
Oliphant, John Hoyt 1943- *St&PR 91*
Oliphant, Margaret 1828-1897 *BioIn 16, FemiCLE*
Oliphant, Martha Carmichael 1935- *WhoE 91*
Oliphant, Naomi Joyce 1953- *IntWWM 90*
Oliphant, Pat *NewYTBS 90*
Oliphant, Pat 1935- *WorAlBi*
Oliphant, Patrick *BioIn 16*
Oliphant, Patrick 1935- *WhoAmA 91*
Oliphant, Robert D. 1949- *St&PR 91*
Oliphant, Timothy Matalebona Abdel-Aziz 1935- *WhoWor 91*
Oliphint, Benjamin Ray 1924- *WhoAm 90*
Oliphint, Robert Erskine 1941- *St&PR 91*
Olitski, Jules 1922- *WhoAm 90, WhoAmA 91, WhoE 91*
Olitsky, Gwen Miller 1942- *WhoWrEP 89*
Olitzky, Kerry Marc 1954- *WhoE 91*
Oliva, Ann Machin 1947- *WhoE 91*
Oliva, Antonia Hernanda de la *EncCoWW*
Oliva, Damaso Andres 1938- *BiDrAPA 89*
Oliva, Deborah A. 1952- *WhoWor 91*
Oliva, Jayne Ellen 1958- *WhoE 91*
Oliva, Lawrence Jay 1933- *WhoAm 90*
Oliva, Pavel 1923- *ConAu 132*
Oliva, Robert Rogelio 1946- *WhoEmL 91*
Oliva, Samuel Nicholas 1953- *WhoEmL 91*
Oliva, Stephen Edward 1946- *WhoEmL 91*
Oliva, Suzanne Marie 1965- *WhoSSW 91*
Oliva, Tony 1940- *Ballpl 90 [port], WhoHisp 91, WorAlBi*
Olivar, Jordan *NewYTBS 90*
Olivares, Julian, Jr. 1940- *WhoHisp 91*
Olivares, Olga 1939- *WhoHisp 91*
Olivares, Rene Eugenio 1941- *WhoE 91*
Olivarez, Graciela 1928- *BioIn 16*
Olivarius-Imlah, MaryPat 1957- *WhoAmW 91*
Olivarri, Leah Pagan 1951- *WhoAmW 91*
Olivas, Guadalupe Soto 1952- *WhoHisp 91*
Olivas, Louis 1947- *WhoHisp 91*
Olivas, Ramon Rodriguez, Jr. 1949- *WhoHisp 91*
Olive, David M. 1952- *WhoEmL 91*
Olive, Diego Eduardo 1949- *WhoHisp 91*
Olive, John 1949- *WhoAm 90*
Olive, Lindsay Shepherd 1917-1988 *BioIn 16*
Olive, Randolph Milan 1947- *St&PR 91*
Oliveira, Celia Regina *BiDrAPA 89*
Oliveira, Cesar Cavalcanti 1941- *WhoWor 91*
Oliveira, Elmar 1950- *IntWWM 90, WhoAm 90*
Oliveira, Helena Silva De 1915- *WhoWor 91*
Oliveira, Manuel J. 1936- *St&PR 91*
Oliveira, Nathan 1928- *BioIn 16, WhoAmA 91*
Olivella, Barry James 1947- *St&PR 91, WhoAm 90*
Olivella, Manuel Zapata *HispWr 90*
Oliver, Adela *WhoAmW 91, WhoE 91*
Oliver, Al 1946- *Ballpl 90 [port]*
Oliver, Alexander 1944- *IntWWM 90*
Oliver, Allen Laws, Jr. 1915- *WhoAm 90*
Oliver, Allen Mennell 1939- *St&PR 91*
Oliver, Anthony 1922- *TwCCr&M 91*
Oliver, Anthony David 1940- *BiDrAPA 89*
Oliver, Bill *BioIn 16*
Oliver, Bob 1943- *Ballpl 90*
Oliver, Bobbie 1949- *WhoAmA 91*
Oliver, Bonnie Bondurant 1933- *WhoAmW 91, WhoWor 91*
Oliver, Bonnie Kliscz 1944- *WhoAmW 91*
Oliver, Bruce Lawrence 1951- *WhoE 91*
Oliver, Burton *AuBYP 90*
Oliver, Byron D. 1942- *St&PR 91*
Oliver, Carla Rae 1947- *WhoAmW 91*
Oliver, Chad 1928- *RGTwCSF*
Oliver, Clifton, Jr. 1915- *WhoSSW 91*
Oliver, Craig *BioIn 16*
Oliver, Dale Hugh 1947- *WhoEmL 91*
Oliver, Daniel 1939- *WhoAm 90*
Oliver, David *BioIn 16*
Oliver, David 1958- *St&PR 91*
Oliver, David Field 1952- *WhoEmL 91*
Oliver, David Rogers, Jr. 1941- *WhoAm 90*
Oliver, Denise A *WhoAmW 91*
Oliver, Diann 1951- *WhoAmW 91*
Oliver, Don L. 1943- *St&PR 91*
Oliver, Donald Lynn 1936- *WhoAm 90*
Oliver, Doug *BioIn 16*
Oliver, Eddy Glenn 1957- *WhoEmL 91*
Oliver, Edith *BioIn 16*
Oliver, Edith 1913- *NotWoAT*
Oliver, Edna May 1883-1942 *WorAlBi*
Oliver, Edward Carl 1930- *St&PR 91*
Oliver, Elena 1942- *WhoHisp 91*
Oliver, Elizabeth Kimball 1918- *WhoAmW 91*
Oliver, Fernando 1949- *WhoHisp 91*
Oliver, Gene 1935- *Ballpl 90*
Oliver, George Benjamin 1938- *WhoAm 90*
Oliver, George Joseph 1947- *WhoEmL 91*
Oliver, George L. 1929- *St&PR 91*
Oliver, Harold Hunter 1930- *WhoWor 91*
Oliver, Harry Maynard, Jr. 1921- *WhoAm 90*
Oliver, Heath 1930- *St&PR 91*
Oliver, Helen Theresa 1949- *WhoAmW 91*
Oliver, Herman 1929- *BiDrAPA 89*
Oliver, Isaac 1560?-1617? *IntDcAA 90*
Oliver, Jack Ertle 1923- *WhoAm 90, WhoE 91*
Oliver, James Willard 1912- *WhoAm 90*
Oliver, Jane *AuBYP 90*
Oliver, Joe 1885-1938 *OxCPMus*
Oliver, Joe Hicks *BiDrAPA 89*
Oliver, John Edward 1951- *WhoWor 91*
Oliver, John Herbert 1934- *St&PR 91*
Oliver, John Jacob, Jr. 1945- *St&PR 91*
Oliver, John Lee 1937- *WhoAm 90*
Oliver, John Preston 1934- *WhoAm 90*
Oliver, John W. 1914-1990 *BioIn 16*
Oliver, Joseph 1885-1938 *BioIn 16*
Oliver, Joyce Anne 1958- *WhoAmW 91, WhoEmL 91, WhoWor 91*
Oliver, Kermit *BioIn 16*
Oliver, King 1885-1938 *BioIn 16, DrBIPA 90, WorAlBi*
Oliver, Larry Kenneth 1939- *St&PR 91*
Oliver, Lisi 1951- *IntWWM 90*
Oliver, Louis *BioIn 16*
Oliver, M. Leon 1943- *St&PR 91*
Oliver, Marguerite Bertoni 1929- *WhoAmW 91*
Oliver, Maria Antonia 1946- *EncCoWW*
Oliver, Mark A. 1958- *St&PR 91*
Oliver, Marvin E *WhoAmA 91*
Oliver, Mary 1935- *WhoAm 90, WhoWrEP 89, WorAu 1980 [port]*
Oliver, Mary Wilhelmina 1919- *WhoAm 90*
Oliver, Melvin James 1910-1988 *BioIn 16*
Oliver, Michael Kelway 1925- *WhoAm 90*
Oliver, Nate 1940- *Ballpl 90*
Oliver, Orson 1943- *St&PR 91*
Oliver, Patricia Leanene 1938- *WhoAmW 91*
Oliver, Ralph David 1958- *St&PR 91*
Oliver, Raymond *NewYTBS 90 [port]*
Oliver, Raymond 1909-1990 *ConAu 132*
Oliver, Raymond Davies 1936- *WhoAm 90*
Oliver, Richard Bruce 1942-1983 *WhoAmA 91N*
Oliver, Richard Wayne 1943- *BiDrAPA 89*
Oliver, Robert 1930- *WhoWor 91*
Oliver, Robert Bruce 1931- *WhoAm 90*
Oliver, Robert Warner 1922- *WhoAm 90*
Oliver, Roger Meredith 1948- *WhoSSW 91*
Oliver, Roland Anthony *BioIn 16*
Oliver, Roland Anthony 1923- *WhoWor 91*
Oliver, Rose Warshaw 1910- *WhoAmW 91, WhoWor 91*
Oliver, Rupert *AuBYP 90*
Oliver, Ruth Ann 1949- *St&PR 91*
Oliver, Sandra 1941- *WhoAmA 91*
Oliver, Sharlyn Chyrel 1948- *WhoAmW 91*
Oliver, Stephen 1950- *IntWWM 90, PenDiMP A*
Oliver, Steven Wiles 1947- *WhoWor 91*
Oliver, Susan *BioIn 16, NewYTBS 90*
Oliver, Susan Jane 1944- *BiDrAPA 89*
Oliver, Sy 1910-1988 *AnObit 1988, BioIn 16, DrBIPA 90, OxCPMus*
Oliver, Terry James 1949- *WhoSSW 91*
Oliver, Thelma *DrBIPA 90*
Oliver, Thomas Anthony 1937- *St&PR 91*
Oliver, Thomas Mitchell, Jr. 1939- *WhoSSW 91*
Oliver, Thomas R. 1941- *St&PR 91*
Oliver, Thomas Sherman 1932- *WhoE 91*
Oliver, Thomas William 1939- *WhoAm 90*
Oliver, Tom 1903-1988 *Ballpl 90*
Oliver, W. Thomas 1942- *St&PR 91*
Oliver, Walter Maurice 1945- *St&PR 91*
Oliver, William Albert, Jr. 1926- *WhoAm 90*
Oliver, William H. 1942- *ODwPR 91, St&PR 91*
Oliver, William John 1925- *WhoAm 90*
Oliver, Wrenshall A *BiDrAPA 89*
Oliver-Pickett, Cheryl Kay 1949- *WhoWrEP 89*
Oliver-Smith, Richard W *BiDrAPA 89*
Olivera, Armando Juan 1949- *St&PR 91*
Olivera, Arturo A 1929- *BiDrAPA 89*
Olivera, Beatriz Maria 1956- *WhoHisp 91*
Olivera, Gerardo Francisco *BiDrAPA 89*
Olivera, Mercedes 1948- *WhoHisp 91*
Oliveras, Rene Martin 1943- *WhoHisp 91*
Oliverez, Manuel *WhoHisp 91*
Oliverez, Manuel Antonio 1959- *WhoSSW 91*
Oliveri, Robert Peter 1942- *WhoE 91*
Oliverio, Alfred P. 1927- *St&PR 91*
Oliverio, Antoinette Frances 1948- *WhoAmW 91*
Oliverio, Donald A. *St&PR 91*
Oliverio, William J. 1938- *St&PR 91*
Olivero, Alberto 1952- *IntWWM 90*
Olivero, Magda 1912- *IntWWM 90, PenDiMP*
Oliveros, Gilda C. 1949- *WhoHisp 91*
Oliveros, Pauline 1932- *IntWWM 90, WhoAm 90*
Oliveto, Eugene C 1941- *BiDrAPA 89*
Oliveto, Frank Louis 1956- *WhoSSW 91*
Olivia, William Brian 1960- *WhoSSW 91*
Olivier, Lord 1907-1989 *AnObit 1989*
Olivier, Adolphus *AmLegL*
Olivier, Donald Andrew 1931- *St&PR 91*
Olivier, Edith 1872-1948 *BioIn 16*
Olivier, Henri Gaston 1954- *WhoSSW 91*
Olivier, Henry R 1930- *BiDrAPA 89*
Olivier, Jason Thomas 1961- *WhoEmL 91, WhoSSW 91*
Olivier, Jean Claude 1936- *WhoWor 91*
Olivier, Laurence 1907-1989 *BioIn 16, ConAu 129, ConTFT 8 [port], WorAlBi*
Olivier, Nancy 1954- *WhoAmW 91*
Oliviera, Nathan *WhoAm 90*
Olivieri, Anthony G. 1934- *St&PR 91*
Olivieri, Daniel Wayne *BiDrAPA 89*
Olivieri, Luis Arturo 1937- *IntWWM 90*
Olivieri, Tom 1965- *BioIn 16*
Olivo, Chi Chi 1926-1977 *Ballpl 90*
Olivo, Diomedes 1919-1977 *Ballpl 90*
Olivo, Efren 1936- *WhoHisp 91*
Olivos, Guillermo D. 1929- *BiDrAPA 89*
Oliwa, Wlodzimierz 1924-1989 *BioIn 16*
Olkhovsky, Paul George 1960- *WhoE 91*
Olkinetzky, Sam 1919- *WhoAm 90, WhoAmA 91*
Olkkola, Judith A. 1948- *WhoAmW 91*
Olko, Robert Steven *BiDrAPA 89*
Olkowska, Krystyna Maria Nardelli 1939- *WhoAm 90*
Ollari, Frank Joseph 1946- *St&PR 91*
Olleman, Roger Dean 1923- *WhoAm 90*
Ollen, Richard Albin 1932- *St&PR 91*
Oller, Anna Kathryn 1916- *WhoAm 90*
Oller, Charles I *BiDrAPA 89*
Oller, Lars-Erik 1939- *WhoWor 91*
Oller, William Maxwell 1924- *WhoAm 90*
Ollers, Edvin 1888-1959 *PenDiDA 89*
Olleson, Edward 1937- *IntWWM 90*
Ollestad, Melvin E. 1942- *St&PR 91*
Ollett, Frederick Beatty, III 1948- *WhoAm 90*
Olley, Randy Isabelle 1946- *WhoE 91*
Olley, Robert Edward 1933- *WhoAm 90*
Ollicot 1845?-1877 *WhNaAH*
Ollikut 1845?-1877 *WhNaAH*
Ollila, Leo W. 1916- *St&PR 91*
Olling, Hans 1954- *WhoWor 91*
Ollis, Johnny R. 1942- *St&PR 91*
Ollis, Linda Neu 1952- *WhoAmW 91*
Ollivier, Francois *PenDiDA 89*
Ollivier, Jacques *PenDiDA 89*
Ollivier, Sophie Paule 1927- *WhoWor 91*
Ollman, Arthur *BioIn 16*
Ollman, Arthur L 1947- *WhoAmA 91*
Ollman, Arthur Lee 1947- *WhoAm 90*
Ollmann, Robert Raymond 1931- *St&PR 91*
Ollodart, Robert M *BiDrAPA 89*

Ollokot 1845?-1877 WhNaAH
Ollokut 1845?-1877 WhNaAH
Ollongren, Alexander Alexandrovich 1928- WhoWor 91
Ollor, Walter Gbute 1950- WhoEmL 91, WhoWor 91
Olman, Abe 1888-1984 BioIn 16, OxCPMus
Olman, Maryellen 1946- WhoAmW 91
Olmedo, Jose C 1922- BiDrAPA 89
Olmedo, Kim Ellen 1959- WhoAmW 91
Olmedo, Mario Ernesto 1955- St&PR 91
Olmedo-Borecky, Stephanie Kathryn 1950- WhoAmW 91
Olmer, Henry 1887-1950 WhoAmA 91N
Olmer, Lionel Herbert 1934- WhoAm 90
Olmes, Donald Marinus 1950- WhoE 91
Olmi, Becky B. 1951- St&PR 91
Olmi, Ermanno 1931- BioIn 16, ConTFT 8
Olmi, Urban A. 1952- St&PR 91
Ol'minskii, M. 1863-1933 BioIn 16
Olmo, Jaime Alberto 1930- WhoSSW 91, WhoWor 91
Olmo, Luis 1919- Ballpl 90
Olmos, Antonio Garcia 1963- WhoHisp 91
Olmos, David R. 1957- WhoHisp 91
Olmos, Edward James BioIn 16, WhoAm 90
Olmos, Edward James 1947- News 90 [port], WhoHisp 91
Olmstead, Cecil Jay 1920- WhoAm 90
Olmstead, David 1943- WhoAm 90
Olmstead, Francis Henry, Jr. 1938- WhoAm 90
Olmstead, Fred 1883-1936 Ballpl 90
Olmstead, Gary Eugene 1956- St&PR 91
Olmstead, Harold M. BioIn 16
Olmstead, Paul Smith 1897- WhoSSW 91
Olmstead, Robert 1954- ConAu 129
Olmstead, Steven W. 1951- St&PR 91
Olmstead, William Edward 1936- WhoAm 90
Olmstead, Williard G. 1944- St&PR 91
Olmsted, Arthur George 1827-1914 AmLegL
Olmsted, Frederick Law 1822-1903 WorAlBi
Olmsted, George Hamden 1901- WhoAm 90
Olmsted, Jerauld Lockwood 1938- WhoAm 90
Olmsted, Joanna Belle 1947- WhoAmW 91
Olmsted, Katherine M 1888-1964 BioIn 16
Olmsted, Martha Ann 1941- WhoSSW 91
Olmsted, Mary Catherine 1959- BiDrAPA 89
Olmsted, Mildred Scott WhoAm 90
Olmsted, Mildred Scott NewYTBS 90
Olmsted, Richard Raymond 1938- WhoAm 90
Olmsted, Robert Walsh 1936- WhoWrEP 89
Olmsted, Sterling Pitkin 1915- WhoAm 90
Olmsted, Suzanne M 1956- WhoAmA 91
Olmsted, Thomas Russell BiDrAPA 89
Olney, James 1933- WhoAm 90, WhoWrEP 89
Olney, John William 1931- BiDrAPA 89
Olney, Martha Louise 1956- WhoE 91
Olney, Nigel BioIn 16
Olney, Richard 1835-1917 BiDrUSE 89, BioIn 16
Olney, Robert C. 1926- WhoAm 90
Olney, Ross R. 1929- AuBYP 90
Olofson, Tom William 1941- WhoAm 90
Olofsson, Georg DcScanL
Olofsson, Klas Tuve 1943- WhoWor 91
O'Lone, Joseph P 1923- BiDrAPA 89
O'Looney, Patricia Anne 1954- WhoAmW 91
Olorunsola, Victor Adeola 1939- WhoAm 90
Olotacara WhNaAH
Olotaraca WhNaAH
Olotoraca WhNaAH
O'Loughlin, Dennis Patrick 1947- St&PR 91
O'Loughlin, Earl T. 1930- WhoAm 90
O'Loughlin, John Kirby 1929- St&PR 91, WhoAm 90
O'Loughlin, Maurice Edwin James 1922- WhoAm 90
O'Loughlin, Silk Ballpl 90
Olowin, Mary Dreisbach BiDrAPA 89
Olowu, Elizabeth BioIn 16
Olpin, Owen 1934- WhoAm 90
Olpin, Robert Spencer 1940- WhoAmA 91
Olrog Hedvall, Yvonne Elisabeth 1939- WhoWor 91
Olschwang, Alan Paul 1942- WhoAm 90, WhoE 91, WhoWor 91
Olsder, Geert Jan 1944- WhoWor 91
Olsen, Alfred Jon 1940- WhoAm 90
Olsen, Allen Richard 1940- St&PR 91
Olsen, Alvin Gordon 1927- WhoAm 90
Olsen, Andy 1931- Ballpl 90
Olsen, Arnold 1916- WhoWor 91
Olsen, Arthur Martin 1909- WhoAm 90
Olsen, Arthur Robert 1910- WhoWor 91
Olsen, August B. St&PR 91
Olsen, Bengt 1959- WhoWor 91
Olsen, Betty Ann 1934-1968 BioIn 16
Olsen, Bobby Gene 1951- WhoSSW 91
Olsen, Brian W. 1952- St&PR 91
Olsen, Byron Donn 1934- St&PR 91
Olsen, Carl Edwin 1902- WhoWor 91
Olsen, Charles J. 1951- St&PR 91
Olsen, Charles T 1938- BiDrAPA 89
Olsen, D. B. 1907-1973 TwCCr&M 91
Olsen, Daniel Paul 1952- WhoEmL 91
Olsen, David Alexander 1937- St&PR 91
Olsen, David George 1941- WhoE 91
Olsen, Donald Bert 1930- WhoAm 90
Olsen, Donald D. 1931- WhoWrEP 89
Olsen, Donald Emmanuel 1919- WhoAm 90, WhoWor 91
Olsen, Douglas Marc 1957- WhoE 91
Olsen, Edward Gustave 1908- WhoAm 90
Olsen, Edward H, Jr. BiDrAPA 89
Olsen, Edward John 1927- WhoAm 90
Olsen, Edwin Joseph 1942- BiDrAPA 89
Olsen, Erik Ronald 1963- WhoSSW 91
Olsen, Ernest Moran 1910- WhoAmA 91
Olsen, Francis Richard 1933- WhoAm 90
Olsen, Frederick L 1938- WhoAmA 91
Olsen, Frederick Milton 1930- St&PR 91
Olsen, George 1893-1971 OxCPMus
Olsen, George Allen 1928- St&PR 91
Olsen, George David 1940- St&PR 91
Olsen, Gregg 1966- Ballpl 90
Olsen, Gregory W. 1954- St&PR 91
Olsen, Hans L. 1944- St&PR 91
Olsen, Hans Peter 1940- WhoAm 90
Olsen, Harold Fremont 1920- WhoAm 90
Olsen, Harris Leland 1947- WhoEmL 91
Olsen, Herb 1905-1973 WhoAmA 91N
Olsen, Homer Edward BiDrAPA 89
Olsen, Humphrey Adoniram 1909- WhoWrEP 89
Olsen, Inger Anna 1926- WhoAmW 91
Olsen, Jack 1925- WhoAm 90
Olsen, James C. 1935- St&PR 91
Olsen, John Alvin 1938- St&PR 91
Olsen, John Brian 1942- St&PR 91
Olsen, John J. EncACom
Olsen, John Robert 1928- St&PR 91
Olsen, John Stuart 1950- WhoSSW 91
Olsen, Jorn C. 1949- St&PR 91
Olsen, Kai 1933- WhoWor 91
Olsen, Kenneth H. BioIn 16
Olsen, Kenneth H. 1926- St&PR 91
Olsen, Kenneth Harry 1926- WhoAm 90, WhoE 91
Olsen, Kenneth Harry 1928- ConAmBL
Olsen, Kenneth O. 1918- St&PR 91
Olsen, Kurt H. 1924- WhoAm 90
Olsen, Laurie ODwPR 91
Olsen, Lawrence G. 1941- St&PR 91
Olsen, Leif H. 1926- St&PR 91
Olsen, Lynne BioIn 16
Olsen, Margaret Ann 1944- WhoWor 91
Olsen, Mari K. ODwPR 91
Olsen, Marilyn B. 1944- ODwPR 91
Olsen, Marvin Elliott 1936- WhoAm 90
Olsen, Melvin E. 1943- St&PR 91
Olsen, Merlin 1940- ConTFT 8 [port], WorAlBi
Olsen, Michael J. 1950- ODwPR 91
Olsen, Miriam Gladys 1923- WhoAmW 91
Olsen, Niels-Erik 1948- WhoWor 91
Olsen, Olaf 1928- WhoWor 91
Olsen, Ole 1892-1963 BioIn 16
Olsen, Paul E. BioIn 16
Olsen, Ray 1937- St&PR 91
Olsen, Rex E. 1935- WhoSSW 91
Olsen, Rex Norman 1925- WhoAm 90
Olsen, Richard Ellison 1941- WhoWrEP 89
Olsen, Richard Galen 1945- WhoSSW 91
Olsen, Richard George 1937- WhoAm 90
Olsen, Richard J. 1938- ODwPR 91
Olsen, Richard James 1938- St&PR 91
Olsen, Richard Leon 1942- BiDrAPA 89
Olsen, Robert B 1945- BiDrAPA 89
Olsen, Robert E. BioIn 16
Olsen, Robert John 1928- WhoE 91, WhoWor 91
Olsen, Roger Milton 1942- WhoAm 90
Olsen, Suzanne 1944- WhoAmW 91
Olsen, Theodore Alan 1953- WhoEmL 91
Olsen, Tillie 1912- WhoAm 90, WhoWrEP 89
Olsen, Tillie 1913- EncAL, FemiCLE, MajTwCW
Olsen, Vern 1918- Ballpl 90
Olsen, Violet 1922- BioIn 16
Olsen, Wanda B BiDrAPA 89
Olsen, William E. 1928- St&PR 91
Olsen Bergman, Ciel 1938- WhoAmA 91
Olsen-Fulero, Lynda Laverne 1947- WhoAmW 91
Olsen-Stenglein, Karen Marie 1953- WhoAmW 91
Olseth, Dale R. 1930- St&PR 91
Olshaker, Bennett 1921- BiDrAPA 89
Olshan, Bernard 1921- WhoAmA 91
Olshan, Karen BioIn 16, WhoAmW 91
Olshan, Kenneth S. 1932- St&PR 91, WhoAm 90
Olshan-Cooper, Debra ODwPR 91
Olshansky, Donald H. 1931- WhoE 91
Olshen, Abraham Charles 1913- St&PR 91
Olshen, Paul Robert 1938- WhoE 91
Olshin, Arnold S. 1940- St&PR 91
Olshonsky, Jay Benjamin 1960- WhoE 91
Olshwanger, Ron BioIn 16
Olsinski, Peter Kevin 1942- WhoE 91
Olsman, Robert C. 1945- St&PR 91
Olson, Alfred E. 1939- St&PR 91
Olson, Allan S. 1941- St&PR 91
Olson, Barbara Jeannette Sloan 1950- WhoSSW 91
Olson, Barbara Martha 1943- WhoAmW 91
Olson, Bettye Johnson 1923- WhoAmA 91
Olson, Bob Moody 1934- WhoAm 90
Olson, Bonnie Breternitz-Waggoner WhoAmW 91, WhoE 91, WhoWor 91
Olson, Bonnie Lee BiDrAPA 89
Olson, Bruce Joseph 1949- St&PR 91
Olson, Carl Eric 1914- WhoE 91, WhoWor 91
Olson, Carolyn Healey 1958- ODwPR 91
Olson, Charles 1910-1970 BioIn 16, MajTwCW
Olson, Charles Eric 1942- WhoE 91
Olson, Charles J. 1945- WhoSSW 91, WhoWor 91
Olson, Charles Lindbergh 1928- St&PR 91, WhoAm 90
Olson, Clarence Elmer, Jr. 1927- WhoAm 90, WhoWrEP 89
Olson, Clayton Leo 1947- WhoWrEP 89
Olson, Clifford Larry 1946- WhoAm 90, WhoEmL 91
Olson, Clinton Louis 1916- WhoAm 90
Olson, Clyde R BiDrAPA 89
Olson, Craig Alan 1960- WhoWor 91
Olson, Craig William 1956- WhoWor 91
Olson, D. Joseph 1941- St&PR 91
Olson, Dale C. 1934- ODwPR 91, WhoAm 90
Olson, Dan Arnold 1957- St&PR 91
Olson, David 1950- ODwPR 91
Olson, David Edwin, Sr. BiDrAPA 89
Olson, David Henry 1933- WhoAm 90
Olson, David Herman 1940- WhoAm 90
Olson, David John 1941- WhoAm 90
Olson, David Mark BiDrAPA 89
Olson, David Ramon 1953- BiDrAPA 89
Olson, David W. ODwPR 91
Olson, Del ODwPR 91
Olson, Diana Craft 1941- WhoAmW 91
Olson, Donald Ernest 1921- WhoAm 90
Olson, Donald Eugene 1934- St&PR 91
Olson, Donald George 1941- WhoWor 91
Olson, Donald Richard 1917- WhoAm 90
Olson, Donald W. 1934- St&PR 91
Olson, Donna Rae 1947- WhoAmW 91
Olson, Dorise Evelyn 1932- WhoAmW 91
Olson, Dorothy May 1938- WhoAmW 91
Olson, Douglas John 1934- WhoAmA 91
Olson, E.K. St&PR 91
Olson, Earl B. WhoAm 90
Olson, Edmund E. 1945- St&PR 91
Olson, Edwin W. BioIn 16
Olson, Elder 1909- BioIn 16, ConAu 31NR, ConAu 12AS [port]
Olson, Elder James 1909- WhoAm 90
Olson, Elizabeth Jeanette 1951- WhoAmW 91
Olson, Eric Ellis 1949- WhoSSW 91
Olson, Ernest Leroy 1916- WhoAm 90
Olson, Eugene R. 1926- St&PR 91
Olson, Eugene Rudolph 1926- WhoAm 90
Olson, Everett Claire 1910- WhoAm 90
Olson, Frances P BiDrAPA 89
Olson, Frank Albert 1932- St&PR 91
Olson, Frederick Irving 1916- WhoAm 90
Olson, Gary Carl 1944- BiDrAPA 89
Olson, Gen 1938- WhoAmW 91
Olson, Gene 1922- AuBYP 90
Olson, Gene Russel 1949- WhoAmA 91
Olson, George E. 1937- St&PR 91
Olson, Gerald L. 1933- WhoAm 90
Olson, Gilbert Arthur 1925- St&PR 91
Olson, Gordon Bennie 1924- WhoAm 90
Olson, Gordon D. 1927- St&PR 91
Olson, Gordon Eugene 1944- WhoE 91
Olson, Harold Roy 1928- WhoE 91
Olson, Harry Andrew, Jr. 1923- St&PR 91, WhoAm 90
Olson, Helen Kronberg BioIn 16
Olson, Hilding Harold 1916- WhoAm 90
Olson, Ivy 1885-1965 Ballpl 90
Olson, Jack B. 1920- WhoAm 90
Olson, Jack Francis 1925- WhoAm 90
Olson, James Chester 1907- WhoAm 90
Olson, James Clifton 1917- WhoAm 90
Olson, James E. 1925-1988 BioIn 16
Olson, James R. 1941- ODwPR 91
Olson, James Richard 1941- WhoAm 90
Olson, James Robert 1940- WhoAm 90, WhoE 91, WhoWor 91
Olson, James Wallace 1947- WhoE 91
Olson, Jane Virginia 1916- WhoAm 90, WhoWrEP 89
Olson, Janice Lynn 1946- WhoAmW 91
Olson, Jay Raymond 1933- St&PR 91
Olson, Jeannine Evelyn WhoAmW 91
Olson, Jeffry Olav 1942- St&PR 91
Olson, John 1941- St&PR 91
Olson, John Blake 1943- WhoSSW 91
Olson, John Charles 1948- BiDrAPA 89
Olson, John Frederick 1939- WhoAm 90, WhoE 91, WhoWor 91
Olson, John Melvin 1929- WhoWor 91
Olson, John Victor 1913- WhoAm 90
Olson, Joseph Olaf WhoAmA 91
Olson, Joseph Robert 1935- St&PR 91
Olson, Judith Mary Reedy 1939- WhoAmW 91
Olson, Julie Ann 1957- WhoAmW 91
Olson, Julie Ann 1958- WhoAmW 91
Olson, Julie Eileen 1959- WhoAmW 91
Olson, Karl 1930- Ballpl 90
Olson, Kathy Rae 1950- WhoAmW 91
Olson, Kay Melchisedech 1948- WhoWrEP 89
Olson, Keith Waldemar 1931- WhoAm 90
Olson, Kenneth A. 1955- St&PR 91
Olson, Kenneth Cornell BiDrAPA 89
Olson, Kenneth Paul 1935- WhoWor 91
Olson, Kirby 1956- WhoWrEP 89
Olson, Kurt Andrew BiDrAPA 89
Olson, Larry Arlen 1942- St&PR 91
Olson, Larry Wayne 1952- BiDrAPA 89
Olson, Laura Maxine 1927- WhoWor 91
Olson, Lawrence 1918- WhoAm 90, WhoWrEP 89
Olson, Leroy Calvin 1926- WhoAm 90
Olson, LeRoy Curtis 1943- BiDrAPA 89
Olson, Loren Alva 1943- BiDrAPA 89
Olson, Lynn WhoWrEP 89
Olson, Lynn Freeman 1938-1987 BioIn 16
Olson, Lynnette Gail 1945- WhoEmL 91
Olson, Mancur Lloyd 1932- WhoAm 90
Olson, Marian Edna 1923- WhoAmW 91
Olson, Marian Katherine 1933- WhoAmW 91
Olson, Mark William 1946- WhoWrEP 89
Olson, Maxine 1931- WhoAmA 91
Olson, Melvin E. 1917- St&PR 91
Olson, Michael J. 1953- St&PR 91
Olson, Michael Steven 1944- St&PR 91
Olson, Milton Joseph 1910- St&PR 91
Olson, Nancy Dian BiDrAPA 89
Olson, Nancy Stoddard 1948- St&PR 91
Olson, Norman Fredrick 1931- WhoAm 90
Olson, O. Lars 1942- WhoWor 91
Olson, Paul Richard 1925- WhoAm 90
Olson, Peter Wesley 1950- WhoE 91
Olson, Ramon L. 1926- St&PR 91
Olson, Randall J. 1947- WhoAm 90
Olson, Rex Melton 1940- WhoSSW 91
Olson, Richard C. ODwPR 91
Olson, Richard David 1944- WhoAm 90
Olson, Richard Dean 1949- WhoAm 90, WhoEmL 91, WhoWor 91
Olson, Richard F. 1927- St&PR 91
Olson, Richard George 1940- WhoAm 90, WhoWrEP 89
Olson, Richard Gustave 1959- WhoE 91
Olson, Richard H. 1925- St&PR 91
Olson, Richard W 1938- WhoAmA 91
Olson, Rick 1950- WhoAmA 91
Olson, Robert WhoSSW 91
Olson, Robert A. BioIn 16
Olson, Robert A. 1933- St&PR 91
Olson, Robert E. 1940- St&PR 91
Olson, Robert Edward 1927- WhoAm 90
Olson, Robert Eugene 1919- WhoAm 90
Olson, Robert Goodwin 1924- WhoAm 90
Olson, Robert Henry 1946- IntWWM 90
Olson, Robert Howard 1934- WhoE 91
Olson, Robert Leonard 1930- WhoAm 90
Olson, Robert Louis 1933- St&PR 91
Olson, Robert Nolan 1937- BiDrAPA 89
Olson, Robert Stanley 1925- St&PR 91
Olson, Robert Wallace 1933- IntWWM 90
Olson, Robert Wyrick 1945- St&PR 91, WhoAm 90
Olson, Roberta Jeanne Marie 1947- WhoAmA 91, WhoE 91
Olson, Rodney D. 1951- St&PR 91
Olson, Roger 1935- WhoE 91
Olson, Roger Grove 1935- St&PR 91
Olson, Ronald Dale 1947- WhoAm 90
Olson, Ronald Kenneth 1943- WhoE 91
Olson, Ronald Wayne 1931- WhoAm 90
Olson, Rue Eileen 1928- WhoAmW 91, WhoWor 91
Olson, Russel Einar 1931- WhoAm 90
Olson, Scott Robert 1958- WhoE 91
Olson, Sigmund Lars 1935- WhoAm 90
Olson, Stanley BioIn 16
Olson, Stanley 1948-1989 ConAu 130
Olson, Stanley William 1914- WhoAm 90
Olson, Stephen Craig 1954- BiDrAPA 89
Olson, Stephen Michael 1948- WhoEmL 91
Olson, Susan Jayne BiDrAPA 89

Olson, Sylvester Irwin 1907- *WhoAm 90*
Olson, Terrence Leonard 1953- *WhoSSW 91*
Olson, Theodore Alexander 1904- *WhoAm 90*
Olson, Thomas Edward 1954- *WhoEmL 91*
Olson, Thomas Francis, II 1948- *WhoAm 90*
Olson, Thomas Michael 1946- *St&PR 91*
Olson, Timothy P 1950- *BiDrAPA 89*
Olson, Toby 1937- *ConAu 31NR, WhoWrEP 89*
Olson, Tom *BioIn 16*
Olson, Val 1933- *St&PR 91*
Olson, Walter G. 1924- *St&PR 91*
Olson, Walter Gilbert 1924- *WhoAm 90*
Olson, Walter Justus, Jr. 1941- *WhoAm 90*
Olson, Walter Theodore 1917- *WhoAm 90*
Olson, Warren Russell 1929- *St&PR 91*
Olson, Wayne Charles 1949- *WhoE 91*
Olson, Wilbert Orin 1947- *WhoEmL 91*
Olson, William Clinton 1920- *WhoAm 90*
Olson, William F. 1928- *St&PR 91*
Olson, William Furman 1928- *WhoAm 90*
Olson, William Henry 1936- *WhoAm 90*
Olson, William Jeffrey 1949- *WhoE 91*
Olsson, Carl Alfred 1938- *WhoAm 90*
Olsson, Curt Gunnar 1927- *WhoWor 91*
Olsson, Curt Olof 1919- *WhoWor 91*
Olsson, Eva Birgitta 1948- *WhoWor 91*
Olsson, Gunnar 1921- *WhoWor 91*
Olsson, Hagar 1893-1978 *DcScanL, EncCoWW*
Olsson, Nils William 1909- *WhoAm 90*
Olsson, Pamela Nicholson *BiDrAPA 89*
Olsson, Peter Alan 1941- *BiDrAPA 89*
Olsson, Sture G. 1920- *St&PR 91*
Olsson, Sture Gordon 1920- *WhoAm 90, WhoSSW 91*
Olstad, Roger Gale 1934- *WhoAm 90*
Olstad, Walter Ballard 1932- *WhoAm 90*
Olsten, Stuart *WhoAm 90*
Olsten, William 1919- *St&PR 91, WhoAm 90*
Olston, Mary Kay 1949- *WhoEmL 91*
Olstowski, Franciszek 1927- *WhoSSW 91, WhoWor 91*
Olszak, Daniel Dominic 1947- *WhoEmL 91*
Olszamowski, Slawomir 1953- *IntWWM 90*
Olszewska, Maria 1892-1969 *PenDiMP*
Olszewski, Deborah D. 1950- *WhoAmW 91*
Olszewski, Edward Paul 1930- *St&PR 91*
Olszewski, Gerald B. *ODwPR 91*
Olszewski, Kevin Trent 1957- *WhoEmL 91*
Olszewski, Laurence Michael 1938- *WhoE 91*
Olszewski, Lawrence J. 1947- *WhoEmL 91*
Olszewski, Liliana 1965- *WhoHisp 91*
Olszewski, Rick Allen 1948- *St&PR 91*
Olszewski, Walter A *BiDrAPA 89*
Olsztynski, James C. 1947- *WhoWrEP 89*
Oltman, C. Dwight 1936- *WhoAm 90*
Oltman, Elizabeth Ann 1963- *WhoAmW 91*
Oltman, Henry George, Jr. 1927- *WhoAm 90*
Oltman, James H. 1930- *St&PR 91*
Oltman, James Harvey 1930- *WhoAm 90*
Oltmanns, Robert J. 1957- *ODwPR 91*
Olton, Roy 1922- *WhoAm 90*
Oltrogge, Cal G. 1945- *WhoE 91*
Oltz, Charles H. 1945- *St&PR 91*
Olubadewo, Joseph Olanrewaju 1945- *WhoSSW 91*
Oludimu, Olufemi Ladipo 1951- *WhoWor 91*
Olum, Paul 1918- *WhoAm 90*
Oluwajuyitan, Jide Matthew 1949- *WhoWor 91*
Oluwek, Arthur 1926- *St&PR 91*
Olver, Frank William John 1924- *WhoE 91*
Olvera, Joe 1944- *WhoWrEP 89*
Olvera, Joe E. 1944- *WhoHisp 91*
Olvera, Jose Jesus 1935- *WhoHisp 91*
Olvey, Daniel Richard 1948- *St&PR 91*
Olwin, John Hurst 1907- *WhoAm 90*
Olwine, Ed 1958- *Ballpl 90*
Olympia, Josie Lim 1944- *BiDrAPA 89*
Olyphant, David 1936- *WhoAm 90*
Olyschlaeger, Helmut 1950- *St&PR 91*
Olzendam, Harriett Steele 1914- *WhoAmW 91*
Olzman, Saul 1920- *St&PR 91, WhoAm 90*
Om, Wendy 1956- *WhoAmW 91*
O'Maggio, Patrick Bernard 1922- *St&PR 91*
O'Mahoney, Robert M. 1925- *WhoAm 90*
O'Maley, David Boyers 1946- *WhoAm 90*
O'Malley, Alice Theresa 1929- *WhoAmW 91*
O'Malley, Bert William 1936- *WhoAm 90*
O'Malley, Beverly Black *BioIn 16*
O'Malley, Brian Eugene 1938- *St&PR 91*
O'Malley, Brian Richard 1937- *St&PR 91, WhoAm 90*
O'Malley, Carlon Martin 1929- *WhoAm 90*
O'Malley, Charles A. 1917-1989 *BioIn 16*
O'Malley, Charles J. *BioIn 16*
O'Malley, D. J. 1867-1943 *BioIn 16*
O'Malley, Denis Michael 1943- *St&PR 91*
O'Malley, Dominick John 1867-1943 *BioIn 16*
O'Malley, Edward 1926- *WhoAm 90*
O'Malley, Edward P *BiDrAPA 89*
O'Malley, Edward V., Jr. 1929- *St&PR 91*
O'Malley, Eugene F. 1901-1989 *BioIn 16*
O'Malley, Eugene Francis 1950- *WhoE 91, WhoEmL 91, WhoWor 91*
O'Malley, Honor *WhoAmW 91, WhoE 91*
O'Malley, James, Jr. 1910- *WhoAm 90*
O'Malley, James Terence 1950- *WhoEmL 91*
O'Malley, John Daniel 1926- *WhoAm 90*
O'Malley, John E. 1927- *St&PR 91*
O'Malley, John Edward 1942- *BiDrAPA 89, WhoAm 90, WhoE 91, WhoWor 91*
O'Malley, John G., Jr. 1914- *St&PR 91*
O'Malley, Kathleen Ann 1955- *WhoAmW 91*
O'Malley, Kevin Francis 1947- *WhoEmL 91*
O'Malley, Marjorie Glaubach 1950- *WhoAmW 91*
O'Malley, Mary Dolling 1889-1974 *BioIn 16*
O'Malley, Michael John 1954- *WhoEmL 91*
O'Malley, Michael Joseph 1941- *St&PR 91*
O'Malley, Patricia *AuBYP 90*
O'Malley, Patrick L. 1911- *St&PR 91*
O'Malley, Peter 1937- *WhoAm 90*
O'Malley, Robert C. 1925- *St&PR 91*
O'Malley, Robert Edmund, Jr. 1939- *WhoAm 90*
O'Malley, Robert Emmet 1923- *WhoAm 90*
O'Malley, Sean 1944- *WhoAm 90*
O'Malley, Shaun F. *WhoAm 90, WhoE 91*
O'Malley, Suzanne Marie *WhoE 91*
O'Malley, Thomas D. 1941- *WhoAm 90*
O'Malley, Thomas Patrick 1930- *WhoAm 90*
O'Malley, Timothy E. 1966- *WhoEmL 91*
O'Malley, Tom 1960- *Ballpl 90*
O'Malley, W. Gresham, III 1933- *St&PR 91*
O'Malley, Walter 1903-1979 *Ballpl 90*
O'Malley, William Charles 1937- *St&PR 91, WhoSSW 91*
O'Malley, William J 1931- *ConAu 31NR*
Oman and Shanti *NewAgMG*
Oman, Carl R. 1892-1989 *BioIn 16*
Oman, Carola 1897-1978 *FemiCLE*
Oman, Deborah Sue 1948- *WhoAmW 91*
Oman, Elizabeth Ann 1940- *WhoWrEP 89*
Oman, Jack Allen 1939- *St&PR 91*
Oman, Julia Trevelyan 1930- *WhoWor 91*
Oman, LaFel Earl 1912- *WhoAm 90, WhoWor 91*
Oman, Richard Heer 1926- *WhoAm 90*
Oman, Sidney Maynard 1928- *WhoSSW 91*
Oman, Wanda Arline McCamey 1926- *WhoAmW 91*
Omana, Julio Alfredo, Sr. 1938- *WhoHisp 91*
Omang, Joanne Brenda 1943- *WhoAm 90*
Omang, Myrna Louise 1934- *St&PR 91*
Omar Khayyam 1048?-1122 *WorAlBi*
Omar, Margit 1941- *WhoAmA 91*
O'Mara, Catherine Anne 1964- *WhoAmW 91*
O'Mara, Deborah Lynn 1957- *WhoWrEP 89*
O'Mara, Ethel Rose 1920- *WhoE 91*
O'Mara, John Aloysius 1924- *WhoAm 90*
O'Mara, Ollie 1891- *Ballpl 90*
O'Mara, Peggy Noreen 1947- *WhoAmW 91, WhoWrEP 89*
O'Mara, Robert Edmund George 1933- *WhoAm 90*
O'Mara, Stephen Paul 1951- *WhoAm 90*
O'Mara, Thomas George 1929- *St&PR 91*
O'Mara, Thomas Patrick 1937- *St&PR 91, WhoAm 90, WhoWor 91*
O'Marie, Carol Anne *TwCCr&M 91*
Omarr, Sydney *EncO&P 3*
Omatu, Sigeru 1946- *WhoWor 91*
O'May, John Gavin 1947- *WhoWor 91*
Ombres, Teresa 1952- *WhoEmL 91*
Ombu, Claudio *WhoWrEP 89*
Omdahl, Lloyd *WhoAm 90*
O'Mealia, Leo 1884-1960 *Ballpl 90, EncACom [port]*
O'Meallie, Kitty 1916- *WhoAm 90, WhoAmA 91, WhoAmW 91, WhoSSW 91*
O'Meally, Robert G 1948- *ConAu 130*
O'Meally, Serge A. 1939- *St&PR 91*
O'Meara, David Collow 1929- *WhoAm 90*
O'Meara, Edward Francis, Jr. 1942- *WhoSSW 91*
O'Meara, James Joseph 1946- *St&PR 91*
O'Meara, John Corbett 1933- *WhoAm 90*
O'Meara, Kathleen 1839-1888 *FemiCLE*
O'Meara, Onorato Timothy 1928- *WhoAm 90*
O'Meara, Patrick O. 1938- *WhoAm 90*
O'Meara, Raymond E. 1949- *St&PR 91*
O'Meara, Terence C 1929- *BiDrAPA 89*
O'Meara, Thomas Franklin 1935- *WhoAm 90*
O'Meara, Walter 1897-1989 *BioIn 16, ConAu 129*
O'Melia, Charles Richard 1934- *WhoAm 90*
O'Melia, Kevin M. 1944- *St&PR 91*
O'Mell, Herbert Sidney 1935- *WhoSSW 91*
Omelsky, Paul Theodore 1943- *BiDrAPA 89*
Omenn, Gilbert Stanley 1941- *WhoAm 90*
Omer, George Elbert, Jr. 1922- *WhoAm 90*
Omer, Osama L M 1943- *BiDrAPA 89*
Omez, Reginald 1895- *EncO&P 3*
Omholt, Bruce Donald 1943- *WhoWor 91*
Omidian, Bahram *BiDrAPA 89*
Omilian, Karen Lee *BiDrAPA 89*
Ominayak, Bernard *BioIn 16*
Ominski, Steve 1952- *BioIn 16*
Ominsky, Alan Jay *BiDrAPA 89*
Ominsky, Harris 1932- *WhoAm 90*
Omland, Tov 1923- *WhoWor 91*
Omlid, Harlan Hauser 1926- *BiDrAPA 89*
Omlor, John Joseph 1935- *WhoAm 90*
Ommaya, Ayub Khan 1930- *WhoAm 90, WhoWor 91*
Ommen, Joke van 1948-1988 *BioIn 16*
Ommodt, Donald Henry 1931- *St&PR 91, WhoAm 90*
Omnell, Karl-Ake *WhoAm 90*
Omohundro, Joseph Roger 1910- *WhoE 91*
Omoiele, Marna Tambura 1948- *WhoWor 91*
Omole, Gabriel Gbolabo 1940- *WhoWor 91*
O'Morain, Sean *WhoWrEP 89*
O'Morchoe, Charles Christopher Creagh 1931- *WhoAm 90*
O'Morchoe, Patricia Jean 1930- *WhoAmW 91*
omowale maxwell, marina ama 1934- *FemiCLE*
Omrani, Shahriar *BiDrAPA 89*
Oms, Alex *Ballpl 90*
Omura, George Adolf 1938- *WhoAm 90*
Omura, James Matsumoto 1912- *WhoWrEP 89*
Omura, Jimmy Kazuhiro 1940- *WhoAm 90*
Omura, Keiichi 1949- *WhoWor 91*
Omurtag, Yildirim 1939- *WhoAm 90*
Omwake, Eo, Jr 1946- *WhoAmA 91*
On Wings of Sound *NewAgMG*
Ona, Celia Mercado *BiDrAPA 89*
Ona, Pedro de 1570-1643? *BioIn 16*
Ona-Sarino, Milagros Felix 1940- *WhoAmW 91, WhoSSW 91, WhoWor 91*
Onady, Alice Amy 1951- *BiDrAPA 89*
Onaga, Corinne Yurie 1952- *WhoAmW 91*
Onak, Thomas Philip 1932- *WhoAm 90*
O'Nan, Martha 1921- *WhoAm 90, WhoWor 91*
Onassis, Aristotle 1906-1975 *WorAlBi*
Onassis, Christina *BioIn 16*
Onassis, Christina 1950-1988 *AnObit 1988*
Onassis, Jacqueline Bouvier Kennedy 1929- *WhoAmW 91, WorAlBi*
Onassis, Jacqueline K. *BioAmW*
Onassis, Jacqueline Kennedy *BioIn 16*
Onate, Claro Orfanel 1940- *BiDrAPA 89*
Onate, Juan De 1549?-1624? *EncCRAm*
Onate, Juan De 1550?-1624? *WhNaAH*
Onate, Santiago 1949- *WhoWor 91*
Oncina, Juan 1925- *IntWWM 90*
Oncken, Clara *AuBYP 90*
Oncken, Henry Kuck 1938- *WhoAm 90*
Oncken, Johann Gerhard 1800-1884 *BioIn 16*
Oncley, John Lawrence 1910- *WhoAm 90*
Onda, Akira 1925- *EncPaPR 91*
Onda, Yutaka 1934- *St&PR 91*
Ondaatje, Christopher *BioIn 16*
Ondaatje, Michael 1943- *BioIn 16, WhoWrEP 89*
Onder, Sevket Yuksel 1936- *WhoWor 91*
Onderdonk, John Adrian 1934-1990 *BioIn 16*
Onderdonk, Julian 1882-1922 *BioIn 16*
Onderdonk, Patricia R. 1950- *ODwPR 91*
Onderdonk, Robert Jenkins 1852?-1917 *BioIn 16*
Onderdonk, Stephen Richter 1944- *St&PR 91*
Onderko, Gregory John *BiDrAPA 89*
Ondersma, David M. 1942- *St&PR 91*
Ondrack, Esther Signe 1940- *St&PR 91*
Ondrejovich, Michael Paul *WhoE 91*
Ondricek, Frantisek 1857-1922 *PenDiMP*
Ondricek, Jan 1832-1900 *PenDiMP*
Ondrusek, David Francis 1955- *WhoSSW 91*
One, Ernest 1929- *St&PR 91*
O'Neal, Carole Kelley 1933- *WhoAmW 91*
O'Neal, Cathy Lynn 1955- *WhoSSW 91, WhoWrEP 89*
O'Neal, Charles E. 1950- *St&PR 91*
O'Neal, Cynthia Marie Engler 1964- *WhoEmL 91*
O'Neal, David Cortland 1937- *WhoAm 90*
O'Neal, Dianne Wiggins 1954- *WhoSSW 91*
O'Neal, Don 1939- *ODwPR 91*
O'Neal, Dorothy Decker 1923- *WhoAmW 91*
O'Neal, Edgar Carl 1939- *WhoAm 90*
O'Neal, Edward A. 1944- *St&PR 91*
Oneal, Elizabeth 1934- *BioIn 16*
O'Neal, Emmet 1921- *St&PR 91*
O'Neal, Frank *EncACom*
O'Neal, Frederick 1905- *DrBlPA 90, WhoAm 90*
O'Neal, Gary R. 1951- *St&PR 91*
Oneal, Glen, Jr. 1917- *WhoE 91, WhoWor 91*
O'Neal, Griffin *BioIn 16*
O'Neal, Gwenelle Marine S. 1948- *WhoE 91*
O'Neal, Harriet Roberts 1952- *WhoAmW 91, WhoWor 91*
O'Neal, Henry L. 1942- *St&PR 91*
O'Neal, J Michael 1952- *BiDrAPA 89*
O'Neal, J. Michael 1952- *WhoE 91*
O'Neal, John H 1948- *BiDrAPA 89*
O'Neal, Julia Ann 1948- *WhoEmL 91*
O'Neal, Kathleen Len 1953- *WhoE 91*
O'Neal, Kelle Snyder 1948- *WhoAmW 91*
O'Neal, Margaret Funderburk 1949- *WhoAmW 91*
O'Neal, Maston E. 1907-1990 *BioIn 16*
O'Neal, Maston E., Jr. *NewYTBS 90*
O'Neal, Michael Ralph 1951- *WhoEmL 91*
O'Neal, Michael Robert 1948- *St&PR 91*
O'Neal, Michael Scott, Sr. 1948- *WhoEmL 91, WhoSSW 91*
O'Neal, Moncure Camper, Jr. 1947- *WhoSSW 91*
O'Neal, Patricia L *BiDrAPA 89*
O'Neal, Randy 1960- *Ballpl 90*
O'Neal, Reagan *WhoWrEP 89*
O'Neal, Roland Lenard 1948- *WhoAmA 91*
O'Neal, Ron 1937- *DrBlPA 90*
O'Neal, Russell E. 1925- *St&PR 91*
O'Neal, Ruth 1915- *WhoAmW 91*
O'Neal, Ryan 1941- *WhoAm 90, WorAlBi*
O'Neal, Sally *BioIn 16*
O'Neal, Steve J. 1951- *St&PR 91*
O'Neal, Susan A. 1962- *WhoAmW 91*
O'Neal, Tatum 1963- *WhoAm 90, WorAlBi*
O'Neal, Tosha Dierdre 1961- *WhoAmW 91*
O'Neal, William B. 1907- *WhoAm 90*
O'Neal, Winston James, Jr. 1948- *WhoSSW 91, WhoWrEP 89*
Oneal, Zibby 1934- *Au&Arts 5 [port], BioIn 16*
O'Neal-Smith, Melba Margo 1951- *WhoAmW 91*
O'Neale, Charles Duncan 1879-1936 *BioIn 16*
O'Neale, Jefferyes Hamett 1734-1801 *PenDiDA 89*
O'Neale, Rosalyn Taylor 1950- *WhoAmW 91*
O'Neale, Sondra A. *BioIn 16*
Onegin, Sigrid 1889-1943 *PenDiMP*
O'Neil, Bruce William 1942- *WhoAmA 91*
O'Neil, Buck 1911- *Ballpl 90*
O'Neil, C. Roderick 1931- *WhoAm 90*
O'Neil, Daniel Joseph 1942- *WhoSSW 91*
O'Neil, Dennis E. *ODwPR 91*
O'Neil, Edward Joseph, Jr. 1930- *St&PR 91, WhoAm 90*
O'Neil, Edward T. 1935- *St&PR 91*
O'Neil, Gilbert William 1930- *St&PR 91*
O'Neil, Herbert Earl 1944- *WhoWor 91*
O'Neil, James Edward 1939- *WhoE 91*
O'Neil, James Joseph 1936- *St&PR 91*
O'Neil, James Peter 1944- *St&PR 91, WhoAm 90*
O'Neil, Jane F 1910- *BiDrAPA 89*
O'Neil, Jane Farrell 1910- *WhoE 91*
O'Neil, John 1915- *WhoAm 90, WhoAmA 91*
O'Neil, John 1942- *ODwPR 91*
O'Neil, John Joseph 1932- *WhoAmA 91*
O'Neil, John Patrick 1921- *St&PR 91, WhoAm 90*
O'Neil, John Patton 1942- *WhoAmA 91*
O'Neil, Joseph C. 1933- *St&PR 91*
O'Neil, Joseph Francis 1934- *WhoAm 90*
O'Neil, Kenneth W. *BioIn 16*
O'Neil, Leo E. 1928- *WhoAm 90*

O'Neil, Louisa Watson Peat 1949- *WhoE 91*
O'Neil, M.G. 1922- *St&PR 91*
O'Neil, Mary Agnes 1926- *WhoAmW 91*
O'Neil, Michael Joseph 1951- *WhoEmL 91*
O'Neil, Mickey 1900-1964 *Ballpl 90*
O'Neil, Patricia Mayer 1946- *St&PR 91*
O'Neil, Patrick Arthur 1946- *St&PR 91*
O'Neil, Paul 1909-1988 *BioIn 16*
O'Neil, Richard J. 1929- *St&PR 91*
O'Neil, Robert H. *St&PR 91*
O'Neil, Robert Marchant 1934- *WhoAm 90, WhoSSW 91, WhoWor 91*
O'Neil, Shane 1947- *WhoAm 90*
O'Neil, Sharon Lund 1942- *WhoSSW 91*
O'Neil, Stephen Edward 1932- *St&PR 91, WhoAm 90*
Oneil, Susan Jean 1952- *WhoAmW 91*
O'Neil, Terence Quinn 1949- *WhoAm 90*
O'Neil, W M 1912- *ConAu 32NR*
O'Neil, Wayne 1931- *WhoAm 90, WhoWrEP 89*
O'Neil, William Andrew 1927- *WhoAm 90*
O'Neil, William Charles, Jr. 1934- *St&PR 91*
O'Neil, William Dennis 1931- *St&PR 91*
O'Neil, William F. 1929- *St&PR 91*
O'Neil, William Francis 1936- *WhoAm 90, WhoE 91*
O'Neil, William J. 1921- *St&PR 91*
O'Neil-Contini, Anita *WhoAmA 91*
O'Neill, Abby Weiss 1956- *ODwPR 91*
O'Neill, Albert Clarence, Jr. 1939- *WhoAm 90*
O'Neill, Ann Marie 1950- *St&PR 91*
O'Neill, Barbara Maxwell 1936- *WhoE 91*
O'Neill, Beverly *WhoAm 90*
O'Neill, Beverly Lewis 1930- *WhoAmW 91*
O'Neill, Brian 1940- *WhoAm 90*
O'Neill, Brian Dennis 1946- *WhoEmL 91*
O'Neill, Brian Edward 1935- *St&PR 91, WhoAm 90, WhoSSW 91*
O'Neill, Brian Francis 1929- *WhoAm 90*
O'Neill, Carlotta Monterey *BioIn 16*
O'Neill, Carlotta Monterey 1888-1970 *BioAmW*
O'Neill, Charles Kelly 1933- *WhoAm 90, WhoWor 91*
O'Neill, Con 1912-1988 *AnObit 1988*
O'Neill, Cornelius Thomas 1935- *WhoSSW 91*
O'Neill, Daniel 1938- *WhoHisp 91*
O'Neill, Daniel J. 1937- *WhoAm 90*
O'Neill, Daniel Patrick 1919- *WhoAm 90*
O'Neill, Dennis W. 1939- *St&PR 91*
O'Neill, Donald E. 1926- *St&PR 91*
O'Neill, Donald Edmund 1926- *WhoAm 90, WhoE 91*
O'Neill, Donald Francis 1939- *St&PR 91*
O'Neill, Ed *BioIn 16*
O'Neill, Edward J. 1942- *WhoE 91*
O'Neill, Emmett 1918- *Ballpl 90*
O'Neill, Eugene 1888-1953 *BioIn 16, ConAu 132, MajTwCW, WorAlBi*
O'Neill, Eugene Francis 1918- *WhoAm 90*
O'Neill, Eugene Gladstone 1888-1953 *WrPh*
O'Neill, Eugene Milton 1925- *WhoAm 90*
O'Neill, Frances *FemiCLE*
O'Neill, Francis Xavier, III 1953- *WhoAm 90*
O'Neill, Frank *SpyFic*
O'Neill, George D. 1926- *St&PR 91*
O'Neill, Gerard Kitchen 1927- *WhoE 91, WhoWor 91*
O'Neill, Grace O'Brien *BioIn 16, NewYTBS 90*
O'Neill, Grover, Jr. 1922- *St&PR 91*
O'Neill, Harry William 1929- *WhoAm 90, WhoE 91*
O'Neill, Hector *WhoHisp 91*
O'Neill, Henrietta 1758-1793 *FemiCLE*
O'Neill, Henry Martin, Jr. 1935- *St&PR 91*
O'Neill, Hester 1908- *AuBYP 90*
O'Neill, Hugh *BiDrAPA 89, BioIn 16*
O'Neill, James Andrew 1946- *St&PR 91*
O'Neill, James Edward 1923- *St&PR 91*
O'Neill, James J. 1934- *St&PR 91*
O'Neill, James Joseph 1941- *WhoE 91*
O'Neill, James P. *BioIn 16*
O'Neill, James Paul 1958- *BiDrAPA 89, WhoE 91*
O'Neill, Jennifer Lee 1948- *WhoAm 90*
O'Neill, John J. 1920- *St&PR 91*
O'Neill, John Joseph 1920- *WhoAm 90*
O'Neill, John Joseph, Jr. 1919- *WhoAm 90*
O'Neill, John Joseph, Jr. 1922- *WhoAm 90*
O'Neill, John Robert 1937- *St&PR 91, WhoAm 90*
O'Neill, John T. 1944- *St&PR 91*
O'Neill, John Thomas 1928- *St&PR 91, WhoAm 90*
O'Neill, June Ellenoff 1934- *WhoAmW 91*
O'Neill, Katherine Templeton 1949- *WhoAmW 91*
O'Neill, Kevin B. 1957- *St&PR 91*
O'Neill, Lawrence Daniel 1946- *WhoWor 91*
O'Neill, Leo *BioIn 16*
O'Neill, Leo C. 1940- *St&PR 91*
O'Neill, Marcella Pecora 1930- *BiDrAPA 89*
O'Neill, Margaret 1935- *WhoAmW 91*
O'Neill, Mary *NewYTBS 90*
O'Neill, Mary Jane 1923- *WhoAmW 91*
O'Neill, Mary L 1908?-1990 *ConAu 130, SmATA 64*
O'Neill, Mary le Duc 1908-1990 *AuBYP 90, BioIn 16*
O'Neill, Maura *ODwPR 91*
O'Neill, Maureen Anne 1948- *WhoAmW 91*
O'Neill, Michael Hugh 1954- *WhoEmL 91*
O'Neill, Michael John 1932- *WhoE 91*
O'Neill, Michael John 1942- *BiDrAPA 89*
O'Neill, Michael Joyce 1922-1989 *BioIn 16*
O'Neill, Mike 1877-1959 *Ballpl 90*
O'Neill, Norah Ellen 1949- *WhoEmL 91*
O'Neill, Patricia Margaret 1948- *WhoAmW 91*
O'Neill, Patrick F. *St&PR 91*
O'Neill, Patrick Henry 1915- *St&PR 91, WhoAm 90*
O'Neill, Patrick T 1955- *BiDrAPA 89*
O'Neill, Paul *NewYTBS 90 [port]*
O'Neill, Paul 1963- *Ballpl 90*
O'Neill, Paul Henry 1935- *St&PR 91, WhoAm 90, WhoE 91, WhoWor 91*
O'Neill, Peter J. *WhoWrEP 89*
O'Neill, Peter J. 1947- *St&PR 91*
O'Neill, Philip Daniel, Jr. 1951- *WhoE 91*
O'Neill, Randal Bruce 1956- *St&PR 91*
O'Neill, Richard Eugene 1942- *St&PR 91*
O'Neill, Richard Michael 1923- *WhoWor 91*
O'Neill, Robert Brendan 1938- *St&PR 91*
O'Neill, Robert Charles 1923- *WhoAm 90*
O'Neill, Robert Edward 1925- *WhoAm 90*
O'Neill, Robert F. 1923- *St&PR 91*
O'Neill, Robert Hugh 1928- *St&PR 91*
O'Neill, Rose Cecil 1874-1944 *BioAmW*
O'Neill, Russell Richard 1916- *WhoAm 90*
O'Neill, Stephen *BiDrAPA 89*
O'Neill, Stephen Vincent 1948- *WhoSSW 91*
O'Neill, Steve 1891-1962 *Ballpl 90*
O'Neill, Terence 1914-1990 *CurBio 90N*
O'Neill, Terence M. 1914-1990 *NewYTBS 90 [port]*
O'Neill, Terence Marne 1914-1990 *BioIn 16*
O'Neill, Thomas Newman, Jr. 1928- *WhoAm 90*
O'Neill, Thomas P. *BioIn 16*
O'Neill, Thomas P. 1953- *St&PR 91*
O'Neill, Thomas P., II 1912- *WhoAm 90*
O'Neill, Thomas P., Jr. 1912- *WorAlBi*
O'Neill, Tip *BioIn 16*
O'Neill, Tip 1858-1915 *Ballpl 90*
O'Neill, W. Paul 1938- *WhoAm 90*
O'Neill, Walter James 1926- *WhoWor 91*
O'Neill, William Atchison 1930- *WhoAm 90, WhoE 91, WhoWor 91*
O'Neill, William Bernard 1942- *WhoE 91*
O'Neill, William Edward 1960- *WhoE 91*
O'Neill, William J., Jr. 1933- *St&PR 91*
O'Neill, William James, Jr. 1933- *WhoAm 90, WhoWor 91*
O'Neill, William Lawrence 1935- *WhoAm 90, WhoWrEP 89*
O'Neill, William M. 1933- *St&PR 91*
O'Neill, William Patrick 1950- *St&PR 91*
O'Neill Bidwell, Katharine Thomas 1937- *WhoAm 90*
O'Neill-Brown, Jacqueline A. 1948- *WhoE 91*
O'Neill of the Marine, Baron 1914-1990 *BioIn 16*
Onek, Margot Piore 1942- *BiDrAPA 89*
Oneka 1640?-1710 *WhNaAH*
Onesti, Silvio J 1926- *BiDrAPA 89*
Onesti, Silvio Joseph 1926- *WhoAm 90, WhoE 91*
Oneto, Tom Laurence 1943- *St&PR 91*
Onetti, Juan Carlos 1909- *BioIn 16, ConAu 32NR, HispWr 90, MajTwCW*
Ong, Charles Chen Chung *WhoWor 91*
Ong, Fen Ching 1927- *St&PR 91*
Ong, John Doyle 1933- *St&PR 91, WhoAm 90*
Ong, Michael King 1955- *WhoE 91*
Ong, Richard M. 1915- *St&PR 91*
Ong, Walter Jackson 1912- *WhoAm 90, WhoWrEP 89*
Ongania, Juan Carlos 1914- *BioIn 16*
Ongaro, Mario Peter 1926- *WhoWor 91*
Ongjoco, Rodolfo C 1934- *BiDrAPA 89*
Ongyert, Werner 1938- *St&PR 91*
O'Nions, Robert Keith 1944- *WhoWor 91*
Onishchuk, Ellen Colleen *BiDrAPA 89*
Onishi, Aiko 1930- *IntWWM 90*
Onishi, Akira 1929- *WhoWor 91*
Onista'poka 1838?-1897 *DcCanB 12*
Onizuka, Ellison S. 1946-1986 *BioIn 16*
Onken, George Marcellus 1914- *WhoAm 90, WhoWor 91*
Onken, Lisa Simon 1954- *WhoAmW 91*
Onken, Richard R. 1951- *St&PR 91*
Onkin, Ronald Harvey 1938- *BiDrAPA 89*
Onkst, James Richard 1939- *WhoSSW 91*
Onley, Ernest Edward, Jr. 1932- *WhoSSW 91*
Onley, M. Francesca 1933- *WhoAmW 91*
Onley, Toni 1928- *WhoAmA 91*
Onn, Hussein Bin 1922-1990 *BioIn 16*
Onne, Joseph *BiDrAPA 89*
Onnen, James H. 1939- *St&PR 91*
Onnou, Alphonse *PenDiMP*
Ono Yoko 1933- *EncJap*
Ono, Allen Kenji 1933- *WhoAm 90*
Ono, Seigen *NewAgMG*
Ono, Takahiko 1951- *WhoWor 91*
Ono, Yasokichi 1933- *WhoWor 91*
Ono, Yoko *BioIn 16, EncPR&S 89*
Ono, Yoko 1933- *WhoAmA 91, WhoAmW 91*
Onoda, John *ODwPR 91*
Onoe, Morio 1926- *WhoWor 91*
Onofrey, John Francis 1935- *St&PR 91*
Onofrio, Janis Lynn 1963- *WhoAmW 91*
Ononye, Daniel Chuka 1948- *WhoEmL 91, WhoWor 91*
Onorato, Anthony J. 1950- *St&PR 91*
Onorato, Anthony Peter 1954- *St&PR 91*
Onorato, Nicholas Anthony 1949- *WhoE 91*
Onorato, Nicholas Louis 1925- *WhoAm 90*
Onorato, Ronald Joseph 1949- *WhoAmA 91, WhoE 91*
Onorato, Susan Dobbs 1964- *WhoAmW 91*
Onque, Gloria C 1931- *BiDrAPA 89*
Onsager, Jerome Andrew 1936- *WhoAm 90*
Onsager, Lars 1903-1976 *DcScB S2*
Onslow, John 1906-1985 *BioIn 16*
Onslow Ford, Gordon M 1912- *WhoAmA 91*
Onslow Ford, Gordon Max 1912- *WhoAm 90*
Onstott, Edward Irvin 1922- *WhoAm 90, WhoWor 91*
Onstott, Joseph E. 1949- *WhoE 91*
Ontai, Laurie A. *ODwPR 91*
Ontiveros, Robert *WhoHisp 91*
Ontiveros, Steve 1951- *Ballpl 90*
Ontiveros, Steve 1961- *Ballpl 90*
Ontjes, David Ainsworth 1937- *WhoAm 90*
Ontko, Gary M. 1954- *St&PR 91*
Ontko, Joseph Andrew 1932- *WhoSSW 91*
Onukwuli, Francis Osita 1955- *WhoSSW 91*
Onyon, Michael Lee 1943- *St&PR 91*
Onyonka, Zachary 1939- *WhoWor 91*
Onyszchuk, Mario 1930- *WhoAm 90*
Oom the Omnipotent *EncO&P 3*
Oommen, George 1942- *WhoAm 90*
Oommen, Kalarickal J 1947- *BiDrAPA 89*
Ooms, Van Doorn 1934- *WhoAm 90*
Oost, Gert 1942- *IntWWM 90*
Oosten, Roger Lester 1937- *WhoSSW 91*
Oosterhof, Darlene Kobes 1945- *WhoAmW 91*
Oosterom, Richard H 1955- *WhoAmA 91*
Op de Coul, Paul Matthijs 1940- *WhoWor 91*
Opacki, Bronislaw 1929- *WhoWor 91*
Opal, John Anthony 1917- *BiDrAPA 89*
Opal, Kenneth Edward 1940- *St&PR 91*
Opala, Marian Peter 1921- *WhoAm 90, WhoSSW 91*
Opalek, Marvin 1939- *St&PR 91*
Opalinski, Fred Stanley 1948- *WhoE 91*
Opalka, Joseph G. 1940- *St&PR 91*
Opalski, Douglas Victor 1942- *WhoE 91*
Opao, Aida A *BiDrAPA 89*
Opar, Patricia Ann 1938- *WhoE 91*
Oparin, Aleksandr Ivanovich 1894-1980 *DcScB S2*
Opass, Edward 1957- *BiDrAPA 89*
Opdycke, Leonard 1895-1977 *WhoAmA 91N*
Opechancanough 1545?-1644 *EncCRAm, WhNaAH*
Opechowski, Jarek F 1956- *BiDrAPA 89*
Opee-O'Wun *DcCanB 12*
Opeka, John Frank 1940- *St&PR 91, WhoAm 90*
Opel, John R. 1925- *St&PR 91, WhoAm 90*
Opelt, Rilla Anne 1939- *WhoAmW 91*
Openden, Lori *WhoAmW 91*
Openshaw, Calvin Reynolds 1921- *WhoAm 90*
Openshaw, John D. 1941- *St&PR 91*
Operhall, Harrie Marie Pollok 1949- *WhoEmL 91*
Opezzi, Marco Pierguido 1943- *WhoWor 91*
Opfer, Warren Arthur 1952- *St&PR 91*
Opgenoorth, Winfried 1939- *BioIn 16*
Opgrande, Jarl L. 1938- *St&PR 91*
Ophaug, Brian Ross 1958- *WhoEmL 91*
Opheim, Janice Elaine 1957- *WhoEmL 91*
Opheim, Roberta Claire 1948- *WhoAmW 91*
Ophiel *EncO&P 3*
Ophir, Dan David 1946- *WhoWor 91*
Ophuls, Marcel 1927- *BioIn 16, ConTFT 8, WhoAm 90*
Opie, Alan 1945- *IntWWM 90*
Opie, Amelia 1769-1853 *FemiCLE*
Opie, Amelia Alderson 1769-1853 *BioIn 16*
Opie, Evarts W., Jr. 1934- *St&PR 91*
Opie, Iona 1923- *SmATA 63 [port]*
Opie, Iona Archibald *BioIn 16*
Opie, John Mart 1936- *WhoAmA 91*
Opie, Peter 1918-1982 *SmATA 63 [port]*
Opie, Peter Mason 1918-1982 *DcNaB 1981*
Opie, William Robert 1920- *WhoAm 90*
Opila, Andy *ODwPR 91*
Opitz, Bernard Francis, Jr. 1947- *WhoE 91, WhoEmL 91, WhoWor 91*
Opitz, John Marius 1935- *WhoAm 90, WhoWor 91*
Opland, Sam 1938- *St&PR 91*
Opler, Lewis Alan 1948- *BiDrAPA 89, WhoE 91*
Oplinger, Clarence G. 1934- *WhoWor 91*
Oplinger, Kathryn Ruth 1951- *WhoAmW 91*
Opothle Yoholo 1798?-1862 *WhNaAH*
Opothleyaholo 1798?-1862 *WhNaAH*
Opothleyohola 1798?-1862 *WhNaAH*
Opothleyoholo 1798?-1862 *WhNaAH*
Opotowsky, Barbara Berger 1945- *St&PR 91*
Opotowsky, Maurice Leon 1931- *WhoAm 90*
Opotowsky, Mel 1931- *St&PR 91*
Opotowsky, Stuart B. 1935- *St&PR 91*
Opotowsky, Stuart Berger 1935- *WhoAm 90, WhoE 91*
Opp, W.R. 1939- *St&PR 91*
Opp, Walter 1931- *WhoWor 91*
Oppedahl, John Fredrick 1944- *WhoAm 90*
Oppedahl, Phillip Edward 1935- *WhoWor 91*
Oppedisano, Suzanne Marie *WhoAmW 91*
Oppegard, Charles R *BiDrAPA 89*
Oppegard, Peter *BioIn 16*
Oppel, Richard Alfred 1943- *WhoAm 90*
Oppel, Theodore W. 1903-1989 *BioIn 16*
Oppen, Mary 1908-1990 *BioIn 16, ConAu 131*
Oppen, Steven Bernard 1946- *WhoE 91*
Oppenheim, Alan Victor 1937- *WhoAm 90*
Oppenheim, Alfred 1915- *WhoAm 90*
Oppenheim, Antoni Kazimierz 1915- *WhoAm 90*
Oppenheim, Austin E. 1925- *St&PR 91*
Oppenheim, David J. 1922- *IntWWM 90*
Oppenheim, David Jerome 1922- *WhoAm 90*
Oppenheim, Dennis A 1938- *WhoAmA 91*
Oppenheim, Dennis Allen 1938- *WhoAm 90*
Oppenheim, E Phillips 1866-1946 *TwCCr&M 91*
Oppenheim, Edward Phillips 1926-1946 *SpyFic*
Oppenheim, Ellen 1951- *WhoEmL 91*
Oppenheim, Garrett 1911- *WhoE 91*
Oppenheim, Irwin 1929- *WhoAm 90*
Oppenheim, James K. 1946- *St&PR 91*
Oppenheim, Judith R. 1946- *WhoAmW 91*
Oppenheim, Justin Sable 1923- *WhoAm 90*
Oppenheim, Lucy Linda 1959- *WhoWrEP 89*
Oppenheim, Martha Kunkel 1935- *WhoAmW 91*
Oppenheim, Mayer *PenDiDA 89*
Oppenheim, Meret 1913-1985 *BiDWomA, BioIn 16*
Oppenheim, Paul Andrew 1955- *WhoEmL 91*
Oppenheim, Rick 1952- *ODwPR 91*
Oppenheim, Robert 1925- *WhoE 91*
Oppenheim, Ruth 1927- *St&PR 91*
Oppenheim, Samuel Edmund *WhoAmA 91*
Oppenheim, Walter M. 1923- *St&PR 91*
Oppenheimer, Alice 1894- *BioIn 16*
Oppenheimer, Andres Miguel 1951- *WhoHisp 91*
Oppenheimer, Bonnie Lou 1955- *WhoSSW 91*
Oppenheimer, David 1834-1897 *DcCanB 12*
Oppenheimer, Deanna Watson *ODwPR 91*
Oppenheimer, Edgar 1885-1952 *BioIn 16*
Oppenheimer, Eric *BiDrAPA 89*
Oppenheimer, Ernest *BiDrAPA 89*

Oppenheimer, Franz Martin 1919- WhoAm 90
Oppenheimer, Hamilton G. 1948- St&PR 91
Oppenheimer, Harry Frederick 1908- BioIn 16, WhoWor 91
Oppenheimer, Heather Leigh 1949- WhoAmW 91
Oppenheimer, J. Robert 1904-1967 BioIn 16
Oppenheimer, J Robert 1904-1967 MajTwCW
Oppenheimer, J. Robert 1904-1967 WorAlBi
Oppenheimer, Jack Hans 1927- WhoAm 90
Oppenheimer, James Richard 1921- WhoAm 90
Oppenheimer, Jane Marion 1911- WhoAm 90
Oppenheimer, Jerry L. 1937- WhoAm 90
Oppenheimer, Jess 1913-1988 BioIn 16, ConTFT 8
Oppenheimer, Joel 1930-1988 BioIn 16
Oppenheimer, Joseph 1927- WhoAm 90
Oppenheimer, Laurence Brian 1952- WhoEmL 91
Oppenheimer, Lillian AuBYP 90
Oppenheimer, Marion BioIn 16
Oppenheimer, Max, Jr. 1917- WhoAm 90
Oppenheimer, Michael 1946- WhoAm 90
Oppenheimer, Selma L 1898- WhoAmA 91N
Oppenheimer, Suzi BioIn 16
Oppenheimer, Suzi 1934- WhoAmW 91, WhoE 91
Oppenheimer, Tamar Mariamne 1925- WhoWor 91
Oppenheimer, Valerie Kincade 1932- WhoAm 90
Oppenlander, Ann 1942- St&PR 91
Oppenlander, Robert 1923- St&PR 91, WhoAm 90
Oppenlander, Robert Kirk 1952- WhoEmL 91
Oppenord, Gilles-Marie 1672-1742 PenDiDA 89
Oppens, Ursula 1944- IntWWM 90
Opper, Frederick Burr 1857-1937 EncACom
Opper, John 1908- WhoAmA 91
Opperman, Amelia 1939- WhoAmW 91
Opperman, Dwight Darwin 1923- WhoAm 90
Oppermann, Rudiger NewAgMG
Oppewall, Jeannine BioIn 16
Oppler, Willy BiDrAPA 89
Oppokov, Georgii Ippolitovich 1888-1938 BioIn 16
Oppong, Kwabena BioIn 16
Oppowa, Rudolf Johann 1928- WhoWor 91
Oppriecht, L. Elliott ODwPR 91
Opre, Thomas Edward 1943- WhoAm 90, WhoWrEP 89
Oprea, Gheorghe 1927- WhoWor 91
Opremcak, Colleen Marie 1956- BiDrAPA 89
Opsahl, David George BiDrAPA 89
Opton, Frank G. 1906-1989 BioIn 16
Opyr, Linda Elena 1953- WhoE 91
Oquendo, Jose 1963- Ballpl 90
Oquendo, Jose Manuel 1963- WhoHisp 91
Oquendo, Juan Lechin 1915- BioIn 16
Oquendo, Maria Antonia 1960- BiDrAPA 89
Oquendo, Regina Gerlach 1955- BiDrAPA 89
Oquendo, Sonia Iris BiDrAPA 89
O'Quinn, Percy C. 1923- St&PR 91
O'Quinn, Ruth Granger 1925- WhoAmW 91
Oquist, Gunnar F. 1941- WhoWor 91
Ora, Sergio S., Jr. 1946- St&PR 91
Orabi, Ismail Ibrahim 1950- WhoE 91
Oraefo, Johnny Ndubuisi 1945- WhoSSW 91
Orakwanen-Takon DcCanB 12
Oram, Arthur T 1916- EncO&P 3
Oram, Daphne Blake 1925- IntWWM 90
Oram, George Arthur, Jr. 1947- WhoE 91
Oram, Hiawyn BioIn 16
Oram, Robert W. 1922- WhoAm 90
Oramas-Oliva, Oscar 1936- WhoWor 91
Oran, Elaine Surick 1946- WhoAmW 91
Oran, Frederic M. 1932- St&PR 91
Oran, Geraldine Ann 1938- WhoAmW 91, WhoSSW 91
Orange, John W. 1949- St&PR 91
Orange, Lenore Joan BiDrAPA 89
Oransky, David 1934- WhoE 91
Oransky, John Joseph 1953- WhoE 91
Oratam WhNaAH
Oratamin WhNaAH
Oratamy WhNaAH
Oratan WhNaAH
Oraton WhNaAH
Orav, Helle Reissar 1925- WhoAmW 91
Oravec, Christian Robert 1937- WhoE 91
O'Rawe, Kevin Dillon 1950- WhoSSW 91
Orazio, Joan Politi 1930- WhoAmW 91
Orb, John Alexander 1919- WhoAm 90
Orbach, Jerry 1935- OxCPMus, WhoAm 90, WorAlBi
Orbach, Raymond Lee 1934- WhoAm 90
Orban, Diana M. 1947- ODwPR 91
Orban, Edmond Henry 1925- WhoAm 90
Orban, Kurt 1916- WhoAm 90
Orbe, Monica Patricia 1968- WhoHisp 91
Orbe, Octavius Anthony 1927- WhoAm 90
Orbell, Craig Lithgow 1949- WhoAm 90
Orben, Jack R. 1938- St&PR 91
Orben, Jack Richard 1938- WhoAm 90
Orben, Robert 1927- ConAu 31NR, WhoAm 90, WhoWrEP 89
Orben, Robert A. 1936- St&PR 91
Orben, Robert Allen 1936- WhoAm 90
Orbis, Victor ConAu 30NR
Orbison, James Graham 1953- WhoEmL 91, WhoWor 91
Orbison, Roy 1936-1988 AnObit 1988, BioIn 16, EncPR&S 89, OxCPMus, WorAlBi
Orbuch, Allen Harold 1928- WhoAm 90
Orbuch, Martin 1932- BiDrAPA 89
Orcagna 1308?-1368? IntDcAA 90
Orcel, Jean 1896-1978 DcScB S2
Orchard, Donna Lee 1931- WhoAmW 91
Orchard, Henry John 1922- WhoAm 90
Orchard, William Henry BiDrAPA 89
Orchin, Milton 1914- WhoAm 90
Orchow, Harold S 1931- BiDrAPA 89
Orcutt, Ben Avis 1914- WhoAmW 91
Orcutt, Donald Adelbert 1926- WhoSSW 91
Orcutt, Guy Henderson 1917- WhoAm 90
Orcutt, James Douglas 1943- WhoSSW 91
Orcutt, Timothy Parkhurst 1939- St&PR 91
Orcutt, William P. 1928- St&PR 91
Orczy, Baroness 1865-1947 FemiCLE, WorAlBi
Orczy, Baroness 1865-1967 TwCCr&M 91
Orczy, Emma Magdalena Rosalia Maria J 1865-1947 SpyFic
Orczy, Emmuska 1865-1947 AuBYP 90, BioIn 16
Orczyk, S.R. 1930- St&PR 91
Ord, Angustias de la Guerra 1815-1880 BioIn 16
Ord, John Robert 1950- St&PR 91
Ord, Kenneth Stephen 1946- St&PR 91
Ord, Lecki BioIn 16
Ordal, Caspar Reuben 1922- WhoAm 90
Ordaz, Gustavo Diaz 1911-1979 BioIn 16
Ordaz, Joel S BiDrAPA 89
Ordaz, Phillip A. 1934- WhoHisp 91
Ordemann, Carl W. 1951- St&PR 91
Ordemann, Marshall Frederick, Jr. 1948- St&PR 91
Orden, Alex 1916- WhoAm 90
Ordentlich, Elena BiDrAPA 89
Ordentlich, Ivan 1934- WhoWor 91
Order, Stanley Elias 1934- WhoAm 90
Order, Trudy 1944- WhoAmA 91
Ordin, Andrea Sheridan WhoAm 90
Ording, Michael K. 1955- WhoEmL 91
Ordiway, M Vernon 1932- BiDrAPA 89
Ordjanian, Nikit 1918- St&PR 91
Ordman, Arnold 1912-1989 BioIn 16
Ordman, Jeannette WhoWor 91
Ordog, Adam 1934- WhoWor 91
Ordona, Truce Taneo 1942- BiDrAPA 89
Ordonez, Ester Belo BiDrAPA 89
Ordonez, Jose Batlle y 1856-1929 BioIn 16
Ordonez, Mario A BiDrAPA 89
Ordonez, Ricardo 1959- WhoHisp 91
Ordonez-Schneider, Marylin BiDrAPA 89
Ordoubadian, Reza 1932- WhoSSW 91
Ordover, Abraham Philip 1937- WhoWor 91
Ordover, Sondra T. BioIn 16
Ordower, Myrna E. WhoAmW 91, WhoWor 91
Orduna-Muslimani, Maria 1959- WhoAmW 91
Ordung, Philip Franklin 1919- WhoAm 90
Orduno, Robert Daniel 1933- WhoAmA 91
Ordway, Ellen 1927- WhoAmW 91
Ordway, Frederick Ira, III 1927- WhoAm 90
Ordway, Janet Eddy 1925- BiDrAPA 89
Ordway, John A 1920- BiDrAPA 89
Ordway, Ronald D. 1941- St&PR 91
Ordway, Ronald Dale 1941- WhoSSW 91
Ordway, Sally 1939- BioIn 16, NotWoAT
Ordynsky, George 1944- WhoWor 91
Ordzhonikidze, Sergo 1886-1937 BioIn 16
Ore, Cecilie 1954- IntWWM 90
Orea, David Amor BiDrAPA 89
Oreamuno, Ricardo Jimenez 1859-1945 BioIn 16
O'Rear, David Arthur 1957- WhoWor 91
O'Rear, Edgar Allen, III 1953- WhoSSW 91
Orear, Jay 1925- WhoAm 90, WhoWrEP 89
Orechio, Frank Anthony 1917- WhoWor 91
Oreffice, Paul Fausto 1927- St&PR 91, WhoAm 90, WhoWor 91
O'Regan, Richard Arthur 1919- WhoAm 90
Oregon NewAgMG
Orehosky, James George 1929- St&PR 91
Oreibi, Misbah Ibrahim 1936- WhoWor 91
O'Reilly, Alejandro BioIn 16
O'Reilly, Anthony J. F. BioIn 16
O'Reilly, Anthony John Francis 1936- WhoAm 90, WhoE 91
O'Reilly, Brendan PenDiMP
O'Reilly, Charles Henry 1913- St&PR 91
O'Reilly, Charles Terrance 1921- WhoAm 90
O'Reilly, David R. St&PR 91
O'Reilly, Eugene F. 1931- St&PR 91
O'Reilly, Frank Warren, Jr. 1921- WhoE 91
O'Reilly, George Robert 1930- St&PR 91
O'Reilly, Graham Henry Meredith 1947- IntWWM 90
O'Reilly, Jackson WhoWrEP 89
O'Reilly, James Christopher 1943- WhoWor 91
O'Reilly, James Timothy 1939- St&PR 91
O'Reilly, Jane 1936- ConAu 31NR
O'Reilly, John 1906- AuBYP 90
O'Reilly, John B 1930- WhoAmA 91
O'Reilly, Katy ODwPR 91
O'Reilly, Larry P. 1946- St&PR 91
O'Reilly, Lawrence Patrick 1937- WhoSSW 91
O'Reilly, Louise 1948- WhoAmW 91
O'Reilly, Mary A. ODwPR 91
O'Reilly, Michael 1912- WhoWor 91
O'Reilly, Myra Faith 1938- WhoWor 91
O'Reilly, Patricia H. 1939- St&PR 91
O'Reilly, Richard Brooks 1941- WhoAm 90
O'Reilly, Richard John 1943- WhoAm 90
O'Reilly, Robert F. 1934- St&PR 91
O'Reilly, Sally 1940- IntWWM 90
O'Reilly, Sue Ann 1950- WhoWrEP 89
O'Reilly, Terence John 1945- WhoAm 90, WhoWor 91
O'Reilly, Terence Joseph 1954- WhoE 91
O'Reilly, Terrence M. 1945- St&PR 91
O'Reilly, Thomas Eugene 1932- WhoE 91
O'Reilly, Timothy P. 1948- St&PR 91
O'Reilly, Toni BioIn 16
O'Reilly, Vincent A. 1944- WhoAm 90
O'Reilly, Vincent M. WhoAm 90
O'Reilly-Keddy, Eve Marie 1957- WhoAmW 91
Orel, Harold 1926- WhoAm 90, WhoWrEP 89
Orell, Larry BioIn 16
Orellana, Elbin Alfredo 1950- BiDrAPA 89
Orellana, Francisco de 1500-1550 BioIn 16
Orellana, Rolando 1942- WhoHisp 91
Orelove, Alex E. 1917- St&PR 91
Orem, Charles Annistone 1929- St&PR 91
Orem, Sandra Elizabeth 1940- WhoAmW 91
Oremland, Fred Donald BiDrAPA 89
Oremland, Jerome D BiDrAPA 89
Oremland, S.L. 1942- St&PR 91
Oremland, Stanley 1943- St&PR 91
Oren, Bruce Clifford 1952- WhoAm 90
Oren, Dan A. 1958- BiDrAPA 89
Oren, Dan Ahiassaf 1958- WhoE 91
Oren, John Birdsell 1909- WhoAm 90
Orenchuk, Peter H. 1956- WhoE 91
Orendain, Antonio 1931- BioIn 16
Orengo, Joe 1914- Ballpl 90
Orengo, Serafin BiDrAPA 89
Orens, Elaine Frances 1929- WhoAmA 91
Orens, Iris S 1925- BiDrAPA 89
Orens, Scott Samuel 1955- BiDrAPA 89
Orensanz, Angel L 1941- WhoAmA 91
Orensanz, Angel Lop 1941- WhoWor 91
Orenshein, Herbert 1931- St&PR 91
Orenstein, Frank 1919- ConAu 30NR
Orenstein, Gloria Feman 1938- WhoAmA 91
Orenstein, Herbert N 1945- BiDrAPA 89
Orenstein, Leo L BiDrAPA 89
Orenstein, Myra Goldstein 1952- WhoAmW 91
Orent, Gerard M. 1931- WhoAm 90
Orentlicher, John 1943- WhoAmA 91, WhoE 91
Orentzel, Jack 1918- St&PR 91
Oresick, Peter 1955- ConAu 30NR
Oresick, Peter Michael 1955- WhoWrEP 89
Oreskes, Irwin 1926- WhoAm 90
Oreskovic, Thomas A. St&PR 91
Oresman, Donald 1925- St&PR 91, WhoAm 90
Oresme, Nicole 1320?-1382 EncO&P 3
Orf, John W. 1950- St&PR 91
Orf, Ted 1945- St&PR 91
Orfalea, Gregory Michael 1949- WhoWrEP 89
Orff, Carl 1895-1982 PenDiMP A
Orff, James Robert 1947- WhoSSW 91
Orfield, Olivia Fuller 1922- WhoWrEP 89
Orford, David Charles 1946- WhoWor 91
Orgad, Ben Zion 1926- IntWWM 90, WhoWor 91
Orgain, Benjamin Darby 1909- WhoAm 90
Orgain, James Robert, Jr. 1917- WhoSSW 91
Organ, Arnold Thomas 1938- St&PR 91
Organski, Abramo Fimo Kenneth 1923- WhoAm 90
Orge, Hasan Yalcin BiDrAPA 89
Orgebin-Crist, Marie-Claire 1936- WhoAm 90
Orgel, Doris 1929- AuBYP 90
Orgel, Leslie Eleazer 1927- WhoAm 90
Orgel, Morris 1910-1989 BioIn 16
Orgel, Shelley 1928- BiDrAPA 89
Orgel, Stephen 1933- WhoWrEP 89
Orgera, Raymond Edward 1948- WhoSSW 91
Orghana WomWR
Orgill, Andrew Alan 1955- WhoWor 91
Orgill, John L. 1931- St&PR 91
Orgon, Edward A. 1945- ODwPR 91
Orgun, Ibrahim N 1929- BiDrAPA 89
Ori, Geno, Jr. 1937- WhoAm 90
Ori, Kan 1933- WhoWor 91
Ori, Peter Francis 1962- WhoSSW 91
Oriaku, Ebere Agwu 1951- WhoSSW 91
Oriani, Richard Anthony 1920- WhoAm 90
Orians, Gordon H 1932- ConAu 30NR
Orians, Gordon Howell 1932- WhoAm 90
Oribe EncJap
Oribe, Ann BiDrAPA 89
Oribe, Manuel 1792-1857 BioIn 16
Orie, Ronald Thomas 1937- St&PR 91
Orient, Anatol BioIn 16
Oriethyia 1951- WhoEmL 91
Origen BioIn 16
Origen 185-254 WrPh P
Origenes, Edna Florentino 1943- BiDrAPA 89
Original Dixieland Jazz Band OxCPMus
Origliosso, James H. 1952- St&PR 91
Origo, Iris 1902-1988 AnObit 1988
Orihel, Thomas Charles 1929- WhoAm 90
O'Riley, Christopher BioIn 16
O'Riley, Patrick Adelbert 1941- WhoWrEP 89
Oring, Michael Sanford 1957- St&PR 91
Oringer, Howard 1942- St&PR 91
Oringer, Kenneth W. 1931- St&PR 91
Oriol e Ybarra, Miguel de BioIn 16
Orioles, The EncPR&S 89
Orioli, Pietro 1458-1496 BioIn 16
O'Riordan, Colin Lucas 1943- IntWWM 90
O'Riordan, Kaye L. 1949- St&PR 91
Oris, Caryl A 1953- BiDrAPA 89
Orisek, Ivan 1945- WhoE 91
O'Risky, Dorothy Sandra 1939- WhoAmW 91
Orjasaeter, Tore 1886-1968 DcScanL
Orjuela, Hector H 1930- ConAu 32NR, HispWr 90
Orkand, Donald Saul 1936- WhoE 91
Orkin, Louis Richard 1915- WhoAm 90
Orkin, Ruth 1921-1985 WhoAmA 91N
Orkis, Lambert Thomas 1946- IntWWM 90
Orko, Riitta Helena 1940- WhoWor 91
Orkow, Alex Frank 1945- WhoEmL 91
Orkwis, Rose Ann Elena 1946- WhoAmW 91
Orland, Frank 1920- BiDrAPA 89
Orland, Frank Jay 1917- WhoAm 90, WhoWor 91
Orland, Henry 1918- IntWWM 90
Orland, Ralph Michael BiDrAPA 89
Orland, Rees M. 1944- St&PR 91
Orland, Ted N WhoAmA 91
Orlander, Michael 1933- St&PR 91
Orlandi Malaspina, Rita 1937- IntWWM 90
Orlando, Adolph Alfred 1943- St&PR 91
Orlando, Andrea Lee 1953- WhoAmW 91
Orlando, Anthony Carl 1935- St&PR 91
Orlando, Anthony Michael 1942- WhoSSW 91
Orlando, Antonini 1933- WhoWor 91
Orlando, Barbara ODwPR 91
Orlando, Donna Morrison 1941- St&PR 91
Orlando, Frances 1954- WhoAmW 91
Orlando, George 1944- WhoAm 90
Orlando, Guido 1906-1988 BioIn 16
Orlando, James, III 1957- BiDrAPA 89
Orlando, Jean M. St&PR 91
Orlando, Joe 1927- EncACom
Orlando, Joseph A. 1927- St&PR 91
Orlando, Joy Ann 1965- WhoAmW 91
Orlando, Kathy Reber 1942- WhoAmW 91
Orlando, Louis Lynn 1931- WhoSSW 91
Orlando, Marianne BioIn 16
Orlando, Tony BioIn 16

Orth, Norbert 1939- *IntWWM 90*
Orthwein, James Busch 1924- *St&PR 91*
Orthwein, William Coe 1924- *WhoAm 90, WhoWor 91*
Ortigoza, Napoleon *BioIn 16*
Ortinau, David Joseph 1948- *WhoEmL 91, WhoSSW 91, WhoWor 91*
Ortino, Hector Ruben 1942- *St&PR 91*
Ortino, Leonard James 1919- *St&PR 91*
Ortique, Revius Oliver, Jr. 1924- *WhoAm 90*
Ortiz, Adalberto 1914- *ConAu 131, HispWr 90*
Ortiz, Alfonso Alex 1939- *WhoAm 90*
Ortiz, Alfredo 1944- *Ballpl 90*
Ortiz, Alfredo Tomas 1948- *WhoHisp 91*
Ortiz, Alicia Milagros 1963- *BiDrAPA 89*
Ortiz, Araceli 1937- *WhoHisp 91*
Ortiz, Augusto 1917- *WhoHisp 91*
Ortiz, Aurelio *BiDrAPA 89*
Ortiz, Beatriz E. 1959- *WhoHisp 91*
Ortiz, Carlos *WhoAmA 91*
Ortiz, Carlos A. 1946- *WhoHisp 91*
Ortiz, Carlos Guillermo 1956- *WhoHisp 91*
Ortiz, Carlos Rafael *BiDrAPA 89*
Ortiz, Carlos Roberto 1946- *St&PR 91, WhoHisp 91*
Ortiz, Charles Leo 1941- *WhoHisp 91*
Ortiz, Clemencia 1942- *WhoHisp 91*
Ortiz, Cristina 1950- *IntWWM 90, PenDiMP*
Ortiz, Daisy 1951- *WhoE 91*
Ortiz, Edward *WhoHisp 91N*
Ortiz, Eugene Denis 1956- *WhoWrEP 89*
Ortiz, Francesca 1964- *WhoAmW 91*
Ortiz, Francis V., Jr. 1926- *WhoHisp 91*
Ortiz, Francis Vincent 1926- *BioIn 16*
Ortiz, Francis Vincent, Jr. 1926- *WhoAm 90*
Ortiz, Frank Holguin 1946- *WhoSSW 91*
Ortiz, George *BioIn 16*
Ortiz, George 1942- *WhoHisp 91*
Ortiz, Irene E *BiDrAPA 89*
Ortiz, Irma 1922- *WhoAmW 91*
Ortiz, Isidro D. 1949- *WhoHisp 91*
Ortiz, Ivan 1949- *WhoE 91*
Ortiz, James A. *WhoHisp 91*
Ortiz, John William 1924- *St&PR 91*
Ortiz, Jose G. 1950- *WhoHisp 91*
Ortiz, Joseph Vincent 1956- *WhoHisp 91*
Ortiz, Juan F *BiDrAPA 89*
Ortiz, Julia Cristina 1955- *WhoHisp 91*
Ortiz, Junior 1959- *Ballpl 90, WhoHisp 91*
Ortiz, Lilia Maria *BiDrAPA 89*
Ortiz, Lori 1950- *St&PR 91*
Ortiz, Luis Malaquias Concha 1859-1921 *BioIn 16*
Ortiz, Luis Tony 1955- *WhoHisp 91*
Ortiz, Manuel, Jr. 1938- *WhoHisp 91*
Ortiz, Maria C. 1959- *WhoHisp 91*
Ortiz, Maria de Los Angeles 1947- *WhoHisp 91*
Ortiz, Maria Elena 1946- *WhoHisp 91*
Ortiz, Maritza 1956- *WhoHisp 91*
Ortiz, Maritza 1958- *WhoHisp 91*
Ortiz, Melba Anabel 1947- *WhoAmW 91*
Ortiz, Miranda Renee 1962- *WhoAmW 91*
Ortiz, Neftali *BiDrAPA 89*
Ortiz, Nelda Jean 1956- *WhoSSW 91*
Ortiz, Norma I. 1955- *WhoHisp 91*
Ortiz, Nydia 1951- *WhoHisp 91*
Ortiz, Olivia Frances 1926- *WhoHisp 91*
Ortiz, Pablo Francis 1948- *WhoHisp 91*
Ortiz, Peter J. *BioIn 16*
Ortiz, Rachael 1941- *WhoHisp 91*
Ortiz, Rafael Montanez 1934- *BioIn 16, WhoAm 90, WhoAmA 91, WhoE 91, WhoHisp 91, WhoWor 91*
Ortiz, Ramon 1813-1896 *BioIn 16*
Ortiz, Raquel 1945- *WhoHisp 91*
Ortiz, Remey S. *WhoHisp 91*
Ortiz, Reynaldo U. 1946- *WhoHisp 91*
Ortiz, Roberto 1915-1971 *Ballpl 90*
Ortiz, Ronald Antonio 1930- *WhoHisp 91*
Ortiz, Roxanne Dunbar 1938- *WhoWrEP 89*
Ortiz, Solomon P. 1937- *BioIn 16, WhoAm 90, WhoSSW 91*
Ortiz, Solomon Porfirio 1937- *WhoHisp 91*
Ortiz, Tino G. *WhoHisp 91*
Ortiz, Vilma 1954- *WhoHisp 91*
Ortiz, William 1947- *IntWWM 90*
Ortiz-Alvarez, Jorge L. 1952- *WhoHisp 91*
Ortiz-Buonafina, Marta 1933- *WhoHisp 91*
Ortiz Cofer, Judith 1952- *BioIn 16*
Ortiz-Cotto, Pablo 1929- *WhoHisp 91*
Ortiz-Daliot, Jose A. *ODwPR 91*
Ortiz de Montellano, Bernard Ramon, V 1938- *WhoHisp 91*
Ortiz de Montellano, Paul Richard *WhoHisp 91*
Ortiz-Franco, Luis 1946- *WhoHisp 91*
Ortiz-Griffin, Julia L. *WhoHisp 91*
Ortiz-Mena, Antonio 1912- *St&PR 91, WhoAm 90, WhoWor 91*
Ortiz-Murias, Alfredo *BioIn 16, WhoHisp 91N*
Ortiz Sanchez, Lourdes 1943- *EncCoWW*
Ortiz-Sotelo, Cesar Augusto 1958- *WhoWor 91*
Ortiz-Suarez, Humberto J. 1941- *WhoHisp 91*
Ortiz-Truscott, Margarita 1942- *WhoAmW 91*
Ortiz-White, Aleene J. 1953- *WhoHisp 91*
Ortleb, Charles *BioIn 16*
Ortlieb, Robert Eugene 1925- *WhoAm 90, WhoAmA 91*
Ortlip, Mary Krueger *WhoAmA 91, WhoSSW 91*
Ortlip, Paul Daniel 1926- *WhoAm 90, WhoAmA 91, WhoWor 91*
Ortman, Eldon E. 1934- *WhoAm 90*
Ortman, George Earl 1926- *WhoAm 90, WhoAmA 91*
Ortman, James *BioIn 16*
Ortman, Laurice W. 1908- *St&PR 91*
Ortmann, Dorothea 1912- *WhoAmW 91, WhoE 91, WhoWor 91*
Ortmayer, Roland *BioIn 16*
Ortmeyer, Dale Herbert 1926- *WhoE 91*
Ortner, Donald Richard 1922- *WhoSSW 91*
Ortner, Everett Howard 1919- *WhoAm 90*
Ortner, Gustav 1935- *WhoWor 91*
Ortner, Mary Joanne 1946- *WhoAmW 91, WhoE 91*
Ortner, Michael 1954- *WhoWor 91*
Ortner, Reinhold 1930- *WhoWor 91*
Ortner, Samuel 1912- *St&PR 91*
Ortner, Sherry B 1941- *ConAu 130*
Ortolani, Benito 1928- *WhoAm 90*
Ortolani, Minot Henry 1929- *WhoAm 90*
Ortolano, Leonard 1941- *WhoAm 90*
Ortoll, Javier *WhoHisp 91*
Orton, Eve *BioIn 16*
Orton, Helen 1872- *AuBYP 90*
Orton, Joe *BioIn 16, MajTwCW*
Orton, Joe 1933-1967 *WorAlBi*
Orton, John Kingsley 1933-1967 *MajTwCW*
Orton, Katharine Wilson 1953- *St&PR 91*
Orton, Lawrence M. 1899-1988 *BioIn 16*
Orton, Robert C. *St&PR 91*
Orton, Robert Clayton 1934- *WhoAm 90*
Orton, Samuel Torrey *BioIn 16*
Orton, Stewart 1915- *WhoAm 90*
Orton, Susan Josephine 1945- *WhoAmW 91*
Ortt, Felix 1866-1959 *EncO&P 3*
Orttung, William Herbert 1934- *WhoAm 90*
Orttung-Morrow, Janet *BiDrAPA 89*
Ortuno, Rene Barrientos 1919-1969 *BioIn 16*
Ortyl, Nicholas Edward, III 1961- *WhoE 91*
Orullian, B. LaRae 1933- *WhoAmW 91*
Orullian, LaRae 1933- *St&PR 91*
Orum, Poul 1919- *TwCCr&M 91B*
Orum, Terrell Beth 1961- *WhoAmW 91*
Orvik, Wallace Duane 1926- *St&PR 91*
Orville, Harold Duvall 1932- *WhoAm 90*
Orville, Richard Edmonds 1936- *WhoAm 90*
Orvin, Donna Clair *BiDrAPA 89*
Orvin, George H 1922- *BiDrAPA 89*
Orvis, I.D. 1924- *St&PR 91*
Orvis, Marianne 1816-1901 *FemiCLE*
Orvos, Robert L. 1932- *St&PR 91*
Orwell, George *ConAu 132, MajTwCW*
Orwell, George 1903-1950 *DcLB 98 [port], RGTwCSF, WorAlBi*
Orwen, Gifford Phillips *WhoAm 90*
Orwig, Cherie Lee 1948- *WhoAmW 91*
Orwoll, Gregg S. K. 1926- *WhoAm 90, WhoWor 91*
Orwoll, Rebecca Lynn 1949- *WhoAmW 91*
Orwoll, Robert Arvid 1940- *WhoSSW 91*
Ory, Edward 1926- *WhoAm 90*
Ory, Kid 1886-1973 *BioIn 16, DrBlPA 90, OxCPMus, WorAlBi*
Ory, Marcia Gail 1950- *WhoAmW 91*
Oryschuk, Roman 1953- *St&PR 91*
Oryshkevich, Roman Sviatoslav 1928- *WhoAm 90*
Orza, Vincent Frank 1950- *WhoSSW 91*
Orzac, Edward Seymour 1917- *WhoWor 91*
Orze, Joseph John 1932- *WhoAmA 91*
Orzech, Ann Dorothy Wagner 1950- *WhoE 91*
Orzechowski, R.J. 1943- *St&PR 91*
Orzechowski, Robert David 1949- *WhoE 91*
Orzeck, Eric A. 1940- *St&PR 91*
Orzeszkowa, Eliza 1841-1910 *EncCoWW*
Orzolek, Walter P. 1933- *St&PR 91*
Osadca, Bohdan S 1919- *BiDrAPA 89*
O'Saile, Charles Murray 1944- *WhoSSW 91*
Osaka, Naoyuki 1946- *WhoWor 91*
Osaki, Toyoko 1930- *WhoWor 91*
Osakwe, Christopher 1942- *WhoAm 90, WhoWor 91*
Osam, Harold Duane 1927- *St&PR 91*
Osamu, Muroi 1934- *WhoWor 91*
Osamu, Takenaka 1940- *WhoWor 91*
Osato, Michael Shoji 1949- *WhoSSW 91*
Osawa, Gengo 1932- *WhoWor 91*
Osawa, Kazuko 1926- *IntWWM 90*
Osawa, Misumi 1926- *WhoWor 91*
Osback, Terry *BiDrAPA 89*
Osbaldeston, Gordon Francis 1930- *WhoAm 90*
Osberg, Allan F. 1924- *St&PR 91*
Osbon, Bradley Sillick 1827-1912 *BioIn 16*
Osborn, Arthur W 1891- *EncO&P 3, EncPaPR 91*
Osborn, Bob 1903-1960 *Ballpl 90*
Osborn, Carolyn Culbert 1934- *WhoWrEP 89*
Osborn, Clifford J. 1917- *St&PR 91*
Osborn, Clifton Earl 1937- *WhoSSW 91*
Osborn, David Dudley 1958- *WhoE 91*
Osborn, Donald Herbert 1936- *St&PR 91*
Osborn, Donald Robert 1929- *WhoAm 90*
Osborn, Donald W. 1931- *St&PR 91*
Osborn, Earl Dodge 1893-1988 *BioIn 16*
Osborn, Edward Collet 1909-1957 *EncO&P 3*
Osborn, Elburt Franklin 1911- *WhoAm 90*
Osborn, Elodie C 1911- *WhoAmA 91*
Osborn, Emily Mary 1834-1913? *BiDWomA*
Osborn, Frank D. 1947- *St&PR 91*
Osborn, Gerald Guy 1947- *BiDrAPA 89*
Osborn, Glenn Richard 1928- *WhoSSW 91, WhoWor 91*
Osborn, Guy A. 1936- *WhoAm 90*
Osborn, Ian Charles 1946- *BiDrAPA 89*
Osborn, Jacqueline Elizabeth 1951- *WhoAmW 91*
Osborn, James E., II 1925- *St&PR 91*
Osborn, James Marshall, Jr. *WhoAm 90*
Osborn, Janet Lynn 1952- *WhoAmW 91*
Osborn, John David 1948- *WhoWor 91*
Osborn, John Edward 1957- *WhoE 91*
Osborn, John Emory 1950- *WhoEmL 91*
Osborn, John S., Jr. 1926- *St&PR 91*
Osborn, John Simcoe, Jr. 1926- *WhoAm 90*
Osborn, June Elaine 1937- *WhoAm 90, WhoAmW 91*
Osborn, Kathleen Anne 1953- *BiDrAPA 89*
Osborn, Kent 1940- *St&PR 91*
Osborn, Kevin Russell 1951- *WhoAmA 91*
Osborn, La Donna Carol 1947- *WhoSSW 91*
Osborn, Leslie A 1906- *BiDrAPA 89*
Osborn, Leslie Andrewartha 1906- *WhoAm 90*
Osborn, Lois D 1915- *SmATA 61 [port]*
Osborn, Malcolm Everett 1928- *WhoWor 91*
Osborn, Marvin Griffing, Jr. 1922- *WhoAm 90*
Osborn, Mary Jane Merten 1927- *WhoAm 90*
Osborn, Michael V 1946- *BiDrAPA 89*
Osborn, Michelle Pynchon 1927- *WhoAmW 91*
Osborn, Paul *BioIn 16*
Osborn, Paul 1901-1988 *AnObit 1988, WorAu 1980 [port]*
Osborn, Retus W, III 1926- *BiDrAPA 89*
Osborn, Robert 1904- *WhoAmA 91*
Osborn, Robert Chesley 1904- *WhoAm 90*
Osborn, Roger Cook 1920- *WhoAm 90*
Osborn, Ronald Edwin 1917- *WhoAm 90*
Osborn, Ruth Gentry *BiDrAPA 89*
Osborn, Sarah 1693-1775 *FemiCLE*
Osborn, Sarah 1714-1796 *FemiCLE*
Osborn, Sarah Haggar 1714-1796 *EncCRAm*
Osborn, Stephen J. 1846-1941 *AmLegL*
Osborn, Susan *NewAgMG*
Osborn, Tap *BioIn 16*
Osborn, Terry Wayne 1943- *WhoAm 90*
Osborn, Thomas Andrew 1836-1898 *BioIn 16*
Osborn, Thomas Ogden 1832-1904 *BioIn 16*
Osborn, William George 1925- *WhoAm 90*
Osborne, Alice 1592-1659 *BiDEWW*
Osborne, Audrey Mae 1935- *WhoAmW 91*
Osborne, Bobbie 1931- *OxCPMus*
Osborne, Bobo 1935- *Ballpl 90*
Osborne, Bruce F. 1942- *St&PR 91*
Osborne, Burl 1937- *WhoAm 90, WhoSSW 91*
Osborne, Carol Ann 1938- *WhoAmW 91*
Osborne, Cary Goodrich 1945- *WhoWrEP 89*
Osborne, Charles 1927- *BioIn 16, IntWWM 90*
Osborne, Cynthia A 1947- *WhoAmA 91*
Osborne, Dallas Hampton 1960- *WhoSSW 91*
Osborne, David *AuBYP 90, MajTwCW*
Osborne, Dee S. 1930- *WhoAm 90*
Osborne, Dorothy 1627-1695 *BiDEWW, BioIn 16, FemiCLE*
Osborne, Elizabeth 1936- *WhoAmA 91, WhoE 91*
Osborne, Frederick Spring, Jr. 1940- *WhoAm 90*
Osborne, Gayla Marlene 1956- *WhoAmW 91*
Osborne, Gayle Ann 1951- *WhoAmW 91, WhoWor 91*
Osborne, Geneva Estelle Massey Riddle 1901-1981 *BioIn 16*
Osborne, George *MajTwCW*
Osborne, George Delano 1938- *WhoE 91*
Osborne, Gerald E. 1938- *WhoSSW 91*
Osborne, Gordon 1906- *St&PR 91*
Osborne, Gregory *BioIn 16, WhoAm 90*
Osborne, Harold 1905-1987 *BioIn 16*
Osborne, Harold Wayne 1930- *WhoAm 90*
Osborne, James Gilbert *BiDrAPA 89*
Osborne, James William 1928- *WhoAm 90*
Osborne, Jeffrey *BioIn 16*
Osborne, Jerry Paul 1944- *WhoWrEP 89*
Osborne, Joe C. 1948- *St&PR 91*
Osborne, John 1929- *MajTwCW, WorAlBi*
Osborne, John Alfred 1936- *BioIn 16*
Osborne, John James 1929- *WhoWor 91*
Osborne, John Walter 1927- *WhoAm 90, WhoWrEP 89*
Osborne, Joseph 1962- *WhoSSW 91*
Osborne, Kenneth Ray 1936- *St&PR 91*
Osborne, Maggie Ellen 1941- *WhoWrEP 89*
Osborne, Mark Lewis 1952- *WhoWor 91*
Osborne, Mary 1921- *BioIn 16*
Osborne, Mary Pope 1949- *BioIn 16*
Osborne, MaryHelen 1936- *WhoAmW 91*
Osborne, Morris Floyd 1931- *WhoSSW 91*
Osborne, Neville 1928- *IntWWM 90*
Osborne, Nigel 1948- *IntWWM 90, PenDiMP A*
Osborne, Raymond Lester *BiDrAPA 89*
Osborne, Raymond Lester, Jr. 1939- *WhoE 91*
Osborne, Richard Cogswell 1944- *St&PR 91, WhoAm 90*
Osborne, Richard De Jongh 1934- *St&PR 91, WhoAm 90, WhoE 91*
Osborne, Richard E. 1932- *St&PR 91*
Osborne, Richard Hazelet 1920- *WhoAm 90*
Osborne, Richard Jay 1951- *WhoAm 90, WhoEmL 91*
Osborne, Richard L. 1942- *St&PR 91*
Osborne, Robert George, II *BiDrAPA 89*
Osborne, Robert Lee 1928- *WhoAmA 91*
Osborne, Robert V. 1916- *St&PR 91*
Osborne, Seward Russell 1946- *WhoE 91*
Osborne, Sheri *BioIn 16*
Osborne, Sonny 1937- *OxCPMus*
Osborne, Stanley de Jongh 1905- *WhoAm 90, WhoWor 91*
Osborne, Stanley J. 1905- *St&PR 91*
Osborne, Theresa Jo 1945- *WhoAmW 91, WhoEmL 91, WhoWor 91*
Osborne, Thomas Cramer 1927- *St&PR 91*
Osborne, Tiny 1893-1969 *Ballpl 90*
Osborne, Tony Roy Stuart 1947- *IntWWM 90*
Osborne, Vincent Edward 1942- *St&PR 91*
Osborne, Walter Daryl 1954- *St&PR 91*
Osborne, Will 1949- *ConAu 132*
Osborne, William Mays 1934- *WhoAm 90*
Osborne, Willis Williams 1935- *St&PR 91*
Osborne, Zebulon L. 1946- *WhoSSW 91*
Osborne-Popp, Glenna Jean 1945- *WhoE 91*
Osbourne, John 1946- *EncPR&S 89*
Osbourne, Ozzy *BioIn 16*
Osbourne, Ozzy 1948- *WorAlBi*
Osbourne, Sharon *BioIn 16*
Osbun, William N. 1914- *St&PR 91*
Osburn, Charles Benjamin 1939- *WhoAm 90*
Osburn, James Octavius 1919- *WhoAm 90*
Osby, Greg *BioIn 16*
Osby, Larissa Geiss 1928- *WhoAm 90, WhoAmA 91*
Osby, Robert Edward 1937- *WhoAm 90*
O'Scanlon, Declan *BiDrAPA 89*
O'Scannlain, Diarmuid Fionntain 1937- *WhoAm 90*
Oscar, Joyce Annette 1956- *WhoAmW 91*
Oscar, Leung Honman 1919- *WhoWor 91*
Oscarsson, Gosta Valentin 1944- *WhoWor 91*
Oscarsson, Victoria Constance Gunhild 1951- *WhoAmA 91*
Osceola *MajTwCW*
Osceola 1803?-1838 *WhNaAH [port]*
Osceola 1804-1838 *BioIn 16*
Oscherwitz, Bernard 1910- *St&PR 91*
Oscherwitz, Mark 1931- *St&PR 91*
Oscherwitz, Millard Samuel 1921- *St&PR 91*
Oscherwitz, Morris G 1937- *BiDrAPA 89*
Oschin, Francine 1943- *WhoAmW 91*
Osdene, Thomas Stefan 1927- *WhoAm 90, WhoWor 91*

Ose, Peggy Jo 1951- *WhoEmL 91*
Ose, Wendy Gross *BiDrAPA 89*
Oseasohn, Robert 1924- *WhoAm 90*
Osei-Tutu, John B *BiDrAPA 89*
Osekowsky, Henry J 1932- *BiDrAPA 89*
Oseland, Bruce J. *BioIn 16*
Oseland, Bruce J. 1946- *ODwPR 91*
Osella, Wayne Alexander 1945- *St&PR 91*
Osenar, Peter R. 1940- *St&PR 91*
Osenlund, Richard K. 1954- *WhoE 91*
Oseola 1803?-1838 *WhNaAH [port]*
Osepchuk, John Moses 1927- *WhoAm 90*
Oser, Bernard Lerussove 1899- *WhoAm 90*
Oser, Marsha *WhoAmW 91*
Oser, Roman Bernard 1930- *St&PR 91, WhoAm 90*
Oser, Ronald Sandor 1945- *WhoE 91*
Osero, Gloria Jean 1950- *WhoAmW 91*
Oseroff, Andrew Bell 1938- *WhoSSW 91*
Oseroff, Charles Jacob *BiDrAPA 89*
Oseroff, Stephen L. 1941- *St&PR 91*
Oses, Joaquin M 1929- *BiDrAPA 89*
Osesr, David Neal 1946- *WhoE 91*
Osfield, Kenneth James 1952- *WhoEmL 91*
Osgood, Barbara Travis 1934- *WhoAmW 91*
Osgood, Charles *BioIn 16*
Osgood, Charles 1933- *WhoAm 90, WhoE 91*
Osgood, Charles Egerton 1916- *WhoWrEP 89*
Osgood, Charles Freeman 1938- *WhoE 91*
Osgood, Edward H. 1916- *St&PR 91*
Osgood, Frances 1811-1850 *FemiCLE*
Osgood, Frank William 1931- *WhoWor 91*
Osgood, Jere 1936- *WhoAmA 91*
Osgood, Lawrence Walter 1946- *WhoEmL 91*
Osgood, Peter G. 1940- *ODwPR 91*
Osgood, Peter Greer 1940- *WhoAm 90, WhoWor 91*
Osgood, Richard M., Jr. 1943- *WhoAm 90*
Osgood, Russell King 1947- *WhoAm 90*
Osgood, Ruth *WhoAmA 91N*
Osgood, Samuel 1748-1813 *BiDrUSE 89*
Osgood, William Edward 1926- *AuBYP 90*
O'Shan, Philip H. 1921- *St&PR 91*
O'Shanick, Gregory John 1953- *BiDrAPA 89*
O'Shaughnessey, Herschel E. *St&PR 91*
O'Shaughnessey, Hugh Peter *BiDrAPA 89*
O'Shaughnessy, John Patrick 1930- *St&PR 91*
O'Shaughnessy, Kathleen Kolbe 1951- *WhoWrEP 89*
O'Shaughnessy, Nelson Jarvis Waterbury 1876-1932 *BioIn 16*
O'Shaughnessy, Patricia Mary 1949- *WhoAmW 91*
O'Shaughnessy, Rosemarie 1940- *WhoAmW 91*
O'Shaughnessy, Roy Joseph *BiDrAPA 89*
O'Shaughnessy, Thomas Michael 1956- *WhoSSW 91*
O'Shaugnessy, Brian 1925- *ConAu 132*
O'Shea, Alice Pauline *BiDrAPA 89*
O'Shea, Arthur Ambrose, Jr. 1934- *WhoSSW 91*
O'Shea, Catherine Large 1944- *WhoWrEP 89*
O'Shea, Eileen Mary 1945- *WhoE 91*
O'Shea, Harriet E. *BioIn 16*
O'Shea, John 1928- *WhoE 91, WhoWor 91*
O'Shea, John Anthony 1939- *WhoWor 91*
O'Shea, John D. 1918- *St&PR 91*
O'Shea, John Edward 1932- *St&PR 91*
O'Shea, John James 1944- *St&PR 91*
O'Shea, John Joseph 1943- *St&PR 91*
O'Shea, John P. 1930- *WhoE 91*
O'Shea, John Stewart 1944- *WhoE 91*
O'Shea, Kathy Ann 1962- *WhoSSW 91*
O'Shea, Lynne Edeen 1945- *WhoAm 90*
O'Shea, Michael John 1937- *St&PR 91*
O'Shea, Neil Patrick 1961- *WhoE 91*
O'Shea, Pat 1931- *AuBYP 90*
O'Shea, Paul C. 1936- *ODwPR 91*
O'Shea, Peter Joseph, Jr. 1937- *WhoAm 90*
O'Shea, Terrence Patrick 1941- *WhoAmA 91*
O'Shea, Thomas Kevin 1948- *WhoEmL 91*
O'Sheal, Frank E *BiDrAPA 89*
Osheowitz, Michael *ODwPR 91*
Osher, Fred Charles *BiDrAPA 89*
Osher, Stanley *BiDrAPA 89*
Osheroff, Douglas Dean 1945- *WhoAm 90*
Osheroff, Marjorie Helen 1948- *WhoE 91*
O'Shields, Richard L. 1926- *St&PR 91*
O'Shields, Richard Lee 1926- *WhoAm 90*
Oshima Nagisa 1932- *EncJap*
Oshima, Michael W. 1957- *WhoE 91*
Oshima, Nagisa 1932- *BioIn 16, WhoWor 91*
Oshima, Shunsaku 1927- *WhoWor 91*
Oshima, Tomoo 1925- *WhoWor 91*
Oshin, Sheldon Burton 1927- *St&PR 91*
Oshins, Gladys Barbara 1935- *WhoAmW 91*
Oshita, Hiroshi *Ballpl 90*
Oshita, Hosen 1926- *St&PR 91*
Oshita, Kazuma 1948- *WhoAmA 91*
Oshita, Koji *BioIn 16*
Oshita, Koji 1928- *WhoAm 90, WhoWor 91*
Oshkosh 1795-1858 *WhNaAH*
Oshkushi 1795-1858 *WhNaAH*
Oshlo, Eric Lee 1947- *WhoSSW 91*
Oshman, Malin Kenneth 1940- *WhoAm 90*
Oshodin, Osayuki Godwin 1950- *WhoWor 91*
Oshop, Robert Wm. 1946- *St&PR 91*
Oshrain, Mindy 1957- *BiDrAPA 89*
Oshrin, Harvey W 1934- *BiDrAPA 89*
Oshry, Harold L. 1918- *St&PR 91*
Oshry, Jay 1939- *St&PR 91*
Osias, Richard Allen 1938- *WhoAm 90, WhoSSW 91, WhoWor 91*
O'Sickey, Joseph Benjamin 1918- *WhoAmA 91*
Osieck, Hans 1910- *IntWWM 90*
Osigweh, Brenda Jean 1957- *WhoAmW 91*
Osigweh, Chimezie Anthony Baylon-Pascal 1955- *WhoSSW 91, WhoWor 91*
Osika, Susan Mary 1947- *BiDrAPA 89*
Osinski, Dan 1933- *Ballpl 90*
Osinski, Margaret Jean 1939- *WhoE 91*
Osinski, Walter A *BiDrAPA 89*
Osinskii, N. 1887-1938 *BioIn 16*
Osipow, Samuel Herman 1934- *WhoAm 90*
Osipuk, Darlene Marie *BiDrAPA 89*
Osis, Karlis 1917- *EncO&P 3, EncPaPR 91*
Osius, Larry Clark 1930- *WhoAm 90*
Oskam, Adrianus 1935- *WhoWor 91*
Oskandy, James Michael 1948- *St&PR 91*
Oskashe 1795-1858 *WhNaAH*
Oskay, Billy *NewAgMG*
Oskey, D. Beth 1921- *WhoAmW 91*
Oski, Frank Aram 1932- *WhoAm 90*
Oskin, David W. 1942- *St&PR 91*
Oskin, David William 1942- *WhoAm 90*
Oskin, Hilbert Edgar 1930- *BiDrAPA 89, WhoE 91*
Oskoshe 1795-1858 *WhNaAH*
Oskowski, Mary C *BiDrAPA 89*
Osler, Dorothy K. 1923- *WhoAmW 91*
Osler, Featherstone Lake 1805-1895 *DcCanB 12*
Osler, Geoffrey F *BiDrAPA 89*
Osler, Gordon Peter 1922- *WhoAm 90*
Osler, Howard Lloyd 1927- *WhoAm 90*
Osler, Julie 1947- *ODwPR 91, WhoE 91*
Osler, William 1849-1919 *BioIn 16*
Oslin, David Wayne 1963- *BiDrAPA 89*
Oslin, K. T. *BioIn 16, WhoNeCM [port]*
Oslin, Kay Toinette *WhoAm 90, WhoAmW 91*
Osman, Betty Barshad 1929- *WhoAmW 91*
Osman, Dewaine Lowell 1934- *St&PR 91*
Osman, Edith Gabriella 1949- *WhoAmW 91, WhoSSW 91*
Osman, Ismail Ibrahim 1943- *WhoWor 91*
Osman, Mahomed Hussen 1947- *WhoWor 91*
Osman, Marvin P 1924- *BiDrAPA 89*
Osman, Mary Ella Williams *WhoAmW 91*
Osman, Mitchel 1943- *BiDrAPA 89*
Osman, Ossama M *BiDrAPA 89*
Osmanczyk, Edmund Jan 1913-1989 *BioIn 16, ConAu 130*
Osmer, Margaret *WhoAm 90*
Osmer, Patrick Stewart 1943- *WhoAm 90*
Osmer, Robert Henry 1952- *WhoSSW 91*
Osmond, Alan 1949- *EncPR&S 89, OxCPMus*
Osmond, Andrew Philip Kingsford 1938- *SpyFic*
Osmond, Dennis Gordon 1930- *WhoAm 90*
Osmond, Donny 1957- *EncPR&S 89, OxCPMus, WorAlBi*
Osmond, Edward 1900- *AuBYP 90*
Osmond, Gordon Condie 1934- *WhoAm 90*
Osmond, Humphrey 1917- *EncO&P 3*
Osmond, Jay 1955- *EncPR&S 89, OxCPMus*
Osmond, Jimmy *BioIn 16*
Osmond, Jimmy 1963- *OxCPMus*
Osmond, Lynn Joyce 1957- *IntWWM 90, WhoAmW 91*
Osmond, Marie 1959- *BioIn 16, EncPR&S 89, OxCPMus, WhoAm 90, WhoAmW 91, WorAlBi*
Osmond, Merrill 1953- *EncPR&S 89, OxCPMus*
Osmond, Robert 1711?-1789 *PenDiDA 89*
Osmond, Wayne 1951- *EncPR&S 89, OxCPMus*
Osmonds, The *EncPR&S 89, OxCPMus*
Osmont, Anne 1872-1953 *EncO&P 3*
Osmycki, Daniel A. 1931- *WhoWor 91*
Osner, George Thomas 1947- *WhoEmL 91*
Osnes, Larry G. 1941- *WhoAm 90*
Osnos, David M. 1932- *St&PR 91*
Osnos, David Marvin 1932- *WhoAm 90, WhoWor 91*
Osnos, Marta *NewYTBS 90*
Osnos, Peter Lionel Winston 1943- *WhoAm 90*
Osnos, Robert J B 1931- *BiDrAPA 89*
Osoff, Jeffrey Arlin 1936- *WhoE 91*
Osofsky, Herbert S. 1934- *WhoSSW 91*
Osofsky, Howard Joseph 1935- *BiDrAPA 89*
Osorio, Hector Jairo 1959- *BiDrAPA 89*
Osorio, Irene Figueroa 1948- *WhoHisp 91*
Osorio, Oscar 1910-1969 *BioIn 16*
Osorio, Rosa 1946- *WhoAmW 91*
Ososami, Olayide Theophilus 1932- *WhoWor 91*
Osowiec, Darlene Ann 1951- *WhoAmW 91*
Ospina Perez, Mariano 1891-1976 *BioIn 16*
Osrin, Raymond Harold 1928- *WhoAm 90*
Ossakow, Susan Amy *BiDrAPA 89*
Ossart, Michel 1938- *WhoWor 91*
Ossenberg, Friedrich-Wilhelm 1940- *WhoWor 91*
Ossenberg, Hella Svetlana 1930- *WhoAmW 91*
Ossenkop, David Charles 1937- *IntWWM 90*
Osser, David Neal 1946- *BiDrAPA 89*
Osserman, Elliott F. 1925-1989 *BioIn 16*
Osserman, Robert 1926- *WhoAm 90*
Osservanza Master *BioIn 16*
Ossewaarde, Anne Winkler 1957- *WhoAmW 91*
Ossian, Michael Steven 1957- *BiDrAPA 89*
Ossio Sanjines, Luis *WhoWor 91*
Ossip, Bobbi Ann 1938- *WhoAmW 91*
Ossip, Jerome J. *BioIn 16*
Ossip, Jerome J. 1920- *WhoE 91*
Ossipoff, Vladimir Nicholas 1907- *WhoAm 90*
Ossmann, Robert E. 1944- *St&PR 91*
Ossoff, Robert Henry 1947- *WhoAm 90, WhoEmL 91, WhoSSW 91*
Ossofsky, Helen Johns *BiDrAPA 89*
Ossofsky, Helen Johns 1921- *WhoAmW 91*
Ossofsky, Jack *BioIn 16*
Ossola, Rinaldo *NewYTBS 90*
Ossoli, Marchesa *BioAmW*
Ossoli, Margaret Fuller 1810-1850 *BioIn 16*
Ossoli, Sarah M Fuller, Marchesa d' 1810-1850 *BioIn 16*
Ossont, Margaret Rebecca 1948- *WhoAmW 91*
Ossorguine, Serge *BioIn 16*
Ossorio, Alfonso 1916-1990 *NewYTBS 90, WhoAmA 91N*
Ossorio, Gualberto 1949- *WhoWor 91*
Ossorio, Joseph Manuel 1947- *BiDrAPA 89*
Ossowiecki, Stefan 1877-1944 *EncPaPR 91*
Ossowiecki, Stephan 1877-1944 *EncO&P 3*
Ostap, Martine Elizabeth 1959- *WhoAmW 91*
Ostapchuk, William John 1943- *WhoE 91*
Ostapowicz, Phillip Gary 1956- *St&PR 91*
Ostaptzeff, Georges 1934- *WhoWor 91*
Ostapuk, David Ray 1948- *WhoEmL 91, WhoWor 91*
Ostar, Allan William 1924- *WhoAm 90, WhoWor 91*
Ostaszewski, Krzysztof Maciej 1957- *WhoSSW 91*
Ostberg, Gustaf 1926- *WhoWor 91*
Ostberg, Henry D. 1928- *St&PR 91*
Ostby, Kevin Charles 1956- *St&PR 91*
Ostby, Ronald 1937- *WhoAm 90*
Ostby, Sandra Josephine 1951- *WhoAmW 91*
Ostdiek, Glen Richard 1930- *St&PR 91*
Osteen, Claude 1939- *Ballpl 90*
Osteen, Harry Montague, Jr. 1941- *WhoAm 90*
Osteen, Helen Cooper 1932- *WhoSSW 91*
Osteen, Hubert Duvall, Jr. 1936- *St&PR 91*
O'Steen, Jacqueline Janda 1953- *WhoSSW 91*
O'Steen, John A. 1944- *St&PR 91*
O'Steen, John Andrew 1944- *WhoAm 90*
O'Steen, Judi K. 1947- *St&PR 91*
O'Steen, Michael 1962- *ConTFT 8*
O'Steen, Wendall Keith 1928- *WhoAm 90*
Ostell, John 1813-1892 *DcCanB 12*
Ostendorf, Carole Glorine 1948- *WhoAmW 91*
Ostendorf, Joan Donahue 1933- *WhoAmW 91*
Ostendorf, Lloyd 1921- *AuBYP 90*
Ostendorf, Lloyd, Jr 1921- *WhoAmA 91*
Ostendorff, William Charles 1954- *WhoSSW 91*
Ostendorp, Gary Lee 1941- *St&PR 91*
Ostenso, Brian T. 1951- *St&PR 91*
Ostenso, Martha 1900-1963 *DcLB 92 [port], FemiCLE*
Oster, A.F. 1930- *St&PR 91*
Oster, Avi Robert 1959- *St&PR 91*
Oster, Clinton Victor 1920- *WhoAm 90*
Oster, Gerald 1918- *WhoAm 90, WhoAmA 91*
Oster, Heidi Joy 1958- *St&PR 91*
Oster, Lewis Henry 1923- *St&PR 91*
Oster, Ludwig Friedrich 1931- *WhoAm 90*
Oster, Martin William 1947- *WhoE 91, WhoEmL 91*
Oster, Merrill James 1940- *WhoAm 90*
Oster, Michael L. 1952- *St&PR 91*
Oster, Patrick 1944- *ConAu 131*
Oster, Patrick Ralph 1944- *WhoAm 90*
Oster, Robert Alan 1944- *St&PR 91*
Oster, Rose Marie Gunhild 1934- *WhoAm 90*
Oster, William P. 1905- *St&PR 91*
Osterback, Vernon L. 1932- *St&PR 91*
Osterberg, Becky 1946- *WhoAmW 91*
Osterberg, Becky W. 1946- *ODwPR 91, St&PR 91*
Osterberg, Mark William 1950- *St&PR 91, WhoAm 90*
Osterberg, Thomas Karl 1953- *WhoWor 91*
Osterbrock, Donald Edward *WhoAm 90*
Ostergaard, G N 1926-1990 *ConAu 131*
Ostergaard, Jerry 1960- *ODwPR 91*
Ostergard, Holly Acklie 1957- *St&PR 91*
Ostergard, Paul Michael 1939- *WhoAm 90, WhoE 91*
Ostergren, Jerald B. 1930- *St&PR 91*
Osterhaus, William Eric 1935- *WhoAm 90*
Osterheld, Robert Keith 1925- *WhoAm 90*
Osterhoff, James M. 1936- *St&PR 91*
Osterhoff, James Marvin 1936- *WhoAm 90*
Osterholm, John Roger 1936- *WhoSSW 91*
Osterhout, Dan R. 1950- *St&PR 91*
Osterhout, Dan Roderick 1950- *WhoAm 90*
Osterhout, Michael Dennis 1948- *WhoAm 90, WhoSSW 91*
Osterhout, Richard A. 1929- *St&PR 91*
Osterhout, Suydam 1925- *WhoAm 90*
Osterhout, Winthrop John Vanleuven 1871-1964 *DcScB S2*
Osterhus, Herman 1932- *St&PR 91*
Osterhus, John E. 1945- *ODwPR 91*
Osterle, John Fletcher 1925- *WhoAm 90*
Osterling, Allen W. 1926- *St&PR 91*
Osterling, Anders Johan 1884-1981 *DcScanL*
Osterloh, Wellington F. 1936- *ODwPR 91*
Osterloh, Wellington Frederick 1936- *St&PR 91*
Osterlund, Kari Johan 1945- *WhoWor 91*
Osterman, Charles Anthony 1933- *WhoSSW 91*
Osterman, Constantine E. 1936- *WhoAmW 91*
Osterman, Debra M *BiDrAPA 89*
Osterman, Susan 1949- *WhoWrEP 89*
Osterman-Olson, Karen 1951- *WhoAmW 91*
Ostermeier, Terry Harlan 1937- *WhoAm 90*
Ostermeier, Wilmer John 1929- *St&PR 91*
Ostermeir-Nostro, Sharon 1962- *WhoAmW 91*
Ostermeyer, Elmer H. 1922- *St&PR 91*
Ostermiller, Wayne Harold 1943- *St&PR 91*
Ostermueller, Fritz 1907-1957 *Ballpl 90*
Ostern, Wilhelm Curt 1923- *WhoAm 90*
Osterndorf, Logan Carl 1917- *WhoE 91*
Osterneck, Guy-Kenneth 1934- *St&PR 91*
Osterreich, Traugott Konstantin 1880-1949 *EncPaPR 91*
Osterritter, John F. 1923- *AuBYP 90*
Ostertag, Robert Louis 1931- *WhoAm 90*
Osterweil, Suzanne 1940- *WhoAmA 91*
Osterweil, Wendy 1953- *WhoWrEP 89*
Osterweis, Steven L. 1912- *St&PR 91*
Osterweis, Steven Levy 1912- *WhoAm 90*
Osteryoung, Janet Gretchen 1939- *WhoAm 90*
Ostfeld, Adrian Michael 1926- *WhoAm 90*
Ostfeld, Alexander Marion 1932- *WhoE 91*
Ostfeld, Leonard S. 1942- *St&PR 91, WhoAm 90*
Ostgulen, R.E. 1951- *St&PR 91*
Osthoff, Wolfgang 1927- *IntWWM 90*
Ostiguy, Jean P.W. 1922- *St&PR 91*
Ostiguy, Jean-Rene 1925- *WhoAmA 91*
Ostler, James B. 1931- *St&PR 91*
Ostler, O. Don 1931- *St&PR 91, WhoAm 90*
Ostling, Paul James 1948- *WhoE 91*
Ostling, Richard Neil 1940- *WhoAm 90*
Ostlund, H. Gote 1923- *WhoAm 90*
Ostlund, Philip D 1928- *BiDrAPA 89*
Ostlund, Sorena Ann 1955- *WhoE 91*
Ostman, Arnold 1939- *PenDiMP*

Ostman, Jan I. C. 1929- *WhoWor 91*
Ostmann, Barbara Gibbs 1948- *WhoEmL 91*
Ostow, Abigail Ruth 1952- *BiDrAPA 89*
Ostow, Mortimer 1918- *BiDrAPA 89, WhoE 91*
Ostoyich, Marie Cross 1958- *WhoE 91*
Ostrach, Michael Sherwood 1951- *St&PR 91*
Ostrach, Simon 1923- *WhoAm 90*
Ostrand, Don R. 1923- *St&PR 91*
Ostrander, David Todd 1928- *St&PR 91*
Ostrander, Frederick 1926- *WhoWrEP 89*
Ostrander, Gregg Alan 1953- *St&PR 91*
Ostrander, Linda Woodaman 1937- *IntWWM 90*
Ostrander, Patricia *BioIn 16*
Ostrander, Robert Edwin 1931- *WhoE 91, WhoWor 91*
Ostrander, Thomas William 1950- *WhoAm 90*
Ostrander, William Lamar 1933- *St&PR 91*
Ostrem, Gunnar Muldrup 1922- *WhoWor 91*
Ostriche, Muriel 1896- *BioIn 16*
Ostriker, Alicia 1937- *ConAu 30NR, FemiCLE, WhoWrEP 89*
Ostriker, Jeremiah Paul 1937- *WhoAm 90*
Ostriker, Richard Alan 1951- *WhoEmL 91*
Ostro, Marc Jeffrey 1949- *WhoAm 90*
Ostroff, Alan M. 1952- *St&PR 91*
Ostroff, Arthur J. 1955- *St&PR 91*
Ostroff, James Jerrard 1951- *WhoE 91*
Ostroff, Robert Barasch 1948- *BiDrAPA 89*
Ostrofsky, Benjamin 1925- *WhoSSW 91*
Ostrogorsky, Michael 1951- *WhoWor 91*
Ostrom, Anthony De Witt 1935- *WhoAm 90*
Ostrom, Bjorn 1946- *WhoWor 91*
Ostrom, Carol Marie 1947- *WhoAmW 91*
Ostrom, Elinor 1933- *WhoAm 90*
Ostrom, John H. 1928- *WhoAm 90*
Ostrom, Mary Beth *BiDrAPA 89*
Ostrom, Meredith Eggers 1930- *WhoAm 90*
Ostrom, Vincent Alfred 1919- *WhoAm 90*
Ostroski, Gerald Basil 1941- *St&PR 91*
Ostroski, Richard J. 1938- *St&PR 91*
Ostrosser, Richard Holbrook 1927- *St&PR 91*
Ostroumova-Lebedeva, Anna Petrovna 1871-1955 *BiDWomA*
Ostrov, Jerome 1942- *WhoE 91*
Ostrove, Michele V. *ODwPR 91*
Ostrove, Paul Stuart 1931- *St&PR 91*
Ostrovsky, Alexander 1823-1886 *NinCLC 30 [port]*
Ostrovsky, Charles Y 1933- *BiDrAPA 89*
Ostrow, Barry Seymour 1941- *BiDrAPA 89*
Ostrow, David Gene 1947- *BiDrAPA 89*
Ostrow, Eileen Joyce 1949- *WhoAmW 91*
Ostrow, Eric H. 1944- *St&PR 91*
Ostrow, Joseph W. 1933- *St&PR 91, WhoAm 90*
Ostrow, Lawrence D *BiDrAPA 89*
Ostrow, Norman S. 1936-1988 *BioIn 16*
Ostrow, Philip Bernard 1918- *WhoAm 90*
Ostrow, Robert W. 1926- *St&PR 91*
Ostrow, Rona Lynn 1948- *WhoAmW 91*
Ostrow, Ronald F. 1944- *St&PR 91*
Ostrow, Ronald J. 1931- *ConAu 130*
Ostrow, Samuel D. 1945- *ODwPR 91*
Ostrow, Samuel David 1945- *WhoAm 90, WhoEmL 91*
Ostrow, Stephen Edward 1932- *WhoAmA 91*
Ostrow, Stosh 1948- *WhoSSW 91*
Ostrow, Stuart 1932- *WhoAm 90*
Ostrowska, Bronislawa 1881-1928 *EncCoWW*
Ostrowski, Dora J *BiDrAPA 89*
Ostrowski, Edward Joseph 1923- *WhoE 91*
Ostrowski, Elena Marina 1962- *WhoAmW 91*
Ostrowski, Helen *ODwPR 91*
Ostrowski, Ivan Daniel 1952- *WhoE 91*
Ostrowski, Jerzy 1938- *WhoWor 91*
Ostrowski, Joe 1916- *Ballpl 90*
Ostrowski, John 1917- *Ballpl 90*
Ostrowski, Lawrence G 1947- *BiDrAPA 89*
Ostrowski, Maria J. 1937- *WhoAmW 91*
Ostrowsky, Laura Ruth 1951- *WhoAmW 91*
Ostrum, Dean Gardner 1922- *WhoAm 90*
Ostry, Bernard 1927- *WhoAm 90*
Ostry, Sylvia *BioIn 16, WhoAm 90*
Ostrzenski, Adam 1940- *WhoE 91*
Ostteen, Bobby Claude 1945- *WhoEmL 91*
Ostuni, Peter W 1908- *WhoAmA 91*
Ostwal, Tilokchand P. 1954- *WhoWor 91*
Ostwald, Arnold 1923-1990 *BioIn 16*
Ostwald, David Frank *IntWWM 90*
Ostwald, Martin 1922- *WhoAm 90*
Ostwald, Peter 1928- *BiDrAPA 89*
Ostwald, Wilhelm 1853-1932 *WorAlBi*

Osty, Eugen 1874-1938 *EncO&P 3*
Osty, Eugene 1874-1938 *EncPaPR 91*
O'Such, Frederick Michael 1937- *St&PR 91*
Osuka, Akira 1934- *WhoWor 91*
O'Sullivan, Alex 1937- *St&PR 91*
O'Sullivan, Daniel Edward 1929- *WhoAm 90*
O'Sullivan, Daniel F. 1941- *St&PR 91*
O'Sullivan, Daniel John 1954- *WhoE 91*
O'Sullivan, Daniel Joseph 1940- *WhoAmA 91*
O'Sullivan, Dennis Ambrose 1848-1892 *DcCanB 12*
O'Sullivan, Dudley Joseph 1935- *WhoWor 91*
O'Sullivan, Edward Joseph 1939- *St&PR 91*
O'Sullivan, Eileen Ann 1956- *WhoAmW 91*
O'Sullivan, Emmet Patrick 1936- *St&PR 91*
O'Sullivan, Eugene Henry 1942- *WhoAm 90*
O'Sullivan, Eugene Joseph 1949- *St&PR 91*
O'Sullivan, Girardin S *BiDrAPA 89*
O'Sullivan, James Lawton 1916- *WhoAm 90*
O'Sullivan, James Noel 1944- *BiDrAPA 89*
O'Sullivan, John 1942- *ConAu 132*
O'Sullivan, John Conor 1932- *WhoWor 91*
O'Sullivan, John Francis 1938- *St&PR 91*
O'Sullivan, John Louis 1813-1895 *BioIn 16*
O'Sullivan, John Patrick, Jr. 1942- *St&PR 91*
O'Sullivan, Judith Roberta 1942- *WhoAm 90*
O'Sullivan, Mary J. 1938- *WhoAm 90*
O'Sullivan, Maureen *BioIn 16*
O'Sullivan, Maureen 1911- *WorAlBi*
O'Sullivan, Paul Kevin 1938- *WhoAm 90*
O'Sullivan, Peter *BioIn 16*
O'Sullivan, Preston Browne 1902-1989 *BioIn 16*
O'Sullivan, Stephen Francis 1944- *St&PR 91*
O'Sullivan, Timothy 1935- *ODwPR 91*
O'Sullivan, Timothy H. 1840-1882 *BioIn 16, WhNaAH*
Osumi, Masato 1942- *WhoWor 91*
Osunde, John Iriowen 1939- *WhoWor 91*
Osvald, Per Hakan 1928- *WhoWor 91*
Osver, Arthur 1912- *WhoAm 90, WhoAmA 91*
Oswald, Charles Wallace 1928- *St&PR 91*
Oswald, Elisabeth *EncCoWW*
Oswald, Ernest John 1943- *WhoWrEP 89*
Oswald, Eva Sue Aden 1949- *WhoAmW 91*
Oswald, George C. 1914- *St&PR 91*
Oswald, George Charles 1914- *WhoAm 90*
Oswald, Gretchen 1945- *St&PR 91, WhoAmW 91*
Oswald, Lee Harvey *BioIn 16*
Oswald, Lee Harvey 1939-1963 *WorAlBi*
Oswald, Marina *BioIn 16*
Oswald, Richard 1705?-1784 *EncCRAm*
Oswald, Robert Stanley 1941- *St&PR 91*
Oswald, Rudolph A. 1932- *WhoAm 90*
Oswald, Stanton S. 1927- *WhoAm 90*
Oswald, Vincent E. 1912- *St&PR 91*
Oswald, Walter Paul 1919- *St&PR 91*
Oswald, William Jack 1927- *WhoWor 91*
Oswalt, Charles Edward 1944- *WhoSSW 91*
Oswold, Thomas J. 1952- *St&PR 91*
Osyczka, Bohdan Danny *WhoAmA 91*
Osza, Debra Evans 1954- *WhoAmW 91*
Osze, Andrew E 1909- *WhoAmA 91*
Ota, Hidemichi 1918- *WhoWor 91*
Ota, Kazuo 1931- *WhoWor 91*
Ota, Leslie H. *BioIn 16*
Otaka, Tadaaki 1947- *IntWWM 90, PenDiMP*
Otake, Takashi 1949- *WhoWor 91*
Otanez, George Arthur *BiDrAPA 89*
Otani, Priscilla H. V. 1952- *WhoAmW 91*
Otani, Soji 1924- *EncO&P 3, EncPaPR 91*
Otani, Yoshihiko 1938- *WhoWor 91*
Otcasek, Christopher *BioIn 16*
Otchy, Thomas G. 1943- *St&PR 91*
Oteiba, Mana Said Al- 1946- *WhoWor 91*
Otemaa, John *BiDrAPA 89*
Otero, Agustin F. 1932- *WhoHisp 91*
Otero, Alejandro 1921- *ArtLatA*
Otero, Antonio Jose 1809-1870 *BioIn 16*
Otero, Carmen 1933- *WhoHisp 91*
Otero, Gregorio N. 1832?-1899? *AmLegL*
Otero, Ingrid 1959- *WhoHisp 91*
Otero, Joaquin Francisco 1934- *WhoHisp 91*
Otero, Joseph A. 1926- *WhoHisp 91*
Otero, Manuel J 1918- *BiDrAPA 89*
Otero, Manuel Ramos 1948- *BioIn 16*
Otero, Mariano S. 1844-1904 *BioIn 16*

Otero, Miguel Antonio 1829-1882 *BioIn 16*
Otero, Miguel Antonio 1859-1944 *BioIn 16, HispWr 90*
Otero, Richard J. 1939- *WhoHisp 91*
Otero, Rolando 1957- *WhoHisp 91*
Otero-Mahjouri, Altagracia *BiDrAPA 89*
Otero-Warren, Maria Adelina Emelia 1882-1965 *BioIn 16*
Otero-Warren, Nina 1882-1965 *BioIn 16*
Otey, Orlando 1925- *WhoAm 90*
Otfinoski, Steven 1949- *BioIn 16*
Othello, Maryann Cecilia 1946- *WhoAmW 91*
Otherday, John 1801-1871 *WhNaAH*
Othersen, Cheryl Lee 1948- *WhoAmW 91*
Othersen, Henry Biemann, Jr. 1930- *WhoAm 90*
Othmer, Donald F. 1904- *BioIn 16*
Othmer, Donald Frederick 1904- *WhoAm 90, WhoE 91, WhoWor 91*
Othmer, Ekkehard *BiDrAPA 89*
Oths, Richard Philip 1935- *WhoAm 90*
Oticica, Helio 1937-1980 *BioIn 16*
Otike, John Peter 1958- *WhoE 91*
Otis, Amos 1947- *Ballpl 90*
Otis, Arthur Brooks 1913- *WhoAm 90*
Otis, Carre *BioIn 16*
Otis, Elisha Graves 1811-1861 *WorAlBi*
Otis, Glenn Kay 1929- *WhoAm 90*
Otis, Harrison Gray 1765-1848 *BioIn 16*
Otis, Harrison Gray 1837-1917 *BioIn 16*
Otis, Henry W. *BioIn 16*
Otis, Jack 1923- *WhoAm 90*
Otis, James 1725-1783 *EncCRAm [port], EncPaPR 91, WorAlBi*
Otis, James, Jr. 1931- *WhoAm 90*
Otis, James D. 1939- *St&PR 91*
Otis, John James 1922- *WhoSSW 91, WhoWor 91*
Otis, John Lee 1945- *BiDrAPA 89*
Otis, Johnny 1921- *EncPR&S 89, OxCPMus*
Otis, Thomas 1931- *St&PR 91*
Otokpa, Augustine Emmanuel Ogaba, Jr. 1945- *WhoWor 91*
O'Toole, Allan Thomas 1925- *WhoAm 90*
O'Toole, Annette 1952- *WorAlBi*
O'Toole, Austin Martin 1935- *St&PR 91, WhoAm 90*
O'Toole, George J A *SpyFic*
O'Toole, J. Dennis *BioIn 16*
O'Toole, James Joseph 1945- *WhoAm 90*
O'Toole, James K 1928- *BiDrAPA 89*
O'Toole, James Michael 1950- *WhoE 91*
O'Toole, James P. 1939- *ODwPR 91*
O'Toole, James St Laurence 1895- *WhoAmA 91*
O'Toole, Jim 1937- *Ballpl 90*
O'Toole, John Dudley 1921- *WhoAm 90*
O'Toole, John E. *BioIn 16*
O'Toole, John E. 1929- *St&PR 91, WhoAm 90*
O'Toole, Joseph W. 1938- *WhoAm 90*
O'Toole, Joseph William 1938- *St&PR 91*
O'Toole, Kelly Ann 1962- *WhoE 91*
O'Toole, Marty 1888-1949 *Ballpl 90*
O'Toole, Michael Bradford 1934- *St&PR 91*
O'Toole, Molly Patricia 1959- *BiDrAPA 89*
O'Toole, Peter *BioIn 16*
O'Toole, Peter 1932- *WhoAm 90, WhoWor 91, WorAlBi*
O'Toole, Robert E 1932- *BiDrAPA 89*
O'Toole, Robert J. 1941- *St&PR 91*
O'Toole, Robert Joseph 1941- *WhoAm 90*
O'Toole, Thomas F. 1934- *St&PR 91*
O'Toole, Thomas M. *BioIn 16*
O'Toole, Timothy S. 1955- *St&PR 91*
O'Toole, Timothy T. 1955- *St&PR 91*
O'Toole, William P. 1942- *St&PR 91*
Otoshi, Tom Yasuo 1931- *WhoWor 91*
Otovo, Earnestine *BiDrAPA 89*
Otrakul, Amphorn 1936- *BiDrAPA 89*
Otremba, Bernard Otto 1944- *WhoE 91*
Otruba, Emery 1934- *St&PR 91*
Otruba, Gustav 1925- *WhoWor 91*
Otrzan, Durda 1953- *WhoWor 91*
Ots, Tony 1942- *St&PR 91*
Otsuka, Eiji 1919- *WhoWor 91*
Otsuka, Megumi 1953- *WhoWor 91*
Otsuki, Tamayo *BioIn 16*
Ott, Alan Wayne 1931- *St&PR 91*
Ott, Carolyn Pipkin 1935- *WhoSSW 91*
Ott, Dana Beth 1952- *WhoAmW 91*
Ott, David Michael 1952- *WhoAm 90*
Ott, Dennis McKay 1946- *St&PR 91*
Ott, Donald W. 1918- *St&PR 91*
Ott, Ed 1951- *Ballpl 90*
Ott, Ernst 1928- *St&PR 91*
Ott, George William, Jr. 1932- *WhoAm 90*
Ott, Geri L. 1950- *WhoSSW 91*
Ott, Gil 1950- *WhoWrEP 89*
Ott, Gilbert Russell, Jr. 1943- *St&PR 91, WhoAm 90, WhoE 91, WhoWor 91*
Ott, Hanns Herbert 1920- *WhoWor 91*
Ott, Holly-Brooks 1956- *WhoAmW 91*
Ott, Jack M. 1931- *WhoSSW 91*

Ott, James F. *St&PR 91*
Ott, James Forgan 1935- *WhoAm 90*
Ott, Jane Joseph 1958- *WhoSSW 91*
Ott, Jerry 1947- *WhoAmA 91*
Ott, John Harlow 1944- *WhoAm 90, WhoSSW 91*
Ott, Joseph 1827- *PenDiDA 89*
Ott, Joseph H. 1929-1990 *BioIn 16*
Ott, Karin 1948- *IntWWM 90*
Ott, Kevin D. 1954- *St&PR 91*
Ott, Mel 1909-1958 *Ballpl 90 [port], BioIn 16, WorAlBi*
Ott, Melvin Dale 1936- *St&PR 91*
Ott, Michael E 1945- *WhoAmA 91*
Ott, Richard E. 1942- *St&PR 91*
Ott, Richard Webster 1948- *WhoSSW 91*
Ott, Rita Ann 1961- *WhoAmW 91*
Ott, Robert B. 1923- *St&PR 91*
Ott, Robert Joseph 1944- *WhoE 91*
Ott, Robert William 1934- *WhoAmA 91*
Ott, Ruth Ann 1936- *WhoSSW 91*
Ott, Sabina 1955- *WhoAmA 91*
Ott, Stanley Joseph 1927- *WhoAm 90, WhoSSW 91*
Ott, Urmas *BioIn 16*
Ott, Walter Richard 1943- *WhoAm 90*
Ott, Wayne Robert 1940- *WhoAm 90, WhoWor 91*
Ott, Wendell Lorenz 1942- *WhoAm 90, WhoAmA 91*
Ott, William A. *BioIn 16*
Ottaviano, Doris Baginski 1938- *WhoAmW 91*
Ottaviano, Jorge V *BiDrAPA 89*
Ottavino, A. George 1918- *St&PR 91*
Ottavino, Gerald A. 1921- *St&PR 91*
Ottaway, Elizabeth Sarah Anne 1956- *WhoWor 91*
Ottaway, James H., Jr. 1938- *St&PR 91*
Ottaway, James Haller, Jr. 1938- *WhoAm 90*
Ottaway, Larry Dean 1948- *WhoSSW 91*
Otte, Daniel 1939- *WhoE 91*
Otte, Paul John 1943- *WhoAm 90*
Otte, Ruth Louise *BioIn 16*
Otte, Stephen 1943- *St&PR 91*
Ottemberg, Amalia 1926- *St&PR 91*
Otten, Charlotte F 1926- *ConAu 131*
Otten, Douglas B. *St&PR 91*
Otten, Gerald Joseph 1932- *St&PR 91*
Otten, Jim 1951- *Ballpl 90*
Otten, Joseph *PenDiMP*
Otten, Julie Anne 1959- *BiDrAPA 89*
Otten, Kurt 1926- *WhoWor 91*
Otten, Ralph Friedrich 1933- *WhoAm 90*
Otten, Robert Bernard 1934- *BiDrAPA 89*
Ottenberg, B Perry 1924- *BiDrAPA 89*
Ottenberg, James Simon 1918- *WhoAm 90*
Ottenberg, Miriam 1914-1982 *BioIn 16*
Ottenheimer, Lilly 1902- *BiDrAPA 89*
Ottenheimer, Richard Joseph 1926- *St&PR 91*
Ottensmeyer, David Joseph 1930- *WhoAm 90*
Ottenstein, Donald 1922- *BiDrAPA 89*
Ottenweller, Albert Henry 1916- *WhoAm 90*
Otter, Anne Sofie Von 1955- *IntWWM 90*
Otter, John M. 1930- *St&PR 91*
Otter, John Martin, III 1930- *WhoAm 90*
Otterbourg, Robert Kenneth 1930- *WhoAm 90, WhoE 91*
Otterloo, Willem van *PenDiMP*
Otterness, Larry James *BiDrAPA 89*
Otterson, Jack Leroy 1950- *WhoWor 91*
Otteson, Evan L 1938- *BiDrAPA 89*
Otteson, Schuyler Franklin 1917- *WhoAm 90*
Ottey, Jean B. 1954- *ODwPR 91*
Otth, Edward John, Jr. 1925- *WhoAm 90*
Ottiano, John William 1926- *WhoAmA 91*
Ottie, Timothy Westerfield 1955- *St&PR 91*
Otting, Frederick P. 1916- *St&PR 91*
Ottinger, Mary Louise 1956- *WhoAmW 91*
Ottley, Charlotte V. M. 1947- *ODwPR 91*
Ottley, Jerold Don 1934- *WhoAm 90*
Ottley, Norman Franklin 1928- *St&PR 91*
Ottley, Peter J. *NewYTBS 90 [port]*
Ottley, Reginald *AuBYP 90*
Ottley, Roi 1906-1960 *EarBlAP*
Ottlik, Geza 1912-1990 *ConAu 132*
Ottman, Jim 1945- *WhoWrEP 89*
Ottman, Josephine Kennedy 1955- *WhoAmW 91*
Ottman, Richard V. *WhoSSW 91*
Ottman, Thomas Wayne 1956- *St&PR 91*
Ottmann, Judi 1959- *WhoAmW 91*
Ottmann, Klaus 1954- *WhoAmA 91, WhoE 91*
Ottmar, Peter H. 1947- *St&PR 91*
Ottney, Nancy Louise 1954- *WhoAmW 91*
Otto, Bruce M. 1936- *St&PR 91*
Otto, Calvin Peter 1930- *WhoSSW 91*
Otto, Catherine Nan 1953- *WhoAmW 91*
Otto, Donald R. 1943- *WhoAm 90*
Otto, Donald W. *BioIn 16*
Otto, Edward D. 1926- *St&PR 91*

Otto, George John 1904- *St&PR 91, WhoAm 90*
Otto, Gilbert Fred 1901- *WhoE 91, WhoWor 91*
Otto, Hansjorg 1938- *WhoWor 91*
Otto, Harry Claude 1957- *WhoE 91*
Otto, Ingolf Helgi Elfried 1920- *WhoSSW 91, WhoWor 91*
Otto, James Warren 1935- *St&PR 91*
Otto, Jean Hammond 1925- *WhoAm 90*
Otto, Jeffery Lee 1955- *WhoEmL 91*
Otto, John Ernest 1938- *WhoAm 90*
Otto, Jrmgard 1912- *IntWWM 90*
Otto, Kenneth Lee 1930- *WhoAm 90*
Otto, Lisa 1919- *IntWWM 90, PenDiMP*
Otto, Lon 1948- *ConAu 130*
Otto, Ludwig 1934- *WhoSSW 91*
Otto, Luise 1819-1895 *EncCoWW*
Otto, Margaret 1909-1976 *AuBYP 90*
Otto, Margaret Amelia 1937- *WhoAm 90, WhoAmW 91*
Otto, Marie 1930- *WhoAmW 91*
Otto, Myron L. 1942- *St&PR 91*
Otto, Nikolaus August 1832-1891 *WorAlBi*
Otto, Ole Thomas 1963- *WhoSSW 91*
Otto, Owen *BiDrAPA 89*
Otto, Richard 1935- *St&PR 91*
Otto, Svend 1916- *BioIn 16*
Otto, Terrance Alden 1954- *BiDrAPA 89*
Otto, Wayne Raymond 1931- *WhoAm 90, WhoWrEP 89*
Otto-Primi, Terre A. 1941- *WhoAmW 91*
Ottolenghi, Abramo C. 1931- *WhoAm 90*
Ottoman, Richard Edward 1910- *WhoWor 91*
Ottosen, Kirsten 1938- *IntWWM 90*
Ottoson, Howard Warren 1920- *WhoAm 90*
Ottoson, Lars Henrik 1922- *WhoSSW 91*
Ottosson, Stig Roland 1947- *WhoWor 91*
Otts, Mark Grafton 1956- *WhoSSW 91*
Otunga, Maurice 1923- *WhoWor 91*
Otuteye, Godfred P. 1946- *St&PR 91*
Otway, Harry John 1935- *WhoWor 91*
Otwell, Ralph Maurice 1926- *WhoAm 90*
Ouaknine, Michel Daniel 1947- *WhoWor 91*
Oualline, Viola Jackson 1927- *WhoAmW 91*
Oubradous, Fernand 1903- *PenDiMP*
Oubre, Hayward Louis *WhoAmA 91*
Ouchi, Atsuyoshi 1919- *St&PR 91*
Ouchi, William G 1943- *ConAu 129*
Ouchi, William George 1943- *WhoAm 90*
Oudaltsova, N. *BiDWomA*
Ouderkirk, Gary D. 1941- *St&PR 91*
Ouderkirk, Mason James 1953- *WhoEmL 91, WhoWor 91*
Oudin, Eugene 1858-1894 *PenDiMP*
Oudry, Jean-Baptiste 1686-1755 *PenDiDA 89*
Ouellet, Ronald *BiDrAPA 89*
Ouellette, Bernard Charles 1936- *St&PR 91, WhoAm 90*
Ouellette, Fernand *BioIn 16*
Ouellette, Fernand 1930- *ConAu 13AS [port]*
Ouellette, Jane Lee Young 1929- *WhoAmW 91, WhoSSW 91, WhoWor 91*
Ouellette, Keith Edward 1951- *WhoSSW 91*
Ouellette, P. Lynn 1956- *BiDrAPA 89*
Ouellette, Reno Roland 1931- *St&PR 91*
Ouellette, Robert Paul 1938- *St&PR 91*
Oughton, Diana 1942-1970 *BioAmW*
Oughton, James Henry, Jr. 1913- *WhoWor 91*
Oughtred, Angus Winn 1942- *St&PR 91*
Oughtred, John W. 1949- *St&PR 91*
Oughtred, William 1575-1660 *WorAlBi*
Ouida 1839-1908 *FemiCLE*
Ouimet, Alphonse 1908-1988 *BioIn 16*
Ouimet, Guy 1954- *St&PR 91*
Ouimet, Luc *BiDrAPA 89*
Ouimet, Richard J. *St&PR 91*
Oujesky, Helen M. 1930- *WhoAmW 91*
Ouko, Robert John 1932-1990 *BioIn 16*
Ould Daddah, Turkia Turkia 1940- *WhoE 91*
Ould Mohamed Mahmoud, Mohamedou 1944- *WhoWor 91*
Oules, Firmin 1904- *WhoWor 91*
Oulet, B. *EncCoWW*
Oulman, Alain *BioIn 16*
Oulton, Richard James 1945- *WhoSSW 91*
Oulton, Therese 1953- *BiDWomA*
Oulundsen, Terry O. *St&PR 91N*
Oundjian, Peter Haig *PenDiMP*
Ounjian, Marilyn J. 1947- *WhoAmW 91, WhoE 91, WhoWor 91*
Ouray 1820?-1880 *WhNaAH*
Ourieff, Arthur J *BiDrAPA 89*
Ourisson, Guy 1926- *WhoWor 91*
Ourivio, Jose Carlos Mello 1933- *WhoWor 91*
Ours, Robert Maurice 1936- *WhoWrEP 89*
Oursler, Charles Fulton 1893-1952 *EncPaPR 91*
Oursler, Fulton *BioIn 16*
Oursler, Fulton 1893-1952 *AuBYP 90*
Oursler, Fulton, Jr. 1932- *WhoAm 90*
Oursler, Tony 1957- *WhoAmA 91*
Oursler, Will 1913- *EncO&P 3*
Ourso, J. Clifford 1937- *St&PR 91*
Ourso, Robert J, Jr. *BiDrAPA 89*
Oury, Anna Caroline Belleville 1808-1880 *BioIn 16*
Oury, Granville Henderson 1825-1891 *AmLegL*
Ousby, W J 1904- *EncO&P 3*
Ouseph, Florence 1949- *BiDrAPA 89*
Ouseph, Valsa *BiDrAPA 89*
Ousky, Lawrence 1942- *St&PR 91*
Ousmane, Semben 1923- *WorAlBi*
Ousmane, Sembene 1923- *BioIn 16, MajTwCW*
Ouspenskaya, Maria 1876-1949 *WorAlBi*
Ouspensky, P D 1878-1947 *EncO&P 3*
Ouspensky, Peter Demianovitch 1878-1947 *EncPaPR 91*
Oussani, James John 1920- *WhoE 91, WhoWor 91*
Ousset, Cecile 1936- *IntWWM 90, PenDiMP*
Ouston, Philip Anfield 1923-1988 *BioIn 16*
Outacity *EncCRAm*
Outcalt, David Lewis 1935- *WhoAm 90*
Outcault, Richard F. 1863-1928 *EncACom*
Outcault, Richard Felton 1863-1928 *BioIn 16*
Outenreath, Robert Lynn 1953- *BiDrAPA 89*
Outhwaite, Lucille Conrad 1909- *WhoAmW 91*
Outhwaite, Stephen J. 1943- *St&PR 91*
Outhwaite, William 1949- *ConAu 130*
Outka, Gene Harold 1937- *WhoAm 90*
Outland, Wendy Helen 1953- *WhoAmA 91*
Outlaw, A. Benjamin *ODwPR 91*
Outlaw, Arthur Robert 1926- *St&PR 91, WhoSSW 91*
Outlaw, Jimmy 1913- *Ballpl 90*
Outlaw, Linda N. 1948- *St&PR 91*
Outlaw, Robert J 1924- *BiDrAPA 89*
Outler, Albert Cook *BioIn 16*
Outram, Dorinda 1949- *ConAu 132*
Outram, John 1934- *BioIn 16*
Outrebon, Jean-Louis-Dieudonne *PenDiDA 89*
Outrebon, Nicolas, I *PenDiDA 89*
Outrebon, Nicolas, II *PenDiDA 89*
Outterbridge, John Wilfred 1933- *WhoAmA 91*
Outwater, John Ogden 1923- *WhoAm 90*
Ouziel, Jacky 1948- *WhoWor 91*
Ouzounian, Richard 1950- *OxCCanT*
Ouzts, Daniel Rhett 1946- *St&PR 91*
Ouzts, David Perry 1962- *IntWWM 90*
Ouzts, John Andrew, III *BiDrAPA 89*
Ouzts, Katharyn J *BiDrAPA 89*
Ouzts, William Truman 1933- *St&PR 91*
Ovacik, Gultekin *BiDrAPA 89*
Ovadia, Anne Brownlee *BiDrAPA 89*
Ovaitt, Frank, Jr. *ODwPR 91*
Ovalle, Ralph K. 1950- *St&PR 91*
Ovando Candia, Alfredo 1918-1982 *BioIn 16*
Ovanesyan, Igor Ter- *BioIn 16*
Ovca, Michael Scott 1954- *St&PR 91*
Ovchinikov, Vladimir 1960- *IntWWM 90*
Ove, Horace 1939- *DrBlPA 90*
Ove, Peter 1930- *WhoAm 90*
Oven, Jacoba Van 1920- *IntWWM 90*
Ovenden, J.A. 1963- *St&PR 91*
Ovenden, Keith William 1943- *WhoWor 91*
Ovens, Raymond 1932- *IntWWM 90*
Over, Jana Thais 1956- *WhoAmW 91*
Over, John F. 1940- *St&PR 91*
Overall, James Carney, Jr. 1937- *WhoAm 90*
Overall, John E. 1929- *WhoAm 90*
Overall, Orval 1881-1947 *Ballpl 90*
Overall, Park *BioIn 16*
Overbagh, Virginia Anne 1944- *WhoAmW 91*
Overbeck, Friedrich 1789-1869 *IntDcAA 90*
Overbeck, Gene Edward 1929- *St&PR 91, WhoAm 90*
Overbeck, Gerta 1898-1979 *BiDWomA*
Overbeck, Henry West 1930- *WhoAm 90*
Overbeck, Joseph C. 1936- *WhoAm 90*
Overbeck, Lois More 1945- *WhoAmW 91*
Overberg, Paul J. 1926- *St&PR 91*
Overberg, Paul Joseph 1926- *WhoAm 90*
Overbey, Charles Brown, Jr. 1915- *BiDrAPA 89*
Overby, Annette *BioIn 16*
Overby, Donald Wesley 1938- *WhoSSW 91*
Overby, George Robert 1923- *WhoAm 90*
Overby, James J. 1926- *St&PR 91*
Overby, Jon Jefferson 1953- *WhoSSW 91*
Overby, Karen Gayle 1963- *WhoSSW 91*
Overby, Lacy Rasco 1920- *WhoAm 90*
Overby, Osmund Rudolf 1931- *WhoAm 90*
Overby, Susan Nye *BiDrAPA 89*
Overcash, Michael Ray 1944- *WhoSSW 91*
Overcash, Reece A., Jr. 1926- *WhoAm 90, WhoSSW 91*
Overcash, Reece Alexander, Jr. 1926- *St&PR 91*
Overdorff, Elvin W., Jr. 1918- *St&PR 91*
Overduijn, Leendert 1901-1976 *BioIn 16*
Overell, William L. 1947- *St&PR 91*
Overend, John James 1928- *St&PR 91*
Overend, Robert Benjamin, Jr. 1943- *WhoWrEP 89*
Overfelt, Eugene 1922- *St&PR 91*
Overgaard, Cordell Jersild 1934- *WhoAm 90*
Overgaard, Gerd Iris 1930- *WhoWor 91*
Overgaard, Mary Ann 1951- *WhoEmL 91*
Overgaard, Mitchell Jersild 1931- *WhoAm 90*
Overgaard, Willard Michele 1925- *WhoAm 90*
Overgard, R. Gail 1941- *St&PR 91*
Overgard, William *BioIn 16*
Overgard, William 1926-1990 *ConAu 131, EncACom*
Overhauser, Albert Warner 1925- *WhoAm 90*
Overhiser, George R. 1921- *St&PR 91*
Overholser, Richard James 1928- *St&PR 91*
Overholser, Stephen *BioIn 16*
Overholser, Wayne D. 1906- *BioIn 16*
Overholser, Winfred, Jr. 1930- *BiDrAPA 89*
Overholt, Gail Claire 1944- *WhoAmW 91*
Overholt, Hugh Robert 1933- *WhoAm 90*
Overholt, Mary Ann 1935- *St&PR 91, WhoAm 90*
Overholt, Richard M. *NewYTBS 90*
Overland, Arnulf 1889-1968 *DcScanL*
Overland, Carlton Edward 1942- *WhoAmA 91*
Overley, Toner M, Jr. 1928- *BiDrAPA 89*
Overlock, Leslie C. *BioIn 16*
Overman, Amegda Nicole Jack 1920- *WhoAmW 91*
Overman, Glenn Delbert 1916- *WhoAm 90*
Overman, Gregg *ODwPR 91*
Overman, Harold Speight, III 1948- *WhoSSW 91*
Overman, Jerry Grey 1949- *WhoSSW 91*
Overman, Lee Slater 1854-1930 *AmLegL*
Overman, Marjorie Moore 1919- *WhoWrEP 89*
Overman, Steven Joe 1943- *WhoSSW 91*
Overmire, Stubby 1919-1977 *Ballpl 90*
Overmyer, Daniel Lee 1935- *WhoAm 90*
Overmyer, John 1844-1919 *AmLegL*
Overmyer, John Eugene 1933- *St&PR 91, WhoAm 90*
Overmyer, Robert D. *St&PR 91*
Overpeck, Lem Franklin 1911- *WhoAm 90*
Overseth, Oliver Enoch 1928- *WhoAm 90*
Overstreet, Carole 1948- *St&PR 91*
Overstreet, Diane Alma 1959- *WhoSSW 91*
Overstreet, Frederick Gordon 1932- *WhoSSW 91*
Overstreet, Jim 1947- *ODwPR 91*
Overstreet, Joe William, Jr. 1954- *St&PR 91*
Overstreet, Raymond Gartin 1949- *BiDrAPA 89*
Overstreet, Rosemarie Elizabeth 1961- *WhoWor 91*
Overstreet, Sarah Gayle 1951- *WhoAmW 91*
Overstrom, Gunnar S., Jr. 1942- *St&PR 91, WhoAm 90*
Overton, Benjamin Frederick 1926- *WhoAm 90, WhoSSW 91*
Overton, Betty Jean 1949- *WhoAmW 91*
Overton, Bill *BioIn 16*
Overton, Bill 1947?- *DrBlPA 90*
Overton, Bruce 1941- *WhoAm 90*
Overton, Carl E. 1917- *St&PR 91*
Overton, Frank William 1938- *St&PR 91*
Overton, George Washington 1918- *WhoAm 90*
Overton, Glen W. *ODwPR 91*
Overton, Gwendolen 1876- *FemiCLE*
Overton, Helen Parke 1920- *WhoAmW 91*
Overton, James Ralph 1947- *WhoSSW 91*
Overton, Jane Taylor 1935- *WhoWrEP 89*
Overton, Jane Vincent Harper 1919- *WhoAm 90, WhoAmW 91*
Overton, Jenny 1942- *BioIn 16*
Overton, Joseph Allen, Jr. 1921- *WhoAm 90*
Overton, Kenneth 1908- *WhoSSW 91, WhoWor 91*
Overton, Lewis M. 1937- *St&PR 91*
Overton, Mary *BiDEWW*
Overton, Nerina 1953- *WhoWor 91*
Overton, Richard A. 1942- *St&PR 91*
Overton, Richard Albert 1942- *WhoAm 90*
Overton, Ronald Ernest 1943- *WhoWrEP 89*
Overton, Rosilyn Gay Hoffman 1942- *WhoAmW 91*
Overtree, Edward L. 1945- *St&PR 91*
Overturf, Elaine Vivian 1937- *St&PR 91*
Overweg, Norbert Ido Albert *WhoE 91*
Ovesen, Carsten 1946- *WhoSSW 91*
Ovesen, Ellis *WhoWrEP 89*
Ovesey, Lionel *BiDrAPA 89*
Oveson, W. Val 1952- *WhoAm 90*
Ovett, Steve *BioIn 16*
Ovezgeldiev, O. *WhoWor 91*
Oviatt, Ross Hannum 1918- *WhoAm 90*
Oviatt, Russell D. 1947- *ODwPR 91*
Oviatt, Sherman B. 1845- *AmLegL*
Ovid 43BC-17AD *WorAlBi*
Ovid 43BC-18?AD *PoeCrit 2 [port]*
Oviedo y Valdes, Gonzalo Fernandez de 1478-1557 *BioIn 16*
Ovington, Mary White 1885-1951 *EncAL*
Ovington, Ray *AuBYP 90*
Ovington, Robert Carl *BiDrAPA 89*
Ovitz, Michael *BioIn 16, WhoAm 90*
Ovitz, Michael 1946- *News 90*
Ovitz, Morris *BiDrAPA 89*
Ovlisen, Mads 1940- *WhoAm 90*
Ovseenko, Vladimir Aleksandrovich A. 1884-1939 *BioIn 16*
Ovshinsky, Iris M. 1927- *St&PR 91*
Ovshinsky, Stanford R. 1922- *St&PR 91*
Ovshinsky, Stanford Robert 1922- *WhoAm 90*
Ovstedal, Barbara *ConAu 130*
Owada, Hisashi 1932- *WhoWor 91*
Owais, Carol Elizabeth Fisk 1952- *BiDrAPA 89*
Owais, Wisam N 1949- *BiDrAPA 89*
Owchinko, Bob 1955- *Ballpl 90*
Owczarek, Jerzy Antoni 1926- *WhoE 91*
Oweiss, Ibrahim Mohamed 1931- *WhoAm 90*
Owen, Alan Robert George 1919- *EncO&P 3, EncPaPR 91*
Owen, Albert Alan 1948- *IntWWM 90*
Owen, Amy 1944- *WhoAm 90, WhoAmW 91*
Owen, B. David 1941- *St&PR 91*
Owen, Barbara 1933- *IntWWM 90*
Owen, Benton B. 1900-1989 *BioIn 16*
Owen, Beti Mary *IntWWM 90*
Owen, Blythe 1898- *IntWWM 90*
Owen, Bob Forbess 1929- *WhoSSW 91*
Owen, Boone B, Jr. *BiDrAPA 89*
Owen, Carol Elaine 1957- *WhoAmW 91, WhoSSW 91*
Owen, Carol Thompson 1944- *WhoAmW 91*
Owen, Carolyn Sutton 1932- *WhoAmW 91*
Owen, Charles Archibald, Jr. 1915- *WhoAm 90*
Owen, Claude Bernard, Jr. 1945- *St&PR 91, WhoAm 90, WhoSSW 91*
Owen, Conan *BioIn 16*
Owen, Curtis L. 1930- *St&PR 91*
Owen, Dan D. 1948- *St&PR 91*
Owen, Daniel B. 1950- *St&PR 91*
Owen, Daniel Bruce 1950- *WhoEmL 91, WhoSSW 91, WhoWor 91*
Owen, Daniel Thomas 1947- *WhoWor 91*
Owen, David 1938- *ConAu 129*
Owen, David Anthony Llewellyn 1938- *WhoWor 91*
Owen, David Dalrymple 1942- *WhoSSW 91*
Owen, David P. 1954- *St&PR 91*
Owen, David Rogers 1914- *WhoAm 90*
Owen, Deborah K. *WhoAmW 91*
Owen, Duncan Shaw, Jr. 1935- *WhoAm 90*
Owen, Eileen Edmunds 1949- *WhoWrEP 89*
Owen, Elspeth 1941- *BioIn 16*
Owen, Eugene E. 1915- *St&PR 91*
Owen, Eugene H. 1929- *St&PR 91*
Owen, Frank 1879-1942 *Ballpl 90*
Owen, Frank 1939- *WhoAmA 91*
Owen, Franklin Pierce 1853-1905 *AmLegL*
Owen, Fred Wynne 1928- *WhoAm 90*
Owen, Frederick 1869-1959 *WhoAmA 91N*
Owen, Gary E. 1945- *St&PR 91*
Owen, George Earle 1908- *WhoAm 90, WhoWor 91*
Owen, George Vale 1869-1931 *EncO&P 3*
Owen, H. Martyn 1929- *WhoE 91*
Owen, Harvey W. 1949- *St&PR 91*
Owen, Henry 1920- *WhoAm 90*
Owen, Iris *EncPaPR 91*
Owen, Iris M. *EncO&P 3*
Owen, J.P. 1954- *St&PR 91*
Owen, James Churchill 1901- *WhoAm 90*
Owen, Jane *FemiCLE*
Owen, Jane *BiDEWW*
Owen, Jean Wivel 1941- *BiDrAPA 89*
Owen, John 1929- *WhoAm 90*
Owen, John Atkinson, Jr. 1924- *WhoAm 90*

Owen, John Douglas 1956- *St&PR 91*
Owen, John H. *WhoAm 90*
Owen, John Laverty 1923- *WhoE 91*
Owen, John R. 1929- *St&PR 91*
Owen, Joseph W *BiDrAPA 89*
Owen, Karen Michelle 1952- *WhoAmW 91*
Owen, Kenneth Dale 1938- *WhoSSW 91*
Owen, Kim Ranell *BiDrAPA 89*
Owen, Larry Gene 1932- *WhoSSW 91, WhoWor 91*
Owen, Larry Lesley 1945- *WhoEmL 91, WhoSSW 91*
Owen, Larry Malcolm 1928- *WhoAm 90*
Owen, Lynn *IntWWM 90*
Owen, Lynn Rasmussen *WhoAm 90*
Owen, Marv 1906- *Ballpl 90*
Owen, Mary Alicia 1858-1935 *FemiCLE*
Owen, Mary Jane 1936- *WhoWrEP 89*
Owen, Melvin Lee 1951- *St&PR 91*
Owen, Michael *WhoAm 90*
Owen, Mickey 1916- *Ballpl 90*
Owen, Nathan R. 1919- *St&PR 91*
Owen, Nathan Richard 1919- *WhoAm 90*
Owen, Patricia Rose 1955- *WhoAmW 91*
Owen, Philip *TwCCr&M 91*
Owen, Randy *BioIn 16*
Owen, Ray David 1915- *WhoAm 90*
Owen, Reginald 1887-1972 *BioIn 16*
Owen, Richard 1804-1892 *WorAlBi*
Owen, Richard 1922- *WhoAm 90, WhoE 91*
Owen, Richard Roberts, Jr. *BiDrAPA 89*
Owen, Robert 1771-1858 *BioIn 16, EncO&P 3, WorAlBi*
Owen, Robert C. 1923- *WhoSSW 91*
Owen, Robert Dale 1801-1877 *EncO&P 3, EncPaPR 91, WorAlBi*
Owen, Robert E. 1943- *St&PR 91*
Owen, Robert Harrison, Jr. 1937- *WhoSSW 91*
Owen, Robert Hubert 1928- *WhoAm 90*
Owen, Robert Roy 1921- *WhoAm 90*
Owen, Robert Vaughan 1920- *WhoE 91*
Owen, Roberts Bishop 1926- *WhoAm 90*
Owen, Roderic *ConAu 129*
Owen, Russell *AuBYP 90*
Owen, Ruth 1885- *AuBYP 90*
Owen, Ruth A. 1950- *St&PR 91*
Owen, Sarah *BioIn 16*
Owen, Sherri Lynne Shaw 1962- *WhoSSW 91*
Owen, Spike 1961- *Ballpl 90*
Owen, Stephen Cooke, Jr. 1933- *WhoAm 90*
Owen, Stephen Lee 1952- *WhoEmL 91*
Owen, Steven James 1952- *WhoEmL 91*
Owen, Sue Ann 1942- *WhoWrEP 89*
Owen, Susan Moore 1944- *BiDrAPA 89*
Owen, Suzanne 1926- *WhoAmW 91*
Owen, T.G. 1945- *St&PR 91*
Owen, Ted 1920- *EncO&P 3*
Owen, Thomas Barron 1920- *WhoAm 90*
Owen, Thomas J. 1934- *St&PR 91*
Owen, Thomas John 1934- *WhoAm 90*
Owen, Thomas Llewellyn 1928- *WhoAm 90, WhoE 91, WhoWor 91*
Owen, Thomas Lon 1945- *WhoEmL 91*
Owen, Thomas P. 1931- *St&PR 91*
Owen, Thomas Walker 1925- *WhoAm 90*
Owen, Timothy Charles 1956- *WhoE 91*
Owen, Tobias Chant 1936- *WhoAm 90*
Owen, Tracy Lynn 1961- *WhoAmW 91*
Owen, Walt 1912- *BioIn 16*
Owen, Walter Shepherd 1920- *WhoAm 90*
Owen, Warren Herbert 1927- *St&PR 91, WhoAm 90*
Owen, Wilfred 1893-1918 *WorAlBi*
Owen, William Cone 1942- *WhoAm 90, WhoSSW 91*
Owen, William D. 1949- *ODwPR 91*
Owen, William Geoffrey 1942- *WhoAm 90*
Owen, William H., III 1948- *St&PR 91*
Owen, William H., Jr. 1930- *St&PR 91*
Owen, William Ivan 1924- *St&PR 91*
Owen, William Parker 1950- *WhoSSW 91*
Owen, William Paschal, Jr. 1952- *BiDrAPA 89*
Owen-Towle, Carolyn Sheets 1935- *WhoAmW 91*
Owens, Alice Watson *WhoSSW 91*
Owens, Anne-Marie *IntWWM 90*
Owens, Barbara Ann 1948- *WhoAmW 91*
Owens, Billy *BioIn 16*
Owens, Bobbie Deane 1935- *WhoAm 90*
Owens, Brick *Ballpl 90*
Owens, Buck *WhoNeCM C [port]*
Owens, Buck 1929- *BioIn 16, WhoAm 90, WorAlBi*
Owens, C. Richard 1930- *St&PR 91*
Owens, Catherine Ura 1957- *WhoSSW 91*
Owens, Charles David 1947- *WhoSSW 91*
Owens, Charles Richard 1930- *WhoAm 90*
Owens, Charles V., Jr. 1927- *St&PR 91*
Owens, Charles Vincent, Jr. 1927- *WhoAm 90*
Owens, Cheryl Laurita 1957- *WhoAmW 91*
Owens, Christopher G. 1961- *WhoWrEP 89*
Owens, Clifford W. 1925- *St&PR 91*
Owens, Craig 1950-1990 *ConAu 132, NewYTBS 90*
Owens, Danielle *BioIn 16*
Owens, David 1925- *BiDrAPA 89*
Owens, David Bruce 1950- *IntWWM 90*
Owens, David Douglas 1939- *WhoSSW 91*
Owens, David Gordon 1945- *WhoEmL 91*
Owens, David J *BiDrAPA 89*
Owens, David Whit 1950- *WhoSSW 91*
Owens, Delia *BioIn 16*
Owens, Donna 1936- *WhoAmW 91*
Owens, Doris Jerkins 1940- *WhoSSW 91*
Owens, Ernest Sibley, III 1945- *WhoE 91*
Owens, Frank Enos 1931- *WhoSSW 91*
Owens, Frank S., Jr. 1931- *St&PR 91*
Owens, Frederick Hammann 1928- *WhoE 91*
Owens, Fredric Newell 1941- *WhoAm 90*
Owens, G. Kay 1942- *WhoSSW 91*
Owens, G.L. 1936- *St&PR 91*
Owens, Gail 1939- *BioIn 16*
Owens, Garland Chester 1922- *WhoAm 90*
Owens, Gary *BioIn 16, WhoAm 90, WhoWor 91*
Owens, Gary Mitchell 1949- *WhoE 91, WhoWor 91*
Owens, Gary R. 1949- *St&PR 91*
Owens, Gary Standifer 1949- *St&PR 91*
Owens, George Ray 1948- *WhoE 91*
Owens, Geraldine Sullivan 1930- *WhoSSW 91*
Owens, Glynn I. 1949- *St&PR 91*
Owens, Gwendolyn Jane 1954- *WhoAmA 91, WhoE 91*
Owens, Harold B. 1926- *WhoSSW 91*
Owens, Harry 1902- *OxCPMus*
Owens, Hettie Catherine 1930- *St&PR 91*
Owens, Howard 1945- *BiDrAPA 89*
Owens, Hugh F. *NewYTBS 90*
Owens, Hugh Franklin 1909- *WhoAm 90*
Owens, J. Howell 1940- *St&PR 91*
Owens, Jack Byron 1944- *WhoAm 90*
Owens, James Cuthbert 1916- *WhoAm 90, WhoWor 91*
Owens, James Hilliard 1920- *St&PR 91*
Owens, James Jacob 1942- *St&PR 91*
Owens, James Robert 1957- *WhoEmL 91*
Owens, James Robert, Jr. 1943- *WhoE 91*
Owens, James William 1950- *St&PR 91*
Owens, Jana Jae 1943- *WhoWor 91*
Owens, Jean Batts 1928- *WhoAmW 91*
Owens, Jeri Eugene *BiDrAPA 89*
Owens, Jesse 1913-1980 *BioIn 16, WorAlBi*
Owens, Jim 1934- *Ballpl 90*
Owens, John Franklin 1935- *WhoSSW 91*
Owens, John Hughes 1945- *WhoSSW 91*
Owens, John Patrick 1927- *WhoE 91*
Owens, Joseph 1908- *WhoAm 90*
Owens, Joseph Henry *BiDrAPA 89*
Owens, Karyn Lynn 1964- *WhoSSW 91*
Owens, Keith E. 1952- *ODwPR 91*
Owens, Lawrence Dale 1954- *WhoEmL 91*
Owens, Lewis E. 1934- *WhoAm 90*
Owens, Lorraine Lucille 1927- *WhoAmW 91*
Owens, Luvie Moore 1933- *WhoAm 90*
Owens, Major Robert Odell 1936- *BlkAmsC [port], WhoAm 90, WhoE 91*
Owens, Mark *BioIn 16*
Owens, Marvin Franklin, Jr. 1916- *WhoAm 90*
Owens, Mary 1935- *WhoAmA 91*
Owens, Millard Fillmore, III 1952- *WhoSSW 91*
Owens, O'dell M. *BioIn 16*
Owens, Patricia S. 1941- *WhoSSW 91*
Owens, Paul Theodore 1952- *St&PR 91*
Owens, Peter Lawrence 1949- *BiDrAPA 89*
Owens, Randy 1945- *WhoSSW 91*
Owens, Richard George 1946- *WhoEmL 91*
Owens, Richard Wilson 1941- *WhoSSW 91*
Owens, Robert G. 1923- *ConAu 132*
Owens, Robert Julian 1942- *St&PR 91*
Owens, Robert W. 1948- *St&PR 91*
Owens, Robin Maria 1956- *WhoSSW 91*
Owens, Rochelle 1936- *BioIn 16, FemiCLE, NotWoAT, WhoAm 90, WhoWrEP 89*
Owens, Rodney Joe 1950- *WhoEmL 91*
Owens, Sandra Renee *BiDrAPA 89*
Owens, Scott *BioIn 16*
Owens, Shelby Jean 1936- *WhoAmW 91*
Owens, Susan Sligh 1954- *WhoSSW 91*
Owens, Susan Weir 1949- *WhoAmW 91*
Owens, Tennys Bowers 1940- *WhoAmA 91*
Owens, Thomas Dew 1953- *BiDrAPA 89*
Owens, Thomas Dunn 1952- *St&PR 91*
Owens, Tracy C *BiDrAPA 89*
Owens, Vanassa Lynn 1953- *WhoAmW 91*
Owens, Wallace, Jr *WhoAmA 91*
Owens, Warren L. 1923- *ODwPR 91*
Owens, Wayne 1937- *WhoAm 90*
Owens, Wilbur Dawson, Jr. 1930- *WhoSSW 91*
Owens, William 1908- *MusmAFA*
Owens, William A. 1905- *BioIn 16*
Owens, William Abbott, Jr. 1914- *WhoAm 90*
Owens, William Arthur 1940- *WhoAm 90*
Owens, William Claiborne 1849-1925 *AmLegL*
Owens, William Don 1939- *WhoAm 90*
Owens, William Raymond 1937- *WhoE 91*
Owens, William Richard 1941- *WhoSSW 91*
Owens, William Ward, Jr. 1944- *WhoE 91*
Owens, Williams Lawrence 1936- *St&PR 91*
Owens, Wyeth Eugene 1928- *BiDrAPA 89*
Owensby, Clyde Norman 1932- *BiDrAPA 89*
Owers, Albert *BiDrAPA 89*
Owers, Brian Charles 1934- *St&PR 91*
Owhi *WhNaAH*
Owings, Francis Barre 1941- *WhoAm 90*
Owings, Francis Miller 1941- *WhoAm 90*
Owings, Malcolm William 1925- *St&PR 91, WhoAm 90*
Owings, Margaret Wentworth 1913- *WhoAm 90, WhoAmW 91*
Owings, Phillip Jeffrey 1944- *St&PR 91*
Owings, Rachel Harriet 1926- *WhoAmW 91*
Owings, Richard Alan 1949- *BiDrAPA 89*
Owings, Robert Mason 1932- *WhoWrEP 89*
Owings, William Donovan 1957- *WhoEmL 91*
Owings, Zelotes H. 1926- *St&PR 91*
Ownbey, Gerald Bruce 1916- *WhoAm 90*
Ownbey, Richard Miles *BiDrAPA 89*
Ownbey, Rick 1957- *Ballpl 90*
Ownby, Charlotte Ledbetter 1947- *WhoAmW 91, WhoSSW 91*
Ownby, Chris *BioIn 16*
Ownby, J. Steve 1939- *WhoAm 90*
Ownes, Owen Ernest 1925- *St&PR 91*
Owsley, David Thomas 1929- *WhoAm 90, WhoAmA 91*
Owsley, Michele Malek 1950- *WhoAmW 91*
Owsley, Robert Warner 1940- *St&PR 91*
Owsley, Tim *EarBlAP*
Owsley, William Clinton, Jr. 1923- *WhoAm 90*
Owsnitzki, Gabriele Anna J. 1957- *WhoAmW 91*
Owyang, King 1945- *St&PR 91*
Ox, Jack 1948- *WhoAmA 91*
Oxenberg, Catherine *BioIn 16*
Oxenburg, Allen Sven 1927- *WhoAm 90*
Oxenbury, Helen 1938- *AuBYP 90, ChlLR 22 [port]*
Oxenden, Ashton 1808-1892 *DcCanB 12*
Oxendine, Glenda Holt 1956- *St&PR 91*
Oxendine, Joseph B. *BioIn 16, WhoAm 90*
Oxenhandler, Neal 1926- *WhoAm 90*
Oxenhorn, Harvey *BioIn 16*
Oxenhorn, Harvey 1952?-1990 *ConAu 131*
Oxenhorn, Joseph *BioIn 16*
Oxenhorn, Sanford *BiDrAPA 89*
Oxenhorn, Sanford 1926- *WhoE 91*
Oxenreiter, Maurice Frank 1924- *WhoAm 90*
Oxenreiter, Robert A. 1936- *St&PR 91*
Oxenreiter, William F., Jr. *St&PR 91*
Oxford, Charles William 1921- *WhoAm 90*
Oxford, Hubert, III 1938- *WhoSSW 91*
Oxford, Lamar Dwight 1949- *WhoSSW 91*
Oxford, Michael Edward 1947- *WhoSSW 91*
Oxford, Robert de Vere, Earl of 1362-1392 *BioIn 16*
Oxford, Robert Harley, Earl of 1661-1724 *BioIn 16*
Oxford, Sharon M. 1939- *WhoAmW 91*
Oxholm, Mary Hall *BioIn 16*
Oxley, Geraldine Motta 1930- *St&PR 91, WhoAm 90*
Oxley, Greg 1948- *St&PR 91*
Oxley, Gregory L. *ODwPR 91*
Oxley, Harrison 1933- *IntWWM 90*
Oxley, John Thurman 1909- *WhoAm 90*
Oxley, Leo L. *BiDrAPA 89*
Oxley, Mary *FemiCLE*
Oxley, Michael Garver 1944- *WhoAm 90, WhoSSW 91*
Oxley, Philip 1922- *St&PR 91, WhoAm 90*
Oxley, Stephen Leo 1948- *BiDrAPA 89*
Oxlie, Mary *BiDEWW, FemiCLE*
Oxman, Bennett N. 1930- *St&PR 91*
Oxman, Bruce 1930- *St&PR 91*
Oxman, David Craig 1941- *WhoAm 90*
Oxman, Harold Leon *BiDrAPA 89*
Oxman, Katja *WhoAmA 91*
Oxman, Mark 1940- *WhoAmA 91*
Oxman, Thomas Elliot 1949- *BiDrAPA 89, WhoE 91*
Oxnam, Robert Bromley 1942- *WhoAm 90*
Oxnard, Charles Ernest 1933- *WhoAm 90*
Oxsen, Jo Ann 1946- *WhoAmW 91*
Oxtoby, John Corning 1910- *WhoAm 90*
Oxtoby, Robert Boynton 1921- *WhoAm 90*
Oyake, Tsuneo 1932- *WhoWor 91*
Oybir, A Fahrettin *BiDrAPA 89*
Oye Mba, Casimir 1942- *WhoWor 91*
Oyefule, Biyi Kayode 1952- *BiDrAPA 89, WhoE 91*
Oyen, Gerald J. 1940- *St&PR 91*
Oyer, Herbert Joseph 1921- *WhoAm 90*
Oyewumi, L Kolawole O *BiDrAPA 89*
Oyler, Benjamin *BioIn 16*
Oyler, Gregory Kenneth 1953- *WhoEmL 91*
Oyler, James R. 1946- *St&PR 91*
Oyler, James Russell, Jr. 1946- *WhoAm 90, WhoWor 91*
Oyler, Ray 1938-1981 *Ballpl 90*
Oyler, William Kent 1958- *St&PR 91*
Oyster, David Fairfax, Jr. 1945- *WhoEmL 91*
Oyte *WhNaAH*
Oytes *WhNaAH*
Oz, Amos 1939- *MajTwCW, WhoWor 91*
Oz, Frank 1944- *SmATA 60 [port]*
Oz, Frank Richard *WhoAm 90*
Oza, Dipak Harshadrai 1954- *WhoE 91*
Oza, Mina K *BiDrAPA 89*
Ozag, David 1962- *WhoE 91, WhoEmL 91*
Ozaki, Koyo 1867-1903 *WorAlBi*
Ozaki, Robert H. *ODwPR 91*
Ozaki, Robert H. 1947- *WhoAm 90*
Ozaki, Robert Harold 1947- *St&PR 91*
Ozaki, Yukio 1944- *Ballpl 90*
Ozal, Turgut *BioIn 16*
Ozal, Turgut 1927- *PolLCME, WhoWor 91*
Ozanne, Charles 1865-1961 *EncPaPR 91*
Ozanne, Charles E 1865-1961 *EncO&P 3*
Ozanne, James Herbert 1943- *St&PR 91*
Ozar, I. 1926- *WhoAm 90*
Ozar, Stuart *BiDrAPA 89*
Ozarin, Lucy D 1914- *BiDrAPA 89*
Ozark, Chilly *WhoWrEP 89*
Ozark, Damian Michael 1954- *WhoEmL 91*
Ozark, Danny 1923- *Ballpl 90*
Ozark, Edward L. 1944- *St&PR 91*
Ozaroff, Gary R. 1933- *WhoAm 90*
Ozato, Keiko 1941- *WhoAmW 91*
Ozawa Seiji 1935- *EncJap*
Ozawa, Ichiro 1942- *WhoWor 91*
Ozawa, Keiya 1953- *WhoWor 91*
Ozawa, Martha Naoko 1933- *WhoAm 90, WhoAmW 91*
Ozawa, Paul M. 1929- *St&PR 91*
Ozawa, Sakihito 1954- *WhoWor 91*
Ozawa, Seiji 1935- *IntWWM 90, PenDiMP, WhoAm 90, WhoE 91, WhoWor 91, WorAlBi*
Ozawa, Susuma 1932- *St&PR 91*
Ozawa, Takayuki 1932- *WhoWor 91*
Ozbek, Rifat *BioIn 16*
Ozbek, Sahver *BiDrAPA 89*
Ozbirn, Willie Paul 1944- *St&PR 91*
Ozbolt, Jesse Q. 1941- *St&PR 91*
Ozbun, James L. *WhoAm 90*
Ozdemir, Refik Munir *BiDrAPA 89*
Ozelli, Tunch 1938- *WhoE 91*
Ozenbaugh, Robert B. 1952- *St&PR 91*
Ozendo, Pierre L. 1950- *St&PR 91*
Ozenfant, Amedee J 1886-1966 *WhoAmA 91N*
Ozer, Jerome S. 1927- *BioIn 16*
Ozer, Judi 1933- *WhoAmA 91*
Ozer, Kerry Jae 1945- *BiDrAPA 89*
Ozer, Mark N 1932- *ConAu 30NR*
Ozer, Marty *BioIn 16*
Ozeray, Madeleine 1910-1989 *AnObit 1989*
Ozerengin, M Feyzi 1922- *BiDrAPA 89*
Ozernoy, Leonid Moissey 1939- *WhoAm 90*
Ozero, Brian John 1932- *WhoE 91*
Ozersky, Sam *BiDrAPA 89*
Ozick, Cynthia *BioIn 16*
Ozick, Cynthia 1928- *BioAmW, ConLC 62 [port], FemiCLE, MajTwCW, WhoAm 90, WhoAmW 91, WhoE 91, WhoWrEP 89, WorAlBi*
Oziemblewski, Felix Walter 1934- *St&PR 91*
Ozier, Irving 1938- *WhoAm 90*
Ozim, Igor 1931- *IntWWM 90, PenDiMP*
Ozimek, Lewis Frank 1922- *St&PR 91*
Ozinga, Kenneth *WhoAm 90*
Ozkan, Avni Dogan 1928- *BiDrAPA 89*
Ozkan, Suha *WhoWor 91*
Ozley, Marvin W. 1934- *St&PR 91*
Ozment, Steven 1939- *WhoAm 90, WhoWrEP 89*
Ozmon, Kenneth Lawrence 1931- *WhoAm 90*
Ozoa, Manuel Suela 1950- *BiDrAPA 89*
Ozolins, Arthur Marcelo 1946- *IntWWM 90*

Ozolins, Janis Alfreds 1919- *IntWWM 90, WhoWor 91*
Ozols, Sandra Lee 1957- *WhoAmW 91, WhoEmL 91, WhoWor 91*
Ozonoff, Ida 1904- *WhoAm 90, WhoAmA 91*
Ozores, Julio N. 1958- *BiDrAPA 89*
Ozosky, Edward Thomas 1947- *WhoE 91*
Ozpak, Mehmet Ziya 1927- *BiDrAPA 89*
Ozturk, Orhan M 1926- *BiDrAPA 89*
Ozu Yasujiro 1903-1963 *EncJap*
Ozvath, Rose Mary Hornik 1951- *WhoAmW 91*
Ozveren, Mustafa Fikret 1952- *WhoWor 91*
Ozzard, Janet Lucile 1927- *WhoAmW 91*
Ozzello, Jann Lorraine 1953- *WhoEmL 91*

P

P, E *BiDEWW*
P-Funk All Stars *EncPR&S 89*
P.W.O. *EncCoWW*
Pa-ta Shan-jen 1624?-1705? *BioIn 16*
Paabo, Maya 1929- *WhoAmW 91*
Paakkala, Timo Antero 1941- *WhoWor 91*
Paal, Peter *DcScanL*
Paalen, Wolfang 1905-1959 *ArtLatA*
Paalz, Anthony L. 1924- *WhoAm 90*
Paalzow, Henriette 1788-1847 *EncCoWW*
Paananen, Eloise Katherine 1923- *WhoWrEP 89*
Paananen, Victor Niles 1938- *WhoAm 90*
Paar, Jack 1918- *WorAlBi*
Paar, Michael Ann 1952- *WhoE 91*
Paasch, Wayne Charles 1951- *WhoEmL 91*
Paasio, Pertti Kullervo 1939- *WhoWor 91*
Paaswell, Robert Emil 1937- *WhoAm 90*
Paau, Danny Shiu Lam 1944- *WhoWor 91*
Paauw, Robert S. 1928- *St&PR 91*
Pabers, Nancy Lynn 1960- *WhoAmW 91*
Pabilonia, Jaime Abaquin 1932- *BiDrAPA 89*
Pablo 1934- *WhoAmA 91*
Pablo, James F. 1923- *St&PR 91*
Pablo, Jeanette Marie 1959- *WhoAmW 91*
Pablos, Rolando 1939- *WhoHisp 91*
Pablos-Duclerc, Yaidi Norah 1954- *BiDrAPA 89*
Pabo, Marcia J *BiDrAPA 89*
Pabon-Price, Noemi 1950- *WhoHisp 91*
Pabst, Alan Joseph 1939- *St&PR 91*
Pabst, Daniel *PenDiDA 89*
Pabst, Margaret *DcCanB 12*
Pabst, Mark L. 1946- *WhoAm 90*
Pabst, Robert D. 1936- *St&PR 91*
Pabst-Wright, Suzanne Marie 1959- *WhoAmW 91*
Paca, William 1740-1799 *EncCRAm*
Pacacha, Pamela Ann 1962- *WhoAmW 91*
Pacala, Leon 1926- *WhoAm 90*
Pacas Castro, Manuel *WhoWor 91*
Pacavira, Manuel Pedro 1939- *WhoWor 91*
Pacchiana, Ronald D. *BioIn 16*
Pace Jubilee Singers *DcAfAmP*
Pace, Alicia Guzman 1949- *WhoHisp 91*
Pace, Annie *BioIn 16*
Pace, Anthony M. 1938- *St&PR 91*
Pace, Anthony M. 1940- *ODwPR 91*
Pace, Bedford *ODwPR 91*
Pace, Bill *BioIn 16*
Pace, Carmelo 1906- *IntWWM 90*
Pace, Carolina Jolliff 1938- *WhoAmW 91, WhoSSW 91*
Pace, Catherine T. *ODwPR 91*
Pace, Charles D. 1935- *St&PR 91*
Pace, Charles Robert 1912- *WhoAm 90*
Pace, Clint W. 1943- *St&PR 91*
Pace, Dale Kent 1939- *WhoE 91*
Pace, David 1944- *ConAu 130*
Pace, De Wanna Williams 1954- *WhoWrEP 89*
Pace, Eric Dwight 1936- *WhoAm 90*
Pace, Frank 1912-1988 *BioIn 16*
Pace, Harry H 1884-1943 *DcAfAmP*
Pace, J. T. *BioIn 16*
Pace, James Robert 1958- *WhoAmA 91*
Pace, Jan Soderman 1951- *WhoSSW 91*
Pace, Joseph Vincent *BiDrAPA 89*
Pace, Judy 1946- *DrBlPA 90*
Pace, L. Vernon 1931- *St&PR 91*
Pace, Leonard 1924- *WhoAm 90*
Pace, Margaret Bosshardt *WhoAmA 91*
Pace, Mary *BiDEWW*
Pace, Michael Randolph 1957- *WhoSSW 91*
Pace, Mildred Mastin 1907- *AuBYP 90*
Pace, Norma *WhoAm 90*
Pace, Norma T. *St&PR 91*
Pace, Paul David 1948- *WhoSSW 91*
Pace, Ralph Wayne 1931- *WhoAm 90*
Pace, Richard Alan 1945- *WhoAm 90*
Pace, Richard Yost 1956- *WhoEmL 91*
Pace, Robert *BioIn 16*
Pace, Stanley C. 1921- *St&PR 91*
Pace, Stanley Carter 1921- *WhoAm 90*
Pace, Stephen S 1918- *WhoAmA 91*
Pace, Stephen Shell 1918- *WhoAm 90*
Pace, Thomas 1951- *WhoEmL 91*
Pace, W.A., Jr. 1932- *St&PR 91*
Pace, William Fleming 1945- *St&PR 91*
Pacella, Bernard L *BiDrAPA 89*
Pacella, John 1924- *St&PR 91*
Pacella, John 1956- *Ballpl 90*
Pacelli, Eugenio 1876-1958 *BioIn 16*
Pacelli, Paul John 1961- *WhoE 91*
Pacello, James 1947- *St&PR 91*
Paces, Vaclav 1942- *WhoWor 91*
Pacey, Steven 1957- *ConTFT 8 [port]*
Pach, Lleni 1943- *BiDrAPA 89*
Pach, Magda F 1884-1950 *WhoAmA 91N*
Pach, Walter 1883-1958 *WhoAmA 91N*
Pach, Zsigmond Pal 1919- *WhoWor 91*
Pacha, Beulah Marie 1933- *St&PR 91*
Pache, Bernard 1934- *WhoWor 91*
Pache, George Roger 1948- *St&PR 91*
Pacheco, Antonio 1942- *BiDrAPA 89*
Pacheco, Catherine Chapman 1927- *ConAu 130*
Pacheco, Deborah Yvonne *BiDrAPA 89*
Pacheco, Efrain Alcides 1934- *WhoHisp 91*
Pacheco, Harry Adrian 1955- *St&PR 91*
Pacheco, Henricus Luis 1947- *HispWr 90*
Pacheco, Henry L. *HispWr 90*
Pacheco, Humberto, Jr. 1940- *WhoWor 91*
Pacheco, Joe B. 1937- *WhoHisp 91*
Pacheco, Jose Emilio 1939- *ConAu 131, HispWr 90*
Pacheco, Luis Novoa 1956- *WhoHisp 91*
Pacheco, Manuel Trinidad 1941- *WhoAm 90, WhoHisp 91, WhoSSW 91*
Pacheco, Richard 1924- *WhoHisp 91*
Pacheco, Richard, Jr. 1927- *WhoHisp 91*
Pacheco, Robert Joseph 1953- *St&PR 91*
Pacheco, Romualdo 1831-1899 *BioIn 16*
Pacheco, Sammy Lawrence 1952- *WhoHisp 91*
Pacheco, Vicente C 1940- *BiDrAPA 89*
Pacheco Aviles, Migdalia 1948- *WhoSSW 91*
Pacheco Pereira, Jose Alvaro Machado 1949- *WhoWor 91*
Pacheco-Perez, Jimmy 1958- *BiDrAPA 89*
Pacheco-Ransanz, Arsenio 1932- *WhoAm 90*
Pacheleque, Calisto 1957- *WhoWor 91*
Pachence, Donald M. 1936- *St&PR 91*
Pacher, Michael 1430?-1498 *IntDcAA 90*
Pachios, Harold Christy 1936- *WhoAm 90*
Pachmakova-Weiss, Ahinora *BiDrAPA 89*
Pachman, Daniel J. 1911- *WhoAm 90*
Pachman, Lauren Merle 1937- *WhoAm 90*
Pachman, Louis J. 1955- *St&PR 91*
Pachmann, Vladimir 1848-1933 *PenDiMP*
Pachmann, Vladimir de 1848-1933 *BioIn 16*
Pachner, William 1915- *WhoAmA 91*
Pachniak, Char K. 1953- *WhoAmW 91*
Pacholewski, Robert Thomas 1951- *St&PR 91*
Pacholick, John Roger 1938- *St&PR 91*
Pacholski, Audrey Phyllis 1961- *WhoAmW 91*
Pacholski, Richard Francis 1947- *WhoAm 90*
Pachon, Harry 1945- *WhoHisp 91*
Pacht, Otto 1902-1988 *BioIn 16*
Pachter, Cyrus 1919- *BiDrAPA 89*
Pachter, Hedwig 19--?-1988 *SmATA 63*
Pachter, Irwin Jacob 1925- *WhoAm 90*
Pachter, Josh 1951- *ConAu 132*
Pachtman, Norman 1939- *St&PR 91*
Paci, Pier F. 1930-1989 *BioIn 16*
Pacific, Joseph Nicholas, Jr. 1950- *WhoEmL 91, WhoWor 91*
Pacifico, Albert Dominick 1940- *WhoAm 90*
Pacik, Peter Thomas 1940- *WhoE 91*
Pacillo, Pat 1963- *Ballpl 90*
Pacini, Carl Joseph 1953- *WhoSSW 91*
Pacino, Al 1940- *WhoAm 90, WorAlBi*
Pacino, Frank George 1930- *WhoAm 90, WhoWor 91*
Pacio Lindin, Dino 1934- *WhoE 91*
Paciocco, P.J. 1938- *St&PR 91*
Paciorek, Tom 1946- *Ballpl 90*
Pack, Allen S. 1930- *St&PR 91, WhoAm 90, WhoSSW 91*
Pack, Allen Thomas 1945- *BiDrAPA 89*
Pack, Harry S. 1943- *St&PR 91*
Pack, Howard Meade 1918- *St&PR 91*
Pack, Jane Robin 1955- *WhoAm 90, WhoAmW 91, WhoE 91*
Pack, Janet Elaine 1952- *WhoWrEP 89*
Pack, John L 1927- *EncO&P 3*
Pack, John R *BiDrAPA 89*
Pack, Leonard Brecher 1944- *WhoAm 90*
Pack, Lola Kathryn Lee 1924- *WhoWrEP 89*
Pack, Ludwig 1929- *WhoWor 91*
Pack, Phoebe Katherine Finley 1907- *WhoAmW 91, WhoWor 91*
Pack, Richard Morris 1915- *WhoAm 90*
Pack, Robert 1929- *AuBYP 90*
Pack, Robert M. 1929- *WhoWrEP 89*
Pack, Spencer J. 1953- *WhoE 91*
Pack, Susan Joan 1951- *WhoAmW 91*
Pack, Walter Frank 1916- *WhoAm 90*
Packa, Donna Rogers 1950- *WhoSSW 91*
Packard, Allison *BioIn 16*
Packard, Barbara Baugh 1938- *WhoAm 90*
Packard, Daniel Mark 1955- *St&PR 91*
Packard, David *BioIn 16*
Packard, David 1912- *ConAmBL, St&PR 91, WhoAm 90, WhoWor 91*
Packard, Edward 1931- *BioIn 16*
Packard, Eleanor M. 1934- *WhoAmW 91*
Packard, Frank L 1877-1942 *TwCCr&M 91*
Packard, Gene 1887-1959 *Ballpl 90*
Packard, George Quincy 1933- *St&PR 91*
Packard, George Randolph 1932- *WhoAm 90*
Packard, J.W. 1926- *St&PR 91*
Packard, James W. 1863-1928 *WorAlBi*
Packard, James Ward *EncABHB 4 [port]*
Packard, John B. 1945- *St&PR 91*
Packard, John Mallory 1920- *WhoAm 90*
Packard, Joyce H. 1925- *WhoAmW 91*
Packard, Marion V. 1908- *WhoAm 90*
Packard, Martin Everett 1921- *St&PR 91, WhoAm 90*
Packard, Matthew Davis 1961- *WhoE 91*
Packard, P. Kim 1938- *St&PR 91*
Packard, Peter Kim 1938- *WhoAm 90*
Packard, Ralph Kempton 1945- *St&PR 91*
Packard, Robert Charles 1919- *WhoAm 90*
Packard, Robert Gay 1924- *WhoAm 90*
Packard, Ronald 1931- *WhoAm 90*
Packard, Russell C 1946- *BiDrAPA 89*
Packard, Sandra Podolin 1942- *WhoAm 90*
Packard, Thomas Norris 1943- *St&PR 91*
Packard, Vance 1914- *WorAlBi*
Packard, Vance Oakley 1914- *WhoAm 90, WhoWor 91, WhoWrEP 89*
Packard, Warren C. 1934- *St&PR 91*
Packard, William Doud *EncABHB 4*
Packard, William I *BiDrAPA 89*
Packard, William S 1950- *BiDrAPA 89*
Packenham, Richard Daniel 1953- *WhoEmL 91*
Packer, Al 1923- *St&PR 91*
Packer, Brad H. 1953- *St&PR 91*
Packer, Clair Lange 1901-1978 *WhoAmA 91N*
Packer, Francis H 1873-1957 *WhoAmA 91N*
Packer, Fred L 1886-1956 *WhoAmA 91N*
Packer, George *BioIn 16*
Packer, Joy 1905-1977 *AuBYP 90*
Packer, Katherine Helen 1918- *WhoAm 90*
Packer, Kerry Francis Bullmore 1937- *WhoWor 91*
Packer, Leo S. 1920- *WhoWor 91*
Packer, Louan *BiDrAPA 89*
Packer, Mark Barry 1944- *WhoAm 90*
Packer, Mary A. 1952- *WhoE 91*
Packer, Max I *BiDrAPA 89*
Packer, Milton Isaac 1919- *St&PR 91*
Packer, Peter D. 1940- *ODwPR 91*
Packer, Raymond Allen 1914- *WhoAm 90*
Packer, Rekha Desai 1955- *WhoAm 90*
Packer, Richard A. 1957- *St&PR 91*
Packer, Robert Clyde 1935- *WhoAm 90*
Packer, Robert R. 1934- *St&PR 91*
Packer, Robert W. 1923-1988 *BioIn 16*
Packer, Samuel *BiDrAPA 89*
Packer, Vin *MajTwCW*
Packer, Vin 1927- *SmATA X [port]*
Packie, Susan 1946- *WhoWrEP 89*
Packles, Joan Beth *BiDrAPA 89*
Packman, Paul Michael 1938- *BiDrAPA 89*
Packo, Joseph John 1925- *WhoWor 91*
Packwood, Bob 1932- *WhoAm 90, WhoWor 91*
Packwood, Richard B. 1944- *St&PR 91*
Paclisanu, Zeno G *BiDrAPA 89*
Paclt, Jaromir 1927- *IntWWM 90*
Pacomio *WhNaAH*
Pacter, Paul Allan 1943- *WhoAm 90*
Pacula, Joanna *BioIn 16*
Pacun, Norman 1932- *WhoAm 90*
Pacy, James Steven 1930- *WhoE 91*
Paczynski, Bohdan 1940- *WhoAm 90*
Padach, Kenneth Michael *BiDrAPA 89*
Padatsu, Pekka Sam 1943- *WhoWor 91*
Padavick, David William 1940- *St&PR 91*

Padberg, Daniel I. BioIn 16
Padberg, Daniel Ivan 1931- WhoAm 90
Padberg, Harriet Ann 1922- WhoAmW 91
Padberg, Helen Swan WhoAmW 91
Padberg, Manfred Wilhelm 1941- WhoWor 91
Paddack, Charles 1937- BiDrAPA 89
Padden, Anthony Aloysius, Jr. 1949- WhoEmL 91, WhoWor 91
Padden, Dick 1870-1922 Ballpl 90
Padden, Preston BioIn 16
Padden, Thomas C. 1951- St&PR 91
Padden, Tom 1908-1973 Ballpl 90
Paddick, Garry E. 1937- St&PR 91
Paddison, Patricia Louise 1951- BiDrAPA 89, WhoE 91
Paddock, Austin Joseph 1908- WhoAm 90
Paddock, Benjamin Henry, III 1928- St&PR 91, WhoAm 90
Paddock, Harold Dewolf 1948- WhoEmL 91
Paddock, James Stephen 1941- St&PR 91
Paddock, Paul Bradley 1942- WhoSSW 91
Paddock, Robert Young 1917- St&PR 91
Paddock, Susan Mary 1946- WhoAmW 91
Paddock, Willard Dryden 1873-1956 WhoAmA 91N
Paddrik, Peter Endel 1947- WhoSSW 91
Pade, Else Marie 1924- IntWWM 90
Pade, Lois BioIn 16
Padeh, Asher S A BiDrAPA 89
Padeloup, Antoine-Michel 1685-1758 PenDiDA 89
Paden, Carolyn Eileen Belknap 1953- WhoAmW 91, WhoEmL 91, WhoWor 91
Paden, Carter N., Jr. 1927- St&PR 91
Paden, Jack 1931- WhoSSW 91
Paden, John N. WhoAm 90
Paden, Lindsay Bernard 1950- BiDrAPA 89
Paden, Lyman R. 1954- WhoEmL 91
Paden, William Reynolds, Jr. 1936- WhoSSW 91
Paderanga, Cayetano Woo, Jr. 1948- WhoWor 91
Paderewski, Clarence Joseph 1908- WhoAm 90
Paderewski, Ignace 1860-1941 WorAlBi
Paderewski, Ignace Jan 1860-1941 BioIn 16
Paderewski, Ignacy 1860-1941 PenDiMP
Padgett, Don 1911-1980 Ballpl 90
Padgett, Ernie 1899-1957 Ballpl 90
Padgett, Ernie 1947- WhoSSW 91
Padgett, George A. 1932- St&PR 91
Padgett, George Arthur 1932- WhoAm 90, WhoE 91
Padgett, Kenneth M. 1944- St&PR 91
Padgett, Lewis 1915-1958 WorAlBi
Padgett, Ron 1942- ConAu 30NR, WhoWrEP 89
Padgett, Shirley Perry 1934- WhoAmW 91
Padgett, Thomas V., Jr. 1921- St&PR 91
Padgett, Valerie Ruth 1949- WhoAmW 91
Padgett, W.D. 1927- St&PR 91
Padgett, William R. 1932- St&PR 91
Padgett-Chandler, David E. 1945- IntWWM 90
Padgette, Linda D. 1946- WhoAmW 91
Padia, Alyssa 1959- WhoAmW 91
Padia, Anna Marie 1945- WhoHisp 91
Padian, Robert Bruce 1952- WhoE 91
Padilla, Alma J. 1944- WhoAmW 91
Padilla, Amado Manuel 1942- WhoHisp 91
Padilla, Americo Francisco BiDrAPA 89
Padilla, David P. 1949- WhoHisp 91
Padilla, Donald G. 1921- WhoAm 90
Padilla, Elaine S. WhoAmW 91
Padilla, Enrique BiDrAPA 89
Padilla, Ernest A. WhoHisp 91
Padilla, George Alonso 1945- WhoHisp 91
Padilla, George Jasso 1934- WhoHisp 91
Padilla, Gilbert 1929- WhoHisp 91
Padilla, Gilberto Cruz 1939- WhoHisp 91
Padilla, Heberto 1932- BioIn 16, ConAu 131, HispWr 90, WhoHisp 91, WorAu 1980 [port]
Padilla, Hernan 1938- WhoHisp 91
Padilla, Isaac F. WhoHisp 91
Padilla, James Earl 1953- WhoE 91, WhoEmL 91
Padilla, Jose Sancho 1889-1960 OxCPMus
Padilla, Juan De 1500?-1542 EncCRAm
Padilla, Laurel ODwPR 91
Padilla, Leocadio Joseph 1927- WhoHisp 91
Padilla, Lorraine Marie 1952- WhoAmW 91, WhoWor 91
Padilla, Luiz Roberto Nunes 1958- WhoWor 91
Padilla, Lydia A. 1950- WhoHisp 91
Padilla, Mary Louise 1943- WhoSSW 91
Padilla, Michael A. WhoHisp 91
Padilla, Patrick J. 1950- WhoHisp 91
Padilla, Paula Jeanette 1953- WhoHisp 91
Padilla, Phyllis Eileen 1952- WhoHisp 91
Padilla, Raymond O. 1951- St&PR 91
Padilla, Raymond V. 1944- ConAu 130, HispWr 90
Padilla, Richard 1949- WhoHisp 91
Padilla, Sally G. 1937- WhoHisp 91
Padilla, Steven Michael 1949- St&PR 91
Padilla, Wanda Marie WhoHisp 91
Padilla, William Joseph 1956- WhoHisp 91
Padin, Dion WhoHisp 91
Padin, Yadira Yumac BiDrAPA 89
Padiyara, Anthony 1921- WhoWor 91
Padla, Dennis Peter BiDrAPA 89
Padley, Susanna BiDEWW
Padlo, Barbara Kellstrom 1947- St&PR 91
Padluck, Diane 1951- ODwPR 91
Padmore, Elaine Marguirite IntWWM 90
Padnes, Stephen C 1942- BiDrAPA 89
Padnes, Stephen Charles 1942- WhoE 91
Padnos, Jeffrey Stephen 1948- St&PR 91
Padnos, Seymour K. 1920- St&PR 91
Padolina-Pamintuan, Helen BiDrAPA 89
Pados, Frank John, Jr. 1944- WhoAm 90
Padouvas, Dimitrios BiDrAPA 89
Padovano, Anthony John 1933- WhoAmA 91, WhoE 91
Padovano, Anthony Thomas 1934- WhoAm 90
Padovano, Louis BiDrAPA 89
Padove, Stuart Jay 1947- WhoEmL 91
Padow, Rhoda B 1945- BiDrAPA 89
Padre Pio EncPaPR 91
Padrick, Comer Woodward, Jr. 1926- WhoSSW 91
Padrick, Joseph Michael 1949- WhoSSW 91
Padro-Yumet, Rafael BiDrAPA 89
Padron, Armando 1959- WhoSSW 91
Padron, D. Lorenzo 1945- WhoHisp 91
Padron, Eduardo 1958- WhoSSW 91
Padron, Eduardo J. WhoHisp 91
Padron, Elida R. 1954- WhoHisp 91
Padron, Esteban A. BiDrAPA 89
Padron, Justo Jorge 1943- IntvSpW [port]
Padron, Maria de Los Angeles 1955- WhoHisp 91
Padron, Peter E. WhoHisp 91
Padron-Gayol, Maria V 1946- BiDrAPA 89
Padros, David 1942- IntWWM 90
Padros, Jaime 1926- IntWWM 90
Padrutt, Hanspeter 1939- WhoWor 91
Padua, Eric 1954- WhoE 91
Padua, Saturnino B, Jr. BiDrAPA 89
Padua, Yolanda Sarabia BiDrAPA 89
Paduano, James A. 1942- St&PR 91, WhoAm 90
Paduano, Mary Ann BioIn 16
Padula, Fred David 1937- WhoAm 90, WhoAmA 91
Padula, Louis J BiDrAPA 89
Padulo, Louis 1936- WhoAm 90, WhoSSW 91
Paeff, Bashka 1893-1979 WhoAmA 91N
Paek, Kee Sung BiDrAPA 89
Paelinck, Honore Coralia 1935- WhoWor 91
Paelinck, Jean-Pierre 1939- WhoWor 91
Paemel, Monika van 1945- EncCoWW
Paeschke, Olaf WhoAm 90
Paese, Augie St&PR 91
Paez, Francisco A. 1936- WhoWor 91
Paez, Jose Antonio 1790-1873 BioIn 16
Paez, Patricio Ramon 1944- BiDrAPA 89
Paez, Raul 1937- BiDrAPA 89
Paffenbarger, Ralph BioIn 16
Paffenbarger, Ralph Seal, Jr. 1922- WhoAm 90
Paffgen, Christa BioIn 16
Paffumi, Ernest Charles 1949- St&PR 91
Pafko, Andy 1921- Ballpl 90
Pafumi, Glenn Robert 1950- WhoE 91
Pagan, Annette Lydia 1950- BiDrAPA 89
Pagan, Dave 1949- Ballpl 90
Pagan, Isobel 1742?-1821 FemiCLE
Pagan, John S. 1929- St&PR 91
Pagan, Jose 1935- Ballpl 90
Pagan, Juan Osvaldo 1939- BiDrAPA 89
Pagan, Rafael D., Jr. 1927- ODwPR 91
Pagan, Richard 1954- WhoAmA 91
Pagan-Agostini, Walter John BiDrAPA 89
Pagan Ferrer, Gloria M. 1921- HispWr 90
Pagan-Gordils, Emilio BiDrAPA 89
Pagan-Pagan, Rafael A BiDrAPA 89
Paganelli, John Dean 1958- WhoE 91
Paganelli, Paolo BioIn 16
Paganelli, Robert Peter 1931- WhoAm 90
Pagani, Albert Louis 1936- WhoWor 91
Paganini, Niccolo 1782-1840 PenDiMP, -A, WorAlBi
Pagano, Barbara Lynne 1945- WhoSSW 91
Pagano, Filippo Frank 1939- WhoSSW 91
Pagano, Gary BiDrAPA 89
Pagano, George Anthony 1952- WhoE 91
Pagano, James Lawrence 1955- WhoEmL 91
Pagano, Joseph Stephen 1931- WhoAm 90
Pagano, Marco 1956- WhoWor 91
Pagano, Matio PenDiDA 89
Pagano, Paul J. 1943- St&PR 91
Pagano, Philip C BiDrAPA 89
Pagano, Ross Joseph 1942- WhoSSW 91
Pagano, Virginia Rooney- 1924-1990 BioIn 16
Paganucci, Paul D. 1931- St&PR 91
Paganucci, Paul Donnelly 1931- WhoAm 90
Paganuzzi, Enrico 1921- IntWWM 90
Pagarigan, Roberto R 1932- BiDrAPA 89
Page, Albert Lee 1927- WhoAm 90
Page, Allan R. 1947- St&PR 91
Page, Anne Eichelberger 1953- WhoAmW 91
Page, Anne Ruth 1949- WhoAmW 91, WhoEmL 91
Page, Barbara B. 1939- St&PR 91
Page, Benjamin Ingrim 1940- WhoAm 90
Page, Benjamin Walker BiDrAPA 89
Page, Bettie BioIn 16
Page, Calvin A. 1922- St&PR 91
Page, Catherine A. ODwPR 91
Page, Catherine Marie 1955- BiDrAPA 89
Page, Charles Hunt 1909- WhoAm 90
Page, Christopher Howard 1952- IntWWM 90
Page, Clarence BioIn 16
Page, Clarence E. 1947- WhoAm 90
Page, Curtis Matthewson 1946- WhoEmL 91
Page, Dale BioIn 16
Page, David K. 1933- St&PR 91
Page, David Keith 1933- WhoAm 90
Page, David L. 1934- St&PR 91
Page, Dennis 1932- WhoWor 91
Page, Dennis Brett 1949- WhoEmL 91
Page, Doris Morrison 1940- WhoSSW 91
Page, Dorothy 1899- FemiCLE
Page, Dozzie Lyons 1921- WhoAmW 91, WhoWor 91
Page, Edgar BioIn 16
Page, Eleanor AuBYP 90, WhoAm 90
Page, Ellis Batten 1924- WhoAm 90, WhoSSW 91, WhoWor 91
Page, Ernest 1927- WhoAm 90
Page, Frederick West 1932- WhoAm 90
Page, Gale Charles 1943- WhoSSW 91
Page, Garrett David 1955- WhoE 91
Page, Genevieve 1927- WhoWor 91
Page, George Keith 1917- WhoAm 90
Page, Geraldine 1924-1987 BioIn 16, NotWoAT, WorAlBi
Page, Grover 1893-1958 WhoAmA 91N
Page, Harrison DrBlPA 90
Page, Harry Robert 1915- WhoAm 90
Page, Herbert William 1923- WhoE 91
Page, Hot Lips 1908-1954 DrBlPA 90, OxCPMus
Page, Irvine Heinly 1901- WhoAm 90
Page, Jack Randall 1956- WhoEmL 91
Page, James Benson BiDrAPA 89
Page, Janet L. 1944- St&PR 91
Page, Janet Louise 1944- WhoAm 90
Page, Janice Ellen 1948- WhoAmW 91
Page, Jean Jepson 1924- WhoAmA 91
Page, Jimmy EncPR&S 89
Page, Jimmy 1944- ConMus 4 [port]
Page, Joe 1917- BioIn 16
Page, Joe 1917-1980 Ballpl 90
Page, John 1744-1808 BioIn 16
Page, John Henry, Jr 1923- WhoAmA 91
Page, Jonathan R. 1946- St&PR 91
Page, Kathleen Marie 1944- WhoSSW 91
Page, Kathy 1958- WhoWor 91
Page, Ken 1954- DrBlPA 90
Page, Kenneth 1927- IntWWM 90
Page, La Don Barbara 1945- WhoAmW 91
Page, Larry Keith 1933- WhoAm 90
Page, Lawanda 1920- DrBlPA 90
Page, Linda Kay 1943- WhoAmW 91
Page, Lorne Albert 1921- WhoAm 90
Page, Lou 1912- AuBYP 90
Page, Louise 1955- FemiCLE
Page, M. Ann 1958- WhoAmW 91
Page, Malcolm 1935- ConAu 31NR
Page, Marco 1909-1968 TwCCr&M 91
Page, Marcus William 1937- WhoAm 90
Page, Marion E. BiDrAPA 89
Page, Marjorie Eileen 1920- WhoAmW 91
Page, Martin Robert 1944- St&PR 91
Page, Melvin Eugene 1944- WhoSSW 91
Page, Merle C 1926- BiDrAPA 89
Page, Michael William 1953- St&PR 91
Page, Michel 1940- WhoAm 90
Page, Mitchell 1951- Ballpl 90
Page, Nadine Cullison 1903- WhoAmW 91
Page, Nicholas John 1964- IntWWM 90
Page, Norman 1930- ConAu 31NR
Page, Oscar C. 1939- WhoAm 90
Page, P. K. 1916- FemiCLE
Page, P K 1916- MajTwCW
Page, P. K. 1916- WhoWrEP 89
Page, P Renauld BiDrAPA 89
Page, Patti 1927- OxCPMus, WorAlBi
Page, Paul Collins 1945- WhoAm 90
Page, Paula 1942- IntWWM 90
Page, Pierre WhoAm 90
Page, Pierre E. 1943- WhoWor 91
Page, Rebecca Lee 1950- St&PR 91
Page, Richard M. 1926- St&PR 91
Page, Richard Max 1926- WhoAm 90
Page, Richard Morton 1932- WhoE 91
Page, Richard S. 1937- WhoAm 90
Page, Richard W. 1947- St&PR 91
Page, Robert E. St&PR 91
Page, Robert Griffith 1921- WhoAm 90
Page, Robert Henry 1927- WhoAm 90, WhoSSW 91, WhoWor 91
Page, Robert Jeffress 1922- WhoAm 90
Page, Robert Lee 1945- WhoSSW 91
Page, Robert Wesley 1927- WhoAm 90, WhoE 91
Page, Robin Gregory 1954- IntWWM 90
Page, Roy Christopher 1932- WhoAm 90
Page, Roy William 1947- St&PR 91, WhoEmL 91
Page, Russell BioIn 16
Page, Russell J. 1942- ODwPR 91
Page, Ruth 1899- WhoAmW 91
Page, Ruth 1900- BioAmW
Page, Ruth W. 1921- WhoWrEP 89
Page, Sally Jacquelyn 1943- WhoWor 91
Page, Shelby H. 1921- WhoAm 90
Page, Stephen Franklin 1940- St&PR 91
Page, Stephen Jeffrey Lawrence 1955- WhoWor 91
Page, Steven 1950- IntWWM 90
Page, Susan WhoWrEP 89
Page, Susannah L. 1954- WhoE 91
Page, Ted 1903-1986 Ballpl 90
Page, Thomas A. 1933- St&PR 91
Page, Thomas Alexander 1933- WhoAm 90
Page, Thomas Nelson 1853-1922 BioIn 16
Page, Thornton Leigh 1913- WhoAm 90
Page, Tim BioIn 16
Page, Ulalia BiDEWW
Page, Vance 1905-1951 Ballpl 90
Page, Walter Hines 1855-1918 BioIn 16
Page, William Howard 1929- WhoWrEP 89
Page, William Noble 1928- St&PR 91
Page, Willis WhoAm 90
Page, Willis 1918- IntWWM 90
Pagel, Augusta BioIn 16
Pagel, Walter T. U. 1898-1983 ConAu 129
Pagel, William Rush 1901- WhoAm 90
Pagella, Maurice Vondy 1946- WhoAm 90
Pagelow, Stephen W. 1950- St&PR 91
Pagels, Carrie Fancett 1958- WhoAmW 91
Pagels, Elaine Hiesey WhoAm 90
Pagels, Elaine Hiesey 1943- WhoWrEP 89
Pagels, Heinz R. 1939-1988 BioIn 16
Pagels, Heinz Rudolf 1939-1988 WhoAm 90
Pagen, William Roland 1921- St&PR 91
Pagendarm, William F. 1949- St&PR 91
Pagenkopf, Andrea L. 1942- WhoAmW 91
Pagenkopf, Robert C. 1929- St&PR 91
Pagenstecher, Gustav 1855-1942 EncO&P 3, EncPaPR 91
Pagenstert, Gottfried 1928- WhoWor 91
Pagent-Fredericks, J Rous-Marten 1905-1963 WhoAmA 91N
Pages, Beltran J 1951- BiDrAPA 89
Pages, Ernest Alexander 1959- WhoHisp 91
Pages, Jean 1907-1977 WhoAmA 91N
Pages, Robert Charles Henri 1931- WhoWor 91
Paget, Allen Maxwell 1919- WhoE 91
Paget, Bridget BiDEWW
Paget, James 1814-1899 BioIn 16
Paget, James Robert 1942- St&PR 91
Paget, Richard M. 1913- St&PR 91
Paget, Violet 1856-1935 BioIn 16
Paget-Lowe, Henry MajTwCW
Paglia, Michael A. 1929- WhoE 91
Pagliaro, Harold Emil 1925- WhoAm 90
Pagliaro, Lynn A. 1940- WhoAm 90
Pagliaro, Salvatore BiDrAPA 89
Pagliaroni, Jim 1937- Ballpl 90
Pagliarulo, Margaret Manchester 1959- WhoAmW 91
Pagliarulo, Mike 1960- Ballpl 90
Paglierani, Ronald Joseph 1947- WhoEmL 91
Pagliero, Keith Michael 1938- WhoWor 91
Paglio, Lydia Elizabeth WhoAm 90, WhoWrEP 89
Pagliughi, Lina 1907-1980 PenDiMP
Pagnamenta, Peter John 1941- WhoWor 91
Pagnard, David A. ODwPR 91
Pagni, Albert Frank 1935- WhoWor 91
Pagni, Patrick John 1942- WhoAm 90
Pagni, Patrick Robert 1949- WhoWor 91
Pagnol, Marcel 1895-1974 MajTwCW
Pagnozzi, Richard Douglas 1947- St&PR 91
Pagter, Carl Richard 1934- St&PR 91, WhoAm 90
Paguiligan, Eufracia Angeles 1942- WhoAmW 91
Pahl, Aleta AuBYP 90
Pahl, Joy L. 1930- St&PR 91
Pahl, Kurt Gardner 1940- St&PR 91
Pahl, Michael Raymond 1947- St&PR 91

Pahl, Stephen Donald 1956- WhoEmL 91
Pahlavan, Kambiz 1943- BiDrAPA 89
Pahlavi, Mohammed Reza 1919-1980 BioIn 16, WorAlBi
Pahlavi, Reza BioIn 16
Pahlmann, William Carroll 1900-1987 BioIn 16
Pahlsson, Birgit Monica 1936- WhoWor 91
Pahtahquahong DcCanB 12
Pahule, Edward Joseph 1957- WhoWrEP 89
Pahwa, Ashok 1955- WhoSSW 91
Pai, Anna Chao 1935- WhoE 91
Pai, Arvind K 1945- BiDrAPA 89
Pai, John S BiDrAPA 89
Pai, Kamalesh Kochikar 1953- BiDrAPA 89
Pai, Mohan 1941- St&PR 91
Pai, Ramesh Upendra Tonse 1924- WhoWor 91
Pai, Ratnakar S. BiDrAPA 89
Paice, Eric 1927?-1989 ConAu 129
Paicopolos, Ernest Michael 1951- WhoE 91
Paidas, George Peter 1946- St&PR 91
Paidosh, Mary Catherine 1946- WhoEmL 91
Paidoussi, Eleftheria R BiDrAPA 89
Paidoussis, Michael Pandeli 1935- WhoAm 90
Paier, Adolf A., Jr. 1938- St&PR 91
Paier, Adolf Arthur 1938- WhoAm 90
Paiewonsky, Ralph 1907- BioIn 16
Paige, Allan Wallace 1854-1913 AmLegL
Paige, Alvin 1934- WhoE 91, WhoWor 91
Paige, Anita Parker 1908- WhoAmW 91, WhoE 91, WhoWor 91
Paige, Connie 1945- ConAu 130
Paige, Elaine 1951- OxCPMus
Paige, Emmett, Jr. BioIn 16
Paige, Eugene Carroll, Jr. 1929- WhoAm 90
Paige, Glenn Durland 1929- WhoAm 90
Paige, Harry W 1922- ConAu 32NR
Paige, Hilliard Wegner 1919- WhoAm 90
Paige, Janis 1922- OxCPMus
Paige, Leroy 1906- WorAlBi
Paige, Leslie Zeldin 1952- WhoEmL 91
Paige, Mabeth Hurd 1870-1961 BioAmW
Paige, Norma 1922- St&PR 91, WhoAm 90
Paige, Norman IntWWM 90
Paige, Richard MajTwCW
Paige, Richard Bruce 1949- WhoAm 90
Paige, Richard D. 1949- St&PR 91
Paige, Richard E. BioIn 16
Paige, Satchel BioIn 16
Paige, Satchel 1906-1982 Ballpl 90 [port]
Paige, Vivian J. 1960- WhoAmW 91
Paige, Wayne Leo 1944- WhoAmA 91
Paik, Kun-Woo 1946- IntWWM 90
Paik, Kwanik Kenneth 1940- WhoAm 90
Paik, Nam June 1932- IntWWM 90, WhoAmA 91
Paikeday, Thomas M. 1926- WhoWor 91
Paikert, Geza Charles NewYTBS 90
Paikin, Lawrence S. 1933- St&PR 91
Paikowsky, Sandra R 1945- WhoAmA 91
Paikowsky, Sandra Roslyn 1945- WhoAm 90
Pailin, David A. 1936- ConAu 129
Paillard, Jean-Francois 1928- IntWWM 90
Pailthorpe, Grace W. 1883-1971 BiDWomA
Pain, Charles Leslie 1913- WhoAm 90
Painchaud, Georges 1940- BiDrAPA 89
Paine, Albert B. 1861-1937 AuBYP 90
Paine, Albert Bigelow 1861-1937 EncPaPR 91
Paine, Andrew J., Jr. 1937- St&PR 91
Paine, Bonnie BioIn 16
Paine, Bruce Edwin 1933- WhoE 91
Paine, C.W. Eliot 1936- St&PR 91
Paine, Charles William Eliot 1936- WhoAm 90
Paine, Christopher Hammon 1935- WhoWor 91
Paine, David M. ODwPR 91
Paine, Heidi BioIn 16
Paine, James Carriger 1924- WhoAm 90, WhoSSW 91
Paine, John BioIn 16
Paine, Lauran 1916- ConAu 31NR
Paine, Lincoln D 1936- BiDrAPA 89
Paine, Louis Burr, Jr. 1932- WhoAm 90
Paine, Nancy Marie 1948- WhoAmW 91
Paine, Phil 1930-1978 Ballpl 90
Paine, R.M. 1914- St&PR 91
Paine, Ralph Delahaye 1871-1925 BioIn 16
Paine, Raymond Lee, Jr. 1937- BiDrAPA 89
Paine, Robert T 1900-1965 WhoAmA 91N
Paine, Robert Treat 1731-1814 EncCRAm
Paine, Robert Treat 1933- WhoAm 90
Paine, Roberta M. 1925- AuBYP 90
Paine, Stephen William 1908- WhoAm 90
Paine, Thomas 1737-1809 BioIn 16, EncCRAm [port], WorAlBi
Paine, Thomas Otten 1921- St&PR 91
Painleve, Paul 1863-1933 BiDFrPL
Paino, F.A. 1939- St&PR 91
Painter, Allen Hall 1907- St&PR 91
Painter, Benjamin David 1924- St&PR 91
Painter, Charles C. WhNaAH
Painter, Charlotte WhoWrEP 89
Painter, Christopher William 1962- IntWWM 90
Painter, David L. 1949- St&PR 91
Painter, Dewey Earl, Sr. 1941- WhoSSW 91
Painter, George Andrew, Jr. 1949- WhoSSW 91
Painter, Jack 1944- St&PR 91
Painter, Jack Timberlake 1930- WhoAm 90
Painter, James Russell 1943- St&PR 91
Painter, John Hoyt 1934- WhoAm 90
Painter, John W. 1929- St&PR 91
Painter, John William 1929- WhoAm 90
Painter, Linda Robinson 1940- WhoAmW 91
Painter, Mary Ella 1920- WhoWor 91
Painter, Paul 1923- BiDrAPA 89
Painter, Ruth Robbins 1910- WhoAmW 91
Painter, Samuel Franklin 1946- WhoEmL 91
Painter, Susan Ellen 1957- WhoE 91
Painter, Thomas Jay 1944- St&PR 91
Painter, William Hall 1927- WhoAm 90
Painter, William Steene 1949- WhoEmL 91
Painton, Ira Wayne 1917- WhoAm 90
Painton, Russell Elliott 1940- St&PR 91, WhoAm 90
Painvin, Jean-Marie 1951- St&PR 91
Pair, Paul Milton 1898- WhoAm 90
Pairpoint, Thomas J. PenDiDA 89
Pais, Abraham 1918- WhoAm 90
Pais, Donald A. BioIn 16
Paisley, David John 1955- WhoE 91
Paisley, Ian R. K. 1926- BioIn 16
Paisley, Ian Richard Kyle 1926- WhoWor 91
Paisley, Larry Greer 1946- WhoAm 90
Paisley, Melvyn BioIn 16
Paisley, Tom BioIn 16
Paisner, Bruce Lawrence 1942- WhoAm 90
Paisner, Martin N. BiDrAPA 89
Paiss, Doris Bell 1929- WhoAmW 91, WhoE 91, WhoWor 91
Pait, Larry Richard 1954- WhoE 91
Pait, Robert McCrae 1943- St&PR 91
Pait, Theodore BiDrAPA 89
Paita, Carlos 1932- IntWWM 90
Paiva, Jose Francisco de 1744-1824 PenDiDA 89
Paiva, Joseph Moura 1955- WhoE 91, WhoWor 91
Paiva-Parada, Antonio G 1927- BiDrAPA 89
Paivio, Allan Urho 1925- WhoAm 90
Paiz, Edgar BiDrAPA 89
Pajak, John Joseph 1935- St&PR 91
Pajari, Karen Louise BiDrAPA 89
Pajari, Roger Nelson 1941- WhoSSW 91
Pajer, Kathleen A 1952- BiDrAPA 89
Pajetta, Giancarlo NewYTBS 90
Pajetta, Guiliano 1915-1988 BioIn 16
Pajot, Gilles-Etienne 1958- WhoWor 91
Pajula, Jaakko Ilmari 1928- WhoWor 91
Pajunen, Grazyna Anna 1951- WhoAmW 91
Pak Song-chol 1913- WhoWor 91
Pak, Hyung Woong 1932- WhoAm 90, WhoWrEP 89
Pakalla, Paul A. 1922- St&PR 91
Paka'panikapi DcCanB 12
Pake, George Edward 1924- WhoAm 90
Pakeeree, Renga A 1948- BiDrAPA 89
Pakel, Stanley Scott 1950- St&PR 91
Pakenham, Antonia MajTwCW
Pakenham, Francis Aungier 1905- BioIn 16
Pakes, Eddy H 1937- BiDrAPA 89
Pakes, Judith Bernice BiDrAPA 89
Pakier, Oscar 1948- BiDrAPA 89
Pakington, Dorothy BiDEWW, FemiCLE
Pakiser, Louis Charles, Jr. 1919- WhoAm 90
Pakkala, Olli K. 1952- WhoWor 91
Pakkala, Teuvo 1862-1925 DcScanL
Pakola, Richard S 1943- BiDrAPA 89
Paksoy, Bulent 1947- WhoWor 91
Pakstis, Edward Joseph BiDrAPA 89
Pakula, Alan J. 1928- BioIn 16, ConAu 130
Pakula, Alan Jay 1928- WhoAm 90, WhoE 91
Pakula, Hannah BioIn 16
Pakula, Randall H. 1924- St&PR 91
Pakull, Barton 1935- BiDrAPA 89
Pal, Earni Satya 1941- BiDrAPA 89
Pal, Joginder BiDrAPA 89
Pal, Lenard 1925- WhoWor 91
Pal, Pratapaditya 1935- WhoAm 90, WhoAmA 91
Pal, Satya 1948- WhoE 91
Palace, Herbert M 1927- WhoE 91
Palacio, June Rose Payne 1940- WhoAmW 91
Palacio, Rhodora Gozon BiDrAPA 89
Palacio, Sergio M BiDrAPA 89
Palacios, Agustin L 1926- BiDrAPA 89
Palacios, Alfredo Lorenzo 1879-1965 BioIn 16
Palacios, Alvar Gonzalez- 1936- BioIn 16
Palacios, Arturo 1961- WhoHisp 91
Palacios, Jeannette C. De 1946- WhoHisp 91
Palacios, Luis E. 1956- WhoHisp 91
Palacios, May Husni 1926- WhoAmW 91
Palacios, Raphael R. WhoHisp 91
Palacioz, Joe John 1948- WhoHisp 91
Palade, George Emil 1912- WhoAm 90, WhoWor 91, WorAlBi
Paladini, Achille BioIn 16
Paladino, Daniel R. WhoAm 90
Paladino, Daniel Ralph 1943- St&PR 91
Paladino, Francis E. 1935- St&PR 91
Paladino, Hugo Robert 1929- St&PR 91
Paladino, Jeannette ODwPR 91
Paladino, Mimmo BioIn 16
Paladino, Robert Christopher 1950- WhoEmL 91
Palagaino, Vincent F. 1940- St&PR 91
Palagi, Pelagio 1775-1860 PenDiDA 89
Palagonia, Chris St&PR 91
Palagonia, Joseph Peter 1957- St&PR 91
Palahniuk, Richard John 1944- WhoAm 90
Palaia, Franc 1949- WhoAmA 91
Palaia, Franc Dominic 1949- WhoE 91
Palais, Donald Gerard 1928- St&PR 91
Palamara, Francis J. 1925- St&PR 91
Palamara, J. Francis 1950- St&PR 91
Palamountain, Bromley 1927- St&PR 91
Palan, Robert V. 1944- St&PR 91
Palanca, Terilyn 1957- WhoAmW 91, WhoEmL 91, WhoWor 91
Palance, Jack 1920- WhoAm 90, WorAlBi
Palanchian, John 1933-1989 BioIn 16
Palaniappan, Vaiapuri BiDrAPA 89
Palao, Paloma 1945- EncCoWW
Palasota, Jim Gerard 1953- WhoSSW 91
Palasota, Pete C 1924- BiDrAPA 89
Palasz, Bogumil 1931- IntWWM 90
Palat, Miroslav Josef Antonin 1927- WhoWor 91
Palate, The DcCanB 12
Palau, Gerald Leo 1956- WhoE 91
Palau, Marta 1934- WhoAmA 91
Palay, Elliot 1948- IntWWM 90
Palay, Gilbert 1827- WhoAm 90
Palay, Jayne Sigman 1935- WhoAmW 91
Palay, Sanford Louis 1918- WhoAm 90, WhoWrEP 89
Palayew, Max Jacob 1930- WhoAm 90
Palazhchenko, Pavel BioIn 16
Palazuelos, Ramon 1929- WhoHisp 91
Palazzi, Joseph Lazarro 1947- WhoAm 90
Palazzi, Joseph Lazzaro 1947- St&PR 91
Palazzi, Thomas 1916- St&PR 91
Palazzini, Pietro 1912- WhoWor 91
Palazzo, Maria Carmen BiDrAPA 89
Palazzo, Tony 1905-1970 AuBYP 90
Palazzola, Guy 1919-1978 WhoAmA 91N
Palazzolo, Carl 1935- WhoAmA 91
Palazzolo, Dominic Paul 1951- WhoEmL 91
Palazzolo, Tom 1937- WhoAm 90
Palcy, Euzhan BioIn 16
Palden Thondup Namgyal 1923- BioIn 16
Paldus, Josef 1935- WhoAm 90
Palecek, Josef 1932- BioIn 16
Paleczny, Raymond John 1940- St&PR 91
Palen, Rufus James 1843-1916 EncABHB 6 [port]
Palencia, Isabel de 1878- EncCoWW
Palencia-Roth, Michael 1946- WhoHisp 91
Palenzona, Peter James 1952- St&PR 91
Paler, Irving H. 1933- St&PR 91
Palerme, Patrick 1957- St&PR 91
Palermo, Anthony Robert 1929- WhoAm 90
Palermo, George B 1925- BiDrAPA 89
Palermo, Joseph 1917- WhoAm 90
Palermo, Joseph Michael 1923- St&PR 91
Palermo, Judy Hancock 1938- WhoAmW 91
Palermo, Louis P. 1944- St&PR 91
Palermo, Nicholas J. 1937- St&PR 91, WhoAm 90
Palermo, Peter M. 1941- St&PR 91
Palermo, Peter M., Jr. 1941- WhoAm 90
Palermo, Regino Valenzona, Jr. 1935- WhoWor 91
Palermo, Robert James 1949- WhoE 91
Palermo, Steve 1949- Ballpl 90
Pales, George Patrick 1950- WhoSSW 91
Pales Matos, Luis 1898-1959 BioIn 16, HispWr 90
Paleschuck, Rita Frank 1928- St&PR 91
Palestrina, Giovanni Pierluigi Da 1525?-1594 WorAlBi
Palevsky, Harry NewYTBS 90
Palevsky, Max 1924- ConAmBL, WhoAm 90
Palewski, Gaston 1901-1984 BiDFrPL
Paley, Aaron BiDrAPA 89
Paley, Albert 1944?- BioIn 16
Paley, Albert Raymond 1944- WhoAm 90, WhoAmA 91
Paley, Alfred Irving 1927- WhoAm 90
Paley, Ann-Marie N 1945- BiDrAPA 89, WhoE 91
Paley, Dianne Marie 1956- WhoWrEP 89
Paley, Elizabeth A. 1966- WhoE 91
Paley, Gerald Larry 1939- WhoAm 90
Paley, Grace 1922- FemiCLE, MajTwCW, WhoAm 90, WhoWrEP 89, WorAlBi
Paley, Herbert M BiDrAPA 89
Paley, James Alan 1946- WhoE 91
Paley, Marc Lance 1961- WhoE 91
Paley, Renee E. ODwPR 91
Paley, Renee E. 1945- WhoAmW 91
Paley, Richard Thomas 1936- WhoWor 91
Paley, Sharon Lisa BiDrAPA 89
Paley, Stephen M BiDrAPA 89
Paley, Vivian Gussin 1929- ConAu 30NR
Paley, William S. St&PR 91N
Paley, William S. 1901- BioIn 16, WhoAm 90, WhoE 91, WhoWor 91, WorAlBi
Paley, William S 1901-1990 ConAu 132, NewYTBS 90 [port], News 91-2, WhoAmA 91N
Paley, William S, Mrs WhoAmA 91N
Palframan, David Seymour 1943- BiDrAPA 89
Palfrey, Sarah AuBYP 90
Palgrave, Francis Turner 1824-1897 BioIn 16
Palgutt, William 1941- St&PR 91
Pali, Robert G. 1946- St&PR 91
Paliani, Mary Ann 1935- WhoAmW 91
Palic, Kevin Michael 1964- WhoE 91
Palica, Erv 1928-1982 Ballpl 90
Palihnich, Nicholas Joseph, Jr. 1939- WhoAm 90
Palik, Thomas Frank 1949- WhoSSW 91
Palileo, Maria Magdalena BiDrAPA 89
Palin, Michael Edward 1943- WhoWor 91
Palincsar, Annemarie Sullivan 1950- WhoAmW 91
Palinkas, James Thomas 1945- St&PR 91
Palinsky, Constance Genevieve 1927- WhoAmW 91
Palinurus MajTwCW
Palisca, Claude Victor 1921- IntWWM 90, WhoAm 90
Palisi, Anthony Thomas 1930- WhoAm 90
Palissy, Bernard 1510-1589? BioIn 16
Palissy, Bernard 1510?-1590? PenDiDA 89
Palit, Helen Mabel Ver Duin 1948- WhoAmW 91
Palitz, Bernard G. 1924- St&PR 91, WhoAm 90
Palitz, Clarence Y., Jr. 1931- St&PR 91
Palitz, Clarence Yale, Jr. 1931- WhoAm 90
Palizzi, Anthony N. 1942- St&PR 91, WhoAm 90
Palk, William John 1946- WhoE 91
Palker, Marc Paul 1952- St&PR 91
Palkhiwala, Bharati Arun BiDrAPA 89
Palkivala, John K. 1933- St&PR 91
Palko, Michael James 1936- St&PR 91, WhoAm 90
Palkowski, Daniel Henry 1955- IntWWM 90
Pall, Ellen 1952- BioIn 16
Palladin, Aleksandr Vladimirovich 1885-1972 DcScB S2
Palladin, Jean-Louis BioIn 16
Palladino, Angela 1929- MusmAFA
Palladino, Arthur 1950- BiDrAPA 89
Palladino, David Ludwig 1954- WhoE 91
Palladino, Eusapia 1854-1918 EncO&P 3, EncPaPR 91
Palladino, Nunzio Joseph 1916- WhoAm 90
Palladino-Craig, Allys 1947- WhoAm 90, WhoAmA 91, WhoAmW 91, WhoSSW 91
Palladio, Andrea 1508-1580 BioIn 16, PenDiDA 89, WorAlBi
Pallai, David Francis 1950- WhoE 91
Pallakoff, Owen E. 1930- St&PR 91, WhoAm 90
Pallan, Richard Nelson 1943- St&PR 91
Pallangyo, Ephata Parmena 1941- WhoWor 91
Pallares, Mariano 1943- WhoHisp 91
Pallares, Pilar 1957- EncCoWW
Pallaron, Ronald K. 1947- WhoAm 90
Pallas, Christopher William 1956- WhoSSW 91
Pallas, David Mark 1957- BiDrAPA 89
Pallasch, B. Michael 1933- WhoAm 90, WhoWor 91
Pallasch, Magdalena Helena 1908- WhoWor 91

Pallaschke, Diethard 1940- WhoWor 91
Pallat, Daniel Jon 1938- St&PR 91
Pallavicini, Federico von Berzeviczy- 1909-1989 BioIn 16
Pallayev, Gaibnazar Pallayevich WhoWor 91
Palle, Giambattista dalle PenDiDA 89
Pallemaerts, Marc 1960- WhoWor 91
Paller, Alan T. 1945- WhoE 91
Paller, Gary 1953- WhoAmA 91
Paller, Jack 1928- St&PR 91
Palley, Reese 1922- WhoAmA 91
Palley, Stephen W. 1945- St&PR 91
Palley, Stephen William BioIn 16
Pallin, Irving M. 1910- WhoAm 90
Pallin, Paddy BioIn 16
Pallini, Frank Charles 1953- WhoSSW 91
Pallister, Janis Louise 1926- WhoWrEP 89
Pallone, Adrian Joseph 1928- WhoAm 90
Pallone, Frank 1951- BioIn 16
Pallone, Frank, Jr. 1951- WhoAm 90, WhoE 91
Pallone, Joseph Charles 1943- St&PR 91
Pallone, Julius Louis 1930- St&PR 91, WhoAm 90
Pallot, E. Albert 1908- WhoAm 90, WhoWor 91
Pallot, William L. 1912- St&PR 91
Pallotta, Gail Cassady 1942- WhoWrEP 89
Pallotta, Gina M. 1958- WhoAmW 91
Pallotta, Michael Vincent 1955- St&PR 91
Pallotti, Marianne Marguerite 1937- WhoAmW 91
Pallucchini, Rodolfo 1908-1989 BioIn 16
Palluzi, Richard Peter 1952- WhoE 91
Pally, Regina 1948- BiDrAPA 89
Palm, Charles H BiDrAPA 89
Palm, Earl W. 1928- St&PR 91
Palm, Erwin Walter 1910-1988 BioIn 16
Palm, Goran 1931- DcScanL
Palm, Robert Gustav 1950- St&PR 91
Palm, Siegfried 1927- IntWWM 90, PenDiMP
Palma WhNaAH
Palma Vecchio 1480-1528 IntDcAA 90
Palma, Arturo Alessandri 1868-1950 BioIn 16
Palma, Dolores Patricia 1951- WhoAm 90, WhoE 91, WhoEmL 91, WhoWor 91
Palma, Manuel Ricardo 1833-1919 BioIn 16
Palma, Marigloria HispWr 90
Palma, Massimo Ugo 1927- WhoWor 91
Palma, Raul Arnulfo 1925- WhoHisp 91
Palma, Ricardo 1833-1919 BioIn 16
Palma, Tomas Estrada 1835-1908 BioIn 16
Palman, Deborah BioIn 16
Palmarez, Sulema E. 1957- WhoHisp 91
Palmas, Angelo 1914- WhoAm 90
Palmatier, George Edward 1946- St&PR 91
Palmatier, Rex V. 1955- St&PR 91
Palmatier, Robert Allen 1926- WhoWrEP 89
Palmatier, William Edwin 1943- St&PR 91
Palmay, Richard Leo 1959- WhoE 91
Palmbaum, Paul J 1933- BiDrAPA 89
Palmberger, Herbert Walter 1943- WhoWor 91
Palme, Michelle Yvonne 1964- WhoEmL 91
Palmeiro, Rafael 1964- Ballpl 90
Palmeiro, Rafael Corrales 1964- WhoHisp 91
Palmen, Michael Allen 1943- BiDrAPA 89
Palmer, A.B. 1924- St&PR 91
Palmer, Ada Margaret 1940- WhoAmW 91
Palmer, Adrian B. 1910- WhoAm 90
Palmer, Alan James 1958- WhoWor 91
Palmer, Alexander Mitchell 1872-1936 BiDrUSE 89
Palmer, Alice Eugenia 1910- WhoAm 90
Palmer, Alice F. 1855-1902 BioAmW
Palmer, Alicia 1763-1822? FemiCLE
Palmer, Allen Ingels 1910-1950 WhoAmA 91N
Palmer, Allen Jay BiDrAPA 89
Palmer, Anne Caldwell 1956- WhoSSW 91
Palmer, Anthony John 1931- IntWWM 90
Palmer, Arnold 1929- WorAlBi
Palmer, Arnold Daniel 1929- WhoAm 90
Palmer, Ashley Joanne 1951- WhoAmW 91
Palmer, Barbara BiDEWW
Palmer, Bert 1924- St&PR 91
Palmer, Bertha 1849-1918 BioAmW
Palmer, Beverly Blazey 1945- WhoAmW 91, WhoEmL 91
Palmer, Brian David 1957- WhoEmL 91
Palmer, Bruce Hamilton 1932- AuBYP 90
Palmer, Bruce Harrison 1955- WhoSSW 91
Palmer, C. Everard 1930- BioIn 16
Palmer, Carol Ann 1949- WhoAmW 91
Palmer, Charlene Noel 1930- WhoWrEP 89
Palmer, Charles L. 1942- St&PR 91
Palmer, Charles Ray 1940- WhoWor 91
Palmer, Charles Robert 1934- St&PR 91, WhoAm 90
Palmer, Charles Robert 1954- WhoSSW 91
Palmer, Charlotte 1762?-1834? FemiCLE
Palmer, Charman F 1922- BiDrAPA 89
Palmer, Chester L., Jr. 1947- WhoSSW 91
Palmer, Cruise 1917- WhoAm 90
Palmer, Curtis Howard 1908- St&PR 91, WhoAm 90
Palmer, Curtis Ray WhoWor 91
Palmer, Daniel David 1845-1913 NewAgE 90
Palmer, Darwin L. 1930- WhoAm 90
Palmer, Dave Richard 1934- WhoAm 90
Palmer, David 1957- Ballpl 90
Palmer, David Bartow 1929- BiDrAPA 89
Palmer, David Walter 1928- WhoWrEP 89
Palmer, Deborah Jean 1947- WhoEmL 91
Palmer, Delos 1891-1961 WhoAmA 91N
Palmer, Dennis Dale 1945- WhoEmL 91
Palmer, Don 1934- BiDrAPA 89
Palmer, Doreen P. BioIn 16
Palmer, Earl BioIn 16
Palmer, Edward Brian 1928- WhoWor 91
Palmer, Edward Lewis 1917- St&PR 91, WhoAm 90
Palmer, Erwin George 1908- WhoAm 90
Palmer, Ethel Susan 1943- WhoAmW 91
Palmer, Felicity 1944- PenDiMP
Palmer, Felicity Joan 1944- IntWWM 90
Palmer, Forrest Charles 1924- WhoAm 90
Palmer, Frank K. 1955- St&PR 91
Palmer, Gary Andrew 1953- WhoAm 90
Palmer, Gary James 1954- WhoSSW 91
Palmer, Geoffrey 1927- ConTFT 8 [port]
Palmer, Geoffrey 1942- WhoWor 91
Palmer, George A. BioIn 16
Palmer, George C., II 1922- St&PR 91
Palmer, George E. 1908- WhoAm 90
Palmer, Gertrude BioIn 16
Palmer, Grace BiDrAPA 89
Palmer, Hans Christian 1933- WhoAm 90
Palmer, Harvey John 1946- WhoAm 90
Palmer, Hazel WhoAm 90
Palmer, Heidi Marie 1955- WhoAmW 91, WhoE 91
Palmer, Helen NewAgE 90
Palmer, Helen Marion 1898-1967 AuBYP 90
Palmer, Henry L. 1819-1909 AmLegL
Palmer, Henry Spencer 1838-1893 DcCanB 12
Palmer, Herbert Bearl 1915- WhoAmA 91
Palmer, Howard Linter St&PR 91N
Palmer, Hubert Bernard 1912- WhoSSW 91
Palmer, Humphrey PenDiDA 89
Palmer, Humphrey 1930- ConAu 31NR
Palmer, Ian Robert 1940- WhoE 91
Palmer, Irene Sabelberg 1923- WhoAm 90
Palmer, James A. 1937- St&PR 91
Palmer, James Daniel 1930- WhoAm 90
Palmer, James Edward 1935- WhoAm 90
Palmer, James Edwin 1934- St&PR 91
Palmer, James M. 1949- St&PR 91
Palmer, Jane ODwPR 91
Palmer, Janet BiDrAPA 89
Palmer, Janet Joyce 1941- WhoE 91
Palmer, Janice Marie 1949- WhoAmW 91
Palmer, Jeffrey Scott 1964- WhoSSW 91
Palmer, Jerry L. 1933- St&PR 91
Palmer, Jim 1945- Ballpl 90 [port], News 91-2 [port], WorAlBi
Palmer, Jo Ann 1932- WhoAmW 91
Palmer, Joanne Melton 1927- WhoSSW 91
Palmer, Joel 1810-1881 AmLegL
Palmer, Joel 1946- WhoEmL 91
Palmer, John 1943- OxCCanT
Palmer, John 1944- EncPaPR 91
Palmer, John A., III 1955- WhoE 91
Palmer, John F. 1928- St&PR 91
Palmer, John Francis 1928- WhoAm 90
Palmer, John Jacob 1939- St&PR 91, WhoAm 90
Palmer, John James Ellis 1913- WhoAm 90
Palmer, John L. 1943- WhoAm 90
Palmer, John Leslie TwCCr&M 91
Palmer, John Marshall 1906- WhoAm 90
Palmer, John Mattern 1933- WhoAm 90
Palmer, John N. 1934- St&PR 91
Palmer, John Robert 1939- WhoSSW 91
Palmer, John W. 1952- WhoE 91
Palmer, Jonathan BiDrAPA 89
Palmer, Julie L 1945- BiDrAPA 89
Palmer, Kelly Page BiDrAPA 89
Palmer, Kenneth Arthur 1939- St&PR 91
Palmer, L Secord BiDrAPA 89
Palmer, Langdon 1928- WhoAm 90
Palmer, Larry Dean 1953- WhoSSW 91
Palmer, Laura BioIn 16
Palmer, Leo E. 1934- WhoAm 90
Palmer, Lilli 1914-1986 WorAlBi
Palmer, Linda Conner 1949- WhoAmW 91
Palmer, Linda Gail 1947- WhoEmL 91
Palmer, Louis Thomas 1937- WhoWor 91
Palmer, Lowell 1947- Ballpl 90
Palmer, Lucie Mackay 1913- WhoAmA 91
Palmer, M. Leslie 1959- WhoAmW 91
Palmer, Mabel 1903- WhoAmA 91
Palmer, Margaret Ochs BioIn 16
Palmer, Marianne Eleanor 1945- WhoSSW 91
Palmer, Martin B. 1957- St&PR 91
Palmer, Mary 1716-1794 FemiCLE
Palmer, Melville Louis 1924- WhoAm 90
Palmer, Meredith Ann 1951- WhoAmA 91
Palmer, Michael Andrew 1942- WhoAmA 91, WhoE 91
Palmer, Michael Charles 1931- WhoE 91
Palmer, Michael E. 1942- St&PR 91
Palmer, Michael S 1942- WorAu 1980
Palmer, Michael Z. 1939- St&PR 91
Palmer, Mildred Eunice 1911- WhoSSW 91
Palmer, Milton Meade 1916- WhoAm 90
Palmer, Nancy G. 1957- WhoSSW 91
Palmer, Nathan Hunt 1936- St&PR 91
Palmer, Nathaniel Brown 1799-1877 WorAlBi
Palmer, Nettie 1885-1964 FemiCLE
Palmer, Nina 1947- WhoAm 90, WhoAmW 91
Palmer, Nina Ann 1953- BiDrAPA 89
Palmer, Norman 1922- St&PR 91
Palmer, Norman Dunbar 1909- WhoAm 90
Palmer, Patricia Ann Texter 1932- WhoWor 91
Palmer, Patrick Edward 1940- WhoAm 90
Palmer, Pete 1938- Ballpl 90
Palmer, Peter 1945- IntWWM 90
Palmer, Philip Edward Stephen 1921- WhoAm 90
Palmer, Philip Isham, Jr. 1929- WhoAm 90, WhoWor 91
Palmer, Potter 1826-1902 WorAlBi
Palmer, Raymond AuBYP 90
Palmer, Raymond A. 1910-1977 EncO&P 3
Palmer, Raymond A. 1939- WhoAm 90
Palmer, Rex M. 1954- St&PR 91
Palmer, Richard Alan 1935- WhoAm 90
Palmer, Richard B. St&PR 91
Palmer, Richard C 1944- BiDrAPA 89
Palmer, Richard Eugene 1920- WhoAm 90, WhoSSW 91
Palmer, Richard Roy 1942- BiDrAPA 89
Palmer, Richard Ware 1919- WhoAm 90, WhoWor 91
Palmer, Robert BioIn 16
Palmer, Robert Baylis 1938- WhoAm 90
Palmer, Robert Bitts 1940- St&PR 91
Palmer, Robert C 1945- BiDrAPA 89
Palmer, Robert Conrad, Jr. 1929- WhoSSW 91
Palmer, Robert D. 1915- St&PR 91
Palmer, Robert Erwin 1934- WhoAm 90
Palmer, Robert Franklin, Jr. 1945- WhoWrEP 89
Palmer, Robert Joseph 1934- WhoAm 90
Palmer, Robert Joseph 1954- WhoEmL 91
Palmer, Robert K. 1946- St&PR 91
Palmer, Robert L. 1929- St&PR 91
Palmer, Robert Lewis 1910- WhoAm 90
Palmer, Robert Roswell 1909- WhoAm 90
Palmer, Robert Towne 1947- WhoEmL 91, WhoWor 91
Palmer, Robie E. BioIn 16
Palmer, Robie Marcus Hooker Mark 1941- WhoAm 90, WhoWor 91
Palmer, Robin 1911- AuBYP 90
Palmer, Roger Farley 1931- WhoAm 90
Palmer, Roger Raymond 1926- WhoAm 90
Palmer, Rolf G 1951- BiDrAPA 89
Palmer, Ronald DeWayne BioIn 16
Palmer, Ronald DeWayne Faisal 1932- WhoAm 90, WhoWor 91
Palmer, Rose 1943- WhoAmW 91
Palmer, Rose Ada 1920- St&PR 91
Palmer, Rudolph Alexis 1952- IntWWM 90
Palmer, Russell Eugene 1934- WhoAm 90
Palmer, Samuel 1805-1881 BioIn 16, IntDcAA 90
Palmer, Samuel Copeland, III 1934- WhoAm 90
Palmer, Sidney M. St&PR 91
Palmer, Sophia 1853-1920 BioIn 16
Palmer, Stephen B. 1927- St&PR 91
Palmer, Stephen Eugene 1896- WhoAm 90
Palmer, Stephen Eugene, Jr. 1923- WhoAm 90
Palmer, Steven W. 1950- St&PR 91
Palmer, Steven William 1950- WhoE 91
Palmer, Stuart 1905-1968 TwCCr&M 91
Palmer, Stuart Hunter 1924- WhoAm 90, WhoWor 91
Palmer, Susan Jane 1940- WhoSSW 91
Palmer, Susann 1923- ConAu 132
Palmer, Ted W. 1933- St&PR 91
Palmer, Thomas A. 1961- WhoE 91
Palmer, Thomas James 1942- WhoSSW 91
Palmer, Thomas Monroe 1931- WhoSSW 91
Palmer, Timothy 1958- ODwPR 91
Palmer, Timothy Trow 1938- WhoE 91
Palmer, Wayne Lewis 1949- WhoE 91, WhoWor 91
Palmer, Willard Aldrich, Jr. 1917- IntWWM 90
Palmer, William A. 1916- St&PR 91
Palmer, William Bailey 1931- WhoAm 90
Palmer, William Hassell 1945- WhoEmL 91
Palmer, William P. 1897-1989 BioIn 16
Palmer, William Ralph 1950- WhoEmL 91
Palmer, Winthrop Bushnell 1899-1988 BioIn 16
Palmer-Hass, Lisa Michelle 1953- WhoAmW 91
Palmeri, Barbara Ann 1951- BiDrAPA 89
Palmeri, Christine 1965- WhoE 91
Palmeri, Diane BioIn 16
Palmeri, Tom BioIn 16
Palmero, Emilio 1895-1970 Ballpl 90
Palmerston, Henry John 1784-1865 BioIn 16
Palmese, Richard Dominick 1947- St&PR 91, WhoAm 90
Palmeter, N. David 1938- WhoAm 90
Palmgren, Donald Gene 1938- WhoAmA 91
Palmieri, Alain John Verron 1941- WhoE 91
Palmieri, Charlie BioIn 16
Palmieri, Clara Jeannette BiDrAPA 89
Palmieri, Edmund L. 1907-1989 BioIn 16
Palmieri, Guy Joseph 1936- St&PR 91
Palmieri, Joanne 1956- WhoAmW 91
Palmieri, Lucien Eugene 1921- WhoE 91
Palmieri, Nicola W. 1935- St&PR 91
Palmieri, Peter C. 1934- St&PR 91
Palmieri, Robert Jeffrey 1952- St&PR 91
Palmieri, Robert Michael 1930- IntWWM 90
Palmieri, Ronald John 1944- BiDrAPA 89
Palmieri, Victor Henry 1930- WhoAm 90
Palmisano, Cynthia Mary 1954- WhoAmW 91
Palmisano, Edwina Margaret 1943- WhoAmW 91
Palmisano, Shirley Ann 1944- WhoAmW 91
Palmiter, Richard DeForest 1942- WhoAm 90
Palmon, Oded 1951- WhoE 91
Palmon, Roberto P BiDrAPA 89
Palmore, James Andrew, Jr. 1940- WhoAm 90
Palmore, John Stanley, Jr. 1917- WhoAm 90
Palmquist, Charles Welles, Jr. 1950- WhoE 91
Palmquist, Donald H. 1934- St&PR 91
Palmquist, Donald Harvey 1934- WhoAm 90
Palmqvist, Sven 1906-1984 ConDes 90
Palmqvist, Sven Ernst Robert PenDiDA 89
Palmroth, John William 1939- St&PR 91
Palms, John Michael 1935- WhoAm 90
Palms, Roger Curtis 1936- WhoAm 90
Palms, Valerie Grace BiDrAPA 89
Palo, Jorma Heikki Ilari 1936- WhoWor 91
Palo, Nicholas Edwin 1945- WhoAm 90
Paloian, Ab 1929- St&PR 91
Palomaki, Mauri Juho 1931- WhoWor 91
Palombi, Barbara Jean 1949- WhoWor 91
Palombi, Joseph John 1941- BiDrAPA 89
Palombo, Arthur James 1923- St&PR 91
Palombo, Bernardo Alfredo 1948- WhoHisp 91
Palombo, Paul Lanny 1964- WhoSSW 91
Palombo, Robert Victor 1942- BiDrAPA 89
Palombo, Stanley R 1934- BiDrAPA 89
Palombo, Tony 1959- St&PR 91
Palomino, Carlos 1950- BioIn 16, WhoHisp 91
Palomino, Ernesto Ramirez 1933- BioIn 16
Palomo, Guillermo E 1927- BiDrAPA 89
Palos, James Joseph 1961- WhoHisp 91
Palotai, Boris 1907-1984 EncCoWW
Palotai, Vilmos PenDiMP
Palotasi, Andras 1941- WhoWor 91
Palotta, Joseph Luke BiDrAPA 89
Palou, Digna 1940?- EncCoWW
Palou, Francisco 1722-1789 WhNaAH
Palou, Ines 1923-1975 EncCoWW
Palovic, Lora 1918- AuBYP 90
Palowicz, Efram O. St&PR 91
Paloyan, Edward 1932- WhoAm 90
Pals, Dean Clifford 1938- WhoSSW 91
Palser, Barbara F. 1916- WhoAm 90
Palsho, Dorothea Coccoli 1947- WhoAmW 91
Palsis, Peter Paul 1937- St&PR 91
Palsson, Gestur 1852-1891 DcScanL
Palsson, Pall 1912- IntWWM 90
Palsson, Thorsteinn 1947- WhoWor 91
Palsson, Tryggvi 1949- WhoWor 91
Palsulich, Ronda Marie 1965- WhoAmW 91
Paltauf, Fritz 1936- WhoWor 91

Palte, Lambertus 1953- *WhoWor 91*
Palter, Robert Monroe 1924- *WhoAm 90*
Paltiel, Rae G. 1946- *St&PR 91*
Paltin, Samuel J 1926- *BiDrAPA 89*
Paltrow, Kenneth G 1933- *BiDrAPA 89*
Paltrowitz, Donna 1950- *BioIn 16, SmATA 61 [port]*
Paltrowitz, Stuart 1946- *BioIn 16, SmATA 61 [port]*
Paluch, Edward Peter 1952- *WhoSSW 91*
Paluchowski, Carol Anne 1953- *WhoEmL 91*
Paluck, Robert John 1947- *WhoAm 90*
Paludan, Jacob 1896-1975 *DcScanL*
Paludan-Muller, Frederik 1809-1876 *DcScanL*
Palumbo, Benjamin Lewis 1937- *WhoE 91*
Palumbo, Diane Irene 1958- *WhoAmW 91*
Palumbo, Dominic Joseph 1945- *WhoE 91*
Palumbo, James F. 1950- *St&PR 91*
Palumbo, James Fredrick 1950- *WhoE 91*
Palumbo, John Christopher 1931- *WhoWor 91*
Palumbo, Joseph H *BiDrAPA 89*
Palumbo, Mario Joseph 1933- *WhoSSW 91*
Palumbo, Michael Nicholas 1960- *WhoWrEP 89*
Palumbo, Nicholas Eugene 1928- *WhoAm 90*
Palumbo, Robert Anthony 1951- *St&PR 91*
Paluszak, Naoko 1957- *WhoSSW 91*
Paluszek, John L. 1933- *ODwPR 91, WhoAm 90*
Paluszny, Maria Janina 1939- *BiDrAPA 89*
Palvino, Jack Anthony 1934- *WhoAm 90*
Palys, Garsutis K *BiDrAPA 89*
Palzer, Keith Allan 1964- *WhoE 91*
Pam, Frank Ulrich 1936- *IntWWM 90*
Pambakian, Robert 1948- *BiDrAPA 89*
Pamdeth, Narayanan Menon 1929- *WhoWor 91*
Pamerleau, William Charles 1933- *St&PR 91*
Pamies i Bertran, Teresa 1919- *EncCoWW*
Pampalon, Alfred 1867-1896 *DcCanB 12*
Pampanini, Andrea Henry A 1940- *St&PR 91*
Pampanini, Rosetta 1896-1973 *PenDiMP*
Pampel, Joseph Philip Stevenson 1932- *WhoE 91*
Pampel, Roland D. 1934- *St&PR 91*
Pampena, Ralph 1937- *St&PR 91*
Pamplin, Peter 1954- *St&PR 91*
Pamplin, Robert B. 1911- *St&PR 91*
Pamplin, Robert Boisseau, Jr. 1941- *WhoAm 90, WhoWor 91*
Pamplin, Robert Boisseau, Sr. 1911- *WhoAm 90, WhoSSW 91*
Pamplona, Sofia Louisa *BiDrAPA 89*
Pampoude, Pavlina 1949- *EncCoWW*
Pampoudi, Pavlina *EncCoWW*
Pampusch, Anita Marie 1938- *WhoAm 90, WhoAmW 91*
Pampy, Edna Theresa 1948- *WhoAmW 91*
Pan Hong *BioIn 16*
P'an, Albert Yuan 1941- *WhoE 91*
Pan, Cheng Tsing *BiDrAPA 89*
Pan, Coda H. T. 1929- *WhoAm 90*
Pan, Elizabeth Lim 1941- *WhoAm 90*
Pan, Francis Kuang-Chung 1904- *WhoWor 91*
Pan, Henry Yue-Ming 1946- *WhoE 91*
Pan, Hermes *NewYTBS 90*
Pan, Hermes 1910- *WhoAm 90*
Pan, Huo-Ping 1921- *WhoWor 91*
Pan, Joshua Jih 1942- *WhoWor 91*
Pan, Jove Mu-Wang 1950- *WhoE 91*
Pan, Kuo-Chen 1962- *WhoEmL 91*
Pan, Loretta Ren-Qiu 1917- *WhoWor 91*
Pan, Steve Chia-tung 1922- *WhoAm 90*
Pan, Theodore *WhoAmA 91*
Pan, Victor Yakovlevich 1939- *WhoE 91*
Pan, Yibiao 1963- *WhoEmL 91*
Panaeva, Avdot'ia 1819?-1893 *EncCoWW*
Panagiotopoulos, Panagiotis Dionysios 1950- *WhoWor 91*
Panagiotopoulos, Vasos-Peter John, II 1961- *WhoE 91*
Panagoulias, Patricia Ann 1951- *WhoAmW 91*
Panahon, Norma C 1943- *BiDrAPA 89*
Panait, Constantin *BioIn 16*
Panangaden, Prakash 1954- *WhoE 91*
Panarale, Joseph Anthony 1936- *St&PR 91*
Panarese, William C. 1929- *WhoAm 90*
Panaretos, John 1948- *WhoWor 91*
Panarites, John P. 1939- *St&PR 91*
Panaro, Victor Anthony 1928- *WhoAm 90*
Panasci, Henry A., Jr. 1928- *St&PR 91*
Panasci, Henry Anthony, Jr. 1928- *WhoAm 90, WhoE 91*
Panassie, Hugues 1912-1974 *OxCPMus*
Panattoni, Marcia J. 1959- *St&PR 91*
Panayi, Laura Polito 1959- *WhoAmW 91*
Panayiotou, Georghios S. 1937- *WhoWor 91*
Panayotopoulos, Andonis Demetre 1947- *WhoWor 91*
Pancer, Joel M. 1937- *St&PR 91*
Pancha, Sancho *EncCoWW*
Panchen Lama, The 1938-1989 *AnObit 1989*
Panchen, Lama X. 1937-1989 *BioIn 16*
Pancner, Ronald Jerry 1935- *BiDrAPA 89*
Pancoast, Duane A. *ODwPR 91*
Pancoast, Edwin C. 1925- *WhoAm 90*
Pancoast, Mary Susan 1944- *WhoAmW 91, WhoSSW 91*
Pancoast, Scott Rutledge 1958- *St&PR 91*
Pancoast, Terrence Russell 1942- *WhoAm 90*
Pancu, Lucia *BiDrAPA 89*
Panczenko, Russell 1947- *WhoAmA 91*
Pandaleon, A. George 1930- *St&PR 91*
Pande, Atul C 1954- *BiDrAPA 89*
Pande, Shashi K *BiDrAPA 89*
Pande, Vinod Kumar *BiDrAPA 89*
Pandelidis, Pandelis Kirk 1927- *BiDrAPA 89*
Pandey, Dhirendra Kumar 1951- *WhoSSW 91*
Pandey, Kailash Nath 1946- *WhoSSW 91*
Pandey, Ramendra Narayan 1951- *WhoSSW 91*
Pandeya, Nirmalendu Kumar 1940- *WhoWor 91*
Pandian, Jothi 1893-1954 *BioIn 16*
Pandick, Thomas O'Donnell 1947- *WhoE 91*
Pandit, Vijay Lakshmi *NewYTBS 90*
Pandit, Vijaya Lakshmi 1900- *WomWR*
Pandit, Vinay Yeshwant 1943- *WhoE 91*
Pandji, Wisaksana 1925- *WhoWor 91*
Pando, Alan Oscar 1931- *WhoAm 90*
Pando, Jeffrey Jerome 1950- *WhoEmL 91*
Pando, Jose Manuel 1848?-1917 *BioIn 16*
Pandolfini, Canzio 1939- *St&PR 91*
Pandolfo, Michael A. 1945- *St&PR 91*
Pandosy, Charles 1824-1891 *DcCanB 12*
Pandozy, Raffaele Martini *WhoAmA 91*
Pandurangi, Ananda Krishna *BiDrAPA 89*
Panduro, Leif 1923-1977 *DcScanL*
Pandya, Ashvinkumar *BiDrAPA 89*
Pandya, Ashvinkumar Ramchandra 1937- *WhoE 91*
Pandya, Jyotsna R 1920- *BiDrAPA 89*
Pandya, Renu R 1955- *BiDrAPA 89*
Pandyan *WomWR*
Pane, Gina 1939- *BiDWomA*
Pane, Joseph Francis 1921- *St&PR 91*
Pane, Michael Anthony 1942- *WhoWor 91*
Pane, Remigio Ugo 1912- *WhoAm 90, WhoWor 91*
Panecasio, Eugene L. 1936- *St&PR 91*
Panek, Jeri Herndon 1939- *WhoAmW 91*
Panek, LeRoy Lad 1943- *ConAu 32NR*
Panelli, Edward Alexander 1931- *WhoAm 90*
Panenka, Jan 1922- *IntWWM 90*
Paneque, Hector E *BiDrAPA 89*
Panerai, Rolando 1924- *IntWWM 90, PenDiMP*
Panes, Jack Samuel 1925- *WhoAm 90*
Paneth, Donald J. 1927- *WhoAm 90, WhoE 91*
Panetta, George 1915-1969 *AuBYP 90*
Panetta, Leon E. *BioIn 16*
Panetta, Leon Edward 1938- *WhoAm 90*
Paney, Harry Edmond 1926- *St&PR 91*
Paneyko, Stephen Hobbs 1942- *St&PR 91, WhoAm 90*
Panfil, John A. 1930- *St&PR 91*
Panfile, Orlando Ernest 1928- *St&PR 91*
Panfilov, Gleb *BioIn 16*
Pang, Herbert George 1922- *WhoAm 90, WhoWor 91*
Pang, Jim, Jr. 1952- *BiDrAPA 89*
Pang, Robert Russell 1956- *BiDrAPA 89*
Pangborn, Edgar 1909-1980 *RGTwCSF*
Pangborn, Jerald L. 1932- *St&PR 91*
Pangburn, Arthur Dewitt 1942- *St&PR 91*
Pangburn, James E. 1930- *WhoSSW 91*
Pangburn, Patricia Dillard 1933- *WhoAmW 91*
Pangerapan, Bob George 1938- *WhoWor 91*
Pangilinan, Nestor S *BiDrAPA 89*
Pangrazi, Robert P. *BioIn 16*
Panhofer, Walter 1910- *IntWWM 90*
Panholzer, Adam Paul 1964- *St&PR 91*
Panholzer, J. Robert 1958- *St&PR 91*
Paniagua, Alejandro D 1927- *BiDrAPA 89*
Panic Brothers, The *WhoNeCM B*
Panic, Milan 1929- *St&PR 91*
Panicali, Dennis 1949- *St&PR 91*
Paniccia, Mario Domenic 1948- *WhoE 91, WhoEmL 91, WhoWor 91*
Panich, Paula Marie 1947- *WhoWrEP 89*
Panichas, George Andrew 1930- *WhoAm 90, WhoWrEP 89*
Panichi, Michele A. 1959- *WhoAmW 91*
Panico, Alison Mary 1967- *WhoAmW 91*
Panico, C. Richard 1941- *St&PR 91*
Panico, Frank S. 1958- *St&PR 91*
Panico, Richard Anthony 1950- *BiDrAPA 89*
Panigrahi, U S 1944- *BiDrAPA 89*
Panik, Michael Joseph 1940- *WhoE 91*
Panish, Brian Joseph 1958- *WhoEmL 91*
Panish, Morton B. 1929- *WhoAm 90*
Panitt, Merrill 1917- *WhoAm 90, WhoWrEP 89*
Panitz, Lawrence 1928- *WhoE 91*
Panitz, Lawrence Herbert 1941- *WhoAm 90, WhoWor 91*
Panizza, Michael 1946- *WhoWor 91*
Panjikaran, Rosamma Scaria *BiDrAPA 89*
Pank, Esther *BioIn 16*
Pankau, Edmund J. 1945- *WhoSSW 91*
Panken, Peter Michael 1936- *WhoAm 90*
Pankey, Edgar Edward 1916- *WhoAm 90*
Pankey, George Atkinson 1933- *WhoAm 90*
Pankey, George Edward 1903- *WhoSSW 91, WhoWor 91*
Pankey, George Stephen 1922- *WhoSSW 91, WhoWor 91*
Pankhurst, Christabel 1880-1958 *BioIn 16, FemiCLE*
Pankhurst, Emmeline 1858-1928 *BioIn 16, FemiCLE, WorAlBi*
Pankhurst, Sylvia 1882-1960 *BiDWomA, BioIn 16, FemiCLE*
Pankin, Boris Dmitrievich 1931- *WhoWor 91*
Pankin, Jayson Darryl 1957- *St&PR 91, WhoWor 91*
Pankin, Mark David 1945- *WhoSSW 91*
Pankok, Bernhard 1872-1943 *PenDiDA 89*
Pankopf, Arthur, Jr. 1931- *WhoAm 90, WhoE 91*
Pankove, Jacques Isaac 1922- *WhoAm 90*
Pankovits, Jim 1955- *Ballpl 90*
Pankow, John *ConTFT 8*
Pankow, Larry Milton *BiDrAPA 89*
Pankow, Wlodzimierz 1946- *WhoWor 91*
Pankowski, Elsie Marie 1933- *WhoWrEP 89*
Pankowsky, Helen Orit 1953- *BiDrAPA 89*
Panman, Sandra 1944- *WhoE 91*
Pannariello, Anthony Louis 1935- *St&PR 91*
Pannell, Berry Coleman 1933- *St&PR 91*
Pannell, Creed White, Jr. 1946- *WhoSSW 91*
Pannell, William Robert 1936- *St&PR 91*
Pannemaker, Willem P. *PenDiDA 89*
Pannenberg, Wolfhart 1928- *BioIn 16*
Panner, Bernard J. 1928- *WhoAm 90*
Panneton, Jacques 1943- *WhoAm 90*
Panni, Marcello 1940- *IntWWM 90*
Pannick, David 1956- *ConAu 130*
Pannier, Alan 1959- *St&PR 91*
Pannier, Clyde Robert 1930- *St&PR 91*
Pannier, Loren C. 1942- *St&PR 91*
Pannill, Fitzhugh Carter, Jr. 1921- *WhoAm 90*
Pannill, William Presley 1940- *WhoSSW 91, WhoWor 91*
Pannini, Gian Paolo 1692?-1765 *IntDcAA 90*
Pannkuk, Paul Allen 1948- *St&PR 91*
Pannone, Richard R. 1942- *St&PR 91*
Pannone, Walter Anthony 1947- *WhoE 91*
Pannozzo, Sharon *BioIn 16*
Pannullo, Deborah Paolino 1953- *WhoAmW 91*
Panny, William Paul 1928- *St&PR 91*
Panoff, Michel Jean 1931- *WhoWor 91*
Panoff, Robert C. 1947- *St&PR 91*
Panofsky, Hans A. 1917-1988 *BioIn 16*
Panoor, Leela Andrews *BiDrAPA 89*
Panopoulos, Mildred Matthews 1930- *WhoWor 91*
Panos, George 1911- *St&PR 91*
Panos, Peter 1933- *St&PR 91*
Panos Schmitt, Athanasia Nancy 1951- *WhoAmW 91*
Panossian, Hagop Vartevar 1946- *WhoEmL 91*
Panou, Georges 1934- *WhoWor 91*
Panova, V. 1915- *AuBYP 90*
Panova, Vera 1905-1973 *EncCoWW, MajTwCW*
Panowicz, Mary Kay 1948- *WhoAmW 91*
Panowski, Eileen Thompson *AuBYP 90*
Panoz, Donald Eugene 1935- *St&PR 91*
Panozzo, Michael Edward 1958- *WhoWrEP 89*
Panshin, Alexei 1940- *RGTwCSF, WhoAm 90, WhoWrEP 89*
Pansini Brothers *EncO&P 3*
Pansini, Michael Samuel 1928- *WhoAm 90*
Panson, Gilbert Stephen 1920- *WhoAm 90*
Pant, Apa 1918- *BioIn 16*
Pant, Govind Ballabh 1887-1961 *BioIn 16*
Pant, Hem Chandra 1943- *WhoWor 91*
Pant, Shri Krishna Chandra 1931- *WhoWor 91*
Pantages, Alexander 1871-1936 *OxCCanT*
Pantages, Louis James 1916- *WhoAm 90*
Pantaleano, Michael Joseph 1941- *St&PR 91*
Pantaleon, Igmedio S *BiDrAPA 89*
Pantaleoni, Hewitt 1929-1988 *BioIn 16*
Pantano, Russell M *BiDrAPA 89*
Pantazelos, Peter G. 1930- *St&PR 91*
Pantel, Glenn Steven 1953- *WhoE 91, WhoEmL 91*
Panteledes, George 1940- *BiDrAPA 89*
Pantelis, Jorge 1932- *WhoHisp 91*
Pantell, Dora F. *AuBYP 90*
Pantell, Richard Keith 1951- *WhoAmA 91*
Panten-Licker, Brigitte 1943- *BiDrAPA 89*
Pantenberg, Michel 1926- *WhoAm 90*
Panter, Barry Michael 1934- *BiDrAPA 89*
Panter, Carol 1936- *AuBYP 90*
Panter, Gary 1950- *WhoAmA 91*
Panter, Peter *St&PR 91*
Panter-Downes, Mollie 1906- *BioIn 16, FemiCLE*
Panther, Jim 1945- *Ballpl 90*
Pantillon, Christophe David 1965- *IntWWM 90*
Pantillon, Pierre Louis 1960- *IntWWM 90*
Pantillon-Stokes, Gwendolyn June 1930- *IntWWM 90*
Pantin, Santiago Iglesias 1872-1939 *BioIn 16*
Pantin, Simon *PenDiDA 89*
Pantina, Donald M. 1933- *St&PR 91*
Pantke, Dawn Eileen 1966- *IntWWM 90*
Pantle, William David 1936- *WhoAm 90*
Pantoja, Rene V. 1960- *WhoHisp 91*
Pantoja, Richard Daniel 1960- *WhoSSW 91*
Pantoja, Yvonne Magno 1926- *WhoAmW 91*
Panton, Jane Ellen 1848-1923 *FemiCLE*
Panton, Verner 1926- *ConDes 90*
Pantschak, Vera *ODwPR 91*
Pantuso, Vincent Joseph 1940- *WhoAm 90*
Pantzer, Alfred Kivu 1925- *WhoWrEP 89*
Pantzer, Kurt Friedrich, Jr. 1928- *WhoAm 90, WhoWor 91*
Panufnik, Andrzej 1914- *IntWWM 90, PenDiMP, -A, WhoWor 91*
Panula, Pertti Aarre Juhani 1952- *WhoWor 91*
Panunzi, Benito 1835?-1886? *ArtLatA*
Panuska, Joseph Allan 1927- *WhoAm 90, WhoE 91*
Panwar, Shivendra Singh 1959- *WhoE 91*
Panza, Nicholas F. 1926- *St&PR 91*
Panza Di Biumo, Giuseppe *BioIn 16*
Panza Di Biumo, Giuseppe 1923- *WhoWor 91*
Panzarino, Connie *BioIn 16*
Panzarino, Peter Joseph, Jr. 1946- *BiDrAPA 89*
Panzella, Victor Donald, Jr. 1942- *WhoE 91*
Panzer, Arnold N. 1932- *St&PR 91*
Panzer, Donald Allen 1930- *St&PR 91*
Panzer, Edward I 1912- *BiDrAPA 89*
Panzer, Mitchell Emanuel 1917- *WhoAm 90*
Panzer, Thomas Phillip 1939- *WhoSSW 91*
Panzer, Wesley John 1945- *WhoEmL 91*
Panzera, Charles 1896-1976 *PenDiMP*
Panzetta, Anthony F 1934- *BiDrAPA 89*
Panzetta, Mary Teresa *BiDrAPA 89*
Panzner, Michael Joseph 1958- *WhoE 91*
Panzone, Lisa Marie Gina 1960- *WhoAmW 91*
Pao, Henry C. 1937- *St&PR 91*
Pao, Y.H. Michael 1944- *St&PR 91*
Pao, Yih-Hsing 1930- *WhoAm 90*
Paolano, Mary 1918- *WhoWrEP 89*
Paoletta, Michael L. 1952- *St&PR 91*
Paoletti, Donald Anthony *BiDrAPA 89*
Paoli, Betty *EncCoWW*
Paoli, Bob 1937- *St&PR 91*
Paoli, Francisco Matos *ConAu 131, HispWr 90*
Paoli, Francisco Matos 1915- *BioIn 16*
Paolillo, William P. 1937- *St&PR 91*
Paolini, Albert, Jr. 1931- *St&PR 91*
Paolini, Angelo 1947- *St&PR 91*
Paolini, Frank Rudolph 1930- *St&PR 91*
Paolini, Gilbert *WhoAm 90*
Paolini, Ronald 1956- *BiDrAPA 89*
Paolini, Shirley Joan *WhoSSW 91, WhoWor 91*
Paolino, Joseph Robert, Jr. 1955- *WhoAm 90, WhoE 91*
Paolino, Richard Francis 1945- *WhoAm 90*
Paolino, Vincent A. 1943- *St&PR 91*
Paolitto, Frank John 1937- *BiDrAPA 89*
Paolo da Verona *PenDiDA 89*
Paolo, Giovanni Di *BioIn 16*
Paolo, Veronese 1528-1588 *BioIn 16*
Paoloni, Joseph A. 1932- *WhoE 91*
Paolozzi, Anthony C. 1945- *St&PR 91*
Paolozzi, Eduardo Luigi 1924- *WhoWor 91*
Paolucci, Anne *WhoWrEP 89*
Paolucci, Anne Attura *WhoAm 90*
Paolucci, Henry *WhoAm 90*

Paolucci, Ronald Vincent 1927- *St&PR 91*
Paolucci, Stephen Joseph 1955- *BiDrAPA 89*
Paolucci, Susan Leigh 1956- *BiDrAPA 89*
Paone, Peter 1936- *WhoAm 90, WhoAmA 91*
Paonessa, Joseph Dominec 1935- *St&PR 91*
Paonessa, Philip John 1951- *WhoE 91*
Pap, Lajos 1883- *EncO&P 3*
Papa, Anthony Emil 1914- *WhoAm 90, WhoWor 91*
Papa, Joseph Ralph 1943- *St&PR 91*
Papa, Katina 1903-1959 *EncCoWW*
Papa, Kenneth E. 1931-1986 *BioIn 16*
Papa, Vincent Thomas 1946- *St&PR 91*
Papacosta, Sofia Theresa 1940- *WhoWor 91*
Papacostas, Savvas Symeon *BiDrAPA 89*
Papadakis, Constantine Nicholas 1946- *WhoEmL 91*
Papadakis, Emmanuel Philippos 1934- *WhoAm 90*
Papadakos, Nicholas Peter 1925- *WhoAm 90, WhoE 91*
Papadakos, Peter J. 1914- *St&PR 91*
Papadat-Bengescu, Hortensia 1876-1955 *EncCoWW*
Papadeas, Timothy George 1959- *WhoSSW 91*
Papadimitriou, Christos *WhoAm 90*
Papadimitriou, Dimitri Basil 1946- *WhoE 91, WhoEmL 91, WhoWor 91*
Papadopoli, Vincent 1952- *WhoE 91*
Papadopoulos, Abraham 1962- *WhoWor 91*
Papadopoulos, Dimitrios, I 1914- *WhoWor 91*
Papadopoulos, Gregory Michael 1958- *WhoWor 91*
Papadopoulos, Selios B. 1941- *St&PR 91*
Papadopoulos, Thomas Constantinos 1957- *WhoWor 91*
Papadopoulou, Alexandra 1867-1906 *EncCoWW*
Papagapitos, George Nicholas 1943- *WhoE 91*
Papageorge, Deno D. 1938- *St&PR 91*
Papageorge, Tod 1940- *WhoAm 90, WhoAmA 91*
Papageorgiou, John Constantine 1935- *WhoAm 90*
Papagiannis, Michael D. 1932- *WhoAm 90*
Papai, Al 1919- *Ballpl 90*
Papaioannou, Evangelia-Lilly 1963- *WhoE 91*
Papaioannou, Ioannis Panayoti 1954- *WhoSSW 91*
Papajani, Janet *AuBYP 90*
Papakostas, Yiannis G *BiDrAPA 89*
Papaleksi, Nikolai Dmitrievich 1880-1947 *DcScB S2*
Papaleo, Joseph 1926- *WhoAm 90*
Papaleo, Joseph 1927- *WhoWrEP 89*
Papaleo, Louis Anthony 1953- *WhoWor 91*
Papalexandrou, Christos Elias 1925- *WhoWor 91*
Papalia, Diane Ellen 1947- *WhoAm 90, WhoAmW 91*
Papaliolios, Costas Demetrios 1931- *WhoAm 90*
Papaloi *EncO&P 3*
Papamarkou, Alexander Plutarch 1930- *WhoAm 90*
Papamihalakis, John 1931- *WhoWor 91*
Papanastassiou, Anastassios A *BiDrAPA 89*
Papandreou, Andreas *BioIn 16*
Papandreou, Andreas George 1919- *WhoWor 91*
Papandreou, Constantine 1939- *WhoWor 91*
Papandreou, Margaret *BioIn 16*
Papanek, Andrew Phillip 1927- *St&PR 91*
Papanek, George O 1931- *BiDrAPA 89*
Papanek, Gustav F. 1926- *WhoAm 90, WhoE 91*
Papanek, Victor 1925- *ConDes 90*
Papanek, Victor 1926- *WhoAm 90*
Papanicolaou, George N. 1883-1962 *WorAlBi*
Papanos, Steve *BiDrAPA 89*
Paparella, Joseph 1909- *Ballpl 90*
Paparella, Michael Francis 1961- *WhoEmL 91*
Paparella, William F. 1949- *St&PR 91*
Paparo, Irving *BioIn 16*
Paparo, Jack *BioIn 16*
Papas, Arthur N 1938- *BiDrAPA 89*
Papas, Bill 1927- *BioIn 16*
Papas, Charles Herach 1918- *WhoAm 90*
Papas, Irene 1926- *ConTFT 8, WorAlBi*
Papashvily, George 1898-1978 *WhoAmA 91N*
Papasian, Jack C 1878-1957 *WhoAmA 91N*
Papastrat, Helen P 1958- *BiDrAPA 89*
Papastrat, Helen Panayota 1958- *WhoE 91*
Papatestas, Angelos E. *BioIn 16*
Papatheodorou, George *BiDrAPA 89*
Papathomas, Thomas Virgil 1949- *WhoE 91*
Papathomopoulos, Evangelos 1925- *BiDrAPA 89*
Papavasiliou, Stathis Spyro 1950- *WhoWor 91*
Papay, Lawrence T. 1936- *WhoAm 90*
Papazian, Dennis R. 1931- *WhoAm 90*
Papazickos, Chris George 1930- *St&PR 91*
Papazissis, Michael George 1935- *WhoWor 91*
Pape, Arthur Edward 1939- *WhoAm 90*
Pape, Barbara Harris 1936- *WhoWor 91*
Pape, Duane M. 1950- *WhoEmL 91*
Pape, E.C. 1937- *St&PR 91*
Pape, Eugene Thomas 1947- *WhoE 91*
Pape, Gerard Joseph 1955- *IntWWM 90*
Pape, Glenn Michael 1954- *WhoEmL 91*
Pape, Harry, Jr. 1939- *WhoAm 90*
Pape, Jean William 1946- *WhoWor 91*
Pape, Jerry Lee 1934- *WhoSSW 91, WhoWor 91*
Pape, Lygia 1929- *ArtLatA*
Pape, Patricia Ann 1940- *WhoAmW 91*
Pape, Patricia Jean 1958- *WhoAmW 91*
Pape, Rachel S E *BiDrAPA 89*
Pape, Sharon Barbara 1947- *WhoWrEP 89*
Pape, William J., II 1931- *St&PR 91*
Papello, Juan *WhoHisp 91*
Papen, Franz von 1878-1969 *BioIn 16*
Papen, Julia Stevenson 1910- *WhoAmW 91*
Papendick, Michael Scott 1957- *WhoEmL 91*
Papenfus, Robert George 1932- *St&PR 91*
Papenthien, Thomas R. 1955- *St&PR 91*
Paper, Herbert Harry 1925- *WhoAm 90*
Paper, Lewis 1928- *St&PR 91, WhoAm 90*
Papera, Gabriel L. 1905- *St&PR 91*
Paperin, Stewart J. 1948- *St&PR 91*
Paperin, Stewart Jules 1948- *WhoAm 90*
Papernik, Daniel S 1937- *BiDrAPA 89, WhoE 91*
Papernik, Joel Ira 1944- *WhoAm 90, WhoE 91*
Paperno, Dmitry 1929- *IntWWM 90*
Paperny, Myra 1932- *BioIn 16*
Papero, James M. 1932- *WhoE 91*
Papes, Lawrence J. 1940- *St&PR 91*
Papes, Theodore Constantine, Jr. 1928- *WhoAm 90*
Papesh, William G. 1943- *St&PR 91*
Papi, Stan 1951- *Ballpl 90*
Papi, Vincent J. 1947- *St&PR 91*
Papianni, James John 1953- *St&PR 91*
Papiano, Neil Leo 1933- *WhoAm 90*
Papiasvili, Avtandil *BiDrAPA 89*
Papier, Maurice Anthony 1940- *WhoAmA 91*
Papiernik, Donald 1937- *St&PR 91*
Papiernik, Serge 1958- *WhoSSW 91*
Papik, James Elvin 1952- *WhoEmL 91*
Papillon, Jean 1661-1723 *PenDiDA 89*
Papillon, Jean Baptiste Michel 1696-1776 *PenDiDA 89*
Papilsky, Shirley Barrie *BiDrAPA 89*
Papineau, David 1947- *ConAu 130*
Papineau, Sandra Lynn 1964- *WhoAmW 91*
Papineau-Couture, Jean 1916- *IntWWM 90, WhoAm 90*
Papini, Patricia Burton 1939- *WhoE 91*
Papish, Frank 1917-1965 *Ballpl 90*
Papish, Irwin Jerome 1929- *BiDrAPA 89*
Papitto, Ralph Raymond 1926- *St&PR 91, WhoAm 90, WhoE 91*
Papkin, Robert David 1933- *WhoAm 90, WhoE 91*
Papo, Iso 1925- *WhoAmA 91*
Papock, Herbert 1917- *St&PR 91*
Papone, Aldo 1932- *St&PR 91, WhoAm 90*
Papouin, Gerard 1947- *WhoWor 91*
Papoulias, Karolos 1929- *WhoWor 91*
Papoulias, Sotiri Aris 1953- *WhoE 91*
Papoulis, Athanasios 1921- *WhoAm 90*
Papp, Joseph *BioIn 16*
Papp, Joseph 1921- *WorAlBi*
Papp, Joseph 1922- *WhoAm 90, WhoE 91*
Papp, Laszlo Andras *BiDrAPA 89*
Papp, Laszlo Andras 1953- *WhoE 91*
Papp, Laszlo George 1929- *WhoAm 90, WhoE 91, WhoWor 91*
Papp, Vincent *WhoWrEP 89*
Pappa, Lena 1932- *EncCoWW*
Pappa, Michael Joseph 1936- *St&PR 91*
Pappadis, Thomas J *BiDrAPA 89*
Pappafava, Lorraine Beddick 1929- *St&PR 91*
Pappafava, Premo John 1926- *St&PR 91*
Pappagianis, Demosthenes 1928- *WhoAm 90*
Pappagianis, George Spiros 1924- *WhoAm 90*
Pappalardo, Rosa Gloria 1932- *WhoE 91*
Pappalardo, Salvatore 1918- *WhoWor 91*
Pappano, Robert Daniel 1942- *St&PR 91, WhoAm 90*
Pappas, Alceste Thetis 1945- *WhoAm 90*
Pappas, Alex L. 1932- *St&PR 91*
Pappas, Charles W. 1931- *St&PR 91*
Pappas, Costas Ernest 1910- *WhoAm 90*
Pappas, Daniel 1947- *St&PR 91*
Pappas, David Christopher 1936- *WhoWor 91*
Pappas, Dean C. 1939- *St&PR 91*
Pappas, Edward Harvey 1947- *WhoEmL 91, WhoWor 91*
Pappas, Effie Vamis 1924- *WhoAmW 91*
Pappas, George 1929- *WhoAmA 91*
Pappas, George Demetrios 1926- *WhoAm 90*
Pappas, George Frank 1950- *WhoAm 90*
Pappas, Hercules Chris 1928- *WhoAm 90*
Pappas, James F. 1962- *St&PR 91*
Pappas, James John 1939- *St&PR 91*
Pappas, John J. *WhoAm 90*
Pappas, Lynn Georgianne *BiDrAPA 89*
Pappas, Margaret 1949- *WhoEmL 91*
Pappas, Milt 1939- *Ballpl 90*
Pappas, Milton J. 1928- *St&PR 91*
Pappas, Nina Kalfas 1928- *WhoSSW 91*
Pappas, Pamela Anne 1953- *BiDrAPA 89*
Pappas, Peter C. *St&PR 91*
Pappas, S. Michael 1957- *St&PR 91*
Pappas, Socrates W 1935- *BiDrAPA 89*
Pappas, Ted Phillip 1934- *WhoAm 90*
Pappas, William John 1934- *St&PR 91, WhoAm 90*
Pappenheim, Bertha 1849-1938 *EncCoWW*
Pappenheim, Else 1911- *BiDrAPA 89*
Pappenheimer, Alwin Max, Jr. 1908- *WhoAm 90*
Pappenheimer, Paul A. 1927- *St&PR 91*
Papper, Emanuel Martin 1915- *WhoAm 90*
Pappin, James David *BiDrAPA 89*
Paprock, John-Brian Kenneth 1961- *WhoWor 91*
Paprocki, Thomas John 1952- *WhoEmL 91*
Papsidero, Joseph Anthony 1929- *WhoAm 90*
Papso, Anna Mae 1943- *St&PR 91*
Papus 1865-1916 *EncO&P 3*
Paque, Claude 1916- *WhoWor 91*
Paquet, Alfons 1881-1944 *BioIn 16*
Paquet, Anselme-Homere 1830-1891 *DcCanB 12*
Paquet, Benjamin 1832-1900 *DcCanB 12*
Paquet, Gilles 1936- *WhoAm 90*
Paquet, Karl Joseph 1937- *WhoWor 91*
Paquette, Daniel *IntWWM 90*
Paquette, Jack Kenneth 1925- *WhoAm 90*
Paquette, Joseph F., Jr. *St&PR 91*
Paquette, Joseph F., Jr. 1934- *WhoAm 90, WhoE 91*
Paquette, Richard R 1940- *BiDrAPA 89*
Paquette, Robert Hector 1933- *St&PR 91*
Paquin, Elzear 1850-1947 *OxCCanT*
Paquin, Marilyn Jean 1940- *WhoAmW 91*
Parac, Frano 1948- *IntWWM 90*
Paracelsus 1493-1541 *EncO&P 3, LitC 14 [port], WorAlBi*
Paracka, Daniel Joseph 1949- *St&PR 91*
Parad, Boris 1946- *WhoEmL 91*
Paradice, Sammy Irwin 1952- *WhoEmL 91, WhoSSW 91, WhoWor 91*
Paradice, William Edward John 1953- *WhoWor 91*
Paradies, Hasko Henrich 1940- *WhoWor 91*
Paradis, Adrian Alexis 1912- *AuBYP 90*
Paradis, Andre 1938- *WhoAm 90*
Paradis, Carmen 1950- *WhoEmL 91*
Paradis, Carol Jeanne 1944- *WhoAmW 91*
Paradis, Jean Pierre 1940- *St&PR 91*
Paradis, John Ronald 1934- *St&PR 91*
Paradis, Maria Theresia von 1759-1824 *BioIn 16, PenDiMP*
Paradis, Marjorie Bartholomew 1886?-1970 *AuBYP 90*
Paradis, Philip M. 1951- *WhoWrEP 89*
Paradis, Steven 1940- *St&PR 91*
Paradise, Louis Vincent 1946- *WhoSSW 91*
Paradise, Michael Emmanuel 1928- *WhoAm 90*
Paradise, Paul L. 1929- *IntWWM 90*
Paradise, Phil 1905- *WhoAmA 91*
Paradise, Phil Herschel 1905- *BioIn 16*
Paradise, Philip Herschel 1905- *WhoAm 90*
Paradise, Robert Richard 1934- *WhoAm 90*
Paradiso, K. L. 1946- *WhoWrEP 89*
Paradissis, Pantelis Pete 1938- *St&PR 91*
Paradjanov, Sergei *BioIn 16*
Parado, Laura Aromin *BiDrAPA 89*
Paragas, Magdalena G *BiDrAPA 89*
Paragon, John *ConTFT 8*
Parak, Fritz Gunther 1940- *WhoWor 91*
Paralez, Linda Lee 1955- *WhoAmW 91*
Paramo, Constanza Gisella 1956- *WhoHisp 91*
Paramo Fabeiro, Ramon 1947- *WhoWor 91*
Paramor, Norrie 1914-1979 *OxCPMus*
Paran, Mark Lloyd 1953- *WhoE 91, WhoWor 91*
Paranal, Roberto Z *BiDrAPA 89*
Paranjpe, Mridula Jayant *BiDrAPA 89*
Paras, Nicholas A. 1942- *St&PR 91*
Paras, Nicholas Andrew 1942- *WhoWor 91*
Paras, Sofia Dimitria 1943- *WhoAmW 91*
Parascos, Edward Themistocles 1931- *WhoE 91, WhoWor 91*
Parashos, Ioanis Andreas *BiDrAPA 89*
Paraskakis, Michael Emanuel 1930- *WhoWor 91*
Paraske, Larin 1833-1904 *EncCoWW*
Paraskeva, Saint *EncO&P 3*
Paraskevas, Stelios 1946- *WhoE 91*
Paraskevin-Young, Connie *BioIn 16*
Paraskos, Peter G. 1928- *St&PR 91*
Parasol, Peter *MajTwCW*
Parasole, Isabetta Catanea *PenDiDA 89*
Parathanassiou, Vangelis *NewAgMG*
Paratje, Mercedes *WhoE 91*
Paratore, Anthony 1946- *IntWWM 90*
Paratore, Joseph D. 1948- *IntWWM 90*
Paravi, Anna Marie 1961- *St&PR 91*
Paravisini-Gebert, Lizabeth 1953- *WhoHisp 91*
Paray, Paul 1886-1979 *PenDiMP*
Parayno, Maximo Alano, Jr. 1932- *BiDrAPA 89*
Parazzini, Sergio Serafino 1951- *WhoWor 91*
Parbhoo, Santilal Parag 1937- *WhoWor 91*
Parbury, Charles Alan 1947- *WhoEmL 91*
Parcells, Bill 1941- *WhoAm 90*
Parcells, Charles A., Jr. 1920- *St&PR 91*
Parcells, Duane 1941- *WorAlBi*
Parcells, Duane Charles 1941- *WhoE 91*
Parcells, Frank Hubbard 1925- *BiDrAPA 89*
Parch, Grace Dolores *WhoAm 90*
Parcher, James Vernon 1920- *WhoAm 90*
Parchman, James Patrick 1951- *WhoEmL 91*
Parchman, R.W. 1944- *St&PR 91*
Pardalos, Panos Miltiades 1954- *WhoE 91*
Pardee, Arthur Beck 1921- *WhoAm 90, WhoE 91*
Pardee, Lenora Maxine 1937- *WhoAmW 91*
Pardee, Margaret 1920- *IntWWM 90*
Pardee, Margaret Ross 1920- *WhoAmW 91*
Pardee, Otway O'Meara 1920- *WhoAm 90, WhoE 91*
Pardee, Scott Edward 1936- *St&PR 91*
Pardee, William Durley 1929- *WhoE 91*
Pardee, William Hearne 1946- *WhoAmA 91*
Pardell, Randy Ian *BiDrAPA 89*
Parden, Robert James 1922- *WhoAm 90*
Pardes, Diane *ODwPR 91*
Pardes, Herbert 1934- *BiDrAPA 89, WhoAm 90*
Pardeshi, Ramsing B *BiDrAPA 89*
Pardey, Herbert O 1808-1865 *OxCCanT*
Pardi, Justin A 1898-1951 *WhoAmA 91N*
Pardington, Ralph Arthur 1938- *WhoAmA 91*
Pardini, John Paul 1937- *St&PR 91*
Pardo, Dominick George 1918- *WhoAm 90*
Pardo, Emilio *ODwPR 91*
Pardo, James William 1964- *WhoHisp 91*
Pardo, Jose Victor *BiDrAPA 89*
Pardo, Manuel P 1935- *BiDrAPA 89*
Pardo, Waldo Eugenio *BiDrAPA 89*
Pardo Bazan, Emilia 1851-1921 *EncCoWW*
Pardo Bazan, Emilia, Condesa de 1852-1921 *BioIn 16*
Pardo-Escandon, Juan 1944- *WhoWor 91*
Pardo y Barreda, Jose 1864-1947 *BioIn 16*
Pardo y Lavalle, Manuel 1834-1878 *BioIn 16*
Pardoe, Julia 1806-1882 *FemiCLE*
Pardoe, Michael Warren 1953- *WhoE 91*
Pardoe, Prescott H. 1928- *St&PR 91*
Pardoe, Thomas 1770-1823 *PenDiDA 89*
Pardoe, William Henry *PenDiDA 89*
Pardoe-Russ, Susan Meredith 1948- *WhoAmW 91*
Pardon, Andre 1953- *WhoWor 91*
Pardon, Barry James 1951- *St&PR 91*
Pardon, Donna Marie 1956- *WhoEmL 91*
Pardon, Earl B 1926- *WhoAmA 91*
Pardue, Barbara I. *ODwPR 91*
Pardue, Dwight Edward 1928- *St&PR 91, WhoAm 90*
Pardue, George Thomas 1942- *WhoSSW 91*
Pardue, Larry Henry *BiDrAPA 89*
Pardue, Mary Lou 1933- *WhoAm 90, WhoAmW 91*
Pardue, Michael Edward 1949- *St&PR 91*
Pardue, William B. 1930- *St&PR 91*

Pardus, Donald G. 1940- *St&PR 91*
Pardus, Donald Gene 1940- *WhoAm 90*
Pare, Ambroise 1510?-1590 *BioIn 16, WorAlBi*
Pare, Bernard 1944- *St&PR 91*
Pare, Richard 1948- *WhoAmA 91*
Paredes, Alfonso *BiDrAPA 89*
Paredes, Alfonso 1926- *WhoAm 90*
Paredes, Americo *BioIn 16*
Paredes, Americo 1915- *HispWr 90, WhoAm 90, WhoHisp 91*
Paredes, Frank C. 1949- *WhoHisp 91*
Paredes, James Anthony 1939- *WhoAm 90*
Paredes, Limon Mariano 1912-1979 *WhoAmA 91N*
Paredes, William C. 1931- *St&PR 91*
Pareek, Udai 1925- *WhoWor 91*
Pareigis, Bodo 1937- *WhoWor 91*
Parein, Louis Jean 1937- *WhoSSW 91*
Pareira, Alan S. 1938- *St&PR 91*
Pareja, Nilo John 1937- *BiDrAPA 89*
Parekh, Bhupendra Kumar 1940- *WhoSSW 91*
Parekh, Hema Ratilal 1952- *WhoAmW 91*
Parekh, Kashmira D *BiDrAPA 89*
Parekh, Kishor Manubhai 1964- *WhoSSW 91*
Parekh, Viraf Keki 1942- *WhoWor 91*
Pareles, Lawrence Miles 1951- *WhoE 91*
Parella, Albert Lucian 1909- *WhoAmA 91*
Parello, Raymond Robert 1955- *St&PR 91*
Parello, Thomas R. 1931- *St&PR 91*
Parens, Henri 1928- *BiDrAPA 89*
Parent, Brian A. 1944- *St&PR 91*
Parent, Calvin L. 1935- *St&PR 91*
Parent, Edward E. 1946- *St&PR 91*
Parent, Freddy 1875-1972 *Ballpl 90*
Parent, Gail 1940- *ConTFT 8*
Parent, James E. 1939- *ODwPR 91, St&PR 91*
Parent, Louis N. 1927- *St&PR 91*
Parent, Louise Marie 1950- *WhoEmL 91*
Parent, Mark L. 1948- *St&PR 91*
Parent, Michael J. 1950- *St&PR 91*
Parent, Michelle Susan 1950- *WhoAmW 91*
Parent, Patrick G. 1930- *St&PR 91*
Parent, Rodolphe Jean 1937- *WhoAm 90*
Parente, Audrey 1948- *WhoWrEP 89*
Parente, Charles Eugene 1940- *WhoAm 90*
Parente, John Richard 1946- *WhoE 91*
Parente, Ralph Angelo, Jr. 1927- *WhoE 91*
Parente, William Joseph 1937- *WhoAm 90*
Parenteau, Pierre Romeo 1941- *BiDrAPA 89*
Parenteau, Rosaire 1940- *BiDrAPA 89*
Parenteau, Shirley 1935- *BioIn 16*
Parenteau, Shirley Laurolyn 1935- *ConAu 33NR*
Parenti, Marco *BioIn 16*
Parenty, Roy J 1927- *BiDrAPA 89*
Parepa de Boyescu, Euphrosyne 1836-1874 *PenDiMP*
Parepa-Rosa, Euphrosyne 1836-1874 *PenDiMP*
Parepally, Shailaja *BiDrAPA 89*
Pares-Avila, Jose Agustin 1964- *WhoHisp 91*
Paret, Peter 1924- *WhoAm 90*
Pareti, Giuseppe 1954- *WhoWor 91*
Pareto, Vilfredo 1848-1923 *BioIn 16, WorAlBi*
Paretsky, David 1918- *WhoAm 90*
Paretsky, Sara *BioIn 16*
Paretsky, Sara 1947- *BestSel 90-3 [port], ConAu 129, FemiCLE, TwCCr&M 91*
Paretsky, Sara N. 1947- *WhoAm 90, WhoAmW 91*
Paretzky, Yvonne Rucker 1949- *WhoAmW 91*
Parfait, Raymond Gilbert 1946- *WhoWor 91*
Parfenoff, Michael S 1926- *WhoAmA 91*
Parfet, William U. 1946- *WhoAm 90*
Parfet, William Upjohn 1946- *St&PR 91*
Parfitt, Hugh Lawson *BiDrAPA 89*
Parfrey, Raymond John 1928- *IntWWM 90*
Pargamin, Laurent 1942- *WhoWor 91*
Pargeter, Edith *TwCCr&M 91*
Pargeter, Edith Mary 1913- *MajTwCW*
Pargh, Andy *BioIn 16*
Pargoff, Robert Michael 1961- *WhoEmL 91, WhoWor 91*
Parhad, Harvey Malcolm 1942- *BiDrAPA 89*
Parhad, Salwa Elias *BiDrAPA 89*
Parham, Charles 1938- *St&PR 91*
Parham, Clarence William, III 1933- *St&PR 91*
Parham, Ellen Speiden 1938- *WhoAmW 91*
Parham, Iris Ann 1948- *WhoSSW 91*
Parham, James C. 1916- *St&PR 91*
Parham, Mary Onn 1927- *St&PR 91*
Parham, Robert Randall 1943- *WhoWrEP 89*
Parham, Ruby Inez Myers 1914- *WhoAmW 91*
Parham, William Howard 1929- *St&PR 91*
Parichy, Dennis *ConTFT 8*
Parichy, John B. 1935- *St&PR 91*
Pariente, Rene Guillaume 1929- *WhoWor 91*
Parietti, Ronald B. 1936- *St&PR 91*
Pariewski, Marta Elena *BiDrAPA 89*
Pariewski, Norma Liliana *BiDrAPA 89*
Parikh, Anil Madhukant 1958- *BiDrAPA 89*
Parikh, Arun Vasudev 1949- *BiDrAPA 89*
Parikh, Bakul Krishnakant *BiDrAPA 89*
Parikh, Kalpana K. *BiDrAPA 89*
Parikh, Link Arvind 1961- *WhoE 91*
Parikh, Nitin 1939- *St&PR 91*
Parikh, Rajesh O *BiDrAPA 89*
Parikh, Ramesh R *BiDrAPA 89*
Parikh, Sagar V *BiDrAPA 89*
Parikh, Sonal Bharat *BiDrAPA 89*
Parikian, Manoug 1920-1987 *PenDiMP*
Parilli, Babe *BioIn 16*
Parin, Gino 1876-1944 *BioIn 16*
Parinello, Robert M. *BiDrAPA 89*
Parini, Gregory John 1947- *St&PR 91*
Parini, Jay 1948- *ConAu 32NR*
Parini, Joseph A. 1931- *St&PR 91*
Parins, Robert James 1918- *WhoAm 90*
Paris, Alain 1947- *IntWWM 90*
Paris, Carol Ann *BiDrAPA 89*
Paris, Cheryl *BioIn 16*
Paris, Demetrius Theodore 1928- *WhoAm 90*
Paris, Donna Francine 1951- *WhoAmW 91*
Paris, Frank Martin 1938- *St&PR 91*
Paris, Harold Persico 1925-1979 *WhoAmA 91N*
Paris, Jean *NewYTBS 90*
Paris, Jeanne C *WhoAmA 91*
Paris, Joel Francis 1940- *BiDrAPA 89*
Paris, Keith 1944- *St&PR 91*
Paris, LeRoy Henry 1957- *WhoSSW 91*
Paris, Lucille M 1928- *WhoAmA 91*
Paris, Margaret Lucy 1937- *WhoE 91*
Paris, Mark Frazer 1942- *WhoSSW 91*
Paris, Matthew Lionel 1938- *WhoWrEP 89*
Paris, Mica *BioIn 16*
Paris, Michael David 1942- *BiDrAPA 89*
Paris, Oscar Hall 1931- *WhoE 91*
Paris, Peter Junior 1933- *WhoAm 90*
Paris, Raymond William 1937- *St&PR 91*
Paris, Robert Serge 1954- *WhoE 91*
Paris, Steven Mark 1956- *WhoE 91, WhoWor 91*
Paris, T. Mark 1946- *ODwPR 91*
Parise, Charles J. *BioIn 16*
Parise, F.S., Jr. 1951- *St&PR 91*
Parise, Goffredo 1929-1986 *ConAu 132*
Pariseau, Patricia 1936- *WhoAmW 91*
Pariseleti, Thomas William 1938- *St&PR 91*
Pariser, Andrew R. *St&PR 91*
Pariser, Bertram 1940- *WhoE 91*
Pariser, David Bruce 1941- *WhoSSW 91*
Pariser, Herbert L 1917- *BiDrAPA 89*
Pariser, M. Charles 1911- *St&PR 91*
Pariser, Roslyn F 1919- *BiDrAPA 89*
Pariser, Selma R. *St&PR 91*
Pariser, Stephen F 1946- *BiDrAPA 89*
Parish, Albert Eugene, Jr. 1957- *WhoSSW 91*
Parish, Barbara Shirk 1942- *WhoWrEP 89*
Parish, Carl Denton 1927- *BiDrAPA 89*
Parish, Carol Marie 1954- *WhoE 91*
Parish, Hayward Carroll 1920- *WhoWor 91*
Parish, James R. 1946- *St&PR 91*
Parish, James Robinson 1946- *WhoAm 90, WhoSSW 91*
Parish, John Cook 1910- *WhoAm 90*
Parish, Lawrence Charles 1938- *WhoE 91*
Parish, Margaret Cecile *AuBYP 90*
Parish, Mary *AuBYP 90*
Parish, Maxfield Frederick 1870-1966 *WorAlBi*
Parish, Mitchell 1900- *BioIn 16*
Parish, Naomi Asnien 1941- *BiDrAPA 89*
Parish, Peggy 1927-1988 *AuBYP 90, BioIn 16, ChILR 22 [port]*
Parish, Robert 1953- *WorAlBi*
Parish, Robert Underwood 1925- *WhoAm 90*
Parish, Steven Errol 1960- *WhoSSW 91*
Parish, W. T. 1873-1946 *EncO&P 3*
Parish, William Henry 1954- *WhoEmL 91*
Parish-Alvars, Elias 1808-1849 *PenDiMP*
Parisi, Angelo *BioIn 16*
Parisi, Francis 1954- *St&PR 91*
Parisi, Franklin J. 1945- *ODwPR 91, St&PR 91*
Parisi, Franklin Joseph 1945- *WhoAm 90*
Parisi, Ico 1916- *ConDes 90*
Parisi, Joseph *BioIn 16*
Parisi, Joseph 1944- *WhoAm 90, WhoWrEP 89*
Parisi, Joseph, Jr. 1952- *St&PR 91*
Parisi, Michael Salvatore 1930- *St&PR 91*
Parisi, Ronald Frederick 1945- *St&PR 91*
Parisier, Carlos 1930- *WhoWor 91*
Pariso, Jean Brunner 1925- *WhoE 91*
Parisot, Pierre *PenDiDA 89*
Parizat Tamang *BioIn 16*
Parizeau, Alice 1930- *BioIn 16*
Parizek, Eldon Joseph 1920- *WhoAm 90*
Parizek, Jaro 1934- *WhoAmA 91*
Parizo, Victor Bruce 1931- *St&PR 91*
Park Chung Hee 1917-1979 *WorAlBi*
Park, Barbara 1947- *AuBYP 90, BioIn 16*
Park, Charles D. 1945- *St&PR 91*
Park, Chung I. 1938- *WhoWrEP 89*
Park, Dabney Glenn, Jr. 1941- *WhoSSW 91*
Park, Daekeun 1958- *WhoE 91*
Park, Daphne Margaret Sybil Desiree 1921- *BioIn 16*
Park, David 1911-1960 *BioIn 16*
Park, David Allen 1919- *WhoAm 90*
Park, Dorothy R. 1925- *St&PR 91*
Park, Edward Cahill, Jr. 1923- *WhoWor 91*
Park, Ernest Littleton, Jr. 1936- *WhoAm 90*
Park, Gerald Desmond 1932- *WhoSSW 91*
Park, Ho-Hyun *BiDrAPA 89*
Park, Hyung Soon 1935- *BiDrAPA 89*
Park, In-Ho *BiDrAPA 89*
Park, In Kyu 1925- *BiDrAPA 89*
Park, In Sook 1938- *BiDrAPA 89*
Park, Inhee H. *BiDrAPA 89*
Park, Jacqueline 1951- *WhoAmW 91*
Park, James Charles 1937- *St&PR 91*
Park, James G. 1930- *St&PR 91*
Park, James Theodore 1922- *WhoAm 90*
Park, Jason Shinho 1930- *BiDrAPA 89*
Park, Jason Y S 1935- *BiDrAPA 89*
Park, Jerry Dee 1936- *St&PR 91*
Park, Jihang 1953- *WhoWor 91*
Park, John Charles 1947- *WhoSSW 91*
Park, Jon Keith 1938- *WhoE 91*
Park, Jonathan S. 1957- *WhoSSW 91, WhoWor 91*
Park, Jordan *MajTwCW*
Park, Jungsoo 1941- *WhoWor 91*
Park, Kevin W. 1955- *BiDrAPA 89*
Park, Kie Jung *BiDrAPA 89*
Park, Kwang Hie *BiDrAPA 89*
Park, Kwang S 1947- *BiDrAPA 89*
Park, Kyung Suk *BiDrAPA 89*
Park, Lee Crandall 1926- *BiDrAPA 89, WhoE 91, WhoWor 91*
Park, Leland Madison 1941- *WhoAm 90, WhoSSW 91*
Park, Leone Hoffman 1919- *St&PR 91, WhoAm 90*
Park, Madeleine F 1891-1960 *WhoAmA 91N*
Park, Marian Ford 1918- *WhoWrEP 89*
Park, Mary Cathryne 1918- *WhoAmW 91*
Park, Merle Florence 1937- *WhoWor 91*
Park, Mikyung 1949- *IntWWM 90*
Park, Phocion Samuel, Jr. 1944- *WhoSSW 91*
Park, Robert S. *St&PR 91*
Park, Roderic Bruce 1932- *WhoAm 90*
Park, Roy H. *BioIn 16*
Park, Roy Hampton, Jr. 1938- *WhoAm 90, WhoE 91, WhoWor 91*
Park, Ruth *BioIn 16*
Park, Ruth 1922- *FemiCLE*
Park, Sam 1942- *St&PR 91*
Park, Samuel Albert 1954- *BiDrAPA 89*
Park, Sanghae *BiDrAPA 89*
Park, Seung-Kyoon 1936- *BiDrAPA 89*
Park, Sootong 1945- *BiDrAPA 89*
Park, Stewart Pearce, Jr. 1936- *St&PR 91*
Park, Sun Ku *BiDrAPA 89*
Park, Sung Ho *BiDrAPA 89*
Park, Sungho 1942- *St&PR 91*
Park, Sungkwon 1959- *WhoSSW 91*
Park, Swan Sang 1963- *WhoSSW 91*
Park, Tae Won *BiDrAPA 89*
Park, Tai Wun *BiDrAPA 89*
Park, Therese S. 1921- *BiDrAPA 89*
Park, Thomas 1908- *WhoAm 90*
Park, Thomas Choonbai *AuBYP 90*
Park, Thomas James, Jr. 1927- *WhoE 91, WhoWor 91*
Park, Thomas Tai Soo 1943- *BiDrAPA 89*
Park, Tong-Jin 1922- *WhoWor 91*
Park, Wee Hyun 1945- *WhoWor 91*
Park, William Herron 1947- *WhoWor 91*
Park, William John 1925- *St&PR 91*
Park, William John 1930- *WhoAm 90*
Park, William Wynnewood 1947- *WhoE 91, WhoEmL 91, WhoWor 91*
Park, Won Hoon 1944- *BiDrAPA 89*
Park, Woong Kil *BiDrAPA 89*
Park, Young Joe 1943- *WhoWor 91*
Park, Youngnam 1943- *BiDrAPA 89*
Parkany, John 1921- *WhoAm 90*
Parkas, Iva Richey 1907- *WhoAmW 91*
Parke, Carol Santel 1965- *WhoE 91*
Parke, Daniel 1652?-1712 *BioIn 16*
Parke, Ephraim Jones 1823-1899 *DcCanB 12*
Parke, Harry G. 1926- *St&PR 91*
Parke, Jo Anne Mark 1941- *WhoE 91*
Parke, Laura La Plante 1960- *WhoSSW 91*
Parke, Madelyn Sara 1951- *WhoAmW 91*
Parke, Margaret Bittner 1901- *AuBYP 90*
Parke, Margaret Jean 1920- *WhoAmW 91*
Parke, Polly 1940- *St&PR 91*
Parke, Richard H. *BioIn 16*
Parke, Robert Leon 1940- *WhoSSW 91*
Parke, Robert Neal 1944- *St&PR 91*
Parke, Walter Simpson 1909- *WhoAmA 91*
Parkening, Christopher 1947- *IntWWM 90, PenDiMP*
Parker, Ace 1912- *Ballpl 90*
Parker, Alan 1944- *BioIn 16, IntWWM 90, WorAlBi*
Parker, Alan John 1944- *WhoAm 90*
Parker, Alan William 1944- *WhoAm 90*
Parker, Alfred 1906-1985 *WhoAmA 91N*
Parker, Alfred 1908-1989 *BioIn 16*
Parker, Alfred Browning 1916- *WhoAm 90*
Parker, Alfred Eustace *AuBYP 90*
Parker, Alice 1925- *BioIn 16, IntWWM 90, WhoAmW 91*
Parker, Allan Edward 1952- *WhoEmL 91*
Parker, Allison *WhoWrEP 89*
Parker, Alyce 1953- *WhoE 91*
Parker, Angelo Pan 1945- *WhoEmL 91*
Parker, Ann 1934- *WhoAm 90, WhoAmA 91*
Parker, Anne Vereen 1937- *WhoAmW 91*
Parker, Arri Sendzimir 1948- *WhoWrEP 89*
Parker, Arthur C. 1881-1955 *BioIn 16*
Parker, Averette M *BiDrAPA 89*
Parker, Barbara Jean 1935- *WhoWor 91*
Parker, Barbara L. 1933- *WhoE 91*
Parker, Barry 1935- *ConAu 31NR*
Parker, Barry John 1938- *WhoWor 91*
Parker, Barry Richard 1935- *WhoWrEP 89*
Parker, Beatrice *BiDrAPA 89*
Parker, Benjamin Lloyd *BiDrAPA 89*
Parker, Bert *MajTwCW*
Parker, Bertha Morris 1890-1980 *AuBYP 90*
Parker, Betty June 1929- *WhoWrEP 89*
Parker, Bettye Jean 1931- *WhoAmW 91*
Parker, Beulah *BiDrAPA 89*
Parker, Beverly J. 1953- *WhoAmW 91*
Parker, Billie Ida 1952- *WhoEmL 91*
Parker, Billy L. 1928- *St&PR 91*
Parker, Bobby Eugene, Sr. 1925- *WhoAm 90*
Parker, Bonnie 1910-1934 *WorAlBi*
Parker, Bonnie 1911-1934 *BioAmW*
Parker, Brant 1920- *EncACom*
Parker, Brent Mershon 1927- *WhoAm 90*
Parker, Brother Michael *ConAu 132*
Parker, Camille Killian 1918- *WhoAm 90, WhoWor 91*
Parker, Carl 1934- *WhoSSW 91*
Parker, Carolyn Johnson 1942- *WhoAmA 91*
Parker, Catherine Langloh 1856-1940 *FemiCLE*
Parker, Cathy Joan 1937- *WhoAmW 91*
Parker, Charles A. *WhoAm 90*
Parker, Charles Albert, Jr. 1956- *WhoSSW 91*
Parker, Charles Brand 1936- *WhoSSW 91*
Parker, Charles Bryden 1926- *St&PR 91*
Parker, Charles E *BiDrAPA 89*
Parker, Charles Edward 1927- *WhoWor 91*
Parker, Charles Owen, II 1931- *St&PR 91, WhoAm 90*
Parker, Charles W., Jr. 1922- *ODwPR 91*
Parker, Charles Walter, Jr. 1922- *WhoAm 90*
Parker, Charlie 1920-1955 *BioIn 16, ConMus 5 [port], DrBIPA 90, OxCPMus, WorAlBi*
Parker, Cheryl Jean 1948- *WhoAmW 91*
Parker, Christine Wright 1957- *WhoSSW 91*
Parker, Clarence R *BiDrAPA 89*
Parker, Clea Edward 1927- *WhoAm 90*
Parker, Clyde Alvin 1927- *WhoAm 90*
Parker, Connie 1944- *WhoSSW 91*
Parker, Corey 1965- *ConTFT 8*
Parker, Cortlandt 1921- *St&PR 91*
Parker, Craig 1957- *St&PR 91*
Parker, Craig Burwell 1951- *IntWWM 90*
Parker, Curtis M. 1949- *St&PR 91*
Parker, Dale I. 1945- *St&PR 91*
Parker, Dallas Robert 1947- *WhoEmL 91*
Parker, Dan 1894-1967 *Ballpl 90*
Parker, Daniel 1781-1844 *BioIn 16*
Parker, Daniel 1925- *WhoAm 90*
Parker, Daniel Louis 1924- *St&PR 91*
Parker, Darryle James 1949- *St&PR 91*
Parker, Dave 1951- *Ballpl 90, BioIn 16, WorAlBi*
Parker, David 1941- *ConAu 132*
Parker, David Bascom 1935- *WhoSSW 91*
Parker, David Eugene 1957- *WhoEmL 91*
Parker, David Joel 1944- *St&PR 91*
Parker, David N. *BioIn 16*

Parker, David Raymond 1943- *WhoAm 90, WhoSSW 91*
Parker, David Robert 1939- *St&PR 91*
Parker, David S. *NewYTBS 90*
Parker, David S. 1919-1990 *BioIn 16*
Parker, David Shannon 1953- *WhoAm 90*
Parker, David Sydney 1927- *WhoWor 91*
Parker, Deborah L. Roberts 1952- *WhoAmW 91, WhoSSW 91*
Parker, Denise *BioIn 16*
Parker, Dianna Lynn 1960- *WhoAmW 91*
Parker, Don *BioIn 16*
Parker, Don 1933- *WhoAm 90*
Parker, Donald Fred 1934- *WhoAm 90*
Parker, Donald Henry 1912- *WhoAm 90*
Parker, Donald Howard 1922- *WhoAm 90*
Parker, Donald LaRue 1935- *WhoAm 90*
Parker, Dorothy 1893-1967 *BioIn 16, FemiCLE, MajTwCW, WorAlBi*
Parker, Dorothy R. 1893-1967 *BioAmW*
Parker, Dorothy Rothschild 1893-1967 *NotWoAT*
Parker, Dorothy Telfair Mills *WhoE 91*
Parker, Douglas G. 1955- *St&PR 91*
Parker, Douglas Martin 1935- *WhoAm 90*
Parker, Edna G. 1930- *WhoAm 90, WhoAmW 91*
Parker, Edna Mae 1910- *WhoWrEP 89*
Parker, Edward Bennington 1868-1929 *BioIn 16*
Parker, Edwin B. 1932- *St&PR 91*
Parker, Edwin Chamberlin 1933- *St&PR 91*
Parker, Eleanor 1922- *WorAlBi*
Parker, Elenore Myrna 1939- *WhoAmW 91, WhoE 91*
Parker, Elizabeth Mary 1849?- *FemiCLE*
Parker, Ellis Jackson, III 1932- *WhoAm 90, WhoE 91, WhoWor 91*
Parker, Ely Samuel 1828-1895 *BioIn 16, WhNaAH*
Parker, Emma *FemiCLE*
Parker, Eugene Newman 1927- *WhoAm 90*
Parker, Everett Carlton 1913- *WhoAm 90*
Parker, Everett Hoitt 1930- *WhoAm 90*
Parker, Fania M. Pockrose *AuBYP 90*
Parker, Fess *BioIn 16*
Parker, Fess 1925- *WorAlBi*
Parker, Frances Carr 1925- *WhoWrEP 89*
Parker, Francis Dunbar 1918- *WhoE 91*
Parker, Frank 1932- *WhoAm 90*
Parker, Frank Joseph 1940- *WhoE 91*
Parker, Frank Leon 1926- *WhoAm 90*
Parker, Frank Thomas 1938- *WhoE 91*
Parker, Franklin 1921- *WhoSSW 91, WhoWrEP 89*
Parker, Franklin Eddy 1925- *WhoAm 90*
Parker, Fred N. 1954- *St&PR 91*
Parker, Frida G *BiDrAPA 89*
Parker, Garth Rockwood 1933- *St&PR 91*
Parker, Geoffrey Alan 1945- *WhoSSW 91*
Parker, George 1929- *WhoAm 90*
Parker, George Anthony 1952- *WhoEmL 91*
Parker, George Earl 1937- *WhoAm 90*
Parker, George Edward 1942- *WhoSSW 91*
Parker, George Edward, III 1934- *WhoAm 90*
Parker, George Frederick 1918- *WhoAm 90*
Parker, George S. 1866-1952 *WorAlBi*
Parker, George Waller 1888-1957 *WhoAmA 91N*
Parker, Gerald M. 1943- *WhoSSW 91, WhoWor 91*
Parker, Gerald William 1929- *WhoAm 90*
Parker, Gilbert 1860-1932 *DcLB 99 [port], OxCCanT*
Parker, Gilbert Selwyn 1928- *WhoE 91*
Parker, Gladys 1910-1966 *EncACom*
Parker, Gordon Rae 1935- *St&PR 91, WhoAm 90*
Parker, Graham *BioIn 16*
Parker, Graham 1951- *EncPR&S 89*
Parker, Gwen Cole 1949- *WhoAmW 91*
Parker, Gwendolyn D. *WhoAmW 91*
Parker, Gwendolyn Hall 1946- *WhoAmW 91*
Parker, Gwendolyn Oliver 1945- *WhoSSW 91*
Parker, H. Lawrence 1926- *WhoAm 90*
Parker, Harlen M *BiDrAPA 89*
Parker, Harold Talbot 1907- *WhoAm 90, WhoWor 91*
Parker, Harriet E *BiDrAPA 89*
Parker, Harry 1947- *Ballpl 90*
Parker, Harry J. 1923- *WhoAm 90*
Parker, Harry Lambert 1935- *WhoAm 90*
Parker, Harry Lee 1944- *WhoSSW 91*
Parker, Harry S., III 1939- *WhoAm 90*
Parker, Harry S, III 1939- *WhoAmA 91*
Parker, Henry Griffith, III 1926- *St&PR 91, WhoAm 90, WhoWor 91*
Parker, Henry Seabury, III 1944- *WhoE 91*
Parker, Hershel 1935- *ConAu 30NR*
Parker, Iola B. 1905- *WhoWrEP 89*
Parker, Israel Frank 1917- *WhoAm 90*
Parker, Ivy M. 1907- *BioIn 16*
Parker, J. Dean *St&PR 91*
Parker, Jack Royal 1919- *WhoAm 90, WhoWor 91*
Parker, Jack S. 1918- *St&PR 91*
Parker, Jack Steele 1918- *WhoAm 90*
Parker, James 1714?-1770 *BioIn 16*
Parker, James 1924- *WhoAm 90*
Parker, James Andrew 1936- *WhoAm 90*
Parker, James Aubrey 1937- *WhoAm 90*
Parker, James Clinton *BioIn 16*
Parker, James Cordell 1940- *WhoSSW 91*
Parker, James Edward *BiDrAPA 89*
Parker, James Howard, Jr. 1954- *WhoSSW 91*
Parker, James L. 1938- *St&PR 91*
Parker, James Terry 1958- *WhoSSW 91*
Parker, James Varner 1925- *WhoAmA 91*
Parker, James William 1938- *WhoAm 90*
Parker, Jane Ellen 1960- *BiDrAPA 89*
Parker, Jean *WhoWrEP 89*
Parker, Jean Elizabeth 1957- *WhoAmW 91*
Parker, Jeffrey Lionel 1953- *WhoEmL 91*
Parker, Jeffrey M. 1949- *St&PR 91*
Parker, Jeffrey Robert 1957- *WhoEmL 91*
Parker, Jennifer Ware 1959- *WhoAm 90*
Parker, Jerry Cowan 1944- *St&PR 91*
Parker, Jim 1934- *IntWWM 90*
Parker, Jimmy Byron 1951- *WhoSSW 91*
Parker, Joan *BioIn 16*
Parker, Joan 1935- *ODwPR 91, WhoAm 90*
Parker, Joel Edward *BiDrAPA 89*
Parker, John 1729-1775 *EncCRAm*
Parker, John 1734-1796 *BioIn 16*
Parker, John Clarence 1935- *WhoAm 90*
Parker, John E. 1900-1989 *BioIn 16*
Parker, John E. 1928- *St&PR 91*
Parker, John Eger 1928- *WhoAm 90*
Parker, John Havelock 1929- *WhoAm 90*
Parker, John Malcolm 1920- *WhoSSW 91*
Parker, John Osmyn 1919- *WhoE 91, WhoWor 91*
Parker, John Randall 1934- *St&PR 91*
Parker, John Theodore, Jr. 1932- *WhoAm 90*
Parker, John Victor 1928- *WhoSSW 91*
Parker, John Wesley, Jr. 1958- *WhoSSW 91*
Parker, John William 1931- *WhoAm 90, WhoWor 91*
Parker, Jon Kimura 1959- *IntWWM 90, PenDiMP*
Parker, Jonathan Edward 1936- *St&PR 91*
Parker, Joseph B., Jr. 1916- *WhoAm 90*
Parker, Joseph Mayon 1931- *WhoAm 90, WhoSSW 91*
Parker, Joseph Raymond 1950- *St&PR 91*
Parker, Josephine Ann 1952- *WhoAmW 91*
Parker, Josephus Derward 1906- *WhoSSW 91, WhoWor 91*
Parker, Josiah 1751-1810 *BioIn 16*
Parker, Joyce Cave 1948- *WhoWrEP 89*
Parker, Joyce Hope 1946- *WhoEmL 91*
Parker, Judith Patricia 1947- *WhoAmW 91*
Parker, Julie A. J. *BiDrAPA 89*
Parker, Julie Ann 1958- *WhoAmW 91*
Parker, Katherine Hover 1960- *WhoSSW 91*
Parker, Kathleen 1948- *WhoAmW 91*
Parker, Keith Krom 1950- *WhoEmL 91*
Parker, Kelly Lynn 1958- *WhoSSW 91, WhoWor 91*
Parker, Kenneth Alan 1945- *St&PR 91*
Parker, Kenneth L 1954- *ConAu 132*
Parker, Kenneth Whitten 1929- *WhoAm 90*
Parker, Kris *BioIn 16*
Parker, Kristy 1957- *BioIn 16*
Parker, Larry *BioIn 16*
Parker, Larry L. 1938- *St&PR 91*
Parker, Lee M. 1939- *ODwPR 91*
Parker, Lee Merkel 1939- *St&PR 91, WhoSSW 91*
Parker, Lenore 1933- *WhoE 91*
Parker, Leonard 1932- *DrBlPA 90*
Parker, Levin Woodland 1923- *WhoSSW 91*
Parker, Lewis E.S. 1941- *St&PR 91*
Parker, Linda Kay McDade 1948- *BiDrAPA 89*
Parker, Linda Louise 1950- *WhoEmL 91*
Parker, Linda Marian Bates 1944- *WhoAmW 91*
Parker, Lorne Frederick *BiDrAPA 89*
Parker, Lucky *BioIn 16*
Parker, Lydia Leach 1948- *WhoSSW 91*
Parker, Margaret Maier 1950- *WhoAmW 91*
Parker, Margot 1937- *BioIn 16*
Parker, Marion Dean Hughes 1911- *WhoAmW 91*
Parker, Marji Wilbur 1931- *WhoAmW 91*
Parker, Mark Judson 1956- *WhoSSW 91*
Parker, Martha Ann 1948- *WhoAmW 91*
Parker, Mary Ann *FemiCLE*
Parker, Mary Ann 1953- *WhoEmL 91*
Parker, Mary Elizabeth Abigail 1966- *WhoEmL 91*
Parker, Mary Evelyn 1920- *WhoAm 90*
Parker, Maryland 1926- *WhoWor 91*
Parker, Maynard Michael 1940- *WhoAm 90, WhoWrEP 89*
Parker, Mel 1949- *WhoAm 90*
Parker, Michael David 1954- *WhoEmL 91*
Parker, Michael George 1950- *WhoE 91*
Parker, Michael Jackson 1950- *IntWWM 90*
Parker, Mike 1949- *BioIn 16, WhoAm 90, WhoSSW 91*
Parker, Milford 1925- *BiDrAPA 89*
Parker, Monroe *BioIn 16*
Parker, Nancy Knowles 1929- *WhoE 91*
Parker, Nancy Snowden Deupree 1934- *WhoSSW 91, WhoWor 91*
Parker, Nancy Winslow 1930- *AuBYP 90, WhoAm 90, WhoAmA 91, WhoWrEP 89*
Parker, Neville E 1928- *BiDrAPA 89*
Parker, Olivia 1941- *WhoAm 90, WhoAmA 91*
Parker, Pamela Ann 1962- *WhoAmW 91*
Parker, Pamela E *BiDrAPA 89*
Parker, Pat 1944- *FemiCLE, WhoWrEP 89*
Parker, Patricia Holmes 1936- *WhoAmW 91*
Parker, Patrick S. 1929- *St&PR 91*
Parker, Patrick Streeter 1929- *WhoAm 90*
Parker, Peter 1804-1888 *BioIn 16*
Parker, Peter Jolle 1936- *WhoE 91*
Parker, Philip Alden 1935- *WhoAm 90*
Parker, Philip Joseph 1944- *BiDrAPA 89*
Parker, Phillip A. 1935- *St&PR 91*
Parker, Pierson 1905- *WhoAm 90*
Parker, Prosper P. 1835- *AmLegL*
Parker, Quanah 1845?-1911 *WhNaAH [port]*
Parker, Quanah 1854?-1911 *BioIn 16*
Parker, R. Burton 1914- *St&PR 91*
Parker, R.J. *St&PR 91*
Parker, R. Joseph 1944- *WhoAm 90*
Parker, Ralph Halstead 1909- *WhoAm 90*
Parker, Ray, Jr. *BioIn 16*
Parker, Ray, Jr. 1954?- *DrBlPA 90, EncPR&S 89*
Parker, Raymond 1922-1990 *BioIn 16, NewYTBS 90, WhoAmA 91N*
Parker, Ree 1929- *WhoSSW 91*
Parker, Richard 1915- *AuBYP 90*
Parker, Richard A. 1930- *St&PR 91*
Parker, Richard Anthony 1905- *WhoAm 90*
Parker, Richard Bennett 1925- *WhoAm 90*
Parker, Richard E. *WhoAm 90*
Parker, Richard G. 1926- *St&PR 91*
Parker, Richard Leroy 1941- *St&PR 91*
Parker, Richard Ralph 1948- *WhoEmL 91*
Parker, Robert *AuBYP 90*
Parker, Robert Allan Ridley 1936- *WhoAm 90*
Parker, Robert Andrew 1927- *WhoAm 90, WhoAmA 91*
Parker, Robert B. 1932- *BioIn 16, MajTwCW, TwCCr&M 91*
Parker, Robert Brown 1932- *WhoAm 90*
Parker, Robert Foster *WhoAm 90*
Parker, Robert Frederic 1907- *WhoAm 90*
Parker, Robert George 1925- *WhoAm 90*
Parker, Robert Hallett 1922- *WhoSSW 91*
Parker, Robert Lee, Jr. 1948- *St&PR 91, WhoAm 90, WhoSSW 91*
Parker, Robert Lee, Sr. 1923- *WhoAm 90, WhoSSW 91*
Parker, Robert LeRoy 1866?- *BioIn 16*
Parker, Robert LeRoy 1929- *IntWWM 90*
Parker, Robert M., Jr. *BioIn 16*
Parker, Robert Marc 1952- *WhoEmL 91*
Parker, Robert Michael 1946- *WhoSSW 91*
Parker, Robert R. 1933- *St&PR 91*
Parker, Roger Keith 1950- *WhoSSW 91*
Parker, Roger T. 1924- *St&PR 91*
Parker, Roy Havelock 1948- *WhoWrEP 89*
Parker, Roy Turnage 1920- *WhoAm 90*
Parker, Ruby Brastow 1947- *WhoAmW 91*
Parker, Sam 1901- *BiDrAPA 89*
Parker, Samuel Murray 1936- *WhoAmA 91*
Parker, Samuel Pressey 1955- *WhoSSW 91*
Parker, Sara Ann 1939- *WhoAm 90, WhoAmW 91, WhoE 91*
Parker, Scott Lane 1946- *WhoAm 90*
Parker, Shelley Smith 1963- *WhoSSW 91*
Parker, Stefanie Lyn 1950- *WhoSSW 91*
Parker, Steve H. 1950- *St&PR 91*
Parker, Steven H. 1953- *ODwPR 91*
Parker, Steven Hamilton 1953- *WhoSSW 91*
Parker, Stewart 1941-1988 *AnObit 1988, BioIn 16, ConAu 32NR*
Parker, Susan *BioIn 16*
Parker, Susan Huggard 1939- *WhoAmW 91*
Parker, Susanna 1955- *BiDrAPA 89*
Parker, Suzanne R 1941- *BiDrAPA 89*
Parker, Sydney Richard 1923- *WhoAm 90*
Parker, Theodore Clifford 1929- *WhoWor 91*
Parker, Thomas 1904-1967 *WhoAmA 91N*
Parker, Thomas Jason 1945- *St&PR 91*
Parker, Thomas L. 1949- *St&PR 91*
Parker, Thomas Lee 1921- *WhoAm 90*
Parker, Tom 1943- *ConAu 130*
Parker, Treela May 1954- *WhoAmW 91*
Parker, Victor 1925- *St&PR 91*
Parker, Virginia Anne 1918- *WhoAmW 91*
Parker, Virginia Lee 1935- *WhoAmW 91*
Parker, Walter Burr 1909- *WhoAm 90*
Parker, Walter K. 1948- *St&PR 91*
Parker, Wes 1939- *Ballpl 90*
Parker, Wesley *BioIn 16*
Parker, Will 1944- *WhoAmA 91*
Parker, William 1943- *IntWWM 90*
Parker, William C. 1927- *ODwPR 91, St&PR 91*
Parker, William Covington 1927- *WhoE 91*
Parker, William Dale 1925- *WhoSSW 91*
Parker, William Glenn 1950- *WhoSSW 91*
Parker, William H., III 1937- *WhoAm 90*
Parker, William Nelson 1919- *WhoAm 90*
Parker, William Riley 1906-1968 *DcLB 103 [port]*
Parker, Willis Lamont 1904- *WhoAm 90*
Parker, Wilma Joan 1941- *WhoAmA 91*
Parker, Woodrow W. 1913- *St&PR 91*
Parker-Grant, Bess M. 1947- *WhoAmW 91, WhoE 91*
Parker-Trowe, Lynda Michele *BiDrAPA 89*
Parkerson, George Robert, Jr. 1927- *WhoAm 90*
Parkes, Bessie Rayner 1829-1925 *BioIn 16, FemiCLE*
Parkes, Duane A., Jr. 1925- *St&PR 91*
Parkes, F. M. *EncO&P 3*
Parkes, James William 1896-1981 *BioIn 16, DcNaB 1981*
Parkes, Kenneth Carroll 1922- *WhoAm 90*
Parkey, Glen *WhoSSW 91*
Parkey, Pauline Nelson 1932- *WhoAmW 91*
Parkey, Robert Wayne 1938- *WhoSSW 91, WhoWor 91*
Parkhill, Harold Loyal 1928- *WhoWor 91*
Parkhill, John *TwCCr&M 91*
Parkhill, Mary J. Lore 1956- *St&PR 91*
Parkhill, Miriam May 1913- *WhoAmW 91*
Parkhurst, Beverly Susler 1944- *WhoAm 90*
Parkhurst, Charles 1913- *WhoAm 90, WhoAmA 91*
Parkhurst, Charles Lloyd 1943- *WhoWor 91*
Parkhurst, Elizabeth Smith 1958- *WhoEmL 91*
Parkhurst, George E 1912- *BiDrAPA 89*
Parkhurst, Jeffrey Day 1959- *WhoEmL 91*
Parkhurst, Lolita 1926- *WhoWrEP 89*
Parkhurst, Louis Gifford, Jr 1946- *WhoWrEP 89*
Parkhurst, Todd Sheldon 1941- *WhoAm 90*
Parkhurst, W. Nicholas 1952- *WhoE 91*
Parkhurst, Wayne Lee 1954- *WhoE 91*
Parkin, David 1940- *ConAu 30NR*
Parkin, Eric 1924- *IntWWM 90*
Parkin, Evelyn Hope 1910- *WhoAmW 91*
Parkin, James Lamar 1939- *WhoAm 90*
Parkin, John Cresswell 1922-1988 *AnObit 1988, BioIn 16*
Parkin, Larry M. 1934- *WhoAm 90*
Parkin, Robert A. 1938- *St&PR 91*
Parkin, Robert Palmer 1927- *BiDrAPA 89*
Parkin, Sharon Kaye 1940- *WhoAmW 91*
Parkin, Simon 1956- *IntWWM 90*
Parkington, John Joseph 1950- *St&PR 91*
Parkins, Frederick Milton 1935- *WhoAm 90*
Parkins, Roger L. 1940- *St&PR 91*
Parkinson, Antoinette 1943- *WhoAmW 91*
Parkinson, Cecil Edward 1931- *WhoWor 91*
Parkinson, Claire Lucille 1948- *WhoAmW 91*
Parkinson, Dale Alwyn George 1941- *St&PR 91*
Parkinson, Dan 1935- *WhoWrEP 89*
Parkinson, David Stuart 1938- *St&PR 91*
Parkinson, Del R. 1948- *IntWWM 90*
Parkinson, Dennis 1927- *WhoAm 90*
Parkinson, Elizabeth Bliss 1907- *WhoAmA 91*
Parkinson, Ethelyn M. 1906- *AuBYP 90*
Parkinson, Ethelyn Minerva 1906- *WhoAm 90*
Parkinson, Frank 1895-1960 *Ballpl 90*
Parkinson, Greg 1950- *WhoAm 90*
Parkinson, J. David 1929- *St&PR 91*
Parkinson, James 1755-1824 *BioIn 16*
Parkinson, James Thomas, III 1940- *WhoE 91*

Parkinson, John 1950- *BiDrAPA 89*
Parkinson, John Alfred 1920- *IntWWM 90*
Parkinson, John David 1929- *WhoAm 90, WhoE 91*
Parkinson, John Dee *BiDrAPA 89*
Parkinson, Joseph L. *BioIn 16*
Parkinson, Joseph L. 1945- *St&PR 91, WhoAm 90*
Parkinson, Leonard Filson 1937- *St&PR 91*
Parkinson, Margaret B. *BioIn 16*
Parkinson, Maria Luisa 1951- *WhoAmW 91, WhoWor 91*
Parkinson, Norman 1913-1990 *BioIn 16, NewYTBS 90*
Parkinson, Paul Andrew 1954- *IntWWM 90*
Parkinson, Philip William 1956- *WhoWor 91*
Parkinson, Richard *BioIn 16*
Parkinson, Thomas Francis 1920- *WhoAm 90, WhoWrEP 89*
Parkinson, Thomas Ignatius, Jr. 1914- *WhoE 91, WhoWor 91*
Parkinson, William Charles 1918- *WhoAm 90*
Parkman, Ebenezer 1703-1782 *BioIn 16*
Parkman, Francis 1823-1893 *BioIn 16, DcCanB 12, WhNaAH*
Parkman, Henriette G *BiDrAPA 89*
Parkman, Paul Douglas 1932- *WhoAm 90*
Parkos, Gregory T. 1930- *WhoAm 90*
Parkos, Gregory Theodore 1930- *St&PR 91*
Parks, Arva Moore 1939- *WhoAmW 91*
Parks, Bert 1914- *WorAlBi*
Parks, Carol Louise 1963- *WhoAmW 91*
Parks, Carrie Anne 1955- *WhoAmA 91*
Parks, Charles C. 1945- *St&PR 91*
Parks, Charles Cropper 1922- *WhoAm 90, WhoAmA 91*
Parks, David Jonathan 1955- *St&PR 91*
Parks, Donna Marie 1959- *WhoAmW 91*
Parks, Ed Horace, III 1948- *WhoEmL 91, WhoSSW 91, WhoWor 91*
Parks, Edgar E. 1929- *St&PR 91*
Parks, Elizabeth Robins 1862-1952 *BioIn 16*
Parks, Floyd Mason 1952- *WhoEmL 91*
Parks, Frank Bernard, Jr. 1930- *St&PR 91*
Parks, George M. *NewYTBS 90*
Parks, George Richard 1935- *WhoAm 90*
Parks, Gilbert R *BiDrAPA 89*
Parks, Gordon *BioIn 16*
Parks, Gordon 1912- *DrBlPA 90*
Parks, Gordon, Jr. 1934-1979 *DrBlPA 90*
Parks, Gordon Roger Alexander Buchanan 1912- *WhoAm 90*
Parks, Harold Francis 1920- *WhoAm 90*
Parks, Henry 1916-1989 *AnObit 1989*
Parks, Henry G. 1916-1989 *BioIn 16*
Parks, Henry G., Jr. 1916- *St&PR 91*
Parks, Herbert L. 1925- *St&PR 91*
Parks, Hildy 1926- *BioIn 16, NotWoAT*
Parks, J. Michael 1950- *WhoAm 90*
Parks, James G. 1924- *St&PR 91*
Parks, James Henry, III 1956- *WhoSSW 91*
Parks, James Robert 1936- *WhoSSW 91*
Parks, James Thomas 1947- *St&PR 91*
Parks, Janet Elaine 1946- *WhoAmW 91, WhoWor 91*
Parks, Jerry *BioIn 16*
Parks, Joanne Gail 1957- *BiDrAPA 89*
Parks, Joe Benjamin 1915- *WhoE 91*
Parks, John Emory 1909- *WhoAm 90*
Parks, John H 1927- *BiDrAPA 89*
Parks, Joseph John, III 1957- *BiDrAPA 89*
Parks, Karyn Ann 1955- *WhoAmW 91*
Parks, Kent E. 1957- *St&PR 91*
Parks, Kimberly Sue 1964- *WhoAmW 91*
Parks, Lenore Yvonne 1963- *BiDrAPA 89*
Parks, Lloyd Lee 1929- *St&PR 91, WhoAm 90, WhoWor 91*
Parks, Louise *NewYTBS 90*
Parks, Lyle Fredrick, Jr. 1956- *BiDrAPA 89*
Parks, Madelyn N. *WhoAm 90*
Parks, Mary Irene 1919- *WhoAmW 91, WhoSSW 91, WhoWor 91*
Parks, Mary Lu 1928- *WhoWrEP 89*
Parks, Matthew William 1925- *WhoE 91*
Parks, Maurice D. 1935- *St&PR 91*
Parks, Melanie Ann 1958- *WhoAmW 91*
Parks, Michael Christopher 1943- *WhoAm 90, WhoWor 91*
Parks, Paul 1923- *WhoE 91, WhoWor 91*
Parks, Richard E. 1928- *St&PR 91*
Parks, Richard L. 1948- *St&PR 91*
Parks, Robert A. 1946- *St&PR 91*
Parks, Robert Henry 1924- *WhoAm 90*
Parks, Robert Myers 1927- *WhoAm 90*
Parks, Robin 1957- *WhoAmW 91*
Parks, Ronald R *BiDrAPA 89*
Parks, Rosa 1913- *BioIn 16, WorAlBi*
Parks, Steven Lillard 1952- *WhoEmL 91*
Parks, Susan Johnson 1951- *WhoE 91*
Parks, Sydney Jo 1950- *St&PR 91*
Parks, Thomas Keith 1951- *WhoE 91*
Parks, Thomas W. 1939- *WhoAm 90*
Parks, Tim 1954- *ConAu 131*
Parks, Van Dyke *BioIn 16*
Parks, Van Dyke 1943- *SmATA 62 [port]*
Parks, Wilda Alice 1940- *WhoAmW 91*
Parks, William 1698-1750 *BioIn 16*
Parks, William A. 1939- *St&PR 91*
Parks, William Allen 1939- *WhoAm 90*
Parks, William H. *AmLegL*
Parks, William Howard 1933- *WhoSSW 91*
Parkyn, John William 1931- *WhoSSW 91*
Parkyns, Mansfield 1823-1894 *BioIn 16*
Parla, JoAnn Oliveros 1948- *WhoHisp 91*
Parlamis, Michael Frank 1940- *WhoE 91*
Parland, Henry 1908-1930 *DcScanL*
Parlato, George S 1934- *BiDrAPA 89*
Parlato, George Salvatore 1934- *WhoE 91*
Parlatore, Anselm 1943- *WhoWrEP 89*
Parlatore, Anselm A *BiDrAPA 89*
Parliament *EncPR&S 89*
Parlin, Charles C., Jr. 1928- *WhoAm 90*
Parlin, Gary V. 1941- *WhoAm 90*
Parlin, Gary Victor 1941- *St&PR 91*
Parlin, Jody A. 1961- *WhoAmW 91*
Parlin, John *AuBYP 90*
Parloff, Michael Leon 1952- *WhoAm 90*
Parlour, Richard R 1927- *BiDrAPA 89*
Parlow, Carol Marian *BiDrAPA 89*
Parly, Ticho 1928- *IntWWM 90*
Parma, Zita von Bourbon- 1892-1989 *BioIn 16*
Parmacek, Robert K. 1931- *St&PR 91*
Parman, Frank *WhoWrEP 89*
Parman, James Frank 1938- *WhoWrEP 89*
Parmanand, Nari 1937- *WhoWor 91*
Parmar, Raji *BiDrAPA 89*
Parmater, Jon Anthony 1944- *WhoSSW 91*
Parmelee, Arthur Hawley, Jr. 1917- *WhoAm 90*
Parmelee, David Freeland 1924- *WhoAm 90*
Parmelee, Dean Xandor 1947- *BiDrAPA 89*
Parmelee, Harold Joseph 1937- *St&PR 91*
Parmelee, Jennifer Beale 1958- *WhoWor 91*
Parmelee, Robert E. 1925- *St&PR 91*
Parmelee, Roy 1907-1981 *Ballpl 90*
Parmenides *WorAlBi, WrPh P*
Parmenter, Charles Stedman 1933- *WhoAm 90*
Parmenter, L. Richard 1949- *St&PR 91*
Parmenter, Robert Haley 1925- *WhoAm 90*
Parmentier, Roger Cyriel 1943- *WhoWor 91*
Parmer 1907- *WhoAm 90*
Parmer, Jess Norman 1925- *WhoAm 90*
Parmerlee, Mark S. 1955- *WhoSSW 91*
Parmese, Barbara Jean 1954- *WhoAmW 91*
Parmet, Harriet Abbey 1928- *WhoAmW 91*
Parmet, Herbert Samuel 1929- *WhoE 91*
Parmet, Mitchell L *BiDrAPA 89*
Parmigianino 1503-1540 *IntDcAA 90*
Parmiter, James Darlin 1934- *WhoAm 90*
Parmley, Loren Francis, Jr. 1921- *WhoAm 90, WhoWor 91*
Parmley, Robert James 1950- *WhoSSW 91*
Parnall, Bill *BioIn 16*
Parnall, Peter 1936- *SmATA 11AS [port]*
Parnas, David Lorge 1941- *WhoAm 90*
Parnas, Leslie 1932- *IntWWM 90*
Parnas, Raymond Irvin 1937- *WhoAm 90*
Parnell, Andrea Hudson 1944- *WhoWrEP 89*
Parnell, Andrew 1954- *IntWWM 90*
Parnell, Charles Stewart 1846-1891 *BioIn 16, WorAlBi*
Parnell, Dale Paul 1928- *WhoAm 90*
Parnell, Francis William, Jr. 1940- *WhoAm 90*
Parnell, Harvey 1880-1936 *BioIn 16*
Parnell, Jack Callihan 1935- *WhoAm 90*
Parnell, Kenneth Eugene *BioIn 16*
Parnell, Lawrence J. *ODwPR 91*
Parnell, Mel 1922- *Ballpl 90, BioIn 16*
Parnell, Michael *WhoWrEP 89*
Parnell, Michael 1934- *ConAu 130*
Parnell, Thomas 1679-1718 *DcLB 95 [port]*
Parnell, Thomas Alfred 1931- *WhoAm 90*
Parnes, Edmund Ira 1936- *WhoSSW 91*
Parnes, Larry 1930-1989 *AnObit 1989*
Parnes, Robert Mark 1946- *WhoE 91*
Parness, Alan Mark 1946- *WhoE 91*
Parness, Andrea Michelle 1956- *WhoAmW 91*
Parness, Charles 1945- *WhoAmA 91*
Parnis, Mollie 1905- *WorAlBi*
Parnok, Sofiia Iakolevna 1885-1933 *EncCoWW*
Paro, Robert T. 1964- *St&PR 91*
Paro, Tom Edward 1923- *St&PR 91, WhoAm 90, WhoE 91*
Parode, Ann 1947- *St&PR 91, WhoEmL 91*
Parodi, Alexandre 1901-1979 *BiDFrPL*
Parodi, Ana Lilia 1954- *BiDrAPA 89, WhoE 91*
Parodi, Filippo 1630-1702 *PenDiDA 89*
Parodi, Luis *WhoWor 91*
Parodi, Oscar S. 1932- *WhoHisp 91*
Parolari, Fred Foley 1929- *St&PR 91*
Parolin, Francesco *PenDiDA 89*
Paront, George John 1943- *WhoE 91, WhoWor 91*
Paros, James Reginald 1950- *WhoSSW 91*
Paroski, Paul *BioIn 16*
Paroski, Paul A., Jr. *NewYTBS 90*
Parotti, Phillip Elliott 1941- *WhoSSW 91*
Paroush, Jacob 1934- *WhoWor 91*
Parque, Richard Anthony 1935- *WhoWrEP 89*
Parquin, Charles *BioIn 16*
Parr, A. H. *ConAu 132*
Parr, Adolf Henry 1900-1990 *ConAu 132*
Parr, Adolph Henry 1900- *AuBYP 90*
Parr, Albert F. W. 1923- *WhoAm 90*
Parr, Carol Cunningham 1941- *WhoAm 90*
Parr, Carolyn Miller 1937- *WhoAm 90, WhoAmW 91*
Parr, Christopher Alan 1941- *WhoSSW 91*
Parr, Doris Ann 1933- *WhoAmW 91, WhoWor 91*
Parr, Eugene Quincy 1925- *WhoWor 91*
Parr, Ferdinand Van Siclen, Jr. 1908- *WhoAm 90*
Parr, Grant Van Siclen 1942- *WhoAm 90, WhoE 91*
Parr, Harry Edward, Jr. 1928- *WhoAm 90*
Parr, James Floyd, Jr. 1929- *WhoE 91*
Parr, James Gordon 1927- *WhoAm 90*
Parr, Katharine 1512-1548 *FemiCLE*
Parr, Katherine 1512-1548 *BioIn 16*
Parr, Larry Michael 1946- *St&PR 91*
Parr, Louisa *FemiCLE*
Parr, Mary Ann 1950- *WhoSSW 91*
Parr, Michael F 1939- *BiDrAPA 89*
Parr, Patricia Ann 1937- *IntWWM 90*
Parr, Robert Ghormley 1921- *WhoAm 90*
Parr, Royse M. 1935- *St&PR 91*
Parr, Royse Milton 1935- *WhoAm 90*
Parr, Samuel E. 1921- *St&PR 91*
Parr, Sandra Hardy 1952- *WhoAmW 91*
Parr, Susan Resneck 1943- *WhoAm 90*
Parr, Susanna *BiDEWW, FemiCLE*
Parr-Davies, Harry 1914-1955 *OxCPMus*
Parra, Carmen 1944- *WhoAmA 91*
Parra, Felix 1845-1919 *ArtLatA*
Parra, Frank *WhoHisp 91*
Parra, Nicanor 1914- *BioIn 16, ConAu 32NR, HispWr 90, MajTwCW, WorAlBi*
Parra, Robert Joseph 1940- *WhoE 91*
Parra, Roberto Enrique 1960- *WhoWor 91*
Parra, Teresa de la 1890-1936 *BioIn 16*
Parrado, Peter Joseph 1953- *WhoSSW 91*
Parraga, Humberto C. *BiDrAPA 89*
Parramore, Barbara Mitchell 1932- *WhoAmW 91*
Parramore, John Andrew, II 1955- *WhoSSW 91*
Parramore, Katherine F. 1959- *WhoAmW 91*
Parramore, Nancy *ODwPR 91*
Parras, Antonio *BiDrAPA 89*
Parratt, Lyman George 1908- *WhoAm 90*
Parratt, Walter 1841-1924 *PenDiMP*
Parratto, Nanette Pamela 1956- *WhoAmW 91*
Parrella, Joseph 1951- *WhoE 91*
Parren, Callirhoe 1861-1940 *EncCoWW*
Parrenin Quartet *PenDiMP*
Parrenin, Jacques *PenDiMP*
Parrent, Joanne Elizabeth 1948- *WhoAmW 91*
Parres, Ramon 1920- *BiDrAPA 89*
Parrett, Jeff 1961- *Ballpl 90*
Parretti, Giancarlo *BioIn 16*
Parrick, Gerald Hathaway 1924- *WhoWor 91*
Parrilla, Ramon H 1946- *BiDrAPA 89*
Parrinello, Diane Davies 1939- *WhoAmW 91*
Parrington, Vernon Louis 1871-1929 *BioIn 16*
Parrino, George 1942- *WhoAmA 91*
Parriott, James Deforis, Jr. 1923- *WhoAm 90*
Parris, Frederick N 1940- *BiDrAPA 89*
Parris, Gail A. 1951- *St&PR 91*
Parris, Nina Gumpert 1927- *WhoAmA 91*
Parris, Paul Augustus, Jr. 1937- *WhoSSW 91*
Parris, Robert 1924- *WhoAm 90*
Parris, Robert B. 1935- *St&PR 91*
Parris, Samuel 1653-1720 *EncCRAm*
Parris, Stanford E. 1929- *WhoAm 90, WhoSSW 91*
Parrish, Alvin Edward 1922- *WhoAm 90*
Parrish, Barry Jay 1946- *WhoAm 90*
Parrish, Carroll E *BiDrAPA 89*
Parrish, Cheryl 1954- *WhoAm 90*
Parrish, Cheryl Ann 1954- *IntWWM 90*
Parrish, Danny Burke 1947- *St&PR 91*
Parrish, David Buchanan 1939- *WhoAmA 91*
Parrish, David D *BiDrAPA 89*
Parrish, David O'Neil 1948- *WhoSSW 91*
Parrish, David Walker, Jr. 1923- *WhoAm 90*
Parrish, Delores M. 1935- *St&PR 91*
Parrish, Douglas D. 1945- *St&PR 91*
Parrish, E. Al 1945- *St&PR 91*
Parrish, Edgar Lee 1948- *WhoE 91*
Parrish, Edward Alton, Jr. 1937- *WhoAm 90*
Parrish, Edward Evans 1791-1874 *BioIn 16*
Parrish, Edward L. 1939- *St&PR 91*
Parrish, Fayrene Elizabeth 1936- *WhoAmW 91*
Parrish, Frank 1929- *TwCCr&M 91*
Parrish, Frank Jennings 1923- *St&PR 91, WhoAm 90, WhoWor 91*
Parrish, Harry Jacob 1922- *St&PR 91*
Parrish, Harry Jacob, II 1950- *St&PR 91*
Parrish, HelenSue 1933- *WhoAmW 91*
Parrish, Henry Howard, Jr. 1944- *WhoSSW 91*
Parrish, Herbert Charles 1919- *WhoAm 90*
Parrish, James Nathaniel 1939- *St&PR 91*
Parrish, James Ogden 1940- *St&PR 91*
Parrish, Jean 1911- *BioIn 16, WhoAmA 91*
Parrish, Jere Paul 1941- *St&PR 91*
Parrish, Jerrold J *BiDrAPA 89*
Parrish, John Bishop 1911- *WhoAm 90*
Parrish, John Brett 1934- *WhoAm 90*
Parrish, John Wayne 1916- *St&PR 91*
Parrish, John Wesley, Jr. 1941- *WhoSSW 91*
Parrish, Lance *BioIn 16*
Parrish, Lance 1956- *Ballpl 90*
Parrish, Larry 1953- *Ballpl 90*
Parrish, Lawrence Wolcott 1936- *St&PR 91*
Parrish, Louis E 1927- *BiDrAPA 89*
Parrish, Marie McAdams 1916- *WhoSSW 91*
Parrish, Mary Jeanne 1924- *WhoAmW 91*
Parrish, Matthew D *BiDrAPA 89*
Parrish, Mattie C. 1921- *St&PR 91*
Parrish, Maxfield 1870-1966 *WhoAmA 91N*
Parrish, Michael Udy 1945- *WhoEmL 91*
Parrish, Morris Holland 1927- *WhoSSW 91*
Parrish, Nancy Elaine Buchele 1948- *WhoAmW 91*
Parrish, Overton Burgin, Jr. 1933- *WhoAm 90, WhoWor 91*
Parrish, R. Alan 1949- *St&PR 91*
Parrish, Richard Brooks 1938- *St&PR 91*
Parrish, Richard L. 1943- *ODwPR 91*
Parrish, Richard Thomas 1946- *St&PR 91*
Parrish, Robert *BioIn 16*
Parrish, Robert Alton 1930- *WhoAm 90*
Parrish, Ronald Keith 1941- *WhoAm 90*
Parrish, Stephen Bennett 1952- *St&PR 91*
Parrish, Stephen L. 1951- *St&PR 91*
Parrish, Stephen Maxfield 1921- *WhoAm 90*
Parrish, Susan H. 1937- *ODwPR 91*
Parrish, T.R. 1954- *St&PR 91*
Parrish, Teresa Brown 1957- *WhoSSW 91*
Parrish, Terry Myles *BiDrAPA 89*
Parrish, Thomas Kirkpatrick, III 1930- *WhoAm 90*
Parrish, Thomas William 1949- *WhoSSW 91*
Parrish, William Earl 1931- *WhoSSW 91*
Parrish-Harra, Carol W. 1935- *NewAgE 90*
Parrot, Kenneth D. 1947- *St&PR 91*
Parrot, Kent Kane 1911- *WhoE 91*
Parrott, Andrew 1947- *IntWWM 90, PenDiMP*
Parrott, B.J. 1951- *St&PR 91*
Parrott, Barbara Telling 1925- *IntWWM 90*
Parrott, Carl Leonard, Jr. 1948- *WhoEmL 91*
Parrott, Charles N. 1950- *St&PR 91*
Parrott, Christopher A. 1949- *St&PR 91*
Parrott, Earl Quinton 1947- *BiDrAPA 89*
Parrott, Edwin A. 1830-1931 *AmLegL*
Parrott, Harold 1909-1987 *Ballpl 90*
Parrott, Ian 1916- *IntWWM 90*
Parrott, Ida T. 1944- *WhoAmW 91*
Parrott, Jerry L. 1947- *ODwPR 91*
Parrott, John William 1948- *St&PR 91*
Parrott, Lawrence Howard 1926- *St&PR 91*
Parrott, Leslie 1922- *WhoAm 90*
Parrott, Mike 1954- *Ballpl 90*
Parrott, Polly Cronyn *BioIn 16*
Parrott, Robert Harold 1923- *WhoAm 90*
Parrott, Tod 1937- *WhoAm 90*
Parrott, Tod H. 1937- *St&PR 91*
Parrott, Wanda Sue 1935- *WhoWrEP 89*
Parrott, Wilbur Lavoisia, III 1948- *WhoE 91*

Parrow, Janice Ann 1954- *WhoAmW 91*
Parry, Albert 1901- *WhoAm 90, WhoWor 91*
Parry, Alexander Lewis, Jr. 1924- *St&PR 91*
Parry, Carol Jacqueline 1941- *WhoAm 90, WhoAmW 91*
Parry, Catherine *FemiCLE*
Parry, Charles G. 1936- *St&PR 91*
Parry, Charles Hubert Hastings 1848-1918 *BioIn 16*
Parry, Ellwood Comly, III 1941- *WhoAmA 91*
Parry, Hugh Jones 1916- *WhoAm 90*
Parry, John 1710?-1782 *PenDiMP*
Parry, John Robert 1941- *WhoAm 90*
Parry, Lance Aaron 1947- *WhoAm 90*
Parry, Marian 1924- *WhoAmA 91*
Parry, Michael David 1951- *St&PR 91*
Parry, Pamela Jeffcott 1948- *WhoAm 90, WhoAmA 91*
Parry, Patricia Gilman 1942- *WhoAmW 91*
Parry, Rawdon Moira Crozier 1949- *St&PR 91, WhoAm 90, WhoWor 91*
Parry, Richard David 1939- *WhoSSW 91*
Parry, Robert T. 1939- *St&PR 91*
Parry, Robert Troutt 1939- *WhoAm 90*
Parry, Ruth Elaine 1952- *WhoAmW 91, WhoE 91*
Parry, Thomas C. 1928- *St&PR 91, WhoAm 90, WhoSSW 91*
Parry, William 1817- *AmLegL*
Parsa, Mahmoud A *BiDrAPA 89*
Parseghian, Ara *BioIn 16*
Parseghian, Ara 1923- *WorAlBi*
Parsell, David Beatty 1941- *WhoSSW 91*
Parsell, Richard Kendrick 1899-1989 *BioIn 16*
Parshall, Dewitt 1864-1956 *WhoAmA 91N*
Parshall, Douglass Ewell 1899- *WhoAm 90*
Parshall, George William 1929- *WhoAm 90*
Parshall, Gerald 1941- *WhoAm 90*
Parshall, Walter Raymond 1905- *WhoAm 90*
Parshalle, Gerald S. 1924- *St&PR 91*
Parshley, Floyd Atwood 1935- *St&PR 91*
Parsia, K Shahi 1937- *BiDrAPA 89*
Parsky, Gerald Lawrence 1942- *WhoAm 90*
Parsky, Robert M. 1937- *St&PR 91*
Parsley, Andrew Gus, Jr. 1953- *WhoSSW 91*
Parsley, Brantley Hamilton 1927- *WhoWor 91*
Parsley, Jacque 1947- *WhoAmA 91*
Parsley, Robert Horace 1923- *WhoAm 90, WhoSSW 91*
Parsley, Steven Dwayne 1959- *WhoEmL 91*
Parslow, Philip Leo 1938- *WhoAm 90*
Parson, Christine Jennifer N. 1943- *WhoE 91*
Parsonage, Chris *BioIn 16*
Parsonage, William Herbert 1936- *WhoE 91*
Parsons, Albert 1848-1887 *EncAL*
Parsons, Alvin L. 1949- *ODwPR 91*
Parsons, Andrew John 1943- *WhoE 91*
Parsons, Betty 1900- *BiDWomA*
Parsons, Betty Bierne 1900-1982 *WhoAmA 91N*
Parsons, Bill 1948- *Ballpl 90*
Parsons, Catherine B. *WhoWrEP 89*
Parsons, Charles Algernon 1854-1931 *WorAlBi*
Parsons, Charles Dacre 1933- *WhoAm 90*
Parsons, Craig A. 1948- *ODwPR 91*
Parsons, David *NewAgMG*
Parsons, David Goode 1911- *WhoAmA 91*
Parsons, Denys 1914- *EncO&P 3, EncPaPR 91*
Parsons, Donald Gladwin 1927- *St&PR 91*
Parsons, Donald H. 1930- *St&PR 91*
Parsons, Donald James 1922- *WhoAm 90*
Parsons, Earl, Jr. 1915- *BiDrAPA 89*
Parsons, Edith Barretto 1878-1956 *WhoAmA 91N*
Parsons, Edmund Morris 1936- *WhoE 91, WhoSSW 91*
Parsons, Edward Lewis 1930- *BiDrAPA 89, WhoE 91*
Parsons, Edwin Spencer 1919- *WhoAm 90*
Parsons, Eileen *ODwPR 91*
Parsons, Eliza *FemiCLE*
Parsons, Elizabeth W. 1910- *St&PR 91*
Parsons, Ellen *BioIn 16*
Parsons, Elmer Earl 1919- *WhoAm 90*
Parsons, Elsie Clews 1875-1971 *BioAmW*
Parsons, Elsie Worthington Clews 1875-1941 *BioIn 16*
Parsons, Eric Keith 1951- *WhoEmL 91*
Parsons, Ernestine 1884-1967 *WhoAmA 91N*
Parsons, Ervin Ivy, Jr. 1928- *WhoAm 90*
Parsons, Estelle 1927- *WhoAm 90, WhoE 91, WorAlBi*
Parsons, Fletcher Ralph 1926- *St&PR 91*
Parsons, Frances M. 1923- *ConAu 129*
Parsons, Frank 1854-1908 *BioIn 16*
Parsons, Frederick Ambrose 1916- *WhoWor 91*
Parsons, Geoffrey 1929- *PenDiMP*
Parsons, Geoffrey Penwill 1929- *IntWWM 90*
Parsons, George Howland 1910- *St&PR 91, WhoWor 91*
Parsons, George Raymond, Jr. 1938- *WhoAm 90*
Parsons, George Williams 1918- *WhoAm 90*
Parsons, Gerald A. 1928- *ODwPR 91*
Parsons, Gerald Joseph 1952- *St&PR 91*
Parsons, Ginger Shellenberger 1950- *WhoAmW 91*
Parsons, Glenn 1933- *ODwPR 91*
Parsons, Gordon John 1926- *St&PR 91*
Parsons, Gram *WhoNeCM A [port]*
Parsons, Gram 1946-1973 *EncPR&S 89, OxCPMus*
Parsons, Helga Lund 1906- *WhoAmW 91*
Parsons, Henry McIlvaine 1911- *WhoAm 90*
Parsons, Irene *WhoAm 90*
Parsons, James 1956- *IntWWM 90*
Parsons, James Bowne 1954- *WhoEmL 91*
Parsons, James Jerome 1915- *WhoAm 90*
Parsons, Jan *BioIn 16*
Parsons, Jeffrey Robinson 1939- *WhoAm 90*
Parsons, Jim *BioIn 16*
Parsons, John T. 1913- *St&PR 91*
Parsons, Judith N. 1942- *WhoAmW 91*
Parsons, Judson Aspinwall, Jr. 1929- *WhoAm 90*
Parsons, Keith I. 1912- *WhoAm 90*
Parsons, Kermit Carlyle 1927- *WhoAm 90*
Parsons, Lauren Denise 1959- *BiDrAPA 89*
Parsons, Leonard Jon 1942- *WhoAm 90*
Parsons, Lewis Eliphalet 1817-1895 *AmLegL*
Parsons, Lloyd Holman 1893-1968 *WhoAmA 91N*
Parsons, Louella 1881-1972 *BioIn 16*
Parsons, Louella 1893-1972 *BioAmW*
Parsons, Louella O. 1893-1972 *WorAlBi*
Parsons, Lucia Gonzalez 1852?-1942 *BioIn 16*
Parsons, Lucy 1853-1942 *EncAL*
Parsons, Lucy E. 1859-1942 *BioAmW*
Parsons, Lynda A. 1941- *WhoAmW 91*
Parsons, Malcolm Barningham 1919- *WhoAm 90*
Parsons, Merribell Maddux *WhoAm 90*
Parsons, Michael John 1935- *WhoAm 90*
Parsons, Patty Leigh 1954- *WhoAmW 91*
Parsons, Paul 1952- *ConAu 132*
Parsons, Peter Harold 1938- *St&PR 91*
Parsons, Radford Royce 1965- *WhoWrEP 89*
Parsons, Richard Chappell 1826-1899 *AmLegL*
Parsons, Richard Curtis 1942- *St&PR 91*
Parsons, Richard D. *BioIn 16*
Parsons, Roger 1926- *WhoWor 91*
Parsons, Russell James 1918- *WhoAm 90*
Parsons, Rymn James 1955- *WhoEmL 91*
Parsons, Sara E. 1864-1949 *BioIn 16*
Parsons, Stuart N. 1942- *St&PR 91*
Parsons, Talcott 1902-1979 *MajTwCW, WorAlBi*
Parsons, Terence 1930-1985 *DcNaB 1981*
Parsons, Terry Diane 1951- *WhoEmL 91*
Parsons, Timothy Richard 1932- *WhoAm 90*
Parsons, Tom 1939- *Ballpl 90*
Parsons, Usher 1788-1868 *BioIn 16*
Parsons, Vinson Adair 1932- *St&PR 91, WhoAm 90*
Parsons, Virginia Mae 1942- *WhoAmW 91*
Parsons, Warren F. 1939- *St&PR 91*
Parsons, William 1909- *WhoAm 90*
Parsons, William A. 1910- *St&PR 91*
Parsons, William E. 1936- *AuBYP 90*
Parsons, William Earl, II 1948- *WhoSSW 91*
Parsons, William Harold 1919- *BiDrAPA 89*
Parsons, William Walter 1912- *WhoAm 90*
Parsons-Salem, Diane Lora 1945- *WhoAmW 91, WhoEmL 91*
Parsont, Mina Raines-Lambe 1935- *WhoAmW 91*
Parsont, Robert E. 1936- *St&PR 91*
Parsont, Robert Edward 1936- *WhoAm 90*
Part, Arvo 1935- *IntWWM 90, PenDiMP A*
Partain, Clarence Leon 1940- *WhoAm 90*
Partain, Eugene Gartly 1930- *WhoAm 90*
Partain, Larry Dean 1942- *WhoAm 90*
Partan, Daniel Gordon 1933- *WhoAm 90*
Partanen, Carl Richard 1921- *WhoAm 90, WhoE 91*
Partap, Mohinder 1938- *BiDrAPA 89*
Partch, Kenneth Paul 1925- *WhoAm 90, WhoWrEP 89*
Partch, Virgil *AuBYP 90*
Partch, Virgil Franklin 1916- *WhoAmA 91N*
Partee, Barbara Hall 1940- *WhoAm 90, WhoAmW 91, WhoWrEP 89*
Partee, Cecil A. 1921- *WhoAm 90*
Partee, Donna Markle 1946- *WhoEmL 91*
Partee, Roy 1917- *Ballpl 90*
Parten, Elizabeth Helen *BiDrAPA 89*
Parten, Joe W. 1927- *St&PR 91*
Parten, Jubal R. 1896- *WhoAm 90*
Parter, Alan S. 1944- *ODwPR 91*
Parter, Seymour Victor 1927- *WhoAm 90*
Partha, Ramaswamy 1959- *WhoWor 91*
Parthasarathi, Aanand 1959- *WhoE 91*
Parthemore, Jacqueline G. 1940- *WhoAmW 91*
Parthenis, Alexander *BiDrAPA 89*
Parthum, Charles Albert 1929- *St&PR 91, WhoAm 90*
Partier, Susan Kalmus 1947- *WhoAmW 91*
Partin, Edward Grady 1924-1990 *BioIn 16*
Partin, Kenneth August 1933- *St&PR 91*
Partin, Robert 1927- *WhoAmA 91*
Partin, Ronald Lee 1946- *WhoEmL 91*
Partinen, Markku Mikael 1948- *WhoWor 91*
Partington, David 1934- *St&PR 91*
Partnoy, Ronald Allen 1933- *WhoAm 90*
Partoll, Alfred Carl 1934- *St&PR 91, WhoAm 90*
Parton, Dolly *BioIn 16*
Parton, Dolly 1946- *OxCPMus, WorAlBi*
Parton, Dolly Rebecca 1946- *WhoAm 90, WhoAmW 91*
Parton, James 1912- *WhoAm 90, WhoWor 91*
Parton, Nike 1922- *WhoAmA 91*
Parton, Ralf 1932- *WhoAmA 91*
Parton, Sara Payson Willis 1811-1872 *BioIn 16*
Parton, William C. 1930- *St&PR 91*
Partridge, Anthony *TwCCr&M 91*
Partridge, B. W. *AuBYP 90*
Partridge, Bruce James 1926- *St&PR 91, WhoAm 90*
Partridge, Connie R. 1941- *WhoAmW 91*
Partridge, David Gerry 1919- *WhoAmA 91*
Partridge, Dixie Lee 1943- *WhoWrEP 89*
Partridge, Dorothy *BiDEWW*
Partridge, Eric 1894-1979 *WorAlBi*
Partridge, Frances 1900- *BioIn 16, ConAu 30NR*
Partridge, George 1740-1828 *BioIn 16*
Partridge, Gerald Latimer 1949- *WhoWor 91*
Partridge, Ian 1938- *IntWWM 90, PenDiMP*
Partridge, J.R. 1935- *St&PR 91*
Partridge, James Rudolph 1823-1884 *BioIn 16*
Partridge, Jennifer 1942- *IntWWM 90, PenDiMP*
Partridge, Jenny 1947- *BioIn 16*
Partridge, John Albert 1924- *WhoWor 91*
Partridge, John Albert 1941- *IntWWM 90*
Partridge, John William 1929- *St&PR 91*
Partridge, Katie Ann 1958- *WhoAmW 91*
Partridge, Lloyd Donald 1922- *WhoAm 90*
Partridge, Robert A 1936- *BiDrAPA 89*
Partridge, Robert Bruce 1940- *WhoAm 90*
Partridge, Roi 1888-1984 *WhoAmA 91N*
Partridge, Ronald Ray 1934- *WhoSSW 91*
Partridge, William Francis 1928- *St&PR 91*
Partridge, William Schaubel 1922- *WhoAm 90*
Partsch, Ernest Walter 1925- *WhoWor 91*
Partz, Felix 1945- *WhoAmA 91*
Paru, Joan Kemeny 1944- *WhoE 91*
Paru, Marden David 1941- *WhoE 91*
Parulekar, Damini Shekhar *BiDrAPA 89*
Parun, Vesna 1922- *EncCoWW*
Parveaux, Albert Rene 1942- *WhoWor 91*
Parviainen, Tapio Juhani 1948- *WhoWor 91*
Parvin, Charles Landon 1948- *WhoE 91*
Parvin, Rose A. 1950- *WhoEmL 91*
Parvizi, Jamshid 1950- *WhoSSW 91*
Parwatikar, Sadashiv D *BiDrAPA 89*
Pary, Raymond *BiDrAPA 89*
Pary, Robert Joseph 1952- *BiDrAPA 89*
Parzen, Emanuel 1929- *WhoAm 90*
Parzen, Herbert 1896-1985 *BioIn 16*
Parzybok, William G. 1942- *St&PR 91*
Parzych, Marilyn *BioIn 16*
Pasachoff, Jay Myron 1943- *WhoAm 90*
Pasachoff, Naomi 1947- *WhoEmL 91*
Pasahow, Lynn Harold 1947- *WhoEmL 91*
Pasak, Mary Jolene 1956- *WhoSSW 91*
Pasakarnis, Pamela Ann 1949- *WhoAmW 91, WhoEmL 91*
Pasamanick, Benjamin 1914- *BiDrAPA 89, WhoAm 90*
Pasamar, Pilar Paz 1933- *EncCoWW*
Pasant, Athanase J. 1918- *St&PR 91*
Pasarell, Emilio J 1891- *HispWr 90*
Pasarow, Reinee Elizabeth 1950- *WhoAmW 91*
Pasbrig, Dave 1944- *St&PR 91*
Pascal, Blaise 1623-1662 *BioIn 16, WorAlBi, WrPh P*
Pascal, Cecil Bennett 1926- *WhoAm 90*
Pascal, Claude *EncCoWW*
Pascal, Claude 1921- *IntWWM 90*
Pascal, David 1918- *WhoAm 90, WhoAmA 91, WhoWor 91*
Pascal, Felipe Antonio 1953- *WhoHisp 91*
Pascal, Francine 1938- *BioIn 16*
Pascal, Francoise 1632-1698 *EncCoWW*
Pascal, Guillermo B. 1906- *EncO&P 3*
Pascal, Harold James 1935- *BiDrAPA 89*
Pascal, Jacqueline 1625-1661 *EncCoWW*
Pascal, Jean-Pierre 1935- *WhoWor 91*
Pascal, Leon *PenDiMP*
Pascal, Robert Joseph 1932- *St&PR 91*
Pascal, Roger 1941- *WhoAm 90*
Pascal-Trouillot, Ertha 1943- *NewYTBS 90 [port], WhoWor 91*
Pascal-Trouillot, Ertha 1944- *WomWR*
Pascale, Daniel Richard 1940- *WhoAm 90*
Pascale, Michael Mauro 1952- *St&PR 91*
Pascale, Richard Tanner 1938- *WhoAm 90*
Pascali, Dan Dumitru 1935- *WhoE 91*
Pascall, James *PenDiDA 89*
Pascaner, Joel Lawrence 1953- *WhoE 91*
Pascanu, Alexandru 1920- *IntWWM 90*
Pascarella, Al *BioIn 16*
Pascarella, Perry James 1934- *WhoAm 90, WhoWrEP 89*
Pascarella, Tina Marie 1956- *WhoE 91*
Pascarzi, George Anthony 1957- *BiDrAPA 89*
Pascasio, Anne 1924- *WhoAm 90*
Pasch, Alan 1925- *WhoAm 90*
Pasch, Herbert A. 1906- *St&PR 91*
Pasch, Maurice Bernard 1910- *WhoAm 90*
Pasch, Peter Alan 1950- *St&PR 91, WhoE 91*
Paschal, Ben 1895-1974 *Ballpl 90*
Paschal, Guy Sherman *BioIn 16*
Paschal, Nancy *AuBYP 90*
Paschall, Douglas Duane 1944- *WhoSSW 91*
Paschall, Jeanette 1921- *WhoAm 90, WhoE 91*
Paschall, Jim R. 1935- *BioIn 16*
Paschall, Jim Roddy 1935- *WhoE 91*
Paschall, Jo Anne 1949- *WhoAmA 91*
Paschall, Lee McQuerter 1922- *WhoAm 90*
Paschall, Pamela Genelle 1949- *WhoAmW 91*
Paschall, Stephen Paul 1947- *WhoE 91*
Paschedag, Theodore 1905- *BioIn 16*
Paschen, Allen Joseph 1927- *St&PR 91*
Paschino, Antonio R *BiDrAPA 89*
Paschke, Allen John 1952- *WhoE 91*
Paschke, Donald Vernon 1929- *IntWWM 90*
Paschke, Ed 1939- *BioIn 16*
Paschke, Edward F. 1939- *WhoAm 90, WhoAmA 91*
Paschyn, Lisa Jasewytsch 1954- *WhoAmW 91*
Pascin, Jules 1885-1930 *BioIn 16*
Pasciuti, Michele Maura 1951- *WhoAmW 91*
Pasco, H. Merrill 1915- *St&PR 91*
Pasco, Hansell Merrill 1915- *WhoAm 90*
Pasco, Richard Edward 1926- *WhoWor 91*
Pasco, Samuel 1834-1917 *AmLegL*
Pascoe, Blair Carl 1932- *St&PR 91*
Pascoe, Christopher J.C. 1934- *St&PR 91*
Pascoe, Donald John 1949- *St&PR 91*
Pascoe, Edward Rudy 1948- *WhoEmL 91*
Pascoe, Herbert 1927- *BiDrAPA 89*
Pascoe, Jerome Kay 1938- *WhoWor 91*
Pascoe, Patricia Hill 1935- *WhoAmW 91, WhoWrEP 89*
Pascoe, Valentine *WhoWrEP 89*
Pascoli, Vittorio 1943- *WhoWor 91*
Pascua-Lim, Elvira *BiDrAPA 89*
Pascual, Camilo 1934- *Ballpl 90*
Pascual, Felicitas Doris 1952- *WhoAmW 91*
Pascual, Frank George 1918- *St&PR 91*
Pascual, Hugo 1935- *WhoHisp 91*
Pascual, Miguel Andre 1953- *St&PR 91*
Pascual, Milagros De V *BiDrAPA 89*
Pascual, Rosa Monica 1961- *WhoAmW 91*
Pascualy, Ofelia Marcella *BiDrAPA 89*
Pascucci, Richard Anthony 1948- *WhoEmL 91*
Pascudniak, Pascal 1935- *SmATA X*
Pasda, Patricia Jeanine *WhoAmW 91*
Pasdar, Adrian *BioIn 16*
Pasdeloup, Jules 1819-1887 *PenDiMP*
Pasek, Jeffrey Ivan 1951- *WhoEmL 91*
Pasek, Judith Eleanor 1955- *WhoAmW 91*

Pasek, Mary A. WhoAmW 91
Pasekoff, Marilyn 1949- WhoAmW 91
Paselk, Richard Alan 1945- WhoEmL 91
Pasem, S Reddy 1946- BiDrAPA 89
Paserman, Hyman Judah-Maier 1949- WhoE 91
Pasero, Tancredi 1893-1983 PenDiMP
Paseur, C. Herbert 1925- St&PR 91
Pasewark, William Robert 1924- WhoAm 90
Pasfield, William Reginald 1909- IntWWM 90
Pash, George Kinnear 1938- St&PR 91
Pasha, Jaseem BiDrAPA 89
Pasha, Shamveel 1958- WhoE 91
Pashall, Ellen Minkoff 1953- BiDrAPA 89
Pashayan, Annette Louise Grynkewich 1953- WhoSSW 91
Pashayan, Charles, Jr. 1941- WhoAm 90
Pashek, Robert Donald 1921- WhoAm 90
Pashgian, M Helen WhoAmA 91
Pashigian, Bedros Peter 1932- WhoAm 90
Pashkin-Boyer, Rona Linda 1946- WhoWor 91
Pashley, Anne 1937- IntWWM 90
Pashnick, Larry 1956- Ballpl 90
Pasho, Philip B. 1941- WhoE 91
Pashupathi, Rudrappa 1929- BiDrAPA 89
Pasicatan, Susan 1941- BiDrAPA 89
Pasik, Donald J. 1957- St&PR 91
Pasik, Lawrence Ira 1945- WhoEmL 91
Pasinetti, Luigi Lodovico 1930- WhoWor 91
Pasinetti, Pier Maria 1913- WhoAm 90
Pasinski, Irene 1923- WhoAmA 91
Pasionaria EncCoWW
Pask, James Bruce 1943- St&PR 91
Pask, Joseph Adam 1913- WhoAm 90
Paskai, Laszlo 1927- WhoWor 91
Paskal, Joseph S. 1937- St&PR 91
Paskalis, Kostas 1929- IntWWM 90
Paskerian, Wayne H. 1940- St&PR 91
Paskert, Dode 1881-1959 Ballpl 90
Paskewitz, Bill, Jr 1953- WhoAmA 91
Paskin, Sylvia BioIn 16
Paskins-Hurlburt, Andrea Jeanne 1943- WhoAmW 91
Paskuda, Georg 1926- IntWWM 90
Paslawsky, Jean Marie 1957- WhoAmW 91
Paslay, Le Roy Clay 1907- WhoAm 90, WhoWor 91
Pasley, Francis C 1931- BiDrAPA 89
Pasley, James Michael 1953- WhoWor 91
Pasman, James S., Jr. 1930- St&PR 91, WhoAm 90
Pasmanick, Kenneth 1924- IntWWM 90, WhoAm 90
Pasmas, Arthur John 1935- St&PR 91
Pasmatzis, Ioannis 1961- WhoWor 91
Pasmore, John L BiDrAPA 89
Pasmore, Victor 1908- IntDcAA 90
Pasnau, Robert O 1934- BiDrAPA 89
Pasnick, Lila Jean BiDrAPA 89
Pasnick, Raymond Wallace 1916- WhoAm 90
Pasolini, Pier Paolo 1922-1975 BioIn 16, MajTwCW
Pasqua, Charles Victor 1927- BiDFrPL
Pasqua, Dan 1961- Ballpl 90
Pasqua, Thomas M, Jr. 1938- ConAu 131
Pasqua, Tom ConAu 131
Pasquale, Douglas M. 1954- St&PR 91
Pasquale, Frank Anthony 1954- WhoE 91, WhoWor 91
Pasquale, Joanne Eileen 1940- WhoAmW 91
Pasquale, Michael Feaster 1947- St&PR 91
Pasquale, Rosemarie Diane 1958- WhoAmW 91
Pasquale, Vincent J. 1939- St&PR 91
Pasqualucci, Fausto 1943- WhoWor 91
Pasquarelli, Joseph J. 1927- WhoE 91, WhoWor 91
Pasquariello, Angela Catherine 1955- WhoAmW 91
Pasquariello, Anthony Michael 1914- WhoAm 90
Pasquariello, John Ray 1929- St&PR 91
Pasquerilla, Frank James 1926- St&PR 91, WhoAm 90
Pasquerilla, Mark E. 1959- St&PR 91
Pasquet, Philippe 1939- WhoWor 91
Pasquier, Joel 1943- WhoAm 90
Pasquier, P. Michel 1939- St&PR 91
Pasquini MajTwCW
Pasquini, Dan E. 1942- St&PR 91
Pasquino, Ralph D. 1936- St&PR 91
Pasricha, Satya P 1927- BiDrAPA 89
Pass, Bobby Clifton 1931- WhoSSW 91
Pass, Carolyn Joan 1941- WhoAmW 91, WhoE 91
Pass, Donald 1930- BioIn 16
Pass, Douglas W. 1953- St&PR 91
Pass, Gail Bernice 1940- WhoAmW 91
Pass, Herman W. 1937- St&PR 91
Pass, Joe BioIn 16
Pass, Ralph P., Jr. 1924- St&PR 91
Pass, Thomas Emery 1945- WhoSSW 91
Pass Kesler, Delores Mercer 1940- WhoAmW 91
Passaconaway 1565?-1665? WhNaAH
Passalacqua, Fernando A BiDrAPA 89
Passalacqua, Kristine Gay 1955- WhoEmL 91
Passalacqua, S.A. 1949- St&PR 91
Passali, Desiderio 1947- WhoWor 91
Passamaneck, Kenneth BiDrAPA 89
Passanisi, Douglas John 1954- WhoEmL 91
Passano, Edward M. 1904- St&PR 91
Passano, Edward Magruder 1904- WhoAm 90
Passano, William M. 1929- St&PR 91
Passante, John A. 1940- St&PR 91
Passantino, George Christopher WhoAmA 91
Passarella, Art 1909-1981 Ballpl 90
Passarelli, Giulio Domenic 1939- WhoE 91
Passarelli, Melanie Susan 1963- WhoE 91
Passarge, Eberhard 1935- WhoWor 91
Passarini, Filippo 1638?-1698 PenDiDA 89
Passaro, Aurora St&PR 91
Passaro, Erasmo Andre BiDrAPA 89
Passaro, Louis St&PR 91
Passavant, Claude PenDiDA 89
Passe, Crispin de PenDiDA 89
Passe, James G. 1951- WhoEmL 91
Passeau, Claude 1909- Ballpl 90
Passeggio, Nicole Phenice 1963- WhoAmW 91
Passer, Ivan BioIn 16
Passer, Ivan 1933- ConTFT 8
Passer, Kevin Mark 1955- BiDrAPA 89
Passer, Morris Harry 1929- St&PR 91, WhoAm 90
Passeri, Mario Carlo 1931- WhoWor 91
Passerini, Andrea 1933- WhoWor 91
Passet, Michael Steven 1951- WhoAm 90
Passey, George Edward 1920- WhoAm 90
Passin, Herbert 1916- WhoAm 90
Passlof, Pat WhoAmA 91
Passman, Otto E. 1900-1988 BioIn 16, WorAlBi
Passman, Terry Elliot 1943- BiDrAPA 89
Passmore, Ben H, Jr. BiDrAPA 89
Passmore, George BioIn 16
Passmore, Howard Clinton, Jr. 1942- WhoAm 90
Passmore, Jan William 1940- WhoAm 90
Passmore, John Murrah, Jr. 1947- WhoEmL 91, WhoSSW 91
Passmore, L. Ray 1942- St&PR 91
Passmore, Ronald C BiDrAPA 89
Passon, Richard Henry 1939- WhoAm 90
Passons, Katherine Dupont 1946- WhoSSW 91
Passow, Aaron Harry 1920- WhoAm 90
Passuntino, Peter Zaccaria 1936- WhoAmA 91
Passwater, Richard Albert 1937- WhoAm 90, WhoE 91, WhoWor 91
Passy, Frederic 1822-1912 WorAlBi
Past, Raymond Edgar 1918- WhoAm 90
Pasta, Giuditta 1797-1865 PenDiMP
Pasta, Giuditta 1798-1865 WorAlBi
Pastan, Harvey Lewis 1927- St&PR 91
Pastan, Linda 1932- FemiCLE, WhoWrEP 89, WorAu 1980 [port]
Pastell, Matthew J. 1928- St&PR 91
Pasten, Laura Jean 1949- WhoAmW 91
Paster, Barry Nathan 1949- St&PR 91
Paster, David Joseph 1945- BiDrAPA 89
Paster, James BioIn 16
Paster, Joseph Phillip 1945- St&PR 91
Paster, Samuel 1902- BiDrAPA 89
Pasterak, George E 1920- BiDrAPA 89
Pasterchik, Carolyn Dorothy Thomas 1936- WhoSSW 91
Pasternac, Andre 1937- WhoE 91
Pasternack, Bruce Arthur 1947- St&PR 91
Pasternack, Douglas Allan 1954- St&PR 91, WhoEmL 91
Pasternack, Robert Francis 1936- WhoAm 90
Pasternack, Stefan A BiDrAPA 89
Pasternak, Alexander 1893-1982 BioIn 16
Pasternak, Andrew V BiDrAPA 89
Pasternak, Boris 1890-1960 ConLC 63 [port], MajTwCW, WorAlBi, WrPh
Pasternak, Boris Leonidovich 1890-1960 BioIn 16
Pasternak, Ceel 1932- WhoWrEP 89
Pasternak, David Joel 1951- WhoEmL 91
Pasternak, Derick Peter 1941- WhoAm 90
Pasternak, Irwin M 1936- BiDrAPA 89
Pasternak, Joseph 1901- WorAlBi
Pasternak, Kathryn Ann 1961- WhoAmW 91
Pasternak, Louis BiDrAPA 89
Pasternak, Rona Eve BiDrAPA 89
Pasterski, Darian Chag 1955- WhoAmW 91
Pasteur, Louis 1822-1895 BioIn 16, WorAlBi
Pastille, William 1954- IntWWM 90
Pastin, Mark Joseph 1949- WhoEmL 91, WhoWor 91
Pastine, Maureen Diane 1944- WhoAmW 91
Paston, Alan Jay 1937- St&PR 91
Paston, George 1860-1936 FemiCLE
Paston, Katherine 1578?-1628 BiDEWW
Paston, Margaret Mauteby 1423-1482 BioIn 16
Pastor, Ed Lopez 1943- WhoHisp 91
Pastor, Harry BioIn 16
Pastor, Larry Howard 1958- BiDrAPA 89
Pastor, Stephen Daniel 1947- WhoWor 91
Pastor, Tony 1837-1908 BioIn 16, OxCPMus
Pastore, Frank 1957- Ballpl 90
Pastore, Frank Richard BiDrAPA 89
Pastore, John Orlando 1907- BioIn 16
Pastore, Joseph Dominic 1938- St&PR 91
Pastore, Joseph Michael, Jr. 1941- WhoAm 90
Pastore, Peter Nicholas 1907- WhoAm 90
Pastore, Peter Nicholas, Jr. 1950- WhoSSW 91
Pastore, Roger C. 1945- St&PR 91
Pastorek, Norman Joseph 1939- WhoE 91, WhoWor 91
Pastorelle, Peter John 1933- WhoAm 90
Pastorelli, Robert BioIn 16
Pastorello, Thomas J. 1957- St&PR 91
Pastorius, Francis Daniel 1651-1720? EncCRAm
Pastorius, Jaco BioIn 16
Pastorius, Jim 1881-1941 Ballpl 90
Pastrano, Willie 1935- BioIn 16
Pastreich, Peter 1938- WhoAm 90
Pastrick, Robert A. BioIn 16
Pastukhiv, Serhij Kindzeriavyj 1924- WhoAm 90
Paszkowski, Jan Krok ConAu 130
Pasztor, Jan BioIn 16
Pasztory Pedroni, Catherine Alcsuti 1910- WhoWor 91
Patachich, Ivan 1922- IntWWM 90
Patacsil, Gregorio Banez, Jr. 1934- WhoWor 91
Patafio, Donald J. 1928- St&PR 91
Patafio, John J. 1926- St&PR 91
Patafio, Robert J. 1924- St&PR 91
Patai, Daphne 1943- ConAu 33NR
Patai, Raphael 1910- BioIn 16, ConAu 33NR, WhoAm 90
Pataki, Andrew 1927- WhoAm 90
Pataki, Caroly Sue BiDrAPA 89
Pataki, Heidi 1940- EncCoWW
Pataki, Istvan 1949- WhoE 91
Pataki, Jolie BiDrAPA 89
Patalano, Robert Michael 1944- St&PR 91
Patallo, Indalecio WhoHisp 91
Patanazzi, Alfonso PenDiDA 89
Patanazzi, Antonio PenDiDA 89
Patanazzi, Francesco PenDiDA 89
Patanazzi, Vincenzo PenDiDA 89
Patane, Franco 1908-1968 PenDiMP
Patane, Giuseppe 1932-1989 AnObit 1989, BioIn 16, PenDiMP
Patanelli, Dolores Jean 1932- WhoAmW 91, WhoE 91
Patarino, Vincent V. 1938- St&PR 91
Patarlageanu, Radu Contantin 1925- WhoWor 91
Patashnik, Ethan 1954- St&PR 91
Patava, M.J. St&PR 91
Patch, David A. 1943- St&PR 91
Patch, David Ellsworth 1936- St&PR 91
Patch, Edith 1876-1954 WomFie [port]
Patch, Lauren Nelson 1951- St&PR 91
Patch, Lorraine Marie 1947- WhoAmW 91
Patch, Margaret Merwin 1894-1987 BioIn 16
Patch, Vernon D BiDrAPA 89
Patch, Vernon Duane 1929- WhoE 91
Patchan, Joseph 1922- WhoAm 90
Patchan, Rita Grace 1950- WhoE 91
Patchell, Thomas A. 1928- St&PR 91
Patchen, Kenneth 1911-1972 MajTwCW
Patchett, Mary Elwyn 1897- AuBYP 90
Patchin, Stephen Ross 1958- St&PR 91
Patchis, Pauline 1940- WhoAmW 91, WhoE 91
Pate, Adlai McMillan, Jr. 1921- WhoAm 90
Pate, Alfred R., Jr. 1933- St&PR 91
Pate, Christine Nelson 1950- WhoAmW 91
Pate, J. Kirby 1949- BiDrAPA 89
Pate, Jacqueline Hail 1930- WhoAmW 91, WhoSSW 91
Pate, James Leonard 1935- St&PR 91, WhoAm 90
Pate, James Wynford 1928- WhoAm 90
Pate, J'Nell Laverne 1938- WhoSSW 91
Pate, Joan Seitz WhoAm 90, WhoAmW 91
Pate, Lauren Ann 1957- BiDrAPA 89
Pate, Mavis Orisca 1925-1972 BioIn 16
Pate, Michael Lynn 1951- WhoEmL 91
Pate, Robert Lynn 1936- St&PR 91
Pate, S Ray, Jr. 1929- BiDrAPA 89
Pate, Sharon Shamburger 1957- WhoAmW 91
Pate, Stephen Gregory 1958- WhoSSW 91
Pate, Steve BioIn 16
Pate, Troy Wendell, Jr. 1931- WhoSSW 91
Pate, William 1960- ODwPR 91
Pate, William August 1942- WhoSSW 91
Pate, William Earl 1953- WhoSSW 91
Patee, Susan 1944- WhoAmW 91
Patek, Freddie 1944- Ballpl 90
Patek, S.E. 1923- St&PR 91
Patel, Achala BiDrAPA 89
Patel, Amita Rajesh BiDrAPA 89
Patel, Anil S. 1939- WhoWor 91
Patel, Arunkumar F BiDrAPA 89
Patel, Arvind Motibhai 1937- WhoAm 90
Patel, Ashok Kantilal 1954- BiDrAPA 89
Patel, Ashokkumar C 1955- BiDrAPA 89
Patel, Ashvin A 1949- BiDrAPA 89
Patel, Ashvin Ambalal 1949- WhoSSW 91
Patel, Bhagwandas Mavjibhai 1938- WhoSSW 91
Patel, Bharat Narandas 1950- BiDrAPA 89
Patel, Bipin L 1955- BiDrAPA 89
Patel, Chandra Kumar Naranbhai 1938- WhoAm 90
Patel, Chandrakant M 1954- BiDrAPA 89
Patel, Charu Kaushik 1953- BiDrAPA 89
Patel, Choudhary B S 1935- BiDrAPA 89
Patel, Dilipkumar BiDrAPA 89
Patel, Dinesh C. 1950- WhoWor 91
Patel, Dorothy BioIn 16
Patel, Ghanshyam Ashabhai 1936- St&PR 91
Patel, Hansraj J. St&PR 91
Patel, Harshad BiDrAPA 89
Patel, Himanshu S BiDrAPA 89
Patel, Hiten C BiDrAPA 89
Patel, Homi Burjor 1949- WhoAm 90
Patel, Jay D BiDrAPA 89
Patel, Jayanti BiDrAPA 89
Patel, Jayantkumar C BiDrAPA 89
Patel, Jaylata Madhusudan BiDrAPA 89
Patel, Jeram 1930- WhoWor 91
Patel, Jyotikaben N 1954- BiDrAPA 89
Patel, Kantibhai Babhaidas 1954- BiDrAPA 89
Patel, Kanubhai C 1945- BiDrAPA 89
Patel, Khandu Bhikhabhai 1939- WhoE 91
Patel, Kirtida Arun BiDrAPA 89
Patel, Laxmanbhai P BiDrAPA 89
Patel, Madhubala A BiDrAPA 89
Patel, Madhuben J 1935- BiDrAPA 89
Patel, Magan C. 1937- St&PR 91
Patel, Mahendra Rambhai 1939- WhoE 91
Patel, Maline BiDrAPA 89
Patel, Malti M 1944- BiDrAPA 89
Patel, Manmohan Nandubhai 1947- WhoWor 91
Patel, Manojbhai P BiDrAPA 89
Patel, Marilyn Hall 1938- WhoAmW 91
Patel, Maya B BiDrAPA 89
Patel, Meenakshi P BiDrAPA 89
Patel, Minaldevi V BiDrAPA 89
Patel, Mona M BiDrAPA 89
Patel, Mukesh D 1955- BiDrAPA 89
Patel, Mukesh P 1957- BiDrAPA 89
Patel, Muni H 1947- BiDrAPA 89
Patel, Nagindas L 1929- BiDrAPA 89
Patel, Nalin G BiDrAPA 89
Patel, Nandini Anil BiDrAPA 89
Patel, Narendra D 1955- BiDrAPA 89
Patel, Narendra Harilal BiDrAPA 89
Patel, Narendrabhai N 1953- BiDrAPA 89
Patel, Navin P 1944- BiDrAPA 89
Patel, Navnitlal P BiDrAPA 89
Patel, Pankaj R BiDrAPA 89
Patel, Piyush D BiDrAPA 89
Patel, Prabhakcr S 1951 BiDrAPA 89
Patel, Pravinchandra C BiDrAPA 89
Patel, Radhika Dilip 1956- BiDrAPA 89
Patel, Rajani J BiDrAPA 89
Patel, Rajendra B 1951- BiDrAPA 89
Patel, Rajesh R 1960- BiDrAPA 89
Patel, Rajeshkumar P. BiDrAPA 89
Patel, Rajnikant Becharbhai 1954- BiDrAPA 89
Patel, Raman D. St&PR 91
Patel, Ramanbhai C 1951- BiDrAPA 89
Patel, Ramesh 1951- St&PR 91
Patel, Ramesh Ganeshbhai 1955- BiDrAPA 89
Patel, Ramesh Punjalal 1948- BiDrAPA 89
Patel, Ranjina K. 1949- WhoSSW 91
Patel, Ray L. 1945- St&PR 91
Patel, Renuka Narain BiDrAPA 89
Patel, Ronald Anthony 1947- WhoAm 90, WhoWor 91
Patel, Sanjay R. 1953- WhoE 91
Patel, Sarla BiDrAPA 89
Patel, Sarla S BiDrAPA 89
Patel, Satishchandra V BiDrAPA 89
Patel, Sharad C BiDrAPA 89
Patel, Shashikant S BiDrAPA 89
Patel, Shila 1956- BiDrAPA 89
Patel, Shodhan A BiDrAPA 89
Patel, Smita H BiDrAPA 89
Patel, Smita K 1956- BiDrAPA 89

Patel, Sudhir 1961- *WhoEmL 91, WhoWor 91*
Patel, Suresh A 1945- *BiDrAPA 89*
Patel, Suresh Maganbhai 1944- *BiDrAPA 89*
Patel, Varsha N *BiDrAPA 89*
Patel, Vikram M *BiDrAPA 89*
Patel, Vinod B 1949- *BiDrAPA 89*
Patel, Vinodkumar C *BiDrAPA 89*
Patel, Virendra Chaturbhai 1938- *WhoAm 90*
Patel, Vit Universal 1941- *BiDrAPA 89*
Patel, Vithalbhai D 1936- *BiDrAPA 89*
Patel-Shrivastava, Saraswatiben *BiDrAPA 89*
Patelis-Siotis, Irene 1957- *BiDrAPA 89*
Patell, James M. *WhoAm 90*
Patenaude, John William 1946- *St&PR 91*
Patenotre, Raymond 1900-1951 *BiDFrPL*
Patent, Dorothy Hinshaw *BioIn 16*
Patent, Dorothy Hinshaw 1940- *AuBYP 90*
Pater, Walter 1839-1894 *BioIn 16*
Paterna, Salvatore A. 1941- *St&PR 91*
Paternina, Alvaro de 1929- *WhoWor 91*
Paterno, Joe *BioIn 16*
Paterno, Joseph 1926- *WorAlBi*
Paternoster, Linda *ODwPR 91*
Paternosto, Cesar Pedro 1931- *WhoAm 90, WhoAmA 91*
Paternotte, William Leslie 1945- *WhoAm 90*
Paterson, Alan Leonard Tuke 1944- *WhoSSW 91*
Paterson, Allen Peter 1933- *WhoAm 90*
Paterson, Andrew B. 1864-1941 *AuBYP 90*
Paterson, Anthony R 1934- *WhoAmA 91*
Paterson, Anthony Ralph 1934- *WhoE 91*
Paterson, Basil Alexander 1926- *WhoAm 90*
Paterson, D.S. 1918- *St&PR 91*
Paterson, Diane *AuBYP 90*
Paterson, Diane 1946- *BioIn 16*
Paterson, Donald G. *BioIn 16*
Paterson, Emily Murray 1855-1934 *BiDWomA*
Paterson, Emma Anne 1846-1886 *BioIn 16*
Paterson, Erik Thomas 1941- *WhoWrEP 89*
Paterson, Isabel 1885-1961 *FemiCLE*
Paterson, James Hunter 1947- *WhoAm 90*
Paterson, Katherine *BioIn 16*
Paterson, Katherine 1932- *AuBYP 90, FemiCLE, MajTwCW*
Paterson, Katherine Womeldorf 1932- *WhoAm 90*
Paterson, Lin Richter 1936- *WhoAmW 91, WhoWrEP 89*
Paterson, Linda 1951- *WhoAmW 91*
Paterson, Mervyn Silas 1925- *WhoWor 91*
Paterson, Paul Charles 1927- *WhoSSW 91*
Paterson, Richard D. 1942- *St&PR 91*
Paterson, Richard Denis 1942- *WhoAm 90*
Paterson, Robert Andrew 1926- *WhoAm 90*
Paterson, Robert Cowans 1928- *St&PR 91, WhoAm 90*
Paterson, Robert Douglas 1920- *St&PR 91*
Paterson, Robert E. 1926- *WhoAm 90*
Paterson, Sheila 1940- *WhoAmW 91*
Paterson, T T 1909- *EncO&P 3*
Paterson, Vicki Switzer 1939- *WhoSSW 91*
Paterson, Warwick Rountree 1941- *WhoWor 91*
Paterson, William 1745-1806 *BioIn 16*
Paterson-Berwick, Sheena 1942- *WhoAm 90*
Patey, Douglas Lane 1952- *WhoE 91*
Patey, Janet Monarch 1842-1894 *PenDiMP*
Patey, John George 1835-1901 *PenDiMP*
Pathak, Hridayesh K 1954- *BiDrAPA 89*
Pathak, Raghunandan Swarup 1924- *WhoWor 91*
Pathak, Sunit Rawly 1953- *WhoSSW 91*
Pathan, Naeem Amanullah 1952- *BiDrAPA 89*
Pathiaux, Genevieve 1941- *WhoWor 91*
Pathiraja, Ananda Priya *BiDrAPA 89*
Pati, Prasanna K 1925- *BiDrAPA 89*
Patibandla, Sree Hari 1958- *BiDrAPA 89*
Patience, Jennifer *BioIn 16*
Patierno, John *BioIn 16*
Patil, Allamprabhu S *BiDrAPA 89*
Patil, Aruna A 1946- *BiDrAPA 89*
Patil, Bhaskar R *BiDrAPA 89*
Patil, Jadhav Fakira 1918- *BiDrAPA 89*
Patil, Jayakumar *BiDrAPA 89*
Patil, Kashinath B 1929- *BiDrAPA 89*
Patil, Pushpa Shyam *BiDrAPA 89*
Patil, Rayangouda C. 1936- *WhoWor 91*
Patil, Rohi *BiDrAPA 89*
Patil, Shyam Tukaram *BiDrAPA 89*
Patil, Smita 1955-1986 *BioIn 16*
Patil, Suresh F 1942- *BiDrAPA 89*
Patil, Veeresh M *BiDrAPA 89*
Patil, Vilas J *BiDrAPA 89*
Patin, Gabriel J. 1929- *St&PR 91*
Patin, Robert White 1942- *St&PR 91*
Patinir, Joachim 1475?-1524? *IntDcAA 90*
Patinkin, Don 1922- *WhoWor 91*
Patinkin, Mandy 1952- *WhoAm 90, WorAlBi*
Patinkin, Mandy 1953?- *BioIn 16*
Patinkin, Mark *BioIn 16*
Patinkin, Mark Alan 1953- *WhoE 91*
Patino, Douglas Xavier 1939- *WhoAm 90*
Patino, Edgar 1941- *BiDrAPA 89*
Patino, Lauro Amezcua 1960- *BiDrAPA 89*
Patino, Simon Iturri 1862-1947 *WorAlBi*
Patison, Barbara *BiDEWW*
Patitucci, John *BioIn 16*
Patitz, Dolores Rose *WhoWrEP 89*
Patitz, Tatjana *BioIn 16*
Patkau, Patricia 1950- *WomArch [port]*
Patkin, Izhar 1955- *WhoAmA 91*
Patkin, Max *BioIn 16*
Patkin, Max 1920- *Ballpl 90*
Patlak, Erwin M 1925- *BiDrAPA 89*
Patler, Louis 1943- *WhoWrEP 89*
Patmagrian, Ethelia M *WhoAmA 91*
Patman, Wright 1893-1976 *EncABHB 7 [port], WorAlBi*
Patmodihardjo, Soeroso 1918- *WhoWor 91*
Patmore, Alan Barry 1940- *WhoAm 90*
Patmore, Brigit 1882-1965 *FemiCLE*
Patmore, Conventry Kersey Dighton 1823-1896 *BioIn 16*
Patmore, Coventry 1823-1896 *DcLB 98 [port]*
Patmore, Geraldine Mary *WhoAmW 91*
Patmore, J. Allan *BioIn 16*
Patmore, John Allan *BioIn 16*
Patmore, Lester Claudius, III 1946- *WhoE 91*
Patmore, Thomas Eugene 1928- *St&PR 91*
Patmos, Adrian Edward 1914- *WhoAm 90*
Patnaik, Kunkun 1964- *WhoE 91*
Patnaik, Promode K. 1939- *WhoSSW 91*
Patnaude, William E. 1937- *WhoAm 90*
Patno, Felix A. 1939- *St&PR 91*
Patnode, J Scott 1945- *WhoAmA 91*
Pato, Carlos Neves 1956- *BiDrAPA 89, WhoE 91*
Pato, Michele Tortora 1956- *BiDrAPA 89*
Paton, Mrs. *EncO&P 3*
Paton, Alan *BioIn 16*
Paton, Alan 1903- *AuBYP 90*
Paton, Alan 1903-1988 *AnObit 1988, MajTwCW, WorAlBi*
Paton, Andrew 1833-1892 *DcCanB 12*
Paton, Angela 1930- *BioIn 16, NotWoAT*
Paton, David 1930- *WhoWor 91*
Paton, Jock Esmond 1952- *St&PR 91*
Paton, Kathi Jean 1953- *WhoE 91*
Paton, Lennox McLean 1928- *WhoWor 91*
Paton, Mary Anne 1802-1864 *PenDiMP*
Paton, Mary Margaret 1918- *WhoAmW 91*
Paton, Samuel T. 1910- *St&PR 91*
Paton, William Bryce 1907-1988 *BioIn 16*
Paton, William Drummond Macdonald 1917- *WhoWor 91*
Paton, William Dunning 1929- *WhoAm 90*
Paton Walsh, Jill 1937- *BioIn 16*
Patra, Eleni 1958- *WhoWor 91*
Patras, James T 1951- *BiDrAPA 89*
Patras, Lucas P. 1921- *WhoWor 91*
Patrell, Oliver L. 1927- *St&PR 91*
Patrell, Oliver Lincoln 1927- *WhoAm 90*
Patriaco, Andrew Domenick 1927- *St&PR 91*
Patric, Cheryl M. *ODwPR 91*
Patrice, Stephen 1927- *St&PR 91*
Patrice, Stephen J. 1960- *St&PR 91*
Patricelli, Robert E. 1939- *WhoAm 90*
Patrichi, Mihai Dimitrie 1911- *St&PR 91*
Patrick, Saint 385?-461 *WorAlBi*
Patrick, Alan K 1942- *WhoAmA 91*
Patrick, Allen Lee 1938- *WhoAm 90*
Patrick, Alvin William 1931- *BiDrAPA 89*
Patrick, Andrew Joseph, IV 1959- *WhoSSW 91*
Patrick, Angela Arlene 1957- *WhoAmW 91*
Patrick, Bernard Sutherland 1927- *WhoSSW 91*
Patrick, Beverly Prior 1849-1873 *BioIn 16*
Patrick, Brenda Jean 1955- *WhoSSW 91*
Patrick, Butch *BioIn 16*
Patrick, Carl Lloyd 1918- *WhoAm 90*
Patrick, Casimir J. F. 1906-1990 *BioIn 16*
Patrick, Cecil Wayne 1943- *WhoSSW 91*
Patrick, Charles Roger 1942- *St&PR 91*
Patrick, Charles William 1937- *WhoAmA 91*
Patrick, Craig 1946- *WhoAm 90*
Patrick, Darryl L 1936- *WhoAmA 91*
Patrick, David *BioIn 16*
Patrick, David Kinnear 1934- *IntWWM 90*
Patrick, David Michael 1947- *IntWWM 90*
Patrick, Debra A. 1965- *WhoAmW 91*
Patrick, Dennis 1918- *WhoAm 90*
Patrick, Dennis Roy *BioIn 16*
Patrick, Dennis Roy 1951- *WhoAm 90*
Patrick, Dick *BioIn 16*
Patrick, Edie 1935- *WhoAmW 91*
Patrick, Eileen 1950- *WhoWrEP 89*
Patrick, Eva Bert 1953- *WhoSSW 91*
Patrick, F. C., Mrs. *FemiCLE*
Patrick, Freddie Benjamin 1953- *WhoSSW 91*
Patrick, Gail Denise 1954- *WhoAmW 91*
Patrick, Genie Hudson 1938- *WhoAmA 91*
Patrick, George Milton 1920- *WhoWor 91*
Patrick, George Thomas 1931- *WhoSSW 91*
Patrick, Georgia O'Brien Lakaytis 1945- *WhoEmL 91*
Patrick, J. Andrew 1963- *WhoE 91*
Patrick, James Duvall, Jr. 1947- *WhoWor 91*
Patrick, James Gus 1946- *WhoSSW 91*
Patrick, James K. 1923- *WhoAm 90*
Patrick, James Nicholas, Sr. 1950- *WhoSSW 91*
Patrick, Jane Austin 1930- *WhoAmW 91, WhoWor 91*
Patrick, John 1905- *WhoWor 91*
Patrick, John 1906- *LiHiK*
Patrick, John Corbin 1905- *WhoAm 90*
Patrick, John Franklin 1933- *WhoE 91*
Patrick, John Joseph 1935- *WhoAm 90, WhoWor 91*
Patrick, John William 1949- *WhoSSW 91*
Patrick, Joseph *St&PR 91*
Patrick, Joseph A. 1910- *St&PR 91*
Patrick, Joseph Alexander 1938- *WhoAmA 91*
Patrick, June Carol 1932- *BiDrAPA 89, WhoAmW 91*
Patrick, Kevin Land 1952- *WhoEmL 91*
Patrick, Kit *WhoWrEP 89*
Patrick, Lance Lyle *BiDrAPA 89*
Patrick, Leslie Dayle 1951- *WhoEmL 91*
Patrick, Lynn Allen 1935- *WhoAm 90*
Patrick, Margaret *BioIn 16*
Patrick, Marie *BioIn 16*
Patrick, Martha McShan 1960- *WhoSSW 91*
Patrick, Marty 1949- *WhoSSW 91*
Patrick, Mary Mills 1850-1940 *BioAmW*
Patrick, Michael Neale 1953- *WhoSSW 91*
Patrick, Michael Wynn 1950- *St&PR 91*
Patrick, Michele Mary 1963- *WhoE 91*
Patrick, Pamela Ann 1963- *WhoAmW 91*
Patrick, Patricia C M 1937- *BiDrAPA 89*
Patrick, Patrick F. 1942- *St&PR 91*
Patrick, Paul A. 1942- *St&PR 91*
Patrick, Philip Howard 1946- *WhoE 91, WhoEmL 91*
Patrick, Q. *TwCCr&M 91*
Patrick, Ransom R 1906-1971 *WhoAmA 91N*
Patrick, Rayford Powell 1939- *WhoSSW 91*
Patrick, Robert 1937- *ConAu 30NR*
Patrick, Robert M. 1934- *St&PR 91*
Patrick, Robert Winton, Jr. 1940- *WhoAm 90, WhoWor 91*
Patrick, Ronald Lee 1937- *St&PR 91*
Patrick, Ruth *WhoAm 90*
Patrick, Sam J. 1937- *WhoWrEP 89*
Patrick, Sandra Farmer- *BioIn 16*
Patrick, Spicer 1791-187-? *AmLegL*
Patrick, Stuart Kavanaugh 1939- *St&PR 91*
Patrick, Sue Ford 1946- *WhoAmW 91*
Patrick, Thelma Joyce 1935- *WhoAmW 91*
Patrick, Thomas D. 1942- *ODwPR 91*
Patrick, Thomas Donald 1942- *WhoE 91*
Patrick, Ueal Eugene 1929- *St&PR 91, WhoAm 90*
Patrick, Van 1916-1974 *Ballpl 90*
Patrick, Vijayalakshmy *BiDrAPA 89*
Patrick, Vincent 1935- *WhoWrEP 89*
Patrick, Walton R. *BioIn 16*
Patrick, Warren R. 1955- *St&PR 91*
Patrick, Warren Russell 1955- *WhoEmL 91*
Patrick, William Anderson 1847-1871 *BioIn 16*
Patrick, William Hardy, Jr. 1925- *WhoAm 90*
Patrick, William Samuel 1927- *WhoSSW 91*
Patrick Morales, Vita Jo 1953- *WhoAmW 91*
Patricof, Alan J. 1934- *St&PR 91*
Patricoski, Paul Thomas 1955- *WhoEmL 91*
Patridge, Timothy Wayne 1951- *WhoSSW 91*
Patrie, Cheryl Christine 1947- *WhoAmW 91*
Patrikis, Ernest T. 1943- *St&PR 91, WhoE 91*
Patriquin, David Ashley 1927- *WhoAm 90*
Patriquin, Redmond L. 1938- *St&PR 91*
Patrishkoff, David John 1952- *WhoEmL 91*
Patrizio, Louis A *BiDrAPA 89*
Patron, Irving 1912- *St&PR 91*
Patron, Juan B. 1855-1884 *BioIn 16*
Patron, Juan Bautista 1850-1884 *AmLegL*
Patry, Marcel Joseph 1923- *WhoAm 90*
Patryn, Elaine Lillian 1937- *WhoAmW 91*
Patst, Edmund G. 1916- *WhoAm 90*
Patt, Nurit Hale *BiDrAPA 89*
Patt, Stephen Lee 1938- *BiDrAPA 89*
Pattaratornkosohn, Santi 1949- *BiDrAPA 89*
Patte, Christian 1935- *WhoAm 90*
Pattee, Dailey *BioIn 16*
Pattee, Gordon *BioIn 16*
Pattee, Gordon Burleigh 1948- *WhoE 91*
Patten, Bebe Harrison 1913- *WhoAm 90, WhoWor 91*
Patten, Bebe Rebecca 1950- *WhoAmW 91*
Patten, Casey 1876-1935 *Ballpl 90*
Patten, Charles Anthony 1920- *WhoAm 90, WhoWor 91*
Patten, Charles Robertson, Jr. 1941- *St&PR 91*
Patten, Clyde Gowell 1930- *St&PR 91*
Patten, Cynthia Marie 1956- *WhoAmW 91*
Patten, Eileen Dunlevy *WhoE 91*
Patten, Elizabeth Bryan *BioIn 16*
Patten, Ethel Doudine 1942- *WhoAmW 91*
Patten, Gary N. 1947- *St&PR 91*
Patten, Gerland Paul 1907- *WhoAm 90*
Patten, James 1936- *IntWWM 90*
Patten, John Talbot 1947- *BiDrAPA 89*
Patten, John W. 1930- *St&PR 91*
Patten, Lanny R. 1934- *St&PR 91*
Patten, Lisa 1963- *WhoE 91*
Patten, Paul Raymond 1947- *WhoSSW 91*
Patten, Ronald James 1935- *WhoAm 90*
Patten, Scott Burton *BiDrAPA 89*
Patten, Stanley Fletcher, Jr. 1924- *WhoAm 90*
Patten, Thomas Henry, Jr. 1929- *WhoAm 90*
Patten, William Russell 1954- *WhoSSW 91*
Patterson, Mrs. *FemiCLE*
Patterson, Alan Bruce 1953- *WhoEmL 91*
Patterson, Alicia 1906-1963 *BioIn 16*
Patterson, Andrew B 1929- *BiDrAPA 89*
Patterson, Ann 1947- *BioIn 16*
Patterson, Anthony Curtis 1958- *BiDrAPA 89*
Patterson, Arthur Kenneth 1933- *St&PR 91*
Patterson, Aubrey B. 1942- *St&PR 91*
Patterson, Aubrey Burns, Jr. 1942- *WhoAm 90*
Patterson, Austin H. *AmLegL*
Patterson, Barry S. 1951- *St&PR 91*
Patterson, Becky *WhoWrEP 89*
Patterson, Beverley Pamela Grace 1956- *WhoAmW 91*
Patterson, Beverly Ann Gross 1938- *WhoAmW 91*
Patterson, Blair 1947- *St&PR 91*
Patterson, Boyd Crumrine *BioIn 16*
Patterson, Burns, III 1942- *St&PR 91*
Patterson, Carrick Heiskell 1945- *St&PR 91*
Patterson, Carroll Dean 1939- *BiDrAPA 89*
Patterson, Casey *BioIn 16*
Patterson, Charles *BioIn 16*
Patterson, Charles Darold 1928- *WhoAm 90*
Patterson, Charles Edward 1842-1913 *AmLegL*
Patterson, Charles K. 1933- *St&PR 91*
Patterson, Charles Robert 1875-1958 *WhoAmA 91N*
Patterson, Charles W 1940- *BiDrAPA 89*
Patterson, Charles Ward *BiDrAPA 89*
Patterson, Charles Wilson 1935- *WhoWrEP 89*
Patterson, Christopher Malone 1952- *WhoEmL 91*
Patterson, Cindy L. 1956- *WhoAmW 91*
Patterson, Clair Cameron 1922- *WhoAm 90*
Patterson, Clarinda Gibson 1950- *WhoSSW 91*
Patterson, Clayton Ian 1948- *WhoAmA 91, WhoE 91*
Patterson, Curtis Ray 1944- *WhoAmA 91*
Patterson, Daniel Watkins *WhoAm 90*
Patterson, Daniel Y 1940- *BiDrAPA 89*
Patterson, Daryl 1943- *Ballpl 90*
Patterson, David E. 1938- *St&PR 91*
Patterson, David Larry 1949- *WhoSSW 91*
Patterson, David Llewhelin Hood 1942- *WhoWor 91*
Patterson, David M. 1945- *St&PR 91*
Patterson, David Nolte 1941- *IntWWM 90*
Patterson, David Sands 1937- *WhoE 91*
Patterson, David Williams 1953- *WhoEmL 91*
Patterson, Dawn Marie *WhoAmW 91, WhoWor 91*
Patterson, Deborah-Lea 1951- *WhoAmW 91*
Patterson, Dick 1929- *ConTFT 8 [port]*

Patterson, Dirk Campbell 1954- *St&PR 91*
Patterson, Donald George, Jr. 1944- *WhoSSW 91*
Patterson, Donald Lee 1947- *IntWWM 90, WhoEmL 91*
Patterson, Donald S 1916- *BiDrAPA 89*
Patterson, Donis Dean 1930- *WhoAm 90*
Patterson, Doyle 1918- *St&PR 91, WhoAm 90*
Patterson, Duane Allen 1931- *St&PR 91*
Patterson, Dwight Fleming, Jr. 1939- *WhoSSW 91*
Patterson, Earl S 1927- *BiDrAPA 89*
Patterson, Edward 1920- *WhoAm 90, WhoE 91, WhoWor 91*
Patterson, Edward J. 1916- *St&PR 91*
Patterson, Edward Scott 1957- *WhoE 91*
Patterson, Eleanor 1884-1948 *BioAmW*
Patterson, Eleanor Medill 1881-1948 *BioIn 16*
Patterson, Elizabeth Johnston 1939- *WhoAm 90, WhoAmW 91, WhoSSW 91*
Patterson, Ellen *BiDrAPA 89*
Patterson, Ellen Anne 1960- *St&PR 91*
Patterson, Ellmore Clark 1913- *WhoAm 90*
Patterson, Eugene Corbett 1923- *WhoAm 90, WhoSSW 91*
Patterson, Eugene Tad 1947- *BiDrAPA 89*
Patterson, Florence Ghoram 1936- *WhoAmW 91*
Patterson, Floyd 1935- *WorAlBi*
Patterson, Francine *AuBYP 90*
Patterson, Frank 1928- *St&PR 91*
Patterson, Frank Henry, Jr. 1930- *WhoSSW 91*
Patterson, Frederick D. *BioIn 16*
Patterson, Frederick Douglas 1901- *WorAlBi*
Patterson, G.S. 1909- *St&PR 91*
Patterson, Gary Wayne 1947- *WhoEmL 91*
Patterson, Geoffrey 1943- *BioIn 16*
Patterson, George 1824-1897 *DcCanB 12*
Patterson, George S. 1900-1989 *BioIn 16*
Patterson, Glenn Wayne 1938- *WhoAm 90*
Patterson, Gordon Neil 1908- *WhoAm 90*
Patterson, Grady Leslie, Jr. 1924- *WhoAm 90, WhoSSW 91*
Patterson, Grady Siler, Jr. 1928- *WhoSSW 91*
Patterson, Guy K. 1922- *St&PR 91*
Patterson, Guy Kelly 1951- *BiDrAPA 89*
Patterson, Harlan Ray 1931- *WhoAm 90, WhoWor 91*
Patterson, Harry 1929- *ConAu 33NR, MajTwCW*
Patterson, Henry *ConAu 33NR, MajTwCW, TwCCr&M 91*
Patterson, Henry 1929- *SpyFic*
Patterson, Henry S., II 1922- *St&PR 91*
Patterson, Herbert M. 1919- *St&PR 91*
Patterson, Herman Fitch 1928- *WhoSSW 91*
Patterson, J.B. 1927- *St&PR 91*
Patterson, J. O. 1912-1989 *BioIn 16*
Patterson, James Aris 1935- *WhoSSW 91*
Patterson, James G. 1943- *St&PR 91*
Patterson, James Hardy 1935- *WhoSSW 91, WhoWor 91*
Patterson, James Martle 1952- *WhoSSW 91*
Patterson, James Milton 1927- *WhoAm 90*
Patterson, James Oglethorpe 1912-1989 *BioIn 16*
Patterson, James Thomas 1908-1989 *BioIn 16*
Patterson, James Thurston 1944- *WhoSSW 91*
Patterson, James William 1940- *WhoAm 90*
Patterson, James Willis 1946- *WhoSSW 91*
Patterson, Janet 1947- *IntWWM 90*
Patterson, Jerry Eugene 1931- *WhoAm 90*
Patterson, Jerry Neal 1937- *WhoSSW 91*
Patterson, Joan Esther 1932- *BiDrAPA 89*
Patterson, John C *BiDrAPA 89*
Patterson, John Franklin 1950- *WhoE 91*
Patterson, John H. 1844-1922 *WorAlBi*
Patterson, John Henry 1844-1922 *BioIn 16*
Patterson, John Malcolm 1921- *WhoAm 90*
Patterson, John Oliver *BioIn 16*
Patterson, John Pershing 1933- *WhoAm 90*
Patterson, John R. 1950- *St&PR 91*
Patterson, John Thomas 1873-1960 *DcScB S2*
Patterson, Joseph F. 1946- *ODwPR 91*
Patterson, Joseph H. 1939- *WhoSSW 91*
Patterson, Joseph Medill 1879-1946 *BioIn 16, EncACom, WorAlBi*
Patterson, Joseph Redwine 1927- *WhoAm 90*
Patterson, Katherine Hulen 1947- *WhoAmW 91*
Patterson, Kenneth Ray 1947- *St&PR 91*
Patterson, Kevin *BioIn 16*
Patterson, Leland Francis 1937- *WhoE 91*
Patterson, Lillie *BioIn 16*
Patterson, Lillie G. *AuBYP 90*
Patterson, Lindsay 1937- *DrBlPA 90*
Patterson, Lloyd C 1917- *BiDrAPA 89*
Patterson, Louise Thompson 1901- *EncAL*
Patterson, Lucy Phelps 1931- *WhoAmW 91*
Patterson, Lydia Ross 1936- *WhoAmW 91*
Patterson, Margaret Winchester *BioIn 16*
Patterson, Maria Jevitz 1944- *WhoAmW 91*
Patterson, Marjorie Scott Sellers 1925- *WhoAmW 91*
Patterson, Mark Roland 1951- *WhoEmL 91*
Patterson, Marla Katherine 1950- *WhoAmW 91*
Patterson, Mary-Margaret Sharp 1944- *WhoAm 90*
Patterson, Mary Marvin Breckinridge 1905- *BioIn 16, WhoAm 90*
Patterson, Melroy, Jr. 1960- *WhoE 91*
Patterson, Merrill Reeves 1902- *WhoAm 90*
Patterson, Michael E. *St&PR 91*
Patterson, Nick James 1947- *WhoE 91*
Patterson, Norman W. *NewYTBS 90*
Patterson, Norman William 1917-1990 *BioIn 16*
Patterson, Olga *BiDrAPA 89*
Patterson, Orlando 1940- *WorAu 1980 [port]*
Patterson, Oscar, III 1945- *WhoSSW 91*
Patterson, P. J. *WhoWor 91*
Patterson, P. J. 1950- *WhoAmW 91*
Patterson, Pamela Jane 1951- *WhoAmW 91*
Patterson, Pat *Ballpl 90*
Patterson, Patricia 1941- *WhoAmA 91*
Patterson, Patricia Lynn 1946- *WhoSSW 91*
Patterson, Patricia Sue 1944- *WhoWrEP 89*
Patterson, Patrick J. 1925- *St&PR 91*
Patterson, Paul H. 1943- *WhoAm 90*
Patterson, Paul Leslie 1947- *IntWWM 90*
Patterson, Perry William 1949- *WhoE 91*
Patterson, Philip Stephen 1950- *WhoSSW 91*
Patterson, Polly Reilly 1912- *WhoAmW 91, WhoE 91*
Patterson, Ralph Brunell 1949- *St&PR 91*
Patterson, Randall Wright 1954- *WhoEmL 91*
Patterson, Ray Albert 1922- *WhoSSW 91*
Patterson, Raymond F *BiDrAPA 89*
Patterson, Raymond Richard 1929- *WhoWrEP 89*
Patterson, Reba *WhoE 91*
Patterson, Remington Perrigo 1926- *WhoAm 90*
Patterson, Richard *ConTFT 8*
Patterson, Richard A. *BioIn 16*
Patterson, Richard Brown 1937- *St&PR 91, WhoAm 90*
Patterson, Richard Henry 1931- *BiDrAPA 89*
Patterson, Rickey Lee 1952- *WhoEmL 91, WhoSSW 91*
Patterson, Robert Arthur 1915- *WhoAm 90, WhoWor 91*
Patterson, Robert Bruce 1953- *WhoSSW 91*
Patterson, Robert Dennis 1937- *BiDrAPA 89*
Patterson, Robert Eugene 1932- *St&PR 91*
Patterson, Robert Hobson, Jr. 1927- *St&PR 91, WhoAm 90*
Patterson, Robert Hudson 1936- *WhoAm 90*
Patterson, Robert Logan 1940- *WhoAm 90*
Patterson, Robert Lynn 1939- *WhoSSW 91*
Patterson, Robert Porter 1891-1952 *BiDrUSE 89*
Patterson, Robert Porter, Jr. 1923- *WhoAm 90*
Patterson, Robert S. 1941- *St&PR 91*
Patterson, Robert Stanton 1941- *WhoSSW 91*
Patterson, Robert Youngman, Jr. 1921- *WhoAm 90*
Patterson, Roger 1950- *St&PR 91*
Patterson, Roger Lewis 1939- *WhoWor 91*
Patterson, Ronald Paul 1941- *WhoAm 90*
Patterson, Ronald Roy 1942- *WhoAm 90, WhoSSW 91*
Patterson, Rosemarie Robert 1964- *WhoEmL 91*
Patterson, Roy 1876-1953 *Ballpl 90*
Patterson, Roy 1926- *WhoAm 90*
Patterson, Roy 1942- *St&PR 91*
Patterson, Russel Hugo, Jr. 1929- *WhoAm 90*
Patterson, Russell 1894-1977 *EncACom [port]*
Patterson, Russell 1928- *IntWWM 90*
Patterson, Russell 1930- *WhoAm 90*
Patterson, S.E., Mrs. *EncO&P 3*
Patterson, Sam Garmon 1945- *WhoSSW 91*
Patterson, Samuel Charles 1931- *WhoAm 90*
Patterson, Samuel Findley 1842- *AmLegL*
Patterson, Scot G. 1953- *WhoWrEP 89*
Patterson, Scott 1931- *BiDrAPA 89*
Patterson, Seth Lynn 1953- *WhoAm 90*
Patterson, Shirley Abbott 1923- *WhoAmA 91, WhoE 91*
Patterson, Solon P. 1935- *St&PR 91*
Patterson, Steve 1957- *WhoAm 90*
Patterson, Thomas H. 1941- *St&PR 91*
Patterson, Timothy Dale 1949- *WhoWrEP 89*
Patterson, Trudy Jenkins 1951- *WhoEmL 91*
Patterson, Vanessa Leigh *WhoAmW 91*
Patterson, Veronica Shantz 1945- *WhoWrEP 89*
Patterson, Vivian Jane 1937- *WhoSSW 91*
Patterson, W. Morgan 1925- *WhoAm 90*
Patterson, William *BioIn 16*
Patterson, William Bradford 1921- *WhoAm 90*
Patterson, William Joseph 1941- *WhoAmA 91*
Patterson, William Kent 1941- *St&PR 91*
Patterson, William L. 1891-1980 *EncAL*
Patterson, William Morrow 1941- *BiDrAPA 89*
Patterson, William Orr, Jr. *BiDrAPA 89*
Patterson, William Robert 1924- *WhoAm 90*
Patterson, William Wayne 1943- *St&PR 91, WhoAm 90*
Patteson, Okey L. 1898-1989 *BioIn 16*
Patteson, Roy Kinneer, Jr. 1928- *WhoAm 90*
Patti, Adelina 1843-1919 *BioIn 16, PenDiMP*
Patti, Andrew S. 1940- *WhoAm 90*
Patti, Frances Marie 1934- *WhoAmW 91*
Patti, Josephine Marie 1934- *WhoAmW 91*
Patti, Sandi *BioIn 16, WhoAmW 91*
Patti, Tom *WhoAmA 91*
Patti, Tony Stephen 1958- *WhoE 91*
Pattie, James O. 1804?-1850? *BioIn 16*
Pattie, James Ohio 1804?-1851? *WhNaAH*
Pattie, Jane Anne 1935- *WhoAmW 91*
Pattie, Kenton Harman 1939- *WhoSSW 91*
Pattillo, Albert Dixon 1908- *BiDrAPA 89*
Pattillo, David B. 1928- *St&PR 91*
Pattillo, Manning Mason, Jr. 1919- *WhoAm 90*
Pattillo, Nickles Keat 1947- *WhoSSW 91*
Pattin, Marty 1943- *Ballpl 90*
Pattinson, John Gilbert 1938- *IntWWM 90*
Pattis, S. William 1925- *WhoAm 90*
Pattishall, Beverly Wyckliffe 1916- *WhoAm 90, WhoWor 91*
Pattison, Abbott 1916- *WhoAmA 91*
Pattison, Abbott Lawrence 1916- *WhoAm 90*
Pattison, David Harry 1939- *WhoWor 91*
Pattison, E Mansell 1933- *BiDrAPA 89*
Pattison, Edward Worthington 1932- *WhoAm 90*
Pattison, James Allen 1928- *St&PR 91*
Pattison, Joseph H 1927- *BiDrAPA 89*
Pattison, Mark 1813-1884 *BioIn 16*
Pattison, Robert 1945- *ConAu 129*
Pattison, William Brien 1932- *WhoAm 90*
Pattison-Lehning, Barbara Jeanne 1936- *WhoAmW 91*
Pattiz, Norman J. 1943- *St&PR 91*
Patton, Alton DeWitt 1935- *WhoAm 90*
Patton, Andy 1952- *WhoAmA 91*
Patton, Bob J. 1925- *WhoSSW 91*
Patton, Carl Vernon 1944- *WhoAm 90*
Patton, Carlton Clement 1936- *WhoAm 90*
Patton, Charley 1887-1934 *OxCPMus*
Patton, Darla June Eaton 1948- *WhoAmW 91*
Patton, Deanna Kay 1953- *WhoEmL 91*
Patton, Denise Pretzer 1957- *WhoEmL 91*
Patton, Diana Lee Wilkoc 1940- *WhoAm 90*
Patton, Earnest 1935- *MusmAFA*
Patton, Elda C *BiDrAPA 89*
Patton, G. Thomas, Jr. 1929- *St&PR 91*
Patton, Gary Clark 1959- *BiDrAPA 89*
Patton, George Erwin 1920- *WhoAm 90*
Patton, George S. 1885-1945 *BioIn 16*
Patton, George S., Jr. 1885-1945 *WorAlBi*
Patton, George Smith 1923- *WhoAm 90*
Patton, Henry H. 1913- *St&PR 91*
Patton, James Lewis 1928- *St&PR 91*
Patton, James M. *St&PR 91*
Patton, James Richard, Jr. 1928- *WhoAm 90, WhoSSW 91, WhoWor 91*
Patton, Janet Clara 1945- *WhoAmW 91*
Patton, Jennifer 1943- *St&PR 91*
Patton, Joelle Delbourgo 1953- *WhoAm 90*
Patton, John Michael 1947- *WhoE 91*
Patton, Judith Wood 1953- *WhoSSW 91*
Patton, Karen Ann *WhoAmA 91*
Patton, Kevin Conor 1947- *WhoEmL 91*
Patton, Larry *BioIn 16*
Patton, Macon G. 1936-1989 *BioIn 16*
Patton, Martha Jane 1946- *WhoEmL 91*
Patton, Michael J 1938- *BiDrAPA 89*
Patton, Michael Quinn 1945- *WhoWrEP 89*
Patton, Mitchell 1931- *St&PR 91*
Patton, Richard Bolling 1929- *St&PR 91, WhoAm 90*
Patton, Richard G. 1928- *St&PR 91*
Patton, Richard W. 1929- *St&PR 91*
Patton, Rita Williams 1949- *BiDrAPA 89*
Patton, Robert Frederick 1927- *WhoAm 90, WhoWor 91*
Patton, Robert W *BiDrAPA 89*
Patton, Ronald C. 1947- *St&PR 91*
Patton, Ronald F. 1935- *St&PR 91*
Patton, Shari K. 1951- *WhoAmW 91*
Patton, Stephen Currie 1963- *WhoE 91*
Patton, Stuart 1920- *WhoAm 90*
Patton, Thomas Earl 1940- *WhoAm 90*
Patton, Thomas F. 1903- *St&PR 91*
Patton, Thomas F. 1925- *St&PR 91*
Patton, Thomas H, Jr. 1916- *BiDrAPA 89*
Patton, Thomas James 1948- *WhoEmL 91*
Patton, Thomas Kirkby 1954- *WhoSSW 91*
Patton, Tom 1954- *WhoAmA 91*
Patton, Walter H. 1917- *WhoSSW 91*
Patton, Wendell Melton, Jr. 1922- *WhoAm 90*
Patton, William A. 1937- *St&PR 91*
Patton, William B., Jr. *BioIn 16*
Patton, William S. 18--?-1865? *AmLegL*
Pattou, Brace 1923- *ODwPR 91*
Pattullo, Andrew 1917- *WhoAm 90*
Pattullo, George Robson 1879-1967 *BioIn 16*
Pattulo, Thomas Dufferin 1873-1956 *BioIn 16*
Patty, Ann Elizabeth 1951- *WhoWrEP 89*
Patty, Claibourne Watkins, Jr. 1934- *WhoAm 90*
Patty, Clarence Wayne 1932- *WhoAm 90*
Patty, Frank L. 1908- *St&PR 91*
Patty, R. Bruce 1935- *WhoAm 90*
Patty, William A 1889-1961 *WhoAmA 91N*
Pattyn, Remi C. 1922- *St&PR 91*
Pattyn, Remi Ceasar 1922- *WhoAm 90*
Pattyn, Roland Louis 1937- *St&PR 91*
Paturis, Emmanuel Michael 1933- *WhoSSW 91, WhoWor 91*
Patwa, Vinod Kumar *BiDrAPA 89*
Paty, Donald Winston 1936- *WhoAm 90*
Paty, Melissa Brown 1951- *WhoAmW 91*
Patz, Arnall 1920- *WhoAm 90*
Patz, Edward Frank 1932- *WhoAm 90*
Patzak, Julius 1898-1974 *PenDiMP*
Patzer, Emmons Michael 1954- *WhoEmL 91*
Patzig, Guenther 1926- *WhoWor 91*
Patzke, Richard J. 1941- *St&PR 91*
Patzke, Richard Joseph 1941- *WhoAm 90, WhoSSW 91*
Pau, Hans 1918- *WhoWor 91*
Pau, Maria de la *PenDiMP*
Pau-Llosa, Ricardo 1954- *HispWr 90*
Pau-Llosa, Ricardo Manuel 1954- *WhoHisp 91*
Pauel, Hermann G. *PenDiDA 89*
Pauer, Ernst 1826-1905 *PenDiMP*
Pauerstein, Carl Joseph 1932- *WhoAm 90*
Paugh, James Joseph, Jr. 1934- *St&PR 91*
Paugh, Richard David 1949- *WhoE 91*
Paugh, Thomas Francis 1929- *WhoAm 90, WhoWrEP 89*
Pauig, Maximo *BiDrAPA 89*
Pauk, Gyorgy 1936- *IntWWM 90, PenDiMP*
Pauk, Laronna 1960- *WhoAmW 91*
Pauk, Zdenek D 1932- *BiDrAPA 89*
Pauken, Thomas Weir 1944- *WhoSSW 91*
Pauker, Neil E 1947- *BiDrAPA 89*
Pauker, Samuel L *BiDrAPA 89*
Pauker, Samuel Levin 1948- *WhoE 91*
Paukstelis, Vytautas 1931- *St&PR 91*
Paukstis, Charles A. 1935- *St&PR 91*
Paul VI, Pope 1897-1978 *BioIn 16, ConAu 30NR*
Paul, Saint *WorAlBi*
Paul, the Apostle *BioIn 16*
Paul, Aileen *WhoWrEP 89*
Paul, Aileen 1917- *AuBYP 90*
Paul, Alice 1885-1977 *BioAmW, WorAlBi*
Paul, Alice 1936- *WhoAmW 91, WhoE 91*
Paul, Alida Ruth 1953- *WhoSSW 91*
Paul, Ara Garo 1929- *WhoAm 90*
Paul, Art 1925- *ConDes 90*
Paul, Arthur 1925- *WhoAm 90, WhoAmA 91*
Paul, Barbara *ConAu 130*
Paul, Barbara 1931- *ConAu 132*
Paul, Billy *DrBlPA 90*
Paul, Biraja Bilash 1933- *WhoWor 91*
Paul, Boris Dupont 1901- *WhoAmA 91N*
Paul, Bruno 1874-1968 *PenDiDA 89*
Paul, Carol Lynn 1945- *WhoAmW 91*

Paul, Carolyn M. 1932- *WhoAmW 91*
Paul, Charles R. 1947- *ODwPR 91*
Paul, Charlotte 1916-1989 *BioIn 16, ConAu 129*
Paul, Charlotte P. 1941- *WhoAmW 91*
Paul, Christian Thomas 1926- *WhoAm 90*
Paul, Courtland Price 1927- *WhoAm 90*
Paul, David L. 1939- *BioIn 16*
Paul, David Lewis 1939- *WhoAm 90*
Paul, David Tyler 1934- *WhoWrEP 89*
Paul, David Tyler 1934-1988 *BioIn 16*
Paul, Denis Francis 1940- *WhoE 91*
Paul, Denny K. 1941- *St&PR 91*
Paul, Dieter 1939- *WhoWor 91*
Paul, Donald Ross 1939- *WhoAm 90*
Paul, Doris Jessie 1903- *WhoWrEP 89*
Paul, Douglas Allan 1949- *St&PR 91*
Paul, Edward Mark 1957- *BiDrAPA 89*
Paul, Eldor Alvin 1931- *WhoAm 90*
Paul, Elias 1919- *WhoAm 90*
Paul, Ellen Louise 1948- *WhoAmW 91*
Paul, Elliot 1891-1958 *TwCCr&M 91*
Paul, Eve W. 1930- *WhoAm 90*
Paul, Frank 1924- *WhoAm 90*
Paul, Fritz Werner 1942- *WhoWor 91*
Paul, Gabe 1910- *Ballpl 90*
Paul, Gabriel 1910- *WhoAm 90, WhoWor 91*
Paul, George James 1927- *St&PR 91*
Paul, Gerald 1924- *St&PR 91*
Paul, Glenn 1957- *WhoE 91*
Paul, Gordon Lee 1935- *WhoAm 90*
Paul, Gordon Wilbur 1933- *WhoSSW 91*
Paul, Grace 1908- *WhoWor 91*
Paul, Helmut 1940- *St&PR 91*
Paul, Henry Allan 1946- *BiDrAPA 89*
Paul, Herbert Morton *WhoAm 90, WhoE 91, WhoWor 91*
Paul, Herman Louis, Jr. 1912- *WhoE 91, WhoWor 91*
Paul, Howard Steven 1946- *BiDrAPA 89*
Paul, Hugo B *BiDrAPA 89*
Paul, Jack 1928- *St&PR 91*
Paul, Jacques-Pierre Peminuit *DcCanB 12*
Paul, James Anthony 1948- *St&PR 91*
Paul, James Caverly Newlin 1926- *WhoAm 90*
Paul, James R. *BioIn 16*
Paul, James Robert 1934- *WhoAm 90, WhoSSW 91*
Paul, James T. 1918- *St&PR 91*
Paul, James William 1945- *WhoAm 90*
Paul, Jan *BioIn 16*
Paul, Jay Snyder 1945- *WhoWrEP 89*
Paul, Jean-Claude *BioIn 16*
Paul, Jeffrey William 1946- *St&PR 91*
Paul, Jerome Edward 1942- *St&PR 91*
Paul, Joel Richard 1955- *WhoEmL 91*
Paul, John Eugene 1917- *WhoAm 90*
Paul, John Joseph 1918- *WhoAm 90*
Paul, Johnny 1912- *BioIn 16*
Paul, Jon F. 1953- *St&PR 91*
Paul, Julian 1917- *St&PR 91*
Paul, Justus Fredrick 1938- *WhoAm 90*
Paul, K-Lynn 1937- *BiDrAPA 89*
Paul, Karen 1944- *WhoE 91*
Paul, Ken 1938- *WhoAmA 91*
Paul, Lee Gilmour 1907- *WhoAm 90*
Paul, Les 1915- *BioIn 16*
Paul, Les 1916- *OxCPMus*
Paul, Leslie Allen 1905-1985 *DcNaB 1981*
Paul, Louis 1919- *BiDrAPA 89*
Paul, Louis Anthony 1958- *WhoE 91*
Paul, Madhulatha A *BiDrAPA 89*
Paul, Malanie Dawne 1942- *BiDrAPA 89*
Paul, Margaret A *BiDrAPA 89*
Paul, Martin Ambrose 1910- *WhoAm 90*
Paul, Mary Melchior 1952- *WhoAmW 91*
Paul, Michael Ian 1939- *BiDrAPA 89*
Paul, Mike 1945- *Ballpl 90*
Paul, Nikolaus *PenDiDA 89*
Paul, Norman L 1926- *BiDrAPA 89*
Paul, Oglesby 1916- *WhoAm 90*
Paul, Patricia Christine 1954- *WhoWrEP 89*
Paul, Philip F. 1941- *St&PR 91*
Paul, Probir Kumar 1954- *BiDrAPA 89*
Paul, R.A. 1938- *St&PR 91*
Paul, Richard A. 1946- *St&PR 91*
Paul, Richard Dorsel 1927- *St&PR 91*
Paul, Richard Stanley 1941- *WhoAm 90*
Paul, Robert 1931- *WhoSSW 91*
Paul, Robert Arthur 1937- *St&PR 91, WhoAm 90, WhoE 91*
Paul, Robert Carey 1950- *WhoWor 91*
Paul, Robert D. 1928- *St&PR 91*
Paul, Robert David 1928- *WhoAm 90*
Paul, Robert Dennis 1941- *WhoAm 90*
Paul, Robert G. 1942- *St&PR 91*
Paul, Rodman W. 1912- *BioIn 16*
Paul, Roland Arthur 1937- *St&PR 91, WhoAm 90*
Paul, Ronald N. 1934- *St&PR 91*
Paul, Ronald Neale 1934- *WhoAm 90*
Paul, Ronald Stanley 1923- *St&PR 91, WhoAm 90*
Paul, Roslyn Croog 1942- *WhoSSW 91*
Paul, Sandra K. 1938- *WhoWrEP 89*
Paul, Sheri *ConAu 30NR*
Paul, Sherman 1920- *WhoAm 90*
Paul, Stephen Howard 1947- *WhoEmL 91*
Paul, Steven Everett 1937- *IntWWM 90*
Paul, Steven Marc *BiDrAPA 89*
Paul, Susan L. 1944- *WhoAmW 91*
Paul, T.R. 1932- *St&PR 91*
Paul, Thomas Wayne 1950- *WhoE 91, WhoWor 91*
Paul, Tibor 1909-1973 *PenDiMP*
Paul, Vincent de 1581-1660 *BioIn 16*
Paul, William 1926- *WhoAm 90*
Paul, William A. J. 1905-1988 *BioIn 16*
Paul, William Alex 1930- *St&PR 91*
Paul, William Bruce 1943- *WhoWrEP 89*
Paul, William D, Jr 1934- *WhoAmA 91*
Paul, William Dewitt, Jr. 1934- *WhoAm 90*
Paul, William Erwin 1936- *WhoAm 90*
Paul, William F. *WhoAm 90*
Paul, William George 1930- *St&PR 91, WhoAm 90*
Paul, Wolfgang 1913- *WhoWor 91, WorAlBi*
Paul-Boncour, Joseph Alexandre Alfred 1873-1972 *BiDFrPL*
Paul-Hus, Gilles A *BiDrAPA 89*
Paul-Michelini, Joan B. 1934- *WhoAmW 91*
Paulauskas, Edmund Walter 1937- *WhoSSW 91, WhoWor 91*
Paulding, James Kirke 1778-1860 *BiDrUSE 89, BioIn 16*
Paulding, James Y. 1927- *St&PR 91*
Pauleau, Yves Marius 1942- *WhoWor 91*
Paulen, Jacques Roderick 1925- *WhoSSW 91*
Paules, Dean La Mar 1931- *WhoE 91*
Paules, Eugene Henry 1924- *WhoE 91*
Paulette, Gene 1892-1966 *Ballpl 90*
Pauley, Jane *BioIn 16, NewYTBS 90 [port]*
Pauley, Jane 1950- *WhoAm 90, WhoAmW 91, WorAlBi*
Pauley, Judy Ruth 1943- *WhoAmW 91*
Pauley, Rhoda Anne 1939- *WhoAmW 91*
Pauley, Robert Reinhold 1923- *WhoAm 90*
Pauley, Scott Douglas *BiDrAPA 89*
Pauley, Stanley Frank 1927- *St&PR 91, WhoAm 90*
Paulhan, Jean *EncCoWW*
Paulhus, Norman Gerard, Jr. 1950- *WhoE 91, WhoWor 91*
Pauli, Andrew Denzil *BiDrAPA 89*
Pauli, Erica Deuber- *BioIn 16*
Pauli, Hanna 1864-1940 *BiDWomA*
Pauli, Hannes G. 1924- *WhoWor 91*
Pauli, Hansjorg 1931- *IntWWM 90*
Pauli, Hertha 1909-1972 *EncCoWW*
Pauli, Hertha Ernestine 1909-1973 *AuBYP 90*
Pauli, Wolfgang 1900-1958 *WorAlBi*
Paulie 1947- *WhoWrEP 89*
Paulik, Mary Theresa 1939- *WhoAmW 91*
Paulikas, George Algis 1936- *WhoAm 90*
Paulin, Arthur *St&PR 91*
Paulin, Edward J. 1947- *St&PR 91*
Paulin, Guy *NewYTBS 90*
Paulin, Henry Sylvester 1927- *WhoAm 90*
Paulin, Richard Calkins 1928- *WhoAmA 91*
Paulina *WhNaAH*
Pauline *EncCoWW*
Pauline *WhNaAH*
Pauline, Lawrence Joseph 1932- *WhoE 91*
Pauline, Roseann Judith 1957- *WhoAmW 91*
Pauling, Linus 1901- *MajTwCW*
Pauling, Linus C. 1901- *BioIn 16, WorAlBi*
Pauling, Linus C, Jr. *BiDrAPA 89*
Pauling, Linus Carl 1901- *WhoAm 90, WhoWor 91*
Paulk, Michael W. 1945- *St&PR 91*
Paulk, William 1929- *WhoWrEP 89*
Paull, Barberi P. 1948- *IntWWM 90*
Paull, Grace A. 1898- *AuBYP 90*
Paull, Irwin Leff 1946- *WhoSSW 91*
Paull, J. Will 1922- *St&PR 91*
Paull, James Bartlett 1945- *St&PR 91*
Paull, Rachel Krebs 1933- *WhoAmW 91*
Paull, Richard Allen 1930- *WhoAm 90*
Paull, Theodore 1920- *St&PR 91*
Paullus, Lucius Aemilius 229?BC-160BC *BioIn 16*
Paulmeno, Linda *ODwPR 91*
Paulmeno, Roger Gene 1949- *WhoE 91*
Paulo, Michele Ann 1963- *WhoAmW 91*
Paulos, John Allen *BioIn 16*
Pauls, Charles W. 1946- *St&PR 91*
Pauls, Cherry-Willow 1946- *IntWWM 90*
Pauls, Dayton Frank 1910- *WhoAm 90*
Pauls, John P. 1937- *St&PR 91*
Pauls, Theodore D. 1951- *St&PR 91*
Paulsel, Lee 1936- *St&PR 91*
Paulsen, Annamarie S *BiDrAPA 89*
Paulsen, Brendan Patrick *AuBYP 90*
Paulsen, Brian Oliver 1941- *WhoAmA 91*
Paulsen, Darlyne Evelyn 1936- *WhoSSW 91*
Paulsen, Darrell R. 1937- *St&PR 91*
Paulsen, Douglas Frank 1952- *WhoEmL 91*
Paulsen, Eric Lynn 1951- *St&PR 91*
Paulsen, Eugene August 1922- *WhoAm 90*
Paulsen, Frank Robert 1922- *WhoAm 90*
Paulsen, Gary *BioIn 16*
Paulsen, Gary 1939- *AuBYP 90, ConAu 30NR*
Paulsen, James A 1922- *BiDrAPA 89*
Paulsen, John Andrew 1960- *St&PR 91*
Paulsen, John Quincy 1928- *St&PR 91*
Paulsen, Jorgen Wittenborg 1931- *WhoWor 91*
Paulsen, Joseph Charles, V 1925- *WhoE 91*
Paulsen, Norman, Jr. 1926- *ODwPR 91*
Paulsen, Norman Deitrich 1929- *WhoWrEP 89*
Paulsen, Pat 1927- *WhoAm 90*
Paulsen, Philip K. *BioIn 16*
Paulsen, Randall Howard 1945- *BiDrAPA 89*
Paulsen, Robert A. 1917- *St&PR 91*
Paulsen, Serenus Glen 1917- *WhoAm 90*
Paulsen, Stanley K. 1935- *St&PR 91*
Paulsen, Stephen W. 1948- *St&PR 91*
Paulsen, Suzanne M 1932- *BiDrAPA 89*
Paulsen, Vivian 1942- *WhoAm 90*
Paulsen, William Paul 1922- *WhoE 91*
Paulshus, Deborah Lee 1955- *WhoAmW 91*
Paulson, Alan Charles 1947- *WhoWrEP 89*
Paulson, Allen Eugene 1922- *WhoSSW 91*
Paulson, Belden Henry 1927- *WhoAm 90*
Paulson, Bernard Arthur 1928- *WhoAm 90*
Paulson, Cindy Patrice 1949- *WhoEmL 91*
Paulson, David Alan *BiDrAPA 89*
Paulson, Donald Erwin 1934- *St&PR 91*
Paulson, Donald Robert 1943- *WhoAm 90*
Paulson, Eric *ODwPR 91*
Paulson, Gerald C. 1935- *St&PR 91*
Paulson, Howard E. 1926- *St&PR 91*
Paulson, Jack *AuBYP 90*
Paulson, James Marvin 1923- *WhoAm 90*
Paulson, Jeannette *WhoAmW 91*
Paulson, Jerome S. 1945- *St&PR 91*
Paulson, John Alfred 1955- *WhoAm 90, WhoE 91*
Paulson, John D. 1915- *St&PR 91*
Paulson, John Doran 1915- *WhoAm 90*
Paulson, Leroy Arthur 1942- *St&PR 91*
Paulson, Loretta Nancy 1943- *WhoAmW 91, WhoE 91*
Paulson, Louis 1930- *WhoE 91*
Paulson, Marvel P. 1920- *St&PR 91*
Paulson, Moses 1897- *WhoAm 90, WhoWor 91*
Paulson, Paul Joseph 1932- *WhoAm 90*
Paulson, Peter John 1928- *WhoAm 90*
Paulson, Robert C. 1944- *St&PR 91*
Paulson, Ronald 1930- *ConAu 33NR*
Paulson, Ronald Howard 1930- *WhoAm 90*
Paulson, S. Lawrence *ODwPR 91*
Paulson, Stanley Fay 1920- *WhoAm 90*
Paulson, Stanley Lawrence 1947- *WhoE 91*
Paulson, Thomas L. 1949- *St&PR 91*
Paulson-Ehrhardt, Patricia Helen 1956- *WhoEmL 91*
Paulson-Ellis, Jeremy David 1943- *WhoWor 91*
Paulston, Christina Bratt 1932- *WhoAm 90*
Paulucci, Jeno F. *BioIn 16*
Paulucci, Jeno F. 1918- *St&PR 91*
Paulucci, Jeno Francisco 1918- *ConAmBL*
Paulus, Friedrich 1890-1957 *WorAlBi*
Paulus, Harold Edward 1929- *WhoAm 90*
Paulus, John David 1943- *WhoAm 90*
Paulus, John Douglas 1917- *St&PR 91, WhoWor 91*
Paulus, John Joseph 1907- *St&PR 91*
Paulus, John R. 1935- *St&PR 91*
Paulus, Michael John 1957- *WhoEmL 91*
Paulus, Norma Jean Petersen 1933- *WhoAm 90*
Paulus, Stephen Harrison 1949- *IntWWM 90, WhoAm 90*
Pauly, Bruce Henry 1920- *WhoAm 90*
Pauly, D. Tod 1954- *St&PR 91*
Pauly, Gregory E. 1926- *St&PR 91*
Pauly, Gregory N. 1951- *St&PR 91*
Pauly, Ira B 1930- *BiDrAPA 89*
Pauly, John Edward 1927- *WhoAm 90*
Pauly, Max Johann Friedrich 1907-1946 *BioIn 16*
Pauly, Nelson Anthony 1914- *St&PR 91*
Pauly, Rosa 1894-1975 *PenDiMP*
Paumanabhan, Valayapettai Srinivasan 1933- *WhoWor 91*
Paumgarten, Nicholas B. 1945- *St&PR 91*
Paumgarten, Nicholas Biddle 1945- *WhoAm 90*
Paumgartner, Balthasar 1551-1600 *BioIn 16*
Paumgartner, Bernhard 1887-1971 *PenDiMP*
Paumgartner, Gustav 1933- *WhoWor 91*
Paumgartner, Magdalena Balthasar 1555-1642 *BioIn 16*
Paunina *WhNaAH*
Paupini, Giuseppe 1907- *WhoWor 91*
Pauquette, Lynn Johnston 1941- *WhoE 91*
Paus, Eva Antonia 1954- *WhoE 91*
Pausa, Carol L. 1951- *St&PR 91*
Pausa, Clements Edward 1930- *St&PR 91, WhoAm 90*
Pausig, Ralph W. 1934- *St&PR 91*
Paustian, Joan Paulette 1948- *WhoE 91*
Paustian, Jodie Lee 1957- *WhoAmW 91*
Pauth, Patricia Ruth 1936- *WhoAmW 91*
Pautsch, Bruce L. 1951- *St&PR 91*
Pauwels, Charles Achille 1938- *St&PR 91*
Pauwels, Henri 1923- *WhoWor 91*
Pauwels, Louis 1920- *EncO&P 3*
Pauwels, Louis Francois 1920- *BiDFrPL*
Pauwels, Rudolf Paul 1937- *WhoWor 91*
Pavalon, Eugene Irving 1933- *WhoWor 91*
Pavan, Pietro 1903- *WhoWor 91*
Pavao, Leonel Maia 1934- *WhoAm 90*
Pavarotti, Luciano *BioIn 16*
Pavarotti, Luciano 1935- *IntWWM 90, PenDiMP, WhoAm 90, WhoWor 91, WorAlBi*
Pavek, Bryn Carpenter 1955- *WhoAmW 91*
Pavek, Charles Christopher 1955- *WhoE 91*
Pavel, Elmer Lewis 1918- *WhoSSW 91*
Pavelchek, Walter Raymond 1925- *WhoAm 90*
Pavelic, Ante 1889-1959 *BioIn 16*
Pavelka, Elaine Blanche *WhoAmW 91*
Pavelka, Leonard R. 1924- *St&PR 91*
Pavelka, Martha C. 1927- *St&PR 91*
Pavelka, Robert F. 1953- *St&PR 91*
Pavels, Victor 1919- *St&PR 91*
Pavelski, Patrick M. 1942- *St&PR 91*
Pavenstedt, Eleanor *BiDrAPA 89*
Paverenst, Anne *BiDEWW*
Pavese, Cesare 1908-1950 *EuWr 12, WorAlBi*
Pavey, George Madison, Jr. 1919- *WhoSSW 91*
Pavia, Mario J. 1950- *St&PR 91*
Pavia, Michael Raymond, Jr. 1955- *WhoEmL 91*
Pavic, Milorad 1929- *ConLC 60 [port]*
Pavilanis, Vytautas 1920- *WhoAm 90*
Pavillard, Michele Aline 1952- *BiDrAPA 89*
Paviour, Paul 1931- *IntWWM 90*
Pavitt, Keith Leslie 1937- *WhoWor 91*
Pavkov, Janet Ruth 1939- *WhoAmW 91*
Pavkovic, Aleksandar 1950- *WhoWor 91*
Pavkovic, Ivan *BiDrAPA 89*
Pavkovic, Ivan 1927- *WhoAm 90*
Pavlechko, Thomas John 1962- *IntWWM 90*
Pavlescak, Rik 1962- *WhoEmL 91*
Pavletich, Don 1938- *Ballpl 90*
Pavlica, Jovanka 1929- *BiDrAPA 89*
Pavlich, Walter David 1955- *WhoWrEP 89*
Pavlick, Harvey Naylor 1942- *WhoWor 91*
Pavlick, Pamela Kay 1944- *WhoAmW 91, WhoSSW 91*
Pavlick, Walter E. 1934- *St&PR 91*
Pavlick, Walter Eugene 1934- *WhoAm 90*
Pavlidis, Dimitris 1950- *WhoEmL 91*
Pavlidis, Panos 1904- *WhoWor 91*
Pavlik, Alan Edward *WhoWrEP 89*
Pavlik, Edward John 1946- *WhoSSW 91*
Pavlik, Elsa M. 1943- *WhoAmW 91*
Pavlik, James William 1937- *WhoAm 90*
Pavlik, Jenny *BioIn 16*
Pavlik, Lynda McElroy 1939- *WhoAmW 91*
Pavlik, Raymond K. 1940- *St&PR 91*
Pavlik, William Bruce 1932- *WhoAm 90*
Pavlinac, Dennis M *BiDrAPA 89*
Pavliv, Mark Alexander 1951- *WhoE 91, WhoWor 91*
Pavlo, Annemarie E *BiDrAPA 89*
Pavlo, E. Lionel *BioIn 16*
Pavloff, Jonathan T. 1949- *St&PR 91*
Pavlov, Ivan 1849-1936 *WorAlBi*
Pavlov, Yuri *BioIn 16*
Pavlova, Anna 1882-1931 *WorAlBi*
Pavlova, Karolina 1807-1893 *EncCoWW*
Pavlovic, Miodrag 1928- *WorAu 1980 [port]*
Pavlovich, Chkalov Valery 1904-1938 *BioIn 16*
Pavlovich, Constantine 1779-1831 *BioIn 16*
Pavlovich, Paul Branibor 1932- *WhoE 91*
Pavlow, Shara Toursh 1950- *WhoAmW 91*
Pavlus, Craig S. 1946- *St&PR 91*
Pavoni, Mary Michelle 1944- *WhoAmW 91*
Pavony, William H. 1940- *St&PR 91, WhoAm 90*
Pavsek, Daniel Allan 1945- *WhoAm 90*
Pawa, Debra Sue 1953- *WhoE 91*
Pawel, Ernst 1920- *ConAu 131*
Pawel, Michael Alan 1946- *BiDrAPA 89*
Pawelec, William John 1917- *WhoE 91*
Pawhuska *WhNaAH*
Pawlak, Mark Joseph 1948- *WhoWrEP 89*

Pawlak, Stanislaw Michal 1933- *WhoWor 91*
Pawlcyn, Cindy *BioIn 16*
Pawley, Thomas D., III 1917- *EarBlAP*
Pawlick, Joseph Lawrence 1942- *St&PR 91*
Pawlik, James David 1958- *WhoEmL 91*
Pawlikowska-Jasnorzewska, Maria 1891-1945 *EncCoWW*
Pawloski, Andrzej 1925- *ConDes 90*
Pawlowski, Diane R. 1944- *WhoWrEP 89*
Pawlowski, Emil J *BiDrAPA 89*
Pawlowski, John J. 1925- *St&PR 91*
Pawlowski, Joseph P. 1941- *St&PR 91*
Pawlson, Leonard Gregory 1943- *WhoAm 90*
Pawluczyk, Sonia *BiDrAPA 89*
Pawluk, Orest M *BiDrAPA 89*
Pawnee Killer *WhNaAH*
Pawson, Robin L. 1948- *St&PR 91*
Pawula, Kenneth John 1935- *WhoAm 90*
Paxihos *WhNaAH*
Paxinos *WhNaAH*
Paxinos, Esther F. 1935- *St&PR 91*
Paxinosa *WhNaAH*
Paxman, Gale Freeman 1957- *WhoAmW 91*
Paxnos *WhNaAH*
Paxnous *WhNaAH*
Paxon, Bill 1954- *WhoAm 90, WhoE 91*
Paxon, L. William 1954- *BioIn 16*
Paxowan *WhNaAH*
Paxsinos *WhNaAH*
Paxson, Edgar Samuel 1852-1919 *WhNaAH*
Paxson, James Malone 1912- *St&PR 91*
Paxson, Lowell *BioIn 16*
Paxson, Lowell White 1935- *WhoAm 90, WhoSSW 91*
Paxson, Wesley C. 1923- *St&PR 91*
Paxton, Alice Adams 1914- *WhoAmW 91, WhoE 91, WhoWor 91*
Paxton, Dan R. 1947- *St&PR 91*
Paxton, Harold William 1927- *WhoAm 90*
Paxton, Harry Theodore 1915- *WhoWor 91*
Paxton, James Fred 1932- *St&PR 91*
Paxton, James L., Jr. 1908- *St&PR 91*
Paxton, John 1923- *ConAu 129*
Paxton, John Van Middlesworth 1938- *WhoE 91*
Paxton, John W. 1937- *St&PR 91*
Paxton, John Wesley 1937- *WhoAm 90*
Paxton, Joseph 1801-1865 *BioIn 16*
Paxton, Laura Belle-Kent 1942- *WhoAmW 91*
Paxton, Mike 1953- *Ballpl 90*
Paxton, R. Robert 1920- *St&PR 91*
Paxton, Robert Barnet *BiDrAPA 89*
Paxton, Robert Owen 1932- *WhoAm 90*
Paxton, Tom 1937- *ConMus 5 [port], OxCPMus, WhoAm 90*
Paxton, Walter Blake 1944- *St&PR 91*
Paxton, William G. 1939- *St&PR 91*
Paxton, William Perce, II 1941- *St&PR 91*
Payack, Paul J J 1950- *ConAu 31NR*
Payack, Paul Joseph John 1950- *WhoE 91*
Paycheck, Johnny 1941- *WorAlBi*
Paydos, Charles J. 1940- *St&PR 91, WhoAm 90*
Payepot *WhNaAH*
Payer, Carolyn Ann 1934- *WhoAmW 91*
Payer, Stephen C. 1935- *St&PR 91*
Payes, Wm. J. 1906- *St&PR 91*
Payette, Thomas M. 1932- *St&PR 91*
Payette, Thomas Martin 1932- *WhoAm 90*
Payette, William 1913-1989 *BioIn 16*
Payeur, Richard 1960- *BiDrAPA 89*
Paykel, Eugene S 1934- *BiDrAPA 89*
Paylor, Larry E. 1943- *St&PR 91*
Payment, Robert C. 1934- *St&PR 91*
Payn, Graham 1918- *OxCPMus*
Payn, Stephen B 1909- *BiDrAPA 89*
Payn, Stephen Bert 1909- *WhoE 91*
Payne *WhNaAH*
Payne, Alan *MajTwCW*
Payne, Alan 1932- *SmATA X [port]*
Payne, Alan 1941- *ODwPR 91*
Payne, Alan Lafayette 1929- *St&PR 91*
Payne, Alma Smith *AuBYP 90*
Payne, Ancil Horace 1921- *WhoAm 90*
Payne, Anita Hart 1926- *WhoAmW 91*
Payne, Anthony Edward 1936- *IntWWM 90*
Payne, B. Darwin 1937- *WhoSSW 91*
Payne, Bennie 1907- *DrBlPA 90*
Payne, Bernal C., Jr. 1941- *SmATA 60 [port]*
Payne, Bettie Selden Watford 1948- *WhoE 91*
Payne, Billie Jean 1932- *WhoSSW 91*
Payne, Blanche 1896-1972 *BioIn 16*
Payne, Bruce 1911- *St&PR 91, WhoAm 90*
Payne, Carl *BioIn 16*
Payne, Carla *BioIn 16*
Payne, Carter *BioIn 16*
Payne, Charles E *BiDrAPA 89*
Payne, Charles E. 1944- *St&PR 91*
Payne, Charles M. 1873-1964 *EncACom*
Payne, Clare Hudson 1952- *WhoEmL 91*
Payne, Connie Sue 1946- *WhoEmL 91*
Payne, Dan *BioIn 16*
Payne, David B. 1936- *WhoAm 90*
Payne, David Hoag *BiDrAPA 89*
Payne, David LeBaron 1927- *WhoSSW 91*
Payne, Dean Alan 1948- *WhoE 91*
Payne, Deborah Ann 1952- *WhoAmW 91*
Payne, Deborah Anne 1952- *WhoAmW 91, WhoE 91*
Payne, Diana J. 1946- *WhoE 91*
Payne, Don Charles 1940- *BiDrAPA 89*
Payne, Donald 1934- *WhoAm 90, WhoE 91*
Payne, Donald M. *BioIn 16*
Payne, Donald Milford 1934- *BlkAmsC [port]*
Payne, Donald Ray 1947- *WhoSSW 91*
Payne, Duncan Macrae 1941- *St&PR 91*
Payne, Edgar Alwin 1882-1947 *BioIn 16*
Payne, Edmund C 1923- *BiDrAPA 89*
Payne, Edward Carlton 1928- *WhoAm 90*
Payne, Elizabeth Anne 1960- *WhoSSW 91*
Payne, Elizabeth Eleanore 1945- *WhoAmW 91*
Payne, Elsie Palmer 1884-1971 *BioIn 16*
Payne, Emmy *AuBYP 90*
Payne, Fernandus 1881-1977 *DcScB S2*
Payne, Frances Anne 1932- *WhoAm 90*
Payne, Fred J. 1922- *WhoSSW 91, WhoWor 91*
Payne, Fred R. 1953- *WhoSSW 91*
Payne, Fred Ray 1931- *WhoSSW 91*
Payne, Freda 1944- *DrBlPA 90*
Payne, Frederick Blake *BioIn 16*
Payne, Frederick Warren 1949- *WhoEmL 91*
Payne, Gareld Gene 1931- *WhoWor 91*
Payne, George Frederick 1941- *WhoAm 90*
Payne, Gerald Oliver 1930- *WhoAm 90*
Payne, Graham Stuart 1945- *St&PR 91*
Payne, Harry Charles 1947- *WhoAm 90, WhoE 91*
Payne, Harry Morse, Jr. 1922- *WhoAm 90*
Payne, Henry Clay 1843-1904 *BiDrUSE 89*
Payne, Ilene Delores 1946- *WhoAmW 91*
Payne, Jack 1899-1969 *OxCPMus*
Payne, James Leroy 1936- *St&PR 91, WhoAm 90*
Payne, James Parker 1944- *WhoSSW 91*
Payne, James R., Jr. 1916- *St&PR 91*
Payne, Jennifer Lynn 1965- *WhoAmW 91*
Payne, John 1877?-195-? *DcAfAmP*
Payne, John 1912-1989 *AnObit 1989, BioIn 16, ConTFT 8, WorAlBi*
Payne, John Barton 1855-1935 *BiDrUSE 89*
Payne, John D 1934- *WhoAmA 91*
Payne, John Dundee *BiDrAPA 89*
Payne, John Spencer 1953- *WhoSSW 91*
Payne, John W. 1940- *St&PR 91*
Payne, Juanita Brinkley 1939- *WhoSSW 91*
Payne, Kenyon Thomas 1918- *WhoAm 90*
Payne, L Marlene 1947- *BiDrAPA 89*
Payne, Ladell 1933- *WhoAm 90*
Payne, Laurence 1919- *TwCCr&M 91*
Payne, Lawrence Edward 1923- *WhoAm 90*
Payne, Leslie J. 1907-1981 *MusmAFA*
Payne, Leslie Julian 1945- *WhoE 91*
Payne, Lewis Franklin *BioIn 16, WhoAm 90, WhoSSW 91*
Payne, Linda Cohen 1953- *WhoAmW 91*
Payne, Lorraine Marie 1952- *WhoAmW 91*
Payne, Lynda Sue 1944- *WhoSSW 91*
Payne, Mabel Louise 1949- *WhoAmW 91*
Payne, Maggi *NewAgMG*
Payne, Maggi 1945- *IntWWM 90*
Payne, Maggi D. 1945- *WhoEmL 91*
Payne, Martha G. *St&PR 91*
Payne, Mary *WhoWrEP 89*
Payne, Maxwell Carr, Jr. 1927- *WhoAm 90*
Payne, Melissa Anne 1964- *WhoAmW 91*
Payne, Melvin M. *NewYTBS 90 [port]*
Payne, Melvin Monroe 1911- *WhoAm 90*
Payne, Michael David 1941- *WhoAm 90, WhoWrEP 89*
Payne, Michael Wilkinson 1963- *WhoSSW 91*
Payne, Mitchell W. 1956- *St&PR 91*
Payne, Otis Edd 1939- *BiDrAPA 89*
Payne, Patricia 1942- *IntWWM 90*
Payne, Patricia Anne 1946- *WhoE 91*
Payne, Peggy 1949- *WhoWrEP 89*
Payne, Rachel Ann 1932- *SmATA X [port]*
Payne, Richard *BiDrAPA 89*
Payne, Richard A. 1934- *ODwPR 91*
Payne, Richard Allen 1934- *St&PR 91*
Payne, Robert 1911-1983 *ConAu 31NR*
Payne, Robert Somers 1938- *St&PR 91*
Payne, Robert Walter 1925- *WhoAm 90*
Payne, Roger 1739-1797 *PenDiDA 89*
Payne, Ronald D. 1947- *St&PR 91*
Payne, Rufus Floyd 1909- *WhoSSW 91*
Payne, Sherry Neuwirth *AuBYP 90*
Payne, Sidney Stewart 1932- *WhoAm 90*
Payne, Terence L. 1946- *St&PR 91*
Payne, Theresa Mae 1955- *WhoAmW 91*
Payne, Thomas 1920- *WhoAm 90*
Payne, Thomas J. 1922- *St&PR 91*
Payne, Tyson Elliott, Jr. 1927- *WhoAm 90*
Payne, Virginia Jenkins *BiDrAPA 89*
Payne, Walter Fitch 1936- *St&PR 91*
Payne, William Bruce 1943- *St&PR 91*
Payne, William Clark, Sr. 1929- *WhoSSW 91*
Payne, William Douglas 1910- *St&PR 91*
Payne, William Haydon 1939- *WhoAm 90*
Payne, William Jackson 1925- *WhoAm 90*
Payne, William Joseph 1932- *St&PR 91*
Payne, William Spencer 1926- *WhoAm 90*
Payne, Winfield Scott 1917- *WhoWor 91*
Payne Palacio, June Rose 1940- *WhoAmW 91*
Payne-Parsons, Sharon Lee 1945- *WhoAmW 91*
Paynter, Alan H. 1938- *St&PR 91*
Paynter, Harry Alvin 1923- *WhoAm 90*
Paynter, John Frederick 1931- *IntWWM 90*
Paynter, John Philip 1928- *WhoAm 90*
Payot, Turia Mau *BioIn 16*
Payro, Roberto J 1867-1928 *HispWr 90*
Payro, Roberto Jorge 1867-1928 *BioIn 16*
Pays, Amanda *BioIn 16*
Payseur, Victoria Felland *WhoAmW 91*
Payson, Henry Edwards *BiDrAPA 89*
Payson, Henry Edwards 1925- *WhoAm 90*
Payson, Joan Whitney 1903-1975 *WorAlBi*
Payson, John Whitney 1940- *WhoAmA 91, WhoSSW 91*
Payson, Ken A. 1930- *St&PR 91*
Payson, Tony A *BiDrAPA 89*
Payte, Joseph Michael 1946- *St&PR 91*
Payton, Antoinette Shields 1926- *WhoAmW 91*
Payton, Benjamin Franklin 1932- *WhoAm 90*
Payton, Bob *BioIn 16*
Payton, Carolyn Robertson 1925- *WhoAm 90*
Payton, Christopher Charles 1957- *WhoWor 91*
Payton, Edgar Lee 1950- *WhoEmL 91*
Payton, James Bayard 1947- *BiDrAPA 89*
Payton, Jimmy *Ballpl 90*
Payton, Jimmy C. *BioIn 16*
Payton, Lew 1873- *EarBlAP*
Payton, Michael J. 1956- *ODwPR 91*
Payton, Nancy Anne 1948- *WhoE 91*
Payton, Randolph Randi 1954- *WhoWrEP 89*
Payton, Roger E. 1956- *St&PR 91*
Payton, Roger Edward 1956- *WhoAm 90*
Payton, Thomas W. 1946- *St&PR 91*
Payton, Thomas William 1946- *WhoAm 90*
Payton, Walter 1954- *BioIn 16, WorAlBi*
Paz, George Gabriel *BiDrAPA 89*
Paz, Gil *ConAu 131, HispWr 90*
Paz, Maria V *BiDrAPA 89*
Paz, Octavio 1914- *BioIn 16, ConAu 32NR, DcLB Y90 [port], HispWr 90, MajTwCW, News 91-2 [port], PoeCrit 1 [port], WhoAm 90, WhoSSW 91, WhoWor 91, WorAlBi*
Paz, Rudy J. 1938- *WhoHisp 91*
Paz Estenssoro, Victor 1907- *BioIn 16, WhoWor 91*
Paz Soldan, Miguel Mateo 1945- *WhoEmL 91, WhoWor 91*
Paz Zamora, Jaime 1939- *WhoWor 91*
Pazandak, Carol Hendrickson *WhoAmW 91*
Pazdar, Donna Jean 1949- *WhoAmW 91*
Pazder, Lawrence H *BiDrAPA 89*
Pazdera, John Paul 1948- *WhoE 91*
Pazdral, George Howard *BiDrAPA 89*
Pazevic, Jon-Pierre 1962- *WhoEmL 91*
Pazicky, Edward P. 1946- *St&PR 91*
Pazik, George James 1921- *WhoAm 90*
Pazirandeh, Mahmood 1932- *WhoWor 91*
Pazmany, Zoltan 1929- *WhoSSW 91*
Paznekas, Susan Jennifer 1949- *WhoAmW 91*
Pazner, Sherman S *BiDrAPA 89*
Pazos, Carlos Agustin 1956- *WhoSSW 91*
Pazur, John Howard 1922- *WhoAm 90*
Pazy, Amnon Joseph 1936- *WhoWor 91*
Pazzaglia, Alberto Giuseppe 1940- *WhoWor 91*
Pazzaglia, Peggy Jo 1954- *BiDrAPA 89*
Pazzi, Maria Maddalena de' 1566-1607 *EncCoWW*
p'Bitek, Okot 1931-1982 *MajTwCW*
Pcilka, Olena *EncCoWW*
P'Cock *NewAgMG*
Peabody, Amelia 1890-1984 *WhoAmA 91N*
Peabody, Cecilia Ann *BiDrAPA 89*
Peabody, Charles W. 1941- *St&PR 91*
Peabody, Elizabeth P. 1804-1894 *BioAmW*
Peabody, Elizabeth Palmer 1804-1894 *FemiCLE, WorAlBi*
Peabody, George 1795-1869 *BioIn 16, EncABHB 6 [port], WorAlBi*
Peabody, George A *BiDrAPA 89*
Peabody, George F. 1852-1938 *WorAlBi*
Peabody, George Francis 1912- *WhoAm 90*
Peabody, Josephine 1874-1922 *FemiCLE*
Peabody, Josephine Preston 1874-1922 *BioIn 16, NotWoAT*
Peabody, Judith Dunnington 1930- *WhoAmW 91*
Peabody, Lucy Whitehead McGill 1861-1949 *BioIn 16*
Peabody, Maryanne 1946- *WhoAmW 91*
Peabody, Myra Agnes 1912- *WhoWrEP 89*
Peabody, Oliver William Bourn 1799-1848 *BioIn 16*
Peabody, Richard Myers 1951- *WhoWrEP 89*
Peabody, William Tyler, Jr. 1921- *WhoAm 90*
Peace, Barbara Lou Jean 1939- *WhoAmW 91*
Peace, Bernie 1933- *WhoAmA 91*
Peace, Dale Conrad 1942- *BiDrAPA 89*
Peace, H.W., II 1935- *St&PR 91*
Peace, H. W., II 1935- *WhoAm 90, WhoSSW 91*
Peace, Lisa Burk 1960- *WhoAmW 91*
Peace, Richard 1933- *ConAu 131*
Peace, William Henry, III 1938- *WhoWor 91*
Peach, David George 1935- *WhoSSW 91*
Peach, James L., Sr. 1944- *WhoSSW 91*
Peach, Kenneth D. 1903-1988 *BioIn 16*
Peach, William Bernard 1918- *WhoAm 90*
Peachena 1948- *DrBlPA 90*
Peacher, Douglas John 1912- *WhoAm 90*
Peacher, Terry Gene 1942- *BiDrAPA 89*
Peaches and Herb *EncPR&S 89*
Peachey, Cathy Jean 1949- *WhoAmW 91*
Peachey, Georgia A. 1928- *WhoAmW 91, WhoE 91*
Peachey, Lee DeBorde 1932- *WhoAm 90*
Peachey, Sidney R. 1922- *St&PR 91*
Peaco, Joyce Lorane *WhoAmW 91*
Peacock, A. Ward 1929- *St&PR 91*
Peacock, Albert Leonard, Jr. 1954- *WhoSSW 91*
Peacock, Alvin Ward 1929- *WhoAm 90*
Peacock, Andrew Sharp 1939- *WhoWor 91*
Peacock, Bruce Anthony 1951- *St&PR 91*
Peacock, C. Robert 1931- *St&PR 91*
Peacock, Carlos *ConAu 132*
Peacock, Cliffton 1953- *WhoAmA 91*
Peacock, Erle Ewart, Jr. 1926- *WhoAm 90*
Peacock, George Rowatt 1923- *St&PR 91, WhoAm 90*
Peacock, Graham Rex 1938- *WhoWor 91*
Peacock, James Daniel 1930- *WhoAm 90*
Peacock, James Harry 1928- *St&PR 91*
Peacock, John Edward Dean 1919- *WhoAm 90*
Peacock, John Kevin 1941- *WhoE 91*
Peacock, Johnny 1910-1981 *Ballpl 90*
Peacock, Judith Ann 1939- *WhoAmW 91*
Peacock, Lamar Batts 1920- *WhoAm 90*
Peacock, LaRita Williams 1954- *WhoAmW 91*
Peacock, Lelon James 1928- *WhoAm 90*
Peacock, Lowell 1926- *WhoAm 90*
Peacock, Lowell L. 1926- *St&PR 91*
Peacock, Lucy 1947- *IntWWM 90*
Peacock, Markham Lovick, Jr. 1903- *WhoAm 90*
Peacock, Mary Willa 1942- *WhoAm 90*
Peacock, Molly 1947- *ConLC 60 [port], WhoWrEP 89*
Peacock, Paul Frederick 1962- *WhoE 91*
Peacock, Peter Bligh 1921- *WhoAm 90*
Peacock, Robert Richard 1928- *WhoE 91*
Peacock, Robert S. 1925- *St&PR 91*
Peacock, Robert William 1950- *WhoSSW 91*
Peacock, Shawn Brian 1960- *WhoE 91*
Peacock, Stan 1957- *WhoSSW 91*
Peacock, Stewart S. 1928- *St&PR 91*
Peacock, Thomas Love 1785-1866 *BioIn 16, DcLB 96 [port]*
Peacock, Valerie Lynn 1962- *WhoAmW 91*
Peacock, William T., Jr. *ODwPR 91*
Peacos, Nancy B. 1954- *WhoE 91*
Peairs, Richard Hope 1929- *WhoAm 90*
Peak *NewAgMG*
Peak, Daniel T 1928- *BiDrAPA 89*
Peak, Elizabeth Jayne 1952- *WhoAmA 91*
Peak, James Bennett 1940- *WhoSSW 91*
Peak, James Hamilton 1962- *BiDrAPA 89*
Peak, Kenneth Raymond 1945- *St&PR 91*
Peak, Myra Lee 1954- *WhoAmW 91*
Peak, Pamela Elaine 1957- *WhoSSW 91*
Peak, Robert *WhoAmA 91*
Peake, Albert Louis 1927- *St&PR 91*
Peake, Channing 1910- *WhoAmA 91*
Peake, Charles Franklin 1933- *WhoE 91*
Peake, Clifford M. 1927- *WhoAm 90, WhoE 91*
Peake, Darryl Lee 1952- *WhoEmL 91*
Peake, John L. *BiDrAPA 89*
Peake, Junius W. 1931- *WhoE 91*

Peake, Kirby 1915- *WhoAm 90*
Peake, Lorraine Elizabeth Fowler 1954- *WhoSSW 91*
Peake, Mervyn 1911-1968 *MajTwCW*
Peake, Rebecca Mote *BiDrAPA 89*
Peake, Richard Henry, Jr. 1934- *WhoSSW 91*
Peake, Thomas Rhea 1939- *WhoWrEP 89*
Peake-Dickerman, Luise Eitel 1925- *IntWWM 90*
Peal, James A *BiDrAPA 89*
Peal, Stanley *BiDrAPA 89*
Peal, Stanley 1913- *WhoE 91*
Peale, Anna Claypoole 1791-1878 *BiDWomA*
Peale, Charles Willson 1741-1827 *EncCRAm*
Peale, Charles Wilson 1741-1827 *IntDcAA 90, WorAlBi*
Peale, James 1934- *WhoE 91*
Peale, Norman Vincent *BioIn 16*
Peale, Norman Vincent 1898- *AuBYP 90, MajTwCW, WhoAm 90, WhoE 91, WhoWor 91, WorAlBi*
Peale, Ruth Stafford 1906- *WhoAm 90, WhoAmW 91*
Peale, Sarah M. 1800-1885 *BioAmW*
Peale, Sarah Miriam 1800-1885 *BiDWomA, BioIn 16*
Peale, Stanton Jerrold 1937- *WhoAm 90*
Pealor, Dennis L. 1952- *St&PR 91*
Peanasky, Robert Joseph 1927- *WhoAm 90*
Peapples, George Alan 1940- *WhoAm 90, WhoWor 91*
Pearce, Alice *ODwPR 91*
Pearce, Alison Margaret 1953- *IntWWM 90*
Pearce, Betty McMurray 1926- *WhoAmW 91, WhoSSW 91, WhoWor 91*
Pearce, Carol Ann *WhoWrEP 89*
Pearce, Charles A. 1923- *St&PR 91*
Pearce, Charles Abraham 1923- *WhoAm 90*
Pearce, Charles Wellington 1927- *WhoAm 90, WhoSSW 91*
Pearce, Christopher Thomas 1941- *WhoWor 91*
Pearce, Dickey 1836-1908 *Ballpl 90 [port]*
Pearce, Donald Joslin 1924- *WhoAm 90*
Pearce, Doris Parsons 1929- *WhoSSW 91*
Pearce, Drue 1951- *WhoAmW 91*
Pearce, E.L. 1945- *St&PR 91*
Pearce, Earl Robert 1940- *WhoAm 90*
Pearce, Edward H 1901-1990 *NewYTBS 90*
Pearce, Elvina Truman 1931- *IntWWM 90*
Pearce, Floyd Earl *WhoWrEP 89*
Pearce, Frances Jean 1954- *WhoAmW 91*
Pearce, G. Martin 1942- *St&PR 91*
Pearce, George 1888-1935 *Ballpl 90*
Pearce, George Geoffrey 1943- *IntWWM 90*
Pearce, George Hamilton 1921- *WhoAm 90*
Pearce, H.R. 1919- *St&PR 91*
Pearce, Harry Jonathan 1942- *WhoAm 90*
Pearce, Hubert *EncPaPR 91*
Pearce, J. Winston 1907-19--? *ConAu 130*
Pearce, James Dunn 1930- *WhoSSW 91*
Pearce, James Walker 1951- *WhoSSW 91*
Pearce, James Wishart 1916- *WhoAm 90*
Pearce, Jane E 1914- *BiDrAPA 89*
Pearce, Janet Dinkel 1943- *WhoAm 90, WhoAmW 91*
Pearce, Jennifer Sue 1954- *WhoSSW 91*
Pearce, Joan DeLap 1930- *WhoAmW 91*
Pearce, John K, Jr. 1935- *BiDrAPA 89*
Pearce, John Kenneth 1935- *WhoE 91*
Pearce, Julia Lee Anne 1940- *WhoAmW 91*
Pearce, Llewellyn Gregory, Jr. 1948- *WhoSSW 91*
Pearce, Lupe 1942- *WhoHisp 91*
Pearce, Luther W *BiDrAPA 89*
Pearce, Mary E 1932- *ConAu 31NR*
Pearce, Mary McCallum 1906- *WhoAmW 91*
Pearce, Michael L. 1933- *St&PR 91*
Pearce, Patricia Lee *BiDrAPA 89*
Pearce, Patricia R 1924- *BiDrAPA 89*
Pearce, Paul Francis 1928- *WhoAm 90*
Pearce, Philippa *AuBYP 90*
Pearce, Philippa 1920- *BioIn 16*
Pearce, Philippa 1921- *FemiCLE*
Pearce, Richard 1943- *ConTFT 8*
Pearce, Richard William, Jr. 1941- *St&PR 91*
Pearce, Robert Michael 1942- *BiDrAPA 89*
Pearce, Roy Harvey 1919- *WhoAm 90, WhoWrEP 89*
Pearce, Stephen Wade 1954- *WhoEmL 91*
Pearce, Susan M. *ODwPR 91*
Pearce, Theodore Delaney 1934- *WhoSSW 91*
Pearce, Tony Scot 1955- *IntWWM 90*
Pearce, William 1920- *WhoAm 90*
Pearce, William Joseph 1925- *WhoAm 90*
Pearce, William Martin 1913- *WhoAm 90*
Pearce-Percy, Henry Thomas 1947- *WhoWor 91*
Pearcey, Leonard Charles 1938- *IntWWM 90*
Peard, Frances Mary 1835-1923 *FemiCLE*
Peare, Catherine Owens 1911- *AuBYP 90*
Pearen, Allan Edward 1939- *St&PR 91*
Pearincott, Joseph Verghese 1929- *WhoE 91, WhoWor 91*
Pearl, Alan Howard *BiDrAPA 89*
Pearl, Carleton Day 1943- *St&PR 91*
Pearl, Daniel S *BiDrAPA 89*
Pearl, Eric *WhoWrEP 89*
Pearl, Helen Zalkan 1938- *WhoAmW 91*
Pearl, Julie Chaikin 1960- *WhoAmW 91*
Pearl, Leslie S. *BioIn 16*
Pearl, Marilyn *WhoAmA 91*
Pearl, Mary Corliss 1950- *WhoE 91*
Pearl, Melvin E. 1936- *WhoAm 90*
Pearl, Minnie *ConAu 129*
Pearl, Minnie 1912- *BioIn 16, WorAlBi*
Pearl, Norman H 1923- *BiDrAPA 89*
Pearl, Richard Alan 1943- *WhoE 91*
Pearl, Richard Maxwell 1913- *AuBYP 90*
Pearlman, Chester A, Jr. *BiDrAPA 89*
Pearlman, Chester Arthur, Jr. 1934- *WhoAm 90*
Pearlman, Daniel L. *ODwPR 91*
Pearlman, David Samuel 1934- *WhoAm 90*
Pearlman, Dorothy Rae Carter 1917- *WhoAmW 91*
Pearlman, Elliot Stuart 1941- *St&PR 91*
Pearlman, Emanuel R. *BioIn 16*
Pearlman, Etta S *WhoAmA 91*
Pearlman, Florence Sadoff 1928- *WhoAmW 91*
Pearlman, Henry 1895-1974 *WhoAmA 91N*
Pearlman, Ira Weiss 1921- *BiDrAPA 89*
Pearlman, Jack *BiDrAPA 89*
Pearlman, Jerry K. 1939- *St&PR 91*
Pearlman, Jerry Kent *BioIn 16*
Pearlman, Jerry Kent 1939- *WhoAm 90*
Pearlman, Jordan Arthur 1937- *St&PR 91*
Pearlman, Louis Jay 1954- *WhoE 91, WhoEmL 91, WhoWor 91*
Pearlman, Marianne Spencer 1945- *WhoE 91*
Pearlman, Mary Irene *BiDrAPA 89*
Pearlman, Meyer 1917- *St&PR 91*
Pearlman, Michael 1942- *BiDrAPA 89*
Pearlman, P.A. 1911- *St&PR 91*
Pearlman, Peter Steven 1946- *WhoE 91, WhoWor 91*
Pearlman, Richard Lee 1943- *BiDrAPA 89, WhoE 91*
Pearlman, Ronald Alan 1940- *WhoAm 90*
Pearlman, Sidney Burton 1940- *St&PR 91*
Pearlman, Sidney Simon 1932- *WhoAm 90*
Pearlman, Stuart 1939- *ODwPR 91*
Pearlman, Theodore 1933- *BiDrAPA 89*
Pearlman, Vicki *ODwPR 91*
Pearlman, William D. 1943- *WhoWrEP 89*
Pearlmutter, Anne Frances 1940- *WhoAmW 91*
Pearlmutter, Florence Nichols 1914- *WhoAmW 91*
Pearlson, Fredda S. 1949- *WhoWrEP 89*
Pearlson, Godfrey David 1950- *BiDrAPA 89, WhoE 91*
Pearlson, Susan E *BiDrAPA 89*
Pearlstein, Alix *WhoAmA 91*
Pearlstein, Arne Jacob 1952- *WhoEmL 91*
Pearlstein, Brenda 1943- *WhoAmW 91*
Pearlstein, Howard J. 1949- *ODwPR 91*
Pearlstein, Joel P. 1936- *St&PR 91*
Pearlstein, Leo 1920- *ODwPR 91*
Pearlstein, Philip 1924- *WhoAm 90, WhoAmA 91*
Pearlstein, Seymour 1923- *WhoAm 90, WhoAmA 91*
Pearlstein, Teri *BiDrAPA 89*
Pearlstine, Norman 1942- *St&PR 91, WhoAm 90, WhoE 91*
Pearman, Hal *ODwPR 91*
Pearman, Katharine K 1893-1961 *WhoAmA 91N*
Pearman, Mary Ann 1934- *WhoAmW 91*
Pearman, Reginald James 1923- *WhoAm 90, WhoE 91*
Pearman, Sara Jane 1940- *WhoAmA 91*
Pearman, William Robert 1930- *WhoAm 90*
Pearn, John Hemsley 1940- *WhoWor 91*
Pearn, Victor 1950- *WhoWrEP 89*
Pearne, George Reginald 1948- *WhoEmL 91, WhoWor 91*
Pears, Iain 1955- *ConAu 130*
Pears, Peter 1910-1986 *PenDiMP*
Pearsall, Edward R. 1954- *IntWWM 90*
Pearsall, George Wilbur 1933- *WhoAm 90*
Pearsall, Henry Batterman 1934- *St&PR 91, WhoAm 90*
Pearsall, Herbert Rowland 1949- *BiDrAPA 89*
Pearsall, Mary Helen 1948- *WhoSSW 91*
Pearsall, Otis Pratt 1932- *WhoAm 90*
Pearsall, Ronald 1927- *ConAu 31NR*
Pearsall, Rosellen Dee 1945- *WhoAmW 91*
Pearsall, Thomas Edward 1925- *WhoAm 90*
Pearsall, Willard H., Jr. 1923- *St&PR 91*
Pearsall, William Wright 1929- *St&PR 91*
Pearse, Gabriela 1963- *FemiCLE*
Pearse, John J 1911- *BiDrAPA 89*
Pearse, Madeline Isabel 1937- *WhoE 91*
Pearse, Robert Francis 1916- *WhoE 91*
Pearse, Warren Harland 1927- *WhoAm 90*
Pearson, Alan A. 1945- *St&PR 91*
Pearson, Albert Marchant 1916- *WhoAm 90*
Pearson, Albie 1934- *Ballpl 90*
Pearson, Allen Day 1925- *WhoAm 90*
Pearson, Andrew 1783-1872 *BioIn 16*
Pearson, Andrew Russell 1897-1969 *MajTwCW*
Pearson, Anthony John 1944- *WhoAm 90*
Pearson, Arliene Marian 1954- *WhoE 91*
Pearson, Becky Durham 1963- *WhoSSW 91*
Pearson, Belinda K. 1931- *St&PR 91*
Pearson, Belinda Kemp 1931- *WhoAm 90*
Pearson, Calvin Holbrook 1954- *WhoEmL 91*
Pearson, Carol Eve *BiDrAPA 89*
Pearson, Charles Thomas, Jr. 1929- *WhoAm 90*
Pearson, Clarence Edward 1925- *WhoAm 90*
Pearson, Clifton 1948- *WhoAmA 91*
Pearson, Clinton Charles 1950- *WhoEmL 91*
Pearson, Daniel Bester, III 1949- *BiDrAPA 89*
Pearson, Daniel Bester, Jr. 1915- *BiDrAPA 89*
Pearson, Daniel S. 1930- *WhoAm 90*
Pearson, David 1932- *ODwPR 91*
Pearson, David H. 1932- *WhoSSW 91*
Pearson, David Petri 1926- *WhoAm 90*
Pearson, David Waldron 1936- *BiDrAPA 89*
Pearson, Deborah Ann 1957- *WhoAmW 91*
Pearson, Diana 1956- *ODwPR 91*
Pearson, Donald Emanual 1914- *WhoAm 90*
Pearson, Donald Melvin 1917- *WhoAm 90*
Pearson, Douglas John 1950- *WhoE 91*
Pearson, Douglas N. *WhoAm 90*
Pearson, Drew *MajTwCW*
Pearson, Drew 1897-1969 *BioIn 16, WorAlBi*
Pearson, Emma Maria 1828?-1893 *FemiCLE*
Pearson, Frank Dixon 1945- *St&PR 91*
Pearson, Frederick Young 1941- *St&PR 91*
Pearson, Gary Dean 1952- *WhoEmL 91, WhoWor 91*
Pearson, Gary Thomas 1951- *St&PR 91*
Pearson, Gayle *AuBYP 90*
Pearson, Gayle 1947- *BioIn 16*
Pearson, George Burton, Jr. 1905- *WhoE 91*
Pearson, George D. 1919- *St&PR 91*
Pearson, Gerald Leon 1925- *WhoAm 90*
Pearson, Glen Thomas, Jr. *BiDrAPA 89*
Pearson, Glenn Ellis 1956- *BiDrAPA 89*
Pearson, H.J.S. 1921- *St&PR 91*
Pearson, Henry C 1914- *WhoAmA 91*
Pearson, Henry Charles 1914- *WhoAm 90*
Pearson, Ike 1917-1985 *Ballpl 90*
Pearson, James Blackwood, Jr. 1949- *WhoE 91*
Pearson, James Boyd, Jr. 1930- *WhoAm 90*
Pearson, James C 1930- *BiDrAPA 89*
Pearson, James Edward 1956- *WhoWor 91*
Pearson, James Eugene 1939- *WhoAm 90, WhoAmA 91*
Pearson, James Lawrence 1938- *St&PR 91*
Pearson, James Richard 1928- *St&PR 91*
Pearson, Janaan K. 1920- *St&PR 91*
Pearson, Jane 1734-1816 *FemiCLE*
Pearson, Jean Elizabeth 1945- *WhoWrEP 89*
Pearson, Jerry Allen 1936- *St&PR 91*
Pearson, Jim Berry 1924- *WhoAm 90*
Pearson, Jim Berry, Jr. 1948- *WhoSSW 91*
Pearson, Joanne M *BiDrAPA 89*
Pearson, John 1923- *WhoAm 90, WhoWor 91*
Pearson, John 1930- *SpyFic*
Pearson, John 1940- *WhoAmA 91*
Pearson, John Edgar 1927- *St&PR 91, WhoAm 90*
Pearson, John Edward 1932- *BiDrAPA 89*
Pearson, John R. Anthony 1930- *WhoWor 91*
Pearson, John S., III 1950- *St&PR 91*
Pearson, John Thomas 1944- *St&PR 91*
Pearson, Joseph T, Jr 1876-1951 *WhoAmA 91N*
Pearson, Judy *ODwPR 91*
Pearson, Jules Michael 1908- *WhoWrEP 89*
Pearson, Karl Gustav 1908- *WhoAm 90*
Pearson, Keith M. 1921- *St&PR 91*
Pearson, Kit *BioIn 16*
Pearson, Kristine Ann 1956- *WhoEmL 91*
Pearson, Larry Lester 1942- *WhoAm 90*
Pearson, Lester 1897-1972 *WorAlBi*
Pearson, Lionel Ignacius Cusack 1908-1988 *BioIn 16*
Pearson, Louise Mary 1919- *WhoAmW 91*
Pearson, Margit 1950- *St&PR 91*
Pearson, Margit Linnea 1950- *WhoAm 90*
Pearson, Mark Landell 1940- *WhoE 91*
Pearson, Michael Roy 1945- *BiDrAPA 89*
Pearson, Monte 1909-1978 *Ballpl 90*
Pearson, Nathan W. 1911- *St&PR 91*
Pearson, Nathan Williams 1911- *WhoAm 90*
Pearson, Nathan Williams 1951- *IntWWM 90*
Pearson, Norman 1928- *WhoAm 90, WhoE 91, WhoWor 91*
Pearson, Olof Hjalmer 1913- *WhoAm 90*
Pearson, P. A. 1939- *WhoAmW 91, WhoSSW 91*
Pearson, Paul A., Jr. 1955- *WhoE 91*
Pearson, Paul Brown 1905- *WhoAm 90*
Pearson, Paul Guy 1926- *WhoAm 90*
Pearson, Paul Hammond *WhoAm 90*
Pearson, Paul Holding 1940- *St&PR 91, WhoAm 90*
Pearson, Phillip Theodore 1932- *WhoAm 90*
Pearson, Ralph Gottfrid 1919- *WhoAm 90*
Pearson, Ralph M 1883-1958 *WhoAmA 91N*
Pearson, Richard Esher 1928- *WhoE 91*
Pearson, Richard J. 1925- *St&PR 91*
Pearson, Richard Jarvis 1925- *WhoAm 90*
Pearson, Richard Joseph 1938- *WhoAm 90*
Pearson, Robert *BioIn 16*
Pearson, Robert 1937- *WhoAm 90*
Pearson, Robert Edwin 1923- *WhoSSW 91*
Pearson, Robert Greenlees 1917- *WhoAm 90*
Pearson, Robert Lawrence 1939- *WhoAm 90*
Pearson, Robert Walter 1962- *WhoE 91*
Pearson, Roger 1927- *WhoAm 90*
Pearson, Roger Lee 1940- *WhoAm 90*
Pearson, Ronald Lee 1949- *St&PR 91*
Pearson, Roy Laing 1939- *WhoSSW 91*
Pearson, Roy Messer, Jr. 1914- *WhoAm 90*
Pearson, Scott Duff 1962- *WhoE 91*
Pearson, Stanley Peter 1926- *St&PR 91*
Pearson, Stephen Funk 1950- *IntWWM 90*
Pearson, Steven V. 1935- *St&PR 91*
Pearson, Susan 1946- *AuBYP 90*
Pearson, Susan K. 1954- *BiDrAPA 89*
Pearson, Susanna *FemiCLE*
Pearson, Suzanne Carol 1965- *WhoEmL 91*
Pearson, Sylvia Anne 1942- *WhoE 91*
Pearson, T R 1956- *ConAu 130*
Pearson, Thomas F. 1936- *St&PR 91*
Pearson, Thomas S 1949- *ConAu 132*
Pearson, Tonja Lee 1950- *WhoAmW 91*
Pearson, Tony Alan 1954- *WhoSSW 91*
Pearson, Tracey Campbell 1956- *SmATA 64 [port]*
Pearson, Wallace H. 1925- *St&PR 91*
Pearson, Walter Donald 1916- *WhoAm 90*
Pearson, Walter Howard 1946- *WhoEmL 91*
Pearson, Welton Dennis 1906- *WhoE 91*
Pearson, Willard 1915- *WhoAm 90*
Pearson, William James 1938- *St&PR 91*
Pearson, William Rowland 1923- *WhoE 91*
Pearson, William S 1926- *BiDrAPA 89*
Pearson, William Whildey 1925- *St&PR 91*
Peart, Jerry Linn 1948- *WhoAmA 91*
Peary, Robert E. 1856-1920 *WorAlBi*
Peary, Robert Edwin 1856-1920 *BioIn 16*
Peary, Stephen Kenneth 1939- *St&PR 91*
Peasback, David R. *WhoAm 90*
Peasback, David Raymond 1933- *St&PR 91*
Pease, Burton R. 1925- *St&PR 91*
Pease, Carol Helene 1949- *WhoAmW 91, WhoEmL 91*
Pease, Clarence Frank 1923- *WhoAm 90*
Pease, David G 1932- *WhoAmA 91*
Pease, David Gordon 1932- *WhoAm 90, WhoE 91*
Pease, Denise Louise 1953- *WhoAmW 91*
Pease, Donald James 1931- *WhoAm 90*
Pease, Doris Owen 1921- *WhoAmW 91*
Pease, Douglas Edward 1942- *St&PR 91*
Pease, Eleanor Thompson 1923- *WhoAmW 91*
Pease, Howard 1894-1974 *AuBYP 90*
Pease, James Lewis, Jr. 1921- *St&PR 91*

Pease, James Norman, Jr. 1921- *WhoAm 90*
Pease, John H. 1943- *St&PR 91*
Pease, Josephine Van Dolzen *AuBYP 90*
Pease, Julie Keller 1956- *BiDrAPA 89*
Pease, L. D. 1828-1892 *AmLegL*
Pease, Norma Maxine Feltz 1925- *WhoAmW 91*
Pease, Robert A. 1940- *St&PR 91*
Pease, Roger Fabian Wedgwood 1936- *WhoAm 90*
Pease, Steven L. 1943- *St&PR 91*
Pease, W.H. 1918- *St&PR 91*
Pease, Warren Stewart 1915- *St&PR 91*
Pease, Willard H. 1960- *St&PR 91*
Pease-Windy Boy, Janine *BioIn 16*
Peaslee, Amos J. 1923-1989 *BioIn 16*
Peaslee, Charlotte Hoffman 1931- *WhoE 91*
Peaslee, Margaret Mae Hermanek 1935- *WhoAm 90, WhoAmW 91*
Peaslee, Maurice Keenan 1950- *WhoEmL 91*
Peaslee, Richard Cutts 1930- *IntWWM 90, WhoE 91*
Peaslee, Robert L. *St&PR 91*
Peasley, Theodore Lucas 1926- *WhoAm 90*
Peat, Andrew Brian 1952- *WhoWor 91*
Peat, F. David 1938- *ConAu 132*
Peat, Kenneth L. 1947- *St&PR 91*
Peat, Laurey A. 1950- *ODwPR 91*
Peat, Leslie *BioIn 16*
Peat, Maclyn Ray 1927- *St&PR 91*
Peat, Randall Dean 1935- *WhoAm 90*
Peatick, George E *BiDrAPA 89*
Peatman, William Burling 1939- *WhoWor 91*
Peattie, Donald Culross 1898-1964 *AuBYP 90, BioIn 16*
Peattie, Elia 1862-1935 *FemiCLE*
Peattie, Lisa Redfield 1924- *WhoAm 90*
Peattie, Louise Redfield 1900-1965 *BioIn 16*
Peattie, Noel Roderick 1932- *WhoWrEP 89*
Peavey, Hartley Davis 1941- *WhoAm 90*
Peavler, Nancy Jean 1951- *WhoAmW 91*
Peavy, Dan Cornelius 1939- *WhoSSW 91*
Peavy, Homer Louis, Jr. 1924- *WhoWor 91*
Peavy, J.H. 1917- *St&PR 91*
Peavy, Lanny 1938- *St&PR 91*
Peavy, Linda 1943- *ConAu 31NR, WhoWrEP 89*
Peavy, Linda Sellers 1943- *BioIn 16*
Pebbles *BioIn 16*
Pebly, Robert Roth 1929- *St&PR 91*
Pecano, Donald Carl 1948- *WhoAm 90*
Pecar, Philip David 1930- *WhoAm 90*
Pecchenino, J Ronald 1932- *WhoAmA 91*
Pecci, Jose Danilo 1915- *WhoWor 91*
Pecen, Nancy E *BiDrAPA 89*
Pecevich, Mark *BiDrAPA 89*
Pech, Rose Ann 1942- *WhoAmW 91*
Pech-Petel, Christiane 1930- *WhoWor 91*
Pechauer, John Naeve 1937- *St&PR 91*
Peche, Dagobert 1887-1923 *PenDiDA 89*
Peche, Dale C 1928- *WhoAmA 91*
Peche de Madeleine, Auteur du *EncCoWW*
Pechersky, Aleksandr 1909- *BioIn 16*
Pechilis, William John 1924- *WhoAm 90*
Pechman, Joseph A. 1918-1989 *BioIn 16, ConAu 129*
Pechmann, James Christopher 1954- *WhoEmL 91*
Pechota, Vratislav Henry 1928- *WhoE 91*
Pechova, Al'beta *EncCoWW*
Pechstein, Henry P *BiDrAPA 89*
Pechter, Richard Scott 1945- *St&PR 91*
Pechter, Steven Jerome 1958- *WhoEmL 91*
Pechukas, Philip 1942- *WhoAm 90*
Pechulis, Ann 1948- *WhoAmW 91*
Peck, A. John, Jr. 1940- *St&PR 91*
Peck, Abraham 1945- *WhoAm 90*
Peck, Abraham Joseph 1946- *WhoEmL 91*
Peck, Alan H 1942- *BiDrAPA 89*
Peck, Andrew F. *St&PR 91N*
Peck, Andrew F. 1926-1989 *BioIn 16*
Peck, Anne Elliott Roberts 1935- *WhoAmW 91*
Peck, Anne Merriman 1884- *AuBYP 90*
Peck, Annie Smith 1850-1935 *BioAmW*
Peck, Arthur 1926- *BiDrAPA 89*
Peck, Austin H., Jr. 1913- *WhoAm 90*
Peck, Bernard Sidney 1915- *WhoAm 90*
Peck, Charles E, III 1920- *BiDrAPA 89*
Peck, Charles Edward 1925- *St&PR 91, WhoAm 90, WhoE 91*
Peck, Clair L., Jr. 1920- *St&PR 91*
Peck, Curtiss Steven 1947- *WhoEmL 91, WhoWor 91*
Peck, Dallas Lynn 1929- *WhoAm 90*
Peck, Daniel Farnum 1927- *WhoAm 90*
Peck, David Hill 1951- *WhoEmL 91*
Peck, David W. *NewYTBS 90 [port]*
Peck, David W 1902-1990 *ConAu 132*
Peck, David Warner 1902- *WhoAm 90*
Peck, David Warner, Jr. 1932- *St&PR 91*
Peck, Deana S. 1947- *WhoEmL 91*
Peck, Delbert E. 1924- *St&PR 91*
Peck, Dennis 1914- *IntWWM 90*
Peck, Dianne Kawecki 1945- *WhoAmW 91, WhoSSW 91*
Peck, Donald Vincent 1930- *WhoAm 90*
Peck, Dwight Clark 1945- *WhoWor 91*
Peck, Edward *WhoAmA 91N*
Peck, Edward Lionel 1929- *WhoAm 90*
Peck, Edwin Cady, Jr. 1942- *BiDrAPA 89*
Peck, Edwin Russell 1931- *WhoAm 90*
Peck, Ellie Enriquez 1934- *WhoAmW 91, WhoHisp 91*
Peck, Frances *FemiCLE*
Peck, Fred Neil 1945- *St&PR 91, WhoE 91, WhoEmL 91, WhoWor 91*
Peck, Fremont C. *BioIn 16*
Peck, Garnet Edward 1930- *WhoAm 90*
Peck, George *BioIn 16, NewYTBS 90*
Peck, George 1931-1990 *ConAu 130*
Peck, George Williams, IV 1932- *St&PR 91*
Peck, Gregory 1916- *BioIn 16, WhoAm 90, WhoWor 91, WorAlBi*
Peck, Hal 1917- *Ballpl 90*
Peck, Harris B 1915- *BiDrAPA 89*
Peck, James Edward 1907- *WhoAmA 91*
Peck, James Irving, IV 1948- *WhoEmL 91*
Peck, James Landis 1920- *St&PR 91*
Peck, James Mason, Jr. 1945- *WhoEmL 91*
Peck, James Stevenson 1923- *WhoAm 90*
Peck, Jane Cary 1932-1990 *ConAu 132*
Peck, Jane Clark 1946- *WhoE 91*
Peck, John Leslie 1947- *WhoSSW 91*
Peck, John Mason 1789-1858 *BioIn 16*
Peck, John S 1924- *BiDrAPA 89*
Peck, John W. 1913- *WhoAm 90*
Peck, John W. 1944- *St&PR 91*
Peck, John Weld 1944- *St&PR 91*
Peck, Joseph Richard 1947- *St&PR 91*
Peck, Judith 1930- *WhoAmA 91*
Peck, Kathryn Chandler 1954- *WhoWrEP 89*
Peck, Lee Barnes 1942- *WhoAmA 91*
Peck, Louis Provost 1918- *WhoAm 90, WhoE 91*
Peck, M. Scott *BioIn 16*
Peck, Marie Johnston 1932- *WhoAmW 91, WhoWrEP 89*
Peck, Maryly VanLeer 1930- *WhoAm 90*
Peck, Michael Alan 1949- *WhoEmL 91*
Peck, Morgan Scott *BioIn 16*
Peck, Morgan Scott 1936- *BiDrAPA 89*
Peck, Paul Arthur 1926- *WhoAm 90*
Peck, Phyllis Hainline 1921- *WhoAmW 91*
Peck, Ralph Brazelton 1912- *WhoAm 90*
Peck, Richard *BioIn 16*
Peck, Richard E 1936- *ConAu 31NR*
Peck, Richard Earl 1936- *WhoAm 90*
Peck, Richard Ellis 1946- *WhoSSW 91*
Peck, Richard Hyde 1941- *WhoSSW 91*
Peck, Richard Wayne 1934- *WhoAm 90, WhoWrEP 89*
Peck, Robert Curtiss 1957- *BiDrAPA 89*
Peck, Robert Daniel 1922- *WhoE 91*
Peck, Robert David 1929- *WhoAm 90*
Peck, Robert Newton 1928- *AuBYP 90, BioIn 16, ConAu 31NR, SmATA 62 [port]*
Peck, Robert Stephen 1953- *WhoEmL 91*
Peck, Russell A. 1933- *WhoAm 90*
Peck, Russell James 1945- *IntWWM 90*
Peck, Shiela Roy *ODwPR 91*
Peck, Susan 1948- *WhoAmW 91*
Peck, Templeton 1908- *WhoAm 90*
Peck, Thomas A. 1917- *St&PR 91*
Peck, Timberly Padden *ODwPR 91*
Peck, William Arno 1933- *WhoAm 90*
Peck, William Henry 1932- *WhoAmA 91*
Peck, Winifred 1882-1962 *FemiCLE*
Pecka *EncCoWW*
Peckar, Paul Joshua 1939- *BiDrAPA 89*
Peckauskaite, Marija *EncCoWW*
Peckenpaugh, Angela J. 1942- *WhoWrEP 89*
Peckenpaugh, Robert E. 1926- *St&PR 91*
Peckenpaugh, Robert Earl 1926- *WhoAm 90*
Pecker, Jean-Claude 1923- *WhoWor 91*
Peckerman, Joseph 1946-1988 *BioIn 16*
Peckford, Alfred Brian 1942- *WhoAm 90*
Peckham, Charles Allen 1949- *WhoEmL 91*
Peckham, Donald Eugene 1922- *WhoAm 90*
Peckham, Gary R. 1947- *St&PR 91*
Peckham, Howard Henry 1910- *WhoAm 90*
Peckham, John Munroe, III 1933- *WhoE 91*
Peckham, Margaret 1939- *IntWWM 90*
Peckham, Nicholas 1940- *WhoAmA 91*
Peckham, Richard *AuBYP 90*
Peckham, Robert 1785-1877 *BioIn 16*
Peckham, Robert Dabney 1946- *WhoSSW 91*
Peckham, Robert Francis 1920- *WhoAm 90*
Peckinpah, Betty *AuBYP 90*
Peckinpah, Sam 1925- *WorAlBi*
Peckinpah, Sam 1925-1984 *BioIn 16*
Peckinpaugh, Roger 1891-1977 *Ballpl 90 [port]*
Peckitt, William 1731-1795 *PenDiDA 89*
Pecknold, John Cecil 1941- *BiDrAPA 89*
Peckolick, Alan 1940- *WhoAm 90*
Peckosh, Paul Joseph 1945- *St&PR 91*
Pecora, Ferdinand 1882-1971 *BioIn 16*
Pecora, Robert 1938- *WhoAm 90*
Pecoraro, Frank J. 1934- *St&PR 91*
Pecorini, Domenico 1962- *WhoWor 91*
Pecorino, Donna Marie 1956- *WhoAmW 91*
Pecos, Bill *WhoWrEP 89*
Pecot, Charles Matthew 1934- *St&PR 91*
Pecot, David Edward 1939- *St&PR 91*
Pecsenye, Timothy 1952- *WhoEmL 91*
Pecsok, John Gilbert 1930- *WhoAm 90*
Pecsok, Robert Louis 1918- *WhoAm 90*
Pector, Elizabeth Ann 1958- *WhoAmW 91*
Peczkowski, James Joseph 1960- *WhoEmL 91*
Pedalino, Joseph S. 1938- *WhoE 91*
Pedalino, Michael Donald 1931- *WhoE 91*
Pedas, Theodore Alex 1936- *St&PR 91*
Peddicord, K. SiAnne 1948- *WhoSSW 91*
Peddicord, Roland Dale 1936- *WhoAm 90*
Peddle, M. *FemiCLE*
Pedemonte, Liliana M *BiDrAPA 89*
Pedemonte, Walter A *BiDrAPA 89*
Peden, Dona 1952- *WhoAmA 91*
Peden, Irene 1925- *BioIn 16*
Peden, Irene Carswell 1925- *WhoAm 90*
Peden, James Gwyn, Jr. 1953- *BiDrAPA 89*
Peden, James K, Jr. 1916- *BiDrAPA 89*
Peden, John Carl 1944- *St&PR 91*
Peden, Katherine Graham 1926- *WhoAm 90*
Peden, Robert F., Jr. 1911- *WhoSSW 91*
Pedersen, Arne Niels 1933- *WhoWor 91*
Pedersen, Bent 1942- *WhoWor 91*
Pedersen, Brent Martin 1937- *WhoE 91*
Pedersen, Brian 1949- *BiDrAPA 89*
Pedersen, Carolyn H 1942- *WhoAmA 91*
Pedersen, Charles 1904-1989 *AnObit 1989*
Pedersen, Charles J. 1904- *WorAlBi*
Pedersen, Charles J. 1904-1989 *BioIn 16*
Pedersen, Eigil Steen 1937- *WhoWor 91*
Pedersen, Ellis Hans 1948- *WhoWor 91*
Pedersen, Elsa Kienitz 1915- *AuBYP 90*
Pedersen, Erik 1941- *St&PR 91*
Pedersen, Gary 1953- *IntWWM 90*
Pedersen, Gary L. 1951- *St&PR 91*
Pedersen, Gilbert John 1909- *WhoAm 90*
Pedersen, Jean 1934- *WhoWrEP 89*
Pedersen, Jeffrey Thomas 1959- *WhoEmL 91*
Pedersen, Joan Shepherd 1948- *WhoE 91*
Pedersen, John Richard 1926- *St&PR 91*
Pedersen, Joyce Helena 1928- *WhoAmW 91*
Pedersen, Keld Fuhr 1940- *WhoWor 91*
Pedersen, Knud *DcScanL*
Pedersen, Knud-Erik 1955- *WhoWor 91*
Pedersen, Knud George 1931- *WhoAm 90*
Pedersen, Knut 1859-1952 *MajTwCW*
Pedersen, Lars Bo 1958- *WhoWor 91*
Pedersen, Leslie *BiDrAPA 89*
Pedersen, Miriam Swydan 1954- *WhoE 91*
Pedersen, Ole Albaek 1952- *WhoWor 91*
Pedersen, Paul 1935- *IntWWM 90*
Pedersen, Paul Richard 1935- *WhoAm 90*
Pedersen, Peer 1925- *St&PR 91*
Pedersen, Poul Ove 1937- *WhoWor 91*
Pedersen, Richard Foote 1925- *WhoAm 90*
Pedersen, Robert K. 1919- *St&PR 91*
Pedersen, Ronald P. 1941- *St&PR 91*
Pedersen, Stuart 1925- *St&PR 91*
Pedersen, Thor 1945- *WhoWor 91*
Pedersen, Wesley 1922- *ODwPR 91*
Pedersen, Wesley Niels 1922- *WhoAm 90, WhoE 91, WhoWor 91*
Pedersen, William *BioIn 16*
Pedersen, William Francis 1908- *WhoAm 90*
Pederson, Carrie Ann 1957- *WhoAmW 91*
Pederson, Cynthia Sue 1956- *WhoWrEP 89*
Pederson, Dennis F. 1938- *St&PR 91*
Pederson, Frank C. 1944- *St&PR 91*
Pederson, Jan Meyer *BiDrAPA 89*
Pederson, Jerome E. 1943- *St&PR 91*
Pederson, Mai 1960- *WhoAmW 91*
Pederson, Michele Marie 1962- *WhoAmW 91*
Pederson, Thoru Judd 1941- *WhoAm 90*
Pederson, Tony Weldon 1950- *WhoAm 90, WhoSSW 91*
Pederson, Vernon R. 1919- *WhoAm 90*
Pederson, William David 1946- *WhoEmL 91, WhoSSW 91, WhoWor 91*
Pederson, William F. *NewYTBS 90*
Pederson, William Marion *BiDrAPA 89*
Pederson-Krag, Geraldine H *BiDrAPA 89*
Pederson-Krag, Geraldine Huanayra 1901- *EncO&P 3*
Pediaditakis, Nicholas 1928- *BiDrAPA 89*
Pedian, Ara 1931- *St&PR 91*
Pedian, Haig 1924- *St&PR 91*
Pedicin, Michael, Jr. 1945- *WhoE 91*
Pedicini, Louis J. 1926- *St&PR 91*
Pedicini, Louis James 1926- *WhoAm 90*
Pedigo, James M 1933- *BiDrAPA 89*
Pedigo, Leon 1932- *St&PR 91*
Pedley, John Griffiths 1931- *WhoAm 90*
Pedlosky, Joseph 1938- *WhoAm 90*
Pedoe, Daniel 1910- *WhoAm 90, WhoWrEP 89*
Pedolsky, Alan Robert 1946- *WhoEmL 91, WhoWor 91*
Pedone, Joseph Lawrence 1947- *St&PR 91*
Pedota, Jack *BioIn 16*
Pedowicz, Lee Richard 1952- *WhoE 91*
Pedowitz, James M. 1915- *St&PR 91, WhoAm 90*
Pedowitz, Robin *BiDrAPA 89*
Pedraja, Rafael R. 1929- *WhoAm 90*
Pedram, Marilyn Beth 1937- *WhoAmW 91*
Pedras, Rui Manuel 1958- *WhoWor 91*
Pedraza, Angela *BiDrAPA 89*
Pedraza, Edgard *BiDrAPA 89*
Pedraza, Francisco 1933- *WhoAm 90*
Pedreno Munoz, Andres 1953- *WhoWor 91*
Pedrero Diez-Caneja, Paloma 1957- *EncCoWW*
Pedretti, Erica 1930- *EncCoWW*
Pedretty, Catherine Partain 1928- *WhoAmW 91*
Pedrique, Al 1960- *Ballpl 90*
Pedro I 1798-1834 *WorAlBi*
Pedro I, Emperor of Brazil 1798-1834 *BioIn 16*
Pedro II, Emperor of Brazil 1825-1891 *BioIn 16*
Pedro, Nicholas Julius, Jr. 1949- *WhoSSW 91*
Pedrotti, Franco 1934- *BioIn 16*
Pedrotti, Leno Stephano 1927- *WhoAm 90*
Pedroza, Javier Sergio 1953- *WhoHisp 91*
Pedulla, Joseph Peter 1954- *WhoE 91*
Peebler, Charles David, Jr. 1936- *WhoAm 90*
Peebler, Robert Paul 1947- *WhoSSW 91*
Peebles, Allene Kay 1938- *WhoAmW 91*
Peebles, Anthony Gavin Ian 1946- *IntWWM 90*
Peebles, Carter David 1934- *WhoAm 90*
Peebles, Charles Ross 1959- *IntWWM 90*
Peebles, David D. *BioIn 16*
Peebles, Donald L. 1938- *St&PR 91*
Peebles, E. B., III 1943- *WhoSSW 91*
Peebles, Florence 1874-1956 *BioIn 16*
Peebles, J M 1822-1922 *EncO&P 3*
Peebles, James David 1949- *WhoSSW 91*
Peebles, Laura Hebner 1956- *WhoSSW 91*
Peebles, Linda Mae 1950- *WhoAmW 91*
Peebles, Lucretia Neal Drane 1950- *WhoAmW 91, WhoWor 91*
Peebles, Marvin L. 1944- *WhoWrEP 89*
Peebles, Mary Josephine 1950- *WhoEmL 91*
Peebles, Peyton Zimmerman, Jr. 1934- *WhoSSW 91*
Peebles, Rex Charles 1953- *WhoSSW 91*
Peebles, Robert Alvin 1947- *WhoAm 90*
Peebles, Roy B 1899-1957 *WhoAmA 91N*
Peebles, Ruth Addelle 1929- *WhoAmW 91*
Peechatka, Walter Norman 1939- *WhoAm 90*
Peeden, Paula Zarbock 1958- *WhoAmW 91*
Peek, Charles B. *BiDrAPA 89*
Peek, Duane Francis 1951- *WhoSSW 91*
Peek, Elizabeth Taylor 1948- *WhoAm 90*
Peek, Merle 1938- *AuBYP 90*
Peek, Richard Maurice 1927- *IntWWM 90*
Peek, Samuel Millard 1956- *WhoSSW 91*
Peek, Walter Alva 1927- *St&PR 91*
Peek, Walter D., II 1958- *St&PR 91*
Peel, Deborah C 1951- *BiDrAPA 89*
Peel, Jesse R 1940- *BiDrAPA 89*
Peel, John 1939- *OxCPMus*
Peel, John David Yeadon 1941- *WhoWor 91*
Peel, Paul 1860-1892 *DcCanB 12*
Peel, Robert 1788-1850 *BioIn 16, WorAlBi*
Peel, William Laurie, Jr. 1952- *WhoSSW 91*
Peele, George 1558?-1597? *BioIn 16*
Peele, Jon R. 1943- *St&PR 91*
Peele, Kathleen O'Rourke *BioIn 16*
Peele, Roger 1930- *BiDrAPA 89, WhoAm 90, WhoWrEP 89*
Peele, Stanley 1932- *WhoSSW 91*
Peeler, Joseph David 1895- *WhoAm 90, WhoWor 91*
Peeler, Ray Doss, Jr. 1929- *WhoSSW 91*
Peeler, Scott Loomis, Jr. 1947- *WhoEmL 91*

Peeler, Stuart Thorne 1929- *St&PR 91, WhoAm 90*
Peeler, William James 1927- *WhoWor 91*
Peeling, William Brian 1930- *WhoWor 91*
Peemeecheekag *DcCanB 12*
Peeney, James Doyle 1933- *WhoAm 90, WhoE 91*
Peeples, Adam 1850?-1914 *AmLegL*
Peeples, Audrey Rone 1939- *WhoAmW 91*
Peeples, Barbara C. 1927- *ODwPR 91*
Peeples, Lisa Lea 1960- *WhoSSW 91*
Peeples, Maija 1942- *WhoAmA 91*
Peeples, Minor, Jr. 1921- *St&PR 91*
Peeples, Samuel A. 1917- *BioIn 16*
Peeples, William Dewey, Jr. 1928- *WhoAm 90, WhoSSW 91*
Peer, George J. 1925- *St&PR 91*
Peer, George Joseph 1925- *WhoAm 90*
Peer, Henk Wilhelmus 1947- *WhoWor 91*
Peerbhoy, Zehra M 1937- *BiDrAPA 89*
Peerce, Jan 1904-1984 *PenDiMP, WorAlBi*
Peerce, Larry *WhoAm 90*
Peerce, Stuart Bernard 1931- *WhoAm 90*
Peerhossaini, Mohammad Hassan 1951- *WhoWor 91*
Peerman, Dean Gordon 1931- *WhoAm 90*
Peers, Donald 1908-1973 *OxCPMus*
Peers, Michael Geoffrey 1934- *WhoAm 90*
Peerschke, Ellinor Irmagard Barbara 1954- *WhoAmW 91*
Peerthum, Satteeanund 1941- *WhoWor 91*
Peery, Sidney *St&PR 91N*
Peery, Thomas Martin 1909- *WhoAm 90*
Peery, Troy A., Jr. 1946- *St&PR 91*
Peeslake, Gaffer *ConAu 132, MajTwCW*
Peet, Bill *BioIn 16*
Peet, Charles D., Jr. 1935- *WhoAm 90*
Peet, Creighton 1899-1977 *AuBYP 90*
Peet, Creighton Houck 1938- *St&PR 91*
Peet, Greg J. 1953- *St&PR 91*
Peet, John *BioIn 16*
Peet, John Carlisle, Jr. 1928- *St&PR 91, WhoAm 90*
Peet, Rex Leroy 1949- *WhoSSW 91*
Peet, Richard Clayton 1928- *WhoWor 91*
Peet, William Bartlett 1915- *AuBYP 90*
Peete, Calvin *NewYTBS 90*
Peete, Rodney *BioIn 16*
Peete, William Pettway Jones 1921- *WhoAm 90*
Peeters, Clara 1594?-1657? *BioIn 16*
Peeters, Flor 1903-1986 *PenDiMP*
Peeters, Jacques Josef 1942- *WhoWor 91*
Peeters, Paul 1953- *IntWWM 90*
Peeters, Paul Alexander 1935- *WhoWor 91*
Peeters, Randall Louis 1945- *WhoEmL 91*
Peeters, Rene Adrien Marie-Louise 1933- *WhoWor 91*
Peeters, Theo J. 1937- *WhoWor 91*
Peetoom, Frans 1913- *WhoWor 91*
Peets, Orville 1884-1968 *WhoAmA 91N*
Peetz, Robert William 1947- *WhoSSW 91*
Peever, Arthur Jay 1933- *WhoAm 90*
Peevey, Michael R. 1938- *WhoAm 90*
Peevy, Donn Milliard 1949- *WhoSSW 91*
Peffer, Craig Dion 1934- *St&PR 91*
Pefley, Charles Saunders 1943- *WhoSSW 91*
Pegado, Carlos Alberto 1958- *WhoWor 91*
Pegeas, Ines Duke 1945- *WhoE 91*
Pegels, C. Carl 1933- *WhoAm 90*
Pegeron, Jean-Paul 1949- *BiDrAPA 89*
Pegg, David C. 1938- *St&PR 91*
Pegis, Anton George 1920- *WhoAm 90*
Pegle, Yolanda 1934- *EncCoWW*
Pegler, Westbrook 1894-1969 *Ballpl 90, BioIn 16*
Pegler, Wolfgang Otto 1938- *WhoWor 91*
Pegli, Yolanda *EncCoWW*
Pegram, George Braxton 1876-1958 *DcScB S2*
Pegram, John Braxton 1938- *WhoAm 90*
Pegreffi, Elisa *PenDiMP*
Peguero, Julio Antonio 1951- *WhoSSW 91*
Peguy, Charles 1873-1914 *WorAlBi*
Peguy, Charles Pierre 1873-1914 *BiDFrPL*
Pehfield, Janet Harbison 1916- *WhoAmW 91*
Pehl, Erich Ludwig 1939- *WhoWor 91*
Pehlke, Robert Donald 1933- *WhoAm 90*
Pehrson, Arthur G. 1929- *St&PR 91*
Pehrson, Barbara J. 1928- *WhoWrEP 89*
Pehrson, Gordon Oscar, Jr. 1943- *WhoAm 90*
Pehrson, Joseph Ralph 1950- *IntWWM 90*
Pehrson, Peter Alvin 1939- *St&PR 91*
Pei, I. M. 1917- *BioIn 16*
Pei, I M 1917- *CurBio 90 [port], News 90 [port], WhoAmA 91*
Pei, I. M. 1917- *WorAlBi*
Pei, Ieoh Ming 1917- *WhoAm 90, WhoWor 91*
Pei, Ming L. 1923- *WhoAm 90, WhoWor 91*
Peifer, Charles L. 1950- *St&PR 91*
Peifer, Chris Alan 1948- *St&PR 91, WhoAm 90*
Peiffer, Gerald M. 1948- *St&PR 91*
Peii, Ahmad Osni 1930- *WhoAmA 91*
Peiker, Edwin W., Jr. 1931- *St&PR 91*
Peil, James Francis 1934- *WhoAm 90*
Peimbert, Manuel 1941- *WhoAm 90*
Pein, Georg 1775-1834 *PenDiDA 89*
Peinado, Arnold B., Jr. 1931- *WhoHisp 91*
Peinado, Arnold Benicio, Jr. 1931- *WhoSSW 91*
Peinado, Luis Armando 1929- *WhoHisp 91*
Peinecke, Ralph George 1925- *St&PR 91*
Peinemann, Edith 1939- *IntWWM 90*
Peins, Rudolph M., Jr. 1929- *St&PR 91*
Peiperl, Adam 1935- *WhoAm 90, WhoAmA 91, WhoWor 91*
Peirce, Brooke 1922- *WhoAm 90*
Peirce, Carol Marshall 1922- *WhoAm 90*
Peirce, Carole 1943- *WhoAmW 91*
Peirce, Charles S. 1839-1914 *WorAlBi*
Peirce, David Lear 1928- *St&PR 91*
Peirce, Frederick Fairbanks 1953- *WhoEmL 91*
Peirce, George Leighton 1933- *WhoAm 90*
Peirce, Georgia Wilson 1960- *WhoAmW 91, WhoE 91, WhoWor 91*
Peirce, Henry Augustus 1808-1885 *BioIn 16*
Peirce, John Wentworth 1912- *WhoAm 90*
Peirce, John Wentworth 1946- *WhoEmL 91*
Peirce, Kenneth B. 1943- *St&PR 91*
Peirce, Kenneth B., Jr. 1943- *WhoAm 90*
Peirce, Neal R. 1932- *WhoAm 90, WhoE 91*
Peirce, Robert L. 1946- *ODwPR 91*
Peirce, Roger D. 1937- *St&PR 91*
Peirce, Waldo 1884-1970 *WhoAmA 91N*
Peirce, William R. 1934- *St&PR 91*
Peirotes, Yves Jean-Marie 1940- *WhoWor 91*
Peirson, Edward L. 1936- *St&PR 91*
Peisen, Conan Eric 1960- *WhoWor 91*
Peiser, Robert Alan 1948- *WhoAm 90*
Peisinger, Jon R. 1947- *St&PR 91*
Peisinger, Jon Robert 1947- *WhoAm 90*
Peisley, Mary 1717-1757 *FemiCLE*
Peisner, Arthur M. 1941- *St&PR 91*
Peisner, Arthur Mann 1941- *WhoAm 90*
Peiss, Clarence Norman 1922- *WhoAm 90*
Peissel, Michel 1937- *ConAu 30NR*
Peitersen, Erik 1931- *WhoWor 91*
Peitso, Martti Samuli 1924- *WhoWor 91*
Peitz, Earl Francis 1930- *St&PR 91*
Peitz, Heinie 1870-1943 *Ballpl 90*
Peixoto, Floriano 1839-1895 *BioIn 16*
Peixotto, Benjamin Franklin 1834-1890 *BioIn 16*
Peixotto, Ernest Dishman 1929- *WhoAm 90*
Peizer, Maurice Samuel 1912- *WhoE 91*
Pejovich, Ted *ConAu 131*
Pejovich, Theodore Peter 1945- *ConAu 131*
Pekar, Harvey 1939- *EncACom*
Pekar, Ronald Walter 1942- *WhoAmA 91*
Pekarek, Elizabeth Mary *BiDrAPA 89*
Pekarsky, Mel 1934- *BioIn 16, WhoAmA 91*
Pekarsky, Melvin Hirsch 1934- *WhoAm 90*
Pekich, Elizabeth Krams 1948- *WhoE 91*
Pekich, Stephen 1941- *St&PR 91*
Pekie, W.R. 1909- *St&PR 91*
Pekin, D. James 1938- *St&PR 91*
Pekinel, Guher 1953- *PenDiMP*
Pekinel, Suher 1953- *PenDiMP*
Pekkanen, John 1939- *BioIn 16*
Pekkanen, Toivo 1902-1957 *DcScanL*
Pekkanen, Tuomo Antero 1934- *WhoWor 91*
Pekny, Frank P. 1943- *St&PR 91*
Pekor, Allan J. *St&PR 91*
Pekow, Charles 1954- *WhoE 91*
Pekow, Eugene 1930- *St&PR 91, WhoAm 90*
Pekruhn, John Edward 1915- *WhoAm 90*
Pekrul, Kimberly Ann 1960- *WhoWrEP 89*
Pelaccio, Jack 1945- *BiDrAPA 89*
Peladeau, Marius Beaudoin 1935- *WhoAm 90, WhoAmA 91*
Peladeau, Pierre *BioIn 16*
Peladeau, Pierre 1925- *St&PR 91, WhoAm 90*
Pelaez, Amelia 1897-1968 *ArtLatA*
Pelaez, Armantina R. 1948- *WhoAmW 91, WhoWor 91*
Pelafigue, Lauren Brown 1954- *WhoSSW 91*
Pelandini, Thomas F. 1938- *ODwPR 91*
Pelandini, Thomas Francis 1938- *WhoAm 90*
Pelanek, Philip S. 1943- *St&PR 91*
Pelant, Robert Kenneth 1956- *WhoSSW 91*
Pelat, Roger-Patrice *BioIn 16*
Pelavin, Daniel Alan 1948- *WhoE 91*
Pelavin, Sol Herbert 1941- *WhoWor 91*
Pelayo, Marcelino Menendez y 1856-1912 *BioIn 16*
Pelc, Jo Ann 1956- *WhoAmW 91*
Pelchat, Rodney James 1953- *BiDrAPA 89*
Pelcyger, Iran 1937- *WhoE 91*
Pelcyger, Martin Edward 1943- *St&PR 91*
Pelczar, Michael Joseph, Jr. 1916- *WhoAm 90*
Pelczar, Otto 1934- *WhoWor 91*
Pelczarski, Karen Ann 1960- *WhoAmW 91*
Pele 1940- *BioIn 16, WhoAm 90, WorAlBi*
Peleckis, Anthony J. 1937- *St&PR 91*
Peled, Abraham 1945- *WhoAm 90*
Peled, David 1944- *St&PR 91*
Peled, Nina 1948- *WhoAmW 91*
Peleda, Lazdynu *EncCoWW*
Pelejo-Such, Purita P. 1938- *WhoAmW 91*
Pelekoudas, Chris 1918-1984 *Ballpl 90*
Pelepchan, Walter V. 1931- *St&PR 91*
Pelet, Jean-Jacques 1777-1858 *BioIn 16*
Pelham, Aviva 1948- *IntWWM 90*
Pelham, Donald 1927- *St&PR 91*
Pelham, Frances *BiDEWW*
Pelham, Peter 1695?-1751 *EncCRAm*
Peli, Pinchas Hacohen 1930-1989 *BioIn 16*
Pelikan, Anton *PenDiDA 89*
Pelikan, Emanuel *PenDiDA 89*
Pelikan, Franz *PenDiDA 89*
Pelikan, Franz Anton 1786-1858 *PenDiDA 89*
Pelikan, Jaroslav Jan 1923- *WhoAm 90*
Pelikan, Joseph *PenDiDA 89*
Pelino, David Franklin *BiDrAPA 89*
Pelissier, Edouard-Pierre 1937- *WhoWor 91*
Pelissier, H. G. 1874-1913 *OxCPMus*
Pelkey, Clarence E. 1935- *St&PR 91*
Pelkowski, Lawrence Joseph 1947- *St&PR 91*
Pell, Arthur Robert 1920- *WhoAm 90*
Pell, Claiborne 1918- *WhoAm 90, WhoE 91, WhoWor 91, WorAlBi*
Pell, David 1946- *St&PR 91*
Pell, Derek 1947- *WhoE 91*
Pell, Derinda Smith 1949- *WhoSSW 91*
Pell, Douglas Kent 1964- *WhoSSW 91*
Pell, Ernest Eugene 1937- *WhoAm 90, WhoWor 91*
Pell, John Alward 1926- *St&PR 91, WhoAm 90*
Pell, Jonathan Laurence 1949- *WhoAm 90*
Pell, Pyrma Daphne Tilton 1909- *WhoAmW 91*
Pell, Wilbur Frank, III 1945- *WhoEmL 91*
Pell, Wilbur Frank, Jr. 1915- *WhoAm 90*
Pella, Milton Orville 1914- *WhoAm 90*
Pellagrini, Eddie 1918- *Ballpl 90*
Pellan, Alfred 1906-1988 *BioIn 16*
Pelland, Gilles 1931- *WhoWor 91*
Pellathy, Stephan I *BiDrAPA 89*
Pellaton, Johny Edgar Roger 1936- *St&PR 91*
Pellatt, Apsley 1791-1863 *PenDiDA 89*
Pelle, Marie-Paule *BioIn 16*
Pellecchia, Martha L. 1933- *St&PR 91*
Pellechia, Nicholas D. 1945- *St&PR 91*
Pellegrin, Diana Jeanne 1945- *WhoAmW 91*
Pellegrin, Jonathan G. 1944- *St&PR 91*
Pellegrini, Adrian Joseph 1957- *BiDrAPA 89*
Pellegrini, Anna Maria 1944- *WhoAm 90*
Pellegrini, Benjamin J. 1935- *St&PR 91*
Pellegrini, Benjamin John 1935- *WhoAm 90*
Pellegrini, Bernadette 1966- *WhoAmW 91*
Pellegrini, Ernesto P. 1932- *IntWWM 90*
Pellegrini, Joe Louis 1931- *St&PR 91*
Pellegrini, Lora Marie 1960- *WhoAmW 91*
Pellegrini, Louis 1919- *St&PR 91*
Pellegrini, Maria 1939- *IntWWM 90*
Pellegrini, Maria 1947- *WhoAmW 91*
Pellegrini, Ralph Patrick 1933- *St&PR 91*
Pellegrini, Ruby Louise 1962- *WhoWrEP 89*
Pellegrini, Umberto 1930- *WhoWor 91*
Pellegrino, di Mariano *BioIn 16*
Pellegrino, Charles R. 1953- *WhoWrEP 89*
Pellegrino, Edmund Daniel 1920- *WhoAm 90*
Pellegrino, Lauren Mary 1963- *WhoAmW 91*
Pellegrino, Peter 1934- *WhoE 91*
Pellegrino, Victoria Grazziella 1962- *WhoAmW 91*
Pellepoix, Louis Darquier de 1897-1980 *BioIn 16*
Peller, Karol 1937- *WhoWor 91*
Peller, Marci Terry 1949- *WhoAmW 91*
Peller, Marion 1943- *WhoAmW 91*
Peller, Mary Ellen Cheney 1951- *WhoAmW 91*
Pellerin, Fernand Jean 1923- *WhoWor 91*
Pellerin, Patrick L., Jr. 1943- *ODwPR 91*
Pellerite, James John 1926- *IntWWM 90*
Pellerito, Lynn A. *ODwPR 91*
Pellerzi, Leo Maurice 1924- *WhoAm 90*
Pellet, John David 1949- *St&PR 91*
Pellet, Robert O. 1932- *ODwPR 91*
Pelletan, Camille Charles 1846-1915 *BiDFrPL*
Pelletier, Arthur Louis 1947- *St&PR 91*
Pelletier, Claude Henri 1941- *WhoE 91, WhoWor 91*
Pelletier, Claude Patrick 1933- *St&PR 91*
Pelletier, Denise 1929-1976 *OxCCanT [port]*
Pelletier, Gilles 1925- *OxCCanT*
Pelletier, Jean 1935- *WhoAm 90, WhoE 91*
Pelletier, John *PenDiDA 89*
Pelletier, John 1949- *St&PR 91*
Pelletier, Kenneth R. 1946- *NewAgE 90*
Pelletier, Laurie Anne 1962- *WhoSSW 91*
Pelletier, Louis Conrad 1940- *WhoAm 90*
Pelletier, Madeleine 1874-1939 *BiDFrPL*
Pelletier, Norma-Jean T. 1952- *St&PR 91*
Pelletier, Robert P.C. 1930- *St&PR 91*
Pelletier, S. William 1924- *WhoAm 90*
Pelletier, Stephen D. 1953- *St&PR 91*
Pelletier, Stephen Gerald 1955- *WhoE 91*
Pelletier, Wilfrid *PenDiMP*
Pelletreau, Robert Halsey 1935- *WhoAm 90, WhoWor 91*
Pellett, Kent Louis 1904- *WhoWrEP 89*
Pellett, Thomas Lawrence, II 1958- *WhoEmL 91*
Pellett, Thomas Rowand 1925- *St&PR 91, WhoAm 90*
Pellettier, John Ritchie 1945- *BiDrAPA 89*
Pellettieri, Michael Joseph 1943- *WhoAmA 91, WhoE 91*
Pelletz, S.J. 1932- *St&PR 91*
Pelleve, Denis-Pierre *PenDiDA 89*
Pelleve, Etienne-Dominique *PenDiDA 89*
Pellew, John C. 1903- *WhoAm 90*
Pellew, John Clifford 1903- *WhoAmA 91*
Pelli, Cesar 1926- *WhoAm 90, WhoAmA 91, WhoE 91*
Pelli, Moshe 1936- *ConAu 132*
Pellicano, Edward George 1942- *BiDrAPA 89*
Pellicciotti, Joseph Michael 1950- *WhoEmL 91*
Pellicciotti, Patricia M. *WhoAmW 91*
Pellicer, Carlos 1899-1977 *HispWr 90*
Pellico, Enrique Alejandro 1951- *WhoWor 91*
Pellicone, Marie *WhoAmA 91*
Pellicone, William 1915- *WhoAmA 91*
Pellington, J. Richard 1922- *WhoWrEP 89*
Pellioni, Paul Clement 1953- *St&PR 91*
Pellipario, Nicolo *PenDiDA 89*
Pellizzari, Edo D. 1942- *St&PR 91*
Pellman, Dennis E. 1947- *St&PR 91*
Pelloquin, Gary 1951- *St&PR 91*
Pelloutier, Fernand Leonce Emile 1867-1901 *BiDFrPL*
Pellow, Terri Ann 1954- *BiDrAPA 89*
Pellowe, Arthur John 1943- *BiDrAPA 89*
Pellowski, Anne 1933- *AuBYP 90*
Pellowski, Michael 1949- *BioIn 16*
Pelner, Norman *BiDrAPA 89*
Pelonero, Anthony Leonard *BiDrAPA 89*
Peloquen, James Lloyd, Jr. *BiDrAPA 89*
Peloquin, Alfred Leo 1921- *WhoAm 90*
Peloquin, Lori Jeanne 1957- *WhoAmW 91*
Peloquin, Robert Dolan 1929- *St&PR 91*
Pelosi, Anthony Andrew 1942- *BiDrAPA 89*
Pelosi, Charles J. 1945- *St&PR 91*
Pelosi, Evelyn Tyminski 1938- *WhoAmW 91*
Pelosi, Marino 1942- *St&PR 91*
Pelosi, Nancy 1941- *WhoAm 90, WhoAmW 91*
Peloso, John F. X. 1934- *WhoE 91*
Pelotte, Donald Edmond 1945- *WhoAm 90*
Pelou, Jean-Louis 1950- *WhoWor 91*
Pelphrey, Michael Wayne 1946- *WhoEmL 91*
Pels, Albert 1910- *WhoAmA 91*
Pels, Donald A. 1928- *St&PR 91*
Pels, Donald Arthur 1928- *WhoAm 90*
Pels, Gertrude Jaeckel *AuBYP 90*
Pels, Jule H. 1914- *St&PR 91*
Pelster, Patrick J. 1950- *St&PR 91*
Pelt, Alvin DeAundra 1956- *BiDrAPA 89*
Pelt, Joost *BioIn 16*
Pelta, Ely David *BiDrAPA 89*
Peltason, Jack Walter 1923- *WhoAm 90, WhoWor 91*
Peltcs, Raymond A. 1932- *St&PR 91*
Peltier, Donna *ODwPR 91*
Peltier, Eugene Joseph 1910- *WhoAm 90*
Peltier, Philippe 1937- *WhoWor 91*
Peltier, Robert Leonard 1939- *St&PR 91*
Peltier, William H. 1935- *St&PR 91*
Pelton, Elmer L. 1925- *St&PR 91*
Pelton, Elois Bleidt 1939- *WhoAmW 91*
Pelton, James Rodger 1945- *WhoAm 90, WhoSSW 91*
Pelton, John Forrester 1924- *WhoAm 90*
Pelton, John Stafford 1946- *St&PR 91*
Pelton, Richard McKay 1938- *St&PR 91*
Pelton, Russell Gilbert 1914- *WhoAm 90*

Pelton, Russell Meredith, Jr. 1938- *WhoAm 90*
Pelton, Terry Lynn 1950- *WhoAmW 91*
Pelton, Timothy John 1956- *WhoWrEP 89*
Pelton, Virginia Lue 1928- *WhoAmW 91*
Pelton, William Harvey 1946- *WhoWor 91*
Peltonen, Johannes Vihtori *DcScanL*
Peltonen, Keijo Kalervo 1939- *WhoWor 91*
Pelty, Barney 1880-1938 *Ballpl 90*
Peltz, Alan Howard 1944- *St&PR 91, WhoAm 90*
Peltz, Lisa 1962- *WhoAmW 91*
Peltz, Morris L 1930- *BiDrAPA 89*
Peltz, Nelson 1942- *WhoAm 90*
Peltz, Robert Dwight 1951- *WhoSSW 91*
Peltz, William L *BiDrAPA 89*
Peltzman, Barbara Ruth 1950- *WhoEmL 91*
Peltzman, Sam 1940- *WhoAm 90*
Peltzman, Steven Martin 1946- *St&PR 91*
Pelullo, Leonard A. *BioIn 16*
Peluso, Gerald William 1953- *St&PR 91*
Peluso, Marta E 1951- *WhoAmA 91*
Peluso, Renee Irene 1958- *WhoAmW 91*
Pelz, Caroline Duncombe *WhoAmW 91*
Pelz, Elayne Frances 1954- *WhoAmW 91*
Pelz, Herman H. 1931- *WhoE 91*
Pelz, Joel Thomas 1955- *WhoEmL 91*
Pelz, Robert L. 1918- *St&PR 91*
Pelz, Robert Leon 1918- *WhoAm 90*
Pelzel, Ronald George 1940- *St&PR 91*
Pelzer, Carol Cole 1944- *WhoSSW 91*
Pelzer, Gerald Edward 1938- *St&PR 91*
Pelzer, William 1947- *St&PR 91*
Pemberton, Bradley Powell 1952- *WhoEmL 91*
Pemberton, Charles Edward, Jr. 1942- *WhoSSW 91*
Pemberton, Dironda Lynn 1950- *WhoAmW 91*
Pemberton, Elizabeth Fay 1957- *WhoAmW 91*
Pemberton, Harrison Joseph 1925- *WhoAm 90*
Pemberton, James A. *St&PR 91*
Pemberton, Jeffery Kenneth 1931- *WhoAm 90*
Pemberton, Jeffrey K. 1931- *St&PR 91*
Pemberton, Jenny C. 1937- *St&PR 91*
Pemberton, Joanne Jody 1952- *WhoAmW 91*
Pemberton, John, III 1928- *WhoAm 90*
Pemberton, John de Jarnette, Jr. 1919- *WhoAm 90*
Pemberton, Joseph Despard 1821-1893 *DcCanB 12*
Pemberton, Lanny Vannard 1941- *St&PR 91*
Pemberton, Melissie Collins 1907- *WhoAmW 91*
Pemberton, Nan *ConAu 130*
Pemberton, Scott Bender 1951- *WhoAm 90*
Pemberton, Val R. 1925- *St&PR 91*
Pemberton, Vernal B. *BioIn 16*
Pemberton, William Erwin 1940- *WhoWrEP 89*
Pemberton, William L. 1926- *St&PR 91*
Pembroke, Anne Clifford, Countess of 1590-1676 *BioIn 16*
Pembroke, Eugene K. 1928- *St&PR 91*
Pembroke, John J. 1945- *St&PR 91*
Pembroke, Mary, Countess of 1561-1621 *FemiCLE*
Pembroke, Mary S Herbert, Countess of 1561-1621 *BioIn 16*
Pembroke, Richard Heber, Jr. 1910- *BiDrAPA 89*
Peminuit Paul, Jacques-Pierre 1800-1895 *DcCanB 12*
Pemmaraju, Uma Devi 1958- *WhoE 91*
Pempel, T.J. 1942- *ConAu 30NR*
Pemrick, Alfred E. 1929- *St&PR 91*
Pen, Eddie P. S. 1940- *WhoSSW 91*
Pena, Albar A. 1931- *WhoHisp 91*
Pena, Alejandro 1959- *Ballpl 90, WhoHisp 91*
Pena, Alvaro *WhoHisp 91*
Pena, Amado Maurilio 1943- *BioIn 16*
Pena, Amado Maurilio, Jr 1943- *WhoAmA 91*
Pena, Anthony 1953- *WhoE 91*
Pena, Antonio 1931- *WhoWor 91*
Pena, Antonio 1936- *WhoWor 91*
Pena, Antonio Francisco 1957- *WhoAm 90*
Pena, Carmen Aida 1941- *WhoHisp 91*
Pena, Celinda Marie 1961- *WhoHisp 91*
Pena, Daniel Steven 1945- *WhoSSW 91*
Pena, Domingo 1947- *WhoE 91*
Pena, Eduardo 1935- *WhoHisp 91*
Pena, Elena L 1937- *BiDrAPA 89*
Pena, Elizabeth 1959- *WhoHisp 91*
Pena, Englantina Canales 1927- *WhoHisp 91*
Pena, Ervie 1934- *WhoHisp 91*
Pena, Estela M. 1935- *WhoHisp 91*
Pena, Federico *BioIn 16*
Pena, Federico 1947- *WhoHisp 91*
Pena, Federico Fabian 1947- *WhoAm 90*
Pena, Fernando, Jr. 1937- *WhoHisp 91*
Pena, G Antonio 1935- *BiDrAPA 89*
Pena, George A. *WhoHisp 91*
Pena, Heather Maria 1955- *WhoAmW 91*
Pena, Hilario S. 1910- *WhoHisp 91*
Pena, John J., Jr. 1954- *WhoHisp 91*
Pena, Johnny 1939- *St&PR 91*
Pena, Jose 1942- *Ballpl 90*
Pena, Jose Manuel 1956- *BiDrAPA 89*
Pena, Juan-Paz 1942- *WhoHisp 91*
Pena, Larry *BioIn 16*
Pena, Manuel *WhoHisp 91*
Pena, Manuel, Jr. 1924- *WhoHisp 91*
Pena, Modesta Celedonia 1929- *WhoSSW 91*
Pena, Orlando 1933- *Ballpl 90*
Pena, Peco 1942- *IntWWM 90*
Pena, Ramon Richard 1947- *WhoE 91*
Pena, Raymundo *WhoHisp 91*
Pena, Raymundo Joseph 1934- *WhoAm 90, WhoSSW 91*
Pena, Richard 1948- *WhoEmL 91*
Pena, Roberto 1937-1982 *Ballpl 90*
Pena, Romeo Altamirano 1948- *WhoSSW 91*
Pena, Roque Saenz 1851-1914 *BioIn 16*
Pena, Steve Andrew 1955- *WhoHisp 91*
Pena, Teresita D 1935- *BiDrAPA 89*
Pena, Tonita 1895-1949 *WhoAmA 91N*
Pena, Tony 1957- *Ballpl 90, WhoHisp 91*
Pena, Victor A 1936- *BiDrAPA 89*
Pena-Ariet, Marie Elena *BiDrAPA 89*
Pena-Ariet, Rosendo V *BiDrAPA 89*
Pena Gomez, Jose Francisco *BioIn 16*
Pena-Ramos, Abelardo *BiDrAPA 89*
Penaherrera, Blasco Manuel 1934- *WhoWor 91*
Penaloza, Charles Aaron 1948- *WhoHisp 91*
Penaluna, James Elliot 1957- *WhoEmL 91*
Penalver, Rafael A. *BioIn 16*
Penalver Ballina, Rafael A. *BioIn 16*
Penaranda, Elizabeth Anne 1943- *WhoAmW 91*
Penaranda, Frank E. 1939- *WhoHisp 91*
Penasales, Sergio Villar 1935- *WhoWor 91*
Penasson, Pierre *PenDiMP*
Penati, Enrico 1940- *WhoWor 91*
Penbera, Joseph John 1947- *WhoAm 90*
Penberthy, William John, Jr. 1949- *WhoE 91*
Pence, Christopher Cyrus 1950- *WhoEmL 91*
Pence, George M., III 1961- *St&PR 91*
Pence, George M., Jr. 1924- *St&PR 91*
Pence, Jay C. 1950- *St&PR 91*
Pence, John Gerald 1936- *WhoAmA 91*
Pence, Margaret R. 1928- *St&PR 91*
Pence, Robert Dudley 1928- *WhoAm 90, WhoWor 91*
Pence, Robert V. 1928- *St&PR 91*
Pence, Robert W. 1954- *St&PR 91*
Pence, Ronald M *BiDrAPA 89*
Pencek, Mary Faith Russo 1958- *WhoAmW 91*
Pencheva, Stanka 1929- *EncCoWW*
Penchina, Steven *BioIn 16*
Penchoff, David Neil 1954- *WhoE 91*
Pencovic, Francis Heindswater *EncO&P 3*
Pencsak, Patricia Susanne 1963- *WhoAmW 91*
Penczner, Paul Joseph 1916- *WhoAmA 91*
Pendall, Maria Helga 1944- *WhoAmW 91*
Pendarves, Thomasina 1618- *BiDEWW*
Pendarvis, China Clark *ConAu 129*
Pendell, Judyth Wickett 1942- *WhoAmW 91, WhoE 91*
Pendell, Sue Davis 1946- *WhoAmW 91*
Pendell-Frantz, Peggy Metzka 1947- *WhoEmL 91*
Pender, David M. 1947- *St&PR 91*
Pender, Huey Paul 1936- *WhoSSW 91*
Pender, John Hurst 1930- *St&PR 91*
Pender, Lydia 1907- *SmATA 61 [port]*
Pender, Lydia Podger 1907- *AuBYP 90*
Pender, Marilyn 1899-1976 *SpyFic*
Pender, Pollard Eugene 1931- *St&PR 91, WhoAm 90*
Pender, Richard Anthony 1957- *WhoE 91*
Pender, Richard F. 1949- *ODwPR 91*
Penderecki, Krzysztof 1933- *IntWWM 90, PenDiMP A, WhoAm 90, WhoWor 91*
Pendered, Mary Lucy 1858-1940 *FemiCLE*
Pendergast, Charlotte Arla 1950- *St&PR 91*
Pendergast, Edward Gaylord 1938- *St&PR 91, WhoAm 90*
Pendergast, Robert W. 1939- *ODwPR 91*
Pendergast, Russell A. 1936- *ODwPR 91*
Pendergast, Warren Josef 1959- *BiDrAPA 89*
Pendergast, William Ross 1931- *WhoAm 90*
Pendergast-Savage, Linda *ODwPR 91*
Pendergraft, Lee Owen 1951- *WhoSSW 91*
Pendergraft, Norman Elveis 1934- *WhoAmA 91*
Pendergrass, Ewell Dean 1945- *WhoSSW 91*
Pendergrass, Henry Pancoast 1925- *WhoAm 90*
Pendergrass, John A. 1925- *WhoAm 90*
Pendergrass, John Ambrose 1925- *WhoE 91*
Pendergrass, John Ambrose 1954- *WhoEmL 91*
Pendergrass, John R. 1935- *St&PR 91*
Pendergrass, Karen *BioIn 16*
Pendergrass, Kenneth Lee 1952- *WhoEmL 91*
Pendergrass, Marshall L. 1946- *St&PR 91*
Pendergrass, Teddy *BioIn 16*
Pendergrass, Teddy 1950- *DrBlPA 90, EncPR&S 89, WhoAm 90*
Pendergrast, William Jefferson, Jr. 1946- *WhoSSW 91*
Penders, James Robert 1927- *St&PR 91*
Penders, Thomas M *BiDrAPA 89*
Pendexter, Harold E., Jr. 1934- *St&PR 91*
Pendle, Karin A. 1939- *IntWWM 90*
Pendlebury, Ralph 1929- *St&PR 91*
Pendleton, Andrea Kailo 1948- *WhoAmW 91, WhoE 91*
Pendleton, Barbara 1924- *St&PR 91*
Pendleton, Barbara Jean 1924- *WhoAm 90*
Pendleton, Brian Franklin 1950- *WhoEmL 91*
Pendleton, Carolyn M. 1941- *WhoAmW 91*
Pendleton, Carolyn Madge 1941- *St&PR 91*
Pendleton, Clarence M. 1930-1988 *AnObit 1988*
Pendleton, Clarence M., Jr. *BioIn 16*
Pendleton, Cornelius W. 1859-1936 *AmLegL*
Pendleton, David 1937- *DrBlPA 90*
Pendleton, Don *WhoWrEP 89*
Pendleton, Don 1927- *TwCCr&M 91*
Pendleton, Edmund *ODwPR 91*
Pendleton, Edmund 1721-1803 *EncCRAm*
Pendleton, Elmer Dean, Jr. 1927- *WhoAm 90, WhoE 91, WhoWor 91*
Pendleton, Eugene Barbour, Jr. 1913- *WhoAm 90*
Pendleton, Gail Ruth 1937- *WhoAmW 91, WhoE 91*
Pendleton, Gary Herman 1947- *WhoSSW 91*
Pendleton, George Cassety 1845-1913 *AmLegL*
Pendleton, George Hunt 1825-1889 *BioIn 16*
Pendleton, James Dudley 1930- *WhoWrEP 89*
Pendleton, James Lowrie 1931- *BiDrAPA 89*
Pendleton, Jim 1924- *Ballpl 90, BioIn 16*
Pendleton, Mary Caroline *WhoAmA 91*
Pendleton, Mary Catherine 1940- *WhoAmW 91*
Pendleton, Moses 1949- *BioIn 16*
Pendleton, Moses Robert Andrew 1949- *WhoAm 90*
Pendleton, Othniel Alsop 1911- *WhoWor 91*
Pendleton, Stephanie Barker 1948- *WhoE 91*
Pendleton, Sumner Alden 1918- *WhoAm 90*
Pendleton, Terry 1960- *Ballpl 90*
Pendleton, Thelma Brown 1911- *WhoAmW 91*
Pendleton, Thomas Hale 1936- *WhoSSW 91*
Pendleton, William B. 1949- *St&PR 91*
Pendleton, William M. 1931- *St&PR 91*
Pendleton-Parker, Billie Geraldine 1952- *WhoSSW 91*
Pendley, David Harold 1942- *St&PR 91*
Pendley, Donald L. 1950- *ODwPR 91*
Pendley, Donald Lee 1950- *WhoE 91*
Pendley, Steve S. 1937- *St&PR 91*
Pendley, William Tyler 1936- *WhoAm 90*
Pendower, Jacques 1899-1976 *SpyFic*
Pendrak, Joseph John 1929- *St&PR 91*
Pendrill, Viviana *WhoHisp 91*
Pendry, John Brian 1943- *WhoWor 91*
Pendzimaz, Robert Edward 1964- *WhoEmL 91*
Pene du Bois, William 1916- *BioIn 16*
Penebacker, John *BioIn 16*
Penedo, Luis Filipe do Cruzeiro G. 1941- *WhoWor 91*
Penegar, Kenneth Lawing 1932- *WhoAm 90*
Penelhum, Terence 1929- *EncPaPR 91*
Penelhum, Terence Michael 1929- *EncO&P 3*
Penelope, Julia 1941- *WhoE 91*
Penessiti, Samuel D. 1921- *St&PR 91*
Penetrante, Aristides E 1934- *BiDrAPA 89*
Penfield, Frederic Courtland 1855-1922 *BioIn 16*
Penfield, Robert Stephen 1946- *WhoE 91*
Penfold, Jamie 1961- *BiDrAPA 89*
Penfold, Marge 1942- *St&PR 91*
Peng Zhen 1902- *WhoWor 91*
Peng, Frederick Che-Ching 1934- *WhoWor 91*
Peng, Hsin 1952- *WhoE 91*
Peng, Kevin Kong-Hsiung 1943- *WhoWor 91*
Peng, Liang-Chuan 1936- *WhoSSW 91, WhoWor 91*
Pengel, Johan Adolf 1916- *BioIn 16*
Pengelly, John Henry 1935- *St&PR 91*
Penghlis, Thaao *ConTFT 8 [port]*
Pengidore, D.A. 1957- *St&PR 91*
Pengilly, Brian William 1930- *WhoAm 90*
Penglase, Frank Dennis 1940- *St&PR 91, WhoAm 90*
Penguin Cafe Orchestra *NewAgMG*
Penguins, The *EncPR&S 89*
Penhaligon, David Charles 1944-1986 *BioIn 16*
Penherski, Zbigniew 1935- *IntWWM 90*
Penhoet, Edward 1940- *WhoAm 90*
Penhorwood, Herbert Frederick 1937- *St&PR 91*
Penhune, John Paul 1936- *WhoAm 90*
Peniazek, Ziszko *BiDrAPA 89*
Penicaud, Jean *PenDiDA 89*
Penicaud, Jean, II *PenDiDA 89*
Penicaud, Jean, III *PenDiDA 89*
Penicaud, Leonard 1470?-1543 *PenDiDA 89*
Penicaud, Pierre *PenDiDA 89*
Peniche, Edward Albert 1925- *WhoSSW 91*
Penick, George Dial, Jr. 1948- *WhoAm 90*
Penick, Joe Edward 1920- *WhoAm 90*
Penick, John Edgar 1944- *WhoWrEP 89*
Penick, Michael Hayes 1944- *WhoAm 90*
Penick, Richard Joseph, Jr. 1947- *WhoSSW 91*
Penikett, Antony David John 1945- *WhoAm 90*
Penington, David Geoffrey 1930- *WhoWor 91*
Penington, Mary 1623-1682 *FemiCLE*
Penington, Mary 1625?-1682 *BiDEWW*
Penisten, Gary Dean 1931- *St&PR 91, WhoAm 90*
Penka, Eloise Marie 1960- *WhoAmW 91*
Penkava, Robert Ray 1942- *WhoAm 90, WhoWor 91*
Penkoff, Ronald Peter 1932- *WhoAmA 91*
Penkova, Reni 1935- *IntWWM 90*
Penland, Arnold Clifford, Jr. 1933- *IntWWM 90, WhoSSW 91*
Penland, John Thomas 1930- *WhoAm 90*
Penland, K.V. *St&PR 91*
Penland, Nancy Gallup *BiDrAPA 89*
Penland, Paul Stephan 1949- *WhoEmL 91*
Penley, David Allan 1952- *St&PR 91*
Penley, Stephen S. 1949- *St&PR 91*
Penman, Eugene John 1943- *St&PR 91*
Penman, Gordon Reese 1956- *WhoEmL 91*
Penman, Loren A. 1953- *WhoE 91*
Penman, Sheldon 1930- *WhoAm 90*
Penn Family *EncCRAm*
Penn, Anne 1899-1976 *SpyFic*
Penn, Anthony A. 1945- *St&PR 91*
Penn, Arthur 1852-1929 *BioIn 16*
Penn, Arthur 1922- *BioIn 16, ConAu 130, WorAlBi*
Penn, Arthur Hiller 1922- *WhoAm 90*
Penn, Charles Ehrig 1922- *St&PR 91*
Penn, E.W. *St&PR 91*
Penn, Edwin Allen 1939- *WhoAm 90*
Penn, Harold 1928- *St&PR 91*
Penn, Harold Ray, Jr. 1948- *WhoSSW 91*
Penn, Harry 1939- *BiDrAPA 89*
Penn, Hugh Franklin 1917- *WhoSSW 91*
Penn, Irving 1917- *WhoAm 90, WhoAmA 91*
Penn, Jean Cox 1944- *WhoWrEP 89*
Penn, Jeffrey Raymond *BiDrAPA 89*
Penn, Jeffrey Scott 1962- *WhoE 91*
Penn, John *ConAu 129, -31NR*
Penn, John 1729-1795 *EncCRAm*
Penn, John 1740-1788 *EncCRAm*
Penn, John Garrett 1932- *WhoAm 90*
Penn, Lynn Sharon 1943- *WhoAmW 91*
Penn, Michael *ConMus 4 [port]*
Penn, Patricia A. *WhoAmW 91*
Penn, Patricia W. 1953- *WhoAmW 91*
Penn, Pennetta *WhoWrEP 89*
Penn, Richard 1735-1811 *EncCRAm*
Penn, Ruth Bonn *AuBYP 90*
Penn, Sean *BioIn 16*
Penn, Sean 1960- *WhoAm 90, WorAlBi*
Penn, Stanley William 1928- *WhoAm 90*
Penn, Thomas 1703-1775 *EncCRAm*
Penn, William 1621-1670 *EncCRAm*
Penn, William 1644-1718 *EncCRAm [port], WhNaAH, WorAlBi*
Penna, Ignez Jansen *BiDrAPA 89*
Penna, Lawrence Arthur 1949- *WhoAm 90*
Penna, Manoel W D S *BiDrAPA 89*
Pennal, Hugh A 1920- *BiDrAPA 89*
Pennanen, Eila 1916- *DcScanL*
Pennario, Leonard 1924- *WhoAm 90*

Pennebaker, D. A. *BioIn 16*
Pennebaker, Donn Alan 1925- *WhoE 91*
Pennebaker, E. Vachel 1941- *St&PR 91*
Pennekamp, Frederick H. 1948- *St&PR 91*
Pennel, Lisa Spring Potts 1960- *WhoEmL 91*
Pennell, Abby Reed *BioAmW*
Pennell, Danny Joe 1945- *WhoEmL 91*
Pennell, Elizabeth Robins 1855-1936 *FemiCLE*
Pennell, Jack 1934- *St&PR 91*
Pennell, Nicholas 1939- *OxCCanT*
Pennell, Richard H. 1926- *St&PR 91*
Pennell, Willard H 1925- *BiDrAPA 89*
Pennell, William Brooke 1935- *WhoAm 90*
Penneman, Robert Allen 1919- *WhoAm 90*
Penner, Edgar 1933- *BiDrAPA 89*
Penner, Hans Henry 1934- *WhoAm 90*
Penner, Harold U 1923- *BiDrAPA 89*
Penner, Harry Harold Hamilton 1945- *WhoAm 90*
Penner, Helen 1937- *WhoWrEP 89*
Penner, Joe 1905-1941 *WorAlBi*
Penner, Jonathan David 1940- *WhoWrEP 89*
Penner, Klaus-Christian 1948- *St&PR 91*
Penner, Lucille Recht *AuBYP 90*
Penner, Peter 1925- *ConAu 129*
Penner, Roland 1924- *WhoAm 90*
Penner, Rudolph Gerhard 1936- *WhoAm 90*
Penner, Stanford Solomon 1921- *WhoAm 90*
Penner, Vernon DuBois 1939- *WhoWor 91*
Penner, William A. 1933- *WhoAm 90*
Pennewitz, David *PenDiDA 89*
Penney, Alexandra *WhoAmW 91*
Penney, Alphonsus Liguori 1924- *WhoAm 90*
Penney, Bradford Arnold 1950- *WhoE 91*
Penney, Charles Rand 1923- *WhoAm 90, WhoAmA 91, WhoE 91, WhoWor 91*
Penney, Christian Freeland N.F.G.T.E. 1908- *WhoWor 91*
Penney, Edmund F. 1926- *ConAu 132*
Penney, Edward Thomas 1935- *WhoAm 90*
Penney, Jacqueline 1930- *WhoAmA 91*
Penney, James 1910-1982 *WhoAmA 91N*
Penney, James C. 1875-1971 *WorAlBi*
Penney, Jeffrey Freeman 1954- *BiDrAPA 89*
Penney, Jerre Franklin 1951- *St&PR 91*
Penney, Linda Friedberg *ODwPR 91*
Penney, Nancy Sanford 1934- *WhoAmW 91*
Penney, R. Andrew 1955- *ODwPR 91*
Penney, Sherry Hood 1937- *WhoAm 90, WhoAmW 91, WhoE 91*
Penneys, Edith T 1920- *BiDrAPA 89*
Pennick, Loraine Anne 1954- *WhoAmW 91*
Penniman, Clara 1914- *WhoAm 90*
Penniman, Howard Rae 1916- *WhoAm 90, WhoWor 91*
Penniman, Nicholas Griffith, IV 1938- *St&PR 91, WhoAm 90*
Penniman, Richard *BioIn 16*
Penniman, W. David 1937- *BioIn 16, WhoAm 90*
Penning, Richard Ted 1955- *WhoEmL 91*
Penninger, Frieda Elaine 1927- *WhoAmW 91*
Penninger, William Holt, Jr. 1954- *WhoEmL 91*
Penningroth, Robert Paul 1939- *BiDrAPA 89*
Pennington, A. A. 1825-1885 *AmLegL*
Pennington, Ann 1894-1971 *OxCPMus*
Pennington, Beverly Melcher 1931- *WhoAmW 91*
Pennington, Bruce Carter 1932- *ODwPR 91*
Pennington, Christopher Royston 1946- *WhoWor 91*
Pennington, Clarence 1925- *St&PR 91*
Pennington, Dorothy Agnes 1944- *WhoSSW 91*
Pennington, Edward Joel 1858-1911 *EncABHB 4*
Pennington, Eliberto Escamilla 1958- *WhoHisp 91*
Pennington, Elizabeth 1732-1759 *FemiCLE*
Pennington, Ernest L. 1936- *ODwPR 91*
Pennington, Estill Curtis 1950- *WhoAmA 91*
Pennington, George Alvin 1947- *St&PR 91*
Pennington, Huey B., Jr. 1947- *St&PR 91*
Pennington, Jay C *BiDrAPA 89*
Pennington, Jeanne Rose 1955- *WhoAmW 91*
Pennington, John *PenDiMP*
Pennington, John E. 1942- *ODwPR 91*
Pennington, Lee 1939- *ConAu 31NR, LiHiK*
Pennington, Loyd Donald 1928- *St&PR 91*
Pennington, Mary Anne 1943- *WhoAm 90, WhoAmA 91, WhoSSW 91*
Pennington, Mary Helen *BiDrAPA 89*
Pennington, Phillip E 1923- *BiDrAPA 89*
Pennington, Richard M. 1926- *St&PR 91*
Pennington, Richard Maier 1926- *WhoAm 90*
Pennington, Robin Amie 1964- *WhoEmL 91*
Pennington, S. Wayne 1924- *ODwPR 91*
Pennington, Sally 1953- *WhoAmA 91*
Pennington, Sarah *FemiCLE*
Pennington, Theresa Sue 1948- *WhoEmL 91*
Pennington, William Michael 1957- *WhoSSW 91*
Pennisten, John William 1939- *WhoE 91, WhoWor 91*
Pennock, Donald William 1915- *WhoE 91, WhoWor 91*
Pennock, George T. 1912- *St&PR 91*
Pennock, George Tennant 1912- *WhoAm 90*
Pennock, Herb 1894-1948 *Ballpl 90 [port]*
Pennock, James Roland 1906- *WhoAm 90*
Pennoyer, A Sheldon 1888-1957 *WhoAmA 91N*
Pennoyer, Frances *BioIn 16*
Pennoyer, John 1949- *OxCCanT*
Pennoyer, Paul Geddes, Jr. 1920- *WhoAm 90*
Pennoyer, Peter *BioIn 16*
Pennoyer, Robert M. 1925- *WhoAm 90*
Pennoyer, Russell Parsons 1951- *St&PR 91, WhoEmL 91*
Pennuto, James William 1936- *WhoAmA 91*
Penny, Anne 1731-1784 *FemiCLE*
Penny, Aubrey John Robert 1917- *WhoAmA 91*
Penny, Brian John 1947- *IntWWM 90*
Penny, Charles Richard 1934- *St&PR 91, WhoAm 90*
Penny, Don *BioIn 16*
Penny, Donald Charles 1935- *WhoAmA 91*
Penny, Donald Gordon 1955- *WhoE 91*
Penny, Fanny 1847-1939 *FemiCLE*
Penny, Jimmy Autrey, Jr. 1933- *WhoSSW 91*
Penny, Josephine B. 1925- *WhoAmW 91*
Penny, Mary 1951- *IntWWM 90*
Penny, Roger Pratt 1936- *St&PR 91, WhoAm 90*
Penny, Timothy Joseph 1951- *WhoAm 90*
Penny, William 1809-1892 *DcCanB 12*
Pennybacker, Anna J. 1861-1938 *BioAmW*
Pennybacker, Miles 1901- *St&PR 91*
Pennyman, Mary *BiDEWW*
Pennyman, Mary 1630-1701 *FemiCLE*
Pennypacker, Henry Sutton 1937- *St&PR 91*
Pennypacker, James S 1951- *WhoAmA 91*
Penrod, James Wilford 1934- *WhoAm 90*
Penrod, Kenneth Earl 1916- *WhoAm 90*
Penrose, Charles, Jr. 1921- *WhoAm 90*
Penrose, Clement Biddle 1927- *St&PR 91*
Penrose, Cynthia C. 1939- *WhoAmW 91*
Penrose, Edith Tilton 1914- *WhoWor 91*
Penrose, Lee Miller 1907-1977 *BioIn 16*
Penrose, Roger *BioIn 16*
Penrose, Roland Algernon 1900-1984 *DcNaB 1981*
Penrose, Timothy Nicholas 1949- *IntWWM 90*
Penry, Nancy Sandberg 1955- *WhoAmW 91*
Penry, Walter P. 1933- *St&PR 91*
Pensack, Robert *BiDrAPA 89*
Pense, Alan Wiggins 1934- *WhoAm 90*
Pense, Kevin M.E. 1951- *St&PR 91*
Pension, Frank Anthony 1935- *WhoE 91*
Pension-Smith, Matthew Omololu 1945- *WhoWor 91*
Penske, Roger *BioIn 16*
Pensler, Sanford Nolan 1956- *St&PR 91*
Penson, Edward Martin 1927- *WhoAm 90, WhoSSW 91*
Pensyl, William Edward 1913- *WhoSSW 91*
Penta, Lily Kim 1960- *WhoAmW 91*
Pentak, Stephen 1951- *WhoAmA 91*
Pentcheff, Nicolas 1911- *WhoE 91*
Pentecost, Eric John 1956- *WhoWor 91*
Pentecost, Hugh 1903-1989 *BioIn 16, TwCCr&M 91*
Pentecost, Richard L *BiDrAPA 89*
Pentek, Marion Stanton 1931- *WhoAmW 91*
Pentelovitch, Robert Alan 1955- *WhoAmA 91*
Pentland, Barbara Lally 1912- *WhoAm 90*
Pentland, Barbarba 1912- *IntWWM 90*
Pentlarge, Victor H 1925- *BiDrAPA 89*
Pentler, Glenn Irving 1953- *St&PR 91*
Pentler, Irving Edward 1923- *St&PR 91*
Pentler, Marcelene Marion 1928- *St&PR 91*
Pentlin, Susan Lee 1947- *WhoAmW 91, WhoEmL 91*
Penton, David Noel 1941- *WhoSSW 91*
Penton, Howard A., Jr. 1931- *St&PR 91*
Penton, Lilymae 1933- *St&PR 91*
Penton, Lilymae Joanne 1933- *WhoAmW 91*
Pentony, Alfred B. 1926- *St&PR 91*
Penttila, Timo Jussi 1931- *WhoWor 91*
Penttinen, Risto Pekka K. 1942- *WhoWor 91*
Penty, Arthur Joseph 1875-1937 *BioIn 16*
Pentz, Donald Robert 1940- *WhoAmA 91*
Pentz, Gene 1953- *Ballpl 90*
Pentz, Judith Eve *BiDrAPA 89*
Pentz, Paul G 1935- *BiDrAPA 89*
Pentzien, Roger Jay 1946- *BiDrAPA 89*
Pentzlin, Karl Ludwig 1951- *WhoWor 91*
Penuelas, Marcelino Company 1916- *WhoAm 90*
Penwell, William Frank 1932- *St&PR 91, WhoAm 90*
Penz, Anton Jacob 1906- *WhoAm 90*
Penza, Patricia German 1957- *WhoAmW 91*
Penzel, Carl Gene 1934- *WhoWor 91*
Penzell, Andrew Wade 1945- *WhoSSW 91*
Penzer, Mark 1932- *WhoAm 90, WhoWrEP 89*
Penzias, Arno 1933- *WorAlBi*
Penzias, Arno Allan *BioIn 16*
Penzias, Arno Allan 1933- *St&PR 91, WhoAm 90, WhoE 91, WhoWor 91*
Penzien, Charles Henry 1945- *St&PR 91*
Penzien, Joseph 1924- *WhoAm 90*
Penzl, Herbert 1910- *WhoAm 90*
Peo-peo-mox-mox *WhNaAH*
Peo-peo-mux-mux *WhNaAH*
Peopeo Moxmox *WhNaAH*
Peopeomoxmox *WhNaAH*
Peoples, James Daniel 1936- *St&PR 91*
Peoples, James R. 1949- *St&PR 91*
Peoples, John, Jr. 1933- *WhoAm 90*
Peoples, John Arthur, Jr. 1926- *WhoAm 90*
Peoples, Thomas Edward 1915- *WhoAm 90*
Pep, Willie 1922- *BioIn 16*
Pepe, Dominick 1955- *St&PR 91*
Pepe, Donna T. *ODwPR 91*
Pepe, Frank A. 1931- *WhoAm 90, WhoE 91*
Pepe, John Michael 1939- *St&PR 91*
Pepe, Michael James 1938- *WhoAm 90*
Pepe, Raymomd A. 1942- *St&PR 91*
Pepe, Russell Charles 1954- *WhoE 91*
PEPECE *ConAu 131, HispWr 90*
Peper, Christian B. 1910- *St&PR 91*
Peper, Christian Baird 1910- *WhoAm 90, WhoWor 91*
Peper, George Frederick 1950- *WhoAm 90, WhoWrEP 89*
Peper, Martin C 1930- *BiDrAPA 89*
Pepera, John A. 1945- *St&PR 91*
Pepich, Bruce Walter 1952- *WhoAmA 91*
Pepin, Carolan *ODwPR 91, WhoAmW 91*
Pepin, David Anthony 1963- *WhoSSW 91*
Pepin, Debbie Neuhauser 1953- *WhoAmW 91*
Pepin, E. Lyle 1941- *St&PR 91*
Pepin, Jean-Luc 1924- *WhoAm 90*
Pepin, John Nelson 1946- *WhoE 91*
Pepin, Randall John 1953- *WhoEmL 91*
Pepin, Yvonne Mary 1956- *WhoAmW 91*
Pepine, Carl John 1941- *WhoAm 90*
Pepinsky, Pauline Nichols 1919- *WhoAmW 91*
Pepitone, Byron Vincent 1918- *WhoAm 90*
Pepitone, Joe 1940- *Ballpl 90*
Pepler, Hilary D. C. *BioIn 16*
Peplinski, James L. 1921- *St&PR 91*
Peplow, William Edward 1934- *St&PR 91*
Peppard, Blaylock A 1952- *WhoAmA 91*
Peppard, George 1928- *WhoAm 90, WorAlBi*
Peppe, Patrick V. *BioIn 16*
Peppel, Heidi Karen Ross 1960- *WhoEmL 91*
Pepper, Adeline *WhoAmW 91, WhoE 91*
Pepper, Allan Michael 1943- *WhoAm 90*
Pepper, Art 1925-1982 *BioIn 16, OxCPMus*
Pepper, Bert *BiDrAPA 89*
Pepper, Beverly 1924- *BiDWomA, BioIn 16, WhoAm 90, WhoAmA 91*
Pepper, Charles Hovey 1864-1950 *WhoAmA 91N*
Pepper, Claude *BioIn 16*
Pepper, Claude 1900-1989 *AnObit 1989*
Pepper, David M. 1949- *WhoAm 90, WhoEmL 91, WhoWor 91*
Pepper, Dorothy Mae 1932- *WhoAmW 91*
Pepper, Frank S 1910-1988 *SmATA 61*
Pepper, Franklin Jay 1935- *BiDrAPA 89*
Pepper, Gerald Edward 1938- *St&PR 91*
Pepper, Gordon Terry 1934- *WhoWor 91*
Pepper, Harry S. 1891-1970 *OxCPMus*
Pepper, Jane G. *BioIn 16*
Pepper, John Ennis 1938- *St&PR 91*
Pepper, John Ennis, Jr. 1938- *WhoAm 90*
Pepper, John Randolph 1954- *WhoE 91*
Pepper, John Roy 1937- *WhoWor 91*
Pepper, Jonathan Charles 1951- *WhoE 91*
Pepper, Kathleen Daly *WhoAmA 91*
Pepper, Laurin 1931- *Ballpl 90*
Pepper, Louis Henry 1924- *St&PR 91, WhoAm 90*
Pepper, Mary Janice 1942- *WhoAmW 91, WhoSSW 91, WhoWor 91*
Pepper, Max P *BiDrAPA 89*
Pepper, May S. 1868- *EncO&P 3*
Pepper, Michael 1942- *WhoWor 91*
Pepper, Pete *ODwPR 91*
Pepper, Ray 1905- *Ballpl 90*
Pepper, Robert *BioIn 16*
Pepper, Sam James 1949- *St&PR 91*
Pepper, Sanford R. *BiDrAPA 89*
Pepper, Stephen C 1891-1972 *ConAu 32NR*
Pepper, Thomas Mark 1939- *WhoE 91*
Pepper, Tom Hartwell 1943- *BiDrAPA 89*
Peppercorn, Lisa Margot 1913- *IntWWM 90*
Pepperdene, Margaret Williams 1919- *WhoAm 90*
Pepperell, William 1696-1759 *EncCRAm*
Peppers, Jeffrey Dwight 1951- *WhoSSW 91*
Peppers-Johnson, Mary Lynne 1960- *WhoWrEP 89*
Peppet, Russell Frederick 1939- *WhoAm 90*
Peppin, Gene Francis 1943- *St&PR 91*
Pepple, David Ralph 1943- *St&PR 91*
Pepple, Otis Darrell 1921- *St&PR 91*
Peppler, Charles A. 1945- *ODwPR 91*
Peppler, Michael Damien *BiDrAPA 89*
Peppler, Nils Fredrik Wilhelm 1923- *WhoAm 90*
Peppler, William Norman 1925- *WhoAm 90*
Pepples, Ernest 1935- *WhoAm 90*
Pepples, Ernest C. 1935- *St&PR 91*
Peprah, Robert Martin *BiDrAPA 89*
Pepski, Kathleen Patrice 1955- *St&PR 91*
Pepyne, Edward Walter 1925- *WhoAm 90*
Pepys, Samuel 1633-1703 *BioIn 16, DcLB 101 [port], WorAlBi*
Pera, Isabella 1945- *WhoAmA 91*
Peracchio, Aldo Anthony 1935- *WhoE 91*
Peradotto, John Joseph 1933- *WhoAm 90*
Perahia, Murray 1947- *BioIn 16, IntWWM 90, PenDiMP, WhoAm 90, WhoWor 91*
Peraino, Robert Anthony 1944- *WhoE 91*
Peraino, Roy T. 1928- *St&PR 91, WhoAm 90, WhoE 91*
Perakis, Emmanuel Adam 1958- *BiDrAPA 89*
Perales, Alonso S. 1898-1960 *BioIn 16*
Perales, Cesar A. 1940- *WhoHisp 91*
Perales, J Alberto 1932- *BiDrAPA 89*
Perales, Mercedes Judith *BiDrAPA 89*
Perales, Mirta Raya *WhoHisp 91*
Peralta, Frank Carlos 1946- *WhoHisp 91*
Peralta, Jose Ramon 1926- *WhoSSW 91*
Peralta, Manuel *BioIn 16*
Peralta, Pedro De 1584?-1666 *EncCRAm*
Peranteau, Michael 1951- *WhoAmA 91*
Perard, Victor S 1867-1957 *WhoAmA 91N*
Perates, John W. 1895-1970 *MusmAFA*
Peratrovich, Roy *BioIn 16*
Peratt, Karen Lee 1954- *WhoE 91*
Perault, Peter Zander 1947- *BiDrAPA 89*
Peraza, Oswaldo 1962- *Ballpl 90*
Perbeck, Leif Gustav 1944- *WhoWor 91*
Percas de Ponseti, Helena 1921- *WhoAm 90*
Percelay, Eliot Erwin 1932- *BiDrAPA 89*
Percher, Philippe Marie Loys 1935- *WhoWor 91*
Perchick, Morton Kenneth 1937- *St&PR 91*
Perchik, Benjamin Ivan 1941- *WhoSSW 91, WhoWor 91*
Perchorowicz, John Thomas 1948- *WhoEmL 91*
Percier, Charles *PenDiDA 89*
Percier, Charles 1764-1838 *BioIn 16*
Percival, Evelyn M. 1953- *WhoAmW 91*
Percival, Harold W. *NewAgE 90*
Percival, John 1683-1748 *BioIn 16*
Percival, Marilyn Tindall *BioIn 16*
Percival, Roger B. 1926- *St&PR 91*
Percival, S. Piers Bassnett 1937- *WhoWor 91*
Percoco, Thelma Ann 1935- *WhoSSW 91*
Perconte, Jack 1954- *Ballpl 90*
Percoto, Caterina 1812-1887 *EncCoWW*
Percus, Jerome Kenneth 1926- *WhoAm 90, WhoE 91*
Percy, Ann Buchanan 1940- *WhoAm 90, WhoAmA 91*
Percy, Anne *ODwPR 91*
Percy, Charles H. 1919- *BioIn 16, WorAlBi*
Percy, Charles Harting 1919- *AuBYP 90, WhoAm 90*

Percy, Elizabeth *BioIn 16*
Percy, Hugh Algernon *BioIn 16*
Percy, Keith Edward 1945- *WhoWor 91*
Percy, Rachel 1930- *SmATA 63 [port]*
Percy, Rick *BioIn 16*
Percy, Thomas 1729-1811 *BioIn 16, DcLB 104 [port]*
Percy, Walker 1916-1990 *BioIn 16, ConAu 131, CurBio 90N, DcLB Y90N [port], MajTwCW, NewYTBS 90 [port], News 90, WorAlBi*
Percy, William Alexander 1834?-1888 *AmLegL*
Perdieu, Sue *BioIn 16*
Perdigao, H Gunther 1931- *BiDrAPA 89*
Perdigao, Maria Madalena Azeredo 1923- *IntWWM 90*
Perdigo, Luisa Marina 1947- *WhoHisp 91*
Perdomo, Eduardo *WhoHisp 91*
Perdomo, Roberto 1934- *BiDrAPA 89*
Perdue, David A., Jr. 1949- *WhoSSW 91*
Perdue, Franklin P. *WhoAm 90*
Perdue, Franklin Parsons 1920- *ConAmBL*
Perdue, Garland Day 1926- *WhoAm 90*
Perdue, Georgia Persinos 1938- *WhoE 91*
Perdue, Hub 1882-1968 *Ballpl 90*
Perdue, James Everett 1916- *WhoAm 90*
Perdue, Mary Henderson 1941- *WhoAmW 91*
Perdue, Richard M. *ODwPR 91*
Perdue, Robert Edward, Jr. 1924- *WhoE 91*
Perdue, Sheri Lynn 1965- *WhoSSW 91*
Perdue, T. Ramon 1932- *St&PR 91*
Perdue, Theda 1949- *WhoAmW 91*
Perdunn, Richard Francis 1915- *WhoAm 90*
Perdutto, James Vincent 1928- *St&PR 91*
Perduyn, John P. 1939- *ODwPR 91, St&PR 91*
Pere, Rifat Mustafa *BiDrAPA 89*
Perea, Francisco 1830-1913 *BioIn 16*
Perea, Jaime *BiDrAPA 89*
Perea, Pedro 1852-1906 *BioIn 16*
Perea, Sylvia Jean 1941- *WhoHisp 91*
Perea, Toribio 1944- *WhoHisp 91*
Perec, Ann Marie 1964- *WhoAmW 91*
Perec, Georges 1936-1982 *BioIn 16, WorAu 1980 [port]*
Pereda, Delfina Haydee 1921- *WhoHisp 91*
Pereda, Francisco E 1923- *BiDrAPA 89*
Pereda, Francisco Eugenio 1923- *WhoHisp 91*
Pereda, John *WhoHisp 91*
Peregoff, Lee Steven 1959- *WhoSSW 91*
Peregoy, George Weems *MajTwCW*
Peregoy, Richard Pierce 1934- *WhoSSW 91*
Peregrin, Magda Elizabeth 1923- *WhoAmA 91*
Peregrina, La *EncCoWW*
Peregrinus De Maricourt, Petrus 1220?- *WorAlBi*
Perehudoff, William W 1919- *WhoAmA 91*
Pereira da Silva 1939- *WhoWor 91*
Pereira, A. Nicolau Gracias 1926- *WhoWor 91*
Pereira, Abraham *BioIn 16*
Pereira, Aristides Maria 1923- *WhoWor 91*
Pereira, Azamor Tenorio 1927- *WhoWor 91*
Pereira, Bartolomeu Simoes *BioIn 16*
Pereira, Carl W. 1939- *St&PR 91*
Pereira, Enrique A. *WhoHisp 91*
Pereira, I Rice 1901-1971 *WhoAmA 91N*
Pereira, Irene 1907-1971 *BiDWomA*
Pereira, Isabel T *BiDrAPA 89*
Pereira, Ismael *BioIn 16*
Pereira, Joao Torres 1953- *WhoWor 91*
Pereira, John 1950- *St&PR 91*
Pereira, Jorgina Antunes 1944- *WhoAmW 91*
Pereira, Jose Alfaia Pinto *WhoWor 91*
Pereira, Julio Cesar 1944- *WhoHisp 91*
Pereira, Kenneth John 1957- *WhoE 91*
Pereira, Linda Christine 1966- *WhoAmW 91*
Pereira, Milton Alan 1935- *BiDrAPA 89*
Pereira, Patricia Sue 1960- *WhoAmW 91*
Pereira, Paul J. 1946- *St&PR 91*
Pereira, Selwyn Jack *BiDrAPA 89*
Pereira, Sergio 1944- *WhoHisp 91*
Pereira, Teresinha Alves 1934- *WhoWrEP 89*
Pereira, Thales 1952- *BioIn 16*
Pereira-Ogan, Jorge Arturo *BiDrAPA 89*
Pereiras Garcia, Manuel 1950- *WhoHisp 91*
Perella, Joseph R. *BioIn 16, NewYTBS 90*
Perella, Joseph Robert 1941- *St&PR 91, WhoAm 90*
Perella, Susanne Brennan 1936- *WhoAm 90*
Perelle, Ira B. 1925- *WhoAm 90*
Perelli-Minetti, Antonio, Jr. 1922- *BiDrAPA 89*
Perellon, Carlos Diez 1957- *WhoE 91*
Perelman, Jeffrey *St&PR 91*
Perelman, Leon Joseph 1911- *St&PR 91, WhoAm 90, WhoE 91, WhoWor 91*
Perelman, Melvin 1930- *St&PR 91, WhoAm 90*
Perelman, Ronald Owen 1943- *BioIn 16, St&PR 91, WhoAm 90, WhoE 91*
Perelman, S J 1904-1979 *MajTwCW*
Perelman, S. J. 1904-1979 *WorAlBi*
Perelman, Samuel W. 1935- *St&PR 91*
Perelman, Sophie Schneebalg- 1914-1988 *BioIn 16*
Perelmuter-Perez, Rosa 1948- *WhoHisp 91*
Perelson, Alan Stuart 1947- *WhoEmL 91*
Perenchio, Andrew Jerrold 1930- *WhoAm 90*
Perenyi, Eleanor 1918- *BioIn 16*
Perera, Clifford C 1942- *BiDrAPA 89*
Perera, Everistus Winsley Nihal 1950- *WhoWor 91*
Perera, George A. 1911- *WhoAm 90*
Perera, Gihan Nissanka 1965- *WhoWor 91*
Perera, Hettiaratchige Lionel 1944- *WhoWor 91*
Perera, Lawrence Thacher 1935- *WhoAm 90, WhoWor 91*
Perera, Philip Daniel 1952- *BiDrAPA 89*
Perera, Thomas Biddle 1938- *WhoWrEP 89*
Perera Molina, Ramos 1939- *EncPaPR 91*
Perera-Pfeifer, Isabel *WhoHisp 91*
Peres, Asher 1934- *WhoWor 91*
Peres, Kenneth Edwin, Jr. *BiDrAPA 89*
Peres, Shimon 1923- *BioIn 16, PolLCME, WhoWor 91*
Peres Cortez, Carlos O *BiDrAPA 89*
Peress, Gilles 1946- *WhoAm 90, WhoAmA 91*
Peress, Maurice 1930- *WhoAm 90*
Peress, Mwafak S. 1937- *St&PR 91*
Peressini, Richard 1928- *St&PR 91*
Peressini, William E. 1956- *St&PR 91*
Peretsky, Burton 1946- *ODwPR 91*
Peretta, Amedeo 1949- *WhoWor 91*
Peretti, E.A. James 1943- *St&PR 91*
Peretti, Elsa *BioIn 16*
Peretti, Elsa 1940- *WhoAmW 91*
Peretti, Ettore Alex James 1913- *WhoAm 90*
Peretti, Marilyn Gay 1935- *WhoAmW 91*
Peretz, David 1933- *BiDrAPA 89*
Peretz, Isaac Leib 1852?-1915 *WorAlBi*
Peretz, Martin 1939- *WhoAm 90*
Perey, Bernard Jean Francois 1930- *WhoAm 90*
Pereyra-Suarez, Charles Albert 1947- *WhoEmL 91*
Pereyra-Suarez, Esther 1925- *WhoHisp 91*
Perez Celis *BioIn 16*
Perez Prado *BioIn 16*
Perez, Alan Garcia *BioIn 16*
Perez, Albert Pena 1940- *WhoHisp 91*
Perez, Alberto Julian 1948- *WhoHisp 91*
Perez, Alejandro 1940- *WhoHisp 91*
Perez, Alicia S. 1931- *WhoHisp 91*
Perez, Alonzo 1956- *WhoHisp 91*
Perez, Ana C. 1954- *WhoAmW 91*
Perez, Ana Maria *BiDrAPA 89*
Perez, Anna *BioIn 16, WhoAmW 91*
Perez, Arturo *WhoHisp 91*
Perez, Atilano V. 1937- *WhoSSW 91*
Perez, Barbara *BioIn 16*
Perez, Bernardo Matias 1939- *WhoHisp 91*
Perez, Betty Weiss *WhoAmA 91*
Perez, Carla *BiDrAPA 89*
Perez, Carlos 1950- *WhoHisp 91*
Perez, Carlos A. 1934- *WhoAm 90, WhoHisp 91*
Perez, Carlos Andres *BioIn 16*
Perez, Carlos Andres 1922- *News 90 [port], WhoWor 91*
Perez, Carlos Jesus 1959- *WhoHisp 91*
Perez, Carmen *WhoHisp 91*
Perez, Carmen Gonzalez 1956- *WhoHisp 91*
Perez, Carolyn Delfina 1951- *WhoHisp 91*
Perez, Cecilia C.A. 1946- *WhoAmW 91*
Perez, Clara Teresita *BiDrAPA 89*
Perez, Danny Edward 1963- *WhoHisp 91*
Perez, Dario 1941- *WhoHisp 91*
Perez, David Douglas 1937- *WhoHisp 91*
Perez, David William 1956- *WhoEmL 91*
Perez, Donna Jean 1949- *WhoSSW 91*
Perez, Edgar 1948- *WhoHisp 91*
Perez, Edgardo Luis 1951- *BiDrAPA 89*
Perez, Edward Lopez 1933- *WhoSSW 91*
Perez, Elio 1938- *WhoHisp 91*
Perez, Elva A. *WhoHisp 91*
Perez, Emiliano 1935- *WhoHisp 91*
Perez, Emilio 1940- *WhoHisp 91*
Perez, Enrique *BiDrAPA 89*
Perez, Enrique David 1934- *St&PR 91*
Perez, Enrique Manuel 1957- *WhoHisp 91*
Perez, Ernest 1957- *St&PR 91*
Perez, Esther Perurena 1927- *BiDrAPA 89*
Perez, Eustolia *WhoHisp 91*
Perez, F. Xavier 1956- *St&PR 91*
Perez, Francisco Luis 1950- *WhoHisp 91*
Perez, Francisco R. 1938- *WhoHisp 91*
Perez, Galo Rene 1923- *WhoWor 91*
Perez, George *WhoHisp 91*
Perez, Gerald S. A. 1943- *WhoAm 90*
Perez, Gilbert Bernal 1950- *WhoHisp 91*
Perez, Gilberto Guillermo 1943- *WhoHisp 91*
Perez, Ginger Sprinkle 1962- *WhoAmW 91*
Perez, Guido Oscar 1938- *WhoHisp 91*
Perez, Gustavo 1928- *WhoHisp 91*
Perez, Helio C. *BiDrAPA 89*
Perez, James Benito *WhoHisp 91*
Perez, Jane R. 1943- *WhoHisp 91*
Perez, Jeffrey Joseph 1952- *WhoSSW 91*
Perez, Jorge L. 1962- *WhoHisp 91*
Perez, Jorge Luis 1945- *WhoSSW 91*
Perez, Jorge Luis 1953- *WhoSSW 91*
Perez, Jose 1944- *BiDrAPA 89*
Perez, Jose Miguel *WhoHisp 91*
Perez, Jose R., Jr. 1948- *WhoHisp 91*
Perez, Joseph Dominique 1942- *WhoSSW 91*
Perez, Joseph E. 1946- *WhoHisp 91*
Perez, Josephine 1941- *BiDrAPA 89*
Perez, Juan *EncCRAm*
Perez, Juan Ovidio 1954- *WhoHisp 91*
Perez, Julie Anna 1961- *WhoAmW 91*
Perez, Julio E. 1958- *WhoHisp 91*
Perez, Julio Edgardo 1950- *WhoHisp 91*
Perez, Kathleen Irma 1951- *WhoAmW 91*
Perez, Laura Alonso 1962- *WhoHisp 91*
Perez, Leander *BioIn 16*
Perez, Leo 1958- *WhoHisp 91*
Perez, Leopoldo Luis 1946- *BiDrAPA 89*
Perez, Lillian 1957- *WhoAmW 91*
Perez, Lombardo *WhoHisp 91*
Perez, Louis Anthony 1939- *WhoE 91*
Perez, Louis G. 1946- *WhoHisp 91*
Perez, Luis 1928- *WhoHisp 91*
Perez, Luis 1940- *WhoHisp 91*
Perez, Luis A. 1947- *WhoHisp 91*
Perez, Luis Alberto *BiDrAPA 89*
Perez, Luis Alberto 1956- *WhoEmL 91, WhoHisp 91*
Perez, Lydia Tena 1955- *WhoHisp 91*
Perez, Manuel 1939- *WhoHisp 91*
Perez, Margaret 1949- *WhoHisp 91*
Perez, Maria E. 1928- *WhoHisp 91*
Perez, Mariano Martin 1964- *WhoHisp 91*
Perez, Mariano Ospina 1891-1976 *BioIn 16*
Perez, Mario 1940- *BiDrAPA 89, WhoE 91*
Perez, Mario Alberto 1958- *WhoHisp 91*
Perez, Maritza E. 1947- *WhoHisp 91*
Perez, Maritza Ivonne 1957- *WhoHisp 91*
Perez, Mark Richard 1951- *WhoSSW 91*
Perez, Marlene 1959- *WhoHisp 91*
Perez, Marta R. 1951- *WhoSSW 91*
Perez, Martin *WhoHisp 91*
Perez, Marty 1947- *Ballpl 90*
Perez, Mary A. 1934- *WhoHisp 91*
Perez, Melido 1966- *Ballpl 90*
Perez, Melido T. 1966- *WhoHisp 91*
Perez, Minerva 1955- *WhoHisp 91*
Perez, Nicasia Sibayan *BiDrAPA 89*
Perez, Oscar Ernesto *BiDrAPA 89*
Perez, Pascual 1957- *Ballpl 90*
Perez, Pascual Gross 1957- *WhoHisp 91*
Perez, Pedro L. *WhoHisp 91*
Perez, Pedro M *BiDrAPA 89*
Perez, Peter Manuel 1940- *WhoAm 90*
Perez, Rafael *WhoHisp 91*
Perez, Ralph Jose 1962- *WhoSSW 91*
Perez, Richard Lee 1940- *WhoHisp 91*
Perez, Richard Raymond 1934- *St&PR 91, WhoHisp 91*
Perez, Robert *WhoHisp 91*
Perez, Robert Michael 1953- *WhoE 91*
Perez, Romulo 1954- *WhoHisp 91*
Perez, Ronald A. 1949- *WhoHisp 91*
Perez, Salvador Stephen 1965- *WhoHisp 91*
Perez, Severo, Jr. 1941- *WhoHisp 91*
Perez, Stephen Manuel 1947- *WhoHisp 91*
Perez, Tony 1942- *Ballpl 90 [port], BioIn 16, WhoHisp 91*
Perez, Toraldo Casimiro, Jr. 1936- *WhoHisp 91*
Perez, Victor Martin 1956- *BiDrAPA 89*
Perez, Vincent 1938- *WhoAmA 91*
Perez, Vincent R. 1938- *WhoHisp 91*
Perez, Waldo D. 1946- *WhoHisp 91*
Perez, Yorkis Miguel 1967- *WhoHisp 91*
Perez-Aguilera, Jose Raul 1961- *WhoHisp 91*
Perez-Blanco, Horacio 1951- *WhoHisp 91*
Perez Buendia, Pedro 1937- *WhoWor 91*
Perez-Captoe, Juan M. 1938- *WhoHisp 91*
Perez-Colon, Roberto 1949- *WhoHisp 91*
Perez-Comas, Adolfo 1941- *WhoWor 91*
Perez-Cruet, Jorge 1931- *WhoWor 91*
Perez-Cruet, Jorge F 1931- *BiDrAPA 89*
Perez de Ayala, Ramon 1880-1962 *BioIn 16*
Perez de Cuellar, Javier 1920- *WhoWor 91, WorAlBi*
Perez del Rio, Jose Joaquin 1941- *WhoHisp 91*
Perez-Enriquez, Juan A *BiDrAPA 89*
Perez Esquivel, Adolfo 1931- *WhoWor 91*
Perez Farfante, Isabel C. 1916- *WhoAmW 91, WhoHisp 91*
Perez Ferreira, Emma Victoria 1925- *WhoWor 91*
Perez Firmat, Gustavo 1950- *WhoHisp 91*
Perez-Firmat, Gustavo Francisco 1950- *WhoAm 90*
Perez Galdos, Benito 1843-1920 *BioIn 16, HispWr 90*
Perez Gil Salazar, Eugenio 1923- *St&PR 91*
Perez-Gimenez, Juan Manuel 1941- *WhoAm 90, WhoSSW 91*
Perez-Gomez, Alberto 1949- *ConAu 130, HispWr 90*
Perez-Gutierrez, Mariano 1932- *IntWWM 90*
Perez-Hernandez, Manny *WhoHisp 91*
Perez Jimenez, Marcos 1914- *BioIn 16*
Perez-Lacey, Catalina M 1947- *BiDrAPA 89*
Perez-Lazo, Pedro Francisco 1934- *WhoWor 91*
Perez-Lopez, Rene 1945- *WhoHisp 91*
Perez-Marchand, Monelisa L 1918- *HispWr 90*
Perez Marin, Andres 1961- *WhoHisp 91*
Perez Mascayano, Jose Joaquin 1801-1889 *BioIn 16*
Perez-Mendez, Victor 1923- *WhoAm 90, WhoHisp 91*
Perez Mon, Coynthia 1958- *WhoHisp 91*
Perez-Montfort, Ruy 1951- *WhoWor 91*
Perez-Munoz, Ibzan 1950- *BiDrAPA 89*
Perez-Noy, Antonio L 1950- *BiDrAPA 89*
Perez-Reyes, Mario 1928- *BiDrAPA 89*
Perez-Rocha, Luz Marina *BiDrAPA 89*
Perez Sanchez, Alfonso Emilio 1935- *WhoWor 91*
Perez-Spencer, Eloisa 1935- *WhoAmW 91*
Perez-Stable, Maria Adelaida 1954- *WhoHisp 91*
Perez-Stansfield, Maria Pilar *WhoHisp 91*
Perez-Tulla, Maritza Ivonne 1957- *WhoHisp 91*
Perez y Mena, Andres I. 1948- *WhoHisp 91*
Perfetti, Peter James 1950- *St&PR 91*
Perfilio, Andrew Mark *BiDrAPA 89*
Pergam, Albert Steven 1938- *WhoAm 90*
Pergament, Lisa Diane 1960- *WhoAmW 91*
Pergander, Mary Sue 1955- *WhoAmW 91*
Pergola, Charles A. 1933- *St&PR 91*
Pergolesi, Giovanni Battista 1710-1736 *PenDiMP A*
Pergolesi, Michelangelo *PenDiDA 89*
Pergrin, David E. *BioIn 16*
Perhach, James Lawrence 1943- *WhoAm 90*
Perhacs, Marylouise Helen 1944- *WhoAmW 91*
Perham, Margery Freda 1895-1982 *DcNaB 1981*
Perham, Roy Gates 1916- *WhoAmA 91, WhoE 91, WhoWor 91*
Perham, Sidney 1819-1907 *AmLegL*
Peri, Barbara A. 1925- *WhoAmW 91*
Peri, Gabriel 1902-1941 *BiDFrPL*
Peri, Jacopo 1561-1633 *PenDiMP A*
Peri Rossi, Cristina 1941- *ConAu 131, HispWr 90*
Perich, Robert Charles 1954- *WhoEmL 91, WhoWor 91*
Pericles 499BC-429BC *BioIn 16*
Pericola, Julius Louis 1929- *St&PR 91*
Pericoli, Tullio 1936- *BioIn 16*
Perier, Yvon *WhoWor 91*
Peries, Lester James 1919- *BioIn 16*
Perigo, Willis Earl 1921- *St&PR 91*
Perigyi, Jo-Ann Katherine 1953- *WhoAmW 91*
Perilla *EncCoWW*
Perilla, Bob *ODwPR 91*
Perillo, Giulio 1946- *St&PR 91*
Perillo, Louis Joseph 1952- *BiDrAPA 89*
Perilman, Jules Bryan 1946- *WhoE 91*
Perilstein, Roger S 1950- *BiDrAPA 89*
Perilstein, William 1933- *St&PR 91*
Periman, Larry E. 1939- *St&PR 91*
Perin, Charles Henry, Jr. 1954- *WhoEmL 91*
Perin, Donald Wise, Jr. 1915- *WhoAm 90*
Perin, Reuben L., Jr. 1938- *St&PR 91*
Perin, Robert Jean 1947- *WhoE 91*
Perinchief, Robert Y. 1931- *IntWWM 90*
Perine, Martha L. 1948- *St&PR 91*
Perine, Maxine Harriet 1918- *WhoWor 91*
Perine, Robert Heath 1922- *WhoAmA 91*
Perini, David B. 1937- *St&PR 91, WhoAm 90*
Perini, Joseph Richard, Jr. 1930- *St&PR 91*
Perini, Patricia Paul 1944- *WhoAmW 91*

Perino Del Vaga 1501-1547 *IntDcAA 90, PenDiDA 89*
Perino, Gary R. 1953- *ODwPR 91*
Periola, Virginia K 1955- *BiDrAPA 89*
Periolat, Lee Michael *BiDrAPA 89*
Perissin, Aldo Arrigo 1938- *WhoWor 91*
Perito, John E *BiDrAPA 89*
Peritsky, Martin Michael 1946- *St&PR 91*
Peritz, Abraham D. 1940- *St&PR 91*
Peritz, Abraham Daniel 1940- *WhoAm 90*
Perivier, Jean-Claude 1946- *WhoWor 91*
Perkel, Robert Simon 1925- *WhoSSW 91*
Perkel, Steven Emory 1947- *WhoE 91*
Perkin, James Russell Conway 1928- *WhoAm 90*
Perkin, Joan 1926- *ConAu 131*
Perkin, Reginald Lewis 1930- *WhoAm 90*
Perkin, William Henry 1838-1907 *WorAlBi*
Perkins, A Alan 1915- *WhoAmA 91*
Perkins, A. William 1925- *WhoE 91*
Perkins, Ann 1915- *WhoAmA 91*
Perkins, Anne Scarlett 1937- *WhoAmW 91*
Perkins, Anthony *BioIn 16*
Perkins, Anthony 1932- *WhoAm 90, WorAlBi*
Perkins, B. Webster 1933- *St&PR 91*
Perkins, Benjamin 1904- *MusmAFA*
Perkins, Benjamin Franklin 1922- *St&PR 91*
Perkins, Beverly Ann 1953- *WhoAmW 91*
Perkins, Bill *ODwPR 91*
Perkins, Bobby Frank 1929- *WhoAm 90*
Perkins, Bradford 1925- *WhoAm 90*
Perkins, Bradley John 1960- *WhoE 91*
Perkins, Broderick 1954- *Ballpl 90*
Perkins, Bruce Devereau 1954- *WhoSSW 91*
Perkins, Carl 1932- *EncPR&S 89, OxCPMus*
Perkins, Carl Christopher 1954- *WhoAm 90, WhoSSW 91*
Perkins, Carol Louise 1946- *BiDrAPA 89*
Perkins, Carroll M. 1929- *St&PR 91*
Perkins, Carroll Mason 1929- *WhoAm 90*
Perkins, Charles *ODwPR 91*
Perkins, Charles Lincoln 1961- *WhoE 91*
Perkins, Cheryl Alice 1956- *WhoAmW 91*
Perkins, Chris Steele- 1947- *BioIn 16*
Perkins, Christina Wray 1946- *WhoAmW 91*
Perkins, Clarence James 1935- *WhoAmA 91*
Perkins, Constance M 1913- *WhoAmA 91*
Perkins, Cy 1896-1963 *Ballpl 90*
Perkins, David 1928- *WhoAm 90*
Perkins, David Dexter 1919- *WhoAm 90*
Perkins, David Layne, Sr. 1925- *WhoAm 90*
Perkins, David Miles 1949- *St&PR 91*
Perkins, David S. 1938- *ODwPR 91*
Perkins, Deborah Anne 1954- *WhoAmW 91*
Perkins, Dee Ann 1968- *WhoAmW 91*
Perkins, Dennis Edward 1944- *St&PR 91*
Perkins, Diana 1958- *BiDrAPA 89*
Perkins, Donald A. 1929- *St&PR 91*
Perkins, Donald S. 1927- *St&PR 91*
Perkins, Dorothy A. 1926- *WhoAm 90, WhoAmW 91*
Perkins, Dwight Clark 1914- *St&PR 91*
Perkins, Dwight Heald 1934- *WhoAm 90, WhoE 91*
Perkins, E. Lawrence 1927- *St&PR 91*
Perkins, Edward A. 1928- *WhoAm 90*
Perkins, Edward J. 1928- *WhoAm 90, WhoWor 91*
Perkins, Elizabeth *BioIn 16*
Perkins, Eric Ross 1950- *WhoE 91*
Perkins, Esther Roberta 1927- *WhoAmW 91, WhoWor 91*
Perkins, Eugene Oral 1923- *WhoWor 91*
Perkins, Faelton C., Jr. 1920- *St&PR 91*
Perkins, Floyd Jerry 1924- *WhoWor 91*
Perkins, Frances 1882-1965 *BiDrUSE 89, BioAmW, BioIn 16, WorAlBi*
Perkins, Frank C. 1941-1990 *BioIn 16*
Perkins, Frank Overton 1938- *WhoAm 90*
Perkins, Frederick Myers 1928- *WhoAm 90*
Perkins, G. Frederick 1936- *St&PR 91*
Perkins, G Holmes 1904- *WhoAmA 91*
Perkins, George Frederick, Jr. 1936- *WhoAm 90*
Perkins, George Holmes 1904- *WhoAm 90*
Perkins, George Walbridge 1862-1920 *BioIn 16*
Perkins, George William, II 1926- *WhoAm 90*
Perkins, Gordon P. 1937- *St&PR 91*
Perkins, Henry Crawford 1935- *WhoAm 90*
Perkins, Herbert Albert 1943- *BiDrAPA 89*
Perkins, Herbert Asa 1918- *WhoAm 90*
Perkins, Holly Ann 1955- *BiDrAPA 89*
Perkins, Homer G. 1916- *St&PR 91*
Perkins, J Morris 1929- *BiDrAPA 89*
Perkins, Jack Edwin 1943- *WhoAm 90*
Perkins, James Alfred 1911- *WhoAm 90*
Perkins, James Ashbrook 1941- *WhoWrEP 89*
Perkins, James Bradley 1954- *WhoSSW 91*
Perkins, James Caldwell 1952- *WhoE 91*
Perkins, James Eliab *NewYTBS 90*
Perkins, James Eliab 1905-1990 *BioIn 16*
Perkins, James Francis 1924- *WhoSSW 91, WhoWor 91*
Perkins, James Lewis 1942- *St&PR 91*
Perkins, James Patrick 1939- *WhoAm 90*
Perkins, James Wood 1924- *WhoAm 90*
Perkins, John Allen 1919- *WhoAm 90*
Perkins, John Bryan Ward- 1912-1981 *DcNaB 1981*
Perkins, John M. *AmLegL*
Perkins, John P. 1948- *St&PR 91*
Perkins, Judy Annette 1962- *WhoSSW 91*
Perkins, Julie Anne Rate 1935- *WhoAmW 91*
Perkins, K. 1926- *BioIn 16*
Perkins, Karon Elaine 1959- *WhoEmL 91*
Perkins, Ken *BioIn 16*
Perkins, Laures T. *St&PR 91*
Perkins, Lawrence Bradford 1907- *WhoAm 90*
Perkins, Lawrence Leonard 1918- *St&PR 91*
Perkins, Leeman Lloyd 1932- *IntWWM 90*
Perkins, Len *BioIn 16*
Perkins, Lois Bouthillier 1937- *WhoAmA 91*
Perkins, Lucy Fitch 1865-1937 *BioAmW*
Perkins, Lynn Marie 1963- *WhoAmW 91*
Perkins, Mable H 1880-1974 *WhoAmA 91N*
Perkins, Malcolm Donald 1914- *WhoAm 90*
Perkins, Marion 1908-1961 *WhoAmA 91N*
Perkins, Marlin 1905-1986 *BioIn 16*
Perkins, Marvin A. 1934- *St&PR 91*
Perkins, Marvin E 1920- *BiDrAPA 89*
Perkins, Marvin Earl 1920- *WhoAm 90, WhoWor 91*
Perkins, Mary Lynn 1954- *WhoAmW 91*
Perkins, Maxwell E. 1884-1947 *WorAlBi*
Perkins, Merle Lester 1919- *WhoAm 90, WhoWrEP 89*
Perkins, Michael 1942- *WhoWrEP 89*
Perkins, Nancy Jane 1949- *WhoAmW 91, WhoEmL 91, WhoWor 91*
Perkins, Nina Rosalie 1953- *WhoSSW 91*
Perkins, Paul Thomas 1939- *St&PR 91*
Perkins, Paula Michelle 1955- *WhoAmW 91*
Perkins, Peter 1930- *St&PR 91*
Perkins, Philip G 1952- *BiDrAPA 89*
Perkins, Philip R *WhoAmA 91N*
Perkins, R. Marlin 1905-1986 *AuBYP 90*
Perkins, Ralph Linwood 1914- *WhoAm 90*
Perkins, Ray 1941- *WhoAm 90, WhoSSW 91*
Perkins, Robert *BioIn 16*
Perkins, Robert Austin 1934- *WhoAm 90*
Perkins, Robert Eugene 1931 *WhoAmA 91*
Perkins, Robert James 1943- *BiDrAPA 89*
Perkins, Robert Louis 1931- *WhoAm 90*
Perkins, Robert P. 1952- *St&PR 91*
Perkins, Robert Peter 1952- *WhoAm 90, WhoEmL 91*
Perkins, Roger Allan 1943- *WhoE 91*
Perkins, Ronald Dee 1935- *WhoAm 90*
Perkins, Sam G. 1931- *St&PR 91*
Perkins, Scott *ODwPR 91*
Perkins, Stanley Lvan 1930- *St&PR 91*
Perkins, Steven Curtis 1949- *WhoEmL 91*
Perkins, Tammy Jo 1959- *WhoAmW 91*
Perkins, Thomas E. 1925- *St&PR 91*
Perkins, Thomas James 1932- *WhoAm 90*
Perkins, Thomas Keeble 1932- *WhoAm 90*
Perkins, Van L. 1930- *WhoAm 90*
Perkins, Wesley A 1925- *BiDrAPA 89*
Perkins, Whitney Trow 1921- *WhoAm 90*
Perkins, William Allan, Jr. 1925- *WhoAm 90*
Perkins, William H., Jr. 1921- *WhoAm 90*
Perkins, William Horace, Jr. 1931- *St&PR 91*
Perkins, William O'Neil 1815-1895 *AmLegL*
Perkins-Carpenter, Betty Lou 1931- *WhoAmW 91*
Perkins-Ripley, Lucy Fairfield *WhoAmA 91N*
Perkinson, Coleridge Taylor 1932- *DrBlPA 90*
Perkinson, Diana Agnes Zouzelka 1943- *WhoAm 90*
Perkinson, James Edward 1956- *St&PR 91*
Perkinson, Robert Ronald 1945- *WhoEmL 91*
Perko, Kenneth Albert, Jr. 1943- *WhoE 91*
Perko, Margaret Ruth 1915- *WhoWrEP 89*
Perkoff, Gerald Thomas 1926- *WhoAm 90*
Perkovic, Robert Branko 1925- *WhoAm 90, WhoWor 91*
Perkovich, Robert 1951- *WhoEmL 91*
Perkowitz, Sidney 1939- *WhoSSW 91*
Perkowski, Harry 1922- *Ballpl 90*
Perkowski, John F. *BioIn 16*
Perks, Barbara Ann Marcus 1937- *WhoAmW 91, WhoWor 91*
Perks, Marcia Kay 1949- *St&PR 91*
Perks, Mary Edna Wilkins 1940- *WhoSSW 91*
Perl, Charles G. 1942- *WhoSSW 91*
Perl, Eliezer 1945- *BiDrAPA 89*
Perl, Jeffrey Michael 1952- *WhoSSW 91*
Perl, Lila *AuBYP 90, BioIn 16*
Perl, Mark 1946- *BiDrAPA 89*
Perl, Martin Lewis 1927- *WhoAm 90*
Perl, Teri 1926- *WhoAmW 91*
Perlah, Philip Michael 1945- *WhoEmL 91*
Perlberg, Jules Martin 1931- *WhoAm 90*
Perlberg, William 1933- *St&PR 91*
Perle, Eugene Gabriel 1922- *WhoAm 90, WhoE 91*
Perle, George 1915- *IntWWM 90, WhoAm 90*
Perle, Richard Norman 1941- *WhoAm 90*
Perlemuter, Vlado 1904- *IntWWM 90, PenDiMP*
Perler, Arthur Harmon 1950- *WhoE 91*
Perler, Dennis Scott 1946- *WhoE 91*
Perles, Alfred 1897-1990? *ConAu 130*
Perless, Ellen 1941- *WhoAm 90, WhoAmW 91*
Perless, Robert 1938- *WhoAmA 91*
Perless, Robert L. 1938- *WhoAm 90*
Perley, J. Dwight 1911- *WhoSSW 91*
Perley, John Stephen 1937- *St&PR 91*
Perley, Moses Henry 1804-1862 *DcLB 99*
Perlgut, Mark R. 1942- *ODwPR 91*
Perli, Lisa *PenDiMP*
Perlick, Nancy Beth 1944- *WhoAmW 91*
Perlik, Charles *BioIn 16*
Perlik, William R. 1925- *WhoAm 90*
Perlin, Arthur Saul 1923- *WhoAm 90*
Perlin, Bernard 1918- *WhoAmA 91*
Perlin, Gary Laurence 1951- *St&PR 91*
Perlin, Louis *BiDrAPA 89*
Perlin, Marc Gerald 1948- *WhoEmL 91*
Perlin, Rae *WhoAmA 91*
Perlin, Ruth Rudolph *WhoAmA 91*
Perlin, Seymour *BiDrAPA 89*
Perlin, Seymour 1925- *WhoAm 90*
Perlis, Alan J. *NewYTBS 90*
Perlis, Alan J. 1922-1990 *BioIn 16*
Perlis, Donald M. 1941- *WhoAm 90*
Perlis, Michael Fredrick 1947- *WhoWor 91*
Perlis, Michael Stephen 1953- *WhoAm 90*
Perlis, Sanford J 1926- *BiDrAPA 89*
Perliss, Herbert 1936- *BiDrAPA 89*
Perll, Rita Dobel 1920- *BiDrAPA 89*
Perlman, Barry Bruce 1945- *BiDrAPA 89*
Perlman, Barry Stuart 1939- *WhoAm 90*
Perlman, Bennard Bloch 1928- *WhoAmA 91, WhoE 91*
Perlman, Brett Alan 1959- *WhoSSW 91*
Perlman, Daniel Hessel 1935- *WhoAm 90*
Perlman, David 1918- *WhoAm 90*
Perlman, David 1920- *WhoAm 90*
Perlman, David B. 1954- *St&PR 91*
Perlman, Ely 1913-1988 *BioIn 16*
Perlman, Hirsch *WhoAmA 91*
Perlman, I. Lee 1930- *St&PR 91*
Perlman, Itzhak 1945- *BioIn 16, IntWWM 90, PenDiMP, WhoAm 90, WhoE 91, WhoWor 91*
Perlman, Jerald Lee 1947- *WhoEmL 91*
Perlman, Joel Leonard 1943- *WhoAmA 91, WhoE 91*
Perlman, John Niels 1946- *WhoWrEP 89*
Perlman, John Richard 1956- *WhoSSW 91*
Perlman, Karen Ann 1959- *St&PR 91*
Perlman, Karen Susan 1943- *WhoAmW 91*
Perlman, Katherine Lenard 1928- *WhoAmW 91*
Perlman, Lawrence 1938- *St&PR 91, WhoAm 90, WhoWor 91*
Perlman, Leonard G. 1932- *WhoAm 90*
Perlman, Mark 1923- *WhoAm 90, WhoWrEP 89*
Perlman, Mark A 1950- *WhoAmA 91*
Perlman, Matthew Saul 1936- *WhoAm 90*
Perlman, Michael Ellis 1954- *WhoSSW 91*
Perlman, Michael S 1939- *BiDrAPA 89*
Perlman, Philip 1927- *St&PR 91*
Perlman, Radia *BioIn 16*
Perlman, Raymond 1923- *WhoAm 90*
Perlman, Rhea *BioIn 16, WhoAm 90, WhoAmW 91*
Perlman, Rhea 1948- *WorAlBi*
Perlman, Richard Brian 1951- *WhoEmL 91*
Perlman, Richard Wilfred 1923- *WhoAm 90*
Perlman, Ron *BioIn 16*
Perlman, Ron 1950- *ConTFT 8*
Perlman, Samuel *BioIn 16*
Perlman, Sandra Lee 1944- *WhoAmW 91*
Perlman, Scott David 1957- *St&PR 91*
Perlman, Sharon Toby 1948- *WhoAmW 91*
Perlman, Stanley M. 1930- *St&PR 91*
Perlman, Steven Mark 1953- *St&PR 91*
Perlman, Susan Gail 1950- *WhoWrEP 89*
Perlmuth, William Alan 1929- *WhoAm 90*
Perlmutter, Alan Jay 1947- *WhoEmL 91*
Perlmutter, Alvin Howard 1928- *WhoAm 90*
Perlmutter, Barbara S. 1941- *St&PR 91*
Perlmutter, David Michael 1938- *WhoAm 90*
Perlmutter, Diane F. 1945- *WhoAmW 91, WhoE 91, WhoWor 91*
Perlmutter, Donna *WhoAm 90, WhoAmW 91*
Perlmutter, Frank 1912- *WhoE 91*
Perlmutter, Ilisse Robin *BiDrAPA 89*
Perlmutter, Ilisse Robin 1951- *WhoE 91*
Perlmutter, Jack 1920- *WhoAm 90, WhoAmA 91, WhoWor 91*
Perlmutter, Jerome Herbert 1924- *WhoAm 90, WhoWor 91, WhoWrEP 89*
Perlmutter, Jona A 1934- *BiDrAPA 89*
Perlmutter, Louis 1934- *WhoAm 90*
Perlmutter, Marion 1948- *WhoAmW 91*
Perlmutter, Mark 1943- *St&PR 91*
Perlmutter, Mark Leeds 1949- *WhoEmL 91*
Perlmutter, Merle 1936- *WhoAmA 91*
Perlmutter, Nathan Martin 1947- *WhoE 91*
Perlmutter, Philip 1925- *WhoWrEP 89*
Perlmutter, Richard Alan 1949- *BiDrAPA 89*
Perlmutter, Ruben George 1958- *WhoE 91*
Perlmutter, William *AuBYP 90*
Perlo, Solomon 1944- *BiDrAPA 89*
Perloff, Harvey S 1915-1983 *ConAu 129*
Perloff, Joseph Kayle 1924- *WhoAm 90*
Perloff, Marjorie G 1931- *WhoAmA 91*
Perloff, Marjorie Gabrielle 1931- *WhoAm 90*
Perloff, Robert 1921- *WhoAm 90, WhoWor 91*
Perloff, Susan *ODwPR 91*
Perlongo, Daniel James 1942- *WhoAm 90*
Perlov, Dadie 1929- *WhoAm 90*
Perlow, Katharina Rich *WhoAmA 91*
Perlowitz, Harry *BiDrAPA 89*
Perlowitz, Valerie Wienslaw 1962- *WhoAmW 91*
Perls, Frank 1910-1975 *WhoAmA 91N*
Perls, Klaus G 1912- *WhoAmA 91*
Perls, Laura 1905-1990 *NewYTBS 90*
Perlstadt, Sidney Morris 1907- *WhoAm 90*
Perlstein, Abraham P 1926- *BiDrAPA 89*
Perlstein, Jill *BioIn 16*
Perlstein, Paul Mark 1947- *WhoEmL 91*
Perlstein, Robert *BioIn 16*
Perlstein, Shaul 1941- *WhoE 91*
Perlstein, Susan S 1946- *BiDrAPA 89*
Perlsweig, Mark Steven 1961- *BiDrAPA 89*
Perlswig, Ellis A 1923- *BiDrAPA 89*
Perman, Esther D. *ODwPR 91*
Perman, Gerald 1923- *BiDrAPA 89*
Perman, Gerald Paul 1947- *BiDrAPA 89, WhoE 91*
Perman, Joshua M 1916- *BiDrAPA 89*
Perman, Norman Wilford 1928- *WhoAm 90*
Permar, Mary Elizabeth 1956- *WhoAmW 91, WhoEmL 91*
Permesly, Lester Scott 1945- *BiDrAPA 89*
Permut, Robert 1945- *BiDrAPA 89*
Permut, Stephen Robert 1945- *WhoE 91*
Permutt, Solbert 1925- *WhoAm 90*
Perna, Doris *BiDrAPA 89*
Perna, Frank, Jr. 1938- *WhoAm 90*
Perna, Nicholas S. 1942- *St&PR 91*
Perna, Thomas Joseph 1950- *St&PR 91*
Perna-Elias, Frank 1952- *WhoE 91*
Pernel, Orrea 1906- *IntWWM 90*
Pernety, Antoine Joseph 1716-1801 *EncO&P 3*
Perni, Jaya Ramaiah *BiDrAPA 89*
Perni, Raja Kumari *BiDrAPA 89*
Pernick, Alan S. 1936- *St&PR 91*
Pernick, Leonard Jacob 1929- *St&PR 91*
Pernick, Sandra Rose 1944- *WhoAmW 91*
Pernoll, Martin Lester 1939- *WhoWrEP 89*
Pernot-Masson, Anne-Catherine 1955- *WhoWor 91*
Pernotto, James Angelo 1950- *WhoAmA 91*
Pernotto, Stephen John 1947- *St&PR 91*
Pernsteiner, Carol Ann *WhoAmW 91*
Pero, Joseph John 1939- *St&PR 91, WhoAm 90*
Perocier-Aguirre, Marieanne *BiDrAPA 89*
Peron, Eva 1919-1952 *BioIn 16*
Peron, Eva Duarte De 1919-1952 *WorAlBi*
Peron, Isabel *BioIn 16*
Peron, Isabel 1931- *WomWR*
Peron, Isabel De 1931- *WorAlBi*
Peron, Juan Domingo 1895-1974 *BioIn 16*

Peron, Yves-Marie 1939- *BioIn 16*
Peron Sosa, Juan 1895-1974 *WorAlBi*
Peronard, Guy 1942- *St&PR 91*
Perone, Denise M *BiDrAPA 89*
Perone, Joseph Peter 1950- *WhoWor 91*
Perosa, Sergio 1933- *WhoWor 91*
Perosch, Tony Anthony George 1930- *WhoWor 91*
Perot, H. Ross 1930- *BioIn 16*
Perot, H Ross 1930- *ConAmBL*
Perot, H. Ross 1930- *WhoAm 90*
Perot, Henry Ross 1930- *WhoSSW 91, WhoWor 91*
Perotti, Anthony Robert 1958- *WhoE 91*
Perotto, Richard 1941- *St&PR 91*
Perouse, Jean-F de Galaup, Comte de la 1741-1788? *EncCRAm*
Perovic, Aleksandar *BiDrAPA 89*
Perovich, Robert Michael *BiDrAPA 89*
Perovsky-Petrovo-Solovovo, Count *EncO&P 3*
Perovsky-Petrovo-Solovovo, Count 1868-1954 *EncPaPR 91*
Perowne, Barry 1908-1985 *TwCCr&M 91*
Perowne, Stewart 1901-1989 *AnObit 1989, BioIn 16*
Perpeet, Wilhelm Edmund Ernst 1915- *WhoWor 91*
Perpetua, Saint *BioIn 16*
Perpetua, Vibia 181?-203 *EncCoWW*
Perpich, Joseph G 1941- *BiDrAPA 89*
Perpich, Rudy *BioIn 16*
Perpich, Rudy George 1928- *WhoAm 90, WhoWor 91*
Perr, Herbert M 1921- *BiDrAPA 89*
Perr, Irwin 1928- *WhoAm 90*
Perr, Irwin N 1928- *BiDrAPA 89*
Perr, Jane Victoria 1955- *BiDrAPA 89*
Perr, Julius P. 1931- *St&PR 91*
Perranoski, Ron 1936- *Ballpl 90*
Perrault, Charles 1628-1703 *AuBYP 90, BioIn 16, WorAlBi*
Perrault, Dorothy Ann Jacques 1937- *WhoAmW 91*
Perrault, Georges Gabriel 1934- *WhoWor 91*
Perrault, Patsy Ann 1939- *WhoAmW 91*
Perrault, Pierre 1957- *WhoAmA 91*
Perrault, Raymond 1926- *WhoAm 90*
Perrault, Richard P 1916- *BiDrAPA 89*
Perreal, Jean 1455?-1530 *IntDcAA 90*
Perreard, Suzanne Louise Butler *AuBYP 90*
Perreault, Gerard 1940- *BiDrAPA 89*
Perreault, Jeanne 1929- *WhoAm 90, WhoAmW 91, WhoE 91*
Perreault, John 1937- *WhoAmA 91*
Perreault, Paul Frederick 1929- *St&PR 91*
Perreault, William Daniel, Jr. 1948- *WhoAm 90*
Perreiah, Alan Richard 1937- *WhoAm 90*
Perrella, James Elbert 1935- *St&PR 91*
Perret, Donna C 1949- *WhoAmA 91*
Perret, Ferdinand 1888-1960 *WhoAmA 91N*
Perret, Gene *BioIn 16*
Perret, Joseph A. 1929- *St&PR 91*
Perret, Joseph Aloysius 1929- *WhoAm 90*
Perret, Nell Foster 1916-1986 *WhoAmA 91N*
Perreten, Frank Arnold 1927- *WhoWor 91*
Perrett, Betty Eileen Patricia 1922- *IntWWM 90*
errett, Danielle Gillian 1958- *IntWWM 90*
errett, Galen J 1875-1949 *WhoAmA 91N*
errett, Jon Brian 1940- *St&PR 91*
erretta, Nancy Vrooman 1940- *WhoAmW 91*
erretti, Peter N., Jr. 1932- *WhoE 91*
errewe, Pamela Lynn 1955- *WhoAmW 91*
rri, Carol Sue 1946- *WhoWrEP 89*
rri, Colleen 1936- *BioIn 16*
rri, Joseph 1949- *St&PR 91*
rriand, Charlotte 1903- *PenDiDA 89*
rrich, Jerry Robert 1947- *WhoAm 90, WhoEmL 91*
rrick, Cynthia Alice 1962- *WhoAmW 91*
rricone, Bernard 1929-1990 *NewYTBS 90*
rricone, Joseph Stephan 1945- *St&PR 91*
rriello, David G. 1939- *St&PR 91*
rrier, Donald Glenn 1945- *WhoAm 90*
rrier, Henri Francis Marc 1914- *WhoWor 91*
rrigo, Lyle Donovan 1930- *WhoWor 91*
rriman, A. E., Mrs. *EncO&P 3*
rrin, Alice 1867-1934 *FemiCLE*
rrin, Bill K. 1938- *WhoAm 90, WhoWor 91*
rin, C Robert 1915- *WhoAmA 91*
rin, Charles John 1940- *WhoWor 91*
rin, Charles Robert 1915- *WhoE 91*
rin, Donald William 1947- *St&PR 91*
rin, Edward Burton 1931- *WhoAm 90*
rin, Gail 1938- *WhoAm 90*
rin, Helen Joyce 1915- *BiDrAPA 89*
rin, Horace *BioIn 16*

Perrin, James 1930- *WhoAm 90*
Perrin, John 1930- *WhoWor 91*
Perrin, John Paul 1943- *WhoAm 90*
Perrin, Kenneth Crossett 1914- *IntWWM 90*
Perrin, Kenneth Lynn 1937- *WhoAm 90, WhoE 91*
Perrin, Michael 1905-1988 *AnObit 1988*
Perrin, Michel 1931- *WhoWor 91*
Perrin, Noel 1927- *ConAu 31NR, WhoAm 90*
Perrin, Pierette *PenDiDA 89*
Perrin, Robert Maitland 1950- *St&PR 91*
Perrin, Roy Albert, Jr. 1940- *WhoSSW 91*
Perrin, Sarah Ann 1904- *WhoAmW 91, WhoSSW 91, WhoWor 91*
Perrin, Thomas, Jr. 1937- *St&PR 91*
Perrin, Timothy Alton 1949- *WhoWrEP 89*
Perrin, Vic *BioIn 16*
Perrin-Gouron, Gerard Pierre Marie V 1934- *WhoWor 91*
Perrine, Laurence 1915- *WhoAm 90, WhoWrEP 89*
Perrine, Lynn Marie 1949- *WhoAmW 91*
Perrine, Mary 1913- *AuBYP 90*
Perrine, Patricia Sue *BiDrAPA 89*
Perrine, Richard Leroy 1924- *WhoAm 90*
Perrine, Valerie *BioIn 16*
Perrine, Valerie 1943- *WhoAm 90, WorAlBi*
Perrine, William Everett 1933- *St&PR 91, WhoAm 90*
Perrine, William W. *St&PR 91*
Perring, George 1884-1960 *Ballpl 90*
Perrino, Albert Carl 1934- *St&PR 91*
Perrins, Lesley 1953- *BioIn 16*
Perris, Andrew Arthur 1968- *WhoEmL 91*
Perris, Elizabeth L. 1951- *WhoAmW 91*
Perritt, Pol 1892-1947 *Ballpl 90*
Perron, Dave *BioIn 16*
Perron, Eric 1950- *St&PR 91*
Perron, Pierre O. 1939- *WhoAm 90*
Perron, Robert Truman 1938- *WhoE 91*
Perrone, Charles A. 1951- *ConAu 132*
Perrone, Jeff 1953- *WhoAmA 91*
Perrone, Jerome Frank 1938- *St&PR 91*
Perrone, Nicholas 1930- *WhoAm 90*
Perrone, Robert W. 1929- *St&PR 91*
Perrone, Susanne Saeli 1953- *WhoAmW 91*
Perrone, Thomas John 1941- *WhoE 91*
Perrone, Vincenzo 1927- *WhoWor 91*
Perros, Theodore Peter 1921- *WhoAm 90*
Perrot, Bernard *PenDiDA 89*
Perrot, Luce *BiDEWW*
Perrot, Nicolas 1644-1718 *EncCRAm, WhNaAH*
Perrot, Paul N 1926- *WhoAmA 91*
Perrot, Paul Norman 1926- *WhoAm 90, WhoSSW 91*
Perrotta, Anthony Paul 1936- *WhoAm 90*
Perrotta, Charles, Jr. *BiDrAPA 89*
Perrotta, Fioravante Gerald 1931- *WhoAm 90, WhoE 91*
Perrotta, Robert John 1947- *St&PR 91*
Perrotti, Joseph 1913- *St&PR 91*
Perrotti, Pasquale G. 1930- *St&PR 91*
Perrotto, Bernard *PenDiDA 89*
Perrucci, Robert 1931- *WhoAm 90*
Perruchoud, Andre Paul 1942- *WhoWor 91*
Perruchoud, Jean-Yves 1952- *WhoWor 91*
Perry, A. Michael 1936- *WhoAm 90*
Perry, Alan Stoddard 1923- *St&PR 91*
Perry, Anna Haas 1943- *WhoAmW 91*
Perry, Anne 1938- *TwCCr&M 91*
Perry, Anne Marie Litchfield 1943- *WhoAmW 91*
Perry, Anne Waters 1933- *WhoAmW 91*
Perry, Anthony John 1919- *WhoAm 90*
Perry, Antoinette 1888-1946 *BioIn 16, NotWoAT*
Perry, Aubrey Harrison, Jr. 1922- *St&PR 91*
Perry, Barbara Fisher *ConAu 30NR*
Perry, Barbara R. 1944- *St&PR 91*
Perry, Beth 1928- *WhoWrEP 89*
Perry, Billy Dwight 1933- *WhoAm 90*
Perry, Bradford Benton 1958- *BiDrAPA 89*
Perry, Bradley Wilbur 1938- *WhoE 91*
Perry, Brenda L. 1948- *WhoAmW 91*
Perry, Brian M. 1959- *St&PR 91*
Perry, Bruce Duncan *BiDrAPA 89*
Perry, Carlos J G 1932- *BiDrAPA 89*
Perry, Carrie Saxon *BioIn 16, WhoAm 90, WhoAmW 91, WhoE 91*
Perry, Chana *BioIn 16*
Perry, Charles David 1955- *WhoSSW 91*
Perry, Charles E. 1932- *WhoWrEP 89*
Perry, Charles E. 1937- *WhoAm 90*
Perry, Charles Norvin 1928- *WhoE 91*
Perry, Charles O 1929- *WhoAmA 91*
Perry, Charles Owen 1929- *WhoAm 90*
Perry, Charlotte 1890-1983 *BioIn 16, NotWoAT*
Perry, Chris Nicholas 1945- *WhoAm 90*
Perry, Christopher L. 1938- *ODwPR 91*

Perry, Christopher Richard 1932- *WhoWor 91*
Perry, Clarence R. 1930- *St&PR 91*
Perry, Clifford W. *St&PR 91*
Perry, Craig Crane 1948- *WhoE 91*
Perry, Cynthia Judith 1956- *BiDrAPA 89*
Perry, Cynthia Norton Shepard 1928- *WhoAm 90, WhoAmW 91, WhoWor 91*
Perry, Dale Lynn 1947- *WhoAm 90, WhoEmL 91*
Perry, David A. *St&PR 91*
Perry, David Arnold *BiDrAPA 89*
Perry, David Lewis 1940- *St&PR 91, WhoAm 90*
Perry, Dianne Foster 1948- *WhoAmW 91*
Perry, Donald A. *ODwPR 91*
Perry, Donald A. 1938- *WhoAm 90*
Perry, Donald Charles 1925- *WhoSSW 91*
Perry, Donald Dean 1939- *WhoAmA 91*
Perry, Donald J *BiDrAPA 89*
Perry, Douglas *WhoAm 90*
Perry, Dunman, Jr. 1926- *St&PR 91*
Perry, Edson Clifton 1929- *IntWWM 90*
Perry, Edward *PenDiDA 89*
Perry, Edward Samuel 1937- *WhoAmA 91*
Perry, Erik David 1952- *WhoE 91*
Perry, Erma Jackson McNeil *WhoAm 90*
Perry, Ernest Lee 1944- *WhoSSW 91*
Perry, Eston Lee 1936- *WhoAm 90*
Perry, Evelyn Reis *WhoWor 91*
Perry, Felton *DrBlPA 90*
Perry, Frank *BioIn 16, NewAgMG*
Perry, Frank 1923- *WhoAmA 91*
Perry, Frank 1930- *WhoAm 90*
Perry, Gaylord 1938- *Ballpl 90 [port], WorAlBi*
Perry, George Edward, Jr. 1936- *WhoAm 90*
Perry, George Lewis 1934- *WhoAm 90*
Perry, George Wilson 1929- *St&PR 91, WhoSSW 91*
Perry, Gerald 1960- *Ballpl 90*
Perry, Gerald F 1919- *BiDrAPA 89*
Perry, Glen Howard 1942- *St&PR 91*
Perry, Gordon E. 1932- *WhoAm 90*
Perry, Grace 1927-1987 *FemiCLE*
Perry, Greg Milton 1961- *WhoSSW 91*
Perry, Guy LaVerde 1905- *St&PR 91*
Perry, Harold Otto 1921- *WhoAm 90*
Perry, Harold R. 1916- *WhoAm 90*
Perry, Harold Tyner 1926- *WhoWor 91*
Perry, Harvey Chace 1949- *St&PR 91*
Perry, Harvey Parnell 1944- *St&PR 91*
Perry, Helen Frances *St&PR 91*
Perry, Hope Craig 1929- *WhoAmW 91*
Perry, J Christopher 1948- *BiDrAPA 89*
Perry, J. Warren 1921- *WhoAm 90*
Perry, Jack Richard 1945- *St&PR 91*
Perry, Jacquelin 1918- *WhoAm 90, WhoAmW 91*
Perry, James A. 1932- *St&PR 91*
Perry, James B. 1952- *WhoEmL 91*
Perry, James Benn 1950- *WhoAm 90*
Perry, James DeWolf 1941- *WhoE 91*
Perry, James Frederick 1945- *WhoSSW 91*
Perry, James Martin 1953- *St&PR 91*
Perry, James Nelson 1932- *St&PR 91, WhoAm 90*
Perry, James R. 1935- *St&PR 91*
Perry, Janet 1947- *IntWWM 90*
Perry, Jean Louise 1950- *WhoAmW 91*
Perry, Jesse Laurence, Jr. 1919- *WhoSSW 91*
Perry, Jim 1936- *Ballpl 90*
Perry, Joan Anne 1951- *WhoAmW 91*
Perry, John 1914- *AuBYP 90*
Perry, John Curtis 1930- *WhoE 91*
Perry, John Guy 1948- *WhoE 91*
Perry, John Holliday, Jr. 1917- *WhoAm 90*
Perry, John Hoyt 1848-1928 *AmLegL*
Perry, John Richard 1943- *WhoAm 90*
Perry, John Wilson 1925- *WhoE 91*
Perry, Joseph Quenton, Jr. 1942- *WhoE 91*
Perry, Joyce Lee 1945- *WhoAmW 91*
Perry, Judith Laura 1939- *WhoAmW 91*
Perry, Judy 1947- *BiDrAPA 89*
Perry, Julia Kay 1960- *WhoAmW 91*
Perry, Kathryn M. 1927- *St&PR 91*
Perry, Kathryn Powers 1948- *WhoAmA 91*
Perry, Keith 1931- *ConTFT 8 [port]*
Perry, Ken *ODwPR 91*
Perry, Kenneth E. 1920- *St&PR 91*
Perry, Kenneth Moore 1932- *St&PR 91, WhoSSW 91*
Perry, Kenneth W. 1932- *St&PR 91*
Perry, Kenneth Walter 1932- *WhoAm 90, WhoSSW 91, WhoWor 91*
Perry, Kenneth Wilbur 1919- *WhoAm 90*
Perry, Kimberly Jean 1955- *WhoAmW 91*
Perry, Lallah Miles 1926- *WhoAmA 91*
Perry, Landsford Wilder 1955- *St&PR 91*
Perry, Lawrence P. 1932- *St&PR 91*
Perry, Lee Rowan 1933- *WhoAm 90, WhoWor 91*
Perry, Leona E *BiDrAPA 89*
Perry, Lewis Curtis 1938- *WhoAm 90*
Perry, Lilla 1848-1933 *BiDWomA*

Perry, Lincoln Frederick 1949- *WhoAmA 91*
Perry, Louis B. 1918- *St&PR 91*
Perry, Louis Barnes 1918- *WhoAm 90*
Perry, Lynne *St&PR 91*
Perry, Malcolm Blythe 1930- *WhoAm 90*
Perry, Malcolm Oliver 1929- *WhoAm 90*
Perry, Margaret 1933- *WhoAm 90*
Perry, Margaret N. 1940- *WhoAm 90, WhoAmW 91, WhoSSW 91*
Perry, Marion J.H. 1943- *WhoWrEP 89*
Perry, Mark 1951- *WhoEmL 91*
Perry, Mark Sherman 1956- *WhoE 91*
Perry, Marsha Gratz 1936- *WhoAmW 91*
Perry, Marvin Banks, Jr. 1918- *WhoAm 90*
Perry, Marvin Chapman, II 1948- *IntWWM 90*
Perry, Mary Chase 1867-1961 *PenDiDA 89*
Perry, Mary Chase 1868-1961 *BioIn 16*
Perry, Mary Dean 1928- *WhoAmW 91*
Perry, Mary-Ellen 1932- *WhoAmW 91*
Perry, Matilda Toni *WhoAmW 91*
Perry, Matthew C. 1794-1858 *WorAlBi*
Perry, Matthew Calbraith 1794-1858 *BioIn 16, EncJap*
Perry, Mervyn Francis 1923- *WhoAm 90*
Perry, Michael C 1933- *EncO&P 3*
Perry, Michael Charles 1933- *EncPaPR 91*
Perry, Michael Clinton 1945- *WhoAm 90*
Perry, Michael D. 1946- *St&PR 91*
Perry, Michael David 1946- *WhoAm 90*
Perry, Murvin Henry 1922- *WhoAm 90*
Perry, Nancy Estelle 1934- *WhoAmW 91*
Perry, Nancy Jo 1931- *WhoAmW 91*
Perry, Nancy Ling 1947-1974 *WorAlBi*
Perry, Nina Diamond 1956- *WhoWrEP 89*
Perry, Norman 1941- *St&PR 91*
Perry, Norman L. 1928- *St&PR 91*
Perry, Norman Robert 1929- *WhoAm 90*
Perry, Oliver H. 1815-1882 *AmLegL*
Perry, Oliver Hazard 1785-1819 *WorAlBi*
Perry, Osgood Endecott 1930- *St&PR 91*
Perry, Pat 1959- *Ballpl 90*
Perry, Patrick James 1948- *St&PR 91*
Perry, Paul Alverson 1929- *WhoAm 90*
Perry, Paul G *BiDrAPA 89*
Perry, Paul William 1942- *St&PR 91*
Perry, Percival 1916- *WhoAm 90*
Perry, Peter Patrick 1932- *WhoWor 91*
Perry, Phyllis J 1933- *SmATA 60 [port]*
Perry, Ralph Barton, III 1936- *St&PR 91, WhoAm 90*
Perry, Ralph Foster, Jr. 1927- *St&PR 91*
Perry, Randolph Hugh 1951- *WhoSSW 91*
Perry, Raymond 1876-1960 *WhoAmA 91N*
Perry, Regenia Alfreda 1941- *WhoAmA 91*
Perry, Reuben *BioIn 16*
Perry, Richard 1944- *BioIn 16*
Perry, Richard Alan 1953- *St&PR 91*
Perry, Richard Allan 1948- *WhoE 91*
Perry, Richard E. 1929- *St&PR 91*
Perry, Richard Irwin 1942- *BiDrAPA 89, WhoE 91*
Perry, Ritchie 1942- *TwCCr&M 91*
Perry, Ritchie John Allen 1942- *SpyFic*
Perry, Robert Haynes 1933- *WhoSSW 91*
Perry, Robert Joseph 1932- *WhoAm 90*
Perry, Robert Joseph 1934- *WhoAm 90*
Perry, Robert M. 1931- *St&PR 91*
Perry, Robert Michael 1931- *WhoAm 90*
Perry, Robert S. 1942- *St&PR 91*
Perry, Robin L. 1917- *WhoWrEP 89*
Perry, Rod 1941?- *DrBlPA 90*
Perry, Roger Lawrence 1923- *St&PR 91*
Perry, Rose Theresa 1961- *WhoAmW 91*
Perry, Rotraud Mezger 1927- *WhoE 91*
Perry, Ruth 1892- *ConAu 131*
Perry, Samuel Wesley, III 1940- *BiDrAPA 89*
Perry, Sara D. 1947- *BiDrAPA 89*
Perry, Scott 1891-1959 *Ballpl 90*
Perry, Seymour Monroe 1921- *WhoAm 90*
Perry, Shauneille 1929- *DrBlPA 90*
Perry, Stanislaus Francis 1823-1898 *DcCanB 12*
Perry, Stephen F. 1929- *St&PR 91*
Perry, Susan 1946- *WhoWrEP 89*
Perry, Thomas 1947- *ConAu 130*
Perry, Thomas Bernard 1948- *St&PR 91*
Perry, Thomas Kennedy 1952- *WhoWrEP 89*
Perry, Vincent Aloysius *WhoAm 90*
Perry, W. Brian 1963- *BiDrAPA 89*
Perry, Will *SpyFic*
Perry, William *BioIn 16*
Perry, William 1962- *WorAlBi*
Perry, William E. *WhoSSW 91*
Perry, William H. 1918- *St&PR 91*
Perry, William J. 1927- *St&PR 91*
Perry, William James 1927- *WhoAm 90*
Perry-Camp, Jane 1936- *IntWWM 90*
Perry-Daniel, Annie Vee 1940- *WhoAmW 91*
Perryman, Dwayne B., III 1963- *ConTFT 8*

Perryman, Elizabeth Kay 1940- *WhoAmW 91*
Perryman, Polly 1947- *WhoAmW 91*
Perryman, Thelma Diane 1952- *WhoAmW 91*
Perryman, Thomas Ruben 1952- *WhoSSW 91*
Perryman, Tom *WhNaAH*
Perryman, Willie 1911-1985 *BioIn 16*
Persad, Toolsie 1960- *St&PR 91*
Persaile, Kerri Bullard 1960- *WhoAmW 91*
Persaud, Ronald Godwin *BiDrAPA 89*
Persaud, Trivedi Vidhya Nandan 1940- *WhoAm 90*
Persaud, Vyas 1957- *BiDrAPA 89*
Persavich, Warren D. 1952- *St&PR 91*
Persavich, Warren Dale 1952- *WhoAm 90*
Persch, Wilbert John 1941- *St&PR 91*
Perschbacher, Debra Bassett 1956- *WhoAmW 91*
Perschetz, Arthur D. 1943- *St&PR 91*
Perschmann, Lutz Ingo 1940- *WhoSSW 91*
Perse, Saint-John *MajTwCW*
Perse, St.-John 1887-1975 *WorAlBi*
Perse, Teri L. *BiDrAPA 89*
Persell, Caroline Hodges 1941- *WhoAm 90*
Persell, Charles B. 1909-1988 *BioIn 16*
Persell, William Dailey 1943- *WhoE 91*
Persellin, Robert Harold 1930- *WhoAm 90*
Persels, Jimmy Burdette 1944- *WhoSSW 91*
Pershan, Marion *WhoAmA 91, WhoE 91*
Pershan, Richard Henry 1930- *WhoAm 90*
Pershing, Cyndie 1957- *ODwPR 91*
Pershing, David Walter 1948- *WhoAm 90*
Pershing, John J. 1860-1948 *BioIn 16, WorAlBi*
Pershing, Richard Wilson 1927- *St&PR 91*
Pershing, Robert George 1941- *WhoAm 90*
Persiani, Fanny 1812-1867 *PenDiMP*
Persichetti, Vincent 1915-1987 *BioIn 16*
Persico, Alphonse *BioIn 16*
Persico, Joseph Edward 1930- *WhoAm 90, WhoWrEP 89*
Persing, Joel Howard 1953- *St&PR 91*
Persinger, Garnet Lasure 1940- *WhoSSW 91*
Persinger, Louis 1887-1966 *PenDiMP*
Perske, Robert 1927- *BioIn 16*
Persky, Alan D *BiDrAPA 89*
Persky, Alan D. 1934- *WhoE 91*
Persky, Allan Lee 1943- *WhoSSW 91*
Persky, Joseph H. 1914- *St&PR 91*
Persky, Lester 1927- *WhoAm 90*
Persky, Mordecai 1931- *WhoAm 90, WhoWrEP 89*
Persky, Murray 1923- *BiDrAPA 89*
Persky, Robert S 1930- *WhoAmA 91*
Persky, Robert Samuel 1930- *WhoWrEP 89*
Persky, Stewart Alan 1952- *WhoEmL 91*
Persky, Victoria Weyler 1945- *WhoAmW 91*
Persoff, Nehemiah 1920- *WorAlBi*
Person, Curtis S., Jr. 1934- *WhoSSW 91*
Person, Donald Ames, Sr. 1938- *WhoAm 90*
Person, Dorothy Evelyn 1924- *WhoAmW 91*
Person, Ethel S 1934- *BiDrAPA 89*
Person, Evert Bertil 1914- *WhoAm 90*
Person, Philip 1919- *WhoE 91*
Person, Robert John 1927- *WhoAm 90*
Person, William Thomas 1900- *AuBYP 90*
Person, Willis Bagley 1928- *WhoSSW 91*
Personick, Stewart David 1947- *WhoAm 90*
Persons, Albert C. 1915- *BioIn 16*
Persons, Carol Ann *BiDrAPA 89*
Persons, John Wade 1953- *WhoEmL 91*
Persons, Oscar N. 1939- *WhoAm 90*
Persons, Stow Spaulding 1913- *WhoAm 90*
Persons, Timothy David 1951- *WhoE 91*
Persons, Wallace R. *BioIn 16*
Persons, Wallace R. 1909- *St&PR 91*
Perssion, Leo B *BiDrAPA 89*
Persson, Phyllis-Ann 1945- *WhoE 91*
Persson, Sigurd 1914- *ConDes 90*
Persson, Sten Erik Bertil 1937- *WhoWor 91*
Persson, Stig Y. 1941- *St&PR 91*
Persson-Melin, Signe 1925- *ConDes 90*
Persyko, Isaac 1906- *BiDrAPA 89*
Pertegaz, Manuel *BioIn 16*
Pertel, Susan *BioIn 16*
Perthou, Alison Chandler 1945- *WhoAmW 91, WhoWor 91*
Perti, Rajesh Kumar 1935- *WhoWor 91*
Pertica, Bill 1897-1967 *Ballpl 90*
Pertile, Aureliano 1885-1952 *PenDiMP*
Pertini, Sandro 1896-1990 *BioIn 16, NewYTBS 90 [port]*
Pertl, Audrey *St&PR 91*
Pertrakis, Harry Mark 1923- *WorAu 1980 [port]*
Pertschuk, Louis Philip 1925- *WhoWor 91*
Pertschuk, Michael 1933- *WhoWrEP 89*
Pertschuk, Michael J *BiDrAPA 89*
Perttula, Norman K. 1927- *St&PR 91*
Perttunen, Paula Marja 1956- *WhoWor 91*
Pertuz, Danilo Jimeno 1917- *St&PR 91*
Perty, Maximilian *EncO&P 3*
Perty, Maximillan 1804-1884 *EncPaPR 91*
Pertz, Stuart K. 1936- *St&PR 91*
Peru, Rosita *WhoAmW 91*
Perucic, Jasna 1947- *WhoWor 91*
Perugini, Kate 1838-1929 *BiDWomA*
Perugino 1450?-1524 *IntDcAA 90*
Perullo, Ralph F. 1941- *St&PR 91*
Perumallu, Tripuraneni L 1939- *BiDrAPA 89*
Perun, John Joseph, Jr. 1963- *WhoE 91*
Peruo, Marsha 1951- *WhoAmA 91*
Perusse, Roland Irving 1921- *WhoAm 90*
Perutz, Gerald E.A. 1929- *St&PR 91*
Perutz, Max F. 1914- *WorAlBi*
Perutz, Max Ferdinand 1914- *WhoAm 90, WhoWor 91*
Peruzzi, Elio 1927- *IntWWM 90*
Peruzzo, Albert Louis 1951- *WhoEmL 91, WhoWor 91*
Pervaiz, Mehtab Max 1954- *WhoE 91*
Pervelis, George H. 1934- *St&PR 91*
Pervin, William Joseph 1930- *WhoAm 90*
Pery, Angela Olivia 1897-1981 *DcNaB 1981*
Peryon, Mary Charleen D. 1931- *WhoAmW 91*
Perzanowski, Stan 1950- *Ballpl 90*
Perzley, Alan Harris 1955- *WhoEmL 91*
Perzow, Sydney M *BiDrAPA 89*
Pesaran, Mohammad Hashem 1946- *WhoWor 91*
Pesaresi, Daniel J. 1939- *St&PR 91*
Pesavento, Joseph Amedeo 1936- *WhoE 91*
Pesce, Antonino L *BiDrAPA 89*
Pesce, Cheryl J. 1952- *St&PR 91*
Pesce, Gaetano 1939- *ConDes 90*
Pesce, Ulises Jorge 1943- *BiDrAPA 89*
Pesce, Victor S. 1925- *St&PR 91*
Pesch, Alan James 1941- *St&PR 91*
Pesch, Leroy 1931- *BioIn 16*
Pesch, Leroy Allen 1931- *WhoAm 90, WhoSSW 91, WhoWor 91*
Pesch, William Allan 1948- *WhoE 91*
Peschau, John B, Jr. 1909- *BiDrAPA 89*
Peschel, Frederick M. 1918- *WhoSSW 91*
Peschel, Stephen Stanley 1955- *St&PR 91*
Peschka, Thomas Alan 1931- *St&PR 91, WhoAm 90*
Peschmann, Kristian R. 1940- *St&PR 91*
Pesci, Frank Bernard, Sr. 1929- *WhoE 91*
Pesci, Joe 1943- *ConTFT 8*
Pesci, Paula Marie *BiDrAPA 89*
Pesciotta, Barbara Phyllis 1936- *WhoAmW 91*
Pescosolido, William Bulkeley 1932- *WhoWor 91*
Peseenz, Tulio F. *ConAu 131, HispWr 90*
Pesek, Cyril Paul, Jr. 1932- *St&PR 91*
Pesek, Diana Lynn 1950- *WhoAmW 91*
Pesek, Libor 1933- *IntWWM 90, PenDiMP, WhoWor 91*
Peselow, Eric D 1950- *BiDrAPA 89*
Peshewah 1761?-1841 *WhNaAH*
Peshkin, Alan 1931- *WhoAm 90*
Peshkin, Murray 1925- *WhoAm 90*
Peshkin, Samuel David 1925- *WhoAm 90, WhoWor 91*
Pesikoff, Richard B 1940- *BiDrAPA 89*
Pesin, Ella 1956- *ODwPR 91*
Pesin, Meyer 1902-1989 *BioIn 16*
Peske, Edgar Derek 1939- *WhoE 91*
Peskin, Henry Martin 1937- *WhoE 91*
Peskin, Kenneth *WhoE 91*
Peskin, Martin Rudolph 1949- *St&PR 91*
Peskin, Mervyn Max *BiDrAPA 89*
Peskin, Sidney F. 1914- *St&PR 91*
Peskin-Jacobs, Marjorie Ruth 1952- *WhoAmW 91*
Pesko, Zoltan 1937- *IntWWM 90, WhoWor 91*
Peskoe, Sondra Helane 1955- *WhoAmW 91, WhoE 91, WhoWor 91*
Pesky, Johnny 1919- *Ballpl 90*
Peslar, Norman George 1942- *St&PR 91*
Pesmen, Sandra 1931- *WhoAm 90*
Pesner, Carole Manishin 1937- *WhoAmA 91*
Pesonen, Jori Eino 1925- *WhoWor 91*
Pesotta, Rose 1896-1965 *EncAL, FemiCLE*
Pesqueira, Ralph Raymond *WhoHisp 91*
Pesqueira, Richard E. 1937- *WhoHisp 91*
Pess, Daniel M. 1952- *St&PR 91*
Pessagno, Richard Anthony 1960- *WhoSSW 91*
Pessar, Linda Faith *BiDrAPA 89*
Pessemier, Robert Campbell 1956- *WhoWrEP 89*
Pessen, Edward 1920- *WhoAm 90, WhoWrEP 89*
Pessi, Yrjo 1926- *WhoWor 91*
Pessin, Joseph *BiDrAPA 89*
Pessoa, Fernando 1888-1935 *BioIn 16, WorAlBi*
Pessoa, Michelle Marie 1966- *WhoE 91*
Pessolano, Linda 1946- *WhoWrEP 89*
Pessoni, Douglas Herbert 1941- *St&PR 91*
Pestaina, Karen Helena 1963- *WhoAmW 91*
Pestalozzi, Johann Heinrich 1746-1827 *DcLB 94 [port], WorAlBi*
Pestana, Carlos 1936- *WhoAm 90*
Pestana, Mary Helen 1961- *WhoAmW 91*
Pestel, Vera Efimovna 1886?-1952 *BiDWomA*
Pester, Jack C. 1935- *St&PR 91*
Pester, Jack Cloyd 1935- *WhoAm 90*
Pesterfield, Linda Carol 1939- *WhoSSW 91*
Pestillo, Peter John 1938- *St&PR 91*
Pestritto, Anthony Charles 1926- *St&PR 91*
Peszke, Michael A 1932- *BiDrAPA 89*
Peszke, Michael Alfred 1932- *WhoE 91*
Pet Shop Boys *ConMus 5 [port]*
Pet, Donald David 1936- *BiDrAPA 89*
Pet-Edwards, Julia Johanna Agricola 1955- *WhoSSW 91*
Peta Nocona 1812?-1862? *WhNaAH*
Peta, James Joseph 1942- *St&PR 91*
Petaccio, Anthony M. 1932- *St&PR 91*
Petacque, Art 1924- *WhoAm 90*
Petain, Francis Daniel 1946- *WhoWor 91*
Petain, Henri Philippe 1856-1951 *BioIn 16, WorAlBi*
Petain, Henri Philippe Benoni Omer J. 1856-1951 *BiDFrPL*
Petalesharo 1787?-1832? *WhNaAH*
Petancic, Adolf August 1937- *St&PR 91*
Petch, Howard Earle 1925- *WhoAm 90*
Petch, Steve 1952- *OxCCanT*
Petculescu, Pia Radu *BiDrAPA 89*
Peteet, John Raymond 1947- *BiDrAPA 89*
Petek, William Louis 1942- *St&PR 91*
Petel, Georg 1601?-1634 *PenDiDA 89*
Peteler, Jennings C *BiDrAPA 89*
Peteler, Philip E. 1920- *St&PR 91*
Petenbrink, Nancy Ann 1950- *WhoEmL 91*
Peter I 1672-1725 *WorAlBi*
Peter and Gordon *EncPR&S 89*
Peter III, Emperor of Russia 1728-1762 *BioIn 16*
Peter of Abano 1250-1318 *EncO&P 3*
Peter, Paul & Mary *ConMus 4 [port]*
Peter, Paul and Mary *OxCPMus*
Peter Porcupine 1763-1835 *BioIn 16*
Peter, the Apostle *BioIn 16*
Peter I, the Great, Emperor of Russia 1672-1725 *BioIn 16*
Peter, Arnold Philimon 1957- *WhoEmL 91*
Peter, Carl Joseph 1932- *WhoAm 90*
Peter, David C. 1950- *BiDrAPA 89*
Peter, Edward Compston, II 1929- *WhoAm 90*
Peter, Frances Marchbank *WhoAm 90*
Peter, Friedrich Gunther 1933- *WhoAmA 91*
Peter, George 1922- *WhoAmA 91*
Peter, H. G. *EncACom*
Peter, Hugh 1598-1660 *EncCRAm*
Peter, John Edward 1934- *WhoSSW 91*
Peter, Laurence J. *BioIn 16*
Peter, Laurence J 1919-1990 *ConAu 130, NewYTBS 90 [port]*
Peter, Laurence Johnston 1919- *WhoWrEP 89*
Peter, Lawrence J. 1919-1990 *WorAlBi*
Peter, Phillips Smith 1932- *St&PR 91, WhoAm 90, WhoE 91, WhoWor 91*
Peter, Premkumar 1938- *BiDrAPA 89*
Peter, Richard Ector 1943- *WhoAm 90*
Peter, Sarah W. 1800-1877 *BioAmW*
Peter, T.H. 1916- *St&PR 91*
Peterdi, Gabor F 1915- *WhoAmA 91*
Peterfreund, Emanuel 1924- *BiDrAPA 89*
Peterfreund, Herbert 1913- *WhoAm 90*
Peterfreund, Norman 1920- *St&PR 91*
Peterfreund, Sheldon Paul 1917- *WhoAm 90*
Peterfreund, Stuart 1945- *ConAu 30NR*
Peterfreund, Stuart Samuel 1945- *WhoWrEP 89*
Peterhansel, Carole Louise 1939- *WhoE 91*
Peterinck, Francois-Joseph *PenDiDA 89*
Petering, Janice Faye 1950- *WhoAmW 91*
Petering, Ralph Edwin 1908- *WhoAm 90*
Petering, Roland Vernon 1910- *St&PR 91*
Peterka, Richard A. 1927- *St&PR 91*
Peterkin, Allan David *BiDrAPA 89*
Peterkin, DeWitt, Jr. 1913- *WhoAm 90*
Peterkin, Elliot Clark 1939- *WhoE 91*
Peterkin, George A., Jr. 1927- *St&PR 91*
Peterkin, George Alexander, Jr. 1927- *WhoAm 90*
Peterkin, Julia 1880-1961 *BioAmW, FemiCLE*
Peterle, Tony John 1925- *WhoAm 90*
Peterman, Bruce E. 1931- *St&PR 91*
Peterman, Bruce Edgar 1931- *WhoAm 90*
Peterman, Donna C. 1947- *ODwPR 91*
Peterman, Jack Maurice 1931- *St&PR 91*
Peterman, Parker C. 1927- *St&PR 91*
Petermeier, Norman Bruce 1941- *St&PR 91*
Peternell, Ben C. 1945- *St&PR 91*
Peternell, Ben Clayton 1945- *WhoAm 90*
Peters, Aileen *ODwPR 91*
Peters, Alan *PenDiDA 89*
Peters, Alan 1929- *WhoAm 90*
Peters, Alan Edmond *BiDrAPA 89*
Peters, Alexander 1923- *SmATA X*
Peters, Alfred Vout 1867- *EncO&P 3*
Peters, Alton Emil 1935- *WhoAm 90*
Peters, Andrew Dalzell 1954- *WhoE 91*
Peters, Arthur King 1919- *WhoAm 90*
Peters, Arthur W. 1942- *St&PR 91*
Peters, Augustus Winniett 1927- *St&PR 91*
Peters, Aulana Louise 1941- *WhoAm 90*
Peters, Barbara Humbird 1948- *WhoAmW 91, WhoEmL 91, WhoWor 91*
Peters, Barbara Jean 1948- *WhoEmL 91, WhoSSW 91*
Peters, Barbara Nancy 1956- *WhoAmW 91*
Peters, Bernadette *BioIn 16*
Peters, Bernadette 1948- *WhoAm 90, WhoAmW 91, WorAlBi*
Peters, Bill *TwCCr&M 91*
Peters, Bobbie Jo 1947- *WhoSSW 91*
Peters, Bonnie Sigmon 1952- *WhoSSW 91*
Peters, Boyd Leon 1951- *WhoWor 91*
Peters, Brock 1927- *DrBlPA 90, WhoAm 90, WorAlBi*
Peters, Calvin Ronald 1940- *WhoSSW 91*
Peters, Carl W 1897-1980 *WhoAmA 91N*
Peters, Carol Beattie Taylor 1932- *WhoAmW 91, WhoE 91*
Peters, Carolyn *BioIn 16*
Peters, Charles 1926- *BioIn 16, CurBio 90 [port]*
Peters, Charles Denfield 1945- *WhoE 91, WhoEmL 91, WhoWor 91*
Peters, Charles Given, Jr. 1926- *WhoAm 90*
Peters, Charles L. 1933- *St&PR 91*
Peters, Charles Merrell 1953- *WhoAm 90*
Peters, Charles Paul 1952- *BiDrAPA 89*
Peters, Charles William 1927- *WhoAm 90*
Peters, Charlotte Lestyan 1942- *WhoAmW 91*
Peters, Chester Evan 1922- *WhoAm 90*
Peters, Christine Marie 1949- *WhoAmW 91*
Peters, Clarice *WhoWrEP 89*
Peters, D.C. 1915- *St&PR 91*
Peters, Dale David 1944- *St&PR 91*
Peters, David B 1903- *BiDrAPA 89*
Peters, David C. 1950- *St&PR 91*
Peters, David Michael 1940- *St&PR 91, WhoE 91*
Peters, David Thomas 1926- *St&PR 91*
Peters, Dean Frank 1965- *WhoE 91*
Peters, Denis L *ODwPR 91*
Peters, Denis J. 1933- *St&PR 91*
Peters, Dennis Gail 1937- *WhoAm 90*
Peters, Diane 1940- *WhoAmA 91*
Peters, DiDi *BioIn 16*
Peters, Donald Cameron 1915- *WhoAm 90*
Peters, Donald Delbert 1940- *WhoSSW 91*
Peters, Donald Eugene 1948- *WhoSSW 91*
Peters, Donald H. 1940- *St&PR 91*
Peters, Donald Mullen 1950- *WhoEmL 91*
Peters, Donald Walter 1956- *BiDrAPA 89*
Peters, Dorothy Marie 1913- *WhoWor 91*
Peters, Douglas Cameron 1955- *WhoEmL 91, WhoWor 91*
Peters, Douglas D. 1936- *St&PR 91*
Peters, Edward Murray 1936- *WhoAm 90*
Peters, Elizabeth 1927- *BioIn 16, TwCCr&M 91*
Peters, Ellen Ash 1930- *WhoAm 90, WhoAmW 91, WhoE 91*
Peters, Ellis *MajTwCW*
Peters, Ellis 1913- *TwCCr&M 91*
Peters, Farnsley Lewellyn 1929- *WhoAm 90*
Peters, Frances Elizabeth 1915- *WhoAmW 91*
Peters, Francis C 1902-1977 *WhoAmA 91N*
Peters, Frank Albert 1931- *WhoE 91*
Peters, Frank Lewis, Jr. 1930- *WhoAm 90*
Peters, Frederick P. *BioIn 16, NewYTBS 90*
Peters, Frederick Whitten 1946- *WhoEmL 91*
Peters, Garry Lowell 1952- *WhoAm 90*
Peters, Gary 1937- *Ballpl 90, BioIn 16*
Peters, Gene Aloysius 1934- *WhoE 91*
Peters, Geoffrey Wright 1945- *WhoEmL 91*
Peters, Glenn W. 1948- *St&PR 91*
Peters, Gordon Benes 1931- *IntWWM 90, WhoAm 90*
Peters, Helge 1937- *WhoWor 91*

Peters, Henry A Augustus 1920- *BiDrAPA 89*
Peters, Henry Augustus 1920- *WhoAm 90*
Peters, Henry Buckland 1916- *WhoAm 90*
Peters, Henry John 1924- *WhoAm 90*
Peters, Howard Nevin 1938- *WhoAm 90*
Peters, Isadore D *BiDrAPA 89*
Peters, Jacobus Franciscus M 1931- *WhoWor 91*
Peters, James *St&PR 91*
Peters, James Alexander 1928- *WhoAm 90*
Peters, James Horsfield 1811?-1891 *DcCanB 12*
Peters, James M. 1935- *St&PR 91*
Peters, James Robert 1950- *St&PR 91*
Peters, Jane Catherine 1939- *WhoAmW 91*
Peters, Jane Kastl 1954- *WhoAmW 91*
Peters, Janet J. 1930- *WhoAmW 91*
Peters, Jeffrey Lee 1953- *BiDrAPA 89, WhoE 91*
Peters, Jerome Charles Miller 1951- *BiDrAPA 89*
Peters, Joan Karen 1945- *WhoWrEP 89*
Peters, Joann 1933- *WhoSSW 91*
Peters, Johanna McLennan 1932- *IntWWM 90*
Peters, Johannes Reinier 1940- *WhoWor 91*
Peters, John Albin *BiDrAPA 89*
Peters, John Basil 1952- *WhoEmL 91, WhoWor 91*
Peters, John E 1917- *BiDrAPA 89*
Peters, John Edward 1931- *WhoAm 90*
Peters, John Raymond 1926- *WhoAm 90*
Peters, Jon *BioIn 16*
Peters, Jon 1947- *WhoAm 90*
Peters, Joseph Edwin 1938- *St&PR 91*
Peters, Judith Rochelle 1951- *WhoAmW 91*
Peters, Judy Gale 1941- *WhoAmW 91*
Peters, Karen C. 1947- *St&PR 91*
Peters, Karen Ronell 1944- *WhoAmW 91*
Peters, Kelly Boyte 1958- *WhoAmW 91*
Peters, Kenneth Maxwell 1935- *WhoE 91*
Peters, Klaus 1937- *WhoE 91*
Peters, Kristen *BioIn 16*
Peters, Kurt Rudolph, Jr. *BiDrAPA 89*
Peters, Lana *WhoWrEP 89*
Peters, Larry Dean 1938- *WhoAmA 91*
Peters, Lauralee Milberg 1943- *WhoAm 90*
Peters, Lauren *ODwPR 91*
Peters, Laurie Jean 1943- *BiDrAPA 89, WhoAmW 91*
Peters, Lawrence Carl *BiDrAPA 89*
Peters, Lawrence H. 1945- *WhoSSW 91*
Peters, Leon, Jr. 1923- *WhoAm 90*
Peters, Leone J. *BioIn 16*
Peters, Leone J. 1911- *St&PR 91*
Peters, Lori Susan 1958- *WhoSSW 91*
Peters, Lorraine A. *St&PR 91*
Peters, Louise *WhoWrEP 89*
Peters, Ludovic 1931-1984 *SpyFic*
Peters, Maria Liberia- 1942- *BioIn 16*
Peters, Marilynn Joanne *BiDrAPA 89*
Peters, Mark 1940- *WhoAm 90*
Peters, Martha Hamm *DcCanB 12*
Peters, Mary E. 1911-1989 *BioIn 16*
Peters, Mary Robin *BiDrAPA 89*
Peters, Max Stone 1920- *WhoAm 90*
Peters, Mercedes *WhoAmW 91, WhoE 91, WhoWor 91*
Peters, Merle A. 1936- *St&PR 91*
Peters, Michael *BioIn 16*
Peters, Michael 1948?- *DrBlPA 90*
Peters, Michael Arthur 1943- *WhoAm 90*
Peters, Michael Bartley 1943- *WhoAm 90*
Peters, Michael Morris 1937- *WhoE 91*
Peters, Mike 1943- *WorAlBi*
Peters, Molly Samuel 1958- *WhoAmW 91*
Peters, Nancy *BiDrAPA 89*
Peters, Pamela Sue 1956- *WhoAmW 91*
Peters, Paul R. 1920- *St&PR 91*
Peters, Penny *ODwPR 91*
Peters, Ralph Edgar 1923- *WhoE 91, WhoWor 91*
Peters, Ralph Frew 1929- *St&PR 91, WhoAm 90*
Peters, Ralph L., Jr. 1947- *WhoSSW 91*
Peters, Ralph Martin 1926- *WhoAm 90*
Peters, Raymond Eugene 1933- *WhoWor 91*
Peters, Raymond Robert 1942- *WhoAm 90*
Peters, Richard H. 1920- *St&PR 91*
Peters, Richard Morse 1922- *WhoAm 90*
Peters, Ricky 1955- *Ballpl 90*
Peters, Rob *BioIn 16*
Peters, Robert 1924- *DcLB 105 [port], WhoWrEP 89*
Peters, Robert C. 1941- *St&PR 91*
Peters, Robert H 1928- *BiDrAPA 89*
Peters, Robert Henry 1944- *WhoSSW 91*
Peters, Robert J. 1940- *St&PR 91*
Peters, Robert Lee 1920- *WhoAm 90*
Peters, Robert Lynn, Jr. 1919- *St&PR 91*
Peters, Robert Nisley 1923- *St&PR 91, WhoAm 90*
Peters, Roberta 1930- *IntWWM 90, WhoAm 90, WhoAmW 91, WorAlBi*
Peters, Robin Lynn 1957- *WhoEmL 91*
Peters, Robyn Goldman 1942- *WhoAmW 91*
Peters, Ronald Arthur 1943- *WhoE 91*
Peters, Rudolph Albert 1889-1982 *DcNaB 1981*
Peters, Rusty 1914- *Ballpl 90*
Peters, S. H. *ConAu 131, MajTwCW*
Peters, Sharon V. 1939- *ODwPR 91*
Peters, Stephen 1907?-1990 *ConAu 130*
Peters, Stephen 1946- *St&PR 91*
Peters, Tamara Susan 1959- *WhoAmW 91*
Peters, Ted Hopkins 1943- *WhoSSW 91*
Peters, Teresa Widner 1959- *WhoAmW 91*
Peters, Thomas Guy 1945- *WhoSSW 91*
Peters, Thomas J. *BioIn 16*
Peters, Thomas Samuel 1941- *WhoE 91*
Peters, Tommaso Enrico *PenDiDA 89*
Peters, Uwe Henrik 1930- *BiDrAPA 89*
Peters, Vera Constance Aster Hess 1945- *WhoAmW 91*
Peters, Vickie Jann 1951- *WhoAmW 91, WhoWrEP 89*
Peters, Virginia 1924- *WhoAm 90*
Peters, William 1921- *WhoAm 90, WhoWrEP 89*
Peters, William F 1924- *BiDrAPA 89*
Peters, William Henry 1928- *WhoAm 90*
Peters, William P. 1950- *WhoAm 90*
Peters, Windell Franklin 1941- *WhoSSW 91*
Petersburg, Lauri Loth 1956- *WhoAmW 91*
Petersdorf, Robert George 1926- *WhoAm 90*
Peterse, Jan Gerardus 1947- *WhoWor 91*
Petersen, Allen R. 1954- *St&PR 91*
Petersen, Anne Cheryl 1944- *WhoAm 90, WhoAmW 91*
Petersen, Arne Herlov 1943- *WhoWor 91*
Petersen, Arnold 1885-1976 *EncAL*
Petersen, August Charles 1952- *WhoSSW 91*
Petersen, Barbara A. 1945- *IntWWM 90*
Petersen, Christopher A *BiDrAPA 89*
Petersen, Cliff *BioIn 16*
Petersen, Conrad William 1924- *St&PR 91*
Petersen, Daniel Lee 1948- *St&PR 91*
Petersen, Daniel Ronald 1933- *St&PR 91*
Petersen, David *AuBYP 90*
Petersen, David 1946- *SmATA 62 [port]*
Petersen, David L. *WhoAm 90*
Petersen, Donald E. *BioIn 16*
Petersen, Donald E. 1926- *WorAlBi*
Petersen, Donald Eugene 1926- *ConAmBL, EncABHB 5 [port], WhoAm 90, WhoWor 91*
Petersen, Edgar N. 1938- *St&PR 91*
Petersen, Forrest S. *NewYTBS 90*
Petersen, Forrest Silas 1922- *WhoAm 90*
Petersen, Frank Gerhard 1933- *WhoWor 91*
Petersen, Franklin G 1940- *WhoAmA 91*
Petersen, Franklin George 1940- *WhoE 91*
Petersen, Gordon W 1937- *BiDrAPA 89*
Petersen, Gwenn Boardman 1924- *SmATA 61*
Petersen, Hjalmar 1890-1968 *BioIn 16*
Petersen, James Niels 1954- *WhoEmL 91*
Petersen, Jane 1876-1975 *BiDWomA*
Petersen, Janice L 1950- *BiDrAPA 89*
Petersen, Jean Snyder 1931- *WhoAm 90*
Petersen, John James 1944- *St&PR 91*
Petersen, John Mark 1950- *St&PR 91*
Petersen, John William 1921- *St&PR 91*
Petersen, Jon Q. 1950- *St&PR 91*
Petersen, Kenneth C. 1936- *St&PR 91*
Petersen, Kenneth Clarence 1936- *WhoAm 90*
Petersen, Lee 1946- *WhoEmL 91*
Petersen, Lee Bennett, Jr. 1951- *St&PR 91*
Petersen, Marie Anne 1942- *WhoAm 90*
Petersen, Marie C. 1923- *St&PR 91*
Petersen, Mark E. 1900-1984 *ConAu 132*
Petersen, Mark Lowry 1963- *WhoSSW 91*
Petersen, Marshall Arthur 1938- *St&PR 91, WhoAm 90*
Petersen, Martin Eugene 1931- *WhoAm 90*
Petersen, Mary Beth 1954- *WhoE 91*
Petersen, Maureen Jeanette Miller 1956- *WhoAmW 91, WhoWor 91*
Petersen, Michael Frederic 1955- *St&PR 91*
Petersen, Michael J. 1945- *St&PR 91*
Petersen, Michael Mack 1952- *WhoSSW 91*
Petersen, Niels Helveg 1939- *WhoWor 91*
Petersen, Nils Holger 1946- *IntWWM 90*
Petersen, Nis 1897-1943 *DcScanL*
Petersen, Norman Richard, Jr. 1933- *WhoAm 90*
Petersen, P. J. 1941- *BioIn 16*
Petersen, P J 1941- *ConAu 30NR*
Petersen, Pat *BioIn 16*
Petersen, Patricia H. 1945- *IntWWM 90*
Petersen, Paul David 1946- *WhoE 91*
Petersen, Phil Brent *BiDrAPA 89*
Petersen, Ralph A. 1923- *St&PR 91*
Petersen, Raymond J. 1919- *St&PR 91*
Petersen, Raymond Joseph 1919- *WhoAm 90*
Petersen, Richard Herman 1934- *WhoAm 90*
Petersen, Richard J. 1941- *St&PR 91*
Petersen, Robert C. 1931- *WhoE 91*
Petersen, Robert Charles 1951- *WhoE 91*
Petersen, Robert V. 1926- *WhoAm 90*
Petersen, Roland 1926- *WhoAm 90*
Petersen, Roland Conrad 1926- *WhoAmA 91*
Petersen, Russell J. 1937- *WhoAm 90*
Petersen, Sidney R. 1930- *St&PR 91*
Petersen, Susan Jane 1944- *WhoAm 90*
Petersen, Sven Gjevert 1935- *WhoWor 91*
Petersen, Toni 1933- *WhoAm 90, WhoAmA 91*
Petersen, Ulrich 1927- *WhoAm 90*
Petersen, Warren R. 1946- *St&PR 91*
Petersen, Will 1928- *WhoAmA 91*
Petersen, William Lawrence 1950- *WhoEmL 91*
Petersen, William Otto 1926- *WhoAm 90*
Petersen, Wolfgang 1941- *ConTFT 8*
Petersen-Frey, Roland 1937- *St&PR 91, WhoWor 91*
Petersham, Maud 1890-1971 *AuBYP 90*
Petersham, Miska 1888-1959 *WhoAmA 91N*
Petersham, Miska 1888-1960 *AuBYP 90*
Petersik, John T 1915- *BiDrAPA 89*
Petersmeyer, Charles Wrede 1919- *WhoAm 90*
Petersmeyer, Gregg *WhoAm 90*
Petersmeyer, Nancy Q. *BiDrAPA 89*
Petersmeyer, Nancy Quayle 1954- *WhoE 91*
Petersohn, Steven Jeffrey 1957- *WhoE 91*
Peterson, A. D. C. 1908-1988 *BioIn 16*
Peterson, A E S 1908-1984 *WhoAmA 91N*
Peterson, Alan C. 1938- *St&PR 91*
Peterson, Alexander Duncan Campbell 1908-1988 *BioIn 16*
Peterson, Alfred H. 1938- *St&PR 91*
Peterson, Alfred H. 1946- *St&PR 91*
Peterson, Amanda *BioIn 16*
Peterson, Andrew F. 1958- *St&PR 91*
Peterson, Andrew Norman 1952- *St&PR 91*
Peterson, Ann Sullivan 1928- *WhoAm 90*
Peterson, Annamarie Jane 1936- *WhoAmW 91*
Peterson, Anne Virginia 1948- *WhoAmW 91*
Peterson, April Lynn 1966- *WhoAmW 91*
Peterson, Arthur J. 1941- *St&PR 91*
Peterson, Arthur L 1917- *BiDrAPA 89*
Peterson, Arthur Laverne 1926- *WhoAm 90, WhoWor 91*
Peterson, Audrey *ConAu 131*
Peterson, Barbara Ann 1942- *WhoAmW 91, WhoWor 91*
Peterson, Barbara Jo 1943- *WhoAmW 91*
Peterson, Billye Louise Newton 1947- *WhoSSW 91*
Peterson, Brooke Alan 1949- *WhoEmL 91*
Peterson, Bruce Bigelow 1935- *WhoAm 90*
Peterson, Bruce Edward 1943- *St&PR 91*
Peterson, C.B., Jr. 1913- *St&PR 91*
Peterson, Caleb 1917-1988 *DrBlPA 90*
Peterson, Cap 1942-1980 *Ballpl 90*
Peterson, Carl Eric 1944- *WhoAm 90*
Peterson, Carl J. 1937- *St&PR 91*
Peterson, Carl L. 1933- *St&PR 91*
Peterson, Carl R 1935- *BiDrAPA 89*
Peterson, Carl Rudolf 1907- *WhoAm 90*
Peterson, Carol Ann 1947- *WhoE 91*
Peterson, Carolann *BioIn 16*
Peterson, Carolyn *ODwPR 91*
Peterson, Charles E. 1936- *St&PR 91*
Peterson, Charles Emil 1906- *WhoAm 90*
Peterson, Charles Gordon 1926- *WhoAm 90*
Peterson, Charles Hayes 1938- *WhoAm 90, WhoWor 91*
Peterson, Charles John 1933- *WhoAm 90*
Peterson, Charles Lee 1941- *St&PR 91*
Peterson, Charles Loren 1938- *WhoAm 90*
Peterson, Charles S. 1927- *BioIn 16*
Peterson, Charles T. 1937- *St&PR 91*
Peterson, Charles Warner, III 1948- *WhoE 91*
Peterson, Chase N. 1929- *WhoAm 90*
Peterson, Chesley *BioIn 16*
Peterson, Chester, Jr. 1937- *WhoWrEP 89*
Peterson, Chester Gibe 1922- *WhoE 91*
Peterson, Chris Robert 1961- *WhoWor 91*
Peterson, Clarence Wilford 1924- *St&PR 91*
Peterson, Claudette 1953- *IntWWM 90*
Peterson, Conrad Alyn 1934- *St&PR 91*
Peterson, Cordell Quentin 1941- *St&PR 91*
Peterson, Courtland Harry 1930- *WhoAm 90*
Peterson, Craig *ODwPR 91*
Peterson, Cynthia Jane 1948- *St&PR 91*
Peterson, D. Wayne 1936- *WhoSSW 91*
Peterson, Dale Howard, Jr. 1949- *WhoE 91*
Peterson, Dan W. 1930- *St&PR 91*
Peterson, David Andreas 1939- *WhoAm 90*
Peterson, David Charles 1949- *WhoAm 90*
Peterson, David Dalvey 1931- *St&PR 91*
Peterson, David Frederick 1937- *WhoAm 90*
Peterson, David Reid 1949- *WhoEmL 91*
Peterson, David Robert *BioIn 16*
Peterson, David Robert 1943- *WhoAm 90, WhoE 91, WhoWor 91*
Peterson, David Thomas 1951- *WhoSSW 91*
Peterson, David Winfield 1913- *WhoAmA 91*
Peterson, Delaine C. 1936- *St&PR 91*
Peterson, Delmont Russell 1918- *St&PR 91*
Peterson, Dennis Edwin 1938- *St&PR 91*
Peterson, Diane Lynn 1955- *WhoAmW 91*
Peterson, Donald A. 1935- *St&PR 91*
Peterson, Donald Robert 1923- *WhoAm 90*
Peterson, Donald Robert 1929- *WhoAm 90, WhoWrEP 89*
Peterson, Donald Walter 1925- *St&PR 91*
Peterson, Dorothy 1932- *WhoAmA 91*
Peterson, Duwayne J. 1932- *St&PR 91*
Peterson, Dwight A. 1933- *St&PR 91*
Peterson, Edward Adrian 1941- *WhoAm 90*
Peterson, Edward Alfred 1928- *WhoAm 90*
Peterson, Edward Dale 1929- *WhoAm 90*
Peterson, Edward Nohl 1930- *WhoE 91*
Peterson, Edwin J. 1930- *WhoAm 90*
Peterson, Edwin P *BiDrAPA 89*
Peterson, Ellen Lenore 1949- *WhoEmL 91*
Peterson, Ellsworth Lorin 1924- *St&PR 91*
Peterson, Elmor Lee 1938- *WhoSSW 91*
Peterson, Eric 1946- *OxCCanT*
Peterson, Eric Clinton 1944- *WhoWrEP 89*
Peterson, Eric Robert 1944- *WhoE 91*
Peterson, Eric Webster 1945- *BiDrAPA 89*
Peterson, Esther *BioIn 16*
Peterson, Esther 1906- *WhoAm 90*
Peterson, Evan Tye 1925- *WhoAm 90*
Peterson, Floyd Delner 1907- *WhoAm 90*
Peterson, Franklynn Don 1938- *WhoWrEP 89*
Peterson, Fred McCrae 1936- *WhoAm 90*
Peterson, Fritz 1942- *Ballpl 90*
Peterson, Gale Eugene 1944- *WhoAm 90*
Peterson, Gale Roy 1948- *WhoEmL 91*
Peterson, Gary 1945- *BiDrAPA 89*
Peterson, Gary Andrew 1940- *WhoAm 90*
Peterson, Gary Glenn 1953- *WhoEmL 91*
Peterson, George Emanuel, Jr. 1931- *St&PR 91, WhoAm 90*
Peterson, George Harold 1931- *WhoAm 90*
Peterson, George P. 1930- *WhoAm 90*
Peterson, Gerald Alvin 1931- *WhoAm 90*
Peterson, Gerald C 1938- *BiDrAPA 89*
Peterson, Glade 1928-1990 *BioIn 16*
Peterson, Glen Nathan 1945- *BiDrAPA 89*
Peterson, Glenn Richard 1948- *BiDrAPA 89*
Peterson, Gordon Edmond, II 1951- *WhoWor 91*
Peterson, Grant 1954- *BioIn 16*
Peterson, Greg J. 1956- *St&PR 91*
Peterson, Gregg Lee 1943- *WhoAm 90*
Peterson, Gregor G. 1932- *St&PR 91*
Peterson, Gregor Goss 1932- *WhoAm 90*
Peterson, Gregory 1954- *ODwPR 91*
Peterson, Gregory Alan 1952- *BiDrAPA 89*
Peterson, Gwen Entz 1938- *WhoAmA 91*
Peterson, H. William 1922- *WhoE 91, WhoWor 91*
Peterson, Hal 1948- *IntWWM 90*
Peterson, Hans 1922- *AuBYP 90*
Peterson, Harding 1929- *WhoAm 90*
Peterson, Harold Albert 1908- *WhoAm 90*
Peterson, Harold Albert 1946- *St&PR 91*
Peterson, Harold L. 1922- *AuBYP 90*
Peterson, Harold Oscar 1909- *WhoAm 90*
Peterson, Harold Patrick 1935- *WhoAmA 91*
Peterson, Harries-Clichy 1924- *WhoAm 90*
Peterson, Harry E. 1921- *St&PR 91*
Peterson, Harry N. *BioIn 16*
Peterson, Harry Valdemar 1927- *WhoWor 91*
Peterson, Hazel Agnes *WhoAmW 91*
Peterson, Heidi Aarlien 1961- *WhoEmL 91*
Peterson, Herbert W 1932- *BiDrAPA 89*
Peterson, Holger Martin 1912- *WhoSSW 91*
Peterson, Horthon L. 1924- *St&PR 91*
Peterson, Howard Cooper 1939- *WhoWor 91*
Peterson, Howard George Finnemore 1951- *WhoAm 90*
Peterson, Howard John 1951- *WhoAm 90*
Peterson, Hubert H. 1913- *St&PR 91*

Peterson, J. Dwight 1897- St&PR 91, WhoAm 90
Peterson, J. Renee 1966- WhoAmW 91
Peterson, James AuBYP 90
Peterson, James Algert 1915- WhoAm 90
Peterson, James Charles 1949- WhoEmL 91
Peterson, James Douglas 1948- WhoEmL 91
Peterson, James Gary 1937- St&PR 91
Peterson, James Kenneth 1934- WhoAm 90
Peterson, James Lincoln 1942- WhoAm 90
Peterson, James Robert 1927- WhoAm 90
Peterson, James Robert 1932- WhoSSW 91
Peterson, Jane 1876-1965 WhoAmA 91N
Peterson, Jane Scanland 1935- WhoAmW 91
Peterson, Jane White 1941- WhoAmW 91
Peterson, Janet Bolster 1937- WhoAmW 91
Peterson, Jeannie Ellen 1940- WhoWor 91
Peterson, Jerome Sidney 1903-1987 BioIn 16
Peterson, Jimmy L. 1947- WhoSSW 91
Peterson, John BiDrAPA 89
Peterson, John A. 1934- St&PR 91
Peterson, John Christian 1951- WhoEmL 91
Peterson, John D. 1933- St&PR 91
Peterson, John Dargavel 1961- WhoEmL 91
Peterson, John David 1946- IntWWM 90
Peterson, John Douglas 1939- WhoAm 90, WhoAmA 91
Peterson, John Edgar, Jr. 1916- WhoSSW 91
Peterson, John Edward 1944- St&PR 91
Peterson, John Eric 1914- WhoAm 90
Peterson, John Frederick 1953- St&PR 91
Peterson, John Lawrence 1924- AuBYP 90
Peterson, John Oscar 1929- WhoE 91
Peterson, John P WhoAmA 91N
Peterson, John Robert 1953- WhoSSW 91
Peterson, Joleen Phyllis 1964- WhoAmW 91
Peterson, Karl Lee 1919- WhoAm 90
Peterson, Kathleen Ann 1951- WhoAmW 91
Peterson, Kathy Marie 1951- WhoAmW 91
Peterson, Kenneth Allen, Sr. 1939- WhoWor 91
Peterson, Kenneth James 1935- St&PR 91
Peterson, Kent 1925- Ballpl 90
Peterson, Kent Wright 1943- WhoAm 90, WhoSSW 91
Peterson, Kirk Charles 1949- WhoAm 90
Peterson, Kristin 1954- WhoAmA 91
Peterson, Larry D 1935- WhoAmA 91
Peterson, Lawrence Peter 1946- BiDrAPA 89
Peterson, Lawrence Robert 1949- WhoAm 90
Peterson, Len 1917- OxCCanT [port]
Peterson, Leroy 1930- WhoWor 91
Peterson, Leslie Ernest 1928- WhoAm 90
Peterson, Leslie R. 1923- St&PR 91
Peterson, Leslie Raymond 1923- WhoAm 90, WhoWor 91
Peterson, Lester G. 1941- St&PR 91
Peterson, Linda Gay 1949- BiDrAPA 89
Peterson, Linda Mercado BiDrAPA 89
Peterson, Lisa Lee 1959- WhoAmW 91
Peterson, Lois Irene 1935- WhoAmW 91
Peterson, Lois Sirry 1934- St&PR 91
Peterson, Lorna Ingrid 1956- WhoAmW 91
Peterson, Lorraine 1940- BioIn 16
Peterson, Louis 1922- DrBlPA 90
Peterson, Louis Robert 1923- WhoAm 90
Peterson, Lowell 1950- WhoEmL 91, WhoWor 91
Peterson, Lynn Marie 1953- WhoAmW 91
Peterson, M. J. 1949- WhoE 91
Peterson, M. Roger 1929- WhoAm 90
Peterson, Margaret 1902- BioIn 16
Peterson, Margaret H BiDrAPA 89
Peterson, Maria Caroline 1950- WhoAmW 91
Peterson, Marilyn Ethel 1926- WhoWrEP 89
Peterson, Mark Christopher Robert 1957- IntWWM 90
Peterson, Mark Warren 1947- WhoEmL 91
Peterson, Mark William 1951- BiDrAPA 89
Peterson, Martha Angell 1945- WhoEmL 91
Peterson, Martin L. 1954- WhoEmL 91
Peterson, Mary Alice 1933- WhoAmW 91
Peterson, Melvin Norman Adolph 1929- WhoAm 90
Peterson, Mendel Lazear 1918- WhoAm 90
Peterson, Merrill Daniel 1921- WhoAm 90
Peterson, Michael Owen 1947- St&PR 91
Peterson, Mildred Othmer 1902- WhoAm 90
Peterson, Miriam Mears 1942- WhoSSW 91
Peterson, Monica WhoAmW 91
Peterson, Monica 1938- DrBlPA 90
Peterson, N. Curtis, Jr. 1922- WhoAm 90
Peterson, Nad A. 1926- St&PR 91, WhoAm 90
Peterson, Nadeen 1934- WhoAm 90, WhoAmW 91
Peterson, Nancy Ann 1947- WhoAmW 91
Peterson, Nancy Carol 1949- WhoEmL 91
Peterson, Neal H BiDrAPA 89
Peterson, Norma Jo 1938- WhoAmW 91
Peterson, Norvell Louis, Sr. 1909- BiDrAPA 89
Peterson, O. James, III 1935- St&PR 91
Peterson, Oscar 1925- BioIn 16, DrBlPA 90, OxCPMus, WorAlBi
Peterson, Oscar Emmanuel 1925- WhoAm 90, WhoWor 91
Peterson, Oscar James, III 1935- WhoAm 90
Peterson, Oscar W. 1887-1951 BioIn 16
Peterson, Oscar William 1887-1951 MusmAFA
Peterson, Osler Leopold 1946- WhoEmL 91
Peterson, Pamela Wynne 1949- WhoAmW 91
Peterson, Patti McGill 1943- WhoAm 90, WhoAmW 91
Peterson, Paul Elliott 1940- WhoAm 90
Peterson, Paul Kenneth 1915- WhoAm 90
Peterson, Paul Quayle 1912- WhoAm 90
Peterson, Paul T. 1947- St&PR 91
Peterson, Paula Maria 1961- WhoAmW 91
Peterson, Perry 1908-1958 WhoAmA 91N
Peterson, Peter G. BioIn 16
Peterson, Peter G. 1926- WhoAm 90
Peterson, Peter George 1926- BiDrUSE 89
Peterson, Philip Everett 1922- WhoAm 90
Peterson, Polly Wietzke 1939- WhoAmW 91, WhoSSW 91
Peterson, Ralph 1924- St&PR 91, WhoAm 90
Peterson, Ralph E. 1934- WhoAm 90
Peterson, Ralph Edward 1932- WhoAm 90
Peterson, Ralph Randall 1944- St&PR 91
Peterson, Raymond Louis 1931- St&PR 91
Peterson, Raynold LaVern 1948- St&PR 91
Peterson, Renno Louis 1948- WhoSSW 91
Peterson, Richard Allan 1938- St&PR 91
Peterson, Richard Allen 1942- WhoAm 90
Peterson, Richard Allen 1955- WhoWor 91
Peterson, Richard Carson 1953- WhoAm 90
Peterson, Richard Elton 1941- WhoAm 90
Peterson, Richard Hamlin 1914- WhoAm 90
Peterson, Richard Lee 1945- WhoSSW 91
Peterson, Richard S. 1930- St&PR 91
Peterson, Richard William 1925- WhoAm 90
Peterson, Robert 1924- WhoWrEP 89
Peterson, Robert A. 1925- St&PR 91
Peterson, Robert Allen 1941- WhoE 91
Peterson, Robert Allen 1944- WhoAm 90
Peterson, Robert Anthony, Jr. 1956- WhoE 91
Peterson, Robert Austin 1925- WhoAm 90
Peterson, Robert Byron St&PR 91
Peterson, Robert D. St&PR 91N
Peterson, Robert Dean 1936- St&PR 91
Peterson, Robert Herrman 1925- BiDrAPA 89
Peterson, Robert L. 1931- St&PR 91
Peterson, Robert Leroy 1934- WhoE 91
Peterson, Robert Stephen 1947- WhoSSW 91
Peterson, Robert Thomas 1950- St&PR 91
Peterson, Robin Tucker 1937- WhoAm 90
Peterson, Roderick William 1921- WhoAm 90
Peterson, Rodney Delos 1932- WhoAm 90
Peterson, Roger Dean, Jr. 1965- WhoEmL 91
Peterson, Roger E. 1937- St&PR 91
Peterson, Roger Eric 1937- WhoAm 90
Peterson, Roger Tory 1908- WhoAm 90, WhoAmA 91
Peterson, Roger William 1936- St&PR 91
Peterson, Roland Oscar 1932- WhoAm 90
Peterson, Ronald A. 1949- St&PR 91
Peterson, Ronald Arthur 1938- WhoE 91, WhoWor 91
Peterson, Ronald H. 1944- St&PR 91
Peterson, Ross King 1947- BiDrAPA 89
Peterson, Rudolph A. 1904- St&PR 91, WhoAm 90
Peterson, Russell Francis AuBYP 90
Peterson, Russell Wilbur 1916- WhoAm 90
Peterson, Sally Lu 1942- WhoAmW 91
Peterson, Scott ODwPR 91
Peterson, Scott Clifford 1953- WhoEmL 91
Peterson, Sharon Marie 1947- WhoWrEP 89
Peterson, Shirley D. 1941- WhoAm 90
Peterson, Sophia 1929- WhoAmW 91
Peterson, Spiro 1922- WhoAm 90
Peterson, Stanley Lee 1949- WhoEmL 91, WhoWor 91
Peterson, Stephen W 1949- BiDrAPA 89
Peterson, Sue BioIn 16
Peterson, Susan Harnly 1925- WhoAmA 91
Peterson, Susan Kathryn 1964- WhoAmW 91
Peterson, Susan Vietzke 1960- WhoAmW 91
Peterson, Sushila Jane 1952- WhoAmW 91
Peterson, Terence Joseph 1959- WhoSSW 91
Peterson, Thage G. 1933- WhoWor 91
Peterson, Theodore Bernard 1918- WhoAm 90
Peterson, Thomas 1959- IntWWM 90
Peterson, Thomas Michael 1959- WhoEmL 91
Peterson, Tim BioIn 16
Peterson, Tom BioIn 16
Peterson, Ursula Kullack 1933- WhoSSW 91
Peterson, Vicki Jenkins 1949- WhoAmW 91
Peterson, Virgil W. 1904-1989 BioIn 16
Peterson, Wallace Carroll, Sr. 1921- WhoAm 90
Peterson, Walter Fritiof 1920- WhoAm 90
Peterson, Walter Scott 1944- WhoE 91
Peterson, Wayne Turner 1927- IntWWM 90
Peterson, Willard James 1938- WhoAm 90
Peterson, William C. 1930- St&PR 91
Peterson, William Canova 1945- WhoSSW 91
Peterson, William Dwight 1954- BiDrAPA 89, WhoE 91
Peterson, William Frank 1922- WhoE 91, WhoWor 91
Peterson, William Michael 1942- St&PR 91
Peterson, William Palmer 1953- WhoEmL 91, WhoWor 91
Peterson, William R. 1943-1990 ConAu 132
Peterson, Willis Lester 1932- WhoAm 90
Peterson-Nedry, Judith A. 1947- WhoWrEP 89
Peterson Perez, Emily Lynn 1951- WhoAmW 91
Peterson Q.C., Leslie Raymond 1923- WhoWor 91
Peterson-Tapia, Yvonne BiDrAPA 89
Peterson-Vita, Elizabeth Ann 1955- WhoEmL 91
Petesch, Natalie L.M. WhoWrEP 89
Petesch, Natalie L M 1924- ConAu 12AS [port]
Pethel, James 1936- IntWWM 90
Pethel, Stanley Robert 1950- IntWWM 90
Petheo, Bela Francis 1934- WhoAmA 91
Pether, Donald A. 1948- St&PR 91
Pether, Henry E. 1867-1932 OxCPMus
Petherbridge, Deanna 1939- BiDWomA
Pethick, Christopher John 1942- WhoAm 90
Pethick-Lawrence, Emmeline 1867-1954 FemiCLE
Peticolas, Warner Leland 1929- WhoAm 90
Petiet, Carole Anne 1952- WhoAmW 91
Petievich, Gerald 1944- TwCCr&M 91
Petijt, Maria 1623-1677 EncCoWW
Petika, David M. 1945- WhoAm 90
Petillo, M. Joann 1959- WhoAmW 91
Petion, Alexandre 1770-1818 BioIn 16
Petiot, Michel L. 1936- St&PR 91
Petipa, Marius 1818-1910 WorAlBi
Petit, Allison ODwPR 91
Petit, Brenda Joyce 1939- WhoSSW 91
Petit, Eugene Claudius- 1907-1989 BioIn 16
Petit, Jacob 1796-1865 PenDiDA 89
Petit, James Michael 1948- BiDrAPA 89
Petit, Lynn Ann 1948- WhoAmW 91
Petit, Maria Luisa 1943- WhoWor 91
Petit, Michel W. 1943- St&PR 91
Petit, Nicolas 1732-1791 PenDiDA 89
Petit, Nicolas 1736-1798 PenDiDA 89
Petit, Parker H. 1939- St&PR 91
Petit, Parker Holmes 1939- WhoAm 90, WhoWor 91
Petit, Philippe 1949- BioIn 16
Petit, Pierre 1922- IntWWM 90, WhoWor 91
Petit, Pierre Roger 1952- BiDrAPA 89
Petit, Roland 1924- WhoWor 91
Petitclair, Pierre 1813-1860 DcLB 99, OxCCanT
Petite Bande, La PenDiMP
Petite, Michael James 1937- BiDrAPA 89
Petitjean, Jean WhoWrEP 89
Petito, Victor Thomas, Jr. 1936- WhoSSW 91
Petitpierre, Aristide PenDiDA 89
Petitpierre, Eduard 1941- WhoWor 91
Petitt, Gerald William 1945- St&PR 91
Petitt, Phil A. 1933- St&PR 91
Petitt, Richard George 1948- WhoAm 90
Petitt, Vicki Lynn 1960- WhoE 91
Petivan, Victoria A BiDrAPA 89
Petkash, David Gabriel BiDrAPA 89
Petkov, Dimiter 1939- IntWWM 90
Petkova, Vanya 1942- EncCoWW
Petkus, Donald Allen 1941- St&PR 91
Petlin, Irving 1934- WhoAmA 91
Petliura, Symon Vasyl'ovych 1879-1926 BioIn 16
Petlock, Martin R. 1943- WhoSSW 91
Petluck, Shelley Rae 1949- BiDrAPA 89
Petmecky, William Maier 1937- St&PR 91
Peto, Andrew BiDrAPA 89
Peto, Ulrike Elizabeth 1944- WhoAmW 91
Petok, Samuel 1922- WhoAm 90
Petosa, Jason Joseph 1939- WhoAm 90
Petracek, Michael Ray 1946- WhoAm 90, WhoSSW 91
Petraglia, Philip Francis 1933- St&PR 91
Petraitis, Karel Colette 1945- WhoE 91
Petrakakis, Georgios 1952- WhoWor 91
Petrakis, Harry Mark 1923- ConAu 30NR, WhoAm 90, WhoWrEP 89
Petrakis, Julia Ward 1936- WhoAmW 91, WhoWor 91
Petrakis, Nicholas Louis 1922- WhoAm 90
Petrakis-Pawson, Stella Rose 1948- WhoAmW 91
Petralia, Elaine Phyllis 1960- WhoE 91
Petralia, Ronald Sebastian 1954- WhoAm 90
Petralli, Geno 1959- Ballpl 90
Petrancosta, Salvatore Marco 1947- WhoE 91
Petrarca, Pamela Beth 1956- WhoAmW 91
Petrarch 1304-1374 WorAlBi, WrPh
Petrarcha, Francesco 1304-1374 WrPh
Petraro, Vincent L. 1956- WhoE 91
Petras, James Frank 1937- WhoWrEP 89
Petras, Kathleen Ann 1958- WhoAmW 91
Petrasich, John Moris 1945- WhoWor 91
Petrassi, Goffredo 1904- IntWWM 90, PenDiMP A
Petrat, Betteann BioIn 16
Petrausch, R. J. 1945- ODwPR 91
Petrauskas, Helen O. 1944- WhoAmW 91
Petre, Charles W PenDiMP
Petre, Donna Marie 1947- WhoAmW 91
Petre, Leonardus Josephus 1943- IntWWM 90
Petrecca, Vincent R. 1940- St&PR 91
Petree, William Horton 1920- WhoAm 90
Petrek, William Joseph 1928- WhoAm 90
Petrella, Mary A. 1962- St&PR 91
Petrelli, Joseph Lawrence 1951- St&PR 91
Petremont, Clarice M WhoAmA 91N
Petrenko, Viktor BioIn 16
Petrequin, Harry Joseph, Jr. 1929- WhoAm 90, WhoE 91
Petres, Stephen 1903- BiDrAPA 89
Petretti, Kenneth Alfred 1949- WhoE 91
Petrey, A. D. 1930- WhoSSW 91
Petrey, Charles Louis 1944- St&PR 91
Petrey, Roderick Norman 1941- WhoAm 90
Petri, David 1962- PenDiMP
Petri, Egon 1881-1962 PenDiMP
Petri, Elio 1929-1982 BioIn 16
Petri, Enrico Lodovico 1929- WhoWor 91
Petri, Hanne 1929- PenDiMP
Petri, Lennart 1914- WhoWor 91
Petri, Michala 1958- IntWWM 90, PenDiMP
Petri, Olavus DcScanL
Petri, Peter Alexander 1946- WhoE 91
Petri, Thomas Everet 1940- WhoAm 90
Petri-Raben, Trude PenDiDA 89
Petric, Ivo 1931- IntWWM 90
Petric, Marion Lorna 1965- WhoAmW 91
Petric, Vlada ConAu 129
Petric, Vladimir 1928- ConAu 129
Petrich, Beatrice Ann 1925- WhoAm 90
Petrich, John Michael BiDrAPA 89
Petrich, Scott Lane 1946- St&PR 91
Petricioli Iturbide, Gustavo 1928- WhoWor 91
Petrick, Alfred, Jr. 1926- WhoAm 90
Petrick, Charles Donald 1928- St&PR 91
Petrick, Ernest Nicholas 1922- WhoAm 90
Petrick, Robert BioIn 16
Petrides, George Athan 1916- WhoAm 90
Petrie, Bruce Robert 1960- WhoEmL 91
Petrie, Catherine 1947- BioIn 16
Petrie, Cordia Greer 1872-1964 LiHiK
Petrie, Daniel Mannix 1920- WhoAm 90
Petrie, Donald Archibald 1921- St&PR 91, WhoAm 90
Petrie, Donald Joseph 1921- WhoAm 90
Petrie, Elizabeth M. WhoAm 90
Petrie, Eric Cameron 1954- BiDrAPA 89

Petrie, Ferdinand Ralph 1925- WhoAm 90, WhoAmA 91, WhoWrEP 89
Petrie, Garth F. 1938- WhoSSW 91
Petrie, George Whitefield, III 1912- WhoSSW 91
Petrie, Gregory Steven 1951- WhoEmL 91
Petrie, Henry W. 1857-1925 OxCPMus
Petrie, Howard Lane 1953- WhoE 91
Petrie, Hugh Gilbert 1937- WhoAm 90, WhoWor 91
Petrie, James Stanton 1936- WhoAm 90
Petrie, John Daniel St&PR 91N
Petrie, Lowell E. 1947- St&PR 91
Petrie, Michael J. 1956- St&PR 91
Petrie, Milton 1902?- BioIn 16
Petrie, Milton J. WhoE 91
Petrie, Paul James 1928- WhoE 91
Petrie, Peter Charles 1932- WhoWor 91
Petrie, Rhona TwCCr&M 91
Petrie, Robin NewAgMG
Petrie, Roy H. 1940- WhoAm 90
Petrie, Sylvia Spencer 1931- WhoAmA 91, WhoE 91
Petrie, Trent BioIn 16
Petrie, William 1912- WhoAm 90
Petrie, William M 1946- BiDrAPA 89
Petrik, Eugene Vincent 1932- WhoAm 90
Petrik, Jack 1929- St&PR 91
Petrik, Robert J. St&PR 91
Petrikin, Kathleen Marie 1955- WhoAmW 91
Petrilla, Raymond J. 1951- St&PR 91
Petrilli, Anthony 1941- BiDrAPA 89
Petrillo, Carl Edward 1940- WhoAm 90
Petrillo, Frank 1934- St&PR 91
Petrillo, James C. 1892-1984 BioIn 16
Petrillo, James Steven 1928- St&PR 91
Petrillo, Leonard Philip 1941- St&PR 91
Petrina, Anthony J. WhoAm 90
Petrina, Anthony J. 1935- St&PR 91
Petrine, Deborah Leigh Martin 1955- WhoAmW 91
Petrinjak, Darko 1954- IntWWM 90
Petrinovich, Lewis F. 1930- WhoAm 90
Petrinowitsch, Harry 1957- St&PR 91
Petris, Warren Raymond 1948- WhoE 91
Petro, Frances C. BioIn 16
Petro, George C 1946- BiDrAPA 89
Petro, James Michael 1948- WhoEmL 91
Petro, Jane A. 1946- WhoE 91
Petro, Janos 1937- IntWWM 90
Petro, Joseph, Jr 1932- WhoAmA 91
Petro, Pete P. 1925- St&PR 91
Petro, William Michael 1935- St&PR 91
Petrobelli, Pierluigi 1932- IntWWM 90
Petrocchi, Linda Ann 1958- WhoAmW 91
Petrocelli, Frank John, Jr. 1933- St&PR 91
Petrocelli, John M. 1930- St&PR 91
Petrocelli, Marge BioIn 16
Petrocelli, Rico 1943- Ballpl 90
Petroczi, Kata Szidonia 1662-1708 EncCoWW
Petrone, David M. 1944- WhoAm 90
Petrone, Joseph John BiDrAPA 89
Petrone, William Francis 1949- WhoE 91, WhoWor 91
Petrongolo, Anthony 1927- St&PR 91
Petroni, Paolo G. 1942- WhoWor 91
Petronilla 1136?-1162 WomWR
Petronio, Anthony J. WhoAm 90
Petronis, Daina O. 1962- ODwPR 91
Petronius Arbiter WorAlBi
Petrosino, Rocco 1911- St&PR 91
Petroske, James L BiDrAPA 89
Petroski, Catherine BioIn 16
Petroski, Catherine 1939- WhoWrEP 89
Petroski, Henry BioIn 16
Petroski, Henry 1942- WhoWrEP 89
Petrosky, Michael 1955- WhoSSW 91
Petrossian, Christian 1942- WhoWor 91
Petrou, David Michael 1949- ODwPR 91
Petrou, Nicholas V. 1917- WhoAm 90
Petrou, Pierre J. 1914- WhoAm 90
Petrou, Pierre Jean 1914- St&PR 91
Petrov, Ivan 1920- IntWWM 90, PenDiMP
Petrov, Nicolas 1933- WhoE 91
Petrov, Nikolai 1943- IntWWM 90
Petrov, Nikolay 1943- PenDiMP
Petrov, Osip 1806-1878 PenDiMP
Petrov, Rem Victorovitch 1930- WhoWor 91
Petrov, Vadim 1932- IntWWM 90
Petrovic, Alexandre Gabriel 1925- WhoWor 91
Petrovic, Danica 1945- IntWWM 90
Petrovic, Dragutin WhoWrEP 89
Petrovic, William M. 1950- St&PR 91
Petrovich, Janice 1946- WhoHisp 91
Petrovich, Mirjana 1924- BiDrAPA 89
Petrovics, Emil 1930- IntWWM 90
Petrovska, Marija 1926- WhoSSW 91
Petrovykh, Maria 1908-1979 EncCoWW
Petrucci, Anthony 1932- ODwPR 91
Petrucci, Judith B. 1941- WhoAmW 91
Petrucci, Judy BioIn 16
Petrucelli, Joseph A. St&PR 91
Petrucelli, Rocco Joseph, II 1943- WhoAm 90, WhoWor 91
Petrucelly, Jeffrey Paul 1946- WhoEmL 91
Petruchik, Peter 1930- St&PR 91
Petruno, Frank D. 1932- St&PR 91
Petruny, Francis Michael 1933- WhoE 91
Petrus Andreas PenDiDA 89
Petrus de Abano 1250-1318 EncO&P 3
Petrus, David A. 1939- St&PR 91
Petrus, Earl Paul 1935- BiDrAPA 89
Petrus, Joan Kline 1941- WhoAmW 91
Petrus, Joseph P 1919- BiDrAPA 89, WhoE 91
Petrus, Placidus Sujitno 1951- WhoWor 91
Petrus, Robert Thomas 1957- WhoE 91
Petrushka, Edward Michael 1934- WhoAm 90
Petrushka, Shabtai Arieh 1903- IntWWM 90
Petruska, Alexander 1925- IntWWM 90
Petruska, Marilyn Rose 1955- WhoAmW 91
Petrusky, John W. 1935- WhoE 91, WhoWor 91
Petruzates, Arthur Paul 1925- St&PR 91
Petruzella, Daniel Francis 1937- St&PR 91
Petruzzelli, Nicholas Michael WhoE 91
Petruzzello, Michael J. ODwPR 91
Petruzzi, Christopher Robert 1951- WhoWor 91
Petry, Alice Hall 1951- ConAu 130
Petry, Ann 1908- MajTwCW, WhoWrEP 89
Petry, Ann 1911- FemiCLE
Petry, Ann Lane 1908- HarlReB [port]
Petry, Ann Lane 1911- BioIn 16
Petry, Ann Lane 1912- AuBYP 90
Petry, Dan 1958- Ballpl 90
Petry, Herbert Charles, Jr. 1917- WhoAm 90
Petry, John P. 1935- St&PR 91
Petry, Paul J. 1936- St&PR 91
Petry, Ray C. 1903- WhoAm 90
Petry, Richard F. 1948- St&PR 91
Petry, Roger L. 1923- WhoAm 90
Petry, Ruth Vidrine 1947- WhoAmW 91
Petry, Thomas Edwin 1939- St&PR 91
Pett, John Lyman 1948- WhoAm 90
Pett, Saul 1918- WhoWrEP 89
Pett, Stephen 1949- WhoWrEP 89
Pettaway, Charles Henry, Jr. 1951- IntWWM 90
Pettaway, James BioIn 16
Pette, Nicholas M. 1890-1988 BioIn 16
Pettee, George S 1904?-1989 ConAu 130
Pettee, George Sawyer BioIn 16
Pettegrew, Jeffrey W. BioIn 16
Pettegrew, Robert Levern, Jr. 1929- St&PR 91
Pettelle, Edwin W. 1925- St&PR 91
Pettengill, Gordon Hemenway 1926- WhoAm 90
Pettengill, John Clarence 1925- St&PR 91
Pettengill, Kroger 1922- WhoAm 90
Petterkvist, Lovisa EncCoWW
Petters, Louise 1934- St&PR 91
Pettersen, George Richard 1924- WhoAm 90
Pettersen, Kjell Will 1927- WhoAm 90, WhoWor 91
Pettersen, Michael Scott 1952- WhoEmL 91
Petterson, Donald K. 1930- WhoAm 90, WhoWor 91
Petterson, Rodney Russell 1932- St&PR 91
Pettersson, Gunnar Karl 1921- WhoWor 91
Pettersson, Stefan 1948- WhoWor 91
Petteruto, Raymond Ottaviano 1932- WhoE 91
Pettet, William 1942- WhoAmA 91
Petteway, Samuel Bruce 1924- WhoAm 90
Pettey, Susan Marie 1949- WhoAmW 91
Petteys, Merrie Leslie 1950- IntWWM 90, WhoSSW 91
Petti, Annmarie 1955- WhoAmW 91
Petti, Richard James 1949- WhoE 91
Petti, Theodore A 1942- BiDrAPA 89
Petti, William John 1916- St&PR 91
Petti, William John, Jr. 1949- St&PR 91
Petti, Yvette Marie 1963- WhoAmW 91
Pettibone, John Wolcott 1942- WhoAmA 91
Pettibone, Peter John 1939- WhoAm 90, WhoE 91, WhoWor 91
Pettibone, Richard H 1938- WhoAmA 91
Pettibone, Roger B. 1938- St&PR 91
Pettiette, Alison Yvonne 1952- WhoAmW 91, WhoEmL 91
Pettiford, Oscar 1922-1960 BioIn 16, WorAlBi
Pettiglio, Michael 1957- WhoE 91
Pettigrew, Dana Mary 1951- WhoAmW 91
Pettigrew, Edward Thomas, Jr. 1925- St&PR 91
Pettigrew, Karen Beth 1948- WhoAmW 91
Pettigrew, L. Eudora 1928- WhoAm 90, WhoAmW 91
Pettigrew, Susan Jill 1956- WhoAmW 91
Pettigrew, Thomas F. BioIn 16
Pettigrew, Thomas Fraser 1931- ConAu 30NR, WhoAm 90
Pettigrew, Virgil Bernard 1922- St&PR 91
Pettijohn, Francis John 1904- WhoAm 90
Pettijohn, Fred Phillips 1917- WhoAm 90
Pettijohn, Joyce Lorraine 1955- WhoAmW 91
Pettijohn, Ted M. 1962- WhoSSW 91
Pettinari, Catherine Jean 1943- WhoAmW 91
Pettinato, Anthony J., Jr. 1946- St&PR 91
Pettinella, Ferd Anthony 1926- St&PR 91
Pettinella, Nicholas A. 1942- St&PR 91
Pettinella, Pamela 1953- ODwPR 91
Pettinga, Cornelius Wesley 1921- WhoAm 90
Pettinos, Lewis McMakin 1932- St&PR 91
Pettipiece, Clayton 1929- BiDrAPA 89
Pettis, Gary 1958- Ballpl 90
Pettis, Michael Alan 1958- WhoE 91
Pettis, Roderick Whalen BiDrAPA 89
Pettis-Roberson, Shirley McCumber WhoAm 90
Pettise, Stephen Thomas 1941- St&PR 91
Pettit, Arthur E. BioIn 16
Pettit, Bob 1932- WorAlBi
Pettit, Charlotte Rosemary 1943- WhoSSW 91
Pettit, Dale Alexander 1940- WhoAm 90
Pettit, David Robin 1936- IntWWM 90
Pettit, David Starling 1942- WhoSSW 91
Pettit, Florence H. AuBYP 90
Pettit, Frederick Sidney 1930- WhoAm 90
Pettit, Ghery DeWitt 1926- WhoAm 90
Pettit, Henry Corbin 1863-1913 AmLegL
Pettit, Horace 1903- WhoE 91, WhoWor 91
Pettit, Hubert Cleveland 1944- WhoE 91
Pettit, Joanne Marie 1942- WhoAmW 91
Pettit, John Upfold 1820-1881 AmLegL
Pettit, John W. 1942- WhoAm 90
Pettit, Lawrence Kay 1937- WhoAm 90
Pettit, Manson B BiDrAPA 89
Pettit, Margaret Esta 1926- WhoAmW 91
Pettit, Mary P. AuBYP 90
Pettit, Michael Edwin 1950- WhoWrEP 89
Pettit, Peter Acker 1955- WhoEmL 91
Pettit, Robert Gayle, III 1945- WhoSSW 91
Pettit, Roger Lee 1946- WhoEmL 91
Pettit, Sara L. 1944- WhoAmW 91
Pettit, Steven W. 1944- St&PR 91
Pettit, Thomas Henry 1929- WhoAm 90, WhoWor 91
Pettit, Walter Finch 1918- WhoAm 90
Pettit, Wendy Jean 1945- WhoAmW 91
Pettit, Wesley K. 1956- St&PR 91
Pettit, William Dutton, Jr. 1949- WhoAm 90
Pettit, William F, Jr. 1942- BiDrAPA 89
Pettit, William Thomas 1931- WhoAm 90
Pettitt, Barbara Jean 1952- WhoAmW 91
Pettitt, Denise A. 1959- BiDrAPA 89
Pettitt, Jay S. 1926- WhoAm 90
Pettitt, Roger Carlyle 1927- WhoAm 90
Petts, Dale G. 1950- St&PR 91
Pettus, Barbara Wyper 1947- WhoE 91
Pettus, Francis Leigh 1858-1901 AmLegL
Pettus, Jane M 1908- WhoAmA 91
Pettus, Joseph Hodson 1947- WhoAm 90
Pettus, Katherine BiDEWW
Pettus, Mary 1947- ODwPR 91
Pettus, Noreen Louise 1962- WhoAmW 91
Petty, Anne C. WhoWrEP 89
Petty, Bruce 1930- St&PR 91
Petty, Charles R. WhoSSW 91
Petty, Charles Sutherland 1920- WhoAm 90
Petty, David Herbert 1917- St&PR 91
Petty, Frederick 1944- BiDrAPA 89
Petty, George BioIn 16
Petty, George G. 1940- St&PR 91
Petty, George Oliver 1939- WhoAm 90
Petty, Guy James 1951- WhoWor 91
Petty, Jesse 1894-1971 Ballpl 90
Petty, John Robert 1930- St&PR 91, WhoAm 90
Petty, Joyce Jones 1945- WhoAmW 91
Petty, Keith 1920- St&PR 91
Petty, Kenneth H. 1928- St&PR 91
Petty, Leonora K BiDrAPA 89
Petty, Mark E. 1955- St&PR 91
Petty, Mark Eliot 1955- WhoE 91
Petty, Maurice BioIn 16
Petty, Milana Mc Lead 1954- WhoWrEP 89
Petty, Olive Scott 1895- WhoSSW 91, WhoWor 91
Petty, Peggy Joyce 1932- WhoAmW 91
Petty, Priscilla Hayes 1940- WhoAmW 91, WhoWor 91
Petty, Richard BioIn 16
Petty, Richard 1937- WorAlBi
Petty, Robert C. 1938- St&PR 91
Petty, Ronald F. 1947- ODwPR 91
Petty, Ronald Franklin 1947- WhoE 91, WhoEmL 91, WhoWor 91
Petty, Scott, Jr. 1937- St&PR 91, WhoSSW 91
Petty, Stephen Marrs 1943- BiDrAPA 89
Petty, Terry D. 1935- St&PR 91
Petty, Thomas A 1918- BiDrAPA 89
Petty, Thomas Lee 1932- WhoAm 90
Petty, Tom 1952- WhoAm 90
Petty, Tom 1953- EncPR&S 89
Petty, Tom, and the Heartbreakers EncPR&S 89
Petty, Travis Hubert 1928- St&PR 91, WhoAm 90, WhoSSW 91, WhoWor 91
Petty, Wendy M. ODwPR 91
Petty, William 1623-1687 BioIn 16
Petty, William Calvin, III 1940- WhoE 91
Pettyjohn, Carol LaVonne 1940- WhoAmW 91
Petuchowski, Jakob Josef 1925- WhoAm 90
Petursson, Esra Seraja 1918- BiDrAPA 89
Petursson, Hallgrimur 1614-1674 DcScanL
Petursson, Hannes 1931- DcScanL
Petway, Bruce 1886-1941 Ballpl 90
Petykiewicz, Sandra Dickey 1953- WhoAmW 91
Petz, Edwin V. 1935- WhoAm 90
Petz, Edwin Virgil 1935- St&PR 91
Petzal, David Elias 1941- WhoAm 90, WhoWor 91, WhoWrEP 89
Petzel, Florence Eloise 1911- WhoAmW 91, WhoWor 91
Petzing, James Edward 1932- WhoSSW 91
Petzinger, William Charles 1960- WhoWrEP 89
Petzold, Carol Stoker WhoAmW 91
Petzold, Robert George 1917- WhoAm 90
Petzold, Robert W. 1940- St&PR 91
Petzold, Rudy H. 1933- St&PR 91
Petzoldt, Hans 1551-1633 PenDiDA 89
Petzoldt, Leander 1934- WhoWor 91
Petzolt, Hans 1551-1633 PenDiDA 89
Peugeot, Roland 1926- WhoWor 91
Peurifoy, John Emil 1907-1955 BioIn 16
Pevar, Linda Susan 1942- WhoAmW 91
Pevear, Richard AuBYP 90
Pevec, Anthony Edward 1925- WhoAm 90
Peveler, James J. 1936- St&PR 91
Peven, Michael David 1949- WhoAmA 91
Pevenstein, Robert Lewis 1946- St&PR 91
Peverelli, Gerard Joseph 1954- St&PR 91
Peverill, John Arthur 1957- WhoSSW 91
Peverly, Linda Pauline Vaughan 1941- WhoAmW 91
Pevitt, Christine Anne 1945- WhoAm 90
Pevney, Joseph BioIn 16
Pevnick, Jeffrey Stephen 1948- BiDrAPA 89
Pevovar, Eddy Howard 1953- WhoE 91
Pevsner, Aihud 1925- WhoAm 90
Pevsner, Antoine 1886-1962 IntDcAA 90
Pevsner, Nikolaus 1902-1983 MajTwCW
Pevsner, Nikolaus Bernhard Leon 1902-1983 DcNaB 1981
Pevsner, Stella BioIn 16
Pevtchin, Guy Jean-Pierre 1920- WhoWor 91
Pew, Becky Ann 1948- BiDrAPA 89
Pew, John G., Jr. St&PR 91
Pew, Robert Anderson 1936- WhoAm 90
Pew, Robert C. 1923- St&PR 91
Pew, Thomas Richard 1959- St&PR 91
Pew, Thomas W., Jr 1938- WhoAm 90
Pew, Walter C. BioIn 16
Pewe, Troy Lewis 1918- WhoAm 90
Pewewardy, Cornel NewAgMG
Pewitt, Edward Gale 1932- WhoAm 90
Pewitt, James Dudley 1930- WhoAm 90
Pewsey, Brian G. 1935- St&PR 91
Peyer, Bernhard 1885-1963 DcScB S2
Peyer, Gervase de PenDiMP
Peyman, Douglas Alastair Ralph 1920- WhoSSW 91
Peyre, Henri 1901-1988 BioIn 16
Peyre, Henri Maurice 1901- WhoWrEP 89
Peyrefitte, Alain Antoine 1925- BiDFrPL
Peyregne, Andre 1949- IntWWM 90
Peyrelevade, Jean 1939- WhoWor 91
Peyrol-Bonheur, J. BiDWomA
Peyron, Barthelemi PenDiDA 89
Peyronnin, Joseph Felix, III 1947- WhoAm 90
Peyser, Carol Efron 1953- BiDrAPA 89
Peyser, Ellen Rees 1942- BiDrAPA 89
Peyser, Herbert S 1924- BiDrAPA 89
Peyser, Herbert Stanley 1924- WhoE 91
Peyser, Joseph Leonard 1925- WhoAm 90
Peyser, Robert F. 1932- St&PR 91
Peyton, Bertha Menzler 1871-1947 WhoAmA 91N
Peyton, Charles Randolph 1958- WhoSSW 91
Peyton, Craig NewAgMG
Peyton, Donald Leon 1925- WhoAm 90
Peyton, Helen E. 1921- WhoWrEP 89
Peyton, John Francis 1924- WhoAm 90
Peyton, John Rowzee 1752-1798 BioIn 16

Peyton, K. M. *ConAu 32NR*
Peyton, K. M. 1929- *AuBYP 90*
Peyton, K M 1929- *SmATA X [port]*
Peyton, Kathleen 1929- *SmATA 62 [port]*
Peyton, Kathleen Wendy *AuBYP 90*
Peyton, Kathleen Wendy 1929- *ConAu 32NR*
Peyton, Mary Johanna 1946- *WhoAmW 91*
Peyton, Patrick 1908- *BioIn 16*
Peyton, Preston Carlton 1952- *WhoSSW 91*
Peyton, Robert Glen 1940- *St&PR 91*
Peyton, William Maupin 1932- *St&PR 91, WhoAm 90, WhoWor 91*
Pezhman, Majid *BiDrAPA 89*
Pezor, Laurence Jonh, Jr. *BiDrAPA 89*
Pezza, James Joseph 1922- *St&PR 91*
Pezzani, Angelo M. *St&PR 91*
Pezzarossi, A Guillermo *BiDrAPA 89*
Pezzati, Pietro 1902- *WhoAmA 91, WhoE 91*
Pezzella, Jerry James, Jr. 1937- *WhoAm 90, WhoWor 91*
Pezzi, Shelley 1956- *WhoHisp 91*
Pezzia, Nancy Gallardo *BiDrAPA 89*
Pfaehler, G Thomas *BiDrAPA 89*
Pfaelzer, Mariana R. 1926- *WhoAmW 91*
Pfaelzer, Muriel Z. 1926- *WhoAmW 91*
Pfaelzer, Penny 1947- *ODwPR 91*
Pfaender, Jay A. 1942- *St&PR 91*
Pfaff, Alan Rae 1935- *WhoAm 90*
Pfaff, David Noel 1934- *WhoSSW 91*
Pfaff, Donald W. 1939- *WhoAm 90*
Pfaff, Frederick A. 1962- *St&PR 91*
Pfaff, George Otto 1926- *WhoAm 90*
Pfaff, Judy 1946- *BiDWomA, WhoAmA 91*
Pfaff, Tom Martin 1924- *St&PR 91*
Pfaff, William Wallace 1930- *WhoAm 90*
Pfaffenroth, Sara Beekey 1941- *WhoWor 91*
Pfafflin, Sheila Murphy 1934- *WhoAmW 91*
Pfaffman, William Scott 1954- *WhoAmA 91*
Pfaffmann, Carl 1913- *WhoAm 90*
Pfahl, Charles Alton, III 1946- *WhoAmA 91*
Pfahler, Larry Lee 1943- *BiDrAPA 89*
Pfaltzgraff, Robert Louis, Jr. 1934- *WhoAm 90*
Pfalz, Lisalotte von der *EncCoWW*
Pfalzer, Gerald Martin 1945- *WhoEmL 91*
Pfalzer, Zacharias *PenDiDA 89*
Pfalzgrafin, Elisabeth Charlotte 1652-1722 *EncCoWW*
Pfander, Wilhelm 1937- *St&PR 91*
Pfannenstiel, Max Jakob 1902-1976 *DcScB S2*
Pfannkuch, Robert Blaine 1935- *WhoAm 90*
Pfarrer, Donald Hudson 1934- *WhoE 91*
Pfau, Beth A *BiDrAPA 89*
Pfau, George H., Jr. 1924- *St&PR 91*
Pfau, George Harold, Jr. 1924- *WhoAm 90*
Pfau, Johann Ernst *PenDiDA 89*
Pfau, Ludwig *PenDiDA 89*
Pfau, Rebecca Houle 1959- *WhoAmW 91*
Pfau, Richard Anthony 1942- *WhoAm 90*
Pfautsch, George E. 1935- *St&PR 91*
Pfeffer, Arnold 1936- *WhoAm 90*
Pfeffer, Arnold Z *BiDrAPA 89*
Pfeffer, Big Jeff 1882-1954 *Ballpl 90*
Pfeffer, Bruce Paul 1944- *BiDrAPA 89*
Pfeffer, Christian Jackson 1942- *WhoSSW 91*
Pfeffer, Cynthia R 1943- *BiDrAPA 89*
Pfeffer, Cynthia Roberta 1943- *WhoE 91*
Pfeffer, David H. 1935- *WhoAm 90*
Pfeffer, Deborah Lynn *BiDrAPA 89*
Pfeffer, Edward Israel 1914- *WhoAm 90*
Pfeffer, Franz 1926- *WhoWor 91*
Pfeffer, Fred 1860-1932 *Ballpl 90*
Pfeffer, James Lawrence 1951- *St&PR 91*
Pfeffer, Jeff 1888-1972 *Ballpl 90*
Pfeffer, Jeffrey 1946- *WhoAm 90*
Pfeffer, Leo 1910- *WhoAm 90*
Pfeffer, Mary Graves 1951- *WhoAmW 91*
Pfeffer, Michael A. 1945- *St&PR 91*
Pfeffer, Patricia Irene Hendryx 1930- *WhoAmW 91*
Pfeffer, Paul 1938- *BiDrAPA 89*
Pfeffer, Peter John 1941- *St&PR 91*
Pfeffer, Philip Maurice 1945- *St&PR 91, WhoAm 90*
Pfeffer, Richard Lawrence 1930- *WhoAm 90*
Pfeffer, Robert 1935- *WhoAm 90*
Pfeffer, Rubin Harry 1951- *WhoAm 90*
Pfeffer, Susan Beth 1948- *BioIn 16, ConAu 31NR*
Pfeffer-Hurwitz, Judith 1934- *BiDrAPA 89*
Pfefferbaum, Adolf 1943- *BiDrAPA 89*
Pfefferbaum, Betty 1946- *BiDrAPA 89*
Pfefferkorn, Blanche 1884-1961 *BioIn 16*
Pfeifenberger, Werner 1941- *WhoWor 91*
Pfeifer, Carl M 1935- *BiDrAPA 89*
Pfeifer, Catherine Ilse 1961- *WhoAmW 91*
Pfeifer, David E. *WhoAm 90*
Pfeifer, Hans-Wolfgang 1931- *WhoWor 91*
Pfeifer, Jim 1948- *St&PR 91*
Pfeifer, John W. 1941- *St&PR 91*
Pfeifer, Keith Machold 1949- *WhoE 91*
Pfeifer, Lou Ann 1955- *ODwPR 91*
Pfeifer, Marcuse 1936- *WhoAmA 91*
Pfeifer, Marcuse Lucile 1936- *WhoE 91*
Pfeifer, Martin S. 1932- *St&PR 91*
Pfeifer, Michael David 1937- *WhoSSW 91*
Pfeifer, Norman Franklin 1942- *St&PR 91*
Pfeifer, Walter C. 1926- *St&PR 91*
Pfeiff, Hope Marlene 1959- *WhoEmL 91*
Pfeiffer, Albert 1935- *St&PR 91*
Pfeiffer, Astrid Elizabeth 1934- *St&PR 91, WhoAm 90, WhoSSW 91*
Pfeiffer, Carl C. 1908-1988 *BioIn 16*
Pfeiffer, Carl E. 1930- *WhoSSW 91*
Pfeiffer, Christine Janet 1951- *WhoAmW 91*
Pfeiffer, Eckhard *BioIn 16*
Pfeiffer, Emily Jane 1827-1890 *FemiCLE*
Pfeiffer, Emily Jane Davis 1827-1890 *BioIn 16*
Pfeiffer, Eric A 1935- *BiDrAPA 89*
Pfeiffer, Eric Armin 1935- *WhoAm 90*
Pfeiffer, Everett H. 1934- *WhoE 91*
Pfeiffer, Fritz 1889-1960 *WhoAmA 91N*
Pfeiffer, Gerald Eugene 1951- *WhoEmL 91*
Pfeiffer, Heinrich H 1874- *WhoAmA 91N*
Pfeiffer, J. Douglas 1927- *WhoWrEP 89*
Pfeiffer, James Thomas 1945- *WhoE 91*
Pfeiffer, Jane Cahill 1932- *WhoAm 90, WhoAmW 91, WhoWor 91*
Pfeiffer, Joachim 1950- *WhoWor 91*
Pfeiffer, John David 1931- *WhoAm 90*
Pfeiffer, John Edward 1914- *WhoAm 90*
Pfeiffer, John Howard 1923- *St&PR 91*
Pfeiffer, John William 1937- *WhoAm 90, WhoWrEP 89*
Pfeiffer, Leonard, IV *WhoE 91*
Pfeiffer, Martin James, Jr. 1960- *WhoE 91*
Pfeiffer, Max Adolf *PenDiDA 89*
Pfeiffer, Michelle *BioIn 16*
Pfeiffer, Michelle 1957- *ConTFT 8 [port], News 90 [port], WorAlBi*
Pfeiffer, Michelle 1958- *CurBio 90 [port]*
Pfeiffer, Norma *BioIn 16*
Pfeiffer, Ralph Aloysius, Jr. 1927- *WhoAm 90, WhoSSW 91*
Pfeiffer, Robert J. 1920- *St&PR 91*
Pfeiffer, Robert John 1920- *WhoAm 90*
Pfeiffer, Roxane Javid 1953- *BiDrAPA 89*
Pfeiffer, Werner Bernhard 1937- *WhoAm 90, WhoAmA 91*
Pfeiffer, William Edward 1946- *WhoEmL 91*
Pfeifle, Kathleen 1950- *ODwPR 91*
Pfeifle, William George 1944- *WhoSSW 91*
Pfeil, Enzio Graf Von 1953- *WhoWor 91*
Pfeil, John Frederick 1949- *WhoWrEP 89*
Pfeil, Kenneth Carl 1948- *St&PR 91*
Pfeil, Richard J. 1932- *St&PR 91*
Pfeil, Richard John 1932- *WhoAm 90*
Pfeil, Robert L. 1924- *St&PR 91*
Pfeil, Ronald Harmon 1949- *WhoE 91*
Pfeister, James L. 1951- *St&PR 91*
Pfeister, Raymond Lynn 1946- *WhoEmL 91*
Pfeister, Suzanne E. *St&PR 91*
Pfender, Emil 1925- *WhoAm 90*
Pfendt, Anton N. 1955- *St&PR 91*
Pfening, Fred D., III 1949- *St&PR 91*
Pfenninger, Judith Ann 1960- *WhoEmL 91*
Pfenninger, Karl H. 1944- *WhoAm 90*
Pfeufer, Carl 1910-1980 *EncACom*
Pfeuffer, Heidi Christine 1947- *WhoAmW 91*
Pfeuffer, Robert John 1925- *WhoAm 90*
Pfiefer, Norm *St&PR 91*
Pfiester, Jack 1878-1953 *Ballpl 90*
Pfingstl, Hans 1938- *St&PR 91*
Pfingston, Roger Carl 1940- *WhoWrEP 89*
Pfirman, Charles 1891-1937 *Ballpl 90*
Pfirrman, Melvin T. 1931- *St&PR 91*
Pfischner, Fred L. 1908- *St&PR 91*
Pfischner, Robert D. 1922- *St&PR 91*
Pfister, Alfred J. 1933- *St&PR 91*
Pfister, Charles *PenDiDA 89*
Pfister, Dan 1936- *Ballpl 90*
Pfister, Daniel 1952- *IntWWM 90, WhoE 91*
Pfister, Dean William 1932- *St&PR 91, WhoAm 90*
Pfister, Dennis Francis 1926- *St&PR 91*
Pfister, Donald Henry 1945- *WhoAm 90, WhoE 91*
Pfister, Edward Joseph 1934- *WhoSSW 91*
Pfister, Harold Francis 1947- *WhoAmA 91*
Pfister, James Joseph 1946- *WhoAm 90, WhoWor 91*
Pfister, Jean Jacques 1878-1949 *WhoAmA 91N*
Pfister, Karstin Ann 1955- *WhoAmW 91*
Pfister, Marcus *AuBYP 90*
Pfister, Max 1932- *WhoWor 91*
Pfister, Murray Charles 1939-1990 *WhoAm 90*
Pfister, Roswell Robert 1938- *WhoAm 90*
Pfister, Walter J., Jr. 1929- *ODwPR 91*
Pfisterer, Hermann R. 1934- *St&PR 91*
Pfitzenmaier, Denise Diane 1958- *St&PR 91*
Pfitzner, Hans 1869-1949 *PenDiMP A*
Pfizenmaier, Richard *BioIn 16*
Pflanze, Otto Paul 1918- *WhoAm 90*
Pflaster, Robert John 1943- *WhoSSW 91*
Pflasterer, James Lee 1929- *St&PR 91*
Pflaum, Susanna Whitney 1937- *WhoAm 90*
Pflaum, William C. *ODwPR 91*
Pfleger, Michael *BioIn 16*
Pfleider, Shirley Jean 1952- *WhoAmW 91*
Pflieger, John H., Jr. 1956- *St&PR 91*
Pflieger, Larry Leonard 1923- *St&PR 91*
Pflimlin, Pierre Eugene Jean 1907- *BiDFrPL*
Pflueger, Edward Maximilian 1905- *WhoAm 90*
Pflug, Shirley L 1933- *BiDrAPA 89*
Pflugbeil, Kurt *BioIn 16*
Pfluger, Curtis C. 1927- *St&PR 91*
Pflum, William John 1924- *WhoE 91*
Pflumm, Clarence H. 1902- *St&PR 91*
Pfnister, Allan Orel 1925- *WhoAm 90*
Pfnur, Vinzenz 1937- *WhoWor 91*
Pfohl, Bruce Michael 1951- *BiDrAPA 89*
Pfohl, Karl 1826-1894 *PenDiDA 89*
Pforr, Mary Martha 1948- *WhoE 91*
Pforr, William John 1947- *WhoE 91*
Pforzheimer, Carl H., Jr. 1907- *St&PR 91*
Pforzheimer, Carl Howard, Jr. 1907- *WhoAm 90, WhoWor 91*
Pforzheimer, Harry, III 1954- *ODwPR 91*
Pfost, Dale Robert 1957- *WhoEmL 91*
Pfountz, Harold J. 1943- *St&PR 91*
Pfouts, Ralph William 1920- *WhoAm 90, WhoSSW 91, WhoWor 91*
Pfrang, Edward Oscar 1929- *WhoAm 90*
Pfrender, Richard E *BiDrAPA 89*
Pfriem, Bernard 1916- *WhoAmA 91*
Pfriem, Bernard Aldine 1916- *WhoAm 90*
Pfriender, Robert C. 1954- *St&PR 91*
Pfrommer, James Michael 1957- *BiDrAPA 89*
Pfund, Edward Theodore, Jr. 1923- *WhoWor 91*
Pfund, Harry William 1900- *WhoAm 90*
Pfund, Rose Toshiko 1929- *WhoAmW 91*
Pfunder, Malcolm Gilkey 1919- *WhoAm 90*
Pfundt, William N. *St&PR 91*
Pfuntner, Allan Robert 1946- *WhoEmL 91*
Phair, David 1921- *St&PR 91*
Phalen, George E. 1923- *St&PR 91*
Phalen, Gregory Gerald 1928- *St&PR 91*
Phalon, Philip Anthony 1929- *St&PR 91, WhoAm 90*
Pham van Dong 1906- *WhoWor 91*
Pham Xuan An *BioIn 16, NewYTBS 90*
Pham, Chat V *BiDrAPA 89*
Pham, Giao Ngoc 1941- *BiDrAPA 89*
Pham, Hung 1912-1988 *BioIn 16*
Pham, Kinh Dinh 1956- *WhoWor 91*
Pham, Tuan Quang 1933- *BiDrAPA 89*
Pham, Tung Ngoc 1954- *WhoSSW 91*
Pham, Van Dong *BioIn 16*
Phan, Thai Tien 1945- *BiDrAPA 89, WhoSSW 91*
Phan, Tu *BiDrAPA 89*
Phan-Tan, Tai 1939- *WhoWor 91*
Phanariotou-Philippou, Athena D. 1912-1935 *EncCoWW*
Phansalkar, Arvind G 1944- *BiDrAPA 89*
Phantom, D. S. *WhoWrEP 89*
Pharamond, Jean-Claude 1947- *St&PR 91*
Phares, Alain Joseph 1942- *WhoAm 90*
Phares, Denver Allen 1951- *WhoSSW 91*
Phares, Donald M. 1931- *WhoAm 90*
Phares, E. Jerry 1928- *WhoAm 90*
Phares, Elwood Willis 1930- *St&PR 91*
Phares, Lynn Levisay 1947- *WhoAmW 91*
Phares, Marguerite Linton 1917- *WhoAmW 91*
Pharis, Claudia Cecilia 1944- *WhoAmW 91*
Pharis, Mark 1947- *WhoAmA 91*
Pharis, Mary Evans 1938- *WhoAmW 91*
Pharis, Ruth McCalister 1934- *WhoAmW 91*
Pharis, William Leonard 1928- *WhoAm 90*
Phariss, Bruce Wallace *BiDrAPA 89*
Pharr, Cynthia 1948- *ODwPR 91*
Pharr, Doris Ann 1951- *WhoAmW 91*
Pharr, Gwendolyn Epps 1948- *WhoSSW 91*
Pharr, Michael Milton 1940- *WhoAm 90*
Pharr, Rachel Elizabeth Caroline 1957- *IntWWM 90*
Pharris, Ann Marie 1950- *WhoAmW 91*
Phears, Bill *BioIn 16*
Pheasant, Merle E., Jr. 1945- *St&PR 91*
Pheifer, Roberta Lynne Stolper 1945- *WhoE 91*
Phelah, Linn Lovejoy 1906- *WhoE 91*
Phelan, Andrew L. 1943- *WhoE 91*
Phelan, Art 1887-1964 *Ballpl 90*
Phelan, Arthur Joseph 1915- *WhoAm 90*
Phelan, Carole Mary Ross 1925- *WhoAmW 91*
Phelan, Charlotte Robertson 1917- *WhoAm 90*
Phelan, Ellen Denise 1943- *WhoAmA 91*
Phelan, Francis J. 1925- *WhoWrEP 89*
Phelan, Harold Leon 1934- *WhoAm 90*
Phelan, Jack P. 1941- *St&PR 91*
Phelan, James Bernard 1941- *WhoWor 91*
Phelan, James Francis 1950- *St&PR 91*
Phelan, John Densmore 1914- *WhoAm 90, WhoWor 91*
Phelan, John J. 1931- *St&PR 91*
Phelan, John J., Jr. 1931- *WhoAm 90*
Phelan, John W J 1930- *BiDrAPA 89*
Phelan, Josephine *AuBYP 90*
Phelan, Karen Barbara 1953- *WhoAmW 91*
Phelan, Linn Lovejoy 1906- *WhoAmA 91*
Phelan, Martin DuPont 1913- *WhoAm 90*
Phelan, Mary Claire 1943- *WhoAmW 91*
Phelan, Mary Elizabeth 1958- *WhoEmL 91*
Phelan, Mary Kay 1914- *AuBYP 90*
Phelan, Mary M. *ODwPR 91*
Phelan, Nancy 1913- *FemiCLE*
Phelan, Patrick Joseph 1950- *WhoE 91*
Phelan, Phyllis White 1951- *WhoAmW 91, WhoEmL 91, WhoWor 91*
Phelan, Richard J. 1937- *BioIn 16*
Phelan, Richard John 1937- *WhoAm 90*
Phelan, Richard Magruder 1921- *WhoAm 90*
Phelan, Richard Paul 1939- *WhoE 91*
Phelan, Robert Allan 1949- *St&PR 91*
Phelan, Robert J. 1947- *St&PR 91*
Phelan, Robin Eric 1945- *WhoEmL 91*
Phelan, Sandra L. *ODwPR 91*
Phelan, Terry Wolfe 1941- *BioIn 16*
Phelan, Thomas 1925- *WhoAm 90, WhoWor 91*
Phelan, Thomas Anthony 1928- *WhoWrEP 89*
Phelan, Thomas Joseph, Jr. 1933- *St&PR 91*
Phelip, Christian 1937- *WhoWor 91*
Phelix, Bernard Robert 1942- *WhoSSW 91*
Phelon, William A. 1871-1925 *Ballpl 90*
Phelps, Almira Hart 1793-1884 *BioAmW*
Phelps, Ashton, Jr. 1945- *WhoAm 90*
Phelps, Babe 1908- *Ballpl 90*
Phelps, Bernard Marnigs 1934- *WhoSSW 91*
Phelps, Betsy *BioIn 16*
Phelps, C. Kermit *BioIn 16*
Phelps, Charles A. 1820-1902 *AmLegL*
Phelps, Charles B. 1788-1858 *AmLegL*
Phelps, Christine Elizabeth 1959- *WhoAmW 91*
Phelps, Dean, Jr. 1944- *St&PR 91*
Phelps, Deanne Elayne 1949- *WhoSSW 91*
Phelps, Donald Eugene 1931- *WhoSSW 91*
Phelps, Ed 1879-1942 *Ballpl 90*
Phelps, Edith Catlin 1875-1961 *WhoAmA 91N*
Phelps, Edward John 1822-1900 *BioIn 16*
Phelps, Edwin J., Jr. 1935- *St&PR 91*
Phelps, Eliakim *EncO&P 3*
Phelps, Elizabeth S. 1815-1852 *BioAmW*
Phelps, Elizabeth Stuart 1844-1911 *FemiCLE*
Phelps, Elizabeth Wooster 1815-1852 *FemiCLE*
Phelps, Erin Margaretta 1951- *WhoAmW 91*
Phelps, Flora Louise Lewis 1917- *WhoAm 90, WhoAmW 91, WhoE 91*
Phelps, George E. 1943- *St&PR 91*
Phelps, Greg Alan 1957- *WhoSSW 91*
Phelps, James E. *WhoAm 90*
Phelps, James E. 1922- *St&PR 91*
Phelps, Joe Frank 1944- *WhoSSW 91*
Phelps, John Ray 1946- *WhoSSW 91*
Phelps, Joseph William 1927- *St&PR 91*
Phelps, Judson Hewett 1942- *WhoAm 90*
Phelps, Ken 1954- *Ballpl 90*
Phelps, Lewis McKinnie 1943- *ODwPR 91, St&PR 91*
Phelps, Malcom Elza 1905- *WhoAm 90*
Phelps, Margaret *AuBYP 90*
Phelps, Mason 1925- *St&PR 91*
Phelps, Michael Edward 1939- *WhoAm 90*
Phelps, Michael Everett Joseph 1947- *WhoAm 90*
Phelps, Michael Joseph 1948- *St&PR 91*
Phelps, Nan *WhoAmA 91N*
Phelps, Norman Thomas 1913- *WhoE 91*
Phelps, Orme Wheelock 1906- *WhoAm 90*
Phelps, Paul Michael 1933- *St&PR 91, WhoAm 90*
Phelps, Paulding 1933- *WhoAm 90*
Phelps, Peter Whittenhall *NewYTBS 90*
Phelps, Phelps 1897-1981 *BioIn 16*
Phelps, Ray 1903-1971 *Ballpl 90*
Phelps, Richard J. 1928- *St&PR 91*
Phelps, Richard Stevens 1938- *WhoE 91*
Phelps, Richards 1941- *WorAlBi*

Phelps, Robert 1922-1989 *BioIn 16, ConAu 129*
Phelps, Robert Frederick, Jr. 1956- *WhoEmL 91*
Phelps, Robert S. 1939- *WhoAm 90*
Phelps, Seth Ledyard 1824-1885 *BioIn 16*
Phelps, Shirley Jenkins *BiDrAPA 89*
Phelps, Stanford N. 1934- *St&PR 91*
Phelps, Steve L. 1958- *WhoSSW 91*
Phelps, Stewart J. 1933- *St&PR 91*
Phelps, Suzanne 1946- *WhoAmW 91*
Phelps, Timothy Hunt 1953- *WhoE 91*
Phelps, William Cunningham 1934- *WhoAm 90*
Phelps, William H. 1902-1988 *BioIn 16*
Phelps, William L. 1955- *St&PR 91*
Phelps, William Walter 1839-1894 *BioIn 16*
Phelps, William Wines 1792-1872 *AmLegL*
Phemister, Robert David 1936- *WhoAm 90*
Phemister, Thomas Alexander 1940- *WhoAm 90*
Phenix, Philip Henry 1915- *WhoAm 90*
Pheretima *WomWR*
Pherigo, William L. 1941- *St&PR 91*
Pheterson, Alexander David *BiDrAPA 89*
Phibbs, Clifford Matthew 1930- *WhoAm 90, WhoWor 91*
Phibbs, Harry Albert 1933- *WhoAm 90*
Phibbs, Mary Ellen 1924- *WhoAmW 91*
Phibbs, Philip Monford 1931- *WhoAm 90*
Phibbs, Roderic Henry 1930- *WhoAm 90*
Phidias 500BC-430BC *WorAlBi*
Phiebig, Albert Jakob 1908- *WhoE 91*
Phifer, Cynthia Ann 1960- *WhoAmW 91*
Phifer, J. Reese 1916- *St&PR 91*
Phifer, Samuel Hudson 1923- *WhoE 91*
Phifer, Virginia Hudson 1951- *St&PR 91*
Philaletha, Eirenaeus *EncO&P 3*
Philalethes, Eirenaeus *EncO&P 3*
Philalethes, Eugenius 1622-1666 *EncO&P 3*
Philander, Dennis Alan 1944- *BiDrAPA 89*
Philbin, Edward James 1932- *WhoAm 90*
Philbin, John Arthur 1934- *WhoAm 90*
Philbin, Tom 1934- *BioIn 16*
Philbrick, Donald Lockey 1923- *WhoAm 90*
Philbrick, Julian W. *St&PR 91*
Philbrick, Kathilyn Durnford 1948- *WhoAmW 91*
Philbrick, Kemuel Luke *BiDrAPA 89*
Philbrick, Lawrence Emery 1947- *St&PR 91*
Philbrick, Loretta J. 1934- *St&PR 91*
Philbrick, Margaret Elder 1914- *WhoAm 90, WhoAmA 91*
Philbrick, Otis 1888-1973 *WhoAmA 91N*
Philbrick, Ralph 1934- *WhoAm 90*
Philbrick, Thomas Leslie 1929- *WhoAm 90*
Philbrook, Clem 1917- *AuBYP 90*
Philby, Kim 1912-1988 *AnObit 1988, BioIn 16*
Philby, Rhoda Singleton 1939- *WhoSSW 91*
Philen, James Gilbert, Jr. 1904- *St&PR 91*
Philion, James Robert 1944- *St&PR 91*
Philip 1639?-1676 *WhNaAH [port]*
Philip, King *EncCRAm*
Philip, King 1639?-1676 *WhNaAH [port]*
Philip II, King of Spain 1527-1598 *BioIn 16*
Philip III, King of Spain 1578-1621 *BioIn 16*
Philip IV, King of Spain 1605-1665 *BioIn 16*
Philip V, King of Spain 1683-1746 *BioIn 16*
Philip of Pokanoket 1639?-1676 *WhNaAH [port]*
Philip, Prince 1921- *BioIn 16, WhoWor 91*
Philip, Sachem of the Wampanoags *BioIn 16*
Philip, A. G. Davis 1929- *WhoAm 90, WhoWor 91*
Philip, A.G. Davis 1929- *WhoWrEP 89*
Philip, Andre 1902-1970 *BiDFrPL*
Philip, Craig E. 1953- *St&PR 91*
Philip, Hoffman 1872-1951 *BioIn 16*
Philip, James 1837-1911 *WhNaAH*
Philip, Lotte Brand 1910- *WhoAmA 91N*
Philip, Marlene Nourbese 1947- *WhoWor 91*
Philip, Peter Van Ness 1925- *WhoAm 90*
Philip, Robert Marshall 1945- *IntWWM 90*
Philip, Thomas Peter 1933- *WhoAm 90*
Philip, Thomas Winslow 1962- *WhoE 91*
Philip, William W 1946- *BiDrAPA 89*
Philip, William Warren 1926- *St&PR 91, WhoAm 90*
Philipbar, Charles W. 1935- *St&PR 91*
Philipbar, William Bernard 1925- *St&PR 91*
Philipbar, William Bernard, Jr. 1925- *WhoAm 90*
Philipe, Anne 1917- *EncCoWW*
Philipp, Anita Marie 1948- *WhoSSW 91*
Philipp, Isidore 1863-1958 *PenDiMP*
Philipp, Robert 1895-1981 *WhoAmA 91N*
Philipp, Walter Viktor 1936- *WhoAm 90*
Philippakis, Ioannis Nicolas 1966- *WhoWor 91*
Philippbar, Deborah DeBarr 1951- *WhoAmW 91*
Philippe, duc d'Orleans 1747-1793 *BioIn 16*
Philippe, Charles Louis 1874-1909 *BioIn 16*
Philippe, Jean Claude 1948- *WhoWor 91*
Philippe, Rault-Doumax 1945- *WhoWor 91*
Philippeaux, Eddy Jean 1952- *WhoE 91*
Philippi, Dieter Rudolph 1929- *WhoE 91*
Philipps, Edward William 1938- *St&PR 91, WhoAm 90*
Philipps, Louis Edward 1906- *WhoAm 90*
Philippsen, John Newman 1952- *St&PR 91*
Philips, Arthur Carlton 1881-1942 *BioIn 16*
Philips, B. Calvin 1941- *St&PR 91*
Philips, Barbara Murray 1928- *WhoAmW 91*
Philips, Christine Ann 1938- *WhoSSW 91*
Philips, Connie *ODwPR 91*
Philips, Constantinos L. 1934- *St&PR 91*
Philips, David Evan 1926- *WhoAm 90, WhoWor 91*
Philips, Dorothy M. *St&PR 91*
Philips, George 1931- *St&PR 91, WhoAm 90, WhoE 91*
Philips, Irving *BiDrAPA 89*
Philips, James B. 1907-1987 *EncO&P 3*
Philips, James Davison 1920- *WhoSSW 91*
Philips, Jane Bronson *BioIn 16*
Philips, Jesse 1914- *St&PR 91, WhoAm 90*
Philips, Joan *BiDEWW*
Philips, John 1676-1708 *DcLB 95 [port]*
Philips, John Douglass 1932- *IntWWM 90*
Philips, Judith *BiDEWW*
Philips, Judson *TwCCr&M 91*
Philips, Judson 1903-1989 *AnObit 1989*
Philips, Judson Pentecost 1903-1989 *BioIn 16*
Philips, Katherine 1632-1664 *BiDEWW, FemiCLE*
Philips, Katherine Fowler 1631-1664 *BioIn 16*
Philips, Marianne 1886-1951 *EncCoWW*
Philips, Robert N 1923- *BiDrAPA 89*
Philipsborn, John David 1919- *WhoAm 90*
Philipsborn, Thomas D. 1926- *St&PR 91*
Philipse, Margaret Hardenbrook *EncCRAm*
Philipson, Herman Louis, Jr. 1924- *WhoAm 90*
Philipson, Lennart Carl 1929- *WhoWor 91*
Philipson, Morris 1926- *WhoWrEP 89*
Philipson, Sherri Wagman 1961- *WhoE 91*
Philipson, Willard Dale 1930- *WhoAm 90*
Phillabaum, Leslie Ervin 1936- *WhoAm 90, WhoWrEP 89*
Phillabaum, Stephen Day 1948- *WhoEmL 91*
Philley, Dave 1920- *Ballpl 90*
Phillimore, Mercy *EncO&P 3*
Phillipes, Debra L. 1960- *WhoEmL 91*
Phillippe, Deacon 1872-1952 *Ballpl 90 [port]*
Phillippi, Wendell Crane 1918- *WhoAm 90*
Phillipps, Adelaide 1833-1882 *BioAmW*
Phillips, Adolfo 1941- *Ballpl 90*
Phillips, Adran Abner 1924- *St&PR 91, WhoAm 90*
Phillips, Adrian *NewYTBS 90*
Phillips, Aileen Paul 1917- *WhoWrEP 89*
Phillips, Al 1935- *St&PR 91*
Phillips, Alfred Moore 1847-1896 *DcCanB 12*
Phillips, Alice Jane 1947- *WhoAmA 91*
Phillips, Alice Tinker 1946- *BiDrAPA 89*
Phillips, Allan Burton *BiDrAPA 89*
Phillips, Allan Robert 1914- *WhoWor 91*
Phillips, Almarin 1925- *WhoAm 90*
Phillips, Amy 1958- *WhoAmW 91*
Phillips, Andre'e P. 1939- *St&PR 91*
Phillips, Ann Terry 1813-1886 *BioAmW*
Phillips, Anthony *NewAgMG*
Phillips, Anthony F. 1937- *St&PR 91*
Phillips, Anthony Francis 1937- *WhoAm 90*
Phillips, Anthony George 1943- *WhoAm 90*
Phillips, Arthur 1941- *BiDrAPA 89*
Phillips, Arthur 1948- *St&PR 91*
Phillips, Asa Emory, Jr. 1911- *WhoWor 91*
Phillips, Asa R., Jr. 1932- *St&PR 91*
Phillips, Barbara Ruth 1936- *WhoAmW 91*
Phillips, Barry 1929- *WhoAm 90*
Phillips, Benjamin Murphy, IV 1953- *St&PR 91*
Phillips, Berry W. 1943- *St&PR 91*
Phillips, Bertrand D 1938- *WhoAmA 91*
Phillips, Bessie Gertrude Wright *WhoE 91, WhoWor 91*
Phillips, Betty Jean Nanney 1935- *WhoSSW 91*
Phillips, Betty Lou *BioIn 16, WhoAmW 91, WhoWor 91*
Phillips, Bill 1868-1941 *Ballpl 90*
Phillips, Billy J. 1926- *St&PR 91*
Phillips, Bluebell *ConAu 131*
Phillips, Bluebell S. *ConAu 131*
Phillips, Bluebell Stewart 1904- *ConAu 131*
Phillips, Bonnie 1942- *WhoAmA 91*
Phillips, Brian Roger 1939- *St&PR 91*
Phillips, Bubba 1930- *Ballpl 90*
Phillips, C Albert 1933- *BiDrAPA 89*
Phillips, Calbert Inglis 1925- *WhoWor 91*
Phillips, Carlton V. 1924- *St&PR 91*
Phillips, Carlton Vernon 1924- *WhoWor 91*
Phillips, Carol Ann 1949- *BiDrAPA 89*
Phillips, Carol Fenton 1932- *WhoAmW 91*
Phillips, Carole Cherry 1938- *WhoE 91*
Phillips, Carolyn Ann 1952- *St&PR 91*
Phillips, Carolyn Patricia 1949- *WhoAmW 91*
Phillips, Catharine 1727-1794 *FemiCLE*
Phillips, Cecil B. 1924- *St&PR 91*
Phillips, Cecil Barton 1924- *WhoAm 90*
Phillips, Channing E. 1928-1987 *BioIn 16*
Phillips, Charles A. Speas 1922- *WhoAm 90*
Phillips, Charles Alan 1939- *WhoAm 90*
Phillips, Charles Albert *St&PR 91*
Phillips, Charles Claiborne 1946- *WhoEmL 91*
Phillips, Charles Franklin 1910- *WhoAm 90*
Phillips, Charles Franklin, Jr. 1934- *WhoAm 90*
Phillips, Charles Gorham 1921- *WhoAm 90*
Phillips, Charles S. *ODwPR 91*
Phillips, Cherie 1950- *WhoAmW 91, WhoE 91*
Phillips, Cheryl Reaves 1952- *WhoSSW 91*
Phillips, Christopher Hallowell 1920- *WhoAm 90, WhoWor 91*
Phillips, Chynna *BioIn 16*
Phillips, Clifton J. 1919- *WhoAm 90*
Phillips, Colette Alice-Maude 1954- *WhoAmW 91*
Phillips, Constance Gaiser 1949- *WhoAmW 91*
Phillips, Craig 1922- *WhoAm 90*
Phillips, Craig Austin 1950- *WhoE 91*
Phillips, Craig Joel 1957- *WhoEmL 91*
Phillips, Cushing, Jr. 1923- *WhoSSW 91*
Phillips, Cyril 1915- *BiDrAPA 89*
Phillips, Cyrus Eastman, IV 1944- *WhoE 91*
Phillips, Daniel Anthony 1938- *St&PR 91, WhoE 91*
Phillips, Daniel Miller 1933- *WhoAm 90*
Phillips, Darlene Ann 1951- *WhoAmW 91*
Phillips, Darrell Eugene 1958- *WhoSSW 91*
Phillips, Dave 1943- *Ballpl 90*
Phillips, David Atlee *BioIn 16*
Phillips, David Atlee 1922-1988 *SpyFic*
Phillips, David Atlee, Jr. 1952- *WhoEmL 91*
Phillips, David Beltran 1946- *St&PR 91*
Phillips, David Colin 1940- *WhoAm 90, WhoWor 91*
Phillips, David George 1931- *WhoE 91*
Phillips, David Graham 1867-1911 *BioIn 16*
Phillips, David Harper 1961- *WhoEmL 91*
Phillips, David J *BiDrAPA 89*
Phillips, David John 1937- *St&PR 91*
Phillips, David Lee *BiDrAPA 89*
Phillips, David Lee 1948- *WhoEmL 91*
Phillips, David Lowell 1952- *WhoE 91*
Phillips, Debra Sue 1957- *WhoAmW 91*
Phillips, Dennis *TwCCr&M 91*
Phillips, Derwyn Fraser 1930- *St&PR 91, WhoAm 90*
Phillips, Dewayne K 1929- *BiDrAPA 89*
Phillips, Dick 1931- *Ballpl 90*
Phillips, Dick 1933- *WhoAmA 91*
Phillips, Don Franklin, Jr. 1959- *WhoSSW 91*
Phillips, Don Irwin 1945- *WhoEmL 91*
Phillips, Donald Arthur 1945- *WhoAm 90*
Phillips, Donald E. 1932- *St&PR 91*
Phillips, Donald John 1930- *WhoAm 90*
Phillips, Donald K. *BioIn 16*
Phillips, Dorothy Kay 1945- *WhoAmW 91*
Phillips, Dorothy W 1906-1977 *WhoAmA 91N*
Phillips, Douglas Edward 1943- *St&PR 91*
Phillips, Douglass Martin 1929- *St&PR 91*
Phillips, Duncan 1886-1966 *WhoAmA 91N*
Phillips, Dutch, Jr 1944- *WhoAmA 91*
Phillips, Dwight Wilburn 1951- *WhoEmL 91*
Phillips, Earl Norfleet, Jr. 1940- *St&PR 91, WhoAm 90*
Phillips, Eddie 1901-1968 *Ballpl 90*
Phillips, Edith Schaffer *NewYTBS 90*
Phillips, Edward Everett 1927- *St&PR 91, WhoAm 90*
Phillips, Edwin Allen 1915- *WhoAm 90, WhoWrEP 89*
Phillips, Edwin Charles 1917- *St&PR 91, WhoAm 90*
Phillips, Edwin J *BiDrAPA 89*
Phillips, Elaine Lee 1950- *WhoAmW 91*
Phillips, Elizabeth Faye 1934- *WhoAmW 91*
Phillips, Elizabeth Jane 1830-1904 *OxCCanT*
Phillips, Elizabeth Joan 1938- *WhoAm 90, WhoAmW 91*
Phillips, Elizabeth Snedeker 1911- *WhoAmW 91*
Phillips, Ellen Haygood 1947- *WhoAmW 91*
Phillips, Elliott H. 1919- *St&PR 91*
Phillips, Elliott Hunter 1919- *WhoAm 90*
Phillips, Elliott R 1949- *BiDrAPA 89*
Phillips, Ellis Laurimore, Jr. 1921- *WhoAm 90*
Phillips, Emily Susan 1960- *WhoAmW 91*
Phillips, Ermadean Joy 1942- *WhoSSW 91*
Phillips, Esther 1935-1984 *DrBlPA 90, EncPR&S 89*
Phillips, Esther Campbell *BiDrAPA 89*
Phillips, Ethel C. 1908- *WhoAm 90*
Phillips, Euan Hywel 1928- *WhoAm 90*
Phillips, Faye Eileen Zuckerman 1954- *WhoSSW 91*
Phillips, Flip 1915- *BioIn 16*
Phillips, Frances *ODwPR 91*
Phillips, Frances Isabelle 1912- *WhoE 91*
Phillips, Frances Marie 1918- *WhoAm 90*
Phillips, Frank 1873-1950 *WorAlBi*
Phillips, Fred Ronald 1940- *St&PR 91*
Phillips, Frederic J *BiDrAPA 89*
Phillips, Frederick Clayton 1915- *St&PR 91*
Phillips, Frederick Falley 1946- *WhoEmL 91*
Phillips, Gabriel 1933- *WhoE 91*
Phillips, Gary Lee 1948- *WhoHisp 91*
Phillips, Gary Lee 1954- *St&PR 91*
Phillips, Gene E. *St&PR 91*
Phillips, Geneva Ficker 1920- *WhoAmW 91, WhoWor 91*
Phillips, George M *BiDrAPA 89*
Phillips, George Michael 1947- *WhoAm 90*
Phillips, George Richard 1930- *WhoSSW 91*
Phillips, Gerald Baer 1925- *WhoAm 90*
Phillips, Gerald C. 1922- *St&PR 91*
Phillips, Gerald David 1940- *WhoSSW 91*
Phillips, Gifford 1918- *WhoAmA 91*
Phillips, Gil 1929- *St&PR 91*
Phillips, Glenn A. 1934- *St&PR 91*
Phillips, Graham Holmes 1939- *WhoAm 90, WhoE 91*
Phillips, Harriet Newton 1819-1901 *BioIn 16*
Phillips, Harvey Gene 1929- *IntWWM 90, WhoAm 90*
Phillips, Haven Howell *BiDrAPA 89*
Phillips, Helen 1913- *BiDWomA, WhoAmA 91*
Phillips, Henry Weldon 1917- *WhoWor 91*
Phillips, Herbert Alvin, Jr. 1928- *St&PR 91, WhoAm 90*
Phillips, Howard W. 1930- *St&PR 91*
Phillips, Howard William 1930- *WhoAm 90*
Phillips, Irv 1905- *ConAu 31NR*
Phillips, Irving W 1905- *WhoAmA 91*
Phillips, Ivan Edward 1926- *WhoAm 90*
Phillips, J Campbell 1873-1949 *WhoAmA 91N*
Phillips, J Gordon 1927- *St&PR 91*
Phillips, J. Theo 1927- *St&PR 91*
Phillips, Jack *MajTwCW*
Phillips, Jack 1921- *Ballpl 90*
Phillips, James 1929- *WhoAmA 91*
Phillips, James A. 1928- *St&PR 91*
Phillips, James Atlee *TwCCr&M 91*
Phillips, James Charles 1933- *WhoAm 90*
Phillips, James D. 1933- *WhoAm 90, WhoWor 91*
Phillips, James Davis 1935- *WhoAm 90*
Phillips, James Edward *BiDrAPA 89*
Phillips, James Edward 1928- *St&PR 91, WhoSSW 91*
Phillips, James H *BiDrAPA 89*
Phillips, James H., III 1939- *St&PR 91*
Phillips, James Kenneth 1929- *St&PR 91*
Phillips, James Lee 1934- *BiDrAPA 89*
Phillips, James Lee 1942- *WhoSSW 91*

Phillips, James Linford 1943- *WhoAm 90, WhoSSW 91*
Phillips, James M. 1916- *St&PR 91*
Phillips, James M 1946- *WhoAmA 91*
Phillips, James Macilduff 1916- *WhoE 91*
Phillips, James McJunkin 1929- *WhoE 91*
Phillips, James Sylvester 1930- *St&PR 91*
Phillips, James W. 1930- *St&PR 91*
Phillips, Janet *FemiCLE*
Phillips, Janet Colleen 1933- *WhoAm 90*
Phillips, Janet E. *BioIn 16*
Phillips, Janice *St&PR 91*
Phillips, Jay Allen 1947- *BiDrAPA 89*
Phillips, Jayne Anne 1952- *BioIn 16, FemiCLE, MajTwCW, WorAu 1980 [port]*
Phillips, Jean B. *ODwPR 91*
Phillips, Jean Susan 1942- *IntWWM 90*
Phillips, Jennifer 1942- *FemiCLE*
Phillips, Jerry Juan 1935- *WhoAm 90*
Phillips, Jill Meta 1952- *WhoAm 90*
Phillips, Jimmy E. 1934- *St&PR 91*
Phillips, John 1719-1795 *WorAlBi*
Phillips, John 1920- *St&PR 91*
Phillips, John Benbow, Jr. 1933- *St&PR 91*
Phillips, John Bertram 1906-1982 *DcNaB 1981*
Phillips, John Bomar 1947- *WhoEmL 91*
Phillips, John Burton 1935- *WhoAm 90*
Phillips, John David 1920- *WhoAm 90*
Phillips, John David 1942- *WhoSSW 91*
Phillips, John Davisson 1906- *WhoAm 90*
Phillips, John Drury 1925- *WhoE 91*
Phillips, John F. 1938- *St&PR 91*
Phillips, John G. 1922- *St&PR 91*
Phillips, John Howell 1814-1878 *AmLegL*
Phillips, John Paul 1932- *WhoWor 91*
Phillips, John Pierson 1925- *WhoAm 90*
Phillips, John Richard 1934- *WhoAm 90*
Phillips, John Sanburn 1861-1949 *BioIn 16*
Phillips, John Wendell 1929- *St&PR 91*
Phillips, Josef Clayton 1908- *WhoAm 90*
Phillips, Joseph Donald *BiDrAPA 89*
Phillips, Joseph Douglas 1938- *WhoE 91*
Phillips, Joseph L. 1928- *St&PR 91*
Phillips, Joy Eugenia 1938- *WhoSSW 91*
Phillips, Joyce Martha 1952- *WhoAmW 91*
Phillips, Judith *WhoAmW 91*
Phillips, Julia Miller 1944- *WhoAm 90*
Phillips, Julianne *BioIn 16*
Phillips, Katharine Anne 1955- *BiDrAPA 89*
Phillips, Kathy A. 1955- *WhoSSW 91*
Phillips, Kathy Conlan 1946- *WhoWrEP 89*
Phillips, Kelley L *BiDrAPA 89*
Phillips, Kelly Lyn 1965- *WhoAmW 91*
Phillips, Ken *BioIn 16*
Phillips, Kenneth Edwin 1946- *WhoSSW 91*
Phillips, Kenneth Higbie 1940- *WhoAm 90*
Phillips, Kenneth Lockhart 1924- *St&PR 91*
Phillips, Kenneth Paul *BiDrAPA 89*
Phillips, Kenneth Wayne 1941- *St&PR 91, WhoAm 90*
Phillips, Kevin Price 1940- *WhoAm 90, WhoWrEP 89*
Phillips, Kurt 1956- *St&PR 91*
Phillips, Kyle Meredith 1934-1988 *BioIn 16*
Phillips, Larry 1948- *WhoSSW 91*
Phillips, Larry Duane 1948- *WhoWor 91*
Phillips, Larry Edward 1942- *WhoAm 90*
Phillips, Larry Scott 1962- *WhoSSW 91*
Phillips, Laughlin 1924- *WhoAm 90, WhoAmA 91, WhoE 91*
Phillips, Laura *BioIn 16*
Phillips, Lawrence C. 1938- *WhoSSW 91*
Phillips, Lawrence Disel 1943- *St&PR 91*
Phillips, Lawrence S. 1927- *St&PR 91*
Phillips, Layn R. 1952- *WhoSSW 91*
Phillips, Lena M. 1881-1955 *BioAmW*
Phillips, Lenora Hoppers *BiDrAPA 89*
Phillips, Leo Harold, Jr. 1945- *WhoE 91, WhoEmL 91, WhoWor 91*
Phillips, Leon 1914-1988 *SmATA X*
Phillips, Leslie *BioIn 16*
Phillips, Leverett C. 1946- *WhoSSW 91*
Phillips, Linda Darnell Elaine 1940- *WhoAmW 91, WhoSSW 91*
Phillips, Linda Morand *BioIn 16*
Phillips, Linda Thomas 1940- *St&PR 91*
Phillips, Lisa *BioIn 16*
Phillips, Lloyd 1949- *ConTFT 8*
Phillips, Logan B. 1923- *St&PR 91*
Phillips, Lois Plowden 1927- *WhoAmW 91, WhoWor 91*
Phillips, Lou Diamond *BioIn 16*
Phillips, Louis James 1942- *WhoWrEP 89*
Phillips, Loyal 1905- *WhoAm 90*
Phillips, Lyman C. 1939- *St&PR 91*
Phillips, Margaret *BiDrAPA 89*
Phillips, Margaret Corinna 1950- *IntWWM 90*
Phillips, Margaret Imogene 1926- *WhoWrEP 89*
Phillips, Marian McCamy 1948- *WhoSSW 91*
Phillips, Marilyn 1948- *IntWWM 90*
Phillips, Marilyn Chenault 1949- *WhoAmW 91*
Phillips, Marion Grumman 1922- *WhoAmW 91*
Phillips, Marjorie 1894-1985 *WhoAmA 91N*
Phillips, Marjorie 1895- *BiDWomA*
Phillips, Mark *ConAu 130*
Phillips, Mark 1948- *BioIn 16*
Phillips, Mark Anthony Peter 1948- *WhoWor 91*
Phillips, Mark Francis 1958- *WhoSSW 91*
Phillips, Martha *BioIn 16*
Phillips, Martha Huggins 1950- *WhoAmW 91*
Phillips, Mary C. 1911- *St&PR 91*
Phillips, Mary Geisler 1881-1964 *AuBYP 90*
Phillips, Mary Genevieve 1903-1980 *BioIn 16*
Phillips, Maryann Katherine 1930- *WhoAmW 91*
Phillips, Matt *WhoAmA 91*
Phillips, Maureen M. 1950- *St&PR 91*
Phillips, Meredith Bowen 1943- *WhoWrEP 89*
Phillips, Michael 1937- *WhoAmA 91, WhoSSW 91*
Phillips, Michael Joseph 1937- *WhoWrEP 89*
Phillips, Michael Lynn 1952- *WhoSSW 91, WhoWor 91*
Phillips, Michael Robert 1949- *BiDrAPA 89*
Phillips, Michael W. 1941- *St&PR 91*
Phillips, Michelle *BioIn 16*
Phillips, Mike 1950- *Ballpl 90*
Phillips, Mildred *AuBYP 90*
Phillips, Miriam Ernestine 1918- *WhoAmW 91*
Phillips, Montague Fawcett 1885-1969 *OxCPMus*
Phillips, Nancy Chambers 1941- *WhoAmW 91*
Phillips, Nicholas Richard 1935- *St&PR 91*
Phillips, Oliver Clyde, Jr. 1929- *WhoAm 90*
Phillips, Owen Martin 1930- *WhoAm 90*
Phillips, Pamela Kim 1958- *WhoAmW 91*
Phillips, Patricia Diane 1963- *WhoSSW 91*
Phillips, Paul F *BiDrAPA 89*
Phillips, Paul Kenneth 1951- *BiDrAPA 89*
Phillips, Paul Schuyler 1956- *IntWWM 90*
Phillips, Pearl Raphelita 1941- *WhoAmW 91, WhoE 91*
Phillips, Ped Wesley 1943- *St&PR 91*
Phillips, Peggy Nell 1941- *WhoSSW 91*
Phillips, Penelope Anne 1943- *IntWWM 90*
Phillips, Peter Charles Bonest 1948- *WhoAm 90*
Phillips, Peter Lawrence 1942- *WhoWor 91*
Phillips, Philip B 1915- *BiDrAPA 89*
Phillips, Phyllis Catherine 1935- *WhoAmW 91*
Phillips, Priscilla Moulton 1918- *WhoE 91*
Phillips, Ralph Saul 1913- *WhoAm 90*
Phillips, Ralph Wilbur 1918- *WhoAm 90*
Phillips, Randall Clinger 1924- *WhoAm 90*
Phillips, Randel Eugene 1947- *WhoEmL 91*
Phillips, Raymond Foy 1935- *WhoSSW 91*
Phillips, Reginald Francis 1954- *St&PR 91*
Phillips, Renee Ann 1951- *WhoAmW 91*
Phillips, Richard *MajTwCW*
Phillips, Richard Ellsworth 1924- *St&PR 91*
Phillips, Richard H 1922- *BiDrAPA 89*
Phillips, Richard Hart 1922- *WhoE 91*
Phillips, Richard Lee 1948- *WhoEmL 91*
Phillips, Richard Myron 1931- *WhoAm 90*
Phillips, Richard Raymond 1950- *WhoE 91*
Phillips, Richard Wendell, Jr. 1929- *WhoAm 90*
Phillips, Rick 1956- *ODwPR 91*
Phillips, Robert 1938- *ConAu 13AS [port], DcLB 105 [port]*
Phillips, Robert Allen 1941- *WhoE 91*
Phillips, Robert D 1925- *BiDrAPA 89*
Phillips, Robert Glenn 1954- *WhoAm 90*
Phillips, Robert H. *NewYTBS 90*
Phillips, Robert Haskell 1942- *WhoSSW 91*
Phillips, Robert J 1946- *WhoAmA 91*
Phillips, Robert James, Jr. 1955- *WhoSSW 91, WhoWor 91*
Phillips, Robert M 1914- *BiDrAPA 89*
Phillips, Robert M. 1938- *St&PR 91*
Phillips, Robert Quaife 1925- *WhoAm 90, WhoWor 91*
Phillips, Robert Schaeffer 1938- *WhoWrEP 89*
Phillips, Robert T M *BiDrAPA 89*
Phillips, Robert Thomas 1940- *St&PR 91*
Phillips, Robert W. 1934- *ODwPR 91*
Phillips, Robin 1942- *OxCCanT*
Phillips, Roderick 1947- *ConAu 131*
Phillips, Roger 1939- *St&PR 91, WhoAm 90*
Phillips, Roger E 1907- *BiDrAPA 89*
Phillips, Roland L. 1937-1987 *BioIn 16*
Phillips, Ronald 1942- *St&PR 91*
Phillips, Ronald Frank 1934- *WhoAm 90*
Phillips, Ronald Hart 1932- *WhoSSW 91*
Phillips, Ronald Lewis 1940- *WhoAm 90*
Phillips, Roscoe Wendell, Jr. 1927- *WhoAm 90*
Phillips, Rufus Colfax, III 1929- *WhoAm 90*
Phillips, Russell Alexander, Jr. 1937- *WhoAm 90*
Phillips, Russell Evan 1947- *BiDrAPA 89*
Phillips, Ruth C. 1935- *WhoAmW 91*
Phillips, S. Dave 1942- *St&PR 91*
Phillips, Sam *BioIn 16*
Phillips, Sam 1923- *ConMus 5*
Phillips, Samuel C. 1921-1990 *BioIn 16*
Phillips, Samuel Cochran 1921-1990 *NewYTBS 90 [port]*
Phillips, Samuel Field 1824-1903 *AmLegL*
Phillips, Sharon Kathy 1960- *WhoAmW 91*
Phillips, Shawn *NewAgMG*
Phillips, Sian *WhoWor 91*
Phillips, Sian 1934- *ConTFT 8 [port]*
Phillips, Sid 1907-1973 *OxCPMus*
Phillips, Sidney Frederick 1933- *WhoAm 90*
Phillips, Sidney Hornor, Jr. *BiDrAPA 89*
Phillips, Simon *BioIn 16*
Phillips, Spencer Kleckner 1914- *WhoWor 91*
Phillips, Stanley F. 1925- *St&PR 91*
Phillips, Stephen Clifton 1952- *St&PR 91*
Phillips, Susan Elizabeth 1947- *WhoWrEP 89*
Phillips, Susan Lynn 1955- *WhoAmW 91*
Phillips, Susan M. 1944- *WhoAm 90*
Phillips, Sylvia Elaine 1958- *WhoSSW 91*
Phillips, T. Stephen 1941- *WhoAm 90*
Phillips, Taylor 1933- *Ballpl 90*
Phillips, Ted Ray 1948- *WhoAm 90*
Phillips, Terence Martyn 1946- *WhoE 91*
Phillips, Teresia Constantia 1709-1765 *FemiCLE*
Phillips, Theodore Locke 1933- *WhoAm 90*
Phillips, Thomas C. 1935- *St&PR 91*
Phillips, Thomas L. 1924- *St&PR 91, WhoAm 90, WhoE 91*
Phillips, Thomas L., Jr. 1955- *WhoE 91*
Phillips, Thomas M. 1937- *St&PR 91*
Phillips, Thomas Marion 1916- *WhoAm 90*
Phillips, Thomas Porter 1940- *WhoAm 90, WhoWor 91*
Phillips, Thomas Royal 1949- *WhoAm 90*
Phillips, Thomas W, Jr. *BiDrAPA 89*
Phillips, Timothy A. 1960- *WhoE 91*
Phillips, Tony 1937- *WhoAmA 91*
Phillips, Tony 1959- *Ballpl 90*
Phillips, V Rachel 1955- *BiDrAPA 89*
Phillips, Virginia L. 1923- *St&PR 91*
Phillips, Walter John 1922- *St&PR 91*
Phillips, Walter Mills, III 1947- *WhoWor 91*
Phillips, Walter Ray 1932- *WhoAm 90*
Phillips, Ward *MajTwCW*
Phillips, Warren G *BiDrAPA 89*
Phillips, Warren H. *BioIn 16*
Phillips, Warren H. 1926- *St&PR 91*
Phillips, Warren Henry 1926- *WhoAm 90, WhoE 91*
Phillips, Wayne 1925-1988 *BioIn 16*
Phillips, Wayne Francis *BiDrAPA 89*
Phillips, Wendell 1811-1884 *BioIn 16, WhNaAH*
Phillips, Wendell E., II 1945- *St&PR 91*
Phillips, Willard 1784-1873 *BioIn 16*
Phillips, William *WhoAm 90, WhoWrEP 89*
Phillips, William 1878-1968 *BioIn 16*
Phillips, William A *BiDrAPA 89*
Phillips, William Ault 1946- *WhoWor 91*
Phillips, William Charles 1947- *WhoE 91, WhoWor 91*
Phillips, William E. 1930- *St&PR 91*
Phillips, William Eugene 1930- *WhoAm 90*
Phillips, William G. *BioIn 16, NewYTBS 90*
Phillips, William G. 1920- *St&PR 91*
Phillips, William G. 1924?-1990 *ConAu 130*
Phillips, William George 1920- *WhoAm 90, WhoSSW 91*
Phillips, William Joseph 1938- *IntWWM 90*
Phillips, William Ray, Jr. 1931- *St&PR 91, WhoAm 90*
Phillips, Winfred Marshall 1940- *WhoAm 90, WhoSSW 91*
Phillips, Yale Gilbert 1929- *St&PR 91*
Phillips-Jones, Linda *WhoAmW 91*
Phillips-Madson, Robyn Lynn 1953- *WhoAmW 91*
Phillipson, John Samuel 1917- *WhoAm 90*
Phillipson, Richard William, Jr. 1944- *WhoSSW 91*
Phillis, Frederick C. 1941- *ODwPR 91*
Phillis, John Whitfield 1936- *WhoAm 90*
Phillis, Marilyn Hughey 1927- *WhoAmA 91*
Phillis, Thomas James 1930- *St&PR 91*
Phillis, Yannis Anastasios 1950- *WhoWor 91*
Phillpot, Clive James 1938- *WhoAm 90, WhoAmA 91*
Phillpotts, Eden 1862-1960 *TwCCr&M 91*
Philo-Philippa *BiDEWW*
Philogene, Bernard J. R. 1940- *WhoAm 90*
Philon, James L. 1928- *St&PR 91*
Philosophie eines Weibes, Verfasserin d. *EncCoWW*
Philp, Francis Higginson 1930- *St&PR 91, WhoWor 91*
Philp, Francis Higginson 1930-1990 *BioIn 16*
Philp, Richard Nilson 1943- *WhoAm 90*
Philpot, Desaussure F, Jr. *BiDrAPA 89*
Philpot, Donald Ray 1938- *St&PR 91*
Philpot, Kathryn Ann 1958- *WhoAmW 91*
Philpott, Albert Lee 1919- *WhoAm 90, WhoSSW 91*
Philpott, Harry Melvin 1917- *WhoAm 90*
Philpott, Joe Curtis 1931- *St&PR 91*
Philpott, Larry La Fayette 1937- *WhoAm 90*
Philpott, William H 1919- *BiDrAPA 89*
Phin 1863-1940 *SmATA X [port]*
Phinizy, Kimberly Anne 1964- *WhoSSW 91*
Phinney, Beth *WhoAmW 91*
Phinney, Jean Swift 1933- *WhoAmW 91*
Phinney, Judith F. 1941- *St&PR 91*
Phinney, Marianne 1954- *WhoAmW 91*
Phinney, W.S. 1921- *St&PR 91*
Phinney, William Charles 1930- *WhoAm 90*
Phipps, Allen Mayhew 1938- *WhoAm 90*
Phipps, Charles Howard 1926- *WhoSSW 91*
Phipps, Cornelius Mark 1921- *WhoWor 91*
Phipps, Darleen Marie 1929- *WhoAmW 91*
Phipps, Delores Cheryl 1946- *WhoAmW 91*
Phipps, Diana *BioIn 16*
Phipps, George Howard 1943- *St&PR 91*
Phipps, Gerald H. 1915- *St&PR 91*
Phipps, Gerald Hughes 1915- *WhoAm 90*
Phipps, Graham Howard 1937- *IntWWM 90*
Phipps, Henry 1839-1930 *WorAlBi*
Phipps, Jeffrey P. 1947- *St&PR 91*
Phipps, Jennifer 1934- *OxCCanT*
Phipps, John Randolph 1919- *WhoAm 90*
Phipps, Michael Charles 1944- *WhoAm 90*
Phipps, Ogden Mills 1940- *WhoAm 90*
Phipps, Susie Jones 1950- *WhoAmW 91*
Phipps, Tony Randell 1953- *WhoSSW 91*
Phipps, William E 1930- *ConAu 30NR*
Phips, William 1650-1695 *EncCRAm*
Phipson, Joan *AuBYP 90*
Phister, Montgomery, Jr. 1926- *WhoAm 90*
Phitaksphraiwan, Phuangnoi 1927- *WhoWor 91*
Phiz 1851-1882 *BioIn 16*
Phizo, Angami *BioIn 16*
Phizo, Angami Zapu *NewYTBS 90*
Phlegar, Benjamin Focht 1921- *WhoAm 90*
Phleger, Fred B. 1909- *AuBYP 90, WhoWrEP 89*
Phleger, Marjorie Temple *BioIn 16*
Pho, Robert W.H. 1940- *WhoWor 91*
Phocas, George John 1927- *WhoAm 90, WhoE 91, WhoWor 91*
Phoebus, Tom 1942- *Ballpl 90*
Phoenix, Anne *BiDEWW*
Phoenix, Donald R. 1937- *St&PR 91*
Phoenix, John 1823-1861 *BioIn 16*
Phoenix, P.J. 1928- *St&PR 91*
Phoenix, River *BioIn 16*
Phoenix, River 1970- *News 90 [port], WorAlBi*
Phoenix, Sonja Grant 1941- *WhoSSW 91*
Phoenix, William *EncO&P 3*
Phoonsen, Pieter Laurens 1691-1742 *BioIn 16*
Phoumi Vongvichit *WhoWor 91*
Phoun Sipaseut 1920- *WhoWor 91*
Phoungcherdchoo, Panom 1937- *BiDrAPA 89*
Phranc *BioIn 16*

Phrydas, Irene A *BiDrAPA 89*
Phull, B K *BiDrAPA 89*
Phun, Khieng Ly *BiDrAPA 89*
Phyfe, Duncan 1768-1854 *PenDiDA 89, WorAlBi*
Phyfe, William Lee *BioIn 16*
Phypers, Dean P. 1929- *St&PR 91*
Phypers, Dean Pinney 1929- *WhoAm 90*
Pi, Edmond Hsin-Tung 1948- *BiDrAPA 89*
Pi y Margall, Francisco 1824-1901 *BioIn 16*
Piacentini, John Carl 1957- *WhoE 91*
Piacentino, Edward Joseph 1945- *WhoSSW 91*
Piacenza, Louis Anthony 1927- *St&PR 91*
Piaf, Edith 1915-1963 *BioIn 16, OxCPMus, WorAlBi*
Piaget, Jean 1896-1980 *ConAu 31NR, MajTwCW, WorAlBi*
Piaggio, Rinaldo 1937- *WhoWor 91*
Piaker, Philip Martin 1921- *WhoAm 90*
Pialat, Maurice *BioIn 16*
Pialat, Maurice 1925- *ConTFT 8*
Pian, Carlson Chao-Ping 1945- *WhoE 91*
Pian, Rulan Chao 1922- *IntWWM 90, WhoAm 90*
Pian, Theodore Hsueh-Huang 1919- *WhoAm 90, WhoE 91*
Pian, Thomas Richard 1953- *WhoE 91*
Piana, Dominique 1956- *IntWWM 90*
Piana, Edward Robert 1930- *St&PR 91*
Piana, Emil G *BiDrAPA 89*
Pianalto, Sandra 1954- *St&PR 91*
Pianetti, Catherine Natalie 1909- *WhoAmW 91*
Pianka, Eric Rodger 1939- *WhoAm 90*
Pianka, Uri *PenDiMP*
Pianka, Uri 1937- *WhoAm 90*
Piano, Renzo 1937- *BioIn 16*
Piano, Vincent C. 1922- *St&PR 91*
Piano, Vincent Carmine 1922- *WhoE 91*
Piantadosi, Louis Joseph 1932- *WhoAm 90*
Piantadosi, Sheila Helena 1959- *WhoE 91*
Piantedosi, Thomas 1951- *St&PR 91*
Piantini, Carlos 1927- *WhoWor 91*
Piantoni, Mario Alberto 1942- *WhoWor 91*
Piapot 1816-1908 *WhNaAH [port]*
Piard, Gilles Pierre 1946- *WhoWor 91*
Piasecka, Jadwiga E M 1935- *BiDrAPA 89*
Piasecki, Frank Nicholas 1919- *St&PR 91, WhoAm 90*
Piaseczny, Carol A. 1952- *ODwPR 91*
Piassick, Allen Charles 1935- *St&PR 91*
Piaszczyk, Christopher Mark 1953- *WhoE 91*
Piatak, Donald J. 1929- *St&PR 91*
Piatek, Dariusz Piotr *BiDrAPA 89*
Piatek, Francis John 1944- *WhoAmA 91*
Piatetski-Shapiro, Ilya 1929- *WhoWor 91*
Piatigorsky, Gregor 1903-1976 *PenDiMP, WorAlBi*
Piatnitskii, Iosif Aronovich 1882-1939 *BioIn 16*
Piatnitskii, Osip Aronovich 1882-1939 *BioIn 16*
Piatnochka, Ruth Ann 1955- *WhoWrEP 89*
Piatt, Jack Boyd 1928- *WhoAm 90, WhoE 91*
Piatt, Sarah Morgan 1836-1919 *FemiCLE*
Piatt, Wiley 1874-1946 *Ballpl 90*
Piatt, William McKinney, III 1918- *WhoAm 90*
Piatti, Alfredo 1822-1901 *PenDiMP*
Piatti, Celestino 1922- *AuBYP 90*
Piazza, Barry Lynn 1956- *WhoSSW 91*
Piazza, Duane Eugene 1954- *WhoWor 91*
Piazza, Eugene U 1930- *BiDrAPA 89*
Piazza, Felipe 1951- *St&PR 91*
Piazza, John *WhoSSW 91*
Piazza, Marguerite 1926- *WhoAm 90, WhoAmW 91*
Piazza, Michael A. *ODwPR 91*
Piazzetta, Giovanni Battista 1683-1754 *IntDcAA 90*
Pibulsonggram, Nitya 1941- *WhoWor 91*
Piburn, Marvin F, Jr. 1949- *BiDrAPA 89*
Pic, Ronald John 1953- *WhoSSW 91*
Pica, Christopher C. 1959- *WhoE 91*
Pica, Rae 1953- *WhoWrEP 89*
Picabia, Francis 1879-1953 *IntDcAA 90*
Picachy, Lawrence Trevor 1916- *WhoWor 91*
Picano, Felice 1944- *ConAu 13AS [port], WhoWrEP 89*
Picard, Barbara Leonie 1917- *AuBYP 90*
Picard, Claire *BiDrAPA 89*
Picard, Dennis J. *WhoAm 90*
Picard, Donald Russell 1949- *WhoSSW 91*
Picard, Elizabeth Ann August 1921- *WhoE 91*
Picard, Jacques Jean 1934- *WhoWor 91*
Picard, Jean 1931- *WhoWor 91*
Picard, John Livingston 1956- *WhoWor 91*
Picard, Laurent 1927- *WhoAm 90, WhoWor 91*
Picard, Priscilla Aoki 1959- *WhoAmW 91*
Picard, R.R. 1932- *St&PR 91*
Picard, Raymond H. 1942- *St&PR 91*
Picard, Raymond Jean 1914-1989 *BioIn 16*
Picard, Thomas Henry 1959- *BiDrAPA 89*
Picard, Thomas Joseph, Jr. 1933- *WhoWor 91*
Picard-Ami, Luis A 1927- *BiDrAPA 89*
Picardi, Robert E. 1952- *St&PR 91*
Picardo, Mary Ann *BiDrAPA 89*
Picarelli, John G. 1943- *St&PR 91*
Picasso, Jacqueline *BioIn 16*
Picasso, Pablo 1881-1973 *BioIn 16, IntDcAA 90, PenDiDA 89, WorAlBi*
Picasso, Paloma *BioIn 16*
Picasso, Paloma 1949- *News 91-1 [port], WhoHisp 91*
Picazo, Benjamin T. 1941- *St&PR 91*
Picazo, Eugenio Acevedo 1938- *WhoWor 91*
Piccard, Auguste 1884-1962 *WorAlBi*
Piccard, Jacques Ernest Jean 1922- *WhoWor 91*
Piccardi, Michelle Marie 1966- *WhoAmW 91*
Piccaver, Alfred 1884-1958 *PenDiMP*
Picchi, Mario 1927- *WhoWor 91*
Picchio, Lou *BiDrAPA 89*
Picchione, N. Everett 1928- *St&PR 91*
Picchione, Nicholas, II 1954- *WhoE 91*
Picciano, Lana *WhoAmA 91*
Picciarelli, Vivian *BioIn 16*
Piccillo, Joseph 1941- *WhoAm 90, WhoAmA 91*
Piccinali, Jean Pierre 1940- *WhoWor 91*
Piccini, Assis Pedro Perin 1948- *WhoWor 91*
Piccininni, Stephen Ignatius 1952- *WhoEmL 91*
Piccininno, Gregory Louis 1965- *WhoE 91*
Piccinni, Niccolo 1728-1800 *PenDiMP A*
Piccinni, Paolo 1952- *WhoWor 91*
Picciolo, Rob 1953- *Ballpl 90*
Piccione, Anthony 1939- *WhoWrEP 89*
Piccioni, Constance Elisabeth 1908- *WhoAmW 91*
Picciotto, Maurice Ralph *BiDrAPA 89*
Piccirilli, Furio 1868-1949 *WhoAmA 91N*
Piccola, Mary Teresa 1950- *WhoAmW 91*
Piccoli, David Anthony 1953- *WhoE 91*
Piccoli, Michel 1925- *WhoWor 91*
Piccolo, Joseph Anthony 1953- *WhoE 91*
Piccolo, Richard 1943- *WhoAmA 91*
Piccolpasso, Cipriano 1524-1579 *PenDiDA 89*
Picha, Kenneth George 1925- *WhoAm 90*
Pichardo, Javier A 1913- *BiDrAPA 89*
Piche, James Roland 1937- *WhoSSW 91*
Piche, Matthew Warren 1928- *St&PR 91*
Piche, Ron 1935- *Ballpl 90*
Piche, Stephanie Emilie 1959- *WhoAmW 91*
Pichel, Julian 1924- *BiDrAPA 89*
Pichelman, Peter Paul 1952- *St&PR 91*
Picher, Claude 1927- *WhoAmA 91*
Picheta *ArtLatA*
Pichette, Claude 1936- *WhoAm 90*
Pichler, Gunter *PenDiMP*
Pichler, Gunter 1940- *IntWWM 90*
Pichler, Johann Adam *PenDiDA 89*
Pichler, Johann Hanns 1936- *WhoWor 91*
Pichler, Joseph A. 1939- *St&PR 91*
Pichler, Joseph Anton 1939- *WhoAm 90*
Pichler, Karoline 1769-1843 *EncCoWW*
Pichlmayr, Ina Johanna 1932- *WhoWor 91*
Pichois, Claude 1925- *ConAu 132*
Pichois, Claude P. 1925- *WhoWor 91*
Pichot, Gerard Francoi 1943- *WhoWor 91*
Pichot, J. Thomas 1955- *BiDrAPA 89*
Pichot, Pierre J 1918- *BiDrAPA 89*
Picht-Axenfeld, Edith Maria 1914- *IntWWM 90*
Picinich, Val 1896-1942 *Ballpl 90*
Piciocchi-Maisonrouge, Ketty Alexandra 1958- *WhoEmL 91*
Picirilli, Robert Eugene 1932- *WhoAm 90*
Pick, Arthur Joseph, Jr. 1931- *WhoAm 90*
Pick, Charlie 1888-1954 *Ballpl 90*
Pick, Chuck *BioIn 16*
Pick, Derrald Walter 1946- *St&PR 91*
Pick, Douglas Martin 1959- *WhoEmL 91*
Pick, George G. 1931- *St&PR 91*
Pick, Jan 1924- *BiDrAPA 89*
Pick, John C. *WhoAm 90*
Pick, Karl-Heinz 1929- *IntWWM 90*
Pick, Michael Claude 1931- *WhoAm 90*
Pick, Philip J. 1941- *St&PR 91*
Pick, Richard A. *BioIn 16*
Pick, Rubin *BiDrAPA 89*
Pick, Ruth 1913- *WhoAm 90*
Pick de Weiss, Susan Emily 1952- *WhoEmL 91*
Pick-Jacobs, Elly *ODwPR 91*
Pickands, James, III 1931- *WhoE 91*
Pickar, David 1948- *BiDrAPA 89*
Pickard, Alan Henry 1942- *IntWWM 90*
Pickard, Frank Clemence, III 1944- *St&PR 91*
Pickard, Franklin G.T. 1933- *St&PR 91*
Pickard, Geoffrey L. 1937- *ODwPR 91*
Pickard, George Lawson 1913- *WhoAm 90*
Pickard, John Benedict 1928- *WhoAm 90, WhoWrEP 89*
Pickard, Julian Lee, III 1942- *St&PR 91*
Pickard, Myrna Rae 1935- *WhoAm 90, WhoSSW 91*
Pickard, Nancy 1945- *TwCCr&M 91*
Pickard, Paul F. 1946- *ODwPR 91*
Pickard, Richard Vernon 1943- *St&PR 91*
Pickard, Robert Louis 1926- *St&PR 91*
Pickard, Sherman A. *WhoSSW 91*
Pickel, Stuart M *BiDrAPA 89*
Pickell, John Leroy 1934- *WhoWrEP 89*
Pickell, Lloyd C. 1946- *St&PR 91*
Pickell, Timothy Vernon 1952- *WhoEmL 91*
Picken, Bruce F *BiDrAPA 89*
Picken, George 1898-1971 *WhoAmA 91N*
Picken, Joseph Clarke 1943- *St&PR 91*
Pickenhain, Lothar 1920- *WhoWor 91*
Pickens, Alexander Legrand 1921- *WhoAm 90, WhoWor 91*
Pickens, Allen Arthur 1940- *WhoAm 90*
Pickens, Alton 1917- *WhoAmA 91*
Pickens, Andrew 1739-1817 *EncCRAm*
Pickens, Andrew Trice, III 1943- *BiDrAPA 89*
Pickens, Buford Lindsay 1906- *WhoAm 90*
Pickens, David Richard, Jr. 1920- *WhoAm 90*
Pickens, Earl Franklin 1934- *St&PR 91*
Pickens, F. W. 1805-1869 *BioIn 16*
Pickens, Francis Wilkinson 1805-1869 *BioIn 16*
Pickens, Franklin Ace 1936- *WhoSSW 91*
Pickens, Harry Richard 1947- *St&PR 91*
Pickens, Jack G. 1921- *St&PR 91*
Pickens, Jimmy Burton 1935- *WhoSSW 91*
Pickens, Kel Norris 1949- *WhoWrEP 89*
Pickens, Marshall Ivey 1904- *WhoAm 90*
Pickens, Robert Bruce 1926- *WhoAm 90*
Pickens, Robert Fulton 1931- *St&PR 91*
Pickens, Robert Houston 1940- *WhoSSW 91*
Pickens, Rupert Tarpley, III 1940- *WhoSSW 91*
Pickens, Sunday June *BiDrAPA 89*
Pickens, T. Boone, Jr. *BioIn 16*
Pickens, T. Boone, Jr. 1928- *WorAlBi*
Pickens, Thomas Boone 1928- *ConAmBL*
Pickens, Thomas Boone, Jr. 1928- *St&PR 91, WhoAm 90*
Pickens, Willard E. 1940- *St&PR 91*
Pickens, William 1881-1954 *BioIn 16*
Pickens, William Rogers, Jr. 1947- *WhoSSW 91*
Pickens, William Stewart 1940- *WhoSSW 91, WhoWor 91*
Picker, Arnold M. 1913-1989 *BioIn 16*
Picker, Ghislaine L. 1934- *WhoWor 91*
Picker, Harvey 1915- *WhoAm 90*
Picker, Jean Sovatkin *NewYTBS 90*
Picker, Jean Sovatkin 1921-1990 *BioIn 16*
Picker, Martin 1929- *IntWWM 90*
Picker, Nelly 1916- *WhoAmW 91*
Picker, Walter James 1929- *WhoAm 90*
Pickerell, Albert George 1912- *WhoAm 90*
Pickerell, James Howard 1936- *WhoAm 90*
Pickerell, Rodney R. 1938- *WhoWrEP 89*
Pickering, Allen A. 1954- *St&PR 91*
Pickering, Amelia *FemiCLE*
Pickering, AvaJane 1951- *WhoAmW 91, WhoEmL 91, WhoWor 91*
Pickering, Charles Denton 1950- *WhoEmL 91*
Pickering, E. *BiDWomA*
Pickering, Edward Charles 1846-1919 *EncO&P 3, EncPaPR 91*
Pickering, Howard William 1935- *WhoAm 90*
Pickering, Hugh Russell *BiDrAPA 89*
Pickering, James Henry, III 1937- *WhoAm 90*
Pickering, John Harold 1916- *WhoAm 90*
Pickering, Judith M. 1942- *St&PR 91*
Pickering, Margaret Hastings 1932- *WhoAmW 91*
Pickering, Ollie 1870-1952 *Ballpl 90*
Pickering, Robert E. 1952- *St&PR 91*
Pickering, Robert Earl, Jr. 1952- *WhoAm 90*
Pickering, Robert Easton 1934- *WhoWor 91*
Pickering, Robert Harvey 1937- *WhoWor 91*
Pickering, Terry Allen 1952- *WhoEmL 91*
Pickering, Thomas Clifford 1934- *WhoSSW 91*
Pickering, Thomas Reeve *BioIn 16*
Pickering, Thomas Reeve 1931- *WhoAm 90, WhoWor 91*
Pickering, Timothy 1745-1829 *BiDrUSE 89, BioIn 16, EncCRAm*
Pickering, Urbane 1899-1970 *Ballpl 90*
Pickering, William 1796-1854 *BioIn 16*
Pickering, William Hayward 1910- *WhoAm 90*
Pickering, William Henry 1951- *WhoEmL 91*
Pickett, Betty Horenstein 1926- *WhoAm 90*
Pickett, Bill 1860?-1932 *BioIn 16*
Pickett, Calder Marcus 1921- *WhoAm 90*
Pickett, Christine Sue 1955- *WhoAmW 91*
Pickett, Donald Edward 1968- *WhoSSW 91*
Pickett, Douglas Gene 1953- *WhoEmL 91*
Pickett, Doyle Clay 1930- *WhoAm 90*
Pickett, Edwin G. 1946- *St&PR 91*
Pickett, George Bibb, Jr. 1918- *WhoSSW 91, WhoWor 91*
Pickett, George E. 1825-1875 *WorAlBi*
Pickett, George E. 1953- *St&PR 91*
Pickett, George Eastman 1935- *WhoAm 90*
Pickett, George Edward 1825-1875 *EncPaPR 91*
Pickett, Jarrell Waskom 1890-1981 *BioIn 16*
Pickett, Joan Frances 1955- *St&PR 91*
Pickett, John O., Jr. *WhoAm 90, WhoE 91*
Pickett, John T. *BioIn 16*
Pickett, Joseph 1848-1918 *MusmAFA*
Pickett, L.W. 1930- *St&PR 91*
Pickett, Lawrence Kimball 1919- *WhoAm 90*
Pickett, Nancy Elizabeth 1948- *WhoAmW 91, WhoSSW 91*
Pickett, Norman Lee 1949- *WhoEmL 91*
Pickett, Owen B. 1930- *WhoAm 90, WhoSSW 91*
Pickett, Patricia Ann *BiDrAPA 89*
Pickett, Patricia L. 1952- *WhoAmW 91*
Pickett, Robert C. 1928- *St&PR 91*
Pickett, Robert Clement 1928- *WhoAm 90*
Pickett, Stephen Alan 1953- *WhoSSW 91*
Pickett, Steward T. A. 1950- *WhoE 91*
Pickett, William D. *BioIn 16*
Pickett, William Lee 1941- *WhoAm 90, WhoE 91*
Pickett, William S. 1935- *St&PR 91*
Pickett, Wilson 1941- *DrBlPA 90, EncPR&S 89, OxCPMus, WorAlBi*
Pickett Barnes, Sally 1958- *WhoAmW 91*
Pickford, James Herbert 1925- *WhoSSW 91*
Pickford, Lillian Mary 1902- *WhoWor 91*
Pickford, Mary 1893-1979 *BioIn 16*
Pickford, Mary 1894-1979 *BioAmW*
Pickford, Mary 1938-1979 *WorAlBi*
Pickford, Rollin, Jr *WhoAmA 91*
Pickford, Shirley Roberta Clay 1949- *WhoAmW 91*
Pickhardt, Carl 1908- *WhoAmA 91*
Pickhardt, Carl Emile, Jr. 1908- *WhoAm 90*
Pickhardt, Charles F., Jr. 1937- *St&PR 91*
Pickholtz, Raymond Lee 1932- *WhoAm 90*
Pickholz, Jerome W. 1932- *St&PR 91*
Pickholz, Jerome Walter 1932- *WhoAm 90*
Pickholz, Marvin G. 1942- *WhoAm 90*
Picking, Steven C. 1952- *St&PR 91*
Pickitt, John Leonard 1933- *WhoAm 90*
Pickle, George Edward 1950- *WhoEmL 91*
Pickle, Hal B. 1929- *WhoWrEP 89*
Pickle, Herbert E. 1922- *St&PR 91*
Pickle, James C. 1943- *WhoAm 90*
Pickle, James Jarrell Jake 1913- *WhoAm 90, WhoSSW 91*
Pickle, Jerry Richard 1947- *WhoSSW 91*
Pickle, Linda Williams 1948- *WhoAmW 91*
Pickle, Robert Douglas 1937- *St&PR 91, WhoAm 90*
Pickler, James Joseph 1949- *WhoSSW 91*
Pickles, Anne Couranz 1947- *WhoAmW 91*
Pickover, Gerald 1931- *St&PR 91*
Pickover, Janet Rochelle 1942- *WhoE 91*
Pickrel, Paul 1917- *WhoAm 90*
Pickrel, Susan Gay *BiDrAPA 89*
Pickrell, Patrick Theodore 1950- *WhoSSW 91*
Pickrell, Thomas Richard 1926- *WhoAm 90*
Pickthall, Marjorie 1883-1922 *DcLB 92 [port], FemiCLE*
Pickup, Harry Wilson, III 1947- *IntWWM 90*
Pickus, Albert Pierre 1931- *WhoAm 90*
Pickus, Martin A. 1942- *St&PR 91*
Pico, Andres *BioIn 16*
Pico, Jeff 1966- *Ballpl 90*
Pico, Pio 1801-1894 *BioIn 16*
Pico, Rafael 1912- *WhoAm 90*
Pico, Rosemarie Bernadette 1959- *WhoE 91*
Pico della Mirandola, Giovanni 1463-1494 *EncO&P 3, LitC 15 [port], WorAlBi*
Picon, Hector Tomas, Jr. 1952- *WhoHisp 91*

Picon, Molly 1898- *BioIn 16, NotWoAT, WorAlBi*
Picon-Sales, Mariano 1901-1965 *BioIn 16*
Picon-Varner, Dora Amalia 1950- *WhoAmW 91*
Picone, Edith 1917- *WhoAmW 91*
Picone, Joe Al 1942- *St&PR 91*
Picone, Robert 1950- *St&PR 91*
Picornell, Jose 1927- *St&PR 91*
Picott, J. Rupert *BioIn 16*
Picott, J Rupert 1916?-1989 *ConAu 129*
Picott, John Rupert 1916- *WhoAm 90*
Picotte, J. Charles 1941- *St&PR 91*
Picotte, Michael Bernard 1947- *WhoE 91*
Picower, Warren Michael 1934- *WhoAm 90, WhoE 91*
Picozzi, Anthony 1917- *WhoAm 90*
Pictet, Fabien 1958- *WhoWor 91*
Pidal, Ramon Menendez *HispWr 90*
Pidal, Ramon Menendez 1869-1968 *BioIn 16*
Pidany, John 1929- *St&PR 91*
Piddington, J G 1869-1952 *EncO&P 3*
Piddington, Jack H. 1910- *WhoWor 91*
Piddington, John George 1869-1952 *EncPaPR 91*
Piddington, Lesley *EncO&P 3*
Piddington, Sydney 1921- *EncO&P 3*
Piddington Smith, John George 1869-1952 *EncPaPR 91*
Pidgeon, John Anderson 1924- *WhoAm 90, WhoE 91, WhoWor 91*
Pidgeon, Walter 1898-1984 *WorAlBi*
Pidgeon, Walter Paul, Jr. 1942- *WhoE 91*
Pidgeon, Wayne M 1919- *BiDrAPA 89*
Pidot, George B. *BioIn 16*
Pidoux, Jean Marie 1945- *WhoWor 91*
Piech, Felix L. *St&PR 91N*
Piech, Ferdinand *BioIn 16*
Piech, Margaret Ann 1942- *WhoAmW 91, WhoE 91*
Piechowski, Marjorie Pauline 1939- *WhoAmW 91*
Piechuta, Michael Paul 1960- *WhoEmL 91*
Pieck, Wilhelm 1876-1960 *WorAlBi*
Piecuch, Robert Michael 1943- *St&PR 91*
Piecuch, William M. 1933- *ODwPR 91*
Pieczenik, Steve Richard *BiDrAPA 89*
Pieczynski, Joseph William 1934- *St&PR 91*
Pied Piper *ConAu 129*
Pied Pipers, The *OxCPMus*
Piedmo, Doris R. 1929- *St&PR 91*
Piedmo, George Thomas 1928- *St&PR 91*
Piedra, Mariano Martin 1956- *BiDrAPA 89*
Piedra, Rosano Ibarra de *BioIn 16*
Piedrafite, JoAnn Marie 1955- *WhoE 91*
Piehl, Donald Herbert 1939- *WhoAm 90*
Piehl, Fred 1946- *St&PR 91*
Piehl, Walter Jason, Jr 1942- *WhoAmA 91*
Piehler, Henry Ralph 1938- *WhoAm 90, WhoWor 91*
Piehler, Robert L. *ODwPR 91*
Piehler, Wendell Howard 1936- *WhoE 91*
Piekenbrock, Thomas C *BiDrAPA 89*
Piel, Carolyn Forman 1918- *WhoAm 90, WhoAmW 91*
Piel, Denis *BioIn 16*
Piel, Eric Victor 1948- *St&PR 91*
Piel, Gerard 1915- *St&PR 91, WhoAm 90, WhoWrEP 89*
Piel, H. Ronald 1940- *St&PR 91*
Piel, Jonathan B. 1938- *St&PR 91*
Piel, Kenneth Martin 1936- *WhoWor 91*
Piel, William, Jr. 1909- *WhoAm 90*
Piele, Philip Kern 1935- *WhoAm 90*
Pielken, Walter G. 1930- *ODwPR 91*
Pielmeier, John 1949- *ConAu 132*
Pielou, Evelyn C. *WhoAm 90*
Piemont, Joseph Thomas 1923- *St&PR 91*
Pienaar, Domenick Cuthbert 1926-1978 *EncO&P 3*
Pienaar, Louis Alexander 1926- *WhoWor 91*
Piene, Otto 1928- *WhoAm 90, WhoAmA 91*
Piening, Robert O. 1937- *St&PR 91*
Pienkowski, Jan 1936- *BioIn 16*
Piepenburg, Donald R. 1933- *ODwPR 91, St&PR 91*
Piepenburg, Robert 1941- *WhoAmA 91*
Pieper, Daniel Thomas 1945- *St&PR 91*
Pieper, Heinz Paul 1920- *WhoAm 90*
Pieper, John W. 1935- *St&PR 91*
Pieper, John William 1935- *WhoAm 90*
Pieper, Josef 1904- *BioIn 16*
Pieper, Kenneth *ODwPR 91*
Pieper, Oscar Robert 1935- *St&PR 91*
Pieper, Patricia Rita 1923- *WhoAm 90, WhoAmW 91*
Pieper, Raymond F. 1926- *St&PR 91*
Pieper, Raymond Francis 1926- *WhoAm 90*
Pieper, Rudolf *BioIn 16*
Pieper, Samuel J L, Jr. *BiDrAPA 89*
Pieper, William J *BiDrAPA 89*
Pieper, Wylie Bernard 1932- *St&PR 91*
Piepho, Robert Walter 1942- *WhoAm 90*
Piepmeier, Arthur Lee 1918- *WhoSSW 91*
Pier, Nathaniel *BioIn 16*
Pier, Nathaniel H. *NewYTBS 90*
Pieraerts, Edouard Norbert 1932- *WhoWor 91*
Pierart, Marcel Aime 1945- *WhoWor 91*
Pierart, Z. J. *EncO&P 3*
Pieras, Jaime, Jr. 1924- *WhoAm 90, WhoSSW 91*
Pierattini, Robert Alan 1956- *BiDrAPA 89*
Pierce, Alan Kraft 1931- *WhoAm 90*
Pierce, Allan Dale 1936- *WhoAm 90*
Pierce, Ann Trucksess 1931- *WhoAmA 91*
Pierce, Barbara Gugliotta 1948- *WhoEmL 91*
Pierce, Barbara Hanson 1946- *BioIn 16*
Pierce, Barry G 1946- *BiDrAPA 89*
Pierce, Benedict Enol 1942- *WhoAmW 91*
Pierce, Billy 1927- *Ballpl 90 [port]*
Pierce, Bob *WhoSSW 91*
Pierce, Bruce John 1938- *WhoAm 90*
Pierce, Carol Shaffer 1938- *WhoAmW 91*
Pierce, Catherine Maynard 1918- *WhoSSW 91*
Pierce, Charles C. 1930- *St&PR 91*
Pierce, Charles Eliot, Jr. 1941- *WhoAm 90, WhoAmA 91, WhoE 91*
Pierce, Charles R. 1922- *WhoAm 90*
Pierce, Chester M 1927- *BiDrAPA 89*
Pierce, Chester Middlebrook 1927- *WhoAm 90, WhoWor 91*
Pierce, Clyde Walter 1941- *WhoSSW 91*
Pierce, Daniel 1934- *St&PR 91, WhoAm 90, WhoE 91*
Pierce, Daniel Marshall 1928- *WhoAm 90*
Pierce, Danny P *WhoAmA 91*
Pierce, David Lee 1935- *WhoE 91*
Pierce, Deborah Mary 1938- *WhoAmW 91, WhoWor 91*
Pierce, Delilah W 1904- *WhoAmA 91*
Pierce, DeWayne V. 1942- *St&PR 91*
Pierce, Diane 1939- *WhoAmA 91*
Pierce, Don Frederick 1915- *WhoSSW 91*
Pierce, Donald *WhoSSW 91*
Pierce, Donald 1916- *WhoAmA 91*
Pierce, Donald Benjamin 1916- *WhoE 91*
Pierce, Donald Fay 1930- *WhoWor 91*
Pierce, Dustin *BioIn 16*
Pierce, Edgar Harris, Jr. 1948- *WhoSSW 91*
Pierce, Edward 1635?-1695 *BioIn 16*
Pierce, Edward Allen 1947- *WhoSSW 91*
Pierce, Edward Franklin 1927- *WhoAm 90*
Pierce, Elaine Conley 1953- *St&PR 91*
Pierce, Elijah 1892-1984 *MusmAFA*
Pierce, Elizabeth Gay 1907- *WhoAmW 91, WhoE 91, WhoWor 91*
Pierce, Elizabeth R 1898- *WhoAmA 91*
Pierce, Elliot Stearns 1922- *WhoAm 90, WhoE 91, WhoWor 91*
Pierce, Erik J. 1932- *St&PR 91*
Pierce, Francis Casimir 1924- *WhoE 91, WhoWor 91*
Pierce, Francis Edmund, III 1954- *WhoEmL 91*
Pierce, Franklin 1804-1869 *BiDrUSE 89, BioIn 16, WorAlBi*
Pierce, Fred E. 1935- *St&PR 91*
Pierce, Frederick G., II 1955- *St&PR 91*
Pierce, Garrett E. 1944- *St&PR 91*
Pierce, Gary *WhoAmA 91N*
Pierce, Gary Lynn 1942- *St&PR 91*
Pierce, Gary Ronald *BiDrAPA 89*
Pierce, George Foster, Jr. 1919- *WhoAm 90, WhoSSW 91*
Pierce, George N *EncABHB 4*
Pierce, Glenn *ConAu 129, -31NR*
Pierce, Gregory Robert 1952- *WhoE 91*
Pierce, Gretchen Natalie 1945- *WhoAmW 91*
Pierce, Harold Lee 1930- *WhoSSW 91*
Pierce, Harvey R. *St&PR 91*
Pierce, Hilda Rubin *WhoAmW 91*
Pierce, Irwin A. 1929- *St&PR 91*
Pierce, Jack Steven *BiDrAPA 89*
Pierce, James B 1933- *BiDrAPA 89*
Pierce, James Clarence 1929- *WhoAm 90*
Pierce, James E. *BioIn 16*
Pierce, James Franklin 1950- *WhoWor 91*
Pierce, James G. 1925- *St&PR 91*
Pierce, James Robert 1933- *WhoAm 90*
Pierce, James Smith 1930- *WhoAmA 91*
Pierce, Jane Edrel 1947- *WhoE 91*
Pierce, Jane LaPlante 1960- *WhoSSW 91*
Pierce, Jane M. 1806-1863 *BioIn 16*
Pierce, Janet Kathryn 1948- *WhoAmW 91*
Pierce, Janis Vaughn 1934- *WhoAmW 91*
Pierce, John Brian Lloyd 1933- *St&PR 91*
Pierce, John Hewett 1912- *WhoE 91*
Pierce, John M. 1924- *St&PR 91*
Pierce, John Robert 1949- *WhoE 91*
Pierce, John Robinson 1910- *WhoAm 90*
Pierce, Joseph Booth 1950- *BiDrAPA 89*
Pierce, Judith 1930- *IntWWM 90*
Pierce, Judy Marie 1957- *WhoAmW 91, WhoEmL 91*
Pierce, Julian *BioIn 16*
Pierce, Karen *BiDrAPA 89*
Pierce, Keith Robert 1942- *WhoAm 90*
Pierce, Kenneth B. 1943- *St&PR 91*
Pierce, Kenneth H. 1924- *St&PR 91*
Pierce, Kenneth Ray 1934- *WhoAm 90*
Pierce, Kenney J. *St&PR 91*
Pierce, Laurence Alexander 1931- *WhoE 91*
Pierce, Lawrence J. 1952- *St&PR 91*
Pierce, Lawrence Warren 1924- *WhoAm 90, WhoE 91*
Pierce, Letitia Power 1945- *BiDrAPA 89*
Pierce, Lewis Lee 1925- *St&PR 91*
Pierce, Linda Louise 1949- *St&PR 91*
Pierce, Lois M. *St&PR 91*
Pierce, Louis 1929- *WhoAm 90*
Pierce, Margaret Hunter 1910- *WhoAm 90*
Pierce, Marianne Louise 1949- *WhoAmW 91, WhoEmL 91*
Pierce, Marion Armbruster 1910-1988 *BioIn 16*
Pierce, Maris Bryant 1811-1874 *WhNaAH*
Pierce, Martin 1925- *St&PR 91*
Pierce, Marvin *BioIn 16*
Pierce, Mary Cunningham 1908- *AuBYP 90*
Pierce, Meredith Ann 1958- *BioIn 16*
Pierce, Michael E. 1950- *ODwPR 91*
Pierce, Michael Jones 1961- *BiDrAPA 89*
Pierce, Patricia Jobe 1943- *WhoAmA 91*
Pierce, Pauline Day 1917- *WhoE 91*
Pierce, Percy *EncABHB 4*
Pierce, Peter Gladstone, III 1949- *WhoSSW 91*
Pierce, Philip Nason *AuBYP 90*
Pierce, Ponchitta 1942- *DrBlPA 90*
Pierce, Ponchitta Anne 1942- *WhoAm 90*
Pierce, Preston Eugene 1946- *WhoE 91*
Pierce, Ralph 1926- *St&PR 91, WhoAm 90*
Pierce, Randall Scott 1957- *WhoSSW 91*
Pierce, Rebecca Lynn 1950- *WhoEmL 91*
Pierce, Robert E. 1947- *St&PR 91*
Pierce, Robert Lorne *WhoAm 90*
Pierce, Robert Louis 1944- *WhoSSW 91*
Pierce, Robert Nash 1931- *WhoAm 90, WhoSSW 91*
Pierce, Robert Raymond 1914- *WhoWor 91*
Pierce, Roy 1923- *WhoAm 90*
Pierce, S. R., Jr. 1922- *BiDrUSE 89*
Pierce, Samuel R., Jr. *BioIn 16*
Pierce, Samuel Riley, Jr. 1922- *WhoAm 90, WhoE 91, WhoWor 91*
Pierce, Scott 1930- *WhoAm 90, WhoE 91*
Pierce, Suzanne Helene 1953- *WhoE 91*
Pierce, Tamora 1954- *BioIn 16*
Pierce, Thomas Allen 1949- *WhoSSW 91*
Pierce, Tim Shawn 1957- *WhoE 91*
Pierce, Timatha S. 1940- *ODwPR 91*
Pierce, Timothy E. 1941- *WhoWor 91*
Pierce, Tony 1946- *Ballpl 90*
Pierce, Verlon Lane 1949- *WhoSSW 91, WhoWor 91*
Pierce, Walter Smith 1920- *WhoAm 90*
Pierce, Willard G. 1918- *St&PR 91*
Pierce, William C. 1940- *St&PR 91*
Pierce, William Cobb 1940- *WhoAm 90, WhoE 91*
Pierce, William Leigh 1740?-1789 *BioIn 16*
Pierce, William Michael, Jr. 1953- *St&PR 91*
Pierce, William Schuler 1937- *WhoAm 90*
Pierce-Balek, Cynthia E. 1956- *ODwPR 91*
Pierce Buckelew, Carolyn Rose 1946- *WhoAmW 91*
Piercefield, Julian G. 1929- *St&PR 91*
Pierceson, D. Kraig 1948- *St&PR 91*
Piercey, James C. 1947- *St&PR 91*
Piercey, Michael C 1944- *BiDrAPA 89*
Pierch, Peter M., Jr. 1950- *St&PR 91*
Piercy, Bill 1896-1951 *Ballpl 90*
Piercy, George 1854- *AmLegL*
Piercy, Marge *BioIn 16*
Piercy, Marge 1936- *ConLC 62 [port], FemiCLE, MajTwCW, WhoAm 90, WhoAmW 91, WhoE 91, WhoWrEP 89, WorAlBi*
Piercy-Pont, Ann Lisa 1951- *WhoEmL 91*
Piereson, James Eugene 1946- *WhoE 91*
Pieretti, Marino 1920-1981 *Ballpl 90*
Pierfederici, Antonio 1957- *WhoWor 91*
Pierfelice, Robert Allen 1934- *WhoAm 90, WhoE 91*
Piergallini, Alfred A. *BioIn 16*
Piergallini, Alfred A. 1946- *WhoAm 90*
Pieri, Frank John 1957- *BiDrAPA 89*
Pieri, Giovanni Francesco *PenDiDA 89*
Pieri, Laura Ann 1958- *BiDrAPA 89*
Pierik, Marilyn Anne 1939- *WhoAmW 91*
Pierman, Carol J. 1947- *WhoWrEP 89*
Piermatteo, Joseph J. 1932- *St&PR 91*
Piermatti, Patricia Ann 1948- *WhoE 91*
Pierne, Gabriel 1863-1937 *PenDiMP*
Pierno, Anthony Robert 1932- *WhoAm 90*
Piero Della Francesca 1410?-1492 *IntDcAA 90, WorAlBi*
Piero Di Cosimo 1461?-1521? *IntDcAA 90*
Pierola, Nicolas de 1839-1913 *BioIn 16*
Pieronek, Joann F. 1939- *WhoAmW 91*
Pieroni, Leonard J. 1939- *St&PR 91*
Pierotti, James Joseph 1932- *St&PR 91*
Pierotti, Robert Amedeo 1931- *WhoAm 90*
Pierpoint, Robert Charles 1925- *WhoAm 90*
Pierpont, Carleton Langley 1926- *St&PR 91*
Pierpont, Robert 1932- *WhoAm 90, WhoWor 91*
Pierpont, Wilbur K. 1914- *WhoAm 90*
Pierrakos, John C *BiDrAPA 89*
Pierre, Charles Bernard 1946- *WhoE 91*
Pierre, Michael James, Sr. 1940- *WhoE 91*
Pierre, Percy Anthony 1939- *WhoAm 90, WhoSSW 91*
Pierre-Benoist, Jean 1947- *WhoWor 91*
Pierre-Noel, Vergniaud 1910- *WhoAmA 91*
Pierre-Paul, Raymond 1945- *BiDrAPA 89*
Pierrepont, Edwards 1817-1892 *BiDrUSE 89, BioIn 16*
Pierrepont, Peggy *BioIn 16*
Pierret, Alain Marie 1930- *WhoWor 91*
Pierret, Florencia 1932- *IntWWM 90*
Pierro, Robert M 1949- *BiDrAPA 89*
Pierron, George Joseph, Jr. 1947- *WhoEmL 91*
Piers, Robert *MajTwCW*
Piers, Sarah *FemiCLE*
Piers, Sarah *BiDEWW*
Piersall, Jimmy 1929- *Ballpl 90 [port]*
Piersante, Denise 1954- *WhoAmW 91, WhoWor 91*
Piersanti, Steven 1953- *St&PR 91*
Pierskalla, William Peter 1934- *WhoAm 90*
Piersma, Peter M. 1923- *St&PR 91*
Piersol, Jon R. 1939- *IntWWM 90*
Pierson, Albert Chadwick 1914- *WhoAm 90*
Pierson, Anne Bingham 1929- *WhoE 91*
Pierson, Cheryl *BioIn 16*
Pierson, Curt Allan 1930- *St&PR 91*
Pierson, David R. 1923- *St&PR 91*
Pierson, Delbert J. 1947- *St&PR 91*
Pierson, Earl 1920- *St&PR 91*
Pierson, Edward Samuel 1937- *WhoAm 90*
Pierson, Felix 1926- *St&PR 91*
Pierson, George Wilson 1904- *WhoAm 90*
Pierson, H.E. 1951- *St&PR 91*
Pierson, Helen Hale 1941- *WhoAmW 91*
Pierson, Henry L. 1908- *St&PR 91*
Pierson, Herbert Fletcher 1914- *WhoAm 90*
Pierson, James *BioIn 16*
Pierson, James W. 1925- *St&PR 91*
Pierson, Jay Arthur 1959- *IntWWM 90*
Pierson, Jerry D. 1933- *St&PR 91*
Pierson, John Christopher, Sr. 1947- *WhoEmL 91*
Pierson, John Duane *BiDrAPA 89*
Pierson, John Herman Groesbeck 1906- *WhoE 91*
Pierson, John Theodore, Jr. 1931- *WhoAm 90*
Pierson, Kate *BioIn 16*
Pierson, Kathleen Mary 1949- *WhoAmW 91*
Pierson, Margaret Rosalind 1941- *WhoAmW 91*
Pierson, R. Earl 1920- *St&PR 91*
Pierson, Richard Allen 1944- *WhoAm 90, WhoSSW 91*
Pierson, Richard Norris, Jr. 1929- *WhoAm 90*
Pierson, Rita Tidd Anger 1939- *WhoSSW 91*
Pierson, Robert *St&PR 91*
Pierson, Robert C. 1930- *St&PR 91*
Pierson, Robert David 1935- *St&PR 91, WhoAm 90*
Pierson, Samuel D. 1924- *St&PR 91*
Pierson, Sherleigh G. *AuBYP 90*
Pierson, Steven Scott 1945- *BiDrAPA 89*
Pierson, Susan Judith 1959- *St&PR 91*
Pierson, Thomas C. 1922- *IntWWM 90*
Pies, Ronald William *BiDrAPA 89*
Pies, Ronald William 1952- *WhoE 91*
Pieschel, G.M. 1927- *St&PR 91*
Pieschel, Sharon Gunda 1957- *St&PR 91*
Piest, Oskar 1898-1987 *BioIn 16*
Piet, John Frances 1946- *WhoAmA 91*
Piet, Lawrence Frank 1940- *St&PR 91*
Piet, Tony 1906-1981 *Ballpl 90*
Piet, William M. 1943- *St&PR 91*
Pietersen, William Gerard 1937- *WhoAm 90*
Pietila, Reima Frans Ilmari 1923- *WhoWor 91*
Pietila, Vernon W. 1945- *St&PR 91*
Pietrafesa, Robert Delmonico 1922- *WhoE 91*
Pietrangeli, Carlo 1912- *WhoWor 91*
Pietrantoni, Joseph G. *BioIn 16*
Pietras, Philip R. 1949- *St&PR 91*
Pietri, Arturo Uslar *HispWr 90*
Pietri, Arturo Uslar 1906- *BioIn 16*
Pietri, Giovanna C *BiDrAPA 89*
Pietri, Pedro 1943- *ConAu 32NR, HispWr 90*

Pietri, Pedro 1944- *BioIn 16*
Pietri, Pedro Juan 1943- *WhoHisp 91*
Pietrini, Andrew G. 1937- *St&PR 91*
Pietro da Cortona 1596-1669 *IntDcAA 90*
Pietro, di Domenico 1457-1501? *BioIn 16*
Pietro, di Giovanni d'Ambrogio 1409?-1448 *BioIn 16*
Pietro, Giovanni Di *BioIn 16*
Pietro, Joseph A. *St&PR 91*
Pietro, Lorenzo Di 1412?-1480 *BioIn 16*
Pietro, Louis Alexander 1929- *WhoSSW 91*
Pietro, Sano Di 1406-1481 *BioIn 16*
Pietronero, Carlo 1943- *WhoWor 91*
Pietroski, Joseph J. 1938- *St&PR 91*
Pietrowski, Robert Frank, Jr. 1945- *WhoWor 91*
Pietrs, Florence 1921- *WhoAmW 91*
Pietrus, Carol Lynn 1948- *WhoAmW 91*
Pietruski, John Michael 1933- *St&PR 91*
Pietruski, John Michael, Jr. 1933- *WhoAm 90*
Pietrusko, Robert Gerard 1948- *WhoE 91*
Pietruszka, Anthony Francis 1906-1981 *Ballpl 90*
Pietruszka, Walter Mitchell 1941- *WhoSSW 91*
Pietrzak, Alfred Robert 1949- *WhoE 91, WhoEmL 91, WhoWor 91*
Pietrzak, Leonard Walter 1939- *St&PR 91*
Pietrzyk, Donald John 1934- *WhoAm 90*
Pietsch, Richard A. 1925- *St&PR 91*
Pietschmann, Herbert Victor 1936- *WhoWor 91*
Piette, Lawrence Hector 1932- *WhoAm 90*
Piety, Philip A. 1930- *St&PR 91*
Pietzsch, Michael Edward 1949- *WhoEmL 91*
Pieve, Carlos 1929- *WhoHisp 91*
Piez, William 1932- *WhoAm 90*
Pifarre, Juan Jorge 1942- *WhoHisp 91*
Pifer, Alan 1921- *St&PR 91, WhoAm 90*
Pifer, Glenn A. 1953- *St&PR 91*
Pifer, Lewis Weaver 1916- *St&PR 91*
Pifer, Robert Edwin 1925- *St&PR 91*
Piff, Frank Stephen 1940- *St&PR 91*
Piffard, Jeanne 1892- *BiDWomA*
Piffetti, Pietro 1700?-1777 *PenDiDA 89*
Pig, Edward *ConAu 30NR*
Piga, Franco 1927- *WhoWor 91*
Piga, Stephen Mulry 1929- *WhoAm 90*
Pigage, Leo Charles 1913- *WhoAm 90*
Pigalle, Jean-Baptiste 1714-1785 *IntDcAA 90*
Piganiol, Pierre Guy Albert 1915- *WhoWor 91*
Pigaty, John B. 1922- *St&PR 91*
Pigford, Thomas Harrington 1922- *WhoAm 90*
Pigg, H. 1941- *St&PR 91*
Piggford, Roland Rayburn 1926- *WhoAm 90*
Piggott, Audrey Margaret *IntWWM 90*
Piggott, Juliet *AuBYP 90*
Piggott, Leonard R *BiDrAPA 89*
Piggott, Patrick 1915- *IntWWM 90*
Pignatano, Joe 1929- *Ballpl 90*
Pignataro, Louis James 1923- *WhoAm 90*
Pignatelli, Debora Becker 1947- *WhoAmW 91, WhoE 91*
Pignatelli, Samuel A. 1951- *St&PR 91*
Pignato, Damiano J. 1941- *St&PR 91*
Pignato, John Clayton 1938- *WhoE 91*
Pigneguy, John Joseph 1945- *IntWWM 90*
Pigott, Charles McGee 1929- *St&PR 91, WhoAm 90*
Pigott, H. Dale 1947- *WhoSSW 91*
Pigott, Harriet 1775-1846 *FemiCLE*
Pigott, James Calvin 1936- *St&PR 91*
Pigott, John A. 1932- *St&PR 91*
Pigott, Richard Lacy 1955- *St&PR 91*
Pigott, Teresa A 1958- *BiDrAPA 89*
Pigou, A. C. 1877-1959 *BioIn 16*
Pigou, Arthur Cecil 1877-1959 *BioIn 16*
Pigozzi, Raymond Anthony 1928- *WhoAm 90*
Pihera, Lawrence James 1933- *WhoWor 91*
Pihl, Donald Scott 1937- *WhoAm 90*
Pihlaja, Maxine Muriel Mead 1935- *WhoAmW 91*
Piirma, Irja 1920- *WhoAmW 91*
Piirto-Navarre, Jane Marie 1941- *WhoWrEP 89*
Pijan, Barbara Anne 1956- *WhoAmW 91*
Pijanowski, Eugene M 1938- *WhoAmA 91*
Pijls, Roland Joseph 1944- *WhoWor 91*
Pijor, Stanley G. *St&PR 91*
Pijper, Willem 1894-1947 *PenDiMP A*
Pikaart, Len 1933- *WhoAm 90*
Pikarsky, Milton 1924-1989 *BioIn 16*
Pike, Albert 1809-1891 *EncO&P 3, WhNaAH*
Pike, Albert R. 1916- *St&PR 91*
Pike, Albert Raymond 1916- *WhoAm 90*
Pike, Austin Franklin 1819-1886 *AmLegL*
Pike, Bertram Nisson 1927- *St&PR 91*
Pike, Bruce Parker 1933- *St&PR 91*
Pike, Burton 1930- *ConAu 33NR, WhoAm 90*
Pike, Carol Jean 1958- *WhoAmW 91*
Pike, Dana Ann 1965- *WhoAmW 91*
Pike, David Hankins 1943- *WhoSSW 91*
Pike, E. Royston 1896-1980 *BioIn 16*
Pike, Frederick Augustus 1816-1886 *AmLegL*
Pike, George Harold, Jr. 1933- *WhoAm 90*
Pike, Harold A *BiDrAPA 89*
Pike, James A 1913-1969 *EncO&P 3, WorAlBi*
Pike, James Albert 1913-1969 *EncPaPR 91*
Pike, Jeremy 1955- *IntWWM 90*
Pike, John 1911-1979 *WhoAmA 91N*
Pike, John J. 1912- *St&PR 91*
Pike, John W. 1925- *St&PR 91*
Pike, Joyce Lee 1929- *WhoAmA 91*
Pike, Kenneth Lee 1912- *WhoAm 90*
Pike, Larry Ross 1935- *St&PR 91, WhoAm 90*
Pike, Larry Samuel 1939- *WhoAm 90*
Pike, Laurence Bruce 1927- *WhoAm 90*
Pike, Lawrence 1932- *WhoWrEP 89*
Pike, Lucy Grey 1937- *BiDrAPA 89*
Pike, Mary 1824-1908 *FemiCLE*
Pike, Melvin Richard 1950- *WhoSSW 91*
Pike, Milo L. 1930- *St&PR 91*
Pike, Milton 1921- *St&PR 91*
Pike, Morris *BioIn 16*
Pike, Ralph Webster 1935- *WhoSSW 91*
Pike, Robert L. *TwCCr&M 91*
Pike, Robert William 1941- *WhoAm 90*
Pike, Sidney 1927- *WhoSSW 91*
Pike, Thomas Geoffrey 1906-1983 *DcNaB 1981*
Pike, William B 1933- *BiDrAPA 89*
Pike, William Edward 1929- *WhoAm 90*
Pike, William Edward Cathcart 1952- *WhoWor 91*
Pike, William W *BiDrAPA 89*
Pike, Zebulon Montgomery 1779-1813 *WhNaAH, WorAlBi*
Pikelny, Dov Buryl 1933- *WhoE 91*
Piker, Yale I *BiDrAPA 89*
Pikler, Charles *WhoAm 90*
Pikovsky, Eugene 1920- *St&PR 91*
Pikul, Diane *BioIn 16*
Pikul, Frank John 1951- *WhoEmL 91, WhoWor 91*
Pikul, Joseph *BioIn 16*
Pikul, Valentin *NewYTBS 90*
Pikus, Jeffrey Shawn 1968- *WhoEmL 91*
Pikus, Stanton M. 1940- *St&PR 91*
Pilac, Pamela Ann 1954- *WhoWrEP 89*
Pilant, Christine Eynon 1959- *WhoSSW 91*
Pilar, Frank Louis 1927- *WhoAm 90*
Pilarcik, Al 1930- *Ballpl 90*
Pilarczyk, Daniel Edward 1934- *WhoAm 90*
Pilarczyk, Helga 1925- *IntWWM 90, PenDiMP*
Pilarczyk, Richard Robert 1932- *St&PR 91*
Pilard, Patrick 1947- *WhoWor 91*
Pilate, Pontius *WorAlBi*
Pilavin, Selma F 1908- *WhoAmA 91*
Pilbeam, David Roger 1940- *WhoAm 90*
Pilbery, Joseph 1931- *IntWWM 90*
Pilbrow, Douglas Paul 1944- *WhoWor 91*
Pilbrow, Richard *BioIn 16*
Pilcer, Sonia Hanna 1949- *WhoWrEP 89*
Pilch, Frederic Robert 1927- *St&PR 91*
Pilch, Jane Elizabeth 1963- *WhoAmW 91*
Pilch, John Joseph 1936- *WhoE 91*
Pilch, Susan Marie 1954- *WhoE 91*
Pilcher, Benjamin Lee 1938- *WhoSSW 91*
Pilcher, James Brownie 1929- *WhoSSW 91*
Pilcher, Joshua 1790-1843 *WhNaAH*
Pilcher, Rosamunde *BestSel 90-4 [port]*
Pilcher, Rosamunde 1924- *MajTwCW*
Pilcher, Walter Harold 1941- *St&PR 91, WhoAm 90*
Pilchik, Ely Emanuel 1913- *WhoAm 90, WhoWor 91*
Pilchman, Samuel *BiDrAPA 89*
Pildis, Martin James 1946- *BiDrAPA 89*
Pile, James 1943- *WhoAmA 91*
Pile, Robert Bennett 1918- *WhoAm 90*
Pile, Wendell J 1922- *BiDrAPA 89*
Pilecki, Alexander B. 1937- *St&PR 91*
Pileggi, Elizabeth Morgan 1957- *WhoAmW 91*
Pilet, Paul-Emile 1927- *WhoWor 91*
Pilette, Wilfrid Louis 1942- *BiDrAPA 89*
Pilgaard, Eivind 1944- *WhoWor 91*
Pilgrim, Anne *AuBYP 90*
Pilgrim, Dianne H. 1941- *BioIn 16*
Pilgrim, Dianne Hauserman 1941- *WhoAm 90, WhoAmA 91, WhoAmW 91, WhoE 91*
Pilgrim, James F 1941- *WhoAmA 91*
Pilgrim, James Rollins 1947- *WhoSSW 91*
Pilgrim, Lonnie 1928- *WhoSSW 91*
Pilgrim, Raymond Winfred 1936- *WhoAm 90*
Pilgrim-Guracar, Genevieve 1936- *WhoWrEP 89*
Pilibosian, Helene Rose 1933- *WhoWrEP 89*
Pilic, Ivanka *BiDrAPA 89*
Pilkey, Orrin H. 1934- *WhoAm 90*
Pilkey, Orrin H., Jr. *BioIn 16*
Pilkington family *PenDiDA 89*
Pilkington, Miss *FemiCLE*
Pilkington, Alan Ralph 1943- *WhoAm 90*
Pilkington, Alastair 1920- *WhoWor 91*
Pilkington, David Geoffrey 1959- *WhoSSW 91*
Pilkington, Henry 1905-1983 *DcNaB 1981*
Pilkington, John W. 1944- *St&PR 91*
Pilkington, Laetitia 1706?-1750 *FemiCLE*
Pilkington, Laetitia 1712-1750 *BioIn 16*
Pilkington, Mary 1766-1839 *FemiCLE*
Pilkington, Roger Windle 1915- *AuBYP 90*
Pilkington, Theo Clyde 1935- *WhoAm 90*
Pilko, Robert Michael 1952- *WhoSSW 91*
Pill, Cynthia Joan 1939- *WhoAmW 91*
Pill, Stephen Michael 1945- *St&PR 91*
Pilla, Anthony Michael 1932- *WhoAm 90*
Pilla, Felix Mario 1932- *WhoAm 90*
Pillaert, Edna Elizabeth 1931- *WhoAm 90*
Pillai, Ajit Kesava *BiDrAPA 89*
Pillai, Dharmapalan V *BiDrAPA 89*
Pillai, Jeyakumar P. 1952- *BiDrAPA 89*
Pillai, Pushkalai R *BiDrAPA 89*
Pillar, Charles Littlefield 1911- *WhoWor 91*
Pillar, David Gene 1942- *St&PR 91*
Pillar, Heather Reta 1963- *WhoAmW 91*
Pillar, William 1924- *WhoWor 91*
Pillard, Richard C 1933- *BiDrAPA 89*
Pillement, Jean-Baptiste 1728-1808 *PenDiDA 89*
Piller, Vera 1949-1983 *EncCoWW*
Pillers, Robert Harvey 1932- *St&PR 91*
Pillersdorf, Louis *BiDrAPA 89*
Pillette, Duane 1922- *Ballpl 90*
Pillette, Herman 1895-1960 *Ballpl 90*
Pillin, Polia 1909- *WhoAmA 91*
Pilling, Charles Ashworth, Jr. 1932- *St&PR 91*
Pilling, Janet Kavanaugh 1951- *WhoAmW 91, WhoE 91*
Pilling, Loran F *BiDrAPA 89*
Pillinger, David Arthur 1952- *BiDrAPA 89*
Pillinger, James J. 1918- *WhoE 91*
Pilliod, Charles J., Jr. 1918- *WhoWor 91*
Pillips, William John *WhoWrEP 89*
Pilliter, Chas. J. *St&PR 91*
Pillon, Meredith L. 1946- *ODwPR 91*
Pillot, Gene Merrill 1930- *WhoSSW 91*
Pillot, Patricia Lu 1954- *WhoWrEP 89*
Pillow, Bill C. 1936- *WhoSSW 91*
Pillow, Raymond Eugene 1922- *St&PR 91*
Pillow, William Keith, Jr. 1946- *WhoSSW 91*
Pilloy, Wilfrid John 1947- *WhoWor 91*
Pillsburg, Lawrence *St&PR 91*
Pillsbury, Charles A. 1842-1899 *WorAlBi*
Pillsbury, Earl Lyman 1928- *St&PR 91*
Pillsbury, Edmund P. *BioIn 16*
Pillsbury, Edmund P 1943- *WhoAmA 91*
Pillsbury, Edmund Pennington 1943- *WhoAm 90, WhoSSW 91*
Pillsbury, George S. 1921- *St&PR 91*
Pillsbury, George Sturgis 1921- *WhoAm 90*
Pillsbury, Gordon E. 1933- *St&PR 91*
Pillsbury, Julia Marie 1952- *WhoE 91*
Pillsbury, Sarah *BioIn 16*
Pilnick, Allen Edward 1929- *St&PR 91*
Pilon, Germain 1528?-1590 *IntDcAA 90*
Pilon, Jean-Claude *BiDrAPA 89*
Pilon, Jean-Guy 1930- *BioIn 16*
Pilon, John E. 1925- *St&PR 91*
Pilon, Kevin J. *ODwPR 91*
Pilon, Lawrence James 1948- *St&PR 91*
Pilon, Normand *BiDrAPA 89*
Pilosi, Robert N 1934- *BiDrAPA 89*
Pilot-Peters, Norma Lou 1942- *WhoAmW 91*
Pilotti, Michael Alan 1946- *WhoSSW 91*
Pilou, Jeannette 1931- *IntWWM 90*
Pilous, Betty Scheibel 1948- *WhoAmW 91, WhoWor 91*
Pilowsky, Daniel Jaime 1951- *BiDrAPA 89, WhoE 91*
Pilpel, Harriet Fleischl *WhoAm 90, WhoWrEP 89*
Pilpel, Robert H. 1943- *WhoWrEP 89*
Pilsbury, Betty F. 1921- *St&PR 91*
Pilskaln, Harold 1931- *St&PR 91*
Pilsner, Joyce Marion 1925- *WhoAmW 91*
Pilson, Neal Howard 1940- *St&PR 91, WhoAm 90*
Pilsudski, Jozef 1867-1935 *BioIn 16, WorAlBi*
Pilun-Owad, Chaiyut 1948- *WhoEmL 91, WhoWor 91*
Pilz, Alfred Norman 1931- *WhoAm 90*
Pilz, James William 1928- *St&PR 91*
Pim, Kendall Allan 1940- *St&PR 91*
Pimen, Patriarch 1910-1990 *BioIn 16, NewYTBS 90 [port]*
Pimenta, Simon Ignatius 1920- *WhoWor 91*
Pimental, Joseph Richard 1931- *St&PR 91*
Pimentel, Albert A. 1955- *St&PR 91*
Pimentel, David 1925- *WhoAm 90*
Pimentel, David Delbert 1943- *WhoAmA 91*
Pimentel, George C. *BioIn 16*
Pimentel, Lucita Ching *BiDrAPA 89*
Pimiho *WomWR*
Pimiku *WomWR*
Pimisho *WomWR*
Pimpinella, Ronald Joseph 1935- *WhoE 91, WhoWor 91*
Pimsler, Alvin J. 1918- *WhoAm 90*
Pina, Alberto Buffington 1957- *WhoSSW 91*
Pina, Gary 1956- *WhoHisp 91*
Pina, Horacio 1945- *Ballpl 90*
Pina, Jorge 1954- *WhoHisp 91*
Pina, Matilde Lozano 1946- *WhoHisp 91*
Pina, Sheila Martines 1955- *WhoAmW 91*
Pina, Urbano *WhoHisp 91*
Pinac, Andre Louis, III 1955- *WhoSSW 91, WhoWor 91*
Pinard, Alfred P 1924- *BiDrAPA 89*
Pinard, Georges Frank 1961- *BiDrAPA 89*
Pinard, Gilbert D 1940- *BiDrAPA 89*
Pinard, Gilbert Daniel 1940- *WhoAm 90*
Pinard, Jean-Laurent 1945- *WhoWor 91*
Pinard, Raymond R. 1930- *WhoAm 90*
Pinard, Steven C. 1944- *St&PR 91*
Pinardi, Enrico Vittorio 1934- *WhoAmA 91*
Pinay, Antoine 1891- *BiDFrPL*
Pinazza, Beverly Diane 1961- *WhoAmW 91*
Pincay, Laffit, Jr. 1946- *WhoAm 90, WorAlBi*
Pinch, Patricia Ann 1947- *WhoAmW 91*
Pinchard, Elizabeth *FemiCLE*
Pinchback, Elaine 1953- *WhoSSW 91*
Pinchbeck, Christopher *PenDiDA 89*
Pinchbeck, Peter G 1940- *WhoAmA 91*
Pinchbeck, Peter Gerald 1931- *WhoE 91*
Pincher, Henry Chapman 1914- *SpyFic*
Pincherle, Adriana 1906- *BioIn 16*
Pincherle, Alberto 1907- *BioIn 16, ConAu 33NR, MajTwCW*
Pincherle, Alberto 1907-1990 *ConAu 132*
Pinchot, Ann *WhoWrEP 89*
Pinchot, Bronson *BioIn 16*
Pinchot, Bronson 1959- *WhoAm 90, WorAlBi*
Pinchuck, Curt P *BiDrAPA 89*
Pinchuck, Curt Paul 1960- *WhoEmL 91*
Pinchuk, Nicholas Thomas 1946- *St&PR 91*
Pinciaro, Dominick A. *St&PR 91*
Pinckert, Kathy *ODwPR 91*
Pinckert, Warren Emmett, II 1943- *St&PR 91*
Pinckney, Charles 1757-1824 *BioIn 16, EncCRAm, WorAlBi*
Pinckney, Charles C. 1746-1825 *WorAlBi*
Pinckney, Charles Cotesworth 1746-1825 *BioIn 16, EncCRAm*
Pinckney, Eliza 1722?-1793 *FemiCLE*
Pinckney, Eliza L. 1722?-1793 *BioAmW*
Pinckney, Elizabeth Lucas 1722-1793 *EncCRAm*
Pinckney, Francis deSales, II 1964- *WhoSSW 91*
Pinckney, Neal Theodore 1935- *WhoAm 90*
Pinckney, Samuel Marion, III 1947- *WhoE 91*
Pinckney, Stanley 1940- *WhoAmA 91*
Pinckney, Thomas 1750-1828 *BioIn 16, EncCRAm*
Pincock, Garry LaMar 1949- *WhoSSW 91*
Pincock, Richard Earl 1935- *WhoAm 90*
Pincoffs, Edmund Lloyd 1919- *WhoAm 90*
Pincott, Hugh 1941- *EncO&P 3*
Pincus, Ann Terry 1937- *WhoAmW 91*
Pincus, David N *WhoAmA 91*
Pincus, Debbie Sue 1953- *WhoAmW 91*
Pincus, Emile Irving 1948- *BiDrAPA 89*
Pincus, George 1935- *WhoAm 90, WhoE 91*
Pincus, Gregory 1903-1967 *WorAlBi*
Pincus, Harold Alan 1951- *BiDrAPA 89*
Pincus, Howard Jonah 1922- *WhoAm 90*
Pincus, Jeanette Engel 1909- *WhoAmW 91*
Pincus, Joseph 1919- *WhoAm 90*
Pincus, Larry Alan 1952- *BiDrAPA 89*
Pincus, Laura R. 1923- *WhoSSW 91*
Pincus, Lionel I. 1931- *St&PR 91, WhoAm 90, WhoE 91*
Pincus, Mathilde *BioIn 16*
Pincus, Michael Stern 1936- *WhoSSW 91*
Pincus, Randi 1957- *WhoE 91*
Pincus, Simon Howard *BiDrAPA 89*
Pincus, Theodore H. 1933- *ODwPR 91*
Pincus, Theodore Henry 1933- *WhoAm 90*
Pincus, Walter Haskell 1932- *WhoAm 90*
Pincus-Witten, Robert A 1935- *WhoAmA 91*
Pindar 518?BC-438?BC *WorAlBi*

Pindborg, Jens Jorgen 1921- *WhoWor 91*
Pindell, Howardena 1943- *BiDWomA*
Pindell, Howardena Doreen 1943- *WhoAm 90, WhoAmA 91*
Pinder, Bridget *BiDEWW*
Pinder, George Francis 1942- *WhoAm 90*
Pinder, John E. 1947- *St&PR 91*
Pinder, John Humphrey Murray 1924- *WhoWor 91*
Pinder, Richard Dennis 1946- *WhoE 91*
Pinder, T.D. 1952- *St&PR 91*
Pindera, Jerzy Tadeusz 1914- *WhoAm 90*
Pinderhughes, Charles A 1919- *BiDrAPA 89*
Pindling, Lynden Oscar *BioIn 16*
Pindling, Lynden Oscar 1930- *WhoWor 91*
Pindyck, Bruce Eben 1945- *St&PR 91, WhoEmL 91, WhoWor 91*
Pindyck, Mary E. 1946- *St&PR 91*
Pine, Barbara *BioIn 16*
Pine, Carol L. 1945- *ODwPR 91*
Pine, Charles 1943- *WhoSSW 91*
Pine, Charles H. 1845-1915 *AmLegL*
Pine, Charles Joseph 1951- *WhoAm 90, WhoWor 91*
Pine, Courtney *BioIn 16*
Pine, Granville Martin 1915- *WhoAm 90*
Pine, Irving 1909- *BiDrAPA 89*
Pine, Janet Helen 1951- *BiDrAPA 89*
Pine, John Christopher 1922- *WhoWrEP 89*
Pine, Kathleen Paravich 1948- *WhoEmL 91*
Pine, Katie *BioIn 16*
Pine, Max 1934- *St&PR 91*
Pine, Ralph Jonathan 1939- *WhoAm 90*
Pine, Robert 1928- *ConAu 129*
Pine, Robert Houchin 1934- *BiDrAPA 89*
Pine, Sidney R. 1910-1989 *BioIn 16*
Pine, Tillie Schloss 1896- *AuBYP 90*
Pineas, Herman *BiDrAPA 89*
Pineau, Christian 1904- *BiDFrPL*
Pineau, James B. 1957- *St&PR 91*
Pineau, Joy Victoria 1957- *WhoAmW 91*
Pineau, Michel Jean Pierre 1928- *WhoWor 91*
Pineau, Nicolas 1684-1754 *PenDiDA 89*
Pineault, Jacinthe *BiDrAPA 89*
Pineda, Andres, Jr. 1951- *WhoHisp 91, WhoWor 91*
Pineda, Antonio Jesus, Jr. 1948- *WhoHisp 91*
Pineda, Bernardo Gueco 1929- *BiDrAPA 89*
Pineda, Eliza Laoang 1930- *BiDrAPA 89*
Pineda, Gilbert 1948- *WhoHisp 91*
Pineda, Irene Basilio 1939- *WhoAmW 91*
Pineda, Marianna 1925- *WhoAm 90, WhoAmA 91*
Pineda, Mario Rodolfo 1937- *BiDrAPA 89*
Pineda, Vinson Bagtas 1936- *WhoWor 91*
Pineda Botero, Alvaro 1942- *WhoWor 91*
Pineda-Pineda, Luis F *BiDrAPA 89*
Pinegar, Marta Carlson 1955- *WhoAmW 91*
Pineiro-Montes, Carlos 1955- *WhoHisp 91*
Pinel, Philippe 1745-1826 *WorAlBi*
Pinel, Stephen Leigh 1956- *IntWWM 90*
Pineles, Cipe 1910- *ConDes 90*
Pinell, Octavio C *BiDrAPA 89*
Pinelli, Babe 1895-1984 *Ballpl 90*
Pinelli, Patricia Ruth 1929- *WhoAmW 91*
Piner, Dick Henley, Jr. 1929- *St&PR 91*
Pinera, Virgilio 1912- *ConAu 131, HispWr 90*
Pinero, Arthur Wing 1855-1934 *BioIn 16, WorAlBi*
Pinero, Luis Amilcar 1955- *WhoHisp 91*
Pinero, Miguel *BioIn 16*
Pinero, Miguel 1946-1988 *AnObit 1988, HispWr 90*
Pinero, Miguel Antonio Gomez 1946-1988 *WhoHisp 91N*
Pinero-Medina, Francisco J 1939- *BiDrAPA 89*
Pinero-Rivera, Ramon 1945- *BiDrAPA 89*
Pines, Alexander 1945- *WhoAm 90*
Pines, Allan Jay 1945- *WhoEmL 91*
Pines, Burton Yale 1940- *WhoE 91*
Pines, Catherine Deirdre 1955- *WhoAmW 91*
Pines, David 1924- *WhoAm 90*
Pines, Deborah Ann 1946- *BiDrAPA 89*
Pines, Herman 1902- *WhoAm 90*
Pines, Isidore 1937- *St&PR 91*
Pines, Jack 1925- *St&PR 91*
Pines, Jeffrey M 1947- *BiDrAPA 89, WhoE 91*
Pines, Judith Aiello *WhoAmW 91*
Pines, Kapai 1926- *WhoWor 91*
Pines, Lois G. 1940- *WhoAmW 91*
Pines, Mario 1942- *WhoWor 91*
Pines, Ned L. 1905-1990 *BioIn 16*
Pines, Philip Alan 1926- *WhoE 91*
Pines, Wayne L. 1943- *ODwPR 91*
Pines, Wayne Lloyd 1943- *WhoE 91*
Pinet, Frank Samuel 1920- *WhoAm 90*
Ping, Charles Jackson 1930- *WhoAm 90*
Ping, Er Chang, Jr. 1938- *BiDrAPA 89*
Ping-Robbins, Nancy R. 1939- *IntWWM 90*
Pingel, John S. 1916- *St&PR 91*
Pingel, John Spencer 1916- *WhoAm 90*
Pinger, Carol *BioIn 16*
Pinger, Henry Ambrose 1897-1988 *BioIn 16*
Pingili, Janardana R *BiDrAPA 89*
Pingleton, Jared Philip 1956- *WhoEmL 91*
Pingree, Dale Scott 1957- *St&PR 91*
Pingret, Edouard Henri Theophile 1788-1875 *ArtLatA*
Pingry, Julia Ann 1957- *WhoE 91*
Pings, Anthony Claude 1951- *WhoWor 91*
Pings, Cornelius John 1929- *WhoAm 90, WhoWor 91*
Pinheiro, Joao De Deus 1945- *WhoWor 91*
Pinheiro, Marcio Vasconcellos *BiDrAPA 89*
Pinho, Manuel Joaquim Das Neves 1942- *WhoWor 91*
Pinhorn, W.W. 1942- *St&PR 91*
Pini, Anthony *PenDiMP*
Pini, Carl *PenDiMP*
Pini-Corsi, Antonio 1858-1918 *PenDiMP*
Pinick, Byron Dan 1928- *St&PR 91*
Piniella, Lou 1943- *Ballpl 90*
Pinilis, Lawrence S. 1943- *WhoE 91*
Pinilla, Gustavo Rojas 1900-1975 *BioIn 16*
Pininfarina *ConDes 90*
Pinion, Robert A. 1943- *St&PR 91*
Pink Floyd *EncPR&S 89, OxCPMus*
Pink, Fred G. 1934- *St&PR 91*
Pink, Irene K. *BioIn 16*
Pink, Joseph *BioIn 16*
Pink, Olive *BioIn 16*
Pink, Sidney 1916- *BioIn 16*
Pinkard, Maceo 1897-1962 *BioIn 16, OxCPMus*
Pinke, Judith Ann 1944- *WhoWor 91*
Pinkel, Sheila Mae 1941- *WhoAmA 91*
Pinkenburg, Ronald Joseph 1940- *WhoSSW 91*
Pinkerman, John Horton 1914- *WhoAm 90*
Pinkert, Dorothy Minna 1921- *WhoE 91, WhoWor 91*
Pinkert, Joseph S. 1908- *St&PR 91, WhoAm 90*
Pinkerton, Allan 1819-1884 *WorAlBi*
Pinkerton, Clayton 1931- *WhoAmA 91*
Pinkerton, Clayton David 1931- *WhoAm 90*
Pinkerton, Guy Calvin 1934- *St&PR 91, WhoAm 90*
Pinkerton, James Donald 1940- *WhoAm 90*
Pinkerton, James Pearson 1958- *NewYTBS 90 [port]*
Pinkerton, Jan Marian 1951- *WhoE 91*
Pinkerton, Jane *ODwPR 91*
Pinkerton, Jane E. 1940- *St&PR 91*
Pinkerton, Judith Ann 1954- *IntWWM 90*
Pinkerton, Kathrene Sutherland 1887-1967 *AuBYP 90*
Pinkerton, Max Edward 1935- *St&PR 91*
Pinkerton, Richard LaDoyt 1933- *WhoAm 90*
Pinkerton, Robert B. 1941- *St&PR 91*
Pinkerton, Robert Bruce 1941- *WhoAm 90, WhoE 91*
Pinkerton, W. Stewart, Jr. *ODwPR 91*
Pinkerton, Wilbert Alvin, Jr. 1942- *St&PR 91*
Pinkham, Charles T. 1934- *St&PR 91*
Pinkham, Daniel 1923- *IntWWM 90, WhoAm 90*
Pinkham, Eleanor Humphrey 1926- *WhoAmW 91, WhoWor 91*
Pinkham, Frederick Oliver 1920- *WhoAm 90*
Pinkham, Jefferson Francis 1946- *WhoWor 91*
Pinkham, Lydia 1819-1883 *WorAlBi*
Pinkham, Lydia E. 1819-1883 *BioAmW*
Pinkham, Stephen William 1945- *St&PR 91*
Pinkin, James Edward 1947- *WhoAm 90*
Pinkman, Karen N. *WhoAmW 91*
Pinkney, David Henry 1914- *WhoAm 90*
Pinkney, Helen Louise *WhoAmA 91*
Pinkney, Jerry 1939- *BioIn 16, SmATA 12AS [port], WhoAmA 91, WhoE 91*
Pinkney, Josephine E. 1959- *WhoE 91*
Pinkney, William 1764-1822 *BiDrUSE 89, BioIn 16*
Pinkow, David James 1944- *IntWWM 90*
Pinkowicz, Christine Ann 1961- *WhoAmW 91*
Pinks, Lester R. 1935- *St&PR 91*
Pinkstaff, Carlin Adam 1934- *WhoSSW 91*
Pinkstaff, Marlene Arthur 1936- *WhoAmW 91*
Pinkster, Harm 1942- *WhoWor 91*
Pinkston, Al 1917- *Ballpl 90*
Pinkston, Anita Sue 1960- *WhoAmW 91*
Pinkston, Carolyn Joan 1940- *WhoWrEP 89*
Pinkston, John William, Jr. 1924- *WhoAm 90, WhoSSW 91*
Pinkston, Kathleen F *BiDrAPA 89*
Pinkston, Randall *DrBlPA 90*
Pinkus, Hugh David 1954- *St&PR 91*
Pinkus, Paul 1952- *WhoEmL 91*
Pinkwater, Daniel Manus 1941- *WhoAm 90*
Pinkwater, Manus 1941- *AuBYP 90*
Pinnell, Brian C. 1932- *St&PR 91*
Pinnell, David S. 1812-1885 *AmLegL*
Pinnell, Gary Ray 1951- *WhoEmL 91, WhoSSW 91, WhoWor 91*
Pinnell, George Lewis 1921- *WhoAm 90*
Pinnell, Richard Tilden 1942- *IntWWM 90*
Pinnell, W. George 1922- *St&PR 91*
Pinnell, Walter *BioIn 16*
Pinnell, William George 1922- *WhoAm 90*
Pinnell-Stephens, June Alicia 1948- *WhoEmL 91*
Pinner, Jay Martin 1953- *WhoSSW 91*
Pinney, David Gordon 1939- *St&PR 91*
Pinney, Diane Oliver 1941- *WhoAmW 91*
Pinney, Edward L, Jr. 1925- *BiDrAPA 89*
Pinney, George M. 1833- *AmLegL*
Pinney, Robert Joseph 1954- *BiDrAPA 89*
Pinney, Sidney Dillingham, Jr. 1924- *WhoAm 90*
Pinney, Thomas Clive 1932- *WhoAm 90*
Pinney, William Emery 1941- *WhoSSW 91*
Pinnick, Larry V. 1947- *St&PR 91*
Pinnock, Trevor *BioIn 16*
Pinnock, Trevor 1946- *IntWWM 90, PenDiMP, WhoWor 91*
Pinnow, Arno Lee 1941- *WhoWor 91*
Pino, Anthony John 1948- *WhoE 91*
Pino, David James 1941- *IntWWM 90*
Pino, Fernando 1949- *BiDrAPA 89*
Pino, Frank, Jr. 1942- *WhoHisp 91*
Pino, Jose Facundo 1823-1863 *AmLegL*
Pino, Ramon Enrique 1957- *BiDrAPA 89, WhoE 91*
Pino, Vincent S. 1948- *St&PR 91*
Pino Diaz, Rafael Del *BioIn 16*
Pinoak, Justin Willard *ConAu 33NR*
Pinochet Ugarte, Augusto *BioIn 16*
Pinochet Ugarte, Augusto 1915- *WhoWor 91, WorAlBi*
Pinola, Joseph J. 1925- *EncABHB 7 [port], St&PR 91*
Pinola, Joseph John 1925- *WhoAm 90*
Pinola, Richard J. 1946- *St&PR 91*
Pinon, Nelida *BioIn 16*
Pinosky, David G 1929- *BiDrAPA 89*
Pinover, L. Stanley, Jr. 1933- *St&PR 91*
Pinover, Martin D. 1938- *St&PR 91*
Pinschof, Thomas 1948- *IntWWM 90*
Pinsent, Gordon 1930- *OxCCanT [port]*
Pinsent, Robert John 1834-1893 *DcCanB 12*
Pinske, Roy O. 1933- *St&PR 91*
Pinsker, Essie 1918- *WhoAmA 91*
Pinsker, Essie Levine *WhoAmW 91*
Pinsker, Henry 1928- *BiDrAPA 89*
Pinsker, Penny Collias 1942- *WhoAmW 91*
Pinsker, Sanford 1941- *ConAu 31NR*
Pinsker, Sanford Sigmund 1941- *WhoWrEP 89*
Pinski, Gabriel 1937- *BiDrAPA 89, WhoE 91*
Pinsky, Abe 1914- *BiDrAPA 89, WhoE 91*
Pinsky, George A. 1927- *St&PR 91*
Pinsky, Gerald A. 1938- *St&PR 91*
Pinsky, Jack J *BiDrAPA 89*
Pinsky, Robert *BioIn 16*
Pinsky, Robert Neal 1940- *WhoAm 90, WhoWrEP 89*
Pinsky, Sonja Stahl *BiDrAPA 89*
Pinsof, Philip 1911- *St&PR 91*
Pinson, Cathryn Snellings 1918- *WhoSSW 91*
Pinson, Cora *BioIn 16*
Pinson, Ellis Rex, Jr. 1925- *WhoAm 90*
Pinson, John Carver 1931- *WhoAm 90*
Pinson, John Neil 1947- *St&PR 91*
Pinson, Martin Stanley 1945- *St&PR 91*
Pinson, Vada 1936- *Ballpl 90 [port]*
Pinson, Vada 1938- *BioIn 16*
Pinson, William Meredith 1934- *WhoSSW 91*
Pinsonneault, Alan A. 1946- *St&PR 91*
Pinta, Emil Richard *BiDrAPA 89*
Pinta, Harold *ConAu 33NR, MajTwCW*
Pintak, Larry 1955- *ConAu 132*
Pintal, Helen 1951- *BiDrAPA 89*
Pintar, Judith *NewAgMG*
Pintar, Robert George 1927- *St&PR 91*
Pintat Solans, Josep 1925- *WhoWor 91*
Pintauro, Danny *BioIn 16*
Pintchman, Charles 1930- *ODwPR 91*
Pinter, Frank *St&PR 91*
Pinter, Harold 1930- *BioIn 16, ConAu 33NR, MajTwCW, WhoAm 90, WhoWor 91, WorAlBi*
Pinter, J. James 1945- *St&PR 91*
Pinter, Michael Robert 1948- *St&PR 91*
Pinter, Todd 1953- *BiDrAPA 89*
Pinther, Miklos 1940- *WhoAm 90*
Pinti, John 1944- *St&PR 91*
Pinti, Mario 1920- *WhoWor 91*
Pinto *EncO&P 3*
Pinto, Angelo Raphael 1908- *WhoAmA 91, WhoE 91*
Pinto, Antonio Jose Mendonca 1947- *WhoWor 91*
Pinto, Arun Charles 1949- *BiDrAPA 89*
Pinto, Biagio 1911-1989 *WhoAmA 91N*
Pinto, Edgar 1950- *WhoWor 91*
Pinto, Enrique 1937- *WhoWor 91*
Pinto, James Joseph 1937- *St&PR 91*
Pinto, Joaquin 1842-1906 *ArtLatA*
Pinto, Jody 1942- *BiDWomA, WhoAmA 91, WhoE 91*
Pinto, Joseph C. 1946- *St&PR 91*
Pinto, Les *WhoHisp 91*
Pinto, Michael 1938- *St&PR 91*
Pinto, Peter *MajTwCW*
Pinto, R.A. 1927- *St&PR 91*
Pinto, Ralph 1953- *WhoWor 91*
Pinto, Ronald Isaac 1955- *WhoWor 91*
Pinto, Ronald Joseph 1931- *St&PR 91*
Pinto, Thomas *PenDiMP*
Pinto Coelho, Duarte *BioIn 16*
Pinto da Costa, Manuel 1937- *WhoWor 91*
Pinto Diaz, Francisco Antonio 1785-1858 *BioIn 16*
Pinto Garmendia, Anibal 1825-1884 *BioIn 16*
Pintori, Giovanni 1912- *ConDes 90*
Pintoricchio 1454?-1513 *IntDcAA 90*
Pinturicchio 1454?-1513 *IntDcAA 90*
Pinxten, Rik 1947- *ConAu 131*
Pinyan, Hollis Fitzhugh 1931- *St&PR 91*
Pinz, Alexandra 1949- *BiDrAPA 89*
Pinza, Ezio 1892-1957 *OxCPMus, PenDiMP, WorAlBi*
Pinzarrone, Paul 1951- *WhoAmA 91*
Pinzon, Martin Alonso 1441?-1493 *WorAlBi*
Pinzon, Rodolfo P, Jr. 1935- *BiDrAPA 89*
Pinzon, Vicente Yanez 1460?-1523? *WorAlBi*
Pinzon-Umana, Eduardo 1931- *WhoHisp 91*
Pio, Padre 1887-1968 *EncO&P 3, EncPaPR 91*
Pio, Alessandro 1953- *WhoWor 91*
Piola, Domenico *PenDiDA 89*
Pioli, Richard Theodore 1929- *WhoE 91*
Piomelli, Maria-Rosaria 1937- *WhoAm 90*
Piomingo *WhNaAH*
Pione, Frances Elaine 1952- *WhoE 91*
Pionk, Richard C 1938- *WhoAmA 91*
Piontek, Heinz 1925- *WhoWor 91*
Piontkowski, Chester Leonard 1934- *St&PR 91*
Piontnica, Joseph 1928- *St&PR 91*
Pioquinto, Ronald Peter 1941- *WhoE 91*
Piore, Emanuel Ruben 1908- *WhoAm 90*
Piore, Michael J 1940- *ConAu 130*
Piore, Michael Joseph 1940- *WhoE 91*
Piot, Peter 1949- *WhoWor 91*
Piotrovsky, Boris B. *NewYTBS 90*
Piotrowski, Andrew 1939- *ConAu 131*
Piotrowski, Chester Joseph 1938- *St&PR 91*
Piotrowski, Donna Lynn 1960- *WhoAmW 91*
Piotrowski, John Louis 1934- *WhoAm 90*
Piotrowski, Kenneth W 1945- *BiDrAPA 89*
Piotrowski, Linda Susan *BiDrAPA 89, WhoE 91*
Piotrowski, Richard Francis 1945- *WhoAm 90*
Piotrowski, Sonya Pensgen 1966- *WhoEmL 91*
Pious, William L 1907- *BiDrAPA 89*
Piovanelli, Silvano 1924- *WhoWor 91*
Piowaty, Kim Kennelly 1957- *BioIn 16*
Piozzi, Hester Lynch 1741-1821 *BioIn 16, DcLB 104 [port], FemiCLE*
Pipal, Faustin A. 1921- *St&PR 91*
Pipal, Faustin Anthony 1921- *WhoAm 90*
Pipal, George Henry 1916- *WhoAm 90*
Pipal, Marlaina Lisa 1953- *WhoEmL 91*
Pipe, Bernard J 1910- *BiDrAPA 89*
Pipe, Daniel 1955- *IntWWM 90*
Pipelet, Constance *EncCoWW*
Piper, Addison Lewis 1946- *WhoAm 90*
Piper, Anson Conant 1918- *WhoAm 90*
Piper, Carol Adeline 1924- *WhoAmW 91*
Piper, David Towry 1918- *WhoWor 91*
Piper, Don Courtney 1932- *WhoAm 90, WhoE 91*
Piper, Edgar 1937- *WhoSSW 91*
Piper, Edward *BioIn 16*
Piper, Ernyst Reinhard 1952- *WhoWor 91*
Piper, Evelyn 1908- *TwCCr&M 91*
Piper, Frank Ivan 1933- *St&PR 91*
Piper, George Earle 1932- *WhoAm 90, WhoE 91*
Piper, George Eugene, Jr. *BiDrAPA 89*
Piper, H. Beam 1904-1964 *RGTwCSF*
Piper, H.C., Jr. 1917- *St&PR 91*
Piper, Harry Cushing 1917- *WhoAm 90*
Piper, Henry George 1922- *St&PR 91*

Piper, Jane 1916- *WhoAmA 91*
Piper, John G. *BioIn 16*
Piper, Jon L. 1950- *St&PR 91*
Piper, Leonora E. 1857-1950 *EncPaPR 91*
Piper, Leonora E 1859-1950 *EncO&P 3*
Piper, Linda Ammann 1949- *WhoE 91, WhoEmL 91*
Piper, Lloyd Llewellyn, II 1944- *WhoSSW 91*
Piper, Mark Harry 1931- *WhoAm 90*
Piper, Pat Kathryn 1934- *WhoAmW 91*
Piper, Robert Johnston 1926- *WhoAm 90*
Piper, Terry A. 1945- *St&PR 91*
Piper, Thomas L., III 1941- *St&PR 91*
Piper, Thomas Laurence, III 1941- *WhoAm 90*
Piper, Walter Michael 1942- *WhoWor 91*
Piper, William Howard 1933- *WhoAm 90*
Piper, William T. 1881-1970 *WorAlBi*
Pipes, Daniel 1949- *WhoAm 90*
Pipes, Donald *BioIn 16*
Pipes, John R. 1910- *St&PR 91*
Pipes, Marilyn Anne Schmarder 1954- *WhoEmL 91*
Pipes, Paul Bruce 1941- *WhoAm 90*
Pipes, Richard 1923- *WhoAm 90*
Pipes, Richard Edgar 1923- *WhoWrEP 89*
Pipes, Robert Byron 1941- *WhoAm 90*
Pipes, Stanley Howard 1934- *St&PR 91*
Pipes, Wesley O'Feral 1932- *WhoAm 90*
Pipgras, George 1899-1986 *Ballpl 90*
Pipia, Frank Paul *BiDrAPA 89*
Pipkin, Allen Compere, II 1931- *WhoAm 90*
Pipkin, Alva 1931- *WhoWor 91*
Pipkin, Alva Claude 1931- *St&PR 91*
Pipkin, Barbara Dearman 1937- *WhoSSW 91*
Pipkin, Francis Marion 1925- *WhoAm 90*
Pipkin, James Harold, Jr. 1939- *WhoAm 90, WhoWor 91*
Pipkin, John B., II 1935- *St&PR 91*
Pipkin, Julian Thomas, Jr. 1944- *St&PR 91*
Pipkin, Michael Lee 1947- *BiDrAPA 89*
Pipp, Wally 1893-1965 *Ballpl 90*
Pippard, Alfred Brian 1920- *WhoWor 91*
Pippard, Leone *BioIn 16*
Pippart-Brown, Jane T. 1947- *WhoAmW 91*
Pippen, Christie *AuBYP 90*
Pippen, Joseph Franklin, Jr. 1947- *WhoEmL 91*
Pippen, Rodger 1887-1959 *Ballpl 90*
Pippenger, Lynn 1938- *St&PR 91*
Pippin, Horace 1888-1946 *MusmAFA*
Pippin, Kenneth Andrew 1949- *St&PR 91*
Pippin, Robert B. 1948- *ConAu 130*
Pippin, Warren Arnold 1948- *WhoSSW 91*
Pique, Fernando Rafael 1952- *WhoSSW 91*
Piquet, Nelson *BioIn 16*
Piquette, Marice Ann 1954- *WhoWrEP 89*
Pirages, Michael *ODwPR 91*
Piraino, Ann Mae *WhoAmW 91*
Piramal, Dilip Gopikrishna 1949- *WhoWor 91*
Pirandello, Luigi 1867-1936 *WorAlBi*
Piranesi, Giovanni Battista 1720-1778 *IntDcAA 90, PenDiDA 89*
Pirani, Conrad Levi 1914- *WhoAm 90*
Piranian, Poozant 1910- *St&PR 91*
Pirazzi, Sylvia M. 1934- *WhoHisp 91*
Pircher, Leo Joseph 1933- *WhoAm 90*
Pirelli, Leopoldo 1925- *WhoWor 91*
Pires, Antonio Morgado 1925- *WhoWor 91*
Pires, Filipe 1934- *IntWWM 90*
Pires, Kenneth Michael 1956- *St&PR 91*
Pires, Maria Joao 1945- *IntWWM 90*
Pires, Mary Ann 1944- *ODwPR 91*
Pires, Pedro Verona Rodrigues 1934- *WhoWor 91*
Pires-Filho, Ivon D'Almeida 1953- *WhoWor 91*
Pires Goncalves, Leonidas 1921- *WhoWor 91*
Piret, John J. 1938- *St&PR 91*
Piret, Marguerite Alice 1948- *WhoE 91*
Piri, Markku 1955- *ConDes 90*
Piri, Pentti Eino 1935- *WhoWor 91*
Pirie, Hideko *BioIn 16*
Pirie, John Charles 1907-1988 *BioIn 16*
Pirie, Robert B. *NewYTBS 90*
Pirie, Robert B. 1905-1990 *BioIn 16*
Pirie, Robert B. 1933- *St&PR 91*
Pirie, Robert Burns, Jr. 1933- *WhoAm 90*
Pirie, Robert John 1931- *St&PR 91*
Pirie, Robert S. 1934- *St&PR 91, WhoAm 90*
Pirie, William Stewart 1938- *St&PR 91*
Pirilla, Brian Gannon 1954- *WhoE 91*
Pirilli, John 1943- *St&PR 91*
Piriquito, Horacio Casimiro 1960- *WhoWor 91*
Pirkl, James Joseph 1930- *WhoAm 90, WhoAmA 91*
Pirkle, Earl Charnell 1922- *WhoAm 90*
Pirkle, George Emory 1947- *WhoAm 90, WhoEmL 91, WhoWor 91*
Pirkle, John Ward 1937- *WhoAm 90*
Pirlot, Paul Leon 1920- *WhoAm 90*
Pirnie, Malcolm, Jr. 1917- *WhoAm 90*
Pirnot, Thomas Leonard 1943- *WhoE 91*
Piro, Anthony John 1930- *WhoAm 90*
Piro, Frank *BioIn 16*
Piro, James Joseph 1944- *WhoE 91*
Piro, Killer Joe *BioIn 16*
Piro, Louis J 1921- *BiDrAPA 89*
Piro, Lydia A. 1950- *WhoHisp 91*
Piroch, Sigrid *BioIn 16*
Pirodsky, Donald Max 1945- *BiDrAPA 89, WhoE 91*
Pirofsky, Bernard 1926- *WhoAm 90*
Pirofsky, Harvey *BiDrAPA 89*
Piron, Armand 1888-1943 *OxCPMus*
Pirone, Dorothy Ruth *BioIn 16*
Pirone, Thomas Pascal 1936- *WhoAm 90*
Pironio, Eduardo 1920- *WhoWor 91*
Pirosh, Robert 1910-1989 *BioIn 16, ConAu 130*
Pirot, Andreas *PenDiDA 89*
Pirotte, John Keith 1950- *St&PR 91*
Pirotti *PenDiDA 89*
Pirovano, Dorothy Oliver *ODwPR 91*
Pirozynski, Jan 1936- *WhoWor 91*
Pirozzi, Donald Jude 1942- *WhoSSW 91*
Pirozzoli, Alexander 1922- *St&PR 91*
Pirozzoli, Richard William 1948- *St&PR 91*
Pirquet, Hans P. 1934- *St&PR 91*
Pirsch, Carol McBride 1936- *WhoAmW 91*
Pirsch, Peter Joseph 1936- *St&PR 91*
Pirscher, Carl William 1924- *St&PR 91, WhoAm 90*
Pirschl, Gary 1958- *St&PR 91*
Pirsig, Robert M 1928- *MajTwCW*
Pirsig, Robert Maynard 1928- *WhoAm 90, WhoWrEP 89*
Pirtle, Charles Raymond 1927- *St&PR 91*
Pirtle, Jamie L. 1929- *St&PR 91*
Pirzio-Biroli, Corrado 1940- *WhoE 91*
Pisa, John Charles 1944- *St&PR 91*
Pisacane, Ernie John 1937- *WhoWrEP 89*
Pisacane, Louis C., Jr. 1940- *St&PR 91*
Pisacano, Nicholas J. 1924-1990 *BioIn 16*
Pisacano, Nicholas Joseph 1924- *WhoWor 91*
Pisacich, Kevin Walter 1966- *WhoE 91*
Pisacrita, Marie Seliste 1946- *WhoEmL 91*
Pisanelli, Antonietta *BioIn 16*
Pisanello, Antonio 1395?-1455 *IntDcAA 90*
Pisani, Anthony Michael 1943- *WhoE 91, WhoWor 91*
Pisani, Edgard Edouard Marie-Victor 1918- *BiDFrPL*
Pisani, Gerald Y. 1940- *St&PR 91*
Pisani, James John 1946- *WhoE 91*
Pisani, Janet *BiDrAPA 89*
Pisani, Joseph 1938- *WhoAmA 91*
Pisani, Joseph Michael 1919- *WhoAm 90*
Pisani, Robert Louis 1956- *WhoWrEP 89*
Pisanko, Henry Jonathan 1925- *WhoE 91*
Pisano, A. Robert 1943- *WhoAm 90*
Pisano, Andrea 1290?-1349? *IntDcAA 90*
Pisano, Giovanni 1248?-1314? *IntDcAA 90*
Pisano, Nicola *IntDcAA 90*
Pisano, Ronald George 1948- *WhoAm 90, WhoAmA 91*
Pisano, Thomas Stephen 1956- *BiDrAPA 89*
Pisar, Samuel 1929- *WhoWrEP 89*
Pisarra, Joseph Bernard 1937- *WhoE 91*
Pisasale, Roy Frank 1949- *St&PR 91*
Piscatelli, Nancy Marie 1953- *WhoAmW 91*
Piscator, Maria Ley 1900- *WhoAm 90*
Pischel, Michael C. 1942- *St&PR 91*
Pischinger, Franz Felix 1930- *WhoWor 91*
Pischl, Adolph John 1920- *WhoAm 90*
Pischner, Hans 1914- *IntWWM 90*
Pisciotta, Anthony Vito 1921- *WhoAm 90*
Pisciotta, Charles 1933- *St&PR 91*
Pisciotta, Joseph Anthony 1946- *WhoE 91*
Piscitelli, Linda Ann 1948- *WhoE 91*
Piscitello, Denise Emily 1948- *WhoAmW 91*
Piscopo, Albert E. 1944- *St&PR 91*
Piscopo, Joseph A. 1944- *St&PR 91*
Piscopo, Joseph Charles 1951- *WhoAm 90*
Pisculli, Leo M 1934- *BiDrAPA 89*
Pisegna, Anne Kathleen 1950- *WhoE 91*
Piser, Donald H. 1941- *St&PR 91*
Piserchia, Doris 1928- *RGTwCSF*
Pisetsky, Ingrid Buhler 1945- *BiDrAPA 89*
Pisetsky, Joseph E 1909- *BiDrAPA 89*
Pisetsky, Myron M 1935- *BiDrAPA 89*
Pisetzner, Emanuel 1926- *WhoAm 90*
Pisetzner, Melvin K 1942- *BiDrAPA 89*
Pishchugin, Sergey *PenDiMP*
Pishioneri, Frank Vincent 1932- *St&PR 91*
Pishkin, Vladimir 1931- *WhoAm 90*
Pisier, Marie-France 1944- *ConTFT 8*
Pisinski, Stephen D. *ODwPR 91*
Pisk, Paul Amadeus 1893-1990 *IntWWM 90*
Piskacek, Vladimir Richard 1929- *WhoWor 91*
Piskoti, James 1944- *WhoAmA 91*
Piskurich, S.F. 1935- *St&PR 91*
Pisney, Raymond Frank 1940- *WhoAm 90, WhoSSW 91, WhoWor 91*
Pissarro, Camille 1830-1903 *BioIn 16, IntDcAA 90, WorAlBi*
Pissarro, Camille 1831-1903 *ArtLatA*
Pissocra, C.E. 1933- *St&PR 91*
Pister, Karl Stark 1925- *WhoAm 90*
Pistilli, August Donald 1924- *St&PR 91*
Pistilli, Frederick M. *St&PR 91*
Pistilli, Philip 1926- *St&PR 91, WhoAm 90*
Pistilli, Thomas E. 1942- *St&PR 91*
Pistillo, Bernadino Joseph, Jr. 1957- *WhoEmL 91*
Pistner, Stephen Lawrence 1932- *WhoAm 90*
Pistolakis, Nicholas S. 1933- *WhoE 91*
Pistole, Thomas Gordon 1942- *WhoAm 90*
Piston, Walter 1894-1976 *PenDiMP A, WorAlBi*
Pistone, Joseph D. *BioIn 16*
Pistone, Pamela 1955- *WhoE 91*
Pistone, Peggy *BioIn 16*
Pistor, Charles H., Jr. 1930- *St&PR 91*
Pistor, Charles Herman, Jr. 1930- *WhoAm 90*
Pistorius, Anna *AuBYP 90*
Pistorius, George 1922- *WhoAm 90*
Pistorius, Randolph Joseph 1947- *WhoSSW 91*
Pistulka, Donald Joseph 1946- *St&PR 91*
Pisula, Bettysue 1932- *WhoAmW 91*
Piszczor, Joseph Anthony *BiDrAPA 89*
Pita, George Louis 1961- *WhoHisp 91*
Pitaro, Carl D. *WhoE 91*
Pitarresi, Frances Louise 1948- *WhoE 91*
Pitasi, Pamela Joan 1961- *WhoAmW 91*
Pitassy, Caesar L. 1914- *St&PR 91*
Pitassy, Caesar Leopold 1914- *WhoAm 90*
Pitblado, J.B. 1932- *St&PR 91*
Pitcairn, John 1841-1916 *WorAlBi*
Pitcel, Robert Allen 1932- *St&PR 91*
Pitchell, Ann Loretta 1942- *WhoSSW 91*
Pitchell, Robert J. *WhoAm 90*
Pitcher, Barbara Kent Hickey 1921- *WhoAmW 91*
Pitcher, Caroline 1948- *ConAu 132*
Pitcher, Desmond Henry 1935- *WhoWor 91*
Pitcher, Donald Folsom, Jr. 1938- *St&PR 91*
Pitcher, Eric Robert 1959- *WhoSSW 91*
Pitcher, George Willard 1925- *WhoAm 90*
Pitcher, Georgia Ann 1927- *WhoAmW 91*
Pitcher, Griffith Fontaine 1937- *WhoSSW 91*
Pitcher, Helen Ione 1931- *WhoAmW 91*
Pitcher, John Charles 1949- *WhoAmA 91*
Pitcher, Judith Mitchell 1941- *WhoAmW 91*
Pitcher, Max Grow 1935- *WhoAm 90*
Pitcher, Mildred Anne 1960- *WhoWor 91*
Pitcher, Molly 1754-1832 *BioIn 16, EncCRAm*
Pitcher, Thomas B. 1937- *St&PR 91*
Pitchford, David Louis 1959- *WhoE 91*
Pitchford, Dean Stanley 1951- *WhoAm 90*
Pitchford, Richard Valentine 1895-1973 *BioIn 16*
Pitchlynn, Peter Perkins 1806-1881 *WhNaAH*
Pitchon, Daniel Nathan 1947- *WhoE 91*
Pitchumoni, Capecomorin Sankar 1938- *WhoAm 90*
Pitcock, James Kent 1951- *WhoAm 90*
Pitcock, John W. 1948- *St&PR 91*
Pitegoff, Peter Robert 1953- *WhoEmL 91*
Pitel, Robert J. 1931- *St&PR 91*
Pitelka, Frank Alois 1916- *WhoAm 90*
Pitelka, Sandra Lea 1947- *WhoAmW 91*
Piternick, Anne Brearley *WhoAm 90*
Pitfield, Peter Michael 1937- *WhoE 91*
Pitfield, Thomas Baron 1903- *IntWWM 90*
Pitfield, Ward C. 1925- *St&PR 91*
Pithan, Maxine Helen 1931- *WhoAmW 91*
Pitkapaasi, Elin Lydia 1952- *WhoAmW 91*
Pitkin, Donald Stevenson 1922- *WhoAm 90*
Pitkin, Edward Meyer 1949- *St&PR 91*
Pitkin, Edward Thaddeus 1930- *WhoAm 90*
Pitkin, John T *BiDrAPA 89*
Pitkin, Patricia A. 1951- *WhoAm 90*
Pitkin, Richard *PenDiDA 89*
Pitkin, Roy Macbeth 1934- *WhoAm 90*
Pitkin, Ruthanne Batcheller 1944- *WhoE 91*
Pitkin, Walter 1878-1953 *WorAlBi*
Pitkin, William 1925-1990 *BioIn 16*
Pitkoff, Evan 1956- *WhoE 91*
Pitkowsky, Murray 1931- *St&PR 91*
Pitler, Jake 1894-1968 *Ballpl 90*
Pitler, Richard Kalman 1928- *WhoAm 90*
Pitlock, Skip 1947- *Ballpl 90*
Pitluk, Vicki 1955- *ODwPR 91*
Pitman, Charles H. 1935- *WhoAm 90*
Pitman, Debbie Lynn Odom 1949- *WhoWrEP 89*
Pitman, George Rubi 1927- *WhoE 91*
Pitman, James 1901-1985 *DcNaB 1981*
Pitman, Julie Ahrens 1960- *WhoAmW 91*
Pitman, Karin Marie 1961- *WhoAmW 91*
Pitman, Mark Ira 1932- *WhoAm 90*
Pitman, Nancy Smith 1951- *WhoSSW 91*
Pitman, Roger Keith 1943- *BiDrAPA 89*
Pitman, Sharon Gail 1946- *WhoSSW 91*
Pitman-Gelles, Bonnie 1946- *WhoAm 90*
Pitner, Samuel Ellis 1932- *WhoAm 90*
Pitner, Thomas J. 1941- *St&PR 91*
Pitney, Gene 1941- *EncPR&S 89, OxCPMus, WorAlBi*
Pitofsky, Robert 1929- *WhoAm 90, WhoE 91*
Pitoin, Quentin-Claude *PenDiDA 89*
Pitone, Randall E *BiDrAPA 89*
Pitorak, Larry John 1946- *St&PR 91*
Pitot, Henry Clement 1930- *WhoAm 90*
Pitou, Penny 1938- *WhoAmW 91*
Pitovranov, Yevgeniy *BioIn 16*
Pitra, Frantisek 1942- *WhoWor 91*
Pitre, Felix, Jr. 1949- *WhoE 91*
Pitre, Louise *BioIn 16*
Pitrelli, John R 1935- *BiDrAPA 89*
Pitroda, Satyen Gangrao *BioIn 16*
Pitrone, Jean 1920- *AuBYP 90*
Pitrone, Jean Maddern 1920- *WhoAmW 91*
Pitsch, Larry H. 1941- *St&PR 91*
Pitsch, Peter Kenneth 1951- *WhoAm 90*
Pitstick, George R. 1935- *St&PR 91*
Pitstick, Leslie James 1935- *St&PR 91*
Pitt, Bertram 1932- *WhoAm 90, WhoWor 91*
Pitt, Christine A. 1952- *WhoWrEP 89*
Pitt, Donald Alfred 1926- *WhoSSW 91*
Pitt, Earle William 1923- *St&PR 91, WhoAm 90*
Pitt, Elaine 1937- *BiDrAPA 89*
Pitt, Gavin Alexander 1915- *WhoWor 91*
Pitt, George 1938- *WhoAm 90, WhoWor 91*
Pitt, Harvey Lloyd 1945- *WhoAm 90, WhoE 91*
Pitt, John P. *St&PR 91*
Pitt, Joseph Charles 1944- *WhoSSW 91*
Pitt, Lee *ODwPR 91*
Pitt, Marie 1869-1948 *FemiCLE*
Pitt, Percy 1870-1932 *PenDiMP*
Pitt, Robert Healy, II 1924- *WhoAm 90*
Pitt, Suzan *WhoAmA 91*
Pitt, Suzanne Frances 1946- *WhoWrEP 89*
Pitt, Theo. H. 1936- *St&PR 91*
Pitt, William 1708-1778 *WorAlBi*
Pitt, William 1708-1788 *EncCRAm*
Pitt, William 1759-1806 *WorAlBi*
Pitt, William Arthur John, Jr. 1942- *WhoSSW 91*
Pitt-Aikens, Tom 1940- *ConAu 131*
Pitt-Kethley, Fiona 1954- *ConAu 129*
Pittard, Darrell Dennis 1948- *WhoSSW 91*
Pittard, Joe Tom *BiDrAPA 89*
Pittard, Marion Tarlton 1939- *St&PR 91*
Pittas, John Francis 1932- *St&PR 91*
Pittaway, David Bruce 1951- *WhoE 91*
Pittel, Elliot Mark 1952- *BiDrAPA 89*
Pittelkow, Mark Robert 1952- *WhoAm 90*
Pittelli, Joseph F. 1928- *WhoE 91*
Pittendrigh, Colin Stephenson 1918- *WhoAm 90*
Pittenger, Arthur O., Jr. 1936- *WhoE 91*
Pittenger, Bruce R. 1946- *St&PR 91*
Pittenger, Jerrold W. 1942- *St&PR 91*
Pittenger, Pinky 1899-1977 *Ballpl 90*
Pitter, Ruth 1897- *BioIn 16, FemiCLE*
Pitterson, Felix Oswaldo *BiDrAPA 89*
Pitti, Donald Robert 1929- *St&PR 91*
Pitti, Katalin 1953- *IntWWM 90*
Pittinger, Togie 1871-1909 *Ballpl 90*
Pittius, Dolores Genevieve 1932- *WhoAmW 91*
Pittman, Bob *BioIn 16*
Pittman, David Joshua 1927- *WhoAm 90, WhoWor 91*
Pittman, Edward Dale 1930- *WhoSSW 91*
Pittman, Evelyn LaRue 1910- *IntWWM 90*
Pittman, Frank Smith, III *BiDrAPA 89*
Pittman, G.C. 1921- *St&PR 91*
Pittman, Gee Sidney 1960- *WhoE 91*
Pittman, Glen Dean 1937- *BiDrAPA 89*
Pittman, Hobson 1900-1972 *WhoAmA 91N*
Pittman, Irene K 1938- *WhoAmA 91*
Pittman, Jacquelyn 1932- *WhoSSW 91*
Pittman, James Allen, Jr. 1927- *WhoAm 90, WhoSSW 91, WhoWor 91*
Pittman, James Donald 1948- *WhoSSW 91*
Pittman, James Thomas, Jr. 1913- *WhoE 91*
Pittman, John William 1933- *WhoSSW 91*
Pittman, Karen J. 1952- *BioIn 16*
Pittman, Kathryn 1915-1979 *WhoAmA 91N*

Pittman, Key 1872-1940 *BioIn 16*
Pittman, Lari 1952- *WhoAmA 91*
Pittman, Laura Janine 1943- *WhoAmW 91*
Pittman, Mary Gwendolyn B. 1928- *WhoAmW 91*
Pittman, Michael R. 1957- *BiDrAPA 89*
Pittman, Morant 1961- *WhoSSW 91*
Pittman, Natalie Anne 1952- *WhoAmW 91*
Pittman, Pamela Martin 1953- *BiDrAPA 89*
Pittman, Portia M. 1883-1978 *BioAmW*
Pittman, Richard Frank, Jr. 1923- *St&PR 91, WhoAm 90*
Pittman, Richard Harding 1935- *IntWWM 90*
Pittman, Robert Turner 1929- *WhoAm 90*
Pittman, Robert Warren 1953- *WhoAm 90, WhoEmL 91*
Pittman, Rosemary 1916- *MusmAFA*
Pittman, Russell Warren, III 1951- *WhoE 91*
Pittman, Sandy Hill *BioIn 16*
Pittman, Steuart Lansing 1919- *WhoAm 90*
Pittman, Strayer E. *WhoAm 90*
Pittman, Thomas A. *BiDrAPA 89*
Pittman, Tommy David 1948- *St&PR 91*
Pittman, Virgil 1916- *WhoAm 90, WhoSSW 91*
Pittman, Virgil Lee, Jr. 1941- *St&PR 91*
Pittoni, Luke M. 1945- *WhoEmL 91*
Pittore, Carlo *WhoWrEP 89*
Pittore, Carlo 1943- *WhoAmA 91*
Pitts, Ben Ellis 1931- *WhoWor 91*
Pitts, Bill 1934- *WhoAm 90*
Pitts, Bonita JaNell 1964- *WhoAmW 91*
Pitts, Don Duane 1931- *WhoAm 90*
Pitts, Edmund Levi 1839-1898 *AmLegL*
Pitts, Edward G. 1933- *St&PR 91*
Pitts, Eugene, III 1940- *WhoE 91, WhoWrEP 89*
Pitts, Ferris N, Jr. *BiDrAPA 89*
Pitts, Gloria *BiDrAPA 89*
Pitts, Greenfield 1918- *St&PR 91*
Pitts, James Atwater 1940- *WhoAm 90, WhoE 91*
Pitts, James Rafael *BiDrAPA 89*
Pitts, Joe W., III 1960- *WhoSSW 91, WhoWor 91*
Pitts, John Wilson 1926- *St&PR 91*
Pitts, Kenneth E 1924- *BiDrAPA 89*
Pitts, Lewis *BioIn 16*
Pitts, Lucia Mae *EarBlAP*
Pitts, Lucia Mae 1904-1973 *HarlReB*
Pitts, Richard G 1940- *WhoAmA 91*
Pitts, Robert Eugene, Jr. 1948- *WhoAm 90*
Pitts, Robert Joseph 1932- *St&PR 91*
Pitts, S Martel *BiDrAPA 89*
Pitts, S.R. 1937- *St&PR 91*
Pitts, Terence Randolph 1950- *WhoAmA 91*
Pitts, Thomas J. 1957- *St&PR 91*
Pitts, Vincent Joseph 1947- *WhoE 91*
Pitts, Wendy Jo 1956- *WhoAmW 91*
Pitts, Wesley McArthur, Jr. 1949- *BiDrAPA 89*
Pitts, William 1925- *St&PR 91*
Pitts, Zasu 1898-1963 *WorAlBi*
Piturro, Marlene Cohen 1947- *WhoAmW 91*
Pitz, Henry Clarence 1895-1976 *WhoAmA 91N*
Pitz, Peter E. *BioIn 16*
Pitz, Peter E. 1941- *St&PR 91*
Pitz, Wilhelm 1897-1973 *PenDiMP*
Pitzele, Merlyn Stuart 1911- *WhoAm 90*
Pitzer, Betty Braun 1912- *WhoAmW 91*
Pitzer, Donald Elden 1936- *WhoAm 90*
Pitzer, George Lewis 1916- *St&PR 91*
Pitzer, Kenneth Sanborn 1914- *WhoAm 90*
Pitzer, Larry M. 1939- *St&PR 91*
Pitzer, Randolph L. *ODwPR 91*
Piuck, Charlotte Levin 1922- *BiDrAPA 89*
Piunno, Frank R. 1948- *St&PR 91*
Pius II, Pope 1405-1464 *BioIn 16*
Pius XII, Pope 1876-1958 *BioIn 16*
Piva, Giulio 1940- *WhoWor 91*
Piva, Paolo *BioIn 16*
Pivan, David B. 1921- *St&PR 91*
Pivano, Fernanda 1917- *WhoWor 91*
Pivar, Stuart *BioIn 16*
Pivel Devoto, Juan E. 1910- *BioIn 16*
Piven, Frances Fox 1932- *WhoAm 90*
Piven, Joseph 1954- *BiDrAPA 89*
Piven, Peter Anthony 1939- *WhoAm 90*
Pivert, Marceau 1895-1958 *BiDFrPL*
Pivirotto, Richard Roy 1930- *St&PR 91, WhoAm 90*
Pivnick, Ben 1917- *St&PR 91*
Pivnicka, Barbara Milliken 1953- *WhoAmW 91*
Pivnicki, Dimitrije 1918- *BiDrAPA 89*
Pivot, Bernard 1935- *CurBio 90 [port]*
Piwetz, Eileen Falke 1946- *WhoSSW 91*
Piwowarczyk, Linda Ann *BiDrAPA 89*
Pix, Mary 1666-1709? *BiDEWW, FemiCLE*
Pix, Mary 1666-1720 *BioIn 16*
Pixley, John Sherman, Sr. 1929- *WhoAm 90, WhoSSW 91*
Pixner, Stef 1945- *FemiCLE*
Piyaka, Song Keith *BiDrAPA 89*
Piyakarn, Sawat 1936- *WhoWor 91*
Piza, Arthur Luiz 1928- *WhoWor 91*
Pizam, Abraham 1937- *WhoSSW 91*
Pizan, Christine de 1365?-1430? *EncCoWW*
Pizarro, Agueda 1941- *ConAu 131, HispWr 90*
Pizarro, Cecilio D *BiDrAPA 89*
Pizarro, David 1931- *IntWWM 90*
Pizarro, Francisco 1470?-1541 *EncCRAm*
Pizarro, Francisco 1475-1541 *WorAlBi*
Pizarro, Gonzalo 1502?-1548 *WorAlBi*
Pizarro, Juan 1938- *Ballpl 90*
Pizarro, Renato D. 1941- *St&PR 91*
Pizer, Abigail *AuBYP 90*
Pizer, Donald 1929- *WhoAm 90, WhoWrEP 89*
Pizer, Elizabeth Faw Hayden 1954- *IntWWM 90*
Pizer, Evan F 1932- *BiDrAPA 89*
Pizer, Howard Charles 1941- *WhoAm 90*
Pizer, Irwin Howard 1934- *WhoAm 90, WhoWor 91*
Pizer, Laurence Robert 1946- *WhoE 91*
Pizer, Vernon 1918- *AuBYP 90*
Piziak, Veronica Kelly *WhoAmW 91*
Piziali, J. Marvin 1939- *WhoAm 90*
Piziali, Michael H. 1953- *WhoEmL 91*
Pizitz, Frances *BiDrAPA 89*
Pizitz, Richard 1930- *St&PR 91*
Pizitz, Richard Alan 1930- *WhoAm 90*
Pizitz, Silvia *WhoAmA 91*
Pizor, Kathleen Nathana 1949- *WhoAmW 91*
Pizzagalli, Angelo 1934- *WhoAm 90*
Pizzamiglio, Nancy Alice 1936- *WhoAmW 91*
Pizzano, Rudolph 1957- *WhoE 91*
Pizzarelli, Bucky 1926- *BioIn 16*
Pizzat, Joseph 1926- *WhoAmA 91*
Pizzelanti, Anthony Frank *WhoE 91*
Pizzella, Anthony Nicola 1957- *WhoE 91, WhoEmL 91, WhoWor 91*
Pizzetti, Ildebrando 1880-1968 *PenDiMP A*
Pizzigno, Joanne 1956- *WhoSSW 91*
Pizzitola, Samuel Vincent, III 1955- *WhoSSW 91*
Pizzoferrato, Rudolph Cesidio 1931- *St&PR 91*
Pizzolato, Victor William 1932- *St&PR 91*
Pizzorusso, Arnaldo Paolo 1923- *WhoWor 91*
Pizzuto, Frank Alfred 1924- *WhoE 91*
Plà, George L. *WhoHisp 91*
Plaat, Lotte *EncO&P 3*
Plaatie, Sol. T. 1876-1932 *BioIn 16*
Plaatje, Solomon Tshekisho 1876-1932 *BioIn 16*
Plaatjes, Mark *BioIn 16*
Placci, Carlos Alberto 1933- *BiDrAPA 89*
Place, Bradley Eugene 1920- *WhoAmA 91*
Place, Charles Michael 1951- *St&PR 91*
Place, Dale Hubert 1937- *WhoSSW 91*
Place, David Elliott 1921- *WhoAm 90*
Place, Denise Lisette Marie 1961- *WhoAmW 91*
Place, Francis 1771-1854 *BioIn 16*
Place, Geoffrey 1931- *St&PR 91, WhoAm 90*
Place, Jack 1925- *St&PR 91*
Place, Marian Templeton 1910- *AuBYP 90*
Place, Mary Kay *WhoAm 90*
Place, Phillip W. 1946- *St&PR 91*
Place, Sharon Marie 1947- *WhoEmL 91*
Placek, Karel Vaclav 1942- *BiDrAPA 89*
Placek, Marjorie Youngblood 1944- *WhoAmW 91*
Placek, William M. 1948- *St&PR 91*
Placek-Zimmerman, Ellyn Clare 1951- *WhoAmW 91*
Plachta, Deborah N *BiDrAPA 89*
Placidia, Galla 390-450 *WomWR*
Placiente, Siony Araneta 1944- *WhoAmW 91*
Placier, Philip R. 1933- *WhoAm 90*
Placke, James Anthony 1935- *WhoAm 90*
Placzek, Adolf Kurt 1913- *WhoAm 90, WhoAmA 91*
Placzek, George 1905-1955 *DcScB S2*
Plaeger, Frederick Joseph, II 1953- *WhoEmL 91*
Plaetzer, Ross Frederick 1954- *WhoEmL 91*
Plagemann, Bentz 1913- *AuBYP 90*
Plagens, Peter 1941- *WhoAmA 91*
Plagenz, George Richard 1923- *WhoAm 90*
Plager, S. Jay 1931- *WhoAm 90*
Plagge, Irene R. 1936- *St&PR 91*
Plaia, Edward 1941- *WhoE 91*
Plaidy, Jean 1906- *FemiCLE*
Plaidy, Louis 1810-1874 *PenDiMP*
Plain, Belva 1919- *SmATA 62 [port]*
Plain, Gerald Hayes 1940- *IntWWM 90*
Plaine, Lloyd Leva 1947- *WhoAmW 91*
Plair, Wendell Samuel 1921- *WhoE 91*
Plaisance of Antioch *WomWR*
Plaisted, Carole Ann 1939- *WhoAmW 91*
Plaisted, Robert Leroy 1929- *WhoAm 90*
Plaister, Jean *BioIn 16*
Plaistow, Stephen 1937- *IntWWM 90*
Plaja, Guillermo Diaz *ConAu 131, HispWr 90*
Plakans, Shelley Swift 1943- *WhoAmW 91*
Plakidas, Antonios George 1895-1986 *BioIn 16*
Plakun, Eric Martin 1947- *BiDrAPA 89, WhoE 91*
Plambeck, Herbert Henry 1908- *WhoAm 90*
Plamondon, Antoine 1804-1895 *DcCanB 12*
Plamondon, Marc-Aurele 1823-1900 *DcCanB 12*
Planansky, Karel *BiDrAPA 89*
Planchart, Alejandro Enrique 1935- *IntWWM 90, WhoAm 90*
Planchè, Francois de la *PenDiDA 89*
Planche, J. R. 1796-1880 *BioIn 16*
Planche, James Robinson 1796-1880 *BioIn 16*
Plancher, Robert L. 1932- *St&PR 91*
Plancher, Robert Lawrence 1932- *WhoAm 90, WhoE 91*
Planck, John Maurice 1946- *St&PR 91*
Planck, Max K. E. L. 1858-1947 *WorAlBi*
Plancon, Pol 1851-1914 *PenDiMP*
Plane, Donald Ray 1938- *WhoAm 90*
Planer, Lillian H. *BioIn 16, NewYTBS 90*
Plangere, Jules L., Jr. 1920- *St&PR 91*
Plangere, Jules Leon, Jr. 1920- *WhoAm 90*
Planit, Jan Holly 1961- *WhoAmW 91*
Planitzer, Russell E. 1944- *St&PR 91*
Plank, Betsy Ann 1924- *WhoAm 90*
Plank, Dorothy Diane Garling 1962- *WhoAmW 91*
Plank, Douglas Gene 1942- *St&PR 91*
Plank, Eddie 1875-1926 *Ballpl 90 [port]*
Plank, Raymond 1922- *St&PR 91*
Plank, Richard H. 1948- *St&PR 91*
Plank, Roger B. 1956- *St&PR 91*
Plankis, Joseph V. 1943- *St&PR 91*
Plano, Richard James 1929- *WhoAm 90*
Planquette, Robert 1848-1903 *OxCPMus*
Plansker, Dennis H. 1940- *St&PR 91*
Planson, Rollie Joe 1945- *WhoWor 91*
Plant, Albin MacDonough 1937- *WhoAm 90*
Plant, Andrew Martin 1959- *IntWWM 90*
Plant, Arnold I. 1931- *St&PR 91*
Plant, Forrest Albert 1924- *WhoAm 90*
Plant, Gregory E. 1949- *St&PR 91*
Plant, Howard Michael *BiDrAPA 89*
Plant, Maretta Moore 1937- *WhoAmW 91, WhoE 91*
Plant, Michele Susan 1959- *WhoAmW 91*
Plant, Mike *BioIn 16*
Plant, Robert *BioIn 16, EncPR&S 89*
Plant, Valentina Anatolievna 1961- *WhoAmW 91*
Plante, Albert *BiDrAPA 89*
Plante, Claude *BiDrAPA 89*
Plante, D.F. 1946- *St&PR 91*
Plante, David 1940- *MajTwCW*
Plante, Francis 1839-1934 *BioIn 16*
Plante, Gilles J C 1931- *BiDrAPA 89*
Plante, Inge K R *BiDrAPA 89*
Plante, Inge Rudloff 1929- *WhoAm 90*
Plante, Jacques 1929-1986 *WorAlBi*
Plante, James F. *ODwPR 91*
Plante, Joseph H. 1932- *St&PR 91*
Plante, Kathleen Goulder 1944- *WhoSSW 91*
Plante, Patricia R. *WhoAm 90, WhoAmW 91*
Plante, Peter Paul 1920- *WhoAm 90*
Plante, William Madden 1938- *WhoE 91*
Plantin, Arabella *FemiCLE*
Plantin, Christophe 1520?-1589 *BioIn 16*
Plantin, Patrick *BiDrAPA 89*
Plantinga, Alvin 1932- *WhoAm 90, WhoWrEP 89*
Plantrou, Eric 1952- *WhoWor 91*
Plants, Helen Lester 1925- *WhoAmW 91*
Plapp, Bryce Vernon 1939- *WhoAm 90*
Plas, Jeffrey Charles 1957- *BiDrAPA 89*
Plasencia, Philip Edward 1944- *St&PR 91*
Plasha, Michael, Jr. 1933- *St&PR 91*
Plasket, Carol Mueller 1949- *WhoAmW 91*
Plaskett, Gordon G. *St&PR 91*
Plaskett, Thomas G. 1943- *BioIn 16, St&PR 91, WhoAm 90, WhoE 91*
Plasky, Paul 1952- *BiDrAPA 89*
Plass, Jane Paula 1952- *WhoAmW 91*
Plass, Margaret Feurer *BioIn 16*
Plass, Neil Walton 1935- *St&PR 91*
Plasse, Roger *St&PR 91*
Plassman, Brenda Lee 1957- *WhoAmW 91*
Plasson, Michel 1933- *IntWWM 90, PenDiMP*
Plaster, Alice Marie *WhoAmA 91*
Plaster, Richard Emil 1927- *IntWWM 90*
Plaster, Robert W. 1930- *St&PR 91*
Plaster, Susan W. *ODwPR 91*
Plat, Richard Vertin 1929- *St&PR 91, WhoAm 90*
Plate, Andrea 1952- *ConAu 130*
Plate, Andrea Darvi *ConAu 130*
Plate, Robert 1918- *AuBYP 90*
Plate, Walter 1925-1972 *WhoAmA 91N*
Platel, Pierre *PenDiDA 89*
Plater, Frederick Oliver 1949- *WhoEmL 91*
Plater, William Marmaduke 1945- *WhoAm 90*
Plater-Zyberk, Elizabeth 1950- *WomArch*
Plath, Iona 1907- *WhoAmA 91*
Plath, James Walter 1950- *WhoWrEP 89*
Plath, Peter Daniel 1937- *St&PR 91*
Plath, Sylvia *BioIn 16*
Plath, Sylvia 1932-1963 *AuBYP 90, BioAmW, ConLC 62 [port], FemiCLE, MajTwCW, PoeCrit 1 [port], WorAlBi, WrPh*
Platis, Jim George 1927- *WhoWor 91*
Platkin, Mauris M 1913- *BiDrAPA 89*
Platko, John Ralph, II 1962- *WhoE 91*
Platman, Stanley Roy 1934- *BiDrAPA 89*
Platner, Brian *St&PR 91*
Platner, John L. 1932- *St&PR 91*
Platner, John Leland 1932- *WhoAm 90*
Platner, Warren 1919- *ConDes 90, WhoAm 90*
Plato 427BC-347BC *EncPaPR 91, WorAlBi*
Plato 428BC-348BC *WrPh P*
Plato, Sharyll Adelle 1935- *WhoSSW 91*
Platoni, Katherine Theresa 1952- *WhoAmW 91*
Platou, Joanne 1919- *WhoAm 90*
Platowski, Andrew C. 1947- *St&PR 91*
Platt, Alexander Bradford 1935- *WhoAm 90*
Platt, Alice Whitener 1938- *St&PR 91*
Platt, Arthur S *BiDrAPA 89*
Platt, Charles Adams 1932- *WhoAm 90*
Platt, Charles Michael 1949- *WhoAm 90*
Platt, Christopher *ConAu 129*
Platt, Collier *BioIn 16*
Platt, Craig T. 1952- *St&PR 91*
Platt, D C M 1934-1989 *ConAu 129*
Platt, David 1912- *St&PR 91*
Platt, David Michael 1939- *WhoE 91*
Platt, Dennis Edward 1955- *BiDrAPA 89*
Platt, Douglas G. 1944- *St&PR 91*
Platt, Eleanor 1910-1974 *WhoAmA 91N*
Platt, Ellen M *BiDrAPA 89*
Platt, Eugene 1939- *WhoWrEP 89*
Platt, Franklin Dewitt 1932- *WhoAm 90*
Platt, George R. 1954- *St&PR 91*
Platt, Harold 1923- *St&PR 91*
Platt, Harold Kirby 1942- *WhoE 91*
Platt, Harrison Gray 1902- *WhoAm 90*
Platt, Helen Mccormick *BiDrAPA 89*
Platt, Herbert Abraham 1930- *WhoAm 90*
Platt, Jay Christopher 1960- *WhoEmL 91*
Platt, Jerome Joseph 1941- *WhoAm 90, WhoE 91, WhoWor 91*
Platt, Joseph Beaven 1915- *WhoAm 90*
Platt, Kin 1911- *AuBYP 90, BioIn 16*
Platt, Lawrie Pitcher 1942- *ODwPR 91, WhoSSW 91*
Platt, Leslie A. 1944- *WhoE 91*
Platt, Lucian Brewster 1931- *WhoAm 90*
Platt, Michael Elliott 1942- *St&PR 91*
Platt, Nicholas 1936- *WhoAm 90, WhoWor 91*
Platt, Nicolas W. 1953- *St&PR 91*
Platt, Norman 1920- *IntWWM 90*
Platt, Orville Hitchcock 1827-1905 *AmLegL, BioIn 16*
Platt, Paul Marion 1944- *WhoSSW 91*
Platt, Peter Godfrey 1937- *WhoAm 90*
Platt, Ray *NewAgMG*
Platt, Richard Gordon 1930- *St&PR 91*
Platt, Richard Swaby 1928- *IntWWM 90*
Platt, Robert Holmes 1920- *WhoAm 90*
Platt, Robert Thomas 1938- *BiDrAPA 89*
Platt, Samuel 1874-1941? *AmLegL*
Platt, Sherman Phelps, Jr. 1918- *WhoAm 90*
Platt, Steven Irving 1947- *WhoEmL 91*
Platt, Thomas Collier 1925- *WhoAm 90, WhoE 91*
Platt, Thomas Collier, III 1955- *WhoEmL 91*
Platt, Whitey 1920-1970 *Ballpl 90*
Platt, William B. 1906-1990 *BioIn 16*
Platt, William Rady 1915- *WhoAm 90*
Platte, Mary Kay *WhoAmW 91*
Platten, Donald C. 1918- *St&PR 91*
Platten, Donald Campbell 1918- *WhoAm 90*
Platten, Peter M., III 1939- *St&PR 91*
Platters, The *EncPR&S 89, OxCPMus*
Platthy, Jeno 1920- *WhoAm 90, WhoWor 91*
Platti, Rita Jane 1925- *WhoAmW 91*
Plattner, Marc Florea 1945- *WhoE 91*

Plattner, Philip Brent 1947- *BiDrAPA 89*
Plattner, Phyllis 1940- *WhoAmA 91*
Plattner, Richard Serber 1952- *WhoEmL 91*
Platts, A. Monmouth *TwCCr&M 91*
Platts, Martha *BiDEWW*
Platts-Mills, Thomas Alexander E. 1941- *WhoAm 90*
Platz, George Arthur, III 1939- *WhoAm 90*
Platz, Huberto Ricardo 1929- *St&PR 91*
Platz, Robert H. P. 1951- *IntWWM 90*
Platz, Theodore A., Jr. 1927- *St&PR 91*
Platz, William Gregory *BiDrAPA 89*
Platzack, Jan Christer Georg 1943- *WhoWor 91*
Platzker, Marjorie Ann 1942- *WhoAmW 91*
Platzkere, Hal 1940- *ODwPR 91*
Platzman, George William 1920- *WhoAm 90*
Plaue, Rudolf O. 1939- *St&PR 91*
Plausini, Joseph V. 1930- *St&PR 91*
Plaut, Eric A 1927- *BiDrAPA 89*
Plaut, Eric Alfred 1927- *WhoAm 90*
Plaut, Gerhard Wolfgang Eugen 1921- *WhoAm 90*
Plaut, James S 1912- *WhoAmA 91*
Plaut, James Sachs 1912- *WhoAm 90*
Plaut, Martin Edward 1937- *WhoWrEP 89*
Plaut, Nathan Michael 1917- *WhoAm 90*
Plaut, Wofl Gunther 1912- *WhoAm 90*
Plauth, William Henry, Jr. 1930- *WhoAm 90*
Plautus 254?BC-184BC *WorAlBi*
Plavcan, Joseph Michael 1908-1981 *WhoAmA 91N*
Plavin, Zecharia 1956- *IntWWM 90*
Plawecki, Judith Ann 1943- *WhoAmW 91*
Plaxton, Jim 1942- *OxCCanT*
Playe, George Louis 1917- *WhoAm 90*
Player, Gary 1935- *WorAlBi*
Player, Gary Jim 1935- *WhoAm 90, WhoWor 91*
Player, Geraldine 1952- *WhoAmW 91, WhoWor 91*
Player, Thelma B. *WhoAmW 91, WhoE 91*
Player, Theresa Joan 1947- *WhoEmL 91*
Playfair, Guy Lyon 1935- *EncO&P 3, EncPaPR 91*
Playford, John 1623-1686 *OxCPMus*
Playten, Alice *BioIn 16*
Playten, Alice 1947- *ConTFT 8*
Plaza, Francine Grace 1945- *ODwPR 91*
Plaza, Hector Hugo 1950- *WhoWor 91*
Plaza, Sixto 1944- *WhoHisp 91*
Plaza Gutierrez, Leonidas 1865?-1932 *BioIn 16*
Plaza Lasso, Galo 1906-1987 *BioIn 16*
Plazak, Dean J 1927- *BiDrAPA 89*
Plazyk, Judy Lynn 1960- *WhoWrEP 89*
Pleak, Richard Randall 1954- *BiDrAPA 89*
Plear, Scott 1952- *WhoAmA 91*
Pleasance, Donald 1919- *WorAlBi*
Pleasant, Helen Carolyn 1945- *WhoAmW 91*
Pleasant, Richard J. 1944- *St&PR 91*
Pleasant, Robert Dale 1946- *St&PR 91, WhoWor 91*
Pleasants, Carol Novak 1952- *BiDrAPA 89*
Pleasants, Frederick R 1906- *WhoAmA 91N*
Pleasants, Henry 1910- *IntWWM 90, WhoAm 90*
Pleasants, Jack 1874-1923 *OxCPMus*
Pleasence, Donald 1919- *WhoAm 90, WhoWor 91*
Pleasure, Hyman *BiDrAPA 89*
Pleasure, Robert Jonathan 1942- *WhoWor 91*
Pleau, Lawrence Winslow 1947- *WhoAm 90*
Plebani, G.J. 1946- *St&PR 91*
Plecenik, Jeanne Todd 1955- *WhoAmW 91*
Plechaty, William David 1936- *WhoAm 90, WhoSSW 91*
Plechko, Vladimir Yakovlevich 1934- *WhoWor 91*
Pleck, Elizabeth *ConAu 129*
Pleck, Elizabeth H. *ConAu 129*
Pleck, Elizabeth Hafkin 1945- *ConAu 129*
Plectrudis *WomWR*
Pledger, Carolyn Brastow Hughes 1932- *WhoSSW 91*
Pledger, Reginald Harrison, Jr. 1934- *WhoAm 90*
Pledger, Thomas R. 1938- *St&PR 91*
Pledger, Thomas Rolon 1938- *WhoAm 90*
Pleeth, William *PenDiMP*
Pleeth, William 1916- *IntWWM 90*
Pleiman, Roy B. 1919- *St&PR 91*
Pleis, Bill 1937- *Ballpl 90*
Pleissner, Ogden Minton 1905-1983 *WhoAmA 91N*
Pleitez, Jose Alberto *BiDrAPA 89*
Pleitner, Allan Floyd 1951- *St&PR 91*
Plejdrup, Allyn Dean 1935- *St&PR 91*
Plekhanov, Georgi 1856-1918 *WorAlBi*
Plekhanov, Georgii Valentinovich 1856-1918 *BioIn 16*
Plekker, Johannes D *BiDrAPA 89*
Plemiannikov, Roger Vadim *BioIn 16*
Pleming-Yocum, Laura Chalker 1913- *WhoAmW 91, WhoWor 91*
Plemmons, Gerald Thomas 1940- *St&PR 91*
Plena, Jose 1951- *WhoHisp 91*
Plener, Aage 1930- *WhoWor 91*
Plenert, Gerhard Johannes 1948- *WhoEmL 91*
Plens, Ole Emil 1948- *WhoWor 91*
Plenty Coups 1848-1932 *WhNaAH [port]*
Plenty, Royal Homer 1918- *WhoAm 90*
Plesac, Dan 1962- *Ballpl 90*
Plesch, Peter Hariolf 1918- *WhoWor 91*
Pleshette, John 1942- *ConTFT 8*
Pleshette, Suzanne *WhoAm 90, WhoAmW 91*
Pleshette, Suzanne 1937- *BioIn 16, WorAlBi*
Pleskow, Eric Roy *WhoAm 90*
Pleskow, Eric Roy 1924- *St&PR 91*
Pleskow, Raoul 1931- *IntWWM 90*
Pleso, Joseph Frank 1936- *St&PR 91*
Pleso, Lucy Birmingham 1947- *WhoSSW 91*
Plesofsky, Philip *St&PR 91*
Plesons, Dennis J 1949- *BiDrAPA 89*
Pless, John E. 1938- *WhoAm 90*
Pless, Vera 1931- *WhoAmW 91*
Plessen, Elisabeth 1944- *EncCoWW*
Plesset, Marvin R 1911- *BiDrAPA 89*
Plesset, Milton Spinoza 1908- *WhoAm 90*
Plessis-Belair, Michel 1942- *St&PR 91*
Plessner, Yakir 1935- *WhoWor 91*
Pleszko, E.J. 1930- *St&PR 91*
Pletcher, David Mitchell 1920- *WhoAm 90*
Pletcher, Eldon 1922- *WhoAm 90*
Pletcher, Gerry *WhoAmA 91*
Pletcher, Harold D. 1930- *St&PR 91*
Pletcher, Robert O 1904- *BiDrAPA 89*
Pletka, Paul 1946- *WhoAmA 91*
Pletnev, Mikhail 1957- *IntWWM 90*
Pletscher, Josephine Marie *WhoAmA 91*
Plett, Frederick Randall 1946- *St&PR 91, WhoEmL 91*
Pletz, Francis Gregory 1917- *WhoAm 90*
Pletzer, K. Randall 1945- *St&PR 91*
Pletzke, Frank Ted *BiDrAPA 89*
Pleune, F Gordon *BiDrAPA 89*
Pleune, Frederick Gordon 1916- *WhoE 91*
Pleune, Myrtle L 1911- *BiDrAPA 89*
Pleva, Floyd L. 1929- *St&PR 91*
Pleven, Rene 1901- *BiDFrPL*
Plevy, Arthur L. 1936- *WhoE 91*
Plew, Larry Eugene 1947- *WhoSSW 91*
Plewes, Donald E. 1942- *St&PR 91*
Plewes, John Mccauley 1949- *BiDrAPA 89*
Plewes, Steven Arthur 1954- *WhoE 91*
Plewinski, Teresa Maria Sauer *WhoAmW 91*
Plews, Dennis James 1948- *WhoSSW 91*
Plews, Herb 1928- *Ballpl 90*
Pley, Constance *BiDEWW*
Pleyel, Camille 1788-1855 *PenDiMP*
Pleyel, Marie Denise 1811-1875 *PenDiMP*
Pliatska, Dorothea Georges 1935- *IntWWM 90*
Plichta, Thomas Francis 1952- *WhoSSW 91, WhoWor 91*
Plick et Plock *ConAu 129, MajTwCW*
Plieth, Waldfried Johannes Ludwig 1937- *WhoWor 91*
Plimpton, Calvin Hastings 1918- *WhoAm 90*
Plimpton, George 1927- *ConAu 32NR, MajTwCW, WorAu 1980 [port]*
Plimpton, George Ames 1927- *WhoAm 90, WhoE 91, WhoWrEP 89*
Plimpton, Martha *BioIn 16*
Plimpton, Pauline Ames 1901- *WhoAmW 91, WhoE 91, WhoWor 91*
Plimpton, Peggy Lucas 1931- *WhoAmW 91*
Plimpton, Robert James 1938- *WhoWor 91*
Plimpton, Susan Blaine 1943- *St&PR 91*
Plimpton-Hefti, Franziska Stefania 1938- *WhoWor 91*
Plimsoll, Samuel 1824-1898 *BioIn 16*
Pline, Dale S. 1938- *WhoAm 90*
Plinius Secundus, Galius 23?-79 *EncO&P 3*
Plinkiewisch, Helen Edwina 1908- *IntWWM 90*
Pliny the Elder 23?-79 *EncO&P 3, WorAlBi*
Plischke, Elmer 1914- *WhoAm 90*
Plisetskaya, Erika Michael 1929- *WhoAmW 91*
Plisetskaya, Maya *BioIn 16*
Plisetskaya, Maya 1925- *WorAlBi*
Plishka, Paul 1941- *IntWWM 90*
Pliskin, Robert 1917- *WhoE 91*
Pliskin, William Aaron 1920- *WhoAm 90*
Pliskoff, Stanley Stewart 1930- *WhoAm 90*
Pliss, Louise *AuBYP 90*
Plissonnier, Gaston Desire 1913- *BiDFrPL*
Pliszka, Steven Ray 1955- *BiDrAPA 89*
Plitt, Herbert Robert 1929- *St&PR 91*
Plitt, Jeanne Given 1927- *WhoAm 90, WhoAmW 91, WhoSSW 91*
Plitt, Robert A. 1936- *St&PR 91*
Plitzner, Ferdinand 1678-1724 *PenDiDA 89*
Plochmann, Carolyn Gassan 1926- *WhoAmA 91*
Plochocki, Andrew Plato 1936- *WhoE 91*
Plociak, Richard A. 1943- *St&PR 91*
Ploeger, Katherine Marie 1955- *WhoWrEP 89*
Ploeser, Walter Christian 1907- *WhoAm 90*
Ploetz, Lawrence Oliver 1926- *St&PR 91*
Plofker, Leo *BioIn 16*
Plog, Anthony 1947- *IntWWM 90*
Plog, Edward Frank 1952- *WhoE 91*
Plog, Stanley Clement 1930- *St&PR 91*
Ploger, Robert Riis 1915- *WhoAm 90*
Plohr, George William 1933- *St&PR 91*
Plomer, William 1903-1973 *BioIn 16*
Plomer, William Charles Franklin 1903-1973 *MajTwCW*
Plomgren, Ronald Arthur 1934- *St&PR 91*
Plomley, Roy 1914-1985 *DcNaB 1981*
Plommet, Michel Georges 1927- *WhoWor 91*
Plomp, Teunis 1938- *WhoAm 90*
Plonien, Cynthia G. 1953- *WhoWrEP 89*
Plonnies, Luise von 1803-1872 *EncCoWW*
Plonsey, Robert 1924- *WhoAm 90*
Plonus, Martin Algirdas 1933- *WhoAm 90*
Ploof, Willis H *BiDrAPA 89*
Ploog, Detlev W *BiDrAPA 89*
Plopa, Patricia Ann 1949- *WhoAmW 91*
Plopper, Charles George 1944- *WhoAm 90*
Plopper, Michael Gregory 1948- *BiDrAPA 89*
Plosca, Leontin 1941- *BioIn 16*
Plosser, Charles Irving 1948- *WhoE 91*
Plossu, Bernard 1945- *WhoAmA 91*
Plossu, Bernard Pierre 1945- *WhoAm 90*
Plotch, Walter 1932- *WhoE 91*
Plotek, Leopold 1948- *WhoAmA 91*
Plotinsky, Ira Jay *BiDrAPA 89*
Plotinus 205-270 *WorAlBi, WrPh P*
Plotke, Gary Steven *BiDrAPA 89*
Plotke, Hilde G 1912- *BiDrAPA 89*
Plotkin, Daniel Alan *BiDrAPA 89*
Plotkin, Harry Morris 1913- *WhoAm 90*
Plotkin, Irving H. 1941- *St&PR 91*
Plotkin, Kenneth Edward *BiDrAPA 89*
Plotkin, Linda 1938- *WhoAmA 91*
Plotkin, Lynn 1945- *WhoAmA 91*
Plotkin, Manuel D. *WhoAm 90*
Plotkin, Mark *BioIn 16*
Plotkin, Martin 1922- *WhoAm 90*
Plotkin, Stanley Alan 1932- *WhoAm 90*
Plotkin, Sylvia *WhoAmA 91*
Plotnick, Fred *BioIn 16*
Plotnick, Harvey Barry 1941- *WhoAm 90*
Plotnick, Mark Michael 1935- *WhoAm 90*
Plotnick, Robert David 1949- *WhoEmL 91*
Plotnicka, Frumka 1914-1943 *BioIn 16*
Plotnik, Arthur 1937- *WhoAm 90, WhoWrEP 89*
Plotnik, Samuel Martin 1919- *WhoSSW 91*
Plotsky, Harold *BiDrAPA 89*
Plott, Charles R. 1938- *WhoAm 90*
Plott, Charles R. 1961- *WhoSSW 91*
Plott, Dean Bob 1957- *WhoSSW 91*
Plott, Paula 1946- *WhoAmA 91*
Plotts, Matthew Ray 1959- *WhoEmL 91*
Plotz, Charles Mindell 1921- *WhoAm 90*
Plotz, Gregory A. 1949- *St&PR 91*
Plotz, Helen 1913- *BioIn 16*
Plotz, John B. 1921- *St&PR 91*
Plouffe, Robert Louis 1926- *WhoSSW 91*
Plough, Charles Tobias, Jr. 1926- *WhoWor 91*
Plough, Francis Azzo 1923- *St&PR 91*
Plount, Gerald Craig 1946- *WhoSSW 91*
Plourde, E. Raymond 1932- *St&PR 91*
Plourde, Gerard 1916- *St&PR 91, WhoAm 90*
Plourde, Joseph Donald 1936- *WhoAm 90*
Plous, Phyllis *WhoAmA 91*
Plovsky, Gerald Irving *BiDrAPA 89*
Plowden, David *BioIn 16*
Plowden, David 1932- *WhoAmA 91*
Plowman, C. Bruce 1937- *ODwPR 91*
Plowman, Jack Wesley 1929- *WhoAm 90*
Plowman, Piers *MajTwCW*
Plowman, Timothy Charles 1944-1989 *BioIn 16*
Plowright, David Ernest 1930- *BioIn 16*
Plowright, Joan 1929- *BioIn 16*
Plowright, Joan Anne 1929- *WhoWor 91*
Plowright, Rosalind 1949- *PenDiMP*
Plowright, Rosalind Anne 1949- *IntWWM 90*
Ployart, John William 1930- *WhoWor 91*
Ployer, Barbara *PenDiMP*
Plubell, Ann Marie 1950- *St&PR 91, WhoAm 90*
Pluckhan, F.J. 1933- *St&PR 91*
Plucknett, Evaline 1915- *BiDrAPA 89*
Pludermacher, Georges 1944- *PenDiMP*
Plueckhahn, Penny 1941- *St&PR 91*
Pluff, Barbara 1926- *AuBYP 90*
Pluff, Thomas H. 1947- *St&PR 91*
Plugge, Wilfred Robert 1924- *WhoAm 90*
Pluister, Simon 1913- *IntWWM 90*
Plukas, John Michael 1944- *St&PR 91*
Plum, Charles Walden 1914- *WhoAm 90*
Plum, Diane Woodman 1945- *WhoAmW 91*
Plum, Fred 1924- *WhoAm 90*
Plum, J. *ConAu 33NR, MajTwCW*
Plum, Mary Isabelle 1920- *WhoAmW 91*
Plum, Nancy Terhune 1953- *WhoWrEP 89*
Plum, Richard Eugene 1928- *WhoWor 91*
Plum, Samuel *BioIn 16*
Plumb, Charlie 1900-1982 *EncACom*
Plumb, Helga 1939- *WomArch*
Plumb, J. H. 1911- *BioIn 16*
Plumb, James Douglas 1941- *WhoAmA 91*
Plumb, James W. 1934- *ODwPR 91*
Plumb, John Harold 1911- *BioIn 16*
Plumb, Max L. 1921- *St&PR 91*
Plumb, Pamela 1943- *St&PR 91*
Plumb, Preston Bierce 1837-1891 *AmLegL*
Plumb, Robert Charles 1926- *WhoAm 90*
Plumb, Victor Claude 1939- *St&PR 91*
Plumb, William Lansing 1932- *ConDes 90*
Plumbridge, Robin Allan 1935- *St&PR 91*
Plume, Nona Dextrose *WhoWrEP 89*
Plumecocq, Jean Louis 1948- *WhoSSW 91*
Plumer, Edward D. 1944- *St&PR 91*
Plumer, Herbert Charles 1857-1932 *WorAlBi*
Plumeri, Joseph James, II 1943- *WhoAm 90*
Plumez, Jean Paul 1939- *WhoAm 90*
Plumier, Denis 1688-1721 *BioIn 16*
Plumley, Frank Edwin 1949- *St&PR 91*
Plumley, Geraldine Virgil 1942- *WhoE 91*
Plumley, H. Ladd *St&PR 91N*
Plumley, Harold Johnson 1927- *WhoSSW 91*
Plumley, Michael Alan 1950- *St&PR 91, WhoSSW 91*
Plumley, Sarah 1638-1708 *BiDEWW*
Plumly, Anna C. 1925- *St&PR 91*
Plumly, Daniel Harp 1953- *WhoEmL 91*
Plummer, Alice Tolbert 1953- *BiDrAPA 89*
Plummer, Bill 1947- *Ballpl 90*
Plummer, Carlton B *WhoAmA 91*
Plummer, Carlton Byron *WhoE 91*
Plummer, Carol Ann 1944- *WhoSSW 91*
Plummer, Christopher *BioIn 16*
Plummer, Christopher 1927- *OxCCanT [port]*
Plummer, Christopher 1929- *WhoAm 90, WhoWor 91, WorAlBi*
Plummer, Daniel Clarence, III 1927- *WhoAm 90*
Plummer, Donald R. 1946- *St&PR 91*
Plummer, Edward G. 1949- *St&PR 91*
Plummer, Edward G., Jr. 1949- *WhoAm 90*
Plummer, Ernest Lockhart 1940- *WhoE 91*
Plummer, Jack Moore 1940- *WhoSSW 91, WhoWor 91*
Plummer, James D. *WhoAm 90*
Plummer, Joseph Thornton 1941- *WhoAm 90*
Plummer, Kenneth Alexander 1928- *WhoWor 91*
Plummer, Lawrence L. 1933- *St&PR 91*
Plummer, Marcie Stern 1950- *WhoAm 90, WhoAmW 91*
Plummer, Michael Kenneth 1954- *WhoWor 91*
Plummer, Ora Beatrice 1940- *WhoAmW 91*
Plummer, Patricia Lynne Moore *WhoAmW 91*
Plummer, Richard Emmett 1946- *WhoSSW 91*
Plummer, Risque Wilson 1910- *WhoAm 90*
Plummer, Robert Lee 1927- *St&PR 91*
Plummer, Roger L. *BioIn 16*
Plummer, Roger Lawrence 1942- *WhoAm 90*
Plummer, Roger Sherman, Jr. 1922- *WhoWor 91*
Plummer, Walter A. 1916- *St&PR 91*
Plummer, William Francis 1934- *WhoWor 91*
Plummeridge, Charles Terence 1939- *IntWWM 90*
Plumpton, John Martin 1946- *St&PR 91*
Plumptre, Annabella 1761-1838 *FemiCLE*
Plumptre, Anne 1760-1818 *FemiCLE*
Plumptre, Constance 1847?-1929 *FemiCLE*
Plumstead, Mary 1642-1711 *BiDEWW*
Plumtre, Annabella 1761-1838 *FemiCLE*
Plumtre, Anne 1760-1818 *FemiCLE*

Plunguian, Gina *WhoAmA 91N*
Plunk, Eric 1963- *Ballpl 90*
Plunk, Robert Malcolm 1932- *St&PR 91*
Plunk, Stephen D. 1950- *St&PR 91*
Plunket, Daniel Clark 1929- *WhoAm 90*
Plunkett, Anne Marie Cecilia 1932- *WhoAmW 91*
Plunkett, D. Brian 1956- *St&PR 91*
Plunkett, Elaine Lucille 1957- *WhoE 91*
Plunkett, Jack William 1950- *WhoSSW 91*
Plunkett, Jim *BioIn 16*
Plunkett, Jim 1947- *WhoHisp 91*
Plunkett, John L. 1947- *St&PR 91*
Plunkett, John P 1920- *BiDrAPA 89*
Plunkett, Joseph Charles 1933- *WhoWor 91*
Plunkett, Larry Neil 1945- *St&PR 91*
Plunkett, Maryann 1953- *WhoAmW 91*
Plunkett, Melba Kathleen 1929- *WhoAmW 91, WhoWor 91*
Plunkett, Michael Stewart 1937- *St&PR 91, WhoAm 90*
Plunkett, Nancy Geraldine 1925- *WhoWrEP 89*
Plunkett, Paul M. 1908- *St&PR 91*
Plunkett, Richard A. *ODwPR 91*
Plunkett, Richard L. *BioIn 16*
Plunkett, Robert 1919- *WhoAm 90*
Plunkett, Robert Wilson, Jr. 1950- *St&PR 91*
Plunkett, Ruth Anne 1917- *WhoWrEP 89*
Plunkett, Sherman *BioIn 16*
Plunkett, Tammy Jo 1958- *WhoAmW 91*
Plunkett, Thomas F., Jr. 1925- *St&PR 91*
Plunkett, Thomas P. 1950- *St&PR 91*
Plunkett, Walter 1902-1982 *ConDes 90*
Plush, Vincent 1950- *IntWWM 90*
Plusk, Ronald Frank 1933- *St&PR 91, WhoAm 90*
Plusnick, Robert R. *St&PR 91*
Plusquellic, Donald L. 1949- *WhoAm 90*
Plust, Lois Marion 1954- *WhoAmW 91*
Plutarch 46?-120? *BioIn 16, WorAlBi*
Plutzer, Martin D 1944- *BiDrAPA 89*
Plutzky, Max *BiDrAPA 89*
Pluygers, Catherine 1955- *IntWWM 90*
Pluymen, Bert W. 1948- *WhoEmL 91*
Plybon, Jerry *St&PR 91*
Plyler, Charles G 1933- *BiDrAPA 89*
Plyler, Edward C. 1949- *St&PR 91*
Plym, Lawrence J. 1906- *St&PR 91*
Plym, Lawrence John 1906- *WhoAm 90*
Pnazek, Karen Anne 1961- *WhoAmW 91*
Pniakowski, Andrew Frank 1930- *WhoE 91, WhoWor 91*
Po, Claude 1934- *WhoWor 91*
Poad, William James 1930- *St&PR 91*
Poag, John Andrew 1950- *WhoE 91*
Poarch, John Ellis 1935- *BiDrAPA 89*
Poarch, John Thomas, II 1947- *WhoSSW 91*
Poat, Ray 1917- *Ballpl 90*
Poaty-Souchlaty, Alphonse *WhoWor 91*
Pobereskin, Louis Howard 1948- *WhoWor 91*
Poblete, Jocelyn Guia 1960- *WhoAmW 91*
Poblete, Rita Maria Bautista 1954- *WhoAmW 91*
Pobo, Kenneth George 1954- *WhoWrEP 89*
Pocahontas *BioIn 16*
Pocahontas 1595-1617 *BioAmW, EncCRAm, WhNaAH [port], WorAlBi*
Pocalyko, Michael Nicholas 1954- *WhoE 91*
Pocataro 1815?-1884 *WhNaAH*
Pocatello 1815?-1884 *WhNaAH*
Pocatello, General 1815?-1884 *WhNaAH*
Poce, William Arnold 1948- *St&PR 91*
Pocek, Kenneth Louis 1946- *WhoSSW 91*
Poch, David Wyman 1941- *St&PR 91*
Poch, Gerald 1932- *WhoWor 91*
Poch, Gerald A. *St&PR 91*
Poch, Herbert Edward 1927- *WhoE 91*
Pochapin, Pamela Susan 1961- *WhoAmW 91*
Poche, Renard Joseph 1956- *WhoSSW 91*
Poches, Martin Gregory 1953- *St&PR 91*
Pochi, Peter Ernest 1929- *WhoAm 90*
Pochick, Francis Edward 1931- *WhoE 91*
Pochin, Edward 1909-1990 *ConAu 130*
Pochmann, Virginia 1938- *WhoAmA 91*
Pochoda, Elizabeth Turner 1941- *WhoWrEP 89*
Pochoda, Philip M. 1940- *WhoWrEP 89*
Pochon, Alfred *PenDiMP*
Pochyly, Donald Frederick 1934- *WhoAm 90*
Pocino, Mark C. 1944- *St&PR 91*
Pock, Randolph W 1945- *BiDrAPA 89*
Pockell, Leslie M. 1942- *WhoAm 90*
Pocklington, Peter H. *St&PR 91*
Pockriss, Lee Julien 1927- *WhoE 91*
Poco *EncPR&S 89, WhoNeCM A*
Pocock, Douglas C. D. 1935- *ConAu 129*
Pocock, Frederick James 1923- *WhoAm 90*
Pocock, Jack E. 1925- *St&PR 91*
Pocock, John William 1916- *St&PR 91*
Pocock, Lyndol George 1930- *St&PR 91*
Pocock, Mary *BiDEWW*
Pocock, William 1750-1825 *PenDiDA 89*
Pocoroba, Biff 1953- *Ballpl 90*
Pocsik, Ilona *WhoWor 91*
Podagrosi, Jo-Ella *ODwPR 91*
Podagrosi, Katy Blanche 1935- *WhoAmW 91*
Podany, Amy Elizabeth 1961- *WhoAmW 91*
Podany, Clayton James 1943- *St&PR 91*
Podany, Gerald S. 1944- *St&PR 91*
Podaras, Straton C. 1932- *St&PR 91*
Podberesky, Samuel 1946- *WhoEmL 91*
Podbielan, Bud 1924-1982 *Ballpl 90*
Podboy, John Watts 1943- *WhoWor 91*
Podbrey, Maurice 1934- *OxCCanT*
Podd, Marsha Dianne 1951- *WhoAmW 91*
Podell, Lynn Beth 1955- *WhoAm 90*
Podell, Paul Norman *BiDrAPA 89*
Podell, Ronald Mark 1945- *BiDrAPA 89*
Podell, Ronald Mark 1949- *BiDrAPA 89*
Podesta, Anthony Peter 1928- *WhoWor 91*
Podesta, Beulah M. 1923- *St&PR 91*
Podesta, Robert Angelo 1912- *St&PR 91, WhoAm 90*
Podewell, Cathy *BioIn 16*
Podewils, Robert C. *St&PR 91*
Podgajny, Johnny 1920-1971 *Ballpl 90*
Podgor, Ellen Sue 1952- *WhoAmW 91*
Podgorny, George 1934- *WhoAm 90, WhoWor 91*
Podgorny, Richard Joseph 1944- *WhoAm 90*
Podgurski, Charles Vincent 1941- *WhoSSW 91*
Podhajsky, Alois 1864- *BioIn 16*
Podhoretz, Norman 1930- *WhoAm 90, WhoE 91, WhoWrEP 89*
Podhurst, Richard Scott 1956- *WhoSSW 91*
Podis, Eunice 1922- *IntWWM 90*
Podjavorinska, L'udmila *EncCoWW*
Podkowka, John Adam 1940- *WhoE 91*
Podlecki, Anthony Joseph 1936- *WhoAm 90*
Podles, Eleanor Pauline 1920- *WhoAmW 91*
Podlesak, Robert G. 1938- *St&PR 91*
Podlesney, Francis A. 1932- *St&PR 91*
Podlesny, Laura A. 1962- *ODwPR 91*
Podlewski, Henry K 1920- *BiDrAPA 89*
Podlich, William Frederick 1944- *St&PR 91*
Podlipsky, Alexander 1947- *BiDrAPA 89*
Podmokly, Patricia Gayle 1940- *WhoAmW 91*
Podmore, Frank 1856-1910 *EncO&P 3, EncPaPR 91*
Podnieks, Alfons *BiDrAPA 89*
Podnos, Burton 1931- *BiDrAPA 89*
Podobnikar, Ivan G *BiDrAPA 89*
Podolak, Douglas John 1948- *WhoSSW 91*
Podoloff, Donald Alan 1938- *WhoSSW 91*
Podorf, Frederick M. 1949- *WhoE 91*
Podosek, Frank Anthony 1941- *WhoAm 90*
Podpecan, Milan 1936- *WhoWor 91*
Podratz, Wayne Owen 1940- *St&PR 91*
Podrebarac, Francis Albert *BiDrAPA 89*
Podres, Johnny 1932- *Ballpl 90*
Podro, Michael 1931- *ConAu 132*
Podrug, Dinko 1952- *BiDrAPA 89*
Podshadley, Arlon George 1928- *WhoAm 90*
Podufal, Joseph A. 1952- *St&PR 91*
Poduska, Howard John 1920- *St&PR 91*
Poduska, John William, Jr. 1937- *WhoAm 90*
Poduska, T F 1925- *WhoAmA 91*
Podvoiskii, Nikolai Il'ich 1880-1948 *BioIn 16*
Podvoll, Edward M *BiDrAPA 89*
Podwoski, Thomas Alan 1935- *St&PR 91*
Poe, Bryce, II 1924- *WhoAm 90*
Poe, Charles Eugene 1928- *St&PR 91*
Poe, Crawford 1932- *St&PR 91*
Poe, Douglas Allan 1942- *WhoAm 90*
Poe, Earl John, III 1950- *WhoEmL 91*
Poe, Edgar Allan 1809-1849 *BioIn 16, PoeCrit 1 [port], SpyFic, TwCCr&M 91A, WorAlBi*
Poe, Eliza *BioIn 16*
Poe, Eliza A. 1787?-1811 *BioAmW*
Poe, George A. 1921- *St&PR 91*
Poe, Howard Ritter 1934- *St&PR 91*
Poe, Jerry B. 1931- *WhoAm 90*
Poe, Katrine Laura 1958- *WhoWrEP 89*
Poe, Luke Harvey, Jr. 1916- *WhoAm 90, WhoE 91*
Poe, Merry Rex 1957- *WhoAmW 91*
Poe, Nelson Crawford 1932- *St&PR 91*
Poe, Reigh Kessen 1949- *WhoSSW 91*
Poe, Richard Orla 1936- *BiDrAPA 89*
Poe, Richard W. 1928- *St&PR 91*
Poe, Rose Lorene 1926- *WhoWrEP 89*
Poe, Thomas L. 1957- *St&PR 91*
Poe, Virginia 1932- *WhoAmW 91, WhoSSW 91*
Poe, William Frederick 1931- *WhoAm 90, WhoSSW 91*
Poe-Jobe, Carolyn Sue *WhoSSW 91*
Poehailos, Anthony Walter *BiDrAPA 89*
Poehling, Gerhard G. 1914- *St&PR 91*
Poehling, Robert Edward 1944- *St&PR 91*
Poehlmann, Gerhard Manfred 1924- *WhoWor 91*
Poehlmann, Joanna 1932- *WhoAmA 91*
Poehlmann, Luther D. 1955- *St&PR 91*
Poehner, Raymond Glenn 1923- *WhoWor 91*
Poel, William 1852-1934 *BioIn 16*
Poelker, John H. *BioIn 16*
Poellot, Raymond Albert 1955- *WhoWrEP 89*
Poer, Jerry Robert, Jr. 1953- *WhoSSW 91*
Poernbacher, Hans Karl Victor 1929- *WhoWor 91*
Poersch, Enno *BioIn 16, NewYTBS 90*
Poesch, Jessie Jean 1922- *WhoAm 90*
Poeschla, Brian Doering *BiDrAPA 89*
Poet Of Titchfield Street, The *MajTwCW*
Poetker, Frances Louise 1912- *WhoAmW 91*
Poett, John Luke 1840-1895 *BioIn 16*
Poettcker, Henry 1925- *WhoAm 90*
Poettmann, Fred Heinz 1919- *WhoAm 90*
Poeverlein, Hermann Julius Ferdinand 1911- *WhoWor 91*
Pofahl, Jimmy 1917- *Ballpl 90*
Poff, Gregory V. 1948- *St&PR 91*
Poff, John Wayne, Sr. 1937- *St&PR 91*
Poff, N. Thomas 1937- *St&PR 91*
Poff, Richard Harding 1923- *WhoAm 90*
Poff, Robert L. 1952- *St&PR 91*
Poffenberger, Boots 1915- *Ballpl 90*
Poffenberger, Kathryn Ione 1908- *WhoAmW 91*
Poffenberger, Paul Routzahn 1913- *WhoAm 90*
Pofsky, Norma Louise 1945- *WhoE 91*
Pogacar, Srecko *BiDrAPA 89*
Pogach, Allan C. 1944- *St&PR 91*
Pogach, Gerald *WhoAmA 91*
Pogachnik, Robert Charles 1946- *WhoSSW 91*
Pogacnik, Miha 1949- *IntWWM 90*
Pogany, Miklos 1945- *WhoAmA 91*
Poger, Julia Pauline 1962- *WhoAmW 91*
Poggemiller, Randy Lee 1945- *St&PR 91*
Poggio, Eugene C. 1945- *St&PR 91*
Poggio, Gian Franco 1927- *WhoAm 90*
Poggio, Joseph C. 1943- *St&PR 91*
Poggio, Tomaso Armando 1947- *WhoAm 90*
Poggioli, Frances Consolo Mostel 1930- *WhoAmW 91*
Pogmore, James William 1936- *St&PR 91*
Pognonec, Yves Maurice 1948- *WhoSSW 91*
Pogo, Beatriz Teresa Garcia-Tunon 1932- *WhoAm 90*
Pogodin, Arlyne 1947- *WhoAmW 91*
Pogodin, Fredell *ODwPR 91*
Pogoloff, Joseph M. 1932- *St&PR 91*
Pogolotti, Marcelo 1902- *ArtLatA*
Pogorelich, Ivo *BioIn 16*
Pogorelich, Ivo 1958- *IntWWM 90, PenDiMP*
Pogrebin, Letty Cottin *BioIn 16*
Pogrebin, Letty Cottin 1939- *ConAu 33NR, WhoAm 90, WhoWrEP 89*
Pogson, Patricia 1944- *FemiCLE*
Pogue, Annalee 1945- *WhoEmL 91*
Pogue, D. Eric 1949- *St&PR 91*
Pogue, Donald Eric 1949- *WhoAm 90, WhoEmL 91*
Pogue, Forrest Carlisle 1912- *WhoAm 90, WhoSSW 91, WhoWor 91, WhoWrEP 89*
Pogue, John D. 1933- *St&PR 91*
Pogue, Lloyd Welch 1899- *WhoAm 90, WhoE 91, WhoWor 91*
Pogue, Mary Ellen 1904- *WhoAmW 91*
Pogue, Richard Welch 1928- *WhoAm 90*
Pogue, Robert David 1929- *WhoWor 91*
Pogue, Samuel Franklin 1919- *IntWWM 90*
Pogue, Sandy Alexander Gilmer 1950- *WhoE 91*
Pogue, William Reid 1930- *WhoAm 90*
Poher, Alain Emile Louis Marie 1909- *BiDFrPL*
Pohjolainenh, Pauno Antero 1949- *WhoWor 91*
Pohl, Carla 1942- *IntWWM 90*
Pohl, Franz *PenDiDA 89*
Pohl, Frederik 1919- *MajTwCW, RGTwCSF, WhoAm 90, WhoWrEP 89, WorAlBi*
Pohl, Gunther Erich 1925- *WhoAm 90*
Pohl, Hans Ludwig 1929- *EncO&P 3*
Pohl, Hugo David 1878-1960 *WhoAmA 91N*
Pohl, James William 1931- *WhoSSW 91*
Pohl, Johann *PenDiDA 89*
Pohl, John Joseph, Jr. 1927- *WhoSSW 91*
Pohl, Karl Otto 1929- *WhoWor 91*
Pohl, Kathleen Sharon 1951- *WhoWor 91*
Pohl, Mark Ronald 1954- *WhoEmL 91*
Pohl, Oswald 1892-1951 *BioIn 16*
Pohl, Richard Lewis 1946- *BiDrAPA 89*
Pohl, Richard Walter 1916- *WhoAm 90*
Pohl, Robert Bryant 1948- *BiDrAPA 89*
Pohl, Robert Otto 1929- *WhoAm 90*
Pohl, Robert Wichard 1884-1976 *DcScB S2*
Pohl, Ronald Ray 1941- *St&PR 91*
Pohl, Stephan-Andreas 1956- *WhoWor 91*
Pohl, William Francis 1937- *IntWWM 90*
Pohlad, Bobby Ray 1951- *WhoSSW 91*
Pohlad, Carl R. 1915- *St&PR 91*
Pohle, Arthur R. 1929- *St&PR 91*
Pohlers, Horst Wolfram 1943- *WhoWor 91*
Pohlman, Carlyle George 1931- *WhoAm 90*
Pohlman, James A. 1928- *St&PR 91*
Pohlman, James Erwin 1932- *WhoAm 90*
Pohlman, Jerry E. 1942- *St&PR 91*
Pohlman, Julie M. 1959- *WhoAmW 91*
Pohlman, Michael Joseph 1947- *WhoEmL 91*
Pohlman, Randolph Allen 1944- *WhoAm 90*
Pohlman, Richard C. 1942- *St&PR 91*
Pohlmann, Harry William 1929- *St&PR 91*
Pohlmann, Lillian 1902- *AuBYP 90*
Pohlmann, Thomas Edwin 1954- *WhoSSW 91*
Pohlmann, William Albert 1939- *St&PR 91*
Pohlsander, Hans Achim 1927- *WhoAm 90*
Pohlson, Nancy *BioIn 16*
Pohly, Lawrence M. 1943- *St&PR 91*
Pohly, Susan Kay 1946- *WhoAmW 91*
Pohmer, Thomas 1952- *St&PR 91*
Pohn, Gail W. 1938- *St&PR 91*
Poholsky, Tom 1929- *Ballpl 90*
Pohorecky, Larissa Alexandra 1942- *WhoAmW 91*
Pohorelsky, Viktor Vaclav 1949- *WhoEmL 91*
Poian, Edward Licio 1946- *WhoE 91*
Poiani, Eileen Louise 1943- *WhoAmW 91, WhoE 91*
Poidevin, Ronald K. 1939- *St&PR 91*
Poikail, George John 1933- *WhoSSW 91*
Poile, David Robert 1949- *WhoE 91*
Poim, Senta V *BiDrAPA 89*
Poinar, George Orlo, Jr. 1936- *WhoAm 90*
Poincare, Henri 1854-1912 *EncPaPR 91, WorAlBi*
Poincare, Raymond 1860-1934 *BiDFrPL, WorAlBi*
Poincelot, Raymond Paul, Jr. 1944- *WhoE 91*
Poindexter, Buster *BioIn 16, EncPR&S 89*
Poindexter, Edward Haviland 1930- *WhoE 91*
Poindexter, Elinor Fuller *WhoAmA 91*
Poindexter, John Bruce 1944- *WhoAm 90*
Poindexter, John E. 1923- *St&PR 91*
Poindexter, John M. *BioIn 16*
Poindexter, Joseph Boyd 1935- *WhoAm 90, WhoWrEP 89*
Poindexter, W Ray 1921- *BiDrAPA 89*
Poindexter, William Mersereau 1925- *WhoAm 90*
Poindexter, Wm. 1925- *St&PR 91*
Poinier, Arthur Best 1911- *WhoAmA 91*
Poinsard, Jeanne-Marie-Fabienne *EncCoWW*
Poinsard, Paul J 1915- *BiDrAPA 89*
Poinsett, Alexander Caesar 1926- *WhoAm 90*
Poinsett, Joel Roberts 1779-1851 *BiDrUSE 89, BioIn 16*
Poinsett, Richard Wright 1945- *WhoE 91*
Poinsette, Donald Eugene 1914- *WhoWor 91*
Poinso-Chapuis, Germaine 1901-1981 *BiDFrPL*
Point, Nicolas 1799-1868 *BioIn 16, WhNaAH*
Point, Warren 1921- *WhoSSW 91*
Pointel, Philippe Chennevieres- 1820-1899 *BioIn 16*
Pointer Sisters *DrBIPA 90*
Pointer Sisters, The *EncPR&S 89*
Pointer, Anita 1948?- *EncPR&S 89*
Pointer, Bonnie 1953?- *EncPR&S 89*
Pointer, June 1954?- *EncPR&S 89*
Pointer, Norman James 1942- *BiDrAPA 89*
Pointer, Richard W 1955- *ConAu 131*
Pointer, Ruth 1946?- *EncPR&S 89*
Pointer, Sam Clyde, Jr. 1934- *WhoAm 90, WhoSSW 91*
Pointer, Zeb Hill 1914- *WhoSSW 91*
Poiret, Paul 1879-1944 *BioIn 16*
Poirier, Bernard Wilfred 1931- *WhoWor 91*
Poirier, Charles Carroll, III 1936- *St&PR 91*

Poirier, Francois BiDrAPA 89
Poirier, Frank Eugene 1940- WhoAm 90
Poirier, Louis Joseph 1918- WhoAm 90
Poirier, Pierre 1946- St&PR 91
Poirier, Richard 1925- WhoAm 90, WhoWrEP 89
Poirier, Richard Oveila 1947- WhoWor 91
Poirier, Roger Michel BiDrAPA 89
Poirier, Stanislas-Francois DcCanB 12
Poirier, Therese Irene 1954- WhoE 91
Poirion, Daniel 1927- WhoAm 90
Poirot, James Wesley BioIn 16
Poirot, James Wesley 1931- St&PR 91, WhoAm 90
Poirrier, Jean-Jacques 1949- WhoWor 91
Poiry, James R. 1944- St&PR 91
Pois, Joseph 1905- WhoAm 90, WhoE 91, WhoWor 91
Pois, Robert August 1940- WhoAm 90, WhoWrEP 89
Pois, Seth Warren BiDrAPA 89
Poison EncPR&S 89
Poissant, Charles-Albert 1925- St&PR 91, WhoAm 90
Poisson, Simeon-Denis 1781-1840 WorAlBi
Poister, Carol D. ODwPR 91
Poister, John J. 1923- St&PR 91
Poitevent, Deborah Roulhac 1946- WhoSSW 91
Poitevin, Michel Jean-Marie 1944- WhoWor 91
Poitevint, A. Lloyd 1918- St&PR 91
Poitier, Joseph W 1954- BiDrAPA 89
Poitier, Sidney BioIn 16
Poitier, Sidney 1927- DrBIPA 90, News 90 [port], -90-3 [port], WhoAm 90, WorAlBi
Poitiers, Dianne de 1499?-1566 EncCoWW
Poitou, Joseph PenDiDA 89
Poitout, Dominique Gilbert M. 1946- WhoWor 91
Poitra, Patricia Diane 1955- St&PR 91
Poitras, Nancy Lou 1944- WhoAmW 91, WhoWor 91
Poitras, Pierre 1934- St&PR 91, WhoAm 90
Poja, Frank Joseph 1950- St&PR 91
Pojeta, John, Jr. 1935- WhoAm 90
Poka Laenui 1946- WhoWor 91
Poka, Balazs IntWWM 90
Pokagon, Leopold 1775?-1841 WhNaAH
Pokagon, Simon 1830-1899 WhNaAH
Pokempner, Joseph Kres 1936- WhoAm 90
Poker Joe WhNaAH
Pokky, Eric Jon 1957- WhoSSW 91
Pokorni, Orysia 1938- WhoAmW 91
Pokornowski, Barbara Karen 1959- WhoEmL 91
Pokorny, Alex D 1918- BiDrAPA 89
Pokorny, Ann Marie 1927- WhoE 91
Pokorny, Cathy A. ODwPR 91
Pokorny, Gene BioIn 16
Pokorny, Gerold E. 1928- WhoAm 90
Pokorny, Gerold Erwin 1928- St&PR 91
Pokorny, Jan Hird 1914- WhoAm 90
Pokorny, Joseph L. ODwPR 91
Pokorny, L. Robert 1947- St&PR 91
Pokorski, Chris Evan 1964- WhoE 91
Pokorski, Robert J. 1952- St&PR 91
Pokotilow, Manny David 1938- WhoE 91, WhoWor 91
Pokou, Aura WomWR
Pokracki, Francine Jean 1950- BiDrAPA 89
Pokras, Sheila Frances 1935- WhoAmW 91
Pokrovskii, Mikhail Nikolaevich 1868-1932 BioIn 16
Poku, Isaac T. 1951- WhoSSW 91
Pol Pot 1926- WhoWor 91
Pol, Pio Albert 1936- BiDrAPA 89
Pol Roger, Odette BioIn 16
Pola, Elizabeth Grace 1956- WhoAmW 91
Polacco, Giorgio 1873-1960 PenDiMP
Polach, Susan E. 1955- St&PR 91
Polacheck, Hilda Satt 1882-1967 BioIn 16
Polacheck, Jerry H. 1943- St&PR 91
Polak, Elijah 1931- WhoAm 90
Polak, Jacques J. 1914- WhoAm 90
Polak, Julie Stark 1945- WhoWrEP 89
Polak, Paul Ruben BiDrAPA 89
Polak, Werner L. 1936- WhoAm 90
Polakas, Victoria V. 1936- WhoAmW 91
Polakoff, Abe WhoAm 90
Polakoff, David Fredrick 1954- WhoE 91
Polakoff, Keith Ian 1941- WhoAm 90
Polakoff, Murray Emanuel 1922- WhoAm 90
Polakoff, Steven A BiDrAPA 89
Polakoski, Raymond Robert 1947- WhoE 91
Polakovicova, Viera 1953- IntWWM 90
Polan, Annette 1944- WhoAmA 91
Polan, David Jay 1951- WhoEmL 91, WhoWor 91
Polan, H Jonathan BiDrAPA 89
Polan, Lincoln M 1909- WhoAmA 91
Polan, Morris 1924- WhoAm 90
Polan, Nancy Moore WhoAm 90, WhoAmA 91, WhoAmW 91, WhoSSW 91, WhoWor 91
Polan, Simon BiDrAPA 89
Polanco, Carmen Yvette 1952- WhoE 91
Polanco, Richard 1951- WhoHisp 91
Polanco, Vincente Geigel HispWr 90
Poland, Donald A. 1930- ODwPR 91
Poland, Robert Paul 1925- WhoAm 90
Poland, Thomas Mitchell 1949- WhoSSW 91
Poland, Warren S BiDrAPA 89
Polanek, Richard I. 1931- St&PR 91
Polanis, Mark Florian 1944- WhoWor 91
Polanka, William 1925- BiDrAPA 89
Polanski, Benjamin H. 1951- St&PR 91
Polanski, John Benjamin 1943- WhoE 91
Polanski, Roman BioIn 16
Polanski, Roman 1933- WhoAm 90, WhoWor 91, WorAlBi
Polanski, Rudolph G. 1944- St&PR 91
Polanski, S. Michael 1947- St&PR 91
Polansky, Andrew S. ODwPR 91
Polansky, Edwin Herbert 1932- St&PR 91
Polansky, Larry 1954- IntWWM 90
Polansky, Lois B 1939- WhoAmA 91
Polansky, Sharon H. WhoAmW 91
Polansky, Sol 1926- WhoWor 91
Polansky, Steven Jay 1956- WhoEmL 91
Polanyi, John Charles 1929- WhoAm 90, WhoE 91, WhoWor 91
Polanyi, Michael 1891-1976 DcLB 100 [port]
Polanyi, Mihaly 1891-1976 DcScB S2
Polascik, Mary Ann 1940- WhoAmW 91
Polasek, Carla Louise 1958- BiDrAPA 89
Polasek, Edward John 1927- WhoSSW 91
Polaski, Anne Spencer 1952- WhoEmL 91
Polaski, Deborah 1949- IntWWM 90
Polaski, William Albert 1911- WhoE 91
Polatin, Peter Barth BiDrAPA 89
Polavarapu, Prasad Leela 1952- WhoSSW 91
Polavarapu, Venkata Ratnam 1946- BiDrAPA 89
Polay, Bruce 1949- IntWWM 90
Polayes, Irving Marvin 1927- WhoAm 90, WhoE 91
Polcari, Stephen 1945- WhoAmA 91
Polchert, Susan Elizabeth 1956- BiDrAPA 89
Polcino, Anna M 1924- BiDrAPA 89
Polcyn, Steven R., Jr. 1941- ODwPR 91
Poldrugo, Flavio Antonio BiDrAPA 89
Pole, Dick 1950- Ballpl 90
Pole, James T. AuBYP 90
Pole, Kishor Mahadeo 1934- WhoWor 91
Pole, Rekha BiDrAPA 89
Polebaum, Mark Neal 1952- WhoEmL 91
Polec, Stanley Walter 1930- WhoWrEP 89
Poledor, Theodore St&PR 91
Polemis, Augustis 1955- WhoWor 91
Polemitou, Olga Andrea 1950- WhoAmW 91, WhoE 91, WhoWor 91
Polen, David Martin 1943- WhoWor 91
Polen, G. Raymond 1931- St&PR 91
Polen-Dorn, Linda Frances 1945- WhoAmW 91, WhoSSW 91
Polenberg, Howard Michael 1954- WhoE 91
Polenberg, Richard 1937- WhoAm 90
Polenske, Karen Rosel 1937- WhoE 91
Polenske, Richard Emil 1928- St&PR 91
Polenz, Joanna M 1936- BiDrAPA 89
Polenz, Joanna Magda 1936- WhoE 91
Polep, Anne S. 1932- St&PR 91
Polep, Mortimer A. 1925- St&PR 91
Poles, James Stuart 1953- WhoE 91
Poles, Spot 1887-1962 Ballpl 90
Polese, Carolyn 1947- BioIn 16
Polese, Pietro Andrea 1948- WhoWor 91
Poleskie, Stephen Francis 1938- WhoAm 90, WhoAmA 91, WhoWor 91
Polesky, Herbert Fred 1933- WhoAm 90
Polette, Nancy 1930- WhoWrEP 89
Poletti, Charles 1903- WhoAm 90
Poletti, Pietro M BiDrAPA 89
Poletti, Ugo 1914- WhoWor 91
Poletto, Anthony George 1946- WhoE 91
Polevoy, Nancy Tally 1944- WhoAmW 91, WhoE 91, WhoWor 91
Polgar family BioIn 16
Polgar, Jean 1949- St&PR 91
Polgar, Judith BioIn 16
Polgar, Laszlo 1947- IntWWM 90
Polgar, Tibor 1907- IntWWM 90
Polhamus, Sally Nelson 1947- St&PR 91
Polheim, Karl Konrad 1927- WhoWor 91
Polhemus, Robert M 1935- ConAu 130
Polhill, Dennis Lee 1946- WhoEmL 91
Poli, Kenneth Joseph 1921- WhoAm 90
Poliak, Janice BioIn 16
Poliakoff, Gary A. 1944- WhoSSW 91
Polian, Bill 1942- WhoAm 90, WhoE 91
Polianin, A. EncCoWW
Policano, Joseph Daniel 1933- WhoAm 90, WhoWor 91
Policard, Jean-Daniel BiDrAPA 89
Policastro, Nelson C BiDrAPA 89
Police OxCPMus
Police, The EncPR&S 89
Polich, John Elliott 1946- WhoEmL 91
Polichino, Joseph Anthony, Jr. 1948- WhoSSW 91
Policoff, Leonard David 1918- WhoAm 90
Policoff, Susan Lewis 1944- WhoWrEP 89
Polidor, Gus 1961- Ballpl 90
Polidori, Gianni 1923- ConDes 90
Polidoro Caldara da Caravaggio PenDiDA 89
Polidoro da Caravaggio PenDiDA 89
Polidoro, Caroline Ruth 1939- WhoAmW 91
Polikoff, Benet, Jr. 1936- WhoAm 90
Polimene, Frank Anthony 1946- St&PR 91
Polimeni, Joseph O BiDrAPA 89
Polin, Claire WhoAm 90
Polin, Gerald M 1936- BiDrAPA 89
Polin, Gilles 1959- WhoWor 91
Poliner, Randall Edward 1955- St&PR 91
Poling, Charles W 1938- BiDrAPA 89
Poling, Clark V WhoAmA 91
Poling, George Wesley 1935- WhoAm 90
Poling, Harold A. BioIn 16
Poling, Harold A. 1925- St&PR 91
Poling, Harold Arthur 1925- WhoAm 90, WhoWor 91
Poling, John Robert 1951- St&PR 91
Poling, Norma WhoAmW 91
Poling, Rodney A. 1957- BiDrAPA 89
Polinger, David Harris 1927- WhoE 91
Polinsky, Janet Naboicheck 1930- WhoAmW 91
Polio, Dennis C. 1945- St&PR 91
Poliquin, Nicole BiDrAPA 89
Polis, Julian M. 1925- St&PR 91
Polis, Michael Philip 1943- WhoAm 90
Polis, Sheri Helene 1956- WhoAmW 91
Polisano, Enrico Joseph 1949- St&PR 91
Polish Lady, A EncCoWW
Polishan, Paul F. 1945- St&PR 91
Polishan, Paul Frank 1945- WhoAm 90
Polishook, Irwin H. 1935- WhoWor 91
Polishook, Robert D 1941- BiDrAPA 89
Polisi, Joseph W. IntWWM 90
Polisi, Joseph William 1947- WhoAm 90, WhoE 91, WhoWor 91
Polisi, Salvatore Daniel BioIn 16
Polisseni, Eugene R. 1939- St&PR 91
Poliszuk, John Frederick, Jr. 1950- WhoE 91
Politakis, Lazarus 1927- St&PR 91
Politano, Victor Anthony 1919- WhoAm 90
Polite, Carlene Hatcher 1932- WhoWrEP 89
Polite, Edmonia Allen 1922- WhoAmW 91
Polite, Frank C. 1936- WhoWrEP 89
Polite, Joan Yvonne WhoSSW 91
Polite, L. John, Jr. 1921- St&PR 91
Politella, Dario 1921- WhoE 91
Politella, Ellen Sue 1924- WhoAmW 91
Polites, Demetri J 1934- BiDrAPA 89
Politi, Auguste 1855- EncO&P 3
Politi, Beth Kukkonen 1949- WhoEmL 91
Politi, Leo 1908- AuBYP 90, BioIn 16
Politi, Stephen Michael 1948- WhoEmL 91
Politi, Vincenzo 1944- WhoWor 91
Politis, Albert A BiDrAPA 89
Politis, Janice Marie 1955- WhoSSW 91
Politis, John Valentine 1944- WhoE 91
Polito, Edward 1944- St&PR 91
Polito, Joseph Louis 1940- St&PR 91
Politoske, Daniel T. 1935- IntWWM 90
Politowicz-Heires, Theresa 1953- WhoAmW 91
Politte, Eric Glynn 1960- WhoSSW 91
Polity, Leddy S. 1936- WhoE 91
Polity, Leddy Smith 1936- WhoAmW 91
Politz, Larry 1941- BiDrAPA 89
Politzer, Hugh David 1949- WhoAm 90
Politzer, Pedro R BiDrAPA 89
Politzer, Robert Barry 1948- WhoSSW 91
Politzer, Robert L. BioIn 16
Polivchak, Philip Michael 1933- WhoWor 91
Polivka, John M. ODwPR 91
Polivka, John Michael 1953- WhoE 91
Polivnick, Paul 1947- IntWWM 90
Polizos, Polizoes 1925- BiDrAPA 89
Polizzi, D. Michael 1939- St&PR 91
Polizzi, Joseph Anthony 1938- WhoSSW 91
Polizzi, Salvatore BioIn 16
Polk, B. Frank BioIn 16
Polk, Carol Hurwitz 1924- WhoAmW 91
Polk, Charles 1920- WhoAm 90
Polk, Charles Carrington 1894-1990 BioIn 16
Polk, Don 1955- BioIn 16
Polk, Donald L. BioIn 16
Polk, Edwina Rowand 1921- WhoAmW 91
Polk, Frank Fredrick 1908- WhoAmA 91
Polk, Frank Lyon 1871-1943 BioIn 16
Polk, George 1928- St&PR 91
Polk, Hiram Carey, Jr. 1936- WhoAm 90
Polk, James Arnold 1949- WhoSSW 91
Polk, James Hilliard, III 1942- St&PR 91
Polk, James K. BioIn 16
Polk, James K. 1795-1849 BioIn 16, WorAlBi
Polk, James Knox 1795-1849 BiDrUSE 89
Polk, James Ray 1937- WhoAm 90, WhoSSW 91
Polk, John George 1932- St&PR 91, WhoAm 90
Polk, John Robert 1934- St&PR 91
Polk, Lee 1923- WhoAm 90
Polk, Louis Frederick, Jr. 1930- St&PR 91, WhoAm 90
Polk, Lucy J. 1949- St&PR 91
Polk, Mary Jane 1916- WhoWor 91
Polk, Matthew Steele, Jr. 1949- St&PR 91
Polk, Melanie Rosa 1955- WhoAmW 91
Polk, Naomi 1892-1984 MusmAFA
Polk, Oscar DrBIPA 90
Polk, Peggy BiDrAPA 89
Polk, Robert F. 1947- St&PR 91
Polk, Robert Forrest 1947- WhoAm 90
Polk, Ron 1955- BioIn 16
Polk, Samuel T., III 1950- St&PR 91
Polk, Sarah C. 1803-1891 BioAmW
Polk, Sarah Childress 1803-1891 BioIn 16
Polk, Stephen R. 1955- WhoAm 90
Polk, Susan Luzader 1944- WhoAmW 91
Polk, William A. AmLegL
Polk, William J 1938- BiDrAPA 89
Polk, William Merrill 1935- WhoAm 90
Polkes, Alan H 1931- WhoAmA 91N
Polking, Kirk 1925- ConAu 30NR, WhoWrEP 89
Polking, Kirk Dorothy 1925- WhoAmW 91
Polkinghorne, John Charlton 1930- WhoWor 91
Polkinghorne, Patricia Ann 1948- WhoAmW 91
Polkow, Linda Rose 1953- WhoAmW 91
Polkowski, Delphine Theresa 1930- WhoWor 91
Poll, Gerda 1912- BiDrAPA 89
Poll, Heinz 1926- WhoAm 90
Poll, Joan Frances 1950- BiDrAPA 89, WhoE 91
Poll, Martin Harvey WhoAm 90
Poll, Robert E. 1948- St&PR 91
Poll, Robert Eugene, Jr. 1948- WhoAm 90, WhoEmL 91
Poll, Stanley 1939- WhoE 91
Poll, Sylvia BioIn 16
Pollaci, John Michael 1935- St&PR 91
Pollack, Alan Stuart BiDrAPA 89
Pollack, Ann Davidson 1958- WhoAmW 91
Pollack, Ben 1903-1971 OxCPMus
Pollack, Bruce 1951- WhoE 91
Pollack, Burton Paul 1935- St&PR 91
Pollack, Carol Lough 1924- WhoAmW 91
Pollack, Charles H 1939- BiDrAPA 89
Pollack, Charles I. 1962- WhoSSW 91
Pollack, Claire BioIn 16
Pollack, Dale 1950- ConAu 130
Pollack, Daniel 1935- WhoAm 90
Pollack, David Alan 1947- BiDrAPA 89
Pollack, Deborah R. 1955- BiDrAPA 89
Pollack, Florence Zaks WhoAmW 91
Pollack, George Washington 1949- WhoE 91
Pollack, Gerald A. 1929- WhoE 91
Pollack, Gerald Harvey 1940- WhoAm 90
Pollack, Gerald J. 1942- St&PR 91
Pollack, Gerald Leslie 1933- WhoAm 90
Pollack, H. Clinton BioIn 16
Pollack, Henry Nathan 1936- WhoAm 90
Pollack, Herbert NewYTBS 90
Pollack, Herbert 1905-1990 BioIn 16
Pollack, Herbert William 1927- St&PR 91, WhoAm 90
Pollack, Herman 1919- WhoAm 90
Pollack, Howard Joel 1952- IntWWM 90
Pollack, Irwin William BiDrAPA 89
Pollack, Irwin William 1927- WhoAm 90
Pollack, Jane Susan 1945- WhoAmW 91
Pollack, Janet Marcia 1962- WhoAmW 91
Pollack, Jeffrey S. 1953- St&PR 91
Pollack, Jessica 1960- WhoAmW 91
Pollack, Jill Susan 1963- WhoAmW 91
Pollack, Joe 1931- WhoAm 90
Pollack, Joseph 1917- WhoAm 90
Pollack, Joseph 1939- St&PR 91, WhoAm 90
Pollack, Lana 1942- WhoAmW 91
Pollack, Lester 1933- St&PR 91
Pollack, Lew 1896-1946 OxCPMus
Pollack, Linda Ava BiDrAPA 89
Pollack, Louis 1920- WhoAm 90
Pollack, Louis 1921-1970 WhoAmA 91N
Pollack, Mark Harris BiDrAPA 89
Pollack, Mary Louise 1949- WhoAmW 91, WhoWor 91
Pollack, Merrill 1924-1988 BioIn 16
Pollack, Michael B. 1958- St&PR 91
Pollack, Milton 1906- WhoAm 90
Pollack, Norman 1933- WhoAm 90

Pollack, Paul R. 1941- *St&PR 91*
Pollack, Peter 1911-1978 *WhoAmA 91N*
Pollack, Philip 1916- *St&PR 91*
Pollack, Reginald Murray 1924- *WhoAm 90, WhoAmA 91*
Pollack, Richard S. 1949- *WhoE 91, WhoSSW 91*
Pollack, Robert Elliot 1940- *WhoAm 90, WhoE 91*
Pollack, Robert Harvey 1927- *WhoSSW 91*
Pollack, Robert W 1947- *BiDrAPA 89*
Pollack, Ronald Dale *BiDrAPA 89*
Pollack, Ronald Frank 1944- *WhoAm 90*
Pollack, Ronald Max 1944- *WhoE 91*
Pollack, Saul K *BiDrAPA 89*
Pollack, Seymour *BiDrAPA 89*
Pollack, Solomon Robert 1934- *WhoAm 90*
Pollack, Stanley P. 1928- *St&PR 91*
Pollack, Stephen J. 1937- *WhoE 91*
Pollack, Sydney 1934- *BioIn 16, WhoAm 90*
Pollack, Sylvia Byrne 1940- *WhoAmW 91*
Pollack, Virginia Morris *WhoAmA 91N*
Pollack, William L. 1951- *St&PR 91*
Pollack, William Lewis 1951- *WhoE 91*
Pollaiuolo, Antonio 1430?-1498 *IntDcAA 90*
Pollaiuolo, Antonio del 1431?-1498 *PenDiDA 89*
Pollak, Anna 1912- *IntWWM 90*
Pollak, Bernard E. *BioIn 16*
Pollak, David 1917- *St&PR 91*
Pollak, Edward Barry 1934- *WhoAm 90*
Pollak, Felix 1909- *WhoWrEP 89*
Pollak, Henry M. 1931- *St&PR 91*
Pollak, Henry Otto 1927- *WhoE 91*
Pollak, James 1921- *St&PR 91*
Pollak, James Stephen 1940- *WhoAm 90*
Pollak, Louis Heilprin 1922- *WhoAm 90, WhoE 91*
Pollak, Mark 1947- *WhoEmL 91*
Pollak, Martin M. 1927- *St&PR 91*
Pollak, Martin Marshall 1927- *WhoAm 90, WhoE 91*
Pollak, Richard 1934- *WhoAm 90, WhoWrEP 89*
Pollak, Robert Andrew 1938- *WhoE 91*
Pollak, Theresa 1899- *WhoAmA 91*
Pollak, Thomas F. 1950- *St&PR 91*
Pollak, Tim *WhoAm 90*
Pollak, William F. 1942- *St&PR 91*
Pollan, Andrea Stefanie 1961- *WhoE 91*
Pollan, Bert 1929- *WhoAm 90*
Pollan, Tracy *BioIn 16*
Pollan-Cohen, Shirley *WhoWrEP 89*
Polland, Madeleine Angela Cahill 1918- *AuBYP 90*
Pollara, Bernard *WhoAm 90, WhoE 91*
Pollard, A J 1941- *ConAu 132*
Pollard, A. James 1935- *St&PR 91*
Pollard, Anne *BioIn 16*
Pollard, Annie Randolph 1943- *WhoE 91*
Pollard, Anthony Cecil 1929- *IntWWM 90*
Pollard, Braxton 1908- *WhoAm 90*
Pollard, C. William 1938- *St&PR 91*
Pollard, Carl F. 1938- *WhoSSW 91*
Pollard, Carl Faulkner 1938- *St&PR 91*
Pollard, Charles E. 1932- *St&PR 91*
Pollard, Charles William 1938- *WhoAm 90*
Pollard, Clint E. 1949- *St&PR 91*
Pollard, Constance Jo 1949- *WhoEmL 91*
Pollard, David Edward 1927- *WhoAm 90*
Pollard, Donald Pence 1924- *WhoAmA 91*
Pollard, Edward Ellsberg 1945- *WhoE 91*
Pollard, Elizabeth Blitch 1939- *WhoSSW 91*
Pollard, Eric Wilton 1917- *WhoWor 91*
Pollard, Ernest Charles 1906- *WhoWor 91*
Pollard, Franklin Dawes 1934- *WhoWor 91*
Pollard, Fred Don 1931- *WhoAm 90*
Pollard, George Marvin 1909- *WhoAm 90*
Pollard, Jack 1926- *ConAu 30NR*
Pollard, Jenal A. 1961- *WhoAmW 91*
Pollard, John Oliver 1937- *WhoSSW 91*
Pollard, Jonathan *BioIn 16*
Pollard, Joseph Augustine 1924- *St&PR 91, WhoAm 90, WhoWor 91*
Pollard, Kathryn Jane 1951- *WhoAmW 91*
Pollard, Kenneth Hamilton 1943- *WhoSSW 91*
Pollard, Marcia Jean 1951- *WhoAmW 91*
Pollard, Marilyn Bergkamp 1937- *WhoAmW 91*
Pollard, Michael Ross 1947- *WhoE 91, WhoEmL 91, WhoWor 91*
Pollard, Morris 1916- *WhoAm 90*
Pollard, Nicholas Anthony, Sr. 1924- *WhoWor 91*
Pollard, Overton Price 1933- *WhoAm 90*
Pollard, Rebbecca Rae 1952- *WhoAmW 91*
Pollard, Reed 1913- *St&PR 91*
Pollard, Richard F. 1933- *St&PR 91*
Pollard, Sam A., Jr. 1929- *St&PR 91*
Pollard, Scott Elliott *BiDrAPA 89*
Pollard, Shirley 1939- *WhoAmW 91*
Pollard, Stanley Irving 1922- *St&PR 91*
Pollard, Velma 194-?- *FemiCLE*
Pollard, William Sherman, Jr. 1925- *WhoAm 90*
Pollare, Frank L. 1952- *ODwPR 91*
Pollaro, Paul *WhoAmA 91*
Pollart, Dale Flavian 1932- *WhoAm 90*
Pollastri, Paolo 1960- *IntWWM 90*
Pollatsek, Michael E 1937- *BiDrAPA 89*
Polledri, Paolo *BioIn 16*
Pollei, Dane F *WhoAmA 91*
Pollert, William R. 1944- *St&PR 91*
Pollet, Elizabeth 1922- *WhoWrEP 89*
Pollet, Evelyne 1905- *EncCoWW*
Pollet, Howie 1921-1974 *Ballpl 90*
Pollet, Joseph 1898-1979 *WhoAmA 91N*
Pollet, Sylvester 1939- *WhoWrEP 89*
Pollexfen, Jack 1917- *BioIn 16*
Polley, Dale Whitcomb 1949- *St&PR 91, WhoAm 90*
Polley, David E. 1934- *WhoAm 90*
Polley, Edward Herman 1923- *WhoAm 90*
Polley, Frederick 1875- *WhoAmA 91N*
Polley, Howard Freeman 1913- *WhoAm 90*
Polley, Ira 1917- *WhoAm 90*
Polley, Judith 1938- *ConAu 129*
Polley, Lynda Gaye 1942- *WhoSSW 91*
Polley, Max Eugene 1928- *WhoSSW 91*
Polley, Paulette *BioIn 16*
Polley, Richard Donald 1937- *WhoSSW 91, WhoWor 91*
Polley, Terry Lee 1947- *WhoEmL 91, WhoWor 91*
Polli, G. Patrick 1959- *WhoEmL 91*
Pollich, Peter Adam 1928- *St&PR 91*
Pollick, G. David 1947- *WhoAm 90*
Pollicove, Harvey M. 1944- *WhoE 91*
Pollin, Abe 1923- *WhoE 91*
Pollin, Burton R. 1916- *ConAu 129*
Pollin, William *BiDrAPA 89*
Pollina, Michelle Ann 1960- *WhoSSW 91*
Pollina, Ronald J. 1946- *St&PR 91*
Pollinger, Gerald J. *AuBYP 90*
Pollinger, Holly *ODwPR 91*
Pollini, Francis 1930- *WhoAm 90*
Pollini, Maurizio *BioIn 16*
Pollini, Maurizio 1942- *IntWWM 90, PenDiMP*
Pollino, Patrick A. 1942- *ODwPR 91, St&PR 91*
Pollio, Ralph Thomas 1948- *WhoAm 90, WhoWor 91, WhoWrEP 89*
Pollitt, Gertrude Stein *WhoAmW 91*
Pollitt, Jerome Jordan 1934- *WhoAm 90, WhoAmA 91*
Pollitt, John J. 1932- *St&PR 91*
Pollitt, Katha 1949- *MajTwCW, WhoWrEP 89*
Pollitt, R. Eugene 1947- *St&PR 91*
Pollitzer, William Sprott 1923- *WhoAm 90*
Pollmann, Horst 1938- *WhoWor 91*
Pollmer, Wolfgang Gerhard 1926- *WhoWor 91*
Pollnow, Charles Francis 1932- *St&PR 91*
Pollnow, Jan Lee 1944- *St&PR 91*
Pollock, Alexander John 1943- *WhoAm 90*
Pollock, Alice Diane 1939- *WhoAmW 91*
Pollock, Anthony J 1927- *BiDrAPA 89*
Pollock, Bruce 1951- *WhoAmA 91*
Pollock, Bruce Godfrey *BiDrAPA 89*
Pollock, Charles Cecil 1902-1988 *BioIn 16*
Pollock, David Michael 1945- *St&PR 91*
Pollock, Davis Allen 1942- *St&PR 91, WhoAm 90*
Pollock, Don C. 1933- *St&PR 91*
Pollock, Donald David *BiDrAPA 89*
Pollock, Earl Edward 1928- *WhoAm 90*
Pollock, George H. *BioIn 16*
Pollock, George H 1923- *BiDrAPA 89*
Pollock, George Howard 1923- *WhoAm 90*
Pollock, Gerald Arthur 1950- *WhoEmL 91*
Pollock, Gordon *BioIn 16*
Pollock, Harry Winslow 1942- *BiDrAPA 89*
Pollock, Jack Paden 1920- *WhoSSW 91, WhoWor 91*
Pollock, Jackson 1912-1956 *BioIn 16, IntDcAA 90, WhoAmA 91N, WorAlBi*
Pollock, James Arlin 1898-1949 *WhoAmA 91N*
Pollock, James Valiant 1937- *WhoAm 90*
Pollock, John A. *St&PR 91*
Pollock, John Crothers *ODwPR 91*
Pollock, John Crothers, III 1943- *WhoAm 90*
Pollock, John Glennon 1943- *WhoAm 90*
Pollock, John L. *St&PR 91N*
Pollock, John Phleger 1920- *WhoAm 90*
Pollock, Kathleen Rork 1948- *WhoAmW 91*
Pollock, Kenneth L. 1920- *St&PR 91*
Pollock, Kenneth Leslie 1920- *WhoAm 90*
Pollock, Linda Quattrone 1961- *WhoE 91*
Pollock, Louise *ODwPR 91*
Pollock, Luella Rebecca 1920- *WhoAm 90*
Pollock, Marsha Leibo 1942- *WhoAmW 91*
Pollock, Martha Isacson 1951- *WhoAmW 91*
Pollock, Mary *AuBYP 90, ConAu 33NR*
Pollock, Merlin F 1905- *WhoAmA 91*
Pollock, Neal Jay 1947- *WhoE 91*
Pollock, Oliver 1737?-1823 *EncCRAm*
Pollock, Paul Jackson 1912-1956 *BioIn 16*
Pollock, Paul Robert 1950- *St&PR 91*
Pollock, Ray Jean 1931- *WhoSSW 91*
Pollock, Robert Elwood 1936- *WhoAm 90*
Pollock, Robert Middleton 1854-1920 *AmLegL*
Pollock, Ronald Kevin *BiDrAPA 89*
Pollock, Roy Van Horn 1949- *WhoAm 90*
Pollock, Samuel Louis 1908- *BiDrAPA 89*
Pollock, Sharon *BioIn 16*
Pollock, Sharon 1936- *FemiCLE, OxCCanT*
Pollock, Sharon Rose 1955- *WhoAmW 91*
Pollock, Stephen Michael 1936- *WhoAm 90*
Pollock, Stewart Glasson 1932- *WhoAm 90, WhoE 91*
Pollock, Teri Susan *BiDrAPA 89*
Pollock, Thomas Clark 1902-1988 *BioIn 16*
Pollock, Tom *BioIn 16*
Pollock, Vicki Eileen 1956- *WhoAmW 91, WhoEmL 91*
Pollock, Ward Robert 1943- *St&PR 91*
Pollock, William A. 1817-1882 *AmLegL*
Pollock, William K. 1942- *St&PR 91*
Pollock O'Brien, Louise Mary 1948- *WhoAmW 91*
Polner, Alex M. *St&PR 91*
Polner, Eli 1928- *St&PR 91*
Polner, Murray 1928- *SmATA 64 [port]*
Polo, Marco 1254-1323? *BioIn 16*
Polo, Marco 1254-1324 *WorAlBi*
Polo, Roberto 1950- *BioIn 16*
Polock, William A. 1817-1882 *AmLegL*
Pologar, Alan Joseph 1950- *St&PR 91*
Poloma, Margaret Mary 1943- *ConAu 30NR*
Polome, Edgar Charles 1920- *WhoAm 90, WhoWrEP 89*
Polon, Linda Beth 1943- *WhoAmW 91*
Polon, Martin Ishiah 1942- *WhoE 91, WhoWor 91*
Polon, Steven 1919- *St&PR 91*
Polonia, Luis 1964- *Ballpl 90*
Polonio, Pedro 1915- *BiDrAPA 89*
Polonis, Douglas Hugh 1928- *WhoAm 90*
Polonskaia, Elizaveta Grigor'evna 1890-1969 *EncCoWW*
Polonski, Abraham 1903- *BioIn 16*
Polonsky, Abraham 1910- *BioIn 16*
Polonsky, Arthur 1925- *WhoAm 90, WhoAmA 91*
Polonsky, Derek Colin 1945- *BiDrAPA 89*
Polonsky, Leonard S. 1927- *St&PR 91*
Polonsky, Leonard Selwyn 1927- *WhoWor 91*
Polonyi, Albin Stephen 1926- *WhoAm 90*
Polos, Theodore 1922- *BiDrAPA 89*
Poloski, Patricia Elizabeth 1941- *WhoAmW 91*
Polozola, Frank Joseph 1942- *WhoAm 90*
Pols, Louis C.W. 1941- *WhoWor 91*
Polsby, Nelson Woolf 1934- *WhoAm 90, WhoWrEP 89*
Polsen, W. Gary 1948- *St&PR 91*
Polsinelli, Adelaide Claudia Lisa 1960- *WhoAmW 91, WhoE 91*
Polski, Thomas J. *ODwPR 91*
Polsky, Barry 1940- *ODwPR 91*
Polsky, Cynthia 1939- *WhoAmA 91*
Polsky, Cynthia Hazen 1938- *WhoE 91*
Polsky, Donald N. *St&PR 91*
Polsky, Laurence H. 1943- *St&PR 91*
Polsky, Leon Bernard 1931- *WhoAm 90*
Polsky, Robert N 1940- *BiDrAPA 89*
Polson, Gordon Fairlie 1929- *WhoWor 91*
Polster, Carl Conrad 1946- *WhoEmL 91*
Polster, Eugene Louis 1932- *St&PR 91*
Polster, Jerry 1936- *St&PR 91*
Polster, John J. 1956- *St&PR 91*
Polston, Carolyn 1946- *WhoAmW 91*
Poltorak, Alexander 1957- *St&PR 91*
Polukhina, Valentina Platonovna 1936- *WhoWor 91*
Polumbaum, Julia Bruner 1910- *WhoAmW 91*
Polunin, Elizabeth V. 1887- *BiDWomA*
Polunin, Nicholas *WhoAm 90, WhoWor 91*
Polunin, Oleg 1914-1985 *DcNaB 1981*
Polushkin, Maria *AuBYP 90, BioIn 16*
Polutchko, John Andrew 1933- *St&PR 91*
Polverari, Paul *St&PR 91*
Polverino, Frank Francis, II 1950- *WhoE 91*
Polwhele, Elizabeth 1651?-1691 *BiDEWW, FemiCLE*
Polyansky, Igor *BioIn 16*
Polychron, John P. 1936- *St&PR 91*
Polychron, John Philip 1936- *WhoAm 90*
Polydefkis, Dimitri G *BiDrAPA 89*
Polydoris, Nicholas George 1930- *St&PR 91*
Polydoris, Steven Nicholas 1954- *WhoEmL 91, WhoWor 91*
Polydoure, Maria 1902-1930 *EncCoWW*
Polydouri, Maria *EncCoWW*
Polye, Maureen Ann 1956- *WhoAmW 91*
Polymeropoulos, Mihael H *BiDrAPA 89*
Polzer, Joseph 1929- *WhoAmA 91*
Polzien, Paul Adalbert 1918- *WhoWor 91*
Polzin, John Theodore 1919- *WhoWor 91*
Polzin, Mark Frederick 1945- *St&PR 91*
Polzoni, Bob 1950- *ODwPR 91*
Pomada, Elizabeth Luly 1940- *WhoWrEP 89*
Pomara, Nunzio 1950- *BiDrAPA 89*
Pomare, Eleo 1937- *DrBIPA 90*
Pombo, Manuel *WhoHisp 91*
Pomer, Sydney Lawrence 1917- *BiDrAPA 89*
Pomerance, Alan Saul 1926-1989 *BioIn 16*
Pomerance, Carl Bernard 1944- *WhoSSW 91*
Pomerance, Diane Linda 1951- *WhoAmW 91*
Pomerance, Leon 1907-1988 *BioIn 16*
Pomerance, Norman 1926- *WhoAm 90*
Pomerance, Ralph 1907- *WhoAm 90*
Pomeranchuk, Isaak Iakovlevich 1913-1966 *DcScB S2*
Pomeraniec, Lazaro N 1950- *BiDrAPA 89*
Pomerans, Arno *ConAu 129*
Pomerans, Arnold J 1920- *ConAu 129*
Pomerants-Mazurkevich, Dana 1944- *IntWWM 90*
Pomerantz, Andrew S 1945- *BiDrAPA 89*
Pomerantz, Charlotte *BioIn 16*
Pomerantz, Charlotte 1930- *AuBYP 90, WhoWrEP 89*
Pomerantz, Cheryl Jeanne 1949- *WhoAmW 91*
Pomerantz, David *NewAgMG*
Pomerantz, Ernest Harold *WhoE 91*
Pomerantz, Jacob 1907- *WhoSSW 91*
Pomerantz, James Robert 1946- *WhoAm 90, WhoWor 91*
Pomerantz, Jay M 1939- *BiDrAPA 89*
Pomerantz, Jerald Michael 1954- *WhoEmL 91, WhoSSW 91*
Pomerantz, Joel *ODwPR 91*
Pomerantz, Laura 1948- *WhoAmW 91*
Pomerantz, Lawrence Stewart 1943- *St&PR 91*
Pomerantz, M.A. 1930- *St&PR 91*
Pomerantz, Martin 1939- *WhoAm 90*
Pomerantz, Marvin Alvin 1930- *WhoAm 90*
Pomerantz, Paul Robert *BiDrAPA 89*
Pomerantz, Rhoda Silverstein 1937- *WhoAmW 91*
Pomerantz, Richard 1949- *WhoAm 90*
Pomerantz, Samuel H 1911- *BiDrAPA 89*
Pomerantz, Sanford E 1941- *BiDrAPA 89*
Pomeranz, Bud *ODwPR 91*
Pomeranz, Felix 1926- *WhoAm 90, WhoWor 91*
Pomeranz, Howard David *BiDrAPA 89*
Pomeranz, Yeshajahu 1922- *WhoAm 90*
Pomerdy, Caroline Saunders 1960- *WhoAmW 91*
Pomerene, James Herbert 1920- *WhoAm 90*
Pomerenke Dass, Kelly Joan 1961- *WhoAmW 91*
Pomerleau, Robert Raymond 1947- *St&PR 91*
Pomeroy, Claire *WhoWrEP 89*
Pomeroy, Earl 1915- *WhoAm 90*
Pomeroy, Earl Spencer 1915- *BioIn 16*
Pomeroy, Elizabeth W 1938- *ConAu 32NR*
Pomeroy, Frederick George 1924- *WhoAmA 91*
Pomeroy, Harlan 1923- *WhoAm 90*
Pomeroy, Herb *BioIn 16*
Pomeroy, Ira Lewis 1924- *WhoWrEP 89*
Pomeroy, James Calwell, Jr 1945- *WhoAmA 91*
Pomeroy, John Charles 1950- *BiDrAPA 89*
Pomeroy, John Eric 1941- *WhoAm 90*
Pomeroy, Karl F. 1937- *St&PR 91*
Pomeroy, Lee Harris 1932- *WhoAm 90, WhoE 91*
Pomeroy, Lewis Richard *St&PR 91N*
Pomeroy, Lyndon Fayne 1925- *WhoAmA 91*
Pomeroy, Mary Barnas 1921- *WhoAmA 91*
Pomeroy, Pete *AuBYP 90*
Pomeroy, Robert B *BiDrAPA 89*
Pomeroy, Robert L. 1938- *St&PR 91*
Pomeroy, Robert Watson 1902-1989 *BioIn 16*
Pomeroy, Robert Watson, III 1935- *WhoE 91*
Pomeroy, Thomas Wilson, Jr. 1908- *WhoAm 90, WhoE 91*
Pomeroy, Wesley Arthur Carroll 1920- *BiDrAPA 89*
Pomeroy, William Henry, Jr. 1912- *St&PR 91*

Pomeroy, Wyman Burdette 1932- WhoSSW 91
Pomfret, Henrietta Louisa, Countess of 1700?-1761 FemiCLE
Pomfret, John Dana 1928- WhoAm 90
Pomilia, Frank BioIn 16
Pomm, Raymond Martin BiDrAPA 89
Pommer, Kristian 1949- IntWWM 90
Pommer, Richard 1930- WhoAmA 91, WhoE 91
Pommerehne, Werner Wolf 1943- WhoWor 91
Pommier, Jean-Bernard 1944- IntWWM 90, PenDiMP
Pommier de Santi, Patrice Robert 1945- WhoWor 91
Pomo, Roberto Dario 1949- WhoHisp 91
Pomodoro, Arnaldo 1926- WhoWor 91
Pomodoro, Luis Abel 1935- BiDrAPA 89
Pomorska, Krystyna 1928-1986 ConAu 31NR
Pomorski, Stanislaw 1934- WhoAm 90
Pomp, Martin 1946- St&PR 91
Pompa, James Robert 1937- WhoAm 90
Pompa, Susan Joy 1951- WhoAmW 91
Pompadour, Madame De 1721-1764 WorAlBi
Pompadur, I. Martin 1935- WhoAm 90
Pompan, Jack Maurice 1926- WhoE 91
Pompea, Charles E. 1949- St&PR 91
Pompei, Ronald James BiDrAPA 89
Pompeia, Nuria 1938- EncCoWW
Pompeiano, Ottavio 1927- WhoWor 91
Pompeo, Bernard 1926- St&PR 91
Pomper, Philip 1936- WhoAm 90
Pomper, Victor Herbert 1923- St&PR 91, WhoAm 90
Pompian, Richard Owen 1935- WhoE 91, WhoSSW 91, WhoWor 91
Pompidou, Claude BioIn 16
Pompidou, Georges 1911-1974 WorAlBi
Pompidou, Georges Jean Rene 1911-1974 BiDFrPL
Pomponi, Steven Robert 1968- WhoE 91
Pomponio WhNaAH
Pompushko, Rosalie BiDrAPA 89
Pomputius, James Michael 1940- BiDrAPA 89
Pomraning, Gerald Carlton 1936- WhoAm 90
Pomrinse, Simour David 1916- WhoAm 90
Pomroy, James F. 1934- St&PR 91
Pomus, Doc 1925- OxCPMus, WhoE 91, WhoWor 91
Ponath, Roderick Dean 1946- BiDrAPA 89
Ponce, Carlos 1948- WhoHisp 91
Ponce, Christopher B. WhoHisp 91
Ponce, Danny BioIn 16
Ponce, Joseph L. 1927- St&PR 91
Ponce, Juan F BiDrAPA 89
Ponce, Juan Garcia ConAu 131, HispWr 90
Ponce, LuAnne BioIn 16
Ponce, Mary Helen 1938- WhoHisp 91
Ponce, S. Daniel 1948- St&PR 91
Ponce, Tony 1925- WhoHisp 91
Ponce-Adame, MerriHelen 1938- WhoHisp 91
Ponce De Leon, Adolfo I BiDrAPA 89
Ponce de Leon, Juan 1460?-1521 EncCRAm, WhNaAH, WorAlBi
Ponce de Leon, Michael 1922- BioIn 16, WhoAm 90, WhoAmA 91
Ponce Enriquez, Camilo 1912-1976 BioIn 16
Poncelet, Jacqui PenDiDA 89
Ponces de Carvalho, Joao de Deus Ramos 1957- WhoWor 91
Poncet, Sally BioIn 16
Ponchak, Frank George 1934- St&PR 91
Ponchick, Elliott Joel 1945- WhoE 91
Ponchielli, Amilcare 1834-1886 PenDiMP A
Ponchio, Mary Thomas 1954- WhoAmW 91
Pond, Byron Oliver, Jr. 1936- St&PR 91
Pond, Celia Frances Sophia 1956- IntWWM 90
Pond, Clayton 1941- WhoAmA 91
Pond, Dale C. 1946- St&PR 91
Pond, Dale Claude 1946- WhoAm 90
Pond, Dana 1881-1962 WhoAmA 91N
Pond, Daniel James 1949- WhoSSW 91
Pond, Donald Herbert, Jr. 1943- St&PR 91
Pond, Edward 1929- ConDes 90
Pond, Elaine Skinner 1909- WhoAmW 91
Pond, Elizabeth ConAu 129
Pond, Elizabeth Ann WhoWor 91
Pond, Floyd H. 1918- St&PR 91
Pond, Gloria Dibble 1939- WhoAmW 91
Pond, Helen Barbara WhoAm 90
Pond, Jeffrey Genin 1947- St&PR 91
Pond, Jesse Earl 1917- WhoSSW 91
Pond, Martin Allen 1912- WhoAm 90
Pond, Patricia Ann 1948- WhoAmW 91
Pond, Patricia Brown 1930- WhoAm 90
Pond, Peggy Ann 1951- WhoE 91
Pond, Peter 1740-1807 EncCRAm, WhNaAH
Pond, Phyllis Joan 1930- WhoAmW 91
Pond, Richard L. 1911- St&PR 91
Pond, Ronald Arthur 1932- BiDrAPA 89
Pond, Seymour Gates 1896- AuBYP 90
Pond, Thomas Alexander 1924- WhoAm 90, WhoE 91
Pond, Willi Baze 1896-1947 WhoAmA 91N
Ponda, Vikas V 1956- BiDrAPA 89
Ponder, Annell 1932- WhoAmW 91
Ponder, Bruce Anthony John 1944- WhoWor 91
Ponder, Catherine 1927- WhoWor 91
Ponder, Elmer 1893-1974 Ballpl 90
Ponder, Herman 1928- WhoAm 90
Ponder, James Alton 1933- WhoSSW 91, WhoWor 91
Ponder, Kent 1932- WhoWor 91
Ponder, Lester McConnico 1912- WhoAm 90
Ponder, Michael 1948- IntWWM 90
Ponder, Ron J. 1943- St&PR 91
Ponder, Sanford NewAgMG
Ponder, Stewart M 1917- BiDrAPA 89
Ponder, Thomas C. 1921- WhoAm 90
Pondrom, Lee Girard 1933- WhoAm 90
Pone, Gundaris 1932- IntWWM 90
Ponekeosh 1810?-1891 DcCanB 12
Poneman, Daniel 1956- ConAu 130
Pong Sarasin WhoWor 91
Ponge, Francis 1899-1988 AnObit 1988, BioIn 16
Ponge, Lorraine Joyce 1954- WhoE 91
Pongo, Laszlo 1953- WhoWor 91
Pongracz, Ann Cecilia 1953- WhoEmL 91
Pongratz, Olaf Heinz 1937- WhoWor 91
Poniarski, Richard M 1953- BiDrAPA 89
Poniatoff, Alexander Mathew 1892-1980 BioIn 16
Poniatowska, Elena BioIn 16
Poniatowska, Elena 1933- ConAu 32NR, HispWr 90
Poniatowska, Irena 1933- IntWWM 90
Poniatowski, Michel Casimir 1922- WhoWor 91
Poniatowski, Michel Casmir, prince de 1922- BiDFrPL
Ponicsan, Darryl 1939- WhoWrEP 89
Poniewaz, Jeff 1946- WhoWrEP 89
Poniewaz, Kenneth Anthony 1949- St&PR 91
Ponikvar, Dale Leon 1949- WhoE 91
Ponitz, David Henry 1931- WhoAm 90
Ponka, Lawrence John 1949- WhoWor 91
Ponnamperuma, Cyril Andrew 1923- WhoAm 90
Ponne, Nanci Teresa 1958- WhoAmW 91
Ponnelle, Jean-Pierre BioIn 16
Ponnelle, Jean-Pierre 1932-1988 AnObit 1988, ConDes 90
Ponomareff, George 1932- BiDrAPA 89
Ponomarev, Yuri BioIn 16
Ponquinette, Julie C BiDrAPA 89
Pons, Bernard 1926- WhoWor 91
Pons, Francisco B. 1917- St&PR 91
Pons, Helene 1898-1990 BioIn 16, NewYTBS 90
Pons, Helene Weinncheff 1898- NotWoAT
Pons, Juan 1946- IntWWM 90
Pons, Lily 1898-1976 PenDiMP
Pons, Lily 1904-1976 WorAlBi
Pons, Silvia Teresita 1938- WhoAmW 91
Pons, Stanley BioIn 16
Pons Irazazabal, D. Felix 1942- WhoWor 91
Pons-Nunez, Victor Manuel 1935- WhoSSW 91
Ponsardin, Barbe-Nicole Clicquot- 1777-1866 BioIn 16
Ponsdomenech, Saul Eladio BiDrAPA 89
Ponselle, Rosa 1897-1981 BioIn 16, PenDiMP, WorAlBi
Ponser, Marilyn Ruth 1952- WhoAmW 91
Ponsonby, Mary Emily 1817-1877 FemiCLE
Ponsonby, Moore Charles Garrett 1910- WhoAm 90
Ponsonby, Robert Noel 1926- IntWWM 90
Ponsonby, Thomas Arthur 1930-1990 BioIn 16
Ponsonby of Shulbrede, Baron 1930-1990 BioIn 16
Ponsor, Kenneth C. 1936- St&PR 91
Ponsot, Claude F 1927- WhoAmA 91
Ponsot, Marie FemiCLE
Pont, John 1927- WhoAm 90
Pont, Marisara 1941- WhoAmW 91
Pontaoe, Alejandro G 1931- BiDrAPA 89
Pontarelli, Aurelio 1947- WhoE 91
Pontarelli, Thomas 1949- St&PR 91
Ponte, Francesco 1931- WhoWor 91
Ponte, Joseph, Jr. 1948- ODwPR 91
Ponte, Joseph Gonsalves, Jr. 1925- WhoWrEP 89
Ponte, Leonard Perry 1933- St&PR 91
Ponte, Richard 1934- St&PR 91
Ponte, Rui Augusto 1959- WhoE 91
Ponteach 1720?-1769 WhNaAH
Pontecorvo, Gillo BioIn 16
Pontefract, Robert St&PR 91
Pontell, Irwin 1925- St&PR 91
Pontelli, Baccio PenDiDA 89
Ponteri, Joseph R. 1943- St&PR 91
Pontes, Henry A. WhoHisp 91
Pontes-Leca, Carlos De 1938- IntWWM 90
Ponti, Carlo 1913- WhoWor 91, WorAlBi
Ponti, Gio 1891-1979 ConDes 90, PenDiDA 89
Pontiac 1720?-1769 EncCRAm, WhNaAH, WorAlBi
Ponticello, Matthew 1948- WhoWrEP 89
Pontifell, Luke Ives BioIn 16
Pontiflet, Addie Roberson 1943- WhoAmW 91
Pontikes, Kenneth Nicholas 1940- St&PR 91
Pontious, James Carl 1938- WhoE 91
Pontius, Anneliese A 1921- BiDrAPA 89
Pontius, Anneliese Alma 1921- WhoE 91
Pontius, Edward B 1953- BiDrAPA 89
Pontius, Jill K BiDrAPA 89
Pontius, Keith Don 1933- St&PR 91
Pontnica, Joseph 1929- St&PR 91
Ponton, Anne-Marie BiDrAPA 89
Ponton, Lynn Elisabeth 1951- BiDrAPA 89
Ponton, Mark WhoAm 90
Ponton, Richard Edward 1937- WhoAm 90
Pontoppidan, Henrik 1857-1943 DcScanL
Pontormo, Jacopo 1494-1557? IntDcAA 90
Pontormo, Jacopo Da 1494-1557 WorAlBi
Pontriand, Michel 1954- St&PR 91
Ponty, Jean-Luc NewAgMG
Ponty, Jean-Luc 1942- BioIn 16, WhoAm 90
Pontynen, Arthur 1950- WhoAmA 91
Ponzek, Debra BioIn 16
Ponzi, Charles BioIn 16
Ponzi, Charles 188-?-1949 EncABHB 7 [port]
Ponzi, Frank Joseph 1929- WhoWor 91
Ponzillo, Rosa 1897-1981 PenDiMP
Ponzio, Vittorio 1924- WhoWor 91
Ponzo, Santo Joseph 1948- St&PR 91
Poock, Ronald Bernard 1946- St&PR 91
Pooka, I. M. WhoWrEP 89
Pool, Charles W. 1856-1930 AmLegL
Pool, Deanna 1942- WhoAmW 91
Pool, Douglas Stuart 1940- BiDrAPA 89
Pool, Douglas Vernon 1945- St&PR 91, WhoAm 90
Pool, Jean BioIn 16
Pool, Jerome Marvin 1935- St&PR 91
Pool, Judith Graham 1919-1975 BioIn 16
Pool, Michael Lee 1951- BiDrAPA 89
Pool, Norman D. 1942- St&PR 91
Pool, Rachel Ruysch 1664-1750 BioIn 16
Pool, Richard 1919- BioIn 16
Pool, Timothy Kevin 1954- WhoSSW 91
Poole, Abram 1882-1961 WhoAmA 91N
Poole, Alan C. 1914- St&PR 91
Poole, Albert Harrison 1955- WhoEmL 91
Poole, Anita Joyce 1950- WhoSSW 91
Poole, Carolyn Ann 1931- WhoWrEP 89
Poole, David Armstrong 1921- St&PR 91
Poole, Drusilla Rageu 1921-1981 BioIn 16
Poole, Earl Lincoln 1891-1972 WhoAmA 91N
Poole, Earle Gower 1929- St&PR 91, WhoAm 90
Poole, Ed 1874-1919 Ballpl 90
Poole, Elissa 1951- IntWWM 90
Poole, Elizabeth BiDEWW, FemiCLE
Poole, Euna M. 1962- WhoSSW 91
Poole, Fern W. St&PR 91
Poole, Gordon Leicester 1926- WhoAm 90
Poole, Gray 1906- AuBYP 90
Poole, Gwendolyn Burton 1943- WhoAmW 91
Poole, James E. 1924- St&PR 91
Poole, Jay Martin 1934- WhoAm 90, WhoWrEP 89
Poole, Jean Wiggins 1942- WhoAmW 91
Poole, Jillian Hanbury 1930- WhoE 91
Poole, Jim 1895-1975 Ballpl 90
Poole, John B. 1912-1989 BioIn 16
Poole, John Jordan 1906- WhoAm 90
Poole, John Swanson 1946- St&PR 91
Poole, Joy Louise 1955- WhoAmW 91
Poole, Judith M. ODwPR 91
Poole, Kathleen Zada 1953- WhoWrEP 89
Poole, Leslie Donald 1942- WhoAmA 91
Poole, Lynn 1910-1969 AuBYP 90
Poole, Margaret M. 1950- ODwPR 91
Poole, Mary Beth Gaffney 1946- WhoSSW 91
Poole, Nancy Geddes 1930- WhoAmA 91
Poole, Pamela Kay Ticer 1958- WhoSSW 91
Poole, Penelope Jane 1961- IntWWM 90
Poole, Richard Elliott 1931- WhoAmA 91
Poole, Richard William 1927- WhoAm 90, WhoSSW 91
Poole, Ruth Williams Swain 1945- WhoAmW 91
Poole, Thomas Marion 1961- WhoSSW 91
Poole, Vannette Forbes 1944- WhoE 91
Poole, W. Kenneth 1939- St&PR 91
Poole, William Daniel 1932- WhoE 91
Poole, William Ravern 1913- WhoSSW 91
Pooler, Noel Louis 1948- WhoAm 90
Pooley, Beverley John 1934- WhoAm 90
Pooley, Lorraine Elizabeth 1953- WhoWrEP 89
Pooley, Sarah AuBYP 90
Poon, Vivian Wei Man 1961- WhoAmW 91
Poon, Yi-Chong Sarina Chow 1944- WhoAmA 91
Poons, Larry 1937- WhoAmA 91
Poor, Alfred Easton 1951- WhoE 91
Poor, Anne 1918- BiDWomA, WhoAm 90, WhoAmA 91
Poor, Carolyn Sue 1949- WhoSSW 91
Poor, Henry Varnum 1888-1970 WhoAmA 91N
Poor, James Seward 1937- St&PR 91
Poor, Janet Meakin 1929- WhoAmW 91
Poor, Maria C 1954- BiDrAPA 89
Poor, Peter Varnum 1926- WhoAm 90
Poor, Robert John 1931- WhoAmA 91
Poor, Suzanne Donaldson 1933- WhoAmW 91
Poor, William R. 1928- St&PR 91
Poor, William Russell 1928- WhoAm 90
Poorbaugh, Catherine K. 1935- St&PR 91
Poore, Benjamin Perley 1820-1887 BioIn 16
Poore, Edgar E. 1933- St&PR 91
Poore, Gregory R. 1945- St&PR 91
Poore, Nancye P. St&PR 91
Poorman, Omer Wayne 1949- WhoSSW 91
Poorman, Paul Arthur 1930- WhoAm 90
Poorman, Robert Lewis 1926- WhoAm 90
Poortman, J J 1896- EncO&P 3
Poortvliet, Rien BioIn 16
Poortvliet, William George 1931- St&PR 91
Poos, George Ireland 1923- WhoAm 90
Poos, Jacques Francois 1935- WhoWor 91
Poovey, Kirt Robert 1953- WhoEmL 91
Poovey, William Arthur 1913- WhoAm 90
Pop, Emil 1939- WhoWor 91
Pop, Iggy 1947- EncPR&S 89, WhoAm 90
Popa, Robert A. 1931- ODwPR 91
Popa, Vasco 1922- WorAlBi
Pope EncCRAm, WhNaAH
Pope, Ada BioIn 16
Pope, Addison W BiDrAPA 89
Pope, Albert Augustus 1843-1909 EncABHB 4 [port]
Pope, Albert Augustus 1944- WhoE 91
Pope, Alexander 1688-1744 BioIn 16, DcLB 101 [port], -95 [port], WorAlBi, WrPh
Pope, Alexander H. 1929- WhoAm 90
Pope, Alfred BioIn 16
Pope, Amy Elizabeth 1869-1949 BioIn 16
Pope, Andrew Jackson, Jr. 1913- WhoAm 90
Pope, Anne Elizabeth 1942- WhoE 91
Pope, Barbara Spyridon 1951- WhoAm 90, WhoAmW 91
Pope, Bill Jordan 1922- WhoAm 90
Pope, Britt H. 1948- St&PR 91
Pope, C. Larry 1954- St&PR 91
Pope, Cathryn IntWWM 90
Pope, Clarence Cullam, Jr. WhoAm 90
Pope, Clifford Hillhouse 1899-1974 AuBYP 90
Pope, Dave 1925- Ballpl 90
Pope, David 1927- BiDrAPA 89, WhoE 91
Pope, David E. 1920- WhoAm 90
Pope, Donna 1931- WhoAm 90, WhoAmW 91
Pope, Dorothy Hampson 1905- EncO&P 3, EncPaPR 91
Pope, Douglas V. 1945- St&PR 91
Pope, Elizabeth Marie 1917- AuBYP 90
Pope, Ellen 1950- WhoE 91
Pope, Fergus Bailey 1929- BiDrAPA 89
Pope, Generoso, Jr. BioIn 16
Pope, Generoso Paul, Jr. 1927-1988 ConAmBL
Pope, Guy B. 1936- St&PR 91
Pope, Harrison Graham, Jr. 1947- WhoAm 90, WhoWor 91
Pope, Henry BiDrAPA 89
Pope, Ingrid Bloomquist 1918- WhoAmW 91, WhoE 91
Pope, Jack 1913- WhoAm 90
Pope, James Arthur 1942- WhoSSW 91
Pope, James Larry 1948- WhoSSW 91
Pope, Jane L. 1946- BiDrAPA 89
Pope, Jane Laird Miller 1942- WhoAmW 91
Pope, Jane LaRue 1929- WhoAmW 91
Pope, Jeremy James Richard 1943- WhoWor 91
Pope, John 1822-1892 WhNaAH, WorAlBi
Pope, John A. 1933- St&PR 91
Pope, John Alexander 1906-1982 WhoAmA 91N
Pope, John Charles 1949- St&PR 91, WhoAm 90

Pope, John Edward 1953- *BiDrAPA 89*
Pope, John Edwin, III 1928- *WhoAm 90*
Pope, John W.R., Jr. 1931- *St&PR 91*
Pope, Johnnie B., Jr. 1955- *WhoSSW 91*
Pope, Joseph 1803-1895 *DcCanB 12*
Pope, Joyce *AuBYP 90*
Pope, Kate 1957- *ODwPR 91*
Pope, Kerig Rodgers 1935- *WhoAm 90*
Pope, Kirby Keith 1958- *BiDrAPA 89*
Pope, Lawrence *BioIn 16*
Pope, Leavitt Joseph *BioIn 16*
Pope, Leavitt Joseph 1924- *WhoAm 90*
Pope, Lillie 1918- *WhoAmW 91*
Pope, Marion Holden *WhoAmA 91N*
Pope, Marjorie Jean 1947- *WhoSSW 91*
Pope, Mark Andrew 1952- *WhoEmL 91*
Pope, Mark C., III 1924- *St&PR 91*
Pope, Mark L. 1952- *WhoEmL 91*
Pope, Marvin H. 1916- *WhoAm 90, WhoE 91, WhoWor 91*
Pope, Mary *BiDEWW, FemiCLE*
Pope, Mary Ann Irwin 1932- *WhoAmA 91*
Pope, Michael 1924- *St&PR 91, WhoAm 90*
Pope, Michael Alan 1950- *WhoSSW 91*
Pope, Michael Douglas 1927- *IntWWM 90*
Pope, O.V. 1917- *St&PR 91*
Pope, Peter Talbot, Sr. 1934- *St&PR 91*
Pope, Raymond K. 1927- *St&PR 91*
Pope, Richard Downing, Jr. 1930- *St&PR 91*
Pope, Robert Dean 1945- *WhoEmL 91*
Pope, Robert Glynn 1935- *WhoAm 90*
Pope, Roslyn Elizabeth 1938- *WhoAmW 91*
Pope, Seth Alex 1950- *BiDrAPA 89*
Pope, Stephen Bailey 1949- *WhoE 91*
Pope, Steven Francois 1948- *WhoAm 90, WhoEmL 91*
Pope, Suzette Stanley 1925- *WhoAmW 91*
Pope, Theodate 1868-1946 *BioIn 16*
Pope, Theodore C., Jr. 1932- *St&PR 91*
Pope, Thomas A. *BioIn 16*
Pope, Thomas Harrington, Jr. 1913- *WhoAm 90*
Pope, Thomas Jay 1930- *St&PR 91*
Pope, Thomas Maurice 1930- *St&PR 91, WhoAm 90*
Pope, Tony L. *St&PR 91*
Pope, W. Kenneth 1901-1989 *BioIn 16*
Pope, W. Stuart 1921- *IntWWM 90*
Pope, Willard Bissell 1903-1988 *BioIn 16*
Pope, William H. 1936- *St&PR 91*
Pope, William Jackson 1870-1939 *BioIn 16*
Pope, William L. 1960- *WhoSSW 91*
Pope, William Ray 1935- *St&PR 91*
Pope-Hennessy, John *BioIn 16*
Pope-Hennessy, John Wyndham 1913- *WhoAm 90*
Pope-Massetti, Audrey Laura 1951- *WhoAmW 91, WhoWor 91*
Popeck, Raymond John 1951- *WhoE 91*
Popecki, Joseph Thomas 1924- *WhoE 91*
Popehn, Arthur John 1919- *St&PR 91*
Popek, Gregory Alexander 1951- *WhoSSW 91*
Popel, Esther A. B. 1896-1958 *HarlReB*
Popel Shaw, Esther A. B. 1896-1958 *HarlReB*
Popeleski, Janet 1952- *WhoAm 90*
Popelin, Claudius *PenDiDA 89*
Popelka, Robert Joseph 1920- *WhoAm 90*
Popely, Deborah Rank 1956- *ODwPR 91*
Popenoe, Hugh Llywelyn 1929- *WhoSSW 91*
Popenoe, John 1929- *WhoAm 90, WhoSSW 91*
Popera, Susan Louise 1957- *WhoAmW 91*
Popescu, Cara *WhoAmA 91*
Popescu, Dumitru Radu 1935- *WorAu 1980 [port]*
Popescu, Ioan-Iovit 1932- *WhoWor 91*
Popescu, Lou 1946- *WhoSSW 91*
Popeski, Richard Stanley *BiDrAPA 89*
Popham, Arthur Cobb, Jr. 1915- *WhoAm 90*
Popham, Charles Ray 1951- *WhoSSW 91*
Popham, George *EncCRAm*
Popham, Lewis Charles, III 1928- *WhoAm 90*
Popham, Thomas Wayne 1939- *WhoSSW 91*
Popham, Wayne Gordon 1929- *WhoAm 90*
Popiel, Maryann Julia *BiDrAPA 89*
Popielarz, Beverly 1949- *WhoAmW 91*
Popinsky, Arnold Dave 1930- *WhoAmA 91*
Popitz, Heinrich 1925- *WhoWor 91*
Popjak, George Joseph 1914- *WhoAm 90*
Popkey, Herbert Robert 1931- *WhoSSW 91*
Popkin, Elsie Dinsmore 1937- *WhoAmA 91, WhoAmW 91*
Popkin, Mark Anthony 1929- *WhoSSW 91*
Popkin, Michael Harlan 1950- *WhoSSW 91*
Popkin, Michael K 1943- *BiDrAPA 89*
Popkin, Robert N *BiDrAPA 89*
Popkin, Roy Sandor 1921- *WhoAm 90, WhoWrEP 89*
Popkin, Stephen Marc 1951- *BiDrAPA 89*
Popko, Kathleen Marie 1943- *WhoAmW 91*
Popl, Milan 1934- *WhoWor 91*
Pople, John Anthony 1925- *WhoAm 90*
Pople, Peter *PenDiMP*
Pople, Ross 1945- *IntWWM 90*
Popli, Anil Mohan 1948- *WhoWor 91*
Popli, Shankar Dass 1941- *WhoSSW 91*
Poplin, Richard Rufus 1918- *WhoSSW 91*
Poplinger, Richard Ellis 1953- *WhoSSW 91*
Popoff, Frank Peter 1935- *St&PR 91, WhoAm 90, WhoWor 91*
Popofsky, Melvin Laurence 1936- *WhoAm 90*
Popov, Egor Paul 1913- *WhoAm 90*
Popov, Gavriil *BioIn 16*
Popov, Haralan *BioIn 16*
Popova, Liubov 1889-1924 *BiDWomA, BioIn 16*
Popova, Nina 1922- *WhoAm 90*
Popova-Mutafova, Fani 1902-1977 *EncCoWW*
Popovic, Nenad Dushan 1909- *WhoWor 91*
Popovic, Sanya 1962- *WhoAmW 91*
Popovic, Slobodan 1944- *BiDrAPA 89*
Popovic, Tanya *ConAu 130*
Popovic, Tatyana 1928- *ConAu 130*
Popovich, Helen 1935- *WhoAm 90*
Popovich, JoAnn Margaret 1952- *WhoAmW 91*
Popovich, Paul 1940- *Ballpl 90*
Popovici, Adrian 1942- *WhoAm 90*
Popovici, Mary Jo *ODwPR 91*
Popp, Adelheid 1869-1939 *EncCoWW*
Popp, Anthony C. 1927- *St&PR 91*
Popp, Betty 1935- *St&PR 91*
Popp, Carol Adzick 1948- *WhoAmW 91*
Popp, Carol Anne *BiDrAPA 89*
Popp, Charlotte Louise 1946- *WhoAmW 91, WhoE 91, WhoWor 91*
Popp, Johann Georg Christoph *PenDiDA 89*
Popp, Lucia 1939- *IntWWM 90, PenDiMP*
Popp, Nathaniel 1940- *WhoAm 90*
Popp, Pamela Lynn 1962- *WhoAmW 91*
Popp, Ralph William 1934- *St&PR 91*
Popp, Rosanna Katherine 1955- *WhoAmW 91*
Popp, Virginia Gail 1944- *WhoAmW 91*
Poppa, Ryal R. 1933- *St&PR 91*
Poppa, Ryal Robert 1933- *WhoAm 90*
Poppe, Frances Winnie Perez 1942- *WhoEmL 91*
Poppe, Fred Christoph 1923- *WhoAm 90*
Poppe, Frederick C. 1923- *St&PR 91*
Poppe, Gerald Wayne 1952- *WhoSSW 91*
Poppe, Wassily 1918- *WhoAm 90*
Poppel, Harvey Lee 1937- *WhoAm 90*
Poppel, Seth R. *St&PR 91*
Poppel, Seth Raphael 1944- *WhoE 91, WhoWor 91*
Poppele, J.R. *St&PR 91N*
Poppell, Jack Clifford, Sr. 1933- *WhoSSW 91*
Poppen, Janet Klawiter 1941- *WhoAmW 91*
Poppen, Robert G. 1934- *St&PR 91*
Poppensiek, George Charles 1918- *WhoAm 90*
Popper, Arthur N. 1943- *WhoE 91*
Popper, Beatrice Gertrude 1923- *WhoE 91*
Popper, Charles William 1946- *BiDrAPA 89*
Popper, David 1843-1913 *PenDiMP*
Popper, Edward Thomas 1944- *WhoE 91*
Popper, Hans 1903-1988 *AnObit 1988*
Popper, Hans Philipp 1903-1988 *BioIn 16*
Popper, Henry *BioIn 16*
Popper, Karl 1902- *WhoWor 91*
Popper, Karl R 1902- *MajTwCW*
Popper, Martin 1909-1989 *BioIn 16*
Popper, Pamela Anne 1956- *WhoAmW 91*
Popper, Richard H. 1948- *St&PR 91*
Popper, Robert 1932- *WhoAm 90*
Popper, Robert David *St&PR 91*
Popper, Robert David 1927- *WhoE 91*
Popper, Walter Lincoln 1920- *St&PR 91*
Poppers, Paul Jules 1929- *WhoAm 90*
Poppink, Rhea Nelson *BioIn 16*
Poppino, Allen G. 1925- *St&PR 91*
Poppino, Jean Lavonne 1938- *WhoAmW 91*
Poppitz, James 1957- *WhoAmA 91*
Popple, John A. 1945- *St&PR 91*
Popple, John Arthur 1945- *WhoEmL 91*
Popplewell, Richard John 1935- *IntWWM 90*
Poppy, Constance B. 1946- *WhoAmW 91*
Poprick, Mary Ann 1939- *WhoAmW 91, WhoWor 91*
Popul Vuh *NewAgMG*
Popwell, Albert *DrBIPA 90*
Poquette, Tom 1951- *Ballpl 90*
Por-Srur, Barbara *BiDrAPA 89*
Porada, Edith 1912- *WhoAm 90, WhoAmA 91*
Porat, Avner Meir 1939- *St&PR 91*
Poray, Stan P 1888-1948 *WhoAmA 91N*
Porcalla, Perpetua Servino 1935- *WhoWor 91*
Porcaro, Frank 1927- *WhoE 91*
Porcella, Arthur David 1918- *WhoSSW 91*
Porcelli, Joseph V. 1935- *St&PR 91*
Porcelli, Vito Lorenzo 1933- *WhoAm 90*
Porcello, Joseph Edward 1952- *St&PR 91*
Porcello, Leonard Joseph 1934- *WhoAm 90*
Porch, Phillip Pullen 1954- *WhoSSW 91*
Porcher, Connie Mitchell 1950- *WhoAmW 91*
Porcher, William J *BiDrAPA 89*
Porco, Aldo Joseph *BiDrAPA 89*
Porco, Vincent L. 1950- *WhoE 91*
Porcupine *DcCanB 12*
Porden, Eleanor Anne 1795-1825 *FemiCLE*
Pordenone 1483?-1539 *IntDcAA 90*
Pordy, Leon 1919- *St&PR 91, WhoAm 90*
Porechnikov, V. *EncCoWW*
Poretz, Douglas 1945- *ODwPR 91*
Poretz, Douglas H. 1945- *St&PR 91*
Porfido, Stanley M. 1936- *St&PR 91*
Porges, Walter Rudolf 1931- *WhoAm 90*
Pories, Walter Julius 1930- *WhoAm 90*
Porile, Norbert Thomas 1932- *WhoAm 90*
Poris, Ruth Gloria 1929- *WhoAmW 91*
Poritsky, Susan *BiDrAPA 89*
Poritsky, Susan 1950- *WhoE 91*
Porizkova, Anna *BioIn 16*
Porizkova, Paulina *BioIn 16*
Porkert, Manfred 1933- *ConAu 131, WhoWor 91*
Porlock, Martin *TwCCr&M 91*
Porner, Hans J. W. A. 1942- *WhoWor 91*
Porosoff, Harold 1946- *St&PR 91, WhoAm 90*
Porpiglia, Peter John 1953- *WhoSSW 91*
Porpora, Peter 1934- *St&PR 91*
Porporati, Guido 1932- *St&PR 91*
Porras, Belisario 1856-1942 *BioIn 16*
Porreca, Anne Agnes *WhoE 91*
Porreca, Elizabeth Faye 1950- *WhoAmW 91*
Porrett, James D. 1953- *St&PR 91*
Porretta, David Louis 1949- *WhoSSW 91*
Porretta, Emanuele 1942- *St&PR 91*
Porretta, Emanuele Peter 1942- *WhoAm 90*
Porritt, Jonathon 1950- *BioIn 16*
Porro, James Earle 1946- *WhoEmL 91*
Porsche, Ferdinand 1935- *ConDes 90*
Porsman, Frank O 1905- *WhoAmA 91N*
Port, David *BiDrAPA 89*
Port, David H. *St&PR 91*
Port, Louise A. M. *WhoAmW 91*
Port, Sidney Charles 1935- *WhoAm 90*
Port, Sidney Lawrence 1911- *St&PR 91*
Porta, Enzo 1931- *IntWWM 90*
Porta, John E. 1931- *St&PR 91, WhoSSW 91*
Porta, Pier Luigi 1945- *WhoWor 91*
Porta, Siena Gillann 1951- *WhoAmA 91*
Portaas, Herman Theodor *DcScanL*
Portadin, Gary L 1940- *BiDrAPA 89*
Portago, Alfonso de 1928-1957 *BioIn 16*
Portal, Gilbert Marcel Adrien 1930- *WhoAm 90*
Portalatin, Maria 1937- *WhoHisp 91*
Portales, Diego Jose Victor 1793-1837 *BioIn 16*
Portales, Ramon, Sr. 1929- *WhoHisp 91*
Portanier, Francis 1929- *WhoWor 91*
Portanova, Jaye-Jo *BiDrAPA 89*
Portanova, Joseph Domenico 1909-1979 *WhoAmA 91N*
Porte, Barbara Ann *AuBYP 90, BioIn 16*
Porte, Barbara Ann 1943- *BioIn 16*
Porte, Joel Miles 1933- *WhoAm 90*
Porte-Thomas, Barbara Ann *BioIn 16*
Portela, Alfonso Sanchez 1902- *BioIn 16*
Portela, Rafael 1947- *WhoHisp 91*
Portell, Josep *BiDrAPA 89*
Portell, Mario Rodolfo *BioIn 16*
Porteous, Cameron 1937- *OxCCanT [port]*
Porteous, Charles Robert, Jr. 1944- *WhoE 91*
Porteous, Gavin John 1967- *WhoWor 91*
Porteous, L. Robert, Jr. 1923- *St&PR 91*
Porteous, Timothy 1933- *WhoAm 90*
Porter, Albert Wright 1923- *WhoAmA 91*
Porter, Alisan *BioIn 16*
Porter, Andrew 1928- *IntWWM 90*
Porter, Andrew Brian 1928- *WhoWor 91, WhoWrEP 89*
Porter, Anna *ConAu 130*
Porter, Anna Maria 1780-1832 *BioIn 16, FemiCLE*
Porter, Arthur 1910- *WhoAm 90*
Porter, Arthur Reno 1918- *WhoAm 90*
Porter, Arthur Woods 1955- *WhoEmL 91*
Porter, Aubrey L. 1898- *WhoSSW 91*
Porter, Barry Schuyler 1937- *St&PR 91*
Porter, Beatrice 1928- *WhoAmW 91, WhoE 91*
Porter, Ben G. 1933- *ODwPR 91*
Porter, Bern 1911- *BioIn 16, WhoWrEP 89*
Porter, Bernard L. *St&PR 91*
Porter, Blaine Robert Milton 1922- *WhoAm 90*
Porter, Burton Frederick 1936- *WhoAm 90*
Porter, Carol Denise 1948- *WhoE 91*
Porter, Carolyn 1946- *ConAu 131*
Porter, Catherine 1941- *WhoAmW 91*
Porter, Catherine M. 1948- *WhoAmW 91*
Porter, Charles Allan 1932- *WhoAm 90*
Porter, Charles W. 1930- *St&PR 91*
Porter, Christopher John 1952- *WhoEmL 91*
Porter, Chuck 1956- *Ballpl 90*
Porter, Claire *BioIn 16*
Porter, Clyde C. 1938- *St&PR 91*
Porter, Cole 1891-1964 *BioIn 16, OxCPMus*
Porter, Cole 1893-1964 *WorAlBi*
Porter, Connie Jean 1950- *WhoSSW 91*
Porter, Curtis Hunter 1942- *WhoSSW 91*
Porter, Dale L. 1925- *St&PR 91*
Porter, Daniel Reed, III 1930- *WhoAm 90, WhoE 91*
Porter, Darrel 1952- *Ballpl 90*
Porter, Darrell *BioIn 16*
Porter, Darwin 1937- *ConAu 30NR*
Porter, Darwin Fred 1937- *WhoAm 90, WhoE 91, WhoWor 91, WhoWrEP 89*
Porter, Davena Young 1950- *WhoAmW 91*
Porter, David 1780-1843 *WorAlBi*
Porter, David 1912- *WhoAmA 91*
Porter, David Dixon 1813-1891 *WorAlBi*
Porter, David George 1921- *WhoWor 91*
Porter, David Gray 1953- *IntWWM 90*
Porter, David Hugh 1935- *IntWWM 90, WhoAm 90*
Porter, David L. 1938- *St&PR 91*
Porter, David Lindsey 1941- *WhoAm 90*
Porter, Dennis Dudley 1933- *WhoAm 90*
Porter, Dennis Ray 1955- *BiDrAPA 89*
Porter, Dick 1901-1974 *Ballpl 90*
Porter, Dixie Lee 1931- *WhoAmW 91*
Porter, Donald 1939- *WhoWrEP 89*
Porter, Donald Clayton 1914-1988 *SmATA X*
Porter, Donald James 1921- *WhoAm 90*
Porter, Donald Lindsay 1922- *WhoE 91*
Porter, Donna Viola 1950- *WhoAmW 91*
Porter, Doris M. 1929- *WhoAmW 91*
Porter, Dorothy Louise Burnett 1905- *HarlReB*
Porter, Dudley, Jr. 1915- *St&PR 91, WhoAm 90*
Porter, Dwight Johnson 1916- *WhoAm 90*
Porter, Earnest Stevens 1955- *WhoSSW 91*
Porter, Edgar L 1913- *BiDrAPA 89*
Porter, Edwin Stanton 1870-1941 *WorAlBi*
Porter, Eliot 1901- *BioIn 16, WorAlBi*
Porter, Eliot 1901-1990 *ConAu 132, NewYTBS 90 [port]*
Porter, Eliot Furness 1901- *WhoAm 90*
Porter, Eliot Furness 1901-1990 *WhoAmA 91N*
Porter, Elisabeth Scott 1942- *WhoAm 90, WhoAmW 91*
Porter, Ella Blodwen *AuBYP 90*
Porter, Elmer Johnson 1907- *WhoAmA 91*
Porter, Elsa Allgood 1928- *WhoAm 90*
Porter, Eric 1928- *WhoWor 91*
Porter, Eric William 1944- *St&PR 91*
Porter, Fairfield 1907-1975 *WhoAmA 91N*
Porter, Fitz-John 1822-1901 *WorAlBi*
Porter, Frederick M. 1926- *St&PR 91*
Porter, Gareth 1942- *ConAu 130*
Porter, Garry L 1935- *BiDrAPA 89*
Porter, George 1920- *WhoAm 90, WhoWor 91, WorAlBi*
Porter, George E. 1931- *St&PR 91*
Porter, George Homer, III 1933- *WhoSSW 91*
Porter, Gerald Joseph 1939- *WhoAm 90, WhoE 91*
Porter, Glenn 1944- *WhoAm 90, WhoE 91*
Porter, H. Leonard, III 1945- *WhoSSW 91*
Porter, Harlan David *WhoWrEP 89*
Porter, Harry, Jr. 1934- *BiDrAPA 89*
Porter, Harry William, Jr. 1936- *WhoAm 90*
Porter, Hazel Rebecca 1946- *WhoAmW 91*
Porter, Helen Viney 1935- *WhoAm 90*
Porter, Henry *BioIn 16*
Porter, Henry Homes, Jr. *WhoAm 90*
Porter, Horace 1837-1921 *BioIn 16*
Porter, Irwin Freeman 1918- *St&PR 91*
Porter, Irwin W. 1912- *WhoAm 90*
Porter, J. Larry 1954- *WhoSSW 91*
Porter, J. M. 1937- *WhoWrEP 89*
Porter, J. W. 1933- *Ballpl 90*
Porter, J. Winston 1937- *WhoAm 90*
Porter, James Franklin 1935- *WhoSSW 91*
Porter, James John 1946- *WhoWor 91*
Porter, James Kenneth 1934- *WhoSSW 91*

Porter, James Madison 1793-1862 *BiDrUSE 89*
Porter, James Morris 1931- *WhoAm 90*
Porter, James R. 1935- *St&PR 91*
Porter, James Whyte 1937- *IntWWM 90*
Porter, Jane 1776-1850 *BioIn 16, FemiCLE*
Porter, Janet Kay 1945- *WhoEmL 91, WhoWrEP 89*
Porter, Janet Street- *BioIn 16*
Porter, Jeanne Chenault 1944- *WhoAmA 91*
Porter, Jeffrey Alan 1955- *WhoSSW 91*
Porter, Jermain B. 1925- *St&PR 91*
Porter, Joe Ashby 1942- *LiHiK, WhoWrEP 89*
Porter, John D. 1948- *St&PR 91*
Porter, John Edward 1935- *WhoAm 90*
Porter, John F., III 1934- *St&PR 91*
Porter, John Finley, Jr. 1927- *WhoAm 90*
Porter, John Francis, III 1934- *WhoAm 90*
Porter, John H. 1933- *ODwPR 91*
Porter, John H, III 1925- *BiDrAPA 89*
Porter, John Hill 1933- *WhoAm 90*
Porter, John Robert, Jr. 1935- *WhoAm 90, WhoWor 91*
Porter, John Stephen 1932- *WhoAm 90*
Porter, John Weston 1939- *WhoE 91*
Porter, John William 1926- *St&PR 91*
Porter, John Wilson 1931- *WhoAm 90*
Porter, Joseph Thornton 1953- *WhoSSW 91*
Porter, Joyce 1924- *SpyFic, TwCCr&M 91*
Porter, Joyce Klowden 1949- *WhoAmW 91*
Porter, Judith Deborah Revitch 1940- *WhoAm 90*
Porter, Karl Hampton 1939- *WhoAm 90*
Porter, Katherine Anne 1890- *WorAlBi*
Porter, Katherine Anne 1890-1980 *BioAmW, BioIn 16, DcLB 102 [port], FemiCLE, MajTwCW*
Porter, Keith Carlton *BiDrAPA 89*
Porter, Keith Roberts 1912- *WhoAm 90*
Porter, Kendall 1932- *WhoAm 90*
Porter, Kenneth 1943- *BiDrAPA 89*
Porter, Leah LeEarle 1963- *WhoAmW 91*
Porter, Lee 1929- *WhoSSW 91*
Porter, Leon Eugene, Jr. 1953- *WhoEmL 91*
Porter, Liliana 1941- *BioIn 16, WhoAmA 91*
Porter, Liliana Alicia 1941- *WhoAm 90*
Porter, Lynn Keith 1929- *WhoAm 90*
Porter, M. Gilbert 1937- *ConAu 129*
Porter, Margaret Evans 1959- *WhoWrEP 89*
Porter, Margery Madden *BioIn 16*
Porter, Marjorie M *BiDrAPA 89*
Porter, Mark *AuBYP 90*
Porter, Mary Helen 1957- *WhoEmL 91*
Porter, Maxiene Helen Greve *WhoAmW 91*
Porter, Michael 1943- *ODwPR 91*
Porter, Michael A. 1949- *St&PR 91*
Porter, Michael E. 1947- *WhoAm 90*
Porter, Michael Leroy 1947- *IntWWM 90*
Porter, Michael Pell 1940- *WhoWor 91*
Porter, Milton 1911- *WhoAm 90*
Porter, Nora Roxanne 1949- *WhoE 91*
Porter, Patricia Sue 1933- *WhoAmW 91*
Porter, Paul Berggren 1917- *WhoAm 90*
Porter, Peter Buell 1773-1844 *BiDrUSE 89*
Porter, Philip Wayland 1928- *WhoAm 90*
Porter, Pleasant 1840-1907 *WhNaAH*
Porter, Richard Corbin 1931- *WhoAm 90*
Porter, Richard Frank 1943- *WhoE 91*
Porter, Richard James 1950- *WhoAmA 91*
Porter, Richard Kent 1948- *St&PR 91*
Porter, Richard Sterling 1929- *WhoAm 90*
Porter, Robert C. 1912- *St&PR 91*
Porter, Robert Chamberlain 1912- *WhoAm 90, WhoWor 91*
Porter, Robert T 1919- *BiDrAPA 89*
Porter, Robert William 1926- *WhoAm 90, WhoSSW 91*
Porter, Rodney R. 1917-1985 *WorAlBi*
Porter, Rodney Robert 1917-1985 *DcNaB 1981*
Porter, Roger B. *BioIn 16*
Porter, Roger B. 1946- *ConAu 131*
Porter, Roger Blaine 1946- *WhoAm 90*
Porter, Roger John 1942- *WhoAm 90*
Porter, Roger Stephen 1928- *WhoAm 90*
Porter, Ronald Philip 1944- *St&PR 91*
Porter, Rose 1845-1906 *FemiCLE*
Porter, Russell MacKinlay 1924- *WhoWor 91*
Porter, Russell Wayne 1956- *WhoSSW 91*
Porter, Samuel Hamilton 1927- *WhoAm 90*
Porter, Sarah *FemiCLE*
Porter, Scott D. 1947- *St&PR 91*
Porter, Scott Douglas 1959- *WhoE 91*
Porter, Sharon Ann 1953- *WhoEmL 91, WhoWor 91*
Porter, Shirley *WhoAmA 91*
Porter, Stephen G 1952- *BiDrAPA 89*
Porter, Stephen Winthrop 1925- *WhoAm 90*
Porter, Stuart Charles 1947- *St&PR 91*
Porter, Susan Loraine 1941- *IntWWM 90*
Porter, Susan Smith 1954- *WhoAmW 91*
Porter, Sylvia 1913- *WhoAm 90, WhoAmW 91, WhoWrEP 89, WorAlBi*
Porter, Taylor Linden *BiDrAPA 89*
Porter, Thomas J. 1934- *St&PR 91*
Porter, Tom Dean 1928- *St&PR 91*
Porter, Verna Louise 1941- *WhoAmW 91*
Porter, Vicki Sharon 1955- *WhoAmW 91*
Porter, W. Arthur 1941- *WhoAm 90*
Porter, W. Thomas 1934- *St&PR 91*
Porter, Walter Arthur 1924- *WhoAm 90*
Porter, Walter Thomas, Jr. 1934- *WhoAm 90*
Porter, William 1935- *St&PR 91*
Porter, William Glover, Jr. 1923- *WhoAm 90*
Porter, William James 1914-1988 *BioIn 16*
Porter, William Lyman 1934- *WhoAm 90*
Porter, William Moring 1913- *St&PR 91*
Porter, William Sydney 1862-1910 *AuBYP 90, ConAu 131, MajTwCW*
Porter-Davis, Gail Loretta 1952- *WhoAmW 91*
Porter-O'Grady, Timothy 1947- *WhoSSW 91*
Portera, Alan August 1951- *WhoE 91*
Porterfield, Bob 1923-1980 *Ballpl 90*
Porterfield, Dennis 1936- *St&PR 91*
Porterfield, Donald Richard 1934- *St&PR 91*
Porterfield, James H. 1910-1989 *BioIn 16*
Porterfield, James Temple Starke 1920- *WhoAm 90*
Porterfield, John Michael 1956- *WhoSSW 91*
Porterfield, Neil Harry 1936- *WhoAm 90*
Porterfield, Ralph Ira 1946- *WhoEmL 91*
Porterfield, William Wendell 1936- *WhoAm 90*
Portes, Richard David 1941- *WhoWor 91*
Portfolio, Almerindo Gerard 1923- *WhoAm 90*
Porth, Jose Antonio Rodriguez *BioIn 16*
Porthouse, Cyril R. 1911- *St&PR 91*
Porthouse, J. David 1938- *St&PR 91*
Portilla, Jose Antonio, Jr. 1926- *WhoHisp 91*
Portillo, Carol D. 1963- *WhoHisp 91*
Portillo, Estela *ConAu 32NR, HispWr 90*
Portillo, Febe 1945- *WhoHisp 91*
Portillo, Frank 1933- *St&PR 91*
Portillo, Jose Lopez *BioIn 16, HispWr 90*
Portillo, Juan 1945- *WhoHisp 91*
Portillo, Raul M. 1955- *WhoHisp 91*
Portillo Trambley, Estela 1936- *ConAu 32NR, HispWr 90*
Portillo y Pacheco, Jose Lopez *HispWr 90*
Portinari, Candido 1903-1962 *ArtLatA*
Portis, Alan Mark 1926- *WhoAm 90*
Portis, Charles 1933- *WorAu 1980 [port]*
Portman, Brian 1960- *WhoAmA 91*
Portman, Cheryl Beth 1960- *WhoAmW 91*
Portman, Glenn Arthur 1949- *WhoEmL 91, WhoSSW 91, WhoWor 91*
Portman, Jerry A. 1928- *St&PR 91*
Portman, John C. 1924- *WorAlBi*
Portman, John Calvin, Jr. 1924- *St&PR 91*
Portman, Robert George 1942- *St&PR 91*
Portney, Charles Wayne 1950- *BiDrAPA 89*
Portney, David C. *ODwPR 91*
Portney, Robert B 1952- *BiDrAPA 89*
Portnoff, Alexander 1887-1949 *WhoAmA 91N*
Portnoff, Collice Henry 1898- *WhoAm 90*
Portnow, Marjorie Anne *WhoAmA 91*
Portnow, Stanley L 1929- *BiDrAPA 89*
Portnow, Stanley Lewis 1929- *WhoE 91*
Portnoy, Alvin Julian 1931- *St&PR 91*
Portnoy, Ethel 1927- *EncCoWW, WhoWor 91*
Portnoy, Fern C. 1945- *WhoAm 90*
Portnoy, Howard Neil 1946- *WhoE 91*
Portnoy, Isidore 1914- *BiDrAPA 89*
Portnoy, Sara S. 1926- *WhoAm 90*
Portnoy, Theodora Preiss *WhoAmA 91*
Portnoy, William Manos 1930- *WhoAm 90*
Porto, Boris Joseph *BiDrAPA 89*
Porto, James *BioIn 16*
Porto, Joseph Anthony 1955- *WhoEmL 91*
Porto, Joseph H. *BioIn 16*
Portocarrero, Arnie 1931-1986 *Ballpl 90*
Portocarrero, Rene 1912-1986 *ArtLatA*
Portoghese, Philip Salvatore 1931- *WhoAm 90*
Portola, Gaspar de 1723?-1784 *BioIn 16, WorAlBi*
Portola, Gaspar De 1723?-1786 *EncCRAm*
Porton, Fredric C *BiDrAPA 89*
Portugal, Mark 1962- *Ballpl 90*
Portugal, Pamela Rainbear *WhoWrEP 89*
Portuondo, Juan M *BiDrAPA 89*
Portwood, John H. 1928- *St&PR 91*
Portwood, Presley Haver 1947- *WhoEmL 91, WhoSSW 91*
Portwood, Robert E. 1922- *St&PR 91*
Portyrata, Raymond E. 1949- *St&PR 91*
Portzen, Shari Lynn 1963- *WhoE 91*
Porubcansky, Mark Joseph 1954- *WhoWor 91*
Porucznik, Mary Ann 1948- *WhoAmW 91*
Porumbacu, Veronica 1921-1977 *EncCoWW*
Porybny, Zdenek 1945- *WhoWor 91*
Porzio, Anthony Joseph 1927- *St&PR 91*
Porzio, Patrick F. 1937- *St&PR 91*
Porzio, Raymond J 1936- *BiDrAPA 89*
Pos, Robert 1927- *BiDrAPA 89*
Posa-Kane, Maria Monina 1948- *BiDrAPA 89*
Posada, Alejandro E *BiDrAPA 89*
Posada, Jose Guadalupe 1852-1913 *ArtLatA*
Posada-Angel, Juan Carlos 1951- *WhoWor 91*
Posadas, Jorge *BiDrAPA 89*
Posamentier, Alfred Steven 1942- *WhoAm 90*
Posamentier, Evelyn 1951- *WhoWrEP 89*
Posch, Robert J., Jr. 1950- *St&PR 91*
Posch, Robert John, Jr. 1950- *WhoE 91*
Posedel, Bill 1906- *Ballpl 90*
Posedel, Miroslav A 1930- *BiDrAPA 89*
Posell, Edward A *BiDrAPA 89*
Posell, Elsa Z. *AuBYP 90*
Posen, Al 1895-1960 *EncACom*
Posen, Jack Martin 1936- *WhoE 91*
Posen, Marion Jablon 1959- *WhoAmW 91*
Posen, Stephen 1939- *WhoAmA 91*
Posener, Georges 1906-1988 *AnObit 1988*
Poser, Charles Marcel 1923- *WhoAm 90*
Poser, Ernest George 1921- *WhoAm 90*
Poser, Hans August Louis 1907- *WhoWor 91*
Poser, Joan Rapps 1940- *WhoAmW 91*
Poser, Norman Stanley 1928- *WhoAm 90*
Poser, Wolfgang Edgar 1947- *WhoWor 91*
Poserina, John A. 1940- *St&PR 91*
Poses, Frederic M. *BioIn 16*
Poses, Jack I 1899- *WhoAmA 91*
Poses, Jack I, Mrs 1908- *WhoAmA 91*
Posever, Thomas A *BiDrAPA 89*
Posey, Alexander Lawrence 1873-1908 *WhNaAH*
Posey, Carl A 1933- *ConAu 30NR*
Posey, Chester Nelson 1922- *St&PR 91*
Posey, Conrad Strother 1933- *St&PR 91*
Posey, Cum 1891-1946 *Ballpl 90*
Posey, Delma Powell 1937- *WhoSSW 91*
Posey, Earl A. 1928- *St&PR 91*
Posey, Eldon Eugene 1921- *WhoAm 90*
Posey, Elsa 1938- *WhoAmW 91*
Posey, Ernest Noel 1937- *WhoAmA 91*
Posey, Jumetta Gail 1954- *WhoAmW 91*
Posey, Richard E. 1947- *St&PR 91*
Posey, Robert N. 1960- *St&PR 91*
Posey, Roderick Burl 1953- *WhoSSW 91*
Posey, Warren M. 1940- *St&PR 91*
Posford, George 1906-1976 *OxCPMus*
Poshard, Glenn 1945- *BioIn 16, WhoAm 90*
Posillico, Louis Francis 1946- *St&PR 91*
Posillico, Tino John 1956- *WhoE 91*
Posillipo, Anthony J. *BioIn 16*
Posin, Daniel Q. 1909- *WhoAm 90*
Posin, Melvin 1925- *St&PR 91*
Posinovec, Jasminka 1926- *WhoWor 91*
Positano, Jill Marie 1965- *WhoAmW 91*
Poskas, Peter Edward 1939- *WhoAmA 91, WhoE 91*
Poskochil, Rodney Duane 1952- *St&PR 91*
Posluns, Wilfred Murray 1932- *St&PR 91*
Posnack, Emanuel R. 1897-1989 *BioIn 16*
Posnansky, Merrick 1931- *WhoAm 90, WhoWrEP 89*
Posner, Barbara G. 1947- *ODwPR 91*
Posner, Bernard 1916- *WhoE 91*
Posner, Bruce Frederick 1954- *WhoE 91*
Posner, Carol Jean *BiDrAPA 89*
Posner, David S. 1945- *WhoEmL 91*
Posner, Donald 1931- *WhoAm 90, WhoAmA 91*
Posner, Donald Michael 1934- *BiDrAPA 89*
Posner, Edward Charles 1933- *WhoAm 90*
Posner, Eleanor 1942- *WhoAmW 91*
Posner, Enrique Alan 1964- *WhoE 91*
Posner, Ernest Gary 1937- *St&PR 91*
Posner, Froma Topor 1947- *WhoE 91*
Posner, Gary Herbert 1943- *WhoAm 90*
Posner, Helaine J 1953- *WhoAmA 91, WhoE 91*
Posner, Henry, III 1955- *WhoE 91*
Posner, Howard R. 1935- *St&PR 91*
Posner, Jeffry A. 1941- *St&PR 91*
Posner, Jerome Beebe 1932- *WhoAm 90*
Posner, Judith L 1941- *WhoAmA 91*
Posner, Linda Irene 1939- *WhoAmW 91*
Posner, Marc S. *ODwPR 91*
Posner, Martin S 1937- *BiDrAPA 89*
Posner, Nathaniel *BiDrAPA 89*
Posner, Richard Allen 1939- *WhoAm 90*
Posner, Robert B. 1938- *BiDrAPA 89*
Posner, Roy Edward 1933- *St&PR 91, WhoAm 90*
Posner, Samuel 1935- *St&PR 91*
Posner, Seymour *BioIn 16*
Posner, Sidney 1924- *WhoAm 90*
Posner, Tracy 1962- *WhoAmW 91*
Posner, Victor 1918- *WhoSSW 91*
Posner-Cahill, Cheryl Lynn 1950- *WhoSSW 91*
Posniak, Sallie Cecelia 1934- *WhoAmW 91*
Posnick, Adolph 1926- *St&PR 91, WhoAm 90*
Pospisil, Eva Holdridge 1953- *WhoAmW 91*
Pospisil, George Curtis 1945- *WhoAm 90*
Pospisil, Leopold Jaroslav 1923- *WhoAm 90, WhoE 91*
Pospisil, Radomir Bedrich 1938- *WhoWor 91*
Poss, John Claybron 1948- *WhoAm 90*
Poss, Stephen Daniel 1955- *WhoEmL 91*
Possati, Mario 1922- *WhoWor 91*
Possehl, Jerry Roy 1942- *WhoE 91*
Possenbacher, Joseph 1799-1873 *PenDiDA 89*
Possenti, Cheryl Ann 1957- *WhoAmW 91*
Possick, Stanley G 1944- *BiDrAPA 89*
Possinger, Frank *St&PR 91*
Possis, Zinon C. 1923- *St&PR 91*
Possoff, Viktoria M *BiDrAPA 89*
Post, Alan 1914- *WhoAm 90, WhoWor 91*
Post, Anne B *WhoAmA 91*
Post, Avery Denison 1924- *WhoAm 90, WhoE 91*
Post, Barry A. 1943- *St&PR 91*
Post, Boyd Wallace 1928- *WhoAm 90*
Post, Charles W. 1854-1914 *WorAlBi*
Post, Christian Frederick 1710-1785 *EncCRAm*
Post, David Alan 1941- *WhoAm 90, WhoE 91*
Post, David Lyn 1959- *St&PR 91*
Post, Donald Eugene 1936- *WhoSSW 91*
Post, Donna Mae 1951- *WhoE 91*
Post, Elizabeth Lindley 1920- *WhoAm 90*
Post, Emily 1873-1960 *BioAmW, WorAlBi*
Post, Frederick 1962- *WhoE 91*
Post, G. Roger *St&PR 91*
Post, George 1906- *WhoAmA 91*
Post, George Browne 1837-1913 *BioIn 16*
Post, Gerald Joseph 1925- *WhoAm 90*
Post, Glen Fleming, III 1952- *St&PR 91*
Post, Howard Allen 1916- *WhoAm 90, WhoE 91*
Post, Jackie E. 1928- *St&PR 91*
Post, Jackie Jackson 1928- *WhoAm 90*
Post, James W. 1930- *St&PR 91*
Post, Jerald L. 1946- *St&PR 91*
Post, Jerrold M *BiDrAPA 89*
Post, Jonathan Vos 1951- *WhoEmL 91, WhoWrEP 89*
Post, Joseph 1913- *WhoAm 90*
Post, Kenneth W. 1953- *WhoE 91*
Post, Laura L 1960- *BiDrAPA 89*
Post, Luther Norris 1922- *St&PR 91*
Post, Marion 1910- *WhoAmA 91*
Post, Marjorie M. 1887-1973 *BioAmW*
Post, Melville Davisson 1869-1930 *TwCCr&M 91, TwCLC 39 [port]*
Post, Nancy 1957- *WhoAmW 91*
Post, Peter Alton 1944- *WhoSSW 91*
Post, Rey D. 1951- *WhoSSW 91*
Post, Richard Bennett 1936- *WhoE 91*
Post, Richard F., Jr. 1954- *St&PR 91*
Post, Rick Alan 1962- *WhoWrEP 89*
Post, Robert M. 1914- *St&PR 91*
Post, Robert Morton 1942- *BiDrAPA 89*
Post, Seymour C 1924- *BiDrAPA 89*
Post, Stephen L 1927- *BiDrAPA 89*
Post, Wally 1929-1982 *Ballpl 90*
Post, Wiley 1899-1935 *WorAlBi*
Post, William *BioIn 16*
Post, William J. 1950- *St&PR 91*
Post-Beukens, L. 1908- *EncCoWW*
Post-Gorden, Joan Carolyn 1932- *WhoAmW 91*
Post Wolcott, Marion Scott 1910- *BioIn 16*
Postaer, Larry *BioIn 16*
Postal, Andrew 1948- *St&PR 91*
Postan, Michael Moissey 1899-1981 *DcNaB 1981*
Postar, Joseph 1922- *ODwPR 91*
Poste, George Henry 1944- *WhoAm 90*
Postel, Donald M 1922- *BiDrAPA 89*
Postel, Guillaume 1510-1581 *EncO&P 3*
Postel, John William 1953- *WhoSSW 91*
Postel, Wilfred B *BiDrAPA 89*
Postelle, Frederick Arnold 1945- *St&PR 91*
Postema, Pam *BioIn 16*
Postema, Richard Lee 1955- *WhoEmL 91*
Posten, Harry Owen 1928- *WhoE 91*
Poster, Carol 1956- *WhoWrEP 89*
Poster, Don Steven 1950- *WhoSSW 91*
Poster, June *WhoAmA 91*
Poster, Mark F *BiDrAPA 89*

Poster-Taylor, Terri Lee 1952- *WhoAmW 91*
Posteraro, Anthony Francis 1915- *WhoE 91*
Postgate, John Raymond 1922- *WhoWor 91*
Postgate, Raymond 1896-1971 *TwCCr&M 91*
Posthuma, Helen Marie 1920- *WhoAmW 91*
Posthumus, Carol Laytham 1944- *WhoE 91*
Postiglione, Corey M 1943- *WhoAmA 91*
Postl, Anton 1916- *WhoAm 90*
Postle, Beatrice *BiDrAPA 89*
Postle, Robert Ross 1929- *St&PR 91*
Postler, Ermin Joseph 1942- *WhoWor 91*
Postles, Grace Vera 1906- *HarlReB*
Postlethwaite, Carl Albert 1905- *St&PR 91*
Postlewait, Harry Owen 1933- *St&PR 91*
Postlewaite, Charles Chapman 1955- *WhoEmL 91*
Postlewaite, William Marc 1944- *WhoSSW 91*
Postlewate, Charles Willard 1941- *IntWWM 90*
Postma, Hans 1931- *WhoWor 91*
Postma, Herman 1933- *WhoAm 90*
Postma, Jan Klaas Tjipke 1942- *WhoWor 91*
Postma, Paul Gustaaf 1947- *WhoWor 91*
Postman, Leo Joseph 1918- *WhoAm 90*
Postman, Louise Yood *BiDrAPA 89*
Postman, Robert Derek 1941- *WhoWor 91*
Postnikova, Viktoria 1944- *PenDiMP*
Postol, Lawrence Philip 1951- *WhoEmL 91*
Postol, Steven M. 1930- *St&PR 91*
Postolka, Milan 1932- *IntWWM 90*
Poston, David L. 1953- *WhoWrEP 89*
Poston, Gerald Connell 1936- *St&PR 91*
Poston, Gretchen *BioIn 16*
Poston, Gretchen 1932- *WhoAm 90*
Poston, Joe B. 1951- *St&PR 91*
Poston, John Edward 1948- *St&PR 91*
Poston, Martha Lee *AuBYP 90*
Poston, McCracken King, Jr. 1959- *WhoSSW 91*
Poston, Michael Alan 1937- *St&PR 91*
Poston, Tom *BioIn 16*
Poston, Tom 1927- *WhoAm 90, WorAlBi*
Postone, Norman *BiDrAPA 89*
Postrech, Gary Lee 1950- *WhoE 91*
Postruznik, Drazen Ferdinand 1948- *WhoWor 91*
Postyn, Sol 1934- *WhoAm 90*
Posvar, Dean Roger 1941- *St&PR 91*
Posvar, Wesley Wentz 1925- *WhoAm 90, WhoE 91*
Poswolsky, Melvyn 1947- *WhoE 91*
Pot, Pol 1928- *WorAlBi*
Potac, Svatopluk 1925- *WhoWor 91*
Potamkin, Meyer P. 1909- *WhoAm 90*
Potamkin, Victor *BioIn 16*
Potasek, Mary Joyce 1945- *WhoAmW 91, WhoE 91*
Potash, Janice Sue 1955- *WhoAmW 91*
Potash, Jerome 1925- *St&PR 91*
Potash, Marcia 1948- *ODwPR 91*
Potash, Marlin Sue 1951- *WhoE 91*
Potash, Michael D 1933- *BiDrAPA 89*
Potash, Stephen Jon 1945- *WhoAm 90*
Potash, Tod H. 1942- *ODwPR 91*
Potash, Warren *BioIn 16*
Potash, Zena Cathryn 1953- *BiDrAPA 89*
Potate, John Spencer, Sr. 1934- *WhoSSW 91*
Potcova, Nistor, Jr. 1925- *St&PR 91*
Potdar, Anilkumar S 1946- *BiDrAPA 89*
Pote, Harold William 1946- *St&PR 91, WhoAm 90, WhoE 91*
Poteat, Carol Martin 1929- *WhoAmW 91*
Poteat, Edwin McNeill 1892-1955 *BioIn 16*
Poteet, Daniel Powell, II 1940- *WhoAm 90*
Poteet, Dwayne Lee 1959- *WhoWor 91*
Poteete, Robert Arthur 1926- *WhoAm 90, WhoWrEP 89*
Potekin, Barry 1945- *WhoEmL 91*
Potembski, Larry Michael 1958- *St&PR 91*
Potempa, Lester Edward *BiDrAPA 89*
Potempa, Wayne C. 1949- *St&PR 91*
Poten, William F. *BioIn 16*
Potente, Eugene, Jr. 1921- *WhoWor 91*
Potente, Helmut Michael 1939- *WhoWor 91*
Potenza, Joseph Anthony 1941- *WhoAm 90*
Potenza, Joseph Michael 1947- *WhoEmL 91*
Poterat, Edme 1612-1687 *PenDiDA 89*
Potesta, Rudolph M. 1932- *St&PR 91*
Poth, Edward Cornelius 1927- *WhoAm 90, WhoWor 91*
Poth, Gregory E. 1945- *St&PR 91*
Poth, Harry Augustus, Jr. 1911- *St&PR 91*
Poth, Peter Paul 1929- *WhoAm 90*
Poth, Stefan Michael 1933- *St&PR 91, WhoAm 90*
Pothuloori, Manmohan Pratap *BiDrAPA 89*
Potiker, Howard M. 1927- *St&PR 91*
Potiker, Sheila Millman 1929- *St&PR 91*
Potila, Antti 1938- *WhoWor 91*
Potito, Michael Anthony 1952- *WhoEmL 91*
Potkewitz, Irwin 1938- *BiDrAPA 89*
Potkin, Harvey 1935- *St&PR 91*
Potkin, Steven Garth *BiDrAPA 89*
Potkonski, Leopold A 1911- *BiDrAPA 89*
Potocnik, William John 1936- *St&PR 91*
Potofsky, Jacob S. 1894-1979 *WorAlBi*
Potok, Andrew *BioIn 16*
Potok, Chaim 1929- *BioIn 16, MajTwCW, WhoAm 90, WhoWrEP 89, WorAlBi*
Potoker, Edward Martin 1931- *WhoAm 90, WhoWrEP 89*
Potoker, Herbert 1929- *St&PR 91*
Potoreiko, Jean Frances 1940- *WhoE 91*
Potorski, Robert L. 1937- *St&PR 91*
Pototschnik, John 1946- *BioIn 16*
Potsic, William Paul 1943- *WhoAm 90*
Pott, Francis John Dolben 1957- *IntWWM 90*
Pott, John *EncCRAm*
Pott, Nicholas H *BiDrAPA 89*
Pottabathni, Pandu Ranga 1947- *WhoWor 91*
Pottasch, Stuart Robert 1932- *WhoWor 91*
Pottash, A. Carter 1948- *WhoAm 90*
Pottash, A L C 1948- *BiDrAPA 89*
Pottash, Ruben R 1914- *BiDrAPA 89*
Pottash, Ruben Robert 1914- *WhoE 91*
Pottenger, Charles 1950- *St&PR 91*
Potter, Alfred K. 1948- *St&PR 91*
Potter, Alison R *BiDrAPA 89*
Potter, Andrew John 1949- *IntWWM 90*
Potter, Anne Louise 1949- *WhoAmW 91, WhoEmL 91*
Potter, Anthony Grahame 1949- *St&PR 91*
Potter, Anthony Nicholas, Jr. 1942- *WhoSSW 91, WhoWor 91*
Potter, B. *BiDWomA*
Potter, Barbara Ann 1941- *WhoAmW 91*
Potter, Barr Blakeslee 1948- *WhoAm 90*
Potter, Barrett George 1929- *WhoAm 90*
Potter, Beatrix 1866-1943 *BioIn 16, FemiCLE, WorAlBi*
Potter, Bridget *BioIn 16*
Potter, Bronson *AuBYP 90*
Potter, Carole Ann 1940- *WhoAmW 91*
Potter, Charles Arthur, Jr. 1925- *WhoAm 90*
Potter, Charles Jackson 1908- *St&PR 91, WhoAm 90*
Potter, Christopher *PenDiDA 89*
Potter, Clarkson Nott 1928- *WhoAm 90, WhoWrEP 89*
Potter, Clinton Ray 1936- *St&PR 91*
Potter, Coral S. *BioIn 16, NewYTBS 90*
Potter, Cynthia M. 1950- *WhoAmW 91*
Potter, David Samuel 1925- *WhoAm 90*
Potter, Dean Marion 1939- *St&PR 91, WhoAm 90*
Potter, Delcour Stephen, III 1935- *St&PR 91*
Potter, Dennis *BioIn 16*
Potter, Dennis 1935- *ConAu 33NR, MajTwCW, WhoWor 91*
Potter, Dexter Burtion 1840-1917 *AmLegL*
Potter, Donald Albert 1922- *St&PR 91*
Potter, Donald Joseph, Jr. 1949- *WhoSSW 91*
Potter, Douglas Ernest 1930- *St&PR 91*
Potter, Edmund Lysle 1924- *St&PR 91*
Potter, Edward Ralph 1946- *St&PR 91*
Potter, Elaine Clarke 1935- *WhoAmW 91*
Potter, Elizabeth Walker 1957- *WhoAmW 91*
Potter, Eloise Fretz 1931- *WhoWrEP 89*
Potter, Emma Josephine Hill 1921- *WhoAmW 91, WhoE 91*
Potter, Ernest Elliott 1929- *St&PR 91*
Potter, Ernest Luther 1940- *WhoAm 90, WhoSSW 91*
Potter, F. Edward *BioIn 16*
Potter, Faith *ConAu 30NR*
Potter, Frank M., Jr. 1932- *WhoAm 90*
Potter, Frank N 1911- *ConAu 130*
Potter, Fred Leon 1948- *WhoEmL 91*
Potter, Fuller 1910-1990 *BioIn 16, NewYTBS 90*
Potter, Gary Robert 1945- *St&PR 91*
Potter, George Harris 1936- *St&PR 91*
Potter, George William, Jr. 1930- *WhoWor 91*
Potter, Guy Dill 1928- *WhoAm 90*
Potter, Hamilton Fish, Jr. 1928- *WhoAm 90*
Potter, Harry R *BiDrAPA 89*
Potter, Helen Beatrix 1866-1943 *AuBYP 90*
Potter, Howard Spencer 1916-1989 *BioIn 16*
Potter, Jacqueline Riley *WhoWrEP 89*
Potter, James Craig 1943- *WhoAm 90*
Potter, James Douglas 1944- *WhoAm 90*
Potter, Janet Marie 1967- *WhoAmW 91*
Potter, Jeremy 1922- *ConAu 30NR*
Potter, Joan *BioIn 16*
Potter, John Francis 1925- *WhoAm 90*
Potter, John Leith 1923- *WhoAm 90*
Potter, John R. 1945- *St&PR 91*
Potter, John William 1918- *WhoAm 90*
Potter, June Anita 1938- *WhoAmW 91*
Potter, Karl Harrington 1927- *WhoAm 90*
Potter, Keith 1946- *St&PR 91*
Potter, Kenneth *WhoAmA 91*
Potter, Kenneth 1926- *WhoAmA 91*
Potter, Kenneth C. 1939- *St&PR 91*
Potter, Lillian Florence 1912- *WhoAmW 91*
Potter, Lois Dorais 1941- *WhoWor 91*
Potter, Marian 1915- *AuBYP 90*
Potter, Mark *WhoWrEP 89*
Potter, Marshall Richard 1948- *WhoE 91*
Potter, Mary 1900-1981 *BiDWomA*
Potter, Mary 1920- *WhoWor 91*
Potter, Maxwell G 1926- *BiDrAPA 89*
Potter, Michael Allen 1961- *WhoE 91*
Potter, Miriam Clark 1886-1965 *AuBYP 90*
Potter, Nancy Dutton 1946- *WhoAmW 91*
Potter, Nels 1911- *Ballpl 90*
Potter, Patricia Ann 1951- *BiDrAPA 89, WhoE 91*
Potter, Pennie Charlolette 1952- *WhoSSW 91*
Potter, Peter Edward 1935- *WhoE 91*
Potter, Ralph Benajah, Jr. 1931- *WhoAm 90*
Potter, Rebecca Lynn 1951- *BiDrAPA 89*
Potter, Reese H 1908- *BiDrAPA 89*
Potter, Richard Clifford 1946- *WhoEmL 91*
Potter, Rita Jean 1951- *WhoEmL 91*
Potter, Robert A. 1951- *St&PR 91*
Potter, Robert Burdette 1922- *WhoE 91*
Potter, Robert Dale 1945- *WhoSSW 91, WhoWor 91*
Potter, Robert Daniel 1923- *WhoAm 90, WhoSSW 91*
Potter, Robert Ducharme 1905-1978 *AuBYP 90*
Potter, Robert Ellis 1937- *WhoSSW 91, WhoWor 91*
Potter, Robert Gene 1939- *St&PR 91*
Potter, Robert J. 1932- *St&PR 91*
Potter, Robert Joseph 1932- *WhoAm 90, WhoSSW 91*
Potter, Robert L. 1933- *St&PR 91*
Potter, Robert S. 1920-1988 *BioIn 16*
Potter, Robert Wallace, Jr. 1947- *WhoEmL 91*
Potter, Rosemary Lee 1938- *WhoAmW 91*
Potter, Stephen 1900-1969 *AuBYP 90, MajTwCW*
Potter, Steven P. *BioIn 16*
Potter, Susanna 1659- *BiDEWW*
Potter, Ted 1933- *WhoAmA 91*
Potter, Trevor Alexander McClurg 1955- *WhoE 91*
Potter, Wayne Allen 1944- *St&PR 91*
Potter, William Bartlett 1938- *St&PR 91, WhoAm 90, WhoE 91*
Potter, William Everett 1905-1988 *BioIn 16*
Potter, William Gray, Jr. 1950- *WhoAm 90*
Potter, William Harvey, Jr. 1947- *WhoSSW 91*
Potter, William J 1883-1964 *WhoAmA 91N*
Potter, William James 1948- *WhoE 91, WhoEmL 91, WhoWor 91*
Potter, William Rayner 1936- *WhoWor 91*
Potter, William Z 1945- *BiDrAPA 89*
Potter-Hill, Lynne A. 1955- *WhoAmW 91*
Potterf, Raymond Dewayne *BiDrAPA 89*
Potterfield, Peter Lounsbury 1949- *WhoWrEP 89*
Potthast, John 1944- *WhoE 91*
Potthoff, Richard Frederick 1932- *WhoSSW 91*
Pottie, Roswell Francis 1933- *WhoAm 90*
Pottier and Stymus *PenDiDA 89*
Pottier, Auguste *PenDiDA 89*
Pottinger, David Russell 1965- *WhoSSW 91*
Pottle, Bruce W. 1939- *St&PR 91*
Pottle, Frederick A. 1897-1987 *DcLB 103 [port]*
Pottle, Martin K. 1942- *ODwPR 91*
Pottmeyer, Hermann Josef 1934- *WhoWor 91*
Pottmeyer, Wayne G. 1947- *St&PR 91*
Pottorff, James Arthur 1959- *St&PR 91*
Pottorff, Jo Ann 1936- *WhoAmW 91*
Potts, Annie *BioIn 16*
Potts, Barbara Joyce 1932- *WhoAm 90, WhoAmW 91*
Potts, Bernard 1915- *WhoE 91*
Potts, Byron Keith 1929- *WhoAm 90*
Potts, Charles 1943- *WhoWrEP 89*
Potts, Charles A *WhoAmA 91N*
Potts, Charles Henry 1952- *WhoSSW 91*
Potts, Darla Lynn 1958- *WhoAmW 91*
Potts, David Malcolm 1935- *WhoAm 90*
Potts, Douglas Gordon 1927- *WhoAm 90*
Potts, Erwin Rea 1932- *WhoAm 90*
Potts, Floyd 1922- *WhoSSW 91*
Potts, Frisso J 1914- *BiDrAPA 89*
Potts, Gerald Neal 1933- *WhoAm 90*
Potts, Gilbert E. 1951- *WhoWor 91*
Potts, Harold Francis, Jr. 1955- *St&PR 91, WhoE 91*
Potts, Hugh Eustis 1902-1990 *BioIn 16*
Potts, Jack Lovell *BiDrAPA 89*
Potts, Jackie Stearns *WhoAmW 91*
Potts, James Murray 1921- *WhoE 91*
Potts, Jean 1910- *TwCCr&M 91*
Potts, Jerry 1840?-1896 *DcCanB 12, WhNaAH [port]*
Potts, Kenneth C *BiDrAPA 89*
Potts, Kevin T. 1928- *WhoAm 90*
Potts, Leo Joseph 1931- *BiDrAPA 89*
Potts, Nancy Dee Needham 1947- *WhoEmL 91*
Potts, Paul 1911-1990 *ConAu 132*
Potts, Ramsay Douglas 1916- *WhoAm 90, WhoE 91, WhoWor 91*
Potts, Richard W. 1937- *St&PR 91*
Potts, Rinehart Skeen 1927- *WhoE 91*
Potts, Robert Charles 1939- *BiDrAPA 89*
Potts, Robert Henderson 1924- *WhoAm 90*
Potts, Robert Paul 1947- *WhoEmL 91*
Potts, Stephen Deaderick 1930- *WhoAm 90*
Potts, Thomas Howard 1949- *St&PR 91*
Potts, Tom 1947- *ODwPR 91*
Potts, William James, Jr. *BioIn 16*
Potts-Guin, Marilyn *BioIn 16*
Potuto, Josephine R. 1947- *WhoEmL 91*
Potvin, Alfred Raoul 1942- *WhoAm 90*
Potvin, Anne *BiDrAPA 89*
Potvin, Denis 1953- *WorAlBi*
Potvin, Philip N. 1946- *St&PR 91*
Potvin, Pierre 1932- *WhoAm 90*
Potvin, Raymond Herve 1924- *WhoAm 90*
Potvlieghe, Ghislain Hugo 1936- *IntWWM 90*
Potwin, Connie Marie 1962- *WhoE 91*
Potwin, John Martin 1943- *St&PR 91*
Potzick, James Edward 1941- *WhoE 91*
Pou, Emily Hotchkiss Quinn *WhoAm 90*
Pou, Jose Manuel *BiDrAPA 89*
Pou, Linda Alice 1942- *WhoAmW 91*
Pou, Maria Amelia 1962- *WhoSSW 91*
Poucher, George E 1913- *BiDrAPA 89*
Poucher, W. A. 1891-1988 *BioIn 16*
Poucher, William Arthur 1891-1988 *BioIn 16*
Pouget, Gerard Marcel Rene 1938- *WhoWor 91*
Pouget, Jean-Joseph Emile 1860-1931 *BiDFrPL*
Pouget, Marie 1949- *WhoHisp 91*
Pough, Frederick Harvey 1906- *AuBYP 90, WhoAm 90*
Pough, Richard Hooper 1904- *WhoAm 90*
Poughkeepsie Seer, The 1862-1910 *EncO&P 3*
Pougnet, Jean 1907-1968 *PenDiMP*
Pouishnoff, Lev 1891-1959 *PenDiMP*
Poujade, Pierre-Marie 1920- *BiDFrPL*
Poul, Franklin 1924- *WhoAm 90*
Poulakakis, George M 1930- *BiDrAPA 89*
Poulard Prad, Giovanni *PenDiDA 89*
Poulenc, Francis 1899-1963 *BioIn 16, PenDiMP A, WorAlBi*
Poulet, Gaston 1892-1974 *PenDiMP*
Poulet, Gerard 1938- *PenDiMP*
Poulet, Virginia Maniglier *AuBYP 90*
Pouleur, Hubert Gustave 1948- *WhoWor 91*
Poulin, A., Jr. 1938- *ConAu 32NR, WhoWrEP 89*
Poulin, Gerald Conrad 1942- *St&PR 91*
Poulin, Jacques 1938- *BioIn 16*
Poulin, Louis Gilles 1959- *WhoSSW 91*
Poulin, Marie-Paule 1945- *WhoAm 90*
Poulin, Roland *WhoAmA 91*
Poulin, Yves *BiDrAPA 89*
Poulin-Kloehr, Lisa 1956- *WhoAmW 91, WhoE 91*
Pouliot, Adrien *BioIn 16*
Pouliot, Assunta Gallucci 1937- *WhoAmW 91, WhoWor 91*
Pouliot, Gaston J. 1929- *St&PR 91*
Pouliot, Reynald 1947- *WhoSSW 91*
Poulo, George A. 1923- *WhoE 91*
Poulos, Basilios Nicholas 1941- *WhoAmA 91*
Poulos, Clara Jean 1941- *WhoAmW 91*
Poulos, James Thomas 1938- *WhoWor 91*
Poulos, Michael J. 1931- *St&PR 91*
Poulos, Michael James 1931- *WhoAm 90, WhoSSW 91*
Poulose, Queeny *BiDrAPA 89*
Poulsen, Fern Sue 1959- *WhoAmW 91*
Poulsen, Henning 1912- *BiDrAPA 89*
Poulsen, Jens 1943- *WhoWor 91*
Poulsen, Keld Berg 1945- *WhoWor 91*
Poulsen, Olaf 1943- *WhoWor 91*

Poulson, Donald Frederick 1910-1989 *BioIn 16*
Poulson, Howard D. *WhoAm 90*
Poulson, Robert Dean 1927- *WhoAm 90*
Poulter, Eileen Margaret 1928- *IntWWM 90*
Poulton, Bruce Robert 1927- *WhoAm 90, WhoSSW 91*
Poulton, Charles Edgar 1917- *WhoAm 90*
Poulton, Diana 1903- *PenDiMP*
Poulton, Donna Lee 1945- *WhoEmL 91*
Poulton, Edward Bagnall 1856-1943 *DcScB S2*
Poulton, Robert *IntWWM 90*
Pouncey, Melinda Alice 1949- *WhoAmW 91*
Pouncey, Peter Richard 1937- *WhoAm 90, WhoE 91, WhoWor 91*
Pouncy, Mattie Hunter 1924- *WhoWrEP 89*
Pound, Ezra 1885-1972 *BioIn 16, MajTwCW, WorAlBi, WrPh*
Pound, Glenn Simpson 1914- *WhoAm 90*
Pound, Louise 1872-1958 *FemiCLE*
Pound, Nancy E. 1952- *WhoAmW 91*
Pound, Richard *BioIn 16*
Pound, Richard William Duncan 1942- *WhoAm 90*
Pound, Robert Vivian 1919- *WhoAm 90*
Pounder, C.C.H. 1952- *ConTFT 8, DrBlPA 90*
Pounder, Richard A. 1946- *WhoAm 90*
Poundmaker 1842?-1886 *WhNaAH [port]*
Pounds, Billy Dean 1930- *WhoSSW 91*
Pounds, Carol Jeanne 1955- *WhoSSW 91*
Pounds, Rebecca L. 1961- *St&PR 91*
Pounds, William Frank 1928- *WhoAm 90*
Poundstone, John Walker 1940- *WhoSSW 91*
Poundstone, Robert Bruce 1933- *BiDrAPA 89*
Poundstone, William Nicholas 1925- *St&PR 91*
Poungui, Ange-Edouard 1942- *WhoWor 91*
Pounian, Albert Kachouni 1924- *WhoAmA 91*
Pountney, David 1947- *IntWWM 90*
Poupard, Henri-Pierre 1901-1989 *BioIn 16*
Poupard, James J. 1932- *WhoAm 90*
Poupard, Paul 1930- *WhoWor 91*
Poupelet, Jane 1878-1932 *BiDWomA*
Poupeney, Mollie *WhoAmA 91*
Pour-El, Marian Boykan *WhoAm 90, WhoAmW 91*
Pourchot, Mary Ellen 1923- *WhoWrEP 89*
Pourciau, Lester John 1936- *WhoAm 90*
Pournelle, Jerry 1933- *ConAu 30NR, RGTwCSF*
Pournelle, Jerry Eugene 1933- *WhoAm 90*
Pousada, Lidia 1957- *WhoAmW 91*
Pousette-Dart, Joanna 1947- *WhoAmA 91*
Pousette-Dart, Nathaniel J 1886-1965 *WhoAmA 91N*
Pousette-Dart, Richard 1916- *WhoAm 90, WhoAmA 91*
Poussaint, Alvin Francis 1934- *BiDrAPA 89, WhoAm 90*
Poussaint, Renee Francine 1944- *WhoAmW 91*
Poussart, Denis Jean-Marie 1940- *WhoAm 90*
Poussin, Nicholas 1594-1665 *WorAlBi*
Poussin, Nicolas 1594?-1665 *BioIn 16, IntDcAA 90*
Pousson, Camille Maria 1953- *BiDrAPA 89*
Poutasse, Edmund Joseph 1931- *WhoE 91*
Pouteau, Jean L M *BiDrAPA 89*
Poutrain, Maximilian *BioIn 16*
Poveda, Carlos Manuel, III 1963- *WhoHisp 91*
Poveda Burbano, Alfredo *BioIn 16*
Povell, Roy Albert 1929- *WhoAm 90*
Povey, Charles *BioIn 16*
Povey, Thomas George 1920- *WhoE 91, WhoWor 91*
Povich, Ilissa Kimball 1959- *WhoE 91*
Povich, Maury *BioIn 16*
Povich, Shirley *BioIn 16*
Povich, Shirley 1905- *Ballpl 90*
Povich, Shirley Lewis 1905- *WhoAm 90*
Povish, Kenneth Joseph 1924- *WhoAm 90*
Povondra, Robert M. 1938- *St&PR 91*
Pow, Jill Ann *WhoAmW 91*
Pow, Richard B. 1934- *St&PR 91*
Powalski, Jan *EncCoWW*
Powanda, William Charles 1940- *WhoE 91*
Powasheek 1813?-1843? *WhNaAH*
Powchik, Peter *BiDrAPA 89*
Powderly, Robert G. 1947- *St&PR 91*
Powders, Donna Jo 1942- *WhoWrEP 89*
Powdrill, Gary Leo 1945- *WhoWor 91*
Powell, Adam Clayton 1908-1972 *BioIn 16*
Powell, Adam Clayton, Jr. 1908-1972 *BlkAmsC [port], WorAlBi*
Powell, Alan 1928- *WhoAm 90*
Powell, Albert Henry *BiDrAPA 89*
Powell, Albert M, Jr. *BiDrAPA 89*
Powell, Allen Peter *BiDrAPA 89*
Powell, Andrew J *BiDrAPA 89*
Powell, Anice Carpenter 1928- *WhoAm 90, WhoAmW 91, WhoSSW 91*
Powell, Ann 1951- *BioIn 16*
Powell, Annabelle Council 1953- *WhoEmL 91*
Powell, Anthony 1905- *BioIn 16, ConAu 32NR, MajTwCW*
Powell, Anthony 1935- *ConDes 90*
Powell, Anthony Dymoke 1905- *WhoWor 91*
Powell, Arlene Karr *IntWWM 90*
Powell, Barbara 1929- *WhoAmW 91*
Powell, Barbara Jean 1949- *WhoWrEP 89*
Powell, Barry Bruce 1942- *WhoAm 90*
Powell, Betsy Sue 1963- *WhoAmW 91*
Powell, Betty Jo 1938- *BiDrAPA 89*
Powell, Beverly Jo 1940- *WhoWrEP 89*
Powell, Bill Jake 1936- *WhoAm 90*
Powell, Bob 1917?-1967 *EncACom*
Powell, Bolling Raines, Jr. 1910- *WhoAm 90*
Powell, Boog 1941- *Ballpl 90 [port]*
Powell, Bruce 1952- *WhoE 91*
Powell, Bud 1924-1966 *BioIn 16, OxCPMus, WorAlBi*
Powell, C. Wesley *St&PR 91N*
Powell, Carl E. 1945- *St&PR 91*
Powell, Carol Christine 1941- *WhoAmW 91, WhoWor 91*
Powell, Carol W 1925- *BiDrAPA 89*
Powell, Carolyn Smith 1939- *WhoSSW 91*
Powell, Carolyn Wilkerson 1920- *WhoAmW 91*
Powell, Cecil F. 1903-1969 *WorAlBi*
Powell, Charles Roland 1940- *WhoSSW 91*
Powell, Claire 1954- *IntWWM 90*
Powell, Clinton Cobb 1918- *WhoAm 90*
Powell, Colin 1937- *News 90 [port]*
Powell, Colin J. 1937- *WorAlBi*
Powell, Colin L. *BioIn 16*
Powell, Colin Luther 1937 *NewYTBS 90 [port], WhoAm 90*
Powell, Cornelius Patrick 1931- *St&PR 91*
Powell, Curtis Everett 1961- *WhoSSW 91*
Powell, Cynthia Anne 1958- *WhoWrEP 89*
Powell, Dan T 1950- *WhoAmA 91*
Powell, Daniel Thomas 1947- *St&PR 91*
Powell, Darrell M. 1950- *St&PR 91*
Powell, David *WhoAm 90*
Powell, David Alexander *BiDrAPA 89*
Powell, David G. *ODwPR 91*
Powell, David Greatorex 1933- *St&PR 91, WhoAm 90*
Powell, David L. 1951- *St&PR 91*
Powell, David Raymond 1956- *WhoSSW 91*
Powell, David Thomas, Jr. 1941- *WhoSSW 91*
Powell, Dawn 1897-1965 *FemiCLE*
Powell, Dennis 1963- *Ballpl 90*
Powell, Dennis Darrel 1952- *WhoSSW 91*
Powell, Diana Kearny 1910- *WhoAmW 91, WhoWor 91*
Powell, Diane Elaine 1955- *WhoAmW 91*
Powell, Diane Hannacy *BiDrAPA 89*
Powell, Dick 1904-1963 *OxCPMus, WorAlBi*
Powell, Dionne R. *BiDrAPA 89*
Powell, Doane 1881-1951 *WhoAmA 91N*
Powell, Don Graber 1939- *WhoAm 90, WhoSSW 91*
Powell, Don Watson 1938- *WhoAm 90*
Powell, Donald D. *BioIn 16*
Powell, Donald George 1932- *St&PR 91*
Powell, Drexel Dwane, Jr. 1944- *WhoAm 90*
Powell, Earl 1924- *DrBlPA 90*
Powell, Earl 1924-1966 *BioIn 16*
Powell, Earl Alexander, III 1943- *WhoAmA 91*
Powell, Edmund William 1922- *WhoAm 90*
Powell, Edward C. 1932- *St&PR 91*
Powell, Edward Earle 1935- *WhoSSW 91*
Powell, Edward Lee, I 1958- *WhoEmL 91*
Powell, Eleanor 1910- *OxCPMus*
Powell, Eleanor 1912-1982 *WorAlBi*
Powell, Elizabeth 1943- *WhoAmW 91*
Powell, Ellis T 1869-1922 *EncO&P 3*
Powell, Enid Levinger 1931- *WhoWrEP 89*
Powell, Ernestine Breisch 1906- *WhoAmW 91, WhoWor 91*
Powell, Evan 1881- *EncO&P 3*
Powell, Evan Arnold 1937- *WhoAm 90*
Powell, Everett G. 1934- *WhoSSW 91*
Powell, Felix 1878-1942 *OxCPMus*
Powell, Frank James 1934- *St&PR 91*
Powell, Garry Wayne 1945- *BiDrAPA 89*
Powell, George A. 1926- *St&PR 91*
Powell, George E., Jr. 1926- *St&PR 91*
Powell, George Everett, III 1948- *St&PR 91, WhoAm 90*
Powell, George Lyndon 1937- *WhoSSW 91*
Powell, George Van Tuyl 1910- *WhoAm 90*
Powell, Gerald Wayne 1957- *BiDrAPA 89*
Powell, Gordon 1947- *WhoAmA 91*
Powell, Grosvenor 1932- *ConAu 129*
Powell, H. Robert 1926- *St&PR 91*
Powell, Hampton Oliver 1911- *WhoAm 90*
Powell, Harold 1932- *WhoSSW 91*
Powell, Harold Fryburg 1932- *WhoAm 90*
Powell, Harvard Wendell 1915- *WhoAm 90*
Powell, Hosken 1955- *Ballpl 90*
Powell, Huw David 1959- *WhoE 91*
Powell, Ida Berger 1936- *WhoSSW 91*
Powell, Ivor Blake 1943- *WhoWor 91*
Powell, Jack *Ballpl 90*
Powell, Jack 1874-1944 *Ballpl 90*
Powell, Jack, Jr. *ODwPR 91*
Powell, Jake 1908-1948 *Ballpl 90*
Powell, James *PenDiDA 89*
Powell, James 1932- *TwCCr&M 91*
Powell, James Bobbitt 1938- *St&PR 91, WhoAm 90, WhoSSW 91, WhoWor 91*
Powell, James Dixie 1938- *WhoSSW 91*
Powell, James Henry 1928- *WhoAm 90*
Powell, James Lawrence 1936- *WhoAm 90*
Powell, James Leon 1957- *WhoSSW 91*
Powell, James Lester 1955- *WhoSSW 91*
Powell, James Matthew 1930- *WhoAm 90*
Powell, James Meyers, Jr. *BiDrAPA 89*
Powell, James Vernon, Jr. 1922- *WhoSSW 91*
Powell, Jane 1929- *BioIn 16, OxCPMus, WorAlBi*
Powell, Jay R. 1935- *St&PR 91*
Powell, Jeffrey David 1946- *St&PR 91*
Powell, Jerry T. 1933- *WhoAm 90*
Powell, Jerry W. 1950- *St&PR 91*
Powell, Jim Wayne 1952- *WhoSSW 91*
Powell, John Edward, Jr. 1955- *WhoE 91*
Powell, John Hardman *PenDiDA 89*
Powell, John Hardman 1827-1895 *BioIn 16*
Powell, John Preston *BiDrAPA 89*
Powell, John Wesley 1834-1902 *WhNaAH*
Powell, Joseph Edward 1952- *WhoWrEP 89*
Powell, Joseph Lester 1943- *WhoAm 90*
Powell, Joy Lee 1936- *WhoAmW 91, WhoSSW 91, WhoWor 91*
Powell, June Annette *BiDrAPA 89*
Powell, Karan Hinman 1953- *WhoAmW 91*
Powell, Karin Maria *BiDrAPA 89*
Powell, Kenneth Edward 1952- *WhoEmL 91*
Powell, Kenneth F 1923- *EncO&P 3*
Powell, Kent D. 1946- *St&PR 91*
Powell, Kent Leighton 1935- *BiDrAPA 89*
Powell, Kit 1937- *IntWWM 90*
Powell, Larson Merrill 1932- *WhoE 91*
Powell, Lawrence Clark 1906- *BioIn 16*
Powell, Lee Jackson 1939- *St&PR 91*
Powell, Leslie Charles, Jr. 1927- *WhoAm 90*
Powell, Lewis F., Jr. 1907- *WorAlBi*
Powell, Lewis Franklin, III 1952- *WhoEmL 91*
Powell, Lewis Franklin, Jr. 1907- *WhoAm 90, WhoE 91*
Powell, Lillian Marie 1927- *WhoE 91*
Powell, Lois Cecile 1941- *WhoE 91*
Powell, Lori Jean 1962- *WhoE 91*
Powell, Louis 1923- *WhoAm 90*
Powell, Louise Matilda 1871-1943 *BioIn 16*
Powell, Loyd Earl, Jr. 1928- *WhoAm 90*
Powell, Lydia Bond 1892-1978 *WhoAmA 91N*
Powell, M. Elaine 1954- *WhoAmW 91, WhoSSW 91*
Powell, Marcia *ODwPR 91*
Powell, Marjorie Ann 1933- *WhoAmW 91*
Powell, Mary Louise Wells 1935- *WhoAmW 91*
Powell, Maud 1868-1920 *BioAmW, PenDiMP*
Powell, Maxwell M. 1916- *St&PR 91*
Powell, Mel *WhoAm 90*
Powell, Mel 1923- *BioIn 16, IntWWM 90*
Powell, Melanie K. 1957- *WhoAmW 91*
Powell, Melchior Daniel 1935- *WhoWor 91*
Powell, Michael 1905-1990 *BioIn 16, ConAu 130, CurBio 90N, NewYTBS 90 [port]*
Powell, Michael Calvin 1954- *WhoEmL 91*
Powell, Miles, Jr. 1926- *St&PR 91*
Powell, Norborne Berkeley 1914- *WhoAm 90*
Powell, Norman Jimmie 1932- *St&PR 91*
Powell, Norman R. 1939- *St&PR 91*
Powell, Pamela Sue *WhoAmW 91*
Powell, Paul A. 1912- *St&PR 91*
Powell, Paul Byrne 1927- *St&PR 91*
Powell, Peggy Jean 1933- *WhoAmW 91*
Powell, Peggy Nance 1940- *WhoAmW 91*
Powell, Philip 1921- *WhoWor 91*
Powell, Philip Gordon 1951- *WhoSSW 91*
Powell, Philip Wayne 1913-1987 *BioIn 16*
Powell, Ray 1888-1962 *Ballpl 90*
Powell, Richard Cortland 1953- *WhoE 91, WhoWor 91*
Powell, Richard Gordon 1918- *WhoAm 90*
Powell, Richard Pitts 1908- *WhoAm 90, WhoWor 91, WhoWrEP 89*
Powell, Richard Wayne 1958- *BiDrAPA 89*
Powell, Robert C 1948- *BiDrAPA 89*
Powell, Robert Charles 1948- *WhoEmL 91*
Powell, Robert Ellis 1936- *WhoAm 90*
Powell, Robert Everett 1934- *WhoSSW 91*
Powell, Robert J. 1948- *St&PR 91*
Powell, Robert M 1926- *BiDrAPA 89*
Powell, Robert Morgan 1934- *St&PR 91*
Powell, Robert Wendell, Jr. 1930- *St&PR 91, WhoAm 90*
Powell, Roberta A. 1952- *WhoEmL 91*
Powell, Roger Gant 1949- *WhoE 91*
Powell, Rosalie 1947- *WhoAmW 91*
Powell, Ruth Ann 1939- *WhoAmW 91*
Powell, S. Mark 1959- *WhoSSW 91*
Powell, Sandra Theresa 1944- *St&PR 91, WhoAm 90*
Powell, Scott Ashley 1953- *WhoEmL 91*
Powell, Scott R. 1948- *St&PR 91*
Powell, Sharon Lee 1940- *WhoAmW 91*
Powell, Shirley Jean 1946- *WhoSSW 91*
Powell, Stanley, Jr. 1917- *WhoAm 90*
Powell, Susan Wolfe 1942- *WhoAmW 91*
Powell, Talmage 1920- *TwCCr&M 91*
Powell, Taylor *WhoWrEP 89*
Powell, Thomas Edward, III 1936- *St&PR 91*
Powell, Tia P M *BiDrAPA 89*
Powell, Velma E L *BiDrAPA 89*
Powell, Violet *BioIn 16*
Powell, Virginia E 1927- *BiDrAPA 89*
Powell, W. E., Jr. *BioIn 16*
Powell, W. H. *EncO&P 3*
Powell, W. Kindred, Jr. 1946- *WhoSSW 91*
Powell, Walter Allen 1933- *WhoSSW 91*
Powell, Wayne Bruce 1950- *WhoSSW 91*
Powell, Wellington 1899-1989 *BioIn 16*
Powell, Willard Rees 1926- *WhoAm 90*
Powell, William 1892-1984 *WorAlBi*
Powell, William Arnold, Jr. 1929- *St&PR 91, WhoAm 90, WhoSSW 91, WhoWor 91*
Powell, William Council, Sr. 1948- *WhoSSW 91*
Powell, William Ingram 1933- *St&PR 91*
Powell, William Robert 1936- *St&PR 91*
Powell, William Rossell, Jr. 1926- *WhoAm 90*
Powell, William S *BiDrAPA 89*
Powell, Williams Albert 1935- *St&PR 91*
Powell, Zakiya *BioIn 16*
Powell-Smith, Vincent 1939- *ConAu 30NR*
Powelson, James S. 1931- *St&PR 91*
Powelson, John Palen 1920- *WhoAm 90*
Powelson, Keith D 1922- *BiDrAPA 89*
Powelson, Rosemary A *WhoAmA 91*
Powelson, Stephen *BioIn 16*
Power, Benjamin John 1942- *WhoWor 91*
Power, Cornelius Michael 1913- *WhoAm 90*
Power, Daniel Joseph 1950- *WhoEmL 91*
Power, Dennis Michael 1941- *WhoAm 90*
Power, Effie Louise 1873-1969 *AuBYP 90*
Power, Eileen Edna 1889-1940 *BioIn 16*
Power, Elizabeth Henry 1953- *WhoAmW 91*
Power, Eugene Barnum 1905- *WhoAm 90*
Power, F. William 1925- *St&PR 91, WhoAm 90*
Power, Ian D. 1954- *St&PR 91*
Power, J. David, III *BioIn 16*
Power, James Moore 1925- *St&PR 91*
Power, Jo-Ann 1944- *St&PR 91*
Power, Joanne 1949- *WhoAmW 91*
Power, Joel R. 1939- *ODwPR 91*
Power, John Bruce 1936- *WhoAm 90*
Power, John George 1932- *St&PR 91*
Power, John Richard 1940- *WhoE 91*
Power, Jonathan Richard A. 1941- *WhoWor 91*
Power, Joseph Edward 1938- *WhoAm 90*
Power, Joyce Helene 1946- *WhoAmW 91*
Power, Jules 1921- *WhoAm 90*
Power, Karen Elizabeth 1966- *WhoAmW 91*
Power, M S 1935- *ConAu 130*
Power, Marian Traina 1940- *WhoAmW 91*
Power, Marjorie 1947- *WhoWrEP 89*
Power, Mark 1937- *WhoAm 90, WhoAmA 91*
Power, Mary Susan 1935- *WhoAm 90*
Power, Michael Joseph 1834-1895 *DcCanB 12*
Power, Norma Jean 1928- *WhoAmW 91*
Power, Richard Dunstan 1948- *St&PR 91*
Power, Robert Harbison 1926- *WhoAm 90*
Power, S Brenda Joan 1941- *WhoAmA 91*
Power, Sean *BioIn 16*
Power, Stephen H. 1939- *St&PR 91*
Power, Susan Cantrell 1944- *WhoAmW 91*
Power, Ted 1955- *Ballpl 90*
Power, Thomas Edward 1946- *WhoSSW 91*
Power, Thomas F. 1916-1988 *BioIn 16*

Power, Thomas Francis, Jr. 1940- *St&PR 91, WhoAm 90*
Power, Thomas Joseph 1830-1893 *DcCanB 12*
Power, Thomas Michael 1940- *WhoAm 90*
Power, Tyrone 1913-1958 *WorAlBi*
Power, Vic 1931- *Ballpl 90*
Power, William Randy 1954- *BiDrAPA 89*
Powers, Allen Edward 1939- *St&PR 91, WhoAm 90*
Powers, Arthur 1947- *WhoSSW 91*
Powers, Arthur Jay 1926- *St&PR 91*
Powers, Arthur Sutherland 1947- *St&PR 91*
Powers, Ben *DrBlPA 90*
Powers, Bertram Anthony 1922- *WhoE 91*
Powers, Bill 1931- *BioIn 16*
Powers, Bruce Raymond 1927- *WhoAm 90, WhoE 91*
Powers, Charles Henri 1945- *WhoAm 90*
Powers, Darden 1932- *WhoAm 90*
Powers, Daryle Lynn 1960- *WhoAmW 91*
Powers, David Alton 1948- *WhoSSW 91*
Powers, David Leusch 1939- *WhoE 91*
Powers, Dennis Alpha 1938- *WhoAm 90*
Powers, Dennis W. 1942- *St&PR 91*
Powers, Diane 1943- *St&PR 91*
Powers, Don Arba Horace 1850-1917 *AmLegL*
Powers, Donald T 1950- *WhoAmA 91*
Powers, Doris Hurt 1927- *WhoAmW 91*
Powers, Douglas F *BiDrAPA 89*
Powers, Dudley 1911- *WhoAm 90*
Powers, Edward *BioIn 16*
Powers, Edward Alton 1927- *WhoAm 90*
Powers, Edward D. 1932- *St&PR 91*
Powers, Edward Latell 1919- *WhoAm 90*
Powers, Edwin Malvin 1915- *WhoE 91*
Powers, Ernest Michael 1942- *WhoAm 90, WhoWor 91*
Powers, Eula Evelina *BiDrAPA 89*
Powers, Francis Gary 1929-1977 *WorAlBi*
Powers, Francis Henry 1940- *St&PR 91*
Powers, Frederick Wayne 1951- *St&PR 91*
Powers, George Harold 1919- *BiDrAPA 89*
Powers, Georgia M. 1923- *WhoSSW 91*
Powers, Gerald William 1940- *WhoE 91*
Powers, Harris Pat 1934- *WhoAm 90*
Powers, Henry Martin 1932- *St&PR 91*
Powers, Henry Martin, Jr. 1932- *WhoAm 90*
Powers, Hiram 1805-1873 *WorAlBi*
Powers, Horace Henry 1835-1913 *AmLegL*
Powers, J. F. 1917- *BioIn 16*
Powers, J F 1917- *MajTwCW*
Powers, James Bascom 1924- *WhoAm 90*
Powers, James Farl 1917- *BioIn 16, WhoAm 90, WhoWrEP 89*
Powers, James Francis 1938- *St&PR 91, WhoAm 90*
Powers, James T. 1862-1943 *OxCPMus*
Powers, Janice Gwyn 1959- *WhoSSW 91*
Powers, Jefrey R. 1959- *St&PR 91*
Powers, Jessica *BioIn 16*
Powers, Jimmy *Ballpl 90*
Powers, JoAnne Patricia 1953- *WhoAmW 91*
Powers, John A. 1926- *St&PR 91*
Powers, John Austin 1926- *WhoAm 90*
Powers, John Edward 1930- *St&PR 91*
Powers, John G., Jr. 1930- *WhoAm 90*
Powers, John J. *St&PR 91*
Powers, John Joseph 1918- *WhoSSW 91*
Powers, John Joseph 1935- *St&PR 91*
Powers, John Kieran 1947- *WhoE 91, WhoWor 91*
Powers, John Michael, Jr. 1951- *St&PR 91*
Powers, John R. 1896-1977 *WorAlBi*
Powers, John R. 1945- *WhoAm 90, WhoWrEP 89*
Powers, John W. 1938- *St&PR 91*
Powers, Joshua B. *BioIn 16*
Powers, Kathleen Anne 1941- *WhoAmW 91*
Powers, Larry K. 1942- *St&PR 91*
Powers, Laura Beth 1950- *WhoAmW 91*
Powers, Lawrence M. 1931- *St&PR 91*
Powers, Leslie Lynne 1948- *BiDrAPA 89*
Powers, Llewellyn 1836-1908 *AmLegL*
Powers, Mala 1931- *ConAu 129, WhoAm 90*
Powers, Marcus E. 1929- *St&PR 91*
Powers, Marcus Eugene 1929- *WhoAm 90*
Powers, Marie Mintzer 1955- *WhoSSW 91*
Powers, Marilyn 1925-1976 *WhoAmA 91N*
Powers, Mark Hugh *BiDrAPA 89*
Powers, Mary Ann 1959- *WhoAmW 91*
Powers, Mary Swift 1885-1959 *WhoAmA 91N*
Powers, Michael Francis *BioIn 16*
Powers, Michael Kevin 1948- *WhoE 91*
Powers, Mike 1870-1909 *Ballpl 90*
Powers, N. Thompson 1929- *WhoAm 90*
Powers, Nan Margaret 1956- *WhoSSW 91*
Powers, Nancy Louisa 1948- *WhoEmL 91*
Powers, Nora *ConAu 130*
Powers, Odell E. *St&PR 91*
Powers, Paul Joseph 1935- *St&PR 91, WhoAm 90*
Powers, Pauline Smith 1941- *BiDrAPA 89*
Powers, Philip Hemsley 1937- *WhoSSW 91*
Powers, Philip Nathan 1912-1988 *BioIn 16*
Powers, Ralph A., Jr. 1936- *St&PR 91*
Powers, Rebecca Elizabeth 1947- *WhoAmW 91*
Powers, Richard Dale 1927- *WhoAm 90*
Powers, Richard Edward *BiDrAPA 89*
Powers, Richard Ralph 1940- *WhoAm 90*
Powers, Richard T. 1947- *St&PR 91*
Powers, Robert A. 1918- *St&PR 91*
Powers, Robert Allan 1926- *St&PR 91, WhoAm 90*
Powers, Ronald Clair 1934- *WhoAm 90*
Powers, Ronald George 1934- *WhoWor 91*
Powers, Samuel Joseph, Jr. 1917- *WhoAm 90*
Powers, Shirley Marie 1930- *WhoAmW 91*
Powers, Stefanie 1942- *BioIn 16, WhoAm 90, WorAlBi*
Powers, Stephen L 1944- *BiDrAPA 89*
Powers, Theodore Richard 1932- *St&PR 91*
Powers, Theodore Taylor 1867-1938 *AmLegL*
Powers, Thomas E. 1808-1876 *AmLegL*
Powers, Thomas E. 1929- *St&PR 91*
Powers, Thomas Lynwood 1947- *WhoSSW 91*
Powers, Thomas Moore 1940- *WhoAm 90, WhoWrEP 89*
Powers, Thomas Warren 1935- *WhoAm 90*
Powers, W Alex 1940- *WhoAmA 91*
Powers, Walter E. 1941- *St&PR 91*
Powers, William Edmonds 1907-1989 *BioIn 16*
Powers, William Jennings 1930- *WhoAm 90*
Powers, William Joseph 1951- *WhoEmL 91*
Powers, William Shotwell 1910- *WhoAm 90*
Powers-Craig, Pamela Elisabeth 1962- *WhoAmW 91*
Powerscourt, Sheila *ConAu 130*
Powhatan 1547?-1618 *WhNaAH*
Powhatan 1550?-1618 *EncCRAm*
Powis, Alfred *BioIn 16*
Powis, Alfred 1930- *St&PR 91, WhoAm 90*
Powlen, David Michael 1953- *WhoEmL 91*
Powles, David Edward 1948- *BiDrAPA 89*
Powles, John G. 1936- *St&PR 91*
Powles, Raymond Leonard 1938- *WhoWor 91*
Powles, William E 1919- *BiDrAPA 89*
Powley, Donald 1955- *WhoAmA 91*
Powley, George Reinhold 1916- *WhoAm 90*
Powley, Harrison E., III 1943- *IntWWM 90*
Powlus, Lee Carson 1960- *WhoE 91*
Pownall, James Richard 1951- *WhoE 91, WhoWor 91*
Pownall, Malcolm Wilmor 1933- *WhoAm 90*
Pownall, Thomas 1722-1805 *EncCRAm*
Pownall, Thomas G. 1922- *St&PR 91*
Powning, Maynard W. 1931- *St&PR 91*
Powolny, Michael 1871-1954 *PenDiDA 89*
Powser, John D. 1946- *St&PR 91*
Powsner, Daniel Joseph 1948- *BiDrAPA 89, WhoE 91*
Powsner, Seth M 1953- *BiDrAPA 89*
Powys, Caroline 1738-1817 *FemiCLE*
Powys, Elizabeth *BiDEWW*
Powys, John Cowper 1872-1963 *MajTwCW*
Powys, Llewelyn 1884-1939 *DcLB 98 [port]*
Poyant, Dennis Richard 1950- *WhoE 91*
Poydasheff, Robert S. 1930- *St&PR 91*
Poydock, Mary Eymard 1910- *WhoAm 90*
Poyer, David 1949- *ConAu 30NR, WhoWrEP 89*
Poyer, Joseph John 1939- *SpyFic*
Poyner, James Marion 1914- *WhoAm 90*
Poynor, James Madison, Jr. 1931- *WhoWor 91*
Poynter, Daniel Frank 1938- *WhoWrEP 89*
Poynter, Marion Knauss 1926- *WhoAm 90, WhoAmW 91, WhoE 91*
Poynter, Melissa Venable 1949- *WhoAmW 91, WhoSSW 91*
Poynter, Nelson 1903-1978 *BioIn 16*
Poynton, John Charles 1931- *EncPaPR 91*
Poyntz, Anne B. *FemiCLE*
Poyntz, Francis *PenDiDA 89*
Poyntz, Mary *BiDEWW*
Poythress, David Bryan 1943- *WhoAm 90*
Poythress, Stephanie Lynn 1964- *WhoAmW 91*
Poza, Ernesto J. 1950- *WhoEmL 91*
Poza, Margarita 1948- *WhoHisp 91*
Pozdro, John Walter 1923- *IntWWM 90, WhoAm 90*
Pozen, Robert Charles 1946- *St&PR 91*
Pozen, Walter 1933- *WhoAm 90*
Pozil, Paul L. 1938- *St&PR 91*
Poznanski, Andrew Karol 1931- *WhoAm 90*
Poznanski, Elva O 1933- *BiDrAPA 89*
Poznanski, Elva Orlow 1933- *WhoAm 90*
Pozner, Vladimir 1934- *BestSel 90-3 [port]*
Pozniakoff, Rita Oppenheim 1949- *WhoAmW 91*
Pozos, Anthony Martin 1940- *St&PR 91*
Pozsgay, Imre *BioIn 16*
Pozsgay, Imre 1933- *CurBio 90 [port]*
Pozycki, Harry Steven, Jr. 1947- *WhoEmL 91*
Pozza, Duane Charles 1953- *St&PR 91*
Pozza, Ronald William 1964- *WhoE 91*
Pozzatti, Rudy O 1925- *WhoAmA 91*
Pozzatti, Rudy Otto 1925- *WhoAm 90*
Pozzi, Antonia 1912-1938 *EncCoWW*
Pozzi, Bruce *ODwPR 91*
Pozzi, Catherine 1882-1934 *EncCoWW*
Pozzi, Lucio 1935- *News 90 [port], WhoAmA 91*
Pozzilli, Paolo Paride 1951- *WhoWor 91*
Pozzo, Andrea 1642-1709 *IntDcAA 90*
Pozzo, Jorge 1926- *WhoWor 91*
Pozzo, Modesta 1555-1592 *EncCoWW*
Prabhakaran, Nagarajan 1955- *WhoSSW 91*
Prabhavati Gupta *WomWR*
Prabhu, Catherine Dudley 1941- *WhoE 91*
Prabhu, Manjeshwar R *BiDrAPA 89*
Prabhu, Nileshwar Damodar 1931- *WhoWor 91*
Prabhu, Ravindranath Gopala 1952- *WhoWor 91*
Prabhudesai, Sarita M *BiDrAPA 89*
Prabhupada, Swami 1896-1977 *WorAlBi*
Prabhupada, A. C. Bhaktivedanta 1896-1977 *BioIn 16*
Prachar, Karl 1925- *WhoWor 91*
Prachner, Gottfried 1920- *WhoWor 91*
Pracht, Irena 1927- *WhoAmW 91*
Praczukowski, Edward Leon 1930- *WhoAmA 91*
Prada, Alberto Armando 1962- *WhoWor 91*
Prada, Antonio J. 1946- *WhoHisp 91*
Prada, German Virgilio *BiDrAPA 89*
Prada, Manuel Gonzalez *HispWr 90*
Prada, Manuel Gonzalez 1844-1918 *BioIn 16*
Prada Oropeza, Renato 1937- *ConAu 32NR, HispWr 90*
Prade, Jean Noel 1946- *WhoSSW 91, WhoWor 91*
Praderio, Nestor Hugo *BiDrAPA 89*
Pradhan, Ashwini *BiDrAPA 89*
Pradhan, Goraksha Bahadur N. 1929- *WhoWor 91*
Pradhan, Pemala Suhas *BiDrAPA 89*
Pradhan, Prakash V *BiDrAPA 89*
Pradier, Jerome Martin 1947- *WhoSSW 91*
Prado, Antonio G. 1945- *St&PR 91*
Prado, Bessie A. 1953- *WhoHisp 91*
Prado, Cesar, Jr. 1945- *WhoHisp 91*
Prado, Faustino Lucio 1946- *WhoHisp 91*
Prado, Gerald M. 1946- *St&PR 91, WhoAm 90*
Prado, Huberto W 1940- *BiDrAPA 89*
Prado, Jesus M. *WhoHisp 91*
Prado, Jorge Del 1910- *BioIn 16*
Prado, Luis Antonio 1948- *WhoHisp 91*
Prado, Marta 1951- *WhoHisp 91*
Prado, Monica *ODwPR 91*
Prado, Neilton Gonccalve 1940- *WhoWor 91*
Prado, Oscar G *BiDrAPA 89*
Prado, Pedro 1886-1952 *BioIn 16, ConAu 131, HispWr 90*
Prado, Perez 1916-1989 *OxCPMus*
Prado, Vasco 1914- *ArtLatA*
Prado Ugarteche, Manuel 1889-1967 *BioIn 16*
Prados, John William 1929- *WhoAm 90*
Pradt, Louis A. 1931- *St&PR 91*
Praed, Rosa 1851-1935 *FemiCLE*
Praed, Winthrop Mackworth 1802-1839 *DcLB 96 [port]*
Praeger, Donald Lewis 1933- *WhoAm 90, WhoE 91*
Praeger, Frederick A. 1915- *St&PR 91, WhoAmA 91*
Praeger, Frederick Amos 1915- *WhoAm 90*
Praeger, Herman Albert, Jr. 1920- *WhoWor 91*
Praeger, Mary Wallace 1908- *WhoAmW 91*
Praet, Peter 1949- *WhoWor 91*
Praetorius, William Albert, Sr. 1924- *WhoAm 90*
Prag, Shula Mamie 1958- *WhoE 91*
Pragacz, Susan Ann 1952- *WhoAmW 91*
Prager, David 1918- *WhoAm 90*
Prager, David A 1913- *WhoAmA 91*
Prager, Iris J. 1944- *St&PR 91*
Prager, Jane Price *BiDrAPA 89*
Prager, Mindy Ellen 1961- *BiDrAPA 89*
Prager, Paul G. 1941- *St&PR 91*
Prager, Stanley Edward 1955- *WhoE 91*
Prager, Stephen 1928- *WhoAm 90*
Prager, Susan Westerberg 1942- *WhoAm 90*
Prager, Ulrich 1916- *WhoWor 91*
Prager-Benett, Nancy Ann 1945- *WhoAmW 91*
Prague German Quartet *PenDiMP*
Prah, Pamela M. 1963- *WhoE 91*
Prahl, Richard D. 1945- *St&PR 91*
Prahl-Andersen, Birte 1939- *WhoWor 91*
Prahler, Richard Joseph 1946- *St&PR 91*
Prairie Sage, The *WhoWrEP 89*
Prairie, Celia Esther Freda 1940- *WhoE 91*
Prairie, James R. 1926- *St&PR 91*
Prais, John Peter 1945- *St&PR 91*
Prakap, William A. 1955- *St&PR 91*
Prakapas, Eugene Joseph 1932- *WhoAmA 91, WhoE 91*
Prakash, Aruna Kasturi 1958- *WhoSSW 91*
Prakash, Corazon A P *BiDrAPA 89*
Prakash, Narayan 1956- *BiDrAPA 89*
Prakash, Om 1933- *BiDrAPA 89*
Prakash, Prabha *BiDrAPA 89*
Prakash, Ravi 1941- *WhoAm 90*
Prakash, Rudra 1951- *BiDrAPA 89*
Prakash, Satya 1938- *WhoAm 90*
Prakash, Shanti 1928- *WhoE 91*
Prakash, Shashi *BiDrAPA 89*
Prakash, Surya G.K. 1953- *WhoEmL 91*
Prakash, Ved 1932- *WhoWor 91*
Prakken, Lawrence W. 1908-1987 *BioIn 16*
Prakup, Barbara Lynn 1957- *WhoAmW 91*
Prall, Ivan E. *BioIn 16*
Prall, Robert C 1918- *BiDrAPA 89*
Pralong, Sandra 1958- *WhoAmW 91*
Pramanik, Pushpita Dalal *BiDrAPA 89*
Pramberg, James Cook 1955- *WhoSSW 91*
Pramer, David 1923- *WhoAm 90*
Pramesa, Johnny 1925- *Ballpl 90*
Pramuk, Albert S. 1927- *St&PR 91*
Pramuk, Edward Richard 1936- *WhoAmA 91*
Pran Dith *BioIn 16*
Pran, Peter Christian 1935- *WhoAm 90*
Prance, Ghillean Tolmie 1937- *WhoWor 91*
Prance, June E. *WhoWrEP 89*
Prandtl, Ludwig 1875-1953 *WorAlBi*
Prang, Louis 1824-1909 *BioIn 16*
Prange, Arthur Jergen, Jr. 1926- *BiDrAPA 89, WhoAm 90*
Prange, Henry C. 1927- *St&PR 91*
Prange, Henry Carl 1927- *WhoAm 90*
Prange, Marnie 1953- *WhoWrEP 89*
Prange, Raymon A. 1921- *St&PR 91*
Prange, Sally Bowen 1927- *WhoAmA 91*
Pranger, Margaret A 1922- *BiDrAPA 89*
Pranke, Susan Ann 1957- *WhoAmW 91*
Pranses, Anthony Louis 1920- *WhoAm 90*
Pranske, Alfred A. 1926- *St&PR 91*
Prantera, Amanda 1942- *ConAu 130*
Prantl, Pavel 1945- *IntWWM 90*
Pranzo, Gary G. *BioIn 16*
Pranzo, Gary G. 1932- *WhoAm 90*
Pras, Robert Thomas 1941- *St&PR 91*
Prasad, Ananda Shiva 1928- *WhoAm 90*
Prasad, Brij 1942- *St&PR 91*
Prasad, C. M. 1948- *BiDrAPA 89*
Prasad, Indirarani D 1952- *BiDrAPA 89*
Prasad, Jamuna 1915- *EncPaPR 91*
Prasad, Jonnalagadda Venkata Rama 1953- *WhoSSW 91*
Prasad, Kali 1901- *EncO&P 3*
Prasad, Karipineni *BiDrAPA 89*
Prasad, Lakshman *BiDrAPA 89*
Prasad, Prem S 1935- *BiDrAPA 89*
Prasad, R Bhawani 1949- *BiDrAPA 89*
Prasad, Renuka N *BiDrAPA 89*
Prasad, Sankarshan 1933- *St&PR 91*
Prasad, Vemireddi S. K. 1948- *BiDrAPA 89*
Prasad, Yarlagadda Krishna 1945- *BiDrAPA 89*
Prasetio, Gunawan 1943- *WhoWor 91*
Prashker, Betty A. *WhoWrEP 89*
Prass, Richard E. 1931- *St&PR 91*
Prasse, Ronald D. 1938- *St&PR 91*
Prassel, Frank G. 1912- *St&PR 91*
Prasser, Donald O *BiDrAPA 89*
Prast, Leslie Louise 1946- *WhoAmW 91*
Prast, Robert F. 1939- *St&PR 91*
Prat de la Riba, Enric 1870-1917 *BioIn 16*
Prata, Enrico Alfonso 1945- *WhoE 91*
Prata Barros, Mario Alberto De 1953- *WhoWor 91*
Pratarotti, Antonio *BiDrAPA 89*
Prater, Charles Dwight 1917- *WhoAm 90*
Prater, Dave 1937-1988 *BioIn 16*
Prater, John *AuBYP 90*
Prater, John Edward 1938- *St&PR 91*
Prater, John Forrest *BiDrAPA 89*
Prater, Larry Michael 1944- *BiDrAPA 89*
Prater, N. H. *BioIn 16*

Prater, Nilon Houston 1928- *St&PR 91*
Prater, Robert W. 1930- *St&PR 91*
Prater, Ruby Marian 1915- *WhoWrEP 89*
Prater, William J. *BioIn 16*
Prater-Harvey, Peggy 1949- *St&PR 91*
Prather, Donna Lynn 1946- *BiDrAPA 89*
Prather, Gerald L. 1935- *WhoAm 90*
Prather, John Gideon, Jr. 1946- *WhoEmL 91*
Prather, John William *BiDrAPA 89*
Prather, Lenore Loving 1931- *WhoAm 90, WhoAmW 91*
Prather, Ray *BioIn 16*
Prather, Richard S 1921- *TwCCr&M 91*
Prather, Samuel W. 1937- *St&PR 91*
Prather, Susan L. *ODwPR 91*
Prather, Susan Lynn *WhoAmW 91*
Prather, William Chalmers 1921- *WhoWor 91*
Prather, William E. 1947- *WhoSSW 91*
Prati, Renato S, Jr. 1936- *BiDrAPA 89*
Pratley, Geoffrey Charles 1940- *IntWWM 90*
Prato, Nancy Rutter Henry 1935- *WhoAmW 91*
Pratola, Stephanie 1952- *WhoAmW 91*
Pratolini, Vasco 1913- *BioIn 16*
Prats, Christopher Thomas 1941- *WhoHisp 91*
Prats, Jorge Luis 1956- *IntWWM 90*
Prats, Juan Prim y 1814-1870 *BioIn 16*
Pratt, Alan John 1927- *WhoWor 91*
Pratt, Albert 1911- *WhoAm 90*
Pratt, Alice Reynolds 1922- *WhoAmW 91, WhoWor 91*
Pratt, Arnold W. 1920- *WhoAm 90*
Pratt, Babe 1916-1988 *BioIn 16*
Pratt, Billy Kenton 1948- *WhoSSW 91*
Pratt, Burt Carlton 1911- *WhoAm 90*
Pratt, Cary Lynn 1958- *WhoSSW 91*
Pratt, Charles *BioIn 16*
Pratt, Charles 1830-1891 *WorAlBi*
Pratt, Charles Cade 1943- *WhoAm 90*
Pratt, Christine 1961- *WhoAmW 91*
Pratt, Christopher J. *ODwPR 91*
Pratt, Christopher J. 1949- *St&PR 91*
Pratt, Dallas 1914- *WhoAmA 91*
Pratt, Dan Edwin 1924- *WhoAm 90*
Pratt, Dana Joseph 1926- *WhoAm 90*
Pratt, David D. 1936- *St&PR 91*
Pratt, David Terry 1934- *WhoAm 90*
Pratt, Davis *AuBYP 90*
Pratt, Del 1888-1977 *Ballpl 90 [port]*
Pratt, Diane Adele 1951- *WhoAmW 91*
Pratt, Donald Henry 1937- *St&PR 91, WhoAm 90*
Pratt, Donald Lynn 1942- *WhoE 91*
Pratt, Douglas Frederick 1954- *WhoE 91*
Pratt, Dudley 1897-1975 *WhoAmA 91N*
Pratt, E J 1882-1964 *DcLB 92 [port]*
Pratt, Edmund T., Jr. 1927- *St&PR 91, WhoAm 90, WhoE 91*
Pratt, Edward Taylor, Jr. 1923- *WhoAm 90*
Pratt, Edwin Vincent *BiDrAPA 89*
Pratt, Elizabeth Southwick *WhoAmA 91N*
Pratt, Ellen Marcella Morin 1931- *WhoAmW 91*
Pratt, Felix 1780-1859 *PenDiDA 89*
Pratt, Frances 1913- *WhoAmA 91*
Pratt, Frank Graham, Jr. 1944- *BiDrAPA 89*
Pratt, George 1932- *St&PR 91*
Pratt, George C. 1914-1988 *BioIn 16*
Pratt, George Cheney 1928- *WhoAm 90, WhoE 91*
Pratt, George Malcolm 1935- *IntWWM 90*
Pratt, J G 1910-1979 *EncO&P 3*
Pratt, Jack E., Jr. *WhoAm 90*
Pratt, Jerry *BioIn 16*
Pratt, John Adams, Jr. 1930- *St&PR 91*
Pratt, John Clark 1932- *WhoWrEP 89*
Pratt, John Edward 1945- *WhoWor 91*
Pratt, John Helm 1910- *WhoAm 90*
Pratt, John L. 1906-1968 *AuBYP 90*
Pratt, John Lee 1879-1975 *EncABHB 5 [port]*
Pratt, John M *BiDrAPA 89*
Pratt, John P *BiDrAPA 89*
Pratt, John Winsor 1931- *WhoAm 90*
Pratt, Joseph Gaither 1910-1979 *EncPaPR 91*
Pratt, Lawrence Arthur 1907- *WhoAm 90, WhoWor 91*
Pratt, Margaret Wade 1925- *WhoAmW 91, WhoE 91, WhoWor 91*
Pratt, Marjorie Jean 1936- *WhoWrEP 89*
Pratt, Martha Lee 1957- *WhoAmW 91*
Pratt, Matthew 1734-1805 *EncCRAm*
Pratt, Matthew 1928- *WhoAm 90*
Pratt, Michael Theodore 1943- *WhoAm 90*
Pratt, Murray Fletcher 1897-1956 *AuBYP 90*
Pratt, Orson, Sr. 1811-1881 *AmLegL*
Pratt, Paul W. 1946- *WhoWrEP 89*
Pratt, Philip 1924-1989 *BioIn 16*
Pratt, Philip Chase 1920- *WhoAm 90*
Pratt, R Nicoll, Jr. 1950- *BiDrAPA 89*
Pratt, Rachel Brock *EarBlAP*
Pratt, Richard *BioIn 16*
Pratt, Richard Henry 1840-1924 *WhNaAH*
Pratt, Richard Houghton 1934- *WhoAm 90*
Pratt, Richardson 1923- *BioIn 16*
Pratt, Richardson, Jr. 1923- *WhoAm 90, WhoE 91*
Pratt, Robert A. 1907-1987 *BioIn 16*
Pratt, Robert Cranford 1926- *WhoAm 90*
Pratt, Robert Leonard 1947- *WhoE 91*
Pratt, Robert Marshall 1916-1987 *BioIn 16*
Pratt, Robert Wayne 1967- *WhoSSW 91*
Pratt, Robert Windsor 1950- *WhoEmL 91*
Pratt, Ronald *ODwPR 91*
Pratt, Sharran M. 1940- *WhoAmW 91*
Pratt, Sherwood L. 1932- *St&PR 91*
Pratt, Stephen Philip 1947- *IntWWM 90*
Pratt, Suzanne Garrett 1948- *WhoAmW 91*
Pratt, Terrence Wendall 1940- *WhoAm 90*
Pratt, Vaughan Ronald 1944- *WhoWor 91*
Pratt, Vernon Gaither 1940- *WhoAmA 91*
Pratt, Walter E. 1927- *St&PR 91*
Pratt, Willard 1940- *BioIn 16*
Pratt, William Crouch, Jr. 1927- *WhoAm 90, WhoWrEP 89*
Pratt-Khodabandehloo, Meredith Leigh 1962- *WhoE 91*
Pratte, Deborah Miriam 1952- *WhoEmL 91*
Pratte, Lise *St&PR 91*
Pratte, Louis 1926- *WhoE 91*
Prattis, Charles Maurice 1940- *WhoE 91*
Pratts, Joseph Louis 1960- *IntWWM 90*
Pratty, James S *BiDrAPA 89*
Praus, Douglas James 1960- *BiDrAPA 89*
Prausnitz, Frederik 1920- *PenDiMP*
Prausnitz, Frederik William 1920- *IntWWM 90*
Prausnitz, John Michael 1928- *WhoAm 90*
Pravda, Marvin 1936- *BiDrAPA 89*
Praveenlal, Kuttichira 1955- *BiDrAPA 89*
Praver, Jack 1930- *BiDrAPA 89*
Pravila, Ion *EncCoWW*
Prawer, Harvey Edwin 1938- *St&PR 91*
Prawer, Siegbert Salomon 1925- *WhoWor 91*
Prawiranegara, Sjafruddin 1911-1989 *BioIn 16*
Prawl, Nancy Irene 1942- *WhoAmW 91*
Praxilla *EncCoWW*
Praxiteles *WorAlBi*
Pray, Glen A. *St&PR 91*
Pray, Janet Lorraine 1939- *WhoAmW 91*
Pray, Lloyd Charles 1919- *WhoAm 90*
Pray, Merle Evelyn 1931- *WhoAmW 91*
Pray, Monroe, Jr. *BiDrAPA 89*
Pray, Ralph Marble, III 1938- *WhoAm 90*
Prchal, Vera Marie L *BiDrAPA 89*
Pre, Jacqueline du *PenDiMP*
Preas, Stephen Graham 1947- *BiDrAPA 89*
Preate, Ernest D., Jr. 1940- *WhoAm 90, WhoE 91*
Preate, Ernest D., Sr. 1909- *WhoAm 90*
Prebil, James M. *St&PR 91*
Preble, James J. 1923- *WhoAm 90*
Preble, Laurence George 1939- *WhoAm 90*
Preble, Michael Andrew 1947- *WhoAmA 91*
Preble, Robert C., Jr. 1922- *St&PR 91*
Preblud, Stephen R. *BioIn 16*
Prebluda, Harry Jacob 1911- *WhoAm 90*
Precht, Christian 1706-1779 *PenDiDA 89*
Preckwinkle, George Thomas 1917- *St&PR 91*
Preckwinkle, George Wilburn 1956- *St&PR 91*
Precopio, Frank Mario 1925- *WhoAm 90*
Precourt, Frank Arnold 1929- *St&PR 91*
Precourt, George Augustine 1934- *WhoAm 90, WhoE 91*
Precourt, Jay A. 1937- *St&PR 91*
Pred, Nancy G. 1958- *WhoAmW 91*
Preddy, Raymond Randall 1940- *WhoAm 90, WhoSSW 91*
Predmore, Marian Corinne 1923- *WhoAmW 91*
Predock, Antoine Samuel 1936- *WhoAm 90*
Preece family *BioIn 16*
Preece, David John 1952- *WhoE 91*
Preece, Howard G 1926- *BiDrAPA 89*
Preece, Patricia 1900- *BiDWomA*
Preece, Rodney John 1939- *WhoAm 90*
Preece, Timothy F. 1927- *St&PR 91*
Preece, Warren Eversleigh 1921- *WhoAm 90*
Preede, Nydia 1926- *WhoAmA 91*
Preedy, George *TwCCr&M 91*
Preeg, Ernest Henry 1934- *WhoAm 90*
Preer, Evelyn 1896-1932 *BioIn 16, DrBlPA 90, NotWoAT*
Prefer, Alan 1948- *WhoE 91*
Pregardien, Christoph 1956- *IntWWM 90*
Pregelj, Andrej 1944- *WhoWor 91*
Pregerson, Harry 1923- *WhoAm 90*
Pregl, Fritz 1869-1930 *WorAlBi*
Pregliasco, Janice Lynn 1956- *WhoEmL 91*
Pregnolato, John Anthony 1939- *St&PR 91*
Pregulman, Mervin 1922- *St&PR 91*
Prehn, Ronald Scott 1953- *WhoEmL 91, WhoSSW 91*
Preibisz, Joanne Magdalena *BiDrAPA 89*
Preide, Ruben 1929- *BiDrAPA 89*
Preis, Alfred 1911- *WhoAmA 91*
Preis, Karen 1944- *BiDrAPA 89*
Preis, Paul H. 1933- *St&PR 91*
Preiser, Gert Richard 1928- *WhoWor 91*
Preiser, Stanley 1927- *WhoAm 90*
Preiser, Uriel Zeev 1959- *WhoE 91*
Preiser, Wolfgang Friedrich Ernst 1941- *WhoAm 90*
Preisinger, John Joseph, Jr. 1923- *BiDrAPA 89*
Preiskel, Barbara Scott 1924- *WhoAm 90*
Preiskel, Robert Howard 1922- *WhoAm 90*
Preisman, Richard C 1940- *BiDrAPA 89*
Preiss, Alexandru Petre 1952- *WhoAmA 91*
Preiss, Byron *BioIn 16*
Preiss, David C. 1950- *WhoE 91*
Preiss, David Lee 1935- *WhoAm 90*
Preiss, Frederick Alfred 1938- *WhoE 91*
Preiss, Jack 1932- *WhoAm 90*
Preiss, Lola 1933- *ODwPR 91*
Preiss, Marilyn Briton 1941- *WhoAmW 91*
Preiss, Mitchell Paul 1956- *WhoE 91*
Preissensin, Albrecht *PenDiDA 89*
Preisser, Bernhard F. 1947- *St&PR 91*
Preissler, Daniel 1636-1733 *PenDiDA 89*
Preissova, Gabriela 1862-1946 *EncCoWW*
Prejean, Dalton *BioIn 16*
Prekop, Martin D. 1940- *WhoAm 90*
Prekop, Martin Dennis 1940- *WhoAmA 91*
Prelack, Steven 1957- *St&PR 91*
Prell, Michael Jack 1944- *WhoAm 90*
Preller, Gustav Schoeman 1875-1943 *BioIn 16*
Prelog, Vladimir 1906- *WhoAm 90, WhoWor 91*
Prelutsky, Jack *AuBYP 90, BioIn 16*
Prem Tinsulanonda 1920- *WhoWor 91*
Prem, Frank Herbert, Jr. 1932- *WhoAm 90, WhoE 91*
Prem, Konald Arthur 1920- *WhoAm 90*
Premack, David 1925- *WhoAm 90*
Premack, Irwin Joseph 1927- *WhoSSW 91*
Premadasa, Ranasinghe *BioIn 16*
Premadasa, Ranasinghe 1924- *WhoWor 91*
Premeaux, Lanette Lea 1957- *WhoAmW 91, WhoE 91*
Premer, Isaac Wayne 1923- *St&PR 91*
Premice, Josephine 1926- *DrBlPA 90*
Preminger, Erik Lee 1944- *ConAu 132*
Preminger, Norbert *BiDrAPA 89*
Preminger, Otto 1905-1986 *WorAlBi*
Preminger, Otto 1906-1986 *BioIn 16*
Premo, Paul Mark 1942- *WhoAm 90*
Premont, Paul 1936- *St&PR 91, WhoAm 90*
Prempas, Louis Nicholas 1928- *WhoE 91*
Prempe, Agyeman I *BioIn 16*
Prempree, Thongbliew 1935- *WhoSSW 91*
Premru, Raymond Eugene 1934- *IntWWM 90*
Premsela, Benno 1920- *ConDes 90*
Prendergast, Carol Uhlich 1937- *WhoAmW 91*
Prendergast, Charles E 1868-1948 *WhoAmA 91N*
Prendergast, George Aloysius 1933- *WhoE 91*
Prendergast, James Luke 1800-1895 *DcCanB 12*
Prendergast, James Thomas 1921- *St&PR 91*
Prendergast, Kathleen Veronica 1937- *WhoE 91*
Prendergast, Maurice 1858-1924 *IntDcAA 90*
Prendergast, Maurice Brazil 1859-1924 *BioIn 16*
Prendergast, Michael H. 1913-1990 *BioIn 16, NewYTBS 90 [port]*
Prendergast, Mike 1888-1967 *Ballpl 90*
Prendergast, Thomas A. 1933- *St&PR 91*
Prensky, Arthur Lawrence 1930- *WhoAm 90*
Prensner, Richard William 1933- *St&PR 91*
Prent, Mark 1947- *WhoAmA 91*
Prentice, Ann Ethelynd 1933- *WhoAm 90*
Prentice, Bryant H., III 1940- *St&PR 91*
Prentice, David Ramage 1943- *WhoAm 90, WhoAmA 91*
Prentice, Eugene Miles, III 1942- *WhoE 91, WhoWor 91*
Prentice, Glenn David *BiDrAPA 89*
Prentice, Irving John 1951- *St&PR 91*
Prentice, James Stuart 1944- *WhoAm 90*
Prentice, Margarita 1931- *WhoHisp 91*
Prentice, Norman Macdonald 1925- *WhoAm 90*
Prentice, P. I. 1899-1989 *BioIn 16*
Prentice, Pierrepont Isham 1899-1989 *BioIn 16*
Prentice, Rena 1955- *St&PR 91*
Prentice, Stanley E *BiDrAPA 89*
Prentice, Thomas Archer 1952- *WhoSSW 91*
Prentice, Tim 1930- *WhoAm 90*
Prenting, Theodore Otto 1933- *WhoE 91*
Prentiss, Augustin Mitchell, Jr. 1915- *WhoAm 90*
Prentiss, Elizabeth P. 1818-1878 *BioAmW*
Prentiss, John James 1818-1890 *AmLegL*
Prentiss, Paula 1939- *BioIn 16, WorAlBi*
Prentiss, Robert Noble 1943- *St&PR 91*
Prentiss, Tina M. 1911- *WhoWrEP 89*
Prenzlauer, Steven Lee 1961- *BiDrAPA 89*
Preparata, Franco Paolo 1935- *WhoAm 90*
Prepetit, Emmanuel A *BiDrAPA 89*
Preradovic, Paula von 1887-1951 *EncCoWW*
Presas, Arturo *WhoHisp 91*
Presberg, Burton Alan 1961- *BiDrAPA 89*
Presbrey, Richard B 1921- *BiDrAPA 89*
Presby, J. Thomas 1940- *WhoAm 90*
Preschlack, John Edward 1933- *WhoAm 90*
Prescod, Horace J *BiDrAPA 89*
Prescod, Marsha *FemiCLE*
Prescod, Samuel Jackman 1806-1871 *BioIn 16*
Prescott, Ben W. 1935- *St&PR 91*
Prescott, Bobby 1930- *Ballpl 90*
Prescott, Bruce Henry 1940- *WhoWor 91*
Prescott, Carter A. *ODwPR 91*
Prescott, Cecil H 1925- *BiDrAPA 89*
Prescott, Charles Young 1938- *WhoAm 90*
Prescott, David Marshall 1926- *WhoAm 90*
Prescott, E. Livingston *FemiCLE*
Prescott, Frank Clarke 1859-1934 *AmLegL*
Prescott, Geoffrey Hickson 1933- *WhoWor 91*
Prescott, Gerald James *St&PR 91*
Prescott, Gerald W. 1899-1988 *BioIn 16*
Prescott, Jack *ConAu 130*
Prescott, John Hernage 1935- *WhoAm 90, WhoE 91*
Prescott, John Mack 1921- *WhoAm 90*
Prescott, John Sherwin 1927- *St&PR 91*
Prescott, Kathryn F *BiDrAPA 89*
Prescott, Kenneth Wade 1920- *WhoAmA 91*
Prescott, Lawrence Malcolm 1934- *WhoWor 91*
Prescott, Leslie Susan 1968- *WhoE 91*
Prescott, Orville 1906- *AuBYP 90, WhoAm 90*
Prescott, Peter Sherwin 1935- *WhoAm 90*
Prescott, Roberta Weinstein 1937- *WhoAmW 91*
Prescott, Roger B., Jr. 1923- *St&PR 91*
Prescott, Samuel 1751-1777 *EncCRAm*
Prescott, Thomas Gene *St&PR 91*
Prescott, Thomas Mayhew 1951- *IntWWM 90*
Prescott, William 1726-1795 *EncCRAm, WorAlBi*
Prescott, William Glenn 1936- *BiDrAPA 89, WhoAm 90*
Prescott, William Hickling 1796-1859 *BioIn 16*
Prescott Thomas, John Desmond 1942- *WhoWor 91*
Present, Beryl M. 1921- *St&PR 91*
Present, Gordon S. 1917- *St&PR 91*
Present, James Robert 1947- *St&PR 91*
Present, Raphael 1921- *St&PR 91*
Presgrove, Sharon Ruth 1946- *WhoAmW 91*
Preska, Margaret Louise Robinson 1938- *WhoAm 90, WhoAmW 91*
Presko, Joe 1928- *Ballpl 90*
Preskorn, Sheldon H *BiDrAPA 89*
Preslar, Len Broughton, Jr. 1947- *WhoAm 90, WhoSSW 91*
Presley, Delma E 1939- *ConAu 31NR*
Presley, Edward J. 1936- *St&PR 91*
Presley, Elvis 1935-1977 *BioIn 16, OxCPMus, WorAlBi*
Presley, Elvis Aron 1935-1977 *EncPR&S 89*
Presley, Janet Passidomo 1952- *WhoAmW 91*
Presley, Jim 1961- *Ballpl 90*
Presley, Lisa Marie *BioIn 16*
Presley, Pricilla Beaulieu *BioIn 16*
Presley, Priscilla 1945- *WorAlBi*
Presley, Priscilla 1946- *ConTFT 8*
Presley, Priscilla Beaulieu 1945- *CurBio 90 [port]*
Presley, Ronald Wayne 1941- *WhoSSW 91*
Presley, Vivian Mathews 1952- *WhoAmW 91*
Presnar, Carol Ann 1959- *St&PR 91*

Presnar, Mark Steven 1952- St&PR 91
Presnell, Harve 1933- ConTFT 8
Presnell, Nadean Elizabeth 1936- WhoAmW 91
Presnell, W. Dale 1943- St&PR 91
Press, Aida Kabatznick 1926- WhoAmW 91
Press, Caren Sue 1956- WhoEmL 91
Press, Charles 1922- WhoAm 90
Press, Diane Kay 1958- BiDrAPA 89
Press, Edward 1913- WhoAm 90
Press, Frank 1924- ConAu 130, WhoAm 90, WhoE 91, WhoWor 91
Press, Gary BioIn 16
Press, Jay 1946- BiDrAPA 89
Press, Jeffery Bruce 1947- WhoE 91
Press, Linda Seghers 1950- WhoAmW 91
Press, Michael Warner 1947- St&PR 91, WhoAm 90
Press, Michele Robin 1958- BiDrAPA 89
Press, Michelle 1940- WhoAm 90, WhoAmW 91
Press, Samuel E 1942- BiDrAPA 89
Press, Simone Naomi Juda 1943- WhoWrEP 89
Press, William Henry 1948- WhoAm 90
Pressberg, Gail 1949- WhoAmW 91
Pressburger, Emeric 1902-1988 AnObit 1988
Presseisen, Barbara Zemboch 1936- WhoE 91
Pressense, Francis Dehaut de 1853-1914 BiDFrPL
Presser, Dorothy Ann 1929- WhoSSW 91
Presser, Elena 1940- WhoAmA 91
Presser, Harriet Betty 1936- WhoAm 90
Presser, Jackie BioIn 16
Presser, Josef 1907-1967 WhoAmA 91N
Presser, Stephen Bruce 1946- WhoAm 90
Presser, Stephen Lee 1944- WhoWor 91
Pressey, Walter M. 1944- St&PR 91
Pressler, Herman Paul 1902- WhoAm 90
Pressler, Herman Paul, III 1930- WhoSSW 91
Pressler, Larry 1942- WhoAm 90, WhoWor 91
Pressler, Menahem 1923- IntWWM 90, WhoAm 90
Pressler, Philip Bernard 1946- WhoE 91
Pressley, Daniel 1918-1971 MusmAFA
Pressley, Joyce Carolyn 1953- WhoAmW 91, WhoWor 91
Pressley, Lucius Crawford, Jr. 1928- BiDrAPA 89
Pressley, Tara Elizabeth 1960- BiDrAPA 89
Pressly, John Brycent 1944- WhoSSW 91
Pressly, Nancy Lee 1941- WhoAmA 91
Pressly, Thomas James 1919- WhoAm 90
Pressly, William Laurens 1944- WhoAmA 91
Pressman, Adele Rhea BiDrAPA 89
Pressman, Edward BioIn 16
Pressman, Harold B. 1913- St&PR 91
Pressman, Howard Ira 1948- BiDrAPA 89
Pressman, Jacob 1919- BioIn 16
Pressman, Lisa Jo 1963- WhoAmW 91
Pressman, Mary A BiDrAPA 89
Pressman, Maurie D 1922- BiDrAPA 89
Pressman, Paul S 1929- BiDrAPA 89
Pressman, Thelma 1921- WhoAmW 91
Pressmar, Carl Francis 1933- WhoSSW 91
Pressnell, Tot 1906- Ballpl 90
Pressouyre, Leon 1935- WhoWor 91
Pressprich, William O. 1956- St&PR 91
Prest, Thomas Peckett 1810-1879 BioIn 16
Prestage, James Jordan 1926- WhoAm 90
Prestage, Jewel Limar 1931- WhoAm 90, WhoAmW 91
Prestanski, Harry T. 1947- ODwPR 91
Prestbo, John Andrew 1941- WhoAm 90, WhoWrEP 89
Prestegaard, Peter 1942- WhoAm 90
Prestel, Bernhard Marc 1944- WhoWor 91
Prestera, Lauretta Anne 1947- WhoAmW 91
Prestes, Luis Carlos NewYTBS 90
Prestes, Luis Carlos 1898-1990 BioIn 16
Presthus, Robert Granning 1917- WhoAm 90
Presti, Ida 1924-1967 PenDiMP
Presti, Susan Marie 1959- WhoAmW 91
Prestini, James 1908- ConDes 90
Prestini, James Libero 1908- WhoAm 90, WhoAmA 91
Prestipino, Anthony Charles 1947- St&PR 91
Prestmark, Vagn 1933- WhoWor 91
Preston, Alan Jonathan 1929- BiDrAPA 89
Preston, Alice Bolam 1889-1958 WhoAmA 91N
Preston, Andrew Joseph 1922- WhoAm 90, WhoE 91, WhoWor 91
Preston, Ann L WhoAmA 91
Preston, Beth Brown 1953- WhoE 91
Preston, Billy 1946- DrBIPA 90, WorAlBi
Preston, Bruce Marshall 1949- WhoWor 91
Preston, Carol AuBYP 90
Preston, Cecilia Marie Rodgers 1954- WhoAmW 91
Preston, Charles B. 1928- St&PR 91
Preston, Charles Brian 1937- WhoWor 91
Preston, Charles George 1940- WhoWor 91
Preston, Colleen Ann 1955- WhoEmL 91
Preston, David Michael 1930- WhoAm 90
Preston, Deborah 1953- WhoAmW 91
Preston, Edna Mitchell AuBYP 90
Preston, Eugene Francis 1929- St&PR 91
Preston, Faith 1921- WhoAm 90
Preston, Fran ODwPR 91
Preston, Frances W. WhoAmW 91
Preston, Frank N. 1928- St&PR 91
Preston, Frank W. 1896-1989 BioIn 16
Preston, Frankie Lynn 1956- WhoSSW 91
Preston, Frederick Willard 1912- WhoAm 90
Preston, George Nelson 1938- WhoAmA 91
Preston, Gordon Craig BiDrAPA 89
Preston, Harriet Brown 1892-1961 WhoAmA 91N
Preston, Harriet Waters 1836-1911 FemiCLE
Preston, Hubert M. 1933- St&PR 91
Preston, Ivy Kinross 1914- ConAu 30NR
Preston, J A DrBIPA 90
Preston, James Clarence 1926- WhoAm 90
Preston, James E. 1933- WhoAm 90, WhoE 91
Preston, James Edward 1933- St&PR 91
Preston, James Harry 1860-1938 AmLegL
Preston, James M 1874-1962 WhoAmA 91N
Preston, Jane H 1920- BiDrAPA 89
Preston, John 1945- ConAu 130, WhoWrEP 89
Preston, John Charles BiDrAPA 89
Preston, Katherine Keenan 1950- IntWWM 90
Preston, Kelly BioIn 16
Preston, Kelly 1963?- ConTFT 8
Preston, Kendall, Jr. 1927- WhoAm 90
Preston, Kenneth W. ODwPR 91
Preston, Kevin Mark 1956- WhoEmL 91
Preston, Lee Egan 1930- WhoAm 90
Preston, Lewis BioIn 16
Preston, Lewis T. 1926- St&PR 91
Preston, Lewis Thompson 1926- WhoAm 90, WhoE 91
Preston, Lillian Elvira 1918- BioIn 16
Preston, Loyce Elaine 1929- WhoAmW 91, WhoWor 91
Preston, Malcolm 1919- WhoAm 90
Preston, Malcolm H 1920- WhoAmA 91
Preston, Marcia 1944- WhoWrEP 89
Preston, Margaret 1820-1897 FemiCLE
Preston, Margaret J. 1820-1897 BioAmW
Preston, Mark 1957- BiDrAPA 89
Preston, Melvin Alexander 1921- WhoAm 90
Preston, Meredith 1952- ODwPR 91
Preston, Nancy Lynn 1960- WhoAmW 91
Preston, Noel Gary 1947- St&PR 91, WhoSSW 91
Preston, Norman Wyckoff 1932- St&PR 91
Preston, Penny Hatcher 1953- WhoAmW 91
Preston, Richard ConAu 131
Preston, Richard Arthur 1910- WhoAm 90
Preston, Richard E BiDrAPA 89
Preston, Robert 1918- OxCPMus
Preston, Robert 1918-1987 BioIn 16, WorAlBi
Preston, Robert A. 1945- WhoE 91
Preston, Robert Bruce 1926- WhoAm 90
Preston, Robert Frank 1943- St&PR 91
Preston, Russell Edward WhoE 91
Preston, Samuel Hulse 1943- WhoAm 90
Preston, Seymour Stotler, III 1933- St&PR 91, WhoAm 90, WhoE 91
Preston, Simon 1938- PenDiMP
Preston, Simon John 1938- IntWWM 90
Preston, Sondra Kay 1947- WhoWrEP 89
Preston, Susan Jean 1950- WhoAmW 91
Preston, Thomas 1537-1598 BioIn 16
Preston, Thomas Edgar BiDrAPA 89
Preston, Thomas L. 1934- ODwPR 91
Preston, Thomas Ronald 1936- WhoAm 90
Preston, Wendy Ann 1956- WhoAmW 91, WhoE 91
Preston, William BiDrAPA 89
Preston, William 1742-1818 BioIn 16
Preston, William 1816-1887 BioIn 16
Preston, William Allen 1936- St&PR 91
Preston, William Ballard 1805-1862 BiDrUSE 89
Preston, William Hubbard 1920- WhoAm 90
Preston, William L. 1922- St&PR 91
Preston, William Russell 1925- St&PR 91
Preston-Stubbs, Tish 1952- WhoAmW 91
Prestopino, Frank 1949- St&PR 91
Prestopino, Gregorio 1907- WhoAmA 91N
Prestopino, Robert Joseph 1937- St&PR 91
Prestopnik, Thomas James 1942- WhoSSW 91
Prestowitz, Clyde Vincent 1941- WhoAm 90
Prestridge, Pamela Adair 1945- WhoAmW 91, WhoEmL 91, WhoSSW 91, WhoWor 91
Prestrud, Stuart Holmes 1919- St&PR 91
Prestwidge, Kathleen Joyce 1927- WhoAmW 91
Prestwood, Alvin Tennyson 1929- WhoAm 90, WhoSSW 91, WhoWor 91
Prestwood, Deborah Lynn 1952- WhoAmW 91
Prestwood, John C., Jr. 1953- St&PR 91
Presvelou, Clio 1929- WhoWor 91
Preswick, Barry Edward 1947- St&PR 91
Pretenders, The EncPR&S 89
Preti, Mattia 1613-1699 IntDcAA 90
Pretina, Michael John, Jr. 1940- WhoWor 91
Pretlow, Carol Jocelyn 1946- WhoAmW 91
Preto-Rodas, Richard Anthony 1936- WhoAm 90
Pretre, Georges 1924- IntWWM 90, PenDiMP
Pretto, Franklin David 1946- WhoEmL 91
Prettyman, Elijah Barrett, Jr. 1925- WhoAm 90
Prettyman, Kathleen Collins BioIn 16
Prettyman, Keith Arthur 1951- St&PR 91
Pretzinger, Donald Leonard 1923- WhoAm 90
Preuil, William PenDiMP
Preuning, Andreas PenDiDA 89
Preuning, Kunz PenDiDA 89
Preuning, Matthaus PenDiDA 89
Preuning, Paul PenDiDA 89
Preuning, Stefan PenDiDA 89
Preus, David Walter 1922- WhoAm 90
Preus, Jacob Aall Ottesen 1920- WhoAm 90
Preuschoft, Holger 1932- WhoWor 91
Preusler, Robert Charles 1948- WhoSSW 91
Preuss, Clifford W. 1931- St&PR 91
Preuss, Eva Silvia 1955- WhoAmW 91
Preuss, Fritz Richard 1917- WhoWor 91
Preuss, Hans G 1923- BiDrAPA 89
Preuss, Mary Herge 1937- WhoE 91
Preuss, Paul 1942- ConAu 130
Preuss, Roger 1922- WhoAmA 91
Preuss, Roger Emil 1922- WhoAm 90, WhoWor 91
Preuss, Ronald Stephen 1935- WhoWor 91
Preuss-Ticknor, Jennie BiDrAPA 89
Preusser, E.F. 1946- St&PR 91
Preusser, Robert Ormerod 1919- WhoAmA 91
Preussler PenDiDA 89
Preussler, Otfried 1923- AuBYP 90
Prevatt, Harriet Lee 1931- IntWWM 90
Prevedi, Bruno 1928- IntWWM 90
Preven, David W 1937- BiDrAPA 89
Prevert, Jacques 1900-1977 MajTwCW
Previato, Emma 1952- WhoE 91
Previdi, Melissa WhoE 91
Previdi, Peter P. 1943- St&PR 91
Previn, Andre 1929- BioIn 16, OxCPMus, PenDiMP, -A, WhoAm 90, WhoWor 91, WorAlBi
Previn, Andre George 1929- IntWWM 90
Previtali, Fernando 1907-1985 PenDiMP
Previtali, Giovanni 1935-1988 BioIn 16
Previte, Barbara D BiDrAPA 89
Previte, Richard 1935- St&PR 91
Previti, Peter 1952- WhoSSW 91
Previts, Gary John 1942- WhoAm 90
Prevor, Barry J. 1963- St&PR 91
Prevor, Michael 1936- St&PR 91
Prevor, Sydney 1936- St&PR 91
Prevost, Abbe 1697-1763 WorAlBi
Prevost, Andre IntWWM 90
Prevost, Andre 1934- PenDiMP A
Prevost, Edward James 1941- WhoAm 90
Prevost, Germain PenDiMP
Prevost, James A BiDrAPA 89
Prevost, Mary Lynn WhoAmW 91
Prevost, Oscar 1845-1895 DcCanB 12
Prevost, Robert 1927-1982 OxCCanT
Prevost, Robert Roland 1937- St&PR 91
Prevost, Stephen M. 1938- St&PR 91
Prevost, Verbie Lovorn 1943- WhoSSW 91
Prevost, Winthrop Warren 1917- WhoE 91
Prevost/Linton, Charles 1949- WhoAm 90
Prevoznik, Stephen Joseph 1929- WhoAm 90
Prewin, Andreas Ludwig 1929- IntWWM 90
Prewit, Doris M. 1929- WhoSSW 91
Prewitt, Charles Thompson 1933- WhoAm 90
Prewitt, Dudley B. 1919- St&PR 91
Prewitt, Keith Edward 1963- WhoSSW 91
Prewitt, Kenneth 1936- WhoAm 90
Prewitt, Merle Rainey 1928- WhoSSW 91
Prewitt, Taylor Archie, III 1938- WhoSSW 91
Prewoznik, Jerome Frank 1934- WhoAm 90, WhoWor 91
Prey, Hermann 1929- IntWWM 90, PenDiMP
Prey, William Taylor 1954- BiDrAPA 89
Preyer, Robert Otto 1922- WhoAm 90
Preysz, Louis Robert Fonss, III 1944- WhoSSW 91, WhoWor 91
Prezant, Bradley Dennis 1953- WhoEmL 91
Prezeau, Louis E. 1943- St&PR 91
Preziosi, Donald A 1941- WhoAmA 91
Prezzano, Wilbur J. 1940- St&PR 91
Prezzi, Wilma M 1915- WhoAmA 91N
Priatna, Aloysius Budiarto 1949- WhoWor 91
Priaulx, Allan 1940- WhoAm 90
Priaulx, David Lloyd 1949- WhoSSW 91
Pribadi, Krishnahari BiDrAPA 89
Pribble, Easton 1917- WhoAm 90, WhoAmA 91
Priber, Christian EncCRAm
Priber, Christian Gottlieb WhNaAH
Pribor, Hugo Casimer 1928- WhoWor 91
Pribyl, Vilem 1925- IntWWM 90, PenDiMP
Price, Alan 1926- WhoAm 90
Price, Alan 1942- OxCPMus
Price, Alan Anthony 1928- SpyFic
Price, Alan Roger 1942- WhoE 91
Price, Alan Thomas 1949- WhoSSW 91
Price, Albert M. 1927- St&PR 91
Price, Alexander 1913- WhoE 91
Price, Alfred Lee 1935- St&PR 91
Price, Alice I. 1949- WhoAmW 91
Price, Alvin Audis 1917- WhoAm 90
Price, Andrea Renee 1959- WhoAmW 91
Price, Angela Lynn 1965- WhoAmW 91
Price, Ann Lisbeth 1950- BiDrAPA 89
Price, Anna Mae Johns 1959- IntWWM 90
Price, Anne Atchison 1943- WhoSSW 91
Price, Anne Kirkendall 1922- WhoAmA 91
Price, Anthony 1928- ConAu 33NR, TwCCr&M 91, WorAlBi
Price, Arlen Ray 1931- WhoSSW 91
Price, Arthur Earl BiDrAPA 89
Price, Arthur R. 1951- WhoAm 90
Price, B. Byron WhoAm 90, WhoSSW 91
Price, Barbara Ann 1951- WhoAmW 91
Price, Barbara Gillette 1938- WhoAmA 91
Price, Bart M. 1922- St&PR 91
Price, Bradford F. 1956- St&PR 91
Price, Byron 1891-1981 BioIn 16
Price, Carole Runyan 1937- WhoAmW 91
Price, Caroline Leona 1947- WhoSSW 91
Price, Charles 1846-1905 AmLegL
Price, Charles H. 1931- BioIn 16
Price, Charles H., II 1931- WhoAm 90, WhoWor 91
Price, Charles Steven 1955- WhoEmL 91
Price, Charles T. WhoAm 90
Price, Charles T. 1847-1933 BioIn 16
Price, Charles U. 1916- WhoAm 90
Price, Cheryl St&PR 91
Price, Chester B 1885-1962 WhoAmA 91N
Price, Christie Speir 1954- WhoEmL 91
Price, Christine Hilda 1928-1980 AuBYP 90
Price, Clayton S 1874-1950 WhoAmA 91N
Price, Dalias Adolph 1913- WhoAm 90
Price, Daniel Martin 1955- WhoE 91
Price, David 1940- ConAu 130
Price, David B., Jr. BioIn 16
Price, David Edgar 1914- WhoAm 90
Price, David Eugene 1940- WhoAm 90, WhoSSW 91
Price, David Paul 1925- St&PR 91
Price, David Robert 1940- St&PR 91, WhoAm 90
Price, Deborah Ann BiDrAPA 89
Price, Debra 1958- WhoAmW 91
Price, Dennis Lee 1930- WhoSSW 91
Price, Don K. 1910- WhoAm 90
Price, Donald Albert 1919- WhoAm 90
Price, Donald E. 1928- St&PR 91
Price, Donald Ray 1939- WhoAm 90
Price, Donald W 1932- BiDrAPA 89
Price, Doris EarBIAP
Price, Doris C WhoAmA 91
Price, Doris D. HarlReB
Price, Douglas Armstrong 1950- WhoSSW 91
Price, Douglas B 1923- BiDrAPA 89
Price, E Alan 1918- EncO&P 3
Price, E.H., Jr. 1918- St&PR 91
Price, Earnest, Jr. 1919- WhoSSW 91
Price, Edgar Hilleary, Jr. 1918- WhoAm 90, WhoWor 91
Price, Edward Dean 1919- WhoAm 90
Price, Edwin F BiDrAPA 89
Price, Elizabeth 1668?- BiDEWW
Price, Eugenia BioIn 16
Price, Eva Jane 1855-1900 BioIn 16
Price, Evan John 1840-1899 DcCanB 12
Price, Florence Beatrice 1888-1953 DcAfAmP

Price, Francis D., Jr. 1949- *St&PR 91*
Price, Frank 1930- *WhoAm 90, WhoWor 91*
Price, Frederic Newlin 1884-1963 *WhoAmA 91N*
Price, Frederick *BioIn 16*
Price, Gail Elizabeth 1940- *WhoAmW 91*
Price, Garrett 1897-1979 *WhoAmA 91N*
Price, Gary L. 1944- *St&PR 91*
Price, Gary Layton 1947- *St&PR 91*
Price, George 1901- *WhoAm 90, WhoAmA 91*
Price, George C. *BioIn 16*
Price, George Cadle 1919- *WhoWor 91*
Price, George R 1922- *EncO&P 3*
Price, George Robert 1922-1975 *EncPaPR 91*
Price, Geraldine G *BiDrAPA 89*
Price, Gilbert 1942- *DrBIPA 90*
Price, Glanville 1928- *ConAu 132*
Price, Gordon A. 1947- *St&PR 91, WhoAm 90*
Price, Harrison Alan 1921- *WhoAm 90*
Price, Harrison Lee 1957- *WhoSSW 91*
Price, Harry 1881-1948 *EncO&P 3, EncPaPR 91*
Price, Harry S., Jr. 1910- *St&PR 91*
Price, Harry Steele, Jr. 1910- *WhoAm 90*
Price, Helen Laura 1930- *WhoAmW 91*
Price, Henry Habberley 1899-1984 *EncO&P 3, EncPaPR 91*
Price, Henry Locher 1922- *WhoAm 90*
Price, Herbert E. *St&PR 91*
Price, Herbert H, III 1953- *BiDrAPA 89*
Price, Hickman 1911-1989 *BioIn 16*
Price, Hollister Anne Cawein 1954- *WhoAmW 91, WhoEmL 91, WhoWor 91*
Price, Homer L. 1924- *St&PR 91*
Price, Humphrey Wallace 1954- *WhoWor 91*
Price, I. Edward 1942- *WhoAm 90*
Price, Irving *BioIn 16*
Price, Irving L., Jr. 1917- *WhoAm 90*
Price, Irving Lanouette 1884-1976 *ConAmBL*
Price, Jacqueline S. 1952- *WhoAmW 91*
Price, James Audie 1954- *WhoEmL 91*
Price, James Edward 1941- *WhoE 91*
Price, James Eldridge 1952- *WhoSSW 91*
Price, James Gordon 1926- *WhoAm 90*
Price, James Huddleston 1950- *St&PR 91*
Price, James Lee 1950- *WhoEmL 91*
Price, James Ligon 1915- *WhoSSW 91*
Price, James Melford 1921- *WhoWor 91*
Price, James Ray 1939- *St&PR 91*
Price, Janet 1938- *IntWWM 90*
Price, Janet Hartka 1947- *WhoEmL 91*
Price, Janis *WhoAmW 91*
Price, Jeannine Alleenica 1949- *WhoAmW 91*
Price, Jerome Charles-Joseph 1933- *St&PR 91*
Price, Jerome J. 1933- *St&PR 91*
Price, Jim 1941- *Ballpl 90*
Price, Joan Webster 1931- *WhoAmA 91*
Price, Joanne 1938- *WhoAmW 91*
Price, Joe 1935- *WhoAm 90, WhoAmA 91*
Price, Joe 1956- *Ballpl 90*
Price, Joe D. *BioIn 16*
Price, Joe Sealy 1933- *WhoSSW 91*
Price, Joel Robert *BiDrAPA 89*
Price, John Douglas 1952- *WhoEmL 91*
Price, John Franklyn 1932- *WhoAm 90*
Price, John G. *AmLegL*
Price, John Henry, Jr. 1926- *St&PR 91*
Price, John J. 1951- *St&PR 91*
Price, John Martin 1936- *St&PR 91*
Price, John Ronald 1951- *WhoSSW 91*
Price, John Roy 1938- *St&PR 91*
Price, John Roy, Jr. 1938- *WhoAm 90*
Price, John Vincent *BiDrAPA 89*
Price, John William 1927- *WhoAm 90*
Price, Joy A. 1950- *BiDrAPA 89*
Price, Karen Bynum 1947- *BiDrAPA 89*
Price, Karl S. 1921- *WhoAm 90*
Price, Keith 1950- *St&PR 91*
Price, Keith Murray 1937- *WhoAm 90*
Price, Ken 1945- *ODwPR 91*
Price, Kenneth *PenDiDA 89*
Price, Kenneth 1935- *WhoAmA 91*
Price, Kenneth L. 1938- *St&PR 91*
Price, King Graham 1932- *BiDrAPA 89*
Price, Larry C. 1954- *WhoAm 90*
Price, Leigh 1941- *WhoAmW 91*
Price, Leontyne *BioIn 16*
Price, Leontyne 1927- *DrBIPA 90, IntWWM 90, PenDiMP, WhoAm 90, WhoWor 91, WorAlBi*
Price, Leslie Kenneth *WhoAmA 91*
Price, Linda Anne 1961- *WhoAmW 91*
Price, Linda Jordan 1954- *WhoEmL 91*
Price, Linda Margaret 1946- *WhoAmW 91*
Price, Lionel D.D. 1946- *WhoWor 91*
Price, Lloyd 1933- *EncPR&S 89*
Price, Lloyd F 1945- *BiDrAPA 89*
Price, Lloyd M. 1931- *WhoAm 90*
Price, Lucile Brickner Brown 1902- *WhoAmW 91, WhoWor 91*
Price, Margaret 1941- *PenDiMP*
Price, Margaret Ann 1951- *WhoE 91*
Price, Margaret Berenice 1941- *IntWWM 90*
Price, Margaret E 1888- *WhoAmA 91N*
Price, Marian Whitlow 1943- *WhoSSW 91*
Price, Marilyn *BiDrAPA 89*
Price, Marilyn Jeanne 1948- *WhoAmW 91*
Price, Marion Woodrow 1914- *WhoAm 90*
Price, Mark Ford 1946- *WhoWor 91*
Price, Mark Michael 1920- *WhoWor 91*
Price, Martin 1920- *WhoAm 90*
Price, Martin Burton 1928- *St&PR 91, WhoAm 90*
Price, Maureen Gail 1951- *WhoEmL 91, WhoSSW 91*
Price, Mauricia 1925- *WhoWrEP 89*
Price, Melvin 1905-1988 *BioIn 16*
Price, Michael Benjamin 1940- *WhoAmA 91*
Price, Michael F. 1951- *St&PR 91*
Price, Michael J 1946- *BiDrAPA 89*
Price, Minnie 1877-1957 *WhoAmA 91N*
Price, Monroe Edwin 1938- *WhoAm 90*
Price, Nancy Chance 1953- *WhoAmW 91*
Price, Nancy P. 1932- *WhoAmW 91*
Price, Neil David *BiDrAPA 89*
Price, Nina Mae 1882-1974 *BioAmW*
Price, Norman Mills 1877-1951 *WhoAmA 91N*
Price, Olive M. 1903- *AuBYP 90*
Price, Oscar A. 1931- *St&PR 91*
Price, Otis 1943- *St&PR 91*
Price, Pamela Odell 1945- *WhoEmL 91*
Price, Patrick H. *WhoAm 90*
Price, Paul Buford 1932- *WhoAm 90*
Price, Paul Edward 1934- *St&PR 91*
Price, Paul Marnell 1959- *WhoE 91*
Price, Paula Lea *BiDrAPA 89*
Price, Peter *BioIn 16*
Price, Philip 1898-1989 *BioIn 16*
Price, Philip Adams 1917- *St&PR 91*
Price, Phillip Vincent 1949- *WhoEmL 91*
Price, Phyllis Elizabeth 1949- *WhoAmW 91*
Price, Polly Selders 1922- *WhoWrEP 89*
Price, Powell B. 1947- *St&PR 91*
Price, Ray 1926- *WhoAm 90, WorAlBi*
Price, Ray G. *BioIn 16*
Price, Raymond Alexander 1933- *WhoAm 90*
Price, Raymond K., Jr. *ODwPR 91*
Price, Reine Irene 1950- *WhoAmW 91*
Price, Renata Frances 1946- *WhoAmW 91, WhoE 91*
Price, Reynolds 1933- *BioIn 16, ConLC 63 [port], WhoAm 90, WhoWrEP 89, WorAlBi*
Price, Richard *PenDiDA 89*
Price, Richard 1941- *WhoAm 90, WhoWor 91*
Price, Richard 1949- *BioIn 16, WhoWrEP 89*
Price, Richard Fabian 1935- *BiDrAPA 89*
Price, Richard Foard 1930- *St&PR 91, WhoSSW 91*
Price, Richard Galen 1956- *IntWWM 90*
Price, Richard H. *BioIn 16*
Price, Rita F *WhoAmA 91*
Price, Robert 1929- *WhoAm 90*
Price, Robert 1932- *BioIn 16, St&PR 91, WhoAm 90*
Price, Robert D. 1924- *St&PR 91*
Price, Robert Eben 1931- *WhoAm 90*
Price, Robert Edmunds 1926- *WhoE 91, WhoWor 91*
Price, Robert Edward 1956- *WhoSSW 91*
Price, Robert Ira 1921- *WhoAm 90*
Price, Robert McCollum 1930- *WhoAm 90*
Price, Robert W 1920- *BiDrAPA 89*
Price, Robert Wayne 1945- *WhoSSW 91*
Price, Rosalie Pettus *WhoAmA 91, WhoAmW 91, WhoSSW 91, WhoWor 91*
Price, S. David 1943- *WhoWrEP 89*
Price, Sammy 1908- *BioIn 16*
Price, Sara J *WhoAmA 91*
Price, Selma Brown 1915- *WhoAmW 91*
Price, Shelby Milburn Junior 1938- *IntWWM 90*
Price, Sherri Ann 1953- *WhoAmW 91*
Price, Sol 1932- *St&PR 91*
Price, Stan *BioIn 16*
Price, Stefanie Jean 1958- *WhoAmW 91*
Price, Stephen N 1933- *BiDrAPA 89*
Price, Sterling 1809-1867 *WhNaAH*
Price, Steven 1962- *WhoE 91, WhoEmL 91*
Price, Susan Laura *BiDrAPA 89*
Price, Teresa A. 1965- *WhoAmW 91*
Price, Thomas Benjamin 1920- *WhoAm 90*
Price, Thomas Emile 1921- *WhoAm 90*
Price, Timothy F. 1953- *St&PR 91*
Price, Timothy Wayne 1953- *WhoSSW 91*
Price, Tony *BioIn 16*
Price, Trevor R P 1943- *BiDrAPA 89*
Price, Trevor Robert Pryce 1943- *WhoE 91*
Price, V. B. 1940- *WhoWrEP 89*
Price, Vergie Gayle 1954- *WhoSSW 91*
Price, Vicki Jean 1955- *WhoE 91*
Price, Vincent 1911- *BioIn 16, WhoAmA 91, WorAlBi*
Price, Vincent Leonard 1911- *WhoAm 90*
Price, W. James 1924- *St&PR 91*
Price, Walter *St&PR 91*
Price, Walter Ernest 1948- *WhoE 91*
Price, Walter Lee 1914- *WhoSSW 91*
Price, Warren, III 1943- *WhoAm 90*
Price, Willadene 1914- *AuBYP 90*
Price, Willard 1887-1963 *BioIn 16*
Price, Willard De Mille 1887- *AuBYP 90*
Price, William 1938- *WhoWrEP 89*
Price, William Anthony *BiDrAPA 89*
Price, William Anthony 1938- *WhoSSW 91*
Price, William James 1918- *WhoAm 90*
Price, William James, IV 1924- *WhoAm 90*
Price, William Joseph 1930- *St&PR 91*
Price, William Sloane 1939- *St&PR 91*
Price, William Thompson 1846-1920 *LiHiK*
Price, Willis Joseph 1931- *WhoAm 90*
Price, Woodruff Murray 1935- *St&PR 91, WhoAm 90*
Price Boday, Mary Kathryn 1945- *WhoAmW 91, WhoEmL 91, WhoWor 91*
Price-Gallo, Paola *BiDrAPA 89*
Price Jones, Penelope Gwyneth 1948- *IntWWM 90*
Price-Lee Fatt, Patricia Ann 1954- *WhoAmW 91*
Price-Mars, Jean 1875-1969 *EncO&P 3*
Price-Owen, Anne Louise 1947- *WhoWor 91*
Price-Rabah, Kelly Ann 1963- *WhoAmW 91*
Pricer, Wilbur David 1935- *WhoAm 90*
Prichard, Charles Rollins, Jr. *St&PR 91N*
Prichard, Edgar Allen 1920- *WhoAm 90, WhoWor 91*
Prichard, Elizabeth Robinson 1915- *WhoAmW 91*
Prichard, Gail A *BiDrAPA 89*
Prichard, John Franklin 1907- *WhoSSW 91, WhoWor 91*
Prichard, John Robert Stobo 1949- *WhoAm 90, WhoE 91, WhoWor 91*
Prichard, Katharine Susannah 1883-1969 *ConAu 33NR, FemiCLE, MajTwCW*
Prichard, Nancy Beville 1952- *WhoAmW 91*
Prichard, Peter S. 1944- *WhoAm 90, WhoE 91*
Prichard, Robert Williams 1923- *WhoAm 90*
Prickett, F. Daniel 1946- *St&PR 91*
Prickett, Nancy Miriam 1950- *WhoAmW 91*
Prickett, Robert Lee 1945- *WhoSSW 91*
Prickett, Tom, Jr. 1921- *WhoSSW 91*
Prickett, Walter L 1930- *BiDrAPA 89*
Prickett, Will Smith, Jr. 1950- *St&PR 91*
Pricola, Vito 1925- *St&PR 91, WhoAm 90*
Prida, Dolores 1943- *BioIn 16, WhoHisp 91*
Priddat, Birger Peter 1950- *WhoWor 91*
Priddle, Roland 1933- *WhoAm 90*
Priddy, Bob 1939- *Ballpl 90*
Priddy, Charles Horne 1925- *St&PR 91*
Priddy, Frances Rosaleen 1931- *AuBYP 90*
Priddy, Gerry 1919-1980 *Ballpl 90*
Priddy, Jerry F. 1937- *St&PR 91*
Priddy, Robert Allen *BioIn 16*
Priddy, Robert Eugene 1927- *St&PR 91*
Priddy, Robert L. 1946- *St&PR 91*
Priddy, Robert Lynn 1946- *WhoAm 90*
Priddy, Thomas Wayne 1938- *WhoSSW 91*
Pride, Alfred Melville 1897-1988 *BioIn 16*
Pride, Benjamin David 1952- *WhoE 91*
Pride, Charles E. *ODwPR 91*
Pride, Charley *BioIn 16*
Pride, Charley 1938- *ConMus 4 [port], DrBIPA 90, OxCPMus*
Pride, Charley 1939- *WorAlBi*
Pride, Douglas Spencer 1959- *WhoE 91*
Pride, Fleetwood Martin 1948- *WhoSSW 91*
Pride, Harvey, Jr. 1947- *St&PR 91*
Pride, Kenneth Rodney 1953- *WhoWor 91*
Pride, Portia Duke 1964- *WhoAmW 91*
Prideaux, Gary Dean 1939- *WhoAm 90*
Prideaux, John Denys Charles Anstice 1944- *WhoWor 91*
Pridemore, Larry Edward 1938- *St&PR 91*
Pridgen, Gary L. 1945- *St&PR 91*
Pridgeon, James Stephen 1948- *WhoWor 91*
Pridmore, Roy Davis 1925- *WhoAm 90*
Priebe, Karl 1914-1976 *WhoAmA 91N*
Priebe, Louis V. *ODwPR 91*
Priebe, Richard K. 1942- *WhoSSW 91*
Priebe, Richard O. 1927- *ODwPR 91, St&PR 91*
Priebe, Robert John 1928- *St&PR 91*
Priebe, Waldemar Antoni 1948- *WhoSSW 91*
Priegues, Lauren Jorgensen 1962- *WhoE 91*
Prielipp, Pauline Louise 1957- *WhoAmW 91*
Priem, Ted L. 1940- *St&PR 91*
Prier, Ronald Eugene 1950- *BiDrAPA 89*
Priesand, Sally 1946- *WorAlBi*
Priesand, Sally Jane 1946- *WhoAm 90*
Priesol, Anthony Joseph 1941- *St&PR 91*
Priest, Alan 1898-1968 *WhoAmA 91N*
Priest, Andrea 1956- *ODwPR 91*
Priest, Christopher 1943- *RGTwCSF*
Priest, Emerson B. 1922- *St&PR 91*
Priest, Eva Louise 1935- *WhoAmW 91*
Priest, George L. 1947- *WhoAm 90*
Priest, Gordon Webb, Jr. 1947- *WhoEmL 91*
Priest, Hartwell Wyse 1901- *WhoAm 90, WhoAmA 91, WhoWor 91*
Priest, Melville Stanton 1912- *WhoAm 90, WhoWor 91*
Priest, Michael Richard *BiDrAPA 89*
Priest, Robert George 1933- *WhoWor 91*
Priest, T 1928- *WhoAmA 91*
Priest-Mackie, Nancy Ray 1934- *WhoSSW 91*
Priester, Dudley B. 1923- *St&PR 91*
Priester, Gayle Boller 1912- *WhoE 91*
Priestley, Brian 1946- *ConAu 129*
Priestley, Douglas Allen 1945- *St&PR 91*
Priestley, Hugh Michael 1942- *WhoWor 91*
Priestley, J. B. 1894- *WorAlBi*
Priestley, J.B. 1894-1984 *ConAu 33NR, DcLB 100 [port], MajTwCW, TwCCr&M 91*
Priestley, John Boynton 1894-1984 *DcNaB 1981*
Priestley, Joseph 1733-1804 *BioIn 16, WorAlBi*
Priestley, Mary 1925- *IntWWM 90*
Priestley, Michael Linn 1953- *WhoEmL 91*
Priestley, Opal Lee 1904- *WhoWrEP 89*
Priestley, Ronald 1949- *WhoE 91*
Priestly, Lee Shore 1904- *AuBYP 90*
Priestman, Brian 1927- *IntWWM 90*
Priestner, Edward B. 1936- *St&PR 91*
Priestner, Edward Bernard 1936- *WhoAm 90*
Priesz, Connie Joan 1956- *WhoAmW 91*
Prieto, Carlos 1937- *IntWWM 90, WhoAm 90*
Prieto, Corine 1946- *WhoAmW 91*
Prieto, Joaquin 1786-1854 *BioIn 16*
Prieto, Jorge *BioIn 16*
Prieto, Jose *BiDrAPA 89*
Prieto, Manuel Bulnes 1799-1866 *BioIn 16*
Prieto, Mariana 1912- *AuBYP 90*
Prieto, Pete *BioIn 16*
Prieto, Robert 1954- *St&PR 91, WhoE 91*
Prieto F., Luis B. 1902- *BioIn 16*
Prietto, Carole Anne 1962- *WhoAmW 91*
Prieur, Andre *PenDiMP*
Prieur, Jean-Louis *PenDiDA 89*
Prieur, Jean Luc 1953- *WhoWor 91*
Prieux, Pierre 1952- *WhoWor 91*
Priewasser, Erich 1941- *WhoWor 91*
Prigent, Pierre 1945- *WhoWor 91*
Prigge, Roger Leroy 1935- *St&PR 91*
Prigmore, Charles Samuel 1919- *WhoAm 90, WhoSSW 91, WhoWor 91*
Prigmore, L.T. 1920- *St&PR 91*
Prigmore, Maralee Sands 1930- *WhoAmW 91*
Prigogine, Ilya 1917- *ConAu 131, WhoAm 90, WhoSSW 91, WhoWor 91, WhoWrEP 89*
Prill, Arnold *WhoAm 90*
Prillaman, Bob Maurice 1933- *WhoSSW 91*
Prillaman, Leslie I. 1943- *St&PR 91*
Prillwitz, Diane Patricia 1958- *WhoAmW 91*
Prim, Ray 1906- *Ballpl 90*
Prim y Prats, Juan 1814-1870 *BioIn 16*
Prima, Louis 1911-1978 *OxCPMus*
Prima, Louis 1912-1978 *WorAlBi*
Primack, Leonard 1936- *WhoE 91*
Primakow, Max J *BiDrAPA 89*
Primanis, George *BiDrAPA 89*
Primatesta, Raul Francisco 1919- *WhoWor 91*
Primaticcio, Francesco 1505-1570 *IntDcAA 90*
Primavera, Anne Marilyn 1944- *WhoAmW 91*
Primavera, Denise Luella 1955- *WhoE 91*
Primavera, Elise 1954- *BioIn 16*
Primavera, Joanne Martina 1940- *WhoAmW 91*
Primavera, William J. 1940- *ODwPR 91*
Prime, Cecil T. 1909-1979 *AuBYP 90*
Prime, George Michael *BiDrAPA 89*
Prime, Penelope Benson 1954- *WhoSSW 91*

Prime, William Cowper 1825-1905 *BioIn 16*
Prime-Stevenson, Edward Irenaeus 1868-1942 *BioIn 16*
Primeaux, Henry, III 1941- *WhoSSW 91*
Primelo, Ralph Albert *BiDrAPA 89*
Primero, Remedios C *BiDrAPA 89*
Primi, Don Alexis 1947- *WhoEmL 91*
Primis, Lance Roy 1946- *WhoAm 90*
Primm, Annelle *BiDrAPA 89*
Primm, Darlene Bell 1960- *WhoAmW 91*
Primm, Jules Richard 1923- *WhoSSW 91*
Primm, Marcus Lee 1941- *St&PR 91*
Primo, Albert Thomas 1935- *WhoAm 90*
Primo, Marie Nash 1928- *WhoAmW 91*
Primo, Quintin Ebenezer, Jr. 1913- *WhoAm 90*
Primo de Rivera, Jose Antonio 1903-1936 *BioIn 16*
Primo de Rivera, Miguel 1870-1930 *BioIn 16*
Primoff, Bertram S. *BioIn 16*
Primorac, Zarko-Tadija's 1937- *WhoWor 91*
Primps, William Guthrie 1949- *WhoE 91, WhoWor 91*
Primrose, Archibald Philip 1847-1929 *BioIn 16*
Primrose, Diana *FemiCLE*
Primrose, Diana *BiDEWW*
Primrose, George Henry 1852-1919 *OxCCanT*
Primrose, Tracey *ODwPR 91*
Primrose, William 1903-1982 *PenDiMP*
Primus, Constance Louise Merrill 1931- *IntWWM 90*
Primus, Mary Jane Davis 1924- *WhoWor 91*
Primus, Pearl 1919- *BioIn 16, DrBIPA 90*
Primuth, David J. 1938- *St&PR 91*
Primuth, Eric Mark 1959- *WhoEmL 91*
Prin, Alice Ernestine 1901-1953? *BioIn 16*
Prina, Louis Edgar 1917- *WhoAm 90*
Prina, Stephen James 1954- *WhoAmA 91*
Prince *BioIn 16*
Prince 1958- *DrBIPA 90, OxCPMus, WhoAm 90*
Prince 1959- *EncPR&S 89, WorAlBi*
Prince Mohamed Bolkiah 1947- *WhoWor 91*
Prince, Alan Norton 1939- *St&PR 91*
Prince, Alan Theodore 1915- *WhoAm 90*
Prince, Andrew Steven 1943- *WhoAm 90*
Prince, Anna L. *WhoSSW 91, WhoWor 91*
Prince, Antoinette Odette 1946- *WhoAmW 91*
Prince, Arnold 1925- *WhoAmA 91*
Prince, Bernadine A 1930- *BiDrAPA 89*
Prince, Bill G. *WhoSSW 91*
Prince, Billy *BioIn 16*
Prince, Billy Don 1942- *WhoSSW 91*
Prince, Bob 1916-1985 *Ballpl 90*
Prince, Carl E. 1934- *WhoAm 90*
Prince, Catherine Moran 1945- *WhoAmW 91*
Prince, Charles William 1951- *WhoSSW 91*
Prince, Clayton *BioIn 16*
Prince, Cynthia Ann 1953- *WhoAmW 91*
Prince, Daniel Lloyd 1955- *WhoAm 90*
Prince, E. Ted 1947- *St&PR 91*
Prince, Edward Rudolph, Jr. 1929- *St&PR 91*
Prince, Eugene Edward 1932- *St&PR 91*
Prince, Faith *ConTFT 8*
Prince, Frances Anne Kiely 1923- *WhoWor 91*
Prince, Garnett B., Jr. 1949- *WhoAm 90*
Prince, Gary A. 1954- *St&PR 91*
Prince, Gary Michael 1948- *BiDrAPA 89*
Prince, George Edward 1921- *WhoSSW 91*
Prince, George Richard 1944- *St&PR 91*
Prince, Gregory Smith, Jr. 1939- *WhoAm 90*
Prince, Hal *ConTFT 8*
Prince, Harold *BioIn 16*
Prince, Harold 1928- *WorAlBi*
Prince, Harold S. 1928- *ConTFT 8 [port], WhoAm 90*
Prince, Jacquelynne Bolander 1955- *WhoAmW 91*
Prince, James William 1953- *BiDrAPA 89*
Prince, Jerome 1907-1988 *BioIn 16*
Prince, Jimmy Dale 1948- *WhoSSW 91*
Prince, John Dyneley 1868-1945 *AmLegL*
Prince, Julius S. 1911- *WhoAm 90, WhoE 91, WhoWor 91*
Prince, Kelli Elizabeth 1966- *WhoEmL 91*
Prince, Kenneth C. 1912- *WhoAm 90*
Prince, Kenneth Stephen 1950- *WhoEmL 91*
Prince, Larry L. *WhoAm 90, WhoSSW 91*
Prince, Leon M. 1911-1990 *BioIn 16*
Prince, Martin 1937- *St&PR 91*
Prince, Mary *BiDEWW*
Prince, Mary 1788?-1833? *FemiCLE*
Prince, Milton S. 1912- *WhoAm 90*
Prince, Morris David 1926- *WhoAm 90*
Prince, Morton 1854-1929 *EncO&P 3*
Prince, Morton Bronenberg 1924- *WhoAm 90*
Prince, Nancy 1799- *FemiCLE*
Prince, Patricia Ann 1948- *WhoE 91*
Prince, Philip Steven 1933- *St&PR 91*
Prince, R. E. *AmLegL*
Prince, Richard 1949- *BioIn 16*
Prince, Richard Edmund 1949- *WhoAmA 91*
Prince, Robb L. 1941- *St&PR 91*
Prince, Robb Lincoln 1941- *WhoAm 90*
Prince, Robert George 1929- *WhoSSW 91*
Prince, Robert Leon *BiDrAPA 89*
Prince, Robert M, Jr. *BiDrAPA 89*
Prince, Roger Charles 1950- *WhoE 91*
Prince, Ronald Stanford 1931- *St&PR 91*
Prince, Russell Bruce 1938- *BiDrAPA 89*
Prince, Thomas *WhoSSW 91*
Prince, Thomas 1687-1758 *EncCRAm*
Prince, Thomas Eugene 1947- *St&PR 91*
Prince, Thomas F. 1934- *St&PR 91*
Prince, Thomas Richard 1934- *WhoAm 90, WhoWor 91*
Prince, Walter Franklin 1863-1934 *EncO&P 3, EncPaPR 91*
Prince, Warren Victor 1911- *WhoWor 91*
Prince, William H. 1914- *WorAlBi*
Prince, William Meade 1893-1951 *WhoAmA 91N*
Prince, William Taliaferro 1929- *WhoAm 90*
Prince-Joseph, Bruce 1925- *IntWWM 90*
Princing, Thomas Tim 1938- *WhoAm 90*
Princip, Gavrillo 1895-1918 *WorAlBi*
Principal, Victoria *BioIn 16*
Principal, Victoria 1945- *WorAlBi*
Principal, Victoria 1950- *WhoAm 90, WhoAmW 91*
Princz, Daniel 1953- *WhoSSW 91*
Princz, Judith *WhoAmW 91*
Prindiville, Jim *BioIn 16*
Prindiville, Jim 1941- *WhoAmA 91*
Prindiville, Robert A. 1935- *St&PR 91*
Prindiville, Robert Andrew 1935- *WhoAm 90*
Prindiville, Terry Spencer 1935- *St&PR 91*
Prindl, Andreas Robert 1939- *WhoWor 91*
Prindle, Cheryl H. 1960- *WhoAmW 91*
Prindle, William Roscoe 1926- *WhoAm 90*
Prine, Andrew Lewis 1936- *WhoAm 90*
Prine, Anne M. *ODwPR 91*
Prine, Charles W., Jr. 1926- *St&PR 91, WhoAm 90*
Prine, John 1946- *WhoAm 90*
Prineas, Ronald James 1937- *WhoSSW 91*
Pring, Katherine 1940- *IntWWM 90*
Pring, Martin 1580-1626 *EncCRAm*
Pringle, Aileen 1895-1989 *BioIn 16*
Pringle, Barbara Carroll 1939- *WhoAmW 91*
Pringle, Clifford 1904-1989 *BioIn 16*
Pringle, Colombe *BioIn 16*
Pringle, David L. 1946- *St&PR 91*
Pringle, Dora Roberta 1921- *WhoAmW 91*
Pringle, Edward E. 1914- *WhoAm 90*
Pringle, Edward Graves 1941- *WhoAm 90*
Pringle, Eleanor W 1940- *BiDrAPA 89*
Pringle, Elisa M. 1959- *St&PR 91*
Pringle, George Overton 1923- *WhoSSW 91*
Pringle, James W. 1862- *AmLegL*
Pringle, Jan S. *ODwPR 91*
Pringle, Joan *DrBIPA 90*
Pringle, John Alan 1949- *WhoSSW 91*
Pringle, John William Sutton 1912-1982 *DcNaB 1981*
Pringle, Laurence P. 1935- *AuBYP 90*
Pringle, Lewis Gordon 1941- *St&PR 91, WhoAm 90*
Pringle, Mia Lilly Kellmer 1920-1983 *DcNaB 1981*
Pringle, Oran Allan 1923- *WhoAm 90*
Pringle, Peter Kilner 1941- *WhoSSW 91*
Pringle, Robert Maxwell 1936- *WhoAm 90, WhoWor 91*
Pringle, Thomas Walker 1957- *WhoE 91*
Pringle, William Allen 1841-1896 *DcCanB 12*
Pringsheim, Klaus 1883-1972 *PenDiMP*
Pringy, Madame de 16--?-17--? *EncCoWW*
Prinjinski, Thomas Joseph 1955- *WhoEmL 91*
Prinkki, Aulikki *EncCoWW*
Prinn, Charles Edward, III 1940- *St&PR 91*
Prino, Mary Katherine 1958- *WhoSSW 91*
Prinos, Monique E. 1957- *WhoAmW 91*
Prinotto, Luigi *PenDiDA 89*
Prins, David 1930- *WhoAm 90*
Prins, LaVonne Kay 1957- *WhoAmW 91*
Prins, Richard Greenway 1936- *St&PR 91*
Prins, Robert Jack 1932- *WhoAm 90, WhoWor 91*
Prinsell, Jeffrey Robert 1953- *WhoSSW 91*
Prinsky, Robert *St&PR 91*
Prinster, Anthony F. 1941- *St&PR 91*
Prinster, Leo T. 1928- *St&PR 91*
Printemps, Yvonne 1894-1977 *PenDiMP*
Printemps, Yvonne 1895-1977 *OxCPMus*
Printup, Susan Marie 1953- *WhoEmL 91*
Printz, Bonnie Allen *WhoAmA 91*
Printz, Bonnie Allen 1946- *WhoEmL 91*
Printz, Johan Bjornsson 1592-1663 *EncCRAm, WhNaAH*
Prinz, Helen 1928- *IntWWM 90*
Prinz, Joachim 1902-1988 *BioIn 16*
Prinz, Kenneth A. *St&PR 91*
Prinz, Robert William 1950- *WhoE 91*
Prinz, Steven Mark *BiDrAPA 89*
Prinz, Wolfram 1929- *WhoWor 91*
Prinze, Freddie 1954-1977 *WorAlBi*
Prinzivalli, Joseph Anthony, Jr. 1955- *WhoE 91*
Prio Socarras, Carlos 1903-1977 *BioIn 16*
Priola, Donald Victor 1938- *WhoAm 90*
Prioleau, H. Frost 1929- *St&PR 91*
Prioli, Mary Grace 1916- *WhoAmW 91*
Priolo, Louis Paul 1954- *WhoSSW 91*
Priolo, Toby A. 1939- *St&PR 91*
Prior, A. Dale 1955- *WhoSSW 91*
Prior, Allan *TwCCr&M 91*
Prior, Boyd Thelman 1926- *WhoSSW 91*
Prior, Claude 1918- *IntWWM 90*
Prior, Cornelius B., Jr. 1934- *St&PR 91*
Prior, Harris King 1911-1975 *WhoAmA 91N*
Prior, James Michael Leathes 1927- *WhoWor 91*
Prior, John Alan 1913- *WhoAm 90*
Prior, Katherine Faith 1949- *WhoE 91*
Prior, Martin Giles 1947- *WhoSSW 91*
Prior, Matthew 1664-1721 *DcLB 95 [port]*
Prior, Ole 1935- *WhoSSW 91*
Prior, Patrick *BioIn 16*
Prior, Peter N. 1933- *St&PR 91*
Prior, Richard Marion 1942- *WhoSSW 91*
Priore, Frank Vincent 1946- *WhoWrEP 89*
Priore, Roger L. 1938- *WhoAm 90*
Priori, Jorge *BiDrAPA 89*
Priory, Joseph Downs 1944- *WhoAm 90*
Priory, Richard Baldwin 1946- *St&PR 91*
Prip, Janet 1950- *WhoAmA 91*
Prip, John A 1922- *WhoAmA 91*
Prisant, L. Michael 1949- *WhoSSW 91*
Prisant, M. Barden 1960- *WhoE 91*
Prisant, Millard B. 1935- *St&PR 91*
Prisbrey, Tressa 1896-1988 *MusmAFA*
Prischak, Isabel J. 1936- *St&PR 91*
Prischak, Joseph J. 1931- *St&PR 91*
Prisching, Manfred 1950- *WhoWor 91*
Prisco, Douglas Louis 1945- *WhoE 91, WhoEmL 91*
Prisk, Patricia 1944- *WhoAmW 91*
Priske, Daniel G. 1928- *St&PR 91*
Prislupsky, Vladimir *BioIn 16*
Prismanova, Anna 1898-1960 *EncCoWW*
Pristach, Cynthia Ann *BiDrAPA 89*
Pritchard, Alan S., Jr. 1941- *St&PR 91*
Pritchard, Barbara Ellen 1952- *WhoAmW 91*
Pritchard, Claudius Hornby, Jr. 1927- *WhoAm 90*
Pritchard, Constance Jenkins 1950- *WhoSSW 91*
Pritchard, Dalton Harold 1921- *WhoAm 90*
Pritchard, David Faulkner 1935- *St&PR 91*
Pritchard, Donald William 1922- *WhoAm 90*
Pritchard, Edward Arthur 1943- *WhoAm 90*
Pritchard, Gwyn Charles 1948- *IntWWM 90*
Pritchard, Harmon Otis, Jr. 1930- *St&PR 91*
Pritchard, Huw Owen 1928- *WhoAm 90*
Pritchard, James Bennett 1909- *WhoAm 90*
Pritchard, Joel 1925- *WhoAm 90*
Pritchard, John 1921- *PenDiMP*
Pritchard, John 1921-1989 *AnObit 1989*
Pritchard, John Michael 1921-1989 *BioIn 16, IntWWM 90*
Pritchard, Lois Ruth Breur 1946- *WhoAmW 91, WhoEmL 91, WhoWor 91*
Pritchard, Mary D'Ercole 1940- *WhoAmW 91*
Pritchard, Marylou 1948- *St&PR 91*
Pritchard, Melissa Brown 1948- *WhoWrEP 89*
Pritchard, Michael Gregg 1949- *WhoEmL 91*
Pritchard, Parm Frederick 1914- *WhoWrEP 89*
Pritchard, Paul Clement 1944- *WhoAm 90*
Pritchard, Paul Michael 1938- *WhoSSW 91*
Pritchard, Raymond John 1931- *WhoSSW 91*
Pritchard, Robert Starling 1929- *WhoE 91*
Pritchard, Sarah Margaret 1955- *WhoAmW 91*
Pritchard, Wilbur Louis 1923- *WhoAm 90, WhoE 91*
Pritchard, William Baker 1950- *WhoE 91*
Pritchard, William Roy 1924- *WhoAm 90*
Pritchard, William Shelton, Jr. 1924- *WhoSSW 91*
Pritchard, William Winther 1951- *WhoAm 90*
Pritchett, Anna Marie White 1941- *WhoWor 91*
Pritchett, Charles Herman 1907- *WhoAm 90*
Pritchett, Charles M. 1926- *St&PR 91*
Pritchett, David Ollis 1953- *WhoSSW 91*
Pritchett, Elizabeth Estell 1955- *BiDrAPA 89*
Pritchett, Larry Walter 1933- *WhoSSW 91*
Pritchett, Lois Jane *WhoSSW 91*
Pritchett, Louis Alexander 1931- *WhoAm 90*
Pritchett, Robert Lee 1948- *St&PR 91*
Pritchett, Scott Luther 1963- *WhoSSW 91*
Pritchett, Thomas Carroll 1952- *WhoSSW 91*
Pritchett, Thomas Ronald 1925- *WhoAm 90*
Pritchett, V S 1900- *ConAu 31NR, MajTwCW*
Pritchett, Victor Sawdon 1900- *WhoAm 90, WhoWor 91*
Pritchitt, Jim *ODwPR 91*
Pritikin, Nathan *BioIn 16*
Pritikin, Roland I. 1906- *WhoAm 90*
Pritsker, A. Alan B. 1933- *WhoAm 90*
Pritt, Charlotte J. 1949- *WhoAmW 91*
Pritt, Marianne Patterson 1952- *WhoEmL 91*
Pritt, Terry Gray 1957- *BiDrAPA 89*
Prittie, Terence Cornelius Farmer 1913-1985 *DcNaB 1981*
Pritts, Roger L. 1944- *St&PR 91*
Pritts, William E., II 1939- *St&PR 91*
Pritz, Peter J. 1928- *St&PR 91*
Pritz, William J. 1925- *St&PR 91*
Pritzker Family *ConAmBL*
Pritzker, Abram Nicholas 1896-1986 *ConAmBL*
Pritzker, Donald Nicholas 1932-1972 *ConAmBL*
Pritzker, Jack Nicholas 1904-1979 *ConAmBL*
Pritzker, Jay A. 1922- *St&PR 91*
Pritzker, Jay Arthur 1922- *ConAmBL, WhoAm 90*
Pritzker, Leon 1922- *WhoAm 90*
Pritzker, Nicholas J. *WhoAm 90*
Pritzker, Nicholas J. 1945- *ConAmBL*
Pritzker, Robert A. 1926- *St&PR 91*
Pritzker, Robert Alan 1926- *ConAmBL*
Pritzker, Thomas J. 1950- *St&PR 91*
Pritzker, Thomas Jay 1950- *ConAmBL*
Pritzlaff, John, Jr 1925- *WhoAmA 91*
Pritzlaff, John, Jr, Mrs *WhoAmA 91*
Pritzlaff, John Charles, Jr. 1925- *WhoAm 90*
Privat, Jeannette Mary 1938- *WhoAm 90*
Privat, John Pierre 1934- *St&PR 91*
Privett, Roy Frank 1926- *WhoE 91*
Privette, William Herbert 1949- *WhoWrEP 89*
Privitera, Charles R, Jr. *BiDrAPA 89*
Privitera, Michael, Jr. *BiDrAPA 89*
Privitera, Michael Russell, Jr. 1952- *WhoE 91*
Privitera, Vincent John *BiDrAPA 89*
Privitera, William John *BiDrAPA 89*
Privitere, Louis Philip 1925- *St&PR 91*
Privott, Jo A. 1953- *WhoAmW 91*
Priyatna, Abdurrasyid 1929- *WhoWor 91*
Prizer, Charles John 1924- *WhoAm 90*
Prizzi, Jack Anthony 1935- *WhoAm 90*
Pro Arte Quartet *PenDiMP*
Pro, John Dennis *BiDrAPA 89*
Pro-Landazuri, Jose Miguel 1947- *WhoSSW 91*
Proano, Augusto *BiDrAPA 89*
Proano, Pablo Roberto 1955- *BiDrAPA 89*
Proba *EncCoWW*
Proba, Betitia *EncCoWW*
Proba, Falconia *EncCoWW*
Proba, Faltonia *EncCoWW*
Probasco, Calvin Henry Charles 1926- *WhoAm 90*
Probasco, Scott Livingston 1928- *WhoAm 90*
Probelski, Kathy B. *St&PR 91*
Prober, Mark Alan *BiDrAPA 89*
Probert, Bob *BioIn 16*
Probert, Walter 1925- *WhoAm 90*
Probes, Lawrence Morris 1952- *BiDrAPA 89*
Probst, David S. 1939- *St&PR 91*
Probst, Dominique Henri 1954- *IntWWM 90*
Probst, Gerald Graham 1923-1989 *BioIn 16*
Probst, John William 1951- *WhoSSW 91*
Probst, Lawrence F., Jr. 1925- *St&PR 91*
Probst, Mark 1925- *ConAu 130, ConLC 59 [port]*
Probst Dinerstein, Enrique *BiDrAPA 89*
Probstein, Ronald Filmore 1928- *WhoAm 90, WhoWor 91*

Proby, John Joshua 1751-1828 *BioIn 16*
Proby, Lucien C., III *ODwPR 91*
Probyn, Clive Trevor 1944- *WhoWor 91*
Procario, Rudolph F *BiDrAPA 89*
Procel, Guillermo, Jr. 1947- *WhoHisp 91*
Proch, Robert L. 1952- *St&PR 91*
Prochal, Sheryl Lynn 1958- *WhoEmL 91*
Prochaska, Mark Lawrence 1957- *BiDrAPA 89*
Prochaska, Richard Robert 1946- *WhoSSW 91*
Prochazka, Jan *AuBYP 90*
Prochazka, Zdenek Horymir 1915- *IntWWM 90*
Prochnow, Douglas Lee 1952- *WhoEmL 91*
Prochnow, Herbert Victor 1897- *WhoAm 90*
Prochnow, Herbert Victor, Jr. 1931- *WhoAm 90*
Prochownik, Walter A 1923- *WhoAmA 91*
Procidano, Mary Elizabeth 1954- *WhoAmW 91, WhoEmL 91*
Prock, Markus *BioIn 16*
Procknow, Donald E. 1923- *St&PR 91*
Prockop, Darwin Johnson 1929- *WhoAm 90*
Prockop, Leon Denton 1934- *WhoAm 90*
Procol Harum *EncPR&S 89*
Procope, Ernesta G. *BioIn 16*
Procope, Ernesta Gertrude *WhoAmW 91*
Procopio, Dimple Ozella 1940- *WhoAmW 91*
Procopio, Joseph Guydon 1940- *St&PR 91*
Procopio, Maria Concetta 1964- *WhoE 91*
Procopius, of Caesarea 500?-565? *BioIn 16*
Procter, Adelaide 1825-1864 *FemiCLE*
Procter, Adelaide Anne 1825-1864 *BioIn 16*
Procter, Bryan Waller 1787-1874 *DcLB 96 [port]*
Procter, Dod 1892-1972 *BiDWomA*
Procter, Gordon 1924- *WhoWor 91*
Procter, Henry 1763?-1822 *WhNaAH*
Procter, John Ernest 1918- *WhoAm 90*
Procter, Maurice 1906-1973 *TwCCr&M 91*
Procter, Michael Robert 1951- *IntWWM 90*
Procter, Norma 1928- *IntWWM 90, PenDiMP*
Procter, William C. 1862-1934 *WorAlBi*
Proctor, A Phimister 1862-1950 *WhoAmA 91N*
Proctor, Barbara Gardner *WhoAm 90, WhoAmW 91*
Proctor, Bobby L. 1933- *St&PR 91*
Proctor, Brian Dale 1957- *BiDrAPA 89*
Proctor, Charles Lafayette, II 1954- *WhoSSW 91*
Proctor, Chris *NewAgMG*
Proctor, David Ray 1956- *WhoSSW 91*
Proctor, Deborah Suzanne 1951- *WhoAmW 91*
Proctor, Donald Frederick 1913- *WhoAm 90*
Proctor, Everitt *AuBYP 90*
Proctor, Fletcher Dutton 1860-1911 *AmLegL*
Proctor, Henry 1763?-1822 *WhNaAH*
Proctor, Jesse Harris, Jr. 1924- *WhoAm 90*
Proctor, John Douglas 1949- *St&PR 91*
Proctor, John Franklin 1931- *WhoAm 90*
Proctor, John Howard 1931- *WhoWor 91*
Proctor, Kenneth Donald 1944- *WhoAm 90*
Proctor, Kenneth W., Jr. 1929- *St&PR 91*
Proctor, Lester T., Jr. 1927- *St&PR 91*
Proctor, Lou *Ballpl 90*
Proctor, Mark Alan 1948- *WhoSSW 91*
Proctor, Mark Robinson *BiDrAPA 89*
Proctor, Nigel 1938- *WhoWor 91*
Proctor, Pamela Lloyd 1960- *WhoE 91*
Proctor, Patricia Ann Pezanowski 1958- *WhoAmW 91*
Proctor, Paul Dean 1918- *WhoAm 90*
Proctor, Randall Wesley 1928- *St&PR 91, WhoAm 90, WhoWor 91*
Proctor, Redfield 1831-1908 *BiDrUSE 89*
Proctor, Richard C 1921- *BiDrAPA 89*
Proctor, Richard Owen 1935- *WhoAm 90*
Proctor, Robert Remmington 1936- *WhoSSW 91*
Proctor, Robert Swope 1922- *WhoAm 90*
Proctor, Sallie Earle 1950- *WhoAmW 91*
Proctor, Samuel 1919- *WhoAm 90*
Proctor, Samuel D. *BioIn 16*
Proctor, Stanley Matthew 1920- *St&PR 91*
Proctor, Terrell William 1934- *WhoSSW 91, WhoWor 91*
Proctor, Vivian Clare *BiDrAPA 89*
Proctor, William Con 1925- *St&PR 91*
Proctor, William Lee 1933- *WhoAm 90*
Proctor, William Zinsmaster 1902- *WhoAm 90*
Procul Harum *OxCPMus*
Prod, Raymond John 1931- *St&PR 91*
Prodan, James Christian 1947- *IntWWM 90*
Prodanovic, A. Andy 1956- *St&PR 91*
Proden, Douglas N *BiDrAPA 89*
Prod'Hom, L. Samuel 1926- *WhoWor 91*
Proefrock, Carl Kenneth 1928- *WhoAm 90*
Proefrock, Vicki Gaither 1947- *WhoAmW 91*
Proell, Annemarie 1953- *WorAlBi*
Proesch, Gilbert *BioIn 16*
Proescher, Ward Hornblower 1935- *WhoWor 91*
Profeta, Laurentiu 1925- *IntWWM 90*
Profeta, Nicholas J. 1929- *St&PR 91*
Proffer, Ellendea Catherine 1944- *WhoWrEP 89*
Proffit, William Robert 1936- *WhoAm 90*
Proffitt, David T. 1948- *St&PR 91*
Proffitt, Jack Maurice 1926- *WhoSSW 91*
Proffitt, John B. 1939- *St&PR 91*
Proffitt, John Matthew Gladney 1948- *WhoAm 90*
Proffitt, John R., Sr. 1897- *St&PR 91*
Proffitt, John Richard 1930- *WhoE 91*
Proffitt, John Roscoe, Jr. 1924- *St&PR 91*
Proffitt, Joyce Harrison 1925- *St&PR 91*
Proffitt, Merlyn L. 1930- *St&PR 91*
Proffitt, Nicholas *SpyFic*
Proffitt, Nicholas 1943- *ConAu 131*
Proffitt, Paula Annette *BiDrAPA 89*
Proffitt, William Lloyd 1929- *WhoAm 90*
Profio, Winston Clarke 1931- *St&PR 91*
Profita, Karen Jensen 1959- *WhoAmW 91*
Profitt, David T. 1948- *St&PR 91*
Profughi, Terence C. 1946- *St&PR 91*
Profumo, John D. *BioIn 16*
Progar, Dorothy 1924- *WhoAm 90, WhoSSW 91*
Progelhof, Richard Carl 1936- *WhoAm 90, WhoSSW 91*
Progoff, Ira 1921- *EncO&P 3*
Progulske-Fox, Ann 1951- *WhoAmW 91*
Prohaska, Elena Anastasia 1946- *WhoAmA 91*
Prohaska, Jaro 1891-1965 *PenDiMP*
Prohaska, John William 1929- *St&PR 91*
Prohaska, Ray 1901-1981 *WhoAmA 91N*
Prokai, Bela 1937- *WhoWor 91*
Prokasy, William Frederick 1930- *WhoAm 90*
Prokhorov, Aleksandr 1916- *WorAlBi*
Prokhorov, Aleksandr Mikhailovich 1916- *WhoWor 91*
Prokofiev, Lina 1898-1989 *BioIn 16*
Prokofiev, Sergei 1891-1953 *WorAlBi*
Prokofiev, Sergey 1891-1953 *BioIn 16, PenDiMP A*
Prokop, Bill P. *St&PR 91*
Prokop, Leanne Eliason 1960- *WhoEmL 91*
Prokop, Michael Stephen 1953- *WhoWrEP 89*
Prokopenko, Joseph Ivanovich 1939- *WhoWor 91*
Prokopis, Emmanuel Charles 1942- *WhoAm 90*
Prokopoff, Stephen 1929- *WhoAmA 91*
Prokopoff, Stephen Stephen 1929- *WhoAm 90*
Prokopovich, S. Richard 1948- *WhoE 91*
Prokopy, John Alfred 1926- *WhoE 91*
Prokosch, Frederic 1908-1989 *AnObit 1989, BioIn 16*
Prokoshkin, Yuri Dmitrievich 1929- *WhoWor 91*
Prokoski, Francine J. 1948- *St&PR 91*
Prol, John H. 1937- *St&PR 91*
Proler, Herman 1927- *St&PR 91*
Proll, Douglas A. 1950- *St&PR 91*
Proll, George Simon 1931- *WhoE 91*
Proly, Mike 1950- *Ballpl 90*
Prom, Stephen George 1954- *WhoEmL 91, WhoSSW 91*
Prominski, John Eugene 1924- *St&PR 91*
Promisel, Nathan E. 1908- *WhoAm 90*
Promislo, Daniel 1932- *WhoWor 91*
Promutico, Jean 1936- *WhoAmA 91*
Pronko, Michael J 1934- *BiDrAPA 89*
Prontnicki, Janice 1960- *WhoAmW 91*
Pronzini, Bill *BioIn 16*
Pronzini, Bill 1943- *ConAu 32NR, TwCCr&M 91*
Pronzini, Bill John 1943- *WhoAm 90, WhoWrEP 89*
Proost, Robert Lee 1937- *WhoAm 90*
Proper, Dean D. 1936- *St&PR 91*
Proper, Steven Al 1947- *WhoSSW 91*
Propersi, August J 1926- *WhoAmA 91*
Propes, Major Thomas 1957- *WhoSSW 91*
Prophet, The *MajTwCW*
Prophet, Elizabeth Clare *BioIn 16*
Prophet, Elizabeth Clare *EncPaPR 91*
Prophet, Elizabeth Clare 1940- *NewAgE 90*
Prophet, Mark *EncPaPR 91*
Propp, Gail Dane Gomberg 1944- *WhoAmW 91*
Propper, Michael Welles *BiDrAPA 89*
Propper, Milton 1906-1962 *TwCCr&M 91*
Propper, Norman Sherwin 1923- *WhoSSW 91*
Propst, Catherine Lamb 1946- *WhoAmW 91*
Propst, John Leake 1914- *St&PR 91, WhoAm 90*
Propst, Nell Brown 1925- *WhoWrEP 89*
Proschan, Frank 1921- *WhoAm 90*
Prose, Francine 1947- *BioIn 16, WorAu 1980 [port]*
Prosen, Harry 1930- *BiDrAPA 89, WhoAm 90*
Prosen, Melvin *BiDrAPA 89*
Prosen, Rose Mary *WhoWrEP 89*
Proshansky, Harold Milton 1920- *WhoAm 90, WhoE 91*
Prosio, Gerald Anthony 1948- *St&PR 91*
Proskauer, Joseph Meyer 1877-1971 *BioIn 16*
Proske, Paul Edward 1932- *St&PR 91*
Proske, Robert J. 1946- *St&PR 91*
Prosky, Robert 1930- *WorAlBi*
Prosky, Robert Joseph 1930- *WhoAm 90*
Prosperi, Robert 1942- *St&PR 91*
Pross, Lester Fred 1924- *WhoAmA 91*
Prosser, C. Ladd 1907- *WhoAm 90*
Prosser, Daniel Feigal 1949- *WhoSSW 91*
Prosser, Deborah L. 1954- *WhoAmW 91*
Prosser, Eleanor Alice 1922- *WhoAm 90*
Prosser, Franklin Pierce 1935- *WhoAm 90*
Prosser, H.L. 1944- *ConAu 33NR*
Prosser, Harold Lee 1944- *WhoWrEP 89*
Prosser, John Martin 1932- *WhoAm 90, WhoWor 91*
Prosser, John Warren, Jr. 1945- *St&PR 91*
Prosser, Linda 1955- *ODwPR 91*
Prosser, Lisa Lynn 1955- *WhoAmW 91*
Prosser, Lizann 1954- *WhoE 91*
Prosser, Moorman P 1910- *BiDrAPA 89*
Prosser, Robert L. 1931- *St&PR 91*
Prosser, Thomas James 1936- *St&PR 91*
Prosswimmer, R. Alan 1930- *St&PR 91*
Prost, Alain Marie Pascal 1955- *WhoWor 91*
Prostano, Emanuel T. 1931- *WhoAm 90*
Prosterman, Roy L. 1935- *WhoAm 90*
Proszynski, Stanislaw Tadeusz Konrad 1926- *IntWWM 90*
Prota, Patrick A. 1943- *St&PR 91*
Protagoras 485?BC-410?BC *WorAlBi*
Protas, Ron *WhoAm 90*
Protero, Dodi 1935- *IntWWM 90*
Prothero, Charles Leslie 1932- *St&PR 91*
Prothero, Charles Leslie, III 1932- *WhoAm 90*
Prothero-Smith, Joy Eddette 1952- *WhoAmW 91*
Protheroe, Alan Hackford 1934- *WhoWor 91*
Prothet, Richard 1948- *WhoWor 91*
Prothro, Doc 1893-1971 *Ballpl 90*
Prothro, Esther Jamieson 1913- *WhoWrEP 89*
Prothro, Gerald D. *BioIn 16*
Prothro, Joe N. *WhoSSW 91*
Prothrow-Stith, Deborah *BioIn 16*
Protic, Dushica Babich 1958- *WhoAmW 91*
Protiva, Miroslav 1921- *WhoWor 91*
Protschka, Josef 1944- *IntWWM 90*
Protti, Aldo 1920- *IntWWM 90*
Proud, Ernest Leroy, Jr. 1933- *St&PR 91*
Proud, G. O'Neil 1913- *WhoAm 90*
Proudeit, Isabel 1898- *AuBYP 90*
Proudfoot, Peter Reginald 1936- *WhoWor 91*
Proudfoot, Vincent Bruce 1930- *WhoWor 91*
Proudhon, P.-J. 1809-1865 *BioIn 16*
Proudhon, Pierre-Joseph 1809-1865 *BioIn 16, WorAlBi*
Proudlock, Annabella Phyllis 1943- *WhoWor 91*
Prough, Paul Leroy, Jr. 1946- *WhoAm 90, WhoE 91*
Prough, Russell Allen 1943- *WhoAm 90*
Proujan, Carl 1929- *WhoE 91*
Proulx, Amedee Wilfrid 1932- *WhoE 91*
Proulx, Jean-Baptiste 1846-1904 *OxCCanT*
Proulx, Norman Raymond 1947- *St&PR 91*
Proust, Marcel 1871-1922 *BioIn 16, MajTwCW, WorAlBi*
Prout, Carl Wesley 1941- *WhoWor 91*
Prout, Curtis 1915- *WhoAm 90*
Prout, Curtis T *BiDrAPA 89*
Prout, George Russell, Jr. 1924- *WhoAm 90*
Prout, Gerald R. *ODwPR 91*
Prout, Gerald Robert 1949- *WhoE 91*
Prout, Margaret Millicent 1875-1963 *BiDWomA*
Prout, Marilyn Eileen 1961- *St&PR 91*
Prout, Ralph Eugene 1933- *WhoAm 90*
Prouty, Jack Warren 1946- *St&PR 91*
Prouty, Morton Dennison, Jr. 1918- *WhoAm 90*
Prouve, Emile Victor 1858-1943 *PenDiDA 89*
Prouvost, Gaetane 1954- *IntWWM 90*
Prouza, Zdenek 1955- *IntWWM 90*
Provancher, Leon 1820-1892 *DcCanB 12*
Provder, Carl 1933- *WhoAmA 91*
Provence, Herbert H., Jr. *BioIn 16*
Provencher, Roger Arthur 1923- *WhoAm 90*
Provencher, Stephen Wilfred 1942- *WhoWor 91*
Provencher, Thomas J. 1938- *St&PR 91*
Provencher-Kambour, Frances 1947- *WhoAmW 91, WhoWor 91*
Provencio, Dolores *WhoHisp 91*
Provencio, Ricardo B. 1947- *WhoHisp 91*
Provensen, Alice Rose Twitchell *WhoAm 90*
Provensen, Martin 1916-1987 *BioIn 16*
Provenzano, Tony Pro 1917-1988 *BioIn 16*
Prover, Stephen Erwin 1941- *BiDrAPA 89*
Proverbio, Eduardo 1928- *WhoWor 91*
Province, Martin Robert 1956- *WhoSSW 91*
Provines, Michael Jack 1947- *St&PR 91*
Provis, Dorothy Louise 1926- *WhoAmW 91*
Provist, d'Alain *ConAu 130, MajTwCW*
Provist, d'Alain 1906-1989 *SmATA X*
Provorny, Frederick Alan 1946- *WhoE 91, WhoEmL 91, WhoWor 91*
Provost, David Emile 1949- *St&PR 91*
Provost, Eleanor 1947- *WhoAmW 91*
Provost, Rhonda Marie 1948- *WhoAmW 91, WhoEmL 91*
Provost, Serge 1952- *IntWWM 90*
Provost, Thomas Taylor 1938- *WhoAm 90*
Provost, Wally 1922- *WhoAm 90*
Provvidenza, Michele 1953- *WhoWor 91*
Prowell, Roy Walters, Jr. 1945- *WhoEmL 91, WhoWor 91*
Prowler, Harley *MajTwCW*
Prown, Jules David 1930- *WhoAmA 91*
Prowse, Anne *BiDEWW*
Prowse, Anne Locke *BioIn 16*
Prowse, Juliet 1937- *WorAlBi*
Prox, Robert F., Jr. 1926- *St&PR 91*
Proxmire, William *BioIn 16*
Proxmire, William 1915- *ConAu 31NR, EncABHB 7 [port], WhoWor 91, WorAlBi*
Proyas, Alex *BioIn 16*
Proye, Charles Andre 1938- *WhoWor 91*
Proyect, Martin H. 1932- *WhoAm 90*
Proysen, Alf *AuBYP 90*
Proysen, Alf 1914-1970 *DcScanL*
Prozan, Lawrence Ira 1961- *WhoEmL 91*
Prozan, Michael William 1959- *WhoEmL 91*
Pruce, Marta M *BiDrAPA 89*
Prucha, Francis Paul *BioIn 16*
Prucha, John James 1924- *WhoAm 90*
Prudden, George Alan 1953- *WhoE 91*
Prudden, John Fletcher 1920- *St&PR 91*
Prude, Agnes George de Mille 1905- *ConAu 30NR*
Prude, O. Cooper 1936- *St&PR 91*
Prude, Walter F. *BioIn 16*
Pruden, Laura A. *EncO&P 3*
Pruden, Peter DeWitt, III 1945- *St&PR 91*
Prudent, Robert Michael 1962- *BiDrAPA 89*
Prudenti, Anthony J. *NewYTBS 90 [port]*
Prudenti, Anthony J. 1928-1990 *BioIn 16*
Prud'homme, Albert Frederic 1952- *WhoWor 91*
Prudhomme, Jules Joseph Louis 1927- *WhoWor 91*
Prudhomme, Lisa Ann 1960- *WhoAmW 91*
Prudhomme, Michael P. 1943- *ODwPR 91, St&PR 91*
Prudhomme, William Charles 1950- *St&PR 91*
Prud'hommeaux, Rene *AuBYP 90*
Prud'hon, Pierre Paul 1758-1823 *IntDcAA 90*
Prudic, Joan *BiDrAPA 89*
Prudo-Chelbosz, Raymond *BiDrAPA 89*
Pruess, Joanna *BioIn 16*
Pruet, Chesley 1915- *WhoSSW 91*
Prueter, Michael Harry 1948- *WhoEmL 91*
Pruett, Carl Russell 1955- *WhoSSW 91*
Pruett, Donnie Ray 1948- *WhoAmW 91*
Pruett, Edwin Clark 1946- *St&PR 91*
Pruett, Helen Gorham 1919- *WhoAmW 91*
Pruett, Hub 1900-1982 *Ballpl 90*
Pruett, J. William 1930- *ODwPR 91*
Pruett, James Worrell 1932- *WhoAm 90*
Pruett, Jeanne *WhoAm 90*
Pruett, Jerome 1941- *IntWWM 90*
Pruett, Kyle D 1943- *ConAu 131*
Pruett, Kyle Dean 1943- *BiDrAPA 89, WhoE 91*
Pruett, Rhea Roelie Hofman 1955- *WhoAmW 91*
Pruett, Samuel H. 1932- *St&PR 91*
Prufer, Curt Max *BioIn 16*
Pruger, Robert Joseph 1948- *St&PR 91*
Prugh, Dane G. *NewYTBS 90*
Prugh, Dane Gaskill 1918- *BiDrAPA 89, WhoAm 90*
Prugh, David Clayton 1921- *WhoAm 90*

Prugh, George Shipley 1920- *WhoAm 90*
Prugovecki, Eduard 1937- *WhoAm 90*
Pruiett, Tex 1883-1953 *Ballpl 90*
Pruim, E.G. 1933- *St&PR 91*
Pruis, John J. 1923- *WhoAm 90*
Pruitt, Alice Fay 1943- *WhoAmW 91*
Pruitt, Anne Loring 1929- *WhoAm 90*
Pruitt, Basil Arthur, Jr. 1930- *WhoAm 90*
Pruitt, Bruce Alan 1953- *WhoSSW 91*
Pruitt, Cindy Kay 1957- *WhoAmW 91*
Pruitt, David Burton 1948- *BiDrAPA 89*
Pruitt, Dean Garner 1930- *WhoAm 90*
Pruitt, Dorothy J. Gooch 1935- *WhoAmW 91*
Pruitt, Gary E. 1950- *St&PR 91*
Pruitt, George Albert 1946- *WhoAm 90, WhoE 91*
Pruitt, Ina 1905- *WhoAmW 91*
Pruitt, J. Doug 1945- *WhoEmL 91, WhoWor 91*
Pruitt, John, III *BiDrAPA 89*
Pruitt, John D 1933- *BiDrAPA 89*
Pruitt, John Van Buren, III 1952- *WhoE 91*
Pruitt, Lynn 1937- *WhoAmA 91*
Pruitt, Michael Paul 1953- *BiDrAPA 89*
Pruitt, Nancy Louise 1953- *WhoAmW 91*
Pruitt, Patricia Nordan 1945- *WhoSSW 91*
Pruitt, Raymond Donald 1912- *WhoAm 90*
Pruitt, Ron 1951- *Ballpl 90*
Pruitt, Tamara Ann 1935- *St&PR 91*
Pruitt, Thomas Pitts, Jr. 1922- *St&PR 91*
Pruitt, Vernon Kent 1934- *St&PR 91*
Prume *DcCanB 12*
Pruneau, Tom 1945- *St&PR 91*
Prunella, Warren James 1941- *WhoAm 90*
Prunier, Chantal 1956- *WhoAmW 91*
Prunier, J Edward L 1920- *BiDrAPA 89*
Prunier, Paul George 1949- *BiDrAPA 89*
Prunty, Marshall E., Jr. 1925- *St&PR 91*
Prunty, Robert Earl 1926- *St&PR 91*
Prunty, William S 1929- *BiDrAPA 89*
Prupas, Melvern Irving 1926- *WhoE 91*
Prus, Francis Vincent 1927- *St&PR 91*
Prus, Victor Marius 1917- *WhoAm 90*
Prusa, James Graham 1948- *WhoAm 90, WhoEmL 91*
Prusek, Jaroslav 1906- *ConAu 129*
Prusia, Paul Duwane 1938- *WhoE 91*
Prusiner, Stanley Ben 1942- *WhoAm 90*
Pruski, Richard John 1946- *WhoAm 90*
Pruskin, Steven Lowell 1957- *WhoE 91*
Pruslin, Fred Howard 1951- *WhoE 91*
Pruslin, Stephen 1940- *PenDiMP*
Prusmack, John J *BiDrAPA 89*
Prusnofsky, Leslie 1951- *BiDrAPA 89*
Prusoff, William Herman 1920- *WhoAm 90*
Pruss, Mario Eduardo *BiDrAPA 89*
Prussia, Leland Spencer 1929- *St&PR 91*
Prussin, Barbara Kahn 1942- *WhoAmW 91*
Prussin, Jeffrey A. 1943- *WhoSSW 91*
Prussin, Rebecca Ann 1951- *BiDrAPA 89*
Prussing *WhoAm 90, WhoAmW 91*
Prussing, Ellis Moulton 1919- *St&PR 91*
Prussing, Laurel Lunt 1941- *WhoAmW 91*
Prust, George Morton 1932- *St&PR 91*
Prust, Susan Luzader 1954- *WhoWrEP 89*
Pruter, Karl Hugo 1920- *WhoAm 90*
Pruter, Margaret Franson *WhoAmW 91*
Prutkovsky, Semyon 1923- *WhoE 91*
Prutzman, Penelope Elizabeth 1944- *WhoAmW 91*
Prutzmann, Hans-Adolf 1901-1945 *BioIn 16*
Pruvost, Pierre Eugene Marie Joseph 1890-1967 *DcScB S2*
Pruyn, Fellowes Morgan 1909-1988 *BioIn 16*
Pruyn, Robert Hewson 1815-1882 *AmLegL, BioIn 16*
Pruyn, William J. 1922- *WhoAm 90, WhoE 91*
Pruyn, William James 1922- *St&PR 91*
Pruzan, Irene 1949- *IntWWM 90, WhoAmW 91, WhoWor 91*
Pruzan, Paul Stephen 1940- *St&PR 91*
Pruzansky, Joshua Murdock 1940- *WhoE 91, WhoWor 91*
Pruzensky, William Michael 1936- *WhoE 91, WhoSSW 91*
Pry, Lamont Alfred 1921-1987 *MusmAFA*
Pryatel, Holly Ann 1948- *WhoAmW 91*
Pryatel, William B, Jr. 1949- *BiDrAPA 89*
Pryce, Edward Lyons 1914- *WhoAm 90*
Pryce, John Maxwell 1936- *IntWWM 90*
Pryce-Jones, Alan 1908- *BioIn 16*
Pryde, Marion Jackson 1911- *WhoWrEP 89*
Prydz, Alvilde 1846-1922 *EncCoWW*
Pryjmak, Peter Gothart 1949- *WhoE 91, WhoWor 91*
Pryme, Ian Fraser 1944- *WhoWor 91*
Pryor, Ainslie *AuBYP 90*
Pryor, Alan Mark 1949- *WhoAm 90*
Pryor, Arthur 1870-1942 *BioIn 16, OxCPMus*
Pryor, Arthur 1944- *WhoSSW 91*
Pryor, Bonnie *AuBYP 90*
Pryor, Bonnie H. 1942- *ConAu 130*
Pryor, Brenda Rogers 1952- *St&PR 91, WhoAmW 91*
Pryor, Carol Graham *WhoAmW 91*
Pryor, Dale *St&PR 91*
Pryor, David *BioIn 16*
Pryor, David Hampton 1934- *WhoAm 90, WhoSSW 91, WhoWor 91*
Pryor, Duaine 1930- *St&PR 91*
Pryor, Frank Pierson 1920- *WhoAm 90*
Pryor, Gerald W. 1931- *St&PR 91*
Pryor, Greg 1949- *Ballpl 90*
Pryor, Gwenneth Ruth 1941- *IntWWM 90*
Pryor, Harold S. 1920- *WhoAm 90*
Pryor, Henry 1808-1892 *DcCanB 12*
Pryor, Howard Dayne, II 1965- *WhoSSW 91*
Pryor, Hubert 1916- *WhoAm 90, WhoWor 91, WhoWrEP 89*
Pryor, Jerry Dennis 1952- *WhoWor 91*
Pryor, John 1805-1892 *DcCanB 12*
Pryor, John Joseph *BioIn 16*
Pryor, Joseph Ehrman 1918- *WhoAm 90*
Pryor, Karen Wylie 1932- *WhoAmW 91*
Pryor, Laurel Mae 1956- *WhoAmW 91*
Pryor, Lori Lou 1964- *WhoAmW 91*
Pryor, Mark Wayne 1958- *WhoWrEP 89*
Pryor, Millard H., Jr. 1933- *St&PR 91*
Pryor, Millard H., Sr. 1901- *St&PR 91*
Pryor, Paul 1927- *Ballpl 90*
Pryor, Peter Malachia 1926- *WhoE 91*
Pryor, Peter Patrick 1946- *WhoAm 90*
Pryor, Rain *BioIn 16*
Pryor, Richard *BioIn 16*
Pryor, Richard 1940- *DrBIPA 90, WhoAm 90, WorAlBi*
Pryor, Richard Walter 1932- *WhoAm 90, WhoWor 91*
Pryor, Shepherd Green, IV 1946- *WhoAm 90, WhoEmL 91*
Pryor, W. Lee, III 1933- *St&PR 91*
Pryor, William Austin 1929- *WhoAm 90*
Pryor, William Bernard 1950- *WhoEmL 91*
Pryor, William Lee 1926- *WhoSSW 91, WhoWor 91*
Prysock, Arthur *DrBIPA 90*
Prystowsky, Harry 1925- *WhoAm 90*
Prystowsky, Rose P *BiDrAPA 89*
Prytz, Holger 1928- *IntWWM 90*
Prywes, Noah Shmarya *WhoAm 90*
Pryzma, Mary Anne *BiDrAPA 89*
Przelomski, Anastasia Nemenyi 1918- *WhoAm 90, WhoAmW 91*
Przemieniecki, Janusz Stanislaw 1927- *WhoAm 90*
Przetacznik, Frank 1929- *WhoE 91*
Przybylowicz, Carolyn Lyon 1947- *WhoAmW 91, WhoEmL 91, WhoWor 91*
Przybylowicz, Edwin Paul 1933- *St&PR 91, WhoAm 90*
Przybyszewska, Dagny Juel 1867-1901 *EncCoWW*
Przybyszewska, Stanislawa 1901-1935 *BioIn 16, EncCoWW*
Przybyszewski, Anthony R. 1943- *St&PR 91*
Przybyszewski, Stanislaw 1868-1927 *BioIn 16*
Psacharopoulos, Nikos 1928-1989 *BioIn 16, ConTFT 8*
Psaila, Justin S 1928- *BiDrAPA 89*
Psaila, Walter 1930- *St&PR 91*
Psaltis, John Costas 1940- *St&PR 91, WhoAm 90*
Psarouthakis, John 1932- *St&PR 91, WhoAm 90, WhoWor 91*
Psarras, Ernest Con 1925- *St&PR 91*
Psaty, Martin Melville 1917- *WhoE 91*
Psiharis, Nicholas 1915- *WhoE 91*
Psiloreiti, Petroula *EncCoWW*
Psomas, Marselo Ignatio 1957- *WhoEmL 91, WhoSSW 91*
Psomiades, Harry John 1928- *WhoAm 90*
Psomiades, Paul 1939- *WhoWor 91*
Psychedelic Furs *EncPR&S 89*
Pszczolkowski, Robert E. 1946- *WhoAm 90*
Pszenny, Lawrence John 1943- *St&PR 91*
Ptacek, William H. *WhoAm 90*
Ptak, Edwin A. 1951- *St&PR 91*
Ptak, Frank S. 1943- *WhoAm 90*
Ptak, Robert Charles 1946- *St&PR 91*
Ptalis, Donald L. 1942- *St&PR 91*
Ptashkin, Barry Irwin 1944- *WhoWor 91*
Ptashne, Mark Steven 1940- *WhoAm 90*
Ptaszynska, Marta 1943- *IntWWM 90*
Pteleon *ConAu 33NR, MajTwCW*
Ptolemy 75?- *WorAlBi*
Pu Jie *BioIn 16*
Pu Yi 1906-1967 *BioIn 16*
Pu-su-wan *WomWR*
Puapua, Tomasi 1938- *WhoWor 91*
Puaux, Frederic 1953- *WhoWor 91*
Pubillones, Jorge 1954- *WhoSSW 91*
Pubillones, Manuel G *BiDrAPA 89*
Public Enemy *ConMus 4*
Public Image Ltd. *EncPR&S 89*
Puccetti, Roland Peter 1924- *WhoAm 90, WhoWrEP 89*
Pucci, Emilio 1914- *ConDes 90, WhoWor 91, WorAlBi*
Pucci, Fiore M. *St&PR 91*
Pucci, Francesco *PenDiDA 89*
Puccia, J. Mark 1956- *St&PR 91*
Pucciarelli, Albert John 1950- *WhoAm 90, WhoE 91*
Puccinelli, Alvin Emil 1938- *St&PR 91*
Puccinelli, George 1906-1956 *Ballpl 90*
Puccinelli, Raimondo 1904-1986 *WhoAmA 91N*
Puccinelli, Roger A. 1934- *St&PR 91*
Puccini, Arthur Victor 1932- *St&PR 91*
Puccini, Giacomo 1858-1924 *BioIn 16, PenDiMP A, WorAlBi*
Puccio, Jane Anne 1946- *WhoE 91*
Puccio, Peter James 1938- *St&PR 91*
Pucel, Robert Albin 1926- *WhoAm 90*
Pucelik, Robert Edward *BiDrAPA 89*
Puchalski, Christina Maria *BiDrAPA 89*
Puchalski, Lawrence C. 1938- *St&PR 91*
Pucheu, Pierre Firmin 1900-1943 *BiDFrPL*
Puchnowski, Wlodzimierz Lech 1932- *IntWWM 90*
Puchta, Charles George 1918- *WhoAm 90*
Puchtler, Holde 1920- *WhoAmW 91*
Pucie, Charles R., Jr. 1943- *ODwPR 91*
Puck, Theodore Thomas 1916- *WhoAm 90*
Puck, Wolfgang 1949- *News 90 [port]*
Pucker, Bernard H 1937- *WhoAmA 91*
Pucker, Bernard Harvey 1937- *WhoE 91*
Puckett, Allen E. 1919- *St&PR 91*
Puckett, Allen Emerson 1919- *WhoAm 90*
Puckett, Allen Weare 1942- *WhoAm 90*
Puckett, Barbara Chandley 1935- *WhoAmW 91*
Puckett, Bobette Linn 1959- *WhoAmW 91*
Puckett, Christine Starling 1922- *WhoAmW 91*
Puckett, Dennis Eugene 1938- *WhoAm 90*
Puckett, Elsbeth Camille 1946- *WhoSSW 91*
Puckett, Howard Louis 1940- *WhoSSW 91*
Puckett, James Butler 1947- *WhoSSW 91*
Puckett, James Manuel, Jr. 1916- *WhoSSW 91, WhoWor 91*
Puckett, James Richard 1929- *St&PR 91*
Puckett, Kirby 1961- *Ballpl 90, WhoAm 90, WorAlBi*
Puckett, Loyd 1928- *St&PR 91*
Puckett, Lute *MajTwCW*
Puckett, Richard Edward 1932- *WhoWor 91*
Puckett, Robert Hugh 1935- *WhoAm 90*
Puckett, Robert Lee 1931- *WhoSSW 91*
Puckett, Ruby Parker 1932- *WhoSSW 91*
Puckette, Stephen Elliott 1927- *WhoAm 90*
Puckler-Muskau, Hermann, Furst von 1785-1871 *BioIn 16*
Pucko, Diane B. 1940- *ODwPR 91*
Pucko, Diane Bowles 1940- *WhoAmW 91*
Puckorius, Theodore D. 1930- *St&PR 91*
Puddington, Arch 1944- *WhoE 91*
Puddington, Ira Edwin 1911- *WhoAm 90*
Puddy, Keith 1938- *IntWWM 90*
Puddy, Robert James 1927- *WhoSSW 91*
Puddy, Walter E 1925- *BiDrAPA 89*
Puder, Susan Jane 1948- *WhoE 91*
Pudney, Betty Ann 1931- *WhoAmW 91*
Pudney, Gary Laurence 1934- *WhoAm 90*
Pudovkin, V. 1893-1953 *WorAlBi*
Pudvin, J.E. 1928- *St&PR 91*
Puebla, Claudio Gabriel 1950- *WhoWor 91*
Puelicher, John A. 1920- *St&PR 91*
Puello, Andres D. 1932- *WhoHisp 91*
Puening, Dennis T. 1948- *St&PR 91*
Puente, Dorothea Montalvo *BioIn 16*
Puente, John George 1930- *St&PR 91, WhoAm 90*
Puente, Jose Garza 1949- *WhoWor 91*
Puente, Tito 1920- *OxCPMus*
Puente, Tito 1923- *WhoHisp 91*
Puente, Tito Anthony 1923- *IntWWM 90*
Puente, Victor *WhoHisp 91*
Puentes, Ana Cristina 1952- *WhoE 91*
Puentes, Charles Theodore, Jr. 1933- *WhoHisp 91*
Puentes, Roberto Santos 1929- *WhoHisp 91*
Puentes, Sonia 1940- *WhoAmW 91*
Puerner, Paul Raymond 1927- *WhoWor 91*
Puertolas Villanueva, Soledad 1947- *EncCoWW*
Puett, Albert W. 1834?- *AmLegL*
Puett, Garnett G 1959- *WhoAmA 91*
Puetz, John David 1951- *WhoEmL 91*
Puetz, Robert W. 1941- *St&PR 91*
Pufahl, John K 1942- *WhoAmA 91*
Puff, Jean Ellingwood 1924- *WhoAmW 91, WhoE 91*
Puffer, Barbara Warzecha 1951- *WhoAmW 91*
Puffer, James C. *BioIn 16*
Puffer, Nancy Placek 1933- *WhoAmW 91*
Puffer, Richard Judson 1931- *WhoAm 90*
Puffer, Sheila Marilyn 1953- *WhoAmW 91*
Puffett, Derrick Robert 1946- *IntWWM 90*
Puga, Rafael *WhoHisp 91*
Puga, William Fernando *BiDrAPA 89*
Pugatch, Donald *BiDrAPA 89*
Pugatch, Ernest 1928- *St&PR 91*
Pugay, Jeffrey Ibanez 1958- *WhoEmL 91*
Puget, Pierre 1620-1694 *IntDcAA 90*
Pugh, Andrew Tucker 1959- *WhoE 91*
Pugh, Arthur James 1937- *St&PR 91*
Pugh, Claudia Ann 1947- *WhoAmW 91*
Pugh, Daniel Duncan 1938- *BiDrAPA 89*
Pugh, Edmund Wright, Jr. 1920- *WhoAm 90*
Pugh, Edward, Jr. 1963- *WhoEmL 91, WhoSSW 91*
Pugh, Elizabeth Louise *BiDrAPA 89*
Pugh, Ellen 1920- *AuBYP 90*
Pugh, Emerson William 1929- *WhoAm 90*
Pugh, George Willard 1925- *WhoAm 90*
Pugh, Grace Huntley 1912- *WhoAmA 91*
Pugh, Helen Pedersen 1934- *WhoWor 91*
Pugh, James H., Jr. 1937- *St&PR 91*
Pugh, Jim *BioIn 16*
Pugh, June Blankenship 1938- *WhoAmW 91*
Pugh, Keith E., Jr. 1937- *WhoAm 90*
Pugh, Kenneth Duane 1937- *St&PR 91*
Pugh, Lawrence R. 1933- *WhoAm 90, WhoE 91*
Pugh, Loranzo Dow 1906- *MusmAFA*
Pugh, Marion Stirling 1911- *WhoAm 90*
Pugh, Melanie Sybil 1964- *WhoE 91*
Pugh, Nelda Jordan 1935- *WhoAmW 91*
Pugh, Philip F H 1917- *BiDrAPA 89*
Pugh, Raeford T., Jr. *BiDrAPA 89*
Pugh, Revella 1947- *WhoEmL 91*
Pugh, Richard Conelley 1934- *WhoAm 90*
Pugh, Richard Crawford 1929- *WhoAm 90*
Pugh, Robert Gahagan 1924- *WhoAm 90*
Pugh, Robert Gahagan, Jr. 1954- *WhoSSW 91*
Pugh, Robert L. 1931- *WhoAm 90, WhoWor 91*
Pugh, Roderick Wellington 1919- *WhoAm 90*
Pugh, Roger V. 1929- *St&PR 91*
Pugh, Russell Oris 1927- *IntWWM 90*
Pugh, Samuel Franklin 1904- *WhoWrEP 89*
Pugh, Sheenagh 1950- *FemiCLE*
Pugh, Velda Denise *BiDrAPA 89*
Pugh, William W. 1811- *AmLegL*
Pugh, William Worthington 1922- *St&PR 91*
Pugin, A. W. N. 1812-1852 *BioIn 16*
Pugin, Augustus Charles 1762-1832 *PenDiDA 89*
Pugin, Augustus Welby Northmore 1812-1852 *BioIn 16, PenDiDA 89*
Puglia, Frank 1892?-1975 *BioIn 16*
Puglies, Louis John *BioIn 16*
Pugliese, Abel Orlando *WhoWor 91*
Pugliese, Anthony Paul 1942- *WhoE 91*
Pugliese, Joseph Sebastian 1943- *St&PR 91*
Pugliese, Maria A *BiDrAPA 89*
Pugliese, Richard Gerard *BiDrAPA 89*
Pugliese, Robert A *BiDrAPA 89*
Pugliese, Robert Francis 1933- *St&PR 91, WhoAm 90, WhoE 91*
Puglisi, Angela Aurora 1949- *WhoAmW 91, WhoEmL 91, WhoWrEP 89*
Puglisi, Anthony Joseph 1949- *St&PR 91, WhoAm 90*
Pugmire, Robert Harris 1927- *St&PR 91*
Pugno, Raoul 1852-1914 *BioIn 16, PenDiMP*
Pugsley, Alfred Grenvile 1903- *WhoWor 91*
Pugsley, Edwin *BioIn 16*
Pugsley, Frank Burruss 1920- *WhoAm 90*
Pugsley, Richard John 1938- *IntWWM 90*
Puhala, James Joseph 1942- *St&PR 91, WhoAm 90*
Puhalla, Cyril M J 1948- *BiDrAPA 89*
Puhalla, Dennis John 1949- *WhoE 91*
Puhalla, Robert Thomas, Jr. 1966- *WhoE 91*
Puhani, Josef 1944- *WhoWor 91*
Puharich, Andrija 1918- *EncO&P 3*
Puharich, Henry K 1918- *EncPaPR 91*
Puhl, Michael Earl 1948- *St&PR 91*
Puhl, Terry 1956- *Ballpl 90*
Puhvel, Jaan 1932- *ConAu 31NR, WhoAm 90*
Puhvel, Martin 1933- *WhoWor 91*
Puhvel, Sirje Madli 1939- *WhoAmW 91*
Pui, Ching-Hon 1951- *WhoSSW 91*
Puiforcat, Jean 1897-1945 *PenDiDA 89*
Puig, Angela Renee 1966- *WhoE 91*
Puig, Jose Gerardo *BiDrAPA 89*
Puig, Manuel *BioIn 16*

Puig, Manuel 1932- *WorAlBi*
Puig, Manuel 1932-1990 *ConAu 32NR, CurBio 90N, HispWr 90, MajTwCW, NewYTBS 90 [port]*
Puig, Nicolas 1952- *WhoHisp 91*
Puig, Vicente P. *WhoHisp 91*
Puig-Antich, Joaquim 1944- *BiDrAPA 89*
Puiggari, Jose Luis 1954- *WhoWor 91*
Puisieux, Marie Madeleine d'Arsant de 1720-1798 *EncCoWW*
Pujadas, Thomas Edward 1953- *WhoEmL 91*
Pujals, Humberto A., Jr. 1952- *WhoHisp 91*
Pujmanova, Marie 1893-1958 *EncCoWW*
Pujo, Arsene P. 1861-1939 *EncABHB 6*
Pujo, Maurice 1872-1955 *BiDFrPL*
Pujol, Alfredo Gaspar 1954- *BiDrAPA 89*
Pujol, Elliott 1943- *WhoAmA 91*
Pujol, Emilio 1886-1980 *PenDiMP*
Pujols, Luis 1955- *Ballpl 90*
Pukel, Sanford Jay 1945- *WhoSSW 91*
Pukkila, Tarmo Mikko 1946- *WhoWor 91*
Pukl, Joseph Michael, Jr. 1953- *WhoSSW 91*
Pulakos, A.C. 1926- *St&PR 91*
Pulakos, George A. 1964- *St&PR 91*
Pulas, Elaine Comer 1952- *WhoAmW 91*
Pulaski, Casimir 1747-1779 *WorAlBi*
Pulaski, Casimir 1748?-1779 *EncCRAm*
Pulaski, John B. 1939- *St&PR 91*
Pulcheria 399-453 *WomWR*
Pulcheria, Saint 399-453 *BioIn 16*
Pulci, Antonia 1452?- *EncCoWW*
Pulcrano, James Thomas 1957- *St&PR 91*
Pulda, Arnold M. 1926- *St&PR 91*
Puleo, Charlie 1955- *Ballpl 90*
Puleo, Frederick William 1951- *St&PR 91*
Puleo, William Joseph 1955- *St&PR 91*
Pulfer, Leslie Louis 1932- *WhoWor 91*
Pulford, Robert Edward 1938- *St&PR 91*
Pulgram, Ernst 1915- *WhoAm 90*
Pulgram, William L. 1921- *BioIn 16*
Puliafico, G. Albert 1927- *St&PR 91*
Puliafito, Carmen Anthony 1951- *WhoE 91, WhoWor 91*
Pulido, Miguel Lazaro 1934- *WhoSSW 91*
Pulido, Richard 1960- *WhoHisp 91*
Pulido, Victor Ismael 1961- *WhoHisp 91*
Pulier, Myron Leopold 1941- *BiDrAPA 89, WhoE 91*
Pulis, R.S. 1944- *St&PR 91*
Pulitano, Concetta Norigenna 1941- *WhoAmW 91*
Pulito, Frank *BiDrAPA 89*
Pulitzer, Emily S Rauh 1933- *WhoAm 90, WhoAmW 91*
Pulitzer, Joseph 1847-1911 *BioIn 16, WorAlBi*
Pulitzer, Joseph 1885-1955 *BioIn 16*
Pulitzer, Joseph, Jr. 1913- *WhoAm 90*
Pulitzer, Michael Edgar 1930- *St&PR 91, WhoAm 90*
Pulitzer, Peter *BioIn 16*
Pulitzer, Roxanne *BioIn 16*
Pulitzer, Sam Clarence *St&PR 91N*
Pulitzer, Samuel C. *BioIn 16*
Pulitzer, Sidney C. 1934- *St&PR 91*
Pulizzi, Matthew S. 1943- *St&PR 91*
Pulkkinen, Erkki Juhani 1944- *WhoWor 91*
Pulkkinen, Pekka Juhani 1947- *WhoWor 91*
Pulkrabek, Larry Alster 1939- *St&PR 91*
Pulkrabek, Roger John 1937- *St&PR 91*
Pull, Georges 1810-1889 *PenDiDA 89*
Pullar, D.R. 1939- *St&PR 91*
Pullen, Desmond Peter 1947- *WhoE 91*
Pullen, Don *BioIn 16*
Pullen, Edwin Wesley 1923- *WhoAm 90*
Pullen, James Joel 1945- *BiDrAPA 89*
Pullen, Janet Kaye 1954- *St&PR 91*
Pullen, Jo Ann *WhoE 91*
Pullen, Keats A., Jr. 1916- *WhoAm 90*
Pullen, Myrick W, Jr. 1915- *BiDrAPA 89*
Pullen, Penny Lynne 1947- *WhoAmW 91*
Pullen, Phillip Arden 1926- *St&PR 91*
Pullen, Richard Owen 1944- *WhoE 91, WhoSSW 91*
Pullen, Rickie Lee *BiDrAPA 89*
Puller, Lewis B. 1898-1971 *WorAlBi*
Pulley, Franklin Dean 1956- *WhoSSW 91*
Pulley, Robert Miller 1952- *WhoSSW 91*
Pulleyblank, Edwin George 1922- *WhoAm 90*
Pulleyn, Robert Francis 1902-1990 *BioIn 16*
Pulleyn, Samuel Robert 1946- *WhoAm 90*
Pulli, Frank 1935- *Ballpl 90*
Pulliainen, Erkki Ossi Olavi 1938- *WhoWor 91*
Pulliam, Eugene C. *BioIn 16*
Pulliam, Eugene Smith 1914- *WhoAm 90*
Pulliam, Francine S. 1937- *WhoAmW 91*
Pulliam, Harry 1869-1909 *Ballpl 90*
Pulliam, Harry Clay 1869-1909 *BioIn 16*
Pulliam, Judith Harris 1934- *WhoAmW 91, WhoSSW 91*
Pulliam, Keshia Knight 1979- *DrBlPA 90*
Pulliam, Larry J. 1960- *WhoSSW 91*
Pulliam, Michael L. *St&PR 91*
Pulliam, Robert Floyd 1920- *St&PR 91*
Pulliam, Sandra Brandt 1959- *WhoSSW 91*
Pulliam, Steve Cameron 1948- *WhoSSW 91*
Pulliam, Susan Elise 1953- *WhoAmW 91*
Pullin, Charles Russell 1923- *St&PR 91*
Pullin, Tanya Gaye 1957- *WhoE 91*
Pullinen, Laila 1933- *BiDWomA*
Pulling, Nathaniel Hosler 1920- *WhoE 91*
Pulling, R. Bruce 1933- *WhoAm 90*
Pulling, Ronald Wilson, Sr. 1919- *WhoAm 90*
Pulling, Thomas L. 1939- *St&PR 91*
Pulling, Thomas Leffingwell 1939- *WhoAm 90*
Pullman, Anthony J. 1945- *St&PR 91*
Pullman, Bruce John 1957- *WhoWor 91*
Pullman, George M. 1831-1897 *WorAlBi*
Pullman, Maynard Edward 1927- *WhoAm 90*
Pullman, Philip 1946- *BioIn 16*
Pullman, Philip Nicholas 1946- *WhoWor 91*
Pullmer, Lewis Zeph 1952- *BiDrAPA 89*
Pullo, Barbara Jean 1935- *WhoAmW 91*
Pullon, Kelley Layne 1962- *WhoAmW 91*
Pulos, Arthur J 1917- *ConDes 90*
Pulos, Arthur Jon 1917- *WhoAm 90, WhoAmA 91*
Puls, Kenneth Allen 1962- *IntWWM 90*
Puls, Richard John 1925- *WhoWor 91*
Puls-Jager, Elizabeth Anne 1934- *WhoAmW 91*
Pulsifer, Edgar D. 1934- *St&PR 91*
Pulsifer, Roy 1931- *WhoSSW 91*
Pulver, Mitchell Paul 1952- *BiDrAPA 89*
Pulver, Sydney E 1927- *BiDrAPA 89, WhoE 91*
Pulvermacher, Louis C. 1928- *WhoWor 91*
Pumariega, Andres Julio 1953- *BiDrAPA 89*
Pumo, Dorothy Ellen 1951- *WhoAmW 91*
Pumper, Robert William 1921- *WhoAm 90*
Pumphrey, Janet Kay 1946- *WhoAmW 91, WhoE 91, WhoEmL 91*
Pumphrey, Roger Dwight *BiDrAPA 89*
Pumpin, Cuno 1939- *WhoWor 91*
Punak, Debra Lynn 1959- *WhoAmW 91*
Punch, Howard Dean 1925- *St&PR 91*
Punches, Dennis 1936- *St&PR 91*
Punct, Carl Christoph *PenDiDA 89*
Pundmann, William Roland 1946- *WhoEmL 91*
Pundole, K.N. 1949- *St&PR 91*
Pundsack, Fred L. 1925- *St&PR 91, WhoAm 90*
Pundt, Helen Marie *AuBYP 90*
Puner, Helen W. 1915-1989 *BioIn 16, ConAu 129, SmATA 63*
Pung, Rosalyn Alyce 1948- *WhoAmW 91*
Punia, Charles *BioIn 16*
Punia, Constance Edith *WhoAmA 91*
Puniello, Carmine John 1942- *WhoE 91*
Punjwani, Sohail Shabanali *BiDrAPA 89*
Punnett, Milton B. 1930- *St&PR 91*
Punshon, E R 1872-1956 *TwCCr&M 91*
Punt, Jonathan Arthur 1948- *WhoWor 91*
Punti, Rosita *BiDrAPA 89*
Punto, Giovanni 1746-1803 *PenDiMP*
Punwani, Dharam V. 1942- *St&PR 91*
Punzo, Vincent Christopher 1934- *WhoAm 90*
Puotila, Ritva 1935- *ConDes 90*
Puotinen, Arthur Edwin 1941- *WhoAm 90*
Pupin, Michael Idvorsky 1858-1935 *BioIn 16*
Pupino, Genevieve M *BiDrAPA 89*
Pupo, Jorge I. 1960- *WhoHisp 91*
Pupo, Raul 1946- *St&PR 91*
Pupo-Mayo, Gustavo Alberto 1955- *WhoHisp 91*
Puppala, Shyam Mohan 1949- *BiDrAPA 89*
Pura, William Paul 1948- *WhoAmA 91*
Pural, Dennis Michael 1938- *St&PR 91*
Purbeck, Elizabeth *FemiCLE*
Purbeck, Jane *FemiCLE*
Purce, Jill 1947- *EncO&P 3*
Purcell, Ann 1941- *WhoAmA 91*
Purcell, Ann Marie C. 1957- *WhoAmW 91*
Purcell, Arthur Henry 1944- *WhoAm 90*
Purcell, Bradford M. 1929- *St&PR 91*
Purcell, Bradford Moore 1929- *WhoAm 90*
Purcell, Carolyn Therese 1960- *WhoE 91*
Purcell, Dale 1919- *WhoAm 90*
Purcell, Edward M. 1912- *WorAlBi*
Purcell, Edward Mills 1912- *WhoAm 90, WhoE 91, WhoWor 91*
Purcell, Elaine Irene 1946- *WhoAmW 91*
Purcell, Francis J. 1911-1989 *BioIn 16*
Purcell, George Richard 1921- *WhoE 91, WhoWor 91*
Purcell, Henry 1659-1695 *PenDiMP A, WorAlBi*
Purcell, Henry, III 1929- *WhoSSW 91*
Purcell, James Edward 1932- *St&PR 91*
Purcell, James Francis 1920- *St&PR 91, WhoAm 90*
Purcell, James Lawrence 1929- *WhoAm 90*
Purcell, Jennifer Estelle 1954- *WhoEmL 91*
Purcell, John Howell *BiDrAPA 89*
Purcell, John N. 1937- *St&PR 91*
Purcell, John Wallace *AuBYP 90*
Purcell, John William, II 1948- *WhoSSW 91*
Purcell, Kenneth 1928- *WhoAm 90*
Purcell, Martin James 1918- *WhoAm 90*
Purcell, Mary Hamilton *WhoAmW 91*
Purcell, Mary Louise Gerlinger 1923- *WhoAmW 91*
Purcell, Micki Nolan 1953- *WhoAmW 91*
Purcell, Nancy Lou 1934- *WhoAmW 91*
Purcell, Norris Duane 1940- *BiDrAPA 89*
Purcell, P.J. *St&PR 91*
Purcell, Patricia 1925- *IntWWM 90*
Purcell, Patrick B. 1943- *St&PR 91, WhoAm 90*
Purcell, Patrick Joseph 1947- *WhoAm 90*
Purcell, Paul E. 1959- *WhoWrEP 89*
Purcell, Philip J. 1943- *St&PR 91*
Purcell, Philip James 1943- *WhoAm 90, WhoE 91*
Purcell, Richard Fick 1924- *WhoAm 90*
Purcell, Robert E. *St&PR 91*
Purcell, Robert Harry 1935- *WhoAm 90*
Purcell, Robert Harry 1943- *St&PR 91*
Purcell, Royal 1921- *WhoWrEP 89*
Purcell, Sally 1944- *FemiCLE*
Purcell, Steven Richard 1927- *WhoAm 90, WhoE 91, WhoWor 91*
Purcell, Thomas R. 1935- *St&PR 91*
Purcell, William Hugh 1942- *St&PR 91, WhoAm 90*
Purcell, William Paul 1935- *WhoAm 90*
Purcell, William Paxson, III 1953- *WhoEmL 91, WhoSSW 91*
Purcell, William Riker 1947- *WhoEmL 91*
Purchard, Paul R 1929- *BiDrAPA 89*
Purchatzke, Gerald D 1942- *BiDrAPA 89*
Purcifull, Dan Elwood 1935- *WhoAm 90*
Purcifull, Robert Otis 1932- *WhoAm 90, WhoSSW 91*
Purdeli, Abd as-Satar 1946- *WhoWor 91*
Purdie, Alexander M. 1945- *St&PR 91*
Purdie, Thomas 1843-1916 *DcScB S2*
Purdin, John 1942- *Ballpl 90*
Purdom, Paul 1929- *ODwPR 91*
Purdom, Paul Walton, Jr. 1940- *WhoAm 90*
Purdom, Robert Don 1926- *St&PR 91*
Purdom, Thomas Edward 1936- *WhoE 91*
Purdom, Thomas James 1937- *WhoAm 90*
Purdon, Eric 1913-1989 *ConAu 130*
Purdon, Eric S. 1913-1989 *BioIn 16*
Purdon, Eric Sinclaire 1913- *WhoWrEP 89*
Purdon, Richard Alan 1948- *WhoWor 91*
Purdum, Ralph S. *BioIn 16*
Purdum, Rebecca 1959- *BioIn 16, WhoAmA 91*
Purdum, Robert L. 1935- *St&PR 91, WhoAm 90, WhoE 91, WhoWor 91*
Purdy, Alan Harris 1923- *WhoAm 90*
Purdy, Alan MacGregor 1940- *WhoAm 90*
Purdy, Bruce Barton 1917- *St&PR 91*
Purdy, Captain Jim *AuBYP 90*
Purdy, Carol *AuBYP 90*
Purdy, Charles Robert 1937- *WhoAm 90*
Purdy, Claire Lee 1906- *AuBYP 90*
Purdy, David Lawrence 1928- *St&PR 91*
Purdy, Donald R 1924- *WhoAmA 91*
Purdy, Dwight H 1941- *ConAu 131*
Purdy, Frazier Rodney 1929- *WhoAm 90*
Purdy, Helen Carmichael 1920- *WhoAmW 91*
Purdy, Henry Carl 1937- *WhoAmA 91*
Purdy, James 1923- *MajTwCW, WhoAm 90, WhoWrEP 89*
Purdy, Laurence Henry 1926- *WhoAm 90*
Purdy, Patrick *BioIn 16*
Purdy, Ralph William 1924- *WhoAm 90*
Purdy, Richard Little 1904-1990 *ConAu 132*
Purdy, Robin Christopher 1951- *St&PR 91*
Purdy, Susan 1942- *WhoWrEP 89*
Purdy, Susan Gold 1939- *AuBYP 90*
Purdy, William Crossley 1930- *WhoAm 90*
Purdy, William Marshall 1940- *WhoAm 90, WhoWor 91*
Purens, Ilmars Uldis 1947- *WhoWrEP 89*
Purg, Franc 1955- *WhoWor 91*
Puri, Geetha 1957- *BiDrAPA 89*
Puri, Madan Lal 1929- *WhoAm 90*
Puri, Pratap 1938- *WhoSSW 91*
Puri, Rajendra Kumar 1932- *WhoSSW 91*
Puri, Shamlal 1951- *ConAu 130, WhoWor 91*
Puricelli, Marjorie Gibson 1923- *WhoAmW 91*
Purin, Thomas 1941- *WhoSSW 91*
Purinton, Arthur L., II 1942- *St&PR 91*
Purinton, Michael Ray 1947- *WhoSSW 91*
Puris, Martin Ford 1939- *WhoAm 90*
Puritano, Vincent 1930- *WhoAm 90*
Purkey, Bob 1929- *Ballpl 90, BioIn 16*
Purkey, Ruth Elane 1936- *WhoAmW 91*
Purkhiser, Stephen Dale 1955- *WhoEmL 91*
Purkinje, Jan Evangelista 1787-1869 *WorAlBi*
Purkiser, Westlake Taylor 1910- *WhoAm 90*
Purkiss, Richard Allen 1941- *St&PR 91*
Purl, O. Thomas 1924- *WhoAm 90*
Purmort, Lou *BioIn 16*
Purmort, William R, Jr. 1908- *BiDrAPA 89*
Purnell, Charles Rea 1922- *WhoAm 90*
Purnell, Harry Sylvester 1933- *St&PR 91*
Purnell, John H. 1941- *WhoAm 90*
Purnell, John Harris 1941- *St&PR 91*
Purnell, Maurice Eugene, Jr. 1940- *WhoAm 90*
Purnhagen-Schaal, Jeanne E. 1920- *St&PR 91*
Purohit Swami, Shri 1882-1936? *EncO&P 3*
Purohit, Jaswant S *BiDrAPA 89*
Purohit, Radha Krishna 1936- *WhoWor 91*
Purpur, George Franklin, Jr. 1925- *WhoE 91*
Purpura, Dominick P. 1927- *WhoAm 90*
Purpura, Joseph Matthew 1950- *WhoEmL 91*
Purpura, Peter Joseph 1939- *WhoAm 90*
Purrer, Siegfried 1949- *WhoWor 91*
Purrington, Edward Cobb 1929- *WhoE 91*
Purrington, Suzanne Townsend 1938- *WhoAmW 91*
Pursch, Joseph A *BiDrAPA 89*
Purse, Charles Roe 1960- *WhoEmL 91*
Purse, Robert Allgood 1930- *St&PR 91*
Pursel, Harold Max, Sr. 1921- *WhoWor 91*
Pursel, Jach *EncPaPR 91, NewAgE 90*
Pursel, Peny *NewAgE 90*
Pursell, Carl Duane 1932- *WhoAm 90*
Pursell, Carroll Wirth 1932- *WhoAm 90*
Pursell, William Whitney 1926- *WhoSSW 91*
Purser, Donald Joseph 1954- *WhoEmL 91*
Purser, John R. 1935- *ODwPR 91*
Purser, John Whitley 1942- *IntWWM 90*
Purser, Philip 1925- *TwCCr&M 91*
Purser, Sarah Henrietta 1848-1943 *BiDWomA*
Purser, Stuart Robert 1907-1986 *WhoAmA 91N*
Purser, Susan Joy Richardson 1949- *WhoSSW 91*
Pursey, Derek Lindsay 1927- *WhoAm 90*
Pursey, Stephen Kennett 1952- *WhoWor 91*
Pursifull, Carmen Maria 1930- *WhoWrEP 89*
Pursley, A.N. 1941- *St&PR 91*
Pursley, Michael Bader 1945- *WhoAm 90*
Pursley, Michael Gene 1958- *WhoSSW 91*
Pursley, Ricky Anthony 1954- *WhoEmL 91*
Purtell, Billy 1886-1962 *Ballpl 90*
Purtell, Lawrence Patrick 1946- *WhoE 91*
Purtell, Michael John 1963- *WhoE 91*
Purtell, Regina 1866-1950 *BioIn 16*
Purtill, Richard L. 1931- *BioIn 16*
Purtle, Carol Jean 1939- *WhoAmA 91*
Purtle, John Ingram 1923- *WhoAm 90*
Purtzer, John Charles 1937- *BiDrAPA 89*
Purugganan, Sylvia Marie *BiDrAPA 89*
Puruhito 1943- *WhoWor 91*
Purves, Alan Carroll 1931- *WhoAm 90, WhoWrEP 89*
Purves, Libby 1950- *ConAu 130*
Purves, William Kirkwood 1934- *WhoAm 90*
Purvin, Robert L. 1917- *St&PR 91*
Purvin, Robert Leman 1917- *WhoAm 90*
Purvin, Theodore V. 1918- *St&PR 91*
Purvines, Verne E., Jr. 1945- *St&PR 91*
Purvis, Alexander 1925- *St&PR 91*
Purvis, Archie C., Jr. 1939- *St&PR 91*
Purvis, Darwin W. 1933- *St&PR 91*
Purvis, Eve Poulson *BioIn 16*
Purvis, George 1842- *DcCanB 12*
Purvis, George Allen 1933- *St&PR 91*
Purvis, George Frank, Jr. 1914- *St&PR 91, WhoAm 90*
Purvis, George Porter, III 1942- *WhoWor 91*
Purvis, Hoyt Hughes 1939- *WhoSSW 91*
Purvis, James P. *BioIn 16*
Purvis, John Anderson 1942- *WhoWor 91*
Purvis, Michael Blaikie 1952- *St&PR 91, WhoE 91*
Purvis, Robert Burl 1937- *St&PR 91*
Purvis, Wendy Kim 1964- *WhoAmW 91*
Purvis-Lively, Cathy Lynn 1960- *WhoSSW 91*
Puryear, Alvin Nelson 1937- *WhoAm 90*
Puryear, Douglas A, III 1938- *BiDrAPA 89*
Puryear, Martin 1941- *WhoAm 90, WhoAmA 91*
Pusateri, Lawrence Xavier 1931- *WhoAm 90*

Puscheck, Herbert Charles 1936- *WhoAm 90*
Puschel, Philip P. 1938- *St&PR 91*
Pusey, E. B. 1800-1882 *BioIn 16*
Pusey, Edward Bouverie 1800-1882 *BioIn 16*
Pusey, Ellen Pratt 1928- *WhoAmW 91*
Pusey, Gregory S. 1952- *St&PR 91*
Pusey, William Webb, III 1910- *WhoAm 90*
Push, Brother 1764-1824 *WhNaAH*
Pushkar *NewAgMG*
Pushkarev, Boris S. 1929- *WhoAm 90*
Pushkin, Aleksandr Sergeevich 1799-1837 *BioIn 16*
Pushkin, Alexander 1799-1837 *NinCLC 27 [port], SmATA 61 [port], WorAlBi*
Pushman, Hovsep 1877-1966 *WhoAmA 91N*
Pushmataha 1764-1824 *WhNaAH*
Pusin, Max N 1917- *BiDrAPA 89*
Puskar, Gregory Paul 1956- *WhoSSW 91*
Puskar, Kathryn Rose 1946- *WhoAmW 91*
Puskar, Michael 1932- *St&PR 91*
Puskar, Milan 1934- *St&PR 91*
Puskar, Patricia Ann *St&PR 91*
Puskas, Elek 1942- *WhoE 91*
Pussel, Franz, Jr. 1942- *St&PR 91*
Pussilano, James Timothy 1923- *St&PR 91*
Pustilnik, David Daniel 1931- *WhoE 91*
Pustilnik, Jean Todd 1932- *WhoE 91*
Pustovar, Paul Thomas 1951- *WhoEmL 91*
Pustroem, Aksel W *BiDrAPA 89*
Pustrom, Einar *BiDrAPA 89*
Pusz, Ryszard Jan 1948- *IntWWM 90*
Putansu, Patricia Joan 1934- *WhoAmW 91*
Puteaux, Louis-Francois-Laurent 1780-1864 *PenDiDA 89*
Puth, John W. 1929- *St&PR 91*
Puth, John Wells 1929- *WhoAm 90, WhoWor 91*
Puthoff, Harold E. *WhoSSW 91*
Puthoff, Harold E. 1936- *EncO&P 3*
Puthuff, Steven Henry 1940- *WhoE 91*
Puthumana, Joseph Philip 1925- *BiDrAPA 89*
Putka, Andrew Charles 1926- *WhoAm 90*
Putman, Andree *BioIn 16*
Putman, Andree 1925- *ConDes 90*
Putman, Anthony O'Neal 1945- *St&PR 91, WhoEmL 91*
Putman, Brenda 1890-1975 *WhoAmA 91N*
Putman, Dale Cornelius 1927- *WhoAm 90*
Putman, Glen W. 1940- *ODwPR 91*
Putman, Guy H., III 1950- *St&PR 91*
Putman, Houston Paul, III 1956- *BiDrAPA 89*
Putman, Linda Murray 1953- *WhoEmL 91*
Putman, Paul 1929- *St&PR 91*
Putman, Robert M. 1952- *St&PR 91*
Putnam, Alice 1916- *SmATA 61 [port]*
Putnam, Allan Ray 1920- *WhoWor 91*
Putnam, Ashley 1952- *IntWWM 90, PenDiMP*
Putnam, Barbara Deyo 1926- *WhoAmW 91*
Putnam, Bonnie Bean 1955- *WhoAmW 91*
Putnam, Borden Roger, Jr. 1922- *WhoAm 90*
Putnam, Brenda 1890-1975 *BiDWomA*
Putnam, C.E. 1906- *St&PR 91*
Putnam, Calvin Richard 1924- *WhoAm 90*
Putnam, Carleton 1901- *WhoAm 90*
Putnam, Charles Duane 1928- *St&PR 91*
Putnam, Constance Elizabeth 1943- *WhoAmW 91*
Putnam, Dale Nielsen 1931- *St&PR 91*
Putnam, Donald B. 1932- *St&PR 91*
Putnam, Frank William 1917- *WhoAm 90*
Putnam, Frederic L., Jr. 1925- *St&PR 91*
Putnam, Frederic Ward 1839-1915 *WhNaAH*
Putnam, Frederick Warren, Jr. 1917- *WhoAm 90*
Putnam, George 1926- *St&PR 91*
Putnam, George Endicott 1921- *WhoE 91*
Putnam, George Palmer 1814-1872 *WorAlBi*
Putnam, George W., Jr. 1920- *WhoAm 90*
Putnam, Glendora Mc Ilwain *WhoAm 90*
Putnam, Harold Barnes 1916- *WhoSSW 91*
Putnam, Howard Dean 1937- *St&PR 91*
Putnam, Israel 1718-1790 *BioIn 16, EncCRAm, WorAlBi*
Putnam, John B, Mrs 1903- *WhoAmA 91N*
Putnam, John G., Jr. 1929- *St&PR 91*
Putnam, Kenneth J. 1938- *St&PR 91*
Putnam, Leon Joseph 1928- *WhoAm 90*
Putnam, Mark *ODwPR 91*
Putnam, Mark Ambrose *BiDrAPA 89*
Putnam, Mary Traill 1810-1898 *FemiCLE*
Putnam, Michael Courtney Jenkins 1933- *WhoAm 90*
Putnam, Milton J. 1920-1989 *BioIn 16*
Putnam, Nicholas H, Jr. 1947- *BiDrAPA 89*
Putnam, Nol 1934- *WhoAmA 91*
Putnam, Pat 1953- *Ballpl 90*
Putnam, Peter Brock 1920- *WhoAm 90*
Putnam, Peter L 1936- *BiDrAPA 89*
Putnam, Philip Conrad 1954- *WhoEmL 91*
Putnam, Richard Johnson 1913- *WhoAm 90*
Putnam, Richard Worcester 1945- *WhoEmL 91*
Putnam, Robert E. 1933- *WhoAm 90, WhoWrEP 89*
Putnam, Terri *WhoWrEP 89*
Putnam, Thomas P. *St&PR 91*
Putnam, William Shields 1955- *WhoSSW 91*
Putney, Charles Robert 1946- *WhoE 91*
Putney, Freeman Theodore, Jr. 1933- *St&PR 91*
Putney, John A. 1939- *St&PR 91*
Putney, John Alden, Jr. 1939- *WhoAm 90*
Putney, John W. 1946- *WhoE 91*
Putney, Mark William 1929- *St&PR 91, WhoAm 90*
Putney, Mary Engler 1933- *WhoAmW 91*
Putney, Nancy Hoddinott 1960- *WhoSSW 91*
Putnik, Radomir 1847-1917 *BioIn 16*
Putnoky-Krako, Janice 1951- *St&PR 91*
Putsep, Ervin Peeter 1921- *WhoWor 91*
Putt, William Donald 1937- *St&PR 91*
Putter, Irving 1917- *WhoAm 90*
Putterman, David 1901-1979 *BioIn 16*
Putterman, Florence Grace 1927- *WhoAm 90, WhoAmA 91*
Putterman, Lawrence E. 1948- *St&PR 91*
Putterman, Louis G. 1952- *WhoE 91*
Putterman, Seymour 1931- *St&PR 91*
Puttnam, David 1941- *BioIn 16*
Puttnam, David Terence 1941- *WhoAm 90, WhoWor 91*
Puttonen, Matti Kalervo 1930- *WhoWor 91*
Putz, Christine 1950- *WhoAmW 91*
Putz, Ruth-Margret 1931- *IntWWM 90*
Putz, Walter Edwin 1924- *St&PR 91*
Putze, Louis 1916- *WhoAm 90*
Putzel, Constance Kellner 1922- *WhoAm 90*
Putzel, William L. 1918- *WhoAm 90*
Putzell, Edwin J., Jr. 1913- *St&PR 91*
Putzell, Edwin Joseph, Jr. 1913- *WhoAm 90*
Putzer, Agnes G. 1933- *St&PR 91*
Putzrath, Resha Mae 1949- *WhoAmW 91, WhoE 91*
Puustinen, Heikki Juhani 1922- *WhoWor 91*
Puverel, Roland Marie Pierre 1913- *WhoWor 91*
Puvis de Chavannes, Pierre 1824-1898 *BioIn 16, IntDcAA 90*
Puvvada, Rao Vema 1948- *BiDrAPA 89*
Puyana, Rafael 1931- *IntWWM 90, PenDiMP*
Puyau, Francis Albert 1928- *WhoAm 90*
Puz, Richard 1936- *St&PR 91*
Puzik, Zofia *BioIn 16*
Puzinas, James Joseph 1960- *St&PR 91*
Puzo, Joseph Pascal 1947- *WhoWor 91*
Puzo, Mario 1920- *MajTwCW, WhoWor 91, WhoWrEP 89, WorAlBi*
Puzo, Michael John 1952- *WhoEmL 91*
Puzzele, James Albert 1951- *WhoE 91*
Puzzuoli, Gina Michelle 1951- *BiDrAPA 89*
Pwashimizu, Yukio 1943- *WhoWor 91*
Py, Gilbert 1933- *IntWWM 90*
Pyant, Paul 1953- *ConTFT 8 [port]*
Pyat, Felix 1810-1889 *BioIn 16*
Pyatt, Everett Arno 1939- *WhoAm 90*
Pyatt, Kedar Davis, Jr. 1933- *St&PR 91*
Pyatt, Melvyn Roy 1946- *WhoWor 91*
Pyck, Johan Edmondus 1935- *WhoWor 91*
Pye, August Kenneth 1931- *WhoAm 90, WhoSSW 91*
Pye, Gordon Bruce 1933- *WhoAm 90*
Pye, Jael Henrietta 1736?-1782 *FemiCLE*
Pye, Lucian W. 1921- *BioIn 16*
Pye, Lucian Wilmot 1921- *WhoAm 90*
Pye, Mort 1918- *WhoAm 90, WhoE 91*
Pyeatt, Madelyn *BioIn 16*
Pyett, Roger H. 1929- *St&PR 91*
Pyfer, John Frederick, Jr. 1946- *WhoEmL 91*
Pykare, Nina 1932- *ConAu 130*
Pyke, Helen Ann 1941- *WhoSSW 91*
Pyke, John S., Jr. 1938- *St&PR 91*
Pyke, John Secrest, Jr. 1938- *WhoAm 90*
Pyke, R. A. 1940- *ODwPR 91*
Pyke, Ronald 1931- *WhoAm 90*
Pyke, Thomas Nicholas, Jr. 1942- *WhoAm 90*
Pykett, Ian Lewis 1953- *WhoE 91*
Pylant, Jeffrey Davis 1954- *WhoE 91*
Pylant, Stanley Doyle 1952- *IntWWM 90*
Pyle, Albert Jocelyn *BioIn 16*
Pyle, Ernie 1900-1945 *BioIn 16, WorAlBi*
Pyle, Ewald 1910- *Ballpl 90*
Pyle, Franklin Ross 1951- *St&PR 91*
Pyle, Gerald Fredric 1937- *WhoSSW 91*
Pyle, Howard 1853-1911 *AuBYP 90, ChlLR 22 [port]*
Pyle, J. Howard 1906-1987 *BioIn 16*
Pyle, Kenneth Birger 1936- *WhoAm 90, WhoWrEP 89*
Pyle, Kent C. 1958- *St&PR 91*
Pyle, Michael Terry 1938- *WhoSSW 91*
Pyle, Philip E. 1943- *WhoE 91*
Pyle, Richard L 1931- *BiDrAPA 89*
Pyle, Robert Edgar 1927- *WhoAm 90*
Pyle, Robert M., Jr. 1938- *St&PR 91*
Pyle, Robert Milner, Jr. 1938- *WhoAm 90*
Pyle, Robert Noble 1926- *WhoAm 90*
Pyle, Roger Gail 1933- *WhoSSW 91*
Pyle, Ronald Loyd 1948- *WhoSSW 91*
Pyle, Ronald M. 1940- *St&PR 91*
Pyle, Sallyanne *BiDrAPA 89*
Pyle, Susan Clinard 1960- *WhoAmW 91*
Pyle, Thomas Francis, Jr. 1941- *St&PR 91*
Pyle, Thomas O. *BioIn 16*
Pyle, Timothy Richard 1964- *WhoE 91*
Pyles, Alan N. 1958- *WhoE 91*
Pyles, Carol DeLong 1948- *WhoAmW 91*
Pyles, Charles Ray 1937- *St&PR 91*
Pyles, Robert Phillip 1931- *WhoE 91*
Pyles, Robt Lindsay 1936- *BiDrAPA 89*
Pyles, Rodney Allen 1945- *WhoAm 90*
Pyles, Susan Kay 1954- *WhoAmW 91*
Pylinski, Albert, Jr. 1953- *WhoE 91*
Pylipow, Stanley Ross 1936- *WhoAm 90*
Pylko, Thaddeus 1931- *St&PR 91*
Pylko, Timothy Joseph 1956- *BiDrAPA 89*
Pylypyszyn, Peter Paul 1950- *WhoE 91*
Pym, Baron 1922- *WhoWor 91*
Pym, Barbara *BioIn 16*
Pym, Barbara 1913-1980 *FemiCLE, MajTwCW*
Pynchon, Thomas *BioIn 16*
Pynchon, Thomas 1937- *ConLC 62, MajTwCW, WhoWrEP 89, WorAlBi*
Pynchon, William 1590?-1662 *EncCRAm*
Pyndus, Philip Richard 1921- *St&PR 91*
Pyne, Benjamin *PenDiDA 89*
Pyne, Eben W. 1917- *St&PR 91*
Pyne, Louisa 1832-1904 *PenDiMP*
Pyne, Mable Mandeville 1903-1969 *AuBYP 90*
Pynn, Helen West 1936- *WhoAmW 91*
Pynn, Thomas Damon 1944- *WhoE 91*
Pynoos, Robert Sidney *BiDrAPA 89*
Pyper, George Earl 1927- *IntWWM 90*
Pyra, Thomas Marion 1952- *St&PR 91*
Pyros, John 1931- *WhoWrEP 89*
Pysell, Glen Allen 1942- *WhoSSW 91*
Pysz, Donna Marie 1952- *WhoAmW 91*
Pytell, Robert Henry 1926- *WhoAm 90*
Pythagoras 560?BC-480?BC *WrPh P*
Pythagoras 582?BC-497?BC *WorAlBi*
Pytheas *WorAlBi*
Pytheas, of Massalia *BioIn 16*
Python, Monty *MajTwCW*
Pytko, D. Victor *ODwPR 91*
Pytlak, Frankie 1908-1977 *Ballpl 90*
Pytlak, Hanna *BiDrAPA 89*
Pytte, Agnar 1932- *WhoAm 90, WhoWor 91*
Pyun, Matthew Sung Kwan 1937- *WhoWor 91*
Pyzdek, Thomas 1948- *WhoEmL 91*

Q

Q, Stacey *BioIn 16*
Q-Petersen, Jon 1950- *St&PR 91*
Qaboos Bin Said Bin Taymour 1940- *WhoWor 91*
Qabus Bin Said 1940- *PolLCME*
Qaddafi, Muammar 1942- *PolLCME*
Qaddafi, Muammar Muhammed *WhoWor 91*
Qadeer, Abdul 1940- *WhoE 91*
Qadeer, Abdul, Sheikh *BiDrAPA 89*
Qadeer, Saad Abdul 1962- *WhoWor 91*
Qadir, Aftab 1947- *BiDrAPA 89*
Qadir, Ghulam 1947- *BiDrAPA 89*
Qadri, Muntzra Khatoon 1938- *BiDrAPA 89*
Qanoongo, Shahnawaz Kahn 1957- *BiDrAPA 89*
Qasim, Sayed Zahoor 1926- *WhoWor 91*
Qassem, Abdul Karim 1914-1963 *PolLCME*
Qassem, Marwan 1938- *WhoWor 91*
Qayyum, Mohammad Usman 1955- *BiDrAPA 89*
Qazi, Humayun 1943- *WhoWor 91*
Qazi, Khizir Hayat A. 1945- *WhoWor 91*
Qazilbash, Imtiaz Ali 1934- *WhoWor 91*
Qian Changzhao 1899-1988 *BioIn 16*
Qian Qichen 1928- *WhoWor 91*
Qian Xuesen 1911- *BioIn 16*
Qian Zhongshu *ConAu 130, MajTwCW*
Qianlong, Emperor 1736-1795 *PenDiDA 89*
Qiao Shi *BioIn 16*
Qiao Shi 1924- *WhoWor 91*
Qin Ben Li *BioIn 16*
Qin Jiwei 1914- *WhoWor 91*
Qin Shi Huang 259BC-210BC *BioIn 16*
Qing *PenDiDA 89*
Qoboza, Percy *BioIn 16*
Qoboza, Percy 1938-1988 *AnObit 1988*
Quaal, Albert Lawrence 1933- *St&PR 91*
Quaal, Ward Louis 1919- *WhoAm 90, WhoWor 91*
Quackenboss, Daniel G. *AmLegL*
Quackenbush, James E. 1929- *St&PR 91*
Quackenbush, Robert 1929- *WhoAmA 91*
Quackenbush, Robert Mead 1929- *AuBYP 90, WhoE 91*
Quade, Dana 1935- *WhoSSW 91*
Quade, David Jon 1954- *WhoEmL 91*
Quade, Quentin Lon 1933- *WhoAm 90*
Quade, Victoria Catherine 1953- *WhoAm 90*
Quadri, Fazle Rab 1948- *WhoEmL 91, WhoWor 91*
Quadrino, Umberto 1946- *WhoWor 91*
Quadros, Janio *BioIn 16*
Quadt, Raymond Adolph 1916- *WhoAm 90*
Quadt, Suzanne Marie 1947- *WhoAmW 91, WhoWor 91*
Quagliano, Anthony John 1941- *WhoWrEP 89*
Quagliata, John 1941- *St&PR 91, WhoAm 90*
Quagliata, Narcissus 1942- *WhoAmA 91*
Quaiapan *WhNaAH*
Quaid, Dennis *BioIn 16*
Quaid, Dennis 1954- *WorAlBi*
Quaid, Dennis William 1954- *WhoAm 90*
Quaid, Randy 1950- *WhoAm 90, WorAlBi*
Quaid, Randy 1953- *BioIn 16*
Quaij, Stephen 1947- *BioIn 16*
Quaij, Timothy 1947- *BioIn 16*
Quail, Kenneth Thomas 1952- *WhoE 91*
Quain, Kay D. *BioIn 16*
Quain, Mitchell I. 1951- *WhoAm 90*
Quaintance, Douglas R. 1955- *St&PR 91*
Quainton, Anthony Cecil Eden 1934- *WhoAm 90, WhoWor 91*
Quaison-Sackey, Egya A *BiDrAPA 89*
Quakenbush, John Stephen 1956- *WhoWor 91*
Qualben, Paul A 1924- *BiDrAPA 89*
Qualchiah *WhNaAH*
Qualchin *WhNaAH*
Qualen, Michael A. 1945- *St&PR 91*
Qualey, Carlton C. 1904-1988 *BioIn 16*
Quallen, John Douglas 1962- *WhoEmL 91*
Qualley, Charles Albert 1930- *WhoAm 90*
Qualls, C Brandon 1940- *BiDrAPA 89*
Qualls, Charles Lee 1964- *WhoEmL 91*
Qualls, Charles Robert 1936- *St&PR 91*
Qualls, Corethia 1948- *WhoAmW 91*
Qualls, John H. *ODwPR 91*
Qualls, Robert C. *St&PR 91*
Qualls, Robert L. 1933- *St&PR 91, WhoAm 90*
Qualls, Robert M. 1950- *St&PR 91*
Qualter, Terence Hall 1925- *WhoAm 90*
Qualtere, Thomas Anthony 1955- *BiDrAPA 89*
Qualtrough, Mary Louise 1941- *WhoAmW 91*
Quam, Robert Charles 1934- *St&PR 91*
Quamme, Jack O. 1927- *St&PR 91, WhoAm 90*
Quan, Francis Wayne *BiDrAPA 89*
Quan, John Joseph 1951- *WhoWor 91*
Quan, Lawrence 1951- *WhoSSW 91*
Quanah *WhNaAH*
Quande, Bruce *BioIn 16*
Quandt, Elizabeth 1922- *WhoAmA 91*
Quandt, Richard Emeric 1930- *WhoAm 90*
Quandt, Russell Jerome 1919-1970 *WhoAmA 91N*
Quandt, William Bauer 1941- *WhoAm 90*
Quann, Joan Louise 1935- *WhoE 91*
Quant, Mary 1934- *BioIn 16, ConDes 90, WhoWor 91, WorAlBi*
Quantrill, William C. 1839-1865 *WorAlBi*
Quantrille, Joe *BioIn 16*
Quantz, Albert Theodore, Jr. 1939- *St&PR 91*
Quaranta, Gianni *BioIn 16*
Quaranta, Ronald Anthony 1967- *WhoEmL 91*
Quarles, Albert Merold 1910- *WhoAm 90*
Quarles, Benjamin 1905- *BioIn 16*
Quarles, Carroll Adair, Jr. 1938- *WhoAm 90*
Quarles, Denise Marie 1950- *WhoAmW 91, WhoEmL 91*
Quarles, James Cliv 1921- *WhoAm 90*
Quarles, James Linwood, III 1946- *WhoEmL 91*
Quarles, John M. 1940- *St&PR 91*
Quarles, Joseph V. 1908- *St&PR 91*
Quarles, Leo Thompson 1944- *St&PR 91, WhoAm 90*
Quarles, Mary Virginia 1940- *WhoAmW 91*
Quarles, Norma 1936- *DrBIPA 90*
Quarles, Pamela Anne 1954- *BiDrAPA 89*
Quarles, Ralph B. 1944- *St&PR 91*
Quarles, Steven Princeton 1942- *WhoWor 91*
Quarles, Ursula *BiDEWW*
Quaroni, Ludovico 1911-1987 *BioIn 16*
Quarrington, Glenn Austin 1949- *St&PR 91*
Quarrington, Paul *BioIn 16*
Quarrington, Paul 1953- *ConAu 129*
Quarry, Mary Ann 1953- *WhoAmW 91*
Quarry, Nick *ConAu 30NR, TwCCr&M 91*
Quartaro, Linda Schmidt 1963- *WhoAmW 91*
Quartel, Donald Robert, Jr. 1950- *WhoE 91*
Quartermain, Robert A. 1955- *St&PR 91*
Quarterman, Elsie 1910- *WhoAmW 91*
Quartermass, Martin *ConTFT 8*
Quartetto Fiorentino *PenDiMP*
Quartetto Italiano *PenDiMP*
Quarti, Eugenio 1867-1931 *PenDiDA 89*
Quartin, Leonard J. 1920- *St&PR 91*
Quarton, Gardner C *BiDrAPA 89*
Quarton, Jean Elsa Rulf 1942- *WhoAmW 91*
Quarton, William Barlow 1903- *WhoAm 90*
Quasarano, Joe *BioIn 16*
Quasebarth, Werner Horton 1931- *St&PR 91*
Quasha, Alan G. 1950- *WhoSSW 91*
Quasha, Alan Grant 1949- *St&PR 91*
Quasha, William Howard 1912- *WhoWor 91*
Quasimodo, Salvatore 1901-1968 *EuWr 12, MajTwCW, WorAlBi*
Quasius, Chiyoko Taninari 1948- *WhoAmW 91*
Quasius, Sharron G 1948- *WhoAmA 91*
Quast, Florence Edwina 1937- *WhoAmW 91*
Quast, Richard Donald 1930- *St&PR 91*
Quast, William James 1938- *St&PR 91*
Quat, Helen S 1918- *WhoAmA 91*
Quate, Calvin Forrest 1923- *WhoAm 90*
Quatrain, John *WhoWrEP 89*
Quatro, Suzi 1950- *EncPR&S 89*
Quattlebaum, Donald Anderson 1953- *St&PR 91*
Quattlebaum, James Tindal 1933- *BiDrAPA 89*
Quattlebaum, Walter Emmett, Jr. 1922- *WhoWor 91*
Quattlebaum, William Franklin 1953- *WhoSSW 91*
Quattro, Julie *ODwPR 91*
Quattrocchi, Edmondo 1889-1966 *WhoAmA 91N*
Quattrocchi, John Anthony 1962- *WhoE 91*
Quave, Gerald J. 1933- *St&PR 91*
Quave, Obra L. 1935- *WhoSSW 91*
Quay, Herbert C. 1927- *ConAu 33NR*
Quay, Jennifer 1964- *ODwPR 91*
Quay, Stephen 1947- *BioIn 16*
Quay, Steven Carl 1950- *WhoEmL 91*
Quay, Thomas Emery 1934- *WhoAm 90*
Quay, Timothy 1947- *BioIn 16*
Quayes, Mohamed Mijarul 1960- *WhoWor 91*
Quayle, Anthony 1913-1989 *AnObit 1989, BioIn 16, ConAu 130, CurBio 90N, WorAlBi*
Quayle, Bruce 1923- *ODwPR 91*
Quayle, Corinne *BioIn 16*
Quayle, Dan *BioIn 16*
Quayle, Danforth 1947- *BiDrUSE 89*
Quayle, James Danforth 1947- *WhoAm 90, WhoE 91, WhoWor 91*
Quayle, Marilyn *BioIn 16*
Quayle, Marilyn 1949- *WhoAm 90, WhoAmW 91, WhoE 91*
Quaytman, Harvey 1937- *WhoAmA 91*
Quaytman, Miles Sheldon 1950- *BiDrAPA 89*
Quealy, William Harrison 1913- *WhoAm 90*
Quebedeaux, Richard 1944- *ConAu 30NR*
Queen *EncPR&S 89, OxCPMus*
Queen Anne *PenDiDA 89, WhNaAH*
Queen, C.V. 1903- *St&PR 91*
Queen, Daniel 1934- *WhoE 91, WhoWor 91*
Queen, Ellery *ConAu 32NR, MajTwCW, TwCCr&M 91, WorAlBi*
Queen, Ellery, Jr. *AuBYP 90*
Queen, Gary W. 1947- *WhoAm 90*
Queen, Gary Wayne 1947- *St&PR 91*
Queen, James W. 1940- *St&PR 91*
Queen, Mary Jane *St&PR 91*
Queen, Mel 1918-1982 *Ballpl 90*
Queen, Mel 1942- *Ballpl 90*
Queen, Shelly Ann 1951- *WhoEmL 91*
Queen, Susan Elizabeth *BiDrAPA 89*
Queenan, John Thomas 1933- *WhoAm 90*
Queenan, Joseph Martin, Jr. 1950- *WhoAm 90, WhoWrEP 89*
Queenan, Linda Joyce *WhoWrEP 89*
Queeny, John F. 1859-1933 *WorAlBi*
Queffelec, Anne 1948- *IntWWM 90, PenDiMP*
Quehl, Gary Howard 1938- *WhoAm 90*
Queiroz, Dinah Silveira de *BioIn 16*
Queiroz, Rachel de *BioIn 16*
Quek, Swee-San Susan 1949- *WhoWor 91*
Quelch, John Anthony 1951- *WhoE 91*
Queler, Eve 1936- *IntWWM 90, PenDiMP*
Quelle, Frederick William, Jr. 1934- *WhoAm 90*
Queller, Donald Edward 1925- *WhoAm 90*
Quellin, Arnold 1653-1686 *BioIn 16*
Quellmalz, Frederick 1912- *ODwPR 91*
Quellmalz, Henry 1915- *St&PR 91, WhoE 91, WhoWor 91*
Quellmalz, Marion Lynch 1916- *St&PR 91*
Quello, James Henry 1914- *WhoAm 90*
Quemuel, Conchita H *BiDrAPA 89*
Quemuel, Ruperto S 1926- *BiDrAPA 89*
Quen, Jacques M 1928- *BiDrAPA 89*
Queneau, Paul Etienne 1911- *WhoAm 90*
Queneau, Raymond 1903-1976 *ConAu 32NR, EuWr 12, MajTwCW*
Quenelle, John Duff 1946- *WhoWrEP 89*
Quennell, Peter 1905- *WhoWor 91*
Quenneville, Kathleen 1953- *WhoEmL 91*
Quenneville, Robert *BiDrAPA 89*
Quenon, Robert Hagerty 1928- *WhoAm 90*
Quentel, Charles E., III 1927- *St&PR 91*
Quentel, Holt 1961- *WhoAmA 91*
Quentel, Paul F. 1912- *WhoWor 91*
Quentin, Patrick 1912-1987 *TwCCr&M 91*
Quenzel, Heinrich Paul 1932- *WhoWor 91*
Quenzer, Clinton Quenton 1935- *St&PR 91*
Queoff, Pamela Frances 1952- *WhoAmW 91*

Queralt, Michael 1962- WhoE 91
Querbes, Betty-Lane Shipp WhoAmW 91
Quercia, Jacopo della 1374?-1438 IntDcAA 90
Quern, Arthur Foster 1942- St&PR 91
Querner, Christine 1954- WhoSSW 91
Querner, James Clayton 1953- WhoSSW 91
Querner, Ursula 1921- BiDWomA
Querry, Ronald Burns 1943- WhoWrEP 89
Quertermus, Carl John, Jr. 1943- WhoSSW 91
Quervelle, Antoine-Gabriel 1789-1856 PenDiDA 89
Query, Cecil Arthur 1932- St&PR 91
Query, David Leon 1949- WhoSSW 91
Query, Joy Marves Neale WhoAm 90
Quesnay, Francois 1694-1774 BioIn 16
Quesnel, Joseph 1746-1809 DcLB 99 [port], OxCCanT
Quest, Charles Francis 1904- WhoAm 90, WhoAmA 91
Quest, Donald Richard 1938- St&PR 91
Quest, Dorothy 1909- WhoAmA 91
Quest, Olga W. Hall- 1899-1986 BioIn 16
Questel, Mae 1908- WhoAm 90
Quester, Aline Olson 1943- WhoE 91
Quester, George Herman 1936- WhoAm 90
Question Mark 1945- EncPR&S 89
Question Mark and the Mysterians EncPR&S 89
Queston, Joanna 1951- ConAu 131
Questrom, Allen I. St&PR 91
Questrom, Allen I. 1941- WhoAm 90, WhoSSW 91
Queuille, Henri 1884-1970 BiDFrPL
Queveda, Ben WhoHisp 91
Quevedo, Ermel B. 1947- WhoEmL 91
Quevedo, Sylvestre Grado 1949- WhoHisp 91
Quevedo Y Villegas, Francisco Gomez De 1580-1645 WorAlBi
Quezada, Abel BioIn 16
Quezada-Diamondstein, Maria Del Socorro 1949- WhoWor 91
Quezon Y Molina, Manuel Luis 1878-1944 WorAlBi
Quiambao, Felicinita Y BiDrAPA 89
Quiason, Arturo G BiDrAPA 89
Quiason, Emmeline P BiDrAPA 89
Quiat, Bette Ellen 1952- WhoEmL 91
Quiat, Gerald M. 1924- WhoAm 90
Quiat, Mindy S. 1956- St&PR 91
Quick, Carolyn May 1938- WhoAmW 91
Quick, Diana 1946- ConTFT 8
Quick, Edward Raymond 1943- WhoAm 90, WhoAmA 91
Quick, Jack Beaver 1947- WhoWor 91
Quick, Jim 1943- Ballpl 90
Quick, Joe Cecil 1935- St&PR 91
Quick, John Biery 1918- St&PR 91
Quick, Joseph Haslam 1909- St&PR 91
Quick, Leslie Charles, III 1953- WhoAm 90
Quick, Perry Day 1945- WhoE 91
Quick, Peter 1956- St&PR 91
Quick, Richard T 1933- BiDrAPA 89
Quick, Robert 1948- St&PR 91
Quick, Robert E., Jr. ODwPR 91
Quick, Roy Dixon, Jr. 1951- WhoEmL 91, WhoSSW 91
Quick, Thomas Clarkson 1955- WhoAm 90
Quickel, James J. 1932- St&PR 91
Quickel, Kenneth E., Jr. 1939- WhoAm 90
Quidd, David Andrew 1954- WhoEmL 91, WhoSSW 91
Quidde, Ludwig 1858-1941 WorAlBi
Quidort, David George 1935- St&PR 91
Quie, Paul Gerhardt 1925- WhoAm 90
Quiet Riot EncPR&S 89
Quigg, Donald James 1916- WhoAm 90
Quigg, James R., Jr. 1933- St&PR 91
Quigg, Jane BioIn 16
Quiggins, Richard Stone, II 1947- St&PR 91
Quiggle, John E. 1938- ODwPR 91
Quigley, Austin Edmund 1942- WhoAm 90
Quigley, Behnaz Zolghadr 1944- WhoAmW 91
Quigley, Brian Desmond 1928- BiDrAPA 89
Quigley, Catherine M. BioIn 16
Quigley, Ernie Ballpl 90
Quigley, Jack Allen 1914- WhoAm 90
Quigley, Joan EncO&P 3
Quigley, Joan 1927- BestSel 90-3 [port]
Quigley, John Bernard 1940- WhoAm 90
Quigley, John Charles, II 1945- WhoSSW 91
Quigley, John Lester, Jr. 1936- St&PR 91
Quigley, John Michael 1942- WhoAm 90
Quigley, Joseph Milton 1922- WhoAm 90
Quigley, Joseph V. 1931- St&PR 91
Quigley, Linnea BioIn 16, ConTFT 8
Quigley, Margaret A. 1952- St&PR 91
Quigley, Martin Schofield 1917- WhoAm 90
Quigley, Michael Allen 1950- WhoAmA 91
Quigley, Michael J., III 1940- St&PR 91
Quigley, Robert Alan 1943- St&PR 91, WhoAm 90
Quigley, Robert J. 1929- St&PR 91
Quigley, Robin L 1947- WhoAmA 91
Quigley, Ruth Helen 1935- WhoAmW 91
Quigley, Stephen Howard 1951- WhoE 91
Quigley, Thomas J. 1923- WhoAm 90
Quigley, W. H. 1926- St&PR 91
Quigley-Wolf, Anna Marie Helen 1950- WhoAmW 91
Quiles, Paul 1942- BiDFrPL
Quilici, Frank 1939- Ballpl 90
Quilico, Gino BioIn 16
Quilico, Gino 1955- IntWWM 90
Quilico, Louis BioIn 16
Quilico, Louis 1929- IntWWM 90
Quilico, Louis 1931- WhoAm 90
Quill, Mike 1905-1966 EncAL
Quill, Monica TwCCr&M 91
Quill, Stephen F. 1940- St&PR 91
Quillan, Eddie 1907- WhoE 91
Quillen, Cecil Dyer 1937- St&PR 91
Quillen, Cecil Dyer, Jr. 1937- WhoAm 90
Quillen, Hotense BioIn 16
Quillen, James Henry 1916- WhoAm 90, WhoSSW 91
Quillen, Lloyd Douglas 1943- WhoSSW 91
Quillen, William Tatem 1935- WhoAm 90
Quiller, Stephen Frederick 1946- WhoAmA 91
Quillerette, Antoinette BioIn 16
Quillet, Vitus Dean 1943- St&PR 91
Quillian, William Fletcher, Jr. 1913- WhoAm 90
Quilligan, Edward James 1925- WhoAm 90
Quillin, Ellen 1892- WomFie [port]
Quillinan, Robert Joseph 1947- St&PR 91
Quillman, James Edward 1946- St&PR 91
Quilter, Joan Mary 1928- WhoAmW 91
Quilty, Phyllis Margaret 1952- WhoWor 91
Quilty, Rafe ConAu 132
Quimby, Fred William 1945- WhoEmL 91
Quimby, George Irving 1913- WhoAm 90, WhoWor 91
Quimby, Hugh Allen 1946- WhoSSW 91
Quimby, Phineas P. 1802-1866 EncO&P 3
Quimby, Phineas Parkhurst EncPaPR 91
Quimby, Robert Sherman 1916- WhoAm 90
Quimby, Terry BioIn 16
Quimby, William Robert 1936- WhoWrEP 89
Quin, Ah BioIn 16
Quin, Ann 1936-1973 FemiCLE
Quin, Arden 1913- ArtLatA
Quin, Joseph Marvin 1947- St&PR 91, WhoAm 90
Quin, Louis DuBose 1928- WhoAm 90
Quin, Whayne Sherman 1937- WhoE 91
Quin-Harkin, Janet 1941- Au&Arts 6 [port], ConAu 33NR
Quina, Richard D. 1924- St&PR 91
Quinby, Alan R. 1931- ODwPR 91
Quinby, Charles Edward, Jr. 1943- WhoAm 90
Quinby, William A. 1941- WhoAm 90
Quincy, Anna 1812-1899 FemiCLE
Quincy, Josiah 1744-1775 EncCRAm
Quincy, Margaret 1806- FemiCLE
Quincy, Sophia 1805- FemiCLE
Quincy, Susan 1798-1884 FemiCLE
Quindel, Darlene Jean 1944- WhoAmW 91
Quindlen, Anna BioIn 16
Quindlen, John Joseph 1932- St&PR 91, WhoAm 90
Quine, Hector 1926- IntWWM 90
Quine, Judy BioIn 16
Quine, Richard 1920-1989 AnObit 1989, BioIn 16, ConTFT 8
Quine, Willard Van Orman 1908- WhoAm 90
Quiney, Thomas 1589-1655? BioIn 16
Quiniton, Michael Wayne 1950- St&PR 91
Quinkent 1819- WhNaAH
Quinlan, Claire 1929- WhoAmW 91
Quinlan, Donald Paul 1931- St&PR 91
Quinlan, J. Michael BioIn 16
Quinlan, James E. 1938- St&PR 91
Quinlan, John Edward, Jr. 1946- St&PR 91
Quinlan, John J. 1925- St&PR 91
Quinlan, John Michael 1936- St&PR 91, WhoAm 90
Quinlan, Joseph Michael 1941- WhoAm 90
Quinlan, Kathleen M BiDrAPA 89
Quinlan, Liz W. 1937- WhoAmW 91
Quinlan, Michael R. BioIn 16
Quinlan, Michael Robert 1944- WhoAm 90
Quinlan, Patricia AuBYP 90
Quinlan, Robert J. 1930- ODwPR 91
Quinlan, Thomas E., Jr. 1922- WhoAm 90
Quinlisk, Warren 1924- St&PR 91
Quinly, James Carlton 1931- St&PR 91
Quinn, Aidan BioIn 16
Quinn, Alfred Otto 1915- WhoAm 90
Quinn, Andrew Peter, Jr. 1923- WhoAm 90
Quinn, Anthony BioIn 16
Quinn, Anthony 1915- HispWr 90, WorAlBi
Quinn, Anthony Rudolph Oaxaca 1915- WhoAm 90, WhoHisp 91, WhoWor 91
Quinn, Art Jay 1936- WhoSSW 91
Quinn, Aysha 1945- WhoAmA 91
Quinn, Barbara Ann 1933- WhoAmW 91
Quinn, Bayard Elmer 1915- WhoAm 90
Quinn, Bernetta Viola 1915- WhoWrEP 89
Quinn, Betty Nye 1921- WhoAm 90
Quinn, Bob 1937- BioIn 16
Quinn, Brian Grant 1950- WhoAmA 91
Quinn, C. Edward 1926-1989 BioIn 16
Quinn, C Edward 1926-1989 ConAu 129
Quinn, Cameron Paige 1957- WhoE 91
Quinn, Carl Robert 1934- St&PR 91
Quinn, Carl S. 1931- WhoAm 90, WhoSSW 91
Quinn, Caroline G. 1949- St&PR 91
Quinn, Carroll Thomas 1946- WhoE 91
Quinn, Charles C. 1924- St&PR 91
Quinn, Charles Nicholas 1930- WhoAm 90
Quinn, Charles Vincent 1961- WhoE 91
Quinn, Cheri Lynne 1949- WhoAmW 91
Quinn, Christine Agnes 1946- WhoAmW 91
Quinn, Claire Koffler 1959- WhoAmW 91
Quinn, Clifton Lee 1924- BiDrAPA 89
Quinn, Colin BioIn 16
Quinn, Colin Kerry 1960- BiDrAPA 89
Quinn, Daniel Joseph 1945- St&PR 91
Quinn, Daniel Lonergan 1954- WhoE 91
Quinn, David Beers 1909- WhoWor 91
Quinn, David Phillip 1956- WhoEmL 91
Quinn, David W. WhoAm 90
Quinn, David W. 1942- St&PR 91
Quinn, Denise C BiDrAPA 89
Quinn, Dennis B. 1928- WhoAm 90
Quinn, Diana Kristine BiDrAPA 89
Quinn, Donald Edward, II 1947- St&PR 91
Quinn, Edward Francis, III 1944- WhoE 91
Quinn, Edward J. BioIn 16
Quinn, Edward James 1942- St&PR 91
Quinn, Edward Leigh 1931- St&PR 91
Quinn, Edward W. 1941- St&PR 91
Quinn, Emily Steifle 1946- WhoAmW 91
Quinn, Eugene Frederick 1935- WhoAm 90
Quinn, Francis A. 1921- WhoAm 90
Quinn, Francis Xavier 1932- WhoSSW 91
Quinn, Gary Michael BiDrAPA 89
Quinn, Gerald V. 1952- WhoE 91
Quinn, Henrietta Reist 1918- WhoAmA 91
Quinn, Hugh Joseph 1933- WhoAm 90
Quinn, J.C. ConTFT 8
Quinn, Jack WhoAm 90
Quinn, Jack 1883-1946 Ballpl 90 [port]
Quinn, James Amos 1939- WhoE 91
Quinn, James Francis 1949- WhoSSW 91
Quinn, James Hockley McKee 1916- WhoAm 90
Quinn, James Joseph 1936- IntWWM 90
Quinn, James Leonard 1928- WhoAm 90
Quinn, James P. 1941- St&PR 91
Quinn, Jane Bryant BioIn 16
Quinn, Jane Bryant 1930- WorAlBi
Quinn, Jane Bryant 1939- WhoAm 90, WhoAmW 91
Quinn, Jarus William 1930- WhoAm 90, WhoE 91
Quinn, Jeri Nichols BioIn 16
Quinn, Joe 1864-1940 Ballpl 90
Quinn, John Albert 1932- WhoAm 90
Quinn, John Brian Patrick 1943- WhoAm 90
Quinn, John C., Jr. 1921- St&PR 91
Quinn, John Collins 1925- St&PR 91, WhoAm 90, WhoSSW 91, WhoWrEP 89
Quinn, John F. 1935- St&PR 91
Quinn, John Frederick 1957- WhoE 91
Quinn, John J. 1933- WhoAm 90, WhoSSW 91
Quinn, John J. 1944- St&PR 91
Quinn, John J. 1945- St&PR 91
Quinn, John Joseph 1944- WhoAm 90
Quinn, John Matthew 1933- St&PR 91
Quinn, John R. 1929- WhoAm 90
Quinn, Joseph F. 1931- St&PR 91
Quinn, Joseph Francis 1962- BiDrAPA 89
Quinn, Joseph Michael 1937- WhoAm 90
Quinn, Joseph R. 1932- WhoAm 90
Quinn, Julia Province 1919- WhoAmW 91, WhoSSW 91, WhoWor 91
Quinn, Katha BioIn 16
Quinn, Kathleen May 1949- BiDrAPA 89
Quinn, Kathryn BioIn 16
Quinn, Kelly 1962- WhoAmW 91
Quinn, Kevin A. 1941- St&PR 91
Quinn, Kevin Patrick 1968- WhoEmL 91
Quinn, Kevin Vincent 1954- BiDrAPA 89
Quinn, Leacy Griffin 1901- WhoSSW 91
Quinn, Leon James 1938- BiDrAPA 89
Quinn, Linda BioIn 16
Quinn, Lloyd 1917- St&PR 91
Quinn, Longworth M. BioIn 16
Quinn, Louis BioIn 16
Quinn, Martin Vincent 1948- St&PR 91
Quinn, Mary Hope 1941- WhoAmW 91
Quinn, Matthew J. WhoAm 90
Quinn, Michael Alfred 1946- WhoEmL 91
Quinn, Michael Desmond 1936- WhoE 91
Quinn, Michael J. 1943- St&PR 91
Quinn, Michael J. 1947- St&PR 91
Quinn, Michael William 1949- WhoSSW 91
Quinn, Noel Joseph 1915- WhoAmA 91
Quinn, Patricia Anne 1949- WhoEmL 91
Quinn, Patricia Therese 1958- WhoE 91
Quinn, Patrick John 1943- St&PR 91
Quinn, Patrick John 1946- WhoWor 91
Quinn, Patrick Michael 1934- WhoAm 90
Quinn, Paul J., Jr. 1932- St&PR 91
Quinn, Philip Lawrence 1940- WhoAm 90
Quinn, Revanell 1920- St&PR 91
Quinn, Richard ODwPR 91
Quinn, Rita Marie 1929- WhoAmW 91
Quinn, Robert Hayes 1902-1962 WhoAmA 91N
Quinn, Robert Henry 1919- WhoAm 90
Quinn, Robert J. 1926- St&PR 91
Quinn, Robert K. 1934- St&PR 91
Quinn, Robert M. 1941- St&PR 91
Quinn, Robert William 1912- WhoWor 91
Quinn, Rupert Gregory 1930- St&PR 91
Quinn, Sally BioIn 16
Quinn, Sally 1941- WhoAm 90, WhoAmW 91, WhoWrEP 89
Quinn, Simon TwCCr&M 91
Quinn, Susan Gibson 1958- WhoAmW 91
Quinn, Teresa Moss 1952- WhoAmW 91
Quinn, Theodora K. ConAu 32NR
Quinn, Thomas Joseph, Jr. 1951- WhoE 91
Quinn, Thomas Michael 1940-1989 BioIn 16
Quinn, Thomas Patrick, Jr 1938- WhoAmA 91
Quinn, Timothy Charles, Jr. 1936- WhoE 91
Quinn, Tom BioIn 16
Quinn, Tracy A. ODwPR 91
Quinn, Vincent K. 1931- St&PR 91
Quinn, William 1929- WhoAmA 91
Quinn, William Francis 1919- WhoAm 90
Quinn, William J. 1948- St&PR 91
Quinn, William John 1911- WhoAm 90
Quinn, William Wilson 1907- WhoAm 90, WhoE 91
Quinn-Cordero, Mary 1955- WhoE 91
Quinn-Musgrove, Sandra Lavern 1935- WhoSSW 91
Quinn-Skoros, Judith 1949- WhoAmW 91
Quinnan, Edward Michael 1935- WhoAm 90
Quinnan, Gerald Vincent, Jr. 1947- WhoE 91
Quinnan, Joseph Edward 1944- St&PR 91
Quinnapin WhNaAH
Quinnell, A J 1941- SpyFic
Quinnell, Bruce A. 1949- St&PR 91
Quinnell, Bruce Andrew 1949- WhoAm 90
Quinnette, Patricia Ann 1939- WhoAmW 91
Quinney, John Waunnacon 1797-1855 WhNaAH
Quinones, Angel 1944- WhoAm 90
Quinones, Carlos Ramon 1951- St&PR 91
Quinones, John Manuel 1952- WhoHisp 91
Quinones, Jose Enrique 1951- BiDrAPA 89
Quinones, Jose G 1933- BiDrAPA 89
Quinones, Juan Gomez- BioIn 16
Quinones, Luis 1963- Ballpl 90
Quinones, Matthew Mark 1927- BiDrAPA 89
Quinones, Pedro A. St&PR 91
Quinones, Rey 1963- Ballpl 90
Quinones, Samuel 1949- WhoHisp 91
Quinones Amezquita, Mario Rafael 1933- WhoWor 91
Quinones-D'Brassis, R. Rafael 1937- WhoWor 91
Quinot, Raymond 1920- WhoWor 91
Quinsac, Annie-Paule 1945- WhoAmA 91
Quinsey, Mary Beth 1948- ConAu 132
Quinsler, William Thomson 1924- WhoAm 90
Quinson, Bruno Andre 1938- WhoAm 90, WhoE 91
Quint, Alan Steven 1943- BiDrAPA 89
Quint, Ira 1930- WhoAm 90
Quint, Stephen David 1944- BiDrAPA 89
Quintana, Carlos Narcis 1965- WhoHisp 91
Quintana, Carmen Gloria BioIn 16
Quintana, Edward M. WhoHisp 91
Quintana, Edward M. 1908- St&PR 91
Quintana, Edward M., Mrs. 1915- St&PR 91
Quintana, Francisco J 1923- BiDrAPA 89

Quintana, Henry, Jr. 1952- *WhoHisp 91*
Quintana, Humberto *WhoE 91*
Quintana, Humberto 1948- *BiDrAPA 89*
Quintana, Leroy V. *BioIn 16*
Quintana, Leroy V. 1944- *ConAu 131, HispWr 90, WhoHisp 91*
Quintana, Maria del Rosario 1958- *WhoAmW 91*
Quintana, Sammy Joseph 1949- *WhoHisp 91*
Quintana, Yamile 1940- *WhoHisp 91*
Quintanilla, Antonio Paulet 1927- *WhoWor 91*
Quintanilla, Guadalupe C. 1937- *WhoHisp 91*
Quintanilla, Isabel 1938- *BiDWomA*
Quintanilla, Jaime 1929- *BiDrAPA 89*
Quintanilla, Maria Aline Griffiths y D. *BioIn 16*
Quintanilla, Mario A *BiDrAPA 89*
Quintanilla, Michael Ray 1954- *WhoHisp 91*
Quintela, Abel R. 1946- *WhoHisp 91*
Quintela, Richard Gerard 1964- *WhoHisp 91*
Quinter, Ken John 1931- *St&PR 91*
Quintero, Janneth Ivon 1960- *WhoHisp 91*
Quintero, Jess *WhoHisp 91*
Quintero, Jesus Marciano 1961- *WhoHisp 91*
Quintero, Jose 1924- *ConTFT 8, HispWr 90, WhoAm 90, WhoHisp 91*
Quintero, Juan A. *BioIn 16*
Quintero Arce, Carlos 1920- *WhoAm 90*
Quintin *WhNaAH*
Quinton, Anthony Meredith 1925- *WhoWor 91*
Quinton, Arthur Robert 1924- *WhoAm 90*
Quinton, Everett *BioIn 16*
Quinton, Michael Wayne 1950- *St&PR 91*
Quintrell, Thomas A. 1920- *WhoAm 90*
Quirarte, Jacinto 1931- *BioIn 16, ConAu 32NR, HispWr 90, WhoAm 90, WhoAmA 91, WhoHisp 91*
Quiray, Lourdes Ferrer *BiDrAPA 89*
Quirico, Francis Joseph 1911- *WhoAm 90*
Quirin, Albert Joseph 1948- *St&PR 91*
Quiring, Wayne R. 1927- *St&PR 91*
Quirk, Barbara Long 1935- *WhoAmW 91*
Quirk, Charles Patrick, Jr. 1941- *St&PR 91*
Quirk, Donna Hawkins 1955- *WhoAmW 91*
Quirk, Francis Joseph 1907-1974 *WhoAmA 91N*
Quirk, Frank J. 1941- *St&PR 91*
Quirk, Frank Joseph 1941- *WhoAm 90*
Quirk, Gail Elizabeth Manz 1929- *WhoAmW 91*
Quirk, Jamie 1954- *Ballpl 90*
Quirk, John James 1943- *St&PR 91, WhoAm 90*
Quirk, Lawrence Joseph 1923- *WhoWrEP 89*
Quirk, Michael James *St&PR 91*
Quirk, Peter Richard 1936- *WhoAm 90*
Quirk, Randolph 1920- *WhoWor 91*
Quirk, Thomas Charles, Jr 1922- *WhoAmA 91*
Quirk, Thomas J., II 1938- *St&PR 91*
Quiroga, Alicia Espinosa *WhoAmW 91*
Quiroga, Dario O. 1941- *St&PR 91*
Quiroga, Elena 1921- *EncCoWW*
Quiroga, Francisco Gracia *WhoHisp 91*
Quiroga, Horacio 1878-1937 *BioIn 16, ConAu 131, HispWr 90, MajTwCW*
Quiroga, Indalecio Ruiz 1937- *WhoHisp 91*
Quiroga, Jorge Humberto 1950- *WhoHisp 91*
Quiroga, Jose A. 1959- *WhoHisp 91*
Quiroga, Nydia Mayolo 1943- *BiDrAPA 89*
Quiros, Daniel Oduber 1921- *BioIn 16*
Quiroz, Antonio Castro 1933- *WhoSSW 91*
Quiroz, Jesse M. 1939- *WhoHisp 91*
Quirt, Walter 1902-1968 *WhoAmA 91N*
Quisenberry, Dan 1953- *Ballpl 90*
Quisenberry, Daniel Raymond 1954- *WhoAm 90*
Quisenberry, Richard Keith 1934- *WhoAm 90*
Quisenberry, Robert B. 1936- *St&PR 91*
Quisenberry, Robert Max 1956- *WhoEmL 91*
Quisgard, Liz Whitney 1929- *WhoAm 90, WhoAmA 91*
Quisling, Stewart W 1942- *BiDrAPA 89*
Quisling, Vidkun 1887-1945 *BioIn 16, WorAlBi*
Quispel, Anton 1917- *WhoWor 91*
Quist, Carolyn Wilson 1959- *WhoEmL 91*
Quist, Edwin Arnold, Jr. 1951- *IntWWM 90, WhoAm 90*
Quist, George R. 1920- *St&PR 91*
Quist, Jeanette Fitzgerald 1948- *WhoAmW 91*
Quist, Scott Milton 1953- *St&PR 91*
Quistad, Gary Bennet 1947- *WhoEmL 91*
Quistgaard, Johan Waldemar De Rehling 1877-1962 *WhoAmA 91N*
Quisumbing, Remedios Excond *BiDrAPA 89*
Quiter, James Robert 1953- *WhoEmL 91*
Quitevis, Minda Altea 1937- *WhoAmW 91*
Quitkin, Frederic M 1937- *BiDrAPA 89*
Quitmeier, William Michael 1951- *WhoEmL 91*
Quittmeyer, Charles Loreaux 1917- *WhoAm 90*
Quittmeyer, Robert Theodore 1920- *St&PR 91*
Quivar, Florence *BioIn 16*
Quivar, Florence 1944- *IntWWM 90*
Quixley, Jim 1931- *BioIn 16*
Quogan, Anthony *WhoWrEP 89*
Quoirez, Francoise 1935- *BioIn 16, EncCoWW, MajTwCW, WhoWor 91*
Quoyeser, Clement Louis 1899- *St&PR 91*
Quraishi, Ali Akhtar 1936- *WhoWor 91*
Quraishi, Mohammed Sayeed 1924- *WhoAm 90, WhoWor 91*
Qurashi, Mazhar Mahmood 1925- *WhoWor 91*
Qureshi, Arshad Hasan 1940- *St&PR 91*
Qureshi, Azam Sajjad 1942- *St&PR 91*
Qureshi, Moeen Ahmad 1930- *St&PR 91*
Qureshi, Mohammad Akram 1935- *WhoWor 91*
Qureshi, Mohammed Jamil 1939- *WhoWor 91*
Qureshi, Shahid *St&PR 91*
Qureshi, Shamim Iqbal 1942- *BiDrAPA 89*
Qureshi, Shams M 1950- *BiDrAPA 89*
Qutub, Musa Yacub 1940- *WhoAm 90*
Quwatli, Shukri Al- 1891-1967 *PolLCME*
Qvarnstrom, S Birger 1897- *EncO&P 3*

R

R, S BiDEWW
R.E.M. ConMus 5 [port]
R-va, Zenaida EncCoWW
Ra, Carol Fae 1939- WhoWrEP 89
Raab, Ada Dennett WhoAmA 91N
Raab, Charles 1912?-1952? EncACom
Raab, Cornel E. 1946- St&PR 91
Raab, Ernst BiDrAPA 89
Raab, Ernst S 1933- BiDrAPA 89
Raab, G. Kirk 1935- St&PR 91
Raab, Gail B 1934- WhoAmA 91
Raab, Harry Frederick, Jr. 1926- WhoE 91, WhoWor 91
Raab, Herbert Norman 1925- WhoE 91
Raab, Hilary Albert, Jr. 1942- St&PR 91
Raab, Ira Jerry 1935- WhoAm 90, WhoE 91, WhoWor 91
Raab, Johann Philipp 1736-1802 PenDiDA 89
Raab, Johann Valentin 1777-1839 PenDiDA 89
Raab, John Joseph 1936- St&PR 91
Raab, Kurt 1941-1988 AnObit 1988
Raab, Leonard Frederick 1939- St&PR 91
Raab, Martin D. 1932- St&PR 91
Raab, Selwyn 1934- WhoAm 90
Raab, Sheldon 1937- WhoAm 90
Raab, Susan Salzman 1958- WhoAmW 91
Raab, Walter F. 1924- St&PR 91
Raab, Walter Ferdinand 1924- WhoAm 90, WhoE 91, WhoWor 91
Raab, Yaron Roni 1964- WhoSSW 91
Raabe, Gerhard Karl 1948- WhoE 91
Raabe, James A. 1952- St&PR 91
Raabe, John 1930- St&PR 91
Raach, Frederick Raymond 1914- WhoAm 90
Raacke, Peter 1928- ConDes 90
Raad, Virginia 1925- IntWWM 90, WhoAm 90
Raaen, John Carpenter, Jr. 1922- WhoAm 90
Raaf, John Elbert 1905- WhoAm 90
Raaf, John Hart 1941- WhoAm 90
Raaff, Anton 1714?-1797 PenDiMP
Raaflaub, Kurt A. 1941- WhoAm 90
Raaflaub, Vernon Arthur 1938- WhoWor 91
Raagas, Edita M BiDrAPA 89
Raasoch, John William 1946- BiDrAPA 89
Raatz, Patricia Anne Tirrell 1946- WhoWrEP 89
Raba, Ernest A, Jr. BiDrAPA 89
Rabadeau, Mary Frances 1948- WhoE 91
Rabadjija, Mirjana BiDrAPA 89
Raban, Jonathan BioIn 16
Rabanne, Paco 1934- ConDes 90
Rabassa, Albert Oscar 1936- WhoHisp 91
Rabassa, Gregory 1922- BioIn 16, HispWr 90, WhoAm 90, WhoHisp 91
Rabat, Guy 1943- St&PR 91
Rabb, Bernard Paul 1939- WhoAm 90
Rabb, Bruce 1941- WhoAm 90, WhoWor 91
Rabb, Carlos C., Jr. 1924- WhoAm 90
Rabb, Cheryl Kay 1945- WhoSSW 91
Rabb, Ellis 1930- WhoAm 90
Rabb, George B. 1930- WhoAm 90
Rabb, Harriet Schaffer 1941- WhoAm 90
Rabb, Irving W WhoAmA 91
Rabb, Irving W, Mrs WhoAmA 91
Rabb, Irving William 1913- WhoE 91
Rabb, Jeannette WhoAmA 91
Rabb, Madeline M WhoAmA 91
Rabb, Madeline Murphy 1945- BioIn 16
Rabb, Maurice F. BioIn 16
Rabb, Maxwell M. 1910- WhoAm 90, WhoWor 91
Rabb, Nancy 1938- St&PR 91
Rabb, Richard Avery 1943- St&PR 91
Rabb, Stephen M. 1944- St&PR 91
Rabb, Theodore K. 1937- WhoAm 90
Rabb, Virg Sullivan 1932- St&PR 91
Rabbat, Guy 1943- WhoAm 90
Rabbio, Salvatore Frank 1963- WhoSSW 91
Rabbit, Eddie 1941- WorAlBi
Rabbit, John Michael 1941- St&PR 91
Rabbit, Running WhoAmA 91
Rabbitt, Eddie 1941- ConMus 5 [port]
Rabbitt, Eddie 1944- BioIn 16
Rabbitt, Edward Charles 1952- WhoEmL 91
Rabbitt, Edward Thomas 1941- WhoAm 90
Rabe, Berniece Louise 1928- WhoWrEP 89
Rabe, David 1940- WorAlBi
Rabe, David William 1940- WhoAm 90
Rabe, Diane Marie 1959- St&PR 91
Rabe, Edward Frederic, Jr. BiDrAPA 89
Rabe, Folke 1935- IntWWM 90
Rabe, J.B.E. PenDiDA 89
Rabe, Olive AuBYP 90
Rabe, Peter SpyFic, TwCCr&M 91
Rabe, Richard Frank 1919- WhoWor 91
Rabe, Robert L. NewYTBS 90
Rabe, Rudolph F. 1841- AmLegL
Rabelais, Francois 1490?-1533 WorAlBi
Raben, Gail 1945- WhoAmW 91
Rabenstein, Albert Louis 1931- WhoE 91
Raber, Donald R. 1943- St&PR 91
Raber, Marvin 1937- WhoE 91
Raberge, Allan C. 1930- St&PR 91
Rabes, C.-A. Lennart 1938- IntWWM 90
Rabi, Isidor I. 1896-1988 AnObit 1988
Rabi, Isidor Isaac BioIn 16
Rabi, Isidor Isaac 1898-1988 WorAlBi
Rabideau, Peter Wayne 1940- WhoAm 90
Rabier, Jacques-Rene 1919- WhoWor 91
Rabier, Patrick Jean 1951- WhoE 91
Rabil, Richard Joseph 1956- WhoSSW 91
Rabin, Allan Howard 1937- BiDrAPA 89
Rabin, Barry Edward 1942- BiDrAPA 89
Rabin, Bruce Stuart 1941- WhoAm 90
Rabin, Claire Low 1948- WhoWor 91
Rabin, Herbert 1928- WhoAm 90, WhoE 91
Rabin, Joseph Harry 1927- WhoWor 91
Rabin, Kenneth H. 1943- ODwPR 91
Rabin, Michael O. 1931- WhoAm 90
Rabin, Paul I. 1938- St&PR 91
Rabin, Pauline Lou 1933- BiDrAPA 89
Rabin, Ronald Allan BiDrAPA 89
Rabin, Stanley Arthur 1938- St&PR 91, WhoAm 90, WhoSSW 91
Rabin, Todd Martin 1953- WhoE 91
Rabin, Yitzhak 1922- PolLCME, WhoWor 91
Rabindranath Tagore 1861-1941 BioIn 16
Rabineau, Louis 1924- WhoAm 90
Rabiner, Charles J 1932- BiDrAPA 89
Rabiner, Edwin L 1929- BiDrAPA 89
Rabiner, Lawrence Richard 1943- WhoAm 90
Rabiner, Susan 1948- WhoAm 90, WhoWrEP 89
Rabinkow, Shlomo Barukh 1882?-1941? BioIn 16
Rabino, Isaac 1938- WhoE 91
Rabinovich, Harris 1938- BiDrAPA 89
Rabinovich, Raisa 1937- BiDrAPA 89
Rabinovich, Raquel 1929- WhoAmA 91
Rabinovich, Rhea Sanders WhoAmA 91
Rabinovich, Sergio 1928- WhoAm 90
Rabinovici, Benjamin M. 1922- St&PR 91
Rabinovitch, Benton Seymour 1919- WhoAm 90
Rabinovitch, Donald F. 1946- St&PR 91
Rabinovitch, Gerald I 1947- BiDrAPA 89
Rabinovitch, Ralph David 1917- BiDrAPA 89
Rabinovitch, William Avrum 1936- WhoAmA 91
Rabinovitz, Jason 1921- WhoAm 90
Rabinovitz, Joel 1939- WhoAm 90
Rabinow, Jacob 1910- WhoAm 90
Rabinowicz, Ernest 1926- WhoAm 90
Rabinowitch, David 1943- WhoAmA 91
Rabinowitch, Royden Leslie 1943- WhoAmA 91
Rabinowitch, Victor 1934- WhoAm 90
Rabinowitz, Alan James 1949- WhoEmL 91
Rabinowitz, Allan Charles 1933- St&PR 91
Rabinowitz, Arthur Hugh BiDrAPA 89
Rabinowitz, Beryl St&PR 91
Rabinowitz, Chanina Aaron 1954- WhoE 91
Rabinowitz, Edward BiDrAPA 89
Rabinowitz, Harry 1916- IntWWM 90
Rabinowitz, Hyman Reuven 1893- BioIn 16
Rabinowitz, Isaac 1909-1988 BioIn 16
Rabinowitz, Israel St&PR 91
Rabinowitz, Jack Grant 1927- WhoAm 90
Rabinowitz, Jay Andrew 1927- WhoAm 90
Rabinowitz, Jesse Charles 1925- WhoAm 90
Rabinowitz, Marvin 1939- St&PR 91, WhoAm 90
Rabinowitz, Michael Abraham 1940- WhoE 91
Rabinowitz, Peter Alan 1944- WhoAm 90
Rabinowitz, Rebecca Susan 1953- WhoAmW 91, WhoEmL 91, WhoWor 91
Rabinowitz, Rubin 1919- St&PR 91
Rabinowitz, Samuel Nathan 1932- WhoAm 90
Rabinowitz, Sandy 1954- BioIn 16
Rabinowitz, Sarah Tarko 1948- WhoE 91
Rabinowitz, Seymour 1932- BiDrAPA 89
Rabinowitz, Sholem Yakov 1859-1916 BioIn 16
Rabinowitz, Stanley 1917- BioIn 16
Rabinowitz, Stanley Samuel 1917- WhoAm 90
Rabinowitz, Terry BiDrAPA 89
Rabinowitz, Victor 1911- WhoE 91
Rabinowitz, Wilbur M. 1918- WhoE 91
Rabinowitz, Wilbur Melvin 1918- St&PR 91
Rabinowitz, William 1925- WhoAm 90
Rabins, Michael Jerome 1932- WhoSSW 91
Rabins, Peter Vincent 1947- BiDrAPA 89
Rabison, Samuel 1947- BiDrAPA 89
Rabitz, Herschel Albert 1944- WhoAm 90
Rabjohn, Norman 1915- WhoAm 90
Rabkin, Leo 1919- WhoAm 90, WhoAmA 91
Rabkin, Mitchell Thornton 1930- WhoAm 90
Rabkin, Richard 1932- BiDrAPA 89
Rablen, Elizabeth C 1924- BiDrAPA 89
Rablen, Madeline Jean 1914- WhoAmW 91
Rabo, Jule Anthony WhoAm 90
Raboff, Ernest Lloyd AuBYP 90
Raboin, Mary Ann 1954- WhoSSW 91
Rabold, Robert Eh 1939- St&PR 91
Rabon, Timothy Alan 1954- St&PR 91, WhoSSW 91
Rabon, William James, Jr. 1931- WhoSSW 91
Raborg, Frederick Ashton, Jr. 1934- WhoWrEP 89
Raborn, Thomas Philip 1938- St&PR 91
Raborn, William F., Jr. 1905-1990 NewYTBS 90
Raborn, William Francis 1905-1990 BioIn 16
Raborn, William Francis, Jr. 1905- WhoAm 90
Raborn, William Francis, Jr. 1905-1990 CurBio 90N
Rabosky, Joseph George 1944- WhoE 91
Raboy, David Geoffrey 1952- WhoE 91
Raboy, Mac 1916-1967 EncACom
Raboy, S. Caesar 1936- St&PR 91, WhoAm 90, WhoE 91
Rabson, Alan Saul 1926- WhoAm 90
Rabstejnek, George J. 1932- St&PR 91
Rabstejnek, George John 1932- WhoE 91
Rabuck, Steven Kent 1953- WhoEmL 91
Rabuka, Sitiveni 1948- BioIn 16
Rabuka, Sitiveni Ligamamada 1948- WhoWor 91
Rabun, John Brewton, Jr. 1946- WhoAm 90, WhoE 91, WhoEmL 91, WhoWor 91
Raburn, Josephine 1929- WhoAmW 91
Raby, Albert A. BioIn 16
Raby, Elaine Miller 1938- WhoWrEP 89
Raby, Nancy E. WhoAmW 91
Raby, William Louis 1927- WhoAm 90
Racamond, Julien 1885-1966 BiDFrPL
Racanelli, Vincent J BiDrAPA 89
Racanelli, Vito Peter 1950- St&PR 91
Racaniello, Vincent Raimondi 1953- WhoE 91
Raccah, Dominique Marcelle 1956- WhoWrEP 89
Raccah, Paul Mordechay 1933- WhoAm 90
Racchini, Robert L. 1945- St&PR 91
Race, Anne Rinker 1925- BiDrAPA 89
Race, David H. 1929- St&PR 91
Race, Ernest 1913-1963 PenDiDA 89
Race, G. William 1950- BiDrAPA 89
Race, George Justice 1926- WhoAm 90
Race, James Quinn 1949- WhoSSW 91
Race, Lila Eunice Bunch 1902- WhoWrEP 89
Race, Peter Kempton 1931- St&PR 91
Race, Robert Russell 1907-1984 DcNaB 1981
Race, Steve 1921- IntWWM 90
Racek, Thomas 1927- St&PR 91
Racenstein, Jody Meg 1963- WhoAmW 91
Racer, James Harold 1939- St&PR 91
Rachals, Richard 1910- St&PR 91

RachBeisel, Jill *BiDrAPA 89*
Rachel, Louise 1951- *WhoWrEP 89*
Rachell, Yank *BioIn 16*
Rachelle, Joseph Leo 1942- *WhoSSW 91*
Rachelle, Tamar 1959- *WhoAm 90*
Rachels, Jean *WhoSSW 91*
Rachelson, Joyce Ann 1946- *WhoEmL 91*
Rachette, Jean *PenDiDA 89*
Rachfalski, Thomas Andrew 1956- *WhoE 91*
Rachie, Cyrus 1908- *WhoAm 90*
Rachilde 1860-1953 *EncCoWW*
Rachins, Alan *BioIn 16*
Rachinski, Howard Dale 1951- *WhoEmL 91, WhoWor 91*
Rachkov, Albert Ivanovich 1927- *WhoWor 91*
Rachleff, Jack 1913- *St&PR 91*
Rachleff, Owen Spencer 1934- *WhoAm 90*
Rachlin, Carol K 1919- *SmATA 64*
Rachlin, Harvey 1951- *BioIn 16, WhoWrEP 89*
Rachlin, Harvey Brant 1951- *WhoAm 90*
Rachlin, Jack 1923- *St&PR 91*
Rachlin, Lauren David 1929- *WhoE 91*
Rachlin, Nahid *SmATA 64*
Rachlin, Nahid 1944- *WhoWrEP 89*
Rachlin, Stephen L 1939- *BiDrAPA 89*
Rachlin, Stephen Leonard 1939- *WhoE 91*
Rachlis, Eugene 1920-1986 *BioIn 16*
Rachmaninoff, Sergei 1873-1943 *BioIn 16, WorAlBi*
Rachmaninoff, Sergey *PenDiMP*
Rachmaninov, Sergey *PenDiMP*
Rachmiel, George J. 1940- *St&PR 91*
Rachmiel, Marshall Emmanuel 1945- *WhoE 91*
Rachmilewitz, Eliezer Aviva 1935- *WhoWor 91*
Rachow, Louis August 1927- *WhoAm 90, WhoE 91*
Rachwalski, Frank Joseph, Jr. 1945- *St&PR 91*
Racic, Robert Walter 1949- *St&PR 91*
Racicot, Cathy Lee 1950- *WhoAmW 91*
Racicot, Marc F. 1948- *WhoAm 90*
Racila, John Joseph, Jr. 1930- *WhoWor 91*
Racina, Thom 1946- *WhoAm 90*
Racine, Antoine 1822-1893 *DcCanB 12*
Racine, Francois-Nicolas-Henri 1737-1794 *BioIn 16*
Racine, Jean 1639?-1699 *WorAlBi*
Racine, Jean Dorine 1944- *WhoAmW 91*
Racine, Pierre 1909- *BiDFrPL*
Racioppo, Stephen Gerard 1952- *WhoE 91*
Raciti, Cherie 1942- *WhoAm 90, WhoAmA 91*
Rack, Leonard 1928- *BiDrAPA 89, WhoE 91*
Rackerby, Thomas K. 1947- *St&PR 91*
Rackers, Cleta Louise 1950- *WhoAmW 91*
Rackers, Thomas William 1955- *WhoEmL 91, WhoSSW 91*
Rackl, Donald George 1955- *St&PR 91*
Rackleff, Owen Spencer 1934- *WhoAm 90*
Rackler, Jean Hope 1939- *WhoWrEP 89*
Rackley, Audie Neal 1934- *WhoAm 90, WhoWrEP 89*
Rackley, Frank Bailey, Jr. 1944- *St&PR 91*
Rackmil, Milton R. 1903- *WorAlBi*
Rackoff, Raymond 1922- *St&PR 91*
Rackow, David Lee *BiDrAPA 89*
Rackow, Leon L *BiDrAPA 89*
Rackow, Sylvia 1931- *WhoWrEP 89*
Rackus, George 1927- *WhoAmA 91*
Raclin, Ernestine Morris 1927- *WhoAm 90*
Racoma, Agapito Baclaan 1948- *BiDrAPA 89*
Racusin, Robert J 1946- *BiDrAPA 89*
Racusin, Robert Jerrold 1946- *WhoE 91*
Racy, Ali Jihad *NewAgMG*
Racy, John Cecil 1932- *BiDrAPA 89*
Racz, Andre 1916- *WhoAm 90, WhoAmA 91*
Racz, Victoria Elizabeth 1955- *WhoEmL 91*
Raczek, Stanley W 1945- *BiDrAPA 89*
Raczkiewicz, Mac A. 1942- *St&PR 91*
Rada, Alexander 1923- *WhoWor 91*
Rada, Richard T 1938- *BiDrAPA 89*
Radach, Calvin L. 1928- *St&PR 91*
Radack, Frank Charles 1940- *WhoSSW 91*
Radadia, Chraganbhai Gordhanbhai 1955- *WhoWor 91*
Radakovich, Peter 1948- *St&PR 91*
Radan, George Tivadar 1923- *WhoAmA 91, WhoE 91*
Radandt, Friedhelm K. 1932- *WhoAm 90*
Radant, Allen David *BiDrAPA 89*
Radatz, Dick 1937- *Ballpl 90*
Radavich, David Allen 1949- *WhoWrEP 89*
Radbourn, Charles 1853-1897 *BioIn 16*
Radbourn, Old Hoss 1854-1897 *Ballpl 90 [port]*
Radcliff, Rip 1906-1962 *Ballpl 90*
Radcliff, William Franklin 1922- *WhoAm 90*
Radcliff-Umstead, Douglas 1944- *WhoAm 90*
Radcliffe, Alex 1905- *Ballpl 90*
Radcliffe, Ann 1764-1823 *FemiCLE, WorAlBi*
Radcliffe, Ann Ward 1764-1823 *BioIn 16*
Radcliffe, Beverly Louise 1942- *WhoAmW 91*
Radcliffe, Clifford *BioIn 16*
Radcliffe, Courtney Lane 1962- *WhoEmL 91*
Radcliffe, Donnie *ConAu 132*
Radcliffe, Eleanor Schroeder 1914- *WhoWrEP 89*
Radcliffe, Frederick Roberts, Jr. 1939- *St&PR 91*
Radcliffe, George Grove 1924- *St&PR 91, WhoAm 90*
Radcliffe, Gerald Eugene 1923- *WhoWor 91*
Radcliffe, Janette *WhoWrEP 89*
Radcliffe, Lee Ewing 1935- *BiDrAPA 89*
Radcliffe, Mary Ann 1746?-1810? *BioIn 16, FemiCLE*
Radcliffe, Mary Anne *BioIn 16*
Radcliffe, Maud Elizabeth Furse *EncO&P 3*
Radcliffe, Phyllis E. 1926- *St&PR 91*
Radcliffe, Redonia *ConAu 132*
Radcliffe, Redonia Wheeler *WhoAm 90*
Radcliffe, Robert D. 1934- *St&PR 91*
Radcliffe, Russel Vernon 1942- *WhoE 91*
Radcliffe, S. Victor 1927- *WhoAm 90*
Radcliffe, Sarah 1960- *WhoWor 91*
Radcliffe, Ted 1902- *Ballpl 90*
Radclyffe Hall, Marguerite 1880-1943 *EncPaPR 91*
Raddatz, Robert H. 1926- *St&PR 91*
Radde, Heinz Wolfgang Kurt 1942- *WhoWor 91*
Radder, Joseph Henry 1920- *WhoE 91*
Raddi-Walsh, Antoinette Marie 1954- *WhoAmW 91*
Radding, Andrew 1944- *WhoE 91*
Radding, Edward 1941- *St&PR 91*
Radecki, Anthony Eugene 1939- *St&PR 91, WhoAm 90*
Radecki, Martin John 1948- *WhoAmA 91*
Radecki, Thomas Edward *BiDrAPA 89*
Radegunde 520-587 *EncCoWW*
Radejko, Mykola 1920- *WhoWor 91*
Radek, Gerald A. 1940- *St&PR 91*
Radek, Karl 1885-1939 *BioIn 16*
Radeka, Veljko 1930- *WhoAm 90*
Radel, Glenn Arthur 1927- *St&PR 91*
Radell, George Martin 1933- *St&PR 91*
Radell, Nicholas John 1930- *St&PR 91, WhoAm 90*
Rademacher, Franz 1906-1973 *BioIn 16*
Rademacher, Hollis W. 1935- *St&PR 91*
Rademacher, Hollis William 1935- *WhoAm 90*
Rademacher, Richard Glenn 1937- *St&PR 91*
Rademacher, Richard Joseph 1937- *WhoAm 90*
Rademaker, Chris Theodorus 1934- *St&PR 91*
Rademakers, Fons 1920- *ConTFT 8*
Rademan, Alan Nathan H *BiDrAPA 89*
Raden, Koestedjo 1916- *WhoWor 91*
Raden, Louis 1929- *WhoWor 91*
Rader, Charles George 1946- *WhoAm 90*
Rader, Chovine Richardson, Jr. 1942- *St&PR 91*
Rader, Darwin Joe 1951- *St&PR 91*
Rader, Dave 1948- *Ballpl 90*
Rader, Dotson Carlyle 1942- *WhoAm 90*
Rader, Doug *BioIn 16*
Rader, Doug 1944- *Ballpl 90*
Rader, Douglas Lee 1944- *WhoAm 90*
Rader, Edward Earl 1945- *WhoSSW 91*
Rader, Elizabeth 1951- *WhoAmW 91*
Rader, George S *BiDrAPA 89*
Rader, Hannelore 1937- *WhoAmW 91*
Rader, John J. 1950- *St&PR 91*
Rader, K.C. 1948- *St&PR 91*
Rader, Lloyd Edwin *BiDrAPA 89*
Rader, Louis T. 1911- *WhoAm 90*
Rader, Margaret O. 1914- *St&PR 91*
Rader, Melodee Ann 1961- *WhoAmW 91*
Rader, Ralph Wilson 1930- *WhoAm 90*
Rader, Randall Ray 1949- *WhoAm 90*
Rader, Rhoda Caswell 1945- *WhoE 91*
Rader, Stephen David 1934- *BiDrAPA 89*
Radermacher, Frank James 1953- *St&PR 91*
Radermacher, Reinhard Ludwig Wilhelm 1928- *WhoWor 91*
Rades, William L 1943- *WhoAmA 91*
Radest, Howard Bernard 1928- *WhoAm 90*
Radetzky, Joseph Wenzel 1766-1858 *WorAlBi*
Radewagen, Fred 1944- *WhoAm 90*
Radey, Richard Greger 1933- *St&PR 91, WhoAm 90*
Radfar, Fereydoon *BiDrAPA 89*
Radfar, Soraya Z. Z. *BiDrAPA 89*
Radford, Arthur W. 1896-1973 *WorAlBi*
Radford, Bill Lee 1930- *WhoSSW 91*
Radford, G. Lahrye 1943- *St&PR 91*
Radford, Linda Robertson 1944- *WhoAmW 91*
Radford, Mary Frances 1952- *WhoEmL 91*
Radford, Peter Weston 1949- *St&PR 91*
Radford, Richard Francis, Jr. 1939- *WhoWrEP 89*
Radford, Thomas *PenDiDA 89*
Radford, Winifred Eva 1901- *IntWWM 90*
Radford-Hill, Sheila Audrey 1949- *WhoEmL 91*
Radha Krshna Temple *NewAgMG*
Radha, Sivananda *EncO&P 3*
Radhakrishnan, S. 1888-1975 *BioIn 16*
Radhakrishnan, Sarvepalli 1888-1975 *BioIn 16*
Radiance *NewAgMG*
Radican, Robert Edward 1936- *WhoE 91*
Radican, Theresa Fusco 1937- *WhoE 91*
Radice, Anne-Imelda 1948- *WhoAm 90, WhoAmW 91*
Radice, Anne-Imelda Marino 1948- *WhoAmA 91*
Radice, Frank J. 1949- *WhoWor 91*
Radice, Lawrence J *BiDrAPA 89*
Radice, Michael Daniel 1946- *St&PR 91*
Radice, Robert 1946- *WhoSSW 91*
Radice, Shirley Rosalind 1935- *WhoAmW 91*
Radice, Steven A. 1948- *St&PR 91*
Radies, Norman W. 1952- *St&PR 91*
Radigan, Frank Xavier 1933- *WhoE 91*
Radigan, Joseph Richard 1939- *St&PR 91, WhoAm 90, WhoE 91*
Radigue, Elaine *NewAgMG*
Radigue, Eliane 1932- *IntWWM 90*
Radiguet, Raymond 1903-1923 *BioIn 16*
Radin, Alex 1921- *WhoAm 90*
Radin, Dan 1929- *WhoAmA 91*
Radin, Dean I 1952- *EncPaPR 91*
Radin, Joel Joseph 1940- *WhoE 91*
Radin, Laura Levine 1944- *WhoAmW 91*
Radin, Norman Samuel 1920- *WhoAm 90*
Radin, Robert Paul 1942- *BiDrAPA 89*
Radin, Robert Vernon *BiDrAPA 89*
Radin, Roy 1950-1983 *BioIn 16*
Radin, Ruth Yaffe *AuBYP 90*
Radin, Ruth Yaffe 1938- *BioIn 16*
Radin, Sherwin S 1923- *BiDrAPA 89*
Radin, Sherwin Seth 1923- *WhoE 91*
Radis, Michael William 1946- *WhoE 91*
Radisavljevic, Branko Slobodan 1948- *BiDrAPA 89*
Radischev, Aleksandr 1749-1802 *WorAlBi*
Radisson, Pierre Esprit 1636-1710 *EncCRAm, WhNaAH, WorAlBi*
Radji, Parviz C 1936- *ConAu 131*
Radke, Marilyn S 1951- *BiDrAPA 89*
Radke, Vincent James 1948- *WhoSSW 91*
Radlauer, Edward 1921- *AuBYP 90, ConAu 30NR*
Radlauer, Ruth Shaw 1926- *ConAu 30NR*
Radle, Elizabeth *BiDrAPA 89*
Radle, William D. 1932- *St&PR 91*
Radler, Franklin David 1942- *WhoAm 90*
Radler, Louis 1931- *St&PR 91*
Radler, Warren S. 1936- *WhoAm 90*
Radley, Jean-Pierre Alexandre 1932- *WhoAm 90, WhoE 91*
Radley, Sheila *ConAu 131*
Radley, Sheila 1928- *TwCCr&M 91*
Radley, Virginia Louise 1927- *WhoAm 90*
Radloff, Wayne *BioIn 16*
Radmacher, Camille J. 1917-1989 *BioIn 16*
Radman, Deborah M. *ODwPR 91*
Radmer, Michael John 1945- *St&PR 91, WhoAm 90, WhoEmL 91, WhoWor 91*
Radmin, Nancye *BioIn 16*
Radmore, Barbara Joy 1925- *BiDrAPA 89*
Radnay, Paul Andrew 1913- *WhoAm 90*
Radner, Ephraim 1921- *WhoAm 90*
Radner, Gilda 1946-1989 *AnObit 1989, BioIn 16, ConAu 129, ConTFT 8*
Radner, Roy 1927- *WhoAm 90, WhoE 91*
Radner, Sidney Hollis 1919- *WhoE 91, WhoWor 91*
Radnofsky, Kenneth Alan 1953- *IntWWM 90*
Radnoti, Miklos 1909-1944 *BioIn 16*
Rado, Emil Richard 1931- *WhoWor 91*
Rado, Eva 1928- *BiDrAPA 89*
Rado, Francis A. 1950- *St&PR 91*
Rado, Ladislav Leland 1909- *WhoAm 90*
Rado, Peter Thomas 1928- *St&PR 91*
Rado, Richard 1906-1989 *AnObit 1989*
Rado, Tony 1950- *St&PR 91*
Radock, Michael 1917- *WhoAm 90*
Radocy, Rudolf Ernest 1938- *IntWWM 90*
Radoczy, Albert 1914- *WhoAmA 91*
Radoff, Leonard Irving 1927- *WhoAm 90*
Radojcsics, Anne Parsons 1929- *WhoAmW 91*
Radojevic, Danilo *WhoAm 90*
Radomisli, Aylin 1938- *BiDrAPA 89*
Radomski, Jack London 1920- *WhoAm 90*
Radomski, Robyn *ODwPR 91*
Radomski, Robyn L. 1954- *St&PR 91*
Radomski, Robyn Lynn 1954- *WhoAm 90, WhoEmL 91*
Radomski, Theodore John 1933- *BiDrAPA 89*
Radomsky, Michael 1952- *St&PR 91*
Radon, Jenik Richard 1946- *WhoE 91, WhoEmL 91, WhoWor 91*
Rados, Alexander Stephen 1928- *St&PR 91*
Radosavljevic, Sasa 1962- *WhoWor 91*
Radosh, Ronald 1937- *WhoE 91*
Radoslovich, Matteo 1882-1972 *MusmAFA*
Radosta, John S. *BioIn 16*
Radovan, Mary B. 1922- *St&PR 91*
Radovanovic, Zoran 1940- *WhoWor 91*
Radovic, Carol Ann 1940- *WhoAmW 91*
Radovich, Donald 1932- *WhoAmA 91*
Radovich, John Michael 1948- *WhoEmL 91*
Radt, Richard Louis 1932- *St&PR 91, WhoAm 90*
Radtke, Bruce Michael 1951- *WhoWrEP 89*
Radtke, Eldon *St&PR 91*
Radtke, H. Helmut *BioIn 16*
Radtke, H. Helmut 1946- *St&PR 91, WhoAm 90*
Radtke, Heidrun 1946- *WhoWor 91*
Radtke, James Paul 1951- *St&PR 91*
Radtke, Muriel Marie 1938- *WhoE 91*
Radtke, Richard C. 1938- *ODwPR 91*
Radu, Maria *EncCoWW*
Raduchel, William James 1946- *WhoEmL 91*
Radvany, Craig Joseph 1949- *WhoEmL 91*
Radvic, Stephan 1940- *WhoWor 91*
Radwan, Lawrence A. 1943- *St&PR 91*
Radwanski, George 1947- *WhoAm 90*
Radwanski, Thomas Michael 1949- *WhoSSW 91*
Radway, Laurence Ingram 1919- *WhoAm 90*
Radwill, Arthur Scott 1948- *St&PR 91*
Radwin, Howard M. 1931- *WhoAm 90*
Rady, Elsa 1943- *WhoAmA 91*
Radycki, J Diane 1946- *WhoAmA 91*
Radzilowsky, Michael 1949- *WhoEmL 91*
Radzinowicz, Leon 1906- *WhoWor 91*
Radzinowicz, Mary Ann 1925- *WhoAm 90*
Radzins, Edmund 1919- *St&PR 91*
Radziunas, Eileen *BioIn 16*
Radziwill, Lee *BioIn 16*
Radzykewycz, Dan Theodore 1942- *WhoSSW 91*
Rae, Barbara Joyce 1930- *WhoAmW 91*
Rae, Bruce *BioIn 16*
Rae, Carla Jean 1959- *WhoSSW 91*
Rae, Caroline Anne 1961- *IntWWM 90*
Rae, Charles Bodman 1955- *IntWWM 90*
Rae, Charlotte 1926- *WhoAm 90*
Rae, Douglas Whiting 1939- *WhoAm 90*
Rae, E. Ann 1944- *WhoAm 90*
Rae, Earl F. 1929- *St&PR 91*
Rae, Henrietta 1859-1928 *BiDWomA*
Rae, Hugh C 1935- *TwCCr&M 91*
Rae, John 1796-1872 *BioIn 16*
Rae, John 1813-1893 *DcCanB 12*
Rae, John Bell 1911-1989 *BioIn 16*
Rae, Matthew Sanderson, Jr. 1922- *WhoAm 90, WhoWor 91*
Rae, Michael 1948- *WhoE 91*
Rae, Michelle Lauren 1968- *WhoWrEP 89*
Rae, Nicol C 1960- *ConAu 131*
Rae, Robert Andrew 1944- *St&PR 91*
Rae, Robert Keith *NewYTBS 90 [port]*
Rae-Gerrard, Colleen Margaret 1938- *IntWWM 90*
Rae-Grant, Naomi Ingrid *BiDrAPA 89*
Rae-Grant, Quentin A F 1929- *BiDrAPA 89*
Raebeck, Barry Scott 1952- *WhoSSW 91*
Raeber, Joseph G. 1924- *WhoWor 91*
Raeburn, Andrew Harvey 1933- *WhoAm 90*
Raeburn, Boyd 1913-1966 *OxCPMus*
Raeburn, Henry 1756-1823 *IntDcAA 90*
Raeburn, John Hay 1941- *WhoAm 90*
Raeburn, Vicki Pearthree 1947- *WhoAmW 91*
Raedeke, Linda Dismore 1950- *WhoEmL 91*
Raeder, Erich 1876-1960 *WorAlBi*
Raeder, James Hamilton 1940- *St&PR 91*
Raeder, Myrna Sharon 1947- *WhoAmW 91*
Raedler, Dorothy Florence 1917- *WhoAm 90*
Raedt-De Canter, Eva 1900-1975 *EncCoWW*
Raeff, Marc 1923- *WhoWrEP 89*
Raekallio, Matti Juhani 1954- *IntWWM 90*
Rael, Anthya *PenDiMP*
Rael, Juan Jose 1948- *WhoHisp 91*
Raemer, Harold Roy 1924- *WhoAm 90*
Raeper, William 1959- *ConAu 131*
Raes, Godfried-Willem 1952- *IntWWM 90*
Raes, Jean *PenDiDA 89*
Raeschild, Sheila 1936- *WhoWrEP 89*

Raese, Joachim *BiDrAPA 89*
Raese, Michelle *BioIn 16*
Raether, Edward W. 1936- *St&PR 91*
Raeuchle, Ernest T. 1928- *St&PR 91*
Raezer, Sallie Stewart 1951- *WhoAmW 91, WhoWor 91*
Rafael, Don *WhoWrEP 89*
Rafael, Gideon 1913- *ConAu 129*
Rafael, Ruth Kelson 1929- *WhoAm 90*
Rafaeli, Ada 1949- *WhoWor 91*
Rafaels, Diane 1940- *WhoAmW 91*
Rafaelsen, Ole J *BiDrAPA 89*
Rafajko, Robert Richard 1931- *WhoAm 90*
Rafalski, Andrew S. 1946- *WhoE 91*
Rafalski, Jan Antoni 1947- *WhoE 91*
Rafalsky, Stephen Mark 1942- *WhoWrEP 89*
Rafanan, Manuel O 1940- *BiDrAPA 89*
Rafanelli, Kenneth Robert 1937- *WhoAm 90*
Rafe, Stephen C. 1937- *ConAu 132*
Rafeedie, Edward 1929- *WhoAm 90*
Rafelson, Bob *BioIn 16*
Rafelson, Bob 1933- *WhoAm 90*
Rafelson, Max Emanuel, Jr. 1921- *WhoAm 90*
Raff, Beverly Stein 1933- *WhoAmW 91*
Raff, Daniel Martin Gorodetsky 1951- *WhoE 91*
Raff, David 1945- *WhoE 91*
Raff, Gilbert 1928- *St&PR 91, WhoAm 90*
Raff, Joseph Allen 1933- *WhoAm 90, WhoWor 91*
Raff, Raymond J. 1918- *St&PR 91*
Raff, Robert *BioIn 16*
Raff, Sandra Beth 1947- *WhoAmW 91*
Raffa, Charles *BioIn 16*
Raffa, Joseph 1947- *WhoWrEP 89*
Raffa, Peter Eugene 1926- *St&PR 91*
Raffa, Sam *BioIn 16*
Raffael, Joseph 1933- *WhoAm 90, WhoAmA 91*
Raffael, Judith K *WhoAmA 91*
Raffaele, John Eugene 1948- *St&PR 91*
Raffaelli, Piero 1949- *IntWWM 90*
Raffai, Sarolta 1930- *EncCoWW*
Raffald, Elizabeth 1733-1781 *FemiCLE*
Raffalow, Janet Terry 1947- *WhoEmL 91*
Raffanti, Dano 1948- *IntWWM 90*
Raffay, Stephen Joseph 1927- *WhoAm 90*
Raffe, Minda Lynn 1954- *WhoEmL 91*
Raffe, W G 1888-1950? *EncO&P 3*
Raffel, Angela 1919- *WhoAmW 91*
Raffel, Burton 1928- *ConAu 30NR*
Raffel, Burton Nathan 1928- *WhoWrEP 89*
Raffel, Charles Michael 1950- *WhoE 91*
Raffel, David Nathan 1929- *WhoSSW 91*
Raffel, Jan 1935- *WhoWor 91*
Raffel, Jeffrey Allen 1945- *WhoE 91*
Raffel, Jerome 1925- *St&PR 91*
Raffel, Kenneth C. 1943- *St&PR 91*
Raffel, Leroy B. 1927- *WhoAm 90*
Raffel, Louis B. 1933- *ODwPR 91, WhoAm 90*
Raffensberger, Ken 1917- *Ballpl 90*
Raffensperger, Charlotte F *BiDrAPA 89*
Rafferty, Carolyn Banks 1941- *WhoWrEP 89*
Rafferty, Donald Brian *BiDrAPA 89*
Rafferty, Frank Thomas 1925- *BiDrAPA 89, St&PR 91*
Rafferty, Genevieve Kennedy 1922- *WhoAmW 91*
Rafferty, George A 1951- *BiDrAPA 89*
Rafferty, J. Patrick 1947- *IntWWM 90*
Rafferty, Janice Aloysia 1930- *WhoE 91*
Rafferty, Joanne M. *St&PR 91*
Rafferty, Joanne Miller 1948- *WhoAmA 91*
Rafferty, John T. 1932- *St&PR 91*
Rafferty, Kevin Patrick 1955- *WhoWrEP 89*
Rafferty, Larry E. 1942- *WhoWrEP 89*
Rafferty, Michael Griffin, Jr. 1935- *St&PR 91*
Rafferty, Nancy Schwarz 1930- *WhoAm 90*
Rafferty, Paul G., Jr. 1943- *ODwPR 91*
Rafferty, William Bernard 1912- *WhoAm 90*
Rafferty, William Steven 1952- *St&PR 91*
Raffetto, Michael *BioIn 16, NewYTBS 90*
Raffi *BioIn 16*
Raffi, Charles Louis, Jr. 1927- *St&PR 91*
Raffi, Rhonda Curtin 1953- *St&PR 91*
Raffin, Bennett Lyon 1918- *St&PR 91*
Raffin, Deborah *BioIn 16*
Raffin, Thomas A. 1947- *WhoAm 90*
Raffle, Stephen M 1940- *BiDrAPA 89*
Raffles, Ralph Leslie Stamford 1920- *WhoWor 91*
Raffles, Thomas Stamford 1781-1826 *BioIn 16*
Raffo, Luigi M. 1928- *WhoWor 91*
Raffo, Steve 1912- *WhoAmA 91, WhoE 91*
Rafi, Mohammed 1944- *WhoWor 91*
Rafkin, Alan 1928- *WhoAm 90*
Rafols, Alberto Pedro 1942- *IntWWM 90*
Rafols-Saavedra, Rafael *BiDrAPA 89*
Rafos, Stuart A. 1945- *St&PR 91*
Rafoth, Mary Ann 1957- *WhoAmW 91*
Rafoth, Steven Frank 1947- *St&PR 91*
Rafroidi, Patrick 1930-1989 *ConAu 132*
Rafsanjani, Ali Akbar *BioIn 16*
Rafsanjani, Hashemi *BioIn 16*
Rafshoon, Gerald Monroe 1934- *WhoAm 90*
Rafsky, Jessica C 1924- *WhoAmA 91*
Rafson, Harold 1927- *St&PR 91*
Rafson, Roger Harvey 1958- *WhoE 91*
Raft, Elizabeth V *BiDrAPA 89*
Raft, George 1895-1980 *WorAlBi*
Raftery, John Thomas *BiDrAPA 89*
Raftery, Joseph P. 1938- *St&PR 91*
Raftis, Alkis 1942- *WhoWor 91*
Raftis, George S. *St&PR 91*
Raftis, Spiros 1925- *St&PR 91*
Rafuls, William Anthony 1954- *BiDrAPA 89*
Ragains, Charles C. 1943- *ODwPR 91*
Ragals, William Charles, Jr. 1939- *St&PR 91, WhoAm 90*
Ragan, Charles L 1953- *BiDrAPA 89*
Ragan, David 1925- *WhoAm 90*
Ragan, Elaine Sanford 1955- *WhoSSW 91*
Ragan, Elizabeth Hoffman 1916- *WhoAmW 91*
Ragan, Harold James 1928- *WhoSSW 91*
Ragan, Hugh A. 1942- *WhoSSW 91*
Ragan, James 1944- *WhoWrEP 89*
Ragan, James Thomas 1929- *WhoAm 90*
Ragan, Kenneth Don 1938- *BiDrAPA 89*
Ragan, Kenneth E. 1924- *WhoAm 90*
Ragan, Larry T. 1950- *St&PR 91*
Ragan, Mary Alice 1961- *WhoAmW 91*
Ragan, Pat 1888-1956 *Ballpl 90*
Ragan, Paul Wilhelm *BiDrAPA 89*
Ragan, Paul Wilhelm 1955- *WhoE 91*
Ragan, Roy Allen 1929- *WhoWrEP 89*
Ragan, Samuel Talmadge 1915 *WhoAm 90, WhoWor 91, WhoWrEP 89*
Ragan, Seaborn Bryant Timmons 1929- *WhoWor 91*
Ragan, Susan McLaren 1952- *WhoAmW 91*
Ragana, Satrijos 1877-1930 *EncCoWW*
Ragans, E. Carlyle *WhoAm 90*
Ragatz, Thomas George 1934- *WhoAm 90*
Ragazzini, John R. 1912-1988 *BioIn 16*
Ragen, Brooks Geer 1933- *St&PR 91*
Ragen, Naomi 1949- *ConAu 130*
Ragent, Boris 1924- *WhoAm 90*
Rager, Charles E. 1928- *St&PR 91*
Rager, John Ewing, III 1956- *WhoE 91*
Ragetly, Paul Rene 1944- *WhoWor 91*
Ragghianti, Carlo Ludovico 1910-1987 *BioIn 16*
Ragghianti, Marie 1943?- *BioAmW*
Raggi, Reena 1951- *WhoAmW 91*
Raggio, Louise Ballerstedt 1919- *WhoAm 90*
Raggio, Olga *WhoAmA 91*
Raggio, Olga 1926- *WhoAm 90, WhoAmW 91*
Raggio, William J. 1926- *St&PR 91*
Raghavan, K. 1923- *WhoWor 91*
Raghavan, Veena 1938- *WhoAmW 91*
Ragheb, Magdi 1946- *WhoWor 91*
Ragheb, Youssef 1941- *WhoWor 91*
Raghu, Surya 1956- *WhoE 91*
Raghunath, Nagavedu D 1954- *BiDrAPA 89*
Raghupathi, P. S. 1945- *WhoAm 90, WhoEmL 91*
Ragin, Derek Lee 1958- *IntWWM 90*
Ragins, Naomi *BiDrAPA 89*
Ragins, Naomi 1926- *WhoAmW 91, WhoE 91*
Raginsky, Nina *WhoAmA 91*
Ragir, Meyer J. *St&PR 91*
Ragir, Norma L. *St&PR 91*
Raglan, Fitzroy James H. Somerset, Baron 1788-1855 *BioIn 16*
Raglan, Fitzroy James Henry Somerset 1788-1855 *WorAlBi*
Ragland, Alwine Mulhearn 1913- *WhoAmW 91*
Ragland, Bob 1938- *WhoAmA 91*
Ragland, Douglas Lee 1947- *St&PR 91*
Ragland, Jack Whitney 1938- *WhoAm 90, WhoAmA 91*
Ragland, James B. 1917- *St&PR 91*
Ragland, James Black 1917- *WhoAm 90*
Ragland, John C. 1939- *St&PR 91*
Ragland, Larry 1948- *DrBlPA 90*
Ragland, Sherman Leon, II 1962- *WhoE 91*
Ragle, Joanne Feiger 1948- *WhoAmW 91*
Ragley, Michele Ann Garrick 1948- *WhoEmL 91*
Ragley, Phyllis 1950- *WhoEmL 91*
Ragnarsson, Hjalmar Helgi 1952- *IntWWM 90*
Ragnarsson, Ragnar John 1945- *WhoWor 91*
Rago, Ann D'Amico 1957- *WhoE 91*
Rago, Dorothy Ashton 1925- *WhoE 91*
Rago, John Thomas 1955- *WhoE 91*
Rago, Nicholas A. 1942- *WhoAm 90*
Rago, Peter 1936- *WhoE 91*
Ragogna, Andrew Robert 1948- *St&PR 91*
Ragolta, Eduardo *BiDrAPA 89*
Ragona, Andrew *BioIn 16*
Ragona-Sides, Laurene Cecilia 1955- *WhoAmW 91*
Ragone, David Vincent 1930- *WhoAm 90, WhoE 91, WhoWor 91*
Ragone, Lourdes Margarita 1939- *WhoHisp 91*
Ragone, Therese Victoria 1935- *WhoAmW 91*
Ragonetti, Louis William 1944- *BiDrAPA 89*
Ragovin, Cathie S *BiDrAPA 89*
Ragsdale, Bertha Mae 1925- *WhoAmW 91*
Ragsdale, Carl Vandyke 1925- *WhoAm 90*
Ragsdale, Hugh Appleton 1938- *WhoSSW 91*
Ragsdale, James Marcus 1938- *WhoE 91*
Ragsdale, Richard Elliot 1943- *St&PR 91*
Ragsdale, Richard Elliott 1943- *WhoAm 90, WhoSSW 91*
Ragsdale, Sharon Dorise 1953- *WhoAmW 91*
Ragsdill, Roy Russell, Jr. 1946- *BiDrAPA 89*
Ragucci, Ruth Helena 1933- *BiDrAPA 89*
Rague, William J. 1931- *St&PR 91*
Raguin, Virginia C 1941- *WhoAmA 91*
Raguin, Virginia Chieffo 1941- *WhoE 91*
Ragusa, Isa 1926- *WhoAmA 91*
Ragusa, Joseph F. 1954- *St&PR 91*
Ragusa, Olga Maria 1922- *WhoAm 90*
Raguseo, Lorraine 1955- *ODwPR 91*
Raguseo, Lorraine Anne 1955- *WhoAmW 91*
Raguso, Sam L., Jr. 1941- *St&PR 91*
Raguthu, Simhachalam *BiDrAPA 89*
Rahal, Bobby *BioIn 16*
Rahall, Nick Joe, II 1949- *WhoAm 90, WhoSSW 91*
Rahardjo, Raden Wido 1950- *WhoWor 91*
Rahbar, Zita Ina 1937- *WhoAmW 91, WhoWor 91*
Rahbek, Karen Margrethe 1775-1829 *EncCoWW*
Rahbek Printz, Louis Martin 1933- *WhoWor 91*
Rahdert, George Karl 1950- *WhoSSW 91*
Rahdert, Richard F 1935- *BiDrAPA 89*
Rahe, Lin Christine 1950- *WhoSSW 91*
Raheja, Hari Chand *BiDrAPA 89*
Rahel, Bluwstein 1890-1931 *EncCoWW*
Rahenkamp, Eric Edward 1961- *WhoSSW 91*
Rahenkamp, John Edward 1937- *WhoAm 90*
Rahill, Margaret Fish 1919- *WhoAmA 91*
Rahilly, Paul 1934?- *BioIn 16*
Rahim, Abdur *BiDrAPA 89*
Rahimian, Hooshang 1938- *BiDrAPA 89*
Rahimtoola, Shahbudin Hooseinally 1931- *WhoAm 90*
Rahja, Jean Marie 1929- *WhoAmW 91*
Rahja, Virginia Helga 1921- *WhoAmA 91*
Rahjes, Doyle Dean 1930- *St&PR 91*
Rahko, Timo Kalevi 1939- *WhoWor 91*
Rahl, Cecilia May N. 1931- *WhoWrEP 89*
Rahl, James Andrew 1917- *WhoAm 90*
Rahm, Alan Stanley 1942- *BiDrAPA 89*
Rahm, Calvin R. 1923- *St&PR 91*
Rahm, Dave *BioIn 16*
Rahm, David Alan 1941- *WhoE 91, WhoWor 91*
Rahm, Susan Berkman 1943- *WhoAmW 91, WhoE 91*
Rahman, Abdul *NewYTBS 90 [port]*
Rahman, Abu Tayeb Rafiqur 1936- *WhoE 91*
Rahman, Aneesur 1927-1987 *BioIn 16*
Rahman, Fazlur 1919-1988 *BioIn 16*
Rahman, Hafiz M Abdur *BiDrAPA 89*
Rahman, Kaleel 1944- *WhoWor 91*
Rahman, Mayeed-Ur *BiDrAPA 89*
Rahman, Mir Shakil-Ur 1956- *WhoWor 91*
Rahman, Mujibar Mir 1941- *WhoSSW 91*
Rahman, Shahzad 1953- *BiDrAPA 89, WhoE 91*
Rahman, Syed Fakhrur 1943- *WhoSSW 91*
Rahman, Syedur A. H. 1936- *WhoWor 91*
Rahman, Yueh-Erh 1928- *WhoAm 90*
Rahmani, Kamran 1955- *BiDrAPA 89*
Rahmann, John Charles 1927- *St&PR 91*
Rahmat-Samii, Yahya 1948- *WhoAm 90*
Rahmig, William Conrad 1936- *WhoAm 90*
Rahming, Norris 1886-1959 *WhoAmA 91N*
Rahn, Alvin Albert 1925- *WhoAm 90*
Rahn, Ernst W. 1934- *St&PR 91*
Rahn, Herbert George 1943- *St&PR 91*
Rahn, Hermann 1912- *WhoAm 90*
Rahn, Joan Elma 1929- *BioIn 16*
Rahn, John 1944- *IntWWM 90*
Rahn, Muriel 1911-1961 *BioIn 16, DrBlPA 90*
Rahn, Richard William 1942- *WhoAm 90, WhoE 91*
Rahon-Paalen, Alice 1916-1987 *ArtLatA*
Rahr, Guido R., Jr. 1928- *St&PR 91*
Rahtz, Don Robert 1951- *WhoSSW 91*
Rahtz, Roger A 1947- *BiDrAPA 89*
Rai, Satvinder Singh 1943- *WhoWor 91*
Raia, Carl Bernard 1931- *WhoSSW 91*
Raia, Sam B., Jr. 1935- *St&PR 91*
Raichman, Jorge Arnaldo 1953- *BiDrAPA 89*
Raider, Ann Michaels 1947- *WhoE 91*
Raider, Donald Gene 1932- *St&PR 91*
Raider, Louis 1913- *WhoSSW 91*
Raif, Joshua 1946- *St&PR 91*
Raiff, Frederic Kaufman 1927- *St&PR 91*
Raiff, Robert M. *St&PR 91*
Raigoza, Jaime 1937- *WhoHisp 91*
Raikes, Charles Fitzgerald 1930- *St&PR 91, WhoAm 90*
Raikes, Robert 1735-1811 *BioIn 16, WorAlBi*
Raikin, Bruno 1912- *IntWWM 90*
Raikos, George K. 1934- *St&PR 91*
Raikow, Radmila Boruvka 1939- *WhoAmW 91*
Rail, James William 1935- *WhoAm 90*
Raila, Doug 1952- *St&PR 91*
Railey, Peggy *BioIn 16*
Railey, Walker *BioIn 16*
Railo, Erkki *BioIn 16*
Railsback, David Phillips 1950- *WhoE 91*
Railton, Ruth 1915- *IntWWM 90*
Railton, William Scott 1935- *WhoAm 90, WhoE 91, WhoWor 91*
Railton-Jones, Roger *ODwPR 91*
Raim, Ellen 1958- *WhoAmW 91*
Raiman, Gail Ann 1951- *WhoAmW 91*
Raimi, Burton Louis 1938- *WhoAm 90*
Raimi, Ralph Alexis 1924- *WhoAm 90*
Raimist, Andrew L. 1963- *WhoEmL 91*
Raimon, Louis Alexandre 1922- *BioIn 16*
Raimond, Rose 1929- *WhoAmW 91*
Raimondi, Albert Anthony 1925- *WhoAm 90*
Raimondi, Gianni 1923- *IntWWM 90*
Raimondi, John 1948- *BioIn 16, WhoAmA 91*
Raimondi, Matthew *PenDiMP*
Raimondi, Peter John, III 1955- *WhoE 91*
Raimondi, Ray R. 1927- *St&PR 91*
Raimondi, Ruggero 1941- *IntWWM 90, PenDiMP, WhoAm 90, WhoWor 91*
Raimondo, Beverly Nickell 1946- *WhoAmW 91*
Rain, Douglas 1928- *OxCCanT*
Rain, Maurice O. 1913- *St&PR 91*
Rain, Robert Eley, Jr. 1918- *WhoAm 90*
Rain, Talbot 1920- *St&PR 91*
Rain-in-the-Face 1835?-1905 *WhNaAH*
Rainard, Robert Lyn 1950- *WhoSSW 91*
Rainbolt, H.E. 1929- *St&PR 91*
Rainbow *EncPR&S 89*
Rainbow, Thomas 1948- *WhoWrEP 89*
Rainbow-Earhart, Kathryn A 1921- *BiDrAPA 89*
Raine, A. Kendall, Jr. 1933- *WhoAm 90*
Raine, Allen 1836-1908 *FemiCLE*
Raine, John, II 1954- *WhoEmL 91*
Raine, Kathleen 1908- *BioIn 16, FemiCLE, MajTwCW*
Raine, Ronald Vance 1937- *St&PR 91*
Rainer of Huy *PenDiDA 89*
Rainer, Alice 1932- *IntWWM 90*
Rainer, Arnulf 1929- *WhoWor 91*
Rainer, Clarice 1932- *IntWWM 90*
Rainer, John, Jr. *NewAgMG*
Rainer, John D *BiDrAPA 89*
Rainer, John David 1921- *WhoE 91*
Rainer, Luise 1909- *BioIn 16, WorAlBi*
Rainer, Rex Kelly 1924- *WhoAm 90*
Rainer, William Gerald 1927- *WhoAm 90*
Raines, Betty Lynn 1957- *WhoAmW 91*
Raines, Bobby Ray 1927- *St&PR 91*
Raines, Boyd W. 1950- *St&PR 91*
Raines, Edwin G. 1945- *St&PR 91*
Raines, Ella 1921-1988 *BioIn 16*
Raines, Elvoy *ODwPR 91*
Raines, Franklin Delano 1949- *WhoAm 90, WhoE 91*
Raines, Howell Hiram 1943- *WhoAm 90*
Raines, Irene Freeze 1924- *WhoSSW 91, WhoWor 91*
Raines, Jack A *BiDrAPA 89*
Raines, James Henry 1950- *WhoSSW 91*
Raines, Jean Lee 1949- *IntWWM 90*
Raines, Jeff 1943- *WhoAm 90, WhoSSW 91, WhoWor 91*
Raines, Jo-Ann Ryan 1948- *WhoAmW 91*
Raines, John D. 1947- *St&PR 91*
Raines, Jonathan Mark 1953- *BiDrAPA 89*
Raines, Kathleen Jane 1946- *WhoWrEP 89*
Raines, Keith R. 1951- *WhoEmL 91*
Raines, Nicholas Groves- *BioIn 16*
Raines, O.L., Jr. 1941- *St&PR 91*
Raines, Phillip Arnold 1955- *WhoSSW 91*
Raines, Raymond Lee 1938- *St&PR 91*

Raines, Rosser R. 1938- St&PR 91
Raines, Tim BioIn 16
Raines, Tim 1959- Ballpl 90, WorAlBi
Raines, Tim D. 1950- WhoSSW 91
Rainess, Alan Edward BiDrAPA 89
Rainess, Errol Jonathan 1947- St&PR 91
Rainey, Charles James 1956- WhoEmL 91
Rainey, Charles Rossman, Jr. 1951- WhoSSW 91
Rainey, Christine Rose 1952- WhoAmW 91
Rainey, Chuck 1954- Ballpl 90
Rainey, Clark O. 1963- St&PR 91
Rainey, Claude Gladwin 1923- WhoAm 90
Rainey, Gertrude 1886-1939 BioAmW
Rainey, Gordon Fryer, Jr. 1940- WhoSSW 91
Rainey, James A. 1929- WhoSSW 91
Rainey, James Lee, Jr. 1929- WhoAm 90
Rainey, Jean Osgood 1925- ODwPR 91, WhoAm 90, WhoAmW 91, WhoE 91
Rainey, Jerry BioIn 16
Rainey, John Marion, Jr. 1942- BiDrAPA 89
Rainey, Joseph H. 1832-1887 WorAlBi
Rainey, Joseph Hayne 1832-1887 BlkAmsC [port]
Rainey, Kenneth Tyler 1936- WhoSSW 91
Rainey, Laurie Hughes 1957- WhoSSW 91
Rainey, Ma 1886-1939 BioIn 16, DrBlPA 90, OxCPMus, WorAlBi
Rainey, Mary Teresa 1955- WhoAmW 91
Rainey, Millicent Ann 1944- WhoAmW 91
Rainey, Priscilla Blosser- BioIn 16
Rainey, Robert Edward 1943- WhoSSW 91
Rainey, W. B. AuBYP 90
Rainey, Wayne BioIn 16
Rainey, William Joel 1946- St&PR 91, WhoAm 90
Rainey, William T. 1958- St&PR 91
Rainford, David John 1946- WhoWor 91
Rainford, Henry James 1930- WhoWor 91
Rainger, Charles William 1933- St&PR 91
Rainger, Ralph 1901-1942 BioIn 16, OxCPMus
Rainie, Harrison McKinley, Jr. 1919- WhoAm 90
Rainier III 1923- WhoWor 91
Rainier III, Prince of Monaco 1923- BioIn 16
Rainier, Robert Paul 1940- WhoAm 90, WhoE 91
Rainis, Eugene Charles 1940- St&PR 91, WhoAm 90
Rainoff, Stephan T. 1931- WhoSSW 91
Rainone, Donald J. 1943- St&PR 91
Rainone, Michael Carmine 1918- WhoE 91
Rainone, Robert E. 1934- St&PR 91
Rains, Alan T., Jr. BioIn 16
Rains, Catherine Burke 1959- WhoAmW 91
Rains, Charles Randel 1957- WhoEmL 91
Rains, Claude 1889-1967 WorAlBi
Rains, Gregory Grant 1958- WhoSSW 91
Rains, Harry H. 1909- St&PR 91
Rains, Harry Hano 1909- WhoAm 90
Rains, Jack Morris 1937- WhoAm 90, WhoSSW 91
Rains, James Ira 1956- WhoEmL 91
Rains, Linda Susan 1948- WhoSSW 91
Rains, Mary Jo 1935- WhoAmW 91, WhoSSW 91
Rains, Merritt Neal 1943- WhoAm 90
Rainsford, Augusta Bernadette 1950- WhoE 91
Rainsford, B. C. WhoAm 90
Rainsford, B.C. 1951- St&PR 91
Rainsford, George Nichols 1928- WhoAm 90
Rainson, Ronald L. 1940- St&PR 91
Rainsong, Tovah 1950- WhoAmW 91
Rainville, Dewey 1923- St&PR 91
Rainville, Douglas L. 1952- St&PR 91
Rainville, Paul WhoAmA 91N
Rainville, William Anthony 1942- St&PR 91
Rainwater, Crawford St&PR 91
Rainwater, James 1917-1986 WorAlBi
Rainwater, Richard E. BioIn 16
Rainwater, Wanda Kaye 1947- WhoSSW 91
Rais Yatim 1942- WhoWor 91
Rais, Mahmoud 1941- WhoWor 91
Raisa, Rosa 1893-1963 PenDiMP
Raisanen, Heikki Martti 1941- WhoWor 91
Raisanen, Jouko 1949- WhoWor 91
Raisani, Kamal Khan BiDrAPA 89
Raisbeck, Gordon 1925- St&PR 91, WhoAm 90
Raisbeck, James David 1936- WhoWor 91
Raiselis, Richard 1951- WhoAmA 91
Raiselis, Susan Warren BiDrAPA 89
Raiser, C. Victor, II 1940- St&PR 91
Raisig, Paul Jones, Jr. 1932- WhoAm 90
Raisler, Herbert A. 1916- St&PR 91
Raisler, Robert K. 1904- St&PR 91
Raisman, Victor Hugo 1905-1989 BioIn 16
Raisner, Joseph Craig 1952- WhoE 91
Raiss, John Carl 1950- BiDrAPA 89
Raith, Francis J. 1932- St&PR 91
Raithel, Michael L. 1947- St&PR 91
Raiti, Lisa Maria 1956- St&PR 91
Raiti, Robert Joseph 1950- St&PR 91
Raitiere, Martin N BiDrAPA 89
Raitio, Pentti 1930- IntWWM 90
Raitt, Albert E, Jr. BiDrAPA 89
Raitt, Bonnie BioIn 16
Raitt, Bonnie 1949- CurBio 90 [port], News 90 [port]
Raitt, Bonnie Lynn 1949- WhoAm 90, WhoAmW 91
Raitt, James Thomas 1953- WhoE 91
Raitt, John 1917- OxCPMus, WorAlBi
Raitt, Terri BioIn 16
Raitz, Glenn Norman 1931- St&PR 91
Raitzin, Misha 1930-1990 BioIn 16, NewYTBS 90
Raitzin, Shirley 1924- St&PR 91
Raives, Ann Leslie 1956- St&PR 91
Raizen, Senta Amon 1924- WhoAmW 91
Raizman, Marc 1926- ODwPR 91
Raj, Shashi BiDrAPA 89
Raj, Sneh 1932- BiDrAPA 89
Raja Rao BioIn 16
Raja, Dhirendra Muljibhai 1939- WhoWor 91
Raja, Muhammad R BiDrAPA 89
Raja, Vijay 1936- WhoE 91
Rajadhyaksha, Krishna Dilip BiDrAPA 89
Rajadhyaksha, Sadashiv Y 1950- BiDrAPA 89
Rajadurai, Nigel Pushparajah 1950- WhoWor 91
Rajagopal, Indira 1938- WhoWor 91
Rajagopal, Subramanyam 1955- BiDrAPA 89
Rajah, Hoossain Goolam Mohyedeen WhoWor 91
Rajakumar, Kanuru U BiDrAPA 89
Rajakumar, Thotakura BiDrAPA 89
Rajan, Jagannath Varada 1933- WhoWor 91
Rajan, Periasamy Karivaratha 1942- WhoSSW 91
Rajan, V K Suresh BiDrAPA 89
Rajan, V.K. Suresh 1951- WhoE 91
Rajaneesh, Acharya 1931-1990 BioIn 16
Rajani, Prem R. 1949- St&PR 91
Rajani, Raj P BiDrAPA 89
Rajappa, Muniyapla T BiDrAPA 89
Rajaram, Sanjaya 1943- WhoAm 90
Rajaratnam, Ranjit C BiDrAPA 89
Rajasekaran, Pakkam R BiDrAPA 89
Rajasekhar, Paul Theodore BiDrAPA 89
Rajchman, Jan Aleksander 1911-1989 BioIn 16
Rajdev, Ashoke 1950- WhoWor 91
Rajendran, Kalaiselvi BiDrAPA 89
Rajendran, Somasundaram 1938- BiDrAPA 89
Rajewsky, Manfred Fedor 1934- WhoWor 91
Rajguru, Sarojini V 1933- BiDrAPA 89
Rajiah, Sam Emerson BiDrAPA 89
Rajic, Negovan 1923- ConAu 130
Rajki, Walter Albert 1925- WhoAm 90
Rajkovic, Dragoljub Stevan 1965- WhoE 91
Rajkumar, Pitamber 1931- WhoWor 91
Rajkumar, Sadananda 1945- BiDrAPA 89
Rajmane, Chandrakant G BiDrAPA 89
Rajna, Thomas 1921- IntWWM 90
Rajneesh, Bhagwan Shree ConAu 30NR
Rajneesh, Bhagwan Shree 1931- EncO&P 3
Rajneesh, Acharya 1931-1990 ConAu 130, -30NR
Rajneesh, Baghwan Shree ConAu 130
Rajneesh, Bhagwan Shree 1931-1990 BioIn 16, News 90
Rajotte, Jean St&PR 91
Rajpara, Suresh P. BiDrAPA 89
Rajsich, Dave 1951- Ballpl 90
Rajter, Ludovit 1906- IntWWM 90
Raju, Datla S 1948- BiDrAPA 89
Raju, G.S.P. 1956- BiDrAPA 89
Raju, Mantena S BiDrAPA 89
Raju, Penumetsa B BiDrAPA 89
Raju, Sanyasi Sagi BiDrAPA 89
Rajvanshi, Anil Kumar 1950- WhoWor 91
Rak, Ian Paley BiDrAPA 89
Rak, William St&PR 91
Rakauskas, William BiDrAPA 89
Rakay, William R. 1955- WhoAm 90
Rakel, Robert Edwin 1932- WhoAm 90
Rakers, Harry B. 1946- St&PR 91
Rakes, Ganas Kaye 1938- WhoAm 90
Rakestraw, Warren Vincent 1940- WhoAm 90
Rakhlin, Natan PenDiMP
Rakhmaninov, Sergey 1873-1943 PenDiMP, -A
Rakic, Pasko 1933- WhoAm 90
Rakich, Dawn Michele 1956- WhoAmW 91
Rakita, Louis 1922- WhoAm 90
Raklovits, Gregory Owens 1959- WhoEmL 91
Rakochevich, Woolay 1939- WhoWor 91
Rakocy, William 1924- WhoAmA 91
Rakoff, Alvin 1927- ConTFT 8
Rakoff, Jed Saul 1943- WhoAm 90
Rakoff, Vivian M 1928- BiDrAPA 89
Rakoff, Vivian Morris 1928- WhoAm 90
Rakolta, John 1923- WhoAm 90
Rakosi, Carl ConAu 32NR
Rakosi, Carl 1903- BioIn 16, WhoWrEP 89, WorAu 1980 [port]
Rakotoarijaona, Desire 1934- WhoWor 91
Rakouskas, Michael Gerard 1944- WhoSSW 91
Rakov, Barbara Streem 1946- WhoAmW 91
Rakovan, Lawrence Francis 1939- WhoAmA 91
Rakover, Beryl ben Duvid 1931- WhoE 91, WhoWor 91
Rakovskii, Khristian Georgievich 1873-1941 BioIn 16
Rakow, Candace Demler 1947- WhoAmW 91, WhoE 91
Rakow, Ed 1936- Ballpl 90
Rakow, Leonard S. 1909-1987 BioIn 16
Rakow, Robert Wesley 1940- BiDrAPA 89
Rakow, Thomas Stewart 1942- St&PR 91
Rakowski, Andrzej 1931- IntWWM 90
Rakowski, Barbara Ann 1948- WhoAmW 91
Rakowski, Daniel A BiDrAPA 89
Rakowski, Mieczyslaw F. 1926- BioIn 16
Rakowski, Mieczyslaw Franciszek 1926- WhoWor 91
Rakowski, Ronald John 1940- WhoE 91
Rakowski, Sharon S. 1948- St&PR 91
Raksin, David 1912- OxCPMus
Rale, Sebastien 1654?-1724 EncCRAm
Ralegh, Elizabeth 1564?- BiDEWW
Ralegh, Walter 1552?-1618 BioIn 16
Ralegh, Walter 1554?-1618 WhNaAH
Raleigh, Alfred 1926- St&PR 91
Raleigh, Cecil Baring 1934- WhoAm 90
Raleigh, Frances Stuart 1952- WhoE 91
Raleigh, Henry Patrick 1931- WhoAm 90, WhoAmA 91, WhoE 91
Raleigh, Jeffrey 1947- ODwPR 91
Raleigh, Richard MajTwCW
Raleigh, Thomas L., Jr. NewYTBS 90
Raleigh, Walter 1552?-1618 BioIn 16, EncCRAm
Raleigh, Walter 1554?-1618 WhNaAH, WorAlBi
Rales, Mitchell BioIn 16
Rales, Mitchell P. 1956- WhoAm 90
Rales, Steven BioIn 16
Rales, Steven M. 1951- WhoAm 90
Ralet, Pierre 1932- WhoWor 91
Raley, Cheri Elaine 1951- WhoAmW 91, WhoWor 91
Raley, Gary Lynn 1946- WhoSSW 91
Raley, Harold Cecil 1934- WhoSSW 91
Raley, James Morris 1950- St&PR 91
Raley, James Morris, Jr. 1950- WhoAm 90
Raley, Mary BioIn 16
Raley, Robert BioIn 16
Raley, Robert L 1924- WhoAmA 91
Raley, Thomas P. 1903- St&PR 91
Raley, Thomas P. 1904- WhoAm 90
Ralf, Torsten 1901-1954 PenDiMP
Ralhan, Vijay Kumar 1941- St&PR 91
Ralke-Kahn, Gina Lin 1958- WhoAmW 91
Rall, Charles O. 1908- St&PR 91
Rall, David Platt 1926- WhoAm 90
Rall, Joseph Edward 1920- WhoAm 90
Rallentando, H. P. MajTwCW
Ralli, Constantine Pandia 1948- WhoEmL 91
Rallo, James Gilbert 1942- WhoWor 91
Ralls, Billy Don 1939- WhoSSW 91
Ralls, Geoffrey Quentin 1949- WhoEmL 91
Ralls, Julius Garrett, Jr. 1952- WhoSSW 91
Ralls, Katherine 1939- WhoAm 90, WhoE 91
Ralls, Rawleigh Hazen, III 1932- WhoWor 91
Ralph, Charles Bradshaw 1944- St&PR 91
Ralph, Deborah Malone 1951- WhoAmW 91
Ralph, Elaine BioIn 16
Ralph, Fritz BioIn 16
Ralph, Gary Keith 1957- BiDrAPA 89
Ralph, James R 1932- BiDrAPA 89
Ralph, James R. 1933- WhoWor 91
Ralph, Jean Dolores 1923- WhoAmW 91
Ralph, Jo Ann M. 1957- WhoAmW 91
Ralph, Julian 1853-1903 BioIn 16
Ralph, Shea 1960- St&PR 91
Ralph, Sheryl Lee BioIn 16, DrBlPA 90
Ralph, Sidney 1916- St&PR 91
Ralph, Thomas Gordon, Jr. 1933- St&PR 91
Ralske, Norman N BiDrAPA 89
Ralston, Anthony 1930- WhoAm 90
Ralston, Carl Conrad 1927- WhoAm 90
Ralston, Clare Chapman 1949- WhoE 91
Ralston, Clarice McDuffie 1932- WhoAmW 91
Ralston, David Michael 1955- WhoAm 90
Ralston, David Thomas, Jr. 1954- WhoE 91
Ralston, Gary Michael 1950- St&PR 91
Ralston, Gilbert Alexander 1912- WhoWor 91
Ralston, Henry James, III 1935- WhoAm 90
Ralston, Hugh James 1958- WhoE 91
Ralston, James A. 1946- St&PR 91
Ralston, James Kenneth 1896-1987 WhoAmA 91N
Ralston, Jan AuBYP 90
Ralston, Jan Elizabeth 1963- WhoAmW 91
Ralston, Joanne 1939- ODwPR 91
Ralston, John D BiDrAPA 89
Ralston, Lloyd Stanley 1919- WhoAm 90
Ralston, Marcia Irene 1951- WhoE 91
Ralston, Richard Hugh 1937- WhoAm 90
Ralston, Robert Grier 1943- WhoE 91
Ralston, Robert Orville, II 1951- WhoEmL 91
Ralston, Thomas Michael 1952- WhoSSW 91
Ralston, William Chapman 1826-1875 EncABHB 6 [port]
Ralstor, Adam WhoWrEP 89
Ram Mohun Roy 1772?-1833 BioIn 16
Ram, Chitta Venkata 1948- WhoSSW 91
Ram, Virginia BioIn 16
Ram Dass, Baba EncO&P 3
Ram Dass, Baba 1931- NewAgE 90
Rama, Swami 1925- EncO&P 3
Rama, Zen Master 1940- NewAgE 90
Rama, Carlos M. 1921- WhoWor 91
Rama, Olga Carol 1918- BiDWomA
Ramacci, Rita BioIn 16
Ramaccioni, Astorre 1929- WhoWor 91
Ramachandran, Gopalasamudram Narayana 1922- WhoWor 91
Ramachandran, Kandethody Madhava 1955- WhoSSW 91
Ramachandran, Krishnan 1946- WhoE 91
Ramachandran, Kunjathan BiDrAPA 89
Ramachandran, Kuppusamy 1933- BiDrAPA 89
Ramachandran, M. G. BioIn 16
Ramachandran, Subramaniam BiDrAPA 89
Ramachandran, V 1937- BiDrAPA 89
Ramachandran, Venkatanarayana Deekshit 1934- WhoAm 90
Ramacharaka, Yogi 1862-1932 EncO&P 3
Ramadan, Paul Rafiq 1931- St&PR 91
Ramadas, Shree 1947- St&PR 91
Ramadei, John A. 1950- St&PR 91
Ramadier, Paul 1888-1961 BiDFrPL
Ramage, Cecil 1895-1988 AnObit 1988
Ramage, Colin Stokes 1921- WhoAm 90
Ramage, John 1748-1802 EncCRAm
Ramage, Lawson P. NewYTBS 90
Ramage, Lawson P. 1909-1990 BioIn 16
Ramage, Robert Thomas 1928- WhoAm 90
Ramahatra, Victor WhoWor 91
Ramaiah, Nataraj 1950- WhoWor 91
Ramaker, Dudley Don 1929- St&PR 91
Ramakrishna, Sri 1836-1886 EncO&P 3
Ramakrishna, Chalakudy V. BiDrAPA 89
Ramakrishnan, Jayant Venkateswara 1959- WhoSSW 91
Ramakrishnan, Venkataswamy 1929- WhoAm 90, WhoWor 91
Ramal, Walter AuBYP 90
Ramaley, Judith Aitken 1941- WhoAmW 91
Ramalingam, Adivarahan 1929- WhoWor 91
Ramalingam, Jayapal 1950- WhoWor 91
Ramamurthy, Gollu Venkateshiah 1940- WhoWor 91
Ramamurthy, Nungavaram Sethuraman 1939- WhoE 91
Ramamurti, Ravi 1952- WhoE 91
Raman, Chandrasekhara V. 1888-1970 WorAlBi
Raman, Chandrasekhara Venkata 1888-1970 BioIn 16
Ramana Maharshi, Sri 1879-1950 EncO&P 3
Ramananda, Kriya NewAgMG
Ramanarayanan, Madhava Prabhu 1945- WhoAm 90, WhoE 91
Ramanathan, Kavasseri Vaidianatha 1932- WhoAm 90
Ramanathan, Muthiah 1936- St&PR 91
Ramanathan, Rohini Balakrishnan 1952- WhoAmW 91
Ramanauskas, Dalia I. 1936- WhoE 91
Ramanauskas, Dalia Irena 1936- WhoAmA 91
Ramanauskas-Marconi, Helene Maria A. 1924- WhoAm 90
Ramani, Dashina V BiDrAPA 89
Ramanujan Aiyangar, Srinivasa 1887-1920 BioIn 16

Ramaprasad, Bindi Ramanna 1942- *WhoAm 90*
Ramaswami Balakrishnan 1943- *BioIn 16*
Ramaswami, Devabhaktuni 1933- *WhoWor 91*
Ramaswamy, Gheetha *BiDrAPA 89*
Ramaswamy, Padmanabhan 1953- *WhoEmL 91*
Ramaswamy, Sundar R *BiDrAPA 89*
Ramaswamy, Trivandrum S *BiDrAPA 89*
Ramat, Charles Samuel 1951- *WhoAm 90*
Ramay, James Charles, Jr. 1951- *WhoSSW 91*
Ramazani, Rouhollah Karegar 1928- *WhoAm 90*
Ramazzotti, Bob 1917- *Ballpl 90*
Ramazzotto, Louis John 1940- *WhoE 91*
Rambach, Peggy Diane 1958- *WhoWrEP 89*
Rambacher, Richard Alan 1950- *WhoSSW 91*
Rambaldi, Jose Ariel 1931- *IntWWM 90*
Rambaud, Frederic Andre 1955- *WhoE 91*
Ramberg, Christina 1946- *WhoAm 90, WhoAmA 91*
Ramberg, Cyvia Myriam 1888-1982 *DcNaB 1981*
Ramberg, Dorothy Cathleen 1923- *WhoAmW 91*
Ramberg, Max 1936- *St&PR 91*
Ramberg, Walter Dodd 1932- *WhoAm 90*
Rambert, Charles Jean Julien 1924- *WhoWor 91*
Rambert, Marie 1888-1982 *DcNaB 1981, WorAlBi*
Rambin, Melvin L. 1941- *St&PR 91*
Rambo, David L. *WhoAm 90*
Rambo, Dee M. 1956- *St&PR 91*
Rambo, George Curtis 1928- *St&PR 91*
Rambo, Joann Weslie 1953- *St&PR 91*
Rambo, John William 1932- *St&PR 91*
Rambo, Lewis Mitchell 1937- *St&PR 91*
Rambo, Sylvia H. 1936- *WhoAm 90, WhoAmW 91, WhoE 91*
Rambow, Gunter 1938- *ConDes 90*
Rambusch, Frank X. 1948- *St&PR 91*
Rambusch, Johann, and Friedrich Volkrath *PenDiDA 89*
Rambusch, Lennard K. 1934- *WhoAm 90*
Rambusch, Viggo Bech 1931- *St&PR 91*
Rambusch, Viggo F.E. 1900- *St&PR 91*
Ramchandani, Dilip *BiDrAPA 89*
Ramdat Misier, Lachmipersad F. 1926- *WhoWor 91*
Ramdin, R.H. 1939- *St&PR 91*
Ramdin, Ron 1942- *ConAu 131*
Rame, David 1904-1987 *BioIn 16*
Rameau, Guy Nichel 1940- *WhoWor 91*
Rameau, Jean Philippe 1683-1764 *PenDiMP A*
Ramee, Louise de la 1839-1908 *BioIn 16*
Ramee, Thomas Mark 1955- *WhoEmL 91*
Ramel, Benita Saga 1928- *WhoWor 91*
Ramel, Stig 1927- *WhoWor 91*
Ramelan, Rahardi 1939- *WhoWor 91*
Ramer, Barry S 1936- *BiDrAPA 89*
Ramer, James LeRoy 1935- *WhoAm 90*
Ramer, John Robert 1934- *St&PR 91*
Ramer, Lawrence J. 1928- *St&PR 91*
Ramer, Lawrence Jerome 1928- *WhoWor 91*
Ramer, Linda Kaye 1951- *BiDrAPA 89*
Ramer, Richard C. 1942- *WhoE 91*
Ramer, Samuel M *BiDrAPA 89*
Rames, Laura Jean *BiDrAPA 89*
Rames, Stanley Dodson 1923- *WhoAmA 91*
Ramesar, Charles Philip *BiDrAPA 89*
Rameses II, King of Egypt *BioIn 16*
Ramesh, Bangalore K *BiDrAPA 89*
Ramesh, Nadamuni Raghavan 1955- *WhoWor 91*
Rameshwar, Anthony Bernard *BiDrAPA 89*
Rameshwar, E R *BiDrAPA 89*
Ramette, Richard Wales 1927- *WhoAm 90*
Ramey, Billy Joe 1926- *St&PR 91*
Ramey, Carl Robert 1941- *WhoE 91*
Ramey, Cecil Edward, Jr. 1923- *WhoAm 90, WhoSSW 91*
Ramey, Darol K. 1930- *St&PR 91*
Ramey, David D *ODwPR 91*
Ramey, Diane Elfriede 1949- *WhoWrEP 89*
Ramey, Henry Jackson, Jr. 1925- *WhoAm 90*
Ramey, Jack Robert 1930- *WhoE 91*
Ramey, John Carter 1933- *WhoSSW 91*
Ramey, Joseph Frederick 1925- *WhoAm 90*
Ramey, Marianne Clifford 1957- *WhoEmL 91*
Ramey, Ray Robey 1928- *St&PR 91*
Ramey, Samuel *BioIn 16*
Ramey, Samuel 1940- *PenDiMP*
Ramey, Samuel 1942- *IntWWM 90*
Ramey, Samuel Edward 1942- *WhoAm 90*
Ramgobin, Ela *BioIn 16*
Ramiah, Kirupananthan 1953- *WhoWor 91*
Ramich, James M. 1945- *St&PR 91*
Ramig, Alexander, Jr. 1941- *WhoAm 90*
Ramik, Otto E 1913- *BiDrAPA 89*
Ramila, Carlos G 1944- *BiDrAPA 89*
Ramin, Gunther 1898-1956 *PenDiMP*
Ramin, Sid 1924- *ConTFT 8*
Ramirez, Alejandro 1946- *IntWWM 90*
Ramirez, Alfredo Carlos *BiDrAPA 89*
Ramirez, Alma 1943- *BiDrAPA 89*
Ramirez, Amelie G. 1951- *WhoHisp 91*
Ramirez, Anthony Michael 1953- *WhoE 91*
Ramirez, Arcadio V 1935- *BiDrAPA 89*
Ramirez, Arthur Leonard *BiDrAPA 89*
Ramirez, Baudelio 1941- *WhoHisp 91*
Ramirez, Benji *BioIn 16*
Ramirez, Berta C. 1942- *WhoHisp 91*
Ramirez, Blandina Cardenas *WhoHisp 91*
Ramirez, Blandina Cardenas 1944- *BioIn 16*
Ramirez, Carlos 1957- *WhoHisp 91*
Ramirez, Carlos A. 1953- *WhoHisp 91*
Ramirez, Carlos D. 1946- *WhoHisp 91*
Ramirez, Carlos M. 1951- *WhoHisp 91*
Ramirez, Celso Lopez 1950- *WhoHisp 91*
Ramirez, Charles 1953- *IntWWM 90*
Ramirez, David Eugene 1952- *WhoHisp 91*
Ramirez, Domingo Victor 1932- *WhoAm 90, WhoHisp 91*
Ramirez, Donald E. 1943- *WhoHisp 91*
Ramirez, Enrique Rene 1930- *WhoHisp 91*
Ramirez, Ernest E. 1940- *WhoHisp 91*
Ramirez, Filomena R. 1944- *WhoHisp 91*
Ramirez, Francisco *BioIn 16*
Ramirez, Gilbert 1921- *WhoHisp 91*
Ramirez, Gladys 1962- *WhoHisp 91*
Ramirez, Guillermo 1934- *WhoHisp 91*
Ramirez, Gus 1953- *WhoHisp 91*
Ramirez, Henry M. 1929- *BioIn 16*
Ramirez, Hugo A. 1942- *WhoHisp 91*
Ramirez, Irene 1962- *WhoHisp 91*
Ramirez, J. Roberto 1941- *WhoHisp 91*
Ramirez, Joan 1961- *WhoHisp 91*
Ramirez, Joan E. 1943- *WhoWrEP 89*
Ramirez, Joel Tito 1923- *BioIn 16, WhoAmA 91, WhoHisp 91*
Ramirez, John 1943- *WhoHisp 91*
Ramirez, John Edward 1953- *WhoHisp 91*
Ramirez, Johnny 1957- *WhoHisp 91*
Ramirez, Jose 1929- *WhoHisp 91*
Ramirez, Jose Lorenzo *BiDrAPA 89*
Ramirez, Jose Lorenzo 1959- *WhoHisp 91*
Ramirez, Jose Luis 1936- *WhoHisp 91*
Ramirez, Jose M. 1955- *WhoHisp 91*
Ramirez, Jose S., Sr. 1919- *WhoHisp 91*
Ramirez, Jose Serafin 1818?-1869 *AmLegL*
Ramirez, Joseph 1937- *WhoHisp 91*
Ramirez, Juan *WhoHisp 91*
Ramirez, Juan, Jr. 1945- *WhoHisp 91*
Ramirez, Julio Jesus 1955- *WhoHisp 91*
Ramirez, Kelli *ODwPR 91*
Ramirez, Kevin Michael 1947- *WhoHisp 91*
Ramirez, Linda Sue 1955- *WhoAmW 91*
Ramirez, Luis 1957- *WhoHisp 91*
Ramirez, Luis Fernando *BiDrAPA 89*
Ramirez, Manuel C *BiDrAPA 89*
Ramirez, Maria Concepcion *WhoAmW 91*
Ramirez, Maria Fiorini 1948- *WhoE 91*
Ramirez, Maria Teresa *BiDrAPA 89*
Ramirez, Mario Efrain 1926- *WhoAm 90, WhoHisp 91*
Ramirez, Martin 1895-1963 *MusmAFA*
Ramirez, Michael *BioIn 16*
Ramirez, Mike 1954- *WhoHisp 91*
Ramirez, Mila Francisco 1956- *St&PR 91*
Ramirez, Olga 1936- *WhoHisp 91*
Ramirez, Olga V *BiDrAPA 89*
Ramirez, Oscar 1946- *WhoHisp 91*
Ramirez, Paul Robert 1950- *WhoE 91*
Ramirez, Peter Armando 1960- *BiDrAPA 89*
Ramirez, Rafael 1958- *Ballpl 90*
Ramirez, Rafael 1959- *WhoHisp 91*
Ramirez, Ralph Henry 1949- *WhoWor 91*
Ramirez, Raul Anthony 1944- *WhoAm 90*
Ramirez, Ricardo 1936- *BioIn 16, WhoAm 90, WhoHisp 91*
Ramirez, Richard G. 1952- *WhoHisp 91*
Ramirez, Rodrigo Igonia 1937- *BiDrAPA 89*
Ramirez, Ruben Ramirez 1953- *WhoHisp 91*
Ramirez, Sara Estela 1881-1910 *BioIn 16*
Ramirez, Stephen 1957- *WhoHisp 91*
Ramirez, Susan E 1946- *ConAu 130, HispWr 90*
Ramirez, Temistocles J *BiDrAPA 89*
Ramirez, Teodoro 1791-1871 *BioIn 16*
Ramirez, Tina *BioIn 16, WhoHisp 91*
Ramirez, William Earl 1951- *WhoWor 91*
Ramirez, William Z. 1954- *WhoHisp 91*
Ramirez-Boulette, Teresa *WhoHisp 91*
Ramirez-Coblazo, Lourdes 1962- *WhoAmW 91*
Ramirez de Arellano, Diana *HispWr 90*
Ramirez de Arellano, Diana 1919- *ConAu 32NR, WhoE 91*
Ramirez de Arellano, Diana Teresa C 1914- *WhoHisp 91*
Ramirez de Arellano, Rafael W 1884- *HispWr 90*
Ramirez de Madrid, M. Francisco *EncCoWW*
Ramirez-Garcia, Mari Carmen 1955- *WhoHisp 91*
Ramirez-Honey, Hector *BiDrAPA 89*
Ramirez Mercado, Sergio 1942- *WhoWor 91*
Ramirez-Ocampo, Jorge 1936- *WhoWor 91*
Ramirez-Rivera, Jose 1929- *WhoAm 90*
Ramirez-Ronda, Carlos Hector 1943- *WhoHisp 91*
Ramirez Vazquez, Pedro 1919- *WhoAm 90*
Ramirez Vega, Adrian Nelson 1934- *WhoHisp 91*
Ramis, Guillermo J. 1945- *WhoHisp 91, WhoSSW 91*
Ramis, Harold Allen 1944- *WhoAm 90*
Ramish, Timothy Edward 1948- *WhoE 91*
Ramji, Alnoor 1953- *BiDrAPA 89*
Ramke, Bin 1947- *ConAu 31NR*
Ramler, Karl Wilhelm 1725-1798 *DcLB 97 [port]*
Ramler, Siegfried *BioIn 16*
Ramm, Friedrich 1744-1808 *PenDiMP*
Ramm, Kent Arthur 1935- *St&PR 91*
Ramm, Richard W. 1949- *St&PR 91*
Ramm Von Marnov, Andrea 1928- *IntWWM 90*
Rammah, Sabir Hamid *BioIn 16*
Rammel, John Marshall 1942- *St&PR 91*
Rammelt, Charles G. 1935- *St&PR 91*
Rammohun Roy, Raja 1772?-1833 *BioIn 16*
Ramo, Simon *BioIn 16*
Ramo, Simon 1913- *WhoAm 90*
Ramo, Virginia M. Smith *WhoAmW 91, WhoWor 91*
Ramon, Ceon 1945- *WhoEmL 91*
Ramon, David A. *WhoAm 90*
Ramon, Jaime *WhoHisp 91*
Ramon, Juan *ConAu 131, HispWr 90, MajTwCW*
Ramon y Cajal, Santiago 1852-1934 *BioIn 16, WorAlBi*
Ramona 1865?-1922 *WhNaAH*
Ramond, Charles Knight, II 1930- *WhoAm 90*
Ramones *EncPR&S 89*
Ramont, Mark S. 1956- *ConTFT 8*
Ramos, Abiud 1930- *WhoSSW 91*
Ramos, Albert A. 1927- *WhoWor 91*
Ramos, Andres C. 1961- *St&PR 91*
Ramos, Andres Carlos 1961- *WhoSSW 91*
Ramos, Andres R. 1914- *St&PR 91*
Ramos, Carmen R 1948- *BiDrAPA 89, WhoAmW 91*
Ramos, Domingo 1958- *Ballpl 90*
Ramos, Elizabeth *BioIn 16*
Ramos, Eva *WhoHisp 91*
Ramos, Fidel 1928- *WhoWor 91*
Ramos, Flor Morales 1915-1990 *WhoHisp 91N*
Ramos, Flordeliza P 1935- *BiDrAPA 89*
Ramos, Francisco E 1939- *BiDrAPA 89*
Ramos, Fred 1959- *WhoHisp 91*
Ramos, Fred M., Jr. 1949- *WhoHisp 91*
Ramos, Graciliano 1892-1953 *BioIn 16*
Ramos, Harold Smith 1928- *WhoSSW 91*
Ramos, Harvey Lee 1938- *St&PR 91*
Ramos, J. E., Jr. 1959- *WhoHisp 91*
Ramos, J. Mario 1956- *WhoAm 90, WhoSSW 91*
Ramos, Jesus A. *WhoHisp 91*
Ramos, John Salias 1942- *WhoHisp 91*
Ramos, Jose Maria Castellano 1945- *WhoWor 91*
Ramos, Jose S. 1950- *WhoHisp 91*
Ramos, Joseph Steven 1943- *WhoHisp 91*
Ramos, Juan Ignacio 1953- *WhoHisp 91*
Ramos, Julianne *WhoAmA 91*
Ramos, Kenneth 1956- *WhoHisp 91*
Ramos, Linda Marie 1961- *WhoAmW 91, WhoWor 91*
Ramos, Lolita J. 1945- *WhoHisp 91*
Ramos, Lucie Ellen Templin 1959- *WhoAmW 91*
Ramos, Manuel 1951- *WhoHisp 91*
Ramos, Manuel Posadas *BiDrAPA 89*
Ramos, Mary Angel 1959- *WhoHisp 91*
Ramos, Melvin John 1935- *WhoAm 90, WhoAmA 91*
Ramos, Olga Leticia 1956- *WhoAmW 91*
Ramos, Pedro 1935- *Ballpl 90*
Ramos, Philip M. *WhoHisp 91*
Ramos, Raul 1946- *WhoHisp 91*
Ramos, Raul, Jr. 1935- *WhoSSW 91*
Ramos, Roberto Prisco Paraiso 1946- *WhoWor 91*
Ramos, Rosa Alicia 1953- *WhoHisp 91*
Ramos, Rufino R 1933- *BiDrAPA 89*
Ramos, Tab 1967- *WhoHisp 91*
Ramos, Teofilo Moses V, Jr. 1957- *BiDrAPA 89*
Ramos, Theodore 1928- *WhoAmA 91*
Ramos, Virginia G 1927- *BiDrAPA 89*
Ramos, William *WhoHisp 91*
Ramos-Blue, Hazel Balatero 1936- *WhoSSW 91*
Ramos-Escobar, Jose Luis 1950- *WhoHisp 91*
Ramos-Garcia, Luis A. 1945- *WhoHisp 91*
Ramos-Irizarry, Andres A *BiDrAPA 89*
Ramos-Lorenzi, Jorge R *BiDrAPA 89*
Ramos Otero, Manuel 1948- *BioIn 16*
Ramos-Polanco, Bernardo 1946- *WhoHisp 91*
Ramos-Rodriguez, Isabel 1958- *WhoSSW 91*
Ramovs, Klemen 1956- *IntWWM 90*
Ramovs, Primoz 1921- *IntWWM 90, WhoWor 91*
Ramp, Horace G. 1931- *St&PR 91*
Ramp, Marjorie Jean Sumerwell 1924- *WhoAmW 91*
Rampa, T Lopsang 1911?-1981 *EncO&P 3*
Rampacek, Charles M. 1943- *WhoAm 90*
Rampal, Jean-Pierre *BioIn 16*
Rampal, Jean-Pierre 1922- *PenDiMP, WorAlBi*
Rampal, Jean-Pierre Louis 1922- *IntWWM 90, WhoAm 90, WhoWor 91*
Rampal, Manohar Lal 1944- *WhoWor 91*
Rampe, John F. 1908- *St&PR 91*
Rampino, Louis J. 1952- *St&PR 91*
Rampino, Marjorie 1949- *WhoAmW 91*
Rampley, Wayne Allan 1948- *WhoSSW 91*
Rampling, Anne 1941- *BioIn 16*
Rampling, Charlotte *BioIn 16*
Rampton, Calvin L. 1913- *BioIn 16*
Rams, Armando Ignacio, Jr. 1962- *WhoHisp 91*
Rams, Dieter *PenDiDA 89*
Rams, Dieter 1932- *ConDes 90, WhoWor 91*
Rams, Harold 1888-1987 *BioIn 16*
Ramsak, Lindsey C. *ODwPR 91*
Ramsamujh, Taje Indralall 1960- *WhoSSW 91*
Ramsaran, James P 1919- *BiDrAPA 89*
Ramsauer, Joseph Francis 1943- *WhoAmA 91*
Ramsaur, Allan Fields 1951- *WhoEmL 91*
Ramsay, Allan 1684?-1758 *DcLB 95 [port]*
Ramsay, Allan 1713-1784 *IntDcAA 90*
Ramsay, Bertram Home 1883-1945 *WorAlBi*
Ramsay, Christopher W. 1959- *WhoEmL 91*
Ramsay, David B. 1941- *St&PR 91*
Ramsay, Donald Allan 1922- *WhoAm 90*
Ramsay, Edith *BioIn 16*
Ramsay, Ernest Canaday 1939- *WhoAm 90*
Ramsay, Ethel Davis 1905- *WhoWrEP 89*
Ramsay, George Bowie, Jr. 1913- *St&PR 91*
Ramsay, Gustavus Remak 1937- *WhoAm 90*
Ramsay, James 1733-1789 *BioIn 16*
Ramsay, James G. *ODwPR 91*
Ramsay, Janice Susan 1952- *WhoAmW 91*
Ramsay, John C 1934- *BiDrAPA 89*
Ramsay, John Erwin 1915- *WhoAm 90*
Ramsay, John Erwin, Jr. 1948- *WhoSSW 91*
Ramsay, Louis Lafayette, Jr. 1918- *St&PR 91, WhoAm 90, WhoWor 91*
Ramsay, Martha 1759-1811 *FemiCLE*
Ramsay, Neal *BioIn 16*
Ramsay, Patricia Leyden 1935- *WhoAmW 91*
Ramsay, Robert Alec 1937- *BiDrAPA 89*
Ramsay, William 1852-1916 *WorAlBi*
Ramsay, WIlliam Morrill 1955- *WhoE 91*
Ramsbacher, Laurie *BiDrAPA 89*
Ramsbottom, Fred *BioIn 16*
Ramsdale, David Alan 1950- *WhoWrEP 89*
Ramsdell, Donald Arthur 1928- *WhoAm 90*
Ramsdell, Lewis Stephen 1895-1975 *DcScB S2*
Ramsdell, Vittz-James 1921- *WhoAm 90*
Ramsdell, Willie 1916-1969 *Ballpl 90*
Ramsden, Anthony Neil 1944- *St&PR 91*
Ramsden, Karen McCoin 1945- *WhoSSW 91*
Ramsden, Katharine Lee 1958- *WhoE 91*
Ramsden, Omar 1873-1939 *PenDiDA 89*
Ramseier, Roger I. *WhoAm 90*
Ramsel, Rob *BioIn 16*
Ramsell, Hilary Keith 1933- *IntWWM 90*
Ramses II, King of Egypt *BioIn 16*
Ramseth, Douglas James 1941- *St&PR 91*
Ramseur, F.H., Jr. 1915- *St&PR 91*
Ramsey, Alexander 1815-1903 *BiDrUSE 89*
Ramsey, Ann 1957- *WhoE 91*
Ramsey, Anne *BioIn 16*
Ramsey, Barbara Jean 1920- *WhoE 91*

Ramsey, Bonnie Jeanne *BiDrAPA 89*
Ramsey, Bruce Mitchell 1956- *WhoEmL 91*
Ramsey, Charles C 1928- *BiDrAPA 89*
Ramsey, Charles Eugene 1923- *WhoAm 90*
Ramsey, Charles Frederic, Jr. 1915- *WhoAm 90, WhoWrEP 89*
Ramsey, Claude 1918- *WhoWor 91*
Ramsey, Claude Swanson, Jr. 1925- *WhoAm 90*
Ramsey, Craig R. 1951- *St&PR 91*
Ramsey, Dale Edwin 1946- *IntWWM 90*
Ramsey, David Allen 1934- *WhoE 91*
Ramsey, David Earl, Jr. *BiDrAPA 89*
Ramsey, David Irving 1944- *St&PR 91*
Ramsey, David Lauren 1951- *St&PR 91*
Ramsey, David Selmer 1931- *WhoAm 90*
Ramsey, Dennis Neil 1952- *WhoE 91*
Ramsey, Diana L. 1949- *WhoE 91*
Ramsey, Donald Robert 1955- *WhoE 91*
Ramsey, Dorothy J 1935- *WhoAmA 91*
Ramsey, Doug 1934- *ConAu 132*
Ramsey, Edlow W. 1909- *St&PR 91*
Ramsey, Elizabeth Mapelsden 1906- *WhoAmW 91*
Ramsey, Febbie Lee 1952- *WhoEmL 91*
Ramsey, Forrest Gladstone, Jr. 1930- *St&PR 91, WhoAm 90, WhoSSW 91*
Ramsey, Frank Allen 1929- *WhoAm 90*
Ramsey, Frank B. 1902- *WhoWrEP 89*
Ramsey, Gordon Clark 1941- *IntWWM 90*
Ramsey, Greg W. 1922- *St&PR 91*
Ramsey, Henry Bascom 1847-1897 *AmLegL*
Ramsey, Inez Linn 1938- *WhoAmW 91, WhoSSW 91, WhoWor 91*
Ramsey, Ira Clayton 1931- *St&PR 91, WhoAm 90, WhoSSW 91*
Ramsey, J. Kevin 1932- *St&PR 91*
Ramsey, Jackson Eugene 1938- *WhoSSW 91*
Ramsey, James B. *BioIn 16*
Ramsey, James Edgar 1928- *WhoSSW 91*
Ramsey, James Kenneth 1924- *WhoSSW 91*
Ramsey, Jarold W. 1937- *WhoWrEP 89*
Ramsey, Jarold William 1937- *WhoAm 90*
Ramsey, Jettie Cecil 1925- *WhoWor 91*
Ramsey, Joanne Marie 1945- *WhoEmL 91*
Ramsey, John C. 1936- *St&PR 91*
Ramsey, John Colt 1951- *WhoSSW 91*
Ramsey, John Hansberry 1941- *WhoAm 90*
Ramsey, Julie D. 1966- *WhoAmW 91*
Ramsey, Kenneth Clive 1933- *St&PR 91*
Ramsey, Liston Bryan 1919- *WhoAm 90, WhoSSW 91*
Ramsey, Lloyd Brinkley 1918- *WhoAm 90*
Ramsey, Lloyd Hamilton 1921- *WhoAm 90*
Ramsey, Lucille Avra 1942- *WhoAmW 91*
Ramsey, Lynn A. *ODwPR 91*
Ramsey, Lynn Allison 1944- *WhoE 91*
Ramsey, Marjorie Elizabeth 1921- *WhoAm 90*
Ramsey, Martha Laurens 1759-1811 *EncCRAm*
Ramsey, Mary Lou 1953- *BiDrAPA 89*
Ramsey, Maude Lou 1950- *WhoE 91*
Ramsey, Michael 1904-1988 *BioIn 16*
Ramsey, Michael Kirby 1948- *WhoWrEP 89*
Ramsey, Mike 1954- *Ballpl 90*
Ramsey, Mitchell Lloyd 1945- *WhoSSW 91*
Ramsey, Norman 1915- *WhoAm 90, WhoE 91, WhoWor 91*
Ramsey, Norman F. 1915- *WorAlBi*
Ramsey, Norman Foster 1915- *BioIn 16*
Ramsey, Norman Park 1922- *WhoAm 90, WhoE 91*
Ramsey, Pamela Pratt 1961- *WhoAmW 91*
Ramsey, Paul 1913-1988 *AnObit 1988, BioIn 16*
Ramsey, Paul Willard 1919- *WhoAm 90*
Ramsey, Peter Christie 1942- *WhoE 91*
Ramsey, Peter Michael 1943- *St&PR 91*
Ramsey, Randall Byron 1957- *WhoEmL 91, WhoSSW 91*
Ramsey, Rebecca Ann *BiDrAPA 89*
Ramsey, Reva Snelson 1934- *WhoAmW 91*
Ramsey, Richard L. 1947- *St&PR 91*
Ramsey, Robert Lee 1929- *WhoAm 90*
Ramsey, Robert Russell, Jr. 1929- *WhoSSW 91*
Ramsey, Roger A. 1938- *St&PR 91*
Ramsey, Sally Ann Seitz 1931- *WhoSSW 91*
Ramsey, Stephen T. 1949- *St&PR 91*
Ramsey, Stpehen M. 1923- *WhoE 91*
Ramsey, Suzanne 1965- *WhoSSW 91*
Ramsey, Ted Alan *BiDrAPA 89*
Ramsey, Terry Lane 1941- *WhoSSW 91*
Ramsey, Thomas H. 1948- *St&PR 91*
Ramsey, Toad 1864-1906 *Ballpl 90*
Ramsey, Vicki Lynn 1959- *WhoSSW 91*
Ramsey, Wiley Fredrick 1940- *WhoSSW 91, WhoWor 91*
Ramsey, William Dale, Jr. 1936- *WhoSSW 91, WhoWor 91*
Ramsey, William Edward 1931- *WhoAm 90*
Ramsey, William F. 1951- *St&PR 91*
Ramsey, William Henry 1945- *WhoE 91*
Ramsey, William McCreery 1931- *IntWWM 90, WhoAm 90*
Ramsey, William P. 1936- *St&PR 91*
Ramsey, William Ray 1926- *WhoAm 90*
Ramsey of Canterbury, Lord 1904-1988 *AnObit 1988*
Ramseyer, Paul Edwards 1927- *WhoAm 90*
Ramseyer, Ronald L. 1942- *St&PR 91*
Ramshaw, Peter Johan *BiDrAPA 89*
Ramsower, Reagan Mays 1952- *WhoSSW 91*
Ramstack, Richard V. 1919- *St&PR 91*
Ramstad, Paul Ellertson 1918- *WhoAm 90*
Ramstein, William Louis 1950- *WhoWor 91*
Ramundo, Araldo 1944- *WhoWor 91*
Ramunno, Thomas Paul 1952- *WhoEmL 91, WhoWor 91*
Ramussen, J.A. 1945- *St&PR 91*
Ramzy, Ayman H N *BiDrAPA 89*
Ran, Josef 1947- *WhoWor 91*
Ran, Shulamit 1949- *WhoAmW 91*
Rana, Hiren T *BiDrAPA 89*
Rana, Kiranjit S., II 1946- *WhoWrEP 89*
Rana, Prabhakar Shumshere Jung Bahadur 1935- *WhoWor 91*
Ranade, Rekha V *BiDrAPA 89*
Ranalli, Daniel 1946- *WhoAmA 91*
Ranalli, Daniel 1948- *WhoAm 90, WhoE 91*
Ranalli, Michael Patrick 1933- *St&PR 91, WhoAm 90*
Ranalli, Ramona Renee 1966- *WhoEmL 91*
Ranalow, Frederick 1873-1953 *PenDiMP*
Ranang, Lars Erik 1942- *WhoWor 91*
Ranard, Donald L. *NewYTBS 90*
Ranasinghe, Anne 1925- *FemiCLE*
Ranaudin, William Sutcliffe 1935- *WhoSSW 91*
Ranavalona I *WomWR*
Ranavalona II *WomWR*
Ranavalona III 1861-1916 *WomWR*
Ranc, Arthur Joseph 1831-1908 *BiDFrPL*
Rancier, Marco 1926- *BiDrAPA 89*
Rancour, Joann Sue 1939- *WhoAmW 91*
RanCour, Paul Albert 1939- *WhoSSW 91, WhoWor 91*
Rancourt, John Herbert 1946- *WhoEmL 91*
Rancurello, Michael David 1954- *BiDrAPA 89*
Rand, A. Barry *BioIn 16*
Rand, Addison 1896- *AuBYP 90*
Rand, Ann *AuBYP 90*
Rand, Anthony Eden 1939- *WhoSSW 91*
Rand, Archie 1949- *WhoAmA 91*
Rand, Ayn 1905- *WorAlBi*
Rand, Ayn 1905-1982 *BioAmW, BioIn 16, MajTwCW, WrPh*
Rand, Barry Steven *BiDrAPA 89*
Rand, Bay 1875-1941 *BiDWomA*
Rand, Calvin Gordon 1929- *WhoAm 90*
Rand, Duncan D. 1940- *WhoAm 90*
Rand, Elizabeth H 1941- *BiDrAPA 89*
Rand, Harry 1913- *ODwPR 91*
Rand, Harry 1947- *WhoAmA 91*
Rand, Harry Israel 1912- *WhoAm 90*
Rand, Harry Zvi 1947- *WhoAm 90, WhoE 91*
Rand, James H. 1859-1944 *WorAlBi*
Rand, James Henry 1943- *WhoAm 90*
Rand, Joella M. 1932- *WhoAmW 91*
Rand, John Born 1921- *WhoAm 90*
Rand, John Fay 1932- *WhoAm 90*
Rand, Kathy S. 1945- *ODwPR 91*
Rand, Kathy Sue 1945- *WhoAm 90*
Rand, Lawrence Anthony 1942- *WhoAm 90*
Rand, Leon 1930- *WhoAm 90*
Rand, Man, Jr. *BioIn 16*
Rand, Martha Elizabeth 1950- *WhoAmW 91, WhoE 91*
Rand, Murdock M. *BioIn 16*
Rand, Paul 1914- *AuBYP 90, BioIn 16, ConDes 90, WhoAmA 91, WhoE 91*
Rand, Phillip Gordon 1934- *WhoAm 90*
Rand, Sam *BioIn 16*
Rand, Sheryl B. 1954- *BiDrAPA 89*
Rand, Sidney Anders 1916- *WhoAm 90*
Rand, Stanley J. 1931- *St&PR 91*
Rand, Steven Jay *WhoAmA 91*
Rand, Ted *BioIn 16*
Rand, Theodore Harding 1835-1900 *DcCanB 12*
Rand, Thomas O. S. 1942- *WhoE 91*
Rand, William 1926- *WhoAm 90*
Rand, William Medden 1938- *WhoE 91*
Randall, Alexander Williams 1819-1872 *BiDrUSE 89*
Randall, Ariane *BioIn 16*
Randall, Benjamin 1749-1808 *BioIn 16*
Randall, Blossom E. *AuBYP 90*
Randall, Bob 1937- *ConAu 30NR, WhoAm 90*
Randall, Bob 1949- *Ballpl 90*
Randall, Bruce Allan 1958- *IntWWM 90*
Randall, C. Walter, Jr. 1914- *St&PR 91*
Randall, Charles E. 1932- *St&PR 91*
Randall, Christine Sheppard 1928- *WhoSSW 91*
Randall, Claire 1919- *WhoAm 90, WhoAmW 91*
Randall, Clifford Wendell 1936- *WhoAm 90*
Randall, Craig 1957- *WhoWor 91*
Randall, Dale Bertrand Jonas 1929- *WhoSSW 91*
Randall, Dean Bowman 1920- *WhoAm 90*
Randall, Deborah 1957- *ConAu 131*
Randall, Diane *ConAu 32NR*
Randall, Edward, III 1927- *St&PR 91*
Randall, Edward Caleb 1860-1935 *EncO&P 3*
Randall, Edward Vincent, Jr. 1932- *St&PR 91*
Randall, Edward Walker 1925- *St&PR 91*
Randall, Edwin Clarence 1949- *WhoE 91*
Randall, Eugene Henry *BiDrAPA 89*
Randall, Florence Engel 1917- *AuBYP 90, BioIn 16*
Randall, Francis B. *BioIn 16*
Randall, Francis Ballard 1931- *WhoAm 90*
Randall, Freddie Donald 1924- *St&PR 91*
Randall, Frederick Alvon 1945- *St&PR 91*
Randall, Gail *BioIn 16*
Randall, Gerald Jean 1931- *St&PR 91*
Randall, Harry 1860-1932 *OxCPMus*
Randall, Henry Thomas 1914- *WhoAm 90*
Randall, Hermine Maria 1927- *WhoAmW 91*
Randall, Howard Morgan 1936- *WhoSSW 91*
Randall, Hugh L. 1942- *St&PR 91*
Randall, Jack J. 1940- *WhoSSW 91*
Randall, James 1917- *BiDrAPA 89*
Randall, James A. 1955- *St&PR 91*
Randall, James Edwin 1924- *WhoAm 90*
Randall, James Grafton 1951- *WhoEmL 91*
Randall, James R. 1924- *WhoAm 90*
Randall, Janet 1919- *AuBYP 90*
Randall, Janet S 1947- *BiDrAPA 89*
Randall, John 1810-1910 *PenDiDA 89*
Randall, John 1905-1984 *BioIn 16*
Randall, John Del 1932- *WhoE 91*
Randall, John Henry 1923- *BiDrAPA 89*
Randall, John L 1933- *EncO&P 3*
Randall, John Stone 1912- *St&PR 91*
Randall, John Turton 1905-1984 *DcNaB 1981*
Randall, Katharine *BioIn 16*
Randall, Kenneth Charles *AuBYP 90*
Randall, Larry D. 1941- *St&PR 91*
Randall, Lee W. 1949- *St&PR 91*
Randall, Lilian M C 1931- *WhoAmA 91*
Randall, Linda L. 1945- *WhoAmW 91*
Randall, Linda Lea 1946- *WhoAmW 91*
Randall, Lolly 1952- *WhoAmW 91*
Randall, Lyman K. 1933- *St&PR 91*
Randall, Lynn Ellen 1946- *WhoAmW 91*
Randall, Malcom 1916- *WhoAm 90, WhoSSW 91*
Randall, Margaret 1936- *BioIn 16*
Randall, Marta 1948- *RGTwCSF*
Randall, Mary *AuBYP 90*
Randall, Michael William 1957- *WhoEmL 91*
Randall, Patricia Mary 1948- *WhoAmW 91, WhoE 91*
Randall, Paula 1895-1985 *WhoAmA 91N*
Randall, Penny Kim 1962- *WhoE 91*
Randall, Priscilla Richmond 1926- *WhoAmW 91*
Randall, Richard Dean 1925- *St&PR 91*
Randall, Richard Harding, Jr. 1926- *WhoAm 90, WhoAmA 91*
Randall, Richard Rainier 1925- *WhoAm 90, WhoE 91*
Randall, Richard William 1931- *WhoE 91, WhoWor 91*
Randall, Richard William 1950- *St&PR 91*
Randall, Robert *AuBYP 90, ConAu 130, MajTwCW*
Randall, Robert Lee 1936- *WhoE 91, WhoWor 91*
Randall, Roger D. 1953- *St&PR 91*
Randall, Ronald F. 1934- *St&PR 91*
Randall, Ruth Elaine Painter 1892-1971 *AuBYP 90*
Randall, Ruth Evelyn 1929- *WhoAmW 91*
Randall, Ruth Jean 1937- *WhoAmW 91*
Randall, Ruth Lewis 1916- *WhoAmW 91*
Randall, Sherri Lee 1959- *WhoAmW 91*
Randall, Stephen James 1944- *WhoAm 90*
Randall, Ted 1914-1985 *BioIn 16*
Randall, Thomas Martin 1786-1859 *PenDiDA 89*
Randall, Tony 1920- *WhoAm 90, WorAlBi*
Randall, Willard Sterne 1942- *WhoAm 90*
Randall, William B. 1921- *WhoAm 90, WhoWor 91*
Randall, William S. 1940- *WhoAm 90*
Randall, William Seymour 1933- *WhoAm 90*
Randall, William Theodore 1931- *WhoAm 90*
Randalls, Jeremy Stuart 1959- *IntWWM 90*
Randazzo, Anthony 1943- *St&PR 91*
Randazzo, Joseph C. 1950- *St&PR 91*
Rande, Mary *BiDEWW*
Randegger, Alberto 1832-1911 *PenDiMP*
Randel, Ronald Dean 1938- *WhoSSW 91*
Randell, James Weeden, Jr. 1940- *WhoE 91*
Randell, Roger T. *St&PR 91*
Randell, Sheila 1930- *IntWWM 90*
Randhawa, Amarjeet Kaur *BiDrAPA 89*
Randhawa, Bikkar Singh 1933- *WhoAm 90*
Randi, James 1928- *EncO&P 3, EncPaPR 91, News 90 [port], WhoAm 90, WhoWrEP 89*
Randich, Gene Martin 1929- *St&PR 91*
Randisi, Robert J 1951- *TwCCr&M 91*
Randle, Annie *EarBlAP*
Randle, Augustus Brown, III 1940- *St&PR 91*
Randle, Donald Robert 1928- *St&PR 91*
Randle, Ellen Eugenia Foster 1948- *WhoAmW 91*
Randle, John Bridges 1945- *WhoSSW 91*
Randle, Lenny 1949- *Ballpl 90*
Randle, Michael Charles 1952- *WhoWor 91*
Randle, Sonja L *BiDrAPA 89*
Randle, Thomas 1958- *IntWWM 90*
Randles, Jenny 1951- *EncO&P 3*
Randles, Ronald Herman 1942- *WhoSSW 91*
Randlett, Mary Willis 1924- *WhoAmA 91*
Randlett, Richard Carl 1931- *St&PR 91*
Randman, Bennett Charles 1949- *IntWWM 90*
Rando, Rae 1956- *WhoAmW 91*
Randolph, A. Philip 1889-1979 *EncAL, WorAlBi*
Randolph, Amanda 1902-1967 *DrBlPA 90*
Randolph, Angus C *BiDrAPA 89*
Randolph, Angus M.C. 1946- *St&PR 91*
Randolph, Arthur Raymond 1943- *WhoAm 90*
Randolph, Asa Philip 1889-1979 *BioIn 16*
Randolph, Barry R. 1958- *St&PR 91*
Randolph, Benjamin *PenDiDA 89*
Randolph, Beverley 1951- *WhoAmW 91*
Randolph, Carl L. 1922- *St&PR 91*
Randolph, Carl Lowell 1922- *WhoAm 90*
Randolph, Christopher Craven 1956- *WhoE 91, WhoWor 91*
Randolph, Christopher S *BiDrAPA 89*
Randolph, Clyde Clifton, Jr. 1928- *WhoWor 91*
Randolph, David 1914- *IntWWM 90, WhoAm 90*
Randolph, David M. 1948- *St&PR 91*
Randolph, Deborah Jean Greenway 1951- *WhoAmW 91*
Randolph, Edmund 1753-1813 *WorAlBi*
Randolph, Edmund Jennings 1753-1813 *BiDrUSE 89, BioIn 16, EncCRAm*
Randolph, Edward 1632?-1703 *EncCRAm*
Randolph, Ellen *ConAu 32NR*
Randolph, Elsie 1904-1981 *OxCPMus*
Randolph, Evonne P. 1941- *WhoAmW 91*
Randolph, F.F. 1927- *St&PR 91*
Randolph, Francis Fitz, Jr. 1927- *WhoAm 90*
Randolph, Harrison 1916- *St&PR 91*
Randolph, Harry E. 1932- *St&PR 91*
Randolph, Jackson H. 1930- *St&PR 91*
Randolph, Jackson Harold 1930- *WhoAm 90*
Randolph, James 1934- *DrBlPA 90*
Randolph, James Glenn 1930- *WhoAm 90*
Randolph, James Harrison, Sr. 1917- *WhoSSW 91*
Randolph, Jane Fitz- *BioIn 16*
Randolph, Jennings, Jr. 1934- *WhoAm 90*
Randolph, Jerry Gresham 1935- *St&PR 91*
Randolph, John 1727?-1784 *EncCRAm*
Randolph, John 1773-1833 *BioIn 16, WorAlBi*
Randolph, John 1915- *ConTFT 8 [port], WhoAm 90*
Randolph, John 1931- *St&PR 91*
Randolph, John Denson 1938- *WhoAm 90, WhoWrEP 89*
Randolph, John Hamilton 1936- *St&PR 91*
Randolph, John Lind 1937- *WhoAm 90*
Randolph, John Maurice 1926- *WhoAm 90*
Randolph, Judson Graves 1927- *WhoAm 90*
Randolph, Lee 1954- *St&PR 91*
Randolph, Lillian 1915?-1980 *DrBlPA 90*
Randolph, Lynn Moore 1938- *WhoAmA 91*

Randolph, Lynwood Parker 1938- *WhoE 91*
Randolph, Marie Jackson- *BioIn 16*
Randolph, Martha Jefferson 1772-1836 *BioIn 16*
Randolph, Mike 1937- *St&PR 91*
Randolph, P B 1825-1875 *EncO&P 3*
Randolph, Patricia Dolvin 1940- *WhoAmW 91*
Randolph, Peter B F 1934- *BiDrAPA 89*
Randolph, Peyton 1721-1775 *BiDrUSE 89, EncCRAm, WorAlBi*
Randolph, Robert DeWitt 1929- *WhoAm 90*
Randolph, Robert Lee 1926- *WhoAm 90*
Randolph, Robert Raymond 1937- *WhoAm 90*
Randolph, Rodger Leon 1931- *St&PR 91*
Randolph, Royal, Jr. *BiDrAPA 89*
Randolph, Shirley Wilson 1945- *WhoAmW 91*
Randolph, Susan C. 1938- *St&PR 91*
Randolph, Thomas 1605-1635 *BioIn 16*
Randolph, Velma Lois 1930- *WhoWrEP 89*
Randolph, Walter R. 1926- *St&PR 91*
Randolph, Willene Joyce 1935- *WhoAmW 91*
Randolph, William 1651-1711 *EncCRAm*
Randolph, William Abbott 1923- *St&PR 91*
Randolph, Willie 1954- *Ballpl 90*
Randour, Paul Alfred 1935- *WhoAm 90*
Randova, Eva 1936- *IntWWM 90*
Rands, Bernard 1934- *WhoAm 90*
Rands, Bernard 1935- *IntWWM 90, PenDiMP A*
Rands, Betty Ann 1931- *WhoAmW 91*
Randt, Clark Thorp 1917- *WhoAm 90*
Randt, Clark Thorp, Jr. 1945- *WhoEmL 91*
Ranelli, John Raymond 1946- *WhoAm 90, WhoE 91, WhoEmL 91, WhoWor 91*
Ranelli, Raymond A. 1947- *WhoAm 90*
Ranes, Chris *WhoAmA 91*
Ranew, Frank, Jr. 1950- *ODwPR 91*
Ranew, Merritt 1938- *Ballpl 90*
Raney, Carolyn *IntWWM 90*
Raney, David Franklin *BiDrAPA 89*
Raney, Donald Raymond 1954- *WhoEmL 91*
Raney, George Neal 1922- *WhoE 91*
Raney, Hollaman Martin 1933- *St&PR 91*
Raney, James Oscar 1935- *BiDrAPA 89*
Raney, John Hurth 1943- *BiDrAPA 89*
Raney, Miriam Day 1922- *WhoAmW 91*
Raney, R.H. 1928- *St&PR 91*
Raney, Suzanne Bryant *WhoAmA 91N*
Ranfft, Klaus Karl Horst 1934- *WhoWor 91*
Ranftl, Robert Matthew 1925- *WhoWor 91*
Rangaiah, Govindappa 1939- *BiDrAPA 89*
Ranganathan, Tanjore 1925-1987 *BioIn 16*
Ranganathan, Thodur M *BiDrAPA 89*
Range, A. J. 1950- *WhoSSW 91*
Range, Robert Louis 1933- *St&PR 91*
Range, Ronald Sinclair 1953- *WhoSSW 91*
Rangel, Charles B. *BioIn 16*
Rangel, Charles Bernard 1930- *BlkAmsC [port], WhoAm 90, WhoE 91*
Rangel, Irma 1931- *WhoHisp 91*
Rangel, Richard 1947- *St&PR 91*
Rangeler, Dwight D. *ODwPR 91*
Rangell, Leo 1913- *BiDrAPA 89, WhoAm 90*
Rangell, Nelson 1920- *BiDrAPA 89*
Rangen, Christopher T. 1953- *St&PR 91*
Ranger, Ken *MajTwCW*
Ranginkaman, Asghar 1946- *WhoWor 91*
Rania, Albert Nunzio 1966- *WhoWrEP 89*
Ranieri, Lewis S. *BioIn 16*
Ranieri, Lorraine Mary 1943- *WhoWrEP 89*
Ranieri, William J. *BioIn 16*
Ranina *EncCoWW*
Ranis, Gustav 1929- *WhoAm 90*
Rank, Douglas Holland *BiDrAPA 89*
Rank, Everett George 1921- *WhoAm 90*
Rank, John Thomas 1947- *WhoEmL 91*
Rank, Larry Gene 1935- *WhoAm 90*
Rank, Maureen Joy 1947- *WhoWrEP 89*
Rankaitis, Susan 1949- *WhoAm 90, WhoAmA 91, WhoAmW 91*
Ranki, Dezso 1951- *IntWWM 90*
Ranki, Gyorgy 1930-1988 *BioIn 16*
Rankin, Alfred Marshall 1913- *St&PR 91, WhoAm 90*
Rankin, Alfred Marshall, Jr. 1941- *St&PR 91, WhoAm 90*
Rankin, Arthur 1816-1893 *DcCanB 12*
Rankin, Arthur McKee 1841-1914 *BioIn 16, OxCCanT*
Rankin, B.M., Jr. 1930- *St&PR 91*
Rankin, Bonnie Lee 1953- *WhoAmW 91*
Rankin, Byron McLean, Jr. 1930- *WhoSSW 91*
Rankin, Clyde Evan, III 1950- *WhoE 91, WhoWor 91*
Rankin, D. J. *WhoSSW 91*
Rankin, Dianne Mary 1947- *WhoAmW 91, WhoE 91*
Rankin, Don *WhoAmA 91*
Rankin, Donald T. *St&PR 91*
Rankin, Dorreen Winnie 1965- *WhoAmW 91*
Rankin, Frances Espy *BiDrAPA 89*
Rankin, Harley, Jr. 1939- *St&PR 91*
Rankin, Helen Cross *WhoAmW 91*
Rankin, Henry Hollis, III 1944- *WhoSSW 91*
Rankin, Herb Lee 1957- *St&PR 91*
Rankin, Ian James 1960- *SpyFic*
Rankin, Isaia 1954-1989 *BioIn 16*
Rankin, James 1923- *WhoAm 90*
Rankin, James A. 1928- *St&PR 91*
Rankin, James Asbury 1928- *WhoAm 90*
Rankin, James Winton 1943- *WhoAm 90*
Rankin, Janet Sloan 1942- *WhoSSW 91*
Rankin, Jeanette 1880-1973 *WorAlBi*
Rankin, Jeannette *BioIn 16*
Rankin, Jeannette 1880-1973 *BioAmW*
Rankin, Joanna Marie 1942- *WhoAmW 91*
Rankin, Jocelyn Davis 1955- *WhoAmW 91*
Rankin, Joe Bruce 1945- *WhoAm 90*
Rankin, John J. 1943- *St&PR 91*
Rankin, Joseph E *BiDrAPA 89*
Rankin, Karl Lott 1898- *WhoAm 90*
Rankin, Kitty V. 1953- *WhoAmW 91*
Rankin, Lonnie *BioIn 16*
Rankin, Neil 1926- *IntWWM 90*
Rankin, Richard Allen 1954- *WhoEmL 91*
Rankin, Richard Francis 1944- *WhoSSW 91*
Rankin, Robert 1915- *WhoAm 90*
Rankin, Robert A., Jr. 1945- *ODwPR 91*
Rankin, Robert Allen, Jr. 1945- *St&PR 91*
Rankin, Robert Arthur 1949- *WhoAm 90, WhoE 91*
Rankin, Robert H. *AuBYP 90*
Rankin, Robert Harry 1909-1990 *ConAu 131*
Rankin, Robert M *BiDrAPA 89*
Rankin, Roger 1943- *St&PR 91*
Rankin, Samuel H., Jr. *WhoAm 90*
Rankin, Susan Jewel 1949- *WhoWrEP 89*
Rankin, Sybil Zoe 1943- *WhoAmW 91*
Rankin, Terry Lee 1949- *WhoSSW 91*
Rankin, Thomas R. *ODwPR 91*
Rankin, W.L. 1937- *St&PR 91*
Rankin, William H. 1849-1913 *Ballpl 90*
Rankin, William J. 1937- *St&PR 91*
Rankine, B. James 1936- *St&PR 91*
Rankine, William J. M. 1820-1872 *WorAlBi*
Rankl, Carl Raymond 1940- *BiDrAPA 89*
Rankl, Karl 1898-1968 *PenDiMP*
Ranks, Anne Elizabeth 1916- *WhoAmW 91*
Ranky, Klara G 1912- *BiDrAPA 89*
Rann, Vollian Burr 1897-1956 *WhoAmA 91N*
Ranney, Austin 1920- *WhoAm 90*
Ranney, George Alfred 1912- *WhoAm 90*
Ranney, Glen Allison 1896-1959 *WhoAmA 91N*
Ranney, Helen Margaret 1920- *WhoAm 90, WhoAmW 91*
Rannie, James *PenDiDA 89*
Rano, Peter Robert 1948- *WhoWor 91*
Ranon, Jose Antonio 1932- *WhoHisp 91*
Ranone, John Louis 1940- *WhoE 91*
Rans, Paul 1946- *IntWWM 90*
Ransby, E.J. 1942- *St&PR 91*
Ransdell, Ronald Eugene 1941- *St&PR 91*
Ransdell, Vernon Gale 1935- *St&PR 91*
Ransford, John Gerard 1940- *St&PR 91*
Ransier, Alonzo Jacob 1834-1882 *BlkAmsC [port]*
Ransil, Bernard Jerome 1929- *WhoE 91, WhoWor 91*
Ransohoff, Doris *AuBYP 90*
Ransohoff, Martin 1927- *WhoAm 90*
Ransohoff, Priscilla Burnett 1912- *WhoE 91, WhoWor 91*
Ransom, Alan Brain 1940- *WhoAm 90*
Ransom, Alan Brian 1940- *St&PR 91*
Ransom, Allen R. 1933- *St&PR 91*
Ransom, Bill 1945- *WhoAm 90, WhoWrEP 89*
Ransom, Birdelle Wycoff 1914- *HarlReB*
Ransom, Bunnie Jackson 1940- *WhoAmW 91, WhoSSW 91*
Ransom, Candice F. 1952- *BioIn 16*
Ransom, Champe 1936- *EncO&P 3*
Ransom, Charles Anderson, Sr. 1952- *WhoSSW 91*
Ransom, Dana *WhoWrEP 89*
Ransom, Diana *BioIn 16*
Ransom, Edward Duane 1914- *WhoAm 90*
Ransom, Harry Howe 1922- *WhoAm 90*
Ransom, Henry Cleveland, Jr 1942- *WhoAmA 91*
Ransom, Howard John 1931- *St&PR 91*
Ransom, Janet Ruth 1951- *WhoAmW 91*
Ransom, Jeremy *BioIn 16*
Ransom, John Crowe 1888-1974 *BioIn 16, MajTwCW, WorAlBi, WrPh*
Ransom, John Paul 1940- *St&PR 91*
Ransom, Margaret Priscilla 1947- *WhoAmW 91, WhoE 91*
Ransom, Marion Theresa 1939- *WhoSSW 91*
Ransom, Richard E. 1932- *WhoAm 90*
Ransom, Robert Edwin 1952- *St&PR 91*
Ransom, Ronald Edward 1931- *WhoSSW 91*
Ransom, Thomas Richard 1934- *St&PR 91*
Ransom, William Harrison 1938- *WhoAm 90*
Ransom, William Henry Howe 1958- *IntWWM 90*
Ransome, Arthur 1884-1967 *ConAu 30NR*
Ransome, Arthur Michell 1884-1967 *AuBYP 90*
Ransome, Ernest Leslie, III *WhoAm 90, WhoE 91*
Ransome, Ernest Leslie, III 1926- *St&PR 91*
Ransome, Percy Allan, Jr. 1923- *St&PR 91*
Ransome, Stephen *TwCCr&M 91*
Ranson, Charles W. 1903-1988 *BioIn 16*
Ranson, Guy Harvey 1916- *WhoAm 90*
Ranson, Jeanette S. 1939- *St&PR 91*
Ranson, Lyle H. 1936- *St&PR 91*
Ranson, Nancy Sussman 1905- *WhoAm 90, WhoAmA 91*
Ranson, Pierre 1736-1786 *PenDiDA 89*
Ranson, William Joseph 1938- *WhoSSW 91*
Ransone, Robin Key 1933- *WhoE 91*
Ransopher, Ivan Allen 1960- *WhoAm 90*
Ransopher, Sara Beth 1949- *WhoSSW 91*
Ranta, Jeffrey Alan 1953- *WhoE 91*
Ranta, Richard Robert 1943- *WhoAm 90*
Ranta Aho, Martha Helen 1923- *WhoAmW 91*
Rantamala, Irmari *DcScanL*
Rantanen, Ulla 1940?- *BiDWomA*
Rantchewaime *WhNaAH*
Rantoul, Talbot *BioIn 16*
Rants, Carolyn Jean 1936- *WhoAmW 91*
Rantzau, Heinrich 1526-1598 *BioIn 16*
Ranu, Harcharan Singh *WhoE 91, WhoWor 91*
Ranucci, Marguerite Cullen *WhoAmW 91*
Ranucci, Renato 1921- *AuBYP 90*
Ranucci, Robert J 1930- *BiDrAPA 89*
Ranum, Orest Allen 1933- *WhoAm 90*
Ranz, James 1921- *WhoAm 90*
Ranz, Jules Malcolm 1941- *BiDrAPA 89*
Ranz, Ronnie Beth *BiDrAPA 89*
Ranzahuer, Guillermo Gonzalez 1928- *WhoAm 90*
Ranzinger, Robert 1940- *St&PR 91, WhoAm 90*
Ranzini, Joseph Louis 1929- *St&PR 91*
Ranzini, Mildred *St&PR 91*
Ranzini, Stephen Lange 1965- *St&PR 91*
Rao, A. Narsimha 1927- *St&PR 91*
Rao, A. Ramamohana 1933- *WhoWor 91*
Rao, A Venkoba 1927- *BiDrAPA 89*
Rao, Adharapurapu *BiDrAPA 89*
Rao, Balakrishna M *BiDrAPA 89*
Rao, Bhanoji 1941- *WhoWor 91*
Rao, Chamaraja A 1939- *BiDrAPA 89*
Rao, Chandragiri Dinaker 1938- *WhoSSW 91*
Rao, Chintamani Nagesa Ramachandra 1934- *WhoWor 91*
Rao, Chitaldroog Ramachandra 1931- *WhoWor 91*
Rao, Desiraju Bhavanarayana 1936- *WhoAm 90*
Rao, Dhananjaya K. 1949- *St&PR 91*
Rao, Doreen 1946- *IntWWM 90*
Rao, Dwarakanath G *BiDrAPA 89*
Rao, K Ramakrishna 1932- *ConAu 130, EncO&P 3*
Rao, Kancherla S 1949- *BiDrAPA 89*
Rao, Kant Srikanth 1950- *WhoE 91*
Rao, Kantamsetti Venkata Rama Prabhakara 1947- *WhoWor 91*
Rao, Koneru Ramakrishna 1932- *EncPaPR 91*
Rao, Krishna Chavali Venkata Gopal 1937- *WhoE 91*
Rao, Kusuma S 1949- *BiDrAPA 89*
Rao, Lalitha K K *BiDrAPA 89*
Rao, Leela *BiDrAPA 89*
Rao, Leela S *BiDrAPA 89*
Rao, Leela Sadashiv 1941- *WhoE 91*
Rao, Madhu B *BiDrAPA 89*
Rao, Maya S *BiDrAPA 89*
Rao, Mulki Padupanambur Umanath 1939- *WhoWor 91*
Rao, Murali S. 1950- *WhoE 91*
Rao, Muralidhara S 1950- *BiDrAPA 89*
Rao, N. V. 1929- *WhoAm 90*
Rao, Nannapaneni Narayana *WhoAm 90*
Rao, Neerada 1939- *BiDrAPA 89*
Rao, Nyapati R 1952- *BiDrAPA 89*
Rao, P. V. Krishna 1947- *EncPaPR 91*
Rao, P. V. Narasimha 1921- *WhoWor 91*
Rao, Padmaja C *BiDrAPA 89*
Rao, Paul Peter 1899-1988 *BioIn 16*
Rao, Peter Alan 1959- *BiDrAPA 89*
Rao, Raja *BioIn 16*
Rao, Raja 1909- *MajTwCW*
Rao, Raja V 1947- *BiDrAPA 89*
Rao, Ramakrishna 1942- *BiDrAPA 89*
Rao, Ramesh P. 1944- *St&PR 91*
Rao, Santapuri D 1947- *BiDrAPA 89*
Rao, Shankararao N 1935- *BiDrAPA 89*
Rao, Shyamala B *BiDrAPA 89*
Rao, Srinivasa K *BiDrAPA 89*
Rao, Syamala K 1929- *BiDrAPA 89*
Rao, Tadikonda Lakshmi Kantha 1946- *WhoWor 91*
Rao, Takkallapelli *BiDrAPA 89*
Rao, Thota V *BiDrAPA 89*
Rao, Uma 1958- *BiDrAPA 89*
Raoufi, Mehdi 1952- *WhoSSW 91*
Rapaccioli, Michel Antoine 1934- *St&PR 91, WhoAm 90*
Rapacz, Richard Joseph 1942- *St&PR 91*
Rapakko, Timo Tapio 1957- *WhoWor 91*
Rapalje, Robert John, Sr. 1945- *WhoSSW 91*
Rapaport, David A. 1942- *St&PR 91*
Rapaport, David Alan 1942- *WhoAm 90*
Rapaport, Elyse Newman 1926- *WhoSSW 91*
Rapaport, Felix Theodosius 1929- *WhoAm 90, WhoWor 91*
Rapaport, Mark Hyman 1955- *BiDrAPA 89*
Rapaport, Robert M. 1931- *WhoAm 90*
Rapaport, Ronald L. 1945- *St&PR 91*
Rapaport, Rosemary 1918- *IntWWM 90*
Rapaport, Ross Jay 1950- *WhoEmL 91*
Rapaport, Samuel I. 1921- *WhoAm 90*
Rapawy, Walter 1944- *St&PR 91*
Rapee, Erno 1891-1945 *OxCPMus*
Raper, Charles Albert 1926- *WhoAm 90*
Raper, Kenneth B. 1908-1987 *BioIn 16*
Raper, Marion Eileen 1938- *IntWWM 90*
Raper, Roy Bruce 1952- *BiDrAPA 89*
Raper, William Burkette 1927- *WhoAm 90*
Rapf, Kurt 1922- *IntWWM 90*
Raphael *EncO&P 3*
Raphael *EncO&P 3*
Raphael 1483-1520 *BioIn 16, IntDcAA 90, WorAlBi*
Raphael 1795-1832 *EncO&P 3*
Raphael 1807-1837 *EncO&P 3*
Raphael 1820-1875 *EncO&P 3*
Raphael 1850-1923 *EncO&P 3*
Raphael, Albert Ash, Jr. 1925- *WhoAm 90*
Raphael, Antonietta 1900-1975 *BiDWomA*
Raphael, Beverley 1934- *BiDrAPA 89*
Raphael, Chaim *TwCCr&M 91*
Raphael, Chester M 1912- *BiDrAPA 89*
Raphael, Clara *EncCoWW*
Raphael, Coleman 1925- *St&PR 91, WhoAm 90*
Raphael, Dan Ambrose 1952- *WhoWrEP 89*
Raphael, Edwin *EncO&P 3*
Raphael, Frederic Michael 1931- *WhoAm 90*
Raphael, Louise Arakelian 1937- *WhoAmW 91, WhoE 91*
Raphael, Martin George 1946- *WhoEmL 91*
Raphael, Maryanne Jeanne D'Arc 1938- *WhoAmW 91*
Raphael, Morris Charles 1917- *WhoWrEP 89*
Raphael, Nan Helene 1955- *WhoE 91*
Raphael, Oriel 1939- *WhoAm 90*
Raphael, Phyllis 1937- *WhoWrEP 89*
Raphael, Raffaello Sanzio 1483-1520 *PenDiDA 89*
Raphael, Sally Jessy *BioIn 16*
Raphael, Sally Jessy 1943- *CurBio 90 [port]*
Raphael Mafai, Antonietta 1900-1975 *BioIn 16*
Raphaelson, Joel 1928- *WhoAm 90*
Raphanel, Ghilaine 1956- *IntWWM 90*
Raphel, Arnold Lewis 1943-1988 *BioIn 16*
Raphel, Gerald 1943- *St&PR 91*
Raphling, David L 1937- *BiDrAPA 89, WhoE 91*
Rapholz, James Lewis, II 1939- *St&PR 91*
Rapicavoli, Emanuele *BiDrAPA 89*
Rapidis, Alexander Demetrius 1948- *WhoWor 91*
Rapier, James Thomas 1837-1883 *BlkAmsC [port]*
Rapier, Pascal Moran 1914- *WhoWor 91*
Rapin, Aimee 1860?- *BiDWomA*
Rapin, Isabelle 1927- *WhoAm 90, WhoAmW 91*
Rapin, Lynn Suzanne 1946- *WhoEmL 91*
Rapinchuk, Jane *BiDrAPA 89*
Rapisarda, Antonino 1923- *BiDrAPA 89*
Rapkin, Chester 1918- *BioIn 16*
Rapkin, Robert M 1940- *BiDrAPA 89*
Rapkin, Robert Michael 1940- *WhoE 91*
Raponi, David Francis 1951- *WhoE 91*
Rapoport, Anatol 1911- *WhoAm 90*
Rapoport, Bernard 1917- *St&PR 91, WhoAm 90*

Rapoport, Bernard Robert 1919- *WhoAm 90*
Rapoport, Daniel 1933- *WhoAm 90, WhoWrEP 89*
Rapoport, Janis 1946- *FemiCLE*
Rapoport, Judith 1933- *WhoAmW 91*
Rapoport, Judith L 1933- *BiDrAPA 89*
Rapoport, Louis *BioIn 16*
Rapoport, Mitchell J. 1950- *St&PR 91*
Rapoport, Morton I. 1934- *WhoAm 90*
Rapoport, Naftalie *BiDrAPA 89*
Rapoport, Nancy L. 1945- *St&PR 91*
Rapoport, Ram Wesley 1937- *BiDrAPA 89*
Rapoport, Ronald Jon 1940- *WhoAm 90*
Rapoport, Sonya *WhoAmA 91*
Rapoport-Levy, Susan Marilyn 1950- *WhoAmW 91, WhoE 91*
Raposeiro, Carlos Alberto 1935- *WhoWor 91*
Raposo, Joseph 1938-1989 *AnObit 1989*
Raposo, Joseph G. 1937-1989 *BioIn 16*
Raposo, Joseph Guilherme 1938-1989 *SmATA 61*
Raposo, Sue Nordlund 1936- *WhoWor 91*
Rapp, C. J. *BioIn 16*
Rapp, Christian F. 1933- *St&PR 91, WhoSSW 91*
Rapp, Dorothy Glaves 1943- *WhoAmW 91*
Rapp, Fred 1929- *WhoAm 90, WhoWor 91*
Rapp, George 1757-1847 *WorAlBi*
Rapp, George, Jr. 1930- *ConAu 130*
Rapp, George Robert 1930- *BioIn 16*
Rapp, George Robert, Jr. 1930- *WhoAm 90*
Rapp, Gerald Duane 1933- *St&PR 91, WhoAm 90, WhoWor 91*
Rapp, Goldie 1892-1966 *Ballpl 90*
Rapp, Ilana Beth 1968- *WhoE 91*
Rapp, James Partick 1947- *St&PR 91*
Rapp, John Buswell 1936- *St&PR 91*
Rapp, Larry P. 1948- *St&PR 91*
Rapp, Lea Bayers 1946- *ODwPR 91, WhoE 91, WhoWrEP 89*
Rapp, Lois *WhoAmA 91*
Rapp, Lois 1907- *WhoE 91*
Rapp, Martha Brune 1950- *WhoAmW 91*
Rapp, Paul Ernest 1949- *WhoE 91*
Rapp, Richard Phillip 1928- *St&PR 91*
Rapp, Richard Tilden 1944- *WhoAm 90*
Rapp, Robert Anthony 1934- *WhoAm 90*
Rapp, Robert Cullen, Jr. 1926- *St&PR 91*
Rapp, Robert David 1950- *WhoWor 91*
Rapp, Sue Carol Storer 1939- *WhoAmW 91*
Rapp, William Edward 1924- *St&PR 91*
Rappa, James E *BiDrAPA 89*
Rappacioli, Fernando Chamorro *BioIn 16*
Rappaport, Andrew S. *BioIn 16*
Rappaport, Bernard S 1943- *BiDrAPA 89*
Rappaport, David *BioIn 16*
Rappaport, David *NewYTBS 90*
Rappaport, Earle Samuel, Jr. 1935- *WhoAm 90*
Rappaport, Fred 1912- *WhoAmA 91*
Rappaport, Gary B. 1937- *St&PR 91*
Rappaport, Gary Burton 1937- *WhoAm 90*
Rappaport, Gary Dennis 1950- *St&PR 91*
Rappaport, Irving 1923- *WhoE 91*
Rappaport, Irwin 1932- *St&PR 91*
Rappaport, Jeffrey A. 1961- *ODwPR 91*
Rappaport, Jonathan Charles 1947- *IntWWM 90*
Rappaport, Leonard *BioIn 16*
Rappaport, Margaret M. 1947- *WhoAmW 91, WhoE 91*
Rappaport, Martin Paul 1935- *WhoAm 90, WhoSSW 91*
Rappaport, Maurice 1926- *BiDrAPA 89*
Rappaport, Michael 1941- *St&PR 91*
Rappaport, Michael S 1949- *BiDrAPA 89*
Rappaport, Richard G 1936- *BiDrAPA 89*
Rappaport, Richard Lawrence 1949- *St&PR 91*
Rappaport, Ronnie Sue 1945- *WhoE 91*
Rappaport, Roy Abraham 1926- *WhoAm 90*
Rappaport, Steve Lee 1948- *WhoE 91*
Rappaport, Steven N. 1948- *St&PR 91, WhoAm 90*
Rappaport, Susan Lisic 1957- *WhoE 91*
Rappaport, Sydelle Leah 1946- *WhoE 91*
Rappaport, Sydney Charles 1919-1988 *BioIn 16*
Rappaport, Yvonne Kindinger 1928- *WhoWor 91*
Rappaport, Zvi Harry 1949- *WhoWor 91*
Rapparlie, Evalyn Barbara 1931- *WhoSSW 91*
Rappe, Kristine Ann 1956- *WhoEmL 91*
Rappeport, Jonas R 1924- *BiDrAPA 89*
Rappleye, Richard K. 1940- *St&PR 91*
Rappolt, William Carl 1945- *WhoAm 90*
Rappoport, Irving Barnett 1917- *St&PR 91*
Rappoport, Kenneth E. *WhoAm 90*
Rappoport, Stanley D. 1930- *St&PR 91*
Rapport, Bruce Michael 1958- *WhoEmL 91*
Rapport, Daniel John 1958- *BiDrAPA 89*
Rapport, Robert 1953- *WhoWor 91*
Rapport, Robin Schuman 1954- *WhoAmW 91*
Rappuhn, Debbie Lynn 1956- *WhoSSW 91*
Rapsomanikis, Antonis 1937- *WhoWor 91*
Rapson, William Howard 1912- *WhoAm 90*
Raquel, Edward M. *WhoHisp 91*
Rare Earth *EncPR&S 89*
Rarick, Jeanne Tosh 1944- *WhoAmW 91*
Rariden, Bill 1888-1942 *Ballpl 90*
Raridon, Richard Jay 1931- *WhoAm 90*
Ras, Zbigniew Wieslaw 1947- *WhoSSW 91*
Ras Romani, Khalil Hassan 1947- *WhoWor 91*
Ras-Work, Terrefe 1936- *WhoWor 91*
Rasala, Malcolm 1946- *WhoWor 91*
Rasalam, Livingstone A *BiDrAPA 89*
Rasalilananda, Gurudev Sri 1931- *WhoWor 91*
Rasanen, Eric Konrad 1946- *St&PR 91*
Rasbach, James Harrison 1932- *St&PR 91*
Rasberry, Sharol Barta 1947- *WhoAmW 91*
Rascals, The *EncPR&S 89*
Rascel, Renato *AuBYP 90*
Rasch, Ellen Myrberg 1927- *WhoAmW 91*
Rasch, Emil Otto 1891-1948 *BioIn 16*
Rasch, Robert Wallace 1947- *WhoAm 90*
Rasch, Robert William 1926- *WhoSSW 91*
Rasch, Rudolf Alexander 1945- *IntWWM 90*
Rasche, Robert Harold 1941- *WhoAm 90*
Rascher, Sigurd 1907- *PenDiMP*
Raschi, Vic 1919- *Ballpl 90*
Raschi, Vic 1919-1988 *BioIn 16*
Raschka, Leslie B *BiDrAPA 89*
Raschko, Patrick P. 1940- *St&PR 91*
Rasco, Francine *BiDrAPA 89*
Rascoe, Burton 1892-1957 *LiHiK*
Rascoe, E Marston 1935- *BiDrAPA 89*
Rascoe, Eric 1932- *St&PR 91*
Rascoe, Stephen Thomas 1924- *WhoAmA 91*
Rascon, Armando 1956- *WhoAmA 91*
Raser, Keith Ann 1959- *BiDrAPA 89*
Rash, Bryson Brennan 1913- *WhoAm 90*
Rash, Harold Stephen 1945- *WhoSSW 91*
Rash, Maloy Ray, Jr. 1922- *St&PR 91*
Rash, Millisa Shoun 1963- *WhoEmL 91*
Rash, Nancy 1940- *WhoAmA 91*
Rash, Nancy Batson Nisbet 1940- *WhoE 91*
Rash, Richard Dale 1958- *St&PR 91*
Rash, Steven Britton 1947- *WhoSSW 91*
Rash, Wayne, Jr. 1948- *WhoE 91*
Rashad, Ahmad *BioIn 16*
Rashad, Ahmad 1949- *WhoAm 90*
Rashad, Phylicia *BioIn 16, WhoAm 90*
Rashad, Phylicia 1948- *DrBlPA 90, WorAlBi*
Rasheed, Abdul M. A. 1953- *WhoSSW 91*
Rasheed, Turki Faisal 1954- *WhoWor 91*
Rasher, Arthur Albert 1948- *WhoSSW 91*
Rashford, Nicholas Seamus 1940- *WhoAm 90, WhoE 91*
Rashid Bin Said Al Maktum 1912- *PolLCME*
Rashid bin Said Al-Maktum, Sheikh 1914- *WhoWor 91*
Rashid ibn Ahmad Al-Mualla, Sheikh 1930- *WhoWor 91*
Rashid, Kenneth D 1935- *BiDrAPA 89*
Rashid, Mohammed Mohsen 1951- *WhoWor 91*
Rashid, Zafar 1950- *WhoAm 90*
Rashid Rida, Muhammad 1865-1935 *BioIn 16*
Rashilla, Richard James, Jr. 1959- *WhoEmL 91*
Rashish, Myer 1924- *WhoAm 90*
Rashkes, Moshe 1928- *WhoWor 91*
Rashkis, Harold A 1920- *BiDrAPA 89*
Rashkis, Shirley R *BiDrAPA 89*
Rashkow, Ronald 1940- *WhoAm 90*
Rashmir, Lewis P. 1925- *St&PR 91*
Rashti, Charlotte Sidney 1962- *WhoE 91*
Rashvand, Habib Falari 1946- *WhoWor 91*
Rasi, Humberto Mario 1935- *WhoAm 90*
Rasiah, Lakshman W *BiDrAPA 89*
Rasic, Elizabeth *BioIn 16*
Rasiej, K. Steve 1926- *St&PR 91*
Rasile, John Anthony 1937- *St&PR 91*
Rasin, Grigory S. *BiDrAPA 89*
Rasin, Rudolph Stephen 1930- *WhoAm 90*
Rask, Hans Christian 1948- *WhoWor 91*
Rask, Kolleen Joanne 1960- *WhoE 91*
Rask, Michael Raymond 1930- *WhoAm 90, WhoWor 91*
Raska, Ruth H 1912- *BiDrAPA 89*
Raskai, Lea 14--?-15--? *EncCoWW*
Raskas, Heschel J. 1941- *St&PR 91*
Raskevicius, V. Leo 1936- *St&PR 91*
Raskin, Abraham Henry 1911- *WhoAm 90*
Raskin, Barbara 1935- *ConAu 129*
Raskin, David 1937- *BiDrAPA 89*
Raskin, David Edward 1938- *BiDrAPA 89*
Raskin, Edith Lefkowitz 1908- *AuBYP 90*
Raskin, Ellen 1928- *WhoWrEP 89*
Raskin, Florence Braaf 1957- *WhoAmW 91*
Raskin, Fred Charles 1948- *St&PR 91, WhoAm 90*
Raskin, Jack 1935- *BiDrAPA 89*
Raskin, Judith 1928-1984 *PenDiMP*
Raskin, Marcus Goodman 1934- *WhoAm 90*
Raskin, Marjorie Jane *BiDrAPA 89*
Raskin, Michael A. 1925- *WhoAm 90*
Raskin, Norman 1923- *BiDrAPA 89*
Raskin, Raymond A 1921- *BiDrAPA 89*
Raskin, Rubin 1918- *St&PR 91*
Raskin, Susan M. *ODwPR 91*
Raskin, Valerie Davis 1958- *BiDrAPA 89*
Raskin, Walter 1913- *St&PR 91*
Raskind, Leo Joseph 1919- *WhoAm 90*
Raskind, Murray Albert 1942- *BiDrAPA 89*
Raskind, Philis *WhoAmA 91*
Rasko, Maximilian A 1884-1961 *WhoAmA 91N*
Rasky, Harry 1928- *ConAu 31NR, WhoAm 90*
Rasley, Alicia Todd 1955- *WhoWrEP 89*
Rasmus, John Avery 1954- *WhoAm 90*
Rasmuson, Edward Bernard 1940- *WhoAm 90*
Rasmuson, Elmer Edwin 1909- *WhoAm 90, WhoWor 91*
Rasmussen, Anna 1898- *EncO&P 3*
Rasmussen, Anton J. *BioIn 16*
Rasmussen, Anton Jesse 1942- *WhoAmA 91*
Rasmussen, Arthur E. 1922- *St&PR 91*
Rasmussen, C.F. *St&PR 91*
Rasmussen, Caren Nancy 1950- *WhoAmW 91*
Rasmussen, Carl John 1948- *WhoEmL 91*
Rasmussen, Catherine Ann 1953- *WhoEmL 91*
Rasmussen, Craig Paul 1950- *WhoE 91*
Rasmussen, D. Scott 1958- *WhoE 91*
Rasmussen, Dale L. 1950- *St&PR 91*
Rasmussen, David George 1943- *WhoAm 90*
Rasmussen, Dennis 1959- *Ballpl 90*
Rasmussen, Dennis Loy 1940- *WhoSSW 91*
Rasmussen, Eric 1952- *Ballpl 90*
Rasmussen, Eric Christian 1960- *WhoWor 91*
Rasmussen, Evie Webb 1952- *WhoAmW 91*
Rasmussen, Gerald Elmer 1935- *WhoE 91*
Rasmussen, Glen Edwin 1949- *St&PR 91*
Rasmussen, Halfdan 1915- *DcScanL*
Rasmussen, Harry Paul 1939- *WhoAm 90*
Rasmussen, Henning Bro 1924- *IntWWM 90*
Rasmussen, Jay A. 1928- *St&PR 91*
Rasmussen, John Atwell 1946- *WhoSSW 91*
Rasmussen, John Oscar 1926- *WhoAm 90*
Rasmussen, Jorgen 1931- *ConDes 90*
Rasmussen, Julie Shimmon 1940- *WhoAmW 91, WhoWor 91*
Rasmussen, Karl Aage 1947- *IntWWM 90*
Rasmussen, Kathleen Anne 1958- *WhoAmW 91, WhoSSW 91*
Rasmussen, Keith George 1928- *St&PR 91*
Rasmussen, Keith George, Jr. *BiDrAPA 89*
Rasmussen, Knud 1879-1933 *WorAlBi*
Rasmussen, Louis Charles 1928- *St&PR 91, WhoAm 90*
Rasmussen, Mervin J. 1928- *St&PR 91*
Rasmussen, Milton P. *BioIn 16*
Rasmussen, Mogens Munk 1941- *WhoWor 91*
Rasmussen, Neal Charles 1936- *St&PR 91*
Rasmussen, Nicholas Roberts 1946- *St&PR 91*
Rasmussen, Norman Carl 1927- *WhoAm 90*
Rasmussen, Peter G. 1954- *St&PR 91*
Rasmussen, Richard Frank 1935- *St&PR 91*
Rasmussen, Richard Jones 1940- *St&PR 91*
Rasmussen, Richard Robert 1946- *WhoEmL 91*
Rasmussen, Robert N. 1930- *St&PR 91*
Rasmussen, Robert Norman *WhoAmA 91*
Rasmussen, Scott William 1956- *WhoWor 91*
Rasmussen, Steen Eiler 1898-1990 *ConAu 132*
Rasmussen, Stephen S. 1952- *St&PR 91*
Rasmussen, Steven Alan *BiDrAPA 89*
Rasmussen, Stuart Ricard 1906- *WhoWor 91*
Rasmussen, Thomas Val, Jr. 1954- *WhoWor 91*
Rasmussen, Timothy Richard *BiDrAPA 89*
Rasmussen, Victor Philip, Jr. 1950- *WhoWor 91*
Rasmussen, Warren W. 1930- *St&PR 91*
Rasmusson, Eugene Martin 1929- *WhoE 91*
Rasmusson, Joseph Gabriel 1957- *St&PR 91*
Rasnic, Carol Daugherty 1941- *WhoSSW 91*
Raso, Margaret Mildred 1933- *WhoE 91*
Rasoaherina *WomWR*
Rasool, Shama *BiDrAPA 89*
Rasor, Dina Lynn 1956- *WhoAm 90*
Rasor, Doris Lee 1929- *WhoAmW 91*
Rasor, Garry Girard 1943- *WhoSSW 91*
Rasor, John C. 1932- *ODwPR 91*
Rasor, Richard Drew 1939- *St&PR 91*
Rasor, Robert L. 1922- *St&PR 91*
Rasor, Robert W 1911- *BiDrAPA 89*
Rasoumovsky, Andrey Kyrilovich *PenDiMP*
Raspante, Anthony *St&PR 91*
Raspberry, J. H. *BioIn 16*
Raspberry, William James 1935- *WhoAm 90*
Rasper, Deborah Young 1950- *WhoAmW 91*
Rasporich, Anthony Walter 1940- *WhoAm 90*
Rasputin, Grigori 1873?-1916 *WorAlBi*
Rasputin, Grigorii Efimovich 1871-1916 *BioIn 16*
Rasputin, Grigory Efimovitch 1871?-1916 *EncO&P 3*
Rass, Rebecca Rivka 1936- *WhoWrEP 89*
Rassbach, Herbert David 1944- *WhoAm 90*
Rasschaert, E.H. *St&PR 91*
Rassekh, Hormoz 1928- *BiDrAPA 89*
Rassias, Themistocles M. 1951- *WhoWor 91*
Rassier, Donald B. 1929- *WhoAm 90*
Rassieur, Charles L. 1931- *St&PR 91*
Rassin, Barry Jonathan 1947- *WhoWor 91*
Rassin, David Keith 1942- *WhoSSW 91*
Rassman, Joel H. 1945- *WhoE 91*
Rassmann, Michael 1936- *WhoAm 90*
Rassnick, Leopold S. 1939- *WhoAm 90*
Rasssem, Mohammed Hassan 1922- *WhoWor 91*
Rast, Gary Fischer 1935- *St&PR 91*
Rast, Mendel Walker 1935- *St&PR 91, WhoAm 90*
Rast, Walter, Jr. 1944- *WhoSSW 91*
Rastall, George Richard 1940- *IntWWM 90*
Rastegar, Farzad Ali 1956- *WhoE 91*
Rastegar, Nader Esmail 1953- *WhoSSW 91*
Rastiello, Michael Kenneth 1921- *WhoE 91*
Rastogi, Anil Kumar 1942- *WhoAm 90*
Rastogi, Kamal Raj *BiDrAPA 89*
Rastogi, Santosh Kumar 1942- *BiDrAPA 89*
Rastrick, Frederick James 1819?-1897 *DcCanB 12*
Rasul, Mujahid *BiDrAPA 89*
Rasulala, Thalmus 1939- *ConTFT 8, DrBlPA 90*
Ratajczak, Helen Vosskuhler 1938- *WhoAmW 91*
Ratajczak, Henryk 1932- *WhoWor 91*
Ratajski, Magda A. 1950- *St&PR 91*
Ratajski, Magda Anne 1950- *WhoSSW 91*
Ratalahti, Heikki *NewYTBS 90*
Ratanakorn, Prasop *BiDrAPA 89*
Ratch, Jerry 1944- *WhoWrEP 89*
Ratchford, Maria P. 1959- *ODwPR 91*
Ratchford, Paul Courtney 1955- *St&PR 91*
Ratchford, Thomas C. 1949- *St&PR 91*
Ratcliff, Carter 1941- *WhoAmA 91*
Ratcliff, David L. 1938- *St&PR 91*
Ratcliff, Gene A. 1930- *St&PR 91*
Ratcliff, Gene Austin 1930- *WhoAm 90*
Ratcliff, H.C. 1944- *St&PR 91*
Ratcliff, Hugh Chalfant, Jr. 1944- *WhoAm 90*
Ratcliff, Joseph Gary 1948- *WhoSSW 91*
Ratcliff, Suellen 1956- *WhoAmW 91*
Ratcliff, Thomas J. *WhoAm 90*
Ratcliff, Walter A. 1930- *St&PR 91*
Ratcliffe, Ann Elizabeth 1963- *WhoAmW 91*
Ratcliffe, C. Kenneth 1920- *St&PR 91*
Ratcliffe, Desmond Hayward 1917- *IntWWM 90*
Ratcliffe, George Jackson, Jr. 1936- *St&PR 91, WhoAm 90, WhoE 91*
Ratcliffe, James P. *MajTwCW*
Ratcliffe, John A. 1939- *St&PR 91*
Ratcliffe, Kathleen Mary 1958- *WhoAmW 91*
Ratcliffe, Myron Fenwick 1902- *St&PR 91*
Ratcliffe, Shirley Pendleton 1932- *WhoAmW 91*
Ratcliffe, Thomas Edward 1911-1988 *BioIn 16*
Rateau, Armand-Albert 1882-1938 *PenDiDA 89*
Rateaver, Bargyla 1916- *WhoWrEP 89*
Ratey, John Joseph *BiDrAPA 89*

Ratey, John Joseph 1948- *WhoE 91*
Rath, Alan T *WhoAmA 91*
Rath, Alfred Gary 1946- *St&PR 91*
Rath, Antoinette Petrillo 1959- *WhoE 91*
Rath, Bernard Emil 1949- *WhoAm 90*
Rath, David 1950- *WhoEmL 91*
Rath, Francis Steven 1955- *WhoE 91, WhoEmL 91, WhoWor 91*
Rath, George Edward 1913- *WhoAm 90*
Rath, Gerald Fred 1943- *WhoAm 90*
Rath, Hildegard *WhoAmA 91*
Rath, Hildegard 1909- *WhoAm 90*
Rath, John Frederic 1946- *IntWWM 90*
Rath, Lillian Victoria 1952- *WhoAmW 91*
Rath, Linda Lorraine 1953- *WhoSSW 91*
Rath, Loretta Ann 1949- *St&PR 91*
Rath, Mari Kaye 1958- *WhoAmW 91*
Rath, Morrie 1886-1945 *Ballpl 90*
Rath, R. John 1910- *WhoAm 90, WhoWor 91*
Rath, Sura Prasad 1950- *WhoSSW 91, WhoWor 91*
Rath, Theodore A. 1904-1989 *BioIn 16*
Rath, Thomas David 1945- *WhoAm 90, WhoE 91*
Rath, Vicky 1952- *St&PR 91*
Rathana-Nakintara, Thaworn 1933- *BiDrAPA 89*
Rathblott, Paul L. 1940- *St&PR 91*
Rathblott, Paul Leon 1940- *WhoAm 90*
Rathbone, Basil 1892-1967 *BioIn 16, WorAlBi*
Rathbone, Donald Earl 1929- *WhoAm 90, WhoWor 91*
Rathbone, Eleanor 1872-1946 *FemiCLE*
Rathbone, Hannah Mary 1798-1878 *FemiCLE*
Rathbone, Isabel Servici 1954- *BiDrAPA 89*
Rathbone, Julian 1935- *TwCCr&M 91*
Rathbone, Perry Townsend 1911- *WhoAm 90, WhoAmA 91*
Rathbun, Benjamin Franklin 1928- *WhoE 91*
Rathbun, Henry Tompkins 1922- *WhoAm 90*
Rathbun, James Ronald 1934- *IntWWM 90*
Rathbun, Jennifer Mary *BiDrAPA 89*
Rathbun, John Malcolm 1946- *BiDrAPA 89*
Rathbun, John Wilbert 1924- *WhoAm 90*
Rathbun, Larry Ray 1938- *St&PR 91*
Rathbun, Linda S. 1947- *St&PR 91*
Rathbun, William A. *ODwPR 91*
Rathbun, William Jay 1931- *WhoAmA 91*
Rathburn, Robert Richard 1947- *WhoSSW 91*
Rathe, Alex Werner 1912- *WhoAm 90*
Rathe, R.J. 1928- *St&PR 91*
Rathenau, Emil 1838-1915 *WorAlBi*
Rathenau, Walther 1867-1922 *BioIn 16*
Rather, Dan *BioIn 16*
Rather, Dan 1931- *WhoAm 90, WhoE 91, WorAlBi*
Rather, Gordon Smeade, Jr. 1939- *WhoSSW 91*
Rather, John Daniel 1823-1910 *AmLegL*
Rather, Lelland Joseph 1913- *WhoAm 90*
Rather, Lucia Porcher Johnson 1934- *WhoAm 90*
Rathert, Fred 1924- *St&PR 91*
Rathfelder, Mary L. 1932- *WhoAmW 91*
Rathgeber, Juergen Oskar 1938- *St&PR 91*
Rathgeber, Mark Edwin 1959- *BiDrAPA 89*
Rathgen, Gunther H. 1928- *WhoWor 91*
Rathje, Frank C. 1924- *St&PR 91*
Rathje, Judy Christine 1952- *WhoAmW 91*
Rathje, Rhonda Jean 1958- *WhoAmW 91*
Rathjens, George William 1925- *WhoAm 90*
Rathke, Debra Ann 1953- *WhoAmW 91*
Rathke, Sheila Wells 1943- *WhoAmW 91*
Rathke, Wayne George 1931- *St&PR 91*
Rathkolb, Oliver Robert 1955- *WhoWor 91*
Rathkopf, Steven *BioIn 16*
Rathle, Henri 1911- *WhoAmA 91*
Rathle, Jacques M *BiDrAPA 89*
Rathman, George H. 1941- *St&PR 91*
Rathman, William Ernest 1927- *WhoAm 90*
Rathmann, George Blatz 1927- *WhoAm 90*
Rathmell, Aretta J 1938- *BiDrAPA 89*
Rathmell, Robert Day 1942- *St&PR 91*
Rathnam, Lincoln Yesu 1949- *WhoE 91*
Rathore, Uma Pandey 1950- *WhoWor 91*
Rathvon, Henry *BioIn 16*
Rathwell, Peter John 1943- *WhoAm 90*
Rati, Robert Dean 1939- *WhoWor 91*
Ratican, Peter J. 1943- *St&PR 91*
Ratican, Peter Jay 1943- *WhoAm 90*
Ratick-Stroud, Sheri 1947- *WhoSSW 91*
Ratico, Helen Louise 1950- *BiDrAPA 89*
Ratiu, Indrei Stephen Pilkington 1946- *WhoWor 91*
Ratiu, Ion 1917- *WhoWor 91*
Ratkai, George 1907- *WhoAmA 91*
Ratke, Donald *BiDrAPA 89*
Ratkewitch, Samuel 1945- *St&PR 91*
Ratliff, Brenda Myers *BiDrAPA 89*
Ratliff, Cecil Wayne 1946- *WhoAm 90, WhoWor 91*
Ratliff, Charles Edward, Jr. 1926- *WhoAm 90*
Ratliff, Donald Lewis 1953- *WhoSSW 91*
Ratliff, Donna Lee 1946- *WhoAmW 91*
Ratliff, Floyd 1919- *WhoAm 90*
Ratliff, Henry Wesley 1947- *BiDrAPA 89*
Ratliff, Leigh Ann 1961- *WhoAmW 91, WhoWor 91*
Ratliff, Marielon Elaine Tatum 1947- *WhoSSW 91*
Ratliff, Maurice Adrian 1931- *IntWWM 90*
Ratliff, Mike Robert 1934- *St&PR 91*
Ratliff, Robin Anne 1953- *WhoE 91*
Ratliff, William D., III 1949- *WhoEmL 91*
Ratliff, William Durrah, Jr. 1921- *WhoAm 90, WhoSSW 91*
Ratnakar, Aspari 1941- *WhoWor 91*
Ratnam, Dasari V 1938- *BiDrAPA 89*
Ratnavale, David N 1928- *BiDrAPA 89*
Ratner, Albert B. 1927- *St&PR 91, WhoAm 90*
Ratner, Carl N. 1943- *St&PR 91*
Ratner, David Louis 1931- *WhoAm 90*
Ratner, David M 1922- *WhoAmA 91*
Ratner, Gerald 1913- *WhoAm 90*
Ratner, Harold 1927- *WhoE 91*
Ratner, Jerald H 1944- *BiDrAPA 89*
Ratner, Joel H. 1938- *St&PR 91*
Ratner, Jonathan 1948- *WhoE 91*
Ratner, Joseph Stuart 1944- *BiDrAPA 89*
Ratner, Leonard Gilbert 1916- *IntWWM 90*
Ratner, Lillian Gross 1932- *WhoAmW 91, WhoE 91*
Ratner, Mark Alan 1942- *WhoAm 90*
Ratner, Max 1907- *St&PR 91*
Ratner, Michael Howard 1942- *St&PR 91*
Ratner, Milton Dunne 1918- *WhoAm 90*
Ratner, Paul 1936- *St&PR 91*
Ratner, Phillip 1944- *St&PR 91*
Ratner, Richard A 1941- *BiDrAPA 89*
Ratner, Robert J. 1950- *St&PR 91*
Ratner, Robert S. 1941- *St&PR 91*
Ratner, Rochelle 1948- *WhoWrEP 89*
Ratner, Sabina Teller 1931- *IntWWM 90*
Ratner, Sidney 1908- *WhoE 91*
Ratner-Gantshar, Barbara Grace 1933- *WhoAmW 91*
Ratnoff, Oscar Davis 1916- *WhoAm 90*
Ratoff, Steven Bernard 1942- *St&PR 91, WhoAm 90*
Ratsiraka, Didier 1936- *WhoWor 91*
Ratt *EncPR&S 89*
Rattan, Pradeep 1949- *BiDrAPA 89*
Rattansi, Pyarally Mohamedally 1930- *WhoWor 91*
Rattazzi, William R. 1950- *St&PR 91*
Ratte, Rena J 1928- *EncO&P 3*
Rattee, David A. 1942- *St&PR 91*
Rattee, Michael Dennis 1953- *WhoWrEP 89*
Ratter, Jack 1925- *St&PR 91*
Ratterman, David Burger 1946- *WhoAm 90*
Ratterree, Tina Gaye 1963- *WhoAmW 91*
Ratti, Eugenia 1933- *IntWWM 90*
Ratti, Giovanni Agostino *PenDiDA 89*
Ratti, Ronald Andrew 1948- *WhoAm 90*
Rattigan, Terence 1911-1977 *MajTwCW*
Rattigan, Terence Mervyn 1911- *WorAlBi*
Rattle, Simon *BioIn 16*
Rattle, Simon 1955- *IntWWM 90, PenDiMP, WhoAm 90, WhoWor 91*
Rattley, Jessie Menifield 1929- *WhoAmW 91, WhoSSW 91*
Rattner, Abraham 1895-1978 *WhoAmA 91N*
Rattner, Bernard 1914- *BiDrAPA 89*
Rattner, Steven *BioIn 16*
Rattner, Steven Lawrence 1952- *WhoAm 90*
Rattner, William Edward 1936- *WhoAm 90*
Ratto, Eugene Joseph 1926- *St&PR 91, WhoAm 90*
Rattoballi, James Philip 1942- *St&PR 91*
Rattray, Douglas C. 1944- *St&PR 91*
Rattray, Maurice, Jr. 1922- *WhoAm 90*
Rattray, Simon *TwCCr&M 91*
Ratty, Tess McBride 1944- *WhoAmW 91*
Ratushinskaia, Irina 1954- *EncCoWW*
Ratushinskaya, Irina *BioIn 16*
Ratushinskaya, Irina 1954- *ConAu 129, WorAu 1980 [port]*
Ratz, Steve 1920- *St&PR 91*
Ratzel, Friedrich 1844-1904 *BioIn 16*
Ratzenberg, Irving 1928- *St&PR 91*
Ratzenberger, John 1947- *WorAlBi*
Ratzenberger, John Dezso 1947- *WhoAm 90*
Ratzer, Steve 1953- *BioIn 16*
Ratzinger, Joseph *BioIn 16*
Ratzinger, Joseph Alois 1927- *WhoWor 91*
Ratzka, Arthur L 1869- *WhoAmA 91N*
Ratzke, Dietrich 1939- *WhoWor 91*
Ratzlaff, Alvin Joseph *BiDrAPA 89*
Ratzlaff, David Edward 1938- *WhoSSW 91*
Ratzlaff, James W. 1936- *St&PR 91*
Ratzlaff, Stanley A. 1935- *St&PR 91*
Ratzlaff, Stanley Abe 1935- *WhoAm 90*
Rau, Adolf Wilhelm Ludwig 1922- *WhoWor 91*
Rau, Alfred 1927- *WhoAm 90*
Rau, Bruce William *BiDrAPA 89*
Rau, David Edward 1956- *WhoAm 90*
Rau, Doug 1948- *Ballpl 90*
Rau, James P. 1943- *St&PR 91*
Rau, John Edward 1948- *St&PR 91, WhoAm 90*
Rau, Lawrence M. 1931- *St&PR 91*
Rau, Lee Arthur 1940- *WhoAm 90*
Rau, Michael Curtis *BioIn 16*
Rau, Naraharisetty L *BiDrAPA 89*
Rau, Ralph Ronald 1920- *WhoAm 90*
Rau, Raymond Lewis 1918- *BiDrAPA 89*
Rau, Robert N. 1927- *St&PR 91*
Rau, William R 1874- *WhoAmA 91N*
Raub, Frieda Wright 1912- *WhoAmW 91*
Raub, Kim P. 1953- *St&PR 91*
Raub, Margaret Jane 1948- *WhoAmW 91*
Raub, William Fine 1939- *WhoAm 90*
Rauba, Raymond E. 1925- *St&PR 91*
Raubitschek, Isabelle Kelly 1914-1988 *BioIn 16*
Rauch, Abraham M. 1919- *St&PR 91*
Rauch, Alfred 1902- *St&PR 91*
Rauch, Charles Davis 1955- *St&PR 91*
Rauch, Charles Frederick, Jr. 1925- *WhoE 91*
Rauch, Charles Joseph 1922- *St&PR 91*
Rauch, Dale Eugene *BiDrAPA 89*
Rauch, Dudley Atkins 1941- *St&PR 91*
Rauch, Ellen Christine 1950- *WhoE 91*
Rauch, Francis Clyde 1938- *St&PR 91*
Rauch, Frank W. 1935- *St&PR 91*
Rauch, George Washington 1919- *WhoAm 90*
Rauch, Harry Ben 1954- *BiDrAPA 89*
Rauch, Herbert Emil 1935- *WhoAm 90*
Rauch, Irmengard 1933- *WhoAm 90, WhoWrEP 89*
Rauch, John G 1890-1976 *WhoAmA 91N*
Rauch, John Harold 1930- *WhoAm 90*
Rauch, John Keiser, Jr. 1930- *WhoAm 90*
Rauch, Joseph B 1965- *ConAu 131*
Rauch, Kathleen 1951- *WhoAmW 91*
Rauch, Lawrence Lee 1919- *WhoAm 90*
Rauch, Lillian H. 1925- *St&PR 91*
Rauch, Lillian Shapero *BioIn 16*
Rauch, Marshall Arthur 1923- *WhoSSW 91*
Rauch, Mary Laurissa 1952- *WhoAmW 91*
Rauch, Melvin *St&PR 91*
Rauch, Paul David 1933- *WhoAm 90, WhoWor 91*
Rauch, Richard A. 1929- *St&PR 91*
Rauch, Roxane Spiller 1935- *WhoAmW 91*
Rauch, Rudolph Stewart, III 1943- *WhoAm 90*
Rauch, Scott Laurence *BiDrAPA 89*
Rauch, Stuart Jay *BiDrAPA 89*
Rauch, Tom *BioIn 16*
Raucheisen, Michael *PenDiMP*
Raucher, Herman 1928- *WhoAm 90, WhoE 91*
Rauchle, Craig William 1955- *St&PR 91*
Raudenbush, Bryan Claude 1968- *WhoEmL 91*
Raudive, Konstantin 1909-1974 *EncO&P 3, EncPaPR 91*
Raue, David Philip 1953- *WhoWor 91*
Raue, Jorg Emil 1936- *WhoAm 90*
Rauenhorst, John *BiDrAPA 89*
Rauf, Barbara Claire 1944- *WhoAmA 91*
Rauf, Robert Charles, Sr. 1944- *WhoSSW 91*
Raufaste, Noel Jean 1941- *WhoE 91*
Raugust, Thomas Anthony 1935- *St&PR 91*
Rauh, B. Michael, Jr. *ODwPR 91*
Rauh, Carl Stephen 1940- *WhoAm 90*
Rauh, John David 1932- *WhoAm 90*
Rauh, Joseph L., Jr. 1911- *WhoAm 90*
Rauh, Richard *St&PR 91*
Rauh, Richard Paul 1948- *WhoEmL 91, WhoWor 91*
Rauh, Thomas Richard 1949- *WhoE 91*
Rauhe, Hermann Wilhelm 1930- *IntWWM 90*
Raul, Alan Charles 1954- *WhoAm 90, WhoEmL 91*
Raulee, Marcus *St&PR 91*
Raulerson, Sylvia Steven 1945- *WhoSSW 91*
Raulinaitis, Pranas Algis 1927- *WhoAm 90*
Raullerson, Calvin Henry 1920- *WhoAm 90*
Raulston, Gilbert Warner 1958- *BiDrAPA 89*
Raulston, J. C. *BioIn 16*
Raulston, Lucy 1936- *WhoSSW 91*
Raum, Arnold 1908- *WhoAm 90*
Raum, Bernard Anthony 1944- *WhoE 91*
Raun, William Robert 1957- *WhoWor 91*
Raunam, George Juri 1937- *St&PR 91*
Rauner, Vincent Joseph 1927- *St&PR 91*
Raunikar, Robert 1931- *WhoAm 90*
Raunio, Matthew Isaac 1957- *WhoEmL 91*
Raup, David Malcolm 1933- *WhoAm 90*
Raupe, Craig *BioIn 16*
Rauppius, Lawrence Hugh 1937- *St&PR 91*
Rauramo, Jaakko Kaarle Mauno 1941- *WhoWor 91*
Raus, Calvin Hugh 1929- *St&PR 91*
Rausch, Conrad *WhoAm 90*
Rausch, George H. 1927- *St&PR 91*
Rausch, Howard 1928- *WhoAm 90, WhoE 91*
Rausch, John Reed 1952- *St&PR 91*
Rausch, Maury K. 1927- *St&PR 91*
Rausch, Walter William 1914- *St&PR 91*
Rausch-Medina, Jessica G 1954- *BiDrAPA 89*
Rauschenberg, Dale Eugene 1938- *WhoE 91, WhoWor 91*
Rauschenberg, Richard A. 1945- *St&PR 91*
Rauschenberg, Robert 1925- *IntDcAA 90, ModArCr 1 [port], News 91-2 [port], WhoAm 90, WhoAmA 91, WhoWor 91, WorAlBi*
Rauschenbusch, Walter 1861-1918 *BioIn 16*
Rauschenplat, A. L. *BioIn 16*
Rauscher, Frank A. 1943- *St&PR 91*
Rauscher, Frank Joseph, Jr. 1931- *WhoWor 91*
Rauscher, Frederick P 1942- *BiDrAPA 89*
Rauscher, John Howard, Jr. 1924- *St&PR 91, WhoAm 90*
Rauscher, Stephen Joseph 1947- *WhoE 91*
Rauscher, Tomlinson Gene 1946- *WhoAm 90*
Rauschning, Hermann 1887-1982 *BioIn 16*
Rauseo, Janet C. 1963- *WhoAmW 91*
Raushenbush, Walter Brandeis 1928- *WhoAm 90*
Rauss, Dennis Michael 1951- *WhoEmL 91*
Rausser, Gordon Clyde 1943- *WhoAm 90*
Raussert, Wilfried 1961- *WhoWor 91*
Rautala, Pekka Juhani 1951- *WhoWor 91*
Rautavaara, Einojuhani 1928- *IntWWM 90*
Rautawaara, Aulikki 1906- *PenDiMP*
Rautbord, Dorothy H 1906- *WhoAmA 91*
Rautenberg, George David 1924- *St&PR 91*
Rautenberg, H. William 1930- *St&PR 91*
Rautenberg, Herbert Gustav 1935- *St&PR 91*
Rautenberg, Leonard J. 1920- *St&PR 91*
Rautenberg, Steven A. 1950- *ODwPR 91*
Rautenfeld, Dirk Berens von 1946- *WhoWor 91*
Rauter, Oscar *PenDiDA 89*
Rautio, Erkki Ilmari 1931- *IntWWM 90*
Rautio, H. Kristene 1947- *St&PR 91*
Rautiola, Norman 1932- *St&PR 91*
Rautoja, Veli Uljas 1928- *WhoWor 91*
Rautsola, Riku Heikki 1954- *WhoWor 91*
Rauwolf, Stephen Leroy 1957- *WhoEmL 91*
Rauzin, Erica Meyer 1949- *WhoWrEP 89*
Rauzzini 1746?-1810 *PenDiMP*
Rava, Paolo Antonio 1950- *WhoWor 91*
Ravachol 1859-1892 *BiDFrPL*
Raval, Dilip N. *St&PR 91*
Ravaris, Charles Lewis 1926- *BiDrAPA 89*
Ravarra, Patricia 1947- *WhoAmA 91*
Ravas, Paul George 1935- *St&PR 91*
Ravasz, Thomas *BioIn 16*
Ravazzolo, Miriano Roberto 1953- *WhoWor 91*
Ravden, Reuben 1918- *BiDrAPA 89*
Rave, Ligia *WhoAm 90*
Raveche, Harold Joseph 1943- *WhoAm 90, WhoE 91*
Ravel, Aviva 1928- *FemiCLE, OxCCanT*
Ravel, Joseph Maurice 1875-1937 *BioIn 16*
Ravel, Maurice 1875-1937 *BioIn 16, PenDiMP A, WorAlBi*
Raveling, Dennis Graff 1939- *WhoAm 90*
Ravelo, Daniel F. 1939- *WhoHisp 91*
Raveloson-Mahasampo, Christopher *WhoWor 91*
Raven, Arlene 1944- *WhoAmA 91*
Raven, Bertram Herbert 1926- *WhoAm 90*
Raven, Gregory K. 1949- *St&PR 91*
Raven, Gregory Kurt 1949- *WhoAm 90*
Raven, J.E. 1951- *St&PR 91*
Raven, Joel F. 1951- *St&PR 91*
Raven, Jonathan Ezra 1951- *WhoEmL 91*
Raven, Ninette Helene Jeanty 1903-1990 *ConAu 132*
Raven, Peter Hamilton 1936- *WhoAm 90*
Raven, Peter Leo 1939- *WhoAm 90*
Raven, Robert Dunbar 1923- *BioIn 16, WhoAm 90*

Raven, Ronald Jacob 1935- *WhoAm 90, WhoE 91, WhoWor 91*
Raven-Riemann, Carolyn Sue 1945- *WhoE 91*
Ravenal, Earl Cedric 1931- *WhoAm 90*
Ravenel, Arthur, Jr. 1927- *WhoAm 90, WhoSSW 91*
Ravenel, Charles D. 1938- *St&PR 91*
Ravenel, Douglas Conner 1947- *WhoE 91*
Ravenel, Henry, Jr. 1934- *St&PR 91*
Ravenel, Shannon 1938- *WhoWrEP 89*
Ravenhill, Alice 1859-1954 *BioIn 16*
Ravenholt, Reimert Thorolf 1925- *WhoAm 90*
Ravens, The *EncPR&S 89*
Ravens, Catherine Elizabeth 1930- *WhoAmW 91*
Ravenscroft, Ellen 1876-1949 *WhoAmA 91N*
Ravenscroft, George 1632-1683 *BioIn 16, PenDiDA 89*
Ravenscroft, Kent 1939- *BiDrAPA 89*
Raventos, Antolin 1925- *WhoAm 90*
Raventos, George 1939- *WhoHisp 91*
Raver, William J. 1947- *St&PR 91*
Ravera, Camilla 1889-1988 *BioIn 16*
Raverat, Gwendolen Mary 1885-1957 *BiDWomA*
Raveson, Sherman Harold 1907-1974 *WhoAmA 91N*
Ravett, Abraham 1947- *WhoAmA 91*
Ravetz, Robert Samuel 1931- *BiDrAPA 89*
Ravi *NewAgMG*
Ravich, Norman J. 1926- *St&PR 91*
Ravich, Robert A *BiDrAPA 89*
Ravichandran, Guruswami K 1951- *BiDrAPA 89*
Ravid, Mordchai 1938- *WhoWor 91*
Ravid, S. Abraham 1951- *WhoE 91*
Ravielli, Anthony 1916- *AuBYP 90*
Raviendran, Dharmaja C *BiDrAPA 89*
Ravier, Jacques-Marie *PenDiDA 89*
Ravilious, Eric *PenDiDA 89*
Ravily, Gilbert 1951- *WhoWor 91*
Ravin, Mona Claire 1939- *WhoAmW 91*
Ravin, Richard M. 1943- *St&PR 91*
Ravinal, Rosemary *ODwPR 91*
Ravinal, Rosemary 1954- *WhoHisp 91*
Ravindra, Dhurjety 1948- *WhoWor 91*
Ravindra, Donthi Krishniah 1941- *WhoWor 91*
Ravindra, Mysore V. 1939- *St&PR 91*
Ravindran, Arun 1944- *WhoE 91*
Ravindran, Vijaya L 1944- *BiDrAPA 89*
Ravine, Harris 1942- *St&PR 91*
Ravines, Eudocio 1897-1969 *BioIn 16*
Raviola, Elio 1932- *WhoAm 90*
Ravipati, Sriramamurthy 1959- *BiDrAPA 89*
Ravis, Howard Shepard 1934- *WhoAm 90*
Ravitch, Diane 1938- *ConAu 31NR, MajTwCW*
Ravitch, Diane Silvers 1938- *WhoAm 90, WhoE 91*
Ravitch, Mark M. 1910-1989 *BioIn 16*
Ravitch, Richard *BioIn 16*
Ravitch, Richard 1933- *WhoE 91*
Ravitsky, Charles 1917- *WhoSSW 91*
Ravitz, Alan I 1948- *BiDrAPA 89*
Ravitz, Elene Becky 1964- *WhoAmW 91*
Ravitz, Leonard J *BiDrAPA 89*
Ravitz, Leonard J., Jr. *WhoAm 90, WhoE 91, WhoWor 91*
Ravitz, Robert Allan 1938- *WhoAm 90*
Ravitz, Tina A. 1954- *St&PR 91*
Raviv, Artur 1946- *WhoAm 90*
Raviv, Gabriel *St&PR 91*
Raviv, Gil 1955- *St&PR 91*
Raviv, Sheila *ODwPR 91*
Ravizza, Eugene A. 1928- *St&PR 91*
Ravlin, Lloyd 1921- *BiDrAPA 89*
Ravnkilde, Adda 1862-1883 *EncCoWW*
Ravrio, Antoine-Andre 1759-1814 *PenDiDA 89*
Ravrio, Louis-Stanislas Lenoir 1783-1846 *PenDiDA 89*
Ravven, Robert M *BiDrAPA 89*
Raw, Isaias 1927- *WhoWor 91*
Raw, Saul David 1946- *WhoE 91*
Rawa, Thomas K *BiDrAPA 89*
Rawal, H. V. 1946- *BiDrAPA 89*
Rawding, F. W. 1930- *BioIn 16*
Rawdon, W Kenner 1934- *BiDrAPA 89*
Rawe, Francis Anthony 1941- *WhoWrEP 89*
Rawitch, Robert Joe 1945- *WhoAm 90*
Rawitscher, Jack Joseph 1932- *WhoAm 90*
Rawitt, Kurt Conrad 1912- *BiDrAPA 89*
Rawitt, Ronald R *BiDrAPA 89*
Rawji, Shiraz Fatehali *BiDrAPA 89*
Rawl, Arthur Julian 1942- *WhoE 91, WhoWor 91*
Rawl, Lawrence G. 1928- *St&PR 91, WhoAm 90, WhoE 91, WhoWor 91*
Rawl, Michael J. 1946- *St&PR 91*
Rawle, William *BioIn 16*
Rawles, Lewis G. 1948- *St&PR 91*
Rawley, Callman *BioIn 16*
Rawley, Callman 1903- *ConAu 32NR*
Rawley, James Albert 1916- *WhoAm 90*
Rawley, Shane 1955- *Ballpl 90*
Rawlings, Boynton Mott 1935- *WhoWor 91*
Rawlings, Carol Smith 1955- *WhoSSW 91*
Rawlings, David Lionel 1943- *St&PR 91*
Rawlings, Hunter Ripley, III 1944- *WhoAm 90, WhoWor 91*
Rawlings, James Scott 1922- *WhoAm 90*
Rawlings, Jerry John 1947- *WhoWor 91*
Rawlings, Johnny 1892-1972 *Ballpl 90*
Rawlings, Joseph Edwin, Jr. *BiDrAPA 89*
Rawlings, Margaret Kinnan 1896-1953 *WorAlBi*
Rawlings, Marjorie 1896-1953 *FemiCLE*
Rawlings, Marjorie Kinnan 1896-1953 *BioAmW, BioIn 16, DcLB 102 [port]*
Rawlings, Mary 1936- *WhoAmW 91*
Rawlings, N. Lewis, Jr. *St&PR 91*
Rawlings, Paul C. 1928- *WhoAm 90*
Rawlings, Robert Hoag 1924- *WhoAm 90*
Rawlings, Robert William 1941- *St&PR 91*
Rawlings, Roy M. 1944- *St&PR 91*
Rawlings, Suzanne Corinne 1955- *WhoEmL 91*
Rawlins, Benjamin W., Jr. 1938- *WhoAm 90*
Rawlins, Carol Lynne Stanley 1940- *WhoAmW 91*
Rawlins, Charles Brodhead 1928- *WhoAm 90*
Rawlins, Christopher J. 1945- *St&PR 91*
Rawlins, Christopher John 1945- *WhoAm 90, WhoE 91*
Rawlins, Emily 1950- *IntWWM 90*
Rawlins, George Mimms, III 1938- *WhoSSW 91*
Rawlins, John Aaron 1831-1869 *BiDrUSE 89*
Rawlins, Joseph Thomas 1936- *IntWWM 90*
Rawlins, Kimberly *BiDrAPA 89*
Rawlins, Lester 1924-1988 *BioIn 16*
Rawlins, Lindley Townsend 1950- *WhoAmW 91*
Rawlins, Michael Crist 1952- *WhoSSW 91*
Rawlins, Patti Lynn 1960- *WhoAmW 91, WhoSSW 91*
Rawlins, Steven Wayne 1956- *WhoEmL 91, WhoSSW 91, WhoWor 91*
Rawlins, Susan Elizabeth 1941- *WhoWrEP 89*
Rawlinson, Helen Ann 1948- *WhoAm 90*
Rawlinson, Jonlane Frederick 1940- *WhoAmA 91*
Rawlinson, Richard A 1931- *BiDrAPA 89*
Rawlinson, Victoria Fairchild 1959- *WhoAmW 91*
Rawls, Benjamin M. 1940- *St&PR 91*
Rawls, Eugenia *WhoAm 90*
Rawls, Eugenia 1916- *BioIn 16, NotWoAT*
Rawls, Frank Macklin 1952- *WhoWor 91*
Rawls, James H. 1952- *St&PR 91*
Rawls, James J 1945- *ConAu 30NR*
Rawls, Kathryn Stark 1950- *WhoSSW 91*
Rawls, Lou 1935- *DrBlPA 90, EncPR&S 89*
Rawls, Lou 1936- *WhoAm 90, WorAlBi*
Rawls, Philip *ConAu 31NR*
Rawls, S. Waite 1948- *St&PR 91*
Rawls, Sol Waite, III 1948- *WhoAm 90*
Rawls, Wilson 1913- *AuBYP 90, BioIn 16*
Rawlyk, George Alexander 1935- *SmATA 64*
Rawn, Stanley Ryle, Jr. 1928- *St&PR 91, WhoAm 90*
Rawnsley, Howard Melody 1925- *WhoAm 90*
Rawnsley, John 1949- *IntWWM 90, PenDiMP*
Rawot, Billie Kay 1951- *WhoEmL 91*
Rawski, Conrad Henry 1914- *WhoAm 90*
Rawski, Evelyn Sakakida 1939- *WhoAm 90, WhoAmW 91*
Rawski, Thomas George 1943- *WhoAm 90*
Rawson, Bruce Strathearn 1935- *WhoAm 90*
Rawson, Charles E. 1925- *St&PR 91*
Rawson, Clayton 1906-1971 *TwCCr&M 91*
Rawson, Eleanor S. *WhoAm 90, WhoWrEP 89*
Rawson, Jim Charles 1947- *WhoSSW 91*
Rawson, Kennett Longley 1911- *WhoAm 90, WhoWor 91*
Rawson, L.J. 1917- *St&PR 91*
Rawson, Merle R. 1924- *St&PR 91, WhoAm 90*
Rawson, Michael James 1957- *St&PR 91*
Rawson, Ralph William 1916- *WhoAm 90*
Rawson, Raymond D. 1940- *WhoAm 90*
Rawson, Robert Orrin 1917- *WhoAm 90*
Rawson, Thomas C. 1952- *St&PR 91*
Rawson, William Robert 1925- *WhoAm 90*
Rawsthorne, Alan 1905-1971 *PenDiMP A*
Rawsthorne, Isabel 1910?- *BiDWomA*
Ray, Albert L *BiDrAPA 89*
Ray, Aldo 1926- *ConTFT 8, WorAlBi*
Ray, Alice Louise Raney Nelson 1934- *WhoAmW 91*
Ray, Anne Moore 1941- *WhoSSW 91*
Ray, Annie Lee 1922- *WhoAmW 91*
Ray, Asok 1946- *WhoE 91*
Ray, Barbara Ann 1952- *WhoAmW 91*
Ray, Beatrice Thomas 1950- *WhoAmW 91*
Ray, Billy Frank 1935- *St&PR 91*
Ray, Bob *BioIn 16*
Ray, Bobbi *WhoWrEP 89*
Ray, Bradley Stephen 1957- *WhoSSW 91*
Ray, Brian Daniel 1954- *WhoSSW 91*
Ray, Bruce David 1955- *WhoWor 91*
Ray, Bryan H. 1945- *St&PR 91*
Ray, C. Eugene 1932- *St&PR 91*
Ray, Carl 1943-1978 *SmATA 63*
Ray, Carol Ann 1959- *WhoSSW 91*
Ray, Carolyn Marie 1933- *WhoAmW 91*
Ray, Charles *BioIn 16*
Ray, Charles 1944- *St&PR 91*
Ray, Charles 1953- *WhoAmA 91*
Ray, Charles Kendall 1928- *WhoAm 90*
Ray, Cherie Delaine 1956- *WhoEmL 91*
Ray, Christopher T 1937- *WhoAmA 91*
Ray, Cread L., Jr. 1931- *WhoAm 90*
Ray, Daniel 1939- *St&PR 91*
Ray, Darrell Morris 1959- *WhoWor 91*
Ray, David A. 1926- *St&PR 91*
Ray, David Christian 1961- *WhoWor 91*
Ray, David Eugene 1932- *WhoAm 90, WhoWrEP 89*
Ray, David K. *WhoSSW 91*
Ray, David Randolph 1946- *WhoSSW 91*
Ray, David Scott 1930- *WhoAm 90*
Ray, Deborah *WhoAmA 91*
Ray, Deborah Kogan 1940- *BioIn 16*
Ray, Deborah Kogan 1941- *WhoWrEP 89*
Ray, Derrell Wayne *BiDrAPA 89*
Ray, Dixy Lee 1914- *WorAlBi*
Ray, Donald Hensley 1952- *WhoAm 90*
Ray, Donald Page 1916- *WhoAm 90*
Ray, Dorathea Hammers 1917- *WhoAmW 91*
Ray, Dorothy Florence 1926- *St&PR 91*
Ray, Douglas Ellsworth 1947- *WhoEmL 91*
Ray, Douglas K. 1947- *St&PR 91*
Ray, Dwight Wiley 1944- *St&PR 91*
Ray, Eddye Robert 1941- *WhoSSW 91*
Ray, Edgar Wayne, Jr. 1941- *WhoAm 90*
Ray, Edward 1932- *St&PR 91*
Ray, Edward John 1944- *WhoAm 90*
Ray, Forrest Theodore, Jr. 1952- *WhoSSW 91*
Ray, Frank Allen 1949- *WhoWor 91*
Ray, Frank David 1940- *WhoAm 90, WhoWor 91*
Ray, G. Cristobal Antonio 1930- *WhoE 91*
Ray, Gary L. 1941- *St&PR 91*
Ray, Gene Anthony 1962- *DrBlPA 90*
Ray, Gene W. 1938- *St&PR 91*
Ray, Gene Wells 1938- *WhoAm 90*
Ray, George A. 1940- *St&PR 91*
Ray, George Allan 1951- *St&PR 91*
Ray, George Einar 1910- *WhoAm 90*
Ray, George H. 1847-1910 *AmLegL*
Ray, George Washington, III 1932- *WhoAm 90*
Ray, Gordon N. 1915-1986 *DcLB 103 [port]*
Ray, Gordon Thompson 1928- *WhoE 91*
Ray, H. M. 1924- *WhoAm 90*
Ray, H. Richard, Jr. 1953- *WhoSSW 91*
Ray, Harold Byrd 1940- *St&PR 91*
Ray, Hugh Massey, Jr. 1943- *WhoAm 90*
Ray, James 1932-1988 *BioIn 16*
Ray, James Earl 1928- *BioIn 16*
Ray, James Enos, Jr. 1874- *AmLegL*
Ray, Jerry *ODwPR 91*
Ray, Jim 1944- *Ballpl 90*
Ray, John Thomas, Jr. 1937- *St&PR 91*
Ray, John Walker 1936- *WhoWor 91*
Ray, John William *BiDrAPA 89*
Ray, Johnnie *NewYTBS 90 [port]*
Ray, Johnnie 1927-1990 *BioIn 16, OxCPMus, WorAlBi*
Ray, Johnny 1957- *Ballpl 90*
Ray, Judy Self 1946- *WhoAmW 91, WhoSSW 91, WhoWor 91*
Ray, Karl Arthur 1939- *BiDrAPA 89*
Ray, Kinley LeRoy, Jr. 1944- *St&PR 91*
Ray, Kurt K. 1952- *St&PR 91*
Ray, Larry Dale *BiDrAPA 89*
Ray, Lewis T *BiDrAPA 89*
Ray, Louis 1949- *WhoE 91*
Ray, Man 1890-1976 *BioIn 16, IntDcAA 90, WorAlBi*
Ray, Marc T. 1953- *WhoSSW 91*
Ray, Marcus H. *BioIn 16*
Ray, Marty A. 1943- *WhoSSW 91*
Ray, Mary Dominic 1913- *IntWWM 90*
Ray, Michael *BioIn 16*
Ray, Michael E. 1945- *St&PR 91*
Ray, Michael L. *WhoAm 90*
Ray, Michele Lynn 1963- *WhoEmL 91*
Ray, Nicholas 1911-1979 *BioIn 16*
Ray, Norman H. *St&PR 91*
Ray, Ophelia *AuBYP 90*
Ray, P C 1916- *EncO&P 3*
Ray, Paul R., Jr. 1943- *WhoAm 90*
Ray, Priscilla *BiDrAPA 89*
Ray, Ralph W. 1923- *St&PR 91*
Ray, Richard Archibald 1936- *WhoAm 90*
Ray, Richard Barney 1940- *St&PR 91*
Ray, Richard Belmont 1927- *WhoAm 90, WhoSSW 91*
Ray, Richard F. 1937- *St&PR 91*
Ray, Rick *BioIn 16*
Ray, Ritz Clyde, Jr. 1935- *BiDrAPA 89*
Ray, Robert 1924- *WhoAmA 91*
Ray, Robert D. 1914- *WhoAm 90*
Ray, Robert D. 1928- *WhoAm 90*
Ray, Robert Edison 1931- *WhoE 91*
Ray, Robert F. 1949- *St&PR 91*
Ray, Robert Franklin 1949- *WhoAm 90*
Ray, Roderick Jack, Jr. 1956- *WhoEmL 91*
Ray, Roger Buchanan 1935- *WhoAm 90*
Ray, Ronald Eric 1941- *WhoAm 90*
Ray, Roy Robert 1902- *WhoAm 90*
Ray, Ruth 1919-1977 *WhoAmA 91N*
Ray, Ruth Alice Yancey 1931- *WhoSSW 91*
Ray, Sara Bradshaw 1964- *WhoAmW 91*
Ray, Satyajit *BioIn 16*
Ray, Satyajit 1921- *WhoWor 91*
Ray, Scott H. 1955- *St&PR 91*
Ray, Shirley G. 1934- *WhoWrEP 89*
Ray, Stephen John 1961- *St&PR 91*
Ray, Su Zane Atkinson 1963- *IntWWM 90*
Ray, Sujit Kumar 1959- *WhoSSW 91*
Ray, Susanne Gettings 1938- *WhoAmW 91*
Ray, Suzanne Judy 1939- *WhoWrEP 89*
Ray, Thomas Kreider *WhoAm 90*
Ray, Thomas Willard *BioIn 16*
Ray, Timothy Britt 1939- *WhoSSW 91*
Ray, W. Harmon 1940- *WhoAm 90*
Ray, Wayne Allen 1949- *WhoAm 90*
Ray, William F. 1915- *St&PR 91, WhoAm 90, WhoE 91, WhoWor 91*
Ray, William Jackson 1945- *WhoAm 90, WhoE 91*
Ray, William Joel 1954- *WhoSSW 91*
Ray-Jones, Tony 1941-1972 *BioIn 16*
Rayancha, Suresh *BiDrAPA 89*
Rayasam, Krishnaiah *BiDrAPA 89*
Raybeck, Michael Joseph 1945- *WhoSSW 91*
Raybin, Harry W. *BioIn 16*
Raybin, James B 1939- *BiDrAPA 89*
Raybon, Patricia A. 1943- *St&PR 91*
Rayburn, A. Kent 1937- *St&PR 91*
Rayburn, Boyd 1942- *WhoAmA 91*
Rayburn, George Marvin 1920- *WhoAm 90*
Rayburn, James L. 1944- *St&PR 91*
Rayburn, Jerry W. 1940- *St&PR 91*
Rayburn, Margaret 1927- *WhoAmW 91*
Rayburn, Sam 1882-1961 *BioIn 16, WorAlBi*
Rayburn, Wendell Gilbert 1929- *WhoAm 90, WhoWor 91*
Rayburn, William B. *BioIn 16*
Raydon, Alexander R *WhoAmA 91*
Raydon, Max E. 1942- *St&PR 91*
Raye, Don 1909 *OxCPMus*
Raye, Don 1946- *WhoEmL 91*
Raye, Martha 1916- *BioIn 16, WorAlBi*
Raye, Robert S. 1940- *St&PR 91*
Rayen, James Wilson 1935- *WhoAmA 91, WhoE 91*
Rayfield, Allan Laverne 1935- *WhoAm 90*
Rayfield, Gordon Elliott 1950- *WhoAm 90*
Rayford, Floyd 1957- *Ballpl 90*
Rayher, John 1946- *WhoE 91*
Raykovics, Kenneth Francis 1954- *WhoE 91*
Rayl, Granville Monroe 1917- *WhoWor 91*
Rayl, India 1956- *WhoAmW 91*
Rayleigh, Lord *EncPaPR 91*
Rayleigh, Lord 1842-1919 *EncO&P 3*
Rayleigh, John W. 1842-1919 *WorAlBi*
Raylesberg, Alan Ira 1950- *WhoEmL 91*
Rayman, Marcel 1923-1944 *BioIn 16*
Rayman, Mark Brooks 1947- *BiDrAPA 89*
Rayman, Warren Samuel 1916- *WhoAm 90*
Raymer, Donald George 1924- *St&PR 91, WhoAm 90*
Raymer, Fred 1875-1957 *Ballpl 90*
Raymer, Lester 1906- *BioIn 16*
Raymes, Frederick 1929- *St&PR 91*
Raymo, Robert Rowland 1925- *WhoAm 90*
Raymon, Paul M. 1927- *St&PR 91*
Raymond, Alex 1909-1956 *EncACom*
Raymond, Alexander 1909-1956 *WhoAmA 91N*
Raymond, Bugs 1882-1912 *Ballpl 90*
Raymond, Charles Allen 1946- *WhoSSW 91*
Raymond, Charles Michael 1953- *WhoSSW 91*
Raymond, Charles Walker, III 1937- *WhoE 91*
Raymond, Christopher John 1961- *WhoE 91*

Raymond, Claude 1937- Ballpl 90
Raymond, Clive 1927- St&PR 91
Raymond, Dan 1937- St&PR 91
Raymond, Dana Merriam 1914- WhoAm 90
Raymond, David A. 1940- St&PR 91
Raymond, Dennis M. 1948- BiDrAPA 89
Raymond, Derek 1931- TwCCr&M 91
Raymond, Donald Laurence 1931- WhoE 91
Raymond, Dorothy Gill 1954- St&PR 91, WhoAmW 91
Raymond, Elfie Stock 1931- WhoAm 90
Raymond, Evelyn L 1908- WhoAmA 91
Raymond, F. Douglas, III 1958- WhoE 91
Raymond, Fred 1900-1954 OxCPMus
Raymond, Gene 1908- WhoAm 90, WorAlBi
Raymond, Geoffrey ODwPR 91
Raymond, Geoffrey Peter 1943- St&PR 91, WhoAm 90
Raymond, George G., Jr. 1921- St&PR 91
Raymond, George Marc 1919- WhoAm 90
Raymond, Gregory Jack 1951- WhoEmL 91
Raymond, Guy 1911- WhoAm 90
Raymond, Harvey Francis 1915- WhoAm 90
Raymond, Henry Jarvis 1820-1869 AmLegL, BioIn 16
Raymond, Ilene Helen 1954- WhoWrEP 89
Raymond, Jack 1918- WhoAm 90, WhoWor 91
Raymond, James C. 1940- WhoWrEP 89
Raymond, James Irving BioIn 16
Raymond, James Patrick 1935- WhoAm 90
Raymond, Jeffery B. 1946- ODwPR 91
Raymond, Jeffrey Thomas 1957- WhoSSW 91
Raymond, Jim EncACom
Raymond, John AuBYP 90
Raymond, John A., Jr. 1918- St&PR 91
Raymond, John M., Jr. 1923- ODwPR 91
Raymond, John Marshall, Jr. 1923- WhoE 91
Raymond, June Ferguson 1931- WhoAmW 91
Raymond, Kenneth Norman 1942- WhoAm 90
Raymond, Kenneth W. 1920- St&PR 91
Raymond, Laurie Watson BiDrAPA 89
Raymond, Lee R. 1938- St&PR 91, WhoAm 90, WhoE 91, WhoWor 91
Raymond, Lilo 1922- WhoAmA 91
Raymond, Linda Gail BiDrAPA 89
Raymond, Lucille J. 1943- St&PR 91
Raymond, Margaret Elizabeth 1960- WhoE 91
Raymond, Margaret Thomsen AuBYP 90
Raymond, Mark Wesley 1950- WhoWrEP 89
Raymond, Maurice A. 1938- WhoAm 90
Raymond, Michael Lyons 1943- St&PR 91
Raymond, Monica E. 1949- WhoWrEP 89
Raymond, Nancy Cox BiDrAPA 89
Raymond, Philip John, Jr. 1946- WhoSSW 91
Raymond, Rhoades Robert 1949- WhoSSW 91
Raymond, Robert AuBYP 90
Raymond, Robert 1906- St&PR 91
Raymond, Roby 1920- ODwPR 91, WhoWrEP 89
Raymond, Samuel 1928- St&PR 91
Raymond, Sandra L. 1944- WhoAmW 91
Raymond, Spencer Henry 1926- WhoAm 90
Raymond, Stanley 1913-1988 AnObit 1988
Raymond, Susan Grant 1943- WhoAmW 91
Raymond, Theodore Alan 1927- St&PR 91
Raymond, Thomas Joseph Cicchino 1917- WhoAm 90
Raymond, William Marshall 1934- St&PR 91
Raymonda, James Earl 1933- St&PR 91, WhoAm 90
Raymore, Sandra Hope 1957- WhoE 91
Raymus, Toni Marie 1957- WhoAmW 91
Raynak, Jan Thomas BiDrAPA 89
Raynak, Rose 1950- WhoEmL 91
Raynard, Shirley May 1942- WhoE 91
Raynaud-Horna, Alfredo M BiDrAPA 89
Raynauld, Andre 1927- WhoAm 90
Rayner, Ada 1901- WhoAmA 91
Rayner, Arno A. 1928- St&PR 91
Rayner, Christopher Shepstone 1946- WhoWor 91
Rayner, Claire 1931- ConAu 30NR
Rayner, Colin Robert 1938- WhoWor 91
Rayner, Donald Edward 1944- St&PR 91
Rayner, Frances BiDWomA
Rayner, Gordon 1935- WhoAmA 91
Rayner, James Edmund 1930- St&PR 91
Rayner, Louise 1832-1924 BiDWomA
Rayner, Margaret BiDWomA
Rayner, Nancy 1827-1855 BiDWomA
Rayner, Richard BioIn 16
Rayner, Robert Martin 1946- WhoE 91
Rayner, Roger Spencer 1955- IntWWM 90
Rayner, Rosa BiDWomA
Rayner, Steve 1953- WhoWor 91
Rayner, Walter Holmes 1926- St&PR 91
Rayner, William 1929- BioIn 16
Rayner, William Alexander 1929- WhoAm 90
Raynes, Anthony E 1940- BiDrAPA 89
Raynes, Bruno 1944- St&PR 91
Raynock, Joseph Francis 1924- St&PR 91
Raynolds, Edward O. 1938- ODwPR 91
Raynolds, Harold, Jr. 1925- WhoAm 90, WhoE 91
Raynor, Geoffrey Vincent 1913-1983 DcNaB 1981
Raynor, John Patrick 1923- WhoAm 90
Raynor, Richard Benjamin 1928- WhoE 91, WhoWor 91
Raynor, Sherry Diane 1930- WhoAmW 91, WhoE 91
Raynor, Susanne 1948- WhoAmW 91
Rayport, Stephen G BiDrAPA 89
Rayport, Stephen Gregory 1955- WhoE 91
Rayski, Abraham 1914- BioIn 16
Rayson, Edwin Hope 1923- WhoAm 90
Rayson, Glendon Ennes 1915- WhoE 91
Rayson, Jack Henry 1931- WhoAm 90
Rayudu, Subbulaxmi BiDrAPA 89
Rayward, Warden Boyd 1939- WhoAm 90
Raz, Hilda 1938- WhoWrEP 89
Raz, Jo Anne WhoWrEP 89
Raz, Robert Eugene 1942- WhoAm 90
Raza, Syed Akhtar BiDrAPA 89
Raza, Syed Tasnim 1946- WhoE 91
Razaf, Andy EarBlAP
Razaf, Andy 1895-1973 BioIn 16, DrBlPA 90, OxCPMus
Razafimahatratra, Victor Cardinal 1921- WhoWor 91
Razani, Javad 1939- BiDrAPA 89
Razenson, Helen Louise 1954- WhoAmW 91, WhoE 91
Razia Iltutmish WomWR
Razin, Andrew 1945- WhoE 91
Razin, Andrew Michael 1945- BiDrAPA 89
Razin, Assaf 1941- WhoWor 91
Raziyya Iltutmish WomWR
Raznoff, Beverly Shultz 1946- WhoSSW 91
Razo, Jose H. 1951- WhoHisp 91
Razoharinoro 1936- WhoWor 91
Razonable, John 1943- WhoHisp 91
Razook, Richard J. WhoHisp 91
Razumovsky, Andrey Kyrilovich 1752-1836 PenDiMP
Razzano, Frank Charles 1948- WhoEmL 91, WhoSSW 91, WhoWor 91
Razzano, Pasquale Angelo 1943- WhoE 91, WhoWor 91
Razze, Gary 1953- St&PR 91
Razzouk, Akram Yacoub BiDrAPA 89
Re, Edward D. 1920- WhoAm 90
Rea, Ann Hadley Kuehn 1962- WhoAmW 91
Rea, Betty 1904-1965 BiDWomA
Rea, David 1949- St&PR 91
Rea, David B. 1926- St&PR 91
Rea, George Bronson 1869-1936 BioIn 16
Rea, Kathryn Pollyanna 1957- WhoAmW 91
Rea, Margaret Eleanore 1935- WhoWor 91
Rea, Michael J. 1949- St&PR 91
Rea, Norma 1958- WhoAmW 91
Rea, Norman H. 1923- St&PR 91
Rea, Patricia Ann 1957- BiDrAPA 89
Rea, Richard A. 1939- St&PR 91
Rea, William Edward 1936- St&PR 91
Rea, William J. WhoAm 90
Rea, William Samuel BiDrAPA 89
Reach, Al 1840-1928 Ballpl 90
Reach, Robert L., Jr. 1948- St&PR 91
Reachi, Santiago 1898- WhoHisp 91
Read, Miss 1913- BioIn 16
Read, Allan Alexander 1923- WhoAm 90
Read, Allen Walker BioIn 16
Read, Arthur William 1930- WhoAm 90
Read, Benjamin Huger 1925- WhoAm 90
Read, Benjamin M. 1853-1927 AmLegL
Read, Beverly Money 1919- WhoSSW 91
Read, Charles Arthur 1919- WhoWor 91
Read, Dave 1938- WhoAmA 91
Read, David Hawes 1935- St&PR 91
Read, David Haxton Carswell 1910- WhoAm 90
Read, David T 1928- BiDrAPA 89
Read, Dennis Raymond 1942- WhoE 91
Read, Donald William 1914- IntWWM 90
Read, Elfreida 1920- AuBYP 90
Read, Ernest 1870-1965 PenDiMP
Read, Fay Ellen BiDrAPA 89
Read, Frank Henry 1934- WhoWor 91
Read, Frank Thompson 1938- WhoAm 90
Read, Frederick Wilson, Jr. 1908- WhoAm 90
Read, Gardner 1913- IntWWM 90
Read, George 1733-1798 BioIn 16, EncCRAm
Read, Gilbert E. 1822-1898 AmLegL
Read, Guy C. ODwPR 91
Read, Harriet Fanning FemiCLE
Read, Helen Appleton 1887-1974 WhoAmA 91N
Read, James 1952- ConTFT 8
Read, James Lamar 1926- BiDrAPA 89
Read, Jamie Nevelle BiDrAPA 89
Read, Jan ConAu 32NR
Read, Jennifer Lynn 1946- WhoSSW 91
Read, Joel WhoAm 90, WhoAmW 91
Read, John Conyers 1947- St&PR 91, WhoAm 90
Read, John Emms 1918- St&PR 91
Read, John Hinton 1917- ConAu 32NR
Read, John Meredith 1837-1896 BioIn 16
Read, John Vincent BiDrAPA 89
Read, Julian O. 1927- ODwPR 91
Read, Lynwood Maynard 1943- St&PR 91
Read, Margaret R BiDrAPA 89
Read, Martha FemiCLE
Read, Maureen Hay 1937- BioIn 16
Read, Nicholas Wallace 1945- WhoWor 91
Read, Opie 1852-1939 BioIn 16
Read, Philip Lloyd 1932- WhoAm 90
Read, Piers Paul 1941- WhoAm 90
Read, Robert Gary 1947- St&PR 91
Read, Stanley Foster 1917- St&PR 91
Read, Stephen Lynn BiDrAPA 89
Read, Susan C. WhoAmW 91
Read, Thomas Lawrence 1938- IntWWM 90
Read, Thomas Leigh, III 1953- WhoSSW 91
Read, Vernon Berry 1936- IntWWM 90
Read, Wallace W. 1932- St&PR 91
Read, William Edgar 1927- WhoAm 90
Read, William Edward 1953- St&PR 91
Read, William J. 1938- St&PR 91
Read, William Lawrence 1926- WhoAm 90
Read, William McClain 1918- WhoAm 90
Read-Wharton, Betty Ann 1953- WhoEmL 91
Reade, Charles 1814-1884 BioIn 16, WorAlBi
Reade, Claire Elizabeth 1952- WhoE 91
Reade, David M. 1927- St&PR 91
Reade, Hamish ConAu 32NR, MajTwCW
Reade, Hamish 1936- BioIn 16
Reade, Harriet BioIn 16
Reade, Julia M 1955- BiDrAPA 89
Reade, Paul Geoffrey 1943- IntWWM 90
Reade, Richard Sill 1913- WhoAm 90
Reade, Robert B. 1918- St&PR 91
Reade, Robert Mellor 1940- WhoAm 90
Reade, Roma 1877-1958 WhoAmA 91N
Reader, Barbara 1955- WhoE 91
Reader, Charles M. 1928- St&PR 91
Reader, Dennis Joel 1939- WhoWrEP 89
Reader, George Gordon 1919- WhoAm 90, WhoE 91
Reader, Martin Seth 1956- WhoE 91
Reader, Mary Rae 1952- WhoAmW 91
Reader, Ralph 1903-1982 OxCPMus
Reader, Richard C. 1949- WhoAm 90
Reader, W J 1920-1990? ConAu 132
Readford, Henry 1841-1901 BioIn 16
Reading, Alan William 1950- WhoWor 91
Reading, Anthony 1933- BiDrAPA 89
Reading, Anthony John 1933- WhoAm 90
Reading, James Edward 1924- WhoAm 90
Reading, William Henry 1956- BiDrAPA 89
Readio, Wilfred A 1895-1961 WhoAmA 91N
Ready, Elizabeth M. 1953- WhoAmW 91
Ready, John E. WhoE 91
Ready, Randy 1960- Ballpl 90
Reagan, Allan L. 1953- St&PR 91
Reagan, Barbara Benton WhoAm 90
Reagan, Bernida 1954- WhoAmW 91
Reagan, Cindy ODwPR 91
Reagan, Floranne R. St&PR 91
Reagan, Harry D. 1933- St&PR 91
Reagan, J. Thomas 1931- St&PR 91
Reagan, James C. 1958- St&PR 91
Reagan, Marie Adele 1926- WhoE 91
Reagan, Mark Edward 1949- St&PR 91
Reagan, Maureen BioIn 16
Reagan, Maureen 1941- WhoAmW 91
Reagan, Michael BioIn 16
Reagan, Michael Daniel 1927- WhoAm 90
Reagan, Nancy 1921- WorAlBi
Reagan, Nancy 1923- BioIn 16, ConAu 33NR
Reagan, Nancy Davis 1921- BioAmW
Reagan, Nancy Davis 1923- WhoAm 90, WhoAmW 91, WhoWor 91
Reagan, Owen Walker, III 1952- WhoEmL 91
Reagan, Patricia Ann BioIn 16
Reagan, Peter L. 1944- St&PR 91
Reagan, Reginald Lee 1910- WhoWor 91
Reagan, Ronald 1911- Ballpl 90, BioIn 16, WorAlBi
Reagan, Ronald Prescott BioIn 16
Reagan, Ronald Wilson 1911- BiDrUSE 89, WhoAm 90, WhoWor 91
Reagan, Sally A. 1945- WhoAmW 91
Reagan, Sydney Chandler 1916- WhoAm 90
Reagan, William Ralph 1935- WhoE 91
Reage, Pauline EncCoWW
Reagin, Leslie Dyer, III 1943- St&PR 91
Reagle, Merl BioIn 16
Reagor, Craig St&PR 91
Reahl, Joseph E 1921- BiDrAPA 89
Reak, B. Bennett 1928- St&PR 91
Real, Cathleen Clare 1934- WhoAmW 91
Real, Francisco X. 1957- WhoWor 91
Real, James Cary 1951- St&PR 91
Real, Lawrence Alan BiDrAPA 89
Real, Manuel Lawrence 1924- WhoAm 90
Real, Margaret Anne 1931- WhoAmW 91
Real, William Jay 1948- St&PR 91
Reale, Nicholas Albert 1922- WhoAmA 91N
Reale, Richard Thomas 1939- St&PR 91
Realmuto, George M 1947- BiDrAPA 89
Reals, Gail BioIn 16
Reals, William Joseph 1920- WhoAm 90
Reals, Willis Braithwaite 1925- St&PR 91, WhoAm 90
Ream, Carolyn 1920- WhoWor 91
Ream, James Terrill 1929- WhoAm 90
Ream, John K. 1934- St&PR 91
Ream, Michael D. 1943- St&PR 91
Ream, Norman Jacob 1912- WhoAm 90
Ream, Richard P. 1943- St&PR 91
Ream, Ronald Lee 1941- St&PR 91
Ream, Ronald O. 1935- St&PR 91
Ream, Vinnie 1847-1914 BioAmW
Ream, W. Lawrence 1932- St&PR 91
Reames, Richard R. 1942- St&PR 91
Reames, Stephen Anthony 1945- WhoSSW 91
Reames, Timothy Paul 1935- St&PR 91, WhoAm 90
Reamey, Gerald Sanford 1948- WhoEmL 91
Reams, Bernard Dinsmore, Jr. 1943- WhoAm 90, WhoWor 91
Reams, Bernard L., Sr 1919- St&PR 91
Reams, Gerald Brock 1925- WhoSSW 91
Reamy, Barbara BioIn 16
Reamy, Elsie Marie 1938- WhoSSW 91
Reamy, William R 1946- BiDrAPA 89
Reaney, Gilbert 1924- IntWWM 90, WhoAm 90
Reaney, James 1926- OxCCanT [port]
Reap, Mary Margaret 1941- WhoAm 90, WhoAmW 91
Reardon, Andrew Fitzpatrick 1945- WhoAm 90
Reardon, Anna Joyce 1910- WhoAmW 91, WhoSSW 91
Reardon, Beans 1897-1984 Ballpl 90
Reardon, Bryan Peter 1928- WhoAm 90
Reardon, Edward Hyland 1942- WhoWrEP 89
Reardon, Edward Joseph 1943- St&PR 91
Reardon, Geralyn Anne 1959- WhoAmW 91, WhoE 91
Reardon, James D 1936- BiDrAPA 89
Reardon, Janet Mauk WhoWrEP 89
Reardon, Jeff 1955- Ballpl 90
Reardon, John 1930-1988 BioIn 16
Reardon, John A. BioIn 16
Reardon, John E. 1943-1988 BioIn 16
Reardon, John Joseph 1938- St&PR 91
Reardon, Joseph John 1936- WhoE 91
Reardon, Kevin F. 1935- St&PR 91
Reardon, Leonard W. 1940- St&PR 91
Reardon, Mark William 1956- WhoEmL 91
Reardon, Mary A WhoAmA 91
Reardon, Mary Agnes 1912- WhoE 91
Reardon, Michael Dennis 1934- WhoE 91
Reardon, Michael James 1956- WhoEmL 91
Reardon, Patrick C. 1937- St&PR 91
Reardon, Paul Cashman 1909-1988 BioIn 16
Reardon, Robert J. 1928- St&PR 91
Reardon, Teresa S. BioIn 16
Reardon, Vince ODwPR 91
Reark, John Benson 1923- WhoSSW 91
Reaser, Donald C. St&PR 91N
Reaser, Freda Bright 1929- WhoAmW 91
Reason, Joseph Paul 1941- WhoAm 90
Reason, Patrick 1817-1852 WhoAmA 91N
Reasoner, Elizabeth Diane 1949- WhoAmW 91
Reasoner, Gregory Alan 1953- WhoWor 91
Reasoner, Harry 1923- WhoAm 90, WhoE 91
Reasoner, Harry Max 1939- WhoAm 90
Reasoner, John William 1940- WhoSSW 91
Reasons, George Hubert 1923- WhoAm 90
Reast, Deborah Stanek 1955- WhoAmW 91
Reategui, Julio Antonio 1956- WhoE 91
Reath, Andrews 1951- WhoSSW 91
Reath, George, Jr. 1939- WhoAm 90, WhoE 91
Reaugh, O.H. 1913- St&PR 91

Reaumur, Rene De 1683-1757 *WorAlBi*
Reaves, Benjamin F. *WhoAm 90*
Reaves, Charles Durham 1935- *WhoAm 90*
Reaves, Curtis Felton 1938- *WhoSSW 91*
Reaves, Frank McLeod 1924- *St&PR 91*
Reaves, Giles *NewAgMG*
Reaves, James Benjamin 1928- *St&PR 91*
Reaves, Michael 1946- *BiDrAPA 89*
Reaves, William B., III 1944- *St&PR 91*
Reaves-Phillips, Sandra *DrBlPA 90*
Reavill, Albert Edgar, Jr. 1937- *St&PR 91*
Reavis, Charles G. 1948- *WhoWrEP 89*
Reavis, Hattie King *DcAfAmP*
Reavis, Viola Lea Schubert 1927- *WhoAmW 91*
Reavley, Thomas Morrow 1921- *WhoAm 90*
Reay, Donald Patterson 1914- *WhoAm 90*
Reay, Jed Allen 1957- *WhoEmL 91*
Reback, Avelina Roque *BiDrAPA 89*
Reback, Richard Neal 1954- *WhoEmL 91*
Reback, Samuel *BiDrAPA 89*
Rebal, Ronald Franklin, Jr. 1948- *BiDrAPA 89*
Rebane, John T. 1946- *St&PR 91, WhoAm 90*
Rebar, Robert William 1947- *WhoAm 90*
Rebarber, Steven Bruce *BiDrAPA 89*
Rebay, Hilla 1890-1967 *BiDWomA, BioIn 16, WhoAmA 91N*
Rebay, Luciano 1928- *WhoAm 90*
Rebbeck, Lester James, Jr 1929- *WhoAmA 91, WhoWor 91*
Rebeck, Barry Martin *BiDrAPA 89*
Rebeck, Daniel S. 1938- *St&PR 91*
Rebeck, Pamela Joan 1949- *WhoEmL 91*
Rebeiz, Constantin Anis 1936- *WhoAm 90, WhoWor 91*
Rebele, Anthony P. 1933- *St&PR 91*
Rebele, David E. 1928- *St&PR 91*
Rebell, Walter 1951- *WhoWor 91*
Rebello, Luiz Francisco 1924- *WhoWor 91*
Rebenack, John Henry 1918- *WhoAm 90*
Rebenfeld, Ludwig 1928- *WhoAm 90*
Rebennack, Mac *EncPR&S 89*
Rebentisch, Susan Webster 1943- *WhoAmW 91*
Reber, Grote 1911- *BioIn 16, WorAlBi*
Reber, Mark 1946- *BiDrAPA 89*
Reber, Mark Albert 1954- *WhoE 91*
Reber, Mick 1942- *WhoAmA 91*
Reber, Shannon Warren 1960- *WhoSSW 91*
Reber, Stanley R. 1943- *St&PR 91*
Reber, Stanley Roy 1943- *WhoAm 90*
Reberger, Frank 1944- *Ballpl 90*
Rebernik, Peter 1950- *WhoWor 91*
Rebhun, Lionel Israel 1926- *WhoAm 90*
Rebicek, Vincent Stass 1922- *WhoE 91*
Rebilas, Janet Marie 1958- *WhoAmW 91*
Rebman, Jay Richard 1959- *WhoEmL 91*
Rebner, Ronald Marshall 1944- *St&PR 91*
Rebolledo, Tey Diana 1937- *WhoHisp 91*
Rebone, William Frederick 1931- *St&PR 91*
Rebong, Efren Espiritu *BiDrAPA 89*
Reboredo, Pedro *WhoHisp 91*
Reboul, Antoine *AuBYP 90*
Reboul, Jaques Regis 1947- *WhoWor 91*
Rebozo, Charles Gregory 1912- *WhoAm 90*
Reburn, John A. 1926- *St&PR 91*
Reby, Morris *BiDrAPA 89*
Recabarren, Luis Emilio 1876-1924 *BioIn 16*
Recabo, Jaime Miguel 1950- *WhoE 91*
Recanati, Dimitri N. 1926- *St&PR 91*
Recanati, Dina *WhoAmA 91*
Recanati, Michael 1957- *St&PR 91*
Recanati, Raphael 1924- *WhoAm 90*
Recasens, Manuel *PenDiMP*
Recasens, Ricardo Cortina 1946- *WhoWor 91*
Recca, Theresa Marie 1948- *WhoAmW 91*
Recchia, Richard 1885-1983 *WhoAmA 91N*
Reccoppa, Lawrence *BiDrAPA 89*
Receveur, Betty Layman 1930- *ConAu 130*
Rech, Charles Louis 1938- *St&PR 91*
Rech, J.H. 1947- *St&PR 91*
Rech, Peter Wilhelm 1943- *WhoWor 91*
Rechard, Ottis William 1924- *WhoAm 90*
Rechard, Paul Albert 1927- *WhoAm 90*
Rechard, Robert Paul 1955- *WhoEmL 91*
Rechatin, Henri *BioIn 16*
Rechberger, Herman 1947- *IntWWM 90*
Rechholtz, Robert August 1937- *St&PR 91, WhoAm 90*
Rechkemmer, Michael Louis 1949- *St&PR 91*
Rechner, Theresa Schuh 1956- *St&PR 91*
Rechnitz, Garry Arthur 1936- *WhoAm 90*
Rechnitzer, Ferdinand Edsted 1894- *AuBYP 90*
Recht, Milton Richard 1948- *WhoE 91*
Rechter, Herbert Leslie 1932- *St&PR 91*
Rechter, Richard P. 1939- *St&PR 91*
Rechtin, Eberhardt 1926- *WhoAm 90*
Rechtin, Lissa Kathleen *BiDrAPA 89*
Rechtschaffen, Bernard 1922- *WhoAm 90*
Rechtzeit, Jack *BioIn 16*
Rechtzigel, Sue Marie 1947- *WhoAmW 91*
Rechy, John *BioIn 16*
Rechy, John 1934- *ConAu 32NR, HispWr 90*
Rechy, John Francisco *WhoAm 90, WhoHisp 91*
Recinos Arguello, Orlando Mauricio 1939- *WhoWor 91*
Recinto, Antonio Recio *BiDrAPA 89*
Recio, Carlos A 1915- *BiDrAPA 89*
Recio, Ruben D., Jr. 1947- *St&PR 91*
Reck, Alma Kehoe 1901- *AuBYP 90*
Reck, Andrew Joseph 1927- *WhoAm 90*
Reck, James Rodney 1938- *St&PR 91*
Reck, Joel M. 1941- *St&PR 91*
Reck, Michael Pierce 1928- *WhoWor 91*
Reck, Norma Jean 1933- *WhoE 91*
Reck, Saul I. 1918- *St&PR 91*
Reck, Thomas Carl 1914- *St&PR 91*
Reck, W. Emerson 1903- *WhoWrEP 89*
Reck, Waldo Emerson 1903- *WhoAm 90*
Reckard, Edgar Carpenter, Jr. 1919- *WhoAm 90*
Reckart, Marla Anne *BiDrAPA 89*
Recke, Elisabeth Charlotte K von der 1754-1833 *EncCoWW*
Recker, Kenneth Joseph 1947- *St&PR 91*
Recker, Ronald William 1949- *St&PR 91*
Reckford, Leo P. 1903-1988 *BioIn 16*
Reckless, Hannah *BiDEWW*
Reckless, John B 1929- *BiDrAPA 89*
Recklinghausen, Marianne Von 1929- *WhoAmA 91*
Reckmeyer, William John 1948- *WhoEmL 91*
Recknagel, Richard Otto 1916- *WhoAm 90*
Reclus, Jean-Jacques Elisee 1830-1905 *BiDFrPL*
Record, John Fordham 1942- *St&PR 91*
Record, Phillip Julius 1929- *WhoAm 90, WhoWor 91*
Record, Rush Hamil 1917- *WhoAm 90*
Records, George Jeffrey 1934- *St&PR 91*
Records, Susan Frances 1943- *WhoAmW 91*
Rectanus, Hans 1935- *IntWWM 90*
Rector, Charles Mitchell, Jr. 1962- *WhoWor 91*
Rector, Clark Ellsworth 1934- *WhoSSW 91*
Rector, Donna Lynn 1959- *WhoSSW 91*
Rector, Elias W. 1849- *AmLegL*
Rector, Floyd Clinton, Jr. 1929- *WhoAm 90*
Rector, Frederick P. 1949- *St&PR 91*
Rector, Harold E. 1946- *St&PR 91*
Rector, Henry Massey 1816-1899 *BioIn 16*
Rector, Joel Kirk 1948- *WhoEmL 91*
Rector, John Michael 1943- *WhoAm 90*
Rector, Liam *WhoSSW 91*
Rector, Liam 1949- *WhoWrEP 89*
Rector, Margaret Hayden 1916- *WhoAmW 91*
Rector, Milton Gage 1918- *WhoAm 90*
Rector, Richard Robert 1925- *WhoAm 90*
Rector, Robert Wayman 1916- *WhoAm 90*
Rector, Thomas Fredrick, Jr. 1949- *WhoSSW 91*
Rector, Walter Tucker 1930- *St&PR 91*
Recupero, John 1931- *St&PR 91*
Recupero, Linda *ODwPR 91*
Recupero, Patricia Ryan *BiDrAPA 89*
Red Bird 1788?-1828 *WhNaAH*
Red Cloud 1822?-1909 *WhNaAH [port]*
Red Crow *DcCanB 12*
Red Crow 1830?-1900 *WhNaAH*
Red Eagle *WhNaAH*
Red Iron 1810?-1884 *WhNaAH*
Red Jacket 1756?-1830 *EncCRAm*
Red Jacket 1758?-1830 *WhNaAH*
Red Shoes 1700?-1746 *WhNaAH*
Red Shoes 1700?-1748 *EncCRAm*
Red Wing 1750?-1825 *WhNaAH*
Red Star, Kevin 1943- *WhoAmA 91*
Reda, Fatma A *BiDrAPA 89*
Redcliffe-Maud, Baron 1906-1982 *DcNaB 1981*
Redcliffe-Maud, Lord *ConAu 129*
Redcliffe-Maud, John *ConAu 129*
Redcliffe-Maud, John Primatt 1906-1982 *ConAu 129*
Redd Ekks 1937- *WhoAmA 91*
Redd, Amasa Mason *BiDrAPA 89*
Redd, Charles Appleton 1954- *WhoEmL 91*
Redd, George Lenard 1952- *WhoSSW 91*
Redd, J. Diane 1945- *WhoAmW 91*
Redd, James Riley, III 1949- *WhoE 91*
Redd, Kathryn Jane 1958- *WhoAmW 91*
Redd, Mary Ann 1956- *WhoAmW 91*
Redd, Radney Markel 1947- *WhoSSW 91*
Redd, Richard James 1931- *WhoAmA 91*
Redda, Kinfe Ken 1948- *WhoSSW 91*
Reddall, Henry Hastings 1893-1989 *WhoAm 90*
Reddan, Harold Jerome 1926- *WhoAm 90*
Reddaway, John 1916-1990 *ConAu 132*
Reddell, Patti Jean 1959- *WhoAmW 91*
Redden, Bette Jo 1936- *WhoAmW 91*
Redden, David Normand 1949- *St&PR 91*
Redden, Edward C. 1923- *St&PR 91*
Redden, F. David 1940- *St&PR 91*
Redden, Jack Allison 1926- *WhoAm 90*
Redden, James Anthony 1929- *WhoAm 90*
Redden, Nigel A. 1950- *WhoAm 90*
Redden, Richard A. 1943- *St&PR 91*
Redden, Roger Duffey 1932- *WhoAm 90*
Redder, Thomas H. 1948- *St&PR 91*
Reddick, Bryan DeWitt 1942- *WhoE 91*
Reddick, Consuelo M 1960- *BiDrAPA 89*
Reddick, Eldon *BioIn 16*
Reddick, Raymond 1932- *St&PR 91*
Reddick, Richard L. 1951- *St&PR 91*
Reddick, Walker Homer 1922- *WhoSSW 91, WhoWor 91*
Reddin, Ronald D. 1947- *St&PR 91*
Redding, David W. 1948- *St&PR 91*
Redding, Dick 1891-1940 *Ballpl 90*
Redding, Edward John 1941- *St&PR 91*
Redding, Edward Patrick 1926- *St&PR 91*
Redding, Estelita Duenas 1942- *BiDrAPA 89*
Redding, Foster Kinyon 1929- *WhoAm 90*
Redding, J. Saunders 1906-1988 *BioIn 16*
Redding, Jay Saunders *WhoWrEP 89*
Redding, Jay Saunders 1906-1988 *BioIn 16*
Redding, John Leslie 1943- *WhoE 91*
Redding, Kenneth 1959- *WhoWor 91*
Redding, Lee Scott 1969- *WhoEmL 91*
Redding, Morris G. 1932- *WhoSSW 91*
Redding, Otis 1941-1967 *BioIn 16, ConMus 5 [port], DrBlPA 90, EncPR&S 89, OxCPMus, WorAlBi*
Redding, P.S. 1938- *St&PR 91*
Redding, Peter Stoddard 1938- *WhoAm 90*
Redding, Robert Hull 1919- *AuBYP 90*
Redding, Rogers Walker 1942- *WhoAm 90*
Redding, Stanley Gordon 1937- *WhoWor 91*
Redding, Thomas K. 1952- *St&PR 91*
Redding, William Howard, Jr. 1936- *St&PR 91*
Reddington, Charles Leonard 1929- *WhoAmA 91*
Reddington, Ivan Lloyd 1935- *WhoSSW 91*
Reddington, Joseph 1947- *WhoAm 90*
Reddington, Patrick Michael 1946- *St&PR 91*
Reddish, James H. 1930- *St&PR 91*
Reddish, John Joseph 1946- *WhoE 91, WhoEmL 91*
Redditt, G. Bruce 1951- *ODwPR 91*
Redditt, Julie Catherine 1940- *BiDrAPA 89*
Redditt, Nina Belle 1923- *WhoAmW 91*
Reddix, Roscoe Chester 1933- *WhoAmA 91*
Reddoch, Mildred Lucas 1916- *WhoSSW 91*
Reddout, Donna Jane 1947- *WhoWrEP 89*
Reddy, Agara Srinivas 1951- *BiDrAPA 89*
Reddy, C. Jagadeswara 1962- *WhoWor 91*
Reddy, D. Raj 1937- *WhoAm 90*
Reddy, Damoder Gummala 1942- *WhoWor 91*
Reddy, Daram Hammanth *BiDrAPA 89*
Reddy, Duttala Obula *BiDrAPA 89*
Reddy, Ellen Louise 1961- *WhoAmW 91*
Reddy, Geetha Devi 1957- *BiDrAPA 89*
Reddy, Gunukula Sudhakar 1952- *WhoEmL 91*
Reddy, Harshavardhan 1948- *BiDrAPA 89*
Reddy, Helen 1941- *WhoAm 90, WorAlBi*
Reddy, Helen 1942- *EncPR&S 89*
Reddy, Jagan Mohan S *BiDrAPA 89*
Reddy, Juvvala M 1946- *BiDrAPA 89*
Reddy, Kamalesh K 1938- *BiDrAPA 89*
Reddy, Kandula A *BiDrAPA 89*
Reddy, Karri Rama 1952- *BiDrAPA 89*
Reddy, Keshavpal Gunna *BiDrAPA 89*
Reddy, Kota Rohini 1945- *BiDrAPA 89*
Reddy, Krishna N 1925- *WhoAmA 91*
Reddy, Krishna Narayana 1925- *WhoAm 90*
Reddy, Kurapati B *BiDrAPA 89*
Reddy, Maureen T. 1955- *ConAu 130*
Reddy, Michael Thomas 1942- *WhoAm 90*
Reddy, Mitta Prathyusha 1949- *BiDrAPA 89*
Reddy, N. Sanjiva 1913- *BioIn 16*
Reddy, Nagamani P *BiDrAPA 89*
Reddy, Nirmala M 1953- *BiDrAPA 89*
Reddy, Nukala R 1945- *BiDrAPA 89*
Reddy, Pannala J M *BiDrAPA 89*
Reddy, Pranahitha B *BiDrAPA 89*
Reddy, Prasad *St&PR 91*
Reddy, Pratap Chandupatla 1944- *WhoSSW 91*
Reddy, Raju C *BiDrAPA 89*
Reddy, Ramakrishna P. 1936- *St&PR 91*
Reddy, Rathidevi M *BiDrAPA 89*
Reddy, Ravinder D. *BiDrAPA 89*
Reddy, Sarala K *BiDrAPA 89*
Reddy, Siva Prasad 1946- *St&PR 91*
Reddy, Srinivas P *BiDrAPA 89*
Reddy, Syamala H.K. 1947- *WhoSSW 91*
Reddy, Tanuja *BiDrAPA 89*
Reddy, Tarakumar B *BiDrAPA 89*
Reddy, Vangala V R 1939- *BiDrAPA 89*
Reddy, Vinutha C *BiDrAPA 89*
Reddy, William Mathew 1947- *WhoSSW 91*
Reddy, Y Stanley P *BiDrAPA 89*
Reddy, Yenamala Ramachandra 1939- *WhoSSW 91, WhoWor 91*
Rede, Deborah F. 1952- *WhoAmW 91*
Rede, George Henry 1952- *WhoHisp 91*
Redebaugh-Levi, Caroline Louise 1910- *WhoWor 91*
Redein, Alex S 1912- *WhoAmA 91*
Redeker, Allan Grant 1924- *WhoAm 90*
Redeker, Jerrald H. 1934- *St&PR 91*
Redeker, Jerrald Hale 1934- *WhoAm 90*
Redeker, Richard A. 1943- *St&PR 91*
Redeker, William E. 1919- *St&PR 91*
Redekopp, Elsa *SmATA 61*
Redemann, Louis C. 1938- *St&PR 91*
Redenbaugh, Keith 1951- *WhoEmL 91*
Redenius, Mary Palmer 1942- *WhoWrEP 89*
Reder, Bernard 1897-1963 *WhoAmA 91N*
Reder, Gerald Richard 1933- *St&PR 91*
Reder, Sanford M 1939- *BiDrAPA 89*
Redeske, James Floyd 1939- *St&PR 91*
Redetzki, Horst E. 1937- *St&PR 91*
Redfearn, Donald D. 1952- *St&PR 91*
Redfern, John D. 1936- *WhoAm 90*
Redfern, John Douglas 1935- *St&PR 91*
Redfern, John J., Jr. 1912- *St&PR 91*
Redfern, John Joseph, III 1939- *St&PR 91*
Redfern, June 1951- *BiDWomA*
Redfern, Paul *BioIn 16*
Redfern, Pete 1954- *Ballpl 90*
Redfield, Edward W 1869-1965 *WhoAmA 91N*
Redfield, James Michael 1935- *WhoAm 90*
Redfield, John H. 1924- *St&PR 91*
Redfield, Lisa Claire 1950- *WhoAmW 91*
Redfield, Robert Horace 1945- *WhoE 91*
Redfield, Rue Jean 1962- *WhoAmW 91*
Redfield, William Cox 1858-1932 *BiDrUSE 89*
Redfield, William F. *BioIn 16*
Redford, Donald Bruce 1934- *WhoAm 90, WhoWrEP 89*
Redford, Dorothy Spruill *BioIn 16*
Redford, Elizabeth 1646?-1729 *BiDEWW, FemiCLE*
Redford, Emmette Shelburn 1904- *WhoAm 90*
Redford, Gary William 1951- *WhoWor 91*
Redford, Lora Bryning *AuBYP 90*
Redford, Robert 1936- *BioIn 16*
Redford, Robert 1937- *WhoAm 90, WhoWor 91, WorAlBi*
Redgate, Christopher Frederick 1956- *IntWWM 90*
Redgate, Teresa Thompson 1943- *WhoSSW 91*
Redgrave, Lady *ConAu 130*
Redgrave, Felicity 1920- *WhoAmA 91*
Redgrave, Lynn *BioIn 16*
Redgrave, Lynn 1943- *WhoAm 90, WhoAmW 91, WorAlBi*
Redgrave, Michael 1908-1985 *WorAlBi*
Redgrave, Michael Scudamore 1908-1985 *DcNaB 1981*
Redgrave, Richard 1804-1888 *BioIn 16*
Redgrave, Vanessa 1937- *BioIn 16, WhoAm 90, WhoAmW 91, WhoWor 91, WorAlBi*
Redgwick, Donald Arthur 1933- *St&PR 91*
Redgwick, Hubert Arthur 1906- *St&PR 91*
Redhage, Darryl Keith 1938- *St&PR 91*
Redhage, James Herbert 1939- *St&PR 91*
Redhe, Sven Olle 1932- *WhoWor 91*
Redhead, Paul Aveling 1924- *WhoAm 90*
Redheffer, Raymond Moos 1921- *WhoAm 90*
Redhouse, John Walter, Jr. 1937- *St&PR 91*
Redican, Lois D. 1944- *WhoAmW 91*
Redick, Eva Jane 1901- *WhoAmW 91*
Redicker, Jane E. *ODwPR 91*
Redig, Christine 1949- *WhoAm 90*
Redig, Dale Francis 1929- *WhoAm 90, WhoWor 91*
Rediger, Delmar Reid 1934- *St&PR 91*
Rediker, Robert Harmon 1924- *WhoAm 90*
Reding, Kurt 1944- *WhoWor 91*
Reding, Michael E *BiDrAPA 89*
Reding, Nicholas Lee 1934- *St&PR 91, WhoAm 90*
Reding, Robert W. 1949- *St&PR 91*
Reding, Thomas M., Jr. 1951- *St&PR 91*
Redinger, James C. 1937- *St&PR 91*
Redinger, James Collins 1937- *WhoAm 90, WhoWor 91*
Redinger, Walter Fred 1942- *WhoAmA 91*
Redington, Rowland Wells 1924- *WhoAm 90*
Redington, Thomas 1943- *ODwPR 91*

Redkey, Edwin Storer 1931- *WhoE 91*
Redlawsk, David Paul 1958- *WhoE 91, WhoEmL 91*
Redleaf, Irene Jacklin 1940- *WhoAmW 91*
Redlener, Irwin *BioIn 16*
Redlener, Neil Barry *BiDrAPA 89*
Redler, Sherry Press 1933- *WhoAmW 91, WhoE 91*
Redlich, Frederick C *BiDrAPA 89*
Redlich, Jhodi *ODwPR 91*
Redlich, Marc 1946- *WhoE 91, WhoEmL 91, WhoWor 91*
Redlich, Norman 1925- *WhoAm 90*
Redlo, Rochelle Marcia 1949- *WhoE 91*
Redman, Barbara Klug 1936- *WhoAm 90*
Redman, Charles Bryson 1926- *St&PR 91*
Redman, Charles Edgar 1943- *WhoAm 90, WhoWor 91*
Redman, Clarence O. 1942- *St&PR 91*
Redman, Clarence Owen 1942- *WhoWor 91*
Redman, Dale Edward 1948- *St&PR 91*
Redman, Don 1900-1964 *BioIn 16, OxCPMus*
Redman, Gloria Diane 1940- *WhoAmW 91*
Redman, James Warren *BiDrAPA 89*
Redman, Peter 1935- *St&PR 91, WhoAm 90*
Redman, Ronald Arley 1931- *WhoE 91*
Redman, Samuel *BioIn 16*
Redman, Timothy Paul 1950- *WhoAm 90*
Redman, William Charles 1923- *WhoAm 90*
Redman, William Henry 1840- *AmLegL*
Redman, William Walter, Jr. 1933- *WhoSSW 91*
Redmann, Beverly Joan 1960- *BiDrAPA 89*
Redmayne, Martin 1910-1983 *DcNaB 1981*
Redmon, Charles F. 1942- *WhoAm 90*
Redmon, Mike 1950- *St&PR 91*
Redmond, Charles Robert 1926- *St&PR 91*
Redmond, Daniel G. *BioIn 16*
Redmond, Daniel Mark 1957- *St&PR 91, WhoE 91*
Redmond, Donald E 1939- *BiDrAPA 89*
Redmond, Donald Eugene, Jr. 1939- *WhoE 91*
Redmond, Douglas Michael 1954- *WhoE 91*
Redmond, Franklin C 1943- *BiDrAPA 89*
Redmond, Gail Elizabeth 1946- *WhoAmW 91, WhoSSW 91, WhoWor 91*
Redmond, Granville 1871-1935 *BioIn 16*
Redmond, J. Woodward 1921- *St&PR 91*
Redmond, James John 1933- *St&PR 91*
Redmond, James Ronald 1928- *WhoAm 90*
Redmond, John Charles 1931- *WhoAm 90, WhoE 91*
Redmond, John L. 1930- *St&PR 91*
Redmond, Kent Clifford 1914- *WhoAm 90*
Redmond, Liam 1913-1989 *AnObit 1989*
Redmond, Lisa Marie 1961- *WhoE 91*
Redmond, Lula Moshoures 1929- *WhoAmW 91*
Redmond, Michael C. 1955- *WhoE 91*
Redmond, Patricia Ann 1950- *WhoEmL 91*
Redmond, Paul Anthony 1937- *St&PR 91, WhoAm 90*
Redmond, Richard Joseph 1946- *St&PR 91*
Redmond, Robert Francis 1927- *WhoAm 90*
Redmond, Rosemary Warrick 1947- *WhoSSW 91*
Redmond, Scott Douglas 1954- *WhoWor 91*
Redmond, William Aloysius 1908- *WhoAm 90*
Redmont, Bernard *ODwPR 91*
Redmont, Bernard Sidney 1918- *WhoAm 90*
Redner, Raymond Daniel 1954- *WhoEmL 91*
Redner, Robert P. 1929- *St&PR 91*
Redner, Ronald Willard 1956- *WhoSSW 91*
Redner, S. Alex 1929- *St&PR 91*
Redo, Saverio Frank 1920- *WhoAm 90*
Redon, Jean Louis 1949- *WhoWor 91*
Redon, Joel 1961- *ConAu 131*
Redon, Odilon 1840-1916 *BioIn 16, IntDcAA 90*
Redondo, Ileana Valdes *BiDrAPA 89*
Redondo, Jose 1830-1878 *BioIn 16*
Redoy, Patrick D. 1941- *St&PR 91*
Redpath, Alan 1949- *St&PR 91*
Redpath, Anne 1895-1965 *BiDWomA*
Redrow, Elinor Mary 1938- *WhoAmW 91*
Redruello, Rosa Inchaustegui 1951- *WhoAmW 91*
Redsell, Peter T. W. *WhoE 91*
Redshaw, Peggy Ann 1948- *WhoAmW 91*
Redstone, Edward S. 1928- *St&PR 91*
Redstone, Louis Gordon 1903- *WhoAm 90, WhoAmA 91*
Redstone, Paul A 1937- *BiDrAPA 89*
Redstone, Sumner *BioIn 16*
Redstone, Sumner Murray 1923- *WhoAm 90, WhoE 91, WhoWor 91*
Redus, Gary 1956- *Ballpl 90*
Redway, Alan Arthur Sydney 1935- *WhoAm 90, WhoE 91*
Redway, Albert Sessions, Jr. 1929- *St&PR 91*
Redwine, Gary Scott 1950- *WhoSSW 91*
Redwood, Christopher William 1939- *IntWWM 90*
Redwood, Richard George 1936- *WhoAm 90*
Redyke, James Henry 1942- *WhoAm 90*
Ree, Jean Van 1943- *IntWWM 90*
Ree, Rhonda 1947- *WhoAmW 91*
Reeb, Harold B. 1936- *St&PR 91*
Reece, Arley 1945- *IntWWM 90*
Reece, Benny Ramon 1930- *WhoWor 91*
Reece, Beth Pauley 1945- *WhoAmW 91*
Reece, Cynthia Ann 1956- *WhoAmW 91*
Reece, David N. 1920- *St&PR 91*
Reece, Gabrielle *BioIn 16*
Reece, Helen Steele *BioIn 16*
Reece, James Adolphus 1919- *St&PR 91*
Reece, Jane *BioIn 16*
Reece, Joe Wilson 1935- *WhoAm 90*
Reece, Kathleen D. 1954- *WhoAmW 91*
Reece, Maynard 1920- *WhoAmA 91*
Reece, Maynard Fred 1920- *WhoAm 90*
Reece, Richard Terrance 1935- *WhoE 91*
Reece, Robert William 1942- *WhoAm 90*
Reece, S. Richard 1933- *St&PR 91*
Reece, Sterling Richard 1933- *WhoAm 90*
Reece, Steve Duane 1955- *WhoEmL 91*
Reece, Wanda G. 1956- *WhoAmW 91*
Reece, Wayne Gail 1935- *WhoWrEP 89*
Reeck, Leland K *BiDrAPA 89*
Reed, Adam Victor 1946- *WhoAm 90*
Reed, Addison Walker 1929- *IntWWM 90*
Reed, Alaina 1946- *DrBlPA 90*
Reed, Albert *DrBlPA 90*
Reed, Alfred *BioIn 16*
Reed, Alfred 1921- *WhoAm 90*
Reed, Alfred Byron 1916- *WhoAm 90, WhoWor 91*
Reed, Alfred Douglas 1928- *WhoSSW 91*
Reed, Alison Touster 1952- *WhoWrEP 89*
Reed, Amy 1960- *WhoAmW 91*
Reed, Anita 1939- *WhoSSW 91*
Reed, Anne Louise Mohan 1890-1936 *BioIn 16*
Reed, Austin F. 1951- *St&PR 91*
Reed, Barbara *BioIn 16*
Reed, Barbara Joan 1937- *WhoE 91*
Reed, Barbara Lee 1942- *WhoAmW 91*
Reed, Berenice Anne 1934- *WhoAmW 91, WhoE 91, WhoWor 91*
Reed, Billy *BioIn 16*
Reed, Bruce Norman 1926- *St&PR 91*
Reed, C. Robert 1936- *St&PR 91*
Reed, C. Robert 1944- *WhoSSW 91*
Reed, Carol 1906-1976 *WorAlBi*
Reed, Carolyn Breeding 1945- *WhoAmW 91*
Reed, Charles Allen 1912- *WhoAm 90*
Reed, Charles Bass 1941- *WhoAm 90, WhoSSW 91, WhoWor 91*
Reed, Charles Emmett 1922- *WhoAm 90*
Reed, Charles Loren, Jr. 1940- *St&PR 91*
Reed, Charles Rufus 1948- *WhoEmL 91*
Reed, Chris *BioIn 16*
Reed, Christopher Robert 1948- *WhoWor 91*
Reed, Cindy *BioIn 16*
Reed, Clarence Raymond 1932- *WhoAm 90*
Reed, Cleota *WhoAmA 91*
Reed, Cleveland Vonchero 1951- *WhoSSW 91*
Reed, Cordell 1938- *St&PR 91, WhoAm 90*
Reed, Curtis Michael 1948- *St&PR 91*
Reed, Dale D. 1931- *St&PR 91*
Reed, Dalpha Mae 1921- *WhoWrEP 89*
Reed, Darrel 1941- *St&PR 91*
Reed, Darwin Cramer 1915- *WhoAm 90*
Reed, David 1946- *WhoAm 90, WhoAmA 91*
Reed, David A. 1950- *St&PR 91*
Reed, David Andrew 1933- *WhoAm 90*
Reed, David Benson 1927- *WhoAm 90, WhoSSW 91*
Reed, David J., Jr. 1936- *St&PR 91*
Reed, David Mark 1947- *WhoSSW 91*
Reed, David Michael *BiDrAPA 89*
Reed, David Patrick 1952- *WhoE 91*
Reed, David Randal 1957- *WhoSSW 91*
Reed, David Scudder 1931- *St&PR 91*
Reed, David Stuart 1950- *WhoWrEP 89*
Reed, Deborah Ann 1957- *BiDrAPA 89*
Reed, Debra Lynn 1956- *St&PR 91*
Reed, Denise Jean 1951- *WhoAmW 91*
Reed, Dennis James 1946- *WhoAmA 91*
Reed, Diane Gray 1945- *WhoAmW 91, WhoSSW 91*
Reed, Diane Marie 1934- *WhoAmW 91*
Reed, Doel 1894- *WhoAmA 91N*
Reed, Donna 1921-1986 *WorAlBi*
Reed, Dorothy 1874-1964 *BioIn 16*
Reed, Earthalee 1945- *WhoE 91*
Reed, Edith Theresa 1927- *WhoAmW 91*
Reed, Eliot *MajTwCW, TwCCr&M 91*
Reed, Elizabeth Wagner 1912- *WhoAmW 91*
Reed, Erin *BioIn 16*
Reed, Ernest 1919-1985 *MusmAFA*
Reed, Esther De Berdt 1746-1780 *EncCRAm*
Reed, Evelyn Ruth 1924- *WhoE 91*
Reed, Everett C. 1916- *St&PR 91*
Reed, Flint Winter 1933- *WhoAmA 91*
Reed, Frank Metcalf, Sr. 1912- *St&PR 91*
Reed, Franklin G *BiDrAPA 89*
Reed, Fredric David 1937- *St&PR 91*
Reed, Fredric Wilson 1913- *WhoAm 90*
Reed, Gail S. 1943- *WhoAmW 91*
Reed, Gareth La Verne 1932- *St&PR 91, WhoAm 90*
Reed, George F. 1935- *St&PR 91*
Reed, George Farrell 1922- *WhoAm 90*
Reed, George Floyd 1935- *WhoE 91*
Reed, George Francis 1928- *WhoAm 90*
Reed, George Franklin 1935- *WhoAm 90*
Reed, George Lindmiller 1937- *WhoSSW 91*
Reed, George Michael 1945- *WhoWor 91*
Reed, Gordon W. 1899- *St&PR 91*
Reed, Gordon Wies 1899- *WhoAm 90*
Reed, Grant E. 1921- *St&PR 91*
Reed, Gwendolyn E 1932- *AuBYP 90*
Reed, H. Carlyle 1915- *WhoAm 90*
Reed, H. Edward 1931- *St&PR 91*
Reed, H. Owen 1910- *IntWWM 90*
Reed, Hal 1921- *WhoAmA 91*
Reed, Harold 1937- *WhoAmA 91*
Reed, Helen Bernice 1917- *WhoAmW 91*
Reed, Henry 1808-1854 *BioIn 16*
Reed, Henry Gooding 1810-1901 *PenDiDA 89*
Reed, Horace Curtis 1917- *WhoAm 90*
Reed, Howard Alexander 1920- *WhoAm 90*
Reed, Howie 1936-1984 *Ballpl 90*
Reed, Ishmael 1938- *BioIn 16, ConLC 60 [port], DcLB DS8 [port], MajTwCW, WorAlBi*
Reed, Ishmael Scott 1938- *WhoWrEP 89*
Reed, J. Ross 1949- *St&PR 91*
Reed, J. Walter 1933- *WhoAm 90*
Reed, Jack Louis 1945- *WhoAm 90*
Reed, James Anthony 1939- *WhoWor 91*
Reed, James Donald 1940- *WhoAm 90*
Reed, James Everette 1944- *WhoSSW 91*
Reed, James Hugh, IV 1949- *St&PR 91*
Reed, James M. 1933- *St&PR 91, WhoAm 90*
Reed, James V. *ODwPR 91*
Reed, James Wesley 1944- *WhoAm 90*
Reed, James Whitfield 1935- *WhoAm 90*
Reed, Jane Garson 1948- *WhoAmW 91, WhoEmL 91, WhoWor 91*
Reed, Janey Orr *BioIn 16*
Reed, Jean Salas 1940- *WhoAmW 91*
Reed, Jeff 1962- *Ballpl 90*
Reed, Jerry 1937- *OxCPMus, WorAlBi*
Reed, Jerry 1955- *Ballpl 90*
Reed, Jesse Floyd 1920- *WhoAmA 91*
Reed, Jim *BioIn 16*
Reed, Jimmy Burl, Sr. 1924- *WhoSSW 91*
Reed, Jody 1962- *Ballpl 90*
Reed, JoEllen 1953- *WhoAmW 91*
Reed, John 1887-1920 *BioIn 16, EncAL, WorAlBi*
Reed, John 1909- *IntWWM 90*
Reed, John Alton 1931- *WhoAm 90*
Reed, John Calvin 1935- *WhoSSW 91*
Reed, John E. 1915- *St&PR 91*
Reed, John F. 1917- *St&PR 91*
Reed, John Francis 1949- *WhoE 91*
Reed, John Franklin 1917- *St&PR 91, WhoAm 90*
Reed, John Frederick 1911- *WhoAm 90*
Reed, John G. 1929- *WhoAm 90*
Reed, John Giveen, Jr. 1930- *St&PR 91*
Reed, John Hathaway 1921- *WhoAm 90*
Reed, John Joseph 1956- *St&PR 91*
Reed, John L. 1928- *WhoE 91*
Reed, John M. 1927- *ODwPR 91*
Reed, John S. *BioIn 16*
Reed, John S. 1939- *WorAlBi*
Reed, John Shedd 1917- *WhoAm 90*
Reed, John Shepard 1939- *St&PR 91, WhoAm 90, WhoE 91, WhoWor 91*
Reed, John Squires, II 1949- *WhoSSW 91*
Reed, John Theodore 1946- *WhoWrEP 89*
Reed, John W. 1918- *WhoAm 90*
Reed, Jon Stanley 1939- *St&PR 91*
Reed, Joseph 1741-1785 *EncCRAm*
Reed, Joseph Howard 1930- *WhoAm 90*
Reed, Joseph Verner, Jr. 1937- *WhoAm 90, WhoE 91*
Reed, Joseph Wayne 1932- *WhoAm 90*
Reed, Joseph Wayne, Jr. 1932- *WhoWrEP 89*
Reed, Joyce Ann Borden 1939- *WhoAm 90*
Reed, Judy Jones 1947- *WhoEmL 91*
Reed, Katherine Marie 1942- *BiDrAPA 89*
Reed, Kathleen Rand 1947- *WhoEmL 91*
Reed, Kathlyn Louise 1940- *WhoAm 90*
Reed, Keith Allen 1939- *WhoAm 90*
Reed, Kenneth G. 1917- *WhoAm 90*
Reed, Kit *WhoAm 90, WhoWrEP 89*
Reed, Larita Diane 1960- *WhoAmW 91*
Reed, Larry Douglas 1939- *St&PR 91*
Reed, Laurie Rogers *BiDrAPA 89*
Reed, Leon S. 1918- *St&PR 91*
Reed, Leon Samuel 1949- *WhoE 91*
Reed, Leonard 1929- *St&PR 91*
Reed, Lester James 1925- *WhoAm 90*
Reed, Lester Willard, Jr. 1932- *WhoSSW 91*
Reed, Lois Mary 1919- *WhoWrEP 89*
Reed, Lou *BioIn 16*
Reed, Lou 1942- *WhoAm 90*
Reed, Lou 1943- *WorAlBi*
Reed, Lou 1944- *EncPR&S 89*
Reed, Louis Grant 1941- *WhoSSW 91*
Reed, Marcia McClaim 1944- *WhoAmW 91*
Reed, Margaret Carol 1935- *WhoAmW 91*
Reed, Mark Henry *BiDrAPA 89*
Reed, Marsha Lee 1953- *WhoAmW 91, WhoSSW 91, WhoWor 91*
Reed, Martha Jane 1955- *WhoSSW 91*
Reed, Mary Lou *WhoAmW 91*
Reed, Merian Lynn 1947- *WhoAmW 91*
Reed, Merl Elwyn 1925- *WhoSSW 91*
Reed, Michael Arthur 1947- *WhoAmA 91*
Reed, Michael Charles 1942- *WhoAm 90*
Reed, Michael Christopher 1958- *BiDrAPA 89*
Reed, Michael John 1940- *WhoAm 90*
Reed, Myrtle 1874-1911 *FemiCLE*
Reed, Nancy Carol 1951- *WhoEmL 91*
Reed, Norman Bruce 1949- *WhoEmL 91, WhoWor 91*
Reed, Norman E., Jr. 1928- *St&PR 91*
Reed, Oliver 1938- *WhoAm 90, WhoWor 91, WorAlBi*
Reed, Pamela *BioIn 16*
Reed, Paul 1956- *WhoWrEP 89*
Reed, Paul Allen 1919- *WhoAm 90, WhoAmA 91*
Reed, Philip B *BiDrAPA 89*
Reed, Philip Dunham 1899-1989 *BioIn 16*
Reed, Presley Orell, Jr. *BiDrAPA 89*
Reed, Ramona Booze 1942- *BiDrAPA 89*
Reed, Raymond Deryl 1930- *WhoAm 90*
Reed, Rex 1938- *ConTFT 8, WhoWrEP 89*
Reed, Rex Raymond 1922- *WhoAm 90*
Reed, Richard B. 1943- *WhoSSW 91*
Reed, Richard John 1922- *WhoAm 90*
Reed, Richard W. 1920- *St&PR 91*
Reed, Robert 1932- *WorAlBi*
Reed, Robert Alan 1942- *St&PR 91, WhoAm 90*
Reed, Robert Daniel 1941- *WhoAm 90*
Reed, Robert Dixon 1927- *St&PR 91*
Reed, Robert G., III 1927- *St&PR 91*
Reed, Robert George, III 1927- *WhoAm 90*
Reed, Robert Leonard 1932- *St&PR 91*
Reed, Robert M *BiDrAPA 89*
Reed, Robert Monroe 1932- *WhoAm 90*
Reed, Robert Stuart 1928- *WhoAm 90*
Reed, Roberta Gable 1945- *WhoAmW 91*
Reed, Roger Harold 1941- *St&PR 91*
Reed, Rolland F. 1929- *St&PR 91*
Reed, Ron 1942- *Ballpl 90*
Reed, Rose Pearl 1868-1925 *BioIn 16*
Reed, Rosemary 1952- *WhoAmW 91, WhoE 91*
Reed, Sally Ann 1947- *WhoWrEP 89*
Reed, Scott 1921- *WhoAm 90*
Reed, Scott Eldridge 1948- *St&PR 91, WhoSSW 91*
Reed, Scott William 1960- *WhoAm 90*
Reed, Seaton A., Jr. 1941- *St&PR 91*
Reed, Sherman Kennedy 1919- *WhoAm 90*
Reed, Sidney George, Jr. 1921- *WhoAm 90*
Reed, Stanley Foster 1917- *WhoAm 90, WhoWor 91*
Reed, Stass *BioIn 16*
Reed, Suanne Michelle *BiDrAPA 89*
Reed, Tara Glover 1957- *WhoSSW 91*
Reed, Terry Allen 1948- *WhoSSW 91*
Reed, Theodore Breckenridge 1918- *St&PR 91*
Reed, Thomas Ansley 1922- *St&PR 91*
Reed, Thomas Care 1934- *WhoAm 90*
Reed, Thomas F. 1944- *St&PR 91*
Reed, Thomas German 1817-1888 *OxCPMus*
Reed, Thomas Milburne 1825-1905 *AmLegL*
Reed, Tony N. 1951- *WhoAm 90*
Reed, Tracy 1949?- *DrBlPA 90*
Reed, Travis Dean 1930- *WhoAm 90*
Reed, Vincent Emory 1928- *WhoAm 90*
Reed, Vivian *DrBlPA 90*
Reed, Wallace Allison 1916- *WhoAm 90, WhoWor 91*
Reed, Walt Arnold 1917- *WhoAmA 91, WhoE 91*
Reed, Walter 1851-1902 *WorAlBi*

Reed, Walter Gurnee Dyer 1952- WhoE 91
Reed, Walter W. 1924- ODwPR 91
Reed, Warren H. BioIn 16
Reed, William A. 1936- WhoE 91
Reed, William B. 1806-1876 BioIn 16
Reed, William Burch 1928- St&PR 91
Reed, William Edward 1914- WhoAm 90, WhoWor 91
Reed, William F. BioIn 16
Reed, William Francis, Jr. 1951- WhoE 91
Reed, William H 1876-1942 PenDiMP
Reed, William L. 1951- St&PR 91
Reed, William LaForest 1912- WhoAm 90
Reed, William Leonard 1910- IntWWM 90
Reed, William Preston, Jr. 1954- St&PR 91
Reed, William Stoneman 1937- WhoE 91
Reed, Willis BioIn 16
Reed, Willis 1942- WhoAm 90, WhoE 91, WorAlBi
Reed, Wrightly Thompson 1945- WhoSSW 91
Reed-Bignall, Nancy Louise 1954- WhoAmW 91
Reed-Gohacki, Nancy Eshleman Hazel 1942- WhoSSW 91
Reed-Mackay, Pauline Reed 1942- St&PR 91
Reede, Fred Allan, Jr. 1956- WhoEmL 91
Reede, Ronald Howard 1960- WhoE 91
Reeder, Charles 1918- WhoSSW 91
Reeder, Charles Benton 1922- WhoAm 90
Reeder, Clifton Lee 1918- WhoAm 90
Reeder, David Scott 1944- St&PR 91
Reeder, Dennis Harry 1946- WhoE 91
Reeder, Donald Lee 1930- St&PR 91
Reeder, Douglas L. 1937- St&PR 91
Reeder, Ellen Dryden 1947- WhoE 91
Reeder, Frank Fitzgerald 1932- WhoWor 91
Reeder, Harley S. 1929- St&PR 91
Reeder, Hubert 1948- WhoWrEP 89
Reeder, Hugh Sidney 1930- St&PR 91
Reeder, James Arthur 1933- WhoSSW 91
Reeder, James Seymour, Jr. 1932- St&PR 91
Reeder, John P., Jr. 1937- WhoAm 90
Reeder, Levi B. 1865-1930 AmLegL
Reeder, Marjorie Jones 1953- WhoSSW 91
Reeder, Milton K. 1956- St&PR 91
Reeder, Neil Edward 1934- St&PR 91
Reeder, Oliver Howard 1916- WhoAm 90
Reeder, Paula B. 1950- St&PR 91
Reeder, Red AuBYP 90
Reeder, Robert Harry 1930- WhoAm 90, WhoWor 91
Reeder, Roger Kent 1950- WhoEmL 91
Reeder, Russell Potter 1902- AuBYP 90
Reeder, Stewart St&PR 91
Reeder, Virginia Lee 1929- WhoAmW 91, WhoWor 91
Reeder, William H. 1939- St&PR 91
Reedus, Glenn ODwPR 91
Reedy, Catherine Irene 1953- WhoE 91
Reedy, Eileen L. 1958- St&PR 91
Reedy, George Edward 1917- WhoAm 90, WhoWrEP 89
Reedy, Harry Lee 1945- WhoE 91
Reedy, Jerry Edward 1936- WhoAm 90, WhoWrEP 89
Reedy, John Joseph 1927- WhoE 91
Reedy, Penelope Michal 1947- WhoWrEP 89
Reedy, Raymond E 1917- BiDrAPA 89
Reef, Arthur 1916- ODwPR 91, WhoAm 90
Reefer, Elizabeth Dross 1951- WhoEmL 91
Reeg, Cloyd Pritchard 1922- WhoAm 90
Reeg, Jay F. 1931- St&PR 91
Reeg, Kurtis Bradford 1954- WhoEmL 91
Reeger, Marie Ann 1956- WhoAmW 91
Reeher, William Floyd 1933- St&PR 91
Reehling, Ronald E. 1935- St&PR 91
Reek, Donald Ashley 1934- WhoE 91
Reekie, Charles Douglas 1924- St&PR 91
Reeks, Richard William 1927- WhoSSW 91
Reel, Jerry Royce 1938- WhoAm 90
Reel, Leidy Rodger, III 1952- St&PR 91
Reels, Donna Marie 1948- WhoAmW 91
Reely, Mary Katharine 1881- AuBYP 90
Reeman, Douglas Edward 1924- SmATA 63 [port]
Reemtsma, Keith 1925- WhoAm 90
Reen, Jeremiah Joseph 1942- WhoAm 90
Reep, Douglas Howard 1953- WhoE 91
Reep, Edward Arnold 1918- WhoAm 90, WhoAmA 91
Rees, Albert 1921- WhoAm 90
Rees, Angharad 1949- ConTFT 8
Rees, Angus Macdonald 1925- St&PR 91
Rees, Ceridwen Joyce Louise 1964- IntWWM 90
Rees, Charles H. G. 1922- WhoAm 90, WhoWor 91
Rees, Clifford Harcourt, Jr. 1936- WhoAm 90
Rees, David BioIn 16
Rees, David 1936- BioIn 16
Rees, David John 1935- BiDrAPA 89
Rees, David Linford 1942- WhoWor 91
Rees, Diane DeMuro 1939- WhoAmW 91
Rees, Dilwyn ConAu 30NR
Rees, Eloise Rodkey 1918- WhoWrEP 89
Rees, Ennis 1925- AuBYP 90
Rees, Frances Irene 1942- WhoAmW 91
Rees, Fred Joseph 1949- IntWWM 90
Rees, Grahame 1937- St&PR 91
Rees, Grover Joseph, III 1951- WhoAm 90
Rees, Helen Christina Easson 1903-1970 AuBYP 90
Rees, Heward 1935- IntWWM 90
Rees, Howard David 1953- WhoE 91
Rees, Linford BiDrAPA 89
Rees, Lloyd 1895-1988 AnObit 1988
Rees, Mary AuBYP 90
Rees, Mina 1902- WhoAm 90
Rees, Nigel 1944- ConAu 132
Rees, Norma S. 1929- WhoAm 90
Rees, Paul Stromberg 1900- WhoAm 90
Rees, Sherrel Jerry Evans 1926- WhoAm 90
Rees, Warren A. 1926- St&PR 91
Rees, William Lehigh 1900-1989 BioIn 16
Rees, William Smith, Jr. 1959- WhoEmL 91
Rees-Mogg, William 1928- WhoWor 91
Rees-Williams, Jonathan 1949- IntWWM 90
Reesby, Carl Edwin 1926- St&PR 91
Reese, Andy 1904-1966 Ballpl 90
Reese, Bernard P., Jr. 1925- St&PR 91
Reese, Bert 1851-1926 EncO&P 3, EncPaPR 91
Reese, Bob 1938- BioIn 16, SmATA X [port]
Reese, Bruce T. 1949- St&PR 91
Reese, Carolyn Johnson 1938- ConAu 30NR, SmATA 64
Reese, Charles Lee 1903-1989 BioIn 16
Reese, Charles S. 1948- St&PR 91
Reese, Dana Elizabeth 1955- WhoAmW 91, WhoWor 91
Reese, Daniel William 1953- WhoE 91
Reese, David L. 1945- St&PR 91
Reese, Deborah Decker 1950- WhoAmW 91, WhoWrEP 89
Reese, Della 1931- OxCPMus, WorAlBi
Reese, Della 1932- DrBlPA 90
Reese, Floyd Curtis BiDrAPA 89
Reese, Francis Edward 1919- WhoAm 90
Reese, Frank L. 1919- St&PR 91
Reese, Glen A. 1939- St&PR 91
Reese, Harold, Jr. 1942- WhoSSW 91
Reese, Harry Browne 1926- WhoAm 90
Reese, Harry Edwin, Jr. 1928- WhoAm 90
Reese, Harvey C, Jr. BiDrAPA 89
Reese, Hayne Waring 1931- WhoAm 90
Reese, Jack Edward 1929- WhoSSW 91
Reese, James D. 1941- St&PR 91
Reese, James R. 1930- St&PR 91
Reese, Jesse C. BioIn 16
Reese, Jimmie 1905- Ballpl 90
Reese, John Henry AuBYP 90
Reese, John R. 1944- St&PR 91
Reese, John Rathbone 1944- WhoAm 90
Reese, John Robert 1939- WhoAm 90
Reese, John Russell 1948- St&PR 91
Reese, Joseph Hammond, Jr. 1928- St&PR 91
Reese, Kenneth Wendell 1930- St&PR 91, WhoAm 90, WhoSSW 91
Reese, Lizette Woodworth 1856-1935 FemiCLE
Reese, Lowell D. 1940- WhoAm 90
Reese, Lydia Jane 1960- WhoAmW 91
Reese, Lymon Clifton 1917- WhoAm 90
Reese, Lyn ConAu 30NR
Reese, Marcia Mitchell WhoAmA 91
Reese, Martha Grace 1953- WhoAmW 91
Reese, Martha K BiDrAPA 89
Reese, Mary BioIn 16
Reese, Matthew Anderson 1927- WhoAm 90
Reese, Michael Joseph 1949- St&PR 91
Reese, Mildred Lyons WhoAmW 91
Reese, Mona Lyn 1951- WhoAmW 91
Reese, Norma Carol 1946- WhoAmW 91
Reese, Paul S. 1951- St&PR 91
Reese, Pee Wee 1918- Ballpl 90 [port]
Reese, Rich 1941- Ballpl 90
Reese, Richard Bruce 1940- St&PR 91, WhoAm 90
Reese, Richard F. 1945- St&PR 91
Reese, Richard Page 1926- WhoWrEP 89
Reese, Robert A 1938- SmATA 60 [port]
Reese, Robert Jenkins 1947- WhoEmL 91
Reese, Roger A. 1945- St&PR 91
Reese, Ronald Craig WhoE 91
Reese, S. Howard 1944- St&PR 91
Reese, Ted M. 1959- WhoEmL 91, WhoWor 91
Reese, Terence BioIn 16
Reese, Terence 1913- ConAu 30NR
Reese, Terry W. 1942- St&PR 91
Reese, Thomas Ford 1943- WhoAmA 91
Reese, Thomas William 1924- St&PR 91
Reese, Virginia Margaret Pearson 1929- WhoSSW 91
Reese, William Albert, III 1932- WhoWor 91
Reese, William Foster 1938- WhoAmA 91
Reese, William G 1917- BiDrAPA 89
Reese, William Lewis 1921- WhoAm 90
Reese, William Willis 1940- WhoE 91
Reese, Willis L. M. NewYTBS 90
Reese, Willis Livingston Mesier 1913-1990 WhoAm 90, WhoE 91
Reeser, Denise Louise 1957- WhoAmW 91
Reeser, Eduard 1908- IntWWM 90
Reeser, Edward V. 1952- St&PR 91
Reeser, James R., Jr. 1939- St&PR 91
Reeser, Jeannie G. WhoHisp 91
Reeser, Lyle Grant 1918- WhoAm 90
Reeser, Michael AuBYP 90
Reeser, Robert D 1931- WhoAmA 91
Reeser, Shirley Schulz 1935- WhoAmW 91
Reesman, Kenneth G. 1921- St&PR 91
Reetz, Robert Russell 1958- WhoE 91
Reeve, Ada 1874-1966 OxCPMus
Reeve, Adrian Grantley 1957- WhoWor 91
Reeve, Agnesa Lufkin 1927- WhoWrEP 89
Reeve, Alison BiDrAPA 89
Reeve, Arthur B 1880-1936 TwCCr&M 91
Reeve, Christopher BioIn 16
Reeve, Christopher 1952- WhoAm 90, WorAlBi
Reeve, Clara 1729-1807 BioIn 16, FemiCLE
Reeve, Don NewAgMG
Reeve, Edgar H. 1945- St&PR 91
Reeve, Elizabeth Anne BiDrAPA 89
Reeve, Eve Lynne Joan 1935- IntWWM 90
Reeve, F.D. 1928- WhoWrEP 89
Reeve, James Key WhoAm 90, WhoAmA 91, WhoWor 91
Reeve, Janet Wheeler 1941- WhoWor 91
Reeve, Joel AuBYP 90
Reeve, John Newton 1947- WhoAm 90
Reeve, Lester E. BioIn 16
Reeve, Peter 1934- WhoAm 90
Reeve, Richard Robert 1948- WhoE 91
Reeve, Ronald Cropper, Jr. 1943- WhoAm 90
Reeve, Scott NewYTBS 90
Reeve, Stephen 1948- IntWWM 90
Reeve, William 1757-1815 OxCPMus
Reeve, William Albert 1842-1894 DcCanB 12
Reeve, Winnifred 1877-1954 FemiCLE
Reeves, A. Sue Windsor 1947- WhoAmW 91
Reeves, Alec H. 1902-1971 BioIn 16
Reeves, Amber 1887-1981 FemiCLE
Reeves, Barbara Ann 1949- WhoAm 90, WhoEmL 91
Reeves, Benjamin Franklin 1922- WhoE 91
Reeves, Betty 1913- IntWWM 90
Reeves, Bobby 1904- Ballpl 90
Reeves, Carla Marianne 1949- WhoAmW 91
Reeves, Charles Banes, Jr. 1923- WhoAm 90
Reeves, Charles Howell 1915- WhoAm 90
Reeves, Charles Monroe, Jr. 1923- St&PR 91
Reeves, Charles Sherman 1927- St&PR 91
Reeves, Charlotte Teel 1955- WhoAmW 91
Reeves, Christopher Reginald 1936- WhoAm 90
Reeves, Clara 1729-1807 BioIn 16
Reeves, Dan 1944- BioIn 16
Reeves, Daniel WhoAmA 91
Reeves, David Nash Scott 1951- WhoSSW 91
Reeves, Dianne BioIn 16
Reeves, Edmund Hoffman, III 1949- WhoE 91
Reeves, Edward James 1947- WhoSSW 91
Reeves, Frances Skinner 1926- St&PR 91
Reeves, Gary Wayne 1955- WhoSSW 91
Reeves, Gene 1930- WhoSSW 91
Reeves, Gene S. 1928- St&PR 91
Reeves, George R. 1826- AmLegL
Reeves, Ginger Ann 1949- WhoWrEP 89
Reeves, Gregory Arthur 1961- WhoE 91
Reeves, Henry A. 1923- ODwPR 91
Reeves, Hubert 1932- ConAu 132
Reeves, J Mason 1898-1973 WhoAmA 91N
Reeves, James 1909- AuBYP 90
Reeves, James Franklin 1946- WhoAmA 91
Reeves, Jim 1924-1964 OxCPMus
Reeves, John Alexander 1938- WhoAmA 91
Reeves, John Drummond 1914- WhoE 91
Reeves, John P. 1934- St&PR 91
Reeves, Joyce AuBYP 90
Reeves, Keanu BioIn 16
Reeves, Keith O. 1944- WhoSSW 91
Reeves, Lucy Mary 1932- WhoAmW 91
Reeves, M EncO&P 3
Reeves, Malcolm M. 1908- St&PR 91
Reeves, Mark Thomas 1955- WhoSSW 91
Reeves, Martha BioIn 16
Reeves, Martha 1941- ConMus 4
Reeves, Marvin Coke 1911- St&PR 91
Reeves, Michael C. 1947- WhoSSW 91
Reeves, Michael Stanley 1935- St&PR 91
Reeves, Miranda BioIn 16
Reeves, Patricia Ruth 1931- WhoAmW 91, WhoE 91
Reeves, Paul Alfred 1932- WhoWor 91
Reeves, Ralph Milton BiDrAPA 89
Reeves, Ray St&PR 91
Reeves, Richard Ackroyd 1927- St&PR 91
Reeves, Richard Allen 1944- WhoE 91
Reeves, Richard Edward 1942- WhoSSW 91
Reeves, Richard Lawrence 1948- WhoSSW 91
Reeves, Robert Edwin 1953- BiDrAPA 89
Reeves, Robert Grier LeFevre 1920- WhoAm 90
Reeves, Robert Harold 1926- St&PR 91
Reeves, Ross Newton, III 1944- St&PR 91
Reeves, Rosser Scott, III 1936- WhoAm 90
Reeves, Roy Russell 1952- WhoEmL 91, WhoWor 91
Reeves, Sims 1818-1900 PenDiMP
Reeves, Susan Elizabeth Buchanan 1940- WhoWrEP 89
Reeves, Talmadge C 1934- BiDrAPA 89
Reeves, Thomas Joseph 1935- WhoAm 90
Reeves, Timothy John 1952- WhoE 91
Reeves, Timothy Scott 1953- WhoWrEP 89
Reeves, W. Colby, Jr. 1945- St&PR 91
Reeves, William Harrison, Jr. 1955- WhoE 91
Reeves-Darby, Vonda Gail 1958- WhoAmW 91
Reeves-Kazelskis, Carolyn 1941- WhoAmW 91
Reeves-Marquardt, Dona Batty 1932- WhoSSW 91
Ref-Ren 1907- WhoWor 91
Reff, Robert Alan 1953- BiDrAPA 89
Reff, Theodore 1930- WhoAmA 91
Refinski, Joseph Anthony 1954- WhoE 91
Refior, Everett Lee 1919- WhoAm 90
Refkin, Randy Scott BiDrAPA 89
Refregier, Anton 1905-1979 WhoAmA 91N
Refsland, Gary Arlan 1944- WhoWor 91
Refsnes, Joseph L. 1926- St&PR 91
Rega, Jose Lopez 1916-1989 BioIn 16
Regal, Robert Denis 1941- WhoWor 91
Regalado, Jacinto E BiDrAPA 89
Regalado, Raul L. 1945- WhoAm 90, WhoEmL 91
Regalbuto, Joe ConTFT 8
Regalmuto, Nancy Marie 1956- WhoAmW 91
Regan, Ann Ellen 1962- WhoAmW 91
Regan, Ann Kennedy 1923- WhoAmW 91
Regan, Bill 1899-1968 Ballpl 90
Regan, Bruce L BiDrAPA 89
Regan, Christopher Peter William 1929- IntWWM 90
Regan, Daniel Joseph 1945- St&PR 91
Regan, David 1935- WhoAm 90
Regan, David Bryan BiDrAPA 89
Regan, David Michael 1955- WhoE 91
Regan, Dennis LeRoy 1957- WhoEmL 91
Regan, Donald T. BioIn 16
Regan, Donald Thomas 1918- BiDrUSE 89, WhoAm 90, WhoWor 91
Regan, Edward Van Buren 1930- WhoE 91
Regan, Ellen Frances 1919- WhoAmW 91
Regan, F. Vincent 1922- St&PR 91
Regan, Francisco Antonio 1941- WhoWor 91
Regan, Frederic Dennis 1921- WhoE 91, WhoWor 91
Regan, Geoffrey 1946- ConAu 129
Regan, Harold 1943- St&PR 91
Regan, John J. 1929- ConAu 131, WhoAm 90
Regan, John James 1916- BiDrAPA 89
Regan, John MacVeigh, Jr. 1921- St&PR 91, WhoAm 90
Regan, Judith Jefferson BiDrAPA 89
Regan, Mardee Haidin 1949- WhoAmW 91
Regan, Michael Anthony 1959- WhoE 91
Regan, Michael James 1947- IntWWM 90
Regan, Muriel 1930- WhoAmW 91
Regan, Nathan 1926- St&PR 91
Regan, Patrick James 1949- St&PR 91
Regan, Patrick Joseph 1947- WhoWor 91
Regan, Paul Edward 1939- St&PR 91
Regan, Paul J., Jr. 1940- St&PR 91
Regan, Peter C. 1940- St&PR 91
Regan, Peter F, III 1924- BiDrAPA 89
Regan, Peter Francis, III 1924- WhoAm 90, WhoE 91
Regan, Phil 1937- Ballpl 90
Regan, Robert Charles 1930- WhoAm 90
Regan, Rod 1950- St&PR 91
Regan, Susan J. 1952- BiDrAPA 89

Regan, Suzanne Marie 1950- *WhoAmW 91*
Regan, Sylvia 1908- *WhoAm 90*
Regan, Walter Joseph, Jr. 1936- *St&PR 91*
Regan, William F. 1926-1988 *BioIn 16*
Regan, William Jerome 1943- *St&PR 91*
Regan, William Joseph, Jr. 1946- *WhoAm 90, WhoSSW 91*
Regan, William Marion 1938- *St&PR 91*
Regan, William Mark 1924- *BiDrAPA 89*
Regar, David Bennett 1939- *St&PR 91*
Regardie, Israel 1907-1985 *BioIn 16, EncO&P 3*
Regaspi, Lisa Ford 1961- *WhoAmW 91*
Regat, Jean-Jacques Albert 1945- *WhoAmA 91*
Regat, Mary E 1943- *WhoAmA 91*
Regazzi, John H. 1921- *St&PR 91*
Regazzi, John Henry 1921- *WhoAm 90, WhoWor 91*
Regeimbal, Neil Robert, Sr. 1929- *WhoAm 90*
Regelbrugge, Roger Rafael 1930- *St&PR 91, WhoAm 90*
Regelin, Louise O. 1940- *WhoAmW 91*
Regenbogen, Ellis Arnold 1946- *St&PR 91*
Regenbogen, Leslie Alan 1932- *St&PR 91*
Regenold, William Thomas *BiDrAPA 89*
Regensburg, Anthony Shepard 1928- *WhoAm 90*
Regensburg, Joseph *PenDiDA 89*
Regensburg, Sophy P 1885-1974 *WhoAmA 91N*
Regensburger, Linda Susan 1953- *WhoEmL 91*
Regenstein, Barry I. 1956- *St&PR 91*
Regenstein, Lewis Graham 1943- *WhoAm 90*
Regenstein, Louis 1912- *St&PR 91, WhoAm 90*
Regensteiner, Else 1906- *WhoAmA 91*
Regensteiner, Else Friedsam 1906- *WhoAm 90*
Regenstreif, Herbert 1935- *WhoE 91, WhoWor 91*
Regenstreif, Samuel Peter 1936- *WhoAm 90*
Reger, Daniel L. 1945- *WhoSSW 91*
Reger, George F. 1928- *St&PR 91*
Reger, Lawrence L 1939- *WhoAmA 91*
Reger, Lawrence Lee 1939- *WhoAm 90*
Reger, Max 1873-1916 *BioIn 16, PenDiMP A*
Reger, Paul A. 1926- *St&PR 91*
Reger, Ronald A. 1949- *St&PR 91*
Reges, Marianna Alice 1947- *WhoAm 90, WhoWor 91*
Regester, Charlotte *WhoAmA 91N*
Regets, Mark Curtis 1956- *WhoE 91*
Reggia, Frank 1921- *WhoAm 90*
Regier, Anna Lee Katherine 1926- *WhoWrEP 89*
Regier, Darcy John 1956- *WhoE 91*
Regier, Darrel Alvin 1944- *BiDrAPA 89*
Regier, Gail *BioIn 16*
Regier, Jon Louis 1922- *WhoAm 90, WhoWor 91*
Regina 1894-1974 *BiDWomA*
Regina, Frank Joseph 1934- *St&PR 91*
Reginald, Daniel 1939- *WhoWor 91*
Reginald, Robert 1948- *WhoAm 90, WhoWrEP 89*
Reginalda, Bathsua *BiDEWW*
Reginato, Peter 1945- *BioIn 16, WhoAmA 91*
Reginato, Robert Joseph 1935- *WhoAm 90*
Regini, Judith L. 1953- *WhoAmW 91*
Regiomontanus 1436-1476 *WorAlBi*
Regirer, Walter Wlodzimierz 1913- *WhoWor 91*
Regis, Ed *ConAu 132*
Regis, Edward, Jr. 1944- *ConAu 132*
Register, Annette Rowan 1931- *WhoAmW 91*
Register, Benjamin Franklin, Jr. 1930- *WhoAm 90*
Register, David S. 1956- *St&PR 91*
Register, John 1939- *BioIn 16*
Register, Penelope Warren 1956- *WhoAmW 91*
Register, Richard Outler 1949- *WhoEmL 91*
Register, Ulma Doyle 1920- *WhoAm 90*
Register, Victoria Smith 1944- *WhoWrEP 89*
Regli, Adolph Casper 1896- *AuBYP 90*
Regn, Gerhard Klaus 1944- *WhoWor 91*
Regnard, Louis *PenDiDA 89*
Regnard, Pierre-Louis *PenDiDA 89*
Regner, Steven Henry 1947- *WhoE 91*
Regnery, Alfred Scattergood 1942- *WhoAm 90*
Regnery, Henry *BioIn 16*
Regnery, Henry 1912- *WhoAm 90*
Regnier, Francois Jean 1933- *WhoWor 91*
Regnier, Marc 1939- *St&PR 91*
Regnier, Philippe Thierry 1960- *WhoWor 91*
Regnier, Robert Dennis 1948- *St&PR 91*
Regnier, Stephen Joseph 1950- *WhoWrEP 89*
Regnis, Michael *BioIn 16*
Rego, Edward John 1948- *St&PR 91*
Rego, Jose Lins do 1901-1957 *BioIn 16*
Rego, Lawrence *WhoHisp 91*
Rego, Mark David *BiDrAPA 89*
Rego, Paula 1935- *BiDWomA*
Rego, Vincent Anthony 1924- *St&PR 91*
Rego Monteiro, Vincente do 1899-1970 *ArtLatA*
Regoli, Robert Michael 1950- *WhoEmL 91*
Regosin, Richard Lloyd 1937- *WhoAm 90*
Regteren, Maria Engelina van 1868-1958 *BiDWomA*
Regueiro, Maria Cristina 1947- *WhoHisp 91*
Reguero, Edward Anthony 1960- *WhoEmL 91*
Reguero, M. A. 1918- *WhoHisp 91*
Reguero, Melodie Huber 1956- *WhoAmW 91, WhoEmL 91, WhoWor 91*
Regula, Ralph 1924- *WhoAm 90*
Regules, Roxanne 1955- *WhoAmW 91*
Regulski, Janice Steele 1928- *WhoAmW 91*
Reh, Thomas Edward 1943- *WhoWor 91*
Reha, Rose Krivisky 1920- *WhoAmW 91, WhoWor 91*
Rehagen-Huff, Andrea Lee 1949- *WhoAmW 91*
Rehan, Ada 1860-1916 *BioIn 16*
Rehan, Ada Delia 1857-1916 *NotWoAT*
Rehark, Russell John 1911- *St&PR 91*
Rehbach, Jeffrey Richard 1953- *IntWWM 90*
Rehberg, Jack D. 1929- *St&PR 91*
Rehberger, Gustav 1910- *WhoAmA 91, WhoE 91, WhoWor 91*
Rehberger, Robert Lee 1949- *WhoEmL 91*
Rehbock, Nancy E. 1959- *WhoWrEP 89*
Rehder, Robert Richard 1930- *WhoAm 90*
Rehe, Stephanie *BioIn 16*
Reher, Raymond Agudo 1948- *WhoSSW 91*
Reher, Sven Helge 1911- *IntWWM 90*
Reherman, Ronald Gilbert 1935- *St&PR 91, WhoAm 90*
Reheuser, Edward F. 1933- *St&PR 91*
Rehfeld, Barry J. 1946- *ConAu 132*
Rehfeldt, Phillip R. 1939- *IntWWM 90*
Rehfuss, Heinz 1917-1988 *BioIn 16, PenDiMP*
Rehfuss, Walter Guy 1936- *St&PR 91, WhoAm 90*
Rehg, Wally 1888-1946 *Ballpl 90*
Rehim, Mohsen Sayed *BiDrAPA 89*
Rehkamp, Thomas Allen 1949- *WhoE 91*
Rehkopf, Charles Frederick 1908- *WhoWor 91*
Rehkugler, Gerald Edwin 1935- *WhoAm 90*
Rehm, Diana Aed 1936- *WhoE 91*
Rehm, Dieter 1938- *WhoWor 91*
Rehm, Jack Daniel 1932- *St&PR 91, WhoAm 90*
Rehm, John Edwin 1924- *WhoWor 91*
Rehm, Leo Frank 1916- *WhoAm 90*
Rehm, Lynn Paul 1941- *WhoSSW 91*
Rehm, Patrice Koch 1954- *WhoAmW 91*
Rehm, Warren Stacey, Jr. 1907- *WhoAm 90*
Rehmani, Masood Zafar *BiDrAPA 89*
Rehmann, Ruth 1922- *EncCoWW*
Rehmann, Theodor William, Jr. 1929- *St&PR 91*
Rehmer, John E. 1952- *WhoEmL 91*
Rehmeyer, Evans M. 1940- *St&PR 91*
Rehmus, Charles Martin 1926- *WhoAm 90*
Rehngren, J Philip 1924- *BiDrAPA 89*
Rehnquist, William 1924- *WorAlBi*
Rehnquist, William H. *BioIn 16*
Rehnquist, William Hubbs 1924- *WhoAm 90, WhoE 91, WhoWor 91*
Rehnstrom, J. Bernard 1930- *St&PR 91, WhoAm 90*
Rehor, David G. 1939- *St&PR 91*
Rehor, David George 1939- *WhoAm 90*
Rehor, Raymond James 1929- *St&PR 91*
Rehr, Bruce R. *St&PR 91N*
Rehr, Roger Bruce 1953- *WhoSSW 91*
Rehrauer, Harold W. 1937- *St&PR 91*
Rehrmann, Eileen Mary 1944- *WhoAmW 91*
Rehwald, R. Thomas 1938- *St&PR 91, WhoAm 90*
Rei Kawakubo *EncJap*
Reiback, Earl M 1943- *WhoAmA 91*
Reibel, Bertram 1901- *WhoAmA 91*
Reibel, Jay Steven 1941- *BiDrAPA 89*
Reibel, Kurt 1926- *WhoAm 90*
Reibel, Martin A. 1942- *St&PR 91*
Reibel, Stephen Paul 1935- *BiDrAPA 89*
Reibling, Lorenz, Jr. 1948- *WhoSSW 91*
Reibman, Jeanette Fichman 1915- *WhoAm 90, WhoAmW 91, WhoE 91*
Reibman-Myers, Francine Lee 1949- *WhoAmW 91*
Reiboldt, James Max 1951- *St&PR 91*
Reibstein, Marc David 1945- *WhoE 91*
Reice, Gerard Charles 1946- *St&PR 91*
Reich, Alan Anderson 1930- *WhoAm 90*
Reich, Bernard 1941- *ConAu 32NR, WhoAm 90*
Reich, Beth R. *BiDrAPA 89*
Reich, Carl 1900-1988 *BioIn 16*
Reich, Charles William 1930- *WhoAm 90*
Reich, David E. 1947- *ODwPR 91*
Reich, David Lee 1930- *WhoAm 90*
Reich, Deborah 1960- *ConAu 130*
Reich, Ebbe Klovedal 1940- *DcScanL*
Reich, Edgar 1927- *WhoAm 90*
Reich, Eileene Elizabeth 1953- *WhoAmW 91*
Reich, Ferenc 1930- *WhoE 91, WhoWor 91*
Reich, Gloria Carolyn 1932- *WhoAmW 91*
Reich, Gunter 1921-1989 *PenDiMP*
Reich, Herb *WhoAm 90, WhoWrEP 89*
Reich, Ismar Meyer 1924- *St&PR 91*
Reich, J.E. 1910- *St&PR 91*
Reich, Jack Egan 1910- *WhoAm 90, WhoWor 91*
Reich, James Harry 1950- *BiDrAPA 89, WhoE 91*
Reich, Jay 1929- *St&PR 91*
Reich, Joanne Lee 1945- *WhoAmW 91*
Reich, Kenneth Irvin 1938- *WhoAm 90*
Reich, Louis Henry 1945- *BiDrAPA 89*
Reich, Manuel D 1956- *BiDrAPA 89*
Reich, Merrill Drury 1930- *WhoE 91*
Reich, Michael William 1956- *WhoE 91*
Reich, Morton Melvyn 1939- *WhoAm 90*
Reich, Nathaniel E *WhoAmA 91*
Reich, Nathaniel Edwin 1907- *WhoAm 90*
Reich, Olive B 1935- *WhoAmA 91*
Reich, Olive Buerk 1935- *WhoAmW 91*
Reich, Otto Juan 1945- *WhoAm 90, WhoWor 91*
Reich, Paul Frank 1929- *WhoSSW 91*
Reich, Pauline Carole 1946- *WhoAm 90*
Reich, Peter 1931- *BiDrAPA 89*
Reich, Peter Maria 1929- *WhoAm 90*
Reich, Richard M. 1947- *St&PR 91*
Reich, Robert *BiDrAPA 89*
Reich, Robert Claude 1929- *WhoWor 91*
Reich, Robert I. 1949- *St&PR 91*
Reich, Robert Sigmund 1913- *WhoAm 90*
Reich, Rose Marie 1937- *WhoAmW 91*
Reich, Seymour D. 1933- *WhoAm 90*
Reich, Sheldon 1931- *ConAu 30NR, WhoAmA 91*
Reich, Steve 1936- *IntWWM 90, PenDiMP A, WhoAm 90, WorAlBi*
Reich, Stuart Herbert 1934- *WhoAm 90, WhoSSW 91*
Reich, Theodore *BiDrAPA 89*
Reich, Walter 1943- *BiDrAPA 89, ConAu 129*
Reich, Wilhelm 1897-1957 *BioIn 16, EncO&P 3, EncPaPR 91, NewAgE 90*
Reich, William Michael 1943- *WhoE 91*
Reicha, Antonin *PenDiMP A*
Reichard, Gladys Amanda 1893-1955 *BioIn 16*
Reichard, Hugo Manley 1918- *WhoAm 90*
Reichard, John F *BiDrAPA 89*
Reichard, John Francis 1924- *WhoAm 90, WhoWor 91*
Reichard, John Louis 1930- *St&PR 91*
Reichard, John Mohr, Jr. 1934- *St&PR 91*
Reichard, Karl Barton, Jr. 1943- *WhoE 91*
Reichard, Raul Alberto 1951- *BiDrAPA 89*
Reichard, Sherwood Marshall 1928- *WhoAm 90, WhoSSW 91*
Reichard, Stephen 1949-1988 *BioIn 16*
Reichard, Stephen Brantley 1949- *WhoAmA 91N*
Reichard, William Thomas 1943- *St&PR 91*
Reichard, William Thomas, III 1943- *WhoAm 90, WhoSSW 91*
Reichard-Zamora, Hector 1910- *WhoHisp 91*
Reichardt, Anne Elizabeth *BiDrAPA 89*
Reichardt, Carl E. *BioIn 16*
Reichardt, Carl E. 1931- *WhoAm 90*
Reichardt, Delbert Dale 1927- *WhoAm 90*
Reichardt, Louise 1779-1826 *BioIn 16*
Reichardt, Rick 1943- *Ballpl 90, BioIn 16*
Reichart, Elisabeth 1953- *ConAu 132*
Reichart, James P. 1949- *St&PR 91*
Reichart, Stuart Richard 1924- *WhoE 91*
Reichbach, Edward Myron 1929- *WhoSSW 91*
Reichbart, Howard Enoch 1943- *WhoSSW 91*
Reiche, Frank Perley 1929- *WhoAm 90*
Reiche, Gwendolyn 1912- *IntWWM 90*
Reichek, Elaine 1943- *WhoAmA 91*
Reichek, Elaine 1950?- *BiDWomA*
Reichek, Jesse 1916- *WhoAm 90, WhoAmA 91*
Reichek, Morton Arthur 1924- *WhoAm 90*
Reichel, Aaron I 1950- *ConAu 130*
Reichel, Myra 1951- *WhoAmA 91*
Reichel, Sabine 1946- *ConAu 132*
Reichel, Walter Emil 1935- *WhoAm 90*
Reichelt, Ferdinand Herbert 1941- *WhoAm 90*
Reichenau, Walter von 1884-1942 *BioIn 16*
Reichenbach *EncPaPR 91*
Reichenbach, George Sheridan 1929- *St&PR 91*
Reichenbach, Karl von 1788-1869 *EncO&P 3*
Reichenbach, M. J. Gertrude 1912- *WhoAmW 91*
Reichenbacher, Thomas Michael 1959- *BiDrAPA 89*
Reichenbecher, Vernon Edgar, Jr. 1948- *WhoSSW 91*
Reichenberg, William D. 1941- *St&PR 91*
Reichenecker, David Robert 1950- *St&PR 91*
Reichenthal, Jeffrey Alan 1945- *BiDrAPA 89*
Reichert, Charles Edward 1947- *WhoSSW 91*
Reichert, Cheryl McBroom 1946- *WhoAmW 91*
Reichert, David 1929- *WhoAm 90*
Reichert, Donald 1929- *St&PR 91*
Reichert, Donald Karl 1932- *WhoAmA 91*
Reichert, Edwin C. 1909-1988 *BioIn 16*
Reichert, Gerald Russell 1948- *WhoEmL 91*
Reichert, Heinz Siegfried 1926- *WhoWor 91*
Reichert, Jack Frank 1930- *St&PR 91, WhoAm 90*
Reichert, James William 1944- *St&PR 91*
Reichert, Leo Edmund, Jr. 1932- *WhoAm 90*
Reichert, Norman Vernon 1921- *WhoAm 90*
Reichert, Nury Vandellos 1929- *WhoAmW 91*
Reichert, Paul B. 1938- *St&PR 91*
Reichert, Robert F. 1945- *St&PR 91*
Reichert-Facilides, Otto Ernst 1925- *WhoAm 90*
Reichgott, Ember Darlene 1953- *WhoAmW 91*
Reichgut, Michael D. 1939- *ODwPR 91*
Reichgut, Michael David 1939- *WhoSSW 91*
Reichhoff, Charles Edward, II 1958- *WhoSSW 91*
Reichhold, Henry H. 1901-1989 *BioIn 16*
Reichle, Frederick Adolph 1935- *WhoAm 90*
Reichle, Gregory Charles 1943- *St&PR 91*
Reichler, Joe 1916-1988 *Ballpl 90*
Reichler, Joseph L. 1915-1988 *BioIn 16*
Reichler, Merton Lawrence 1926- *WhoE 91*
Reichler, Paul *BioIn 16*
Reichler, Robert Jay 1937- *BiDrAPA 89*
Reichley, Robert A. *BioIn 16*
Reichlin, Kay Mayfield *BiDrAPA 89*
Reichlin, Scott Mitchell 1949- *BiDrAPA 89*
Reichlin, Seymour 1924- *WhoAm 90*
Reichman, Allen 1932- *BiDrAPA 89, WhoE 91*
Reichman, Dawn Leslie 1951- *WhoAmW 91*
Reichman, Fred 1925- *WhoAmA 91*
Reichman, Fredrick Thomas 1925- *WhoAm 90*
Reichman, George T. 1937- *St&PR 91*
Reichman, Jack Zev 1950- *WhoE 91*
Reichman, John Ben *BiDrAPA 89*
Reichman, Leah Carol 1951- *WhoAmA 91, WhoAmW 91*
Reichman, Lee Brodersohn 1938- *WhoAm 90*
Reichman, Martin 1957- *BiDrAPA 89*
Reichman, Rose E. *ODwPR 91*
Reichman, Rose Ehrinpreis 1942- *WhoAmW 91*
Reichman, Walter 1938- *WhoAm 90*
Reichman, William Eric 1957- *BiDrAPA 89*
Reichmanis, Elsa 1953- *WhoAmW 91*
Reichmann, Albert *BioIn 16, WhoAm 90, WhoWor 91*
Reichmann, Paul *BioIn 16, WhoAm 90*
Reichmann, Ralph *BioIn 16, WhoAm 90, WhoWor 91*
Reichmann, Renee *WhoAm 90*
Reichmann, Renee *BioIn 16, NewYTBS 90*
Reichold, Richard Philip 1927- *St&PR 91*
Reichsman, Franz K *BiDrAPA 89*
Reichstein, Michele B *BiDrAPA 89*
Reichstein, Tadeus 1897- *WhoAm 90, WhoWor 91*
Reichstein, Tadeusz 1897- *WorAlBi*
Reichstetter, Arthur Charles 1946- *St&PR 91, WhoAm 90*
Reichter, Barbara Fast 1935- *WhoAmW 91*
Reichwein, John H. 1909- *St&PR 91*
Reichwein, John Henry, Jr. 1954- *St&PR 91*

Reicin, Ronald Ian 1942- *WhoAm 90*
Reick, Franklin Gerald 1930- *WhoE 91*
Reick, Robert Alan 1947- *St&PR 91*
Reicker, Frederick A. 1934- *ODwPR 91*
Reickert, Erick A. 1935- *St&PR 91*
Reickert, Erick Arthur 1935- *WhoAm 90, WhoWor 91*
Reid, Alastair 1926- *AuBYP 90*
Reid, Antonio *BioIn 16*
Reid, Aubrey Karl, Jr. 1927- *St&PR 91, WhoAm 90*
Reid, Augustus *BiDrAPA 89*
Reid, Barbara 1936- *St&PR 91*
Reid, Barbara Jean 1943- *WhoE 91*
Reid, Belmont Mervyn 1927- *WhoWor 91*
Reid, Benjamin L. *NewYTBS 90*
Reid, Benjamin Lawrence 1918- *WhoAm 90, WhoWrEP 89*
Reid, Bernadette P. *St&PR 91*
Reid, Beverly Ann 1949- *WhoE 91*
Reid, Bill J. 1931- *St&PR 91*
Reid, Bonnie Lee 1937- *WhoAmW 91, WhoWor 91*
Reid, Bryan S., Jr. 1925- *St&PR 91*
Reid, Carol Ann 1938- *WhoAmW 91*
Reid, Charles 1937- *WhoAmA 91*
Reid, Charles Adams, III 1947- *WhoEmL 91*
Reid, Charles Henry 1929- *WhoE 91*
Reid, Charles P. 1930- *St&PR 91*
Reid, Charles Phillip Patrick 1940- *WhoSSW 91*
Reid, Cheryl Soled 1953- *WhoAmW 91*
Reid, Clarice D. *BioIn 16*
Reid, Cornelius J., Jr. 1924- *St&PR 91*
Reid, Daniel Peter 1948- *WhoWor 91*
Reid, Daphne Maxwell *BioIn 16*
Reid, Daphne Maxwell 1948- *DrBlPA 90*
Reid, David William 1943- *BiDrAPA 89*
Reid, Desmond *MajTwCW*
Reid, Donald David 1916- *WhoWor 91*
Reid, Donna Joyce 1954- *WhoAmW 91*
Reid, Dorothy-Marie 1937- *WhoAmW 91*
Reid, Douglas MacKenzie 1935- *St&PR 91*
Reid, Douglas Stewart, Sr. 1932- *St&PR 91*
Reid, Edward Snover 1930- *WhoAm 90*
Reid, Elizabeth Aub 1926- *BiDrAPA 89, WhoE 91*
Reid, Evans Burton 1913- *WhoAm 90, WhoWor 91*
Reid, F Theodore, Jr. 1929- *BiDrAPA 89*
Reid, Fergus *BioIn 16*
Reid, Fiona 1951- *OxCCanT*
Reid, Frances *BiDrAPA 89*
Reid, Frank M. *BioIn 16*
Reid, Garett H.D. 1939- *St&PR 91*
Reid, Gavin Clydesdale 1946- *WhoWor 91*
Reid, Gene Watkins *BiDrAPA 89*
Reid, George Agnew *WhoAmA 91N*
Reid, George Williams 1925- *WhoAm 90*
Reid, Gilbert 1857-1927 *BioIn 16*
Reid, Gordon MacDonald 1935- *St&PR 91*
Reid, Graham Mack *BiDrAPA 89*
Reid, Harry 1939- *WhoAm 90, WhoWor 91*
Reid, Harvey L. 1928- *St&PR 91*
Reid, Helen Rogers 1882-1970 *BioIn 16*
Reid, Hilda Stewart 1899-1982 *FemiCLE*
Reid, Hoch 1909- *WhoAm 90*
Reid, Inez Smith 1937- *WhoAmW 91, WhoE 91, WhoWor 91*
Reid, Ira DeA. 1901-1968 *EarBlAP*
Reid, Irvin D. *WhoAm 90*
Reid, J. Frederick 1927- *St&PR 91*
Reid, J. Kirk 1946- *St&PR 91*
Reid, Jackson Brock 1921- *WhoAm 90*
Reid, James 1849-1923 *BioIn 16*
Reid, James Dolan 1930- *WhoAm 90*
Reid, James M. 1944- *St&PR 91*
Reid, James S., Jr. 1926- *St&PR 91*
Reid, James Sims, Jr. 1926- *WhoAm 90*
Reid, James William 1932- *St&PR 91*
Reid, Janet Kay 1952- *WhoWrEP 89*
Reid, Jim *BioIn 16*
Reid, Jim Frank 1933- *St&PR 91*
Reid, Joan Evangeline 1932- *WhoAmW 91*
Reid, John *BioIn 16*
Reid, John 1925- *ConDes 90*
Reid, John B. 1932- *ODwPR 91*
Reid, John Curtis 1950- *WhoAm 90*
Reid, John Edward 1948- *WhoEmL 91*
Reid, John M. 1926- *St&PR 91*
Reid, John Madden 1924- *WhoWor 91*
Reid, John Phillip 1930- *WhoAm 90*
Reid, John T. 1940- *St&PR 91*
Reid, Joseph Lee 1923- *WhoAm 90*
Reid, Joseph William 1955- *WhoSSW 91*
Reid, Joyce Edna 1941- *WhoWrEP 89*
Reid, Kate 1930- *OxCCanT [port]*
Reid, Kathaleen 1953- *WhoSSW 91*
Reid, Katherine Louise 1941- *WhoAmW 91, WhoSSW 91*
Reid, Kellie *ODwPR 91*
Reid, Kelly M *BiDrAPA 89*
Reid, L. A. *BioIn 16*
Reid, Langhorne, III 1950- *WhoE 91*
Reid, Laura Marcella 1952- *WhoAmW 91*
Reid, Leslie 1947- *WhoAmA 91*
Reid, Loren Dudley 1905- *WhoAm 90, WhoWor 91*
Reid, Louis Arnaud 1895-1986 *BioIn 16*
Reid, Lynne McArthur 1923- *WhoAm 90*
Reid, Malcolm 1943- *St&PR 91*
Reid, Margaret 1925- *ConAu 130*
Reid, Margaret Elizabeth 1934- *WhoE 91*
Reid, Meta Mayne 1905- *BioIn 16*
Reid, Michael 1938- *WhoAm 90*
Reid, Michael Alan 1958- *IntWWM 90*
Reid, Michele Ilene 1954- *BiDrAPA 89*
Reid, Nanci Glick 1941- *WhoAmW 91*
Reid, Nano 1905-1981 *BiDWomA*
Reid, Natalie 1947- *WhoAmW 91*
Reid, Noal Douglas 1944- *St&PR 91*
Reid, Oscar 1936- *St&PR 91*
Reid, P R 1910-1990 *ConAu 131*
Reid, Parlane John 1937- *BiDrAPA 89*
Reid, Pat *ConAu 131*
Reid, Phillip Roger 1959- *St&PR 91*
Reid, R W 1933-1990? *ConAu 132*
Reid, Ralph Ralston, Jr. 1934- *WhoAm 90*
Reid, Ralph Waldo Emerson 1915- *WhoSSW 91, WhoWor 91*
Reid, Randall 1931- *WhoWrEP 89*
Reid, Richard Joseph 1932- *WhoWor 91*
Reid, Robert 1955- *BioIn 16*
Reid, Robert Allen 1942- *WhoSSW 91*
Reid, Robert C *BiDrAPA 89*
Reid, Robert Clark 1924- *WhoAm 90*
Reid, Robert Dennis 1924- *WhoAmA 91*
Reid, Robert John 1942- *WhoAm 90*
Reid, Robert John 1954- *St&PR 91*
Reid, Robert Lelon 1942- *WhoAm 90*
Reid, Robert Newton 1908- *WhoAm 90*
Reid, Ronald L. 1939- *ODwPR 91*
Reid, Rosemary Anne 1951- *WhoAmW 91*
Reid, Ross 1917- *St&PR 91*
Reid, Ross 1917-1989 *BioIn 16*
Reid, Russell *BioIn 16*
Reid, Russell W S 1943- *BiDrAPA 89*
Reid, Rust Endicott 1931- *WhoAm 90, WhoSSW 91*
Reid, Ruth Hanford 1938- *WhoAmW 91*
Reid, Scott Douglas *BiDrAPA 89*
Reid, Steven J. *St&PR 91*
Reid, Sue Titus 1939- *ConAu 31NR, WhoAmW 91*
Reid, Susan Denise 1940- *BiDrAPA 89*
Reid, Terence C. W. 1941- *WhoAm 90*
Reid, Terrence *St&PR 91*
Reid, Thomas R. 1864- *AmLegL*
Reid, Tim *BioIn 16*
Reid, Tim 1944- *DrBlPA 90, WorAlBi*
Reid, Toy Franklin 1924- *St&PR 91*
Reid, Vernon *BioIn 16*
Reid, Whitelaw 1837-1912 *BioIn 16*
Reid, Whitelaw 1913- *St&PR 91*
Reid, Willard Malcolm 1910- *WhoAm 90*
Reid, William H 1945- *BiDrAPA 89*
Reid, William Hill 1926- *WhoAm 90*
Reid, William Howard 1945- *WhoWor 91*
Reid, William James 1927- *WhoSSW 91*
Reid, William James 1928- *WhoAm 90*
Reid, William James 1941- *WhoSSW 91*
Reid, William Michael 1954- *WhoSSW 91*
Reid, William Paul 1949- *St&PR 91*
Reid, William R *BiDrAPA 89*
Reid, Yolanda A. 1954- *WhoHisp 91*
Reid Banks, Lynne *AuBYP 90*
Reid Banks, Lynne 1929- *Au&Arts 6 [port], BioIn 16*
Reid-Bills, Mae *WhoAmW 91*
Reid Cabral, Donald 1923- *WhoWor 91*
Reid Scott, David Alexander Carroll 1947- *WhoWor 91*
Reida-Allen, Pamela Anne 1944- *WhoAmW 91*
Reidelbach, Michael Joseph, Sr. 1946- *WhoEmL 91*
Reidenbach, William John 1930- *St&PR 91*
Reidenbaugh, Lowell Henry 1919- *WhoAm 90*
Reidenberg, Marcus Milton 1934- *WhoAm 90*
Reider, Arthur Elliot 1936- *BiDrAPA 89*
Reider, Norman 1907- *BiDrAPA 89*
Reider, Robert M. 1925- *St&PR 91*
Reidl, Otto 1939- *St&PR 91*
Reidler, Harry J. 1952- *St&PR 91*
Reidy, Ben T. 1933- *WhoAm 90*
Reidy, Bill 1873-1915 *Ballpl 90*
Reidy, Carolyn Kroll 1949- *St&PR 91, WhoAm 90, WhoAmW 91*
Reidy, Ellen Teresa 1962- *WhoAmW 91*
Reidy, James, Jr. 1929- *St&PR 91*
Reidy, James J. 1941- *St&PR 91*
Reidy, John Joseph, Jr. 1932- *St&PR 91*
Reidy, Joseph J *BiDrAPA 89*
Reidy, Joseph J. 1920- *WhoE 91*
Reidy, Richard J. *St&PR 91*
Reidy, Richard Robert 1947- *WhoEmL 91*
Reidy, Sandra Marie 1950- *WhoE 91*
Reidy, William Edward 1931- *St&PR 91*
Reidy, William P. 1932- *St&PR 91*
Reif, Charles Braddock 1912- *WhoE 91*
Reif, David 1941- *WhoAmA 91*
Reif, David Poynter 1953- *St&PR 91*
Reif, James L 1938- *BiDrAPA 89*
Reif, John Henry 1951- *WhoSSW 91*
Reif, Loralyn 1961- *WhoAmW 91*
Reif, Louis R. 1923- *St&PR 91*
Reif, Louis Raymond 1923- *WhoAm 90*
Reif, Robert C. 1949- *St&PR 91*
Reif, Steven Jay 1947- *WhoSSW 91*
Reif-Lehrer, Liane 1934- *WhoE 91*
Reifel, Ben *NewYTBS 90*
Reifel, Ben 1906-1990 *BioIn 16*
Reifenberg, Joseph Oliver 1960- *WhoEmL 91*
Reifenberg, Thomas P. 1930- *St&PR 91*
Reifenrath, Dorothy Ann 1922- *WhoAmW 91*
Reifers, Richard Francis 1919- *WhoAm 90*
Reiff, Dovie Kate 1931- *WhoAmW 91, WhoSSW 91*
Reiff, Jack W. 1927- *St&PR 91*
Reiff, Patricia Hofer 1950- *WhoAmW 91*
Reiff, Robert Frank 1918-1982 *WhoAmA 91N*
Reiff, Stephanie Ann 1948- *BioIn 16*
Reiff Sodano, Tana 1951- *WhoWrEP 89*
Reiffel, Leonard 1927- *St&PR 91, WhoAm 90*
Reifler, Burton Victor 1944- *BiDrAPA 89*
Reifler, Clifford B 1931- *BiDrAPA 89*
Reifler, Clifford Bruce 1931- *WhoAm 90, WhoE 91*
Reifler, Samuel 1939- *WhoWrEP 89*
Reifman, Robert A 1928- *BiDrAPA 89*
Reifschneider, Darrel 1933- *St&PR 91*
Reifschneider, Robert 1935- *St&PR 91*
Reifslager, Walter E *BiDrAPA 89*
Reifsnyder, Charles Frank 1920- *WhoWor 91*
Reifsnyder, David Alan 1950- *WhoAm 90*
Reifsnyder, Mark W. 1951- *St&PR 91*
Reifsnyder, William Edward 1924- *WhoAm 90*
Reig, June Wilson 1933- *WhoAm 90*
Reigel, Todd L. 1958- *St&PR 91*
Reigel, Todd Lambert 1958- *WhoSSW 91*
Reighard, Homer Leroy 1924- *WhoAm 90*
Reighard, Patton Breon 1949- *WhoEmL 91*
Reignolds, Kate 1836-1911 *BioIn 16, NotWoAT*
Reigot, Betty Polisar 1924- *BioIn 16*
Reigrod, Robert Hull 1941- *WhoAm 90*
Reigstad, Ruth Elaine 1923- *WhoAmW 91*
Reijers, L. Nick 1935- *WhoWor 91*
Reijnst, Bernard Antony 1924- *WhoWor 91*
Reik, Haviva 1914-1944 *BioIn 16*
Reik, Louis E *BiDrAPA 89*
Reiland, Lowell Keith 1948- *WhoAmA 91, WhoE 91*
Reiley, Catherine Conway *AuBYP 90*
Reiley, Mame Carrigan 1952- *WhoAmW 91*
Reiley, Thomas Noel 1938- *WhoE 91*
Reiley, Thomas Phillip 1950- *WhoE 91, WhoEmL 91, WhoWor 91*
Reiling, Cecilia Powers 1926- *WhoAmW 91*
Reiling, Henry Bernard 1938- *WhoAm 90*
Reilley, Dennen 1937- *WhoE 91*
Reilley, Michael J. 1954- *St&PR 91*
Reilly, Bernard Francis 1950- *WhoAmA 91*
Reilly, Charles A. 1947- *St&PR 91*
Reilly, Charles Nelson 1931- *WorAlBi*
Reilly, Colleen Marie 1957- *WhoAmW 91*
Reilly, Cynthia Faithe 1952- *WhoAmW 91*
Reilly, Cynthia Marie 1960- *WhoAmW 91*
Reilly, Daniel Lee *BiDrAPA 89*
Reilly, Daniel Patrick 1928- *WhoAm 90, WhoE 91*
Reilly, David Henry 1936- *WhoAm 90*
Reilly, Donald C. 1950- *St&PR 91*
Reilly, Douglas Kenneth *BiDrAPA 89*
Reilly, Edward Arthur 1943- *WhoAm 90*
Reilly, Edward John 1923- *WhoE 91*
Reilly, Edward Joseph 1916- *WhoWrEP 89*
Reilly, Edward L 1936- *BiDrAPA 89*
Reilly, Edward T., Jr. 1946- *St&PR 91*
Reilly, Elvira 1899-1958 *WhoAmA 91N*
Reilly, Frank Eugene *BiDrAPA 89*
Reilly, Frank Kelly 1935- *WhoAm 90*
Reilly, Frank T. 1928- *St&PR 91*
Reilly, George Love Anthony 1918- *WhoAm 90*
Reilly, Gerard Denis 1906- *WhoAm 90*
Reilly, Helen 1891-1962 *TwCCr&M 91*
Reilly, Jack 1950- *WhoAmA 91*
Reilly, James 1955- *WhoSSW 91*
Reilly, James A. *ODwPR 91*
Reilly, James J. *BioIn 16*
Reilly, James Kevin 1952- *WhoE 91*
Reilly, James P., Jr. 1946- *St&PR 91*
Reilly, James Vincent 1926- *St&PR 91*
Reilly, Jean *BioIn 16*
Reilly, Joan Rita 1947- *WhoAmW 91*
Reilly, John *BioIn 16*
Reilly, John A. 1932- *IntWWM 90*
Reilly, John Joseph 1938- *WhoE 91*
Reilly, John Joseph, Jr. 1928- *WhoAm 90*
Reilly, John L. 1940- *St&PR 91*
Reilly, John Lawrence 1940- *WhoAm 90*
Reilly, John Paul 1943- *St&PR 91, WhoAm 90*
Reilly, John R. 1940- *St&PR 91*
Reilly, John Richard 1928- *WhoAm 90*
Reilly, Kathy Maurer 1949- *St&PR 91*
Reilly, Kevin Anthony 1955- *WhoE 91*
Reilly, Kevin Christopher 1954- *WhoE 91*
Reilly, Lawrence Hugh 1928- *St&PR 91*
Reilly, Lawrence J. 1956- *St&PR 91*
Reilly, Lois Ann Pelcarsky 1941- *WhoAmW 91*
Reilly, Long John 1858-1937 *Ballpl 90*
Reilly, M. Suzanne 1941- *WhoAmW 91*
Reilly, Michael D. 1948- *St&PR 91*
Reilly, Michael J. 1954- *St&PR 91*
Reilly, Michael James 1944- *St&PR 91*
Reilly, Michael Terrence 1958- *WhoE 91*
Reilly, Nancy O. 1951- *WhoWrEP 89*
Reilly, Patrick John 1925- *WhoWor 91*
Reilly, Paul 1912-1990 *ConAu 132*
Reilly, Paul Cameron 1948- *WhoEmL 91*
Reilly, Paul David *BiDrAPA 89*
Reilly, Paul J. 1953- *St&PR 91*
Reilly, Paul Vincent 1952- *St&PR 91*
Reilly, Peter C. 1907- *St&PR 91*
Reilly, Richard 1926- *WhoAmA 91*
Reilly, Richard Michael 1938- *St&PR 91*
Reilly, Rick *BioIn 16*
Reilly, Robert Frederick 1952- *WhoEmL 91, WhoWor 91*
Reilly, Robert James 1945- *St&PR 91, WhoEmL 91*
Reilly, Susan Moira 1948- *WhoAmW 91*
Reilly, Theresa *WhoAmW 91*
Reilly, Thomas A., Jr. 1927- *St&PR 91*
Reilly, Thomas Michael 1941- *St&PR 91*
Reilly, Timothy G. 1950- *St&PR 91*
Reilly, Tommy 1919- *PenDiMP*
Reilly, Vini *NewAgMG*
Reilly, Walter N. *BioIn 16*
Reilly, William A. 1947- *St&PR 91*
Reilly, William D. 1930- *St&PR 91*
Reilly, William Francis 1938- *St&PR 91, WhoAm 90, WhoE 91, WhoWor 91*
Reilly, William K. *MajTwCW*
Reilly, William K. 1940- *BioIn 16*
Reilly, William Kane 1940- *WhoAm 90*
Reilly, William Thomas 1949- *WhoEmL 91*
Reily, George W., III 1905- *St&PR 91*
Reily, Jack P. 1950- *St&PR 91*
Reily, John C. 1907- *St&PR 91*
Reim, Gary Paul 1946- *St&PR 91*
Reim, Martin 1931- *WhoWor 91*
Reiman, Donald H 1934- *ConAu 31NR*
Reiman, Donald Henry 1934- *WhoAm 90, WhoE 91, WhoWor 91*
Reiman, Eric Michael 1956- *BiDrAPA 89*
Reiman, Joey 1953- *WhoSSW 91*
Reiman, Thomas Jay 1949- *St&PR 91*
Reimann, Aribert 1936- *IntWWM 90, PenDiMP A*
Reimann, Arline 1937- *WhoAmA 91*
Reimann, Brigitte 1933-1973 *EncCoWW*
Reimann, Curt William 1932- *WhoAm 90*
Reimann, Joachim Oskar Ferdinand 1951- *WhoSSW 91*
Reimann, Kurt William 1944- *St&PR 91*
Reimann, Ronald Hill 1939- *St&PR 91*
Reimann, William P 1935- *WhoAmA 91*
Reimann, William Page 1935- *WhoAm 90*
Reimer, Bennett 1932- *WhoAm 90*
Reimer, Borge R. 1931- *WhoAm 90*
Reimer, Donald Ross 1934- *BiDrAPA 89*
Reimer, Hans *PenDiDA 89*
Reimer, Marvin W. 1909- *St&PR 91*
Reimer, Ronald Anthony 1945- *WhoSSW 91*
Reimer, Susan Martin 1953- *WhoAmW 91*
Reimers, Arthur John 1926- *St&PR 91*
Reimers, David Dean 1943- *WhoSSW 91*
Reimers, Dieter Hermann 1943- *WhoWor 91*
Reimers, K. Lennart 1928- *IntWWM 90*
Reimherr, Frederick W 1946- *BiDrAPA 89*
Reimherr, John Philip 1948- *BiDrAPA 89*
Reims, Clifford Waldemar 1924- *IntWWM 90*
Reimus, Byron 1952- *ODwPR 91*
Rein, Catherine Amelia 1943- *St&PR 91, WhoAm 90*
Rein, Charles Richard 1940- *WhoSSW 91*
Rein, David M. 1960- *St&PR 91*
Rein, Eric Steven 1956- *WhoEmL 91*
Rein, Martin 1928- *WhoAm 90*
Rein, Mercedes *ConAu 131, HispWr 90*
Rein, William F. 1935- *St&PR 91*
Reina *WhoAmA 91*
Reina 1931- *WhoE 91*
Reina, Joyce Cohen 1931- *WhoAmA 91*
Reina, Nicholas Joseph 1948- *WhoHisp 91*
Reina, Sylvia Guagliardo 1939- *WhoSSW 91*
Reinach, Albert 1929- *St&PR 91*
Reinach, Jacquelyn 1930- *WhoWrEP 89*
Reinach, Joseph Herman 1856-1921 *BiDFrPL*

Reinach, Robert Charles 1945- *BiDrAPA 89*
Reinarz, Karen Nielsen 1941- *WhoAmW 91*
Reinarz, Michel *BioIn 16*
Reinauer, B. Franklin, III 1941- *St&PR 91*
Reinauer, Benjamin Franklin, III 1941- *WhoE 91*
Reinbold, Grace Ann 1941- *WhoWor 91*
Reindel, Frederick Oswald *BiDrAPA 89*
Reindel, William George 1871-1948 *WhoAmA 91N*
Reinders, Jim *BioIn 16*
Reindollar, Robert Mason, Jr. 1918- *WhoAm 90*
Reindorf, Samuel 1914-1988 *WhoAmA 91N*
Reinecke, Manfred G. 1935- *WhoAm 90*
Reinecke, Robert Dale 1929- *WhoAm 90*
Reineman, Joseph Vilsack 1933- *St&PR 91*
Reinemann, Glenn N. 1931- *St&PR 91*
Reinemann, Robert Klaus 1926- *WhoWor 91*
Reiner of Huy *PenDiDA 89*
Reiner, Carl 1922- *WhoAm 90, WorAlBi*
Reiner, Carol Curnow 1959- *WhoAmW 91*
Reiner, Douglas Charles 1951- *WhoSSW 91*
Reiner, Elliot R 1919- *BiDrAPA 89*
Reiner, Fritz 1888-1963 *PenDiMP, WorAlBi*
Reiner, Gladys *WhoAmA 91*
Reiner, James Anthony 1958- *WhoEmL 91*
Reiner, Johann Joseph *PenDiDA 89*
Reiner, Jules 1918- *WhoAmA 91*
Reiner, Marc Houston *BiDrAPA 89*
Reiner, Richard Neal 1952- *BiDrAPA 89*
Reiner, Rob *BioIn 16, WhoAm 90*
Reiner, Rob 1945- *WorAlBi*
Reiner, Rob 1947- *News 91-2 [port]*
Reiner, Robert L. 1955- *St&PR 91*
Reiner, Robert William 1957- *WhoEmL 91*
Reiner, Rori Ellen 1962- *WhoAmW 91*
Reiner, Stephen R. 1940- *St&PR 91*
Reinerman, Alan Jerome 1935- *WhoE 91*
Reiners, Neville Henry 1914- *St&PR 91*
Reiners, Rudolph 1931- *St&PR 91*
Reinert, Norbert Frederick 1928- *WhoAm 90*
Reinert, Pamela Ann 1952- *WhoAmW 91*
Reinert, Paul Clare 1910- *WhoAm 90*
Reinert, Raymond E *BiDrAPA 89*
Reinerts, Aivars Maris 1935- *St&PR 91, WhoAm 90*
Reinertsen, Karen J 1947- *BiDrAPA 89*
Reinertsen, Norman 1934- *St&PR 91, WhoAm 90*
Reinertsen, Raymond Ricky 1949- *WhoE 91*
Reinertson, Lisa 1955- *WhoAmA 91*
Reinertson-Sand, Mary Ann 1959- *WhoAmW 91*
Reines, Frederick 1918- *WhoAm 90*
Reines, Scott Alan 1946- *BiDrAPA 89*
Reinfeld, Albert Ivan 1930- *St&PR 91*
Reinfeld, Fred 1910-1964 *AuBYP 90*
Reinfurt, Frederick L *BiDrAPA 89*
Reinganum, Julie Louise 1955- *WhoAmW 91*
Reinganum, Marc Richard 1953- *WhoEmL 91*
Reingold, Carmel Berman *AuBYP 90*
Reingold, Haim 1910- *WhoAm 90*
Reingold, Michael H. *WhoAm 90*
Reingold, Nathan 1927- *WhoAm 90*
Reinhard, Christopher John 1953- *WhoAm 90*
Reinhard, Elisabeth 1950- *WhoWor 91*
Reinhard, Harold J 1924- *BiDrAPA 89*
Reinhard, Herb F., Jr. 1930- *WhoAm 90, WhoE 91*
Reinhard, J. Pedro 1945- *St&PR 91*
Reinhard, James Stewart 1957- *BiDrAPA 89*
Reinhard, Joao Pedro 1945- *WhoAm 90*
Reinhard, Johnny 1956- *IntWWM 90*
Reinhard, Keith L. 1935- *St&PR 91*
Reinhard, Keith Leon 1935- *WhoAm 90, WhoE 91*
Reinhard, Kuehnl 1936- *WhoWor 91*
Reinhard, Mary Marthe 1929- *WhoAm 90, WhoAmW 91*
Reinhardt, Ad 1913-1967 *WorAlBi*
Reinhardt, Ad F 1913-1967 *WhoAmA 91N*
Reinhardt, Bruce P. 1950- *St&PR 91*
Reinhardt, C. Arthur 1933- *St&PR 91*
Reinhardt, Charles Francis 1933- *WhoAm 90*
Reinhardt, Cheryl Lynn 1960- *WhoAmW 91*
Reinhardt, Django *PenDiMP*
Reinhardt, Django 1910-1953 *BioIn 16, OxCPMus*
Reinhardt, Eric M *BiDrAPA 89*
Reinhardt, F. Carl 1937- *St&PR 91*
Reinhardt, George E., Jr. 1929- *St&PR 91*
Reinhardt, George Frederick 1911-1971 *BioIn 16*
Reinhardt, J. Alec 1942- *St&PR 91*
Reinhardt, John Edward 1920- *WhoAm 90*
Reinhardt, Kendall S. 1939- *St&PR 91*
Reinhardt, Kurt 1920- *WhoWor 91*
Reinhardt, Madge 1925- *WhoWrEP 89*
Reinhardt, Max 1915- *WhoWor 91*
Reinhardt, Nola 1947- *WhoE 91*
Reinhardt, Richard W 1927- *ConAu 31NR*
Reinhardt, Roger F 1923- *BiDrAPA 89*
Reinhardt, Stephen Roy 1931- *WhoAm 90*
Reinhardt, Thomas E. *BiDrAPA 89*
Reinhardt, Uwe Ernst 1937- *WhoAm 90*
Reinhardt, William Parker 1942- *WhoAm 90, WhoE 91*
Reinhardt-Kiss, Ursula 1944- *IntWWM 90*
Reinhart, Andrew Jacob, III 1949- *WhoAm 90*
Reinhart, Art 1899-1946 *Ballpl 90*
Reinhart, Betty Louise 1943- *WhoAmW 91*
Reinhart, Carole Dawn 1941- *IntWWM 90*
Reinhart, Ila Jena 1960- *WhoE 91*
Reinhart, John B 1917- *BiDrAPA 89*
Reinhart, John Frederick 1953- *St&PR 91*
Reinhart, Karen Boyll 1962- *WhoAmW 91*
Reinhart, Kay Ellen 1946- *WhoAmW 91*
Reinhart, Kellee Connely 1951- *WhoAm 90*
Reinhart, Margaret Emily 1908- *WhoAmA 91*
Reinhart, Melvin J 1929- *BiDrAPA 89*
Reinhart, Peter S. 1950- *St&PR 91*
Reinhart, Peter Sargent 1950- *WhoAm 90*
Reinhart, Raymond Barr, Jr. *BiDrAPA 89*
Reinharz, Jehuda 1944- *WhoAm 90*
Reinheimer, Robert, Jr. 1917- *WhoAm 90*
Reinherz, Helen Zarsky 1923- *WhoAm 90*
Reinhold, Henry Theodore *PenDiMP*
Reinhold, Judge 1956- *WorAlBi*
Reinhold, Richard L. 1951- *WhoE 91*
Reinhold, W.B. 1924- *St&PR 91*
Reinhold, Warren R. 1925- *St&PR 91*
Reinholm, Gert 1928- *WhoWor 91*
Reinhorn, Andrei M. 1945- *WhoAm 90, WhoE 91, WhoEmL 91*
Reinhoudt, David Nicolaas 1942- *WhoWor 91*
Reinicke, Peter 1715-1768 *PenDiDA 89*
Reinig, Gerd Ernst 1938- *St&PR 91*
Reinikka, Antti Johannes 1953- *WhoWor 91*
Reining, Beth LaVerne 1921- *WhoAmW 91, WhoWor 91*
Reining, Francis E. 1940- *St&PR 91*
Reining, Karen M. 1960- *WhoAmW 91*
Reining, Maria 1903- *IntWWM 90*
Reining, William Norbert 1940- *St&PR 91*
Reininghaus, Ruth 1922- *WhoAm 90, WhoAmA 91*
Reinisch, June Machover 1943- *WhoAm 90*
Reinitz, Arthur H 1918- *BiDrAPA 89*
Reinitzer, Sigrid Friedrun 1941- *WhoWor 91*
Reinke, Doris Marie 1922- *WhoAmW 91*
Reinke, Fred William 1961- *WhoE 91*
Reinke, Jerome L. 1932- *St&PR 91*
Reinke, Leonard Herman 1918- *WhoAm 90*
Reinke, Ralph Louis 1927- *WhoAm 90*
Reinke, Twila O'Such 1942- *WhoAmW 91*
Reinke, William John 1930- *WhoAm 90*
Reinkemeyer, Agnes 1923-1989 *BioIn 16*
Reinking, Ann H. 1950- *WhoAm 90*
Reinman, Jacob J. 1947- *WhoWrEP 89*
Reinmuth, Oscar MacNaughton 1927- *WhoAm 90*
Reinowski, Paul Rogers 1944- *St&PR 91*
Reins, Ralph Erich 1940- *WhoAm 90*
Reinsberg, John Robert 1956- *WhoE 91*
Reinsberg-Duringsfeld, Ida von 1815-1876 *EncCoWW*
Reinsch, James Leonard 1908- *WhoAm 90, WhoWor 91*
Reinsch, Paul Samuel 1869-1923 *BioIn 16*
Reinschmiedt, Anne Tierney 1932- *WhoAmW 91, WhoSSW 91, WhoWor 91*
Reinsdorf, Jerry 1936- *Ballpl 90*
Reinsdorf, Jerry Michael 1936- *WhoAm 90*
Reinsdorf, Marshall Budd 1956- *WhoE 91*
Reinsfelder, Donald Leo 1931- *St&PR 91*
Reinshagen, Gerlind 1926- *EncCoWW*
Reinsma, Harold Lawrence 1928- *WhoWor 91*
Reinstein, Alan 1947- *WhoAm 90*
Reinstein, Jacques Joseph 1911- *WhoE 91*
Reinstein, Linda *BiDrAPA 89*
Reinstein, Michael Jay 1943- *BiDrAPA 89*
Reinstein, Ronald S. 1948- *WhoEmL 91*
Reinstetle, Dwight Alan 1951- *St&PR 91*
Reinthaler, Richard Walter 1949- *WhoEmL 91*
Reintzel, Warren Andrew 1945- *WhoE 91*
Reinvald, Ilmar 1937- *WhoAm 90*
Reinwald, Arthur Burton 1929- *WhoAm 90*
Reinwart, William C. 1938- *St&PR 91*
Reiring, Janelle 1946- *WhoAmA 91*
Reis, Antonio Do Carmo 1942- *WhoWor 91*
Reis, Arthur Robert, Jr. 1916- *WhoAm 90*
Reis, Bobby 1909-1973 *Ballpl 90*
Reis, Cheryl Dianne *BiDrAPA 89*
Reis, Claude Jay 1949- *BiDrAPA 89*
Reis, Curtis Sanford 1934- *St&PR 91*
Reis, Donald Jeffery 1931- *WhoAm 90, WhoE 91, WhoWor 91*
Reis, Gordon, Jr. *St&PR 91N*
Reis, Joan Sachs 1922- *IntWWM 90*
Reis, Judson P. *BioIn 16*
Reis, Judson Patterson 1942- *WhoAm 90*
Reis, Kurt 1935- *OxCCanT*
Reis, Lee Keller *ODwPR 91*
Reis, Leslee *BioIn 16, NewYTBS 90*
Reis, Maria Theresa *BiDrAPA 89*
Reis, Mario 1953- *WhoAmA 91*
Reis, Muriel Henle *WhoAmW 91*
Reis, Ricardo 1888-1935 *BioIn 16*
Reis, Robert Danforth 1950- *St&PR 91*
Reis, Robert Stanley 1916- *St&PR 91*
Reis, Walter J 1918- *BiDrAPA 89*
Reisacher, Carl Raymond 1958- *WhoE 91*
Reisberg, Barry 1947- *BiDrAPA 89, WhoAm 90, WhoE 91*
Reisberg, Leon Elton 1949- *WhoWor 91*
Reisberg, Richard S. 1941- *WhoAm 90*
Reisbord, Paul S.A. 1943- *St&PR 91*
Reisch, Georg *BioIn 16*
Reischauer, Edwin O. 1910-1990 *BioIn 16, ConAu 132, CurBio 90N, NewYTBS 90 [port]*
Reischauer, Edwin Oldfather 1910- *WhoAm 90*
Reischauer, Edwin Oldfather 1910-1990 *EncJap*
Reischauer, Robert D. 1941- *BioIn 16*
Reische, Alan Lawrence 1939- *WhoE 91*
Reischman, Gene 1918- *St&PR 91*
Reischman, Michael C. 1945- *St&PR 91*
Reischman, Michael Mack 1942- *WhoE 91*
Reise, Barbara *WhoAmA 91N*
Reisen, David Arthur 1942- *BiDrAPA 89*
Reisenauer, Alfred 1863-1907 *BioIn 16*
Reisenberg, John Ralph 1944- *St&PR 91*
Reisenbigler, David Richard 1942- *St&PR 91*
Reisenweber, Michael A. 1949- *St&PR 91*
Reiser, Albert I 1928- *BiDrAPA 89*
Reiser, Brian Sydney 1937- *WhoE 91*
Reiser, Charles Edward, Jr. 1939- *WhoAm 90*
Reiser, David Edward 1946- *BiDrAPA 89*
Reiser, David Emerson 1925- *BiDrAPA 89*
Reiser, Duane Dennis 1955- *St&PR 91*
Reiser, Evelyn Ellis 1941- *WhoE 91*
Reiser, Leroy Franklin, Jr. 1921- *WhoAm 90*
Reiser, Lynn Whisnant 1944- *BiDrAPA 89*
Reiser, Morton F *BiDrAPA 89*
Reiser, Morton Francis 1919- *WhoAm 90, WhoE 91*
Reiser, Pete 1919-1981 *Ballpl 90*
Reiser, Stephen Jay 1942- *St&PR 91*
Reisfeld, Robert Irving, Jr. *BiDrAPA 89*
Reising, Paul Andreas, Jr. *BiDrAPA 89*
Reisinger, George Lambert 1930- *WhoAm 90*
Reisinger, John S. 1936- *St&PR 91*
Reisinger, Nicholas Joseph 1952- *St&PR 91*
Reisinger, Walter C. *BioIn 16*
Reiskin, Allan Burt 1936- *WhoE 91*
Reiskin, Ira Morton 1934- *BiDrAPA 89*
Reiskytl, James Frank 1937- *St&PR 91*
Reisler, Raymond, Sr. 1907- *WhoAm 90*
Reisling, Doc 1874-1955 *Ballpl 90*
Reisman, Andy 1956- *St&PR 91*
Reisman, Anna Lisa 1956- *BiDrAPA 89*
Reisman, Arnold 1927- *WhoAm 90*
Reisman, Arnold 1934- *WhoAm 90*
Reisman, Fredricka Kauffman 1930- *WhoAm 90*
Reisman, George F. 1924- *St&PR 91*
Reisman, Harold Bernard 1935- *St&PR 91*
Reisman, Heather *BioIn 16*
Reisman, Joel Allen 1941- *BiDrAPA 89*
Reisman, Judith A. 1935- *WhoAmW 91*
Reisman, Philip 1904- *WhoAmA 91*
Reisman, Robert E. 1932- *WhoAm 90*
Reisman, Sol Simon *BioIn 16*
Reisman, William M. 1939- *WhoAm 90*
Reismann, Herbert 1926- *WhoAm 90, WhoE 91*
Reisner, Milton *BiDrAPA 89*
Reisner, Richard Hansen 1943- *St&PR 91*
Reisner, Ruth Torrey 1951- *WhoAmW 91*
Reisner, Yale Joseph 1956- *WhoE 91*
Reiss, Albert John, Jr. 1922- *WhoAm 90*
Reiss, Alvin 1932- *WhoAm 90, WhoWrEP 89*
Reiss, Alvin H. 1930- *IntWWM 90, ODwPR 91*
Reiss, Alvin Herbert 1930- *WhoWrEP 89*
Reiss, Carol Shoshkes 1950- *WhoAmW 91*
Reiss, Clifford Earl, II 1942- *St&PR 91*
Reiss, David *BiDrAPA 89*
Reiss, David Mitchel 1951- *BiDrAPA 89*
Reiss, Denis Arnaud 1950- *WhoWor 91*
Reiss, Elaine S. 1940- *St&PR 91*
Reiss, Elaine Serlin 1940- *WhoAm 90, WhoAmW 91*
Reiss, Ernest 1909- *St&PR 91*
Reiss, George Russell, Jr. 1928- *WhoE 91*
Reiss, Harold G 1931- *BiDrAPA 89*
Reiss, Harry *BiDrAPA 89*
Reiss, Howard 1922- *WhoAm 90*
Reiss, James 1941- *WhoWrEP 89*
Reiss, Joel A. 1939-1990 *BioIn 16*
Reiss, Johanna *AuBYP 90*
Reiss, John Barlow 1939- *WhoE 91*
Reiss, John C. 1922- *WhoE 91*
Reiss, John J. *AuBYP 90*
Reiss, Lionel S. 1894-1988 *BioIn 16*
Reiss, Lionel S 1929- *WhoAmA 91N*
Reiss, Luce Lauer *BiDrAPA 89*
Reiss, Marilyn Leitner *AuBYP 90*
Reiss, Martin B 1937- *BiDrAPA 89*
Reiss, Martin H. 1935- *St&PR 91*
Reiss, Martin Harold 1935- *WhoE 91*
Reiss, Paul Jacob 1930- *WhoAm 90, WhoE 91*
Reiss, Randy *BioIn 16*
Reiss, Richard T. 1918- *St&PR 91*
Reiss, Roland 1929- *WhoAmA 91*
Reiss, Russell A. *St&PR 91*
Reiss, Theodore J. 1933- *St&PR 91*
Reiss, Timothy James 1942- *WhoAm 90, WhoWrEP 89*
Reiss-Andersen, Gunnar 1896-1964 *DcScanL*
Reisser, Marsha J. 1948- *IntWWM 90*
Reisser, Micha *BioIn 16*
Reissig, Julio Herrera y *HispWr 90*
Reissig, Julio Herrera y 1875-1910 *BioIn 16*
Reissig, Merle Harris 1927- *St&PR 91*
Reissman, Max 1919- *St&PR 91*
Reissman, Rose *BioIn 16*
Reissmuller, Johann Georg 1932- *WhoWor 91*
Reissner, Eric 1913- *WhoAm 90*
Reissner, Pierre Dale 1928- *WhoWrEP 89*
Reist, Andreas 1955- *WhoE 91*
Reist, Christopher *BiDrAPA 89*
Reist, Pierre C. R. 1926- *WhoAm 90*
Reistad, Alf 1933- *WhoWor 91*
Reistam, Lars A. 1946- *WhoWor 91*
Reister, Raymond Alex 1929- *WhoAm 90*
Reister, Ruth Alkema 1936- *WhoAm 90*
Reister, Thomas Lynn 1944- *WhoE 91*
Reistle, Carl Ernest, Jr. 1901- *WhoAm 90*
Reisz, John A. 1915- *St&PR 91*
Reisz, Karel 1926- *BioIn 16*
Reit, Seymour 1918- *AuBYP 90*
Reitan, Daniel Kinseth 1921- *WhoAm 90, WhoWor 91*
Reitan, Paul Hartman 1928- *WhoAm 90*
Reitan, Rachel Elsa 1964- *WhoAmW 91*
Reitano, Carmen I. *BioIn 16*
Reitci, Rita Krohne *AuBYP 90*
Reite, Martin L 1936- *BiDrAPA 89*
Reitemeier, George 1931- *WhoAm 90*
Reitemeier, Richard Joseph 1923- *WhoAm 90*
Reiten, Idun 1942- *WhoWor 91*
Reiter, Carol Ann 1948- *WhoSSW 91*
Reiter, Edward J. 1939- *St&PR 91*
Reiter, Elaine Mary 1928- *WhoAmW 91*
Reiter, Elliot 1951- *WhoE 91*
Reiter, Frances 1904-1977 *BioIn 16*
Reiter, Jack Martin 1941- *BiDrAPA 89*
Reiter, James D. 1926- *St&PR 91*
Reiter, Joseph Henry 1929- *WhoAm 90, WhoWor 91*
Reiter, Lora K. 1939- *WhoWrEP 89*
Reiter, Robert Edward 1943- *St&PR 91, WhoAm 90*
Reiter, Sharon R *BiDrAPA 89*
Reiter, Stanley 1925- *WhoAm 90*
Reiter, Stephen A 1943- *BiDrAPA 89*
Reiter, Stewart Roy 1957- *BiDrAPA 89*
Reiter, William Martin 1925- *WhoE 91*
Reiter, Wolfgang Leo 1946- *WhoWor 91*
Reiter-Soffer, Domy 1948- *WhoWor 91*
Reith, Carl Joseph 1914- *WhoAm 90*
Reith, Marianne 1955- *WhoEmL 91*
Reither, Francesco Edoardo 1945- *WhoWor 91*
Reitman, Ivan *BioIn 16*
Reitman, Ivan 1946- *WhoAm 90*
Reitman, Jack 1910- *St&PR 91*
Reitman, Jeremy Herman 1945- *St&PR 91*
Reitman, Jerry Irving 1938- *WhoAm 90*
Reitman, Lynne 1949- *BiDrAPA 89*
Reitman, Marc Weil 1951- *BiDrAPA 89*
Reitman, Richard Neill 1948- *WhoE 91*
Reitman, Robert S. 1933- *St&PR 91*
Reitman, Robert Stanley 1933- *WhoAm 90*
Reitman, Sidney 1915-1988 *BioIn 16*
Reitmann, John H 1920- *BiDrAPA 89*
Reitsch, Robert A. 1934- *St&PR 91*
Reitsch, Robert B. 1959- *St&PR 91*
Reitter, Charles Andrew 1956- *WhoAm 90*
Reitz, Barbara Maurer 1931- *WhoAmW 91*
Reitz, Bruce Arnold 1944- *WhoAm 90*
Reitz, Curtis Randall *WhoAm 90*

Reitz, Douglas John Frank 1955- *WhoSSW 91*
Reitz, Edgar *BioIn 16*
Reitz, Jeanne Geiger 1941- *WhoAmW 91*
Reitz, Karl *PenDiMP*
Reitz, Ken 1951- *Ballpl 90*
Reitz, Michelle Mastruserio 1954- *WhoWrEP 89*
Reitz, Richard Elmer 1938- *WhoAm 90, WhoWor 91*
Reitz, Stephanie Karen 1968- *WhoAmW 91*
Reitz, William 1923- *St&PR 91*
Reitzel, Robert 1848-1898 *EncAL*
Reitzenstein, Reinhard 1949- *WhoAmA 91*
Reitzfeld, Robert 1938- *WhoAm 90*
Reive, Alma Irene 1936- *BiDrAPA 89*
Reivich, Ronald S *BiDrAPA 89*
Reizen, Mark *PenDiMP*
Reizian, Lee Malvina 1962- *WhoAmW 91*
Reizis, Rosa *BiDrAPA 89*
Rejane 1857-1920 *BioIn 16*
Rejcha, Antonin 1770-1836 *PenDiMP A*
Rejeski, Philip J. 1958- *St&PR 91*
Rejony, Michel 1953- *WhoWor 91*
Rejtman, Jaime S 1940- *BiDrAPA 89*
Rejto, Gabor 1916- *IntWWM 90*
Reju, Gabrielle-Charlotte 1857-1920 *BioIn 16*
Rekate, Albert C. 1916- *WhoAm 90*
Rekau, Richard Robert 1936- *WhoSSW 91*
Reker, James William 1949- *St&PR 91*
Reker, Les 1951- *WhoAmA 91*
Rekettye, Gabor 1944- *WhoWor 91*
Rekhala, Vijay Kumar *BiDrAPA 89*
Rekoff, Michael George, Jr. 1929- *WhoSSW 91*
Rekola, Mirkka 1931- *DcScanL, EncCoWW*
Rekosh, Jerry 1939- *ODwPR 91*
Rekstad, John Bernhard 1943- *WhoWor 91*
Reksten, Harold E. 1932- *St&PR 91*
Rektorik-Sprinkle, Patricia Jean 1941- *WhoSSW 91*
Rekus, John Francis 1951- *WhoE 91*
Reldan, Robert Ronald 1942- *WhoWor 91*
Rele, Parag Jyotindra 1947- *WhoWor 91*
Relfe, C. Perry 1943- *St&PR 91*
Relich, Mary Margaret 1959- *WhoE 91*
Relier, Jean Pierre 1935- *WhoWor 91*
Religa, Sharilyn Jean 1957- *WhoAmW 91*
Rella, Ettore *BioIn 16*
Rella, Gloria D. *ODwPR 91*
Rella, Joseph Victor 1951- *St&PR 91*
Relle, Ferenc Matyas 1922- *WhoAm 90, WhoWor 91*
Relman, Arnold Seymour 1923- *WhoAm 90*
Relson, Morris 1915- *WhoAm 90*
Relton, William 1930- *IntWWM 90*
Relyea, Michael Stewart 1956- *St&PR 91*
Remak, Jeannette Elizabeth 1952- *WhoAmW 91*
Remaley, Allen Richard 1939- *WhoE 91*
Remaley, Donald Frank 1931- *St&PR 91*
Remaly, Richard Carl 1939- *St&PR 91*
Remar, James 1953- *ConTFT 8*
Remarque, Erich Maria 1898-1970 *BioIn 16, MajTwCW, WorAlBi*
Rematt, Theodore J. *WhoAm 90*
Rembar, Charles 1915- *WhoAm 90*
Rembe, Toni 1936- *WhoAm 90*
Rembert, Donald Mosby 1939- *WhoSSW 91*
Rembert, Paul 1930- *St&PR 91, WhoAm 90*
Rembert, Virginia Pitts 1921- *WhoAm 90, WhoAmA 91*
Rembrandt 1606-1669 *IntDcAA 90*
Rembrandt Harmenszoon van Rijn 1606-1669 *BioIn 16*
Rembrandt Van Rijn 1606-1669 *WorAlBi*
Rembski, Stanislav *WhoAm 90, WhoAmA 91, WhoE 91, WhoWor 91*
Remedios, Alberto 1935- *IntWWM 90, PenDiMP*
Remedios, Ramon 1940- *PenDiMP*
Remeika, Joseph P. *BioIn 16*
Remeikis, Ginta Victoria *BiDrAPA 89*
Remele, Lewis Albert, Jr. 1948- *WhoEmL 91*
Remen, Stephen Martin *BiDrAPA 89*
Remeneski, Shirley Rodriguez 1938- *WhoHisp 91*
Remenick, Seymour 1923- *WhoAm 90, WhoAmA 91*
Remenyi, Ede 1828-1898 *PenDiMP*
Remer, Donald Sherwood 1943- *WhoAm 90*
Remer, James C. 1940- *St&PR 91*
Remer, John Higgins 1925- *St&PR 91*
Remer, Vernon Ralph 1918- *WhoAm 90*
Remeschatis, Frederick A. 1945- *St&PR 91*
Remeta, Esther Marie 1960- *WhoAmW 91*
Remetz, Carol Louise 1956- *WhoAmW 91*
Remi, Georges 1907-1983 *ConAu 31NR*
Remick, D.B. 1941- *St&PR 91*
Remick, Forrest Jerome, Jr. 1931- *WhoAm 90*
Remick, Jerome H. 1869-1931 *BioIn 16*
Remick, Lee 1935- *BioIn 16, WhoAm 90, WhoAmW 91, WorAlBi*
Remick, Martha 1832-1906 *FemiCLE*
Remick, Oscar Eugene 1932- *WhoAm 90, WhoWor 91*
Remick, Ronald Allan 1947- *BiDrAPA 89*
Remien, Richard Henry 1938- *St&PR 91*
Remignanti, Anita Esposito 1953- *WhoAmW 91*
Remillard, Gil 1944- *WhoAm 90*
ReMine, William Hervey, Jr. 1918- *WhoAm 90, WhoWor 91*
Reminger, Richard Thomas 1931- *WhoAm 90, WhoWor 91*
Remington, Deborah 1935- *BiDWomA, BioIn 16*
Remington, Deborah Williams 1935- *WhoAm 90, WhoAmA 91*
Remington, Eliphalet 1793-1861 *WorAlBi*
Remington, Frederic 1861-1909 *BioIn 16, WhNaAH, WorAlBi*
Remington, Frederick B 1927- *BiDrAPA 89*
Remington, Jack Samuel 1931- *WhoAm 90*
Remington, John Addison 1941- *WhoSSW 91*
Remington, Michael John 1945- *WhoE 91*
Remington, Neil David *BiDrAPA 89*
Remington, Richard Delleraine 1931- *WhoAm 90*
Remington, Steven S *BiDrAPA 89*
Remington, Thomas R. 1927- *St&PR 91*
Remington, W. Bruce 1950- *St&PR 91*
Remington, William *BioIn 16*
Remini, Robert Vincent 1921- *WhoAm 90*
Remler, Emily *BioIn 16*
Remler, Emily *NewYTBS 90 [port]*
Remley, Audrey Wright 1931- *WhoAmW 91*
Remley, David Mark 1955- *WhoEmL 91*
Remley, John Frank, III 1941- *St&PR 91*
Remme, John 1935- *ConTFT 8 [port]*
Remmel, Harmon L. *BioIn 16*
Remmell, Robert E. 1931- *St&PR 91*
Remmer, Eugene H. *BioIn 16*
Remmer, Harvey Ira *BiDrAPA 89*
Remmers, Johann J. 1934- *WhoWor 91*
Remmers, William H. 1935- *St&PR 91*
Remmert, John 1954- *St&PR 91*
Remmey, Paul B *WhoAmA 91N*
Remol, Theresa Anne 1952- *WhoAmW 91*
Remolador, Phyllis Lieberman 1950- *WhoAmW 91*
Remolina, Rodrigo V *BiDrAPA 89*
Remon Cantera, Jose Antonio 1908-1955 *BioIn 16*
Remond, Felix 1779- *PenDiDA 89*
Remond, Francois 1745?-1812 *PenDiDA 89*
Remondi, John J. 1937- *St&PR 91*
Remoortel, Edouard van *PenDiMP*
Rempe, James Henry 1930- *St&PR 91*
Rempel, Averno Milton 1919- *WhoAm 90*
Rempel, Rudolph William 1932- *St&PR 91*
Rempel, Ursula Mikulko 1943- *IntWWM 90*
Rempert, Leonard Arthur 1930- *St&PR 91*
Rempfer, Robert Weir 1914- *WhoWor 91*
Remsen, Alfred Soule 1942- *St&PR 91*
Remsen, Ira 1846-1927 *WorAlBi*
Remsen, John 1939- *WhoAmA 91*
Remsing, Gary 1946- *WhoAmA 91*
Remson, Irwin 1923- *WhoAm 90*
Remstein, Alan Samuel 1932- *WhoE 91*
Remus, Dale Howard 1929- *St&PR 91*
Remy, Caroline *EncCoWW*
Remy, Henry 1928- *BiDrAPA 89*
Remy, Jerald Carter 1932- *St&PR 91*
Remy, Jerry 1952- *Ballpl 90*
Remy, Ray *WhoAm 90*
Remy, William Emmett 1909- *WhoSSW 91*
Ren Jianxin *WhoWor 91*
Ren Wanding *BioIn 16*
Ren, Elizabeth Rebecca 1910- *WhoSSW 91*
Ren, Jiyu 1916- *WhoWor 91*
Renahan, James Patrick 1944- *St&PR 91*
Renald, Ching 1908- *WhoWor 91*
Renaldo, John Joseph 1938- *WhoSSW 91*
Renan, Ernest 1823-1892 *BioIn 16*
Renard, David Albert 1949- *WhoEmL 91*
Renard, John Sanders 1938- *St&PR 91*
Renard, Ken *DrBlPA 90*
Renard, Kenneth George 1934- *WhoAm 90*
Renard, Phen J. 1939- *St&PR 91*
Renaud, Bernadette Marie Elise 1945- *WhoAm 90*
Renaud, David J. 1951- *St&PR 91*
Renaud, Ernest E. *BioIn 16*
Renaud, Gilles 1946- *St&PR 91*
Renaud, Jacques 1943- *BioIn 16*
Renaud, Jeanne *BioIn 16*
Renaud, Suzane Marcelle *BiDrAPA 89*
Renaud, William E. Michael 1946- *WhoSSW 91*
Renault, Louis *EncABHB 5*
Renault, Louis 1877-1944 *BioIn 16*
Renault, Mary *DcNaB 1981*
Renault, Mary 1905-1983 *AuBYP 90, BioIn 16, FemiCLE, WorAlBi*
Renberg, Lars Olof 1943- *WhoWor 91*
Renberg, Timothy Stephen 1953- *WhoE 91*
Renbourn, John *NewAgMG*
Rencehausen, Linda Mary 1950- *WhoAmW 91, WhoEmL 91*
Renchard, William S. 1908- *St&PR 91*
Renchard, William Shryock 1908- *WhoE 91*
Renda, Dominic Phillip 1913- *WhoAm 90*
Renda, Randolph Bruce 1926- *WhoAm 90*
Rendal, Camille Lynn 1955- *WhoAmW 91*
Rendall, David 1948- *IntWWM 90*
Rendell, Kenneth W. 1943- *WhoWor 91*
Rendell, Ruth 1930- *BioIn 16, ConAu 32NR, FemiCLE, MajTwCW, TwCCr&M 91, WorAlBi, WorAu 1980 [port]*
Rendell, Ruth Barbara 1930- *WhoAmW 91, WhoWor 91*
Rendell, Stephen 1819-1893 *DcCanB 12*
Rendell-Baker, Leslie 1917- *WhoAm 90*
Render, Arleen *WhoAmW 91*
Render, Helena Willis 1896-1970 *BioIn 16*
Render, Kenneth Ray 1926- *St&PR 91*
Render, Robyn Roberts 1953- *WhoAmW 91*
Rendich, Vincent H. *BioIn 16*
Rendina, Laura Cooper 1902- *AuBYP 90*
Rendinell, D.F. *BiDrAPA 89*
Rendino, Anthony 1926- *St&PR 91*
Rendl, M 1928- *WhoAmA 91*
Rendl-Marcus, Mildred 1928- *WhoAmW 91, WhoE 91, WhoWor 91*
Rendleman, Daniel Carl 1950- *BiDrAPA 89*
Rendleman, Dennis Alan 1956- *WhoEmL 91*
Rendleman, Patricia Proctor 1952- *WhoSSW 91*
Rendleman, Rebecca Lynn *BiDrAPA 89*
Rendleman, Robert Terrence 1945- *St&PR 91*
Rendleman, Ruth 1949- *IntWWM 90*
Rendon, Angel 1953- *BiDrAPA 89*
Rendon, Armando B. 1939- *WhoHisp 91*
Rendon, Enrique 1923-1987 *MusmAFA*
Rendon, Mario Ivan 1938- *BiDrAPA 89, WhoE 91*
Rendon, Ruth Marie 1961- *WhoHisp 91*
Rendtorff, Robert Carlisle 1915- *WhoAm 90*
Rendueles, Robert 1905- *WhoWor 91*
Rendulic, James Ronald 1946- *St&PR 91*
Rene, Denise *BioIn 16*
Rene, France Albert 1935- *WhoWor 91*
Rene-Worms, Georges 1945- *WhoWor 91*
Reneau, Daniel *WhoAm 90, WhoSSW 91*
Reneau, Linda Rae 1948- *WhoWrEP 89*
Reneau, Marvin Bryan 1939- *WhoSSW 91*
Reneau, Susan Campbell 1952- *WhoAmW 91*
Renee 1929- *FemiCLE*
Renee de France, Duchess 1510-1575 *BioIn 16*
Renee, Lisabeth 1952- *WhoAmA 91*
Renee, Paula *WhoAmA 91*
Renegar, Laura Estelle 1964- *WhoAmW 91*
Renehan, John Lewis 1926- *St&PR 91*
Renehan, Robert Francis Xavier 1935- *WhoAm 90*
Reneker, Maxine Hohman 1942- *WhoAm 90*
Rener, Jacqueline Kathleen 1959- *WhoAmW 91*
Renfield, Elinor *BioIn 16*
Renfield, Marilyn Lewis *BiDrAPA 89*
Renforth, John *ODwPR 91*
Renfrew, Andrew Colin 1937- *WhoWor 91*
Renfrew, Charles Byron 1928- *St&PR 91, WhoAm 90*
Renfrew, George Richard 1831-1897 *DcCanB 12*
Renfrew, Glen McGarvie 1928- *WhoAm 90*
Renfrew, Malcolm MacKenzie 1910- *WhoAm 90*
Renfrew, Murray Samuel 1936- *BiDrAPA 89*
Renfro, Charles Gilliland 1943- *WhoAm 90*
Renfro, Edward Eugene, III 1925- *WhoSSW 91*
Renfro, Maxine June 1927- *WhoAmW 91*
Renfro, Sandra *BioIn 16*
Renfroe, Anita Louise 1948- *IntWWM 90*
Renfroe, Delwin D. 1939- *St&PR 91*
Renfroe, Janice Marie 1954- *WhoAmW 91*
Renfroe, L. Edwin *WhoSSW 91*
Renfrow, Edward 1940- *WhoAm 90*
Rengarajan, Sembiam Rajagopal 1948- *WhoEmL 91*
Renger, James Dietrich 1940- *St&PR 91*
Reni, Guido 1575-1642 *BioIn 16, IntDcAA 90*
Renick, Carol Bishop 1956- *WhoAmW 91*
Renick, John Terry 1939- *BiDrAPA 89*
Renick, Marion 1905- *AuBYP 90*
Renick, Michele Diane 1963- *WhoAmW 91*
Renick, Ralph Apperson 1928- *WhoAm 90, WhoSSW 91*
Renick, Rick 1944- *Ballpl 90*
Renick, Susan Garner 1945- *WhoAmW 91*
Renick, Timothy Mark 1959- *WhoSSW 91*
Renick, William R. 1951- *St&PR 91*
Renicker, Robert Nolan 1944- *St&PR 91*
Renier, James J. 1930- *WhoAm 90*
Renier, James Joseph 1930- *St&PR 91*
Renier, Joseph Emile *WhoAmA 91N*
Renier, Noreen *EncO&P 3*
Reniff, Hal 1938- *Ballpl 90*
Renik, Owen Dennis *BiDrAPA 89*
Renikoff, Elizabeth Therese 1964- *WhoAmW 91*
Renius, Karl Theodor 1938- *WhoWor 91*
Renjun, Zou 1927- *WhoWor 91*
Renk, Merry 1921- *WhoAmA 91*
Renka, Richard P 1945- *BiDrAPA 89*
Renkar-Janda, Jarri J. 1951- *WhoAmW 91*
Renkema, David 1955- *WhoWor 91*
Renkens, Madeline A. *WhoAmW 91*
Renker, Howard H. 1906- *St&PR 91*
Renkis, Alan Ilmars 1938- *WhoWor 91*
Renko, Steve 1944- *Ballpl 90*
Renn, Daniel J. 1942- *St&PR 91*
Renn, Donald Walter 1932- *WhoE 91*
Renna, Agostino 1937-1988 *BioIn 16*
Renna, Bill 1924- *Ballpl 90*
Rennagel, Marilyn *BioIn 16*
Rennaker, Wayne E. 1930- *St&PR 91*
Renne, Janice Lynn 1952- *WhoEmL 91*
Renne, Louise Hornbeck 1937- *WhoAmW 91*
Renneisen, Robert M 1946- *ODwPR 91*
Renneker, Richard E 1919- *BiDrAPA 89*
Renner, August N. 1921- *St&PR 91*
Renner, E. Wayne 1947- *St&PR 91*
Renner, Eric 1941- *WhoAmA 91*
Renner, George Richard *WhoAm 90*
Renner, Gerald F. 1934- *St&PR 91*
Renner, Glenn Delmar 1925- *WhoSSW 91*
Renner, Greg *St&PR 91*
Renner, John A, Jr. *BiDrAPA 89*
Renner, John F. 1946- *St&PR 91*
Renner, John Wilson 1924- *WhoAm 90*
Renner, Maximilian 1919- *WhoWor 91*
Renner, Otto 1883-1960 *DcScB S2*
Renner, Otto W., III *ODwPR 91*
Renner, Paul Bradley *BiDrAPA 89*
Renner, S. Edward 1934- *St&PR 91*
Renner, Simon Edward 1934- *WhoAm 90, WhoE 91*
Renner, Thomas C. *BioIn 16*
Renner, Thomas C 1928-1990 *ConAu 130*
Rennert, Dutch 1934- *Ballpl 90*
Rennert, Eric *BiDrAPA 89*
Rennert, Jonathan 1952- *IntWWM 90*
Rennert, Vincent P. 1928- *ODwPR 91*
Rennert, Wolfgang 1922- *IntWWM 90*
Rennick, Dan *WhoAmA 91*
Rennick, Hilda May 1902- *WhoAmW 91*
Rennick, John H 1948- *BiDrAPA 89*
Rennick, Kyme Elizabeth Wall 1953- *WhoAmW 91*
Rennie, Helen *WhoAmA 91*
Rennie, Janice G. 1957- *St&PR 91*
Rennie, John Coyne 1937- *WhoE 91*
Rennie, John Ogilvy 1914-1981 *DcNaB 1981*
Rennie, Michael 1909-1971 *WorAlBi*
Rennie, Robert Richard 1922- *St&PR 91*
Rennie, Rud 1897-1956 *Ballpl 90*
Renninger, Jane Frances 1943- *WhoAmW 91*
Renninger, John H. 1939- *St&PR 91*
Renninger, Katharine Steele 1925- *WhoAmA 91*
Renninger, Martin 1940- *St&PR 91*
Renninger, Mary Karen 1945- *WhoAm 90*
Renno, H. Eugene 1942- *St&PR 91*
Reno *BioIn 16*
Reno, Barbara M. 1946- *St&PR 91*
Reno, Barbara Morrison *ODwPR 91*
Reno, Cheryl *St&PR 91*
Reno, Edward A., Jr. 1943- *St&PR 91*
Reno, Hunter *BioIn 16*
Reno, Janet 1938- *WhoAm 90*
Reno, John Findley 1939- *WhoAm 90*
Reno, Marcus Albert 1834-1889 *WhNaAH*
Reno, Roger 1924- *St&PR 91, WhoAm 90*
Reno, Russell Ronald, Jr. 1933- *WhoAm 90*
Reno, Susan Bennekemper 1954- *WhoWrEP 89*
Renoir, Auguste 1841-1919 *BioIn 16*
Renoir, Jean 1894-1979 *BioIn 16, ConAu 129, WorAlBi*
Renoir, Pierre Auguste 1841-1919 *IntDcAA 90, WorAlBi*
Renola, Josephine 1922- *St&PR 91*

Renouf, Edda 1943- *WhoAm 90, WhoAmA 91*
Renouf, Edward 1906- *WhoAmA 91*
Renouf, Francis Henry 1918- *WhoWor 91*
Renouf, Harold Augustus 1917- *WhoAm 90*
Renoux, Gerard Eugene 1915- *WhoWor 91*
Renquist, Donald Eldon 1931- *St&PR 91*
Rens, Max Joannes Leopold Maria 1947- *WhoWor 91*
Rensberger, Michael J. 1947- *St&PR 91*
Rensberry, Richard J. 1952- *WhoWrEP 89*
Rensch, Joseph R. 1923- *St&PR 91*
Rensch, Joseph Romaine 1923- *WhoAm 90*
Rensch, Roslyn *WhoAmA 91*
Renschler, C. Arnold 1942- *WhoAm 90*
Renschler, Daryl L. 1943- *St&PR 91*
Rense, Paige *BioIn 16, WhoAm 90, WhoAmW 91*
Rense, Paige 1929- *NewYTBS 90 [port]*
Rensel, Harry Truedale, Jr. 1949- *WhoE 91*
Renshaw, Bernard Mattison, Jr. 1955- *WhoSSW 91*
Renshaw, Charles Clark, Jr. 1920- *WhoAm 90, WhoWrEP 89*
Renshaw, Domeena C 1929- *BiDrAPA 89*
Renshaw-Zeason, Cheryl R. 1952- *WhoAmW 91*
Rensi, Edward Henry 1944- *WhoAm 90*
Rensimer, Edward R. 1949- *WhoSSW 91*
Rensink, David G. 1946- *St&PR 91*
Renson, Marcel Gilles 1926- *WhoWor 91*
Renstrom, Roger T. 1940- *ODwPR 91*
Rent, Clyda Stokes 1942- *WhoAm 90, WhoAmW 91*
Rentas, Carlos, Jr. 1951- *WhoE 91*
Rentenbach, Thomas J. 1911- *St&PR 91*
Rentenbach, Thomas Joseph 1911- *WhoAm 90, WhoSSW 91*
Rentenbach, Thomas Michael 1939- *St&PR 91*
Renter, Lois Irene Hutson 1929- *WhoAmW 91*
Renteria, Cheryl Christina 1944- *WhoAmW 91*
Renteria, Deborah Maria 1952- *WhoHisp 91*
Renteria, Esther *WhoHisp 91*
Renteria, Hermelinda 1960- *WhoHisp 91*
Renthal, Ann Lomax *BiDrAPA 89*
Rentmeester, Lawrence Raymond 1939- *St&PR 91*
Rentner, James David 1940- *WhoSSW 91*
Renton, Allan Hopkins 1926- *St&PR 91*
Renton, Hollings C. 1946- *St&PR 91*
Rentrop, Norman Frank 1957- *WhoWor 91*
Rentschler, Frederick Brant 1939- *WhoAm 90*
Rentschler, William Henry 1925- *St&PR 91, WhoAm 90, WhoWor 91*
Rentz, J. Fred 1924- *St&PR 91*
Rentz, Richard Ernest 1916- *St&PR 91*
Rentzel, Catharine Rasmussen 1951- *WhoAmW 91*
Rentzepis, Peter M. 1934- *WhoAm 90*
Rentzhog, Sten Erik 1937- *WhoWor 91*
Rentzsch, Ralph Vernon 1925- *St&PR 91*
Renvall, Johan 1959- *BioIn 16*
Renville, Gabriel 1824-1902 *WhNaAH*
Renville, Joseph 1779?-1846 *WhNaAH*
Renwick, Gloria Rainey *WhoWrEP 89*
Renwick, James 1818-1895 *WorAlBi*
Renwick, James Brevoort 1949- *St&PR 91*
Renwick, William Jonathan Michael 1958- *IntWWM 90*
Renxia, Chang 1904- *WhoWor 91*
Reny, D.R. 1954- *St&PR 91*
Reny, L. Guy 1927- *St&PR 91*
Renyi, Albert *PenDiMP*
Renyi, Alfred 1921-1970 *DcScB S2*
Renyi, Thomas A. 1946- *St&PR 91*
Renz, James W. 1944- *St&PR 91*
Renz, Matthew 1959- *WhoSSW 91*
Renz, William Thomas 1938- *St&PR 91*
Renz, William Tomlinson 1947- *WhoEmL 91*
Renza, John Sebastian, Jr. 1948- *WhoE 91*
Renzetti, Attilio David 1920- *WhoAm 90*
Renzi, Emma 1937- *IntWWM 90*
Renzi, Mary Ann 1945- *BiDrAPA 89*
Renzi, Virgie A. 1936- *St&PR 91*
Renzulli, Franco *BioIn 16*
Renzullo, Vittoria *BiDrAPA 89*
Renzy, Bernard Thomas, III 1937- *WhoE 91*
REO Speedwagon *EncPR&S 89*
Reodica, Romeo E *BiDrAPA 89*
Repa, George 1955- *WhoSSW 91*
Repa, John Theodore 1943- *WhoE 91*
Repak, Michael Joseph 1957- *WhoE 91*
Repasky, Mark Edward 1956- *WhoSSW 91*
Repass, James Caldwell *BiDrAPA 89*
RePass, James Paul 1949- *WhoE 91*
Repass, L. Donald 1938- *St&PR 91*
Repetti, James Randolph 1953- *WhoEmL 91*
Repetto, Robert C. *ConAu 129*
Rephan, Jack 1932- *WhoAm 90*
Repin, Ilya 1844-1930 *IntDcAA 90*
Repko, Cheryl Beatrice 1951- *WhoAmW 91*
Repko, William C. 1949- *St&PR 91*
Repko, William Clarke 1949- *WhoE 91*
Replacements, The *EncPR&S 89*
Replansky, Naomi 1918- *FemiCLE, WhoWrEP 89*
Replinger, Dot 1924- *WhoAmA 91*
Replinger, John Gordon 1923- *WhoAm 90*
Replogle, Andy 1953- *Ballpl 90*
Replogle, David Robert 1931- *St&PR 91*
Replogle, Frederick Allen 1898- *WhoAm 90*
Replogle, John C. 1945- *St&PR 91*
Replogle, Katrinia Sue 1956- *WhoAmW 91*
Repman, Judith Lavine 1954- *WhoSSW 91*
Repoli, Michael Gerald 1948- *WhoAm 90*
Reposa, Carol Coffee 1943- *WhoWrEP 89*
Repoz, Roger 1940- *Ballpl 90*
Repp, Joan Mercedes 1930- *WhoAmW 91*
Repp, William E. 1943- *St&PR 91*
Repp, William S. 1933- *St&PR 91*
Reppel, Carmen 1941- *IntWWM 90*
Repper, George Robert 1954- *WhoEmL 91*
Reppert, Alfred R. 1919- *St&PR 91*
Reppert, D.L. 1943- *St&PR 91*
Reppert, Nancy Lue 1933- *WhoAmW 91, WhoWor 91*
Reppert, Steven Marion 1946- *WhoAm 90*
Reppert, Susanna Rebecca 1962- *WhoAmW 91*
Repplier, Agnes 1855-1950 *BioAmW*
Reppy, John David, Jr. 1931- *WhoAm 90*
Reps, Constance Peck 1921- *WhoAmW 91*
Reps, Paul 1895-1990 *ConAu 132*
Repulski, Rip 1927- *Ballpl 90*
Requarth, Harold William 1925- *St&PR 91*
Requarth, William Henry 1913- *WhoAm 90*
Requena, Javier 1952- *WhoSSW 91*
Requena, Manuel 1802?-1876 *BioIn 16*
Requier-Esnault, Francoise 1944- *WhoWor 91*
Reres, Mary Epiphany 1941- *WhoAm 90*
Rerikh, Nikolai Konstantinovich 1874-1947 *BioIn 16*
Rermgosakul, Adul *BiDrAPA 89*
Resch, Andreas 1934- *EncPaPR 91*
Resch, Cynthia Fortes 1951- *WhoE 91*
Resch, David Scott *BiDrAPA 89*
Resch, Joseph Anthony 1914- *WhoAm 90*
Resch, Joseph Bernard, Jr. 1918- *St&PR 91*
Resch, Mary Louise 1956- *WhoAmW 91*
Resch, Michael F. 1950- *St&PR 91*
Resch, Rita Marie *IntWWM 90*
Reschke, Gary Joe 1954- *WhoE 91*
Reschke, Julia Kruger 1955- *BiDrAPA 89*
Rescia, Richard R. 1930- *IntWWM 90*
Rescigno, Nicola *IntWWM 90*
Rescigno, Xavier 1913- *Ballpl 90*
Rescildo, Ralph J. 1941- *St&PR 91*
Rescorla, Robert Arthur 1940- *WhoAm 90*
Reseda *EncCoWW*
Resek, Kate Frances *WhoAmA 91*
Resek, Robert William 1935- *WhoAm 90*
Resel, Werner 1935- *WhoWor 91*
Resen, Frederick Lawrence 1923- *WhoAm 90*
Reser, Bill J. 1933- *St&PR 91*
Reser, Galen *WhoAm 90*
Reser, Michael R 1953- *St&PR 91*
Resh, S. Pete 1946- *St&PR 91*
Reshotko, Eli 1930- *WhoAm 90*
Resika, Paul 1928- *WhoAm 90, WhoAmA 91*
Resino, Carmen 1941- *EncCoWW*
Resis, Steven Joseph 1960- *BiDrAPA 89*
Reskof, David *BiDrAPA 89*
Resnais, Alain 1922- *BioIn 16, WhoWor 91, WorAlBi*
Resnekov, Leon 1928- *WhoAm 90*
Resnick, Albert B *BiDrAPA 89*
Resnick, Alice Robie 1939- *WhoAm 90, WhoAmW 91*
Resnick, Carol Lyn *WhoAmW 91*
Resnick, Cynthia Bilt 1946- *WhoAmW 91*
Resnick, Debra B. 1955- *WhoAmW 91*
Resnick, Don 1928- *WhoAmA 91, WhoE 91*
Resnick, Eugene V *BiDrAPA 89*
Resnick, Eugene Victor 1923- *WhoE 91*
Resnick, Idrian Navarre 1936- *WhoAm 90*
Resnick, Ira *BioIn 16*
Resnick, Irving *BioIn 16*
Resnick, Jack Marvin 1947- *WhoE 91*
Resnick, Jeffrey Tyler 1956- *St&PR 91*
Resnick, Joel H. 1936- *WhoAm 90*
Resnick, Joyce A. *BiDrAPA 89*
Resnick, Kenneth 1934- *WhoWor 91*
Resnick, Marcia Aylene 1950- *WhoAmA 91*
Resnick, Mark I. 1947- *St&PR 91*
Resnick, Michael Philip *BiDrAPA 89*
Resnick, Milton 1917- *WhoAmA 91*
Resnick, Myron J. 1931- *St&PR 91, WhoAm 90*
Resnick, Phillip Jacob 1938- *BiDrAPA 89*
Resnick, Richard B 1931- *BiDrAPA 89*
Resnick, Richard Boyce 1931- *WhoE 91*
Resnick, Robert 1923- *WhoAm 90*
Resnick, Robert Michael 1944- *WhoSSW 91*
Resnick, Ruth G. 1947- *WhoE 91*
Resnick, Saul 1940- *ODwPR 91, WhoE 91*
Resnick, Seymour 1920- *AuBYP 90*
Resnick, Stephanie 1959- *WhoAmW 91, WhoE 91*
Resnick, Steven Ives *BiDrAPA 89*
Resnick, Steven Ives 1956- *WhoE 91*
Resnick, Sylvia 1927- *ConAu 30NR*
Resnicow, Herbert 1921- *TwCCr&M 91*
Resnik, Anna Garfinkel 1951- *WhoAmW 91*
Resnik, David Alan 1956- *St&PR 91, WhoE 91, WhoEmL 91, WhoWor 91*
Resnik, Frank 1942- *St&PR 91*
Resnik, Frank Edward 1928- *St&PR 91, WhoAm 90*
Resnik, Frank H. 1942- *St&PR 91*
Resnik, Harvey L P 1930- *BiDrAPA 89*
Resnik, Harvey Lewis Paul 1930- *WhoAm 90, WhoWor 91*
Resnik, Judith A. 1949-1986 *BioIn 16*
Resnik, Leslie R. *ODwPR 91*
Resnik, Linda Ilene 1950- *WhoAm 90*
Resnik, Regina 1922- *PenDiMP*
Resnik, Regina 1924- *IntWWM 90, WhoAm 90*
Resnik, Robert 1938- *WhoAm 90*
Resnik, Sol Leon 1930- *WhoWor 91*
Resnikoff, George Joseph 1915- *WhoAm 90*
Resnikoff, Richard Joseph 1949- *BiDrAPA 89*
Resnikoff, Roy Otto 1943- *BiDrAPA 89*
Reso, Anthony 1934- *WhoSSW 91*
Reso, Sidney J. 1935- *St&PR 91*
Resor, Alan Gloyd 1940- *BiDrAPA 89*
Resor, Stanley Rogers 1917- *WhoAm 90*
Respess, James Leonadus, III 1943- *St&PR 91*
Respighi, Ottorino 1879-1936 *PenDiMP A*
Ress, Charles William 1933- *WhoWor 91*
Ress, Erica Leslie 1950- *WhoAmW 91*
Ress, Spike *BioIn 16*
Resse, Harry Eugene 1946- *WhoWrEP 89*
Ressler, Barry 1940- *St&PR 91*
Ressler, Judith A. 1949- *ODwPR 91*
Ressler, Parke Edward 1916- *WhoSSW 91*
Ressler, Theodore Whitson *AuBYP 90*
Ressner, Eric Laurie 1954- *BiDrAPA 89*
Ressner, Philip 1922- *AuBYP 90*
Restak, Richard M 1942- *BiDrAPA 89*
Restall, Lawrence Jerry 1939- *St&PR 91, WhoAm 90*
Restani, Jane A. 1948- *WhoAm 90*
Restany, Pierre 1930- *ConAu 130*
Restarick, Henry Bond 1854-1933 *BioIn 16*
Restell, Madame *BioAmW*
Rester, Alfred Carl, Jr. 1940- *WhoSSW 91*
Rester, George G. 1923- *WhoAm 90, WhoWor 91*
Restif De La Bretonne, Nicholas Edme 1734-1806 *WorAlBi*
Restis, Stamatis Macias 1940- *WhoWor 91*
Restivo, James John, Jr. 1946- *WhoAm 90*
Restless Heart *WhoNeCM*
Reston, James 1909- *ConAu 31NR*
Reston, James B. 1909- *WorAlBi*
Reston, James B, Jr. 1941- *ConAu 31NR*
Reston, James Barrett 1909- *WhoAm 90, WhoWor 91*
Reston, Mary Jo 1937- *WhoE 91*
Restrepo, Carlos Armando 1950- *WhoHisp 91*
Restrepo, Carlos Lleras 1908- *BioIn 16*
Restrepo, Christian 1940- *BiDrAPA 89*
Restrepo, George Anthony, Jr. 1933- *WhoHisp 91*
Restrepo, Margo Kaliner *BiDrAPA 89*
Resweber, Louis J. *ODwPR 91*
Reswick, James Bigelow 1922- *WhoAm 90*
Resz, Charles Dennis 1935- *St&PR 91*
Reszka, Alfons 1924- *WhoAm 90*
Reszke, Edouard de *PenDiMP*
Reszke, Jean de *PenDiMP*
Reszke, Jean de 1850-1925 *BioIn 16*
Reszke, Josephine de *PenDiMP*
Retamar, Roberto Fernandez *ConAu 131, HispWr 90*
Retchitzky, Marcel 1924- *IntWWM 90*
Retey, Janos 1934- *WhoWor 91*
Rethberg, Elisabeth 1894-1976 *PenDiMP*
Retherford, John Clifford 1951- *St&PR 91*
Rethore, Bernard Gabriel 1941- *St&PR 91, WhoAm 90*
Reti, Gabriel Andrew 1930- *St&PR 91*
Reti, Tamas 1951- *WhoWor 91*
Retik, Hector *BiDrAPA 89*
Retizos, Nelin Briones *BiDrAPA 89*
Retla, Robert *AuBYP 90*
Retore, Guy 1924- *WhoWor 91*
Retsas, Spyros 1942- *WhoWor 91*
Rettberg, Barbara Carol 1941- *WhoAmW 91*
Rettberg, John R. 1937- *St&PR 91*
Rettenmeier, Albert Wolfgang 1947- *WhoWor 91*
Rettenmund, Merv 1943- *Ballpl 90*
Retterstol, Nils 1924- *WhoWor 91*
Rettger, Mary Ann 1951- *WhoAmW 91*
Rettie, John Garner 1949- *WhoWrEP 89*
Rettig, Carolyn Faith 1951- *WhoAmW 91, WhoE 91*
Rettig, R. Joseph 1943- *St&PR 91*
Rettig, Richard Allen 1936- *WhoAm 90*
Rettig, Terry 1947- *WhoEmL 91, WhoSSW 91, WhoWor 91*
Rettig, Tommy 1941- *BioIn 16*
Rettinger, Dale G. 1944- *St&PR 91*
Rettinger, Donald Henry 1933- *St&PR 91*
Rettke, Michael C. 1944- *St&PR 91*
Retton, Mary Lou *BioIn 16*
Retton, Mary Lou 1968- *WorAlBi*
Retzel, Frank A. 1948- *IntWWM 90*
Retzer, Howard Earl 1925- *WhoAmA 91*
Retzer, Ken 1934- *Ballpl 90*
Retzer, Mary Elizabeth Helm *WhoAmW 91*
Retzer, William K. 1943- *St&PR 91*
Retzke, Melanie Jayne 1952- *WhoAmW 91*
Retzky, Allan Abraham 1937- *St&PR 91*
Retzler, Kurt E. 1927- *St&PR 91*
Retzler, Kurt Egon 1927- *WhoAm 90*
Reuben, Allan H. 1931-1989 *BioIn 16*
Reuben, Alvin Bernard 1940- *WhoAm 90*
Reuben, Betty Gene 1943- *WhoAmW 91*
Reuben, Carola C. *WhoHisp 91*
Reuben, David R. 1933- *WorAlBi*
Reuben, Don H. 1928- *WhoAm 90, WhoWor 91*
Reuben, Rita S *BiDrAPA 89*
Reubens, Paul *BioIn 16*
Reuber, Grant Louis 1927- *St&PR 91, WhoAm 90*
Reubins, Beatriz Markman 1941- *WhoE 91*
Reubins, Marc S 1947- *BiDrAPA 89*
Reuder, Mary Eileen 1923- *WhoAmW 91, WhoE 91*
Reudink, Douglas Otto John 1939- *WhoAm 90*
Reul, Richard Philip 1921- *WhoWrEP 89*
Reuland, Geo. F. 1909- *St&PR 91*
Reuland, Timothy J. *BioIn 16*
Reulbach, Ed 1882-1961 *Ballpl 90 [port]*
Reuling, Hans Juergen 1943- *WhoWor 91*
Reuling, John A. *BioIn 16*
Reuling, Josine 1899-1961 *EncCoWW*
Reuling, Michael Frederick 1946- *St&PR 91, WhoAm 90*
Reum, W. Robert 1942- *St&PR 91, WhoAm 90*
Reuman, Robert Everett 1923- *WhoAm 90*
Reunanen, Mikko Sakari 1944- *WhoWor 91*
Reuning, Stephen *BioIn 16*
Reurs, John H. *BioIn 16, NewYTBS 90*
Reus, Victor Ivar 1947- *BiDrAPA 89*
Reusche, Robert F. 1927- *St&PR 91*
Reuschel, Paul 1947- *Ballpl 90*
Reuschel, Rick 1949- *Ballpl 90 [port], WorAlBi*
Reuschel, Rick Eugene 1949- *WhoAm 90*
Reuscher, Richard J. 1934- *St&PR 91*
Reuscher, William E. *St&PR 91*
Reuschle, Robert James 1941- *St&PR 91*
Reuschlein, Harold Gill 1904- *WhoAm 90*
Reuse, Ronald 1946- *WhoEmL 91*
Reuss, Henry *BioIn 16*
Reuss, Henry S. 1912- *EncABHB 7 [port], WorAlBi*
Reuss, Jerry 1949- *Ballpl 90, BioIn 16*
Reuss, Lloyd E. 1936- *St&PR 91*
Reuss, Lloyd Edwin Armin 1936- *WhoAm 90*
Reuss, Priscilla A. 1946- *WhoAmW 91*
Reuss, Robert P. 1918- *St&PR 91*
Reuss, Robert Pershing 1918- *WhoAm 90*
Reuss, Theodor *EncO&P 3*
Reuss-Ianni, Elizabeth 1946- *ConAu 130*
Reuter, Carol Joan 1941- *WhoAmW 91, WhoE 91*
Reuter, Ernst 1889-1953 *BioIn 16*
Reuter, Florizel von 1893- *EncO&P 3*
Reuter, Frank Theodore 1926- *WhoAm 90, WhoWrEP 89*
Reuter, Gabriele 1859-1941 *BioIn 16*
Reuter, George Edward 1916- *WhoAm 90*
Reuter, Jeanette Miller 1921- *WhoAmW 91*
Reuter, Konrad Dieter 1951- *WhoWor 91*
Reuter, Laurel J 1943- *WhoAmA 91*
Reuter, Lutz Rainer 1943- *WhoWor 91*
Reuter, Paul Julius, Baron Von 1816-1899 *WorAlBi*
Reuter, Stanley Richard 1943- *St&PR 91*
Reuter, Stewart Ralston 1934- *WhoAm 90*

Reuter, William Lee 1934- *St&PR 91*
Reuter, Wilma Sanborn 1922- *WhoAmW 91*
Reuterskiold, Marianne Astrid 1946- *WhoWor 91*
Reuthe, Marjorie Snyder 1914- *WhoAmW 91*
Reuther, David L 1946- *ConAu 31NR*
Reuther, David Louis 1946- *WhoAm 90, WhoWrEP 89*
Reuther, Hans 1940- *St&PR 91*
Reuther, Rosann White 1943- *WhoAmW 91*
Reuther, Walter P. 1907-1970 *WorAlBi*
Reuther, Walter Philip 1907-1970 *BioIn 16, EncABHB 5 [port]*
Reutinger, Annie 1951- *ODwPR 91*
Reutlingen, Hans von *PenDiDA 89*
Reutter, Eberhard Edmund, Jr. 1924- *WhoAm 90*
Reutter, Mark 1950- *ConAu 129*
Revak, Blairanne 1943- *WhoAmW 91*
Revane, Michael J. 1934- *St&PR 91*
Reveal, Ernest Ira 1915- *WhoAm 90*
Reveaux, Mark M. 1941- *St&PR 91*
Reveillon, Jean-Baptiste *PenDiDA 89*
Revel, Bernard 1885-1940 *BioIn 16*
Revel, Gary Neal 1949- *IntWWM 90, WhoWor 91*
Revel, Harry 1905-1958 *OxCPMus*
Revel, Jean 1684-1751 *PenDiDA 89*
Revel, Ricky Joe 1956- *WhoSSW 91*
Reveles, Robert A. 1932- *WhoHisp 91*
Reveles, Robert Apodaca 1932- *St&PR 91*
Reveley, Louis Ramon 1951- *WhoSSW 91, WhoWor 91*
Reveley, Michael A 1944- *BiDrAPA 89*
Reveley, Michael August 1944- *WhoWor 91*
Reveley, Ted 1944- *BiDrAPA 89*
Reveley, Walter Taylor, III 1943- *WhoAm 90*
Revell, Dennis C. 1958- *ODwPR 91*
Revell, Oliver Burgan 1938- *WhoAm 90*
Revell, Pat Joan 1930- *St&PR 91*
Revelle, Donald Gene 1930- *WhoAm 90*
Revelle, John D. 1946- *St&PR 91*
Revelle, Roger Randall Dougan 1909- *WhoAm 90*
Revelli, Ignazio 1756-1836 *PenDiDA 89*
Revelli, Luigi 1776-1858 *PenDiDA 89*
Revels, Hiram R. 1822-1901 *WorAlBi*
Revels, Hiram Rhodes 1827-1901 *BlkAmsC [port]*
Revena 1927- *SmATA X*
Reventlow, Franziska von 1871-1918 *EncCoWW*
Reventlow, Franziska zu 1871-1918 *BioIn 16*
Rever, Barbara L. 1947- *WhoAmW 91, WhoEmL 91*
Rever, George Wright 1928- *BiDrAPA 89*
Rever, Robert W. 1935- *WhoAm 90*
Revercomb, Everett Eugene 1914- *WhoAm 90*
Revercomb, George Hughes 1929- *WhoAm 90*
Reverdin, Bernard J. 1919- *WhoAm 90*
Revere, Alan 1947- *BioIn 16*
Revere, Anne 1903-1990 *NewYTBS 90 [port]*
Revere, Paul *BioIn 16*
Revere, Paul 1734-1818 *PenDiDA 89*
Revere, Paul 1735-1818 *BioIn 16, EncCRAm [port], WorAlBi*
Revere, Paul 1942- *EncPR&S 89*
Revere, Paul, and the Raiders *EncPR&S 89*
Reverend, Claude *PenDiDA 89*
Reverend, Francois *PenDiDA 89*
Revering, Dave 1953- *Ballpl 90*
Reverman, Philip John, Jr. 1946- *WhoEmL 91*
Reveron, Armando 1889-1954 *ArtLatA*
Reveyron, Joseph 1917- *IntWWM 90*
Revie, Don 1927-1989 *AnObit 1989*
Revier, Dorothy 1908- *BioIn 16*
Reville, Joann M. 1946- *WhoAmW 91*
Revin, Bengt 1940- *WhoWor 91*
Revington, George D, III *WhoAmA 91N*
Revington Burdick, Betty *WhoAmA 91*
Revis, Antony 1947- *WhoE 91*
Revis-Yeoman, Alexis 1957- *WhoAmW 91*
Revitch, Eugene 1909- *BiDrAPA 89*
Revoil, Fanely 1910- *PenDiMP*
Revoile, Charles P. 1934- *St&PR 91*
Revoile, Charles Patrick 1934- *WhoAm 90*
Revolinski, Rebecca *BioIn 16*
Revollo Bravo, Mario 1919- *WhoWor 91*
Revor, Remy 1914- *WhoAmA 91*
Revord, Francis Earle 1929- *St&PR 91*
Revsine, Lawrence 1942- *WhoAm 90*
Revson, Alfred F., Jr. 1926- *St&PR 91*
Revson, Charles H. 1906-1975 *WorAlBi*
Revson, Charles Haskell 1906-1975 *ConAmBL*
Revson, James A. *BioIn 16*
Revuelta, Maria Dolores 1956- *WhoWor 91*
Revzan, Henry Allen 1945- *St&PR 91*
Rew, William Edmund 1923- *WhoSSW 91, WhoWor 91*
Rewak, William John 1933- *WhoAm 90, WhoWor 91*
Rewald, Roman 1953- *WhoEmL 91*
Rewbotham, F. Dickson 1941- *St&PR 91*
Rewend, Christian Friedrich *PenDiDA 89*
Rewey, Pamela Sue 1946- *WhoAmW 91*
Rewey, Richard W 1938- *BiDrAPA 89*
Rex, Christopher Davis 1951- *WhoSSW 91*
Rex, David Lawrence 1935- *WhoSSW 91*
Rex, Melvin D. 1937- *St&PR 91*
Rex, Robert Richmond 1909- *WhoWor 91*
Rexford, Eveoleen *BiDrAPA 89*
Rexine, John Efstratios 1929- *WhoAm 90, WhoWrEP 89*
Rexing, Louis G. 1960- *WhoEmL 91*
Rexroth, Kenneth 1905-1982 *MajTwCW*
Rexroth, Nancy Louise 1946- *WhoAm 90, WhoAmA 91*
Rey, Alfonso M 1923- *BiDrAPA 89*
Rey, Alix C 1940- *BiDrAPA 89*
Rey, Alix Charles 1940- *WhoE 91*
Rey, Carlos Raul 1959- *WhoEmL 91, WhoWor 91*
Rey, Carmen Rosello 1923- *WhoAm 90*
Rey, Charles Fernand 1877-1968 *BioIn 16*
Rey, Daniel *WhoHisp 91*
Rey, Fernando 1917- *ConTFT 8*
Rey, H. A. 1898-1977 *BioIn 16*
Rey, H A 1898-1977 *WhoAmA 91N*
Rey, Hans Augusto 1898-1977 *AuBYP 90, BioIn 16*
Rey, Jean-Jacques Arnold 1937- *WhoWor 91*
Rey, Margaret Elizabeth 1906- *AuBYP 90*
Rey, Margret *BioIn 16*
Rey, Monte 1900-1982 *OxCPMus*
Rey, William Kenneth 1925- *WhoAm 90*
Rey Palenzuela, Javier 1938- *WhoWor 91*
Rey-Rosa, Rodrigo 1958- *ConAu 131*
Reya, Ewald Philipp 1943- *WhoWor 91*
Reyburn, Elva Kling *BioIn 16*
Reyburn, Harold Orbra 1915- *WhoAm 90*
Reycraft, George Dewey 1924- *WhoAm 90*
Reye, George H *BiDrAPA 89*
Reyelts, Paul Courtney 1946- *St&PR 91*
Reyer, Allan Kent 1948- *WhoE 91*
Reyer, Eckhard 1937- *WhoWor 91*
Reyer, Randall William 1917- *WhoAm 90*
Reyering, Sally Ann *BiDrAPA 89*
Reyerson, Dennis Orville 1939- *WhoWrEP 89*
Reyes, Alan Doyle *BiDrAPA 89*
Reyes, Alfonso 1889-1959 *BioIn 16, ConAu 131, HispWr 90*
Reyes, Alfonso Salita, Jr. 1955- *St&PR 91*
Reyes, Alicia Llamado 1933- *WhoWor 91*
Reyes, Antonio 1939- *WhoHisp 91*
Reyes, Aurora C. 1938- *WhoHisp 91*
Reyes, Baltazar V, Jr. *BiDrAPA 89*
Reyes, Ben *WhoHisp 91*
Reyes, Benjamin 1952- *WhoHisp 91*
Reyes, Carlos 1935- *WhoWrEP 89*
Reyes, Carlos Jose 1941- *HispWr 90*
Reyes, Cynthia Paula 1960- *WhoHisp 91*
Reyes, David Edward 1947- *WhoHisp 91*
Reyes, Eddie L. 1965- *WhoEmL 91*
Reyes, Edgardo Puyat 1945- *WhoWor 91*
Reyes, Eduardo 1965- *WhoHisp 91*
Reyes, Edward 1944- *WhoHisp 91*
Reyes, Emilio Alejandro 1959- *WhoHisp 91*
Reyes, F.A. 1940- *St&PR 91*
Reyes, Frank *WhoHisp 91*
Reyes, Guadalupe *BioIn 16*
Reyes, Hernan Macaballug 1933- *WhoWor 91*
Reyes, Jesse G. 1952- *WhoHisp 91*
Reyes, Jose Israel 1941- *WhoHisp 91*
Reyes, Jose N., Jr. 1955- *WhoHisp 91*
Reyes, Leopoldo Guadalupe 1940- *WhoHisp 91*
Reyes, Luis Bedoya 1919- *BioIn 16*
Reyes, Manuel, Jr. 1929- *WhoHisp 91*
Reyes, Nap 1919- *Ballpl 90*
Reyes, Nicholas Carlos 1953- *WhoSSW 91*
Reyes, Nora V 1936- *BiDrAPA 89*
Reyes, Oscar J. 1936- *WhoHisp 91*
Reyes, Rafael 1850?-1921 *BioIn 16*
Reyes, Ramon Villareal 1951- *WhoWor 91*
Reyes, Robert *WhoHisp 91*
Reyes, Rogelio 1931- *WhoHisp 91*
Reyes, Sarah Lorraine 1961- *WhoHisp 91*
Reyes, Vinicio H. 1934- *WhoHisp 91*
Reyes, Walfredo, Jr. *BioIn 16*
Reyes-Davila, Jose M *BiDrAPA 89*
Reyes de Ruiz, Neris B. 1929- *WhoHisp 91*
Reyes-Guerra, Antonio, Jr. 1919- *WhoHisp 91*
Reyes-Guerra, David Richard 1933- *WhoAm 90, WhoHisp 91*
Reyes Laborde, Cesar Antonio 1956- *BiDrAPA 89*
Reyes-Mignosa, Aurora F *BiDrAPA 89*
Reyes Rivera, Louis 1945- *BioIn 16*
Reyes Vargas de Vasquez, Marisol M. 1934- *WhoWor 91*
Reyes-Wilson, Edna Luisa 1952- *WhoAmW 91*
Reyher, Rebecca Hourwich 1897-1987 *BioIn 16*
Reyles, Carlos 1868-1938 *HispWr 90*
Reymond, Claude Jean-Marie 1923- *WhoWor 91*
Reymond, Hubert 1938- *WhoWor 91*
Reymond, Jean *PenDiDA 89*
Reymond, Joseph *PenDiDA 89*
Reymond, Martial, I *PenDiDA 89*
Reymond, Martial, II *PenDiDA 89*
Reymond, Pierre 1513-1584 *PenDiDA 89*
Reymondez, Julio 1909- *BiDrAPA 89*
Reyna, Leo J. 1918- *WhoWor 91*
Reynaga, Jesse Richard 1951- *WhoHisp 91*
Reynal, Timothy Lawrence 1959- *WhoE 91*
Reynalds, Anthony Michael 1952- *WhoWor 91*
Reynard, Carolyn Cole 1934- *WhoAmA 91*
Reynard, Clive Aytoun 1947- *WhoWor 91*
Reynard, Grant T 1887-1967 *WhoAmA 91N*
Reynardus, Jorge E. 1944- *WhoHisp 91*
Reynaud, Jacques *EncCoWW*
Reynaud, Paul 1878-1966 *BiDFrPL, WorAlBi*
Reynders, Noel Ghislaine Louis Joseph 1945- *IntWWM 90*
Reyneri, Nelson Rafael 1939- *WhoSSW 91*
Reynes, Wendy Warner 1944- *WhoAmW 91*
Reyno *DrBIPA 90*
Reynolds family *BioIn 16*
Reynolds, A. William 1933- *St&PR 91, WhoAm 90*
Reynolds, Alan Sidney 1928- *St&PR 91*
Reynolds, Albert Barnett 1931- *WhoAm 90, WhoSSW 91*
Reynolds, Allie 1915- *Ballpl 90, BioIn 16*
Reynolds, Alva-Inez 1933- *WhoAmW 91*
Reynolds, Angus Stuart, Jr. 1936- *WhoE 91*
Reynolds, Ann *WhoWrEP 89*
Reynolds, Ann Meredith 1958- *WhoE 91*
Reynolds, Anna 1936- *IntWWM 90*
Reynolds, Anne *ConAu 32NR*
Reynolds, Arlington G. *AmLegL*
Reynolds, Arthur Simpson 1944- *WhoWor 91*
Reynolds, Barbara *BioIn 16*
Reynolds, Barbara Leonard 1915- *AuBYP 90*
Reynolds, Beatrice Kay 1937- *WhoSSW 91*
Reynolds, Bede 1893?-1989 *ConAu 130*
Reynolds, Ben Jeff 1950- *St&PR 91*
Reynolds, Benedict Michael 1925- *WhoAm 90*
Reynolds, Benjamin James 1952- *WhoWrEP 89*
Reynolds, Billie I. 1929- *WhoAm 90*
Reynolds, Billie Iles 1929- *WhoWrEP 89*
Reynolds, Bob 1947- *Ballpl 90*
Reynolds, Brian Joe 1944- *BiDrAPA 89*
Reynolds, Bruce H. 1939- *St&PR 91*
Reynolds, Burt *BioIn 16*
Reynolds, Burt 1936- *WhoAm 90, WorAlBi*
Reynolds, Butch *BioIn 16*
Reynolds, Butch 1964- *WorAlBi*
Reynolds, C June *BiDrAPA 89*
Reynolds, Carl 1903-1978 *Ballpl 90*
Reynolds, Carl Christiansen 1934- *WhoAm 90*
Reynolds, Carl Robert 1948- *St&PR 91*
Reynolds, Carole Lee *WhoWor 91*
Reynolds, Catherine J. 1964- *ODwPR 91*
Reynolds, Catherine Rossi 1959- *WhoE 91*
Reynolds, Charles A 1842-1876 *WhNaAH*
Reynolds, Charles N. *St&PR 91*
Reynolds, Charles Steven 1952- *WhoSSW 91*
Reynolds, Chester L 1906- *BiDrAPA 89*
Reynolds, Clark Andre 1951- *St&PR 91*
Reynolds, Collins James, III 1937- *WhoAm 90*
Reynolds, Craig 1952- *Ballpl 90*
Reynolds, Dallas Thomas, Jr. 1943- *WhoAm 90*
Reynolds, Dana Drummond 1908- *WhoAm 90, WhoWor 91*
Reynolds, David *WhoWrEP 89*
Reynolds, David George 1933- *WhoAm 90*
Reynolds, David J. 1957- *St&PR 91*
Reynolds, David Parham 1915- *St&PR 91, WhoAm 90*
Reynolds, Debbie *BioIn 16*
Reynolds, Debbie 1932- *OxCPMus, WhoAm 90, WorAlBi*
Reynolds, Denise Annette 1960- *WhoWrEP 89*
Reynolds, Dennis Elroy *BiDrAPA 89*
Reynolds, Diane Hatcher 1945- *WhoSSW 91*
Reynolds, Dixon Jace 1956- *WhoSSW 91, WhoWor 91*
Reynolds, Don William 1926- *WhoSSW 91, WhoWor 91*
Reynolds, Donad William 1929- *St&PR 91*
Reynolds, Donald Blair 1928- *St&PR 91*
Reynolds, Donald R. 1922- *St&PR 91*
Reynolds, Dudley C. 1953- *St&PR 91*
Reynolds, Edward 1926- *WhoAm 90*
Reynolds, Edwin Wilfred, Jr. 1937- *WhoE 91*
Reynolds, Elaine Marie 1963- *WhoAmW 91*
Reynolds, Elizabeth *ConAu 32NR*
Reynolds, Elizabeth M 1941- *BiDrAPA 89*
Reynolds, Ernest West 1920- *WhoAm 90*
Reynolds, Evelyn Crawford 1900?- *HarlReB*
Reynolds, Frances 1729-1807 *FemiCLE*
Reynolds, Frank 1923-1983 *BioIn 16*
Reynolds, Frank Everett 1930- *WhoAm 90*
Reynolds, Frank Harrison 1948- *WhoEmL 91*
Reynolds, Frank Miller 1917- *WhoAm 90*
Reynolds, Frank Russell 1920- *St&PR 91*
Reynolds, Fred T. 1921- *St&PR 91*
Reynolds, G. W. M. 1814-1879 *BioIn 16*
Reynolds, Gardner Mead 1918- *WhoAm 90*
Reynolds, Garnet Lulyan 1940- *WhoAmW 91*
Reynolds, Gary A. *NewYTBS 90*
Reynolds, Gary Alan 1943- *WhoAm 90*
Reynolds, Gary Kemp 1944- *WhoE 91*
Reynolds, Gary N. 1940- *St&PR 91*
Reynolds, Gayle Marie 1943- *WhoAmW 91*
Reynolds, George A 1921- *BiDrAPA 89*
Reynolds, George Lazenby, Jr. 1927- *WhoAm 90*
Reynolds, George N. 1925- *ODwPR 91*
Reynolds, George S. *BioIn 16*
Reynolds, George Thomas 1917- *WhoAm 90*
Reynolds, George William MacArthur 1814-1879 *BioIn 16*
Reynolds, Ginger Fay 1950- *WhoAmW 91*
Reynolds, Glenn Francis 1928- *St&PR 91*
Reynolds, Gregg McClellan 1935- *St&PR 91*
Reynolds, Hanson Shallcross 1933- *WhoAm 90*
Reynolds, Harold 1960- *Ballpl 90*
Reynolds, Harry J., Jr. 1923- *St&PR 91*
Reynolds, Harry Lincoln 1925- *WhoAm 90*
Reynolds, Helen Elizabeth 1925- *WhoAmW 91*
Reynolds, Herbert Hal 1930- *WhoAm 90, WhoSSW 91*
Reynolds, Horace Herman, IV 1958- *WhoEmL 91*
Reynolds, Jack Mason 1927- *St&PR 91, WhoE 91*
Reynolds, Jack W. 1923- *St&PR 91, WhoAm 90*
Reynolds, James 1941- *WhoAm 90, WhoE 91*
Reynolds, James A. 1929- *WhoWrEP 89*
Reynolds, James A. 1938- *St&PR 91*
Reynolds, James Elwood 1926- *WhoAmA 91*
Reynolds, James Glenn 1943- *St&PR 91*
Reynolds, James M. 1922- *St&PR 91*
Reynolds, James White 1948- *WhoSSW 91*
Reynolds, Jennifer C. *ODwPR 91*
Reynolds, Jerry Owen 1944- *WhoAm 90*
Reynolds, Jock *WhoAmA 91*
Reynolds, John 1788-1865 *AmLegL*
Reynolds, John Beauchamp, III 1956- *WhoE 91*
Reynolds, John Charles 1933- *WhoAm 90*
Reynolds, John Dana 1945- *WhoWrEP 89*
Reynolds, John Elliott, III 1952- *WhoSSW 91*
Reynolds, John Francis 1921- *WhoAm 90*
Reynolds, John Hamilton 1794-1852 *DcLB 96 [port]*
Reynolds, John Hamilton 1923- *WhoAm 90*
Reynolds, John Hughes, IV 1940- *WhoSSW 91*
Reynolds, John W. 1921- *WhoAm 90*
Reynolds, Jonathan P. 1947- *St&PR 91*
Reynolds, Joseph Allen, Jr. 1925- *WhoAm 90*
Reynolds, Joseph Lee, III 1928- *St&PR 91*
Reynolds, Joseph Melvin 1924- *WhoAm 90, WhoWor 91*
Reynolds, Joseph Patrick, Jr. 1937- *St&PR 91*
Reynolds, Joshua 1723-1792 *BioIn 16, DcLB 104 [port], IntDcAA 90, LitC 15 [port], WorAlBi*
Reynolds, Karen Jeanne 1940- *IntWWM 90*
Reynolds, Kathryn Anne 1957- *WhoAmW 91*
Reynolds, Kathy P. 1950- *St&PR 91*
Reynolds, Keith Allan 1951- *WhoAm 90*
Reynolds, Keith Robert 1951- *WhoSSW 91*
Reynolds, Ken 1947- *Ballpl 90*

Reynolds, Kenyon L. *ConAu 130*
Reynolds, Klara Boynton 1942- *WhoAmW 91*
Reynolds, Laura Alberta 1931- *WhoSSW 91*
Reynolds, Laurel *BioIn 16*
Reynolds, Leo Thomas 1945- *WhoEmL 91*
Reynolds, Linda Ellen 1956- *WhoE 91*
Reynolds, Lloyd George 1910- *WhoAm 90*
Reynolds, Lloyd J. *BioIn 16*
Reynolds, Lloyd J 1902-1978 *WhoAmA 91N*
Reynolds, Lola Sullivan 1955- *WhoAmW 91*
Reynolds, Lorraine Phyllis 1919- *WhoWrEP 89*
Reynolds, Luther Waldo, Jr. 1935- *WhoAm 90*
Reynolds, Mack 1917- *AuBYP 90*
Reynolds, Marion Frances 1940- *St&PR 91*
Reynolds, Marjorie Harris 1903- *AuBYP 90*
Reynolds, Marjorie Lavers 1931- *WhoAmW 91*
Reynolds, Mark Edward *BiDrAPA 89*
Reynolds, Mark Steven *BiDrAPA 89*
Reynolds, Marshall Truman 1937- *WhoAm 90*
Reynolds, Mary Elizabeth Fontaine 1931- *WhoSSW 91*
Reynolds, Mary Trackett 1913- *WhoAm 90, WhoAmW 91, WhoE 91*
Reynolds, Max J. 1939- *St&PR 91*
Reynolds, Michael Henry 1952- *WhoE 91*
Reynolds, Michael Joseph 1938- *WhoAm 90*
Reynolds, Michael Stafford 1944- *WhoSSW 91*
Reynolds, Moira Davison 1915- *WhoAmW 91, WhoWrEP 89*
Reynolds, Nancy Bradford duPont 1919- *WhoAmW 91, WhoE 91*
Reynolds, Nancy Clark *ODwPR 91*
Reynolds, Nancy Remick 1938- *WhoAmW 91*
Reynolds, Nathaniel Dunton 1950- *WhoSSW 91*
Reynolds, Nila Marie 1948- *WhoSSW 91*
Reynolds, Nina Louise 1934- *WhoAmW 91*
Reynolds, Norman Eben 1919- *WhoAm 90, WhoSSW 91*
Reynolds, Norman Thomas 1942- *BiDrAPA 89*
Reynolds, Pamela Christine Schrom 1945- *WhoWrEP 89*
Reynolds, Patricia Ellen 1934- *WhoAmA 91*
Reynolds, Patrick *BioIn 16*
Reynolds, Patrick Taylor 1962- *BiDrAPA 89*
Reynolds, Paul B. 1915- *St&PR 91*
Reynolds, Paul D., III 1952- *St&PR 91*
Reynolds, Paul Edward 1942- *BiDrAPA 89*
Reynolds, Paul G. 1922- *St&PR 91*
Reynolds, Paul R. 1904-1988 *BioIn 16*
Reynolds, Peter James 1949- *WhoE 91, WhoSSW 91, WhoWor 91*
Reynolds, Philip Reeves 1927- *St&PR 91, WhoAm 90*
Reynolds, Quentin James 1902-1965 *AuBYP 90, BioIn 16*
Reynolds, Quinton *BioIn 16*
Reynolds, R. J. 1959- *Ballpl 90*
Reynolds, R. John 1936- *WhoAm 90*
Reynolds, Ralph William 1905- *WhoAmA 91*
Reynolds, Randolph Nicklas 1941- *St&PR 91, WhoAm 90*
Reynolds, Renny *BioIn 16*
Reynolds, Richard 1913- *WhoAmA 91*
Reynolds, Richard Albee, Jr. 1956- *WhoSSW 91*
Reynolds, Richard Clyde 1929- *WhoAm 90*
Reynolds, Richard J., Jr. 1924- *St&PR 91*
Reynolds, Richard Louis 1953- *WhoSSW 91*
Reynolds, Richard Morgan 1937- *WhoAm 90, WhoE 91*
Reynolds, Richard Paulsen 1946- *WhoWor 91*
Reynolds, Richard Roger 1943- *WhoE 91*
Reynolds, Richard Samuel, III 1934- *St&PR 91, WhoSSW 91*
Reynolds, Robert 1936- *BioIn 16, WhoAmA 91*
Reynolds, Robert Arthur 1932- *St&PR 91*
Reynolds, Robert B 1922- *BiDrAPA 89*
Reynolds, Robert Douglas 1963- *WhoSSW 91*
Reynolds, Robert E. 1957- *St&PR 91*
Reynolds, Robert Gregory 1952- *WhoEmL 91*
Reynolds, Robert H. 1913- *St&PR 91*
Reynolds, Robert Hugh 1937- *WhoWor 91*
Reynolds, Robert Joel 1944- *WhoE 91*
Reynolds, Robert Lester 1917- *WhoAm 90*
Reynolds, Robert Louis 1939- *St&PR 91*
Reynolds, Robert Nelson *BiDrAPA 89*
Reynolds, Robert Richard 1935- *WhoE 91*
Reynolds, Robert Steve 1950- *WhoSSW 91*
Reynolds, Roger *NewAgMG*
Reynolds, Roger Dale 1948- *St&PR 91*
Reynolds, Roger Lee 1934- *IntWWM 90, WhoAm 90*
Reynolds, Ron R. 1939- *WhoSSW 91*
Reynolds, Rosalie Dean 1926- *WhoAmW 91*
Reynolds, Russell Seaman, Jr. 1931- *WhoAm 90*
Reynolds, Ruth Lillian 1922- *St&PR 91*
Reynolds, Sallie Blackburn 1940- *WhoAmW 91*
Reynolds, Scott Walton 1941- *St&PR 91, WhoAm 90*
Reynolds, Sidney Rae 1956- *WhoEmL 91, WhoWrEP 89*
Reynolds, Siimon *BioIn 16*
Reynolds, Stephen Francis 1950- *WhoAmA 91*
Reynolds, Stephen Philip 1948- *WhoAm 90*
Reynolds, Susan *ODwPR 91*
Reynolds, Susan Elizabeth 1950- *WhoAmW 91*
Reynolds, Susan Jean 1954- *WhoAmW 91*
Reynolds, Syd J. 1922- *St&PR 91*
Reynolds, Terrence Edward 1938- *St&PR 91*
Reynolds, Thomas *St&PR 91*
Reynolds, Thomas A., Jr. *St&PR 91*
Reynolds, Thomas Dewitt 1929- *BiDrAPA 89*
Reynolds, Thomas Edward 1954- *WhoSSW 91*
Reynolds, Thomas Morgan 1943- *WhoWor 91*
Reynolds, Tom 1950- *WhoE 91*
Reynolds, Tommy 1941- *Ballpl 90*
Reynolds, Valrae 1944- *WhoAmA 91*
Reynolds, Vernon 1935- *ConAu 132*
Reynolds, Vernon Glenn 1952- *WhoSSW 91*
Reynolds, Wade 1929- *WhoAmA 91*
Reynolds, Warren Jay 1918- *WhoAm 90*
Reynolds, Wayne C. 1940- *St&PR 91*
Reynolds, Wellington W 1904- *BiDrAPA 89*
Reynolds, Wiley Richard 1917- *WhoAm 90*
Reynolds, William *BioIn 16*
Reynolds, William Bradford *BioIn 16*
Reynolds, William Bradford 1942- *WhoAm 90*
Reynolds, William Craig 1933- *WhoAm 90*
Reynolds, William Cumberland, Jr. 1926- *WhoAm 90*
Reynolds, William Everett 1938- *St&PR 91*
Reynolds, William Francis 1930- *WhoAm 90*
Reynolds, William Gray, Jr. 1939- *St&PR 91*
Reynolds, William Harold 1925- *IntWWM 90, WhoAm 90*
Reynolds, William J. 1956- *TwCCr&M 91*
Reynolds, William James 1956- *WhoWrEP 89*
Reynolds, William Leroy 1945- *WhoAm 90*
Reynolds, William T. 1959- *St&PR 91*
Reynolds, Woodson 1942- *WhoSSW 91*
Reynolds, Wynetka Ann 1937- *WhoAm 90, WhoAmW 91*
Reynolds Shaw, Mary Anne 1947- *WhoAmW 91*
Reynoldson, Walter Ward 1920- *WhoAm 90*
Reynosa, Jose *WhoHisp 91*
Reynoso, Abimael Guzman 1934- *BioIn 16*
Reynoso, Alonso de *EncCRAm*
Reynoso, Cruz 1931- *BioIn 16, WhoHisp 91*
Reynoso, Jose S. 1953- *WhoHisp 91*
Reyzen, Mark 1895- *PenDiMP*
Reza Pahlavi *BioIn 16*
Reza, Jesus *WhoHisp 91*
Rezac, Richard 1952- *WhoAmA 91*
Rezai, Shari 1949- *St&PR 91*
Reze, Joseph-Pierre 1814-1899 *DcCanB 12*
Rezeanu, Stefan-Cristian 1959- *WhoWor 91*
Rezentes, Cynthia Kim Len 1952- *WhoAmW 91*
Rezich, George F. 1927- *St&PR 91, WhoAm 90*
Rezits, Joseph 1925- *IntWWM 90*
Reznack, Andrew V. 1931- *St&PR 91*
Rezneck, Daniel Albert 1935- *WhoAm 90*
Reznicek, Bernard William 1936- *WhoE 91*
Reznicek, Michael Joseph *BiDrAPA 89*
Reznick, Jerome 1918- *WhoE 91, WhoWor 91*
Reznick, Robert 1919- *St&PR 91*
Reznicki, Jack *BioIn 16*
Reznik, Bob *ODwPR 91*
Reznik, Michel Gabriel 1933- *WhoWor 91*
Reznikoff, Leon 1900- *BiDrAPA 89*
Rezzonico, Renzo 1929- *WhoWor 91*
Rezzori, Gregor Von 1914- *WorAu 1980 [port]*
Rhaly, Henry Crawford, Jr. 1949- *WhoSSW 91*
Rhame, William T. 1915- *St&PR 91*
Rhame, William Thomas 1915- *WhoAm 90*
Rhasis 825?-925 *EncO&P 3*
Rhatican, William F. *ODwPR 91*
Rhawn, Edward Woodward 1938- *St&PR 91*
Rhazes 825?-925 *EncO&P 3*
Rhea, Albert Lisle 1915- *St&PR 91*
Rhea, Claude Hiram, Jr. 1927- *WhoAm 90, WhoWor 91*
Rhea, John Allan 1936- *WhoSSW 91*
Rhea, Karen Hendrix 1946- *BiDrAPA 89*
Rhea, La Julia 1908- *BioIn 16*
Rhea, Marcia Chandler 1956- *WhoAmW 91*
Rhea, Ronald E. 1939- *St&PR 91*
Rhead, Clifton 1921- *BiDrAPA 89*
Rhead, Frederick Alfred 1857-1933 *PenDiDA 89*
Rhead, Frederick Hurten 1880-1942 *BioIn 16*
Rheam, Micheal C. *St&PR 91*
Rheaume, Myron 1944- *St&PR 91*
Rhedin, Judith A. 1948- *WhoAmW 91*
Rhee, Chung Kwang 1940- *BiDrAPA 89*
Rhee, Dongshick 1920- *BiDrAPA 89*
Rhee, H. Albert 1914- *WhoWor 91*
Rhee, Jin Hong 1939- *WhoWor 91*
Rhee, Jin-Soo 1942- *BiDrAPA 89*
Rhee, Joong Oh 1939- *BiDrAPA 89*
Rhee, Nancy Eloranta 1955- *WhoEmL 91*
Rhee, Susan Byungsook 1937- *WhoAmW 91*
Rhee, Syngman 1875-1965 *WorAlBi*
Rhee, Yang Ho 1943- *WhoWor 91*
Rhees, Raymond C. 1914- *St&PR 91*
Rhees, Rush 1905?-1989? *ConAu 129*
Rhein, Ezra A. 1952- *St&PR 91*
Rhein, John Hancock Willing, III 1931- *St&PR 91*
Rhein, Murray Harold 1912- *WhoAm 90*
Rhein, Timothy James 1941- *St&PR 91*
Rheiner, Carolyn Zuch *BiDrAPA 89*
Rheiner, Philippe 1941- *WhoWor 91*
Rheinfrank, Lamson, Jr. 1940- *St&PR 91*
Rheingold, Arnold M. 1931- *St&PR 91*
Rheingold, Arnold Morton 1931- *WhoAm 90*
Rheinhart, Ronald *BioIn 16*
Rheinheimer, Kurt 1946- *WhoWrEP 89*
Rheinlander, T.W. 1940- *St&PR 91*
Rheinstein, Peter Howard 1943- *WhoAm 90, WhoE 91, WhoWor 91*
Rheinstein-Pittard, Linda Carol 1956- *WhoAmW 91*
Rhem, Durward D. 1927- *St&PR 91*
Rhem, Flint 1901-1969 *Ballpl 90*
Rhem, John Fitzhugh, Jr. 1949- *WhoEmL 91*
Rhemann, Eugene Evans 1941- *WhoSSW 91*
Rhene-Baton 1879-1940 *PenDiMP*
Rhett, John Taylor, Jr. 1925- *WhoAm 90*
Rhett, Robert Barnwell 1800-1876 *BioIn 16*
Rhetts, Paul Fisher 1946- *ODwPR 91, WhoE 91, WhoEmL 91*
Rheuban, William Jay *BiDrAPA 89*
Rhew, Steven S H 1935- *BiDrAPA 89*
Rhey, John S. 1819-1891 *AmLegL*
Rhiel, Billy 1900-1946 *Ballpl 90*
Rhiew, H Benjamin 1939- *BiDrAPA 89*
Rhind, Constance 1959- *WhoE 91*
Rhind, James Thomas 1922- *WhoAm 90, WhoWor 91*
Rhind, John Arthur 1920- *St&PR 91*
Rhind, John Christopher 1934- *WhoAm 90*
Rhind, Lisa Kay 1965- *WhoAmW 91*
Rhine, J B 1895-1980 *EncO&P 3*
Rhine, Jack G. 1933- *St&PR 91*
Rhine, Jennie 1939- *WhoAmW 91*
Rhine, Joseph Banks 1895-1980 *EncPaPR 91, WorAlBi*
Rhine, Louisa Ella Weckesser 1891-1983 *EncO&P 3*
Rhine, Louisa Ellen 1891-1983 *EncPaPR 91*
Rhine, Mark W 1934- *BiDrAPA 89*
Rhinehart, John W *BiDrAPA 89*
Rhinelander, Frederic William Templeton 1931- *WhoAm 90*
Rhinelander, John Bassett 1933- *St&PR 91, WhoAm 90*
Rhinelander, Melvin A. 1950- *St&PR 91*
Rhinelander, Thomas Jackson Oakley *BioIn 16*
Rhinerson, David Keith 1956- *WhoEmL 91*
Rhines, Frederick *WhoAm 90*
Rhines, Peter Broomell 1942- *WhoAm 90*
Rhines, Walden Clark 1946- *St&PR 91*
Rhinesmith, Stephen Headley 1942- *WhoAm 90*
Rho, Lorraine Therese *WhoWrEP 89*
Rhoad, Herbert 1944-1988 *BioIn 16*
Rhoades, Amanda *WhoWrEP 89*
Rhoades, Barbara 1947- *ConTFT 8*
Rhoades, Barbara Lynn 1949- *WhoAmW 91*
Rhoades, Bruce Cecil 1941- *BiDrAPA 89*
Rhoades, Jacqueline Jo 1941- *WhoWrEP 89*
Rhoades, John Skylstead, Sr. 1925- *WhoAm 90*
Rhoades, Katharine Nash 1885-1965 *BiDWomA*
Rhoades, Lawrence Woodruff 1922- *WhoE 91*
Rhoades, Leslie H. 1944- *St&PR 91*
Rhoades, Nancy Ann 1959- *WhoAmW 91*
Rhoades, Robert Edward 1942- *WhoWor 91*
Rhoades, Sam J. 1908- *St&PR 91*
Rhoades, Sylvia Eileen 1936- *WhoAmW 91*
Rhoades, Timothy Gerard 1955- *St&PR 91*
Rhoads, Bob 1879-1967 *Ballpl 90*
Rhoads, D. Dean 1927- *St&PR 91*
Rhoads, Dorothy Mary 1895- *AuBYP 90*
Rhoads, Edward John 1949- *BiDrAPA 89*
Rhoads, Edwin A. 1936- *St&PR 91*
Rhoads, George *BioIn 16*
Rhoads, Geraldine Emeline 1914- *WhoAm 90*
Rhoads, James Berton 1928- *WhoAm 90*
Rhoads, James Darius 1936- *St&PR 91*
Rhoads, John M 1919- *BiDrAPA 89*
Rhoads, Jonathan Evans 1907- *WhoAm 90, WhoE 91, WhoWor 91*
Rhoads, Keating 1949- *St&PR 91*
Rhoads, Nancy Glenn 1957- *WhoAmW 91*
Rhoads, Paul Kelly 1940- *WhoAm 90*
Rhoads, Richard C. 1927- *St&PR 91*
Rhoads, Robert K. 1954- *WhoAm 90*
Rhoads, Sheila Lubin 1946- *WhoAmW 91*
Rhoads, William Charles 1929- *St&PR 91*
Rhoda, William F. 1944- *St&PR 91*
Rhodaberger, W.L. 1950- *St&PR 91*
Rhode, Alfred Shimon 1928- *WhoAm 90*
Rhode, Edward Albert 1926- *WhoAm 90*
Rhode, Gerald Kenneth 1929- *St&PR 91*
Rhode, John 1884-1965 *TwCCr&M 91*
Rhode, Robert Thomas 1954- *WhoWrEP 89*
Rhode, Shari Rene 1951- *WhoEmL 91*
Rhodehamel, Sharon Mae 1944- *WhoAmW 91*
Rhoden, Harold 1923-1989 *BioIn 16*
Rhoden, Jack 1925- *St&PR 91*
Rhoden, Jackson A *BiDrAPA 89*
Rhoden, John W 1918- *WhoAmA 91*
Rhoden, Richard Earl 1948- *BiDrAPA 89*
Rhoden, Rick 1953- *Ballpl 90*
Rhoden, Ron E. 1953- *St&PR 91*
Rhodes, Alfred William 1922- *WhoAm 90*
Rhodes, Allen Franklin 1924- *St&PR 91*
Rhodes, Andrew James 1911- *WhoAm 90*
Rhodes, Ann Louise 1941- *WhoAmW 91, WhoSSW 91*
Rhodes, Ann Marie 1953- *WhoAmW 91*
Rhodes, Anna Margaret 1933- *WhoSSW 91*
Rhodes, Ashby Marshall 1923- *WhoAm 90*
Rhodes, Barry 1947- *WhoE 91*
Rhodes, Beverly Anisowicz 1947- *WhoAmW 91, WhoEmL 91*
Rhodes, Bianca A. 1958- *St&PR 91*
Rhodes, Billie *BioIn 16*
Rhodes, Cecil 1853-1902 *WorAlBi*
Rhodes, Cecil John 1853-1902 *BioIn 16*
Rhodes, Charles Harker, Jr. 1930- *WhoAm 90*
Rhodes, Cherry 1943- *IntWWM 90*
Rhodes, Christine Elise 1952- *WhoAmW 91*
Rhodes, Curtis A 1939- *WhoAmA 91*
Rhodes, Cynthia Strahler 1947- *WhoAmW 91*
Rhodes, Daniel 1911-1989 *BioIn 16*
Rhodes, David *PenDiDA 89*
Rhodes, David Mark 1951- *WhoWrEP 89*
Rhodes, Debra Susanne 1956- *WhoSSW 91*
Rhodes, Dennis 1954- *ODwPR 91*
Rhodes, Donald Robert 1923- *WhoAm 90*
Rhodes, Douglas B. 1934- *St&PR 91*
Rhodes, Dusty 1927- *Ballpl 90, BioIn 16*
Rhodes, Elizabeth Joan 1955- *WhoAmW 91*
Rhodes, Eric Foster 1927- *WhoAm 90, WhoWor 91*
Rhodes, Erik *NewYTBS 90*
Rhodes, Erik 1906-1990 *BioIn 16*
Rhodes, Frank Harold Trevor 1926- *WhoAm 90, WhoE 91, WhoWor 91*
Rhodes, Gary L. 1941- *St&PR 91*
Rhodes, Gary Lynn 1941- *WhoAm 90*
Rhodes, Gene Paul 1955- *WhoSSW 91*

Rhodes, George A 1918-1985 *DrBlPA 90*
Rhodes, George R. 1951- *ODwPR 91*
Rhodes, Ginna Lois 1936- *WhoAmW 91*
Rhodes, Gordon 1907-1960 *Ballpl 90*
Rhodes, Gordon Ellsworth 1927- *St&PR 91*
Rhodes, Hari 1932- *DrBlPA 90*
Rhodes, Helen Louise 1946- *WhoAmW 91*
Rhodes, Helen Mary 1921- *WhoAmW 91*
Rhodes, James C. 1947- *WhoE 91*
Rhodes, James Devers 1955- *WhoSSW 91*
Rhodes, James Melvin 1938- *WhoAmA 91*
Rhodes, James Richard 1945- *WhoWor 91*
Rhodes, James Thomas 1941- *St&PR 91*
Rhodes, Jane 1929- *IntWWM 90, PenDiMP*
Rhodes, Jennifer *BiDrAPA 89*
Rhodes, John 1935- *WhoWor 91*
Rhodes, John Bower 1925- *WhoAm 90*
Rhodes, John Bower, Jr. 1925- *St&PR 91*
Rhodes, John H. 1924- *WhoSSW 91*
Rhodes, John J. 1916- *WorAlBi*
Rhodes, John J., III 1943- *WhoAm 90*
Rhodes, John Jacob 1916- *WhoAm 90*
Rhodes, John Robert, Jr. 1948- *WhoE 91*
Rhodes, Judith Carol 1949- *WhoAmW 91*
Rhodes, Kenneth Anthony, Jr. 1930- *WhoE 91*
Rhodes, Kent 1912- *WhoAm 90*
Rhodes, Laura Derrick 1959- *WhoSSW 91*
Rhodes, Leland *ConAu 31NR*
Rhodes, Lisa J. 1955- *ODwPR 91*
Rhodes, M.H. 1926- *St&PR 91*
Rhodes, Marc Alan 1958- *WhoSSW 91*
Rhodes, Mitchell L. 1940- *WhoAm 90*
Rhodes, Nancy Elizabeth 1946- *WhoEmL 91*
Rhodes, Norman Leonard 1942- *WhoWrEP 89*
Rhodes, Peter Dubose 1940- *WhoSSW 91*
Rhodes, Peter E. 1942- *St&PR 91*
Rhodes, Peter Edward 1942- *WhoAm 90*
Rhodes, Reilly Patrick 1941- *WhoAmA 91*
Rhodes, Richard *BioIn 16*
Rhodes, Richard 1937- *WorAu 1980 [port]*
Rhodes, Richard Lee 1937- *WhoAm 90, WhoE 91, WhoWrEP 89*
Rhodes, Richard Llewelyn 1939- *WhoE 91*
Rhodes, Rondell Horace 1918- *WhoE 91*
Rhodes, Samuel *PenDiMP*
Rhodes, Samuel 1941- *IntWWM 90, WhoAm 90*
Rhodes, Scott Whitney 1959- *WhoE 91*
Rhodes, Stanley Williams 1938- *WhoE 91*
Rhodes, Susan E. 1954- *WhoAmW 91*
Rhodes, Valerie Ruth 1961- *WhoAmW 91*
Rhodes, Victoria Elizabeth 1957- *WhoAmW 91*
Rhodes, William Arthur, Jr. 1948- *WhoSSW 91*
Rhodes, William David 1947- *BiDrAPA 89*
Rhodes, William Reginald 1935- *St&PR 91, WhoAm 90, WhoWor 91*
Rhodes, Zandra *BioIn 16*
Rhodes, Zandra 1940- *ConDes 90*
Rhodig, Lori L. 1958- *WhoAmW 91*
Rhody, Ronald E. 1932- *ODwPR 91*
Rhody, Ronald Edward 1932- *St&PR 91, WhoAm 90*
Rhomberg, Rudolf Robert 1922- *WhoE 91*
Rhondda, Margaret Haig 1883-1958 *FemiCLE*
Rhoten, Carey Douglas 1936- *St&PR 91*
Rhoten, Francis Marion 1906- *St&PR 91*
Rhoton, Albert Loren, Jr. 1932- *WhoAm 90*
Rhudy, Charles S. 1943- *ODwPR 91*
Rhue, Madlyn *BioIn 16*
Rhue, Madlyn 1934- *ConTFT 8*
Rhue, Morton *WhoWrEP 89*
Rhule, Imogene Gretchen 1941- *WhoAmW 91*
Rhulen, W.A. 1931- *St&PR 91*
Rhyee, James T S 1943- *BiDrAPA 89*
Rhyl, Baron 1906-1981 *DcNaB 1981*
Rhymes, Pete Holden 1927- *WhoSSW 91*
Rhyne, Charles Sylvanus 1912- *WhoAm 90, WhoE 91, WhoWor 91*
Rhyne, Charles Sylvanus 1932- *WhoAmA 91*
Rhyne, Dennis Keith *BiDrAPA 89*
Rhyne, Hal 1899-1971 *Ballpl 90*
Rhyne, Janie *BioIn 16*
Rhyne, Neal Herbert 1945- *St&PR 91*
Rhys, David Garel 1940- *WhoWor 91*
Rhys, Jean *BioIn 16*
Rhys, Jean 1890-1979 *FemiCLE*
Rhys, Jean 1894-1979 *MajTwCW, WorAlBi*
Rhys, John Marlow 1935- *IntWWM 90*
Riabov, Darelle Dee Lake 1951- *WhoAmW 91*
Riach, Alan Scott 1957- *WhoWor 91*
Riad, Mahmoud 1917- *ConAu 131*
Riahi, Hasna 1966- *WhoEmL 91*
Rial, Juan R. 1943- *WhoWor 91*
Rials, Stephane Claude Germain Robert 1951- *WhoWor 91*
Rianto, Gunawan 1951- *WhoWor 91*
Riasanovsky, Nicholas Valentine 1923- *WhoAm 90*
Riaz, Abdul Ghafur 1934- *BiDrAPA 89*
Riaz, Riaz Uddin *BiDrAPA 89*
Riba, Enric Prat de la 1870-1917 *BioIn 16*
Riba, Michelle 1949- *BiDrAPA 89*
Riba, Paul F 1912-1977 *WhoAmA 91N*
Ribadeneira, Mario 1933- *WhoAm 90*
Ribak, Louis 1902-1980 *WhoAmA 91N*
Ribakov, Anatolii *BioIn 16*
Ribalta, Francisco 1565-1628 *IntDcAA 90*
Ribant, Dennis 1941- *Ballpl 90*
Ribar, Dixie Lee 1938- *WhoAmW 91*
Ribaric, Marijan 1932- *WhoWor 91*
Ribary, Antal 1924- *IntWWM 90*
Ribas, Joao Carvalhah *BiDrAPA 89*
Ribaudo, Sylvester Thomas 1936- *St&PR 91*
Ribault, Jean 1520?-1565 *WhNaAH*
Ribaut, Jean 1520?-1565 *EncCRAm, WhNaAH, WorAlBi*
Ribb, Terry R. *ODwPR 91*
Ribbans, Geoffrey Wilfrid 1927- *WhoE 91*
Ribbentrop, Joachim von 1893-1946 *BioIn 16, WorAlBi*
Ribble, Anne Hoerner 1932- *WhoAmW 91*
Ribble, John Charles 1931- *WhoAm 90*
Ribble, Marland S. 1932- *St&PR 91*
Ribbs, Willy T. *BioIn 16*
Ribby, Alice Marie 1943- *WhoAmW 91*
Ribeiro, Alfonso 1971- *DrBlPA 90*
Ribeiro, Antonio 1928- *WhoWor 91*
Ribeiro, Arnaldo Joaquim 1957- *WhoWor 91*
Ribeiro, Carlos Silva 1947- *WhoWor 91*
Ribeiro, Frank Henry 1949- *WhoEmL 91*
Ribeiro, Joaquim S.S. 1936- *St&PR 91*
Ribeiro, Lenor D *BiDrAPA 89*
Ribelin, Herman A. 1927- *St&PR 91*
Ribelin, Rosemary Bingham 1933- *WhoAmW 91*
Riben, Staffan Jarl Olof 1941- *WhoWor 91*
Ribera, Jusepe de 1591-1652 *IntDcAA 90*
Ribera Chevremont, Evaristo 1896-1976 *HispWr 90*
Ribero, Michael A. 1956- *St&PR 91*
Ribes, Jacqueline de *BioIn 16*
Ribet, Kenneth A. 1948- *WhoAm 90*
Ribi, Nils Andrew 1955- *St&PR 91*
Ribicoff, Abraham A. 1910- *WhoAm 90, WorAlBi*
Ribicoff, Abraham Alexander 1910- *BiDrUSE 89*
Rible, Morton 1938- *WhoAm 90*
Riblet, William Breeze 1938- *St&PR 91*
Ribman, Ronald Burt 1932- *WhoAm 90*
Ribner, Herbert Spencer 1913- *WhoAm 90*
Ribner, Richard 1917- *BiDrAPA 89*
Ribordy, Denis Eugene 1929- *St&PR 91*
Ribot, Alexandre Felix Joseph 1842-1923 *BiDFrPL*
Ribot, Marc *BioIn 16*
Riboud, Barbara Chase- 1936- *BioIn 16*
Riboud, Marc 1923- *BioIn 16*
Ricard, Andre 1938- *OxCCanT*
Ricardi, Leon Joseph 1924- *WhoAm 90*
Ricardi, Randall Kenneth *BiDrAPA 89*
Ricardo, David 1772-1823 *BioIn 16, WorAlBi*
Ricardo-Campbell, Rita 1920- *WhoAm 90, WhoAmW 91, WhoHisp 91*
Ricardo Garcia, Joaquin 1952- *WhoWor 91*
Ricardson, Larie Kenneth 1941- *St&PR 91*
Ricart, Wilfredo *BioIn 16*
Ricaurte, Eduardo A 1927- *BiDrAPA 89*
Ricca, Carmine P., Jr. 1949- *WhoE 91*
Riccardi, Anthony 1941- *St&PR 91*
Riccardi, Richard V. 1940- *St&PR 91*
Riccardi, Susan 1958- *St&PR 91*
Riccardo, John Joseph 1924- *EncABHB 5 [port]*
Riccardo, Leonard Thomas 1933- *St&PR 91*
Riccards, Michael Patrick 1944- *WhoAm 90, WhoWrEP 89*
Ricci, Anthony Gene 1930- *St&PR 91*
Ricci, Anthony Raymond 1954- *WhoE 91*
Ricci, Carolyne Youngblood 1951- *WhoAmW 91*
Ricci, Caterina de' 1522-1590 *EncCoWW*
Ricci, Debra Patricia 1951- *WhoAmW 91*
Ricci, Douglas M. 1945- *St&PR 91*
Ricci, Franco Maria Marchese 1937- *WhoWor 91*
Ricci, Gian Carlo *BiDrAPA 89*
Ricci, Giovanni Mario 1929- *WhoWor 91*
Ricci, Glenn Anthony 1949- *WhoSSW 91*
Ricci, Gregorio 1853-1925 *WorAlBi*
Ricci, James Walter 1935- *WhoWor 91*
Ricci, Jerri *WhoAmA 91*
Ricci, Linda Rae 1960- *WhoE 91*
Ricci, Naomi C. 1942- *WhoWrEP 89*
Ricci, Robert 1905-1988 *BioIn 16*
Ricci, Robert Ronald 1945- *WhoSSW 91*
Ricci, Ruggiero 1918- *IntWWM 90, PenDiMP, WhoAm 90, WhoWor 91*
Ricci, Russell J 1946- *BiDrAPA 89*
Ricci, Sebastiano 1659?-1734 *IntDcAA 90*
Ricci, Steven Peter 1960- *WhoWrEP 89*
Ricci, Thomas Michael 1937- *St&PR 91*
Ricci, Ulysses 1888-1960 *WhoAmA 91N*
Ricci, Vittore 1923- *WhoWor 91*
Ricci, Walter F 1936- *BiDrAPA 89*
Ricciardelli, Thomas Patrick 1948- *WhoEmL 91*
Ricciardi, Franc M. *St&PR 91N*
Ricciardi, Michael Thomas 1954- *BiDrAPA 89*
Ricciardi, Patrice Joan 1956- *WhoAmW 91*
Ricciardone, John H. *ODwPR 91*
Ricciarelli, Katia 1946- *IntWWM 90, PenDiMP, WhoAm 90, WhoWor 91*
Riccinto, Patrick John, Jr. 1943- *WhoWrEP 89*
Riccio, Andrea Briosco *PenDiDA 89*
Riccio, Edmund Gerald 1942- *St&PR 91*
Riccio, Jerome Michael 1955- *WhoE 91, WhoEmL 91, WhoWor 91*
Riccio, Nicholas D. 1947- *St&PR 91*
Riccio, Robert Joseph 1955- *WhoE 91*
Riccioli, N Frank 1929- *BiDrAPA 89*
Ricciuti, Annette A. 1956- *St&PR 91*
Ricco, Antonio *PenDiDA 89*
Ricco, Edward Robert 1950- *WhoEmL 91*
Riccoboni, Madame 1714- *EncCoWW*
Riccoboni, Marie-Jeanne 1714-1792 *BioIn 16, FemiCLE*
Rice, Abraham Joseph *BioIn 16*
Rice, Alan Harrison 1963- *WhoE 91*
Rice, Albert Richard 1951- *IntWWM 90*
Rice, Alfred 1907-1989 *BioIn 16*
Rice, Alice Hegan 1870-1942 *LiHiK, SmATA 63*
Rice, Anita Marie 1947- *St&PR 91*
Rice, Ann 1933- *WhoAm 90*
Rice, Anne *NewYTBS 90 [port]*
Rice, Anne 1941- *BioIn 16, FemiCLE, WhoAmW 91*
Rice, Anthony Hopkins 1948- *WhoAmA 91*
Rice, Argyll Pryor *WhoAmW 91, WhoE 91*
Rice, Arthur Edmund 1919- *St&PR 91*
Rice, Barbara Menen *WhoAmA 91*
Rice, Barbara Slyder 1937- *WhoAmW 91, WhoSSW 91*
Rice, Ben Herbert, III 1918- *WhoAm 90*
Rice, Blair, III *St&PR 91*
Rice, Bruce Clarence 1947- *St&PR 91*
Rice, Cale Young 1872-1943 *LiHiK*
Rice, Canice Timothy, Jr. 1950- *WhoEmL 91*
Rice, Carolyn J. 1952- *WhoWrEP 89*
Rice, Charles Duane 1910-1971 *AuBYP 90*
Rice, Charles Duncan 1942- *WhoAm 90*
Rice, Charles Edward 1935- *St&PR 91, WhoSSW 91*
Rice, Charles Owen 1908- *BioIn 16*
Rice, Charles T. 1893-1988 *BioIn 16*
Rice, Christine Ruth 1951- *St&PR 91*
Rice, Claire Jane 1959- *WhoAmW 91*
Rice, Clare I. 1918- *WhoAm 90*
Rice, Clark H. 1932- *St&PR 91*
Rice, Clark Hammond, Jr. 1932- *WhoAm 90*
Rice, Clovita 1929- *WhoWrEP 89*
Rice, Craig 1908-1957 *FemiCLE, TwCCr&M 91*
Rice, Damaris S 1927- *BiDrAPA 89*
Rice, Daphne Sweatman 1962- *WhoAmW 91*
Rice, David Ainsworth 1940- *WhoAm 90*
Rice, David Eugene, Jr. 1916- *WhoAm 90, WhoE 91, WhoWor 91*
Rice, David R 1916- *BiDrAPA 89*
Rice, Del 1922-1983 *Ballpl 90*
Rice, Denis Timlin 1932- *WhoAm 90, WhoWor 91*
Rice, Donald Blessing 1939- *St&PR 91, WhoAm 90*
Rice, Donald Ervin 1942- *BiDrAPA 89*
Rice, Donald Lee 1938- *WhoWrEP 89*
Rice, Dorothy Pechman 1922- *WhoAm 90, WhoAmW 91*
Rice, Edward 1918- *BestSel 90-4 [port], BioIn 16*
Rice, Edward 1953- *WhoAmA 91*
Rice, Edward E. 1918- *AuBYP 90*
Rice, Edward Everett 1848-1924 *OxCPMus*
Rice, Elizabeth Fischer 1953- *WhoAmW 91*
Rice, Ellen Frances 1941- *WhoAmW 91*
Rice, Elmer 1892-1967 *MajTwCW, WorAlBi*
Rice, Emanuel 1927- *BiDrAPA 89, WhoE 91*
Rice, Erling E. 1915- *St&PR 91*
Rice, Ethel Ann 1933- *WhoWrEP 89*
Rice, Eve 1951- *AuBYP 90, BioIn 16*
Rice, Ferill Jeane 1926- *WhoAmW 91*
Rice, Frank C. 1943- *St&PR 91*
Rice, Gene E. *BioIn 16*
Rice, Gene E. 1930- *St&PR 91*
Rice, George 1854- *AmLegL*
Rice, George T. 1937- *St&PR 91*
Rice, Glen Edward 1933- *St&PR 91, WhoAm 90*
Rice, Grantland 1880-1954 *Ballpl 90, BioIn 16, WorAlBi*
Rice, Greta Jacquelynn 1959- *WhoAmW 91*
Rice, Hal 1924- *Ballpl 90*
Rice, Harold Israel 1929- *St&PR 91*
Rice, Harold Randolph 1912-1987 *WhoAmA 91N*
Rice, Harry 1901-1971 *Ballpl 90*
Rice, Harry Glen 1954- *WhoSSW 91*
Rice, Harvey W 1934- *BiDrAPA 89*
Rice, Haynes 1932- *WhoAm 90*
Rice, Heide Ingeborg 1950- *WhoAmW 91*
Rice, Howard H. 1932- *ODwPR 91*
Rice, Hugh Thompson, Jr. 1957- *WhoEmL 91*
Rice, Inez 1907- *AuBYP 90*
Rice, J. Andrew 1953- *WhoSSW 91*
Rice, J.T. 1922- *St&PR 91*
Rice, Jack *St&PR 91*
Rice, Jack 1948- *St&PR 91*
Rice, Jack Overton 1929- *BiDrAPA 89*
Rice, Jackson *BioIn 16*
Rice, James Anderson 1932- *St&PR 91*
Rice, James Gordon 1948- *WhoEmL 91*
Rice, James H. 1926- *St&PR 91*
Rice, James Lloyd 1937- *BiDrAPA 89*
Rice, James R 1939- *BiDrAPA 89*
Rice, Jean A. 1932- *ODwPR 91*
Rice, Jeanette Ione 1954- *WhoEmL 91*
Rice, Jennifer Susan 1951- *WhoAmW 91, WhoE 91*
Rice, Jerry *BioIn 16*
Rice, Jerry 1962- *CurBio 90 [port], News 90 [port], WorAlBi*
Rice, Jerry Lee 1962- *WhoAm 90*
Rice, Jim *BioIn 16*
Rice, Jim 1953- *Ballpl 90 [port], WorAlBi*
Rice, Jo 1947- *WhoSSW 91*
Rice, Joel Douglass *BiDrAPA 89*
Rice, John 1920- *Ballpl 90*
Rice, John C. 1936- *St&PR 91*
Rice, John Ray 1949- *WhoEmL 91*
Rice, John Rischard 1934- *WhoAm 90*
Rice, John S. 1816-1885 *AmLegL*
Rice, John Thomas 1931- *WhoAm 90*
Rice, Jordan Todd 1955- *WhoSSW 91*
Rice, Joseph Albert 1924- *BioIn 16, WhoAm 90*
Rice, Joseph J. 1949- *St&PR 91*
Rice, Joseph Lee, III 1932- *St&PR 91, WhoE 91*
Rice, Joy Katharine 1939- *WhoAm 90*
Rice, Joyce *BioIn 16*
Rice, Julian Casavant 1924- *WhoAm 90*
Rice, Julius 1923- *BiDrAPA 89*
Rice, Katherine K 1907- *BiDrAPA 89*
Rice, Kathleen Marie 1960- *WhoAmW 91*
Rice, Kathy Strickland 1947- *WhoSSW 91*
Rice, Kenneth Lloyd 1937- *WhoWor 91*
Rice, Kimberely Anne Furgason 1958- *WhoEmL 91*
Rice, Lacy I., Jr. 1931- *St&PR 91, WhoAm 90*
Rice, Lawrence Harvey 1931- *WhoAm 90*
Rice, Leo C. 1928- *St&PR 91*
Rice, Lester 1927- *WhoAm 90*
Rice, Linda Angel 1939- *IntWWM 90*
Rice, Linda Johnson *WhoAmW 91*
Rice, Linda Tillman 1943- *WhoAmW 91*
Rice, Liston M., Jr. 1927- *St&PR 91*
Rice, Lois Dickson 1933- *WhoAm 90*
Rice, Luther 1783-1836 *BioIn 16*
Rice, M Robert *WhoAmA 91*
Rice, Marian Ruth 1931- *WhoAmW 91*
Rice, Martha Helen 1949- *WhoSSW 91*
Rice, Martin A., Jr. 1952- *WhoSSW 91*
Rice, Marvin Samuel 1936- *St&PR 91*
Rice, Mary Alice *BioIn 16*
Rice, Matilda 1931- *BiDrAPA 89*
Rice, Matthew *BioIn 16*
Rice, Melanie Ailene 1957- *WhoAmW 91*
Rice, Michael 1941-1989 *BioIn 16*
Rice, Michael Dennis 1942- *St&PR 91*
Rice, Michael Lewis 1943- *WhoAm 90*
Rice, Milton J. 1928- *St&PR 91*
Rice, Nancy Newman *WhoAmA 91*
Rice, Norman 1943- *WhoAm 90*
Rice, Norman Lewis 1905- *WhoAmA 91*
Rice, Otis LaVerne 1922- *WhoWor 91*
Rice, Pam Joyce 1966- *WhoEmL 91*
Rice, Patricia Ann 1946- *WhoAmW 91*
Rice, Patricia Anne 1949- *WhoWrEP 89*
Rice, Patricia Birch 1949- *WhoAmW 91*
Rice, Paul D. 1932- *St&PR 91*
Rice, Ramona Gail 1950- *WhoAmW 91, WhoEmL 91, WhoWor 91*
Rice, Rebecca Anne 1952- *WhoAmW 91*
Rice, Reginald 1954- *WhoSSW 91*
Rice, Richard Campbell 1933- *WhoWor 91*
Rice, Richard Clark *BiDrAPA 89*
Rice, Richard Lee 1919- *WhoAm 90*
Rice, Robert Jay 1928- *BiDrAPA 89*
Rice, Robert Lynn *BiDrAPA 89*
Rice, Robert Marshall 1930- *WhoAm 90*
Rice, Roger Douglas 1921- *WhoAm 90*
Rice, Roma Jean 1936- *WhoAm 90*

Rice, Ruth Dianne 1924- WhoAmW 91
Rice, Sam 1890-1974 Ballpl 90 [port]
Rice, Shelley Enid 1950- WhoAmA 91
Rice, Sidney Ellis 1928- St&PR 91
Rice, Stanley Matthew 1927- St&PR 91
Rice, Stanley Travis, Jr. 1942- WhoAm 90, WhoWrEP 89
Rice, Stephen Landon 1941- WhoSSW 91
Rice, Steven Nicholas 1950- BiDrAPA 89
Rice, Stuart Alan 1932- WhoAm 90
Rice, Sue Ann 1934- WhoAmW 91
Rice, Susan Joette 1946- WhoAmW 91, WhoWor 91
Rice, Tamara AuBYP 90
Rice, Ted BioIn 16
Rice, Thomas Dartmouth 1808-1860 OxCPMus
Rice, Tim 1944- OxCPMus
Rice, Timothy Miles Bindon 1944- IntWWM 90, WhoWor 91
Rice, Tony BioIn 16
Rice, Tony, Unit NewAgMG
Rice, Victor 1941- St&PR 91
Rice, Victor A. 1941- BioIn 16
Rice, Walter Herbert 1937- WhoAm 90
Rice, William A. 1919- St&PR 91
Rice, William C. 1955- WhoWrEP 89
Rice, William D. 1934- St&PR 91
Rice, William Edward 1938- WhoAm 90
Rice, William Henry 1931- WhoE 91
Rice, William M. 1816-1900 WorAlBi
Rice, Wm. Thomas 1912- St&PR 91
Rice-Simmons, Cathryn Fatima 1954- WhoAmW 91
Riceman, John Patrick 1941- St&PR 91
Ricetti, Jill Alice 1963- WhoE 91
Rich, Adrienne BioIn 16
Rich, Adrienne 1929- FemiCLE, MajTwCW, WhoAm 90, WhoWrEP 89
Rich, Alan 1924- IntWWM 90, WhoAm 90, WhoWrEP 89
Rich, Albert Clark 1950- WhoSSW 91, WhoWor 91
Rich, Alexander 1924- WhoAm 90
Rich, Anthony M BiDrAPA 89
Rich, Arthur Lowndes 1905- WhoAm 90
Rich, Barbara MajTwCW
Rich, Ben Robert 1925- St&PR 91, WhoAm 90
Rich, Beverly Cook 1924- St&PR 91
Rich, Bradford Whitman 1947- WhoEmL 91
Rich, Buddy 1917-1987 BioIn 16, OxCPMus, WorAlBi
Rich, Changhua Sun 1955- WhoEmL 91
Rich, Charles Anthony 1951- WhoWor 91
Rich, Charles F, Jr. 1937- BiDrAPA 89
Rich, Charles L 1943- BiDrAPA 89
Rich, Charlie 1932- EncPR&S 89, OxCPMus, WorAlBi
Rich, Christine Estelle 1947- WhoWrEP 89
Rich, Clayton 1924- WhoAm 90
Rich, Colman Reynolds 1954- St&PR 91
Rich, Cynthia Gay 1945- WhoAmW 91
Rich, Daniel Catton 1904-1976 WhoAmA 91N
Rich, David A. 1944- St&PR 91
Rich, Dru 1960- ODwPR 91
Rich, Edward William 1950- WhoEmL 91
Rich, Elaine Sommers 1926- AuBYP 90, WhoAmW 91
Rich, Elizabeth 1931- IntWWM 90
Rich, Eric 1921- WhoAm 90
Rich, Frances L 1910- WhoAmA 91
Rich, Frances Luther 1910- WhoAm 90
Rich, Frank Hart 1949- WhoAm 90, WhoWrEP 89
Rich, Frank J. ODwPR 91
Rich, Frederick Walter 1949- St&PR 91
Rich, Garry Lorence 1943- WhoAmA 91
Rich, Giles Sutherland 1904- WhoAm 90
Rich, Harold Mervyn 1915- WhoWor 91
Rich, Harry E. 1940- St&PR 91, WhoAm 90
Rich, Harry P. 1942- St&PR 91
Rich, Harvey Louis 1944- BiDrAPA 89
Rich, Hershel Maurice 1925- WhoSSW 91
Rich, Hilda Atlas 1929- WhoAmW 91
Rich, Irene 1891-1988 BioIn 16
Rich, Irene 1897?- WorAlBi
Rich, James Joseph 1935- St&PR 91
Rich, Jay Alan 1950- BiDrAPA 89
Rich, Jenifer Grace BiDrAPA 89
Rich, John 1925- WhoAm 90
Rich, John Martin 1931- WhoAm 90
Rich, John Tyler 1841-1926 AmLegL
Rich, Joseph David 1939- BiDrAPA 89
Rich, Josephine 1912- AuBYP 90
Rich, Jude T. 1943- WhoAm 90
Rich, Judith G. Hemphill 1947- WhoAmW 91
Rich, Kenneth Malcolm 1946- WhoE 91
Rich, Lee BioIn 16, WhoAm 90
Rich, Leonard Geary 1925- St&PR 91, WhoE 91, WhoWor 91
Rich, Les ODwPR 91
Rich, Lesley Steven 1950- WhoE 91
Rich, Linda Sue 1945- WhoAmW 91
Rich, Linvil Gene 1921- WhoAm 90
Rich, Lorimer 1892-1978 WhoAmA 91N
Rich, Louise 1903- AuBYP 90
Rich, Louise Dickinson 1903- BioIn 16
Rich, Lucille DrBlPA 90
Rich, Lucille Mary 1930- WhoAmW 91
Rich, Marc BioIn 16
Rich, Marc 1934- ConAmBL
Rich, Mark David 1958- WhoWrEP 89
Rich, Mark J. 1948- BioIn 16
Rich, Mark Stephen 1947- WhoE 91
Rich, Mary 1625-1678 BiDEWW, BioIn 16
Rich, Mary Beth 1946- WhoEmL 91
Rich, Michael David 1953- WhoAm 90
Rich, Michael Joseph 1945- WhoEmL 91, WhoWor 91
Rich, Patricia W. ODwPR 91
Rich, Patrick J.J. 1931- St&PR 91
Rich, Penelope 1562?-1605? BiDEWW
Rich, Rebecca BiDEWW
Rich, Robert E. BioIn 16
Rich, Robert E., Jr. 1941- WhoE 91
Rich, Robert E., Sr. WhoAm 90
Rich, Robert E., Sr. 1913- ConAmBL
Rich, Robert F. WhoAm 90
Rich, Robert Graham, Jr. 1930- WhoWor 91
Rich, Robert Lee 1953- WhoSSW 91
Rich, Robert Regier 1941- WhoAm 90, WhoSSW 91, WhoWor 91
Rich, Robert Stephen 1938- WhoAm 90
Rich, Roger Lee, Jr. 1934- WhoAm 90
Rich, Ron 1938- DrBlPA 90
Rich, Ronald B. 1955- St&PR 91
Rich, Rosan 1946- WhoAmW 91
Rich, Ruthanne 1941- IntWWM 90
Rich, S. Judith ODwPR 91, St&PR 91, WhoAm 90, WhoAmW 91
Rich, Sarah M. 1940- WhoAmW 91
Rich, Stuart Stanley BiDrAPA 89
Rich, Theodore 1932- St&PR 91
Rich, Thomas Hewitt 1941- WhoWor 91
Rich, Walter George 1946- St&PR 91
Rich, Wayne Adrian 1912- WhoWor 91
Rich, William W.K. 1939- St&PR 91
Rich, Willis Frank, Jr. 1919- WhoAm 90
Richadson, William Cahill, Jr. 1936- St&PR 91
Richard I 1157-1199 WorAlBi
Richard III 1452-1485 WorAlBi
Richard, Duke of York 1411-1460 BioIn 16
Richard I, King of England 1157-1199 BioIn 16
Richard II, King of England 1367-1400 BioIn 16
Richard III, King of England 1452-1485 BioIn 16
Richard, the Lion Heart 1157-1199 BioIn 16
Richard, Adrienne 1921- AuBYP 90
Richard, Alice WhoWrEP 89
Richard, Alison WhoAm 90
Richard, Anita Louise 1951- WhoAmW 91, WhoEmL 91
Richard, Ann Bertha 1944- WhoAmW 91
Richard, Betti 1916- WhoAm 90
Richard, Cifroyen James 1934- WhoSSW 91
Richard, Cliff BioIn 16
Richard, Cliff 1940- EncPR&S 89, OxCPMus
Richard, Colleen Mary 1964- WhoAmW 91
Richard, Darlene Doloras 1946- WhoAmW 91
Richard, David A. 1945- St&PR 91
Richard, Edward H. 1937- St&PR 91
Richard, Elaine 1930- WhoAmW 91
Richard, Frances Joan 1936- WhoE 91
Richard, Guy 1946- St&PR 91
Richard, Howard 1921- WhoE 91
Richard, Ida W. BioIn 16
Richard, J.R. 1950- Ballpl 90
Richard, Jack 1922- WhoAmA 91
Richard, Jacques-Francois PenDiDA 89
Richard, James Robert AuBYP 90
Richard, Jean Pierre 1943- WhoWor 91
Richard, John Bernard 1932- WhoSSW 91
Richard, Laura Ann 1961- WhoAmW 91
Richard, Lawrence J. 1942- IntWWM 90
Richard, Lee 1948- Ballpl 90
Richard, Mae WhoE 91
Richard, Marlene Joan 1932- WhoAmW 91
Richard, Maurice 1924- WorAlBi
Richard, Michel Paul 1933- WhoWrEP 89
Richard, Neil M. 1925- St&PR 91
Richard, Oliver G., III 1952- St&PR 91
Richard, Paul 1939- WhoAmA 91
Richard, Ralph Stephenson 1919- St&PR 91
Richard, Ralph Zachary WhoSSW 91
Richard, Rita 1928- St&PR 91
Richard, Robert John 1947- WhoAm 90
Richard, Sandra Clayton WhoAmW 91, WhoSSW 91, WhoWor 91
Richard, Scott F. 1946- WhoAm 90
Richard, Shirley A. 1947- St&PR 91
Richard, Susan Mathis 1949- WhoAm 90
Richard, William Ralph, Jr. 1922- WhoAm 90
Richard-Ginori PenDiDA 89
Richardella, Lillie Parker 1952- WhoAmW 91
Richardon, Zuma Benjamin 1927- St&PR 91
Richards, Alfred Newton 1876-1976 DcScB S2
Richards, Ann BioIn 16
Richards, Ann 1933- News 91-2 [port]
Richards, Ann 1947- IntWWM 90
Richards, Ann Willis 1933- WhoAmW 91, WhoSSW 91
Richards, Anna Mary 1870-1952 BiDWomA
Richards, Anthony John 1956- IntWWM 90
Richards, Arnold D 1934- BiDrAPA 89
Richards, Arnold David 1934- WhoE 91
Richards, Arthur V. 1939- St&PR 91, WhoAm 90
Richards, Audrey Isabel 1899-1984 DcNaB 1981
Richards, Beah DrBlPA 90
Richards, Benjamin Franklin, Jr. 1941- WhoE 91
Richards, Bernard PenDiMP
Richards, Bernard 1927- St&PR 91, WhoAm 90
Richards, Bill 1936- WhoAm 90, WhoAmA 91
Richards, Bill 1944- WhoAmA 91
Richards, Bradley James 1958- WhoSSW 91
Richards, Brigid 1950- WhoAmW 91
Richards, Burt 1930- WhoAm 90
Richards, Carmeleete A. 1948- WhoAmW 91
Richards, Carolyn Baxter 1926- WhoWrEP 89
Richards, Cecil L. BioIn 16
Richards, Charles A. 1941- St&PR 91
Richards, Charles II BiDrAPA 89
Richards, Charles Lawrence 1856-1927 AmLegL
Richards, Charles T. 1913- St&PR 91
Richards, Christine-Louise 1910- WhoAmW 91
Richards, Clay TwCCr&M 91
Richards, Curtis Vance 1932- WhoAm 90, WhoSSW 91
Richards, Cyndi WhoWrEP 89
Richards, Darrie Hewitt 1921- WhoAm 90, WhoWor 91
Richards, David Adams 1950- BioIn 16, ConLC 59 [port]
Richards, David Alan 1945- WhoWor 91
Richards, David Gleyre 1935- WhoAm 90
Richards, David John 1948- St&PR 91, WhoSSW 91
Richards, David Kimball 1939- WhoAm 90
Richards, David Zehner 1935- St&PR 91
Richards, Deborah Davis 1943- WhoAmW 91
Richards, Denby 1924- IntWWM 90
Richards, Donald C. 1932- St&PR 91
Richards, Donna Nell 1959- WhoAmW 91
Richards, Doris Jean 1937- St&PR 91
Richards, Earl Jeffrey 1952- WhoWor 91
Richards, Edgar Lester 1942- WhoAm 90
Richards, Edsyl William 1927- St&PR 91
Richards, Edward A. 1946- St&PR 91
Richards, Elias, III 1930- St&PR 91
Richards, Elizabeth Glazier 1959- WhoWrEP 89
Richards, Elizabeth M 1933- BiDrAPA 89
Richards, Ellen Henrietta Swallow 1842-1911 BioIn 16
Richards, Eugene 1944- BioIn 16, WhoAmA 91
Richards, F. S. AmLegL
Richards, Frances 1901-1985 BiDWomA
Richards, Francis TwCCr&M 91
Richards, Fred Tracy 1914- St&PR 91, WhoAm 90
Richards, Frederic Middlebrook 1925- WhoAm 90
Richards, Gale Lee 1918- WhoAm 90
Richards, Gene 1953- Ballpl 90
Richards, George A 1934- BiDrAPA 89
Richards, George Henry 1819?-1896 DcCanB 12
Richards, George Leroy 1926- St&PR 91
Richards, George Thomas 1932- WhoSSW 91
Richards, George Whitfield, III 1941- St&PR 91, WhoE 91
Richards, Gerald A. 1940- St&PR 91
Richards, Gilbert 1927- St&PR 91
Richards, Gilbert F. 1929- WhoWor 91
Richards, Gina Rue 1963- WhoAmW 91
Richards, Glenora 1909- WhoAmA 91
Richards, Gregory Lee 1953- BiDrAPA 89
Richards, Harry 1843-1911 OxCPMus
Richards, Herbert East 1919- WhoAm 90
Richards, Hilda 1936- WhoAm 90
Richards, Hugh Taylor 1918- WhoAm 90
Richards, I. A. 1893-1979 BioIn 16
Richards, Jack AuBYP 90
Richards, James Edward 1952- WhoSSW 91
Richards, James H. 1943- St&PR 91
Richards, James R. 1933- WhoAm 90
Richards, James Ward 1933- WhoE 91
Richards, Jane Aileen 1948- WhoAmW 91
Richards, Jeanne Herron WhoAmA 91
Richards, Jeanne Herron 1923- WhoAm 90
Richards, Jeff 1944- WhoWrEP 89
Richards, Jeffrey 1945- ConAu 30NR
Richards, Jeffrey Harris 1945- BiDrAPA 89
Richards, Jerome Francis WhoE 91
Richards, Jerrold Allen 1949- WhoWrEP 89
Richards, Jerry Lee 1939- WhoAm 90
Richards, Jessie Pollard 1927- WhoAmW 91
Richards, John C BiDrAPA 89
Richards, John F. 1947- St&PR 91
Richards, John L.G. 1941- St&PR 91
Richards, John R. 1920- St&PR 91
Richards, John William, Jr. 1950- WhoSSW 91, WhoWor 91
Richards, Joseph Edward 1921- WhoAmA 91
Richards, Judith G. 1939- WhoAmW 91
Richards, Katherine Mary 1941- WhoAmW 91
Richards, Keith BioIn 16
Richards, Keith 1943- WhoAm 90, WorAlBi
Richards, Kenneth J. 1932- St&PR 91
Richards, LaClaire Lissetta Jones WhoAmW 91, WhoWor 91
Richards, Laura Elizabeth 1850-1943 FemiCLE
Richards, Lawrence K. 1938- BiDrAPA 89
Richards, Leonard Martin 1935- St&PR 91, WhoSSW 91
Richards, Leslie 1950- IntWWM 90
Richards, Linda Ann Judson 1841-1930 BioIn 16
Richards, Lisle Frederick 1909- WhoAm 90
Richards, Lloyd DrBlPA 90
Richards, Mark Danner 1919- St&PR 91
Richards, Marta Alison 1952- WhoAmW 91, WhoSSW 91
Richards, Mary Fallon 1920- WhoWrEP 89
Richards, Mary Lea Johnson 1926-1990 BioIn 16, NewYTBS 90
Richards, Merlon Foss 1920- WhoAm 90
Richards, Michael George 1959- WhoWor 91
Richards, Mildred Ruth 1933- WhoAmW 91
Richards, Mira NewAgE 90
Richards, Norman AuBYP 90
Richards, Norman 1932- BioIn 16, ConAu 31NR
Richards, Norman Blanchard 1924- WhoAm 90
Richards, Owain Westmacott 1901-1984 DcNaB 1981
Richards, Pamela Motter 1950- WhoSSW 91
Richards, Paul 1908-1986 Ballpl 90
Richards, Paul B. BioIn 16
Richards, Paul Linford 1934- WhoAm 90
Richards, Peter G. BioIn 16
Richards, Ramona Pope 1957- WhoWrEP 89
Richards, Reuben Francis 1929- St&PR 91, WhoAm 90, WhoE 91
Richards, Rhoda Root Wagner 1917- WhoAmW 91, WhoE 91
Richards, Richard Davison 1927- WhoAm 90
Richards, Riley Harry 1912- WhoAm 90
Richards, Robert D. 1928- St&PR 91
Richards, Robert E. 1955- St&PR 91
Richards, Robert H.E. 1937- St&PR 91
Richards, Roger T. 1947- St&PR 91
Richards, Roger Thomas 1942- WhoE 91, WhoWor 91
Richards, Ronald Charles William 1923- BioIn 16
Richards, Rupert Merrick 1923- St&PR 91
Richards, Ruth AuBYP 90, BiDrAPA 89
Richards, Sabra WhoAmA 91
Richards, Scott B BiDrAPA 89
Richards, Shirley Mastin 1927- WhoSSW 91
Richards, Stan BioIn 16
Richards, Stanford Harvey 1932- WhoAm 90
Richards, Stanley Harold 1922- St&PR 91
Richards, Stephen C. 1914- St&PR 91
Richards, Stephen F. 1948- St&PR 91
Richards, Stephen I. 1949- St&PR 91
Richards, Susan Marie 1955- WhoAmW 91
Richards, Tally WhoAmA 91

Richards, Theodore W. 1868-1928 *WorAlBi*
Richards, Thomas Carl 1930- *WhoAm 90*
Richards, Thomas Jeffrey 1944- *WhoAm 90, WhoWor 91*
Richards, Thomas Lombard 1934- *St&PR 91*
Richards, Victor 1918- *WhoAm 90*
Richards, Vincent Philip Haslewood 1933- *WhoAm 90*
Richards, Walter A. 1907-1988 *BioIn 16*
Richards, Walter DuBois 1907- *WhoAm 90, WhoAmA 91*
Richards, Warren Lewis *BiDrAPA 89*
Richards, Willard 1804-1854 *BioIn 16*
Richards, William 1793-1847 *BioIn 16*
Richards, William George 1920- *WhoSSW 91*
Richards, William Hayward 1921- *St&PR 91*
Richards, William J. 1927- *St&PR 91*
Richards, William W, Jr. 1941- *BiDrAPA 89*
Richards-Wright, Genevieve Mercedes *WhoE 91*
Richardson, Alice Elinor 1961- *WhoEmL 91*
Richardson, Ann 1660?- *BiDEWW*
Richardson, Arthur W. *BioIn 16*
Richardson, Ashley *BioIn 16*
Richardson, Barbara Connell 1947- *WhoAmW 91, WhoEmL 91*
Richardson, Barbara Jean Acker *WhoAmW 91*
Richardson, Benjamin *PenDiDA 89*
Richardson, Betty *BioIn 16*
Richardson, Betty Joyce 1935- *WhoWrEP 89*
Richardson, Betty Kehl 1938- *WhoAmW 91*
Richardson, Bill 1947- *WhoHisp 91*
Richardson, Bobbi 1945- *WhoAmW 91*
Richardson, Bobby 1935- *Ballpl 90 [port], BioIn 16*
Richardson, Brenda 1942- *WhoAmA 91*
Richardson, Brittain David 1927- *St&PR 91, WhoAm 90*
Richardson, C. Leonard 1926- *St&PR 91*
Richardson, Campbell 1930- *WhoAm 90*
Richardson, Carl C. 1941- *St&PR 91*
Richardson, Carol 1932- *BioIn 16*
Richardson, Carol Elliott *St&PR 91*
Richardson, Carol Warner *BiDrAPA 89*
Richardson, Carole *BioIn 16*
Richardson, Channing Bulfinch 1917- *WhoAm 90*
Richardson, Charles Clifton 1935- *WhoAm 90*
Richardson, Charles Edwin *BiDrAPA 89*
Richardson, Charles M *BiDrAPA 89*
Richardson, Charles Marsh 1925- *WhoE 91*
Richardson, Clinton Dennis 1949- *WhoSSW 91*
Richardson, Clyta Faith 1915- *WhoAm 90*
Richardson, Constance 1905- *WhoAmA 91*
Richardson, Dana Theodore 1949- *St&PR 91*
Richardson, Daniel B. 1928- *St&PR 91*
Richardson, Daniel Charles 1937- *WhoAm 90*
Richardson, David Bacon 1916- *WhoE 91*
Richardson, David I. 1943- *St&PR 91*
Richardson, David John 1943- *WhoAm 90*
Richardson, David Neal 1939- *WhoSSW 91*
Richardson, David Vivian 1941- *IntWWM 90*
Richardson, David Walthall 1925- *WhoAm 90, WhoWor 91*
Richardson, David William 1948- *WhoE 91*
Richardson, Davis Bates 1929- *St&PR 91, WhoAm 90, WhoSSW 91*
Richardson, Dean Eugene 1927- *St&PR 91, WhoAm 90*
Richardson, Deane Weir 1930- *WhoAm 90*
Richardson, Deanna Ruth 1956- *WhoAmW 91*
Richardson, Debbie Jean 1957- *WhoSSW 91*
Richardson, Delroy McCoy 1938- *St&PR 91*
Richardson, Denys 1913-1983 *DcNaB 1981*
Richardson, Diane 1951- *WhoEmL 91, WhoWor 91*
Richardson, Don Forrest 1947- *WhoSSW 91*
Richardson, Don Ramon 1938- *WhoSSW 91*
Richardson, Donald Charles 1937- *WhoWor 91*
Richardson, Donald Edward 1931- *WhoAm 90*
Richardson, Dorothy 1873-1957 *FemiCLE*
Richardson, Dorothy Miller 1873-1957 *BioIn 16*
Richardson, Dorothy Virginia 1937- *WhoAmW 91*
Richardson, Doug *BioIn 16*
Richardson, Douglas Fielding 1929- *WhoAm 90*
Richardson, Earle Stanford 1943- *WhoE 91*
Richardson, Ed R. 1939- *WhoSSW 91*
Richardson, Edgar Preston 1902-1985 *WhoAmA 91N*
Richardson, Edward Ewing 1941- *St&PR 91*
Richardson, Edward James 1954- *WhoAm 90*
Richardson, Egerton 1912-1988 *BioIn 16*
Richardson, Elaine M. 1954- *WhoAmW 91*
Richardson, Eleanor Elizabeth 1948- *WhoAmW 91*
Richardson, Elisha Roscoe 1931- *WhoAm 90*
Richardson, Elizabeth *BiDEWW*
Richardson, Elizabeth Ann 1943- *WhoSSW 91*
Richardson, Elliot 1920- *WorAlBi*
Richardson, Elliot L. *BioIn 16*
Richardson, Elliot Lee 1920- *BiDrUSE 89, WhoAm 90*
Richardson, Emeline Hill 1910- *WhoAmW 91*
Richardson, Emilie White *WhoSSW 91*
Richardson, Esther Harbage Cole 1894- *WhoAm 90*
Richardson, Evelyn H. 1929- *St&PR 91*
Richardson, Everett Vern 1924- *WhoAm 90*
Richardson, Forest *St&PR 91*
Richardson, Frank, Jr 1950- *WhoAmA 91*
Richardson, Frank Charles 1928- *WhoAm 90*
Richardson, Frank H. 1933- *St&PR 91, WhoAm 90*
Richardson, Frank Howard *AuBYP 90*
Richardson, Frank Kellogg 1914- *WhoAm 90*
Richardson, Frederick Joseph 1926- *St&PR 91*
Richardson, Freida Laramy 1912- *WhoAmW 91*
Richardson, George *PenDiDA 89*
Richardson, George A 1912- *BiDrAPA 89*
Richardson, George T. 1924- *St&PR 91*
Richardson, Gilbert Payton 1926- *WhoAm 90*
Richardson, Gordie 1939- *Ballpl 90*
Richardson, Gordon Banning 1937- *WhoWor 91*
Richardson, Grace E. 1938- *ODwPR 91*
Richardson, Graham Frederick 1949- *WhoWor 91*
Richardson, Greg Drexel 1955- *WhoEmL 91*
Richardson, Hardy 1855-1931 *Ballpl 90*
Richardson, Harry A., Jr. 1929- *St&PR 91*
Richardson, Hart Middleton 1943- *WhoAmW 91*
Richardson, Henry H. 1838-1886 *WorAlBi*
Richardson, Henry Handel 1870-1946 *BioIn 16, FemiCLE*
Richardson, Henry Hobson 1838-1886 *PenDiDA 89*
Richardson, Herbert Heath 1930- *WhoAm 90*
Richardson, Herbert Lee *BioIn 16*
Richardson, Howard L. 1909- *St&PR 91*
Richardson, Ian William 1934- *WhoWor 91*
Richardson, Inez M *DcAfAmP*
Richardson, J. P. 1930-1959 *EncPR&S 89*
Richardson, James *BioIn 16*
Richardson, James 1819-1892 *DcCanB 12*
Richardson, James 1950- *WhoE 91, WhoWrEP 89*
Richardson, James A. 1948- *WhoSSW 91*
Richardson, James Abner, III 1908- *WhoAm 90*
Richardson, James Bitting, Jr. 1937- *St&PR 91*
Richardson, James Daniel 1843-1914 *AmLegL*
Richardson, James Fairgrieve 1940- *St&PR 91*
Richardson, James Lewis 1927- *WhoAmA 91N*
Richardson, James Robert 1946- *WhoWrEP 89*
Richardson, Jarrett Wood, III 1947- *BiDrAPA 89*
Richardson, Jean *BioIn 16*
Richardson, Jean 1943- *WhoE 91*
Richardson, Jean Brooks 1940- *WhoSSW 91*
Richardson, Jean McGlenn 1927- *WhoAmW 91*
Richardson, Jeffrey Carl 1953- *WhoE 91, WhoEmL 91, WhoWor 91*
Richardson, Jerome Johnson 1936- *St&PR 91, WhoE 91, WhoSSW 91*
Richardson, Jerry W. 1945- *St&PR 91*
Richardson, Joe Leonard 1933- *St&PR 91*
Richardson, John *NewAgMG*
Richardson, John 1796-1852 *DcLB 99 [port]*
Richardson, John 1921- *WhoAm 90*
Richardson, John Adkins 1929- *WhoAmA 91*
Richardson, John Carroll 1932- *WhoAm 90*
Richardson, John David *BiDrAPA 89*
Richardson, John Joseph 1926- *St&PR 91*
Richardson, John M. 1941- *St&PR 91*
Richardson, John Marshall 1921- *WhoAm 90*
Richardson, John Thomas 1923- *WhoAm 90*
Richardson, Jorge Enrique *BiDrAPA 89*
Richardson, Joseph A., Jr. 1928- *St&PR 91*
Richardson, Joseph Ablett, Jr. 1928- *WhoAm 90*
Richardson, Joseph Blancet 1936- *WhoE 91, WhoWor 91*
Richardson, Joseph E., II 1929- *St&PR 91*
Richardson, Joseph Stephen 1837- *AmLegL*
Richardson, Joseph W. 1939- *WhoE 91*
Richardson, K. Scott 1951- *WhoSSW 91*
Richardson, Keith Edward 1947- *WhoWor 91*
Richardson, Ken Edgar 1952- *WhoWrEP 89*
Richardson, Kenneth Edgar 1952- *WhoSSW 91*
Richardson, L. Janette 1925-1989 *BioIn 16*
Richardson, Laurel Walum 1938- *WhoAm 90*
Richardson, Lawrence, Jr. 1920- *WhoAm 90*
Richardson, Legrand 1923- *St&PR 91*
Richardson, Linda F. 1951- *WhoWrEP 89*
Richardson, Linda Walker 1941- *WhoAmW 91*
Richardson, Lunsford, Jr. 1924- *St&PR 91*
Richardson, Madison F. *BioIn 16*
Richardson, Marilyn 1936- *IntWWM 90*
Richardson, Marilyn Goff 1934- *WhoAmW 91*
Richardson, Marion Wachter 1947- *WhoAmW 91*
Richardson, Mark Allen 1955- *BiDrAPA 89*
Richardson, Mark Childs 1957- *WhoE 91*
Richardson, Mark Wyman 1867-1947 *EncPaPR 91*
Richardson, Martha 1917- *WhoAmW 91*
Richardson, Melissa Ann 1954- *WhoAmW 91*
Richardson, Michael G. 1940- *St&PR 91*
Richardson, Michael Joseph 1939- *BiDrAPA 89*
Richardson, Midge Turk 1930- *WhoAm 90, WhoAmW 91, WhoE 91, WhoWrEP 89*
Richardson, Mildred Tourtillott 1907- *WhoWor 91*
Richardson, Miranda *BioIn 16*
Richardson, Natasha *BioIn 16*
Richardson, Nolan *BioIn 16*
Richardson, Norman E. 1909-1990 *BioIn 16*
Richardson, Owen W. 1879-1959 *WorAlBi*
Richardson, Patrice *BioIn 16*
Richardson, Patricia Fogarty 1933- *WhoAmW 91*
Richardson, Peter Damian 1935- *WhoAm 90*
Richardson, Ralph 1902-1983 *WorAlBi*
Richardson, Ralph David 1902-1983 *DcNaB 1981*
Richardson, Ransom Lloyd *BioIn 16*
Richardson, Raymond J. 1946- *St&PR 91*
Richardson, Regina Jo 1949- *WhoAmW 91*
Richardson, Richard Judson 1935- *WhoAm 90*
Richardson, Richard Thomas 1933- *WhoAm 90*
Richardson, Rita Faye 1951- *WhoAmW 91*
Richardson, Robert Alvin 1951- *WhoSSW 91*
Richardson, Robert B. 1927- *St&PR 91*
Richardson, Robert Charlwood, III 1918- *WhoAm 90*
Richardson, Robert Clinton, III 1957- *WhoE 91*
Richardson, Robert Dale, Jr. 1934- *WhoAm 90, WhoE 91*
Richardson, Robert Edward 1955- *WhoEmL 91*
Richardson, Robert Howard *BiDrAPA 89*
Richardson, Robert Lloyd 1930- *WhoAm 90*
Richardson, Robert William 1935- *WhoAm 90*
Richardson, Roberta Marie 1958- *BiDrAPA 89*
Richardson, Roderick Boyd 1938- *St&PR 91*
Richardson, Roger K. 1909- *St&PR 91*
Richardson, Ron 1951?- *DrBlPA 90*
Richardson, Ronald James 1946- *St&PR 91*
Richardson, Ross Frederick 1928- *WhoAm 90*
Richardson, Rudy James 1945- *WhoAm 90*
Richardson, Rupert Norval 1891- *BioIn 16*
Richardson, Ruth Greene 1926- *WhoAmW 91, WhoE 91*
Richardson, Sally M. 1947- *WhoEmL 91*
Richardson, Sam 1934- *WhoAmA 91*
Richardson, Samuel 1689-1761 *WorAlBi*
Richardson, Sandra Kay 1959- *WhoAmW 91*
Richardson, Sandra Lorraine 1947- *WhoAmW 91*
Richardson, Sarah *FemiCLE*
Richardson, Sharon Louise 1956- *WhoEmL 91*
Richardson, Shirley Maxine 1931- *WhoAmW 91*
Richardson, Susan Lynn 1964- *WhoAmW 91*
Richardson, Sylvia Onesti 1920- *WhoAm 90*
Richardson, Thomas *EarBlAP*
Richardson, Thomas F 1938- *BiDrAPA 89*
Richardson, Thomas Hampton 1941- *WhoWor 91*
Richardson, Thomas Lynn 1955- *WhoSSW 91*
Richardson, Tom 1948- *WhoEmL 91*
Richardson, Tony *BioIn 16*
Richardson, Tony 1928- *WhoWor 91, WorAlBi*
Richardson, Tracy 1892-1949 *BioIn 16*
Richardson, Tracy Lynn 1948- *BiDrAPA 89*
Richardson, William Adams 1821-1896 *BiDrUSE 89*
Richardson, William Blaine 1947- *WhoAm 90*
Richardson, William Carlton 1927- *St&PR 91*
Richardson, William Chase 1940- *WhoAm 90*
Richardson, William M. 1934- *St&PR 91*
Richardson, William Randall 1950- *IntWWM 90*
Richardson, William Rowland 1929- *WhoAm 90*
Richardson, William T 1939- *BiDrAPA 89*
Richardson, William Winfree, III 1939- *WhoSSW 91*
Richardson, Willis 1889-1977 *DrBlPA 90, EarBlAP, SmATA 60 [port]*
Richardson Gonzales, James H. *WhoHisp 91*
Richardt, Mike 1958- *Ballpl 90*
Richars, Elmer D. 1938- *ODwPR 91*
Richart, Frank Edwin, Jr. 1918- *WhoAm 90*
Richart, Gerald R. 1947- *St&PR 91*
Richart, John Douglas 1947- *WhoE 91*
Richart, Victoria Betty 1937- *WhoAmW 91*
Richarz, Irmintraut 1927- *WhoWor 91*
Richason, Benjamin F. 1922-1988 *BioIn 16*
Richbourg, Lance *BioIn 16*
Richbourg, Lance 1897-1975 *Ballpl 90*
Richburg, Michael Vaughn 1955- *WhoSSW 91*
Richeimer, Mary Jane 1913- *WhoAmW 91*
Richeimer, Steven Harry *BiDrAPA 89*
Richel, Alan Lewis 1950- *WhoEmL 91*
Richel, Victor M. 1938- *St&PR 91*
Richelieu, Armand Jean DuPlessis, Duc De 1585-1642 *WorAlBi*
Richelson, Elliott *BiDrAPA 89*
Richelsoph, Martin 1945- *WhoEmL 91*
Richen, Clarence W. *St&PR 91*
Richenberg, Richard Edward 1935- *St&PR 91*
Richenburg, Robert Bartlett 1917- *WhoAm 90, WhoAmA 91*
Richens, Muriel Whittaker *WhoAmW 91*
Richer, Alan Brian 1954- *WhoEmL 91*
Richer, Alvin 1929- *St&PR 91*
Richer, Claude *BiDrAPA 89*
Richer, Jean Herbert 1918- *St&PR 91*
Richer, Laurie Anne *BiDrAPA 89*
Richer, Stephane *BioIn 16*
Richer, Stephen Bruce 1946- *WhoE 91*
Richerson, Hal Bates 1929- *WhoAm 90*
Richerson, Modesta Dorsett 1905- *WhoAmW 91*
Richert, Harvey Miller, II 1948- *WhoSSW 91*
Richert, Joel Conlon 1951- *St&PR 91*
Richert, Maxine Harper 1947- *St&PR 91*
Richert, Pete 1939- *Ballpl 90*
Riches, George Thomas 1932- *St&PR 91*
Riches, Kenneth William 1962- *WhoEmL 91, WhoWor 91*
Riches, Pierre Pietro 1927- *WhoWor 91*
Richesin, Jill Dawn 1964- *WhoAmW 91*
Richeson, Cena Golder 1941- *WhoWrEP 89*

Richeson, Hugh Anthony, Jr. 1947- *WhoEmL 91, WhoSSW 91, WhoWor 91*
Richesson, Edward R. 1933- *St&PR 91*
Richet, Charles 1850-1935 *EncO&P 3*
Richet, Charles Robert 1850-1935 *EncPaPR 91*
Richetelli, Dorinda Marie 1962- *WhoE 91*
Richette, Lisa Aversa 1928- *WhoAm 90*
Richey, Albert L. 1949- *St&PR 91*
Richey, Alvan Edgar, Jr. 1936- *St&PR 91*
Richey, Annie Lou 1934- *WhoWrEP 89*
Richey, Charles Robert 1923- *WhoAm 90*
Richey, Elba Lee 1925- *St&PR 91*
Richey, Leroy Milburn, Jr. 1930- *St&PR 91*
Richey, Phil Horace 1923- *WhoAm 90, WhoWor 91*
Richey, Robert Lee 1923- *WhoAm 90*
Richey, Rodney Paul 1957- *WhoWrEP 89*
Richey, Ronald H. 1950- *St&PR 91*
Richey, Ronald K. 1926- *St&PR 91*
Richey, Ronald Kay 1926- *WhoAm 90, WhoSSW 91*
Richey, Sara Josephine 1950- *WhoAmW 91*
Richey, Thomas Adam 1934- *WhoAm 90*
Richey, Thomas Allen 1949- *WhoEmL 91*
Richey, Valerie Lynne 1959- *WhoEmL 91*
Richfield, Jerome 1920- *WhoAm 90*
Richhart, James W. 1941- *St&PR 91*
Richiardi, Aldo 1923-1985 *BioIn 16*
Richie, Brenda *BioIn 16*
Richie, Jerome Paul 1944- *WhoAm 90*
Richie, John N 1941- *BiDrAPA 89*
Richie, Leroy C. 1941- *WhoAm 90*
Richie, Lew 1883-1936 *Ballpl 90*
Richie, Lionel *BioIn 16*
Richie, Lionel 1949- *DrBlPA 90, EncPR&S 89, WorAlBi*
Richie, Lionel B., Jr. 1949- *WhoAm 90*
Richie, William Donald *BiDrAPA 89*
Richier, Germaine 1904-1959 *BiDWomA, BioIn 16*
Richin, Philippe 1952- *WhoWor 91*
Richker, Michael Steven 1945- *St&PR 91*
Richkind, Kathleen E. 1948- *St&PR 91*
Richkus, Peta Naylor 1947- *WhoAmW 91*
Richlan, Theodora Maria *BiDrAPA 89*
Richler, Mordecai 1931- *BioIn 16, ConAu 31NR, MajTwCW, WhoAm 90, WhoWor 91, WhoWrEP 89, WorAlBi*
Richley, Robert Douglas 1944- *WhoSSW 91*
Richlin, Maurice N. *NewYTBS 90*
Richman, Alan *BioIn 16*
Richman, Alan 1939- *WhoAm 90, WhoE 91, WhoWrEP 89*
Richman, Arthur *Ballpl 90*
Richman, Arthur L. 1921- *St&PR 91*
Richman, Barry Jan 1960- *BiDrAPA 89*
Richman, David 1946- *St&PR 91*
Richman, Deborah *BioIn 16*
Richman, Donald 1922- *WhoAm 90*
Richman, Elise Keltz *BiDrAPA 89*
Richman, Elliot 1941- *WhoWrEP 89*
Richman, Gertrude Gross 1908- *WhoAmW 91*
Richman, H.B. 1928- *St&PR 91*
Richman, Harold Alan 1937- *WhoAm 90*
Richman, Harry 1895-1972 *OxCPMus*
Richman, Herbert J. 1935- *St&PR 91*
Richman, Joan F. 1939- *WhoAm 90, WhoAmW 91*
Richman, John Emmett 1951- *WhoEmL 91*
Richman, John Marshall 1927- *St&PR 91, WhoAm 90, WhoWor 91*
Richman, Jordan Paul 1931- *WhoWrEP 89*
Richman, Larry Leon 1955- *WhoEmL 91*
Richman, Marc Herbert 1936- *WhoAm 90*
Richman, Marcia R. *BioIn 16*
Richman, Mark *ConTFT 8*
Richman, Martin Franklin 1930- *WhoAm 90*
Richman, Marvin Jordan 1939- *WhoAm 90, WhoWor 91*
Richman, Milton 1922-1986 *Ballpl 90*
Richman, Paul 1942- *WhoAm 90*
Richman, Penny A. 1944- *ODwPR 91*
Richman, Peter 1927- *WhoAm 90, WhoE 91*
Richman, Peter Mark 1927- *ConTFT 8 [port], WhoAm 90*
Richman, Phil 1923- *ODwPR 91*
Richman, Phyllis Chasanow 1939- *WhoAm 90, WhoAmW 91*
Richman, Selma 1925- *WhoAmW 91*
Richman, Sheldon Barnett 1944- *WhoWor 91*
Richman, Sheldon Louis 1942- *BiDrAPA 89*
Richman, Sidney L *BiDrAPA 89*
Richman, Stephen Ian 1933- *WhoAm 90, WhoE 91, WhoWor 91*
Richman, Steven Mark 1955- *WhoWrEP 89*
Richman, Sumner 1929- *WhoAm 90*
Richman, Victoria S. 1959- *WhoAmW 91*
Richman, William Sheldon 1921- *St&PR 91, WhoAm 90*
Richmond and Gordon, Duke of 1904-1989 *AnObit 1989*
Richmond, Anthony Henry 1925- *WhoAm 90, WhoWor 91*
Richmond, Brian 1948- *St&PR 91*
Richmond, Bruce E. 1938- *WhoAm 90*
Richmond, Bruce Timothy 1959- *St&PR 91*
Richmond, Charles David 1951- *WhoEmL 91*
Richmond, Charles Ronald 1939- *St&PR 91*
Richmond, Cora L V 1840-1923 *EncO&P 3*
Richmond, Dannie *BioIn 16*
Richmond, Dannie 1935-1988 *AnObit 1988*
Richmond, David Walker 1914- *WhoAm 90*
Richmond, Dina Rae 1929- *WhoAmW 91*
Richmond, Eero L. 1938- *IntWWM 90*
Richmond, Gail Levin 1946- *WhoEmL 91*
Richmond, George E. 1933- *St&PR 91*
Richmond, Gillian 1954- *WhoWor 91*
Richmond, Glenn Hickman, Jr. *BiDrAPA 89*
Richmond, James, Jr. 1940- *St&PR 91*
Richmond, James E. 1938- *St&PR 91*
Richmond, James Ellis 1938- *WhoAm 90*
Richmond, John 1907- *WhoWor 91*
Richmond, John Alan 1949- *BiDrAPA 89*
Richmond, John Allen 1932- *St&PR 91*
Richmond, John William 1955- *WhoSSW 91*
Richmond, Jon 1957- *WhoAm 90*
Richmond, Julius B *BiDrAPA 89*
Richmond, Julius B. 1916- *AuBYP 90*
Richmond, Julius Benjamin 1916- *WhoAm 90*
Richmond, Kenneth 1882-1945 *EncPaPR 91*
Richmond, Kenneth Forbes 1882-1945 *EncO&P 3*
Richmond, L.A. 1944- *St&PR 91*
Richmond, Lawrence 1909-1978 *WhoAmA 91N*
Richmond, Lee 1857-1929 *Ballpl 90*
Richmond, Lewis H *BiDrAPA 89*
Richmond, Louis B. *ODwPR 91*
Richmond, Margaret, Countess of 1441-1509 *FemiCLE*
Richmond, Mark Henry 1931- *WhoWor 91*
Richmond, Martin Barrie 1936- *BiDrAPA 89*
Richmond, Mary 1861-1928 *BioAmW*
Richmond, Mitch *BioIn 16*
Richmond, Nancy M. 1944- *St&PR 91*
Richmond, Phyllis Allen 1921- *WhoAm 90, WhoAmW 91*
Richmond, R.D. 1919- *St&PR 91*
Richmond, Rebekah *WhoAmA 91*
Richmond, Rick Lloyd 1959- *WhoSSW 91*
Richmond, Robert Linn 1920- *WhoAm 90*
Richmond, Rocsan *WhoAmW 91*
Richmond, Samuel Bernard 1919- *WhoAm 90*
Richmond, Sandra 1948- *BioIn 16*
Richmond, Steven Allan 1941- *WhoWrEP 89*
Richmond, Thomas *EncO&P 3*
Richmond, Thomas L. 1933- *ODwPR 91*
Richmond, Tim *BioIn 16*
Richmond, Tony 1942- *BioIn 16*
Richmond, Tyronza R. 1940- *WhoSSW 91*
Richmond, Victor J. 1932- *St&PR 91*
Richmond, Wendell Earl 1927- *St&PR 91*
Richmond, William Frederick, Jr. 1943- *WhoSSW 91*
Richmond, William Patrick 1932- *WhoAm 90*
Richmond, Zoe 1888-1986 *EncPaPR 91*
Richmond, Zoe Blanche Russell 1888- *EncO&P 3*
Richmond-Hawkins, Victoria Kathryn 1949- *WhoEmL 91*
Richnak, Barbara M. 1936- *WhoWrEP 89*
Richner, Clifford 1952- *WhoE 91*
Richolson, Sandra Lehman 1951- *WhoAmW 91*
Richoux, Richard William *BiDrAPA 89*
Richoz, Andre Hilaire 1947- *WhoWor 91*
Richstatter, Thomas 1939- *ConAu 30NR*
Richstein, Abraham Richard 1919- *WhoAm 90*
Richstone, Douglas Orange 1949- *WhoAm 90*
Richstone, Ellen Blair 1951- *St&PR 91*
Richter, Achim 1940- *WhoWor 91*
Richter, Ada *BioIn 16*
Richter, Al 1927- *BioIn 16*
Richter, Alan Marc 1955- *St&PR 91*
Richter, Anne J. 1905-1989 *BioIn 16*
Richter, Barbara Ann 1943- *WhoAmW 91*
Richter, Barry 1953- *St&PR 91*
Richter, Bodo Ludwig Otto 1915-1990 *BioIn 16*
Richter, Burton 1931- *WhoAm 90, WhoWor 91, WorAlBi*
Richter, Charles F. 1900-1985 *WorAlBi*
Richter, Conrad 1890-1968 *AuBYP 90, BioIn 16, MajTwCW*
Richter, Curt Paul 1894-1988 *BioIn 16*
Richter, Cwira *BiDrAPA 89*
Richter, Dieter 1938- *WhoWor 91*
Richter, Dieter Max 1930- *WhoWor 91*
Richter, Donald A. 1932- *WhoAm 90*
Richter, Donald Paul 1924- *WhoAm 90*
Richter, Doris Louise 1935- *WhoAmW 91*
Richter, Earl E. 1923- *St&PR 91*
Richter, Ed *AuBYP 90*
Richter, Elmer Bud 1926- *St&PR 91*
Richter, Elwood William 1923- *St&PR 91*
Richter, Francis C. 1854-1926 *Ballpl 90*
Richter, Frank 1916- *WhoWrEP 89*
Richter, George Robert, Jr. 1910- *WhoAm 90*
Richter, Gerhard *BioIn 16*
Richter, Gisela Marie Augusta 1882-1972 *WhoAmA 91N*
Richter, Glenn Charles 1945- *WhoE 91*
Richter, Gustav 1913- *BioIn 16*
Richter, Hank 1928- *WhoAmA 91*
Richter, Hans 1843-1916 *PenDiMP*
Richter, Hans 1888-1976 *ConAu 30NR, WhoAmA 91N*
Richter, Hans Peter 1925- *ChlLR 21 [port], SmATA 11AS [port]*
Richter, Harry Lenwood, Jr. 1940- *St&PR 91*
Richter, Harvena 1919- *WhoWrEP 89*
Richter, Henry Andrew 1930- *WhoE 91*
Richter, Hildeburg *BiDrAPA 89*
Richter, Howard Anthony 1939- *WhoE 91*
Richter, Irvin E. 1944- *St&PR 91*
Richter, James Arthur 1942- *St&PR 91*
Richter, James Michael 1950- *WhoAm 90, WhoE 91*
Richter, Johann 1763-1825 *WorAlBi*
Richter, Johann Paul Friedrich 1763-1825 *DcLB 94 [port]*
Richter, Judith Anne 1942- *WhoAmW 91*
Richter, Karl 1926-1981 *PenDiMP*
Richter, Ken 1953- *BiDrAPA 89*
Richter, Linda Dale 1949- *WhoAmW 91*
Richter, Marga 1926- *BioIn 16*
Richter, Mary Jane 1937- *WhoAmW 91*
Richter, Maurice 1897-1988 *BioIn 16*
Richter, Maurice N., Jr. 1930- *WhoE 91*
Richter, Mischa *AuBYP 90*
Richter, Norman H. 1938- *St&PR 91*
Richter, Patti Quinn 1959- *WhoSSW 91*
Richter, Paul Robert 1948- *St&PR 91*
Richter, Peter 1922- *BiDrAPA 89*
Richter, R.G. 1945- *St&PR 91*
Richter, Richard Paul 1931- *WhoAm 90*
Richter, Robert E. 1947- *St&PR 91*
Richter, Roberta Brandenburg *WhoAmW 91, WhoWor 91*
Richter, Scott 1943- *WhoAmA 91*
Richter, Sviatoslav 1915- *BioIn 16*
Richter, Sviatoslav Teofilovich 1915- *IntWWM 90*
Richter, Sviatoslav Theofilovich 1915- *WhoWor 91*
Richter, Svyatoslav 1915- *PenDiMP, WorAlBi*
Richter, Walter Henry, III 1958- *WhoE 91*
Richter, Wolfram Franz 1948- *WhoWor 91*
Richter-Haaser, Hans 1912-1980 *PenDiMP*
Richters, Tracy Ann 1960- *WhoAmW 91*
Richthofen, Frieda von 1879-1956 *BioIn 16*
Richthofen, Manfred Von 1892-1918 *WorAlBi*
Richthofen, Wolfram, Freiherr von 1895-1945 *BioIn 16*
Richtmeyer-Truax, Debra 1957- *IntWWM 90*
Richtol, Herbert Harold 1932- *WhoAm 90, WhoE 91*
Richwien, Barry Andrew 1951- *WhoE 91*
Richwine, Samuel Winters, Jr. 1951- *WhoSSW 91*
Ricigliano, James Vincent 1938- *St&PR 91*
Ricioppo, Eric 1955- *ODwPR 91*
Rick, Charles M. 1915- *BioIn 16*
Rick, Charles Madeira, Jr. 1915- *WhoAm 90*
Rick, Richard Langley 1928- *St&PR 91*
Rickard, Carolyn Lucille 1937- *WhoAmW 91*
Rickard, Carroll M. 1929- *St&PR 91*
Rickard, Corwin Lloyd 1926- *WhoAm 90*
Rickard, Cynthia Lee 1953- *WhoEmL 91*
Rickard, Henry Charles 1930- *WhoAm 90*
Rickard, Kathryn Wright 1957- *WhoAmW 91*
Rickard, Norman Edward 1936- *WhoAm 90*
Rickard, Rebecca Ann 1952- *WhoAmW 91*
Rickard, Ruth David 1926- *WhoAmW 91*
Rickard-Riegle, Barbara Katherine 1931- *WhoAmW 91*
Rickards, Catherine Isabella 1916- *WhoWrEP 89*
Rickards, Leonard Myron 1927- *WhoAm 90, WhoSSW 91*
Rickart, Charles Earl 1913- *WhoAm 90, WhoE 91*
Rickart, Tex *Ballpl 90*
Ricke, Bruce *BiDrAPA 89*
Ricke, Dennis Frank 1948- *WhoWor 91*
Ricke, Thomas 1947- *ODwPR 91*
Rickel, E.J. 1925- *St&PR 91*
Rickel, William Albert 1941- *WhoAm 90*
Rickels, Karl 1924- *BiDrAPA 89, WhoAm 90*
Ricken, Norman Michael 1936- *St&PR 91, WhoAm 90, WhoE 91*
Rickenbacher, Karl Anton 1940- *IntWWM 90, PenDiMP*
Rickenbacker, Edward 1890-1973 *WorAlBi*
Rickenbacker, Edward V *EncABHB 5 [port]*
Rickenbaker, Hugh K., Jr. 1922- *ODwPR 91*
Rickenbaugh, Hilda Van Horn 1907- *St&PR 91*
Rickenbaugh, Ralph L. 1906- *St&PR 91*
Ricker, David William 1960- *WhoSSW 91*
Ricker, Gerald William 1947- *WhoE 91*
Ricker, John Boykin, Jr. 1917- *WhoAm 90*
Ricker, Nancy Lee 1940- *WhoAmW 91*
Ricker, Robert S. *WhoAm 90*
Ricker, Ronald Earl *BiDrAPA 89*
Ricker, Sharon Lucille 1964- *WhoEmL 91*
Ricker, William Edwin 1908- *WhoAm 90*
Ricker, William Howard 1955- *WhoEmL 91*
Rickerby, David George 1952- *WhoWor 91*
Rickerd, Donald Sheridan 1931- *WhoAm 90*
Rickershauser, Charles Edwin, Jr. 1928- *St&PR 91*
Rickert, David E. 1951- *St&PR 91*
Rickert, Edwin Weimer 1914- *WhoE 91*
Rickert, Jeanne Martin 1953- *WhoEmL 91*
Rickert, Kenneth Wilson, Jr. 1946- *St&PR 91*
Rickert, Marv 1921-1978 *Ballpl 90*
Rickert, Robert Richard 1936- *WhoE 91*
Rickert, Wm. J. 1924- *St&PR 91*
Rickertsen, Donald LeRoy 1948- *WhoSSW 91*
Ricketson, James Doyle 1932- *St&PR 91*
Ricketson, Richard D. 1936- *St&PR 91*
Ricketts, Barrie L. 1949- *St&PR 91*
Ricketts, Deborah Ann 1952 *WhoAmW 91*
Ricketts, Gary Eugene 1935- *WhoAm 90*
Ricketts, Henry *PenDiDA 89*
Ricketts, Jacob Wilcox *PenDiDA 89*
Ricketts, Joanne Elizabeth *BiDrAPA 89*
Ricketts, John Adrian 1924- *WhoAm 90*
Ricketts, John Benjamin 1954- *WhoSSW 91*
Ricketts, Mac Linscott 1930- *ConAu 130*
Ricketts, Mary Jane Gnegy 1925- *WhoWrEP 89*
Ricketts, Michael Edward 1954- *WhoEmL 91*
Ricketts, Richard *PenDiDA 89*
Ricketts, Shirley C. *St&PR 91*
Ricketts, Steven Walter 1942- *St&PR 91*
Ricketts, Thomas Lee 1942- *WhoSSW 91*
Ricketts, Thomas R. 1931- *St&PR 91*
Ricketts, Thomas Roland 1931- *WhoAm 90*
Rickey, Branch 1881-1965 *Ballpl 90 [port], BioIn 16, WorAlBi*
Rickey, Frank 1888-1953 *Ballpl 90*
Rickey, George W. 1907- *BioIn 16, WhoAmA 91*
Rickey, George Warren 1907- *WhoAm 90*
Rickey, Roberta Natalie 1951- *WhoAmW 91*
Rickhoff, Romayne Goranson 1934- *St&PR 91*
Rickin, Sheila Anne 1945- *WhoAmW 91, WhoE 91, WhoEmL 91, WhoWor 91*
Ricklefs, Merle Calvin 1943- *WhoWor 91*
Rickler, Barbara Nancy *BiDrAPA 89*
Rickler, Kenneth C *BiDrAPA 89*
Rickles, Don 1926- *WorAlBi*
Rickles, Donald Jay 1926- *WhoAm 90*
Rickles, George A 1912- *BiDrAPA 89*
Rickles, William H 1933- *BiDrAPA 89*
Rickless, Herman 1906- *BiDrAPA 89*
Ricklin, Arthur H. 1934- *WhoAm 90*
Rickman, Alan *ConTFT 8*
Rickman, Fred Dempsey, Jr. 1953- *St&PR 91*
Rickman, H P 1918- *ConAu 32NR*
Rickman, Raymond Leon 1956- *WhoSSW 91*
Rickman, Wayne Lee 1957- *WhoSSW 91*
Rickman, William Warren 1942- *St&PR 91*
Rickover, Hyman G. 1900-1986 *WorAlBi*
Ricks, David Artel 1942- *WhoWor 91*

Ricks, Donald Jay 1936- *WhoAm 90*
Ricks, Henry C, Jr. 1918- *BiDrAPA 89*
Ricks, John Howard 1926- *St&PR 91*
Ricks, Joycia Camilla 1949- *WhoEmL 91, WhoSSW 91*
Ricks, Ron 1949- *St&PR 91*
Ricks, Thomas E. 1946- *St&PR 91*
Ricks, Thomas Edwin 1955- *WhoE 91*
Ricky, Ang 1947- *WhoWor 91*
Ricky, Michael Raymond 1950- *WhoE 91*
Rico, Francisco 1942- *WhoWor 91*
Rico, Joseph John 1954- *WhoHisp 91*
Rico, Julie 1957- *WhoHisp 91*
Riconda, Harry 1897-1958 *Ballpl 90*
Ricottilli, John, Jr. 1933- *St&PR 91*
Rida, Muhammad Rashid 1865-1935 *BioIn 16*
Ridabock, Ray 1904-1970 *WhoAmA 91N*
Ridd, John Anthony 1939- *WhoSSW 91*
Ridde, Richard Carl 1957- *WhoE 91*
Riddel, Joseph Neill 1931- *WhoAm 90*
Riddell, Charlotte 1832-1906 *FemiCLE*
Riddell, Charlotte Eliza Lawson Cowan 1832-1906 *BioIn 16*
Riddell, Chris *AuBYP 90*
Riddell, Chris F *BiDrAPA 89*
Riddell, Grahame E. 1946- *St&PR 91*
Riddell, J.F. 1953- *St&PR 91*
Riddell, J. H., Mrs. 1832-1906 *BioIn 16*
Riddell, J.H., Mrs. 1832-1906 *TwCLC 40 [port]*
Riddell, James H. 1925- *St&PR 91*
Riddell, Maria 1772-1812 *FemiCLE*
Riddell, Matthew Donald Rutherford 1918- *WhoAm 90*
Riddell, Michael James 1942- *St&PR 91*
Riddell, Richard Harry 1916- *WhoAm 90*
Riddell, Robert L. *BioIn 16, NewYTBS 90*
Riddell, Tally D. 1946- *St&PR 91*
Ridder, Anton De 1929- *IntWWM 90*
Ridder, Bernard H., Jr. 1916- *St&PR 91*
Ridder, Bernard Herman 1916- *BioIn 16*
Ridder, Bernard Herman, Jr. 1916- *WhoAm 90*
Ridder, Daniel Hickey 1922- *WhoAm 90*
Ridder, Eric 1918- *St&PR 91, WhoAm 90*
Ridder, Herman 1851-1915 *BioIn 16*
Ridder, Herman Henry 1908-1969 *BioIn 16*
Ridder, Joseph B. 1920-1989 *BioIn 16*
Ridder, Katie *BioIn 16*
Ridder, Paul Anthony 1940- *WhoAm 90, WhoSSW 91*
Ridder, Walter T. *NewYTBS 90*
Ridder, Walter Thompson 1917-1990 *BioIn 16*
Ridder, Willem 1930- *St&PR 91*
Ridderbusch, Karl 1932- *IntWWM 90, PenDiMP*
Ridderstrom, Bo 1937- *IntWWM 90*
Riddick, Daniel Howison 1941- *WhoAm 90*
Riddick, Douglas Smith 1942- *WhoSSW 91, WhoWor 91*
Riddick, Eva Jayne 1959- *WhoSSW 91*
Riddick, Frank Adams, Jr. 1929- *WhoAm 90, WhoWor 91*
Riddick, Lark C. 1957- *ODwPR 91*
Riddick, Merrill K. *BioIn 16*
Riddiford, Lynn Moorhead 1936- *WhoAmW 91*
Riddle, Barbara Annette 1949- *WhoSSW 91*
Riddle, Charles Daniel 1945- *WhoSSW 91*
Riddle, Christopher Thomas 1958- *WhoE 91*
Riddle, Constance Christine 1923- *WhoAmW 91, WhoWor 91*
Riddle, David Vernon 1947- *BiDrAPA 89*
Riddle, Dennis Raymond 1933- *St&PR 91*
Riddle, Dennis Raymond 1934- *WhoAm 90, WhoSSW 91*
Riddle, Donald Husted 1921- *WhoAm 90*
Riddle, Elmer 1914-1984 *Ballpl 90*
Riddle, Fay Aycock 1949- *WhoSSW 91*
Riddle, Frederick *PenDiMP*
Riddle, H. Marvin, III 1930- *St&PR 91*
Riddle, Ian 1949- *IntWWM 90*
Riddle, James Frank *BiDrAPA 89*
Riddle, John J *BiDrAPA 89*
Riddle, John Paul 1901-1989 *BioIn 16*
Riddle, John Thomas, Jr 1933- *WhoAmA 91*
Riddle, John Wallace 1864-1941 *BioIn 16*
Riddle, Lawrence Hollister 1954- *WhoSSW 91*
Riddle, Malcolm Graeme 1909- *St&PR 91*
Riddle, Mark Alan 1948- *BiDrAPA 89, WhoE 91*
Riddle, Maxwell 1907- *AuBYP 90, WhoWor 91*
Riddle, Michael Howe 1946- *WhoEmL 91*
Riddle, Morton 1909- *MusmAFA*
Riddle, Nelson 1921-1985 *OxCPMus, WorAlBi*
Riddle, Oscar 1877-1968 *DcScB S2*
Riddle, Pauline Peck 1932- *IntWWM 90*
Riddle, Peter H. 1939- *IntWWM 90*
Riddle, Raymond Erwin 1947- *WhoEmL 91, WhoSSW 91*
Riddle, Sturgis Lee 1909- *WhoAm 90*
Riddle, Theodate Pope 1868-1946 *BioIn 16*
Riddle, Toby *WhNaAH*
Riddle, Veryl Lee 1921- *WhoAm 90*
Riddle, Wayne Clifton 1949- *WhoE 91*
Riddleberger, Denny 1945- *Ballpl 90*
Riddles, Juli Beth 1966- *WhoSSW 91*
Riddles, Libby *BioIn 16*
Riddoch, Peter Roy 1947- *St&PR 91*
Riddolls, W.E. 1916- *St&PR 91*
Ride, Sally 1951- *WorAlBi*
Ride, Sally K. *BioIn 16*
Ride, Sally Kristen 1951- *WhoAm 90, WhoAmW 91*
Rideal, Eric Keightley 1890-1974 *DcScB S2*
Riden, Michael David 1947- *WhoEmL 91, WhoSSW 91*
Ridenhour, Joseph Conrad 1920- *WhoAm 90*
Ridenhour, Norman Graham 1923- *St&PR 91*
Ridenour, James Amburs 1939- *WhoSSW 91*
Ridenour, James Franklin 1932- *WhoE 91*
Ridenour, Windsor Allen 1938- *St&PR 91, WhoSSW 91*
Rideout, Alice 1872- *BiDWomA*
Rideout, David Edward 1937- *WhoAm 90*
Rideout, Janet Litster 1939- *WhoAmW 91*
Rideout, Patricia Irene 1931- *WhoAm 90*
Rideout, Philip Munroe 1936- *WhoAm 90, WhoWor 91*
Rideout, Phyllis McCain 1938- *WhoAmW 91*
Rideout, Roy P. 1947- *St&PR 91*
Rideout, Thomas Gerard 1948- *WhoAm 90, WhoE 91*
Rideout, Thomas P. *BioIn 16*
Rideout, Walter Bates 1917- *WhoAm 90, WhoWrEP 89*
Rider, Brent Taylor 1942- *St&PR 91*
Rider, Gregory Ashford 1949- *WhoEmL 91*
Rider, James Wesley 1935- *WhoSSW 91*
Rider, Kenneth Lloyd 1943- *WhoWor 91*
Rider, Marilyn Ann 1941- *WhoAmW 91*
Rider, Morrette Leroy 1921- *IntWWM 90*
Rider, N. Park 1936- *St&PR 91*
Rider, Quila Owens 1942- *WhoAmW 91*
Ridge, Major 1770-1839 *WhNaAH*
Ridge, Helen Sophie 1932- *WhoAmW 91*
Ridge, John 1803-1839 *WhNaAH*
Ridge, John Drew 1909- *WhoAm 90*
Ridge, Lola 1873-1941 *FemiCLE*
Ridge, Martin 1923- *WhoAm 90*
Ridge, Michele Moore 1947- *WhoE 91*
Ridge, Thomas Joseph 1945- *WhoAm 90, WhoE 91*
Ridgely, Henry duPont 1949- *WhoE 91*
Ridgely, Henry Johnson 1913- *WhoE 91*
Ridgen, Delilah Goodroe 1956- *WhoSSW 91*
Ridgeway, Charles *BioIn 16*
Ridgeway, James Fowler 1936- *WhoAm 90, WhoWrEP 89*
Ridgley, Robert Louis 1934- *St&PR 91, WhoAm 90*
Ridgway, Brunilde Sismondo 1929- *BioIn 16, WhoAm 90*
Ridgway, C. David 1930- *St&PR 91*
Ridgway, Charles Baxter 1923- *WhoSSW 91*
Ridgway, David Wenzel 1904- *WhoWor 91*
Ridgway, George 1758?-1823 *PenDiDA 89*
Ridgway, George M. 1936- *St&PR 91*
Ridgway, George Martin 1936- *WhoWor 91*
Ridgway, Gerald Wesley 1918- *St&PR 91*
Ridgway, Helen Jane 1937- *WhoAmW 91*
Ridgway, Jason *AuBYP 90, TwCCr&M 91*
Ridgway, Job 1759-1813 *PenDiDA 89*
Ridgway, John 1785-1860 *PenDiDA 89*
Ridgway, John William 1960- *WhoSSW 91*
Ridgway, Matthew B. 1895- *WorAlBi*
Ridgway, Ralph *PenDiDA 89*
Ridgway, Rozanne LeJeanne 1935- *WhoAm 90, WhoAmW 91*
Ridgway, Sara R. 1944- *ODwPR 91, St&PR 91*
Ridgway, William 1788-1864 *PenDiDA 89*
Ridilla, Andrea Jayne 1956- *WhoAmW 91*
Riding, Laura 1901- *BioIn 16, FemiCLE, WhoAm 90*
Ridinger, Jay George, VII 1934- *WhoWor 91*
Ridinger, Mary Louise 1945- *WhoWor 91*
Ridings, Dorothy Sattes 1939- *WhoAm 90, WhoAmW 91*
Ridings, Kaye Gordon 1937- *St&PR 91*
Ridings, Susan Elizabeth 1949- *WhoAmW 91*
Ridington, William Robin 1939- *WhoAm 90*
Ridker, Ronald Gene 1931- *WhoE 91*
Ridl, Jack Rogers 1944- *WhoWrEP 89*
Ridlehuber, Hugh Wilson 1934- *BiDrAPA 89*
Ridlen, Lillian May Heigle 1946- *WhoAmW 91, WhoSSW 91*
Ridler, Anne 1912- *BioIn 16, FemiCLE*
Ridler, Gregory L. 1946- *St&PR 91*
Ridley, Adam Nicholas 1942- *WhoWor 91*
Ridley, Betty Ann 1926- *WhoAmW 91, WhoWor 91*
Ridley, Donald Eugene 1927- *St&PR 91*
Ridley, Florida Ruffin 1861-1943 *HarlReB*
Ridley, Gregory D, Jr 1925- *WhoAmA 91*
Ridley, Hazel 1900?- *EncO&P 3*
Ridley, J. Samuel 1949- *WhoAm 90*
Ridley, James L. *WhoSSW 91*
Ridley, James R. 1928- *St&PR 91*
Ridley, James Russell 1928- *WhoAm 90*
Ridley, Mark L. 1957- *WhoWor 91*
Ridley, Nicholas 1929- *WhoWor 91*
Ridloff, Richard 1948- *St&PR 91, WhoAm 90*
Ridlon, James A 1936- *WhoAmA 91*
Ridlon, Jim *BioIn 16*
Ridolfi, Loretta Elizabeth 1933- *WhoAmW 91*
Ridolfo, Alfred Charles 1953- *WhoE 91*
Ridolphi, Lucy Elizabeth 1957- *WhoWrEP 89*
Ridpath, William Marion 1845-1914 *AmLegL*
Ridruejo, Dionisio 1912-1975 *BioIn 16*
Ridwas 1845-1913 *BioIn 16*
Ridzik, Steve 1929- *Ballpl 90*
Rie, Lucie *BioIn 16*
Rie, Lucie 1902- *PenDiDA 89*
Riebe, James Clifford 1942- *St&PR 91*
Riebel, Robert A. 1921- *St&PR 91*
Rieben, Jo *BiDrAPA 89*
Rieber, Edith Finton 1932- *IntWWM 90*
Rieber, Jesse Alvin 1945- *WhoE 91*
Rieber, William Joseph 1949- *WhoWor 91*
Riebeseh1, E. Allan 1938- *WhoE 91, WhoWor 91*
Riebman, Jesse Herman 1929- *St&PR 91*
Riebman, Leon 1920- *St&PR 91, WhoAm 90*
Riebold, Gilbert Adrien 1921- *WhoWor 91*
Riechartz, W. Daniel 1946- *St&PR 91*
Rieche, Klaus Alfred 1937- *WhoWor 91*
Riechmann, Fred B. 1915- *St&PR 91, WhoAm 90*
Rieck, Kristine J. 1942- *St&PR 91*
Rieck, Ray C. 1948- *St&PR 91*
Rieck, William Albert 1942- *WhoE 91*
Riecke, Conrad Charles 1933- *WhoE 91*
Rieckelman, Alice P 1927- *BiDrAPA 89*
Riecken, Ellnora Alma 1934- *WhoAmW 91*
Riecken, Henry William 1917- *WhoAm 90*
Riecker, Gerhard 1926- *WhoWor 91*
Riecker, William H. 1924- *St&PR 91*
Ried, Glenda E. 1933- *WhoWrEP 89*
Riedberger, Jean-Luc Rene Giles 1941- *WhoWor 91*
Riede, David G 1951- *ConAu 131*
Riedeburg, Theodore 1912- *WhoAm 90*
Riedel, Alan F. 1930- *St&PR 91*
Riedel, Alan Ellis 1930- *WhoAm 90*
Riedel, Bernard Edward 1919- *WhoAm 90*
Riedel, Claus Josef 1925- *WhoWor 91*
Riedel, Daniel P. 1939- *St&PR 91*
Riedel, Friedrich Wilhelm 1929- *IntWWM 90*
Riedel, Gottlieb Friedrich 1724-1784 *PenDiDA 89*
Riedel, Herbert Heinz Joachim 1958- *WhoSSW 91*
Riedel, Jack A. 1934- *St&PR 91*
Riedel, John 1940- *St&PR 91*
Riedel, Joyce Lucke 1953- *WhoAmW 91, WhoEmL 91*
Riedel Chihuaria, Ernestine 1930- *IntWWM 90*
Rieder, Nancy Jean 1963- *WhoE 91*
Rieder, Richard Walter 1940- *WhoSSW 91*
Rieder, Ronald F. 1932- *ODwPR 91*
Rieder, Ronald Olrich 1942- *BiDrAPA 89, WhoE 91*
Riederer, Donald Edward 1932- *St&PR 91*
Riederer, Josef 1939- *WhoWor 91*
Riedesel, Donald Weston 1919- *St&PR 91*
Riedesel, William M, II 1946- *BiDrAPA 89*
Riediger, Vernon David 1937- *St&PR 91*
Riedinger, DeMeril A. 1928- *St&PR 91*
Riedinger, James Richard 1921- *St&PR 91*
Riedl, Josef *PenDiDA 89*
Riedl, Rudolf George 1936- *St&PR 91*
Riedl, Steve L. 1955- *St&PR 91*
Riedl, Wm. R. 1940- *St&PR 91*
Riedler, John Florian *BiDrAPA 89*
Riedler, Loreen M. *BiDrAPA 89*
Riedman, Sarah Regal 1902- *AuBYP 90*
Riedy, John P. 1936- *St&PR 91*
Riedy, Mark Joseph 1942- *WhoAm 90*
Riefenstahl, Leni 1902- *WhoWor 91*
Rieff, D.E. 1909- *St&PR 91*
Riefke, Robert Francis 1931- *St&PR 91*
Riefkohl, Gloria Rosangeles 1959- *WhoAmW 91*
Riefler, Donald Brown 1927- *WhoAm 90*
Riegel, Byron William 1938- *WhoAm 90, WhoWor 91*
Riegel, J. Kent 1938- *St&PR 91*
Riegel, Kenneth 1938- *IntWWM 90, PenDiMP*
Riegel, Kurt Wetherhold 1939- *WhoAm 90*
Riegel, Michael Byron 1946- *WhoAmA 91*
Riegel, Warren Francis 1951- *WhoE 91*
Rieger, Audrey F. 1920- *WhoAmW 91*
Rieger, Bela R *BiDrAPA 89*
Rieger, Fritz *PenDiMP*
Rieger, Hank *ODwPR 91*
Rieger, Jan McLane *ODwPR 91*
Rieger, Michael Bernard 1949- *St&PR 91*
Rieger, Mitchell Sheridan 1922- *WhoAm 90, WhoWor 91*
Rieger, Philip Henri 1935- *WhoAm 90*
Rieger, Wolfram 1935- *BiDrAPA 89*
Riegert, Peter 1948- *WorAlBi*
Riegert, Robert Adolf 1923- *WhoAm 90*
Riegle, Donald W., Jr. *BioIn 16*
Riegle, Donald Wayne, Jr. 1938- *WhoAm 90, WhoWor 91*
Riegle, Karen Dewald 1951- *WhoWrEP 89*
Riegle, Linda B. 1947- *WhoAmW 91*
Riegle, Robert Mack 1924- *WhoAmA 91*
Riegler, Josef 1938- *WhoWor 91*
Riegler, Lee Edward 1944- *St&PR 91*
Riegler, Richard Robert 1946- *St&PR 91*
Riehl, Harry Ernest 1943- *St&PR 91*
Riehm, J.W. 1920- *St&PR 91*
Riehm, Sarah Lawrence 1952- *WhoWrEP 89*
Rieke, Blaine Eugene 1933- *St&PR 91*
Rieke, Marc Kimm 1948- *WhoAm 90*
Rieke, Reint Neal 1948- *WhoSSW 91*
Rieke, Ronald Alfred 1951- *WhoWor 91*
Rieke, William Betten 1913- *WhoAm 90*
Rieke, William Oliver 1931- *WhoAm 90*
Rieker, Albert George 1889-1959 *WhoAmA 91N*
Rieker, Anne Ellora 1923- *WhoAmW 91*
Riekert, Lothar Hans 1928- *WhoWor 91*
Riel, Eric Walter 1961- *WhoSSW 91*
Riel, Louis 1817-1864 *WhNaAH*
Riel, Louis 1844-1885 *DcLB 99 [port]*
Riel, Louis David 1844-1885 *WhNaAH [port]*
Rielley, Bernard D. 1937- *St&PR 91*
Rielley, David Joseph, III 1938- *St&PR 91*
Rielly, John Edward 1932- *WhoAm 90*
Rielly, Thomas 1932- *WhoWor 91*
Riely, Caroline Armistead 1944- *WhoAmW 91*
Riely, John 1945- *ConAu 32NR*
Riely, Phyllis Eleanor 1918- *WhoAmW 91*
Rieman, Janece Marie 1929- *St&PR 91*
Rieman, Leticia Linda 1951- *WhoAmW 91*
Rieman, Stephen Ralph 1946- *St&PR 91*
Riemann, Frederick Aloysius 1947- *WhoEmL 91*
Riemann, Georg F. B. 1826-1866 *WorAlBi*
Riemann, Helmut Ernst 1926- *WhoWor 91*
Riemann, Kurt *NewAgMG*
Riemann, Mark L. 1956- *St&PR 91*
Riemanschneider, Tilman 1460?-1531 *IntDcAA 90*
Riemcke, Kathryn Elizabeth 1922- *WhoAmW 91*
Riemenschneider, Albert Louis 1936- *WhoAm 90*
Riemenschneider, Klaus Dieter 1943- *WhoWor 91*
Riemenschneider, Paul Arthur 1920- *WhoAm 90*
Riemer, Delilah 1910- *BiDrAPA 89, WhoAmW 91, WhoE 91*
Riemer, George Arthur 1950- *WhoEmL 91*
Riemer, John Richard 1953- *St&PR 91*
Riemer, Maria D C *BiDrAPA 89*
Riemer, Morris D *BiDrAPA 89*
Riemer, Robert Joseph 1932- *WhoWor 91*
Riemer, Ruby 1924- *WhoWrEP 89*
Riemerschmid, Richard 1868-1957 *PenDiDA 89*
Riemersma, James Karl 1942- *St&PR 91*
Riemke, Richard Allan 1944- *WhoAm 90*
Riendeali, Dennis A. 1956- *St&PR 91*
Riendeau, Dennis A. *St&PR 91*
Rienecker, Ronald J. 1957- *St&PR 91*
Riener, Thomas Clem 1947- *St&PR 91*
Rienhoff, Otto 1949- *WhoWor 91*
Rienner, Lynne Carol 1945- *WhoAm 90, WhoAmW 91*
Rienow, Leona Train 1903?-1983 *AuBYP 90*
Rienow, Robert 1909-1989 *BioIn 16*
Rienstra, Ellen Walker 1940- *WhoWrEP 89*
Rienzi, Anthony Thomas 1920- *WhoAm 90*
Rienzi, Thomas Matthew Michael 1919- *WhoAm 90*
Rienzo, George Ramon *BiDrAPA 89*
Riepe, Dale Maurice 1918- *WhoAm 90*

Riepe, James Sellers 1943- *St&PR 91*
Riepe, Russell Casper 1945- *IntWWM 90*
Rieple, Ted R. 1946- *WhoAm 90*
Rieppel, Ludwig 1861-1960 *WhoAmA 91N*
Riera, Antonio 1950- *WhoE 91*
Riera Guilera, Carme 1948- *EncCoWW*
Rierdan, Jill E. 1945- *WhoAmW 91*
Ries, A.E. *EncCoWW*
Ries, Carole Elizabeth 1940- *WhoAmW 91*
Ries, Daniel Roland 1947- *St&PR 91*
Ries, Edward Richard 1918- *WhoAm 90, WhoSSW 91, WhoWor 91*
Ries, Ferdinand 1784?-1838 *PenDiMP*
Ries, Franz Anton 1755-1846 *PenDiMP*
Ries, Harvey Allen 1943- *BiDrAPA 89*
Ries, Herman Elkan, Jr. 1911- *WhoAm 90*
Ries, John Francis 1923- *St&PR 91*
Ries, Louis *PenDiMP*
Ries, Martin 1926- *WhoAmA 91, WhoE 91*
Ries, Richard K 1947- *BiDrAPA 89*
Ries, Richard Raymond 1953- *WhoWrEP 89*
Ries, Rose 1956- *BiDrAPA 89*
Ries, Therese Feodorovna 1874- *BiDWomA*
Ries, William Campbell 1948- *St&PR 91*
Riesbeck, James E. 1942- *St&PR 91*
Riesberg, Kenneth D. 1939- *St&PR 91*
Riesco, German 1854-1916 *BioIn 16*
Riesco, Nancy 1943- *WhoAmW 91*
Riese, Beatrice *WhoAmA 91*
Riese, Irving *NewYTBS 90*
Riesenbach, Marvin S. 1929- *St&PR 91*
Riesenberg, Felix 1913-1962 *AuBYP 90*
Riesenberg, Robert Alan *BiDrAPA 89*
Riesener, Jean-Henri 1734-1806 *PenDiDA 89*
Riesenfeld, Alphonse 1911-1989 *BioIn 16*
Riesenfeld, Stefan Conrad 1948- *St&PR 91*
Riesenhuber, Heinz Friedrich Ruppert 1935- *WhoWor 91*
Riesenman, John Paul 1955- *BiDrAPA 89*
Riesenmy, Brandon Douglas 1960- *BiDrAPA 89*
Rieser, Leonard Moos 1922- *WhoAm 90*
Rieser, Richard *BioIn 16*
Riesgo, Armando *WhoHisp 91*
Riesman, David 1909- *BioIn 16, WhoAm 90*
Riesman, Evelyn Thompson 1912- *WhoAmW 91*
Riesman, Paul *BioIn 16*
Riesmeyer, R. F. 1948- *St&PR 91*
Riesner, S. Herbert *BioIn 16*
Riess, Bernard F. *EncPaPR 91*
Riess, Cheryl Lynn *BiDrAPA 89*
Riess, Dorothy Young 1931- *WhoAmW 91*
Riess, Gordon Sanderson 1928- *St&PR 91*
Riess, Helen *BiDrAPA 89*
Riess, Lore *WhoAmA 91*
Riessen, Martin Clare 1941- *AuBYP 90*
Riesz, Marcel 1886-1969 *DcScB S2*
Riesz, Peter Charles 1937- *WhoAm 90*
Rieth, Otmar Hans 1916- *St&PR 91*
Rieth, Rodney Dale 1938- *St&PR 91*
Riether, Anne Marie Antoinette *BiDrAPA 89*
Riethle, William Edward, III 1948- *WhoE 91*
Riethman, Robert B. 1947- *St&PR 91*
Rieti, Vittorio *BioIn 16*
Rietjens, Leonardus Henricus T 1929- *WhoWor 91*
Rietman, H Jerome 1927- *BiDrAPA 89*
Rietmulder, Joseph Charles 1963- *WhoE 91*
Rietti, Arturo 1863-1943 *BioIn 16*
Rietveld, Gerrit Thomas 1888-1964 *PenDiDA 89*
Rietveld, Jane 1913- *AuBYP 90*
Rietveld, Wopke Johannes 1937- *WhoWor 91*
Rietz, John T. 1933- *St&PR 91*
Rietz, Kenneth Charles 1941- *WhoWor 91*
Rietz, Robert Andrew 1924- *St&PR 91*
Rieu, Emile Victor 1887-1972 *AuBYP 90*
Rifa'i, Zeid Sameer 1936- *WhoWor 91*
Rifai, Zein Samir 1944- *WhoWor 91*
Rifakes, George Peter 1934- *St&PR 91, WhoAm 90*
Rifbjerg, Klaus 1931- *DcScanL*
Rifbjerg, Klaus Thorvald 1931- *WhoWor 91*
Rife, Donald Lee *BiDrAPA 89*
Rife, Jerry Edwin 1949- *IntWWM 90*
Rife, Jerry Lee 1945- *WhoWor 91*
Rife, Joseph L. 1927- *St&PR 91*
Rife, Marilyn N. 1954- *IntWWM 90*
Rife, Patricia Elizabeth 1957- *WhoAmW 91*
Rifenburgh, Richard Philip 1932- *WhoAm 90*
Riff, Carrie S. 1899- *St&PR 91*
Riffaterre, Michael 1924- *BioIn 16, WhoAm 90*
Riffe, Connie Dianne 1957- *WhoAmW 91*
Riffe, Ernest *ConAu 33NR*
Riffe, Vernal G., Jr. *WhoAm 90*
Riffel, Marlise *BioIn 16*
Riffel, Robert D. 1933- *St&PR 91*
Riffel, Rodney William 1948- *WhoE 91*
Riffert, Robert John 1947- *St&PR 91*
Riffle, Charles E. 1935- *St&PR 91*
Riffone, Dianna Lynn 1965- *WhoAmW 91*
Rifino, Crescenzio 1924- *St&PR 91*
Rifkin, Abraham 1920- *St&PR 91*
Rifkin, Arthur 1937- *BiDrAPA 89, WhoE 91*
Rifkin, Bernard M. 1924- *St&PR 91*
Rifkin, Boris G 1930- *BiDrAPA 89*
Rifkin, Daniel James 1957- *BiDrAPA 89*
Rifkin, Harold 1916- *WhoAm 90*
Rifkin, Harvey Barry *BiDrAPA 89*
Rifkin, Jeremy *BioIn 16*
Rifkin, Jeremy 1945- *ConAu 129, News 90, -90-3*
Rifkin, Jeremy Chicago 1945- *WhoWrEP 89*
Rifkin, Joshua 1944- *IntWWM 90, OxCPMus, PenDiMP*
Rifkin, Larry *ODwPR 91*
Rifkin, Larry Scott 1956- *WhoWor 91*
Rifkin, Lillian *AuBYP 90*
Rifkin, Ned Lee 1949- *WhoAm 90*
Rifkin, William 1920- *St&PR 91*
Rifkind, Arleen B. 1938- *WhoAmW 91*
Rifkind, Malcolm 1946- *WhoWor 91*
Rifkind, Melvyn S. 1925- *ODwPR 91*
Rifkind, Richard Allen 1930- *WhoWor 91*
Rifkind, Robert Singer 1936- *WhoAm 90*
Rifkind, Simon H. 1901- *St&PR 91*
Rifkind, Simon Hirsch 1901- *WhoAm 90*
Rifman, Eileen Nissenbaum 1944- *WhoAmW 91*
Rifner, Lois Jean 1947- *WhoAmW 91*
Rigal, Madam 1750?- *EncCoWW*
Rigamer, Elmore F *BiDrAPA 89*
Rigas, Constantine J *BiDrAPA 89*
Rigas, Harriett Badaker 1934- *WhoAm 90*
Rigat Tortorici, Felipe 1937- *WhoWor 91*
Rigaud, Marie Claude *BiDrAPA 89*
Rigaud, Marie-Claude 1939- *WhoAmW 91*
Rigaux-Bricmont, Benny Patrick 1943- *WhoE 91*
Rigberg, Corey Nyles 1947- *BiDrAPA 89*
Rigby, Elizabeth 1809-1893 *BioIn 16, FemiCLE*
Rigby, Ida Katherine 1944- *WhoAmA 91*
Rigby, Jean 1955- *IntWWM 90*
Rigby, Kenneth 1925- *WhoWor 91*
Rigby, Paul Crispin 1924- *WhoAm 90*
Rigby, Perry Gardner 1932- *WhoAm 90*
Rigby, Richard Norris 1935- *WhoWrEP 89*
Rigby-Leather, Ela Miloszewski *BioIn 16*
Rigby-Leather, Geoffrey *BioIn 16*
Rigden, John S. *BioIn 16*
Rigdon, Ronald Milton 1937- *WhoWor 91*
Rigel, Darrell Spencer 1950- *WhoE 91*
Rigelwood, Diane Colleen 1950- *WhoAmW 91*
Riger, Robert *BioIn 16*
Riger, Robert Paris 1960- *St&PR 91*
Rigg, Diana *BioIn 16*
Rigg, Diana 1938- *WhoAm 90, WhoWor 91, WorAlBi*
Rigg, Gerald B. 1938- *St&PR 91*
Rigg, L Isobel 1919- *BiDrAPA 89*
Rigg, Margaret Ruth 1929- *WhoAmA 91*
Rigg, Matthew Vassar 1947- *WhoSSW 91*
Riggall, Steven O'Neill 1950- *BiDrAPA 89*
Riggan, Ronald Thomas 1947- *St&PR 91*
Riggert, Robert Henry 1948- *WhoEmL 91*
Riggi, Stephen Joseph 1937- *WhoAm 90*
Riggin, Aileen 1906- *BioIn 16*
Riggin, Emory B. 1842-1924 *AmLegL*
Riggin, Lee Pepper 1924- *WhoE 91*
Riggins, John *BioIn 16*
Riggins, Ralph *ODwPR 91*
Riggins, Suzy Lee 1951- *WhoE 91*
Riggio, Anita *AuBYP 90*
Riggio, John 1929- *BioIn 16*
Riggleman, Shirley Evelyn 1934- *WhoAmW 91*
Riggott, Charles Robert 1927- *WhoAm 90*
Riggs, Anna Claire 1944- *WhoAmW 91*
Riggs, Benjamin C 1914- *BiDrAPA 89*
Riggs, Benjamin Clapp, Jr. 1945- *WhoE 91*
Riggs, Bobby *BioIn 16*
Riggs, Byron Lawrence, Jr. 1931- *WhoAm 90*
Riggs, David Lynn 1943- *WhoSSW 91*
Riggs, Dionis Coffin 1898- *WhoWrEP 89*
Riggs, Donald Eugene 1942- *WhoAm 90, WhoWor 91*
Riggs, Douglas A. 1944- *St&PR 91, WhoAm 90*
Riggs, Gail Marie 1941- *WhoE 91*
Riggs, Harvey 1914- *St&PR 91*
Riggs, Henry Earle 1935- *WhoAm 90*
Riggs, Ida Berry *AuBYP 90*
Riggs, J.A., Jr. 1909- *St&PR 91*
Riggs, James A. 1936- *St&PR 91*
Riggs, James Arthur 1936- *WhoAm 90*
Riggs, Jeri Ellen 1955- *BiDrAPA 89*
Riggs, John A., III 1934- *St&PR 91*
Riggs, John Arthur 1946- *WhoEmL 91*
Riggs, Lawrence Wilson 1943- *WhoSSW 91*
Riggs, Leonard, II 1943- *WhoAm 90*
Riggs, Lew 1910-1975 *Ballpl 90*
Riggs, Lorrin Andrews 1912- *WhoAm 90*
Riggs, Lynn 1899-1954 *BioIn 16*
Riggs, Lynn Spencer 1946- *WhoWrEP 89*
Riggs, Mary Kathryn 1935- *WhoAmA 91*
Riggs, Mary Lou 1927- *WhoSSW 91*
Riggs, Randall Stuart *BiDrAPA 89*
Riggs, Robert 1896-1970 *WhoAmA 91N*
Riggs, Robert Edwon 1927- *WhoAm 90*
Riggs, Robin L. 1953- *WhoEmL 91*
Riggs, Ronald L. 1944- *St&PR 91*
Riggs, Rosa Kathleen *BiDrAPA 89*
Riggs, Stephen Return 1812-1883 *WhNaAH*
Riggs, Thomas Jeffries, Jr. 1916- *WhoAm 90*
Riggsbee, Jacqueline Sue 1950- *WhoAmW 91, WhoSSW 91*
Riggsby, Dutchie Sellers 1940- *WhoAmW 91*
Riggulsford, Michael James 1956- *WhoWor 91*
Righetti, Dave 1958- *Ballpl 90*
Righi-Lambertini, Egano 1906- *WhoWor 91*
Righteous Brothers *EncPR&S 89*
Righter, Carroll 1900-1988 *BioIn 16*
Righter, Walter Cameron 1923- *WhoAm 90*
Righthand, Vera Fay 1930- *WhoAmW 91*
Rights, Edith Marie Anderson 1927- *WhoAmW 91*
Rigler, Cy 1882- *Ballpl 90*
Rigler, John Barr 1921- *St&PR 91*
Rigney, Bill 1918- *Ballpl 90*
Rigney, Bill 1919- *BioIn 16*
Rigney, Francis J 1923- *BiDrAPA 89*
Rigney, James Oliver, Jr. 1948- *WhoWrEP 89*
Rigney, Johnny 1914-1984 *Ballpl 90*
Rigney, Topper 1897-1972 *Ballpl 90*
Rignold, Hugo 1905-1976 *PenDiMP*
Rigo, Marion Lee Bennett 1948- *WhoAmW 91, WhoSSW 91*
Rigo, Michael Maurice 1956- *WhoSSW 91*
Rigo, Paul Wilson *BioIn 16*
Rigolin, Enio Antonio 1935- *BiDrAPA 89*
Rigolo, Arthur Emil 1909- *WhoAm 90*
Rigolot, Francois 1939- *WhoAm 90*
Rigor, Conrado Nicolas 1942- *WhoWrEP 89*
Rigot, Gerard *BioIn 16*
Rigout, Marcel 1928- *BiDFrPL*
Rigsbee, Ned L. 1941- *St&PR 91*
Rigsbee, William A. 1926- *St&PR 91*
Rigsbee, William Alton 1926- *WhoAm 90*
Rigsbee, William Mark 1956- *WhoSSW 91*
Rigsby, Edith W *BiDrAPA 89*
Rigsby, Roseanne Carole 1956- *WhoAmW 91*
Rigsby, Sheila G. 1955- *WhoAmW 91*
Rigual, Antonio Ramon 1946- *WhoHisp 91*
Rigutti, Mario 1926- *ConAu 131*
Rihm, Paul Charles 1953- *WhoEmL 91*
Rihm, Wolfgang 1952- *IntWWM 90*
Rihoit, Catherine 1946- *EncCoWW*
Riikola, Michael Edward 1951- *WhoEmL 91*
Riikonen, Nancy Cooper 1938- *WhoAmW 91*
Riis, Jacob A. 1849-1914 *BioIn 16, WorAlBi*
Riis, Povl 1925- *WhoWor 91*
Riisgaard, Steen 1951- *St&PR 91*
Rijavec, Andrej 1937- *IntWWM 90*
Rijks, Derk 1933- *WhoWor 91*
Rijo, Jose 1965- *Ballpl 90, WhoHisp 91*
Rikala, Susan Carol 1955- *St&PR 91*
Rike, Linda Stokes 1949- *WhoSSW 91*
Riker, Andrew Lawrence 1868-1930 *EncABHB 4 [port]*
Riker, H. Charles 1921- *St&PR 91*
Riker, Harland Alexander, Jr. 1928- *St&PR 91*
Riker, Walter F., Jr. 1916- *WhoAm 90*
Riker, William Harrison 1920- *WhoAm 90*
Rikhoff, Jean *WhoWrEP 89*
Rikhoff, Jean 1928- *AuBYP 90*
Rikhye, Doris Catherine Hall 1945- *WhoE 91*
Rikhye, Indar Jit 1920- *WhoE 91*
Rikitake, Tsuneji 1921- *WhoWor 91*
Rikki *AuBYP 90*
Rikleen, Lauren Stiller 1953- *WhoAmW 91*
Riklis, Marcia *WhoAm 90*
Riklis, Meshulam *BioIn 16*
Rikoski, Richard A. 1941- *WhoWor 91*
Rikyu *EncJap*
Riland, W. Kenneth *BioIn 16*
Rilander, Kenneth L. 1949- *St&PR 91*
Rilbe, Ulf Christer 1944- *WhoWor 91*
Rile, Joanne Clarissa 1934- *WhoAm 90*
Rilea, Jack Dwight 1930- *St&PR 91*
Riles, Ernest 1960- *Ballpl 90*
Riles, Wilson Camanza 1917- *WhoAm 90*
Riley, Alice Heiskell *WhoAmW 91*
Riley, Ann Peoples 1947- *WhoWor 91*
Riley, Anthony Gaines, Jr. 1942- *WhoSSW 91*
Riley, Anthony William 1929- *WhoAm 90, WhoWrEP 89*
Riley, Arch Wilson, Jr. 1957- *WhoEmL 91*
Riley, B. Gresham 1938- *WhoAm 90*
Riley, B.J. 1925- *St&PR 91*
Riley, Barbara Polk 1928- *WhoWor 91*
Riley, Barbra 1949- *WhoSSW 91*
Riley, Barbra Bayne 1949- *WhoAmA 91*
Riley, Bernard Joseph 1911-1984 *WhoAmA 91N*
Riley, Bridget 1931- *BiDWomA, BioIn 16*
Riley, Bridget Louise 1931- *WhoWor 91*
Riley, Carl Lambert 1951- *IntWWM 90*
Riley, Carroll Lavern 1923- *WhoAm 90*
Riley, Catherine Irene 1947- *WhoAmW 91, WhoE 91*
Riley, Charles E. 1933- *St&PR 91*
Riley, Charles P. 1950- *St&PR 91*
Riley, Charles P., Jr. 1932- *St&PR 91*
Riley, Cheryl *BioIn 16*
Riley, Clayton 1935- *DrBlPA 90*
Riley, Craig Stewart *WhoSSW 91*
Riley, Daniel Edward 1915- *WhoAm 90*
Riley, Daniel Wayne 1949- *St&PR 91*
Riley, David Clyde 1926- *St&PR 91*
Riley, David D. 1961- *WhoE 91*
Riley, David E. 1961- *St&PR 91*
Riley, David Richard 1940- *WhoSSW 91*
Riley, Denise 1948- *FemiCLE*
Riley, Dennis Daniel 1943- *IntWWM 90*
Riley, Derek Mason 1939- *WhoWor 91*
Riley, Derrell Wayne 1951- *WhoEmL 91*
Riley, Dolores Marie 1941- *WhoAmW 91*
Riley, Dorothy Comstock 1924- *WhoAm 90, WhoAmW 91*
Riley, Dorothy Elaine 1944- *WhoAmW 91*
Riley, E.H. 1934- *St&PR 91*
Riley, Francena 1957- *WhoAmW 91*
Riley, Frank J. 1928- *St&PR 91*
Riley, Frank Joseph 1949- *WhoE 91*
Riley, Fredrick Raynard 1961- *WhoEmL 91*
Riley, G. Micheal 1934- *WhoAm 90*
Riley, Gerard J. 1927- *ODwPR 91*
Riley, Glenda 1938- *WhoAmW 91*
Riley, Harold John, Jr. 1940- *WhoSSW 91*
Riley, Harris DeWitt, Jr. 1924- *WhoAm 90*
Riley, Helene Maria Kastinger 1939- *WhoSSW 91*
Riley, Henry Charles 1932- *St&PR 91, WhoAm 90*
Riley, Howard 1943- *IntWWM 90*
Riley, Ivers W. 1932- *St&PR 91*
Riley, Ivers Whitman 1932- *WhoAm 90*
Riley, Jack 1935- *WhoAm 90*
Riley, James Joseph 1919- *WhoAm 90, WhoE 91, WhoWor 91*
Riley, James Whitcomb 1849-1916 *WorAlBi*
Riley, Jeannie C 1945- *ConAu 129*
Riley, Jeffrey A. 1949- *St&PR 91*
Riley, Joan 1958- *FemiCLE*
Riley, Jocelyn *BioIn 16*
Riley, Jocelyn 1949- *SmATA 60 [port]*
Riley, Jocelyn Carol 1949- *WhoWrEP 89*
Riley, John 1955- *WhoEmL 91*
Riley, John Earl 1922- *St&PR 91*
Riley, John Edmund, Jr. 1952- *WhoSSW 91*
Riley, John Francis 1936- *St&PR 91*
Riley, John Graham 1945- *WhoAm 90*
Riley, John Winchell, Jr. 1908- *WhoAm 90, WhoWor 91*
Riley, Joseph Harry 1922- *WhoAm 90*
Riley, Joseph J. *ODwPR 91*
Riley, Joseph John 1941- *St&PR 91*
Riley, Joshua Dean 1962- *WhoSSW 91*
Riley, Karen E. 1950- *St&PR 91*
Riley, Katherine Margaret 1960- *WhoE 91*
Riley, Kay Evon 1941- *St&PR 91*
Riley, Kenneth *BioIn 16*
Riley, Kevin Charles 1952- *WhoSSW 91*
Riley, Larry *ODwPR 91*
Riley, Larry 1952- *DrBlPA 90*
Riley, Laurie Schatz *ODwPR 91*
Riley, Lawrence Joseph 1914- *WhoAm 90*
Riley, Leslie Walter, Jr. 1926- *WhoAm 90*
Riley, Lisa Marie 1961- *WhoAmW 91*
Riley, Malcolm Wood 1927- *St&PR 91*
Riley, Margaret *BiDrAPA 89*
Riley, Maria 1933- *WhoE 91*
Riley, Marilyn Gledhill 1954- *WhoE 91*
Riley, Matilda White 1911- *BioIn 16, ConAu 132, WhoAm 90, WhoAmW 91*
Riley, Michael 1964- *IntWWM 90*
Riley, Michael David 1945- *WhoWrEP 89*
Riley, Millie Willett 1935- *WhoWrEP 89*
Riley, Monica 1926- *WhoE 91*
Riley, Olive Murle 1932- *St&PR 91*
Riley, Pat *BioIn 16, NewYTBS 90 [port]*
Riley, Pat 1945- *WorAlBi*
Riley, Pat Moffeit, Sr. 1923- *WhoSSW 91*
Riley, Patricia Ann 1956- *WhoSSW 91*

Riley, Patricia Yvonne 1958- *WhoAmW 91*
Riley, Patrick Gavan Duffy 1927- *WhoAm 90*
Riley, Patrick James 1936- *St&PR 91*
Riley, Patrick James 1945- *WhoAm 90*
Riley, Paul 1948- *WhoSSW 91*
Riley, Paul David 1938- *BiDrAPA 89*
Riley, Peter James 1956- *WhoSSW 91*
Riley, R. Wayne 1938- *ODwPR 91*
Riley, Ralph 1924- *WhoWor 91*
Riley, Ramon R. 1935- *St&PR 91*
Riley, Randy James 1950- *WhoAm 90*
Riley, Rebecca *WhoWrEP 89*
Riley, Richard Leon 1932- *BiDrAPA 89*
Riley, Robert Annan, III 1955- *WhoE 91, WhoEmL 91, WhoWor 91*
Riley, Robert Bartlett 1931- *WhoAm 90*
Riley, Robert Edward 1930- *WhoAm 90*
Riley, Robert Richard, Jr. 1948- *WhoSSW 91*
Riley, Ronald P. 1948- *St&PR 91*
Riley, Rosetta M. 1940- *St&PR 91*
Riley, Royal *BioIn 16*
Riley, Stephen Thomas 1908- *WhoAm 90*
Riley, Teddy *BioIn 16*
Riley, Terry 1935- *IntWWM 90, NewAgE 90, WhoAm 90*
Riley, Tex *MajTwCW*
Riley, Thomas L. 1937- *St&PR 91*
Riley, Thomas Leslie 1927- *WhoSSW 91*
Riley, Tim 1960- *ConAu 129*
Riley, Victor J., Jr. 1931- *St&PR 91, WhoAm 90, WhoE 91*
Riley, W. Joseph 1934- *St&PR 91*
Riley, W. Mercedes *BioIn 16*
Riley, Walter *BioIn 16*
Riley, William 1931- *St&PR 91*
Riley, William Bell 1861-1947 *BioIn 16*
Riley, William Franklin 1925- *WhoAm 90*
Riley, William James, Jr. 1946- *WhoWor 91*
Riley, William T *BiDrAPA 89*
Riley-Land, Sarah 1947- *WhoAmA 91*
Riley-Smith, Jonathan *BioIn 16*
Rilke, Rainer Maria 1875-1926 *BioIn 16, ConAu 132, MajTwCW, PoeCrit 2 [port], WorAlBi, WrPh*
Rilke-Westhoff, C. *BiDWomA*
Rill, James F. 1933- *NewYTBS 90 [port]*
Rill, James Franklin 1933- *WhoAm 90, WhoWor 91*
Rilling, Helmuth 1933- *IntWWM 90, PenDiMP*
Rilly, Cheryl Ann 1952- *WhoWrEP 89*
Rima, Ingrid Hahne *WhoAm 90*
Riman, Josef 1925- *WhoWor 91*
Rimando, Estanislao O *BiDrAPA 89*
Rimarcik, Joseph Carl 1939- *St&PR 91*
Rimbach, Evangeline Lois 1932- *WhoAmW 91*
Rimbaud, Arthur 1854-1891 *BioIn 16, WorAlBi*
Rimbaud, Jean Nicolas Arthur 1854-1891 *BioIn 16*
Rimberg, Kjeld 1943- *WhoWor 91*
Rimbotti, Francesco Mauro 1936- *WhoWor 91*
Rimel, Rebecca Webster 1951- *WhoAm 90*
Rimel, Warden M 1930- *BiDrAPA 89*
Rimer, J. Thomas *ConAu 130*
Rimer, John Thomas 1933- *WhoAm 90*
Rimerman, Ira Stephen 1938- *St&PR 91, WhoE 91*
Rimerman, Morton W. 1929- *St&PR 91*
Rimerman, Morton Walter 1929- *WhoAm 90*
Rimes, Myrtle L. 1938- *St&PR 91*
Rimm, Michael Lawrence *BiDrAPA 89*
Rimm, Virginia Mary 1933- *WhoWrEP 89*
Rimmele, Frederick C. 1915- *St&PR 91*
Rimmele, Frederick Charles 1915- *WhoE 91*
Rimmer, Christine L. 1950- *WhoWrEP 89*
Rimmer, Jack 1921- *WhoAm 90*
Rimmer, Kenneth George 1947- *WhoEmL 91*
Rimmer, Stephen King 1948- *St&PR 91*
Rimmer, William 1862-1936 *OxCPMus*
Rimmington, Edith 1902- *BiDWomA*
Rimoin, David Lawrence 1936- *WhoAm 90*
Rimpel, Auguste Eugene, Jr. 1939- *WhoE 91*
Rimpela, Matti Keijo 1942- *WhoWor 91*
Rimrott, Friedrich Paul J. 1927- *WhoAm 90*
Rimsky-Korsakov, Nikolai 1844-1908 *WorAlBi*
Rimsky-Korsakov, Nikolay 1844-1908 *BioIn 16, PenDiMP A*
Rimstad, Wynn H. 1944- *St&PR 91*
Rin, Zengi 1935- *WhoWor 91*
Rinaldi, Alberto 1939- *IntWWM 90*
Rinaldi, Ann 1934- *BioIn 16*
Rinaldi, Frank Robert 1927- *St&PR 91*
Rinaldi, Heidi Abuabara *WhoAmW 91*
Rinaldi, Jack Ismael 1946- *St&PR 91*
Rinaldi, John Frank 1945- *WhoE 91*
Rinaldi, Keith Allen 1962- *WhoE 91*
Rinaldi, Keith Stephen 1952- *WhoE 91*
Rinaldi, Margarita 1935- *IntWWM 90*
Rinaldi, Nicholas Michael 1934- *WhoWrEP 89*
Rinaldi, Ophelia Sandoval 1933- *WhoHisp 91*
Rinaldi, Susan Mary *BiDrAPA 89*
Rinaldini, Luis E. 1953- *St&PR 91*
Rinaldini, Luis Emilio 1953- *WhoAm 90*
Rinaldo des Trois-Echelles du Mayne *EncO&P 3*
Rinaldo, Helen 1922- *WhoAmW 91, WhoE 91, WhoWor 91*
Rinaldo, Matthew John 1931- *WhoAm 90, WhoE 91*
Rinaldo, Michael *ODwPR 91*
Rinaldo, Susan Smith 1957- *BiDrAPA 89*
Rinaman, James Curtis, Jr. 1935- *WhoAm 90*
Rinard, R.E. 1950- *St&PR 91*
Rinauro, Paul D. 1943- *St&PR 91*
Rinck, Edward C 1903- *BiDrAPA 89*
Rinck, Elizabeth Appel 1961- *WhoAmW 91*
Rinck, James Richard 1958- *WhoEmL 91*
Rinck, William E 1934- *BiDrAPA 89*
Rincon, Andy 1959- *Ballpl 90*
Rincon, Humberto 1963- *WhoSSW 91*
Rind, Clementina *BioIn 16*
Rind, Kenneth William 1935- *St&PR 91*
Rind, Sherry 1952- *WhoWrEP 89*
Rinder, George Greer 1921- *WhoAm 90*
Rinderknecht, Riger Raymond 1942- *St&PR 91*
Rindfleisch, Donald L. 1947- *St&PR 91*
Rindfleisch, Jan *WhoAmA 91*
Rindge, Debora Anne 1956- *WhoAmA 91*
Rindisbacher, Peter 1806-1834 *WhNaAH*
Rindlaub, Jean Wade *BioIn 16*
Rindlaub, John W. *BioIn 16*
Rindlaub, John Wade 1934- *WhoAm 90, WhoE 91*
Rindt, Jochen 1942-1970 *BioIn 16*
Rinearson, Peter Mark 1954- *WhoAm 90, WhoEmL 91*
Rineberg, William J. 1937- *St&PR 91*
Rineer, Mary Elizabeth 1948- *WhoSSW 91*
Rinehart, Amy 1880?-1958? *BioIn 16*
Rinehart, Arthur M 1919- *BiDrAPA 89*
Rinehart, Arthur Middleton 1919- *WhoE 91*
Rinehart, Charles R. 1947- *WhoAm 90*
Rinehart, Charles Robert 1947- *St&PR 91*
Rinehart, Dana Gillman 1946- *WhoAm 90*
Rinehart, Gary Lee 1940- *St&PR 91*
Rinehart, Harry Elmer 1921- *WhoSSW 91*
Rinehart, James Forrest 1950- *WhoSSW 91*
Rinehart, James Raymond 1930- *St&PR 91*
Rinehart, Jonathan 1930- *ODwPR 91*
Rinehart, Kathryn Ann 1948- *WhoAmW 91*
Rinehart, Mary 1876-1958 *FemiCLE*
Rinehart, Mary Roberts 1876-1958 *BioAmW, BioIn 16, TwCCr&M 91, WorAlBi*
Rinehart, Michael 1934- *WhoAmA 91*
Rinehart, Nita *WhoAmW 91*
Rinehart, Peggy J. 1950- *St&PR 91*
Rinehart, Raymond G. 1922- *St&PR 91*
Rinehart, Richard H 1958- *BiDrAPA 89*
Rinehart, Steven O. 1946- *St&PR 91*
Rinehart, William Francis 1925- *St&PR 91*
Rinek, Robert Pierson 1952- *St&PR 91*
Rinenberg, Lillian S. 1904-1990 *BioIn 16*
Riner, Ronald Nathan 1949- *WhoEmL 91*
Rines, Robert Harvey 1922- *WhoAm 90, WhoWor 91*
Rines, S. Melvin 1924- *St&PR 91, WhoE 91*
Rines, Stanley E. 1921- *St&PR 91*
Rinesmith, Terry L. 1942- *St&PR 91*
Riney, Hal *BioIn 16*
Riney, Hal Patrick 1932- *WhoAm 90*
Riney, Thomas Charles 1951- *WhoEmL 91*
Rinfret, Jean-Claude 1929- *OxCCanT*
Rinfret, Pierre Andre 1924- *St&PR 91*
Ring, Alfred A. 1905- *WhoSSW 91*
Ring, Alvin Manuel 1933- *WhoAm 90*
Ring, Anne Cecelia 1964- *WhoAmW 91*
Ring, Blanche 1871-1961 *BioIn 16, OxCPMus*
Ring, Chester A., III 1927- *St&PR 91*
Ring, Edward A *WhoAmA 91*
Ring, Gary Norman 1949- *WhoEmL 91*
Ring, Gerald J. 1928- *WhoAm 90*
Ring, Hans 1927- *WhoWor 91*
Ring, Herbert Everett 1925- *WhoWor 91*
Ring, Jackson A. 1940- *St&PR 91*
Ring, James Edward Patrick 1940- *WhoAm 90, WhoE 91*
Ring, James Walter 1929- *WhoAm 90*
Ring, Jimmy 1895-1965 *Ballpl 90*
Ring, John Donald 1959- *WhoE 91*
Ring, Kenneth 1935- *EncPaPR 91*
Ring, Leonard M. 1923- *WhoAm 90, WhoWor 91*
Ring, Malvin Emanuel 1919- *WhoSSW 91*
Ring, Margaret R. *WhoWrEP 89*
Ring, Martin 1918- *St&PR 91*
Ring, Nancy G 1956- *WhoAmA 91*
Ring, Robert G. *St&PR 91*
Ringadoo, Veerasamy 1920- *WhoWor 91*
Ringbeck, Jurgen 1955- *WhoWor 91*
Ringblom, Christopher Nils 1949- *WhoWor 91*
Ringdahl, Irving C 1924- *BiDrAPA 89*
Ringdahl, Robert E. 1924- *St&PR 91*
Ringel, Dean 1947- *WhoEmL 91*
Ringel, Robert Lewis 1937- *WhoAm 90*
Ringelblum, Emanuel 1900-1944 *BioIn 16*
Ringen, Catherine Oleson 1943- *WhoAm 90*
Ringenberg, John Jay 1954- *St&PR 91*
Ringer, James Milton 1943- *WhoAm 90, WhoE 91*
Ringer, Jerome 1935- *ODwPR 91*
Ringer, Jerome M. 1935- *St&PR 91*
Ringer, Larry Joel 1937- *WhoSSW 91*
Ringer, Walter M., III 1947- *St&PR 91*
Ringerwole, Joan Mae 1943- *IntWWM 90*
Ringger, Peter 1923- *EncO&P 3, EncPaPR 91*
Ringgold, Faith *BioIn 16*
Ringgold, Faith 1930- *WhoAmA 91*
Ringgold, Faith 1934- *BiDWomA*
Ringham, Rodger Falk 1920- *WhoAm 90*
Ringhaver, Lance Christian 1939- *St&PR 91*
Ringhaver, Randal *St&PR 91*
Ringhofer, Joseph Frank 1936- *St&PR 91*
Ringius, Carl 1879-1950 *WhoAmA 91N*
Ringkjob, Erik Tuxen 1937- *WhoAm 90*
Ringland, Adrian A., Jr. 1925- *St&PR 91*
Ringland, Charles J. 1933- *St&PR 91*
Ringle, Brett Adelbert 1951- *WhoEmL 91, WhoSSW 91*
Ringleben, Joachim 1945- *WhoWor 91*
Ringlee, Robert James 1926- *WhoAm 90*
Ringler, David S. 1948- *St&PR 91*
Ringler, Joseph Jakob 1730-1804 *PenDiDA 89*
Ringler, Lenore *WhoAm 90*
Ringler, Philipp Joseph *PenDiDA 89*
Ringler, Sharon Mattila 1948- *WhoWrEP 89*
Ringler, William Sylvester 1939- *St&PR 91*
Ringling, John N. 1866-1936 *WorAlBi*
Ringmaster, The *MajTwCW*
Ringness, Charles Obert *WhoAmA 91*
Ringness, Ronald Christian 1949- *St&PR 91*
Ringo, David Leer 1912- *St&PR 91*
Ringo, David Leer 1940- *BiDrAPA 89*
Ringo, James Joseph 1935- *WhoSSW 91*
Ringo, Philip J. 1942- *St&PR 91*
Ringoen, Richard Miller 1926- *St&PR 91, WhoAm 90*
Ringoir, Severin Maria Ghislenus 1931- *WhoWor 91*
Ringold, Alan Lynn 1936- *BiDrAPA 89*
Ringrose, David Robert 1938- *WhoAm 90*
Ringswald, Michael Anthony 1950- *St&PR 91*
Ringuet Le Prince *PenDiDA 89*
Ringuette, Adrien Lanthier 1925- *St&PR 91*
Ringwald, Molly *BioIn 16*
Ringwald, Molly 1968- *WorAlBi*
Ringwall, Curt A. A. 1942- *WhoWor 91*
Ringwood, Gwen 1910-1984 *FemiCLE*
Ringwood, Gwen Pharis 1910-1984 *OxCCanT [port]*
Rini, Donald Anthony 1935- *St&PR 91*
Rini, James Richard 1956- *WhoSSW 91*
Rinier, Harold E *BiDrAPA 89*
Rink, Kathleen Clare 1954- *WhoAmW 91*
Rink, Lawrence Donald 1940- *WhoAm 90*
Rink, Linda 1951- *WhoAmW 91*
Rink, Paul 1912- *AuBYP 90*
Rink, Robert F. 1931- *WhoAm 90*
Rink, Robert Joseph 1942- *St&PR 91*
Rink, Wesley Winfred 1922- *WhoAm 90*
Rinke, Lynn Therese 1955- *WhoAmW 91*
Rinkel, Margaret Elizabeth 1928- *WhoWrEP 89*
Rinkel, Sherman A. 1925- *St&PR 91*
Rinkenberger, Richard Krug 1933- *WhoE 91, WhoWor 91*
Rinker, Andrew, Jr. 1957- *WhoEmL 91*
Rinker, Marshall Edison 1904- *St&PR 91*
Rinker, Marshall Edison, Sr. 1904- *WhoAm 90*
Rinker, Ruby Stewart 1936- *WhoAmW 91*
Rinkevich, Charles Francis 1940- *WhoAm 90*
Rinkey, Benjamin S. 1941- *St&PR 91*
Rinkoff, Barbara Jean 1923-1975 *AuBYP 90*
Rinn, Marvin L. 1933- *St&PR 91*
Rinn, William A 1913- *BiDrAPA 89, WhoE 91*
Rinnert, Kathy J. 1957- *WhoEmL 91*
Rinsch, Charles E. 1932- *St&PR 91*
Rinsch, Charles Emil 1932- *WhoAm 90*
Rinser, Luise 1911- *EncCoWW, WhoWor 91*
Rinsky, Jeffrey H 1950- *BiDrAPA 89*
Rinsky, Joel Charles 1938- *WhoWor 91*
Rinsky, Judith Lynn 1941- *WhoAmW 91, WhoE 91*
Rinsland, Roland DeLano 1933- *WhoE 91*
Rinsley, Donald B 1928- *BiDrAPA 89*
Rinsley, Donald Brendan 1928- *WhoAm 90, WhoWor 91*
Rintala, Paavo 1930- *DcScanL*
Rintelmann, William Fred 1930- *WhoAm 90*
Rintzler, Marius 1932- *IntWWM 90*
Rinzel, Daniel Francis 1942- *WhoAm 90*
Rinzler, Allan 1941- *WhoAm 90*
Rinzler, Carl *BiDrAPA 89*
Rinzler, Carol E. *NewYTBS 90*
Rinzler, Carol Gene Eisen 1941- *WhoAm 90, WhoWrEP 89*
Rinzler, Ralph 1934- *WhoAm 90*
Rio, Carlos Alberto Arroyo del 1893-1969 *BioIn 16*
Rio, Linda Karen 1964- *WhoAmW 91*
Rio, Ralph J. *St&PR 91*
Rioja, Carlos 1946- *WhoWor 91*
Riolo, Anthony *BioIn 16*
Riolo-Quinn, Lisa 1963- *WhoAmW 91*
Riom, Adine 1818-1899 *EncCoWW*
Rion, Fount H., Jr. 1920- *St&PR 91*
Riopel, Louis M. 1933- *St&PR 91*
Riopelle, Arthur Jean 1920- *WhoAm 90*
Riopelle, Jean-Paul 1923- *BioIn 16*
Riopelle, Robert John *BiDrAPA 89*
Riordan, Carol Campbell 1946- *WhoAmW 91*
Riordan, Charles E 1938- *BiDrAPA 89*
Riordan, Dale Patrick 1948- *WhoE 91*
Riordan, Denis J. 1936- *St&PR 91*
Riordan, Elliot Joseph 1955- *WhoE 91*
Riordan, Francis Ellen 1915- *WhoAmW 91*
Riordan, George Nickerson 1933- *WhoAm 90*
Riordan, Hugh D *BiDrAPA 89*
Riordan, J. W. *ConAu 129*
Riordan, James Q. 1927- *St&PR 91*
Riordan, James Quentin 1927- *WhoAm 90*
Riordan, John D. 1951- *St&PR 91*
Riordan, John F. 1903-1988 *BioIn 16*
Riordan, John Francis 1936- *WhoAm 90*
Riordan, John Thomas 1945- *WhoAm 90*
Riordan, Joseph Edward 1953- *St&PR 91*
Riordan, Josephine O'Mahoney *BioIn 16*
Riordan, Michael 1946- *WhoWrEP 89*
Riordan, Paul C. 1944- *St&PR 91*
Riordan, Paul James 1927- *WhoSSW 91*
Riordan, Peter *BioIn 16*
Riordan, Robert F. 1942- *St&PR 91*
Riordan, Sue J. 1942- *ODwPR 91*
Riordan, Thomas Michael 1933- *St&PR 91*
Riordan, Thomas Stoddard 1928- *St&PR 91*
Riordan, William F. 1941- *WhoAm 90*
Rios, Armando C., Jr. 1958- *WhoHisp 91*
Rios, Arturo 1948- *BiDrAPA 89*
Rios, Benjamin Bejarano 1931- *WhoHisp 91*
Rios, Carlos A. 1943- *St&PR 91*
Rios, Carlos Oscar *BiDrAPA 89*
Rios, Dolores Garcia 1964- *WhoHisp 91*
Rios, Domingo Teran De Los *EncCRAm*
Rios, Evelyn Deerwester 1916- *WhoSSW 91*
Rios, Francisco Giner de los 1839-1915 *BioIn 16*
Rios, Freddy *WhoHisp 91*
Rios, Irma Garcia 1938- *WhoHisp 91*
Rios, Isabella *HispWr 90*
Rios, Jesus *Ballpl 90*
Rios, Joe 1957- *WhoHisp 91*
Rios, Joseph A. 1941- *WhoHisp 91*
Rios, Juan 1914- *WhoWor 91*
Rios, Juan Antonio 1888-1946 *BioIn 16*
Rios, Juan F *BiDrAPA 89*
Rios, Julian 1941- *IntvSpW [port]*
Rios, Miguel, Jr. 1941- *WhoHisp 91*
Rios, Peter D. 1949- *WhoHisp 91*
Rios, Sylvia C. 1940- *WhoHisp 91*
Rios-Bustamante, Antonio 1948- *WhoHisp 91*
Rios de Betancourt, Ethel 1926- *WhoHisp 91*
Rios R., Adolfo 1959- *WhoWor 91*
Rios-Rodriguez, Rafael 1956- *WhoHisp 91*
Rioux, Berchmans *BiDrAPA 89*
Rioux, Deena Des 1941- *WhoAmA 91*
Rioux, Pierre August *BiDrAPA 89*
Rioux De Messimy, Deena Des 1941- *WhoAmA 91*
Rip, Arie 1941- *WhoWor 91*
Ripa, Frank 1928- *St&PR 91*
Ripberger, Cynthia Lynn 1957- *WhoEmL 91*
Ripberger, Henry A. 1938- *St&PR 91*
Ripeckyj, Andrew Horyslaw 1950- *BiDrAPA 89*
Riperton, Minnie 1947-1979 *DrBlPA 90, WorAlBi*
Ripich, John J. 1901- *St&PR 91*

Ripich, Louis J *BiDrAPA 89*
Ripken, Billy 1964- *Ballpl 90*
Ripken, Cal, Jr. *BioIn 16*
Ripken, Cal, Jr. 1960- *Ballpl 90*
Ripken, Cal, Sr. 1935- *Ballpl 90*
Ripken, Calvin Edwin, Jr. 1960- *WhoAm 90*
Ripley, Alden Lassell 1896-1969 *WhoAmA 91N*
Ripley, Alexandra *BioIn 16*
Ripley, Allen 1952- *Ballpl 90*
Ripley, Arthur 1895-1961 *BioIn 16*
Ripley, Betty Farrally 1915- *WhoAm 90*
Ripley, Craig Meredith 1961- *St&PR 91*
Ripley, Dorothy 1767-1831 *FemiCLE*
Ripley, Edward Franklin 1927- *WhoAm 90*
Ripley, Elizabeth 1906-1969 *AuBYP 90*
Ripley, George 1415?-1490 *EncO&P 3*
Ripley, George 1802-1880 *BioIn 16, WorAlBi*
Ripley, Jack *TwCCr&M 91*
Ripley, John M. 1941- *ODwPR 91*
Ripley, Mary Moncrieffe Livingston *WhoE 91*
Ripley, Michael David 1952- *ConAu 130*
Ripley, Mike *ConAu 130*
Ripley, Patricia F. 1927- *St&PR 91*
Ripley, Ralph Dwain 1928- *St&PR 91*
Ripley, Randall Butler 1938- *WhoAm 90*
Ripley, Robert 1893-1949 *WorAlBi*
Ripley, Robert L. *EncACom*
Ripley, Robert L 1893-1949 *WhoAmA 91N*
Ripley, Sidney Dillon, II 1913- *WhoAm 90*
Ripley, Stuart McKinnon 1930- *WhoWor 91*
Ripley, Thomas Charles 1946- *St&PR 91*
Ripley, Thomas Lloyd 1950- *BiDrAPA 89*
Ripley, Vickie Corbett 1950- *WhoAmW 91*
Ripley, Warren 1921- *ConAu 33NR*
Ripp, Johann Caspar 1681-1726 *PenDiDA 89*
Ripp, Richard J. *St&PR 91*
Ripp, Stephen *BioIn 16*
Rippberger, Gary Lee 1950- *WhoEmL 91*
Rippe, Peter Marquart 1937- *WhoAm 90, WhoSSW 91*
Rippee, Doyle R. 1948- *St&PR 91*
Rippel, Harry Conrad 1926- *WhoAm 90*
Rippel, Jeffrey Alan 1945- *WhoAm 90*
Rippel, John Charles 1926- *WhoE 91*
Rippel, M 1930- *WhoAmA 91*
Rippel, Morris 1930- *BioIn 16*
Rippentrop, Denice M. Langrock 1948- *IntWWM 90*
Ripper, Rita Jo 1950- *WhoAmW 91*
Ripperger-Suhler, Jane Agnes *BiDrAPA 89*
Rippeteau, Darrel Downing 1917- *WhoAm 90*
Rippey, Clayton 1923- *WhoAmA 91*
Rippey, Donald Taylor 1927- *WhoAm 90*
Rippl, George Allyn 1936- *St&PR 91*
Rippl-Ronai, Jozsef 1861-1927 *PenDiDA 89*
Ripple, Jimmy 1909-1959 *Ballpl 90*
Ripple, Kenneth Frances 1943- *WhoAm 90*
Ripple, Louis J. 1945- *St&PR 91*
Ripple, Ronald *St&PR 91*
Ripplinger, George Raymond, Jr. 1945- *WhoAm 90, WhoEmL 91*
ippon, Michael 1938- *PenDiMP*
ippon, Michael George 1938- *IntWWM 90*
ippon, Ruth Margaret 1927- *WhoAmA 91*
ipps, Lewis S. 1932- *St&PR 91*
ipps, Rodney *WhoAmA 91*
ipps, Van 1958- *St&PR 91*
ippy, Frances Marguerite Mayhew 1929- *WhoAm 90, WhoAmW 91, WhoWor 91*
ippy, James Fred 1892-1977 *BioIn 16*
ippy, Rodney Allen 1968?- *DrBlPA 90*
pstein, Charles Benjamin 1913- *WhoAm 90*
rie, Craig Martin 1943- *WhoAm 90, WhoWor 91*
s, Hans 1914- *WhoAm 90*
s, Howard C. 1915- *St&PR 91*
s, William Krakow 1915- *WhoAm 90*
sbeck, Philip Edward 1939- *WhoAmA 91*
sberg, Gerald Lawrence 1930- *St&PR 91*
sberg, Swede 1894-1975 *Ballpl 90*
sby, Emile D *BiDrAPA 89*
sch, James E. 1943- *WhoAm 90*
sch, Martin Donald 1929- *WhoE 91*
sch, William H. 1938- *St&PR 91*
sdon, Antoinette T *BiDrAPA 89*
sdon, David Lyon 1951- *WhoEmL 91*
don, Nancy Read *ODwPR 91*
e, Carl Halley 1915- *St&PR 91*
e, John Ernest 1954- *WhoAmA 91*
ebero, Bill 1938- *ConAu 130*
ebrough, Doug 1954- *WhoAm 90*
eley, Martha Suzannah Heater 1916- *WhoWor 91*
Riseling, Robert Lowell 1941- *WhoAmA 91*
Risen, Stephen Elkin 1941- *BiDrAPA 89*
Risenburgh, Bernard van, I *PenDiDA 89*
Risenburgh, Bernard van, II 1700?-1765? *PenDiDA 89*
Risenburgh, Bernard van, III *PenDiDA 89*
Riser, Brenda Denice 1962- *WhoAmW 91*
Riser, Sharon Judith 1957- *BiDrAPA 89*
Risgaard, Ernest Milton 1936- *St&PR 91*
Risgin, Jim *BioIn 16*
Rish, Stephen A. 1946- *St&PR 91*
Rishel, James Walter, Jr. 1941- *WhoSSW 91*
Rishel, Joseph J. 1940- *WhoAm 90*
Rishel, Joseph John, Jr 1940- *WhoAmA 91*
Rishel, Mary Ann Malinchak 1940- *WhoWrEP 89*
Rishel, Peggy Lynn 1951- *WhoAmW 91*
Rishel, Richard Clinton 1943- *St&PR 91, WhoAm 90*
Rishel, Thomas Walter 1941- *WhoE 91*
Rishell, Robert Clifford 1917-1976 *WhoAmA 91N*
Rishell, William Arthur 1940- *St&PR 91*
Risher, Edward Henkel 1923- *St&PR 91*
Risher, John Robert, Jr. 1938- *WhoAm 90*
Risher-Flowers, Debra *BiDrAPA 89*
Rishton, Timothy John 1960- *IntWWM 90*
Rishwain, Robert J. 1937- *St&PR 91*
Risi, Dino 1916?- *BioIn 16*
Risi, Louis J., Jr. 1937- *WhoAm 90, WhoWor 91*
Risica, Virginia Jean 1957- *WhoAmW 91*
Risien, Cody 1957- *WhoAm 90*
Rising, Austin 1918- *WhoSSW 91*
Rising, Johan Classon 1617-1672 *EncCRAm*
Rising, Suzanne 1964- *WhoAmW 91*
Risinger, D. Michael 1945- *WhoAm 90*
Risinger, James A. 1948- *St&PR 91*
Risinger, Robert Clair *BiDrAPA 89*
Risjord, Norman K. 1931- *WhoWrEP 89*
Risk, George *BioIn 16*
Risk, Gordon Tucker 1943- *BiDrAPA 89*
Risk, J. Fred 1928- *St&PR 91, WhoAm 90*
Risk, Ken R. 1948- *St&PR 91*
Risk, Sydney 1908-1985 *OxCCanT*
Risk, Thomas Neilson 1922- *WhoWor 91*
Riska, Dan-Olof 1944- *WhoWor 91*
Riske, Douglas 1945- *OxCCanT*
Riske, William Kenneth 1949- *WhoAm 90*
Riskin, Gerald H. *St&PR 91*
Riskin, Jules 1926- *BiDrAPA 89*
Riskind, Kenneth J. 1937- *St&PR 91*
Riskind, Kenneth Jay 1937- *WhoAm 90*
Riskind, Mary *AuBYP 90*
Riskind, Mary 1944- *SmATA 60 [port]*
Riskind, Reuben 1919- *St&PR 91*
Riskind, Robert David 1947- *BiDrAPA 89*
Riskus, Stella B *BiDrAPA 89*
Risley, Edyth C. 1928- *WhoAmW 91*
Risley, Henry Brainard 1946- *WhoE 91*
Risley, John Hollister 1919- *WhoAmA 91*
Risley, John P *BiDrAPA 89*
Risley, Kathryn Hanford 1954- *WhoAmW 91*
Risley, Todd Robert 1937- *WhoAm 90, WhoWor 91*
Risman, Michael 1938- *WhoAm 90*
Risner, Paul Edward 1957- *WhoEmL 91*
Risner, Ray D. 1945- *St&PR 91*
Risnes, Helge Briseid 1948- *WhoWor 91*
Risnes, Marilyn Louise Neitzert 1935- *WhoAmW 91*
Risom, Jens 1916- *ConDes 90*
Risom, Ole Christian 1919- *WhoAm 90*
Risquez, Fernando *BiDrAPA 89*
Riss, E.S. 1949 *St&PR 91*
Riss, Eric 1929- *WhoE 91*
Riss, Murray 1940- *WhoAm 90, WhoAmA 91*
Riss, Robert B. 1927- *St&PR 91*
Riss, Robert Bailey 1927- *WhoAm 90, WhoWor 91*
Risse, Guenter Bernhard 1932- *WhoAm 90*
Risse, Klaus H. 1929- *WhoAm 90*
Risse, Klaus Heinz 1929- *St&PR 91*
Risse, Steven Craig 1951- *BiDrAPA 89*
Risser, Fred A. 1927- *WhoAm 90*
Risser, Fred Dean 1938- *BiDrAPA 89*
Risser, James K 1947- *WhoAmA 91*
Risser, James Vaulx, Jr. 1938- *WhoAm 90*
Risser, Paul Gillan 1939- *WhoAm 90*
Risser, Phares N., III 1941- *St&PR 91*
Rissi, William Thomas 1935- *St&PR 91*
Rissinger, Rollin Paul, Jr. 1943- *St&PR 91*
Rissman, Art *ConAu 30NR*
Rissman, Burton Richard 1927- *WhoAm 90*
Rissman, Susan *ConAu 30NR*
Rissmiller, David J *BiDrAPA 89*
Risso, Harry Francis 1929- *WhoHisp 91*
Risso-Novara, Mariangela 1942- *WhoE 91*
Rist, Harold Ernest 1919- *WhoWor 91*
Rist, James Kevin 1956- *BiDrAPA 89*
Rist, Louis G 1888-1959 *WhoAmA 91N*
Rist, Philip Randall 1956- *WhoEmL 91*
Rist, Ray Charles 1944- *WhoE 91*
Ristagno, Robert C. 1953- *St&PR 91*
Ristaniemi, Pentti Vaino Ilmari 1936- *WhoWor 91*
Ristau, Ronald W. 1953- *St&PR 91*
Ristich, Miodrag 1938- *BiDrAPA 89, WhoE 91*
Ristig, Cheryl Ann 1953- *BiDrAPA 89*
Ristig, Kyle Gregory 1954- *WhoSSW 91*
Ristine, Richard Osborne 1920- *St&PR 91*
Ristino, Robert J. 1943- *WhoE 91*
Ristow, Bruno von Buettner 1940- *WhoAm 90*
Ristow, George Edward 1943- *WhoAm 90*
Ristuccia, Patricia Ann 1954- *WhoAmW 91*
Risucci, Donald Andrew 1957- *WhoE 91*
Riswold, Jim *BioIn 16*
Rita *EncO&P 3*
Rita 1850?-1938 *FemiCLE*
Rita, of Cascia 1381?-1457 *BioIn 16*
Rita, A. *EncO&P 3*
Rita, William Edward 1941- *St&PR 91*
Ritardi, Albert F. 1936- *St&PR 91*
Ritardi, Albert Francis 1936- *WhoAm 90, WhoWor 91*
Ritch, Herald LaVern 1951- *WhoE 91*
Ritch, Kathleen 1943- *St&PR 91, WhoAm 90, WhoAmW 91, WhoE 91*
Ritch, Robert Harry 1942- *WhoWor 91*
Ritchard, Cyril 1897-1977 *OxCPMus, WorAlBi*
Ritchee, Paul O'Neal 1931- *St&PR 91*
Ritcheson, Charles Ray 1925- *WhoAm 90*
Ritchey, Arthur F 1918- *BiDrAPA 89*
Ritchey, Claude 1873-1951 *Ballpl 90*
Ritchey, David 1940- *WhoWrEP 89*
Ritchey, Jeanette Mayer 1945- *WhoSSW 91*
Ritchey, John Herbert 1948- *WhoSSW 91*
Ritchey, John J. 1947- *St&PR 91*
Ritchey, Kenneth James 1926- *St&PR 91*
Ritchey, Michael Lee 1956- *WhoEmL 91*
Ritchey, Paul Andrew 1950- *WhoWor 91*
Ritchey, Sherry Yearick 1947- *WhoAmW 91*
Ritchey, William Michael 1925- *WhoAm 90*
Ritchie, Alan Alfred 1939- *St&PR 91*
Ritchie, Alan Isaac 1941- *St&PR 91*
Ritchie, Alan Joseph 1942- *St&PR 91*
Ritchie, Albert 1939- *WhoAm 90*
Ritchie, Alexander Charles 1921- *WhoAm 90*
Ritchie, Andrew C 1907-1978 *WhoAmA 91N*
Ritchie, Ann 1934- *WhoAmA 91*
Ritchie, Anna Cora Ogden Mowatt 1819-1870 *BioIn 16*
Ritchie, Anne Thackeray 1837-1919 *BioIn 16, FemiCLE*
Ritchie, Barbara Gibbons *AuBYP 90*
Ritchie, Cedric Elmer 1927- *St&PR 91, WhoAm 90, WhoWor 91*
Ritchie, Charles *BioIn 16*
Ritchie, Charles Jackson, Jr. 1933- *St&PR 91, WhoAm 90*
Ritchie, Daniel Lee 1931- *WhoAm 90*
Ritchie, Deborah Campbell 1950- *WhoAmW 91*
Ritchie, E.D. 1926- *St&PR 91*
Ritchie, Earl J. 1944- *St&PR 91*
Ritchie, Elspeth Cameron 1958- *BiDrAPA 89*
Ritchie, Eugene *ODwPR 91*
Ritchie, Fred P. 1924- *St&PR 91*
Ritchie, Garry Harlan 1938- *WhoE 91*
Ritchie, Gary Glen 1953- *St&PR 91*
Ritchie, George G, Jr. 1923- *BiDrAPA 89*
Ritchie, Henry S 1934- *BiDrAPA 89*
Ritchie, Jack 1922-1983 *TwCCr&M 91*
Ritchie, Jay 1936- *Ballpl 90*
Ritchie, Jean 1922- *BioIn 16, ConMus 4*
Ritchie, John Anthony *IntWWM 90*
Ritchie, John Bennett 1924- *WhoAm 90*
Ritchie, John C *BiDrAPA 89*
Ritchie, Karen *WhoAmW 91*
Ritchie, Karen 1943- *St&PR 91*
Ritchie, Karen Sue *BiDrAPA 89*
Ritchie, Karen Sue 1949- *WhoEmL 91*
Ritchie, Kenneth A. *St&PR 91*
Ritchie, Kim 1936- *St&PR 91*
Ritchie, Lisa 1961- *WhoSSW 91*
Ritchie, Lyell Kirk 1955- *WhoSSW 91*
Ritchie, Marie P. 1937- *WhoAmW 91*
Ritchie, Mark A. *BioIn 16*
Ritchie, Michael *BioIn 16*
Ritchie, Michael Brunswick 1938- *WhoAm 90*
Ritchie, Michael Karl 1946- *WhoWrEP 89*
Ritchie, Neil Methuen 1897-1983 *DcNaB 1981*
Ritchie, Norman Robert 1933- *WhoAm 90*
Ritchie, Peggy Lou 1945- *WhoAmW 91*
Ritchie, Richard Lee 1946- *WhoAm 90*
Ritchie, Rita 1930- *AuBYP 90*
Ritchie, Robert C. 1929- *St&PR 91*
Ritchie, Robert Cowan 1938- *WhoAm 90*
Ritchie, Robert F. 1917- *St&PR 91*
Ritchie, Robert Field 1917- *WhoAm 90, WhoSSW 91*
Ritchie, Ronald Jay 1952- *WhoE 91*
Ritchie, Ronald Stuart 1918- *WhoAm 90*
Ritchie, Royal Daniel 1945- *WhoAm 90, WhoE 91*
Ritchie, Simon *ConAu 131*
Ritchie, Thomas 1778-1854 *BioIn 16*
Ritchie, W. 1932- *St&PR 91*
Ritchie, Wally 1965- *Ballpl 90*
Ritchie, Ward 1905- *WhoWrEP 89*
Ritchie, William 1941- *WhoAmA 91*
Ritchie, William Augustus 1903- *BioIn 16*
Ritchie, William Johnston 1813-1892 *DcCanB 12*
Ritchie-Calder, Baron 1906-1982 *DcNaB 1981*
Ritchken, Barbara *BiDrAPA 89*
Ritchlin, Martha Ann 1953- *WhoAmW 91*
Ritchotte, Rita Elizabeth 1926- *WhoAmW 91*
Ritenbaugh, Thomas David 1940- *WhoE 91*
Ritenour, Elston Russell 1953- *WhoEmL 91*
Ritenour, Lee *BioIn 16, NewAgMG*
Riter, Stephen 1940- *WhoAm 90*
Riter, William Wollerton 1838-1922 *AmLegL*
Ritholz, Jules 1925- *WhoAm 90*
Ritins, Ilmars 1937- *St&PR 91*
Ritman, Hans 1960- *WhoWor 91*
Ritman, Louis 1889-1963 *WhoAmA 91N*
Ritondaro, G.H. 1946- *St&PR 91*
Ritsch, Frederick Field 1935- *WhoAm 90*
Ritsch, Lisa Catharina 1961- *WhoAmW 91*
Ritschel, James Allan 1930- *WhoWor 91*
Ritschel, William 1864-1949 *WhoAmA 91N*
Ritsema, Coba 1876-1961 *BiDWomA*
Ritsema, Larry James 1950- *St&PR 91*
Ritson, Donna Diane 1955- *WhoAmW 91*
Ritson, Richard 1931- *St&PR 91*
Ritsos, Giannes *MajTwCW*
Ritsos, Yannis 1909- *EuWr 12, MajTwCW, WorAlBi*
Ritsos, Yannis 1909-1990 *NewYTBS 90*
Ritt, Albert E. 1908- *St&PR 91*
Ritt, Howard Edward 1924- *St&PR 91*
Ritt, Martin *BioIn 16*
Ritt, Martin 1914-1990 *NewYTBS 90 [port]*
Ritt, Martin 1920- *WhoAm 90*
Ritt, Paul Edward 1928- *WhoAm 90*
Ritt, William 1901-1972 *EncACom*
Rittberg, Barry Ray *BiDrAPA 89*
Rittberg, Ellen Pober 1952- *WhoWrEP 89*
Rittberger, Werner Heinz 1927- *WhoWor 91*
Rittelmeyer, Louis F, Jr. 1924- *BiDrAPA 89*
Rittenbach, Karen Joan 1959- *WhoE 91*
Rittenberg, Sydney *BioIn 16*
Rittenberg, Vladimir Ivar 1934- *WhoWor 91*
Rittenhouse, Bruce Dean 1951- *WhoSSW 91*
Rittenhouse, Charles 1909-1982 *OxCCanT*
Rittenhouse, David 1732-1796 *EncCRAm*
Rittenhouse, Joseph Wilson 1917- *WhoAm 90*
Rittenhouse, Laura 1956- *ODwPR 91*
Rittenhouse, Ronni 1947- *WhoAmW 91*
Rittenhouse, Thomas Scott 1941- *St&PR 91*
Rittenmeyer, Dennis C. *WhoAm 90*
Rittenoure, Robert Lynn 1943- *WhoSSW 91*
Ritter, Al *BioIn 16*
Ritter, Alfred 1923- *WhoSSW 91*
Ritter, Alfred F., Jr. 1946- *St&PR 91*
Ritter, Alfred Le Grande 1944- *WhoSSW 91*
Ritter, Ann L. 1933- *WhoAmW 91, WhoE 91, WhoWor 91*
Ritter, Anthony B. 1927- *St&PR 91*
Ritter, Baird Stuart 1928- *BiDrAPA 89*
Ritter, Bruce 1927- *BioIn 16, WhoAm 90*
Ritter, Carolyn S. 1934- *St&PR 91*
Ritter, Charles Edward 1938- *WhoAm 90*
Ritter, Charles W., Jr. 1933- *St&PR 91*
Ritter, Christoph, I *PenDiDA 89*
Ritter, Christoph, II 1548-1616 *PenDiDA 89*
Ritter, Christoph, III 1610-1676 *PenDiDA 89*
Ritter, Dale William 1919- *WhoWor 91*
Ritter, Daniel Benjamin 1937- *WhoAm 90*
Ritter, Darlene Mae 1925- *WhoAmW 91*
Ritter, David Allen 1954- *WhoWor 91*
Ritter, Donald Lawrence 1940- *WhoAm 90, WhoE 91*
Ritter, Erica 1948- *FemiCLE*
Ritter, Erika 1948- *OxCCanT*
Ritter, Eugene Kerfoot 1909- *WhoE 91*
Ritter, F. Richard 1932- *St&PR 91*
Ritter, G. Christopher 1956- *WhoEmL 91*
Ritter, Gerhard A. 1929- *WhoWor 91*
Ritter, Gordon Louis 1942- *St&PR 91*

Ritter, Harwood Hugo, II 1935- St&PR 91
Ritter, Henry L. 1941- St&PR 91
Ritter, Jeffrey Michael 1960- WhoWrEP 89
Ritter, Jeremias 1582-1646 PenDiDA 89
Ritter, Jerry E. 1935- St&PR 91, WhoAm 90
Ritter, Johann Wilhelm 1776-1810 WorAlBi
Ritter, John 1948- WhoAm 90, WorAlBi
Ritter, Julian 1909- WhoAmA 91
Ritter, Julian Strawska Fromm WhoAmA 91
Ritter, Karen Anne 1953- WhoAmW 91
Ritter, Karl 1888-1977 BioIn 16
Ritter, Katrina Dania 1963- WhoAmW 91
Ritter, Keith BioIn 16
Ritter, Lawrence 1922- Ballpl 90, WhoWrEP 89
Ritter, Lawrence S. BioIn 16
Ritter, Lou 1875-1952 Ballpl 90
Ritter, Louise BioIn 16
Ritter, Martha Lyn 1957- WhoSSW 91
Ritter, Norman L. 1934- St&PR 91
Ritter, Norman R. 1929- ODwPR 91
Ritter, Renee Gaylinn WhoAmA 91
Ritter, Robert Forcier 1943- WhoAm 90, WhoEmL 91
Ritter, Robert J. 1959- St&PR 91
Ritter, Robert Joseph 1925- WhoE 91, WhoWor 91
Ritter, Robert Merle BiDrAPA 89
Ritter, Rodger L. 1935- WhoSSW 91
Ritter, Teresa G. 1951- WhoAmW 91
Ritter, Tex 1905-1974 OxCPMus
Ritter, Tex 1907-1974 WorAlBi
Ritter, Thelma 1905-1969 WorAlBi
Ritter, Veda Irene WhoAmW 91
Ritter, William Emerson 1856-1944 BioIn 16, DcScB S2
Ritter, Wolf Christoph 1592-1634 PenDiDA 89
Ritterbeck, Lily B BiDrAPA 89
Rittereiser, Robert P. WhoAm 90
Ritterhoff, Charles William 1921- WhoAm 90, WhoE 91, WhoSSW 91
Ritterhoff, Eric John BiDrAPA 89
Ritterman, Sharen Bruneau 1949- WhoEmL 91
Ritterman, Stuart I. 1937- WhoAm 90, WhoWor 91
Rittgers, Albert Joe 1937- St&PR 91
Rittgers, Donald L. 1947- St&PR 91
Rittgers, Rubye Elizabeth 1928- St&PR 91
Ritthaler, Gerald Irvin 1930- WhoAm 90, WhoWor 91
Ritthausen, Karl Heinrich 1826-1912 DcScB S2
Rittmann, Ronald G. 1949- St&PR 91
Rittmann, Ronald George 1949- WhoAm 90
Rittmaster, Robert 1925- St&PR 91
Rittner, Edmund Sidney 1919- WhoAm 90
Rittner, Fritz Wilhelm 1921- WhoWor 91
Ritts, Christy 1957- St&PR 91
Ritts, Edwin Earl, Jr 1948- WhoAmA 91
Ritts, Herb BioIn 16
Ritts, Herbert I. 1912- St&PR 91
Rittwage, William St&PR 91
Ritvo, David Zvi 1949- BiDrAPA 89
Ritvo, Edward R BiDrAPA 89
Ritvo, Joanne Hassing BiDrAPA 89
Ritvo, Jonathan Isaac 1948- BiDrAPA 89
Ritvo, Rachel Z BiDrAPA 89
Ritvo, Roger Alan 1944- WhoAm 90
Ritvo, Samuel 1917- BiDrAPA 89
Ritz, Esther Leah 1918- WhoAm 90
Ritz, Irving 1928- St&PR 91
Ritz, Joseph P. 1929- WhoWrEP 89
Ritz, Lorna J WhoAmA 91
Ritz, Richard L. 1953- St&PR 91
Ritzel, Bud 1943- St&PR 91
Ritzel, Dennis A. 1937- St&PR 91
Ritzel, Joseph William 1958- St&PR 91
Ritzel, Wolfgang Wilhelm 1913- WhoWor 91
Ritzema, Jean Hart 1948- WhoAmW 91
Ritzer, Philip J. 1942- St&PR 91
Ritzer, Teri Ann WhoAmW 91
Ritzinger, Bernard E. 1930- ODwPR 91
Ritzmann, Maryalice ODwPR 91
Ritzu, Barbara Jean 1951- WhoAmW 91
Riu, Victor 1887-1974 WhoAmA 91N
Riva, Douglas 1951- IntWWM 90
Riva Saleta, Luis Octavio 1949- WhoHisp 91
Rivadavia, Bernardino 1780-1845 BioIn 16
Rivard, Adjutor 1868-1945 DcLB 92 [port]
Rivard, George Arthur 1939- WhoE 91
Rivard, George Henry 1931- St&PR 91
Rivard, Jean 1926- WhoAm 90
Rivard, Jean 1940- St&PR 91
Rivard, John Michael BiDrAPA 89
Rivard, Michael Louis 1956- St&PR 91
Rivard, Paul BiDrAPA 89
Rivard, Paul Edmund 1943- WhoAm 90
Rivard, William Charles 1942- WhoAm 90
Rivas, Adela 1954- BiDrAPA 89
Rivas, David 1953- WhoHisp 91
Rivas, Edgar J. 1933- WhoHisp 91
Rivas, Frank 1938- WhoAm 90, WhoWor 91
Rivas, Mercedes 1931- WhoHisp 91
Rivas, Milagros 1955- WhoHisp 91
Rivas, Ronald K. 1958- WhoHisp 91
Rivaz, Alice EncCoWW
Rivell, Maria Jose 1959- BiDrAPA 89
Rivenbark, Jan Meredith 1950- WhoWor 91
Rivenbark, Judy Stovall BiDrAPA 89
Rivenbark, Rembert Reginald, Jr. 1939- St&PR 91
Rivera, Americo, Jr. 1928- WhoHisp 91
Rivera, Ana Delia 1928- WhoAmW 91
Rivera, Angel Luis 1950- WhoSSW 91
Rivera, Angel Miguel 1955- WhoHisp 91
Rivera, Armando 1952- WhoEmL 91
Rivera, Bombo 1952- Ballpl 90
Rivera, Carmen M. 1962- WhoAmW 91
Rivera, Chita 1933- ConTFT 8, OxCPMus, WhoAm 90, WhoAmW 91, WhoHisp 91, WorAlBi
Rivera, Daniel James 1954- WhoSSW 91
Rivera, Diana Huizar 1953- WhoHisp 91
Rivera, Diego 1886-1957 ArtLatA, BioIn 16, EncAL, IntDcAA 90, WorAlBi
Rivera, Edgardo 1953- WhoHisp 91
Rivera, Edith AuBYP 90
Rivera, Edward WhoHisp 91
Rivera, Edwin A. WhoHisp 91
Rivera, Eida Luz 1957- WhoE 91
Rivera, Elias 1937- BioIn 16
Rivera, Elias J 1937- WhoAmA 91
Rivera, Ezequiel Ramirez 1942- WhoHisp 91
Rivera, Fanny 1953- WhoHisp 91
Rivera, Frank 1939- WhoAmA 91
Rivera, Frank E., Sr. 1928- WhoHisp 91
Rivera, Frida Kahlo 1907-1954 BioIn 16
Rivera, Fructuoso 1784?-1854 BioIn 16
Rivera, George 1955- WhoHisp 91
Rivera, Geraldo BioIn 16
Rivera, Geraldo 1943- AuBYP 90, ConAu 32NR, HispWr 90, WhoAm 90
Rivera, Geraldo Miguel 1943- WhoHisp 91
Rivera, Gregorio BioIn 16
Rivera, Hector 1951- WhoHisp 91
Rivera, Hector A. 1943- WhoHisp 91
Rivera, Henry Michael 1946- WhoHisp 91
Rivera, Jim 1922- Ballpl 90
Rivera, Jose Antonio Primo de 1903-1936 BioIn 16
Rivera, Jose Eustasio 1888-1928 BioIn 16
Rivera, Jose Eustasio 1889-1928 HispWr 90
Rivera, Jose Luis 1946- WhoHisp 91
Rivera, Juan 1953- WhoHisp 91
Rivera, Juan M. 1944- WhoHisp 91
Rivera, Juan Manuel 1943- WhoHisp 91
Rivera, Julia E. 1949- WhoHisp 91
Rivera, Laura E. 1945- WhoHisp 91
Rivera, Louis Reyes 1945- BioIn 16, WhoWrEP 89
Rivera, Lucia 1938- WhoHisp 91
Rivera, Lucy 1937- WhoHisp 91
Rivera, Luis 1964- Ballpl 90
Rivera, Luis Eduardo 1940- WhoHisp 91
Rivera, Luis Ernesto 1950- St&PR 91, WhoHisp 91
Rivera, Luis J. 1953- WhoHisp 91
Rivera, Luis Munoz 1859-1916 BioIn 16
Rivera, Marco Antonio 1945- WhoHisp 91
Rivera, Mario Angel 1941- WhoHisp 91
Rivera, Martin Garcia 1963- WhoHisp 91
Rivera, Mercedes A. 1954- WhoHisp 91
Rivera, Miguel Primo de 1870-1930 BioIn 16
Rivera, Miguel R BiDrAPA 89
Rivera, Miquela C. 1954- WhoHisp 91
Rivera, Miquela Carleen 1954- WhoWrEP 89
Rivera, Oscar R. 1956- WhoEmL 91, WhoSSW 91
Rivera, Rafael Rene 1950- WhoHisp 91
Rivera, Raul 1930- WhoHisp 91
Rivera, Ray WhoHisp 91
Rivera, Richard E. 1947- WhoAm 90
Rivera, Robert A. 1940- St&PR 91
Rivera, Ron WhoHisp 91
Rivera, Samuel 1957- WhoE 91
Rivera, Sandra Lynn 1955- WhoHisp 91
Rivera, Theodore Basiliso 1955- WhoHisp 91
Rivera, Thomas D. 1928- WhoHisp 91
Rivera, Tomas BioIn 16
Rivera, Tomas 1935-1984 ConAu 32NR, HispWr 90
Rivera, Vicki Laura 1945- WhoWrEP 89
Rivera, Victor Manuel 1916- WhoAm 90, WhoHisp 91
Rivera, Victoria A BiDrAPA 89
Rivera, Vincent 1950- WhoHisp 91
Rivera, Walter 1955- WhoHisp 91
Rivera, William McLeod 1934- WhoE 91, WhoHisp 91
Rivera-Alvarez, Miguel-Angel 1952- WhoHisp 91
Rivera-Bustamante, Juan A BiDrAPA 89
Rivera-Carrion, Ruben BiDrAPA 89
Rivera-Castro, Ericka BiDrAPA 89
Rivera-Colon, Lucas 1918- St&PR 91
Rivera-Cruz, Ramon BiDrAPA 89
Rivera-Cuesta, Carmen I BiDrAPA 89
Rivera-Dominguez, Manuel BiDrAPA 89
Rivera-Garcia, Ignacio 1914- WhoHisp 91
Rivera-Gomez, Daniel Rene 1962- WhoSSW 91
Rivera Gracia, Maria Teresa 1946- WhoAmW 91
Rivera Irias, Ariel 1943- WhoWor 91
Rivera-Lara, Ruth M BiDrAPA 89
Rivera-Lopez, Angel 1944- WhoHisp 91
Rivera-Maldonado, Jose H BiDrAPA 89
Rivera-Matos, Noelia 1949- WhoHisp 91
Rivera Mendez, Raul BiDrAPA 89
Rivera-Morales, Iksen BiDrAPA 89
Rivera-Morales, Roberto 1953- WhoHisp 91, WhoSSW 91, WhoWor 91
Rivera-Nieves, Pedro BiDrAPA 89
Rivera-Oktem, Milagros R BiDrAPA 89
Rivera-Ortiz, Gilberto 1932- WhoSSW 91
Rivera-Pagan, Carmen A. 1923- WhoHisp 91
Rivera Perez, Efrain E. WhoHisp 91
Rivera-Perez, Rafael A BiDrAPA 89
Rivera-Rivera, Felix A. 1948- WhoHisp 91
Rivera-Rodas, Hernan 1940- WhoHisp 91
Rivera-Soto, Roberto Andres 1953- St&PR 91
Rivera Y Moncada, Fernando De 1725-1781 EncCRAm
Riverin, Bruno 1941- WhoAm 90, WhoWor 91
Riverman, Rylla Claire 1955- WhoAmW 91
Rivero, Andres 1936- WhoWrEP 89
Rivero, Andres 1960- WhoSSW 91
Rivero, Eliana S. 1940- WhoHisp 91
Rivero, Emilio Adolfo 1947- WhoHisp 91
Rivero, Hector M. WhoHisp 91
Rivero, Jose Antonio 1931- St&PR 91
Rivero, Jose Luis Bustamante y 1894-1989 BioIn 16
Rivero, Karen L. 1957- WhoEmL 91
Riveron, Enrique 1902- WhoAmA 91
Rivers, Bobby BioIn 16
Rivers, Bonnie McFarlane 1945- WhoAmW 91
Rivers, Caryl 1937- WhoE 91, WhoWrEP 89
Rivers, Charles Donald 1936- St&PR 91
Rivers, David BioIn 16
Rivers, Edwin Arthur, Jr. 1955- WhoSSW 91
Rivers, Elfrida ConAu 31NR, MajTwCW
Rivers, Elias Lynch 1924- WhoAm 90
Rivers, Francine 1947- ConAu 130
Rivers, Helene 1916- WhoAmW 91, WhoWor 91
Rivers, Jessie Mae 1933- WhoAmW 91
Rivers, Joan 1933- WhoAm 90, WhoAmW 91, WorAlBi
Rivers, Joan 1937- BioIn 16, WhoWrEP 89
Rivers, Joan Nadia 1944- WhoAmW 91
Rivers, John Minott, Jr. 1945- WhoSSW 91
Rivers, Johnny 1942- EncPR&S 89, WorAlBi
Rivers, Kenneth Allen 1944- BiDrAPA 89
Rivers, L. Mendel 1905-1970 WorAlBi
Rivers, Larry 1923- IntDcAA 90, WorAlBi
Rivers, Larry 1925- WhoAmA 91
Rivers, Louis 1922- DrBlPA 90
Rivers, Malcolm IntWWM 90
Rivers, Marie Bie 1928- WhoAmW 91, WhoWor 91
Rivers, Mercedes M de BiDrAPA 89
Rivers, Mickey 1948- Ballpl 90
Rivers, Olivia Burnett 1919- EncO&P 3
Rivers, Otis Thomas 1961- WhoSSW 91
Rivers, Patrick 1920- ConAu 131
Rivers, Pearl 1849-1896 BioAmW
Rivers, Porter, Jr. 1927- St&PR 91
Rivers, Richard Davis 1934- St&PR 91, WhoAm 90
Rivers, Richard Robinson 1942- WhoAm 90
Rivers, Robert Alfred 1923- WhoAm 90
Rivers, Sam 1930- BioIn 16
Rivers, Victoria Z 1948- WhoAmA 91
Rivers, Wilga M. BioIn 16
Rivers, Wilga Marie 1919- WhoAm 90
Rivers-Bulkeley, Noel Timothy R 1954- BiDrAPA 89
Riverside, John AuBYP 90, MajTwCW
Rives, Amelie 1863-1945 BioAmW
Rives, Barbara Anna Sunderland 1941- IntWWM 90
Rives, Chip BioIn 16
Rives, Harry Clayton 1920- St&PR 91
Rives, John Edgar 1933- WhoSSW 91
Rives, Robert Landon 1933- St&PR 91, WhoAm 90
Rives, Sharon J. 1953- St&PR 91
Rives, Stanley Gene 1930- WhoAm 90
Rives, William Cabell 1793-1868 BioIn 16
Rives, William D. 1943- WhoAm 90
Rives, William Legrande 1940- St&PR 91
Rivet, Diana Wittmer 1931- WhoE 91
Rivet, Jean Francois 1757-1804 BioIn 16
Rivet, Laurie Jean 1955- WhoAmW 91
Rivette, Christopher James 1963- WhoSSW 91
Rivette, Francis Robert 1952- WhoE 91
Rivette, Gerard Bertram 1932- WhoAm 90
Rivette, Jacques 1928- BioIn 16
Rivie, Daniel Juan 1964- WhoHisp 91
Riviello Bazan, Antonio 1926- WhoWor 91
Riviere, Jean-Pierre Marcie- BioIn 16
Riviere, Rosemarie Marcie- BioIn 16
Rivierez, Hector 1913- BioIn 16
Rivin, Nancy ODwPR 91
Rivington, James 1724-1802 BioIn 16, EncCRAm
Rivizzigno, Victoria Lynne 1947- WhoSSW 91
Rivkin, Allen NewYTBS 90
Rivkin, Allen 1903-1990 BioIn 16, ConAu 130
Rivkin, B. 1883-1945 EncAL
Rivkin, Donald Herschel 1924- WhoAm 90
Rivkin, Ellis 1918- WhoAm 90
Rivkin, Jack Leon 1940- WhoAm 90, WhoE 91
Rivkin, Laurence S 1937- BiDrAPA 89
Rivkind, Melvin 1919- St&PR 91
Rivlin, Alice Mitchell 1931- WhoAm 90, WhoAmW 91
Rivlin, Benjamin 1921- WhoAm 90
Rivlin, David BioIn 16
Rivlin, Gerald B. 1929- St&PR 91
Rivlin, Ronald Samuel 1915- WhoAm 90
Rivoyre, Christine de 1921- EncCoWW
Riwkin-Brick, Anna 1908-1970 AuBYP 90
Rix, Donald Melvin 1930- St&PR 91
Rix, John 1947- St&PR 91
Rix, Steven C. 1939- St&PR 91
Rix, Steven Carl 1939- WhoAm 90
Rix, Timothy John 1934- WhoWor 91
Rixey, Eppa 1891-1963 Ballpl 90 [port]
Rixford, Oscar Theodore 1925- St&PR 91
Rixon, James Michael 1945- WhoE 91
Rixon, Robert N. 1948- WhoWrEP 89
Rizal, Jose 1861-1896 NinCLC 27 [port]
Rizam, Ihsan 1939- St&PR 91
Rizer, E. Lloyd 1930- St&PR 91
Rizk, Christine Marie 1953- WhoAmW 91
Rizk, Hikmat Youssef 1947- WhoWor 91
Rizk, Laila Galal 1961- WhoWor 91
Rizk, Magdi Shafik 1937- BiDrAPA 89
Rizk, Nabila 1945- BiDrAPA 89
Rizk, Rida Yousef BiDrAPA 89
Rizkalla, John 1935- ConAu 129
Riznerova, L'udmila 1872-1951 EncCoWW
Riznic, Jovica Radomir 1951- WhoWor 91
Rizo, Marco 1916- WhoHisp 91
Rizopoulos, Andreas Christos 1941- WhoWor 91
Rizos, Jason Dimitri 1923- WhoWor 91
Rizos, John 1950- WhoWor 91
Rizowy, Carlos Guillermo 1949- WhoEmL 91
Rizvi, Syed Mohammed Nasir Raza 1953- WhoWor 91
Rizvi, Tanzeem R. 1949- WhoWor 91
Rizza, Peter Joseph, Jr. 1947- WhoWor 91
Rizzardi, Anton 1919- St&PR 91
Rizzello, Joseph Samuel 1947- WhoAm 90
Rizzetta, Carolyn Teresa 1942- WhoSSW 91
Rizzi, Louis Leon 1932- St&PR 91
Rizzi, Paul C., Jr. 1946- St&PR 91
Rizzi, Ruthann Patricia 1963- WhoEmL 91
Rizzie, Dan 1951- WhoAmA 91
Rizzini, Vittorio 1925- WhoWor 91
Rizzitello, Nicholas Anthony 1953- WhoE 91
Rizzo, Adolfo E 1930- BiDrAPA 89
Rizzo, Anthony Augustine 1928- WhoAm 90
Rizzo, Edward Michael 1945- St&PR 91
Rizzo, Francis 1936- IntWWM 90, WhoAm 90, WhoE 91
Rizzo, Frank A. 1932- St&PR 91
Rizzo, Frank Lazarro BioIn 16
Rizzo, Frank Simon 1944- St&PR 91
Rizzo, James J. 1934- St&PR 91
Rizzo, Jeffrey Francis 1954- St&PR 91
Rizzo, John Anthony 1941- WhoE 91
Rizzo, Johnny 1912-1977 Ballpl 90
Rizzo, Mary Ann Frances 1942- WhoAmW 91, WhoWor 91
Rizzo, Nicholas D 1913- BiDrAPA 89
Rizzo, Paul J. 1928- St&PR 91
Rizzo, Richard David 1944- WhoAm 90
Rizzo, Richard John 1943- St&PR 91
Rizzo, Salvatore Thomas, Jr. 1964- WhoEmL 91
Rizzo, Terrie Lorraine Heinrich 1946- WhoAmW 91, WhoWor 91
Rizzolo, Ralph 1931- WhoSSW 91
Rizzuto, Ana Maria BiDrAPA 89
Rizzuto, Carlo Raffaello 1937- WhoWor 91

Rizzuto, Carmela Rita 1942- WhoWor 91
Rizzuto, James Joseph 1939- WhoWrEP 89
Rizzuto, Phil 1917- Ballpl 90 [port]
Rizzuto, Phil 1918- BioIn 16
Rizzuto, Pietro BioIn 16
Rizzuto, Sharida Ann 1948- WhoWrEP 89
Ro, Ola 1948- WhoWor 91
Roa Bastos, Augusto 1917- ConAu 131, HispWr 90, WorAu 1980 [port]
Roa Bastos, Augusto Antonio BioIn 16
Roach, Abby Meguire 1876-1968 LiHiK
Roach, Alfred J. 1915- St&PR 91
Roach, Bonnie Lee 1957- WhoAmW 91
Roach, Carlton Wayne 1954- WhoSSW 91
Roach, Dinsmore D. 1945- St&PR 91
Roach, Donald A. 1930- St&PR 91
Roach, Donald Arthur 1930- WhoAm 90
Roach, Ed D. WhoSSW 91
Roach, Eugene Gayle 1932- BiDrAPA 89
Roach, Francis L BiDrAPA 89
Roach, Herbert R., Jr. 1946- St&PR 91
Roach, J. Thurston 1941- St&PR 91
Roach, James Edward 1917- St&PR 91
Roach, James R. WhoAm 90
Roach, James Robert 1922- WhoAm 90
Roach, Jill BioIn 16
Roach, John St&PR 91
Roach, John D. C. 1943- BioIn 16, WhoAm 90
Roach, John Hendee, Jr. 1941- WhoAm 90, WhoE 91
Roach, John Marvil 1920- WhoAm 90
Roach, John Robert 1921- WhoAm 90
Roach, John V. 1938- St&PR 91
Roach, John Vinson, II 1938- WhoAm 90, WhoSSW 91, WhoWor 91
Roach, Kenneth Earl 1929- WhoSSW 91
Roach, Margot Ruth 1934- WhoAm 90
Roach, Mark Carlton 1954- St&PR 91, WhoSSW 91
Roach, Max BioIn 16
Roach, Max 1924- WorAlBi
Roach, Max 1925- DrBlPA 90, OxCPMus
Roach, Maxwell Lemuel 1924- WhoAm 90
Roach, Mel 1933- Ballpl 90
Roach, Neil Edward 1938- BiDrAPA 89
Roach, Paul BioIn 16
Roach, Ralph Lee 1957- WhoE 91
Roach, Robert H. 1941- ODwPR 91
Roach, Robert M. 1928- St&PR 91
Roach, Steve NewAgMG
Roach, Thomas Adair 1929- WhoAm 90
Roach, Timothy J. 1947- St&PR 91
Roach, Tom G. 1924- St&PR 91
Roach, Wesley Linville 1931- St&PR 91, WhoAm 90
Roach, William L 1903- BiDrAPA 89
Roach, William Russell 1940- WhoAm 90, WhoWor 91
Roache, Edward Francis 1923- WhoAm 90
Roache, Fiona Alexandria 1961- WhoAmW 91
Roache, Francis Michael 1936- WhoAm 90
Roache, Gregory Paul 1957- St&PR 91
Roache, Milton Oris, Jr. 1922- WhoAm 90
Roache, Patrick Michael, Jr. 1946- WhoE 91, WhoEmL 91
Roachford, Andrew BioIn 16
Roadarmel, Paul Douglas 1942- WhoWrEP 89
Roadcap, Allan Williamson 1923- St&PR 91
Roaden, Arliss Lloyd 1930- WhoAm 90
Roads, Curtis Bryant 1951- IntWWM 90
Roaldset, Elen 1944- WhoWor 91
Roan, John A. 1945- St&PR 91
Roan, Tattie Mae Williams 1928- WhoSSW 91
Roan, Wicaksana M 1936- BiDrAPA 89
Roane, John Selden 1817-1867 BioIn 16
Roane, Mattie J. 1896- BioIn 16
Roar, Leif 1939- IntWWM 90
Roark, Carl Oliver 1948- St&PR 91, WhoAm 90
Roark, George W 1926- BiDrAPA 89
Roark, Glenn E BiDrAPA 89
Roark, Glenn Earnest 1929- WhoSSW 91
Roark, Helen Wills 1905- BioIn 16
Roark, James Frazer, Jr. BiDrAPA 89
Roark, Jimmy Lee 1948- WhoEmL 91
Roark, Neva Jane 1955- BiDrAPA 89
Roark, Roderic Bruce 1949- WhoSSW 91
Roark, Terry Paul 1938- WhoAm 90
Roarke, Mike 1930- Ballpl 90
Roat, Aldon N 1924- BiDrAPA 89
Roath, Alane Elizabeth 1964- WhoAmW 91
Roath, Clinton A, Jr. 1933- BiDrAPA 89
Roath, K.B. 1935- St&PR 91
Roath, Michael S 1939- BiDrAPA 89
oatz WhoAmA 91
ob, Charles Granville 1913- WhoAm 90
ob, Joseph M. 1942- St&PR 91
ob, Joseph Michael 1942- WhoE 91
obach, Michael Charles 1953- WhoSSW 91
obachinski, Chester Mark BiDrAPA 89
obar-Dorin, Filip 1940- WhoWor 91
obards, Donald Lynn 1941- St&PR 91
Robards, Jason, Jr. 1922- WorAlBi
Robards, Jason Nelson, Jr. 1922- WhoAm 90
Robards, Preston Orville, Jr. 1944- WhoSSW 91
Robards, Thomas Frederick 1946- St&PR 91, WhoAm 90
Robaska, P. Gordon 1936- St&PR 91
Robason, Randy Deaton 1953- WhoSSW 91
Robato, Jorge Manach y 1898-1961 BioIn 16
Robb, Adelaide Sherwood BiDrAPA 89
Robb, Bruce 1919- WhoAm 90
Robb, Carole 1943- BiDWomA
Robb, Charles 1938- WhoAmA 91
Robb, Charles S. BioIn 16
Robb, Charles Spittal 1939- WhoAm 90, WhoSSW 91, WhoWor 91
Robb, David Buzby, Jr. 1935- WhoAm 90
Robb, David M. 1903-1990 BioIn 16, ConAu 131
Robb, David Metheny, Jr. 1937- WhoAm 90, WhoAmA 91
Robb, Edward Haupt 1912- St&PR 91
Robb, Felix Compton 1914- WhoAm 90
Robb, Inez Callaway 1901?-1979 BioIn 16
Robb, Isabel Hampton 1859-1910 BioIn 16
Robb, James Alexander 1930- WhoAm 90
Robb, James Willis 1918- WhoAm 90
Robb, Janet L. BioIn 16
Robb, John Harold 1940- St&PR 91
Robb, John Wesley 1919- WhoAm 90
Robb, Lynda Bird Johnson 1943- BioIn 16
Robb, Lynda Johnson 1944- WhoAmW 91
Robb, Nathaniel Heyward, Jr. 1942- WhoAm 90
Robb, Peggy Hight 1924- WhoAmA 91
Robb, Raymond R. 1942- St&PR 91
Robb, Richard Arlin 1942- WhoAm 90
Robb, Richard Irving 1935- WhoWrEP 89
Robb, Sheila J. 1947- St&PR 91
Robb, Thomas Bradley 1932- WhoSSW 91, WhoWrEP 89
Robb, Thomas Merrill 1949- BiDrAPA 89
Robb, Walter E., III 1926- St&PR 91
Robb, Walter Lee 1928- WhoAm 90
Robb-Aquino, Marjorie E BiDrAPA 89
Robbart, Charles Foster 1951- WhoE 91
Robbe-Grillet, Alain 1922- BioIn 16, ConAu 33NR, ConTFT 8, EuWr 13, MajTwCW, TwCCr&M 91B, WhoWor 91, WorAlBi
Robberson, Julia Delores 1931- WhoAmW 91
Robbia, Andrea della 1435-1528 PenDiDA 89
Robbia, Girolamo della 1488-1566 PenDiDA 89
Robbia, Luca della 1399?-1482 PenDiDA 89
Robbiano, Dewey, Jr. 1926- BiDrAPA 89
Robbibaro, Joanne C. 1961- WhoSSW 91
Robbie, J. Michael 1948- WhoAm 90
Robbie, Joe 1916-1990 BioIn 16, NewYTBS 90 [port]
Robbin, Anthony Stuart 1943- WhoAmA 91
Robbin, Barry M. 1948- St&PR 91
Robbin, Catherine IntWWM 90
Robbin, Harry J. 1916- St&PR 91
Robbin, Tony 1943- WhoAmA 91
Robbins, Al 1938-1987 BioIn 16
Robbins, Allen Bishop 1930- WhoAm 90
Robbins, Alvin 1941- BiDrAPA 89
Robbins, Ann Turner 1940- WhoAmW 91
Robbins, Anne Francis WhoAmW 91, WhoWor 91
Robbins, Anthony Lee 1935- WhoAm 90
Robbins, Anthony Shawn BiDrAPA 89
Robbins, Arnold 1931- BiDrAPA 89, WhoE 91
Robbins, Arthur S. St&PR 91
Robbins, Bruce 1948- WhoAmA 91
Robbins, Carole Rita 1937- WhoE 91
Robbins, Caroline 1903- WhoAm 90
Robbins, Carrie BioIn 16
Robbins, Carrie 1943- ConDes 90, NotWoAT
Robbins, Catherine Codispoti 1941- WhoWrEP 89
Robbins, Chandler Seymour 1918- WhoAm 90
Robbins, Charles E. BioIn 16
Robbins, Charles F. 1921- St&PR 91
Robbins, Charles H. D. BioIn 16
Robbins, Christine Patricia 1954- WhoAmW 91
Robbins, Cornelius 1931- WhoAm 90
Robbins, Daniel 1933- WhoAm 90
Robbins, Daniel 1947- IntWWM 90
Robbins, Daniel J 1932- WhoAmA 91
Robbins, Darryl Andrew 1945- WhoEmL 91
Robbins, David Alvin 1947- WhoE 91
Robbins, David Arthur 1944- WhoSSW 91
Robbins, David B 1935- BiDrAPA 89
Robbins, David Bruce 1935- WhoE 91
Robbins, David Clark 1937- WhoE 91
Robbins, David Walter, Jr. 1919- WhoAm 90
Robbins, Donald M. 1935- St&PR 91
Robbins, Donald Michael 1935- WhoAm 90
Robbins, Doren Richard 1949- WhoWrEP 89
Robbins, E. Petri 1940- St&PR 91
Robbins, Earl L. 1921- WhoSSW 91
Robbins, Edward R BiDrAPA 89
Robbins, Edwin 1931- St&PR 91
Robbins, Edwin Boyd 1925- St&PR 91, WhoSSW 91
Robbins, Edwin S 1925- BiDrAPA 89
Robbins, Elliott Charles 1946- St&PR 91
Robbins, Enoch G. 1906- St&PR 91
Robbins, Esther Klein 1933- BiDrAPA 89
Robbins, Eugenia S 1935- WhoAmA 91
Robbins, Frances R BiDrAPA 89
Robbins, Frank 1917- EncACom, WhoAmA 91N
Robbins, Fred P 1915- BiDrAPA 89
Robbins, Frederick C. 1916- WorAlBi
Robbins, Frederick Chapman 1916- WhoAm 90, WhoWor 91
Robbins, Gary Edward 1954- WhoAmA 91
Robbins, Gaylen 1943- St&PR 91
Robbins, George William 1940- St&PR 91
Robbins, George William, III 1940- WhoAm 90
Robbins, Gerald H. 1924- St&PR 91
Robbins, Gordon Daniel 1940- WhoSSW 91
Robbins, H. Zane 1930- ODwPR 91
Robbins, Harold 1912- BioIn 16
Robbins, Harold 1916- MajTwCW, WhoAm 90, WhoWor 91, WhoWrEP 89, WorAlBi
Robbins, Harry C. 1925- St&PR 91
Robbins, Henry Zane 1930- WhoAm 90
Robbins, Honey-Miam 1930- WhoWor 91
Robbins, Howard C BiDrAPA 89
Robbins, Hulda D 1910- WhoAmA 91
Robbins, Hulda Dornblatt 1910- WhoAm 90
Robbins, Ira Paul 1949- WhoEmL 91
Robbins, Jack Alan 1944- WhoE 91
Robbins, James Arnold, Jr. 1957- St&PR 91
Robbins, James Bryce, II 1953- St&PR 91
Robbins, James Edward 1931- WhoWor 91
Robbins, James Oliver 1942- BioIn 16
Robbins, James S BiDrAPA 89
Robbins, James Tate 1945- WhoSSW 91
Robbins, Jane Borsch 1939- WhoAm 90, WhoAmW 91
Robbins, Janet Edith 1955- WhoAmW 91
Robbins, Jeffrey Mark 1944- BiDrAPA 89
Robbins, Jerome BioIn 16, NewYTBS 90
Robbins, Jerome 1918- OxCPMus, WhoAm 90, WhoE 91, WhoWor 91, WorAlBi
Robbins, Jerome Walter 1925- WhoAm 90
Robbins, Jerry Hal 1939- WhoAm 90
Robbins, Joan Nash 1941- WhoAmA 91
Robbins, Joan Raff WhoAmW 91
Robbins, John Alan 1948- WhoE 91
Robbins, John Clapp 1921- WhoAm 90
Robbins, John Michael, Jr. 1947- St&PR 91, WhoAm 90
Robbins, Joseph E. 1922- St&PR 91
Robbins, Joseph H. 1924- St&PR 91
Robbins, Judith Hoffman 1937- WhoAmW 91
Robbins, Julien 1950- IntWWM 90
Robbins, Ken BioIn 16
Robbins, Kenneth Ian 1951- BiDrAPA 89
Robbins, Kenneth L. WhoAm 90
Robbins, Kenneth X 1943- BiDrAPA 89
Robbins, Larry Jack 1935- WhoSSW 91
Robbins, Lawrence Harry 1938- WhoAm 90
Robbins, Lee David 1953- WhoE 91
Robbins, Lee Warren, Jr. 1936- WhoE 91
Robbins, Leroy 1904- WhoAmA 91
Robbins, Lionel 1928- St&PR 91
Robbins, Lionel Charles 1898-1984 BioIn 16, DcNaB 1981
Robbins, Louis Jonathan 1956- WhoSSW 91
Robbins, Louise M. 1928-1987 BioIn 16
Robbins, Marcia 1944- ODwPR 91
Robbins, Maria Polushkin BioIn 16
Robbins, Mark D. 1941- St&PR 91
Robbins, Mark Eugene 1953- BiDrAPA 89
Robbins, Martha Helen 1952- WhoAmW 91, WhoEmL 91, WhoWor 91
Robbins, Martin 1931- WhoWrEP 89
Robbins, Marty 1925-1982 BioIn 16, OxCPMus, WorAlBi
Robbins, Marvin 1936- BiDrAPA 89
Robbins, Matthew ConAu 129
Robbins, Melvin Lloyd 1928- St&PR 91
Robbins, Michael D 1933- BiDrAPA 89
Robbins, Michael Jed 1949- WhoAmA 91, WhoE 91
Robbins, Milan 1934- St&PR 91
Robbins, Nancy Christine 1958- WhoSSW 91
Robbins, Nancy Slinker 1923- WhoAmW 91
Robbins, Nina 1965- WhoAmW 91
Robbins, Orem Olford 1915- St&PR 91
Robbins, Orren Bourne 1932- WhoAm 90, WhoE 91
Robbins, Paul Hebert 1914- WhoAm 90
Robbins, Peter Howard 1956- BiDrAPA 89
Robbins, Philip S 1926- BiDrAPA 89
Robbins, Phyllis B BiDrAPA 89
Robbins, Phyllis B. 1934- St&PR 91
Robbins, Ray Charles 1920- St&PR 91, WhoAm 90, WhoSSW 91
Robbins, Richard Leroy 1953- WhoWrEP 89
Robbins, Richard W. St&PR 91
Robbins, Robert St&PR 91
Robbins, Robert Raymond 1946- WhoEmL 91
Robbins, Rossell Hope 1912-1990 BioIn 16, ConAu 131
Robbins, Ruth 1917?- AuBYP 90
Robbins, Sally Ann 1946- WhoAmW 91
Robbins, Samuel K. 1853- AmLegL
Robbins, Shelley E. ODwPR 91
Robbins, Theodore B BiDrAPA 89
Robbins, Thomas Eugene 1936- MajTwCW
Robbins, Thomas Waters, Jr. 1933- BiDrAPA 89
Robbins, Tim BioIn 16
Robbins, Tom BioIn 16, MajTwCW
Robbins, Tom 1936- BestSel 90-3 [port], ConLC 64 [port], WhoAm 90, WhoWrEP 89
Robbins, Trina 1938- WhoAmA 91
Robbins, Vernon Kay 1939- WhoSSW 91
Robbins, Wallace W. 1910-1988 BioIn 16
Robbins, Warren M 1923- WhoAmA 91
Robbins, Wayne TwCCr&M 91
Robbins, Wayne P. 1944- St&PR 91
Robbins, William Curtis, Jr. 1948- WhoWor 91
Robbins, William Michael 1946- St&PR 91
Robbins, William Randolph 1912- WhoE 91, WhoWor 91
Robbins, William S 1916- BiDrAPA 89
Robbins-Wilf, Marcia 1949- WhoAmW 91, WhoE 91, WhoEmL 91, WhoWor 91
Robboy, Ronald 1950- IntWWM 90
Robe, Jane FemiCLE
Robe, Thurlow Richard 1934- WhoAm 90
Robeck, Gordon Gurney 1923- WhoAm 90
Robek, Mary Frances 1927- WhoAm 90
Robel, Eugene Frank BioIn 16
Roben, George Brock BiDrAPA 89
Robenalt, John Alton 1922- WhoAm 90
Roberds, Richard J. 1933- St&PR 91
Roberge, Bert 1954- Ballpl 90
Roberge, Jill Quigley 1955- WhoAmW 91
Roberge, Leo A 1942- BiDrAPA 89
Roberge, M. Sheila WhoAmW 91
Roberge, Marc-Andre 1955- IntWWM 90
Roberge, Skippy 1917- Ballpl 90
Roberson, Bruce H. 1941- WhoAm 90
Roberson, Carol Ann BioIn 16
Roberson, Carolyn A. 1950- WhoAmW 91
Roberson, Charles R. 1933- St&PR 91
Roberson, Clifford Fulton BiDrAPA 89
Roberson, Donald K. 1936- St&PR 91
Roberson, Donald Thomas 1935- St&PR 91
Roberson, Floyd Irvin 1937- WhoAm 90
Roberson, G. Gale 1933- St&PR 91
Roberson, Glenda F. 1942- WhoAmW 91
Roberson, James O. WhoSSW 91
Roberson, Jerri Ann 1958- WhoSSW 91
Roberson, John Chesley 1937- St&PR 91
Roberson, John R. 1930- BioIn 16, ConAu 129
Roberson, John Ronald 1948- St&PR 91
Roberson, John Royster 1930- WhoE 91
Roberson, Kathleen Leigh 1954- WhoEmL 91
Roberson, Kenneth Thomas 1935- WhoSSW 91
Roberson, Kim Elizabeth 1955- WhoAmW 91
Roberson, Linda 1947- WhoEmL 91
Roberson, Loriann 1955- WhoAmW 91
Roberson, Marian Holbrook 1937- WhoAmW 91
Roberson, Nathan Russell 1930- WhoAm 90
Roberson, Richard W. 1947- St&PR 91
Roberson, Robert Stephen 1942- St&PR 91, WhoSSW 91, WhoWor 91
Roberson, Roger Truman 1941- St&PR 91
Roberson, Samuel Arndt 1939- WhoAmA 91
Roberson, Vicky Sue 1946- WhoAmW 91
Roberson, William 1939- WhoAmA 91
Robert I 1274-1329 WorAlBi
Robert I, King of Scotland 1274-1329 BioIn 16

Robert the Bruce 1274-1329 *BioIn 16*
Robert, Adrian *ConAu 32NR*
Robert, Alain Michel 1941- *WhoWor 91*
Robert, Cameron Terrance 1948- *St&PR 91*
Robert, Daniel Winans 1942- *St&PR 91*
Robert, Francois 1946- *BioIn 16*
Robert, Gilbert Oday 1925- *St&PR 91, WhoAm 90*
Robert, Henry Flood, Jr 1943- *WhoAmA 91*
Robert, Jean *WhoAmA 91*
Robert, Joseph Clarke 1906- *WhoSSW 91*
Robert, Joseph-Gaspard *PenDiDA 89*
Robert, Lawrence Wood, IV 1937- *St&PR 91*
Robert, Randolph B. 1922- *St&PR 91*
Robert, Stephen 1940- *WhoAm 90, WhoE 91*
Robert-Houdin, Jean-Eugene 1805-1871 *BioIn 16*
Robertazzi, Thomas Joseph 1928- *St&PR 91*
Roberti, Ercole de' 1451?-1496 *IntDcAA 90*
Roberti, Mario Andrew 1935- *St&PR 91, WhoAm 90*
Roberti, William Vincent 1946- *WhoAm 90*
Robertiello, Charles Edward 1932- *WhoWor 91*
Robertiello, Richard C 1923- *BiDrAPA 89*
Robertiello, Richard Candela 1923- *WhoE 91*
Roberto, Albert Gene 1943- *WhoE 91*
Roberto, Frank Andre 1947- *BiDrAPA 89*
Roberto, Salvatore Richard 1959- *IntWWM 90*
Roberton, Hugh 1874-1952 *PenDiMP*
Roberts, A. Addison 1915- *St&PR 91*
Roberts, Abigail 1748-1823 *FemiCLE*
Roberts, Adele Marie 1941- *WhoAmW 91, WhoSSW 91*
Roberts, Alan S. 1947- *St&PR 91*
Roberts, Alfred S, Jr. 1921- *BiDrAPA 89*
Roberts, Alfred Wheeler, III 1938- *WhoAm 90*
Roberts, Allene S. *ODwPR 91*
Roberts, Ann M. 1954- *WhoAmW 91*
Roberts, Archibald Edward 1915- *WhoWor 91*
Roberts, Arthur 1852-1933 *OxCPMus*
Roberts, Arthur 1912- *IntWWM 90, WhoAm 90*
Roberts, Arthur C *BiDrAPA 89*
Roberts, Ashley Blair 1924- *St&PR 91*
Roberts, B. H. 1857-1933 *BioIn 16*
Roberts, B. K. 1907- *WhoAm 90, WhoWor 91*
Roberts, Barbara 1936- *WhoAm 90, WhoAmW 91*
Roberts, Barbara Baker 1934- *WhoWrEP 89*
Roberts, Barbara Hahn 1942- *WhoAmW 91*
Roberts, Barbara Jean 1934- *WhoAmW 91*
Roberts, Barbara McCue 1955- *WhoE 91*
Roberts, Bernard 1933- *PenDiMP*
Roberts, Bert C., Jr. 1942- *WhoAm 90, WhoE 91*
Roberts, Betty Jo 1927- *WhoAmW 91*
Roberts, Beverly Nance 1954- *WhoE 91, WhoEmL 91*
Roberts, Beverly Randolph 1948- *WhoEmL 91*
Roberts, Bill *BioIn 16*
Roberts, Bill 1914-1978 *WhoAmA 91N*
Roberts, Bill Glen 1938- *WhoAm 90, WhoSSW 91, WhoWor 91*
Roberts, Bip 1963- *Ballpl 90*
Roberts, Blanche Elizabeth 1955- *WhoAmW 91*
Roberts, Bonnie Leslie 1949- *WhoWrEP 89*
Roberts, Brian 1930- *ConAu 30NR*
Roberts, Brian Leon 1959- *WhoAm 90*
Roberts, Brian Michael 1957- *WhoEmL 91*
Roberts, Brian Richard 1906-1988 *BioIn 16*
Roberts, Brigham Henry 1857-1933 *BioIn 16*
Roberts, Bruce 1930- *BioIn 16*
Roberts, Bruce 1947- *BiDrAPA 89*
Roberts, Bruce Elliott *WhoAmA 91*
Roberts, Bruce G. 1949- *St&PR 91*
Roberts, Burnell R. 1927- *St&PR 91*
Roberts, Burnell Richard 1927- *WhoAm 90*
Roberts, Burton Bennett 1922- *WhoAm 90*
Roberts, C. John 1935- *ODwPR 91*
Roberts, C. Kenneth 1930- *WhoAm 90*
Roberts, Carlos A. *ConAu 129*
Roberts, Carol Antonia 1936- *WhoAmW 91*
Roberts, Carol Joy 1953- *WhoAmW 91*
Roberts, Catherin Ann 1944- *BiDrAPA 89*
Roberts, Catherine Christopher 1905- *AuBYP 90*
Roberts, Cathey Jean *BiDrAPA 89*
Roberts, Cecil Johnson *BioIn 16, NewYTBS 90*
Roberts, Celia Ann 1935- *WhoAmW 91, WhoE 91*
Roberts, Chalmers McGeagh 1910- *BioIn 16, WhoAm 90, WhoE 91*
Roberts, Charles 1887-1968 *OxCPMus*
Roberts, Charles A 1918- *BiDrAPA 89*
Roberts, Charles Corwin 1924- *St&PR 91*
Roberts, Charles E. 1950- *St&PR 91*
Roberts, Charles G D 1860-1943 *DcLB 92 [port]*
Roberts, Charles Patrick 1936- *WhoAm 90*
Roberts, Charles S. 1918- *St&PR 91*
Roberts, Charles Wood, Jr. 1962- *WhoSSW 91*
Roberts, Christian 1944- *ConTFT 8 [port]*
Roberts, Christian Bruce 1947- *WhoSSW 91*
Roberts, Christopher Chalmers 1950- *WhoE 91*
Roberts, Clarence Lewis, Jr. 1934- *St&PR 91*
Roberts, Clark Mournane 1932- *WhoSSW 91*
Roberts, Clyde Francis 1924- *WhoAm 90*
Roberts, Clyde Harry 1923- *WhoAmA 91, WhoE 91*
Roberts, Clyde Lafayette, Jr. 1932- *WhoSSW 91*
Roberts, Colette 1910-1971 *WhoAmA 91N*
Roberts, Colin H 1909-1990 *ConAu 132*
Roberts, Craig *BioIn 16*
Roberts, Curt 1929-1969 *Ballpl 90*
Roberts, Dale 1946- *St&PR 91*
Roberts, Dale H. 1941- *St&PR 91*
Roberts, Dan *ConAu 32NR*
Roberts, Daniel Jarrell 1957- *WhoSSW 91*
Roberts, Daniel Thomas 1960- *WhoE 91*
Roberts, Darryl *BioIn 16*
Roberts, Dave 1944- *Ballpl 90*
Roberts, David Caron 1944- *WhoE 91, WhoWor 91*
Roberts, David Dion 1943- *WhoSSW 91*
Roberts, David Glendenning 1928- *WhoAm 90, WhoE 91*
Roberts, David Harrill 1944- *WhoSSW 91*
Roberts, David J. 1944- *St&PR 91*
Roberts, David James *BioIn 16*
Roberts, David Lee 1934- *St&PR 91*
Roberts, David Stanley *BiDrAPA 89*
Roberts, Davis 1917- *DrBIPA 90*
Roberts, Debbie 1951- *WhoSSW 91*
Roberts, Della 1929- *WhoSSW 91*
Roberts, Delmar L. 1933- *WhoWrEP 89*
Roberts, Dennis H. 1954- *St&PR 91*
Roberts, Dennis J. 1942- *St&PR 91*
Roberts, Derek Harry 1932- *BioIn 16*
Roberts, Diana Kaye 1959- *WhoAmW 91*
Roberts, Diane Hill 1947- *WhoWrEP 89*
Roberts, Don E. 1934- *WhoSSW 91*
Roberts, Donald 1923- *WhoAmA 91*
Roberts, Donald Albert 1935- *WhoE 91*
Roberts, Donald Gaylord 1926- *WhoWor 91*
Roberts, Donald John 1945- *WhoAm 90, WhoEmL 91*
Roberts, Donald Lowell 1938- *IntWWM 90*
Roberts, Donald Munier 1935- *WhoAm 90*
Roberts, Donna J. 1935- *St&PR 91*
Roberts, Dora Sandlin 1939- *WhoSSW 91*
Roberts, Doris 1930- *WhoAm 90, WorAlBi*
Roberts, Doris Emma 1915- *WhoAm 90, WhoAmW 91*
Roberts, Dorothy Bougher 1928- *St&PR 91*
Roberts, Dorothy H. 1928- *St&PR 91*
Roberts, Dorothy Hyman 1928- *WhoAmW 91*
Roberts, Dorothy James *NewYTBS 90*
Roberts, Dorothy James 1903-1990 *BioIn 16, ConAu 131, CurBio 90N*
Roberts, Dorothy Mary Gostwick 1906- *FemiCLE*
Roberts, Douglas Earl 1948- *St&PR 91*
Roberts, Dwight Loren 1949- *WhoEmL 91, WhoWor 91*
Roberts, Dwight V. 1935- *St&PR 91*
Roberts, E. F. 1930- *WhoAm 90*
Roberts, E. Wade 1943- *WhoSSW 91*
Roberts, Earl K. 1928- *St&PR 91*
Roberts, Edward Baer 1935- *WhoAm 90, WhoE 91, WhoWor 91*
Roberts, Edward Calhoun 1937- *WhoAm 90, WhoSSW 91*
Roberts, Edward Dryhurst 1904-1989 *ConAu 129*
Roberts, Edward Graham *WhoAm 90*
Roberts, Edward Joseph 1925- *WhoAm 90*
Roberts, Edwin Albert, Jr. 1932- *WhoAm 90*
Roberts, Eileen Doris Frahm 1933- *WhoAmW 91*
Roberts, Elena *ODwPR 91*
Roberts, Elizabeth Dixon 1925- *WhoAmW 91*
Roberts, Elizabeth Madox 1881-1941 *BioAmW, DcLB 102 [port], FemiCLE, LiHiK*
Roberts, Emma 1793?-1840 *FemiCLE*
Roberts, Eric *BioIn 16*
Roberts, Eric 1956- *WhoAm 90, WorAlBi*
Roberts, Eric Wayne 1963- *WhoE 91*
Roberts, Erica Sue 1960- *WhoAmW 91*
Roberts, Ernst Edward 1926- *St&PR 91, WhoAm 90*
Roberts, Estelle 1889-1970 *EncO&P 3, EncPaPR 91*
Roberts, Etta *EncO&P 3*
Roberts, Eugene Leslie, Jr. 1932- *WhoAm 90, WhoE 91*
Roberts, Frances Cabaniss 1916- *WhoAm 90*
Roberts, Francesca *BioIn 16*
Roberts, Francis Donald 1938- *WhoAm 90*
Roberts, Francis Joseph 1918- *WhoAm 90*
Roberts, Francis Stone 1944- *St&PR 91, WhoAm 90*
Roberts, Frank Emmett 1930- *St&PR 91*
Roberts, Fred, Jr. *BioIn 16*
Roberts, Frederic M. *BioIn 16*
Roberts, Frederick J. 1949- *St&PR 91*
Roberts, Gail Devers *BioIn 16*
Roberts, Garrett W. 1942- *St&PR 91*
Roberts, Gayle Ann 1953- *WhoAmW 91*
Roberts, Gemma 1929- *WhoHisp 91*
Roberts, Gene *WhoAm 90, WhoE 91*
Roberts, George Adam 1919- *St&PR 91, WhoAm 90*
Roberts, George Bernard, Jr. 1939- *WhoAm 90*
Roberts, George Christopher 1936- *WhoWor 91*
Roberts, George Harrison 1944- *St&PR 91*
Roberts, George R. *WhoAm 90*
Roberts, George R. 1943?- *ConAmBL*
Roberts, George T. 1917- *St&PR 91*
Roberts, Gerald David 1931- *BiDrAPA 89*
Roberts, Gerald Jeffrey 1949- *WhoAm 90*
Roberts, Gerard J. 1931- *St&PR 91*
Roberts, Gerry Rea 1940- *WhoAmW 91, WhoSSW 91*
Roberts, Gilbert B. 1941- *WhoAm 90*
Roberts, Gilroy *WhoAmA 91*
Roberts, Granville Oral 1918- *WhoAm 90, WhoSSW 91*
Roberts, Gregory Joseph *BiDrAPA 89*
Roberts, H. Edward *BioIn 16*
Roberts, Harry Morris, Jr. 1938- *WhoAm 90, WhoSSW 91, WhoWor 91*
Roberts, Harry Vivian 1923- *WhoAm 90*
Roberts, Helen Heffron 1888-1985 *BioIn 16*
Roberts, Helen Wyvone 1934- *WhoAmW 91*
Roberts, Helene Emylou 1931- *WhoAmA 91*
Roberts, Henry Reginald 1916- *WhoAm 90*
Roberts, Holly L 1951- *WhoAmA 91*
Roberts, Howard A. 1926- *St&PR 91*
Roberts, Howard Leslie 1922- *St&PR 91*
Roberts, Howard Mahlen 1929- *WhoE 91*
Roberts, Howard Topol 1931- *St&PR 91*
Roberts, Hugh Evan 1923- *WhoAm 90*
Roberts, Hyman Jacob 1924- *WhoSSW 91, WhoWor 91*
Roberts, Ida M. 1942- *ODwPR 91*
Roberts, Ida Marie 1942- *St&PR 91*
Roberts, Irene C. 1944- *St&PR 91*
Roberts, Jack 1920- *BioIn 16*
Roberts, Jack Earle 1928- *WhoAm 90*
Roberts, James Alan 1907-1990 *BioIn 16*
Roberts, James Allen 1934- *WhoAm 90*
Roberts, James Allen 1947- *WhoEmL 91*
Roberts, James C. 1924- *St&PR 91*
Roberts, James Cleveland 1946- *WhoE 91*
Roberts, James E. 1934- *St&PR 91*
Roberts, James Edward 1945- *St&PR 91*
Roberts, James G. 1922- *WhoAm 90*
Roberts, James Hall 1927- *TwCCr&M 91*
Roberts, James Harold, III 1949- *WhoEmL 91*
Roberts, James L. 1942- *WhoAm 90*
Roberts, James Lee 1940- *WhoSSW 91*
Roberts, James Lewis 1951- *WhoE 91*
Roberts, James McGregor 1923- *WhoAm 90*
Roberts, James Milnor, Jr. 1918- *WhoAm 90*
Roberts, James Thomas, Jr. 1939- *WhoSSW 91*
Roberts, James Walter 1950- *BiDrAPA 89*
Roberts, Jane *NewAgE 90*
Roberts, Jane 1929- *EncO&P 3*
Roberts, Jane 1929-1984 *EncPaPR 91*
Roberts, Janet Louise 1925- *WhoWrEP 89*
Roberts, Janet Lynn Lekowski 1958- *WhoSSW 91*
Roberts, Janet Marie 1947- *WhoWrEP 89*
Roberts, Janice Lynn 1959- *WhoAmW 91*
Roberts, Jay 1927- *WhoAm 90*
Roberts, Jean 1926- *OxCCanT*
Roberts, Jean 1947- *WhoAmW 91*
Roberts, Jean Reed 1939- *WhoAmW 91*
Roberts, Jeanne Addison *WhoAm 90*
Roberts, Jeffery David 1943- *WhoWor 91*
Roberts, Joan Ellen 1944- *WhoAmW 91*
Roberts, Joan Margaret 1936- *WhoE 91*
Roberts, John Alexander, Jr. 1937- *WhoWor 91*
Roberts, John Arthur 1930- *WhoWor 91*
Roberts, John Austin 1950- *BiDrAPA 89*
Roberts, John B. 1944- *St&PR 91*
Roberts, John Benjamin, II 1955- *WhoAm 90, WhoWor 91, WhoWrEP 89*
Roberts, John Charles 1938- *St&PR 91*
Roberts, John D. 1918- *WhoAm 90*
Roberts, John Glover, Jr. 1955- *WhoAm 90*
Roberts, John Joseph 1922- *St&PR 91*
Roberts, John K. 1961- *St&PR 91*
Roberts, John K., Jr. 1936- *St&PR 91*
Roberts, John Kenneth, Jr. 1936- *WhoAm 90*
Roberts, John Martin *BiDrAPA 89*
Roberts, John McCartney *BiDrAPA 89*
Roberts, John Milton 1916- *WhoAm 90*
Roberts, John Peter Lee 1930- *IntWWM 90, WhoAm 90*
Roberts, John S. 1953- *St&PR 91*
Roberts, John Taylor 1933- *WhoSSW 91*
Roberts, John Watts 1918- *St&PR 91*
Roberts, Judith Marie 1939- *WhoAmW 91, WhoWor 91*
Roberts, Julia *BioIn 16*
Roberts, Justin 1919- *WhoAm 90*
Roberts, Karen 1935- *WhoAmW 91*
Roberts, Kathleen Joy Doty 1951- *WhoAmW 91, WhoE 91*
Roberts, Kay George *BioIn 16*
Roberts, Kay George 1950- *IntWWM 90*
Roberts, Kay K. 1940- *WhoAmW 91*
Roberts, Kaye Virginia 1958- *WhoAmW 91*
Roberts, Keith Edward, Sr. 1928- *WhoWor 91*
Roberts, Kenneth 1885-1957 *EncPaPR 91, WorAlBi*
Roberts, Kenneth A. 1912-1989 *BioIn 16*
Roberts, Kenneth D. 1933- *St&PR 91*
Roberts, Kenneth J. 1948- *ODwPR 91*
Roberts, Kenneth Lewis 1932- *WhoAm 90, WhoSSW 91*
Roberts, Kenneth S. 1930- *St&PR 91*
Roberts, Kenneth Somers 1930- *WhoAm 90*
Roberts, Kristi Smith 1946- *WhoAmW 91*
Roberts, Larry Michael 1957- *WhoEmL 91*
Roberts, Larry Spurgeon 1935- *WhoAm 90*
Roberts, Lawrence 1941- *WhoSSW 91*
Roberts, Lee R. 1939- *St&PR 91*
Roberts, Leigh M *BiDrAPA 89*
Roberts, Leigh Milton 1925- *WhoAm 90*
Roberts, Len *ConAu 32NR*
Roberts, Leon 1951- *Ballpl 90*
Roberts, Leonard 1947- *ConAu 32NR*
Roberts, Leonard H. 1949- *WhoAm 90, WhoSSW 91*
Roberts, Leonard Robert 1947- *WhoWrEP 89*
Roberts, Leonidas Howard 1921- *WhoSSW 91*
Roberts, Les 1937- *TwCCr&M 91*
Roberts, Lewis Alan *BiDrAPA 89*
Roberts, Lillian 1927- *WhoAmW 91*
Roberts, Lionel *ConAu 32NR*
Roberts, Lisa *BioIn 16*
Roberts, Lorin Watson 1923- *WhoAm 90*
Roberts, Louis A. 1952- *St&PR 91*
Roberts, Louis Douglas 1918- *WhoAm 90*
Roberts, Louis Wright 1913- *WhoAm 90, WhoE 91*
Roberts, Louise Nisbet 1919- *WhoAm 90*
Roberts, Lowell Hurlbut 1940- *WhoE 91*
Roberts, Lucille D *WhoAmA 91*
Roberts, Lynn Springer 1943- *WhoAm 90*
Roberts, Marcus *BioIn 16*
Roberts, Margaret 1833-1919 *FemiCLE*
Roberts, Margaret A 1940- *BiDrAPA 89*
Roberts, Margaret Harold 1928- *WhoAm 90*
Roberts, Margaret Rose 1948- *WhoSSW 91*
Roberts, Marge *BioIn 16*
Roberts, Margot Markels 1945- *WhoAmW 91*
Roberts, Marie Dyer 1943- *WhoAmW 91, WhoWor 91*
Roberts, Marie Elizabeth 1955- *WhoWor 91*
Roberts, Marjorie Helen 1938- *WhoAmW 91*
Roberts, Marjory Louise 1963- *WhoAmW 91*
Roberts, Mark Scott 1951- *WhoWor 91*
Roberts, Marke G. 1961- *WhoSSW 91*
Roberts, Markley 1930- *WhoAm 90, WhoE 91*
Roberts, Mary 1788-1864 *FemiCLE*
Roberts, Mary Belle 1923- *WhoAmW 91*
Roberts, Mary Marjorie S. 1923- *WhoAmW 91*

Roberts, Mary May 1877-1959 *BioIn 16*
Roberts, Mary Shams 1932- *BiDrAPA 89*
Roberts, Mary Vesley 1939- *WhoAmW 91*
Roberts, Matthew G., Jr. 1939- *St&PR 91*
Roberts, Melville Parker, Jr. 1931- *WhoAm 90, WhoWor 91*
Roberts, Merle E. 1928- *St&PR 91*
Roberts, Merrill Joseph 1915- *WhoAm 90*
Roberts, Michael A.F. 1941- *St&PR 91*
Roberts, Michael Murphy 1940- *St&PR 91*
Roberts, Michael Wells 1941- *WhoSSW 91*
Roberts, Michele 1949- *FemiCLE*
Roberts, Mitchell 1913- *St&PR 91*
Roberts, Monroe Lionel 1948- *WhoE 91*
Roberts, Morris Henry, Jr. 1940- *WhoSSW 91*
Roberts, Morton 1927-1964 *WhoAmA 91N*
Roberts, Morton Spitz 1926- *WhoAm 90*
Roberts, Myron 1923- *ConAu 31NR*
Roberts, Nancy 1924- *AuBYP 90, BioIn 16*
Roberts, Nancy 1938- *WhoAmW 91*
Roberts, Neil Fletcher 1914- *WhoAm 90*
Roberts, Newell O *BiDrAPA 89*
Roberts, Nickolena Greco 1951- *WhoSSW 91*
Roberts, Nigra Lea 1935- *WhoAmW 91*
Roberts, Norbert J. *NewYTBS 90*
Roberts, Norbert Joseph 1916- *WhoAm 90*
Roberts, Norman Leslie 1935- *WhoAm 90*
Roberts, Oral *BioIn 16*
Roberts, Oral 1918- *WorAlBi*
Roberts, Patrick Kent 1948- *WhoEmL 91*
Roberts, Paul Anthony 1949- *IntWWM 90*
Roberts, Paul Craig, III 1939- *WhoAm 90, WhoWor 91*
Roberts, Paul E 1934- *BiDrAPA 89*
Roberts, Percival R 1935- *WhoAmA 91N*
Roberts, Pernell *WhoAm 90*
Roberts, Pernell 1930- *WorAlBi*
Roberts, Peter A. 1951- *WhoAm 90, WhoWor 91*
Roberts, Peter James 1942- *WhoSSW 91*
Roberts, Peter Job 1944- *WhoAm 90*
Roberts, Philip Kenneth 1945- *St&PR 91*
Roberts, Philip Richard 1942- *St&PR 91, WhoAm 90, WhoE 91*
Roberts, Priscilla Warren 1916- *WhoAm 90, WhoAmA 91*
Roberts, R. *FemiCLE*
Roberts, Ralph F. 1918- *St&PR 91*
Roberts, Ralph Henry, Jr. 1936- *St&PR 91*
Roberts, Ralph J. 1920- *St&PR 91*
Roberts, Ralph Joel 1920- *WhoAm 90*
Roberts, Randal 1951- *St&PR 91*
Roberts, Ray Crouse, Jr. 1929- *WhoAm 90, WhoSSW 91*
Roberts, Raymond Paul 1923- *St&PR 91*
Roberts, Raymond Url 1949- *WhoSSW 91*
Roberts, Richard 1925- *WhoAmA 91, WhoE 91, WhoWor 91*
Roberts, Richard 1946- *IntWWM 90*
Roberts, Richard Allen 1933- *St&PR 91*
Roberts, Richard B. *ODwPR 91*
Roberts, Richard E. 1944- *St&PR 91*
Roberts, Richard G., Jr. 1939- *St&PR 91*
Roberts, Richard Heilbron 1925- *WhoAm 90*
Roberts, Richard James 1922- *WhoAm 90*
Roberts, Richard S. 1929- *St&PR 91*
Roberts, Richard Stuart 1942- *WhoSSW 91*
Roberts, Richard W 1930- *BiDrAPA 89*
Roberts, Robert, Jr. 1903- *WhoAm 90*
Roberts, Robert C 1942- *ConAu 31NR*
Roberts, Robert Winston 1932- *WhoAm 90*
Roberts, Robin 1926- *Ballpl 90*
Roberts, Robin Calvert 1951- *WhoSSW 91*
Roberts, Roger W. 1931- *St&PR 91*
Roberts, Roland R. *BioIn 16*
Roberts, Roland William 1924- *St&PR 91*
Roberts, Rosalee A. 1943- *ODwPR 91*
Roberts, Ross H. 1938- *St&PR 91*
Roberts, Ross Hooven 1938- *WhoAm 90*
Roberts, Roxann Mae 1941- *WhoE 91*
Roberts, Roy S. *BioIn 16, St&PR 91*
Roberts, Sally Joann 1938- *WhoAmW 91*
Roberts, Samuel *PenDiDA 89*
Roberts, Samuel Smith 1936- *WhoE 91*
Roberts, Sandra Brown 1939- *WhoAmW 91*
Roberts, Saxe Gotha 1935- *St&PR 91*
Roberts, Sean Ashley 1949- *WhoE 91*
Roberts, Seymour M. 1934- *WhoAm 90*
Roberts, Sheila *NewAgMG*
Roberts, Sheila Lynn *BiDrAPA 89*
Roberts, Sheila Powe 1947- *WhoAmW 91*
Roberts, Sidney 1918- *WhoAm 90*
Roberts, Sidney I. 1913- *WhoAm 90*
Roberts, Stanley H. 1917- *St&PR 91*
Roberts, Stephen Earl 1948- *St&PR 91*
Roberts, Stephen Hall 1953- *WhoE 91*
Roberts, Stephen Pritchard 1949- *IntWWM 90*
Roberts, Steven D. 1956- *St&PR 91*
Roberts, Steven K. 1952- *BioIn 16*
Roberts, Steven K 1954- *WhoAmA 91*
Roberts, Steven Victor 1943- *WhoAm 90*
Roberts, Suzanne Helen 1946- *WhoAmW 91*
Roberts, Theodore Goodridge 1877-1953 *DcLB 92 [port]*
Roberts, Theodore H. 1929- *St&PR 91*
Roberts, Theodore Harris 1929- *WhoAm 90*
Roberts, Thomas *PenDiDA 89*
Roberts, Thomas George 1929- *WhoWor 91*
Roberts, Thomas H., Jr. 1924- *St&PR 91*
Roberts, Thomas Morgan 1937- *WhoWor 91*
Roberts, Thomasene Blount 1943- *WhoSSW 91*
Roberts, Timothy George *BiDrAPA 89*
Roberts, Tom 1908- *WhoAmA 91*
Roberts, Tony 1939- *WhoAm 90, WorAlBi*
Roberts, Vera Mowry 1918- *BioIn 16, NotWoAT*
Roberts, Vicki Lynn 1957- *BiDrAPA 89*
Roberts, Violet Kent 1880- *WhoAmA 91N*
Roberts, Virginia *AuBYP 90*
Roberts, Wallace Arthur 1939- *WhoE 91*
Roberts, Walter B., Jr. 1926- *St&PR 91*
Roberts, Walter Herbert Beatty 1915- *WhoAm 90*
Roberts, Walter Orr 1915- *ConAu 131*
Roberts, Walter Orr 1915-1990 *BioIn 16, CurBio 90N, NewYTBS 90 [port]*
Roberts, Walter Ronald 1916- *WhoAm 90*
Roberts, Warren Errol 1933- *WhoAm 90*
Roberts, Wayland Gaines, Jr. 1932- *St&PR 91*
Roberts, Wesley 1953- *IntWWM 90*
Roberts, Wilfred Bob 1921- *IntWWM 90*
Roberts, Willard Eugene 1908- *WhoAm 90*
Roberts, Willard Lincoln 1923-1987 *BioIn 16*
Roberts, William B. 1939- *WhoAm 90*
Roberts, William Bradley 1947- *IntWWM 90*
Roberts, William E. 1952- *St&PR 91*
Roberts, William Edward 1941- *WhoAmA 91*
Roberts, William Everett 1926- *WhoAm 90*
Roberts, William G., III *ODwPR 91*
Roberts, William Hooton, IV 1953- *WhoE 91*
Roberts, William Hugh, III 1936- *WhoSSW 91*
Roberts, William J. 1920- *St&PR 91*
Roberts, William J. 1944- *St&PR 91*
Roberts, William James Cynfab 1938- *WhoWor 91*
Roberts, William L. 1916- *St&PR 91*
Roberts, William Lawrence 1924- *WhoSSW 91*
Roberts, William P 1931- *ConAu 32NR*
Roberts, Willo Davis 1928- *AuBYP 90, TwCCr&M 91*
Roberts, Winifred *IntWWM 90*
Roberts-Atwater, Beverly *WhoAmW 91*
Roberts-King, Catherine Stephanie 1962- *WhoAmW 91*
Robertshaw, Kent Louis *BiDrAPA 89*
Robertshaw, Thomas Stevens 1947- *St&PR 91*
Robertson, A. *BiDWomA*
Robertson, A. Haeworth 1930- *WhoAm 90, WhoWor 91*
Robertson, Abel Alfred Lazzarini, Jr. 1926- *WhoAm 90*
Robertson, Agnes 1833-1916 *BioIn 16*
Robertson, Agnes Kelly 1833-1916 *NotWoAT*
Robertson, Alan Grant 1942- *BiDrAPA 89*
Robertson, Alan M 1920- *BiDrAPA 89*
Robertson, Alexander *PenDiDA 89, PenDiMP*
Robertson, Alice Mary 1854-1931 *BioAmW*
Robertson, Alvin Cyrrale 1962- *WhoAm 90*
Robertson, Andre 1957- *Ballpl 90*
Robertson, Anna Mary *BioAmW*
Robertson, Anne *BioIn 16*
Robertson, Archibald Thomas 1863-1934 *BioIn 16*
Robertson, Armand James, II 1937- *WhoAm 90, WhoWor 91*
Robertson, Beverly Carruth 1922- *WhoAm 90*
Robertson, Bill 1956- *BioIn 16*
Robertson, Bob 1946- *Ballpl 90, BioIn 16*
Robertson, Celeste Bernardine 1947- *WhoWor 91*
Robertson, Charles 1941- *SpyFic*
Robertson, Charles Garland 1941- *St&PR 91*
Robertson, Charles J 1934- *WhoAmA 91*
Robertson, Charley 1907-1981 *LiHiK*
Robertson, Charlie 1897-1984 *Ballpl 90*
Robertson, Charlotte *BiDrAPA 89*
Robertson, Christine 1949- *WhoAmW 91*
Robertson, Christopher W. 1931- *St&PR 91*
Robertson, Cliff 1925- *WhoAm 90, WorAlBi*
Robertson, Dale 1923- *WorAlBi*
Robertson, Darrell 1942- *St&PR 91*
Robertson, Dave 1889-1970 *Ballpl 90*
Robertson, David Leonard 1953- *WhoEmL 91*
Robertson, David Wyatt 1937- *WhoAm 90*
Robertson, Dede *BioIn 16*
Robertson, Dennis Holme 1890-1963 *BioIn 16*
Robertson, Dirk Briscoe 1953- *WhoSSW 91*
Robertson, Donna Lou Nagey 1935- *IntWWM 90*
Robertson, Dorothy Lewis 1912- *AuBYP 90*
Robertson, Duncan 1924- *IntWWM 90*
Robertson, Durant Waite, Jr. 1914- *WhoAm 90*
Robertson, E. Arnot 1903-1961 *BioIn 16, FemiCLE*
Robertson, E Bruce 1955- *WhoAmA 91*
Robertson, Edward D., Jr. 1952- *WhoAm 90*
Robertson, Edward Dunbar, Jr. 1942- *St&PR 91*
Robertson, Edwin 1912- *ConAu 130*
Robertson, Edwin David 1946- *WhoE 91, WhoEmL 91, WhoWor 91*
Robertson, Edwin Oscar 1923- *St&PR 91*
Robertson, Eileen Arnot 1903-1961 *BioIn 16*
Robertson, Eliza Frances 1771-1805 *FemiCLE*
Robertson, Elizabeth Ann 1943- *WhoAmW 91*
Robertson, Ellis *MajTwCW*
Robertson, Elmer Lee, Jr. 1947- *WhoE 91*
Robertson, Ethel Florence Lindesay R 1870-1946 *BioIn 16*
Robertson, Franklin Lee 1934- *St&PR 91*
Robertson, Gavin Douglas 1932- *St&PR 91*
Robertson, Gene 1899-1981 *Ballpl 90*
Robertson, Geoffrey Ronald 1946- *WhoWor 91*
Robertson, George *PenDiDA 89*
Robertson, George 1790-1874 *AmLegL*
Robertson, George Leonard 1922- *WhoAm 90*
Robertson, George Leven 1921- *WhoAm 90*
Robertson, George Louis 1947- *WhoE 91*
Robertson, George O. 1930- *St&PR 91*
Robertson, Gerald Melvin 1943- *BiDrAPA 89*
Robertson, Giles Henry 1913-1987 *BioIn 16*
Robertson, Gregg W. 1934- *St&PR 91*
Robertson, Gregg Westland 1934- *WhoAm 90*
Robertson, Hannah 1724-1800? *FemiCLE*
Robertson, Harry Wilson, III 1936- *WhoSSW 91*
Robertson, Heather Anne Laure 1956- *WhoAmW 91*
Robertson, Henry Howard 1950- *WhoSSW 91*
Robertson, Herbert Chapman, Jr. 1928- *WhoSSW 91*
Robertson, Horace Bascomb, Jr. 1923- *WhoAm 90*
Robertson, Howard Wayne 1947- *WhoWrEP 89*
Robertson, Hugh A 1932?-1988 *DrBlPA 90*
Robertson, Hugh C. *PenDiDA 89*
Robertson, Hugh Duff 1957- *WhoWor 91*
Robertson, Ian 1928- *ConAu 132*
Robertson, Ian Robert 1947- *IntWWM 90*
Robertson, J. M. 1856-1933 *BioIn 16*
Robertson, Jack Clark 1943- *WhoAm 90*
Robertson, Jack Eugene, Sr. 1937- *WhoSSW 91*
Robertson, Jack Westbrook, Jr. 1929- *St&PR 91*
Robertson, Jacqueline Lee 1947- *WhoAmW 91*
Robertson, James 1742-1814 *EncCRAm, WhNaAH*
Robertson, James 1831-1900 *DcCanB 12*
Robertson, James 1912- *IntWWM 90, PenDiMP*
Robertson, James 1938- *WhoAm 90*
Robertson, James B 1929- *BiDrAPA 89*
Robertson, James Cole 1929- *WhoSSW 91*
Robertson, James Colvert 1932- *St&PR 91*
Robertson, James David 1922- *WhoAm 90*
Robertson, James Evans 1924- *WhoAm 90*
Robertson, James Irvin, Jr. 1930- *WhoAm 90, WhoSSW 91*
Robertson, James Wharton 1929- *St&PR 91*
Robertson, James Wilson 1899-1983 *DcNaB 1981*
Robertson, Jaquelin Taylor 1933- *WhoAm 90*
Robertson, Jean 1913-1990 *ConAu 132*
Robertson, Jeanne Chorley 1949- *WhoAmW 91*
Robertson, Jeri Jane 1960- *WhoWrEP 89*
Robertson, Jerry 1943- *Ballpl 90*
Robertson, Jerry Earl 1932- *St&PR 91, WhoAm 90*
Robertson, Jewell Lewis 1911- *WhoAmW 91*
Robertson, Joan E 1942- *WhoAmA 91*
Robertson, Joe E. 1918- *St&PR 91*
Robertson, John *WhoWrEP 89*
Robertson, John 1938- *IntWWM 90*
Robertson, John Archibald Law 1925- *WhoAm 90*
Robertson, John Burr, Jr. 1960- *BiDrAPA 89*
Robertson, John Mackinnon 1856-1933 *BioIn 16*
Robertson, Joseph Edmond 1918- *WhoWor 91*
Robertson, Joseph Gibb 1820-1899 *DcCanB 12*
Robertson, Josephine-Leslie 1948- *WhoAmW 91*
Robertson, Julia Merle *BiDrAPA 89*
Robertson, Julian *BioIn 16*
Robertson, Keith 1914- *AuBYP 90*
Robertson, Kent L. *St&PR 91*
Robertson, Kerry Lee 1950- *WhoE 91*
Robertson, Kim *NewAgMG*
Robertson, Lauri R 1953- *BiDrAPA 89*
Robertson, Leon H. 1934- *St&PR 91, WhoAm 90*
Robertson, Leslie E. *BioIn 16*
Robertson, Leslie Earl 1928- *WhoAm 90, WhoWor 91*
Robertson, Linwood Righter 1940- *St&PR 91, WhoAm 90*
Robertson, Lucretia Speziale 1944- *WhoE 91*
Robertson, M Clark 1955- *ConDes 90*
Robertson, Madonna Maria 1946- *St&PR 91*
Robertson, Margaret Murray 1821-1897 *FemiCLE*
Robertson, Margaret Murray 1823?-1897 *DcCanB 12*
Robertson, Marian Ella 1920- *WhoAmW 91, WhoWor 91*
Robertson, Mary *BioIn 16*
Robertson, Mary E. 1937- *WhoWrEP 89*
Robertson, Mary Ella 1924- *St&PR 91*
Robertson, Mary Elsie 1937- *ConAu 33NR*
Robertson, Maynard Wayne 1945- *WhoSSW 91*
Robertson, Melvina 1934- *WhoAmW 91*
Robertson, Michael Swing 1935 *St&PR 91, WhoAm 90*
Robertson, Minta Carol 1949- *WhoAmW 91*
Robertson, Morgan 1861-1915 *EncPaPR 91*
Robertson, Nan *BioIn 16*
Robertson, Nancy Elizabeth *WhoAmA 91*
Robertson, Nat Clifton 1919- *WhoAm 90*
Robertson, Norman 1927- *St&PR 91*
Robertson, Olivia 1917- *EncO&P 3*
Robertson, Oran B. 1917- *St&PR 91, WhoAm 90*
Robertson, Oscar *BioIn 16*
Robertson, Oscar 1938- *WorAlBi*
Robertson, Oscar Palmer 1938- *WhoAm 90*
Robertson, Pat *BioIn 16, WhoWrEP 89*
Robertson, Pat 1930- *WhoAm 90, WorAlBi*
Robertson, Paul *PenDiMP*
Robertson, Paul Chandler 1902-1961 *WhoAmA 91N*
Robertson, Paula Kay 1959- *IntWWM 90*
Robertson, Phil 1925- *WhoWrEP 89*
Robertson, Philip B *BiDrAPA 89*
Robertson, Philip S. 1937- *St&PR 91*
Robertson, Priscilla 1910-1989 *ConAu 130*
Robertson, Priscilla Smith 1910-1989 *BioIn 16*
Robertson, Rae *PenDiMP*
Robertson, Randolph Boyd 1962- *WhoSSW 91*
Robertson, Raymond Edgar 1922- *BiDrAPA 89*
Robertson, Rich 1944- *Ballpl 90*
Robertson, Richard S. 1908- *St&PR 91*
Robertson, Richard Stuart 1942- *WhoAm 90*
Robertson, Rick Alan 1952- *BiDrAPA 89*
Robertson, Robbie *BioIn 16*
Robertson, Robert A. 1934- *St&PR 91*
Robertson, Robert Gordon 1917- *WhoAm 90*
Robertson, Robert H *BiDrAPA 89*
Robertson, Roy Victor, Jr. 1946- *St&PR 91*
Robertson, Royal 1936- *MusmAFA*
Robertson, Russell Boyd 1932- *WhoAm 90*
Robertson, Rutherford Ness 1913- *WhoWor 91*
Robertson, S. *BiDWomA*
Robertson, Samuel Harry, III 1934- *WhoWor 91*

Robertson, Samuel T 1945- *BiDrAPA 89*
Robertson, Sandra Dee 1953- *WhoAmW 91, WhoSSW 91*
Robertson, Sanford R. 1931- *St&PR 91*
Robertson, Sara Elizabeth 1956- *WhoAmW 91*
Robertson, Sarah M *WhoAmA 91N*
Robertson, Sherry 1919-1970 *Ballpl 90*
Robertson, Stephen Lee 1949- *St&PR 91*
Robertson, Stewart John 1948- *IntWWM 90*
Robertson, Suzanne Marie 1944- *WhoE 91*
Robertson, Sydney R. 1941- *St&PR 91*
Robertson, T. W. 1829-1871 *BioIn 16*
Robertson, Ted Zanderson 1921- *WhoAm 90*
Robertson, Thomas Patrick, Jr. 1938- *WhoWrEP 89*
Robertson, Thomas Sinclair 1942- *WhoAm 90*
Robertson, Thomas William 1829-1871 *BioIn 16*
Robertson, Timothy Brian *BioIn 16*
Robertson, Timothy Joel 1937- *WhoAm 90*
Robertson, Timothy John 1951- *BiDrAPA 89*
Robertson, W.R. 1940- *St&PR 91*
Robertson, Walter, III 1945- *St&PR 91*
Robertson, Walter Spencer, Jr. 1926- *St&PR 91*
Robertson, Warren *BioIn 16*
Robertson, William 1721-1793 *DcLB 104 [port]*
Robertson, William 1818-1882 *BioIn 16*
Robertson, William Alan 1938- *St&PR 91*
Robertson, William Cobb 1926- *St&PR 91*
Robertson, William Franklin 1917- *WhoAm 90*
Robertson, William Howard 1921- *WhoSSW 91, WhoWor 91*
Robertson, William L. *St&PR 91*
Robertson, William Osborne 1925- *WhoAm 90*
Robertson, William Paul 1950- *WhoWrEP 89*
Robertson, William Richard 1941- *St&PR 91, WhoAm 90*
Robertson, William Withers 1941- *WhoAm 90*
Robertson, Wyndham Gay 1937- *WhoSSW 91*
Roberval, Jean de la Rocque, Sieur de 1500?-1560 *EncCRAm*
Robesch, Robert Arthur 1946- *St&PR 91*
Robeson, Barbara Jean 1952- *WhoSSW 91*
Robeson, Eslanda Cardoza Goode 1896-1965 *HarlReB*
Robeson, George 1829-1897 *BiDrUSE 89*
Robeson, Joyce 1939- *WhoWrEP 89*
Robeson, Kenneth *TwCCr&M 91*
Robeson, Kyle 1929- *St&PR 91*
Robeson, Paul 1898-1976 *BioIn 16, DrBlPA 90, OxCPMus, PenDiMP, WorAlBi*
Robeson, Paul Leroy 1898-1976 *EncAL*
Robeson, Paul Leroy Bustill 1898-1976 *DcAfAmP*
Robespierre, Maximilien 1758-1794 *BioIn 16*
Robespierre, Maximilien Francois M.I. De 1758-1794 *WorAlBi*
Robey, Ames 1929- *BiDrAPA 89*
Robey, Ann Brawner 1958- *WhoE 91*
Robey, Don *BioIn 16*
Robey, George 1869-1954 *OxCPMus*
Robey, Kathleen Moran 1909- *WhoAmW 91*
Robfogel, Susan Salitan 1943- *WhoAmW 91*
Robhs, Dwight *ConAu 33NR*
Robichaud, Hedard J. 1911- *WhoAm 90*
Robichaud, Kathleen Johanna Kienzle 1942- *WhoSSW 91*
Robichaud, Louis Joseph 1925- *WhoAm 90*
Robichaud, Phyllis Ivy Isabel 1915- *WhoAm 90, WhoAmW 91, WhoSSW 91, WhoWor 91*
Robichaux, Maurice Joseph, Jr. 1933- *St&PR 91*
Robicheaux, Robert A. 1947- *WhoSSW 91*
Robideau, Jeffrey Thomas 1959- *St&PR 91*
Robidoux, Antoine 1794-1860 *WhNaAH*
Robidoux, Billy Jo 1964- *Ballpl 90*
Robidoux, Edmund Allan 1931- *St&PR 91, WhoAm 90*
Robie, Frederick 1822-1912 *AmLegL*
Robie, William B. 1943- *St&PR 91*
Robillard, Matthew Thomas 1959- *BiDrAPA 89*
Robillard, Renee Jean 1952- *WhoAmW 91*
Robin, B.M. 1938- *St&PR 91*
Robin, Frances Perry 1948- *WhoSSW 91*
Robin, Howard W. 1953- *St&PR 91*
Robin, Jacqueline *PenDiMP*
Robin, Joann Cohan 1928- *IntWWM 90*
Robin, Mado 1918-1960 *PenDiMP*
Robin, Richard Allan *BiDrAPA 89*
Robin, Richard Shale 1926- *WhoAm 90*
Robin, Theodore Tydings, Jr. 1939- *WhoSSW 91*
Robineau, Adelaide Alsop 1865-1929 *PenDiDA 89*
Robiner, Donald Maxwell 1935- *WhoWor 91*
Robinet, Harriette Gillem 1931- *BioIn 16*
Robinett, Betty Wallace 1919- *WhoAm 90, WhoWrEP 89*
Robinett, Deborah Jane 1958- *BiDrAPA 89*
Robinett, Gordon 1935- *St&PR 91*
Robinett, James Kevin *BiDrAPA 89*
Robinett, Nancy Gay 1948- *WhoAm 90*
Robinett, Robena Delite 1953- *WhoWrEP 89*
Robinette, Betsye Hunter 1960- *WhoAmW 91*
Robinette, Frank Leroy 1927- *WhoSSW 91*
Robinette, Hillary, Jr. 1913- *St&PR 91*
Robinette, Janet L. 1951- *St&PR 91*
Robinette, Joseph A. 1939- *ConAu 131*
Robinette, Sheree 1957- *WhoAmW 91*
Robinot, Jean Pierre 1946- *WhoWor 91*
Robinow, Richard M. 1945- *St&PR 91*
Robinowitz, Carolyn Bauer 1938- *BiDrAPA 89, WhoAm 90*
Robinowitz, Joe Reece 1950- *WhoAm 90*
Robins, A. 1917- *St&PR 91*
Robins, Alvin L *BiDrAPA 89*
Robins, Cara Leigh 1963- *WhoAmW 91*
Robins, Charles Matthew 1956- *St&PR 91*
Robins, Charles R., III 1951- *St&PR 91*
Robins, Clive Justin 1953- *WhoSSW 91*
Robins, Corinne 1934- *WhoAmA 91, WhoWrEP 89*
Robins, E.W. 1952- *St&PR 91*
Robins, Edwin Claiborne, Jr. 1943- *St&PR 91, WhoAm 90, WhoSSW 91*
Robins, Edwin Claiborne, Sr. 1910- *WhoAm 90, WhoSSW 91*
Robins, Eli 1921- *BiDrAPA 89, WhoAm 90*
Robins, Elizabeth 1862-1952 *BioIn 16, FemiCLE*
Robins, Frederick Herman 1940- *St&PR 91*
Robins, Gerald Burns 1924- *WhoAm 90, WhoWor 91*
Robins, Irwin Brody 1934- *St&PR 91*
Robins, Jay K 1924- *BiDrAPA 89*
Robins, Jeri Lynn Nagler 1961- *WhoAmW 91*
Robins, Joan *AuBYP 90*
Robins, Joel Allen 1947- *St&PR 91*
Robins, Lee Nelken 1922- *WhoAm 90, WhoAmW 91*
Robins, Margaret D. 1868-1945 *BioAmW*
Robins, Marjorie McCarthy 1914- *WhoAmW 91*
Robins, Martin B. 1956- *St&PR 91*
Robins, Mitchell James 1956- *WhoEmL 91*
Robins, Natalie 1938- *WhoWrEP 89*
Robins, Norman Alan 1934- *St&PR 91, WhoAm 90*
Robins, Richard *PenDiDA 89*
Robins, Richard David 1945- *St&PR 91*
Robins, Richard Dennis 1950- *WhoSSW 91, WhoWor 91*
Robins, Robert Henry 1921- *WhoWor 91*
Robins, Robert Sidwar 1938- *WhoAm 90*
Robins, Roe *WhoWrEP 89*
Robins, Roland Kenith 1926- *WhoAm 90*
Robins, Rosemary Gay 1951- *WhoAmW 91*
Robins, Shauna *WhoWrEP 89*
Robins, Susan Lynne 1953- *WhoAmW 91*
Robins, Toby 1931-1986 *OxCCanT*
Robins, W. Randolph 1945- *St&PR 91*
Robins, William R. 1939- *WhoE 91*
Robinson, Miss *PenDiMP*
Robinson, A. J. 1955- *WhoSSW 91*
Robinson, A. Mary F. 1857-1944 *FemiCLE*
Robinson, Aaron 1915-1966 *Ballpl 90*
Robinson, Abraham 1918-1974 *DcScB S2*
Robinson, Adelbert Carl 1926- *WhoSSW 91*
Robinson, Adjai 1932- *BioIn 16*
Robinson, Alan J. 1924- *St&PR 91*
Robinson, Albert Dean 1939- *WhoE 91*
Robinson, Alcurtis 1940- *St&PR 91*
Robinson, Alexander 1789-1872 *WhNaAH*
Robinson, Alexander Jacob 1920- *WhoWor 91*
Robinson, Alix Ida 1937- *WhoAmW 91*
Robinson, Allan Richard 1932- *WhoAm 90, WhoE 91*
Robinson, Allen 1936- *St&PR 91*
Robinson, Allyn Preston, Jr. 1909- *WhoWor 91*
Robinson, Aminah 1940- *BioIn 16*
Robinson, Anastasia 1692?-1755 *PenDiMP*
Robinson, Andrea *BioIn 16*
Robinson, Angela Tomei 1957- *WhoAmW 91*
Robinson, Angelina Massari 1962- *WhoAmW 91*
Robinson, Ann Turner *PenDiMP*
Robinson, Anne Durrum 1913- *WhoSSW 91*
Robinson, Annettmarie 1940- *WhoAmW 91*
Robinson, Arnold 1929- *St&PR 91*
Robinson, Arthur Howard 1915- *WhoAm 90*
Robinson, Arthur Murray 1924- *St&PR 91*
Robinson, Arthur Napoleon Raymond 1926- *WhoWor 91*
Robinson, Aubrey Eugene, Jr. 1922- *WhoAm 90, WhoE 91*
Robinson, Barbara Paul 1941- *WhoAm 90*
Robinson, Barbara Webb 1927- *AuBYP 90, ConAu 30NR*
Robinson, Benjamin *BiDrAPA 89*
Robinson, Berol 1924- *WhoWor 91*
Robinson, Bestor 1898- *BioIn 16*
Robinson, Betty Wilmas 1927- *BiDrAPA 89*
Robinson, Beverley 1722-1792 *EncCRAm*
Robinson, Bill *BioIn 16*
Robinson, Bill 1878-1949 *BioIn 16, DrBlPA 90, OxCPMus, WorAlBi*
Robinson, Bill 1943- *Ballpl 90*
Robinson, Bill 1949- *BioIn 16*
Robinson, Boardman 1876-1952 *WhoAmA 91N*
Robinson, Bob Leo 1933- *WhoAm 90*
Robinson, Bobby *BioIn 16*
Robinson, Bobby Brick 1930- *WhoSSW 91*
Robinson, Brooks 1913- *St&PR 91*
Robinson, Brooks 1937- *Ballpl 90 [port], BioIn 16, WorAlBi*
Robinson, Brooks Calbert, Jr. 1937- *WhoAm 90*
Robinson, Bruce *BioIn 16*
Robinson, Bruce 1946- *ConAu 131*
Robinson, C. Thomas 1950- *WhoSSW 91*
Robinson, Calvin, Jr. 1950- *WhoEmL 91*
Robinson, Calvin Edward 1937- *St&PR 91*
Robinson, Cari Suzanne 1956- *WhoAmW 91*
Robinson, Carl Terrell 1947- *WhoWor 91*
Robinson, Carlan Marie 1944- *WhoAmW 91*
Robinson, Carlota Nilson 1939- *WhoAmW 91*
Robinson, Carole Ann 1935- *WhoAmW 91*
Robinson, Caroline J. 1963- *WhoAmW 91*
Robinson, Cathaleen Starn 1940- *WhoAmW 91*
Robinson, Catherine Lauer 1948- *WhoAmW 91*
Robinson, Cathy 1951- *WhoAmW 91*
Robinson, Charles 1931- *BioIn 16*
Robinson, Charles Alexander 1900-1965 *AuBYP 90*
Robinson, Charles Alvin 1941- *WhoSSW 91*
Robinson, Charles M. 1941- *St&PR 91*
Robinson, Charles Nelson 1936- *WhoE 91*
Robinson, Charles Oakley, III 1946- *St&PR 91*
Robinson, Charles Raymond 1944- *WhoSSW 91*
Robinson, Charlie *BioIn 16*
Robinson, Charlotte 1924- *WhoAmA 91*
Robinson, Cheryl Ann 1946- *WhoAmW 91*
Robinson, Chester Hersey 1918- *WhoAm 90*
Robinson, Chris 1951- *WhoAmA 91*
Robinson, Christine Marie *WhoSSW 91*
Robinson, Christopher 1806-1889 *BioIn 16*
Robinson, Christopher John 1936- *IntWWM 90*
Robinson, Christopher Thomas 1951- *WhoAm 90*
Robinson, Clark Shove 1917- *WhoAm 90*
Robinson, Cora Guinn 1958- *WhoWrEP 89*
Robinson, Cozy Morris *WhoAmW 91*
Robinson, Crabb 1775-1867 *BioIn 16*
Robinson, Craig 1948- *Ballpl 90*
Robinson, Daniel Baruch 1937- *WhoAm 90*
Robinson, Daniel Raymond 1948- *WhoSSW 91*
Robinson, Daniel Thomas 1925- *WhoAm 90*
Robinson, David *BioIn 16*
Robinson, David 1965- *News 90 [port], WorAlBi*
Robinson, David Adair 1925- *WhoAm 90*
Robinson, David B 1924- *BiDrAPA 89*
Robinson, David Bradford 1937- *WhoSSW 91*
Robinson, David Brooks 1939- *WhoAm 90*
Robinson, David Earl 1948- *WhoAm 90*
Robinson, David Kenneth 1951- *St&PR 91*
Robinson, David L. 1948- *ODwPR 91*
Robinson, David Mason 1932- *WhoAm 90*
Robinson, David Peter Francis 1937- *IntWWM 90*
Robinson, David Roger 1951- *WhoEmL 91*
Robinson, David Weaver 1914- *WhoAm 90*
Robinson, David Wells 1936- *BiDrAPA 89*
Robinson, David Wright 1923- *St&PR 91*
Robinson, David Z. 1927- *WhoAm 90, WhoE 91*
Robinson, Davis Rowland 1940- *WhoAm 90, WhoE 91*
Robinson, Dean Edward *BiDrAPA 89*
Robinson, Dean Wentworth 1929- *WhoAm 90*
Robinson, Delbert Gail *BiDrAPA 89*
Robinson, Denise Gary *BioIn 16*
Robinson, Derek 1932- *SpyFic*
Robinson, Diana *EncPaPR 91*
Robinson, Don 1957- *Ballpl 90*
Robinson, Donald 1913- *WhoE 91*
Robinson, Donald Arlington 1915- *St&PR 91*
Robinson, Donald Keith 1932- *WhoAm 90*
Robinson, Donald Lee 1929- *WhoE 91*
Robinson, Donald Leonard 1936- *WhoAm 90*
Robinson, Donald Peter 1928- *WhoE 91*
Robinson, Donald T. *St&PR 91*
Robinson, Donald Walter *WhoAm 90*
Robinson, Donald Warren 1932- *WhoE 91*
Robinson, Donita Dawn 1961- *WhoSSW 91*
Robinson, Doris Herbert 1942- *WhoAmW 91*
Robinson, Dorothy W. 1929- *BioIn 16*
Robinson, Douglas 1930- *WhoAm 90*
Robinson, Douglas Hill *BiDrAPA 89*
Robinson, Douglas Perry *BiDrAPA 89*
Robinson, Douglas W. 1928- *St&PR 91*
Robinson, Duncan 1943- *WhoAm 90, WhoAmA 91, WhoE 91*
Robinson, Dwight P. 1900-1989 *BioIn 16*
Robinson, E. B., Jr. 1941- *WhoSSW 91*
Robinson, Earl 1910- *EncAL*
Robinson, Earl David 1948- *St&PR 91*
Robinson, Earl Hawley 1910- *IntWWM 90, WhoAm 90*
Robinson, Earl James 1949- *WhoE 91*
Robinson, Eddie *BioIn 16*
Robinson, Eddie 1920- *Ballpl 90*
Robinson, Eddie Day *WhoAm 90*
Robinson, Edgar Allen 1933- *St&PR 91, WhoAm 90*
Robinson, Edith 1862-1928? *BioIn 16*
Robinson, Edna L. 1938- *St&PR 91*
Robinson, Edna Mae *BioIn 16*
Robinson, Edward A. 1932- *St&PR 91*
Robinson, Edward Arlington 1869-1935 *WorAlBi*
Robinson, Edward G. 1893-1973 *WorAlBi*
Robinson, Edward H 1924- *BiDrAPA 89*
Robinson, Edward Joseph 1940- *St&PR 91, WhoAm 90, WhoSSW 91*
Robinson, Edward Lewis 1945- *WhoAm 90*
Robinson, Edward Murray 1959- *St&PR 91*
Robinson, Edward N. 1945- *St&PR 91*
Robinson, Edward William 1867-1924 *AmLegL*
Robinson, Edwin Arlington 1869-1935 *MajTwCW, PoeCrit 1 [port]*
Robinson, Elaine Diane 1940- *WhoAmW 91*
Robinson, Eliot Steele 1942- *St&PR 91*
Robinson, Emma 1814-1890 *FemiCLE*
Robinson, Emma Calloway 1896- *WhoAmW 91*
Robinson, Emyre Barrios 1926- *WhoHisp 91*
Robinson, Enders Anthony 1930- *WhoAm 90, WhoSSW 91, WhoWor 91*
Robinson, Eric 1908-1974 *PenDiMP*
Robinson, Eric 1924- *BioIn 16*
Robinson, Eugene 1934- *WhoAm 90*
Robinson, Evelyn Louise 1933- *WhoAmW 91*
Robinson, F. George 1911- *St&PR 91*
Robinson, F. Mabel 1858- *FemiCLE*
Robinson, Farrel Richard 1927- *WhoAm 90*
Robinson, Faye 1943- *IntWWM 90*
Robinson, Flavia Derossi 1926- *WhoE 91*
Robinson, Florence Claire Crim 1932- *WhoAm 90*
Robinson, Florine Samantha 1935- *WhoAmW 91, WhoE 91, WhoWor 91*
Robinson, Floyd 1936- *Ballpl 90*
Robinson, Floyd Lorain 1935- *WhoSSW 91*
Robinson, Floyd Walter, Jr. 1947- *WhoSSW 91*
Robinson, Forbes 1926-1987 *PenDiMP*
Robinson, Francis Edwin 1909- *WhoWor 91*
Robinson, Frank *BioIn 16*
Robinson, Frank 1935- *Ballpl 90 [port], News 90 [port], WhoAm 90, WhoE 91, WorAlBi*
Robinson, Frank Brooks, Sr. 1931- *WhoE 91*
Robinson, Frank D. 1917- *St&PR 91*
Robinson, Franklin W 1939- *WhoAmA 91*
Robinson, Franklin Westcott 1939- *WhoAm 90, WhoE 91*
Robinson, Fred Colson 1930- *WhoAm 90*

Robinson, G. Wilse 1924- *WhoAm 90*
Robinson, Gail *BioIn 16*
Robinson, Gail 1946- *IntWWM 90*
Robinson, Gail Erlick *BiDrAPA 89*
Robinson, Gail Susan 1953- *WhoE 91*
Robinson, George Cottman, Jr. 1934- *St&PR 91*
Robinson, Geraldine Marlene Helwing 1947- *WhoEmL 91*
Robinson, Gerrard 1834-1891 *PenDiDA 89*
Robinson, Gilbert A. 1928- *ODwPR 91*
Robinson, Gilbert de Beauregard 1906- *WhoAm 90*
Robinson, Girard Edwin *BiDrAPA 89*
Robinson, Glen Parmelee, Jr. 1923- *St&PR 91*
Robinson, Glynne 1934- *WhoAmW 91*, *WhoE 91*
Robinson, Gordon Whiteman 1936- *WhoE 91*
Robinson, Gretchen Elizabeth 1937- *WhoAmW 91*
Robinson, Grove 1935- *WhoAmA 91*
Robinson, Gwynn Herndon 1920- *WhoAm 90*
Robinson, H Basil 1919- *ConAu 131*
Robinson, Hamilton, Jr. 1934- *St&PR 91*
Robinson, Hamilton Burrows Greaves 1910- *WhoAm 90*
Robinson, Hank 1889-1965 *Ballpl 90*
Robinson, Harold Ivens 1951- *WhoSSW 91*
Robinson, Harriet H. 1825-1911 *BioAmW*
Robinson, Harriet Jane 1825-1911 *FemiCLE*
Robinson, Harry Albert 1942- *WhoE 91*
Robinson, Harry L. 1929- *St&PR 91*
Robinson, Harry S. *BioIn 16*
Robinson, Helen *BioIn 16*
Robinson, Helen L. *BioIn 16*
Robinson, Henry Crabb 1775-1867 *BioIn 16*
Robinson, Henry John 1934- *St&PR 91*
Robinson, Henry Peach 1830-1901 *BioIn 16*
Robinson, Herbert 1916- *St&PR 91*
Robinson, Herbert A *BiDrAPA 89*
Robinson, Herbert William 1914- *WhoAm 90*
Robinson, Hobart Krum 1937- *WhoAm 90*
Robinson, Holly *BioIn 16*
Robinson, Howard Olis 1926- *WhoAm 90*
Robinson, Hugh Granville 1932- *St&PR 91*, *WhoSSW 91*
Robinson, Hugh Latham 1929- *St&PR 91*
Robinson, Hugh R. 1922- *WhoAm 90*
Robinson, Humberto 1930- *Ballpl 90*
Robinson, Ingrid B. 1939- *WhoAmW 91*
Robinson, Irwin Jay 1928- *WhoAm 90*, *WhoE 91*
Robinson, J. Cordell 1940- *WhoHisp 91*
Robinson, J. Kenneth *NewYTBS 90*
Robinson, J. Kenneth 1916-1990 *BioIn 16*
Robinson, J. Russel 1892-1963 *BioIn 16*
Robinson, J. Russell 1892-1963 *OxCPMus*
Robinson, Jack 1919-1972 *WorAlBi*
Robinson, Jack A. 1930- *St&PR 91*
Robinson, Jack Albert 1930- *WhoAm 90*
Robinson, Jackie 1919-1972 *Ballpl 90 [port]*, *BioIn 16*
Robinson, Jacob 1921-1944 *BioIn 16*
Robinson, Jacqueline Carter 1944- *WhoAmW 91*
Robinson, Jacques Alan 1947- *WhoAm 90*
Robinson, James *WhoSSW 91*
Robinson, James Allen 1923- *BiDrAPA 89*
Robinson, James Arthur 1932- *WhoAm 90*, *WhoWrEP 89*
Robinson, James C. *St&PR 91*
Robinson, James D., III *BioIn 16*
Robinson, James D., III 1935- *St&PR 91*
Robinson, James David 1951- *IntWWM 90*
Robinson, James Dixon, III 1935- *WhoAm 90*, *WhoE 91*
Robinson, James Edward 1930- *St&PR 91*
Robinson, James Fletcher 1944- *St&PR 91*
Robinson, James Ford 1955- *WhoWrEP 89*
Robinson, James Keith 1916- *WhoWrEP 89*
Robinson, James Kenneth 1943- *WhoAm 90*
Robinson, James LeRoy 1940- *WhoAm 90*, *WhoE 91*
Robinson, James Lowery 1838-1887 *AmLegL*
Robinson, James Victor 1927- *St&PR 91*
Robinson, James Wayne 1946- *St&PR 91*
Robinson, James William 1923- *WhoSSW 91*
Robinson, James William 1934- *St&PR 91*
Robinson, James William 1938- *WhoE 91*
Robinson, Jan 1945- *WhoAmW 91*
Robinson, Jan M. 1933- *AuBYP 90*
Robinson, Jane Hasty 1947- *WhoAmW 91*
Robinson, Janet Andrews 1935- *WhoAmW 91*
Robinson, Janice Marie 1943- *WhoAm 90*
Robinson, Jara Baxter 1935- *WhoSSW 91*
Robinson, Jasper *PenDiDA 89*
Robinson, Jay 1915- *WhoAm 90*, *WhoAmA 91*
Robinson, Jay Luke 1932- *WhoAm 90*
Robinson, Jean Ellison *BiDrAPA 89*
Robinson, Jean Hart *BiDrAPA 89*
Robinson, Jean O. 1934- *AuBYP 90*
Robinson, Jean Ruth 1925- *WhoAm 90*
Robinson, Jeff 1960- *Ballpl 90*, *BioIn 16*
Robinson, Jeff 1961- *Ballpl 90*, *BioIn 16*
Robinson, Jeffery Herbert 1956- *WhoSSW 91*
Robinson, Jeffrey Brian 1946- *St&PR 91*
Robinson, Jennifer Milner 1963- *WhoAmW 91*
Robinson, Jerome Lawrence 1922- *St&PR 91*
Robinson, Jerry 1922- *EncACom*
Robinson, Jerry Allen 1939- *WhoSSW 91*
Robinson, Jerry H. 1932- *WhoAm 90*
Robinson, Jerry Mason 1938- *WhoSSW 91*
Robinson, Jim 1892-1976 *BioIn 16*
Robinson, Joan 1903-1983 *BioIn 16*, *MajTwCW*
Robinson, Joan 1963- *WhoAmW 91*
Robinson, Joan Eileen 1937- *WhoAmW 91*
Robinson, Joan G. 1910- *AuBYP 90*
Robinson, Joan McCuen 1953- *WhoAmW 91*
Robinson, Joan Violet 1903-1983 *DcNaB 1981*
Robinson, John 1935- *WorAlBi*
Robinson, John A. 1935- *St&PR 91*
Robinson, John A. T. 1919-1983 *BioIn 16*
Robinson, John Alan 1930- *WhoAm 90*
Robinson, John Alan 1946- *St&PR 91*
Robinson, John Alexander 1935- *WhoAm 90*
Robinson, John Arthur Thomas 1919-1983 *DcNaB 1981*
Robinson, John Beckwith 1922- *WhoAm 90*
Robinson, John Beverley 1820-1896 *DcCanB 12*
Robinson, John Bowers, Jr. 1946- *St&PR 91*, *WhoAm 90*, *WhoE 91*
Robinson, John Charles 1824-1913 *BioIn 16*
Robinson, John Dale 1941- *BiDrAPA 89*
Robinson, John Delyn 1946- *WhoWrEP 89*
Robinson, John Edmund 1924- *WhoAm 90*
Robinson, John Edwin *BiDrAPA 89*
Robinson, John G *BiDrAPA 89*
Robinson, John Hamilton 1927- *WhoAm 90*
Robinson, John Lewis 1918- *WhoAm 90*
Robinson, John Minor 1910- *WhoAm 90*, *WhoWor 91*
Robinson, John Roland 1907-1989 *BioIn 16*
Robinson, John Welch 1953- *BiDrAPA 89*
Robinson, Jon 1942- *BioIn 16*
Robinson, Joseph A. 1938- *St&PR 91*
Robinson, Joseph Albert 1938- *WhoAm 90*
Robinson, Joseph Edward 1925- *WhoAm 90*
Robinson, Joseph Hiram 1807-1896 *DcCanB 12*
Robinson, Joseph T. 1872-1937 *BioIn 16*
Robinson, Judith E *BiDrAPA 89*
Robinson, Julia Ormes 1953- *WhoEmL 91*
Robinson, Julius Ernest 1951- *WhoSSW 91*
Robinson, Karen Andrea 1953- *WhoAmW 91*
Robinson, Karen Ann 1957- *WhoAmW 91*
Robinson, Karen R. 1948- *WhoAmW 91*
Robinson, Katherine Adrienne *BiDrAPA 89*
Robinson, Katherine Prentis Woodroofe 1939- *WhoWrEP 89*
Robinson, Kathleen Shelley 1948- *WhoWrEP 89*
Robinson, Kathy Sue 1952- *WhoEmL 91*
Robinson, Kaylaine 1933- *WhoWrEP 89*
Robinson, Keith *BioIn 16*
Robinson, Kenneth 1911- *IntWWM 90*
Robinson, Kenneth James 1944- *St&PR 91*
Robinson, Kenneth Larry 1944- *WhoSSW 91*
Robinson, Kenneth Patrick 1933- *St&PR 91*
Robinson, Larry 1951- *WorAlBi*
Robinson, Larry R. 1936- *St&PR 91*
Robinson, Lawrence Brandon 1932- *WhoWor 91*
Robinson, Lawrence Dewitt 1943- *WhoAm 90*
Robinson, Lawrence Vernon, Jr. 1934- *St&PR 91*
Robinson, Lee Harris 1939- *WhoAm 90*
Robinson, Leland Walter 1942- *WhoSSW 91*
Robinson, Leon R 1925- *BiDrAPA 89*
Robinson, Leonard Harrison, Jr. 1943- *WhoAm 90*
Robinson, Leonard J 1924- *BiDrAPA 89*
Robinson, Leonard Wallace 1912- *WhoWrEP 89*
Robinson, Leslie Dawn *BiDrAPA 89*
Robinson, Libby *WhoAmA 91*
Robinson, Lilien Filipovitch 1940- *WhoAmA 91*
Robinson, Lillian Harris *BiDrAPA 89*
Robinson, Linda Gosden 1953- *BioIn 16*, *WhoAm 90*, *WhoAmW 91*, *WhoE 91*
Robinson, Lisa M. *St&PR 91*
Robinson, Lloyd *AuBYP 90*, *MajTwCW*
Robinson, Lloyd O. 1923- *St&PR 91*
Robinson, Lois Hart 1927- *WhoAmW 91*
Robinson, Lorna Jane 1957- *WhoAmW 91*
Robinson, Louie *AuBYP 90*, *BioIn 16*
Robinson, Louise Ann 1956- *WhoAm 90*
Robinson, Lowell Warren 1949- *WhoAm 90*
Robinson, Luther D *BiDrAPA 89*
Robinson, M. John 1938- *St&PR 91*
Robinson, Major *BioIn 16*
Robinson, Marc Alan 1951- *St&PR 91*
Robinson, Marc James 1961- *WhoEmL 91*
Robinson, Marcela *WhoWrEP 89*
Robinson, Margaret Virginia 1951- *WhoAmW 91*
Robinson, Margot *WhoAmA 91*
Robinson, Marguerite Stern 1935- *WhoAm 90*
Robinson, Marie Rachelle G 1919-1988 *WhoAmA 91N*
Robinson, Marietta Sebree 1951- *WhoAmW 91*
Robinson, Marilyn Platt 1936- *WhoAmW 91*
Robinson, Marilynne 1943- *FemiCLE*
Robinson, Mark E. 1955- *St&PR 91*
Robinson, Marlene Beatrice 1934- *WhoAmW 91*
Robinson, Marshall Alan 1922- *WhoAm 90*
Robinson, Martha Stewart 1914- *WhoAm 90*
Robinson, Marvin Stuart 1933- *WhoAm 90*
Robinson, Mary 1758-1800 *FemiCLE*
Robinson, Mary 1945- *WomWR*
Robinson, Mary Ann 1923- *WhoAmA 91*
Robinson, Mary Darby 1758-1800 *BioIn 16*
Robinson, Mary E. Goff 1925- *WhoAmW 91*
Robinson, Mary Jean 1929- *WhoSSW 91*
Robinson, Mary Lou 1926- *WhoAm 90*, *WhoAmW 91*, *WhoSSW 91*
Robinson, Matt 1937- *DrBIPA 90*
Robinson, Mattie Williams 1951- *WhoSSW 91*
Robinson, Maura 1956- *WhoAmA 91*
Robinson, Maurice Richard, Jr. 1937- *WhoAm 90*
Robinson, Max 1939-1988 *AnObit 1988*, *BioIn 16*
Robinson, May Morgan *BioIn 16*
Robinson, Mel Gene 1948- *WhoEmL 91*
Robinson, Melvyn Roland 1933- *WhoWor 91*
Robinson, Merle S *BiDrAPA 89*
Robinson, Michael David 1953- *BiDrAPA 89*
Robinson, Michael F. 1948- *St&PR 91*
Robinson, Michael Finlay 1933- *IntWWM 90*
Robinson, Michael Francis 1954- *WhoE 91*, *WhoEmL 91*
Robinson, Michael Hill 1929- *WhoAm 90*
Robinson, Michael J. 1932- *St&PR 91*
Robinson, Mildred Ann 1938- *WhoAmW 91*
Robinson, Milton *BiDrAPA 89*
Robinson, Milton Bernidine 1913- *WhoAm 90*
Robinson, Minnie Lenetha *WhoAmW 91*
Robinson, Muriel C *BiDrAPA 89*
Robinson, Nan Senior 1932- *WhoAmW 91*
Robinson, Nancy K 1942- *AuBYP 90*
Robinson, Naomi Jean 1951- *WhoE 91*
Robinson, Nathaniel David 1904- *WhoSSW 91*, *WhoWor 91*
Robinson, Neal E. 1951- *St&PR 91*
Robinson, Neil *Ballpl 90*
Robinson, Nell Bryant 1925- *WhoAmW 91*
Robinson, Nicholas Frank 1958- *WhoEmL 91*
Robinson, Norman L. 1926- *St&PR 91*
Robinson, Ormsbee W. 1910- *WhoSSW 91*
Robinson, Orville 1801-1882 *AmLegL*
Robinson, Pamela Elaine 1963- *WhoAmW 91*
Robinson, Patricia Ann 1952- *WhoSSW 91*
Robinson, Patricia B. 1952- *St&PR 91*
Robinson, Patricia Lee 1942- *WhoAmW 91*
Robinson, Paul *BioIn 16*
Robinson, Paul Arnold 1940- *WhoAm 90*
Robinson, Paul Heron, Jr. *BioIn 16*
Robinson, Peter 1932- *WhoAm 90*
Robinson, Peter C. 1938- *St&PR 91*
Robinson, Peter Clark 1938- *WhoAm 90*
Robinson, Phelps M 1928- *BiDrAPA 89*
Robinson, Philip 1946- *ConAu 129*
Robinson, Philip Wylie 1959- *WhoSSW 91*
Robinson, Phillip Dean 1956- *WhoSSW 91*
Robinson, Prezell Russell 1922- *WhoAm 90*
Robinson, R.C. 1940- *St&PR 91*
Robinson, Ray 1920- *AuBYP 90*
Robinson, Ray 1920-1989 *WorAlBi*
Robinson, Ray E. 1932- *IntWWM 90*
Robinson, Raymond Edwin 1932- *WhoAm 90*, *WhoSSW 91*
Robinson, Raymond J. 1956- *St&PR 91*
Robinson, Raymond Kenneth 1920- *WhoAm 90*, *WhoWrEP 89*
Robinson, Regina *BiDrAPA 89*
Robinson, Rex *BioIn 16*
Robinson, Richard 1937- *WhoAm 90*
Robinson, Richard Allen, Jr. 1936- *WhoWor 91*
Robinson, Richard Earl 1903- *WhoAm 90*
Robinson, Richard Edwin 1938- *St&PR 91*
Robinson, Richard Irvine 1930- *St&PR 91*, *WhoAm 90*
Robinson, Richard Kenneth 1932- *St&PR 91*
Robinson, Richard L. 1930- *St&PR 91*
Robinson, Rob 1955- *WhoAmW 91*, *WhoEmL 91*
Robinson, Robert A. *NewYTBS 90*
Robinson, Robert Alexander 1914- *WhoAm 90*
Robinson, Robert Armstrong 1925- *St&PR 91*, *WhoAm 90*, *WhoE 91*, *WhoWor 91*
Robinson, Robert B. 1927- *St&PR 91*
Robinson, Robert Blacque 1927- *WhoAm 90*
Robinson, Robert Edward 1924- *St&PR 91*
Robinson, Robert F. 1914- *St&PR 91*
Robinson, Robert George 1945- *BiDrAPA 89*
Robinson, Robert James 1935- *WhoAm 90*
Robinson, Robert James 1943- *St&PR 91*
Robinson, Robert L. 1936- *WhoAm 90*
Robinson, Robert Shirley 1902- *AuBYP 90*
Robinson, Robert Wade, II 1948- *WhoWor 91*
Robinson, Roger 1940- *DrBIPA 90*
Robinson, Roland 1912- *AuBYP 90*
Robinson, Ron 1962- *Ballpl 90*
Robinson, Ron A. 1945- *St&PR 91*
Robinson, Ronald Alan 1952- *WhoAm 90*
Robinson, Ronald Allen 1943- *St&PR 91*
Robinson, Ronald Franklin 1936- *St&PR 91*
Robinson, Ronald Howard 1945- *WhoEmL 91*
Robinson, Ronald James 1946- *WhoEmL 91*
Robinson, Ronald Michael 1942- *WhoE 91*
Robinson, Roscoe Ross 1929- *WhoAm 90*, *WhoWor 91*
Robinson, Roy S. *St&PR 91*
Robinson, Rudy *BioIn 16*
Robinson, Rumeal *BioIn 16*
Robinson, Russell Marable, II 1932- *WhoSSW 91*
Robinson, Sally Anne 1923- *WhoAmW 91*
Robinson, Sally Kay 1952- *WhoSSW 91*
Robinson, Sally W 1924- *WhoAmA 91*
Robinson, Sally Winston 1924- *WhoAmW 91*, *WhoWor 91*
Robinson, Samuel Charles 1931- *St&PR 91*
Robinson, Samuel Lee 1939- *St&PR 91*
Robinson, Sandra Dee 1960- *WhoAmW 91*
Robinson, Sandra Lawson 1944- *WhoAm 90*, *WhoAmW 91*
Robinson, Sarah Bonham 1939- *WhoAmW 91*
Robinson, Sarah Winn *BiDrAPA 89*
Robinson, Savannah Lina 1956- *WhoSSW 91*
Robinson, Shannon *WhoAmW 91*
Robinson, Sharleen 1950- *WhoAmW 91*
Robinson, Sharon *PenDiMP*
Robinson, Sharon 1949- *IntWWM 90*
Robinson, Shawna *BioIn 16*
Robinson, Sheila Mary 1928- *ConAu 131*
Robinson, Sherman 1942- *WhoAm 90*
Robinson, Sherman Monte 1924- *WhoAm 90*
Robinson, Sidney K. 1943- *ConAu 33NR*
Robinson, Smokey *BioIn 16*, *WhoAm 90*
Robinson, Smokey 1940- *DrBIPA 90*, *EncPR&S 89*, *OxCPMus*
Robinson, Smokey, and the Miracles *EncPR&S 89*
Robinson, Spider 1948- *RGTwCSF*
Robinson, Spike *BioIn 16*
Robinson, Spottswood William, III 1916- *WhoAm 90*
Robinson, Stanford 1904-1984 *PenDiMP*
Robinson, Stanley Daniel 1926- *WhoAm 90*
Robinson, Stephen 1953- *IntWWM 90*
Robinson, Stephen Howard 1933- *WhoAm 90*

Robinson, Stephen Michael 1942- *WhoAm 90*
Robinson, Sugar Chile 1940- *DrBlPA 90*
Robinson, Sugar Ray *BioIn 16*
Robinson, Sugar Ray 1920-1989 *DrBlPA 90*
Robinson, Sugar Ray 1921-1989 *AnObit 1989*
Robinson, Sumner Martin 1928- *WhoAm 90*
Robinson, Susan Hand 1942- *WhoWrEP 89*
Robinson, Svend *BioIn 16*
Robinson, Sylvia *BioIn 16*
Robinson, Taylor *BiDrAPA 89*
Robinson, Theodore 1852-1896 *WhoAmA 91N*
Robinson, Theresa Stone 1954- *WhoAmW 91*
Robinson, Therese Albertine Louise von J 1797-1870 *BioIn 16*
Robinson, Thomas *PenDiDA 89*
Robinson, Thomas Bullene 1917- *WhoAm 90*
Robinson, Thomas Christopher 1944- *WhoAm 90*
Robinson, Thomas George 1929- *St&PR 91*
Robinson, Thomas Pendleton 1878- *AuBYP 90*
Robinson, Thomas V 1938- *WhoAmA 91*
Robinson, Thurston 1915- *WhoAm 90*
Robinson, Tom D. *AuBYP 90*
Robinson, Tommy Franklin 1942- *WhoAm 90, WhoSSW 91*
Robinson, Trina Elizabeth 1957- *WhoSSW 91*
Robinson, V. Yvonne 1939- *WhoAmW 91*
Robinson, Valerie Ruth *BiDrAPA 89*
Robinson, Vaughan 1957- *ConAu 132*
Robinson, Veronica *AuBYP 90*
Robinson, Violet Marie 1935- *WhoAmW 91*
Robinson, Virginia A. 1942- *St&PR 91*
Robinson, Virginia Brown 1941- *WhoE 91*
Robinson, W. Lee 1943- *WhoSSW 91*
Robinson, W. Thomas 1950- *WhoSSW 91*
Robinson, Walter 1950- *WhoAmA 91*
Robinson, Walter George 1911- *WhoAm 90*
Robinson, Walter Stitt, Jr. 1917- *WhoAm 90*
Robinson, Warren Clayton 1928- *WhoE 91*
Robinson, Wilbert 1863-1934 *Ballpl 90 [port]*
Robinson, Wilburn Vaughn 1934- *St&PR 91*
Robinson, Wilkes Coleman 1925- *WhoAm 90*
Robinson, William 1940- *WorAlBi*
Robinson, William A. *BioIn 16*
Robinson, William A. 1934- *WhoAm 90*
Robinson, William Cleaver Francis 1834-1897 *DcCanB 12*
Robinson, William Ellsworth 1861-1918 *BioIn 16*
Robinson, William G. 1928- *ODwPR 91*
Robinson, William Gregory 1928- *St&PR 91*
Robinson, William H. 1937- *St&PR 91*
Robinson, William H, III *BiDrAPA 89*
Robinson, William Ingraham 1909- *WhoAm 90*
Robinson, William P. 1949- *WhoAm 90*
Robinson, William Ralph 1926- *BiDrAPA 89*
Robinson, William Steven 1948- *WhoSSW 91*
Robinson, William Wheeler 1918- *WhoAm 90, WhoWrEP 89*
Robinson, Willie Clarence 1934- *WhoAm 90*
Robinson, Windsor Calvert 1950- *WhoE 91*
Robinson, Winfield F. 1938- *St&PR 91*
Robinson-Costas, Irene 1950- *WhoEmL 91*
Robison, Andrew 1940- *WhoAmA 91*
Robison, Andrew Cliffe, Jr. 1940- *WhoAm 90*
Robison, Barbara Ann 1933- *WhoAmW 91*
Robison, Bob John *ODwPR 91*
Robison, Carolyn Love 1940- *WhoAmW 91*
Robison, Carson J. 1890-1957 *OxCPMus*
Robison, Clarence, Jr. 1924- *WhoSSW 91*
Robison, Clyde Francis 1930- *St&PR 91*
Robison, Corwin Milton, II 1950- *WhoSSW 91*
Robison, David A. 1937- *WhoAm 90*
Robison, David Alan 1937- *St&PR 91*
Robison, Deborah *AuBYP 90*
Robison, Frederick Mason 1934- *WhoAm 90*
Robison, James 1943- *BioIn 16*
Robison, James E. 1915- *St&PR 91*
Robison, James Everett 1915- *WhoAm 90, WhoE 91, WhoWor 91*
Robison, James Smith *BiDrAPA 89*
Robison, John Elder 1952- *WhoE 91*
Robison, Joseph Albert 1948- *WhoEmL 91*
Robison, Joyce June 1945- *WhoAmW 91*
Robison, Judy Kay 1947- *WhoAmW 91*
Robison, Kenneth Gerald 1938- *WhoE 91, WhoWor 91*
Robison, Mason W *BiDrAPA 89*
Robison, Nancy L 1934- *ConAu 30NR*
Robison, Olin Clyde 1936- *WhoAm 90, WhoE 91*
Robison, Paul Frederick 1919- *WhoAm 90*
Robison, Paula *IntWWM 90*
Robison, Paula Judith 1941- *WhoAm 90*
Robison, Richard Harrison 1951- *WhoSSW 91*
Robison, Susan Miller 1945- *WhoAmW 91*
Robison, Ted K. 1944- *St&PR 91*
Robison, William P 1925- *BiDrAPA 89*
Robison, William Robert 1947- *WhoEmL 91*
Robitaille, Olivier 1811-1896 *DcCanB 12*
Robitaille, Theodore 1834-1897 *DcCanB 12*
Robitelle, Clifford C. 1947- *St&PR 91*
Robitz, Mark Kenneth 1951- *WhoEmL 91*
Robkin, Maurice Abraham 1931- *WhoAm 90*
Roble, Carole Marcia 1938- *WhoAmW 91*
Roble, M.A. 1955- *St&PR 91*
Roble, Roger Harold 1941- *St&PR 91*
Robledo, Dan A. 1941- *WhoHisp 91*
Robledo, Roberto Manuel 1951- *WhoHisp 91*
Roblek, Branko 1934- *WhoWor 91*
Robles, Alejandro *WhoHisp 91*
Robles, Arturo 1948- *WhoHisp 91*
Robles, Daniel 1939- *WhoHisp 91*
Robles, Ernest Z. *WhoHisp 91*
Robles, John, Jr. 1941- *WhoHisp 91*
Robles, Julian 1933- *WhoAmA 91*
Robles, Marco A 1905-1990 *CurBio 90N, NewYTBS 90*
Robles, Marco Aurelio 1905-1990 *BioIn 16*
Robles, Marisa 1937- *IntWWM 90, PenDiMP*
Robles, Mauro P., Sr. *WhoHisp 91*
Robles, Mireya 1934- *HispWr 90*
Robles, Rosalie Miranda 1942- *WhoAmW 91, WhoWor 91*
Robles, Salvador Antonio 1943- *WhoSSW 91*
Robles de Araujo, Julian 1954- *WhoWor 91*
Robles Garcia, Yolanda *WhoHisp 91*
Robles-Gorriti, Carlos J *BiDrAPA 89*
Robles Jimenez, Jose Esaul 1925- *WhoAm 90*
Roblin, Andrew 1959- *WhoE 91*
Roblin, Duff 1917- *WhoAm 90*
Robling, Nancy Margaret 1941- *BiDrAPA 89*
Robling, V. Dale 1924- *St&PR 91*
Robnak, David Zach 1957- *St&PR 91*
Robnett, Truman J *BiDrAPA 89*
Robock, Stefan Hyman 1915- *WhoAm 90*
Robohm, Peggy Adler 1942- *WhoAmW 91, WhoE 91*
Robold, Alice Ilene 1928- *WhoAm 90, WhoAmW 91*
Roboson, Christopher 1953- *IntWWM 90*
Robota, Roza 1921-1944 *BioIn 16*
Robotham, Barbara 1936- *IntWWM 90*
Robotham, Lascelles Lister 1923- *WhoWor 91*
Robredo, Raimundo 1925- *WhoWor 91*
Robsjohn-Gibbings, Terence Harold 1905-1976 *PenDiDA 89*
Robsjohn-Gibbings, Terrence Harold 1905-1976 *ConDes 90*
Robson, Alan 1915-1987 *BioIn 16*
Robson, Alan David 1945- *WhoWor 91*
Robson, Barbara Baker 1942- *WhoAmW 91*
Robson, Barbara Smith 1938- *WhoE 91*
Robson, Brian A. 1937- *St&PR 91*
Robson, Deborah Ruth 1948- *WhoAmW 91*
Robson, Dirk 1932- *SpyFic*
Robson, Flora 1902-1984 *DcNaB 1981*
Robson, Geoffrey Robert 1929- *WhoWor 91*
Robson, Henry Charles, Jr. 1947- *WhoSSW 91*
Robson, John 1824-1892 *DcCanB 12*
Robson, John Edwin 1930- *St&PR 91, WhoAm 90*
Robson, Kenneth Stone 1933- *BiDrAPA 89*
Robson, L L 1931-1990 *ConAu 132*
Robson, Lucia St. Clair 1942- *BioIn 16*
Robson, Martin Cecil 1939- *WhoAm 90*
Robson, May 1865-1942 *WorAlBi*
Robson, Peter 1926- *WhoWor 91*
Robson, Stuart 1914- *WhoE 91*
Robson, Susan Lucille 1951- *WhoAmW 91*
Robson, Sybil Ann 1956- *WhoAmW 91*
Robson, Terry Patrick 1943- *WhoSSW 91*
Robson, Thomas Douglas 1948- *WhoAm 90*
Robuchon, Joel 1945- *WhoWor 91*
Robus, Hugo 1885-1964 *WhoAmA 91N*
Robustelli, Andy *BioIn 16*
Robusto, C. Carl 1916- *WhoAm 90*
Roby, Christina Yen *WhoAmW 91*
Roby, Donald Franklin 1929- *St&PR 91, WhoAm 90*
Roby, Kinley Edmund 1929- *WhoWrEP 89*
Roby, Lavelle *DrBlPA 90*
Roby, Ross *BiDrAPA 89*
Robyn, Paul *PenDiMP*
Roca, Blas 1898-1987 *BioIn 16*
Roca, Carlos Manuel 1962- *WhoHisp 91*
Roca, F.H. 1939- *St&PR 91*
Roca, Julio Argentino 1843-1914 *BioIn 16*
Roca, Octavio 1949- *WhoHisp 91*
Roca, Rafael A. 1928- *WhoHisp 91*
Roca, Robert Paul 1952- *BiDrAPA 89, WhoE 91*
Rocafuerte, Vicente 1783-1847 *BioIn 16*
Rocah, Barbara Ellen *BiDrAPA 89*
Rocard, Michel *BioIn 16*
Rocard, Michel Louis Leon 1930- *BiDFrPL, WhoWor 91*
Rocca, Guido 1928-1961 *AuBYP 90*
Roccaforte, William Howard 1953- *BiDrAPA 89*
Roccatagliata, Niccolo *PenDiDA 89*
Rocci, Mario Louis, Jr. 1952- *WhoE 91*
Rocco, Alex *BioIn 16*
Rocco, Maurice 1915-1976 *DrBlPA 90*
Rocco, Mickey 1916- *Ballpl 90*
Rocco, Ron 1953- *WhoAmA 91*
Rocco, Vincent Anthony 1945- *St&PR 91, WhoAm 90*
Rocek, Jan 1924- *WhoAm 90*
Roces, Felix Cadag, Jr. 1936- *WhoWor 91*
Roces, Joaquin 1913-1988 *BioIn 16*
Roch, Ernst 1928- *ConDes 90, WhoAmA 91*
Rocha, Armandino Cordeiro Dos Santos 1934- *WhoWor 91*
Rocha, Fernando Aguero 1917?- *BioIn 16*
Rocha, Fernando Augusto 1958- *WhoWor 91*
Rocha, Glauber 1938-1981 *BioIn 16*
Rocha, Marilyn Eva 1928- *WhoAmW 91*
Rocha, Octavio *WhoHisp 91*
Rocha, Randolfo 1950- *WhoAmA 91*
Rocha, Rene *WhoHisp 91*
Rocha, Rina Garcia *HispWr 90*
Rocha, Veronica Rodrigues 1946- *WhoHisp 91*
Rocha da Costa, Celestino *WhoWor 91*
Rochambeau, Jean B D de Vimeur, Comte de 1725-1807 *EncCRAm*
Rochambeau, Jean Baptiste D, Comte De 1725-1807 *WorAlBi*
Rochard, Henri *ConAu 31NR*
Rochas, Albert De 1837-1914 *EncPaPR 91*
Rochas, Eugene Auguste-Albert D'Aiglun 1837-1914 *EncO&P 3*
Rochat, Jean-Paul 1943- *WhoWor 91*
Rochberg, George *BioIn 16*
Rochberg, George 1918- *IntWWM 90, PenDiMP A, WhoAm 90*
Rochbrune, Alphonse-Barnabe Larocque De *DcCanB 12*
Roche, A. K. *AuBYP 90*
Roche, Antonio 1944- *WhoWor 91*
Roche, Arnaldo 1955- *WhoHisp 91*
Roche, Burke B. 1913- *St&PR 91*
Roche, Burke Bernard 1913- *WhoAm 90*
Roche, David Alan 1946- *WhoAm 90*
Roche, David H. 1947- *St&PR 91*
Roche, Denise Ann 1942- *WhoAmW 91*
Roche, Douglas David 1936- *WhoAm 90*
Roche, E. James 1931- *St&PR 91*
Roche, Gail Connor 1953- *WhoE 91*
Roche, George A. 1941- *St&PR 91*
Roche, George Augustine 1941- *WhoAm 90*
Roche, George Charles, III 1935- *WhoAm 90*
Roche, Gerard R. 1931- *St&PR 91*
Roche, Gerard Raymond 1931- *WhoAm 90*
Roche, James Joseph 1953- *WhoSSW 91*
Roche, James M. 1906- *St&PR 91*
Roche, James McMillan 1934- *WhoAm 90*
Roche, James Michael 1906- *EncABHB 5 [port]*
Roche, Jean 1901- *WhoWor 91*
Roche, Jerome Laurence Alexander 1942- *IntWWM 90*
Roche, John E. 1946- *St&PR 91*
Roche, John Jefferson 1934- *WhoAm 90*
Roche, John P. 1923- *WhoAm 90*
Roche, Juliette 1884-1980? *BiDWomA*
Roche, Kevin *BioIn 16*
Roche, Kevin 1922- *WhoAm 90, WhoWor 91*
Roche, Kevin Joseph 1935- *St&PR 91*
Roche, Lynn Frances 1960- *WhoE 91*
Roche, Marcel 1920- *WhoWor 91*
Roche, Myles John 1941- *St&PR 91*
Roche, P. K. 1935- *BioIn 16*
Roche, Patricia K. 1935- *BioIn 16*
Roche, Patrick W. 1948- *St&PR 91*
Roche, Paul C. 1915- *St&PR 91*
Roche, Paul Hoop, Jr. 1945- *St&PR 91*
Roche, Regina Maria 1764-1845 *BioIn 16, FemiCLE*
Roche, Robert *WhoAmA 91*
Roche, Robert Francis 1942- *St&PR 91*
Roche, Stephen *BioIn 16*
Roche, Stephen Michael 1959- *St&PR 91*
Roche, William Francis 1924- *St&PR 91*
Roche, William J. 1924- *St&PR 91*
Roche, William Joseph 1927- *WhoAm 90*
Roche, Zebulon *BioIn 16*
Rochebouet, Gaetan de Grimaudet de 1813-1899 *BiDFrPL*
Rochefort, Christiane 1917- *EncCoWW*
Rochefort, John Spencer 1924- *WhoAm 90*
Rochefort, Victor 1830-1913 *BiDFrPL*
Rocheleau, Donald 1933- *St&PR 91*
Rocheleau, France D *BiDrAPA 89*
Rocheleau, James Romig 1940- *WhoAm 90*
Rocheleau, Norman J. *St&PR 91*
Rocheleau, Ronald D. 1941- *St&PR 91*
Rocheleau, Serge 1942- *St&PR 91*
Rochell, Carlton Charles 1933- *WhoAm 90*
Rochelle, Norman C. 1933- *St&PR 91*
Rocher, Ludo 1926- *WhoAm 90*
Rocher, Rosemarie Gloria 1936- *WhoE 91*
Roches, Dames des *EncCoWW*
Rochester *DrBlPA 90*
Rochester 1905-1977 *WorAlBi*
Rochester, Diana 1944- *WhoAmW 91*
Rochester, George Dixon 1908- *WhoWor 91*
Rochester, Haydon 1912- *BiDrAPA 89*
Rochester, John Wilmot, Earl of 1647-1680 *BioIn 16*
Rochester, Marc Andrew 1954- *IntWWM 90*
Rochester, Michael Grant 1932- *WhoAm 90*
Rochester, Richard Earle *BiDrAPA 89*
Rochet, Waldeck Emile Eugene 1905-1983 *BiDFrPL*
Rochette, Cleophas 1843?-1895 *DcCanB 12*
Rochette, Denis 1945- *BiDrAPA 89*
Rochette, Louis 1923- *St&PR 91, WhoAm 90*
Rochetto, Evelyn Marie 1906- *WhoWor 91*
Rochford, John M. *BioIn 16*
Rochford, Joseph M 1943- *BiDrAPA 89*
Rochford, Walter 1943- *St&PR 91, WhoAm 90*
Rochfort, Cecil Charles Boyd- 1887-1983 *DcNaB 1981*
Rochin-Rodriguez, Refugio Ismael 1941- *WhoHisp 91*
Rochira, Nancy Mary 1944- *WhoAmW 91*
Rochlin, Dina Z *BiDrAPA 89*
Rochlin, Gregory 1912- *BiDrAPA 89, WhoE 91*
Rochlis, James J. 1916- *St&PR 91*
Rochlis, James Joseph 1916- *WhoAm 90*
Rochman, Alan L. 1945- *St&PR 91*
Rochman, Todd Alvin *BiDrAPA 89*
Rochon, Denise *BiDrAPA 89*
Rochon, Edwin Waterbury 1918- *WhoAm 90, WhoWrEP 89*
Rochon, John Philip 1951- *WhoAm 90*
Rochwarger, Jeffrey Alan 1953- *WhoAm 90*
Rochwarger, Leonard 1925- *St&PR 91, WhoAm 90, WhoWor 91*
Rochwarger, Michelle 1955- *WhoAmW 91*
Rochwerger, Leonard Leslie 1942- *St&PR 91*
Rock 'n' Rollen *BioIn 16*
Rock, Amelia Sirianni *WhoAmW 91*
Rock, Arthur 1926- *St&PR 91, WhoAm 90*
Rock, Barry Lee 1958- *WhoSSW 91*
Rock, Cheryl Lynne Poore 1957- *WhoAmW 91*
Rock, David *BioIn 16*
Rock, Douglas L. *BioIn 16*
Rock, Douglas L. 1947- *St&PR 91*
Rock, Douglas Lawrence 1947- *WhoAm 90, WhoSSW 91*
Rock, Gail *AuBYP 90*
Rock, George David 1919-1988 *BioIn 16*
Rock, Harold L. 1932- *WhoAm 90*
Rock, Heidi Marie 1957- *WhoAmW 91*
Rock, Howard 1911-1976 *BioIn 16*
Rock, John Aubrey 1946- *WhoAm 90*
Rock, John Van Hassel 1939- *St&PR 91*
Rock, Leslie S. 1957- *St&PR 91*
Rock, Lydia G. 1952- *WhoAmW 91*
Rock, Nathaniel 1899-1990 *BioIn 16*
Rock, Nicholas L 1932- *BiDrAPA 89*
Rock, Peter Alfred 1939- *WhoAm 90*
Rock, Phillip Joseph 1937- *WhoAm 90*
Rock, Randy Franklyn 1950- *WhoE 91*
Rock, Sabra Leigh 1952- *WhoAmW 91*
Rock, Thomas P. 1943- *St&PR 91*
Rock, William Booth 1947- *WhoWor 91*
Rock, William F. 1935- *WhoSSW 91*
Rockall, Diane Margaret 1945- *WhoAmW 91*
Rockaway, Harold 1926- *BiDrAPA 89*

Rockburne, Dorothea *WhoAmA 91*
Rockburne, Dorothea 1934- *BiDWomA*
Rockburne, Dorothea G. *WhoAm 90, WhoE 91*
Rocke, William J. 1924- *St&PR 91*
Rockefeller, Abby A. 1874-1948 *BioAmW*
Rockefeller, Blanchette Hooker 1909- *WhoAm 90*
Rockefeller, David 1915- *St&PR 91, WhoAm 90, WhoAmA 91, WhoE 91, WhoWor 91, WorAlBi*
Rockefeller, David, Mrs *WhoAmA 91*
Rockefeller, Edwin Shaffer 1927- *WhoAm 90*
Rockefeller, Frederic Lincoln 1921- *St&PR 91*
Rockefeller, Happy *WhoAm 90*
Rockefeller, Herbert Campbell 1942- *WhoSSW 91*
Rockefeller, James S. 1902- *St&PR 91*
Rockefeller, Jeannette E *BiDrAPA 89*
Rockefeller, John D. 1839-1937 *BioIn 16, WorAlBi*
Rockefeller, John D. 1874-1960 *BioIn 16*
Rockefeller, John D. 1906-1978 *BioIn 16*
Rockefeller, John D., Jr. 1874-1960 *WorAlBi*
Rockefeller, John Davison, III 1906-1978 *WhoAmA 91N*
Rockefeller, John Davison, IV 1937- *WhoAm 90, WhoSSW 91, WhoWor 91, WorAlBi*
Rockefeller, Laurance S. 1910- *WhoAm 90, WhoWor 91, WorAlBi*
Rockefeller, Laurance S, Mrs 1910- *WhoAmA 91*
Rockefeller, Margaretta Fitler Murphy *WhoAm 90*
Rockefeller, Mary French 1910- *WhoAm 90*
Rockefeller, Nelson A. 1908-1979 *BioIn 16, WorAlBi*
Rockefeller, Nelson Aldrich 1908-1979 *BiDrUSE 89, WhoAmA 91N*
Rockefeller, Rodman Clark 1932- *WhoAm 90*
Rockefeller, Sharon Percy 1944- *WhoAmW 91*
Rockefeller, Steven C. *WhoAm 90*
Rockefeller, William *NewYTBS 90 [port]*
Rockefeller, William 1918-1990 *BioIn 16*
Rockefeller, Winthrop 1912-1973 *BioIn 16, WhoAmA 91N*
Rockefeller, Winthrop 1948- *BioIn 16*
Rockemann, David Douglas 1954- *WhoEmL 91, WhoWor 91*
Rockenbach, Wayne R. 1943- *St&PR 91*
Rocker, Laura Hannah 1952- *BiDrAPA 89*
Rocker, Rudolf 1873-1958 *EncAL*
Rockett, Rita *BioIn 16*
Rockett, Rocky Lynn 1951- *WhoEmL 91*
Rockey, Ernest Arthur *St&PR 91*
Rockey, Jay 1928- *ODwPR 91*
Rockfeld, Michael 1951- *WhoE 91*
Rockhill, William Woodville 1854-1914 *BioIn 16*
Rockhold, William L. 1932- *St&PR 91*
Rockland, Barry 1943- *St&PR 91*
Rockland, Lawrence H 1932- *BiDrAPA 89*
Rockland, Michael Aaron 1935- *ConAu 32NR*
Rocklen, Kathy Hellenbrand 1951- *St&PR 91, WhoAmW 91, WhoEmL 91*
Rockler, Walter J. 1920- *WhoAm 90*
Rocklin, I.J. 1907- *St&PR 91*
Rocklin, Raymond 1922- *WhoAmA 91*
Rockman, Gregory *BioIn 16*
Rockman, Ilene Frances 1950- *WhoAmW 91*
Rockmore, Daniel Nahum 1961- *WhoE 91*
Rockmore, Sylvie Marie 1945- *WhoAmW 91, WhoE 91*
Rockne, Anton Julius 1870-1950 *AmLegL*
Rockne, Knute 1888-1931 *BioIn 16, WorAlBi*
Rocko, Chester Joseph 1952- *St&PR 91*
Rockoff, Alvin J. 1927- *St&PR 91*
Rockoff, S. David 1931- *WhoAm 90*
Rockoff, Sheila G. 1945- *WhoAmW 91*
Rockola, David C. 1897- *St&PR 91*
Rockowitz, Noah E. 1949- *St&PR 91*
Rockrise, George Thomas 1916- *WhoAm 90*
Rockstein, Morris 1916- *WhoAm 90*
Rocksvold, Phyllis Jean 1947- *WhoEmL 91*
Rockwell, Alvin John 1908- *WhoAm 90*
Rockwell, Anne 1934- *AuBYP 90*
Rockwell, Bruce McKee 1922- *St&PR 91, WhoAm 90*
Rockwell, Burton Lowe 1920- *WhoAm 90*
Rockwell, David Maury 1953- *WhoSSW 91*
Rockwell, Don A 1938- *BiDrAPA 89*
Rockwell, Don Arthur 1938- *WhoAm 90, WhoWor 91*
Rockwell, Elizabeth Dennis 1921- *WhoAmW 91, WhoSSW 91*
Rockwell, Elizabeth K *BiDrAPA 89*
Rockwell, Enid 1951- *BiDrAPA 89*
Rockwell, George 1922- *St&PR 91*
Rockwell, George Barcus 1926- *WhoAm 90*
Rockwell, Harlow 1910-1988 *BioIn 16*
Rockwell, Henry T. 1914- *ODwPR 91*
Rockwell, James Mitchell 1928- *WhoAm 90*
Rockwell, Jerome Corry 1950- *IntWWM 90*
Rockwell, John Sargent 1940- *IntWWM 90, WhoAm 90*
Rockwell, Julius 1805-1888 *AmLegL*
Rockwell, Landon Gale 1914- *WhoAm 90*
Rockwell, Norman 1894-1978 *BioIn 16, WhoAmA 91N, WorAlBi*
Rockwell, Norman 1927- *St&PR 91, WhoE 91*
Rockwell, Orrin Porter 1813-1878 *BioIn 16*
Rockwell, Phillip E. 1952- *WhoSSW 91*
Rockwell, Richard Dean 1955- *St&PR 91*
Rockwell, Richard Thornton 1946- *WhoEmL 91*
Rockwell, Robert Biddle 1938- *BiDrAPA 89*
Rockwell, Robin Markle 1939- *WhoSSW 91*
Rockwell, Ronald James, Jr. 1937- *WhoAm 90*
Rockwell, S. Kent 1944- *St&PR 91*
Rockwell, Teed *NewAgMG*
Rockwell, Theodore 1922- *EncPaPR 91, WhoAm 90*
Rockwell, Thomas C *BiDrAPA 89*
Rockwell, W.J. Kenneth 1931- *BiDrAPA 89*
Rockwell, Willard F., Jr. 1914- *St&PR 91*
Rockwell, Willard Frederick, Jr. 1914- *WhoAm 90*
Rockwood, Frederick Whitney 1947- *St&PR 91*
Rockwood, Ruth 1906-1989 *BioIn 16*
Rockwood, Ruth H. 1906- *WhoAm 90*
Rockwood, S.D. 1943- *St&PR 91*
Rockwood, William A., Jr. 1947- *St&PR 91*
Rocour, Jean Luc 1935- *WhoWor 91*
Roda 1926- *WhoAmA 91*
Roda, Jan 1952- *BiDrAPA 89*
Rodale, Ardath *BioIn 16*
Rodale, Jerome Irving 1899-1971 *NewAgE 90*
Rodale, Robert *NewYTBS 90 [port]*
Rodale, Robert 1930- *NewAgE 90, St&PR 91*
Rodale, Robert 1930-1990 *ConAu 132*
Rodan, Don 1950- *WhoAmA 91*
Rodan, Mendi 1929- *IntWWM 90, WhoWor 91*
Rodbard, Betty *WhoAmA 91*
Rodbell, Clyde A. 1927- *St&PR 91*
Rodbell, Martin 1925- *WhoAm 90*
Rodbell, Sidney Philip 1946- *St&PR 91*
Rodby, Craig Robert 1949- *St&PR 91*
Rodby, John Leonard 1944- *IntWWM 90*
Rodby, Michael Kevin 1955- *WhoEmL 91*
Rodchenko, Aleksandr Mikhailovich 1891-1956 *BioIn 16*
Rodd, Allan Keith 1932- *St&PR 91*
Rodd, Kylie 1912- *AuBYP 90*
Rodd, Kylie Tennant 1912-1988 *MajTwCW*
Rodd, Thomas 1913- *WhoAm 90*
Rodda, Luca 1960- *WhoWor 91*
Rodda, Richard E. 1945- *IntWWM 90*
Rodda, Terrence 1944- *WhoSSW 91*
Roddam, Franc *BioIn 16*
Rodde, Anne-Marie 1946- *IntWWM 90*
Rodden, John 1956- *ConAu 131*
Roddenberry, Bonnie Lindquist 1948- *WhoEmL 91*
Roddenberry, Eugene Wesley 1921- *WhoAm 90*
Roddenberry, Gene 1921- *Au&Arts 5 [port], BioIn 16*
Roddenberry, Ralph J. 1925- *St&PR 91*
Roddewig, Richard John 1948- *WhoEmL 91*
Roddey, Alyce 1932- *WhoE 91*
Roddey, J.G. Richards 1937- *St&PR 91*
Roddick, Anita *BioIn 16*
Roddick, David B. 1948- *St&PR 91*
Roddick, David Bruce 1948- *WhoEmL 91*
Roddick, John William, Jr. 1926- *WhoAm 90*
Roddin, Michael Ian 1955- *WhoWrEP 89*
Roddis, Louis Harry, Jr. 1918- *WhoAm 90, WhoSSW 91*
Roddis, Richard Stiles Law 1930- *WhoAm 90*
Roddy, Dorothy Hodges 1939- *WhoSSW 91*
Roddy, Edith Jeannette *WhoAmA 91N*
Roddy, Edward 1931- *St&PR 91*
Roddy, Edward Joseph 1941- *WhoE 91*
Roddy, Floyd A. 1920- *WhoSSW 91*
Roddy, Francis L. 1931- *St&PR 91*
Roddy, James T. 1942- *WhoAm 90*
Roddy, Lee 1921- *BioIn 16*
Roddy, Marita 1954- *WhoAmW 91*
Roddy, Robert *BiDrAPA 89*
Rode, Albert 1930- *St&PR 91*
Rode, Clifford J. 1941- *St&PR 91*
Rode, Edith 1879-1956 *EncCoWW*
Rode, Francis Warren, III 1942- *St&PR 91*
Rode, Helge 1870-1937 *DcScanL*
Rode, James D. 1948- *St&PR 91*
Rode, James Dean 1948- *WhoAm 90*
Rode, Leif 1926- *WhoAm 90, WhoWor 91*
Rode, Meredith Eagon 1938- *WhoAmA 91*
Rodeck, Willard Martin 1929- *St&PR 91*
Rodefeld, Gary H. 1953- *St&PR 91*
Rodefeld, James A. 1938- *St&PR 91*
Rodefer, Joanne Marie 1953- *WhoSSW 91*
Rodefer, Karl Douglas 1950- *WhoSSW 91*
Rodehaver, Mark William *BiDrAPA 89*
Rodeheaver, Olah Anita 1923- *WhoAmW 91*
Rodeheffer, Jonathan Paul 1942- *WhoSSW 91*
Rodeiro, Jose Manuel 1949- *WhoAmA 91, WhoHisp 91*
Rodel, Arthur 1898-1945 *BioIn 16*
Rodell, Elizabeth Goodson *BioIn 16*
Rodell, Fred 1920- *WhoSSW 91*
Roden, Anthony 1937- *IntWWM 90*
Roden, Chie Sato 1947- *IntWWM 90*
Roden, Mary Suzanne 1939- *WhoSSW 91*
Roden, Valerie-Clark 1963- *WhoE 91*
Roden, William Frost 1922- *St&PR 91*
Rodenbaugh, Marcia Louise 1942- *WhoAmW 91*
Rodenberg, Clinton F. 1944- *St&PR 91*
Rodenberg, Richard Theodore 1920- *St&PR 91*
Rodenberger, Charles Alvard 1926- *WhoAm 90*
Rodenberger, Philip Drew 1944- *BiDrAPA 89*
Rodenbiker, Jo Ann 1954- *WhoAmW 91*
Rodenbough, Dean *ODwPR 91*
Rodenbush, Rebecca Lynn 1948- *WhoAmW 91*
Rodengen, Jeffrey Lee 1949- *WhoWor 91*
Rodenhauser, Paul 1937- *BiDrAPA 89*
Rodenhouse, Curtis W. 1954- *St&PR 91*
Rodenkirch, John Jeffrey 1950- *St&PR 91*
Rodenstein, Howard R. 1954- *WhoE 91*
Rodenwaldt, Gerhart 1886-1945 *BioIn 16*
Roder, Ronald E. 1948- *St&PR 91, WhoEmL 91*
Roderburg, Theodor Kjell 1929- *WhoWor 91*
Roderich, Hans Harold 1926- *St&PR 91*
Roderick, Bruce Anthony 1958- *St&PR 91*
Roderick, David M. *BioIn 16*
Roderick, David M. 1924- *St&PR 91*
Roderick, David Milton 1924- *WhoAm 90, WhoE 91, WhoWor 91*
Roderick, Edward Earl 1932- *St&PR 91*
Roderick, Regis Leo 1940- *WhoE 91*
Roderick, Richard Michael 1948- *St&PR 91, WhoAm 90, WhoE 91*
Roderick, Robert Gene 1944- *WhoSSW 91*
Roderick, Robert Lee 1925- *WhoAm 90*
Roderick, Sue Schock 1937- *WhoAmW 91*
Roderick-Jones, Alan *BioIn 16*
Roderick Jones, Richard Trevor 1947- *IntWWM 90*
Rodericks, Charles Manuel, Jr. 1952- *WhoEmL 91*
Rodewald, Kate *BioIn 16*
Rodewald, Paul Gerhard 1899- *WhoAm 90*
Rodewald, Russell Allen *BiDrAPA 89*
Rodewald, William Young 1928- *WhoAm 90*
Rodewig, John Stuart 1933- *St&PR 91*
Rodger, George 1908- *BioIn 16*
Rodgers, Alice Lynn 1942- *WhoAmW 91*
Rodgers, Andre 1934- *Ballpl 90*
Rodgers, Antoinette Yvetta 1959- *WhoAmW 91*
Rodgers, B.D. 1924- *St&PR 91*
Rodgers, Barry Earle 1940- *WhoE 91*
Rodgers, Betty L. 1930- *St&PR 91*
Rodgers, Bill 1947- *BioIn 16*
Rodgers, Bob 1938- *BioIn 16*
Rodgers, Buck *BioIn 16*
Rodgers, Buck 1938- *Ballpl 90, WhoAm 90, WhoE 91*
Rodgers, Calbraith Perry *BioIn 16*
Rodgers, Carolyn M. 1942- *ConAu 13AS [port]*
Rodgers, Carolyn M 1945- *WorAu 1980*
Rodgers, Daniel Tracy 1942- *WhoAm 90*
Rodgers, Debra Elaine *BiDrAPA 89*
Rodgers, Diana Louise 1962- *WhoAmW 91*
Rodgers, Eugene 1939- *ConAu 132, WhoAm 90*
Rodgers, Francis G. *BioIn 16*
Rodgers, Frank 1927- *WhoAm 90*
Rodgers, Frank Judson, Jr. 1930- *St&PR 91*
Rodgers, Gary Wayne 1947- *WhoSSW 91*
Rodgers, George D. 1933- *St&PR 91*
Rodgers, J.L. 1925- *St&PR 91*
Rodgers, Jack A 1938- *WhoAmA 91*
Rodgers, James Foster 1951- *WhoAm 90*
Rodgers, James Turner 1934- *St&PR 91*
Rodgers, James W. 1907-1989 *BioIn 16*
Rodgers, Jim *WhoAm 90, WhoE 91*
Rodgers, Jimmie *WhoNeCM C [port]*
Rodgers, Jimmie 1879-1933 *OxCPMus*
Rodgers, Jimmie 1897-1933 *WorAlBi*
Rodgers, Joan 1960- *IntWWM 90*
Rodgers, Joe M. 1933- *BioIn 16*
Rodgers, John 1914- *WhoAm 90*
Rodgers, John C, Jr. 1943- *BiDrAPA 89*
Rodgers, John Ex 1935- *St&PR 91, WhoAm 90*
Rodgers, John J. 1939- *ODwPR 91*
Rodgers, John J. 1940- *St&PR 91*
Rodgers, Joseph F. 1932- *St&PR 91*
Rodgers, Lawrence Rodney 1920- *WhoAm 90*
Rodgers, Leslie Clegg 1952- *WhoAmW 91*
Rodgers, Louis Dean 1930- *WhoWor 91*
Rodgers, Mary 1932- *OxCPMus*
Rodgers, Mary Columbro 1925- *WhoAm 90, WhoAmW 91, WhoWor 91, WhoWrEP 89*
Rodgers, Nancy Lucille 1934- *WhoAmW 91*
Rodgers, Nile *BioIn 16*
Rodgers, Paul 1933- *WhoAm 90*
Rodgers, Peter *BioIn 16*
Rodgers, R. Wayne 1928- *St&PR 91*
Rodgers, Richard 1902-1979 *BioIn 16, OxCPMus, PenDiMP A, WorAlBi*
Rodgers, Robert Allen 1939- *WhoE 91*
Rodgers, Rod *DrBIPA 90*
Rodgers, Rowland *St&PR 91*
Rodgers, Royce W. 1933- *St&PR 91*
Rodgers, Sarah Louise 1953- *IntWWM 90*
Rodgers, Stephen *BioIn 16*
Rodgers, Terry C 1917- *BiDrAPA 89*
Rodgers, Thomas Albert 1941- *BiDrAPA 89, WhoE 91*
Rodgers, Thomas H. 1944- *St&PR 91*
Rodgers, Thomas J. 1946- *St&PR 91*
Rodgers, Thomas Paul 1950- *WhoEmL 91*
Rodgers, Victoria Martinez- *BioIn 16*
Rodgers, Will 1879-1935 *WorAlBi*
Rodgers, William, Jr. 1950- *St&PR 91*
Rodgers, William Henry 1947- *WhoAm 90*
Rodgers, William M. 1926- *WhoAm 90*
Rodgers, William Michael 1926- *St&PR 91*
Rodgerson, Dewey A. 1928- *St&PR 91*
Rodgin, David W 1928- *BiDrAPA 89*
Rodgman, Alan 1924- *WhoAm 90*
Rodham, Robert D. 1939-1988 *BioIn 16*
Rodhe, Gosta 1912- *EncO&P 3*
Rodi, D. Richard 1917- *WhoE 91*
Rodia, Simon 1875 1965 *MusmAFA*
Rodia, Simon 1879-1965 *BioIn 16*
Rodic, Stanko *BiDrAPA 89*
Rodich, Michael E. 1952- *St&PR 91*
Rodie, Edward B. 1921- *St&PR 91*
Rodieck, Patricia Anna 1938- *WhoWrEP 89*
Rodier, D.G. *St&PR 91*
Rodimer, Frank Joseph 1927- *WhoAm 90, WhoE 91*
Rodimon, Stanley J. 1939- *WhoAm 90*
Rodin, Auguste 1840-1917 *BioIn 16, IntDcAA 90, WorAlBi*
Rodin, Ernst Anton 1925- *WhoAm 90, WhoWor 91*
Rodin, Gary Michael 1946- *BiDrAPA 89*
Rodin, Geraldine W. 1938- *St&PR 91*
Rodin, Judith Seitz 1944- *WhoAm 90, WhoAmW 91*
Rodin, Jules S *BiDrAPA 89*
Rodin, Leonard M 1942- *BiDrAPA 89*
Rodin, Leonard Steven 1952- *St&PR 91*
Rodin-Novak, Sheila Karen 1947- *WhoAmW 91*
Rodino, Peter W. *BioIn 16*
Rodino, Peter W., Jr. 1909- *WorAlBi*
Rodino, Peter Wallace, Jr. 1909- *WhoAm 90, WhoE 91*
Rodino, Vincent Louis 1929- *WhoE 91*
Rodis, Isadore 1903- *BiDrAPA 89*
Rodis, Monica 1953- *WhoAmW 91*
Rodisch, Robert Joseph 1919- *WhoAm 90*
Roditis, George Christofis 1949- *WhoWor 91*
Rodman, Alan George 1933- *WhoE 91*
Rodman, Alpine Clarence 1952- *WhoEmL 91, WhoWor 91*
Rodman, Angela Faye 1963- *WhoAmW 91*
Rodman, Bella 1903- *AuBYP 90*
Rodman, Constance Anne 1946- *BiDrAPA 89*
Rodman, Cynthia Willett 1960- *WhoAmW 91*
Rodman, Dennis *BioIn 16, NewYTBS 90 [port]*
Rodman, Eric *MajTwCW*
Rodman, F Robert 1934- *BiDrAPA 89*
Rodman, F. Robert 1934- *BioIn 16*
Rodman, Francis Robert 1934- *BioIn 16*
Rodman, George Bush 1911- *WhoAm 90*
Rodman, George Robinson 1948- *WhoEmL 91*
Rodman, Harry Eugene 1913- *WhoAm 90*

Rodman, James Purcell 1926- *WhoAm 90, WhoWor 91*
Rodman, John Anthony 1943- *WhoSSW 91*
Rodman, John Gray 1951- *WhoE 91*
Rodman, Judy *WhoNeCM [port]*
Rodman, Leroy E. 1914- *St&PR 91*
Rodman, Leroy Eli 1914- *WhoAm 90*
Rodman, Michael R. 1949- *St&PR 91*
Rodman, Morton Joseph 1918- *WhoAm 90*
Rodman, Oliver H. P. *AuBYP 90*
Rodman, Peter Warren 1943- *WhoAm 90, WhoE 91*
Rodman, Ruth M 1928- *WhoAmA 91*
Rodman, Selden 1909- *WhoAmA 91*
Rodman, Seldon 1909- *AuBYP 90*
Rodman, Sue Arlene 1951- *WhoAmW 91, WhoEmL 91, WhoWor 91*
Rodman, Sumner 1915- *WhoAm 90*
Rodne, Kjell John 1948- *WhoEmL 91*
Rodner, Kim 1931- *WhoAm 90*
Rodney, Caesar 1728-1784 *EncCRAm, WorAlBi*
Rodney, Caesar Augustus 1772-1824 *BiDrUSE 89*
Rodney, George Albert 1921- *WhoAm 90*
Rodney, Goon Swee Khiang 1948- *WhoWor 91*
Rodney, Joel Morris 1937- *WhoAm 90*
Rodney, Michael Francis 1953- *WhoE 91*
Rodney, Red *BioIn 16*
Rodney, Walter *BioIn 16*
Rodnick, Amie Bowman 1953- *WhoAmW 91*
Rodnick, Eliot Herman 1911- *WhoAm 90*
Rodnite, Andrew John 1935- *WhoSSW 91*
Rodo, Jose Enrique 1871-1917 *BioIn 16*
Rodolitz, Gary Michael 1950- *WhoE 91, WhoWor 91*
Rodon, Francisco 1934- *BioIn 16*
Rodoreda Fiol, Jose Maria 1952- *WhoWor 91*
Rodoreda i Gurgui, Merce 1909-1983 *EncCoWW*
Rodos, Joseph Jerry 1933- *WhoWor 91*
Rodov, Liya I *BiDrAPA 89*
Rodovich, Arlene Guyotte 1935- *WhoAmW 91*
Rodowicz, Henry A. 1930- *St&PR 91*
Rodowsky, Colby F. 1932- *BioIn 16*
Rodowsky, Lawrence Francis 1930- *WhoAm 90, WhoE 91*
Rodrigo, Joaquin *BioIn 16*
Rodrigo, Joaquin 1901- *PenDiMP A*
Rodrigo, Thomas James 1950- *WhoHisp 91*
Rodrigue, Christine M. 1952- *WhoEmL 91*
Rodrigue, George Pierre 1931- *WhoAm 90*
Rodrigue, J. Raphael 1931- *St&PR 91*
Rodrigues, Antonio S. *WhoHisp 91*
Rodrigues, David M. *WhoHisp 91*
Rodrigues, Douglas E. 1958- *WhoE 91*
Rodrigues, Joe E. 1936- *St&PR 91*
Rodrigues, Jose Honorio 1913-1987 *BioIn 16*
Rodrigues, Luiz Antonio Belletti 1959- *WhoWor 91*
Rodrigues, Percy 1924- *DrBlPA 90*
Rodriguez, Albert Ray 1960- *WhoHisp 91*
Rodriguez, Albert S. *WhoHisp 91*
Rodriguez, Alex *WhoHisp 91*
Rodriguez, Alexander R H 1945- *BiDrAPA 89*
Rodriguez, Alfonso Camarillo 1938- *WhoHisp 91*
Rodriguez, Alfredo *WhoHisp 91*
Rodriguez, Amador *WhoHisp 91*
Rodriguez, Ana Milagros 1949- *WhoHisp 91*
Rodriguez, Andres F. 1929- *WhoHisp 91*
Rodriguez, Angel *BioIn 16*
Rodriguez, Angel Alfredo 1941- *WhoHisp 91*
Rodriguez, Angel Edgardo 1949- *WhoHisp 91*
Rodriguez, Angel R. 1934- *WhoHisp 91*
Rodriguez, Ariel A. 1947- *WhoHisp 91*
Rodriguez, Armando M. 1921- *BioIn 16, WhoHisp 91*
Rodriguez, Armando Osorio 1929- *WhoHisp 91*
Rodriguez, Art A. 1958- *WhoHisp 91*
Rodriguez, Augusto 1954- *WhoHisp 91*
Rodriguez, Aurelio 1947- *Ballpl 90, WhoHisp 91*
Rodriguez, Aurora 1940- *WhoHisp 91*
Rodriguez, Barbara Matilde 1954- *BiDrAPA 89*
Rodriguez, Bartolo G. *WhoHisp 91*
Rodriguez, Beatriz *BioIn 16, WhoAm 90*
Rodriguez, Beatriz 1951- *WhoHisp 91*
Rodriguez, Ben *WhoHisp 91*
Rodriguez, Benjamin 1938- *WhoHisp 91*
Rodriguez, Benjamin, Jr. 1943- *WhoHisp 91*
Rodriguez, Carlos Eduardo 1941- *WhoHisp 91*
Rodriguez, Carlos J. 1941- *WhoHisp 91*
Rodriguez, Carlos Rafael 1913- *WhoWor 91*
Rodriguez, Carlos Rafael Rodriguez *BioIn 16*
Rodriguez, Carmen Marta 1943- *WhoAmW 91*
Rodriguez, Carmen N. 1957- *WhoHisp 91*
Rodriguez, Charles F. 1938- *WhoHisp 91*
Rodriguez, Chi Chi *BioIn 16*
Rodriguez, Chi Chi 1935- *WhoHisp 91*
Rodriguez, Chipita *BioIn 16*
Rodriguez, Ciro D. 1946- *WhoHisp 91*
Rodriguez, Clara Elsie 1944- *WhoHisp 91*
Rodriguez, Cristino 1941- *WhoSSW 91*
Rodriguez, Daniel R. *WhoHisp 91*
Rodriguez, Diego 1937- *BiDrAPA 89*
Rodriguez, Dionicio *BioIn 16*
Rodriguez, Domingo 1939- *WhoHisp 91*
Rodriguez, Domingo Antonio *WhoHisp 91*
Rodriguez, Ed 1952- *Ballpl 90*
Rodriguez, Edgar Ronald 1951- *WhoE 91*
Rodriguez, Edmundo 1935- *WhoHisp 91*
Rodriguez, Eduardo A. 1955- *St&PR 91*
Rodriguez, Eduardo L. 1944- *WhoHisp 91*
Rodriguez, Eladio R. 1937- *St&PR 91*
Rodriguez, Elias *WhoHisp 91*
Rodriguez, Eliott 1956- *WhoHisp 91*
Rodriguez, Elisa 1936- *WhoHisp 91*
Rodriguez, Elizabeth 1953- *WhoHisp 91*
Rodriguez, Ellie 1946- *Ballpl 90*
Rodriguez, Elmer Arturo 1934- *WhoHisp 91*
Rodriguez, Eloy 1947- *WhoHisp 91*
Rodriguez, Enrique MacIver 1845-1922 *BioIn 16*
Rodriguez, Ernesto Angelo 1947- *WhoHisp 91*
Rodriguez, Eugene 1940- *WhoHisp 91*
Rodriguez, Eva I. 1948- *WhoHisp 91*
Rodriguez, Fatima 1967- *WhoEmL 91*
Rodriguez, Federico G. 1939- *WhoHisp 91*
Rodriguez, Felipe *WhoHisp 91*
Rodriguez, Felix 1921-1989 *BioIn 16*
Rodriguez, Felix I. *BioIn 16*
Rodriguez, Ferdinand 1928- *WhoAm 90, WhoHisp 91*
Rodriguez, Fernando C 1950- *BiDrAPA 89*
Rodriguez, Fernando V *BiDrAPA 89*
Rodriguez, Frances *BiDrAPA 89*
Rodriguez, Francisco 1943- *Ballpl 90*
Rodriguez, Francisco 1959- *WhoHisp 91*
Rodriguez, Francisco J *BiDrAPA 89*
Rodriguez, Fred 1949- *WhoHisp 91*
Rodriguez, Galindo 1955- *WhoHisp 91*
Rodriguez, Geno 1940- *WhoAm 90, WhoAmA 91*
Rodriguez, Gilbert 1941- *WhoHisp 91*
Rodriguez, Gloria Garza 1948- *WhoHisp 91*
Rodriguez, Guillermo, Jr. 1968- *WhoHisp 91*
Rodriguez, Hector R. 1938- *WhoHisp 91*
Rodriguez, Henry, Jr. 1955- *WhoHisp 91*
Rodriguez, Heriberto, III 1958- *WhoHisp 91*
Rodriguez, Hiram *WhoHisp 91*
Rodriguez, Hugo A. 1950- *WhoHisp 91*
Rodriguez, Isaac *BioIn 16*
Rodriguez, Israel I. 1937- *WhoHisp 91*
Rodriguez, Jacinto 1932- *WhoHisp 91*
Rodriguez, Jacqueline Caridad 1967- *WhoHisp 91*
Rodriguez, James 1956- *WhoHisp 91*
Rodriguez, Jesse 1942- *WhoHisp 91*
Rodriguez, Jesus Gene 1952- *WhoHisp 91*
Rodriguez, Jesus Jorge 1946- *WhoHisp 91*
Rodriguez, Joe D. 1943- *WhoHisp 91*
Rodriguez, Joel De Jesus 1957- *WhoE 91*
Rodriguez, John 1958- *WhoHisp 91*
Rodriguez, John C., Jr. 1930- *WhoHisp 91*
Rodriguez, Jorge 1950- *WhoHisp 91*
Rodriguez, Jorge 1956- *WhoHisp 91*
Rodriguez, Jorge Alessandri 1896-1986 *BioIn 16*
Rodriguez, Jorge Luis 1944- *WhoHisp 91*
Rodriguez, Jorge Luis 1957- *WhoHisp 91, WhoWor 91*
Rodriguez, Jose 1949- *WhoHisp 91*
Rodriguez, Jose Enrique 1933- *WhoHisp 91*
Rodriguez, Jose Gabriel 1945- *WhoEmL 91*
Rodriguez, Jose R. 1959- *WhoHisp 91*
Rodriguez, Joseph 1942- *St&PR 91*
Rodriguez, Joseph H. *WhoHisp 91*
Rodriguez, Joseph H. 1930- *WhoAm 90, WhoE 91*
Rodriguez, Joseph Martin 1937- *St&PR 91*
Rodriguez, Juan Alfonso 1941- *WhoAm 90, WhoHisp 91, WhoWor 91*
Rodriguez, Juan Antonio, Jr. 1946- *WhoHisp 91*
Rodriguez, Juan Carlos 1951- *BiDrAPA 89*
Rodriguez, Juan E *BiDrAPA 89*
Rodriguez, Juan Esteban Montero 1879?-1948 *BioIn 16*
Rodriguez, Juan G. 1920- *WhoHisp 91*
Rodriguez, Juan Guadalupe 1920- *WhoSSW 91*
Rodriguez, Judith 1936- *FemiCLE*
Rodriguez, Julia Garced 1929- *WhoHisp 91*
Rodriguez, Julian Saenz 1938- *WhoHisp 91*
Rodriguez, Kenneth *BioIn 16*
Rodriguez, Kenneth Leigh 1959- *WhoHisp 91*
Rodriguez, Kyrsis Raquel 1948- *WhoHisp 91*
Rodriguez, Leonard 1944- *WhoWor 91*
Rodriguez, Leonardo 1938- *WhoHisp 91*
Rodriguez, Leonor J 1928- *BiDrAPA 89*
Rodriguez, Lilian Teresa 1969- *WhoAmW 91*
Rodriguez, Lorenzo *BiDrAPA 89*
Rodriguez, Lorraine Ditzler 1920- *WhoAmW 91*
Rodriguez, Louis J. 1933- *WhoHisp 91*
Rodriguez, Louis Joseph 1933- *WhoAm 90*
Rodriguez, Luis 1944- *WhoHisp 91*
Rodriguez, Luis Francisco 1951- *WhoEmL 91*
Rodriguez, Luis Francisco 1953- *WhoHisp 91*
Rodriguez, Lula *WhoHisp 91*
Rodriguez, Manuel *WhoHisp 91*
Rodriguez, Manuel Diaz 1868-1927 *BioIn 16*
Rodriguez, Manuel J. 1935- *WhoHisp 91*
Rodriguez, Maria A. 1953- *WhoAmW 91*
Rodriguez, Maria Carla 1954- *WhoHisp 91*
Rodriguez, Maria del Pilar *WhoHisp 91*
Rodriguez, Maria Margarita 1954- *WhoHisp 91*
Rodriguez, Maria Martinez 1945- *WhoHisp 91*
Rodriguez, Maria Teresa 1951- *WhoAmW 91*
Rodriguez, Maria Teresa 1953- *WhoHisp 91*
Rodriguez, Marianne 1940- *St&PR 91*
Rodriguez, Mario J. 1932- *WhoHisp 91*
Rodriguez, Mark Gregory 1957- *WhoHisp 91*
Rodriguez, Mauricio Armando 1949- *WhoE 91*
Rodriguez, Mauro 1942- *BiDrAPA 89*
Rodriguez, Meriemil 1940- *WhoHisp 91*
Rodriguez, Michael Reynaldo 1957- *WhoHisp 91*
Rodriguez, Miguel 1931- *WhoAm 90*
Rodriguez, Milton 1951- *WhoHisp 91*
Rodriguez, Moises Gonzalo 1956- *BiDrAPA 89*
Rodriguez, Moses 1952- *WhoEmL 91*
Rodriguez, Nancy E. 1953- *WhoHisp 91*
Rodriguez, Nicasio Borges 1912- *WhoHisp 91*
Rodriguez, Noelis Gonzalez 1934- *WhoSSW 91*
Rodriguez, Osmarino Amancio *BioIn 16*
Rodriguez, Pablo 1955- *WhoHisp 91*
Rodriguez, Patricia Ann 1958- *WhoHisp 91*
Rodriguez, Paul *BioIn 16*
Rodriguez, Paul E. 1956- *WhoHisp 91*
Rodriguez, Paul Henry 1937- *WhoHisp 91, WhoSSW 91*
Rodriguez, Pedro Asencio 1948- *BiDrAPA 89*
Rodriguez, Pedro F 1944- *BiDrAPA 89*
Rodriguez, Peter 1926- *BioIn 16, WhoHisp 91*
Rodriguez, Placido *BioIn 16*
Rodriguez, Plinio A. 1942- *WhoHisp 91*
Rodriguez, Rachel *BioIn 16*
Rodriguez, Ralph *WhoHisp 91*
Rodriguez, Ralph 1943- *St&PR 91*
Rodriguez, Ramon *WhoHisp 91*
Rodriguez, Ramon Joe 1934- *WhoHisp 91*
Rodriguez, Raul G 1942- *BiDrAPA 89*
Rodriguez, Raul G. 1952- *WhoHisp 91*
Rodriguez, Raymond Mendoza 1924- *WhoHisp 91*
Rodriguez, Rene Mauricio 1946- *WhoHisp 91*
Rodriguez, Richard *BioIn 16*
Rodriguez, Richard 1944- *HispWr 90, WhoHisp 91*
Rodriguez, Richard Fajardo 1945- *WhoHisp 91*
Rodriguez, Rick 1954- *WhoHisp 91*
Rodriguez, Rick 1960- *Ballpl 90*
Rodriguez, Rigoberto 1953- *BiDrAPA 89*
Rodriguez, Rigoberto J *BiDrAPA 89*
Rodriguez, Rita D. 1956- *WhoHisp 91*
Rodriguez, Rita M. 1942- *WhoHisp 91*
Rodriguez, Robert L. 1948- *St&PR 91*
Rodriguez, Roberto 1943- *Ballpl 90*
Rodriguez, Roberto R. 1942- *WhoHisp 91*
Rodriguez, Rodd *WhoHisp 91*
Rodriguez, Rodney Tapanes 1946- *WhoHisp 91*
Rodriguez, Rodolfo *BiDrAPA 89*
Rodriguez, Rolando A *BiDrAPA 89*
Rodriguez, Rolando Damian 1957- *WhoHisp 91*
Rodriguez, Rolando Xavier *BiDrAPA 89*
Rodriguez, Roman 1951- *BiDrAPA 89, WhoAm 90*
Rodriguez, Ronald 1954- *WhoHisp 91*
Rodriguez, Rosa M. 1955- *WhoHisp 91*
Rodriguez, Ruben *WhoHisp 91*
Rodriguez, Rudy, Jr. *WhoHisp 91*
Rodriguez, Ruth Ann 1949- *WhoAmW 91*
Rodriguez, Santiago *BioIn 16*
Rodriguez, Sergio 1930- *WhoHisp 91*
Rodriguez, Simon Yldefonso 1928- *WhoHisp 91*
Rodriguez, Solange B. 1962- *WhoAmW 91*
Rodriguez, Sylvan Robert, Jr. 1948- *WhoHisp 91*
Rodriguez, Sylvia B. 1947- *WhoHisp 91*
Rodriguez, Tamara Mercedes 1947- *WhoE 91*
Rodriguez, Tom Blackburn *WhoHisp 91*
Rodriguez, Tomas Manuel 1959- *WhoSSW 91*
Rodriguez, Tony *WhoHisp 91*
Rodriguez, Valerio Sierra 1922- *WhoHisp 91*
Rodriguez, Victor *WhoHisp 91*
Rodriguez, Vincent Angel 1921- *WhoAm 90, WhoHisp 91*
Rodriguez, Virginia 1939- *ODwPR 91*
Rodriguez, Walter Enrique 1948- *WhoHisp 91*
Rodriguez, Ward Arthur 1948- *WhoHisp 91*
Rodriguez-Alcala, Hugo 1917- *HispWr 90*
Rodriguez-Alvarez, Antonio 1919- *WhoWor 91*
Rodriguez-Borges, Carlina 1952- *WhoHisp 91*
Rodriguez-Boulan, Maria Teresa 1946- *BiDrAPA 89*
Rodriguez-Camilloni, Christian 1947- *WhoWor 91*
Rodriguez-Camilloni, Humberto Leonardo 1945- *WhoAm 90, WhoHisp 91, WhoSSW 91*
Rodriguez-Campoamor, Hernan 1921- *WhoWor 91*
Rodriguez Chevres, Angel Marcelo 1949- *BiDrAPA 89*
Rodriguez-Chomat, Jorge 1945- *WhoSSW 91*
Rodriguez-Delfino, Alejandro *BiDrAPA 89*
Rodriguez-del Valle, Nuri 1945- *WhoHisp 91*
Rodriguez-Diaz, Juan E. 1941- *WhoSSW 91, WhoWor 91*
Rodriguez-Dufau, Oscar Roberto 1945- *WhoWor 91*
Rodriguez-Erdmann, Franz 1935- *WhoAm 90, WhoHisp 91*
Rodriguez-Feo, Raul 1949- *BiDrAPA 89*
Rodriguez-Florido, Jorge Julio 1943- *WhoHisp 91*
Rodriguez-Frank, Laura Virginia 1955- *BiDrAPA 89*
Rodriguez-Fuentes, Diana L 1919- *BiDrAPA 89*
Rodriguez Gacha, Jose Gonzalo *BioIn 16*
Rodriguez-Gomez, Angel Luis *BiDrAPA 89*
Rodriguez Graf, Barbara Ann 1956- *WhoHisp 91*
Rodriguez Hernandez, Aurea E. 1948- *WhoHisp 91*
Rodriguez-Holguin, Jeanette 1954- *WhoHisp 91*
Rodriguez-Howard, Mayra *WhoHisp 91*
Rodriguez Lara, Guillermo 1923- *BioIn 16*
Rodriguez-Leal, Jose Maria 1923- *WhoHisp 91*
Rodriguez-Llauger, Annabelle *BiDrAPA 89*
Rodriguez Monegal, Emir 1921-1985 *ConAu 131, HispWr 90*
Rodriguez-Munoz, Andres *BiDrAPA 89*
Rodriguez-Negron, Enrique *WhoHisp 91*
Rodriguez O, Jaime E 1940- *ConAu 30NR*
Rodriguez O., Jaime E. 1940- *HispWr 90*
Rodriguez-O, Jaime E. 1940- *WhoHisp 91*
Rodriguez-Paez, Teresita *BiDrAPA 89*
Rodriguez-Pagan, Juan Antonio 1942- *WhoHisp 91*
Rodriguez Pedotti, Andres 1924- *WhoWor 91*
Rodriguez-Perez, Manuel *BiDrAPA 89*
Rodriguez Porth, Jose Antonio *BioIn 16*
Rodriguez-Quesada, Wilfredo *BiDrAPA 89*
Rodriguez-Ramirez, Edelmiro *BiDrAPA 89*
Rodriguez-Rivera, Angel Luis 1947- *WhoE 91*
Rodriguez-Robles, Alberto *BiDrAPA 89*
Rodriguez Roche, Jose Antonio 1955- *WhoHisp 91*
Rodriguez Rodriguez, Carlos Rafael *BioIn 16*
Rodriguez-Roque, Victor Bernabe 1935- *WhoHisp 91*
Rodriguez-Sains, Rene S. 1952- *WhoE 91, WhoEmL 91*

Rodriguez-Santiago, Jose R BiDrAPA 89
Rodriguez-Sardinas, Orlando 1938- WhoHisp 91
Rodriguez-Sierra, Jorge Fernando 1945- WhoHisp 91
Rodriguez Suarez, Roberto 1923- WhoHisp 91
Rodriguez-Tellez, Jaime BiDrAPA 89
Rodriguez-Trias, Juan 1925- BiDrAPA 89
Rodriguez-Velez, Juan Jose BiDrAPA 89
Rodriguez-Villa, Fernando 1952- BiDrAPA 89
Rodriguez Villegas, Hernan 1942- WhoWor 91
Rodriguez-Winter, Duane A 1954- BiDrAPA 89
Rodriquez, Charles Joseph 1932- St&PR 91
Rodriquez, Ernesto Angelo 1947- WhoAmA 91
Rodriquez, Jack Vitale BiDrAPA 89
Rodriquez, Rodrigo 1937- WhoWor 91
Rodstein, Richard Michael 1954- St&PR 91
Rodtchenko, Alexander 1891-1956 PenDiDA 89
Rodulfo, Lillie M. 1947- WhoHisp 91
Rodwell, John Dennis 1946- WhoE 91
Rodwin, Lloyd 1919- WhoAm 90
Rody, Elizabeth J. BiDrAPA 89
Rodysill, Jerome O. 1929- St&PR 91
Rodysill, Jerome Otto 1929- WhoAm 90
Rodzianko, Paul 1945- WhoE 91, WhoWor 91
Rodzinski, Arthur 1892-1958 PenDiMP
Rodzinski, Artur 1892-1958 WorAlBi
Roe, Alan 1928-1989 BioIn 16
Roe, Albert S. 1914-1988 BioIn 16
Roe, Allie Jones 1950- WhoAmW 91
Roe, Benson Bertheau 1918- WhoAm 90
Roe, Betty Eileen 1930- IntWWM 90
Roe, Betty Joyce 1944- WhoSSW 91, WhoWrEP 89
Roe, Byron Paul 1934- WhoAm 90
Roe, Charles Richard 1940- WhoAm 90
Roe, D.H. 1946- St&PR 91
Roe, David BioIn 16
Roe, David 1938- St&PR 91
Roe, David 1946- WhoAm 90, WhoE 91, WhoWor 91
Roe, Dorothy M. 1925- St&PR 91
Roe, Fred, Jr. 1954- St&PR 91
Roe, Ina Lea 1930- WhoWrEP 89
Roe, Isabelle BioIn 16
Roe, Jadel Lyn 1950- WhoEmL 91
Roe, Jo Ann WhoWrEP 89
Roe, John H. 1939- WhoAm 90
Roe, Kenneth Andrew 1916- WhoAm 90
Roe, Kenneth Keith 1945- WhoAm 90
Roe, Kenneth Mark 1949- St&PR 91
Roe, Lou D. 1936- St&PR 91
Roe, Lynn Markham 1945- WhoSSW 91
Roe, Michael Henry 1944- WhoSSW 91
Roe, Norman J.E. 1922- St&PR 91
Roe, Preacher 1915- Ballpl 90
Roe, Radie Lynn 1962- WhoAmW 91
Roe, Ramona Jeraldean 1942- WhoSSW 91
Roe, Raymond Lyle, Jr. 1930- St&PR 91
Roe, Richard C. 1930- St&PR 91, WhoAm 90
Roe, Robert A. 1924- WhoAm 90, WhoE 91
Roe, Thomas 1581?-1644 BioIn 16
Roe, Thomas Anderson 1927- WhoAm 90
Roe, Thomas Coombe 1914- WhoAm 90
Roe, Tommy 1942- EncPR&S 89
Roe, William Price 1923- WhoAm 90
Roebling, Emily Warren BioIn 16
Roebling, John A. 1806-1869 WorAlBi
Roebling, Mary G 1905- WhoAmA 91
Roebling, Mary Gindhart WhoAm 90
Roebling, Mary Gindhart 1905- St&PR 91
Roebuck, Basil E BiDrAPA 89
Roebuck, Ed 1931- Ballpl 90
Roebuck, John L. 1926- St&PR 91
Roebuck, Joseph Chester 1946- WhoEmL 91
Roebuck, Kim L BiDrAPA 89
Roebuck, Reginald H. 1942- St&PR 91
Roeck, Thomas J. 1944- St&PR 91
Roeck, Thomas J., Jr. 1944- WhoAm 90
Roecker, Roland Drew 1912- BiDrAPA 89
Roecker, W. A. 1942- WhoWrEP 89
Roed, Jorgen 1808-1888 PenDiDA 89
Roed, Jorgen 1935- WhoE 91
Roed, Kenneth J. 1929- ODwPR 91, St&PR 91
Roedde, William Adolph 1925- WhoAm 90
Roedder, Edwin Woods 1919- WhoAm 90
Roedel, Paul R. 1927- St&PR 91
Roedel, Paul Robert 1927- WhoAm 90
Roedelius, Hans-Joachim NewAgMG
Roeder, Charles L. 1936- St&PR 91
Roeder, Clarence L. 1933- St&PR 91
Roeder, Emy 1890-1971 BiDWomA
Roeder, John 1877-1964 MusmAFA
Roeder, Martin 1925- WhoSSW 91
Roeder, Richard Alan 1937- WhoAm 90
Roeder, Robert Charles 1937- WhoSSW 91
Roeder, Robert Gayle 1942- WhoAm 90
Roeder, Ross Eugene 1938- WhoAm 90
Roeder, Stephen Bernhard Walter 1939- WhoAm 90
Roeder, Thomas S. 1943- WhoAm 90
Roederer, Ernesto BiDrAPA 89
Roederer, Juan G. 1929- IntWWM 90
Roederer, Juan Gualterio 1929- WhoAm 90
Roederer, Pierre-Louis L. 1927- St&PR 91
Roederstein, Ottilie W. 1859-1937 BiDWomA
Roediger, Robert Eldon 1928- St&PR 91
Roedner, Barbara J. 1931- St&PR 91
Roeg, Nicholas 1928- WorAlBi
Roeg, Nicolas 1928- BioIn 16
Roeg, Nicolas Jack 1928- WhoAm 90, WhoWor 91
Roegner, George Peter 1932- WhoE 91
Roehl, Joseph E. 1913- WhoAm 90
Roehl, R. Peter 1935- St&PR 91
Roehm, Carolyne BioIn 16
Roehm, Carolyne J. 1951- WhoAm 90, WhoAmW 91
Roehm, Dan Christian 1925- WhoSSW 91
Roehm, MacDonell, Jr. 1939- WhoAm 90
Roehm, Maryanne Evans 1925- WhoAmW 91
Roehm, Priscilla Donaby 1942- WhoSSW 91
Roehmholdt, Mary Elizabeth BiDrAPA 89
Roehrer, Christopher Voigt 1943- St&PR 91
Roehrich, Herbert George BiDrAPA 89
Roehrich, William 1912- WhoAm 90
Roehrig, Charles Burns 1923- WhoAm 90, WhoE 91
Roehrig, Karla Louise 1946- WhoAmW 91
Roehrkasse, Pauline Catherine Holtorf 1909- WhoAmW 91
Roekle, Carol Clayton BiDrAPA 89
Roekle, V.A. 1929- St&PR 91
Roel, Edmundo Lorenzo 1917- WhoHisp 91
Roeland, Lily 1956- St&PR 91
Roelandts, Rik 1948- WhoWor 91
Roelke, Ada 1928- WhoWor 91
Roellig, Leonard Oscar 1927- WhoAm 90
Roelof, Jay T. 1940- St&PR 91
Roelofs, Wendell Lee 1938- WhoAm 90
Roels, Oswald Albert 1921- WhoAm 90
Roembach-Clark, Jeanine Louise 1952- WhoEmL 91
Roemer, Astrid 1947- EncCoWW
Roemer, Buddy BioIn 16, WhoAm 90
Roemer, Buddy 1943- CurBio 90 [port]
Roemer, Charles E. BioIn 16
Roemer, Charles Elson, III 1943- WhoAm 90, WhoSSW 91, WhoWor 91
Roemer, Chester Eugene 1921- WhoAm 90
Roemer, Edward P BiDrAPA 89
Roemer, Elaine Sloane 1938- WhoAmW 91
Roemer, Elizabeth 1929- WhoAm 90
Roemer, James Paul 1947- WhoAm 90
Roemer, Joan BioIn 16
Roemer, Joan 1933- ConAu 132
Roemer, John Alan 1949- WhoE 91
Roemer, Kenneth Morrison 1945- ConAu 32NR
Roemer, Lawrence John 1916?-1989 ConAu 129
Roemer, Milton Irwin 1916- WhoAm 90
Roemer, William F. 1926- BioIn 16
Roemer, William F., Jr. 1926- ConAu 132
Roemer, William Frederick 1933- St&PR 91, WhoAm 90
Roemig, Martin 1923- St&PR 91
Roeming, Robert Frederick 1911- WhoAm 90, WhoWor 91
Roemmele, Brian Karl 1961- WhoE 91, WhoEmL 91, WhoWor 91
Roemmelt, Arthur F BiDrAPA 89
Roen, Duane Harley 1949- WhoEmL 91
Roen, Sheldon R. WhoAm 90
Roenicke, Gary 1954- Ballpl 90
Roenigk, William Joseph 1929- WhoSSW 91
Roenish, Dana D. 1955- WhoAmW 91
Roenke, Karl Guess 1947- WhoE 91, WhoEmL 91
Roentgen, Abraham 1711-1793 PenDiDA 89
Roentgen, David 1743-1807 PenDiDA 89
Roentgen, Wilhelm Konrad 1845-1923 WorAlBi
Roepe, Carl William 1960- WhoSSW 91
Roeper, Annemarie BioIn 16
Roeper, George BioIn 16
Roeper, Nola Charlene 1950- WhoAmW 91
Roepers, Alexander Joost 1959- WhoE 91
Roepke, Nancy Jean 1955- WhoAmW 91
Roerden, Chris 1935- WhoAmW 91
Roerich, Nicholas 1874-1947 BioIn 16
Roerich, Nicholas K. 1874-1947 EncO&P 3
Roes, Nancy Bennett 1954- WhoAmW 91
Roes, Nicholas A. 1952- WhoWor 91, WhoWrEP 89
Roesch, Clarence Henry 1925- WhoAm 90
Roesch, Dorothy Louise 1954- WhoEmL 91
Roesch, Frederick F. 1919- St&PR 91
Roesch, John M. 1934- St&PR 91
Roesch, Kurt 1905- WhoAmA 91N
Roesch, Raymond August 1914- WhoAm 90
Roesch, Robert Arthur 1946- WhoAmA 91
Roesch-Sanchez, Jacquelyn BioIn 16
Roeschlaub, Jean Marian Clinton 1927- WhoAmW 91
Roeschlaub, Robert Sawers 1843-1923 BioIn 16
Roesel, Harri Hans-Joachim 1926- WhoWor 91
Roeseler, Wolfgang Guenther Joachim 1925- WhoSSW 91, WhoWor 91
Roesgen, William Newell 1931- St&PR 91
Roesinger, Anna Loretta 1951- WhoAmW 91
Roesink, Dick 1944- WhoWor 91
Roeske, Arlys Mae 1934- WhoAmW 91
Roesler, John Reed 1954- WhoEmL 91
Roesler, Mark Allen 1955- St&PR 91
Roesler, Max A. 1933- St&PR 91
Roesler, Norbert Leonhard Hugo 1901- WhoAmA 91N
Roesler, Robert Harry 1927- WhoAm 90
Roesler, Thomas Allen 1945- BiDrAPA 89
Roesli, Rully M.A. 1948- WhoWor 91
Roesner, Kendra Dorothy 1949- WhoEmL 91
Roesner, Larry August 1941- WhoAm 90
Roesner, Peter Lowell 1937- St&PR 91, WhoAm 90
Roess, Roger Peter 1947- WhoAm 90
Roessel, Mary Hasbah BiDrAPA 89
Roesser, Jean Wolberg 1930- WhoAmW 91
Roesser, Karl 1952- WhoSSW 91
Roesser, William D. 1902- St&PR 91
Roesset, Jose M. WhoAm 90
Roessle, Erwin Hugo 1936- St&PR 91
Roessler, Ernest C. 1941- St&PR 91
Roessler, Freidrich 1870-1937 BioIn 16
Roessler, George D. St&PR 91
Roessler, Len 1931- St&PR 91
Roessler, P. Dee 1941- WhoAmW 91
Roessler, Robert L BiDrAPA 89
Roessler, Ronald James 1939- St&PR 91, WhoAm 90
Roessling, Bernhardt Emil 1892-1961 EncO&P 3
Roessner, Gilbert George 1918- St&PR 91, WhoAm 90, WhoSSW 91
Roessner, Roland Gommel 1911- WhoAm 90
Roeth, John Ivan 1936- St&PR 91
Roethel, David Albert Hill 1926- WhoAm 90
Roethenmund, Otto Emil 1928- WhoAm 90
Roethke, Robert R. 1924- St&PR 91
Roethke, Theodore 1908-1963 BioIn 16, MajTwCW, WorAlBi, WrPh
Roethle, John Donald 1933- WhoWor 91
Roethlisberger, Doris BioIn 16
Roetman, Orvil M. 1925- WhoAm 90
Roets, Lois Schelle 1937- WhoWrEP 89
Roett, Riordan 1938- WhoE 91
Roettger, Dorye 1932- IntWWM 90, WhoAmW 91
Roettger, Roger D. 1934- St&PR 91
Roettger, Wally 1902-1951 Ballpl 90
Roettiers, Jacques 1707-1784 PenDiDA 89
Roettiers, Jacques-Nicolas 1736- PenDiDA 89
Roettinger, Ruth Locke 1904- WhoAmW 91
Roetzel, Danny Nile 1952- WhoEmL 91
Roetzer, Ralph Juergen 1937- WhoSSW 91, WhoWor 91
Roever, Dave BioIn 16
Roever, J. M. AuBYP 90
Roever, Luis Conrad 1919- WhoAm 90
Rofe, Barbara Dale 1946- WhoAmW 91, WhoSSW 91
Rofe, Husein 1922- EncO&P 3
Rofes, Eric E. 1954- BioIn 16
Roff, Alan Lee 1936- WhoWor 91
Roff, George J 1939- BiDrAPA 89
Roff, J. Hugh, Jr. 1931- St&PR 91
Roff, John Hugh, Jr. 1931- WhoAm 90, WhoSSW 91
Roff, William Robert 1929- WhoAm 90
Roffe, Shirley BiDrAPA 89
Roffey, Leane Elizabeth 1949- WhoAmW 91, WhoWor 91
Roffey, Robert Cameron, Jr. 1935- St&PR 91
Roffman, Richard H. 1916- ODwPR 91
Roffman, Rosaly De Maios 1937- WhoWrEP 89
Roffwarg, Howard P 1932- BiDrAPA 89
Rofman, E Samuel 1940- BiDrAPA 89
Rofman, Ethan Samuel 1940- WhoE 91
Rofrano, Thomas Aquinas 1959- WhoE 91, WhoSSW 91
Rogal, Charles Robert 1954- WhoE 91
Rogalin, Roger Richard 1949- WhoAm 90
Rogalski, Edward J. 1942- WhoAm 90
Rogalski, Lois Ann 1947- WhoAmW 91, WhoE 91, WhoEmL 91
Rogalski, Walter 1923- WhoAmA 91
Rogan, Barbara 1951- BioIn 16
Rogan, Bullet Joe 1889-1967 Ballpl 90
Rogan, Charles Joseph, Jr. 1951- WhoSSW 91
Rogan, Eleanor Groeniger 1942- WhoAmW 91
Rogan, John B. BioIn 16
Rogan, Johnny 1953- ConAu 130
Rogan, Michael Horsley 1949- St&PR 91
Rogan, Robert William WhoSSW 91, WhoWor 91
Rogan, Theodora 1944- WhoWor 91
Rogari, Joseph C. St&PR 91
Rogari, Joseph J. St&PR 91
Rogas, Edward, Jr. 1940- St&PR 91
Rogasky, Barbara 1933- ConAu 130
Rogat, Morris Edward 1908- WhoAm 90
Rogati, Orpheus A 1911- BiDrAPA 89
Rogatnick, Joseph Hirsch 1917- WhoAm 90
Rogatz, Peter 1926- WhoAm 90
Rogawski, Alexander S BiDrAPA 89
Rogdakis, Constantine Michael 1954- WhoE 91
Roge, Pascal 1951- PenDiMP
Rogel, Mary Josephine 1951- WhoAmW 91
Rogel, Todd Stephen 1952- WhoSSW 91
Rogell, Billy 1904- Ballpl 90
Rogell, Irma Rose WhoAmW 91
Rogeness, Graham Arthur 1938- BiDrAPA 89
Roger ConAu 132
Roger of Helmarshausen PenDiDA 89
Roger, F. Nejes 1942- St&PR 91
Roger, Jean Gerard 1933- WhoWor 91
Rogerio, JoAnn 1967- WhoHisp 91
Rogers, Adela 1894-1988 BioIn 16
Rogers, Adrian BioIn 16
Rogers, Adrian Pierce 1931- WhoAm 90
Rogers, Adrianne Ellefson 1933- WhoAmW 91
Rogers, Alan Wayne 1963- WhoWrEP 89
Rogers, Alex DrBlPA 90
Rogers, Alex C. EarBlAP
Rogers, Anne 1933- OxCPMus
Rogers, Anthony Crawford Nugent 1938- WhoWor 91
Rogers, Archibald Coleman 1917- WhoAm 90
Rogers, Arthur Merriam, Jr. 1941- WhoAm 90
Rogers, Asa PenDiDA 89
Rogers, Aysel BiDrAPA 89
Rogers, Barbara 1937- WhoAmA 91
Rogers, Benjamin F. BioIn 16
Rogers, Bernard Laurence 1924- St&PR 91
Rogers, Bernard William 1921- WhoAm 90
Rogers, Bette R. 1930- St&PR 91
Rogers, Betty Gravitt 1945- WhoAmW 91
Rogers, Beverly R. 1941- BiDrAPA 89
Rogers, Boody 1904- EncACom
Rogers, Brenda Gayle 1949- WhoAmW 91
Rogers, Brien Burdick 1933- St&PR 91
Rogers, Bruce 1870-1957 BioIn 16, WhoAmA 91N
Rogers, Bryan Allen 1925- WhoAm 90
Rogers, Bryan Leigh 1941- WhoAm 90, WhoAmA 91
Rogers, Buddy BioIn 16
Rogers, Buddy 1904- BioIn 16
Rogers, C. B. 1930- WhoAm 90, WhoSSW 91
Rogers, Carl R. 1902-1987 BioIn 16, MajTwCW
Rogers, Carol Lombard 1944- WhoE 91
Rogers, Carter 1955- St&PR 91, WhoEmL 91
Rogers, Cedric 1915- AuBYP 90
Rogers, Charles 1904- WorAlBi
Rogers, Charles B 1911- WhoAmA 91
Rogers, Charles Edwin 1929- WhoAm 90
Rogers, Charles Waylon 1936- WhoSSW 91
Rogers, Clare Ruth 1947- BiDrAPA 89
Rogers, Clarence Birkenshaw, Jr. 1929- WhoAm 90
Rogers, Colonel Hoyt 1906- WhoWor 91
Rogers, Craig Alan 1959- WhoSSW 91
Rogers, Craig Steven BiDrAPA 89
Rogers, D. Michael 1951- WhoSSW 91
Rogers, David WhoAm 90
Rogers, David Anthony 1939- WhoWor 91
Rogers, David Earl 1943- St&PR 91
Rogers, David Elliott 1926- WhoAm 90
Rogers, David Hughes 1947- WhoAm 90
Rogers, David Lynn 1958- WhoSSW 91
Rogers, David Thomas 1942- St&PR 91
Rogers, Deborah Lynn 1951- WhoAmW 91

Rogers, Deborah Susan *BiDrAPA 89*
Rogers, Diane Elizabeth 1948- *WhoAmW 91*
Rogers, Dolores McManus 1936- *WhoAmW 91*
Rogers, Don Lee 1931- *St&PR 91*
Rogers, Donald B 1924- *BiDrAPA 89*
Rogers, Donald Burl 1936- *WhoAm 90*
Rogers, Donald Joseph 1945- *WhoWrEP 89*
Rogers, Donald Onis 1938- *WhoAm 90*
Rogers, Donald Patrick 1947- *WhoSSW 91*
Rogers, Donald Sheldon 1921- *WhoAm 90*
Rogers, E. W. 1863-1913 *OxCPMus*
Rogers, Edmund Pendleton, III 1941- *St&PR 91, WhoAm 90*
Rogers, Edward H., III 1956- *St&PR 91*
Rogers, Edward Maurice, Jr. 1958- *WhoAm 90*
Rogers, Edward S. 1933- *St&PR 91*
Rogers, Edward Samuel 1933- *WhoAm 90*
Rogers, Edwin D 1915- *BiDrAPA 89*
Rogers, Elizabeth Barlow 1936- *WhoAm 90*
Rogers, Eric M. *NewYTBS 90*
Rogers, Estera *BiDrAPA 89*
Rogers, Eugene Charles 1932- *St&PR 91, WhoAm 90*
Rogers, Eugene Jack 1921- *WhoAm 90*
Rogers, Faith Elaine 1945- *WhoWrEP 89*
Rogers, Floyd D. 1938- *St&PR 91*
Rogers, Frances Arlene 1923- *WhoAmW 91*
Rogers, Francis Dennis 1942- *St&PR 91*
Rogers, Fred *BioIn 16*
Rogers, Fred 1928- *WorAlBi*
Rogers, Fred Baker 1926- *WhoAm 90*
Rogers, Fred McFeely 1928- *WhoAm 90*
Rogers, Gayle Johnson 1949- *WhoSSW 91*
Rogers, Genesia Liu *BiDrAPA 89*
Rogers, George 1762-1815 *PenDiDA 89*
Rogers, George A 1924- *BiDrAPA 89*
Rogers, George H. *AmLegL*
Rogers, Ginger 1911- *BioAmW, OxCPMus, WhoAm 90, WhoAmW 91, WorAlBi*
Rogers, Glenn B. 1938- *St&PR 91*
Rogers, Glenn Robert 1943- *St&PR 91*
Rogers, Glenna Joan 1947- *WhoAmW 91*
Rogers, Harold Dallas 1937- *WhoAm 90, WhoSSW 91*
Rogers, Hartsell O. *St&PR 91*
Rogers, Harvey DeLano 1946- *WhoEmL 91*
Rogers, Heidi 1963- *WhoAmW 91*
Rogers, Helen Evelyn Wahrgren 1924- *WhoAmW 91*
Rogers, Helen Sfikas 1953- *WhoEmL 91*
Rogers, Helen Spelman 1913?-1990 *ConAu 132*
Rogers, Henry C. 1914- *ODwPR 91, WhoAm 90*
Rogers, Henry H. 1840-1909 *WorAlBi*
Rogers, Herbert F. 1925- *WhoAm 90*
Rogers, Houston *BioIn 16*
Rogers, Howard Gardner *BioIn 16*
Rogers, Howard Gardner 1915- *WhoAm 90*
Rogers, Howard H. 1926- *WhoAm 90*
Rogers, Howard Jeffords 1955- *St&PR 91*
Rogers, Irene 1932- *WhoAmW 91, WhoE 91, WhoWor 91*
Rogers, Isabel Wood 1924- *WhoAm 90, WhoAmW 91*
Rogers, J. Donald, Jr. 1944- *WhoSSW 91*
Rogers, Jack *BioIn 16*
Rogers, Jack A. 1945- *St&PR 91*
Rogers, Jack Eugene 1957- *WhoSSW 91*
Rogers, Jack M 1932- *BiDrAPA 89*
Rogers, Jackie *BioIn 16*
Rogers, Jacqueline 1960- *WhoAmW 91*
Rogers, Jacqueline A 1938- *BiDrAPA 89*
Rogers, James Albert 1944- *WhoAm 90*
Rogers, James Allen 1947- *BiDrAPA 89*
Rogers, James Douglas 1942- *WhoSSW 91*
Rogers, James E., Jr. 1947- *St&PR 91*
Rogers, James Edward 1945- *WhoAm 90*
Rogers, James Eugene, Jr. 1947- *WhoAm 90*
Rogers, James Frederick 1935- *WhoAm 90*
Rogers, James Gardiner 1952- *WhoE 91*
Rogers, James Keith 1931- *St&PR 91*
Rogers, James Michael *BiDrAPA 89*
Rogers, James P. 1951- *St&PR 91*
Rogers, James Robert 1947- *WhoSSW 91*
Rogers, James Thomas 1941- *WhoWor 91*
Rogers, Jane Hooks 1941- *WhoAmW 91*
Rogers, Janet L. 1950- *WhoEmL 91*
Rogers, Jansie 1939- *WhoAmW 91*
Rogers, Jean 1919- *BioIn 16*
Rogers, Jeffrey Craig 1951- *St&PR 91*
Rogers, Jerry J. 1930- *St&PR 91*
Rogers, Jill Suzanne 1968- *WhoAmW 91*
Rogers, Jim *BioIn 16*
Rogers, Jimmy C. 1934- *St&PR 91*
Rogers, Joan Gerdau 1938- *St&PR 91*
Rogers, Joe E. 1933- *St&PR 91*
Rogers, Joel Townsley 1896-1984 *TwCCr&M 91*
Rogers, John 1648-1721 *BioIn 16*
Rogers, John 1760-1816 *PenDiDA 89*
Rogers, John 1829-1904 *PenDiDA 89*
Rogers, John 1906-1985 *WhoAmA 91N*
Rogers, John, Jr. *BioIn 16*
Rogers, John Alvin 1946- *WhoSSW 91*
Rogers, John Arnold 1945- *St&PR 91*
Rogers, John D. 1940- *WhoSSW 91*
Rogers, John F. W. 1956- *WhoAm 90*
Rogers, John Fletcher *BiDrAPA 89*
Rogers, John H. 1837-1874 *AmLegL*
Rogers, John H 1921- *WhoAmA 91*
Rogers, John James William 1930- *WhoAm 90*
Rogers, John Patrick 1928- *WhoAm 90*
Rogers, John R *BiDrAPA 89*
Rogers, John S. 1930- *WhoAm 90*
Rogers, John W. 1933- *WhoAm 90*
Rogers, John W., Jr. *WhoAm 90*
Rogers, John Willard 1908- *WhoAm 90*
Rogers, Jon Martin 1942- *WhoSSW 91*
Rogers, Jordan Thomas 1921- *WhoAm 90*
Rogers, Joseph *BioIn 16*
Rogers, Joseph Leroy 1956- *WhoEmL 91*
Rogers, Joseph Shepperd *WhoAmA 91*
Rogers, Juanita 1934-1985 *MusmAFA*
Rogers, Judith Long 1955- *WhoAmW 91*
Rogers, Judith W. *WhoAmW 91, WhoE 91*
Rogers, Judy Ann 1954- *WhoAmW 91*
Rogers, Julie Dowdle 1949- *WhoAmW 91*
Rogers, Justin Towner, Jr. 1929- *St&PR 91, WhoAm 90*
Rogers, Karl David 1959- *St&PR 91*
Rogers, Keith Lindsay 1957- *BiDrAPA 89*
Rogers, Kenneth Cannicott 1929- *WhoAm 90*
Rogers, Kenneth Dyer 1921- *WhoAm 90*
Rogers, Kenneth Norman 1931- *WhoAm 90*
Rogers, Kenneth Ray 1938- *WhoAm 90*
Rogers, Kenneth Thomas 1947- *BiDrAPA 89*
Rogers, Kenny 1937- *OxCPMus*
Rogers, Kenny 1938- *BioIn 16, ConTFT 8 [port], WorAlBi*
Rogers, Kipp Alan *BioIn 16, NewYTBS 90*
Rogers, Krista Jane Fritz 1956- *WhoAmW 91*
Rogers, Lance Holland 1955- *WhoSSW 91*
Rogers, Lawrence A. 1947- *St&PR 91*
Rogers, Lawrence H., II 1921- *WhoAm 90*
Rogers, Lawrence S. 1913- *WhoAm 90*
Rogers, Lee Frank 1934- *WhoAm 90*
Rogers, Lee Jasper 1955- *WhoE 91, WhoEmL 91, WhoWor 91*
Rogers, Leo Joseph, Jr. 1936- *St&PR 91, WhoAm 90*
Rogers, Leonard John 1931- *WhoWor 91*
Rogers, Lesley-Jane 1962- *IntWWM 90*
Rogers, Linda Ann 1959- *WhoSSW 91*
Rogers, Lisa Henning 1959- *WhoEmL 91*
Rogers, Lockhart Burgess 1917- *WhoAm 90*
Rogers, Lon Brown 1905- *WhoSSW 91*
Rogers, Lorene Lane 1914- *WhoAm 90*
Rogers, M. Weldon, III 1941- *St&PR 91*
Rogers, Mae Davis 1938- *WhoAmW 91*
Rogers, Malcolm P 1943- *BiDrAPA 89*
Rogers, Margaret Ellen Jonsson 1938- *WhoAmW 91, WhoSSW 91, WhoWor 91*
Rogers, Margaret Esther 1873-1961 *WhoAmA 91N*
Rogers, Margaret Gay 1937- *WhoSSW 91*
Rogers, Margaret Ruriko 1968- *WhoAmW 91*
Rogers, Margarette Ann 1937- *WhoSSW 91*
Rogers, Mark Charles 1942- *WhoAm 90*
Rogers, Marlene Ellen *BiDrAPA 89*
Rogers, Martha *BioIn 16*
Rogers, Martha 1952- *WhoAmW 91*
Rogers, Mary 1931- *AuBYP 90*
Rogers, Mary J. 1882-1955 *BioAmW*
Rogers, Meyric Reynold 1893-1972 *WhoAmA 91N*
Rogers, Michael *BiDrAPA 89*
Rogers, Michael Bruce 1945- *WhoEmL 91, WhoWor 91*
Rogers, Michael Kane 1939- *St&PR 91*
Rogers, Michael Ray 1951- *St&PR 91*
Rogers, Millard Foster, Jr. 1932- *WhoAm 90, WhoAmA 91*
Rogers, Mimi *BioIn 16*
Rogers, Morton S. *BioIn 16*
Rogers, N. Stewart 1930- *St&PR 91*
Rogers, Nat S. *BioIn 16*
Rogers, Nat S. 1919- *St&PR 91*
Rogers, Natalie 1928- *WhoAmW 91*
Rogers, Nathaniel Sims 1919- *WhoAm 90*
Rogers, Nicholas R 1938- *BiDrAPA 89*
Rogers, Nigel 1935- *PenDiMP*
Rogers, Nigel David 1935- *IntWWM 90*
Rogers, Norman R 1914- *BiDrAPA 89*
Rogers, Otto Donald 1935- *WhoAmA 91*
Rogers, P J *WhoAmA 91*
Rogers, Pamela 1927- *AuBYP 90*
Rogers, Patrick John Francis 1948- *IntWWM 90*
Rogers, Pattiann 1940- *DcLB 105 [port], WhoWrEP 89*
Rogers, Paul *AuBYP 90*
Rogers, Paul 1950- *BioIn 16*
Rogers, Paul Grant 1921- *WhoAm 90*
Rogers, Paul William 1926- *St&PR 91*
Rogers, Peggy Jean 1944- *WhoAmW 91*
Rogers, Peter *BioIn 16*
Rogers, Peter 1933- *BioIn 16*
Rogers, Peter Norman 1938- *St&PR 91, WhoAm 90*
Rogers, Peter Philips 1937- *WhoAm 90*
Rogers, Peter Thomas 1952- *St&PR 91*
Rogers, Peter Vance 1955- *St&PR 91*
Rogers, Peter Wilfrid 1933- *WhoAmA 91*
Rogers, Philip Dean 1949- *WhoSSW 91*
Rogers, Phillip O. 1913- *St&PR 91*
Rogers, Poe Nelson 1928- *St&PR 91*
Rogers, Ralph B. 1909- *St&PR 91, WhoAm 90, WhoSSW 91*
Rogers, Ralph Withrow 1932- *St&PR 91*
Rogers, Ray *BioIn 16*
Rogers, Richard 1933- *BioIn 16*
Rogers, Richard A *BiDrAPA 89*
Rogers, Richard Dean 1921- *WhoAm 90*
Rogers, Richard George 1933- *WhoWor 91*
Rogers, Richard Hilton 1935- *WhoAm 90*
Rogers, Richard Hunter 1939- *WhoAm 90*
Rogers, Richard Mead 1942- *St&PR 91, WhoE 91*
Rogers, Richard R. 1943- *St&PR 91*
Rogers, Richard Raymond 1943- *WhoAm 90*
Rogers, Rita Ruth 1925- *BiDrAPA 89*
Rogers, Rita S. *BioIn 16*
Rogers, Robert 1731-1795 *BioIn 16, EncCRAm, WhNaAH, WorAlBi*
Rogers, Robert Burnett 1931- *WhoAm 90*
Rogers, Robert Burnett 1935- *St&PR 91*
Rogers, Robert D. 1936- *WhoAm 90, WhoSSW 91*
Rogers, Robert David 1936- *St&PR 91*
Rogers, Robert Ernest 1928- *WhoAm 90*
Rogers, Robert F. 1931-1989 *BioIn 16*
Rogers, Robert Gordon 1919- *WhoAm 90*
Rogers, Robert Mark 1933- *WhoAm 90*
Rogers, Robert Reed 1929- *WhoWor 91*
Rogers, Robert Stockton 1896- *WhoAmA 91N*
Rogers, Robert Wentworth 1914- *WhoAm 90, WhoWrEP 89*
Rogers, Robert Willis 1912- *WhoWrEP 89*
Rogers, Rodney Albert 1926- *WhoAm 90*
Rogers, Ronald J. 1943- *ODwPR 91*
Rogers, Ronald Lee 1949- *BiDrAPA 89*
Rogers, Ronald W. 1955- *St&PR 91*
Rogers, Rosemary 1932- *MajTwCW, WhoAm 90, WhoWrEP 89, WorAlBi*
Rogers, Roy 1912- *BioIn 16, EncACom, WorAlBi*
Rogers, Ruth Frances 1925- *WhoAmW 91*
Rogers, Rutherford David 1915- *WhoAm 90*
Rogers, Samuel 1763-1855 *DcLB 93 [port]*
Rogers, Samuel B. *ODwPR 91*
Rogers, Samuel M. 1917- *St&PR 91*
Rogers, Seleta Justine 1950- *WhoAmW 91*
Rogers, Sharon *BioIn 16*
Rogers, Sharon J. 1941- *WhoAm 90, WhoAmW 91, WhoE 91*
Rogers, Sheldon 1920- *BiDrAPA 89*
Rogers, Shorty 1924- *OxCPMus, WorAlBi*
Rogers, Si Randall 1945- *St&PR 91*
Rogers, Simeon *PenDiDA 89*
Rogers, Stanley William, Jr. 1956- *WhoE 91*
Rogers, Stearns Walter 1934- *WhoSSW 91*
Rogers, Stephen 1912- *St&PR 91*
Rogers, Stephen R. 1912- *WhoAm 90*
Rogers, Stephen Richard 1959- *WhoSSW 91*
Rogers, Steve 1945- *WhoAmA 91*
Rogers, Steve 1949- *Ballpl 90*
Rogers, Sultan 1922- *MusmAFA*
Rogers, Susan 1949- *WhoAmW 91*
Rogers, Suzanne *BioIn 16*
Rogers, Sydney Michael, Jr. 1925- *St&PR 91*
Rogers, Tamara Ann 1947- *WhoAmW 91*
Rogers, Theodore Courtney 1934- *WhoAm 90, WhoE 91, WhoWor 91*
Rogers, Thomas Charles 1952- *WhoEmL 91*
Rogers, Thomas Francis 1923- *WhoAm 90*
Rogers, Thomas McLemore 1948- *St&PR 91*
Rogers, Thomas N.R. *WhoWrEP 89*
Rogers, Thomas Paul 1932- *St&PR 91*
Rogers, Thomas Sydney 1954- *WhoEmL 91*
Rogers, Timmie 1915?- *DrBlPA 90*
Rogers, Timothy Folk 1947- *WhoSSW 91*
Rogers, Timothy S. 1950- *St&PR 91*
Rogers, Tom 1895-1936 *Ballpl 90*
Rogers, Trumbull 1939- *WhoWrEP 89*
Rogers, Vance Donald 1917- *WhoAm 90*
Rogers, Vera Barbara *St&PR 91*
Rogers, Virgil M. *NewYTBS 90*
Rogers, Virgil Madison 1898-1990 *BioIn 16*
Rogers, Vivian Alicia 1919- *WhoSSW 91*
Rogers, Walter Allyn *BioIn 16*
Rogers, Walter B. *ODwPR 91*
Rogers, Warren Joseph, Jr. 1922- *WhoAm 90*
Rogers, Warren Samuel *BiDrAPA 89*
Rogers, Wayne 1933- *WhoAm 90*
Rogers, Will 1879-1935 *BioIn 16*
Rogers, Will C., III *BioIn 16*
Rogers, William *PenDiDA 89*
Rogers, William Cecil 1919- *WhoAm 90*
Rogers, William D *BiDrAPA 89*
Rogers, William Dill 1927- *WhoAm 90*
Rogers, William Fenna, Jr. 1912- *WhoSSW 91, WhoWor 91*
Rogers, William Garland 1896-1978 *AuBYP 90*
Rogers, William H. 1929- *St&PR 91*
Rogers, William Henry 1821?-1894 *DcCanB 12*
Rogers, William P. 1913- *WorAlBi*
Rogers, William Pierce *BioIn 16*
Rogers, William Pierce 1913- *BiDrUSE 89, WhoAm 90*
Rogers, William Raymond 1932- *WhoAm 90*
Rogers, William Z. 1950- *St&PR 91*
Rogers, Wilma Messer 1931- *WhoAmW 91*
Rogers Dalemans, Louise 1921- *WhoWor 91*
Rogers-Lafferty, Sarah 1956- *WhoAmA 91*
Rogerson, Craig Allan 1956- *WhoSSW 91*
Rogerson, Donald *BioIn 16*
Rogerson, Kenneth Francis 1948- *WhoSSW 91*
Rogerson, Kent Edward *BiDrAPA 89*
Rogerson, Larry Richard 1943- *St&PR 91*
Rogerson, Lynda Gail 1948- *WhoWrEP 89*
Rogerson, William Durie 1934- *St&PR 91*
Rogerwick, Edward Anthony 1938- *WhoE 91*
Roges, Domingo Jesus 1938- *WhoSSW 91*
Rogg, Lionel 1936- *IntWWM 90, PenDiMP*
Rogge, Alma 1894-1969 *EncCoWW*
Rogge, Clint 1889-1969 *Ballpl 90*
Rogge, Helmut 1945- *WhoWor 91*
Rogge, Hermann 1928- *St&PR 91*
Rogge, Scott Debow 1948- *BiDrAPA 89*
Rogge, Timothy Alan 1946- *BiDrAPA 89*
Roggenburk, Garry 1940- *Ballpl 90*
Rogger, Hans Jack 1923- *WhoAm 90*
Roggiano, Alfredo Angel 1919- *WhoHisp 91*
Roggow, Diane Lynn 1957- *WhoAmW 91*
Rogich, Sig *BioIn 16*
Rogin, Bernard S. *BioIn 16*
Rogin, Ellen Barbara *BiDrAPA 89*
Rogin, Gilbert Leslie 1929- *WhoAm 90, WhoWrEP 89*
Roginski, Edward Martin *BioIn 16*
Rogler, Margarette 1924- *BiDrAPA 89*
Rogliano, Aldo Thomas 1925- *WhoAm 90*
Rogna, Lawrence G. 1946- *St&PR 91*
Rognan, Lloyd Norman *WhoAmA 91*
Rogner, Heinz *PenDiMP*
Rognoni, Paulina Amelia 1947- *WhoWor 91*
Rogo, D. Scott 1950-1990 *EncO&P 3, EncPaPR 91*
Rogoff, Jerome Howard *BiDrAPA 89*
Rogoff, Jerome Howard 1938- *WhoAm 90*
Rogoff, Mai-Lan Alicia 1946- *BiDrAPA 89*
Rogolsky, Robert L. 1922- *St&PR 91*
Rogos, Roger B. 1940- *St&PR 91*
Rogosheske, Walter Frederick 1914- *WhoAm 90*
Rogosin, Lionel 1924- *BioIn 16*
Rogovin, Gerald A. 1927- *ODwPR 91*
Rogovin, Mark 1946- *WhoAmA 91*
Rogovin, Milton 1909- *WhoAmA 91*
Rogovin, Mitchell 1930- *WhoE 91*
Rogovin, Saul 1922- *Ballpl 90*
Rogow, Bruce Joel 1945- *WhoE 91*
Rogow, Louis Michael 1944- *WhoE 91*
Rogow, Roberta *BioIn 16*
Rogow, Zack 1952- *WhoWrEP 89*
Rogoway, Sam *BioIn 16*
Rogowicki, John T. 1941- *St&PR 91*
Rogowitz, Bernice Ellen 1951- *WhoE 91*
Rogowski, John P 1931- *BiDrAPA 89*
Rogozinski, Tina Marie 1962- *WhoAmW 91*
Rogstad, Astri 1943- *WhoWor 91*
Rogstad, Mark Roland 1957- *WhoEmL 91, WhoWor 91*
Rogue, Patrick Jean *BiDrAPA 89*
Rogula, James LeRoy 1933- *St&PR 91, WhoAm 90*
Rogus, Pamela L. 1952- *WhoAmW 91*
Rogus, Patricia Susan 1953- *WhoE 91*
Rogus, Robert Ronald 1941- *St&PR 91*
Roguska, Donna Christine Hensley 1961- *WhoSSW 91*
Roh Tae Woo 1932- *WhoWor 91*
Roh, Jeong-Ho 1962- *WhoE 91*

Roh, Juliane 1909-1987 *BioIn 16*
Roh, Milan Samuel 1931- *St&PR 91*
Roh, Tae Woo *BioIn 16*
Rohan, Annemarie R 1911- *BiDrAPA 89*
Rohan, Criena 1925-1963 *FemiCLE*
Rohan, James Sidney 1947- *BiDrAPA 89*
Rohan, Virginia Bartholome 1939- *WhoE 91*
Rohan-Soubise, Anne de 1584-1646 *EncCoWW*
Rohan-Vargas, Fred 1949- *WhoHisp 91*
Rohani *NewAgMG*
Rohatgi, Reeta *BiDrAPA 89*
Rohatyn, Felix G. 1928- *BioIn 16, St&PR 91*
Rohatyn, Felix George 1928- *WhoAm 90*
Rohda, Rodney Raymond 1942- *St&PR 91, WhoAm 90*
Rohde, Claris Johannes 1948- *WhoWor 91*
Rohde, David William 1944- *WhoAm 90*
Rohde, George *St&PR 91*
Rohde, Gilbert 1894-1944 *PenDiDA 89*
Rohde, Heinrich Ludwig 1683-1755 *PenDiDA 89*
Rohde, Johan *PenDiDA 89*
Rohde, John Hans 1929- *WhoE 91*
Rohde, Linda Dianne 1945- *St&PR 91*
Rohde, Patricia Green 1948- *WhoEmL 91*
Rohde, Ruth Bryan Owen 1885-1954 *BioIn 16*
Rohde, Theordore Arthur 1929- *St&PR 91*
Rohde, Thomas Lee *BiDrAPA 89*
Rohde, William Arthur 1945- *BiDrAPA 89*
Rohe, Daniel Edward 1951- *WhoEmL 91*
Rohe, George 1875-1957 *Ballpl 90*
Rohe, Jamie M. 1945- *WhoEmL 91*
Rohe, Ludwig Mies van der 1886-1969 *BioIn 16*
Rohe, Maria Theresa 1959- *WhoAmW 91*
Roheim, Judy M 1933- *BiDrAPA 89*
Roher, Daniel S. 1926- *ODwPR 91*
Roher, Marjorie Mae 1963- *WhoE 91*
Rohira, Lal *BiDrAPA 89*
Rohla, Trudi 1949- *ODwPR 91*
Rohland, Paul 1884-1953 *WhoAmA 91N*
Rohlf, Marvin Eugene 1927- *St&PR 91*
Rohlffs, Duke 1937- *St&PR 91*
Rohlfing, Christian 1916- *WhoAmA 91*
Rohlfing, Duane H. 1933- *St&PR 91*
Rohlfs, Charles 1853-1936 *PenDiDA 89*
Rohlfs, Gerhard 1892-1986 *BioIn 16*
Rohlig, Harald Ernst 1926- *WhoSSW 91*
Rohlig, Harald Ernst Hermann 1926- *IntWWM 90*
Rohlin, Toby L. 1944- *St&PR 91*
Rohling, Horst Rudolf 1929- *WhoWor 91*
Rohlman, Eugene G. 1944- *ODwPR 91*
Rohloff, Heidi M. *St&PR 91*
Rohm, Benita Jill 1953- *WhoEmL 91*
Rohm, C. E. Tapie, Jr. 1947- *WhoEmL 91*
Rohm, Charles Edward 1935- *St&PR 91, WhoAm 90*
Rohm, Eberhard Heinrich 1940- *WhoE 91*
Rohm, Ernst 1887-1934 *BioIn 16, WorAlBi*
Rohm, Jessica Dee 1956- *WhoAm 90*
Rohm, Robert 1934- *WhoAmA 91*
Rohm, Robert Hermann 1934- *WhoAm 90, WhoE 91*
Rohm, Walter 1925- *BiDrAPA 89*
Rohman, David Gordon 1928- *WhoAm 90*
Rohmann, Paul Henry 1918- *WhoWrEP 89*
Rohmer, Eric *BioIn 16*
Rohmer, Eric 1920- *WhoAm 90, WhoWor 91, WorAlBi*
Rohmer, Harriet *BioIn 16*
Rohmer, Mary M. *ODwPR 91*
Rohmer, Sax *EncO&P 3*
Rohmer, Sax 1883-1959 *SpyFic, TwCCr&M 91, WorAlBi*
Rohn, Elizabeth G. 1948- *WhoAmW 91*
Rohn, Elizabeth Gregor 1948- *St&PR 91*
Rohn, William James Anthony 1937- *St&PR 91*
Rohner, Gerrit John 1922- *St&PR 91*
Rohner, Paul E. 1937- *St&PR 91*
Rohner, Ralph John 1938- *WhoAm 90*
Rohner, Ronald P 1935- *ConAu 32NR*
Rohner, Thomas John, Jr. 1936- *WhoAm 90*
Rohr, Billy 1945- *Ballpl 90*
Rohr, Daniel C. 1946- *WhoAm 90*
Rohr, David Baker 1933- *WhoAm 90*
Rohr, Davis Charles 1929- *WhoAm 90*
Rohr, Donald Gerard 1920- *WhoAm 90, WhoE 91*
Rohr, Herbert John 1932- *BiDrAPA 89*
Rohr, James E. 1948- *St&PR 91*
Rohr, James Edward 1948- *WhoAm 90*
Rohr, John McLean *BiDrAPA 89*
Rohrabacher, Dana 1947- *BioIn 16, WhoAm 90*
Rohrbach, June Emma 1948- *WhoSSW 91*
Rohrbach, Michael Hartnett 1941- *WhoSSW 91*
Rohrbach, Nelson Johnstone, Jr. 1940- *St&PR 91*
Rohrbach, Peter Thomas 1926- *WhoWrEP 89*
Rohrbach, Richard Paul 1930- *St&PR 91*
Rohrbach, Thomas 1931- *St&PR 91*
Rohrbach, W. Thomas 1947- *St&PR 91*
Rohrbach, Walter Allen 1934- *St&PR 91*
Rohrbacher, Fred P. 1939- *St&PR 91*
Rohrback, John T. 1946- *St&PR 91*
Rohrbaugh, Jack Arden 1939- *St&PR 91*
Rohrbaugh, John Charles 1925- *St&PR 91*
Rohrbaugh, John Willard 1946- *WhoE 91*
Rohrbaugh, Lewis H. 1908-1989 *BioIn 16*
Rohrbaugh, Paul Gregory 1958- *WhoSSW 91*
Rohrbaugh, Robert Mark 1956- *BiDrAPA 89*
Rohrberger, Mary 1929- *WhoWrEP 89*
Rohrberger, Mary Helen 1929- *WhoSSW 91*
Rohrbough, Linda Jandecka 1947- *WhoAmW 91*
Rohren, Brenda Marie Anderson 1959- *WhoAmW 91*
Rohrer, Alan Harry *BiDrAPA 89*
Rohrer, Edna 1942- *WhoAmW 91*
Rohrer, Heather Hall *BiDrAPA 89*
Rohrer, Heinrich 1933- *WhoAm 90, WhoWor 91, WorAlBi*
Rohrer, Jeffrey Thomas 1952- *St&PR 91*
Rohrer, Joanne Elaine 1956- *St&PR 91*
Rohrer, Josephine N. 1924- *St&PR 91*
Rohrer, Lila Borg 1929- *WhoWrEP 89*
Rohrer, Paul George 1945- *WhoEmL 91*
Rohrer, Reed Beaver 1954- *WhoEmL 91, WhoWor 91*
Rohrer, Richard C., Jr. 1946- *St&PR 91*
Rohrer, Richard Raymond 1958- *St&PR 91*
Rohrer, Ronald Alan 1939- *WhoAm 90*
Rohrer, Warren 1927- *WhoAmA 91*
Rohrich, Clarence George 1920- *St&PR 91*
Rohrich, Eugene S. 1922- *St&PR 91*
Rohrich, Robert D. 1915- *St&PR 91*
Rohrich, Thomas R. 1948- *St&PR 91*
Rohrich, Wilfried 1936- *WhoWor 91*
Rohrl, Manfred 1935- *IntWWM 90*
Rohrlich, George Friedrich 1914- *WhoAm 90, WhoE 91*
Rohrlich, Jay B 1941- *BiDrAPA 89*
Rohrman, Joseph Anthony 1950- *WhoEmL 91*
Rohrman, Nicholas Leroy 1937- *WhoAm 90*
Rohrmann, Guenter 1939- *St&PR 91*
Rohrmoser, Rodolfo 1938- *WhoWor 91*
Rohrs, Gustav Werner 1931- *WhoAm 90*
Rohrs, Wilhelm Hermann 1932- *WhoWrEP 89*
Rohs, Robert G 1950- *BiDrAPA 89*
Rohs, Thomas Joseph 1941- *St&PR 91*
Rohsenow, Warren M. 1921- *St&PR 91*
Rohsenow, Warren Max 1921- *WhoAm 90*
Rohtbart, Meyer 1945- *BiDrAPA 89*
Rohwedder, Donald Charles 1928- *St&PR 91*
Rohwer, Jens 1914- *IntWWM 90*
Rohwetter, Carl B. 1931- *St&PR 91*
Roider, Karl Andrew, Jr. 1943- *WhoSSW 91*
Roig I Fransitorra Montserrat 1946- *EncCoWW*
Roig, Miguel 1921-1989 *BioIn 16*
Roig Fransitorra, Montserrat 1946- *WhoWor 91*
Roiger, Lori Ann 1962- *WhoAmW 91*
Roiland, Gary K. 1948- *St&PR 91*
Roiphe, Anne Richardson 1935- *BioIn 16*
Roiphe, Herman 1924- *BiDrAPA 89, WhoE 91*
Roiphe, Jean Olivia 1958- *BiDrAPA 89, WhoE 91*
Roisler, Glenn Harvey 1952- *WhoEmL 91, WhoSSW 91, WhoWor 91*
Roisman, Josef *PenDiMP*
Roitman, Judith 1945- *WhoAmW 91*
Roitman, Norton A 1951- *BiDrAPA 89*
Roitsch, Paul Albert 1926- *WhoE 91, WhoWor 91*
Roitt, Ivan Maurice 1927- *WhoWor 91*
Roiz, Myriam 1938- *WhoWor 91*
Roizin, Leon *BiDrAPA 89*
Roizin, Leon 1912- *WhoAm 90, WhoWor 91*
Roizman, Bernard 1929- *WhoAm 90, WhoWor 91*
Rojahn, Theodore C. 1938- *St&PR 91*
Rojankovsky, Feodor 1891-1970 *AuBYP 90*
Rojankovsky, Feodor Stepanovich 1891-1970 *WhoAmA 91N*
Rojas, A. R. *HispWr 90*
Rojas, Arnold R. 1896- *BioIn 16*
Rojas, Arnold R. 1896?-1988 *HispWr 90, WhoHisp 91N*
Rojas, Carlos 1928- *WhoAm 90*
Rojas, Cookie 1939- *Ballpl 90, WhoHisp 91*
Rojas, David Alberto *BiDrAPA 89*
Rojas, Francisco Gomez Sandoval y 1552-1625 *BioIn 16*
Rojas, Guillermo 1938- *HispWr 90, WhoHisp 91*
Rojas, John Stephen 1956- *IntWWM 90*
Rojas, Jose Ignacio 1957- *WhoEmL 91*
Rojas, Kristine Briggs 1947- *WhoAmW 91*
Rojas, Larry *BioIn 16*
Rojas, Luis Diaz 1964- *WhoHisp 91*
Rojas, Manuel 1896-1973 *BioIn 16, HispWr 90*
Rojas, Maximo *BiDrAPA 89*
Rojas, Minnie 1938- *Ballpl 90*
Rojas, Paul 1912- *WhoHisp 91*
Rojas, Ricardo 1882-1957 *BioIn 16*
Rojas, Richard Raimond 1931- *WhoAm 90*
Rojas Avalos, Fernando 1935- *WhoWor 91*
Rojas Bouey, Carmen Gloria 1947- *WhoWor 91*
Rojas-Davis, Eli S *BiDrAPA 89*
Rojas de Negri, Rodrigo *BioIn 16*
Rojas-Garcia, Alvaro *BiDrAPA 89*
Rojas Pinilla, Gustavo 1900-1975 *BioIn 16*
Rojcewicz, Stephen J, Jr. 1943- *BiDrAPA 89*
Rojcewicz, Stephen Joseph, Jr. 1943- *WhoE 91*
Rojek, Christine 1949- *WhoAmA 91*
Rojek, Stan 1919- *Ballpl 90*
Rojo, Vicente 1932- *WhoAmA 91*
Roka, Attila Michael 1935- *St&PR 91*
Rokach, Abraham Jacob 1948- *WhoEmL 91*
Rokeach, Barrie 1947- *WhoAmA 91*
Rokeach, Milton *BioIn 16*
Rokely, John Kraft 1946- *St&PR 91*
Roker, Al 1955?- *DrBIPA 90*
Roker, Renny *DrBIPA 90*
Roker, Roxie *DrBIPA 90*
Roker, Roxie 1929- *ConTFT 8*
Rokicki, James Richard 1942- *St&PR 91*
Rokkanen, Seppo Olavi 1945- *WhoWor 91*
Rokop, Joseph 1924- *St&PR 91*
Rokossovski, Konstantin 1896-1968 *WorAlBi*
Rokus, Josef Wilhelm 1942- *St&PR 91*
Rokytovsky, P *EncCoWW*
Rol, Gustavo Adolfo 1906-1987 *EncPaPR 91*
Rol, Maurice William 1958- *BiDrAPA 89*
Roland, Betty 1903- *FemiCLE*
Roland, Billy Ray 1926- *WhoSSW 91, WhoWor 91*
Roland, Catherine Dixon 1936- *WhoAmW 91, WhoSSW 91*
Roland, Charles Gordon 1933- *WhoAm 90*
Roland, Claude-Robert 1935- *IntWWM 90*
Roland, Craig Williamson 1935- *WhoAm 90*
Roland, Donald Edward 1942- *WhoAm 90*
Roland, Eleanor Joyce 1940- *WhoAmW 91*
Roland, Frank H. 1935- *St&PR 91*
Roland, Gilbert 1905- *BioIn 16, WhoHisp 91, WorAlBi*
Roland, Jay 1905-1960 *WhoAmA 91N*
Roland, Jeanne-Marie Phlipon 1754-1793 *EncCoWW*
Roland, Jim 1942- *Ballpl 90*
Roland, Jimmy Dale 1959- *WhoEmL 91*
Roland, John Peter Francis 1953- *WhoE 91*
Roland, Mary 1907-1988 *SmATA X*
Roland, Melissa Montgomery 1961- *WhoSSW 91*
Roland, Miriam Woodall 1942- *BiDrAPA 89*
Roland, Neil David 1951- *WhoSSW 91*
Roland-Scherzer, Lisa Joy 1956- *WhoAmW 91*
Rolander, Carl Arthur, Jr. 1920- *WhoAm 90*
Rolandi, Gianna 1952- *WhoAm 90*
Rolant, Rene *ConAu 32NR*
Rold, Tracy Louis 1950- *WhoEmL 91*
Roldan, Amalia Perez *BiDrAPA 89*
Roldan, Charles Robert 1940- *WhoHisp 91*
Rolde, Alexandra K 1936- *BiDrAPA 89*
Rolde, Edward J *BiDrAPA 89*
Rolen, Stanley Robert 1934- *WhoE 91*
Rolett, Ellis Lawrence 1930- *WhoAm 90*
Roletti, Antonio Maria *PenDiDA 89*
Rolewicz, Robert John 1954- *WhoEmL 91*
Rolf of Mannheim *EncPaPR 91*
Rolf, David 1938- *ConAu 130*
Rolf, Frank Henry 1926- *St&PR 91*
Rolf, Howard Leroy 1928- *WhoAm 90*
Rolf, Ida P. 1896-1979 *NewAgE 90*
Rolf, Marie 1950- *IntWWM 90*
Rolf, Randolph K. 1942- *St&PR 91, WhoAm 90*
Rolfe, Bari 1916- *ConAu 32NR, WhoWrEP 89*
Rolfe, Belinda 1960- *WhoAmW 91*
Rolfe, Gerald T. 1936- *St&PR 91*
Rolfe, John 1585-1622 *EncCRAm, WhNaAH*
Rolfe, Michael N. 1937- *WhoAm 90, WhoWor 91*
Rolfe, Paula Grace 1942- *WhoSSW 91*
Rolfe, Red 1908-1969 *Ballpl 90*
Rolfe, Robin Ann 1949- *WhoAm 90*
Rolfe, Stanley Theodore 1934- *WhoAm 90*
Rolfe, Steven S *BiDrAPA 89*
Rolfe Johnson, Anthony 1940- *IntWWM 90, PenDiMP*
Rolfes, Louis Raymond 1925- *St&PR 91*
Rolfs, Robert T. 1926- *St&PR 91*
Rolfs, Thomas John 1922- *St&PR 91*
Rolin, Dominique 1913- *EncCoWW*
Roll, Barbara Honeyman 1910- *WhoAmW 91*
Roll, Deborah Marie 1954- *WhoE 91*
Roll, Edgar A. 1929- *WhoAm 90*
Roll, Gerald A. 1933- *St&PR 91*
Roll, Irwin C. 1925- *St&PR 91*
Roll, Irwin Clifford 1925- *WhoAm 90*
Roll, Marguerite S. 1927- *WhoAmW 91*
Roll, Michael 1946- *IntWWM 90*
Roll, Richard W. *BioIn 16, WhoAm 90*
Roll, William George 1926- *EncPaPR 91*
Roll, William George, Jr. 1926- *EncO&P 3*
Rolla, Janos 1944- *IntWWM 90*
Rolland, Albert *St&PR 91*
Rolland, Albert 1919- *WhoWor 91*
Rolland, Donna Josephine 1952- *WhoAmW 91*
Rolland, Ian McKenzie *BioIn 16*
Rolland, Ian McKenzie 1933- *St&PR 91, WhoAm 90, WhoWor 91*
Rolland, John Steven 1948- *BiDrAPA 89*
Rolland, Kenneth S. 1930- *St&PR 91*
Rolland, Lucien G. 1916- *St&PR 91, WhoAm 90*
Rolland, Michel Didier 1949- *St&PR 91*
Rolland, Peter George 1930- *WhoAm 90*
Rolland, Romain 1866-1944 *BioIn 16, WorAlBi*
Rolland, Ruick S 1926- *BiDrAPA 89*
Rolland, Solange Chaput- *BioIn 16*
Rollans, James O. 1942- *ODwPR 91, WhoAm 90*
Rollans, James Ora 1942- *St&PR 91*
Rollberg, Jeanne Norton 1957- *WhoAmW 91*
Rolle, Andrew 1922- *WhoWrEP 89*
Rolle, Andrew F. 1922- *WhoAm 90*
Rolle, Esther *WhoAm 90, WhoAmW 91*
Rolle, Esther 1922- *DrBIPA 90*
Rolle, Esther 1933- *WorAlBi*
Rolle, Richard, of Hampole 1290?-1349 *BioIn 16*
Rolle, William C., Jr. 1933- *ODwPR 91*
Rollefson, Anna Mae Maxine 1924- *WhoWrEP 89*
Rollefson, Richard Carl 1948- *WhoAm 90*
Rollenhagen, Kristoph Justus 1961- *WhoE 91*
Roller, Duane Henry DuBose 1920- *WhoAm 90*
Roller, George G. 1947- *St&PR 91*
Roller, Herbert Alfred 1927- *WhoAm 90*
Roller, Marion Bender *WhoAmA 91*
Roller, Maurice L. 1946- *St&PR 91*
Roller, Robert Douglas, III 1928- *WhoAm 90*
Roller, Russell Kenneth 1938- *WhoAmA 91*
Roller, Thomas Benjamin 1950- *WhoE 91*
Roller, Warren Leon 1929- *WhoAm 90*
Rollerson, Stanley J. *WhoE 91*
Rollet, Henry Didier 1939- *WhoWor 91*
Rollhaeuser, Heinz Friedrich Wilhelm 1919- *WhoWor 91*
Rollhaus, Philip E. 1934- *St&PR 91*
Rollhaus, Philip Edward, Jr. 1934- *WhoAm 90, WhoWor 91*
Rolli, John Mario Albert 1942- *WhoSSW 91*
Rollier, Jack Albert 1940- *St&PR 91*
Rollin, Bernard Elliot 1943- *WhoAm 90*
Rollin, Betty 1936- *WhoAm 90*
Rollin, Grant E. 1947- *St&PR 91*
Rolling Stones, The *EncPR&S 89, OxCPMus*
Rolling Thunder *EncPaPR 91*
Rolling, Ruby Elizabeth 1965- *WhoEmL 91*
Rollinghoff, Martin 1941- *WhoWor 91*
Rollings, Alane *WhoWrEP 89*
Rollini, Adrian 1904-1956 *OxCPMus*
Rollini, Arthur *BioIn 16*
Rollins, Albert Williamson 1930- *WhoSSW 91*
Rollins, Alfred Brooks, Jr. 1921- *WhoAm 90*
Rollins, Charlemae 1897-1979 *AuBYP 90, BioIn 16*
Rollins, Donna L. 1959- *WhoAmW 91*
Rollins, Edward *ODwPR 91*
Rollins, Edward Ashton 1828-1885 *AmLegL*
Rollins, Edward Henry 1824-1889 *AmLegL*
Rollins, Gary Wayne 1944- *WhoSSW 91*
Rollins, H. G. 1840- *AmLegL*
Rollins, Henry Moak 1921- *WhoAm 90*
Rollins, Howard, Jr. 1950- *WorAlBi*
Rollins, Howard E 1951- *DrBIPA 90*
Rollins, J. Leslie *BioIn 16*
Rollins, Jack 1914- *WhoAm 90*
Rollins, James Austin 1931- *WhoSSW 91*
Rollins, Jay Neil 1960- *WhoSSW 91*

Rollins, Jo Lutz 1896-1989 *WhoAmA 91N*
Rollins, John P 1918- *BiDrAPA 89*
Rollins, John W. 1916- *St&PR 91*
Rollins, O. Wayne 1912- *St&PR 91*
Rollins, Rex Ronald, Jr. 1946- *St&PR 91*
Rollins, Rich 1938- *Ballpl 90*
Rollins, Richard L. 1936- *St&PR 91*
Rollins, Richard William 1930- *St&PR 91*
Rollins, Robert L, Jr. 1932- *BiDrAPA 89*
Rollins, Sherrie Sandy 1958- *WhoAm 90*
Rollins, Sonny *BioIn 16*
Rollins, Sonny 1929- *OxCPMus*
Rollins, Sonny 1930- *DrBlPA 90, WhoAm 90, WorAlBi*
Rollins, Tim 1955- *WhoAmA 91*
Rollins-Smith, Louise Ann 1948- *WhoSSW 91*
Rollinson, Mark 1935- *WhoSSW 91*
Rollinson, Simeon Harrison, III 1939- *St&PR 91*
Rollman, Steven Allan 1947- *WhoSSW 91*
Rollman-Branch, Hilda S 1912- *BiDrAPA 89*
Rollman-Shay, Charlotte 1947- *WhoAmA 91*
Rollman-Shay, Ed 1947- *WhoAmA 91*
Rollo, F. David 1939- *St&PR 91*
Rollo, Frank David 1939- *WhoAm 90*
Rollock, Barbara T 1924- *SmATA 64 [port]*
Rolloff, Langworthy Carol Lemay 1942- *WhoWrEP 89*
Rollos, Philip *PenDiDA 89*
Rolls, Barbara Jean 1945- *WhoE 91*
Rolls, Charles S. 1877-1910 *WorAlBi*
Rolls, John Allison 1941- *WhoAm 90*
Rolls, Mary *FemiCLE*
Rolls, Robert Earl 1942- *St&PR 91*
Rollwagen, Jack R. 1935- *WhoE 91*
Rollwagen, John A. 1940- *WhoAm 90*
Rolly, Ronald Joseph 1937- *WhoAmA 91*
Rollyson, Carl *ConAu 129*
Rollyson, Carl 1948- *WhoWrEP 89*
Rollyson, Carl E, Jr. 1948- *ConAu 129*
Rollyson, Carl Edmund, Jr. 1948- *WhoEmL 91*
Rolnick, Diane Michelle 1964- *WhoAmW 91*
Rolnick, Neil B. 1947- *IntWWM 90*
Rolnik, Zachary Jacob 1961- *WhoE 91*
Rolnitzky, Julius *BioIn 16*
Rolo, Andre 1910- *BiDrAPA 89*
Rolo, Luis Bernardo 1924- *WhoWor 91*
Roloff, Elisabeth 1937- *IntWWM 90*
Roloff, Hans-Gert 1932- *WhoWor 91*
Roloff, John Scott 1947- *WhoAmA 91*
Roloff, Michael 1937- *ConAu 130, WhoAm 90, WhoWrEP 89*
Roloff, Roger Raymond 1947- *IntWWM 90*
Rolofson, Kristine Nancy 1951- *WhoWrEP 89*
Rolontz, Robert 1920- *WhoAm 90*
Rolph, Alice *BiDEWW*
Rolph, Juanita Lu 1937- *WhoWrEP 89*
Rolston, Holmes, III 1932- *ConAu 32NR, WhoWor 91*
Rolston, Kenneth Stuart 1928- *WhoAm 90*
Rolston, Patricia Kleinpeter 1921- *WhoSSW 91*
Rolston, Richard Gerard 1947- *WhoE 91*
Rolston, Robert L. *St&PR 91*
Rolt, Elizabeth 1747- *FemiCLE*
Roltair, Henry 1853-1910 *BioIn 16*
Rolvaag, O. E. 1876-1931 *WorAlBi*
Rolvaag, Ole E 1876-1931 *DcScanL*
Rolvaag, Ole Edvart 1876-1931 *BioIn 16*
Rolwing, Francis David 1934- *St&PR 91*
Rolwing, Robert Eugene 1926- *St&PR 91*
Rom, Anita Bloch 1951- *WhoWor 91*
Rom, Martin 1946- *WhoAm 90, WhoEmL 91*
Roma, John R. 1940- *St&PR 91*
Romack, Anthoni Re *BiDrAPA 89*
Romack, Sophie Marie 1945- *WhoAmW 91*
Romagosa, Elmo Lawrence 1924- *WhoAm 90*
Romagosa, Jerome J. 1917- *WhoSSW 91*
Romaguera, Mariano Antonio 1928- *WhoWor 91*
Romahi, Seif Ahmed Wady 1938- *WhoWor 91*
Romain, Gerard *BiDrAPA 89*
Romain, Josette *BiDrAPA 89*
Romain, Margaret Ann 1940- *WhoAmW 91*
Romaine, Henry S. 1933- *St&PR 91*
Romaine, Henry Simmons 1933- *WhoAm 90, WhoSSW 91*
Romaine, Ralph O. 1918- *St&PR 91*
Romains, Jules 1885-1972 *BioIn 16, EncO&P 3, EncPaPR 91, MajTwCW*
Roman Nose 1830-1868 *WhNaAH*
Roman, Agustin A. 1928- *WhoAm 90*
Roman, Alfred Victor 1940- *WhoE 91*
Roman, Andy, Jr. 1965- *WhoHisp 91*
Roman, Basil D 1919- *BiDrAPA 89*
Roman, Belinda 1962- *WhoHisp 91*
Roman, Donato 1939- *BiDrAPA 89*
Roman, Ed *BioIn 16*
Roman, Ernan 1950- *WhoE 91*
Roman, Freddie 1937- *BioIn 16*
Roman, Frederick *St&PR 91*
Roman, Gilbert 1940- *WhoHisp 91*
Roman, Gilberto *NewYTBS 90*
Roman, Herschel Lewis 1914-1989 *BioIn 16*
Roman, John Joseph 1950- *WhoE 91*
Roman, John Joseph, Jr. 1954- *WhoEmL 91*
Roman, Kenneth 1930- *ODwPR 91*
Roman, Kenneth, Jr. 1930- *WhoAm 90, WhoE 91*
Roman, Kenneth J. 1930- *St&PR 91*
Roman, Linda Anne 1947- *WhoAmW 91*
Roman, Manuel W 1934- *BiDrAPA 89*
Roman, Mary Broumas 1932- *WhoAmW 91*
Roman, Nancy Grace 1925- *WhoAm 90*
Roman, Petre 1946- *WhoWor 91*
Roman, Roberto 1940- *WhoHisp 91*
Roman, Ronald Peter 1945- *WhoSSW 91*
Roman, Shirley *WhoAmA 91*
Roman, Stephen B. *BioIn 16*
Roman, Stephen B. 1921-1988 *AnObit 1988*
Roman, Stephen E. 1947- *St&PR 91*
Roman, Valerie Ann 1956- *WhoAmW 91*
Roman, W.S. 1943- *St&PR 91*
Roman, William Edward 1955- *WhoAm 90*
Roman-Barber, Helen 1946- *WhoAm 90*
Roman-Barber, Helen E. 1946- *WhoAmW 91*
Roman-Whatts, Fred *BiDrAPA 89*
Romanansky, Marcia Canzoneri 1941- *WhoAmW 91*
Romanchenko, Vladimir Aleksandrovich 1932- *WhoWor 91*
Romanelli, Samuel Aaron 1757-1814 *BioIn 16*
Romanello, Kaarenlee 1956- *WhoAmW 91*
Romanello, Marguerite Marie 1939- *WhoAmW 91*
Romani, John Henry 1925- *WhoAm 90*
Romani, Juana H. C. 1869-1924 *BiDWomA*
Romani, Paul Nicholas 1943- *WhoE 91, WhoWor 91*
Romanick, Ron 1960- *Ballpl 90*
Romanik, R.L. 1951- *BiDrAPA 89*
Romanillos Vega, Jose Luis 1932- *IntWWM 90*
Romaniuk, Jerzy 1943- *IntWWM 90*
Romaniuk, William G. 1949- *St&PR 91*
Romano, Andrew Anthony 1940- *St&PR 91*
Romano, Antonio *BioIn 16*
Romano, Benito 1949- *BioIn 16, WhoAm 90*
Romano, Clare Camille *WhoAmA 91*
Romano, Daniel 1927- *St&PR 91*
Romano, David 1954- *IntWWM 90*
Romano, Dominic Frank 1947- *St&PR 91*
Romano, Donald R. 1934- *St&PR 91*
Romano, Emanuel Glicen 1897- *WhoAmA 91N*
Romano, Frank *BioIn 16*
Romano, Frank Dominick 1937- *St&PR 91*
Romano, Frank J. 1941- *WhoWrEP 89*
Romano, Giulio 1499?-1546 *BioIn 16*
Romano, Gregory *ODwPR 91*
Romano, Henry Schuberth, Jr. 1948- *WhoEmL 91*
Romano, Janet Elizabeth *BiDrAPA 89*
Romano, Jo Ann Patrice 1963- *WhoAmW 91*
Romano, John 1908- *BiDrAPA 89, WhoAm 90, WhoWor 91*
Romano, John Joseph 1942- *WhoAm 90*
Romano, Johnny 1934- *Ballpl 90*
Romano, Joseph Anthony 1946- *WhoE 91*
Romano, Lalla 1909- *EncCoWW*
Romano, Marjorie Jean 1933- *WhoE 91*
Romano, Mary D. *BioIn 16*
Romano, Nick Joseph 1951- *WhoWrEP 89*
Romano, Octavio I. 1932- *HispWr 90*
Romano, Paul Edward 1934- *WhoWor 91*
Romano, Paula Josephine 1940- *WhoAmW 91*
Romano, Richard James 1948- *WhoE 91*
Romano, Salvatore Michael 1925- *WhoAmA 91*
Romano, Sharon Marie 1952- *WhoAmW 91*
Romano, Vincent J. 1928- *St&PR 91*
Romano, William John 1948- *ODwPR 91*
Romano-V, Octavio I. 1932- *BioIn 16*
Romano-V., Octavio I. 1932- *WhoHisp 91*
Romanoff, Douglas Preston 1950- *WhoSSW 91*
Romanoff, Marjorie Reinwald 1923- *WhoAmW 91*
Romanoff, Milford Martin 1921- *WhoAm 90, WhoWor 91*
Romanones, Aline Griffith *BioIn 16*
Romanos, Daniel R *BiDrAPA 89*
Romanos, John, Jr. 1942- *WhoAm 90*
Romanos, William J, Jr. *BiDrAPA 89*
Romanoski, Alan Joseph *BiDrAPA 89*
Romanov, Natasha Galitzine *BioIn 16*
Romanov, Nikolai 1868-1918 *BioIn 16*
Romanov, Vasili 1907-1989 *BioIn 16*
Romanov-Pena, Juan, II *WhoE 91*
Romanow, Gabriela Dreyer 1956- *WhoE 91*
Romanow, Richard Brian 1953- *WhoEmL 91*
Romanow, Roy 1939- *ConAu 132*
Romanowitz, Byron Foster 1929- *WhoAm 90*
Romanowski, Thomas Andrew 1925- *WhoAm 90*
Romans, Bieiris de *EncCoWW*
Romans, Charles John 1891-1973 *WhoAmA 91N*
Romans, Donald B. 1931- *St&PR 91*
Romans, Donald Bishop 1931- *WhoAm 90*
Romans, John Niebrugge 1942- *WhoAm 90*
Romans, Van Anthony 1944- *WhoAmA 91*
Romansky, Monroe James 1911- *WhoAm 90, WhoWor 91*
Romansky, Stephen Hess *BiDrAPA 89*
Romant-Solis, Janice Anne 1944- *WhoAmW 91*
Romanzini *PenDiMP*
Romary, O. Jules *ODwPR 91*
Romauldi, James Philip 1929- *WhoAm 90*
Rombach, C. Scott 1937- *ODwPR 91*
Rombauer, Irma S. 1877-1962 *WorAlBi*
Romberg, Jacquelyn 1944- *St&PR 91*
Romberg, Leslie Holmes 1941- *WhoAmW 91*
Romberg, Sigmund 1887-1951 *BioIn 16, OxCPMus, WorAlBi*
Romberg, Wayne D. 1946- *St&PR 91*
Rombola, Anthony Mario Stephen 1953- *WhoE 91*
Rombough, Bartlett B. 1924- *St&PR 91, WhoAm 90*
Rombout, Luke 1933- *WhoAmA 91*
Rombrich, Johann Christoph *PenDiDA 89*
Rombs, Vincent Joseph 1918- *WhoWor 91*
Rome, Anthony *AuBYP 90, ConAu 30NR, TwCCr&M 91*
Rome, Dan H. 1949- *BiDrAPA 89*
Rome, Donald Lee 1929- *WhoAm 90*
Rome, Edye *ODwPR 91*
Rome, Gerald Francis 1926- *St&PR 91*
Rome, Harold 1908- *OxCPMus, WorAlBi*
Rome, Harold Jacob 1908- *WhoAm 90*
Rome, Herbert Mark 1926- *St&PR 91, WhoAm 90*
Rome, Howard P 1910- *BiDrAPA 89*
Rome, Jeffrey D *BiDrAPA 89*
Rome, John L. 1954- *St&PR 91*
Rome, Lee Howard 1950- *BiDrAPA 89*
Rome, Merit Sarah Ramzy *BiDrAPA 89*
Rome de Lisle, Jean Baptiste Louis 1736-1790 *BioIn 16*
Romeika, David John 1953- *WhoE 91*
Romein-Verschoor, Annie 1895-1978 *EncCoWW*
Romeis, Ronald Alan 1947- *WhoE 91*
Romeling, W B 1909- *WhoAmA 91*
Romen, Werner 1939- *WhoWor 91*
Romeo, Carmen V. 1943- *WhoAm 90*
Romeo, Garet Martin 1938- *St&PR 91*
Romeo, James Joseph 1955- *WhoE 91*
Romeo, Lisa Chipolone 1959- *ODwPR 91*
Romeo, Lucille Marmolejo 1944- *WhoAmW 91*
Romeo, Luigi 1926- *WhoAm 90*
Romeo, Nancy C. 1956- *WhoAmW 91*
Romeo, Pasquale M 1933- *BiDrAPA 89*
Romeo, Paul Peter 1949- *WhoEmL 91*
Romer, Alfred Sherwood 1894-1973 *DcScB S2*
Romer, Istvan 1962- *IntWWM 90*
Romer, Joseph *BioIn 16*
Romer, L. *BiDWomA*
Romer, Markus 1942- *IntWWM 90*
Romer, Patricia 1953- *IntWWM 90*
Romer, Rene Antonio 1929- *WhoWor 91*
Romer, Robert Horton 1931- *WhoAm 90*
Romer, Roy R. 1928- *WhoAm 90, WhoWor 91*
Romero, Alberto C. 1950- *WhoHisp 91*
Romero, Armando Paul 1943- *St&PR 91*
Romero, Arturo 1948- *WhoEmL 91*
Romero, Cesar 1907- *WhoHisp 91, WorAlBi*
Romero, Concha 1945- *EncCoWW*
Romero, Ed 1957- *Ballpl 90*
Romero, Ed L. *WhoHisp 91*
Romero, Emilio Felipe *BiDrAPA 89*
Romero, Emilio Felipe 1946- *WhoHisp 91, WhoSSW 91*
Romero, Eugenio 1837-1920 *BioIn 16*
Romero, Fernando L 1932- *BiDrAPA 89*
Romero, Frederick Armand 1948- *WhoWor 91*
Romero, Gilbert E. *WhoHisp 91*
Romero, Hernando *BiDrAPA 89*
Romero, Javier, Jr. 1954- *WhoWor 91*
Romero, Joaquin 1946- *St&PR 91*
Romero, Jose Ruben 1890-1952 *BioIn 16, ConAu 131, HispWr 90*
Romero, Jose T 1939- *WhoAmA 91*
Romero, Juan Carlos 1937- *WhoHisp 91*
Romero, Judy 1954- *WhoHisp 91*
Romero, Leo 1950- *WhoHisp 91*
Romero, Leon A. 1951- *WhoHisp 91*
Romero, Leota V. 1921- *WhoHisp 91*
Romero, Lino Andres *BiDrAPA 89*
Romero, Lucille Bernadette 1955- *WhoHisp 91*
Romero, Martin E. *WhoHisp 91*
Romero, Megan H 1942- *WhoAmA 91*
Romero, Nancy Lynn 1958- *WhoAmW 91*
Romero, Orlando 1945- *HispWr 90*
Romero, Orlando Arturo 1945- *WhoHisp 91*
Romero, Oscar A. 1917-1980 *BioIn 16*
Romero, Oscar Herney 1941- *BiDrAPA 89*
Romero, Patricia W 1935- *ConAu 31NR*
Romero, Paul Anthony, Sr. 1961- *WhoHisp 91*
Romero, Paulo Armando 1943- *WhoHisp 91*
Romero, Phil Andrew 1949- *WhoHisp 91*
Romero, Phillip Earl *BiDrAPA 89*
Romero, Rafael 1850-1919 *AmLegL*
Romero, Raul R. 1953- *IntWWM 90*
Romero, Raymond G. 1954- *WhoHisp 91*
Romero, Richard Joseph 1955- *WhoHisp 91*
Romero, Rolf Franz Jose 1915- *WhoWor 91*
Romero, Ronaldo *BioIn 16*
Romero, Silvia Divinetz *BiDrAPA 89*
Romero, Theresa Hazeldine 1959- *WhoAmW 91*
Romero, Tino 1935- *WhoHisp 91*
Romero, Victor L 1943- *BiDrAPA 89*
Romero Barcelo, Carlos 1932- *BioIn 16*
Romero-Barcelo, Carlos Antonio 1932- *WhoAm 90, WhoHisp 91, WhoSSW 91, WhoWor 91*
Romero-Bosch, Jose Manuel 1951- *BiDrAPA 89*
Romero Sancho, Santiago 1947- *WhoWor 91*
Romero Serrano, Marina 1908- *EncCoWW*
Romero Wheeler, Rosanna Marie 1953- *WhoAmW 91*
Romersa, Anthony Joseph 1945- *WhoEmL 91*
Romeu, Joost A 1948- *WhoAmA 91*
Romey, Roberta 1953- *WhoAmW 91*
Romey, William Dowden 1930- *WhoAm 90*
Romick, Joyce Trudeau 1939- *WhoAmW 91*
Romig, Alton Dale, Jr. 1953- *WhoEmL 91*
Romig, Charles Stuart 1946- *St&PR 91*
Romig, Edgar Dutcher 1921- *WhoE 91*
Romig, George C. 1931- *St&PR 91*
Romig, Karl A. 1926- *St&PR 91*
Romig, Michael Victor 1943- *St&PR 91*
Romig, Molly Jane 1962- *WhoAmW 91*
Romig, Phillip Richardson 1938- *WhoAm 90*
Romijn, Johanna Maria Kooyker- 1927- *BioIn 16*
Romine, Kevin 1961- *Ballpl 90*
Romine, Thomas Beeson, Jr. 1925- *WhoAm 90, WhoSSW 91, WhoWor 91*
Rominger, Barton D. 1932- *ODwPR 91*
Rominiecki, Ronald R. 1953- *St&PR 91*
Romito, Larry Drake 1944- *WhoSSW 91*
Romjue, John Lawson 1936- *WhoWrEP 89*
Romley, Derek Vanderbilt 1935- *WhoE 91, WhoWor 91*
Romm, Diane Linda 1948- *WhoE 91*
Romm, Herman 1921- *BiDrAPA 89*
Rommel, Ed 1897-1970 *Ballpl 90*
Rommel, Erwin 1891-1944 *WorAlBi*
Rommel, Ryan Gene 1954- *WhoSSW 91*
Rommer, James Andrew 1952- *WhoE 91*
Rommetveit, Ragnar 1924- *WhoWor 91*
Rommey, Marion G. 1897-1988 *BioIn 16*
Romney, Carl F. 1924- *WhoAm 90*
Romney, George 1734-1802 *IntDcAA 90*
Romney, George Wilcken 1907- *BiDrUSE 89, EncABHB 5 [port]*
Romney, Hervin A R 1941- *WhoAmA 91*
Romney, Mary Lou 1930- *BioIn 16*
Romney, Seymour Leonard 1917- *WhoAm 90*
Romo, Eloise R. 1948- *WhoHisp 91*
Romo, Enrique 1947- *Ballpl 90*
Romo, Gene David 1947- *WhoAm 90*
Romo, Paul J. 1936- *WhoHisp 91*
Romo, Ric 1958- *WhoHisp 91*
Romo, Ricardo 1943- *WhoHisp 91*
Romo, Rolando 1947- *WhoHisp 91*
Romo, Vincente 1943- *Ballpl 90*
Romoff, Ira Z. 1947- *WhoE 91*
Romoff, Jeffrey Alan 1945- *WhoAm 90*
Romoff, Joyce Weizer 1954- *WhoAmW 91*
Romonosky, John 1929- *Ballpl 90*
Romoser, George Kenneth 1929- *WhoAm 90*

Rompf, Clifford G., Jr. 1930- St&PR 91
Rompis, Oscar 1944- WhoWor 91
Rompis, Robert James 1951- WhoWor 91
Romppanen, Eino Antti WhoAmA 91
Romrell, Larry E. 1939- St&PR 91
Romrell, Randall L. 1944- St&PR 91
Romsdahl, Marvin Magnus 1930- WhoSSW 91
Romsek, Thomas Anton 1938- St&PR 91
Romtvedt, David William 1950- WhoWrEP 89
Romualdez, Eduardo Z. 1909- WhoWor 91
Romualdez Marcos, Imelda BioIn 16
Romualdi, James Philip 1929- WhoAm 90
Romzek, Barbara Sue 1948- WhoAmW 91
Ron, Amir BiDrAPA 89
Rona, Donna C. 1954- WhoWrEP 89
Rona, George 1924- WhoAm 90
Rona, Peter 1942- St&PR 91
Rona, Peter Arnold 1934- WhoSSW 91
Ronaca, Margherita 1600?-1657? EncCoWW
Ronald, Allan Ross 1938- WhoAm 90
Ronald, F. Eugene, Jr. 1930- St&PR 91
Ronald, Landon 1873-1938 PenDiMP
Ronald, Pauline Carol 1945- WhoAmW 91
Ronald, Peter 1926- WhoAm 90
Ronald, Thomas Iain 1933- St&PR 91
Ronald, William 1926- WhoAm 90, WhoAmA 91
Ronalds, Leigh 1923- St&PR 91
Ronan, Elena Vinade WhoAmW 91
Ronan, Peter William 1944- St&PR 91
Ronan, William J. 1912- St&PR 91
Ronan, William John 1912- WhoAm 90, WhoWor 91
Ronat, Judith G 1935- BiDrAPA 89
Ronayne, Michael Richard, Jr. 1937- WhoAm 90, WhoE 91
Ronberg, Gary M. ODwPR 91
Ronc, Michael Joseph 1944- WhoWor 91
Ronca, Luciano Bruno 1935- WhoAm 90
Roncal, Rogelio B 1939- BiDrAPA 89
Roncalli, Angelo Giuseppe 1881-1963 BioIn 16
Ronchetti, Joseph Franklin 1940- WhoAm 90
Ronchi, Giorgio WhoAm 90
Ronco, Bradley Eugene 1946- St&PR 91
Rond, Philip C BiDrAPA 89
Rondeau, Clement Robert 1928- WhoSSW 91
Rondeau, Doris Jean 1941- WhoWor 91
Rondeau, Edmond Paul 1945- WhoSSW 91
Rondeau, Eugene Thomas BiDrAPA 89
Rondell, Thomas 1933- ODwPR 91
Rondepierre, Edmond 1930- St&PR 91
Rondepierre, Edmond Francois 1930- WhoAm 90
Rondileau, Adrian 1912- WhoAm 90
Rondinelli, Dennis August 1943- WhoSSW 91
Rone, B.J. 1942- St&PR 91
Rone, Charles Curtis 1946- St&PR 91
Rone, Elizabeth BiDEWW
Rone, Jemera BioIn 16
Rone, William Eugene, Jr. 1926- WhoAm 90, WhoWrEP 89
Ronel, Samuel H. 1936- St&PR 91
Rones, Louis 1913- St&PR 91
Ronettes, The EncPR&S 89
Roney, Daryl Douglas 1952- WhoEmL 91
Roney, Harold Arthur 1899-1986 WhoAmA 91N
Roney, John Harvey 1932- WhoWor 91
Roney, Michele Marie 1964- WhoAmW 91
Roney, Paul H. 1921- WhoAm 90, WhoSSW 91
Roney, Stephen Christopher 1951- St&PR 91
Roney, Thomas F. 1945- St&PR 91
Roney, William C., Jr. 1924- St&PR 91
Roney-Dougal, Serena M. 1951- EncPaPR 91
Ronfard, Jean-Pierre 1929- OxCCanT
Rong, Yuhang 1962- WhoEmL 91
Rongieras-d'Usseau, Emmanuel Jean 1958- WhoWor 91
Rongo, Lucille Lynn 1958- WhoAmW 91
Roni, Luigi 1942- IntWWM 90
Roniger, Joseph J BiDrAPA 89
Roniger, Richard Ray 1942- BiDrAPA 89
Roningen, Vernon Oley 1939- WhoE 91
Ronis, Robert Jeremy BiDrAPA 89
Ronish, Cheryl Ann 1957- WhoAmW 91
Ronk, G.E. 1925- St&PR 91
Ronk, Glenn Emery 1925- WhoAm 90
Ronkartz, Patricia Ellen 1959- WhoAmW 91
Ronn, Joshua Imrich 1915- St&PR 91
Ronne, Edith Maslin 1919- WhoE 91
Ronnebeck, Arnold H 1885-1947 WhoAmA 91N
Ronnel, Jacob 1956- WhoWor 91
Ronner, Henriette 1821-1909 BiDWomA
Ronnfeldt, Jacquiline Caroline 1950- WhoAmW 91
Ronnike, Folke WhoWor 91
Ronning, Gerald F BiDrAPA 89
Ronns, Edward TwCCr&M 91
Ronsard, Pierre De 1524-1585 WorAlBi
Ronson, Raoul R. 1931- WhoE 91, WhoWor 91
Ronson, Susan 1940- WhoE 91
Ronstadt, Karl Graves 1929- St&PR 91
Ronstadt, Linda BioIn 16
Ronstadt, Linda 1946- EncPR&S 89, OxCPMus, WorAlBi
Ronstadt, Linda Marie 1946- WhoAm 90, WhoAmW 91, WhoHisp 91
Rontal, Joseph 1909- St&PR 91
Rontgen, Joachim 1906- IntWWM 90
Ronty, Bruno George 1922- WhoE 91, WhoWor 91
Ronzi, Giuseppina 1800-1853 PenDiMP
Ronzi De Begnis, Giuseppina 1800-1853 PenDiMP
Ronzoni, Carlo V 1920- BiDrAPA 89
Roobol, Norman Richard 1934- WhoAm 90
Rood, David S. 1940- WhoAm 90
Rood, Don D. 1930- St&PR 91, WhoAm 90
Rood, Edwin Paul, Jr. 1945- WhoSSW 91
Rood, Frank William 1905- WhoWrEP 89
Rood, George Ashley 1936- St&PR 91
Rood, Henry F. 1906- St&PR 91
Rood, Hope Thornton Thompson 1933- WhoAmW 91
Rood, Jim 1934- St&PR 91
Rood, Joel Francis 1937- WhoSSW 91
Rood, John 1906-1974 WhoAmA 91N
Rood, Kay WhoAmA 91
Rood, Rodney Wilbur 1915- WhoAm 90
Roof, Betty Sams 1926- WhoAmW 91
Roof, Phil 1941- Ballpl 90
Roofner, M. Robert 1946- St&PR 91
Rooijde, Dorthy M. G. 1946- IntWWM 90
Rook, Edward F 1870-1960 WhoAmA 91N
Rook, Pearl Newton 1923- WhoWrEP 89
Rook, Rex L BiDrAPA 89
Rooke, Allen Driscoll, Jr. 1924- WhoSSW 91
Rooke, Daphne 1914- AuBYP 90
Rooke, David Lee 1923- WhoAm 90
Rooke, Denis Eric 1924- WhoWor 91
Rooke, Donald Bruce 1929- St&PR 91
Rooke, Fay Lorraine 1934- WhoAmA 91
Rooker, Jim 1941- Ballpl 90
Rooker, Michael BioIn 16
Rooker, Paul George 1943- St&PR 91
Rooks, Charles Shelby 1924- WhoAm 90
Rooks, George 1951- WhoWrEP 89
Rooks, John F Girard 1933- BiDrAPA 89
Rooks, Wendell H BiDrAPA 89
Rooley, Anthony 1944- IntWWM 90, PenDiMP
Roomann, Hugo 1923- St&PR 91, WhoAm 90, WhoWor 91
Roomberg, Lila Goldstein 1929- WhoAm 90
Roome, Peter D. 1937- St&PR 91
Rooney, Andrew 1919- WorAlBi
Rooney, Andrew A. BioIn 16
Rooney, Andrew A 1919- MajTwCW
Rooney, Andrew Aitken 1919- WhoAm 90, WhoE 91, WhoWrEP 89
Rooney, Andy BioIn 16, MajTwCW
Rooney, Anne 1959- WhoWor 91
Rooney, Art 1901-1988 BioIn 16, WorAlBi
Rooney, Bryan St&PR 91
Rooney, Carol Bruns 1940- WhoAmW 91, WhoWor 91
Rooney, Daniel M. 1932- WhoE 91
Rooney, David B BiDrAPA 89
Rooney, Francis C., Jr. 1921- St&PR 91
Rooney, Francis Charles, Jr. 1921- WhoAm 90
Rooney, Francix Xavier 1927- WhoWor 91
Rooney, Gail Schields 1947- WhoAmW 91
Rooney, Jeffrey L. 1942- St&PR 91
Rooney, John E. 1942- St&PR 91
Rooney, John Edward 1942- WhoAm 90
Rooney, John Henry, Jr. 1952- St&PR 91
Rooney, John Joseph 1915- WhoAm 90
Rooney, John Lossin 1940- WhoWor 91
Rooney, Joseph Hutton 1933- St&PR 91
Rooney, Joseph W. St&PR 91
Rooney, Kevin Davitt 1944- WhoAm 90
Rooney, Kevin Michael 1948- WhoE 91
Rooney, Laurence A. 1938- St&PR 91
Rooney, M. Shawn 1946- St&PR 91
Rooney, Martin Michael 1943- St&PR 91
Rooney, Mary Susan 1959- WhoE 91
Rooney, Michael J. 1941- St&PR 91, WhoE 91
Rooney, Mickey 1920- WhoAm 90, WorAlBi
Rooney, Mickie 1920- OxCPMus
Rooney, Patrick Edward 1946- St&PR 91
Rooney, Paul George 1925- WhoAm 90
Rooney, Paul Monroe 1918- WhoAm 90
Rooney, Phillip Bernard 1944- St&PR 91
Rooney, Sharon 1958- ODwPR 91
Rooney, Steven D. 1947- St&PR 91
Rooney, Terence R. 1951- ODwPR 91
Rooney, Thomas David 1946- St&PR 91
Rooney, Thomas Michael 1947- St&PR 91
Rooney, William Richard 1938- WhoAm 90
Rooney-Pagano, Virginia 1924-1990 BioIn 16
Roop, Connie 1951- BioIn 16
Roop, James J. 1949- ODwPR 91, WhoAm 90
Roop, John W BiDrAPA 89
Roop, Peter 1951- BioIn 16
Roop, Ralph G. 1915- St&PR 91
Roop, Ralph Goodwin 1915- WhoAm 90, WhoSSW 91
Roope, Thomas Charles 1930- St&PR 91
Roorand, Ulo 1924- BiDrAPA 89
Roorbach, Douglas E. 1959- WhoWrEP 89
Roorbach, George B. 1926- St&PR 91
Roorbach, George Brett 1926- WhoE 91
Roorda, John Francis, Jr. 1923- WhoAm 90
Roos, Ann AuBYP 90
Roos, Audrey 1912-1982 TwCCr&M 91
Roos, Casper 1925- WhoAm 90
Roos, Constance C 1949- BiDrAPA 89
Roos, Daniel 1939- WhoAm 90
Roos, Fred BioIn 16
Roos, Frederick Ried 1934- WhoAm 90
Roos, James Michael 1944- IntWWM 90
Roos, Joanna 1901-1989 BioIn 16
Roos, Karen Louise 1956- WhoAmW 91
Roos, Kelley TwCCr&M 91
Roos, Marianne Louise 1955- WhoEmL 91
Roos, Philip 1930- WhoAm 90
Roos, Sonya Ingrid 1940- WhoAmW 91
Roos, Stephen 1945- AuBYP 90, BioIn 16, ConAu 31NR
Roos, Thomas Bloom 1930- WhoAm 90
Roos, Warren Samuel 1955- WhoE 91
Roos, William 1911- TwCCr&M 91
Roos, William Joseph 1921- St&PR 91
Roosa, Robert V. 1918- St&PR 91
Roose, Charlene JoAnn 1950- WhoAmW 91
Roose, Christina 1944- WhoWrEP 89
Roose, Lawrence J. 1912-1989 BioIn 16
Roose, Steven Paul 1948- BiDrAPA 89
Roose-Church, Lisa Ann 1964- WhoWrEP 89
Roosen, Carol H. 1931- St&PR 91
Roosen, Mia Westerlund 1942- WhoAmA 91
Roosen, Willem W 1925- BiDrAPA 89
Roosenboom, Derk St&PR 91
Roosevelt, Alice Hathaway Lee 1861-1884 BioIn 16
Roosevelt, Anna BioAmW
Roosevelt, Anna Eleanor 1884-1962 AuBYP 90
Roosevelt, Anna Eleanor 1906-1975 BioAmW
Roosevelt, Archibald 1918-1990 BioIn 16
Roosevelt, Archibald B. 1918-1990 NewYTBS 90 [port]
Roosevelt, Archibald Bulloch, Jr. 1918-1990 ConAu 131
Roosevelt, Archie ConAu 131
Roosevelt, Edith Kermit 1861-1948 BioAmW
Roosevelt, Edith Kermit Carow 1861-1948 BioIn 16
Roosevelt, Eleanor 1884-1962 BioIn 16, FemiCLE, WorAlBi
Roosevelt, Eleanor R. 1884-1962 BioAmW
Roosevelt, Elliott 1910-1990 ConAu 132, NewYTBS 90 [port]
Roosevelt, Franklin D. 1882-1945 BioIn 16
Roosevelt, Franklin D. 1914-1988 BioIn 16
Roosevelt, Franklin Delano 1882-1945 BiDrUSE 89, WorAlBi
Roosevelt, Heidi 1878-1962 BiDWomA
Roosevelt, James 1907- WhoAm 90
Roosevelt, Joseph Willard 1918- IntWWM 90
Roosevelt, Sara Delano 1855-1941 BioAmW
Roosevelt, Selwa Showker 1929- WhoE 91
Roosevelt, Theodore 1858-1919 BiDrUSE 89, BioIn 16, WorAlBi
Roosevelt, Theodore, IV 1942- St&PR 91, WhoAm 90
Roosevelt, W. Emlen 1917- St&PR 91
Roosjen, Sierd Keimpe 1942- WhoWor 91
Roosma, Hubert 1929- WhoE 91
Roosmaa, Valde WhoWor 91
Roosth, Joseph Howard BiDrAPA 89
Root, Alan BioIn 16
Root, Alan Charles 1925- WhoAm 90
Root, Allen William 1933- WhoAm 90
Root, Ann Renee 1959- WhoAmW 91
Root, Arthur 1921- BiDrAPA 89
Root, Benjamin Allen, Jr. 1952- BiDrAPA 89
Root, Carl E. 1922- St&PR 91
Root, Charlie 1899-1970 Ballpl 90
Root, Deane Leslie 1947- IntWWM 90, WhoE 91
Root, Donna Greenberg 1950- ODwPR 91
Root, Edward Lakin 1940- WhoE 91
Root, Edward W, Mrs WhoAmA 91N
Root, Edward Wales 1884-1956 WhoAmA 91N
Root, Elihu 1845-1937 BioIn 16, WorAlBi
Root, Elihu 1845-1939 BiDrUSE 89
Root, Franklin Russell 1923- WhoE 91
Root, George Frederick 1820-1895 OxCPMus
Root, Gerald William 1934- WhoE 91
Root, J. Stephen 1948- WhoAm 90
Root, John BioIn 16
Root, John Alan 1933- St&PR 91
Root, John Wellborn 1850-1891 WorAlBi
Root, Joseph Pomeroy 1826-1885 BioIn 16
Root, Joyce Lynne 1946- BiDrAPA 89
Root, Kathleen Jean 1964- WhoAmW 91
Root, Larry Donald 1936- St&PR 91, WhoAm 90
Root, Lawrence Gordon 1948- BiDrAPA 89
Root, Linus B 1931- BiDrAPA 89
Root, Louis D., Jr. 1922- St&PR 91
Root, Lynal A. 1930- St&PR 91, WhoAm 90
Root, Margaret G. 1937- ODwPR 91
Root, Mark Woodson BiDrAPA 89
Root, Michael John 1951- WhoWor 91
Root, Nathan J. 1911- St&PR 91
Root, Nile 1926- WhoWor 91
Root, Nina J. 1934- WhoAm 90
Root, Oren 1911- WhoAm 90
Root, Peter T. 1951- St&PR 91
Root, Phyllis AuBYP 90
Root, Phyllis 1949- BioIn 16
Root, Raymond Francis 1948- WhoSSW 91
Root, Richard Bruce 1936- WhoAm 90
Root, Robert Adam BiDrAPA 89
Root, Shelton L. 1923-1986 BioIn 16
Root, Stanley William, Jr. 1923- WhoAm 90
Root, Steven E. 1951- St&PR 91
Root, Stuart Dowling 1932- WhoAm 90
Root, Stuart W. 1942- St&PR 91
Root, Sylvia Ann 1947- WhoE 91
Root, Thomas L. BioIn 16
Root, William Alden 1923- WhoAm 90
Root, William Lucas 1919- WhoAm 90
Root, William Pitt 1941- WhoAm 90, WhoWrEP 89
Root-Bernstein, Robert Scott 1953- ConAu 132
Roote, Tom Stafford, Jr. 1934- WhoSSW 91
Rootering, Jan-Hendrik 1950- IntWWM 90
Rootes, Charles W. 1927- St&PR 91
Rootham, William L. 1923- WhoAm 90
Rootness, Thomas Martin 1947- St&PR 91
Roots, Garrison 1952- WhoAmA 91
Roots, John McCook BioIn 16
Roots, Peter Charles 1921- WhoWor 91
Rootstein, Adel BioIn 16
Rooy, Anton van PenDiMP
Rooy, James Allen 1956- WhoEmL 91
Ropa-Gaizutis, Wanda 1955- WhoEmL 91
Ropchan, Jim R. 1950- WhoWor 91
Rope, Ellen Mary 1855-1934 BiDWomA
Ropek, Jiri 1922- IntWWM 90
Roper, Bert E. 1923- St&PR 91
Roper, Burns Worthington 1925- St&PR 91
Roper, Clyde Forrest Eugene 1937- WhoAm 90
Roper, Daniel C. 1867-1943 BiDrUSE 89
Roper, David J. 1937- St&PR 91
Roper, Eugene T. 1936- St&PR 91
Roper, Francis John 1933- WhoWor 91
Roper, John Edgar 1962- WhoWrEP 89
Roper, John Lonsdale, III 1927- St&PR 91, WhoAm 90, WhoSSW 91
Roper, John W 1929- BiDrAPA 89
Roper, Laroy R. 1943- St&PR 91
Roper, Laura Wood AuBYP 90
Roper, Louis L. 1931- St&PR 91
Roper, Margaret 1505-1544 BioIn 16, FemiCLE
Roper, Maryann 1949- WhoAmW 91
Roper, Milard King, Jr. 1948- WhoEmL 91
Roper, Norman Allen 1936- St&PR 91
Roper, Peter D L 1922- BiDrAPA 89
Roper, Richard Antony Lionel 1921- IntWWM 90
Roper, Rosemary Anne 1954- WhoE 91
Roper, Walter William 1945- St&PR 91
Roper, William Alford, Jr. 1946- St&PR 91
Roper, William H. 1929- St&PR 91
Roper, William L 1897-1990 ConAu 130
Roper, William Lee 1948- WhoAm 90
Roper-Ericson, Kathie Irene 1954- WhoSSW 91
Ropes, John Milton 1924- WhoAm 90
Ropes, John S. 1938- St&PR 91
Ropiequet, John Lee 1947- WhoEmL 91
Ropkey, Ann Samonial 1917- WhoWor 91
Ropp, Ann L. 1939- WhoAmW 91
Ropp, Carrie Lynn 1961- WhoAmW 91
Ropp, Theodore 1911- WhoAm 90
Roppel, Ulrich 1948- WhoWor 91
Roppolo, John Wayne 1939- WhoSSW 91

Roppolo, Sharon T. 1944- St&PR 91
Roque, Barbara Boyd 1943- WhoAmW 91
Roque, Francis Xavier 1928- WhoAm 90
Roque, Roberto Dizon 1929- WhoWor 91
Roque, Victor A. 1946- St&PR 91
Roquemore, Anne Mickler 1950- WhoWrEP 89
Roquemour, Grayson 1942- WhoAmW 91
Rorat, Edwarda WhoE 91
Rorem, C. Rufus 1894-1988 BioIn 16
Rorem, Clarence Rufus 1894-1988 BioIn 16
Rorem, Ned 1923- BioIn 16, ConAu 32NR, IntWWM 90, WhoAm 90, WhoE 91, WhoWrEP 89
Rorer, Leonard George 1932- WhoWor 91
Rorer, Sarah Tyson 1849-1937 BioAmW
Rorer, William Herbert, III 1936- WhoAm 90
Rorex, Jeanne Walker BioIn 16
Rorex, Robert Albright 1935- WhoAmA 91
Rorick, Alan Green 1918- WhoAm 90
Rorick, Nicholas Richard 1941- WhoE 91
Rorick, William Calvin 1941- IntWWM 90
Rorie, Conrad Jonathan 1930- WhoE 91
Rorie, Durwood G., Jr. 1933- St&PR 91
Rorig, Kurt Joachim 1920- WhoAm 90
Rorimer, James J 1905-1966 WhoAmA 91N
Rorimer, Louis 1947- WhoEmL 91
Rorison, James Albert 1962- WhoSSW 91
Rorison, Margaret Lippitt 1925- WhoAmW 91, WhoSSW 91, WhoWor 91
Rork, Allen W. 1944- St&PR 91
Rork, Allen Wright 1944- WhoE 91
Rorke, Edwin Grant 1923- St&PR 91
Rorke, Edwin Grant, Jr. 1923- WhoAm 90
Rorke, Kevin H. 1949- St&PR 91
Rorke, Lucy Balian 1929- WhoAm 90
Rorke, Marcia Lynne 1942- WhoAmW 91
Rorschach, Carol Ann 1940- St&PR 91
Rorschach, Hermann 1884-1922 WorAlBi
Rorschach, Richard Gordon 1928- WhoAm 90
Rorschach, Robert Louis 1922- St&PR 91
Rorty, Richard NewYTBS 90
Rorty, Richard McKay 1931- WhoAm 90
Ros, Amanda McKittrick 1860-1939 FemiCLE
Ros, Edmundo 1910- OxCPMus
Ros, Emy Paz Raval BiDrAPA 89
Ros, Ernest A. 1925- St&PR 91
Ros-Fabregas, Emilio 1955- IntWWM 90
Ros-Lehtinen, Ileana 1952- WhoAm 90, WhoAmW 91, WhoHisp 91, WhoSSW 91
Ros-Lethinen, Ileana BioIn 16
Ros-Marba, Antoni 1937- PenDiMP
Rosa, Alexis Gomez HispWr 90
Rosa, Carl 1842-1889 PenDiMP
Rosa, Clarence Henry 1912- WhoAm 90
Rosa, Daniel C. 1951- St&PR 91
Rosa, Donald J. 1949- St&PR 91
Rosa, Elaine Maria 1940- WhoAmW 91
Rosa, Evelyn de la 1954- IntWWM 90
Rosa, Heidi 1958- BiDrAPA 89
Rosa, Javier de la BioIn 16
Rosa, Joao Guimaraes BioIn 16
Rosa, Kenneth J. 1926- St&PR 91
Rosa, Margarita 1953- WhoAmW 91, WhoHisp 91
Rosa, Raymond Ulric 1927- WhoAm 90
Rosa, Robby BioIn 16
Rosa, Rosa 1884-1980? BiDWomA
Rosa, Salvator 1615-1673 IntDcAA 90
Rosa, Vicky Lynn 1953- WhoAmW 91
Rosa-Nieves, Cesareo 1901-1974 HispWr 90
Rosabal, Nelson John 1943- St&PR 91
Rosado, Patricia Virginia 1958- WhoAmW 91
Rosado, Peggy Moran 1946- WhoAmW 91
Rosado, Victor M BiDrAPA 89
Rosalbe EncCoWW
Rosaldo, Renato BioIn 16
Rosaldo, Renato Ignacio, Jr. 1941- WhoAm 90, WhoHisp 91
Rosales, Francisco A 1942- ConAu 131, HispWr 90
Rosales, Israel BiDrAPA 89
Rosales, John Albert 1956- WhoHisp 91
Rosales, Maria E. 1961- WhoHisp 91
Rosales, Pat BioIn 16
Rosalie EncCoWW
Rosalsky, Andrew James 1948- WhoSSW 91
Rosamond, John Bell 1936- WhoAm 90, WhoSSW 91
Rosamond, Samuel M., Jr. 1937- St&PR 91
Rosamond, Sandra Pauline 1947- WhoAmW 91, WhoSSW 91
Rosamond, William Henry 1949- WhoSSW 91
Rosan, Robert Carl 1927- BiDrAPA 89
Rosan, Shira Judith 1950- WhoE 91
Rosand, David 1938- WhoAm 90, WhoAmA 91
Rosanjin, Kitaioji 1883-1959 PenDiDA 89
Rosanova, Carole Ann BiDrAPA 89
Rosanova, O. BiDWomA
Rosar, Buddy 1914-1979 Ballpl 90
Rosar, Virginia Wiley 1926- WhoAmW 91
Rosario, Alejandro Jose Villanueva 1924- WhoWor 91
Rosario, Aurea Esther BiDrAPA 89
Rosario, Robert 1951- WhoHisp 91
Rosario Green, Maria del 1941- ConAu 130, HispWr 90
Rosario-Leon, Nelson R BiDrAPA 89
Rosario-Leon, Nelson-Ricardo 1952- WhoE 91
Rosario-Pagan, Miguel A BiDrAPA 89
Rosario Rodriguez, Jose Angel 1946- WhoHisp 91
Rosas, Jose Leopold 1944- WhoHisp 91
Rosas, Juan Manuel Jose Domingo Ortiz de 1793-1877 BioIn 16
Rosas, Laura 1957- WhoHisp 91
Rosas, Mel 1950- WhoAmA 91
Rosas, Salvador Miguel 1950- WhoHisp 91
Rosatelli, Dennis 1948- St&PR 91
Rosati, Beth A. 1964- WhoAmW 91
Rosati, Phillis C. 1925- St&PR 91
Rosati, R.S. 1939- St&PR 91
Rosato, Francis Ernest 1934- WhoAm 90
Rosato, Jeanine Lucy 1960- WhoE 91
Rosato, Mark Gustavo 1955- BiDrAPA 89
Rosatti, John BioIn 16
Rosazza, Peter Anthony 1935- WhoAm 90
Rosbaud, Hans 1895-1962 PenDiMP
Rosberg, Carl Gustaf 1923- WhoAm 90
Rosberg, David William 1919- WhoAm 90
Rosberg, Rose WhoWrEP 89
Rosberger, Henry 1913- BiDrAPA 89
Rosborough, E. Marie 1951- WhoSSW 91
Rosborough, George S., Jr. 1918- St&PR 91
Rosborough, Joseph Robert 1911- WhoWor 91
Rosbottom, Ronald Carlisle 1942- WhoAm 90
Rosbrow-Reich, Susan R. 1946- WhoAmW 91
Rosca, Ninotchka BioIn 16
Rosch, John Thomas 1939- WhoAm 90
Rosch, Paul John 1927- WhoAm 90, WhoWor 91
Rosche, Mary Ellen 1949- WhoAmW 91, WhoE 91
Roscher, Georg Michael PenDiDA 89
Roscher, Nina Matheny 1938- WhoAmW 91
Roscher, Wilhelm 1817-1894 BioIn 16
Roscher, Wolfgang 1927- WhoWor 91
Roschman, Georgiann 1940- St&PR 91
Roschwalb, Jerold 1935- WhoE 91
Roscia, John J. 1920- WhoAm 90
Roscoe, Martin 1952- IntWWM 90
Roscoe, Sheila BioIn 16
Roscoe, Stanley Nelson 1920- WhoAm 90
Roscopf, Charles Buford 1928- WhoAm 90
Rosdeitcher, Sidney S. 1936- WhoAm 90
Rose Marie 1925- WorAlBi
Rose Quartet PenDiMP
Rose, Adam Zachary 1948- WhoAm 90
Rose, Albert NewYTBS 90 [port]
Rose, Albert 1910- WhoAm 90
Rose, Andrew James Evans 1946- WhoEmL 91
Rose, Anita Carroll 1922- WhoAmW 91, WhoE 91, WhoWor 91
Rose, Anthony C. 1925- St&PR 91
Rose, Arnold 1863-1946 PenDiMP
Rose, Arthur Morris 1943- WhoE 91
Rose, Axl BioIn 16
Rose, Barbara 1937- WhoAmA 91
Rose, Barbara 1952- BiDrAPA 89
Rose, Barbara Blanchard 1927- WhoAmW 91
Rose, Barbara Elaine 1951- WhoAmW 91, WhoSSW 91
Rose, Barry Michael 1934- IntWWM 90
Rose, Bernard 1916- PenDiMP
Rose, Bernard William George 1916- IntWWM 90
Rose, Billy 1899-1966 OxCPMus, WorAlBi
Rose, Bruce A. 1933- St&PR 91
Rose, C. Robert F. 1938- St&PR 91
Rose, Camille Davied BioIn 16
Rose, Candace Korner 1956- WhoAmW 91
Rose, Carolyn Bruce 1930- WhoWor 91
Rose, Cecilia 1925- WhoAmW 91
Rose, Charles WhoAm 90, WhoE 91
Rose, Charles Alexander 1932- WhoSSW 91
Rose, Charles C. 1934- St&PR 91
Rose, Charles Grandison, III 1939- WhoAm 90, WhoSSW 91
Rose, Charles Jon 1952- WhoEmL 91
Rose, Cheryl Lee 1964- WhoEmL 91
Rose, Cheryl Romprey 1949- WhoAmW 91
Rose, Christine Brooke- 1923- BioIn 16
Rose, Cynthia Pearl 1936- BiDrAPA 89
Rose, D. W. 1925- St&PR 91
Rose, Daniel 1929- WhoAm 90, WhoWor 91
Rose, Daniel Asa 1949- WhoWrEP 89
Rose, David NewYTBS 90 [port]
Rose, David 1910- WhoAmA 91
Rose, David 1910-1990 OxCPMus
Rose, David E. 1944- St&PR 91
Rose, David H. 1955- St&PR 91
Rose, David Semel 1957- WhoE 91
Rose, Deborah Elizabeth 1956- WhoAmW 91
Rose, Deborah Jane 1954- WhoAmW 91
Rose, Deborah S 1943- BiDrAPA 89
Rose, Denise Beye 1953- WhoAmW 91
Rose, Diane BiDrAPA 89
Rose, Donald Frederick 1940- WhoSSW 91
Rose, Donald James 1944- WhoAm 90
Rose, Donald McGregor 1933- WhoAm 90
Rose, Earl Alexander 1946- IntWWM 90
Rose, Edgar 1926- St&PR 91, WhoAm 90
Rose, Edith Sprung 1924- WhoAmW 91
Rose, Eduard PenDiMP
Rose, Edward WhNaAH
Rose, Edward W., III BioIn 16
Rose, Elaine Olga 1943- WhoAmW 91
Rose, Eleanor WhoWrEP 89
Rose, Elihu 1933- WhoAm 90
Rose, Elizabeth 1941- WhoAmW 91
Rose, Eric Allen 1951- WhoAm 90
Rose, Eugene V. 1937- WhoAm 90
Rose, Evans, Jr. 1932- WhoAm 90
Rose, Florella AuBYP 90
Rose, Frank Anthony 1920- WhoAm 90
Rose, Frank Stevens 1935- WhoAm 90
Rose, Fred 1897-1954 BioIn 16, OxCPMus
Rose, Frederick Phineas 1923- WhoAm 90
Rose, G. Sue 1948- WhoSSW 91
Rose, Gail Elaine 1949- WhoAmW 91, WhoEmL 91
Rose, Garland P. 1944- St&PR 91
Rose, George 1920-1988 BioIn 16
Rose, George Maclean 1829-1898 DcCanB 12
Rose, George McNeil 1846-1924 AmLegL
Rose, Gerald Alvin 1950- WhoE 91
Rose, Gervase R. 1936- St&PR 91
Rose, Gilbert J 1923- BiDrAPA 89
Rose, Gilbert Jacob 1923- WhoE 91
Rose, Gilbert Paul 1939- WhoWrEP 89
Rose, Glenn Richard 1927- St&PR 91
Rose, Gregory 1948- IntWWM 90, PenDiMP
Rose, Gregory Mancel 1953- WhoEmL 91
Rose, Gregory Mark 1956- WhoSSW 91
Rose, Guy 1867-1925 BioIn 16
Rose, H. Chapman NewYTBS 90 [port]
Rose, H. Chapman 1907-1990 BioIn 16
Rose, H. Stewart 1933- St&PR 91
Rose, Hanna Toby 1909-1976 WhoAmA 91N
Rose, Herman 1909- WhoAm 90, WhoAmA 91
Rose, Horace Chapman 1907-1990 WhoAm 90
Rose, Howard Claude 1934- St&PR 91
Rose, Howard L. 1924- St&PR 91
Rose, Israel Harold 1917- WhoAm 90
Rose, Iver 1899-1972 WhoAmA 91N
Rose, Jack Wesley 1932- WhoSSW 91
Rose, Jackie Michelle 1954- WhoAmW 91
Rose, James E., Jr. 1942- St&PR 91
Rose, James McKinley, Jr. 1927- WhoAm 90
Rose, James T. BioIn 16
Rose, James Turner 1935- WhoAm 90, WhoWor 91
Rose, James Victor 1925- St&PR 91
Rose, James W. 1935- WhoAm 90, WhoSSW 91
Rose, Janet Lucille 1954- WhoAmW 91
Rose, Jeffrey Raymond 1946- WhoAm 90
Rose, Jerman W 1918- BiDrAPA 89
Rose, Jerome V 1923- BiDrAPA 89
Rose, Jerzy Edwin 1909- WhoAm 90
Rose, Joanna Semel 1930- WhoAmW 91
Rose, Joel 1948- ConAu 129, WhoWrEP 89
Rose, John PenDiDA 89
Rose, John 1948- IntWWM 90
Rose, John A. 1940- WhoSSW 91
Rose, John Charles 1924- WhoAm 90
Rose, John Luke 1933- IntWWM 90
Rose, John Robert 1937- WhoSSW 91
Rose, John Schaefer WhoSSW 91
Rose, John Thomas 1943- WhoAm 90
Rose, John Wilson 1949- St&PR 91
Rose, Jonathan Chapman 1941- WhoAm 90
Rose, Jonathan Ira 1950- St&PR 91
Rose, Judy Sizemore 1939- WhoSSW 91
Rose, Jules Freed 1936- WhoE 91
Rose, June H. 1949- WhoAmW 91
Rose, Jurgen 1937- BioIn 16
Rose, Justin 1932- St&PR 91
Rose, Karen Evans 1959- WhoAmW 91
Rose, Kenneth Leon 1936- St&PR 91
Rose, Larry BioIn 16
Rose, Lawrence Joseph 1941- WhoAm 90
Rose, Leatrice WhoAmA 91
Rose, Leonard 1918-1984 PenDiMP
Rose, Louise Blecher 1943- WhoWrEP 89
Rose, Lynne Catherine McCloskey 1951- WhoE 91
Rose, Major W. Rampling EncPaPR 91
Rose, Marian Jean 1953- WhoSSW 91
Rose, Mark Allen 1939- WhoAm 90, WhoWrEP 89
Rose, Mark Edward 1963- St&PR 91
Rose, Martha Rea 1938- WhoAmW 91
Rose, Martin Engelbert 1947- WhoWor 91
Rose, Mary Anne 1949- WhoAmA 91
Rose, Mason H., IV 1915- WhoAm 90
Rose, Matthew Adam 1959- WhoAmA 91
Rose, Merrill 1955- ODwPR 91
Rose, Michael 1940- ODwPR 91
Rose, Michael D. 1942- St&PR 91
Rose, Michael David 1942- WhoAm 90, WhoSSW 91
Rose, Michael Dean 1937- WhoAm 90
Rose, Michael E. 1947- St&PR 91
Rose, Michael Elvin 1947- WhoAm 90
Rose, Michael I 1936- BiDrAPA 89
Rose, Michael I. 1945- WhoEmL 91
Rose, Michael Simon 1937- WhoWor 91
Rose, Milton C. 1904- St&PR 91
Rose, Milton Curtiss 1904- WhoAm 90
Rose, Nancy 1934- BioIn 16
Rose, Noel Richard 1927- WhoAm 90
Rose, Otto J. 1929- St&PR 91
Rose, Patricia Anthone 1930- WhoWrEP 89
Rose, Paul E. 1947- St&PR 91
Rose, Paul Edward 1947- WhoAm 90, WhoWor 91
Rose, Paul Haran BiDrAPA 89
Rose, Pete 1941- Ballpl 90 [port], BioIn 16, News 91-1 [port], WorAlBi
Rose, Peter 1961- IntWWM 90
Rose, Peter Edward 1941- WhoAm 90
Rose, Peter Henry 1935- WhoAmA 91
Rose, Peter Isaac 1933- WhoAm 90
Rose, Peter Shepard 1940- WhoAm 90
Rose, Petey BioIn 16
Rose, Phyllis ConAu 30NR
Rose, Phyllis 1942- BioIn 16, WhoAm 90, WhoWrEP 89
Rose, Porter Brawley 1942- St&PR 91
Rose, R. Nelson BioIn 16
Rose, Reginald 1920- WhoAm 90, WhoWrEP 89
Rose, Richard BioIn 16
Rose, Richard 1933- WhoWor 91
Rose, Richard 1950- ODwPR 91
Rose, Richard 1955- OxCCanT
Rose, Richard Channon 1947- St&PR 91
Rose, Richard L. 1936- St&PR 91
Rose, Richard Lindsay 1949- WhoSSW 91
Rose, Richard Loomis 1936- WhoAm 90
Rose, Richard S BiDrAPA 89
Rose, Robert Carlisle 1917- WhoAm 90
Rose, Robert Charles 1943- St&PR 91
Rose, Robert E. 1939- WhoAm 90
Rose, Robert Ernest 1938- St&PR 91
Rose, Robert L. 1931- St&PR 91
Rose, Robert Lawrence 1945- WhoAm 90
Rose, Robert M 1936- BiDrAPA 89
Rose, Robert Michael 1937- WhoAm 90
Rose, Robert Neal 1951- WhoE 91, WhoWor 91
Rose, Robert Perry 1953- BiDrAPA 89
Rose, Robert R., Jr. 1915- WhoAm 90
Rose, Robin Carlise 1946- WhoAmA 91
Rose, Roger A 1940- BiDrAPA 89
Rose, Ronald K H 1920- EncO&P 3
Rose, Ronald Kriss Hume 1919- EncPaPR 91
Rose, Roslyn 1929- WhoAmA 91
Rose, Rowland G. 1916- St&PR 91
Rose, Rubye Blevins WhoAm 90
Rose, Sam M. BioIn 16
Rose, Samuel 1941- WhoAmA 91
Rose, Selwyn H. 1933- WhoWor 91
Rose, Seth Edward 1951- WhoSSW 91
Rose, Sheila Phillips 1952- WhoAmW 91
Rose, Shiela Anne 1954- WhoAmW 91
Rose, Shirley 1921- WhoWor 91
Rose, Sidney BiDrAPA 89
Rose, Sidney 1907- WhoE 91
Rose, Stephanie WhoAmA 91
Rose, Stephen C. 1936- ConAu 129
Rose, Steven Marc 1949- WhoEmL 91
Rose, Susan BioIn 16
Rose, Susan Carol 1942- WhoAmW 91, WhoSSW 91, WhoWor 91
Rose, Susan Porter 1941- WhoAm 90
Rose, Thomas A. 1962- WhoE 91
Rose, Thomas Albert 1942- WhoAm 90, WhoAmA 91
Rose, Thomas G. 1957- St&PR 91
Rose, Velma Annette 1953- WhoAmW 91
Rose, Vincent 1880-1944 OxCPMus
Rose, Vincent Harold 1931- St&PR 91
Rose, Wayne Myron 1946- St&PR 91
Rose, Wendy 1948- FemiCLE

Rose, Wendy Elizabeth 1948- *WhoWrEP 89*
Rose, Wesley 1918-1990 *BioIn 16*
Rose, William Allen, Jr. 1938- *WhoAm 90, WhoE 91, WhoWor 91*
Rose, William Louis 1925- *St&PR 91*
Rose, William S. 1928-1989 *BioIn 16*
Rose, Zeke 1932- *ODwPR 91, St&PR 91*
Rose, Zeldon E. 1932- *St&PR 91, WhoAm 90*
Rose-Ackerman, Susan 1942- *WhoAm 90, WhoE 91*
Rose-Hayes, Karla Lavon 1947- *WhoAmW 91*
Rose Pierce, Marjorie Virginia 1926- *WhoAmW 91*
Roseberg, Carl Andersson 1916- *WhoAm 90, WhoAmA 91, WhoWor 91*
Roseberry, Eric Norman 1930- *IntWWM 90*
Roseberry, Richard Lee 1953- *WhoE 91*
Roseberry, Wendy Lou 1955- *WhoWor 91*
Rosebery, Archibald P Primrose, Earl of 1847-1929 *BioIn 16*
Rosebery, Dean Arlo 1919- *WhoAm 90*
Rosebery, Richard J. 1935- *St&PR 91*
Roseboro, Johnny 1933- *Ballpl 90*
Rosebush, James Scott 1949- *WhoAm 90*
Rosecan, Arthur Scott 1957- *BiDrAPA 89*
Rosecan, Jeffrey Sanford 1952- *BiDrAPA 89*
Rosecrans, William Starke 1819-1898 *BioIn 16, WorAlBi*
Rosedahl, David Evans 1947- *St&PR 91*
Rosefield, Herbert Aaron, Jr. 1943- *WhoSSW 91*
Rosefielde, Alan Paul 1946- *WhoSSW 91*
Rosefsky, Quinn B 1941- *BiDrAPA 89*
Rosegger, Gerhard 1930- *WhoAm 90*
Rosehart, Robert George 1943- *WhoAm 90*
Roseland, Harry Herman 1866-1950 *WhoAmA 91N*
Roseliep, Robert Edward 1934- *St&PR 91*
Roselin, Alvin M. 1931- *ODwPR 91*
Roselinsky, Alan 1945- *St&PR 91*
Rosell, Sharon Lynn 1948- *WhoAmW 91, WhoEmL 91*
Rosella, John Daniel 1938- *WhoWor 91*
Roselle, David Paul 1939- *WhoAm 90*
Roselle, Richard Drew 1949- *WhoE 91*
Roselle, Robert Paul 1925- *St&PR 91, WhoAm 90*
Roselle, William Charles 1936- *WhoAm 90, WhoE 91*
Roselli, Luciana *AuBYP 90*
Rosellini, Mario Renaldo, Jr. 1938- *WhoE 91*
Rosello, Dave 1950- *Ballpl 90*
Roseman, Bill 1891- *MusmAFA*
Roseman, George H. 1937- *St&PR 91*
Roseman, Kenneth 1939- *BioIn 16*
Roseman, Kenneth Mark 1954- *WhoSSW 91*
Roseman, Lawrence S. 1929- *WhoE 91*
Roseman, Mill 1921- *St&PR 91*
Roseman, Saul 1921- *WhoAm 90*
Roseman, Stanley 1945- *WhoAmA 91*
Roseman, Susan Carol 1950- *WhoAmA 91*
Rosemarin, Carey Stephen 1950- *WhoEmL 91*
Rosemberg, Eugenia 1918- *WhoAm 90*
Roseme, Sharon Day 1953- *WhoEmL 91*
Rosemergy, Sylvia Elouise 1941- *WhoSSW 91*
Rosemond, Bruce W. 1934- *St&PR 91*
Rosemond, Clinton 1883-1966 *DrBIPA 90*
Rosemond, Henri Ch. *EarBIAP*
Rosemont, Franklin 1943- *WhoWrEP 89*
Rosemont, Norman 1924- *WhoAm 90*
Rosemore, Fredric Michael 1923- *St&PR 91*
Rosen, Al 1924- *Ballpl 90, BioIn 16*
Rosen, Alan *BioIn 16*
Rosen, Albert 1925- *PenDiMP*
Rosen, Albert 1930- *IntWWM 90*
Rosen, Albert J. *BioIn 16*
Rosen, Albert Leonard 1924- *WhoAm 90*
Rosen, Alvin 1926- *BiDrAPA 89*
Rosen, Andrea *BioIn 16*
Rosen, Andrew Mayer 1951- *St&PR 91, WhoAm 90*
Rosen, Anne *BioIn 16*
Rosen, Arnold M 1942- *BiDrAPA 89*
Rosen, Arthur Jonah 1935- *WhoE 91*
Rosen, B. Joshua 1954- *WhoE 91*
Rosen, B. Walter 1931- *WhoE 91*
Rosen, Benedict P. 1936- *St&PR 91*
Rosen, Benedict Phillip 1936- *WhoAm 90*
Rosen, Benjamin M. *BioIn 16*
Rosen, Benjamin Maurice 1933- *WhoAm 90, WhoSSW 91*
Rosen, Benson 1942- *WhoAm 90*
Rosen, Bernard 1920- *WhoAm 90, WhoE 91*
Rosen, Bernard 1927- *St&PR 91*
Rosen, Bernard H. 1922- *WhoAm 90*
Rosen, Bertram H 1933- *BiDrAPA 89*
Rosen, Bertram Howard 1933- *WhoE 91*
Rosen, Beth Dee 1945- *WhoAmW 91*
Rosen, Bruce David 1946- *St&PR 91*
Rosen, Bruce Ira 1945- *BiDrAPA 89*
Rosen, Carol M *WhoAmA 91*
Rosen, Carol Zwick 1932- *WhoAmW 91*
Rosen, Charles 1878-1950 *WhoAmA 91N*
Rosen, Charles 1927- *IntWWM 90, PenDiMP*
Rosen, Charles, II 1925- *WhoAm 90*
Rosen, Charles Welles 1927- *WhoAm 90*
Rosen, Cheryl Hope 1963- *WhoE 91*
Rosen, Daniel Allan 1952- *WhoSSW 91*
Rosen, David 1880-1960 *WhoAmA 91N*
Rosen, David Bruce 1958- *St&PR 91*
Rosen, David Henry 1945- *BiDrAPA 89, WhoWrEP 89*
Rosen, David Lee 1929- *BiDrAPA 89*
Rosen, Dolly 1950- *St&PR 91*
Rosen, Donald Edward 1956- *BiDrAPA 89*
Rosen, Emanuel Herbert *BiDrAPA 89*
Rosen, Esther *St&PR 91*
Rosen, Esther Yovits 1916- *WhoE 91*
Rosen, Evelyn *BiDrAPA 89*
Rosen, Floyd Leonard *BiDrAPA 89*
Rosen, Gary Benard 1955- *BiDrAPA 89*
Rosen, Gary Mitchell 1953- *WhoEmL 91*
Rosen, George 1910-1977 *ConAu 31NR*
Rosen, George 1920- *WhoAm 90*
Rosen, Gerald 1938- *ConAu 30NR*
Rosen, Gerald Harris 1933- *WhoAm 90*
Rosen, Gerald M. 1940- *St&PR 91*
Rosen, Gerald Robert 1930- *WhoAm 90, WhoWrEP 89*
Rosen, Goody 1912- *Ballpl 90, BioIn 16*
Rosen, Haiim Baruch 1922- *WhoWor 91*
Rosen, Harold *BiDrAPA 89*
Rosen, Harvey *ODwPR 91*
Rosen, Harvey Elliot 1939- *BiDrAPA 89*
Rosen, Harvey Sheldon 1949- *WhoE 91*
Rosen, Herbert Irving 1922- *St&PR 91, WhoAm 90*
Rosen, Howard 1914- *WhoE 91*
Rosen, Howard 1929- *St&PR 91*
Rosen, Howard B 1938- *BiDrAPA 89*
Rosen, Howard Robert 1960- *WhoWor 91*
Rosen, Hy 1923- *WhoAmA 91*
Rosen, Hy 1940- *WhoAm 90*
Rosen, Hyman J. 1923- *WhoE 91*
Rosen, Ira A 1936- *BiDrAPA 89*
Rosen, Irving 1928- *St&PR 91*
Rosen, Irving M *BiDrAPA 89*
Rosen, Irving Marcus 1918- *WhoE 91*
Rosen, Israel 1911- *WhoAmA 91*
Rosen, Jack *BioIn 16*
Rosen, James Alan 1930- *WhoE 91*
Rosen, James Mahlon 1933- *WhoAmA 91*
Rosen, Jay H. 1948- *St&PR 91*
Rosen, Jay Martin 1937- *St&PR 91*
Rosen, Jeffrey J. 1949- *WhoEmL 91*
Rosen, Jeffrey Stuart 1946- *WhoE 91*
Rosen, Jerome 1921- *WhoAm 90*
Rosen, Jerome 1939- *IntWWM 90*
Rosen, Jerome William 1921- *IntWWM 90*
Rosen, Joan Fischman *WhoAmA 91*
Rosen, Joel Elliot 1944- *BiDrAPA 89*
Rosen, Joseph D *BiDrAPA 89*
Rosen, Joseph E., Mrs. *WhoAmW 91*
Rosen, Judah Ben 1922- *WhoAm 90*
Rosen, Judith Berenice 1933- *IntWWM 90*
Rosen, Jules *BiDrAPA 89*
Rosen, Karen 1946- *WhoAmW 91*
Rosen, Kathy Meryl Strauss 1956- *WhoE 91*
Rosen, Kay *WhoAmA 91*
Rosen, Kenneth Martin 1940- *WhoE 91*
Rosen, Kenneth Roy 1950- *St&PR 91*
Rosen, Lawrence J. 1943- *St&PR 91*
Rosen, Lee *ODwPR 91*
Rosen, Leo 1906-1989 *BioIn 16*
Rosen, Leon N.M.N. 1924- *WhoE 91*
Rosen, Leonard J 1946- *BiDrAPA 89*
Rosen, Leonard William 1917- *St&PR 91*
Rosen, Leslie April 1954- *WhoAmW 91*
Rosen, Lillian 1928- *SmATA 63*
Rosen, Lionel Wayne *BiDrAPA 89*
Rosen, Louis 1918- *WhoAm 90*
Rosen, Manuel Morrison 1926- *WhoAm 90*
Rosen, Marcella 1934- *St&PR 91*
Rosen, Marcella Jung 1934- *WhoAm 90*
Rosen, Mark Lawrence 1948- *St&PR 91*
Rosen, Marvin 1942- *BiDrAPA 89*
Rosen, Marvin 1947- *St&PR 91*
Rosen, Matthew Stephen 1943- *WhoWor 91*
Rosen, Maurice M. 1920- *St&PR 91*
Rosen, Mel *BioIn 16*
Rosen, Michael *BioIn 16*
Rosen, Michael 1946- *ConAu 32NR*
Rosen, Michael Howard 1943- *WhoE 91*
Rosen, Michael J. 1945- *WhoAm 90*
Rosen, Michael J 1954- *ConAu 132, WhoWrEP 89*
Rosen, Michael Jay 1954- *WhoEmL 91*
Rosen, Milton William 1915- *WhoAm 90*
Rosen, Morris 1932- *WhoWor 91*
Rosen, Mortimer Gilbert 1931- *WhoAm 90*
Rosen, Myor 1917- *WhoAm 90*
Rosen, Nathan 1914- *St&PR 91, WhoE 91*
Rosen, Nathan Aaron 1955- *WhoEmL 91*
Rosen, Nathan David 1915- *WhoSSW 91*
Rosen, Nathan N. *BioIn 16*
Rosen, Nathaniel Kent 1948- *IntWWM 90, WhoAm 90, WhoE 91*
Rosen, Neal 1951- *ODwPR 91*
Rosen, Neil Douglas *BiDrAPA 89*
Rosen, Norma *WhoWrEP 89*
Rosen, Norma Gangel 1925- *BioIn 16*
Rosen, Norman Edward 1938- *WhoAm 90*
Rosen, Ora M. *NewYTBS 90*
Rosen, Ora M. 1935-1990 *BioIn 16*
Rosen, Ora Mendelsohn 1935- *WhoAm 90*
Rosen, Paul *EncO&P 3*
Rosen, Philip 1922- *WhoAm 90*
Rosen, R D *ConAu 30NR*
Rosen, Rhoda 1933- *WhoAmW 91*
Rosen, Richard 1917- *WhoAm 90*
Rosen, Richard 1949- *ConAu 30NR, TwCCr&M 91*
Rosen, Richard Lewis 1943- *WhoAm 90*
Rosen, Richard Michael 1948- *BiDrAPA 89*
Rosen, Robert Arnold 1936- *St&PR 91, WhoAm 90, WhoE 91*
Rosen, Robert Joseph 1956- *IntWWM 90*
Rosen, Robert L. *St&PR 91*
Rosen, Robert Meyers 1941- *WhoE 91*
Rosen, Robert Stanley 1936- *WhoSSW 91*
Rosen, Robert Stephen 1947- *WhoE 91*
Rosen, Ronald 1944- *BiDrAPA 89*
Rosen, Ronald Haiam 1933- *WhoE 91*
Rosen, Ronald Martin *BiDrAPA 89*
Rosen, Sam 1920- *WhoAm 90, WhoE 91*
Rosen, Samuel Howard *BiDrAPA 89*
Rosen, Sarah *BioIn 16*
Rosen, Sheldon 1943- *OxCCanT*
Rosen, Sherman David 1930- *St&PR 91*
Rosen, Sherrill Lynn 1955- *WhoAmW 91*
Rosen, Sherwin 1938- *WhoAm 90*
Rosen, Sidney 1926- *BiDrAPA 89, WhoE 91*
Rosen, Sidney Marvin 1939- *WhoWor 91*
Rosen, Simon Peter 1933- *WhoAm 90*
Rosen, Sindey 1913- *St&PR 91*
Rosen, Stanley Howard 1929- *WhoAm 90*
Rosen, Stanley W. 1932- *St&PR 91*
Rosen, Steven H. 1942- *EncPaPR 91*
Rosen, Steven Raun *BiDrAPA 89*
Rosen, Susan Elizabeth *BiDrAPA 89*
Rosen, Todd Neal 1958- *BiDrAPA 89*
Rosen, William 1926- *WhoAm 90*
Rosen, William G. 1921- *WhoWor 91*
Rosen, William Warren 1936- *WhoAm 90, WhoSSW 91*
Rosen, Wilma Friedman *BiDrAPA 89*
Rosen, Winifred 1943- *ConAu 32NR*
Rosen-Supnick, Elaine Renee 1951- *WhoAmW 91*
Rosenada, Jose 1907-1989 *WhoHisp 91N*
Rosenau, Blanche Gottardo 1918- *WhoAmW 91*
Rosenau, James Nathan 1924- *WhoAm 90, WhoWrEP 89*
Rosenau, Pauline Marie 1943- *WhoE 91*
Rosenau, Steven L. 1948- *St&PR 91*
Rosenauer, Artur 1940- *WhoWor 91*
Rosenbach, Ulrike Nolden 1943- *BiDWomA*
Rosenbaum, Alan Howard *BiDrAPA 89*
Rosenbaum, Allen 1937- *WhoAmA 91*
Rosenbaum, Ann Pharmakis 1949- *WhoAmW 91*
Rosenbaum, Arlene 1944- *WhoAmW 91*
Rosenbaum, Arthur Elihu 1935- *WhoAm 90*
Rosenbaum, Arthur Saul 1953- *WhoE 91*
Rosenbaum, Barbara Amdur 1952- *WhoAmW 91*
Rosenbaum, Belle Sara 1922- *WhoAmW 91, WhoE 91*
Rosenbaum, Bent 1948- *WhoWor 91*
Rosenbaum, Carl Peter 1930- *BiDrAPA 89*
Rosenbaum, Daniel Jesse 1956- *WhoE 91*
Rosenbaum, Edward E. 1915- *BioIn 16, WhoAm 90*
Rosenbaum, Eileen 1936- *AuBYP 90*
Rosenbaum, Eli Menachem 1955- *WhoE 91, WhoEmL 91*
Rosenbaum, Emanuel *St&PR 91*
Rosenbaum, Evelyn Eller *WhoAmA 91*
Rosenbaum, Glen *BioIn 16*
Rosenbaum, Greg Alan 1952- *St&PR 91*
Rosenbaum, H. K. 1916- *St&PR 91*
Rosenbaum, Harold 1950- *IntWWM 90*
Rosenbaum, Harold Dennis 1921- *WhoAm 90*
Rosenbaum, Hattie Clark *BioIn 16*
Rosenbaum, Herbert E *BiDrAPA 89*
Rosenbaum, Irving M. 1921- *WhoAm 90*
Rosenbaum, Jacob I. 1927- *St&PR 91, WhoAm 90*
Rosenbaum, James Michael 1944- *WhoAm 90*
Rosenbaum, Jerrold Frank 1947- *BiDrAPA 89*
Rosenbaum, Joan H *WhoAmA 91*
Rosenbaum, Joan Hannah 1942- *WhoAm 90, WhoAmW 91, WhoE 91*
Rosenbaum, Jonathan 1943- *ConAu 130*
Rosenbaum, Lee Robert 1948- *BiDrAPA 89*
Rosenbaum, Linda Jean 1952- *WhoAmW 91*
Rosenbaum, Maj-Britt 1937- *BiDrAPA 89*
Rosenbaum, Martin Michael 1923- *St&PR 91*
Rosenbaum, Meyer 1900- *St&PR 91*
Rosenbaum, Michael A. *ODwPR 91*
Rosenbaum, Milton 1910- *BiDrAPA 89*
Rosenbaum, Paul Leonard 1937- *WhoE 91*
Rosenbaum, Ralph Ernest 1952- *WhoE 91*
Rosenbaum, Richard Merrill 1931- *St&PR 91, WhoAm 90*
Rosenbaum, Robert Abraham 1915- *WhoAm 90, WhoE 91*
Rosenbaum, Ronald John Joseph 1939- *BiDrAPA 89*
Rosenbaum, S. Mark 1947- *WhoE 91*
Rosenbaum, Samuel 1919- *BioIn 16*
Rosenbaum, Sheldon A. 1948- *WhoE 91*
Rosenbaum, Steven Ira 1946- *WhoAm 90*
Rosenbaum, Susan Jane *BiDrAPA 89*
Rosenbaum, Sylvia P. *WhoWrEP 89*
Rosenbaum, Victor 1941- *IntWWM 90*
Rosenbaum, William John 1945- *WhoSSW 91*
Rosenberg, Aaron Edward 1937- *WhoAm 90*
Rosenberg, Abraham 1950- *WhoSSW 91*
Rosenberg, Alan Paul 1944- *WhoE 91*
Rosenberg, Alan Robert *BiDrAPA 89*
Rosenberg, Alan Stewart 1930- *WhoAm 90*
Rosenberg, Alex 1926- *WhoAm 90*
Rosenberg, Alex Jacob 1919- *WhoAm 90, WhoAmA 91, WhoE 91, WhoWor 91*
Rosenberg, Alexander 1946- *ConAu 132*
Rosenberg, Alfred 1893-1946 *BioIn 16*
Rosenberg, Alison P. 1945- *WhoAm 90*
Rosenberg, Alison Podell 1945- *WhoAmW 91*
Rosenberg, Allan J 1920- *BiDrAPA 89*
Rosenberg, Allen E. 1935- *St&PR 91*
Rosenberg, Arnold 1941- *St&PR 91*
Rosenberg, Arthur James 1926- *St&PR 91, WhoAm 90*
Rosenberg, Asher Earl 1944- *BiDrAPA 89*
Rosenberg, Barnett 1944- *St&PR 91*
Rosenberg, Barr Marvin 1942- *WhoAm 90*
Rosenberg, Beatrice 1908-1989 *BioIn 16*
Rosenberg, Benjamin *St&PR 91*
Rosenberg, Bernard *St&PR 91*
Rosenberg, Bernard 1928- *WhoAm 90*
Rosenberg, Bernard 1938- *WhoAmA 91*
Rosenberg, Bernard Allan 1952- *BiDrAPA 89*
Rosenberg, Bernd 1941- *WhoWor 91*
Rosenberg, Brigitte R *BiDrAPA 89*
Rosenberg, Bruce Alan 1934- *WhoAm 90, WhoWrEP 89*
Rosenberg, Carole 1936- *WhoAmW 91, WhoE 91*
Rosenberg, Carole Halsband 1936- *WhoAmA 91*
Rosenberg, Chaim M *BiDrAPA 89*
Rosenberg, Charles Ernest 1936- *WhoAm 90, WhoWrEP 89*
Rosenberg, Charles Michael 1945- *WhoAm 90, WhoAmA 91*
Rosenberg, Claude Newman, Jr. 1928- *WhoAm 90*
Rosenberg, Cy *St&PR 91*
Rosenberg, Dan 1944- *St&PR 91*
Rosenberg, David *BioIn 16*
Rosenberg, David 1934- *St&PR 91*
Rosenberg, David Howard 1941- *WhoAm 90*
Rosenberg, David L 1928- *BiDrAPA 89*
Rosenberg, David Scott 1961- *BiDrAPA 89*
Rosenberg, Dennis Melville Leo 1921- *WhoAm 90, WhoWor 91*
Rosenberg, Donald *BioIn 16*
Rosenberg, Donald M. 1933- *St&PR 91*
Rosenberg, Donald Martin 1933- *WhoAm 90*
Rosenberg, Edgar *BioIn 16*
Rosenberg, Edgar 1925- *WhoAm 90*
Rosenberg, Edith Esther 1928- *WhoAmW 91*
Rosenberg, Eduardo German 1939- *St&PR 91*
Rosenberg, Edwin M 1940- *BiDrAPA 89*
Rosenberg, Ellen Small 1950- *WhoAmW 91*
Rosenberg, Elliott David 1923- *St&PR 91*
Rosenberg, Ethel *AuBYP 90*
Rosenberg, Ethel *EncAL*
Rosenberg, Ethel 1915-1953 *BioAmW, WorAlBi*
Rosenberg, Ethel 1916-1953 *BioIn 16*
Rosenberg, Ethel Clifford 1915- *BioIn 16*
Rosenberg, Evelyn *BioIn 16*
Rosenberg, Frank Blaustein 1958- *WhoEmL 91*
Rosenberg, Frank Louis 1940- *St&PR 91*
Rosenberg, Gary Aron 1940- *WhoAm 90*

Rosenberg, Gary Burton 1947- BiDrAPA 89
Rosenberg, Gary Marc 1950- WhoEmL 91
Rosenberg, George A. 1945- ODwPR 91
Rosenberg, Gerald Burton 1948- WhoE 91
Rosenberg, Glenda Lerner 1939- WhoAmW 91
Rosenberg, Gustave G. 1900-1988 BioIn 16
Rosenberg, Harold 1906-1978 WhoAmA 91N
Rosenberg, Harry 1940- WhoAm 90
Rosenberg, Harvey J BiDrAPA 89
Rosenberg, Henri 1950- WhoWor 91
Rosenberg, Henry A., Jr. 1929- St&PR 91, WhoAm 90, WhoE 91
Rosenberg, Herb 1942- WhoAmA 91
Rosenberg, Irene Vera 1936- WhoAmW 91
Rosenberg, Irwin H. 1935- BioIn 16
Rosenberg, Jack 1915-1988 BioIn 16
Rosenberg, Jack Eli 1941- BiDrAPA 89
Rosenberg, Jacob Joseph 1947- WhoE 91
Rosenberg, Jakob 1893-1980 WhoAmA 91N
Rosenberg, Jane 1949- BioIn 16, WhoAmA 91
Rosenberg, Jay Frank 1942- WhoAm 90, WhoWrEP 89
Rosenberg, Jeffrey Stephen 1954- St&PR 91
Rosenberg, Jerome B. St&PR 91N
Rosenberg, Jerome I. 1931- WhoAm 90
Rosenberg, Jerome Laib 1921- WhoAm 90
Rosenberg, Jerome Roy 1926- WhoWor 91
Rosenberg, Jerome Willard 1930- WhoAm 90
Rosenberg, Jerry BioIn 16
Rosenberg, Jerry Martin 1935- WhoAm 90, WhoWrEP 89
Rosenberg, Jo 1948- WhoAmW 91
Rosenberg, John David 1929- WhoAm 90, WhoWrEP 89
Rosenberg, John Edward 1953- WhoEmL 91
Rosenberg, John George 1954- BiDrAPA 89
Rosenberg, John K. 1945- St&PR 91
Rosenberg, Jonathan Micah 1951- WhoE 91
Rosenberg, Judith M. 1964- WhoAmW 91
Rosenberg, Julian D. BioIn 16
Rosenberg, Julius EncAL
Rosenberg, Julius 1918-1953 WorAlBi
Rosenberg, Kenneth 1946- St&PR 91
Rosenberg, Kenneth 1956- BiDrAPA 89
Rosenberg, Larry J. 1943- WhoE 91
Rosenberg, Lawrence E 1944- BiDrAPA 89
Rosenberg, Leo Henry 1896-1988 BioIn 16
Rosenberg, Leon E. 1933- WhoAm 90
Rosenberg, Leon Irving 1952- BiDrAPA 89
Rosenberg, Leon Joseph 1918- WhoAm 90
Rosenberg, Leonard BioIn 16
Rosenberg, Leslie Karen 1949- WhoAmW 91
Rosenberg, Liz BioIn 16
Rosenberg, Louis 1898- WhoAm 90
Rosenberg, Louis Aaron 1912- WhoE 91
Rosenberg, Lynn Stephanie 1962- WhoAmW 91
Rosenberg, Manuel 1930- St&PR 91, WhoAm 90, WhoE 91
Rosenberg, Mark Jeffrey BiDrAPA 89
Rosenberg, Mark Michael BiDrAPA 89
Rosenberg, Marsha D 1941- BiDrAPA 89
Rosenberg, Marshal Ernest 1936- WhoSSW 91
Rosenberg, Maurice 1919- WhoAm 90, WhoWrEP 89
Rosenberg, Maxine B. 1939- BioIn 16
Rosenberg, Maxine Berta 1939- AuBYP 90
Rosenberg, Mervin 1925- BiDrAPA 89
Rosenberg, Michael 1928- St&PR 91
Rosenberg, Michael 1937- WhoAm 90
Rosenberg, Michael 1949- WhoE 91
Rosenberg, Michael Joseph 1928- WhoE 91
Rosenberg, Monica Yvonne BioIn 16
Rosenberg, Mordechai 1933- St&PR 91
Rosenberg, Morton Yale 1932- WhoAm 90
Rosenberg, Nancy 1931- AuBYP 90
Rosenberg, Nancy Sherman 1931- WhoWrEP 89
Rosenberg, Nathan 1927- WhoAm 90
Rosenberg, Norman 1916- WhoAm 90
Rosenberg, Norman Jack 1930- WhoAm 90
Rosenberg, Paul 1910- WhoAm 90, WhoE 91
Rosenberg, Paul B. 1932- St&PR 91
Rosenberg, Paul Edward 1947- BiDrAPA 89, WhoE 91
Rosenberg, Per 1953- IntWWM 90
Rosenberg, Philip H 1910- BiDrAPA 89
Rosenberg, Pierre BioIn 16
Rosenberg, Priscilla Elliott 1952- WhoEmL 91
Rosenberg, Ralph S. 1931- St&PR 91
Rosenberg, Raymond 1922- St&PR 91
Rosenberg, Richard M. BioIn 16
Rosenberg, Richard Morris 1930- St&PR 91, WhoAm 90
Rosenberg, Robert Alan 1934- WhoAm 90
Rosenberg, Robert Brinkmann 1937- WhoAm 90
Rosenberg, Robert C. 1934- St&PR 91
Rosenberg, Robert Craig 1951- WhoE 91
Rosenberg, Robert Donald 1947- BiDrAPA 89
Rosenberg, Robert M. BioIn 16
Rosenberg, Robert M. 1938- St&PR 91
Rosenberg, Robert Melvin 1926- WhoAm 90
Rosenberg, Robert Michael 1938- WhoAm 90
Rosenberg, Roger Newman 1939- WhoAm 90
Rosenberg, Ronald C 1947- BiDrAPA 89
Rosenberg, Ronald I. 1936- St&PR 91
Rosenberg, Ronnie Gale BiDrAPA 89
Rosenberg, Rudy 1930- St&PR 91, WhoE 91
Rosenberg, Ruth Helen Borsuk 1935- WhoAm 90
Rosenberg, Saemy WhoAmA 91N
Rosenberg, Sally Jane BiDrAPA 89
Rosenberg, Sally Katherine 1946- WhoSSW 91
Rosenberg, Samuel 1896-1972 WhoAmA 91N
Rosenberg, Samuel Nathan 1936- WhoAm 90
Rosenberg, Sandra 1942- WhoAmW 91
Rosenberg, Saul Allen 1927- WhoAm 90
Rosenberg, Scott Frederic 1951- WhoEmL 91
Rosenberg, Seymour 1917- St&PR 91
Rosenberg, Seymour 1926- WhoAm 90
Rosenberg, Sheli Zysman 1942- WhoAm 90
Rosenberg, Sigmond St&PR 91
Rosenberg, Stanton L 1930- BiDrAPA 89
Rosenberg, Stephen N 1941- ConAu 30NR
Rosenberg, Steven Aaron 1940- WhoAm 90
Rosenberg, Stuart 1927- WhoAm 90
Rosenberg, Stuart E. NewYTBS 90
Rosenberg, Stuart E. 1922-1990 BioIn 16, ConAu 131
Rosenberg, Susan L. ODwPR 91
Rosenberg, Suzanne 1915- BioIn 16
Rosenberg, Sydney J. BioIn 16
Rosenberg, Sydney J. 1914- St&PR 91, WhoAm 90
Rosenberg, Terry 1954- WhoAmA 91
Rosenberg, Theodore T. 1909- St&PR 91
Rosenberg, Victor BioIn 16
Rosenberg, Victor I. 1936- WhoE 91, WhoWor 91
Rosenberg, Victor Laurence 1944- WhoE 91, WhoWor 91
Rosenberg, William 1916- St&PR 91
Rosenberg, Zena 1918- St&PR 91
Rosenberger, Carol 1935- WhoAm 90
Rosenberger, Donald Markley 1913- WhoAm 90
Rosenberger, Ernst Hey 1931- WhoAm 90
Rosenberger, Francis Coleman 1915- WhoWrEP 89
Rosenberger, Frank Joseph 1947- St&PR 91
Rosenberger, Franz Ernst 1933- WhoSSW 91
Rosenberger, John W. BiDrAPA 89
Rosenberger, John Weaver 1934- WhoE 91
Rosenberger, Joseph SpyFic
Rosenberger, Marcus L. St&PR 91
Rosenberger, Walter Emerson 1918- WhoAm 90
Rosenberry, Frank A. 1937- St&PR 91
Rosenblatt, Aaron A. 1958- St&PR 91
Rosenblatt, Adolph 1933- WhoAmA 91
Rosenblatt, Albert Martin 1936- WhoAm 90, WhoE 91
Rosenblatt, Alice 1948- St&PR 91
Rosenblatt, Allan D 1926- BiDrAPA 89
Rosenblatt, Arthur Isaac 1931- WhoAm 90
Rosenblatt, Charles B. 1926- St&PR 91
Rosenblatt, Cy Hart 1954- WhoSSW 91
Rosenblatt, David Sidney 1953- WhoSSW 91
Rosenblatt, Edward Milton 1952- WhoEmL 91
Rosenblatt, Elaine Rochelle 1949- WhoAmW 91
Rosenblatt, Ellen A BiDrAPA 89
Rosenblatt, Gerd Matthew 1933- WhoAm 90
Rosenblatt, Harvey 1933- BiDrAPA 89
Rosenblatt, Harvey 1939- St&PR 91
Rosenblatt, Howard Marshall 1947- WhoSSW 91
Rosenblatt, Jack Elliot BiDrAPA 89
Rosenblatt, Jack Elliot 1949- WhoE 91
Rosenblatt, Jay BioIn 16
Rosenblatt, Joan Raup 1926- WhoAmW 91, WhoE 91
Rosenblatt, Joel 1944- WhoE 91
Rosenblatt, Joseph 1933- WhoAm 90
Rosenblatt, Julia Carlson 1940- WhoE 91, WhoWor 91
Rosenblatt, Laurie Ann 1959- BiDrAPA 89
Rosenblatt, Leonard 1929- St&PR 91, WhoAm 90
Rosenblatt, Lester 1920- WhoAm 90, WhoWor 91
Rosenblatt, Louis 1928- WhoAm 90
Rosenblatt, Louise Michel 1904- WhoAmW 91
Rosenblatt, Malcolm Lee 1930- BiDrAPA 89
Rosenblatt, Marc Saul 1950- St&PR 91
Rosenblatt, Michael 1947- WhoAm 90
Rosenblatt, Murray 1926- WhoAm 90
Rosenblatt, Nancy Crooker BiDrAPA 89
Rosenblatt, Paul 1928- WhoAm 90, WhoWrEP 89
Rosenblatt, Paul Gerhardt 1928- WhoAm 90
Rosenblatt, Peter Ronald 1933- WhoAm 90
Rosenblatt, Robert John 1956- WhoE 91
Rosenblatt, Roger WhoAm 90
Rosenblatt, Roger Alan 1945- WhoAm 90
Rosenblatt, Ruth 1934- WhoWrEP 89
Rosenblatt, Samuel 1907-1989 BioIn 16
Rosenblatt, Seymour BiDrAPA 89
Rosenblatt, Sidney Donald St&PR 91
Rosenblatt, Sol 1929- St&PR 91
Rosenblatt, Stanley Abraham 1937- WhoE 91
Rosenblatt, Stephen Paul 1935- WhoAm 90
Rosenblatt, Steven BiDrAPA 89
Rosenblatt, Suzanne Maris 1937- WhoAmA 91
Rosenbleeth, Richard Marvin 1932- WhoAm 90
Rosenblith, Walter Alter 1913- WhoAm 90
Rosenbloom, Arlan Lee 1934- WhoAm 90
Rosenbloom, Arthur H. BioIn 16
Rosenbloom, Charles 1935- BiDrAPA 89
Rosenbloom, Daniel 1930- St&PR 91, WhoAm 90
Rosenbloom, H. David 1941- WhoAm 90
Rosenbloom, J L BiDrAPA 89
Rosenbloom, Jerry S 1939- ConAu 129
Rosenbloom, Judy R. 1944- ODwPR 91
Rosenbloom, Milton M. 1907-1989 BioIn 16
Rosenbloom, Mindy Sharon 1960- BiDrAPA 89
Rosenbloom, Morris Victor 1915- WhoAm 90, WhoWor 91
Rosenbloom, Richard H. 1939- St&PR 91
Rosenbloom, Richard Selig 1933- WhoAm 90
Rosenbloom, Sanford M. 1928- WhoAm 90
Rosenbloom, William BiDrAPA 89
Rosenblueth, Emilio 1926- WhoAm 90
Rosenblum, Arnold 1935- St&PR 91
Rosenblum, Art NewAgE 90
Rosenblum, Art 1927- WhoE 91
Rosenblum, Barbara 1943-1988 BioIn 16
Rosenblum, Barnett BiDrAPA 89
Rosenblum, Bruce S BiDrAPA 89
Rosenblum, Donald Edward 1929- WhoAm 90
Rosenblum, Edward G. 1944- WhoWor 91
Rosenblum, Harold Arthur 1923- WhoAm 90
Rosenblum, Harvey 1943- St&PR 91
Rosenblum, James Philip 1935- BiDrAPA 89
Rosenblum, Jay 1933-1989 BioIn 16, WhoAmA 91N
Rosenblum, Jerald E. 1935- St&PR 91
Rosenblum, John William 1944- WhoAm 90
Rosenblum, Joseph 1952- St&PR 91
Rosenblum, Lila S. ODwPR 91
Rosenblum, Louis 1925- BiDrAPA 89
Rosenblum, M. Edgar 1932- ConTFT 8 [port]
Rosenblum, Marshall 1947- WhoE 91
Rosenblum, Martin Jack 1946- WhoWrEP 89
Rosenblum, Martin Jerome 1948- WhoEmL 91, WhoSSW 91, WhoWor 91
Rosenblum, Marvin 1926- WhoAm 90
Rosenblum, Mort 1943- ConAu 30NR
Rosenblum, Mort Lee 1943- WhoWor 91
Rosenblum, Muni Edward 1933- WhoAm 90
Rosenblum, Myron 1925- WhoAm 90
Rosenblum, Peter 1941- WhoE 91
Rosenblum, Richard Stephen 1940- WhoAmA 91
Rosenblum, Robert BioIn 16
Rosenblum, Robert 1927- WhoAm 90, WhoAmA 91, WhoE 91
Rosenblum, Ruth BiDrAPA 89
Rosenblum, Sandra P. 1928- IntWWM 90
Rosenblum, Stephen BiDrAPA 89
Rosenblum, Victor Gregory 1925- WhoAm 90
Rosenblum, William Franklin, Jr. 1935- St&PR 91
Rosenbluth, Marshall Nicholas 1927- WhoAm 90
Rosenbluth, Morton 1924- WhoAm 90, WhoWor 91
Rosenbluth, Sidney Alan 1933- WhoAm 90
Rosenboom, David C. 1947- IntWWM 90
Rosenborg, Ralph Mozart 1913- WhoAm 90, WhoE 91
Rosenburg, John M. 1918- AuBYP 90
Rosenburg, Robert Kemper 1920- WhoWrEP 89
Rosenburgh, Dwayne Maurice 1960- WhoE 91
Rosenbury, W. Mark 1947- St&PR 91
Rosenbusch, Jurg Peter 1938- WhoWor 91
Rosencrans, Ernest 1929- BiDrAPA 89
Rosencrans, Evan William 1926- WhoAm 90
Rosencrans, Gordon William 1923- St&PR 91
Rosencrans, Steven Ira 1938- WhoSSW 91
Rosencrantz, Elliot BiDrAPA 89
Rosencrantz, Lawrence 1945- St&PR 91, WhoAm 90
Rosendahl, Bruce BioIn 16
Rosendale, Albert F BiDrAPA 89
Rosendale, Donald P. 1936- ODwPR 91
Rosendale, Richard BiDrAPA 89
Rosendhal, Jeffrey David 1941- WhoAm 90
Rosendin, Raymond J. WhoHisp 91
Rosendin, Raymond Joseph 1929- St&PR 91, WhoAm 90
Rosene, Linda Roberts 1938- WhoAmW 91
Rosene, Ralph Walfred 1938- WhoSSW 91
Rosener, James David 1955- WhoE 91
Rosenfeld, A Victor 1916- St&PR 91
Rosenfeld, Alvin A 1945- BiDrAPA 89, WhoE 91
Rosenfeld, Arie 1963- WhoAm 90
Rosenfeld, Arnold Solomon 1933- WhoAm 90, WhoWrEP 89
Rosenfeld, Arthur H. 1930- WhoAm 90
Rosenfeld, Azriel 1931- WhoAm 90
Rosenfeld, Barbara Rae BiDrAPA 89
Rosenfeld, David Neil BiDrAPA 89
Rosenfeld, Edward Julius 1943- WhoE 91
Rosenfeld, Ernest BioIn 16
Rosenfeld, Eugene David 1917-1988 BioIn 16
Rosenfeld, Frederick Lee 1945- WhoE 91
Rosenfeld, Gerald 1946- WhoAm 90
Rosenfeld, Harold E. 1951- St&PR 91
Rosenfeld, Harry Morris 1929- WhoE 91
Rosenfeld, Herbert St&PR 91
Rosenfeld, Irene Kantor 1919- WhoAmW 91
Rosenfeld, Irwin Ira 1951- BiDrAPA 89
Rosenfeld, Isaac 1918-1956 BioIn 16
Rosenfeld, J. A. 1932- St&PR 91
Rosenfeld, Jonathan Eliot BiDrAPA 89
Rosenfeld, Joseph 1907- WhoWor 91
Rosenfeld, Lyle Martin 1953- WhoE 91
Rosenfeld, Mark K. 1946- St&PR 91
Rosenfeld, Mark Kenneth 1946- WhoAm 90
Rosenfeld, Martin 1950- WhoE 91
Rosenfeld, Michael ODwPR 91
Rosenfeld, Monroe H. 1862-1918 BioIn 16, OxCPMus
Rosenfeld, Norman H. 1919- St&PR 91
Rosenfeld, Richard Joel 1940- WhoAmA 91
Rosenfeld, Robert BiDrAPA 89
Rosenfeld, Robert Lee BiDrAPA 89
Rosenfeld, Robert Maurice 1928- St&PR 91
Rosenfeld, Ronald Marvin 1932- WhoAm 90
Rosenfeld, Sam 1920- AuBYP 90
Rosenfeld, Samuel L 1931- WhoAmA 91
Rosenfeld, Sharon 1954- WhoAmA 91
Rosenfeld, Stephen Samuel 1932- WhoAm 90, WhoE 91
Rosenfeld, Steven Ira 1949- WhoE 91, WhoEmL 91
Rosenfeld, Walter David, Jr. 1930- WhoAm 90, WhoE 91
Rosenfeld, William Peter 1936- St&PR 91
Rosenfeld, William Stuart 1945- BiDrAPA 89
Rosenfelder, Alfred S. 1916- St&PR 91
Rosenfelder, Michael 1935- St&PR 91
Rosenfeldt, Michael Bruce 1951- WhoSSW 91
Rosenfelt, Frank Edward 1921- WhoAm 90
Rosenfield, Allan 1933- WhoAm 90
Rosenfield, Andrew M. 1951- WhoEmL 91
Rosenfield, Ann Baker 1961- WhoAmW 91
Rosenfield, Howard Theodore 1946- BiDrAPA 89

Rosenfield, James H. 1929- *St&PR 91*
Rosenfield, James Harold 1929- *WhoAm 90, WhoE 91*
Rosenfield, Jay *BioIn 16*
Rosenfield, Jay 1948- *St&PR 91*
Rosenfield, Jay Gary 1948- *WhoAm 90*
Rosenfield, John M 1924- *WhoAmA 91*
Rosenfield, John Max 1924- *WhoAm 90, WhoWor 91*
Rosenfield, Maurice Lillman 1909- *St&PR 91*
Rosenfield, Richard L. *BioIn 16*
Rosenfield, Robert Lee 1934- *WhoAm 90*
Rosenfield, Sigurd Arthur 1920- *St&PR 91*
Rosenfield-Adams, Annette 1956- *WhoSSW 91*
Rosengaard, Poul Erik 1934- *St&PR 91*
Rosengard, David Ely 1927- *BiDrAPA 89*
Rosengard, Richard Jay 1956- *BiDrAPA 89*
Rosengarten, Clae *BioIn 16*
Rosengarten, Leonard M 1918- *BiDrAPA 89*
Rosengarten, Richard Atkinson 1920- *St&PR 91*
Rosengarten, Sheldon 1946- *WhoSSW 91*
Rosengren, Gunnar Arvid 1943- *WhoWor 91*
Rosengren, Karl Erik 1932- *WhoWor 91*
Rosengren, William R. 1934- *WhoAm 90*
Rosengren, William Roy 1934- *St&PR 91*
Rosenhan, Alvin Kirk 1940- *WhoSSW 91*
Rosenhaus, Steven L. 1952- *IntWWM 90*
Rosenheck, Robert Alan 1947- *BiDrAPA 89*
Rosenheim, Daniel Edward 1949- *WhoAm 90*
Rosenheim, Donald Edwin 1926- *WhoAm 90*
Rosenheim, Edward Weil 1918- *WhoAm 90*
Rosenheim, Howard Harris 1915- *WhoAm 90*
Rosenheim, Lucile G. 1902-1990 *ConAu 132*
Rosenheim, Margaret Keeney 1926- *WhoAm 90*
Rosenheim, Paul 1944- *WhoE 91*
Rosenhouse, Irwin *WhoAm 90*
Rosenhouse, Irwin 1924- *WhoAmA 91*
Rosenhouse, Michael Allan 1946- *WhoE 91*
Rosenker, Mark V. 1946- *ODwPR 91, WhoAm 90, WhoE 91*
Rosenkilde, Carl Edward 1937- *WhoWor 91*
Rosenkoetter, Gerald E. 1927- *St&PR 91*
Rosenkoetter, Gerald Edwin 1927- *WhoAm 90*
Rosenkrantz, Barbara Gutmann 1923- *WhoAmW 91*
Rosenkrantz, Carol M. 1947- *St&PR 91*
Rosenkrantz, Daniel J. 1943- *WhoAm 90*
Rosenkranz, Barry M *BiDrAPA 89*
Rosenkranz, George 1916- *WhoWor 91*
Rosenkranz, Herbert S. 1933- *WhoAm 90*
Rosenkranz, Morty 1928- *St&PR 91*
Rosenkranz, Robert Bernard 1939- *WhoE 91*
Rosenkranz, Stanley William 1933- *WhoAm 90*
Rosenlicht, Maxwell Alexander 1924- *WhoAm 90*
Rosenlicht, Nicholas 1954- *BiDrAPA 89*
Rosenman, David E *BiDrAPA 89*
Rosenman, John Brown 1941- *WhoWrEP 89*
Rosenman, Leonard 1924- *OxCPMus*
Rosenman, Mark Hirsch 1943- *WhoE 91*
Rosenmann, Carl Jay 1950- *BiDrAPA 89*
Rosenmutter, Gary Michael *BiDrAPA 89*
Rosenn, Daniel Wohl 1942- *BiDrAPA 89*
Rosenn, Harold 1917- *WhoAm 90, WhoE 91, WhoWor 91*
Rosenn, Keith Samuel 1938- *WhoAm 90*
Rosenn, Max 1910- *WhoAm 90, WhoE 91*
Rosenne, Meir 1931- *WhoWor 91*
Rosenow, Edward Carl, III 1934- *WhoAm 90*
Rosenow, Edward Carl, Jr. 1909- *WhoAm 90*
Rosenow, John Edward 1949- *WhoEmL 91*
Rosenow, John Henry 1913- *WhoAm 90*
Rosenow, Ulf F. 1935- *WhoWor 91*
Rosenquist, Glenn Carl 1931- *WhoAm 90*
Rosenquist, James 1933- *WhoAmA 91, WorAlBi*
Rosenquist, James Albert 1933- *WhoAm 90*
Rosenquist, Kay-Sune 1937- *WhoWor 91*
Rosenquist, Peter Bechan 1960- *BiDrAPA 89*
Rosenquit, Bernard 1923- *WhoAm 90, WhoAmA 91*
Rosensaft, Lester Jay 1958- *WhoE 91, WhoEmL 91, WhoWor 91*
Rosensaft, Menachem Zwi 1948- *WhoAm 90, WhoE 91, WhoWor 91*
Rosenschein, Guy Raoul 1953- *WhoWor 91*
Rosenshein, Neil Abbot 1947- *WhoAm 90*
Rosenshine, Allen *BioIn 16*
Rosenshine, Allen Gilbert 1939- *St&PR 91, WhoAm 90, WhoE 91*
Rosensteel, George T. 1947- *WhoAm 90*
Rosensteel, John William 1940- *St&PR 91*
Rosensteele, James William 1948- *St&PR 91*
Rosenstein, Allen Bertram 1920- *WhoAm 90, WhoWor 91*
Rosenstein, Arthur 1930- *St&PR 91*
Rosenstein, Beryl Joel 1937- *WhoE 91*
Rosenstein, David H. 1933- *St&PR 91*
Rosenstein, David Hillel 1934- *BiDrAPA 89*
Rosenstein, David L. *ODwPR 91*
Rosenstein, Diana Shirley 1953- *WhoAmW 91, WhoE 91*
Rosenstein, Donald Lee 1958- *BiDrAPA 89*
Rosenstein, Earl 1932- *St&PR 91*
Rosenstein, Henri 1941- *WhoWor 91*
Rosenstein, Irwin Lawrence 1936- *St&PR 91*
Rosenstein, James Alfred 1939- *WhoAm 90*
Rosenstein, Kenneth Ivan 1953- *BiDrAPA 89*
Rosenstein, Neil Howard 1926- *St&PR 91*
Rosenstein, Perry 1926- *St&PR 91*
Rosenstein, Richard B 1932- *BiDrAPA 89*
Rosenstein, Richard Kenneth 1951- *WhoEmL 91*
Rosenstein, Robert Bryce 1954- *WhoEmL 91*
Rosenstiel, Leonie *WhoWrEP 89*
Rosenstiel, Leonie 1947- *ConAu 30NR*
Rosenstock, Francyne N. 1951- *WhoWrEP 89*
Rosenstock, Harvey Allan *BiDrAPA 89*
Rosenstock, Harvey Allan 1940- *WhoSSW 91*
Rosenstock, Stanley C. 1923- *St&PR 91*
Rosenstrach, Jerry *St&PR 91*
Rosensweig, Ronald Ellis 1932- *WhoAm 90*
Rosensweig, Stanley Harold 1918- *WhoAm 90*
Rosensweig, Tod 1950- *St&PR 91*
Rosental, Alex Jorge 1945- *WhoSSW 91*
Rosenthal, A. M. *BioIn 16*
Rosenthal, Aaron 1914- *WhoAm 90*
Rosenthal, Abraham Michael 1922- *WhoAm 90, WhoE 91, WhoWor 91, WhoWrEP 89*
Rosenthal, Alan H, Mrs *WhoAmA 91*
Rosenthal, Alan J 1938- *BiDrAPA 89*
Rosenthal, Alan Sayre 1926- *WhoAm 90*
Rosenthal, Alan Stephen 1939- *WhoAm 90*
Rosenthal, Albert Harold 1914- *WhoAm 90*
Rosenthal, Albert Jay 1928- *WhoAm 90*
Rosenthal, Albert Joseph 1919- *WhoAm 90*
Rosenthal, Amnon 1934- *WhoAm 90*
Rosenthal, Anthony J 1940- *BiDrAPA 89*
Rosenthal, Arnold H. 1933- *WhoAm 90*
Rosenthal, Arnold R. 1942- *St&PR 91*
Rosenthal, Arthur 1937- *St&PR 91*
Rosenthal, Arthur Jesse 1919- *WhoAm 90*
Rosenthal, Bernard Gordon 1922- *WhoAm 90*
Rosenthal, Bette Lee 1951- *WhoSSW 91*
Rosenthal, Bobbi 1959- *WhoAmW 91*
Rosenthal, Charles M. 1935- *St&PR 91*
Rosenthal, Charles Michael 1935- *WhoAm 90*
Rosenthal, Clifford Neal 1945- *WhoEmL 91*
Rosenthal, David 1876-1949 *WhoAmA 91N*
Rosenthal, David 1943- *St&PR 91*
Rosenthal, David Elliot 1937- *WhoE 91*
Rosenthal, David H. 1945- *WhoWrEP 89*
Rosenthal, David Harry 1965- *WhoEmL 91*
Rosenthal, David Keith *BiDrAPA 89*
Rosenthal, David Michael 1961- *WhoE 91, WhoWor 91*
Rosenthal, Deborah Maly 1950- *WhoAmA 91*
Rosenthal, Donald B. 1937- *WhoAm 90*
Rosenthal, Doris *WhoAmA 91N*
Rosenthal, Douglas Eurico 1940- *WhoAm 90, WhoWrEP 89*
Rosenthal, Earl Edgar 1921- *WhoAm 90, WhoAmA 91*
Rosenthal, Elizabeth Robbins 1943- *WhoAmW 91*
Rosenthal, Ely Manuel 1922- *WhoAm 90*
Rosenthal, Eric Talbot 1950- *WhoE 91*
Rosenthal, Evelyn Daoud *WhoAmW 91*
Rosenthal, Franz 1914- *WhoAm 90*
Rosenthal, Fred *BiDrAPA 89*
Rosenthal, Gary Mark 1954- *WhoE 91*
Rosenthal, Gertrude 1903-1989 *BioIn 16, WhoAmA 91N*
Rosenthal, Glenn Thomas 1935- *WhoSSW 91*
Rosenthal, Gloria M 1928- *WhoAmA 91*
Rosenthal, Harold Leslie 1922- *WhoAm 90*
Rosenthal, Harry *BioIn 16*
Rosenthal, Harvey *BiDrAPA 89*
Rosenthal, Helen Nagelberg 1926- *WhoAmW 91*
Rosenthal, Herbert M 1913- *BiDrAPA 89*
Rosenthal, Herbert M. 1922- *St&PR 91*
Rosenthal, Howard Lewis 1939- *WhoAm 90*
Rosenthal, Hubert Daniel Jean 1933- *WhoWor 91*
Rosenthal, Ira Maurice 1920- *WhoAm 90*
Rosenthal, Irving 1931- *St&PR 91*
Rosenthal, Irwin Gerald 1933- *WhoE 91*
Rosenthal, Jack *BioIn 16*
Rosenthal, Jack 1930- *WhoAm 90, WhoWor 91*
Rosenthal, Jacob 1935- *WhoAm 90, WhoWrEP 89*
Rosenthal, James D. 1932- *WhoAm 90*
Rosenthal, James Edward 1942- *St&PR 91*
Rosenthal, Jane Lisa 1955- *BiDrAPA 89*
Rosenthal, Jean 1912-1969 *BioIn 16, NotWoAT*
Rosenthal, Jesse Samuel 1949- *BiDrAPA 89*
Rosenthal, Joel 1946- *WhoAm 90*
Rosenthal, John W 1928- *WhoAmA 91*
Rosenthal, Jonathan 1955- *St&PR 91*
Rosenthal, Jonathan D *BiDrAPA 89*
Rosenthal, Joseph Aaron 1929- *WhoAm 90*
Rosenthal, Judith-Ann Saks *WhoAmA 91*
Rosenthal, Judith Ellen Lindner 1954- *WhoEmL 91*
Rosenthal, Julian Bernard 1908- *WhoAm 90*
Rosenthal, Larry 1912- *Ballpl 90*
Rosenthal, Lawrence Michael 1935- *WhoWor 91*
Rosenthal, Leighton A. 1915- *WhoAm 90*
Rosenthal, Leon Dorotinsky *BiDrAPA 89*
Rosenthal, Louis S. 1928- *St&PR 91*
Rosenthal, Lucy Gabrielle *WhoAm 90, WhoWor 91*
Rosenthal, M. L. 1917- *BioIn 16, WhoWrEP 89*
Rosenthal, Macha Louis 1917- *BioIn 16, WhoAm 90*
Rosenthal, Manuel 1904- *IntWWM 90, PenDiMP*
Rosenthal, Marc 1946- *St&PR 91*
Rosenthal, Mark 1945- *ConAu 130*
Rosenthal, Mark A 1946- *SmATA 64 [port]*
Rosenthal, Mark L. 1945- *BioIn 16, WhoAmA 91*
Rosenthal, Martha Newman 1956- *WhoAmW 91*
Rosenthal, Martin 1929- *BiDrAPA 89*
Rosenthal, Martin Alek 1928- *St&PR 91*
Rosenthal, Maurice J 1919- *BiDrAPA 89*
Rosenthal, Mena W. *BioIn 16*
Rosenthal, Michael A. 1955- *St&PR 91*
Rosenthal, Michael P. *BioIn 16*
Rosenthal, Michael Robert 1946- *BiDrAPA 89*
Rosenthal, Michael Ross 1939- *WhoAm 90*
Rosenthal, Milton Frederick 1913- *WhoAm 90*
Rosenthal, Miriam B *BiDrAPA 89*
Rosenthal, Mitchell S *BiDrAPA 89*
Rosenthal, Mitchell Stephen 1935- *WhoWor 91*
Rosenthal, Moriz 1862-1946 *BioIn 16, PenDiMP*
Rosenthal, Morris M *BiDrAPA 89*
Rosenthal, Murray Hal 1944- *BiDrAPA 89*
Rosenthal, Myron Martin 1930- *WhoAm 90, WhoE 91, WhoSSW 91, WhoWor 91*
Rosenthal, Nina *BioIn 16*
Rosenthal, Nora *BioIn 16*
Rosenthal, Norman *BioIn 16*
Rosenthal, Norman Edward 1950- *BiDrAPA 89*
Rosenthal, Pamela Susan 1959- *WhoAmW 91*
Rosenthal, Peter 1946- *WhoAm 90*
Rosenthal, Rachel 1926- *BioIn 16, WhoAmA 91*
Rosenthal, Randolph 1912- *BiDrAPA 89, WhoE 91*
Rosenthal, Richard A. 1933- *St&PR 91*
Rosenthal, Richard H. 1933- *St&PR 91*
Rosenthal, Richard J 1939- *BiDrAPA 89*
Rosenthal, Richard L. 1916- *St&PR 91*
Rosenthal, Richard Laurence 1915- *WhoAm 90*
Rosenthal, Richard Nelson *BiDrAPA 89*
Rosenthal, Robert *BioIn 16*
Rosenthal, Robert 1926-1989 *BioIn 16*
Rosenthal, Robert 1933- *WhoAm 90, WhoWrEP 89*
Rosenthal, Robert 1937- *St&PR 91*
Rosenthal, Robert C. 1933- *St&PR 91*
Rosenthal, Robert Jon 1948- *WhoAm 90*
Rosenthal, Robert Seth *BiDrAPA 89*
Rosenthal, Roy Douglas 1945- *BiDrAPA 89*
Rosenthal, Ruth Beth 1948- *BiDrAPA 89*
Rosenthal, Samuel Robert 1899- *WhoAm 90*
Rosenthal, Saul H 1936- *BiDrAPA 89*
Rosenthal, Seymour 1921- *WhoAmA 91*
Rosenthal, Shirley Florence Lord *WhoAm 90, WhoE 91*
Rosenthal, Sol 1934- *WhoAm 90*
Rosenthal, Sol Roy *WhoAm 90*
Rosenthal, Stanley Lawrence 1929- *WhoAm 90*
Rosenthal, Stephen 1935- *WhoAmA 91*
Rosenthal, Stephen 1955- *BiDrAPA 89*
Rosenthal, Steven Siegmund 1949- *WhoEmL 91*
Rosenthal, Stuart *BiDrAPA 89*
Rosenthal, Stuart A. *WhoAm 90*
Rosenthal, Stuart Alan 1945- *St&PR 91*
Rosenthal, Stuart Allan 1948- *WhoEmL 91*
Rosenthal, Susan Barbara 1946- *WhoSSW 91*
Rosenthal, Tomme N. 1926- *St&PR 91*
Rosenthal, Tony 1914- *WhoAm 90, WhoAmA 91*
Rosenthal, Warren Weil 1923- *St&PR 91*
Rosenthal, William 1934- *BiDrAPA 89*
Rosenthal, William Forshaw 1933- *WhoAm 90*
Rosenthal, William J. 1920- *WhoAm 90*
Rosenthal, Yani Benjamin 1965- *WhoWor 91*
Rosenus, Alan Harvey 1940- *WhoWrEP 89*
Rosenwald, Carol 1933- *WhoAmA 91*
Rosenwald, Charles 1962- *WhoSSW 91*
Rosenwald, E. John, Jr. 1930- *St&PR 91, WhoAm 90*
Rosenwald, James *BioIn 16*
Rosenwald, Lessing Julius 1891-1979 *WhoAmA 91N*
Rosenwald, Richard J 1924- *BiDrAPA 89*
Rosenwald, Seth R. 1958- *BiDrAPA 89*
Rosenwald, William 1903- *WhoAm 90*
Rosenzweig, Daphne Lange 1941- *WhoAmA 91*
Rosenzweig, David 1940- *WhoAm 90*
Rosenzweig, Franz 1886-1929 *BioIn 16*
Rosenzweig, Harlan Jay 1947- *WhoAm 90*
Rosenzweig, Harvey 1924- *St&PR 91*
Rosenzweig, Herschel D 1937- *BiDrAPA 89*
Rosenzweig, Leonard 1903- *BiDrAPA 89*
Rosenzweig, Mark Richard 1922- *WhoAm 90*
Rosenzweig, Martin H *BiDrAPA 89*
Rosenzweig, Marvin W *BiDrAPA 89*
Rosenzweig, Norman 1924- *BiDrAPA 89, WhoWor 91*
Rosenzweig, Phyllis D 1943- *WhoAmA 91, WhoWrEP 89*
Rosenzweig, Richard S. 1935- *St&PR 91*
Rosenzweig, Robert Myron 1931- *WhoAm 90*
Rosenzweig, Roy Alan 1950- *WhoSSW 91*
Rosenzweig, Saul 1907- *WhoAm 90*
Rosenzweig, William M 1940- *BiDrAPA 89*
Roser, Ce *WhoAmA 91*
Roser, Elena Mosteferis 1952- *WhoAmW 91*
Roser, Harold C. *BioIn 16*
Roser, Herman E. *NewYTBS 90*
Roser, Michael R. 1948- *WhoEmL 91*
Roser, Wiltrud *AuBYP 90*
Rosett, Arthur Irwin 1934- *WhoAm 90*
Rosett, Jacqueline Berlin 1945- *WhoAmW 91*
Rosett, Richard Nathaniel 1928- *WhoAm 90*
Rosette, Fabian R. 1948- *WhoHisp 91*
Rosetti, Ana 1950- *EncCoWW*
Rosetti, Scotty Rester 1942- *WhoSSW 91*
Rosetto, Ronald Lewis 1955- *WhoE 91*
Rosevear, Robert Allan 1915- *IntWWM 90*
Roseveare, Helen *BioIn 16*
Roseveare, Martin Pearson 1898-1985 *DcNaB 1981*
Rosewall, Ken *BioIn 16*
Rosewall, Ken 1934- *WorAlBi*
Rosewoman, Michele *BioIn 16*
Rosfjord, Thomas James 1946- *WhoE 91*
Roshco, Martin S 1936- *BiDrAPA 89*
Roshel, John Albert, Jr. 1941- *WhoWor 91*
Rosher, Grace *EncO&P 3*
Roshkind, David Michael 1950- *WhoSSW 91*
Roshon, George Kenneth 1942- *WhoE 91*
Roshong, Dee Ann Daniels 1936- *WhoAmW 91, WhoWor 91*
Rosi, Eugene Joseph 1931- *WhoAm 90*
Rosi, Francesco *BioIn 16*
Rosiak, Michael 1942- *WhoE 91*
Rosica, Gabriel Adam 1940- *St&PR 91, WhoAm 90*

Rosica, Marilyn Barbara 1937- *WhoE 91*
Rosicky, Bohumir 1922- *WhoWor 91*
Rosicky, John Anton 1940- *St&PR 91*
Rosier, James Louis 1932- *WhoAm 90, WhoWrEP 89*
Rosier, Patricia *BioIn 16*
Rosier, Peter *BioIn 16*
Rosilier, Glenn D. 1948- *St&PR 91*
Rosillo, Ronald H *BiDrAPA 89*
Rosillo, Salvador Edmundo 1936- *WhoHisp 91*
Rosin, Dale G. *BiDrAPA 89*
Rosin, David Aaron 1938- *BiDrAPA 89*
Rosin, Harry 1897-1973 *WhoAmA 91N*
Rosin, Lindsay Zweig 1954- *WhoEmL 91, WhoSSW 91*
Rosin, Morris 1924- *WhoSSW 91*
Rosing, Vladimir 1890-1963 *PenDiMP*
Rosini, Joseph 1939- *WhoE 91*
Rosini, Neil Justin 1951- *WhoEmL 91*
Rosinski, Edwin Francis 1928- *WhoAm 90*
Rosinski, Herbert 1903-1962 *BioIn 16*
Rosinski, Jeanne *BioIn 16*
Rosinski, Leonard Daniel 1951- *St&PR 91*
Rosinski, Martin A. 1927-1988 *BioIn 16*
Rosinski, Martin J. 1938- *St&PR 91*
Rosinski, Patrice Ann 1945- *WhoEmL 91*
Rosinski, Thaddeus Julian 1930- *St&PR 91, WhoE 91*
Roskam, Edward Elias Charles Iben 1932- *WhoWor 91*
Roskam, Jan 1930- *WhoAm 90*
Roskam, Verlyn Ronald 1929- *St&PR 91*
Roskell, Penelope *IntWWM 90*
Roskens, Ronald William 1932- *WhoAm 90*
Roskies, Arthur 1927- *St&PR 91*
Roskies, Ethel 1933- *WhoAm 90*
Roskill, Mark W. 1933- *WhoE 91*
Roskill, Mark Wentworth 1933- *WhoAmA 91*
Roskill, Stephen Wentworth 1903-1982 *DcNaB 1981*
Roskin, Gerald 1931- *BiDrAPA 89*
Roskin, Joan Kogel *BiDrAPA 89*
Roskin, Lewis Ross 1920- *WhoAm 90*
Roskind, Stanley C 1938- *BiDrAPA 89*
Roskind, Susan Reimer 1951- *WhoAmW 91, WhoSSW 91, WhoWor 91*
Rosko, Michael Daniel 1949- *WhoE 91*
Roskos, Donald Paul 1945- *WhoAm 90*
Roskos, S Richard 1942- *BiDrAPA 89*
Roskoski, Robert, Jr. 1939- *WhoAm 90*
Roskothen, Michael S. 1936- *WhoAm 90*
Roskoz, Jack Houston 1938- *St&PR 91*
Rosky, Burton Seymour 1927- *WhoAm 90*
Rosky, Theodore S. 1937- *St&PR 91*
Rosky, Theodore Samuel 1937- *WhoAm 90*
Rosler, Lee 1923- *WhoAm 90*
Rosler, Martha 1943- *BiDWomA, WhoAmA 91*
Rosley-Griffin, Joan Evelyn 1958- *WhoAmW 91*
Roslow, Sydney 1910- *WhoSSW 91, WhoWor 91*
Rosma, Charles B. *EncO&P 3*
Rosman, Jonathan Paul *BiDrAPA 89*
Rosman, Lowell Douglas 1930- *BiDrAPA 89*
Rosman-Bakehouse, Mary Pat 1956- *WhoAmW 91*
Rosmarin, David *BiDrAPA 89*
Rosmarin, Susan Gresser 1954- *St&PR 91*
Rosmundsson, Olafur Ingi 1941- *WhoWor 91*
Rosner, Bennett L 1936- *BiDrAPA 89*
Rosner, Bennett Leonard 1936- *WhoE 91*
Rosner, Bernat 1932- *St&PR 91*
Rosner, Carl Heinz 1929- *St&PR 91*
Rosner, Caryl J. 1952- *ODwPR 91*
Rosner, Charles E. 1944- *WhoAm 90*
Rosner, Donna *ODwPR 91*
Rosner, Fred 1935- *ConAu 32NR, WhoAm 90*
Rosner, Henry 1928- *BiDrAPA 89*
Rosner, Jonathan Lincoln 1941- *WhoAm 90*
Rosner, Jorge 1921- *WhoAm 90*
Rosner, Laurie 1948- *ODwPR 91*
Rosner, Lawrence 1912- *St&PR 91*
Rosner, M. Norton 1931- *WhoAm 90*
Rosner, Marsha Rich 1950- *WhoAmW 91*
Rosner, Richard 1941- *BiDrAPA 89, WhoE 91*
Rosner, T. *WhoAm 90*
Rosness, Betty June 1924- *WhoAmW 91, WhoWor 91*
Rosnick, Lyle Eugene 1948- *BiDrAPA 89*
Rosoff, Aviva Margolit 1961- *WhoAmW 91*
Rosoff, Elaine Bernadette 1938- *WhoAmW 91*
Rosoff, Leonard 1912- *WhoAm 90*
Rosoff, Stanley Jacob *BiDrAPA 89*
Rosoff, William A. 1943- *WhoAm 90, WhoE 91, WhoWor 91*
Rosofsky, Seymour 1924- *WhoAmA 91N*
Rosolio, Daniel 1927- *WhoWor 91*
Rosomoff, Hubert Lawrence 1927- *WhoAm 90*
Rosovsky, Henry *St&PR 91*
Rosovsky, Henry 1927- *WhoAm 90*
Rosow, H Michael 1907- *BiDrAPA 89*
Rosow, I. Peter 1937- *WhoAm 90*
Rosow, Jerome Morris 1919- *WhoAm 90*
Rosowicz, Theodore John 1945- *St&PR 91*
Rosowski, Robert B. 1940- *St&PR 91*
Rosowski, Robert Bernard 1940- *WhoAm 90*
Ross, Mrs. *FemiCLE*
Ross, Adrian 1859-1933 *OxCPMus*
Ross, Adrian E. 1912- *St&PR 91, WhoE 91, WhoWor 91*
Ross, Alan Dale 1956- *WhoE 91*
Ross, Alan Otto 1921- *WhoAm 90*
Ross, Albion 1906-1988 *BioIn 16*
Ross, Alexander 1783-1856 *WhNaAH*
Ross, Alexander 1908- *WhoAm 90, WhoAmA 91*
Ross, Alexander Milton 1832-1897 *DcCanB 12*
Ross, Alexander S. 1929- *St&PR 91*
Ross, Allan *BioIn 16*
Ross, Allan Anderson 1939- *IntWWM 90, WhoAm 90*
Ross, Allan Michael 1939- *WhoAm 90*
Ross, Alvin 1920-1975 *WhoAmA 91N*
Ross, Andrea Patricia *WhoWrEP 89*
Ross, Angus 1927- *SpyFic, TwCCr&M 91*
Ross, Ann Clarke 1943- *WhoE 91*
Ross, Arthur 1910- *St&PR 91, WhoAm 90*
Ross, Arthur Leonard 1924- *WhoE 91*
Ross, Ashley M. 1938- *St&PR 91*
Ross, Austin, Jr. 1929- *WhoAm 90*
Ross, Barbara *ODwPR 91*
Ross, Barbara Jean 1955- *WhoAmW 91*
Ross, Barnaby *AuBYP 90, MajTwCW, TwCCr&M 91*
Ross, Barry Joel 1948- *St&PR 91*
Ross, Beatrice Brook 1927- *WhoAm 90*
Ross, Bernard 1916- *WhoAm 90*
Ross, Bernard Harris 1927- *WhoAm 90*
Ross, Bernard L. *ConAu 33NR, MajTwCW*
Ross, Betsy 1752-1836 *EncCRAm, WorAlBi*
Ross, Betsy G. 1752-1836 *BioAmW*
Ross, Betty Grace 1931- *WhoAmW 91*
Ross, Betty Witten 1930- *WhoE 91*
Ross, Blair Arthur 1927- *St&PR 91*
Ross, Bradford Jay 1959- *WhoE 91*
Ross, Brenda Marie 1944- *WhoSSW 91*
Ross, Brian Elliott 1948- *WhoAm 90*
Ross, Bruce 1954- *ODwPR 91*
Ross, Buck 1915-1978 *Ballpl 90*
Ross, C Chandler *WhoAmA 91N*
Ross, C. Ian 1942- *St&PR 91*
Ross, Cameron M. 1952- *St&PR 91*
Ross, Carolyn Thayer 1948- *WhoAm 90*
Ross, Charles 1937- *WhoAm 90, WhoAmA 91, WhoE 91*
Ross, Charles Gregory 1959- *WhoSSW 91*
Ross, Charles Harold 1940- *St&PR 91*
Ross, Charles Robert 1920- *WhoAm 90*
Ross, Charles Worthington, IV 1933- *WhoAm 90*
Ross, Charlotte Pack 1932- *WhoAmW 91*
Ross, Chet 1917- *Ballpl 90*
Ross, Christopher A. 1951- *BiDrAPA 89*
Ross, Christopher Jonathan 1954- *WhoWor 91*
Ross, Christopher Wade Stelyan 1943- *WhoAm 90, WhoWor 91*
Ross, Clare Romano 1922- *BioIn 16*
Ross, Clarissa *ConAu 32NR*
Ross, Claude Gordon Anthony 1917- *WhoE 91*
Ross, Clay Whitten *BiDrAPA 89*
Ross, Clifford 1952- *WhoAmA 91*
Ross, Cloteen S. 1939- *St&PR 91*
Ross, Coleman DeVane 1943- *WhoE 91, WhoWor 91*
Ross, Colin Andrew *BiDrAPA 89*
Ross, Connie Sue 1947- *WhoEmL 91*
Ross, Conrad H 1931- *WhoAmA 91*
Ross, Craig Allan *BiDrAPA 89*
Ross, D Gwendolyn *BiDrAPA 89*
Ross, Dan *ConAu 32NR*
Ross, Dana *ConAu 32NR*
Ross, Dana Fuller 1914-1988 *SmATA X*
Ross, Daniel Geoffrey *BiDrAPA 89*
Ross, Daniel Robert 1955- *WhoWor 91*
Ross, Dave *AuBYP 90*
Ross, David *ODwPR 91*
Ross, David 1896-1975 *BioIn 16*
Ross, David 1929- *WhoE 91, WhoWrEP 89*
Ross, David 1949- *AuBYP 90, BioIn 16*
Ross, David Alexander 1819-1897 *DcCanB 12*
Ross, David Anthony 1949- *WhoAmA 91*
Ross, David Charles 1955- *WhoSSW 91*
Ross, David Eugene 1949- *IntWWM 90*
Ross, David Ewall 1945- *St&PR 91*
Ross, David Michael *BiDrAPA 89*
Ross, Deborah Rosalie *BiDrAPA 89*
Ross, Debra Ann 1956- *WhoAmW 91*
Ross, Debra Benita 1956- *WhoAmW 91, WhoEmL 91, WhoWor 91*
Ross, Delmer Gerrard 1942- *WhoAm 90*
Ross, Deloy C. 1925- *St&PR 91*
Ross, Dennis Andrew 1952- *WhoE 91, WhoEmL 91*
Ross, Dennis B. *BioIn 16*
Ross, Diana *BioIn 16*
Ross, Diana 1944- *DrBlPA 90, EncPR&S 89, OxCPMus, WhoAm 90, WhoAmW 91, WhoWor 91, WorAlBi*
Ross, Dolores Anne 1952- *WhoAmW 91, WhoE 91*
Ross, Don 1914- *Ballpl 90*
Ross, Don Carl 1927- *St&PR 91*
Ross, Donald, Jr. 1941- *WhoAm 90*
Ross, Donald C *BiDrAPA 89*
Ross, Donald Edward 1930- *WhoE 91, WhoWor 91*
Ross, Donald James 1926- *WhoAm 90*
Ross, Donald Jay 1948- *BiDrAPA 89*
Ross, Donald Keith 1925- *St&PR 91, WhoAm 90, WhoE 91, WhoWor 91*
Ross, Donald Kenneth 1925- *WhoAm 90*
Ross, Donald Robert 1953- *BiDrAPA 89*
Ross, Donald Roe 1922- *WhoAm 90*
Ross, Doris D. 1946- *St&PR 91*
Ross, Doris G. 1919- *WhoAmW 91, WhoE 91, WhoWor 91*
Ross, Dorthy Marcussen 1933- *WhoWrEP 89*
Ross, Douglas 1948- *WhoE 91*
Ross, Douglas Allan 1937- *WhoAmA 91*
Ross, Douglas Taylor 1929- *St&PR 91, WhoAm 90*
Ross, Duncan 1941- *BiDrAPA 89*
Ross, Edward 1937- *WhoAm 90, WhoWor 91*
Ross, Edward John 1935- *WhoE 91*
Ross, Edward Joseph 1934- *WhoAm 90, WhoE 91*
Ross, Edward W. 1920- *St&PR 91*
Ross, Edwin Francis 1917- *WhoAm 90*
Ross, Elinor 1932- *IntWWM 90, WhoAm 90*
Ross, Elinor Parry 1932- *WhoSSW 91*
Ross, Elisabeth K *BiDrAPA 89*
Ross, Elisabeth Kubler- *BioIn 16*
Ross, Elise *PenDiMP*
Ross, Elise 1947- *IntWWM 90*
Ross, Elise J. 1943- *St&PR 91*
Ross, Elise Jane 1943- *WhoAm 90*
Ross, Elizabeth A *BiDrAPA 89*
Ross, Elizabeth Ann 1944- *WhoSSW 91*
Ross, Ellen *FemiCLE*
Ross, Else Barasch 1917- *BiDrAPA 89*
Ross, Eunice Latshaw 1923- *WhoAmW 91*
Ross, Flora Amelia 1842-1897 *DcCanB 12*
Ross, Francine Helen 1952- *WhoAmW 91, WhoE 91*
Ross, Frank *AuBYP 90*
Ross, Frank *NewYTBS 90*
Ross, Frank 1904-1990 *BioIn 16*
Ross, Frank Howard, III 1946- *WhoEmL 91, WhoWor 91*
Ross, Fred *BioIn 16*
Ross, Fred Elliott *BiDrAPA 89*
Ross, Gail *BiDrAPA 89*
Ross, Gail Sharon 1946- *WhoAmW 91*
Ross, Gary 1947- *Ballpl 90*
Ross, George 1730-1779 *EncCRAm*
Ross, George Everett 1947- *St&PR 91*
Ross, George Martin 1933- *WhoAm 90*
Ross, George William 1940- *WhoAm 90*
Ross, Gerald Elliott 1941- *WhoE 91*
Ross, Gerald Fred 1930- *WhoAm 90, WhoSSW 91*
Ross, German Reed *WhoAm 90*
Ross, Gilbert 1903- *IntWWM 90*
Ross, Gilbert I. 1902- *St&PR 91*
Ross, Gilbert Stuart 1930- *WhoAm 90*
Ross, Glen Ernest 1929- *WhoWrEP 89*
Ross, Gloria F 1923- *WhoAmA 91*
Ross, Gloria Frankenthaler 1923- *WhoE 91*
Ross, Glynn 1914- *WhoAm 90*
Ross, Glynn William 1914- *IntWWM 90*
Ross, Guy Matthews, Jr. 1933- *WhoAm 90*
Ross, Hans-Georg 1939- *WhoWor 91*
Ross, Harold 1892-1951 *WorAlBi*
Ross, Harold Wallace 1892-1951 *BioIn 16*
Ross, Harry F. 1912- *St&PR 91*
Ross, Harry L. *St&PR 91*
Ross, Harvey M *BiDrAPA 89*
Ross, Harvey M. 1927- *St&PR 91*
Ross, Hazel 1934- *WhoAmW 91*
Ross, Herbert *BioIn 16*
Ross, Herbert *BioIn 16*
Ross, Herbert David 1925- *WhoAm 90*
Ross, Hervey Shaw 1929- *WhoSSW 91*
Ross, Horatio 1801-1886 *BioIn 16*
Ross, Howard 1943- *St&PR 91*
Ross, Howard D 1928- *BiDrAPA 89*
Ross, Howard Lee 1948- *WhoE 91*
Ross, Hugh Alan 1924- *WhoAm 90*
Ross, Hugh C. 1929- *St&PR 91*
Ross, Hugh C. M. *NewYTBS 90 [port]*
Ross, Hugh C. M. 1898-1990 *BioIn 16*
Ross, Hugh Courtney 1923- *WhoAm 90*
Ross, Ian M. 1927- *BioIn 16*
Ross, Ian Munro 1927- *WhoAm 90, WhoE 91*
Ross, Idajane McDowell 1919- *WhoAm 90*
Ross, Irwin 1919- *WhoE 91*
Ross, Ishbel 1897-1975 *BioIn 16*
Ross, J. Andrew 1949- *WhoWor 91*
Ross, J. Pat 1929- *St&PR 91*
Ross, Jack F *BiDrAPA 89*
Ross, Jack L 1932- *BiDrAPA 89*
Ross, Jack Lewis 1932- *WhoAm 90*
Ross, Jacob John, Jr. 1939- *WhoAm 90*
Ross, Jaime 1946- *WhoAmA 91*
Ross, James 1933- *WhoWor 91*
Ross, James 1953- *WhoE 91*
Ross, James Adrian 1936- *St&PR 91*
Ross, James Barrett 1930- *WhoAm 90*
Ross, James Donald 1948- *St&PR 91*
Ross, James E. 1921- *WhoE 91*
Ross, James Elmer 1931- *WhoAm 90*
Ross, James Francis 1931- *WhoAm 90, WhoWrEP 89*
Ross, James H. *St&PR 91*
Ross, James H. 1938- *WhoAm 90*
Ross, James Matthew 1931- *WhoAmA 91*
Ross, James Neil, Jr. 1940- *WhoE 91*
Ross, James Ulric 1941- *WhoSSW 91*
Ross, Janet Anne Duff Gordon 1842-1927 *BioIn 16*
Ross, Janice Koenig 1926- *WhoAmA 91*
Ross, Jayne M. 1956- *St&PR 91*
Ross, Jeannette Luisi 1954- *WhoE 91*
Ross, Jeffrey Allan 1947- *WhoAm 90, WhoEmL 91*
Ross, Jeffrey M *BiDrAPA 89*
Ross, Jeffrey Tennyson 1954- *IntWWM 90*
Ross, Jerrold 1935- *WhoAm 90*
Ross, Jerry 1926-1955 *OxCPMus*
Ross, Jerry L. *BioIn 16*
Ross, Jesse 1921- *St&PR 91*
Ross, Jimmy Douglas 1936- *WhoAm 90*
Ross, Joan M 1931- *WhoAmA 91*
Ross, Joan Marie 1931- *WhoE 91*
Ross, Joe *BioIn 16*
Ross, Joe 1954- *ODwPR 91*
Ross, John *BioIn 16*
Ross, John 1790-1866 *WhNaAH [port]*
Ross, John 1926- *WhoAm 90*
Ross, John, Jr. 1928- *WhoAm 90*
Ross, John Joseph 1927- *WhoAm 90*
Ross, John M. *EarBlAP*
Ross, John Mershon 1931- *St&PR 91, WhoAm 90*
Ross, John Michael 1919- *WhoAm 90*
Ross, John Munder 1945- *WhoE 91*
Ross, John Raymond 1923- *WhoAm 90*
Ross, John T 1921- *WhoAmA 91*
Ross, John Thompson, Jr. 1942- *WhoAm 90*
Ross, Jonathan 1916- *TwCCr&M 91*
Ross, Joseph 1934- *BiDrAPA 89*
Ross, Joseph Charles, Jr. 1925- *St&PR 91*
Ross, Joseph Comer 1927- *WhoAm 90*
Ross, Joseph E. 1923- *WhoAm 90*
Ross, Joseph Foster 1910- *WhoAm 90*
Ross, Judith Paris 1939- *WhoAm 90, WhoAmW 91, WhoWor 91*
Ross, Judy 1942- *BioIn 16*
Ross, Julie 1956- *ODwPR 91*
Ross, Julie A. K. *ODwPR 91*
Ross, June Rosa Pitt 1931- *WhoAmW 91*
Ross, Katharine 1943- *WhoAm 90, WorAlBi*
Ross, Katharine Colace *FemiCLE*
Ross, Kathleen Anne 1941- *WhoAmW 91*
Ross, Kathleen B. Henrich 1947- *WhoAmW 91*
Ross, Kenneth E. 1952- *St&PR 91*
Ross, Kenneth Scott 1925- *St&PR 91*
Ross, Kenton Eugene 1930- *WhoAm 90*
Ross, L. C. 1947- *St&PR 91*
Ross, L. Michael 1954- *WhoE 91*
Ross, Lanny 1906-1988 *BioIn 16*
Ross, Laura *AuBYP 90*
Ross, Leabelle I *BiDrAPA 89*
Ross, Leabelle I. 1905- *WhoAmW 91*
Ross, Lee A. 1945- *WhoWrEP 89*
Ross, Leona Curtis 1953- *WhoWrEP 89*
Ross, Leonard Ellis 1930- *WhoAm 90*
Ross, Leonard Lester 1927- *WhoAm 90*
Ross, Leonard Stanley 1928- *WhoE 91*
Ross, Lesa Moore 1959- *WhoAmW 91*
Ross, Lewis *NewAgMG*
Ross, Linda Anne 1951- *WhoAmW 91*
Ross, Lisa Joan 1957- *WhoEmL 91*
Ross, Lois Ina 1947- *WhoAmW 91*
Ross, Lorraine G. 1935- *WhoAmW 91*
Ross, Louis 1901-1963 *WhoAmA 91N*
Ross, Louis Albert *BiDrAPA 89*
Ross, Louis Julius 1928- *St&PR 91*
Ross, Louis R. 1932- *St&PR 91*
Ross, Louis Robert 1932- *WhoAm 90*
Ross, Louise L. 1928- *St&PR 91*
Ross, Luther Wayne *BiDrAPA 89*
Ross, Mabel *BiDrAPA 89*
Ross, Madelyn Ann 1949- *WhoAm 90, WhoAmW 91*
Ross, Maggie *FemiCLE*
Ross, Manuel 1932- *BiDrAPA 89*

Ross, Marc Louis 1960- *WhoE 91*
Ross, Marcia J. 1956- *WhoAmW 91*
Ross, Margaret T *BiDrAPA 89*
Ross, Marilyn *ConAu 32NR*
Ross, Marilyn Ann 1939- *WhoWrEP 89*
Ross, Marilyn Heimberg 1939- *ConAu 31NR*
Ross, Marilyn Jane 1944- *WhoAmW 91*
Ross, Marion *WhoAm 90*
Ross, Martin 1862-1915 *BioIn 16*
Ross, Mary Cowell 1910- *WhoAmW 91*
Ross, Mary Jane 1961- *WhoAmW 91*
Ross, Mary T. *St&PR 91*
Ross, Mason Greene 1944- *St&PR 91*
Ross, Mathew 1917- *BiDrAPA 89*
Ross, Matthew 1953- *WhoEmL 91*
Ross, Melvin B *BiDrAPA 89*
Ross, Melvin Gerald, Jr. 1954- *WhoSSW 91*
Ross, Michael Aaron 1941- *WhoAm 90*
Ross, Michael Franklin 1945- *WhoEmL 91*
Ross, Michael Frederick 1950- *WhoE 91, WhoEmL 91, WhoWor 91*
Ross, Michael I. 1926- *St&PR 91*
Ross, Michael Ray 1949- *WhoEmL 91*
Ross, Milton E. 1919- *St&PR 91*
Ross, Miriam Dewey 1927- *WhoAmW 91*
Ross, Monica 1950?- *BiDWomA*
Ross, Monte 1932- *WhoAm 90*
Ross, Morton M. 1925- *St&PR 91*
Ross, Murray George 1910- *WhoAm 90*
Ross, Murray L. 1947- *St&PR 91*
Ross, Nancy Jane 1943- *WhoSSW 91*
Ross, Nancy Scandrett 1932- *WhoAmW 91*
Ross, Nathaniel *BiDrAPA 89*
Ross, Nell Triplett 1922- *WhoAmW 91*
Ross, Nellie Tayloe 1876-1977 *WorAlBi*
Ross, Norman Alan 1942- *WhoAm 90*
Ross, Norman Alexander 1922- *WhoAm 90*
Ross, Norman E. 1941- *St&PR 91*
Ross, Norman Everett 1930- *WhoE 91*
Ross, Norman Kimball 1947- *WhoSSW 91*
Ross, Otho Bescent, III 1951- *WhoWor 91*
Ross, Pat *BioIn 16*
Ross, Pat 1943- *AuBYP 90*
Ross, Patricia 1899- *AuBYP 90*
Ross, Patricia Ann 1935- *WhoAmW 91*
Ross, Patricia Cleland 1950- *St&PR 91*
Ross, Patrick C. 1929- *St&PR 91*
Ross, Patrick Conroy 1929- *WhoAm 90*
Ross, Patti Jayne 1946- *WhoAmW 91, WhoSSW 91*
Ross, Paul 1927- *WhoAm 90*
Ross, Percy Nathan 1916- *WhoAm 90*
Ross, Philip Drew 1952- *WhoEmL 91*
Ross, Prudence Leith *ConAu 132*
Ross, Ramon R 1930- *SmATA 62 [port]*
Ross, Randal Glenn *BiDrAPA 89*
Ross, Randall Martin *BiDrAPA 89*
Ross, Randolph Ernest 1955- *WhoEmL 91, WhoWor 91*
Ross, Randy Keith 1959- *WhoSSW 91*
Ross, Raymond Louis 1949- *WhoE 91*
Ross, Raymond Samuel 1925- *WhoWrEP 89*
Ross, Rhoda 1941- *WhoAmW 91*
Ross, Rhoda Honore 1941- *WhoAmA 91*
Ross, Richard 1932- *WhoE 91*
Ross, Richard 1937- *St&PR 91*
Ross, Richard Deloy 1953- *St&PR 91*
Ross, Richard Francis 1935- *WhoAm 90*
Ross, Richard Jay 1947- *BiDrAPA 89*
Ross, Richard L. 1928- *St&PR 91*
Ross, Richard L. 1935- *St&PR 91*
Ross, Richard M., Jr. 1929- *St&PR 91*
Ross, Richard Morrow, Jr. 1929- *WhoAm 90*
Ross, Richard Starr 1924- *WhoAm 90*
Ross, Robert C. 1945- *ODwPR 91*
Ross, Robert E. 1944- *WhoWrEP 89*
Ross, Robert Edward 1929- *St&PR 91*
Ross, Robert Grierson, II 1950- *WhoEmL 91*
Ross, Robert John 1956- *WhoEmL 91*
Ross, Robert Lewis 1947- *BiDrAPA 89*
Ross, Robert Page 1942- *St&PR 91*
Ross, Robert S. 1920- *St&PR 91*
Ross, Robert Thomas 1924- *WhoAm 90*
Ross, Robin Laune *BiDrAPA 89*
Ross, Robinette Davis 1952- *WhoAmW 91, WhoE 91, WhoWor 91*
Ross, Roderic Henry 1930- *St&PR 91, WhoAm 90*
Ross, Ronald 1857-1932 *WorAlBi*
Ross, Ronald 1929- *St&PR 91*
Ross, Roseanna Gaye 1949- *WhoWrEP 89*
Ross, Russell *EncACom*
Ross, Russell 1929- *WhoAm 90*
Ross, Russell Marion 1921- *WhoAm 90*
Ross, Sandra Elaine Polk 1942- *WhoAmW 91*
Ross, Sayre 1928- *St&PR 91*
Ross, Scott *BioIn 16*
Ross, Scott Francis 1936- *WhoSSW 91*
Ross, Sean Darrow 1962- *WhoE 91*
Ross, Sheila Maureen Holmes 1951- *WhoAmW 91*
Ross, Sheldon 1925- *WhoAmA 91*
Ross, Sheldon Jules 1924- *WhoAm 90*
Ross, Sherman 1919- *WhoAm 90*
Ross, Sheryl Jean 1954- *WhoEmL 91*
Ross, Shirley 1915- *OxCPMus*
Ross, Stanford G. 1931- *WhoAm 90*
Ross, Stanley 1914- *WhoAm 90*
Ross, Stanley Ralph 1940- *WhoAm 90*
Ross, Stephen 1948- *St&PR 91*
Ross, Stephen A. *BioIn 16*
Ross, Stephen Alan 1944- *WhoAm 90*
Ross, Stephen B. 1944- *ODwPR 91*
Ross, Steven Charles 1947- *WhoEmL 91*
Ross, Steven Gary 1954- *BiDrAPA 89, WhoE 91*
Ross, Steven J. *BioIn 16*
Ross, Steven J. 1927- *St&PR 91, WhoAm 90, WhoE 91*
Ross, Steven L. 1942- *WhoAm 90*
Ross, Steven S. 1958- *St&PR 91*
Ross, Steven Sander 1946- *WhoAm 90, WhoWrEP 89*
Ross, Stuart B. 1937- *St&PR 91, WhoAm 90*
Ross, Stuart Dunning 1936- *WhoE 91*
Ross, Stuart Tennent 1907- *WhoAm 90*
Ross, Sueellen 1941- *WhoAmA 91*
Ross, Susan *WhoWrEP 89*
Ross, Susan Kohn 1945- *WhoEmL 91*
Ross, Suzanne Iris 1948- *WhoAmW 91, WhoEmL 91*
Ross, Suzanne Jeannette 1960- *WhoAmW 91*
Ross, Sylvia Patterson 1942- *WhoSSW 91*
Ross, Ted *DrBlPA 90*
Ross, Ted 1931- *St&PR 91*
Ross, Terence William 1935- *WhoWor 91*
Ross, Theodore John 1924- *WhoWrEP 89*
Ross, Thomas B. 1929- *ODwPR 91*
Ross, Thomas Bernard 1929- *St&PR 91, WhoAm 90*
Ross, Thomas Edward 1942- *WhoSSW 91*
Ross, Thomas Hugh 1927- *WhoE 91, WhoWor 91*
Ross, Thomas McCallum 1931- *WhoE 91*
Ross, Thomas R. *St&PR 91*
Ross, Thomas Warren 1950- *WhoEmL 91, WhoSSW 91*
Ross, Tony 1938- *BioIn 16*
Ross, Virginia R. *WhoAmW 91*
Ross, W. A. 1926- *St&PR 91*
Ross, W Donald 1913- *BiDrAPA 89*
Ross, W E D 1912- *ConAu 32NR*
Ross, W. G. *OxCPMus*
Ross, Walter Beghtol 1936- *IntWWM 90*
Ross, Warren Reinhard 1926- *WhoAm 90*
Ross, Wendy Clucas 1942- *WhoAm 90*
Ross, Wilbur Louis, Jr. 1937- *St&PR 91, WhoE 91*
Ross, Wilda *AuBYP 90*
Ross, Wilda 1915- *BioIn 16*
Ross, William B *BiDrAPA 89*
Ross, William Dee, Jr. 1921- *WhoWor 91*
Ross, William Jarboe 1930- *WhoAm 90, WhoWor 91*
Ross, William Thomas 1927- *St&PR 91*
Ross, William Warfield 1926- *WhoAm 90*
Ross, Wyatt Gene 1942- *WhoSSW 91*
Ross, Z. H. *ConAu 130*
Ross, Zola Helen *BioIn 16*
Ross, Zola Helen 1912- *AuBYP 90*
Ross, Zola Helen 1912-1989 *ConAu 130*
Ross-Breggin, Virginia Faye 1951- *WhoWrEP 89*
Ross-Jacobs, Ruth Ann 1934- *WhoAmW 91, WhoSSW 91*
Ross-Pancost, Francine 1951- *IntWWM 90*
Ross-Rhoades, Vicki Ann 1957- *WhoAmW 91*
Rossa, Glynn Michael 1937- *St&PR 91*
Rossa, Robert Frank 1942- *WhoSSW 91*
Rossano, August Thomas 1916- *WhoAm 90*
Rossano, Kenneth R. 1934- *St&PR 91*
Rossant, James Stephane 1928- *WhoAm 90*
Rossant, Murray J. *BioIn 16*
Rossardi, Orlando 1938- *WhoHisp 91*
Rossario, Edward Jose *BiDrAPA 89*
Rossbach, Paul Robert 1946- *WhoSSW 91*
Rossbach, William 1928- *St&PR 91*
Rossbacher, Lisa Ann 1952- *WhoAmW 91*
Rossberg, Robert Howard 1926- *WhoAm 90*
Rosse, James Nelson 1931- *WhoAm 90*
Rosse, Mark 1950- *BiDrAPA 89*
Rosse, Maryvonne 1917- *WhoAmA 91*
Rosse, Richard Barnett *BiDrAPA 89*
Rosse, Wendell Franklyn 1933- *WhoAm 90*
Rosseels, Maria 1916- *EncCoWW*
Rossel, Sven H. 1943- *WhoWrEP 89*
Rossel-Majdan, Hildegard 1921- *IntWWM 90*
Rosseland, Wanda Jane 1949- *WhoWrEP 89*
Rossell, Christine Ann 1960- *WhoE 91*
Rossell, Elizabeth Harlicka 1942- *WhoE 91*
Rossell, John Ellis, III 1948- *WhoAm 90*
Rosselli, Alberto 1921-1976 *ConDes 90*
Rosselli, Amelia 1930- *EncCoWW*
Rosselli, Francis Ralph 1952- *WhoE 91*
Rosselli, Humberto 1923- *BiDrAPA 89*
Rosselli, Rita *BioIn 16*
Rossellini, Isabella *BioIn 16*
Rossellini, Isabella 1952- *WhoAm 90*
Rossellini, Roberto 1906-1977 *BioIn 16, WorAlBi*
Rossellino, Antonio 1427-1479 *IntDcAA 90*
Rossellino, Bernardo 1409-1464 *IntDcAA 90*
Rossello, Juan A *BiDrAPA 89*
Rossello, Randolph Joseph 1962- *St&PR 91*
Rosselot, Max B. 1913- *WhoE 91, WhoWor 91*
Rosselot, Mim 1954- *WhoSSW 91*
Rosselot, Richard G. 1934- *St&PR 91*
Rossen, James R. 1935- *St&PR 91*
Rossen, Jordan 1934- *WhoAm 90*
Rossen, Robert 1908-1966 *WorAlBi*
Rossen, Susan F *WhoAmA 91*
Rossen, Ted 1920- *St&PR 91*
Rosser, Andrea Louise 1958- *WhoE 91*
Rosser, Charles D. 1935- *WhoAm 90*
Rosser, Darryl 1951- *St&PR 91*
Rosser, David Pendleton 1945- *WhoSSW 91*
Rosser, Donna Colwell 1954- *WhoWrEP 89*
Rosser, James Milton 1939- *WhoAm 90*
Rosser, John Barkley 1907- *WhoAm 90*
Rosser, Nancy Lee 1942- *BiDrAPA 89*
Rosser, Paul C. 1934- *St&PR 91*
Rosser, Richard Franklin 1929- *WhoAm 90*
Rosser, Tim *BioIn 16*
Rosser, Willie Ruth Seals 1935- *WhoAmW 91*
Rosset, Barnet Lee, Jr. 1922- *WhoAm 90*
Rosset, Joseph 1706-1786 *PenDiDA 89*
Rosset, Lisa Krug 1952- *WhoAm 90, WhoWrEP 89*
Rossetti, Christina 1830-1894 *FemiCLE*
Rossetti, Christina Georgina 1830-1894 *BioIn 16*
Rossetti, Dante Gabriel 1828-1882 *BioIn 16, EncO&P 3, IntDcAA 90, WorAlBi*
Rossetti, Elizabeth Eleanor Siddal 1829-1862 *BioIn 16*
Rossetti, Joseph Paul 1938- *WhoAm 90*
Rossetti, Louis A. 1934- *St&PR 91*
Rossetti, Lucy 1843-1894 *BiDWomA*
Rossetti, Mark Joseph 1946- *WhoE 91*
Rossetti, Paul 1948- *St&PR 91*
Rossetti, Richard P. 1946- *St&PR 91*
Rossetti, Ronald Louis 1943- *St&PR 91*
Rossetti, Veronica Theresa 1963- *WhoE 91*
Rossetti, William Michael 1829-1919 *BioIn 16*
Rossey, Paul William 1926- *WhoAm 90, WhoWor 91*
Rossi, Agnelo 1913- *WhoWor 91*
Rossi, Alan Juan 1948- *St&PR 91*
Rossi, Albert Joseph *BiDrAPA 89*
Rossi, Aldo 1931- *BioIn 16, WhoAm 90, WhoWor 91*
Rossi, Alice S. 1922- *BioIn 16, WhoAm 90*
Rossi, Amadeo Joseph 1954- *WhoEmL 91*
Rossi, Anthony Gerald 1935- *WhoAm 90*
Rossi, Barbara *WhoAmA 91*
Rossi, Bruno *ConAu 31NR*
Rossi, Bruno 1905- *WhoAm 90, WhoWor 91*
Rossi, Cristina Peri *ConAu 131, HispWr 90*
Rossi, Cynthia Ann 1954- *WhoAmW 91, WhoEmL 91*
Rossi, David Thomas 1957- *WhoEmL 91*
Rossi, Diana M. 1948- *WhoAmW 91*
Rossi, Dominick F., Jr. 1941- *WhoAm 90*
Rossi, Edith Marta *BiDrAPA 89*
Rossi, Erno Delano 1936- *WhoWrEP 89*
Rossi, Francis Vincent 1925- *WhoE 91*
Rossi, Franco *PenDiMP*
Rossi, Frank Arthur 1937- *WhoAm 90*
Rossi, Gail *BioIn 16*
Rossi, Guido Antonio 1944- *WhoWor 91*
Rossi, Gustavo Alberto 1942- *WhoHisp 91*
Rossi, Harald Hermann 1917- *WhoAm 90*
Rossi, Harry 1919- *St&PR 91, WhoAm 90*
Rossi, Jean-Baptiste 1931- *BioIn 16*
Rossi, Jerome R. 1943- *WhoAm 90*
Rossi, Joseph H. 1950- *St&PR 91*
Rossi, Joseph Henry 1950- *WhoEmL 91*
Rossi, Joseph O *WhoAmA 91, WhoE 91*
Rossi, Lawrence N 1944- *BiDrAPA 89*
Rossi, Linda D'Amario *BioIn 16*
Rossi, Linda Elaine 1950- *WhoAmW 91*
Rossi, Linda Jean 1956- *WhoAmW 91*
Rossi, Louis D. 1944- *St&PR 91*
Rossi, Louis Peter 1945- *WhoE 91*
Rossi, Luis Heber 1948- *WhoHisp 91*
Rossi, Luke 1947- *IntWWM 90*
Rossi, Mario 1902- *IntWWM 90, PenDiMP*
Rossi, Mario Alexander 1931- *WhoAm 90*
Rossi, Michael Dudley 1950- *WhoEmL 91*
Rossi, Nick 1924- *IntWWM 90*
Rossi, Opilio 1910- *WhoWor 91*
Rossi, Peter Henry 1921- *WhoAm 90*
Rossi, Pietro *BioIn 16*
Rossi, Ralph L. 1928- *St&PR 91, WhoAm 90, WhoE 91*
Rossi, Richard A. 1943- *ODwPR 91*
Rossi, Robert N. *BioIn 16*
Rossi, Roberto A. S. 1943- *St&PR 91*
Rossi, Rosalie Clara 1940- *WhoAmW 91*
Rossi, Steven 1954- *ODwPR 91*
Rossi, Tino 1907-1983 *OxCPMus*
Rossi, William Matthew 1954- *WhoEmL 91*
Rossi Di Montelera, Luigi 1946- *WhoWor 91*
Rossi-Espagnet, Gianfranco 1947- *St&PR 91, WhoAm 90*
Rossi-Lemeni, Nicola 1920- *IntWWM 90, PenDiMP*
Rossides, Eugene Telemachus 1927- *WhoAm 90*
Rossides, Zenon *NewYTBS 90 [port]*
Rossides, Zenon 1895-1990 *BioIn 16*
Rossiensky, Jean-Paul 1941- *WhoWor 91*
Rossier, Jean Pierre 1944- *WhoWor 91*
Rossif, Frederic *BioIn 16*
Rossignol, Jean-Francois 1943- *St&PR 91*
Rossington Collins Band *EncPR&S 89*
Rossington, David Ralph 1932- *WhoAm 90*
Rossini, Carlotta 1944- *WhoAmW 91*
Rossini, Gioacchino 1792-1868 *WorAlBi*
Rossini, Gioachino 1792-1868 *PenDiMP A*
Rossinot, Andre 1945- *BiDFrPL*
Rossio, Robert D. 1929- *St&PR 91*
Rossitch, Eugene 1934- *St&PR 91*
Rossiter, Alexander, Jr. 1936- *WhoAm 90*
Rossiter, Bruce *St&PR 91*
Rossiter, Charles M. 1942- *WhoWrEP 89*
Rossiter, Frank Raymond 1937- *IntWWM 90*
Rossiter, Jane *ConAu 32NR*
Rossiter, John *TwCCr&M 91*
Rossiter, Lyle Harold, Jr. *BiDrAPA 89*
Rossiter, Martin Edward 1940- *WhoWor 91*
Rossiter, Phyllis Jo 1938- *WhoWrEP 89*
Rossiter, Roger James 1913-1976 *DcScB S2*
Rossiter, Vincent Emmett, Sr. 1914- *St&PR 91*
Rosskamm, Alan 1950- *St&PR 91, WhoAm 90*
Rosskamm, Martin 1915- *St&PR 91*
Rossler, Willis Kenneth, Jr. 1946- *WhoSSW 91*
Rossler, Wolf 1650?-1717 *PenDiDA 89*
Rossley, Paul Robert 1938- *St&PR 91, WhoAm 90*
Rossman, Claude 1881-1928 *Ballpl 90*
Rossman, Cynthia A. 1956- *St&PR 91*
Rossman, Francine Pitts 1950- *WhoSSW 91*
Rossman, Janet Kay 1954- *WhoE 91*
Rossman, Max 1903- *BiDrAPA 89*
Rossman, Parker 1919- *WhoWrEP 89*
Rossman, Paul Gordon *BiDrAPA 89*
Rossman, Richard Alan 1939- *WhoAm 90*
Rossman, Ruth Scharff *WhoAm 90, WhoAmA 91*
Rossman, Stuart T. 1954- *WhoAm 90*
Rossman, Toby Gale 1942- *WhoAmW 91*
Rossman, William Byron *BiDrAPA 89*
Rossman, William J. 1941- *St&PR 91*
Rossmann, Michael George 1930- *WhoAm 90*
Rossmann, Pavel 1933- *WhoWor 91*
Rossmeisl, Leslie A. 1961- *St&PR 91*
Rossmiller, George Eddie 1935- *WhoAm 90*
Rossner, Judith 1935- *BestSel 90-3 [port], MajTwCW, WhoAm 90, WhoWrEP 89*
Rosso, David John 1938- *WhoAm 90*
Rosso, Domenico del *PenDiDA 89*
Rosso, Fernando *BiDrAPA 89*
Rosso, Fiorentino 1494-1540 *IntDcAA 90*
Rosso, Jean-Pierre 1940- *WhoWor 91*
Rosso, Linda Schraufnagl 1955- *ODwPR 91*
Rosso, Louis T. 1933- *St&PR 91, WhoAm 90*
Rosso, Medardo 1858-1928 *IntDcAA 90*
Rosso, Ronal George *BiDrAPA 89*
Rosso de Irizarry, Carmen 1947- *WhoSSW 91*
Rosso Fiorentino, Giovanni Battista R. 1495-1540 *PenDiDA 89*
Rossoff, Mack *BioIn 16*
Rosson, Barry Allen 1946- *BiDrAPA 89*
Rosson, Glenn Richard 1937- *WhoAm 90*
Rosson, Hal 1895-1988 *AnObit 1988*
Rosson, Harold 1895-1988 *BioIn 16*

Rosson, William Mimms 1922- *St&PR 91*
Rosson-Davis, Barbara Ann 1946- *WhoWrEP 89*
Rossotti, Barbara Jill Margulies 1940- *WhoAm 90, WhoAmW 91*
Rossotti, Charles C. *St&PR 91*
Rossotti, Charles O. 1941- *St&PR 91*
Rossotti, Charles Ossola 1941- *WhoAm 90, WhoSSW 91*
Rossovich, Rick *BioIn 16*
Rossow, Judy *BioIn 16*
Rossow, Rachel Lee Wheeler 1939- *WhoAmW 91*
Rosston, Edward William 1918- *WhoAm 90*
Rossum, Ralph Arthur 1946- *WhoAm 90*
Rosswall, Per Thomas 1941- *WhoWor 91*
Rossy, Richard Paul 1949- *St&PR 91*
Rost, Alice E *BiDrAPA 89*
Rost, Andrew J. 1908- *St&PR 91*
Rost, Jan *PenDiDA 89*
Rost, Michele Pauline 1956- *WhoEmL 91*
Rost, Miles Ernest 1891-1961 *WhoAmA 91N*
Rost, Peter 1959- *WhoEmL 91*
Rost, Stephen H. 1949- *St&PR 91*
Rost, William Joseph 1926- *WhoAm 90*
Rostafinski, Michael Jan *BiDrAPA 89*
Rostain, Anthony Leon 1952- *BiDrAPA 89*
Rostain, Hana *BiDrAPA 89*
Rostal, Max 1905- *IntWWM 90, PenDiMP*
Rostan, John P., III 1943- *St&PR 91*
Rostan, R. D. 1944- *St&PR 91*
Rostand, Edmond 1868-1918 *MajTwCW, TwCLC 37 [port], WorAlBi*
Rostand, Jean Cyrus 1894-1977 *DcScB S2*
Rostand, Michel 1895- *WhoAmA 91N*
Roste, Ola 1950- *WhoWor 91*
Rostel, Jan *PenDiDA 89*
Rosten, Irwin 1924- *WhoAm 90*
Rosten, Leo Calvin 1908- *WhoAm 90*
Rosten, Michael Leonard 1963- *WhoSSW 91*
Rostenbach, Kevin Victor 1959- *WhoEmL 91*
Rostenkowski, Dan *BioIn 16*
Rostenkowski, Dan 1928- *WhoAm 90, WorAlBi*
Roster, Fred Howard 1944- *WhoAmA 91*
Roster, Laila Bergs 1944- *WhoAmA 91*
Roster, Michael 1945- *WhoEmL 91*
Rosthip, Chinda 1933- *WhoWor 91*
Rostick, Edward Anthony 1930- *St&PR 91*
Rostkowski, John Robert 1943- *BiDrAPA 89*
Rostkowski, Margaret I. 1945- *BioIn 16*
Rostkowski-Kizon, Valerie Jean 1961- *WhoE 91*
Rostky, George Harold 1926- *WhoAm 90, WhoWrEP 89*
Rostoker, David 1933- *WhoE 91*
Rostoker, William 1924- *WhoAm 90*
Roston, Arnold 1923- *WhoAm 90*
Roston, Diane Marlene 1955- *BiDrAPA 89*
Roston, Murray 1928- *WhoWor 91*
Roston, Robert A. 1926- *St&PR 91*
Rostopchina, Evdokiia 1811-1858 *EncCoWW*
Rostov, Charles I. *BioIn 16*
Rostovsky, Nikita D. Lobanov- *BioIn 16*
Rostow, Edna Greenberg *WhoE 91*
Rostow, Elspeth Davies *WhoAm 90*
Rostow, Eugene Victor 1913- *BioIn 16, WhoAm 90*
Rostow, W. W. 1916- *BioIn 16*
Rostow, Walt Whitman 1916- *BioIn 16, WhoAm 90*
Rostropovich, Mstislav 1927- *BioIn 16, IntWWM 90, PenDiMP, WorAlBi*
Rostropovich, Mstislav Leopoldovich 1927- *WhoAm 90, WhoE 91, WhoWor 91*
Rosuck, Jordan I. 1937- *St&PR 91*
Rosvoll, Randi Veie 1928- *WhoAm 90*
Roswaenge, Helge 1897-1972 *PenDiMP*
Roswick, Elmer Julius 1919- *St&PR 91*
Roswick, John T. 1946- *St&PR 91*
Roswig, Bernard J. 1939- *ODwPR 91*
Roswitha *EncCoWW*
Roszak, Theodore 1907-1981 *WhoAmA 91N*
Roszell, Douglas King 1941- *BiDrAPA 89*
Roszkowski, Stanley Julian 1923- *WhoAm 90*
Rota, Gian-Carlo 1932- *WhoAm 90, WhoWor 91*
Rota, Nino 1911-1979 *OxCPMus*
Rotach, Werner E. *WhoAm 90*
Rotan, Walter 1912- *WhoAmA 91*
Rotberg, Eugene H. 1930- *St&PR 91*
Rotberg, Eugene Harvey 1930- *WhoAm 90*
Rotberg, Jack 1949- *BiDrAPA 89*
Rotberg, Robert Irwin 1935- *WhoAm 90, WhoE 91*
Rotch, William 1929- *WhoAm 90*
Rotch, William B. *BioIn 16*
Rotchford, Edward Joseph 1945- *WhoSSW 91*
Rotchford, Patricia Kathleen 1945- *WhoWor 91*
Rote, Andrew Bendler 1928- *St&PR 91*
Rote, Carey Clements 1957- *WhoSSW 91*
Rote, William Edwin 1938- *WhoE 91*
Rotella, Guy Louis 1947- *WhoE 91*
Rotella, Mimmo 1918- *BioIn 16*
Rotella, Salvatore G. 1934- *WhoAm 90*
Roteman, Carol Barbara 1946- *WhoAmW 91*
Roten, Robert Darrel 1946- *St&PR 91*
Rotenberg, Carl Theodore 1941- *BiDrAPA 89*
Rotenberg, Helen *BioIn 16*
Rotenberg, Judi *WhoAmA 91*
Rotenberg, Larry Abraham *BiDrAPA 89*
Rotenberg, Marc Steven 1960- *WhoE 91*
Rotenberg, Mark Benjamin 1954- *WhoEmL 91*
Rotenberg, Sheldon 1917- *IntWWM 90, WhoAm 90*
Rotenberg, Stella 1916- *EncCoWW*
Rotenstreich, Jon W. 1943- *St&PR 91*
Rotenstreich, Jon Wallace 1943- *WhoSSW 91*
Roter, Benjamin *St&PR 91*
Rotermund, Maynard A. *BioIn 16*
Rotert, Charles Henry, Jr. 1933- *St&PR 91, WhoAm 90*
Rotert, Denise Anne 1949- *WhoAmW 91*
Rotfeld, Berl *BioIn 16*
Rotfeld, Herbert Jack 1950- *WhoSSW 91*
Rotfeld, Steve *BioIn 16*
Rotgun, Lawrence Martin 1945- *WhoSSW 91*
Roth, Adam M. *BiDrAPA 89*
Roth, Adam Micah 1956- *WhoE 91*
Roth, Allan Robert 1931- *WhoAm 90, WhoE 91*
Roth, Alvin Eliot 1951- *WhoAm 90*
Roth, Andrew J *BiDrAPA 89*
Roth, Ann *ConDes 90*
Roth, Arnold 1929- *AuBYP 90*
Roth, Arthur 1925- *SmATA 11AS [port]*
Roth, Arthur J 1925- *AuBYP 90*
Roth, Barbara 1916- *WhoAmW 91*
Roth, Barbara Edeson 1955- *WhoAmW 91*
Roth, Barry Howard 1947- *BiDrAPA 89*
Roth, Barry N. 1949- *ODwPR 91*
Roth, Batya 1954- *WhoAmW 91*
Roth, Ben 1910-1960 *WhoAmA 91N*
Roth, Bernard Allen 1932- *St&PR 91*
Roth, Bernard B. 1915- *St&PR 91*
Roth, Bernhard A. *AuBYP 90*
Roth, Braggo 1892-1936 *Ballpl 90*
Roth, Brenda C. 1956- *ODwPR 91*
Roth, Charles E 1934- *ConAu 30NR*
Roth, Christian Francis *BioIn 16*
Roth, Daniel Benjamin 1929- *WhoAm 90*
Roth, David *PenDiMP*
Roth, David 1942- *WhoAmA 91*
Roth, David Lee *EncPR&S 89*
Roth, David Lee 1955- *WorAlBi*
Roth, David Robert 1936- *IntWWM 90*
Roth, David Samuel 1953- *BiDrAPA 89*
Roth, Deborah C 1949- *BiDrAPA 89*
Roth, Delena E. *ODwPR 91*
Roth, Donald *BioIn 16*
Roth, Dover 1928- *BiDrAPA 89*
Roth, Duane A. 1957- *WhoWrEP 89*
Roth, Duane J. 1949- *St&PR 91*
Roth, Edwin Isaac 1935- *BiDrAPA 89*
Roth, Edwin Morton 1927- *WhoAm 90*
Roth, Elisabeth Dietlind Wilma 1947- *WhoWor 91*
Roth, Elizabeth Elam *WhoAmW 91*
Roth, Ellen Carlstein *St&PR 91*
Roth, Eugene 1935- *WhoWor 91*
Roth, Francis H. 1938- *St&PR 91*
Roth, Frank 1940- *WhoAmA 91*
Roth, Gabriel *NewAgMG*
Roth, Gary Francis 1947- *WhoE 91*
Roth, George Stanley 1946- *WhoAm 90*
Roth, Gerald Bart 1941- *St&PR 91*
Roth, Guenther *BioIn 16*
Roth, Hadden Wing 1930- *WhoWor 91*
Roth, Hal *BioIn 16, ODwPR 91*
Roth, Harold *BioIn 16*
Roth, Harold 1934- *WhoAm 90*
Roth, Harold Philmore 1915- *WhoAm 90, WhoE 91*
Roth, Harvey Paul 1933- *St&PR 91, WhoAm 90*
Roth, Helene 1943- *St&PR 91*
Roth, Henry 1906- *BioIn 16, MajTwCW, WorAlBi*
Roth, Henry H. 1933- *WhoWrEP 89*
Roth, Herbert, Jr. 1928- *WhoAm 90*
Roth, Herbert Fredrick 1930- *WhoAm 90*
Roth, Herman *BioIn 16*
Roth, Herman 1901-1989 *NewYTBS 90 [port]*
Roth, Holly 1916-1964 *SpyFic, TwCCr&M 91*
Roth, Howard M. 1935- *St&PR 91*
Roth, I. 1940- *St&PR 91*
Roth, Ivan 1935- *St&PR 91*
Roth, J. Ronald 1942- *WhoE 91*
Roth, Jack 1927- *WhoAmA 91*
Roth, Jack Joseph 1920- *WhoAm 90*
Roth, James F. *BioIn 16*
Roth, James Frank 1925- *WhoAm 90*
Roth, James Seymour 1934- *WhoAm 90*
Roth, Jane Richards 1935- *WhoAm 90, WhoAmW 91*
Roth, Janet Helene *BiDrAPA 89*
Roth, Jeffrey David 1953- *BiDrAPA 89*
Roth, Jim Craig 1934- *St&PR 91*
Roth, John *NewAgMG*
Roth, John Andrew 1942- *WhoAm 90*
Roth, John Austin 1934- *WhoSSW 91*
Roth, John K. *BioIn 16*
Roth, John King 1940- *WhoAm 90, WhoWrEP 89*
Roth, John Paul 1922- *WhoAm 90*
Roth, John Reece 1937- *WhoAm 90*
Roth, John Roger 1939- *WhoAm 90*
Roth, Joyce Wolf 1954- *WhoE 91*
Roth, Judith Paris 1949- *WhoWrEP 89*
Roth, June 1926-1990 *BioIn 16, ConAu 132*
Roth, June Doris Spiewak 1926- *WhoAm 90, WhoWrEP 89*
Roth, Katalin Eve 1948- *WhoE 91*
Roth, Kevin *NewAgMG*
Roth, Klaus Friedrich 1925- *WhoWor 91*
Roth, Laura Maurer 1930- *WhoAm 90*
Roth, Lawrence Max 1936- *WhoAm 90*
Roth, Leland M 1943- *WhoAmA 91*
Roth, Lewis Phillip 1937- *St&PR 91, WhoAm 90*
Roth, Loren Dennis 1943- *St&PR 91*
Roth, Loren Henry 1939- *BiDrAPA 89*
Roth, M. Augustine 1926- *WhoAmW 91*
Roth, Marie Mercury 1926- *WhoAmW 91*
Roth, Mark 1951- *WorAlBi*
Roth, Marlen Deanne 1949- *WhoAmW 91*
Roth, Martha 1938- *WhoWrEP 89*
Roth, Martin *BiDrAPA 89*
Roth, Martin G. 1937- *St&PR 91*
Roth, Marvin *BioIn 16*
Roth, Michael 1931- *WhoAm 90*
Roth, Michael I. 1945- *St&PR 91, WhoAm 90*
Roth, Michael William 1952- *WhoE 91*
Roth, Moira 1933- *WhoAmA 91*
Roth, Muriel Parker *BioIn 16, NewYTBS 90*
Roth, Myron Alfred 1917- *WhoAm 90*
Roth, Nathan 1910- *BiDrAPA 89, WhoE 91*
Roth, Paul Frederick 1933- *WhoAm 90*
Roth, Paul William 1960- *WhoEmL 91*
Roth, Peter T. 1957- *St&PR 91*
Roth, Philip *BioIn 16*
Roth, Philip 1933- *Ballpl 90, BestSel 90-3 [port], MajTwCW, WhoAm 90, WhoE 91, WhoWor 91, WhoWrEP 89, WorAlBi*
Roth, Phillips E *BiDrAPA 89*
Roth, Phyllis Irene 1937- *WhoE 91*
Roth, Raymond Edward 1918- *WhoAm 90*
Roth, Regina Sarah 1950- *WhoAmW 91*
Roth, Richard 1904-1987 *BioIn 16*
Roth, Richard 1946- *WhoAmA 91*
Roth, Richard, Jr. 1933- *St&PR 91, WhoAm 90*
Roth, Richard J. 1936- *WhoAm 90*
Roth, Richard Joseph 1941- *St&PR 91*
Roth, Richard Lee 1931- *WhoAm 90*
Roth, Richard Lee 1942- *BiDrAPA 89*
Roth, Richard Leslie 1951- *WhoEmL 91*
Roth, Robert A. 1943- *WhoE 91*
Roth, Robert Earl 1937- *WhoAm 90*
Roth, Robert George 1925- *St&PR 91*
Roth, Robert W. 1923- *St&PR 91*
Roth, Robert William 1953- *WhoSSW 91*
Roth, Roger Z. 1938- *St&PR 91*
Roth, Rubi 1905- *WhoAmA 91*
Roth, Russell Robert 1946- *St&PR 91, WhoAm 90*
Roth, Sally 1960- *WhoAmW 91*
Roth, Sandor *PenDiMP*
Roth, Sanford Harold 1934- *WhoAm 90*
Roth, Sanford Irwin 1932- *WhoAm 90*
Roth, Schawkie *NewAgMG*
Roth, Sheidon 1938- *BiDrAPA 89*
Roth, Sheldon Robert 1936- *St&PR 91*
Roth, Shellie 1943- *ODwPR 91*
Roth, Sherri *BioIn 16*
Roth, Sol 1927- *WhoAm 90*
Roth, Stacia Lynn 1960- *WhoAmW 91*
Roth, Stanley 1929- *St&PR 91*
Roth, Stanley W. 1932- *WhoE 91*
Roth, Steven David 1956- *BiDrAPA 89, WhoE 91*
Roth, Susan 1948- *WhoAmW 91*
Roth, Toby 1938- *WhoAm 90*
Roth, Walter L. 1921- *St&PR 91*
Roth, Walton T 1939- *BiDrAPA 89*
Roth, Wesley A. 1932- *St&PR 91*
Roth, William George 1938- *WhoAm 90*
Roth, William Matson 1916- *WhoAm 90*
Roth, William Stanley 1929- *WhoWor 91*
Roth, William V., Jr. 1921- *WhoAm 90, WhoE 91, WhoWor 91*
Roth, Wolfgang 1910-1988 *BioIn 16*
Roth-Maier, Dora Anna 1940- *WhoWor 91*
Rotha, Paul 1907-1984 *DcNaB 1981*
Rothaus, Paula Montgomery 1952- *WhoAmW 91*
Rothbard, Abe 1918- *St&PR 91*
Rothbard, Harold 1920- *St&PR 91*
Rothbard, Murray Newton 1926- *BioIn 16*
Rothbard, Richard Dale *BiDrAPA 89*
Rothbard, Richard Wintman 1947- *St&PR 91*
Rothbart, Glen 1938- *St&PR 91*
Rothbaum, Barbara Olasov 1960- *WhoE 91*
Rothbaum, Ira *WhoAm 90*
Rothbaum, Kenneth L 1947- *BiDrAPA 89*
Rothbaum, Michael 1936- *St&PR 91*
Rothbaum, Stephen E. *BioIn 16*
Rothbein, Renee 1924- *WhoAmA 91*
Rothbein, Sylvia 1951- *WhoAmW 91*
Rothberg, Abraham 1922- *BioIn 16, WhoAm 90, WhoWrEP 89*
Rothberg, David A. 1954- *St&PR 91*
Rothberg, Eugene *BioIn 16*
Rothberg, Gerald 1937- *WhoAm 90, WhoE 91*
Rothberg, Joan O. 1941- *WhoAmW 91*
Rothberg, Joseph Morris 1936- *WhoE 91*
Rothberg, June Simmonds 1923- *WhoAm 90*
Rothberg, Karen Parker 1942- *WhoAmW 91*
Rothberg, Sol 1910- *St&PR 91, WhoAm 90*
Rothberg-Smoke, F. Dee 1940- *WhoAmW 91*
Rothberger, Sue Ellen 1944- *WhoAmW 91*
Rothblatt, Donald Noah 1935- *WhoAm 90*
Rothblatt, Emma Alden 1918- *WhoWor 91*
Rothblatt, Marv 1927- *BioIn 16*
Rothblum, Egon Gotthilf 1915- *WhoWor 91*
Rothchild, Donald 1928- *ConAu 31NR*
Rothchild, Edward S. *BioIn 16*
Rothchild, Ellen N 1929- *BiDrAPA 89*
Rothchild, Herbert E. 1921- *St&PR 91*
Rothchild, Howard Leslie 1929- *WhoAm 90*
Rothchild, Joseph F. 1918- *St&PR 91*
Rothe, Anna 1850-1907 *EncO&P 3*
Rothe, David H. 1939- *IntWWM 90*
Rothe, Edward Norman 1942- *WhoAm 90*
Rothe, Eric Vaughn 1957- *IntWWM 90*
Rothe, Eugenio M. 1956- *BiDrAPA 89*
Rothe, Guenter Hans 1928- *WhoSSW 91*
Rothe, Gunter Max 1941- *WhoWor 91*
Rothe de Valibona, Rima Gretel 1931- *WhoHisp 91*
Rothenberg, Alan I. 1939- *WhoAm 90*
Rothenberg, Albert 1930- *BiDrAPA 89, WhoAm 90, WhoE 91*
Rothenberg, Allen W. 1929- *WhoAm 90*
Rothenberg, Barbara 1933- *WhoAmA 91*
Rothenberg, Elliot Calvin 1939- *WhoAm 90, WhoWor 91*
Rothenberg, Frederick M. 1942- *WhoSSW 91*
Rothenberg, Gilbert A. 1930- *St&PR 91*
Rothenberg, Gunther Erich 1923- *WhoAm 90*
Rothenberg, Irving 1916- *St&PR 91*
Rothenberg, Jerome 1931- *WhoAm 90*
Rothenberg, Jerome Dennis 1931- *WhoWrEP 89*
Rothenberg, Joseph Howard 1940- *WhoE 91*
Rothenberg, Joseph Lawrence 1940- *St&PR 91*
Rothenberg, Lee M. 1927- *St&PR 91*
Rothenberg, Leonard 1940- *St&PR 91*
Rothenberg, Leslie Steven 1941- *WhoAm 90*
Rothenberg, Mark 1949- *St&PR 91*
Rothenberg, Michael *ODwPR 91*
Rothenberg, Michael B *BiDrAPA 89*
Rothenberg, Norma *ODwPR 91*
Rothenberg, Paul A 1915- *BiDrAPA 89*
Rothenberg, Robert Edward 1908- *WhoAm 90, WhoWor 91*
Rothenberg, Robert P. 1936- *ODwPR 91*
Rothenberg, Robert Philip 1936- *WhoAm 90*
Rothenberg, Saundra Hamm 1943- *WhoAmW 91*
Rothenberg, Steven Alan 1952- *WhoEmL 91*
Rothenberg, Susan *BioIn 16*
Rothenberg, Susan 1945- *BiDWomA, WhoAm 90, WhoAmA 91, WhoAmW 91*
Rothenberger, Anneliese 1924- *IntWWM 90, PenDiMP*
Rothenberger, Harold A. 1943- *St&PR 91*
Rothenburg, Paul Michael 1942- *WhoE 91*
Rothenstein, William 1872-1945 *BioIn 16*
Rothenstreich, Mindi Cheryl 1962- *WhoAmW 91*
Rother, Anita *ODwPR 91*
Rother, John Charles 1947- *WhoAm 90*

Rother, Stanley 1935-1981 *BioIn 16*
Rotheram Borus, Mary J. 1949- *WhoAmW 91*
Rotherham, Jean 1922- *WhoAmW 91*
Rothermel, Dan Hiester 1943- *IntWWM 90*
Rothermel, Daniel Krott 1938- *St&PR 91, WhoAm 90*
Rothermel, Harold C *BiDrAPA 89*
Rothermel, Joan Ashley *BioIn 16*
Rothermel, Richard Lloyd 1926- *WhoWor 91*
Rothermel, Rodman S. 1932- *St&PR 91*
Rothermere, Harold Harmsworth, Viscount 1868-1940 *WorAlBi*
Rothermund, Cathy Lou 1955- *WhoAmW 91*
Rothery, Agnes Edwards 1888- *AuBYP 90*
Rothfarb, Ruth *BioIn 16*
Rothfeld, Michael B. 1947- *St&PR 91, WhoAm 90*
Rothfeld, Neil S. 1936- *St&PR 91*
Rothfield, Lawrence I. 1927- *WhoAm 90*
Rothfield, Naomi Fox 1929- *WhoAm 90, WhoAmW 91*
Rothfus, John Arden 1932- *WhoAm 90*
Rothfuss, Earl Levering 1952- *IntWWM 90*
Rothfuss, Robert Allen 1928- *St&PR 91*
Rothgarn, Mildred 1935- *WhoAmW 91*
Rothgeb, Russell 1936- *St&PR 91*
Rothhammer, Francisco 1940- *WhoWor 91*
Rothholz, Peter L. 1929- *ODwPR 91*
Rothholz, Peter Lutz 1929- *WhoAm 90*
Rothing, Frank John 1924- *WhoAm 90*
Rothko, Mark 1903-1970 *BioIn 16, IntDcAA 90, WhoAmA 91N, WorAlBi*
Rothkopf, Michael H. 1939- *WhoE 91*
Rothkopf, Robert Henry 1945- *St&PR 91*
Rothlein, Gerard John, Jr. 1943- *St&PR 91, WhoAm 90*
Rothlein, Lee Alan 1944- *St&PR 91*
Rothman, Andrew L. *ODwPR 91*
Rothman, Bernard 1932- *WhoE 91*
Rothman, Bernard 1938- *St&PR 91*
Rothman, Claire L. *BioIn 16*
Rothman, David Bill 1952- *WhoEmL 91, WhoSSW 91*
Rothman, Deanna 1938- *WhoAmW 91*
Rothman, Elaine Paula 1959- *WhoWor 91*
Rothman, Esther Pomeranz 1919- *WhoAmW 91*
Rothman, Frank 1926- *St&PR 91, WhoAm 90*
Rothman, Frank George 1930- *WhoAm 90*
Rothman, Gerald 1937- *St&PR 91*
Rothman, Hal 1958- *ConAu 130*
Rothman, Harry I. *BioIn 16*
Rothman, Henry Isaac 1943- *WhoAm 90*
Rothman, Herbert L 1937- *BiDrAPA 89*
Rothman, Howard 1953- *WhoWrEP 89*
Rothman, Howard Joel 1945- *WhoAm 90, WhoEmL 91*
Rothman, Irvin Douglass 1923- *WhoSSW 91*
Rothman, Irwin *BiDrAPA 89*
Rothman, James Edward 1950- *WhoAm 90*
Rothman, John 1948- *WhoE 91*
Rothman, Jonathan Stuart *BiDrAPA 89*
Rothman, Judith Lee 1940- *WhoAmW 91*
Rothman, Julius Lawrence 1920- *WhoWor 91*
Rothman, Marc Irwin 1952- *BiDrAPA 89*
Rothman, Martin 1946- *St&PR 91*
Rothman, Melvin L. 1930- *WhoAm 90*
Rothman, Patricia Mary 1946- *WhoAmW 91*
Rothman, R. H. 1941- *St&PR 91*
Rothman, Richard Brian 1953- *BiDrAPA 89*
Rothman, Sara 1929- *WhoAmW 91*
Rothman, Seymour J 1938- *BiDrAPA 89*
Rothman, Sidney *WhoAmA 91*
Rothman, Stephanie 1936- *WhoAm 90*
Rothman, Stewart Neil 1930- *WhoWor 91*
Rothman, Tony 1953- *ConAu 33NR*
Rothman, William B. *St&PR 91*
Rothman-Denes, Lucia Beatriz 1943- *WhoAmW 91*
Rothmeier, Steven George *BioIn 16*
Rothmeier, Steven George 1946- *St&PR 91, WhoAm 90*
Rothmere, Lord 1898-1978 *WorAlBi*
Rothmuller, Marko 1908- *PenDiMP*
Rothmuller, Marko Aron 1908- *IntWWM 90*
Rothney, John Watson Murray 1906-1989 *BioIn 16*
Rothney, William B *BiDrAPA 89*
Rotholz, Rina *WhoAmA 91*
Rothovius, Iska 1926- *WhoE 91*
Rothrock, Carol Simon 1953- *WhoAmW 91*
Rothrock, Ilse Skipsna 1928-1981 *WhoAmA 91N*
Rothrock, Irvin A 1926- *BiDrAPA 89*
Rothrock, Jack 1905-1980 *Ballpl 90*
Rothrock, Jan Campbell 1935- *WhoAmW 91, WhoSSW 91, WhoWor 91*
Rothrock, Mark Allan 1953- *BiDrAPA 89*
Rothschild family *BioIn 16*
Rothschild, Lord *NewYTBS 90 [port]*
Rothschild, Alan Friend 1925- *WhoAm 90*
Rothschild, Amalie 1916- *WhoAmA 91*
Rothschild, Amalie Randolph 1945- *WhoAmW 91*
Rothschild, Amalie Rosenfeld 1916- *WhoAm 90*
Rothschild, Ann Hatfield *BioIn 16*
Rothschild, Anthony Joseph *BiDrAPA 89*
Rothschild, Anthony Joseph 1953- *WhoE 91*
Rothschild, Beatrice de *BioIn 16*
Rothschild, Bernhard A., Jr. 1913- *St&PR 91*
Rothschild, Bruce Stephen 1954- *BiDrAPA 89*
Rothschild, Carolyn Anita 1939- *WhoAmA 91, WhoE 91*
Rothschild, Charles Joseph, Jr. 1921- *St&PR 91, WhoAm 90*
Rothschild, Diane 1943- *WhoAm 90, WhoAmW 91*
Rothschild, Donna Maria Beatrice de *BioIn 16*
Rothschild, Dorothy de *BioIn 16*
Rothschild, Eric de *BioIn 16*
Rothschild, Ernest Leo 1922- *WhoAm 90*
Rothschild, F Salomon *BiDrAPA 89*
Rothschild, Friedrich 1899- *EncPaPR 91*
Rothschild, George William 1917- *WhoAm 90*
Rothschild, Guy de *ConAu 129*
Rothschild, Herbert 1892-1976 *WhoAmA 91N*
Rothschild, Herbert 1921- *WhoE 91*
Rothschild, James Alan 1946- *WhoE 91*
Rothschild, Jeffrey L. 1945- *St&PR 91*
Rothschild, John D 1940- *WhoAmA 91*
Rothschild, John David 1940- *WhoWor 91*
Rothschild, Joseph 1931- *WhoAm 90*
Rothschild, Judith *WhoAmA 91*
Rothschild, Larry 1954- *BioIn 16*
Rothschild, Leigh Mitchell 1951- *WhoSSW 91*
Rothschild, Lincoln 1902-1983 *WhoAmA 91N*
Rothschild, Lionel Nathan 1808-1879 *WorAlBi*
Rothschild, Loren Robert 1938- *St&PR 91, WhoAm 90*
Rothschild, Marie-Helene de *BioIn 16*
Rothschild, Mayer Anselm 1743-1812 *WorAlBi*
Rothschild, Michael 1942- *WhoAm 90*
Rothschild, Miriam Louisa 1908- *WhoWor 91*
Rothschild, Nathan Mayer 1777-1836 *WorAlBi*
Rothschild, Nathaniel Mayer Victor 1910-1990 *BioIn 16, ConAu 131*
Rothschild, Olimpia de *BioIn 16*
Rothschild, Paul H. 1937- *St&PR 91*
Rothschild, Philippe de 1902-1988 *AnObit 1988*
Rothschild, Randolph Schamberg 1909- *IntWWM 90*
Rothschild, Rona R. 1941- *St&PR 91*
Rothschild, Steven James 1944- *WhoAm 90*
Rothschild, Steven M. 1945- *WhoAm 90*
Rothschild, Victor Henry, II 1908- *WhoAm 90, WhoWor 91*
Rothschild, Walter 1926- *BiDrAPA 89*
Rothschild, Walter Galeski 1956- *WhoSSW 91*
Rothschild, Walter Nathan 1892-1960 *WorAlBi*
Rothschild, William Baron 1948- *BiDrAPA 89*
Rothstein, Alan D 1930- *BiDrAPA 89*
Rothstein, Anne Louise 1943- *WhoE 91*
Rothstein, Arnold Marton *BiDrAPA 89*
Rothstein, Arthur 1915-1985 *BioIn 16, WhoAmA 91N*
Rothstein, Aser 1918- *WhoAm 90*
Rothstein, Barbara Jacobs 1939- *WhoAm 90, WhoAmW 91*
Rothstein, David 1901-1989 *BioIn 16*
Rothstein, David A 1935- *BiDrAPA 89*
Rothstein, Eric 1936- *WhoAm 90, WhoWrEP 89*
Rothstein, Eugene Leonard 1927- *St&PR 91*
Rothstein, Fred H. *WhoAm 90*
Rothstein, Gerald Alan 1941- *St&PR 91, WhoE 91*
Rothstein, L. *St&PR 91*
Rothstein, Lawrence I. 1952- *St&PR 91*
Rothstein, Leonard M 1925- *BiDrAPA 89*
Rothstein, Marilyn E. 1938- *WhoWrEP 89*
Rothstein, Mark Alan 1949- *WhoEmL 91*
Rothstein, Martin C. *BioIn 16*
Rothstein, Morton 1926- *WhoAm 90*
Rothstein, Richard J. 1948- *ODwPR 91*
Rothstein, Robert 1921- *St&PR 91*
Rothstein, Ron *WhoAm 90*
Rothstein, Samuel 1921- *WhoAm 90*
Rothuizen, Jasper Warner 1939- *WhoWor 91*
Rothwell, Albert Falcon 1926- *WhoAm 90*
Rothwell, Evelyn 1911- *PenDiMP*
Rothwell, James Harold 1945- *St&PR 91*
Rothwell, Robert Clark 1939- *St&PR 91*
Rothwell, T. A. 1931- *St&PR 91*
Rothwell, Timothy Gordon 1951- *WhoAm 90*
Rothwell, Warren Randall 1917- *St&PR 91*
Rotier, Peter 1888- *WhoAmA 91N*
Rotko, Michael 1938- *St&PR 91*
Rotman, Arthur 1926- *WhoAm 90*
Rotman, Jesse L. 1947- *ODwPR 91*
Rotman, Jesse Louis 1947- *WhoAm 90*
Rotman, Morris B. 1918- *ODwPR 91*
Rotman, Morris Bernard 1918- *WhoAm 90*
Rotman, Walter 1922- *WhoAm 90*
Rotner, Robert Alan 1944- *WhoAm 90, WhoE 91*
Rotolo, Joseph A. 1931- *WhoAm 90*
Rotondi, Charles A. 1949- *St&PR 91*
Rotondi, Marie A. 1924- *St&PR 91*
Rotondi, Paul C. 1924- *St&PR 91*
Rotondo, Dean John 1954- *BiDrAPA 89*
Rotsuith *EncCoWW*
Rotta, Frank 1934- *ODwPR 91, St&PR 91*
Rottas, Ray 1927- *WhoAm 90*
Rotte, Bruce Edward 1942- *St&PR 91*
Rottem, Shlomo 1939- *WhoWor 91*
Rottenberg, Dan 1942- *WhoE 91*
Rottenberg, Simon 1916- *WhoE 91*
Rottensteiner, Franz 1942- *ConAu 33NR*
Rotter, Arlene F. 1926- *St&PR 91*
Rotter, Hans 1932- *WhoWor 91*
Rotter, Hershel 1924- *St&PR 91*
Rotter, Jerome Israel 1949- *WhoEmL 91*
Rotter, Julian B. 1916- *BioIn 16*
Rotter, Merrill Richard *BiDrAPA 89*
Rotter, Paul Talbott 1918- *WhoAm 90, WhoWor 91*
Rotter, Robert Reynold 1946- *St&PR 91*
Rotter, Shlomo 1947- *WhoWor 91*
Rotter, William R. 1953- *St&PR 91*
Rotterdam, Paul Z 1939- *WhoAmA 91*
Rottersman, William *BiDrAPA 89*
Rottler, Terry Robert 1951- *WhoEmL 91*
Rottman, Ellis 1930- *WhoAm 90*
Rottman, Gordon Leroy 1947- *WhoWrEP 89*
Rottman, Howard 1922- *St&PR 91*
Rottura, Joseph Peter 1949- *WhoSSW 91*
Rotunda, Donald Theodore 1945- *WhoE 91, WhoWor 91*
Rotunda, Ronald Daniel 1945- *WhoAm 90, WhoEmL 91*
Rotunno, Giuseppe 1923- *ConTFT 8*
Rotunno, Joseph R. 1928- *St&PR 91*
Rotz, John Robert 1950- *St&PR 91*
Rotzien, Mary Kathryn 1952- *WhoAmW 91*
Rotzinger-Padden, Karin Marie 1962- *WhoWrEP 89*
Rotzoll, Kim Brewer 1935- *WhoAm 90*
Rotzsch, Hans-Joachim 1929- *IntWWM 90*
Rotzsch, Helmut Karl Werner 1923- *WhoWor 91*
Rou, Henry Jennings, II 1935- *St&PR 91*
Rouanet, Sergio Paulo 1934- *WhoWor 91*
Rouault, Georges 1871-1958 *BioIn 16, IntDcAA 90 [port]*
Roub, Bryan R. 1941- *St&PR 91*
Roub, Bryan Roger 1941- *WhoAm 90*
Rouba, Duane Edward 1954- *WhoE 91*
Roubicek, Erwin J 1929- *BiDrAPA 89*
Roubik, Susanne Eileen 1959- *WhoAmW 91*
Roubiliac, Louis Francois 1702?-1762 *BioIn 16, IntDcAA 90*
Roubitchek, Donald A. 1950- *St&PR 91*
Roubo, Jacob 1739-1791 *PenDiDA 89*
Roubos, Gary Lynn 1936- *St&PR 91, WhoAm 90, WhoE 91*
Roucek, Joseph S 1902- *ConAu 32NR*
Rouch, Jean *BioIn 16*
Rouchell, Alvin Martin *BiDrAPA 89*
Roud, Richard 1929-1989 *AnObit 1989, BioIn 16*
Rouda, Mitchell Bruce 1957- *WhoAm 90*
Roudabush, Aaron Paul 1965- *WhoEmL 91*
Roudebush, George M. 1894- *WhoAm 90*
Roudebush, Marion E 1912- *BiDrAPA 89*
Rouder, Willa 1950- *IntWWM 90*
Roudy, Yvette 1929- *BiDFrPL*
Roudybush, Alexandra 1911- *WhoAmW 91, WhoWor 91*
Roudybush, Franklin 1906- *WhoWor 91*
Roueche, Berton 1911- *WhoAm 90, WhoWrEP 89*
Roueche, John Edward, II 1938- *WhoAm 90, WhoWor 91*
Rouff, Benjamin 1914- *St&PR 91*
Rougelot, Rodney S. 1933- *St&PR 91*
Rougemont, Michel 1946- *WhoWor 91*
Rough, Gaylord Earl 1924- *WhoAm 90*
Roughton, Francis John Worsley 1899-1972 *DcScB S2*
Roughton, Ralph Emerson, Jr. 1932- *BiDrAPA 89*
Rougier-Chapman, Alwyn Spencer Doug- 1939- *St&PR 91*
Rougraff, Maurice E. 1926- *St&PR 91*
Rouhana, William J. 1952- *St&PR 91*
Rouhban, Badaoui Michel 1951- *WhoWor 91*
Rouhi, Rouhollah A *BiDrAPA 89*
Rouilard, Richard *BioIn 16*
Rouillard Johnson, Holly 1960- *WhoAmW 91*
Rouin, Carole Christine 1939- *WhoAmW 91*
Roukema, Margaret Scafati 1929- *WhoAm 90, WhoAmW 91, WhoE 91*
Roukema, Richard 1927- *BiDrAPA 89*
Roukes, Nicholas M 1925- *WhoAmA 91*
Roulac, Stephen E. 1945- *WhoAm 90*
Rouleau, Carolyn Fernan 1950- *WhoAmW 91*
Rouleau, Joseph 1929- *IntWWM 90*
Rouleau, Monique Lucille 1964- *WhoE 91*
Rouleau, Yves 1922- *BiDrAPA 89*
Roulet, Jean-Francois 1947- *WhoWor 91*
Roulet, Marcel *BioIn 16*
Roulet, Norman L 1932- *BiDrAPA 89*
Roulier, Joy Roulier 1960- *WhoWrEP 89*
Roulier, Richard 1947- *St&PR 91*
Roulson, Lee C. 1943- *St&PR 91*
Roulston, John Frank Clement 1941- *WhoWor 91*
Roulston, Thomas Henry 1933- *WhoAm 90, WhoWor 91*
Roumas, James Charles 1926- *WhoE 91*
Roumier, Francois *PenDiDA 89*
Round, Lawrence Allen 1928- *St&PR 91*
Round, Nicholas Grenville 1938- *WhoWor 91*
Rounding, Virginia 1956- *WhoWor 91*
Rounds, Barbara Lynn 1934- *BiDrAPA 89*
Rounds, Donald Edwin 1926- *WhoAm 90*
Rounds, Glen 1906- *AuBYP 90*
Rounds, John S. 1927- *St&PR 91*
Rounds, Kathleen Linda 1948- *WhoWrEP 89*
Rounds, Kevin Thomas 1951- *WhoAm 90*
Rounds, Robert A *BiDrAPA 89*
Roundtree, Eugene Van Nostrand 1927- *St&PR 91*
Roundtree, Jacqueline Washington 1949- *WhoEmL 91*
Roundtree, Phil Robert *St&PR 91*
Roundtree, Richard 1942- *DrBlPA 90, WhoAm 90*
Rounick, Jack A. 1935- *St&PR 91, WhoAm 90*
Rounsaville, Bruce James 1949- *BiDrAPA 89*
Rounsaville, Donna Drinkard 1942- *WhoWor 91*
Rounsaville, Guy, Jr. 1943- *St&PR 91*
Rounsaville, Michael Wayne 1954- *WhoSSW 91*
Rountree, Asa 1927- *WhoAm 90*
Rountree, Frank Cox 1944- *St&PR 91*
Rountree, Janet Caryl 1937- *WhoAm 90*
Rountree, Jeanie Sue 1960- *WhoSSW 91*
Rountree, John Griffin Richardson 1936- *WhoSSW 91*
Rountree, Michael Allen 1942- *St&PR 91*
Rountree, Neva Dixon 1943- *ODwPR 91, WhoAm 90, WhoSSW 91*
Rountree, Robert Benjamin 1924- *St&PR 91*
Rountree, Sue *BioIn 16*
Rountree, W Dekle, Jr. 1941- *St&PR 91*
Rountree, William C. 1941- *St&PR 91*
Rountree, William F., Jr. 1944- *St&PR 91*
Roup, Brenda Jacobs 1948- *WhoAmW 91*
Roupe, James Paul 1957- *WhoE 91*
Roura, Samuel Elias *BiDrAPA 89*
Rourk, Thomas Lee 1935- *St&PR 91*
Rourke, Arlene Carol 1944- *WhoAmW 91, WhoSSW 91, WhoWor 91*
Rourke, Charles Kane 1932- *St&PR 91*
Rourke, Constance M. 1885-1941 *BioAmW*
Rourke, John A. 1930- *ODwPR 91*
Rourke, Michael J. 1934- *ODwPR 91, St&PR 91*
Rourke, Michael James 1934- *WhoAm 90*
Rourke, Mickey *NewYTBS 90 [port], WhoAm 90*
Rourke, Mickey 1956- *WorAlBi*
Rous, Peyton 1879-1970 *WorAlBi*
Rous, Robert Kenneth 1944- *St&PR 91*
Rous, Stephen Norman 1931- *WhoAm 90, WhoE 91, WhoWor 91*
Rousakis, John Paul 1929- *WhoAm 90, WhoSSW 91*
Rousch, Bernard L 1936- *BiDrAPA 89*
Rouse, Allen Lee 1937- *WhoAm 90*
Rouse, Andrew Miles 1928- *WhoAm 90*
Rouse, Charles Richard 1954- *WhoSSW 91*

Rouse, Charlie 1924-1988 *AnObit 1988*, *BioIn 16*
Rouse, Christopher Chapman 1949- *IntWWM 90*
Rouse, Clyde Carlos, Jr. 1952- *BiDrAPA 89*
Rouse, Doris Jane 1948- *WhoAm 90*
Rouse, Eloise Meadows 1931- *WhoWor 91*
Rouse, Garry Paget 1941- *WhoWor 91*
Rouse, George Lothrop 1846-1922 *AmLegL*
Rouse, Irving 1913- *WhoAm 90*
Rouse, James R. 1942- *St&PR 91*
Rouse, James W. *BioIn 16*
Rouse, John Dashiell 1950- *BiDrAPA 89*
Rouse, John Jay 1955- *WhoE 91*
Rouse, John W., Jr. 1937- *St&PR 91*
Rouse, John Wilson, Jr. 1937- *WhoAm 90*
Rouse, Margaret 1633?-1706 *BiDEWW*
Rouse, Richard Hunter 1933- *WhoAm 90*
Rouse, Richard Oliver, Jr. 1920- *WhoAm 90*
Rouse, Robert A. 1949- *St&PR 91*
Rouse, Robert Sumner 1930- *WhoAm 90*
Rouse, Roscoe, Jr. 1919- *WhoAm 90*
Rouse, Roy Dennis 1920- *WhoAm 90*
Rouse, Ted D. 1935- *St&PR 91*
Rouse, Terrie Suzitte 1952- *WhoAmW 91*
Rouse, Thomas Clay 1943- *WhoSSW 91*
Rouse, William Bradford 1947- *WhoAm 90*
Rouse, William S. 1931- *St&PR 91*
Rousell, Charles H 1946- *BiDrAPA 89*
Rousell, Ralph Henry 1933- *WhoWor 91*
Roush, Ann Marie 1937- *WhoAmW 91*
Roush, David P. 1957- *St&PR 91*
Roush, Edd 1893-1988 *Ballpl 90 [port]*, *BioIn 16*
Roush, Rex L. 1928- *St&PR 91*
Roush, Robert Warren 1930- *St&PR 91*
Rouskas, Basil Panagiotis 1943- *WhoE 91*
Rouson, Vivian Reissland 1929- *WhoAmW 91*
Rousos, Anthony P 1915- *BiDrAPA 89*
Roussakis, Nicolas 1934- *WhoAm 90*
Roussan, Matei Stephan 1922- *WhoAm 90*
Rousse, David Edmond 1953- *St&PR 91*
Rousseau, Arthur William 1948- *BiDrAPA 89*
Rousseau, Cecile *BiDrAPA 89*
Rousseau, Eugene 1932- *IntWWM 90*
Rousseau, Eugene Ellsworth 1932- *WhoAm 90*
Rousseau, Eva Rice 1944- *WhoE 91*
Rousseau, Francois-Eugene 1827-1891 *PenDiDA 89*
Rousseau, George Sebastian 1941- *WhoAm 90*
Rousseau, Henri 1844-1910 *IntDcAA 90*, *WorAlBi*
Rousseau, Henri Julien Felix 1844-1910 *BioIn 16*
Rousseau, Irene Victoria *WhoAmA 91*, *WhoE 91*
Rousseau, Jacques Ambroise 1933- *St&PR 91*
Rousseau, Jean-Jacques 1712-1778 *LitC 14 [port]*, *WhNaAH*, *WorAlBi*, *WrPh*
Rousseau, Jeannine Marie 1941- *WhoAm 90*
Rousseau, John F. 1943- *St&PR 91*
Rousseau, Leodor Edgar 1933- *St&PR 91*
Rousseau, Mews *BiDrAPA 89*
Rousseau, Monique J *BiDrAPA 89*
Rousseau, Rita Ann 1949- *WhoAmW 91*
Rousseau, Roger *BiDrAPA 89*
Rousseau, Ronald Joseph 1935- *St&PR 91*
Rousseau, Ronald William 1943- *WhoAm 90*
Rousseau, Theodore 1812-1867 *IntDcAA 90*
Rousseau, Theodore, Jr 1912-1974 *WhoAmA 91N*
Rousseau, William H. *St&PR 91*
Rousseau-Vermette, Mariette *WhoAmA 91*
Roussel, Albert 1869-1937 *PenDiMPA*
Roussel, Athina *BioIn 16*
Roussel, Barbara R. 1937- *WhoAmW 91*
Roussel, Claude Patrice 1930- *WhoAmA 91*
Roussel, Ker Xavier 1867-1944 *BioIn 16*
Roussel, Louis J., Jr. *WhoSSW 91*
Roussel, Louis Richard 1930- *WhoAm 90*
Roussel, Nelly 1878-1922 *EncCoWW*
Roussel, Norman Lucien 1934- *WhoE 91*
Roussel, Peter 1942- *ODwPR 91*
Roussel, Pierre 1723-1782 *PenDiDA 89*
Roussel, Thierry *BioIn 16*
Rousselet, Louis 1845-1929 *BioIn 16*
Roussell, Vanessa Lynn 1952- *WhoAmW 91*
Rousselle, Aline 1939- *ConAu 130*
Rousselot, Edouard *WhoWor 91*
Rousselot, John H. *St&PR 91*
Rousset, Elias Karl *PenDiDA 89*
Roussey, Robert Stanley 1935- *WhoWor 91*
Roussimoff, Andre *BioIn 16*
Roussin, Richard A. 1932- *St&PR 91*
Rousso, Eli L. 1920- *St&PR 91*
Rousso, Henry 1954- *WhoWor 91*
Rousso, Judith 1947- *BiDrAPA 89*
Rousso, Lee *BioIn 16*
Rousso, Marc *BioIn 16*
Rout, Kathleen Joan Kinsella 1942- *WhoAmW 91*
Rout, Leslie B. 1936-1987 *BioIn 16*
Routamo, Reino Edvard 1931- *WhoWor 91*
Route, Deborah A. 1953- *WhoWrEP 89*
Routh, Donald Kent 1937- *WhoAm 90*
Routh, Francis John 1927- *IntWWM 90*
Routh, Martha 1743-1817 *FemiCLE*
Routhier, Adolphe-Basile 1839-1920 *DcLB 99 [port]*
Routhier, Francois *WhoAm 90*
Routhier, Roland Maurice 1926- *St&PR 91*
Routien, John Broderick 1913- *WhoAm 90*
Routon, David F 1931- *WhoAmA 91*
Routson, Clell Dennis 1946- *St&PR 91*
Routson, Susan Hutchins 1943- *WhoAmW 91*
Routt, William W 1937- *BiDrAPA 89*
Routtenberg, Max J. 1909-1987 *BioIn 16*
Routti, Jorma Tapio 1938- *WhoWor 91*
Routzahn, Deborah Marie 1963- *WhoWor 91*
Rouvier, Pierre Maurice 1842-1911 *BiDFrPL*
Rouvinen, Hannu Matti 1951- *WhoWor 91*
Roux, Alexandre *PenDiDA 89*
Roux, Ambroise Marie Casimir 1921- *WhoAm 90*, *WhoWor 91*
Roux, Gus Louis, III 1954- *WhoEmL 91*
Roux, Hubert 1934- *WhoWor 91*
Roux, Jean-Louis 1923- *OxCCanT*, *WhoAm 90*
Roux, Joseph Edward 1958- *WhoSSW 91*
Roux, Michel *BioIn 16*
Roux, Michel 1924- *IntWWM 90*
Roux, Mildred Anna 1914- *WhoAmW 91*
Roux-Alezais, Henry 1938- *WhoWor 91*
Roux-Buisson, Isabelle Lucie 1957- *WhoWor 91*
Rouxel, Vincent Yves 1948- *St&PR 91*
Rouzade, Leonie 1839-1916 *EncCoWW*
Rovansek, Gary John 1942- *St&PR 91*
Roveda, John Gregory 1938- *St&PR 91*
Rovegno, George F. 1948- *St&PR 91*
Rovelli, Fausto 1918- *WhoWor 91*
Rovelstad, Mathilde Verner 1920- *WhoAm 90*
Rovelstad, Robert W. 1918- *St&PR 91*
Rovelstad, Trygue A *WhoAmA 91N*
Rover, Edward Frank 1938- *WhoAm 90*
Rover, Harold V. 1924- *St&PR 91*
Rovere, George D. 1933-1988 *BioIn 16*
Rovere, Raphael A *BiDrAPA 89*
Roversi, Paolo *BioIn 16*
Roverud, Eleanor 1912- *WhoWor 91*
Rovetti, Paul F 1939- *WhoAmA 91*
Rovin, Leo 1914- *St&PR 91*
Rovin, Sheldon 1932- *WhoAm 90*
Rovine, Arthur William 1937- *WhoAm 90*, *WhoWor 91*
Rovinsky, Joseph Judah 1927- *WhoAm 90*
Rovinsky, Serafima *BiDrAPA 89*
Rovira, F Victor 1941- *BiDrAPA 89*
Rovira, Luis Dario 1923- *WhoAm 90*
Rovner, Arkady 1940- *WhoWrEP 89*
Rovner, Barry W 1954- *BiDrAPA 89*
Rovner, David Richard 1930- *WhoAm 90*
Rovner, Ilana Kara Diamond 1938- *WhoAm 90*, *WhoAmW 91*
Rovner, Leonard Irving *WhoE 91*
Rovno, David A *BiDrAPA 89*
Row, David 1949- *WhoAmA 91*
Row, Lisa Ann 1959- *WhoAmW 91*
Row, Orion Y. 1915- *St&PR 91*
Rowady, Edward P. 1928- *St&PR 91*
Rowan, Amy Beth *BiDrAPA 89*
Rowan, Barry Lee 1956- *WhoEmL 91*
Rowan, Bruce Clayton 1952- *St&PR 91*
Rowan, Carl Thomas 1925- *BioIn 16*, *WhoAm 90*, *WhoWrEP 89*
Rowan, Dan 1922-1987 *WorAlBi*
Rowan, David C. 1930- *St&PR 91*
Rowan, Dennis Michael 1938- *WhoAmA 91*
Rowan, Donald James 1941- *WhoE 91*
Rowan, Edward Beatty 1898-1946 *WhoAmA 91N*
Rowan, Edward L. 1940- *WhoE 91*
Rowan, Edward Leslie 1940- *BiDrAPA 89*
Rowan, Edward Walter 1947- *St&PR 91*
Rowan, Frances Physioc 1908- *WhoAmA 91*
Rowan, George Edward *BiDrAPA 89*
Rowan, Gerald Burdette 1916- *WhoAm 90*
Rowan, Herman 1923- *WhoAmA 91*
Rowan, Hester *ConAu 131*
Rowan, Hugh *BioIn 16*
Rowan, Jack 1887-1966 *Ballpl 90*
Rowan, James P. 1933- *St&PR 91*
Rowan, John M. 1829- *AmLegL*
Rowan, John Robert 1919- *WhoAm 90*, *WhoSSW 91*
Rowan, Kathy Catsinas 1957- *ODwPR 91*
Rowan, Keith P. *ODwPR 91*
Rowan, Lynne Estelle 1947- *WhoAmW 91*
Rowan, Michael Terrance 1958- *WhoSSW 91*
Rowan, Patrick 1937- *WhoAmA 91*
Rowan, Rena Jung 1928- *WhoAm 90*
Rowan, Richard Lamar 1931- *WhoAm 90*
Rowan, William Patrick 1951- *IntWWM 90*
Rowand, Edward W. 1942- *St&PR 91*
Rowand, Joseph Donn 1942- *WhoAmA 91*
Rowane, William Anthony, II 1959- *BiDrAPA 89*
Rowark, Maureen 1933- *WhoAm 90*
Rowcliffe, Judith L. 1954- *ODwPR 91*
Rowden, Frances Arabella *FemiCLE*
Rowden, Marcus Aubrey 1928- *WhoAm 90*
Rowden, Phillip Charles 1950- *BiDrAPA 89*
Rowden, William Henry 1930- *WhoAm 90*
Rowder, William Louis 1937- *WhoAm 90*
Rowe, A Prescott 1938- *ODwPR 91*
Rowe, A. Prescott 1938- *St&PR 91*
Rowe, Alan M. 1956- *St&PR 91*
Rowe, Alan Thomas 1931- *WhoAm 90*
Rowe, Allan D. 1951- *St&PR 91*
Rowe, Arthur Edgar 1929- *St&PR 91*, *WhoAm 90*, *WhoWor 91*
Rowe, Beverly Hope 1933- *WhoWrEP 89*
Rowe, Bobby Lewis 1932- *WhoSSW 91*
Rowe, Bonnie Gordon 1922- *WhoWor 91*
Rowe, Bruce Machin 1936- *WhoWor 91*
Rowe, C J 1944- *ConAu 132*
Rowe, Charles Alfred 1934- *WhoAm 90*, *WhoAmA 91*
Rowe, Charles Spurgeon 1925- *WhoAm 90*
Rowe, Cheryl June 1955- *BiDrAPA 89*
Rowe, Christopher Cornell *BiDrAPA 89*
Rowe, Clair Devere 1924- *WhoAm 90*
Rowe, Clarence J *BiDrAPA 89*
Rowe, Clarence John 1916- *WhoAm 90*
Rowe, Corinne *WhoAmA 91N*
Rowe, David John 1936- *WhoAm 90*
Rowe, David Knox *BioIn 16*
Rowe, David Knox 1924?-1989 *ConAu 129*
Rowe, Deborah Lynn 1953- *WhoAmW 91*
Rowe, Donald Allen 1937- *WhoAm 90*
Rowe, Donald Edward 1929- *WhoAm 90*, *WhoWor 91*
Rowe, Dorothy E. *BioIn 16*
Rowe, Edgar Riley 1922- *WhoSSW 91*
Rowe, Elizabeth 1674-1737 *BioIn 16*, *FemiCLE*
Rowe, Elizabeth Singer 1674-1737 *DcLB 95 [port]*
Rowe, Elizabeth Webb 1957- *WhoE 91*
Rowe, Evelyn Karla 1943- *WhoAmW 91*
Rowe, Fanny 1913-1988 *AnObit 1988*
Rowe, Fanny Bickart 1927- *WhoAmW 91*
Rowe, Frank 1921-1985 *ConAu 130*
Rowe, Frederic Lee 1957- *BiDrAPA 89*
Rowe, Frederick Martin 1925- *WhoAm 90*
Rowe, Galen Otto 1937- *WhoAm 90*
Rowe, Geneva Lassiter 1927- *WhoAmW 91*
Rowe, George Giles 1921- *WhoAm 90*
Rowe, Guy 1894-1969 *WhoAmA 91N*
Rowe, Harris 1923- *St&PR 91*
Rowe, Harrison Edward 1927- *WhoAm 90*
Rowe, Henry Theodore, Jr. 1932- *WhoSSW 91*
Rowe, Herbert Joseph 1924- *WhoAm 90*
Rowe, Jack 1857-1911 *Ballpl 90*
Rowe, Jack Field 1927- *St&PR 91*, *WhoAm 90*
Rowe, James Harrison, Jr. 1942- *WhoSSW 91*
Rowe, James N. *BioIn 16*
Rowe, James W. 1923- *WhoAm 90*, *WhoE 91*
Rowe, James Walter 1923- *St&PR 91*
Rowe, John Franklin 1814-1880 *AmLegL*
Rowe, John Howland 1918- *WhoAm 90*
Rowe, John J. 1951- *St&PR 91*
Rowe, John Westel 1924- *WhoAm 90*
Rowe, John William 1941- *St&PR 91*
Rowe, John William 1945- *WhoAm 90*, *WhoE 91*
Rowe, Jonathan *BioIn 16*
Rowe, Josiah Pollard 1928- *St&PR 91*
Rowe, Kenneth *BioIn 16*
Rowe, Kevin S. 1938- *WhoAm 90*
Rowe, Leo Stanton 1871-1946 *BioIn 16*
Rowe, Lisa Dawn 1966- *WhoAmW 91*
Rowe, Mae Irene 1927- *WhoAmW 91*
Rowe, Marieli Dorothy *WhoAmW 91*
Rowe, Mary Sue 1940- *WhoAmW 91*
Rowe, Max L. 1921- *WhoAm 90*
Rowe, Melanie *WhoWrEP 89*
Rowe, Michael George 1940- *St&PR 91*
Rowe, Myra 1927- *WhoWrEP 89*
Rowe, Nathaniel Hawthorne 1931- *WhoAm 90*
Rowe, Nellie Mae 1900-1982 *MusmAFA*
Rowe, Nick *BioIn 16*
Rowe, O Reagan, Jr. 1929- *St&PR 91*
Rowe, Peter Grimmond 1945- *WhoAm 90*
Rowe, Reginald M 1920- *WhoAmA 91*
Rowe, Richard Justin 1949- *WhoEmL 91*
Rowe, Richard Lloyd 1926- *WhoAm 90*
Rowe, Richard R. 1933- *WhoAm 90*
Rowe, Richard Roy 1933- *St&PR 91*
Rowe, Richard Wesley 1954- *WhoSSW 91*
Rowe, Rick *BioIn 16*
Rowe, Robert Gammell, III 1954- *WhoEmL 91*
Rowe, Robert Lester 1942- *WhoWor 91*
Rowe, Roger Vosburgh 1924- *St&PR 91*
Rowe, Ruth Wanda 1954- *WhoAmW 91*
Rowe, Sandra *BioIn 16*
Rowe, Sandra Mims 1948- *WhoAm 90*, *WhoAmW 91*
Rowe, Schoolboy 1910-1961 *Ballpl 90*
Rowe, Sheila Johnson 1959- *WhoSSW 91*
Rowe, Susan *BioIn 16*
Rowe, Terry Ann 1953- *WhoE 91*
Rowe, Thomas Dudley, Jr. 1942- *WhoAm 90*
Rowe, Timothy Julius 1958- *WhoSSW 91*
Rowe, Timothy Owen 1944- *BiDrAPA 89*
Rowe, Todd Anthony *BiDrAPA 89*
Rowe, Verald Keith 1914- *WhoAm 90*
Rowe, Viola Carson 1903-1969 *AuBYP 90*
Rowe, William 1942- *ConAu 131*
Rowe, William Davis 1937- *WhoAm 90*
Rowe, William John 1936- *WhoE 91*
Rowe, William Leonard 1931- *WhoAm 90*
Rowe, William Morford, Jr. 1937- *WhoWrEP 89*
Rowe, Winthrop A. 1845?-1919 *AmLegL*
Rowe-Ham, David 1935- *WhoWor 91*
Rowe-Maas, Betty Lu 1925- *WhoWor 91*
Rowecki, Stefan 1895-1944 *BioIn 16*
Rowekamp, Barry Lewis 1955- *WhoWor 91*
Rowell, Bama 1916- *Ballpl 90*
Rowell, Charles Frederick 1935- *WhoAm 90*
Rowell, Chester Harvey 1867-1948 *BioIn 16*
Rowell, David Benton 1939- *WhoE 91*
Rowell, Edward Morgan 1931- *WhoAm 90*, *WhoWor 91*
Rowell, Eve *BiDrAPA 89*
Rowell, Gayle L *BiDrAPA 89*
Rowell, Geoffrey 1943- *ConAu 129*
Rowell, George G. 1919- *St&PR 91*
Rowell, Harry B., Jr. 1941- *St&PR 91*
Rowell, Harry Brown, Jr. 1941- *WhoAm 90*
Rowell, James Keith 1959- *WhoSSW 91*
Rowell, Lester John, Jr. 1932- *St&PR 91*, *WhoAm 90*, *WhoE 91*
Rowell, Margit *WhoAmA 91*
Rowell, Melissa C. *St&PR 91*
Rowell, Pamela Sue 1960- *WhoE 91*
Rowell, Theodore H., Jr. 1932- *St&PR 91*
Rowen, Harold Charles 1931- *St&PR 91*, *WhoAm 90*
Rowen, Harvey Allen 1943- *WhoAm 90*
Rowen, Henry Stanislaus 1925 *WhoAm 90*
Rowen, Hobart 1918- *WhoAm 90*
Rowen, Kathlyn Lamper 1949- *BiDrAPA 89*
Rowen, Marshall *WhoAm 90*
Rowen, Meryl Gordon *BiDrAPA 89*
Rowen, Michael J. 1956- *St&PR 91*
Rowen, Rose Lee 1917- *WhoAmW 91*, *WhoE 91*
Rowen, Ruth Halle 1918- *WhoAm 90*, *WhoAmW 91*, *WhoE 91*, *WhoWor 91*
Rowena 1944- *BioIn 16*
Rowicki, Witold 1914-1989 *AnObit 1989*, *BioIn 16*, *PenDiMP*
Rowinski, Ludwig Joseph 1929- *WhoAm 90*
Rowitch, Jerome 1926- *BiDrAPA 89*
Rowjee, Zehra I *BiDrAPA 89*
Rowland, Albert Westley 1915- *WhoAm 90*
Rowland, Allen Ray 1944- *St&PR 91*
Rowland, Anne *WhoAmA 91*
Rowland, Arthur Ray 1930- *WhoAm 90*, *WhoSSW 91*
Rowland, Benjamin J R 1904-1972 *WhoAmA 91N*
Rowland, Christopher *PenDiMP*
Rowland, Christopher Selwyn 1946- *IntWWM 90*
Rowland, Christopher V, Jr. 1934- *BiDrAPA 89*
Rowland, David Jack 1921- *WhoSSW 91*
Rowland, Debran Maxinee 1963- *WhoAmW 91*
Rowland, Dermot F. 1937- *St&PR 91*
Rowland, Donald M. 1926- *St&PR 91*
Rowland, Elden Hart 1915-1982 *WhoAmA 91N*
Rowland, Esther Edelman 1926- *WhoAm 90*
Rowland, Florence 1900- *AuBYP 90*
Rowland, Frank Sherwood *BioIn 16*

Rowland, Frank Sherwood 1927- *WhoAm 90*
Rowland, Herbert L. 1925- *ODwPR 91*
Rowland, Herbert Leslie 1925- *WhoAm 90*
Rowland, Hugh *St&PR 91N*
Rowland, Ida 1904- *HarlReB*
Rowland, Ivan Wendell 1910- *WhoAm 90*
Rowland, James Richard 1940- *WhoAm 90*
Rowland, James Roy 1926- *WhoAm 90, WhoSSW 91*
Rowland, Jan Brownstein 1958- *WhoAmW 91*
Rowland, Jan Reagan 1944- *WhoSSW 91*
Rowland, Janet Miller 1961- *WhoAmW 91*
Rowland, Joan Charlotte 1930- *IntWWM 90*
Rowland, John G. 1957- *WhoAm 90, WhoE 91*
Rowland, Landon Hill 1937- *St&PR 91, WhoAm 90*
Rowland, Leslie Wiggins 1958- *WhoAmW 91*
Rowland, Lewis Phillip 1925- *WhoAm 90*
Rowland, Mike *NewAgMG*
Rowland, Pants 1879-1969 *Ballpl 90*
Rowland, Patricia Brittingham 1941- *WhoAmW 91*
Rowland, Ralph Thomas 1920- *WhoAm 90*
Rowland, Robert Joseph, Jr. 1938- *WhoE 91*
Rowland, Roland W. *BioIn 16*
Rowland, Ronald John 1936- *WhoWor 91*
Rowland, Sherry *BioIn 16*
Rowland, Suzanne Bushinsky 1961- *WhoE 91*
Rowland, Theodore Justin 1927- *WhoAm 90*
Rowland, Thomas W. 1948- *St&PR 91*
Rowland, Thomas William 1942- *St&PR 91*
Rowland, Thomas William 1948- *WhoAm 90*
Rowland, Timothy Norwood 1947- *BiDrAPA 89, WhoE 91*
Rowland, Tiny *BioIn 16*
Rowland, William Lachell 1946- *St&PR 91*
Rowland-Jones, Simon *PenDiMP*
Rowlands, David Thomas 1930- *WhoAm 90*
Rowlands, Gena *BioIn 16*
Rowlands, Gena 1934- *WorAlBi*
Rowlands, Gena 1936- *WhoAm 90, WhoAmW 91*
Rowlands, Martyn 1923- *ConDes 90*
Rowlands, Marvin Lloyd, Jr. 1926- *WhoAm 90*
Rowlands, Maxim John Paul 1958- *IntWWM 90*
Rowlands, T. Dewi 1939- *WhoAm 90*
Rowlandson, Mary *BiDEWW*
Rowlandson, Mary 1635?-1677? *FemiCLE*
Rowlandson, Mary 1635?-1678? *WhNaAH*
Rowlandson, Mary White 1635?-1682? *EncCRAm*
Rowlandson, Thomas 1756-1827 *IntDcAA 90*
Rowlenson, Richard C. 1949- *St&PR 91*
Rowles, Charles A. 1915- *WhoAm 90*
Rowles, John Mark 1949- *BiDrAPA 89*
Rowles, Peter Alexander 1954- *St&PR 91*
Rowles, Russana Louise 1956- *WhoEmL 91*
Rowlett, Bobby N. 1952- *St&PR 91*
Rowlett, Dale K. 1955- *St&PR 91*
Rowlett, David B *BiDrAPA 89*
Rowlett, David Branch, III 1946- *BiDrAPA 89*
Rowlett, Ralph Morgan 1934- *WhoAm 90*
Rowlett, Randall R. *BiDrAPA 89*
Rowlette, Roger Lee 1952- *WhoEmL 91*
Rowlette, Ronna 1942- *WhoAmW 91*
Rowley, Ames Dorrance *MajTwCW*
Rowley, Beverley Davies 1941- *WhoAm 90*
Rowley, Carol S. 1943- *WhoAmW 91*
Rowley, Charles G. 1936- *St&PR 91*
Rowley, Charles Kershaw 1939- *WhoSSW 91*
Rowley, Craig M. 1925- *St&PR 91*
Rowley, Deborah Ann 1950- *WhoEmL 91*
Rowley, F Lawrence *BiDrAPA 89*
Rowley, Frank Selby, Jr. 1913- *WhoSSW 91*
Rowley, H. L. 1945- *St&PR 91*
Rowley, James Walton 1925- *WhoAm 90*
Rowley, Janet Davison 1925- *WhoAm 90, WhoAmW 91*
Rowley, Jill DeOn 1955- *IntWWM 90*
Rowley, John F. *WhoAm 90*
Rowley, John Vail 1932- *WhoE 91*
Rowley, L. Dale 1939- *St&PR 91*
Rowley, Michael Fitzgerald 1949- *St&PR 91*
Rowley, Michele Betrice 1952- *BiDrAPA 89*
Rowley, Peter Templeton 1929- *WhoAm 90*
Rowley, R. Casey 1932- *St&PR 91*
Rowley, Rae Carol 1924- *WhoAmW 91*
Rowley, Susan Peet 1947- *BiDrAPA 89*
Rowley, Trevor 1942- *ConAu 131*
Rowley, William 1585?-1642? *BioIn 16*
Rowley, William Robert 1943- *WhoAm 90*
Rowlings, Donald George 1929- *WhoAm 90*
Rowlingson, John Clyde 1948- *WhoAm 90, WhoSSW 91*
Rowlinson, John Shipley 1926- *WhoWor 91*
Rownak, John Joseph, Jr. 1946- *St&PR 91*
Rowney, John A. 1945- *St&PR 91*
Rowney, John Adalbert 1945- *WhoE 91*
Rowntree, Ellen B 1941- *BiDrAPA 89*
Roworth, Christine 1948- *WhoWor 91*
Rowse, A. L. 1903- *BioIn 16*
Rowse, Alfred Leslie 1903- *BioIn 16, WhoWor 91*
Rowse, Joyann 1944- *WhoSSW 91*
Rowson, Richard Cavanagh 1926- *WhoAm 90*
Rowson, Susanna 1762-1824 *FemiCLE*
Rowson, Susanna H. 1762?-1824 *BioAmW*
Rowson, Susanna Haswell 1762-1824 *BioIn 16, NotWoAT*
Rowswell, Rosey *Ballpl 90*
Rowton, Eugene E. 1931- *St&PR 91*
Rowzie, Kathi *WhoE 91*
Roxborough, Elsie *EarBlAP*
Roxburgh, Stuart Thomas Dalrymple 1950- *WhoWor 91*
Roxbury, Theodore Joseph 1933- *WhoWor 91*
Roxe, Joseph D. 1936- *St&PR 91*
Roxy Music *EncPR&S 89, OxCPMus*
Roy, Allan George 1937- *St&PR 91*
Roy, Asim 1948- *WhoWor 91*
Roy, Bruno 1941- *BiDrAPA 89*
Roy, Camille 1870-1943 *DcLB 92 [port]*
Roy, Catherine Elizabeth 1948- *WhoAmW 91, WhoEmL 91, WhoWor 91*
Roy, Charles Robert 1930- *St&PR 91, WhoAm 90*
Roy, Chunilal 1935- *WhoAm 90, WhoWor 91*
Roy, Clarence Leslie 1927- *WhoAm 90*
Roy, Claude 1915- *BioIn 16*
Roy, David Tod 1933- *WhoAm 90, WhoWor 91*
Roy, Della Martin 1926- *WhoAm 90, WhoAmW 91*
Roy, Dev Kumar 1951- *WhoSSW 91*
Roy, Donald Edward 1929- *WhoAm 90*
Roy, Elsijane Trimble 1916- *WhoAm 90, WhoAmW 91, WhoSSW 91*
Roy, Gabrielle 1909-1983 *FemiCLE, MajTwCW*
Roy, Gary Paul 1948- *WhoSSW 91*
Roy, Gaston Eugene *BiDrAPA 89*
Roy, Gordon J. 1949- *St&PR 91*
Roy, Harold Edward 1921- *WhoWor 91*
Roy, Harry 1900-1971 *OxCPMus*
Roy, Helen Antoinette 1933- *St&PR 91*
Roy, Henri A. 1947- *WhoAm 90*
Roy, James DeWall 1940- *St&PR 91*
Roy, James Stapleton 1935- *WhoAm 90*
Roy, Jean-Yves *BiDrAPA 89*
Roy, Jean Zellers 1930- *WhoAmW 91*
Roy, Jeffrey 1955- *St&PR 91*
Roy, Jessie Hailstalk 1895-1986 *BioIn 16*
Roy, John L. 1929- *St&PR 91*
Roy, John Reid *BiDrAPA 89*
Roy, Joseph R. 1943- *ODwPR 91*
Roy, Jules 1907- *BioIn 16*
Roy, Kathleen Anne 1964- *WhoAmW 91*
Roy, Klaus George 1924- *IntWWM 90*
Roy, Kuldip Kumar 1935- *WhoWor 91*
Roy, Louise *BioIn 16*
Roy, M. N. 1893-1954 *BioIn 16*
Roy, Manabendra Nath 1893-1954 *BioIn 16*
Roy, Marc-Andre *BiDrAPA 89*
Roy, Matt *BioIn 16*
Roy, Michael *BiDrAPA 89*
Roy, Norman E. 1926- *WhoAm 90*
Roy, Norman Ernest 1926- *St&PR 91*
Roy, P. Norman 1934- *St&PR 91, WhoAm 90*
Roy, Panna *BiDrAPA 89*
Roy, Patricia Jane 1956- *WhoAmW 91*
Roy, Patrick 1965- *WorAlBi*
Roy, Paul Henri 1924- *WhoAm 90*
Roy, Philip Franklin 1921- *St&PR 91*
Roy, Pradeep K. 1953- *BiDrAPA 89*
Roy, Radha Raman 1921- *WhoAm 90*
Roy, Ram Mohun 1772?-1833 *BioIn 16*
Roy, Ramashray 1927- *WhoWor 91*
Roy, Raymond Serge 1942- *WhoAm 90*
Roy, Real O. 1938- *St&PR 91*
Roy, Rene Ronald 1943- *BiDrAPA 89*
Roy, Reuben S, Jr. 1933- *BiDrAPA 89*
Roy, Richard 1955- *St&PR 91*
Roy, Robert Douglas 1956- *BiDrAPA 89*
Roy, Ronald Dwayne 1956- *WhoE 91*
Roy, Rose Mary 1949- *WhoEmL 91*
Roy, Rustum 1924- *WhoAm 90*
Roy, Samar N. 1949- *WhoE 91*
Roy, Samir *BiDrAPA 89*
Roy, Sanat Kumar *BiDrAPA 89*
Roy, Will 1937- *IntWWM 90*
Roy, William 1911-1977 *EncO&P 3*
Roy, William Robert 1926- *WhoAm 90*
Roy-Byrne, Peter Paul 1951- *BiDrAPA 89*
Royal, Billy W 1927- *BiDrAPA 89*
Royal, Darrell K. 1924- *WhoAm 90*
Royal, Janice Marie 1964- *WhoAmW 91*
Royal, Jennifer *BioIn 16*
Royal, Orren L 1926- *BiDrAPA 89*
Royal, Richard P *WhoAmA 91*
Royal, Wilbert Lawrence 1948- *WhoE 91*
Royal, William Henry 1924- *WhoWor 91*
Royale, A. *ConAu 130*
Royall, Anne 1769-1854 *FemiCLE*
Royall, Anne Newport 1769-1854 *BioAmW, BioIn 16*
Royall, George P., Jr. 1937- *ODwPR 91*
Royall, Kenneth Claiborne 1894- *BiDrUSE 89*
Royall, Robert Venning, Jr. 1934- *St&PR 91, WhoAm 90*
Royals, Charlie *BioIn 16*
Royalty, Arlen Ray 1959- *WhoSSW 91*
Royalty, Robert Malcolm 1933- *WhoAm 90*
Roybal, Edward R. 1916- *BioIn 16, WhoAm 90, WhoHisp 91*
Roybal-Allard, Lucille 1941- *WhoHisp 91*
Royce, Barbara *ODwPR 91*
Royce, Barrie Saunders Hart 1933- *WhoAm 90*
Royce, Frederick H. 1863-1933 *WorAlBi*
Royce, Henry 1863-1933 *BioIn 16*
Royce, Joseph *BioIn 16*
Royce, Josiah 1855-1916 *BioIn 16, EncO&P 3, EncPaPR 91, WorAlBi, WrPh P*
Royce, Kenneth 1920- *SpyFic, TwCCr&M 91*
Royce, Paul C. 1928- *WhoAm 90*
Royce, Rachel *BioIn 16*
Royce, Raymond Watson 1936- *WhoAm 90*
Royce, Robert Alan 1949- *WhoE 91*
Royce, Robert Coolidge 1930- *St&PR 91*
Royce, Robert Farnham 1931- *WhoSSW 91*
Royce, Sarah 1819-1891 *FemiCLE*
Royce, Toni *BioIn 16*
Roychoudhuri, Chandrasekhar 1942- *WhoE 91, WhoSSW 91, WhoWor 91*
Roycroft, David J. 1946- *ODwPR 91*
Roycroft, Elizabeth Anne 1960- *WhoSSW 91*
Roycroft, Howard Francis 1930- *WhoAm 90*
Roycroft, Richard Wallace 1963- *WhoSSW 91*
Royde-Smith, Naomi 1875-1964 *FemiCLE*
Royden, Agnes Maude 1876-1956 *BioIn 16*
Royden, Halsey Lawrence 1928- *WhoAm 90*
Royden, Maude 1876-1956 *FemiCLE*
Royds, Caroline 1953- *BioIn 16*
Royds, Robert Bruce 1944- *WhoE 91*
Roye, Nancy L. 1923- *St&PR 91*
Roye, Paladine H. *BioIn 16*
Roye, Sherry Renee 1960- *WhoAmW 91, WhoSSW 91*
Royer, Charles Theodore 1939- *WhoAm 90*
Royer, Clemence Augustine Audouard 1830-1902 *EncCoWW*
Royer, David Lee 1950- *St&PR 91*
Royer, Donald E. 1949- *WhoAm 90*
Royer, Henry 1931- *St&PR 91, WhoAm 90*
Royer, Jean-Francois 1921- *BiDFrPL*
Royer, Kathleen Rose 1949- *WhoAmW 91*
Royer, Kenneth W. 1928- *St&PR 91*
Royer, Mona Lee 1944- *WhoAmA 91*
Royer, Robert Lewis 1928- *St&PR 91, WhoAm 90, WhoSSW 91*
Royer, Ronald *BioIn 16*
Royer, Thomas Jerry 1943- *WhoWor 91*
Royko, Mike 1932- *WhoAm 90, WhoWrEP 89, WorAlBi*
Royko, Raymond Thomas 1946- *St&PR 91*
Roylance, Lynn Michelle 1951- *WhoAmW 91*
Roylance, Peter James 1928- *WhoE 91*
Roylance, Richard G. 1915- *St&PR 91*
Roylance, William M. 1865-1925 *AmLegL*
Royle, Max *BioIn 16*
Royle, Trevor 1945- *ConAu 31NR*
Royola, Samuel Aranas 1915- *BiDrAPA 89*
Roys, David Shannon 1939- *BiDrAPA 89*
Royse, Charles David 1954- *St&PR 91*
Roysher, Hudson 1911- *WhoAmA 91*
Royster, Constance Laurel 1949- *WhoAmW 91*
Royster, David Calvin 1952- *WhoSSW 91*
Royster, Jerry 1952- *Ballpl 90*
Royster, Vermont *BioIn 16*
Royster, Vermont 1914- *WhoAm 90*
Royston, Christopher Michael 1950- *WhoEmL 91*
Royston, Richard John 1931- *WhoAm 90*
Rozakis, Gregory *BioIn 16*
Rozakis, Gregory 1943?-1989 *ConAu 129*
Rozakis, Robert H. 1951- *WhoWrEP 89*
Rozan, Gerald H *BiDrAPA 89*
Rozanczyk, Gary A. 1952- *St&PR 91*
Rozanova, Olga Vladimirovna 1886-1918 *BiDWomA*
Rozanski, Cynthia Leann 1965- *WhoAmW 91*
Rozanski, Edward Casimir 1915- *WhoWor 91*
Rozanski, Jules 1912- *BiDrAPA 89*
Rozansky, Gerald I *BiDrAPA 89*
Rozario, Patricia *IntWWM 90*
Rozas, Carlos Luis 1944- *WhoHisp 91*
Roze, Marie 1846-1926 *PenDiMP*
Rozeboom, Lora Lyn 1956- *WhoAmW 91*
Rozel, Samuel Joseph 1935- *St&PR 91, WhoAm 90*
Rozell, Herbert 1931- *WhoSSW 91*
Rozell, Joseph Gerard 1959- *WhoEmL 91, WhoWor 91*
Rozelle, Alvin 1926- *WorAlBi*
Rozelle, Donna C. *ODwPR 91*
Rozelle, Lee Theodore 1933- *WhoAm 90, WhoWor 91*
Rozelle, Pete 1926- *WhoAm 90*
Rozema, Dave 1956- *Ballpl 90*
Rozen, Jerome George, Jr. 1928- *WhoAm 90*
Rozenbaum, Najman 1945- *WhoWor 91*
Rozenblum, Maurice J. 1935- *St&PR 91*
Rozenblum, Raquel L. *St&PR 91*
Rozendal, Sylvus 1928- *BioIn 16*
Rozendale, David S. 1934- *WhoAm 90*
Rozendale, David Swan 1935- *St&PR 91*
Rozental, Alberto *BiDrAPA 89*
Rozett, Oscar *BiDrAPA 89*
Rozett, Walter P. 1923- *St&PR 91*
Rozett, Walter Philip 1923- *WhoAm 90*
Rozewicz, Tadeusz 1921- *MajTwCW*
Rozhdestvensky, Gennadi 1931- *PenDiMP*
Rozhdestvensky, Gennadi Nikolaevich 1931- *WhoWor 91*
Rozhdestvensky, Gennady Nikolayevich 1931- *IntWWM 90*
Rozhdestvensky, Robert Ivanovich 1932- *WhoWor 91*
Rozich, Ileene Shaffer 1932- *WhoWor 91*
Rozier, Robert L *WhoAmA 91*
Rozina *EncCoWW*
Rozman, Gilbert Friedell 1943- *WhoAm 90*
Rozman, Joseph John 1944- *WhoAmA 91*
Rozman, Sheryl Ann 1956- *WhoAmW 91*
Rozo-Sanmiguel, Alvaro 1924- *BiDrAPA 89*
Rozran, Jack Louis 1939- *WhoWor 91*
Rozsa, Elizabeth 1907- *BiDrAPA 89*
Rozsa, Laszlo 1943- *IntWWM 90*
Rozsa, Miklos 1907- *BioIn 16, ConTFT 8, IntWWM 90, OxCPMus, PenDiMP A*
Rozsa, Nick *BioIn 16*
Rozsnyai, Zoltan *NewYTBS 90*
Rozsnyai, Zoltan Frank 1927- *WhoAm 90*
Rozycki, William Eugene 1940- *St&PR 91*
Rozzell, George McAllaster 1926- *WhoSSW 91*
Rozzi 1921- *WhoAmA 91*
Rozzi, Santa Caputo 1950- *WhoAmW 91*
Rozzini, Paul Joseph 1940- *St&PR 91*
Ru, Ju-Chieh 1935- *St&PR 91*
Ru Dusky, Basil Michael 1933- *WhoAm 90*
Rua, Milton Francisco 1919- *WhoSSW 91, WhoWor 91*
Ruaix, Antonia Eulalia *BiDrAPA 89*
Ruan, John, III 1943- *St&PR 91*
Ruane, James Joseph 1949- *WhoEmL 91*
Ruane, John Patrick, Jr. 1939- *St&PR 91*
Ruano, Jose *WhoHisp 91*
Ruark, Donna McLeod 1958- *WhoAmW 91*
Ruark, Gibbons 1941- *ConAu 31NR, WhoWrEP 89*
Ruark, John Edward 1951- *BiDrAPA 89*
Ruark-Hearst, Margo Lynn 1956- *WhoAmW 91*
Rub, Louis John 1915- *WhoAm 90*
Rubach, Peggy 1947- *WhoAmW 91*
Ruban, Gerhard 1926- *WhoWor 91*
Rubano, Gregory Lynn 1949- *WhoE 91*
Rubash, Karen A 1958- *BiDrAPA 89*
Rubash, Norman Joseph 1932- *St&PR 91, WhoAm 90*
Rubashkin, Boris 1945- *BiDrAPA 89*
Rubati, Pasquale *PenDiDA 89*
Rubatscher, Maria Veronika 1900- *EncCoWW*
Rubayi, Salah 1942- *WhoWor 91*
Rubb, Peggy-Grace Plourd 1931- *WhoAmW 91, WhoE 91, WhoWor 91*
Rubbia, Carlo 1934- *WhoAm 90, WhoWor 91, WorAlBi*
Rubbra, Edmund 1901-1986 *PenDiMP A*
Rube, David Mendil 1960- *BiDrAPA 89*

Rube, Pierre A BiDrAPA 89
Rubeck, Mark 1951- WhoEmL 91
Rubel, Arthur 1940- WhoE 91
Rubel, Arthur Joseph 1924- WhoAm 90
Rubel, C Adrian 1904-1978 WhoAmA 91N
Rubel, David Michael 1917- WhoAm 90
Rubel, Martin 1934- BiDrAPA 89
Rubel, Matthew Evan 1957- WhoE 91
Rubeli, Paul E. 1943- WhoAm 90
Rubell, Steve BioIn 16
Rubell, Steve 1944-1989 AnObit 1989
Rubello, David Jerome 1935- WhoAmA 91
Ruben, Abe Gwynne 1933- WhoSSW 91
Ruben, Alan Miles 1931- WhoAm 90
Ruben, Albert 1918- WhoAmA 91
Ruben, Ann Moliver 1925- WhoSSW 91, WhoWrEP 89
Ruben, Brent David 1944- WhoAm 90
Ruben, David Alan 1947- BiDrAPA 89
Ruben, Gary A. 1924- WhoAm 90
Ruben, Harvey L 1941- BiDrAPA 89, WhoE 91
Ruben, Irwin 1946- BiDrAPA 89
Ruben, Lawrence 1926- St&PR 91, WhoAm 90, WhoWor 91
Ruben, Leonard 1921- WhoAm 90
Ruben, Marilyn BioIn 16
Ruben, Regina Lansing 1950- WhoAmW 91
Ruben, Richards 1925- WhoAmA 91
Ruben, Robert J. 1923- St&PR 91
Ruben, Robert Joseph 1923- WhoAm 90
Ruben, Samuel 1900-1988 BioIn 16
Ruben, William Samuel 1927- St&PR 91, WhoAm 90
Rubenchik, Aleksander Markovich 1947- WhoWor 91
Rubendall, Charles Wesley, II 1950- WhoEmL 91
Rubendall, Donald 1913- St&PR 91
Rubendall, Howard L. 1910- BioIn 16
Rubenfaer, Leon Marc BiDrAPA 89
Rubenfeld, Joseph 1927- St&PR 91
Rubenfeld, Louis Allen 1941- St&PR 91
Rubenfeld, Michael 1948- St&PR 91
Rubenfeld, Stanley Irwin 1930- WhoAm 90
Rubenis, Nellija BiDrAPA 89
Rubenovitz, Herman Harry 1883-1966 BioIn 16
Rubenow, Jon Carl BiDrAPA 89
Rubenowitz, Sigvard 1925- WhoWor 91
Rubens, Bernice BioIn 16
Rubens, Bernice 1923- ConAu 33NR, MajTwCW
Rubens, Bernice 1928- FemiCLE, WorAu 1980 [port]
Rubens, Charles, II 1930- WhoAm 90
Rubens, Harley Glenn 1946- BiDrAPA 89
Rubens, Leonard PenDiMP
Rubens, Lori Van 1954- BiDrAPA 89
Rubens, Paul A. 1875-1917 OxCPMus
Rubens, Peter Paul 1577-1640 IntDcAA 90, WorAlBi
Rubens, Robert David 1943- WhoWor 91
Rubens, Sidney Michel 1910- WhoAm 90
Rubenson, James R. 1937- St&PR 91
Rubenson, Lynn Beth 1952- WhoE 91
Rubenstein, Alan 1955- WhoSSW 91
Rubenstein, Albert Harold 1923- WhoAm 90
Rubenstein, Ann BioIn 16
Rubenstein, Arthur Harold 1937- WhoAm 90
Rubenstein, Barry J. 1950- St&PR 91
Rubenstein, Bernard 1937- IntWWM 90, WhoAm 90, WhoSSW 91
Rubenstein, Bruce Edward BiDrAPA 89
Rubenstein, David Aaron 1954- WhoEmL 91
Rubenstein, Edith Barbi 1953- BiDrAPA 89
Rubenstein, Edward 1924- WhoAm 90
Rubenstein, Elaine J. 1949- WhoWrEP 89
Rubenstein, Eleanor Tessler 1922- WhoE 91
Rubenstein, Elyse Shari 1957- BiDrAPA 89, WhoE 91
Rubenstein, Farrell 1930- WhoAm 90
Rubenstein, Harry BiDrAPA 89
Rubenstein, Howard J. 1932- ODwPR 91
Rubenstein, Howard Joseph 1932- WhoAm 90
Rubenstein, Howard Martin 1946- BiDrAPA 89
Rubenstein, Hy David 1956- WhoEmL 91
Rubenstein, Jack BioIn 16
Rubenstein, Jerome Max 1927- WhoAm 90
Rubenstein, Joshua Seth 1954- WhoEmL 91
Rubenstein, Lee Aaron 1956- WhoE 91
Rubenstein, Leonard Mark 1946- St&PR 91
Rubenstein, Lewis W. 1908- WhoAm 90, WhoAmA 91
Rubenstein, M. D. 1924- St&PR 91
Rubenstein, Marc A 1935- BiDrAPA 89
Rubenstein, Margo Ann 1955- WhoAmW 91
Rubenstein, Melvin 1921- BiDrAPA 89
Rubenstein, Meridel 1948- WhoAmA 91
Rubenstein, Nancy Beth 1947- BiDrAPA 89
Rubenstein, Nancy Lee WhoAmW 91
Rubenstein, Ralph BiDrAPA 89
Rubenstein, Richard 1946- St&PR 91
Rubenstein, Richard E 1938- ConAu 32NR
Rubenstein, Richard Lowell 1924- WhoAm 90
Rubenstein, Robert 1926- BiDrAPA 89
Rubenstein, Robert Joel BiDrAPA 89
Rubenstein, Sharon Lynn 1945- WhoWrEP 89
Rubenstein, Stanley E. 1930- ODwPR 91
Rubenstein, Stanley Ellis 1930- WhoAm 90
Rubenstein, Steven B. 1959- St&PR 91
Rubenstein, Steven Paul 1951- WhoAm 90
Rubenstein, Thomas Walter 1955- WhoEmL 91
Ruberman, Louise BiDrAPA 89
Rubert, Shirley Laney 1927- BiDrAPA 89
Rubertone, Donna J. 1958- St&PR 91
Rubes, Susan 1925- OxCCanT
Rubey, Steven Allen 1941- BiDrAPA 89
Rubey, Tony 1952- WhoAmA 91
Rubi, Marques de EncCRAm
Rubiano, Tannia BioIn 16
Rubicam, Harry Cogswell 1902- AuBYP 90
Rubicam, Raymond 1892-1978 WorAlBi
Rubicam, Shannon BioIn 16
Rubidge, Frederick Preston 1806-1897 DcCanB 12
Rubidoux WhoAmA 91
Rubien, Judith Ann 1956- St&PR 91
Rubies, Antonio Planells 1943- WhoWor 91
Rubin, A Lawrence BiDrAPA 89
Rubin, Alan A. 1926- WhoAm 90
Rubin, Alan J. 1926- St&PR 91
Rubin, Alan J. 1934- WhoAm 90
Rubin, Alfred Peter 1931- WhoE 91
Rubin, Aliza Sass BioIn 16
Rubin, Alvin Benjamin 1920- WhoAm 90, WhoSSW 91
Rubin, Arline Barbara 1942- WhoAmW 91
Rubin, Arnold 1937-1988 BioIn 16
Rubin, Arnold Gary 1937-1988 WhoAmA 91N
Rubin, Arnold Jesse 1924- WhoAm 90
Rubin, Arthur Herman 1927- WhoE 91, WhoWor 91
Rubin, B. Norman 1917- St&PR 91
Rubin, Barbara Jean 1945- WhoAmW 91
Rubin, Barry 1950- ConAu 32NR
Rubin, Barry Alan 1945- WhoE 91
Rubin, Barry C. 1950- WhoSSW 91
Rubin, Barry Mitchel 1950- WhoAm 90
Rubin, Benjamin H. 1962- St&PR 91
Rubin, Bernard 1926- BiDrAPA 89
Rubin, Blake Douglas 1955- WhoEmL 91
Rubin, Bruce S. 1947- ODwPR 91
Rubin, Carl Bernard 1920- WhoAm 90
Rubin, Cathy Ann 1948- WhoAmW 91
Rubin, Charles Elliott 1947- WhoAm 90
Rubin, Cheryl ODwPR 91
Rubin, Daniel John 1949- St&PR 91
Rubin, David Lee 1939- ConAu 33NR, WhoSSW 91
Rubin, David Lee 1943- WhoAm 90
Rubin, David M. 1945- WhoWrEP 89
Rubin, David Robert 1933- WhoAm 90
Rubin, David S 1949- WhoAmA 91
Rubin, David Samuel 1952- WhoEmL 91
Rubin, David Stephen 1944- WhoSSW 91
Rubin, Debra Jill 1958- WhoAmW 91
Rubin, Diana Kwiatkowski 1958- WhoWrEP 89
Rubin, Diane Marie 1951- WhoAmW 91
Rubin, Donald S. 1934- St&PR 91
Rubin, Donald Vincent 1937- WhoAmA 91
Rubin, Edward 1912- WhoAm 90
Rubin, Edward P, Jr. 1931- BiDrAPA 89
Rubin, Edward Stephen 1941- WhoAm 90
Rubin, Edwin Manning 1927- WhoAm 90
Rubin, Emanuel BiDrAPA 89
Rubin, Emanuel 1928- WhoAm 90
Rubin, Emily ODwPR 91
Rubin, Eric 1955- St&PR 91
Rubin, Eugene BiDrAPA 89
Rubin, Eugene Harold 1949- BiDrAPA 89
Rubin, Frederick Alan 1933- WhoE 91
Rubin, George F. 1943- St&PR 91
Rubin, Gerald Mayer 1950- WhoAm 90
Rubin, Gerrold Robert 1940- WhoAm 90
Rubin, Gustav 1913- WhoAm 90
Rubin, Hal Ira BiDrAPA 89
Rubin, Harold Richard 1927- St&PR 91
Rubin, Harris B. 1932- WhoAm 90
Rubin, Harry 1926- WhoAm 90
Rubin, Harry M. 1952- St&PR 91
Rubin, Harry Meyer 1952- WhoAm 90
Rubin, Henri WhoAm 90
Rubin, Henry Park 1943- IntWWM 90, WhoSSW 91
Rubin, Herbert E 1908- BiDrAPA 89
Rubin, Hy 1905-1960 WhoAmA 91N
Rubin, Ida Ely WhoAmA 91
Rubin, Irvin I. 1919- WhoE 91
Rubin, Irving 1911- St&PR 91
Rubin, Irving 1916- WhoAm 90, WhoWor 91
Rubin, Irwin 1930- WhoAmA 91, WhoE 91
Rubin, Izhak 1942- WhoAm 90
Rubin, J Barry 1939- BiDrAPA 89
Rubin, Jacob Carl 1926- WhoAm 90, WhoE 91
Rubin, Jane Lockhart Gregory 1944- WhoE 91
Rubin, Jason ODwPR 91
Rubin, Jay NewYTBS 90
Rubin, Jean Estelle 1926- WhoAm 90
Rubin, Jeffrey 1947- BiDrAPA 89
Rubin, Jeffrey Seth 1943- St&PR 91
Rubin, Jeffrey Zachary 1941- WhoAm 90, WhoE 91
Rubin, Jenae Carol 1958- WhoSSW 91
Rubin, Jennifer BioIn 16
Rubin, Jerome Sanford 1925- St&PR 91, WhoAm 90, WhoWor 91
Rubin, Jerry BioIn 16
Rubin, Jesse 1932- BiDrAPA 89
Rubin, Joan 1932- WhoE 91
Rubin, Joel 1926- St&PR 91
Rubin, Joel Edward 1928- WhoE 91
Rubin, Joseph Ezra V 1947- BiDrAPA 89
Rubin, Joseph Ezra Victor 1947- WhoE 91
Rubin, Joseph H. 1942- St&PR 91
Rubin, Julius 1909- BiDrAPA 89
Rubin, Karen Beth 1951- WhoAmW 91
Rubin, Kenneth 1922- BiDrAPA 89
Rubin, Kenneth Allen 1947- WhoEmL 91
Rubin, Kenneth Jay 1948- BiDrAPA 89
Rubin, Larry Bruce 1958- WhoEmL 91, WhoWor 91
Rubin, Larry Jerome 1930- WhoWrEP 89
Rubin, Laurie BioIn 16
Rubin, Laurie 1956- BioIn 16
Rubin, Lawrence 1933- St&PR 91, WhoAmA 91
Rubin, Lawrence Edward 1933- WhoAm 90
Rubin, Lawrence Gilbert 1925- WhoAm 90, WhoWor 91
Rubin, Lawrence Ira 1945- WhoEmL 91
Rubin, Leah Plonchak 1957- WhoWor 91
Rubin, Lee Anthony 1951- WhoAm 90
Rubin, Leonard Jay 1939- BiDrAPA 89
Rubin, Lore R 1928- BiDrAPA 89
Rubin, Louis Decimus, Jr. 1923- WhoAm 90, WhoWrEP 89
Rubin, Lowell Jay BiDrAPA 89
Rubin, Mahlon 1924- St&PR 91
Rubin, Marcel 1905- IntWWM 90
Rubin, Mark Evan 1947- St&PR 91
Rubin, Mark Stephen 1946- WhoSSW 91
Rubin, Martin N. 1928- WhoWor 91
Rubin, Martin Neil BiDrAPA 89
Rubin, Matonah A BiDrAPA 89
Rubin, Melvin Lynne 1932- WhoAm 90
Rubin, Meyer I. 1918- St&PR 91
Rubin, Michael 1946- St&PR 91
Rubin, Michael D. 1944- ODwPR 91
Rubin, Michael Greg 1953- WhoE 91
Rubin, Michele Barrie 1944- WhoE 91
Rubin, Mitchell Frederick 1960- WhoE 91
Rubin, Nancy 1944- ConAu 129
Rubin, Nancy Ruth Zimman 1944- WhoAmW 91, WhoE 91
Rubin, Norman Julius 1923- WhoE 91
Rubin, Norman L BiDrAPA 89
Rubin, Paul Harold 1942- WhoE 91
Rubin, Paulette Maisus BiDrAPA 89
Rubin, Peggy Miller 1953- St&PR 91
Rubin, Philip 1927- WhoAm 90
Rubin, Phillip Herbert 1925- WhoE 91
Rubin, Richard 1952- WhoE 91
Rubin, Richard Allan 1942- WhoAm 90
Rubin, Richard B BiDrAPA 89
Rubin, Richard I. 1903- St&PR 91
Rubin, Richard Lee 1946- WhoSSW 91
Rubin, Richard Lewis 1946- BiDrAPA 89
Rubin, Richard Lloyd 1945- BiDrAPA 89
Rubin, Robert AuBYP 90
Rubin, Robert E. 1938- St&PR 91
Rubin, Robert Edward 1938- WhoAm 90
Rubin, Robert Irving 1922- St&PR 91
Rubin, Robert Joseph 1946- WhoAm 90
Rubin, Robert Melvin 1925- St&PR 91
Rubin, Robert S. 1931- St&PR 91
Rubin, Robert Samuel 1931- WhoAm 90
Rubin, Robert T 1936- BiDrAPA 89
Rubin, Ron BioIn 16
Rubin, Ronald Glen 1955- BiDrAPA 89
Rubin, Rose Mohr 1939- WhoSSW 91
Rubin, Samuel 1901-1978 WhoAmA 91N
Rubin, Samuel E BiDrAPA 89
Rubin, Samuel Harold 1916- WhoAm 90
Rubin, Sandra WhoAmA 91
Rubin, Seymour Jeffrey 1914- WhoAm 90, WhoE 91
Rubin, Sheldon 1938- St&PR 91
Rubin, Stanley B. 1928- St&PR 91
Rubin, Stanley Creamer 1917- WhoAm 90
Rubin, Stanley Gerald 1938- WhoAm 90
Rubin, Stephen Edward 1941- WhoAm 90
Rubin, Steven 1947- St&PR 91
Rubin, Steven Edward BiDrAPA 89
Rubin, Steven Ellis 1953- WhoE 91
Rubin, Stuart A. 1958- St&PR 91
Rubin, Theodore I 1923- BiDrAPA 89
Rubin, Theodore Isaac 1923- WhoAm 90
Rubin, Thomas A. 1947- St&PR 91
Rubin, Tillie Eva 1919- WhoAmW 91
Rubin, Vera Cooper 1928- WhoAm 90, WhoAmW 91
Rubin, William 1927- WhoAm 90, WhoAmA 91
Rubin, William David 1953- WhoSSW 91
Rubin, William Stanley BioIn 16
Rubin, Wladyslaw 1917- WhoWor 91
Rubin, Zick 1944- WhoAm 90
Rubine, Arthur BioIn 16
Rubiner, Walter J. 1930- St&PR 91
Rubinfeld, Abraham Norman 1952- St&PR 91
Rubinfeld, Daniel Lee 1945- WhoAm 90
Rubinfien, David 1921- St&PR 91
Rubinfien, Leo H 1953- WhoAmA 91
Rubinger, Joshua H BiDrAPA 89
Rubinger, Robert S. 1942- St&PR 91
Rubington, Norman 1921- WhoAmA 91
Rubini, Eileen 1948- WhoAmW 91
Rubini, Giovanni Battista 1794-1854 PenDiMP
Rubini, Michel NewAgMG
Rubini, Nancy Beth 1956- St&PR 91
Rubini, Roberto 1930- St&PR 91
Rubino, Anthony August 1931- St&PR 91
Rubino, Frank 1919- St&PR 91
Rubino, Joe BioIn 16
Rubino, Kathy 1959- WhoAmW 91
Rubino, Mary Ann 1965- WhoAmW 91
Rubino, Richard Gregory 1926- St&PR 91
Rubino, Robert Carl 1935- St&PR 91
Rubinoff, Ira 1938- WhoAm 90, WhoWor 91
Rubinovitz, Samuel 1929- St&PR 91, WhoAm 90
Rubinow, David Russell 1949- BiDrAPA 89
Rubinow, Leo BiDrAPA 89
Rubins, David Kresz 1902-1985 WhoAmA 91N
Rubinson, Laurna 1945- WhoEmL 91
Rubinstein, Alina A 1945- BiDrAPA 89
Rubinstein, Alvin Zachary 1927- WhoAm 90
Rubinstein, Anton 1829-1894 BioIn 16, PenDiMP, WorAlBi
Rubinstein, Anton Grigoryevich 1829-1894 EncPaPR 91
Rubinstein, Arthur 1887-1982 PenDiMP, WorAlBi
Rubinstein, Artur 1887-1982 BioIn 16
Rubinstein, Benjamin B BiDrAPA 89
Rubinstein, Benjamin B. BioIn 16
Rubinstein, Boris 1946- BiDrAPA 89
Rubinstein, Charlotte Streifer 1921- WhoAmA 91
Rubinstein, David 1927- BiDrAPA 89
Rubinstein, David Herbert 1942- BiDrAPA 89
Rubinstein, Elaine Perle 1953- WhoEmL 91
Rubinstein, Eric M BiDrAPA 89
Rubinstein, Erica ODwPR 91
Rubinstein, Eva 1933- WhoAm 90
Rubinstein, Frank 1922- St&PR 91
Rubinstein, G. Edward 1949- WhoE 91
Rubinstein, Gerardo BiDrAPA 89
Rubinstein, Helena 1870-1965 BioAmW, BioIn 16, WorAlBi
Rubinstein, Hyman S 1904- BiDrAPA 89
Rubinstein, Hyman Solomon 1904- WhoAm 90
Rubinstein, Ida Lvovna 1885-1960 BioIn 16
Rubinstein, Jerold H. 1938- St&PR 91
Rubinstein, Joan BiDrAPA 89
Rubinstein, Joel Franklin BiDrAPA 89
Rubinstein, John Arthur 1946- WhoAm 90
Rubinstein, John B. 1946- St&PR 91
Rubinstein, Joseph E BiDrAPA 89
Rubinstein, Lionel E. 1908-1989 BioIn 16
Rubinstein, Lucien 1924-1990 BioIn 16
Rubinstein, Lucien J. NewYTBS 90
Rubinstein, M Scott 1927- BiDrAPA 89
Rubinstein, Margot Susan 1957- BiDrAPA 89
Rubinstein, Mark 1942- BiDrAPA 89
Rubinstein, Martin J 1926- BiDrAPA 89
Rubinstein, Moshe Fajwel 1930- WhoAm 90
Rubinstein, Nikolay 1835-1881 PenDiMP
Rubinstein, Renate 1929- EncCoWW
Rubinstein, Richard N BiDrAPA 89
Rubinstein, Richard Paul 1947- St&PR 91
Rubinstein, Robert E. 1943- BioIn 16
Rubinstein, Samuel 1949- WhoWor 91
Rubinstein, Shira Hope 1957- BiDrAPA 89
Rubinstein, Shirley Joy 1927- WhoAmW 91, WhoE 91

Rubinstein, Steven David 1952- *St&PR 91*
Rubinstein, Susan R *WhoAmA 91*
Rubinstein, Virginia G *BiDrAPA 89*
Rubinstein, William Morris 1923- *St&PR 91*
Rubinstein, Yeva G 1939- *BiDrAPA 89*
Rubio, Alberto *BiDrAPA 89*
Rubio, Elenita Ignacio 1943- *WhoWor 91*
Rubio, Lorenzo Sifuentes 1952- *WhoHisp 91*
Rubio, Mauricio 1921- *BiDrAPA 89*
Rubio, Nancy Beth Elder 1953- *BiDrAPA 89*
Rubio, Pedro Antonio 1944- *WhoSSW 91, WhoWor 91*
Rubio, Ramon Mario *BiDrAPA 89*
Rubio, Robert B. 1955- *WhoSSW 91*
Rubio-Boitel, Fernando Fabian 1945- *WhoHisp 91*
Rubio Mane, Jorge Ignacio 1904-1988 *BioIn 16*
Rubis, Stacy *ODwPR 91*
Ruble, Ann 1953- *WhoAmW 91, WhoEmL 91*
Ruble, Duane Russell 1943- *St&PR 91*
Ruble, Randall Tucker 1932- *WhoAm 90*
Rublev, Andrei 1360?-1430? *IntDcAA 90*
Rubloff, Burton 1912- *WhoAm 90*
Rublowsky, John M. 1928- *AuBYP 90, SmATA 62*
Rubottom, Roy Richard, Jr. 1912- *WhoAm 90*
Rubovits-Seitz, Philip F D 1921- *BiDrAPA 89*
Rubovits-Seitz, Randi 1946- *BiDrAPA 89*
Rubright, James Alfred 1946- *WhoSSW 91*
Rubright, Royal Cushing 1909- *WhoAm 90*
Ruby, Burton Bennett 1919- *St&PR 91, WhoAm 90*
Ruby, Charles Leroy 1900- *WhoWor 91*
Ruby, Harry 1895-1974 *BioIn 16, OxCPMus, WorAlBi*
Ruby, Jack *BioIn 16*
Ruby, Jack 1911?-1967 *WorAlBi*
Ruby, Jay William 1935- *WhoE 91*
Ruby, Kenneth Jay 1951- *BiDrAPA 89, WhoE 91*
Ruby, Laura 1945- *WhoAmA 91*
Ruby, Lois 1942- *BioIn 16*
Ruby, Mike *WhoAm 90*
Ruby, Russell 1911- *WhoAm 90*
Ruby, Sally Anne 1944- *WhoWor 91*
Rubylee 1928- *WhoAmA 91*
Rucci, Anthony Joseph 1950- *St&PR 91*
Rucci, Carlos A 1939- *BiDrAPA 89*
Ruch, Charles E 1932- *BiDrAPA 89*
Ruch, Charles P. 1938- *WhoAm 90*
Ruch, John S. 1939- *ODwPR 91*
Ruch, Peggy Ann F. 1940- *WhoAmW 91*
Ruch, Richard H. 1930- *St&PR 91*
Ruch, Richard Hurley 1930- *WhoAm 90*
Ruch, Sandra J. *ODwPR 91*
Ruch, William Vaughn 1937- *WhoE 91, WhoWor 91*
Ruchelman, Leonard Isadore 1933- *WhoSSW 91*
Ruchin, Cecile Ann 1936- *WhoAmW 91*
Ruchlis, Hyman 1913- *AuBYP 90*
Ruchman, Allan B. 1953- *WhoAm 90*
Ruchman, Isaac 1909- *WhoSSW 91*
Rucier, Robin Arthur 1951- *St&PR 91*
Rucinski, Walter Paul 1944- *St&PR 91*
Ruck, Berta 1878-1978 *BioIn 16, FemiCLE*
Ruck, David Carl 1953- *BiDrAPA 89*
Ruck, Heribert 1930- *WhoWor 91*
Ruck, Kenneth Allen 1934- *St&PR 91*
Ruck-Pauquet, Gina *AuBYP 90*
Ruckel, John Marvin 1948- *WhoSSW 91*
Ruckelshaus, William D. 1932- *St&PR 91*
Ruckelshaus, William Doyle 1932- *WhoAm 90, WhoSSW 91*
Rucker, Adin Henry, Jr. 1937- *St&PR 91*
Rucker, Charles Thomas 1931- *WhoAm 90*
Rucker, Dave 1957- *Ballpl 90*
Rucker, Edward W., IV 1953- *IntWWM 90*
Rucker, Harrison Campbell 1930- *WhoAmA 91*
Rucker, James William 1936- *WhoWor 91*
Rucker, James William 1946- *WhoSSW 91*
Rucker, Jo Anne 1931- *WhoSSW 91*
Rucker, Johnny 1917-1985 *Ballpl 90*
Rucker, Max Ramon 1932- *St&PR 91*
Rucker, Morton S 1923- *BiDrAPA 89*
Rucker, Nap 1884-1970 *Ballpl 90*
Rucker, Richard Sim 1947- *WhoEmL 91*
Rucker, Thomas 1532?-1606 *PenDiDA 89*
Rucker, Wilie J., Jr. 1920- *St&PR 91*
Rucker, Winfred Ray 1920- *WhoAm 90*
Ruckert, Ann Johns 1945- *WhoAmW 91, WhoEmL 91*
Rucki, Judith A. *ODwPR 91*
Rucki, Robin Lynn 1961- *WhoAmW 91*
Ruckman, Frederick L. 1949- *St&PR 91*
Ruckman, Ivy 1931- *BioIn 16, ConAu 30NR*
Ruckman, Mark Warren 1954- *WhoE 91*
Ruda, Edwin 1922- *WhoAmA 91*
Ruda, Jerome 1943- *St&PR 91*
Ruda, Jose Maria 1924- *WhoWor 91*
Ruda, Neil Michael 1957- *WhoSSW 91*
Rudach, Mazal *BioIn 16*
Rudacille, Sharon Victoria 1950- *WhoAmW 91*
Rudaitis, Loretta Gloria 1956- *WhoAmW 91*
Rudall-Moore, Mollie Elaine 1934- *WhoAm 90*
Rudavsky, Elana Leah 1954- *BiDrAPA 89*
Rudbach, Jon Anthony 1937- *St&PR 91*
Rudberg, Sten 1917- *WhoWor 91*
Rudberg, Stig Yngve 1920- *WhoWor 91*
Rudd, A. C. *BioIn 16*
Rudd, Buck Alan 1941- *WhoSSW 91*
Rudd, Carolyn Elaine 1949- *WhoAmW 91*
Rudd, Charles Leo 1936- *St&PR 91*
Rudd, Dale Frederick 1935- *WhoAm 90*
Rudd, David Owen 1955- *WhoEmL 91*
Rudd, David William 1931- *WhoE 91*
Rudd, Eldon *WhoAm 90*
Rudd, Gerald Ray 1929- *St&PR 91, WhoAm 90*
Rudd, Howard F., Jr. 1944- *WhoSSW 91*
Rudd, Hynda L. 1936- *WhoAmW 91*
Rudd, Margaret Caroline 1745?-1794? *FemiCLE*
Rudd, Michael 1936- *WhoAm 90*
Rudd, Nicholas 1943- *WhoAm 90*
Rudd, Paul Ryan 1940- *WhoAm 90*
Rudd, Robert Michael 1939- *WhoSSW 91*
Rudd, Robert William 1919- *WhoAm 90*
Rudd, Roswell 1935- *BioIn 16*
Rudd, Tony *BioIn 16*
Ruddell, Gary Ronald 1948- *WhoAm 90*
Ruddell, Thomas A. 1936- *ODwPR 91*
Rudden, David Philip 1935- *St&PR 91*
Rudden, Eileen Marie 1950- *WhoAmW 91*
Rudden, Marie G 1951- *BiDrAPA 89*
Rudder, Kenneth Wayne 1949- *WhoSSW 91*
Rudder, William H 1922- *BiDrAPA 89*
Ruddick, Bruce R. 1915- *BiDrAPA 89*
Ruddick, J. Perry 1936- *St&PR 91, WhoAm 90*
Ruddle, Francis Hugh 1929- *WhoAm 90*
Ruddle, Richard Dickson 1948- *WhoE 91*
Ruddley, John 1912- *WhoAmA 91*
Ruddock, Margot 1907-1951 *FemiCLE*
Ruddon, Raymond Walter, Jr. 1936- *WhoAm 90*
Ruddy, E. Peter, Jr. 1940- *WhoAm 90, WhoE 91*
Ruddy, Frank S. 1937- *WhoAm 90, WhoE 91, WhoWor 91*
Ruddy, Kenneth Edward 1925- *St&PR 91*
Rudee, Mervyn Lea 1935- *WhoAm 90*
Rudel, Hans Ulrich 1916-1982 *BioIn 16*
Rudel, Julius 1921- *IntWWM 90, PenDiMP, WhoAm 90*
Rudel, Lawrence Lee 1941- *WhoSSW 91*
Rudelic-Fernandez, Zvjezdana Dana 1959- *WhoWor 91*
Rudelius, William 1931- *WhoAm 90*
Rudell, Fredrica 1946- *WhoEmL 91*
Rudell, Milton Wesley 1920- *WhoAm 90*
Rudelli, Mercedes *BiDrAPA 89*
Ruden, Violet Howard *WhoAmW 91*
Rudenius, Arne Rolf 1938- *WhoWor 91*
Rudensky, Morris 1898-1988 *BioIn 16*
Rudensky, Red 1898-1988 *BioIn 16*
Rudenstine, Angelica Zander *WhoAmA 91*
Rudenstine, Neil Leon 1935- *WhoAm 90*
Ruder, Avima Merise 1941- *WhoAmW 91*
Ruder, Brian 1954- *St&PR 91*
Ruder, David S. *BioIn 16*
Ruder, David Sturtevant 1929- *WhoAm 90*
Ruder, Emil 1914-1970 *ConDes 90*
Ruder, Jay Stanley 1955- *WhoEmL 91*
Ruder, Lois Jean Rodriguez 1951- *WhoHisp 91*
Ruder, Melvin Harvey 1915- *WhoAm 90*
Ruder, Phillip 1939- *WhoAm 90*
Ruder, William 1921- *ODwPR 91, St&PR 91, WhoAm 90*
Ruderman, Armand Peter 1923- *WhoAm 90*
Ruderman, David Stephen 1950- *BiDrAPA 89*
Ruderman, Gill H. 1943- *BioIn 16*
Ruderman, Jerome *BiDrAPA 89*
Ruderman, Ronald 1943- *St&PR 91*
Ruderman, Warren 1920- *St&PR 91*
Ruders, Poul 1949- *IntWWM 90*
Rudestam, Rolf C. *ODwPR 91*
Rudet, Jacqueline 1962?- *FemiCLE*
Rudge, Christopher 1937- *St&PR 91*
Rudge, William Edwin 1908-1989 *BioIn 16*
Rudhe, Ulf Gustaf 1919- *WhoWor 91*
Rudhyar, Dane 1895-1985 *EncO&P 3, NewAgE 90*
Rudi, Joe 1946- *Ballpl 90*
Rudiakov, Michael *PenDiMP*
Rudiakov, Michael 1934- *IntWWM 90*
Rudick, M. J. 1938- *St&PR 91*
Rudie, Donald Duane 1935- *St&PR 91*
Rudie, Evelyn *WhoAmW 91*
Rudin, Anne Noto 1924- *WhoAm 90, WhoAmW 91*
Rudin, Arnold James 1934- *WhoWrEP 89*
Rudin, Edward 1922- *BiDrAPA 89*
Rudin, Mary Ellen *BioIn 16*
Rudin, Walter 1921- *WhoAm 90*
Ruding, Herman Onno 1939- *WhoWor 91*
Rudinger, George 1911- *WhoE 91*
Rudinger, Warren Craig 1945- *St&PR 91*
Rudins, Leonids 1928- *WhoE 91*
Rudisill, Richard 1932- *WhoAm 90*
Rudisill, Robert Grant 1922- *St&PR 91*
Rudisill, Robert Mack, Jr. 1945- *WhoAm 90, WhoEmL 91, WhoWor 91*
Ruditz, Stanley H. *St&PR 91*
Rudkin, Margaret Fogarty 1897-1967 *ConAmBL*
Rudko, Frances Howell 1935- *WhoAmW 91*
Rudkoff, Douglass McFerrin 1925- *WhoAmW 91*
Rudland, Malcolm 1941- *IntWWM 90*
Rudley, Lloyd Dave *BiDrAPA 89*
Rudley, Lloyd Dave 1955- *WhoE 91*
Rudloff, Jacques 1917- *WhoWor 91*
Rudloff, Linda Stuart 1945- *WhoSSW 91*
Rudloff, Robert William, Jr. 1958- *WhoE 91*
Rudloff, William Joseph 1941- *WhoSSW 91*
Rudman, Christina Gesina 1943- *WhoWor 91*
Rudman, Daniel S. 1945- *WhoEmL 91*
Rudman, Frances *St&PR 91*
Rudman, Herbert Charles 1923- *WhoAm 90*
Rudman, Joan *WhoAmA 91*
Rudman, Mark 1948- *WhoWrEP 89*
Rudman, Masha Kabakow 1933- *WhoE 91*
Rudman, Michael P. 1950- *St&PR 91*
Rudman, Richard James 1927- *St&PR 91*
Rudman, Warren B. *BioIn 16*
Rudman, Warren Bruce 1930- *NewYTBS 90 [port], WhoAm 90, WhoE 91, WhoWor 91*
Rudmin, Joseph Webster 1942- *WhoSSW 91*
Rudner, Benjamin *BiDrAPA 89*
Rudner, Rita *BioIn 16*
Rudner, Sara 1944- *WhoAm 90*
Rudney, Harry 1918- *WhoAm 90*
Rudnick, Alan A. *WhoAm 90*
Rudnick, Alan A. 1947- *St&PR 91*
Rudnick, Alice Ann 1947- *BiDrAPA 89*
Rudnick, Barry F *BiDrAPA 89*
Rudnick, David Lawrence 1940- *St&PR 91*
Rudnick, Ellen A. 1950- *St&PR 91*
Rudnick, Ellen Ava *WhoAm 90, WhoAmW 91*
Rudnick, Franklin David 1941- *BiDrAPA 89*
Rudnick, Herman D 1918- *BiDrAPA 89*
Rudnick, Irene Krugman 1929- *WhoAmW 91*
Rudnick, Isadore 1917- *WhoAm 90*
Rudnick, M. J. 1948- *St&PR 91*
Rudnick, Paul David 1940- *WhoAm 90*
Rudnick, Pauline L *BiDrAPA 89*
Rudnik, Mary Chrysantha 1929- *WhoAmW 91*
Rudo, Andrew Brent 1950- *BiDrAPA 89*
Rudo, Marvin 1921- *BiDrAPA 89*
Rudofker, Robert C. 1934- *St&PR 91*
Rudofsky, Bernard 1905-1988 *BioIn 16*
Rudolf 1788-1831 *PenDiMP*
Rudolf, German *BioIn 16*
Rudolf, Leslie E. 1927- *WhoAm 90*
Rudolf, Max 1902- *IntWWM 90, PenDiMP, WhoAm 90, WhoWor 91*
Rudolf, Walter F. 1931- *WhoWor 91*
Rudolph, Abraham Morris 1924- *WhoAm 90*
Rudolph, Andrew Henry 1943- *WhoWor 91*
Rudolph, Arnold Jack 1918- *WhoAm 90*
Rudolph, Arthur 1928- *St&PR 91*
Rudolph, Carl J. 1945- *St&PR 91*
Rudolph, Deborah Ann 1958- *WhoAmW 91*
Rudolph, Dick 1887-1949 *Ballpl 90*
Rudolph, Don 1931-1968 *Ballpl 90*
Rudolph, Elaine Taylor 1926- *WhoAmW 91*
Rudolph, Frederick 1920- *WhoAm 90*
Rudolph, Frederick W. 1929- *St&PR 91*
Rudolph, Frederick William 1929- *WhoAm 90*
Rudolph, George Cooper 1951- *WhoEmL 91*
Rudolph, Gerald Allen 1928- *WhoAm 90*
Rudolph, Gilbert Lawrence 1946- *WhoEmL 91*
Rudolph, Hans-Joachim 1926- *WhoWor 91*
Rudolph, Howard Emerson 1933- *WhoAm 90*
Rudolph, Joseph 1917- *BiDrAPA 89*
Rudolph, Ken 1946- *Ballpl 90*
Rudolph, Lavere Christian 1921- *WhoAm 90*
Rudolph, Lee Norman 1948- *WhoE 91*
Rudolph, Lloyd Irving 1927- *WhoAm 90*
Rudolph, Malcolm R. 1924- *St&PR 91*
Rudolph, Malcolm Rome 1924- *WhoAm 90*
Rudolph, Marguerita 1908- *AuBYP 90*
Rudolph, Paul 1918- *BioIn 16*
Rudolph, Ralph A. 1926- *St&PR 91*
Rudolph, Richard 1948- *WhoSSW 91, WhoWor 91*
Rudolph, Richard Casper 1909- *WhoAm 90*
Rudolph, Richard Hinman 1921- *WhoAm 90*
Rudolph, Robert E. 1936- *St&PR 91*
Rudolph, Robert R 1909- *BiDrAPA 89*
Rudolph, Robert R. 1937- *St&PR 91*
Rudolph, Sondra 1934- *WhoAmW 91*
Rudolph, Stephen E. 1945- *St&PR 91*
Rudolph, Susanne Hoeber 1930- *WhoAm 90*
Rudolph, Theodore J. *St&PR 91*
Rudolph, Wallace Morton 1930- *WhoAm 90*
Rudolph, Wilma *BioIn 16*
Rudolph, Wilma 1940- *WorAlBi*
Rudomin, Esther *AuBYP 90*
Rudominer, Arnold B. *BiDrAPA 89*
Rudominer, Howard Steven 1943- *BiDrAPA 89*
Rudorfer, Fanny *BiDrAPA 89*
Rudorfer, Matthew Victor 1951- *BiDrAPA 89*
Rudow, Vivian Adleberg Vickie 1936- *IntWWM 90*
Rudquist, Jerry Jacob 1934- *WhoAmA 91*
Rudrud, Judy L. 1952- *St&PR 91*
Rudstein, David Stewart 1946- *WhoAm 90*
Rudulph, Milnor *AmLegL*
Rudwall, John C. 1929- *St&PR 91*
Rudy, Ann Lizette 1957- *WhoAmW 91*
Rudy, Dorothy L. 1924- *WhoWrEP 89*
Rudy, George Warren 1911- *St&PR 91*
Rudy, Lester H *BiDrAPA 89*
Rudy, Lester Howard 1918- *WhoAm 90*
Rudy, Mikhail 1953- *IntWWM 90*
Rudy, Raymond Bruce, Jr. 1931- *St&PR 91, WhoAm 90*
Rudy, Ruth Corman 1938- *WhoAmW 91*
Rudy, Sylvia June 1939- *St&PR 91*
Rudy, Victor David *BiDrAPA 89*
Rudy, Willis 1920- *WhoAm 90*
Rudzinski, Aleksander W. 1900-1989 *BioIn 16*
Rudzinski, John J. *St&PR 91*
Rudzinski, Kenneth William 1947- *WhoE 91*
Rudzinski, Witold 1913- *IntWWM 90*
Rudzinski, Zbigniew 1935- *IntWWM 90*
Rudzki, Robert A. 1953- *WhoE 91*
Rue, C. J. 1945- *St&PR 91*
Rue, Carl C. 1938- *St&PR 91*
Rue, David S 1941- *BiDrAPA 89*
Rue, Joe 1897-1984 *Ballpl 90*
Rue, Joseph I. 1926- *St&PR 91*
Rue, Leonard Lee 1926- *AuBYP 90*
Rue, Leslie W 1944- *ConAu 30NR*
Rue, Robert Reeve 1948- *WhoE 91*
Rue, T. Steve 1946- *St&PR 91*
Ruebe, Bambi Lynn 1957- *WhoAmW 91*
Ruebhausen, Oscar Melick 1912- *WhoAm 90*
Ruebhausen, Zelia P. *NewYTBS 90*
Ruebhausen, Zelia P. 1914-1990 *BioIn 16*
Rueck, Jon Michael 1940- *WhoAm 90*
Rueda, Juan Luis *BiDrAPA 89*
Rueda-Vasquez, Eduardo *BiDrAPA 89*
Rueden, Henry Anthony 1949- *WhoEmL 91, WhoWor 91*
Ruedenberg, Klaus 1920- *WhoAm 90*
Ruedin, James Messer, Sr. 1928- *St&PR 91*
Ruedinger, Donald Joseph *BiDrAPA 89*
Ruedisili, Chester Henry 1910- *WhoAm 90*
Ruedrich, Stephen L 1951- *BiDrAPA 89*
Rueff, Jacques Leon 1896-1978 *BiDFrPL*
Rueff, Mildred Mae 1923- *WhoSSW 91*
Rueger, Lauren John 1921- *WhoAm 90*
Ruegg, Donald George 1924- *WhoAm 90*
Ruegg, Robert George *BiDrAPA 89*
Ruegger, Philip Theophil, III 1949- *WhoEmL 91*
Ruehl, Jeanette Louise 1957- *WhoAmW 91*
Ruehl, Mercedes *BioIn 16*
Ruehle, Charles Joseph 1943- *WhoE 91, WhoWor 91*
Ruehr, Ben B. 1933- *St&PR 91*
Ruehr, Henry L 1920- *BiDrAPA 89*
Ruel, Jean M 1938- *BiDrAPA 89*
Ruel, Muddy 1896-1963 *Ballpl 90*
Ruell, Patrick *ConAu 32NR, TwCCr&M 91*
Ruellan, Alain Jean 1943- *WhoWor 91*
Ruellan, Andree 1905- *WhoAm 90, WhoAmA 91*
Ruello, Samuel Angus 1931- *WhoAm 90*
Ruelos, Emilio Bunvan *BiDrAPA 89*

Ruelos, Nellie *BiDrAPA 89*
Ruemelin, Charles R. *St&PR 91*
Ruemelin, Robert J. *St&PR 91*
Ruesch, Heinz-Wolfgang 1960- *WhoWor 91*
Ruesch, Jurgen 1909- *BiDrAPA 89*
Ruesink, Albert William 1940- *WhoAm 90*
Ruest, Sue Ellen 1944- *WhoAmW 91*
Rueth, Alora Lynn 1958- *WhoWrEP 89*
Ruether, Dutch 1893-1970 *Ballpl 90*
Ruether, Rosemary Radford 1936- *WhoAmW 91*
Ruetschlin, Tracey Marie 1961- *WhoAmW 91*
Ruettgers, Michael C. 1942- *St&PR 91*
Ruettgers, Michael Cadet 1942- *WhoAm 90*
Ruetz, George J. 1925- *St&PR 91*
Ruetz, James Peter 1957- *St&PR 91*
Ruetz, William Joseph 1949- *St&PR 91*
Rueve, Charles E. 1937- *St&PR 91*
Ruf, Dave G., Jr. 1938- *St&PR 91*
Ruf, John Frederic 1937- *WhoAm 90*
Rufa, Robert Henry 1943- *WhoAm 90*
Rufajzen, Oswald 1922- *BioIn 16*
Rufe, R. Kane 1930- *St&PR 91*
Rufe, Redding Kane 1930- *WhoAm 90*
Rufeh, Firooz 1937- *WhoE 91*
Rufener, Jayne Michelle 1964- *WhoAmW 91*
Ruff, Billy *BioIn 16*
Ruff, Charles F. C. 1939- *WhoAm 90*
Ruff, Christopher *BioIn 16*
Ruff, Darryl Everett John 1938- *WhoWor 91*
Ruff, Edward C. 1939- *St&PR 91*
Ruff, George E 1928- *BiDrAPA 89*
Ruff, Howard J. *BioIn 16*
Ruff, Howard Joseph 1930- *WhoAm 90, WhoWrEP 89*
Ruff, James Edward 1936- *BiDrAPA 89*
Ruff, Jean-Paul A. 1934- *St&PR 91*
Ruff, John Thomas 1954- *WhoSSW 91*
Ruff, Katheryn Lorene 1954- *WhoAmW 91*
Ruff, Larry Wayne 1948- *WhoSSW 91*
Ruff, Lorraine *ODwPR 91*
Ruff, Marie Nancy 1934- *St&PR 91*
Ruff, Richard *BioIn 16*
Ruff, Robert Louis 1950- *WhoEmL 91, WhoWor 91*
Ruff, Thomas 1958- *BioIn 16*
Ruffalo, Alan Michael 1943- *St&PR 91*
Ruffalo, James Anthony 1949- *St&PR 91*
Ruffalo, Maria Therese 1963- *WhoAmW 91*
Ruffer, David Gray 1937- *WhoAm 90*
Ruffer, Michael *BioIn 16*
Ruffian, M. *ConAu 129, MajTwCW*
Ruffin, Albert 1961- *WhoSSW 91*
Ruffin, Bruce 1963- *Ballpl 90*
Ruffin, Bruce E. 1944- *St&PR 91*
Ruffin, Cathy Hoke 1961- *WhoSSW 91*
Ruffin, Craige 1902- *St&PR 91, WhoWor 91*
Ruffin, Edmund 1794-1865 *BioIn 16*
Ruffin, Glenn Bernice 1926- *BiDrAPA 89*
Ruffin, Joseph B 1928- *BiDrAPA 89*
Ruffin, Julian M. 1946- *St&PR 91*
Ruffin, Margaret Elaine 1936- *WhoAmW 91*
Ruffin, Mark Anthony 1956- *WhoWrEP 89*
Ruffin, Paul Dean 1941- *WhoWrEP 89*
Ruffin, Roger Sherman 1927- *WhoAm 90*
Ruffin, William C, Jr. *BiDrAPA 89*
Ruffing, Anne Elizabeth *WhoAm 90, WhoAmA 91*
Ruffing, Red 1904-1986 *Ballpl 90 [port]*
Ruffino, Anthonette 1948- *WhoSSW 91*
Ruffino, Anthony Michael 1935- *WhoE 91*
Ruffins, Reynold 1930- *BioIn 16*
Ruffle, Joan Madeline 1945- *WhoE 91*
Ruffle, John Frederick 1937- *WhoAm 90*
Ruffley, Herbert Elsworth 1929- *St&PR 91*
Ruffman, Jill Valerie 1958- *WhoAmW 91*
Ruffner, Charles Louis 1936- *WhoSSW 91*
Ruffner, Frederick G., Jr. 1926- *WhoAm 90, WhoWor 91*
Ruffner, Frederick Gale, Jr. 1926- *St&PR 91*
Ruffner, Ginny Martin 1952- *WhoAmA 91*
Ruffner, J David *BiDrAPA 89*
Ruffner, John Merle 1927- *St&PR 91*
Ruffo, Joseph Martin 1941- *WhoAmA 91*
Ruffo, Titta 1877-1953 *PenDiMP*
Ruffolo, Jeff 1957- *ODwPR 91*
Ruffolo, Lisa M. 1956- *WhoWrEP 89*
Ruffus, Stephen 1949- *WhoWrEP 89*
Rufino, Ernesto Baltazar, Jr. 1941- *WhoWor 91*
Rufolo, Joseph William 1947- *WhoE 91*
Rufolo, Regina S. 1961- *St&PR 91*
Rufus-Isaacs, Antony *BioIn 16*
Rufus-Isaacs, Heide *BioIn 16*
Rugaber, Walter Feucht, Jr. 1938- *WhoAm 90, WhoSSW 91*
Rugambwa, Laurean 1912- *WhoWor 91*
Ruge, Daniel August 1917- *WhoAm 90*
Ruge, Michael Helmuth 1962- *WhoEmL 91*
Ruge, Neil Marshall 1913- *WhoAm 90*
Rugen, Karen 1949- *ODwPR 91*
Rugendas, Johann Moritz 1802-1858 *ArtLatA*
Ruger, William Batterman 1916- *St&PR 91, WhoAm 90*
Rugeroni, Ian *WhoAm 90*
Rugg, James Moncrieff 1923- *St&PR 91*
Rugg, Janet Vera 1949- *WhoAmW 91*
Rugg, Marjorie Alice 1916- *WhoAmW 91*
Rugg, William P. 1927- *St&PR 91*
Rugge, Hugo Robert 1935- *WhoAm 90*
Rugge, Sue 1941- *BioIn 16*
Rugger, Gerald Klein 1916- *St&PR 91*
Ruggeri, Bernardo 1951- *WhoWor 91*
Ruggeri, Cinzia 1945- *ConDes 90*
Ruggero, Pedro Alberto *BiDrAPA 89*
Ruggia, James Charles 1954- *WhoWrEP 89*
Ruggiano, John Robert *BiDrAPA 89*
Ruggieri, Bernard J. 1926- *WhoAm 90*
Ruggieri, Helen 1938- *WhoWrEP 89*
Ruggieri, John Thomas 1956- *St&PR 91*
Ruggieri, Oreste *PenDiDA 89*
Ruggieri, Pamela Joy 1944- *WhoAmW 91*
Ruggiero, Angelo *BioIn 16*
Ruggiero, Anthony William 1941- *St&PR 91, WhoAm 90*
Ruggiero, Charles Howard 1947- *IntWWM 90*
Ruggiero, Edward Michael 1939- *WhoSSW 91*
Ruggiero, John A. 1936- *St&PR 91*
Ruggiero, John Salvator 1931- *WhoAm 90*
Ruggiero, Laurence J 1948- *WhoAmA 91*
Ruggiero, Laurence Joseph 1948- *WhoAm 90, WhoSSW 91*
Ruggiero, Linda Sue 1952- *WhoAmW 91*
Ruggiero, Mary Tina 1958- *WhoAmW 91*
Ruggiero, Matthew John 1932- *WhoAm 90*
Ruggiero, Richard Salvador 1944- *WhoE 91*
Ruggiero, Salvatore 1914-1988 *BioIn 16*
Ruggles, A. D. *EncO&P 3*
Ruggles, Charles 1886-1970 *WorAlBi*
Ruggles, Connie Patricia 1940- *WhoAmW 91*
Ruggles, David J. 1936- *St&PR 91*
Ruggles, Donald Francis 1936- *St&PR 91*
Ruggles, Henry Joseph 1813-1906 *BioIn 16*
Ruggles, James A *BiDrAPA 89*
Ruggles, Joanne Beaule 1946- *WhoAmA 91*
Ruggles, Richard 1916- *WhoAm 90*
Ruggles, Robert Thomas 1931- *St&PR 91*
Ruggles, Rudy Lamont 1909- *WhoAm 90*
Ruggles, Rudy Lamont, Jr. 1938- *WhoAm 90*
Ruggles, Timothy 1711-1795 *EncCRAm*
Rugh, Belle Dorman 1908- *AuBYP 90*
Rugh, James B. 1945- *WhoE 91*
Rugh, John F. 1934- *St&PR 91*
Rugh, William Arthur 1936- *WhoAm 90*
Rugh, Wilson John, II 1944- *WhoAm 90*
Rugina, Anghel N. 1913- *WhoE 91*
Rugman, Alan Michael 1945- *WhoE 91*
Rugo, Paul R. 1933- *WhoAm 90*
Rugo, Steven Alfred 1953- *WhoEmL 91*
Rugoff, Donald S. 1927-1989 *BioIn 16*
Rugoff, Milton 1913- *WhoAm 90*
Rugolo, Lawrence 1931- *WhoAmA 91*
Rugolo, Pete 1915- *OxCPMus*
Rugolo, Pete 1916- *WorAlBi*
Rugowski, James Anthony 1946- *BiDrAPA 89*
Rugstad, Gunnar 1921- *IntWWM 90*
Ruhe, Barnaby Sieger 1946- *WhoAmA 91*
Ruhe, David Sieger 1914- *WhoWor 91*
Ruhe, Edward L. 1923-1989 *BioIn 16*
Ruhemann, Martin 1903- *BioIn 16*
Ruhenstroth-Bauer, Gerhard Rudolf 1913- *WhoWor 91*
Ruhig, Alexander S *BiDrAPA 89*
Ruhkala, Peter D. 1940- *St&PR 91*
Ruhl, Douglas L. 1948- *St&PR 91*
Ruhl, John Benjamin 1957- *WhoEmL 91*
Ruhl, Robert Charles 1941- *St&PR 91*
Ruhl, Ronald F. 1947- *St&PR 91*
Ruhl, Steven 1954- *WhoWrEP 89*
Ruhland, Elizabeth A. *WhoWrEP 89*
Ruhle, Vern 1951- *Ballpl 90*
Ruhlman, Herman Cloyd, Jr. 1949- *WhoWor 91*
Ruhlman, Jon Randall 1927- *St&PR 91*
Ruhlman, Terrell Louis 1926- *WhoAm 90*
Ruhlmann, Jacques-Emile 1879-1933 *PenDiDA 89*
Ruhm, Christopher John 1955- *WhoE 91*
Ruhm, Jane *BioIn 16*
Ruhm, Thomas Francis 1935- *WhoE 91, WhoWor 91*
Ruhmann, Roger Lowell 1941- *WhoAm 90*
Ruibal, Charles Adrian 1947- *WhoAm 90*
Ruibal, Salvador 1953- *WhoHisp 91*
Ruijgh, Cornelis Jord 1930- *WhoWor 91*
Ruis, Helmut 1940- *WhoWor 91*
Ruis, Janet Wood 1945- *WhoSSW 91*
Ruis, Stanley W. 1936- *St&PR 91*
Ruis, Thomas Paul 1947- *WhoAm 90*
Ruisch, Matheus Johannes 1933- *WhoWor 91*
Ruisdael, Jacob van 1628?-1682? *IntDcAA 90, WorAlBi*
Ruisi, Christopher Salvatore 1949- *St&PR 91*
Ruisi, Helen Suydam 1951- *WhoE 91*
Ruisinger, Charles A., Jr. 1931- *St&PR 91*
Ruitenberg, Nicholas 1957- *St&PR 91*
Ruiter, Adriaan 1934- *WhoWor 91*
Ruiter-Feenstra, Pamela S. 1961- *IntWWM 90*
Ruiz, Andrew Michael 1941- *WhoHisp 91*
Ruiz, Anthony *WhoHisp 91*
Ruiz, Antonio 1897-1964 *ArtLatA*
Ruiz, Armando 1957- *WhoHisp 91*
Ruiz, Cesar Laureola *BiDrAPA 89*
Ruiz, Chico 1938- *Ballpl 90*
Ruiz, Darlene Elizabeth *WhoHisp 91*
Ruiz, Dolores M. 1958- *WhoHisp 91*
Ruiz, Dorothy Ann 1934- *St&PR 91*
Ruiz, Edmundo J 1917- *BiDrAPA 89*
Ruiz, Edward F. *WhoHisp 91*
Ruiz, Emilio 1957- *WhoHisp 91*
Ruiz, Fernando Ray 1939- *BiDrAPA 89*
Ruiz, Frank Anthony 1954- *WhoSSW 91*
Ruiz, Frederick R. 1943- *WhoHisp 91*
Ruiz, Henry N. 1936- *WhoHisp 91*
Ruiz, Hildebrando 1945- *WhoHisp 91*
Ruiz, J. Anthony *WhoHisp 91*
Ruiz, Jesus, Jr. 1939- *WhoHisp 91*
Ruiz, Joaquin 1951- *WhoHisp 91*
Ruiz, Jose Garcia 1947- *WhoEmL 91, WhoWor 91*
Ruiz, Jose Martinez *HispWr 90*
Ruiz, Julio Vernon 1947- *BiDrAPA 89*
Ruiz, Leticia 1957- *WhoHisp 91*
Ruiz, Lisbeth J. 1949- *WhoHisp 91*
Ruiz, Manuel, Jr. 1905- *WhoAm 90*
Ruiz, Maria Cristina 1952- *WhoHisp 91*
Ruiz, Norberto 1954- *WhoHisp 91*
Ruiz, Oscar Antonio *BiDrAPA 89*
Ruiz, Pedro 1936- *BiDrAPA 89, WhoHisp 91*
Ruiz, Peter Ricardo *BiDrAPA 89*
Ruiz, Peter Virgil, II 1951- *WhoHisp 91*
Ruiz, Ramon Eduardo *BioIn 16*
Ruiz, Ramon Eduardo 1921- *ConAu 30NR, HispWr 90, WhoAm 90, WhoHisp 91*
Ruiz, Raul 1941- *BioIn 16*
Ruiz, Rene A. 1929-1982 *BioIn 16*
Ruiz, Reynaldo 1940- *WhoHisp 91*
Ruiz, Richard A. 1950- *WhoHisp 91*
Ruiz, Robert J. 1949- *WhoHisp 91*
Ruiz, Roberto 1925- *WhoHisp 91*
Ruiz, Roberto C. *WhoHisp 91*
Ruiz, Roberto-Jesus *BiDrAPA 89*
Ruiz, Rosemary L. *WhoHisp 91*
Ruiz, Rosie *BioIn 16*
Ruiz, Ruben O, Jr. 1945- *BiDrAPA 89*
Ruiz, Ruby R. 1949- *WhoHisp 91*
Ruiz, Samuel *BiDrAPA 89*
Ruiz, Vicki L. 1955- *WhoHisp 91*
Ruiz, William C. 1944- *WhoHisp 91*
Ruiz Castaneda, Maria del Carmen 1926- *WhoAm 90*
Ruiz-Castillo, Javier 1944- *WhoWor 91*
Ruiz-Conforto, Tracie *BioIn 16*
Ruiz-Contreras, Anita *WhoHisp 91*
Ruiz de Castilla, Terry Marie 1953- *WhoSSW 91*
Ruiz-de-Conde, Justina 1909- *WhoAm 90, WhoHisp 91*
Ruiz-Fornells, Enrique S. 1925- *WhoHisp 91*
Ruiz-Gadea, Ada-Luvy D. *BiDrAPA 89*
Ruiz-Julia, Angela M. 1940- *WhoHisp 91*
Ruiz-Ramon, Francisco Jose 1930- *WhoAm 90*
Ruiz-Valera, Phoebe Lucile 1950- *WhoAmW 91, WhoHisp 91, WhoWor 91*
Ruk-Focic, Bozena 1937- *IntWWM 90*
Rukadikar, Arunlalit H 1944- *BiDrAPA 89*
Rukadikar, Mary Arunlalit 1944- *BiDrAPA 89*
Rukeyser, Louis R. 1933- *WorAlBi*
Rukeyser, Louis Richard 1933- *WhoAm 90, WhoE 91*
Rukeyser, M. S., Jr. *BioIn 16*
Rukeyser, M. S., Jr. 1931- *WhoAm 90*
Rukeyser, Merryle S. 1897-1988 *BioIn 16*
Rukeyser, Muriel 1913-1980 *AuBYP 90, FemiCLE, MajTwCW, WorAlBi*
Rukeyser, Robert J. 1942- *ODwPR 91*
Rukeyser, Robert James 1942- *St&PR 91, WhoAm 90*
Rukeyser, William Simon 1939- *WhoAm 90*
Rukstad, Michael George 1954- *WhoE 91*
Rul, Christiaan Francois 1952- *WhoWor 91*
Ruland, Donald Bert 1942- *St&PR 91*
Ruland, Maurice B *BiDrAPA 89*
Rulau, Russell 1926- *WhoWor 91*
Rule, Brendan Gail Lonergan 1937- *WhoAm 90*
Rule, Charles Frederick 1955- *WhoAm 90*
Rule, Colter *BiDrAPA 89*
Rule, Elton H. *NewYTBS 90 [port]*
Rule, Elton H. 1916-1990 *BioIn 16*
Rule, Geraldine Levingston 1924- *WhoSSW 91*
Rule, Jane 1931- *BioIn 16, ConAu 30NR, FemiCLE*
Rule, John Corwin 1929- *WhoAm 90*
Rule-Hoffman, Richard Carl 1947- *WhoEmL 91*
Rulfo, Juan 1918-1986 *BioIn 16, HispWr 90, MajTwCW*
Rulis, Raymond Joseph 1924- *WhoAm 90*
Rulla, Luigi M *BiDrAPA 89*
Rullan, Pilar M. 1941- *WhoHisp 91*
Rulli, Carmen Joseph 1925- *WhoE 91*
Rulon-Miller, Robert, Jr. 1952- *St&PR 91*
Rulon-Miller, William Lippincott 1948- *St&PR 91*
Rulseh, Ted *ODwPR 91*
Rumage, Sarah Agnes 1956- *WhoEmL 91*
Ruman, Robert S. 1942- *St&PR 91*
Rumbaugh, James H 1939- *BiDrAPA 89*
Rumbaugh, James H. 1939-1989 *BioIn 16*
Rumbaugh, Margaret Gutjahr 1961- *WhoAmW 91*
Rumbaugh, Max Elden, Jr. 1937- *WhoAm 90, WhoWor 91*
Rumbaugh, Melvin Dale 1929- *WhoAm 90*
Rumbaugh, Paul Ernest 1919- *St&PR 91*
Rumbaut, Luis *WhoHisp 91*
Rumbaut, Michelle 1963- *WhoAmW 91*
Rumbaut, Ruben D 1922- *BiDrAPA 89*
Rumbel, Nancy *NewAgMG*
Rumberger, Regina 1921- *WhoAmW 91*
Rumble, Thomas Reid 1943- *BiDrAPA 89, WhoE 91*
Rumbough, Stanley Maddox, Jr. 1920- *St&PR 91, WhoAm 90, WhoSSW 91*
Rumens, Carol 1944- *ConAu 131, FemiCLE, WorAu 1980*
Rumer, Ralph Raymond, Jr. 1931- *WhoAm 90*
Rumford, Beatrix Tyson 1939- *WhoAm 90, WhoAmA 91*
Rumford, Benjamin Thompson 1753-1814 *WorAlBi*
Rumford, Kennerley *PenDiMP*
Rumford, Marie Anne P Paulze, Countess 1758-1836 *BioIn 16*
Rumi, Jalal al-Din *EncO&P 3*
Rumill, Ed *Ballpl 90*
Rumilly, Bernard Sebastian 1935- *WhoE 91*
Rumkowski, Mordechai Chaim 1877-1944 *BioIn 16*
Ruml, Jiri *BioIn 16*
Rumler, Robert Hoke 1915- *WhoAm 90*
Rummage, Stephen Michael 1955- *WhoEmL 91*
Rumman, Wadi 1926- *WhoAm 90*
Rummans, Teresa Anne *BiDrAPA 89*
Rummel, Charles Garman 1912- *St&PR 91*
Rummel, Charles Garmin 1912- *WhoAm 90*
Rummel, Jack 1950- *ConAu 132*
Rummel, Robert Wiland 1915- *WhoAm 90*
Rummerfield, Benjamin Franklin 1917- *WhoWor 91*
Rummler, Randy Ord 1960- *BiDrAPA 89*
Rummler, William R. 1940- *St&PR 91*
Rumor, Mariano *NewYTBS 90*
Rumor, Mariano 1915-1990 *BioIn 16, CurBio 90N*
Rumore, Franklin A 1942- *BiDrAPA 89*
Rumowicz, Edmund Stanley 1930- *WhoE 91*
Rump, Richard G. *ODwPR 91*
Rumpeltin, Frank E. 1945- *St&PR 91*
Rumpf, Christian 1938- *WhoWor 91*
Rumpf, Ewald Wolfgang 1943- *WhoWor 91*
Rumpf, Francois Max Edouard 1941- *WhoWor 91*
Rumpf, John Louis 1921- *WhoAm 90*
Rumpff, Barbara Bryant 1951- *WhoAmW 91*
Rumph, Lee C. 1921- *WhoAm 90*
Rumpp, Johannes 1702-1755 *PenDiDA 89*
Rumpza, Robert J. 1951- *ODwPR 91*
Rumrill, Harry Barlow *BioIn 16*
Rumsey, David Maciver 1944- *WhoAmA 91*
Rumsey, Victor Henry 1919- *WhoAm 90*
Rumsfeld, Donald 1932- *BiDrUSE 89*
Rumsfeld, Donald H. 1932- *WhoAm 90, WhoWor 91*
Rumyantsev, Nelly 1963- *WhoAmW 91*
Rumzie, Kenneth Hubbard 1931- *St&PR 91*
Run-D.M.C. *ConMus 4 [port], EncPR&S 89*
Runac, Pamela Joan 1948- *WhoAmW 91*
Runaways, The *EncPR&S 89*
Runcie, Robert *BioIn 16*

Runcie, Robert Alexander Kennedy 1921- WhoAm 90, WhoWor 91
Runciman, James Cochran Stevenson 1903- BioIn 16
Runciman, Lex 1951- WhoWrEP 89
Runciman, Steven 1903- BioIn 16, WhoWor 91
Rund, Douglas Andrew 1945- WhoWor 91
Runde, James A. 1946- WhoAm 90
Runde, William C. 1929- St&PR 91
Rundell, C. A., Jr. 1931- St&PR 91
Rundell, James Ray 1957- BiDrAPA 89
Rundell, Maria Eliza 1745-1826 FemiCLE
Rundell, Philip 1743-1827 PenDiDA 89
Runden, Ingrid Eve 1952- BiDrAPA 89
Rundgren, Bengt 1931- IntWWM 90
Rundgren, Todd 1948- EncPR&S 89, WhoAm 90, WorAlBi
Rundle, Frank L 1928- BiDrAPA 89
Rundle, John Belting 1950- WhoEmL 91
Rundle, Juliet Walker 1938- WhoAmW 91
Rundle, Philip Sterling 1953- St&PR 91
Rundle, Robert Terrill 1811-1896 DcCanB 12
Rundlett, Donald Hodgman 1935- WhoWor 91
Rundquist, Howard Irving 1929- WhoAm 90
Rundquist, Lee Allison 1951- WhoSSW 91
Rundquist, Richard Allyn 1927- St&PR 91
Rundstedt, Gerd Von 1875-1953 WorAlBi
Runeberg, Fredrika Charlotta 1807-1879 EncCoWW
Runeberg, Johan Ludvig 1804-1877 DcScanL
Runeby, Nils Olof 1931- WhoWor 91
Runes, Richard Norton 1944- WhoWor 91
Runfola, Daniel 1950- WhoE 91
Rung, Richard Allen 1929- WhoAm 90
Runge, Albert Louis 1921- St&PR 91
Runge, Donald E. 1938- St&PR 91
Runge, Donald Edward 1938- WhoAm 90
Runge, Ed 1918- Ballpl 90
Runge, Erika Maria 1939- EncCoWW
Runge, John Scott 1927- St&PR 91
Runge, Kay Kretschmar 1946- WhoEmL 91
Runge, Mary Munson 1928- WhoAm 90
Runge, Paul 1958- Ballpl 90
Runge, Peter-Christoph 1933- IntWWM 90
Runge, Philipp Otto 1777-1810 IntDcAA 90
Rungius, Carl 1869-1959 WhoAmA 91N
Runia, Klaas 1926- WhoWor 91
Runk, Fred J. 1942- St&PR 91
Runk, John W. 1938- St&PR 91
Runk, Lee H. 1940- St&PR 91
Runk, Lee Hammond 1940- WhoAm 90
Runk, Renwick J, Jr. BiDrAPA 89
Runkel, Francis J. 1949- St&PR 91
Runkle, Ethel Mona 1921- WhoAmW 91
Runkle, Martin Davey 1937- WhoAm 90
Runkle, Mary Arvella 1934- WhoWrEP 89
Runkle, Robert S. 1936- St&PR 91
Runkle, Walter Davis 1936- St&PR 91
Runnalls, John 1924- WhoAm 90
Runnells, Clive 1926- WhoSSW 91
Runnells, David L. 1945- St&PR 91
Runnells, James Edward 1928- Ballpl 90
Runnells, Tom BioIn 16
Runnels, Charles Duke 1953- St&PR 91
Runnels, G. Tyler 1956- St&PR 91
Runnels, Gathel O 1926- BiDrAPA 89
Runnels, Hardin R., Jr. 1820-1875 AmLegL
Runnels, Jerry Spencer 1940- St&PR 91
Runnels, Pamala Dianne 1950- WhoAmW 91
Runnels, Pete 1928- Ballpl 90
Runner, David Clark 1948- IntWWM 90
Running Crane DcCanB 12
Running, Joseph Martin, Jr. 1945- WhoSSW 91
Runnion, Cynthia Prosser 1948- St&PR 91
Runnion, Howard J., Jr. 1930- WhoAm 90
Runnion, Howard Jackson 1930- St&PR 91
Runnqvist, Jan Arvid 1929- WhoWor 91
Runquist, Alfonse William 1945- WhoEmL 91
Runte, Roseann 1948- WhoAmW 91
Runvinskis, Elsa BiDrAPA 89
Runyan, Charles Alan 1951- WhoEmL 91
Runyan, Donald Ralph 1945- WhoEmL 91
Runyan, John Stephen 1938- WhoAm 90
Runyan, John William, Jr. 1924- WhoAm 90
Runyan, Roger A. 1952- St&PR 91
Runyan, William Marion 1924- St&PR 91
Runyon, Alfred Damon 1880-1946 BioIn 16
Runyon, Catherine 1947- SmATA 62
Runyon, Damon 1880-1946 BioIn 16
Runyon, Damon 1884-1946 Ballpl 90, WorAlBi
Runyon, Gerri Lewis 1949- WhoAmW 91
Runyon, Guy Eric 1945- WhoE 91
Runyon, Linda BioIn 16
Runyon, Marvin Travis 1924- WhoAm 90, WhoSSW 91
Runyon, Mary Lucille 1927- WhoAmW 91
Runyon, William B. 1957- ODwPR 91
Runze, Klaus 1930- IntWWM 90
Runzheimer, Lee 1942- St&PR 91
Ruocchio, Patricia Jeanne 1958- WhoWrEP 89
Ruof, Richard Alan 1932- WhoE 91
Ruoff, Andrea 1939- WhoE 91
Ruoff, Andrew Christian, III 1919- WhoAm 90
Ruoff, Arthur Louis 1930- WhoAm 90
Ruoff, Axel D. 1957- IntWWM 90
Ruoff, Michael Rolf 1944- WhoWor 91
Ruoff, Paul Allyn 1944- BiDrAPA 89
Ruolz PenDiDA 89
Ruona, Arthur Ernest 1920- WhoWor 91
Ruona, Luanne BiDrAPA 89
Ruonck, Ellen Ava 1950- St&PR 91
Ruono, Jose WhoHisp 91
Ruoti, Maria Clemente 1619?-1690 EncCoWW
Ruoti, Rocco Richard 1942- BiDrAPA 89
Ruotolo, Onorio 1888-1966 BioIn 16
Rupard, G Marion, Sr. 1905- St&PR 91
Ruparel, Meera Kiran 1946- BiDrAPA 89
Rupe, Carol Anne 1958- WhoE 91
Rupel, Dennis F BiDrAPA 89
Rupert, Elizabeth Anastasia 1918- WhoAm 90
Rupert, Hoover 1917- WhoAm 90
Rupert, J. Paul 1942- St&PR 91
Rupert, John Edward 1927- WhoAm 90
Rupert, Karen Martin 1961- St&PR 91
Rupke, Jerry I. 1938- St&PR 91
Ruple, William 1947- St&PR 91
Rupley, David Carroll, Jr. BiDrAPA 89
Rupley, John Wayne 1946- St&PR 91
Rupley, Theodore J. 1939- WhoAm 90
Rupley, William Henry, III 1945- WhoSSW 91
Rupnik, Louis John 1942- St&PR 91
Rupp, Adolph 1901-1977 WorAlBi
Rupp, David Carroll 1935- WhoSSW 91
Rupp, Dean Edward 1941- St&PR 91
Rupp, Dennis Jay 1952- St&PR 91
Rupp, George Erik 1942- WhoAm 90, WhoSSW 91, WhoWor 91
Rupp, George W. 1949- St&PR 91
Rupp, Geraldlynn Sue 1946- WhoAmW 91
Rupp, Glenn N. 1944- St&PR 91
Rupp, James M. 1935- St&PR 91
Rupp, John Norris 1913- WhoAm 90
Rupp, Marwood Fred 1927- WhoSSW 91
Rupp, Peter E. BioIn 16
Rupp, Ralph Russell 1929- WhoAm 90
Rupp, Richard W. 1918- St&PR 91
Rupp, Sharen Lynn 1941- WhoSSW 91
Rupp, Sheron Adeline 1943- WhoAmA 91, WhoAmW 91
Rupp, William John 1927- WhoAm 90
Ruppel, George Robert 1911- WhoAm 90
Ruppel, Howard James, Jr. 1941- WhoWor 91
Ruppel, Joseph Paul 1919- St&PR 91
Ruppel, Stephen Allen 1951- WhoEmL 91
Ruppel, Wayne D. 1940- St&PR 91
Ruppelli, Todd P. 1927- St&PR 91
Ruppenthal, Karl M. 1917- WhoAm 90
Ruppersberg, Allen 1944- WhoAmA 91
Ruppert, Barbara Lee 1949- WhoAmW 91
Ruppert, David Paul 1934- St&PR 91
Ruppert, Donald Gerald 1960- WhoSSW 91
Ruppert, Gary Lee 1944- St&PR 91
Ruppert, Jacob 1867-1939 WorAlBi
Ruppert, Jake 1867-1939 Ballpl 90
Ruppert, James K. 1949- WhoWrEP 89
Ruppert, John Lawrence 1953- WhoEmL 91
Ruppert, Raimund Albert Laurentius 1936- WhoWor 91
Ruppert, Richard Dale 1931- WhoAm 90
Ruppert, Susan Donna 1953- WhoAmW 91
Ruppert, William Ernest 1947- St&PR 91
Rupprecht, Carol Schreier 1939- WhoAmW 91
Rupprecht, Nancy Ellen 1948- WhoAmW 91
Rupprecht, Sandra E. 1947- St&PR 91
Ruprecht, Archibald L BiDrAPA 89
Ruprecht, Mary Margaret Wyant 1934- WhoAmW 91
Ruquist, Richard BioIn 16
Rurik WorAlBi
Rurode, Louise Joyce 1948- WhoWrEP 89
Rury, Kevin Val 1957- WhoSSW 91
Rus, Jan, III 1948- WhoWor 91
Rusak, Halina R WhoAmA 91
Rusak, Halina Rodko WhoAmW 91
Ruscetta, Harold Pasquale, Jr. 1945- WhoE 91
Rusch, Bruce R. 1943- St&PR 91
Rusch, Hugh Leonard 1902- WhoAm 90
Rusch, James Allen BiDrAPA 89
Rusch, Jonathan Jay 1952- WhoEmL 91
Rusch, Kenneth H 1923- BiDrAPA 89
Rusch, Thomas William 1946- WhoAm 90, WhoWor 91
Rusch-Feja, Diann Dorothy 1951- WhoWor 91
Rusch Walton, Sandra Lee 1957- WhoAmW 91
Ruscha, Edward BioIn 16
Ruscha, Edward 1937- WhoAm 90
Ruscha, Edward Joseph 1937- WhoAmA 91
Rusche, Sue 1938- WhoAmW 91
Ruschp, Sepp BioIn 16, NewYTBS 90
Rusciano, Anthony 1944- WhoE 91
Rusciano, Eugene A. 1925- St&PR 91
Ruscica, Dorothy P. 1934- St&PR 91
Ruscitti, Donald R. St&PR 91
Rusco, Linda Suzanne 1951- WhoAmW 91
Ruse, Paul William, Jr. 1943- WhoAm 90, WhoE 91
Rusen, Jorn 1938- WhoWor 91
Ruser, John William 1955- WhoE 91
Rush EncPR&S 89
Rush, Alvin 1926- WhoAm 90
Rush, Andrew 1931- WhoAmA 91
Rush, Andrew Wilson 1931- WhoAm 90
Rush, Art BioIn 16
Rush, Augustus John, Jr. 1942- BiDrAPA 89
Rush, Avery, Jr. 1922- St&PR 91
Rush, Barbara 1930- WorAlBi
Rush, Benjamin 1746-1813 EncCRAm [port], WorAlBi
Rush, Bob 1925- Ballpl 90
Rush, Bobby BioIn 16
Rush, Catherine Patricia 1944- WhoAmW 91
Rush, David 1934- WhoAm 90
Rush, David H. 1918- St&PR 91
Rush, David Kenneth 1910- BioIn 16
Rush, Donald E. 1934- St&PR 91
Rush, Douglas Kevin 1950- WhoEmL 91
Rush, Elena Pribyl 1962- WhoSSW 91
Rush, Fletcher Grey, Jr. 1917- WhoAm 90
Rush, Herbert G 1933- BiDrAPA 89
Rush, Herman 1929- St&PR 91
Rush, Herman E. 1929- WhoAm 90
Rush, J H 1911- EncO&P 3
Rush, James Warner BioIn 16
Rush, Janet Sue 1957- WhoSSW 91
Rush, Jean C 1933- WhoAmA 91
Rush, Jeffrey S. 1950- WhoWrEP 89
Rush, John Lawrence 1934- St&PR 91
Rush, Jon N 1935- WhoAmA 91
Rush, Joseph H. 1911- EncPaPR 91
Rush, Julianne 1968- WhoAmW 91
Rush, Kenneth 1910- WhoAm 90
Rush, Kent Thomas 1948- WhoAmA 91
Rush, Martin Aa, Jr. BiDrAPA 89
Rush, Mary Ellen Rheutan 1947- WhoSSW 91
Rush, Peter 1949- ODwPR 91
Rush, Rebecca 1779?- FemiCLE
Rush, Rebecca Lynn 1948- St&PR 91
Rush, Richard BioIn 16
Rush, Richard 1780-1859 BiDrUSE 89
Rush, Sean Charles 1951- WhoE 91
Rush, Stephen Jon 1958- IntWWM 90
Rush, William John 1936- WhoAm 90
Rush, William Louis 1955- WhoWrEP 89
Rush, William Marshall 1887-1950 AuBYP 90
Rushby-Smith, John 1936- IntWWM 90
Rushdie, Salman BioIn 16, NewYTBS 90 [port]
Rushdie, Salman 1947- ConAu 33NR, MajTwCW, WhoWor 91, WorAlBi
Rushen, Frank Joseph 1940- St&PR 91
Rusher, Albert L. 1897- St&PR 91
Rusher, Derwood H., II 1954- WhoEmL 91
Rusher, William A. 1923- BioIn 16
Rusher, William Allen 1923- WhoAm 90, WhoE 91
Rushford, Donald Lawrence 1930- St&PR 91, WhoAm 90
Rushford, Eloise Johnson WhoAmW 91
Rushia, Mary Anna BiDrAPA 89
Rushin, Steve BioIn 16
Rushing, Allen Ingram 1949- St&PR 91
Rushing, Dorothy Marie 1925- WhoAmW 91
Rushing, Francis W 1939- ConAu 31NR
Rushing, Henry H. 1943- St&PR 91
Rushing, Jane Gilmore 1925- WhoAm 90, WhoWrEP 89
Rushing, Jimmy 1902-1972 OxCPMus
Rushing, Jimmy 1903-1972 WorAlBi
Rushing, Joe Bob 1921- WhoAm 90
Rushing, Roy Eugene 1943- St&PR 91
Rushing, Stephen Orren 1943- BiDrAPA 89
Rushing, Tammy Maureen 1959- WhoSSW 91
Rushing, Zella Ann 1940- St&PR 91
Rushinsky, Michael J. 1933- St&PR 91
Rushmore, Helen 1898- AuBYP 90
Rushmore, Robert BioIn 16
Rushnell, Squire D. 1938- St&PR 91
Rushnell, Squire Derrick 1938- WhoAm 90, WhoE 91
Rushton, Brian Mandel 1933- WhoAm 90
Rushton, Brian Mandell 1933- St&PR 91
Rushton, Brian Norman 1932- WhoWor 91
Rushton, Darrell M. St&PR 91
Rushton, David William 1945- IntWWM 90
Rushton, Jared BioIn 16
Rushton, John R, III BiDrAPA 89
Rushton, Julian 1941- ConAu 132
Rushton, Julian Gordon 1941- IntWWM 90
Rushton, Theodore Allan 1938- WhoWrEP 89
Rushton, W A H 1901-1980 EncO&P 3
Rushton, William J., III 1929- St&PR 91
Rushton, William James, III 1929- WhoAm 90
Rushworth, Robert Aitken 1924- WhoAm 90
Rusie, Amos Ballpl 90 [port]
Rusie, Amos 1871-1942 BioIn 16
Rusiecki, Wanda A. 1954- WhoAmW 91
Rusin, Edward A. 1922- WhoAm 90
Rusine, James Michael 1948- St&PR 91
Rusing, Michael John 1957- WhoEmL 91
Rusiniak, Yvonne Lubov 1945- WhoWrEP 89
Rusinyak, Lawrence Russell 1948- St&PR 91
Rusk, Barbara Joan 1926- St&PR 91
Rusk, David Dean 1909- BiDrUSE 89
Rusk, Dean 1909- BioIn 16, WhoAm 90, WorAlBi
Rusk, Gary H 1943- BiDrAPA 89
Rusk, Howard 1901-1989 AnObit 1989
Rusk, Howard A 1901-1989 ConAu 130, CurBio 90N
Rusk, Howard Archibald 1901-1989 BioIn 16
Rusk, Jeremiah McLain 1830-1893 BiDrUSE 89
Rusk, John D., Jr. ODwPR 91
Rusk, John Michael 1935- BiDrAPA 89
Rusk, Nance J. 1957- WhoWrEP 89
Rusk, Ralph L. 1888-1962 DcLB 103 [port]
Rusk, Richard BioIn 16
Rusk, Thomas Norman BiDrAPA 89
Rusk, Willard C. 1921- St&PR 91
Ruska, Ernest 1906-1988 WorAlBi
Ruska, Ernst 1906-1988 AnObit 1988, BioIn 16
Ruskal, Mary Beth 1944- WhoAmW 91, WhoE 91
Ruskin, Ariane 1935- AuBYP 90
Ruskin, Asa P. 1929-1989 BioIn 16
Ruskin, John 1819-1900 BioIn 16, ConAu 129, EncO&P 3, EncPaPR 91, WorAlBi
Ruskin, Joseph Richard 1924- WhoAm 90
Ruskin, Lewis J 1905-1981 WhoAmA 91N
Ruskin, Paul E BiDrAPA 89
Ruskin, Robert Edward 1916- WhoWor 91
Ruskin, Samuel H BiDrAPA 89
Ruskin, Susan E BiDrAPA 89
Ruskin, Uzi 1945- WhoAm 90
Ruslander, Harold Simon 1904- St&PR 91
Ruslanov, Sviatoslav ConAu 132
Rusling, Barbara Neubert 1945- WhoSSW 91
Rusling, Thomas Griswold 1941- St&PR 91
Rusnock, John A. 1939- St&PR 91
Rusonis, Elisa Jo Slater 1961- WhoAmW 91
Ruspoli, Maria Pia BioIn 16
Ruspoli, Palma BiDrAPA 89
Ruspoli, Sforza BioIn 16
Russ, Charles P., III 1944- St&PR 91
Russ, Donald Bernard BiDrAPA 89
Russ, Helene Gizelle 1957- WhoAmW 91
Russ, Joanna 1937- ConAu 31NR, FemiCLE, MajTwCW, RGTwCSF, WhoAm 90, WhoWrEP 89
Russ, John C. 1949- St&PR 91
Russ, Jonathan Jay BiDrAPA 89
Russ, Lavinia 1904- AuBYP 90
Russ, Lawrence 1950- WhoEmL 91, WhoWrEP 89
Russ, Lisa WhoWrEP 89
Russ, Mark Jack BiDrAPA 89
Russ, Michael 1952- IntWWM 90
Russ, Robert Dale 1933- WhoAm 90
Russ, Sherman B. 1937- St&PR 91
Russ, Zack, Jr. 1923- BiDrAPA 89
Russac, Randall Joseph 1947- WhoSSW 91
Russack, Harvey Noel 1946- WhoE 91
Russack, Richard A. 1938- ODwPR 91
Russak, Ben BioIn 16
Russak, Sidney 1925- BiDrAPA 89
Russakoff, L Mark 1944- BiDrAPA 89
Russakoff, L. Mark 1944- WhoE 91
Russamano, Dean Michael 1956- St&PR 91

Russavage, Janet Marie 1962- WhoAmW 91
Russaw, Joyce Belynda 1952- WhoAmW 91
Russe, Conrad Thomas Campbell 1954- WhoSSW 91
Russe, Henry Paul 1928- WhoAm 90
Russek, Edward BiDrAPA 89
Russek, Franklin David 1942- BiDrAPA 89
Russek, Henry I NewYTBS 90 [port]
Russek, Henry I. 1911-1990 BioIn 16, ConAu 131
Russel, John Joe 1948- WhoSSW 91
Russel, Marjorie Ellen 1944- WhoAmW 91
Russel, Robert Lee, Jr. 1955- WhoE 91
Russell, A. A., Jr. 1927- St&PR 91
Russell, Adononisaw J. 1852-1932 AmLegL
Russell, Albert Edward 1941- St&PR 91
Russell, Albert Milton BiDrAPA 89
Russell, Alden BioIn 16
Russell, Allan 1893-1972 Ballpl 90
Russell, Allan David 1924- WhoAm 90
Russell, Allen Stevenson 1915- WhoAm 90
Russell, Andrew Thomas 1944- BiDrAPA 89
Russell, Armand King 1932- IntWWM 90
Russell, Armistead Goode 1913- St&PR 91
Russell, Attie Yvonne 1923- WhoAmW 91
Russell, Audrey 1906-1989 AnObit 1989, ConAu 129
Russell, Axel 1922- BiDrAPA 89
Russell, Barry William 1950- WhoSSW 91
Russell, Benjamin 1761-1845 BioIn 16
Russell, Benjamin F. 1844-1900? AmLegL
Russell, Bernice K. 1961- WhoAmW 91
Russell, Bertrand 1872-1970 BioIn 16, DcLB 100 [port], MajTwCW, WorAlBi, WrPh P
Russell, Betty Corene 1933- St&PR 91
Russell, Beverly 1941- St&PR 91
Russell, Bill BioIn 16
Russell, Bill 1934- WhoAm 90, WorAlBi
Russell, Bill 1948- Ballpl 90
Russell, Brenda BioIn 16
Russell, Bruce Alexander 1903-1963 WhoAmA 91N
Russell, Carol Ann 1943- WhoAmW 91
Russell, Carolann Marie 1951- WhoWrEP 89
Russell, Catherine Marie 1910- WhoAmW 91
Russell, Catherine Stout 1955- WhoAmW 91
Russell, Charles A. 1933- St&PR 91
Russell, Charles Allyn 1920- WhoE 91
Russell, Charles Edward 1860-1941 BioIn 16
Russell, Charles Hinton 1903-1989 BioIn 16
Russell, Charles M. 1864-1926 BioIn 16
Russell, Charles Marion 1864-1926 WhNaAH
Russell, Charles Mead, Jr. 1937- St&PR 91
Russell, Charles Roberts 1914- WhoAm 90
Russell, Charles Stevens 1926- WhoAm 90
Russell, Charles Taze 1852-1916 WorAlBi
Russell, Charles Wells 1856-1927 BioIn 16
Russell, Charlie L 1932- DrBlPA 90
Russell, Charlotte Sananes 1927- WhoAmW 91
Russell, Cheryl Anne 1952- WhoEmL 91
Russell, Colette Marie 1957- WhoAmW 91
Russell, Colin Archibald 1928- ConAu 30NR
Russell, Craig NewYTBS 90
Russell, Cristine Elaine 1953- WhoAmW 91
Russell, Dan M., Jr. 1913- WhoAm 90
Russell, David Allison 1935- WhoAm 90
Russell, David Emerson 1922- WhoSSW 91
Russell, David L. 1942- WhoAm 90, WhoSSW 91
Russell, David Lawson 1921- WhoAm 90, WhoWor 91
Russell, David Williams 1945- WhoEmL 91, WhoWor 91
Russell, Dean Franklin, Jr. 1957- WhoSSW 91
Russell, Dean Wall 1960- WhoEmL 91
Russell, Don 1899-1986 BioIn 16
Russell, Donald A. 1935- St&PR 91
Russell, Donald G. 1953- ODwPR 91
Russell, Donald H 1913- BiDrAPA 89
Russell, Donald L. 1943- St&PR 91
Russell, Donald Ray 1926- St&PR 91
Russell, Donald Stuart 1906- WhoAm 90
Russell, Dora 1894-1986 FemiCLE
Russell, Dora Winifred Black 1894-1986 BioIn 16
Russell, Dorothy Stuart 1895-1983 DcNaB 1981
Russell, Douglas Campbell 1945- WhoWor 91
Russell, Edward D. 1920- St&PR 91
Russell, Edward Frederick Langley 1895-1981 DcNaB 1981
Russell, Edwin F. 1914- St&PR 91
Russell, Edwin Fairman 1914- WhoAm 90
Russell, Edwin L. 1945- St&PR 91
Russell, Elizabeth 1528-1609 FemiCLE
Russell, Elizabeth Ann 1955- WhoAmW 91
Russell, Elizabeth G. 1958- WhoAmW 91, WhoEmL 91
Russell, Elizabeth Irene 1959- WhoAmW 91
Russell, Eric Frank 1905-1978 EncO&P 3, RGTwCSF
Russell, Eric Jay 1950- WhoEmL 91
Russell, Erin G 1950- BiDrAPA 89
Russell, Erk BioIn 16
Russell, Fay Lee 1944- WhoSSW 91
Russell, Findlay Ewing 1919- WhoAm 90
Russell, Francia BioIn 16
Russell, Francia 1938- WhoAm 90, WhoAmW 91
Russell, Francis 1910- WhoWrEP 89
Russell, Francis 1910-1989 BioIn 16
Russell, Francis Henry 1904-1989 BioIn 16
Russell, Frank Eli 1920- WhoAm 90
Russell, Frank S. 1926- St&PR 91
Russell, Franklin 1926- AuBYP 90
Russell, Fred McFerrin 1906- St&PR 91, WhoAm 90, WhoSSW 91
Russell, Frederick Stratten 1897-1984 DcNaB 1981
Russell, Gaylord L. 1942- St&PR 91
Russell, Gene 1942- St&PR 91
Russell, George A. 1949- St&PR 91
Russell, George Albert 1921- WhoAm 90
Russell, George Albert 1947- St&PR 91
Russell, George Allan BioIn 16
Russell, George Allen 1923- IntWWM 90, WhoAm 90
Russell, George E., Jr. 1944- St&PR 91
Russell, George Keith 1937- WhoE 91
Russell, George W 1867-1935 EncO&P 3
Russell, George William 1867-1935 BioIn 16
Russell, Gerald F M BiDrAPA 89
Russell, Glen Allan 1925- WhoAm 90
Russell, Gordon 1892-1980 ConDes 90, PenDiDA 89
Russell, Grace Jarrell Williams 1924- WhoWrEP 89
Russell, Grant Neil 1953- St&PR 91
Russell, Gregory Keith 1957- WhoSSW 91
Russell, Harold BioIn 16
Russell, Harold 1914- ConAu 129
Russell, Harriet Shaw 1952- WhoAmW 91, WhoEmL 91
Russell, Harry A. 1919- St&PR 91
Russell, Heather Anne 1965- WhoAmW 91
Russell, Helen Crocker 1896-1966 WhoAmA 91N
Russell, Helen Diane 1936- WhoAmA 91, WhoE 91
Russell, Helen Ross 1915- WhoWrEP 89
Russell, Henry 1812-1900 OxCPMus, PenDiMP
Russell, Henry Edwards St&PR 91N
Russell, Henry G. 1912-1990 BioIn 16
Russell, Henry N. 1877-1957 WorAlBi
Russell, Henry Norris 1877-1957 BioIn 16
Russell, Herman Jerome 1930- WhoAm 90
Russell, Ian 1947- IntWWM 90
Russell, Inez Snyder 1951- WhoAmW 91, WhoSSW 91, WhoWor 91
Russell, Irwin E. 1926- St&PR 91
Russell, Jack 1905- Ballpl 90
Russell, James Alvin, Jr. 1917- WhoAm 90, WhoSSW 91
Russell, James Christopher 1948- WhoWor 91
Russell, James E. 1943- St&PR 91
Russell, James F. 1941- St&PR 91
Russell, James Franklin, Jr. 1935- St&PR 91
Russell, James Michael 1946- WhoSSW 91
Russell, James Miller 1959- BiDrAPA 89
Russell, James Miller, III 1935- St&PR 91
Russell, James Reagan 1935- IntWWM 90
Russell, James Sargent 1903- WhoWor 91
Russell, James Webster, Jr. 1921- WhoAm 90
Russell, Jane 1921- BioIn 16, WorAlBi
Russell, Jane Terrill 1945- WhoAmW 91
Russell, Janelle Diner 1957- WhoEmL 91
Russell, Jeanne Y. St&PR 91
Russell, Jeff 1961- Ballpl 90
Russell, Jeffrey Burton 1934- WhoAm 90
Russell, Jerry Don 1954- WhoSSW 91
Russell, Jesse E. BioIn 16
Russell, Jim 1918-1987 Ballpl 90
Russell, Jim 1933- BioIn 16
Russell, Jimmy R. BioIn 16
Russell, John 1710-1771 BioIn 16
Russell, John 1821- AmLegL
Russell, John 1919- WhoAm 90
Russell, John 1961- Ballpl 90
Russell, John A BiDrAPA 89
Russell, John A 1908- BiDrAPA 89
Russell, John A. 1931- St&PR 91
Russell, John Adams 1940- WhoWor 91
Russell, John D 1903- BiDrAPA 89
Russell, John David 1928- WhoAm 90
Russell, John F BiDrAPA 89
Russell, John Francis 1929- WhoSSW 91
Russell, John G. 1928- St&PR 91
Russell, John Jewett 1927- St&PR 91
Russell, John Laurel 1916- WhoAmA 91
Russell, John M. 1942- St&PR 91
Russell, John St. Clair, Jr. 1917- WhoAm 90
Russell, John W. WhoAm 90
Russell, John William 1952- WhoE 91
Russell, Jonathan 1771-1832 BioIn 16
Russell, Joseph 1922- St&PR 91
Russell, Joseph James 1854-1922 AmLegL
Russell, Josiah Cox 1900- WhoAm 90, WhoWor 91
Russell, Joyce Anne Rogers 1920- WhoAm 90
Russell, Katharine A. 1948- St&PR 91
Russell, Katharine Anne 1948- WhoEmL 91
Russell, Keith BioIn 16
Russell, Keith P. 1945- St&PR 91
Russell, Keith Palmer 1916- WhoAm 90
Russell, Ken 1927- BioIn 16, IntWWM 90, WhoAm 90, WorAlBi
Russell, Kenneth Calvin 1936- WhoAm 90
Russell, Kimberly BioIn 16
Russell, Kitty Elizabeth 1953- WhoAmW 91
Russell, Kurt BioIn 16
Russell, Kurt 1951- WorAlBi
Russell, Kurt Von Vogel 1951- WhoAm 90
Russell, Laura 1945- WhoAmW 91
Russell, Leon 1942- EncPR&S 89
Russell, Leonard H. 1927- St&PR 91
Russell, Lillian 1861-1922 BioAmW, BioIn 16, NotWoAT, OxCPMus, WorAlBi
Russell, Louise 1931- WhoAmW 91
Russell, Louise Bennett 1942- WhoAm 90, WhoE 91
Russell, Luis 1902-1963 OxCPMus
Russell, Lynn Darnell 1937- WhoSSW 91
Russell, Marie Bernadette 1962- WhoSSW 91
Russell, Mark 1932- WhoAm 90
Russell, Martin 1934- TwCCr&M 91
Russell, Mary Annette Beauchamp 1866-1941 BioIn 16
Russell, Marybeth BioIn 16
Russell, Mattie Underwood 1915-1988 BioIn 16
Russell, Maud BioIn 16
Russell, Maud 1893?-1989 ConAu 130
Russell, Michael James 1958- WhoE 91, WhoEmL 91, WhoWor 91
Russell, Michael K. 1939- St&PR 91
Russell, Michael R. 1942- St&PR 91
Russell, Michael Thomas 1950- St&PR 91
Russell, Miranda BioIn 16
Russell, Morgan 1886-1953 WhoAmA 91N
Russell, Neil Arthur 1942- WhoWor 91
Russell, Nipsey 1923- DrBlPA 90
Russell, Olive Nelson 1905- IntWWM 90
Russell, Oris Stanley 1922- WhoWor 91
Russell, Paul BioIn 16
Russell, Paul Edgar 1924- WhoAm 90
Russell, Paul J. 1945- ODwPR 91
Russell, Paul Lawrence 1947- WhoAm 90
Russell, Paul Libbey BiDrAPA 89
Russell, Paul Snowden 1925- WhoAm 90
Russell, Pee Wee 1906-1969 BioIn 16, OxCPMus, WorAlBi
Russell, Peggy Taylor 1927- WhoSSW 91, WhoWor 91
Russell, Peter 1921- WorAu 1980 [port]
Russell, Philip C 1933- WhoAmA 91
Russell, Philip King 1932- WhoAm 90
Russell, Phillip Ray 1953- WhoSSW 91
Russell, R. Dana 1906- WhoAm 90
Russell, Rachel 1636-1723 BiDEWW, FemiCLE
Russell, Randall L. C. 1945- St&PR 91, WhoE 91
Russell, Ray 1924- WhoAm 90
Russell, Raymond WhoAmA 91
Russell, Reb 1889-1973 Ballpl 90
Russell, Rebecca Palmer 1965- WhoAmW 91
Russell, Richard B. 1897-1971 WorAlBi
Russell, Richard Bruce 1949- WhoEmL 91
Russell, Richard Doncaster 1929- WhoAm 90
Russell, Richard Frederick 1950- St&PR 91
Russell, Richard G. 1943- St&PR 91
Russell, Richard Joel 1895-1971 DcScB S2
Russell, Richard John 1953- WhoE 91
Russell, Richard L 1932- BiDrAPA 89
Russell, Richard Olney, Jr. 1932- WhoAm 90
Russell, Rip 1915-1976 Ballpl 90
Russell, Robert Alan 1946- WhoSSW 91
Russell, Robert Anderson 1927- St&PR 91
Russell, Robert Emerson, Jr. 1937- WhoWor 91
Russell, Robert Gilmore 1928- WhoAm 90, WhoWor 91
Russell, Robert Hilton 1927- WhoAm 90
Russell, Robert J. 1942- St&PR 91
Russell, Robert John 1938- WhoE 91
Russell, Robert K. BioIn 16
Russell, Robert Larry 1942- St&PR 91
Russell, Robert Leonard 1916- WhoWor 91
Russell, Robert M. 1925- St&PR 91
Russell, Robert Price 1939- WhoAmA 91
Russell, Robin Irvine 1936- WhoWor 91
Russell, Roger Allen 1952- WhoSSW 91
Russell, Rosalind 1911-1976 WorAlBi
Russell, Russell ConAu 130
Russell, Sharman Apt 1954- WhoWrEP 89
Russell, Sheila FemiCLE
Russell, Solveig Paulson 1904- AuBYP 90
Russell, Stanley G., Jr. WhoAm 90
Russell, Stella Pandell WhoAmA 91
Russell, Steven Turner 1950- WhoEmL 91
Russell, T. Alan 1944- St&PR 91
Russell, Ted McKinnies 1943- WhoE 91, WhoWor 91
Russell, Terence Lee 1943- WhoAm 90
Russell, Theodore Pease 1820-1899 BioIn 16
Russell, Theresa BioIn 16
Russell, Thomas Edgie, III 1942- St&PR 91, WhoE 91
Russell, Thomas Fletcher 1951- WhoEmL 91
Russell, Thomas Frank 1924- St&PR 91, WhoAm 90
Russell, Thomas Lyon 1946- WhoWrEP 89
Russell, Thomas Triplett 1910- WhoAm 90
Russell, Thomas William Fraser 1934- WhoAm 90
Russell, Thomas Wright, Jr. 1916- WhoAm 90
Russell, Thomas Wynne 1941- WhoE 91
Russell, Timothy 1951- WhoWrEP 89
Russell, Timothy Paul 1950- WhoWor 91
Russell, Timothy Ross 1942- WhoE 91
Russell, Timothy Wells 1955- IntWWM 90
Russell, Tomas Morgan 1934- WhoAm 90
Russell, Victoria BiDrAPA 89
Russell, Virginia Willis 1913- WhoAmW 91
Russell, Vivian Mary 1952- WhoWor 91
Russell, Wallace Dee 1933- St&PR 91
Russell, Wanda Yvonne 1944- WhoSSW 91
Russell, Wiliam Douglas 1949- St&PR 91
Russell, William Arthur, Jr. 1947- WhoE 91, WhoWor 91
Russell, William Douglas 1962- WhoSSW 91
Russell, William Edward 1944- St&PR 91
Russell, William F. 1805?- AmLegL
Russell, William H. 1812-1872 WorAlBi
Russell, William Howard 1820-1907 BioIn 16
Russell, William Joseph 1941- WhoAm 90
Russell, William Richard, Jr. 1930- St&PR 91
Russell, William Steven 1948- St&PR 91, WhoAm 90
Russell, William Thomas, III 1958- St&PR 91
Russell, William Worthington 1859-1944 BioIn 16
Russell, Willy 1947- ConLC 60 [port]
Russell-Hunter, William Devigne 1926- WhoAm 90, WhoWor 91
Russell of Kingston, John Russell, Earl 1792-1878 BioIn 16
Russell-Smith, Enid 1903-1989 ConAu 129
Russell-Wood, Anthony John R. 1939- WhoAm 90
Russiano, John 1942- WhoAm 90
Russianoff, Leon BioIn 16
Russin, Darius Giles 1953- WhoWor 91
Russin, F. Stanley 1951- St&PR 91
Russin, Jonathan 1937- WhoAm 90
Russin, Robert I 1914- WhoAmA 91
Russin, Robert Isaiah 1914- WhoAm 90
Russinger, Laurentius PenDiDA 89
Russinovich, Nicholas S BiDrAPA 89
Russler, David James 1948- St&PR 91
Russman, Thomas Anthony 1944- WhoSSW 91
Russo, A. Sam 1931- St&PR 91
Russo, Alexander Peter 1922- WhoAm 90, WhoAmA 91
Russo, Anthony BioIn 16
Russo, Anthony F 1942- BiDrAPA 89
Russo, Anthony J. 1938- St&PR 91
Russo, Anthony J. 1953- ODwPR 91
Russo, Bill 1928- OxCPMus
Russo, Charline Smith 1950- WhoEmL 91

Russo, Christine Lou 1958- WhoSSW 91
Russo, Christopher John 1958- WhoE 91
Russo, Cynthia Louise 1958- WhoSSW 91
Russo, David Francis 1944- WhoSSW 91
Russo, Elizabeth BioIn 16
Russo, Frank Raymond, Jr. 1958- WhoSSW 91
Russo, Fred Anthony 1941- St&PR 91
Russo, Gregory T. 1949- St&PR 91
Russo, Irma Haydee Alvarez de 1942- WhoAmW 91, WhoWor 91
Russo, Joe Duane 1947- St&PR 91
Russo, John Francis 1949- WhoEmL 91
Russo, John N. 1936- St&PR 91
Russo, Jose 1942- WhoAm 90
Russo, Joseph Donald 1935- St&PR 91
Russo, Joseph Frank 1924- WhoAm 90
Russo, Karen Marie 1948- WhoE 91
Russo, Kathleen Marie 1947- WhoSSW 91
Russo, Laura ODwPR 91
Russo, Lori H. ODwPR 91
Russo, Marisabina AuBYP 90, BioIn 16
Russo, Marius 1914- Ballpl 90
Russo, Martin A. 1944- WhoAm 90
Russo, Michael Arnold 1959- WhoE 91
Russo, Michael John 1960- WhoEmL 91
Russo, Michael L. 1948- St&PR 91
Russo, Michele 1909- WhoAmA 91
Russo, Nicholas Joseph, II 1948- WhoEmL 91
Russo, Patti Ann 1943- St&PR 91
Russo, Paul A. 1943- WhoAm 90
Russo, Peter Francis 1932- St&PR 91, WhoAm 90
Russo, Peter John 1946- WhoE 91
Russo, Richard 1949- WhoWrEP 89
Russo, Richard A. 1945- St&PR 91
Russo, Richard Paul 1954- ConAu 129
Russo, Robert Ritter 1926- WhoWor 91
Russo, Rosemary 1951- WhoAmW 91
Russo, Roy Lawrence 1935- WhoAm 90
Russo, Sally Fulton Haley WhoAmA 91
Russo, Sharon Kay 1948- WhoAmW 91
Russo, Thomas Anthony 1943- WhoAm 90
Russo, Thomas Joseph 1941- WhoAm 90
Russo, Vito NewYTBS 90
Russo, Vivian Alfonsina 1949- WhoAmW 91
Russo, William J. 1950- ODwPR 91
Russoli, Franco 1923-1977 WhoAmA 91N
Russon, David 1944- WhoWor 91
Russow, Edmund August Friedrich 1841-1897 BioIn 16
Russudan WomWR
Russwurm, John B. BioIn 16
Rust, David E WhoAmA 91
Rust, David Edward 1929- WhoAm 90
Rust, Edward B., Jr. 1950- St&PR 91
Rust, Edwin C 1910- WhoAmA 91
Rust, James Henry, Jr. 1928- WhoE 91
Rust, John Boyd, III 1946- BiDrAPA 89
Rust, Mathias BioIn 16
Rust, Mildred D 1928- BiDrAPA 89
Rust, Patricia Joan 1958- WhoAmW 91
Rust, Philip C. 1944- St&PR 91
Rust, Rachel Louise 1955- WhoAmW 91, WhoSSW 91
Rust, Robert Francis 1927- WhoSSW 91
Rust, Robert Warren 1928- WhoSSW 91
Rust, Rod 1928- WhoAm 90, WhoE 91
Rust, William C. WhoAm 90
Rust, William J. 1929- St&PR 91
Rust, William James 1929- WhoAm 90
Rusta B WhoWrEP 89
Rustagi, Jagdish Sharan 1923- WhoAm 90
Rustagi, Narendra Kumar 1953- WhoE 91
Rustagi, Prevesh Kumar BiDrAPA 89
Rustagi, Raghuvir Sharan 1936- WhoE 91
Rustam-Zade, S. A. WhoWor 91
Rustand, Jon Arthur 1963- WhoSSW 91
Rusten, Elmer Mathew 1902- WhoWor 91
Rusterholz, Kenneth George 1928- WhoAm 90
Rustgi, Moti Lal 1929- WhoAm 90
Rusthoven, Peter James 1951- WhoAm 90
Rustin, Bayard 1910-1987 BioIn 16, EncAL, WorAlBi
Rustin, Catherine Ann 1956- WhoSSW 91
Rustin, Terry Aubrey BiDrAPA 89
Rustvold, Katherine Jo 1950- WhoAmA 91
Rusudan WomWR
Rusudani WomWR
Ruszkai, Stephen John 1966- WhoE 91
Rut, Josef 1926- IntWWM 90
Ruta, Peter Paul 1918- WhoAmA 91, WhoE 91
Rutan, Burt BioIn 16
Rutan, Dick BioIn 16
Rutan, Elbert L. 1943- WhoAm 90
Rutan, Everett John, III 1952- WhoE 91
Rutan, Richard Glenn 1938- WhoAm 90
Rutan, Thomas Carl 1954- WhoSSW 91
Rutenberg-Rosenberg, Sharon Leslie 1951- WhoAm 90, WhoAmW 91
Rutenburg, Selma Hyde 1924- BiDrAPA 89
Ruter, Christiaan Frederik 1938- WhoWor 91
Rutes, Walter Alan 1928- WhoAm 90
Rutford, Robert Hoxie 1933- WhoAm 90, WhoSSW 91
Rutgers, Katharine Phillips 1910- WhoAmW 91, WhoE 91
Rutgers van der Loeff-Basenau, An 1910- EncCoWW
Ruth, Alpheus Landis 1915- WhoAm 90
Ruth, Amy BiDrAPA 89
Ruth, Babe 1895-1948 Ballpl 90 [port], BioIn 16
Ruth, Charles Wallace 1922- St&PR 91
Ruth, Cynthia Moore BiDrAPA 89
Ruth, Daniel John 1949- WhoAm 90
Ruth, Douglas D BiDrAPA 89
Ruth, Franklin William, Jr. 1917- WhoAm 90
Ruth, George Herman 1895-1948 BioIn 16, WorAlBi
Ruth, Irma 1929- WhoAmW 91
Ruth, James Perry 1946- WhoAm 90
Ruth, Jan-Erik Uno 1944- WhoWor 91
Ruth, John Homer 1936- WhoAm 90
Ruth, JoLinda S. 1956- WhoE 91, WhoWor 91
Ruth, Kevin Jack 1960- WhoE 91
Ruth, Lois-Jean 1931- WhoAmW 91
Ruth, Marsha Diane 1950- WhoAmW 91
Ruth, Roger A. 1950- WhoSSW 91
Ruth, Sheila 1951- WhoAmA 91
Ruth, Volker 1932- WhoWor 91
Ruth, William Edward 1926- WhoAm 90
Ruthchild, Geraldine Quietlake WhoAmW 91
Ruthenberg, Charles E. 1882-1927 EncAL
Ruthenberg, Donald Burton 1930- WhoAm 90
Rutherfoord, James Kincanon 1946- WhoSSW 91
Rutherford, Brett 1947- WhoWrEP 89
Rutherford, Charles BioIn 16
Rutherford, Donald W. S. 1939- St&PR 91
Rutherford, Douglas 1915-1988 TwCCr&M 91
Rutherford, Eric D. 1929- St&PR 91
Rutherford, Ernest 1871-1937 WorAlBi
Rutherford, G. W. 1920- St&PR 91
Rutherford, Harold Phillip 1951- WhoEmL 91, WhoSSW 91, WhoWor 91
Rutherford, Howard Don 1936- WhoSSW 91
Rutherford, J. H. 1930- St&PR 91
Rutherford, James Lee 1954- BiDrAPA 89
Rutherford, John Sherman, III 1938- WhoAm 90
Rutherford, Joseph Franklin 1869-1942 WorAlBi
Rutherford, Katherine Swan BiDrAPA 89
Rutherford, Leo Herschel 1929- St&PR 91
Rutherford, Margaret 1892-1972 WorAlBi
Rutherford, Mark 1831-1913 BioIn 16
Rutherford, Mildred L. 1852-1928 BioAmW
Rutherford, Paul Harding 1938- WhoAm 90
Rutherford, Ralph DeWitt, Jr. 1949- WhoSSW 91
Rutherford, Rana Hunter 1952- St&PR 91
Rutherford, Reid 1952- WhoEmL 91
Rutherford, Robert Barry 1931- WhoAm 90
Rutherford, Romilly T. 1908- St&PR 91
Rutherford, Sally Jane 1959- St&PR 91
Rutherford, Samuel J. 1928- St&PR 91
Rutherford, William Drake 1939- WhoAm 90, WhoE 91
Ruthling, Ford 1933- WhoAmA 91
Ruthman, Thomas R. 1933- St&PR 91
Ruthven, Alexander Patric Greysteil Hore 1939- BioIn 16
Ruthven, Dick 1951- Ballpl 90
Ruthven, Douglas Morris 1938- WhoAm 90
Ruthven, John Aldrich 1924- WhoAmA 91
Rutigliano, Barbara A. 1951- St&PR 91
Rutigliano, Sam 1932- BioIn 16
Rutins, Karlis Visvaldis 1937- WhoE 91, WhoWor 91
Rutishauser, Robert Gray 1931- St&PR 91
Rutkin, Lynne 1950- WhoE 91
Rutkin, Seymour 1927- WhoAm 90
Rutkovsky, Lisa Ellen 1962- WhoAmW 91
Rutkovsky, Paul Michael 1947- WhoWrEP 89
Rutkowski, David John 1951- St&PR 91
Rutkowski, Joseph Richard 1954- IntWWM 90
Rutkowski, Katherine Sharon 1951- WhoE 91
Rutland, George Patrick 1932- WhoAm 90, WhoE 91
Rutland, Lilli Ida 1918- WhoAmA 91
Rutland, Robert Allen 1922- WhoAm 90
Rutledge, Arthur Clayton, Jr. 1944- St&PR 91
Rutledge, Brett TwCCr&M 91
Rutledge, Brian Aaron 1951- WhoAm 90, WhoE 91
Rutledge, Calvin BioIn 16
Rutledge, Carol Marie Brunner 1938- WhoAmW 91
Rutledge, Charles Ozwin 1937- WhoAm 90
Rutledge, Cheryl Juanita 1946- IntWWM 90
Rutledge, E. Peter 1940- St&PR 91
Rutledge, Edward 1749-1800 EncCRAm, WorAlBi
Rutledge, Eileen Marie 1958- St&PR 91
Rutledge, Felix Noah 1917- WhoAm 90
Rutledge, Ivan Cate 1915- WhoAm 90
Rutledge, James Joseph 1948- WhoSSW 91
Rutledge, John 1739-1800 BioIn 16, EncCRAm
Rutledge, John H. 1950-1987 BioIn 16
Rutledge, John Paul 1943- BiDrAPA 89
Rutledge, John William 1923- WhoAm 90, WhoWor 91
Rutledge, Paul Edmund, III 1953- St&PR 91
Rutledge, Perry 1930- St&PR 91
Rutledge, Robert William 1950- WhoSSW 91
Rutledge, Roger Keith 1946- WhoEmL 91
Rutledge, William J. 1932- St&PR 91
Rutman, Charles BioIn 16
Rutman, Leo 1935- ConAu 30NR
Rutman, Mark C. 1930- ODwPR 91
Rutman, Mark Charles 1930- WhoAm 90
Rutman, Neil 1953- IntWWM 90
Rutman, Robert Jesse 1919- WhoAm 90
Rutman, Sheldon Mark 1931- WhoSSW 91
Rutman, Susan H. 1948- WhoAmW 91
Rutner, Mickey 1920- BioIn 16
Rutrick, Daniel 1946- BiDrAPA 89
Rutsala, Vern 1934- WhoWrEP 89
Rutsch, Alexander WhoAmA 91
Rutschman, Edward Raymond 1946- IntWWM 90
Rutsky, Albert 1928- BiDrAPA 89
Rutsky, Lester 1924- WhoWrEP 89
Rutstein, David W. 1944- St&PR 91, WhoAm 90
Rutstein, Sheldon 1934- St&PR 91
Rutstein, Stanley Harold 1941- WhoAm 90
Rutt, Carl Nelson 1944- BiDrAPA 89
Rutt, Jan Curtis 1944- WhoE 91
Ruttan, Susan 1950- WorAlBi
Ruttan, Vernon Wesley 1924- WhoAm 90
Rutten, Martin Gerard 1910-1970 DcScB S2
Rutten, Rand John 1954- WhoEmL 91
Ruttenberg, Alan Samuel BiDrAPA 89
Ruttenberg, Bertram A 1922- BiDrAPA 89
Ruttenberg, Derald H. 1916- WhoAm 90
Ruttenberg, Harold Joseph 1914- St&PR 91, WhoAm 90
Ruttenberg, Harold S. 1941- St&PR 91
Ruttenberg, Harvey Nolan 1942- WhoSSW 91
Ruttenberg, Reid 1936- St&PR 91
Ruttenberg, Rhoda BiDrAPA 89
Ruttenberg, Stanley Harvey 1917- WhoAm 90
Rutter, Deborah Frances 1956- WhoAmW 91
Rutter, Elizabeth J. 1937- St&PR 91
Rutter, Elizabeth Jane 1937- WhoAm 90
Rutter, Frances Tompson 1920- WhoAm 90
Rutter, Itala T.C. 1940- WhoAmW 91
Rutter, James E. 1933- WhoE 91
Rutter, John 1945- IntWWM 90
Rutter, Nathaniel Westlund 1932- WhoAm 90
Rutter, Peter 1943- BiDrAPA 89
Rutter, Thomas H. 1950- St&PR 91
Rutterer, Paul James 1948- St&PR 91
Rutterer, Paul James Matthew 1948- WhoAm 90
Rutti, Carl 1949- IntWWM 90
Ruttinger, Jacquelyn 1940- WhoAmA 91
Ruttner, Albert A. ODwPR 91
Ruttner, Albert A. 1937- WhoAm 90
Rutty, John 1698-1775 BioIn 16
Rutups, Haralds 1922- IntWWM 90
Rutz, Karen Elisabeth 1954- WhoAmW 91
Rutz, Rebecca Ruth 1948- WhoSSW 91
Rutz, Richard Emil, Jr. 1952- WhoEmL 91
Rutz, Richard Frederick 1919- WhoAm 90
Rutzen, Arthur BioIn 16
Rutzen, Arthur Cooper, Jr. 1947- WhoAm 90
Rutzky, Ivy Sky 1948- WhoAmA 91
Rutzky, Lloyd BioIn 16
Ruud, Arne Conrad 1926- WhoE 91
Ruud, Millard Harrington 1917- WhoAm 90
Ruuhinen, Erkki BioIn 16
Ruuhinen, Erkki 1943- ConDes 90
Ruusuvuori, Aarno Emil 1925- WhoWor 91
Ruvalcaba-Flores, Rosemary 1959- WhoHisp 91
Ruvane, John Austin 1935- WhoAm 90
Ruvelson, Alan K. 1915- St&PR 91
Ruvolo, Felix 1912- WhoAm 90
Ruvolo, Felix Emmanuele 1912- WhoAmA 91
Ruwe, Dean Melvin 1938- St&PR 91, WhoAm 90
Ruwe, L. Nicholas 1933-1990 BioIn 16, NewYTBS 90 [port]
Ruwe, Lester Nicholas 1933-1990 WhoAm 90
Ruyle-Hullinger, Elizabeth Smith 1946- WhoAmW 91, WhoEmL 91
Ruys, Chris ODwPR 91
Ruysbrock, Jan van 1293-1381 EncO&P 3
Ruysbroek, Jan van 1293-1381 EncO&P 3
Ruysch, Rachel 1664-1750 BioIn 16, IntDcAA 90
Ruysser, Bernard J. 1919- St&PR 91
Ruza, Martin B. 1920- St&PR 91
Ruza, Stanley Wolfe 1919- St&PR 91
Ruzdjak, Vladimir 1922- IntWWM 90
Ruzic, David Neil 1958- WhoEmL 91
Ruzic, Neil Pierce 1930- WhoAm 90, WhoWrEP 89
Ruzicano, Raymond Stephen BiDrAPA 89
Ruzick, S., Jr. 1945- St&PR 91
Ruzicka, Annette Marie 1960- WhoAmW 91
Ruzicka, Jeffrey F. 1942- WhoAm 90
Ruzicka, Jeffrey Friser 1942- St&PR 91
Ruzicka, Leopold 1887-1976 DcScB S2
Ruzicka, Mary Helen 1945- WhoE 91
Ruzicka, Rudolf 1941- IntWWM 90
Ruzicka, Rudolph 1883-1978 WhoAmA 91N
Ruzicka, Vicki 1945- WhoAmW 91
Ruzickova, Zuzana 1927- WhoWor 91
Ruzickova, Zuzana 1928- IntWWM 90, PenDiMP
Ruzimatov, Faruk BioIn 16
Ruzinsky, Ellen Fern 1961- WhoAmW 91
Ruzo, Luis Octavio 1949- WhoEmL 91
Ruzu WhoAmA 91
Ruzumna, Richard A BiDrAPA 89
Rwegellera, George G C 1936- BiDrAPA 89
Ryall, Jo-Ellyn M 1949- BiDrAPA 89
Ryals, Clyde de Loache 1928- WhoAm 90
Ryals, Shirley A. 1933- St&PR 91
Ryan, Alice J. 1959- St&PR 91
Ryan, Alison 1964- ODwPR 91
Ryan, Allan Andrew, Jr. 1945- WhoAm 90
Ryan, Andrew Jack BiDrAPA 89
Ryan, Anne 1889-1954 BiDWomA
Ryan, Arthur F. 1942- St&PR 91
Ryan, Arthur Frederick 1942- WhoAm 90, WhoE 91
Ryan, Arthur Norman 1938- St&PR 91, WhoAm 90
Ryan, Arthur S. 1945- St&PR 91
Ryan, Barbara Battle 1928- WhoWrEP 89
Ryan, Barry J. 1949- St&PR 91
Ryan, Barry Ronelle 1934- St&PR 91
Ryan, Bernard Francis 1936- St&PR 91
Ryan, Blondy 1906-1959 Ballpl 90
Ryan, Bruce Kenneth St&PR 91
Ryan, Buddy BioIn 16
Ryan, Buddy 1934- WhoAm 90, WhoE 91
Ryan, Carl Ray 1938- WhoAm 90
Ryan, Carol Eileen 1944- BiDrAPA 89
Ryan, Caroline Menslage 1939- WhoAmW 91
Ryan, Cathy Kaman 1953- WhoAmW 91
Ryan, Charles Barbour 1950- WhoSSW 91
Ryan, Charles E. 1940- ODwPR 91
Ryan, Charles Edward 1940- WhoAm 90
Ryan, Charles Patrick, Jr. 1939- St&PR 91
Ryan, Cheli Duran AuBYP 90
Ryan, Cheyney BioIn 16
Ryan, Christopher J. St&PR 91
Ryan, Christopher Robert 1946- WhoSSW 91
Ryan, Clarence Augustine, Jr. 1931- WhoAm 90, WhoWor 91
Ryan, Colleen BiDrAPA 89
Ryan, Connie 1920- Ballpl 90
Ryan, Cornelius Michael 1933- WhoAm 90
Ryan, Cornelius O'Brien 1917- WhoAm 90
Ryan, Daniel Leo 1930- WhoAm 90
Ryan, Daniel N. 1930- St&PR 91
Ryan, Daniel Nolan 1930- WhoAm 90
Ryan, Daniel P. 1940- St&PR 91
Ryan, David Michael 1939- WhoAmA 91
Ryan, Deborah Bohlmann 1952- WhoSSW 91
Ryan, Dennis Patrick 1946- St&PR 91
Ryan, Desmond 1943- ConAu 130
Ryan, Diane Phyllis 1954- WhoE 91
Ryan, Donald Francis 1929- St&PR 91
Ryan, Donald Kevin 1952- WhoEmL 91
Ryan, Donald Patrick 1930- St&PR 91
Ryan, Dorothy Barger 1942- WhoE 91
Ryan, DyAnne DiSalvo- 1954- BioIn 16
Ryan, Edward J., Jr. 1953- WhoWor 91
Ryan, Edward J., Jr. 1957- St&PR 91
Ryan, Edward L. St&PR 91
Ryan, Edward V. 1928- St&PR 91
Ryan, Edwin L., Jr. 1930- St&PR 91

Ryan, Eileen Patricia 1957- *BiDrAPA 89, WhoE 91*
Ryan, Elaine Marie 1958- *WhoE 91*
Ryan, Eleanore A. *WhoAmW 91*
Ryan, Eliz Ann 1947- *WhoSSW 91*
Ryan, Elizabeth *WhoAmA 91*
Ryan, Ellen Bouchard 1947- *WhoAm 90*
Ryan, Ellen M *BiDrAPA 89*
Ryan, Ellie Louise 1945- *WhoAmW 91*
Ryan, Frances Mary 1920- *WhoAm 90*
Ryan, Francis J. 1947- *IntWWM 90*
Ryan, Francis Patrick 1944- *WhoWor 91*
Ryan, Frank J. 1931- *WhoAm 90*
Ryan, Frank J. 1935- *ODwPR 91*
Ryan, Frank J. 1938- *ODwPR 91*
Ryan, Frank T. 1939- *ODwPR 91*
Ryan, Frederick Joseph, Jr. 1955- *WhoAm 90*
Ryan, George 1934- *WhoAm 90*
Ryan, George William *BioIn 16*
Ryan, George William 1939- *WhoWor 91*
Ryan, Gerald A. 1935- *St&PR 91*
Ryan, Gerard Spencer 1926- *WhoAm 90*
Ryan, Harold J. 1945- *St&PR 91*
Ryan, Hewitt Fitts 1928- *BiDrAPA 89*
Ryan, Hewson Anthony 1922- *WhoAm 90*
Ryan, Holly Anne 1945- *WhoAmW 91*
Ryan, Howard Chris 1916- *WhoAm 90*
Ryan, Hugh 1832-1899 *DcCanB 12*
Ryan, Hugh M. 1944- *ODwPR 91*
Ryan, Ione Jean Alohilani 1926- *WhoAmW 91*
Ryan, Irene 1903-1973 *WorAlBi*
Ryan, J. Richard 1929- *St&PR 91*
Ryan, Jack 1869-1952 *Ballpl 90*
Ryan, Jack 1878-1958 *Ballpl 90*
Ryan, James A 1840?-1896 *DcCanB 12*
Ryan, James C. 1938- *St&PR 91*
Ryan, James Edwin 1919- *WhoAm 90*
Ryan, James Francis 1928- *WhoAm 90*
Ryan, James Franklin 1948- *WhoAm 90*
Ryan, James H *BiDrAPA 89*
Ryan, James Joseph 1929- *WhoAm 90*
Ryan, James Leo 1932- *WhoAm 90*
Ryan, James Martin 1954- *WhoE 91*
Ryan, James Neal 1931- *St&PR 91*
Ryan, James R. 1948- *ODwPR 91*
Ryan, James Thomas 1931- *St&PR 91*
Ryan, James Vincent *BioIn 16, NewYTBS 90*
Ryan, James Walter 1935- *WhoAm 90, WhoWor 91*
Ryan, Jane Frances 1950- *WhoEmL 91*
Ryan, Jane Touhey Hammes 1925- *WhoSSW 91*
Ryan, Janice E. *WhoAmW 91*
Ryan, Jeanette Mines 1948- *SmATA X [port]*
Ryan, Jerry William 1928- *WhoAm 90*
Ryan, Jill Wyan 1947- *WhoE 91*
Ryan, Jimmy 1863-1923 *Ballpl 90 [port]*
Ryan, Joan Aho *ODwPR 91*
Ryan, Joan Sue 1948- *WhoEmL 91*
Ryan, John C. *BioIn 16*
Ryan, John D. 1864-1933 *WorAlBi*
Ryan, John David *BioIn 16*
Ryan, John F *BiDrAPA 89*
Ryan, John Francis 1946- *St&PR 91*
Ryan, John Francis, III 1953- *St&PR 91*
Ryan, John Franklin 1848-1936 *AmLegL*
Ryan, John Franklin 1925- *WhoAm 90*
Ryan, John Gerald 1952- *St&PR 91*
Ryan, John J. *ODwPR 91*
Ryan, John J. *BioIn 16*
Ryan, John J. 1948- *St&PR 91*
Ryan, John Lester, Jr. 1936- *St&PR 91*
Ryan, John P. 1938- *ConTFT 8*
Ryan, John T., Jr. 1912- *St&PR 91*
Ryan, John Thomas, III 1943- *St&PR 91, WhoAm 90*
Ryan, John Thomas, Jr. 1912- *WhoAm 90, WhoWor 91*
Ryan, John William 1929- *WhoAm 90*
Ryan, John William 1937- *WhoAm 90, WhoWor 91*
Ryan, John William, Jr. 1940- *WhoAm 90*
Ryan, Joseph B., Jr. 1931- *St&PR 91*
Ryan, Joseph Bloomfield, Jr. 1931- *WhoAm 90*
Ryan, Joseph Edwin 1929- *St&PR 91*
Ryan, Joseph Thomas 1913- *WhoAm 90*
Ryan, Joseph W., Jr. 1948- *WhoEmL 91*
Ryan, Judith Andre 1936- *WhoAm 90*
Ryan, Keith William 1922- *WhoWor 91*
Ryan, Kenneth John 1926- *WhoAm 90*
Ryan, Kenneth Robert, Jr. 1947- *WhoSSW 91*
Ryan, Kevin James 1940- *St&PR 91*
Ryan, Kevin Matthew 1939- *WhoAm 90*
Ryan, Larry Robert 1950- *BiDrAPA 89*
Ryan, Lawrence Thomas, Jr. 1952- *WhoEmL 91*
Ryan, Lehan Jerome 1935- *WhoAm 90*
Ryan, Leo Vincent 1927- *WhoAm 90*
Ryan, Leonard Eames 1930- *WhoAm 90, WhoWor 91*
Ryan, Loretta Ann 1955- *WhoAmW 91*
Ryan, Louis Farthing 1947- *St&PR 91, WhoAm 90*
Ryan, M. Paton *WhoAm 90*
Ryan, Margaret 1950- *WhoWrEP 89*
Ryan, Marisa *BioIn 16*
Ryan, Marleigh Grayer 1930- *WhoAm 90, WhoAmW 91*
Ryan, Martin David 1947- *WhoE 91*
Ryan, Mary A. 1940- *WhoAm 90, WhoAmW 91, WhoWor 91*
Ryan, Mary E 1953- *SmATA 61 [port]*
Ryan, Mary Elizabeth 1953- *WhoWrEP 89*
Ryan, Mary Elizabeth 1962- *WhoE 91*
Ryan, Maureen Ann 1957- *WhoE 91*
Ryan, Meg *BioIn 16*
Ryan, Michael 1950- *WhoE 91*
Ryan, Michael 1952- *WhoE 91*
Ryan, Michael A. 1949- *St&PR 91*
Ryan, Michael Beecher 1936- *WhoAm 90*
Ryan, Michael E. 1938- *St&PR 91*
Ryan, Michael Edmond 1938- *WhoAm 90*
Ryan, Michael J. 1952- *St&PR 91*
Ryan, Michael Joseph 1945- *WhoEmL 91*
Ryan, Michael Joseph 1953- *WhoWrEP 89*
Ryan, Michael Louis 1945- *WhoEmL 91, WhoWor 91*
Ryan, Michael O. 1945- *WhoE 91*
Ryan, Mike 1941- *Ballpl 90*
Ryan, Mike, II 1951- *WhoEmL 91*
Ryan, Nancy D. *BioIn 16*
Ryan, Nancy Marie *WhoWrEP 89*
Ryan, Nancy Marie 1938- *WhoAmW 91, WhoE 91*
Ryan, Neal D 1952- *BiDrAPA 89*
Ryan, Noel 1925- *WhoAm 90*
Ryan, Nolan *BioIn 16*
Ryan, Nolan 1947- *Ballpl 90 [port], WhoAm 90, WorAlBi*
Ryan, Pat *WhoWrEP 89*
Ryan, Patricia *WhoAm 90*
Ryan, Patricia Ellen 1956- *BiDrAPA 89*
Ryan, Patrick 1949- *ODwPR 91*
Ryan, Patrick G. 1937- *St&PR 91, WhoAm 90*
Ryan, Patrick J. 1937- *St&PR 91*
Ryan, Patrick J. 1938- *WhoAm 90*
Ryan, Patrick John 1937- *WhoAm 90*
Ryan, Patrick Michael 1937- *St&PR 91, WhoAm 90*
Ryan, Patrick Michael 1944- *WhoAm 90*
Ryan, Paul F. 1938- *St&PR 91*
Ryan, Paul J. 1925- *St&PR 91*
Ryan, Paul Ryder, Jr. 1932- *WhoAm 90, WhoE 91, WhoWor 91*
Ryan, Peter John 1922- *WhoAm 90*
Ryan, Peter M. 1948- *St&PR 91*
Ryan, Philip Browne 1942- *WhoE 91*
Ryan, Philip G. 1945- *ODwPR 91*
Ryan, Philip Glennon 1945- *WhoE 91, WhoEmL 91*
Ryan, Raymond D. 1922- *WhoAm 90*
Ryan, Reade Haines, Jr. 1937- *WhoAm 90, WhoWor 91*
Ryan, Regina Claire 1938- *WhoAm 90*
Ryan, Richard E 1950- *WhoAmA 91*
Ryan, Richard G. 1953- *St&PR 91*
Ryan, Richard James 1937- *WhoAm 90*
Ryan, Richard K. 1937- *St&PR 91*
Ryan, Richard Matthew 1945- *St&PR 91*
Ryan, Robert 1909-1973 *WorAlBi*
Ryan, Robert 1913-1973 *BioIn 16*
Ryan, Robert Collins 1953- *WhoWor 91*
Ryan, Robert L. 1935- *ODwPR 91*
Ryan, Robert Leslie 1943- *WhoAm 90*
Ryan, Robert Seibert 1922- *WhoAm 90*
Ryan, Roger Neville 1934- *WhoAm 90*
Ryan, Ronald Eugene 1945- *WhoEmL 91*
Ryan, Rosy 1898-1980 *Ballpl 90*
Ryan, Ruth M *BiDrAPA 89*
Ryan, Sandra Belcher 1943- *WhoAmW 91*
Ryan, Sarah Bucknell 1960- *WhoEmL 91*
Ryan, Sheena Ross 1944- *WhoWor 91*
Ryan, Sheila Benson 1964- *WhoSSW 91*
Ryan, Sherry Lynn 1944- *WhoAmW 91*
Ryan, Stephen F. 1935- *St&PR 91*
Ryan, Stephen Joseph, Jr. 1940- *WhoAm 90*
Ryan, Steven James *BiDrAPA 89*
Ryan, Suzanne Irene 1939- *WhoAmW 91, WhoE 91*
Ryan, T. Claude 1898-1982 *BioIn 16*
Ryan, Theresa Ann Julia 1962- *WhoAmW 91*
Ryan, Therese Eileen 1952- *WhoAmW 91*
Ryan, Thomas E. 1931- *ODwPR 91*
Ryan, Thomas E 1944- *BiDrAPA 89*
Ryan, Thomas Edward 1931- *St&PR 91*
Ryan, Thomas F. 1851-1928 *WorAlBi*
Ryan, Thomas J. 1930- *St&PR 91*
Ryan, Thomas Joseph 1945- *WhoAm 90*
Ryan, Thomas M. 1948- *St&PR 91*
Ryan, Thomas P. *St&PR 91*
Ryan, Thomas Patrick, Jr. 1929- *WhoAm 90, WhoE 91*
Ryan, Thomas Timothy, Jr. 1945- *WhoAm 90*
Ryan, Thomas W. *St&PR 91*
Ryan, Thomas W. 1947- *WhoAm 90*
Ryan, Tom 1922- *BioIn 16*
Ryan, Tom Kreusch 1926- *WhoAm 90*
Ryan, Tony *BioIn 16*
Ryan, Tula Fleshman 1927- *WhoAmW 91*
Ryan, Veronica 1956- *BiDWomA*
Ryan, Victoria Brosokas 1950- *WhoSSW 91*
Ryan, William Anthony 1926- *St&PR 91*
Ryan, William C 1930- *BiDrAPA 89*
Ryan, William Edward 1936- *WhoAmA 91*
Ryan, William Francis 1925- *WhoAm 90*
Ryan, William Frank 1924- *WhoAm 90, WhoWor 91*
Ryan, William George 1951- *BiDrAPA 89*
Ryan, William Herbert 1937- *WhoSSW 91*
Ryan, William James *BiDrAPA 89*
Ryan, William John, Jr. 1954- *WhoE 91*
Ryan, William Joseph 1932- *WhoAm 90, WhoWor 91*
Ryan, William Paul 1930- *St&PR 91*
Ryan, William R. 1911- *St&PR 91, WhoAm 90, WhoE 91*
Ryan-White, Jewell 1943- *WhoAmW 91*
Ryang, Myung Kim 1948- *BiDrAPA 89*
Ryans, William Thomas, Jr. 1958- *WhoSSW 91*
Ryant, Bradley Erven 1935- *WhoE 91*
Ryant, Mary Louise 1942- *WhoAmW 91*
Ryba, Mike 1903-1971 *Ballpl 90*
Ryback, Ralph Simon 1940- *BiDrAPA 89*
Ryback, William Allan 1946- *WhoEmL 91*
Rybak, Michael Dennis 1951- *WhoEmL 91*
Rybak, Wlodzimierz Stefan 1922- *BiDrAPA 89*
Rybakov, Anatolii Naumovich *BioIn 16*
Rybakov, Anatoly Naumovich 1911- *WorAu 1980 [port]*
Rybalka, Michel 1933- *WhoAm 90*
Rybar, Peter 1913- *IntWWM 90*
Rybar, Valerian S. *NewYTBS 90 [port]*
Rybar, Valerian S. 1918-1990 *BioIn 16*
Rybarczyk, Heidi Mary 1957- *WhoAmW 91*
Rybczynski, Witold Marian 1943- *WhoAm 90*
Rybensky, Jaroslav *PenDiMP*
Ryberg, Eric Sven 1964- *WhoE 91*
Ryberg, Jean E. 1932- *St&PR 91*
Ryberg, Percy E 1908- *BiDrAPA 89*
Rybicki, Alexander Andrew, Jr. 1944- *St&PR 91*
Rybicki, Clarice Annette 1959- *WhoEmL 91*
Rybnick, William 1920- *St&PR 91*
Rybolt, Robert Marsh 1913- *WhoAm 90*
Rybolt, Thomas R 1954- *SmATA 62*
Ryburn, Betty Cornett 1935- *WhoAmW 91*
Ryburn, Samuel McChesney 1914- *WhoAm 90, WhoWor 91*
Rycheck, Jayne Bogus *WhoAmW 91*
Rychecky, Helen Rose 1922- *WhoAmW 91*
Rychlak, Joseph Frank 1928- *WhoAm 90*
Ryckman, DeVere Wellington 1924- *WhoAm 90*
Ryckman, Lawrence G. 1955- *St&PR 91*
Ryckoff, Irving M *BiDrAPA 89*
Rycroft, Donald C. 1938- *St&PR 91*
Rycroft, Donald Cahill 1938- *WhoAm 90*
Rycroft, Eric Brian 1948- *IntWWM 90*
Rycus, Mitchell Julian 1932- *WhoAm 90*
Ryczek, Edward Frank 1938- *St&PR 91*
Rydberg, Abraham Viktor 1828-1895 *DcScanL*
Rydberg, Sven 1933- *WhoWor 91*
Ryde, Hans Bengt 1931- *WhoWor 91*
Rydell, Bobby 1942- *WorAlBi*
Rydell, Chris *BioIn 16*
Rydell, Forbes *TwCCr&M 91*
Rydell, Mark *BioIn 16*
Rydell, Roger P. 1955- *ODwPR 91*
Rydell, Sheila Veronica 1964- *WhoAmW 91*
Ryden, Bengt Gunnar 1936- *WhoWor 91*
Ryden, Hope *AuBYP 90*
Ryden, John Graham 1939- *St&PR 91, WhoAm 90*
Ryden, Katherine 1947- *St&PR 91*
Ryden, Kenneth Glenn 1945- *WhoAmA 91*
Ryden, Mats Lennart Edvard 1929- *WhoWor 91*
Ryden, T. E. 1936- *St&PR 91*
Rydenfelt, Sven 1911- *ConAu 132*
Ryder, Albert Pinkham 1847-1917 *BioIn 16, IntDcAA 90, WorAlBi*
Ryder, Bruce David 1955- *WhoEmL 91*
Ryder, C. C. 1947- *St&PR 91*
Ryder, Chauncey Foster 1868-1949 *WhoAmA 91N*
Ryder, Florence *BioIn 16*
Ryder, Frank A. 1939- *St&PR 91*
Ryder, Georgia A. 1924- *IntWWM 90*
Ryder, Harl Edgar 1938- *WhoAm 90*
Ryder, Henry Clay 1928- *WhoAm 90*
Ryder, Jack 1871-1936 *Ballpl 90*
Ryder, Jack McBride 1928- *WhoAm 90*
Ryder, Jeanne 1952- *IntWWM 90*
Ryder, Jim *BioIn 16*
Ryder, Joanne *BioIn 16*
Ryder, John Douglas 1907- *WhoAm 90*
Ryder, Jonathan *MajTwCW, TwCCr&M 91, WorAu 1980*
Ryder, M. Lynn 1937- *St&PR 91*
Ryder, Mahler Bessinger 1937- *WhoAmA 91*
Ryder, Paul Allan 1964- *WhoE 91*
Ryder, Raymond Teele 1957- *WhoSSW 91*
Ryder, Sandra Smith 1949- *WhoAmW 91, WhoSSW 91, WhoWor 91*
Ryder, Stephen Willis, Jr. 1923- *St&PR 91*
Ryder, Thomas Michael 1934- *WhoAm 90*
Ryder, William P. 1936- *ODwPR 91*
Ryder, Winona *BioIn 16*
Ryder, Winona 1971- *ConTFT 8 [port], News 91-2 [port]*
Rydholm, Ralph Williams 1937- *St&PR 91, WhoAm 90*
Rydin, Bo Goran 1932- *WhoWor 91*
Rydl, Kurt 1947- *IntWWM 90*
Rydman, John Alan 1950- *WhoSSW 91*
Rydquist, Dean B. 1959- *WhoSSW 91*
Rydz, John S. 1925- *St&PR 91, WhoAm 90*
Rydzewski, Robert Stanley 1956- *St&PR 91*
Rydzinski, Joyce Weg 1952- *BiDrAPA 89*
Rye, Curtis LaVerne 1929- *St&PR 91*
Rye, Joe T. 1938- *St&PR 91*
Rye, Margareta 1935- *WhoWor 91*
Rye, Maria 1829-1903 *BioIn 16*
Rye, Walter L., Jr. 1930- *St&PR 91*
Ryerse, Dorance D., Jr. 1932- *St&PR 91*
Ryerse, William C. 1929- *St&PR 91*
Ryerson, Gary 1948- *Ballpl 90*
Ryerson, Jay W. 1935- *St&PR 91*
Ryerson, Joseph Leslie 1918- *WhoAm 90*
Ryerson, Kevin *EncPaPR 91, NewAgE 90*
Ryerson, Margery 1886-1989 *BioIn 16*
Ryerson, Mitch *WhoAmA 91*
Ryerson, W. Newton 1902- *WhoE 91, WhoWor 91*
Ryerson, William Newton 1945- *WhoE 91*
Ryga, George *BioIn 16*
Ryga, George 1932-1987 *OxCCanT [port]*
Rygh, Ole B. 1944- *St&PR 91*
Rygh, Sigurd 1905- *WhoWor 91*
Rygiewicz, Paul Thaddeus 1952- *WhoEmL 91*
Rygor, Stanley 1926- *St&PR 91*
Rygwalski, Dennis Michael 1946- *WhoE 91*
Ryherd, Geraldine Schneider 1929- *WhoAmW 91*
Ryherd, Larry Earl 1940- *WhoAm 90*
Ryker, Charles Edwin 1920- *WhoAm 90*
Ryker, Norman J., Jr. 1926- *St&PR 91, WhoAm 90*
Rykhoek, Philip M. 1956- *St&PR 91*
Rykiel, Sonia *BioIn 16*
Rykiel, Sonia 1930- *ConDes 90, CurBio 90 [port]*
Rykov, Aleksei Ivanovich 1881-1938 *BioIn 16*
Rykwert, Joseph 1926- *WhoAm 90*
Ryland, Caius T. 1826-1897 *AmLegL*
Ryland, Greaner Neal 1941- *St&PR 91, WhoAm 90*
Ryland, Robert Knight 1873-1951 *WhoAmA 91N*
Ryland, Robin Smith- *BioIn 16*
Ryland, William Hugh 1934- *St&PR 91*
Rylander, Edith May 1935- *WhoWrEP 89*
Rylander, Henry Grady, Jr. 1921- *WhoAm 90*
Rylander, Robert Allan 1947- *WhoEmL 91*
Rylands, Enriqueta Augustina 1843-1908 *BioIn 16*
Rylands, George 1902- *BioIn 16*
Rylant, Cynthia *BioIn 16*
Rylant, Cynthia 1954- *AuBYP 90*
Ryle, Joseph Donald 1910- *WhoAm 90*
Ryle, Martin 1918-1984 *DcNaB 1981*
Rylee, R. T. 1930- *St&PR 91*
Ryles, Gerald Fay 1936- *WhoAm 90*
Ryles, John Arnold 1945- *St&PR 91*
Rylko, Walter Russell 1948- *WhoE 91*
Rylyk, Andrew 1950- *WhoAm 90, WhoWor 91*
Rymal, Joseph 1821-1900 *DcCanB 12*
Ryman, Lloyd James 1917- *WhoAm 90*
Ryman, Robert 1930- *WhoAmA 91*
Ryman, Robert Tracy 1930- *WhoAm 90*
Ryman, Roger Gerald 1932- *St&PR 91*
Rymar, Julian Wencel 1919- *St&PR 91*
Rymer, Charles A *BiDrAPA 89*
Rymer, Pamela Ann 1941- *WhoAm 90, WhoAmW 91*
Rymer, R. A. 1939- *St&PR 91*
Rymer, S. Bradford, Jr. 1915- *WhoAm 90*
Rymer, Thomas 1643?-1713 *DcLB 101 [port]*
Rymland, Howard Jerome 1928- *WhoE 91*
Rymuza, Jeffrey Zdzislaw 1948- *WhoSSW 91*
Ryn, Claes G. 1943- *ConAu 129*
Ryn, Claes Gosta 1943- *WhoAm 90*
Rynders, Leo Julian 1912- *WhoWor 91*
Ryndress, Shirley Ann 1929- *WhoAmW 91*

Rynearson, Edward King 1939- *BiDrAPA 89*
Rynearson, Gary M. 1940- *St&PR 91*
Rynearson, Robert 1932- *BiDrAPA 89*
Rynes, Ralph Edmond 1954- *WhoSSW 91*
Ryngaert, Ward Laurentius Johannes 1951- *WhoWor 91*
Rynier, Donald Lee *BiDrAPA 89*
Rynkiewicz, Robert Peter 1954- *WhoE 91*
Rynn, Nathan 1923- *WhoAm 90*
Rynne, David John 1940- *St&PR 91*
Rynning, Elvind Pryoz 1943- *St&PR 91*
Ryno, Gary M. 1940- *St&PR 91*
Ryno, H Bruce 1949- *St&PR 91*
Rynone, Richard T. 1957- *St&PR 91*
Ryokan 1758-1831 *EncJap*
Ryon, John Lesley, Jr. 1926- *St&PR 91*
Ryon, Laurie Grace 1962- *WhoSSW 91*
Ryon, Margaret Stevens 1951- *WhoAmW 91*
Ryon, Mortimer 1929- *St&PR 91, WhoAm 90*
Rypczyk, Candice Leigh 1949- *WhoAmW 91*
Rypdal, Terry *NewAgMG*
Rypel, Thaddeus Chester 1949- *WhoWrEP 89*
Rypinski, Arthur Donald 1955- *WhoE 91*
Rypka, Eugene Weston 1925- *WhoWor 91*
Rypkema, Richard G. 1939- *St&PR 91*
Ryrie, William Sinclair 1928- *St&PR 91*
Rysanek, Leonie *BioIn 16*
Rysanek, Leonie 1926- *IntWWM 90, PenDiMP, WhoAm 90, WhoWor 91*
Rysanek, Lotte 1928- *IntWWM 90, PenDiMP*
Rysbrack, John Michael 1693-1770 *BioIn 16*
Rysbrack, Michael 1693-1770 *BioIn 16*
Rysbrack, Michael 1694-1770 *IntDcAA 90*
Rysdon, Kent Lee 1940- *St&PR 91*
Ryser, Frank Ronald 1942- *St&PR 91*
Ryser, Hugues Jean-Paul 1926- *WhoAm 90*
Ryskamp, Bruce Edward 1941- *St&PR 91*
Ryskamp, Carroll Joseph 1930- *WhoE 91, WhoWor 91*
Ryskamp, Charles *BioIn 16*
Ryskamp, Charles Andrew 1928- *WhoAm 90, WhoE 91, WhoWor 91*
Ryskamp, Kenneth Lee 1932- *WhoAm 90, WhoSSW 91*
Ryskulov, Turar 1894-1937? *BioIn 16*
Rystedt, Ingela Gunilla 1933- *WhoWor 91*
Rystrom, Eric Lewis 1957- *BiDrAPA 89*
Rysz, Lili 1955- *BiDrAPA 89, WhoE 91*
Rytand, David A. 1909- *WhoAm 90*
Rytel, Krystyna D *BiDrAPA 89*
Rytych, Barbara Elizabeth 1949- *WhoAmW 91*
Ryu, Chun Kee 1939- *BiDrAPA 89*
Ryu, Jaiyoung 1951- *WhoSSW 91*
Ryum, Ulla 1937- *EncCoWW*
Ryun, Jim 1947- *WorAlBi*
Ryuytel, Arnold Fedorovich 1928- *WhoWor 91*
Ryves, Eliza 1750-1797 *FemiCLE*
Ryynanen, Eva 1915- *BiDWomA*
Ryzhkov, Nikolai 1929- *BioIn 16*
Ryzhkov, Nikolai Ivanovich 1929- *WhoWor 91*
Ryzl, Milan 1928- *EncO&P 3, EncPaPR 91*
Ryznar, Caroline Lucille 1950- *WhoAmW 91*
Rzad, James Joseph 1948- *St&PR 91*
Rzadkowolsky, Anna *BiDrAPA 89*
Rzeminski, Peter Joseph 1947- *WhoEmL 91*
Rzepecki, Isabela 1930- *BiDrAPA 89*
Rzepka, Peter 1928- *St&PR 91*
Rzewnicki, Janet C. 1953- *WhoAm 90, WhoAmW 91, WhoE 91*
Rzewski, Frederic 1938- *PenDiMP*
Rzewski, Frederic Anthony 1938- *IntWWM 90*

S

S., Milka *EncCoWW*
S., Svend Otto *ConAu 132*
S.S. *MajTwCW*
Sa, Khun *BioIn 16*
Sa, Kong Il *BioIn 16*
Sa Barbosa, Maria Ferreira 1946- *WhoWor 91*
Saa, Alfonso H *BiDrAPA 89*
Saab, Deanne Keltum 1945- *WhoAmW 91*
Saab, Ghassan M. 1944- *St&PR 91*
Saad Al-Abdallah Al-Salim Al-Sabah *WhoWor 91*
Saad, Edward Theodore 1923- *WhoE 91*
Saad, Elizabeth L. 1940- *St&PR 91*
Saad, Joyce Ray 1954- *WhoAmW 91*
Saad, Kamal N. 1931- *St&PR 91*
Saad, Maged Hanna 1937- *BiDrAPA 89*
Saad, Theodore S. 1920- *St&PR 91*
Saad, Theodore Shafick 1920- *WhoAm 90, WhoE 91*
Saad-Lipshitz, Natan Mayer 1953- *St&PR 91*
Saada, Adel Selim 1934- *WhoAm 90*
Saadatnejadi, Mohamed M 1932- *BiDrAPA 89*
Saadawi, Nawal el- 1932- *WorAu 1980 [port]*
Saade, Jose A. 1947- *St&PR 91*
Saadian, Javid 1953- *WhoEmL 91*
Saag, James B. 1930- *St&PR 91*
Saal, Elias 1952- *St&PR 91*
Saal, Hubert Daniel 1924- *WhoAm 90*
Saal, Jocelyn 1947- *BioIn 16*
Saalfeld, Clem J. 1942- *St&PR 91*
Saalfield, James A. 1946- *St&PR 91*
Saalfield, James Albert 1946- *WhoE 91*
Saalman, Howard 1928- *WhoAm 90*
Saam, Byrum 1914- *Ballpl 90*
Saar, Alison M 1956- *WhoAmA 91*
Saar, Betye 1926- *BiDWomA, BioIn 16, WhoAm 90, WhoAmA 91*
Saar, James 1949- *ConAu 131*
Saarel, Douglas A. 1939- *WhoAm 90*
Saari, Bruce Bernard 1950- *WhoWor 91*
Saari, Donald Gene 1940- *WhoAm 90*
Saari, Jouko Erik Sakari 1944- *IntWWM 90*
Saari, Leonard Mathew 1938- *St&PR 91, WhoAm 90*
Saari, Lise Margaret 1953- *WhoEmL 91*
Saari, Peter H 1951- *WhoAmA 91*
Saari, Seppo Ilari 1948- *IntWWM 90*
Saarikoski, Pentti 1937-1983 *DcScanL*
Saarinen, Arthur W., Jr. 1927- *St&PR 91*
Saarinen, Arthur William, Jr. 1927- *WhoAm 90*
Saarinen, Eero 1910-1961 *BioIn 16, PenDiDA 89, WhoAmA 91N, WorAlBi*
Saarinen, Eliel 1873-1950 *BioIn 16, PenDiDA 89*
Saarinen, Lilian 1912- *WhoAmA 91*
Saario, Vaino Sakari 1942- *WhoWor 91*
Saario, Vieno Voitto 1912- *WhoWor 91*
Saarlas, Maido 1930- *WhoE 91*
Saas, William J. 1940- *St&PR 91*
Saask, Aapo 1943- *WhoWor 91*
Saatchi, Charles *BioIn 16*
Saatchi, Charles 1943- *WhoAm 90, WhoWor 91*
Saatchi, Maurice *BioIn 16*
Saatchi, Maurice 1946- *WhoAm 90, WhoWor 91*
Saathoff, Gregory Brian 1957- *BiDrAPA 89*
Saaty, Thomas Lorie 1926- *WhoAm 90, WhoE 91*
Saavedra, Bautista 1870-1939 *BioIn 16*
Saavedra, Cecile B. 1947- *St&PR 91*
Saavedra, Charles James 1941- *WhoAm 90*
Saavedra, Daniel Ortega *BioIn 16*
Saavedra, Edgardo 1963- *WhoHisp 91*
Saavedra, Henry *WhoHisp 91*
Saavedra, Jesus M *BiDrAPA 89*
Saavedra, Kleber 1945- *WhoHisp 91*
Saavedra, Leonel Orlando 1950- *WhoHisp 91*
Saavedra, Lillian Tatari 1944- *BiDrAPA 89*
Saavedra, Louis 1933- *WhoHisp 91*
Saavedra, Miguel de Cervantes 1547-1616 *BioIn 16*
Saavedra, Ro 1952- *WhoAmW 91*
Saba, Gabriel N. 1930- *WhoWor 91*
Saba, Joseph Philip 1947- *WhoE 91*
Saba, Michel Samir 1943- *WhoWor 91*
Saba, Richard 1946- *WhoAmA 91, WhoE 91*
Sabah, Abdullah al-Salem al- 1895-1965 *BioIn 16*
Sabah, Jaber al-Ahmad al-Jaber al- 1926- *BioIn 16*
Sabah, Jaber al-Ahmed al- *NewYTBS 90 [port]*
Sabala, James A. 1954- *St&PR 91*
Sabalesky, Doreen Ann 1958- *BiDrAPA 89*
Sabanayagam, Muthiah K 1941- *BiDrAPA 89*
Sabanayagam, Muthukrishna 1940- *BiDrAPA 89*
Sabanci, Sakip 1933- *WhoWor 91*
Sabar, Yona 1939- *ConAu 30NR*
Sabaroff, Rose Epstein 1918- *WhoAm 90*
Sabas, Marilu *BiDrAPA 89*
Sabata, Victor De *PenDiMP*
Sabate, Nuria Alicia *BiDrAPA 89*
Sabatell, Henry Paul 1937- *St&PR 91*
Sabatella, Elizabeth Maria 1940- *WhoAmW 91*
Sabatella, Joseph John 1931- *WhoAmA 91*
Sabates, Felix Nabor 1930- *WhoAm 90*
Sabath, Jerrold 1947- *St&PR 91*
Sabath, Kenneth Michael 1956- *WhoWor 91*
Sabath, Leon David 1930- *WhoAm 90*
Sabath, Robert Edward 1943- *St&PR 91*
Sabatier, Paul 1854-1941 *WorAlBi*
Sabatier, Robert 1923- *WhoWor 91*
Sabatine, Jean Ann 1941- *WhoWrEP 89*
Sabatine, John W. 1932- *WhoSSW 91*
Sabatini, Albert *BiDrAPA 89*
Sabatini, Alma 1922-1988 *BioIn 16*
Sabatini, Denise *BioIn 16*
Sabatini, Francis P. 1947- *St&PR 91*
Sabatini, Frank Carmine 1932- *WhoAm 90*
Sabatini, Gabriela *BioIn 16*
Sabatini, Nelson John 1940- *WhoAm 90*
Sabatini, Raphael 1896-1985 *WhoAmA 91N*
Sabato, Ernesto 1911- *ConAu 32NR, HispWr 90, MajTwCW, WhoWor 91*
Sabato, Ernesto R. 1911- *BioIn 16*
Sabato, Osvaldo D *BiDrAPA 89*
Sabattani, Aurelio 1912- *WhoWor 91*
Sabau, Carmen Sybile 1933- *WhoAmW 91*
Sabbag, Allen L. 1944- *St&PR 91*
Sabbagh, Sheraine Kay 1959- *WhoAmW 91*
Sabbath, Joseph C *BiDrAPA 89*
Sabbatino, Joseph A *BiDrAPA 89*
Sabbatino, Pat Joseph 1942- *St&PR 91*
Sabbato, Robert, Jr. *ODwPR 91*
Sabbeth, Daniel Paul 1941- *BiDrAPA 89*
Sabbeth, Stephen 1947- *St&PR 91*
Sabbeth, Stephen J. 1947- *WhoAm 90*
Sabean, Joel Arthur 1947- *WhoEmL 91*
Sabeata *WhNaAH*
Sabel, Barbara S *BiDrAPA 89*
Sabel, Bernhard August Maria 1957- *WhoWor 91*
Sabel, Bradley Kent 1948- *WhoAm 90*
Sabel, Charles F 1947- *ConAu 129*
Sabel, David G. 1952- *St&PR 91*
Sabel, Ivan R. 1945- *St&PR 91*
Sabel, Mark 1920- *St&PR 91*
Sabel, Richard Aaron 1933- *St&PR 91*
Sabel, Robert Hunter 1924- *WhoAm 90*
Sabela, Simon 1931- *DrBlPA 90*
Sabelis, Huibert 1942- *WhoAmA 91*
Sabell, Wallace S. 1951- *St&PR 91*
Sabella, Ernie *ConTFT 8*
Sabella, John A. 1959- *St&PR 91*
Sabelli, Hector C 1937- *BiDrAPA 89*
Sabellicus, Georgius *EncO&P 3*
Saben, Laurence Ross *BiDrAPA 89*
Saber, Terry Ann 1953- *St&PR 91*
Saberhagen, Bret 1964- *Ballpl 90, WhoAm 90, WorAlBi*
Saberhagen, Fred 1930- *ConAu 33NR, MajTwCW, RGTwCSF*
Sabers, Richard Wayne 1938- *WhoAm 90*
Sabersky, Rolf Heinrich 1920- *WhoAm 90*
Sabesan, Shardha K *BiDrAPA 89*
Sabet, Habib *BioIn 16, NewYTBS 90*
Sabet-Sharghi, Farid *BiDrAPA 89*
Sabeti, Mohebat 1949- *BiDrAPA 89*
Sabharwal, Ranjit Singh 1925- *WhoAm 90, WhoWor 91*
Sabiani, Simon *BioIn 16*
Sabiani, Simon Pierre 1887-1956 *BiDFrPL*
Sabicas *BioIn 16, NewYTBS 90 [port]*
Sabin, Albert B. 1906- *WorAlBi*
Sabin, Albert Bruce 1906- *WhoAm 90*
Sabin, Arnold Leonard 1926- *WhoAm 90, WhoWor 91*
Sabin, Arthur J. 1930- *WhoWrEP 89*
Sabin, Clifford G. 1908- *St&PR 91*
Sabin, Florence Rena 1871-1953 *BioAmW, BioIn 16*
Sabin, Gary B. 1954- *St&PR 91*
Sabin, James Evan 1939- *BiDrAPA 89*
Sabin, James Stephen 1946- *BiDrAPA 89*
Sabin, James Thomas 1943- *St&PR 91, WhoAm 90*
Sabin, John Merrill 1954- *WhoEmL 91*
Sabin, Julia Leigh 1959- *WhoAmW 91*
Sabin, Louis 1930- *WhoE 91*
Sabin, William Albert 1931- *WhoAm 90*
Sabina, Frank James 1951- *WhoWrEP 89*
Sabina, Maria Magdalena 1889-1985 *EncPaPR 91*
Sabine, Elizabeth *BioIn 16*
Sabine, Gordon Arthur 1917- *WhoAm 90*
Sabine, William H W 1903- *EncO&P 3*
Sabines, Jaime 1925?- *HispWr 90*
Sabines, Luis 1917- *WhoHisp 91, WhoSSW 91*
Sabino, Francis V. 1935- *St&PR 91*
Sabio, John Manuel 1955- *WhoSSW 91*
Sabir, Surriya Akhtar 1938- *BiDrAPA 89*
Sabisch, Christian 1955- *ConAu 129*
Sabiston, David Coston, Jr. 1924- *WhoAm 90, WhoWor 91*
Sablan, Suzanne Barbara 1962- *WhoAmW 91*
Sable, Barbara Kinsey 1927- *IntWWM 90, WhoAmW 91, WhoWrEP 89*
Sable, David *ODwPR 91*
Sable, Henry Zodoc 1918- *WhoAm 90*
Sable, John E. 1939- *St&PR 91*
Sable, Madeleine de 1598?-1678 *EncCoWW*
Sable, Martin Howard 1924- *WhoAm 90*
Sable, Ronald K. 1941- *St&PR 91*
Sable, Victor 1911- *BioIn 16*
Sableman, Mark Stephen 1951- *WhoEmL 91*
Sabliere, Marguerite Hessein de la 1640-1693 *EncCoWW*
Sablik, Martin John 1939- *WhoSSW 91*
Sabloff, Jeremy Arac 1944- *WhoAm 90*
Sablok, Anil Kumar 1960- *WhoSSW 91*
Sablon, Jean 1906- *OxCPMus*
Sablonniere, Blanche de la 1855?- *OxCCanT*
Sablotny, Elbert Theodore 1922- *St&PR 91*
Sablotsky, Noreen 1955- *St&PR 91*
Sablotsky, Steven 1955- *St&PR 91*
Sablow, Rhoda Lillian *WhoAmA 91*
Sablowksy, Robert 1938- *St&PR 91*
Sabo, Alex Nicholas *BiDrAPA 89*
Sabo, Betty Jean 1928- *WhoAmA 91*
Sabo, Chris *BioIn 16*
Sabo, Chris 1962- *Ballpl 90*
Sabo, Jack Charles 1936- *WhoE 91*
Sabo, Mark Andrew 1950- *St&PR 91*
Sabo, Martin Olav 1938- *WhoAm 90*
Sabo, Richard Steven 1934- *WhoAm 90*
Sabo, Walter Richard, Jr. 1954- *WhoAm 90*
Saboeiro, Gregory Roy 1961- *WhoEmL 91*
Sabol, Albert Thomas 1952- *St&PR 91*
Sabol, Paul William 1926- *St&PR 91*
Sabol, Susan Ann 1957- *WhoAmW 91*
Sabolcik, Gene 1951- *WhoSSW 91*
Sabonis, Arvidas *BioIn 16*
Saboor, Syed Abdul 1935- *BiDrAPA 89*
Sabosik, Patricia Elizabeth 1949- *WhoAm 90, WhoAmW 91*
Sabot, Lawrence M 1933- *BiDrAPA 89*
Sabot, Richard Henry 1944- *WhoE 91*
Saboungi, Marie-Louise Jean 1948- *WhoAmW 91*
Saboupin, Rodney Wood 1949- *WhoEmL 91*
Sabourin, Dennis M. 1940- *St&PR 91*
Sabourin, Jean-Guy 1934- *OxCCanT*
Sabourin, Richard 1942- *St&PR 91*
Sabra, Abdalhamid Ibrahim 1924- *WhoAm 90*
Sabran, Eleonore de 1750- *BioIn 16*
Sabroff, Albert Edward 1934- *St&PR 91*
Sabrosky, Alan Ned 1941- *WhoE 91*
Sabsevitz, Abraham Meyer 1907- *WhoAm 90*
Sabsevitz, Meyer 1907- *St&PR 91*
Sabshin, Edith G *BiDrAPA 89*

Sabshin, Melvin 1925- *BiDrAPA 89, WhoAm 90*
Sabu 1924-1963 *BioIn 16*
Sabuco de Nantes Barrera, Oliva 1562-1622? *EncCoWW*
Sabumei, Benais *WhoWor 91*
Saburo, Matsuoka 1915- *WhoWor 91*
Saby, John Sanford 1921- *WhoAm 90*
Sacagawea 1784?-1812? *WhNaAH*
Sacagawea 1786-1884 *BioIn 16*
Sacagawea 1787?-1812? *WorAlBi*
Sacajawea 1784?-1812? *WhNaAH*
Sacajawea 1786?-1812? *BioAmW*
Sacajawea 1787?-1812? *WorAlBi*
Sacastru, Martin *HispWr 90, MajTwCW*
Sacastru, Martin 1914- *BioIn 16*
Sacca, Harriet Wands 1919- *WhoAmW 91*
Sacchet, Edward M. 1936- *WhoAm 90*
Sacchetta, Pasquale Joseph 1964- *WhoE 91*
Sacchetti, Richard Henry 1942- *WhoE 91*
Sacchetti, Richard Peter *St&PR 91*
Sacchi, Andrea 1599?-1661 *IntDcAA 90*
Sacci, Rocco A. *ODwPR 91*
Saccio, Joseph D 1934- *BiDrAPA 89*
Saccio, Leonard John 1911- *WhoAm 90*
Sacco, Ernesto 1940- *WhoWor 91*
Sacco, John Michael 1952- *WhoE 91*
Sacco, Joseph *BioIn 16*
Sacco, Joseph *BioIn 16*
Sacco, Nicola *EncAL*
Sacco, Nicola 1891-1927 *BioIn 16, WorAlBi*
Sacco, P. Peter 1928- *IntWWM 90*
Sacco, Rachel Rognrud 1956- *WhoAmW 91*
Sacco, Thomas Anthony 1953- *WhoSSW 91*
Saccoccio, August J. 1937- *St&PR 91*
Saccoman, Patricia Linden 1933- *WhoAmW 91*
Sacdalan, Felipe Jordan 1916- *WhoWor 91*
Sacerdote, George S. 1945- *St&PR 91*
Sacerdote, Manuel Ricardo 1943- *St&PR 91, WhoAm 90*
Sacerdote, Peter M. 1937- *St&PR 91, WhoAm 90*
Sacha, Robert Frank 1946- *WhoAm 90*
Sachar, Abram Leon 1899- *WhoAm 90*
Sachar, Howard Morley 1928- *WhoAm 90*
Sachar, Louis 1954- *AuBYP 90, BioIn 16, ConAu 33NR, SmATA 63*
Sacharow, Stanley 1935- *WhoE 91*
Sachdev, Anil 1954- *WhoWor 91*
Sachdev, G. S. *NewAgMG*
Sachdev, Janek Raj *BiDrAPA 89*
Sachdev, Mohindar Singh 1928- *WhoAm 90*
Sachdev, Sunil H *BiDrAPA 89*
Sachdev, Vidya Sagar 1927- *WhoWor 91*
Sachdeva, Yesh Paul 1945- *WhoEmL 91*
Sacher, Angela Anton 1954- *WhoSSW 91*
Sacher, Michael C. 1934- *St&PR 91*
Sacher, Paul 1906- *IntWWM 90, PenDiMP*
Sacher, Philipp Alexander 1959- *WhoWor 91*
Sacher, S. Mark *BiDrAPA 89*
Sacher, Steven Jay 1942- *WhoAm 90, WhoE 91*
Sachez-Scott, Milcha *HispWr 90*
Sachinvala, Kersasp B *BiDrAPA 89*
Sachinvala, Neena 1945- *BiDrAPA 89*
Sachkar, Catharine Mollica 1921- *St&PR 91*
Sachman, Douglas Philip 1951- *St&PR 91*
Sachs, A M *WhoAmA 91*
Sachs, Alan Arthur 1947- *WhoAm 90*
Sachs, Albie 1933- *BioIn 16*
Sachs, Allan M. 1921-1989 *BioIn 16*
Sachs, Arthur Samuel 1927- *St&PR 91*
Sachs, Benjamin K. 1930- *WhoAm 90*
Sachs, Bernice Cohen 1918- *BiDrAPA 89, WhoAm 90*
Sachs, Blanche 1933- *WhoWrEP 89*
Sachs, Clinton Ticu 1916- *BiDrAPA 89*
Sachs, David 1933- *WhoAm 90*
Sachs, David Morton *BiDrAPA 89*
Sachs, David Stanley 1942- *St&PR 91*
Sachs, Elizabeth-Ann 1946- *BioIn 16*
Sachs, Gary Steven 1955- *BiDrAPA 89*
Sachs, Harvey 1946- *IntWWM 90*
Sachs, Howard Frederic 1925- *WhoAm 90*
Sachs, Howard George 1942- *St&PR 91*
Sachs, Irving H. 1917- *St&PR 91*
Sachs, Irwin M. 1932- *St&PR 91*
Sachs, James H 1907-1971 *WhoAmA 91N*
Sachs, Jeffrey D. *BioIn 16*
Sachs, Jerry *WhoAm 90*
Sachs, John P. 1926- *St&PR 91, WhoAm 90*
Sachs, Judith 1947- *BioIn 16*
Sachs, Keith Lee 1945- *St&PR 91*
Sachs, Ken 1914- *St&PR 91*
Sachs, Klaus-Jurgen 1929- *IntWWM 90*
Sachs, Lorraine Phyllis 1936- *WhoAmW 91*
Sachs, Louis S. 1928- *St&PR 91*
Sachs, Marilyn 1927- *BioIn 16*
Sachs, Michael David 1961- *WhoAm 90*
Sachs, Nancy Lyn 1957- *St&PR 91*
Sachs, Nelly 1891-1970 *EncCoWW, WorAlBi*
Sachs, Oscar *BiDrAPA 89*
Sachs, Paul J 1878-1965 *WhoAmA 91N*
Sachs, Paul Steven *BiDrAPA 89*
Sachs, Robert A. 1942- *St&PR 91*
Sachs, Robert Green 1916- *WhoAm 90*
Sachs, Robert H. 1939- *St&PR 91*
Sachs, Ronald Allen 1953- *BiDrAPA 89*
Sachs, Samuel, II 1935- *WhoAm 90, WhoAmA 91*
Sachs, Sidney S. 1916- *St&PR 91*
Sachs, Sidney Stanley 1916- *WhoAm 90*
Sachs, Stephen Carl 1955- *St&PR 91*
Sachse, Barbara Kay 1961- *WhoAmW 91*
Sachse, Elinor Yudin 1940- *WhoAmW 91*
Sachse, Janice R 1908- *WhoAmA 91*
Sachsse, Lothar 1921- *WhoWor 91*
Sachtleben, Alan T. 1942- *St&PR 91, WhoAm 90*
Sachtler, Wolfgang Max Hugo 1924- *WhoAm 90*
Sacino, Dick F. 1930- *St&PR 91*
Sacino, Sherry Wheatley 1959- *WhoAmW 91*
Sack, Alan Lawrence 1926- *St&PR 91*
Sack, Brian George 1923- *WhoWor 91*
Sack, Bruce Michael *BiDrAPA 89*
Sack, Burton Marshall 1937- *St&PR 91, WhoAm 90*
Sack, David Andrew *BiDrAPA 89*
Sack, Edgar Albert 1930- *WhoAm 90*
Sack, Erna 1898-1972 *PenDiMP*
Sack, Joseph Harry 1946- *BiDrAPA 89*
Sack, Lawrence C *BiDrAPA 89*
Sack, Marshall Barnett 1951- *BiDrAPA 89*
Sack, Michael Roland 1957- *WhoE 91*
Sack, Peter Gordon 1943- *BiDrAPA 89*
Sack, R. G. 1933- *St&PR 91*
Sack, R. J. 1903- *St&PR 91*
Sack, Robert David 1939- *WhoAm 90*
Sack, Robert Ira 1957- *BiDrAPA 89*
Sack, Robert Leroy 1942- *BiDrAPA 89*
Sack, Ron W. 1966- *WhoEmL 91*
Sack, Sylvan Hanan 1932- *WhoAm 90*
Sack, Thomas F. 1927- *St&PR 91*
Sack, William H 1934- *BiDrAPA 89*
Sackeim, Harold 1951- *WhoAm 90*
Sackel, Sol 1924- *St&PR 91*
Sacken, Thomas Patrick 1944- *BiDrAPA 89*
Sackett, Dennis Anthony 1950- *St&PR 91*
Sackett, Donna Coulson 1949- *WhoWrEP 89*
Sackett, Ernest L. 1928- *WhoWrEP 89*
Sackett, Frederic Moseley 1868-1941 *BioIn 16*
Sackett, Gary G. 1940- *St&PR 91*
Sackett, Hugh F. 1930- *WhoE 91*
Sackett, Mary Lou 1949- *WhoAmW 91*
Sackett, Richard 1934- *St&PR 91*
Sackett, Ross DeForest 1930- *WhoAm 90*
Sackett, Susan 1943- *WhoWrEP 89*
Sackett, Susan Deanna 1943- *WhoAmW 91*
Sackett, Vincent A 1945- *BiDrAPA 89*
Sackett, Walter James, Jr. 1932- *St&PR 91*
Sackett, William Tecumseh, Jr. 1921- *WhoAm 90*
Sackeyfio, Alexander H 1947- *BiDrAPA 89*
Sackin, Erwin R. 1915- *St&PR 91*
Sackin, Eugene M. 1920- *St&PR 91*
Sackin, H David 1931- *BiDrAPA 89*
Sackin, Stanley Owen 1936- *WhoSSW 91*
Sackler, Arthur Brian 1950- *WhoEmL 91*
Sackler, Arthur M. 1913-1987 *BioIn 16*
Sackler, Howard 1929-1982 *ConAu 30NR*
Sackler, Joseph L *BiDrAPA 89*
Sackler, Mortimer D *BiDrAPA 89*
Sackler, Raymond R *BiDrAPA 89*
Sacklow, Harriette Lynn 1944- *WhoAmW 91, WhoE 91*
Sacklow, Stewart Irwin 1942- *WhoAm 90, WhoE 91*
Sackman, Nicholas 1950- *IntWWM 90*
Sackmann, Peter Carver 1942- *St&PR 91*
Sackner, Marvin Arthur 1932- *WhoAm 90*
Sacknoff, Michael David 1947- *WhoE 91*
Sacks, Albert Martin 1920- *WhoAm 90*
Sacks, Beverly *WhoAmA 91*
Sacks, Charles B *BiDrAPA 89*
Sacks, David G. 1924- *St&PR 91, WhoAm 90, WhoE 91*
Sacks, David Gregory 1950- *WhoE 91*
Sacks, Diane Jessica *BiDrAPA 89*
Sacks, Herbert S 1926- *BiDrAPA 89*
Sacks, Herbert Simeon 1926- *WhoAm 90, WhoE 91*
Sacks, Ira Stephen 1948- *WhoEmL 91*
Sacks, Jeffrey H 1946- *BiDrAPA 89*
Sacks, Jeffrey Howard 1946- *WhoE 91*
Sacks, Julian Harold *BiDrAPA 89*
Sacks, Lawrence *BiDrAPA 89*
Sacks, Mark I. 1965- *St&PR 91*
Sacks, Maury Eli *BiDrAPA 89*
Sacks, Michael H 1940- *BiDrAPA 89*
Sacks, Norman Paul 1914- *WhoAm 90*
Sacks, Oliver 1933- *MajTwCW, WhoWrEP 89, WorAu 1980 [port]*
Sacks, Ray *WhoAmA 91*
Sacks, Richard A. 1949- *ODwPR 91*
Sacks, Richard Paul 1937- *WhoE 91*
Sacks, Robert Steven *BiDrAPA 89*
Sacks, Roslyn 1932- *St&PR 91*
Sacks, Steven Irwin *BiDrAPA 89*
Sacks, Temi J. *WhoAm 90*
Sacks, Temi J. 1947- *ODwPR 91*
Sacksteder, Frederick Henry 1924- *WhoAm 90*
Sacksteder, James Louis *BiDrAPA 89*
Sacksteder, John Dennis 1926- *WhoAm 90*
Sackton, Frank Joseph 1912- *WhoAm 90*
Sacktor, Bertram 1922-1988 *BioIn 16*
Sackville, John Frederick 1745-1799 *BioIn 16*
Sackville, Margaret 1882-1963 *FemiCLE*
Sackville, Thomas 1536-1608 *BioIn 16, WorAlBi*
Sackville-West, V. 1892-1962 *BioIn 16, MajTwCW*
Sackville-West, Victoria 1892-1962 *BioIn 16*
Sackville-West, Vita 1892-1962 *FemiCLE*
Sacon, Kiyoshi Kinoshita 1931- *WhoWor 91*
Sacon, Leonard 1938- *St&PR 91*
Sacona, Harry M. 1927- *St&PR 91*
Sacre, Antonio Charo 1935- *BiDrAPA 89*
Sacre, Mary Alice 1933- *WhoAmW 91*
Sacuto, Enrica *BiDrAPA 89*
Sada Kaur *WomWR*
Sadai, Yizhak 1935- *IntWWM 90*
Sadaka, Ronald Nicholas 1957- *WhoSSW 91*
Sadani, Sunderlal Lal 1955- *WhoWor 91*
Sadao, Shoji 1927- *WhoAm 90*
Sadat, Anwar 1918-1981 *BioIn 16*
Sadat, Anwar Al- 1918-1981 *PolLCME*
Sadat-Mansouri, Abolfazl *BiDrAPA 89*
Sadauskas, J. Linas *BiDrAPA 89*
Sadavoy, Joel *BiDrAPA 89*
Sadd, William Wheeler 1935- *WhoAm 90, WhoSSW 91*
Saddam Hussein *BioIn 16*
Saddik, Fouad Wade 1947- *BiDrAPA 89*
Saddlemyer, Ann 1932- *WhoAm 90, WhoAmW 91, WhoWrEP 89*
Saddler, Allen 1923- *BioIn 16*
Saddler, Donald 1918- *ConTFT 8*
Saddler, Donald Edward 1920- *WhoAm 90*
Saddock, Harry G. 1929- *WhoAm 90, WhoE 91*
Saddock, Harry George 1929- *St&PR 91*
Sade *BioIn 16*
Sade 1959- *DrBIPA 90*
Sade 1960?- *EncPR&S 89*
Sade, Marquis De 1740-1814 *WorAlBi*
Sade, Donald Stone 1937- *WhoAm 90*
Sadecki, Ray 1940- *Ballpl 90*
Sadek, Adel 1943- *BiDrAPA 89*
Sadek, Amal Ahmad Mokhtar 1937- *IntWWM 90*
Sadek, George 1928- *WhoAmA 91*
Sadek, Ibrahim Said 1949- *WhoSSW 91*
Sadek, Mike 1946- *Ballpl 90*
Sader, Carol Hope 1935- *WhoAmW 91*
Sader, Neil Steven 1958- *WhoEmL 91*
Sader, Ronald Joseph 1934- *St&PR 91*
Sadick, Barbara Ann 1952- *WhoAmW 91*
Sadie, Julie Anne 1948- *IntWWM 90*
Sadie, Stanley 1930- *IntWWM 90*
Sadie, Stanley John 1930- *WhoWor 91*
Sadik, Marvin Sherwood 1932- *WhoAm 90, WhoAmA 91*
Sadik-Khan, Orhan Idris 1929- *WhoAm 90*
Sadikot, Susan *BiDrAPA 89*
Sadilek, Vladimir 1933- *WhoWor 91*
Sadiyev, Makhtai Ramazanovich 1929- *WhoWor 91*
Sadja, Elliott Daniel 1919- *St&PR 91*
Sadja, Lee York 1948- *BiDrAPA 89*
Sadker, David 1942- *WhoE 91*
Sadker, Myra Pollack 1943- *WhoWrEP 89*
Sadkin, Herbert *BioIn 16*
Sadle, Amy Ann 1940- *WhoAmW 91*
Sadle, Amy Ann Brandon 1940- *WhoAmA 91*
Sadler, Arleamon 1947- *WhoE 91*
Sadler, Barbara Ann 1955- *WhoE 91*
Sadler, Barry *BioIn 16*
Sadler, Barry 1940- *ConAu 129*
Sadler, Catherine Edwards 1952- *SmATA 60 [port]*
Sadler, Charles Benjamin, Jr. 1939- *WhoSSW 91, WhoWor 91*
Sadler, Charles Randolph 1928- *WhoE 91*
Sadler, Chuck *BioIn 16*
Sadler, David Gary 1939- *WhoAm 90*
Sadler, Graham Hydrick 1931- *WhoAm 90, WhoSSW 91*
Sadler, H Harrison *BiDrAPA 89*
Sadler, Harold G. *WhoAm 90*
Sadler, John 1720-1789 *PenDiDA 89*
Sadler, John Edward, Jr. 1938- *BiDrAPA 89*
Sadler, John Zell *BiDrAPA 89*
Sadler, Mark *TwCCr&M 91, WhoWrEP 89*
Sadler, Mark 1924- *BioIn 16*
Sadler, Mary Kathryn 1953- *WhoAmW 91*
Sadler, Natalie Jones *BiDrAPA 89*
Sadler, Norma Jean 1944- *WhoWrEP 89*
Sadler, Richard T. 1926- *St&PR 91*
Sadler, Richard Thomas 1926- *WhoAm 90*
Sadler, Robert Alexander 1938- *St&PR 91*
Sadler, Robert K. *St&PR 91*
Sadler, Robert Livingston 1935- *St&PR 91, WhoAm 90*
Sadler, Stuart Ragland 1948- *WhoSSW 91*
Sadler, Theodore R., Jr. 1930- *WhoAm 90*
Sadlier, Anna Teresa 1854-1932 *FemiCLE*
Sadlier, Mary Anne 1820-1903 *DcLB 99 [port], FemiCLE*
Sadlo, Milos 1912- *IntWWM 90, PenDiMP*
Sadlon, Lynn T. 1956- *ODwPR 91*
Sadlon, Richard Dale 1933- *St&PR 91*
Sadlowski, Dennis Allen 1940- *St&PR 91*
Sadock, Benjamin J 1933- *BiDrAPA 89*
Sadock, Benjamin James 1933- *WhoAm 90*
Sadock, Virginia A 1938- *BiDrAPA 89*
Sadock, William M. 1925- *St&PR 91*
Sadoff, Ira 1945- *WhoWrEP 89*
Sadoff, Micky 1944- *WhoAmW 91*
Sadoff, Robert L 1936- *BiDrAPA 89*
Sadoff, Robert Leslie 1936- *WhoAm 90, WhoWor 91*
Sadovnikoff, Vsevolod 1918- *BiDrAPA 89*
Sadow, Harvey S. 1922- *St&PR 91, WhoAm 90*
Sadow, Leo *BiDrAPA 89*
Sadow, Todd Forrest *BiDrAPA 89*
Sadowey, John Peter 1925- *St&PR 91*
Sadowitz, Jo Kremer 1946- *BiDrAPA 89*
Sadowitz, Paul *BiDrAPA 89*
Sadowska, Barbara 1940-1986 *EncCoWW*
Sadowska, Maria 1924- *BiDrAPA 89*
Sadowski, A. J. 1938- *St&PR 91*
Sadowski, Anthony James 1938- *WhoAm 90*
Sadowski, Bob 1938- *Ballpl 90*
Sadowski, Carol Johnson 1929- *WhoAmA 91*
Sadowski, Chester Philip 1946- *St&PR 91*
Sadowski, Denise A. 1958- *WhoAmW 91*
Sadowski, John Stanley 1948- *WhoE 91, WhoEmL 91, WhoWor 91*
Sadowsky, Marc Mahlon 1956- *BiDrAPA 89*
Sadowsky, William *BiDrAPA 89*
Sadoyama, Nancy Artis 1947- *WhoAmW 91*
Sadr, Houman *WhoWor 91*
Sadr, Musa Al- 1928-1978? *PolLCME*
Sadre-Mashayekh, Mahin *BiDrAPA 89*
Sadri, Manouchehr *BiDrAPA 89*
Sadruddin, Moe 1943- *WhoWor 91*
Sadun, Alfredo Arrigo 1950- *WhoWor 91*
Sadwin, Arnold 1926- *BiDrAPA 89, WhoE 91*
Sadwith, Geoffrey Richard 1946- *St&PR 91*
Sadwith, Howard Marvin 1916- *St&PR 91*
Sadykov, T. *WhoWor 91*
Saeden, Erik 1924- *IntWWM 90*
Saeed, Anjum 1954- *WhoWor 91*
Saeed, Mohammad 1948- *BiDrAPA 89*
Saeed, Mohammad 1950- *WhoWor 91*
Saef, Karen Bailis 1954- *WhoAmW 91*
Saefke, Steven Charles 1945- *St&PR 91*
Saegebarth, Klaus Arthur 1929- *WhoAm 90*
Saeger, William T. 1931- *St&PR 91*
Saegert, Gerald Fitzgerald 1918- *St&PR 91*
Saegesser, Donald Arlen 1933- *St&PR 91*
Saeks, Richard Ephraim 1941- *WhoAm 90*
Saelens, Deborah Lynn 1955- *WhoAmW 91*
Saemann, Robert Alan 1964- *St&PR 91*
Saenger, Bruce Walter 1943- *WhoWor 91*
Saenger, Eugene Lange 1917- *WhoAm 90*
Saenger, Theodore Jerome 1928- *WhoAm 90*
Saenredam, Pieter 1597-1665? *IntDcAA 90*
Saens, Camille Saint- 1835-1921 *BioIn 16*
Saens, Charles Camille Saint- 1835-1921 *BioIn 16*
Saent-Johns, Geraldine McCormick 1930- *WhoWor 91*
Saenz, Alonzo A. 1940- *WhoHisp 91*
Saenz, Carlos Antonio 1951- *WhoSSW 91*
Saenz, Carol June 1944- *WhoAmW 91*
Saenz, Dalmiro *HispWr 90*
Saenz, Dalmiro A. 1926- *HispWr 90*
Saenz, Diana Eloise 1949- *WhoHisp 91*
Saenz, Jose Carlos 1938- *WhoHisp 91*
Saenz, Lydia 1953- *WhoAmW 91*
Saenz, Marc B. 1950- *WhoHisp 91*

Saenz, Marta 1928- BiDrAPA 89
Saenz, P. Alex 1950- WhoHisp 91
Saenz, Rodolfo Forero 1934- WhoE 91
Saenz Pena, Roque 1851-1914 BioIn 16
Saenz-Schroeder, Martha BioIn 16
Saetone MajTwCW
Saeverud, Harald 1896- IntWWM 90
Saez, Pedro Justo WhoHisp 91
Saez, Richard 1936- WhoE 91
Safa, Cynthia Shaklee 1960- WhoAmW 91
Safa, Helen M. Icken 1930- ConAu 30NR
Safadi, Gabriel 1963- BiDrAPA 89
Safan, Craig 1948- ConTFT 8 [port]
Safar, Mahmood Mohammad 1940- WhoWor 91
Safar, Serge Elie 1926- WhoWor 91
Safarik-Grimming, Jana Eliska 1938- BiDrAPA 89
Safars, Berta 1928- WhoAmW 91
Safarty, Regina 1932- IntWWM 90
Safavi, Roknedin BiDrAPA 89
Safaya, Vijay Kumar 1949- WhoWor 91
Safdar, Ali 1950- BiDrAPA 89
Safdie, Moshe 1938- BioIn 16, WhoAm 90, WhoWor 91
Safe, Kenneth Shaw, Jr. 1929- WhoE 91, WhoWor 91
Safeer, Neil I. 1939- St&PR 91
Safenowitz, Milton 1927- St&PR 91, WhoAm 90
Safer, Daniel J 1934- BiDrAPA 89, WhoE 91
Safer, Edward George 1927- St&PR 91
Safer, Elaine Berkman 1937- WhoE 91
Safer, John 1922- WhoAm 90, WhoAmA 91, WhoWor 91
Safer, Leslie F. 1950- WhoSSW 91
Safer, Morley BioIn 16
Safer, Morley 1931- WhoAm 90, WhoE 91
Saferite, Linda Lee 1947- WhoAmW 91
Saferstein, Harvey I. 1943- WhoAm 90
Saff, Donald Jay 1937- WhoAmA 91
Saffeir, Harvey J. 1929- St&PR 91
Saffeir, Harvey Joseph 1929- WhoAm 90
Saffell, Tom 1921- Ballpl 90
Saffell, Virginia Marie 1923- WhoAmW 91
Saffels, Dale Emerson 1921- WhoAm 90
Saffer, Alfred 1918- WhoAm 90
Saffer, Morris Barry 1940- WhoAm 90
Saffer, Sheldon P. 1926- St&PR 91
Safferman, Allan Zachary 1959- BiDrAPA 89
Safferman, Robert Samuel 1932- WhoAm 90
Saffert, Paul M. 1945- St&PR 91
Safferthal, Rolf Richard 1951- WhoWor 91
Saffiotti, Umberto 1928- WhoAm 90
Saffir, Herbert Seymour 1917- WhoAm 90, WhoWor 91
Saffir, Kurt 1929-1988 BioIn 16
Saffir, Leonard 1930- ODwPR 91, WhoAm 90
Saffle, Michael Benton 1946- IntWWM 90
Saffle, Sherry Wood 1959- WhoAmW 91
Saffman, Philip G. 1931- WhoAm 90
Saffo, Mary Beth 1948- WhoAmW 91, WhoEmL 91
Safford, Dan Scott 1950- WhoWrEP 89
Safford, John Lugton 1947- WhoSSW 91
Saffran, Bernard 1936- WhoAm 90
Saffran, Judith 1923- WhoAmW 91
Saffran, Kalman 1947- WhoAm 90
Saffran, Murray 1924- WhoAm 90
Saffron, Dorothy BiDrAPA 89
Saffron, Morris Harold 1905- WhoE 91
Safft, Stuart J. 1941- St&PR 91
Safi, Deborah Cavazos 1953- WhoAmW 91, WhoSSW 91
Safian, Gail R. 1947- ODwPR 91
Safian, Shelley Carole 1954- WhoAmW 91
Safiano, Sebastian 1928- WhoSSW 91
Safier, Jozef BiDrAPA 89
Safier, Stanley BiDrAPA 89
Safilios-Rothschild, Constantina 1936- ConAu 31NR
Safiol, George E. 1932- St&PR 91, WhoAm 90, WhoE 91
Safir, Andrew Jeffrey 1948- WhoAm 90
Safire, William BioIn 16
Safire, William 1929- ConAu 31NR, WhoAm 90, WhoE 91, WhoWor 91, WhoWrEP 89, WorAlBi
Safley, James Robert 1943- WhoAm 90
Safonov, Vasily 1852-1918 PenDiMP
Safra, Edmund J. WhoAm 90
Safra, Zvi 1952- WhoE 91
Safran, Alexander 1910- BioIn 16
Safran, Claire WhoAm 90, WhoWrEP 89
Safran, Edward Myron 1937- WhoAm 90
Safran, Gordon Howard 1935- St&PR 91
Safran, Marc A BiDrAPA 89
Safran, Nadav WhoAm 90
Safran, Perry Renfrow 1950- WhoEmL 91, WhoSSW 91
Safran, Verna WhoWrEP 89
Safran, William 1930- ConAu 32NR
Safranek, Doug BioIn 16
Safransky, Norma Frances BiDrAPA 89
Safransky, Sy 1945- WhoWrEP 89
Safron, Monte M. 1955- St&PR 91
Safronchuk, Vasiliy Stepanovich 1925- WhoWor 91
Saft, Virginia C 1928- BiDrAPA 89
Sag, Nancy Sue 1947- WhoE 91
Sagaev, Dimiter 1915- IntWWM 90
Sagal, Katey BioIn 16
Sagal-Mutrynowski, Laurie Mae 1950- WhoAmW 91
Sagalkin, Sanford 1942- WhoAm 90
Sagalyn, James M. 1945- St&PR 91
Sagalyn, Raphael BioIn 16
Sagan, Carl 1934- BioIn 16, MajTwCW, WorAlBi
Sagan, Carl Edward 1934- WhoAm 90, WhoE 91, WhoWor 91, WhoWrEP 89
Sagan, Dorion 1959- ConAu 131
Sagan, Francoise EncCoWW, MajTwCW
Sagan, Francoise 1935- BioIn 16, WhoWor 91, WorAlBi
Sagan, Hans 1928- WhoSSW 91
Sagan, John 1921- WhoAm 90
Sagan, Kathyrne V. 1952- WhoWrEP 89
Sagan, Miriam Anna 1954- WhoWrEP 89
Saganash 1781-1841 WhNaAH
Saganic, Livio Michele 1950- WhoAmA 91
Sagar, Virendra 1946- WhoWor 91
Sagasta, Praxedes Mateo BioIn 16
Sagaunash 1781-1841 WhNaAH
Sagawa, Shirley Sachi 1961- WhoAmW 91, WhoE 91
Sagawa, Yoneo 1926- WhoAm 90
Sage, Andrew G. C., II 1926- St&PR 91
Sage, Andrew Gregg Curtin, II 1926- WhoAm 90
Sage, Andrew Patrick, Jr. 1933- WhoAm 90, WhoWor 91
Sage, Bill B WhoAmA 91
Sage, Jeanette Bonner 1945- WhoAmW 91
Sage, Jeremy BioIn 16
Sage, John A. 1935- St&PR 91
Sage, Jonathan 1953- ConAu 129
Sage, Juniper AuBYP 90, SmATA X [port]
Sage, Kay 1898-1963 BiDWomA, WhoAmA 91N
Sage, Margaret Olivia 1828-1918 WorAlBi
Sage, Michael AuBYP 90
Sage, Mildred Devereux WhoAm 90
Sage, Myron Alvin 1920- St&PR 91
Sage, Peter J. 1941- St&PR 91
Sage, Phyllis Ann 1955- BiDrAPA 89
Sage, Russell 1816-1906 WorAlBi
Sage, Sandy Wisener 1950- WhoEmL 91
Sagebiel, Craig Douglas 1948- WhoSSW 91
Sagel, Jim 1947- ConAu 131, HispWr 90
Sageman, Sharon L 1953- BiDrAPA 89
Sagen, Johan, Jr. 1946- WhoWor 91
Sagendorf, Bud 1915- EncACom, WhoAm 90
Sager, Al Carl WhoWor 91
Sager, Alan Robert 1942- BiDrAPA 89
Sager, Carole Bayer 1944- ConMus 5 [port]
Sager, Carole Bayer 1947- WhoAm 90
Sager, Clifford J BiDrAPA 89
Sager, Donald Jack 1938- WhoAm 90
Sager, Donna Layne 1956- WhoWrEP 89
Sager, Ethel BiDrAPA 89
Sager, Gilbert Landis 1947- WhoE 91
Sager, Harry Charles 1930- St&PR 91
Sager, Henry S BiDrAPA 89
Sager, Jo Ann ODwPR 91
Sager, Jo Ann 1956- WhoAmW 91
Sager, Jonathan Ward 1954- WhoEmL 91
Sager, Joyce Toshiye Tanimoto 1950- WhoAmW 91
Sager, Martin Steven BiDrAPA 89
Sager, Mike BioIn 16
Sager, Patricia Wells 1930- St&PR 91
Sager, Richard St&PR 91
Sager, Roderick Cooper 1923- WhoAm 90
Sager, Ronald D BiDrAPA 89
Sager, Ruth 1918- BioIn 16, WhoAm 90, WhoAmW 91
Sager, William F. 1918- WhoAm 90
Sagerholm, Frithiof Norris, Jr. 1925- WhoE 91
Sagerholm, James Alvin 1927- WhoAm 90
Sagerman, Ronald 1932- BiDrAPA 89
Sagert, Horst 1934- ConDes 90
Sagesser, Rene Walter 1949- WhoWor 91
Saget, Bob BioIn 16
Saggese, Aldo E. 1928- St&PR 91
Saggese, JoAnn 1960- WhoE 91
Saghir, Marcel T BiDrAPA 89
Sagi, Eli Abraham 1946- BiDrAPA 89
Sagi, Gyorgy A BiDrAPA 89
Sagi, Gyorgy Andras 1954- WhoE 91
Saginaw, Rose Blas 1926- WhoAmW 91
Sagiova, Marketa 1901- IntWWM 90
Sagiroglu, Mehmet 1951- WhoWor 91
Sagle, Robert Franklin 1930- WhoAm 90
Sagman, Doron BiDrAPA 89
Sagness, Richard Lee 1937- WhoAm 90
Sago, Paul Edward 1931- WhoAm 90
Sagola, Mario J. TwCCr&M 91
Sagra, Ramon de la 1798-1871 ArtLatA
Sagstuen, Warren Richard 1945- WhoEmL 91
Sagvik, Stellan 1952- IntWWM 90
Sah, Chih-Tang 1932- WhoAm 90
Sah, Raaj Kumar 1952- WhoE 91
Saha, Asis Kumar 1941- WhoSSW 91, WhoWor 91
Saha, Meghnad 1893-1956 BioIn 16
Saha, Pabitra Kumar 1949- WhoSSW 91
Sahadeo, Arlene Viswassee BiDrAPA 89
Sahag, John BioIn 16
Sahagian, Marco Zarikian 1951- WhoWor 91
Sahagun, Bernardino de BioIn 16
Sahakian, Henry D. 1937- St&PR 91
Sahandy, Parviz 1934- BiDrAPA 89
Sahanek, Tatana 1922- WhoAm 90, WhoAmW 91, WhoE 91
Sahasranaman, Bhagirathy BiDrAPA 89
Sahatdjian, Haig Aram 1922- St&PR 91
Sahatdjian, Victor S. 1949- St&PR 91
Sahatjian, Steven 1964- St&PR 91
Sahgal, Nayantara 1927- FemiCLE
Sahgal, Pavan 1949- St&PR 91, WhoWrEP 89
Sahgal, Ranjit 1951- WhoE 91
Sahinoglu, Orhan 1933- WhoWor 91
Sahl, Michael 1934- IntWWM 90
Sahl, Mort BioIn 16
Sahl, Mort 1927- WorAlBi
Sahl, Morton Lyon 1927- WhoAm 90
Sahl, Richard Joachim 1919- WhoWor 91
Sahl, Robert Alan 1956- BiDrAPA 89
Sahlberg, Adelbert Hayden 1924- St&PR 91
Sahlberg, Robert Donald 1926- St&PR 91, WhoAm 90
Sahler, Helen Gertrude WhoAmA 91N
Sahli, Brenda Payne 1942- WhoAmW 91
Sahli, Don 1962- BioIn 16
Sahli, Edward Augustus, Jr. 1936- St&PR 91
Sahlie, Richard Scott 1929- St&PR 91
Sahliger, Herbert 1920- BioIn 16
Sahlin, Leland John 1925- St&PR 91
Sahlin, Nils Gosta 1900-1988 BioIn 16
Sahlins, Marshall D. WhoAm 90
Sahlman, Charles Wesley 1926- St&PR 91
Sahlstrand, James Michael 1936- WhoAmA 91
Sahlstrand, Margaret Ahrens 1939- WhoAmA 91
Sahlstrom, Elmer Bernard 1918- WhoAm 90
Sahlul, Ali Ahmad WhoWor 91
Sahly, Donald R. WhoAm 90
Sahm, Peter R. 1934- WhoWor 91
Sahmie, Ida 1960- MusmAFA
Sahn, John G. 1946- St&PR 91
Sahneuti DcCanB 12
Sahni, Anil Manoharlal 1937- WhoWor 91
Sahnyateh DcCanB 12
Sahoo, Prasanna 1951- WhoSSW 91
Sahota, Gurcharn Singh 1940- WhoE 91
Sahr, Morris G. 1928- WhoSSW 91
Sahrbeck, Everett William 1910- WhoAmA 91
Sai Baba EncO&P 3
Sai, Zaiju 1927- WhoWor 91
Sai-Halasz, George Anthony 1943- WhoE 91
Sai Hung, Henri Li 1951- WhoWor 91
Saia, Albert Steve 1933- St&PR 91
Saia, Jorge WhoAmA 91
Saia, Vincent Joseph 1958- St&PR 91
Saibini, John 1921- St&PR 91
Saibou, Ali WhoWor 91
Saich, Anthony James 1953- WhoWor 91
Saicho 767-822 EncJap
Said Bin Taymur 1910-1972 PolLCME
Said, Abdul Aziz 1930- WhoAm 90
Said, Edward W. BioIn 16
Said, Edward W. 1935- WhoAm 90, WhoWrEP 89
Said, Fahad bin Mahmoud al- 1944- WhoWor 91
Said, Fahr bin Taimur al- 1928- WhoWor 91
Said, John BiDrAPA 89
Said, Mohsin M. 1954- WhoEmL 91
Said, Nuri 1888-1958 PolLCME
Said, Tewfik 1955- BiDrAPA 89
Saidel, Donald R 1945- BiDrAPA 89
Saidenberg, Daniel 1906- WhoAm 90, WhoAmA 91
Saidenberg, Eleanore B 1911- WhoAmA 91
Saidenberg, Lawrence Daniel 1934- St&PR 91
Saidenberg, Rebecca Marshall 1958- WhoE 91
Saidi, Ahmad 1904- WhoSSW 91, WhoWor 91
Saidman, Gary K. 1952- WhoEmL 91
Saidt, Bus BioIn 16
Saied, J. Robert St&PR 91
Saier, Vic 1891-1967 Ballpl 90
Saif, Laila Abou BioIn 16
Saifer, Mark Gary 1938- St&PR 91
Saiger, George Max 1940- BiDrAPA 89
Saigo Takamori 1827-1877 EncJap
Saigol, M Younus 1945- BiDrAPA 89
Saigol, Muhammad Younus 1945- WhoWor 91
Saiia, Barbara Ann 1950- WhoAmW 91
Saikaku 1642-1693 EncJap
Saiki, Lorel Keiko 1954- WhoAmW 91
Saiki, Patricia 1930- WhoAm 90, WhoAmW 91
Saikkonen, Pekka Juhani 1946- WhoWor 91
Saikowski, Ronald Alexander 1950- WhoSSW 91
Sail, Lawrence 1942- ConAu 132
Sailer, Christopher Aldrich 1946- St&PR 91
Sailer, Henry Powers 1929- WhoAm 90
Sailer, Jerrold D. 1956- St&PR 91
Sailer, Lynne Barger 1956- WhoAmW 91
Saillon, Alfred 1944- WhoWor 91
Sailly, Francis Antoine 1942- WhoWor 91
Sailor, Dennis I. 1939- St&PR 91
Sailors, Susanne Creech 1913- WhoAmW 91
Saiman, Martin S. 1932- WhoAm 90
Saimei-tenno WomWR
Sain, Johnny 1917- Ballpl 90
Sain, Michael Kent 1937- WhoAm 90
Sain, Robert Leonard BiDrAPA 89
Sainani, Ram Hariram 1925- St&PR 91, WhoE 91, WhoWor 91
Sainburg, Richard B. 1924- St&PR 91
Saindon, Alfred Louis 1923- St&PR 91
Saine, Carroll Lee 1934- St&PR 91, WhoAm 90, WhoSSW 91
Sainer, Arthur 1924- WhoAm 90, WhoWrEP 89
Sainer, Leonard 1909- St&PR 91
Saini, B. S. 1948- BiDrAPA 89
Saini, Bakhtavar Singh 1932- WhoWor 91
Saini, Gulshan Rai 1924- WhoE 91
Saini, Rajendar Mohan 1940- WhoE 91
Saini, Tejinder Singh BiDrAPA 89
Saini, Vasant Durgadas 1952- WhoE 91
Sainju, Mohan Man 1941- WhoWor 91
Saino, Catherine Claire 1963- WhoEmL 91
Saino, Joseph Neuhoff 1933- St&PR 91
Sainsbury, John Davan 1927- WhoWor 91
Sainsbury, Lionel 1958- IntWWM 90
Saint Teresa of Jesus 1515- EncCoWW
Saint, Dora Jessie 1913- BioIn 16, WhoWor 91
Saint, Eva Marie 1924- WhoAm 90, WorAlBi
Saint, Lawrence 1885-1961 WhoAmA 91N
Saint, Paul Michael 1949- WhoE 91
St Amand, Joseph 1925- WhoAmA 91
St. Amand, Normand Gerard 1939- St&PR 91
St. Amand, Pierre 1920- WhoAm 90
St. Amant, Kathleen 1947- WhoSSW 91
Saint-Andre, Martin BiDrAPA 89
St. Andrews, Barbara Fitterer WhoAmW 91
Saint-Ange, Jacques-Louis DeLaHamayde De 1780- PenDiDA 89
Saint-Arnaud, Louis 1946- St&PR 91
St Aubin de Teran, Lisa 1953- FemiCLE
St. Clair, Arthur 1734-1818 BiDrUSE 89, WorAlBi
St. Clair, Arthur 1736-1818 EncCRAm, WhNaAH
St Clair, Beverly Page 1949- BiDrAPA 89
St. Clair, Byron Wagner 1924- St&PR 91
St. Clair, Carolyn Sue 1957- WhoAmW 91
St. Clair, David 1932- EncO&P 3
St. Clair, Dexter TwCCr&M 91
St Clair, Doris E 1937- BiDrAPA 89
St. Clair, Guy 1940- WhoE 91
St. Clair, Hal Kay 1925- WhoAm 90
St Clair, Harvey R 1921- BiDrAPA 89
St. Clair, James Draper 1920- WhoAm 90
St. Clair, Jane Catherine 1946- WhoEmL 91
St. Clair, Jane Elizabeth 1944- WhoAmW 91
St. Clair, Jesse Walton, III 1954- WhoSSW 91
St. Clair, Jesse Walton, Jr. 1930- St&PR 91, WhoAm 90
St. Clair, John Norman 1905- St&PR 91
St. Clair, Margaret 1911- RGTwCSF
St Clair, Michael 1912- WhoAmA 91
St. Clair, Philip 1944- WhoWrEP 89
St Clair, Ray Lawrence 1947- BiDrAPA 89
St. Clair, Rita BioIn 16
St. Clair, Rita Erika WhoAm 90
St. Clair, Robert Neal 1934- WhoSSW 91
St Clair, Rosalia FemiCLE
St. Clair, Scott Andrew 1951- WhoEmL 91
St. Clair, Thomas McBryar 1935- WhoAm 90
St. Claire, Frank Arthur 1949- WhoSSW 91, WhoWor 91
St. Claire, Randy 1960- Ballpl 90

St. Claire, Roxanne 1957- ODwPR 91
St. Clare, Dexter TwCCr&M 91
St. Clement, Courtney Tolson 1951- WhoE 91, WhoEmL 91
St. Cloud, Alden WhoWrEP 89
St. Columbia, Rhonda Scheider 1964- WhoSSW 91
Saint-Come, Monique EncCoWW
Saint-Cricq, Jean-Georges 1948- WhoWor 91
St. Croix, Judie Ann 1948- WhoEmL 91
St Cyr, Bernard 1934- BiDrAPA 89
St. Cyr, Cyprian MajTwCW
St. Cyr, Henry P. 1944- St&PR 91
St. Cyr, Napoleon Joseph 1924- WhoWrEP 89
St. Cyr, Virginia C. 1928- WhoAmW 91
Saint-Denis, Michel 1897-1971 OxCCanT
St Denis, Paul Andre 1938- WhoAmA 91
St. Denis, Ruth 1877-1968 BioAmW
St. Denis, Ruth 1877-1968 WorAlBi
St. Dennis, Jerry A. 1942- WhoAm 90
St. Denys, Louis Juchereau De 1676-1744 EncCRAm
Saint-Exupery, Antoine de 1900-1944 ConAu 132, EuWr 12, MajTwCW, WorAlBi
St. Florian, Friedrich Gartler 1932- WhoAm 90
St Florian, Friedrich Gartler 1932- WhoAmA 91
Saint-Gaudens, Augustus 1848-1907 BioIn 16, WorAlBi
St Gaudens, Homer 1879-1958 WhoAmA 91N
Saint-Genys, Marquise de BioIn 16
St. George, Arthur ConAu 31NR
St. George, Judith 1931- BioIn 16, SmATA 12AS [port]
St. George, Margaret WhoWrEP 89
St. George, Nicholas James 1939- St&PR 91, WhoAm 90, WhoSSW 91
St. George, William Ross 1924- WhoAm 90
Saint-Georges Chaume, Xavier 1922- WhoWor 91
St. Gerard, Michael BioIn 16
St. Germain, Comte de 1710?-1780? EncO&P 3
St. Germain, Fernand BioIn 16
St Germain, Fernand 1928- EncABHB 7 [port]
St. Germain, Fernand Joseph WhoAm 90
Saint-Germain, Jean-Joseph de 1719-1791 PenDiDA 89
St. Germain, Jean Mary WhoAmW 91, WhoE 91
St. Goar, Edward 1955- WhoAm 90
St. Goar, Herbert 1916- St&PR 91, WhoAm 90
St Helier, Ivy 1890-1971 OxCPMus
St. Hilaire, Donald 1944- St&PR 91
St. Hilaire, Sheila Barbara 1951- St&PR 91
Saint-Jacques, Alfred Joseph 1956- WhoWrEP 89
St. Jacques, Alphonse 1925- St&PR 91
Saint-Jacques, Bernard 1928- WhoAm 90, WhoWrEP 89
Saint-Jacques, R. P. de EncO&P 3
St. Jacques, Raymond 1930- DrBIPA 90, WhoAm 90
St. Jacques, Raymond 1930-1990 NewYTBS 90 [port]
St. Jacques, Robert H. 1924- St&PR 91, WhoAm 90
St. James, Dana Juan 1955- WhoE 91
St. James, Lionel David 1926- WhoWor 91
St. James, Lyn BioIn 16
St. James, Lyn 1947- WhoAmW 91
St. James, Susan 1946- ConTFT 8, WhoAm 90, WorAlBi
Saint-Jean, Comte de EncCoWW
St. Jean, Andre 1947- St&PR 91
St. Jean, Catherine Avery 1950- WhoAmW 91
St. Jean, Denis L. 1933- St&PR 91
St. Jean, Joseph, Jr. 1923- WhoAm 90
St Jean, Pierre 1833-1900 DcCanB 12
St John, Adam 1952- WhoAmA 91
St. John, Adam 1952- WhoWor 91
St. John, Adrian, II 1921- WhoAm 90, WhoWor 91
St. John, Anthony Paul 1937- WhoAm 90
St. John, B. D. 1931- St&PR 91
St. John, Bill D. 1931- WhoAm 90, WhoSSW 91
St. John, Billy Eugene 1932- WhoAm 90
St. John, Bonnie BioIn 16
St. John, Bonnie BioIn 16
St John, Bruce 1916- WhoAmA 91N
St. John, Christopher DrBIPA 90
St John, Christopher 1875?-1960 FemiCLE
St. John, Dale W. 1924- St&PR 91
St. John, David TwCCr&M 91
St. John, Harold Bernard 1931- BioIn 16
St. John, Howard C. WhoAm 90
St. John, Jill 1940- BioIn 16, WhoAm 90, WorAlBi
St. John, John St&PR 91
St. John, John 1921- WhoAm 90
St. John, John Gerald 1948- St&PR 91
St John, Kathleen Louise 1942- IntWWM 90
St. John, Lisa ConAu 130
St. John, Margaret Kay 1953- WhoAmW 91
St. John, Mary FemiCLE
St. John, Mary Ann 1958- WhoAmW 91
St John, Mary Elizabeth BiDrAPA 89
St. John, Nancy Marie 1953- WhoAmW 91
St. John, Nicole ConAu 32NR
St. John, Philip AuBYP 90, MajTwCW
St. John, Richard Joseph 1936- St&PR 91
St John, Robert 1929- BiDrAPA 89
St. John, Robert 1941- St&PR 91
St. John, Robert William 1951- WhoE 91
St John, Terry N 1934- WhoAmA 91
St. John, Vincent 1876-1929 EncAL
St John, William T BiDrAPA 89
St. John, Wylly Folk 1908-1985 AuBYP 90
St. John de Crevecoeur, J. Hector 1735-1813 BioIn 16
St. John-Foster, Keith Edward BioIn 16
St. John Sommer, Mary Margaret 1940- WhoAmW 91
St. John Thomas, David ConAu 30NR
St. Johns, Adela Rogers 1894-1988 BioIn 16, WorAlBi
St. Just, Edward Charles Grenfell, Baron 1870-1941 BioIn 16
St. Landau, Norman 1925- WhoAm 90, WhoE 91, WhoWor 91
St. Laurent, Henry A. 1925- St&PR 91
St. Laurent, Henry Alexander 1925- St&PR 91
St Laurent, Jacques 1933- BiDrAPA 89
St. Laurent, Yves BioIn 16
St. Laurent, Yves BioIn 16
St. Laurent, Yves 1936- ConDes 90, WhoWor 91
St. Laurent, Yves 1936- WorAlBi
St. Leger, Barry 1737-1789 EncCRAm
St Leger, Evelyn 1861-1944 FemiCLE
Saint-Louis, Acedius 1938- WhoWor 91
St. Louis, Eileen Marie 1957- WhoAmW 91
Saint-Marcoux, Micheline Coulombe 1938- IntWWM 90
St. Marie, Satenig 1927- WhoAm 90
St. Mark, Carole F. WhoAm 90, WhoAmW 91
St. Martin, Alexis BioIn 16
St Martin, David A BiDrAPA 89
Saint-Martin, Jacques Edouard 1934- WhoWor 91
Saint-Martin, Louis Claude de 1743-1803 EncO&P 3
Saint-Martin Perman Junot d'Abrantes, L. 1784-1838 EncCoWW
St. Mary, Edward Sylvester 1941- WhoAm 90
St Maur, Kirk WhoAmA 91
Saint-Maurice, N.-H.-E. Faucher De DcCanB 12
St-Onge, Denis Alderic 1929- WhoAm 90
St. Onge, Guylaine BioIn 16
St. Onge, Hubert Jules 1946- WhoWor 91
St. Onge, John Lionel 1934- WhoE 91
St Oswald, Baron 1916-1984 DcNaB 1981
St. Peter, John M. 1942- St&PR 91
St. Peter, Lori Ann 1960- WhoAmW 91
Saint-Phalle, Niki de BioIn 16
Saint-Phalle, Niki de 1930- BiDWomA
St Pierre, Aimee Claire 1947- BiDrAPA 89
St. Pierre, Barry Joseph 1946- St&PR 91
St. Pierre, George Roland, Jr. 1930- WhoAm 90
St.-Pierre, Jacques 1920- WhoAm 90
St. Pierre, Richard William 1940- St&PR 91
St Pierre, Roderick G 1907- BiDrAPA 89
St. Pierre, Ronald Leslie 1938- WhoAm 90
Saint-Preux, J M Y Carl BiDrAPA 89
St. Romain, Janice Marie 1955- WhoSSW 91
St. Rose, Edwina Losey 1952- WhoAmW 91
Saint-Saens, Camille 1835-1921 BioIn 16, PenDiMP A, WorAlBi
Saint-Saens, Charles Camille 1835-1921 BioIn 16, EncPaPR 91
St. Sauveur, John Harold 1932- St&PR 91
Saint-Simon, Claude de Rouvroy, comte de 1760-1825 BioIn 16
St Tamara WhoAmA 91
St. Tamara WhoAmW 91
St. Thomas, James W. 1927- St&PR 91
St. Thomas, William H. 1901- St&PR 91
St. Vrain, Ceran de Hault de Lassus de 1802-1870 BioIn 16
Sainte-Marie, Buffy 1941- WorAlBi
Ste Marie, Stephen Bruce 1948- St&PR 91
Sainton, Prosper 1813-1890 PenDiMP
Sainton-Dolby, Charlotte PenDiMP
Saintsbury, George 1845-1933 BioIn 16
Sainz, Gustavo 1940- ConAu 131, HispWr 90
Saionji Kimmochi 1849-1940 EncJap
Saisselin, Remy Gilbert 1925- WhoAm 90
Saitas, Vasiliki 1961- WhoEmL 91
Saito, Albert Yutaka BiDrAPA 89
Saito, Frank Kiyoji 1945- WhoEmL 91
Saito, Joichi 1935- St&PR 91
Saito, Kiyomi 1950- WhoAmW 91, WhoWor 91
Saito, Michiko 1946- AuBYP 90
Saito, Moto BioIn 16
Saito, Nobuo 1932- WhoWor 91
Saito, Paul Makoto 1936- WhoAm 90
Saito, R. 1950- St&PR 91
Saito, Seiji 1933- WhoAmA 91, WhoE 91
Saito, Taiichi 1931- WhoWor 91
Saito, Yoshitaka 1926- WhoWor 91
Saitoh, Mamoru 1935- WhoWor 91
Saitoti, George WhoWor 91
Saitoti, Tepilit Ole 1949- BioIn 16
Saitta, Peter Andrew 1942- St&PR 91
Saiyed, Humaira Fatima 1958- BiDrAPA 89
Saiz-Ruiz, Jeronimo BiDrAPA 89
Saizan, Paula Theresa 1947- WhoAmW 91, WhoEmL 91
Sajak, Pat BioIn 16
Sajak, Pat 1947- WhoAm 90, WorAlBi
Sajatovic, Martha 1961- BiDrAPA 89
Sajja, S Prasad 1949- BiDrAPA 89
Sajjad, Riffat BiDrAPA 89
Sajwani, Faisal Ali 1957- WhoWor 91
Sajwani, Taher Mohd 1955- WhoWor 91
Sak, Peter Joseph 1933- St&PR 91
Sakada, Daryll M. 1941- St&PR 91
Sakaguchi, Shukichi 1926- WhoWor 91
Sakai, Hiroko 1939- WhoAmW 91
Sakai, James T. 1926- St&PR 91
Sakai, Katsuo 1942- WhoWor 91
Sakai, Magara 1903-1983 BioIn 16
Sakai, Tomio 1950- St&PR 91
Sakai, Toshihiko 1943- WhoWor 91
Sakai, Yoshiro 1935- WhoWor 91
Sakakibara, Yasuo 1929- WhoWor 91
Sakalauskas, Vitautas Vladovich 1933- WhoWor 91
Sakamaki, Leigh BiDrAPA 89
Sakamoto Ryuichi 1952- EncJap
Sakamoto, Frederick A 1943- BiDrAPA 89
Sakamoto, Ichitaro 1926- WhoWor 91
Sakamoto, Ryuichi NewAgMG
Sakamoto, Tadanobu 1931- WhoWor 91
Sakaoka, Yasue 1933- WhoAmA 91
Sakara, Marilyn Judith 1949- WhoEmL 91
Sakaris, Kay Waters BioIn 16
Sakarissa 1730?-1810? WhNaAH
Sakashita, Kiyoshi 1933- ConDes 90
Sakata, Lenn 1954- Ballpl 90
Sakata, Shoichi 1911-1970 DcScB S2
Sakauye, Kenneth Mark 1948- BiDrAPA 89
Sakbani, M. Michael WhoWor 91
Sakell, Edith B. 1939- WhoAmW 91
Sakell, Leonidas 1946- WhoE 91
Sakharov, Andrei 1921-1989 AnObit 1989, News 90, WorAlBi
Sakharov, Andrei D 1921-1989 ConAu 130, CurBio 90N
Sakharov, Andrei Dmitrievich 1921-1989 BioIn 16
Sakharov, Elena Bonner BioIn 16
Saki ConAu 130, MajTwCW
Saki 1870-1916 WorAlBi
Saki, Masayasu 1946- WhoWor 91
Sakires, Nicholas James 1928- St&PR 91
Sakita, Bunji 1930- WhoAm 90
Sakiz, Edouard 1926- WhoWor 91
Sakkal, Mamoun 1950- WhoEmL 91
Saklad, Maurice J. 1915-1989 BioIn 16
Saklad, Sarah M BiDrAPA 89
Saklad, Stephen Ross 1953- WhoSSW 91
Saklani, Chand BioIn 16
Sakles, Constantine J 1934- BiDrAPA 89
Saklofsky, Robert Frederick 1930- St&PR 91
Sakmann, Charles Albert, III 1954- WhoE 91
Sakofsky, Harvey Yale BiDrAPA 89
Sakol, Jonathan H. 1942- WhoAm 90
Sakosits, John Joseph 1934- St&PR 91
Sakoutis, Steve 1930- St&PR 91
Sakow, Henry A BiDrAPA 89
Sakowicz, Richard 1939- St&PR 91
Sakowitz, Robert 1938- St&PR 91
Sakowitz, Robert Tobias 1938- WhoAm 90
Saks, Arnold 1931- WhoAm 90
Saks, Bonnie Rae BiDrAPA 89
Saks, Gene WhoAm 90
Saks, Gene 1921- WorAlBi
Saks, Judith-Ann 1943- WhoAmA 91, WhoAmW 91
Saks, Michael J. BioIn 16
Saks, Stephen Howard 1941- WhoAm 90
Sakse, Andrea Louise BiDrAPA 89
Sakse, Anna 1905-1981 EncCoWW
Sakuma, Masahide NewAgMG
Sakurai, Jo Mary 1918- WhoAmA 91
Sakurai, Kunihiro 1940- WhoWor 91
Sakurai, Kunitomo 1933- WhoWor 91
Sakurai, Nobushige 1945- St&PR 91
Sakurai, Takejiroh 1939- WhoWor 91
Sakuta, Manabu 1947- WhoEmL 91, WhoWor 91
Sakuyama, Shunji 1940- WhoAmA 91, WhoE 91
Sal, Jack 1954- WhoAmA 91
Sala, Antonio 1935- WhoHisp 91
Sala, George Augustus Henry 1828-1896 BioIn 16
Sala, Jim ODwPR 91
Sala, Luis Francisco 1919- WhoWor 91
Salabe, Giovanni Battista 1932- WhoWor 91
Salabert, Maria Teresa 1948- WhoHisp 91
Salabounis, Manuel 1935- WhoWor 91
Salacrou, Armand 1899-1989 AnObit 1989
Salacuse, Jeswald William 1938- WhoAm 90, WhoE 91
Saladin 1138?-1193 WorAlBi
Saladin, Sultan of Egypt And Syria 1137-1193 BioIn 16
Saladin, Lois J 1933- BiDrAPA 89
Saladino, Anthony Joseph 1959- WhoSSW 91
Saladino, John A. 1954- St&PR 91
Saladino, John F 1939- ConDes 90
Saladino, Tony 1943- WhoAmA 91
Saladrigas, Carlos Augusto 1948- WhoHisp 91
Salaff, Peter PenDiMP
Salafia, Linda Mary 1946- WhoAmW 91
Salaga, Vivian Odell 1946- WhoEmL 91
Salah, Ahmed Ben BioIn 16
Salah, Anton 1953- St&PR 91
Salahuddin Abdul Aziz Shah 1926- WhoWor 91
Salam, Abdus 1926- BioIn 16, WhoAm 90, WhoWor 91, WorAlBi
Salam, Debera Jean 1957- WhoAmW 91
Salama, Abdel Aziz A 1932- BiDrAPA 89
Salama, Claude 1936- St&PR 91
Salama, Ezzeldin M BiDrAPA 89
Salama, Guy 1930- St&PR 91
Salama, Hannu 1936- DcScanL
Salama, Mona Sadek F BiDrAPA 89
Salama, Samir A BiDrAPA 89
Salama, Sheila 1943- BiDrAPA 89
Salamacha, Judy Anne 1944- WhoAmW 91
Salaman, Esther Sarah IntWWM 90
Salamanca, Concha de EncCoWW
Salamanca, Daniel 1869?-1935 BioIn 16
Salamanca, Lucy ConAu 130
Salamanca, Lucy 1900?-1989 SmATA X
Salamanca, Rosalba BiDrAPA 89
Salamasina BioIn 16
Salamon, Isaac 1933- St&PR 91
Salamon, Itamar 1934- BiDrAPA 89, WhoE 91
Salamon, Joseph 1952- WhoE 91
Salamon, Linda Bradley 1941- WhoAm 90, WhoAmW 91
Salamon, Martin A BiDrAPA 89
Salamon, Michael Jacob 1951- WhoEmL 91, WhoWor 91
Salamon, Miklos Dezso Gyorgy 1933- WhoAm 90
Salamon, Myron Ben 1939- WhoAm 90
Salamon, Renay 1948- WhoAmW 91, WhoE 91, WhoEmL 91, WhoWor 91
Salamone, Anthony A. 1944- St&PR 91
Salamone, Debbie 1965- WhoAmW 91
Salamone, Jean G. 1929- St&PR 91
Salamone, Jean Smith 1929- St&PR 91
Salamone, Joseph Charles 1939- WhoAm 90
Salamone, Thomas W. 1944- St&PR 91
Salamovich, Sofia 1946- BiDrAPA 89
Salan, Beryl R. 1936- St&PR 91
Salan, Irving 1911- BiDrAPA 89
Salan, Raoul Albin Louis 1899-1984 BiDFrPL
Saland, Linda Carol 1942- WhoAmW 91
Saland, Stephanie WhoAm 90
Salandra, John A. 1952- WhoE 91
Salane, Douglas Edward 1952- WhoEmL 91
Salanga, Emilia Raval BiDrAPA 89
Salanguit, Filipinas A BiDrAPA 89
Salans, Carl Fredric 1933- WhoAm 90, WhoWor 91
Salans, Lester Barry 1936- WhoAm 90
Salant, Abner Samuel 1930- WhoAm 90
Salant, Mindi 1956- WhoAmW 91
Salant, Nathan Nathaniel 1955- WhoE 91
Salant, Richard S. 1914- BioIn 16, WorAlBi
Salant, Walter S. 1911- WhoAm 90, WhoE 91
Salanter, Israel 1810-1883 BioIn 16
Salantrie, Frank 1926- WhoWrEP 89
Salarrue 1899-1975 BioIn 16
Salas, Alan Robert 1956- WhoEmL 91
Salas, Alejandro WhoHisp 91
Salas, Antonio 1795-1860 ArtLatA
Salas, Floyd 1931- HispWr 90

Salas, Floyd Francis 1931- WhoHisp 91, WhoWrEP 89
Salas, Francisco Jose WhoHisp 91
Salas, Gloria Gamido BiDrAPA 89
Salas, Gumecindo 1941- WhoHisp 91
Salas, Marcos 1944- WhoHisp 91
Salas, Mariano Picon- 1901-1965 BioIn 16
Salas, Marilyn Sue 1943- WhoAmW 91, WhoWor 91
Salas, Mark 1961- Ballpl 90
Salas, Max E. 1953- WhoHisp 91
Salas, Peter 1965- WhoHisp 91
Salas, Rafael M. BioIn 16
Salas, Rafael M 1928-1987 ConAu 129
Salas, Ramon 1815?-1880 ArtLatA
Salas, Ramon Antonio BiDrAPA 89
Salas, Randall Nouel 1945- WhoWor 91
Salaspuro, Jukka Veikko 1946- WhoWor 91
Salassi, Otto R. 1939- BioIn 16
Salat, Joseph A. 1915- St&PR 91
Salata, Gerard A. 1944- St&PR 91
Salata Julian, Elaine 1960- WhoE 91
Salathe, John, Jr. 1928- St&PR 91, WhoAm 90
Salatich, Donald C. 1946- St&PR 91
Salatich, John Smyth 1926- WhoSSW 91
Salatich, William G. 1922- St&PR 91
Salatka, Charles Alexander 1918- WhoAm 90, WhoSSW 91
Salaverria, Helena Clara 1923- WhoAmW 91
Salay, Carolyn Jeanne WhoAmW 91, WhoSSW 91, WhoWor 91
Salay, Cindy Rolston 1955- WhoAmW 91
Salazar, Alberto BioIn 16
Salazar, Alberto 1958- WhoHisp 91
Salazar, Alfredo BioIn 16
Salazar, Angel 1961- Ballpl 90
Salazar, Antonio De Oliveira 1889-1970 WorAlBi
Salazar, Barbara M. 1949- WhoWrEP 89
Salazar, Berette Anne BiDrAPA 89
Salazar, Carmen 1940- WhoHisp 91
Salazar, Daniel Reynolds 1942- WhoWor 91
Salazar, David Henry 1942- WhoHisp 91
Salazar, Debra 1952- WhoAmW 91
Salazar, Diego 1945- WhoHisp 91
Salazar, Edward 1944- WhoHisp 91
Salazar, Enrique Camarena BioIn 16
Salazar, Eulogio BioIn 16
Salazar, Fred James, Jr. 1942- WhoHisp 91
Salazar, Gentil 1936- BiDrAPA 89
Salazar, Gertrude 1936- WhoHisp 91
Salazar, Helen Aquila 1944- WhoHisp 91
Salazar, I. C. WhoHisp 91
Salazar, J Octavio BiDrAPA 89
Salazar, Jorge BiDrAPA 89
Salazar, Kenneth Vincent 1948- WhoHisp 91
Salazar, Luis 1956- Ballpl 90
Salazar, Luis Garcia 1956- WhoHisp 91
Salazar, Miriam Larios 1962- WhoHisp 91
Salazar, Nilda B BiDrAPA 89
Salazar, Raymond Anthony 1947- WhoHisp 91
Salazar, Ruben 1928-1970 BioIn 16
Salazar, Steve 1965- WhoHisp 91
Salazar, Tony 1959- WhoHisp 91
Salazar Arrue, Salvador 1899-1975 BioIn 16
Salazar Bondy, Sebastian 1924-1965 HispWr 90
Salazar-Carrillo, Jorge 1938- WhoHisp 91, WhoSSW 91, WhoWor 91
Salazar Lopez, Jose 1910- WhoAm 90, WhoWor 91
Salazar-Navarro, Hernando 1931- WhoHisp 91
Salbaing, Pierre Alcee 1914- WhoAm 90
Salber, Eva J. BioIn 16
Salber, Eva Juliet 1916- WhoAm 90, WhoAmW 91
Salber, Hubert Wilhelm 1928- WhoWor 91
Salberg, Batsheva 1953- WhoAmW 91
Salce, Ludwig 1934- WhoE 91
Salcedo, Augusto Bernardino Leguia y BioIn 16
Salcedo, Jose Jesus 1960- WhoHisp 91
Salcedo, Luis Martin 1940- BiDrAPA 89
Salcedo Fernandez Del Castillo, Tomas 1946- WhoWor 91
Salch, Steven Charles 1943- WhoAm 90
Salchert, Brian Arthur 1941- WhoWrEP 89
Salci, Larry Eugene 1946- WhoAm 90
Salcido, Silvia Astorga WhoHisp 91
Salcudean, Martha Eva 1934- WhoAm 90
Saldan, Nicholas 1955- WhoEmL 91
Saldana, Alicia Mata BiDrAPA 89
Saldana, Elsa Antonia 1950- WhoAmW 91
Saldana, Fred, Jr. WhoHisp 91
Saldana, Mariana WhoHisp 91
Saldana, Oscar Eduardo BiDrAPA 89
Saldana, Theresa BioIn 16
Saldana-Luna, Pura 1944- WhoHisp 91
Saldarriaga, Alexander 1960- WhoSSW 91
Saldate, Macario, IV 1941- WhoHisp 91
Saldich, Robert Joseph 1933- St&PR 91
Saldin, Thomas R. 1946- St&PR 91, WhoAm 90
Saldinger, Joel S 1930- BiDrAPA 89
Saldivar, Ramon 1949- WhoHisp 91
Saldivia, Aida Yolanda BiDrAPA 89
Sale, Marilyn Mills 1928- WhoAm 90, WhoWrEP 89
Sale, Richard 1911- TwCCr&M 91
Sale, Roger 1932- ConAu 33NR
Sale, Sara Lee 1954- WhoAmW 91
Sale, Tom S. 1942- WhoSSW 91, WhoWor 91
Sale, William Merritt 1929- WhoAm 90
Saleda, Marion Eugene 1935- St&PR 91
Saleeby, Raymond G. 1945- St&PR 91
Saleeby, Robert W. 1951- WhoWor 91
Saleem, Ab 1940- St&PR 91
Saleem, Shahnaz BiDrAPA 89
Saleem, Syed Mohammed 1940- WhoWor 91
Saleemi, Muhammad Saleem 1949- WhoWor 91
Saleh, Dennis 1942- WhoWrEP 89
Saleh, Jaime 1941- WhoWor 91
Saleh, Mohammed 1939- WhoWor 91
Saleh, Saida Shamsuddin 1936- BiDrAPA 89
Saleh, Wadih 1910- EncO&P 3
Salem, Anton Salim 1931- St&PR 91
Salem, Carlito Ariel Capili 1946- WhoWor 91
Salem, Charles Louis 1935- St&PR 91
Salem, Dorothy Carlson 1946- WhoAmW 91
Salem, E. 1936- St&PR 91
Salem, Edward S BiDrAPA 89
Salem, George Richard 1953- WhoAm 90
Salem, Mamdouh Mohamed 1918-1988 AnObit 1988
Salem, Raphael 1898-1963 DcScB S2
Salem, Richard Joseph 1947- WhoSSW 91
Salem, Samuel 1923- St&PR 91
Salem, Suhayl Shukri 1937- WhoWor 91
Salem, Susanne Frances 1945- WhoEmL 91
Salem Farrell, Sandra BioIn 16
Salembier, Henri 1753?-1820 PenDiDA 89
Salembier, Richard Van Zandt, Jr. 1931- St&PR 91
Salembier, Valerie BioIn 16
Salembier, Valerie Birnbaum 1945- WhoAm 90, WhoAmW 91
Salembier, Walter Charles 1940- St&PR 91
Salemi, Joseph R. 1941- St&PR 91
Salemme, Antonio 1892- WhoAmA 91
Salemme, Lucia 1919- WhoAmA 91
Salemme, Martha 1912- WhoAmA 91
Salemo, Robert James 1954- WhoE 91
Salemson, Harold J. BioIn 16
Salenger, Lucy Lee 1938- WhoAmW 91
Salengro, Roger Henri Charles 1890-1936 BiDFrPL
Salentine, Thomas James 1939- St&PR 91
Salerian, Alen Johannes BiDrAPA 89
Salerno, Al 1931- Ballpl 90
Salerno, Charles 1916- WhoAmA 91
Salerno, Darryl J 1952- ODwPR 91
Salerno, Frederic V. 1943- WhoAm 90
Salerno, Harry Edward 1953- WhoE 91
Salerno, James Leonard 1930- St&PR 91
Salerno, Leon Alexander 1933- St&PR 91
Salerno, Louis J. 1915-1988 BioIn 16
Salerno, Marie ODwPR 91
Salerno, Michael J. 1936- St&PR 91
Salerno, Nicholas Andrew 1936- WhoWrEP 89
Salerno, Nicholas James 1927- St&PR 91
Salerno, Peter Thomas 1941- St&PR 91
Salerno, Philip Adams 1953- WhoSSW 91
Salerno-Sonnenberg, Nadja BioIn 16
Sales, A. R. 1948- WhoAm 90
Sales, Eugenio de Araujo 1920- WhoWor 91
Sales, Francisca F BiDrAPA 89
Sales, Gary Nelson BiDrAPA 89
Sales, James Bohus 1934- WhoAm 90, WhoSSW 91, WhoWor 91
Sales, Kathleen C BiDrAPA 89
Sales, Michel 1928- WhoAm 90
Sales, Soupy BioIn 16
Sales, Soupy 1926- WorAlBi
Salese, Irene 1930- St&PR 91
Salesses, John Joseph 1933- WhoAm 90
Salet, Eugene Albert 1911- WhoSSW 91, WhoWor 91
Saletu, Bernd 1942- BiDrAPA 89
Salewski, Ruby Marie Graf 1932- WhoAmW 91
Salfi, Thomas Apa 1931- St&PR 91
Salgado, Alfredo Garcia 1951- St&PR 91
Salgado, Annivar 1954- WhoHisp 91
Salgado, Carmelita Garcia 1939- WhoWor 91
Salgado, John, III 1956- WhoHisp 91
Salgado, Luis J. 1953- WhoHisp 91
Salgado, Maria Antonia 1933- WhoHisp 91
Salgado, Ruwan Navindra 1963- WhoE 91
Salgado, Sebastiao BioIn 16
Salganik, Amy Ellen 1956- WhoE 91
Salgo, Peter Lloyd 1949- WhoE 91, WhoWor 91
Salgueiro, Alex 1954- WhoSSW 91
Salgueiro, Carmen Escude WhoAmW 91
Salguero, Carlos Eduardo 1929- St&PR 91, WhoAm 90
Salguero, Carlos H BiDrAPA 89
Salguero, Richard Arturo 1954- St&PR 91
Salgunan, Nambi 1943- BiDrAPA 89
Salha, Rhett Herman 1959- St&PR 91
Salhany, Gary T. 1954- St&PR 91
Salhany, Lucille WhoAmW 91
Salhias de Tournemir, Elizaveta 1815-1892 EncCoWW
Sali Vongkhamsao WhoWor 91
Salib, Magdy Guirguis BiDrAPA 89
Salib, Theresa Boutros 1951- WhoWor 91
Saliba, Jacob 1913- St&PR 91, WhoAm 90
Saliba, John H. 1938- St&PR 91
Saliba, Philip E. 1931- WhoAm 90
Saliba, Richard Jameel 1957- WhoSSW 91
Saliba, Tony BioIn 16
Salice, Barbara Farenga 1944- WhoAmW 91
Salick, Bernard 1939- St&PR 91
Saliege, Jules Gerard 1870-1956 BioIn 16
Salieri, Antonio 1750-1825 PenDiMP A
Saliga, Marie T. 1934- St&PR 91
Saligman, Harvey 1938- WhoAm 90
Salih, Ali Abdullah 1942- PolLCME, WhoWor 91
Salih, Halil Ibrahim 1939- WhoSSW 91
Salih, Hassan Ali 1934- BiDrAPA 89
Salik, Julian Oswald 1909- WhoAm 90
Salim, Salim Ahmed 1942- WhoWor 91
Salim, Yusuf BiDrAPA 89
Salin, William N. 1931- St&PR 91
Salina, David M. St&PR 91
Salinas, Baruj 1935- WhoAmA 91
Salinas, Dora 1936- WhoAmW 91
Salinas, Harry Roger 1949- WhoHisp 91
Salinas, Jimmy 1949- WhoSSW 91
Salinas, Lorina WhoHisp 91
Salinas, Luciano, Jr. 1950- WhoHisp 91
Salinas, Lucila Mercedes 1953- WhoSSW 91
Salinas, Luis Lauro, II 1952- WhoSSW 91
Salinas, Luis Omar 1937- BioIn 16, ConAu 131, HispWr 90, WhoHisp 91
Salinas, Lupe 1948- WhoHisp 91
Salinas, Maria Elena WhoHisp 91
Salinas, Norberto WhoHisp 91
Salinas, Porfirio 1910-1973 BioIn 16
Salinas, R. Rolando 1951- BiDrAPA 89
Salinas, Raul G. 1946- WhoHisp 91
Salinas, Ricardo 1961- WhoHisp 91
Salinas, Simon 1955- WhoHisp 91
Salinas, Trinidad Cervantes 1940- St&PR 91
Salinas de Gortari, Carlos BioIn 16
Salinas de Gortari, Carlos 1948- WhoSSW 91, WhoWor 91
Salinas Izaguirre, Saul F. 1932- WhoHisp 91
Salinas-Norman, Bobbi WhoHisp 91
Salindong-Dario, Nemecia R BiDrAPA 89
Saline, Lindon Edgar 1924- WhoAm 90
Salinger, Gerhard Ludwig 1934- WhoAm 90
Salinger, J. D. 1919- BioIn 16, DcLB 102 [port]
Salinger, J D 1919- MajTwCW
Salinger, J. D. 1919- WorAlBi
Salinger, James A. 1922- St&PR 91
Salinger, Jerome David 1919- BioIn 16, WhoWrEP 89
Salinger, Marion Casting 1917- WhoAmW 91
Salinger, Michael Alvin 1956- WhoE 91
Salinger, Pierre 1925- WorAlBi
Salinger, Pierre Emil George 1925- WhoAm 90, WhoWrEP 89
Salinger, Robert Jules BiDrAPA 89
Salinger, Ruth Angier 1931- WhoAmW 91
Salinger, Steven Alan 1954- WhoE 91
Salinsky, Cathy Joan 1953- WhoAmW 91
Saliola, Frances 1921- St&PR 91
Salisachs, Mercedes 1916- EncCoWW
Salisbury, Alan Blanchard 1937- WhoSSW 91
Salisbury, Alicia Laing 1939- WhoAmW 91
Salisbury, Carla Ann 1964- WhoE 91
Salisbury, Charlotte Y. 1914- ConAu 129
Salisbury, David Francis 1947- WhoEmL 91
Salisbury, Donald Charles 1946- WhoSSW 91
Salisbury, Douglas Lee 1946- St&PR 91, WhoAm 90
Salisbury, Ellsworth C., Jr. WhoE 91
Salisbury, Frank Boyer 1926- WhoAm 90
Salisbury, Franklin Cary 1910- WhoAm 90
Salisbury, Harrison E 1908- ConAu 30NR, MajTwCW, WorAlBi
Salisbury, Harrison Evans 1908- BioIn 16, WhoAm 90
Salisbury, Helen Holland 1923- WhoE 91
Salisbury, Helen Margaret 1923- WhoSSW 91
Salisbury, Ian Patrick 1925- IntWWM 90
Salisbury, Irving Daniel 1936- WhoE 91
Salisbury, Jenny Olivia 1959- WhoAmW 91
Salisbury, John ConAu 33NR
Salisbury, John Eagan 1931- St&PR 91
Salisbury, John Francis 1930- St&PR 91
Salisbury, Joshua Milton 1963- WhoEmL 91
Salisbury, Kevin M. 1935- St&PR 91
Salisbury, Kevin Mahon 1935- WhoAm 90
Salisbury, Marianne Hart 1929- St&PR 91
Salisbury, Mary Ann WhoAmW 91
Salisbury, Patricia Dianne 1951- WhoAmW 91
Salisbury, R Gascoyne-Cecil, Marquis of 1830-1903 BioIn 16
Salisbury, Ralph James 1926- WhoWrEP 89
Salisbury, Ray 1942- ConAu 31NR
Salisbury, Robert Cameron 1943- WhoAm 90
Salisbury, Robert Cecil, Earl of 1563-1612 BioIn 16
Salisbury, Robert Holt 1930- WhoAm 90
Salishchev, Konstantin Alekseyevich 1905-1989 BioIn 16
Salisian, Neal S. 1938- St&PR 91
Salit, Norman 1896-1960 BioIn 16
Salit, Vivian L. 1928- WhoE 91
Salita, Christine Theresa 1951- WhoAmW 91
Saliterman, Laura Shrager 1946- WhoAmW 91
Salitore, Robert Angelo 1948- St&PR 91
Salituri, Jeff Robert 1950- WhoSSW 91
Salius, Michael W. 1947- St&PR 91
Salivar, Charles Joseph 1923- St&PR 91
Salizzoni, Frank L. 1938- St&PR 91
Salizzoni, Frank Louis 1938- WhoAm 90, WhoE 91
Salk, Jonas NewYTBS 90 [port]
Salk, Jonas 1914- BioIn 16
Salk, Jonas E. 1914- WorAlBi
Salk, Jonas Edward 1914- WhoAm 90, WhoWor 91
Salk, Jonathan Daniel BiDrAPA 89
Salk, Lee 1926- WhoAm 90
Salkeld, Bill 1917-1967 Ballpl 90
Salkeld, Robert 1920- IntWWM 90
Salkeld, Robert J 1932- ConAu 31NR
Salkeld, Roger BioIn 16
Salkever, David Simeon 1944- WhoE 91
Salkey, Andrew 1928- BioIn 16
Salkin, Jay Harvey 1939- St&PR 91
Salkin, Maureen Ada 1943- WhoE 91
Salkin, Paul 1932- BiDrAPA 89
Salkind, Alvin J. 1927- WhoAm 90
Salkind, Milton 1916- WhoAm 90
Salkind, Neil J. 1947- WhoAm 90
Salkind, Neil Joseph 1947- WhoWrEP 89
Salko, Henry BioIn 16
Salkowski, Claire J. 1952- WhoE 91
Sall, David Leonard BiDrAPA 89
Sall, Robert Dayton BiDrAPA 89
Sall, Ronald Martin 1941- St&PR 91
Sallade, Victoria Lee 1953- WhoEmL 91
Sallagar, Walter Hermann 1935- IntWWM 90
Sallah, Majeed 1920- WhoWor 91
Salle, David BioIn 16
Salle, David 1952- WhoAm 90, WhoAmA 91
Sallee, Bill 1929- WhoSSW 91
Sallee, Charles H. BioIn 16
Sallee, Marilyn 1948- WhoWrEP 89
Sallee, Roger Kent 1948- St&PR 91
Sallee, Slim 1885-1950 Ballpl 90 [port]
Sallee, Wesley William 1951- WhoEmL 91
Sallen, David Urban 1952- WhoEmL 91
Sallen, Ira Bruce 1954- WhoE 91, WhoWor 91
Sallen, Melvin J. 1928- St&PR 91
Saller, K F 1902- EncO&P 3
Salles, Jaime Carlos 1930- WhoHisp 91
Salles, Maurice 1943- WhoWor 91
Sallet, Dirse Wilkis 1936- WhoAm 90
Salley, J. Ronald 1939- St&PR 91
Salley, James W. 1923- St&PR 91
Salley, James William, Jr. 1949- St&PR 91
Salley, John BioIn 16
Salley, John Jones 1926- WhoAm 90
Sallick, Lucy Ellen 1937- WhoAmA 91
Sallick, Richard M BiDrAPA 89
Sallin, Sandra Friedman 1940- WhoAmW 91
Sallinen, Aulis 1935- IntWWM 90, PenDiMP A
Sallis, Peter 1921- ConTFT 8 [port]
Sallis, Susan 1929- BioIn 16
Sallman, Jeanne L. BioIn 16

Sallnow, Michael 1949-1990 ConAu 131
Sallot, Lynne ODwPR 91
Salloum, Antoine Abdullah 1913- WhoWor 91
Salloway, Stephen Paul BiDrAPA 89
Sallus, Marc Leonard 1954- WhoEmL 91
Sallye, Frederick Isaac, I 1949- WhoSSW 91
Salm, Constance de EncCoWW
Salm, Peter 1919- WhoWrEP 89
Salm, Peter 1919-1990 ConAu 132
Salm, Rick D. 1952- St&PR 91
Salm, Walter Gene 1933- WhoE 91
Salm-Dyck, La comtesse de EncCoWW
Salma, Emanuel A. 1908-1989 BioIn 16
Salmaggi, Felix W. BioIn 16, NewYTBS 90
Salman, Arslan 1947- WhoWor 91
Salmans, Charles G. ODwPR 91
Salmans, Charles Gardiner 1945- WhoAm 90, WhoEmL 91
Salmans, James Lee 1935- St&PR 91
Salmen, Larry James 1947- St&PR 91
Salmen, Stanley 1914- St&PR 91
Salmen, Walter 1926- ConAu 132
Salmeron, Jose Luis 1948- WhoWor 91
Salmeron y Alonso, Nicolas 1838-1908 BioIn 16
Salmi, Albert NewYTBS 90 [port]
Salmi, Albert 1928-1990 BioIn 16
Salmi, Ernest W. BioIn 16
Salmina, Ida EncCoWW
Salminen, Matti 1945- IntWWM 90
Salminen, Matti Juhani 1932- WhoWor 91
Salminen, Sally Alina Ingeborg Duhrkop- 1906-1976 EncCoWW
Salmins, Ida EncCoWW
Salmoiraghi, Gian Carlo 1924- BiDrAPA 89, WhoAm 90, WhoWor 91
Salmon, Charles R. 1927- St&PR 91
Salmon, Chico 1940- Ballpl 90
Salmon, Christopher David Baker 1940- IntWWM 90
Salmon, Eugene Richard 1931- WhoWor 91
Salmon, Garland Russell 1930- St&PR 91
Salmon, James Alan BiDrAPA 89
Salmon, Joan Bernadette 1957- WhoAmW 91
Salmon, John Hearsey McMillan 1925- WhoAm 90, WhoWrEP 89
Salmon, Joseph Thaddeus 1927- WhoAm 90
Salmon, Joyce Martine 1946- WhoAmW 91
Salmon, Judith Elaine 1940- WhoSSW 91
Salmon, Louis 1923- WhoAm 90, WhoWor 91
Salmon, Lucy Maynard 1853-1927 BioAmW
Salmon, Phyllis Ward 1948- WhoAmW 91
Salmon, Raymond Merle 1931- WhoAmA 91
Salmon, Robert L. 1920- St&PR 91
Salmon, Robin Robertson 1952- WhoSSW 91
Salmon, Thomas Martin Branden 1945- WhoWor 91
Salmon, Vincent 1912- WhoAm 90
Salmon, Walter Lawrence, Jr. 1930- St&PR 91
Salmon, Watt T BiDrAPA 89
Salmon, Wesley Charles 1925- WhoAm 90
Salmon, William Cooper 1935- WhoAm 90
Salmon, William Gordon 1946- St&PR 91
SalmonCampbell, Joan BioIn 16
Salmond, Felix 1888-1952 PenDiMP
Salmond, Norman 1858-1914 PenDiMP
Salmons, Arthur W. 1944- St&PR 91
Salmons, Hugh I. 1940- St&PR 91
Salmons, Joanna 1931- WhoAmW 91
Salo, Jarmo Antero 1947- WhoWor 91
Salo, John E. 1947- St&PR 91
Salo, Matti Antero 1933- WhoWor 91
Salokar, Rebecca Mae 1956- WhoSSW 91
Salom, Pedro G. 1856-1945 EncABHB 4 [port]
Saloman, Ora Frishberg 1938- IntWWM 90
Salome Alexandra WomWR
Salome, Lou Andreas- 1861-1937 BioIn 16
Salome, William C., III 1929- St&PR 91
Salomon, Adam 1818-1881 BioIn 16
Salomon, Allan 1939- St&PR 91
Salomon, Gerhard 1930- WhoWor 91
Salomon, J Eugene 1928- St&PR 91
Salomon, Johann Peter 1745-1815 PenDiMP
Salomon, Lawrence 1940- WhoAmA 91
Salomon, Louis Etienne Felicite Lysius 1815-1888 BioIn 16
Salomon, Lucy 1925- BiDrAPA 89, WhoE 91
Salomon, Muriel 1933- WhoAmW 91
Salomon, Nancy Kelly 1958- WhoAmW 91
Salomon, Richard 1912- WhoAm 90
Salomon, Richard Adley 1953- WhoEmL 91
Salomon, Roger Blaine 1928- WhoAm 90
Salomon, Ronald Murray BiDrAPA 89
Salomon, Sidney BioIn 16
Salomone, A. William 1915-1989 BioIn 16
Salomone, Arcangelo William 1915-1989 BioIn 16
Salomone, J. G. 1940- St&PR 91
Salomone, Paul A. BioIn 16
Salomone, William Gerald 1948- WhoSSW 91
Salomons, Anni BioIn 16
Salomons, Annie 1885-1980 EncCoWW
Salon, Dayton D BiDrAPA 89
Salonen, Esa-Pekka 1958- IntWWM 90, PenDiMP, WhoWor 91
Salonen, Frans Uuno DcScanL
Salonen, Heikki Olavi 1933- WhoWor 91
Saloner, Garth 1955- WhoE 91
Salonga, Fred Talens 1935- St&PR 91
Saloom, Joseph Michael 1950- WhoSSW 91
Saloom, Kaliste Joseph, Jr. 1918- WhoWor 91
Salop, Arnold 1923- WhoE 91
Salopek, Daniel F. 1938- St&PR 91
Salote Topou III 1900-1965 WomWR [port]
Salote Tupou, Queen of Tonga 1900-1965 BioIn 16
Salovaara, Juhani 1943- ConDes 90
Saloway, Kenneth Richard 1948- St&PR 91
Salpeter, Edwin Ernest 1924- WhoAm 90
Salpeter, Max PenDiMP
Salpeter, Miriam Mark 1929- WhoAm 90
Salrin, Robert E. 1927- St&PR 91
Salsberg, Arthur Philip 1929- WhoAm 90
Salsburg, Bertha R. 1929- WhoE 91
Salsburg, Kevyn Anne 1951- WhoEmL 91
Salsbury, Glenna Ruth 1937- WhoAmW 91
Salsbury, Larry G. 1940- St&PR 91
Salsbury, Phillip James 1942- St&PR 91
Salsbury, Sherrod 1915- St&PR 91
Salsbury, Stephen Matthew 1931- WhoAm 90
Salsinger, H.G. 1887-1958 Ballpl 90
Salska, Agnieszka 1940- WhoWor 91
Salt, Charles 1810-1864 PenDiDA 89
Salt, John 1937- WhoAmA 91
Salt, Ralph 1782-1846 PenDiDA 89
Salta, Linda Jean 1950- WhoAmW 91
Salta, Steven Anthony 1955- WhoEmL 91
Salta, Wendy Ann Kehl 1942- WhoAmW 91
Saltamachia, Joe G. 1930- St&PR 91
Saltarelli, Eugene A. 1923- WhoAm 90
Saltarelli, Martin O. 1935- St&PR 91
Salten, David George 1913- WhoAm 90
Salten, Felix AuBYP 90
Saltenberger, Pamela Guay 1944- St&PR 91
Salter, Barry Martin BiDrAPA 89
Salter, Diana G. 1956- WhoAmW 91
Salter, Douglas Neel 1940- WhoAm 90
Salter, Edwin 1824-1888 AmLegL
Salter, Edwin Carroll 1927- WhoAm 90
Salter, George 1907-1967 WhoAmA 91N
Salter, Hannah BiDEWW
Salter, Helen de Gaudrion Verrall 1883-1959 EncPaPR 91
Salter, Helen Woollgar de Gaudrion V. 1883-1959 EncO&P 3
Salter, James 1925- ConLC 59 [port], NewYTBS 90 [port]
Salter, John Randall 1898-1978 WhoAmA 91N
Salter, Lester Herbert 1918- WhoAm 90
Salter, Lionel Paul 1914- IntWWM 90
Salter, Margery 1952- WhoAmW 91
Salter, Maxwell Hillary 1920- St&PR 91
Salter, Michael Laurie 1949- St&PR 91
Salter, Nina BioIn 16
Salter, Richard 1943- IntWWM 90
Salter, Richard Jay 1955- WhoEmL 91
Salter, Richard Mackintire 1940- WhoAmA 91
Salter, Robert Mundhenk, Jr. 1920- WhoAm 90
Salter, Ronald Scott 1964- WhoSSW 91
Salter, Timothy 1942- IntWWM 90
Salter, W H 1880-1969 EncO&P 3
Salter, William Henry 1880-1969 EncPaPR 91
Salterberg, Susan Kay 1960- WhoWrEP 89
Salterio, Joseph Louis, Jr. 1944- St&PR 91
Saltford, Herbert Wetherbee 1911- WhoWrEP 89
Saltich, Jack L. 1943- St&PR 91
Saltiel, David Michael 1954- WhoEmL 91
Saltiel, Natalie 1927- WhoAmW 91
Saltman, Anne Bregy 1951- WhoAmW 91
Saltman, David 1912- WhoWor 91
Saltman, Jack 1936- ConAu 129
Saltman, Judith 1947- SmATA 64
Saltman, Stuart Ivan 1940- WhoWor 91
Saltmarche, Kenneth Charles 1920- WhoAmA 91
Saltmarsh, H. F. 1881-1943 EncO&P 3, EncPaPR 91
Saltmarsh, P. David 1939- St&PR 91
Salton, Gerard 1927- WhoAm 90
Salton, Linda M. 1949- St&PR 91
Saltonstall, David 1935- WhoE 91
Saltonstall, Dudley 1738-1796 EncCRAm
Saltonstall, Elizabeth 1900-1990 WhoAmA 91N
Saltonstall, Rebecca 1947- BiDrAPA 89
Saltonstall, Rosamond 1612- BiDEWW
Saltonstall, William G 1905?-1989 ConAu 130
Saltonstall, William Gurdon 1905-1989 BioIn 16
Saltsgiver, Thomas M. 1939- St&PR 91
Salturelli, Lynn Strawn 1943- WhoAmW 91
Saltus, Scott M. 1953- St&PR 91
Saltwell, E.R. 1924- St&PR 91
Saltz, Bruce L BiDrAPA 89
Saltz, Carole Pogrebin 1949- WhoAm 90, WhoAmW 91
Saltz, Ivan Kenneth 1949- WhoSSW 91
Saltz, James G. 1932- St&PR 91
Saltz, Jerry 1951- WhoAmA 91
Saltz, Ralph 1948- St&PR 91, WhoAm 90
Saltzberg, Barney AuBYP 90
Saltzberg, Burton Reuben 1933- WhoAm 90
Saltzberg, Edward Charles 1947- WhoEmL 91
Saltzburg, Stephen Allan 1945- WhoAm 90
Saltzgaver, Jack 1905-1978 Ballpl 90
Saltzman, Barry 1931- WhoAm 90
Saltzman, Benjamin Nathan 1914- WhoAm 90
Saltzman, Charles BiDrAPA 89
Saltzman, Charles E. 1903- St&PR 91
Saltzman, Charles Eskridge 1903- WhoAm 90
Saltzman, Glenn Alan 1935- WhoAm 90
Saltzman, Harry 1915- WhoAm 90
Saltzman, Irene Cameron 1927- WhoAmW 91, WhoWor 91
Saltzman, Joseph 1939- WhoAm 90
Saltzman, Linda Renee 1951- WhoAmW 91
Saltzman, Marvin 1931- WhoAmA 91
Saltzman, Nancy Elise 1965- WhoAmW 91
Saltzman, Philip 1928- WhoAm 90
Saltzman, Robert P. 1942- St&PR 91
Saltzman, Robert Paul 1942- WhoSSW 91
Saltzman, Sidney 1926- WhoAm 90
Saltzman, Steven L. 1945- WhoSSW 91
Saltzman, William 1916- WhoAm 90, WhoAmA 91
Salucci, Anthony 1942- St&PR 91
Saluck, Leonard H. 1930- WhoE 91
Salus, Karl BiDrAPA 89
Salus, Sydney 1920- BiDrAPA 89
Salutin, Rick 1942- ConAu 131, OxCCanT
Saluzzi, Dino BioIn 16
Saluzzo-Roero, Diodata 1775-1849 EncCoWW
Salvador, Dorothea 1935- WhoAmW 91
Salvador, Sal 1925- WhoAm 90, WhoWor 91
Salvadore, Michael A. St&PR 91
Salvadori, Tedfilo Alexander 1899- WhoWor 91
Salvadori, Vieri R 1943- WhoAmA 91
Salvage, Paul R. 1939- WhoE 91
Salvaggio, Caterina Ellen 1963- WhoE 91
Salvaggio, John Edmond 1933- WhoAm 90
Salvaggio, Tony J. 1931- St&PR 91
Salvant, Patricia Jean 1939- WhoAmW 91
Salvati, Dominic P. 1934- St&PR 91
Salvatierra, Richard C. 1920- WhoHisp 91
Salvatore, Anthony Joseph 1938- MusmAFA
Salvatore, Donna Ann 1953- WhoAmW 91
Salvatore, Michael Joseph 1934- WhoWrEP 89
Salvatore, Nancy Barbara 1953- WhoAmW 91
Salvatore, Nicholas 1943- ConAu 32NR
Salvatore, Nicholas D. 1941- St&PR 91
Salvatore, Nick ConAu 32NR
Salvatore, Ramon 1944- IntWWM 90
Salvatore, Victor 1885-1965 WhoAmA 91N
Salvatori, Grace Ford BioIn 16, NewYTBS 90
Salvatori, Vincent L. 1932- St&PR 91
Salvatti, Wayne A. 1956- WhoWor 91
Salvendy, Gavriel 1938- WhoAm 90
Salverson, Carol Ann 1944- WhoWor 91
Salverson, Laura 1890-1970 FemiCLE
Salverson, Laura Goodman 1890-1970 DcLB 92 [port]
Salvesen, Bonnie Forbes 1944- WhoAmW 91, WhoWor 91
Salvesen, Lawrence C 1929- BiDrAPA 89
Salveson, Jack 1914-1974 Ballpl 90
Salveson, Melvin Erwin 1919- WhoAm 90, WhoWor 91
Salvey, Janine Lichacz 1954- ODwPR 91
Salviati, Antonio 1816-1890 PenDiDA 89
Salviati, Francesco 1510?-1563 IntDcAA 90, PenDiDA 89
Salvigsen, Stanley D. BioIn 16
Salvino, Carmen BioIn 16
Salvino, S. M. 1928- St&PR 91, WhoAm 90
Salvo, Brenda Jean BiDrAPA 89
Salvo, Joseph Charles, Jr. 1941- St&PR 91
Salvo, Manny 1913- Ballpl 90
Salvucci, Hector 1930- BiDrAPA 89
Salvucci, Suzanne Mary 1962- WhoAmW 91
Salwak, Dale Francis 1947- WhoEmL 91
Salwarowski, Jerzy Hubert 1946- IntWWM 90
Salwen, Bertram B. 1920-1988 BioIn 16
Salwen, Edward 1924- St&PR 91
Salwen, Richard 1942- St&PR 91
Salyard, Lann Biddle 1956- BiDrAPA 89
Salyer, Gary 1938- St&PR 91
Salyer, Robert L. 1949- St&PR 91
Salyers, David B. 1940- ODwPR 91
Salyers, Thomas Edwin 1963- WhoSSW 91
Salz, Leon A. St&PR 91
Salzarulo, Leonard Michael 1927- WhoAm 90
Salzberg, Betty Joan 1944- WhoAmW 91
Salzberg, Harry L. 1948- St&PR 91
Salzberg, Irving Garry 1951- WhoE 91
Salzberg, Steven BiDrAPA 89
Salzedo, Carlos 1885-1961 PenDiMP
Salzedo, Leonard 1921- IntWWM 90
Salzer, John Michael 1917- WhoAm 90
Salzer, Louis William 1918- WhoWor 91
Salzer-Falisey, Rosemary 1948- WhoSSW 91
Salzman, Andrea BioIn 16
Salzman, Anne Meyersburg 1928- WhoAmW 91
Salzman, Arthur George 1929- WhoAm 90
Salzman, Bernard BiDrAPA 89
Salzman, Carl 1938- BiDrAPA 89
Salzman, David Elliot 1943- WhoAm 90
Salzman, Eric 1933- IntWWM 90
Salzman, Herbert NewYTBS 90 [port]
Salzman, Herbert 1916- WhoAm 90
Salzman, Leon 1915- BiDrAPA 89, WhoE 91
Salzman, Marilyn Jean 1939- WhoAmW 91
Salzman, Mark BioIn 16
Salzman, Neil ODwPR 91
Salzman, Siegmund 1869-1945 AuBYP 90
Salzman, Stephen Philip 1937- St&PR 91
Salzmann, George Stephen 1948- WhoE 91
Salzmann, Richard R. BioIn 16
Salzmann, Zdenek 1925- WhoE 91
Salzstein, Richard Alan 1959- WhoAm 90
Sam and Dave EncPR&S 89
Sam the Sham and the Pharaohs EncPR&S 89
Sam, David 1933- WhoAm 90
Sam, Joseph 1923- WhoAm 90
Sama, Robert F. 1931- St&PR 91
Samaan, Naguib Abdelmalik 1925- WhoAm 90, WhoWor 91
Samachson, Dorothy 1914- AuBYP 90
Samachson, Joseph 1906- AuBYP 90
Samachson, Joseph 1906-1980 BioIn 16
Samad, Isa A 1922- BiDrAPA 89
Samad, Zahida BiDrAPA 89
Samadi, Aziz Rahman 1932- WhoSSW 91
Samakow, D. C. 1952- St&PR 91
Samalin, Edwin 1935- WhoWor 91
Saman l'Esbatx, Prudence de EncCoWW
Samaniego, Alvaro 1931- BiDrAPA 89
Samaniego, Mariano G. 1844-1907 BioIn 16
Samansky, Arthur W. 1942- ODwPR 91
Samant, Arvind R BiDrAPA 89
Samanta, Subarna Kumar 1953- WhoE 91
Samantar, Mohammed Ali 1931- WhoWor 91
Samara, Brenda Mary 1941- WhoAmW 91
Samaran, Max Leon 1939- WhoWor 91
Samaranayake, Silverine D BiDrAPA 89
Samaranch, Juan Antonio BioIn 16
Samaranch, Juan Antonio 1920- WhoWor 91
Samaras, Antonis 1951- WhoWor 91
Samaras, Charalambos George 1933- WhoWor 91
Samaras, George Nicholas 1944- St&PR 91
Samaras, Lucas 1936- WhoAmA 91
Samaras, Zoe 1935- WhoWor 91
Samaraweera, Albert B 1920- BiDrAPA 89
Samaraweera, Shera BiDrAPA 89
Samardich, Gordon R. St&PR 91
Samargya, Michael J. 1934- St&PR 91
Samarian, Ron 1952- BiDrAPA 89
Samaritani, Pier Luigi 1942- IntWWM 90
Samaritani, Pier Luigi 1942- WhoWor 91
Samaroff, Olga 1882-1948 BioIn 16

Samartini, James Rogers 1935- *St&PR 91, WhoAm 90*
Samaset 1590?-1653? *WhNaAH*
Samat, Ramkishin Kanu 1945- *WhoE 91*
Samay, Z. Lance 1944- *WhoWor 91*
Samayoa, John F. 1930- *St&PR 91*
Sambajon, Emilia Tolibas *BiDrAPA 89*
Sambajon, Galileo A *BiDrAPA 89*
Sambaluk, Nicholas Wayne 1955- *WhoSSW 91*
Sambandham, Masilamani 1949- *WhoSSW 91*
Samber, David Mark 1949- *St&PR 91*
Samber, Richard Allan 1938- *St&PR 91*
Samberg, Eslee *BiDrAPA 89*
Sambin, Hugues 1515?-1600? *PenDiDA 89*
Sambito, Joe 1952- *Ballpl 90*
Samble, Jane *BiDEWW*
Sambonet, Roberto 1924- *ConDes 90*
Sambor, S. F. *EncO&P 3*
Sambor, Stephan Fomitch *EncPaPR 91*
Samborski, Anne Hedvig 1917- *BiDrAPA 89*
Sambs, James Michael 1937- *BiDrAPA 89*
Sambuchi, Ed L. *BioIn 16*
Sambunaris, Angelo 1957- *BiDrAPA 89*
Samburg, Grace *WhoAmA 91*
Sameh, Ahmed Hamdy 1939- *WhoAm 90*
Samek, Edward L. 1936- *St&PR 91*
Samek, Michael Johann 1920- *WhoAm 90*
Samel, Jeffrey 1952- *WhoEmL 91*
Samela, Lorraine Ann 1947- *WhoAmW 91*
Samelson, Charles F 1917- *BiDrAPA 89*
Samelson, Lincoln Russell 1926- *St&PR 91, WhoAm 90, WhoWor 91*
Samenfeld-Specht, James Allan *BiDrAPA 89*
Samenow, Stanton E 1941- *ConAu 129*
Samerjan, George E 1915- *WhoAmA 91*
Samet, Harry 1932- *St&PR 91, WhoSSW 91*
Samet, Jack I. 1940- *WhoAm 90*
Samet, Joseph 1949- *WhoEmL 91*
Samet, L. Reyner 1905-1989 *BioIn 16*
Samet, Norman T 1923- *BiDrAPA 89*
Samford, John S. P. 1950- *St&PR 91*
Samford, John Singleton Pitts 1950- *WhoSSW 91*
Samford, Judith Lee 1939- *WhoAmW 91*
Samford, Karen Elaine 1941- *WhoSSW 91*
Samford, Thomas Drake, III 1934- *WhoAm 90*
Samford, Yetta Glenn, Jr. 1923- *WhoAm 90*
Sami, Sherif F *BiDrAPA 89*
Samide, M. R. 1944- *St&PR 91*
Samigli, E. *MajTwCW*
Samii, Abdol Hossein 1930- *WhoE 91*
Samii, Mary Alice 1951- *WhoAmW 91*
Samiian, Barazandeh 1939- *WhoAmW 91*
Samilowitz, Hazel Faye 1940- *BiDrAPA 89, WhoE 91*
Samimi, Mansour 1946- *WhoSSW 91*
Samios, Nicholas *BiDrAPA 89*
Samios, Nicholas Peter 1932- *WhoAm 90*
Samis, Gust A. 1936- *St&PR 91*
Samis, Michael Stephen 1953- *WhoAm 90*
Samler, Jacob D 1931- *BiDrAPA 89*
Samloff, I. Michael 1932- *WhoAm 90*
Samm, Mary 1667-1680 *BiDEWW*
Samman, George 1946- *WhoAm 90*
Sammarco, Maria Therese 1963- *BiDrAPA 89*
Sammarco, Paul William 1948- *WhoEmL 91, WhoWor 91*
Sammartino, Peter 1904- *WhoAm 90*
Sammartino, Sylvia 1903- *WhoAm 90, WhoAmW 91*
Sammataro, John Anthony 1931- *St&PR 91*
Sammet, Jean E. *WhoAm 90, WhoAmW 91*
Sammis, S. Fraser 1928- *WhoAm 90*
Sammler, Walter Gottfried Karl 1934- *WhoWor 91*
Sammon, Kevin Michael 1942- *WhoSSW 91*
Sammon, Peter Francis 1938- *St&PR 91*
Sammond, John Stowell 1928- *WhoAm 90*
Sammons, Albert 1886-1957 *PenDiMP*
Sammons, Charles G. 1898-1988 *BioIn 16*
Sammons, Dennis M. 1948- *St&PR 91*
Sammons, Doreleena Ann 1954- *WhoAmW 91*
Sammons, Jack Michael 1955- *WhoSSW 91*
Sammons, James E. 1933- *St&PR 91*
Sammons, Jeffrey T. 1949- *BioIn 16*
Sammons, John Paul 1946- *ODwPR 91*
Sammons, Robert Ardel 1945- *BiDrAPA 89*
Sammons, Ronald Colin 1943- *St&PR 91*
Samms, Emma 1960- *WorAlBi*
Sammuramat *WomWR [port]*
Sammuramat, Queen *BioIn 16*
Samner, David *St&PR 91*
Samojlowicz, Adrian Aleksander 1938- *WhoE 91*
Samolis, John Richard 1947- *St&PR 91*
Samonek, Kenneth John 1950- *St&PR 91*
Samora, Joanne *WhoHisp 91*
Samora, Joseph E., Jr. 1955- *WhoHisp 91*
Samora, Julian 1920- *BioIn 16, HispWr 90, WhoAm 90, WhoHisp 91*
Samoset 1590?-1653? *WhNaAH*
Samosud, Samuil 1884-1964 *PenDiMP*
Samotulka, Theodosy *BiDrAPA 89*
Samouilidis, Leonidas 1930- *BiDrAPA 89*
Samoy, Achille Gustave 1918- *WhoWor 91*
Samozvantsev, Andrei Michailovich 1949- *WhoWor 91*
Sampas, Dorothy M. 1933- *WhoAmW 91, WhoWor 91*
Sampat, Sushila Juli 1945- *BiDrAPA 89*
Sampath, Hugh McCrorie 1926- *BiDrAPA 89*
Sampath, Lakshmi Narsingh 1939- *WhoSSW 91*
Sampayo, Hector M *BiDrAPA 89*
Sampedro, Hortensia Edelmira 1950- *WhoEmL 91*
Sampedro, Jose Luis 1917- *IntvSpW [port], WhoWor 91*
Sampel, James Richard 1932- *St&PR 91*
Sampel, Pamela J. 1959- *WhoAmW 91*
Samper, J. Phillip 1934- *BioIn 16, St&PR 91, WhoHisp 91*
Samper, Joseph Phillip 1934- *WhoAm 90*
Samperi, Frank V. 1933- *WhoWrEP 89*
Sampey, James J. 1933- *St&PR 91*
Sampias, Ernest Joseph 1951- *WhoAm 90*
Sample, Albert Race *BioIn 16*
Sample, Beverly A. 1944- *WhoAmW 91*
Sample, Billy 1955- *Ballpl 90*
Sample, Constance Jeanne 1950- *WhoAmW 91*
Sample, Dale 1945- *St&PR 91*
Sample, Frederick Palmer 1930- *WhoAm 90*
Sample, John Philip 1946- *WhoSSW 91*
Sample, Joseph Scanlon 1923- *WhoAm 90*
Sample, Judith Neuer 1943- *WhoAmW 91*
Sample, Karen Ann 1949- *WhoAmW 91*
Sample, Michael M. 1952- *St&PR 91*
Sample, Nathaniel Welshire 1918- *WhoAm 90*
Sample, Paul 1896-1974 *WhoAmA 91N*
Sample, Steven Browning 1940- *WhoAm 90, WhoWor 91*
Sample, Theodore Glenn, Jr. 1955- *WhoWor 91*
Sample, Wendy Elizabeth 1956- *WhoAmW 91*
Samples, Darwin H. 1930- *St&PR 91*
Samples, Jerry Wayne 1947- *WhoEmL 91*
Samples, Martina 1942- *WhoAmW 91, WhoSSW 91*
Sampley, Howard Russell 1952- *BiDrAPA 89*
Sampley, Samuel Barry 1940- *WhoSSW 91*
Sampliner, Robert B *BiDrAPA 89*
Sampo, Ronald Lee 1932- *St&PR 91*
Sampou, Andre Peter 1931- *St&PR 91*
Sampras, Pete *BioIn 16*
Sampsell, Charles K. 1924- *St&PR 91*
Sampsell, Robert Bruce 1941- *St&PR 91, WhoAm 90*
Sampson, Anthony 1926- *BioIn 16*
Sampson, Anthony Terrell Seward 1926- *WhoWor 91*
Sampson, Arthur Francis 1926-1988 *BioIn 16*
Sampson, Bonnie P. 1942- *WhoAmW 91*
Sampson, Carol Ann 1942- *WhoWrEP 89*
Sampson, Curtis A. 1933- *St&PR 91*
Sampson, Deborah 1760-1827 *BioAmW, EncCRAm*
Sampson, Deborah K. 1951- *WhoAmW 91*
Sampson, Edgar 1907-1973 *DrBlPA 90, OxCPMus*
Sampson, Edward Coolidge 1920- *WhoE 91*
Sampson, Emma Speed 1868-1947 *LiHiK*
Sampson, Frank 1928- *WhoAmA 91*
Sampson, Gary Philip 1943- *WhoWor 91*
Sampson, Harold Y. 1921- *St&PR 91*
Sampson, Harvey, Jr. 1929- *St&PR 91*
Sampson, Herschel Wayne 1944- *WhoSSW 91*
Sampson, John Eugene 1941- *St&PR 91*
Sampson, John Patterson 1837- *EarBlAP*
Sampson, John Pierce 1940- *St&PR 91*
Sampson, June Elisabeth 1946- *WhoAmW 91*
Sampson, Kurt D. 1963- *St&PR 91*
Sampson, Lawrence M 1939- *BiDrAPA 89*
Sampson, Louis *BiDrAPA 89*
Sampson, Mark J 1956- *BiDrAPA 89*
Sampson, Mikki Lynn 1950- *WhoAmW 91*
Sampson, Patsy Hallock 1932- *WhoAm 90, WhoAmW 91*
Sampson, R Neil 1938- *ConAu 31NR*
Sampson, R. W. 1921- *St&PR 91*
Sampson, Ralph *BioIn 16*
Sampson, Robert Carl, Jr. *BiDrAPA 89*
Sampson, Robert Carl, Jr. 1948- *WhoE 91*
Sampson, Robert Neil 1938- *WhoAm 90*
Sampson, Roger M. 1933- *WhoAm 90*
Sampson, Ronald Gary 1942- *St&PR 91*
Sampson, Ruth Louise 1947- *WhoEmL 91*
Sampson, Samuel Franklin 1934- *WhoAm 90*
Sampson, Steven Curtis 1958- *St&PR 91*
Sampson, Thyra Ann 1948- *WhoAmW 91*
Sampson, Vincent Louis 1946- *St&PR 91*
Sampson-Landers, Carole 1946- *WhoAmW 91*
Samra, Rise Jane 1952- *WhoAmW 91*
Samra, Victor M., Jr. 1941- *St&PR 91*
Samrock, Carl 1941- *ODwPR 91*
Sams, Alexander Hammond 1965- *WhoSSW 91*
Sams, David E., Jr. *WhoAm 90*
Sams, David E., Jr. 1943- *St&PR 91*
Sams, Doris Laverne 1926- *WhoAmW 91*
Sams, Emmett Sprinkle 1920- *WhoSSW 91*
Sams, Eric 1926- *IntWWM 90*
Sams, James Farid 1932- *WhoE 91*
Sams, John Roland 1922- *WhoAm 90*
Sams, Kenneth Dorsey 1951- *St&PR 91*
Sams, Mary Ann Pacella 1933- *WhoAmW 91*
Sams, Robert Eugene 1939- *BiDrAPA 89*
Sams, Ross Martin, Jr. 1927- *St&PR 91*
Sams, William Ernest, III 1942- *WhoSSW 91*
Samsel, Maebell Scroggins 1940- *WhoSSW 91*
Samsel, Philip Paul 1950- *St&PR 91*
Samsia *WomWR*
Samson, Allen L. 1939- *St&PR 91*
Samson, Allen Lawrence 1939- *WhoAm 90*
Samson, Alvin 1917- *WhoAm 90*
Samson, Bruce A. *WhoAm 90*
Samson, Charles Harold, Jr. 1924- *WhoAm 90*
Samson, David A. *ODwPR 91*
Samson, David Richard 1944- *BiDrAPA 89*
Samson, Edme 1810-1891 *PenDiDA 89*
Samson, Emile 1837-1913 *PenDiDA 89*
Samson, Frederick Eugene, Jr. 1918- *WhoAm 90*
Samson, James A. 1949- *St&PR 91*
Samson, Jim 1946- *ConAu 129*
Samson, John *BioIn 16*
Samson, M. S. 1941- *St&PR 91*
Samson, Richard Max 1946- *WhoAm 90*
Samson, Solomon B. 1947- *St&PR 91*
Samson, Stuart *BiDrAPA 89*
Samson, Thomas I. 1931- *St&PR 91*
Samson, Thomas James 1946- *IntWWM 90*
Samsonov, Aleksandr 1859?-1914 *WorAlBi*
Samstag, Gordon 1906- *WhoAmA 91*
Samstag, Nicholas 1903-1968 *AuBYP 90*
Samter, Max 1908- *WhoAm 90, WhoWor 91*
Samton, Sheila White *AuBYP 90*
Samuel *EncPaPR 91*
Samuel, Arthur L. *NewYTBS 90*
Samuel, Athanasius Yeshue 1907- *WhoAm 90*
Samuel, Charlene 1956- *WhoAmW 91*
Samuel, Cynthia Ann 1947- *WhoAm 90*
Samuel, Dan Judah 1925- *WhoE 91, WhoWor 91*
Samuel, Geoffrey Brian 1946- *IntWWM 90*
Samuel, Gerhard 1924- *IntWWM 90, WhoAm 90*
Samuel, Harold 1879-1937 *BioIn 16, PenDiMP*
Samuel, Harold E. 1924- *IntWWM 90*
Samuel, Harry Cecil 1927- *IntWWM 90*
Samuel, Henri *BioIn 16*
Samuel, Howard David 1924- *WhoAm 90, WhoE 91*
Samuel, James W. 1957- *ODwPR 91*
Samuel, Joseph H. 1925- *St&PR 91*
Samuel, Juan 1960- *Ballpl 90*
Samuel, Juan Milton Romero 1960- *WhoHisp 91*
Samuel, K. 1953- *St&PR 91*
Samuel, Raphael 1946- *WhoE 91, WhoEmL 91*
Samuel, Richard I. 1940- *St&PR 91*
Samuel, Robert Thompson 1944- *WhoWor 91*
Samuel, Roger Z *BiDrAPA 89*
Samuel, Winston *BiDrAPA 89*
Samueli, Henry 1954- *WhoEmL 91*
Samuelly, Israel 1927- *BiDrAPA 89*
Samuelly, Michaela 1931- *BiDrAPA 89*
Samuels, Abram 1920- *WhoAm 90*
Samuels, Alan Bart 1956- *WhoSSW 91*
Samuels, Alfred Putnam, Jr. 1926- *WhoWrEP 89*
Samuels, Andrew Albert, Jr. 1937- *St&PR 91*
Samuels, Arthur S 1925- *BiDrAPA 89*
Samuels, Barbara *AuBYP 90*
Samuels, Brenda Ellian 1948- *WhoAmW 91*
Samuels, Cheryl Troy Metzger 1945- *WhoE 91*
Samuels, Cynthia K. *AuBYP 90, BioIn 16*
Samuels, Cynthia Kalish 1946- *WhoAmW 91, WhoEmL 91*
Samuels, David *NewAgMG*
Samuels, Donald 1943- *St&PR 91*
Samuels, Douglas Scott 1954- *BiDrAPA 89*
Samuels, Ernest 1903- *WhoAm 90*
Samuels, Gerald 1927- *WhoAmA 91, WhoE 91*
Samuels, Gertrude *AuBYP 90*
Samuels, Gloria 1926- *WhoAmW 91*
Samuels, Helen 1931- *St&PR 91*
Samuels, J. Victor 1940- *St&PR 91*
Samuels, Janet Irene 1957- *WhoEmL 91*
Samuels, Janet Lee 1953- *WhoAmW 91, WhoWor 91*
Samuels, John C. *ODwPR 91*
Samuels, John Stockwell, III 1933- *WhoAm 90, WhoAmA 91*
Samuels, Kathleen 1952- *WhoAmW 91*
Samuels, Leslie Eugene 1929- *WhoE 91, WhoWor 91*
Samuels, Louis P. 1922- *St&PR 91*
Samuels, Marwyn Stewart 1942- *WhoE 91*
Samuels, Michele L. *ODwPR 91*
Samuels, Michele Lauren 1962- *WhoAmW 91*
Samuels, Morton 1925- *St&PR 91*
Samuels, Myra Lee 1940- *WhoAmW 91*
Samuels, Nathaniel 1908- *WhoAm 90*
Samuels, Norman 1937- *WhoAm 90, WhoE 91*
Samuels, Richard Mel 1943- *WhoE 91, WhoWor 91*
Samuels, Robert 1957- *St&PR 91*
Samuels, Robert Hestal 1926- *WhoSSW 91*
Samuels, Robert T. 1934- *WhoAm 90*
Samuels, Robert Walter 1929- *St&PR 91*
Samuels, Ronald Larry 1946- *St&PR 91*
Samuels, Sandor E. 1950- *St&PR 91*
Samuels, Seymour, Jr. 1912- *WhoSSW 91*
Samuels, Sheldon Wilfred 1929- *WhoAm 90*
Samuels, Sherwin L. 1935- *St&PR 91, WhoAm 90*
Samuels, Solon D 1907- *BiDrAPA 89*
Samuels, Stephanie J. *BiDrAPA 89*
Samuels, Stephen Howard 1949- *WhoE 91*
Samuels, Steven Charles 1963- *BiDrAPA 89*
Samuels, Ted *BioIn 16*
Samuels, Valerie Bryant 1952- *WhoAmW 91*
Samuels, Walter 1950- *St&PR 91*
Samuels, William Mason 1929- *WhoAm 90*
Samuels, William Oscar 1945- *BiDrAPA 89*
Samuelsen, Roy 1933- *WhoAm 90*
Samuelson, Albert F 1929- *BiDrAPA 89*
Samuelson, Alberta W *BiDrAPA 89*
Samuelson, Bernard J. 1942- *St&PR 91*
Samuelson, Charles Harry 1929- *WhoSSW 91*
Samuelson, Derrick W. 1929- *St&PR 91*
Samuelson, Derrick William 1929- *WhoAm 90*
Samuelson, Fred Binder 1925- *WhoAmA 91*
Samuelson, Georgia Jamie 1950- *WhoWrEP 89*
Samuelson, Jacqueline K. 1953- *WhoEmL 91*
Samuelson, Joan *BioIn 16*
Samuelson, Kenneth Lee 1946- *WhoE 91, WhoEmL 91*
Samuelson, Lance Denzel 1944- *St&PR 91*
Samuelson, Marie Gayle 1956- *WhoAmW 91*
Samuelson, Marvin Lee 1931- *WhoAm 90, WhoSSW 91*
Samuelson, Paul A. 1915- *WorAlBi*
Samuelson, Paul Anthony 1915- *WhoAm 90, WhoE 91, WhoWor 91*
Samuelson, Robert William 1933- *St&PR 91*
Samuelson, Stephen Daryl *BiDrAPA 89*
Samuelson, Sylvia Heller *WhoE 91*
Samuelson, Thomas W *BiDrAPA 89*
Samuelsson, Arne 1933- *St&PR 91*
Samuelsson, Bengt 1934- *WorAlBi*
Samuelsson, Bengt Ingemar 1934- *WhoAm 90, WhoWor 91*
Samus, Mila 1937- *BiDrAPA 89*
Samz, Jane Dede *WhoAm 90, WhoAmW 91, WhoWor 91*
San Diego Chicken *Ballpl 90*
San Yu 1919- *WhoWor 91*
San, Nguyen Duy 1932- *BiDrAPA 89, WhoWor 91*
San, Wai-Lam 1921- *WhoWor 91*
Sanabria, Luis Angel 1950- *WhoHisp 91*
Sanabria, Robert 1931- *WhoAmA 91*
Sanabria, Sherry Zvares 1937- *WhoAmA 91*
Sanabria, Tomas V. 1953- *WhoHisp 91*

Sanabria Martinez, Victor 1899-1952 *BioIn 16*
Sanada, Ikkan 1950- *WhoE 91*
Sanada, Nadshi 1928- *WhoWor 91*
San Agustin, Eleazar S *BiDrAPA 89*
San Agustin, Joe Taitano 1930- *WhoWor 91*
Sananman, Michael Lawrence 1939- *WhoE 91, WhoWor 91*
San Antonio, Joel 1952- *St&PR 91*
San Antonio, Karen 1963- *ODwPR 91*
Sanator, Robert Joseph 1930- *St&PR 91*
Sanaullah, Andrew Suleman 1916- *WhoWor 91*
Sanayei, Masoud 1954- *WhoE 91*
Sanazaro, Paul Joseph 1922- *WhoAm 90*
Sanberg, Paul Ronald 1955- *WhoWrEP 89*
Sanborn, Anna Lucille 1924- *WhoAmW 91*
Sanborn, B. X. *TwCCr&M 91*
Sanborn, Charles Prescott 1834-1889 *AmLegL*
Sanborn, David *BioIn 16*
Sanborn, Doreen Kay 1948- *WhoAmW 91, WhoWor 91*
Sanborn, Dorothy Chappell 1920- *WhoAmW 91*
Sanborn, Duane *AuBYP 90*
Sanborn, Herbert J 1907- *WhoAmA 91*
Sanborn, Irving *Ballpl 90*
Sanborn, Jim 1945- *BioIn 16*
Sanborn, John Page 1844-1926 *AmLegL*
Sanborn, Kate 1839-1917 *FemiCLE*
Sanborn, L. T. 1928- *St&PR 91*
Sanborn, Margaret 1915- *St&PR 91*
Sanborn, Paul Joseph 1946- *WhoE 91*
Sanborn, Richard John Jay 1954- *WhoEmL 91*
Sanborn, Robert B. 1929- *WhoAm 90*
Sanborn, Robert Charles 1914- *St&PR 91*
Sanborn, Sheree-Maria 1958- *WhoAmW 91*
Sanborn, Stephen 1941- *St&PR 91*
Sanborn, Terry L. 1943- *St&PR 91*
Sanborn, Theodore 1921- *St&PR 91*
Sanborn, Theodore S. 1921- *WhoAm 90*
Sanborn, Tonia *BioIn 16*
Sanborn, Walter D., III 1943- *St&PR 91*
Sancetta, Constance Antonina 1949- *WhoAmW 91*
Sancha, Tom Luis 1947- *WhoWor 91*
Sanches, Ruy Ramirez 1925- *WhoWor 91*
Sanches Perez, Elias *WhoHisp 91*
Sanchez, Adolfo Erik 1935- *WhoHisp 91*
Sanchez, Albert 1936- *WhoHisp 91*
Sanchez, Andrew J, Jr. 1926- *BiDrAPA 89*
Sanchez, Antonio 1954- *WhoSSW 91*
Sanchez, Antonio L. 1954- *WhoHisp 91*
Sanchez, Antonio M. 1932- *WhoHisp 91*
Sanchez, Antonio R. 1916- *BioIn 16*
Sanchez, Antonio R., Sr. *St&PR 91*
Sanchez, Antonio R., Sr. 1916- *WhoHisp 91*
Sanchez, Arantxa *BioIn 16*
Sanchez, Armand J. 1933- *WhoHisp 91*
Sanchez, Arnaldo Ochoa *BioIn 16*
Sanchez, Arthur Ronald 1948- *WhoHisp 91*
Sanchez, Arturo E. 1949- *WhoHisp 91*
Sanchez, Beatrice Rivas 1941- *WhoAmA 91, WhoAmW 91*
Sanchez, Carlos Antonio 1960- *WhoHisp 91*
Sanchez, Carol Ashton-Evans 1943- *WhoAmW 91, WhoSSW 91, WhoWor 91*
Sanchez, Celerino 1944- *Ballpl 90*
Sanchez, Christina J. 1963- *WhoHisp 91*
Sanchez, Cynthia J. 1962- *WhoHisp 91*
Sanchez, D. Jean 1948- *WhoAmW 91*
Sanchez, Daniel J. 1964- *WhoHisp 91*
Sanchez, Daniel R. 1936- *WhoHisp 91*
Sanchez, David Alan 1933- *WhoAm 90, WhoHisp 91*
Sanchez, Dolores *WhoHisp 91*
Sanchez, Don *WhoHisp 91*
Sanchez, Dorothy L. 1938- *WhoHisp 91*
Sanchez, Edith 1956- *WhoHisp 91*
Sanchez, Eduardo A *BiDrAPA 89*
Sanchez, Edwin 1955- *WhoHisp 91*
Sanchez, Elba I. 1947- *WhoHisp 91*
Sanchez, Elisa Garza 1955- *BiDrAPA 89*
Sanchez, Enrique 1932- *WhoHisp 91*
Sanchez, Ernest *WhoHisp 91*
Sanchez, Eugenio 1951- *WhoSSW 91*
Sanchez, Fameliza 1940- *WhoHisp 91*
Sanchez, Fausto H. 1953- *WhoHisp 91*
Sanchez, Federico A. 1935- *WhoHisp 91*
Sanchez, Felix A. 1936- *St&PR 91*
Sanchez, Fernando *BioIn 16*
Sanchez, Fernando Victor 1953- *St&PR 91, WhoHisp 91*
Sanchez, Florencio 1875-1910 *BioIn 16, HispWr 90, TwCLC 37 [port]*
Sanchez, Francisco P. 1960- *WhoWrEP 89*
Sanchez, Gabriel *WhoHisp 91*
Sanchez, George I 1906-1972 *HispWr 90*
Sanchez, George Isdore 1906-1972 *BioIn 16*
Sanchez, Gilbert 1938- *WhoAm 90, WhoHisp 91*
Sanchez, Gilbert Anthony 1930- *WhoHisp 91*
Sanchez, Gonzalo Jose 1932- *WhoHisp 91*
Sanchez, Hector J 1932- *BiDrAPA 89*
Sanchez, Henry Orlando 1937- *WhoHisp 91*
Sanchez, Homero Rodolfo *BiDrAPA 89*
Sanchez, Hortensia O. 1947- *WhoSSW 91*
Sanchez, Isaac C. 1941- *WhoHisp 91*
Sanchez, Jacquelyn Roesch- *BioIn 16*
Sanchez, Janice Patterson 1948- *WhoAmW 91*
Sanchez, Javier A. 1960- *WhoHisp 91*
Sanchez, Jerry 1945- *WhoHisp 91*
Sanchez, Jesus Ramirez 1950- *WhoHisp 91*
Sanchez, Joe M. 1933- *WhoHisp 91*
Sanchez, John Charles 1950- *WhoHisp 91*
Sanchez, Jonathan *WhoHisp 91*
Sanchez, Jose M. 1943- *WhoHisp 91*
Sanchez, Jose R *BiDrAPA 89*
Sanchez, Jose Ramon 1951- *WhoHisp 91*
Sanchez, Juan Francisco 1928- *WhoHisp 91*
Sanchez, Julian *WhoHisp 91*
Sanchez, Julian Claudio 1938- *WhoHisp 91*
Sanchez, Laura Balverde- *BioIn 16*
Sanchez, Laura Elena *BiDrAPA 89*
Sanchez, Leda A *BiDrAPA 89*
Sanchez, Leonard R. 1942- *WhoHisp 91*
Sanchez, Leonedes Monarrize Worthington 1951- *WhoEmL 91, WhoWor 91*
Sanchez, Leveo V. *WhoHisp 91*
Sanchez, Lorenzo 1943- *WhoHisp 91*
Sanchez, Luis 1953- *Ballpl 90*
Sanchez, Luis Alberto 1900- *BioIn 16*
Sanchez, Luis Humberto 1951- *WhoHisp 91*
Sanchez, Luis Rafael 1936- *BioIn 16, HispWr 90*
Sanchez, Luis Tomas *BiDrAPA 89*
Sanchez, Manuel *BioIn 16*
Sanchez, Manuel 1947- *WhoEmL 91, WhoHisp 91*
Sanchez, Manuel A. 1959- *St&PR 91*
Sanchez, Manuel Tamayo, Jr. 1949- *WhoHisp 91*
Sanchez, Marcia Odalys 1962- *WhoAmW 91*
Sanchez, Maria *BioIn 16*
Sanchez, Maria C. 1926-1989 *WhoHisp 91N*
Sanchez, Marie-Alice *BiDrAPA 89*
Sanchez, Mario 1908- *MusmAFA*
Sanchez, Marisabel 1963- *WhoHisp 91*
Sanchez, Marisabel 1964- *WhoAmW 91*
Sanchez, Marta *WhoAm 90, WhoHisp 91*
Sanchez, Mary B. 1930- *WhoHisp 91*
Sanchez, Mary Lowe 1914- *WhoAmA 91*
Sanchez, Michael M. 1953- *ODwPR 91*
Sanchez, Miguel R. 1950- *WhoHisp 91*
Sanchez, Nancy Eileen 1956- *WhoWrEP 89*
Sanchez, Nelson *WhoHisp 91*
Sanchez, Nelson D *BiDrAPA 89*
Sanchez, Norma R. 1939- *WhoHisp 91*
Sanchez, Orlando 1956- *Ballpl 90*
Sanchez, Oscar Arias *BioIn 16 HispWr 90*
Sanchez, Osmundo, Jr. 1939- *WhoSSW 91*
Sanchez, Patricia Irene *WhoHisp 91*
Sanchez, Pedro 1831-1904 *AmLegL*
Sanchez, Pedro Antonio 1940- *WhoHisp 91*
Sanchez, Phillip V. 1929- *WhoHisp 91*
Sanchez, Phillip Victor 1929- *BioIn 16*
Sanchez, Poncho *BioIn 16*
Sanchez, Poncho 1951- *WhoHisp 91*
Sanchez, Porfirio 1932- *WhoHisp 91*
Sanchez, Rafael C. 1919- *WhoHisp 91*
Sanchez, Rafael Camilo 1919- *WhoAm 90*
Sanchez, Ramiro 1948- *WhoHisp 91*
Sanchez, Ramon Antonio 1947- *WhoHisp 91*
Sanchez, Ray F. 1927- *WhoHisp 91*
Sanchez, Raymond G. 1941- *WhoAm 90, WhoHisp 91*
Sanchez, Raymond L. 1964- *WhoHisp 91*
Sanchez, Ricardo 1941- *BioIn 16, ConAu 32NR, HispWr 90, WhoHisp 91, WhoWrEP 89*
Sanchez, Rick *WhoHisp 91*
Sanchez, Rick Dante 1940- *WhoHisp 91*
Sanchez, Robert Alfred 1938- *WhoHisp 91*
Sanchez, Robert Charles 1956- *WhoHisp 91*
Sanchez, Robert Fortune 1934- *BioIn 16, WhoAm 90*
Sanchez, Robert Francis 1938- *WhoAm 90*
Sanchez, Roberto G. 1922- *WhoHisp 91*
Sanchez, Roberto Luis 1957- *WhoHisp 91*
Sanchez, Roberto R. 1948- *WhoHisp 91*
Sanchez, Rosaura 1941- *WhoHisp 91*
Sanchez, Rozier Edmond 1931- *WhoHisp 91*
Sanchez, Sergio Arturo 1950- *WhoHisp 91*
Sanchez, Shiree 1957- *WhoHisp 91*
Sanchez, Simon *BiDrAPA 89*
Sanchez, Sonia 1934- *DcLB DS8 [port], DrBlPA 90, FemiCLE, MajTwCW*
Sanchez, Sonia 1935- *BioIn 16*
Sanchez, Sylvia Deleon 1951- *St&PR 91*
Sanchez, Teresa Barbero 1934- *EncCoWW*
Sanchez, Thomas 1944- *ConAu 32NR, HispWr 90, WhoHisp 91*
Sanchez, Thorvald 1933- *WhoAmA 91*
Sanchez, Victoria Wagner 1934- *WhoAmW 91*
Sanchez, Vivian Eugenia 1963- *WhoHisp 91*
Sanchez, Walter A. 1958- *WhoHisp 91*
Sanchez, William Arthur 1936- *St&PR 91*
Sanchez, William Q. 1951- *WhoHisp 91*
Sanchez-Atzel, Alejandro 1964- *WhoEmL 91*
Sanchez-Boudy, Jose 1928- *BioIn 16, WhoHisp 91*
Sanchez Campo, Evagrio 1947- *WhoWor 91*
Sanchez Cerro, Luis M. 1889-1933 *BioIn 16*
Sanchez-Cotan, Juan 1561-1627 *IntDcAA 90*
Sanchez de Pedro y Crespo, Miguel 1949- *WhoWor 91*
Sanchez Fair, Debra *ODwPR 91*
Sanchez Flores, Daniel 1960?-1990 *ConAu 132*
Sanchez Garcia, Alfonso 1881-1953 *BioIn 16*
Sanchez-Grey Alba, Esther 1931- *WhoHisp 91*
Sanchez-H., Jose 1951- *WhoHisp 91*
Sanchez-Korrol, Virginia *ConAu 131, HispWr 90, WhoHisp 91*
Sanchez-Lacay, Jose Arturo *BiDrAPA 89*
Sanchez-Leal, Henry Richard *BiDrAPA 89*
Sanchez-Longo, Luis P. 1925- *WhoHisp 91*
Sanchez-Lopez, Paula M *BiDrAPA 89*
Sanchez-Lugo, Manuel 1934- *WhoAm 90*
Sanchez-Mejorada, Rodrigo 1950- *WhoWor 91*
Sanchez Portela, Alfonso 1902- *BioIn 16*
Sanchez Sanchez, Luis Alberto 1940- *WhoWor 91*
Sanchez-Scott, Milcha *ConAu 131, WhoHisp 91*
Sanchez-Sinencio, Edgar 1944- *WhoHisp 91*
Sanchez Triana, Ernesto 1959- *WhoWor 91*
Sanchez-Way, Ruth Dolores 1940- *WhoHisp 91*
Sanchidrian, Maria Del Carmen 1954- *WhoAmW 91*
Sanchini, Dominick J. *NewYTBS 90*
Sancho, Gloria Precious Manneh 1960- *WhoAmW 91*
Sancho, Robert *WhoHisp 91*
Sancho, Rosemarie 1949- *WhoAmW 91*
Sand, George *EncCoWW*
Sand, George 1804-1876 *BioIn 16, FemiCLE, WorAlBi*
Sand, George X. *AuBYP 90, WhoWrEP 89*
Sand, Gregory Anthony 1945- *WhoE 91*
Sand, Heinie 1897-1958 *Ballpl 90*
Sand, John F., Jr. 1932- *ODwPR 91*
Sand, Jules *EncCoWW*
Sand, Leonard *BioIn 16*
Sand, Leonard B. 1928- *WhoAm 90, WhoE 91*
Sandage, Allan Rex 1926- *WhoAm 90*
Sandage, Charles Harold 1902- *WhoAm 90*
Sandage, Elizabeth Anthea 1930- *WhoAmW 91*
Sandage, Scott James *BiDrAPA 89*
Sandahl, Bonnie Beardsley 1939- *WhoAmW 91*
Sandak, Cass R. 1950- *BioIn 16*
Sandal, Ejvind 1943- *WhoWor 91*
Sandalls, William Thomas, Jr. 1944- *St&PR 91, WhoAm 90*
Sandalow, Terrance 1934- *WhoAm 90*
Sanday, Juan *St&PR 91*
Sandbach, Margaret 1812-1852 *FemiCLE*
Sandback, Frederick Lane 1943- *WhoAm 90, WhoAmA 91*
Sandbank, Henry 1932- *WhoAm 90*
Sandbek, Raymond Earl 1941- *WhoSSW 91*
Sandberg, Arthur Gunnar 1916- *WhoWor 91*
Sandberg, Diana Pardew 1957- *BiDrAPA 89*
Sandberg, Gary Melvin Michael 1957- *WhoWrEP 89*
Sandberg, Hans Torbjorn 1946- *WhoWor 91*
Sandberg, Irwin David 1935- *St&PR 91, WhoAm 90*
Sandberg, Irwin Walter 1934- *WhoAm 90*
Sandberg, Jack Thomas 1923- *St&PR 91*
Sandberg, Job B. B. 1946- *St&PR 91*
Sandberg, Joel E. 1950- *St&PR 91*
Sandberg, Larry S *BiDrAPA 89*
Sandberg, Richard A. 1942- *St&PR 91*
Sandberg, Richard J. 1927- *St&PR 91*
Sandberg, Robert Alexis 1914- *WhoAm 90*
Sandberg, Ryne *BioIn 16*
Sandberg, Ryne 1959- *Ballpl 90, WhoAm 90, WorAlBi*
Sandberg, Sharon Kay 1959- *WhoAmW 91*
Sandberg, Stevan A. 1952- *St&PR 91*
Sandberg, W. Gary 1946- *St&PR 91*
Sandberg, Willem 1897-1984 *ConDes 90*
Sandbo, John H. 1931- *St&PR 91*
Sandborg, Shirlee J. 1934- *WhoAmW 91*
Sandbrook, John Richard 1946- *WhoWor 91*
Sandbulte, Arend John 1933- *St&PR 91, WhoAm 90*
Sandburg, Carl 1878-1967 *AuBYP 90, BioIn 16, EncAL, MajTwCW, PoeCrit 2 [port], WorAlBi*
Sandburg, Charles *AuBYP 90, MajTwCW*
Sandburg, Charles A. *MajTwCW*
Sandburg, Helga *BioIn 16*
Sandburg, Helga 1918- *AuBYP 90, WhoAm 90, WhoWrEP 89*
Sandburg, Lillian S. *BioAmW*
Sandburg, Richard Rex 1925- *St&PR 91*
Sande, Barbara 1939- *WhoAmW 91, WhoWor 91*
Sande, Ervin Elder 1932- *St&PR 91*
Sande, Gunvald 1918- *St&PR 91*
Sande, Rhoda *WhoAmA 91*
Sande, Ronald Gene 1941- *St&PR 91*
Sande, Theodore Anton 1933- *WhoAm 90*
Sandefer, Norma Steele 1958- *WhoAmW 91*
Sandefur, James Tandy 1947- *WhoE 91*
Sandefur, Thomas E., Jr. *St&PR 91*
Sandefur, Thomas Edwin, Jr. 1939- *WhoSSW 91*
Sandel, Cora 1880-1974 *DcScanL, EncCoWW, FemiCLE*
Sandel, James Leon 1949- *WhoSSW 91*
Sandelin, Karl R. 1928- *St&PR 91*
Sandell, Richard Arnold 1937- *WhoAm 90*
Sandelman, Sanford Melvyn 1925- *St&PR 91*
Sandeman, Robert *BioIn 16*
Sandemose, Aksel 1899-1965 *DcScanL*
Sanden, John Howard 1935- *WhoAmA 91*
Sander, Allan Nils 1948- *WhoSSW 91*
Sander, Denise Olivia 1960- *WhoAmW 91*
Sander, Donald F 1928- *BiDrAPA 89*
Sander, Frank Ernest Arnold 1927- *WhoAm 90*
Sander, Fred Martin 1937- *BiDrAPA 89*
Sander, Gary H. 1949- *St&PR 91*
Sander, Jil *BioIn 16*
Sander, Lawrence D. *WhoWrEP 89*
Sander, Lincoln Raymond 1939- *St&PR 91*
Sander, Linda Dian 1947- *WhoAmW 91*
Sander, Louis W 1918- *BiDrAPA 89*
Sander, Ludwig 1906-1975 *WhoAmA 91N*
Sander, Malvin Gustav 1946- *St&PR 91, WhoAm 90*
Sander, Margaretta Bushnell 1948- *WhoE 91*
Sander, Peter 1933- *IntWWM 90*
Sander, Raymond John 1944- *WhoAm 90*
Sander, Robert A. *BioIn 16*
Sander, Steve David 1953- *WhoEmL 91*
Sander, Volkmar 1929- *WhoAm 90*
Sandera, Frank Moss 1936- *WhoSSW 91*
Sandercox, Robert Allen 1932- *WhoAm 90*
Sanderfoot, Thomas Aloysius 1954- *WhoEmL 91*
Sanderlin, Eva Slover 1924- *WhoWrEP 89*
Sanderlin, George 1915- *WhoWrEP 89*
Sanderlin, M. L. 1946- *St&PR 91*
Sanderlin, Owenita Harrah 1916- *WhoWrEP 89*
Sanderling, Kurt 1912- *IntWWM 90, PenDiMP*
Sanderling, Thomas 1942- *IntWWM 90, PenDiMP*
Sanderman, Dick 1956- *IntWWM 90*
Sanders, Aaron Perry 1924- *WhoAm 90*
Sanders, Alan Roger *BiDrAPA 89*
Sanders, Alex 1926- *EncO&P 3*
Sanders, Angelus Cornelia 1944- *WhoE 91*
Sanders, Anita Marie 1953- *WhoAmW 91, WhoE 91*
Sanders, Anthony Bown 1951- *WhoEmL 91*
Sanders, Arthur Hardie 1924- *WhoE 91*
Sanders, Augusta Swann 1932- *WhoAmW 91*
Sanders, Barbara *BioIn 16*
Sanders, Barbara Jane 1936- *WhoAmW 91*
Sanders, Barry *BioIn 16*
Sanders, Benjamin Elbert 1918- *WhoAm 90*
Sanders, Bernard *BioIn 16, EncAL*
Sanders, Bernard 1941- *WhoE 91*
Sanders, Beth Mehne 1960- *WhoAmW 91*
Sanders, Bryan Henry 1937- *St&PR 91*

Sanders, C. B. 1831- *EncO&P 3*
Sanders, Carl Julian 1912- *WhoAm 90*
Sanders, Carol 1944- *WhoWor 91*
Sanders, Celestine G. *EncO&P 3*
Sanders, Charles Addison 1932- *St&PR 91, WhoAm 90, WhoSSW 91*
Sanders, Charles Franklin 1931- *WhoAm 90*
Sanders, Charles G. 1943- *St&PR 91*
Sanders, Charles L. *NewYTBS 90*
Sanders, Charles L. 1932?-1990 *ConAu 132*
Sanders, Charles Martin, Jr. 1939- *St&PR 91*
Sanders, Chris *BioIn 16*
Sanders, Dale 1953- *WhoWor 91*
Sanders, Daphne *TwCCr&M 91*
Sanders, David F. *BioIn 16*
Sanders, David Griffin 1928- *BiDrAPA 89*
Sanders, David James 1952- *WhoEmL 91*
Sanders, David Marvin 1953- *WhoSSW 91*
Sanders, David S 1926- *BiDrAPA 89*
Sanders, Debra Faye 1952- *WhoWrEP 89*
Sanders, Deion *BioIn 16*
Sanders, Donald C 1930- *BiDrAPA 89*
Sanders, Donald Neil 1927- *WhoWor 91*
Sanders, Dwain Dupree 1947- *St&PR 91*
Sanders, Elissa Meryl *BiDrAPA 89*
Sanders, Elmer Blair 1923- *St&PR 91*
Sanders, Eric 1946- *WhoWor 91*
Sanders, Ernest H. 1918- *IntWWM 90*
Sanders, Esther Jeannette 1926- *WhoWrEP 89*
Sanders, Eugene Thomas 1950- *St&PR 91*
Sanders, Evelyn Beatrice 1931- *WhoAmW 91*
Sanders, Franklin D. 1935- *St&PR 91, WhoAm 90*
Sanders, Fred Joseph 1928- *WhoAm 90*
Sanders, Frederick 1923- *WhoAm 90*
Sanders, Gary Glenn 1944- *WhoWor 91*
Sanders, Gary Wayne 1949- *WhoAm 90, WhoEmL 91*
Sanders, George 1906-1972 *WorAlBi*
Sanders, Georgia Elizabeth 1933- *WhoSSW 91*
Sanders, Gladys Shultz *BioIn 16*
Sanders, H. R., Jr. 1932- *St&PR 91*
Sanders, Harold Barefoot, Jr. 1925- *WhoAm 90, WhoSSW 91*
Sanders, Hassel Marteen 1930- *St&PR 91, WhoAm 90*
Sanders, Helen Cook 1938- *WhoSSW 91*
Sanders, Herbert 1909-1988 *BioIn 16*
Sanders, Herbert Harvey 1909- *WhoAmA 91N*
Sanders, Howard 1941- *WhoAm 90, WhoWor 91*
Sanders, Howard R. 1947- *St&PR 91*
Sanders, Irwin Taylor 1909- *WhoAm 90*
Sanders, Jack Ford 1918- *WhoAm 90*
Sanders, Jack Thomas 1935- *WhoAm 90*
Sanders, Jacquelyn Seevak 1931- *WhoAmW 91*
Sanders, James Alvin 1927- *WhoAm 90*
Sanders, James Joseph 1946- *St&PR 91*
Sanders, James Worthington 1946- *WhoEmL 91*
Sanders, James Wright 1950- *WhoSSW 91*
Sanders, Jared Young 1869-1944 *AmLegL*
Sanders, Jay William 1924- *WhoAm 90*
Sanders, Jean Marie 1939- *WhoAmW 91*
Sanders, Jeff Davis 1931- *WhoSSW 91*
Sanders, Jerry Dwight 1943- *WhoSSW 91*
Sanders, Joann Johnson 1935- *WhoSSW 91*
Sanders, Joanne 1949- *WhoAmW 91*
Sanders, John David 1938- *WhoSSW 91*
Sanders, John Derek 1933- *IntWWM 90*
Sanders, John Grayson 1940- *St&PR 91*
Sanders, John Lassiter 1927- *WhoAm 90*
Sanders, John Moncrief 1936- *WhoAm 90*
Sanders, John Theodore 1941- *WhoAm 90*
Sanders, Joop A 1922- *WhoAmA 91*
Sanders, Joseph Stanley 1942- *WhoAm 90*
Sanders, Joyce E. 1943- *WhoAmW 91*
Sanders, Karl 1930- *St&PR 91*
Sanders, Kathy Marie *BiDrAPA 89*
Sanders, Keith R. 1939- *WhoAm 90*
Sanders, Ken 1941- *Ballpl 90*
Sanders, Kenton Morris 1950- *WhoAm 90, WhoEmL 91*
Sanders, Kinney L. 1934- *St&PR 91*
Sanders, Larry Otto *BiDrAPA 89*
Sanders, Lawrence 1920- *BioIn 16, ConAu 33NR, MajTwCW, TwCCr&M 91, WhoAm 90, WhoWrEP 89, WorAlBi*
Sanders, Leisha L. 1962- *WhoWrEP 89*
Sanders, Leonard Marion, Jr. 1929- *WhoWrEP 89*
Sanders, Leslie Catherine 1944- *ConAu 129*
Sanders, Linda 1950- *WhoAmW 91*
Sanders, Madeline Sandy 1943- *WhoAmW 91*
Sanders, Marguerite Dees 1914- *WhoSSW 91*
Sanders, Mark E. *BioIn 16*
Sanders, Marlene *BioIn 16*
Sanders, Marlene 1931- *WhoAm 90, WhoAmW 91*
Sanders, Marthame Elliot, Jr. 1939- *St&PR 91*
Sanders, Marvin Cecil 1934- *WhoSSW 91*
Sanders, Mary Louise *WhoAmW 91*
Sanders, Mellissa *BioIn 16*
Sanders, Neal H. 1949- *ODwPR 91*
Sanders, Nicholas *BiDrAPA 89*
Sanders, Noah *MajTwCW*
Sanders, Paul Hampton 1909- *WhoAm 90*
Sanders, Pharoah 1940- *BioIn 16, DrBIPA 90, WhoAm 90*
Sanders, Phyllis Aden 1919- *WhoAmW 91*
Sanders, R Michael *BiDrAPA 89*
Sanders, R Wyman 1931- *BiDrAPA 89*
Sanders, Randy W. 1948- *St&PR 91*
Sanders, Ray 1916-1983 *Ballpl 90*
Sanders, Raymond Carter, Jr. 1942- *WhoAm 90*
Sanders, Raymond Wayne 1951- *WhoSSW 91*
Sanders, Rhea 1923- *WhoAmA 91, WhoE 91*
Sanders, Richard Douglas 1957- *BiDrAPA 89*
Sanders, Richard Kinard 1940- *WhoAm 90*
Sanders, Richard Scott 1950- *St&PR 91*
Sanders, Rivka Ann *BiDrAPA 89*
Sanders, Robert Lee 1933- *St&PR 91*
Sanders, Robert Martin 1928- *WhoAm 90*
Sanders, Roger Cobban 1936- *WhoAm 90*
Sanders, Roger J. 1953- *St&PR 91*
Sanders, Ronald 1932- *WhoAm 90, WhoWrEP 89*
Sanders, Rose M. 1945- *BioIn 16*
Sanders, Russell Edward 1949- *WhoSSW 91*
Sanders, Russell Ronald 1956- *WhoEmL 91*
Sanders, Ruth Manning 1895 1988 *BioIn 16*
Sanders, S. Vernon 1947- *IntWWM 90*
Sanders, Scoot R. 1945- *BioIn 16*
Sanders, Scott Russell 1945- *WhoWrEP 89*
Sanders, Sharon *WhoWrEP 89*
Sanders, Sharon Michelle 1955- *WhoEmL 91*
Sanders, Sheldon Morton 1937- *WhoE 91*
Sanders, Stephanie Ann 1954- *WhoAmW 91*
Sanders, Stephen Brian *BiDrAPA 89*
Sanders, Steve *WhoAm 90*
Sanders, Steven Gill 1936- *WhoSSW 91, WhoWor 91*
Sanders, Stuart Braidwood 1956- *BiDrAPA 89*
Sanders, Ted *BioIn 16*
Sanders, Ted Joe 1933- *BiDrAPA 89*
Sanders, Teressa Irene 1951- *WhoEmL 91*
Sanders, Thomas Joseph, Sr. 1942- *WhoAm 90*
Sanders, Thompson *BioIn 16*
Sanders, Tommy *BioIn 16*
Sanders, Vernon Charles 1930- *St&PR 91*
Sanders, Wallace Wolfred, Jr. 1933- *WhoAm 90*
Sanders, Walter Jeremiah, III 1936- *WhoAm 90*
Sanders, Wanda Marie *BioIn 16*
Sanders, Ward Louis 1946- *WhoE 91*
Sanders, Wayne R. 1947- *WhoAm 90*
Sanders, Wendell Rowan 1933- *BiDrAPA 89*
Sanders, Wes *BioIn 16*
Sanders, William Eugene 1933- *WhoSSW 91*
Sanders, William Eugene, Jr. 1934- *WhoAm 90*
Sanders, William Evan 1919- *WhoAm 90*
Sanders, William George 1932- *WhoAm 90*
Sanders, William Vernon 1949- *WhoE 91*
Sanders, Winston P. *AuBYP 90, MajTwCW*
Sanders-Brahms, Helma 1940- *BioIn 16*
Sandersen, Elaine M. 1941- *WhoAmW 91*
Sanderson, Allen Ross 1952- *WhoSSW 91*
Sanderson, Charles Howard 1925- *WhoAmA 91*
Sanderson, Dana Lynn 1960- *BiDrAPA 89*
Sanderson, David Odell 1956- *WhoSSW 91*
Sanderson, Dennis Darrell 1944- *St&PR 91*
Sanderson, Edward French 1947- *WhoE 91*
Sanderson, Elijah 1751-1825 *PenDiDA 89*
Sanderson, Fred Hugo 1914- *WhoAm 90*
Sanderson, Gary Warner 1934- *St&PR 91, WhoAm 90*
Sanderson, George Edmond 1951- *St&PR 91*
Sanderson, Ivan T 1911-1973 *EncO&P 3*
Sanderson, Ivan Terence 1911-1973 *AuBYP 90*
Sanderson, Jack T. 1936- *St&PR 91*
Sanderson, Jacob 1757-1810 *PenDiDA 89*
Sanderson, James Michael 1954- *WhoSSW 91*
Sanderson, James Richard 1925- *WhoAm 90*
Sanderson, Joe Frank 1925- *St&PR 91*
Sanderson, John M., Jr. 1938- *St&PR 91*
Sanderson, Julia 1887-1975 *OxCPMus*
Sanderson, Keith Wayne 1945- *WhoEmL 91*
Sanderson, Lesley Mary 1965- *WhoEmL 91*
Sanderson, Lester E. 1920- *St&PR 91*
Sanderson, Michael O. 1942- *WhoAm 90*
Sanderson, Richard *BioIn 16*
Sanderson, Richard D. 1941- *St&PR 91*
Sanderson, Richard Elmer 1936- *WhoAm 90*
Sanderson, Robert *PenDiDA 89*
Sanderson, Robert C. 1939- *St&PR 91*
Sanderson, Robert G. 1941- *St&PR 91*
Sanderson, Sandra B. 1943- *St&PR 91*
Sanderson, Sara Lee 1942- *WhoAmW 91*
Sanderson, Scott 1956- *Ballpl 90*
Sanderson, Sibyl 1865-1903 *PenDiMP*
Sanderson, Timothy Alonzo 1946- *BiDrAPA 89*
Sanderson, Warren 1931- *WhoAmA 91, WhoE 91*
Sanderson, Wilfrid 1878-1935 *OxCPMus*
Sanderson, William *BioIn 16*
Sanderson, William Woodrow, Jr. 1954- *WhoEmL 91*
Sandes, Flora *BioIn 16*
Sandeson, William Seymour 1913- *WhoAm 90, WhoAmA 91*
Sandfield *DcCanB 12*
Sandford, Cedric Thomas 1924- *ConAu 32NR*
Sandford, Dean 1929- *St&PR 91*
Sandford, Eugene Halsey 1933- *WhoSSW 91*
Sandford-Smith, John Henry 1937- *WhoWor 91*
Sandfort, Peter H., Jr. 1944- *St&PR 91*
Sandgren, Clyde Dahlman 1910- *WhoAm 90*
Sandgren, Ernest Nelson 1917- *WhoAmA 91*
Sandground, Mark Bernard, Sr 1932- *WhoAmA 91*
Sandholm, Lars-Erik 1929- *WhoWor 91*
Sandhu, Bachittar Singh 1935- *WhoWor 91*
Sandhu, Hartej Singh 1943- *BiDrAPA 89*
Sandhu, Jagveer Singh *BiDrAPA 89*
Sandhu, Rajinder Singh *BiDrAPA 89*
Sandhu, Sarabjit Singh *BiDrAPA 89*
Sandhu, Tejinder *BiDrAPA 89*
Sandidge, Kanita Durice 1947- *WhoAmW 91, WhoWor 91*
Sandifer, James Roy 1945- *WhoE 91*
Sandifer, Linda Prophet 1951- *WhoWrEP 89*
Sandifer, Myron Guy, Jr. *BiDrAPA 89*
Sandifer, Wallace L. 1926- *St&PR 91*
Sandiford, Kimberly Elyse 1965- *WhoAmW 91*
Sandiford, Lloyd Erskine 1937- *WhoWor 91*
Sandiford, Rodger James 1948- *WhoWor 91*
Sandifur, Ann Elizabeth 1949- *IntWWM 90*
Sandifur, C. Paul, Jr. 1941- *St&PR 91*
Sandifur, C. Paul, Sr. 1903- *St&PR 91*
Sandige, John Milton 1817-1870 *AmLegL*
Sandilands, Mary *BiDEWW*
Sandilands, Roger James 1945- *WhoWor 91*
Sandin, A. Bonnie 1942- *WhoAmW 91*
Sandin, Caroline Towley 1915- *WhoAmW 91*
Sandin, Joan 1942- *BioIn 16*
Sandin, Rodolfo Santos 1941- *BiDrAPA 89*
Sandin, W. T. 1934- *St&PR 91*
Sandino, Augusto Cesar 1895-1934 *BioIn 16*
Sandison, Janet *AuBYP 90*
Sanditen, Edgar Richard 1920- *St&PR 91, WhoAm 90*
Sandland, Paul 1941- *St&PR 91*
Sandler, Aaron E. 1926- *St&PR 91*
Sandler, Alan P 1944- *BiDrAPA 89*
Sandler, Albert Nathan 1930- *WhoWor 91*
Sandler, Allen H *BiDrAPA 89*
Sandler, Allen Haydon 1944- *WhoE 91*
Sandler, Asir *BioIn 16*
Sandler, Barbara 1943- *WhoAmA 91*
Sandler, Benjamin 1957- *WhoHisp 91*
Sandler, Bernice Resnick 1928- *WhoAmW 91*
Sandler, Dale P. 1951- *WhoAmW 91*
Sandler, Fulton William 1923- *St&PR 91*
Sandler, Gerald H. 1934- *St&PR 91*
Sandler, Gerald Howard 1934- *WhoE 91*
Sandler, Herbert M. 1931- *St&PR 91, WhoAm 90*
Sandler, Irving 1925- *ConAu 31NR*
Sandler, Irving Harry 1925- *WhoAm 90, WhoAmA 91, WhoWrEP 89*
Sandler, Kenneth Bruce 1942- *WhoE 91*
Sandler, Kenneth R 1944- *BiDrAPA 89*
Sandler, Lawrence David 1949- *BiDrAPA 89*
Sandler, Lee Neil 1950- *BiDrAPA 89*
Sandler, Leonard H. 1926-1988 *BioIn 16*
Sandler, Lucy Freeman 1930- *ConAu 31NR, WhoAm 90, WhoWrEP 89*
Sandler, Marion O. 1930- *St&PR 91*
Sandler, Marion Osher 1930- *WhoAm 90, WhoAmW 91*
Sandler, Nat Harold 1937- *BiDrAPA 89*
Sandler, Philip Jay 1942- *BiDrAPA 89*
Sandler, Richard *BioIn 16*
Sandler, Robert Michael 1942- *WhoAm 90*
Sandler, Roberta 1943- *WhoWrEP 89*
Sandler, Scott Eric 1954- *St&PR 91*
Sandler, Stanley Irving 1940- *WhoAm 90*
Sandler, Steven *BiDrAPA 89*
Sandler, Thomas R. 1946- *WhoAm 90*
Sandler, Wayne Cary *BiDrAPA 89*
Sandles, Ellen Joan 1960- *WhoAmW 91*
Sandles, Faith Meyer 1942- *WhoAmW 91*
Sandlin, Darlyne Koretos 1945- *ODwPR 91*
Sandlin, David Thomas 1956- *WhoAmA 91*
Sandlin, Doris Jean 1932- *St&PR 91*
Sandlin, George Wilson 1912- *WhoSSW 91*
Sandlin, James Randolph 1957- *WhoSSW 91*
Sandlin, Joseph Ernest 1919- *WhoAm 90*
Sandlin, Richard Mancel 1937- *WhoAm 90*
Sandlin, Tim 1950- *WhoWrEP 89*
Sandlin, Walker Patterson, Jr. 1919- *WhoSSW 91*
Sandman, Alan 1947- *WhoAmA 91*
Sandman, Alan Richard 1945- *BiDrAPA 89*
Sandman, James Joseph 1951- *WhoEmL 91*
Sandman, Jo 1931- *WhoAmA 91*
Sandman, Lester Mark 1951- *BiDrAPA 89*
Sandman, Paul William 1947- *St&PR 91*
Sandman, Robert Earl 1920- *St&PR 91*
Sandman, Robert L. 1927- *St&PR 91*
Sandmeyer, Robert Lee 1929- *WhoAm 90*
Sandmire, James E. *BioIn 16*
Sandner, Frank X., Jr. 1918- *St&PR 91*
Sandner, John Francis 1941- *WhoAm 90*
Sando, Arthur R. *ODwPR 91*
Sando, Ernest 1950- *ODwPR 91*
Sando, Nobundo 1932- *WhoWor 91*
Sando, William Jasper 1927- *WhoSSW 91*
Sandok, Burton Alan 1937- *WhoAm 90*
Sandol, Maynard 1930- *WhoAmA 91*
Sandom, J. Gregory 1956- *WhoE 91*
Sandon, Nicholas John 1948- *IntWWM 90*
Sandona, Janet 1957- *St&PR 91*
Sandonato, Claudia Ellen 1947- *WhoEmL 91*
Sandor, David B. *ODwPR 91*
Sandor, George Nason 1912- *WhoAm 90*
Sandor, Gyorgy *WhoAm 90*
Sandor, Gyorgy 1912- *IntWWM 90, PenDiMP*
Sandor, Jean-Marie 1943- *WhoWor 91*
Sandor, Kenneth V. 1947- *St&PR 91*
Sandor, Leslie Thomas 1927- *St&PR 91*
Sandorfy, Camille 1920- *WhoAm 90*
Sandorse-Lovey, Donna Irene 1957- *WhoAmW 91*
Sandoval, Alejandro 1896-1989 *MusmAFA*
Sandoval, Alicia Catherine 1943- *WhoHisp 91*
Sandoval, Don 1966- *WhoHisp 91*
Sandoval, Donald A. 1935- *WhoHisp 91*
Sandoval, Edward C. *WhoHisp 91*
Sandoval, Edward P. 1960- *WhoHisp 91*
Sandoval, Emiliana P *BiDrAPA 89*
Sandoval, Epifanio Gloria, Jr. *BiDrAPA 89*
Sandoval, Ernie 1948- *WhoHisp 91*
Sandoval, Frances *BioIn 16*
Sandoval, George 1932-1989 *WhoHisp 91N*
Sandoval, Howard Kenneth 1931- *WhoHisp 91*
Sandoval, Joe G. 1937- *WhoHisp 91*
Sandoval, Joseph *WhoHisp 91*
Sandoval, Mercedes 1949- *WhoHisp 91*
Sandoval, Moises 1930- *BioIn 16, WhoHisp 91*
Sandoval, Olivia Medina 1946- *WhoHisp 91*
Sandoval, R. Christoph 1949- *WhoHisp 91*
Sandoval, Raul M. 1957- *WhoHisp 91*
Sandoval, Rodolfo 1942- *WhoHisp 91*
Sandoval, Rudolph 1929- *WhoHisp 91*
Sandoval, Secundino 1933- *BioIn 16*

Sandoval y Rojas, Francisco Gomez 1552-1625 BioIn 16
Sandoz, Mari 1896-1966 BioAmW, FemiCLE, MajTwCW
Sandoz, Marie 1901-1966 AuBYP 90
Sandoz, Rodney Joseph 1939- St&PR 91
Sandquist, Carol Patricia 1957- WhoAmW 91
Sandquist, Elroy Charles, Jr. 1922- WhoAm 90
Sandquist, Eric G. 1935- St&PR 91
Sandrap, Jean Pierre 1944- WhoWor 91
Sandred, Karl Inge 1925- WhoWor 91
Sandresky, Margaret Vardell 1921- IntWWM 90
Sandrich, Jay H. 1932- WhoAm 90
Sandridge, Sidney Edwin 1927- WhoAm 90
Sandritter, G Lee BiDrAPA 89
Sandrock, E. Thomas 1951- St&PR 91
Sandrock, Otto 1930- WhoWor 91
Sandrock, Scott Paul 1953- WhoEmL 91
Sandrow, Edward Theodore 1905?-1975 BioIn 16
Sandrow, Hope 1951- WhoAmA 91
Sands, Barry J. 1939- WhoAm 90
Sands, Bob 1950- WhoSSW 91
Sands, Brian Frederick 1957- BiDrAPA 89, WhoE 91
Sands, Charles Douglas 1964- WhoE 91
Sands, Dave TwCCr&M 91
Sands, David Lee 1956- WhoE 91
Sands, Diana 1934-1973 DrBIPA 90
Sands, Don W. 1926- St&PR 91
Sands, Don William 1926- WhoAm 90, WhoSSW 91
Sands, Donald Edgar 1929- WhoSSW 91
Sands, Edith Sylvia Abeloff WhoAm 90, WhoWrEP 89
Sands, Edward Theodore 1913- St&PR 91
Sands, Ethel 1873-1962 BiDWomA
Sands, I. Jay WhoAm 90, WhoE 91
Sands, Jerome D., Jr. 1939- St&PR 91
Sands, Joel Brian BiDrAPA 89
Sands, John Eliot 1941- WhoAm 90
Sands, Julian BioIn 16
Sands, Julian 1958- ConTFT 8
Sands, Lisa Gwyn 1961- WhoE 91
Sands, Marvin 1924- WhoAm 90
Sands, Matthew Linzee 1919- WhoAm 90
Sands, Melody Gail 1955- WhoWrEP 89
Sands, Oktarsars Harjo WhNaAH
Sands, Raoul L. 1928- St&PR 91
Sands, Richard BioIn 16
Sands, Richard 1956- WhoWor 91
Sands, Robert C. 1947- St&PR 91
Sands, Robert Edward 1946- BiDrAPA 89
Sands, Sharon Louise 1944- WhoAmW 91
Sands, Thomas Allen 1935- WhoSSW 91
Sands, Velma Ahda WhoAmW 91
Sands, W Wayne BiDrAPA 89
Sands, William L 1924- BiDrAPA 89
Sandskaer, Carlos Cesar 1949- WhoWor 91
Sandson, Gerald B 1937- BiDrAPA 89
Sandson, John I. 1927- WhoAm 90
Sandstad, Kenneth D. 1946- WhoAm 90, WhoSSW 91
Sandstead, Harold Hilton 1932- WhoAm 90
Sandstrom, Alice Wilhelmina 1914- WhoAmW 91
Sandstrom, Dale Vernon 1950- WhoEmL 91, WhoWor 91
Sandstrom, Donald Bruce 1930- St&PR 91
Sandstrom, Robert Edward 1946- WhoWor 91
Sandstrom, Scott 1954- WhoE 91
Sandstrom, Sven-Erik 1942- IntWWM 90
Sandstrom, Ulf Teddy 1952- WhoSSW 91
Sandt, John J BiDrAPA 89
Sandt, Sherry Kay 1962- WhoAmW 91
Sandusky, Billy Ray 1945- WhoAmA 91
Sandvi, Muhammad A BiDrAPA 89
Sandvig, Kirsten 1950- WhoWor 91
Sandvik, Gudmund 1925- WhoWor 91
Sandweg, Darryl John 1949- WhoAm 90
Sandweiss, Jack 1930- WhoAm 90
Sandweiss, Martha A. 1954- WhoAmW 91
Sandweiss, Martha Ann 1954- WhoAmA 91
Sandweiss, Samuel H BiDrAPA 89
Sandwell, B K 1876-1954 DcLB 92 [port]
Sandwell, Peter Gerard BiDrAPA 89
Sandwich, The Earl of 1839-1916 EncO&P 3
Sandy, Cynthia Sue 1959- WhoAmW 91
Sandy, Milton Larimore, Sr. 1916- St&PR 91
Sandy, Stephen 1934- WhoAm 90
Sandy, Stephen Merrill 1934- WhoWrEP 89
Sandy, Steven C. 1942- St&PR 91
Sandy, William H. 1929- St&PR 91
Sandy, William Haskell 1929- WhoAm 90, WhoWor 91
Sandys, George 1578-1644 EncCRAm
Sanefuji, Takashi 1937- WhoWor 91
Saner, Joseph P. 1934- St&PR 91
Saner, Reginald Anthony 1931- WhoAm 90
Sanese, Ralph, Jr. 1953- St&PR 91
Saneto, Russell Patrick 1950- WhoEmL 91
Sanetti, Stephen Louis 1949- WhoE 91
Sanfacon, Cheryl Lynn BiDrAPA 89
Sanfelici, Arthur Hugo 1934- WhoAm 90, WhoWrEP 89
Sanfelippo, Peter Michael 1938- WhoAm 90
Sanfield, Steve AuBYP 90
Sanfield, Steve 1937- WhoWrEP 89
SanFilippo, Marianne 1944- WhoAmW 91
Sanfilippo, Peter Sebastian BiDrAPA 89
San Filippo, Rosario P. 1899-1989 BioIn 16
Sanfilippo, Susan Jo BiDrAPA 89
San Fillipo, Mariane 1944- St&PR 91
Sanford, Agnes 1897-1976 SmATA 61
Sanford, Annette 1929- ConAu 130
Sanford, Barbara H. 1927- WhoAm 90
Sanford, Bascom N. 1917- St&PR 91
Sanford, Carl Thomas 1932- St&PR 91
Sanford, Charles David 1939- St&PR 91
Sanford, Charles Steadman, Jr. 1936- St&PR 91, WhoAm 90, WhoE 91, WhoWor 91
Sanford, David Boyer 1943- WhoAm 90, WhoWrEP 89
Sanford, David Hawley 1937- WhoAm 90
Sanford, David Newton 1952- WhoEmL 91
Sanford, Diane Lynn 1956- WhoAmW 91
Sanford, Donald G. 1938- WhoSSW 91
Sanford, Edmund Eyers 1959- St&PR 91
Sanford, Edward F 1925- BiDrAPA 89
Sanford, Frank Wadsworth 1955- St&PR 91
Sanford, Fred 1919- Ballpl 90
Sanford, G. Foster, Jr. 1902- St&PR 91
Sanford, Geraldine A. 1928- WhoWrEP 89
Sanford, Harriet BioIn 16
Sanford, Henry Shelton 1823-1891 BioIn 16
Sanford, Isabel 1917- WorAlBi
Sanford, Isabel Gwendolyn WhoAm 90, WhoAmW 91
Sanford, Isabell 1917- DrBIPA 90
Sanford, Jack 1929- Ballpl 90
Sanford, James B. AmLegL
Sanford, Janet Carol 1930- St&PR 91
Sanford, Jay Philip 1928- WhoAm 90
Sanford, John 1904- WorAu 1980 [port]
Sanford, John B. 1904- BioIn 16
Sanford, John Eliot 1830-1907 AmLegL
Sanford, Joseph P. 1937- St&PR 91
Sanford, Julie Lynn 1957- BiDrAPA 89
Sanford, Katherine 1915- BioIn 16
Sanford, Katherine Koontz 1915- WhoAmW 91
Sanford, Maria L. 1836-1920 BioAmW
Sanford, Marion 1904-1986? BiDWomA
Sanford, Midge BioIn 16
Sanford, Mollie 1838-1915 FemiCLE
Sanford, Nell Dunn 1936- BioIn 16
Sanford, Nevitt BioIn 16
Sanford, Paul Everett 1917- WhoAm 90
Sanford, Robert Glasgow, Jr. 1955- WhoSSW 91
Sanford, Robert Preston 1959- St&PR 91
Sanford, Robert Wadsworth 1920- St&PR 91
Sanford, Roy Leon 1946- WhoAm 90
Sanford, Ruth B. 1925- St&PR 91
Sanford, Ruth Eileen 1925- WhoAmW 91
Sanford, Sarah J. 1949- WhoAm 90
Sanford, Susan Haspel 1944- WhoAmW 91
Sanford, Terry 1917- WhoAm 90, WhoSSW 91, WhoWor 91, WhoWrEP 89
Sanford, Valerius 1923- WhoAm 90
Sanford, William Anthony 1933- St&PR 91
Sanford, William Eli 1838-1899 DcCanB 12
Sanford-Harris, Judith Leslie 1953- WhoAmW 91
Sanfuentes, Juan Luis 1858-1930 BioIn 16
Sang, Andreas Friedrich PenDiDA 89
Sang, Barry Ray 1951- WhoSSW 91
Sang, Evadne BiDrAPA 89
Sangal, Rahul 1955- BiDrAPA 89
Sangalang, J C BiDrAPA 89
Sangalli, Scott Robert 1950- St&PR 91
Sangani, Kishor R BiDrAPA 89
Sangani, Sashmikant P 1937- BiDrAPA 89
Sangani, Vipul Raiyabhai 1952- BiDrAPA 89
Sangastiano, Raymond Paul 1952- WhoE 91
Sangdhal, Christopher W. 1953- BiDrAPA 89
Sanger, Alexander C. 1947- St&PR 91
Sanger, Ann Winters 1950- WhoE 91
Sanger, David John 1947- IntWWM 90
Sanger, Eleanor 1929- WhoAm 90, WhoAmW 91
Sanger, Ellin Gail 1955- WhoE 91
Sanger, Elliott M. 1897-1989 BioIn 16, ConAu 129
Sanger, Frances Ella AuBYP 90
Sanger, Frederick 1918- BioIn 16, WhoAm 90, WhoWor 91, WorAlBi
Sanger, Grant 1908-1989 BioIn 16
Sanger, Herbert Shelton, Jr. 1936- WhoAm 90
Sanger, Josef BiDrAPA 89
Sanger, Margaret 1879-1966 BioIn 16, EncAL, FemiCLE
Sanger, Margaret 1883-1966 WorAlBi
Sanger, Margaret H. 1879-1966 BioAmW
Sanger, Marjory Bartlett 1920- AuBYP 90
Sangha, Jangbir 1945- St&PR 91
Sanghavi, D. K. 1938- St&PR 91
Sanghavi, Devendra Kantilal 1939- WhoE 91
Sanghera, Kanwal 1942- BiDrAPA 89
Sanghi, Harishankar Lal 1937- BiDrAPA 89
Sanghi, Jodh K 1925- BiDrAPA 89
San Giacomo, Laura BioIn 16
Sangiacomo, Roxann M BiDrAPA 89
Sangiamo, Albert WhoAmA 91
Sangiocomo, Thomas G. 1949- St&PR 91
Sangiorgi, Mario 1922- WhoWor 91
San Giovanni, Francine E BiDrAPA 89
Sangiovanni-Vincentelli, Alberto Luigi 1947- WhoAm 90
Sangiuliano, Iris Agatha WhoAmW 91
Sanglier, Michele Jeanne Fernande 1950- WhoWor 91
Sangmeister, George E. 1931- BioIn 16
Sangmeister, George Edward 1931- WhoAm 90
Sangnier, Francois-Marie Marc 1873-1950 BiDFrPL
Sangree, Walter Hinchman 1926- WhoAm 90
Sangster, Charles 1822-1893 DcCanB 12, DcLB 99 [port]
Sangster, Donald Burns 1911-1967 BioIn 16
Sangster, James Allan 1954- St&PR 91
Sangster, Margaret 1838-1912 FemiCLE
Sangster, Robert Edmund 1936- WhoWor 91
Sangthong, Kriengsak 1948- WhoWor 91
Sanguillen, Manny 1944- Ballpl 90
Sanguinet, Robert Charles 1957- WhoE 91
Sanguineti, Edoardo 1930- WhoWor 91
Sanguineti, Vincenzo R BiDrAPA 89
Sanguineti, Vittorio 1940- St&PR 91
Sanguinetti, Alexandre 1913-1981 BiDFrPL
Sanguinetti, Eugene F 1917- WhoAmA 91
Sanguinetti, Eugene Frank 1917- WhoAm 90
Sanguinetti, Julio Maria BioIn 16
Sanguinetti, Julio Maria 1936- WhoWor 91
Sani, Robert LeRoy 1935- WhoAm 90
Sani Bako, Mahamane WhoWor 91
Sanii, A. E. 1936- St&PR 91
Sanikop, Rajendra B BiDrAPA 89
Sanislo, Stephen V., Jr. 1956- St&PR 91
Sanjar, Mansour R 1933- BiDrAPA 89
Sanjian, Avedis Krikor 1921- WhoAm 90
Sanjines, Jorge 1936- BioIn 16
Sanjiva Reddy, N. 1913- BioIn 16
San Jose, George L. 1954- WhoHisp 91
San Juan, Javier 1951- St&PR 91
San Juan, Vivian 1957- WhoAmW 91
Sanjurjo, Carmen Hilda 1952- WhoHisp 91
Sankar, Devarakonda Venkata Siva 1927- WhoE 91
Sankara, Thomas BioIn 16
Sankaran, Sivarama Krishnan 1945- WhoWor 91
Sankey, Clayton David 1947- WhoEmL 91
Sankey, Ira David 1840-1908 BioIn 16
Sankey, John 1920- St&PR 91
Sankey, Kenneth 1946- St&PR 91
Sankey, Vernon L. 1949- St&PR 91
Sankhyan, Anek Ram 1951- WhoWor 91
Sankner, Sheri Warren 1959- WhoE 91, WhoWor 91
Sankowsky, Itzhak 1908- WhoAmA 91
Sankpill, James Conrad 1939- WhoSSW 91
Sankpill, L. Alan 1942- St&PR 91
Sankpill, Linda Lucas 1945- WhoAmW 91
Sanks, Charles Randolph, Jr. 1928- WhoAm 90, WhoE 91, WhoWor 91
Sanks, Robert Leland 1916- WhoAm 90
Sanladerer, Loren K. 1936- St&PR 91
San Luis, Edward Charles 1933- WhoE 91
San Martin, Jose de 1778?-1850 BioIn 16, WorAlBi
San Martin, Juan Zorrilla de 1855-1931 BioIn 16
San Martin, Ramon Grau 1877-1969 BioIn 16
San Miguel, Xavier 1954- BiDrAPA 89
Sann, Ted BioIn 16
Sanna, Lucy Jean 1948- WhoAmW 91
Sannappa, Bisineer Sharanappa BiDrAPA 89
Sannella, Lee Sherman 1916- St&PR 91
Sannella, Maria Amelia 1942- WhoAmW 91
Sanner, George Elwood 1929- WhoE 91
Sanner, Royce Norman 1931- St&PR 91, WhoAm 90
Sannwald, William Walter 1940- WhoAm 90
Sano, di Pietro 1406-1481 BioIn 16
Sano, Hideo 1926- WhoWor 91
Sano, Keiji 1920- WhoWor 91
Sanocki, Edward John, Jr. 1950- WhoE 91
Sanoff, Henry 1934- WhoSSW 91
Sanor, David Roy 1950- WhoSSW 91
San Pedro, Enrique 1926- WhoAm 90
Sanquist, Nancy Jean 1947- WhoAmW 91
Sanroma, Jesus Maria 1902-1984 PenDiMP
San Roman, Jose Perez BioIn 16
Sans, Diego Cosme BiDrAPA 89
Sans, Nick 1949- St&PR 91
Sansalone, Elena ODwPR 91
Sansaverino, Joseph Frank 1937- St&PR 91
Sansay, Leonora FemiCLE
Sansbury, Olin Bennett, Jr. 1937- WhoAm 90
Sanscrainte, Willard Allen, Jr. 1960- WhoEmL 91
Sansevere, Lawrence Michael 1957- WhoE 91
Sanseverino, Raymond Anthony 1947- WhoEmL 91
Sanseverino, Vincenzo 1951- St&PR 91
Sansfacon, Chantal BiDrAPA 89
Sanslone, William Robert 1931- WhoE 91
Sansolo, Jack 1943- WhoAm 90
Sansom, George Bailey 1883-1965 EncJap
Sansom, Gillian Rosemary 1935- IntWWM 90
Sansom, Jane BiDEWW
Sansom, William 1912-1976 MajTwCW
Sanson, Barbara Elizabeth 1955- WhoEmL 91
Sanson, Charles-Henri BioIn 16
Sanson, Phil 1941- St&PR 91
Sanson, Raul Eduardo David de 1942- WhoWor 91
Sanson, Raymond R. 1950- ODwPR 91
Sanson, Rudolph J., Jr. 1937- St&PR 91
Sansone, John C. 1955- St&PR 91
Sansone, Joseph Daniel 1943- WhoE 91
Sansone, Joseph F 1922- WhoAmA 91
Sansone, Leonard 1917-1956 EncACom
Sansone, Marleen Barbara 1942- WhoAmW 91
Sansone, Mary 1916- BioIn 16
Sansone, Philip Andrew BiDrAPA 89
Sansone, Randy Alan 1953- BiDrAPA 89
Sansone, Robert 1942- WhoAm 90
Sansone, Steven Anthony 1953- WhoSSW 91
San Soucie, Patricia Molm 1931- WhoAmA 91
Sansovino, Andrea 1467?-1529 IntDcAA 90
Sansovino, Jacopo 1486-1570 IntDcAA 90
Sanstead, Wayne Godfrey 1935- WhoAm 90
Sansweet, Stephen Jay 1945- WhoAm 90
Sant, John Talbot 1932- St&PR 91, WhoAm 90
Sant, Joni Rose 1963- WhoAmW 91
Sant, William Webster 1927- St&PR 91
Sant' Angelo, Giorgio BioIn 16
Sant Jordi, Rosa de EncCoWW
Santa Maria ConAu 30NR
Santa, Ferenc 1927- WorAu 1980 [port]
Santa, Sharon Aichele 1953- St&PR 91
Santa, Wilfredo G BiDrAPA 89
Santa Ana, Benjamin P 1932- BiDrAPA 89
Santa Anna, Antonio Lopez de 1794?-1876 BioIn 16, WorAlBi
Santa Cruz, Andres 1792-1865 BioIn 16
Santa Cruz, Nicomedes 1925- HispWr 90
Santa Maria, Andres de 1860-1945 ArtLatA
Santa Maria, Philip Joseph, III 1945- WhoEmL 91
Santa Maria, Zeke Polanco 1942- WhoHisp 91
Santa Maria Gonzalez, Domingo 1825-1889 BioIn 16
Santacana, Guido E. 1952- WhoAm 90
Santacaterina, Luis 1932- St&PR 91
Santacroce, David Anthony 1951- WhoE 91
Santacroce, Donald Paul 1932- St&PR 91
Santaella, Fernando F 1930- BiDrAPA 89
Santaella, Irma 1924- WhoHisp 91
Santaella, Irma Vidal 1924- WhoAmW 91, WhoWor 91
Santaella, Pablo Livinally ArtLatA
Santala, Ilpo BioIn 16
Santalainen, Timo Juhani 1946- WhoWor 91
Santalla, Eusebio L BiDrAPA 89

Santalo, Lois *AuBYP 90*
Santalucia, Michael P. 1943- *St&PR 91*
Santamaria, Henry, Jr. 1948- *WhoHisp 91*
Santamaria, Jaime 1911- *WhoHisp 91*
Santamaria, Phillip Hunt 1940- *St&PR 91*
Santana *EncPR&S 89, OxCPMus*
Santana, Altagracia *BiDrAPA 89*
Santana, Anthony *WhoHisp 91*
Santana, Carlos 1947- *BioIn 16, EncPR&S 89, WhoAm 90, WhoHisp 91*
Santana, Carlota *WhoHisp 91*
Santana, Elida *WhoHisp 91*
Santana, Franklin A. 1948- *ODwPR 91*
Santana, Juan Jose 1942- *WhoHisp 91*
Santana, Pedro 1801-1864 *BioIn 16*
Santana, Pepe 1942- *WhoHisp 91*
Santana, Rafael 1958- *Ballpl 90*
Santana, Rafael Francisco 1958- *WhoHisp 91*
Santana, Robert Joseph 1914- *WhoE 91*
Santana, Sharon Lynn 1957- *WhoE 91*
Santana, Victor Manuel, Jr. 1962- *WhoHisp 91*
Santana-Garcia, Maritza *BiDrAPA 89*
Santander, Francisco de Paula 1792-1840 *BioIn 16*
Santandrea, Mary Frances 1952- *WhoAmW 91*
Santangeli, Frank 1934- *WhoAm 90*
Santangelo, Arlene E. 1947- *St&PR 91*
Santangelo, Betty J. 1950- *WhoEmL 91*
Santangelo, Cesare Federico 1956- *WhoE 91*
Santangelo, Charles Edward 1927- *St&PR 91*
Santangelo, Gerard 1930- *St&PR 91*
Sant'Angelo, Giorgio *BioIn 16*
Sant'Angelo, Giorgio 1933-1989 *AnObit 1989, ConDes 90*
Santangelo, Joseph Anthony 1954- *St&PR 91*
Santangelo, Mario Vincent 1931- *WhoWor 91*
Santarella, Joseph Michael 1939- *WhoSSW 91*
Santarelli, Carlo Henry, Jr. 1950- *St&PR 91*
Santarelli, Donald Eugene 1937- *WhoAm 90*
Santarelli, Marino J. 1951- *St&PR 91*
Santarello, Piero Enrico 1942- *WhoWor 91*
Santarlasci, Stephen M. 1952- *WhoWrEP 89*
Santarlasci, Stephen Michael 1952- *WhoE 91*
Santarone, Pat *BioIn 16*
Santavicca, Donald Gene 1943- *St&PR 91*
Santayana, George 1863-1952 *BioIn 16, TwCLC 40 [port], WorAlBi, WrPh P*
Sante, Luc *BioIn 16*
Sante, William Arthur, II 1943- *St&PR 91, WhoAm 90*
Santee, Richard Ellis, Jr. 1951- *WhoE 91*
Santeiro, Luis Grau 1947- *WhoHisp 91*
Santello, Vicki 1956- *WhoAmW 91*
Santemma, Jon Noel 1937- *WhoE 91*
Santer, Jean Jacques 1937- *WhoWor 91*
Santhakumar, Sankunni *BiDrAPA 89*
Santi, Nello *BioIn 16*
Santi, Nello 1931- *IntWWM 90*
Santiago, Alfredo 1953- *WhoHisp 91*
Santiago, Americo *WhoHisp 91*
Santiago, Benito 1965- *Ballpl 90, WhoHisp 91*
Santiago, Danny *BioIn 16*
Santiago, Edgardo G. 1949- *WhoHisp 91*
Santiago, George 1929- *WhoHisp 91*
Santiago, Gloria B. *WhoHisp 91*
Santiago, Irma Delia *BiDrAPA 89*
Santiago, Isaura Santiago 1946- *WhoHisp 91*
Santiago, Ismael *WhoHisp 91*
Santiago, Jaime A. *WhoHisp 91*
Santiago, Jose 1940- *Ballpl 90*
Santiago, Jose Maria *BiDrAPA 89*
Santiago, Jose William 1956- *BiDrAPA 89*
Santiago, Marcosa Juliano *BiDrAPA 89*
Santiago, Miguel A. *WhoHisp 91*
Santiago, Milly 1954- *WhoHisp 91*
Santiago, Ramon 1943- *WhoAmA 91*
Santiago, Ramona A. 1952- *WhoAmW 91*
Santiago, Rebecca Velasco 1944- *BiDrAPA 89*
Santiago, Ricardo 1952- *WhoSSW 91*
Santiago, Roberto *BioIn 16*
Santiago, Roberto 1963- *WhoHisp 91*
Santiago, Rosa Emilia 1935- *WhoWor 91*
Santiago, Saundra *WhoHisp 91*
Santiago, Teresa *WhoHisp 91*
Santiago, Virgilio G 1924- *BiDrAPA 89*
Santiago-Aviles, Jorge Juan 1944- *WhoHisp 91*
Santiago-Lugo, Haydee *BiDrAPA 89*
Santiago-Negron, Salvador 1942- *WhoHisp 91*
Santiago-Noa, Victor Manuel 1944- *BiDrAPA 89, WhoE 91*
Santiago-Rodriguez, Liduvina 1937- *WhoSSW 91*
Santiago Y Ruiz De Porras, Carlos R 1933- *BiDrAPA 89*
Santiccioli, Aldo Bruno *BiDrAPA 89*
Santiesteban, Humberto 1934- *WhoHisp 91*
Santillan, Antonio 1936- *WhoWor 91*
Santilli, Paul Thomas 1929- *St&PR 91*
Santillo, Carl John 1949- *St&PR 91*
Santillo, Josephine 1943- *WhoE 91*
Santillo, Rosemary Ross 1948- *WhoAmW 91*
Santina, Henry Della 1914- *WhoSSW 91*
Santini, Gilles Francois-Marie 1947- *WhoWor 91*
Santini, John Amedeo 1926- *WhoAm 90*
Santini, Rosemarie *WhoWrEP 89*
Santini, William Andrew, Jr. 1931- *St&PR 91*
Santini, Zachary M. 1949- *St&PR 91*
Sant'Ismael, Ilia di *EncCoWW*
Santisteban, Carlos *WhoHisp 91*
Santisteban, Iggy 1954- *WhoSSW 91*
Santley, Charles 1834-1922 *PenDiMP*
Santley, Joseph 1889-1971 *OxCPMus*
Santley, Thomas S. 1935- *ODwPR 91*
Santlofer, Jonathan 1946- *WhoAmA 91*
Santman, Leon Duane 1930- *WhoAm 90*
Santmyer, Helen Hooven 1895-1986 *ConAu 33NR, MajTwCW*
Santo, Bela *PenDiMP*
Santo, James Matthew 1941- *St&PR 91*
Santo, James R. 1937- *St&PR 91*
Santo, Nancy 1928- *WhoAmW 91, WhoE 91*
Santo, Ron 1940- *Ballpl 90 [port]*
Santoli, Joan Murphy 1961- *WhoAmW 91*
Santoli, Joseph Ralph 1957- *WhoEmL 91*
Santoliquido, Rocco 1854-1930? *EncO&P 3*
Santolucito, Joseph Anthony 1946- *WhoAm 90*
Santomasso, Antoinette Therese 1949- *WhoE 91*
Santomauro, Mary Elizabeth 1935- *WhoWrEP 89*
Santomero, Anthony M. 1946- *WhoAm 90, WhoE 91*
Santona, Gloria 1950- *WhoEmL 91*
Santoni, Ronald Ernest 1931- *WhoAm 90*
Santonio, Joel San 1952- *St&PR 91*
Santop, Louis 1890-1942 *Ballpl 90*
Santora, A. J. *BioIn 16*
Santora, Philip Jay 1944- *BiDrAPA 89*
Santora, Robert William 1927- *WhoE 91*
Santorelli, Thomas J. 1941- *St&PR 91*
Santori, Rafael Edward 1937- *WhoSSW 91*
Santorine, Adolph William, Jr. 1958- *St&PR 91*
Santorini, Al 1948- *Ballpl 90*
Santoro, Alex 1936- *WhoWor 91*
Santoro, Anthony R. *WhoAm 90*
Santoro, Carlo Maria 1935- *WhoWor 91*
Santoro, Carmelo James 1941- *WhoAm 90*
Santoro, Claudio 1919-1989 *AnObit 1989*
Santoro, Edward R. 1934- *St&PR 91*
Santoro, John R. 1939- *St&PR 91*
Santoro, Michael Anthony 1954- *WhoEmL 91*
Santoro, Paul M. 1949- *St&PR 91*
Santoro, Vincenzo 1939- *WhoWor 91*
Santoro, William D *BiDrAPA 89*
Santoro-Putnam, Karen Ann 1954- *WhoAmW 91*
Santos, Adele Naude 1938- *WhoAm 90*
Santos, Al 1951- *BiDrAPA 89*
Santos, Alberto *St&PR 91*
Santos, Antonio H. Ribeiro 1943- *WhoWor 91*
Santos, David E. *ODwPR 91*
Santos, Dianne S. 1941- *St&PR 91*
Santos, Domiciano E *BiDrAPA 89*
Santos, Eduardo 1888-1974 *BioIn 16*
Santos, Ernesto Agustin 1958- *WhoSSW 91*
Santos, Fermin Mario *BiDrAPA 89*
Santos, George Wesley 1928- *WhoAm 90*
Santos, Igmidio Ambrocio *BiDrAPA 89*
Santos, Jean Anne 1959- *WhoAmW 91*
Santos, Joaquim Jorge 1951- *WhoWor 91*
Santos, Joe 1931- *WhoHisp 91*
Santos, Jose A *BiDrAPA 89*
Santos, Jose Eduardo Dos 1942- *BioIn 16*
Santos, Jose Miguel Costa 1946- *WhoWor 91*
Santos, Jose Ramon *BiDrAPA 89*
Santos, Joseph 1916- *St&PR 91*
Santos, Laura Marie 1965- *WhoAmW 91*
Santos, Luzviminda R. *BiDrAPA 89*
Santos, Marcelino Dos 1929- *BioIn 16*
Santos, Nelson Pereira Dos 1928- *BioIn 16*
Santos, Reydel 1954- *WhoHisp 91*
Santos, Robert Frederick 1934- *St&PR 91*
Santos, Rogelio R. 1943- *WhoHisp 91*
Santos, Rufino V 1936- *BiDrAPA 89*
Santos, Sherod 1948- *ConAu 132, WhoWrEP 89*
Santos, Silvio *BioIn 16*
Santos-Alborna, Gipsy 1965- *WhoHisp 91*
Santos-Hernandez, Erick F 1942- *BiDrAPA 89*
Santos-Martinez, Jesus 1924- *WhoSSW 91*
Santos-Pizzaro, Priscila R *BiDrAPA 89*
Santos Silva, Loreina 1933- *BioIn 16*
Santosa, Rahajoe Imam 1950- *WhoWor 91*
Santosuosso, Joseph Ralph 1942- *WhoAm 90*
Santovenia, Nelson 1961- *Ballpl 90*
Santovenia, Nelson Gil 1961- *WhoHisp 91*
Santoyo, Elsa Margarita 1953- *WhoE 91*
Santrizos, Mario P. 1933- *ODwPR 91*
Santry, Arthur Joseph, Jr. 1918- *St&PR 91, WhoAm 90*
Santry, Barbara Lea 1948- *WhoAmW 91*
Santry, J. E. 1934- *St&PR 91*
Santschi, Peter Hans 1943- *WhoSSW 91*
Santucci, Michael Louis 1949- *WhoEmL 91*
Santucci, Patricia Ann 1942- *BiDrAPA 89*
Santucci, Peter A. 1927- *BiDrAPA 89*
Santuccio, John A. *WhoE 91*
Santulli, Andrew Philip 1947- *St&PR 91*
Santulli, Richard T. *BioIn 16*
Santulli, Robert B 1947- *BiDrAPA 89*
Santulli, Thomas Vincent 1915- *WhoAm 90*
Santulli, Vincent F. 1942- *St&PR 91*
Santunione, Orianna 1934- *IntWWM 90*
Santy, Albert Christy 1948- *WhoE 91*
Santy, Patricia Anne *BiDrAPA 89*
Sanudo, Marin *BioIn 16*
Sanusi, Marina *BiDrAPA 89*
Sanuto, Marino *BioIn 16*
Sanvitale, Francesca 1928- *EncCoWW*
Sanyal, Somes Chandra 1933- *WhoWor 91*
Sanyour, Michael Louis 1930- *St&PR 91*
Sanyour, Michael Louis, Jr. 1930- *WhoAm 90*
Sanytyi *DcCanB 12*
Sanz, Eleutherio Llorente 1926- *WhoHisp 91*
Sanz, Manuel Ortuno *BiDrAPA 89*
Sanz, Wanda Lis 1958- *BiDrAPA 89*
Sanzari, Paul V. 1949- *St&PR 91*
Sanzio, Raffaello 1483-1520 *BioIn 16*
Sanzogno, Nino 1911-1983 *PenDiMP*
Sao, Maria da Conceicao 1946- *WhoAmW 91*
Sapala, Elizabeth M 1943- *BiDrAPA 89*
Sapan, Joshua *BioIn 16*
Sapan, Joshua Ward 1950- *WhoE 91*
Sapanski, John William 1930- *St&PR 91, WhoAm 90*
Saper, Leslie David 1957- *WhoSSW 91*
Saper, Ronald L. 1950- *WhoAm 90*
Sapera, Leonard Joseph 1940- *WhoSSW 91*
Sapers, Carl Martin 1932- *WhoAm 90*
Saperstein, Alan 1949- *WhoE 91*
Saperstein, David 1937- *ConAu 130*
Saperstein, David Allan 1937- *WhoAm 90*
Saperstein, David Dorn 1946- *WhoEmL 91*
Saperstein, Jerome Louis 1917- *BiDrAPA 89*
Saperstein, Joan Weingast 1952- *BiDrAPA 89*
Saperstein, Lee Waldo 1943- *WhoAm 90*
Saperstein, Marc Eli 1944- *WhoAm 90*
Saperston, Howard Truman, Sr. 1899- *WhoAm 90*
Sapeta, Robert G. 1947- *St&PR 91*
Saphir, Richard Louis 1933- *WhoE 91*
Saphire, Gary Steven 1952- *WhoE 91*
Saphire, Lawrence M 1931- *WhoAmA 91*
Saphire, Naomi Carroll 1938- *WhoAmW 91*
Sapico, Francisco Lejano 1940- *WhoAm 90*
Sapien, Darryl Rudolph 1950- *WhoAmA 91*
Sapiens, Alexander 1946- *WhoHisp 91*
Sapienza, John Thomas 1913- *WhoAm 90*
Sapieyevski, Anne Lindbergh *AuBYP 90*
Sapieyevski, Jerzy 1945- *IntWWM 90*
Sapin, Cory Roberta 1951- *WhoAmW 91*
Sapinsky, Joseph Charles 1923- *WhoAm 90*
Sapinsley, Lila Manfield 1922- *WhoAmW 91*
Sapio, David A. 1945- *St&PR 91*
Sapir, Edward 1884-1939 *BioIn 16, DcLB 92 [port]*
Sapir, Paul E *BiDrAPA 89*
Sapir, Philip 1916- *BiDrAPA 89*
Sapir, Richard *TwCCr&M 91*
Sapir, Richard 1936-1987 *SpyFic*
Sapir, Richard, and Warren Murphy *SpyFic*
Sapiro, Miriam Elizabeth 1960- *WhoE 91*
Sapirstein, Fran *BioIn 16*
Sapirstein, Milton R 1914- *BiDrAPA 89*
Sapoch, Betty *BioIn 16*
Sapoff, Meyer 1927- *WhoE 91, WhoWor 91*
Sapolsky, Harvey Morton 1939- *WhoAm 90*
Saponaro, Joseph Anthony 1939- *St&PR 91*
Sapone, Michel *BioIn 16*
Saporito, Jim *NewAgMG*
Saporito, Rhenda C. 1950- *WhoAmW 91*
Saporta, Jack 1927- *WhoWor 91*
Saporta, Jose Alberto, Jr. 1956- *BiDrAPA 89*
Saporta, Marc 1923- *WhoWor 91*
Saporta, Vicki *BioIn 16*
Sapos, Mary Ann *WhoAmW 91*
Sapoznikoff, John Barry 1939- *BiDrAPA 89*
Sapp, A Eugene 1936- *St&PR 91*
Sapp, A. Eugene, Jr. 1936- *WhoAm 90, WhoSSW 91*
Sapp, Allan D. 1956- *St&PR 91*
Sapp, Betty Oldham 1941- *WhoAm 90*
Sapp, Clayton H. *St&PR 91*
Sapp, Donald Gene 1927- *WhoWor 91*
Sapp, Eva Jo 1944- *WhoWrEP 89*
Sapp, James Winston, Jr. 1932- *BiDrAPA 89*
Sapp, Kathy Cambridge 1955- *WhoAmW 91*
Sapp, Neil Carleton 1939- *WhoSSW 91*
Sapp, Peggy Brotherton 1942- *WhoAmW 91*
Sapp, Richard Cassell 1928- *WhoAm 90*
Sapp, Sharon Ann 1952- *WhoAmW 91*
Sapp, Stanley C. 1961- *St&PR 91*
Sapp, Walter W. 1930- *St&PR 91*
Sapp, Walter William 1930- *WhoAm 90*
Sapp, William Darlo 1932- *St&PR 91*
Sapp, William Rothwell 1943- *WhoAmA 91*
Sappelstein, Ralph 1930- *St&PR 91*
Sappenfield, Charles Madison 1930- *WhoAm 90*
Sappenfield, Diane Hastings 1940- *WhoAmW 91*
Sappenfield, Mary Frances 1937- *WhoAmW 91*
Sappenfield, Rita Cummins 1929- *WhoAmW 91*
Sapper 1888-1937 *TwCCr&M 91*
Sapper, Agnes 1852-1929 *EncCoWW*
Sapper, Alan Louis Geoffrey 1931- *WhoWor 91*
Sapper, Eugene Herbert 1929- *WhoHisp 91*
Sapper, Laurence Joseph 1922-1989 *ConAu 129*
Sapper, Neil Gary 1941- *WhoSSW 91*
Sapper, Richard *PenDiDA 89*
Sapper, Richard 1932- *ConDes 90*
Sapperstein, Ralph 1930- *St&PR 91*
Sappho *WorAlBi*
Sappho 612?BC- *FemiCLE*
Sappho 620?BC- *EncCoWW*
Sappia, Alfred E. 1930- *St&PR 91*
Sappington, Cheryl Elizabeth 1949- *WhoAmW 91*
Sappington, Michael Lee 1949- *St&PR 91*
Sappington, Thomas Edward 1955- *WhoSSW 91*
Sappir, Mark Zelig 1952- *WhoE 91*
Sapra, Ravi Kant 1939- *BiDrAPA 89*
Sapriel, Sheryl-Hope 1957- *WhoAmW 91*
Sapsford, Ralph Neville 1938- *WhoWor 91*
Sapsowitz, Sidney H. 1936- *St&PR 91, WhoAm 90*
Sapszon, Ferenc *IntWWM 90*
Sapundziju, Riza *WhoWor 91*
Sapuppo, Victor 1938- *St&PR 91*
Saqr bin Muhammad Al-Qasimi, Sheikh 1920- *WhoWor 91*
Saqui, Soqui *PenDiDA 89*
Sara, St. *EncO&P 3*
Sarabasa, Albert Gonzalez, Jr. 1952- *WhoHisp 91*
Sarabia, Fermin *BiDrAPA 89*
Sarabia, Horace 1938- *WhoHisp 91*
Sarabia, Louis 1942- *WhoHisp 91*
Saracchi family *PenDiDA 89*
Saracchi, Costanzo *PenDiDA 89*
Saracchi, Gabriele *PenDiDA 89*
Saracchi, Gasparo *PenDiDA 89*
Saracchi, Giovanni Ambrogio *PenDiDA 89*
Saracchi, Michele *PenDiDA 89*
Saracchi, Pietro Antonio *PenDiDA 89*
Saracchi, Raffaello *PenDiDA 89*
Saracchi, Simone Stefano *PenDiDA 89*
Saraceni, Elyse *BioIn 16*
Saraceni, Remo 1935- *BioIn 16*
Sarachene, Joseph Eugene 1960- *BiDrAPA 89*
Sarachman, Theodore N. 1932-1987 *BioIn 16*
Saracino, Arthur Michael 1949- *St&PR 91*
Saracino, Luigi *BiDrAPA 89*
Saracoglu, Rusdu *BioIn 16*
Saracoglu, Rusdu 1948- *WhoWor 91*
Sarada, Thyagaraja 1929- *WhoAmW 91*
Saraf, Dilip Govind 1942- *WhoWor 91*

Saraf, Kishore R 1940- *BiDrAPA 89*
Sarafian, Karl 1918- *WhoSSW 91*
Saragat, Giuseppe 1898- *WhoWor 91*
Saragat, Giuseppe 1898-1988 *AnObit 1988, BioIn 16*
Sarah, Duchess of York 1959- *BioIn 16*
Sarah, Robyn 1949- *ConAu 31NR*
Sarai, Tibor K. 1919- *IntWWM 90*
Saraiva de Azevedo, Manuela 1911- *EncCoWW*
Saralegui, Cristina Maria 1948- *WhoAmW 91, WhoHisp 91*
Saram, Rohan de *PenDiMP*
Saran, Avtar S *BiDrAPA 89*
Saran, Brij Mohan *BiDrAPA 89*
Saran, Deo 1955- *WhoWor 91*
Saran, Nihal *BiDrAPA 89*
Saran, Parmatma 1943- *ConAu 129*
Saran, Sam H. 1924- *St&PR 91*
Saran, Shabd 1931- *BiDrAPA 89*
Saranasena, Gamage 1933- *WhoWor 91*
Sarandon, Susan *BioIn 16*
Sarandon, Susan 1946- *WorAlBi*
Sarandon, Susan Abigail 1946- *WhoAm 90, WhoAmW 91*
Sarangi, Sunil Kumar 1949- *WhoWor 91*
Sarante, Galateia 1920?- *EncCoWW*
Saranti, Galateia *EncCoWW*
Sarantides, Stylianos 1936- *WhoWor 91*
Sarapata, Susan Lee 1950- *WhoEmL 91*
Sarapo, Donato Frank 1925- *WhoAm 90*
Sarasa, Jose *BiDrAPA 89*
Sarasate, Pablo de 1844-1908 *PenDiMP*
Sarasate y Navascuez, Pablo de 1844-1908 *PenDiMP*
Sarashina *BioIn 16*
Sarasin, Jennifer 1947- *BioIn 16*
Sarasohn, Cecilia Lester *BioIn 16*
Sarason, Esther Kroop 1918- *WhoAmW 91*
Sarason, Henry 1896-1979 *WhoAmA 91N*
Sarason, Seymour Bernard 1919- *BioIn 16*
Saraste, Jukka-Pekka 1956- *IntWWM 90*
Sarasua, Martha Marion *BiDrAPA 89*
Sarasy, Phyllis Powell 1930- *AuBYP 90*
Sarat, Austin D. 1947- *WhoAm 90*
Sarati, Carmen M. 1931- *WhoHisp 91*
Saravay, Stephen M *BiDrAPA 89*
Saravay, Stephen Martin 1938- *WhoE 91*
Saravia, Aparicio 1855-1904 *BioIn 16*
Saravia, George G *BiDrAPA 89*
Sarazen, Richard Allen 1933- *WhoAm 90, WhoE 91*
Sarazin, Bernard 1929- *WhoWor 91*
Sarbanes, Paul Spyros 1933- *WhoAm 90, WhoE 91, WhoWor 91*
Sarbello, Michael Charles 1943- *St&PR 91*
Sarbin, Hershel B. 1924- *St&PR 91*
Sarbin, Hershel Benjamin 1924- *WhoAm 90*
Sarbu, Eugene 1950- *IntWWM 90*
Sarchet-Waller, Paul Robert 1947- *WhoWor 91*
Sarcia, James F. 1931- *St&PR 91*
Sarcopski, Sharon A. Coleman 1951- *WhoAmW 91*
Sard, George D. 1953- *ODwPR 91*
Sardachuk, Grant R. 1958- *St&PR 91*
Sardas, Jacques Raphael 1930- *St&PR 91, WhoAm 90*
Sardeau, Helene 1899-1968 *WhoAmA 91N*
Sardeau, Helene 1899-1969 *BiDWomA*
Sardella, Stephen *BioIn 16*
Sarden, Claudia 1958- *WhoWrEP 89*
Sardi, Emilio 1943- *WhoWor 91*
Sardi, Ivan 1930- *IntWWM 90*
Sardilli, David Bruce 1945- *WhoAm 90*
Sardina, Adolfo F. 1933- *BioIn 16, WhoAm 90, WhoWor 91*
Sardinias, Eligio 1907-1988 *AnObit 1988*
Sardinias, Eligio 1910-1988 *BioIn 16*
Sardoff, Philip Y. 1937- *ODwPR 91*
Sardone, Vincent Paul 1953- *St&PR 91*
Sardou, Victorien 1831-1908 *EncO&P 3*
Sarduy, Severo *BioIn 16*
Sarduy, Severo 1937- *HispWr 90*
Sareini, Suzanne 1951- *WhoEmL 91*
Sarellano, Luis Humberto 1947- *WhoHisp 91*
Saren, Drucilla 1947- *WhoEmL 91*
Saret, Alan Daniel 1944- *WhoAmA 91*
Sarett, Herbert Paul 1916- *WhoSSW 91*
Saretzky, Simon 1908- *St&PR 91*
Sarezky, Michael Neil *BiDrAPA 89*
Sarf, Peter Francis 1922- *St&PR 91*
Sarfati, Frederique 1960- *WhoWor 91*
Sarfatti, Margherita 1883-1961 *EncCoWW*
Sarfaty, Wayne Allen 1951- *WhoE 91, WhoWor 91*
Sargan, John Denis 1924- *WhoWor 91*
Sargant, William 1907-1988 *AnObit 1988*
Sargeant, Ernest James 1918- *WhoAm 90*
Sargeant, Nancy Reardon 1933- *WhoWrEP 89*
Sargeant, Thomas Lee *BiDrAPA 89*
Sargent, Albert John, III 1947- *BiDrAPA 89*
Sargent, Amy 1962- *WhoE 91*
Sargent, Anneila Isabel *WhoAmW 91*
Sargent, Ben 1948- *BioIn 16, WhoAm 90*
Sargent, Benson Collins 1943- *WhoAm 90*
Sargent, Bernard Victor 1928- *WhoWor 91*
Sargent, Carl Robert 1952- *St&PR 91*
Sargent, Charles Jackson 1929- *WhoSSW 91*
Sargent, Charles Lee 1937- *St&PR 91, WhoWor 91*
Sargent, David Jasper 1931- *WhoAm 90*
Sargent, David R. 1920- *St&PR 91*
Sargent, David Stansfeld 1944- *BiDrAPA 89*
Sargent, Diana Rhea 1939- *WhoAmW 91*
Sargent, Douglas A *BiDrAPA 89*
Sargent, Epes 1813-1880 *EncO&P 3*
Sargent, Ernest Douglas 1931- *WhoAm 90*
Sargent, Francis Williams, Jr. 1946- *WhoE 91*
Sargent, Frank *BioIn 16*
Sargent, Henry B., Jr. 1934- *St&PR 91*
Sargent, Henry Barry, Jr. 1934- *WhoAm 90*
Sargent, Herbert E. *St&PR 91*
Sargent, J McNeil *WhoAmA 91*
Sargent, James Cunningham 1916- *WhoAm 90*
Sargent, John Allston 1909-1989 *BioIn 16*
Sargent, John Allston, Jr. 1937- *WhoAm 90*
Sargent, John Garibaldi 1860-1939 *BiDrUSE 89*
Sargent, John Michael 1943- *WhoE 91*
Sargent, John Singer 1856-1925 *BioIn 16, IntDcAA 90, WorAlBi*
Sargent, John T. 1924- *St&PR 91*
Sargent, Jonathan Everett 1816-1890 *AmLegL*
Sargent, Joseph Denny 1929- *WhoAm 90*
Sargent, Joseph Dudley 1937- *WhoAm 90*
Sargent, Malcolm 1895-1967 *PenDiMP*
Sargent, Margaret Holland 1927- *WhoAmA 91*
Sargent, Pamela *BioIn 16*
Sargent, Pamela 1948- *WhoAmW 91*
Sargent, Peter B. 1952- *St&PR 91*
Sargent, Richard 1932- *WhoAmA 91*
Sargent, Robert George 1937- *WhoAm 90*
Sargent, Robert Strong 1912- *WhoWrEP 89*
Sargent, Sarah 1937- *BioIn 16*
Sargent, Seth Richard 1941- *St&PR 91*
Sargent, Shirley 1927- *AuBYP 90*
Sargent, Thomas Andrew 1933- *WhoAm 90*
Sargent, Wallace Leslie William 1935- *WhoWor 91*
Sargent, William Copley 1928- *St&PR 91*
Sargent, William Leroy 1947- *St&PR 91*
Sarger, Rene 1917-1988 *BioIn 16*
Sargon, Simon A. 1938- *IntWWM 90*
Sargunam, Issac Prince 1941- *WhoSSW 91*
Sari, Colleen E. 1955- *BiDrAPA 89*
Sari, Keith J. 1948- *St&PR 91*
Sari, Leslie Donald 1944- *St&PR 91*
Sarian, Jirair Nerses 1915- *WhoWor 91*
Sarich, Ralph Tony 1938- *WhoWor 91*
Saricks, Ambrose 1915- *WhoAm 90*
Saricks, Joyce Goering 1948- *WhoAmW 91*
Sarid-Segal, Ofra 1958- *BiDrAPA 89*
Saridis, George Nicholas 1931- *WhoAm 90*
Sariego, Paul David 1959- *WhoE 91*
Sarigumba, Rosalina L 1940- *BiDrAPA 89*
Sarin, Alok 1958- *BiDrAPA 89*
Sarin, Madhu 1945- *WomArch [port]*
Sarini, N. J. 1927- *St&PR 91*
Sarino, Edgardo Formantes 1940- *WhoWor 91*
Sariputra, Rahul *NewAgMG*
Saris, Linda Ellen 1952- *St&PR 91*
Sarkar, Dilip 1957- *WhoSSW 91*
Sarkar, Jadunath 1870-1958 *BioIn 16*
Sarkar, Probhat Ranjan *EncO&P 3*
Sarkar, Satyabrata 1928- *WhoWor 91*
Sarkar, Subal Kumar 1945- *WhoE 91*
Sarkar, Subrata Kumar 1936- *WhoWor 91*
Sarkar-Crooks, Patricia Anne *BiDrAPA 89*
Sarkari, Bahadur 1943- *BiDrAPA 89*
Sarker, Shila *BiDrAPA 89*
Sarkesian, Sam Charles 1927- *WhoAm 90*
Sarkett, Joann Lynn 1959- *WhoWrEP 89*
Sarkett, John A. *ODwPR 91*
Sarkia, Kaarlo 1902-1945 *DcScanL*
Sarkis 1909-1977 *WhoAmA 91N*
Sarkis, Elias Henry 1952- *BiDrAPA 89*
Sarkisian, Cherilyn *WhoAmW 91*
Sarkisian, Paul 1928- *WhoAmA 91*
Sarkisian, Richard Gabriel 1952- *WhoE 91*
Sarkissian, Miran P. *ODwPR 91*
Sarkissoff, Jean-Paul 1922- *WhoWor 91*
Sarkisyan, Fadei Tachatovich 1923- *WhoWor 91*
Sarkowski, Michael S. 1949- *St&PR 91*
Sarlat, Noah 1918- *WhoAm 90*
Sarle, Charles Richard 1944- *WhoE 91*
Sarle, William A. 1948- *St&PR 91*
Sarles, Peter Mason 1926- *WhoAm 90*
Sarles, Richard M 1935- *BiDrAPA 89*
Sarli, Robert J. 1950- *St&PR 91*
Sarlin, Morton B 1931- *BiDrAPA 89*
Sarlo, Arnold F. 1927- *St&PR 91*
Sarlow, Michael-Tyler Curtis 1952- *WhoWor 91*
Sarma, Atul Chandra 1939- *WhoSSW 91*
Sarma, Narasimhulu R *BiDrAPA 89*
Sarma, P S B 1941- *BiDrAPA 89*
Sarmanian, Peter 1934- *St&PR 91*
Sarmanto, Auvo Kaleva 1935- *WhoWor 91*
Sarmento, Mario Augusto 1936- *WhoSSW 91*
Sarmiento, Cresencio B 1933- *BiDrAPA 89*
Sarmiento, Domingo Faustino 1811-1888 *BioIn 16*
Sarmiento, Manny 1956- *Ballpl 90*
Sarmiento De Biscotti, Luz Socorro 1954- *WhoHisp 91*
Sarmientos-De Leon, Jorge Alvaro 1931- *WhoWor 91*
Sarmousakis, Gregory 1930- *BiDrAPA 89*
Sarna, Jeanne Anne Norman 1952- *WhoAmW 91*
Sarna, Nahum Mattathias 1923- *WhoAm 90*
Sarna, Thomas S. 1941- *St&PR 91*
Sarnat, Bernard George 1912- *WhoAm 90*
Sarnat, David Isaac 1942- *WhoSSW 91*
Sarner, Charles Alan 1933- *BiDrAPA 89*
Sarner, George 1931- *St&PR 91*
Sarner, James George 1949- *St&PR 91*
Sarner, Steven W 1954- *BiDrAPA 89*
Sarnes, Martin Howard 1940- *BiDrAPA 89*
Sarnese, Alphonse Michael 1939- *WhoAm 90*
Sarney, George W. 1939- *St&PR 91*
Sarney Costa, Jose 1930- *WhoWor 91*
Sarni, Bill 1927-1983 *Ballpl 90*
Sarni, Vincent A. 1928- *St&PR 91*
Sarni, Vincent Anthony 1928- *WhoAm 90, WhoE 91*
Sarnie, Richard Walter 1963- *WhoE 91*
Sarno, Carla Ann *BiDrAPA 89*
Sarno, Gerald D. 1928- *St&PR 91*
Sarno, Patricia Ann 1947- *WhoAmW 91, WhoWor 91*
Sarno, Sam 1946- *St&PR 91*
Sarnoff, Albert 1925- *St&PR 91, WhoAm 90*
Sarnoff, Arthur *BioIn 16*
Sarnoff, Arthur Saron 1912- *WhoAmA 91*
Sarnoff, Charles A 1928- *BiDrAPA 89*
Sarnoff, David 1891-1971 *WorAlBi*
Sarnoff, Dorothy *WhoE 91*
Sarnoff, Irving *BiDrAPA 89*
Sarnoff, Jane 1937- *AuBYP 90*
Sarnoff, Jeffrey Ray *BiDrAPA 89*
Sarnoff, Lili-Charlotte Dreyfus 1916- *WhoAmW 91, WhoWor 91*
Sarnoff, Lolo 1916- *WhoAmA 91*
Sarnoff, Paul 1918- *WhoE 91*
Sarnoff, Stanley J. *NewYTBS 90*
Sarnoff, Stanley J. 1917-1990 *BioIn 16*
Sarnoff, Stanley Jay *St&PR 91N*
Sarnoff, Stanley Jay 1917- *WhoAm 90*
Sarnoff, Stanley Jay 1917-1990 *ConAu 131*
Sarnoff, Thomas Warren 1927- *WhoAm 90*
Sarnoff, William 1929- *St&PR 91, WhoAm 90*
Sarnowski, Stanley John 1940- *St&PR 91*
Sarnowski, Thomas John 1938- *WhoAm 90*
Saroff, Marie S. 1928- *WhoE 91*
Sarofim, Adel Fares 1934- *WhoAm 90*
Sarony, Leslie 1897-1985 *DcNaB 1981, OxCPMus*
Saros, Carmen Nydia 1936- *WhoAmW 91*
Saros, Gust A. 1924- *St&PR 91*
Saros, Steven Emery 1947- *St&PR 91*
Sarosi, Balint 1925- *IntWWM 90*
Sarosiek, James J. 1946- *St&PR 91*
Sarot, Irving 1910-1990 *BioIn 16*
Saroufim, Mounir Albert 1952- *WhoWor 91*
Sarov, Israel *BioIn 16*
Saroyan, Aram *BioIn 16*
Saroyan, Aram 1943- *ConAu 30NR*
Saroyan, William 1908- *WorAlBi*
Saroyan, William 1908-1981 *ConAu 30NR, MajTwCW*
Sarpalius, Bill 1948- *BioIn 16, WhoAm 90, WhoSSW 91*
Sarpaneva, Timo 1926- *ConDes 90, PenDiDA 89*
Sarpaneva, Timo Tapani 1926- *WhoWor 91*
Sarpel, Gunseli 1945- *WhoAmW 91*
Sarpy, Leon 1907- *WhoAm 90*
Sarracino, Cooney 1933- *WhoHisp 91*
Sarrade-Loucheur, Bernard Louis 1945- *WhoWor 91*
Sarraf, Roberta Jean 1945- *WhoAmW 91, WhoE 91, WhoWor 91*
Sarramon, Jean-Pierre Fernand Louis 1938- *WhoWor 91*
Sarran, Wallace E., Jr. 1928- *St&PR 91*
Sarratori, Debbie *BioIn 16*
Sarraut, Albert 1872-1962 *BiDFrPL*
Sarraut, Maurice 1869-1943 *BiDFrPL*
Sarraute, Nathalie 1900- *EncCoWW, EuWr 12, MajTwCW, WhoWor 91*
Sarrazin, Albertine 1937-1967 *EncCoWW*
Sarrazin, Bernard P. 1937- *St&PR 91*
Sarrazin, Guy *ODwPR 91*
Sarrazin, Hubertus O. 1942- *St&PR 91*
Sarrazin, Yvette *ODwPR 91*
Sarrien, Jean-Marie Ferdinand 1840-1915 *BiDFrPL*
Sarrigiannis, Maria 1917- *BiDrAPA 89*
Sarris, Alexander Hippocrates 1948- *WhoWor 91*
Sarris, Andrew George 1928- *WhoAm 90, WhoWrEP 89*
Sarris, John George *BiDrAPA 89*
Sarro, John Joseph 1943- *WhoE 91*
Sarro, Sinikka 1945- *ODwPR 91*
Sarro-Burbano, Ramon *BiDrAPA 89*
Sarry, Christine 1946- *WhoAm 90*
Sarson, Evelyn Patricia *WhoWrEP 89*
Sarson, Evelyn Patricia 1937- *WhoAm 90*
Sarson, John Christopher 1935- *WhoAm 90*
Sarsony, Robert 1938- *WhoAmA 91*
Sarsten, Gunnar E. 1937- *St&PR 91*
Sarsten, Gunnar Edward 1937- *WhoAm 90*
Sartain, E. P. 1963- *St&PR 91*
Sartain, Emily 1841-1927 *BiDWomA*
Sartain, James Edward 1941- *WhoWor 91*
Sartain, Robert Lee 1939- *WhoSSW 91*
Sartain, William Franklin 1921- *WhoSSW 91*
Sartelli, Deborah Nelson 1953- *WhoAmW 91*
Sarten, Irine Champion 1943- *WhoAmW 91*
Sarto, Gloria Elizabeth 1929- *WhoAm 90*
Sarton, May 1912- *BioAmW, BioIn 16, FemiCLE, MajTwCW, WhoAm 90, WhoAmW 91*
Sartor, Anthony Joseph 1943- *WhoAm 90*
Sartor, Curtis Joseph 1954- *WhoSSW 91*
Sartor, Daniel Ryan, Jr. 1932- *WhoAm 90*
Sartorelli, Alan Clayton 1931- *WhoAm 90*
Sartoretti, Christine 1943- *IntWWM 90*
Sartori, Giovanni 1924- *WhoAm 90*
Sartori, Helfred Edwin 1939- *WhoE 91*
Sartori, Joseph 1858-1946 *EncABHB 7 [port]*
Sartori, Silvio 1957- *St&PR 91*
Sartorio, George Robert 1953- *WhoE 91*
Sartre, Jean-Paul 1905-1980 *BiDFrPL, BioIn 16, EuWr 12, MajTwCW, WorAlBi, WrPh, -P*
Sartzetakis, Christos 1929- *WhoWor 91*
Saru, George 1920- *WhoAmA 91*
Sarubbi, Thomas F. 1922- *St&PR 91*
Sarubin, Myra Norma 1940- *WhoAmW 91*
Saruk, Cynthia M *BiDrAPA 89*
Sarungu, Simon Tiranda 1932- *WhoWor 91*
Sarvay, Thomas Long, Jr. 1938- *BiDrAPA 89*
Sarvepalli Radhakrishnan 1888-1975 *BioIn 16*
Sarver, Edward James 1945- *WhoE 91*
Sarver, Eugene 1943- *WhoE 91*
Sarver, Jerry L. 1938- *St&PR 91*
Sarver, Linton Lane 1941- *WhoSSW 91*
Sarver, Mary Virginia 1941- *WhoSSW 91*
Sarver, Robert Dean 1938- *St&PR 91*
Sarvet, Barry David 1962- *BiDrAPA 89*
Sarvetnick, H. 1929- *St&PR 91*
Sarvig, Ole 1921-1981 *DcScanL*
Sarwer-Foner, Gerald Jacob 1924- *BiDrAPA 89, WhoAm 90*
Sas, Louis J. 1937- *St&PR 91*
Sasahara, Arthur Asao 1927- *WhoAm 90, WhoWor 91*
Sasaki, Carol *BioIn 16*
Sasaki, Clarence Takashi 1941- *WhoAm 90, WhoE 91*
Sasaki, Hideo 1919- *WhoAm 90*
Sasaki, Itaru 1935- *WhoWor 91*
Sasaki, Jane E *BiDrAPA 89*
Sasaki, Koichi 1943- *St&PR 91*
Sasaki, Kyohei 1918- *WhoAm 90*
Sasaki, Muneo 1941- *WhoWor 91*
Sasaki, Patricia Ann 1950- *WhoWor 91*
Sasaki, Robert K. 1941- *St&PR 91*
Sasaki, Tatsuo 1944- *WhoWor 91*
Sasaki, Tazu 1932- *AuBYP 90*
Sasaki, Toshio 1946- *WhoAmA 91*
Sasaki-Black, Karen Yukari *BiDrAPA 89*
Sasayama, Takao 1937- *WhoE 91*
Sasdi, George P. 1934- *St&PR 91, WhoAm 90*
Saseen, Sharon Louise 1949- *WhoSSW 91*
Sasek, Gloria Burns 1926- *WhoAmW 91, WhoSSW 91*
Sasek, Susan Kaye 1958- *WhoAmW 91*

Sasenick, Joseph Anthony 1940- WhoAm 90
Sashin, Jerome I. BioIn 16
Sashin, Jerome I 1940- BiDrAPA 89
Sasiadek, John D. 1943- St&PR 91
Sasloff, Alan I. 1935- St&PR 91
Saslofsky, Harry Israel 1935- WhoE 91
Saslow, George 1906- BiDrAPA 89, WhoAm 90
Saslow, Jerome A. 1938- St&PR 91
Sasmor, James Cecil 1920- WhoSSW 91, WhoWor 91
Sasmor, Jeannette Louise 1943- WhoAmW 91
Sass, Anna Maria BiDrAPA 89
Sass, Arthur Harold 1928- WhoE 91, WhoWor 91
Sass, David Werner 1935- WhoE 91
Sass, Else Kai 1912-1987 BioIn 16
Sass, Lorna J. BioIn 16
Sass, Robert William 1933- St&PR 91
Sass, Sylvia 1951- IntWWM 90, PenDiMP
Sass-Glaser, Ruth 1919?- BioIn 16
Sassacus 1560?-1637 EncCRAm, WhNaAH
Sasseen, George Thiery 1928- WhoSSW 91
Sasseen, Robert Francis 1932- WhoAm 90
Sassen, Anne 1958- IntWWM 90
Sassen, Saskia 1947- WhoHisp 91
Sassenrath, Julius Marlin 1923- WhoAm 90
Sasser, Bob 1951- St&PR 91
Sasser, Bruce Kent 1949- WhoE 91
Sasser, Charles Eugene 1946- St&PR 91
Sasser, Edward Rhone 1937- St&PR 91
Sasser, James Ralph 1936- WhoAm 90, WhoSSW 91, WhoWor 91
Sasser, Jim 1936- NewYTBS 90 [port]
Sasser, Jonathan Drew 1956- WhoEmL 91, WhoSSW 91
Sasser, Mackey 1962- Ballpl 90
Sasser, Sam Michael BiDrAPA 89
Sasser, William David 1962- WhoSSW 91, WhoWor 91
Sassetta 1392?-1450 IntDcAA 90
Sassetta, Stefano Di Giovanni 1392-1450? BioIn 16
Sasseville, Marc BiDrAPA 89
Sassi, Henry D. St&PR 91
Sassin, James Michael 1958- WhoSSW 91
Sasso, Anthony B. 1933- St&PR 91
Sasso, Cassandra Gay 1946- WhoAm 90
Sasso, Eleanor Catherine 1934- WhoAmW 91
Sasso, John BioIn 16
Sasson, Deborah 1955- IntWWM 90
Sasson, Michel 1935- WhoAm 90
Sasson Khadouri, Hakham BioIn 16
Sassone, Eugene Joseph 1953- WhoE 91
Sassone, Marco 1942- WhoAmA 91
Sassone, Ralph John 1926- St&PR 91
Sassoon, Adrian David 1961- WhoWor 91
Sassoon, Andre Gabriel 1936- WhoE 91
Sassoon, Siegfried 1886-1967 BioIn 16, MajTwCW, WorAlBi
Sassoon, Vidal 1928- WhoAm 90
Sassou-Nguesso, Denis WhoWor 91
Sastry, G M 1934- BiDrAPA 89
Sastry, Gayathri BiDrAPA 89
Sastry, Shankaranarayana 1938- WhoWor 91
Sasvari, George S. 1924- WhoSSW 91
Sata, Lindbergh S 1928- BiDrAPA 89
Sataloff, Robert Thayer 1949- IntWWM 90
Sataniski EncCoWW
Satank 1810?-1871 WhNaAH
Satanowski, Robert Zdzislaw 1918- IntWWM 90
Satanta 1830-1878 WhNaAH
Satava, George Louis 1946- St&PR 91
Satchel, Dorethea Browning 1942- WhoAmW 91
Satchell, Carol Alexis 1945- WhoWrEP 89
Satchell, Cynthia Vale 1957- BiDrAPA 89
Satchell, David NewAgMG
Satchell, Roy C. 1929- St&PR 91
Satcher, David 1941- St&PR 91
Satchidananda, Swami 1914- EncO&P 3, NewAgE 90
Satchler, George Raymond 1926- WhoAm 90
Satchwell, John BioIn 16
Sateja, John Joseph 1952- St&PR 91
Satel, Sally Louise 1956- BiDrAPA 89
Satell, Margaret Cox 1947- WhoAmW 91
Sater, Gail Beseth 1949- WhoAmW 91
Saterbo, Richard Dean 1929- WhoSSW 91
Sateren, Leland Bernhard 1913- IntWWM 90
Satern, Miriam Nella 1951- WhoAmW 91
Saternow, Pauline Virginia 1946- WhoEmL 91
Satersmoen, Theodore 1923- BiDrAPA 89
Satha-Anand, Chaiwat 1955- WhoWor 91
Sathananthan, Sivapragasam 1957- WhoSSW 91
Sathe, Sharad Somnath 1940- WhoAm 90
Satheesachandran, Chiyyarath V BiDrAPA 89
Sather, Glen Cameron 1943- WhoAm 90
Sather, John Henry 1921- WhoAm 90
Sathianathan, Inpeswaran BiDrAPA 89
Sathre, Leroy 1936- WhoSSW 91
Sathya Sai Baba 1926- EncPaPR 91
Sati Beg WomWR
Satian, Sarkis 1938- WhoE 91
Satie, Erik 1866-1925 BioIn 16, PenDiMP A, WorAlBi
Satin, David G 1933- BiDrAPA 89
Satin, Joseph 1920- WhoAm 90
Satin, Mark Ivor 1946- WhoE 91
Satinover, Jeffrey 1947- BiDrAPA 89
Satinover, Jeffrey Burke 1947- WhoAm 90, WhoE 91
Satinover, Terry Klieman 1936- WhoAmW 91
Satinskas, Henry A. 1936- St&PR 91
Satinskas, Henry Anthony 1936- WhoAm 90
Satinsky, Barnett 1947- WhoEmL 91
Satinsky, Victor Paul BiDrAPA 89
Satir, Virginia M. 1916-1988 BioIn 16
Satish, Sheo 1948- WhoWor 91
Satisky, Donald B. 1938- St&PR 91
Satlin, Andrew 1954- BiDrAPA 89, WhoE 91
Satloff, Aaron 1934- BiDrAPA 89, WhoE 91
Satlow, Marcia Faith Elaine 1949- WhoAmW 91
Sato Eisaku 1901-1975 EncJap
Sato, Eisaku 1901-1975 WorAlBi
Sato, Eunice Noda 1921- WhoAm 90
Sato, Frank Saburo 1929- WhoAm 90
Sato, Gordon Hisashi 1927- WhoAm 90
Sato, Haruo 1935- WhoWor 91
Sato, Hideo 1942- WhoWor 91
Sato, Hiroko 1942- WhoWor 91
Sato, Hiroshi 1918- WhoAm 90
Sato, Isao BioIn 16
Sato, Junzo 1937 WhoWor 91
Sato, Kazunori St&PR 91
Sato, Kazuya 1942- WhoSSW 91
Sato, Kazuyoshi 1930- WhoE 91
Sato, Kitaru 1939- St&PR 91
Sato, Koji 1938- WhoWor 91
Sato, Makiko 1947- WhoAmW 91
Sato, Masaaki 1941- WhoAmA 91
Sato, Masachiyo 1926- WhoWor 91
Sato, Masuko 1938- WhoWor 91
Sato, Motoaki 1929- WhoSSW 91
Sato, Nobuyuki 1929- WhoWor 91
Sato, Noriaki 1928- WhoWor 91
Sato, Norie 1949- WhoAmA 91
Sato, Shizuo BioIn 16
Sato, Shozo 1933- WhoWor 91
Sato, Tadashi 1923- WhoAmA 91
Sato, Takuya 1935- BiDrAPA 89
Sato, Tsuyoshi 1943- WhoAm 90
Satoh, Jiro 1935- WhoWor 91
Satoh, Somei NewAgMG
Satoh, Tsugihiko 1925- WhoWor 91
Satoh, Yoshiharu 1928- St&PR 91, WhoAm 90
Satolli, Roberto 1948- WhoWor 91
Satonaka, Hideto 1933-1989 BioIn 16
Satorsky, Cyril WhoAmA 91
Satou, Alan Hanry BiDrAPA 89
Satovsky, Abraham 1907- WhoAm 90
Satowaki, Joseph Asajiro 1904- WhoWor 91
Satran, George 1931- BiDrAPA 89
Satre, Philip Glen 1949- WhoAm 90
Satre, Wendell Julian 1918- St&PR 91
Satriani, Joe BioIn 16
Satriani, Joe 1957?- ConMus 4 [port]
Satriano, Tom 1940- Ballpl 90
Sattee, Andrew L. 1920- WhoAm 90
Sattel, Leonard 1924- BiDrAPA 89
Satten, Joseph 1921- BiDrAPA 89
Satten, Neal Richard BiDrAPA 89
Satten, Neal Richard 1949- WhoE 91
Satter, Marlene Yvonne 1952- WhoWrEP 89
Satter, Ruth BioIn 16
Satterfield, Ben 1945- WhoWrEP 89
Satterfield, Carol Mink 1941- WhoSSW 91
Satterfield, Charles MajTwCW
Satterfield, Charles Nelson 1921- WhoAm 90
Satterfield, David E. 1920-1988 BioIn 16
Satterfield, James H 1921- BiDrAPA 89
Satterfield, John Edward 1931- WhoAmA 91
Satterfield, Mark Edward 1955- WhoSSW 91
Satterfield, Mary McAden 1911- WhoAmW 91
Satterfield, Michael Steven 1955- WhoSSW 91
Satterfield, Richard T BiDrAPA 89
Satterfield, Robert Wayne 1926- St&PR 91
Satterfield, Russell L. 1911- St&PR 91
Satterfield, Sharon Burgan BiDrAPA 89
Satterlee, W. Bryan, Jr. 1934- St&PR 91
Satterlund, Frederic Paul 1956- St&PR 91
Satterly, Jack 1906- WhoAm 90
Satterthwaite, Cameron B. 1920- WhoAm 90
Satterthwaite, Helen Foster 1928- WhoAmW 91
Satterthwaite, James Sheafe BioIn 16
Satterthwaite, Joseph C. NewYTBS 90
Satterwhite, Cynthia Bennett 1955- WhoSSW 91
Satterwhite, Debra Dawn 1949- WhoAmW 91
Satterwhite, James BioIn 16
Satterwhite, Mark Alan 1947- WhoSSW 91
Satterwhite, William T. 1933- St&PR 91
Satti, Venkata Subbi Reddy 1939- BiDrAPA 89
Satti, Venkata Subbireddy 1939- WhoE 91
Sattin, Albert 1931- BiDrAPA 89
Sattin, Lonnie DrBlPA 90
Sattin, Tina DrBlPA 90
Sattler, Carol Ann 1946- WhoAmW 91
Sattler, Helen Roney BioIn 16
Sattler, Helen Roney 1921- AuBYP 90, ConAu 31NR, WhoWrEP 89
Sattler, John E. 1919- ODwPR 91
Sattler, Lee A. 1920- St&PR 91
Satuloff, Barth 1945- WhoSSW 91
Satuloff, Robert Lawrence 1942- WhoE 91
Saturday, Karen Renee 1961- WhoAmW 91
Saturday, Larry C. 1947- WhoSSW 91
Saturen, Ben 1948- WhoAmA 91
Saturnesky, Ruth WhoAmA 91
Satya Sai Baba 1926- EncO&P 3
Satyanand, David BiDrAPA 89
Satyshur, Rosemarie Frances DiMauro 1955- WhoAmW 91
Satz, Janet M 1933- WhoAmA 91
Satz, Louis K. 1927- WhoAm 90
Satz, Michael Ellis 1948- WhoE 91
Satz, Phyllis Robyne Sdoia 1935- WhoAmW 91, WhoSSW 91
Sau Sanchez, Victoria 1930- EncCoWW
Sauceda, Richard 1965- WhoHisp 91
Saucedo, Robert 1932- WhoAm 90
Saucier, Albert Pierre, Jr. 1959- WhoSSW 91
Saucier, Kevin 1956- Ballpl 90
Saucke, M. M. 1927- St&PR 91
Sauckel, Fritz 1894-1946 BioIn 16
Saud Al-Faisal, Prince 1941- WhoWor 91
Sauder, Elizabeth Lynn 1949- St&PR 91
Sauder, Erie Joseph 1904- WhoAm 90
Sauder, Michael Hockensmith 1948- WhoSSW 91
Sauder, Richard Eugene 1923- St&PR 91
Sauer, Carl Andrew 1960- WhoSSW 91
Sauer, Colin PenDiMP
Sauer, Conrad Frederick, III 1923- St&PR 91
Sauer, David Andrew 1948- WhoE 91
Sauer, Douglas C. 1943- St&PR 91
Sauer, Elisabeth Ruth 1948- WhoEmL 91
Sauer, Emil von 1862-1942 PenDiMP
Sauer, Frank James 1946- WhoSSW 91
Sauer, Gordon Chenoweth 1921- WhoAm 90, WhoWor 91
Sauer, Hank 1917- Ballpl 90
Sauer, Harold 1918- St&PR 91
Sauer, Harold John 1953- WhoEmL 91
Sauer, Harry John, Jr. 1935- WhoAm 90
Sauer, J George 1916- St&PR 91
Sauer, Jane Gottlieb 1937- WhoAmA 91
Sauer, Jean Covert 1931- BiDrAPA 89
Sauer, Jeffery Joseph 1956- WhoEmL 91
Sauer, John Robert 1936- WhoSSW 91
Sauer, Jonathan Deininger 1918- WhoAm 90
Sauer, Kenneth 1931- WhoAm 90
Sauer, Louis E. 1915- St&PR 91
Sauer, Mary Julia 1949- WhoAmW 91, WhoE 91
Sauer, Richard John 1939- WhoE 91
Sauer, Robert H 1934- BiDrAPA 89
Sauer, Walter R. 1936- St&PR 91
Sauerberg, Robert Allen 1930- St&PR 91
Sauerbrey, Ellen Elaine Richmond 1937- WhoAmW 91, WhoE 91
Sauerbruch, Tilman 1946- WhoWor 91
Sauereisen, Phil F. 1930- St&PR 91
Sauerhaft, Stan 1926- ODwPR 91, WhoAm 90
Sauerhoff, Jeffrey M. 1949- St&PR 91
Sauers, Clayton Henry 1926- St&PR 91
Sauers, Edward S. 1941- St&PR 91
Sauers, Harry Lechner 1938- BiDrAPA 89
Sauey, William R. 1927- St&PR 91
Saufley, William Edward 1956- St&PR 91, WhoAm 90
Saugen, Janet Norma 1935- WhoWor 91
Saugstad, Olaf WhoAmA 91N
Sauguet, Henri 1901-1989 BioIn 16
Saul WorAlBi
Saul, Adele Scott BioIn 16
Saul, Ann ODwPR 91
Saul, B. Francis, II 1932- WhoAm 90
Saul, Barbara Ann 1940- WhoAmW 91
Saul, Bradley Scott 1960- WhoEmL 91, WhoWor 91
Saul, Connie Cline 1954- WhoAmW 91, WhoSSW 91
Saul, Deborah Mangum 1963- WhoAmW 91
Saul, Franklin Robert 1929- St&PR 91, WhoAm 90
Saul, George Brandon, II 1928- WhoAm 90
Saul, John BioIn 16
Saul, John 1942- BestSel 90-4 [port]
Saul, John Woodruff, III 1942- WhoAm 90, WhoWrEP 89
Saul, Kenneth Louis 1923- WhoAm 90
Saul, Leslie St&PR 91
Saul, Marjorie Ruth C 1953- BiDrAPA 89
Saul, Mark E. 1948- WhoWor 91
Saul, Nancy Goodwine 1952- WhoAmW 91
Saul, Norman Eugene 1932- WhoAm 90
Saul, Peter 1934- WhoAm 90, WhoAmA 91
Saul, Ralph Southey 1922- St&PR 91, WhoAm 90
Saul, Richard B 1935- BiDrAPA 89
Saul, Ronald John 1947- St&PR 91
Saul, Shura 1920- WhoE 91
Saul, Thomas Patious 1953- WhoSSW 91
Saul, W. James 1923- St&PR 91
Saulesco, Mircea Petre 1926- IntWWM 90
Saulino, John Louis 1944- St&PR 91
Saulness, Fiona 1956- WhoAmW 91
Saulnier, Jon St&PR 91
Saulniers, Alfred Hervey 1945- WhoE 91, WhoEmL 91
Sauls, Frederick Inabinette 1934- WhoAmA 91
Saulsbury, Olin Baker 1934- WhoSSW 91
Saulson, Harold 1953- WhoAmA 91
Saum, Elizabeth Pape 1930- WhoAmW 91
Saumier, Andre 1933- WhoAm 90
Saunby, John Brian 1933- WhoAm 90
Saunders, Alan J. 1943- St&PR 91
Saunders, Alan Keith 1947- WhoAm 90
Saunders, Albert Henry, II 1950- St&PR 91
Saunders, Alexander Hall 1941- WhoSSW 91
Saunders, Alexander W. 1941- St&PR 91
Saunders, Allen 1899-1986 EncACom
Saunders, Amos Charles 1934- WhoE 91
Saunders, Anne Z. 1928- WhoSSW 91
Saunders, Antoinette Mercier 1947- WhoAmW 91
Saunders, Antony Jefferis 1945- IntWWM 90
Saunders, Arlene 1935- IntWWM 90, WhoAm 90
Saunders, Aulus Ward 1904- WhoAmA 91
Saunders, Barry Wayne 1944- WhoSSW 91
Saunders, Beatrice Nair 1915- WhoAmW 91
Saunders, Betty Huey 1909- WhoE 91, WhoWor 91
Saunders, Blanche 1906-1964 AuBYP 90
Saunders, Brenda M. 1947- WhoSSW 91
Saunders, Caleb AuBYP 90, MajTwCW
Saunders, Carol Silver 1953- WhoAmW 91
Saunders, Catherine Hoover 1948- WhoE 91
Saunders, Catherine Ruggie 1951- WhoWrEP 89
Saunders, Charles Baskerville, Jr. 1928- WhoAm 90
Saunders, Charles Edward 1932- St&PR 91
Saunders, Cicely BioIn 16
Saunders, Clara Rosman WhoAmA 91N
Saunders, Dero Ames 1913- WhoAm 90, WhoWrEP 89
Saunders, Dickson M. 1920- St&PR 91
Saunders, Donald H. 1935- St&PR 91
Saunders, Donald Herbert 1935- WhoAm 90
Saunders, Donald Leslie 1935- WhoAm 90
Saunders, Doris Evans 1921- WhoAm 90, WhoWrEP 89
Saunders, Douglas J. 1942- St&PR 91
Saunders, Edgar Bogue, Jr. 1933- St&PR 91
Saunders, Edith Dariel Chase 1922- WhoAmA 91
Saunders, Edward Watts 1860-1921 AmLegL
Saunders, Elizabeth BiDEWW
Saunders, Ernest Walter 1935- BioIn 16
Saunders, Evalina Loretta 1938- WhoE 91
Saunders, F. Guy 1940- St&PR 91
Saunders, Francis J. 1927- ConAu 131
Saunders, Francis Miller 1916- St&PR 91
Saunders, Frank ConAu 131
Saunders, Frank A. BioIn 16
Saunders, Frank Henry 1934- WhoWor 91
Saunders, Frederick Albert 1875-1963 DcScB S2
Saunders, George Lawton, Jr. 1931- WhoAm 90, WhoWor 91
Saunders, George Wendell 1917- WhoE 91

Saunders, Gillian Marguerite 1956- *WhoWor 91*
Saunders, Gregory T. 1956- *St&PR 91*
Saunders, Harold E. 1925- *St&PR 91*
Saunders, Harold Henry 1930- *WhoAm 90*
Saunders, Helen 1885-1963 *BiDWomA*
Saunders, Herbert G. 1937- *St&PR 91*
Saunders, Hilary 1956- *IntWWM 90*
Saunders, Hilary Aiden St. George *TwCCr&M 91*
Saunders, J. B. 1901- *St&PR 91*
Saunders, J Boyd 1937- *WhoAmA 91*
Saunders, Jackie *ODwPR 91*
Saunders, James Harwood 1948- *WhoWor 91*
Saunders, James Henry 1923- *WhoAm 90*
Saunders, James S. 1943- *St&PR 91*
Saunders, Jennelle Carroll *BiDrAPA 89*
Saunders, John Charles 1949- *St&PR 91*
Saunders, John D. 1926- *St&PR 91*
Saunders, John Harvey 1939- *WhoAm 90*
Saunders, John Howard 1957- *WhoSSW 91*
Saunders, John Louis 1937- *WhoSSW 91*
Saunders, John Martin 1916- *WhoWor 91*
Saunders, John R *BiDrAPA 89*
Saunders, John Richard 1925- *WhoE 91*
Saunders, John William, Jr. 1935- *WhoSSW 91*
Saunders, Joseph Arthur 1926- *St&PR 91, WhoE 91, WhoWor 91*
Saunders, Joseph Francis 1950- *WhoAm 90*
Saunders, Joyce Carol 1938- *WhoAmW 91*
Saunders, Karen Estelle 1941- *WhoAmW 91, WhoWor 91*
Saunders, Katharine Christine 1965- *WhoEmL 91*
Saunders, Kathryn A. 1920- *WhoAmW 91*
Saunders, Keith C. 1942- *St&PR 91*
Saunders, Kenneth D. 1927- *WhoAm 90*
Saunders, Laurel Barnes 1926- *WhoAmW 91*
Saunders, Lonna Jeanne *WhoWor 91*
Saunders, Lonna Jeanne 1952- *WhoEmL 91*
Saunders, Lucy Leatherbee 1957- *WhoAmW 91*
Saunders, Margaret Marshall 1861-1947 *DcLB 92 [port], FemiCLE*
Saunders, Mary Noel 1935- *St&PR 91*
Saunders, Michael Edwin 1950- *WhoE 91*
Saunders, Neil 1918- *IntWWM 90*
Saunders, Owen 1904- *WhoWor 91*
Saunders, Patricia Gene 1946- *WhoAmW 91*
Saunders, Paul *PenDiDA 89*
Saunders, Paul Christopher 1941- *WhoAm 90*
Saunders, Peter Paul 1928- *St&PR 91, WhoAm 90*
Saunders, Phyllis S. 1942- *WhoAmW 91*
Saunders, Raymond Jennings 1934- *WhoAm 90, WhoAmA 91*
Saunders, Rebecca Ann 1949- *WhoAmW 91*
Saunders, Rhona E. *ODwPR 91*
Saunders, Richard Faye 1919- *St&PR 91*
Saunders, Richard Gayne, Jr. 1951- *St&PR 91*
Saunders, Richard Henry, III 1949- *WhoE 91*
Saunders, Richard P. *NewYTBS 90*
Saunders, Richard T. *ODwPR 91*
Saunders, Robert Leonard 1948- *WhoEmL 91*
Saunders, Robert Mallough 1915- *WhoAm 90*
Saunders, Robert Samuel 1951- *WhoE 91, WhoWor 91*
Saunders, Robert Walter 1959- *WhoSSW 91*
Saunders, Roger A. *BioIn 16*
Saunders, Roger Alfred 1929- *WhoAm 90*
Saunders, Ron 1954- *WhoSSW 91*
Saunders, Rubie Agnes 1929- *WhoAm 90, WhoWrEP 89*
Saunders, Russell Joseph 1937- *WhoAm 90*
Saunders, Ruth Lynch 1927- *WhoAmW 91*
Saunders, Sally Love 1940- *WhoAm 90, WhoAmW 91, WhoWrEP 89*
Saunders, Sam Cundiff 1931- *WhoAm 90*
Saunders, Samuel Paul 1914- *St&PR 91*
Saunders, Stephen Darall 1941- *WhoSSW 91*
Saunders, Steven Hirsch 1955- *St&PR 91*
Saunders, Stuart John 1931- *WhoWor 91*
Saunders, Stuart Thomas, Jr. 1941- *St&PR 91, WhoAm 90*
Saunders, Susan Presley 1956- *WhoAmW 91*
Saunders, Suzanne 1947- *BioIn 16*
Saunders, Ted Elliott 1952- *WhoSSW 91*
Saunders, Thomas R. 1946- *St&PR 91*
Saunders, Toni Lynne 1949- *WhoAmW 91, WhoEmL 91*
Saunders, Trevor John 1934- *WhoWor 91*
Saunders, V. Lamoine 1941- *St&PR 91*
Saunders, Wade 1949- *WhoAmA 91*
Saunders, Ward Bishop, Jr. 1919- *WhoAm 90*
Saunders, William Hundley, Jr. 1926- *WhoAm 90*
Saunders, William John 1943- *St&PR 91*
Saunders, William Lockwood 1911- *WhoAm 90*
Saunders-Henderson, Martha Mae 1924- *WhoE 91*
Saunders-Spencer, Brenda Dee 1962- *WhoAmW 91*
Saunier, Bernard-Marie 1948- *WhoWor 91*
Saunier, Claude-Charles 1735-1807 *PenDiDA 89*
Saunier, Jacques 1948- *WhoWor 91*
Saunier-Seite, Alice Louise 1925- *BiDFrPL*
Sauntry, Susan Schaefer 1943- *WhoAmW 91*
Saupe, William A. 1928- *St&PR 91*
Saur, Ronald Garlin 1950- *WhoSSW 91*
Saura, Carlos *BioIn 16*
Saura, Carlos 1932- *ConAu 131, HispWr 90*
Sauret, Emile 1852-1920 *PenDiMP*
Sause, Helen L. *BioIn 16*
Sause, William T. 1916- *St&PR 91*
Sausedo, Ann Elizabeth 1929- *WhoAmW 91*
Sausedo, Robert A. *WhoHisp 91*
Sausen, Allen A. 1948- *St&PR 91*
Sauser-Hall, Frederic 1887-1961 *MajTwCW*
Sausville, Albert Joseph 1949- *St&PR 91*
Sautarel, Francois Michel 1947- *WhoWor 91*
Sauter, Charles H. 1942- *St&PR 91*
Sauter, Eddie 1914-1981 *BioIn 16, OxCPMus*
Sauter, Eric 1948- *TwCCr&M 91*
Sauter, Franz Fabian 1933- *WhoWor 91*
Sauter, John Valentine 1939- *WhoSSW 91*
Sauter, Paul Jonathan 1962- *WhoE 91*
Sauter, Roy Jacob 1930- *St&PR 91*
Sauter, Van Gordon *BioIn 16*
Sauter, Walter August 1925- *St&PR 91*
Sauter-Bailliet, Theresia 1932- *WhoWor 91*
Sautet, Claude 1924- *BioIn 16*
Sautter, Hermann 1938- *WhoWor 91*
Sautter, R. Craig 1947- *WhoWrEP 89*
Sautter, Richard Daniel 1926- *WhoAm 90*
Sautuola, Maria de 1870-1946 *BioIn 16*
Sauvage, Charles-Gabriel *PenDiDA 89*
Sauvage, Jean Andre 1945- *WhoWor 91*
Sauvage, Leo *BioIn 16*
Sauvage, Michael 1948- *WhoWor 91*
Sauvageau, Philippe 1940- *WhoWor 91*
Sauvageau, Yves 1946-1970 *OxCCanT*
Sauvageot, Ludel *BioIn 16*
Sauve, Georges 1925- *WhoWor 91*
Sauve, Jacqueline Annmary 1943- *WhoAmW 91*
Sauve, Jeanne 1922- *WhoAm 90, WhoAmW 91, WhoE 91, WhoWor 91*
Sauvey, Donald 1924- *WhoAm 90*
Sauvier, Maria Consuela *BiDrAPA 89*
Sauzo, Richard *WhoHisp 91*
Savabi, Fatemeh 1948- *WhoEmL 91*
Savage, Adrienne Elizabeth 1928- *St&PR 91*
Savage, Alan Clyde 1942- *St&PR 91*
Savage, Albert Russell 1847-1917 *AmLegL*
Savage, Archie *DrBIPA 90*
Savage, Arthur L. *WhoAm 90*
Savage, Augusta 1900-1962 *WhoAmA 91N*
Savage, Augusta Christine 1892-1962 *BiDWomA*
Savage, Beryl *BioIn 16*
Savage, Blair deWillis 1941- *WhoAm 90*
Savage, Blake *ConAu 131*
Savage, Blake 1914-1990 *BioIn 16*
Savage, Bob 1921- *Ballpl 90*
Savage, Carlton Raymond 1897-1990 *ConAu 131*
Savage, Charles 1918- *BiDrAPA 89*
Savage, Charles Roscoe 1832-1909 *WhNaAH*
Savage, Christopher William 1956- *WhoE 91*
Savage, Dave 1948- *St&PR 91*
Savage, David *BioIn 16*
Savage, Donald C. *WhoAm 90, WhoWrEP 89*
Savage, Donald George 1925- *St&PR 91*
Savage, Donna Marie 1953- *WhoAmW 91*
Savage, Edward Warren, Jr. 1933- *WhoAm 90*
Savage, Ernest 1918- *TwCCr&M 91*
Savage, Ethel Mary Dell 1881-1939 *BioIn 16*
Savage, Frank *BioIn 16*
Savage, Frank 1938- *WhoAm 90*
Savage, Fred *BioIn 16*
Savage, Fred 1976- *ConTFT 8 [port], News 90 [port]*
Savage, Gale Eleanor *WhoAmW 91*
Savage, George Alfred 1914- *St&PR 91*
Savage, Graham 1886-1981 *DcNaB 1981*
Savage, Grant Theodore 1954- *WhoSSW 91*
Savage, Gus *BioIn 16*
Savage, Gus 1925- *BlkAmsC [port], WhoAm 90*
Savage, Harry 1936- *ODwPR 91*
Savage, Herbert Rosser 1919- *St&PR 91*
Savage, James Amos 1949- *WhoSSW 91*
Savage, James Cathey, III 1947- *WhoE 91*
Savage, James Francis 1939- *WhoAm 90*
Savage, Jerry 1936- *WhoAmA 91*
Savage, John Edmund 1939- *WhoAm 90*
Savage, John William, Jr. 1951- *WhoEmL 91*
Savage, Jon *ConAu 129*
Savage, Joseph George *WhoE 91*
Savage, Katharine James 1905-1989 *SmATA 61*
Savage, Leonard Jimmie 1917-1971 *DcScB S2*
Savage, Lloyd Calvin 1923- *IntWWM 90*
Savage, M. *FemiCLE*
Savage, Marcia A. *WhoAm 90, WhoAmW 91*
Savage, Mary Helen 1956- *WhoAmW 91*
Savage, Minot Judson 1841-1918 *EncO&P 3*
Savage, Naomi 1927- *WhoAm 90, WhoAmA 91*
Savage, Neve Richard 1944- *WhoAm 90*
Savage, Patricia Werner 1949- *WhoAmW 91, WhoE 91*
Savage, Paul *BioIn 16*
Savage, Randall Ernest 1939- *WhoAm 90*
Savage, Raymond C. 1938- *St&PR 91*
Savage, Richard 1697?-1743 *DcLB 95*
Savage, Richard Mark 1950- *WhoSSW 91*
Savage, Richard Nigel 1948- *WhoWor 91*
Savage, Richard R. 1925- *St&PR 91*
Savage, Robert Heath 1929- *WhoAm 90*
Savage, Robert J. 1951- *St&PR 91*
Savage, Robert L. 1937- *WhoSSW 91*
Savage, Robin Gordon 1960- *WhoE 91*
Savage, Roger 1941- *WhoAmA 91*
Savage, Sarah 1664-1752 *BiDEWW, FemiCLE*
Savage, Stephen Edman 1940- *WhoE 91*
Savage, Stephen Leon 1942- *IntWWM 90*
Savage, Stephen William 1953- *WhoE 91*
Savage, Ted 1937- *Ballpl 90*
Savage, Terry L. 1952- *St&PR 91*
Savage, Thomas *BioIn 16*
Savage, Thomas 1915- *ConAu 132*
Savage, Thomas A. *BioIn 16*
Savage, Thomas Hixon 1928- *WhoAm 90*
Savage, Thomas Joseph 1947- *WhoAm 90*
Savage, Thomas U. 1948- *WhoWrEP 89*
Savage, Wallace Hamilton 1912- *WhoAm 90*
Savage, Walter P 1928- *BiDrAPA 89*
Savage, William Edward 1940- *WhoE 91*
Savage, William Lyttleton *BioIn 16*
Savage, William Russell *ODwPR 91*
Savage, William Woodrow 1914- *WhoAm 90*
Savage, Xyla Ruth 1937- *WhoAm 90*
Savageau, Michael Antonio 1940- *WhoAm 90*
Savak, Gregory E. 1951- *WhoSSW 91*
Savala, Leonard *WhoHisp 91*
Savalas, Telly *BioIn 16*
Savalas, Telly 1924- *WorAlBi*
Savalas, Telly Aristoteles 1926- *WhoAm 90*
Savalia, Harsukh J 1954- *BiDrAPA 89*
Savannah Jack *WhNaAH*
Savannah, Sheila *BioIn 16*
Savant, Marilyn Mach Vos *BioIn 16*
Savard, Edward Victor 1939- *WhoSSW 91*
Savard, Ghislaine *BiDrAPA 89*
Savard, Pierre 1936- *WhoWrEP 89*
Savard, Serge 1946- *WhoAm 90, WhoE 91*
Savarese, E. W. *St&PR 91*
Savarese, John *BioIn 16*
Savarese, Joseph A., Jr. 1924- *St&PR 91*
Savarese, Louis A. 1926- *St&PR 91*
Savariego, Bernardo *BiDrAPA 89*
Savariego, Samuel *WhoHisp 91*
Savarino, Samuel Joseph 1958- *WhoE 91*
Savarkar, Vinayak Damodar 1883-1966 *BioIn 16*
Savary, Alain 1918-1988 *AnObit 1988, BioIn 16*
Savary, Alain Francois 1918-1988 *BiDFrPL*
Savary-Ogden, Geraldine 1929- *WhoAmW 91*
Savaryn, Peter 1926- *WhoAm 90*
Savas, Emanuel S. 1931- *WhoAm 90*
Savas, Jo-Ann 1934- *WhoAmA 91*
Savaskan, Sinan Carter 1954- *IntWWM 90*
Saveanu, Radu Vasile 1955- *BiDrAPA 89*
Savedge, Anne Creery 1947- *WhoSSW 91*
Savedoff, Jamie Phillip 1948- *WhoE 91*
Savedra, Jo Ann 1960- *WhoHisp 91*
Savedra, Ruben 1932- *WhoHisp 91*
Saveeah *DcCanB 12*
Saveland, Robert Nelson 1921- *WhoWrEP 89*
Savelkoul, Donald Charles 1917- *WhoAm 90*
Savell, Edward Lupo 1921- *WhoAm 90*
Savellano, Leticia *BiDrAPA 89*
Savellano, Romeo L *BiDrAPA 89*
Savelli, Angelo 1911- *WhoAm 90*
Saven, Bjorn Erik 1950- *WhoAm 90, WhoEmL 91, WhoWor 91*
Savenor, Betty Carmell 1927- *WhoAmA 91*
Saver, Gordon *BiDrAPA 89*
Saveriano, G. J. 1922- *St&PR 91*
Saverin, Ronald F. 1950- *St&PR 91*
Saverine, Bob 1941- *Ballpl 90*
Savery, Constance 1897- *AuBYP 90*
Savery, William 1721-1788 *PenDiDA 89*
Savesky, Robert S. 1940- *St&PR 91*
Saveth, Edward Norman 1915- *WhoAm 90, WhoWrEP 89*
Savett, Marc I 1948- *BiDrAPA 89*
Savi, Ethel 1865-1954 *FemiCLE*
Saviano, Carl R 1940- *BiDrAPA 89, WhoE 91*
Saviano, John Paul 1940- *St&PR 91*
Savicky, Randolph Philip 1953- *WhoE 91, WhoWrEP 89*
Saviers, F. Grant 1944- *WhoAm 90*
Savignac, Antonio Enriquez *BioIn 16*
Savile of Rufford, John S Lumley, Baron 1818-1896 *BioIn 16*
Savill, Patrick Stanley 1909- *IntWWM 90*
Saville, Curtis 1946- *BioIn 16*
Saville, Dudley Albert 1933- *WhoAm 90*
Saville, Eric Joseph 1919- *St&PR 91*
Saville, Katherine 1667-1755 *BiDEWW*
Saville, Kathleen 1956- *BioIn 16*
Saville, Ken 1949- *WhoAmA 91*
Saville, Lynn Adele 1950- *WhoAmW 91*
Saville, Royce Blair 1948- *WhoEmL 91*
Saville, Thorndike, Jr. 1925- *WhoAm 90*
Saville, Wendy 1949- *BiDrAPA 89*
Saville-Troike, Muriel Renee 1936- *WhoAm 90*
Savimbi, Jonas 1934- *BioIn 16*
Savin, Daniel Maynard 1960- *BiDrAPA 89*
Savin, Kenneth Philip 1952- *WhoE 91*
Savin, Robert Shevryn 1925- *St&PR 91*
Savin, Ronald Richard 1926- *WhoWor 91*
Savin, Samuel Marvin 1940- *WhoAm 90*
Savinelli, Emilio Alfred 1930- *WhoAm 90*
Savini, Donato Anthony 1939- *St&PR 91*
Savini, Richard *BioIn 16*
Savinkov, Boris 1879-1925 *BioIn 16*
Savino, April *BioIn 16*
Savino, Beatriz *WhoHisp 91*
Savino, Evelyn Goldstein Buhler 1916- *WhoAmW 91*
Savino, Frank John 1930- *St&PR 91*
Savino, John *BiDrAPA 89*
Savino, Peter J. 1942- *WhoAm 90*
Savino, Salvatore M. 1943- *St&PR 91*
Savino-Jones, Marie Dauphine 1961- *WhoAmW 91*
Savinsky, Dennis Michael *BiDrAPA 89*
Saviori, John Conley 1922- *St&PR 91*
Saviskas, Judson P. 1953- *St&PR 91*
Savit, Carl H. 1922- *BioIn 16*
Savit, Carl Hertz 1922- *WhoAm 90*
Savitch, Jessica 1947-1983 *BioAmW, BioIn 16*
Savitskaya, Svetlana *BioIn 16*
Savitske, M. B. 1941- *St&PR 91*
Savitsky, Daniel 1921- *WhoAm 90, WhoE 91*
Savitsky, David R. 1948- *St&PR 91*
Savitsky, Elias *BiDrAPA 89*
Savitsky, John 1910- *MusmAFA*
Savitsky, Stephen J. 1945- *St&PR 91*
Savitsky, Yevgeny Y. 1910-1990 *BioIn 16*
Savitt, Jan 1908-1948 *OxCPMus*
Savitt, Jan 1912-1948 *BioIn 16*
Savitt, Robert A *BiDrAPA 89*
Savitt, Sam *WhoAmA 91*
Savitt, Sam 1917- *AuBYP 90*
Savitt, Sidney Allan 1920- *WhoAm 90*
Savitt, Susan Schenkel 1943- *WhoWor 91*
Savitz, Frieda 1931-1985 *WhoAmA 91N*
Savitz, Harriet May 1933- *AuBYP 90, ConAu 32NR*
Savitz, Joel Lawrence 1944- *BiDrAPA 89*
Savitz, Lily 1933- *IntWWM 90*
Savitz, Maxine Lazarus 1937- *WhoAmW 91*
Savitz, Richard J. 1946- *St&PR 91*
Savitz, S Alan *BiDrAPA 89*
Savitz, Sam 1915- *St&PR 91*
Savitz, Samuel J. 1936- *WhoAm 90*
Savitzky, David C *BiDrAPA 89*
Savko, Ed *BioIn 16*
Savla, Lalit 1938- *BiDrAPA 89*
Savodnik, Irwin *BiDrAPA 89*
Savoie, L. 1943- *St&PR 91*
Savoie, Leonard Norman 1928- *St&PR 91, WhoAm 90*
Savoie, Louise de 1476-1531 *EncCoWW*
Savoie, Philip Oscar 1939- *St&PR 91*

Savoie, Terrence Maurice 1946- WhoWrEP 89
Savoldi, Gloria Root AuBYP 90
Savolt, Louann Sue 1942- WhoAmW 91
Savona, Michael Richard 1947- WhoEmL 91, WhoWor 91
Savonarola, Girolamo 1452-1498 BioIn 16, WorAlBi
Savonuzzi, Giovanni 1912- BioIn 16
Savopoulos, Haris 1954- WhoWor 91
Savory, Harry BioIn 16
Savory, Teo 1907-1989 ConAu 31NR
Savoy, Chyrl Lenore 1944- WhoAmA 91
Savoy, Douglas Eugene 1927- WhoAm 90, WhoWor 91, WhoWrEP 89
Savoy, Harold 1924- St&PR 91
Savoy, Jacqueline Sandra 1951- WhoAmW 91
Savoy, James Cunningham 1930- WhoAm 90
Savoy, Marguerite de 1523-1574? EncCoWW
Savoy, Suzanne Marie 1946- WhoEmL 91
Savrann, Richard Allen 1935- WhoAm 90
Savren, Shelley 1949- WhoWrEP 89
Savrin, Louis 1927- WhoAm 90
Savyckyj, Jurij 1944- BiDrAPA 89
Saw Maung WhoWor 91
Sawabini, Nabil George 1951- WhoAm 90, WhoE 91
Sawabini, Wadi Issa 1917- WhoAm 90
Sawada, Ikune 1936- WhoAmA 91
Sawada, Nobuaki 1922- WhoWor 91
Sawada, Toshio 1933- WhoWor 91
Sawada, Tsuguo 1941- WhoWor 91
Sawai, Atsuhiro 1939- WhoWor 91
Sawai, Noboru 1931- WhoAmA 91
Sawallisch, Wolfgang 1923- IntWWM 90, PenDiMP, WhoWor 91
Sawamura, Eiji 1915-1945 Ballpl 90
Saward, Ernest W. 1914-1989 BioIn 16
Sawatski, Carl 1927- Ballpl 90
Sawayama, Toshitami 1934- WhoWor 91
Sawchuck, Terry 1929-1970 WorAlBi
Sawchuk, Ronald John 1940- WhoAm 90
Sawczyk, Josephine BiDrAPA 89
Sawdei, Milan A. 1946- St&PR 91
Sawdey, Richard M. 1943- St&PR 91
Sawdey, Richard Marshall 1943- WhoAm 90
Sawer, David 1961- IntWWM 90
Sawers, Peter Ritchie 1933- St&PR 91
Sawey, George Vincent 1928- St&PR 91
Sawh, Lall Ramnath 1951- WhoWor 91
Sawhill, Isabel V 1937- ConAu 130
Sawhill, Isabel Van Devanter 1937- WhoAm 90
Sawhill, John Crittenden 1936- WhoAm 90
Sawi, Ahmed Lotfi BiDrAPA 89
Sawicki, Craig Randall 1959- St&PR 91
Sawicki, Holly 1954- WhoAmW 91
Sawicki, Katherine Rivas 1929- WhoAmW 91
Sawicki, Norma Jean AuBYP 90
Sawicki, Thomas 1945- St&PR 91, WhoAm 90
Sawicz, Edward J. St&PR 91
Sawin, Nancy Churchman 1917- WhoAm 90
Sawinski, Vincent John 1925- WhoAm 90
Sawiris, Milad Youssef 1922- WhoAm 90
Sawiya DcCanB 12
Sawka, Jan 1946- ConDes 90
Sawka, Jan A 1946- WhoAmA 91
Sawkar, Venkatesh T. 1944- BiDrAPA 89
Sawle, William S., III 1924- St&PR 91
Sawrotnow, Parfeny Pavlovich 1924- WhoE 91
Sawtell, Stephen M. 1931- WhoAm 90
Sawtelle, Carl S. 1927- WhoE 91, WhoWor 91
Sawyer, Alan R 1919- WhoAmA 91
Sawyer, Amos BioIn 16
Sawyer, Anne V. ODwPR 91
Sawyer, Barbara Jean 1920- WhoWrEP 89
Sawyer, Blanche Melton 1932- WhoAmW 91
Sawyer, Bruce P. 1939- St&PR 91
Sawyer, C. Wilson 1945- St&PR 91
Sawyer, Carrie M. EncO&P 3
Sawyer, Celia Mae 1946- WhoAmW 91
Sawyer, Charles 1887-1979 BiDrUSE 89
Sawyer, Charles Glenn 1922- WhoAm 90
Sawyer, Charles Henry 1906- WhoAmA 91
Sawyer, Charles Henry 1915- WhoAm 90
Sawyer, Christopher Glenn 1950- WhoSSW 91
Sawyer, Constance Bragdon 1926- WhoAmW 91
Sawyer, Corinne Holt 1924- WhoWrEP 89
Sawyer, David Neal 1940- WhoSSW 91
Sawyer, Diane BioIn 16
Sawyer, Diane 1945- WhoAm 90, WhoAmW 91, WhoE 91, WorAlBi
Sawyer, Donald D. 1933- WhoWor 91
Sawyer, Donald Keith, Jr. 1930- St&PR 91
Sawyer, Dorothy Straker 1924- WhoAmW 91
Sawyer, Dwight Wesley 1933- St&PR 91
Sawyer, Eddie 1910- Ballpl 90
Sawyer, Forrest WhoAm 90
Sawyer, Frederick W. 1950- St&PR 91
Sawyer, Gene 1910- WhoAmW 91
Sawyer, George A. 1931- St&PR 91
Sawyer, Gregory Dean BiDrAPA 89
Sawyer, Helen WhoAmA 91
Sawyer, Helen Alton WhoAm 90, WhoAmW 91
Sawyer, Howard Jerome 1929- WhoAm 90
Sawyer, J Clay 1954- BiDrAPA 89
Sawyer, James L BiDrAPA 89
Sawyer, Jane Orrock 1944- WhoAmW 91
Sawyer, John WhoAm 90
Sawyer, John B 1933- BiDrAPA 89
Sawyer, John Edward 1917- WhoAm 90
Sawyer, John R 1953- WhoAmA 91
Sawyer, Katherine H. 1908- WhoAmW 91
Sawyer, Lisa Marie 1961- WhoE 91
Sawyer, Maria Artemis Papageorge WhoAmA 91
Sawyer, Marshall W. 1907- St&PR 91
Sawyer, Martha H. 1942- ODwPR 91
Sawyer, Michael Gifford 1948- BiDrAPA 89
Sawyer, Nancy Elizabeth 1961- WhoAmW 91
Sawyer, Philip Ayer WhoAmA 91N
Sawyer, Philip John 1948- IntWWM 90
Sawyer, Philip Nicholas 1925- WhoE 91
Sawyer, Philip R., Jr. 1947- St&PR 91
Sawyer, Phyllis Rose 1923- WhoAmW 91
Sawyer, Raymond Terry 1943- WhoAm 90
Sawyer, Rick 1948- Ballpl 90
Sawyer, Robert G. 1938- St&PR 91
Sawyer, Robert McLaran 1929- WhoAm 90
Sawyer, Robert William 1880-1959 BioIn 16
Sawyer, Ruth 1880-1970 AuBYP 90, BioAmW
Sawyer, Samuel Locke 1922- St&PR 91
Sawyer, Sydney White 1960- WhoAmW 91
Sawyer, Thomas C. ODwPR 91
Sawyer, Thomas C. 1945- WhoAm 90
Sawyer, Thomas Edgar 1932- WhoWor 91
Sawyer, Thomas William 1933- WhoAm 90
Sawyer, Warren Allen BioIn 16
Sawyer, Wells M 1863- WhoAmA 91N
Sawyer, Wilbur Henderson 1921- WhoAm 90
Sawyer, William 1920- WhoAmA 91
Sawyer, William Dale 1929- WhoAm 90
Sawyerr, Akilagpa 1939- WhoWor 91
Sawyers, Elizabeth Joan 1936- WhoAm 90, WhoAmW 91
Sawyers, John Lazelle 1925- WhoAm 90, WhoWor 91
Sawyers, June 1957- WhoWrEP 89
Sax, Albert M 1931- BiDrAPA 89
Sax, Barbara Louise 1934- BiDrAPA 89
Sax, Helen Spigel 1915- WhoAm 90
Sax, Joseph Lawrence 1936- WhoAm 90
Sax, Karl 1892-1973 DcScB S2
Sax, Leonard B. 1917- St&PR 91
Sax, Mary Randolph 1925- WhoAmW 91, WhoWor 91
Sax, Robert A. 1930- St&PR 91
Sax, Sam Morris, II 1942- WhoSSW 91
Sax, Spencer Meridith 1955- WhoEmL 91
Sax, Stanley P. 1925- St&PR 91
Sax, Stanley Paul 1925- WhoAm 90
Sax, Steve NewYTBS 90 [port]
Sax, Steve 1960- Ballpl 90
Sax, W Peter 1922- BiDrAPA 89
Saxbe, William 1916- BiDrUSE 89
Saxbe, William Bart 1916- WhoAm 90
Saxberg, Borje Osvald 1928- WhoAm 90
Saxby, Joseph PenDiMP
Saxby, Joseph Anthony 1910- IntWWM 90
Saxby, Lewis Weyburn, Jr. 1924- St&PR 91
Saxe, Adrian A 1943- WhoAmA 91
Saxe, Chaylie Louis 1918- St&PR 91
Saxe, Earl BiDrAPA 89
Saxe, Elizabeth Lee 1934- WhoAmW 91
Saxe, H Laurence 1951- St&PR 91
Saxe, Henry 1937- WhoAmA 91
Saxe, Isobel ConAu 30NR
Saxe, John Godfrey 1816-1887 AuBYP 90
Saxe, Jon S. 1936- St&PR 91
Saxe, Louis P 1920- BiDrAPA 89
Saxe, Maurice, Comte de 1696-1750 BioIn 16
Saxe, Melinda BioIn 16
Saxe, Natalie 1923- WhoE 91
Saxe, R. Daniel, Jr. 1927- St&PR 91
Saxe, Richard Baxter, Jr. 1923- WhoSSW 91
Saxe, Thelma Richards 1941- WhoE 91
Saxena, Anil BiDrAPA 89
Saxena, Arjun Nath 1932- WhoE 91, WhoWor 91
Saxena, Ashok 1948- WhoSSW 91
Saxena, Brij B. WhoAm 90
Saxena, Shekhar 1956- BiDrAPA 89
Saxena, Subhash Chandra WhoSSW 91
Saxer, Richard Karl 1928- WhoAm 90
Saxhaug, Gunnar 1944- WhoWor 91
Saxman, Anna Esther 1949- WhoAmW 91
Saxo Grammaticus DcScanL
Saxon, Alex ConAu 32NR, TwCCr&M 91
Saxon, Andrew John 1949- BiDrAPA 89
Saxon, Brody 1947- St&PR 91
Saxon, Charles 1920-1988 AnObit 1988
Saxon, Charles D. 1920-1988 BioIn 16
Saxon, Charles David 1920-1988 WhoAmA 91N
Saxon, David Stephen 1920- WhoAm 90
Saxon, Dirk WhoWrEP 89
Saxon, Edward G. 1959- St&PR 91
Saxon, Frances Shiver 1928- WhoAmW 91
Saxon, Franklin N. 1952- St&PR 91
Saxon, Grady Sue Loftin WhoSSW 91
Saxon, James 1954- WhoE 91
Saxon, James J. 1914-1980 EncABHB 7 [port]
Saxon, Jamie ODwPR 91
Saxon, John A. TwCCr&M 91
Saxon, Joseph George 1920- BiDrAPA 89
Saxon, Pauline BioIn 16
Saxon, Richard BioIn 16
Saxon, Steven Dee 1955- St&PR 91
Saxonhouse, W. Jack 1941- WhoE 91
Saxton, Beryl 1934- IntWWM 90
Saxton, Carolyn Virginia 1948- WhoAmW 91
Saxton, Ernest W. 1942- ODwPR 91
Saxton, H. James 1943- WhoAm 90, WhoE 91
Saxton, Josephine 1935- FemiCLE
Saxton, La Verne Young 1921- WhoWrEP 89
Saxton, Pamela L. 1952- St&PR 91
Saxton, Paul Allen 1938- St&PR 91
Saxton, Ralph Arthur 1955- WhoSSW 91
Saxton, Richard W 1949- BiDrAPA 89
Saxton, Robert 1953- IntWWM 90, PenDiMP A
Saxton, Robert F. 1922- St&PR 91
Saxton, Thomas Marvin 1951- St&PR 91
Saxton, William Marvin 1927- WhoAm 90
Saxtorph, Gertrude Margreta 1902- WhoAmW 91
Say Phouthang WhoWor 91
Say, Allen 1937- BioIn 16, ChILR 22 [port], ConAu 30NR
Say, Jean Baptiste 1767-1832 BioIn 16
Say, Leon Jean-Baptiste 1826-1896 BiDFrPL
Say, Marlys Mortensen 1924- WhoAmW 91, WhoWor 91
Say, Peggy BioIn 16
Sayad, Homer Elisha 1915- WhoAm 90
Sayad, Pamela Miriam 1949- WhoEmL 91
Sayampanathan, Sathiamoorthy Ramalingam 1921- WhoWor 91
Sayano, Reizo Ray 1937- WhoAm 90
Sayao, Bidu 1902- PenDiMP
Sayatovic, Wayne Peter 1946- St&PR 91, WhoAm 90
Sayavedra, Leo WhoHisp 91
Sayayli, Salih Munassir al- WhoWor 91
Sayed, Albert Joseph 1949- BiDrAPA 89
Sayed, Mustafa Kamal 1946- WhoWor 91
Sayeed, Mufti Muhammad 1936- WhoWor 91
Sayeed, Usman Ahmed 1939- WhoWor 91
Sayeg, Shiva 1961- WhoEmL 91
Sayegh, Glenda Faye 1953- WhoSSW 91
Sayegh, Paul S. 1943- St&PR 91
Sayen, William Henry 1921- WhoE 91
Sayer, Jane M. 1942- WhoAmW 91
Sayer, Leo 1948- OxCPMus
Sayer, Michael 1935- WhoAm 90
Sayer, Paul 1955- ConAu 132
Sayer, Robert John 1925- BiDrAPA 89
Sayers, Charles Marshall 1892- AuBYP 90
Sayers, Chera Lee 1959- WhoAmW 91, WhoSSW 91
Sayers, Dorothy 1893-1957 FemiCLE
Sayers, Dorothy L. 1893-1957 BioIn 16, DcLB 100 [port], MajTwCW, TwCCr&M 91, WorAlBi
Sayers, Frances Clarke 1897-1989 AuBYP 90, BioIn 16, ConAu 129, SmATA 62
Sayers, Fred BioIn 16
Sayers, Gale 1943- BioIn 16, WhoAm 90, WorAlBi
Sayers, Hazel Jean 1927- WhoAmW 91
Sayers, John H 1930- BiDrAPA 89
Sayers, Martin Peter 1922- WhoAm 90
Sayers, Peig 1873-1958 FemiCLE
Sayers, Randall William 1952- WhoEmL 91
Sayers, Richard 1908-1989 AnObit 1989
Sayers, Richard E. 1937- St&PR 91
Sayers, Richard James 1947- WhoAm 90
Sayers, Vera Winifred 1912- IntWWM 90
Sayetta, Thomas Charles 1937- WhoSSW 91
Sayfie, Eugene Joe 1934- WhoSSW 91
Sayka, Anthony 1957- WhoWor 91
Saykally, Richard James 1947- WhoAm 90
Sayko, Gene J. 1939- WhoWrEP 89
Sayle, Alexei 1952- ConTFT 8
Sayle, John Gilbert 1939- St&PR 91
Sayler, John William, Jr. 1935- St&PR 91
Sayles, Edward Dayton 1929- St&PR 91
Sayles, Edward Thomas 1952- WhoE 91
Sayles, Eva 1928- WhoAmA 91, WhoE 91
Sayles, John 1950- BioIn 16, WorAlBi
Sayles, John Thomas 1950- WhoAm 90
Sayles, Leonard Robert 1926- WhoAm 90
Sayles, Thomas D., Jr. 1932- St&PR 91
Sayles, Thomas Dyke, Jr. 1932- WhoAm 90
Saylor, Brian Michael 1942- St&PR 91
Saylor, David J. 1952- St&PR 91
Saylor, Jimmy D. 1950- WhoEmL 91
Saylor, John W. 1945- St&PR 91
Saylor, Lynn Leon 1940- WhoE 91
Saylor, Peter M. 1941- WhoAm 90
Saylors, Jo BioIn 16
Saylors, Jo An 1932- WhoAmA 91
Sayn-Wittgenstein, Carolyne de 1819-1887 BioIn 16
Sayre, David 1924- WhoAm 90
Sayre, Eleanor Axson 1916- WhoAmA 91
Sayre, Francis Bowes, Jr. 1915- WhoAm 90
Sayre, J. L. 1936- St&PR 91
Sayre, John Marshall 1921- WhoAm 90, WhoWor 91
Sayre, John Nevin 1884-1977 BioIn 16
Sayre, Kenneth Malcolm 1928- WhoAm 90
Sayre, Larry W. 1948- St&PR 91
Sayre, Philip Russell 1932- St&PR 91
Sayre, Robert Freeman 1933- WhoAm 90, WhoWrEP 89
Sayre, Robert H. 1922- WhoAm 90, WhoWor 91
Sayre, Robert Heysham 1939- St&PR 91
Sayre, Robert Marion 1924- WhoAm 90, WhoWor 91
Sayre, Stephen 1736-1818 EncCRAm
Sayre, Warren Grover 1844-1931 AmLegL
Sayre, William Heysham 1933- St&PR 91, WhoAm 90
Sayres, William Cortlandt 1927- WhoAm 90
Saywell, William George Gabriel 1936- WhoAm 90
Sazama, James F. 1942- St&PR 91
Sazama, Kathleen 1941- WhoAmW 91
Sazegar, Morteza 1933- WhoAm 90, WhoAmA 91
Sazer, Gary Neil 1946- WhoE 91
Sazerac, Bernard PenDiDA 89
Sazerac, Louis PenDiDA 89
Sazerat, Pierre-Leon PenDiDA 89
Sazima, Gregory Charles 1961- BiDrAPA 89
Sazima, Henry John 1927- WhoAm 90
Sbarbaro, Andrea BioIn 16
Sbarbaro, Richard D. 1946- St&PR 91
Sbarbaro, Richard Donald 1946- WhoAm 90
Sbarbaro, Robert Arthur 1933- St&PR 91, WhoAm 90
Sbardella, Edward F BiDrAPA 89
Sbarge, Raphael 1964- ConTFT 8
Sbarra, Donald 1930- St&PR 91
Sbarra, Robert Anthony 1934- WhoE 91
Sbarri, Manno di Bastiano 1536-1576 PenDiDA 89
Sbordon, William G. 1928- WhoAm 90
Sbordone, James R. 1945- WhoAm 90
Sbragia, Gary W. 1941- WhoWor 91
Sbriglio, Robert Patrick BiDrAPA 89
Sbriglio, Robert Patrick 1953- WhoE 91, WhoWor 91
Sbuttoni, Michael James 1953- WhoE 91
Scaasi, Arnold 1932?- BioIn 16
Scaasi, Arnold Martin WhoAm 90
Scacchi, Greta BioIn 16
Scaccia, Carmelo Anthony 1930- St&PR 91
Scaduto, Al 1928- EncACom
Scafe, Kenneth R. 1936- St&PR 91
Scafetta, Joseph, Jr. 1947- WhoSSW 91
Scaffidi, Judith Ann 1950- WhoAmW 91
Scaffidi, Marie Ann 1961- St&PR 91
Scaggs, Boz BioIn 16
Scaggs, Boz 1944- EncPR&S 89, WhoAm 90, WorAlBi
Scaggs, Howard Irwin 1921- WhoAm 90
Scaggs, Roger T. 1939- St&PR 91
Scaglione, Aldo Domenico 1925- WhoAm 90
Scaglione, Cecil F. ODwPR 91
Scagliotti, Maria Cristina BiDrAPA 89
Scagnetti, Jack 1924- AuBYP 90
Scagnetti, Jack James 1924- WhoWrEP 89
Scaia, Mary Julie 1953- WhoAmW 91, WhoE 91, WhoEmL 91
Scaife, Issable BiDEWW
Scaife, William Arthur 1947- WhoSSW 91
Scal, Howard N 1918- BiDrAPA 89
Scala, Alessandra 1475-1506 EncCoWW

Scala, Donna Jean 1951- WhoE 91
Scala, James 1934- St&PR 91, WhoAm 90
Scala, Joseph 1940- WhoAmA 91
Scala, Joseph Anthony, Jr. 1940- WhoAm 90
Scala, Ralph John 1949- St&PR 91
Scala, Robert Andrew 1931- WhoE 91
Scalabrino, Edwin BioIn 16
Scalamandre, Franco 1898-1988 BioIn 16
Scalchunes, William 1935- St&PR 91
Scalcucci, Frank S. 1943- St&PR 91
Scalea, Donald David 1953- BiDrAPA 89
Scalercio, Eugene Nicholas 1940- St&PR 91
Scales, Althea E. 1951- WhoWrEP 89
Scales, Caroline 1873-1898 DcCanB 12
Scales, Diann Roylette 1945- WhoAmW 91
Scales, Eric John BiDrAPA 89
Scales, George 1900-1976 Ballpl 90
Scales, James Pinckney 1831- AmLegL
Scales, James Ralph 1919- WhoAm 90
Scales, Jeffrey M. 1953- St&PR 91
Scales, Junius Irving 1920- EncAL
Scales, Peter Craig 1949- WhoEmL 91
Scalessa, Donald Francis 1942- WhoSSW 91
Scaletta, Helen Marguerite 1927- WhoWor 91
Scalf, Donald Lee 1935- WhoSSW 91
Scalf, Susan Hamlett 1958- WhoSSW 91
Scali, John Alfred 1918- WhoAm 90
Scali, Sam WhoAm 90
Scalia, Antonin 1936- WhoAm 90, WhoE 91, WhoWor 91, WorAlBi
Scalia, John Cazes 1947- WhoE 91
Scalia, Rebeka J. 1942- St&PR 91
Scalia, William Charles 1944- St&PR 91
Scalies, Charles Joseph 1940- St&PR 91
Scaliger, Joseph Juste 1540-1609 BioIn 16
Scaliger, Joseph Justus 1540-1609 WorAlBi
Scaling, G. Wilson, II 1938- WhoAm 90
Scalise, George BioIn 16
Scalise, George Martin 1934- WhoAm 90
Scalise, Margaret Mary 1952- BiDrAPA 89
Scalise, Nicholas Peter 1932- WhoAmA 91, WhoE 91
Scalisi, Nicholas Anthony 1947- WhoAm 90
Scall, P. 1936- St&PR 91
Scallen, Thomas K. 1926- St&PR 91
Scalley, John J. 1930- WhoAm 90
Scallorn, Glenda Jean BiDrAPA 89
Scally, M. Anthony WhoE 91
Scally, Sean Patrick 1960- WhoE 91
Scalzo, Michael Angelo 1950- WhoE 91
Scamman, John Philip BiDrAPA 89
Scamman, W. Douglas, Jr. 1941- WhoAm 90
Scammel, Harry Glenn 1948- WhoEmL 91
Scammell, Barry Edward 1941- St&PR 91
Scammell, Geoffrey Vaughan 1925- WhoWor 91
Scammon, Richard Montgomery 1915- WhoAm 90
Scanavino, N. H. Marco 1953- WhoWor 91
Scandalios, John George 1934- WhoAm 90
Scandary, E. Jane 1923- WhoAmW 91
Scandinaro, David W BiDrAPA 89
Scandling, William Fredric 1922- WhoAm 90
Scandlyn, Kathie Dunn 1950- WhoSSW 91
Scandura, Joseph Michael 1932- WhoAm 90
Scandura, Teresa Anne 1960- WhoAmW 91, WhoSSW 91
Scanga, Italo 1932- WhoAm 90, WhoAmA 91
Scanhan, Thomas Moore 1935- St&PR 91
Scanlan, Doc 1881-1949 Ballpl 90
Scanlan, James Patrick 1927- WhoAm 90
Scanlan, John B BiDrAPA 89
Scanlan, John Douglas 1927- WhoAm 90, WhoWor 91
Scanlan, John E., Jr. 1961- St&PR 91
Scanlan, John Michael 1937- BiDrAPA 89
Scanlan, Katherine Ann 1940- WhoAmW 91
Scanlan, P. Douglas St&PR 91
Scanlan, Richard Thomas 1928- WhoAm 90
Scanlan, Sharon Ann 1948- WhoAmW 91
Scanlan, Thomas Joseph 1945- WhoAm 90, WhoE 91
Scanlan, Thomas M. 1935- St&PR 91
Scanlin, Francis G. 1929- St&PR 91
Scanling, Frederick Hamilton 1942- WhoSSW 91
Scanlon, Barry Francis BiDrAPA 89
Scanlon, C. K. M. TwCCr&M 91
Scanlon, Charles Joseph 1915- WhoAm 90
Scanlon, David G. 1921-1990 ConAu 132
Scanlon, Dorothy Therese 1928- WhoAmW 91
Scanlon, Edward F. 1918- WhoAm 90
Scanlon, Everett Robert 1921- St&PR 91
Scanlon, Gregory S. 1949- WhoEmL 91
Scanlon, James Thomas 1946- St&PR 91
Scanlon, Jane Cronin 1922- WhoAm 90
Scanlon, John P. ODwPR 91
Scanlon, Lawrence Joseph 1951- WhoEmL 91
Scanlon, Owen J. BioIn 16
Scanlon, Peter Redmond 1931- WhoAm 90, WhoE 91
Scanlon, Rosemary 1939- WhoAm 90
Scanlon, Susan J. 1949- St&PR 91
Scanlon, Terrence Maurice 1939- WhoAm 90, WhoE 91
Scanlon, Thomas Michael 1909- WhoAm 90
Scanlon, Wilson G 1914- BiDrAPA 89
Scannapieco, Pasquale Joseph 1942- WhoE 91
Scannell, Dale Paul 1929- WhoAm 90
Scannell, Gerard F. BioIn 16
Scannell, John Gordon 1914- WhoAm 90
Scannell, Philip Lawrence, Jr. 1919- St&PR 91
Scannell, Robert E. 1939- St&PR 91
Scannell, Stacy Monee 1960- BiDrAPA 89
Scannell, Timothy Joseph 1954- WhoE 91
Scannell, Vernon BioIn 16
Scannell, William Edward 1934- WhoWor 91
Scanni, Pat 1942- WhoE 91
Scanniello, Stephen BioIn 16
Scannon, Patrick Jerome 1947- St&PR 91
Scantland, Donald Maurice 1931- St&PR 91
Scantlebury, Velma Patricia 1955- WhoAmW 91
Scar, Howard S. 1930- St&PR 91
Scaralia, John Anthony 1954- WhoE 91
Scaramella, Thomas Jerry BiDrAPA 89
Scaramuzzi, Franco 1926- WhoWor 91
Scaravaglione, Concetta 1900-1975 BiDWomA
Scaravaglione, Concetta Maria 1900-1975 WhoAmA 91N
Scarbath, Horst G. 1938- WhoWor 91
Scarberry, Alma Sioux 1899-1990 BioIn 16, ConAu 131
Scarbery, Randy 1952- Ballpl 90
Scarbinsky, Mark Joseph 1949- St&PR 91
Scarboro, Edwin Mosgrove 1931- St&PR 91
Scarborough, Alexander Alan 1923- WhoSSW 91
Scarborough, Carl Arthur 1940- St&PR 91
Scarborough, Charles Bishop, III 1943- WhoAm 90, WhoWor 91
Scarborough, Clarence Virgil 1945- WhoSSW 91
Scarborough, Claude Mood, Jr. 1929- WhoSSW 91
Scarborough, Danny BioIn 16
Scarborough, Isabel Willena 1898- WhoWrEP 89
Scarborough, Jack William 1946- WhoSSW 91
Scarborough, James S BiDrAPA 89
Scarborough, Jon Dale 1935- WhoE 91
Scarborough, Lee F BiDrAPA 89
Scarborough, Lonnie T, Jr. BiDrAPA 89
Scarborough, Ray 1917-1982 Ballpl 90
Scarborough, Robert Joseph Bowman 1928- St&PR 91
Scarborough, Robert Henry, Jr. 1923- WhoAm 90
Scarborough, Ruth Ellen 1917- WhoAmW 91
Scarborough, Walter A. Jr. 1940- BiDrAPA 89
Scarborough, Yancey Wilcox, Jr. 1922- St&PR 91
Scarborow, Anne BiDEWW
Scarbrough, Arlan Earl 1936- St&PR 91
Scarbrough, Cleve Knox, Jr. 1939- WhoAm 90, WhoAmA 91, WhoSSW 91
Scarbrough, Dawn Denise 1962- WhoAmW 91
Scarbrough, Ernest Earl 1947- WhoWor 91
Scarbrough, George Addison 1915- WhoWrEP 89
Scarbrough, Patsy Ann Wurth 1947- WhoEmL 91
Scarbrough, Wayne E. 1947-1990 BioIn 16
Scarce, Mac 1949- Ballpl 90
Scarcella, Erminia 1945- BiDrAPA 89
Scarcella, Giuseppe 1922- BiDrAPA 89
Scardigli, Gualfredo 1922- WhoWor 91
Scardina, Frank Joseph 1948- WhoAm 90
Scardina, Ray Gerard 1955- BiDrAPA 89
Scardino, Albert 1948- ConAu 129
Scardino, Albert James 1948- WhoAm 90
Scardino, Dorothy BioIn 16
Scardino, Gerard Anthony 1957- BiDrAPA 89
Scardino, James J. 1953- St&PR 91
Scardino, Joseph BiDrAPA 89
Scarf, Frederick L. BioIn 16
Scarf, Herbert Eli 1930- WhoAm 90, WhoE 91
Scarf, Maggie 1932- WhoWrEP 89
Scarf, Margaret 1932- WhoAm 90
Scarface Charley 1837?-1896 WhNaAH
Scarfaced Charley 1837?-1896 WhNaAH
Scarfe, Alan 1946- OxCCanT
Scarfe, Alan John 1946- WhoE 91
Scarff, Edward L. 1930- WhoAm 90
Scarff, S. Thomas 1942- WhoAm 90
Scarfia, Michael Louis 1928- St&PR 91
Scarfo, Louis Joseph 1948- WhoE 91
Scarino, Marianne Cannava 1951- WhoWrEP 89
Scarito, Kathryn Veronica 1945- WhoEmL 91
Scarizza, Spartaco BiDrAPA 89
Scarlata, Antonia Ellen L. 1944- WhoE 91
Scarlatti, Alessandro 1660-1725 PenDiMP A, WorAlBi
Scarlatti, Domenico 1685-1757 WorAlBi
Scarlett, Harold Owen WhoAm 90
Scarlett, John Archibald 1951- St&PR 91
Scarlett, John Donald 1923- WhoAm 90
Scarlett, Susan ConAu 31NR
Scarman, Leslie George BioIn 16
Scarminach, Charles Anthony 1944- St&PR 91
Scarnati, Richard Alfred 1940- BiDrAPA 89
Scarne, John 1903- WhoAm 90
Scarne, Paul Thomas 1947- WhoAm 90, WhoWor 91
Scarne, Steffi Norma 1925- WhoAmW 91
Scarola, John 1947- WhoEmL 91
Scaros, Constantine St&PR 91
Scaros, Constantine E. 1945- WhoAm 90
Scarouady WhNaAH
Scarpa, Antonio 1942- WhoAm 90
Scarpa, Carlo 1906-1978 ConDes 90
Scarpa, Dorothea 1926- WhoAmA 91
Scarpa, Tobia 1935- ConDes 90
Scarpa, Vincenzo EncPaPR 91
Scarpelli, Dante Giovanni 1927- WhoAm 90
Scarpelli, Kevin Thomas 1940- St&PR 91
Scarpino, Pasquale Valentine 1932- WhoAm 90
Scarpitta, Salvatore 1919- WhoAmA 91
Scarpitti, Frank Roland 1936- WhoAm 90
Scarpone, Frank R. 1947- St&PR 91
Scarr, Deryck 1939- ConAu 132
Scarr, Sandra BioIn 16
Scarr, Sandra Wood 1936- WhoAm 90
Scarritt, James Richard 1935- WhoAm 90
Scarritt, Russ 1903- Ballpl 90
Scarrow, Pamela Kay 1949- WhoAmW 91
Scarry, Donald Michael 1941- WhoE 91
Scarry, Huck ConAu 130
Scarry, Patricia 1924- AuBYP 90
Scarry, Richard 1919- AuBYP 90, BioIn 16
Scarry, Richard McClure 1919- WhoAm 90
Scarry, Richard McClure, Jr. 1953- ConAu 130
Scarry, Shannon J BiDrAPA 89
Scarsdale, Richard Bouten 1931- St&PR 91
Scarsdale, Sybil S. 1933- St&PR 91
Scarsdale, William M. 1952- St&PR 91
Scarsella, Les 1913-1958 Ballpl 90
Scarth, John Campbell 1924- WhoAm 90
Scarton, Bennie, Jr. 1936- WhoAm 90
Scasta, David Lynn 1949- BiDrAPA 89, WhoE 91
Scatchard, George 1892-1973 DcScB S2
Scatena, Lorraine Borba 1924- WhoAmW 91
Scates, Alice Yeomans 1915- WhoAmW 91
Scaunas, Simona 1965- IntWWM 90
Scavarda, Donald Robert 1928- IntWWM 90
Scavetta, Joseph F 1941- BiDrAPA 89
Scavone, Alison Patricia 1959- WhoE 91
Scavullo, Blaise Carlo 1947- BiDrAPA 89
Scavullo, Charles, Jr. 1953- St&PR 91
Scavullo, Francesco 1929- WhoAm 90
Scearce, William Russell 1930- WhoWrEP 89
Scearse, Patricia Dotson 1931- WhoAm 90
Scedrov, Andre 1955- WhoE 91
Scelba, Anthony 1947- WhoE 91
Scelsa, Joseph Vincent 1945- WhoE 91
Scelsi, Giacinto 1905-1988 AnObit 1988, BioIn 16
Scemiophris WomWR
Scemons, Donna J. WhoAmW 91
Scepanski, Jordan Michael 1942- WhoAm 90
Scerbo, Frances Carolyn Garrott 1932- WhoAmW 91
Scerbo, Francis Barry 1943- WhoWor 91
Scerbo, Joseph E. 1934- St&PR 91
Scerpella, Marino WhoHisp 91
Scerra, Robert A. 1955- St&PR 91
Schaack, Philip Anthony 1921- WhoAm 90
Schaad, Anne Phyllis 1955- WhoE 91
Schaaf, Barbara Carol WhoAmW 91
Schaaf, Bradford Perkins 1942- St&PR 91
Schaaf, Carl Hart 1912- WhoAm 90
Schaaf, Douglas Allan 1955- WhoEmL 91
Schaaf, Eric William 1956- WhoE 91
Schaaf, Frederick Carl 1954- WhoWrEP 89
Schaaf, Kathryn Ann 1954- WhoAmW 91
Schaaf, M. B. Goffstein BioIn 16
Schaaf, Nine van der 1882-1973 EncCoWW
Schaaf, Rachelle Vander BioIn 16
Schaaf, Richard Edmund 1949- WhoWrEP 89
Schaake, Paul E. 1946- St&PR 91
Schaal, Daniel A., Jr. 1941- St&PR 91
Schaal, John Eric 1943- St&PR 91
Schaal, Paul 1943- Ballpl 90
Schaal, Peter 1935- WhoWor 91
Schaal, William L. St&PR 91
Schaap, James Calvin 1948- WhoWrEP 89
Schaap, Richard Jay 1934- WhoAm 90, WhoWrEP 89
Schaap, William Herman 1940- WhoE 91
Schaar, Frances Elizabeth 1911- WhoWrEP 89
Schaar, Jacqueline K. 1933- ODwPR 91
Schaar, John H 1928- ConAu 31NR
Schaar, Victoria Lynn 1959- WhoAmW 91
Schaar, William Henry 1938- St&PR 91
Schab, Margo Pollins 1945- WhoAmA 91
Schabacker, Betty Barchet 1925- WhoAmA 91
Schabarum, Peter F. 1929- WhoHisp 91
Schaber, Gordon Duane 1927- WhoAm 90
Schaberg, S Donald 1938- St&PR 91
Schabot, Catherine Mary 1938- WhoAmW 91
Schachman, Howard Kapnek 1918- WhoAm 90
Schachne, Gary 1950- St&PR 91, WhoE 91
Schachner, Abraham 1953- WhoE 91
Schachner, E. Douglas M. 1935- St&PR 91
Schachner, Robert Wahl 1940- WhoSSW 91
Schacht, Al 1892-1984 Ballpl 90
Schacht, Edward Lewis BiDrAPA 89
Schacht, Henry B. 1934- St&PR 91
Schacht, Henry Brewer 1934- WhoAm 90
Schacht, Henry Mevis 1916- WhoAm 90
Schacht, Hjalmar 1877-1970 BioIn 16, WorAlBi
Schacht, Jochen Heinrich 1939- WhoAm 90
Schacht, Letty Gail 1937- WhoE 91
Schacht, Mervyn BiDrAPA 89
Schacht, Richard 1941- ConAu 31NR
Schacht, Richard Lawrence 1941- WhoAm 90, WhoWrEP 89
Schacht, Ronald Stuart 1932- WhoAm 90
Schacht, William Eugene 1941- WhoWor 91
Schachte, John Jacob 1933- St&PR 91
Schachtel, Barbara Harriet Levin 1921- WhoAmW 91
Schachtel, Irving I. NewYTBS 90
Schachtel, Irving I. 1909-1990 BioIn 16
Schachter, Esther Roditti 1933- WhoAmW 91
Schachter, Gustav 1926- WhoE 91
Schachter, Harry 1933- WhoAm 90
Schachter, Hindy Lauer 1945- WhoWrEP 89
Schachter, Joseph 1925- BiDrAPA 89, WhoE 91
Schachter, Judith S 1928- BiDrAPA 89
Schachter, Julius 1936- WhoAm 90
Schachter, Justine Ranson 1927- WhoAmA 91
Schachter, Max 1913- WhoAm 90
Schachter, Meri BiDrAPA 89
Schachter, Michael B 1941- BiDrAPA 89
Schachter, Michael Ben 1941- WhoE 91
Schachter, Oscar 1915- WhoAm 90, WhoE 91
Schachter, Oscar H. 1933- St&PR 91
Schachter, Sheldon Jay 1943- St&PR 91
Schachter, Sherman O 1926- BiDrAPA 89
Schachter-Shalomi, Zalman 1924- NewAgE 90
Schachtschneider, Herbert 1919- IntWWM 90
Schack, Arthur Martin 1945- WhoEmL 91
Schack, Benedikt 1758-1826 PenDiMP
Schack, David Paul 1957- WhoEmL 91
Schack, Elisabeth PenDiMP
Schack, Hans Egede 1820-1858 DcScanL
Schack, Ricardo BiDrAPA 89
Schack, William BioIn 16
Schackman, Lynn Debra 1953- BiDrAPA 89
Schacknow, Max BioIn 16
Schacknow, Rosalind Koss 1925- St&PR 91
Schacter, Bernice Zeldin 1943- WhoAmW 91
Schactman, Barry Robert 1930- WhoAmA 91
Schad, James L. 1917- WhoAm 90

Schad, Theodore George, Jr. 1927- St&PR 91, WhoAm 90, WhoSSW 91, WhoWor 91
Schad, Theodore MacNeeve 1918- WhoAm 90, WhoE 91, WhoWor 91
Schade, Ardith Ann 1945- WhoAmW 91
Schade, Charlene Joanne 1935- WhoAmW 91
Schade, Edward P. 1941- St&PR 91
Schade, John ODwPR 91
Schade, Robert Richard 1948- WhoWor 91
Schade, Robert S. 1926- St&PR 91
Schadlbauer, Friedrich Guenther 1939- WhoWor 91
Schadler, Margaret Horsfall 1931- WhoAmW 91
Schadler, Thomas E. 1951- St&PR 91
Schadow, Johann Gottfried PenDiDA 89
Schadrack, Frederick Charles 1926- St&PR 91
Schadt, Robert Russell 1936- St&PR 91
Schadt, Rudi Wilhelm 1957- WhoWor 91
Schaeberle, Robert K. 1953- WhoE 91
Schaeberle, Robert M. 1923- St&PR 91
Schaecher, Francis P. 1948- St&PR 91
Schaecher, Susan Marie 1957- WhoEmL 91
Schaechter, Judith 1961- WhoAmA 91
Schaechter, Moselio 1928- WhoAm 90
Schaedel, Elroy W. 1931- St&PR 91
Schaefer, Adolph O. 1901-1989 BioIn 16
Schaefer, Adolph O., Jr. 1932- WhoAm 90
Schaefer, C. Barry 1939- St&PR 91, WhoAm 90
Schaefer, Carl Fellman 1903- WhoAm 90, WhoAmA 91
Schaefer, Carl George Lewis WhoAm 90
Schaefer, Carl Walter, II 1934- WhoE 91
Schaefer, Carla Jo 1952- WhoAmW 91
Schaefer, Charles James, III 1926- WhoAm 90, WhoWor 91
Schaefer, Charles V., Jr. 1914- St&PR 91
Schaefer, Dan L. 1936- WhoAm 90
Schaefer, David Scott BiDrAPA 89
Schaefer, Donald A. 1925- WhoAm 90
Schaefer, Donald Ernest 1932- WhoSSW 91
Schaefer, Donald L 1926- BiDrAPA 89
Schaefer, Edward Donald 1944- WhoE 91
Schaefer, Edward J. 1901- St&PR 91
Schaefer, Edward John 1901- WhoAm 90
Schaefer, Ephraim A. 1926- St&PR 91
Schaefer, Erhardt H. 1928- St&PR 91
Schaefer, F. W. Dietmar 1928-1989 BioIn 16
Schaefer, Fred H. 1944- St&PR 91
Schaefer, Gail 1938- WhoAmA 91
Schaefer, George 1920- ConTFT 8 [port]
Schaefer, George A. 1945- St&PR 91
Schaefer, George Anthony 1928- ConAmBL, St&PR 91, WhoAm 90
Schaefer, George Julius, Sr. 1914- St&PR 91
Schaefer, George Louis 1920- WhoAm 90
Schaefer, Germany 1877-1919 Ballpl 90
Schaefer, Gordon E. 1932- WhoAm 90
Schaefer, Hans 1906- EncO&P 3
Schaefer, Hans-Eckart 1936- WhoWor 91
Schaefer, Hans Michael 1940- St&PR 91
Schaefer, Harold W. 1909-1988 BioIn 16
Schaefer, Harry G. 1936- St&PR 91
Schaefer, Harry George 1936- WhoAm 90
Schaefer, Helen Schwarz 1933- WhoAmW 91
Schaefer, Henry 1930- St&PR 91
Schaefer, Jack Warner 1907- AuBYP 90, WhoAm 90
Schaefer, Jacob WhoAm 90
Schaefer, Jacob Wernli 1919- WhoAm 90
Schaefer, James M. BioIn 16
Schaefer, Jimmie Wayne, Jr. 1951- WhoAm 90, WhoWor 91
Schaefer, John L. 1935- St&PR 91
Schaefer, John Paul 1934- WhoAm 90
Schaefer, Jon Patrick 1948- WhoWor 91
Schaefer, Julius J. BioIn 16
Schaefer, Lawrence James 1953- BiDrAPA 89
Schaefer, Lois Elizabeth 1924- WhoAm 90
Schaefer, Louis 1859- AmLegL
Schaefer, Marilyn Louise 1933- WhoAmW 91
Schaefer, Mary Ann 1942- WhoAmW 91
Schaefer, Mary B. 1932- WhoAmW 91
Schaefer, Mary Jesse 1963- WhoAmW 91
Schaefer, Michael R. 1949- St&PR 91
Schaefer, Otto BiDrAPA 89
Schaefer, P. James 1918- St&PR 91
Schaefer, Pamela Joy 1949- WhoAmW 91
Schaefer, Patricia 1930- WhoAmW 91
Schaefer, Rhoda Pesner 1947- WhoE 91
Schaefer, Robert 1928- St&PR 91
Schaefer, Robert A. 1961- St&PR 91
Schaefer, Robert L. 1939- St&PR 91
Schaefer, Robert Walter 1941- St&PR 91
Schaefer, Robert Wayne 1934- WhoAm 90
Schaefer, Ronald H 1939- WhoAmA 91
Schaefer, Rowland 1916- St&PR 91
Schaefer, Rudolph J. 1863-1923 WorAlBi
Schaefer, Ruth Marion 1923- IntWWM 90
Schaefer, Scott Jay 1948- WhoAmA 91
Schaefer, Scott Michael 1955- St&PR 91
Schaefer, Steven John 1957- WhoEmL 91
Schaefer, Steven Joseph 1950- WhoSSW 91
Schaefer, Susan Marie 1952- WhoAmW 91
Schaefer, Terry William 1946- St&PR 91
Schaefer, Theodore Peter 1933- WhoAm 90
Schaefer, Thomas Carl 1939- St&PR 91
Schaefer, Thomas Lewitt 1944- St&PR 91
Schaefer, Thomas Reuben 1950- St&PR 91
Schaefer, Vernon Joseph 1919- WhoWrEP 89
Schaefer, William A. 1918- IntWWM 90
Schaefer, William David 1928- WhoAm 90
Schaefer, William Donald BioIn 16
Schaefer, William Donald 1921- WhoAm 90, WhoE 91, WhoWor 91
Schaeffer, Albrecht 1885-1950 BioIn 16
Schaeffer, Barbara Hamilton 1926- WhoAmW 91, WhoSSW 91, WhoWor 91
Schaeffer, Bernard S BiDrAPA 89
Schaeffer, Boguslaw Julien 1929- IntWWM 90
Schaeffer, Edwin Frank, Jr. 1930- St&PR 91, WhoAm 90
Schaeffer, Francis A. BioIn 16
Schaeffer, Frank E. 1928- St&PR 91
Schaeffer, Geraldine BiDrAPA 89
Schaeffer, Glen St&PR 91
Schaeffer, Glenn William 1953- WhoAm 90, WhoEmL 91
Schaeffer, Karren Telford 1952- WhoAmW 91
Schaeffer, Kate WhoAmA 91
Schaeffer, Kenneth Peter 1957- WhoE 91
Schaeffer, Martha J 1948- WhoAmA 91
Schaeffer, Nancy E. 1949- IntWWM 90
Schaeffer, Peter N. 1951- St&PR 91
Schaeffer, Phillip A 1935- BiDrAPA 89
Schaeffer, Pierre Henri Marie 1910- IntWWM 90, WhoWor 91
Schaeffer, Piotr Mikolaj 1958- IntWWM 90
Schaeffer, R. 1945- St&PR 91
Schaeffer, Rebecca BioIn 16
Schaeffer, Reiner Horst 1938- WhoAm 90
Schaeffer, Richard J 1934- BiDrAPA 89
Schaeffer, Ronald Carl 1959- WhoSSW 91
Schaeffer, Shirley Ann 1955- WhoEmL 91
Schaeffer, Steven Lee 1949- WhoE 91
Schaeffer, Susan 1941- FemiCLE
Schaeffer, Susan Fromberg BioIn 16
Schaeffer, Susan Fromberg 1941- MajTwCW, WhoAmW 91, WhoWrEP 89, WorAu 1980 [port]
Schaeffer, Wayne G. 1946- St&PR 91
Schaeffer, Wendell Gordon 1917- WhoWor 91
Schaefgen, Philip P. 1958- WhoSSW 91
Schaefler, Leon 1903- WhoAm 90
Schaen, Frederic Warren 1937- St&PR 91
Schaen, Lawrence L. 1929- St&PR 91
Schaen, Robert P. 1926- St&PR 91
Schaenen, Lee Joel 1925- WhoAm 90
Schaengold, Richard BiDrAPA 89
Schaer, Werner 1940- St&PR 91
Schaerf, Frederick 1951- BiDrAPA 89
Schaerf, Frederick Warren 1951- WhoSSW 91
Schafenacker, James A. 1930- St&PR 91
Schafer, Alice Pauline 1899-1980 WhoAmA 91N
Schafer, Carl Walter 1936- WhoAm 90, WhoE 91, WhoWor 91
Schafer, Carolyn Marie Ground 1955- WhoAmW 91
Schafer, Curtin E. 1935- St&PR 91
Schafer, Dieter 1935- WhoWor 91
Schafer, Donald W 1919- BiDrAPA 89
Schafer, Edward Hetzel 1913- WhoAm 90, WhoWrEP 89
Schafer, Fritz 1945- WhoWor 91
Schafer, Garland Jeffrey 1953- WhoEmL 91
Schafer, George 1928- ODwPR 91
Schafer, James Henry 1945- WhoAm 90
Schafer, John Francis 1921- WhoAm 90
Schafer, John Stephen 1934- WhoAm 90
Schafer, Kenneth C. 1907- St&PR 91
Schafer, Klaus Peter 1943- WhoWor 91
Schafer, Lawrence 1940- OxCCanT
Schafer, Michael Eugene 1940- WhoAm 90
Schafer, Michael Frederick 1942- WhoAm 90
Schafer, Neil Joseph 1945- St&PR 91
Schafer, Pamela R BiDrAPA 89
Schafer, Raymond Murray 1933- IntWWM 90, WhoAm 90
Schafer, Ronald William 1938- WhoAm 90
Schafer, Seymour Jay 1933- WhoE 91
Schafer, Steven Harris 1954- WhoEmL 91
Schafer, Thomas Wilson 1939- St&PR 91, WhoAm 90
Schafer, Walter L. 1929- St&PR 91
Schafer, Wilhelm 1912-1981 DcScB S2
Schaff, Adam 1913- WhoWor 91
Schaff, Louise E. AuBYP 90
Schaff, Mary Ruth BiDrAPA 89
Schaff, Paula Kay 1945- WhoAmW 91
Schaff, Philip H., Jr. 1920- St&PR 91
Schaffalitzky de Muckadell, Ove B. 1944- WhoWor 91
Schaffel, Larry S. 1933- ODwPR 91
Schaffel, Lewis WhoAm 90
Schaffeld, Daniel J. 1957- St&PR 91
Schaffer, Alan L. 1942- St&PR 91
Schaffer, Bonnie Lynn 1957- WhoAmW 91
Schaffer, Carole Sue BiDrAPA 89
Schaffer, Charles B 1945- BiDrAPA 89
Schaffer, David Edwin 1929- WhoE 91
Schaffer, David Irving 1935- WhoAm 90
Schaffer, Debra S 1936- WhoAmA 91
Schaffer, Diane Maximoff 1946- WhoAmW 91
Schaffer, Dietrich PenDiDA 89
Schaffer, Donald E BiDrAPA 89
Schaffer, Dora BiDrAPA 89
Schaffer, Edmund John 1925- WhoAm 90
Schaffer, Ellen Gore 1949- WhoE 91
Schaffer, Franklin Edwin 1924- WhoAm 90
Schaffer, Irene Elizabeth 1923- St&PR 91
Schaffer, Irving 1922- St&PR 91
Schaffer, Jimmie 1936- Ballpl 90
Schaffer, Joel Lance 1945- WhoWor 91
Schaffer, Juan Jorge 1930- WhoE 91
Schaffer, Kathryn Lois 1945- WhoWor 91
Schaffer, Leslie 1925- BiDrAPA 89
Schaffer, Linda C BiDrAPA 89
Schaffer, Michael J. 1944- WhoE 91
Schaffer, Miriam Ellen 1955- WhoAmW 91
Schaffer, Monroe 1917- St&PR 91
Schaffer, Neil M. 1959- St&PR 91
Schaffer, Peter 1940- St&PR 91
Schaffer, Robert W. St&PR 91
Schaffer, Rose WhoAmA 91N
Schaffer, Scott A. St&PR 91
Schaffer, Shirley 1921- BiDrAPA 89
Schaffer, Ulrich 1942- ConAu 31NR
Schaffer, Walker William 1936- St&PR 91
Schaffernoth, Joe 1937- Ballpl 90
Schaffert, Lori Anne 1966- WhoEmL 91
Schaffhausen, Paul Vincent 1929- St&PR 91
Schaffhauser, Robert J. 1938- St&PR 91
Schaffner, Bernard P. 1936- St&PR 91
Schaffner, Bertram Henry 1912- BiDrAPA 89
Schaffner, Caroline 1901- BioIn 16
Schaffner, Caroline Hannah 1901- NotWoAT
Schaffner, Charles Etzel 1919- WhoAm 90
Schaffner, Clara Dekiss BiDrAPA 89
Schaffner, Fenton 1920- WhoAm 90
Schaffner, Franklin J. 1920-1989 AnObit 1989, BioIn 16
Schaffner, Fred C. 1926- St&PR 91
Schaffner, George A., II 1921- St&PR 91
Schaffner, J Luray WhoAmA 91
Schaffner, Karl NewAgMG
Schaffner, Kurt Walter 1931- WhoWor 91
Schaffner, Robert Jay, Jr. 1949- WhoE 91
Schaffner, Robert Thomas, Jr. 1937- WhoE 91
Schaffner, Valerie Lynn 1959- WhoAmW 91
Schaffran, Thomas Foxhall 1941- St&PR 91
Schaffrath, Ludwig 1924- PenDiDA 89
Schaffstall, Charles Francis 1926- St&PR 91
Schaffzin, Richard Alan 1944- St&PR 91
Schafroth, Lucretia Nicole 1962- WhoE 91
Schaible, Grace Berg WhoAm 90
Schaible, John Edward 1938- St&PR 91
Schaible, Ronald David 1947- WhoE 91
Schaich, Georg Eberhard 1940- WhoWor 91
Schaider, Elisabeth A BiDrAPA 89
Schaider, Renate 1943- EncCoWW
Schaie, Klaus Warner 1928- WhoAm 90
Schaik-Willing, Jeanne Gabrielle van 1885-1984 EncCoWW
Schainholz, Jay D. 1959- St&PR 91
Schairer, George Swift 1913- WhoAm 90
Schairer, John Frank 1904-1970 DcScB S2
Schairer, John Otto BiDrAPA 89
Schaitel, Jeanne Marie 1952- WhoAmW 91
Schajer, Gary Stephen 1952- WhoEmL 91
Schake, Lowell Martin 1938- WhoAm 90
Schake, Robert H. 1932- St&PR 91
Schakel, Carl BioIn 16
Schakne, Norman R 1927- BiDrAPA 89
Schakne, Robert BioIn 16
Schakne, Robert 1926-1989 ConAu 129
Schakovskoy, Zinaida 1906- EncCoWW
Schaleben, Arville 1907- WhoAm 90
Schalekamp, Jacob Cornelis 1942- WhoWor 91
Schalk, Barbara Ann WhoAmW 91
Schalk, Beverly VanDyke 1959- WhoAmW 91
Schalk, Eugene Norbert 1932- St&PR 91
Schalk, Franz 1863-1931 PenDiMP
Schalk, Josef 1857-1911 PenDiMP
Schalk, Ray 1892-1970 Ballpl 90 [port]
Schalk, Roy 1908- Ballpl 90
Schalk, Thomas William 1952- St&PR 91
Schalk, Willi BioIn 16
Schalk, Willi 1940- St&PR 91
Schalker, David Edwin 1936- BiDrAPA 89
Schalkowsky, Samuel 1925- St&PR 91
Schall, Amy Elizabeth 1964- WhoAmW 91
Schall, Fred R. 1948- St&PR 91
Schall, Hero 1942- WhoWor 91
Schall, William L. 1939- St&PR 91
Schallenkamp, Kay 1949- WhoAm 90
Schaller, Christopher L. WhoE 91
Schaller, Daryl Richard 1943- St&PR 91, WhoAm 90
Schaller, Dieter A. 1929- WhoWor 91
Schaller, George B. 1933- AuBYP 90
Schaller, George Beals 1933- WhoAm 90, WhoWrEP 89
Schaller, H. W. 1905- St&PR 91
Schaller, James E. 1940- St&PR 91
Schaller, Jane Green 1934- WhoAm 90, WhoAmW 91
Schaller, Lyle E 1923- ConAu 131
Schaller, Warren Edward 1931-1988 BioIn 16
Schallert, William Joseph 1922- WhoAm 90
Schallhorn, Susan Kelley 1945- WhoSSW 91
Schalliol, James Paul 1942- BiDrAPA 89
Schalliol, Thomas Edgar 1951- WhoEmL 91
Schallock, Art 1924- Ballpl 90
Schally, Andrew V. 1926- WorAlBi
Schally, Andrew Victor 1926- WhoAm 90, WhoSSW 91, WhoWor 91
Schalm, Paul John, III 1936- WhoE 91
Schalon, Edward I. 1920- St&PR 91
Schalow, Gayle Jean 1951- WhoAmW 91
Scham, Arnold 1941- BiDrAPA 89
Scham, Manuel J BiDrAPA 89
Schamber, J. G. 1938- St&PR 91
Schamberger, Beatrice M H BiDrAPA 89
Schamberger, William George, Jr. 1943- WhoSSW 91
Schambra, Philip Ellis 1934- WhoAm 90
Schamel, Cheryl 1947- WhoAmW 91
Schanbaum, Gene T. 1928- St&PR 91
Schanberg, Saul Murray 1933- WhoAm 90
Schanberg, Sydney H 1934- CurBio 90 [port]
Schanberg, Sydney Hillel 1934- WhoAm 90, WhoE 91
Schanck, Francis Raber, Jr. 1907- WhoAm 90
Schanck, Jordan Thomas 1931- St&PR 91
Schane, Murray David BiDrAPA 89
Schang, Kenneth William 1941- St&PR 91
Schang, Wally 1889-1965 Ballpl 90
Schank, Bernard Lynn 1921- WhoSSW 91
Schank, Lee H. 1935- St&PR 91
Schank, Roger C. 1946- BioIn 16, ConAu 132
Schank, Roger Carl 1946- WhoAm 90
Schanker, Jacob Zalman 1941- WhoE 91
Schanker, Louis 1903-1981 WhoAmA 91N
Schankman, Alan Robert 1947- WhoEmL 91, WhoWor 91
Schanne, Frank J. 1941- St&PR 91
Schannep, John Dwight 1934- WhoAm 90
Schannon, Robert Neil 1949- BiDrAPA 89
Schanstra, Carla Ross 1954- WhoAmW 91, WhoWrEP 89
Schantz, Daniel Dean 1942- WhoWrEP 89
Schantz, Gregory Allen 1963- WhoSSW 91
Schantzenbach, William Kerchner 1941- St&PR 91
Schanz, Charley 1919- Ballpl 90
Schanz, Geri L. ODwPR 91
Schanzlin, Patricia Roberts 1944- WhoAmW 91
Schanzmeyer, Lawrence P. 1946- WhoAm 90
Schanzmeyer, Lawrence Patrick 1946- St&PR 91
Schap, Louis R. 1928- St&PR 91
Schaper, Gerald Lee 1934- St&PR 91
Schaper, Johann 1621-1670 PenDiDA 89
Schaper, Laurence T. 1936- St&PR 91
Schaper, Richard J. 1957- St&PR 91
Schapery, Richard Allan 1935- WhoAm 90
Schapira, Henri Jacques BiDrAPA 89
Schapira, Morey R. 1949- St&PR 91
Schapira, Morey Rael 1949- WhoEmL 91
Schapire, Hans M BiDrAPA 89
Schapiro, Donald 1925- WhoAm 90
Schapiro, Edith K. 1929- St&PR 91

Schapiro, Ellen Eardley 1937- *BiDrAPA 89*
Schapiro, George Arnold 1946- *St&PR 91*
Schapiro, Herb 1929- *WhoAm 90*
Schapiro, Ivor *BiDrAPA 89*
Schapiro, Jaime 1939- *WhoSSW 91*
Schapiro, Jerome B. 1930- *St&PR 91*
Schapiro, Jerome Bentley 1930- *WhoE 91, WhoWor 91*
Schapiro, Leonard Bertram 1908-1983 *DcNaB 1981*
Schapiro, Mary *WhoAm 90*
Schapiro, Meyer 1904- *EncAL, WhoAm 90, WhoAmA 91*
Schapiro, Miriam 1923- *BiDWomA, BioIn 16, WhoAm 90, WhoAmA 91*
Schapiro, Morris A. 1903- *St&PR 91, WhoAm 90*
Schapiro, Nancy 1929- *WhoWrEP 89*
Schapiro, Raya Czerner 1934- *BiDrAPA 89*
Schapiro, Rolf Lutz 1933- *WhoE 91*
Schapiro, Ruth Goldman 1926- *WhoAm 90, WhoAmW 91, WhoE 91*
Schapiro, Salo Reizen 1945- *BiDrAPA 89*
Schaplowsky, Ellen H. 1946- *St&PR 91*
Schapp, Rebecca Maria 1956- *WhoEmL 91*
Schappell, Arthur W 1917- *BiDrAPA 89*
Schappes, Morris U 1907- *WhoWrEP 89*
Schaps, David *BioIn 16*
Schar, Stuart 1941- *WhoAmA 91*
Schara, Charles G. 1952- *St&PR 91*
Schara, Charles Gerard 1952- *WhoAm 90*
Scharabi, Mohamed 1938- *WhoWor 91*
Scharbert, Josef 1919- *WhoWor 91*
Schardein, Sandra Wild 1946- *WhoWrEP 89*
Schardt, Cyndi Diane 1958- *WhoE 91*
Scharein, Art 1905-1969 *Ballpl 90*
Scharein, George 1914-1981 *Ballpl 90*
Scharett, Ann Elizabeth 1941- *WhoAmW 91*
Scharf, Charles F. 1949- *St&PR 91*
Scharf, Charles Selden *BiDrAPA 89*
Scharf, Eric Greene 1958- *WhoE 91*
Scharf, Irwin 1935- *St&PR 91*
Scharf, Joachim-Hermann 1921- *WhoWor 91*
Scharf, Joel Stewart 1934- *St&PR 91*
Scharf, Kenny 1958- *WhoAmA 91*
Scharf, Kurt 1902-1990 *BioIn 16*
Scharf, Linda Elaine 1956- *WhoE 91*
Scharf, Michael 1942- *WhoAm 90*
Scharf, Robert D *BiDrAPA 89*
Scharf, Stephan Paul 1962- *IntWWM 90*
Scharf, Steven 1953- *St&PR 91*
Scharf, William 1927- *WhoAm 90, WhoAmA 91, WhoE 91*
Scharfe, Charles Louis 1923- *St&PR 91*
Scharfe, Hartmut Ewald Fritz 1930- *WhoAm 90*
Scharfenberg, Doris Ann 1917- *WhoAm 90*
Scharfenberg, Joachim 1927- *WhoWor 91*
Scharfer, Philip Jay 1948- *BiDrAPA 89*
Scharff, Constance Kramer *WhoAmA 91, WhoE 91*
Scharff, Daniel W. 1959- *St&PR 91*
Scharff, David Edward 1941- *BiDrAPA 89*
Scharff, Matthew Daniel 1932- *WhoAm 90*
Scharff, Monroe Bernard 1923- *WhoE 91, WhoWor 91*
Scharff, Morris Fraenkel 1929- *St&PR 91*
Scharffenberger, George T. 1919- *St&PR 91*
Scharffenberger, George Thomas 1919- *WhoAm 90, WhoE 91*
Scharffenberger, William J. 1921- *St&PR 91, WhoAm 90, WhoSSW 91*
Scharfman, Beth Karen *BiDrAPA 89*
Scharfman, Edward L 1950- *BiDrAPA 89*
Scharfman, Herbie *BioIn 16*
Scharfman, Melvin A 1928- *BiDrAPA 89*
Scharfsten, Alan J. 1953- *St&PR 91*
Scharlach, Andrew Edmund 1951- *WhoEmL 91*
Scharlau, Charles Edward 1927- *St&PR 91*
Scharlau, Charles Edward, III 1927- *WhoAm 90, WhoSSW 91*
Scharlemann, Robert Paul 1929- *WhoAm 90*
Scharold, Mary L 1943- *BiDrAPA 89*
Scharold, Mary Louise 1943- *WhoAmW 91*
Scharp, Anders 1934- *WhoAm 90*
Scharpenberg, Margot 1924- *EncCoWW*
Scharpf, Tad 1946- *St&PR 91*
Scharrer, Berta 1906- *BioIn 16*
Scharrer, Berta Vogel 1906- *WhoAm 90, WhoAmW 91*
Scharrer, Irene 1888-1971 *PenDiMP*
Scharringhausen, Michael Charles 1950- *WhoSSW 91*
Schartel, Elisabeth 1919- *IntWWM 90*
Scharten-Antink, Margo Sybranda Everdina 1869-1957 *EncCoWW*
Schartner, Albert Lyman 1931- *WhoE 91*
Scharvogel, Johann Julius 1854-1938 *PenDiDA 89*
Schary, Dore 1905-1980 *WorAlBi*
Schary, Ed 1925- *St&PR 91*
Schary, Emanuel 1924- *WhoAm 90, WhoAmA 91*
Schary, Saul 1904-1978 *WhoAmA 91N*
Schatell, Brian *BioIn 16*
Schatten, William E. 1928- *St&PR 91*
Schattinger, James Henry 1935- *St&PR 91*
Schattinger, Joan Myers 1936- *WhoAmW 91*
Schattke, Wolfgang 1937- *WhoWor 91*
Schattner, Edward *BiDrAPA 89*
Schattner, Robert L. 1938- *St&PR 91*
Schatton, Norman P. 1917- *St&PR 91*
Schatz, Bernard Elliott *BiDrAPA 89*
Schatz, Deborah Legow 1958- *WhoE 91*
Schatz, E. Gary 1929- *St&PR 91*
Schatz, Gottfried 1936- *WhoWor 91*
Schatz, Irvin I *BiDrAPA 89*
Schatz, Irwin Jacob 1931- *WhoAm 90*
Schatz, James Edward 1946- *WhoEmL 91*
Schatz, Mona Claire Struhsaker 1950- *WhoEmL 91*
Schatz, Paul Jacob Leonard, Jr. 1942- *WhoSSW 91*
Schatz, Pauline 1923- *WhoAmW 91*
Schatz, S. Michael 1921- *WhoAm 90*
Schatzberg, Alan F 1944- *BiDrAPA 89*
Schatzberg, Alan Frederic 1944- *WhoAm 90*
Schatzberg, Jerry 1927- *BioIn 16*
Schatzberg, Jerry Ned 1927- *WhoAm 90*
Schatzberg, Richard K. *St&PR 91*
Schatzberg, Theodore 1929- *St&PR 91*
Schatzberger, Lesley Ann 1953- *IntWWM 90*
Schatzeder, Dan 1954- *Ballpl 90*
Schatzer, John William 1961- *WhoSSW 91*
Schatzki, George 1933- *WhoAm 90*
Schatzow, Michael 1949- *WhoEmL 91*
Schaub, Frank Howard, IV 1962- *WhoE 91*
Schaub, Harry C. 1929- *St&PR 91*
Schaub, Harry Carl 1929- *WhoE 91*
Schaub, James Hamilton 1925- *WhoAm 90*
Schaub, Julie Nettie 1952- *WhoSSW 91*
Schaub, Marilyn McNamara 1928- *WhoAm 90, WhoAmW 91*
Schaub, Pete *BioIn 16*
Schaub, Philip D. *ODwPR 91*
Schaub, Raymond C. 1929- *St&PR 91*
Schaub, Sherwood Anhder, Jr. 1942- *WhoAm 90, WhoWor 91*
Schaubel, Howard James 1916- *WhoWor 91*
Schaubert, Stephen Jay 1946- *WhoAm 90*
Schaubhut, C. W. *BioIn 16*
Schaubroeck, Armand P. *St&PR 91*
Schaubroeck, Bruce *St&PR 91*
Schauder, Juliusz Pawel 1899-1943 *DcScB S2*
Schaudies, Jesse P., Jr. 1954- *WhoSSW 91*
Schauenberg, Susan Kay 1945- *WhoAmW 91*
Schauer, Albert Christian 1942- *St&PR 91*
Schauer, Catharine Guberman 1945- *WhoAmW 91*
Schauer, Frederick Franklin 1946- *WhoAm 90*
Schauer, Hans 1926- *WhoWor 91*
Schauer, Louis Frank 1928- *WhoAm 90*
Schauer, Rube 1891-1957 *Ballpl 90*
Schauer, Thomas Alfred 1927- *WhoWor 91*
Schauer, Thomas Lee 1935- *St&PR 91*
Schauer, Wilbert Edward, Jr. 1926- *WhoAm 90*
Schauerte-Maubouet, Helga Elisabeth 1957- *IntWWM 90*
Schauf, Victoria 1943- *WhoAmW 91*
Schaufele, Roger Donald 1928- *WhoAm 90*
Schauffler, Harvey Elliott, Jr. 1918- *WhoWor 91*
Schaufler, Robin Gordon 1957- *WhoAmW 91*
Schaufuss, Peter *BioIn 16*
Schaufuss, Peter 1950- *WhoAm 90, WhoWor 91*
Schaum, J. Michael 1949- *St&PR 91*
Schaumann, Sigrid Maria 1877-1979 *BiDWomA*
Schaumburg, Donald Roland 1919- *WhoAmA 91*
Schaumburg, Herbert Howard 1932- *WhoAm 90*
Schaumburg, Ronald G. 1936- *St&PR 91*
Schaumburger, Joseph Zalmon 1930- *WhoE 91*
Schaumer, Leo L. 1901- *St&PR 91*
Schaupp, Richard 1936- *St&PR 91*
Schaut, Joseph William 1928- *WhoAm 90*
Schautz, Carol A. *WhoAmW 91*
Schauwecker, Margaret Liddie 1934- *WhoAmW 91*
Schave, Douglas Jay 1945- *BiDrAPA 89*
Schaw, Janet 1731?-1801 *BioIn 16*
Schaw, Janet 1737?- *FemiCLE*
Schawk, Clarence W. 1926- *St&PR 91*
Schawlow, Arthur L. 1921- *WorAlBi*
Schawlow, Arthur Leonard 1921- *WhoAm 90, WhoWor 91*
Schaye, Edward Zach *BiDrAPA 89*
Schaye, Paul Leo 1952- *WhoE 91*
Schcoley, Virginia G. 1946- *St&PR 91*
Schealer, John Milton 1920- *AuBYP 90*
Schear, Herbert 1908- *St&PR 91*
Schechner, Richard 1934- *WhoAm 90*
Schechner, Sheridan 1905- *WhoAm 90*
Schechter, A. A. 1907-1989 *BioIn 16*
Schechter, Abel Alan 1907-1989 *BioIn 16*
Schechter, Allen Edward 1935- *St&PR 91, WhoAm 90*
Schechter, Arthur Louis 1939- *WhoSSW 91*
Schechter, Ben 1935- *AuBYP 90*
Schechter, Bernard Alvin 1923- *St&PR 91*
Schechter, Betty Goodstein 1921- *AuBYP 90*
Schechter, Daniel Philip 1942- *WhoAm 90*
Schechter, George *BioIn 16*
Schechter, Geraldine Poppa 1938- *WhoAmW 91*
Schechter, Harold A. 1944- *St&PR 91*
Schechter, Hope Mendoza 1921- *BioIn 16*
Schechter, Janet B *BiDrAPA 89*
Schechter, John Mendell 1946- *IntWWM 90*
Schechter, John Michael *BiDrAPA 89*
Schechter, Justin Owen 1955- *BiDrAPA 89*
Schechter, Loren 1940- *BiDrAPA 89*
Schechter, Mark Abraham *BiDrAPA 89*
Schechter, Marshall D 1921- *BiDrAPA 89*
Schechter, Mathilde Roth 1859-1924 *BioIn 16*
Schechter, Miriam 1950- *BiDrAPA 89*
Schechter, Robert P. *St&PR 91*
Schechter, Robert Samuel 1929- *WhoAm 90*
Schechter, Saul 1933- *St&PR 91*
Schechter, Sol 1916- *WhoSSW 91*
Schechter, Solomon 1847-1915 *BioIn 16*
Schechter, Stephen Lloyd 1945- *WhoAm 90*
Schechter, Stuart 1958- *WhoEmL 91*
Schechter, William 1934- *ODwPR 91*
Schechtman, Irving S. 1933- *St&PR 91*
Schechtman, Saul *IntWWM 90*
Scheck, Marianne 1914- *IntWWM 90*
Scheck, Michael 1939- *WhoSSW 91*
Scheckner, Sy 1924- *WhoAm 90*
Schecter, Joel R. 1947- *WhoWrEP 89*
Schecter, Peggy Smoler 1958- *WhoAmW 91*
Schectman, Herbert A. 1930- *St&PR 91, WhoAm 90*
Schectman, Stephen Barry 1947- *WhoE 91, WhoEmL 91*
Schedler, Gilbert Walter 1935- *WhoWrEP 89*
Schedler, Spencer Jaime 1933- *WhoE 91, WhoWor 91*
Scheeder, Louis William 1946- *WhoAm 90*
Scheel, Mark W. 1943- *WhoWrEP 89*
Scheel, Nels Earl 1925- *WhoAm 90*
Scheel, Paul Joseph 1933- *St&PR 91*
Scheel, Signe 1860-1942 *BiDWomA*
Scheel, Walter 1919- *WhoWor 91*
Scheele, Karl Wilhelm 1742-1786 *WorAlBi*
Scheele, Lee Norwood 1946- *St&PR 91*
Scheele, Leonard A. *BiDrAPA 89*
Scheele, Paul Drake 1922- *WhoAm 90, WhoWor 91*
Scheele, Roy Martin 1942- *WhoWrEP 89*
Scheele, William Earl 1920- *AuBYP 90*
Scheeler, Charles 1925- *WhoAm 90*
Scheeler, James Arthur 1927- *WhoAm 90*
Scheeler, John *BioIn 16*
Scheeler, Milford C. 1949- *St&PR 91*
Scheeler, Milford Charles, Jr. 1949- *St&PR 91*
Scheemaeckers, Hendrik *BioIn 16*
Scheemaeckers, Peter 1691-1781 *BioIn 16*
Scheer, Carl 1936- *WhoAm 90*
Scheer, George F. 1917- *AuBYP 90*
Scheer, Julian *St&PR 91*
Scheer, Julian 1926- *AuBYP 90*
Scheer, Julian Weisel 1926- *WhoAm 90*
Scheer, Milton David 1922- *WhoAm 90*
Scheer, R. Scott 1938- *WhoE 91*
Scheer, Ruth C. 1940- *St&PR 91*
Scheer, Sherie 1940- *WhoAmA 91*
Scheer, Stefanie *BioIn 16*
Scheer, Thomas N. 1934- *St&PR 91*
Scheerenberger, Richard Charles 1930- *WhoAm 90*
Scheeringa, Michael Scott *BiDrAPA 89*
Scheers, Susan Adams 1946- *WhoE 91*
Scheetz, Mary JoEllen 1926- *WhoAm 90, WhoAmW 91*
Scheetz, Thomas S. 1935- *St&PR 91*
Scheff, Burton Harold 1935- *St&PR 91*
Scheff, Fritzi 1879-1954 *OxCPMus*
Scheff, Steven R. 1937- *St&PR 91*
Scheffe, Henry 1907-1977 *DcScB S2*
Scheffel, Pablo G. 1946- *St&PR 91*
Scheffel, Renee Lee *BiDrAPA 89*
Scheffing, Bob 1913-1985 *Ballpl 90*
Scheffler, Israel *WhoAm 90*
Scheffler, Linda W. 1936- *WhoAmW 91*
Scheffler, Samuel 1951- *WhoAm 90*
Scheffler, Stuart Jay 1950- *WhoEmL 91*
Scheffman, David Theodore 1943- *WhoAm 90, WhoSSW 91*
Scheflen, Ann *ODwPR 91*
Schefold, Bertram 1943- *WhoWor 91*
Schefold, Dian 1936- *WhoWor 91*
Scheftel, Herbert 1907- *St&PR 91*
Schefter, Robert J. 1937- *St&PR 91*
Scheftner, Gerold 1937- *WhoAm 90*
Scheftner, William A *BiDrAPA 89*
Schehr, Lawrence Robins 1954- *WhoSSW 91*
Schehrer, Rudolf G. 1939- *WhoWor 91*
Scheianu, Constantin Sturza- 1797-1877 *BioIn 16*
Scheib, Carl 1927- *Ballpl 90, BioIn 16*
Scheib, Ida *AuBYP 90*
Scheibe, Karl Edward 1937- *WhoAm 90*
Scheibel, Arnold 1923- *BiDrAPA 89*
Scheibel, Arnold Bernard 1923- *WhoAm 90*
Scheibel, Jim 1947- *WhoAm 90*
Scheibel, Kenneth Maynard 1920- *WhoAm 90, WhoWor 91*
Scheiber, Donald Edwin 1926- *St&PR 91*
Scheiber, Stephen C 1938- *BiDrAPA 89*
Scheiber, Stephen Carl 1938- *WhoAm 90, WhoWor 91*
Scheibl, Jerome Alois 1930- *St&PR 91*
Scheible, Douglas Laverne 1962- *St&PR 91*
Scheible, R. G. *St&PR 91*
Scheibling, Norman John 1932- *St&PR 91*
Scheibner, Henry W. 1913- *St&PR 91*
Scheich, John F. 1942- *WhoE 91, WhoWor 91*
Scheichenbauer, Mario 1931- *ConDes 90*
Scheid, Francis 1920- *WhoAm 90*
Scheid, Paul 1938- *IntWWM 90*
Scheid, Wolfgang 1932- *WhoWor 91*
Scheid-Raymond, Linda Anne 1953- *WhoAmW 91*
Scheide, Richard Gilson 1929- *St&PR 91, WhoAm 90, WhoE 91*
Scheidel, Thomas Maynard 1931- *WhoAm 90*
Scheideler, Albert L. 1926- *St&PR 91*
Scheider, Roy 1932- *WorAlBi*
Scheider, Roy Richard 1935- *WhoAm 90*
Scheidhauer, Lynn Irene 1955- *WhoWrEP 89*
Scheidlinger, Saul 1918- *BioIn 16*
Scheidt, Karl 1934- *St&PR 91*
Scheidt, Lois Ann 1959- *WhoAmW 91*
Scheie, Harold G. *NewYTBS 90 [port]*
Scheie, Harold G. 1909-1990 *BioIn 16*
Scheier, Edwin 1910- *BioIn 16*
Scheier, Mary 1910- *BioIn 16*
Scheifele, Richard Paul 1934- *St&PR 91, WhoAm 90*
Scheifly, John Edward 1925- *WhoAm 90*
Scheimberg, Bernardo S *BiDrAPA 89*
Scheimer, Janice Schaefer 1948- *WhoAmW 91*
Scheimer, Louis 1928- *WhoAm 90*
Schein, Boris Moiseyevich 1938- *WhoSSW 91*
Schein, Edgar H. *BioIn 16*
Schein, Eugenie *WhoAmA 91*
Schein, Gabriel 1900- *BiDrAPA 89*
Schein, Harvey L. 1927- *WhoAm 90*
Schein, Jacob M. *BioIn 16*
Schein, Jerome 1923- *WhoWrEP 89*
Schein, Jonah Walter 1945- *BiDrAPA 89, WhoE 91*
Schein, Joseph 1915- *BiDrAPA 89*
Schein, Martin Warren 1925- *WhoAm 90*
Schein, Philip Samuel 1939- *WhoAm 90*
Schein, Sally Joy 1930- *WhoAmW 91*
Schein, Steven M. 1949- *St&PR 91*
Schein, Virginia Ellen 1943- *WhoAmW 91*
Schein, W. M. 1958- *St&PR 91*
Scheinbaum, David 1951- *WhoAm 90*
Scheinbaum, Mark Ira 1947- *WhoSSW 91*
Scheinberg, Audrey C *BiDrAPA 89*
Scheinberg, Peritz 1920- *WhoAm 90*
Scheinblum, Richie 1942- *Ballpl 90, BioIn 16*
Scheindlin, Raymond Paul 1940- *WhoAm 90*
Scheine, Arnold J. 1937- *St&PR 91*
Scheiner, David Charles 1945- *St&PR 91*
Scheiner, Leon 1937- *St&PR 91*
Scheiner, Michele 1952- *BiDrAPA 89*
Scheinert, Lindsey Gray 1950- *St&PR 91*
Scheinfeld, James D. 1926- *St&PR 91*
Scheinfeld, James David 1926- *WhoAm 90, WhoWor 91*
Scheinholtz, Leonard Louis 1927- *WhoAm 90*

Scheinin, Theodor Mikael 1924- *WhoWor 91*
Scheinkman, Alan David 1950- *WhoE 91*
Scheinkman, Jose Alexandre 1948- *WhoAm 90*
Scheinman, David A. 1942- *St&PR 91*
Scheinman, Stanley Bruce 1933- *WhoAm 90*
Scheirer, George A 1895-1959 *WhoAmA 91N*
Scheiring, Michael J. 1949- *WhoE 91, WhoWor 91*
Scheitler, Melissa Stout 1949- *St&PR 91, WhoEmL 91*
Scheitlin, Constance Joy 1949- *WhoSSW 91*
Schelar, Virginia M. 1924- *WhoAmW 91*
Schelbert, Heidi 1934- *WhoWor 91*
Scheld, Karl A. 1930- *St&PR 91*
Scheld, Karl Anton 1930- *WhoAm 90*
Schelde, Per 1945- *WhoE 91*
Scheldt, Judi Winsome 1946- *WhoAmW 91*
Scheler, Werner 1923- *WhoWor 91*
Schell, Allan Carter 1934- *WhoAm 90, WhoE 91*
Schell, Anne McCall 1942- *WhoAmW 91*
Schell, Braxton 1924- *WhoAm 90*
Schell, Edgar Thomas 1931- *WhoAm 90*
Schell, Erwin Haskell, Jr. *BiDrAPA 89*
Schell, James Munson 1944- *WhoAm 90*
Schell, John Le Roy 1919- *WhoAm 90*
Schell, Jonathan 1943- *BioIn 16*
Schell, Jonathan Edward 1943- *WhoWrEP 89*
Schell, Joseph Otis 1914- *WhoAm 90*
Schell, Maria 1926- *WorAlBi*
Schell, Mark Alexander Frederick 1951- *WhoSSW 91*
Schell, Mark Edward 1957- *St&PR 91*
Schell, Maximilian 1930- *WhoAm 90, WhoWor 91, WorAlBi*
Schell, Michael 1961- *IntWWM 90*
Schell, Orville H. 1940- *AuBYP 90*
Schell, Rolfe F 1916- *WhoWrEP 89*
Schell, Scott Thomas *BiDrAPA 89*
Schell, Thomas Charles 1951- *WhoE 91*
Schell, William P. 1822- *AmLegL*
Schellack, Rodney Scott 1954- *St&PR 91*
Schelle, Michael 1950- *IntWWM 90*
Schellenberg, August 1932- *OxCCanT*
Schellenberg, Ernest 1932- *St&PR 91*
Schellenberg, Karl Abraham 1931- *WhoAm 90*
Schellenberg, Peter Joseph 1931- *WhoE 91*
Schellenberg, Walter 1910-1952 *BioIn 16*
Schellenberger, Robert Earl 1932- *WhoSSW 91*
Schellenberger, Rudolph Harry 1926- *WhoE 91*
Schellenger, James P. 1919- *St&PR 91*
Schellens, Arlette Julie Lucie 1955- *WhoWor 91*
Scheller, Ernest, Jr. 1929- *St&PR 91*
Scheller, Sanford Gregory 1931- *St&PR 91, WhoAm 90*
Scheller, William *BioIn 16*
Schellhas, Edward William 1920- *St&PR 91*
Schellhase, Jodi Ann 1966- *WhoE 91*
Schellhous, Nancy Shick 1940- *WhoAmW 91*
Schelli, Jacob *PenDiDA 89*
Schellie, Coralee Ann 1931- *WhoAmW 91*
Schellin, Beth *BioIn 16*
Schellin, Robert William 1910-1985 *WhoAmA 91N*
Schelling, Ernest 1876-1939 *BioIn 16*
Schelling, Friedrich 1775-1854 *NinCLC 30 [port], WrPh P*
Schelling, Friedrich Von 1775-1854 *WorAlBi*
Schelling, John P. 1924- *St&PR 91*
Schelling, John Paul 1924- *WhoAm 90*
Schelling, Joyce Elaine 1937- *WhoAmW 91*
Schelling, Thomas Crombie 1921- *WhoAm 90, WhoE 91*
Schellingerhoudt, Elizabeth Whitner L. 1960- *WhoSSW 91*
Schellink, J. *PenDiDA 89*
Schellman, John A. 1924- *WhoAm 90*
Schellmann, Hans-Joachim Werner Egbert 1944- *WhoWor 91*
Schellpeper, Gene H. 1941- *St&PR 91*
Schelm, Roger Leonard 1936- *WhoAm 90, WhoE 91*
Schelp, Richard Herbert 1936- *WhoSSW 91*
Schelske, Claire L. 1932- *WhoAm 90*
Schelzel, Sharon Sullivan 1949- *WhoAmW 91*
Scheman, Andrew Joseph 1953- *WhoE 91*
Scheman, Blanche 1917- *WhoAmW 91*
Scheman, L. Ronald 1931- *WhoE 91*
Scheman, Rita Susan 1950- *WhoAmW 91*
Schembechler, Bo *BioIn 16*
Schembechler, Bo 1929- *News 90 [port], -90-3 [port], WhoAm 90*
Schemineck, Herb 1947- *St&PR 91*
Scheminske, Dennis *ODwPR 91*
Schemmel, Thomas G *BiDrAPA 89*
Schemmer, Benjamin F. 1932- *WhoAm 90*
Schenck, A. W., Jr. 1916- *St&PR 91*
Schenck, Andrew Craig 1941- *WhoAm 90*
Schenck, Benjamin Robinson 1938- *St&PR 91, WhoAm 90*
Schenck, Carlos Hugh 1951- *BiDrAPA 89*
Schenck, Frederick A. 1928- *WhoAm 90*
Schenck, Henry Paul 1929- *WhoE 91*
Schenck, Herbert Holtzclaw 1911- *WhoE 91*
Schenck, Jack Lee 1938- *St&PR 91, WhoAm 90*
Schenck, Jane E. 1949- *WhoAmW 91*
Schenck, John Franklin, III 1921- *St&PR 91*
Schenck, Philip Knight 1944- *WhoE 91, WhoWor 91*
Schenck, Robert Cumming 1809-1890 *BioIn 16*
Schenck, Steven James 1948- *St&PR 91*
Schenck, Susan Jane 1949- *WhoE 91*
Schenck, William Clinton 1947- *WhoAmA 91*
Schenck, William Ziegler 1945- *WhoEmL 91*
Schend, Valerie A. 1957- *WhoAmW 91*
Schendel, Mira 1919-1988 *ArtLatA*
Schene, Arthur V. 1916- *St&PR 91*
Schenendorf, Ronald 1950- *BiDrAPA 89*
Schengber, John S 1932- *BiDrAPA 89*
Schengrund, Cara-Lynne 1941- *WhoAmW 91*
Schenk, David Eric 1962- *BiDrAPA 89*
Schenk, Joseph Bernard 1953- *WhoAmA 91*
Schenk, Karl-Ernst 1929- *WhoWor 91*
Schenk, Manfred 1930- *IntWWM 90*
Schenk, Norman Frederick 1949- *St&PR 91*
Schenk, Otto 1930- *IntWWM 90*
Schenk, Quentin Frederick 1922- *WhoAm 90*
Schenk, Teresa *ODwPR 91*
Schenk, Worthington George, Jr. 1922- *WhoAm 90*
Schenk von Stauffenberg, Klaus Philipp 1907-1944 *BioIn 16*
Schenk-Ziebelman, Cynthia Marian 1954- *WhoAmW 91*
Schenkar, Joan *BioIn 16*
Schenkel, Barbara Ann 1951- *WhoEmL 91*
Schenkel, John Lawrence *BiDrAPA 89*
Schenkel, Steven Solomon *BiDrAPA 89*
Schenkel, Susan 1946- *WhoAmW 91*
Schenken, Carl G. 1949- *St&PR 91*
Schenker, Alexander Marian 1924- *WhoAm 90*
Schenker, Eric 1931- *WhoAm 90*
Schenker, Jonathan 1951- *ODwPR 91*
Schenker, Joseph George 1933- *WhoWor 91*
Schenker, Leo 1922- *WhoAm 90*
Schenker, Leon 1959- *WhoE 91*
Schenker, Steven 1929- *WhoAm 90*
Schenkkan, Robert 1953- *ConAu 132*
Schenkler, Bernard 1948- *WhoEmL 91*
Schenkman, John Boris 1936- *WhoAm 90*
Schenkman, Richard D *BiDrAPA 89*
Schensted, M. A. 1943- *St&PR 91*
Schenz, Hank 1919- *Ballpl 90*
Schepens, Luc John 1940- *WhoE 91*
Schepers, Donald Herbert 1951- *WhoWor 91*
Schepis, Anthony Joseph 1927- *WhoAmA 91*
Schepis, Diane Jo 1962- *WhoAmW 91*
Schepis, Giovanni 1894-1963 *EncO&P 3*
Schepis, Guy A. *St&PR 91*
Schepis, Joseph Michael 1953- *St&PR 91*
Schepker, Donald Joseph 1949- *St&PR 91*
Schepman, Berne Adair 1926- *St&PR 91, WhoAm 90*
Schepp, Brad Jeffrey 1955- *WhoWrEP 89*
Scheppach, Raymond Carl, Jr. 1940- *WhoAm 90*
Schepps, Phil J. 1918- *St&PR 91*
Schepps, Victoria Hayward 1956- *WhoEmL 91*
Scheps, Clarence 1915- *WhoAm 90*
Scheps, Marc 1932- *WhoWor 91*
Scher, Allen Myron 1921- *WhoAm 90*
Scher, Ann I. 1956- *WhoAmW 91*
Scher, Anne J. 1952- *ODwPR 91*
Scher, Barry F. 1942- *ODwPR 91*
Scher, Barry Frederick 1942- *WhoE 91*
Scher, Coby Allyn 1942- *WhoSSW 91*
Scher, Ellen Judith 1953- *WhoAmW 91*
Scher, Herbert Irwin 1928- *St&PR 91*
Scher, Howard Dennis 1945- *WhoEmL 91*
Scher, Irving 1933- *WhoAm 90*
Scher, Jill *BioIn 16*
Scher, Martin M. 1922- *St&PR 91*
Scher, Maryonda *BiDrAPA 89*
Scher, Norman *BiDrAPA 89*
Scher, Norman A. 1937- *St&PR 91*
Scher, Paula *AuBYP 90*
Scher, Paula 1948- *BioIn 16*
Scher, Roberta Snyder 1945- *WhoSSW 91*
Scher, Stanley Jules 1929- *WhoAm 90*
Scher, Stephen Karl 1934- *St&PR 91*
Scher, Steven Paul 1936- *WhoAm 90*
Scheraga, Harold Abraham 1921- *WhoAm 90*
Scheraga, Joel Dov 1955- *WhoE 91*
Scherb, Joan C. 1937- *St&PR 91*
Scherb, Peter 1944- *St&PR 91*
Scherba, Elaine Louise 1949- *WhoAm 90, WhoAmW 91*
Scherba, Elaine P. 1949- *St&PR 91*
Scherba, John E. 1928- *St&PR 91*
Scherber, Anthony L. 1934- *St&PR 91*
Scherchen, Hermann 1891-1966 *PenDiMP*
Schere, Jonathan Lawrence 1938- *WhoAm 90*
Scherer, Alfredo Vicente 1903- *WhoWor 91*
Scherer, Anita 1938- *WhoAmW 91*
Scherer, Carol Louise 1945- *WhoAmW 91*
Scherer, Donald Richard 1939- *WhoAm 90*
Scherer, Frederic Michael 1932- *WhoAm 90, WhoE 91*
Scherer, George Howard 1927- *St&PR 91*
Scherer, Gordon H. 1906-1988 *BioIn 16*
Scherer, Harold N., Jr. 1929- *St&PR 91*
Scherer, Harold Nicholas, Jr. 1929- *WhoAm 90*
Scherer, Harvey Daniel 1944- *BiDrAPA 89, WhoE 91*
Scherer, Herbert Grover 1930- *WhoAmA 91*
Scherer, J. Peter 1949- *St&PR 91*
Scherer, Jeanne Catherine 1928- *WhoAmW 91*
Scherer, Karla 1937- *WhoAmW 91*
Scherer, Lester B 1931- *ConAu 132*
Scherer, Marcia Joslyn 1948- *WhoAmW 91*
Scherer, Maurice 1920- *WhoAm 90, WhoWor 91*
Scherer, Otto E. 1915- *St&PR 91*
Scherer, Patricia Ann 1948- *WhoWor 91*
Scherer, Peter R. 1956- *St&PR 91*
Scherer, Robert B. 1941- *St&PR 91*
Scherer, Robert Davisson 1929- *WhoAm 90*
Scherer, Robert Frederic 1955- *WhoSSW 91*
Scherer, Robert Grainger 1929- *St&PR 91*
Scherer, Roger Henry 1935- *St&PR 91*
Scherer, Ron 1944- *ODwPR 91*
Scherer, Roy *BioIn 16*
Scherer, Susan M. *BiDrAPA 89*
Scherer, Theodore M. 1934- *St&PR 91*
Scherer, Victor Richard 1940- *WhoWor 91*
Scherer, Wallace B 1913- *EncO&P 3*
Scherf, Christopher N. 1950- *WhoAm 90*
Scherf, Margaret 1908-1979 *AuBYP 90, TwCCr&M 91*
Scherff, Richard Lee 1937- *WhoAm 90, WhoE 91*
Scherffius, Stephen Wilson 1949- *BiDrAPA 89*
Scherfig, Hans 1905-1979 *DcScanL*
Schergens, Becky Lou 1940- *WhoAmW 91, WhoSSW 91*
Scherger, Mozelle Spainhour 1916- *WhoAmW 91*
Scherich, Edward Baptiste 1923- *WhoAm 90*
Scherich, Erwin Thomas 1918- *WhoAm 90, WhoWor 91*
Scherker, Michael *BioIn 16, NewYTBS 90*
Scherl, Allen I. 1940- *St&PR 91*
Scherl, Donald J 1935- *BiDrAPA 89*
Scherl, Donald Jacob *WhoAm 90, WhoE 91*
Scherle, Volker 1941- *St&PR 91*
Scherler, Barbara 1938- *IntWWM 90*
Scherman, Debra Davidson 1962- *WhoE 91*
Scherman, Fred 1944- *Ballpl 90*
Scherman, Katharine 1915- *AuBYP 90*
Scherman, Susan Louise 1953- *WhoWrEP 89*
Scherman, Thomas 1917-1979 *PenDiMP*
Schermann, Raphael 1879- *EncO&P 3*
Schermer, George *BioIn 16*
Schermer, Harry Angus 1942- *St&PR 91, WhoAm 90*
Schermer, Judith Kahn 1949- *WhoAmW 91*
Schermer, Lloyd G. 1927- *St&PR 91, WhoAm 90*
Schermerhorn, Clifton Seth *BiDrAPA 89*
Schermerhorn, Debra Carol 1961- *WhoAmW 91*
Schermerhorn, John Watson 1920- *WhoAm 90*
Schermerhorn, Kenneth DeWitt 1929- *IntWWM 90, WhoAm 90, WhoSSW 91*
Schermerhorn, Lee Van Dyke, Jr. 1928- *St&PR 91*
Schermerhorn, Neal Y. 1936- *St&PR 91*
Schermers, Henry Gerhard 1928- *WhoWor 91*
Scherokman, Barbara Jeanne 1949- *WhoAmW 91*
Scherpenberg, Theodore Anthony 1924- *St&PR 91*
Scherpereel, Richard Charles 1931- *WhoAmA 91*
Scherpf, Joseph Charles 1943- *St&PR 91*
Scherr, Allan Lee 1940- *WhoAm 90*
Scherr, Barbara Nadle 1946- *St&PR 91*
Scherr, Bill *BioIn 16*
Scherr, David Edward 1948- *St&PR 91*
Scherr, Harry, III 1944- *St&PR 91*
Scherr, Jim *BioIn 16*
Scherr, Lawrence 1928- *WhoAm 90*
Scherr, Marvin Gerald 1940- *WhoE 91*
Scherr, Paul *ODwPR 91*
Scherrer, Bill 1958- *Ballpl 90*
Scherrer, Charles Lee 1948- *St&PR 91*
Scherrer, Everett John 1942- *St&PR 91*
Scherrer, Laetitia *BioIn 16*
Scherrer, Leonor *BioIn 16*
Scherrer, Paul Hermann 1890-1969 *DcScB S2*
Scherry, Eugene Bernard 1931- *St&PR 91*
Schersten, H. Donald 1919- *WhoAm 90*
Schertle, Alice 1941- *AuBYP 90*
Schertz, Morris 1929- *WhoAm 90*
Schertzer, Stephen Jonathan *BiDrAPA 89*
Schertzinger, Victor 1880-1941 *OxCPMus*
Scherwinski, Darrell H. 1938- *St&PR 91*
Scherz, Bruno 1938- *BiDrAPA 89*
Scherzer, Anna S M 1948- *BiDrAPA 89*
Scherzer, Daniel Jay 1962- *BiDrAPA 89*
Scherzer, Harry S. 1935- *St&PR 91*
Scherzer, Rosalie *EncCoWW*
Scherzer, Suzana 1931- *WhoWor 91*
Scheske, Jan *ODwPR 91*
Schessl, Franz *PenDiMP*
Schetky, Diane H 1940- *BiDrAPA 89*
Schetky, Diane Heiskell 1940- *WhoE 91*
Schetky, Laurence McDonald 1922- *St&PR 91*
Schetlick, William G. 1924- *St&PR 91*
Schetlin, Eleanor M. 1920- *WhoAmW 91, WhoE 91, WhoWor 91*
Schettino, Robert *ODwPR 91*
Schetz, John Joseph 1946- *BiDrAPA 89*
Schetz, Joseph Alfred 1936- *WhoAm 90*
Scheu, Leonard 1904- *WhoAmA 91*
Scheuber, Theodor Schmidt 1934- *St&PR 91*
Scheuch, Donald Ralph 1918- *St&PR 91*
Scheuch, Richard 1921- *WhoAm 90*
Scheuer, James Haas 1920- *WhoAm 90, WhoE 91*
Scheuer, Lothar Erwin Andreas 1928- *WhoWor 91*
Scheuer, Paul Josef 1915- *WhoAm 90*
Scheuerer, Janie Lynn 1954- *WhoE 91*
Scheuerl, Hans Jurgen 1919- *WhoWor 91*
Scheuerle, Angela Elizabeth 1962- *WhoEmL 91*
Scheuerle, Paul Norman 1926- *IntWWM 90*
Scheuerman, Carl Edward 1943- *St&PR 91*
Scheuerman, Lola Kathryn 1939- *WhoAmW 91*
Scheuermann, Milton George, Jr. 1933- *WhoSSW 91*
Scheuermann, Mona 1946- *WhoAmW 91*
Scheufele, W. Joseph 1948- *St&PR 91*
Scheuing, Eberhard Eugen 1939- *WhoE 91*
Scheuing, Richard A. 1927- *St&PR 91*
Scheurenbrand, Kim Rene 1960- *WhoAmW 91*
Scheurer, Charles B. 1941- *St&PR 91*
Scheurer, Elizabeth Jeanne 1930- *WhoAmW 91*
Scheurer-Kestner, Auguste 1833-1899 *BiDFrPL*
Scheurich, Paul 1883-1945 *PenDiDA 89*
Scheuring, Garry J. 1939- *St&PR 91*
Scheuring, Garry Joseph 1939- *WhoAm 90*
Scheuring, Helen 1940- *WhoAmW 91, WhoWor 91*
Scheutzow, Monet Dorothy 1953- *WhoAmW 91*
Scheve, Kenneth Edward 1946- *St&PR 91*
Scheve, Larry Gerard 1950- *WhoEmL 91*
Schevill, James 1920- *ConAu 12AS [port]*
Schevill, James Erwin 1920- *WhoAm 90, WhoWrEP 89*
Scheving, Lawrence Einar 1920- *WhoAm 90*
Schewe, Bruce Victor 1956- *WhoEmL 91*
Schewel, Rosel Hoffberger 1928- *WhoAmW 91*
Schewel, Stanford 1918- *WhoAm 90*
Schexnayder, Brian 1953- *IntWWM 90*
Schexnayder, Brian Edward 1953- *WhoAm 90*
Schexnayder, Donald Alfred 1940- *BiDrAPA 89*
Schexnayder, Lisa W *BiDrAPA 89*
Schey, John Anthony 1922- *WhoAm 90*
Scheye, Klaus G. 1923- *St&PR 91*
Scheyer, Ernst 1900- *WhoAmA 91*

Scheyer, Stuart R. 1930- *St&PR 91*
Scheyrer, Gerda 1925- *IntWWM 90*
Schiaffino, Silvio Stephen 1927- *WhoAm 90*
Schiaffo, Alfred D. 1920-1988 *BioIn 16*
Schiano, Barry Edward 1963- *WhoE 91*
Schiaparelli, Elsa 1890-1973 *WorAlBi*
Schiaparelli, Elsa 1896-1973 *BioIn 16*
Schiaparelli, Giovanni Virginio 1835-1910 *WorAlBi*
Schiappa, Janice Miller 1950- *WhoAmW 91*
Schiappacasse, DeeAnn Lynn 1951- *WhoAmW 91*
Schiavelli, Melvyn David 1942- *WhoAm 90*
Schiavi, Anthony Romeo 1950- *WhoEmL 91*
Schiavi, Felice 1931- *IntWWM 90*
Schiavi, Raul C 1930- *BiDrAPA 89*
Schiavi, Raul Constante 1930- *WhoE 91*
Schiavi, Rosemary Filomena 1947- *WhoAmW 91*
Schiavina, Laura M 1917- *WhoAmA 91*
Schiavina, Laura Margaret 1917- *WhoAm 90*
Schiavone, Andrew Anthony, Jr. *BiDrAPA 89*
Schiavone, George Joseph 1948- *WhoE 91*
Schiavone, James 1929- *St&PR 91*
Schiavone, John Michael 1957- *WhoE 91*
Schiazza, Guido Domenic 1930- *WhoE 91*
Schibler, Ueli 1947- *WhoWor 91*
Schiciano, Joseph S. 1927- *St&PR 91*
Schick, Alice 1946- *AuBYP 90*
Schick, Alice Edith 1927- *WhoSSW 91*
Schick, Edgar Brehob 1934- *WhoAm 90*
Schick, Eleanor 1942- *AuBYP 90*
Schick, Elliot 1924- *St&PR 91*
Schick, Frank L 1918- *ConAu 132*
Schick, Harry L. 1927- *St&PR 91*
Schick, Harry Leon 1927- *WhoAm 90*
Schick, Irvin Henry 1924- *WhoE 91, WhoWor 91*
Schick, Jacob 1877-1937 *WorAlBi*
Schick, James Baldwin Mc Donald 1940- *WhoWrEP 89*
Schick, Jane *BiDrAPA 89*
Schick, Joseph Carl 1930- *St&PR 91*
Schick, Maria Seraphina Suzanna M. *PenDiDA 89*
Schick, Thomas Edward 1941- *St&PR 91, WhoAm 90, WhoSSW 91*
Schickel, Richard 1933- *WhoWrEP 89, WorAu 1980 [port]*
Schickele, Peter 1935- *ConMus 5 [port], IntWWM 90, WhoAm 90*
Schickele, Rene 1883-1940 *BioIn 16*
Schicker, Dona Roberta 1939- *WhoSSW 91*
Schicker, Glenn Earl 1950- *WhoWrEP 89*
Schickler, Robert Dennis 1951- *WhoE 91*
Schickler, W. J. 1934- *St&PR 91*
Schickler, William John 1934- *WhoE 91*
Schidlof, Peter *PenDiMP*
Schidlovsky, John 1948- *WhoWor 91*
Schidlowski, Juan Carlos *BioIn 16*
Schidlowski, Manfred 1933- *WhoWor 91*
Schiebel, Herman Max 1909- *WhoSSW 91*
Schieber, Allen Dale 1948- *St&PR 91*
Schieber, Anna 1867-1945 *EncCoWW*
Schieber, Eric Charles 1959- *BiDrAPA 89*
Schieber, Paul H. 1955- *WhoE 91*
Schieber, Sylvester Joseph 1946- *WhoE 91*
Schiebler, Gerold Ludwig 1928- *WhoAm 90*
Schiebler, Theodor Heinrich 1923- *WhoWor 91*
Schiebold, Hans 1938- *WhoAmA 91*
Schieder, Joseph Eugene 1908- *WhoAm 90*
Schiefelbusch, Richard L. 1918- *WhoAm 90*
Schiefer, Johannes *WhoAmA 91N*
Schieferdecker, G. Peter 1925- *St&PR 91*
Schieferdecker, Ivan E 1935- *WhoAmA 91*
Schieffelin, Bayard *BioIn 16*
Schieffelin, George Richard 1930- *WhoE 91, WhoSSW 91, WhoWor 91*
Schieffelin, Laurie Graham 1941- *WhoAm 90, WhoWrEP 89*
Schieffelin, Thomas Lawrence 1936- *WhoSSW 91*
Schieffelin, W. J., III 1922- *St&PR 91*
Schieffelin, William Jay 1922-1989 *BioIn 16*
Schieffer, Bob *WhoAm 90*
Schieffer, Joseph H. 1951- *WhoEmL 91*
Schiefner, Dieter 1939- *WhoSSW 91*
Schieke, Herman Edward, Jr. 1937- *St&PR 91*
Schieken, Richard Merrill 1939- *WhoSSW 91*
Schield, Marshall Lew 1946- *St&PR 91*
Schield, Michael F. 1948- *St&PR 91*
Schield, William H., Jr. 1926- *St&PR 91*
Schiele, Burtrum C *BiDrAPA 89*
Schiele, Daniel R 1941- *BiDrAPA 89*
Schiele, Egon 1890-1918 *IntDcAA 90*
Schiele, Henry F. 1922- *St&PR 91*
Schiele, Herbert S, Jr. 1924- *BiDrAPA 89*
Schiele, James E. 1929- *St&PR 91*
Schiele, Paul Ellsworth, Jr. 1924- *WhoWor 91*
Schiele, Roy L. 1943- *St&PR 91*
Schieler, Calvin Louis 1932- *St&PR 91*
Schier, Donald Stephen 1914- *WhoAm 90*
Schier, Flint *BioIn 16*
Schier, Mary Jane 1939- *WhoAmW 91*
Schierholz, William Francis, Jr. 1921- *WhoAm 90*
Schierholz, Wm. F., Jr. 1921- *St&PR 91*
Schiering, Charles Edward 1923- *St&PR 91*
Schiering, Harry Calvin 1924- *St&PR 91*
Schierl, Paul J. 1935- *St&PR 91*
Schierl, Paul Julius 1935- *WhoAm 90*
Schierling, Charlotte Anna 1911- *EncO&P 3*
Schierlinger, Kevin Nickolas 1955- *WhoEmL 91*
Schierow, Linda-Jo 1947- *WhoAmW 91*
Schiesel, Jane *AuBYP 90*
Schieser, Hans Alois 1931- *WhoAm 90*
Schiesl, Joseph P. 1952- *St&PR 91*
Schiess, Betty Bone 1923- *WhoAmW 91*
Schiess, Kenneth R. 1947- *St&PR 91*
Schiessler, Robert Walter 1918- *WhoAm 90*
Schiesswohl, Cynthia Rae Schlegel 1955- *WhoAmW 91, WhoWor 91*
Schieszler, Augustus J. 1918- *St&PR 91*
Schieszler, Joseph F. 1939- *St&PR 91*
Schietinger, James Frederick 1946- *WhoAmA 91*
Schieve, Catherine James 1949- *BiDrAPA 89*
Schiever, Ernst *PenDiMP*
Schiewe, Robert George 1944- *St&PR 91*
Schifano, Angelo J. *BioIn 16*
Schifelbein-Jordan, Karen *BioIn 16*
Schiff, Alan Dana 1950- *St&PR 91*
Schiff, Albert John 1942- *WhoAm 90*
Schiff, Alexander 1899-1990 *BioIn 16*
Schiff, Andras 1953- *IntWWM 90, PenDiMP*
Schiff, Arthur *St&PR 91*
Schiff, Daniel 1929- *BiDrAPA 89*
Schiff, David Tevele 1936- *WhoAm 90, WhoE 91*
Schiff, Donald Wilfred 1925- *WhoAm 90*
Schiff, Dorothy 1903-1989 *AnObit 1989, BioAmW, BioIn 16, ConAu 129*
Schiff, Edward J 1922- *BiDrAPA 89*
Schiff, Eugene Roger 1937- *WhoAm 90*
Schiff, Gert 1926-1990 *NewYTBS 90*
Schiff, Gert K A 1926- *WhoAmA 91*
Schiff, Graenum R 1929- *BiDrAPA 89*
Schiff, Gunther Hans 1927- *WhoAm 90*
Schiff, Heinrich 1951- *IntWWM 90, PenDiMP*
Schiff, Isaac 1944- *WhoAm 90*
Schiff, Jacob Henry 1847-1920 *EncABHB 6 [port]*
Schiff, Jacques Charles, Jr. 1931- *WhoE 91*
Schiff, Jayne Nemerow 1945- *WhoAmW 91, WhoE 91, WhoEmL 91*
Schiff, Jean 1929- *WhoAmA 91*
Schiff, Jerome Arnold 1931- *WhoAm 90*
Schiff, John J. 1916- *St&PR 91*
Schiff, John Jefferson, Jr. 1916- *WhoAm 90*
Schiff, Joseph *WhoAm 90*
Schiff, Laurence E *BiDrAPA 89*
Schiff, Laurence Elliot 1950- *WhoE 91*
Schiff, Laurie 1960- *WhoAmW 91*
Schiff, Leonard Isaac 1915-1971 *DcScB S2*
Schiff, Leonard Norman 1938- *WhoE 91*
Schiff, Lonny *WhoAmA 91*
Schiff, Marlene Sandler *WhoAmW 91*
Schiff, Martin 1922- *WhoAm 90, WhoWor 91*
Schiff, Matthew M 1943- *BiDrAPA 89*
Schiff, Michael Stephen 1949- *WhoSSW 91*
Schiff, Morton 1934- *St&PR 91*
Schiff, Samuel B 1928- *BiDrAPA 89*
Schiff, Sheldon K *BiDrAPA 89*
Schiff, Stefan Otto 1930- *WhoAm 90*
Schiff, Steven H. 1947- *BioIn 16*
Schiff, Steven Harvey 1947- *WhoAm 90*
Schiff, Susan *BiDrAPA 89*
Schiff-Mayer, Morisa *BiDrAPA 89*
Schiffel, D. D. 1943- *St&PR 91*
Schiffel, Suzanne Driscoll 1946- *WhoAmW 91*
Schiffer, Claudia *BioIn 16*
Schiffer, Daniel L. 1943- *St&PR 91*
Schiffer, Fredric *BiDrAPA 89*
Schiffer, Hubert *PenDiDA 89*
Schiffer, Irvine 1917- *BiDrAPA 89*
Schiffer, Jean Marie 1962- *WhoAmW 91*
Schiffer, John Paul 1930- *WhoAm 90*
Schiffer, Randolph B 1948- *BiDrAPA 89*
Schiffer, Randolph Brenton 1948- *WhoE 91*
Schiffer, Robert L. *AuBYP 90*
Schiffer, Selma *AuBYP 90*
Schiffermuller, Willard John 1935- *WhoSSW 91*
Schiffler, Ludger 1937- *WhoWor 91*
Schiffmacher, C. Ellis 1908-1988 *BioIn 16*
Schiffman, Alan Theodore 1942- *WhoE 91*
Schiffman, Bonnie 1950- *BioIn 16*
Schiffman, David 1926- *WhoE 91*
Schiffman, Gerald 1926- *WhoAm 90, WhoE 91, WhoWor 91*
Schiffman, Harold 1928- *IntWWM 90*
Schiffman, Harold Fosdick 1938- *WhoAm 90*
Schiffman, Jeffrey Howard *BiDrAPA 89*
Schiffman, Joseph Harris 1914- *WhoAm 90, WhoE 91, WhoWor 91*
Schiffman, Louis F. 1927- *WhoWor 91*
Schiffman, Mark Joel 1946- *WhoE 91*
Schiffman, Mia Helen 1953- *WhoAmW 91*
Schiffman, Nancy Elizabeth 1937- *WhoAmW 91*
Schiffman, Peter Allen *BiDrAPA 89*
Schiffman, Robert Stanley 1944- *St&PR 91*
Schiffman, Saul S. 1914- *St&PR 91*
Schiffman, Shirlee 1942- *WhoAmW 91*
Schiffman, Susan Stolte 1940- *WhoAmW 91*
Schiffman, Suzanne *BioIn 16*
Schiffman, Yale Marvin 1938- *WhoSSW 91*
Schiffmann, Elliott 1927- *WhoE 91*
Schiffmann, Robert *BioIn 16*
Schiffmann, Robert Frank 1935- *WhoE 91*
Schiffner, Charles Robert 1948- *WhoEmL 91*
Schiffrin, Andre 1935- *WhoAm 90*
Schiffrin, Milton Julius 1914- *WhoSSW 91, WhoWor 91*
Schiflett, Mary Fletcher Cavender 1925- *WhoAmW 91*
Schifman, Edward Joseph 1949- *WhoEmL 91, WhoWor 91*
Schifrin, Lalo 1932- *OxCPMus*
Schifter, Catherine Crutchfield 1950- *WhoAmW 91*
Schifter, Richard 1923- *WhoAm 90*
Schikaneder, Emanuel 1751-1812 *PenDiMP*
Schikofsky, Heinz Gerd 1938- *WhoWor 91*
Schilbach, Christhart S *BiDrAPA 89*
Schilbrack, Karen Gail 1949- *WhoWor 91*
Schild, Albert 1920- *WhoAm 90, WhoE 91*
Schild, Joyce Anna 1931- *WhoAmW 91*
Schild, Wayne L. 1945- *St&PR 91*
Schilde, Barbara D. 1933- *WhoAmW 91*
Schilder, J. Michael 1943- *St&PR 91*
Schilder, Mark *BioIn 16*
Schilder, Stephen *BiDrAPA 89*
Schildgen, Gordon Wayne 1943- *St&PR 91*
Schildhaus, Andrew 1915-1988 *BioIn 16*
Schildhaus, Donald Ira 1933- *WhoE 91*
Schildhouse, Burton *St&PR 91*
Schildkraut, Carl Louis 1937- *WhoAm 90*
Schildkraut, Joseph *BiDrAPA 89*
Schildkraut, Joseph 1896-1964 *WorAlBi*
Schildkraut, Joseph Jacob 1934- *WhoAm 90*
Schildkrout, Barbara Ellen *BiDrAPA 89*
Schildkrout, Elliot 1947- *BiDrAPA 89*
Schildkrout, Mollie S *BiDrAPA 89*
Schildt, Ernst Runar 1888-1925 *DcScanL*
Schildwachter, Fred Henry, III 1949- *St&PR 91*
Schilke, Clifford H *BiDrAPA 89*
Schillaci, Miriam *BioIn 16*
Schillawski, Norman D. 1952- *WhoE 91*
Schille, Alice 1869-1955 *BiDWomA*
Schiller, Alfred George 1918- *WhoAm 90*
Schiller, Alice Ann 1950- *WhoAmW 91*
Schiller, Allan 1943- *IntWWM 90*
Schiller, Arthur A. 1910- *WhoAm 90*
Schiller, Barbara 1928- *AuBYP 90*
Schiller, Beatrice *WhoAmA 91*
Schiller, Dan 1951- *ConAu 131*
Schiller, Donald Charles 1942- *WhoAm 90*
Schiller, F.C.S. 1864-1937 *EncO&P 3*
Schiller, Ferdinand Canning Scott 1864-1937 *EncPaPR 91*
Schiller, Francine Sandra 1941- *WhoSSW 91*
Schiller, Friedrich 1759-1805 *DcLB 94 [port]*
Schiller, Friedrich Von 1759-1805 *WorAlBi, WrPh*
Schiller, Gabrielle Antonia 1962- *WhoAmW 91*
Schiller, Ginnell M. 1955- *St&PR 91*
Schiller, Herbert I. 1919- *WhoWrEP 89*
Schiller, Herbert Irving 1919- *WhoAm 90*
Schiller, Herbert Miles 1943- *WhoSSW 91*
Schiller, Jerome Paul 1934- *WhoAm 90*
Schiller, Jerry A. 1932- *St&PR 91, WhoAm 90*
Schiller, Jo Anne 1938- *WhoAmW 91*
Schiller, Karl August 1911- *WhoWor 91*
Schiller, Lawrence Julian 1936- *WhoAm 90*
Schiller, Lynne Ann 1966- *WhoAmW 91*
Schiller, Madeline 1842?-1911 *PenDiMP*
Schiller, Marvin 1933- *St&PR 91*
Schiller, Matthew Eugene 1952- *WhoE 91*
Schiller, Maurice A 1906- *BiDrAPA 89*
Schiller, Michael 1933- *St&PR 91*
Schiller, Neal Leander 1949- *WhoEmL 91*
Schiller, Peter Harkai *WhoAm 90*
Schiller, Pieter Jon 1938- *WhoAm 90, WhoE 91*
Schiller, Robert Achille 1918- *WhoAm 90*
Schiller, Thomas George 1956- *St&PR 91*
Schiller, William Charles 1923- *St&PR 91*
Schiller, William E. *NewYTBS 90*
Schiller, William E. 1909-1990 *BioIn 16*
Schiller, William Richard 1937- *WhoAm 90*
Schillhammer, Richard W. 1914- *St&PR 91*
Schillhammer, William R., Jr. 1924- *St&PR 91*
Schilling, Albert Henry 1943- *WhoAm 90*
Schilling, Allan Dale 1942- *St&PR 91*
Schilling, Carl F. 1923- *St&PR 91*
Schilling, Charles Henry 1918- *WhoAm 90*
Schilling, Charles Walter 1915- *IntWWM 90*
Schilling, Chuck 1937- *Ballpl 90*
Schilling, Deborah Jan 1951- *WhoAmW 91*
Schilling, Don *BioIn 16*
Schilling, Franklin Charles, Jr. 1958- *WhoE 91*
Schilling, Janet Naomi 1939- *WhoAmW 91*
Schilling, John Albert 1917- *WhoAm 90*
Schilling, John Michael 1951- *WhoAm 90*
Schilling, John Wharton 1946- *WhoSSW 91*
Schilling, Kenneth Lee 1946- *St&PR 91*
Schilling, Leslie *BioIn 16*
Schilling, Mona Lee C. 1944- *WhoHisp 91*
Schilling, Ralph Franklin 1921- *WhoAm 90*
Schilling, Richard Merlin 1937- *St&PR 91*
Schilling, Stacey Lynn 1964- *WhoAmW 91*
Schilling, William Richard 1933- *WhoSSW 91, WhoWor 91*
Schillinger, Beat 1945- *St&PR 91*
Schillinger, Brent Mark 1953- *WhoSSW 91*
Schillinger, Edwin Joseph 1923- *WhoAm 90*
Schillings, Max von 1868-1933 *PenDiMP A*
Schilpp, Paul Arthur 1897- *WhoAm 90*
Schilt, Alexander Frank 1941- *WhoAm 90*
Schilt, Stephen Neal 1950- *BiDrAPA 89*
Schilthuis, Willem C. *BioIn 16, NewYTBS 90*
Schiltz, Hugo 1927- *WhoWor 91*
Schiltz, James *St&PR 91*
Schiltz, Jane Ann 1955- *WhoAmW 91*
Schiltz, Joyce Dorothy 1949- *WhoSSW 91*
Schiltz, Kenneth *St&PR 91*
Schiltz, Marlin *St&PR 91*
Schiltz, Richard *St&PR 91*
Schily, Otto 1932- *BioIn 16*
Schilz, Len Robert 1950- *St&PR 91*
Schimansky, Donya Dobrila *WhoAmA 91*
Schimberg, Armand Bruce 1927- *WhoAm 90, WhoWor 91*
Schimberg, Henry Aaron 1933- *St&PR 91, WhoAm 90*
Schimberni, Mario 1923- *WhoAm 90*
Schimbor, Mark Anderson 1945- *St&PR 91*
Schimel, John L *BiDrAPA 89*
Schimel, John L. 1916- *WhoE 91*
Schimel, Louis Leo 1950- *BiDrAPA 89*
Schimelpfenig, Clarence William, Jr. 1930- *WhoSSW 91*
Schimelpfenig, Danny Alfred 1945- *St&PR 91*
Schimelpfenig, Glen Herbert 1929- *St&PR 91*
Schimenti, Joseph Theodore 1961- *WhoSSW 91*
Schimer, John Francis 1934- *St&PR 91*
Schimidt, Eric 1960- *St&PR 91*
Schimizzi, Ned Vincent 1936- *WhoE 91, WhoWor 91*
Schimke, Robert Tod 1932- *WhoAm 90*
Schiml, Marga 1945- *IntWWM 90*
Schimmel, Abbe 1933- *WhoE 91*
Schimmel, Allan 1940- *St&PR 91, WhoAm 90*
Schimmel, Annemarie 1922- *ConAu 132*
Schimmel, Bella F *BiDrAPA 89*
Schimmel, Bruce Andrew 1952- *WhoE 91*
Schimmel, Caroline Fearey 1944- *WhoAm 90*
Schimmel, Morris Joseph *BiDrAPA 89*
Schimmel, Norbert 1904-1990 *BioIn 16, NewYTBS 90*
Schimmel, Paul Reinhard 1940- *WhoAm 90*
Schimmel, Robert H. 1937- *St&PR 91*

Schimmel, William Michael 1946- *IntWWM 90*
Schimmelbusch, Werner H 1937- *BiDrAPA 89*
Schimmelpenninck, Mary Anne 1778-1856 *FemiCLE*
Schimmelpfennig, Jorg 1955- *WhoWor 91*
Schimmenti, Michael Ronald 1932- *St&PR 91*
Schimmer, John, Jr. 1933- *WhoSSW 91*
Schimpf, John J. 1949- *St&PR 91*
Schimpf, John Joseph 1949- *WhoAm 90*
Schimpf, Klaus 1923- *WhoWor 91*
Schimpff, Stephen Callender 1941- *WhoAm 90*
Schinagl, Erich F. 1932- *St&PR 91*
Schinagl, Erich Friedrich 1932- *WhoAm 90*
Schinagle, Allan Charles 1930- *WhoWor 91*
Schinagle, Martha Sue *BiDrAPA 89*
Schinazi, Raymond Felix 1950- *WhoSSW 91*
Schinbeckler, Roland Lee 1950- *WhoAm 90*
Schindel, Arnold 1923- *WhoE 91*
Schindel, Donald A. 1933- *St&PR 91*
Schindel, Donald Marvin 1932- *WhoAm 90, WhoWor 91*
Schindel, Ronnie Susan Levine 1939- *WhoAmW 91*
Schindelin, Juergen Wolfgang 1928- *WhoWor 91*
Schinderle, Robert Frank 1923- *WhoAm 90*
Schindewolf, Darcy Doyle 1947- *St&PR 91*
Schindler, Adolf Eduard 1936- *WhoWor 91*
Schindler, Albert Isadore 1927- *WhoAm 90*
Schindler, Alexander Moshe 1925- *WhoAm 90, WhoE 91*
Schindler, Anton 1795-1864 *PenDiMP*
Schindler, Barbara K 1944- *BiDrAPA 89*
Schindler, Daniel Mark 1955- *WhoSSW 91*
Schindler, David William 1940- *WhoAm 90*
Schindler, Dennis 1944- *St&PR 91*
Schindler, Gayle Ann 1950- *WhoAmW 91*
Schindler, Haim 1916- *WhoWor 91*
Schindler, Hollis 1930- *IntWWM 90*
Schindler, Joel Marvin 1950- *WhoEmL 91*
Schindler, Judith Kay 1941- *WhoAmW 91*
Schindler, Mark 1921- *St&PR 91*
Schindler, Marvin Samuel 1932- *WhoAm 90*
Schindler, Norbert 1918- *WhoWor 91*
Schindler, Oskar 1908-1974 *BioIn 16*
Schindler, Peter D 1931- *BiDrAPA 89*
Schindler, Peter David 1931- *WhoAm 90, WhoE 91*
Schindler, R M 1887-1953 *WhoAmA 91N*
Schindler, Ralph Joseph, Jr. 1948- *St&PR 91*
Schindler, Ronald Louis 1944- *WhoSSW 91*
Schindler, Rudolph Michael 1887-1953 *BioIn 16*
Schindler, S. D. *BioIn 16*
Schindler, Stanley Fred 1929- *St&PR 91*
Schindler, William Stanley 1933- *WhoAm 90*
Schindler-Mahler, Alma Maria 1879-1964 *BioIn 16*
Schine, G David 1927- *St&PR 91*
Schine, Gerard David 1927- *WhoAm 90*
Schine, Jerome Adrian 1926- *WhoSSW 91*
Schingler, Steve Lee 1952- *St&PR 91*
Schink, Frank Edward 1922- *WhoAm 90*
Schink, James Harvey 1943- *WhoAm 90*
Schink, Richard Robert 1942- *St&PR 91*
Schinkel, Karl Friedrich 1781-1841 *PenDiDA 89*
Schinman, Henry Lawrence 1943- *St&PR 91*
Schinske, John Louis 1957- *WhoSSW 91*
Schinsky, William Charles 1946- *WhoAmA 91*
Schintzius, Dwayne *BioIn 16*
Schinz, Fred William 1950- *WhoSSW 91*
Schinzel, Donald Leo 1935- *St&PR 91*
Schinzer, Michael H. 1957- *St&PR 91*
Schioler, Annette *PenDiMP*
Schiotling, Johannes 1730-1799 *PenDiDA 89*
Schiotz, Aksel 1906-1975 *PenDiMP*
Schiotz, Fredrik Axel 1901-1989 *BioIn 16*
Schipa, Tito 1888-1965 *PenDiMP*
Schipa, Tito 1889-1965 *BioIn 16*
Schiper, Ignacy 1884-1943 *BioIn 16*
Schipizky, Frederick Alexander 1952- *IntWWM 90*
Schippel, Eliana M. 1942- *WhoHisp 91*
Schippel, John E. 1934- *St&PR 91*
Schipper, Cynthia Zvanut 1948- *ODwPR 91*
Schipper, Merle Solway *WhoAmA 91*
Schippers, David Philip 1929- *WhoAm 90*
Schippers, Thomas 1930-1977 *PenDiMP, WorAlBi*
Schira, Cynthia 1934- *WhoAmA 91*
Schirach, Baldur von 1907-1974 *BioIn 16*
Schiraldi, Calvin 1962- *Ballpl 90*
Schiralli, Evelyn Eleanor 1941- *WhoE 91*
Schirber, Jane Packard *BioIn 16*
Schirch, Carol Ann 1937- *WhoAmW 91*
Schirm, Karen Marie 1946- *WhoWrEP 89*
Schirmang, William Peter 1923- *St&PR 91*
Schirmer, Astrid 1942- *IntWWM 90*
Schirmer, Henry William 1922- *WhoAm 90*
Schirmer, Howard August, Jr. 1942- *St&PR 91, WhoAm 90*
Schirmer, Robert H. 1940- *St&PR 91*
Schirn, Janet Sugerman *WhoAm 90*
Schirner, Wayne Arthur 1945- *WhoSSW 91*
Schiro, C Herbert 1934- *BiDrAPA 89*
Schiro-Geist, Chrisann 1946- *WhoAmW 91*
Schirra, Wally *BioIn 16*
Schirra, Walter M., Jr. 1923- *WorAlBi*
Schirra, Walter Marty, Jr. 1923- *WhoAm 90, WhoWor 91*
Schisgal, Murray Joseph 1926- *WhoAm 90*
Schisler, Floyd 1926- *St&PR 91*
Schisler, George Milford, Jr. 1957- *WhoEmL 91*
Schisler, Richard Carl 1945- *WhoE 91*
Schissel, Luke James 1939- *WhoSSW 91*
Schivek, Elaine Rona 1930- *WhoE 91*
Schjeldahl, Peter 1942- *WhoAmA 91*
Schjerfbeck, Helene Sofia 1862-1946 *BiDWomA [port]*
Schkeeper, Peter A., II 1944- *St&PR 91*
Schkeeper, Peter Albert, II 1944- *WhoE 91*
Schlachter, Gail Ann 1943- *ConAu 31NR*
Schlachter, Nina Kram *BiDrAPA 89*
Schlacks, Deborah Davis 1956- *WhoAmW 91*
Schlactenhaufen, John E. 1939- *St&PR 91*
Schlader, David Anthony 1958 *WhoEmL 91*
Schlader, Donald Richard 1933- *St&PR 91*
Schlaepfer, Thomas Edward *BiDrAPA 89*
Schlaerth, Sally Anne Gallagher 1928- *WhoAmW 91*
Schlafer, Donald Hughes 1948- *WhoAm 90*
Schlaff, Frederick 1941- *BiDrAPA 89*
Schlafly, Hubert Joseph 1919- *St&PR 91*
Schlafly, Hubert Joseph, Jr. 1919- *WhoAm 90*
Schlafly, Phyllis 1924- *MajTwCW, WorAlBi*
Schlafly, Phyllis S. 1924- *BioAmW*
Schlafly, Phyllis Stewart 1924- *WhoAm 90, WhoAmW 91, WhoWrEP 89*
Schlagel, Clarence R. 1928- *St&PR 91*
Schlagel, Richard H. 1925- *WhoAm 90*
Schlagenhaft-Edwards, Pam Lynn 1960- *WhoAmW 91*
Schlagenhauf, George K, Jr. 1932- *BiDrAPA 89*
Schlagenhauff, Reinhold E 1923- *BiDrAPA 89*
Schlager, David S *BiDrAPA 89*
Schlager, Franz Michael 1945- *BiDrAPA 89*
Schlageter, Albert Leo 1894-1923 *BioIn 16*
Schlageter, Robert William 1925- *WhoAm 90, WhoAmA 91, WhoSSW 91*
Schlaich, Klaus Dieter *WhoWor 91*
Schlaifer, Charles *BiDrAPA 89*
Schlaifer, Charles 1909- *WhoAm 90*
Schlaikjer, Jes 1897-1982 *WhoAmA 91N*
Schlain, Barbara E. 1948- *St&PR 91*
Schlain, Barbara Ellen 1948- *WhoAmW 91*
Schlais, Rudolph Anthony, Jr. 1940- *WhoAm 90*
Schlam, Murray J 1911- *WhoAmA 91*
Schlang, Alan Leslie 1942- *St&PR 91*
Schlang, David 1912- *WhoE 91*
Schlang, Elliott L. 1934- *St&PR 91*
Schlang, Joseph *BioIn 16*
Schlang, Joseph 1911- *WhoAm 90, WhoE 91*
Schlanger, Eugene Joseph 1925- *St&PR 91*
Schlanger, Jacob L. 1951- *St&PR 91*
Schlanger, Jeff 1937- *WhoAmA 91, WhoE 91*
Schlanger, Norman R. 1937- *St&PR 91*
Schlanger, Warren W *BiDrAPA 89*
Schlant, Robert Carl 1929- *WhoAm 90, WhoSSW 91*
Schlarb, Roger James 1943- *St&PR 91*
Schlarman, Stanley Gerard 1933- *WhoAm 90*
Schlater, Herb 1919- *St&PR 91*
Schlatter, Charlie *BioIn 16*
Schlatter, Christian Lebrecht 1937- *WhoWor 91*
Schlatter, Donald Allan 1929- *St&PR 91*
Schlatter, Francis 1855-1895 *EncO&P 3*
Schlatter, Francis 1856-1896? *BioIn 16*
Schlatter, George *BioIn 16*
Schlatter, Konrad 1935- *St&PR 91, WhoAm 90*
Schlauch, Paul John 1942- *WhoAm 90*
Schlauch, Robert W 1946- *BiDrAPA 89*
Schlauch, Robert William 1946- *WhoE 91*
Schlauch, Walter F. 1941- *St&PR 91*
Schlayer, Mary Elizabeth 1915-1987 *ConAu 129*
Schlecht, William Rogers 1955- *WhoEmL 91*
Schlechte, David William 1949- *WhoEmL 91*
Schlechty, John L. 1955- *WhoEmL 91*
Schleck, Robert W. *BioIn 16*
Schleck, Roth Stephen 1915- *WhoAm 90*
Schleck, Thomas T. 1947- *St&PR 91*
Schlecker, Barry S. 1940- *St&PR 91*
Schlee, Thomas Daniel 1957- *IntWWM 90*
Schlee, Valentina *BioIn 16*
Schlee, Walter 1942- *WhoWor 91*
Schleede, Glenn R. 1933- *St&PR 91*
Schleede, Glenn Roy 1933- *WhoAm 90*
Schleef, Helen Ida 1914- *WhoWrEP 89*
Schleeh, Hans Martin 1928- *WhoAmA 91*
Schlefer, Ellen King *BiDrAPA 89*
Schlegel, August Wilhelm 1767-1845 *DcLB 94 [port]*
Schlegel, Beverly Faye 1950- *WhoAmW 91*
Schlegel, David Edward 1927- *WhoAm 90*
Schlegel, Friedrich von 1772-1829 *BioIn 16, WorAlBi*
Schlegel, John Frederick 1944- *WhoAm 90*
Schlegel, Jorgen Ulrik 1918- *WhoWor 91*
Schlegel, Michael T. 1951- *WhoE 91*
Schlegel, Robert Philip 1929- *St&PR 91*
Schlegel, Rolf 1942- *WhoWor 91*
Schlegel, Rudolf *IntWWM 90*
Schlegel Schelling, Dorothea Caroline 1763-1809 *EncCoWW*
Schlegelmilch, Margaret Elizabeth 1918- *WhoAmW 91*
Schleger, Hans 1898-1976 *ConDes 90*
Schleger, Peter Ralph 1944- *WhoE 91, WhoWor 91*
Schlehuser, Stephen Lawrence 1941- *WhoE 91*
Schlei, Admiral 1878-1958 *Ballpl 90*
Schlei, Norbert Anthony 1929- *WhoAm 90*
Schleicher, Dennis J. 1945- *St&PR 91*
Schleicher, Heinz Anton 1938- *WhoWor 91*
Schleicher, Henry E. 1936- *ODwPR 91*
Schleicher, Joel Arthur 1952- *WhoAm 90*
Schleicher, Nora Elizabeth 1952- *WhoAmW 91*
Schleicher, Rowell A. 1899- *St&PR 91*
Schleiden, Matthias Jacob 1804-1881 *WorAlBi*
Schleidt, Wolfgang Matthias 1927- *WhoWor 91*
Schleiermacher, Friedrich 1768-1834 *WorAlBi*
Schleifer, Carl B 1928- *BiDrAPA 89*
Schleifer, Constance Louise 1955- *WhoE 91*
Schleifer, Ronald 1948- *WhoAm 90*
Schleifer, Steven Jay *BiDrAPA 89*
Schleifer, Steven Jay 1950- *WhoE 91*
Schleiff, Henry Stephan 1948- *St&PR 91*
Schleiff, Henry Stephen *BioIn 16*
Schleimer, Helen Lilli 1960- *BiDrAPA 89*
Schleimer, Joseph 1930- *WhoE 91, WhoWor 91*
Schlein, Charles *BioIn 16*
Schlein, Dov C. *WhoAm 90*
Schlein, Dov C. 1947- *St&PR 91*
Schlein, Mark H. 1946- *WhoSSW 91*
Schlein, Miriam *WhoAmW 91*
Schlein, Miriam 1926- *AuBYP 90*
Schlein, Stephen 1944- *St&PR 91*
Schleiss, Franz *PenDiDA 89*
Schleitwiler, David Martin 1951- *WhoEmL 91*
Schlembach, John Michael 1947- *WhoWor 91*
Schlemm, Anny 1929- *IntWWM 90*
Schlemm, Betty Lou 1934- *WhoAmA 91, WhoE 91*
Schlemmer, Alfred E., Jr. 1931- *St&PR 91*
Schlemmer, Nancy L. 1936- *St&PR 91*
Schlemmer, Oskar 1888-1943 *IntDcAA 90*
Schlemmer, Roger P. 1933- *St&PR 91*
Schlemowitz, Abram 1911- *WhoAmA 91*
Schlender, William Elmer 1920- *WhoAm 90*
Schlenger, Donald Lee 1950- *St&PR 91*
Schlenker, Ralph F. 1928- *St&PR 91*
Schlenker, Ralph P. 1945- *St&PR 91*
Schlensker, David Richard 1961- *WhoEmL 91*
Schlensker, Gary Chris 1950- *WhoAm 90, WhoEmL 91*
Schlerath, Bernfried H. 1924- *WhoWor 91*
Schlesch, Ronald Duane 1929- *St&PR 91*
Schlesinger, Abraham 1906-1988 *BioIn 16*
Schlesinger, Albert R. 1941- *St&PR 91*
Schlesinger, Albert Reuben 1941- *WhoAm 90*
Schlesinger, Arthur, Jr. 1917- *WhoAm 90, WhoWor 91, WhoWrEP 89*
Schlesinger, Arthur M., Jr. 1917- *MajTwCW, SmATA 61 [port], WorAlBi*
Schlesinger, B. Frank 1925- *WhoAm 90*
Schlesinger, Benjamin 1928- *WhoWrEP 89*
Schlesinger, David Harvey 1939- *WhoAm 90*
Schlesinger, Edward Bruce 1913- *WhoAm 90*
Schlesinger, Herbert J 1921- *BiDrAPA 89*
Schlesinger, Hilde *BiDrAPA 89*
Schlesinger, James 1929- *BiDrUSE 89*
Schlesinger, James G. 1943- *St&PR 91*
Schlesinger, James R. 1929- *WorAlBi*
Schlesinger, James Rodney 1929- *WhoAm 90, WhoWor 91*
Schlesinger, Jeanne Carolyn 1928- *WhoE 91*
Schlesinger, John 1926- *BioIn 16*
Schlesinger, John Richard 1926- *WhoAm 90, WhoWor 91*
Schlesinger, Joseph *BiDrAPA 89*
Schlesinger, Joseph Abraham 1922- *WhoAm 90*
Schlesinger, Judith Diane 1945- *WhoEmL 91*
Schlesinger, Judith Susan 1950- *WhoAmW 91*
Schlesinger, Lee 1926- *St&PR 91*
Schlesinger, Lora 1937- *WhoAmW 91*
Schlesinger, Otto J. 1924- *St&PR 91*
Schlesinger, Otto J., III 1949- *St&PR 91*
Schlesinger, Regine 1951- *WhoAmW 91*
Schlesinger, Robert Walter 1913- *WhoAm 90*
Schlesinger, Rudolf Berthold 1909- *WhoAm 90, WhoWor 91*
Schlesinger, Sanford Joel 1943- *WhoE 91, WhoWor 91*
Schlesinger, Stephen Lyons 1940- *WhoAm 90*
Schlesinger, Steven Roger 1944- *WhoAm 90*
Schlesinger, Victor H. 1925- *St&PR 91*
Schlesinger, William *BioIn 16*
Schless, Arthur Paul *BiDrAPA 89*
Schless, Guy Lacy 1929- *WhoWor 91*
Schless, James Murray 1918- *WhoSSW 91*
Schless, Phyllis Ross *WhoAm 90*
Schlessel, Richard Benjamin *BiDrAPA 89*
Schlessel, Walter *St&PR 91*
Schlesser, Michael A 1951- *BiDrAPA 89*
Schlessinger, Bernard S. 1930- *WhoAm 90, WhoSSW 91*
Schlessinger, June Hirsch 1933- *WhoSSW 91*
Schlessinger, Nathan 1924- *BiDrAPA 89*
Schlette, Sharon Elizabeth 1945- *WhoAmW 91, WhoWor 91*
Schleunes, Brenda Pursel 1939- *WhoSSW 91*
Schleuse, William 1932- *BiDrAPA 89*
Schleusener, Richard August 1926- *WhoAm 90*
Schleussner, Robert, Mrs. *WhoE 91*
Schlevssner, Robert, Jr., Mrs. *WhoAmW 91*
Schley, Charles C. 1923- *St&PR 91*
Schley, Gerhard 1934- *WhoWor 91*
Schley, James Powrie 1956- *WhoWrEP 89*
Schley, Michael D. 1955- *St&PR 91*
Schley, Michael Dodson 1955- *WhoAm 90*
Schley, Reeve, III 1936- *WhoAm 90*
Schleyer, Marvin 1934- *St&PR 91*
Schleyer, Paul von Rague 1930- *WhoAm 90, WhoWor 91*
Schlezinger, Nathan S 1908- *BiDrAPA 89*
Schlicher, Karl Theodore 1905-1989 *WhoAmA 91N*
Schlichter, Art *BioIn 16*
Schlichtig, Jean-Georges 1736-1782? *PenDiDA 89*
Schlichting, Harold E. 1915- *AuBYP 90*
Schlichting, Mary Southworth *AuBYP 90*
Schlichting, Philip F. 1937- *St&PR 91*
Schlick, Barbara 1943- *IntWWM 90*
Schlick, Benjamin *PenDiDA 89*
Schlick, Tamar 1961- *WhoE 91*
Schlick, Thomas Leroy 1950- *WhoEmL 91*
Schlickau, George Hans 1922- *WhoAm 90*
Schlicting, Michael 1953- *BioIn 16*
Schlieben, George Thomas 1946- *St&PR 91*
Schliefer, Edward Isadore 1933- *WhoE 91*
Schlieffen, Alfred, Graf Von 1833-1913 *WorAlBi*
Schlieman, Mable Storie 1932- *WhoAmW 91*
Schliemann, Heinrich 1822-1890 *BioIn 16, WorAlBi*
Schliemann, Peter C. 1945- *St&PR 91*
Schlier, Christoph Georg 1930- *WhoWor 91*
Schlier, Paula 1899- *EncCoWW*

Schlies, Edward A 1945- *BiDrAPA 89*
Schlig, Joseph 1927- *WhoE 91*
Schlimbach, Walter Otto 1903- *St&PR 91*
Schlindwein, James A. 1929- *WhoSSW 91*
Schlingensiepen, Georg Hermann 1928- *WhoWor 91*
Schlinger, Alexander Peter 1948- *WhoEmL 91*
Schlipf, Betty Jean 1943- *WhoAmW 91*
Schlipf, Frederick A. 1941- *WhoWrEP 89*
Schlissel, Carla H. 1957- *WhoE 91*
Schlissel, Theodore 1940- *St&PR 91*
Schlitt, Klaus 1938- *WhoWor 91*
Schlitter, Helga *WhoAmA 91*
Schlitzkus, Jolly Maddox 1940- *WhoSSW 91*
Schlobohm, Josefina T *BiDrAPA 89*
Schlobohm, Philip George *BiDrAPA 89*
Schlobohm, Raymond William 1943- *WhoE 91*
Schloegel, George Anthony 1940- *St&PR 91, WhoAm 90*
Schloeman, James Michael 1942- *St&PR 91*
Schloemann, Ernst Fritz 1926- *WhoAm 90*
Schloemer, Paul George 1928- *St&PR 91, WhoAm 90*
Schloen, Lloyd Henry 1946- *St&PR 91*
Schloendorff, Volker 1939- *ConTFT 8*
Schloerb, Paul Richard 1919- *WhoAm 90*
Schloesser, Harvey L 1921- *BiDrAPA 89*
Schloifer, Eckart 1941- *IntWWM 90*
Schlom, Jeffrey Bert 1942- *WhoAm 90*
Schlomann, James Martin 1949- *St&PR 91*
Schlondorff, Volker *BioIn 16*
Schlondorff, Volker 1939- *WhoWor 91*
Schloop, Clinton P. 1942- *St&PR 91*
Schlorff, Donald Joseph 1955- *St&PR 91*
Schlosberg, Carl Martin 1936- *WhoAmA 91*
Schlosnagle, Carol 1950- *ODwPR 91*
Schloss, Arleen P 1943- *WhoAmA 91*
Schloss, B. Stephen 1954- *St&PR 91*
Schloss, Bert James 1944- *BiDrAPA 89*
Schloss, Carolyn Dina 1963- *WhoAmW 91*
Schloss, Edith *WhoAmA 91*
Schloss, Eugene M., Jr. 1932- *St&PR 91*
Schloss, Ezekiel 1912-1987 *BioIn 16*
Schloss, Fredlyn D. 1936- *St&PR 91*
Schloss, Henry *St&PR 91*
Schloss, Howard Michael 1952- *St&PR 91*
Schloss, Jo Ann Bock 1932- *WhoAmW 91, WhoWor 91*
Schloss, Lawrence James 1947- *WhoEmL 91*
Schloss, Leo 1914-1988 *BioIn 16*
Schloss, Mary Lou *BioIn 16*
Schloss, Max 1933- *St&PR 91*
Schloss, Milton J. 1913- *St&PR 91*
Schloss, Morley *BioIn 16*
Schloss, Richard Steven *BiDrAPA 89*
Schloss, Richard Steven 1957- *WhoE 91*
Schloss, Samuel Leopold 1926- *St&PR 91*
Schloss, Samuel Leopold, Jr. 1926- *WhoAm 90*
Schlossberg, Edwin *BioIn 16*
Schlossberg, Edwin Arthur 1945- *WhoE 91*
Schlossberg, Louis 1923- *WhoAm 90*
Schlossberg, Rose Kennedy *BioIn 16*
Schlossberg, Stephen 1921- *WhoAm 90*
Schlosser, Allan *ODwPR 91*
Schlosser, Anne Griffin 1939- *WhoAmW 91*
Schlosser, Eleanor Florence *WhoAmW 91*
Schlosser, Frank Roger 1941- *St&PR 91*
Schlosser, George McGarraugh 1907- *WhoAm 90*
Schlosser, Herbert S. 1926- *St&PR 91, WhoAm 90*
Schlosser, John R. 1919- *St&PR 91*
Schlosser, Mary Ann 1947- *BiDrAPA 89*
Schlosser, Mary Ann 1960- *WhoAmW 91*
Schlosser, Max *BiDrAPA 89*
Schlosser, Peter Friedrich 1935- *WhoWor 91*
Schlosser, Scott *St&PR 91*
Schlossman, George Bradley 1954- *WhoEmL 91*
Schlossman, Howard Harvey 1915- *BiDrAPA 89, WhoE 91*
Schlossman, John Isaac 1931- *WhoAm 90*
Schlotelburg, Susanne 1959- *BioIn 16*
Schlotfeldt, Rozella May 1914- *WhoAm 90, WhoAmW 91*
Schloth, Edward C. 1929- *St&PR 91*
Schlotman, Virginia B. 1919- *WhoE 91*
Schlott, Mary Camille 1932- *WhoAmW 91*
Schlott, Richard William, III 1939- *WhoE 91*
Schlotterback, David Lee 1932- *St&PR 91*
Schlotterbeck, Walter Albert 1926- *WhoAm 90*
Schlotthauer, Karl-Heinz 1950- *WhoWor 91*
Schlottman, Richard A. *St&PR 91*
Schlotz, Randy Craig 1947- *WhoSSW 91*
Schlough, Paul W. 1937- *St&PR 91*
Schluchter, Wolfgang Gerhard 1938- *WhoWor 91*
Schluechter, Ellen 1938- *WhoWor 91*
Schlueter, Donald Herman *WhoSSW 91*
Schlueter, John J. 1939- *St&PR 91*
Schlueter, June 1942- *ConAu 32NR*
Schlueter, Linda Lee 1947- *WhoEmL 91, WhoSSW 91, WhoWor 91*
Schlueter, Paul 1933- *ConAu 32NR*
Schluger, James H *BiDrAPA 89*
Schlumberger, Jean 1877-1968 *BioIn 16*
Schlumberger, Robert Ernest 1951- *WhoSSW 91*
Schlund, Brandon *BioIn 16*
Schlunegger, Urs Peter 1934- *WhoWor 91*
Schlusnus, Heinrich 1888-1952 *PenDiMP*
Schlussel, Joseph Lazar 1935- *WhoE 91*
Schlussel, Yvette Rebecca 1956- *WhoE 91*
Schluter, Peter Mueller 1933- *St&PR 91, WhoAm 90, WhoE 91*
Schluter, Poul Holmskov 1929- *WhoWor 91*
Schlutter, Lois Cochrane 1953- *WhoAmW 91, WhoEmL 91*
Schmadeka, Delores 1933- *WhoWrEP 89*
Schmader, Michael T. 1948- *St&PR 91*
Schmaehl, Winfried Arthur 1942- *WhoWor 91*
Schmal, Robert James 1927- *St&PR 91*
Schmal, Timothy James 1956- *WhoEmL 91*
Schmalbruch, T. Dankward 1932- *St&PR 91*
Schmale, Matthias 1962- *WhoWor 91*
Schmalenberger, Jerry L. 1934- *WhoAm 90*
Schmalensee, Diane H. 1946- *St&PR 91*
Schmalensee, Richard Lee 1944- *WhoAm 90*
Schmalfuss, Peter 1937- *IntWWM 90*
Schmall, Arthur J. 1927- *St&PR 91*
Schmall, Marylee Younger 1933- *WhoE 91*
Schmalstieg, Linda Ash *BiDrAPA 89*
Schmalstieg, Walter Lee, Jr. *BiDrAPA 89*
Schmalstieg, William Riegel 1929- *WhoAm 90, WhoWor 91*
Schmaltz, Kathleen Mary 1958- *WhoAmW 91*
Schmaltz, Lawrence Gerard 1957- *WhoSSW 91*
Schmaltz, Richard R. 1940- *St&PR 91*
Schmaltz, Roy Edgar 1937- *WhoAmA 91*
Schmaltz, Vernon J. 1948- *WhoE 91*
Schmalz, Carl, Jr 1926- *WhoAmA 91*
Schmalz, Carl Nelson, Jr. 1926- *WhoAm 90, WhoE 91*
Schmalz, Randall John 1952- *WhoEmL 91*
Schmalz, Robert L. 1940- *St&PR 91*
Schmalz, Roman 1927- *St&PR 91*
Schmalz, William A. 1921- *St&PR 91*
Schmalzried, Marvin E. 1924- *St&PR 91*
Schmalzried, Marvin Eugene 1924- *WhoAm 90*
Schmalzriedt, Egidius 1935- *WhoWor 91*
Schman, Daniel C 1941- *BiDrAPA 89*
Schmandt, Jurgen 1929- *WhoSSW 91*
Schmandt, Ray 1896-1969 *Ballpl 90*
Schmandt-Besserat, Denise 1933- *WhoAm 90, WhoAmA 91*
Schmank, James R. 1953- *St&PR 91*
Schmanski, Andrew Frank 1948- *St&PR 91*
Schmaus, Siegfried H. A. 1915- *WhoE 91, WhoWor 91*
Schmechel, Warren P. 1927- *WhoAm 90*
Schmechel, Warren Paul 1927- *St&PR 91*
Schmeck, George M. 1934- *St&PR 91*
Schmeckebier, Laurence E 1906- *WhoAmA 91N*
Schmedes, Erik 1866-1931 *PenDiMP*
Schmeer, Arline Catherine 1929- *WhoAmW 91*
Schmehl, Kenneth Gordan 1942- *St&PR 91*
Schmeidler, Blanche J *WhoAmA 91N*
Schmeidler, Carol Beth 1958- *WhoE 91*
Schmeidler, Gertrude Raffel 1912- *EncO&P 3, EncPaPR 91*
Schmeiser, Stephen George 1943- *WhoSSW 91*
Schmeling, Gareth 1940- *WhoAm 90*
Schmeling, Max 1905- *BioIn 16*
Schmelkin, Benjamin 1910- *WhoWor 91*
Schmeltzer, David 1930- *WhoAm 90*
Schmeltzer, Edward 1923- *WhoAm 90*
Schmeltzle, Dale R. 1954- *St&PR 91*
Schmelz, Brenda Lea 1958- *WhoAmW 91*
Schmelz, Gus 1850-1925 *Ballpl 90*
Schmelz, Julius Wirth 1931- *St&PR 91*
Schmelzer, Francine *St&PR 91*
Schmelzer, Henry Louis Phillip 1943- *St&PR 91, WhoAm 90*
Schmelzer, John Kevin 1957- *WhoEmL 91*
Schmelzer, Joseph John, III 1946- *St&PR 91*
Schmelzle, Christian George 1944- *St&PR 91*
Schmemann, Serge 1945- *WhoWor 91*
Schmerer, Susan Ann 1946- *WhoEmL 91*
Schmerge, Albert G. *BioIn 16*
Schmergel, Gabriel 1940- *WhoAm 90*
Schmerler, Alan 1946- *BiDrAPA 89, WhoE 91*
Schmerling, Erwin Robert 1929- *WhoAm 90*
Schmertmann, John Henry 1928- *WhoAm 90*
Schmertz, Eric Joseph 1925- *WhoAm 90, WhoWor 91*
Schmertz, Herbert 1930- *ODwPR 91, St&PR 91, WhoAm 90*
Schmertz, Mildred Floyd 1925- *WhoAm 90*
Schmertzler, Alvin Louis 1925- *WhoE 91*
Schmetterer, Robert Allen 1943- *WhoAm 90*
Schmetzer, Alan David 1946- *BiDrAPA 89, WhoEmL 91*
Schmickler, Wolfgang Wilhelm 1946- *WhoWor 91*
Schmid, Dr. *EncCoWW*
Schmid, Andrew Michael, Jr. 1957- *WhoE 91*
Schmid, Anton 1900-1942 *BioIn 16*
Schmid, Beppo 1901-1956 *BioIn 16*
Schmid, Calvin Eric 1950- *WhoE 91*
Schmid, Charles W. *BioIn 16*
Schmid, David Anthony *BiDrAPA 89*
Schmid, Erich 1907- *IntWWM 90*
Schmid, Frank Richard 1924- *WhoAm 90*
Schmid, Hans 1920- *IntWWM 90*
Schmid, Hans Fred 1933- *St&PR 91*
Schmid, Hermann Arnold *BiDrAPA 89*
Schmid, John G. 1908- *St&PR 91*
Schmid, Josef 1901-1956 *BioIn 16*
Schmid, Lynette Sue *BiDrAPA 89*
Schmid, Patricia Ann 1948- *WhoAmW 91*
Schmid, Paul A. 1912- *St&PR 91*
Schmid, Paul Albert, III 1943- *St&PR 91*
Schmid, Richard Alan 1934- *WhoAmA 91*
Schmid, Richard Jay 1929- *St&PR 91*
Schmid, Robert Armand 1913-1988 *BioIn 16*
Schmid, Ron Jay 1945- *St&PR 91*
Schmid, Ronald E. *ODwPR 91*
Schmid, Rudi 1922- *WhoAm 90, WhoWor 91*
Schmid, Rudolf 1946- *WhoSSW 91*
Schmid, Warren Walter 1936- *WhoSSW 91*
Schmid, Wilfried 1943- *WhoAm 90*
Schmidbaur, Hubert 1934- *WhoWor 91*
Schmidek, Henry Hans-Heinz 1937- *WhoAm 90*
Schmidhaeuser, Eberhard Karl 1920- *WhoWor 91*
Schmidhofer, Ernst Siegfried 1911- *BiDrAPA 89*
Schmidlin, Emil A. *BioIn 16*
Schmidlin, Paul Robert 1948- *WhoEmL 91*
Schmidpeter, Alfred 1929- *WhoWor 91*
Schmidt, Adolph William 1904- *WhoAm 90*
Schmidt, Albert Daniel 1925- *St&PR 91, WhoAm 90*
Schmidt, Alexander MacKay 1930- . *WhoAm 90*
Schmidt, Alfred Otto 1906- *WhoE 91*
Schmidt, Alvin J. *BioIn 16*
Schmidt, Annerose 1936- *IntWWM 90*
Schmidt, Annie M. G. 1911- *BioIn 16*
Schmidt, Annie M G 1911- *ChlLR 22 [port], EncCoWW*
Schmidt, Arno 1914-1979 *BioIn 16*
Schmidt, Arnold Alfred 1930- *WhoAmA 91, WhoE 91*
Schmidt, Arthur Louis 1927- *WhoSSW 91*
Schmidt, Baldwin Stephen 1942- *St&PR 91*
Schmidt, Barbara Ellyn 1954- *WhoAmW 91*
Schmidt, Barbara Maria 1962- *WhoEmL 91*
Schmidt, Benedict Joseph 1956- *WhoEmL 91*
Schmidt, Benno C., Jr. 1942- *WorAlBi*
Schmidt, Benno Charles 1913- *St&PR 91, WhoAm 90*
Schmidt, Benno Charles, Jr. 1942- *WhoAm 90, WhoE 91, WhoWor 91*
Schmidt, Berlie Louis 1932- *WhoAm 90*
Schmidt, Betty J. 1938- *WhoAmW 91*
Schmidt, Blaine Galen 1916- *WhoAm 90*
Schmidt, Bob 1933- *Ballpl 90*
Schmidt, Boss 1880-1932 *Ballpl 90*
Schmidt, Butch 1886-1952 *Ballpl 90*
Schmidt, C.L. Mike 1940- *WhoSSW 91*
Schmidt, C. Oscar, Jr. *St&PR 91*
Schmidt, Carl Brandon 1941- *IntWWM 90*
Schmidt, Carol Suzanne 1936- *WhoAmW 91*
Schmidt, Charles 1939- *WhoAmA 91, WhoE 91*
Schmidt, Charles J. *WhoSSW 91*
Schmidt, Charles Lynn 1936- *St&PR 91*
Schmidt, Charles Wilson 1928- *WhoAm 90*
Schmidt, Charlie *EncACom*
Schmidt, Chauncey E. 1931- *St&PR 91*
Schmidt, Chauncey Everett 1931- *WhoAm 90*
Schmidt, Chester W, Jr. 1934- *BiDrAPA 89*
Schmidt, Clarence 1897-1978 *MusmAFA*
Schmidt, Claude Henri 1924- *WhoAm 90*
Schmidt, Cyril James 1939- *WhoAm 90*
Schmidt, Dale Russell 1948- *WhoEmL 91*
Schmidt, Dave 1957- *Ballpl 90*
Schmidt, David Robert 1954- *St&PR 91*
Schmidt, Deborah Thyng 1955- *WhoE 91*
Schmidt, Debra Podraza 1957- *WhoAmW 91*
Schmidt, Diane Joy 1953- *WhoWrEP 89*
Schmidt, Donald L. 1945- *St&PR 91*
Schmidt, Douglas W 1942- *ConDes 90*
Schmidt, E. Richard 1939- *St&PR 91*
Schmidt, Edith Taglicht *BioIn 16*
Schmidt, Edward Conrad 1932- *St&PR 91*
Schmidt, Edward Craig 1947- *WhoEmL 91, WhoWor 91*
Schmidt, Edward Frank 1941- *St&PR 91*
Schmidt, Edward William 1946- *WhoAmA 91*
Schmidt, Edwin H *BiDrAPA 89*
Schmidt, Elaine Lois *BiDrAPA 89*
Schmidt, Erika 1913- *IntWWM 90*
Schmidt, Ferdinand 1923- *WhoWor 91*
Schmidt, Ferenc Joseph 1921- *St&PR 91, WhoAm 90*
Schmidt, Franklin W. 1914- *St&PR 91*
Schmidt, Fred 1922- *WhoAm 90*
Schmidt, Freddy 1916- *Ballpl 90*
Schmidt, Frederick Lee 1937- *WhoAmA 91*
Schmidt, Frederick Louis 1922- *WhoAmA 91*
Schmidt, George *BioIn 16*
Schmidt, George 1926- *WhoAm 90*
Schmidt, George P. 1894-1989 *BioIn 16, ConAu 130*
Schmidt, George Raymond, Jr. 1957- *WhoSSW 91*
Schmidt, George T. 1942- *WhoE 91*
Schmidt, Gernot Gustav 1931- *WhoWor 91*
Schmidt, Glenda Bottoms 1949- *WhoAmW 91*
Schmidt, Glenn W. 1943- *St&PR 91*
Schmidt, Gordon Williams 1950- *WhoEmL 91*
Schmidt, Grant 1949- *WhoEmL 91*
Schmidt, Gregory Linn 1945- *BiDrAPA 89*
Schmidt, Gregory Michael 1964- *WhoEmL 91*
Schmidt, Gustav Friedrich 1938- *WhoWor 91*
Schmidt, Guy L. 1933- *St&PR 91*
Schmidt, Hans-Jurgen 1933- *WhoWor 91*
Schmidt, Harold Eugene 1925- *WhoAm 90, WhoSSW 91*
Schmidt, Harvey 1929- *OxCPMus*
Schmidt, Harvey Martin 1925- *WhoWor 91*
Schmidt, Helmut 1918- *BioIn 16, WorAlBi*
Schmidt, Helmut 1928- *EncO&P 3*
Schmidt, Helmut Heinrich Wilhelm 1928- *EncPaPR 91*
Schmidt, Helmut S 1939- *BiDrAPA 89*
Schmidt, Henry 1873-1926 *Ballpl 90*
Schmidt, Herman J. 1917- *St&PR 91, WhoAm 90*
Schmidt, Hermann 1902- *WhoWor 91*
Schmidt, Hugo 1929- *WhoAm 90*
Schmidt, Ingrid E *BiDrAPA 89*
Schmidt, Jakob Edward 1906- *WhoAm 90, WhoWor 91*
Schmidt, James Craig 1927- *WhoAm 90*
Schmidt, James Harvey 1953- *WhoSSW 91*
Schmidt, James Richard 1933- *St&PR 91*
Schmidt, Janet Lynn 1949- *St&PR 91*
Schmidt, Janet Marie 1963- *WhoAmW 91*
Schmidt, Jean Marie 1938- *WhoAmW 91*
Schmidt, Joanne Harper 1938- *WhoAmW 91, WhoSSW 91*
Schmidt, Joel 1937- *ConAu 130*
Schmidt, John Edward 1946- *WhoAm 90*
Schmidt, John J. 1928- *St&PR 91*
Schmidt, John Joseph 1928- *WhoWor 91*
Schmidt, John Nicholas 1947- *St&PR 91*
Schmidt, John Richard 1929- *WhoAm 90*
Schmidt, John Wesley 1917- *WhoAm 90*
Schmidt, Joseph 1904-1942 *PenDiMP*
Schmidt, Julius 1923- *WhoAm 90, WhoAmA 91*
Schmidt, June D. 1948- *St&PR 91*
Schmidt, Justin Orvel 1947- *WhoEmL 91*
Schmidt, Karl 1873-1954 *PenDiDA 89*
Schmidt, Karl J. 1953- *St&PR 91*
Schmidt, Karl Patterson 1890-1957 *DcScB S2*
Schmidt, Karyn Beth 1951- *WhoAmW 91*
Schmidt, Katalin 1930- *BiDrAPA 89, WhoE 91*
Schmidt, Katherine 1898-1978 *WhoAmA 91N*

Schmidt, Kathryn Ann 1958- *WhoAmW 91*
Schmidt, Kenneth A. 1937- *St&PR 91*
Schmidt, Kenneth G. *ODwPR 91*
Schmidt, Kenneth Paul 1954- *WhoEmL 91*
Schmidt, Klaus Dieter 1930- *WhoAm 90, WhoE 91*
Schmidt, Klaus Franz 1928- *WhoAm 90, WhoE 91*
Schmidt, L. Lee, Jr. 1937- *WhoAm 90*
Schmidt, Lail William, Jr. 1936- *WhoWor 91*
Schmidt, Laura Lemieux 1933- *WhoE 91*
Schmidt, Laverne Frederick 1940- *St&PR 91*
Schmidt, Leon Herbert 1909-1989 *BioIn 16*
Schmidt, Leonard J 1936- *BiDrAPA 89*
Schmidt, Loraine *BiDrAPA 89*
Schmidt, Louis Bernard, Jr. 1922- *WhoWor 91*
Schmidt, Lynn Anne 1958- *WhoAmW 91*
Schmidt, Maarten 1929- *WhoWor 91*
Schmidt, Manfred 1928- *IntWWM 90*
Schmidt, Mark Edward 1957- *BiDrAPA 89*
Schmidt, Mary Jane *BioIn 16*
Schmidt, Mary May 1949- *WhoAmW 91, WhoE 91*
Schmidt, Mary Morris 1926- *WhoAmA 91, WhoAmW 91*
Schmidt, Matthew 1959- *ODwPR 91*
Schmidt, Michael *BioIn 16*
Schmidt, Michael Jack 1949- *WhoAm 90*
Schmidt, Mike 1949- *Ballpl 90 [port], BioIn 16, WorAlBi*
Schmidt, Milton J *BiDrAPA 89*
Schmidt, Milton Otto 1910- *WhoAm 90*
Schmidt, Nancy J. 1936- *WhoAm 90*
Schmidt, Ole 1928- *IntWWM 90*
Schmidt, Oscar *BioIn 16*
Schmidt, Paul Gerhard 1937- *WhoWor 91*
Schmidt, Paul Joseph 1925- *WhoWor 91*
Schmidt, Paul Wickham 1948- *WhoEmL 91*
Schmidt, Pavel 1933- *WhoWor 91*
Schmidt, Peter Gustav 1921- *St&PR 91, WhoAm 90*
Schmidt, Peter R. 1934- *St&PR 91*
Schmidt, Randall Bernard 1942- *WhoAmA 91*
Schmidt, Richard E. 1932- *St&PR 91*
Schmidt, Richard Edward 1932- *WhoAm 90*
Schmidt, Richard Frederick 1930- *WhoAm 90*
Schmidt, Richard H., Jr. 1936- *St&PR 91*
Schmidt, Richard Harry 1940- *WhoSSW 91*
Schmidt, Richard Marten, Jr. 1924- *WhoAm 90*
Schmidt, Robert 1927- *WhoAm 90*
Schmidt, Robert Charles, Jr. 1942- *WhoAm 90*
Schmidt, Robert L. 1942- *St&PR 91*
Schmidt, Robert Milton 1944- *WhoAm 90*
Schmidt, Robert Paul 1921- *St&PR 91*
Schmidt, Robert W. 1916- *St&PR 91*
Schmidt, Ronald V. *BioIn 16*
Schmidt, Rose Marie 1952- *WhoSSW 91*
Schmidt, Russel Alan, II 1953- *WhoEmL 91, WhoWor 91*
Schmidt, Ruth Ann 1930- *WhoAm 90, WhoAmW 91*
Schmidt, Ruth Caroline 1922- *WhoAmW 91*
Schmidt, Sandra Kay 1941- *WhoAmW 91*
Schmidt, Scott Alan 1960- *WhoSSW 91*
Schmidt, Stephanie Elizabeth 1954- *WhoAmW 91*
Schmidt, Stephen Christopher 1920- *WhoAm 90*
Schmidt, Stephen Wilfred 1944- *St&PR 91*
Schmidt, Ted Otto 1957- *WhoSSW 91*
Schmidt, Terry Lane 1943- *WhoAm 90*
Schmidt, Theodore August 1927- *St&PR 91*
Schmidt, Thomas Carson 1930- *WhoAm 90*
Schmidt, Thomas Frank 1944- *WhoWor 91*
Schmidt, Thomas Lee 1948- *WhoEmL 91*
Schmidt, Tom V. 1939- *WhoWrEP 89*
Schmidt, Trudeliese 1943- *IntWWM 90*
Schmidt, Uwey Karl-Heinz 1939- *WhoWor 91*
Schmidt, Violet Danielson 1920- *St&PR 91*
Schmidt, Wallace Alan 1948- *WhoEmL 91*
Schmidt, Walter 1887-1973 *Ballpl 90*
Schmidt, Wendy Sue 1959- *WhoAmW 91*
Schmidt, Werner A. 1925- *WhoE 91*
Schmidt, Werner Albert 1925- *IntWWM 90*
Schmidt, Werner F *BiDrAPA 89*
Schmidt, Werner H. 1935- *ConAu 131*
Schmidt, Wilhelm 1845-1938 *BioIn 16*
Schmidt, Willard 1928- *Ballpl 90*
Schmidt, William C. 1938- *WhoAm 90*
Schmidt, William Fredric 1928- *St&PR 91, WhoAm 90, WhoE 91*
Schmidt, Winsor Chase, Jr. 1949- *WhoSSW 91*
Schmidt-Duisburg, Margarete Dina Alwina 1906- *IntWWM 90*
Schmidt-Eichstaedt, Gerd 1941- *WhoWor 91*
Schmidt-Hartmann, Eva 1946- *WhoWor 91*
Schmidt-Isserstedt, Hans 1900-1973 *PenDiMP*
Schmidt-Lackner, Susan 1956- *BiDrAPA 89*
Schmidt-Matthiesen, Heinrich 1923- *WhoWor 91*
Schmidt-Melchiors, Thomas A.F. 1958- *WhoWor 91*
Schmidt-Nielsen, Bodil Mimi 1918- *WhoAm 90*
Schmidt-Nielsen, Knut 1915- *WhoAm 90, WhoSSW 91*
Schmidt-Trenz, Hans-Joerg Josef Maria 1959- *WhoWor 91*
Schmidtgall, William Harold 1946- *St&PR 91*
Schmidtke, Heinz 1925- *WhoWor 91*
Schmidtke, John Herbert 1946- *WhoEmL 91*
Schmidtlein, Andrew John 1932- *St&PR 91*
Schmidtmann, Lucie Ann 1963- *WhoAmW 91*
Schmiedeberg, Oswald 1838-1921 *DcScB S2*
Schmieder, Carl 1938- *WhoWor 91*
Schmieder, Frank J. 1941- *St&PR 91*
Schmieder, Frank Joseph 1941- *WhoAm 90*
Schmieder, Wolfgang 1901- *IntWWM 90*
Schmiedeskamp, Kathy D. 1958- *St&PR 91*
Schmiege, Gustav R, Jr. 1932- *BiDrAPA 89*
Schmiege, Marilyn 1955- *IntWWM 90*
Schmiege, Robert 1941- *St&PR 91, WhoAm 90*
Schmiege, Sandra Kay 1953- *WhoWor 91*
Schmiel, Edgar Herman 1921- *WhoAm 90*
Schmilovici, Ina *WhoAmW 91*
Schmisek, John Michael, Jr. 1946- *WhoEmL 91*
Schmit, Crazy 1866-1940 *Ballpl 90*
Schmit, Gerard M 1934- *BiDrAPA 89*
Schmit, Lucien Andre, Jr. 1928- *WhoAm 90*
Schmit, Raymond J. 1934- *St&PR 91*
Schmit, Thomas S. 1943- *St&PR 91*
Schmitmeyer, Debra A. 1951- *WhoAmW 91*
Schmits, G Michael 1949- *BiDrAPA 89*
Schmitt, Barb *WhoAmW 91*
Schmitt, Betty J. 1936- *WhoWrEP 89*
Schmitt, Carl 1888-1985 *BioIn 16*
Schmitt, Carveth Joseph Rodney 1934- *WhoWor 91*
Schmitt, Charles B. 1933-1986 *BioIn 16*
Schmitt, Conrad V *BiDrAPA 89*
Schmitt, Florent 1870-1958 *PenDiMP A*
Schmitt, Francis Otto 1903- *WhoAm 90*
Schmitt, Gary D. 1957- *St&PR 91*
Schmitt, George Frederick, Jr. 1939- *WhoAm 90*
Schmitt, George Herbert 1939- *WhoAm 90*
Schmitt, Harrison 1935- *WorAlBi*
Schmitt, Harrison Hagan 1935- *WhoAm 90*
Schmitt, Horst 1925-1989 *BioIn 16*
Schmitt, Jeffrey L. *St&PR 91*
Schmitt, John Edward 1938- *St&PR 91, WhoAm 90*
Schmitt, Karl Michael 1922- *WhoAm 90*
Schmitt, Lisa Marie 1963- *WhoAmW 91*
Schmitt, Louis Charles 1946- *St&PR 91*
Schmitt, Madeline Hubbard 1943- *WhoAmW 91*
Schmitt, Marie 1947- *WhoAmW 91*
Schmitt, Marilyn Low 1939- *WhoAmA 91*
Schmitt, Mark F. 1923- *WhoAm 90*
Schmitt, Mark James 1950- *WhoEmL 91*
Schmitt, Philip Julian 1954- *BiDrAPA 89*
Schmitt, R Larry 1936- *BiDrAPA 89*
Schmitt, Raymond F, Jr. 1935- *BiDrAPA 89*
Schmitt, Raymond J. 1934- *St&PR 91*
Schmitt, Robert Edward 1948- *St&PR 91*
Schmitt, Robert F. 1934- *St&PR 91*
Schmitt, Robert J *BiDrAPA 89*
Schmitt, Robert Lee 1948- *WhoE 91*
Schmitt, Robert W *BiDrAPA 89*
Schmitt, Roger Michael Laurence 1952- *WhoEmL 91*
Schmitt, Roland W. *BioIn 16*
Schmitt, Roland Walter 1923- *St&PR 91, WhoAm 90, WhoE 91, WhoWor 91*
Schmitt, Stephen Richard 1948- *WhoEmL 91*
Schmitt, Thomas E. *WhoAm 90*
Schmitt, William Howard 1936- *WhoAm 90*
Schmitt, William Robert 1948- *St&PR 91*
Schmitt, Wolfgang R. 1944- *St&PR 91*
Schmitt, Wolfgang Rudolph 1944- *WhoAm 90*
Schmitt-Noble, Cynthia Lynn 1956- *WhoSSW 91*
Schmitt-Walter, Stefan 1947- *WhoWor 91*
Schmitter, Charles Harry 1928- *WhoAm 90*
Schmitthoff, Clive M 1903-1990 *ConAu 132*
Schmitz, Albert 1933- *WhoWor 91*
Schmitz, Aron Hector 1861-1928 *MajTwCW*
Schmitz, Carl Ludwig 1900-1967 *WhoAmA 91N*
Schmitz, Charles Edison 1919- *WhoSSW 91, WhoWor 91*
Schmitz, David F. 1956- *ConAu 132*
Schmitz, Dennis 1937- *WhoWrEP 89*
Schmitz, Dennis Mathew 1937- *WhoAm 90*
Schmitz, Dolores Jean 1931- *WhoAmW 91*
Schmitz, Edward Henry 1929- *St&PR 91, WhoWor 91*
Schmitz, James Carl 1948- *St&PR 91*
Schmitz, James H. 1911-1981 *RGTwCSF*
Schmitz, John Michael *BiDrAPA 89*
Schmitz, Johnny 1920- *Ballpl 90*
Schmitz, Nicholas W *BiDrAPA 89*
Schmitz, Ralph K. 1932- *St&PR 91*
Schmitz, Robert Allen 1941- *WhoAm 90*
Schmitz, Roger Anthony 1934- *WhoAm 90*
Schmitz, Stephen L. 1953- *St&PR 91*
Schmitz, Stephen Louis 1953- *WhoEmL 91*
Schmitz, Walter Douglas 1930- *St&PR 91, WhoAm 90*
Schmitz, Wolfgang 1949- *WhoWor 91*
Schmoe, Wilfred P. 1927- *St&PR 91*
Schmoelling, Johannes *NewAgMG*
Schmoke, Kurt *BioIn 16*
Schmoke, Kurt 1949- *WhoAm 90, WhoE 91*
Schmokel, Wolfe William 1933- *WhoE 91*
Schmolka, Leo Louis 1939- *WhoAm 90*
Schmoll, Betty Lee 1936- *WhoAmW 91*
Schmoll, Harry F., Jr. 1939- *WhoE 91*
Schmoller, Gustav von 1838-1917 *BioIn 16*
Schmoller, Hans 1916-1985 *ConDes 90*
Schmoller, Hans Peter 1916-1985 *BioIn 16*
Schmolling, Paul 1930- *WhoE 91*
Schmoyer, Terrence K. 1939- *St&PR 91*
Schmucker, Ruby Elvy Ladrach 1923- *WhoAmW 91*
Schmucker, Toni 1921- *WhoWor 91*
Schmucker, William Albert 1931- *St&PR 91*
Schmuckler, Stanley Lloyd 1925- *St&PR 91*
Schmude, Judy Gail 1939- *WhoAmW 91*
Schmuhl, Marian Hobbs 1945- *WhoWrEP 89*
Schmuhl, Thomas Roeger 1946- *WhoE 91*
Schmuhl, William John, Jr. 1943- *St&PR 91*
Schmukler, Anita Gloria *BiDrAPA 89*
Schmults, Edward Charles 1931- *St&PR 91, WhoAm 90*
Schmutz, Arthur Walter 1921- *WhoAm 90*
Schmutz, Dana May 1938- *WhoAmW 91*
Schmutzhart, Berthold Josef 1928- *WhoAm 90, WhoAmA 91*
Schmutzhart, Slaithong Chengtraku 1934- *WhoE 91*
Schmutzhart, Slaithong Chengtrakul 1934- *WhoAmA 91*
Schmutzler, David Lee 1939- *St&PR 91*
Schmuz-Baudiss, Theodor Hermann *PenDiDA 89*
Schnaas, Francisco J 1947- *BiDrAPA 89*
Schnabel, Artur 1882-1951 *BioIn 16, PenDiMP*
Schnabel, E. Eugene 1936- *St&PR 91*
Schnabel, Harold Bernard 1928- *WhoE 91*
Schnabel, Jacqueline *BioIn 16*
Schnabel, John Henry 1915- *WhoAm 90*
Schnabel, Julian 1951- *WhoAm 90, WhoAmA 91*
Schnabel, Karl 1909- *WorAlBi*
Schnabel, Karl Ulrich 1909- *IntWWM 90, PenDiMP, WhoAm 90*
Schnabel, Robert Victor 1922- *WhoAm 90*
Schnabel, Rockwell Anthony 1936- *St&PR 91, WhoAm 90, WhoWor 91*
Schnabel, Stefan Artur 1912- *WhoAm 90*
Schnabel, Walter 1927- *St&PR 91*
Schnabl, Alexandrine Martina Augusta 1882-1957 *EncCoWW*
Schnack, Gayle Hemingway Jepson 1926- *WhoAmW 91, WhoWor 91*
Schnack, George F 1917- *BiDrAPA 89*
Schnack, Harold Clifford 1918- *WhoWor 91*
Schnack, Larry Gene 1937- *WhoAm 90*
Schnacke, Robert Howard 1913- *WhoAm 90*
Schnackenberg, Robert C *BiDrAPA 89*
Schnackenberg, Roy 1934- *WhoAm 90, WhoAmA 91*
Schnadelbach, R.T. 1939- *St&PR 91*
Schnader, Donald Dixon 1935- *St&PR 91*
Schnadig, Lawrence K. 1908- *St&PR 91*
Schnaiberg, Allan 1939- *WhoAm 90*
Schnaitman, William Kenneth 1926- *WhoAm 90*
Schnakenberg, Donald G. 1939- *WhoE 91*
Schnakenberg, Henry 1892-1970 *WhoAmA 91N*
Schnakenburg, Barry Allen 1947- *St&PR 91*
Schnakenburg, Otto H. 1916- *St&PR 91*
Schnall, Edith Lea 1922- *WhoAm 90, WhoE 91, WhoWor 91*
Schnall, Herbert K. 1928- *St&PR 91*
Schnap, Isidore 1906- *BiDrAPA 89*
Schnaper, Nathan 1918- *BiDrAPA 89*
Schnapf, Abraham *NewYTBS 90*
Schnapf, Abraham 1921-1990 *BioIn 16*
Schnapf, Donald Jeffrey 1946- *WhoE 91, WhoWor 91*
Schnapp, Diana Corley 1946- *WhoEmL 91*
Schnapp, John Berthold 1928- *WhoE 91*
Schnapp, Roger Herbert 1946- *WhoEmL 91, WhoWor 91*
Schnapp, Russell Lawrence 1955- *WhoEmL 91*
Schnapp, Stuart Michael 1953- *WhoE 91*
Schnapper, Dominique 1934- *ConAu 130*
Schnarr, Richard A. 1929- *St&PR 91*
Schnatterly, Stephen E. 1938- *WhoAm 90*
Schnaus, Peter 1936- *IntWWM 90*
Schnaut, Gabriele 1953- *IntWWM 90*
Schnautz, Nancy Lee *BiDrAPA 89*
Schnebel, Robert 1943- *St&PR 91*
Schnebelen, Pierre 1935- *WhoWor 91*
Schnebly, Diane Dee 1961- *WhoAmW 91*
Schneck, Dale A. 1947- *St&PR 91*
Schneck, Daniel Julio 1941- *WhoSSW 91*
Schneck, Ernest 1929- *St&PR 91*
Schneck, Jerome M 1920- *BiDrAPA 89, WhoAm 90, WhoWor 91*
Schneck, Marcus Herb 1956- *WhoE 91*
Schneck, Michael K *BiDrAPA 89*
Schneck, Paul E *BiDrAPA 89*
Schneck, Peter T. *BioIn 16*
Schneck, Stuart Austin 1929- *WhoAm 90*
Schneck, William Joseph 1943- *St&PR 91*
Schneckenburger, Karen Lynne 1949- *WhoAmW 91, WhoEmL 91, WhoSSW 91*
Schnee, Amanda Meryl MacNab 1945- *WhoAmW 91*
Schnee, David Z. 1941- *WhoE 91*
Schnee, Jack 1928- *BiDrAPA 89*
Schneebacher, Alexander T. 1944- *St&PR 91*
Schneebalg-Perelman, Sophie 1914-1988 *BioIn 16*
Schneebaum, Steven Marc 1948- *WhoE 91*
Schneebaum, Tobias 1921- *WhoAmA 91*
Schneebaum, Tobias 1922- *WhoWrEP 89*
Schneeberg, Helen Bassen 1920- *WhoAmW 91*
Schneeberger, Don Roy 1930- *St&PR 91*
Schneeman, Carolee 1939- *BiDWomA*
Schneeman, Peter Henry 1937- *WhoWrEP 89*
Schneemann, Carolee 1939- *WhoAmA 91, WhoWrEP 89*
Schneemelcher, Wilhelm 1914- *WhoWor 91*
Schneer, Henry Irving 1916- *BiDrAPA 89*
Schneevoigt, Georg 1872-1947 *PenDiMP*
Schneeweiss, Daniel Norman *BiDrAPA 89*
Schneewind, Jerome Borges 1930- *WhoAm 90*
Schneid, Gary Frederic 1946- *WhoE 91*
Schneidau, Tom Rodger 1942- *St&PR 91*
Schneideman, Robert Ivan 1926- *WhoAm 90*
Schneider Brothers *EncO&P 3*
Schneider, Adele Goldberg 1924- *WhoAmW 91*
Schneider, Alan 1917- *WhoWor 91*
Schneider, Alan Louis 1958- *BiDrAPA 89*
Schneider, Alan Neil 1916- *WhoWor 91*
Schneider, Alex 1927- *EncPaPR 91*
Schneider, Alexander 1908- *IntWWM 90, PenDiMP, WhoAm 90*
Schneider, Alexander J N 1911- *BiDrAPA 89*
Schneider, Alfred Reuben 1926- *St&PR 91*
Schneider, Allan Stanford 1940- *WhoAm 90*
Schneider, Andrew 1942- *ConAu 132*
Schneider, Arnold 1953- *WhoEmL 91*
Schneider, Arthur 1947- *WhoSSW 91*
Schneider, Arthur Paul 1930- *WhoAm 90*
Schneider, Arthur Sanford 1929- *WhoAm 90*
Schneider, Barbara Jean 1962- *WhoAmW 91*
Schneider, Barbara S. 1933- *WhoAmW 91*

Schneider, Ben Ross, Jr. *WhoWrEP 89*
Schneider, Benjamin 1938- *WhoAm 90, WhoE 91*
Schneider, Bob R. *St&PR 91*
Schneider, Bobby Dean 1937- *WhoSSW 91*
Schneider, Brenda L. 1946- *St&PR 91*
Schneider, C. Rex 1937- *WhoWrEP 89*
Schneider, Calvin 1924- *WhoWor 91*
Schneider, Calvin Dwaine 1931- *WhoSSW 91*
Schneider, Carl W. 1932- *WhoAm 90*
Schneider, Carol 1964- *WhoAmW 91*
Schneider, Charles 1881-1962 *PenDiDA 89*
Schneider, Charles Frederick 1955- *WhoE 91*
Schneider, Charles I. 1923- *WhoAm 90*
Schneider, Charles R. 1940- *St&PR 91*
Schneider, Cheryl Judith 1954- *WhoAmW 91*
Schneider, Chester Louis 1922- *BiDrAPA 89, WhoE 91*
Schneider, Christian Gottfried 1710-1773 *PenDiDA 89*
Schneider, Christine Lynn 1960- *WhoAmW 91*
Schneider, Cindy 1959- *ODwPR 91*
Schneider, Claudine Cmarada 1947- *WhoAm 90, WhoAmW 91, WhoE 91*
Schneider, Conrad H. 1931- *WhoWor 91*
Schneider, Cyril M. 1929- *WhoAm 90*
Schneider, Dan 1942- *Ballpl 90*
Schneider, Dan 1948- *St&PR 91*
Schneider, Daniel 1927- *WhoE 91*
Schneider, Daniel E *BiDrAPA 89*
Schneider, Daniel Max 1948- *WhoEmL 91*
Schneider, David 1918- *IntWWM 90*
Schneider, David M. 1937- *St&PR 91*
Schneider, David Miller 1937- *WhoAm 90*
Schneider, David Theodore 1949- *WhoE 91*
Schneider, Debra Ann 1963- *WhoAmW 91*
Schneider, Dennis Eugene 1957- *WhoEmL 91, WhoWor 91*
Schneider, Dennis Ray 1952- *WhoSSW 91*
Schneider, Dietrich 1919- *WhoWor 91*
Schneider, Donald Alfred 1951- *St&PR 91*
Schneider, Donald Frederic 1939- *WhoAm 90*
Schneider, Donald Wike 1930- *St&PR 91*
Schneider, Duane Bernard 1937- *WhoAm 90, WhoWrEP 89*
Schneider, Eberhard Georg 1941- *WhoWor 91*
Schneider, Edward Lewis 1940- *WhoAm 90*
Schneider, Eloise Covell 1923- *WhoAmW 91*
Schneider, Emory Hugh 1940- *St&PR 91*
Schneider, Ernest Emil 1925- *WhoE 91*
Schneider, Eugene John 1952- *BiDrAPA 89*
Schneider, F. Russell 1920- *WhoAm 90*
Schneider, Francis M. H. 1951- *IntWWM 90*
Schneider, Frank John 1923- *WhoAm 90*
Schneider, Fred *BioIn 16*
Schneider, Frederick P. 1926- *St&PR 91*
Schneider, Frederick William 1923- *St&PR 91*
Schneider, Frederick William, Jr. 1923- *WhoAm 90*
Schneider, Friedrich Georg 1949- *WhoWor 91*
Schneider, Gene W. 1926- *St&PR 91, WhoAm 90*
Schneider, George T. *WhoAm 90*
Schneider, Gerald A *BiDrAPA 89*
Schneider, Gerald Edward 1940- *WhoAm 90*
Schneider, Gerhard 1930- *St&PR 91*
Schneider, Hannes *BioIn 16*
Schneider, Harold J. 1931- *St&PR 91*
Schneider, Harold Joel 1923- *WhoAm 90*
Schneider, Harold K. *BioIn 16*
Schneider, Harold N. 1950- *St&PR 91*
Schneider, Harold Norman 1950- *WhoAm 90*
Schneider, Harry *St&PR 91N*
Schneider, Harry 1908-1989 *BioIn 16*
Schneider, Harvey B. 1922- *St&PR 91*
Schneider, Herbert Carpenter 1945- *WhoE 91*
Schneider, Herbert Joseph 1938- *WhoE 91*
Schneider, Herbert William 1930- *WhoAm 90*
Schneider, Herman 1905- *AuBYP 90*
Schneider, Hermann 1935- *WhoWor 91*
Schneider, Hortense 1833-1920 *PenDiMP*
Schneider, Howard 1935- *WhoAm 90*
Schneider, Howard M. 1943- *St&PR 91*
Schneider, Howard Stewart 1945- *WhoAm 90*
Schneider, Ira 1939- *WhoAmA 91*
Schneider, Irving 1925- *BiDrAPA 89*
Schneider, Jack Ward 1943- *WhoSSW 91*
Schneider, James G. 1925- *St&PR 91*
Schneider, James Gordon 1925- *WhoAm 90*
Schneider, Jan 1933- *WhoAm 90*
Schneider, Janet M. 1950- *WhoAm 90, WhoAmA 91*
Schneider, Janice Linnea 1938- *WhoAmW 91*
Schneider, Jean Marie 1929- *WhoAmW 91*
Schneider, Jeanette Elaine *BiDrAPA 89*
Schneider, Jeffrey M. 1955- *St&PR 91*
Schneider, Jo Anne 1919- *WhoAmA 91*
Schneider, JoAnne 1919- *WhoAm 90*
Schneider, Joel Alan 1938- *WhoSSW 91*
Schneider, John Arnold 1926- *WhoAm 90*
Schneider, John B. 1935- *St&PR 91*
Schneider, John Hoke 1931- *WhoAm 90*
Schneider, John Phillip, Jr. 1959- *WhoSSW 91*
Schneider, Jon David 1939- *St&PR 91*
Schneider, Jorge 1938- *BiDrAPA 89*
Schneider, Joseph Alan *BiDrAPA 89*
Schneider, Joseph R. 1929- *St&PR 91*
Schneider, Judith Ann 1944- *WhoAmW 91*
Schneider, Jules Edouard 1930- *St&PR 91*
Schneider, Julia L *BiDrAPA 89*
Schneider, Julie 1944- *WhoAmA 91*
Schneider, Jurgen 1936- *WhoAm 90*
Schneider, Karl Friedrich 1931- *WhoE 91*
Schneider, Keith Hilary 1956- *WhoAm 90*
Schneider, Kenneth Paul 1948- *WhoEmL 91*
Schneider, Klaus Dieter 1941- *WhoWor 91*
Schneider, Larry R. 1946- *St&PR 91*
Schneider, Lawrence Alan 1949- *WhoEmL 91*
Schneider, Laz Levkoff 1939- *WhoSSW 91*
Schneider, Leila Marie *WhoAmW 91*
Schneider, Lewis 1941- *St&PR 91*
Schneider, Lewis Michael 1935- *WhoE 91*
Schneider, Linda Ann 1945- *WhoAmW 91*
Schneider, Lisa Dawn 1954- *WhoAmA 91, WhoE 91*
Schneider, Lloyd Rhynehart 1949- *WhoWor 91*
Schneider, Lon S 1953- *BiDrAPA 89*
Schneider, Lori Beth 1960- *WhoAmW 91*
Schneider, Louise Carol *BiDrAPA 89*
Schneider, Mahlon Craig 1939- *St&PR 91*
Schneider, Mark 1946- *WhoAm 90*
Schneider, Mark Lewis 1941- *WhoAm 90*
Schneider, Mary Katherine 1944- *WhoE 91*
Schneider, Maryann W. 1946- *St&PR 91*
Schneider, Maryann Wellman 1946- *WhoAm 90*
Schneider, Melvin 1927- *St&PR 91*
Schneider, Michael Gerard 1957- *St&PR 91*
Schneider, Michael Ira 1936- *St&PR 91*
Schneider, Michael Joseph 1938- *WhoAm 90*
Schneider, Michael Wilmarth 1942- *St&PR 91*
Schneider, Michelle 1952- *WhoAmW 91*
Schneider, Mildred F *BiDrAPA 89*
Schneider, Mischa *PenDiMP*
Schneider, Mona *BiDrAPA 89*
Schneider, Myles Shelley *BiDrAPA 89*
Schneider, Nancy Reynolds 1942- *WhoSSW 91*
Schneider, Nina 1913- *AuBYP 90*
Schneider, Noel 1920- *WhoAmA 91*
Schneider, Norman M. 1911- *WhoAm 90*
Schneider, Owen B 1943- *BiDrAPA 89*
Schneider, Pam Horvitz 1951- *WhoEmL 91*
Schneider, Paul H. 1916- *St&PR 91*
Schneider, Paul L. 1954- *St&PR 91*
Schneider, Penny Lois 1954- *WhoAmW 91*
Schneider, Pete 1895-1957 *Ballpl 90*
Schneider, Peter 1939- *IntWWM 90*
Schneider, Petr 1933- *WhoWor 91*
Schneider, Phyllis Jean 1953- *WhoSSW 91*
Schneider, Phyllis Leah 1947- *WhoAm 90, WhoAmW 91*
Schneider, Ralph Saul 1928- *WhoAm 90*
Schneider, Raymond Clinton 1920- *WhoAm 90, WhoWor 91*
Schneider, Richard C. 1925- *St&PR 91*
Schneider, Richard Durbin 1937- *WhoAmA 91*
Schneider, Richard Graham 1930- *WhoAm 90*
Schneider, Richard Harold 1947- *WhoSSW 91*
Schneider, Richard Theodore 1927- *WhoSSW 91*
Schneider, Richard William 1946- *WhoAm 90*
Schneider, Robert Edward 1950- *St&PR 91, WhoAm 90*
Schneider, Rolf 1932- *ConAu 130*
Schneider, Rudi 1908-1957 *EncO&P 3, EncPaPR 91*
Schneider, Sandra Lee 1944- *WhoAmW 91*
Schneider, Scott Anthony *BiDrAPA 89*
Schneider, Stanley F. *BioIn 16*
Schneider, Stephen Gary 1945- *St&PR 91*
Schneider, Stephen Henry *BioIn 16*
Schneider, Stephen Henry 1945- *WhoAm 90*
Schneider, Stephen Scott *BiDrAPA 89*
Schneider, Steven Eric *BiDrAPA 89*
Schneider, Steven Eric 1952- *WhoE 91*
Schneider, Steven Matthew *BiDrAPA 89*
Schneider, Susan Lee 1957- *WhoAmW 91*
Schneider, Susan W 1954- *BiDrAPA 89*
Schneider, Susan Willey Byrd 1954- *WhoE 91*
Schneider, Tamara Roman 1952- *WhoAmW 91*
Schneider, Urs 1939- *IntWWM 90*
Schneider, Valerie Lois 1941- *WhoAmW 91, WhoSSW 91*
Schneider, Virginia Dee 1914- *WhoWrEP 89*
Schneider, Walter O. *St&PR 91*
Schneider, Willi 1903-1971 *EncO&P 3, EncPaPR 91*
Schneider, William Charles 1923- *WhoAm 90, WhoE 91*
Schneider, William George 1915- *WhoAm 90*
Schneider, William George 1919- *WhoAm 90*
Schneider, William George, Jr. 1941- *WhoAm 90, WhoE 91*
Schneider, William Henry 1934- *WhoAm 90*
Schneider, William James 1943- *WhoSSW 91*
Schneider, Yvette E. *WhoWrEP 89*
Schneider, Zola Dincin *WhoE 91*
Schneider-Braus, Kathleen 1953- *BiDrAPA 89*
Schneider-Criezis, Susan Marie 1953- *WhoAmW 91*
Schneider-Dice, Nanette 1920- *BiDrAPA 89*
Schneider-Maunoury, Michel 1931- *St&PR 91, WhoAm 90, WhoE 91*
Schneider-Siemssen, Gunther 1926- *IntWWM 90*
Schneider Town, Janis Elma 1950- *WhoAmW 91*
Schneidereith, C. Wm., Jr. 1938- *St&PR 91*
Schneiderhan, Wolfgang 1915- *IntWWM 90, PenDiMP*
Schneiderman, Charles I. 1943- *WhoE 91*
Schneiderman, David Abbott 1947- *WhoAm 90, WhoE 91, WhoEmL 91*
Schneiderman, Dorothy 1919- *WhoAmA 91*
Schneiderman, Edward Steven 1944- *WhoE 91*
Schneiderman, Gerald *St&PR 91*
Schneiderman, Gerald 1933- *BiDrAPA 89*
Schneiderman, Howard A. *NewYTBS 90*
Schneiderman, Howard Allen 1927- *WhoAm 90*
Schneiderman, Irwin 1923- *St&PR 91, WhoAm 90*
Schneiderman, Leonard 1928- *WhoAm 90*
Schneiderman, Michael Goodman 1939- *WhoAm 90*
Schneiderman, Richard S 1948- *WhoAmA 91*
Schneiderman, Richard Steven 1948- *WhoAm 90*
Schneiderman, Rose 1884-1972 *WorAlBi*
Schneiders, Anne Elizabeth 1938- *WhoAmW 91*
Schneidman, Barbara Sue 1944- *BiDrAPA 89*
Schneidman, Louis *BiDrAPA 89*
Schneidmuhl, Abraham Moses *BiDrAPA 89*
Schneier, Donna Frances 1938- *WhoAmA 91*
Schneier, Franklin Richard *BiDrAPA 89*
Schneier, Marc Malvin 1955- *WhoEmL 91*
Schneiman, Maurice 1909- *BiDrAPA 89*
Schneir, Steven Richard *BiDrAPA 89*
Schnek, Ariane Louise *BiDrAPA 89*
Schnell, Carlton Bryce 1932- *WhoAm 90*
Schnell, Donald F. 1932- *St&PR 91*
Schnell, Gary Keith *BiDrAPA 89*
Schnell, George Adam 1931- *WhoAm 90*
Schnell, Gertrude Helen 1934- *WhoAmW 91*
Schnell, Harry *BioIn 16*
Schnell, John Arthur 1933- *St&PR 91*
Schnell, Martin *PenDiDA 89*
Schnell, Richard Dale 1930- *BiDrAPA 89*
Schnell, Roger Thomas 1936- *WhoWor 91*
Schnell-Itten, Dora 1904- *IntWWM 90*
Schnelle, Helmut Otto 1932- *WhoWor 91*
Schnelle, Karl Benjamin, Jr. 1930- *WhoAm 90*
Schneller, Carney Joe 1941- *WhoWor 91*
Schneller, George Charles 1921- *WhoWor 91*
Schneller, Johanna *BioIn 16*
Schneller, Leo *BiDrAPA 89*
Schneller, Sylvia Johns 1940- *BiDrAPA 89*
Schnepf, Max Owen 1941- *WhoWrEP 89*
Schnepfe, Marian Moeller 1923- *WhoAmW 91*
Schnepper, Jeff 1947- *WhoEmL 91*
Schnepper, Robert Franklin 1920- *St&PR 91*
Schneps, Henry G. 1946- *St&PR 91*
Schneps, Jack 1929- *WhoAm 90*
Schnering, Otto Y. 1891-1953 *WorAlBi*
Schnering, Philip Blessed 1917- *WhoAm 90*
Schnering, Philip Scott 1947- *WhoE 91*
Schnetzler, Anne-Marie Fracassi 1940- *WhoAmW 91*
Schneyer, Charlotte Alper 1923- *WhoAm 90, WhoAmW 91*
Schnick, Thomas H. 1940- *St&PR 91*
Schnidrig, Herman Edward 1930- *St&PR 91*
Schniewind, Carl O 1900-1957 *WhoAmA 91N*
Schniewind, Henry Ernest, Jr. 1938- *BiDrAPA 89*
Schnip, John I. 1927- *St&PR 91*
Schnipper, Lowell Elliot 1943- *WhoAm 90*
Schnirring, William Richard 1929- *St&PR 91*
Schnitman, Harriet 1957- *WhoAmW 91*
Schnitt, Jack 1955- *St&PR 91*
Schnitt, Jerome M *BiDrAPA 89*
Schnitter, Beate 1929- *WomArch [port]*
Schnittke, Alfred 1934- *IntWWM 90, PenDiMPA*
Schnittmann, Sascha S 1913- *WhoAmA 91N*
Schnitzer, Arlene 1929- *WhoAmA 91*
Schnitzer, Arlene Director 1929- *WhoAmW 91*
Schnitzer, Bruce W. 1944- *St&PR 91*
Schnitzer, Christine A. 1955- *WhoWrEP 89*
Schnitzer, Howard Joel 1934- *WhoAm 90*
Schnitzer, Iris Taymore 1943- *WhoAmW 91, WhoE 91*
Schnitzer, Jeshaia 1918- *WhoE 91*
Schnitzer, Jordan Director 1951- *WhoEmL 91*
Schnitzer, Klaus A *WhoAmA 91*
Schnitzer, Leonard Elliott 1924- *St&PR 91*
Schnitzer, Martin Colby 1925- *WhoAm 90*
Schnitzer, Moshe 1921- *WhoWor 91*
Schnitzer, Robert C. 1906- *WhoAm 90*
Schnitzler, Arthur 1862-1931 *WorAlBi*
Schnoes, Robert F. 1926- *St&PR 91*
Schnog, Rene Herbert 1949- *WhoE 91*
Schnoll, Steven 1946- *St&PR 91*
Schnoor, Edward T *BiDrAPA 89*
Schnoor, Jerald Lee 1950- *WhoAm 90*
Schnoor, Steven R. 1952- *St&PR 91*
Schnorf, James Roy 1954- *St&PR 91*
Schnorr von Carolsfeld, Ludwig 1836-1865 *BioIn 16, PenDiMP*
Schnorr von Carolsfeld, Malvina 1825-1904 *PenDiMP*
Schnorrenberg, Barbara Brandon 1931- *WhoAmW 91*
Schnorrenberg, John Martin 1931- *WhoAmA 91*
Schnuck, Craig 1948- *WhoAm 90*
Schnur, David B 1949- *BiDrAPA 89*
Schnur, James Oliver 1936- *WhoSSW 91*
Schnur, Jerome *NewYTBS 90*
Schnur, Jerome 1923-1990 *BioIn 16*
Schnure, Dorothy 1953- *ODwPR 91*
Schnurer, Anthony T *BiDrAPA 89*
Schnurr, Constance Burke 1932- *WhoWrEP 89*
Schnurr, Elinore *WhoAmA 91*
Schnurr, Kenneth Eugene 1933- *St&PR 91*
Schnurr, William Bernhardt *WhoWrEP 89*
Schnurre, Wolfdietrich 1920- *WhoWor 91*
Schnurre, Wolfdietrich 1920-1989 *AnObit 1989, ConAu 129, SmATA 63*
Schoales, Dudley Nelson *BioIn 16*
Schober, Brian 1951- *IntWWM 90*
Schober, Charles C 1924- *BiDrAPA 89*
Schober, Charles Coleman, III 1924- *WhoSSW 91*
Schober, Dorothy Florence 1910- *WhoAmW 91*
Schober, Gary Michael 1953- *WhoEmL 91*
Schober, Glenn E. 1938- *WhoAm 90*
Schober, Robert Charles 1940- *WhoWor 91*
Schobinger, Juan 1928- *WhoWor 91*
Schoch, Arn Edward 1955- *St&PR 91*
Schoch, Bernadette Helen 1930- *WhoAmW 91*
Schoch, Clarissa Anthony 1935- *WhoAmW 91*
Schoch, Gerhard Konrad 1936- *WhoWor 91*
Schoch, Jacqueline Louise 1929- *WhoAmW 91*
Schoch, Laurence William 1934- *St&PR 91*
Schochet, Barry P. 1951- *WhoSSW 91*
Schochor, Jonathan 1946- *WhoWor 91*
Schock, Dixie *BioIn 16*
Schock, Elaine Irene 1946- *WhoAmW 91*

Schooley, Virginia Geist 1946- *WhoAmW 91*
Schoolfield, Henry Palmer, Jr. 1928- *WhoWrEP 89*
Schools, Charles Hughlette 1929- *WhoSSW 91, WhoWor 91*
Schoon, Susan Wylie 1948- *WhoAm 90*
Schoonbaert, Lydia Margareta Achillea 1930- *WhoWor 91*
Schoonhoven, Ray James 1921- *WhoAm 90*
Schoonmaker, Eric Michael 1960- *WhoE 91*
Schoonmaker, Jeanette S 1937- *BiDrAPA 89*
Schoonmaker, John B *BiDrAPA 89*
Schoonmaker, Samuel Vail, III 1935- *WhoAm 90*
Schoonover, Garry Gene 1950- *WhoSSW 91*
Schoonover, Hugh James 1942- *WhoSSW 91*
Schoonover, Jack Ronald 1934- *WhoSSW 91, WhoWor 91*
Schoonover, Jason 1946- *ConAu 129*
Schoonover, Jean Way *WhoAm 90, WhoAmW 91*
Schoonover, Jean Way 1920- *ODwPR 91*
Schoonover, Rodney Lee 1950- *St&PR 91*
Schoonover, Stephen C 1947- *BiDrAPA 89*
Schoonover, Thomas F. 1929- *St&PR 91*
Schoop, Ernest R. *WhoHisp 91*
Schooping, Fred W. 1942- *St&PR 91*
Schoor, Gene 1921- *AuBYP 90*
Schoor, Gerald W. 1934- *St&PR 91*
Schoor, Howard M. 1939- *WhoWor 91*
Schoor, Michael Mercier 1942- *WhoWor 91*
Schopbach, Robert R 1919- *BiDrAPA 89*
Schopenhauer, Arthur 1788-1860 *BioIn 16, WorAlBi, WrPh P*
Schopf, J. William 1941- *BioIn 16*
Schopick, David J. *BiDrAPA 89*
Schopler, John Henry 1930- *WhoAm 90*
Schoppe, Amalie 1791-1858 *EncCoWW*
Schoppe, Siegfried Georg 1944- *WhoWor 91*
Schoppenhorst, William 1931- *St&PR 91*
Schopper, Herwig Franz 1924- *WhoWor 91*
Schopper, Michael 1942- *IntWWM 90*
Schoppmeyer, Martin William 1929- *WhoAm 90, WhoSSW 91, WhoWor 91*
Schor, Joseph Martin 1929- *St&PR 91, WhoAm 90, WhoE 91*
Schor, Laurence 1942- *WhoE 91*
Schor, Lynda 1938- *WhoWrEP 89*
Schor, Mary Ann McCarthy *WhoAmW 91*
Schor, Olga Seemann 1951- *WhoAmW 91, WhoWor 91*
Schor, Robin Cheryl 1953- *BiDrAPA 89, WhoE 91*
Schor, Sandra 1932?-1990 *ConAu 132*
Schor, Sandra M. *NewYTBS 90*
Schor, Stanley Sidney 1922- *WhoAm 90*
Schor, Tony 1964- *ODwPR 91*
Schore, Arthur Howard *BiDrAPA 89*
Schorer, Calvin E 1919- *BiDrAPA 89*
Schorer, Mark 1908-1977 *DcLB 103 [port]*
Schork, Rudolph Joseph, Jr. 1933- *WhoAm 90*
Schorling, William Harrison 1949- *WhoWor 91*
Schorm, Evald 1931- *BioIn 16*
Schornack, John James 1930- *WhoAm 90*
Schornstein, Herman 1929- *BiDrAPA 89*
Schorr, Alan Edward 1945- *WhoAm 90*
Schorr, Alvin Louis 1921- *WhoAm 90*
Schorr, Bayla 1943- *BiDrAPA 89*
Schorr, Bruce Alan 1941- *WhoSSW 91*
Schorr, Daniel Louis 1916- *WhoAm 90*
Schorr, Friedrich 1888-1953 *PenDiMP*
Schorr, Justin 1928- *WhoAmA 91*
Schorr, Lisbeth Bamberger 1931- *WhoAm 90, WhoAmW 91*
Schorr, Mark 1953- *TwCCr&M 91*
Schorr, Martin Mark 1923- *WhoWor 91*
Schorr, Marvin Gerald 1925- *St&PR 91*
Schorr, Norman A. *WhoE 91*
Schorr, Phillip Andrew 1936- *St&PR 91, WhoAm 90*
Schorr, Robert Barton 1945- *BiDrAPA 89*
Schorr, Stephen I. 1945- *St&PR 91*
Schorr, Thelma M. 1924- *St&PR 91, WhoAm 90, WhoAmW 91*
Schorre, Charles 1925- *WhoAmA 91*
Schorre, Louis Charles, Jr. 1925- *WhoAm 90*
Schorsch, Ismar 1935- *BioIn 16, WhoAm 90*
Schorsch, John Louis 1943- *BiDrAPA 89*
Schorske, Carl Emil 1915- *WhoAm 90*
Schorzman, Glen Walter 1945- *WhoSSW 91*
Schosheim, John Paul 1950- *BiDrAPA 89*
Schotanus, Eugene Leroy 1937- *St&PR 91, WhoAm 90*
Schotland, Donald Lewis 1930- *WhoAm 90*
Schotland, Roy Arnold 1933- *WhoAm 90*
Schotsky, Samuel A. 1943- *St&PR 91*
Schott, Edward E. 1931- *St&PR 91*
Schott, Emil H. 1902- *St&PR 91*
Schott, Francis H. 1926- *St&PR 91*
Schott, Gene 1913- *Ballpl 90*
Schott, George E. 1936- *WhoAm 90*
Schott, Howard Mansfield 1923- *IntWWM 90*
Schott, John 1936- *WhoAm 90, WhoE 91*
Schott, John William 1940- *BiDrAPA 89*
Schott, Joseph Lawrence 1933- *WhoSSW 91*
Schott, Louis Ried 1949- *WhoE 91*
Schott, Marcia Whitney *BioIn 16*
Schott, Marge *BioIn 16*
Schott, Marge 1928- *WhoAm 90, WhoAmW 91*
Schott, Melvin 1925- *St&PR 91*
Schott, Merna Fisher 1951- *WhoSSW 91*
Schott, Michael B. 1948- *St&PR 91*
Schott, Penelope Scambly 1942- *WhoWrEP 89*
Schott, Stephen Harold 1961- *WhoWor 91*
Schotta, Charles 1935- *WhoAm 90*
Schottelkotte, Albert Joseph 1927- *St&PR 91, WhoAm 90*
Schottelkotte, William F. 1945- *St&PR 91*
Schottenfeld, Alvin C. 1916- *St&PR 91*
Schottenfeld, David 1931- *WhoAm 90*
Schottenfeld, Milton 1923- *St&PR 91*
Schottenfeld, Richard Steven 1949- *BiDrAPA 89, WhoE 91*
Schottenfeld, Steven Richard 1954- *St&PR 91*
Schottenheimer, Martin Edward 1943- *WhoAm 90*
Schottenstein, Jerome M. 1926- *St&PR 91*
Schotter, Andrew Roye 1947- *WhoAm 90*
Schottl, Luisa H 1935- *BiDrAPA 89*
Schottland, Charles Irwin 1906- *WhoAm 90*
Schottland, M 1935- *WhoAmA 91*
Schottmayer, Georg 1924- *WhoWor 91*
Schottstaedt, Mary F G *BiDrAPA 89*
Schotz, Eli Martin 1943- *BiDrAPA 89*
Schotz, Jeffrey Michael 1957- *WhoE 91*
Schotz, Jon P. 1955- *St&PR 91*
Schou, Michael Johan 1949- *WhoSSW 91*
Schough, Sven-Gunnar 1948- *WhoWor 91*
Schoultz, A.C., III 1940- *St&PR 91*
Schoultz, Solveig Margareta von 1907- *EncCoWW*
Schoultz, Solveig von 1907- *DcScanL*
Schouman, Aert 1710-1792 *PenDiDA 89*
Schounau, Walter 1936- *WhoWor 91*
Schouten, Cees 1927- *WhoWor 91*
Schouten, Gabriel *BioIn 16*
Schouten, Ronald 1953- *BiDrAPA 89*
Schouten, Sybo Adrianus 1940- *EncPaPR 91*
Schow, Russell Stewart 1949- *St&PR 91*
Schow, Terry D. 1948- *WhoEmL 91*
Schowalter, Ellen Lefferts 1937- *WhoE 91*
Schowalter, John Erwin 1936- *BiDrAPA 89, WhoAm 90*
Schowalter, Toni Lee 1948- *WhoE 91*
Schowalter, William Raymond 1929- *WhoAm 90*
Schowe, Sheral Lee Speaks 1953- *WhoAmW 91*
Schowen, Richard Lyle 1934- *WhoAm 90*
Schowengerdt, Louis W. *WhoAm 90*
Schoyer, David Kennedy 1946- *St&PR 91, WhoEmL 91*
Schrack, Joseph Earl 1890-1973 *WhoAmA 91N*
Schrade, Rolande Maxwell Young *WhoAmW 91*
Schrader, Arnold C. 1933- *St&PR 91*
Schrader, David Alan 1954- *WhoEmL 91*
Schrader, David Dillon 1952- *IntWWM 90*
Schrader, Franz 1891-1962 *DcScB S2*
Schrader, Harry Christian, Jr. 1932- *WhoAm 90*
Schrader, Henry Carl 1918- *WhoAm 90, WhoE 91, WhoSSW 91*
Schrader, James M. 1955- *St&PR 91*
Schrader, Jerry Lee *BiDrAPA 89*
Schrader, Keith William 1938- *WhoAm 90*
Schrader, Lawrence Edwin 1941- *WhoAm 90*
Schrader, Lee Frederick 1933- *WhoAm 90*
Schrader, Lynwood 1930- *St&PR 91, WhoAm 90*
Schrader, Margaret Anne 1954- *WhoEmL 91*
Schrader, Martin Harry 1924- *WhoAm 90*
Schrader, Nancy Lee 1949- *WhoE 91*
Schrader, Paul *BioIn 16*
Schrader, Paul Joseph 1946- *WhoAm 90*
Schrader, Thomas F. 1950- *St&PR 91, WhoAm 90*
Schrader, William Cutler 1933- *WhoAm 90*
Schrader, William Joseph 1929- *WhoAm 90*
Schrader-Moore, Sandra 1959- *WhoSSW 91*
Schrady, David Alan 1939- *WhoAm 90*
Schraeger, Maurice 1907- *St&PR 91*
Schraer, Rosemary S. J. 1924- *WhoAm 90, WhoAmW 91, WhoWor 91*
Schraff, Anne Elaine 1939- *AuBYP 90*
Schraff, Paul Albert 1949- *WhoEmL 91*
Schrag, Adele Frisbie 1921- *WhoAm 90*
Schrag, Crystal Blythe 1965- *WhoAmW 91*
Schrag, Edward A., Jr. 1932- *WhoAm 90*
Schrag, Karl 1912- *WhoAm 90, WhoAmA 91*
Schrag, Peter 1931- *WhoAm 90, WhoWrEP 89*
Schrage, Howell Evan *BiDrAPA 89*
Schrage, Martin Henry 1941- *WhoE 91*
Schrage, Paul Daniel 1935- *St&PR 91, WhoAm 90*
Schrage, Rose 1942- *WhoAmW 91*
Schrager, Harley Dean 1947- *St&PR 91*
Schrager, Jeffrey Jerome 1961- *WhoE 91*
Schrager, Mindy Rae 1958- *WhoAmW 91, WhoEmL 91, WhoWor 91*
Schrager, Stuart 1957- *St&PR 91*
Schraibman, Sandra Marguerite Milner 1947- *WhoE 91*
Schram, Donald Edward 1925- *St&PR 91*
Schram, James L. 1947- *St&PR 91*
Schram, John P. *St&PR 91*
Schram, Martin Jay 1942- *WhoAm 90*
Schram, Peter Charles *BiDrAPA 89*
Schram, Ronald 1942- *St&PR 91*
Schram, William S *BiDrAPA 89*
Schram, William Thomas 1949- *St&PR 91*
Schram-McRae, Norma 1957- *WhoAmW 91*
Schrameck, John Manning 1936- *WhoAm 90*
Schramek, Lynn Beth 1956- *WhoAmW 91*
Schramek, Tomas 1944- *WhoAm 90*
Schramel, Douglas J *BiDrAPA 89*
Schramm, Alfred 1943- *WhoWor 91*
Schramm, Bernard Charles, Jr. 1928- *WhoAm 90*
Schramm, Darrell G.H. 1943- *WhoWrEP 89*
Schramm, David Arden 1947- *WhoSSW 91*
Schramm, David Norman 1945- *WhoAm 90*
Schramm, Frederick Cullen 1942- *St&PR 91*
Schramm, George Palmer 1927- *WhoSSW 91*
Schramm, Gregory Paul 1953- *WhoSSW 91*
Schramm, Howard Murfee, Jr. 1942- *St&PR 91*
Schramm, Jane Marie 1960- *WhoAmW 91*
Schramm, John Clarendon 1908- *WhoAm 90*
Schramm, Kathleen Ann *BiDrAPA 89*
Schramm, Marilyn Jean 1951- *WhoAmW 91*
Schramm, Rachel Fleischmann 1929- *WhoWrEP 89*
Schramm, Richard Carl 1958- *BiDrAPA 89*
Schramm, Richard M. 1940- *St&PR 91*
Schramm, Susan Anne 1952- *WhoE 91*
Schramm, Tex *BioIn 16*
Schramm, Texas E. 1920- *WhoAm 90, WhoSSW 91*
Schramm, Theodore A 1926- *BiDrAPA 89*
Schramm, W.M. *St&PR 91*
Schramm, Werner Alfred 1939- *WhoWor 91*
Schramm, Wilbur Lang 1907-1987 *BioIn 16*
Schramme, Larry G. 1940- *St&PR 91*
Schrandt, David T. 1947- *St&PR 91*
Schrank, Holly L. 1941- *WhoAmW 91*
Schrank, Joseph 1900-1984 *AuBYP 90*
Schrantz, G. Mons 1936- *St&PR 91*
Schranz, Karoly *PenDiMP*
Schratz, Paul R. 1915- *BioIn 16*
Schratz, Walter Alfred 1922- *WhoE 91*
Schraut, Kenneth Charles 1913- *WhoAm 90*
Schrauth, William Lawrence 1935- *WhoAm 90*
Schray, Laurie 1957- *BiDrAPA 89*
Schrayer, Diane Wightman 1943- *St&PR 91*
Schreadley, Richard Lee 1931- *WhoAm 90, WhoSSW 91*
Schreck, Gordon Dalton 1943- *WhoSSW 91*
Schreck, Helen Elina 1949- *WhoE 91*
Schreck, James F. 1940- *St&PR 91*
Schreck, Michael H *WhoAmA 91*
Schreck, Richard Henry 1934- *St&PR 91*
Schreckengost, Ossee 1875-1914 *Ballpl 90*
Schreckengost, Viktor 1906- *WhoAmA 91*
Schrecker, Bruno *PenDiMP*
Schreckinger, Sy Edward 1937- *WhoAm 90*
Schrecongost, James Ray 1946- *St&PR 91*
Schredelseker, Klaus 1943- *WhoWor 91*
Schreffler, Samuel John 1945- *St&PR 91*
Schregenberger, Martin Niklaus Wilhelm 1947- *WhoWor 91*
Schrei, Rudolph L. 1909- *St&PR 91*
Schreiber, Alan Marc 1947- *St&PR 91*
Schreiber, Alfred L. *ODwPR 91*
Schreiber, Alice Mildred 1927- *WhoAmW 91*
Schreiber, Allan Charles 1941- *St&PR 91, WhoAm 90*
Schreiber, Caron *ODwPR 91*
Schreiber, Charles J. *ODwPR 91*
Schreiber, Charlotte Elizabeth Bertie G. 1812-1895 *BioIn 16*
Schreiber, Clayton John 1946- *St&PR 91*
Schreiber, David C. 1938- *ODwPR 91*
Schreiber, Edward 1943- *WhoWor 91*
Schreiber, Edward Joseph 1946- *WhoEmL 91*
Schreiber, Eileen Sher *WhoAmA 91*
Schreiber, Eileen Sher 1925- *WhoAmW 91*
Schreiber, Eliot Bruce 1956- *WhoEmL 91*
Schreiber, Elliot S. 1947- *ODwPR 91*
Schreiber, Elliot Steven 1947- *WhoE 91*
Schreiber, Ernest H 1934- *BiDrAPA 89*
Schreiber, Eugene Ralph 1939- *WhoE 91*
Schreiber, Flora Rheta *BioIn 16*
Schreiber, Fred James, Jr. 1922- *WhoAm 90*
Schreiber, Frederick Carl 1922-1979 *BioIn 16*
Schreiber, George Richard 1922- *WhoAm 90*
Schreiber, Georges 1904-1977 *WhoAmA 91N*
Schreiber, James G. 1949- *St&PR 91*
Schreiber, James Ralph 1946- *WhoEmL 91*
Schreiber, Jeffrey Lee 1952- *WhoEmL 91*
Schreiber, Johannes 1927- *WhoWor 91*
Schreiber, Julius 1908- *BiDrAPA 89*
Schreiber, Kenneth Alan 1946- *BiDrAPA 89*
Schreiber, Klaus W *BiDrAPA 89*
Schreiber, Kurt Gilbert 1946- *St&PR 91, WhoAm 90*
Schreiber, Lawrence J 1934- *BiDrAPA 89*
Schreiber, Le Anne *BioIn 16*
Schreiber, Leonard Irwin 1914- *St&PR 91*
Schreiber, Marc Elliot 1951- *St&PR 91*
Schreiber, Marguerite *BioIn 16*
Schreiber, Marilynn Kay 1940- *WhoSSW 91*
Schreiber, Mark 1960- *WhoWrEP 89*
Schreiber, Mark Traudt *BiDrAPA 89*
Schreiber, Martin 1923- *WhoAmA 91*
Schreiber, Max Benjamin *BioIn 16*
Schreiber, Maxine Ellen 1945- *WhoAmW 91*
Schreiber, Melvyn Hirsh 1931- *WhoAm 90*
Schreiber, Moses 1762?-1839 *BioIn 16*
Schreiber, Otto J *BiDrAPA 89*
Schreiber, Ralph W. *BioIn 16*
Schreiber, Raymond Gary 1940- *St&PR 91*
Schreiber, Robert F 1937- *BiDrAPA 89*
Schreiber, Robert R. 1942- *St&PR 91*
Schreiber, Ron 1934- *WhoWrEP 89*
Schreiber, Roy *BioIn 16*
Schreiber, Sally Ann 1951- *WhoEmL 91*
Schreiber, Sanford Jay 1931- *BiDrAPA 89*
Schreiber, Scott H. 1953- *St&PR 91*
Schreiber, Selma Emdin 1918- *St&PR 91, WhoAmW 91*
Schreiber, Sol Joseph 1916- *St&PR 91*
Schreiber, Steven L. 1942- *WhoE 91, WhoWor 91*
Schreiber, Suydam Van Zandt 1939- *St&PR 91*
Schreiber, Suzanne E. 1936- *WhoWrEP 89*
Schreiber, Terry *BioIn 16*
Schreiber, Thelma 1918- *St&PR 91*
Schreiber, Thomas John 1948- *BiDrAPA 89*
Schreiber, William Francis 1925- *WhoAm 90*
Schreiber, William Mark 1948- *WhoEmL 91*
Schreibman, Rochelle Rita *BiDrAPA 89*
Schreibman, Ron 1949- *ODwPR 91*
Schreier, Leonard 1934- *WhoAm 90*
Schreier, Max N. *WhoAm 90*
Schreier, Morton 1931- *St&PR 91*
Schreier, Peter 1935- *IntWWM 90, PenDiMP, WhoAm 90*
Schreier, Sandy *BioIn 16*
Schreier, Thomas Stephen 1936- *WhoWor 91*
Schreiner, Albert William 1926- *WhoAm 90*
Schreiner, Beverly Ethel 1931- *WhoAmW 91*
Schreiner, Carol Anne *BiDrAPA 89*
Schreiner, George E. 1922- *WhoAm 90*
Schreiner, Joan Mau 1944- *WhoAmW 91*
Schreiner, John Christian 1933- *WhoAm 90*

Schreiner, Olive 1855-1920 *BioIn 16, FemiCLE*
Schreiner, Richard August 1964- *WhoE 91*
Schreiner, Robert George 1925- *St&PR 91, WhoAm 90*
Schreiner, Robert K. 1948- *St&PR 91*
Schreiner, Susan 1950- *ODwPR 91*
Schreiner, Werner Emil 1921- *WhoWor 91*
Schreiter, Johannes 1930- *PenDiDA 89*
Schreiver, George August *WhoAmA 91N*
Schreivogel, Paul A. *BioIn 16*
Schremmer, Eckart G. 1934- *WhoWor 91*
Schrempf, Robert J. 1932- *St&PR 91*
Schremser, Donna Barrett 1949- *WhoSSW 91*
Schrenck-Notzing, Albert von 1862-1929 *EncO&P 3, EncPaPR 91*
Schrenk, Willi Juergen 1945- *WhoEmL 91*
Schrero, Ruth Lieberman *WhoAmA 91, WhoAmW 91*
Schreter, Michael M. 1940- *St&PR 91*
Schreter, Robert K 1945- *BiDrAPA 89*
Schrett, Roy F. 1937- *St&PR 91*
Schretter, Louis Frank 1937- *St&PR 91*
Schretzmann, Charles F. 1943- *WhoAm 90*
Schretzmann, Charles Francis 1943- *St&PR 91*
Schretzmann, Joseph Gustav 1952- *St&PR 91*
Schretzmann, Rudolph Charles 1907- *WhoE 91*
Schreuer, Christoph Herbert 1944- *WhoWor 91*
Schreurs, Dale Kenneth 1931- *St&PR 91*
Schreve, Robert Paul 1939- *WhoSSW 91*
Schrevel, Joseph Desire 1939- *WhoWor 91*
Schreyer, Greta L 1923- *WhoAmA 91*
Schreyer, Nancy Kraft 1952- *WhoAmW 91*
Schreyer, William A. 1928- *St&PR 91*
Schreyer, William Allen 1928- *WhoAm 90, WhoE 91*
Schreyer-Thomson, Camella Joy 1949- *WhoAmW 91, WhoEmL 91*
Schreyvogel, Charles 1861-1912 *WhNaAH*
Schriber, Jonathan David 1951- *WhoE 91*
Schriber, Margrit 1939- *EncCoWW*
Schriber, Thomas Jude 1935- *WhoAm 90*
Schrichte, Dellzell 1962- *WhoWrEP 89*
Schrick, Edward Arthur 1948- *WhoE 91*
Schricker, Joanie Marie 1962- *WhoAmW 91*
Schrieffer, John R. 1931- *WorAlBi*
Schrieffer, John Robert 1931- *WhoAm 90, WhoWor 91*
Schriener, Judy A. 1949- *WhoWrEP 89*
Schrier, Allan M. *BioIn 16*
Schrier, Arnold 1925- *WhoAm 90, WhoWrEP 89*
Schrier, Clarence M *BiDrAPA 89*
Schrier, Robert William 1936- *WhoAm 90*
Schrier, Stan 1935- *St&PR 91*
Schriesheim, Alan 1930- *WhoAm 90*
Schriever, Bernard Adolph 1910- *WhoAm 90*
Schriever, Fred M. 1930- *St&PR 91*
Schriever, Fred Martin 1930- *WhoAm 90*
Schrift, Michael Joel 1953- *BiDrAPA 89*
Schrift, Shirley *WhoAmW 91*
Schriftgiesser, Karl 1903-1988 *BioIn 16*
Schrijver, Robert William 1948- *WhoEmL 91*
Schrijvers, Jan Frans 1935- *BiDrAPA 89*
Schrimper, Vernon L. 1933- *St&PR 91, WhoAm 90*
Schrimpf, Sherry Ann 1957- *St&PR 91*
Schriner, John David 1955- *WhoSSW 91*
Schriver, Byron, Jr. 1936- *St&PR 91*
Schriver, Pop 1866-1932 *Ballpl 90*
Schriver, Roland H. 1938- *St&PR 91*
Schrobilgen, Linda *BioIn 16*
Schrock, Harold Arthur 1915- *WhoAm 90*
Schrock, Rosalind 1937- *WhoAmW 91*
Schrock, Virgil Edwin 1926- *WhoAm 90*
Schrocke, Helmut Heinrich 1922- *WhoWor 91*
Schroder, Dieter Karl 1935- *WhoAm 90*
Schroder, Friedrich 1910-1972 *OxCPMus*
Schroder, Gerhard *NewYTBS 90 [port]*
Schroder, Gerhard 1910-1989 *BioIn 16, CurBio 90N*
Schroder, Gisela *BiDrAPA 89*
Schroder, J. Michael 1937- *WhoWor 91*
Schroder, Jaap 1925- *IntWWM 90, PenDiMP*
Schroder, Josef 1937- *WhoWor 91*
Schroder, Kirk Theodore 1962- *WhoSSW 91*
Schroder, Raymond A. 1926- *WhoAm 90*
Schroder, Ricky *BioIn 16*
Schroder-Devrient, Wilhelmine 1805-1860 *PenDiMP*
Schroder-Feinen, Ursula 1935- *IntWWM 90*
Schrodinger, Erwin 1887-1961 *BioIn 16, WorAlBi*
Schrodt, Ariel G. 1927- *St&PR 91*
Schrodt, Christopher J *BiDrAPA 89*
Schrodt, George Randolph 1928- *WhoAm 90*
Schrodt, George Randolph, Jr. 1955- *BiDrAPA 89*
Schroeck, R D 1949- *WhoAmA 91*
Schroedel, Herman L. 1931- *St&PR 91*
Schroedel, Huberta Gowen Wolf 1943- *WhoAmW 91*
Schroeder, Aaron Harold 1926- *WhoAm 90*
Schroeder, Alfred Christian 1915- *WhoAm 90*
Schroeder, Betty Louise 1937- *WhoAmW 91*
Schroeder, Bill 1958- *Ballpl 90*
Schroeder, Binette 1939- *BioIn 16*
Schroeder, Carole Gibson 1943- *WhoAmW 91*
Schroeder, Charles E. 1935- *St&PR 91*
Schroeder, Charles Edgar 1935- *WhoAm 90*
Schroeder, Charles Henry 1942- *WhoAm 90*
Schroeder, Cheryl Ann 1960- *WhoWrEP 89*
Schroeder, Christopher Matthew 1964- *WhoE 91*
Schroeder, Cynthia R. 1949- *WhoAmW 91*
Schroeder, Dana J. 1956- *WhoAmW 91*
Schroeder, David Alan 1941- *BiDrAPA 89*
Schroeder, David Harold 1940- *WhoWor 91*
Schroeder, David Lawrence 1954- *St&PR 91*
Schroeder, Deborah M. 1952- *WhoAmW 91*
Schroeder, Don R. 1948- *St&PR 91*
Schroeder, Donald Carl 1957- *WhoEmL 91*
Schroeder, Donald Perry 1930- *WhoAm 90*
Schroeder, Douglas Fredrick 1935- *WhoAm 90*
Schroeder, Dwight Jon 1953- *BiDrAPA 89*
Schroeder, Ellen Barbara *BiDrAPA 89*
Schroeder, Eric 1904- *WhoAmA 91N*
Schroeder, Eva Pamela *BiDrAPA 89*
Schroeder, Fred Erich Harald 1932- *WhoAm 90*
Schroeder, Frederick John 1947- *WhoE 91*
Schroeder, Frederick John, Jr. 1934- *St&PR 91*
Schroeder, Gary Steven 1951- *WhoWrEP 89*
Schroeder, H.B.W. *St&PR 91*
Schroeder, Harold T 1913- *BiDrAPA 89*
Schroeder, Harry William, Jr. 1952- *WhoSSW 91*
Schroeder, Heinz R 1918- *BiDrAPA 89*
Schroeder, Herbert *St&PR 91*
Schroeder, Herman Elbert 1915- *WhoAm 90*
Schroeder, Horst Wilhelm 1941- *WhoAm 90*
Schroeder, Jay 1961- *BioIn 16*
Schroeder, John 1954- *WhoEmL 91*
Schroeder, John C *BiDrAPA 89*
Schroeder, John H. 1920- *St&PR 91*
Schroeder, John Louis 1930- *WhoAm 90*
Schroeder, John Speer 1937- *WhoAm 90*
Schroeder, Jon Robert 1946- *St&PR 91*
Schroeder, Joseph James 1960- *WhoSSW 91*
Schroeder, Karen Ruth 1946- *WhoAmW 91*
Schroeder, Karl John *BiDrAPA 89*
Schroeder, Karl Vincent 1953- *BiDrAPA 89*
Schroeder, Kathleen Audrey 1959- *WhoWrEP 89*
Schroeder, Keith Carl 1936- *St&PR 91*
Schroeder, L. Clifford 1931- *St&PR 91*
Schroeder, Lawrence R. 1941- *St&PR 91*
Schroeder, Leila Obier 1925- *WhoWor 91*
Schroeder, Lesley A *BiDrAPA 89*
Schroeder, Lynn Ellen *BiDrAPA 89*
Schroeder, Manfred Franz 1930- *St&PR 91*
Schroeder, Margaret Louise 1957- *WhoWrEP 89*
Schroeder, Martha Saenz- *BioIn 16*
Schroeder, Mary Esther 1947- *WhoAmW 91*
Schroeder, Mary Murphy 1940- *WhoAm 90, WhoAmW 91*
Schroeder, Mike F. 1957- *WhoWrEP 89*
Schroeder, Milton Robert 1940- *WhoAm 90*
Schroeder, Oliver Charles, Jr. 1916- *ConAu 30NR*
Schroeder, Pat 1940- *NewYTBS 90 [port]*
Schroeder, Patricia *BioIn 16*
Schroeder, Patricia 1953- *WhoAmW 91*
Schroeder, Patricia Elaine 1954- *WhoAmW 91*
Schroeder, Patricia Scott 1940- *WhoAm 90, WhoAmW 91*
Schroeder, Reinhold 1956- *WhoEmL 91*
Schroeder, Richard Philip 1951- *WhoE 91*
Schroeder, Rita Molthen 1922- *WhoAmW 91, WhoWor 91*
Schroeder, Robert *NewAgMG*
Schroeder, Robert Anthony 1912- *WhoAm 90, WhoWor 91*
Schroeder, Robert Engle 1929- *WhoWrEP 89*
Schroeder, Ronald Thomas 1948- *St&PR 91, WhoAm 90*
Schroeder, Stephanie Lynn 1962- *WhoSSW 91*
Schroeder, Steven Alfred 1939- *WhoAm 90*
Schroeder, Steven Clifford 1958- *St&PR 91*
Schroeder, Steven Michael 1953- *BiDrAPA 89*
Schroeder, Sydney O 1918- *BiDrAPA 89*
Schroeder, Terri Lea 1955- *WhoAmW 91, WhoEmL 91*
Schroeder, Terry 1957?- *BioIn 16*
Schroeder, W.F. 1932- *St&PR 91*
Schroeder, Wallace William 1924- *St&PR 91*
Schroeder, Walter Warren 1948- *St&PR 91*
Schroeder, Wayne Harold 1944- *WhoWor 91*
Schroeder, William A. 1911- *St&PR 91*
Schroeder, William Henry 1929- *St&PR 91*
Schroeder, William John 1944- *St&PR 91*
Schroeder, William Paul 1953- *WhoSSW 91*
Schroeder, William Robert 1945- *WhoEmL 91*
Schroeer, Dietrich 1938- *WhoAm 90*
Schroepfer, George John, Jr. 1932- *WhoAm 90, WhoWor 91*
Schroer, Barbara Claire 1958- *WhoAmW 91*
Schroer, Edmund A. 1928- *St&PR 91*
Schroer, Edmund Armin 1928- *WhoAm 90*
Schroer, Gene Eldon 1927- *WhoWor 91*
Schroeter, Arnold L. 1936- *WhoAm 90*
Schroeter, Joachim Johannes 1931- *WhoWor 91*
Schroeter, Louis C. 1929- *WhoAm 90*
Schroeter, Louis Clarence 1929- *St&PR 91*
Schroll, Al 1933- *Ballpl 90*
Schroller, Christine Marie 1950- *WhoAmW 91*
Schrom, Elizabeth Ann 1941- *WhoAmW 91, WhoWor 91*
Schrom, Gerard Killard 1947- *WhoE 91, WhoEmL 91*
Schrom, Ken 1954- *Ballpl 90*
Schrom, Michael 1951- *WhoE 91*
Schropfer, David Waldron 1939- *WhoE 91*
Schropp, James Howard 1943- *WhoWor 91*
Schropp, Mary Lou 1947- *WhoAmW 91*
Schrorer, Herbert Wolffram 1943- *WhoWor 91*
Schrot, John Joseph, Jr. 1950- *WhoEmL 91*
Schrotberger, Gloria Mae 1929- *WhoAmW 91*
Schrote, John Ellis 1936- *WhoAm 90, WhoE 91*
Schroth, C. William 1948- *St&PR 91, WhoE 91*
Schroth, Evelyn Mary 1919- *WhoAmW 91*
Schroth, James L. 1933- *St&PR 91*
Schroth, Peter William 1946- *WhoE 91, WhoWor 91*
Schroth, Thomas Nolan 1920- *WhoAm 90*
Schrott, John D. 1947- *St&PR 91*
Schrotta, Werner 1935- *WhoWor 91*
Schroy, Carter Brett 1947- *WhoSSW 91*
Schroyer, William Keith 1955- *WhoEmL 91*
Schruben, John Henry 1926- *WhoAm 90*
Schrumpf, Robyn Lynn 1959- *WhoAmW 91, WhoWor 91*
Schrunk, John Thomas 1947- *St&PR 91*
Schrupp, Anne Nicolai *ODwPR 91*
Schrut, Albert H *BiDrAPA 89*
Schrut, Sherry 1928- *WhoAmA 91*
Schryver, Richard E. 1931- *St&PR 91*
Schu, Rick 1962- *Ballpl 90*
Schuba, Kenneth F. 1929- *St&PR 91*
Schubart, Christian Friedrich Daniel 1739-1791 *DcLB 97 [port]*
Schubart, Mark Allen 1918- *WhoAm 90*
Schubauer, James W. 1934- *St&PR 91*
Schubauer, James William 1934- *WhoAm 90*
Schubel, Howard C., Jr. 1932- *St&PR 91*
Schubel, Jerry Robert 1936- *WhoAm 90*
Schubert, Anthony S 1938- *BiDrAPA 89*
Schubert, Anthony Stephen 1938- *WhoE 91*
Schubert, Barbara Schuele 1939- *WhoAm 90*
Schubert, Daniel S P 1935- *BiDrAPA 89*
Schubert, Dieter 1947- *SmATA 62 [port]*
Schubert, Edmund F., Jr. 1936- *St&PR 91*
Schubert, Elaine Elisabeth 1947- *St&PR 91*
Schubert, Franz 1797-1828 *BioIn 16, PenDiMP A, WorAlBi*
Schubert, Glendon 1918- *WhoAm 90*
Schubert, Guenther Erich 1930- *WhoWor 91*
Schubert, Helen C. *WhoAmW 91*
Schubert, Helga 1940- *EncCoWW*
Schubert, James Ronald 1932- *St&PR 91*
Schubert, John Edward 1912- *WhoAm 90*
Schubert, Joseph H. 1938- *St&PR 91*
Schubert, Kathryn Ilyne 1941- *WhoAmW 91*
Schubert, Lisa Lynn 1961- *WhoAmW 91*
Schubert, Martin William 1935- *WhoE 91, WhoWor 91*
Schubert, Nancy Ellen 1945- *WhoAmW 91, WhoEmL 91, WhoWor 91*
Schubert, Richard Francis 1936- *WhoAm 90*
Schubert, Robert William, Jr. 1952- *WhoWor 91*
Schubert, Rolf B. 1938- *St&PR 91*
Schubert, Rudolph G. 1927- *St&PR 91*
Schubert, Ruth Carol Hickok 1927- *WhoAmW 91*
Schubert, Ulrich 1946- *WhoWor 91*
Schubert, William Kuenneth 1926- *WhoAm 90*
Schubert, William L. 1943- *St&PR 91*
Schubert-Gabrys, Ingrid 1953- *SmATA 62 [port]*
Schuble, Heinie 1906- *Ballpl 90*
Schubler, Johann Jakob 1689-1741 *PenDiDA 89*
Schubmehl, James Q. *BiDrAPA 89*
Schubmehl, Quinton D 1920- *BiDrAPA 89*
Schuch, Airton Correa 1942- *WhoWor 91*
Schuch, Diane Jean 1942- *WhoAmW 91*
Schuch, Ernst von 1846-1914 *PenDiMP*
Schuchard, Georg *PenDiDA 89*
Schuchardt, Daniel Norman 1937- *St&PR 91*
Schuchart, John Albert 1929- *St&PR 91*
Schuchart, John Albert, Jr. 1929- *WhoAm 90*
Schuchart, Wayne Joseph 1949- *St&PR 91*
Schuchinski, Luis 1937- *WhoE 91*
Schucht, John F. 1944- *St&PR 91*
Schuchter, Wilhelm 1911-1974 *PenDiMP*
Schuck, Carl Joseph 1915- *WhoAm 90*
Schuck, Marjorie Massey 1921- *WhoWrEP 89*
Schuck, Peter H. 1940- *ConAu 129, WhoAm 90*
Schuck, Robert Nelson 1936- *St&PR 91*
Schuck, Victoria 1909- *WhoAm 90, WhoAmW 91, WhoE 91, WhoWor 91*
Schuckard, John Daryle 1947- *St&PR 91*
Schucker, Charles 1908- *WhoAmA 91, WhoE 91*
Schuckit, Marc Alan 1944- *BiDrAPA 89*
Schuckman, Nancy Lee 1939- *WhoAmW 91*
Schudel, Hansjoerg 1937- *WhoAm 90*
Schudel, Thomas 1937- *IntWWM 90*
Schudel, Willem Joost 1944- *WhoWor 91*
Schuder, Raymond Francis 1926- *WhoSSW 91*
Schuder, Suzie E *BiDrAPA 89*
Schudmak, Mel Edward 1948- *St&PR 91*
Schudson, Charles B 1950- *ConAu 130*
Schudy, Patricia Hellingen 1939- *WhoWrEP 89*
Schuebelin, Peter Walter 1940- *WhoWor 91*
Schuele, Alban W. 1944- *St&PR 91*
Schuele, Alban Wilhelm 1944- *WhoAm 90*
Schuele, Donald Edward 1934- *WhoAm 90*
Schueler, Carrol Guerrant 1949- *St&PR 91*
Schueler, James Robert 1947- *St&PR 91*
Schueler, Jon R 1916- *WhoAmA 91*
Schueler, Jon Rudolf 1916- *WhoE 91*
Schueler, Klaus Wilhelm 1940- *WhoWor 91*
Schueler, Ron 1948- *Ballpl 90*
Schueling, Donna Eileen 1958- *WhoSSW 91*
Schuelke, Arthur Roy 1947- *WhoSSW 91*
Schuelke, Constance Patricia 1953- *WhoSSW 91*
Schueller, Thomas George 1936- *WhoAm 90*
Schuemann, Douglas L. 1939- *St&PR 91*
Schuenke, Donald J. 1929- *St&PR 91*
Schueppert, George L. 1938- *St&PR 91*
Schueppert, George Louis 1938- *WhoAm 90*
Schuerch, Conrad 1918- *WhoAm 90*
Schuerger, Thomas Robert 1925- *WhoE 91*
Schuering, Mark Allen 1953- *WhoEmL 91*
Schuerman, Janice Constance 1947- *St&PR 91*
Schuerman, John Richard 1938- *WhoAm 90*
Schuermann, David C. 1943- *St&PR 91*
Schuessler, John T. 1950- *St&PR 91*

Schuessler, Karl Frederick 1915- *WhoAm 90*
Schuessler, Mary Ann Petery 1936- *WhoAmW 91*
Schuessler, Morgan McGueen 1935- *St&PR 91*
Schuessler, Morgan McQueen 1935- *WhoAm 90*
Schuessler, Richard D. 1942- *St&PR 91*
Schuessler, Richard Jay 1938- *WhoE 91*
Schuessler, Robert F. 1939- *St&PR 91*
Schuessler, Suzanne Wright 1959- *WhoAmW 91*
Schuessler, Walter E. 1913- *St&PR 91*
Schuessler Fiorenza, Elisabeth 1938- *WhoAm 90, WhoAmW 91*
Schuetrumpf, Robert Gilbert 1953- *WhoE 91*
Schuette, Bill 1953- *WhoAm 90*
Schuette, Frederick Max 1924- *WhoAm 90*
Schuette, Henry William 1923- *St&PR 91*
Schuette, Janice J. *St&PR 91*
Schuette, John H., Jr. 1924- *St&PR 91*
Schuette, Michael 1937- *WhoAm 90*
Schuette, Oswald Francis 1921- *WhoAm 90*
Schuette, Timothy Mark 1955- *St&PR 91*
Schuetz, Arnim Friedrich 1946- *WhoE 91*
Schuetze, Frederik Edwin 1947- *IntWWM 90*
Schuetze, Joy Louise Talbert 1953- *IntWWM 90*
Schuetzenduebel, Wolfram Gerhard 1932- *WhoSSW 91*
Schuetzinger, C E 1909- *EncO&P 3*
Schuff, Karen Elizabeth 1937- *WhoWrEP 89*
Schug, Kenneth Robert 1924- *WhoAm 90*
Schug, Linda Louise 1951- *St&PR 91*
Schuh, G Edward 1930- *ConAu 30NR*
Schuh, George Edward 1930- *WhoAm 90*
Schuh, Stephen Joseph 1952- *WhoEmL 91*
Schuh, Terrence John 1942- *St&PR 91*
Schuhmann, Reinhardt, Jr. 1914- *WhoAm 90*
Schuitema, Paul 1897-1973 *ConDes 90*
Schuk, Linda Lee 1946- *WhoAmW 91*
Schuk, Rosalind 1949- *WhoAmW 91*
Schukai, Robert Joseph 1938- *St&PR 91*
Schuker, Eleanor S 1941- *BiDrAPA 89*
Schuker, Eleanor Sheila 1941- *WhoE 91*
Schuker, Jill Anita 1946- *ODwPR 91*
Schuker, Louis A. *BioIn 16, NewYTBS 90 [port]*
Schuker, Stephen Alan 1939- *WhoAm 90*
Schuknecht, Harold Frederick 1917- *WhoAm 90*
Schulberg, Arnold L. 1952- *WhoE 91*
Schulberg, Budd *BioIn 16*
Schulberg, Budd 1914- *WhoAm 90, WhoWrEP 89, WorAlBi*
Schulberg, Jay *BioIn 16*
Schulberg, Jay William 1939- *WhoAm 90, WhoE 91*
Schuldenrein, Joseph 1949- *WhoE 91*
Schuldiner, Arthur P. 1930- *St&PR 91*
Schuldner, Edward *BioIn 16*
Schuldner, Tiberius H. 1940- *St&PR 91*
Schuldt, George D. *WhoSSW 91*
Schuldt, Michael Bruce 1951- *WhoWrEP 89*
Schuldt, Robert R. 1930- *St&PR 91*
Schule, Bernard E. 1909- *IntWWM 90*
Schule, Donald Kenneth 1938- *WhoAmA 91*
Schuler, Alison Kay 1948- *WhoAmW 91, WhoWor 91*
Schuler, Burton Silverman 1950- *WhoSSW 91*
Schuler, C. Barr 1940- *St&PR 91*
Schuler, Carla Egly 1959- *WhoAmW 91*
Schuler, Carol Sue 1953- *WhoEmL 91*
Schuler, Else Lasker- 1869-1945 *BioIn 16*
Schuler, Gary Claude 1938- *WhoAm 90*
Schuler, Gerhard 1922- *IntWWM 90*
Schuler, Heinz Friedrich 1945- *WhoWor 91*
Schuler, Herbert F. 1940- *St&PR 91*
Schuler, Jack William 1940- *St&PR 91, WhoAm 90, WhoWor 91*
Schuler, John Albert 1942- *St&PR 91*
Schuler, John Neville 1927- *St&PR 91*
Schuler, Joseph F., Jr. 1961- *WhoEmL 91*
Schuler, Maureen Patricia 1932- *WhoAmW 91*
Schuler, Melvin Albert 1924- *WhoAmA 91*
Schuler, Melvin L. 1944- *St&PR 91*
Schuler, Michael Aloysius 1950- *St&PR 91*
Schuler, Michael Harold 1940- *WhoAm 90*
Schuler, Paul A. 1933- *St&PR 91*
Schuler, Robert Hugo 1926- *WhoAm 90*
Schuler, Robert Jordan 1939- *WhoWrEP 89*
Schuler, Ruth Wildes 1933- *WhoWrEP 89*
Schuler, Steven T. 1951- *St&PR 91*
Schuler, Theodore Anthony 1934- *WhoSSW 91*
Schuler, Thomas D. 1951- *WhoE 91*
Schuler, William C. 1920- *St&PR 91*
Schuler, Wolfgang A. 1942- *WhoWor 91*
Schulert, Arthur Robert 1922- *WhoSSW 91, WhoWor 91*
Schulhof, Hugh Tuck 1936- *St&PR 91*
Schulhof, Michael P. *BioIn 16*
Schulhof, Michael Peter 1942- *WhoAm 90, WhoE 91, WhoWor 91*
Schulian, John 1945- *ConAu 129, WhoAm 90*
Schulian, Nielsen *WhoAm 90*
Schulke, Flip *BioIn 16*
Schulke, Herbert Ardis, Jr. 1923- *WhoAm 90*
Schull, Joseph 1910-1980 *OxCCanT*
Schuller, Britta Zecher 1962- *WhoE 91*
Schuller, Deborah R *BiDrAPA 89*
Schuller, Diane Ethel 1943- *WhoE 91*
Schuller, Grete *WhoAmA 91N*
Schuller, Gunther 1925- *IntWWM 90, OxCPMus, PenDiMP A*
Schuller, Gunther Alexander 1925- *WhoAm 90*
Schuller, Ivan Kohn 1946- *WhoAm 90*
Schuller, Kevin Carl 1948- *St&PR 91*
Schuller, Kirby B. 1953- *St&PR 91*
Schuller, Louis 1924- *BiDrAPA 89*
Schuller, Mary Ann 1952- *WhoWrEP 89*
Schuller, Nancy Shelby 1942- *WhoAmA 91*
Schuller, Robert H. 1926- *WorAlBi*
Schuller, Robert Harold *BioIn 16*
Schuller, Robert Harold 1926- *WhoAm 90*
Schuller, Stephen Arthur 1951- *WhoEmL 91, WhoSSW 91*
Schullery, Paul 1948- *ConAu 30NR*
Schullian, Dorothy *BioIn 16*
Schully, Sherwin H. 1918- *St&PR 91*
Schulman, Alan Michael 1946- *WhoEmL 91*
Schulman, Arthur *BioIn 16*
Schulman, Bob *BioIn 16*
Schulman, Bob 1933- *ODwPR 91*
Schulman, Brian Martin 1946- *BiDrAPA 89, WhoE 91*
Schulman, Bruce David 1950- *WhoE 91*
Schulman, David *BiDrAPA 89*
Schulman, Grace *BioIn 16*
Schulman, Harold 1930- *WhoAm 90*
Schulman, Harry David 1951- *WhoSSW 91*
Schulman, Herbert J 1928- *BiDrAPA 89*
Schulman, Howard 1957- *ODwPR 91*
Schulman, Ivan A 1931- *ConAu 131*
Schulman, Jacob 1915-1987 *WhoAmA 91N*
Schulman, Janet Carol 1933- *WhoAm 90*
Schulman, Jerome L 1925- *BiDrAPA 89*
Schulman, Joanne 1952- *WhoEmL 91*
Schulman, Joseph Daniel 1941- *WhoAm 90*
Schulman, Mary 1910- *WhoWrEP 89*
Schulman, Melvin Louis 1921- *St&PR 91*
Schulman, Michael 1941- *BioIn 16*
Schulman, Paul Martin 1940- *WhoAm 90*
Schulman, Robert 1924- *WhoAmA 91*
Schulman, Robert Ivan 1946- *WhoAm 90*
Schulman, Robert M 1934- *BiDrAPA 89*
Schulman, Robert P. 1927- *St&PR 91*
Schulman, Robert W 1947 *BiDrAPA 89*
Schulman, Rose *BioIn 16*
Schulman, Sandra Jean 1954- *WhoAmW 91*
Schulman, Sarah M. 1958- *WhoWrEP 89*
Schulman, Sidney 1923- *WhoAm 90*
Schulman, Stuart M. 1953- *WhoE 91*
Schulman, Tammy Beth 1960- *WhoAmW 91, WhoWor 91*
Schulmerich, Wes 1901-1985 *Ballpl 90*
Schulsinger, Marcus Fini *BiDrAPA 89*
Schulsinger, Michael Alan 1952- *WhoWor 91*
Schulson, Susan 1941- *WhoAmA 91*
Schult, R.W. 1949- *St&PR 91*
Schulte, Arthur D 1906- *WhoAmA 91*
Schulte, Arthur D, Mrs *WhoAmA 91*
Schulte, Bernard J. 1929- *St&PR 91*
Schulte, David Michael 1946- *WhoAm 90*
Schulte, Francis B. 1926- *WhoAm 90, WhoSSW 91*
Schulte, Fred 1901-1983 *Ballpl 90*
Schulte, Fred C. 1946- *St&PR 91*
Schulte, Fred S. 1942- *St&PR 91*
Schulte, Fredrick Steven 1942- *WhoAm 90*
Schulte, Helen Irene Denne 1889-1971 *BioIn 16*
Schulte, Henry Clyde 1921- *St&PR 91*
Schulte, Henry Frank 1924- *WhoAm 90*
Schulte, Henry John, III *BiDrAPA 89*
Schulte, Jeffrey Lewis 1949- *WhoE 91*
Schulte, Jerome Frank 1931- *St&PR 91*
Schulte, Jerome John, Jr. *BiDrAPA 89*
Schulte, John K. 1932- *ODwPR 91*
Schulte, John W. 1949- *St&PR 91*
Schulte, Joseph W. 1941- *St&PR 91*
Schulte, Josephine Helen 1929- *WhoSSW 91*
Schulte, Mary Ann 1953- *WhoAmW 91*
Schulte, Patrick Leo 1933- *St&PR 91*
Schulte, Rainer 1937- *WhoWrEP 89*
Schulte, Richard Frank 1935- *WhoAm 90*
Schulte, Robert Daniel 1956- *BiDrAPA 89*
Schulte, Robert N. 1949- *St&PR 91*
Schulte, Wildfire 1882-1949 *Ballpl 90*
Schulte Holthausen, Heinrich Wilhelm 1935- *WhoWor 91*
Schulteis, Herm C. 1928- *St&PR 91*
Schultek, Robert D. 1951- *St&PR 91*
Schulter-Ellis, Frances Pierce 1923- *WhoAm 90, WhoE 91*
Schultes, Richard Evans 1915- *WhoAm 90*
Schultheis, Edwin Milford 1928- *WhoE 91, WhoWor 91*
Schultheis, Gary B *BiDrAPA 89*
Schultheis, Michael James 1932- *WhoWor 91*
Schulthies, Ronald A. 1943- *St&PR 91*
Schulties, Charles Walter 1936- *St&PR 91, WhoAm 90*
Schults, Carol Anne 1961- *WhoAmW 91*
Schults, Robert David 1955- *BiDrAPA 89*
Schultz, Albert Barry 1933- *WhoAm 90*
Schultz, Allen M. 1932- *St&PR 91*
Schultz, Alvin Leroy 1921- *WhoWor 91*
Schultz, Amy Tomblinson 1962- *WhoAmW 91*
Schultz, Andrew Schultz, Jr. 1913- *WhoAm 90*
Schultz, Arthur J., III 1943- *ODwPR 91*
Schultz, Arthur Joseph, Jr. 1918- *WhoAm 90*
Schultz, Arthur Warren 1922- *St&PR 91, WhoWor 91*
Schultz, B. Cameron 1965- *WhoE 91*
Schultz, Barney 1926- *Ballpl 90*
Schultz, Betty Littlejohn 1945- *WhoEmL 91*
Schultz, Bob 1923-1979 *Ballpl 90*
Schultz, Buddy 1950- *Ballpl 90*
Schultz, Carl Herbert 1925- *St&PR 91, WhoAm 90*
Schultz, Caroline Reel *WhoAmA 91*
Schultz, Charles L. 1928- *St&PR 91*
Schultz, Clarence Carven, Jr. 1924- *WhoSSW 91*
Schultz, Daniel Joseph 1951- *St&PR 91*
Schultz, Darrell Homer 1936- *St&PR 91*
Schultz, Deborah Ann 1949- *WhoAmW 91*
Schultz, Dick *BioIn 16*
Schultz, Don Louis *BiDrAPA 89*
Schultz, Donald H *BiDrAPA 89*
Schultz, Dorothy Teresa *WhoAmW 91*
Schultz, Douglas George 1947- *WhoAm 90, WhoAmA 91, WhoE 91*
Schultz, Dutch 1902-1935 *WorAlBi*
Schultz, Dwight *BioIn 16*
Schultz, Earl Robert 1931- *BiDrAPA 89*
Schultz, Edward Anson 1952- *WhoWor 91*
Schultz, Edward Irving 1948- *WhoE 91, WhoEmL 91*
Schultz, Eileen Hedy *WhoAm 90*
Schultz, Emily Celestia 1907- *WhoAmW 91*
Schultz, Estelle Peterson 1935- *WhoAmW 91*
Schultz, Finis W. 1937- *St&PR 91*
Schultz, Frank 1938- *St&PR 91*
Schultz, Franklin M. 1917- *WhoAm 90*
Schultz, Fred Russell 1947- *BiDrAPA 89*
Schultz, Frederick Carl 1929- *St&PR 91*
Schultz, Frederick H. *BioIn 16*
Schultz, Frederick Henry 1929- *WhoAm 90*
Schultz, George E. 1921- *St&PR 91*
Schultz, George J. *ODwPR 91*
Schultz, Gerald Emil 1929- *St&PR 91*
Schultz, Gerald Ernest 1941- *WhoAm 90*
Schultz, Gwen Manette *WhoWor 91*
Schultz, H.W. 1934- *St&PR 91*
Schultz, Harold A 1907- *WhoAmA 91*
Schultz, Harry 1938- *WhoE 91*
Schultz, Harry Louis 1929- *WhoAm 90*
Schultz, Herbert Victor, Jr. 1935- *WhoE 91*
Schultz, Howie 1922- *Ballpl 90*
Schultz, Irwin M 1924- *BiDrAPA 89*
Schultz, J. Carl, Jr. *BioIn 16*
Schultz, Jackson L. 1925- *St&PR 91*
Schultz, James Clement 1934- *St&PR 91, WhoAm 90*
Schultz, James H. 1948- *St&PR 91*
Schultz, James Willard 1859-1947 *AuBYP 90, BioIn 16, WhNaAH*
Schultz, Jan Edward 1934- *St&PR 91*
Schultz, Jan Roger 1942- *WhoE 91*
Schultz, Janet Darlene 1942- *WhoAmW 91*
Schultz, Jay Ward 1937- *St&PR 91*
Schultz, Jaynie 1960- *WhoSSW 91*
Schultz, Jean Eunice 1929- *BiDrAPA 89*
Schultz, Jeffrey Eric 1948- *WhoEmL 91*
Schultz, Jerome Samson 1933- *WhoAm 90*
Schultz, Joe, Jr. 1918- *Ballpl 90*
Schultz, Joe, Sr. 1893-1941 *Ballpl 90*
Schultz, John *BioIn 16*
Schultz, John Bernard 1948- *WhoAmA 91*
Schultz, John Christian 1840-1896 *DcCanB 12*
Schultz, John D *BiDrAPA 89*
Schultz, Jurgen 1934- *WhoWor 91*
Schultz, Karen Lee 1953- *WhoAmW 91*
Schultz, Kathleen *BioIn 16*
Schultz, Kathryn L 1907- *BiDrAPA 89*
Schultz, L. Ron 1932- *St&PR 91*
Schultz, L. Scott 1952- *WhoE 91*
Schultz, Leslie Brown 1936- *WhoAmW 91*
Schultz, Leslie P. 1918- *WhoAm 90*
Schultz, Leslie Page 1918- *St&PR 91*
Schultz, Linda Kathryn 1961- *WhoAmW 91*
Schultz, Linda Michelle 1960- *WhoAmW 91*
Schultz, Loraine E *BiDrAPA 89*
Schultz, Louis William 1927- *WhoAm 90*
Schultz, Lucy J. 1962- *WhoAmW 91*
Schultz, Lynette Carol 1951- *WhoSSW 91*
Schultz, Marcy Lynn 1957- *WhoAmW 91*
Schultz, Marilyn Le Ellen Smith 1936- *WhoWor 91*
Schultz, Mark Stuart 1951- *BiDrAPA 89*
Schultz, Mary Elizabeth 1958- *WhoAmW 91*
Schultz, Mary Suzanne 1932- *WhoSSW 91*
Schultz, Michael 1938- *WhoAm 90*
Schultz, Michael A *DrBlPA 90*
Schultz, Michael Edward 1953- *WhoWrEP 89*
Schultz, Nancy Lusignan 1956- *WhoWrEP 89*
Schultz, Pamela Busch 1951- *WhoAmW 91*
Schultz, Pamela Kay 1947- *WhoAmW 91*
Schultz, Paul Oesterle 1958- *WhoSSW 91*
Schultz, Peter G. *BioIn 16*
Schultz, Philip 1945- *WhoAm 90, WhoWrEP 89*
Schultz, Phyllis May 1933- *WhoAmW 91*
Schultz, Richard Carlton 1927- *WhoAm 90*
Schultz, Richard Dale 1929- *WhoAm 90*
Schultz, Richard I. 1932- *St&PR 91*
Schultz, Richard Otto 1930- *WhoAm 90*
Schultz, Robert Jordan 1930- *WhoAm 90*
Schultz, Robert Vernon 1936- *WhoWor 91*
Schultz, Ruby Ethel 1934- *WhoAmW 91*
Schultz, Ruth Anne 1953- *WhoAmW 91*
Schultz, Samuel Jacob 1914- *WhoAm 90*
Schultz, Saunders 1927- *WhoAmA 91*
Schultz, Shelly Irene 1953- *WhoAmW 91, WhoWor 91*
Schultz, Sigrid Lillian 1893-1980 *BioIn 16*
Schultz, Stanley George 1931- *WhoAm 90*
Schultz, Stephen Otto 1951- *WhoEmL 91*
Schultz, Stephen Warren 1946- *WhoAmA 91*
Schultz, Steven Lee *BiDrAPA 89*
Schultz, T. Paul 1940- *WhoAm 90*
Schultz, Terry Allen 1946- *WhoEmL 91, WhoWor 91*
Schultz, Theodore Edward 1945- *St&PR 91, WhoAm 90*
Schultz, Theodore John 1922- *WhoAm 90*
Schultz, Theodore W. 1902- *WorAlBi*
Schultz, Theodore William 1902- *WhoAm 90, WhoWor 91*
Schultz, Thomas A. 1957- *St&PR 91*
Schultz, Thomas S. 1944- *WhoE 91*
Schultz, Trevor S. 1942- *St&PR 91*
Schultz, Warren Robert 1949- *WhoEmL 91*
Schultz, William A., Jr. 1949- *WhoEmL 91*
Schultz, William Louis 1923- *WhoAm 90*
Schultz, Willis Jackson, Jr. 1953- *WhoE 91*
Schultz-Ross, Roy Andrew 1961- *BiDrAPA 89*
Schultze, Carl Edward *EncACom*
Schultze, Charles 1924- *WorAlBi*
Schultze, Charles Louis 1924- *WhoAm 90*
Schultze, Ernst Eugene 1944- *WhoWor 91*
Schultze, Helmuth W. 1927- *St&PR 91*
Schultze, Kristian *NewAgMG*
Schultze, Robert William 1939- *St&PR 91*
Schultze, Ronald D. 1937- *St&PR 91*
Schultze, Sharon Edel 1939- *WhoAmW 91*
Schulweis, Harold M. 1925- *BioIn 16*
Schulz, Al 1889-1931 *Ballpl 90*
Schulz, Anne Markham 1938- *WhoAmA 91*
Schulz, Arthur *BioIn 16*
Schulz, August Joseph 1932- *BiDrAPA 89*
Schulz, Barbara 1954- *WhoAmW 91*
Schulz, Bonnie Lou 1951- *WhoAmW 91*
Schulz, Bruno 1892-1942 *BioIn 16*
Schulz, Carol Doris 1953- *WhoAmW 91*
Schulz, Charles 1922- *EncACom*
Schulz, Charles M. *BioIn 16*
Schulz, Charles M. 1922- *WorAlBi*
Schulz, Charles Monroe 1922- *AuBYP 90, WhoAm 90, WhoAmA 91*
Schulz, Clarence G 1922- *BiDrAPA 89*
Schulz, Dale Valdyn *St&PR 91*
Schulz, David A 1933- *ConAu 30NR*
Schulz, David Alan 1952- *WhoEmL 91*
Schulz, David M. 1945- *St&PR 91*
Schulz, Edwin Lee 1954- *WhoSSW 91*
Schulz, George D. 1938- *St&PR 91*
Schulz, Gerhard *PenDiMP*
Schulz, Henry E. 1921- *WhoSSW 91*

Schulz, Horst D. 1942- *WhoWor 91*
Schulz, Jakob Albert *BiDrAPA 89*
Schulz, James F. 1940- *St&PR 91*
Schulz, James Henry 1936- *WhoE 91*
Schulz, James Lawrence 1937- *St&PR 91*
Schulz, John Carl 1942- *St&PR 91*
Schulz, Juergen 1927- *WhoAmA 91*
Schulz, Karen Gayle 1959- *WhoAmW 91, WhoEmL 91*
Schulz, Kathleen Marie 1942- *WhoE 91*
Schulz, Keith Donald 1938- *WhoAm 90*
Schulz, Ken 1920- *WhoAmA 91*
Schulz, Klaus 1928- *WhoWor 91*
Schulz, Klaus Robert 1927- *WhoWor 91*
Schulz, Michael Anthony, Jr. 1934- *WhoSSW 91*
Schulz, Moriah *BioIn 16*
Schulz, Otto 1902- *St&PR 91*
Schulz, Otto G. 1930- *St&PR 91*
Schulz, Patricia Lynn 1957- *WhoAmW 91*
Schulz, Rainer Walter 1942- *WhoWor 91*
Schulz, Ralph Richard 1928- *St&PR 91, WhoAm 90*
Schulz, Rex, Sr. 1934- *WhoSSW 91*
Schulz, Richard Burkart 1920- *WhoAm 90, WhoSSW 91*
Schulz, Robert A. 1942- *St&PR 91*
Schulz, Robert Emil 1929-1978 *WhoAmA 91N*
Schulz, Robert Francis 1936- *St&PR 91*
Schulz, Rockwell Irwin 1929- *WhoAm 90*
Schulz, Roy James 1944- *WhoSSW 91*
Schulz, Rudolph Walter 1930- *WhoAm 90*
Schulz, S Charles 1945- *BiDrAPA 89*
Schulz, Susanna *BioIn 16*
Schulz, Walter 1912- *WhoWor 91*
Schulz, William C. *St&PR 91*
Schulz, William Frederick 1949- *WhoAm 90, WhoE 91, WhoWor 91*
Schulz, William J. 1946- *St&PR 91*
Schulze, Arthur Edward 1938- *WhoSSW 91*
Schulze, Arthur Robert 1931- *St&PR 91*
Schulze, Arthur Robert, Jr. 1931- *WhoAm 90*
Schulze, Don 1962- *Ballpl 90*
Schulze, Enika Hermine 1938- *WhoWrEP 89*
Schulze, Erwin E. 1925- *St&PR 91*
Schulze, Erwin Emil 1925- *WhoAm 90*
Schulze, Franz 1927- *WhoAmA 91*
Schulze, Franz, Jr. *WhoWrEP 89*
Schulze, Franz, Jr. 1927- *WhoAm 90*
Schulze, Herbert Ernest, Jr. 1932- *St&PR 91*
Schulze, Howard Dean 1929- *WhoSSW 91*
Schulze, Howard L. 1942- *St&PR 91*
Schulze, Ingeborg 1933- *BiDrAPA 89*
Schulze, John 1915- *WhoAmA 91*
Schulze, Kenneth W 1951- *WhoWrEP 89*
Schulze, Klaus *BioIn 16, NewAgMG*
Schulze, Mark Levon 1958- *WhoWor 91*
Schulze, Martin Samuel Paul 1928- *WhoWor 91*
Schulze, Max Henry 1939- *St&PR 91*
Schulze, Paul 1934- *WhoAmA 91*
Schulze, Richard Taylor 1929- *WhoAm 90, WhoE 91*
Schulze, Richard W. 1937- *ODwPR 91*
Schulze, Richard Wilfred 1937- *St&PR 91, WhoAm 90*
Schulze, Robert Oscar 1922- *WhoAm 90*
Schulze, Tascha Jon 1950- *WhoAmW 91*
Schulze, Winfried 1942- *WhoWor 91*
Schulze-Kossens, Richard *BioIn 16*
Schulze-Smidt, Bernhardine 1846-1911? *EncCoWW*
Schum, Stephen J. 1956- *St&PR 91*
Schumacher, Bruno Anselm 1936- *WhoWor 91*
Schumacher, Charles W. 1915- *St&PR 91*
Schumacher, Cynthia Jo 1928- *WhoAmW 91*
Schumacher, Cynthia Lynn *BiDrAPA 89*
Schumacher, Daniel 1663-1728 *PenDiDA 89*
Schumacher, Diane K. 1953- *St&PR 91*
Schumacher, Edward G. *BioIn 16*
Schumacher, Edward W. 1916- *St&PR 91*
Schumacher, Emery Robert 1935- *St&PR 91*
Schumacher, Emil 1912- *BioIn 16*
Schumacher, Evelyn A 1919- *ConAu 130*
Schumacher, Frederick Carl 1911- *WhoAm 90*
Schumacher, Frederick Richmond 1930- *WhoWor 91*
Schumacher, Garry 1901-1978 *Ballpl 90*
Schumacher, Gebhard Friederich Bernhard 1924- *WhoAm 90*
Schumacher, Genny *WhoWrEP 89*
Schumacher, Hal 1910- *Ballpl 90 [port]*
Schumacher, Harry Ralph 1933- *WhoAm 90, WhoE 91*
Schumacher, Henry Jerold 1934- *WhoAm 90*
Schumacher, Howard S. 1935- *St&PR 91*
Schumacher, James Delbert 1931- *WhoWor 91*
Schumacher, John C. 1935- *St&PR 91*
Schumacher, John Christian 1935- *WhoWor 91*
Schumacher, John N 1927- *ConAu 131*
Schumacher, John W 1919- *BiDrAPA 89*
Schumacher, Jon Lee 1937- *WhoAm 90*
Schumacher, Jon Robert 1937- *St&PR 91*
Schumacher, Joseph Charles 1911- *WhoAm 90*
Schumacher, Julie Alison 1958- *WhoWrEP 89*
Schumacher, Kathleen Miles 1954- *WhoAmW 91*
Schumacher, Kurt Edward 1956- *WhoSSW 91*
Schumacher, Lynn Ingraham 1956- *WhoAmW 91*
Schumacher, Martin 1695-1781 *PenDiDA 89*
Schumacher, Norbert 1936- *St&PR 91*
Schumacher, Paul Maynard 1951- *WhoEmL 91*
Schumacher, Randal P *ODwPR 91*
Schumacher, Ray Fred 1942- *WhoSSW 91*
Schumacher, Richard H. 1955- *St&PR 91*
Schumacher, Robert Denison 1933- *St&PR 91, WhoAm 90*
Schumacher, Robert Kent 1924- *WhoAm 90*
Schumacher, Walter H. 1924- *St&PR 91*
Schumacher, Weldon David 1936- *WhoWor 91*
Schumacher, William Emil *BiDrAPA 89*
Schumack, Edward James 1940- *BiDrAPA 89*
Schumack, Joan Maria 1953- *WhoAmW 91, WhoWrEP 89*
Schumack, Ray 1927- *ODwPR 91*
Schumaker, Dale H. 1933- *St&PR 91, WhoAm 90*
Schumaker, Larry Lee 1939- *WhoSSW 91*
Schumaker, W. James *St&PR 91*
Schuman, Allan L. 1937- *WhoAm 90*
Schuman, Arnold Joseph *BiDrAPA 89*
Schuman, Daniel C. 1941- *WhoE 91*
Schuman, Diana C. 1947- *WhoE 91*
Schuman, Edwin Z. 1929- *WhoAm 90*
Schuman, Frank Albert 1944- *St&PR 91*
Schuman, George Alfred 1947- *WhoE 91*
Schuman, Harold R 1925- *BiDrAPA 89*
Schuman, Howard 1928- *WhoAm 90*
Schuman, Jack 1919- *St&PR 91*
Schuman, Patricia 1954- *IntWWM 90*
Schuman, Patricia Glass 1943- *WhoAmW 91*
Schuman, Robert 1886-1963 *WorAlBi*
Schuman, Robert James *BiDrAPA 89*
Schuman, Robert James 1956- *WhoE 91*
Schuman, Robert Jean-Baptiste Nicolas 1886-1963 *BiDFrPL*
Schuman, Sid W., Jr. *St&PR 91*
Schuman, William 1910- *BioIn 16, PenDiMP A*
Schuman, William Howard 1910- *IntWWM 90, WhoAm 90, WhoWor 91*
Schuman, William John, Jr. 1930- *WhoE 91*
Schumann, Clara 1819-1896 *BioIn 16, PenDiMP*
Schumann, Elisabeth 1885-1952 *BioIn 16*
Schumann, Elisabeth 1888-1952 *PenDiMP*
Schumann, Frederick John 1904- *WhoAm 90*
Schumann, Gerhard 1911- *BioIn 16*
Schumann, James Michael 1944- *WhoSSW 91*
Schumann, Karen Lynn 1941- *WhoAmW 91*
Schumann, Katja *BioIn 16*
Schumann, Malcolm E. 1942- *St&PR 91*
Schumann, Maurice 1911- *BiDFrPL, WhoWor 91*
Schumann, Merlin J. 1943- *St&PR 91*
Schumann, P. Richard *St&PR 91*
Schumann, Robert 1810-1856 *BioIn 16, PenDiMP A, WorAlBi*
Schumann, Robert Alexander 1810-1856 *EncPaPR 91*
Schumann, Robert M 1920- *BiDrAPA 89*
Schumann, William F. 1939- *St&PR 91*
Schumann, William H. 1950- *St&PR 91*
Schumann, William Henry, III 1950- *WhoAm 90*
Schumann-Heink, Ernestine 1861-1936 *BioIn 16, PenDiMP*
Schumer, Charles E. *BioIn 16*
Schumer, Charles Ellis 1950- *WhoAm 90, WhoE 91*
Schumer, Irwin P. 1931- *St&PR 91*
Schumer, William 1926- *WhoAm 90*
Schumitz, Elizabeth Dorothy 1935- *WhoAmW 91, WhoE 91*
Schumm, Christine Lynn 1960- *WhoAmW 91*
Schumm, Joseph J., Jr. 1944- *St&PR 91*
Schumm, Stanley Alfred 1927- *WhoAm 90*
Schumpert, Tom 1941- *St&PR 91*
Schumpeter, Joseph 1883-1950 *WorAlBi*
Schumpeter, Joseph Alois 1883-1950 *BioIn 16*
Schuna, Arthur Allen 1950- *WhoEmL 91*
Schuncke, Gottfried Michael 1929- *IntWWM 90*
Schundler, Bruce E. 1948- *St&PR 91*
Schundler, Michael F. 1955- *St&PR 91*
Schundler, Robert Jeffrey 1945- *St&PR 91*
Schuneman, Norman Douglas 1942- *St&PR 91*
Schuneman, Robert A. 1934- *IntWWM 90*
Schunemann, Wolfgang Bernward 1947- *WhoWor 91*
Schunk, Dale Hansen 1946- *WhoEmL 91*
Schunk, Robert 1948- *IntWWM 90*
Schuntermann, Peter 1934- *BiDrAPA 89*
Schuon, Karl Albert 1913-1984 *AuBYP 90*
Schupack, Andrew Larry 1953- *St&PR 91, WhoE 91*
Schupack, Mark Barry 1931- *WhoAm 90, WhoE 91*
Schupack, Melvyn B 1934- *BiDrAPA 89*
Schupak, Donald 1943- *St&PR 91, WhoAm 90, WhoWor 91*
Schupak, Leslie Allen 1945- *WhoAm 90*
Schuplinsky, Walter 1921-1990 *WhoAmA 91N*
Schupp, Albert O. 1932- *St&PR 91*
Schupp, Ferdie 1891-1971 *Ballpl 90*
Schupp, Volker 1943- *WhoWor 91*
Schuppanzigh, Ignaz 1776-1830 *PenDiMP*
Schuppe, John *PenDiDA 89*
Schur, Helen 1909- *BiDrAPA 89*
Schur, Leon Milton 1923- *WhoAm 90*
Schur, Maxine *ConAu 129*
Schur, Maxine 1948- *BioIn 16*
Schur, Maxine Rose 1948- *ConAu 129*
Schur, Susan Dorfman 1940- *WhoAmW 91*
Schur, Susan E. 1939- *WhoAm 90*
Schur, Walter Robert 1914- *WhoE 91, WhoWor 91*
Schure, Alexander 1921- *WhoAm 90, WhoE 91*
Schure, Matthew 1948- *WhoAm 90, WhoE 91*
Schure, Teri *WhoAmW 91*
Schurgast, Anselm W 1921- *BiDrAPA 89*
Schurgast, Anselm Wolfgang 1921- *WhoE 91*
Schurger, Robert J. 1929- *St&PR 91*
Schuricht, Carl 1880-1967 *PenDiMP*
Schurman, Anna-Maria van 1607-1678 *EncCoWW, FemiCLE*
Schurman, Donald Glenn 1933- *WhoAm 90*
Schurman, Jacob Gould 1854-1942 *BioIn 16*
Schurman, Joseph Rathborne 1924- *WhoAm 90, WhoE 91*
Schurman, Kim *BiDrAPA 89*
Schurmann, Gerard 1924- *IntWWM 90*
Schurmann, Gerard 1928- *PenDiMP A*
Schurmann, Gregor R. 1957- *WhoWor 91*
Schurmeier, L. Jon 1937- *WhoAm 90, WhoWor 91*
Schurr, Cathleen *BioIn 16*
Schurr, Jerry M 1940- *WhoAmA 91*
Schurr, Michael Randolph 1952- *WhoEmL 91*
Schurr, Thierry Marie 1957- *WhoWor 91*
Schurrer, Suzanne Barbara 1945- *WhoAmW 91*
Schurter, Dennis Dean 1942- *WhoSSW 91*
Schurz, Carl 1829-1906 *BiDrUSE 89, BioIn 16, EncPaPR 91, WhNaAH, WorAlBi*
Schurz, Franklin D., Jr. 1931- *St&PR 91*
Schurz, Franklin Dunn, Jr. 1931- *WhoAm 90*
Schurz, James Montgomery 1933- *St&PR 91*
Schurz, Scott Clark 1936- *WhoAm 90*
Schuselka, Elfi 1940- *WhoAmA 91*
Schusler, Herbert Henry, II 1936- *WhoSSW 91*
Schusselin, Omar 1938- *BiDrAPA 89*
Schussheim, Zelo *BioIn 16*
Schussler, Irwin 1943- *BiDrAPA 89, WhoSSW 91, WhoWor 91*
Schussler, Samuel 1936- *St&PR 91*
Schussler, Theodore 1934- *WhoAm 90, WhoE 91, WhoWor 91*
Schust, Ralph Henry 1904-1988 *BioIn 16*
Schuster, Allan D. *St&PR 91*
Schuster, Carl 1904- *WhoAmA 91N*
Schuster, Carlotta *BiDrAPA 89*
Schuster, Carlotta Lief 1936- *WhoE 91*
Schuster, Charles Roberts 1930- *WhoAm 90*
Schuster, Cita Fletcher 1929- *WhoAmA 91*
Schuster, Daniel B *BiDrAPA 89*
Schuster, Donna Norine 1883-1953 *WhoAmA 91N*
Schuster, Dwight W *BiDrAPA 89*
Schuster, Elaine 1947- *WhoAm 90*
Schuster, Eugene I. 1936- *St&PR 91*
Schuster, Eugene Ivan 1936- *WhoAmA 91*
Schuster, Eula Elaine 1936- *WhoAmW 91*
Schuster, Franklin P., Jr. 1927- *BiDrAPA 89*
Schuster, Gary F. 1942- *St&PR 91*
Schuster, Gary Francis 1942- *WhoAm 90*
Schuster, George Ernest 1881-1982 *DcNaB 1981*
Schuster, Grae Lee *BiDrAPA 89*
Schuster, Ingeborg Ida 1937- *WhoAmW 91*
Schuster, James Morton 1958- *BiDrAPA 89, WhoE 91*
Schuster, John Carl 1940- *St&PR 91*
Schuster, Lee R. 1934- *St&PR 91*
Schuster, Marvin Meier 1929- *BiDrAPA 89*
Schuster, Mary Patricia 1931- *WhoE 91*
Schuster, Melvin L. 1925- *St&PR 91*
Schuster, Monis 1931- *St&PR 91*
Schuster, Moris 1952- *WhoWor 91*
Schuster, Neil Dennis 1952- *WhoE 91*
Schuster, Paula C. *ODwPR 91*
Schuster, Philip Frederick, II 1945- *WhoEmL 91, WhoWor 91*
Schuster, Richard John 1944- *St&PR 91*
Schuster, Richard Louis 1945- *WhoE 91*
Schuster, Robert Parks 1945- *WhoAm 90, WhoEmL 91, WhoWor 91*
Schuster, Seymour 1926- *WhoAm 90*
Schuster, Sharon Lee 1939- *WhoAmW 91*
Schuster, Steven D. 1956- *St&PR 91*
Schuster, Timothy S 1937- *BiDrAPA 89*
Schuster, Todd Mervyn 1933- *WhoAm 90*
Schuster-Eakin, Cynthia Anne 1952- *WhoEmL 91*
Schusterman, Gerrie Marva 1928- *WhoAmA 91*
Schut, Jacob 1928- *BiDrAPA 89*
Schute, E. F. *ArtLatA*
Schuth, Mary McDougle 1942- *WhoAmW 91, WhoSSW 91*
Schutkeker, Bruno G *BiDrAPA 89*
Schutt, Leonard D. 1926- *St&PR 91*
Schutt, Walter Eugene 1917- *WhoWor 91*
Schutt, Wayne R. 1938- *St&PR 91*
Schutta, Henry Szczesny 1928- *WhoAm 90*
Schutte, Alden Frederick 1940- *WhoE 91*
Schutte, Giles W. 1931- *St&PR 91, WhoAm 90, WhoE 91, WhoWor 91*
Schutte, Howard J. 1909- *St&PR 91*
Schutte, Paula Marion 1941- *WhoAmW 91, WhoWor 91*
Schutte, Ron 1956- *St&PR 91*
Schutte, Thomas Frederick 1935- *WhoAm 90, WhoAmA 91*
Schutte, William Metcalf 1919- *WhoAm 90, WhoWrEP 89*
Schutter, David John 1945- *WhoEmL 91*
Schutting, Jutta 1937- *EncCoWW*
Schutz, Alfred 1899-1959 *BioIn 16*
Schutz, Anton 1894-1977 *WhoAmA 91N*
Schutz, David Charles 1938- *BiDrAPA 89*
Schutz, Dieter *NewAgMG*
Schutz, Donald Frank 1934- *WhoAm 90*
Schutz, Estelle 1907- *WhoAmA 91*
Schutz, Heinrich 1585-1672 *BioIn 16, PenDiMP A*
Schutz, Helga 1937- *EncCoWW*
Schutz, Helmut Georg 1938- *WhoWor 91*
Schutz, James E. 1950- *St&PR 91*
Schutz, John Adolph 1919- *WhoAm 90, WhoWor 91*
Schutz, John Edwin 1935- *St&PR 91*
Schutz, John Howard 1933- *WhoAm 90*
Schutz, Karl-Heinz 1926- *WhoWor 91*
Schutz, Matthew *BioIn 16*
Schutz, Prescott Dietrich 1948-1990 *WhoAmA 91N*
Schutz, Richard P. 1951- *WhoEmL 91*
Schutz, Robert Henry 1926- *WhoSSW 91*
Schutz, Robert J. 1946- *St&PR 91*
Schutz, Rudolf M. 1929- *WhoWor 91*
Schutz, Trudi *ODwPR 91*
Schutze, Gladys Henrietta 1884-1946 *FemiCLE*
Schutzenhofer, Joseph William 1936- *St&PR 91*
Schutzenhofer, Karen Kelly 1950- *WhoAmW 91*
Schutzer, George Jeffrey 1955- *WhoEmL 91*
Schutzer, Ulysses *BiDrAPA 89*
Schutzman, Bernard Michael 1932- *BiDrAPA 89*
Schutzman, Elias 1925- *WhoAm 90*
Schutzman, Frans 1915- *WhoWor 91*
Schutzman, Leonard 1946- *St&PR 91, WhoAm 90*
Schuur, Diane *BioIn 16, WhoAmW 91*
Schuur, Robert George 1931- *WhoAm 90*
Schuyff, Peter 1956- *BioIn 16*
Schuyler Knobloch And Bickhardt *WhoNeCM [port]*
Schuyler, Catherine V. 1734-1803 *BioAmW*
Schuyler, Daniel Merrick 1912- *WhoAm 90, WhoWor 91*
Schuyler, Dean 1942- *BiDrAPA 89, WhoE 91*
Schuyler, Eugene 1840-1890 *BioIn 16*

Schuyler, George S. 1895-1977 *EarBlAP*
Schuyler, Jack 1911- *WhoSSW 91*
Schuyler, James Marcus 1923- *WhoAm 90, WhoWrEP 89*
Schuyler, Jane 1943- *WhoAmW 91, WhoE 91, WhoWor 91*
Schuyler, Louisa Lee 1837-1926 *BioIn 16*
Schuyler, Michael Robert 1949- *WhoEmL 91*
Schuyler, Peter 1657-1724 *WhNaAH*
Schuyler, Philip 1913- *WhoAmA 91N*
Schuyler, Philip John 1733-1804 *BioIn 16, EncCRAm, WhNaAH*
Schuyler, Philippa 1931-1967 *DrBlPA 90*
Schuyler, Robert L. 1936- *St&PR 91*
Schuyler, Robert Len 1936- *WhoAm 90*
Schuyler, William L. 1952- *St&PR 91*
Schuz, Ernst Paul Theodor 1924- *WhoWor 91*
Schvehla, Thomas Joseph 1954- *BiDrAPA 89*
Schwab, Albert *St&PR 91*
Schwab, Carl Edwin 1929- *St&PR 91*
Schwab, Carol Ann 1953- *WhoAmW 91, WhoEmL 91, WhoSSW 91*
Schwab, Charles 1938?- *ConAmBL*
Schwab, Charles M. 1862-1939 *WorAlBi*
Schwab, Charles R. *WhoAm 90*
Schwab, Curtis A. 1932- *St&PR 91*
Schwab, David S 1937- *BiDrAPA 89*
Schwab, Donald Ira *BiDrAPA 89*
Schwab, Ernest Roe 1950- *WhoEmL 91*
Schwab, Evan Lynn 1938- *WhoAm 90*
Schwab, George David 1931- *WhoAm 90, WhoE 91*
Schwab, Glenn Orville 1919- *WhoAm 90*
Schwab, Harold Lee 1932- *WhoE 91, WhoWor 91*
Schwab, Hermann Caspar 1920- *WhoAm 90*
Schwab, Israel 1935- *St&PR 91*
Schwab, John Harris 1927- *WhoAm 90*
Schwab, John J 1923- *BiDrAPA 89*
Schwab, John Joseph 1923- *WhoAm 90*
Schwab, Joseph J. 1909-1988 *BioIn 16*
Schwab, Leonard C. 1922- *St&PR 91*
Schwab, Marilyn 1929- *BiDrAPA 89*
Schwab, Mark Francis 1953- *WhoEmL 91*
Schwab, Martin J. 1922- *St&PR 91*
Schwab, Martin Jay 1922- *WhoAm 90*
Schwab, Michael Joel *BiDrAPA 89*
Schwab, Morris *St&PR 91*
Schwab, Morton E *BiDrAPA 89*
Schwab, Paul A. 1929- *St&PR 91*
Schwab, Paul Josiah 1932- *BiDrAPA 89*
Schwab, Philip Walter 1940- *St&PR 91*
Schwab, Ralph G. 1932- *St&PR 91*
Schwab, Reiko 1931- *WhoSSW 91*
Schwab, Richard D. 1926- *St&PR 91*
Schwab, Roland Friedrich 1930- *St&PR 91, WhoWor 91*
Schwab, Stephen Wayne 1956- *WhoEmL 91*
Schwab, Susan Carol *WhoAm 90*
Schwab, Winthrop DeV 1918- *St&PR 91*
Schwab-Stone, Mary Eleanor 1949- *BiDrAPA 89*
Schwabacher, Ethel K. 1903-1984 *BioIn 16, WhoAmA 91N*
Schwabe, Albert, II 1932- *WhoSSW 91*
Schwabe, Annette Marie 1958- *WhoE 91*
Schwabe, Arthur David 1924- *WhoAm 90*
Schwabe, Calvin Walter 1927- *WhoAm 90*
Schwabe, George Blaine, III 1947- *WhoEmL 91, WhoSSW 91*
Schwabe, John Bennett, II 1946- *WhoEmL 91, WhoWor 91*
Schwabe, John Leonard 1919- *WhoAm 90*
Schwabe, Mario R 1940- *BiDrAPA 89*
Schwabe, Samuel Heinrich 1789-1875 *WorAlBi*
Schwaber, Evelyne *BiDrAPA 89*
Schwabl, Franz 1938- *WhoWor 91*
Schwabsky, Barry 1957- *WhoAmA 91*
Schwacha, George 1908-1986 *WhoAmA 91N*
Schwacke, Ginger Wishik 1957- *BiDrAPA 89*
Schwadron, Abraham A. 1925-1987 *BioIn 16*
Schwaeber, Marlene Robin 1966- *WhoAmW 91*
Schwager, George Willard 1911- *WhoSSW 91*
Schwager, John L. 1948- *St&PR 91*
Schwager, Michael 1946- *WhoE 91*
Schwager, Myron August 1937- *IntWWM 90*
Schwager, Robert Solomon 1935- *St&PR 91*
Schwager, Ronny Joel 1950- *St&PR 91*
Schwager, Thomas Edward 1951- *St&PR 91*
Schwahn, Frank Stephen 1953- *WhoSSW 91*
Schwaiger, Brigitte 1949- *EncCoWW*
Schwaiger, Walt N. 1937- *St&PR 91*
Schwalb, Neil Stanford 1943- *BiDrAPA 89*
Schwalb, Susan 1944- *WhoAmA 91*
Schwalbe, Jim P. 1944- *St&PR 91*
Schwalbe, Kelly *ODwPR 91*
Schwalje, Earl G. 1921- *AuBYP 90*
Schwalje, Joseph Louis 1922- *WhoAm 90*
Schwalje, Marjory C. *AuBYP 90*
Schwall, Don 1936- *Ballpl 90*
Schwaller, Anthony E. *BioIn 16*
Schwaller, John Frederick 1948- *WhoSSW 91*
Schwaller, Shirley Files 1946- *WhoSSW 91*
Schwalm, Fritz Ekkehardt 1936- *WhoAm 90*
Schwalm, J.J. 1937- *St&PR 91*
Schwam, Jeffrey S *BiDrAPA 89*
Schwam, Marvin Albert 1942- *WhoAm 90, WhoE 91*
Schwamb, Donald F., Jr. 1940- *St&PR 91*
Schwamb, Donald Frederick 1952- *St&PR 91*
Schwamm, Ellen *BioIn 16*
Schwan, Herman Paul 1915- *WhoAm 90*
Schwan, Judith Alecia 1925- *WhoAm 90, WhoAmW 91*
Schwan, LeRoy Bernard 1932- *WhoWor 91*
Schwanbeck, Bodo 1935- *IntWWM 90*
Schwandt, Stephen 1947- *SmATA 61 [port]*
Schwanhardt, Georg *PenDiDA 89*
Schwanhardt, Georg 1601-1667 *PenDiDA 89*
Schwanhardt, Heinrich *PenDiDA 89*
Schwank, Friedrich Johann 1947- *WhoWor 91*
Schwanke, Robert Louis 1930- *St&PR 91, WhoAm 90*
Schwankhaus, Marcia Jane *BiDrAPA 89*
Schwann, Theodor 1810-1882 *WorAlBi*
Schwann, William 1913- *IntWWM 90*
Schwann, William Joseph 1913- *WhoAm 90*
Schwantes, William Ray 1932- *St&PR 91*
Schwantner, Joseph 1943- *WhoAm 90*
Schwanz, H Lee 1923- *WhoWrEP 89*
Schwanz, Herman Lee 1923- *WhoAm 90*
Schwarberg, Guenther 1926- *ConAu 130*
Schwarberg, Thomas Marcell, Jr. 1933- *WhoSSW 91*
Schwarcz, June Theresa 1918- *WhoAmA 91*
Schwarcz, Samuel *BioIn 16*
Schwarcz, Susan Kolodny 1954- *WhoAmW 91*
Schwardt, Susan Kelly 1936- *WhoAmW 91*
Schwark, Mary Beth 1954- *BioIn 16*
Schwarting, Anne Angevine 1945- *WhoAmW 91*
Schwarting, Arthur Ernest 1917- *WhoAm 90*
Schwartz, A Herbert 1932- *BiDrAPA 89*
Schwartz, A.J. 1947- *St&PR 91*
Schwartz, Aaron Robert 1926- *WhoAm 90*
Schwartz, Abba P. 1916-1989 *BioIn 16*
Schwartz, Adrienne Claire *WhoAmA 91*
Schwartz, Aimee 1953- *BiDrAPA 89, WhoE 91*
Schwartz, Alan *St&PR 91*
Schwartz, Alan David 1950- *St&PR 91*
Schwartz, Alan E. 1925- *St&PR 91, WhoAm 90*
Schwartz, Alan Jay 1946- *WhoE 91*
Schwartz, Alan Stuart 1943- *WhoAm 90*
Schwartz, Alan Uriel 1933- *WhoAm 90*
Schwartz, Alfred 1922- *WhoAm 90*
Schwartz, Alice M. *St&PR 91*
Schwartz, Allen 1930- *WhoAm 90*
Schwartz, Allen G. 1934- *WhoAm 90*
Schwartz, Alvin 1927- *AuBYP 90, BioIn 16*
Schwartz, Alyse Bett 1960- *WhoAmW 91*
Schwartz, Amy 1954- *BioIn 16*
Schwartz, Andrew 1943- *BiDrAPA 89*
Schwartz, Anna J. 1915- *WhoAm 90*
Schwartz, Anthony 1940- *WhoAm 90, WhoE 91*
Schwartz, Arnold 1929- *WhoAm 90*
Schwartz, Arnold C. 1932- *St&PR 91*
Schwartz, Arthur 1900-1984 *BioIn 16, OxCPMus, WorAlBi*
Schwartz, Arthur Edward 1955- *WhoEmL 91*
Schwartz, Arthur H. *NewYTBS 90*
Schwartz, Arthur H 1936- *BiDrAPA 89*
Schwartz, Arthur Leonard 1941- *WhoAm 90*
Schwartz, Arthur M 1919- *BiDrAPA 89*
Schwartz, Arthur Robert 1947- *WhoAm 90*
Schwartz, Aubrey E 1928- *WhoAmA 91*
Schwartz, Aubrey Earl 1928- *WhoAm 90*
Schwartz, Barbara Ann 1948- *WhoAmA 91*
Schwartz, Barbara Harriet *BiDrAPA 89*
Schwartz, Barry 1942- *ConAmBL*
Schwartz, Barry J 1929- *BiDrAPA 89*
Schwartz, Barry Jay 1929- *WhoE 91*
Schwartz, Bella *WhoAmA 91*
Schwartz, Benjamin F. 1909-1990 *BioIn 16*
Schwartz, Bernard 1905- *St&PR 91*
Schwartz, Bernard 1923- *WhoAm 90*
Schwartz, Bernard 1927- *WhoAm 90*
Schwartz, Bernard L. 1925- *St&PR 91, WhoAm 90, WhoE 91*
Schwartz, Bernard S *BiDrAPA 89*
Schwartz, Bertram 1934- *St&PR 91*
Schwartz, Blanche *BioIn 16*
Schwartz, Bruce Jan *BiDrAPA 89*
Schwartz, Buky 1932- *WhoAmA 91*
Schwartz, C. Edward 1940- *WhoAm 90, WhoE 91*
Schwartz, Carl A 1923- *BiDrAPA 89*
Schwartz, Carl E 1935- *WhoAmA 91*
Schwartz, Carl Edward 1935- *WhoAm 90*
Schwartz, Carl R E 1955- *BiDrAPA 89*
Schwartz, Carol A. 1953- *WhoAmW 91*
Schwartz, Carol Levine 1927- *WhoE 91*
Schwartz, Carol Levitt 1944- *WhoAmW 91*
Schwartz, Charles, Jr. 1922- *WhoAm 90, WhoSSW 91*
Schwartz, Charles A 1936- *BiDrAPA 89*
Schwartz, Charles D. 1948- *WhoE 91*
Schwartz, Charles Elias 1952- *BiDrAPA 89, WhoE 91*
Schwartz, Charles Frederick 1916- *WhoAm 90, WhoE 91*
Schwartz, Charles P., Jr. 1927- *St&PR 91*
Schwartz, Charles Phineas, Jr. 1927- *WhoAm 90*
Schwartz, Charles Walsh 1914- *AuBYP 90*
Schwartz, Corinne O'Hare 1929- *WhoAmW 91*
Schwartz, Craig 1953- *St&PR 91*
Schwartz, Dale Marvin 1942- *WhoAm 90, WhoSSW 91*
Schwartz, Daniel Bennett 1929- *WhoAm 90*
Schwartz, Daniel Ian 1965- *WhoE 91*
Schwartz, Daniel M. 1956- *St&PR 91*
Schwartz, Daniel P 1925- *BiDrAPA 89*
Schwartz, Daniel W 1933- *BiDrAPA 89*
Schwartz, David *BioIn 16*
Schwartz, David 1916-1989 *ConAu 130*
Schwartz, David 1935- *BiDrAPA 89*
Schwartz, David Elving 1954- *WhoEmL 91*
Schwartz, David Howard 1957- *WhoE 91*
Schwartz, David M. *BioIn 16*
Schwartz, David M. 1948- *St&PR 91*
Schwartz, David Stough 1931- *St&PR 91*
Schwartz, Dean A. 1962- *St&PR 91*
Schwartz, Delmore 1913-1966 *MajTwCW, WorAlBi*
Schwartz, Donald 1927- *WhoAm 90*
Schwartz, Donald A 1926- *BiDrAPA 89*
Schwartz, Donald D 1929- *BiDrAPA 89*
Schwartz, Donald E. 1930-1988 *BioIn 16*
Schwartz, Donald Franklin 1935- *WhoAm 90*
Schwartz, Doris Ruhbel 1915- *WhoAm 90, WhoAmW 91*
Schwartz, Douglas Wright 1929- *WhoAm 90*
Schwartz, Earl D 1942- *BiDrAPA 89*
Schwartz, Edward Arthur 1937- *St&PR 91, WhoAm 90*
Schwartz, Edward F. 1927- *St&PR 91*
Schwartz, Edward Lester 1910- *WhoE 91*
Schwartz, Edward Malcolm 1928- *WhoAm 90*
Schwartz, Edward R. 1910- *St&PR 91*
Schwartz, Eleanor Brantley 1937- *WhoAm 90, WhoAmW 91*
Schwartz, Eli 1921- *WhoAm 90*
Schwartz, Elizabeth Reeder 1912- *AuBYP 90*
Schwartz, Ellen Rae 1949- *WhoWrEP 89*
Schwartz, Elliott S *WhoAmA 91*
Schwartz, Elliott S. 1936- *IntWWM 90*
Schwartz, Elliott Shelling 1936- *WhoAm 90*
Schwartz, Elon Nardi *BiDrAPA 89*
Schwartz, Emanual K. 1912-1973 *EncO&P 3*
Schwartz, Estar Alma 1950- *WhoAmW 91*
Schwartz, Esther Ipp 1904-1988 *BioIn 16*
Schwartz, Esther Latterman 1938- *WhoAmW 91*
Schwartz, Eugene M 1927- *WhoAmA 91*
Schwartz, Felice N. 1925- *WhoAmW 91*
Schwartz, Fran B. 1950- *ODwPR 91*
Schwartz, Francine *BiDrAPA 89*
Schwartz, Frederic W. 1916- *St&PR 91*
Schwartz, Frederick G. 1928- *St&PR 91*
Schwartz, Gail Leslie 1952- *BiDrAPA 89*
Schwartz, Gary Alan 1952- *St&PR 91*
Schwartz, Gary David 1940- *WhoWor 91*
Schwartz, George Edwin 1924- *St&PR 91, WhoAm 90*
Schwartz, George Leopold 1891-1983 *DcNaB 1981*
Schwartz, Gerald 1927- *WhoWor 91*
Schwartz, Gerald S. 1947- *ODwPR 91*
Schwartz, Gerald Wilfred 1941- *WhoAm 90, WhoWor 91*
Schwartz, Gerri E. *WhoAmW 91*
Schwartz, Gordon Francis 1935- *WhoAm 90*
Schwartz, Harold *NewYTBS 90*
Schwartz, Harold 1920- *WhoAm 90*
Schwartz, Harold Albert 1913- *WhoAm 90*
Schwartz, Harold I 1947- *BiDrAPA 89*
Schwartz, Harold Lloyd 1936- *WhoWor 91*
Schwartz, Harry *St&PR 91N*
Schwartz, Harry 1919- *WhoAm 90*
Schwartz, Harry Kane 1934- *WhoAm 90*
Schwartz, Harvey Joel 1951- *BiDrAPA 89, WhoE 91*
Schwartz, Henry 1927- *WhoAmA 91*
Schwartz, Henry G., Jr. 1938- *St&PR 91*
Schwartz, Henry Gerard 1909- *WhoAm 90*
Schwartz, Herbert Charles 1926- *WhoAm 90*
Schwartz, Herbert Marshall 1947- *WhoSSW 91*
Schwartz, Herman 1916- *St&PR 91*
Schwartz, Hilda 1923- *St&PR 91*
Schwartz, Howard L 1937- *BiDrAPA 89*
Schwartz, Howard S. 1946- *St&PR 91*
Schwartz, Ilene 1942- *WhoAmW 91*
Schwartz, Ilsa Roslow 1941- *WhoAmW 91*
Schwartz, Ilze K 1935- *BiDrAPA 89*
Schwartz, Irving Donn 1927- *WhoAm 90*
Schwartz, Irving Leon 1918- *WhoAm 90*
Schwartz, Irwin H. 1948- *WhoEmL 91*
Schwartz, Isaac Joseph 1885-1971 *LiHiK*
Schwartz, Jack 1938- *WhoAm 90*
Schwartz, Jack Theodore 1914- *WhoAm 90*
Schwartz, Jacob T. 1930- *WhoAm 90*
Schwartz, Jacques Paul 1928- *WhoAm 90*
Schwartz, James 1923- *St&PR 91*
Schwartz, James D., Jr. 1950- *St&PR 91*
Schwartz, James Frederick 1929- *WhoAm 90*
Schwartz, James Harris 1932- *WhoAm 90*
Schwartz, James Peter 1919- *WhoWor 91*
Schwartz, Jane Susan 1955- *WhoAmW 91*
Schwartz, Jane T *BiDrAPA 89*
Schwartz, Janet Harriet *BiDrAPA 89*
Schwartz, Janet Singer 1951- *WhoE 91*
Schwartz, Jean 1878-1956 *BioIn 16, OxCPMus*
Schwartz, Jean Retta 1934- *BiDrAPA 89*
Schwartz, Jeffrey 1952- *WhoWrEP 89*
Schwartz, Jeffrey Byron 1940- *WhoWor 91*
Schwartz, Jeffrey I *BiDrAPA 89*
Schwartz, Jeffrey Michael 1951- *BiDrAPA 89*
Schwartz, Jesse M. 1947- *St&PR 91*
Schwartz, Joel L. 1940- *BioIn 16*
Schwartz, Joel Louis 1940- *BiDrAPA 89*
Schwartz, Joel Richard 1957- *BiDrAPA 89*
Schwartz, John Burnham *BioIn 16*
Schwartz, John Burnham 1965- *ConAu 132, ConLC 59 [port]*
Schwartz, John James 1919- *WhoAm 90, WhoE 91*
Schwartz, John L *BiDrAPA 89*
Schwartz, John Norman 1945- *WhoAm 90*
Schwartz, Jonathan *BioIn 16*
Schwartz, Jonathan H 1950- *BiDrAPA 89*
Schwartz, Jonathan Ralph 1947- *BiDrAPA 89, WhoE 91*
Schwartz, Joseph 1911- *WhoAm 90*
Schwartz, Joseph 1925- *WhoAm 90, WhoWrEP 89*
Schwartz, Joseph Alan *BiDrAPA 89*
Schwartz, Joseph Elias *BiDrAPA 89*
Schwartz, Joseph J. 1899-1975 *BioIn 16*
Schwartz, Joyce Gensberg 1950- *WhoAmW 91*
Schwartz, Judy *BiDrAPA 89*
Schwartz, Judy Ellen 1946- *WhoAmW 91*
Schwartz, Jules Jacob 1932- *WhoAm 90*
Schwartz, Julia Maynard 1957- *BiDrAPA 89*
Schwartz, Julius 1907- *AuBYP 90*
Schwartz, Kenneth Ernst 1922- *WhoWor 91*
Schwartz, Kenneth J. *BiDrAPA 89*
Schwartz, Kenneth Jay *WhoE 91*
Schwartz, Kessel 1920- *WhoAm 90, WhoWrEP 89*
Schwartz, L.M. 1910- *St&PR 91*
Schwartz, Larry 1922- *WhoSSW 91*
Schwartz, Laurence M 1936- *BiDrAPA 89*
Schwartz, Laurens R. 1951- *WhoEmL 91*
Schwartz, Laurie Koller 1947- *WhoAmW 91*
Schwartz, Lawrence 1935- *WhoWor 91*
Schwartz, Lawrence B. 1929- *St&PR 91*
Schwartz, Lawrence H 1924- *BiDrAPA 89*
Schwartz, Lee Scott 1955- *BiDrAPA 89*
Schwartz, Leo 1903-1990 *BioIn 16*
Schwartz, Leon 1922- *WhoAm 90*
Schwartz, Leonard *BiDrAPA 89*
Schwartz, Leonard 1925- *WhoE 91*
Schwartz, Leonard 1926- *WhoE 91*
Schwartz, Leonard E. 1943- *WhoAm 90*
Schwartz, Leslie Harry 1946- *BiDrAPA 89*
Schwartz, Lester 1928- *BiDrAPA 89*
Schwartz, Lillian 1927- *WhoAmA 91*

Schwartz, Lillian Feldman 1927- *WhoAm 90, WhoAmW 91, WhoE 91*
Schwartz, Lionel A 1922- *BiDrAPA 89*
Schwartz, Lloyd 1941- *WhoWrEP 89*
Schwartz, Lloyd Marvin 1923- *WhoAm 90*
Schwartz, Lois L *BiDrAPA 89*
Schwartz, Lonn R. 1946- *St&PR 91*
Schwartz, Lou *BioIn 16*
Schwartz, Louis A *BiDrAPA 89*
Schwartz, Louis Brown 1913- *WhoAm 90*
Schwartz, Louis Martin 1926- *St&PR 91*
Schwartz, Lynne Sharon 1939- *WhoAm 90, WhoWrEP 89, WorAu 1980 [port]*
Schwartz, M. David *WhoAm 90*
Schwartz, Manfred 1909-1970 *WhoAmA 91N*
Schwartz, Marc D *BiDrAPA 89*
Schwartz, Marjorie Watson 1905- *WhoAmA 91*
Schwartz, Marshall Zane 1945- *WhoAm 90, WhoEmL 91*
Schwartz, Martin 1923- *St&PR 91*
Schwartz, Martin 1933- *WhoE 91*
Schwartz, Martin Weber 1944- *WhoE 91*
Schwartz, Marvin 1922- *WhoAm 90*
Schwartz, Marvin D 1926- *WhoAmA 91*
Schwartz, Mary Kay 1941- *WhoAmW 91*
Schwartz, Mel M. 1929- *WhoE 91*
Schwartz, Melvin 1932- *BioIn 16, WhoAm 90, WhoWor 91, WorAlBi*
Schwartz, Melvin 1934- *BiDrAPA 89*
Schwartz, Melvin L 1925- *BiDrAPA 89*
Schwartz, Melvin S. *BioIn 16*
Schwartz, Meyer 1904- *WhoAm 90*
Schwartz, Michael 1937- *WhoAm 90*
Schwartz, Michael 1952- *BiDrAPA 89*
Schwartz, Michael 1959- *BioIn 16*
Schwartz, Michael Alan 1944- *BiDrAPA 89, WhoE 91*
Schwartz, Michael Allen 1946- *WhoE 91*
Schwartz, Michael Brian *BiDrAPA 89*
Schwartz, Michael Harris *BiDrAPA 89*
Schwartz, Michael I. 1939- *St&PR 91*
Schwartz, Michael Joel 1941- *WhoE 91*
Schwartz, Michael N 1938- *BiDrAPA 89*
Schwartz, Michael Robinson 1940- *WhoAm 90*
Schwartz, Michael Steven 1953- *WhoEmL 91*
Schwartz, Milton 1923- *St&PR 91*
Schwartz, Milton Lewis 1920- *WhoAm 90*
Schwartz, Mischa 1926- *WhoAm 90*
Schwartz, Modest Euphemia 1915- *WhoAmW 91*
Schwartz, Mona 1953- *WhoAmW 91*
Schwartz, Morris 1901- *St&PR 91*
Schwartz, Muriel A. *MajTwCW*
Schwartz, Murray Louis 1920- *WhoAm 90*
Schwartz, Murray M. 1931- *WhoAm 90, WhoE 91*
Schwartz, Nan Louise 1953- *WhoEmL 91*
Schwartz, Nate *St&PR 91*
Schwartz, Nathan R. 1913- *St&PR 91*
Schwartz, Neena Betty 1926- *WhoAm 90*
Schwartz, Neil D. 1942- *St&PR 91*
Schwartz, Norman David 1950- *St&PR 91*
Schwartz, Norman Donald 1945- *WhoE 91*
Schwartz, Norman L. 1935- *WhoAm 90*
Schwartz, Patricia Luz Testa *BiDrAPA 89*
Schwartz, Paul Jeffrey 1957- *BiDrAPA 89*
Schwartz, Paul Marc *WhoWor 91*
Schwartz, Paul Norman 1946- *St&PR 91*
Schwartz, Pedro 1935- *WhoWor 91*
Schwartz, Pepper *BioIn 16*
Schwartz, Perry H. 1938- *St&PR 91, WhoAm 90*
Schwartz, Perry Lester 1939- *WhoAm 90*
Schwartz, Peter A. *St&PR 91*
Schwartz, Peter A. 1943- *WhoAm 90*
Schwartz, Peter Edward 1941- *WhoAm 90*
Schwartz, Philip 1930- *WhoWor 91*
Schwartz, Philip C. 1925- *St&PR 91*
Schwartz, Philip L. 1940- *St&PR 91*
Schwartz, R. Malcolm 1934- *WhoAm 90*
Schwartz, Raymond Lawrence 1913- *WhoSSW 91*
Schwartz, Richard 1929- *WhoAm 90*
Schwartz, Richard A 1935- *BiDrAPA 89*
Schwartz, Richard Alan 1951- *WhoSSW 91*
Schwartz, Richard Brenton 1941- *WhoAm 90, WhoWor 91*
Schwartz, Richard D. 1944- *St&PR 91*
Schwartz, Richard Derecktor 1925- *WhoAm 90*
Schwartz, Richard Gary 1947- *WhoSSW 91*
Schwartz, Richard H 1938- *BiDrAPA 89*
Schwartz, Richard M. 1939- *St&PR 91*
Schwartz, Richard S 1948- *BiDrAPA 89*
Schwartz, Richard Stanton 1948- *WhoE 91*
Schwartz, Richard Theophile 1904- *WhoE 91*
Schwartz, Robert *BiDrAPA 89*
Schwartz, Robert 1939- *WhoAm 90*
Schwartz, Robert 1946- *St&PR 91*
Schwartz, Robert D 1935- *BiDrAPA 89*
Schwartz, Robert Donald 1924- *WhoSSW 91*
Schwartz, Robert G. 1928- *BioIn 16, St&PR 91*
Schwartz, Robert George 1928- *WhoE 91, WhoWor 91*
Schwartz, Robert Glenn 1956- *WhoSSW 91*
Schwartz, Robert J. 1917- *St&PR 91*
Schwartz, Robert N. 1917- *ODwPR 91*
Schwartz, Robert Nash 1917- *WhoAm 90*
Schwartz, Robert Philip *BiDrAPA 89*
Schwartz, Robert R. 1941- *St&PR 91*
Schwartz, Robert S. 1947- *WhoAm 90*
Schwartz, Robert William 1944- *WhoE 91, WhoWor 91*
Schwartz, Roberta Christine *WhoWrEP 89*
Schwartz, Roger Alan 1945- *WhoWor 91*
Schwartz, Ronald Bruce *BiDrAPA 89*
Schwartz, Ronald Herman 1956- *WhoSSW 91*
Schwartz, Ronald Michael *BiDrAPA 89*
Schwartz, Rosalye Ann 1936- *WhoAmW 91*
Schwartz, Roselind Shirley Grant 1922- *WhoAmW 91*
Schwartz, Rosemarie K. *St&PR 91*
Schwartz, Roy Richard 1943- *St&PR 91*
Schwartz, Ruth *WhoAmA 91*
Schwartz, Ruth Wainer *WhoAmW 91*
Schwartz, Samuel 1927- *St&PR 91, WhoAm 90*
Schwartz, Sanford Louis 1950- *St&PR 91*
Schwartz, Sanford Mark 1951- *St&PR 91*
Schwartz, Seymour Ira 1928- *WhoAm 90*
Schwartz, Seymour N. 1937- *St&PR 91*
Schwartz, Sheila 1929- *ConAu 30NR*
Schwartz, Shirley Eckwall 1935- *WhoAm 90, WhoAmW 91, WhoWor 91*
Schwartz, Sing-Si 1954- *WhoAmA 91*
Schwartz, Sol 1925- *St&PR 91*
Schwartz, Sorell Lee 1937- *WhoE 91*
Schwartz, Stephan A 1942- *ConAu 130*
Schwartz, Stephen 1948- *OxCPMus*
Schwartz, Stephen A. 1943- *EncPaPR 91*
Schwartz, Stephen Alfred 1948- *WhoEmL 91*
Schwartz, Stephen Allan 1949- *WhoAm 90*
Schwartz, Stephen Blair 1934- *WhoAm 90*
Schwartz, Stephen C. 1942- *St&PR 91*
Schwartz, Stephen L 1935- *BiDrAPA 89*
Schwartz, Stephen Marc 1944- *WhoE 91*
Schwartz, Steven 1947- *St&PR 91*
Schwartz, Steven D 1910- *BiDrAPA 89*
Schwartz, Steven Gary 1954- *WhoEmL 91*
Schwartz, Steven Harvey 1948- *WhoE 91*
Schwartz, Steven M. 1948- *ODwPR 91*
Schwartz, Steven R 1950- *WhoWrEP 89*
Schwartz, Stuart 1925- *St&PR 91*
Schwartz, Stuart R *BiDrAPA 89*
Schwartz, Susan Elisabeth Braloff 1956- *WhoE 91*
Schwartz, Sylvan, Jr. 1946- *St&PR 91*
Schwartz, Ted 1947- *St&PR 91*
Schwartz, Terry Walter 1950- *WhoWrEP 89*
Schwartz, Theodore B. 1918- *WhoAm 90*
Schwartz, Therese 1928- *WhoAmA 91*
Schwartz, Thomas Alan 1951- *St&PR 91*
Schwartz, Thomas D. 1932- *WhoAm 90*
Schwartz, Tony *BioIn 16*
Schwartz, Tony 1923- *WhoWrEP 89*
Schwartz, Valerie Breuer 1912- *WhoAmW 91, WhoE 91*
Schwartz, Vicki Anne 1954- *WhoAmW 91*
Schwartz, Victor Israel *BiDrAPA 89*
Schwartz, Werner W. 1914- *St&PR 91*
Schwartz, Wilbert F. 1941- *St&PR 91*
Schwartz, William 1927- *BiDrAPA 89*
Schwartz, William 1933- *WhoAm 90, WhoE 91, WhoWor 91*
Schwartz, William Allen 1938- *WhoAm 90*
Schwartz, William B., Jr. 1921- *WhoAm 90*
Schwartz, William Benjamin 1922- *WhoAm 90*
Schwartz, William Carleton 1933- *WhoAm 90*
Schwartzberg, Allan Z 1930- *BiDrAPA 89*
Schwartzberg, Allan Zelig 1930- *WhoAm 90, WhoE 91*
Schwartzberg, Linda Kay 1949- *WhoAmW 91*
Schwartzberg, Martin M. 1935- *St&PR 91, WhoAm 90, WhoE 91*
Schwartzburg, David Curtiss 1936- *St&PR 91*
Schwartze, Therese 1851-1918 *BiDWomA*
Schwartzel, Charlotte A. 1949- *WhoSSW 91*
Schwartzer, Alice 1942- *EncCoWW*
Schwartzer, Joseph Simon 1948- *BiDrAPA 89*
Schwartzhoff, James P. 1937- *St&PR 91*
Schwartzhoff, James Paul 1937- *WhoAm 90*
Schwartzlow, Jerry Ernest 1941- *St&PR 91*
Schwartzman, Alan 1923- *WhoAm 90*
Schwartzman, Andrew Jay *BioIn 16*
Schwartzman, Andrew Jay 1946- *WhoAm 90, WhoE 91*
Schwartzman, Bonnie *ODwPR 91*
Schwartzman, Daniel 1909-1977 *WhoAmA 91N*
Schwartzman, David 1924- *WhoAm 90*
Schwartzman, Jack 1912- *WhoE 91, WhoWor 91*
Schwartzman, Leon 1931- *WhoAm 90, WhoE 91*
Schwartzman, Lois Phoebe 1937- *WhoWrEP 89*
Schwartzman, Michael Isaac 1945- *WhoEmL 91*
Schwartzman, Peter 1936- *St&PR 91*
Schwartzman, William *BiDrAPA 89*
Schwartzreich, Edward Sylvan 1942- *BiDrAPA 89*
Schwartzstein, Daniel *St&PR 91*
Schwartzstein, Marvin 1931- *St&PR 91*
Schwartztol, Holly Wechsler 1946- *WhoEmL 91*
Schwartzwald, David W. 1949- *St&PR 91*
Schwary, Ronald Louis 1944- *WhoAm 90*
Schwarz, Anton Josef 1927- *St&PR 91*
Schwarz, Arturo Samuele 1924- *WhoWor 91*
Schwarz, Barbara Ruth Ballou 1930- *WhoAmW 91*
Schwarz, Berthold E 1924- *BiDrAPA 89*
Schwarz, Berthold Eric 1924- *EncPaPR 91*
Schwarz, Carol Cameron 1933- *BiDrAPA 89*
Schwarz, Charles W. 1926- *St&PR 91*
Schwarz, Daniel R 1941- *ConAu 131*
Schwarz, Daniel Tracy 1938- *WhoAm 90*
Schwarz, Earle Jay 1952- *WhoEmL 91*
Schwarz, Egon 1922- *WhoAm 90*
Schwarz, Eitan Daniel *BiDrAPA 89*
Schwarz, Ekkehart Richard Johannes 1938- *WhoE 91*
Schwarz, Elizabeth Dorian *BiDrAPA 89*
Schwarz, Eric R. 1954- *St&PR 91*
Schwarz, Esther Doris 1933- *WhoE 91*
Schwarz, Felix Conrad 1906- *WhoAmA 91*
Schwarz, Frank Henry 1894-1951 *WhoAmA 91N*
Schwarz, Fred Charles 1913- *ConAu 32NR*
Schwarz, Frederic George 1926- *WhoAm 90*
Schwarz, Frederick August Otto, Jr. 1935- *WhoAm 90*
Schwarz, Gabriel A *BiDrAPA 89*
Schwarz, Gene 1941- *St&PR 91*
Schwarz, George Carl 1935- *BiDrAPA 89*
Schwarz, Gerard *BioIn 16*
Schwarz, Gerard 1947- *IntWWM 90, PenDiMP*
Schwarz, Gerard Ralph 1947- *WhoAm 90*
Schwarz, Gerta *BiDrAPA 89*
Schwarz, H. Marshall 1936- *St&PR 91*
Schwarz, Hanna 1943- *IntWWM 90*
Schwarz, Harold P *BiDrAPA 89*
Schwarz, Harold Poust 1943- *WhoE 91*
Schwarz, Harry 1949- *WhoSSW 91*
Schwarz, Heinrich 1894-1974 *WhoAmA 91N*
Schwarz, Heinz Herbert 1924- *BiDrAPA 89*
Schwarz, I Gene 1930- *BiDrAPA 89*
Schwarz, James Nicholas 1945- *St&PR 91*
Schwarz, Janet Marie 1950- *WhoE 91*
Schwarz, John H. 1938- *St&PR 91*
Schwarz, John Henry 1941- *WhoAm 90*
Schwarz, Joseph Edmund 1929- *WhoAm 90*
Schwarz, Josephine Lindeman 1908- *WhoAm 90*
Schwarz, Joyce A. *WhoWrEP 89*
Schwarz, Judith 1944- *WhoAmA 91*
Schwarz, Kathleen Marie 1958- *BiDrAPA 89*
Schwarz, Louis Jay 1946- *WhoE 91*
Schwarz, Luis H *BiDrAPA 89*
Schwarz, M. Roy 1936- *WhoAm 90*
Schwarz, Mary DuBois *BioIn 16*
Schwarz, Maurice, Jr. 1910- *St&PR 91*
Schwarz, Michael 1952- *WhoEmL 91*
Schwarz, Myrtle Cooper 1900- *WhoAmA 91*
Schwarz, Patricia Ann 1921- *IntWWM 90*
Schwarz, Patricia Tzuanos 1948- *WhoAmW 91*
Schwarz, Peter Karl 1944- *WhoE 91*
Schwarz, Ralph Jacques 1922- *WhoAm 90*
Schwarz, Ray Paul 1948- *WhoSSW 91*
Schwarz, Richard Howard 1931- *WhoAm 90*
Schwarz, Richard Michael *BiDrAPA 89*
Schwarz, Richard William 1925- *WhoAm 90*
Schwarz, Rudolf 1905- *IntWWM 90, PenDiMP*
Schwarz, Ruth Newman *BioIn 16*
Schwarz, Sanford 1920- *WhoAm 90*
Schwarz, Shirley Jean 1935- *WhoAmW 91*
Schwarz, Sibylle 1621-1638 *EncCoWW*
Schwarz, Stephen William 1940- *WhoAm 90*
Schwarz, Thomas Ralph 1936- *St&PR 91*
Schwarz, Walter F. *St&PR 91*
Schwarz, Wolfgang 1926- *WhoAm 90*
Schwarz, Wolfgang Karl 1934- *WhoWor 91*
Schwarzbart, Gunter 1932- *WhoSSW 91*
Schwarzbart, Ignacy Isaac 1888-1961 *BioIn 16*
Schwarzbaum, Henry 1956- *WhoWor 91*
Schwarzburg-Hohnstein, Countess of 1640-1672 *EncCoWW*
Schwarzchild, Steven S. 1924-1989 *BioIn 16*
Schwarzenbach, Alfons Pieter 1953- *WhoWor 91*
Schwarzenbach, Annemarie 1908-1942 *EncCoWW*
Schwarzenbach, Dieter 1936- *WhoWor 91*
Schwarzenbach, Gerold Karl 1904-1978 *DcScB S2*
Schwarzenbek, Eugene E. 1943- *St&PR 91*
Schwarzenburg, Elisabeth 1933- *IntWWM 90*
Schwarzenegger, Arnold *BioIn 16*
Schwarzenegger, Arnold 1947- *News 91-1 [port], WorAlBi*
Schwarzenegger, Arnold Alois 1947- *WhoAm 90*
Schwarzer, Thomas Philip 1938- *WhoSSW 91*
Schwarzer, William W. 1925- *WhoAm 90*
Schwarzkopf, Dietrich Guenter 1927- *WhoWor 91*
Schwarzkopf, Elisabeth 1915- *IntWWM 90, PenDiMP, WorAlBi*
Schwarzkopf, H. Norman 1934- *WhoAm 90*
Schwarzkopf, Hartmut 1940- *WhoWor 91*
Schwarzkopf, Lyall Arthur 1931- *WhoAm 90*
Schwarzkopf, Richard M. 1939- *St&PR 91*
Schwarzkopf, Steven Bernard *BiDrAPA 89*
Schwarzmann, Stephen Theodore 1945- *WhoEmL 91*
Schwarzmueller, Lynne Marie 1953- *WhoAmW 91*
Schwarzrock, Shirley Pratt 1914- *WhoAmW 91, WhoWor 91*
Schwarzschild, Arthur 1930-1987 *BioIn 16*
Schwarzschild, Martin 1912- *WhoAm 90*
Schwarzschild, William Harry, Jr. 1903- *WhoAm 90*
Schwarztrauber, Sayre Archie 1929- *WhoWor 91*
Schwarzwalder, Daniel Robert 1948- *St&PR 91, WhoE 91*
Schwarzwalder, John Carl 1917- *WhoAm 90*
Schwass, Gary L. 1945- *St&PR 91, WhoAm 90*
Schwatka, Frederick 1849-1892 *DcCanB 12*
Schwatka, Mark Andrew 1950- *WhoAm 90*
Schwebel, Andrew I. 1943- *WhoAm 90*
Schwebel, Jack P. 1925- *St&PR 91, WhoSSW 91*
Schwebel, Milton 1914- *WhoAm 90*
Schwebel, Renata Manasse 1930- *WhoAmA 91, WhoE 91*
Schwebel, Stephen Myron 1929- *WhoAm 90, WhoE 91*
Schweber, Silvan Samuel 1928- *WhoAm 90*
Schwed, Pedro E. 1931- *St&PR 91*
Schwed, Peter 1911- *ConAu 31NR, WhoAm 90, WhoWrEP 89*
Schwedel, Alan R. 1942- *St&PR 91*
Schwedel, Nat N 1910- *St&PR 91*
Schwedhelm, Raymond Gustav 1944- *St&PR 91*
Schwedler, Donald James 1923- *St&PR 91*
Schwedler, William A 1942-1982 *WhoAmA 91N*
Schween, Peter H *BiDrAPA 89*
Schweers, John Ray 1945- *St&PR 91*
Schweers, Ronald Glenn 1936- *St&PR 91*
Schwefel, Charles Albert 1955- *WhoE 91*
Schwefel, Hans-Paul 1940- *WhoWor 91*
Schwegel, Richard C. 1953- *IntWWM 90*
Schwehm, Jerry Kenneth *WhoSSW 91*
Schwei, Mark Gerard 1953- *BiDrAPA 89*
Schwei, Russell Paul 1959- *St&PR 91*
Schweibert, Raymond H *BiDrAPA 89*
Schweich, Robert Joseph 1934- *WhoAm 90*
Schweichler, Mary Ellen 1931- *WhoE 91*
Schweickart, Jim 1950- *WhoAm 90*
Schweickart, Russell L. 1935- *WhoWor 91*
Schweid, Daniel Edson *BiDrAPA 89*
Schweid, Jeffrey Marc 1952- *WhoSSW 91*
Schweig, Hal *ODwPR 91*
Schweig, Margaret Berris 1928- *WhoAmW 91*
Schweig, Noel A 1930- *BiDrAPA 89*
Schweiger, Anthony Walter 1941- *WhoE 91*

Schweiger, Debra Jean 1953- *WhoAmW 91*
Schweigert, B. S. 1921-1989 *BioIn 16*
Schweigert, Lynette Aileen 1949- *WhoEmL 91*
Schweighofer, Anton 1930- *WhoWor 91*
Schweighofer, Jurgen 1921- *EncO&P 3*
Schweik, Robert C 1927- *ConAu 31NR*
Schweikart, Dieter 1942- *IntWWM 90*
Schweiker, Richard 1926- *BiDrUSE 89*
Schweiker, Richard S. 1926- *WorAlBi*
Schweiker, Richard Schultz 1926- *WhoAm 90*
Schweikert, Norman Carl 1937- *IntWWM 90, WhoAm 90*
Schweikhart, Kenneth Arthur 1938- *St&PR 91*
Schweikle, Carl F. 1928- *St&PR 91*
Schweinfurth, Ulrich 1925- *WhoWor 91*
Schweinhart, Richard A. 1949- *St&PR 91*
Schweinhart, Richard Alexander 1949- *WhoAm 90*
Schweinhaut, Margaret Collins *WhoAmW 91, WhoE 91*
Schweinle, Frieda E. 1952- *WhoAmW 91*
Schweinshaut, Louise K. 1918- *St&PR 91*
Schweinshaut, Max, Jr. 1918- *St&PR 91*
Schweiss, Ruth Keller *WhoAmA 91*
Schweitzer, Albert 1875-1965 *BioIn 16, PenDiMP, WorAlBi*
Schweitzer, Byrd Baylor *AuBYP 90*
Schweitzer, Carl Lawrence 1929- *St&PR 91*
Schweitzer, Conrad 1928- *St&PR 91, WhoSSW 91*
Schweitzer, Darrell Charles 1952- *WhoWrEP 89*
Schweitzer, Don Alan 1941- *WhoAm 90*
Schweitzer, Frank Weaver 1932- *St&PR 91*
Schweitzer, George Keene 1924- *WhoAm 90*
Schweitzer, Gertrude Honig 1911-1989 *BioIn 16*
Schweitzer, H. George 1927- *WhoAm 90*
Schweitzer, Iris *BioIn 16*
Schweitzer, John Stephens 1929- *St&PR 91*
Schweitzer, Laurence R 1937- *BiDrAPA 89*
Schweitzer, M. Peter 1910- *WhoAm 90*
Schweitzer, M R 1911- *WhoAmA 91*
Schweitzer, N. Tina 1941- *WhoAm 90, WhoAmW 91, WhoE 91*
Schweitzer, Pierre-Paul 1912- *WhoAm 90*
Schweitzer, Sandra Lynn 1952- *WhoEmL 91*
Schweitzer, Theodore Gottlieb, III 1942- *WhoWor 91*
Schweitzer, Thomas Fred *WhoE 91, WhoWor 91*
Schweitzer, Ulrich 1920- *WhoAm 90*
Schweizer, Alfred 1941- *IntWWM 90*
Schweizer, Karl Wolfgang 1946- *WhoE 91*
Schweizer, Paul A. 1913- *St&PR 91*
Schweizer, Paul Douglas 1946- *WhoAm 90, WhoAmA 91*
Schweizer, Raymond C. 1921- *St&PR 91*
Schweizer, William Stuart 1944- *St&PR 91*
Schweke, Mark A. 1951- *St&PR 91*
Schwelb, Frank Ernest 1932- *WhoE 91*
Schwellenbach, Lewis Baxter 1894-1948 *BiDrUSE 89*
Schweller, Susan *ODwPR 91*
Schwemer, Cullen R 1935- *BiDrAPA 89*
Schwemm, Henry Christian, Jr. 1941- *St&PR 91*
Schwemm, John B. 1934- *St&PR 91*
Schwemm, John Butler 1934- *WhoAm 90*
Schwender, Charles F. 1937- *St&PR 91*
Schweninger, Ann Rozzelle 1951- *WhoAmA 91*
Schweninger, Irma 1939- *WhoSSW 91*
Schwenk, Harold S. 1941- *St&PR 91*
Schwenk, Richard C. *St&PR 91*
Schwenk, Rosalind M. *BioIn 16*
Schwenk, Wendy Ann 1962- *WhoAmW 91*
Schwenk-Berman, Laura Leacock 1956- *WhoAmW 91*
Schwenker, Carl Emerson 1933- *WhoSSW 91*
Schwenn, Lee William 1925- *WhoAm 90*
Schwenzer, Kristine Ann 1957- *WhoWrEP 89*
Schweppe, J.L. 1921- *St&PR 91*
Schweppe, John Shedd 1917- *WhoAm 90*
Schwerdfeger, Jean-Ferdinand-Joseph 1734-1818 *PenDiDA 89*
Schwerin, Doris 1922- *SmATA 64 [port], WhoWrEP 89*
Schwerin, Horace S. 1914- *WhoAm 90*
Schwerin, Karl Henry 1936- *WhoAm 90*
Schwerin, Paul H. 1932- *St&PR 91*
Schwerin, Stuart Lawrence 1941- *WhoAm 90*
Schwering, Felix Karl 1930- *WhoAm 90*
Schwerm, Gerald 1933- *WhoAm 90*
Schwerman, Jack F. 1952- *St&PR 91*
Schwerner, Armand 1927- *WhoWrEP 89*
Schwerner, Michael Henry 1939-1964 *BioIn 16*
Schwert, George William, III 1950- *WhoE 91*
Schwert, Pius 1892-1941 *Ballpl 90*
Schwertfeger, Floyd Edward 1915- *WhoAm 90*
Schwertfeger, Richard 1935- *WhoWor 91*
Schwertfeger, Robert E. 1943- *St&PR 91*
Schwertfeger, Ruth 1941- *ConAu 132*
Schwertly, Gary W. 1947- *St&PR 91*
Schwertner, Marjorie Frank 1924- *WhoAmW 91*
Schwertner, Ray 1948- *St&PR 91*
Schwertsik, Kurt 1935- *IntWWM 90*
Schwerzmann, Urs *BioIn 16*
Schwesig, Claude Rudolph Emil 1945- *WhoE 91*
Schwesinger, Edmund Arno, Jr. 1939- *WhoE 91*
Schwichtenberg, Jon I. 1934- *St&PR 91*
Schwicker, Dale Henry 1939- *WhoSSW 91*
Schwidder, Ernst 1931- *WhoAmA 91*
Schwied, Ellis Michael 1950- *BiDrAPA 89*
Schwieger, C Robert 1936- *WhoAmA 91*
Schwieger, John H. 1913-1988 *BioIn 16*
Schwieger, John Henry 1913- *St&PR 91*
Schwier, Frederick W. 1923- *St&PR 91*
Schwier, Frederick Warren 1923- *WhoAm 90*
Schwier, James W. 1928- *St&PR 91*
Schwier, Priscilla Lamb Guyton 1939- *WhoAmW 91, WhoWor 91*
Schwiering, Conrad 1916- *WhoAmA 91N*
Schwilck, Gene Leroy 1925- *WhoAm 90*
Schwille, Michael Edward 1936- *WhoSSW 91*
Schwimmer, David 1913- *WhoAm 90, WhoWor 91*
Schwimmer, Jeffrey Lawrence *BiDrAPA 89*
Schwimmer, Walter 1903- *WhoAm 90*
Schwimmer, Walter 1903-1989 *ConAu 129*
Schwin, Robert Lowell *BiDrAPA 89*
Schwind, Hans-Dieter 1936- *WhoWor 91*
Schwind, Michael Angelo 1924- *WhoAm 90, WhoE 91*
Schwinden, Ted 1925- *WhoWor 91*
Schwindt, G.A. 1933- *St&PR 91*
Schwindt, Robert F. 1929- *St&PR 91*
Schwing, Ann Taylor 1946- *WhoEmL 91*
Schwing, Charles Edward 1929- *WhoAm 90*
Schwinge, Elaine A *BiDrAPA 89*
Schwinger, Hermann 1640-1683 *PenDiDA 89*
Schwinger, Julian 1918- *WhoAm 90, WhoWor 91*
Schwinger, Julian S. 1918- *WorAlBi*
Schwinghamer, Robert John 1928- *WhoAm 90*
Schwinghammer, Arch C.L. 1926- *St&PR 91*
Schwinn, Robert James 1930- *WhoAm 90, WhoE 91, WhoWor 91*
Schwintzer, Christa Rose 1940- *WhoE 91*
Schwippert, Guustaaf Arthur 1935- *WhoWor 91*
Schwirian, Ann 1934- *WhoWrEP 89*
Schwitalla, Stephen Edward 1953- *WhoAm 90*
Schwitter, Frank Joseph 1933- *WhoE 91*
Schwitters, Kurt 1887-1948 *BioIn 16, IntDcAA 90, WorAlBi*
Schwitters, Roy Frederick 1944- *WhoAm 90*
Schwob, Antoinette 1906- *MusmAFA*
Schwoebel, John Joseph 1942- *WhoE 91*
Schwoebel, Richard F. 1941- *St&PR 91*
Schwoerer, Carol Ann 1943- *St&PR 91*
Schwoerer, Lois Green 1927- *WhoE 91*
Schwope, Mary Kathryn 1917- *WhoAmW 91*
Schworer-Kohl, Gretel 1951- *IntWWM 90*
Schwotzer, Gregg Adam 1949- *WhoE 91*
Schwyn, Charles Edward 1932- *WhoAm 90*
Schwyn, James Milton 1938- *St&PR 91*
Schydlowsky, Daniel Moises 1940- *WhoE 91*
Schyve, Paul Milton 1944- *BiDrAPA 89*
Sciabica, Vincent Samuel 1959- *WhoSSW 91*
Scialabba, Arthur Joseph 1966- *WhoE 91*
Scialabba, Fred Patrick 1949- *WhoE 91*
Scialdone, Eugene B. 1945- *ODwPR 91*
Scialfa, Patti *BioIn 16*
Scialla, Vittorio 1952- *WhoWor 91*
Scialli, John V 1953- *BiDrAPA 89*
Sciama, Dennis William 1926- *WhoWor 91*
Sciame, Joseph 1941- *WhoE 91*
Sciammarella, Cesar Augusto 1926- *WhoWor 91*
Sciammas, Jacques D. 1956- *St&PR 91*
Scianandre, Dominick Thomas 1949- *St&PR 91*
Sciance, Carroll Thomas 1939- *WhoSSW 91*
Sciarini, James F. 1931- *St&PR 91*
Sciascia, Leonardo *BioIn 16*
Sciascia, Leonardo 1921- *WhoWor 91*
Sciascia, Leonardo 1921-1989 *AnObit 1989, ConAu 130, MajTwCW, TwCCr&M 91B*
Sciba, JoAnn 1946- *WhoAmW 91*
Scibetta, Barbara Smith 1949- *ConAu 129*
Scibetta, Richard C *BiDrAPA 89*
Scibilia, Laurie Jean 1960- *WhoAmW 91*
Scibilia, Philip Chester 1940- *WhoWor 91*
Scibor-Marchocki, Romuald Ireneus 1926- *WhoWor 91*
Scicchitano, Edward Vincent 1931- *WhoE 91*
Scicluna, Ronnie Nazarene *WhoWor 91*
Scicluna, William Leslie 1921- *WhoWor 91*
Scicutella, John Vincent 1949- *St&PR 91*
Scielzo, Nicholas Henry 1941- *St&PR 91*
Scifres, Don R. *WhoAm 90*
Scilligo, Pio Felice 1928- *WhoWor 91*
Scimeca, Margaret R 1933- *BiDrAPA 89*
Scimeca, Michael M 1947- *BiDrAPA 89*
Scimeca, Michael Mariano 1947- *WhoE 91*
Scimeca, William Hannon 1953- *BiDrAPA 89*
Scimecca, Joseph A. 1940- *ConAu 129*
Scimone, Claudio 1934- *IntWWM 90, PenDiMP*
Scindia, Vijayaraje *BioIn 16*
Sciolino, Michael Salvatore 1931- *WhoE 91*
Sciolino, Susan Frances 1957- *WhoAmW 91*
Scionti, Isabel *BioIn 16*
Sciorra, Annabella *BioIn 16*
Scioscia, Mary 1926- *SmATA 63 [port]*
Scioscia, Mike 1958- *Ballpl 90*
Sciotti, Elissa Emilia 1956- *WhoE 91*
Scipio, Beverly Yvette 1951- *WhoAmW 91*
Scipio, Louis Albert, II 1922- *WhoAm 90*
Scipio Africanus, Publius Cornelius 236BC-183BC *WorAlBi*
Scipione, Marianne 1946- *St&PR 91*
Scipione, Richard Stephen 1937- *St&PR 91, WhoAm 90*
Scippa, Antonio 1942- *St&PR 91*
Scirica, Anthony Joseph 1940- *WhoE 91*
Scism, Daniel Reed 1936- *WhoAm 90*
Scisson, Brenda *ODwPR 91*
Scisson, Sidney E. 1917- *St&PR 91, WhoAm 90*
Scissors, Richard Curtis 1935- *WhoAm 90*
Scites, Janice L. 1950- *St&PR 91*
Scitovsky, Anne Aickelin 1915- *WhoAm 90, WhoAmW 91*
Sciubba, James John 1942- *WhoE 91*
Sciulli, Frank 1938- *WhoAm 90*
Sciullo, John J. 1931- *WhoAm 90*
Sciutti, Graziella 1927- *IntWWM 90, PenDiMP*
Sciutto, Mary Spelman *BiDrAPA 89*
Scivally, Bart Murnane 1944- *WhoSSW 91*
Scivetti, Frank 1942- *St&PR 91*
Sclafani, Accursio Peter 1947- *WhoE 91*
Sclafani, Frances Ann 1949- *WhoAm 90, WhoAmW 91*
Sclar, Charles Bertram 1925- *WhoAm 90*
Sclar, Stanley 1942- *St&PR 91*
Sclarow, Barbara Harriet 1946- *WhoAmW 91*
Sclater, James Stanley 1943- *IntWWM 90*
Sclater, John George 1940- *WhoAm 90*
Sclater, Ranald Douglas 1923- *St&PR 91, WhoAm 90*
Scliar, Moacyr 1937- *WorAu 1980 [port]*
Scobee, Dick 1939-1986 *BioIn 16*
Scobee, Francis R. 1939-1986 *BioIn 16*
Scobee, June *BioIn 16*
Scobell, George Albert 1930- *St&PR 91*
Scobey, Brad Preston 1957- *WhoSSW 91*
Scobey, Jack Leroy 1956- *BiDrAPA 89*
Scobey, Raphael G. 1918-1989 *BioIn 16*
Scobie, David G. 1947- *St&PR 91*
Scobie, Itha 1950- *WhoWrEP 89*
Scobie, Stephen *BioIn 16*
Scocozza, Matthew Vincent 1948- *WhoAm 90, WhoE 91, WhoEmL 91*
Scodari, Nicholas F. 1927- *St&PR 91*
Scoffier, Jean Pierre 1930- *WhoWor 91*
Scoffone, A. Vincent 1943- *St&PR 91, WhoAm 90*
Scoffone, Roy S. 1938- *St&PR 91*
Scofield, Gary Lee 1944- *St&PR 91*
Scofield, Gordon Lloyd 1925- *WhoAm 90*
Scofield, John *BioIn 16*
Scofield, John B 1925- *BiDrAPA 89*
Scofield, John D. 1908- *St&PR 91*
Scofield, Jonathan *ConAu 31NR*
Scofield, Martin 1945- *ConAu 132*
Scofield, Milton N. 1911- *St&PR 91*
Scofield, Oscar R. 1941- *St&PR 91*
Scofield, Paul 1922- *BioIn 16, WhoWor 91, WorAlBi*
Scofield, Penrod 1933- *SmATA 62*
Scofield, Richard *BioIn 16*
Scofield, Rupert Wallace 1949- *WhoE 91*
Scofield, Sandra Kay 1947- *WhoAmW 91*
Scofield, William B. 1928- *St&PR 91*
Scoggan, John Kenneth 1953- *St&PR 91*
Scoggin, Margaret Clara 1905-1968 *BioIn 16*
Scoggins, Don 1938- *ODwPR 91*
Scoggins, Roy T. *St&PR 91N*
Scoggins, Tracy *BioIn 16*
Scogland, William Lee 1949- *WhoEmL 91*
Scogna, Flavio Emilio 1956- *IntWWM 90*
Scola, David Anthony 1953- *BiDrAPA 89*
Scola, Ettore 1931- *ConTFT 8*
Scola, Ralph Joseph 1943- *WhoWor 91*
Scola, Richard J. 1942- *St&PR 91*
Scolari, Massimo 1943- *BioIn 16*
Scolari, Peter *BioIn 16*
Scoles, Clyde Sheldon 1949- *WhoAm 90*
Scoles, Eugene Francis 1921- *WhoAm 90*
Scollard, Cynthia McNutt 1954- *WhoAmW 91*
Scollard, Diane Louise 1945- *WhoAmW 91*
Scollard, Jeannette Reddish *WhoWor 91*
Scollard, Patrick John 1937- *St&PR 91, WhoAm 90*
Scollard, William E. 1926- *WhoAm 90*
Scolnick, Edward Mark 1940- *WhoAm 90, WhoE 91*
Sconfitto, Gerard Carl 1942- *WhoE 91*
Sconiers, Daryl 1958- *Ballpl 90*
Sconyers, Hal W. 1928- *St&PR 91*
Sconyers, Jeff 1935- *WhoE 91, WhoSSW 91*
Sconyo, Philip 1951- *WhoE 91*
Sconzert, Alan C *BiDrAPA 89*
Sconzo, Joseph *BiDrAPA 89*
Scoon, Paul 1935- *WhoWor 91*
Scopa, Frank J. 1923- *St&PR 91*
Scopaz, John M. 1948- *St&PR 91*
Scopaz, John Matthew 1948- *WhoAm 90*
Scopelianos, Margaret Anthou 1959- *WhoAmW 91*
Scopes, Gary Martin 1947- *WhoAm 90*
Scopes, John T. 1900-1970 *WorAlBi*
Scopinich-Buhler, Jill Lorie 1945- *WhoAmW 91, WhoEmL 91*
Scoppettone, Sandra 1936- *AuBYP 90, BioIn 16*
Scoppettone, Sandra Valerie 1936- *WhoWrEP 89*
Scordelis, Alexander Costicas 1923- *WhoAm 90*
Scordelis, Byron A. *BioIn 16*
Scordino, Felice 1933- *WhoWor 91*
Score, Herb 1933- *Ballpl 90*
Scoresby, William 1789-1857 *EncO&P 3*
Scorsese, Martin *BioIn 16*
Scorsese, Martin 1942- *WhoAm 90, WhoWor 91, WorAlBi*
Scorsine, John Magnus 1957- *WhoEmL 91*
Scorti, Michael Joseph 1941- *St&PR 91*
Scortia, Thomas N. 1926- *RGTwCSF*
Scorza, Carlo *BioIn 16*
Scorza, Manuel *BioIn 16*
Scorza, Manuel 1928-1983 *ConAu 131, HispWr 90*
Scorza, Thomas J. 1948- *ConAu 132*
Scot, Dred 1795?-1858 *WorAlBi*
Scot, Elizabeth 1729-1789 *FemiCLE*
Scotch, David Solomon 1938- *WhoE 91, WhoWor 91*
Scotford, David Matteson 1921- *WhoAm 90*
Scothorn, Donald L. 1929- *St&PR 91*
Scotland, Jay *AuBYP 90, MajTwCW*
Scotland, Jay 1932- *SmATA X [port]*
Scotland, Leslie Hubert 1943- *WhoWor 91*
Scott *ConAu 31NR*
Scott, Adrian *BioIn 16*
Scott, Alan James 1934- *WhoWor 91*
Scott, Alastair *ConAu 32NR*
Scott, Alastair Ian 1928- *WhoAm 90*
Scott, Alexander Robinson 1941- *WhoAm 90*
Scott, Alfred James 1913- *WhoAm 90*
Scott, Alice H. *WhoAm 90, WhoAmW 91*
Scott, Alicia 1810-1900 *FemiCLE*
Scott, Alistair John 1946- *WhoWor 91*
Scott, Alma Ham 1885-1972 *BioIn 16*
Scott, Amanda *WhoWrEP 89*
Scott, Amy Annette 1916- *WhoWor 91*
Scott, Amy Annette Holloway 1916- *WhoAmW 91*
Scott, Amy Holloway 1922- *WhoAmW 91*
Scott, Andrea Kay 1948- *WhoAmW 91, WhoWor 91*
Scott, Andrea Lynne 1962- *WhoAmW 91*
Scott, Andrew 1928- *St&PR 91, WhoAm 90*
Scott, Anita Irma 1949- *WhoAmW 91*
Scott, Ann 1926- *AuBYP 90*
Scott, Ann Besser 1933- *WhoAmW 91*
Scott, Ann Harvey 1939- *WhoAmW 91*
Scott, Ann Herbert 1926- *BioIn 16*
Scott, Anne Byrd Firor 1921- *WhoAm 90, WhoAmW 91*
Scott, Antoinette 1948- *WhoSSW 91*
Scott, Arden 1938- *WhoAmA 91, WhoE 91*
Scott, Arnold D. 1942- *St&PR 91*

Scott, Audrey Ebba 1935- WhoAm 90
Scott, B Nibbelink 1944- WhoAmA 91
Scott, Barbara Ann BioIn 16
Scott, Barbara Ann 1937- WhoAmW 91
Scott, Barbara Ann Heim 1959- WhoAmW 91
Scott, Barbara S. 1948- WhoWrEP 89
Scott, Basil Yearwood 1925- WhoE 91
Scott, Benjamin L. 1949- WhoAm 90
Scott, Bertha 1884-1965 WhoAmA 91N
Scott, Beth 1922- ConAu 132
Scott, Beth O'Briant 1960- WhoAmW 91
Scott, Betty Lea WhoE 91
Scott, Bill ConAu 132
Scott, Bill 1949- WhoE 91
Scott, Blaine W., III 1927- St&PR 91
Scott, Blaine Wahab, III 1927- WhoE 91, WhoWor 91
Scott, Bob Gerald 1938- St&PR 91, WhoAm 90
Scott, Bobby NewYTBS 90
Scott, Bradley Neil 1950- St&PR 91
Scott, Bradley Sterling 1948- WhoEmL 91, WhoWor 91
Scott, Brian Edward 1936- St&PR 91
Scott, Brian Walter 1935- WhoWor 91
Scott, Byron BioIn 16
Scott, C. A. 1865-1934 FemiCLE
Scott, C A 1940- WhoAmA 91
Scott, C Paul 1943- BiDrAPA 89
Scott, C. Paul 1943- WhoE 91
Scott, Campbell 1930- WhoAm 90, WhoAmA 91
Scott, Carol Seeley 1921- WhoAmW 91
Scott, Carole Eileen 1944- WhoSSW 91
Scott, Caroline 1784-1857 FemiCLE
Scott, Catherine Dorothy 1927- WhoAmW 91
Scott, Charles 1739-1813 BioIn 16
Scott, Charles 1933- St&PR 91
Scott, Charles David 1929- WhoAm 90
Scott, Charles Edward 1935- WhoAm 90
Scott, Charles F. BioIn 16
Scott, Charles J. 1946- BioIn 16
Scott, Charles Kennedy 1876-1965 PenDiMP
Scott, Charles Lewis 1924- WhoAm 90
Scott, Charles R. 1928- St&PR 91
Scott, Charles S. 1921-1989 BioIn 16
Scott, Charles Wesley 1932- WhoSSW 91
Scott, Charley 1923- WhoAm 90
Scott, Cheryl Faye 1947- WhoE 91
Scott, Christopher 1927- EncPaPR 91
Scott, Christopher 1930- WhoSSW 91
Scott, Christopher S. O'D. 1927- EncO&P 3
Scott, Clyde Eugene 1884-1959 WhoAmA 91N
Scott, Cora Annett AuBYP 90
Scott, Cyril 1879-1970 EncO&P 3
Scott, Daniel T. 1944- WhoE 91
Scott, Daniel Thomas 1944- St&PR 91
Scott, David 1806-1849 EncO&P 3
Scott, David Bytovetzski 1919- WhoAm 90
Scott, David Charles 1915- St&PR 91
Scott, David Francis 1946- IntWWM 90
Scott, David Henry Tudor 1948- WhoWor 91
Scott, David Howard 1956- WhoSSW 91
Scott, David Knight 1940- WhoAm 90, WhoWor 91
Scott, David McClure 1930- WhoAm 90
Scott, David Oscar 1952- WhoEmL 91
Scott, David Warren 1950- WhoSSW 91
Scott, David William 1940- WhoAm 90, WhoWor 91
Scott, David William 1943- WhoAm 90
Scott, David Winfield 1916- WhoAmA 91
Scott, Deborah Emont WhoAmA 91
Scott, Dixon 1881-1915 DcLB 98 [port]
Scott, Dolores H. 1927- WhoAmW 91
Scott, Donald Allison 1929- WhoAm 90
Scott, Donald John 1940- WhoAm 90
Scott, Donald L. 1933- St&PR 91
Scott, Donald P. 1934- St&PR 91
Scott, Donald Rector 1905- WhoAm 90
Scott, Donald Wayne 1946- St&PR 91
Scott, Donna J 1949- BiDrAPA 89
Scott, Dorothy Marie 1921- WhoAmW 91
Scott, Douglas Kenneth 1946- WhoSSW 91
Scott, Douglas Michael IntWWM 90
Scott, Douglas Walter 1949- WhoEmL 91
Scott, Duncan Campbell 1862-1947 DcLB 92 [port], WhNaAH
Scott, Ed 1874-1933 Ballpl 90
Scott, Eddie Elmer 1939- WhoSSW 91
Scott, Edgar BioIn 16
Scott, Edward Hofert 1929- St&PR 91
Scott, Edward Robert Dalton 1947- WhoEmL 91
Scott, Edward William, Jr. 1938- WhoAm 90
Scott, Eileen Diane 1953- WhoAmW 91
Scott, Eldred H. 1903- St&PR 91
Scott, Eleanor Meyer 1933- WhoAmW 91
Scott, Elizabeth 1708?-1776 FemiCLE
Scott, Elizabeth Ann 1951- WhoWrEP 89
Scott, Elmore Nimrod 1926- St&PR 91
Scott, Eric B. 1942- St&PR 91
Scott, Ernie BioIn 16
Scott, Eugene Lytton 1937- WhoE 91
Scott, Evelyn 1893-1963 BioAmW, BioIn 16, FemiCLE
Scott, Everett 1892-1960 Ballpl 90 [port]
Scott, Everett B. 1931- St&PR 91
Scott, F. R. 1899-1985 BioIn 16
Scott, Francis Reginald 1899-1985 BioIn 16
Scott, Frank Edward 1920- St&PR 91, WhoAm 90
Scott, Franklin Daniel 1901- WhoAm 90
Scott, Frederick George 1861-1944 DcLB 92 [port]
Scott, Frederick Isadore, Jr. 1927- WhoAm 90
Scott, Gail FemiCLE
Scott, Gail Elizabeth 1954- WhoAmW 91
Scott, Gary Kuper 1933- WhoAm 90
Scott, Gary LeRoy 1954- WhoEmL 91, WhoSSW 91
Scott, Gene Dwight 1942- St&PR 91
Scott, George 1944- Ballpl 90
Scott, George C. 1927- WorAlBi
Scott, George Campbell 1927- WhoAm 90
Scott, George Edmond 1924- WhoAm 90
Scott, George Ernest 1924- WhoAm 90
Scott, George Gallmann 1928- WhoSSW 91
Scott, George Gilbert 1811-1878 BioIn 16
Scott, George Hahn 1941- WhoAm 90
Scott, George Larkham, IV 1947- WhoEmL 91
Scott, Gerald Delano 1940- WhoSSW 91
Scott, Gerald Francis 1958- WhoEmL 91
Scott, Gerald Joseph 1947- WhoWrEP 89
Scott, Geraldine 1934- St&PR 91
Scott, Gertrude R. ODwPR 91
Scott, Glenn E. 1918- St&PR 91
Scott, Gloria 1927- WhoE 91
Scott, Gloria Dean Randle 1938- WhoAmW 91
Scott, Gloria R. BioIn 16
Scott, Gregory Atkins 1960- WhoSSW 91
Scott, Guthrie Michael 1907-1983 DcNaB 1981
Scott, Gwendolyn L BiDrAPA 89
Scott, H. Glen 1923- St&PR 91
Scott, Harold 1935- DrBlPA 90
Scott, Harold Bartlett 1917- WhoAm 90
Scott, Harold Bartlett, Jr. 1917- St&PR 91
Scott, Harold Lee, Jr. 1949- WhoAm 90
Scott, Harriett Anne 1819-1894 FemiCLE
Scott, Harvey H. 1912- St&PR 91
Scott, Harvey Whitefield 1838-1910 BioIn 16
Scott, Hazel 1920-1981 DrBlPA 90, OxCPMus
Scott, Helen G. BioIn 16
Scott, Henderson 1929- St&PR 91
Scott, Henry E 1900-1990 WhoAmA 91N
Scott, Henry Edwards, Jr. NewYTBS 90
Scott, Henry Lawrence 1908- WhoAm 90, WhoWor 91
Scott, Henry Thomas, Jr. 1927- WhoSSW 91
Scott, Henry William, Jr. 1916- WhoAm 90
Scott, Herbert Lee 1933- St&PR 91
Scott, Homer Albert, Jr. 1935- WhoAm 90
Scott, Honoria FemiCLE
Scott, Hope BioIn 16
Scott, Howard Winfield, Jr. 1935- WhoE 91
Scott, Hubert Randolph BiDrAPA 89
Scott, Hugh 1900- WhoAm 90
Scott, Hugh D., Jr. 1900- WorAlBi
Scott, Hugh Lenox 1853-1934 WhNaAH
Scott, Hugh Patrick 1938- WhoAm 90
Scott, I. B. 1930- WhoAm 90
Scott, Irene Feagin 1912- WhoAm 90
Scott, Isaac Alexander, Jr. 1934- WhoWor 91
Scott, Isadore Meyer 1912- WhoAm 90
Scott, J. D. 1931- WhoAm 90, WhoSSW 91
Scott, Jack 1892-1959 Ballpl 90
Scott, Jack Denton 1915- AuBYP 90, BioIn 16
Scott, Jack P. 1946- St&PR 91
Scott, Jack S. 1922-1987 TwCCr&M 91
Scott, James 1649-1685 BioIn 16
Scott, James 1922- MusmAFA
Scott, James Brown 1866-1943 BioIn 16
Scott, James C. 1948- St&PR 91
Scott, James Edward 1947- WhoSSW 91
Scott, James Frazier 1934- WhoWrEP 89
Scott, James Henry 1942- WhoE 91
Scott, James Hobbs, III 1938- St&PR 91
Scott, James Lawrence 1949- WhoSSW 91
Scott, James Lester, Jr. BiDrAPA 89
Scott, James M. 1934- St&PR 91
Scott, James Owen 1936- St&PR 91
Scott, James Raymond 1937- WhoAm 90
Scott, James Robert 1943- St&PR 91
Scott, James Sylvester 1885-1938 OxCPMus
Scott, James Thomas BiDrAPA 89
Scott, James White 1926- WhoAm 90
Scott, Jane 1931- BioIn 16
Scott, Jane Elizabeth 1962- WhoSSW 91
Scott, Jane Harrington 1931- WhoWrEP 89
Scott, Jane M. FemiCLE
Scott, Janice Gail 1949- WhoEmL 91
Scott, Janice Marie 1955- WhoAmW 91
Scott, Janice Veronica 1958- WhoAmW 91
Scott, Jay 1949- WhoAm 90
Scott, Jeffrey Emerson 1943- WhoE 91
Scott, Jennifer N. S. 1960- WhoAmW 91
Scott, Jerod Luke 1958- BiDrAPA 89
Scott, Jerry Earl 1955- WhoSSW 91
Scott, Jim NewAgMG
Scott, Jim 1888-1957 Ballpl 90
Scott, Joan Wallach 1941- WhoAmW 91
Scott, John 1907- WhoAmA 91
Scott, John 1950- WhoAmA 91
Scott, John 1956- PenDiMP
Scott, John Andrew 1952- WhoAm 90
Scott, John Anthony 1916- AuBYP 90
Scott, John Arthur Guillum 1910-1983 DcNaB 1981
Scott, John Beldon 1946- WhoAmA 91
Scott, John Brooks 1931- WhoAm 90
Scott, John Campbell 1949- WhoEmL 91
Scott, John Carver, Jr. 1918- WhoE 91
Scott, John Clark, Jr. 1953- WhoE 91
Scott, John E. 1939- St&PR 91
Scott, John Edward 1920- WhoAm 90
Scott, John Edward Smith 1936- WhoAm 90, WhoWor 91
Scott, John Fredrik 1936- WhoAmA 91
Scott, John Gavin 1956- IntWWM 90
Scott, John Glenn 1948- WhoSSW 91
Scott, John J 1905- BiDrAPA 89
Scott, John Joseph 1950- WhoEmL 91
Scott, John Lenard 1921- WhoAm 90, WhoE 91, WhoWor 91
Scott, John Roland 1937- St&PR 91, WhoWor 91
Scott, John T. 1919- St&PR 91
Scott, John Tarrell 1940- WhoAmA 91
Scott, John Troy 1947- WhoE 91
Scott, John W. 1908- St&PR 91
Scott, John Walter 1823-1899 AmLegL
Scott, John Walter 1919- WhoAm 90
Scott, John William 1935- WhoAm 90
Scott, Jonathan 1914- WhoAmA 91
Scott, Jonathan 1958- ConAu 132
Scott, Jonathan L. 1930- St&PR 91
Scott, Jonathan LaVon 1930- WhoAm 90
Scott, Jonnie Melia Dean 1957- WhoWrEP 89
Scott, Joseph AuBYP 90
Scott, Joseph M. 1945- St&PR 91
Scott, Joseph Vernon 1926- St&PR 91
Scott, Joyce Alaine 1943- WhoAm 90
Scott, Judith Johnson 1948- WhoEmL 91
Scott, Julius S., Jr. 1925- WhoAm 90
Scott, K. BiDWomA
Scott, Karen Ann 1957- WhoAmW 91
Scott, Karyn G. 1964- ODwPR 91
Scott, Kathleen A. ODwPR 91
Scott, Kathleen Annette 1943- WhoAmW 91
Scott, Kathleen Mueller 1945- St&PR 91
Scott, Keith Wesley BiDrAPA 89
Scott, Kem Wayne 1948- St&PR 91
Scott, Kenneth C. 1940- St&PR 91
Scott, Kenneth Elsner 1926- WhoAm 90
Scott, Kenneth Eugene 1928- WhoAm 90
Scott, Kenneth Pleasant, Jr. 1946- WhoSSW 91
Scott, Kenneth Robert 1939- St&PR 91
Scott, Kenneth W BiDrAPA 89
Scott, Kerrigan Davis 1941- WhoSSW 91, WhoWor 91
Scott, Larry WhoSSW 91
Scott, Larry Edwin 1948- St&PR 91
Scott, Larry Zant 1952- WhoSSW 91
Scott, Lary R. 1936- WhoAm 90
Scott, Lawrence Rowe 1956- WhoEmL 91
Scott, Lawrence Vernon 1917- WhoAm 90
Scott, Lee Hansen 1926- WhoAm 90
Scott, Lenore AuBYP 90
Scott, Lenore Dorsen 1940- WhoAmW 91
Scott, Leslie 1921-1969 DrBlPA 90
Scott, Leslie 1961- WhoWor 91
Scott, Linda Lorraine 1948- WhoSSW 91
Scott, Lindsay 1960- BioIn 16
Scott, Lois Alison 1960- WhoAmW 91
Scott, Louis Edward 1923- St&PR 91, WhoAm 90
Scott, Louis R. 1927- St&PR 91
Scott, Lurell Vaden 1942- St&PR 91
Scott, Lynn Edward 1933- St&PR 91
Scott, M. Lee 1910- St&PR 91
Scott, Malora Courtney 1949- WhoAmW 91
Scott, Marcia 1931- BiDrAPA 89
Scott, Margaret Louise 1925- WhoAmW 91
Scott, Margaret Simon 1934- WhoAmW 91
Scott, Marian 1906- WhoAmA 91
Scott, Marianne Florence 1928- WhoAm 90, WhoAmW 91
Scott, Mark E. 1953- WhoEmL 91
Scott, Martha 1914- WorAlBi
Scott, Martha F 1916- WhoAmA 91
Scott, Martha Sue 1961- WhoAmW 91
Scott, Mary 1751-1793 FemiCLE
Scott, Mary 1752?-1793 BioIn 16
Scott, Mary Davies 1944- WhoAmW 91
Scott, Mary Elizabeth 1951- WhoAmW 91
Scott, Mary Jane Gomez 1944- WhoE 91
Scott, Mary Jane W 1949- ConAu 129
Scott, Mary Shy 1929- WhoAmW 91
Scott, Maud BioIn 16
Scott, Maurice FitzGerald 1924- WhoWor 91
Scott, Meckinley WhoSSW 91
Scott, Michael 1175?-1234? EncO&P 3
Scott, Michael 1905-1989 AnObit 1989
Scott, Michael 1907-1983 ConAu 130
Scott, Michael 1924-1989 BioIn 16, ConAu 129
Scott, Michael 1952- BioIn 16
Scott, Michael David 1963- WhoE 91
Scott, Michael Dennis 1945- WhoAm 90, WhoEmL 91
Scott, Michael Ray 1948- WhoEmL 91
Scott, Michael Warren 1955- WhoAm 90
Scott, Mickey 1947- Ballpl 90
Scott, Mike 1955- Ballpl 90, WorAlBi
Scott, Mimi Koblenz 1940- WhoE 91
Scott, Molly NewAgMG
Scott, Morgan E BiDrAPA 89
Scott, Munroe 1927- ConAu 130
Scott, Nancy Ellen 1960- WhoAmW 91, WhoE 91, WhoWor 91
Scott, Nathan Alexander, Jr. 1925- WhoAm 90
Scott, Neil R 1936- BiDrAPA 89
Scott, Nellie Chavarria 1956- WhoAmW 91
Scott, Oz 1950?- DrBlPA 90
Scott, Patricia B.R. 1949- BiDrAPA 89
Scott, Patricia Jean 1946- WhoEmL 91
Scott, Patricia Jeanne 1942- WhoWrEP 89
Scott, Patrick J 1848-1899 DcCanB 12
Scott, Paul 1920-1978 ConAu 33NR, ConLC 60 [port], MajTwCW
Scott, Peggy Joyce 1949- WhoSSW 91
Scott, Pete 1898-1953 Ballpl 90
Scott, Peter 1909-1989 AnObit 1989, ConAu 129
Scott, Peter 1938-1989 BioIn 16
Scott, Peter Bryan 1947- WhoEmL 91
Scott, Peter Francis 1927- WhoAm 90
Scott, Peter Hamilton 1936- St&PR 91
Scott, Peter John 1920- St&PR 91
Scott, Peter L. St&PR 91
Scott, Peter Markham 1909-1989 BioIn 16
Scott, Philip Leslie 1958- BiDrAPA 89
Scott, Ralph 1927- BioIn 16
Scott, Ralph C. 1921- WhoAm 90, WhoWor 91
Scott, Ralph D. BioIn 16
Scott, Randall Abell BiDrAPA 89
Scott, Randolph 1898-1987 BioIn 16, WorAlBi
Scott, Randolph 1929- WhoSSW 91
Scott, Raymond 1910- OxCPMus
Scott, Raymond Peter William 1924- WhoAm 90
Scott, Richard Albert, Jr. 1957- WhoE 91
Scott, Richard E. 1942- St&PR 91
Scott, Richard Lee 1953- WhoSSW 91
Scott, Robert Allyn 1939- WhoAm 90, WhoE 91, WhoWor 91
Scott, Robert Charles 1943- BiDrAPA 89
Scott, Robert Cooper 1930- WhoAm 90
Scott, Robert Cortez 1947- WhoSSW 91
Scott, Robert D., III 1942 St&PR 91
Scott, Robert Edwin, Jr. 1940- St&PR 91
Scott, Robert F BiDrAPA 89
Scott, Robert F. 1868-1912 WorAlBi
Scott, Robert Heatlie 1905-1982 DcNaB 1981
Scott, Robert Hugh 1943- WhoE 91
Scott, Robert Kent 1936- WhoAm 90
Scott, Robert Lane 1922- WhoAm 90
Scott, Robert Lee 1908- AuBYP 90
Scott, Robert Lee 1928- WhoAm 90
Scott, Robert Lee, Jr. 1908- WhoAm 90
Scott, Robert Montgomery 1929- WhoAm 90, WhoAmA 91, WhoE 91, WhoWor 91
Scott, Robert Willard 1940- WhoAm 90, WhoE 91
Scott, Roberta Lee 1942- WhoE 91
Scott, Roderic MacDonald 1916- WhoAm 90
Scott, Rodney 1953- Ballpl 90
Scott, Rognvald Johnston 1933- WhoWor 91
Scott, Roland Boyd 1909- WhoAm 90, WhoWor 91
Scott, Ronald Bodley 1906-1982 DcNaB 1981
Scott, Ronald Fraser 1929- WhoAm 90
Scott, Ronald H. 1932- St&PR 91
Scott, Ronald John 1936- WhoE 91

Scott, Roney TwCCr&M 91
Scott, Ronnie 1927- OxCPMus
Scott, Rose 1847-1925 FemiCLE
Scott, Roy 1935- WhoWor 91
Scott, Roy A. 1940- St&PR 91
Scott, Russell William 1957- WhoE 91
Scott, Sally Elisabeth 1948- AuBYP 90
Scott, Sam 1940- WhoAmA 91
Scott, Sandra Smith 1942- WhoSSW 91
Scott, Sandy 1943- WhoAmA 91
Scott, Sarah 1723-1795 BioIn 16, FemiCLE
Scott, Sharon Kay 1940- St&PR 91
Scott, Sheila 1927-1988 AnObit 1988, BioIn 16
Scott, Sherry Lee 1950- WhoAmW 91
Scott, Sidney Buford 1933- WhoSSW 91
Scott, Stanley DeForest 1926- WhoE 91
Scott, Stanley S. ODwPR 91
Scott, Stanley Southall 1933- WhoAm 90
Scott, Steve BioIn 16
Scott, Steven Donald 1941- WhoAm 90
Scott, Stuart John 1949- IntWWM 90
Scott, Stuart Nash 1906- WhoAm 90
Scott, Susan Ellen 1964- WhoAmW 91
Scott, Susan Jane Boyle 1947- WhoAmW 91
Scott, Susan Rice 1942- WhoAmW 91
Scott, Sylvia Rachel Jeanne 1949- WhoAmW 91
Scott, Taryn WhoWrEP 89
Scott, Terri Renae 1959- WhoAmW 91
Scott, Terry Lee 1950- WhoSSW 91
Scott, Theodore R. 1924- WhoAm 90
Scott, Thomas Clevenger 1936- WhoAm 90
Scott, Thomas Emerson, Jr. 1948- WhoAm 90, WhoSSW 91
Scott, Thomas Seaton 1826-1895 DcCanB 12
Scott, Thomas Wright 1948- WhoAm 90
Scott, Timothy Dwight 1950- St&PR 91
Scott, Timothy Leighton 1944- St&PR 91
Scott, Tom BioIn 16
Scott, Tom Keck 1931- WhoAm 90
Scott, Tom William 1902-1988 BioIn 16
Scott, Tony NewAgMG
Scott, Tony 1951- Ballpl 90
Scott, Valerie Don 1949- WhoAmW 91
Scott, Vanessa 1955- IntWWM 90
Scott, Verne Harry 1924- WhoAm 90
Scott, Victor Richard 1950- St&PR 91
Scott, W Clifford 1903- BiDrAPA 89
Scott, W. N. ConAu 132
Scott, W. Russell, Jr. 1937- St&PR 91
Scott, Waldron 1929- WhoAm 90, WhoE 91
Scott, Walt 1894-1970 EncACom
Scott, Walter 1771-1832 DcLB 93 [port], EncPaPR 91, WorAlBi
Scott, Walter 1919- WhoAmA 91
Scott, Walter Coke 1919- WhoAm 90
Scott, Walter Decker 1915- WhoAm 90
Scott, Walter Dill 1931- WhoAm 90
Scott, Walter Gerard, Jr. 1941- St&PR 91
Scott, Walter M. 1906-1989 ConTFT 8
Scott, Walter Neil 1935- WhoE 91
Scott, Walter Ray 1913- WhoWrEP 89
Scott, Walter Winfield 1867- AmLegL
Scott, Warwick TwCCr&M 91
Scott, Wendell NewYTBS 90
Scott, Will 1921- St&PR 91
Scott, Willard BioIn 16
Scott, Willard Herman 1934- WhoAm 90
Scott, William NewYTBS 90 [port]
Scott, William 1913-1989 AnObit 1989, BioIn 16
Scott, William Alexander 1902-1934 BioIn 16
Scott, William Alexander, Jr. 1943- WhoSSW 91
Scott, William Bell 1811-1890 EncO&P 3
Scott, William Beverley 1917- WhoAm 90
Scott, William Clement, III 1934- WhoAm 90
Scott, William Coryell 1920- WhoAm 90
Scott, William Fred 1953- WhoAm 90, WhoSSW 91
Scott, William Gavin 1925- WhoAm 90
Scott, William H. BioIn 16
Scott, William Henry 1921- ConAu 132
Scott, William Joseph, Jr. 1945- WhoEmL 91
Scott, William Lloyd 1915- WhoAm 90
Scott, William M W BiDrAPA 89
Scott, William N 1923- ConAu 132
Scott, William P. 1930- St&PR 91
Scott, William Richard 1932- WhoAm 90
Scott, William Thomas BioIn 16, NewYTBS 90
Scott, William W., Jr. 1944- St&PR 91
Scott, Winfield 1786-1866 WhNaAH, WorAlBi
Scott Brown, Denise 1931- BioIn 16
Scott-Conner, Carol Elizabeth Hoffman 1946- WhoSSW 91
Scott-Drennan, Lynne Ellen 1944- WhoWrEP 89
Scott Fernandez, M. Cristina 1952- WhoAmW 91
Scott-Finan, Nancy Isabella 1949- WhoAmW 91
Scott-Gibson, Herbert Nathaniel 1928-1981 WhoAmA 91N
Scott-Heron, Gil 1949- DrBIPA 90
Scott-Johnson, Barbara Ann 1949- WhoAmW 91
Scott-Kilvert, Ian 1917-1989 AnObit 1989
Scott-Maxwell, Florida Pier 1884-1979 BioIn 16
Scott-McBride, Nancy Forsyth 1940- WhoWrEP 89
Scott-Wood, George 1903-1978 OxCPMus
Scotte, Brandon WhoWrEP 89
Scotti, Antonio 1866-1936 PenDiMP
Scotti, Ciro 1985-1987 BioIn 16
Scotti, Diana S. 1962- WhoAmW 91
Scotto, Frank 1911-1989 BioIn 16
Scotto, Joseph V. 1934- St&PR 91
Scotto, Laura Frances 1962- WhoAmW 91
Scotto, Renata 1933- IntWWM 90, PenDiMP, WorAlBi
Scotto, Renata 1935- WhoAm 90, WhoWor 91
Scotto, Vincent 1876-1952 OxCPMus
Scotton, Bruce Warren BiDrAPA 89
Scoular, Robert Frank 1942- WhoAm 90, WhoWor 91
Scourby, Alexander 1913-1985 WorAlBi
Scouten, Arthur Hawley 1910- WhoWor 91
Scouten, William Henry 1942- WhoAm 90
Scovel, Harry 1869-1905 BioIn 16
Scovel, Henry Sylvester 1869-1905 BioIn 16
Scovell, Brian 1935- ConAu 130
Scovell, E. J. 1907- BioIn 16, FemiCLE
Scovell, Edith Joy 1907- BioIn 16
Scovil, Doug BioIn 16
Scovil, H. Raymond 1925- WhoE 91
Scovil, Samuel K. 1923- St&PR 91
Scovil, Samuel Kingston 1923- WhoAm 90
Scovill, Mark Allen 1958- WhoSSW 91
Scovill, Polly DcCanB 12
Scoville, James Griffin 1940- WhoAm 90
Scoville, John J. 1935- St&PR 91
Scoville, Jonathan Armstrong 1937- WhoAmA 91
Scoville, Ralph Dalton 1946- BiDrAPA 89
Scoville, Ronald Robert 1927- St&PR 91
Scoville, Wayne W. 1937- St&PR 91
Scovotti, Jeanette 1936- IntWWM 90
Scowcroft, Brent BioIn 16
Scowcroft, Brent 1925- NewYTBS 90
Scowcroft, Jerome Chilwell 1947- WhoEmL 91
Scowcroft, John A. 1955- St&PR 91
Scoza, Robert H. 1947- St&PR 91
Scozzaro, Phillip 1933- BiDrAPA 89
Scrafano, C. J. BioIn 16
Scragg, George Henry, Jr. 1934- WhoSSW 91
Scragg, Thomas William 1940- IntWWM 90, WhoWor 91
Scragg, William W. 1941- St&PR 91
Scranton, George W. 1811-1861 WorAlBi
Scranton, Robert J. 1940- St&PR 91
Scranton, William Maxwell 1921- St&PR 91, WhoAm 90
Scranton, William W. 1917- WorAlBi
Scrase, Arthur 1911-1988 BioIn 16
Scremin, Anthony James 1941- WhoSSW 91
Screpetis, Dennis 1930- WhoE 91, WhoWor 91
Screvane, Paul Rogers 1914- WhoAm 90
Screven, James Odingsell 1925- WhoAm 90
Screven, William 1629-1713 BioIn 16
Scriabin, Aleksandr 1872-1915 WorAlBi
Scribante, Adrian J. 1930- St&PR 91
Scriber, Betty Pratt 1953- WhoAmW 91
Scribner, Barbara Colvin 1926- WhoAm 90
Scribner, Belding Hibbard 1921- WhoAm 90
Scribner, Bobette Gilpatric 1947- WhoAmW 91
Scribner, Brenda Carol BiDrAPA 89
Scribner, Charles 1821-1871 WorAlBi
Scribner, Charles, III 1951- WhoAm 90, WhoAmA 91
Scribner, Charles, Jr. BioIn 16
Scribner, Charles, Jr. 1921- WhoAm 90
Scribner, Fred Clark, Jr. 1908- St&PR 91, WhoAm 90
Scribner, Kimball 1917- SmATA 63 [port]
Scribner, Margaret Ellen 1948- WhoEmL 91
Scribner, Ralph Warren 1928- St&PR 91
Scribner, Richard Orestes 1936- WhoAm 90
Scribner, Ronald Kent 1948- WhoSSW 91
Scriggins, Larry Palmer 1936- WhoAm 90
Scrignar, Chester B 1934- BiDrAPA 89
Scrim, Russel C. 1918- St&PR 91
Scrimgeour, James Richard 1938- WhoWrEP 89
Scrimshaw, Nevin Stewart 1918- WhoAm 90
Scrimsher, Lila Gravatt 1897-1974 AuBYP 90
Scripps, Charles E. 1920- St&PR 91
Scripps, Charles Edward 1920- WhoAm 90
Scripps, E. W. 1854-1926 BioIn 16, WorAlBi
Scripps, Edward Willis BioIn 16
Scripps, Edward Wyllis 1854-1926 BioIn 16
Scripps, Edward Wyllis 1909- WhoAm 90
Scripps, Ellen Browning 1836-1932 BioAmW, BioIn 16, WorAlBi
Scripps, James Edmund 1835-1906 BioIn 16
Scripps, John P. 1912-1989 BioIn 16
Scripps, Virginia BioIn 16
Scritsmier, Jerome Lorenzo 1925- WhoWor 91
Scriven, L E, II 1931- WhoAm 90
Scriven, Michael John 1928- EncO&P 3, EncPaPR 91
Scrivener, Michael 1948- ConAu 130
Scrivener, Noel Bernard 1946- WhoWor 91
Scrivens, Dilwyn 1938- WhoWor 91
Scriver, Charles Robert 1930- WhoAm 90
Scriver, Robert Macfie 1914- WhoAm 90, WhoAmA 91
Scrivner, Barbara E. 1931- WhoAmW 91
Scro, Anthony Francis 1943- WhoE 91
Scro, Jerome R. St&PR 91
Scroeder, Darrell H. 1923- St&PR 91
Scroggie, Lucy Ethelyn 1935- WhoAmW 91
Scroggie, Wayne Lee 1949- WhoWor 91
Scroggins, Carol D. 1933- St&PR 91
Scroggins, Carol Dean 1933- WhoSSW 91
Scroggins, Deborah Lane 1961- WhoAm 90
Scroggins, Nancy E.J. 1950- WhoAmW 91
Scroggins, Richard Muir 1932- St&PR 91
Scruby, Brian C. ODwPR 91
Scruggs, Betty Joyce Clenney 1928- WhoSSW 91
Scruggs, Charles G. 1923- WhoAm 90
Scruggs, Earl 1924- OxCPMus
Scruggs, Earl Eugene 1924- WhoAm 90
Scruggs, Edwin Noel, Jr. 1953- WhoSSW 91
Scruggs, Ima Sue 1936- St&PR 91
Scruggs, Jack Gilbert 1930- St&PR 91
Scruggs, Jan C. BioIn 16
Scruggs, Jennifer Juliette 1966- WhoAmW 91
Scruggs, John Dudley 1911- WhoAm 90
Scruggs, John Floyd 1955- WhoE 91
Scruggs, Kenneth Mason 1941- WhoSSW 91
Scruggs, Mollie Sue 1957- WhoAmW 91
Scruggs, Paul Cecil 1937- WhoSSW 91
Scruggs, Richard T. 1915- St&PR 91
Scruggs, Richard Turner, Jr. 1948- WhoSSW 91
Scruggs, Steven Dennis 1946- WhoE 91
Scruggs, William Lindsay 1836-1912 BioIn 16
Scrugham, Nancy Lee 1954- WhoAmW 91
Scruitsky, Robert Lee 1963- WhoE 91
Scruton, George Stephen 1926- St&PR 91
Scruton, Irene E. 1955- St&PR 91
Scrutton, Keith Robert 1932- St&PR 91
Scucchi, Robie, Jr 1944- WhoAmA 91
Scucci, Mary Kay 1958- WhoAmW 91
Scudamore, John 1542-1623 BioIn 16
Scudamore, Pauline 1936- ConAu 129
Scudder, David Witherspoon 1936- St&PR 91
Scudder, Edward Wallace, Jr. 1911- WhoAm 90
Scudder, Geoffrey George Edgar 1934- WhoAm 90
Scudder, Ida Sophia 1870-1960 BioAmW
Scudder, Janet 1869-1940 BiDWomA
Scudder, Lance Alan 1965- WhoSSW 91
Scudder, Lorraine Helen 1952- WhoEmL 91
Scudder, Richard B. 1913- WhoAm 90
Scudder, Thayer 1930- WhoAm 90
Scudder, Townsend 1900-1988 BioIn 16
Scudder, Vida Dutton 1861-1954 EncAL
Scudder, Virgil E. ODwPR 91
Scuderi, Filomena Perone 1930- WhoAmW 91
Scudery, Madeleine de 1607-1701 EncCoWW, FemiCLE
Scudieri, Lorraine Alberto 1940- WhoAmW 91, WhoE 91
Sculati, Marvin A. 1932- St&PR 91
Sculfort, Maurice Charles 1925- WhoAm 90
Scull, Alvis J 1916- BiDrAPA 89
Scull, Andrew 1947- ConAu 33NR
Scull, Dorothy Mae 1948- WhoAmW 91
Scull, Sandra Sue 1953- WhoE 91
Sculley, David W. 1946- WhoAm 90, WhoE 91
Sculley, John BioIn 16
Sculley, John 1939- St&PR 91, WhoAm 90, WorAlBi
Sculley, Mary E. 1952- St&PR 91
Sculley, Max Dean 1943- WhoSSW 91
Sculley, Patrick David 1947- WhoSSW 91
Sculley, Sheryl BioIn 16
Scullin, Frederick James, Jr. 1939- WhoAm 90
Scullin, Leo BioIn 16
Scullion, Annette Murphy 1926- WhoAmW 91
Scullion, William Joseph 1932- St&PR 91
Scully, Annie Z. 1960- WhoE 91
Scully, Geoffrey Ballenger 1959- St&PR 91
Scully, James Henry, Jr. 1944- BiDrAPA 89
Scully, James Joseph 1937- WhoWrEP 89
Scully, John A. 1931- St&PR 91
Scully, John C. 1932- St&PR 91
Scully, John Carroll 1932- WhoAm 90, WhoE 91
Scully, John Edward 1943- St&PR 91
Scully, John Pendleton 1914- WhoE 91
Scully, John Robert 1949- WhoEmL 91, WhoWor 91
Scully, John Thomas 1931- WhoAm 90
Scully, Julia BioIn 16
Scully, Monya Frances 1921- WhoE 91
Scully, Paul Glenn 1924- St&PR 91
Scully, Robert G. 1926- St&PR 91
Scully, Roger Tehan 1948- WhoE 91, WhoWor 91
Scully, Sean 1945?- BioIn 16
Scully, Sean Paul 1945- WhoAm 90
Scully, Tamara Annalora 1957- WhoAmW 91
Scully, Vin 1927- Ballpl 90, WorAlBi
Scully, Vincent Edward 1927- WhoAm 90
Scully, Vincent Joseph 1920- BioIn 16
Scullywest, Elizabeth Mary 1953- WhoAmW 91
Sculthorpe, Peter 1929- PenDiMP A
Sculthorpe, Peter Joshua 1929- IntWWM 90, WhoWor 91
Sculti, Leon 1934- St&PR 91
Scuralli, Joseph P. St&PR 91
Scurci, Daniel James 1925- St&PR 91
Scurlock, Arch Chilton 1920- St&PR 91, WhoAm 90, WhoSSW 91
Scurlock, John C. WhoSSW 91
Scurlock, Robert Edward 1933- St&PR 91
Scurria, Philip Louis 1959- BiDrAPA 89
Scurry, Richardson Gano 1938- St&PR 91
Scurry, Richardson Gano, Jr. 1938- WhoAm 90
Scurry, Rod 1956- Ballpl 90
Scutchfield, F. Douglas 1942- WhoAm 90
Scutt, Gerald Arthur 1929- St&PR 91
Szech, Marilyn J. 1948- St&PR 91
Seaberg, Ladd M. 1946- St&PR 91
Seaberg, Steve 1930- WhoAmA 91
Seaberry, Macarthur 1948- WhoSSW 91
Seaborg, David Michael 1949- WhoEmL 91
Seaborg, Glenn E. WhoAm 90
Seaborg, Glenn T. 1912- St&PR 91, WorAlBi
Seaborg, Glenn Theodore 1912- WhoAm 90, WhoWor 91
Seaborn, J.L. 1923- St&PR 91
Seaborn, John Robert 1940- St&PR 91
Seaborn, Louis Augustus, Jr. 1932- St&PR 91
Seabourn, Bert Dail 1931- WhoAmA 91
Seabourn, Connie 1951- WhoAmA 91
Seabourn, Danny 1951- St&PR 91
Seabra-Veiga, Lisa Ruth 1956- WhoAmW 91
Seabrook, John Martin 1917- St&PR 91, WhoAm 90
Seabrook, William 1886-1945 EncO&P 3
Seabrooks, John R. 1947- St&PR 91
Seabrooks, Nettie Harris 1934- WhoAmW 91
Seaburg, Lisa S. 1956- WhoAmW 91
Seaburg, Paul Allen 1934- WhoAm 90
Seabury, Candi Pynes 1947- WhoAmW 91
Seabury, Francis William 1868-1946 AmLegL
Seabury, Paul NewYTBS 90
Seabury, Paul 1923-1990 ConAu 132
Seabury, Richard Williams, III 1937- St&PR 91
Seabury, Samuel 1729-1796 EncCRAm
Seabury, Samuel 1801-1872 BioIn 16
Seacole, Mary 1805-1881 FemiCLE
Seacrest, Joe Rushton 1920- WhoAm 90
Seader, Junior DeVere 1927- WhoAm 90
Seaga, Edward P. G. BioIn 16
Seaga, Edward Philip George 1930- WhoWor 91
Seagal, Harry 1922- BiDrAPA 89
Seager, Daniel Albert 1920- WhoAm 90
Seager, Donald Alfred 1947- WhoAm 90
Seager, Samuel Nathan 1928- St&PR 91
Seager, Stephen Brett BiDrAPA 89

›agle, Victor Ryland 1945- *WhoSSW 91*
›agondollar, Lewis Worth 1920- *WhoAm 90*
›agram, Norman Meredith 1934- *WhoAm 90*
›agrave, James Edward 1949- *St&PR 91*
›agrave, Richard Augustus 1928- *St&PR 91*
›agraves, Marilyn Kaye 1951- *WhoAmW 91, WhoSSW 91*
›al, Arlene B. 1946- *WhoAmW 91*
›al, B.G. 1934- *St&PR 91*
›al, Gregory Scott *BiDrAPA 89*
›al, John Charles 1950- *WhoAm 90*
›al, John S., Jr. 1944- *WhoE 91, WhoWor 91*
›al, Joseph K 1955- *BiDrAPA 89*
›al, Leo W., Jr. 1924- *St&PR 91*
›al, Lester Paul 1932- *St&PR 91*
›al, Michael 1930- *WhoWor 91*
›al, Robert Hutcheson 1923- *St&PR 91, WhoSSW 91*
›al, Thomas F. 1953- *St&PR 91*
›ale, Arthur L *BiDrAPA 89*
›ale, Ervin *BioIn 16*
›ale, Ervin 1910?-1990 *ConAu 130*
›ale, J. William 1943- *St&PR 91*
›ale, James Lawrence, Jr. 1949- *WhoSSW 91, WhoWor 91*
›ale, Jan Epton 1939- *WhoWrEP 89*
›ale, Joseph Lloyd 1919- *WhoWrEP 89*
›ale, Thomas M. 1923- *St&PR 91*
›ale, William Edward 1941- *BioIn 16, WhoAm 90*
›ale, William Tyler 1957- *WhoE 91*
›ales, Franklyn *DrBlPA 90*
›ales, Sugar Ray *BioIn 16*
›all, Stephen Albert 1940- *WhoAm 90*
›alock, Ronald F. 1934- *St&PR 91*
›als and Crofts *EncPR&S 89*
›als, Betty 1944- *WhoAmW 91*
›als, Dan *WhoNeCM [port]*
›als, Ernest C. 1937- *St&PR 91*
›als, Henry Chaim 1924- *St&PR 91*
›als, J. Dennis 1942- *WhoE 91*
›als, Jim 1941- *EncPR&S 89*
›als, Linda 1951- *WhoAmW 91*
›als, Ryan Brown 1920- *WhoSSW 91*
›als, Woodrow 1917- *WhoAm 90*
›alth 1788?-1866 *WhNaAH*
›aly, Albert Henry 1917- *WhoAm 90, WhoWor 91*
›aly, George 1835-1901 *BioIn 16*
›aly, George Paul 1926- *St&PR 91*
›aly, Joan Rice 1942- *BiDrAPA 89*
›aly, John Roland *BiDrAPA 89*
›aly, Ruby *WhoWrEP 89*
›aly, Tom 1909- *WhoAm 90*
›aman, Alfred Barrett 1945- *WhoE 91*
›aman, Alfred Jarvis 1912- *WhoAm 90*
›aman, Alonzo D *EncABHB 4*
›aman, Augusta 1879-1950 *AuBYP 90*
›aman, Barbara 1935- *WhoAm 90*
›aman, Byron James 1923- *St&PR 91, WhoAm 90*
›aman, Catherine Hawes Coleman 1923- *WhoSSW 91*
›aman, Charles *BiDrAPA 89*
›aman, Cheryl 1945- *BiDrAPA 89*
›aman, Christopher 1942- *IntWWM 90, PenDiMP, WhoWor 91*
›aman, Daryl Kenneth 1922- *St&PR 91, WhoAm 90*
›aman, David M. *AuBYP 90*
›aman, Dick *BioIn 16*
›aman, Donald Peter 1922- *SpyFic*
›aman, Donald Roy 1925- *St&PR 91, WhoAm 90*
›aman, Drake F *WhoAmA 91*
›aman, Elizabeth C. *BioAmW*
›aman, Elwood Armstrong 1916- *BioIn 16*
›aman, Gerald Roberts 1934- *IntWWM 90, WhoWor 91*
›aman, Gideon *BiDrAPA 89*
›aman, Irving, Jr. 1923- *St&PR 91, WhoAm 90*
›aman, James A. 186-?- *AmLegL*
›aman, James David 1930- *St&PR 91*
›aman, James Richard 1941- *St&PR 91*
›aman, Janet W. 1934- *St&PR 91*
›aman, John Gates 1919- *WhoSSW 91*
›aman, Peter B. 1952- *St&PR 91*
›aman, Peter Bailey 1951- *WhoE 91*
›aman, Richard Norman 1949- *WhoEmL 91*
›aman, Robert Lee 1942- *WhoAm 90*
›aman, William Bernard 1917- *WhoAm 90*
›aman, William Casper 1925- *WhoAm 90*
›amands, Craig Neil *BiDrAPA 89*
›amans, Andrew *BioIn 16*
›amans, Andrew Charles 1937- *WhoE 91, WhoWrEP 89*
›amans, Beverly Benson 1928- *WhoAmA 91*
›amans, Robert C., Jr. 1918- *St&PR 91*
Seamans, Robert Channing, Jr. 1918- *WhoAm 90*
Seamans, William 1925- *WhoAm 90*
Seames, Clarann *WhoAmA 91*
Seami *EncJap*
Seamon, Edward 1932- *ConTFT 8 [port]*
Seanor, Susan Tanner 1961- *WhoSSW 91*
Seapker, Janet Kay 1947- *WhoAmW 91, WhoSSW 91*
Sear, Morey Leonard 1929- *WhoAm 90, WhoSSW 91*
Searage, Ray 1955- *Ballpl 90*
Searby, Richard Henry 1931- *WhoWor 91*
Searchers, The *OxCPMus*
Searcy, Alan Winn 1925- *WhoAm 90*
Searcy, Chris Jackson 1953- *WhoSSW 91*
Searcy, Christian Dietrich 1947- *WhoEmL 91*
Searcy, James F. 1938- *St&PR 91*
Searcy, Jarrell D. 1934- *WhoAm 90*
Searcy, Margaret Zehmer 1926- *BioIn 16*
Searcy, Stephen Wayne 1952- *WhoSSW 91*
Searcy, William Michael 1943- *St&PR 91*
Searfoss, David William 1951- *St&PR 91*
Searight, Mary Dell 1918- *WhoWor 91*
Searight, Patricia Adelaide *WhoAmW 91*
Searing, Marjory Ellen 1945- *WhoAm 90*
Searing, Susan Ellis 1950- *WhoAmW 91*
Searl, Jacalyn Joy 1953- *WhoAmW 91*
Searl, Linda *BioIn 16*
Searl, Margaret *BiDEWW*
Searle, Charles Frederick 1931- *St&PR 91*
Searle, Daniel C. 1926- *St&PR 91*
Searle, Eleanor Millard 1926- *WhoAm 90*
Searle, George Baldwin 1933- *St&PR 91*
Searle, Humphrey 1915- *PenDiMPA*
Searle, Humphrey 1915-1982 *DcNaB 1981*
Searle, James 1733-1797 *EncCRAm*
Searle, James Elmhurst 1929- *WhoWor 91*
Searle, John Gideon 1901-1978 *ConAmBL*
Searle, Margaret Ann 1944- *WhoAmW 91*
Searle, Norma Doris 1925- *WhoAmW 91*
Searle, Philip Ford 1924- *WhoAm 90*
Searle, Q.R. 1937- *St&PR 91*
Searle, Robert A. 1944- *St&PR 91*
Searle, Rodney Newell 1920- *WhoAm 90*
Searle, Ronald 1920- *WhoAm 90*
Searle, Stewart A. 1923- *WhoAm 90*
Searle, Verna 1919- *ConAu 132*
Searle, William Louis 1928- *St&PR 91, WhoAm 90*
Searles, Anna Mae Howard 1906- *WhoAmW 91, WhoSSW 91*
Searles, Charles *WhoAmA 91*
Searles, David Sewall, Jr. 1946- *WhoSSW 91*
Searles, Dewitt Richard 1920- *WhoAm 90*
Searles, Harold F *BiDrAPA 89*
Searles, Jerry Lee *WhoWor 91*
Searles, John Rumney, Jr. 1912- *WhoSSW 91*
Searles, Michael M. 1949- *St&PR 91*
Searles, Richard Walker 1931- *St&PR 91*
Searles, Stephen *WhoAmA 91*
Searles, T.M., Jr. 1921- *St&PR 91*
Searles, Thomas Daniel 1937- *WhoE 91*
Searls, David 1947- *ODwPR 91*
Searls, Eileen Haughey 1925- *WhoAmW 91*
Searls, Frederick Taylor 1912- *WhoAm 90*
Searls, Hank *BioIn 16*
Searls, Melvin William, Jr. 1935- *WhoAm 90*
Searns, Robert Michael 1946- *WhoEmL 91*
Sears, Al *NewYTBS 90*
Sears, Al 1910-1990 *BioIn 16*
Sears, Bonnie Lou House 1945- *WhoSSW 91*
Sears, Bradford George 1915- *WhoAm 90*
Sears, Curtis Thornton, Jr. 1938- *WhoSSW 91*
Sears, David Ripley *BiDrAPA 89*
Sears, Deborah G 1954- *BiDrAPA 89*
Sears, Derek William George 1948- *WhoSSW 91*
Sears, Donald J. 1935- *St&PR 91*
Sears, Edward Milner, Jr. 1944- *WhoAm 90*
Sears, Elizabeth Ann 1949- *IntWWM 90*
Sears, Ernest Robert 1910- *WhoAm 90*
Sears, George Ames 1926- *WhoAm 90*
Sears, George W., Jr. 1917- *St&PR 91*
Sears, H James T 1937- *BiDrAPA 89*
Sears, Isaac 1730?-1786 *BioIn 16, EncCRAm*
Sears, James Thomas 1951- *WhoSSW 91*
Sears, John Patrick 1940- *WhoAm 90*
Sears, John Winthrop 1930- *WhoAm 90, WhoE 91*
Sears, Lucius J., Jr. 1916- *St&PR 91*
Sears, Mariann 1957- *WhoEmL 91*
Sears, Mary Helen 1929- *WhoE 91*
Sears, Max 1925- *St&PR 91*
Sears, Raymond Andrew *BioIn 16*
Sears, Richard C. 1936- *St&PR 91*
Sears, Richard Duane 1940- *WhoSSW 91*
Sears, Richard W. 1863-1914 *WorAlBi*
Sears, Richard Warren, Jr. 1942- *St&PR 91*
Sears, Robert Needham 1915- *St&PR 91*
Sears, Robert Richardson 1908-1989 *BioIn 16*
Sears, Robert Stephen 1950- *WhoSSW 91*
Sears, Roger Donald 1959- *WhoEmL 91*
Sears, Stanton Gray 1950- *WhoAmA 91*
Sears, Victoria C 1929- *BiDrAPA 89*
Sears, Wesley Dyer 1916- *St&PR 91*
Sears, William Gratz 1860-1949 *AmLegL*
Sears, William Gray 1910- *WhoAm 90*
Sears, William H. 1830-1891 *AmLegL*
Sears, William R. 1913- *BioIn 16*
Sears, William Rees 1913- *WhoAm 90*
Sears, William Robert 1920- *WhoAm 90*
Sears, Zenas *BioIn 16*
Sears, Ziggy *Ballpl 90*
Seary, Lawrence Anthony 1951- *WhoE 91*
Sease, Gene Elwood 1931- *WhoAm 90*
Sease, John William 1920- *WhoAm 90*
Seasholtz, Joanne Marie 1953- *WhoAmW 91*
Seasholtz, Sara Irene 1953- *WhoEmL 91*
Season, James Hobson 1944- *WhoE 91*
Seastrom, Victor 1879-1960 *BioIn 16*
Seastrunk, Jay Walter, II *BiDrAPA 89*
Seath, Olga Winnifred Hanna 1899- *WhoWrEP 89*
Seathl 1788?-1866 *WhNaAH*
Seaton, Douglass 1950- *IntWWM 90, WhoSSW 91*
Seaton, Earle Edward 1924- *WhoWor 91*
Seaton, Edward Lee 1943- *WhoAm 90*
Seaton, Frederick Andrew 1909-1974 *BiDrUSE 89*
Seaton, John Richard 1934- *St&PR 91*
Seaton, Kenneth Duncan 1929- *WhoAm 90*
Seaton, Lloyd, Jr. 1929- *WhoAm 90*
Seaton, Louis Goermer 1906-1988 *BioIn 16*
Seaton, Richard Melvin 1913- *WhoAm 90*
Seaton, Robert Finlayson 1930- *St&PR 91, WhoAm 90*
Seaton, Stanley L *BiDrAPA 89*
Seaton, Tom 1887-1940 *Ballpl 90*
Seaton, W.B. 1925- *St&PR 91*
Seaton, W. B. 1925- *WhoAm 90*
Seaton, William Richmond 1951- *WhoSSW 91*
Seaton, William Winston 1785-1866 *BioIn 16*
Seator, Lynette Hubbard 1929- *WhoWrEP 89*
Seator, Pamela 1950- *BiDrAPA 89*
Seats, Harlon *WhoSSW 91*
Seats, Peggy Chisolm 1951- *WhoAmW 91*
Seats, Tom 1911- *Ballpl 90*
Seattle 1788?-1866 *WhNaAH*
Seatz, Lloyd Frank 1919- *WhoAm 90*
Seaver, Danny Wade 1954- *WhoSSW 91*
Seaver, Esther *WhoAmA 91N*
Seaver, James Everett 1918- *WhoAm 90, WhoWrEP 89*
Seaver, Lloyd B. *BioIn 16*
Seaver, Richard Carlton 1922- *St&PR 91, WhoAm 90*
Seaver, Robert I *BiDrAPA 89*
Seaver, Thomas 1944- *WorAlBi*
Seaver, Tom *BioIn 16*
Seaver, Tom 1944- *Ballpl 90 [port]*
Seaver, W. Burleigh 1944- *St&PR 91*
Seavey, Ava Beth 1954- *WhoAmW 91*
Seavey, Richard Curtis 1956- *St&PR 91*
Seavy, Mary Ethel Ingle 1910- *WhoAmW 91*
Seavy, Mary Lynn 1942- *WhoWrEP 89*
Seawall, Richard Magnus 1951- *WhoE 91*
Seaward, Edward Thomas 1923- *WhoSSW 91*
Seawell, Donald R. 1912- *St&PR 91*
Seawell, Donald Ray 1912- *WhoAm 90, WhoWor 91*
Seawell, Molly 1860-1916 *FemiCLE*
Seawell, Thomas Robert 1936- *WhoAm 90, WhoAmA 91*
Seawell, William Thomas 1918- *WhoAm 90*
Seaworth, Mary Ellen 1947- *WhoEmL 91*
Seawright, James L., Jr. 1936- *WhoAm 90*
Seawright, James L, Jr 1936- *WhoAmA 91*
Seawright, Toni *BioIn 16*
Seaxburh *WomWR*
Seay, Audrey Boschen 1930- *WhoAmW 91*
Seay, Charles Ledbetter, III 1924- *WhoSSW 91*
Seay, Dick 1906- *Ballpl 90*
Seay, Dudley G. 1922- *St&PR 91*
Seay, Frank H. 1938- *WhoSSW 91*
Seay, Lella Delores 1946- *WhoAmW 91*
Seay, Margaret J *BiDrAPA 89*
Seay, Mary Burt 1953- *WhoAmW 91*
Seay, Solomon S. 1899- *BioIn 16*
Seay, Thomas Patrick 1941- *St&PR 91, WhoAm 90*
Sebastian 1947- *WhoAmA 91*
Sebastian, C Simon 1949- *BiDrAPA 89*
Sebastian, George E *BiDrAPA 89*
Sebastian, Georges 1903-1989 *BioIn 16*
Sebastian, James *BioIn 16*
Sebastian, Jeanne *AuBYP 90*
Sebastian, Jill C 1950- *WhoAmA 91*
Sebastian, John 1944- *WorAlBi*
Sebastian, John Victor 1942- *St&PR 91*
Sebastian, Joseph A 1930- *BiDrAPA 89*
Sebastian, Lee *MajTwCW*
Sebastian, Michael James 1930- *St&PR 91, WhoAm 90, WhoSSW 91*
Sebastian, Paul E. 1934- *St&PR 91*
Sebastian, Peter 1926- *WhoAm 90*
Sebastian, Praxedes S *BiDrAPA 89*
Sebastian, Richard Lee 1942- *WhoAm 90*
Sebastian, T C 1943- *BiDrAPA 89*
Sebastian, Thomas Anthony 1947- *St&PR 91*
Sebastian, Timothy 1952- *SpyFic*
Sebastiani, August 1913-1980 *BioIn 16*
Sebastiani, Susan Marie 1954- *WhoAmW 91*
Sebastiani-Cuneo, Mary Ann 1947- *WhoAmW 91*
Sebastiano del Piombo 1485?-1547 *IntDcAA 90*
Sebastiano, Frank Anthony 1945- *St&PR 91*
Sebby, Steven Dale 1957- *WhoEmL 91, WhoWor 91*
Sebeck, Karen Pleasy 1946- *WhoAmW 91*
Sebeknefru *WomWR*
Sebela, Vicki Dawn 1964- *WhoAmW 91, WhoEmL 91, WhoWor 91*
Sebelius, Helen 1953- *WhoAmA 91*
Sebell, Adolph Leon 1918- *St&PR 91*
Sebell, Tellervo 1915- *IntWWM 90*
Sebenius, James Kimble 1953- *WhoE 91*
Sebeok, Thomas Albert 1920- *WhoAm 90, WhoWrEP 89*
Seberg, Jean 1938-1979 *BioAmW, BioIn 16*
Sebes, Joseph 1915-1990 *ConAu 131*
Sebesky, Douglas C. 1951- *St&PR 91*
Sebesta, Charles Joseph, Jr. 1940- *WhoAm 90*
Sebestyen, Andras 1917- *IntWWM 90*
Sebestyen, Istvan 1947- *WhoEmL 91, WhoWor 91*
Sebestyen, Janos 1931- *IntWWM 90*
Sebestyen, Ouida 1924- *BioIn 16*
Sebestyen, Ouida Glenn 1924- *WhoAmW 91*
Sebok, Gyorgy 1922- *WhoAm 90*
Sebold, Duane David 1945- *WhoAm 90*
Sebold, Russell Perry, III 1928- *WhoAm 90*
Sebottendorf, Rudolf Freiherr von 1875-1945 *EncO&P 3*
Sebra, Bob 1961- *Ballpl 90*
Sebree, Charles 1914-1985 *DrBlPA 90*
Sebrell, William Henry, Jr. 1901- *WhoAm 90*
Sebren, Lucille Griggs 1922- *WhoAmW 91*
Sebring, Jimmy 1882-1909 *Ballpl 90*
Sebring, Joseph Bernard 1947- *St&PR 91*
Sebring, Marjorie Marie Allison 1926- *WhoAmW 91*
Secada, Maria G *BiDrAPA 89*
Seccafico, John 1948- *WhoE 91*
Secchia, Peter F. *WhoWor 91*
Secco-Suardo, Baldo 1917- *WhoWor 91*
Sechen, Glenn Charles 1947- *WhoEmL 91*
Sechen, Robert Nicholas 1952- *WhoEmL 91, WhoSSW 91*
Secher, Herbert Pierre 1924- *WhoAm 90*
Sechrest, Linda Anne 1936- *WhoSSW 91*
Sechrest, Thomas Lee 1949- *WhoSSW 91*
Sechrest, William B. 1942- *WhoAm 90, WhoSSW 91*
Sechriest, John Hugh 1938- *WhoE 91*
Sechriest, Walter Stimpson, Jr. 1934- *WhoSSW 91*
Sechrist, Chalmers F., Jr. 1930- *WhoAm 90*
Sechrist, Elizabeth 1903- *AuBYP 90*
Seckel, Carol Ann 1949- *WhoAmW 91*
Seckel, Paul Bernhard 1918- *WhoAmA 91*
Seckinger, Emilia Posada *WhoHisp 91*
Seckinger, Harold Eugene 1926- *WhoSSW 91*
Seckinger, Raymond Paul 1926- *BiDrAPA 89*
Seckler, Dorothy Gees 1910- *WhoAmA 91*
Seckman, John Randolph, III 1962- *WhoSSW 91*
Secondari, Helen Jean Rogers *WhoAm 90*
Secoquian, Mary Lou 1953- *St&PR 91*
Secor, Donald Terry, Jr. 1934- *WhoAm 90*
Secor, E. Christine *BioIn 16*
Secor, Glen Michael 1960- *WhoE 91*
Secor, Jay Ketchum 1960- *WhoE 91*
Secor, Richard A. 1930- *St&PR 91*
Secor, William B. 1931- *St&PR 91*
Secord, Mack D. 1931- *ODwPR 91*
Secory, Frank 1912- *Ballpl 90*
Secrest, Fred Gilbert 1922- *St&PR 91*
Secrest, John Cary 1922- *WhoAm 90*
Secrest, Larry 1941- *St&PR 91*

Secrest, Leslie Harold 1942- *BiDrAPA 89*
Secrest, Ronald Dean 1951- *WhoEmL 91*
Secrest, Stephen Frederick 1947- *WhoEmL 91*
Secret, Robert John Spencer *IntWWM 90*
Secretan, Lance H. K. 1939- *ConAu 130*
Secretariat 1970-1989 *News 90*
Secrist, Patricia Aljoe 1950- *ODwPR 91*
Secrist, Richard A. 1945- *St&PR 91*
Secrist-Schmedes, Barbera Shaw 1952- *IntWWM 90*
Sectzer, Jose Cesar 1949- *WhoHisp 91*
Secunda, Arthur 1927- *WhoAm 90, WhoAmA 91*
Secunda, Eugene 1934- *ODwPR 91, WhoAm 90*
Secunda, Holland 1927- *WhoAm 90*
Secunda, Lazarus 1910- *BiDrAPA 89*
Secunda, Steven K 1940- *BiDrAPA 89*
Secunde, Nadine *IntWWM 90*
Seda, Eliezer Elliott 1955- *WhoE 91*
Seda, Wilfredo *WhoHisp 91*
Sedaghatpour, Nasser *BiDrAPA 89*
Sedaka, Neil 1939- *BioIn 16, ConMus 4 [port], EncPR&S 89, OxCPMus, WhoAm 90, WorAlBi*
Sedam, Glenn J., Jr. 1937- *WhoAm 90*
Sedano, Dora 1902- *EncCoWW*
Sedberry, Donald C. 1934- *St&PR 91*
Sedberry, Margaret M 1925- *BiDrAPA 89*
Seddon, Anne Marie *St&PR 91*
Seddon, George *PenDiDA 89*
Seddon, George 1727?-1801 *PenDiDA 89*
Seddon, John Pollard 1827-1906 *PenDiDA 89*
Seddon, Margaret Rhea *BioIn 16*
Seddon, Margaret Rhea 1947- *WhoAmW 91*
Seddon, Melvin E. *St&PR 91*
Seddon, Robert Edward 1942- *St&PR 91*
Seddon, Thomas *PenDiDA 89*
Sedelmaier, J. J. 1956- *WhoE 91*
Sedelmaier, John Josef 1933- *WhoAm 90*
Sedelmaier, Josef *BioIn 16*
Sedelow, Sally Ann Yeates 1?31- *WhoAm 90*
Sedelow, Walter Alfred, Jr. 1928- *WhoAm 90*
Seder, Arthur Raymond, Jr. 1920- *WhoAm 90*
Seder, Herschel Lewis 1918- *St&PR 91*
Seder, Lawrence Richard 1935- *WhoE 91*
Seder, Steve Dennis 1955- *St&PR 91, WhoEmL 91*
Sederbaum, William 1914- *WhoAm 90*
Sederer, Lloyd I 1945- *BiDrAPA 89, WhoE 91*
Sedergren, Muriel Dwyer 1942- *WhoAmW 91*
Sederholm, Don 1930- *WhoWrEP 89*
Seders, Francine Lavinal 1932- *WhoAmA 91*
Sedges, John *MajTwCW*
Sedgwick, Alexander 1930- *WhoAm 90*
Sedgwick, Anne Douglas 1873-1935 *FemiCLE*
Sedgwick, Arthur George 1844-1915 *BioIn 16*
Sedgwick, Catharine M. 1789-1867 *BioAmW*
Sedgwick, Catharine Maria 1789-1867 *FemiCLE*
Sedgwick, Donald W. 1945- *WhoSSW 91*
Sedgwick, Edie 1943-1971 *BioAmW*
Sedgwick, Ellery, Jr. 1908- *St&PR 91*
Sedgwick, Henry D. 1928- *St&PR 91*
Sedgwick, Kyra *BioIn 16*
Sedgwick, Pamela Dwight 1753-1807 *BioIn 16*
Sedgwick, Phillip Westel, III 1947- *WhoSSW 91*
Sedgwick, Rae 1944- *WhoAmW 91*
Sedgwick, Robert P 1918- *BiDrAPA 89*
Sedgwick, Theodore 1746-1813 *BioIn 16*
Sedgwick, William Thomas 1952- *WhoSSW 91*
Sedgwick-Hirsch, Carol Elizabeth 1922- *WhoAmW 91*
Sedillo, Pablo 1935- *WhoHisp 91*
Sedivka, Jan Boleslav 1917- *IntWWM 90*
Sedki, Atef 1930- *WhoWor 91*
Sedky, Cherif 1943- *WhoWor 91*
Sedlacek, Evelyn Ann 1919- *WhoAmW 91*
Sedlacek, John 1925- *St&PR 91*
Sedlacek, Keith Wayne 1944- *BiDrAPA 89, WhoE 91*
Sedlacek, Michael J 1959- *BiDrAPA 89*
Sedlacek, Warren Richard 1925- *St&PR 91*
Sedlack, Robert J. 1935- *St&PR 91*
Sedlacko, John Robert 1934- *St&PR 91*
Sedlak, Eric William 1958- *WhoEmL 91*
Sedlak, Joseph Anthony, III 1952- *WhoEmL 91*
Sedlak, Richard 1944- *WhoWor 91*
Sedlak, Valerie Frances 1934- *WhoAmW 91, WhoE 91, WhoWor 91*
Sedlarz, Karl H. 1937- *St&PR 91*
Sedler, Herbert L. 1930- *St&PR 91*
Sedler, Mark Jeffrey 1952- *BiDrAPA 89*
Sedler, Michael Dean 1955- *WhoEmL 91*
Sedlin, Elias David 1932- *WhoAm 90*
Sedlock, Joy 1958- *WhoAmW 91, WhoWor 91*
Sedlock, Thomas 1937- *BiDrAPA 89*
Sedman, Elizabeth *BiDEWW*
Sedoc, Edwin Johan 1938- *WhoWor 91*
Sedor, Daniel Wayne 1956- *St&PR 91*
Sedor, Robert Steven 1954- *St&PR 91*
Seduski, Maryann 1950- *WhoAmW 91*
Sedwick, Frank 1924- *WhoAm 90*
Sedwick, Robert Curtis 1926- *WhoAm 90*
See, Alan Jeffery 1959- *WhoSSW 91*
See, Andrew Bruce 1949- *WhoEmL 91*
See, Carolyn *BioIn 16*
See, Henry Wesselman 1923- *St&PR 91*
See, James Vernon 1922- *WhoSSW 91*
See, John R. 1949- *St&PR 91*
See, Karen Mason 1952- *WhoAmW 91*
See, Sarah Gavin 1922- *WhoAmW 91*
See-yat 1788?-1866 *WhNaAH*
Seeba, Hinrich Claassen 1940- *WhoAm 90*
Seebach, Dieter 1937- *WhoWor 91*
Seebach, Karl Josef 1912- *WhoWor 91*
Seebart, George E. 1928- *St&PR 91, WhoAm 90*
Seebass, Alfred Richard, III 1936- *WhoAm 90*
Seebass, Tilman 1939- *IntWWM 90*
Seebeck, William B. 1950- *ODwPR 91*
Seeber, Henry Kenneth 1947- *St&PR 91*
Seeber, Orville Alexander 1913- *St&PR 91*
Seeberg, Peter 1925- *DcScanL*
Seeberger, Edward J. 1951- *St&PR 91*
Seebert, Kathleen Anne 1949- *WhoAmW 91, WhoWor 91*
Seebold, Donald J. 1922- *St&PR 91*
Seebree, Charles *EarBlAP*
Seeburg, Karin Neville *BiDrAPA 89*
Seeburger, John 1923- *St&PR 91*
Seed, Allen H. *BioIn 16*
Seed, H. Bolton 1922-1989 *BioIn 16*
Seed, Harris Waller 1927- *St&PR 91*
Seed, John *BioIn 16*
Seed, John Charles 1943- *BiDrAPA 89*
Seed, Suzanne *AuBYP 90*
Seed, Suzanne Liddell 1940- *WhoAmA 91*
Seeder, Richard Owen 1947- *WhoEmL 91*
Seedlock, Robert Francis 1913- *WhoAm 90, WhoE 91, WhoWor 91*
Seedor, Marie M. *BioIn 16*
Seeds, Bob 1907- *Ballpl 90*
Seeds, George M 1929- *BiDrAPA 89*
Seeds, Stanley Morrell 1930- *St&PR 91*
Seefehlner, Egon Hugo 1912- *IntWWM 90, WhoWor 91*
Seefeld, Sandra Leah 1945- *IntWWM 90*
Seefeldt, Carol 1935- *WhoE 91*
Seefried, Irmgard 1919-1988 *AnObit 1988, BioIn 16, PenDiMP*
Seefried, P.A. *PenDiDA 89*
Seefried, Philip W. 1935- *St&PR 91*
Seefried-Matejkova, Ludmila 1938- *BiDWomA*
Seegal, Herbert Leonard 1915- *St&PR 91, WhoAm 90*
Seegar, Sara *NewYTBS 90*
Seegal, Richard Lawrence 1937- *WhoE 91*
Seeger, Charles 1886-1979 *BioIn 16, EncAL*
Seeger, Charles Ronald 1931- *WhoAm 90*
Seeger, Christine Anne *BiDrAPA 89*
Seeger, Gregory Lawler 1951- *BiDrAPA 89*
Seeger, Gunter *BioIn 16*
Seeger, Horst 1926- *IntWWM 90*
Seeger, Melinda Wayne 1940- *WhoAmW 91*
Seeger, Michael 1933- *IntWWM 90, WhoAm 90*
Seeger, Murray Amsdell 1929- *WhoWor 91*
Seeger, Peggy 1935- *BioIn 16, OxCPMus*
Seeger, Pete *BioIn 16*
Seeger, Pete 1919- *ConAu 33NR, ConMus 4 [port], EncAL, OxCPMus, WhoAm 90, WorAlBi*
Seeger, Ruth Crawford 1901-1953 *BioIn 16*
Seeger, Ruth Porter 1901-1953 *AuBYP 90*
Seeger, Walter August, Jr. 1932- *St&PR 91*
Seegers, George Edwin 1942- *WhoE 91*
Seegers, Paul R. 1930- *WhoSSW 91*
Seegers, Walter Henry 1910- *WhoAm 90*
Seegman, Irvin P. 1921- *St&PR 91, WhoAm 90*
Seegmiller, Don *BioIn 16*
Seegmiller, Ray Reuben 1935- *St&PR 91*
Seegmiller, Wan 1926- *St&PR 91*
Seegmiller, William Henry 1843-1923 *AmLegL*
Seegretc, Carole Ruth 1947- *WhoAmW 91*
Seehafer, Herbert Milton 1930- *St&PR 91*
Seeherman, Julian 1929- *WhoAm 90*
Seekers, The *OxCPMus*
Seekings, Sara Margaret 1953- *WhoAmW 91*
Seekins, Anna Marie 1948- *WhoAmW 91*
Seel, Jeffery W. 1947- *St&PR 91*
Seel, Martin Anthony 1933- *St&PR 91*
Seeland, Irene B 1938- *BiDrAPA 89*
Seelander, John Marshall 1940- *St&PR 91*
Seelbach, Charles William 1923- *WhoE 91, WhoWor 91*
Seelbach, Chuck 1948- *Ballpl 90*
Seelenfreund, Alan 1936- *WhoAm 90*
Seelenfreund, Alan Jay 1936- *St&PR 91*
Seeler, Richard W. 1919- *St&PR 91*
Seeler, Robert S. *WhoAm 90*
Seeler, Robert S. 1935- *St&PR 91*
Seeley, Blossom 1891-1974 *OxCPMus*
Seeley, Chester L. 1913- *St&PR 91*
Seeley, David William 1944- *WhoSSW 91*
Seeley, Frederick Cooley 1942- *St&PR 91*
Seeley, Harry Wilbur, Jr. 1917- *WhoAm 90*
Seeley, Jeane McWorkman 1916- *WhoAmW 91*
Seeley, John Robert 1834-1895 *BioIn 16*
Seeley, Kimberley Ann 1960- *WhoAmW 91*
Seeley, Mabel 1903- *FemiCLE, TwCCr&M 91*
Seeley, Maryann Del Visco 1948- *WhoAmW 91*
Seeley, Paul David 1949- *IntWWM 90*
Seeley, Rebecca Zahm 1935- *WhoAmW 91*
Seeley, Robert Harry 1922- *St&PR 91*
Seeley, Rod Ralph 1945- *WhoAm 90*
Seelhammer, Cynthia Mae 1957- *WhoAmW 91*
Seelig, Gerard Leo 1926- *WhoAm 90*
Seelig, Leonard Robert 1956- *WhoSSW 91*
Seelig, Steven Alfred 1944- *WhoE 91*
Seelinger, Tatiana *BioIn 16*
Seelman, Gerald William 1936- *St&PR 91*
Seelman, Robert Norman 1934- *St&PR 91*
Seeloff, Gregory Scott 1954- *WhoEmL 91*
Seely, Alice Warder 1942- *BioIn 16*
Seely, Anne Lofgren 1947- *WhoAmW 91*
Seely, Dennis Jack 1952- *WhoSSW 91*
Seely, James Michael 1932- *WhoAm 90*
Seely, Karen Ann 1955- *WhoAmW 91*
Seely, Martha Ann 1952- *WhoAmW 91*
Seely, Michael 1945- *ODwPR 91*
Seely, Robert Daniel 1923- *WhoAm 90, WhoWor 91*
Seely, Thomas Johnston *BiDrAPA 89*
Seelye, Edward E 1924- *BiDrAPA 89*
Seelye, Ned H. *WhoHisp 91*
Seelye, Sarah Emma 1841-1898 *BioAmW*
Seeman, Bernard 1911- *WhoE 91*
Seeman, Charles Alan 1953- *St&PR 91*
Seeman, Fred 1924- *St&PR 91*
Seeman, Helene Zucker 1950- *WhoAmA 91*
Seeman, Kenneth 1938- *BiDrAPA 89*
Seeman, Mary Violette 1935- *BiDrAPA 89*
Seeman, Melvin 1918- *WhoAm 90*
Seeman, Philip 1934- *WhoAm 90*
Seeman, William Henry 1955- *St&PR 91*
Seemann, Charles Henry, Jr. 1946- *IntWWM 90*
Seemann, Ernest Albright 1929- *WhoAm 90*
Seemann, Jeffrey Randall 1955- *WhoEmL 91*
Seemann, Klaus Dieter 1932- *WhoWor 91*
Seemann-Kocon, Renata *BiDrAPA 89*
Seemayer, Deryl Leslie 1953- *WhoE 91*
Seemiller, Mark Louis 1957- *St&PR 91*
Seerey, Pat 1923-1986 *Ballpl 90*
Seerey-Lester, John 1945- *BioIn 16*
Seerey-Lester, John Vernon 1945- *WhoAmA 91*
Seers, Dudley 1920-1983 *ConAu 129*
Sees, Mary Carolyn 1931- *WhoSSW 91*
Seese, Perry Gray *BiDrAPA 89*
Seeser, James W. 1943- *St&PR 91*
Seessel, Thomas Vining 1937- *WhoAm 90*
Seethaler, Albin J. 1941- *St&PR 91*
Seethaler, William Charles 1937- *WhoWor 91*
Seetoo, Amy Dah Sun 1946- *WhoWor 91*
Seevak, Sheldon 1929- *WhoAm 90*
Seevers, Charles Junior 1925- *WhoAm 90, WhoWor 91*
Seevers, Gary Leonard 1937- *WhoAm 90*
Seewald, Carol Sandra 1947- *WhoAmW 91*
Sefcik, James Francis 1943- *WhoAm 90, WhoSSW 91*
Seferiades, Giorgos Stylianou 1900-1971 *MajTwCW*
Seferis, George *MajTwCW*
Seferis, George 1900-1971 *EuWr 12*
Seferis, Giorgos 1900-1971 *WorAlBi*
Seferis, James Constantine 1950- *WhoWor 91*
Seff, Ronald Leon 1947- *BiDrAPA 89*
Seffrin, John Reese 1944- *WhoAm 90*
Seffrin, Nickolaus Johannes 1931- *WhoWor 91*
Sefrna, Ann Barnett 1949- *WhoAmW 91*
Seftick, Ronald Gregory 1952- *St&PR 91*
Sefton, Henry Francis 1808?-1892 *DcCanB 12*
Sefton, Thomas W. 1917- *St&PR 91*
Segade-Lugaro, Lila 1940- *BiDrAPA 89*
Segal, Aaron Lee 1938- *WhoWor 91*
Segal, Arlene Esta 1937- *WhoAmW 91*
Segal, Arthur Maxwell *BiDrAPA 89*
Segal, Avrom Carl 1934- *BiDrAPA 89*
Segal, Barbara Handler *BioIn 16*
Segal, Barbara Jean 1953- *WhoAmA 91*
Segal, Barry Michael *BiDrAPA 89*
Segal, Bernard 1907-1984 *BioIn 16*
Segal, Bernard Gerard 1907- *WhoAm 90, WhoE 91*
Segal, Bernard Louis 1929- *WhoAm 90*
Segal, Bernice G. 1929-1989 *BioIn 16*
Segal, Boris M *BiDrAPA 89*
Segal, Charles 1898- *WhoSSW 91*
Segal, Charles Mitchell 1921- *WhoE 91*
Segal, Charles Paul 1936- *WhoAm 90, WhoWrEP 89*
Segal, Claire *ODwPR 91*
Segal, D. Robert 1920- *WhoAm 90, WhoWor 91*
Segal, David 1940- *WhoAmA 91, WhoE 91*
Segal, David P. 1931- *St&PR 91*
Segal, Donald Henry Gilbert 1928- *WhoE 91, WhoWor 91*
Segal, Elliott Gerald 1937- *BiDrAPA 89*
Segal, Eric Bruce 1942- *St&PR 91*
Segal, Erich 1937- *MajTwCW, WhoWrEP 89*
Segal, Evan J. *St&PR 91*
Segal, George 1924- *BioIn 16, WhoAm 90, WhoAmA 91, WorAlBi*
Segal, George 1934- *WhoAm 90, WorAlBi*
Segal, Geraldine Rosenbaum 1908- *WhoAmW 91*
Segal, Harold Lewis 1924- *WhoAm 90*
Segal, Harry L. 1900-1990 *BioIn 16*
Segal, Henry A *BiDrAPA 89*
Segal, Herb 1924- *St&PR 91*
Segal, Herbert Erwin 1941- *WhoSSW 91*
Segal, Irving Ezra 1918- *WhoAm 90, WhoE 91*
Segal, Irving Randall 1914- *WhoAm 90*
Segal, Jack 1934- *WhoAm 90*
Segal, Jerome J. 1929- *St&PR 91*
Segal, JoAn Smyth 1930- *WhoAm 90*
Segal, Joel Michael 1933- *WhoAm 90*
Segal, Jonathan Bruce 1946- *WhoAm 90, WhoWrEP 89*
Segal, Jonathan Henry *BiDrAPA 89*
Segal, Jonathan L. 1952- *WhoEmL 91*
Segal, Kathleen Rita 1952- *WhoAmW 91*
Segal, Lester *BiDrAPA 89*
Segal, Linda Gale 1947- *WhoAmW 91*
Segal, Lore 1928- *SmATA 11AS [port], WhoAm 90, WhoWrEP 89, WorAu 1980 [port]*
Segal, Lore Groszmann *BioIn 16*
Segal, Marilyn *BiDrAPA 89*
Segal, Martin *BioIn 16*
Segal, Martin E. 1916- *St&PR 91*
Segal, Martin Eli 1916- *WhoAm 90, WhoWor 91*
Segal, Maurice S. 1907-1988 *BioIn 16*
Segal, Mendal 1914- *St&PR 91*
Segal, Merton Joseph 1929- *St&PR 91*
Segal, Michael *BioIn 16*
Segal, Morey M *BiDrAPA 89*
Segal, Morton 1931- *ODwPR 91*
Segal, Paul 1944- *WhoWor 91*
Segal, Perry M 1934- *BiDrAPA 89*
Segal, Perry Roy 1951- *BiDrAPA 89*
Segal, Peter Wyman 1943- *WhoE 91*
Segal, Philip A., Jr. 1926- *St&PR 91*
Segal, Philip L. 1931- *St&PR 91*
Segal, Phyllis Gordon *BiDrAPA 89*
Segal, Richard Avery *BiDrAPA 89*
Segal, Robert B. 1944- *St&PR 91*
Segal, Robert M 1925- *ConAu 32NR*
Segal, Robert Mandal 1915- *WhoAm 90, WhoE 91*
Segal, Robert Martin 1935- *WhoAm 90*
Segal, Ronald 1938- *St&PR 91*
Segal, Ronald Michael 1932- *WhoWor 91*
Segal, Sanford Leonard 1937- *WhoE 91*
Segal, Scott 1964- *BiDrAPA 89*
Segal, Scott Daniel *BiDrAPA 89*
Segal, Sheldon Jerome 1926- *WhoAm 90*
Segal, Stephen Martin 1938- *WhoAm 90, WhoE 91*
Segal, Tama 1949- *WhoAmA 91*
Segal, Uri 1944- *PenDiMP*
Segal, Valerie Judith 1950- *WhoAmW 91*
Segal, Vivienne 1897- *BioIn 16, NotWoAT, OxCPMus*
Segalas, Hercules A. 1935- *BioIn 16*
Segalas, Hercules Anthony 1935- *WhoAm 90*
Segale, Blandina 1850-1941 *BioIn 16*
Segalen, Martine 1940- *ConAu 130*
Segall, Errol Alan 1949- *BiDrAPA 89*
Segall, Harold Abraham 1918- *WhoAm 90*
Segall, James Arnold 1956- *WhoEmL 91, WhoSSW 91*
Segall, Jean Florin *BiDrAPA 89*
Segall, Joel 1923- *WhoAm 90, WhoE 91*

Segall, John Louis 1926- St&PR 91, WhoAm 90
Segall, Lasar 1891-1957 ArtLatA
Segall, Laura Jeanne 1958- WhoAmW 91
Segall, Marshall H. 1930- WhoAm 90
Segall, Maurice 1929- WhoAm 90, WhoE 91, WhoWor 91
Segall, Ronald Neil 1957- WhoE 91
Segall, Samson 1920- St&PR 91
Segall, Thomas Allan BiDrAPA 89
Segall, William Edwin WhoSSW 91
Segalove, Harvey P. BiDrAPA 89
Segalove, Ilene Judy 1950- WhoAmA 91
Segan, Ken Akiva 1950- WhoAmA 91
Segantini, Giovanni 1858-1899 IntDcAA 90
Segar, Charles 1903- Ballpl 90
Segar, E. C. 1894-1938 EncACom
Segar, E C 1894-1938 SmATA 61 [port]
Segar, Mary Lou 1936- WhoAmW 91
Segar, William Elias 1923- WhoAm 90
Segarnick, David J. ODwPR 91
Segarra, Jose Enrique 1945- WhoHisp 91
Segarra, Ninfa 1950- WhoHisp 91
Segars, Alvin John 1953- St&PR 91
Segatta, Joseph John 1930- St&PR 91
Segatto, Bernard Gordon 1931- WhoAm 90
Segawa, Masaya 1936- WhoWor 91
Segawa, Yasuo 1932- BioIn 16
Sege, Thomas Davis 1926- St&PR 91, WhoAm 90
Segel, J.M. 1931- St&PR 91
Segel, Joseph M. 1931- WhoAm 90
Segel, Richard M. 1940- St&PR 91
Segel, Ronald George 1935- WhoAm 90
Segeler, Curt George BioIn 16
Segelin, Bernard 1921- St&PR 91
Segelken, John Maurice 1948- WhoEmL 91
Segenreich, Harry M BiDrAPA 89
Seger, Bob BioIn 16
Seger, Bob 1945- EncPR&S 89, WhoAm 90
Seger, Charles Frederick, III 1943- St&PR 91
Seger, Forrest M BiDrAPA 89
Seger, George Wilbur 1938- St&PR 91
Seger, Hermann PenDiDA 89
Seger, Martha Romayne 1932- WhoAm 90, WhoAmW 91, WhoWor 91
Seger, Ron BioIn 16
Segerson, Joan Elizabeth 1951- WhoAm 90
Segerstam, Leif 1944 PenDiMP
Segersten, Robert Hagy 1941- WhoAm 90
Segerstrom, Jane Archer 1930- WhoWrEP 89
Seges, Philip George 1934- WhoAm 90
Seges, Phillip G. 1934- St&PR 91
Segger, Martin Joseph 1946- WhoAm 90, WhoAmA 91
Seggerman, Harry Gurney Atha 1927- WhoAm 90
Seggerman, M.K. St&PR 91
Seggerman, Marianne Gurney Catharine 1954- WhoAmW 91
Seggev, Meir 1939- WhoE 91
Seghers, Anna 1900-1983 EncCoWW
Seghers, Hercules 1589?-1638? IntDcAA 90
Seghi, Peter Richard 1946- WhoEmL 91
Segil, Larraine Diane 1948- WhoAmW 91, WhoEmL 91
Seglem, Christopher King 1946- St&PR 91
Seglias, Lynda Johnson 1947- WhoE 91
Seglin, Melvin N 1926- BiDrAPA 89
Segnar, Sam F. 1927- WhoAm 90
Segnar, Samuel Frederick 1927- St&PR 91
Segner, Edmund Peter, III 1953- WhoAm 90, WhoEmL 91
Segnitz, Philip Warren 1930- WhoE 91
Segnr, Edmund Peter, III 1953- St&PR 91
Sego, Trina Ann 1965- WhoAmW 91
Segovia, Andres 1893-1987 BioIn 16, PenDiMP
Segovia, Andres 1894-1987 WorAlBi
Segovis, Elizabeth Wilson 1948- WhoAmW 91
Segraves, John Walter 1925- St&PR 91
Segraves, Robert Taylor 1941- BiDrAPA 89
Segraves, Steven Deane 1959- BiDrAPA 89
Segre, Claudio 1932- WhoWor 91
Segre, Emilio BioIn 16
Segre, Emilio 1905-1989 AnObit 1989
Segre, Emilio G. 1905-1989 WorAlBi
Segre, Mariangela Bertani 1927- WhoAmW 91
Segresser, Felipe 1698-1762 EncCRAm
Segrest, David Shelton 1946- WhoSSW 91
Segreto, Mary Christine BiDrAPA 89
Segui, Diego 1937- Ballpl 90
Seguin, Carlos A 1907- BiDrAPA 89
Seguin, David Gerard 1943- WhoE 91
Seguin, Gilles 1939- St&PR 91
Seguin, Jean 1939- WhoWor 91
Seguin, Jean-Pierre 1951- WhoAmA 91
Seguin, Juan N. 1806-1889? BioIn 16
Seguin, M. PenDiDA 89
Seguin, Philippe Daniel Alain 1943- BiDFrPL
Seguin, Robert Edgar 1960- WhoWor 91
Segun, Mabel 1930- FemiCLE
Segur, La Comtesse de EncCoWW
Segur, Eleanor Corinne 1923- WhoAmA 91
Segur, Sophie de 1799-1874 EncCoWW
Segura, Denise A. WhoHisp 91
Segura, Phyllis Lola 1943- WhoE 91
Segura, Robert Andrew 1961- WhoE 91
Segura-Bustamante, Alina BiDrAPA 89
Seguy, Georges 1927- BiDFrPL
Segy, Ladislas 1904- ConAu 30NR
Segy, Ladislas 1904-1988 BioIn 16, WhoAmA 91N
Seher, Russell John 1923- St&PR 91
Seheult, Malcolm McDonald Richardson 1949- WhoEmL 91, WhoWor 91
Sehgal, Amar Nath 1922- WhoWor 91
Sehgal, Raghbir Kumar 1937- St&PR 91
Sehgal, Suren N. 1932- WhoE 91
Sehgal, Vitasta Bazaz 1942- BiDrAPA 89
Sehlin, Arthur Andrew 1931- St&PR 91
Sehn, Marvin Daniel 1951- WhoEmL 91
Sehn, Susan Cleary 1943- BiDrAPA 89
Sehnert, Charles Fredrick 1931- St&PR 91
Sehon, Alec 1924- WhoAm 90
Sehorn, Marshall Estus 1934- WhoSSW 91, WhoWor 91
Sehovic, Enver 1938- WhoWor 91
Sehr, Steven BiDrAPA 89
Sehring, Adolf 1930- WhoAmA 91
Sehring, Hope Hutchison WhoE 91
Sei Shonagon EncJap
Sei Shonagon 966?-1017? ClMLC 6
Seib, Charles Bach 1919- WhoAm 90
Seib, Elizabeth June 1936- WhoAmW 91
Seib, Philip 1949- ConAu 129
Seibel, Fred O 1886-1968 WhoAmA 91N
Seibel, George Henry, Jr. 1921- WhoWor 91
Seibel, John Carl 1955- St&PR 91
Seibel, Kathleen Marie 1954- BiDrAPA 89
Seibel, Mary Ann 1945- WhoAmW 91
Seibel, Mary Ann 1950- WhoAmW 91
Seibel, Mildred L. 1920- St&PR 91
Seibel, Monroe 1933- St&PR 91
Seibel, Philip A 1954- BiDrAPA 89
Seiber, Matyas 1905-1960 PenDiMP A
Seiber, Patricia Wilson 1950- WhoSSW 91
Seiberlich, Carl Joseph 1921- WhoAm 90, WhoWor 91
Seiberling, John Frederick 1918- WhoAm 90
Seibert, Earl Henry, Jr. 1952- WhoE 91
Seibert, Earl W. BioIn 16
Seibert, Edward P. 1939- St&PR 91
Seibert, Jakob 1939- WhoWor 91
Seibert, Mark Eric 1957- WhoEmL 91
Seibert, Mary Lee 1942- WhoE 91
Seibert, Robin A. 1956- St&PR 91
Seibert, Russell Jacob 1914- WhoAm 90
Seibert, Scott E. 1939- St&PR 91
Seibert, Steven Wayne 1955- WhoEmL 91
Seibert, Venita 1878- LiHiK
Seibert, Wilson A., Jr. 1927- WhoAm 90
Seibold, Dean Phillip 1940- WhoAm 90
Seibold, Philip W., Jr. 1937- St&PR 91
Seibold, Ronald Lee 1945- WhoEmL 91
Seibold, Socks 1896-1965 Ballpl 90
Seibold, Wayne Dean 1928- St&PR 91
Seibt, Alfred K. St&PR 91
Seibyl, John Peter 1958- BiDrAPA 89
Seid, Alex Loy 1945- WhoEmL 91
Seid, Allan Lloyd BiDrAPA 89
Seid, Eva 1950- WhoAmW 91
Seid, Jay D. 1960- St&PR 91
Seid, Ruth BioAmW
Seid, Ruth 1913- WhoAm 90, WhoWrEP 89
Seide, Charles 1915-1980 WhoAmA 91N
Seide, Diane 1930- ConAu 31NR
Seide, Leonard M. 1929- St&PR 91
Seide, Paul 1926- WhoAm 90
Seide, Paul A 1949- WhoAmA 91
Seidel, Alexander Carl-Victor 1897-1979 WhoAmA 91N
Seidel, Andrew David 1949- WhoSSW 91
Seidel, Arthur Harris 1923- WhoAm 90
Seidel, Barry S. 1956- St&PR 91
Seidel, Darrell Edwin St&PR 91N
Seidel, David Allen 1947- WhoE 91
Seidel, Dianne Marie 1959- WhoAmW 91
Seidel, Donald R 1931- BiDrAPA 89
Seidel, Frederick Lewis 1936- WhoAm 90, WhoWrEP 89
Seidel, Glenda Lee 1936- WhoAmW 91
Seidel, Helmut 1954- WhoWor 91
Seidel, Ina 1885-1974 BioIn 16, EncCoWW
Seidel, Jan 1908- IntWWM 90
Seidel, Marianne 1943- BiDrAPA 89
Seidel, Max Alfred 1940- WhoWor 91
Seidel, Rachel Gilman BiDrAPA 89
Seidel, Richard Maurice 1926- St&PR 91
Seidel, Robert B. 1926- St&PR 91
Seidel, Selvyn 1942- WhoE 91, WhoWor 91
Seidel, Susan Hauptman 1949- WhoAm 90
Seidel, William P. 1931- St&PR 91
Seidel-Zoller, Rosemarie 1950- WhoWor 91
Seidell, Atherton 1878-1961 BioIn 16
Seidelman, James Edward 1926- AuBYP 90
Seidelman, Marsha Joyce 1957- WhoAmW 91
Seidelman, Susan BioIn 16
Seidelman, Susan 1952- CurBio 90 [port], WhoAm 90, WhoAmW 91
Seideman, Ruth Evelyn Young 1934- WhoAmW 91
Seidemann, Hans BioIn 16
Seidemann, Maria 1944- EncCoWW
Seiden, Anne Maxwell 1936- BiDrAPA 89
Seiden, Arthur WhoAmA 91, WhoE 91
Seiden, Eric A. 1965- WhoSSW 91
Seiden, George 1942- BiDrAPA 89
Seiden, Henry 1928- St&PR 91, WhoAm 90, WhoE 91, WhoWor 91
Seiden, Katie WhoAmA 91
Seiden, Leslie 1943- BiDrAPA 89
Seiden, Steven A. 1936- St&PR 91
Seiden, Steven Arnold 1936- WhoAm 90
Seiden, Steven Jay 1960- WhoE 91
Seidenbaum, Art 1930-1990 ConAu 132
Seidenbaum, Art David 1930- WhoAm 90, WhoWrEP 89
Seidenberg, Anne Miriam 1960- BiDrAPA 89
Seidenberg, Henry 1923- BiDrAPA 89
Seidenberg, Ivan G. 1946- St&PR 91
Seidenberg, Jacob Jean 1930- WhoSSW 91
Seidenberg, Robert BiDrAPA 89
Seidenfaden, Gunnar 1908- WhoWor 91
Seidenfeld, Arthur Jay 1951- St&PR 91
Seidenfeld, Glenn Kenneth 1914- WhoAm 90
Seidenfeld, Glenn Kenneth, Jr. 1944- WhoAm 90
Seidenfrau, Steven 1945- St&PR 91
Seidensticker, Edward George 1921- WhoAm 90, WhoWor 91
Seidensticker, John Christian, IV 1944- WhoE 91
Seidensticker, Louis Peter 1930- St&PR 91
Seidensticker, Robert Beach 1929- St&PR 91
Seidenthal, L.H. St&PR 91N
Seider, J. Paul 1926- St&PR 91
Seider, Rhoda Levy 1936- WhoE 91
Seiderer, Franz Rolf 1933- WhoWor 91
Seiderman, Maurice BioIn 16
Seiders, Joseph Robert 1948- St&PR 91, WhoAm 90
Seiders, Lori Ann 1955- WhoAmW 91
Seides, S Warren 1932- BiDrAPA 89
Seidewitz, Edwin Von 1962- WhoE 91
Seidl, Anton 1850-1898 PenDiMP
Seidl, Claire 1951- WhoAmA 91
Seidl, Fredrick William 1940- WhoAm 90
Seidl, Gerald Dorsey 1933- St&PR 91
Seidl, John Michael 1939- St&PR 91, WhoAm 90
Seidl-Hohenveldern, Ignaz Christian 1918- WhoWor 91
Seidle, Joseph Worrell 1946- St&PR 91
Seidler, Doris WhoAmA 91
Seidler, Doris 1912- WhoAm 90
Seidler, Edouard A. 1932- WhoWor 91
Seidler, Harry 1923- WhoWor 91
Seidler, Horst Gunther 1944- WhoWor 91
Seidler, I. Marshall 1934- WhoAm 90
Seidler, James F. 1942- St&PR 91
Seidler, Lee J. 1935- St&PR 91
Seidler, M. Bonnie 1942- WhoAmW 91
Seidler, Tor 1952- BioIn 16
Seidler, William Dickson 1920-1988 BioIn 16
Seidman, Ellen Shapiro 1948- WhoAmW 91
Seidman, Graham Zalman 1932- WhoWor 91
Seidman, Harold 1911- WhoAm 90
Seidman, Hugh 1940- WhoWrEP 89
Seidman, L. William 1921- St&PR 91
Seidman, Lewis William 1921- WhoAm 90
Seidman, Marshall Jacob 1925- WhoSSW 91
Seidman, Miriam Rosalind 1923- WhoE 91
Seidman, Morris 1929- St&PR 91
Seidman, Stuart Ivan 1957- WhoE 91
Seidman, Sue Rindsberg 1936- WhoE 91
Seidman, Theodore M. 1924- St&PR 91
Seidner, Diane ConAu 31NR
Seidner, Frederic J. 1931- ODwPR 91
Seidner, Frederic Jay 1931- WhoAm 90
Seidner-Edelson, Suellen 1952- WhoAmW 91, WhoEmL 91
Seif, Sue Solomon 1946- WhoAmW 91
Seif, Walter L., Jr. 1931- WhoE 91
Seifer, David 1932- St&PR 91
Seifer, Judith Huffman 1945- WhoEmL 91
Seifer, Ronald Leslie 1942- WhoSSW 91
Seiferheld, David Froehlich 1904- WhoAm 90
Seiferle, Rebecca Ann 1951- WhoWrEP 89
Seifert, Bo Leopold 1945- WhoWor 91
Seifert, Cheryl Etta 1952- WhoAmW 91
Seifert, Debra ODwPR 91
Seifert, Eugene 1923- St&PR 91
Seifert, George 1940- WhoAm 90
Seifert, Gerd-Heinrich 1931- IntWWM 90
Seifert, Hans-Joachim 1930- WhoWor 91
Seifert, Horst Hans 1937- St&PR 91
Seifert, Jaroslav 1901-1986 MajTwCW
Seifert, Laurence Curt 1938- WhoAm 90
Seifert, Otto Erich 1912- IntWWM 90
Seifert, Sharon Kay 1944- WhoSSW 91
Seifert, Stephen Wayne 1957- WhoEmL 91
Seifert, Thomas Lloyd 1940- WhoAm 90, WhoWor 91
Seifert, William John, Jr. 1950- St&PR 91
Seifert, William Walther 1920- WhoAm 90
Seiff, Arthur N. 1901-1988 BioIn 16
Seiffert, Peter PenDiMP
Seiffert, Peter 1955- IntWWM 90
Seifried, F Stanley 1935- BiDrAPA 89
Seifried, Harold Edwin 1946- WhoE 91
Seifullina, Lidia 1889-1954 EncCoWW
Seig, Ann Barbara BiDrAPA 89
Seigel, Allen S. 1942- WhoE 91
Seigel, Arthur Michael 1944- WhoE 91
Seigel, Charles Jay 1941- WhoE 91
Seigel, Charles Meyers 1958- WhoE 91
Seigel, Harold O. 1924- St&PR 91
Seigel, Hersch 1927- St&PR 91
Seigel, Jerrold Edward 1936- WhoAm 90
Seigel, Max H. BioIn 16
Seigel, Michael H. 1947- St&PR 91
Seigel, Morton David BiDrAPA 89
Seigel, Robert Alan 1938- WhoSSW 91
Seigel, Stuart Evan 1933- WhoAm 90
Seigen NewAgMG
Seigenthaler, John Lawrence 1927- WhoAm 90, WhoWor 91
Seigfried, Edgar Martin 1932- St&PR 91
Seigle, Eliot Brandon BiDrAPA 89
Seigle, Harold T. 1908- St&PR 91
Seigle, John William 1929- WhoAm 90
Seigle, Mark Steven 1958- St&PR 91
Seigle, Richard D 1951- BiDrAPA 89
Seigler, David Stanley 1940- WhoAm 90
Seigler, Ruth Queen 1942- WhoAmW 91
Seigler, William David 1934- St&PR 91
Seignoret, Clarence Henry Augustus 1919- WhoWor 91
Seignouret, Francois 1768-1853? PenDiDA 89
Seikaly, Mouin Gerios 1954- WhoSSW 91
Seikel, George R. 1933- WhoWor 91
Seikel, Oliver Edward 1937- St&PR 91, WhoAm 90
Seikus, Patti Rae 1953- WhoAmW 91
Seil, David E 1936- BiDrAPA 89
Seil, Fredrick John 1933- WhoAm 90
Seiler, Albert C. 1924- St&PR 91
Seiler, Amy Hart 1950- WhoE 91
Seiler, Charlotte Woody 1915- WhoAmW 91
Seiler, Conrad EarBlAP
Seiler, Daniel S. St&PR 91
Seiler, Earnest Edward, III 1960- BiDrAPA 89
Seiler, Elaine Ann 1940- WhoAmW 91, WhoE 91
Seiler, Jacob Martin BioIn 16
Seiler, Jane F. 1959- WhoAmW 91
Seiler, John Gray, Jr. 1933- St&PR 91
Seiler, Mark J. 1958- St&PR 91
Seiler, Otto J. 1929- WhoWor 91
Seiler, Peter NewAgMG
Seiler, Robert D. 1953- St&PR 91
Seiler, Robert Edward 1925- WhoAm 90
Seiler, Robert Ramsey, Jr. 1928- WhoSSW 91
Seiler, Roslyn Lila 1930- WhoAmW 91
Seilheimer, Robert 1939- St&PR 91
Seilliere de Laborde, Ernest-Antoine 1937- WhoWor 91
Seils, William G. 1935- St&PR 91
Seils, William George 1935- WhoAm 90
Seim, Stuart S. St&PR 91
Sein, Shu May 1934- BiDrAPA 89
Seiner, Jerome Allan 1932- WhoE 91
Seinfeld, Jerry BioIn 16
Seinfeld, John Hersh 1942- WhoAm 90
Seinsheimer, Joseph Fellman, III 1940- St&PR 91
Seinsheimer, Joseph Fellman, Jr. 1913- St&PR 91, WhoAm 90
Seinuk, Ysrael A. 1931- WhoHisp 91
Seip, Tom D. 1950- St&PR 91
Seipler, Maurice Russell 1926- St&PR 91
Seipold, Charles F. 1948- St&PR 91
Seipp, Walter 1925- WhoWor 91
Seireg, Ali Abdel Hay 1927- WhoAm 90
Seisser, Tod BioIn 16
Seitchik, Richard J. St&PR 91
Seitel, Fraser P. 1946- ODwPR 91, St&PR 91

Seitel, Fraser Paul 1946- *WhoAm 90*
Seitelberger, Franz 1916- *WhoWor 91*
Seitelman, Jeffrey Kevin 1952- *BiDrAPA 89*
Seitelman, Margot *BioIn 16*
Seiter, James Julian 1941- *St&PR 91*
Seith, Alex R. 1934- *St&PR 91*
Seith, Alex Robert 1934- *WhoAm 90*
Seitlin, Robert Louis 1915- *WhoSSW 91*
Seitschek, Viktor Rudolf 1943- *WhoWor 91*
Seittelman, Elizabeth Edith 1922- *WhoAm 90*
Seittelman, Estelle *WhoE 91*
Seitz, Anne Marie 1939- *WhoWor 91*
Seitz, David Frederick 1944- *St&PR 91*
Seitz, David J *BiDrAPA 89*
Seitz, Donn Philip 1948- *St&PR 91*
Seitz, Frederick 1911- *WhoAm 90*
Seitz, G.L. 1909- *St&PR 91*
Seitz, Howard Alexander 1907- *WhoAm 90*
Seitz, Jacqueline 1936- *BioIn 16*
Seitz, Joel Neil 1941- *St&PR 91*
Seitz, Laura Ruth 1951- *WhoEmL 91*
Seitz, M.N. 1945- *St&PR 91*
Seitz, Martin 1895-1988 *BioIn 16*
Seitz, Melvin Christian, Jr. 1939- *St&PR 91*
Seitz, Nicholas Joseph 1939- *WhoAm 90, WhoWrEP 89*
Seitz, Reynolds C. 1909- *WhoAm 90*
Seitz, Robert J., Jr. 1953- *ODwPR 91*
Seitz, Robert John, Jr. 1953- *WhoE 91*
Seitz, Roger Michael 1937- *WhoAm 90*
Seitz, Tadd C. 1941- *St&PR 91*
Seitz, Tycho 1933- *WhoWor 91*
Seitz, Victoria Ann 1956- *WhoSSW 91*
Seitz, Wesley Donald 1940- *WhoAm 90*
Seitz, William Chapin 1914-1974 *WhoAmA 91N*
Seitzer, Kevin 1962- *Ballpl 90*
Seitzer, Robert Harris 1916- *WhoE 91*
Seitzinger, Harry Otis 1928- *St&PR 91, WhoAm 90*
Seivewright, Robert Peter 1954- *IntWWM 90*
Seiwa Genji Clan *EncJap*
Seixas, Judith S. 1922- *AuBYP 90*
Seja, Austra *EncCoWW*
Sejour, Victor 1817-1874 *DrBlPA 90, EarBlAP*
Sejourne-Daitch, Chantal Marie 1952- *BiDrAPA 89*
Sekar, Vimala 1951- *BiDrAPA 89*
Sekas, Gus N. 1932- *St&PR 91*
Sekas, Nicholas 1963- *St&PR 91*
Sekeba, Drake Simwogerere 1944- *WhoWor 91*
Sekerka, Robert Floyd 1937- *WhoAm 90*
Sekharan, Chandra 1928- *BiDrAPA 89*
Sekhon, Gurmit Singh *BiDrAPA 89*
Sekhon, Harbir Sinah *BiDrAPA 89*
Seki, Hideo 1905- *EncPaPR 91*
Seki, Hiroharu 1927- *WhoWor 91*
Seki, Masahiro 1934- *WhoWor 91*
Sekiguchi, Mutsuo 1932- *WhoWor 91*
Sekiguchi, Seiya 1932- *WhoWor 91*
Sekimoto, Tadahiro 1926- *St&PR 91, WhoWor 91*
Sekin, Darrell Joseph 1926- *WhoSSW 91*
Sekiya, Gerald Yoshinori 1942- *WhoWor 91*
Sekiyama, Morihiro 1936- *BiDrAPA 89*
Sekka, Johnny 1939- *DrBlPA 90*
Seklecki, Gail Ann 1947- *WhoE 91*
Sekler, Eduard Franz 1920- *WhoAm 90, WhoE 91, WhoWrEP 89*
Sekoll, June Louise 1931- *WhoSSW 91, WhoWrEP 89*
Sekowski, Cynthia Jean 1953- *WhoAmW 91*
Sektberg, Willard *BioIn 16*
Sekula, Edward Joseph, Jr. 1937- *WhoAm 90*
Sekuler, Eliot *ODwPR 91*
Sekuler, Robert William 1939- *WhoAm 90*
Sekulic, Ante 1920- *WhoWor 91*
Sela, Michael 1924- *WhoWor 91*
Selak, Barbara S. *WhoWrEP 89*
Selak, Robert Allen 1954- *WhoEmL 91*
Selander, Lucy Mae 1946- *WhoAmW 91*
Selbach, Kip 1872-1956 *Ballpl 90*
Selbach, Scott C. 1955- *St&PR 91*
Selber, Arlene Bork 1942- *WhoSSW 91*
Selber, Leonard 1934- *St&PR 91*
Selberg, Ingrid Maria 1950- *WhoWor 91*
Selberherr, Siegfried 1955- *WhoEmL 91, WhoWor 91*
Selbin, Joel 1931- *WhoSSW 91*
Selbit, P. T. 1881-1938 *BioIn 16*
Selbst, Ronald A 1927- *BiDrAPA 89*
Selbst, Stanton Creson 1935- *WhoE 91*
Selby, Cecily Cannan 1927- *WhoAm 90, WhoAmW 91*
Selby, Clark Linwood, Jr. 1936- *WhoSSW 91, WhoWor 91*
Selby, Hubert, Jr. 1928- *ConAu 33NR, WhoAm 90*
Selby, Jerome M. 1948- *WhoWor 91*
Selby, John Horace 1919- *WhoSSW 91*
Selby, John Rodney 1929- *St&PR 91*
Selby, Katherine *WhoWrEP 89*
Selby, Kathryn Shauna 1962- *IntWWM 90*
Selby, Nancy Chizek 1935- *WhoAmW 91, WhoSSW 91*
Selby, Philip 1948- *IntWWM 90*
Selby, Roger Lowell 1933- *WhoAm 90, WhoAmA 91*
Selby, Roy Clifton, Jr. 1930- *WhoSSW 91*
Selby, Stephen P. 1940- *St&PR 91*
Selby Wright, Ronald 1908- *WhoWor 91*
Selby-Wright, Sonya *NewYTBS 90*
Selchow, Richard P. *BioIn 16*
Selchow, Roger Hoffman 1911- *WhoAmA 91, WhoE 91*
Selco, Jodye I. 1957- *WhoAmW 91*
Selden, Annie Alexander 1938- *WhoAmW 91, WhoSSW 91*
Selden, Catherine *FemiCLE*
Selden, George *AuBYP 90, ConAu 130*
Selden, George 1929-1989 *BioIn 16, SmATA X*
Selden, George B *EncABHB 4*
Selden, John 1584-1654 *BioIn 16*
Selden, John 1934- *WhoSSW 91*
Selden, Joseph Wixson 1916- *WhoSSW 91*
Selden, Margery Juliet Stomne *IntWWM 90*
Selden, Neil R 1931- *SmATA 61*
Selden, Richard Thomas 1922- *WhoAm 90*
Selden, Robert Wentworth 1936- *WhoAm 90*
Selden, Samuel 1899-1979 *AuBYP 90*
Selden, William Kirkpatrick 1911- *WhoAm 90*
Seldes, George 1890- *BioIn 16, WhoAm 90*
Seldes, Gilbert Vivian 1893-1970 *BioIn 16*
Seldes, Marian *BioIn 16, WhoAm 90*
Seldes, Marian 1928- *NotWoAT*
Seldin, Donald Wayne 1920- *WhoAm 90*
Seldis, Henry J 1925-1978 *WhoAmA 91N*
Selditch, Alan Daniel 1926- *WhoWor 91*
Seldman, L. William 1921- *NewYTBS 90 [port]*
Seldner, Elaine Carlson 1949- *WhoE 91*
Seldom Scene, The *ConMus 4 [port]*
Seldon, Willa Esther 1960- *WhoE 91*
Seleb, Marcie Robertson 1958- *WhoSSW 91*
Selecman, Charles Edward 1928- *WhoAm 90*
Selee, Frank 1859-1909 *Ballpl 90*
Selegue, John Paul 1952- *WhoSSW 91*
Selenow, Harvey Steven 1943- *St&PR 91*
Seles, Monica *NewYTBS 90 [port]*
Seleshi, Ermias 1952- *BiDrAPA 89*
Selesnick, Rose Goodman 1926- *WhoAmW 91*
Seletsky, Burton 1935- *WhoSSW 91*
Seley, Jason 1919-1983 *WhoAmA 91N*
Self, Adrian Geoffrey 1952- *IntWWM 90*
Self, Alla Kay 1946- *WhoSSW 91*
Self, Charles Edwin 1934- *WhoAm 90*
Self, Craig Baldwin 1952- *WhoE 91*
Self, Edwin Forbes 1920- *WhoAm 90, WhoWrEP 89*
Self, Geoffrey Robert 1930- *IntWWM 90*
Self, George Doyle 1943- *St&PR 91*
Self, Glen 1938- *St&PR 91*
Self, James C. 1919- *St&PR 91*
Self, James Cuthbert 1919- *WhoAm 90*
Self, James Reed 1944- *WhoAm 90*
Self, Joseph Morrison 1929- *WhoWor 91*
Self, Lee Vann 1940- *WhoSSW 91*
Self, Lizabeth *BioIn 16*
Self, Madison Allen 1921- *WhoAm 90*
Self, Margaret Cabell 1902- *AuBYP 90*
Self, Mark Edward 1955- *WhoEmL 91, WhoSSW 91, WhoWor 91*
Self, Peggy Joyce 1938- *WhoSSW 91*
Self, Raymond Weaver *WhoAm 90*
Self, Stanley David *BiDrAPA 89*
Self, William Edwin 1921- *WhoAm 90*
Self, William Lee 1932- *WhoSSW 91*
Selfe, Robert W. 1943- *WhoAm 90*
Selfman, David 1936- *BiDrAPA 89*
Selfon, Rosanne Nancy 1948- *WhoAmW 91*
Selfridge, George Dever 1924- *WhoAm 90*
Selfridge, Harry G. 1864-1947 *WorAlBi*
Selfridge, Steven G. 1955- *St&PR 91*
Selgas, Alfred Michael 1943- *WhoHisp 91*
Selhorst, L.O. 1933- *St&PR 91*
Selhorst, Lawrence O'Hare 1933- *WhoAm 90*
Selib, Stanley Zalmen 1929- *WhoE 91*
Selig, Allan H. 1934- *WhoAm 90*
Selig, Don *BiDrAPA 89*
Selig, J Daniel 1938- *WhoAmA 91N*
Selig, Julian W, Jr. 1934- *BiDrAPA 89*
Selig, Karl-Ludwig 1926- *WhoAm 90, WhoWor 91, WhoWrEP 89*
Selig, Kenneth Mishara *BiDrAPA 89*
Selig, Kenneth Mishara 1950- *WhoE 91*
Selig, Leon Morange 1933- *WhoWor 91*
Selig, Manfred *WhoAmA 91*
Selig, Manfred, Mrs *WhoAmA 91*
Selig, S. Stephen, III 1943- *St&PR 91*
Seliger, Charles 1926- *WhoAm 90, WhoAmA 91*
Seligman, Charles 1893-1978 *WhoAmA 91N*
Seligman, Daniel 1924- *WhoAm 90, WhoWrEP 89*
Seligman, Dorothy Halle *AuBYP 90*
Seligman, Edwin Robert Anderson 1861-1939 *BioIn 16*
Seligman, Fred *BiDrAPA 89*
Seligman, Garry Alan 1949- *BiDrAPA 89*
Seligman, George Benham 1927- *WhoE 91*
Seligman, Irving *BioIn 16*
Seligman, Joseph 1819-1880 *EncABHB 6 [port]*
Seligman, Mac 1918- *St&PR 91*
Seligman, Mac 1928- *ODwPR 91*
Seligman, Morris J *BiDrAPA 89*
Seligman, Muriel 1922- *WhoAmW 91*
Seligman, Raphael David 1919- *WhoWor 91*
Seligman, Roslyn *BiDrAPA 89*
Seligman, Rudolph Frank 1943- *WhoAm 90*
Seligman, Scott D. *ODwPR 91*
Seligman, Thomas Knowles 1944- *WhoAm 90, WhoAmA 91*
Seligmann, Gustav Leonard 1934- *WhoSSW 91*
Seligmann, Herbert J 1891-1984 *WhoAmA 91N*
Seligmann, Kurt 1900-1962 *WhoAmA 91N*
Seligson, Carl H. 1935- *WhoAm 90*
Seligson, Charles D. 1942- *St&PR 91*
Seligson, Jose L 1947- *BiDrAPA 89*
Seligson, Jose Luis 1947- *WhoE 91*
Seligson, M. Ross 1949- *WhoWor 91*
Seligson, Robert Allen 1932- *WhoAm 90*
Seligson, Theodore H. 1930- *WhoAm 90*
Selika, Marie 1849?-1937 *BioIn 16*
Selimi, Fehime 1954- *EncCoWW*
Selin, Ivan 1937- *WhoAm 90, WhoE 91, WhoWor 91*
Seline, Helen Crabb *BiDrAPA 89*
Selinger, Neil R *BiDrAPA 89*
Selinske, Charles E. 1933- *St&PR 91*
Selinsky, Herman 1901- *BiDrAPA 89*
Selis, John Leon 1936- *St&PR 91*
Seliskar, Denise Martha 1953- *WhoE 91*
Selk, Eleanor Hutton 1918- *WhoAmW 91*
Selk, Gail Barbara 1937- *WhoAmW 91*
Selke, Charles Richard 1947- *WhoSSW 91*
Selke, Eloise Wildenthal 1924- *WhoAmW 91*
Selke, William August 1922- *St&PR 91*
Selke-Kern, Barbara Ellen 1950- *WhoAmW 91, WhoEmL 91, WhoSSW 91*
Selkirk, George 1908-1987 *Ballpl 90*
Selkirk, James Kirkwood 1938- *WhoAm 90*
Selkirk, Jane *AuBYP 90*
Selko, Soll Leonard 1923- *St&PR 91*
Selkoe, Dennis J. 1943- *WhoAm 90*
Selkowitz, Arthur 1943- *WhoAm 90*
Selky, John Lee 1937- *St&PR 91*
Sell, Alan Philip Frederick 1935- *WhoWor 91*
Sell, David Frank 1930- *IntWWM 90*
Sell, Donald A. 1935- *St&PR 91*
Sell, Donald Arthur 1935- *WhoAm 90*
Sell, Douglas P. 1948- *St&PR 91*
Sell, Edward Scott, Jr. 1917- *St&PR 91, WhoAm 90*
Sell, Floyd E. 1933- *St&PR 91*
Sell, Jill 1950- *WhoWrEP 89*
Sell, Joan Isobel 1936- *WhoAmW 91, WhoSSW 91*
Sell, Kenneth Walter 1931- *WhoAm 90*
Sell, Leo L 1927- *BiDrAPA 89*
Sell, Mercer B, Jr. 1922- *BiDrAPA 89*
Sell, Neil I. 1941- *St&PR 91*
Sell, Steven Ray 1941- *St&PR 91*
Sell, Winifred Anne 1949- *WhoSSW 91*
Sella, Alvin Conrad 1924- *WhoAmA 91*
Sella, Edward Gerard 1933- *WhoE 91*
Sella, Emmanuel 1924- *WhoE 91*
Sella, George John, Jr. 1928- *St&PR 91, WhoAm 90, WhoE 91*
Sellars, James Allen 1958- *WhoWor 91*
Sellars, James Edward *IntWWM 90*
Sellars, John Dennis 1948- *WhoEmL 91*
Sellars, Nigel Anthony 1954- *WhoWrEP 89*
Sellars, Peter 1958- *IntWWM 90*
Sellars, Roy Henry 1964- *WhoWor 91*
Sellars, Victor Carol Gene 1929- *WhoWor 91*
Sellars, Wilfrid 1912-1989 *BioIn 16*
Sellars, Wilfrid Stalker 1912-1989 *ConAu 129*
Selldorff, J. Thomas 1928- *St&PR 91*
Sellecca, Connie *BioIn 16*
Sellecca, Connie 1955- *WorAlBi*
Selleck, Margaret 1892- *WhoAmA 91N*
Selleck, Tom *BioIn 16*
Selleck, Tom 1945- *WhoAm 90, WorAlBi*
Seller, Michael Scott *BiDrAPA 89*
Seller, Robert Herman 1931- *WhoAm 90*
Seller, William Frank 1934- *St&PR 91*
Sellers, Alan *St&PR 91*
Sellers, Barbara Jackson 1940- *WhoAmW 91*
Sellers, Bettie Mixon 1926- *WhoWrEP 89*
Sellers, Bobby Eugene 1937- *BiDrAPA 89*
Sellers, Dennis Aaron 1956- *WhoWrEP 89*
Sellers, Donald W 1928- *BiDrAPA 89*
Sellers, Fred Evans 1941- *WhoSSW 91*
Sellers, Fred Wilson 1942- *St&PR 91*
Sellers, Georgeanna 1955- *WhoSSW 91*
Sellers, Gregory Jude 1947- *WhoEmL 91, WhoWor 91*
Sellers, Howard E. 1925- *St&PR 91*
Sellers, Jacquelyn Marie 1958- *IntWWM 90*
Sellers, James Earl 1926- *WhoAm 90*
Sellers, James McBrayer 1895- *WhoAm 90*
Sellers, Jane Whitt 1953- *WhoEmL 91*
Sellers, Jeff 1964- *Ballpl 90*
Sellers, Jerry D. 1939- *St&PR 91*
Sellers, John 1924- *DrBlPA 90*
Sellers, John Lewis 1934- *WhoAmA 91, WhoE 91*
Sellers, Mark Russell 1963- *WhoE 91*
Sellers, Mark Thomas 1964- *WhoSSW 91*
Sellers, Marlene 1933- *WhoAmW 91*
Sellers, Peter 1925-1980 *BioIn 16, WorAlBi*
Sellers, Peter Hoadley 1930- *WhoAm 90*
Sellers, Peter Richard Henry 1925-1980 *EncPaPR 91*
Sellers, Philip A. 1920- *St&PR 91*
Sellers, Randall V. 1952- *BiDrAPA 89*
Sellers, Richard Lynn 1954- *WhoSSW 91*
Sellers, Richard Wesley 1938- *St&PR 91*
Sellers, Shirley Nesbit 1926- *WhoAmW 91*
Sellers, Sidney Levingston, IV 1953- *WhoEmL 91*
Sellers, Wallace O. 1929- *St&PR 91*
Sellers, William E. 1934- *St&PR 91*
Sellers, William Freeman 1929- *WhoAmA 91*
Sellers, Wm D, Jr. 1913- *St&PR 91*
Sellers-Bok, Margaret *BiDrAPA 89*
Sellery, J'nan Morse 1928- *WhoWrEP 89*
Selles, Jean-Philippe 1948- *WhoWor 91*
Sellew, Ann Parker *BiDrAPA 89*
Sellew, Catharine Freeman 1922- *AuBYP 90*
Sellick, John F. 1934- *St&PR 91*
Sellick, Phyllis 1911- *PenDiMP*
Sellick, Phyllis Doreen 1911- *IntWWM 90*
Sellier, Henri Charles 1883-1943 *BiDFrPL*
Sellier, Louis 1885-1978 *BiDFrPL*
Sellin, David 1930- *WhoAmA 91, WhoE 91*
Sellin, Eric 1933- *WhoAm 90, WhoWrEP 89*
Sellin, Theodore 1928- *WhoAm 90*
Sellin, Thorsten 1896- *BioIn 16*
Sellinger, Scott Michael 1953- *St&PR 91*
Sellings, David *BioIn 16*
Sellitto, Larry Audeno 1955- *WhoE 91*
Sellman, Charles Harwood 1934- *St&PR 91*
Sellman, James E. 1947- *BiDrAPA 89*
Sellman, Wayne Steven 1940- *WhoE 91*
Sellmann, Dieter 1941- *WhoWor 91*
Sello, Allen Ralph 1939- *WhoAm 90*
Sellon, John A. 1910- *St&PR 91*
Sellon, Martha Ann *FemiCLE*
Sellon, Perry Kimball *BioIn 16*
Sells, Boake Anthony 1937- *St&PR 91, WhoAm 90*
Sells, Bruce Howard 1930- *WhoAm 90*
Sells, Dan 1939- *St&PR 91*
Sells, Dave 1946- *Ballpl 90*
Sells, Harold E. 1928- *St&PR 91, WhoAm 90, WhoE 91*
Sells, Harold Robert 1917- *WhoWor 91*
Sells, Joyce Green 1946- *WhoSSW 91*
Sells, Luther Ray 1936- *WhoSSW 91*
Sells, Marcia Lynn *NewYTBS 90 [port]*
Sells, Sam R., II 1933- *St&PR 91*
Sells, Saul B. 1913-1988 *BioIn 16*
Sells, William A. 1933- *St&PR 91*
Sellstrom, Barbara 1928- *St&PR 91*
Selm, Robert Prickett 1923- *WhoWor 91*
Selma, Dick 1943- *Ballpl 90*
Selman, David H. 1933- *St&PR 91*
Selman, Forrest B *BiDrAPA 89*
Selman, Glenda Chaffin 1950- *WhoSSW 91*
Selman, Harold Wayne 1949- *BiDrAPA 89*
Selman, Helen Collins *WhoAmW 91*
Selman, Ireson Walton 1913-1988 *BioIn 16*
Selman, Jay Edward *BiDrAPA 89*
Selman, Kelly *WhoAmW 91*
Selman, LaRue W. 1927- *BioIn 16*
Selman, Murray 1926- *St&PR 91, WhoAm 90*

Selman, Richard David 1946- BiDrAPA 89
Selman, T.C. 1950- St&PR 91
Selmeier, Richard James 1943- WhoAm 90
Selmonsky, Jill Sharon 1964- WhoAmW 91
Selnau, Edward Walter 1929- St&PR 91
Selonick, James Bennett 1925- St&PR 91
Selonke, Irene A WhoAmA 91N
Selous, Edmund 1857-1934 DcScB S2
Selsam, Milicent Ellis WhoWrEP 89
Selsam, Millicent 1912- AuBYP 90
Selser, Christopher 1950- WhoAmA 91
Selski, William E. 1953- WhoE 91
Selsor, Jeff 1961- St&PR 91
Selsted, Walter T. BioIn 16
Seltman, Gary Myron 1951- BiDrAPA 89
Seltser, Raymond 1923- WhoAm 90
Seltz, Alfred Carl 1931- St&PR 91
Seltz, Paul H. 1921- St&PR 91
Seltzberg, Roni Lynn BiDrAPA 89
Seltzer, Alan Mark 1958- BiDrAPA 89
Seltzer, Chester E. 1915-1971 ConAu 131, HispWr 90
Seltzer, Craig H. 1954- St&PR 91
Seltzer, David BioIn 16
Seltzer, David Alan 1948- BiDrAPA 89
Seltzer, Dov 1932- IntWWM 90
Seltzer, Earl Charles 1922- WhoAm 90
Seltzer, Edward Charles 1927- St&PR 91
Seltzer, Ellen 1958- WhoAmW 91
Seltzer, Herbert A. 1907-1989 BioIn 16
Seltzer, Jeffrey Lloyd 1956- WhoE 91, WhoEmL 91, WhoWor 91
Seltzer, Joanne 1929- WhoWrEP 89
Seltzer, Joanne 1949- BiDrAPA 89
Seltzer, Joanne Lynn 1946- WhoAmA 91, WhoEmL 91
Seltzer, Laurence D 1936- BiDrAPA 89
Seltzer, Leo 1910- WhoAm 90
Seltzer, Leon Zee 1914- WhoAm 90
Seltzer, Matthew D. St&PR 91
Seltzer, Mildred June 1921- WhoAm 90
Seltzer, Phyllis 1928- WhoAmA 91
Seltzer, Phyllis Estelle 1928- WhoAm 90
Seltzer, Robert J. ODwPR 91
Seltzer, Robert Stephen 1935- WhoE 91
Seltzer, Ronald 1931- WhoAm 90
Seltzer, Ronald Anthony 1935- WhoAm 90
Seltzer, Ronni Lee 1952- BiDrAPA 89, WhoE 91
Seltzer, Samuel Marvin 1926- St&PR 91
Seltzer, Vicki Lynn 1949- WhoAm 90, WhoAmW 91, WhoWor 91
Seltzer-Rank family PenDiDA 89
Selvadurai, Antony Patrick Sinnappa 1942- WhoAm 90
Selvaggio, Pierro BioIn 16
Selvera, Norma Brito WhoHisp 91
Selvey, Henry Arthur 1940- BiDrAPA 89
Selvig, Forrest Hall 1924- WhoAmA 91
Selvig, William Norman 1932- St&PR 91
Selvin, Hanan C. 1921-1989 BioIn 16
Selvin, Nancy 1943- BioIn 16, WhoAmA 91
Selvon, Sam MajTwCW
Selvon, Samuel 1923- MajTwCW
Selvy, Barbara 1938- WhoAmW 91
Selwood, Pierce Taylor 1939- WhoAm 90
Selwyn, Beatrice Josephine 1942- WhoAmW 91, WhoSSW 91
Selwyn, David Morton 1951- IntWWM 90
Selwyn, Donald 1936- WhoAm 90
Selwyn, Francis 1935- TwCCr&M 91
Selwyn, Philip Alan 1945- WhoE 91
Selwyn, Sydney 1934- WhoWor 91
Selwyn Lloyd, John Selwyn Brooke, Baron 1904-1978 BioIn 16
Selya, Bruce Marshall 1934- WhoAm 90, WhoE 91
Selz, Allen 1931- WhoE 91
Selz, B.T. 1940- St&PR 91
Selz, Bernard 1940- WhoAm 90
Selz, Peter H 1919- WhoAmA 91
Selz, Peter Howard 1919- WhoAm 90
Selzer, Arthur 1911- WhoAm 90
Selzer, Gerard Bruno 1945- BiDrAPA 89
Selzer, Melvin L 1925- BiDrAPA 89
Selzer, Michael A 1934- BiDrAPA 89
Selzer, Michael David 1947- WhoSSW 91
Selzer, Richard BioIn 16
Selzer, Richard Alan 1928- WhoAm 90
Selzer, William Henry 1925- St&PR 91
Selzler, Bernard John 1939- WhoWrEP 89
Selznick, David O. 1902-1965 WorAlBi
Selznick, Irene Mayer NewYTBS 90 [port]
Selznick, Irene Mayer 1907- BioIn 16, NotWoAT, WhoAm 90
Selznick, Irene Mayer 1907-1990 ConAu 132
Sem-Jacobsen, Carl Wilhelm 1912- BiDrAPA 89
Semak, David P. 1948- St&PR 91
Semak, Michael 1934- WhoAmA 91
Semak, Michael William 1934- WhoAm 90
Seman, Constantin 1943- St&PR 91
Semans, James Hustead 1910- WhoAmA 91
Semans, Truman Thomas 1926- WhoAm 90
Semard, Pierre 1887-1942 BiDFrPL
Semark, Philip Norman 1945- WhoAm 90
Semas, Leonard Allen 1947- WhoEmL 91
Semas, Philip Wayne 1946- WhoAm 90
Semba, Susan Commander 1952- WhoEmL 91
Sembat, Marcel Etienne 1862-1922 BiDFrPL
Sembene, Ousmane 1923- BioIn 16, DrBIPA 90
Sember, Joseph Alexander 1923- St&PR 91
Sembera, Carroll 1941- Ballpl 90
Sembler, Melvin 1932- WhoWor 91
Sembrich, Marcella 1858-1935 PenDiMP
Semchishen, Orest M 1932- WhoAmA 91
Semchyshyn, George O 1937- BiDrAPA 89
Semedo, Julio 1942- WhoWor 91
Semegen, Patrick W. 1946- St&PR 91
Semegen, Patrick William 1946- WhoAm 90
Semel, Charles David 1942- BiDrAPA 89
Semel, Terry 1943- WhoAm 90
Semelsberger, Kenneth J. 1936- St&PR 91, WhoAm 90
Semeniuk, Charmaine I 1953- BiDrAPA 89
Semenov, Grigorii Mikhailovich 1890-1946 BioIn 16
Semenov, Nikolay 1896-1986 WorAlBi
Semente, Gloria Rose 1933- WhoE 91
Semer, Jerry Martin BiDrAPA 89
Semerad, Roger Dale 1940- WhoAm 90
Semerjian, Evan Yervant 1940- WhoAm 90
Semerjian, Harry 1933- IntWWM 90
Semerjian, Helena Brown 1936- WhoE 91
Semhon, Gerard 1936- St&PR 91
Semiler, Bulent BioIn 16
Seminario, Rafael F BiDrAPA 89
Seminick, Andy 1920- Ballpl 90
Semino, Houshang BiDrAPA 89
Semiramis BioIn 16
Semke, L.K. 1936- St&PR 91
Semkiw, Peter Martin BiDrAPA 89
Semkov, Jerzy 1928- IntWWM 90
Semkow, Jerzy 1928- PenDiMP
Semkow, Jerzy Stanislaw 1928- WhoAm 90, WhoE 91, WhoWor 91
Semler, Dean R. 1929- St&PR 91
Semler, Jerry D. 1937- St&PR 91, WhoAm 90, WhoWor 91
Semler, Johannes 1923- WhoWor 91
Semlitz, Linda J BiDrAPA 89
Semloh 1898- SmATA X [port]
Semlow, Bruce E. 1938- St&PR 91
Semlyen, Adam 1923- WhoAm 90
Semmel, Bernard 1928- WhoAm 90, WhoWrEP 89
Semmel, David Robert 1957- St&PR 91
Semmel, Joan 1932- BiDWomA, WhoAmA 91
Semmelmeyer, Kristin Leigh 1958- WhoE 91
Semmelweis, Ignac Fulop 1818-1865 BioIn 16
Semmelweis, Ignaz Philipp 1818-1865 WorAlBi
Semmens, James Pike 1919- WhoSSW 91
Semmer, John Richard 1943- WhoSSW 91
Semmer, Lorraine Bobbie 1950- WhoSSW 91
Semmes, Raphael 1809-1877 WorAlBi
Semon, Warren Lloyd 1921- WhoAm 90
Semonche, John E 1933- ConAu 30NR
Semones, Charles 1937- LiHiK
Semones, James King 1948- WhoSSW 91, WhoWor 91
Semones, Jeanne Angela BiDrAPA 89
Semonian, Robert Alexander 1939- WhoAm 90, WhoE 91, WhoWor 91
Semonin, William J. 1930- St&PR 91
Semonoff, Ralph Perlow 1918- WhoAm 90
Semonsky, Charles 1940- BiDrAPA 89
Semos, Chris Victor 1936- WhoSSW 91
Semowich, Charles John WhoAmA 91
Semper, Gottfried PenDiDA 89
Semper, Gottfried 1803-1879 BioIn 16
Sempier, Burt N. 1931- St&PR 91
Semple, Cecil Snowdon 1917- WhoAm 90, WhoE 91
Semple, Ellen Churchill 1863-1932 LiHiK
Semple, H. W. B. BioIn 16
Semple, Harton Singer NewYTBS 90
Semple, Harton Singer 1920-1990 BioIn 16
Semple, Jack Lionel St&PR 91N
Semple, Jock 1903-1988 BioIn 16
Semple, Lloyd Ashby 1939- WhoAm 90
Semple, Lorenzo, Jr. ConAu 129
Semple, Maggie BioIn 16
Semple, Margaret Olivia 1954- WhoWor 91
Semple, Muriel Virginia 1915- WhoAmW 91, WhoWor 91
Semple, Nathaniel Meacon 1946- WhoE 91
Semple, Robert Baylor 1910-1988 BioIn 16
Semple, Robert Baylor, Jr. 1936- WhoAm 90
Semple, Robert Warren 1950- St&PR 91
Semple, William Tunstall 1946- WhoE 91
Sempliner, John Alexander 1953- WhoWor 91
Semproch, Ray 1931- Ballpl 90
Semprun, Jorge 1923- WorAu 1980 [port]
Semprun y Maura, Jorge 1923- WorAu 1980 [port]
Semrad, John B. 1923- St&PR 91
Semrad, Myron L. 1945- St&PR 91
Semrad, Myron Leslie 1945- WhoSSW 91
Semrad, R. Anthony 1935- St&PR 91
Semrau, Stanley Robert BiDrAPA 89
Semrod, T. Joseph BioIn 16
Semrod, T. Joseph 1936- WhoAm 90, WhoE 91
Semrod, Theodore Joseph 1936- St&PR 91
Semyonov, Julian 1931- WhoWor 91
Sen no Rikyu 1522-1591 EncJap
Sen Soshitsu EncJap
Sen, Amartya Kumar 1933- WhoWor 91
Sen, Ashish Kumar 1942- WhoAm 90
Sen, Colleen Taylor 1944- WhoAmW 91
Sen, Gautam 1951- WhoSSW 91
Sen, Mrinal BioIn 16
Sen, Pranab Kumar 1937- WhoSSW 91
Sen, Sandip BiDrAPA 89
Sen, Sudhir BioIn 16
Sen, Sudhir 1906-1989 ConAu 129
Sena, Carol Little 1946- BiDrAPA 89
Sena, Diane M. 1950- St&PR 91
Sena, Estevan S. 1945- WhoHisp 91
Sena, Richard Alan 1947- WhoE 91
Sena, Robert John 1946- BiDrAPA 89
Sena, Tom BioIn 16
Senack, Marsha Mariam 1949- WhoAmW 91
Senak, Mark BioIn 16
Senanayake, Edward M BiDrAPA 89
Senapati, Hemant Kumar BiDrAPA 89
Senati DcCanB 12
Senator, Rochelle B. 1939- WhoAmW 91
Senator, Ronald 1926- IntWWM 90
Senatore, Rosemary 1949- WhoAmW 91
Senay, David T. 1956- ODwPR 91
Senay, Edward C 1927- BiDrAPA 89
Senay, Pierrette BiDrAPA 89
Sencer, Walter 1921- BiDrAPA 89
Sendak, Jack AuBYP 90
Sendak, Maurice BioIn 16
Sendak, Maurice 1928- AuBYP 90, MajTwCW, WorAlBi
Sendak, Maurice Bernard 1928- WhoAm 90, WhoAmA 91, WhoWrEP 89
Sendax, Victor Irven 1930- WhoAm 90, WhoWor 91
Sendecki, Vladislav NewAgMG
Sendell, Stuart Daniel 1942- St&PR 91
Sender, Henry Herman 1925- WhoSSW 91
Sender, Ramon 1902-1982 HispWr 90, MajTwCW
Sender, Ramon Jose 1901-1982 BioIn 16
Sender, Ruth M 1926- SmATA 62 [port]
Sender, Ruth Minsky BioIn 16
Sender, Sidney 1917- WhoE 91
Sender, Toni 1888-1964 BioIn 16
Sender Barayon, Ramon 1934- ConAu 130, HispWr 90
Senderling, Jon Townsend WhoAm 90
Senderowitz, Stephen Jay 1949- WhoEmL 91
Sendgraff, Mary Lou 1935- WhoAmW 91
Sendic, Raul 1925-1989 BioIn 16
Sendlein, Lyle V. A. 1933- WhoSSW 91
Sendler, David A. 1938- WhoWrEP 89
Sendler, David Alan 1938- WhoAm 90
Sendler, Irena 1916- BioIn 16
Sendrovic, Israel 1947- St&PR 91, WhoAm 90
Sendzimir, Tadeusz 1894-1989 BioIn 16
Sene, Claude, I 1724-1792 PenDiDA 89
Sene, Gerard BioIn 16
Sene, Jean-Baptiste-Claude 1747-1803 PenDiDA 89
Seneca the Younger 3?BC-65AD WorAlBi
Seneca, Joe ConTFT 8 [port], DrBIPA 90
Seneca, Lucius Annaeus 4?BC-65AD ClMLC 6 [port]
Seneca, Lucius Annus 4?BC-65AD WrPh P
Senecal, Eugene Gerald 1943- St&PR 91
Senecal, Eva 1905- DcLB 92
Senecal-Tremblay, Francois WhoAm 90
Senechal, Lester John 1934- WhoE 91
Senechal, Michel 1927- PenDiMP
Senechal, Philip J. 1946- St&PR 91
Senegal, Bently Benjamin 1958- WhoSSW 91
Seneker, Stanley A. WhoAm 90
Senelick, Laurence P 1942- WhoWrEP 89
Senenky, Joseph P BiDrAPA 89
Senensky, Ralph BioIn 16
Sener, Joseph W., Jr. 1926- St&PR 91
Sener, Joseph Ward, Jr. 1926- WhoAm 90
Seneriches, Juliana S 1943- BiDrAPA 89
Senese, Donald Joseph 1942- WhoAm 90
Senesh, Hannah 1921-1944 BioIn 16
Senesino 1680?-1759? PenDiMP
Senesy, John J. WhoSSW 91
Seneterre, Alain Guy 1935- WhoWor 91
Senf, Randall L. 1947- St&PR 91
Senft, Dexter E. 1952- St&PR 91
Senft, Mason George 1942- WhoE 91, WhoWor 91
Senftle, Frank Edward 1921- WhoE 91
Seng, Ann Frances 1936- WhoAmW 91
Seng, Cynthia D 1957- BiDrAPA 89
Seng, Hout BioIn 16
Seng, John J. 1957- ODwPR 91
Seng, Michael Leroy BiDrAPA 89
Seng, Minnie Anna 1909- WhoE 91
Seng, Thomas N. 1947- St&PR 91
Sengai Gibon 1750-1837 EncJap
Sengbush, Lynn Rae 1946- WhoSSW 91
Senger, Alan F. ODwPR 91
Senger, Harry L 1931- BiDrAPA 89
Senger, John David 1922- WhoWor 91
Senger, Leslie Walter 1945- WhoEmL 91, WhoWor 91
Senger Und Etterlin, Frido von 1891- BioIn 16
Senghor, Leopold Sedar 1906- BiDFrPL, MajTwCW, WorAlBi
Sengpiehl, June Shirley WhoWrEP 89
Sengstack, David Kells 1922- IntWWM 90
Sengstacke, John H. 1912- St&PR 91
Sengstacke, John Herman Henry 1912- WhoAm 90
Sengstacke, Robert A. 1943- St&PR 91
Sengstock, Charles A., Jr. 1932- ODwPR 91
Sengupta, Ashoke Kumar 1943- BiDrAPA 89
Sengupta, Dipendra Chandra 1955- WhoSSW 91
Sengupta, Indra Narayan 1931- WhoWor 91
Sengupta, Jharna Dana 1954- WhoSSW 91
Sengwe, Ngoni Francis 1949- WhoWor 91
Senhauser, Donald Albert 1927- WhoAm 90
Senica, James Peter 1951- WhoEmL 91
Senich, Donald 1929- WhoAm 90
Senich, Linda Lea 1953- WhoEmL 91
Senie, Harriet 1943- WhoAmA 91, WhoE 91
Senior, David 1948- St&PR 91, WhoAm 90
Senior, Derek 1912-1988 BioIn 16
Senior, Enrique F. 1943- St&PR 91
Senior, Enrique Francisco 1943- WhoAm 90
Senior, George Livingston 1929- St&PR 91
Senior, Jane Elizabeth Hughes 1828-1877 BioIn 16
Senior, Nassau William 1790-1864 BioIn 16
Senior, Neil Frederick 1947- BiDrAPA 89
Senior, Olive 1943- FemiCLE
Senior, Solomon E. BioIn 16
Senior, Thomas Bryan A. 1928- WhoAm 90
Senior, Walter E. St&PR 91
Senior, William C. 1926- St&PR 91
Seniuk, Christopher 1957- WhoE 91
Senk, Marcyanne Rose 1941- WhoAmW 91
Senker, Richard C. 1953- WhoEmL 91
Senkevitch, Judith Anne Jamison 1943- WhoAmW 91
Senkier, Robert Joseph 1916- WhoAm 90
Senkowski, Ernst 1922- EncPaPR 91
Senler, Vicdan A 1930- BiDrAPA 89
Senn, Charles Liester WhoAm 90
Senn, Glenda Edna Nichols 1950- WhoAmW 91
Senn, Marilyn Helene 1939- WhoAmW 91
Senn, Milton J E 1902-1990 CurBio 90N
Senn, Milton J. E. 1902-1990 NewYTBS 90
Senn, Milton John Edward 1902-1990 BioIn 16
Senn, Nikolaus St&PR 91
Senn, Steve 1950- BioIn 16, SmATA 60 [port]
Senn, William P. 1931- St&PR 91
Senna, Ayrton BioIn 16
Senneby, Annette Catharina Elizabeth 1951- WhoWor 91
Sennels, Richard 1912- IntWWM 90
Sennesh, Louise BiDrAPA 89
Sennet, Murray 1923- St&PR 91
Sennett, Henry Herbert, Jr. 1945- WhoSSW 91
Sennett, John F. St&PR 91
Sennett, John Patrick 1952- WhoWrEP 89
Sennett, Mack 1884-1960 WorAlBi
Sennett, Richard 1943- WhoAm 90
Senney, Walter Franklin 1955- St&PR 91
Sennhauser, John WhoAmA 91N
Sennott, John Stephen 1946- WhoEmL 91
Sennstrom, John Harold 1941- WhoAm 90

Seno, Gary F. 1956- WhoEmL 91
Senquiz, William 1957- WhoHisp 91
Sens, Gloria Jane 1936- WhoAmW 91
Sens, Loretta Susan 1956- WhoAmW 91
Sens, Maurice PenDiMP
Sensabaugh, Mary Elizabeth 1939- WhoAmW 91, WhoSSW 91, WhoWor 91
Senseman, John Howard 1943- St&PR 91
Senseman, Laurence A 1911- BiDrAPA 89
Senseman, Ronald Sylvester 1912- WhoAm 90
Sensemann, Susan 1949- WhoAmA 91
Sensenbrenner, Frank James, Jr. 1943- WhoAm 90
Sensenbrenner, Kenneth Clark 1948- WhoEmL 91
Senseney, Cecil Wayne 1943- WhoSSW 91
Sensenich, Ila Jeanne 1939- WhoAmW 91
Sensenig, David Martin 1921- WhoE 91
Sensenig, John Howard 1930- WhoE 91
Sensenig, Kenneth V. 1936- St&PR 91
Senser, Kenneth David BiDrAPA 89
Senser, Steven H. 1953- St&PR 91
Sensi, Guiseppe Maria 1907- WhoWor 91
Sensibar, Ezra BioIn 16
Sensing, Wilbur Carson, Jr. 1929- St&PR 91
Sensiper, Samuel 1919- WhoAm 90
Sensor, George Michael 1944- St&PR 91
Sensor, Mary Delores 1930- WhoAmW 91, WhoWor 91
Sentak, Gertrude Rose 1945- WhoE 91
Sentandreu, Rafael 1937- WhoWor 91
Sentelle, David Bryan 1943- WhoAm 90
Sentenn, Gregg Allen 1946- BiDrAPA 89
Sentenne, Justine 1936- WhoAm 90, WhoAmW 91
Senter, Alan Zachary 1941- WhoAm 90
Senter, Alice Hanson 1923- WhoWrEP 89
Senter, Allan Z. 1941- St&PR 91
Senter, Douglas M. 1943- WhoAm 90
Senter, Jay BioIn 16
Senter, John PenDiMP
Senter, Lyonel Thomas, Jr. 1933- WhoAm 90, WhoSSW 91
Senter, Meredith S., Jr. 1953- WhoE 91
Senter, Merilyn Patricia 1935- WhoAmW 91
Senter, Michelle Faye 1959- WhoAmW 91
Senter, Roger Campbell 1932- St&PR 91, WhoAm 90, WhoE 91, WhoWor 91
Senter, William Joseph 1921- WhoAm 90
Senter, William Oscar 1910- WhoAm 90
Senti, R. Richard 1946- WhoWrEP 89
Senti, Richard Johann 1935- WhoWor 91
Sentman, David K. 1950- St&PR 91
Sentman, David Keith 1950- WhoAm 90
Sentman, George Armor AuBYP 90
Senturia, Todd Alexander 1965- WhoWor 91
Sentz, Catherine Jeanne 1947- WhoAmW 91
Sentz, Harold Orville 1928- St&PR 91
Senyard, Corley Price, Jr. 1956- WhoSSW 91
Senz, Laurie S. 1957- WhoWrEP 89
Seo, Syng Pyo BiDrAPA 89
Seow, Francis BioIn 16
Seow, Yitkin 1955- IntWWM 90
Sepa, Maria C. 1953- WhoWor 91
Sepa, Roland L. 1929- WhoE 91
Sepahpur, Hayedeh Christina 1958- WhoAmW 91
Sepe, Carole Jaar 1957- WhoE 91
Sepe, Orsolina BiDrAPA 89
Sepeta, Donald William 1950- St&PR 91
Sepetys, Lionginas 1927- WhoWor 91
Sepharial 1864-1929 EncO&P 3
Sepheriades, Georgios MajTwCW
Sepic, Milton Thomas 1940- St&PR 91, WhoAm 90
Sepinwall, Harriet Lipman 1941- WhoE 91
Seplaki, Les 1947- WhoEmL 91
Seplowin, Charles Joseph 1945- WhoAmA 91
Seppa, Heikki Markus 1927- WhoAmA 91
Seppala, Katherine Seaman 1919- WhoAmW 91, WhoWor 91
Seppala, Katherline Annette 1919- St&PR 91
Seppala, Marvin David BiDrAPA 89
Seppala, William Leslie 1946- St&PR 91
Seppala-Holtzman, David Nathan 1950- WhoE 91
Seppanen, Alpo Jaakko 1931- WhoWor 91
Seppinen, Jukka Tapani 1945- WhoWor 91
Seprish, Bernadette Theresa 1949- WhoSSW 91
Seprodi, Judith Catherine 1955- WhoAmW 91
Sepsy, Charles Frank 1924- WhoAm 90
September, Anna EncCoWW
Septimius Severus 146-211 BioIn 16
Septimus, Bernard Mark WhoAm 90
Septimus, Irwin Leonard 1924- St&PR 91
Sepulvado, Joseph Michael 1952- WhoSSW 91
Sepulveda, Isaias 1954- BiDrAPA 89
Sepulveda, John Ulises 1954- WhoHisp 91
Sepulveda, Lora Z BiDrAPA 89
Sepulveda, Miguel A. 1955- WhoHisp 91
Sepulveda, Salvador Antonio 1936- WhoHisp 91
Sepulveda, Sharon WhoHisp 91
Sepulveda Amor, Bernardo 1941- WhoAm 90
Sepulveda-Amor, Javier BiDrAPA 89
Sepulveda-Bailey, Jamie Alice 1945- WhoHisp 91
Sequeira, Luis 1927- BioIn 16, WhoAm 90
Sequin, Carlo H. 1941- WhoAm 90
Sequoia 1770?-1843 WhNaAH [port]
Sequoya 1770?-1843 WhNaAH [port], WorAlBi
Sequoyah 1770?-1843 WhNaAH [port]
Sera, Beatrice del 1515-1585 EncCoWW
Sera, Enrique Jose 1950- WhoHisp 91
Serafin, Barry D. 1941- WhoAm 90
Serafin, David TwCCr&M 91
Serafin, Donald 1938- WhoAm 90
Serafin, Jeanne C. BiDrAPA 89
Serafin, Robert J. 1936- BioIn 16
Serafin, Tullio 1878-1968 PenDiMP
Serafine, Mary Louise 1948- WhoEmL 91
Serafini, Angela 1913- WhoAmW 91
Serafino, Vittorio 1950- WhoWor 91
Serafinowicz, Leokadia 1915- ConDes 90
Seraj, Mohamad 1944- St&PR 91
Seranne, Ann 1914-1988 BioIn 16
Serao, Matilde 1856-1927 EncCoWW
Seraphine, Danny Peter 1948- WhoAm 90
Seratte, Andrea Rae 1954- WhoAmW 91
Serban, Andrei 1943- ConTFT 8, IntWWM 90
Serban, D. EncCoWW
Serban, George BiDrAPA 89
Serban, George 1926- ConAu 129
Serban, George 1927- WhoE 91
Serbia, Victoria Caridad 1948- BiDrAPA 89
Serbin, Mark Dwight 1953- WhoEmL 91
Serbin, Richard Martin 1947- WhoEmL 91
Serbin, Richard Stanley 1944- WhoE 91
Serbus, Pearl Sarah Dieck WhoAmW 91, WhoWor 91
Serby, Michael J BiDrAPA 89
Serchuk, Ivan 1935- WhoE 91, WhoWor 91
Sereboff, Joel Lee 1937- WhoE 91
Serebriakova, Zinaida Eugenievna 1884-1967 BiDWomA
Serebrier, Jose 1938- IntWWM 90, PenDiMP, WhoAm 90
Serebrjakova, Zoya N BiDrAPA 89
Serebrovskii, Aleksandr Sergeevich 1892-1948 DcScB S2
Sereda, Lawrence E 1928- BiDrAPA 89
Sereda, Sheryl Louise 1946- WhoAmW 91
Seredy, Kate 1896-1975 AuBYP 90
Serembe, Gilberto 1955- IntWWM 90
Seremet, Peter M 1947- ODwPR 91
Serena, Bill 1924- Ballpl 90
Serenbetz, Robert 1944- WhoAm 90, WhoE 91
Serenbetz, Warren Lewis 1924- WhoAm 90
Sereni, Enzo 1905-1944 BioIn 16
Sereni, Mario 1928- IntWWM 90
Serenyi, Peter 1931- WhoAm 90, WhoAmA 91, WhoE 91
Seretean, Martin B. 1924- WhoAm 90
Serfaty, Daniel 1954- WhoE 91
Serfaty, Simon Henry 1940- WhoE 91
Serge, Victor 1890-1947 BiDFrPL, BioIn 16
Sergeant, Adeline 1851-1904 FemiCLE
Sergeant, Harriet 1954- ConAu 132
Sergeant, John NewAgMG
Sergeant, John 1710-1749 WhNaAH
Sergeant, Michael John BiDrAPA 89
Sergel, Christopher Roger 1918- WhoAm 90
Sergel, Ruth ConAu 131
Serger, Frederick B 1889-1965 WhoAmA 91N
Serger, Helen 1901-1989 BioIn 16, WhoAmA 91N
Sergey, John Michael, Jr. 1942- WhoAm 90
Serghi, Cella 1907- EncCoWW
Sergio, Elisa 1905-1989 ConAu 129
Sergio, Lisa ConAu 129
Sergio, Lisa 1905-1989 BioIn 16
Serieno, Joseph Paul 1927- St&PR 91
Serieye, Michel P 1932- BiDrAPA 89
Serigny, Eugenia de BioIn 16
Serio, Augustine, Jr. 1945- WhoE 91
Serio, Kathryn Beth 1957- WhoAmW 91
Serio, Veronica Comer 1948- WhoE 91
Serios, Ted EncO&P 3
Serios, Ted 1918- EncPaPR 91
Serious, Yahoo BioIn 16
Serisawa, Sueo 1910- WhoAmA 91
Serizawa, Keisuke 1895-1984 PenDiDA 89
Serjeant, Denis BioIn 16
Serkey, Stephen J. 1945- St&PR 91
Serkin, Peter BioIn 16
Serkin, Peter 1947- IntWWM 90, PenDiMP, WhoAm 90
Serkin, Rudolf 1903- BioIn 16, CurBio 90 [port], IntWWM 90, PenDiMP, WhoAm 90, WhoWor 91, WorAlBi
Serkland, Wayne C. 1943- St&PR 91
Serl, Jon 1894- MusmAFA
Serlachius, Gustaf Fredrik 1935- WhoWor 91
Serle, Seymour Jack 1928- St&PR 91
Serling, Rod 1924-1975 BioIn 16, EncO&P 3, WorAlBi
Serlio, Sebastiano 1475-1554 PenDiDA 89
Serlippens, Robert Al 1926- WhoWor 91
Sermadiras, Gilles BioIn 16
Sermadiras, Patrick BioIn 16
Sermila, Jarmo Kalevi 1939- IntWWM 90
Sermos, Sybil Falk 1938- WhoAmW 91
Serna, Enrique Gonzalo 1946- WhoHisp 91
Serna, Eric 1949- WhoHisp 91
Serna, Ramon Gomez de la HispWr 90
Serna, Raquel Casiano 1929- WhoHisp 91
Sernau, Stephanie Wiley 1961- WhoE 91
Sernesi, Raffaello 1838-1866 BioIn 16
Sernett, Richard Patrick 1938- WhoAm 90
Sernigi, Raffaella de' 1472?-1557 EncCoWW
Sernyak, Michael Joseph BiDrAPA 89
Sernyak, Michael Joseph, Jr. 1961- WhoE 91
Serocky, William Howard 1936- WhoWor 91
Seroka, James Henry 1950- WhoE 91
Serooskerken, Isabella van Tuyll van EncCoWW
Serota, Nicholas BioIn 16
Serota, Nicholas Andrew 1946- WhoWor 91
Serota, Ronald David 1942- BiDrAPA 89
Serota, Susan Perlstadt 1945- WhoAmW 91, WhoEmL 91
Serowka, Juanita Domicella 1946- WhoAmW 91
Serpan, Roger L. 1939- WhoAm 90
Serpe, Diane BioIn 16
Serpe, John S. 1944- St&PR 91
Serpe, Roger A. 1950- St&PR 91
Serpento, B. James 1960- WhoWrEP 89
Serposs, Alan Dennis BiDrAPA 89
Serquina, Florida Javier BiDrAPA 89
Serr, Barbara Jean 1943- WhoAmW 91
Serra, Enrique 1944- WhoHisp 91
Serra, Jeffrey Robert 1956- St&PR 91
Serra, Junipero 1713-1784 BioIn 16, EncCRAm, WhNaAH, WorAlBi
Serra, Luciana 1942- IntWWM 90
Serra, Miguel Jose 1713-1784 BioIn 16
Serra, Patricia Janet 1933- WhoAmW 91
Serra, Richard BioIn 16
Serra, Richard 1939- WhoAm 90, WhoAmA 91
Serra, Roberto 1952- WhoWor 91
Serra, Rudy 1948- WhoAmA 91
Serra-Badue, Daniel 1914- WhoAmA 91
Serra-Badue, Daniel Francisco 1914- WhoAm 90
Serra Mont, Esteban 1948- WhoWor 91
Serra Puche, Jaime Jose 1951- WhoWor 91
Serra y Serra, Narciso 1943- WhoWor 91
Serrahima, Nuria 1937- EncCoWW
Serral, Frederick Amos 1922- WhoAm 90, WhoSSW 91
Serrani, Thom 1947- WhoE 91
Serrano, Alberto C 1931- BiDrAPA 89, WhoE 91
Serrano, Alberto Carlos 1931- WhoHisp 91
Serrano, Andres 1950- WhoAmA 91
Serrano, Arthur Vincent, Jr. 1923- St&PR 91
Serrano, Gustavo 1933- WhoHisp 91
Serrano, Jack 1938- WhoHisp 91
Serrano, Jose 1943- WhoAm 90
Serrano, Jose E. 1945- WhoHisp 91
Serrano, Jose S. 1933- WhoWor 91
Serrano, Jose Simeon 1873-1943 OxCPMus
Serrano, Lucienne J. 1936- ConAu 131
Serrano, Luis 1955- WhoAmA 91
Serrano, Lynnette Maritza 1964- WhoHisp 91
Serrano, Maria Christina 1954- WhoHisp 91
Serrano, Miguel 1917- ConAu 132
Serrano, Myrna 1954- WhoAmW 91
Serrano, Pedro, Jr. 1953- WhoHisp 91
Serrano, Rose Arlene 1950- WhoAmW 91
Serrano, Yolanda BioIn 16
Serrano-Diaz, Mark Anthony 1940- WhoAm 90
Serrano Pinto, German WhoWor 91
Serrano Suner, Ramon 1901- BioIn 16
Serrano Y Bartolome, Joaquina BiDWomA
Serrantino, Salvatore 1932- St&PR 91
Serrao, Amilcar 1951- WhoWor 91
Serrao, Daniel dos Santos Pinto 1928- WhoWor 91
Serrao, Robert Anthony 1931- St&PR 91
Serrata, Lidia 1947- WhoHisp 91
Serrato, Michael A. WhoHisp 91
Serratrice, George Theodore 1927- WhoWor 91
Serravezza, June Carol 1945- BiDrAPA 89
Serravezza, William J. 1945- St&PR 91
Serres, Olivia 1772-1834 FemiCLE
Serrie, Hendrick 1937- WhoSSW 91
Serrie, Jonn NewAgMG
Serrill, J. Edward 1948- St&PR 91
Serrill, Patricia Whitfield 1941- WhoAmW 91
Serrill, Theodore Andrew 1911- WhoSSW 91
Serrin, James Burton 1926- WhoAm 90
Serritella, James Anthony 1942- WhoAm 90
Serrurier-Bovy, Gustave 1858-1910 PenDiDA 89
Serruya, Delia Gladis BiDrAPA 89
Serruya, Roberto Jose BiDrAPA 89
Serstock, Doris Shay 1926- WhoAmW 91, WhoWor 91
Sertl, William John 1946- WhoE 91
Serum, Gary 1956- Ballpl 90
SerVaas, Margaret Ann 1952- WhoAmW 91
Servadei, Annette Elizabeth 1945- IntWWM 90
Servadei, Franco 1951- WhoWor 91
Servadio, Emilio 1904- EncO&P 3, EncPaPR 91
Servais, Donna J. 1946- WhoWrEP 89
Servan-Schreiber, David D 1961- BiDrAPA 89
Servan-Schreiber, Jean-Jacques 1924- BiDFrPL, WhoWor 91
Servedio, Dominick M. 1940- St&PR 91
Servellon, Cesar H BiDrAPA 89
Servi, Leslie David 1955- WhoEmL 91
Service, Alastair 1933- ConAu 130
Service, Grace 1879-1954 BioIn 16
Service, Kenneth P. 1946- ODwPR 91
Service, Pamela F. 1945- SmATA 64 [port]
Service, Robert 1874-1958 DcLB 92 [port]
Service, Robert R. 1879-1935 BioIn 16
Service, Robert W. 1874-1958 AuBYP 90, WorAlBi
Servier, Jean H 1918- EncO&P 3
Servin, Manuel P. 1920- BioIn 16
Servis, Mark Edward 1957- BiDrAPA 89
Servison, Roger Theodore 1945- St&PR 91
Servodidio, Pat A. 1937- St&PR 91
Servodidio, Pat Anthony 1937- WhoAm 90
Servose, Douglas Michael 1953- WhoEmL 91
Servoss, Marcus E. ODwPR 91
Serwadda, William Moses 1931- BioIn 16
Serwatka, Walter D. 1937- St&PR 91
Serwatka, Walter Dennis 1937- WhoAm 90, WhoE 91
Serwer, Alan Michael 1944- WhoAm 90
Serwy, Robert Anthony 1950- WhoEmL 91, WhoWor 91
Sesen, Harriet Roberta 1940- WhoAmW 91
Seshadri, Rajagopal BiDrAPA 89
Sesholtz, Marilyn BiDrAPA 89
Sesing, Peter Joseph 1942- St&PR 91
Seslowsky, Harvey Michael 1942- WhoE 91
Sesnon, Porter 1899- St&PR 91
Sesody, John J. 1946- St&PR 91
Sesonske, Alexander 1921- WhoAm 90
Sessa, Anthony Joseph 1946- WhoE 91
Sessa, Charles Edward 1935- St&PR 91
Sesser, Gary Douglas 1950- WhoEmL 91
Sesshu Toyo 1420-1506 EncJap
Session, Willie Mae 1943- WhoAmW 91
Sessions, Clifton Farr 1931- WhoE 91
Sessions, Frances Pope 1933- BiDrAPA 89
Sessions, George Purd 1931- WhoSSW 91
Sessions, Jean E 1946- WhoAm 90
Sessions, Jean Young BiDrAPA 89
Sessions, Kate Olivia 1857-1940 BioIn 16
Sessions, Larry C. 1952- St&PR 91
Sessions, Milan H. 1821- AmLegL
Sessions, Patty Bartlett BioIn 16
Sessions, Robert Morris 1927- St&PR 91
Sessions, Robert Paul 1926- WhoAm 90
Sessions, Roger BioIn 16
Sessions, Roger 1896-1985 PenDiMP A, WorAlBi
Sessions, Roger Carl 1944- WhoSSW 91
Sessions, Shelley BioIn 16
Sessions, Steven 1949- BioIn 16
Sessions, William Lewis 1953- WhoEmL 91
Sessions, William Steele BioIn 16
Sessions, William Steele 1930- WhoAm 90
Sessle, Barry John 1941- WhoAm 90
Sessler, Alfred A 1909-1963 WhoAmA 91N
Sessler, Andrew Marienhoff 1928- WhoAm 90

Sessoms, Stephanie Thompson 1963- *WhoAmW 91*
Sessoms, Stuart McGuire 1921- *WhoAm 90*
Sessoms, Teresa Lyn 1962- *WhoE 91*
Sessue Hayakawa *EncJap*
Sestak, Joseph, Jr. 1932- *St&PR 91*
Sestak, Tomislav 1931- *IntWWM 90*
Sestak, Zdenek 1925- *IntWWM 90*
Sestakova, Marie Langerova 1951- *IntWWM 90*
Sestile, Cynthia Jeanne 1956- *WhoAmW 91*
Sestina, John E. 1942- *WhoWor 91*
Sestini, Virgil Andrew 1936- *WhoWor 91*
Sesto, Mark Ernest 1955- *WhoSSW 91*
Setangya *WhNaAH*
Setapen, James Anthony 1948- *WhoSSW 91*
Setchell, Martin Philip 1949- *IntWWM 90*
Setchell, Sarah 1803-1894 *BiDWomA*
Sete, Bola *NewAgMG*
Seter, Mordecai 1916- *IntWWM 90*
Seth, Bernie 1957- *WhoWor 91*
Seth, J Cabot 1953- *WhoEmL 91*
Seth, Joseph Bruff 1845-1927 *AmLegL*
Seth, Naveen Kumar 1935- *WhoWor 91*
Seth, Ray 1935- *St&PR 91*
Seth, Ronald 1911-1985 *AuBYP 90, SpyFic*
Seth, Suresh C. 1935- *St&PR 91*
Seth, Vikram 1952- *WhoWrEP 89*
Sethi, Baljit Singh 1948- *WhoE 91*
Sethi, Brij B 1932- *BiDrAPA 89*
Sethi, Deepak 1945- *WhoE 91*
Sethi, Dino Sheriden 1949- *WhoE 91*
Sethi, Indrash C 1931- *BiDrAPA 89*
Sethi, Vidya Sagar *BiDrAPA 89*
Sethna, Beheruz Nariman 1948- *WhoAm 90, WhoSSW 91, WhoWor 91*
Sethna, Jerri P. *BiDrAPA 89*
Sethna, Patarasp Rustomji 1923- *WhoAm 90*
Sethness, Charles Henry, Jr. 1910- *WhoWor 91*
Sethness, Charles Olin 1941- *WhoAm 90*
Sethos *EncO&P 3*
Sethuraman, Salem Venkataraman 1935- *WhoWor 91*
Setien, Miguel Delibes *HispWr 90, MajTwCW*
Setlich-Drozda, Kimberly Kay 1956- *WhoAmW 91, WhoWor 91*
Setlow, Jane Kellock 1919- *WhoAm 90*
Setlow, Neva C 1940- *WhoAmA 91*
Setlow, Richard Burton 1921- *WhoAm 90*
Seto, Robert Mahealani Ming 1936- *WhoWor 91*
Seton, Alexander *EncO&P 3*
Seton, Anya *NewYTBS 90 [port]*
Seton, Anya 1904?- *FemiCLE*
Seton, Charles B. 1910- *WhoAm 90*
Seton, Cynthia Propper 1926-1982 *WorAu 1980*
Seton, Elizabeth A. Bayley 1774-1821 *BioAmW*
Seton, Elizabeth Ann 1774-1821 *BioIn 16, FemiCLE, WorAlBi*
Seton, Ernest Thompson 1860-1946 *DcLB 92 [port] WhNaAH*
Seton, Fenmore Roger 1917- *WhoAm 90, WhoWor 91*
Seton, Paul H *BiDrAPA 89*
Seton-Thompson, Ernest 1860-1946 *WhNaAH*
Seton-Watson, Hugh 1916-1984 *DcNaB 1981*
Seton-Williams, M. V. 1910- *BioIn 16*
Seton-Williams, Marjory Veronica 1910- *BioIn 16*
Setrakian, Berge 1949- *WhoE 91*
Setser, Carole Sue 1940- *WhoAmW 91*
Setser, Donald Wayne 1935- *WhoAm 90*
Setsuko *BioIn 16*
Sett, Ralph Frank 1937- *BiDrAPA 89*
Settel, Kenneth M 1946- *BiDrAPA 89*
Settembrini, Sara Charlotte 1949- *St&PR 91*
Setter, David Mark 1956- *WhoEmL 91*
Setterberg, Carl Georg 1897- *WhoAmA 91N*
Setterberg, Stephen R *BiDrAPA 89*
Setterlin, James Lawrence 1948- *St&PR 91*
Setterstrom, William N. 1942- *St&PR 91*
Settich, John F. *ODwPR 91*
Settis, Salvatore 1941- *WhoWor 91*
Settlage, Calvin F 1921- *BiDrAPA 89*
Settle, Edmund Carr, Jr. 1949- *BiDrAPA 89*
Settle, Frank Alexander, Jr. 1937- *WhoSSW 91*
Settle, Karen R. 1948- *WhoSSW 91*
Settle, Larry D. 1942- *St&PR 91*
Settle, Mary Lee *BioIn 16*
Settle, Mary Lee 1918- *ConLC 61 [port], FemiCLE, WhoAm 90, WhoAmW 91*
Settle, Robert Burton 1934- *WhoE 91*
Settle, Russell O 1904- *BiDrAPA 89*
Settle, Russell Orion, Jr. 1935- *BiDrAPA 89*
Settle, Thomas, Jr. 1831-1888 *AmLegL*
Settle, William Sydnor 1933- *WhoAm 90*
Settlemier, B.R. 1934- *St&PR 91*
Settlemyer, Kenneth Theodore 1935- *WhoE 91*
Settles, Cheryl Lynne 1947- *WhoWrEP 89*
Settles, F. Stan, Jr. 1938- *WhoAm 90*
Settles, G. Patrick 1949- *St&PR 91*
Settles, George *BioIn 16*
Settles, Joseph Hays 1954- *WhoEmL 91*
Settles, Lois Ellen 1933- *WhoSSW 91*
Settles, Thomas Edward 1951- *WhoSSW 91*
Settles, William Frederick 1937- *WhoWrEP 89*
Setton, Kenneth M. 1914- *WhoAm 90, WhoWor 91*
Settoon, William Alden, Jr. 1949- *WhoSSW 91*
Setyadi, Djoni 1942- *WhoWor 91*
Setyonegoro, R Kusumanto *BiDrAPA 89*
Setzer, David Everett 1934- *WhoSSW 91*
Setzer, Doris Wills 1917- *WhoAmW 91*
Setzer, Gene Willis 1918- *WhoAm 90*
Setzer, H.C. 1919- *St&PR 91*
Setzer, Herbert John 1928- *WhoAm 90, WhoE 91, WhoWor 91*
Setzer, Rick A. 1946- *WhoSSW 91*
Setzer, Robert D. 1947- *St&PR 91*
Setzer, Robert L. 1943- *St&PR 91*
Setzler, William Edward 1926- *WhoAm 90*
Seuferer, Stanley Leroy *BiDrAPA 89*
Seuling, Barbara 1937- *AuBYP 90*
Seume, Johann Gottfried 1763-1810 *DcLB 94 [port]*
Seung, Thomas Kaehao 1930- *WhoAm 90, WhoWrEP 89*
Seurat, Georges 1859-1891 *IntDcAA 90, WorAlBi*
Seurat, Georges Pierre 1859-1891 *BioIn 16*
Seurkamp, Mary Pat 1946- *WhoAmW 91*
Seuss, Dr. *AuBYP 90, BioIn 16, ConAu 32NR, MajTwCW*
Seuster, Horst 1930- *WhoWor 91*
Seuter, Abraham 1688?-1747 *PenDiDA 89*
Seuter, Bartholomaus 1678-1754 *PenDiDA 89*
Sevagian, Aram Haig 1932- *WhoAm 90, WhoE 91, WhoWor 91*
Sevall, Joseph Roy, III 1941- *St&PR 91*
Sevandal, Marciana Asis Sagun 1912- *WhoWrEP 89*
Sevareid, Arnold Eric 1912- *WhoAm 90*
Sevareid, Eric 1912- *BioIn 16, WorAlBi*
Sevcenko, Ihor 1922- *WhoAm 90*
Sevcik, Edward J. *St&PR 91*
Sevcik, Melanie Jenice 1958- *WhoSSW 91*
Sevcik, Otakar 1852-1934 *PenDiMP*
Sevdalis, Theophilos G *BiDrAPA 89*
Sevela, Efraim 1928- *ConAu 30NR*
Seven, John Anthony 1926- *St&PR 91*
Sevensma, Eugene S 1918- *BiDrAPA 89*
Sever, Beverly Gerane 1960- *WhoSSW 91*
Sever, Dolores L. 1936- *WhoAmW 91*
Sever, Jana Sue 1963- *WhoAmW 91*
Sever, Shmuel 1933- *WhoWor 91*
Severa, James Dennis 1950- *BiDrAPA 89*
Severaid, Ronald Harold 1951- *WhoWor 91*
Severance, Joan *BioIn 16*
Severance, Malcolm Floyd 1924- *St&PR 91*
Severance, Martha Elaine 1957- *WhoAmW 91*
Severance, Richard Norman 1933- *WhoE 91*
Severe, John Thomas 1951- *WhoSSW 91, WhoWor 91*
Severeid, Hank 1891-1968 *Ballpl 90*
Severin, Dorothy Sherman 1942- *WhoWor 91*
Severin, Hans Karl Friedrich 1920- *WhoWor 91*
Severin, Michael Allen 1943- *St&PR 91*
Severine 1855-1929 *BiDFrPL, EncCoWW*
Severinghaus, Nelson 1929- *St&PR 91*
Severinghaus, Nelson, Jr. 1929- *WhoSSW 91*
Severini, Gino 1883-1966 *IntDcAA 90*
Severini, Joseph John 1931- *St&PR 91*
Severino, Alexandrino Eusebio 1931- *WhoAm 90*
Severino, Dominick Alexander 1914- *WhoAm 90*
Severino, Elizabeth Forrest 1945- *WhoAmW 91*
Severino, Sally K *BiDrAPA 89*
Severinsen, Al 1944- *Ballpl 90*
Severinsen, Doc *BioIn 16*
Severinsen, Doc 1927- *WhoAm 90, WorAlBi*
Severinson, Kenneth J. *WhoAm 90*
Severn, Ann Mary 1832-1866 *BiDWomA*
Severn, David *AuBYP 90*
Severn, Margaret 1901- *BioIn 16*
Severn, Sue 1918- *AuBYP 90*
Severn, William Irving 1914- *AuBYP 90*
Severns, Penny L. 1952- *WhoAmW 91*
Severo, Leanne 1959- *WhoAmW 91*
Severo, Richard 1932- *WhoAm 90*
Severs, Eugene Ryals 1923- *St&PR 91*
Severs, Walter Bruce 1938- *WhoAm 90*
Severs, William Floyd 1932- *WhoE 91*
Severseike, Gary L. 1940- *St&PR 91*
Severson, Herbert H. 1944- *WhoAm 90*
Severson, James Martin 1934- *St&PR 91*
Severson, Jerry W. 1942- *St&PR 91*
Severson, John Robert 1955- *St&PR 91*
Severson, Karen *BioIn 16*
Severson, Larry J 1939- *BiDrAPA 89*
Severson, Patricia Lou 1937- *WhoAmW 91*
Severson, Richard Henry 1932- *St&PR 91*
Severson, Roger A. 1932- *St&PR 91*
Severson, Roger Allan 1932- *WhoAm 90*
Severson, Sherman Wayne *BiDrAPA 89*
Severson, William Conrad 1924- *WhoAmA 91*
Severud, Fred 1899-1990 *BioIn 16*
Severus, Lucius Septimius 146-211 *BioIn 16*
Severus, Sibylle 1937- *EncCoWW*
Severy, Janaki Gayle 1948- *WhoEmL 91*
Severy, Lawrence James 1943- *WhoSSW 91*
Severy, Linda Andrea 1945- *WhoAmW 91*
Sevey, John C. 1913- *St&PR 91*
Sevier, Ernest Youle 1932- *WhoAm 90*
Sevier, Helen *BioIn 16*
Sevier, James Rollins 1918- *St&PR 91*
Sevier, John 1745-1815 *BioIn 16, EncCRAm, WhNaAH*
Sevier, Victor Henry, Jr. 1927- *St&PR 91*
Sevigne, Marquise de 1626-1696 *EncCoWW*
Sevigne, Marie, marquise de 1626-1696 *FemiCLE*
Sevigne, Marie De Rabutin C, Marquise De 1626-1696 *WorAlBi*
Sevigny, Joseph A. 1927- *St&PR 91*
Sevigny, Maurice Joseph, II 1943- *WhoAmA 91*
Sevil, Ismet 1938- *WhoWor 91*
Sevilhano Ribeiro, Vitor 1950- *WhoWor 91*
Sevilla, Aloma Penaranda *BiDrAPA 89*
Sevilla, Carlos Arthur 1935- *WhoHisp 91*
Sevilla, Stanley 1920- *WhoAm 90*
Sevillano, Trinidad *BioIn 16*
Seville, Jack James, Jr. 1938- *WhoWrEP 89*
Seville, Linda Jones 1954- *WhoAmW 91*
Seville, Mary Alice 1942- *WhoAmW 91*
Sevilya, Metin B 1921- *BiDrAPA 89*
Sevin, Bradley H 1943- *BiDrAPA 89, WhoE 91*
Sevin, Dieter Hermann 1938- *WhoSSW 91*
Sevin, Eugene 1928- *WhoAm 90*
Sevin, Irik Peter 1947- *St&PR 91*
Sevold, Gordon James 1926- *WhoAm 90*
Sevy, Barbara Snetsinger 1926- *WhoAmA 91*
Sevy, Roger Warren 1923- *WhoAm 90*
Sewall, Charles L. *WhoAm 90*
Sewall, Edward R. 1927- *St&PR 91*
Sewall, George Popham 1811-1881 *AmLegL*
Sewall, Harold Marsh 1860-1924 *BioIn 16*
Sewall, Marcia *AuBYP 90*
Sewall, Michael O'Malley 1928- *St&PR 91*
Sewall, Richard Benson 1908- *WhoWrEP 89*
Sewall, Samuel 1652-1730 *WorAlBi*
Sewall, Stanley Joseph 1944- *St&PR 91*
Sewall, Tingey H. 1940- *St&PR 91*
Sewall, Warren 1941- *WhoE 91*
Sewall, William Dana 1948- *St&PR 91*
Seward, Anna 1742-1809 *BioIn 16, FemiCLE*
Seward, Charles X. *AmLegL*
Seward, Doyle Adam, Jr. 1956- *WhoWrEP 89*
Seward, Frances M. 1805-1865 *BioAmW*
Seward, Frederick T *BiDrAPA 89*
Seward, Frederick William 1830-1915 *BioIn 16*
Seward, George C. 1910- *St&PR 91*
Seward, George Chester 1910- *WhoAm 90, WhoWor 91*
Seward, Jeffrey James 1953- *WhoEmL 91*
Seward, John E., Jr. 1948- *St&PR 91*
Seward, John Edward, Jr. 1943- *WhoWor 91*
Seward, John Wesley, Jr. 1948- *WhoEmL 91*
Seward, Kathryn Ellen 1926- *WhoAmW 91*
Seward, Ralph Theodore 1907- *WhoAm 90*
Seward, Richard Bevin 1932- *WhoAm 90*
Seward, Richard E. 1947- *BiDrAPA 89*
Seward, Rudy Ray 1944- *WhoSSW 91*
Seward, Steven Le Mar 1946- *WhoEmL 91*
Seward, Troilen Gainey 1941- *WhoSSW 91*
Seward, William H. 1801-1872 *WorAlBi*
Seward, William Henry 1801-1872 *BiDrUSE 89, BioIn 16*
Seward, William Ward, Jr. 1913- *WhoAm 90, WhoWrEP 89*
Sewell, Anna 1820-1878 *BioIn 16, FemiCLE*
Sewell, Ben Gardner 1911- *WhoAm 90*
Sewell, Beverly Jean 1942- *WhoAmW 91*
Sewell, Cecil W. 1946- *St&PR 91*
Sewell, Charles Haslett 1928- *WhoAm 90*
Sewell, Charles Robertson 1927- *WhoWor 91*
Sewell, Daniel D. 1959- *BiDrAPA 89*
Sewell, Darrel L 1939- *WhoAmA 91*
Sewell, Darrel Leslie 1939- *WhoAm 90*
Sewell, Elizabeth 1815-1906 *FemiCLE*
Sewell, Elizabeth 1919- *WhoAmW 91, WhoWrEP 89*
Sewell, Elizabeth Missing 1815-1906 *BioIn 16*
Sewell, Helen Moore 1896-1957 *AuBYP 90*
Sewell, Helen Moore 1897-1957 *WhoAmA 91N*
Sewell, Hobart H 1939- *BiDrAPA 89*
Sewell, Isabel Fowler 1920- *St&PR 91*
Sewell, Jack Vincent 1923- *WhoAmA 91*
Sewell, James Kimberly 1951- *BiDrAPA 89*
Sewell, James Leslie 1903- *WhoAm 90*
Sewell, Joan Marshall 1936- *WhoWrEP 89*
Sewell, Joe 1898- *Ballpl 90 [port]*
Sewell, Joe 1898-1990 *BioIn 16, NewYTBS 90*
Sewell, John Williamson 1935- *WhoAm 90*
Sewell, Laurence S. 1929- *ODwPR 91*
Sewell, Leo 1945- *WhoAmA 91*
Sewell, Luke 1901-1987 *Ballpl 90*
Sewell, Marion Hutcherson 1934- *WhoSSW 91*
Sewell, Mary *FemiCLE*
Sewell, Mary 1797-1884 *FemiCLE*
Sewell, Michael Clay 1957- *WhoSSW 91*
Sewell, Morton Edward 1919- *St&PR 91*
Sewell, Patrick E *BiDrAPA 89*
Sewell, Phyllis Shapiro 1930- *St&PR 91, WhoAm 90, WhoAmW 91*
Sewell, Richard George 1942- *WhoAmA 91*
Sewell, Richard Herbert 1931- *WhoAm 90*
Sewell, Rip 1907- *Ballpl 90*
Sewell, Rip 1907-1989 *BioIn 16*
Sewell, Susan *ODwPR 91*
Sewell, Valerie Roesch 1954- *WhoAmW 91*
Sewell, W. R. Derrick 1931-1987 *BioIn 16*
Sewell, William George, III 1950- *WhoE 91, WhoEmL 91*
Sewell, William Gerald 1941- *St&PR 91*
Sewell, William Hamilton 1909- *BioIn 16, WhoAm 90*
Sewell, William Thomas 1934- *St&PR 91, WhoSSW 91*
Sewell, Winifred 1917- *WhoAm 90*
Sewer, Carolyn Marie 1948- *WhoE 91*
Sewill, Joyce 1917- *BioIn 16*
Sewnauth, Deonarine G 1955- *BiDrAPA 89*
Sewpershad, Lionel 1940- *WhoSSW 91*
Sewright, Charles William, Jr. 1946- *WhoE 91*
Sex Pistols, The *ConMus 5 [port], EncPR&S 89, OxCPMus*
Sexauer, Donald Richard *WhoAmA 91*
Sexauer, James D 1935- *BiDrAPA 89*
Sexauer, Robert S. 1923- *St&PR 91*
Sexsmith, David Randal 1933- *St&PR 91, WhoE 91*
Sexson, Richard Wayne 1949- *WhoEmL 91*
Sexson, Sandra *BiDrAPA 89*
Sexson, Ward Earl 1933- *St&PR 91*
Sexton, Anne *BioIn 16*
Sexton, Anne 1928-1974 *FemiCLE, MajTwCW, PoeCrit 2 [port], WorAlBi*
Sexton, Brendan 1911-1988 *BioIn 16*
Sexton, Carol Burke 1939- *WhoAmW 91*
Sexton, Charlie *BioIn 16*
Sexton, David F. 1943- *St&PR 91*
Sexton, David Farrington 1943- *WhoAm 90*
Sexton, Donald Lee 1932- *WhoAm 90*
Sexton, Edward William, Jr. 1931- *St&PR 91*
Sexton, Emily Stryker 1880-1948 *WhoAmA 91N*
Sexton, George *EncO&P 3*
Sexton, J.F. 1918- *St&PR 91*
Sexton, Jo Ann 1933- *WhoAmW 91*
Sexton, John *BioIn 16*
Sexton, John 1953- *WhoAmA 91*
Sexton, John Edward 1942- *WhoAm 90*
Sexton, John F. 1932- *St&PR 91*
Sexton, John Q. 1937- *St&PR 91*
Sexton, John W., Jr. 1926- *St&PR 91*
Sexton, Joseph Price 1923- *St&PR 91*
Sexton, Mark S. 1956- *St&PR 91*

Sexton, Owen James 1926- *WhoAm 90*
Sexton, Ray Owen 1941- *BiDrAPA 89*
Sexton, Richard 1929- *WhoAm 90, WhoE 91*
Sexton, Steve *NewAgMG*
Sexton, Thomas 1944- *St&PR 91*
Sexton, Thomas Mackin 1919- *St&PR 91*
Sexton, Will *BioIn 16*
Sexton, William Cottrell 1928- *WhoAm 90*
Sextus V, Pope 1521-1590 *EncO&P 3*
Sey, Omar *WhoWor 91*
Seybert, Henry P. 1883-1983 *EncPaPR 91*
Seybert, Janet Rose 1944- *WhoAmW 91, WhoWor 91*
Seybold, Adele Neely 1919- *WhoAmW 91*
Seybold, H. Robert 1949- *St&PR 91*
Seybold, Socks 1870-1921 *Ballpl 90*
Seydel, Scott O'Sullivan 1940- *WhoSSW 91, WhoWor 91*
Seyfarth, Henry Edward 1908- *WhoAm 90*
Seyfert, Ella Maie *AuBYP 90*
Seyfert, Richard Leopold 1915-1979 *WhoAmA 91N*
Seyfert, Theresa 1956- *WhoAmW 91*
Seyferth, Dietmar 1929- *WhoAm 90*
Seyffarth, Linda Jean Wilcox 1948- *WhoAmW 91*
Seyffert, J Robert 1952- *WhoAmA 91*
Seyhoun, Houshang 1920- *WhoWor 91*
Seyle, Robert Harley 1937- *WhoAmA 91*
Seyler, Athene *NewYTBS 90*
Seyler, Patti Lynne Sanders 1953- *WhoSSW 91*
Seymore, William A. 1943- *St&PR 91*
Seymour, Anne 1909-1988 *BioIn 16*
Seymour, Arthur Hallock 1928- *WhoAm 90*
Seymour, Beatrice Kean 1885?-1955 *FemiCLE*
Seymour, Charles, Jr 1912-1977 *WhoAmA 91N*
Seymour, Charles Burch 1932- *St&PR 91*
Seymour, Charles F. 1921- *St&PR 91*
Seymour, Cy 1872-1919 *Ballpl 90 [port]*
Seymour, Elbert H, Jr. *BiDrAPA 89*
Seymour, Everett Hedden, Jr. 1958- *WhoE 91*
Seymour, George Austin 1926- *WhoSSW 91*
Seymour, Gerald 1933- *St&PR 91*
Seymour, Gerald 1941- *TwCCr&M 91*
Seymour, Gerald William Herschel Kean 1941- *SpyFic*
Seymour, Harlan Francis 1950- *WhoSSW 91*
Seymour, Harold 1910- *Ballpl 90*
Seymour, James David 1934- *WhoSSW 91*
Seymour, James G *BiDrAPA 89*
Seymour, Jane *BioIn 16*
Seymour, Jane 1951- *WhoAm 90, WhoAmW 91, WorAlBi*
Seymour, Janet Elizabeth 1960- *WhoE 91*
Seymour, Jeffrey Alan 1950- *WhoEmL 91*
Seymour, John 1738?-1818 *PenDiDA 89*
Seymour, John Herbert 1945- *WhoAm 90*
Seymour, Josephine Evans 1912- *WhoAmW 91*
Seymour, Lynn 1939- *WhoWor 91*
Seymour, Martha Dailey 1944- *WhoSSW 91*
Seymour, Mary Frances 1948- *WhoAmW 91, WhoEmL 91*
Seymour, Mary Powell 1922- *WhoAmW 91*
Seymour, Origen Storrs 1804-1881 *AmLegL*
Seymour, Pearl M. 1929- *WhoAmW 91*
Seymour, Percy *BioIn 16*
Seymour, Peter Mark *BiDrAPA 89*
Seymour, Raymond Benedict 1912- *WhoAm 90, WhoWor 91*
Seymour, Richard Kellogg 1930- *WhoAm 90*
Seymour, Samuel 1797-1823 *WhNaAH*
Seymour, Stephanie Kulp 1940- *WhoAmW 91*
Seymour, Thaddeus 1928- *WhoAm 90*
Seymour, Thomas *PenDiDA 89*
Seymour, Whitney North, Jr. 1923- *WhoAm 90*
Seymour, William Richard 1930- *WhoE 91*
Seymour-Harris, Barbara Laverne 1953- *WhoEmL 91*
Seyrig, Delphine *NewYTBS 90 [port]*
Seyss-Inquart, Arthur 1892-1946 *WorAlBi*
Seyss-Inquart, Artur von 1892-1946 *BioIn 16*
Seznec, Alain 1930- *WhoAm 90*
Sfar, Rachid 1933- *WhoWor 91*
Sfeir, Sami G. 1946- *WhoWor 91*
Sfikas, Peter Michael 1937- *WhoAm 90*
Sforza, Caterina 1463-1509 *BioIn 16*
Sforza, Ippolita 1445-1488 *EncCoWW*
Sforza, Mario Vito 1933- *WhoWor 91*
Sforzo, Robert J. 1947- *WhoE 91, WhoWor 91*
Sforzo, Robert Joseph 1947- *WhoAm 90*
Sgall, Petr 1926- *WhoWor 91*
Sgambati, Catherine Jane 1959- *WhoAmW 91*
Sgarlata, Francesco 1926- *WhoWor 91*
Sgouros, Thomas 1927- *BioIn 16*
Sgro, Joseph Anthony 1937- *WhoAm 90*
Sgroi, Donald Angelo 1943- *WhoE 91*
Sgroi, Joseph Nicholas 1937- *St&PR 91*
Sha Na Na *EncPR&S 89*
Shaaban, Fadel A *BiDrAPA 89*
Shaalan, Mohammed M *BiDrAPA 89*
Shaar, H. Erik *WhoAm 90*
Shaar, Michael Vincent 1933- *St&PR 91*
Shaara, Michael 1929-1988 *BioIn 16*
Shabad, Theodore 1922-1987 *BioIn 16*
Shabashova, Regina *BiDrAPA 89*
Shabat, Richard Gary 1940- *St&PR 91*
Shabazian, Bob *ODwPR 91*
Shabazz, Attallah *BioIn 16*
Shabazz, Menelik *DrBIPA 90*
Shabbethai Tzevi 1626-1676 *BioIn 16*
Shabbir, Mahnaz Mehdi 1959- *WhoAmW 91*
Shabbona 1775-1859 *WhNaAH*
Shabel, Karen Lind 1948- *WhoAmW 91*
Shablin, Lisabeth Teresa 1964- *WhoAmW 91*
Shabona 1775-1859 *WhNaAH*
Shabonee 1775-1859 *WhNaAH*
Shabot, Myron Michael 1945- *WhoEmL 91*
Shabry, Fryderyka R. *BiDrAPA 89*
Shabtai, Yaakov 1934-1981 *WorAu 1980*
Shachnow, Norman Keith *BiDrAPA 89*
Shachoy, Norman James 1937- *WhoAm 90*
Shachtman, Max 1904-1972 *EncAL*
Shachtman, Tom 1942- *BioIn 16*
Shack, Donald D. 1928- *St&PR 91*
Shack, William Alfred 1923- *WhoAm 90*
Shackel, Neal Frederick 1951- *WhoEmL 91*
Shackelford, Alphonso Leon 1920- *WhoSSW 91, WhoWrEP 89*
Shackelford, Barton Warren 1920- *St&PR 91, WhoAm 90*
Shackelford, Bud 1918- *WhoAmA 91*
Shackelford, George Green 1920- *WhoAm 90, WhoSSW 91*
Shackelford, James Hubert 1945- *WhoEmL 91*
Shackelford, John Cooper 1921- *St&PR 91*
Shackelford, Kim R. 1959- *St&PR 91*
Shackelford, Laurel 1946- *WhoAmW 91*
Shackelford, Lottie Holt 1941- *WhoAmW 91, WhoSSW 91*
Shackelford, Mary Jo 1949- *WhoAmW 91*
Shackelford, Shelby 1899-1987 *WhoAmA 91N*
Shackelford, Ted 1946- *ConTFT 8, WhoAm 90, WorAlBi*
Shackelford, Walter McDonald 1945- *WhoSSW 91*
Shackelford, William Edwin 1927- *St&PR 91*
Shackell, Ross Bingham 1936- *WhoWor 91*
Shackett, Thomas Charles 1938- *St&PR 91*
Shackford, Paul R. 1950- *St&PR 91*
Shackford, Paul Raymond 1950- *WhoE 91*
Shackle, George Lennox Sharman 1903- *WhoWor 91*
Shackleford, Covington 1924- *St&PR 91, WhoAm 90*
Shackleford, Ruby P. 1913- *WhoWrEP 89*
Shackleton, Basil 1900?-1978 *EncPaPR 91*
Shackleton, C. C. *MajTwCW*
Shackleton, Clayton Albert 1958- *St&PR 91*
Shackleton, Ernest 1874-1922 *WorAlBi*
Shackleton, Richard James 1933- *WhoE 91, WhoWor 91*
Shackleton, Suzanne M. 1950- *WhoAmW 91*
Shacklock, Constance 1913- *PenDiMP*
Shackman, Daniel R 1941- *BiDrAPA 89*
Shacochis, Bob *BioIn 16*
Shactman, Tom *AuBYP 90*
Shad, Harry G. *BioIn 16*
Shad, John 1923- *St&PR 91, WhoAm 90, WhoWor 91*
Shadbolt, Douglas 1925- *WhoAm 90*
Shadbolt, Jack Leonard 1909- *WhoAmA 91*
Shadd, Isaac D. 1831- *AmLegL*
Shadd, Marlon *BioIn 16*
Shadd, Mary Ann Camberton 1823-1893 *DcCanB 12*
Shaddeau, Carol Sue 1938- *WhoSSW 91*
Shaddix, James W. 1946- *St&PR 91*
Shaddix, W.J. 1928- *St&PR 91*
Shaddle, Alice 1928- *WhoAmA 91*
Shaddock, David Mulford 1958- *WhoSSW 91*
Shaddock, David Robert 1948- *WhoWrEP 89*
Shaddock, Roland Edwin 1925- *St&PR 91*
Shadduck, John Allen 1939- *WhoAm 90*
Shade, Frederick Albert 1944- *IntWWM 90*
Shade, Michael W. 1954- *St&PR 91*
Shade, Nancy Elizabeth 1949- *IntWWM 90*
Shadegg, Stephen *NewYTBS 90*
Shadegg, Stephen 1909-1990 *BioIn 16*
Shadegg, Stephen C. 1909-1990 *ConAu 131*
Shader, Melvin Aaron 1925- *St&PR 91*
Shader, Mickey 1891-1953 *Ballpl 90*
Shader, Richard I 1935- *BiDrAPA 89*
Shader, Richard Irwin 1935- *WhoAm 90, WhoE 91*
Shader Nassoiy, Suzan Lynda 1954- *WhoSSW 91*
Shaderowfsky, Eva Maria 1938- *WhoAmW 91*
Shaderowfsky, Lawrence 1935- *BiDrAPA 89*
Shadid, David Lee 1956- *BiDrAPA 89*
Shadid, Ernest G 1929- *BiDrAPA 89*
Shadid, George D. 1954- *St&PR 91*
Shadid, Larry George 1955- *BiDrAPA 89*
Shadid, Nanay Laporte 1959- *WhoAmW 91*
Shadle, Douglas James 1948- *BiDrAPA 89*
Shadle, Susan Beth 1957- *WhoAmW 91*
Shadler, Jimmy Arthur 1929- *St&PR 91*
Shadley, Meri Louise 1948- *WhoAmW 91*
Shadoan, George Woodson 1933- *WhoAm 90*
Shadoan, Richard A 1930- *BiDrAPA 89*
Shadoan, Shelley Ann 1964- *WhoAmW 91*
Shadoian, Holly Lynn 1952- *WhoE 91*
Shadovitz, David Jay 1954- *WhoWrEP 89*
Shadow, Don *BioIn 16*
Shadowfax *NewAgMG*
Shadows, The *EncPR&S 89, OxCPMus*
Shadrach, Jean H *WhoAmA 91*
Shadwell, Delvenia Gail 1938- *WhoWrEP 89*
Shaeffer, Charles Wayne 1910- *St&PR 91, WhoAm 90*
Shaeffer, Henry Warren 1945- *WhoEmL 91*
Shaeffer, Ruth Gilbert 1923- *WhoE 91*
Shaer, Milton 1923- *St&PR 91*
Shaer, Patricia Ann Blacha 1941- *WhoAmW 91*
Shaevitz, Marjorie Hansen 1943- *WhoAmW 91*
Shaevsky, Mark 1935- *St&PR 91, WhoAm 90*
Shafai, Lotfollah 1941- *WhoAm 90*
Shafarevich, I. R. 1923- *BioIn 16*
Shafarevich, Igor' Rostislavovich 1923- *BioIn 16*
Shafer, B. Lyle 1924- *St&PR 91*
Shafer, Basil Lyle 1924- *WhoAm 90*
Shafer, Burr *WhoAmA 91N*
Shafer, Byron Alvin 1938- *St&PR 91*
Shafer, Christine L *BiDrAPA 89*
Shafer, Eldon Eugene 1933- *WhoAm 90*
Shafer, Everett Earl 1925- *WhoAm 90*
Shafer, Guy C. 1918- *St&PR 91*
Shafer, Ingrid Hedwig 1939- *WhoSSW 91*
Shafer, J. M. 1944- *WhoAm 90*
Shafer, Jack L. 1945- *St&PR 91*
Shafer, Johanna Marie 1945- *WhoAmW 91*
Shafer, John Donald 1936- *WhoSSW 91*
Shafer, Jonathan Stickley 1936- *WhoE 91*
Shafer, Joseph Ernest 1903- *WhoAm 90*
Shafer, Linda Ann 1947- *WhoAmW 91*
Shafer, Linda Carol *BiDrAPA 89*
Shafer, Lorraine Pat 1958- *WhoAmW 91*
Shafer, Marguerite Neuhauser 1888-1976 *WhoAmA 91N*
Shafer, Michael Joe 1948- *St&PR 91*
Shafer, Randall Jay 1965- *St&PR 91*
Shafer, Raymond Philip 1917- *WhoAm 90, WhoE 91*
Shafer, Robert Eugene 1925- *WhoAm 90*
Shafer, Robert L *ODwPR 91*
Shafer, Robert L. 1932- *St&PR 91*
Shafer, Robert Tinsley, Jr. 1929- *WhoSSW 91*
Shafer, Roberta W. Crow 1950- *WhoAmW 91, WhoE 91*
Shafer, Roger Deane 1937- *BiDrAPA 89*
Shafer, Scott Michael 1962- *WhoSSW 91*
Shafey, Moustafa Hassan 1952- *BiDrAPA 89*
Shaff, Alan Martin 1958- *WhoSSW 91*
Shaff, Beverly Gerard 1925- *WhoAmW 91*
Shaff, Gerald H. 1933- *St&PR 91*
Shaff, Robert Myrven 1929- *St&PR 91*
Shaff, Stanley M. 1929- *IntWWM 90*
Shaffer, Alan Lee 1950- *WhoAm 90*
Shaffer, Albert Jay 1953- *St&PR 91*
Shaffer, Allen Grant 1954- *St&PR 91*
Shaffer, Anita Mohrland 1939- *WhoAmW 91, WhoSSW 91*
Shaffer, Anthony *TwCCr&M 91*
Shaffer, Audrey Jeanne 1929- *WhoAmW 91*
Shaffer, Bernard William 1924- *WhoAm 90, WhoE 91*
Shaffer, Carolyn G. 1943- *St&PR 91*
Shaffer, Clifton 1931- *St&PR 91*
Shaffer, David 1936- *BiDrAPA 89, WhoAm 90, WhoWor 91*
Shaffer, David H. 1942- *WhoAm 90, WhoE 91, WhoWor 91*
Shaffer, Dean W. 1926- *St&PR 91*
Shaffer, Deborah *BioIn 16*
Shaffer, Dorothy Browne 1923- *WhoAmW 91*
Shaffer, Edward Harry 1923- *WhoWor 91*
Shaffer, Elaine *PenDiMP*
Shaffer, Ethel Armstrong 1914- *WhoAmW 91*
Shaffer, Fern 1944- *WhoAmA 91*
Shaffer, Frances Annette 1946- *WhoAmW 91*
Shaffer, Fred Whittaker 1932- *St&PR 91*
Shaffer, Gail S. 1948- *WhoAmW 91, WhoE 91*
Shaffer, Harry G., Jr. 1926- *St&PR 91*
Shaffer, Harry George 1919- *WhoAm 90*
Shaffer, Herman Morris 1951- *WhoEmL 91*
Shaffer, Ian Arnold *BiDrAPA 89*
Shaffer, J.M. 1901- *St&PR 91*
Shaffer, James Burgess 1945- *WhoAm 90*
Shaffer, Janice Dawn 1946- *St&PR 91*
Shaffer, Jay Christopher 1947- *WhoEmL 91*
Shaffer, Jay Hammond 1947- *BiDrAPA 89*
Shaffer, Jerome Arthur 1929- *WhoAm 90*
Shaffer, Jill A. 1959- *St&PR 91*
Shaffer, John Christopher 1937- *St&PR 91*
Shaffer, John Robert 1928- *WhoE 91*
Shaffer, Judy Ann 1942- *WhoAmW 91*
Shaffer, Juliet Popper 1932- *WhoAmW 91*
Shaffer, Lawrence Blaine, III 1950- *BiDrAPA 89*
Shaffer, Louise *BioIn 16*
Shaffer, Lyman *AmLegL*
Shaffer, Margaret Minor 1940- *WhoSSW 91*
Shaffer, Mary 1947- *WhoE 91*
Shaffer, Michael L. 1945- *St&PR 91*
Shaffer, Orator 1852- *Ballpl 90*
Shaffer, Oren G. 1942- *St&PR 91*
Shaffer, Oren George 1942- *WhoAm 90*
Shaffer, Paul *BioIn 16*
Shaffer, Paul 1949- *WorAlBi*
Shaffer, Paul E. 1926- *St&PR 91, WhoAm 90*
Shaffer, Peter *BioIn 16, TwCCr&M 91*
Shaffer, Peter 1926- *ConLC 60 [port], MajTwCW, WorAlBi*
Shaffer, Peter Levin 1926- *WhoAm 90, WhoWor 91*
Shaffer, R. James 1931- *St&PR 91*
Shaffer, Richard 1947- *WhoAmA 91*
Shaffer, Richard Carl 1945- *WhoSSW 91*
Shaffer, Richard James 1931- *WhoAm 90*
Shaffer, Richard Paul 1949- *WhoSSW 91*
Shaffer, Robert Lynn 1929- *WhoAm 90*
Shaffer, Roberta Ivy 1953- *WhoAmW 91*
Shaffer, Ronald Lowrey 1951- *WhoWor 91*
Shaffer, Rosalind 1949- *WhoAmA 91*
Shaffer, Rosalind Keating 1896-1990 *ConAu 131*
Shaffer, Russell K. 1933- *WhoAm 90*
Shaffer, Samuel Holmes 1946- *St&PR 91*
Shaffer, Sara Alene 1913- *WhoAmW 91*
Shaffer, Sherrill Lynn 1952- *WhoE 91*
Shaffer, Steve *BioIn 16*
Shaffer, Susan E. 1947- *WhoAmW 91*
Shaffer, Thomas Lindsay 1934- *WhoAm 90*
Shafferman, Howard Haswell 1954- *WhoEmL 91*
Shaffet, Michael 1935- *St&PR 91*
Shaffner, George Van Cleve 1947- *WhoEmL 91*
Shaffner, Randolph Preston 1940- *WhoSSW 91*
Shaffner, Robert Christopher 1944- *St&PR 91*
Shafi, Mansoor 1954- *WhoE 91*
Shafia, Georgia 1936- *St&PR 91*
Shafii, Mohammad *BiDrAPA 89*
Shafir, Grace Chastain 1948- *WhoAmW 91, WhoE 91*
Shafir, Michael 1944- *ConAu 129*
Shafner, Hyim 1938- *BiDrAPA 89*
Shafran, Daniil 1923- *PenDiMP*
Shafran, Hank 1945- *ODwPR 91, WhoAm 90*
Shafritz, David Andrew 1940- *WhoAm 90*
Shaftan, Bernice *WhoWor 91*
Shafter, Albert Jene, Jr. 1924- *WhoAm 90*
Shafter, James McMillen 1816-1892 *AmLegL*
Shafter, William Rufus 1835-1906 *BioIn 16*
Shaftesbury, Anthony A. Cooper, Earl of 1671-1713 *DcLB 101 [port]*
Shaftesbury, Anthony A Cooper, Earl of 1801-1885 *BioIn 16*

Shaftesbury, Anthony Ashley Cooper 1621-1683 *WorAlBi*
Shaftman, Fredrick Krisch 1948- *WhoSSW 91*
Shaftner, Kim K. 1954- *WhoSSW 91*
Shafto, Carl Richard 1948- *BiDrAPA 89*
Shafto, Robert Austin 1935- *St&PR 91, WhoAm 90*
Shagam, Melvin H. 1916- *St&PR 91*
Shagan, Steve 1927- *WhoAm 90*
Shagass, Charles 1920- *BiDrAPA 89, WhoAm 90, WhoE 91*
Shaginian, Marietta 1888-1982 *EncCoWW*
Shaginyan, Mariettta 1888-1982 *ConAu 129*
Shagrithaya, Narayana Balaya 1946- *WhoWor 91*
Shah Jehan 1592-1666 *WorAlBi*
Shah, Amritlal Jivraj 1941- *WhoWor 91*
Shah, Anil V 1934- *BiDrAPA 89*
Shah, Anwar Muhammad Chaudry 1948- *WhoE 91*
Shah, Arun Premchand *BiDrAPA 89*
Shah, Arun Premchand 1954- *WhoE 91*
Shah, Arvind Asharam 1939- *WhoWor 91*
Shah, Asghar Ali *BiDrAPA 89*
Shah, Ashok K *BiDrAPA 89*
Shah, Ashok R *BiDrAPA 89*
Shah, Atul 1948- *BiDrAPA 89*
Shah, Bharat J 1956- *BiDrAPA 89*
Shah, Bhupendra Panalal 1934- *WhoE 91*
Shah, Bipin Chandra 1938- *WhoAm 90*
Shah, Chandresh 1955- *BiDrAPA 89*
Shah, Dina Bharat *BiDrAPA 89*
Shah, Dinesh Kumar 1938- *BiDrAPA 89*
Shah, Girish V 1937- *BiDrAPA 89*
Shah, Girishkumar Popatlal 1956- *BiDrAPA 89*
Shah, Haresh C. 1937- *WhoAm 90*
Shah, Hasmukh J 1938- *BiDrAPA 89*
Shah, Hemendra K. 1945- *St&PR 91*
Shah, Idries 1924- *EncO&P 3*
Shah, Ishwer Chabildas 1938- *WhoE 91*
Shah, Itezaz Hussain 1939- *WhoWor 91*
Shah, Jagdish Vallabhdas *BiDrAPA 89*
Shah, Jyoti Ramesh *BiDrAPA 89*
Shah, Kanti 1947- *St&PR 91*
Shah, Kantilal M 1944- *BiDrAPA 89*
Shah, Kanu V 1926- *BiDrAPA 89*
Shah, Ketki Sharadkumar *BiDrAPA 89*
Shah, Ketki Sharadkumar 1957- *WhoE 91*
Shah, Khawaja Tahir 1943- *WhoWrEP 89*
Shah, Kumar 1949- *St&PR 91*
Shah, Lalit P 1936- *BiDrAPA 89*
Shah, Mahasukhlal H 1934- *BiDrAPA 89*
Shah, Mahendra B *BiDrAPA 89*
Shah, Mahendra Ratilal *BiDrAPA 89*
Shah, Manjula A 1938- *BiDrAPA 89*
Shah, Manoj R 1945- *BiDrAPA 89*
Shah, Maya Nalin 1942- *WhoWor 91*
Shah, Modaser *BiDrAPA 89*
Shah, Muhammad Azher Zafar 1956- *WhoWor 91*
Shah, Mukesh Harilal 1953- *BiDrAPA 89*
Shah, Mukhtar H *BiDrAPA 89*
Shah, Naren Natwarlal 1934- *WhoE 91*
Shah, Narendra C *BiDrAPA 89*
Shah, Navin Chandra 1942- *BiDrAPA 89*
Shah, Navinchandra R 1949- *BiDrAPA 89*
Shah, Nayana 1950- *BiDrAPA 89*
Shah, Nila Ashok *BiDrAPA 89*
Shah, Nurun Nessa 1953- *BiDrAPA 89*
Shah, Panna Lalit *BiDrAPA 89*
Shah, Paresh K *BiDrAPA 89*
Shah, Pareshkumar B *BiDrAPA 89*
Shah, Piyush 1937- *WhoWor 91*
Shah, Pradip Panalal 1953- *WhoWor 91*
Shah, Pramod A 1948- *BiDrAPA 89*
Shah, Pritesh J *BiDrAPA 89*
Shah, R C 1948- *BiDrAPA 89*
Shah, Rajni 1950- *WhoWor 91*
Shah, Ramesh A 1935- *BiDrAPA 89*
Shah, Ramesh Keshavlal 1941- *WhoAm 90*
Shah, Ramesh Premchand 1937- *WhoWor 91*
Shah, Rashmikant K 1948- *BiDrAPA 89*
Shah, Satish C. 1941- *St&PR 91*
Shah, Satish N 1948- *BiDrAPA 89*
Shah, Shirish Kalyanbhai 1942- *WhoE 91*
Shah, Sudhir Vithalbhai 1947- *WhoSSW 91*
Shah, Surendra P. 1937- *St&PR 91*
Shah, Surendra Poonamchand 1936- *WhoAm 90*
Shah, Suresh B 1938- *BiDrAPA 89*
Shah, Swarupchand Mohanlal 1905- *WhoSSW 91*
Shah, Talaxi Dunger 1939- *BiDrAPA 89*
Shah, Vikram Jay 1938- *WhoWor 91*
Shah, Vinaykant D *BiDrAPA 89*
Shah, Vinodbala S 1944- *BiDrAPA 89*
Shah-Jahan, M.M. 1943- *WhoE 91*
Shahabuddin, Mohammad 1940- *WhoE 91*
Shahady, Edward John 1938- *WhoAm 90*
Shahaka 1765?-1815? *WhNaAH*
Shaham, Jacob *BioIn 16*
Shahan, Donald Allan 1950- *St&PR 91*
Shahan, James William 1932- *St&PR 91*
Shahan, Sherry *AuBYP 90*
Shahan, William R. 1939- *St&PR 91*
Shahbakian, Michael B. 1947- *St&PR 91*
Shaheen, Gary Edward 1952- *WhoAmA 91*
Shaheen, John A. 1953- *St&PR 91*
Shaheen, Joseph Maron *BiDrAPA 89*
Shaheen, Michael Edmund, Jr. 1940- *WhoAm 90*
Shaheen, Shaheen Azeez 1928- *WhoAm 90*
Shaheen, Shouky Azeez 1929- *WhoSSW 91*
Shahen, Timothy 1943- *St&PR 91, WhoAm 90*
Shahid, Agha *BiDrAPA 89*
Shahid, Aida Meshki 1959- *WhoAmW 91*
Shahim, Houshang *BiDrAPA 89*
Shahin, Majdi Musa 1936- *WhoWor 91*
Shahin-Itteilag, Nancy 1955- *WhoE 91*
Shahly, Jehan 1928- *WhoAmA 91, WhoE 91*
Shahn, Abby 1940- *WhoAmA 91*
Shahn, Ben 1898-1969 *IntDcAA 90, WhoAmA 91N, WorAlBi*
Shahn, Bernarda Bryson 1903- *WhoAmA 91*
Shahnasarian, Michael 1957- *WhoEmL 91*
Shahnavaz, Houshang 1936- *WhoWor 91*
Shahon, Susan Valerie 1948- *WhoEmL 91*
Shahriar, Mostafa 1953- *WhoSSW 91*
Shahryar, Muhammad Husayn 1905?-1988 *AnObit 1988*
Shahshahani, Ahmad 1947- *WhoEmL 91*
Shahzade, Ann Mary 1928- *WhoAmW 91*
Shaifer, David Wayne 1951- *WhoSSW 91*
Shaifer, Norman 1931- *WhoAm 90*
Shaikh, Abdul Hafeez 1942- *WhoWor 91*
Shaikh, Najmussahar M *BiDrAPA 89*
Shail, Linda Grace 1947- *WhoWrEP 89*
Shain, Benjamin Ned 1953- *BiDrAPA 89*
Shain, Irving 1926- *St&PR 91, WhoAm 90*
Shain, Kenneth Stephen 1952- *WhoEmL 91*
Shain, Myron Raymond 1940- *St&PR 91*
Shain, Philip Warren *BiDrAPA 89*
Shain, Robert A *BiDrAPA 89*
Shain, Russell Earl 1944- *WhoAm 90*
Shain, Steven M. *St&PR 91*
Shain, Yossi 1956- *ConAu 131*
Shainberg, Lawrence 1936- *ConAu 131*
Shaine, Frances *St&PR 91*
Shaine, Theodore Harris 1947- *WhoAm 90*
Shainess, Natalie 1915- *BiDrAPA 89, WhoE 91*
Shainis, Murray J. 1926- *WhoWrEP 89*
Shainis, Murray Joseph 1926- *WhoE 91, WhoWor 91*
Shainman, Irwin 1921- *WhoAm 90*
Shainman, Jack S 1957- *WhoAmA 91*
Shainmark, Steven S 1962- *BiDrAPA 89*
Shair, David I. 1921- *St&PR 91*
Shajar Al Durr *WomWR*
Shaka, George James 1934- *BiDrAPA 89*
Shaka, James Athan *BiDrAPA 89*
Shakabpa, Tsepon Wangchuk Deden *BioIn 16*
Shaked, Gershon 1929- *ConAu 131*
Shaked, Haim 1939- *ConAu 130*
Shakehand *WhNaAH*
Shakely, John Bower 1940- *WhoAm 90, WhoWor 91*
Shaker, Abdullah Jassim al- *BioIn 16*
Shaker, Thomas R. 1926- *St&PR 91*
Shakes *WhNaAH*
Shakespear, Dorothy 1886-1973 *BiDWomA*
Shakespear, Raul 1947- *ConDes 90*
Shakespear, Ronald 1941- *ConDes 90*
Shakespeare, Easton Geoffrey 1946- *WhoE 91*
Shakespeare, Frank 1925- *WhoAm 90, WhoWor 91*
Shakespeare, John William Richmond 1930- *WhoWor 91*
Shakespeare, William 1564-1616 *BioIn 16, EncPaPR 91, WorAlBi*
Shakhmundes, Lev 1933- *WhoWor 91*
Shakin, Elisabeth J *BiDrAPA 89*
Shakir, Saad Adnan *BiDrAPA 89*
Shaklan, Allen Yale 1945- *WhoAm 90, WhoE 91, WhoSSW 91*
Shakno, Robert Julian 1937- *WhoAm 90*
Shaknovich, Alexander 1957- *WhoE 91*
Shakopee *WhNaAH*
Shakopee *WhNaAH*
Shakpadan *WhNaAH*
Shaktman, Diane Merril 1943- *BiDrAPA 89*
Shakur, Assata *BioIn 16*
Shalack, Joan H 1932- *BiDrAPA 89*
Shalala, Donna *BioIn 16*
Shalala, Donna Edna 1941- *WhoAm 90, WhoAmW 91, WhoWor 91*
Shalala, Philip D. 1937- *WhoAm 90*
Shalam, John J. 1933- *St&PR 91*
Shalamanov, Neum *BioIn 16*
Shalamov, Varlam 1907?-1982 *ConAu 129*
Shalamskas, John *BiDrAPA 89*
Shalanca, Philip Anthony 1947- *WhoE 91*
Shaldon, Stanley 1931- *WhoWor 91*
Shalek, Nancy *BioIn 16*
Shaler, Nathaniel Southgate 1841-1906 *BioIn 16*
Shales, Thomas William 1948- *WhoAm 90, WhoE 91*
Shalette, Michael Alan 1935- *St&PR 91, WhoAm 90*
Shalhoub, Michael *WhoWor 91*
Shalhoub, Michael David 1957- *WhoEmL 91*
Shalikashvili, John Malchase 1936- *WhoAm 90*
Shalit, Bernard Lawrence 1920- *WhoE 91, WhoWor 91*
Shalit, Hanoch 1953- *WhoE 91*
Shalit, Mitzi 1923- *WhoE 91*
Shalita, Alan Remi 1936- *WhoAm 90, WhoE 91*
Shalkop, Robert Leroy 1922- *WhoAm 90, WhoAmA 91*
Shallard, Michael 1951- *ConTFT 8 [port]*
Shallberg, Dale F. 1915- *St&PR 91*
Shallberg, Mary Ann Harris 1942- *WhoAmW 91*
Shallcross, Helen Clanahan 1913- *WhoWor 91*
Shallenberger, John B. 1917- *St&PR 91*
Shallenberger, Samuel Andre *BiDrAPA 89*
Shalom, Liliane Winn 1940- *WhoAmW 91*
Shalom, Rose *BiDrAPA 89*
Shalowitz, Erwin Emmanuel 1924- *WhoAm 90*
Shalsha, Lilli C 1909- *BiDrAPA 89*
Shalson, Vaughan H.J. 1946- *St&PR 91*
Shalyapin, Fyodor 1883-1938 *PenDiMP*
Sham, Brad Michael 1949- *WhoSSW 91*
Sham, Lu Jeu 1938- *WhoAm 90*
Shaman, Sanford Sivitz 1946- *WhoAm 90, WhoAmA 91*
Shamas, Barry Neil 1947- *St&PR 91*
Shamash, Jack 1924-1990 *BioIn 16, NewYTBS 90 [port]*
Shamask, Ronaldus *BioIn 16*
Shamask, Ronaldus 1945- *ConDes 90*
Shambarger, James Allen 1950- *St&PR 91*
Shambaugh, Adele E *BiDrAPA 89*
Shambaugh, George Elmer, III 1931- *WhoAm 90*
Shambaugh, Mark P. *St&PR 91*
Shambaugh, Max Paul 1922- *St&PR 91*
Shambaugh, Philip W 1932- *BiDrAPA 89*
Shambaugh, Stephen Ward 1920- *WhoWor 91*
Shamberg, Barbara Ann 1953- *WhoAmW 91, WhoE 91*
Shamberg, Kurt D. *BioIn 16*
Shamberg, Michael *BioIn 16*
Shamblin, A. Kent 1935- *ODwPR 91, St&PR 91*
Shamblin, Arnold Kent 1935- *WhoAm 90*
Shamblin, William J, Jr. *BiDrAPA 89*
Shamburek, Roland Howard 1928- *WhoAm 90*
Shamel, Roger Ervin 1945- *WhoE 91*
Shamers, Irving H. 1923- *WhoAm 90*
Shames, Ervin Richard 1940- *St&PR 91, WhoAm 90*
Shames, Harold 1924- *St&PR 91*
Shames, Henry Joseph 1921- *WhoAm 90*
Shames, Irving Herman 1923- *WhoAm 90*
Shames, Jeffrey L. 1955- *St&PR 91*
Shames, Jordan Nelson 1949- *WhoE 91, WhoEmL 91*
Shames, Sidney J. 1917- *St&PR 91*
Shamgar, Meir 1925- *WhoWor 91*
Shamie, Mohammed Ali *BiDrAPA 89*
Shamimi-Noori, Soroush *BiDrAPA 89*
Shamir, Yitzhak *BioIn 16*
Shamir, Yitzhak 1915- *PolLCME, WhoWor 91*
Shamitoff, Daryl Lawrence 1950- *St&PR 91*
Shamlaty, Ronald W. 1942- *St&PR 91*
Shamlin, Rose 1918- *WhoAmW 91*
Shammas, Anton *BioIn 16*
Shammas, Elia *BiDrAPA 89*
Shamoian, Charles A 1931- *BiDrAPA 89*
Shamoo, Adil Elias 1941- *WhoAm 90*
Shamos, Morris H. 1917- *St&PR 91*
Shamos, Morris Herbert 1917- *WhoAm 90*
Shamp, David Jerome 1922- *St&PR 91*
Shampain, Lawrence R 1956- *BiDrAPA 89*
Shamray, Gerry *BioIn 16*
Shams, Kiumars E *BiDrAPA 89*
Shamsavari, Ali 1944- *WhoWor 91*
Shamshoum, Kamal 1942- *WhoWor 91*
Shamsi, Manazir 1935- *BiDrAPA 89*
Shamsi, Rahim *BiDrAPA 89*
Shamsky, Art 1941- *Ballpl 90*
Shamuyarira, Nathan Marwirakuwa 1930- *WhoWor 91*
Shamy, Carolyn Graham 1939- *WhoE 91*
Shan, Robert Kuocheng 1927- *WhoSSW 91*
Shan Foo, Cheng 1927- *WhoWor 91*
Shanaberg, Peter Howard 1947- *WhoWor 91*
Shanabrook, Linda 1956- *WhoAmW 91*
Shanafelt, P. David 1931- *WhoAm 90*
Shanahan, Bill *BioIn 16*
Shanahan, Brendan 1969- *BioIn 16*
Shanahan, Edmond M. 1926- *St&PR 91*
Shanahan, Eileen 1924- *WhoAmW 91*
Shanahan, Eugene Miles 1946- *WhoAm 90*
Shanahan, James Anthony 1898- *WhoAm 90*
Shanahan, James Patrick 1933- *St&PR 91*
Shanahan, John Edward 1915- *St&PR 91*
Shanahan, Kathleen E 1920- *BiDrAPA 89*
Shanahan, Marie Julie 1958- *WhoAmW 91*
Shanahan, Michael F. 1939- *St&PR 91*
Shanahan, Michael Francis 1939- *WhoAm 90*
Shanahan, Mike *WhoAm 90*
Shanahan, R. Michael 1939- *St&PR 91*
Shanahan, Robert B. 1928- *WhoAm 90*
Shanahan, Thomas Joseph 1932- *St&PR 91*
Shanahan, Thomas M. 1934- *WhoAm 90*
Shanahan, William M 1910- *BiDrAPA 89*
Shanahan, William Stephen 1940- *WhoAm 90*
Shanahan-Busby, Moira 1955- *WhoSSW 91*
Shanard, G.H. 1926- *St&PR 91*
Shanas, Bert Z. 1944- *WhoAm 90*
Shanas, Ethel 1914- *WhoAm 90, WhoAmW 91*
Shanbhag, Shirish Sadanand 1954- *WhoWor 91*
Shanbhag, Suhas Ramdas *BiDrAPA 89*
Shand, Douglas Grosh 1956- *St&PR 91*
Shand, Jimmy 1908- *OxCPMus*
Shand Kydd, Frances *BioIn 16*
Shandell, Kenneth Evan *BiDrAPA 89*
Shander, Ellyn Pearlman 1949- *BiDrAPA 89*
Shandler, Alan Robert 1944- *St&PR 91*
Shandler, Barbara Rochelle 1955- *WhoAmW 91*
Shandling, Garry *BioIn 16*
Shandling, Gary 1950- *WorAlBi*
Shandloff, Nina Beth 1952- *WhoWor 91*
Shands, Courtney, Jr. 1929- *WhoAm 90*
Shands, Kathryn N. 1946- *BiDrAPA 89*
Shands, William R., Jr. 1929- *St&PR 91*
Shands, William Ridley, Jr. 1929- *WhoAm 90*
Shane, Bob 1934- *WhoAm 90*
Shane, Charles N., Jr. 1936- *St&PR 91*
Shane, Donald Eugene 1935- *St&PR 91*
Shane, Harold David 1936- *WhoAm 90*
Shane, Harold Gray 1914- *WhoAm 90*
Shane, J. Lawrence 1935- *St&PR 91*
Shane, Jeffrey N. 1941- *WhoAm 90*
Shane, John Marder 1942- *WhoSSW 91*
Shane, Joseph 1927- *WhoE 91*
Shane, Michael B. 1941- *St&PR 91*
Shane, Morton *BiDrAPA 89*
Shane, Paul E. 1944- *St&PR 91*
Shane, Rita *WhoAm 90*
Shane, Rita Frances 1940- *IntWWM 90*
Shane, Ronald 1953- *WhoAm 90*
Shane, Sheldon Richard 1929- *WhoAm 90*
Shane, Sylvan Myron Elliot 1918- *BioIn 16*
Shane, William R. 1947- *St&PR 91*
Shane, William Whitney 1928- *WhoWor 91*
Shaner, Andrew Lee *BiDrAPA 89*
Shaner, David 1934- *WhoAmA 91*
Shaner, Peyton Nash 1928- *St&PR 91*
Shaner, Richard Clark 1948- *WhoWrEP 89*
Shaner, Roderick *BiDrAPA 89*
Shaner, Stephanie E *BiDrAPA 89*
Shaner, Steven Keister 1961- *IntWWM 90*
Shanet, Howard 1918- *ConAu 130*
Shaney, Kevin Robert 1950- *WhoEmL 91*
Shanfari, Said Ahmad al 1939- *WhoWor 91*
Shanfield, Stephen B 1939- *BiDrAPA 89*
Shang *PenDiDA 89*
Shange, Ntozake *BioIn 16*
Shange, Ntozake 1948- *DrBlPA 90, FemiCLE, MajTwCW, NotWoAT, WhoAm 90, WhoWrEP 89*
Shangraw, Clarence Frank 1935- *WhoAm 90, WhoAmA 91*
Shangraw, Robert Edward 1954- *WhoE 91, WhoEmL 91*
Shangraw, Sylvia Chen 1937- *WhoAmA 91N*
Shangri-Las, The *EncPR&S 89*
Shanin, Teodor 1930- *WhoWor 91*
Shanis, Joseph 1919- *St&PR 91*
Shank, Adele Edling *BioIn 16*
Shank, Adele Edling 1940- *NotWoAT*
Shank, Charles Vernon 1943- *WhoAm 90*
Shank, Clare Brown Williams 1909- *WhoAm 90, WhoAmW 91, WhoSSW 91*
Shank, Cleo Bernard 1927- *St&PR 91*

Shank, Gerald E. 1924- *St&PR 91*
Shank, Kevin Charles *BioIn 16*
Shank, Maurice Edwin 1921- *WhoAm 90*
Shank, Robert Ely 1914- *WhoAm 90*
Shank, Roxanne Crystal 1954- *WhoWor 91*
Shank, Russell 1925- *WhoAm 90*
Shank, Stephen George 1943- *St&PR 91, WhoAm 90*
Shank, Suzanne Adams 1946- *WhoWor 91*
Shank, Theodore *ConAu 129*
Shank, Theodore J 1929- *ConAu 129*
Shank, William Haldeman 1915- *WhoE 91*
Shank, William O. 1924- *St&PR 91, WhoAm 90*
Shankar, R. Sam 1942- *St&PR 91*
Shankar, Ramsewak 1937- *WhoWor 91*
Shankar, Ratnaswamy 1942- *WhoE 91*
Shankar, Ravi *AuBYP 90, NewAgMG*
Shankar, Ravi 1920- *IntWWM 90, PenDiMP, WhoWor 91*
Shankel, Gerald Marvin 1943- *WhoE 91*
Shanken, Williard Jay 1941- *BiDrAPA 89*
Shanker, Albert 1928- *WhoAm 90, WhoE 91, WorAlBi*
Shanker, Daya 1929- *EncPaPR 91*
Shanker, Morris Gerald 1926- *WhoAm 90*
Shankin, Stephen 1943- *St&PR 91, WhoE 91*
Shankland, Charles 1942- *WhoWor 91*
Shanklin, Christopher Bryan 1946- *WhoSSW 91*
Shanklin, Douglas Radford 1930- *WhoSSW 91*
Shanklin, James Gordon 1909-1988 *BioIn 16*
Shanklin, Richard Vair, III 1937- *WhoAm 90*
Shankman, Andrew Stuart *BiDrAPA 89*
Shankman, Arnold M 1945- *ConAu 129*
Shankman, Cheryl Ann 1952- *WhoAmW 91*
Shankman, Florence Vogel 1912- *WhoAm 90*
Shankman, Gary Charles 1950- *WhoAmA 91, WhoE 91*
Shankman, Jack S. *ODwPR 91*
Shankman, K. 1943- *St&PR 91*
Shankman, Minda Rose 1959- *BiDrAPA 89*
Shankman, Robert 1943- *St&PR 91*
Shankman, Sidney *BiDrAPA 89*
Shanks, Ann Zane *WhoAm 90, WhoAmW 91, WhoE 91*
Shanks, Carroll D. *WhoAm 90, WhoSSW 91*
Shanks, Carroll Dean 1927- *St&PR 91*
Shanks, David *WhoAm 90*
Shanks, David C. 1939- *St&PR 91*
Shanks, Donald DeWitt 1923- *IntWWM 90*
Shanks, Donald Gordon 1933- *St&PR 91*
Shanks, Donald Mike 1934- *St&PR 91*
Shanks, Elizabeth *BiDrAPA 89*
Shanks, Eugene B., Jr. *WhoAm 90*
Shanks, Eugene Baylis 1913- *WhoAm 90*
Shanks, Eugene Baylis, Jr. 1947- *St&PR 91*
Shanks, Genevieve Madeline 1923- *WhoAmW 91*
Shanks, Hershel 1930- *WhoAm 90, WhoWrEP 89*
Shanks, Howard 1890-1941 *Ballpl 90*
Shanks, James William 1926- *St&PR 91*
Shanks, Joan P. 1936- *ODwPR 91*
Shanks, Judith Weil 1941- *WhoAmW 91, WhoE 91, WhoWor 91*
Shanks, Kathryn Mary 1950- *WhoAmW 91*
Shanks, Lawrence Edward 1946- *St&PR 91*
Shanks, Lorna Evelyn 1938- *WhoWor 91*
Shanks, Margaret McCloskey 1953- *WhoAmW 91*
Shanks, Michael James 1927-1984 *DcNaB 1981*
Shanks, Stephen Ray 1956- *WhoSSW 91*
Shanley, Bernard Michael 1903- *WhoAm 90*
Shanley, John Patrick *BioIn 16*
Shanley, Kevin 1942- *St&PR 91*
Shanly, Walter 1817-1899 *DcCanB 12*
Shanman, James Alan 1942- *WhoAm 90, WhoE 91, WhoWor 91*
Shanmugham, Revathi *BiDrAPA 89*
Shannahan, Franklin M. 1928- *St&PR 91*
Shannahan, John Henry Kelly 1913- *WhoAm 90*
Shanno, David Francis 1938- *WhoAm 90*
Shannon, Charles 1914- *WhoAmA 91*
Shannon, Cheryl 1945- *St&PR 91*
Shannon, Christina *WhoWrEP 89*
Shannon, Claude E. 1916- *WorAlBi*
Shannon, Claude Elwood 1916- *WhoAm 90*
Shannon, Clayton P. 1934- *St&PR 91*
Shannon, Daniel Gerard 1946- *St&PR 91*
Shannon, David Allen 1920- *WhoAm 90*
Shannon, David H. 1937- *St&PR 91*
Shannon, David Thomas 1933- *WhoAm 90, WhoSSW 91*
Shannon, Del 1939- *EncPR&S 89*
Shannon, Del 1939-1990 *BioIn 16, NewYTBS 90 [port], WorAlBi*
Shannon, Dell *TwCCr&M 91*
Shannon, Don Michael 1948- *WhoWrEP 89*
Shannon, Donald Hawkins 1923- *WhoAm 90*
Shannon, Doris *TwCCr&M 91*
Shannon, Edfred L., Jr. 1926- *WhoAm 90*
Shannon, Edgar Finley, Jr. 1918- *WhoAm 90*
Shannon, F.W.D. 1935- *St&PR 91*
Shannon, George 1952- *BioIn 16*
Shannon, Gerald T. 1923- *St&PR 91*
Shannon, Iris Reed *WhoAm 90, WhoAmW 91*
Shannon, Jacqueline *SmATA 63 [port]*
Shannon, James A. 1904- *WhoAm 90*
Shannon, James Jebusa 1862-1923 *BioIn 16*
Shannon, James Michael 1952- *WhoAm 90, WhoE 91*
Shannon, James Patrick 1921- *WhoAm 90*
Shannon, James William 1938- *St&PR 91*
Shannon, John *BioIn 16*
Shannon, John Sanford 1931- *St&PR 91, WhoAm 90*
Shannon, John W. 1933- *WhoAm 90*
Shannon, Joseph A Eric *BiDrAPA 89*
Shannon, Judith L. 1942- *ODwPR 91, St&PR 91*
Shannon, Judith Lewis 1942- *WhoE 91*
Shannon, Kenneth Francis 1955- *WhoEmL 91*
Shannon, Len Broughton, Jr. 1936- *St&PR 91*
Shannon, Lyle William 1920- *WhoAm 90*
Shannon, Margaret Rita *WhoAm 90*
Shannon, Margaret Sherry 1954- *WhoAmW 91*
Shannon, Martha Alberter 1958- *WhoAmW 91*
Shannon, Michael *BioIn 16*
Shannon, Michael Edward 1936- *St&PR 91, WhoAm 90*
Shannon, Mike 1939- *Ballpl 90*
Shannon, Mike 1951- *Ballpl 90*
Shannon, Mitsuko Perry 1957- *BiDrAPA 89*
Shannon, Monica 1905?-1965 *AuBYP 90*
Shannon, Paul 1876-1939 *Ballpl 90*
Shannon, Philip P. *BioIn 16*
Shannon, Randall Phillip 1953- *IntWWM 90*
Shannon, Red 1895-1970 *Ballpl 90*
Shannon, Rex Byron 1930- *St&PR 91*
Shannon, Robert Allen, Jr. 1945- *St&PR 91*
Shannon, Robert F 1933- *BiDrAPA 89*
Shannon, Robert Rennie 1932- *WhoAm 90*
Shannon, Samuel Leonard 1816-1895 *DcCanB 12*
Shannon, Scott *BioIn 16*
Shannon, Scott Matthew 1956- *BiDrAPA 89*
Shannon, Shad 1955- *WhoWor 91*
Shannon, Spike 1878-1940 *Ballpl 90*
Shannon, Stephen Quinby, Jr. *WhoAm 90*
Shannon, Terry *AuBYP 90*
Shannon, Thomas Alfred 1932- *WhoAm 90*
Shannon, Thomas Bowles 1827-1897 *AmLegL*
Shannon, Timothy Mayze 1948- *WhoSSW 91*
Shannon, William Norman, III 1937- *WhoWor 91*
Shannon, William V. *BioIn 16*
Shannon, William Vincent *BioIn 16*
Shannon McConaghy, Marilyn 1953- *WhoAmW 91*
Shannon-Spalding, Louise May 1961- *WhoAmW 91*
Shannonhouse, Hugh P. 1953- *St&PR 91*
Shannonhouse, Sandra 1947- *WhoAmA 91*
Shanok, Larry F. 1947- *St&PR 91*
Shanok, Larry Frank 1947- *WhoE 91*
Shanor, Donald Read 1927- *ConAu 30NR, WhoAm 90*
Shanor, Leland 1914- *WhoWor 91*
Shansby, John Gary 1937- *WhoAm 90*
Shanshal, Abdul Jabbar Khalil *WhoWor 91*
Shantaram, Vankudre 1901- *WhoWor 91*
Shanteau, Richard E 1945- *BiDrAPA 89*
Shanti *NewAgMG*
Shanti, Wael Mohamed 1946- *WhoWor 91*
Shantz, Bobby 1925- *Ballpl 90*
Shantz, John Edson 1934- *St&PR 91*
Shantzer, Louis 1930- *St&PR 91, WhoAm 90*
Shao, Otis Hung-I 1923- *WhoAm 90*
Shap, Sylvia 1948- *WhoAmA 91*
Shapcott, Ralph Lewis 1927- *St&PR 91*
Shapell, Nathan 1922- *St&PR 91*
Shaper, Christopher Thorne 1955- *WhoE 91*
Shaper, Stephen J. 1936- *St&PR 91*
Shaper, Stephen Jay 1936- *WhoSSW 91*
Shapere, Dudley 1928- *WhoAm 90*
Shapero, Esther Geller *WhoAmA 91*
Shapero, Harold 1920- *IntWWM 90*
Shapero, James Allen 1943- *BiDrAPA 89*
Shapero, Norman 1948- *St&PR 91*
Shapero, Theodore A. 1939- *WhoAm 90*
Shapes, Jeffrey N. 1949- *ODwPR 91*
Shapey, Ralph 1921- *IntWWM 90*
Shapin, Betty 1914- *EncPaPR 91*
Shapira, Dahlia 1939- *WhoWor 91*
Shapira, David 1942- *WhoAm 90*
Shapira, Edith Laura *BiDrAPA 89*
Shapira, Max L. 1944- *St&PR 91*
Shapira, Michael 1942- *WhoAm 90*
Shapiro, Adrian Michael 1950- *WhoAmA 91*
Shapiro, Alan M. 1956- *St&PR 91*
Shapiro, Alexander M. 1929- *BioIn 16*
Shapiro, Alvin M 1929- *BiDrAPA 89*
Shapiro, Alvin N. 1927- *WhoE 91*
Shapiro, Alvin Philip 1920- *WhoAm 90*
Shapiro, Amy Rosemarie 1949- *WhoAmW 91*
Shapiro, Andy *NewAgMG*
Shapiro, Ann R. 1937- *WhoAmW 91*
Shapiro, Annette M. 1955- *WhoE 91*
Shapiro, Arnold G 1951- *BiDrAPA 89*
Shapiro, Arnold L. *BioIn 16*
Shapiro, Arthur K 1923- *BiDrAPA 89, WhoE 91*
Shapiro, Ascher Herman 1916- *WhoAm 90*
Shapiro, Avraham 1918- *WhoWor 91*
Shapiro, Babe 1937- *WhoAm 90, WhoAmA 91*
Shapiro, Barbara J 1934- *ConAu 130*
Shapiro, Barry 1941- *St&PR 91*
Shapiro, Benjamin Louis 1943- *WhoE 91*
Shapiro, Bennett Michaels 1939- *WhoAm 90*
Shapiro, Bernard J. 1930- *St&PR 91*
Shapiro, Beverly Sue 1944- *WhoE 91*
Shapiro, Bruce 1946- *BiDrAPA 89*
Shapiro, Burton Leonard 1934- *WhoAm 90*
Shapiro, Caren Knight 1945- *WhoAmW 91*
Shapiro, Carol Sadie 1939- *WhoAmW 91*
Shapiro, Charlotte Heller *WhoAmW 91*
Shapiro, Cynthia Rose 1946- *WhoAmW 91*
Shapiro, Daniel 1922- *BiDrAPA 89*
Shapiro, Daniel 1926- *BiDrAPA 89*
Shapiro, David 1916- *WhoAm 90, WhoAmA 91*
Shapiro, David 1944- *WhoAmA 91*
Shapiro, David 1947- *BioIn 16, WhoAmA 91*
Shapiro, David 1951- *St&PR 91*
Shapiro, David A 1939- *BiDrAPA 89*
Shapiro, David Israel 1928- *WhoAm 90*
Shapiro, David Lloyd 1957- *WhoE 91*
Shapiro, David Louis 1932- *WhoAm 90*
Shapiro, Debbie 1954- *ConTFT 8*
Shapiro, Debbie Lynn *WhoAm 90, WhoAmW 91*
Shapiro, Dee 1936- *WhoAmA 91, WhoE 91*
Shapiro, Donald L 1931- *BiDrAPA 89*
Shapiro, Doris *BioIn 16*
Shapiro, E. Donald 1931- *WhoAm 90*
Shapiro, Edith T 1935- *BiDrAPA 89*
Shapiro, Edward Muray 1924- *WhoSSW 91, WhoWor 91*
Shapiro, Edward Robert 1941- *BiDrAPA 89, WhoAm 90*
Shapiro, Eli 1916- *WhoAm 90, WhoE 91*
Shapiro, Ellen Louise 1950- *WhoAmW 91*
Shapiro, Ellen Marie 1948- *WhoAmW 91*
Shapiro, Esther 1934- *ConTFT 8*
Shapiro, Feliks *BiDrAPA 89*
Shapiro, Felix Lehman 1932- *BiDrAPA 89*
Shapiro, Fred David 1926- *WhoAm 90*
Shapiro, Fred Louis 1934- *WhoAm 90*
Shapiro, Gail Greenberg 1947- *WhoAm 90*
Shapiro, Gary Joel 1956- *WhoEmL 91*
Shapiro, Gary Michael 1941- *WhoAm 90*
Shapiro, George Howard 1936- *WhoAm 90*
Shapiro, George M. 1919- *WhoAm 90, WhoE 91, WhoWor 91*
Shapiro, Hadassah Ruth 1924- *WhoE 91*
Shapiro, Harold Benjamin 1937- *St&PR 91, WhoAm 90*
Shapiro, Harold D. 1930- *St&PR 91*
Shapiro, Harold David 1927- *WhoAm 90*
Shapiro, Harold M. 1927- *St&PR 91*
Shapiro, Harold T 1935- *ConAu 132*
Shapiro, Harold Tafler 1935- *WhoAm 90, WhoE 91, WhoWor 91*
Shapiro, Harry Dean 1940- *WhoE 91*
Shapiro, Harry L 1902-1990 *CurBio 90N*
Shapiro, Harry Lionel 1902-1990 *BioIn 16, NewYTBS 90*
Shapiro, Harvey 1924- *WhoAm 90, WorAu 1980 [port]*
Shapiro, Harvey Allan 1941- *WhoWor 91*
Shapiro, Harvey Dean 1944- *WhoE 91*
Shapiro, Harvey Harris 1943- *BiDrAPA 89*
Shapiro, Howard Allan 1930- *WhoAm 90*
Shapiro, Howard Irwin 1932- *WhoE 91*
Shapiro, Howard Irwin 1962- *BiDrAPA 89*
Shapiro, Howard S *BiDrAPA 89*
Shapiro, Ira Mark 1956- *BiDrAPA 89*
Shapiro, Irvin *BioIn 16*
Shapiro, Irving 1927- *WhoAmA 91*
Shapiro, Irving Saul 1916- *ConAmBL, WhoAm 90*
Shapiro, Irwin 1911- *AuBYP 90*
Shapiro, Irwin Allen 1936- *WhoE 91*
Shapiro, Irwin Ira 1929- *WhoAm 90*
Shapiro, Isadore 1916- *WhoWor 91*
Shapiro, Israel David 1905- *WhoSSW 91*
Shapiro, Ivan 1928- *WhoAm 90*
Shapiro, Jacob 1897-1947 *WorAlBi*
Shapiro, Jan A. 1949- *WhoAmW 91*
Shapiro, Jed Sickles 1946- *BiDrAPA 89*
Shapiro, Jeffrey Stephen 1949- *BiDrAPA 89*
Shapiro, Jerome E 1927- *BiDrAPA 89*
Shapiro, Jerome Gerson 1924- *WhoAm 90*
Shapiro, Jerome Herbert 1924- *WhoAm 90*
Shapiro, Jerome Leonard 1925- *St&PR 91*
Shapiro, Joan Isabelle 1943- *WhoAmW 91, WhoWor 91*
Shapiro, Joan Rachel 1950- *BiDrAPA 89*
Shapiro, Joel 1934- *IntWWM 90*
Shapiro, Joel 1941- *WhoAmA 91*
Shapiro, Joel Elias 1941- *WhoAm 90*
Shapiro, Judith R. 1942- *WhoAmW 91*
Shapiro, Julian L. 1904- *BioIn 16*
Shapiro, Julian Lawrence *WorAu 1980*
Shapiro, Karl 1913- *MajTwCW, WorAlBi*
Shapiro, Karl Jay 1913- *BioIn 16, WhoAm 90*
Shapiro, Larry Michael 1948- *WhoSSW 91*
Shapiro, Laurence David 1941- *WhoAm 90*
Shapiro, Lee Tobey 1943- *WhoAm 90*
Shapiro, Leo Martin *BiDrAPA 89*
Shapiro, Leon N 1926- *BiDrAPA 89*
Shapiro, Leonard 1928- *St&PR 91*
Shapiro, Lester 1912- *St&PR 91*
Shapiro, Lester E 1914- *BiDrAPA 89*
Shapiro, Louis B 1906- *BiDrAPA 89*
Shapiro, Lucille 1940- *WhoAm 90*
Shapiro, Marc J. 1947- *St&PR 91, WhoAm 90*
Shapiro, Marian Kaplun 1939- *WhoAmW 91*
Shapiro, Marillyn Irene 1925- *WhoAmW 91*
Shapiro, Mark 1946- *WhoSSW 91*
Shapiro, Mark Howard 1940- *WhoAm 90*
Shapiro, Mark L. 1944- *St&PR 91*
Shapiro, Mark Lawrence 1944- *WhoAm 90*
Shapiro, Martin 1933- *WhoAm 90*
Shapiro, Marvin I 1920- *BiDrAPA 89*
Shapiro, Marvin Lincoln 1923- *WhoAm 90*
Shapiro, Marvin Seymour 1936- *WhoAm 90*
Shapiro, Maurice 1873-1911 *BioIn 16*
Shapiro, Maurice Mandel 1915- *WhoAm 90*
Shapiro, Mel *BioIn 16*
Shapiro, Michael 1942- *WhoAm 90*
Shapiro, Michael Edward 1949- *WhoAmA 91*
Shapiro, Michael I. *BioIn 16*
Shapiro, Michael Jeffrey 1951- *IntWWM 90*
Shapiro, Michael Saul *BiDrAPA 89*
Shapiro, Milton J. 1926- *AuBYP 90*
Shapiro, Milton Stanley 1922- *WhoAm 90, WhoWor 91*
Shapiro, Mortimer F 1915- *BiDrAPA 89*
Shapiro, Moses *NewYTBS 90 [port], St&PR 91N*
Shapiro, Moses 1910-1990 *BioIn 16*
Shapiro, Myra Stein 1932- *WhoAmW 91*
Shapiro, Naomi K. 1941- *WhoWrEP 89*
Shapiro, Neil Robert 1962- *WhoE 91*
Shapiro, Norma Sondra Levy 1928- *WhoAm 90, WhoAmW 91*
Shapiro, Norman Richard 1930- *WhoAm 90*
Shapiro, Paul David 1940- *St&PR 91*
Shapiro, Perry 1941- *WhoAm 90*
Shapiro, Peter A. 1956- *BiDrAPA 89*
Shapiro, Philip 1943- *BiDrAPA 89*
Shapiro, Philip Alan 1940- *WhoWor 91*
Shapiro, Phyllis *ODwPR 91*
Shapiro, Phyllis 1922- *WhoAm 90*
Shapiro, Raymond L. 1934- *WhoAm 90*
Shapiro, Raymond Marc *BiDrAPA 89*
Shapiro, Rebecca *AuBYP 90*
Shapiro, Richard 1934- *ConTFT 8*
Shapiro, Richard Alan *BiDrAPA 89*
Shapiro, Richard F. 1937- *St&PR 91*

Shapiro, Richard Gerald 1924- *WhoAm 90*
Shapiro, Richard Stanley 1925- *WhoAm 90*
Shapiro, Robert 1932- *WhoAm 90*
Shapiro, Robert Alan 1946- *WhoAm 90, WhoEmL 91*
Shapiro, Robert B 1936- *BiDrAPA 89*
Shapiro, Robert B. 1938- *St&PR 91*
Shapiro, Robert C 1924- *BiDrAPA 89*
Shapiro, Robert D. 1928- *St&PR 91*
Shapiro, Robert Elliott 1953- *WhoE 91*
Shapiro, Robert Frank 1934- *WhoAm 90*
Shapiro, Robert Lee 1910- *St&PR 91*
Shapiro, Robert M. 1945- *WhoEmL 91*
Shapiro, Robert S 1927- *BiDrAPA 89*
Shapiro, Robert Scott 1950- *BiDrAPA 89*
Shapiro, Robyn Sue 1952- *WhoEmL 91*
Shapiro, Roger L *BiDrAPA 89*
Shapiro, Ronald 1946- *St&PR 91*
Shapiro, Ronald M. 1948- *St&PR 91*
Shapiro, Ronald Maurice 1943- *WhoAm 90*
Shapiro, Ruth 1926- *WhoE 91*
Shapiro, Sam *BioIn 16*
Shapiro, Sam 1914- *WhoAm 90*
Shapiro, Sam Oliver 1902- *St&PR 91*
Shapiro, Samuel 1927- *WhoE 91*
Shapiro, Samuel Bernard 1909- *WhoAm 90*
Shapiro, Sandra 1944- *WhoAmW 91*
Shapiro, Sanford 1933- *BiDrAPA 89*
Shapiro, Sidney 1931- *WhoAm 90*
Shapiro, Sidney Robert 1919- *St&PR 91*
Shapiro, Solomon Marc *BiDrAPA 89*
Shapiro, Stanley *NewYTBS 90*
Shapiro, Stanley 1925-1990 *ConAu 132*
Shapiro, Stanley 1937- *BiDrAPA 89, St&PR 91, WhoAm 90*
Shapiro, Stanley W *BiDrAPA 89*
Shapiro, Stephen M 1941- *BiDrAPA 89*
Shapiro, Steven Ira 1945- *BiDrAPA 89*
Shapiro, Stuart Charles 1944- *WhoAm 90*
Shapiro, Sumner 1923- *St&PR 91*
Shapiro, Sumner 1926- *WhoAm 90*
Shapiro, Sumner L 1926- *BiDrAPA 89*
Shapiro, Theodore 1932- *BiDrAPA 89, WhoAm 90*
Shapiro, Vadim 1959- *WhoE 91*
Shapiro, Victor Lenard 1924- *WhoAm 90, WhoWor 91*
Shapiro, Walter Elliot 1947- *WhoEmL 91*
Shapleigh, Donald Snowden 1948- *St&PR 91*
Shaplen, Robert 1917-1988 *BioIn 16*
Shaplen, Robert Modell 1917- *WhoWrEP 89*
Shapley, Deborah 1945- *WhoE 91*
Shapley, John 1890-1969 *WhoAmA 91N*
Shapley, Lloyd Stowell 1923- *WhoAm 90*
Shapo, Marshall Schambelan 1936- *WhoAm 90*
Shapoff, Stephen H. 1944- *St&PR 91*
Shapolsky, Sam *BioIn 16*
Shapp, Charles M. 1906-1989 *BioIn 16, SmATA 61*
Shapp, Martha Glauber 1910- *WhoAm 90*
Shappel, Cynthia M *BiDrAPA 89*
Shappirio, David Gordon 1930- *WhoAm 90*
Shapshak, Rene *WhoAmA 91N*
Shapson, Edward M. 1948- *ODwPR 91*
Shapson, Edward Michael 1948- *WhoE 91*
Shapson, Milton *BiDrAPA 89*
Shapu, Stephen Nate 1947- *WhoAm 90*
Shar, Albert Oscar 1944- *WhoE 91*
Shara, Farouk al- 1938- *WhoWor 91*
Sharaff, Irene 1910?- *BioIn 16, ConDes 90, NotWoAT*
Sharaga, Leontine *BioIn 16*
Sharan, Rahoul 1961- *St&PR 91*
Sharansky, Natan *BioIn 16*
Sharansky, Natan 1948- *WhoAm 90*
Sharat Chandra, G.S. 1938- *WhoWrEP 89*
Sharbaugh, Amandus Harry 1919- *WhoAm 90*
Sharbaugh, H. Robert 1928- *St&PR 91*
Sharbaugh, Joseph Edward 1947- *St&PR 91*
Sharbaugh, Kathryn Kennedy 1948- *WhoAmW 91*
Sharbel, Jean M. *WhoAmW 91*
Sharber, Ann Boutwell 1948- *St&PR 91*
Sharbo, David Arthur 1940- *BiDrAPA 89*
Shardad *NewAgMG*
Share, Donald Seth 1957- *WhoWrEP 89*
Share, Isaiah A *BiDrAPA 89*
Share, Kenneth 1940- *St&PR 91*
Shareef, Mohammed 1949- *BiDrAPA 89*
Shareff, Karen Rae 1945- *WhoAmW 91*
Sharer, David Roland 1935- *BiDrAPA 89*
Sharer, Elmer Eugene 1933- *St&PR 91*
Sharer, Kevin W. 1948- *WhoAm 90*
Sharett, Alan Richard 1943- *WhoSSW 91, WhoWor 91*
Sharf, Donald Jack 1927- *WhoAm 90*
Sharf, Stephan 1920- *WhoAm 90*
Sharff, Karl Edward 1934- *St&PR 91*
Sharfman, Amalie *AuBYP 90*
Sharfman, Caroline Sharp 1942- *WhoAmW 91*
Sharfman, Herbert 1909- *WhoSSW 91, WhoWor 91*
Sharfman, Mark Phillip 1951- *WhoE 91*
Sharfman, William L. 1942- *ODwPR 91*
Sharfstein, Steven Samuel 1942- *BiDrAPA 89, WhoAm 90, WhoE 91*
Shari, Ruth *ODwPR 91*
Shariat-Panahi, Jaleh 1945- *WhoEmL 91*
Sharick, Merle Dayton, Jr. 1946- *WhoSSW 91*
Sharif, Omar 1932- *BioIn 16, WhoAm 90, WhoWor 91, WorAlBi*
Sharif, Y.N. *St&PR 91*
Sharif-Emami, Jafar 1910- *WhoAm 90, WhoWor 91*
Sharifian, Mehdi *BiDrAPA 89*
Sharify, Nasser 1923- *BioIn 16*
Sharify, Nasser 1925- *WhoAm 90, WhoE 91, WhoWor 91*
Sharin, Samuel 1924- *St&PR 91*
Sharitarish 1790?-1822 *WhNaAH*
Sharits, Paul Jeffrey 1943- *WhoAmA 91*
Shark, Alan Roy 1947- *WhoE 91*
Sharkany, Edward J. 1931- *St&PR 91*
Sharkey, Charles W. 1932- *St&PR 91*
Sharkey, Dennis Michael 1944- *St&PR 91*
Sharkey, John F. 1943- *St&PR 91*
Sharkey, Kenneth George 1938- *St&PR 91*
Sharkey, Ray *BioIn 16*
Sharkey, Robert M. 1941- *ODwPR 91*
Sharlach, Jeffrey R. 1953- *ODwPR 91*
Sharma, Ajay Kumar 1955- *WhoWor 91*
Sharma, Arun *BiDrAPA 89*
Sharma, Balbir Chand *BiDrAPA 89*
Sharma, Bhu Dev 1938- *WhoSSW 91*
Sharma, Ganga Ram 1942- *BiDrAPA 89*
Sharma, Geeta 1951- *BiDrAPA 89*
Sharma, Haseen Banu *BiDrAPA 89*
Sharma, Hem 1943- *BiDrAPA 89*
Sharma, Jagdish Saran 1924- *WhoWor 91*
Sharma, Jyotsana *BiDrAPA 89*
Sharma, Kaushal K. 1949- *BiDrAPA 89*
Sharma, Kul Bhushan 1943- *BiDrAPA 89*
Sharma, Manorama 1945- *WhoEmL 91*
Sharma, Mridulaben N 1943- *BiDrAPA 89*
Sharma, Niranjan M 1944- *BiDrAPA 89*
Sharma, Parashu Ram 1946- *WhoSSW 91*
Sharma, Pradeep 1956- *BiDrAPA 89*
Sharma, Prem Vallabh 1932- *WhoWor 91*
Sharma, Purna Nand *BiDrAPA 89*
Sharma, Rajiv Pandit 1955- *BiDrAPA 89*
Sharma, Ramesh 1953- *WhoE 91*
Sharma, Santosh Devraj 1934- *WhoAmW 91*
Sharma, Sarita *BiDrAPA 89*
Sharma, Shankar Dayal 1918- *WhoWor 91*
Sharma, Shiv 1933- *WhoWor 91*
Sharma, Shiv K. 1941- *St&PR 91, WhoAm 90*
Sharma, Shridhar 1935- *BiDrAPA 89*
Sharma, Som Deo 1937- *WhoWor 91*
Sharma, Sushil 1956- *WhoE 91, WhoWor 91*
Sharma, Timothy L 1940- *BiDrAPA 89*
Sharma, Vanshdeep 1957- *BiDrAPA 89*
Sharma, Venkata K 1947- *BiDrAPA 89*
Sharma, Verinder 1957- *BiDrAPA 89*
Sharma, Vidya D 1931- *BiDrAPA 89*
Sharma, Vinod 1942- *BiDrAPA 89*
Sharman, Bill 1926- *Ballpl 90*
Sharman, Dick 1934- *St&PR 91*
Sharman, Lewis C 1922- *BiDrAPA 89*
Sharman, Richard Lee 1932- *WhoSSW 91*
Sharman, William 1926- *WhoAm 90*
Sharmat, Marjorie Weinman 1928- *AuBYP 90*
Sharmat, Mitchell 1927- *BioIn 16*
Sharmel, Theolyn Pekrul *WhoWrEP 89*
Sharoff, Richard J. 1946- *WhoAm 90, WhoSSW 91*
Sharoff, Richard Joseph 1946- *St&PR 91*
Sharoff, Robert L *BiDrAPA 89*
Sharoff, Victor *AuBYP 90*
Sharon, Ariel *BioIn 16, NewYTBS 90 [port]*
Sharon, Ariel 1928- *WhoWor 91*
Sharon, C. William 1952- *WhoSSW 91*
Sharon, Dennis Paul 1935- *St&PR 91, WhoSSW 91*
Sharon, Jeffrey D. 1949- *St&PR 91*
Sharon, Lorraine *BiDrAPA 89*
Sharon, Mary B 1891-1961 *WhoAmA 91N*
Sharon, Rose *MajTwCW*
Sharon, Russell 1948- *WhoAmA 91*
Sharon, Steven 1960- *WhoE 91*
Sharoubim, Kamel Fahim 1934- *WhoE 91*
Sharouni, Yusuf *ConAu 131*
Sharp, Aaron John 1904- *WhoAm 90*
Sharp, Adda Mai *AuBYP 90*
Sharp, Alfred Jay 1929- *WhoE 91*
Sharp, Allen 1932- *WhoAm 90*
Sharp, Anne 1943- *WhoAmA 91*
Sharp, Anne Catherine 1943- *WhoAm 90, WhoAmW 91*
Sharp, Arthur Glynn 1941- *WhoWrEP 89*
Sharp, Bert Lavon 1926- *WhoAm 90*
Sharp, Bill 1950- *Ballpl 90*
Sharp, Cecil 1859-1924 *OxCPMus*
Sharp, Charles Frederick 1914- *St&PR 91, WhoAm 90*
Sharp, Clay LaValle 1940- *WhoE 91*
Sharp, Daniel Asher 1932- *WhoAm 90, WhoE 91*
Sharp, David Lee 1952- *WhoEmL 91*
Sharp, Donald Young 1937- *St&PR 91*
Sharp, Dorothea 1874-1955 *BiDWomA*
Sharp, Edgar E. 1933- *WhoE 91*
Sharp, Evelyn 1869-1955 *FemiCLE*
Sharp, Evelyn Adelaide 1903-1985 *DcNaB 1981*
Sharp, Gail M. *St&PR 91*
Sharp, George 1917- *St&PR 91*
Sharp, George Kendall 1934- *WhoAm 90*
Sharp, Gerald Bruce 1951- *WhoSSW 91*
Sharp, Gun Algerius 1943- *ODwPR 91*
Sharp, H. Ray 1935- *WhoSSW 91*
Sharp, Helen *ConAu 31NR*
Sharp, Helen Taylor 1937- *WhoSSW 91*
Sharp, Herbert Cecil 1923- *St&PR 91*
Sharp, Isabella 1771-1843 *FemiCLE*
Sharp, Isadore *BioIn 16*
Sharp, Jacob Hunter 1833-1907 *AmLegL*
Sharp, James 1613-1679 *BioIn 16*
Sharp, James 1843-1904 *AmLegL*
Sharp, James Franklin 1938- *WhoAm 90, WhoE 91, WhoWor 91*
Sharp, James R. 1945- *St&PR 91*
Sharp, Jane *BiDEWW, FemiCLE*
Sharp, Jane Ellyn 1934- *WhoAmW 91*
Sharp, Jennifer Mary 1934- *IntWWM 90*
Sharp, Jerrilyn Sue 1957- *WhoAmW 91*
Sharp, Jerry Lee 1934- *St&PR 91*
Sharp, Joane *BiDEWW*
Sharp, John Frederick 1954- *WhoSSW 91*
Sharp, John M., Jr. 1944- *WhoAm 90*
Sharp, Joseph Henry 1859-1953 *WhNaAH*
Sharp, Karl Olin 1936- *St&PR 91*
Sharp, Katharine L. 1865-1914 *BioAmW*
Sharp, Lemuel, III 1951- *St&PR 91*
Sharp, Lewis Inman 1941- *WhoAmA 91*
Sharp, Linda Elizabeth 1948- *WhoAmW 91*
Sharp, Lyle Duane 1931- *St&PR 91*
Sharp, Margery *WhoWor 91*
Sharp, Margery 1905- *AuBYP 90, BioIn 16*
Sharp, Mary Lucille 1938- *WhoAmW 91*
Sharp, Michael C. 1948- *St&PR 91*
Sharp, Michiko Maezawa 1957- *WhoAmW 91*
Sharp, Mitchell William 1911- *WhoAm 90*
Sharp, Pamela A. 1955- *WhoSSW 91*
Sharp, Paul Frederick 1918- *WhoAm 90, WhoSSW 91*
Sharp, Peggy Agostino 1950- *WhoEmL 91*
Sharp, Philip R. 1942- *WhoAm 90*
Sharp, Phillip Allen 1944- *WhoAm 90*
Sharp, Richard L. *BioIn 16*
Sharp, Richard L. 1947- *St&PR 91, WhoAm 90, WhoSSW 91*
Sharp, Robert A. 1932- *St&PR 91*
Sharp, Robert Andrew 1946- *WhoSSW 91*
Sharp, Robert Charles 1936- *St&PR 91*
Sharp, Robert G. 1935- *St&PR 91*
Sharp, Robert Phillip 1911- *WhoAm 90*
Sharp, Robert R. 1945- *St&PR 91*
Sharp, Robert Weimer 1917- *WhoAm 90*
Sharp, Ronald Alan 1945- *WhoAm 90*
Sharp, Ronald William 1929- *IntWWM 90*
Sharp, Russell Alan 1957- *WhoSSW 91*
Sharp, Ruth Ann 1935- *WhoSSW 91*
Sharp, Saundra 1942- *DrBIPA 90*
Sharp, Scott *BioIn 16*
Sharp, Sharon Annette Andrews 1952- *WhoWrEP 89*
Sharp, Stephen Alan 1947- *WhoAm 90*
Sharp, Susan S 1942- *WhoAmA 91*
Sharp, Vernon H 1932- *BiDrAPA 89*
Sharp, W Leland 1906- *BiDrAPA 89*
Sharp, Walter M. 1916- *St&PR 91*
Sharp, Warren Donald 1939- *St&PR 91*
Sharp, William 1855-1905 *BioIn 16, TwCLC 39 [port]*
Sharp, William 1856-1905 *EncO&P 3*
Sharp, William 1900-1961 *WhoAmA 91N*
Sharp, William 1929- *WhoAm 90*
Sharp, William F. 1942- *St&PR 91*
Sharp, William Graves 1859-1922 *BioIn 16*
Sharp, William R. 1936- *St&PR 91*
Sharp, William Wheeler 1923- *WhoSSW 91, WhoWor 91*
Sharp, Willoughby 1936- *WhoAmA 91*
Sharpe, Anne Johnson 1932- *WhoE 91*
Sharpe, Avery *BioIn 16*
Sharpe, Blair 1954- *WhoAmA 91*
Sharpe, Calvin William 1945- *WhoEmL 91*
Sharpe, Charles Richard 1925- *WhoAm 90*
Sharpe, Christopher Grant 1949- *WhoEmL 91*
Sharpe, Clarence *BioIn 16, NewYTBS 90*
Sharpe, Clyde E. 1928- *St&PR 91*
Sharpe, Debra Fetterman 1954- *WhoSSW 91*
Sharpe, Donald Edward 1937- *WhoAm 90*
Sharpe, Edward Cary 1938- *WhoSSW 91*
Sharpe, Gary S. 1953- *ODwPR 91*
Sharpe, George Henry 1828-1900 *AmLegL*
Sharpe, George W. *BioIn 16*
Sharpe, Henry Dexter, Jr. 1923- *St&PR 91, WhoAm 90*
Sharpe, James M. 1950- *St&PR 91*
Sharpe, John Henry 1921- *WhoWor 91*
Sharpe, John I. 1934- *St&PR 91*
Sharpe, John T. 1936- *St&PR 91*
Sharpe, Kathleen Conklin 1955- *WhoAmW 91*
Sharpe, Kathryn Moye 1922- *WhoAmW 91*
Sharpe, Kathy *St&PR 91*
Sharpe, Katrinka *BioIn 16*
Sharpe, Keith Yount 1930- *WhoAm 90*
Sharpe, Larry *BioIn 16*
Sharpe, Leslie Allen 1947- *WhoEmL 91*
Sharpe, Logan Garnett 1952- *St&PR 91*
Sharpe, Louis Kerre 1944- *St&PR 91*
Sharpe, Martha Hayes 1942- *WhoAmW 91*
Sharpe, Michael Douglas 1954- *St&PR 91*
Sharpe, Myron Emanuel 1928- *WhoAm 90, WhoWrEP 89*
Sharpe, Paul Stuart 1946- *St&PR 91*
Sharpe, Richard Samuel 1930- *WhoAm 90*
Sharpe, Robert C. 1954- *BiDrAPA 89*
Sharpe, Robert F., Jr. 1953- *WhoWor 91*
Sharpe, Robert Francis 1921- *St&PR 91, WhoAm 90*
Sharpe, Roland Leonard 1923- *WhoAm 90*
Sharpe, Ronald Morgan 1940- *WhoE 91*
Sharpe, Samuel *BioIn 16*
Sharpe, Sara Buzze 1955- *St&PR 91*
Sharpe, Shelton E, III *BiDrAPA 89*
Sharpe, Tom 1928- *WorAu 1980 [port]*
Sharpe, William Forsyth 1934- *WhoAm 90*
Sharpe, William Norman, Jr. 1938- *WhoAm 90*
Sharpf, Larry K. 1938- *St&PR 91*
Sharples, Virginia Mitchell 1942- *WhoAmW 91*
Sharples, Winston Singleton 1932- *WhoSSW 91*
Sharpless, Eric Cope 1933- *St&PR 91*
Sharpless, K. Barry 1941- *WhoAm 90*
Sharpless, Nansie Sue 1932- *BioIn 16*
Sharpless, Richard Kennedy 1911- *WhoAm 90*
Sharpley, Patricia Haig 1932- *BiDrAPA 89*
Sharps, Donald Lee 1954- *BiDrAPA 89*
Sharpstein, Richard Alan 1950- *WhoSSW 91*
Sharpton, Al *BioIn 16*
Sharpton, Al 1954- *News 91-2 [port]*
Sharpton, Thomas 1949- *WhoEmL 91, WhoWor 91*
Sharrar, Victoria Anne 1958- *WhoAmW 91*
Sharrock, David B. 1936- *St&PR 91*
Sharrock, David F.P. 1931- *St&PR 91*
Sharrow, Marilyn Jane *WhoAmW 91*
Sharrow, Sheba 1926- *WhoAmA 91*
Sharsig, Bill 1855-1902 *Ballpl 90*
Shartle, Mark W. 1948- *St&PR 91*
Sharum, Bernard Joseph 1944- *WhoE 91*
Sharvitt, Uri 1939- *IntWWM 90*
Sharwell, William G. 1920- *St&PR 91*
Sharwell, William Gay 1920- *WhoAm 90, WhoE 91*
Shasberger, Michael David 1952- *IntWWM 90*
Shasha, Alfred A. *St&PR 91*
Shasha, Dennis Elliott 1955- *WhoE 91*
Shashaty, Yolanda Victoria 1950- *WhoAmA 91*
Shashidharan, Veena 1950- *BiDrAPA 89*
Shaskan, Donald 1910- *BiDrAPA 89*
Shaskan, George F., Jr. 1917- *St&PR 91*
Shasteen, Donald Eugene 1928- *WhoAm 90*
Shastid, Jon Barton 1914- *WhoAm 90*
Shastri, Lal Bahadur 1904-1966 *BioIn 16*
Shatalin, Stanislav S. *NewYTBS 90 [port]*
Shatalov, Viktor Fedorovich *BioIn 16*
Shatalow, Vladimir Mihailovich 1917- *WhoAmA 91*
Shatan, Chaim F 1924- *BiDrAPA 89*
Shatan, Chaim Felix 1924- *WhoAm 90*
Shatin, Harry 1910- *WhoAm 90*
Shatkin, Aaron Jeffrey 1934- *WhoAm 90*
Shatkin, Eugene Parker 1924- *BiDrAPA 89*
Shatner, William 1931- *BioIn 16, OxCCanT, WhoAm 90, WorAlBi*
Shatrov, Mikhail *BioIn 16*
Shatsillo, Kornely Fyodorovich 1924- *WhoWor 91*
Shattan, Samuel P 1929- *BiDrAPA 89*
Shatter, Susan Louise 1943- *WhoAmA 91*
Shattil, Siegfried 1914- *St&PR 91*
Shatto, Gloria McDermith 1931- *WhoAm 90, WhoAmW 91, WhoSSW 91*
Shatto, Mayme W. 1936- *WhoAmW 91*

Shatto, Michael Eugene 1941- WhoSSW 91
Shatton, Alexander 1924- WhoE 91
Shattuck, Barbara Zaccheo 1950- WhoAmW 91
Shattuck, Carol ODwPR 91
Shattuck, Cathie Ann 1945- WhoAm 90, WhoAmW 91
Shattuck, Charles Harlen 1910- WhoAm 90
Shattuck, Howard Francis, Jr. 1920- WhoE 91
Shattuck, Paul C. 1944- St&PR 91
Shattuck, Petra Tolle BioIn 16
Shattuck, Roger 1923- SmATA 64 [port]
Shattuck, Roger Whitney 1923- WhoAm 90, WhoWrEP 89
Shattuck, William L. 1909- St&PR 91
Shattuck, William Pitt 1922- WhoSSW 91
Shatz, Stephen Sidney 1937- WhoAm 90
Shatzkin, Leonard 1919- WhoAm 90
Shaub, Harold Arthur 1915- WhoAm 90, WhoE 91
Shauck, Edwin W. 1926- St&PR 91
Shaud, Grant BioIn 16
Shaud, John Albert 1933- WhoAm 90
Shaughnessy, April Marie 1957- WhoAmW 91
Shaughnessy, Charles Stephen, Jr. 1929- St&PR 91, WhoAm 90
Shaughnessy, Edward L 1932- ConAu 130
Shaughnessy, George Albert 1926- WhoE 91
Shaughnessy, James Francis 1923- St&PR 91
Shaughnessy, James J BiDrAPA 89
Shaughnessy, James Michael 1945- WhoAm 90, WhoE 91
Shaughnessy, Marie Kaneko 1924- WhoAmW 91
Shaughnessy, Mary Rose 1931- WhoAmW 91
Shaughnessy, Michael Francis 1951- WhoEmL 91
Shaughnessy, Michael Kevin 1949- St&PR 91, WhoAm 90
Shaughnessy, Molly Clements 1949- St&PR 91
Shaughnessy, Patrick Sherman 1945- St&PR 91
Shaughnessy, Phyllis B. 1934- WhoWrEP 89
Shaughnessy, Robert Michael 1940- St&PR 91
Shaughnessy, Shag 1883-1969 Ballpl 90
Shaughnessy, Stanley H. 1938- WhoAm 90
Shaughnessy, Thomas William 1938- WhoAm 90
Shaul, Janice Lee 1944- St&PR 91
Shaul, Robert 1925- St&PR 91
Shaul, Roger Louis, Jr. 1948- WhoSSW 91
Shaul, Sheldon 1957- BiDrAPA 89
Shaull, Richard 1919- WhoAm 90
Shauman, R. William 1939- St&PR 91
Shaunnessey, Robert Lawrence 1947- St&PR 91
Shaunnessy, George Daniel 1948- WhoAm 90, WhoEmL 91
Shaurette, Glen N BiDrAPA 89
Shaute, Joe 1899-1970 Ballpl 90
Shave, David W BiDrAPA 89
Shavelson, Kenneth M. 1949- St&PR 91
Shavelson, Melville 1917- WhoAm 90
Shaver, Carl H. 1913- St&PR 91
Shaver, Carl Hutchens 1913- WhoAm 90
Shaver, Dennis George 1949- St&PR 91
Shaver, Dorothy 1897-1959 ConAmBL
Shaver, Edwards Boone 1948- WhoEmL 91, WhoSSW 91, WhoWor 91
Shaver, Harold C. 1938- WhoSSW 91
Shaver, James Porter 1933- WhoAm 90
Shaver, James Robert 1867-1949 WhoAmA 91N
Shaver, Jesse M. 1919- St&PR 91
Shaver, Jesse Milton 1919- WhoAm 90
Shaver, Phillip 1944- ConAu 130
Shaver, Richard S. 1907-1975 EncO&P 3
Shaver, Richard William 1940- St&PR 91
Shaver, Robert Harold 1922- WhoAm 90
Shaver, Scott Owen 1956- St&PR 91
Shaver, Sharon Rusch 1952- WhoSSW 91
Shaver, Tami Lee 1958- WhoAmW 91
Shaver, William 1927- St&PR 91
Shavers, Lisa 1963- WhoAmW 91
Shaw, Al 1881-1974 Ballpl 90
Shaw, Alan 1930- St&PR 91, WhoAm 90
Shaw, Alan Eric 1948- WhoEmL 91
Shaw, Alan J. 1949- St&PR 91
Shaw, Alan Roger 1938- WhoAm 90
Shaw, Albert 1857-1947 BioIn 16
Shaw, Alison 1957- ConAu 130
Shaw, Allen D. 1947- St&PR 91
Shaw, Amos F. 1839-1898 AmLegL
Shaw, Andrew, Jr. 1931- WhoAm 90
Shaw, Ann BiDEWW
Shaw, Anna Howard 1847-1919 FemiCLE
Shaw, Arnold BioIn 16
Shaw, Arnold 1909- AuBYP 90, IntWWM 90, WhoWrEP 89
Shaw, Arnold 1909-1989 ConAu 129, SmATA 63
Shaw, Artie 1910- BioIn 16, OxCPMus, WhoAm 90, WorAlBi
Shaw, Barbara Ann 1943- St&PR 91
Shaw, Barry N. 1940- WhoE 91
Shaw, Benjamin BioIn 16
Shaw, Bernard BioIn 16, MajTwCW
Shaw, Bernard 1856-1950 BioIn 16
Shaw, Bernard 1940- WhoAm 90
Shaw, Bernard Heughes 1941- St&PR 91
Shaw, Bob 1933- Ballpl 90
Shaw, Brad W. 1948- WhoWor 91
Shaw, Brewster Hopkinson, Jr. 1945- WhoAm 90
Shaw, Bruce Jennings 1952- WhoSSW 91
Shaw, Bryan P. H. 1921- WhoAm 90
Shaw, Bryce Robert 1930- WhoSSW 91
Shaw, Bynum Gillette 1923- WhoSSW 91, WhoWrEP 89
Shaw, Carl Bradley 1924- WhoWor 91
Shaw, Carol Jean 1952- WhoAmW 91
Shaw, Carole 1936- WhoAm 90, WhoAmW 91
Shaw, Cathleen Malin 1958- WhoAmW 91
Shaw, Charles Green 1892-1974 WhoAmA 91N
Shaw, Charles Lemmon 1924- St&PR 91
Shaw, Charles M 1945- BiDrAPA 89
Shaw, Charlie BioIn 16
Shaw, Christopher Graham 1924- IntWWM 90
Shaw, Clara S. Weeks 1856-1940 BioIn 16
Shaw, Colin Don 1928- WhoWor 91
Shaw, Courtney Ann 1946- WhoAmA 91
Shaw, Daniel 1941- BiDrAPA 89
Shaw, David Lee 1947- WhoSSW 91
Shaw, David Lyle 1943- WhoAm 90
Shaw, David Peter 1941- St&PR 91
Shaw, David Tai-Ko 1938- WhoAm 90
Shaw, David William 1852-1910? AmLegL
Shaw, Denis Martin 1923- WhoAm 90
Shaw, Dennis Frederick 1924- WhoWor 91
Shaw, Don 1944- Ballpl 90
Shaw, Don Wayne 1937- WhoAm 90
Shaw, Donald Edward 1934- WhoAmA 91
Shaw, Donald H. 1922- St&PR 91
Shaw, Donald Hardy 1922- WhoAm 90
Shaw, Donald Ray 1945- WhoEmL 91
Shaw, Donna Marie BiDrAPA 89
Shaw, Dorene Lee 1925- WhoWrEP 89
Shaw, Doris 1921- WhoAm 90
Shaw, Douglas Ian 1954- St&PR 91
Shaw, Douglas R. 1943- St&PR 91
Shaw, Dupee 1859-1938 Ballpl 90
Shaw, E. Joseph St&PR 91
Shaw, Edgar Albert George 1921- WhoAm 90
Shaw, Eleanor Jane 1949- WhoAmW 91
Shaw, Elizabeth BioIn 16
Shaw, Ernest Carl 1942- WhoAmA 91
Shaw, Ernest G. 1929- St&PR 91
Shaw, Eugene Clay, Jr. 1939- WhoAm 90, WhoSSW 91
Shaw, Fiona BioIn 16
Shaw, Flora 1852-1929 FemiCLE
Shaw, Fran Weber 1947- WhoWrEP 89
Shaw, Francis Richard 1942- IntWWM 90
Shaw, Frank 1926- St&PR 91, WhoAm 90
Shaw, Fred L. BioIn 16
Shaw, Frederick 1912- WhoE 91
Shaw, G. Bernard MajTwCW
Shaw, George A. St&PR 91
Shaw, George Bernard 1856-1950 BioIn 16, MajTwCW, WorAlBi, WrPh
Shaw, George D. BioIn 16
Shaw, George Vincent 1928- St&PR 91
Shaw, Gerald Pawling BiDrAPA 89
Shaw, Ghita Milgrom 1929- WhoWor 91
Shaw, Grace Goodfriend WhoAm 90, WhoAmW 91, WhoE 91, WhoWor 91, WhoWrEP 89
Shaw, Harmon Lee 1923- St&PR 91
Shaw, Harold 1923- WhoAm 90
Shaw, Harold Nelson 1865?-1937 OxCCanT
Shaw, Harriet Lessy 1942- ODwPR 91
Shaw, Harry Alexander, III 1937- St&PR 91, WhoAm 90
Shaw, Helen 1913-1985 FemiCLE
Shaw, Helen Lester Anderson 1936- WhoAmW 91
Shaw, Helen Louise Haith 1931- WhoAmW 91
Shaw, Henry A. 1818-1891 AmLegL
Shaw, Henry Davis 1933- St&PR 91
Shaw, Henry Francis 1955- WhoEmL 91
Shaw, Hester BiDEWW, FemiCLE
Shaw, Ian Alexander 1940- WhoAm 90
Shaw, Irwin 1913-1984 BioIn 16, DcLB 102 [port], MajTwCW, WorAlBi
Shaw, Isabel WhoAmA 91
Shaw, Jack Allen 1939- WhoAm 90
Shaw, James BioIn 16
Shaw, James 1832-1906 AmLegL
Shaw, James 1944- WhoSSW 91
Shaw, James Clair BioIn 16
Shaw, James Everett 1948- IntWWM 90
Shaw, James H. 1929- WhoAm 90
Shaw, James Headon 1918- WhoAm 90
Shaw, James Kent 1938- BiDrAPA 89
Shaw, Jane Elizabeth 1939- St&PR 91, WhoAm 90
Shaw, Janet 1937- SmATA 61 [port], WhoWrEP 89
Shaw, Janet Beeler 1937- SmATA X [port]
Shaw, Janine Ann 1955- WhoAmW 91
Shaw, Jerome 1926- St&PR 91, WhoAm 90
Shaw, Jim 1893-1962 Ballpl 90
Shaw, Jim 1952- WhoAmA 91
Shaw, John 1745-1829 PenDiDA 89
Shaw, John Arthur 1922- WhoAm 90
Shaw, John Firth 1948- WhoAm 90
Shaw, John Guy 1950- WhoSSW 91
Shaw, John Malach 1931- WhoAm 90
Shaw, John Marion 1920- WhoSSW 91
Shaw, John Palmer 1948- WhoAmA 91, WhoE 91
Shaw, John Robert 1940- St&PR 91
Shaw, Jon Angus 1937- BiDrAPA 89
Shaw, Joseph Thomas 1919- WhoAm 90
Shaw, Joseph Winterbotham 1935- WhoAmA 91
Shaw, Judith 1944- ODwPR 91
Shaw, Julius C. 1929- WhoAm 90, WhoSSW 91
Shaw, Kailie R BiDrAPA 89
Shaw, Karen 1941- WhoAmA 91
Shaw, Karen Lee 1953- WhoSSW 91
Shaw, Keith Moffatt 1944- WhoWor 91
Shaw, Kendall 1924- WhoAm 90, WhoAmA 91
Shaw, Kenneth, Jr. 1942- St&PR 91
Shaw, Kenneth Alan 1939- WhoAm 90
Shaw, Kenneth Louis 1958- WhoSSW 91
Shaw, Kenneth Roger 1952- WhoSSW 91
Shaw, Kirk Cordell 1944- WhoSSW 91
Shaw, L. Edward, Jr. 1944- St&PR 91, WhoAm 90
Shaw, L Noah BiDrAPA 89
Shaw, Lawrence Hugh 1940- WhoE 91
Shaw, Lawrence Madison 1928- St&PR 91
Shaw, Leander Jerry, Jr. 1930- WhoAm 90
Shaw, Lee Charles 1913- WhoAm 90
Shaw, Leonard Glazer 1934- WhoAm 90
Shaw, Leroy Robert 1923- WhoWrEP 89
Shaw, Leslie Mortimer 1848-1932 BiDrUSE 89
Shaw, Li Kung 1915- WhoWrEP 89
Shaw, Linda WhoAm 90
Shaw, Linda Louise 1938- WhoWrEP 89
Shaw, Lois Williams 1942- WhoAmW 91
Shaw, Luci BioIn 16
Shaw, M. Allan 1940- St&PR 91
Shaw, Madeline Read 1902- WhoWor 91
Shaw, Manford Avis 1906- WhoAm 90
Shaw, Margery Wayne Schlamp 1923- WhoAm 90
Shaw, Marjorie Betts 1938- WhoAm 90
Shaw, Mark 1939- St&PR 91
Shaw, Marlena DrBIPA 90
Shaw, Martha L. 1961- WhoWrEP 89
Shaw, Martha Louise 1959- WhoAmW 91
Shaw, Mary 1854-1929 BioIn 16
Shaw, Mary Ann 1937- WhoAmW 91
Shaw, Mary Brown 1928- St&PR 91
Shaw, Mary Elizabeth Miller BioIn 16
Shaw, Mary G 1854-1929 NotWoAT
Shaw, Mary M. 1943- WhoE 91
Shaw, Mary Todd WhoAmA 91
Shaw, Marybeth 1963- WhoE 91
Shaw, Maurice Kenneth 1939- St&PR 91, WhoAm 90
Shaw, Melvin Phillip 1936- WhoAm 90
Shaw, Melvin Robert 1948- WhoEmL 91
Shaw, Michael 1924- WhoAm 90
Shaw, Michael 1944- WhoSSW 91, WhoWor 91
Shaw, Michael Allan 1940- WhoAm 90
Shaw, Michael Joseph 1946- WhoSSW 91
Shaw, Michael S. 1954- St&PR 91
Shaw, Milton Clayton 1915- WhoAm 90
Shaw, Milton H. 1918- St&PR 91
Shaw, Milton Herbert 1918- WhoAm 90
Shaw, Nancy WhoAmA 91
Shaw, Nancy Berry Keeling 1950- WhoSSW 91
Shaw, Ned W. 1929- St&PR 91
Shaw, Neil McGowan 1929- WhoAm 90
Shaw, Norman E. 1929- St&PR 91
Shaw, Oscar 1889-1967 OxCPMus
Shaw, Oscar M. 1904- St&PR 91
Shaw, Paul Jefferson 1954- WhoAmA 91, WhoE 91
Shaw, Paul Whit 1952- St&PR 91
Shaw, Perry 1937- BiDrAPA 89
Shaw, Philip John 1951- IntWWM 90
Shaw, Pixie Mudge Massey 1944- WhoWor 91
Shaw, R Preston BiDrAPA 89
Shaw, Ray 1934- WhoAm 90, WhoE 91
Shaw, Ray Edward 1946- WhoSSW 91
Shaw, Reesey 1943- WhoAmA 91
Shaw, Renata Vitzthum 1926- WhoAmA 91
Shaw, Richard 1941- WhoAm 90
Shaw, Richard Blake 1941- WhoAmA 91
Shaw, Richard C. ODwPR 91
Shaw, Richard Ervin 1936- St&PR 91
Shaw, Richard John Gildroy 1936- WhoWor 91
Shaw, Richard Leslie 1927- St&PR 91, WhoAm 90
Shaw, Richard Melvin 1947- WhoWor 91
Shaw, Richard Monroe, Jr. 1938- WhoSSW 91
Shaw, Richard Norman 1831-1912 BioIn 16
Shaw, Robert BiDrAPA 89, BioIn 16
Shaw, Robert 1916- PenDiMP
Shaw, Robert 1927-1978 WorAlBi
Shaw, Robert D. 1930- St&PR 91
Shaw, Robert E. 1931- WhoAm 90, WhoSSW 91
Shaw, Robert E. 1946- St&PR 91
Shaw, Robert Fletcher 1910- WhoAm 90
Shaw, Robert Gould 1837-1863 BioIn 16
Shaw, Robert Harold 1919- WhoAm 90
Shaw, Robert Lawson 1916- WhoAm 90
Shaw, Robert Michael 1925- WhoWor 91
Shaw, Robert T. WhoSSW 91
Shaw, Robert W. 1913- St&PR 91
Shaw, Robert William, Jr. 1941- WhoAm 90
Shaw, Ronald Ahrend 1946- WhoAm 90, WhoE 91
Shaw, Ronald G. 1938- St&PR 91
Shaw, Ronald Gordon 1938- WhoE 91
Shaw, Ronda R 1941- BiDrAPA 89
Shaw, Run Run 1907- ConTFT 8 [port]
Shaw, Russell Burnham 1935- WhoAm 90, WhoE 91
Shaw, Russell Clyde 1940- WhoAm 90
Shaw, Samuel E. 1943- St&PR 91
Shaw, Samuel Ervine, II 1933- St&PR 91, WhoAm 90
Shaw, Samuel Robert BioIn 16
Shaw, Sandra Cleave 1946- WhoEmL 91
Shaw, Scott 1964- WhoAm 90
Shaw, Seana H 1938- BiDrAPA 89
Shaw, Sondra A 1944- WhoWrEP 89
Shaw, Spencer 1946- WhoAm 90
Shaw, Stan 1952- DrBIPA 90
Shaw, Stanford Jay 1930- WhoWrEP 89
Shaw, Stanley Miner 1935- WhoAm 90
Shaw, Steven John 1918- WhoAm 90
Shaw, Steven R. 1950- St&PR 91
Shaw, Susan Boyce 1955- WhoEmL 91
Shaw, Susan Coulter 1943- WhoAmW 91
Shaw, Talbert O. WhoAm 90
Shaw, Thelma 1901- WhoSSW 91
Shaw, Thomas Jensen 1942- St&PR 91
Shaw, Timothy Milton 1945- ConAu 30NR
Shaw, Trevor Henry Montague 1933- St&PR 91
Shaw, Valerine R. WhoWrEP 89
Shaw, Virginia Ruth 1952- WhoAmW 91
Shaw, Wayne Ray BiDrAPA 89
Shaw, Wilfred B 1881- WhoAmA 91N
Shaw, William 1924- St&PR 91, WhoAm 90
Shaw, William Frederick 1920- WhoAm 90
Shaw, William H. 1909-1988 BioIn 16
Shaw, William H. 1927- St&PR 91
Shaw, William H 1931- BiDrAPA 89
Shaw, William James 1947- WhoEmL 91, WhoSSW 91
Shaw, William Joseph 1945- St&PR 91
Shaw, William M. 1944- St&PR 91
Shaw, Willie Matthew, III 1958- WhoSSW 91
Shaw, Woody BioIn 16
Shaw, Woody 1944-1989 AnObit 1989
Shaw-Cohen, Lori Eve 1959- WhoAm 90
Shaw-Gallant, Catharine 1944- WhoAmW 91
Shaw-Galvez, Enrique WhoWrEP 89
Shawa, Rashad al- BioIn 16
Shawanahdit, Nancy WhNaAH
Shawber, Lloyd Oberlin 1926- St&PR 91
Shawcross, William Edgerton 1934- St&PR 91
Shawe-Taylor, Desmond 1907- IntWWM 90
Shawhan, Dorothy Sample 1942- WhoAmW 91
Shawhan, Ralph 1903?-1990 ConAu 130
Shawhan, Samuel F. 1932- St&PR 91
Shawhan, Samuel Frazier, Jr. 1932- WhoAm 90, WhoE 91
Shawkey, Bob 1890-1980 Ballpl 90 [port]
Shawn, Allen E. 1948- IntWWM 90
Shawn, Dick BioIn 16
Shawn, Dick 1929-1987 WorAlBi
Shawn, Michael BioIn 16
Shawn, Michael NewYTBS 90 [port]
Shawn, Wallace 1943- WhoAm 90
Shawn, William 1907- WhoAm 90, WorAlBi
Shawnee Prophet WhNaAH

Shawstad, Raymond Vernon 1931- *WhoWor 91*
Shawver, John R *BiDrAPA 89*
Shawzin, Mark Russell 1957- *WhoE 91*
Shay, Doris Walsey *BiDrAPA 89*
Shay, Ed 1947- *WhoAmA 91*
Shay, Francis Joseph 1942- *WhoE 91*
Shay, John E., Jr. 1933- *WhoAm 90*
Shay, Judith *BiDrAPA 89*
Shay, Martin Edward 1948- *WhoAm 90*
Shay, Michele *DrBlPA 90*
Shay, Paul Richard 1954- *St&PR 91*
Shay, Philipp Wendell 1914- *WhoE 91*
Shay, Robert Michael 1936- *St&PR 91, WhoE 91, WhoWor 91*
Shay, Thomas K. 1938- *St&PR 91*
Shaya, Elias Karim *BiDrAPA 89*
Shaye, Robert Kenneth 1939- *St&PR 91, WhoAm 90*
Shayevitz, Jessie Rebecca 1960- *WhoAmW 91*
Shaykin, Leonard P. *BioIn 16*
Shaykin, Leonard P. 1943- *WhoAm 90*
Shayla *NewAgMG*
Shayman, Mark Allen 1954- *WhoE 91*
Shayman, Robert Alan 1955- *WhoSSW 91*
Shayne, Arnie 1929- *WhoAm 90*
Shayne, David 1934- *WhoAm 90*
Shayne, Herbert M. 1926- *St&PR 91*
Shayne, Jane Hirsch 1946- *WhoAmW 91*
Shays, Christopher 1945- *WhoAm 90, WhoE 91*
Shays, Daniel 1747?-1825 *WorAlBi*
Shays, E. Michael 1934- *WhoAm 90*
Shcharansky, Anatoly *BioIn 16*
Shcharansky, Natan 1948- *WorAlBi*
Shchedrin, Rodion Konstantinovich 1932- *WhoWor 91*
Shcherbakova, Galina 193-?- *EncCoWW*
Shcherbitskii, V. V. 1918-1990 *BioIn 16*
Shcherbitskii, Vladimir Vasil'evich 1918-1990 *BioIn 16*
Shcherbitsky, Vladimir V. 1918-1990 *NewYTBS 90 [port]*
Shchredrin, Rodion 1932- *PenDiMP A*
Shea, Andrew John 1934- *St&PR 91*
Shea, Anne Joan 1907- *WhoAmW 91*
Shea, Bernard Charles 1929- *WhoAm 90, WhoWor 91*
Shea, Cheryl Lilley 1953- *WhoE 91*
Shea, Christopher Lane 1959- *WhoWor 91*
Shea, Daniel Bartholomew, Jr. 1936- *WhoAm 90*
Shea, Daniel John, Jr. 1950- *WhoSSW 91*
Shea, Daniel William 1935- *St&PR 91*
Shea, David Michael 1922- *WhoAm 90, WhoE 91*
Shea, Diane Parameros 1962- *WhoE 91*
Shea, Diane Sullivan *WhoAmW 91*
Shea, Dianne Kathleen *BiDrAPA 89*
Shea, Dion Warren Joseph 1937- *WhoAm 90*
Shea, Donald Francis 1925- *WhoAm 90, WhoE 91*
Shea, Donald Richard 1926- *WhoAm 90, WhoWrEP 89*
Shea, Edward Emmett 1932- *WhoAm 90*
Shea, Edward J. *BioIn 16*
Shea, Edward J. 1951- *St&PR 91*
Shea, Estelle Margaret *St&PR 91*
Shea, Everett D., Jr. 1930- *St&PR 91*
Shea, Francis J., Jr. 1938- *WhoE 91*
Shea, Francis M. 1905-1989 *BioIn 16*
Shea, Francis X. 1941- *St&PR 91*
Shea, G. Leonard 1933- *St&PR 91*
Shea, George 1940- *BioIn 16*
Shea, George P. 1938- *St&PR 91*
Shea, Gerald James 1949- *WhoWrEP 89*
Shea, Gregory Michael 1946- *St&PR 91*
Shea, James Russell 1935- *WhoAm 90*
Shea, James William 1936- *WhoAm 90*
Shea, Jeremiah P. 1926- *St&PR 91*
Shea, Jeremiah Patrick 1926- *WhoAm 90*
Shea, John Edward 1943- *WhoE 91*
Shea, John Francis 1928- *St&PR 91*
Shea, John Martin, Jr. 1922- *WhoAm 90, WhoWor 91*
Shea, Joseph William, III 1947- *WhoEmL 91*
Shea, Judith 1948- *WhoAmA 91*
Shea, Katherine L. *BioIn 16*
Shea, Kathleen T. 1950- *St&PR 91*
Shea, Laura Karen 1960- *BiDrAPA 89*
Shea, Martin F. 1923-1989 *BioIn 16*
Shea, Merv 1900-1953 *Ballpl 90*
Shea, Michael 1938- *ConAu 130*
Shea, Michael Alan 1946- *WhoEmL 91*
Shea, Michael Edward 1953- *WhoEmL 91*
Shea, Michael Robert 1943- *WhoAm 90*
Shea, Pat *BioIn 16*
Shea, Patrick 1908- *ConAu 130*
Shea, Richard J. 1936- *St&PR 91*
Shea, Robert F. 1916-1989 *BioIn 16*
Shea, Robert James 1932- *St&PR 91*
Shea, Robert McConnell 1924- *WhoAm 90*
Shea, Shawn *BiDrAPA 89*
Shea, Spec 1920- *Ballpl 90*
Shea, Stephen Michael *BiDrAPA 89*
Shea, Stephen Michael 1926- *WhoAm 90*
Shea, Terence Joseph 1932- *St&PR 91*
Shea, Terry *ODwPR 91*
Shea, Thomas D., Jr. 1931- *St&PR 91*
Shea, Timothy T. 1944- *St&PR 91*
Shea, Victoria Anne 1953- *BiDrAPA 89*
Shea, Walter James 1929- *WhoAm 90*
Shea, William Alfred 1907- *WhoAm 90, WhoE 91*
Shea, William Anthony 1933- *St&PR 91*
Shea, William Francis 1945- *WhoSSW 91*
Shea, William P., III 1942- *BiDrAPA 89*
Shea, William Rene 1937- *WhoAm 90*
Shead, S Ray 1938- *WhoAmA 91*
Sheafer, William L. 1943- *St&PR 91*
Sheaffer, Carey Nelson 1947- *WhoE 91*
Sheaffer, Carol M 1942- *BiDrAPA 89*
Sheaffer, John Jacob, II 1944- *WhoE 91*
Sheaffer, Louis 1912- *DcLB 103 [port], WhoAm 90*
Sheaffer, M.P.A. *WhoWrEP 89*
Sheaffer, Richard Allen 1950- *WhoEmL 91*
Sheaffer, Steven Craig 1956- *WhoSSW 91*
Sheaffer, Theodore Campbell 1902- *St&PR 91*
Sheahan, Donald P. *BioIn 16*
Sheahan, James V. 1937- *ODwPR 91*
Sheahan, John Bernard 1923- *WhoAm 90*
Sheahan, Melody Ann 1959- *WhoAmW 91, WhoSSW 91*
Sheahan, Robert Emmett 1942- *WhoSSW 91*
Sheahen, Allan 1932- *WhoWrEP 89*
Sheahen, Mary Carol 1944- *WhoAmW 91*
Sheahin, John Matthew 1942- *St&PR 91*
Sheaks, Barclay *WhoAmA 91*
Shealy, Clyde Norman 1932- *NewAgE 90, WhoAm 90*
Shealy, David Lee 1944- *WhoSSW 91*
Shealy, Ramon Lee 1940- *St&PR 91*
Shealy, William Walter 1934- *St&PR 91*
Shealy, Y. Fulmer 1923- *WhoWor 91*
Shean, Dave 1878-1963 *Ballpl 90*
Shean, David Charles 1934- *IntWWM 90*
Shean, Timothy Joseph 1945- *WhoSSW 91*
Shear, Allan Levi 1955- *WhoE 91*
Shear, Benjamin D. 1910- *St&PR 91*
Shear, Edward Phillip 1923- *St&PR 91*
Shear, Henry Herbert 1935- *St&PR 91*
Shear, Ione Mylonas 1936- *WhoAmW 91, WhoE 91*
Shear, Jay Maurice 1921- *St&PR 91*
Shear, M Katherine *BiDrAPA 89*
Shear, Nancy J. 1946- *WhoAmW 91*
Shear, Nathaniel 1908- *WhoWor 91*
Shear, Phyllis Marks 1936- *St&PR 91*
Shear, Theodore Leslie, Jr. 1938- *WhoAm 90, WhoWor 91*
Shear, Virginia Marguerite 1950- *WhoE 91*
Shear, William Bruce 1954- *WhoE 91*
Shearar, Jeremy Brown 1931- *WhoWor 91*
Shearburn, Donald E. 1925- *St&PR 91*
Shearcroft, Patrick Fairfax 1945- *WhoWor 91*
Sheard, Michael H 1927- *BiDrAPA 89*
Sheard, Norma Fae Voorhees 1936- *WhoAmW 91*
Sheard, Paul MacKenzie *BiDrAPA 89*
Sheard, Titus 1841-1904 *AmLegL*
Sheard, Wendy Stedman 1935- *WhoAmA 91*
Sheardown, Frank 1922- *BioIn 16*
Shearer, Burt A. 1923- *St&PR 91*
Shearer, Carolyn Juanita 1944- *WhoAmW 91*
Shearer, Charles Livingston 1942- *WhoAm 90*
Shearer, Cynthia Louise 1957- *WhoAmW 91*
Shearer, David Paul 1940- *St&PR 91*
Shearer, Eric Berthold 1922- *WhoE 91*
Shearer, Eugene Eisenhardt 1930- *WhoSSW 91*
Shearer, Harry 1943- *ConTFT 8*
Shearer, Jill 1934- *FemiCLE*
Shearer, John 1947- *AuBYP 90, BioIn 16*
Shearer, John Clyde 1928- *WhoAm 90*
Shearer, Jonathan Turbitt 1945- *WhoEmL 91, WhoSSW 91*
Shearer, Linda *BioIn 16*
Shearer, Linda 1946- *WhoAmA 91*
Shearer, Marcia Cathrine 1933- *WhoAmW 91, WhoE 91*
Shearer, Marshall L, Jr. 1933- *BiDrAPA 89*
Shearer, Martin Pogue 1947- *St&PR 91*
Shearer, Michael Charles 1957- *St&PR 91*
Shearer, Moira 1926- *WorAlBi*
Shearer, Norma 1900-1983 *BioIn 16*
Shearer, Norma 1904-1983 *WorAlBi*
Shearer, Rhonda Roland 1954- *WhoAmA 91*
Shearer, Richard Eugene 1919- *WhoAm 90*
Shearer, Robert Dale 1941- *BiDrAPA 89*
Shearer, Ronald Alexander 1932- *WhoAm 90*
Shearer, Sergio 1939- *WhoHisp 91*
Shearer, Thomas *PenDiDA 89*
Shearer, William Kennedy 1931- *WhoAm 90*
Sheargold, Richard 1911-1988 *EncPaPR 91*
Sheargold, Richard K 1911-1988 *EncO&P 3*
Shearin, Betty Spurlock 1931- *WhoAmW 91*
Shearin, Kathryn Kay 1946- *WhoE 91, WhoEmL 91*
Shearing, George *BioIn 16*
Shearing, George 1919- *OxCPMus, WorAlBi*
Shearing, George Albert 1919- *WhoAm 90*
Shearing, Joseph 1886-1952 *TwCCr&M 91*
Shearman, Sylvester Gardiner 1802-1868 *AmLegL*
Shearman, Thomas B. *BioIn 16*
Shearon, George Buard 1932- *St&PR 91*
Shearouse, Nelson Leroy 1928- *WhoSSW 91*
Sheasby, Edward Gordon 1925- *WhoAm 90*
Sheasby, J. Michael 1936- *St&PR 91*
Sheatsley, Paul Baker 1916-1989 *BioIn 16*
Sheba *WomWR*
Shebalin, Dmitry *PenDiMP*
Sheble, Walter Franklin 1926- *WhoE 91*
Shechter, Ben-Zion 1940- *WhoAm 90, WhoAmA 91*
Shechter, Floyd 1954- *St&PR 91*
Shechter, Laura J 1944- *WhoAmA 91*
Shechter, Laura Judith 1944- *WhoAm 90*
Shechter, Mordechai 1937- *WhoWor 91*
Shechtman, George Henoch 1941- *WhoAmA 91*
Shechtman, Joseph *BiDrAPA 89*
Shechtman, Stephen 1946- *St&PR 91, WhoAm 90, WhoEmL 91*
Sheckard, Jimmy 1878-1947 *Ballpl 90*
Sheckley, Robert 1928- *RGTwCSF*
Shecter, Fredric Michael 1950- *BiDrAPA 89*
Shecter, Leonard 1926-1974 *Ballpl 90*
Shecter, Pearl S 1910- *WhoAmA 91*
Shecter, Pearl Sarah 1910- *WhoE 91*
Shectman, Robin 1948- *WhoWrEP 89*
Shedd, Donald Pomroy 1922- *WhoAm 90*
Shedd, George *BioIn 16*
Shedd, George J 1922- *WhoAmA 91*
Shedd, Hibbard Houston 1847-1905 *AmLegL*
Shedd, John Charles 1947- *WhoEmL 91*
Shedd, John G. 1850-1926 *WorAlBi*
Shedd, Rebecca Lynn 1954- *WhoAmW 91*
Shedd, William Greenough Thayer 1820-1894 *BioIn 16*
Shediac, Rawy Roy 1950- *St&PR 91*
Shedlack, Karen Jean *BiDrAPA 89*
Shedosky, Suzanne *WhoAmA 91*
Shedrick, Genevieve Mitchell *WhoAmW 91*
Shedrick, Mary Bernice 1940- *WhoAmW 91*
Sheean, Vincent 1899-1975 *AuBYP 90, BioIn 16*
Sheed, F.J. *ConAu 129*
Sheed, Francis J. *ConAu 129*
Sheed, Francis Joseph 1897-1981 *ConAu 129*
Sheed, Frank *ConAu 129*
Sheed, Frank J. *ConAu 129*
Sheed, Maisie Ward 1889-1975 *BioAmW*
Sheed, Wilfrid 1930- *ConAu 30NR, MajTwCW*
Sheed, Wilfrid John Joseph 1930- *WhoAm 90*
Sheedy, Ally 1962- *WhoAmW 91, WorAlBi*
Sheedy, Charles E. 1912-1990 *BioIn 16*
Sheedy, Janice Liberator 1951- *WhoE 91*
Sheedy, John Joseph 1948- *St&PR 91*
Sheedy, Katherine A. 1948- *St&PR 91*
Sheedy, Kenneth John 1945- *St&PR 91*
Sheehan, Charles Vincent 1930- *WhoAm 90*
Sheehan, Clyde Alexander *BiDrAPA 89*
Sheehan, Daniel Charles 1947- *St&PR 91*
Sheehan, Daniel Eugene 1917- *WhoAm 90*
Sheehan, Danny *BioIn 16*
Sheehan, David V 1947- *BiDrAPA 89*
Sheehan, Deborah Ann 1953- *WhoAmW 91*
Sheehan, Dennis William 1934- *St&PR 91, WhoAm 90*
Sheehan, Diane 1945- *WhoAmA 91*
Sheehan, Donald Thomas 1911- *WhoAm 90*
Sheehan, Douglas 1949- *ConTFT 8*
Sheehan, Edward James 1935- *WhoAm 90*
Sheehan, Elizabeth Ellen 1940- *WhoAmW 91*
Sheehan, Ethna 1908- *AuBYP 90*
Sheehan, Evelyn 1919- *WhoAmA 91*
Sheehan, George *BioIn 16*
Sheehan, James C. 1946- *St&PR 91*
Sheehan, James John 1937- *WhoAm 90*
Sheehan, James Patrick 1942- *St&PR 91, WhoAm 90, WhoSSW 91*
Sheehan, Jan A. *ODwPR 91*
Sheehan, Joe 1926- *ODwPR 91*
Sheehan, John C 1928- *BiDrAPA 89*
Sheehan, John Clark 1915- *WhoAm 90, WhoWor 91*
Sheehan, John Francis 1906- *WhoAm 90*
Sheehan, John Joseph 1899- *WhoAm 90*
Sheehan, John M. 1929- *WhoE 91*
Sheehan, John Patrick 1933- *St&PR 91*
Sheehan, Kathleen 1954- *WhoSSW 91*
Sheehan, Kathleen S *BiDrAPA 89*
Sheehan, Kevin Edward 1945- *St&PR 91*
Sheehan, Kevin John 1951- *St&PR 91*
Sheehan, Lawrence James 1932- *WhoAm 90*
Sheehan, Louis James 1934- *St&PR 91*
Sheehan, Maura A 1954- *WhoAmA 91*
Sheehan, Michael Francis 1951- *WhoEmL 91*
Sheehan, Michael Gilbert 1952- *WhoEmL 91*
Sheehan, Michael Jarboe 1939- *WhoAm 90, WhoSSW 91*
Sheehan, Monica Mary 1955- *WhoWor 91*
Sheehan, Nancy M. *WhoAm 90*
Sheehan, Neil *BioIn 16, NewYTBS 90 [port]*
Sheehan, Neil 1936- *WhoAm 90, WhoWrEP 89*
Sheehan, Patricia Queenan 1934- *WhoAmW 91*
Sheehan, Patrick J 1942- *BiDrAPA 89*
Sheehan, Patty *BioIn 16*
Sheehan, Richard J. 1934- *St&PR 91*
Sheehan, Robert James, II 1937- *WhoE 91*
Sheehan, Ruth Conroy 1954- *WhoAmW 91*
Sheehan, Shaun M. 1944- *ODwPR 91*
Sheehan, Susan *BioIn 16*
Sheehan, Susan 1937- *WhoAm 90, WhoAmW 91, WorAu 1980 [port]*
Sheehan, Thomas J. 1943- *St&PR 91*
Sheehan, Tom 1894-1982 *Ballpl 90*
Sheehan, Tommy 1877-1959 *Ballpl 90*
Sheehan, Valerie A *BiDrAPA 89*
Sheehan, Virginia Mary 1945- *WhoAmW 91*
Sheehan, William *ODwPR 91*
Sheehan, William Edward, Jr. 1925- *WhoAm 90*
Sheehan, William Francis 1859-1917 *AmLegL*
Sheehan, William G. 1938- *St&PR 91*
Sheehan, William J. 1943- *St&PR 91*
Sheehan, William Joseph 1943- *WhoE 91*
Sheehan, William Patrick 1954- *BiDrAPA 89*
Sheehan, William Patrick 1956- *BiDrAPA 89*
Sheehe, Lillian Carolyn 1915- *WhoAmA 91*
Sheehy, Dennis *BioIn 16*
Sheehy, Edmund Francis, Jr. 1952- *WhoEmL 91*
Sheehy, Edward Joseph 1923- *WhoE 91*
Sheehy, Eugene Paul 1922- *WhoAm 90*
Sheehy, Gail *BioIn 16*
Sheehy, Gail 1936?- *MajTwCW*
Sheehy, Gail 1937- *ConAu 33NR*
Sheehy, Gail Henion 1937- *WhoAm 90, WhoWrEP 89*
Sheehy, Howard Sherman, Jr. 1934- *WhoAm 90*
Sheehy, James William 1949- *WhoSSW 91*
Sheehy, John C. 1918- *WhoAm 90*
Sheehy, John Patrick 1942- *WhoE 91, WhoWor 91*
Sheehy, L Michael 1938- *BiDrAPA 89*
Sheehy, Maryann C. 1954- *WhoAmW 91*
Sheehy, Patrick 1930- *St&PR 91, WhoAm 90, WhoSSW 91, WhoWor 91*
Sheehy, Robert Francis 1950- *St&PR 91, WhoAm 90*
Sheehy, Thomas Daniel 1946- *St&PR 91, WhoAm 90*
Sheehy, William R *BiDrAPA 89*
Sheek, Roy Steven 1952- *WhoSSW 91*
Sheeks, Ben *AmLegL*
Sheel, John F, Jr. 1932- *BiDrAPA 89*
Sheeler, Charles 1883-1965 *BioIn 16, WhoAmA 91N, WorAlBi*
Sheeler, Donald Eugene 1952- *St&PR 91, WhoAm 90*
Sheeley, Rachel Evelyn 1966- *WhoAmW 91*
Sheeley, William F 1917- *BiDrAPA 89*
Sheeline, Paul C. 1921- *St&PR 91*
Sheeline, Paul Cushing 1921- *WhoAm 90*
Sheely, David G. 1958- *St&PR 91*
Sheely, Earl 1893-1952 *Ballpl 90*
Sheen, Charlie *BioIn 16*
Sheen, Charlie 1966- *WhoHisp 91, WorAlBi*
Sheen, Fulton J. 1895-1979 *BioIn 16, MajTwCW*
Sheen, Fulton John 1895-1979 *WorAlBi*

Sheen, John E. 1925- *BiDrAPA 89*
Sheen, Martin 1940- *BioIn 16, WhoAm 90, WhoHisp 91, WorAlBi*
Sheen, Robert Tilton 1909- *WhoAm 90*
Sheer, Martin George 1944- *St&PR 91*
Sheeran, John Francis 1937- *WhoAm 90*
Sheeran, Thomas Joseph 1947- *WhoE 91*
Sheeran, William James 1938- *WhoAm 90, WhoE 91*
Sheeran-Emory, Kathleen Mary 1948- *WhoEmL 91, WhoWor 91*
Sheerer, Mary G. *PenDiDA 89*
Sheerin, Jerry 1933- *WhoAmA 91*
Sheerin, Mira Josephine 1927- *WhoE 91*
Sheerman, Steven *St&PR 91*
Sheesley, Devere L., Jr. 1938- *St&PR 91*
Sheesley, DeVere Lamar, Jr. 1938- *WhoAm 90*
Sheets, Charles Van 1957- *WhoSSW 91*
Sheets, David Lloyd 1945- *WhoEmL 91*
Sheets, Herman Ernest 1908- *WhoAm 90, WhoE 91*
Sheets, John Wesley, Jr. 1953- *WhoEmL 91*
Sheets, Kenneth Ray 1936- *WhoAm 90*
Sheets, Larry 1959- *Ballpl 90*
Sheets, Martha Louise 1923- *WhoAmW 91*
Sheets, Michael Jay 1930- *WhoAm 90, WhoWor 91*
Sheets, Millard 1907-1989 *BioIn 16, WhoAmA 91N*
Sheets, Robin Lauterbach 1943- *ConAu 131*
Sheets, Sue Laura 1929- *WhoAmW 91*
Sheets, Timothy Baskerville *BioIn 16*
Sheetz, Christine Ninfa 1940- *WhoAmW 91, WhoWor 91*
Sheetz, David Patrick 1926- *WhoAm 90*
Sheetz, Maria R. 1948- *WhoSSW 91*
Sheetz, Natalie E. *BioIn 16*
Sheetz, Ralph Albert 1908- *WhoE 91, WhoWor 91*
Sheetz, Richard LaTrelle 1906- *WhoAm 90*
Sheetz, Richard Smedley 1924- *St&PR 91, WhoAm 90*
Shefcik, Kenneth Stanley 1947- *St&PR 91*
Shefelman, Janice Jordan 1930- *BioIn 16*
Shefelman, Tom 1927- *BioIn 16*
Sheff, Albert Gene *BiDrAPA 89*
Sheff, Honey A. 1954- *WhoAmW 91, WhoSSW 91, WhoWor 91*
Sheff, Lawrence 1934- *BiDrAPA 89*
Sheffe, Edward Devereux, III 1950- *WhoE 91*
Sheffel, Irving Eugene 1916- *WhoAm 90*
Sheffer, Albert Lester, II 1929- *WhoE 91*
Sheffer, Donald Alger 1917- *St&PR 91*
Sheffer, Glenn C 1881-1948 *WhoAmA 91N*
Sheffer, H. R. 1926- *BioIn 16*
Sheffer, Ralph Lin, Jr. *St&PR 91*
Sheffer, Sandra J. 1947- *St&PR 91*
Sheffers, Peter Winthrop 1893-1949 *WhoAmA 91N*
Sheffey, Fred Clifton, Jr. 1928- *WhoAm 90*
Sheffey, Hugh White 1815-1889 *AmLegL*
Sheffield, Frank Elwyn 1946- *WhoEmL 91*
Sheffield, Gary *BioIn 16*
Sheffield, Gary 1968- *Ballpl 90*
Sheffield, Horace Lindsey, Jr. 1916- *WhoAm 90*
Sheffield, Lee *BioIn 16*
Sheffield, Leslie Floyd 1925- *WhoAm 90*
Sheffield, Linda Jensen 1949- *WhoSSW 91*
Sheffield, Martin P. 1950- *St&PR 91*
Sheffield, Pappy *BioIn 16*
Sheffield, Scott D. 1952- *St&PR 91*
Sheffield, Walter Jervis 1946- *WhoEmL 91*
Sheffield, William Jennings 1928- *WhoAm 90*
Sheffield, William P. 1919- *St&PR 91*
Sheffler, Larry N. 1939- *St&PR 91*
Sheffner, David Julian *BiDrAPA 89*
Sheffner, Paul Wayne 1948- *BiDrAPA 89*
Shefrin, Harold Marvin 1948- *WhoWor 91*
Sheft, Leonard Alvin 1931- *WhoE 91*
Sheft, Mark David 1953- *WhoEmL 91*
Shefte, James Francis 1943- *St&PR 91*
Sheftel, Beatrice K. 1945- *WhoWrEP 89*
Sheftel, Roger Terry 1941- *WhoE 91, WhoWor 91*
Sheftel, Theodore C *BiDrAPA 89*
Sheftell, Fred David 1941- *BiDrAPA 89*
Sheftman, Howard Stephen 1949- *WhoEmL 91*
Shefts, Joelle *BioIn 16*
Shegogue, Rich *ODwPR 91*
Sheh, Robert Bardhyl 1939- *St&PR 91, WhoAm 90*
Shehata, Hany Ramzy *BiDrAPA 89*
Shehee, A.B. 1926- *St&PR 91*
Shehee, Walter H *BiDrAPA 89*
Sheheen, Robert J. 1943- *WhoSSW 91*
Shehi, George Michael 1949- *BiDrAPA 89*
Shehi, Lyle E, Jr. 1947- *BiDrAPA 89*
Shei, Juliana C. 1948- *WhoAmW 91*
Sheid, Irma Elizabeth 1943- *WhoAmW 91*
Sheih, David Pong S. 1940- *WhoSSW 91*
Sheik, Iqbal *BiDrAPA 89*
Sheikh, Atique Zafar 1940- *WhoWor 91*
Sheikh, Javaid Iqbal 1954- *BiDrAPA 89*
Sheikh, Mehboob Basha 1946- *WhoSSW 91*
Sheikh, Ramsey U. 1930- *St&PR 91*
Sheikh, Tahir M *BiDrAPA 89*
Sheikh-Djavadi, Nasser *BiDrAPA 89*
Sheikha, Sabri Hassan *BiDrAPA 89*
Sheikkariem, Ahmed W. *WhoWor 91*
Sheikman, Michael B 1928- *BiDrAPA 89*
Sheil, Donald Edward 1938- *WhoE 91*
Sheila E *DrBIPA 90*
Sheils, James H. 1912-1989 *BioIn 16*
Sheiman, Ronald Lee 1948- *WhoE 91, WhoWor 91*
Sheimo, Stanton L *BiDrAPA 89*
Sheinbaum, Richard Louis 1935- *St&PR 91*
Sheinbaum, Stanley K. 1920- *WhoWor 91*
Sheinberg, George Charles 1935- *WhoAm 90*
Sheinberg, Israel 1932- *St&PR 91, WhoAm 90*
Sheinberg, Sidney Jay 1935- *WhoAm 90*
Sheinberg, Zena *BioIn 16*
Sheiner, Richard Hugh *BiDrAPA 89*
Sheiner, Sara B *BiDrAPA 89*
Sheinfeld, David 1906- *IntWWM 90, WhoAm 90*
Sheinfeld, Myron M. 1930- *WhoSSW 91*
Sheingold, Abraham 1917- *WhoAm 90*
Sheingold, Robin 1952- *WhoAmW 91*
Sheinin, Lisa Basya J *BiDrAPA 89*
Sheinin, Rose 1930- *WhoAm 90, WhoAmW 91*
Sheinis, Arnold *BiDrAPA 89*
Sheinkman, Betty Frances 1931- *WhoAmW 91*
Sheinkman, Jack 1926- *WhoAm 90*
Sheinkopf, Russell H 1951- *BiDrAPA 89*
Sheinman, Eugene 1929- *St&PR 91*
Sheinwold, Alfred *WhoAm 90*
Sheirr, Olga 1931- *WhoAmA 91*
Shekerjian, Regina Tor *AuBYP 90*
Shekhar, Anantha *BiDrAPA 89*
Shekhar, Chandra 1927- *NewYTBS 90 [port], WhoWor 91*
Shekhar, Vellore Srinivasan 1946- *WhoWor 91*
Shekher, S Chandra *BiDrAPA 89*
Shekhtel, Fyodor *BioIn 16*
Shekim, Walid Othman *BiDrAPA 89*
Shelanski, Michael L. 1941- *WhoAm 90*
Shelat, Nayan Jagdishchandra 1954- *WhoWor 91*
Shelato, Robert 1923- *St&PR 91*
Shelbourne, Cecily *ConAu 31NR*
Shelburne, Fiona Mary 1954- *WhoWor 91*
Shelburne, William Petty, Lord 1737-1805 *EncCRAm*
Shelby, Antonio McGee 1941- *St&PR 91*
Shelby, Carolyn June 1949- *WhoAmW 91*
Shelby, Carroll 1923- *BioIn 16*
Shelby, Don *BioIn 16*
Shelby, Isaac 1750-1826 *EncCRAm, WhNaAH*
Shelby, J Teresa *BiDrAPA 89*
Shelby, James Stanford 1934- *WhoSSW 91, WhoWor 91*
Shelby, Jerome 1930- *St&PR 91, WhoAm 90*
Shelby, John 1958- *Ballpl 90*
Shelby, Joyce Young 1947- *WhoWrEP 89*
Shelby, Kelly Russell 1925- *St&PR 91*
Shelby, Lila 1900- *WhoAmA 91*
Shelby, Nancy Jane 1950- *WhoEmL 91*
Shelby, Reuben 1803-1882 *AmLegL*
Shelby, Richard Craig 1934- *WhoAm 90, WhoSSW 91, WhoWor 91*
Shelby, Robert B 1920- *BiDrAPA 89*
Sheldon, Albert Millard, III 1950- *BiDrAPA 89*
Sheldon, Alice 1915-1987 *FemiCLE*
Sheldon, Alice Hastings Bradley 1915-1987 *MajTwCW*
Sheldon, Brooke Earle 1931- *WhoAm 90, WhoAmW 91*
Sheldon, Charles Harvey 1929- *WhoAm 90*
Sheldon, Charles M. 1857-1946 *BioIn 16*
Sheldon, Clifford George 1942- *St&PR 91*
Sheldon, Courtney Roswell 1920- *WhoE 91*
Sheldon, Curtiss Samuel 1941- *St&PR 91*
Sheldon, Dana M 1924- *BiDrAPA 89*
Sheldon, David Frederick 1929- *WhoAm 90*
Sheldon, Donald Charles 1937- *St&PR 91*
Sheldon, Edgar K. 1938- *ODwPR 91*
Sheldon, Edwin O 1930- *BiDrAPA 89*
Sheldon, Eleanor Harriet Bernert 1920- *WhoAm 90, WhoAmW 91*
Sheldon, Eric 1930- *WhoAm 90*
Sheldon, Frances Dorothy Gigante 1949- *WhoEmL 91*
Sheldon, Gary 1953- *WhoAm 90*
Sheldon, George F. *WhoAm 90*
Sheldon, Georgiana Hortense 1923- *WhoAm 90, WhoAmW 91*
Sheldon, Ian Martin 1956- *WhoWor 91*
Sheldon, Ingrid Kristina 1945- *WhoAmW 91*
Sheldon, Joan Redden 1928- *WhoAmW 91*
Sheldon, John Arthur 1935- *St&PR 91*
Sheldon, John Mahlon 1937- *St&PR 91*
Sheldon, Mary W 1932- *BiDrAPA 89*
Sheldon, Michael Richard 1949- *WhoEmL 91*
Sheldon, Muriel *AuBYP 90*
Sheldon, Nancy Way 1944- *WhoAmW 91, WhoWor 91*
Sheldon, Peter Spafford 1939- *WhoAm 90*
Sheldon, Raccoona *MajTwCW*
Sheldon, Ralph *PenDiDA 89*
Sheldon, Ralph 1537-1613 *PenDiDA 89*
Sheldon, Richard C. *BioIn 16*
Sheldon, Richard Jay 1935- *St&PR 91*
Sheldon, Richard Robert 1932- *WhoAm 90*
Sheldon, Robert E. *ODwPR 91*
Sheldon, Roger Alpha 1922- *WhoE 91*
Sheldon, Rollie 1936- *Ballpl 90*
Sheldon, Ruth Torrant 1931- *BiDrAPA 89*
Sheldon, Sidney 1917- *BioIn 16, ConAu 33NR, ConTFT 8, MajTwCW, WhoAm 90, WhoWrEP 89, WorAlBi*
Sheldon, Susan Frances 1948- *WhoAmW 91*
Sheldon, Terry Edwin 1945- *WhoAm 90*
Sheldon, Thomas Donald 1920- *WhoAm 90, WhoWor 91*
Sheldon, Walter J. 1917- *AuBYP 90*
Sheldon, Wilfrid Percy Henry 1901-1983 *DcNaB 1981*
Sheldon, William *PenDiDA 89*
Sheldon, William R. 1947- *WhoE 91*
Sheldrake, Rupert 1942- *EncO&P 3, EncPaPR 91*
Shelekhov, Gregor Ivanovich 1747-1795 *EncCRAm*
Shelekhov, Grigori Ivanovich 1747-1795 *WhNaAH*
Sheleski, Stanley John 1931- *WhoE 91, WhoWor 91*
Shelesnyak, Moses Chaim 1909- *WhoAm 90*
Sheley, Donald Ray, Jr. 1942- *WhoAm 90*
Shelfer, A. Gordon, Jr. 1943- *St&PR 91, WhoAm 90*
Shelfer, Tad Douglas 1963- *WhoSSW 91*
Shelford, Victor Ernest 1877-1968 *DcScB S2*
Shelhamer, John H. 1947- *St&PR 91*
Shelhamer, Linda K. 1952- *St&PR 91*
Shelhamer, Lloyd 1923- *St&PR 91*
Shelhorse, Mark Edwin 1956- *BiDrAPA 89*
Shelikov, Gregoriivanovich 1747-1795 *WhNaAH*
Sheline, Glenn E. 1918-1989 *BioIn 16*
Sheline, Raymond K. 1922- *WhoAm 90*
Shelkrot, Elliot Louis 1943- *WhoAm 90, WhoE 91*
Shell, Art *BioIn 16, WhoAm 90*
Shell, Bernard Ray 1925- *WhoSSW 91*
Shell, Billy Joe 1925- *WhoAm 90*
Shell, Courtney *WhoWrEP 89*
Shell, Glenn Harmen 1943- *St&PR 91, WhoAm 90*
Shell, Karl 1938- *WhoAm 90*
Shell, Leslie G., III 1946- *St&PR 91*
Shell, Owen G. 1936- *St&PR 91*
Shell, Owen G., Jr. 1936- *WhoAm 90, WhoSSW 91*
Shell, Robert Edward Lee 1946- *WhoEmL 91, WhoSSW 91, WhoWor 91*
Shell, Ted *BioIn 16*
Shell, V Nia *BiDrAPA 89*
Shellaberger, Donna Jean 1920- *WhoAmW 91*
Shelladay, Stephen B. 1801-1870 *AmLegL*
Shelledy, Stephen B. 1801-1870 *AmLegL*
Shellenback, Frank 1898-1969 *Ballpl 90*
Shellenback, Jim 1943- *Ballpl 90*
Shellenbarger, Melanie T. 1953- *WhoAmW 91*
Shellenberger, Verna S. 1915- *WhoWrEP 89*
Shellenberger, Wallace Alyn 1938- *BiDrAPA 89*
Shelley, Carole Augusta 1939- *WhoAm 90, WhoAmW 91*
Shelley, Donna Louise 1945- *WhoAmW 91*
Shelley, Edward Herman, Jr. 1919- *WhoAm 90*
Shelley, Edward M *BiDrAPA 89*
Shelley, Edwin *BioIn 16*
Shelley, Edwin F. *NewYTBS 90*
Shelley, George R. 1930- *WhoE 91*
Shelley, Howard 1950- *IntWWM 90*
Shelley, James LaMar 1915- *WhoAm 90*
Shelley, Louise Isobel 1952- *WhoEmL 91*
Shelley, Mary 1797-1851 *FemiCLE*
Shelley, Mary 1950- *MusmAFA*
Shelley, Mary Michael 1950- *WhoAmW 91*
Shelley, Mary Wollstonecraft 1797-1851 *BioIn 16, WorAlBi*
Shelley, Nancy Kay 1946- *WhoAmW 91*
Shelley, Percy Bysshe 1792-1822 *BioIn 16, DcLB 96 [port], EncPaPR 91, WorAlBi, WrPh*
Shelley, Rulon Gene 1924- *WhoE 91*
Shelley, Sally Swing 1924- *WhoWor 91*
Shelley, Steven Marius 1920- *WhoWor 91*
Shelley, Sue H. 1954- *St&PR 91*
Shelley, Walter Brown 1917- *WhoAm 90*
Shellhase, George Mann *BioIn 16*
Shellhase, Leslie John 1924- *WhoAm 90*
Shellhorn, Ruth Patricia 1909- *WhoAm 90*
Shellnut, Thomas Cochran 1940- *St&PR 91*
Shellow, James Myers 1926- *WhoAm 90*
Shellow, Jill Rachel 1956- *WhoAmW 91*
Shellow, Robert 1929- *WhoAm 90*
Shellow, Ronald A 1933- *BiDrAPA 89*
Shellum, Steven 1954- *WhoWor 91*
Shelly, James Harold 1932- *WhoSSW 91*
Shelly, Maynard Wolfe *WhoAm 90*
Shelly, Walter M. 1933- *WhoSSW 91*
Shelnutt, Eve 1941- *ConAu 132*
Shelnutt, Eve B. 1941- *WhoWrEP 89*
Shelnutt, Robert Curtis 1928- *WhoSSW 91, WhoWor 91*
Shelp, Ronald Kent 1941- *WhoAm 90*
Shelp, Woody *BioIn 16*
Shelpuk, Christopher Alexander 1944- *WhoSSW 91*
Shelquist, Vivian Rampy 1917- *WhoAmW 91*
Shelter, Robert Weldon 1940- *BiDrAPA 89*
Shelton, Anne 1927- *OxCPMus*
Shelton, Anne Elizabeth 1948- *WhoAmW 91, WhoSSW 91*
Shelton, Bennett Frank, Jr. 1938- *WhoSSW 91*
Shelton, Betty Clare 1940- *WhoSSW 91*
Shelton, Bryan Keith 1956- *WhoSSW 91*
Shelton, C. A. *WhoSSW 91*
Shelton, C. R. 1927- *ODwPR 91*
Shelton, Carl F. 1931- *St&PR 91*
Shelton, Charles B., III 1941- *St&PR 91*
Shelton, Cynthia Anne 1965- *WhoEmL 91*
Shelton, David Cochran 1952- *WhoEmL 91*
Shelton, David Houston 1928- *St&PR 91*
Shelton, David Howard 1928- *WhoAm 90*
Shelton, Deborah Jackson 1942- *WhoSSW 91*
Shelton, Delbert A. 1944- *St&PR 91*
Shelton, Donald Charles 1933- *St&PR 91*
Shelton, Dorothy Aubinoe 1927- *WhoAmW 91*
Shelton, Edward Norman, Jr. 1958- *WhoSSW 91*
Shelton, Frank Harvey 1924- *St&PR 91*
Shelton, Frank White, Jr. 1950- *IntWWM 90*
Shelton, Gary Richard 1947- *WhoSSW 91*
Shelton, Gene 1942- *St&PR 91*
Shelton, George Hallett 1933- *St&PR 91*
Shelton, Grady 1928- *St&PR 91*
Shelton, Harry Bernard 1964- *WhoE 91*
Shelton, Harry C. 1929- *St&PR 91*
Shelton, Henry Z *BiDrAPA 89*
Shelton, Hugh Norman Arthur 1925- *IntWWM 90*
Shelton, James Douglas 1939- *WhoE 91*
Shelton, James Joseph 1916- *St&PR 91*
Shelton, James T *BiDrAPA 89*
Shelton, Jammi M. 1947- *WhoAmW 91*
Shelton, Jerrell Wilson 1945- *St&PR 91, WhoEmL 91*
Shelton, Jerry Guy 1953- *WhoSSW 91*
Shelton, Judy McLelland 1958- *WhoAmW 91*
Shelton, Karl Mason 1933- *WhoAm 90*
Shelton, Katherine W. 1943- *WhoAmW 91*
Shelton, Kathleen J. 1946-1990 *ConAu 131*
Shelton, L.C. Buddy 1943- *WhoSSW 91*
Shelton, Larry Brandon 1934- *WhoAm 90, WhoSSW 91*
Shelton, Larry M. 1954- *St&PR 91*
Shelton, Lucy *WhoAmW 91*
Shelton, M. Linda Gale 1952- *WhoAmW 91*
Shelton, Mark Logan 1958- *WhoWrEP 89*
Shelton, Mary Nell 1931- *WhoSSW 91*
Shelton, Melvin Dewey, III *BiDrAPA 89*
Shelton, Nicolina *WhoWrEP 89*
Shelton, Paul G. 1950- *St&PR 91*
Shelton, Peter T 1951- *WhoAmA 91*
Shelton, Reid Leroy 1924- *WhoAm 90*
Shelton, Richard 1933- *WhoWrEP 89*
Shelton, Richard Charles 1954- *BiDrAPA 89*
Shelton, Richard Fottrell 1929- *WhoAm 90*

Shelton, Robert Arthur 1941- *WhoAm 90*
Shelton, Robert Lee 1939- *WhoAmA 91*
Shelton, Robert Neal 1948- *WhoAm 90*
Shelton, Robert Warren 1943- *WhoSSW 91*
Shelton, Ron *BioIn 16*
Shelton, Sally Angela 1944- *WhoAmW 91, WhoE 91*
Shelton, Sandra Lee 1952- *WhoAmW 91*
Shelton, Sloane 1934- *WhoAm 90*
Shelton, Stephani *WhoAm 90*
Shelton, Stephen Eugene 1947- *St&PR 91*
Shelton, Steven R *BiDrAPA 89*
Shelton, Susan Bechtel *BiDrAPA 89*
Shelton, Terri Lizabeth 1955- *WhoE 91*
Shelton, Timothy Edwin 1948- *St&PR 91*
Shelton, Turner Blair 1915- *WhoAm 90*
Shelton, Wanda Carol 1956- *WhoAmW 91*
Shelton, Wayne 1932- *St&PR 91*
Shelton, Wayne Vernon 1932- *WhoAm 90, WhoSSW 91*
Shelton, William Chastain 1916- *WhoWor 91*
Shelton, William Everett 1944- *WhoAm 90*
Shelton, William R 1920- *BiDrAPA 89*
Shelton, William Roy 1919- *AuBYP 90*
Shelton, Winfred N *BiDrAPA 89*
Sheluck, William, Jr. 1940- *St&PR 91*
Shely, Benjamin L. 1933-1990 *WhoAm 90*
Shemancik, John Allen 1948- *St&PR 91*
Shembarger, Donald Eugene 1938- *St&PR 91*
Shemely, Charles Louis 1938- *St&PR 91, WhoAm 90*
Shemer, Martha Evvard 1919- *WhoAmW 91*
Shemesh, Lorraine R 1949- *WhoAmA 91*
Shemiakin, Mikhail Mikhailovich 1908-1970 *DcScB S2*
Shemin, Barry L. 1942- *St&PR 91, WhoAm 90*
Shemin, David 1911- *WhoAm 90*
Shemitz, Sylvan R. 1925- *St&PR 91*
Shemo, John Palmer D 1948- *BiDrAPA 89*
Shemo, John Palmer David 1948- *WhoSSW 91*
Shemo, Mary Carroll 1950- *BiDrAPA 89*
Shemo, Thomas E. 1950- *St&PR 91*
Shemorry, Corinne Joynes 1920- *WhoAmW 91*
Shems, Estherina *BiDrAPA 89*
Shems, Estherina 1932- *WhoE 91*
Shemtob, Richard 1940- *St&PR 91*
Shen Congwen 1902-1988 *BioIn 16*
Shen Jung *WorAu 1980*
Shen Rong *WorAu 1980*
Shen Tong *BioIn 16*
Shen, Benjamin Shih-Ping 1931- *WhoAm 90*
Shen, Bernard *BioIn 16*
Shen, Catherine 1947- *WhoAm 90, WhoAmW 91*
Shen, Chang Huan 1913- *WhoWor 91*
Shen, Chia Theng 1913- *WhoAm 90, WhoWor 91*
Shen, George Clement 1929- *WhoWor 91*
Shen, Grace Chi-mei 1950- *WhoAmW 91*
Shen, Hsieh Wen 1931- *WhoAm 90*
Shen, Nelson Mu-Ching 1946- *WhoWor 91*
Shen, Seng 1944- *BiDrAPA 89*
Shen, Shan-Fu 1921- *WhoAm 90*
Shen, Sinyan 1949- *IntWWM 90*
Shen, Steve Yu-Liang 1946- *WhoE 91*
Shen, Theodore Ping 1945- *St&PR 91, WhoAm 90*
Shen, Thomas To 1926- *WhoE 91*
Shen, Ts'ung wen 1902-1988 *BioIn 16*
Shen, Tsung Ying 1924- *WhoAm 90*
Shen, Winston W 1943- *BiDrAPA 89*
Shen, Yao Tian 1938- *WhoWor 91*
Shen, Yueh 441-513 *BioIn 16*
Shen, Yujin 1949- *WhoE 91*
Shenandoah *WhoNeCM [port]*
Shenandoah, Joanne Lynne 1957- *WhoE 91*
Shenar, Paul 1936- *WhoAm 90*
Shenar, Paul 1936-1989 *ConTFT 8*
Shencup, Steven Robert 1945- *St&PR 91*
Shendock, George Michael 1949- *WhoE 91*
Shendow, Harry S. 1933- *St&PR 91*
Shenefield, John Hale 1939- *WhoAm 90*
Sheneman, Wayne E. 1933- *St&PR 91*
Shengold, Leonard L *BiDrAPA 89*
Shenk, Dale M. *WhoAm 90*
Shenk, John C., Jr. 1926- *St&PR 91*
Shenk, John Christian, Jr. 1926- *WhoAm 90*
Shenk, Mike *BioIn 16*
Shenk, Thomas Eugene 1947- *WhoAm 90*
Shenk, Wilbur, III 1941- *St&PR 91*
Shenk, Willis Weidman 1915- *St&PR 91*
Shenkarow, Barry *WhoAm 90*
Shenker, Morris A. 1907-1989 *BioIn 16*
Shenkir, William Gary 1938- *WhoAm 90*
Shenkle, George Alfred 1921- *St&PR 91*
Shenkler, Leslie Morris 1939- *WhoE 91*
Shenkman, Aaron M. 1940- *St&PR 91*
Shenkman, Sidney 1920-1990 *BioIn 16*
Shenman, Martin M. 1948- *ODwPR 91*
Shennan, James G. 1910- *St&PR 91*
Shennum, Robert Herman 1922- *WhoAm 90*
Shenouda, Anba, III 1923- *WhoWor 91*
Shenoy, Prakash Pundalik 1950- *WhoEmL 91*
Shenoy, Ramakrishnan 1941- *BiDrAPA 89*
Shenoy, Shyamala B *BiDrAPA 89*
Shenoy, Shyamala Baburaya 1948- *WhoE 91*
Shenoy, Sudhakar Venkatraya 1947- *St&PR 91, WhoSSW 91*
Shenoy, Suresh Venkatraya 1950- *WhoE 91*
Shensky, Davida Ann 1951- *WhoSSW 91*
Shenston, Thomas Strahan 1822-1895 *DcCanB 12*
Shenstone, Michael 1928- *WhoWor 91*
Shenstone, William 1714-1763 *DcLB 95 [port]*
Shenton, Martha Elizabeth 1952- *WhoAmW 91*
Sheon, Aaron 1937- *WhoAm 90, WhoAmA 91*
Sheon, Sarah Lynn 1958- *WhoAmW 91*
Sheopuri, Ramesh Chandra 1939- *WhoWor 91*
Sheorn, Keyhill D. 1955- *BiDrAPA 89*
Shepard, A. Courtenay 1939- *St&PR 91, WhoAm 90*
Shepard, Alan B., Jr. *BioIn 16*
Shepard, Alan B., Jr. 1923- *WorAlBi*
Shepard, Alan Bartlett, Jr. 1923- *WhoAm 90, WhoWor 91*
Shepard, Andrew J. 1924- *St&PR 91*
Shepard, Barry 1931- *St&PR 91*
Shepard, Bob *Ballpl 90*
Shepard, Bruce Carl 1946- *WhoSSW 91*
Shepard, Charles Virgil 1940- *WhoSSW 91, WhoWor 91*
Shepard, Christy Carol 1950- *WhoSSW 91*
Shepard, Connie Christine 1947- *WhoAmW 91*
Shepard, Cynthia Lynn 1963- *WhoSSW 91*
Shepard, D. C. 1924- *WhoAm 90*
Shepard, David B. 1942- *St&PR 91*
Shepard, David Hammond 1923- *St&PR 91*
Shepard, David Meredith *BiDrAPA 89*
Shepard, Dean Warren 1930- *St&PR 91*
Shepard, Donald James 1946- *St&PR 91*
Shepard, Earl Alden 1932- *WhoWor 91*
Shepard, Earl Emanuel 1908- *WhoAm 90*
Shepard, Elaine Elizabeth *WhoAm 90*
Shepard, Francis B. 1940- *St&PR 91*
Shepard, Geoffrey C. 1944- *St&PR 91*
Shepard, Geoffrey Carroll 1944- *WhoAm 90*
Shepard, Helen G. *BioAmW*
Shepard, Herschel Elwood 1931- *WhoAm 90*
Shepard, Jack 1932- *Ballpl 90*
Shepard, Jack H. 1933- *St&PR 91*
Shepard, James Dudley 1938- *St&PR 91*
Shepard, James J. 1931- *WhoAm 90*
Shepard, Janie Ray 1954- *WhoAmW 91, WhoSSW 91*
Shepard, Jesse Francis Grierson 1849-1927 *EncO&P 3*
Shepard, John deBerard, Jr. 1949- *IntWWM 90*
Shepard, Jon Max 1939- *WhoAm 90*
Shepard, Kyle Mark 1963- *WhoEmL 91*
Shepard, Leonard *BioIn 16*
Shepard, Leroy Grenville 1920- *St&PR 91*
Shepard, Lewis Albert 1945- *WhoAmA 91*
Shepard, Linda Mary 1949- *WhoAmW 91*
Shepard, Margaret Louisa Vanderbilt 1845-1924 *BioIn 16*
Shepard, Mary Eleanor 1909- *BioIn 16*
Shepard, Mikki Maureen Allison 1951- *WhoAmW 91*
Shepard, Neal *TwCCr&M 91*
Shepard, Paul Cooper 1948- *WhoEmL 91*
Shepard, Paul Howe 1925- *WhoAm 90*
Shepard, Paul M., Jr. 1930- *St&PR 91*
Shepard, Randall Terry 1946- *WhoAm 90, WhoEmL 91*
Shepard, Robert Andrews 1923- *WhoAm 90*
Shepard, Robert Kight 1943- *WhoWor 91*
Shepard, Robert M. 1932- *WhoAm 90*
Shepard, Robert Payne 1953- *WhoEmL 91*
Shepard, Roger Newland 1929- *WhoAm 90*
Shepard, Sam 1943- *BioIn 16, MajTwCW, WhoAm 90, WorAlBi*
Shepard, Samuel E. 1931- *St&PR 91*
Shepard, Stephen Benjamin 1939- *St&PR 91, WhoAm 90*
Shepard, Thomas 1605-1649 *BioIn 16*
Shepard, Thomas Hill 1923- *WhoAm 90*
Shepard, Thomas Rockwell, Jr. 1918- *WhoAm 90*
Shepard, William A *BiDrAPA 89*
Shepard, William H. 1923- *ODwPR 91*
Shepard, William Seth 1935- *WhoAm 90*
Shepardson, Lucille D. 1937- *St&PR 91*
Sheperd, Lois von Behren *BioIn 16*
Shephard, Bruce Dennis 1944- *WhoSSW 91*
Shephard, Jacqueline 1946- *St&PR 91*
Shephard, Juddson E 1918- *BiDrAPA 89*
Shephard, Mark Scott 1951- *WhoE 91*
Shepherd, Abigal *BiDEWW*
Shepherd, Alan J. 1942- *WhoAm 90*
Shepherd, Alice Grant 1949- *St&PR 91*
Shepherd, Bill *BioIn 16*
Shepherd, Burton Hale, Jr. 1956- *WhoSSW 91*
Shepherd, Carl Lee 1952- *WhoAm 90*
Shepherd, Carol Nelson 1952- *WhoEmL 91*
Shepherd, Catherine 1915- *WhoWrEP 89*
Shepherd, Charles David 1953- *WhoSSW 91*
Shepherd, Charles Edward 1920- *St&PR 91*
Shepherd, Charles L. 1928- *St&PR 91*
Shepherd, Christopher Hart 1952- *St&PR 91*
Shepherd, Cybill *BioIn 16*
Shepherd, Cybill 1950- *WhoAm 90, WorAlBi*
Shepherd, Dee A. *BioIn 16*
Shepherd, Dennis Granville 1912- *WhoAm 90*
Shepherd, Donald Ray 1935- *WhoSSW 91*
Shepherd, Elizabeth *AuBYP 90*
Shepherd, Elizabeth Poole 1937- *WhoSSW 91*
Shepherd, Frances Ann 1946- *IntWWM 90*
Shepherd, Gary Gene 1940- *St&PR 91*
Shepherd, Gary Kevin 1957- *WhoWrEP 89*
Shepherd, Gary Lee *BiDrAPA 89*
Shepherd, Gilbert B. 1937- *WhoWor 91*
Shepherd, Gordon Greeley 1931- *WhoAm 90*
Shepherd, Helen Parsons 1923- *WhoAmA 91*
Shepherd, Isaac Barnett 1938- *WhoE 91*
Shepherd, Jack Edwin 1937- *WhoE 91*
Shepherd, James Robley 1945- *WhoE 91*
Shepherd, Jerry 1949- *WhoE 91*
Shepherd, Jesse 1848-1927 *BioIn 16*
Shepherd, Jesse George 1821-1869 *AmLegL*
Shepherd, John *TwCCr&M 91*
Shepherd, John Barrie 1935- *WhoE 91*
Shepherd, John Barron 1933- *St&PR 91*
Shepherd, John Calvin 1925- *WhoAm 90*
Shepherd, John Calvin 1944- *St&PR 91*
Shepherd, John Charles 1947- *IntWWM 90*
Shepherd, John Thompson 1919- *WhoAm 90*
Shepherd, Judy Carlile *WhoWor 91*
Shepherd, Lemuel C, Jr. *NewYTBS 90*
Shepherd, Lemuel C., Jr. 1896-1990 *CurBio 90N*
Shepherd, LeRoy Bryan 1957- *WhoSSW 91*
Shepherd, Mark, Jr. *BioIn 16*
Shepherd, Mark, Jr. 1923- *St&PR 91, WhoAm 90*
Shepherd, Mary Anne 1950- *WhoAmW 91*
Shepherd, Michael *BiDrAPA 89, MajTwCW, TwCCr&M 91, WorAu 1980*
Shepherd, Michael Wayne 1963- *WhoE 91*
Shepherd, Murray C. 1938- *WhoAm 90*
Shepherd, Reginald 1924- *WhoAmA 91*
Shepherd, Robert James 1930- *WhoAm 90*
Shepherd, Stephen Cedric 1952- *WhoSSW 91*
Shepherd, Suzanne Moore 1952- *WhoE 91*
Shepherd, Tamara Ann *BioIn 16*
Shepherd, William Fritz 1943- *WhoAmA 91*
Shepherd, William J. 1926- *St&PR 91*
Shepherd, William M. *BioIn 16*
Shepherd, William Smythe 1916- *St&PR 91*
Shepherd-Stanley, Zoe May 1955- *IntWWM 90*
Shepitko, Larissa *BioIn 16*
Shepler, Cynthia Marie 1956- *WhoSSW 91*
Shepler, Dwight 1905- *WhoAmA 91N*
Shepler, John Edward 1950- *WhoEmL 91*
Shepley, George A. 1922- *St&PR 91*
Shepley, Hugh 1928- *WhoAm 90*
Shepley, James Robinson 1917-1988 *BioIn 16*
Shepley, Lewis Baker 1939- *St&PR 91*
Shepley, Robert Gardiner 1953- *St&PR 91*
Shepp, Alan 1935- *WhoAmA 91*
Shepp, Archie *BioIn 16*
Shepp, Archie 1937- *DrBlPA 90*
Shepp, Bryan Eugene 1932- *WhoAm 90*
Shepp, Lawrence Alan 1936- *WhoAm 90*
Sheppard, Albert Parker, Jr. 1936- *WhoAm 90*
Sheppard, Allen 1932- *WhoWor 91*
Sheppard, Bob *BioIn 16*
Sheppard, C. James 1943- *IntWWM 90*
Sheppard, Carl Dunkle 1916- *WhoAmA 91*
Sheppard, Charles Frank 1935- *St&PR 91*
Sheppard, Charles Wayne *St&PR 91*
Sheppard, Claude-Armand 1935- *WhoAm 90*
Sheppard, David Eugene 1950- *WhoE 91*
Sheppard, Donald *BioIn 16*
Sheppard, Edith 1920- *BiDrAPA 89*
Sheppard, Edward C 1934- *BiDrAPA 89*
Sheppard, Edward Richard 1934- *St&PR 91, WhoE 91*
Sheppard, Elizabeth 1931- *IntWWM 90*
Sheppard, Elizabeth Sara 1830-1862 *FemiCLE*
Sheppard, Gina *BioIn 16*
Sheppard, Harold Lloyd 1922- *WhoSSW 91*
Sheppard, Jack W. 1931- *WhoAm 90*
Sheppard, James C. 1936- *St&PR 91*
Sheppard, John Calhoun 1850-1931 *AmLegL*
Sheppard, John Chester 1925- *St&PR 91*
Sheppard, John Craig 1913-1978 *WhoAmA 91N*
Sheppard, John Frederick 1939- *WhoSSW 91*
Sheppard, John Gavin 1916- *St&PR 91*
Sheppard, John W. *St&PR 91N*
Sheppard, John W., Jr. 1946- *St&PR 91*
Sheppard, Joseph Sherly 1930- *WhoAmA 91*
Sheppard, Louis Clarke 1933- *WhoSSW 91*
Sheppard, Matthew 1951- *St&PR 91*
Sheppard, Matthew Patrick 1951- *WhoE 91*
Sheppard, Nina Akamu *WhoAmA 91*
Sheppard, Philip Macdonald 1921-1976 *DcScB S2*
Sheppard, Posy 1916- *WhoAm 90, WhoE 91, WhoWor 91*
Sheppard, Richard Herbert 1910-1982 *DcNaB 1981*
Sheppard, Thomas Richard 1934- *WhoAm 90*
Sheppard, Walter Lee, Jr. 1911- *WhoE 91*
Sheppard, William J. 1937- *St&PR 91*
Sheppard, William Stevens 1930- *WhoAm 90*
Sheppard, William Vernon 1941- *WhoWor 91*
Sheppe, William Marco, Jr. 1924- *BiDrAPA 89*
Sheppeard, Sarah Y. 1955- *WhoEmL 91*
Sheppeck, Michael Louis 1910- *BiDrAPA 89*
Shepperd, John Ben 1915-1990 *BioIn 16, WhoSSW 91*
Shepperd, John Ray 1961- *WhoSSW 91*
Shepperd, John William 1951- *WhoWor 91*
Shepperd, Wayne Delbert 1947- *WhoEmL 91*
Sheppers, Joseph Theodore, Jr. 1941- *WhoSSW 91*
Shepperson, Geraldine Stish 1940- *WhoAmW 91*
Shepperson, Jacqueline R. 1935- *WhoAmW 91*
Shepperson, Wilbur Stanley 1919- *WhoAm 90*
Sheps, Cecil George 1913- *WhoAm 90*
Sheptyts'kyi, Andrii 1865-1944 *BioIn 16*
Sher, Ada Elizabeth 1948- *WhoSSW 91*
Sher, Allan L. 1931- *WhoAm 90, WhoE 91*
Sher, Barbara 1935- *ConAu 132*
Sher, Daniel 1943- *IntWWM 90, WhoAm 90*
Sher, Elizabeth 1943- *WhoAmA 91*
Sher, Harold T. 1927- *St&PR 91*
Sher, Jack 1913-1988 *BioIn 16*
Sher, Joanna Ruth Hollenberg 1933- *WhoAmW 91, WhoE 91*
Sher, Leopold Zangwill 1953- *WhoEmL 91*
Sher, Linda Rosenberg 1938- *WhoAmW 91*
Sher, Margery Leveen 1947- *WhoAmW 91*
Sher, Michael Buster 1941- *WhoE 91*
Sher, Norman B 1931- *BiDrAPA 89*
Sher, Patricia Ann 1941- *WhoSSW 91*
Sher, Patricia Ryan 1947- *WhoAmW 91*
Sher, Richard B. 1948- *WhoE 91*
Sher, Richard Benjamin 1939- *WhoSSW 91*
Sher, Richard Philip 1950- *WhoEmL 91*
Sher, Stanley Owen 1935- *WhoAm 90*
Sher, Steven J. 1949- *WhoWrEP 89*
Sher, Thomas O. *St&PR 91N*
Shera, Jesse Hauk 1903-1982 *BioIn 16*
Shera, Joyce Ann 1944- *WhoAmW 91*
Sherak, Donald Lawrence *BiDrAPA 89*
Sheram, Benjamin Stanley 1947- *WhoSSW 91*
Sherar, Joseph William 1930- *WhoWor 91*
Sheraton, Mimi *BioIn 16*

Sheraton, Thomas 1751-1806 *BioIn 16, PenDiDA 89, WorAlBi*
Sherba, John *PenDiMP*
Sherbell, Rhoda *WhoAm 90, WhoAmA 91, WhoAmW 91, WhoWor 91*
Sherber, Kenneth 1948- *St&PR 91*
Sherbin, John M., II 1949- *St&PR 91*
Sherblom, Anne Partridge 1949- *WhoAmW 91*
Sherblom, James Peter 1955- *St&PR 91, WhoE 91*
Sherbon, David *BiDrAPA 89*
Sherbourne, Archibald Norbert 1929- *WhoAm 90*
Sherbourne, Janet Lynne 1952- *IntWWM 90*
Sherburn, James R. 1936- *St&PR 91*
Sherburne, Donald Wynne 1929- *WhoAm 90, WhoWrEP 89*
Sherburne, James Robert 1925- *LiHiK*
Sherburne, John P. *BioIn 16*
Sherburne, Mary Lela 1926- *WhoAmW 91*
Sherburne, Robert C. 1920- *St&PR 91*
Sherburne, Zoa 1912- *BioIn 16*
Sherburne, Zoa Morin 1912- *AuBYP 90*
Sherby, Carolyn N. *ODwPR 91*
Sherdel, Bill 1896-1968 *Ballpl 90*
Shere, Dennis 1940- *WhoAm 90*
Shere, Louis 1900-1988 *BioIn 16*
Shere, Norbert L *BiDrAPA 89*
Shereff, Harry 1913- *St&PR 91*
Sherer, Arlene G 1940- *BiDrAPA 89*
Sherer, Billee Jean 1948- *WhoWrEP 89*
Sherer, Frank Audemars, Jr. 1947- *WhoEmL 91*
Sherer, Gabriela F *BiDrAPA 89*
Sherer, Margaret *BioIn 16*
Sherer, Samuel Ayers 1944- *WhoE 91*
Sherer, Thomas E. 1928- *St&PR 91*
Sherf, Arden Frederick 1916- *WhoAm 90*
Sherf, Sandee Croft 1950- *WhoAmW 91, WhoWor 91*
Sherfey, Geraldine Richards 1929- *WhoAmW 91, WhoWor 91*
Sherfey, James Daniel 1934- *St&PR 91*
Sherick, Donald R. 1941- *St&PR 91*
Sherid, Roy 1907-1982 *Ballpl 90*
Sheridan, Alison Mary 1956- *BiDrAPA 89*
Sheridan, Andrew James, III 1944- *WhoSSW 91*
Sheridan, Ann 1915-1967 *WorAlBi*
Sheridan, Charles Steve 1958- *WhoWrEP 89*
Sheridan, Christopher Frederick 1953- *WhoAm 90*
Sheridan, Clare 1885-1970 *BiDWomA*
Sheridan, Clare Consuelo 1885-1970 *FemiCLE*
Sheridan, David *BioIn 16*
Sheridan, Desmond John 1948- *WhoWor 91*
Sheridan, Frances 1724-1766 *FemiCLE*
Sheridan, Frances Chamberlaine 1724-1766 *BioIn 16*
Sheridan, Helen Adler *WhoAmA 91*
Sheridan, Helen Marie 1953- *WhoAmW 91*
Sheridan, James 1903-1989 *BioIn 16*
Sheridan, James Edward 1922- *WhoAm 90*
Sheridan, James Michael 1940- *St&PR 91*
Sheridan, John *Ballpl 90*
Sheridan, John Brian 1947- *WhoAm 90, WhoEmL 91*
Sheridan, Joseph Francis 1960- *St&PR 91*
Sheridan, Joseph L 1918- *BiDrAPA 89*
Sheridan, Joseph Lee 1918- *WhoE 91*
Sheridan, Lee Arthur 1943- *St&PR 91*
Sheridan, Linda Mary 1953- *WhoAmW 91*
Sheridan, Martin F. 1942- *St&PR 91*
Sheridan, Mary Stoebe 1948- *WhoEmL 91*
Sheridan, Pat 1957- *Ballpl 90*
Sheridan, Patrick M. 1940- *St&PR 91*
Sheridan, Patrick Michael 1940- *WhoAm 90, WhoWor 91*
Sheridan, Paul Matthew 1950- *St&PR 91*
Sheridan, Philip 1831-1888 *WorAlBi*
Sheridan, Philip Henry 1831-1888 *BioIn 16, WhNaAH*
Sheridan, R. Champlin 1930- *St&PR 91*
Sheridan, Richard Bert 1918- *WhoAm 90, WhoWor 91*
Sheridan, Richard Brinsley 1751?-1816 *WorAlBi*
Sheridan, Sonia Landy 1925- *WhoAm 90, WhoAmA 91*
Sheridan, Sylvester R 1930- *BiDrAPA 89*
Sheridan, Teresa Weave 1959- *WhoAmW 91*
Sheridan, Thomas Brown 1929- *WhoAm 90*
Sheridan, Thomas R. *NewYTBS 90*
Sheridan, Thomas R. 1929-1990 *BioIn 16*
Sheridan, Timothy Philip 1954- *WhoEmL 91*
Sheridan, Virginia M. 1944- *ODwPR 91*
Sheridan, William Cockburn Russell 1917- *WhoAm 90*
Sheridan, William F 1922- *BiDrAPA 89*
Sherif, Muzafer 1905-1988 *BioIn 16*
Sheriff, Leonard S. 1915- *St&PR 91*
Sheriff, Linda Lepper 1954- *WhoAmW 91*
Sherifis, Michael Eleftheriou 1937- *WhoWor 91*
Sherin, Edwin 1930- *WhoAm 90*
Sherizen, Sanford Marvin 1940- *WhoE 91*
Sherk, Douglas M. 1956- *ODwPR 91*
Sherk, George William 1949- *WhoEmL 91*
Sherk, Louise G *BiDrAPA 89*
Sherkat, Reza *BiDrAPA 89*
Sherkow, Susan P *BiDrAPA 89*
Sherlaw-Johnson, Robert 1932- *IntWWM 90*
Sherling, Clive *BioIn 16*
Sherlock, Emmanell Phillips 1914- *WhoWor 91*
Sherlock, Michael J. 1937- *St&PR 91*
Sherlock, Peter Allen 1960- *St&PR 91*
Sherlock, Philip Manderson 1902- *AuBYP 90, BioIn 16*
Sherlock, Thomas Henry 1924- *WhoE 91*
Sherman, Alan M 1929- *BiDrAPA 89*
Sherman, Alec *PenDiMP*
Sherman, Allan 1924-1973 *AuBYP 90*
Sherman, Althea Rosina 1854-1943 *WomFie [port]*
Sherman, Arlene 1947- *WhoAmW 91*
Sherman, Arnold *St&PR 91*
Sherman, Arthur *BiDrAPA 89*
Sherman, Beatrice Ettinger 1919- *WhoAmW 91*
Sherman, C.L. 1931- *St&PR 91*
Sherman, Carl Leon 1945- *WhoEmL 91*
Sherman, Charles Daniel, Jr. 1920- *WhoAm 90*
Sherman, Charles Edwin 1934- *WhoAm 90*
Sherman, Cindy *BioIn 16*
Sherman, Cindy 1954- *CurBio 90 [port], WhoAm 90, WhoAmA 91*
Sherman, Claire Richter 1930- *WhoAmA 91*
Sherman, D. R. 1934- *BioIn 16*
Sherman, Dana 1953- *WhoEmL 91*
Sherman, Daniel Adam 1948- *BiDrAPA 89, WhoEmL 91*
Sherman, Daniel Michael 1950- *SpyFic*
Sherman, David 1952- *St&PR 91*
Sherman, David Robert 1952- *WhoEmL 91, WhoSSW 91, WhoWor 91*
Sherman, Dean J. 1956- *St&PR 91*
Sherman, Denis Ronald 1934- *BioIn 16*
Sherman, Edward Albert, III 1949- *WhoE 91*
Sherman, Elaine C. 1938- *WhoAm 90, WhoAmW 91*
Sherman, Elizabeth *AuBYP 90*
Sherman, Elizabeth Munves 1955- *St&PR 91*
Sherman, Ellen Ewing 1824-1888 *BioAmW*
Sherman, Ellen Finder *BiDrAPA 89*
Sherman, Ellen Neuwald *BioIn 16*
Sherman, Eugene Jay 1935- *WhoAm 90*
Sherman, Francis 1871-1926 *DcLB 92*
Sherman, Frank H. 1916- *St&PR 91*
Sherman, Fred 1932- *WhoAm 90*
Sherman, Fred S. 1932- *St&PR 91*
Sherman, George M. 1941- *WhoAm 90*
Sherman, Gerald Howard 1932- *WhoE 91*
Sherman, Gordon B. 1927-1987 *ConAmBL*
Sherman, Gordon Rae 1928- *WhoSSW 91*
Sherman, Greta Gail 1951- *WhoAmW 91*
Sherman, Harold 1898- *Ballpl 90*
Sherman, Harold 1898-1987 *EncO&P 3, EncPaPR 91*
Sherman, Harry W. 1930- *St&PR 91*
Sherman, Harry Walker 1930- *WhoSSW 91*
Sherman, Helen Bates 1919- *IntWWM 90*
Sherman, Henrietta Marie 1940- *WhoAmW 91*
Sherman, Hiram 1908-1989 *BioIn 16, ConTFT 8*
Sherman, Holly *ODwPR 91*
Sherman, Howard 1924- *St&PR 91*
Sherman, Howard Kevin 1956- *WhoAm 90*
Sherman, Howard Wig 1947- *St&PR 91*
Sherman, Irving C 1910- *BiDrAPA 89*
Sherman, Irwin William 1933- *WhoAm 90*
Sherman, J. Walter 1917- *St&PR 91*
Sherman, James Richard 1935- *WhoWrEP 89*
Sherman, James Schoolcraft 1855-1912 *BiDrUSE 89*
Sherman, Jane Ehlinger 1941- *WhoE 91*
Sherman, Jay 1958- *BiDrAPA 89*
Sherman, Jerry 1930- *ODwPR 91*
Sherman, Joe 1945- *WhoWrEP 89*
Sherman, John *BioIn 16*
Sherman, John 1823-1900 *BiDrUSE 89, BioIn 16, EncABHB 6 [port], WorAlBi*
Sherman, John, Jr. 1945- *WhoSSW 91*
Sherman, John C. 1932- *St&PR 91*
Sherman, John Clinton 1916- *WhoAm 90*
Sherman, John Foord 1919- *WhoAm 90*
Sherman, John K 1898-1969 *WhoAmA 91N*
Sherman, Jonathan Goodhue 1907-1989 *BioIn 16*
Sherman, Joyce Chestang 1946- *WhoAmW 91*
Sherman, Judith Myers 1944- *BiDrAPA 89*
Sherman, Julius Rahn, Jr. *BiDrAPA 89*
Sherman, Kenneth Charles 1944- *St&PR 91*
Sherman, Kenneth Newton 1958- *WhoEmL 91*
Sherman, Lawrence Charles 1957- *WhoEmL 91*
Sherman, Lawrence M. 1940- *WhoAm 90*
Sherman, Lawrence Yates 1858-1939 *AmLegL*
Sherman, Lee M. 1947- *St&PR 91*
Sherman, Lenore 1920- *WhoAmA 91*
Sherman, Lenore Shustak 1956- *WhoEmL 91*
Sherman, Loretta Sue 1946- *WhoAmW 91*
Sherman, Malcolm Lee 1931- *St&PR 91*
Sherman, Marion Eleanor *BiDrAPA 89*
Sherman, Mark A. 1951- *St&PR 91*
Sherman, Mark Alan 1951- *WhoE 91*
Sherman, Martin 1920- *WhoAm 90*
Sherman, Marvin 1925- *BiDrAPA 89*
Sherman, Mary Angus 1937- *WhoAmW 91*
Sherman, Max Ray 1935- *WhoAm 90*
Sherman, Michael H. 1935- *St&PR 91*
Sherman, Michael Henry 1950- *BiDrAPA 89*
Sherman, Michael Paul 1952- *WhoAm 90*
Sherman, Michael Stuart 1947- *WhoAm 90*
Sherman, Mike 1957- *WhoEmL 91*
Sherman, Mildred Mozelle Clark 1932- *IntWWM 90*
Sherman, Miriam *BiDrAPA 89*
Sherman, Nancy *AuBYP 90*
Sherman, Nat *BioIn 16, NewYTBS 90 [port]*
Sherman, Nathan H. 1898?-1980 *ConAmBL*
Sherman, Neil E. 1942- *St&PR 91*
Sherman, Norman Mark 1948- *WhoAm 90*
Sherman, Patsy O'Connell 1930- *WhoAmW 91*
Sherman, Philip D. 1941- *St&PR 91*
Sherman, R. J. 1934- *ODwPR 91*
Sherman, Richard Beatty 1929- *WhoSSW 91*
Sherman, Richard Freeman 1943- *St&PR 91*
Sherman, Richard L. 1929- *ODwPR 91*
Sherman, Richard M. 1928- *OxCPMus*
Sherman, Richard Max 1940- *St&PR 91*
Sherman, Robert 1950- *WhoEmL 91, WhoWor 91*
Sherman, Robert A. 1942- *St&PR 91, WhoE 91*
Sherman, Robert B. 1925- *OxCPMus*
Sherman, Robert Bernard 1925- *WhoAm 90*
Sherman, Robert Frank 1943- *WhoAm 90*
Sherman, Robert Irving 1923- *St&PR 91*
Sherman, Robert Lee 1929- *BiDrAPA 89*
Sherman, Robert Marc 1954- *WhoSSW 91*
Sherman, Robert Martin 1949- *WhoE 91*
Sherman, Robert Stuart 1939- *WhoSSW 91*
Sherman, Robert T. 1937- *WhoWrEP 89*
Sherman, Roger 1721-1793 *BioIn 16, EncCRAm [port], WorAlBi*
Sherman, Roger 1930- *WhoAm 90*
Sherman, Roger D 1915- *BiDrAPA 89*
Sherman, Roger E. 1934- *St&PR 91*
Sherman, Roger Talbot 1923- *WhoAm 90*
Sherman, Roger William 1938- *BiDrAPA 89*
Sherman, Ronald K. *BioIn 16*
Sherman, Russell 1930- *BioIn 16*
Sherman, Sarai 1922- *WhoAmA 91*
Sherman, Saul Lawrence 1926- *WhoAm 90, WhoWor 91*
Sherman, Scott 1954- *St&PR 91*
Sherman, Scott Bradley 1954- *WhoSSW 91*
Sherman, Sharon *ODwPR 91*
Sherman, Steve Barry 1938- *WhoWrEP 89*
Sherman, T.J. 1906- *St&PR 91*
Sherman, Theodore I. 1926- *St&PR 91*
Sherman, Thomas George 1947- *BiDrAPA 89*
Sherman, Thomas White 1940- *St&PR 91*
Sherman, William Courtney 1923- *WhoAm 90*
Sherman, William D *BiDrAPA 89*
Sherman, William David 1940- *WhoWrEP 89*
Sherman, William H. 1915- *St&PR 91*
Sherman, William T. 1820-1891 *BioIn 16*
Sherman, William Tecumseh 1820-1891 *BiDrUSE 89, EncABHB 6 [port], WhNaAH, WorAlBi*
Sherman, Z Charlotte *WhoAmA 91*
Sherman-Appel, Lori Rae 1955- *WhoAmW 91*
Sherman-Bircher, Ruth Faye 1956- *WhoSSW 91*
Shermoen, Richard Eugene 1930- *WhoAm 90*
Shern, Stephanie Marie 1948- *WhoAmW 91*
Sherner, Stephen D. 1950- *St&PR 91*
Shero, Fred *NewYTBS 90 [port]*
Sheronas, Victor F., Jr. 1941- *St&PR 91*
Sherouse, Elizabeth *BioIn 16*
Sherover-Marcuse, Erica *BioIn 16*
Sherowitz-Sheny, Phyllis J. 1953- *WhoAmW 91*
Sherowski, Henry John 1942- *St&PR 91*
Sherr, Paul E. 1933- *St&PR 91*
Sherr, Paul Edgar 1933- *WhoE 91*
Sherr, Richard Jonathan 1947- *IntWWM 90*
Sherr, Ronald Norman 1952- *WhoAmA 91*
Sherr, Sol 1918- *WhoWor 91*
Sherr, Virginia T 1931- *BiDrAPA 89*
Sherratt, Gerald Robert 1931- *WhoAm 90, WhoWor 91*
Sherratt, Hamlet *PenDiDA 89*
Sherratt, Martha *PenDiDA 89*
Sherratt, Obadiah *PenDiDA 89*
Sherren, Anne Terry 1936- *WhoAmW 91, WhoWor 91*
Sherrer, Charles David 1935- *WhoAm 90*
Sherrer, Dorothy White *BiDrAPA 89*
Sherrer, James Wylie 1935- *St&PR 91*
Sherrerd, John J.F. 1930- *St&PR 91*
Sherrick, Daniel N. 1929- *St&PR 91*
Sherrick, Daniel Noah 1929- *WhoAm 90, WhoSSW 91, WhoWor 91*
Sherriffs, Ronald Everett 1934- *WhoAm 90*
Sherril, Joya *DrBlPA 90*
Sherrill, Betty *BioIn 16*
Sherrill, Fred Lee, Jr. 1934- *St&PR 91*
Sherrill, Hugh Virgil 1920- *St&PR 91, WhoAm 90*
Sherrill, J. Stevens 1853- *AmLegL*
Sherrill, Jackie *BioIn 16*
Sherrill, Joseph H., Jr. 1941- *St&PR 91*
Sherrill, Joseph Newton, Jr. 1929- *St&PR 91*
Sherrill, Kimberly Ann *BiDrAPA 89*
Sherrill, Milton Lewis 1949- *WhoAmA 91*
Sherrill, Nancy Lee 1966- *WhoEmL 91*
Sherrill, Richard C. 1938- *St&PR 91*
Sherrill, Thomas Boykin, III 1930- *WhoAm 90, WhoWor 91*
Sherrington, Charles S. 1857-1952 *WorAlBi*
Sherrington, Paul William 1949- *WhoSSW 91*
Sherrod, Donna Louise 1962- *WhoAmW 91*
Sherrod, Gerald E. 1922- *St&PR 91*
Sherrod, Hilton Byron 1949- *WhoSSW 91*
Sherrod, Philip Lawrence 1935- *WhoAmA 91, WhoE 91*
Sherrod, Robert Lee 1909- *WhoAm 90*
Sherron, Walter Frederick 1931- *St&PR 91*
Sherry, Charles William 1929- *St&PR 91*
Sherry, Donald Lee 1953- *BiDrAPA 89*
Sherry, George Leon 1924- *WhoAm 90, WhoWor 91*
Sherry, James Terence 1946- *WhoE 91, WhoWrEP 89*
Sherry, John Ernest Horwath 1932- *WhoAm 90*
Sherry, John Sebastian 1946- *WhoEmL 91*
Sherry, Kathleen Susan 1954- *WhoAmW 91*
Sherry, Larry 1935- *Ballpl 90*
Sherry, Lee 1948- *WhoSSW 91*
Sherry, Norman 1935- *WhoWor 91*
Sherry, Owen Edward 1918- *St&PR 91*
Sherry, Robert 1943- *WhoSSW 91*
Sherry, Sol 1916- *WhoAm 90*
Sherry, Susan Theresa 1952- *WhoAmW 91*
Sherry, Sylvia *AuBYP 90*
Sherry, William Grant 1914- *WhoAmA 91*
Sherry, William James 1899- *WhoAm 90*
Shershin, Carmen Baytan 1944- *WhoSSW 91*
Shershow, John C 1940- *BiDrAPA 89*
Shershow, John Cutler 1940- *WhoE 91*
Shershow, Lee Wolfe 1942- *BiDrAPA 89*
Shertzer, Bruce Eldon 1928- *WhoAm 90*
Shertzer, Ronald Robert 1941- *WhoSSW 91*
Sherva, Dennis G. 1942- *WhoAm 90*
Shervette, Robert Edward, III *BiDrAPA 89*
Shervheim, Lloyd Oliver 1928- *WhoAm 90*
Shervington, Denese O *BiDrAPA 89*
Shervington, Walter W 1937- *BiDrAPA 89*
Sherwan, Roy Glenn 1930- *WhoWor 91*
Sherwin, Chalmers William 1916- *WhoAm 90*

Sherwin, Duane Oliver *BiDrAPA 89*
Sherwin, George Rhodes 1941- *St&PR 91*
Sherwin, Gilda L 1950- *BiDrAPA 89*
Sherwin, James Leland 1950- *WhoWrEP 89*
Sherwin, James T. 1933- *St&PR 91*
Sherwin, James Terry 1933- *WhoAm 90*
Sherwin, Jonathan S. 1951- *St&PR 91*
Sherwin, Judith Johnson *WhoWrEP 89*
Sherwin, Manning 1902-1974 *OxCPMus*
Sherwin, Michael Dennis 1939- *WhoAm 90*
Sherwin, Richard P. 1948- *St&PR 91*
Sherwin, Richard S *BiDrAPA 89*
Sherwin, Richard Scott 1954- *WhoE 91*
Sherwinter, Julius 1947- *WhoSSW 91*
Sherwood family *BioIn 16*
Sherwood, Aaron Wiley 1915- *WhoAm 90*
Sherwood, Allen Joseph 1909- *WhoAm 90*
Sherwood, Ann *BiDEWW*
Sherwood, Bette Wilson 1920- *WhoAm 90, WhoWor 91*
Sherwood, Carlton M 1895- *EncO&P 3*
Sherwood, Charles D. *AmLegL*
Sherwood, Don Hugh 1935- *WhoAm 90*
Sherwood, Donald 1901- *St&PR 91*
Sherwood, Edward Charles 1941- *WhoSSW 91*
Sherwood, Evelyn Ruth 1929- *WhoWrEP 89*
Sherwood, George Kenneth 1939- *St&PR 91*
Sherwood, George R. 1939- *St&PR 91*
Sherwood, Gretchen Wieting 1953- *WhoEmL 91*
Sherwood, James Blair 1933- *St&PR 91, WhoAm 90, WhoWor 91*
Sherwood, John 1913- *TwCCr&M 91*
Sherwood, Katherine 1952- *WhoAmA 91*
Sherwood, Keith R. 1944- *St&PR 91*
Sherwood, Kenneth N. *BioIn 16*
Sherwood, Kenneth Parker, Jr. 1945- *WhoE 91*
Sherwood, Lawrence B. 1945- *St&PR 91*
Sherwood, Leona *WhoAmA 91*
Sherwood, Louis 1941- *WhoAm 90*
Sherwood, Louis Maier 1937- *WhoAm 90*
Sherwood, Malcolm Harvey, Jr. 1930- *St&PR 91*
Sherwood, Marcia 1944- *ODwPR 91*
Sherwood, Martha 1775-1851 *BioIn 16*
Sherwood, Mary Martha 1775-1851 *FemiCLE*
Sherwood, Midge *WhoAmW 91*
Sherwood, Paul M *BiDrAPA 89*
Sherwood, Rhonda Griffin 1953- *WhoSSW 91*
Sherwood, Richard Edwin 1928- *WhoAm 90*
Sherwood, Robert 1896-1955 *WorAlBi*
Sherwood, Rosina 1854-1948 *BiDWomA*
Sherwood, Rosina Emmet 1854-1948 *WhoAmA 91N*
Sherwood, Sam C., Jr. 1923- *St&PR 91*
Sherwood, Sheila Primps 1959- *ODwPR 91*
Sherwood, Sherry 1902- *WhoAmA 91N*
Sherwood, Thomas Anderson 1942- *St&PR 91*
Sherwood, Thorne 1910- *WhoAm 90*
Sherwood, William Anderson 1875-1951 *WhoAmA 91N*
Shess, Phyllis A. 1948- *ODwPR 91*
Shestack, Alan *BioIn 16*
Shestack, Alan 1938- *WhoAm 90, WhoAmA 91, WhoE 91, WhoWor 91*
Shestack, Jerome Joseph 1925- *WhoAm 90, WhoE 91, WhoWor 91*
Shestack, Melvin Bernard 1931- *WhoAm 90, WhoWrEP 89*
Shester, Alexander A *BiDrAPA 89*
Shestokas, Jill Barbara 1955- *WhoEmL 91*
Sheth, Aruna *BiDrAPA 89*
Sheth, Atul Kumar *BiDrAPA 89*
Sheth, Jagdish Nanchand 1938- *WhoAm 90*
Sheth, Kokila K 1942- *BiDrAPA 89*
Sheth, Nila Amarish *BiDrAPA 89*
Sheth, Nila Amarish 1946- *WhoE 91*
Sheth, Nitin Vasantrai 1955- *BiDrAPA 89*
Sheth, Sarvajna C *BiDrAPA 89*
Shettar, Shashidhar M. 1955- *BiDrAPA 89*
Shettel, Patricia Frances 1934- *WhoAmW 91, WhoE 91*
Shetterly, Robert Browne 1915- *WhoAm 90*
Shetterly, William Howard 1955- *WhoWrEP 89*
Shettle, George Payson *BioIn 16*
Shettles, Landrum Brewer 1909- *WhoAm 90*
Shettsline, Bill 1863-1933 *Ballpl 90*
Shetty, Jayaprakash B *BiDrAPA 89*
Shetty, M. Shankara 1945- *WhoEmL 91*
Shetty, Mulki Radhakrishna 1940- *WhoWor 91*
Shetty, Taranath 1938- *WhoWor 91*
Shetty, Udaya Kumar *BiDrAPA 89*
Shetty, Yeshwanthi *BiDrAPA 89*
Shetty, Yolan Lee 1948- *WhoAmW 91*
Sheuerman, Arnold A, Jr. 1922- *BiDrAPA 89*
Shev, Eleanor Upton Brown- 1924-1989 *BioIn 16*
Shevack, Brett David 1950- *WhoAm 90*
Shevardnadze, Eduard *BioIn 16*
Shevardnadze, Eduard 1928- *WorAlBi*
Shevardnadze, Eduard Amvrosiyevich 1928- *WhoWor 91*
Shevchenko, A. N. *ConAu 129*
Shevchenko, Arkady N 1930- *ConAu 129*
Shevchenko, T. H. 1814-1861 *BioIn 16*
Shevchenko, Taras Hryhorovych 1814-1861 *BioIn 16*
Shevchenko, Valentina Semenovna 1935- *WhoWor 91*
Shevchuck, Harry 1924- *WhoE 91*
Shevel, W. Lee 1932- *St&PR 91*
Shevel, Wilbert Lee 1932- *WhoAm 90*
Shevell, Nancy Ellen 1930- *WhoAmW 91*
Sheviak, Margaret 1911-1989 *BioIn 16*
Shevin, David A. 1951- *WhoWrEP 89*
Shevin, Frederick F 1921- *BiDrAPA 89*
Shevin, Robert Lewis 1934- *WhoAm 90*
Shevitz, Stewart Allen 1945- *BiDrAPA 89*
Shevlin, Robert A. 1960- *St&PR 91*
Shevoroshkin, Vitaly 1932- *WhoAm 90*
Shevrin, Aliza 1931- *ConAu 129*
Shew, Anita Kramer 1944- *WhoAmW 91*
Shew, Harold Allen 1935- *St&PR 91*
Shew, Louis Glen 1932- *St&PR 91*
Shewach, Melvin David 1941- *WhoAm 90*
Shewan, James MacKay 1909-1988 *BioIn 16*
Sheward, Jerry Edward *BiDrAPA 89*
Sheward, Michael C. 1951- *ODwPR 91*
Shewbridge, Deborah Kay 1963- *WhoSSW 91*
Shewchuk, Robert John 1950- *WhoE 91*
Shewhart, Walter Andrew 1891-1967 *DcScB S2*
Shewmake, C.B. 1916- *St&PR 91*
Shewmaker, Jack C. *BioIn 16*
Shewmaker, Jack Clifford 1938- *WhoAm 90*
Shewmon, Paul Griffith 1930- *WhoAm 90*
Shewring, Walter Hayward 1906?-1990 *ConAu 132*
Shey, Jane Elizabeth 1956- *WhoAmW 91*
Shey, Kenneth Robert 1954- *WhoSSW 91*
Sheya *WhoAmA 91*
Shi Fong 1942- *WhoAm 90*
Shi Guoliang *BioIn 16*
Shi, Nansun *BioIn 16*
Shi, Peipu *BioIn 16*
Shiach, Allan G. *BioIn 16*
Shiba, Ellen Keller Moore *BioIn 16*
Shibad, Prabhakar Ramanath 1934- *WhoWor 91*
Shibano, Yuuko *BiDrAPA 89*
Shibata, Akikazu 1935- *WhoWor 91*
Shibata, Heki 1931- *WhoWor 91*
Shibata, Hirofumi 1929- *WhoWor 91*
Shibayama, Kimio 1919- *WhoWor 91*
Shibazaki, Kikuo 1928- *WhoWor 91*
Shibley, George E. *BioIn 16*
Shibley, Gertrude *WhoAmA 91*
Shibley, Raymond Nadeem 1925- *WhoAm 90*
Shibley, Robert Gordon 1946- *WhoAm 90*
Shibli, Mohammed Abdullah 1952- *WhoE 91*
Shibue, Io 1816-1884 *BioIn 16*
Shibuya, Hironobi 1946- *WhoE 91*
Shibuya, Hironobu *ODwPR 91*
Shick, Bradley Ullin 1956- *WhoE 91*
Shick, Eloise K. 1950- *WhoWrEP 89*
Shick, J Fred E 1944- *BiDrAPA 89*
Shick, Richard Arlon 1943- *WhoE 91*
Shickshack *WhNaAH*
Shicoff, Neil 1949- *IntWWM 90*
Shidehara Kijuro 1872-1951 *EncJap*
Shidehara, Francesco Eichi 1935- *WhoWor 91*
Shideler, Howard H. 1932- *St&PR 91*
Shideler, Ross *AuBYP 90*
Shideler, Ross Patrick 1936- *WhoAm 90, WhoWrEP 89*
Shideler, Shirley Ann Williams 1930- *WhoAm 90*
Shiel, M P 1865-1947 *TwCCr&M 91*
Shiel, Thomas William 1941- *WhoE 91*
Shiel, William A. 1950- *St&PR 91*
Shield, James Asa, Jr. 1938- *BiDrAPA 89*
Shield, Joel David 1949- *BiDrAPA 89*
Shield, Lansing P. 1896-1960 *WorAlBi*
Shield, Paul Harold 1942- *BiDrAPA 89, WhoE 91*
Shield, Richard Thorpe 1929- *WhoAm 90*
Shield, William 1748-1829 *OxCPMus*
Shields, Alan J 1944- *WhoAmA 91, WhoE 91*
Shields, Alison R. 1964- *WhoAmW 91*
Shields, Allan Edwin 1919- *WhoAm 90*
Shields, Andre De 1946- *DrBlPA 90*
Shields, Anne Kesler 1932- *WhoAmA 91*
Shields, Anthony Frank 1952- *WhoEmL 91*
Shields, Brooke *BioIn 16*
Shields, Brooke 1965- *WorAlBi*
Shields, Brooke Christa Camille 1965- *WhoAm 90*
Shields, Carol 1935- *FemiCLE*
Shields, David J. 1956- *WhoWrEP 89*
Shields, Del *BioIn 16*
Shields, Ella 1879-1952 *OxCPMus*
Shields, Frank Cox 1944- *WhoWor 91*
Shields, George W. 1951- *WhoSSW 91*
Shields, Gerald N. 1937- *St&PR 91*
Shields, Gordon Adams 1957- *WhoEmL 91*
Shields, H. Richard *WhoAm 90*
Shields, Hal Cline 1933- *WhoSSW 91*
Shields, J. Hugh *St&PR 91*
Shields, James P. 1947- *St&PR 91*
Shields, James William 1915- *St&PR 91*
Shields, Janis Darlene 1957- *WhoAmW 91, WhoEmL 91*
Shields, Jeffrey Patrick 1951- *St&PR 91*
Shields, Jerry *ODwPR 91*
Shields, John C 1921- *BiDrAPA 89*
Shields, John Dillard, Jr. 1946- *WhoSSW 91*
Shields, John Joseph 1938- *St&PR 91, WhoAm 90*
Shields, John Russell 1953- *WhoSSW 91*
Shields, Joyce Lee 1942- *WhoE 91*
Shields, Karena *AuBYP 90*
Shields, Laura Aull *WhoAmW 91*
Shields, Laurie *BioIn 16*
Shields, Lawrence Thornton 1935- *WhoE 91, WhoWor 91*
Shields, Louis P. 1943- *St&PR 91*
Shields, Mary 1955- *WhoAmW 91*
Shields, Molly T. 1961- *WhoAmW 91*
Shields, Nancy Claire 1925- *WhoAmW 91*
Shields, Paul Keith 1949- *WhoSSW 91*
Shields, Ren 1868-1913 *OxCPMus*
Shields, Richard Lee 1955- *WhoSSW 91*
Shields, Rita *AuBYP 90*
Shields, Robert Emmet 1942- *WhoAm 90*
Shields, Robert Michael 1952- *WhoE 91*
Shields, Roger Elwood 1939- *WhoE 91*
Shields, Roy B. 1931- *St&PR 91*
Shields, Steve 1958- *Ballpl 90*
Shields, Tamara West-O'Kelley 1948- *WhoAmW 91*
Shields, Terrell Michael 1954- *WhoSSW 91*
Shields, Thomas Charles 1941- *WhoAm 90*
Shields, Thomas E. 1931- *St&PR 91*
Shields, Thomas Todhunter 1873-1955 *BioIn 16*
Shields, Thomas William 1922- *WhoAm 90*
Shields, Walker Edmund, Jr. 1940- *BiDrAPA 89*
Shields, Walter A. *BioIn 16*
Shields, Walter W. 1935- *WhoWor 91*
Shields, William A., III 1948- *WhoAm 90*
Shields, William M. 1937- *St&PR 91*
Shields, William Maurice 1937- *WhoAm 90*
Shiell, Jerome A 1919- *BiDrAPA 89*
Shiell, John A. 1919- *St&PR 91*
Shielly, Barbara 1944- *St&PR 91*
Shiels, Barbara 1943- *SmATA X [port]*
Shiels, John Morse 1937- *WhoE 91*
Shiels, Robert John 1927- *St&PR 91*
Shiels, Tony *EncO&P 3*
Shiely, J.L., Jr. 1914- *St&PR 91*
Shiely, John Stephen 1952- *WhoAm 90*
Shiely, Joseph Leo, III 1941- *St&PR 91*
Shiener, Gerald Alan 1949- *BiDrAPA 89*
Shientag, Florence Perlow *WhoAm 90*
Shier, Jerome B. 1918- *St&PR 91*
Shier, John Wellington 1923- *St&PR 91*
Shier, Jonathan Fraser 1947- *WhoWor 91*
Shier, Milton 1917- *St&PR 91*
Shierk, Catherine Kim 1956- *WhoAmW 91*
Shierry, Robert Stephen 1932- *St&PR 91*
Shiffer, James David 1938- *St&PR 91, WhoAm 90*
Shiffler, Neil Frederick 1922- *WhoAm 90*
Shiffman, Bernard 1942- *WhoAm 90, WhoE 91*
Shiffman, Bernard M. *BioIn 16*
Shiffrin, Alan Lewis 1947- *BiDrAPA 89*
Shiflet, Donald L. 1947- *St&PR 91*
Shiflett, David *BioIn 16*
Shiflett, Wilma Jean 1942- *WhoSSW 91*
Shifley, Ralph Louis 1910- *WhoAm 90*
Shifrin, Bruce Carl 1947- *WhoEmL 91*
Shifrin, Kenneth Steven 1949- *St&PR 91*
Shifter, Michael Evan 1955- *WhoE 91*
Shigemitsu, Takeo *BioIn 16*
Shigemura, Rose Kamuri *St&PR 91*
Shigemura, Thomas S. *St&PR 91*
Shigenaka, Yoshinobu 1932- *WhoWor 91*
Shigeru, Mori 1937- *St&PR 91*
Shigeta, James 1933- *ConTFT 8*
Shigley, Klaus O. 1945- *St&PR 91*
Shih Huang Ti 259?BC-210BC *WorAlBi*
Shih, Chi-Yang 1935- *WhoWor 91*
Shih, Helen 1953- *WhoAmW 91*
Shih, J. Chung-wen *WhoAm 90*
Shih, Jason Cheng 1942- *WhoSSW 91*
Shih, Joan Chung-Wen *WhoWrEP 89*
Shih, Joan Fai *WhoAmA 91*
Shih, Joan Fai 1932- *WhoAmW 91*
Shih, Ping-Wen 1939- *BiDrAPA 89*
Shih, Stan *BioIn 16*
Shih, Symong 1950- *WhoSSW 91*
Shih, Tom I-Ping 1952- *WhoE 91*
Shih Carducci, Joan Chia-mo 1933- *WhoAmW 91, WhoE 91, WhoWor 91*
Shihata, Ibrahim Fahmy Ibrahim 1937- *WhoAm 90*
Shiina, Motto *BioIn 16*
Shikallamy *WhNaAH*
Shikanai, Nobutaka 1911-1990 *NewYTBS 90 [port]*
Shikelimo *WhNaAH*
Shikellamy *EncCRAm, WhNaAH*
Shikellemus *WhNaAH*
Shikellima *WhNaAH*
Shikellimy *WhNaAH*
Shikhverg, Valery *BiDrAPA 89*
Shiki 1867-1902 *BioIn 16*
Shikiba, Satoshi 1926- *BiDrAPA 89*
Shikiko, Saitoh 1944- *WhoWor 91*
Shikler, Aaron 1922- *WhoAm 90, WhoAmA 91*
Shildneck, Barbara Jean 1937- *WhoAm 90, WhoAmW 91*
Shilepsky, Arnold Charles 1944- *WhoE 91*
Shilinis, Natasha V. 1926- *WhoAmW 91*
Shill, John Kevin *BiDrAPA 89*
Shilladey, Ann 1933- *WhoAmW 91*
Shillea, Thomas John 1947- *WhoAmA 91*
Shillestad, John G. 1934- *St&PR 91*
Shillestad, John Gardner 1934- *WhoAm 90*
Shilling, Donnie Wayne 1946- *St&PR 91*
Shilling, Eric 1920- *IntWWM 90, PenDiMP*
Shilling, Kay Marlene 1953- *BiDrAPA 89, WhoAmW 91*
Shilling, Maurice *BiDrAPA 89*
Shilling, Roy Bryant, Jr. 1931- *WhoAm 90*
Shillingburg, Patricia Moser 1943- *WhoAmW 91*
Shillinglaw, Gordon 1925- *WhoAm 90*
Shillingsburg, Miriam J. *ConAu 130*
Shillingsburg, Miriam Jones 1943- *ConAu 130, WhoAmW 91*
Shillito, Barry James 1921- *St&PR 91*
Shiloh, Adam 1933- *St&PR 91*
Shiloh, Yigal 1937-1987 *BioIn 16*
Shils, Edward B. 1915- *WhoAm 90*
Shilson, Wayne Stuart 1943- *WhoAmA 91*
Shilstone, Sandra Sciacca 1956- *WhoAmW 91*
Shilts, Randy *BioIn 16*
Shim, Dong Yup 1941- *BiDrAPA 89*
Shim, Eunshil 1952- *WhoAmW 91*
Shim, Jae Yong 1939- *BiDrAPA 89*
Shim, S Christopher *BiDrAPA 89*
Shim, Sang Koo 1942- *WhoWor 91*
Shim, Ui-Sup 1944- *WhoWor 91*
Shima, Richard John 1939- *St&PR 91, WhoAm 90*
Shimada, Hitomi 1946- *WhoWor 91*
Shimada, Linda Michi 1963- *WhoAmW 91*
Shimada, Tomiko 1932- *WhoAmW 91*
Shimasaki, Lynn Mitsugi 1953- *St&PR 91*
Shimazu Clan *EncJap*
Shimazu, Kiyonobu 1946- *WhoWor 91*
Shimazu, Takashi 1948- *St&PR 91*
Shimberg, Elaine Fantle 1937- *ConAu 31NR*
Shimeall, Warren Glen 1925- *WhoWor 91*
Shimeda, Takashi 1958- *IntWWM 90*
Shimek, Ronald Lee 1948- *WhoEmL 91*
Shimell, William 1952- *IntWWM 90*
Shimelman, Myer Morris 1942- *BiDrAPA 89*
Shimer, Alice Marie 1926- *WhoE 91*
Shimer, Dale J. 1935- *St&PR 91*
Shimer, Daniel Lewis 1944- *WhoAm 90, WhoWor 91*
Shimer, Zachary 1933- *WhoAm 90*
Shimizu, Akira 1933- *St&PR 91*
Shimizu, Keiichi 1936- *WhoWor 91*
Shimizu, Masahiro 1939- *St&PR 91*
Shimizu, Norihiko 1940- *WhoWor 91*
Shimizu, P.H. *St&PR 91*
Shimizu, Takashi 1953- *IntWWM 90*
Shimizu, Yoshiaki 1936- *WhoAm 90, WhoAmA 91, WhoE 91*
Shimizu, Yoshifusa 1929- *WhoWor 91*
Shimkin, Demitri Boris 1916- *WhoAm 90*
Shimkin, Leon 1907-1988 *BioIn 16*
Shimkin, Michael B. 1912-1989 *BioIn 16*
Shimkos, P. Dan 1949- *St&PR 91*
Shimkus, Cathy *BioIn 16*
Shimm, Cynia Brown 1926- *BiDrAPA 89*
Shimm, Melvin Gerald 1926- *WhoAm 90*
Shimm, Stephen Jay *BiDrAPA 89*
Shimmel, Stephen Miller 1952- *WhoSSW 91*
Shimmin, Kathleen Grace 1939- *WhoAmW 91*

Shimoda, Karen McAlister 1951- WhoE 91
Shimoda, Osamu 1924- WhoAmA 91
Shimoff, Paul Martin 1947- WhoEmL 91
Shimohsa, Tadayoshi 1924- WhoWor 91
Shimoji, Koki 1935- WhoWor 91
Shimomura, Roger Yutaka 1939- WhoAmA 91
Shimotsu, Gary Rikikazu 1961- WhoEmL 91
Shimp, Karen Ann 1959- WhoAmW 91
Shimp, Richard Lee 1942- WhoSSW 91, WhoWor 91
Shimp, Robert Everett, Jr. 1942- WhoAm 90
Shimpi, Snehal A BiDrAPA 89
Shimrat, Niusia NewYTBS 90
Shin, Anthony BiDrAPA 89
Shin, Hyun Chan 1939- BiDrAPA 89
Shin, Ji Jae BiDrAPA 89
Shin, Kwang Shik 1954- WhoWor 91
Shin, Kyun BiDrAPA 89
Shin, Kyung-Joon BiDrAPA 89
Shin, Margaret K 1940- BiDrAPA 89
Shin, So Yung 1941- BiDrAPA 89
Shin, Yong Ae Im 1932- WhoAmW 91
Shin, Yong Shik BiDrAPA 89
Shin, Young J BiDrAPA 89
Shin-Zoulek, Yoon Sook 1946- WhoWor 91
Shinabarger, Bruce Winter 1925- St&PR 91
Shinagel, Fred 1931- St&PR 91
Shinagel, Michael 1934- WhoAm 90
Shinal, Frank A. 1940- St&PR 91
Shinall, Robert Phillip, III 1947- WhoEmL 91
Shinbach, Kent D BiDrAPA 89
Shindell, Sidney 1923- WhoAm 90
Shindelman, Laurence Stephen 1942- BiDrAPA 89
Shinderman, Marc S BiDrAPA 89
Shindler, Colin 1946- WhoWor 91
Shindler, Elaine Rosalie G. 1934- WhoAm 90, WhoAmW 91
Shindler, George Rudolph 1935- St&PR 91
Shindler, Steven Hunt 1954- WhoEmL 91
Shindo, Kaneto 1912- BioIn 16
Shine, Bonnie BioIn 16
Shine, James Patrick 1932- St&PR 91
Shine, John 1946- WhoWor 91
Shine, John T. 1935- St&PR 91
Shine, Kevin Z. 1955- St&PR 91
Shine, Neal James 1930- WhoAm 90
Shine, Richard Patrick 1951- WhoEmL 91, WhoSSW 91
Shine, Ted 1936- DrBlPA 90
Shine, William Walter 1925- WhoAm 90
Shinebourne, Jan 1947- FemiCLE
Shinefield, Henry Robert 1925- WhoAm 90
Shineman, Edward W., Jr. 1915- St&PR 91
Shiner, Farley C. 1956- St&PR 91
Shiner, Joel L. 1919-1988 BioIn 16
Shiner, Robert Lawrence, Jr. 1936- St&PR 91
Shiney, Richard Delmar 1929- St&PR 91
Shingaba W'ossin WhNaAH
Shingabawassin WhNaAH
Shingledecker, Jane Ann 1963- WhoAmW 91
Shingleton, Davis Hall 1951- BiDrAPA 89
Shingleton, Hugh Maurice 1931- WhoAm 90
Shingo, Shigeo NewYTBS 90
Shinholser, Ray BioIn 16
Shinichi, Kano ConAu 132
Shinjo, Yasuhito 1937- St&PR 91
Shinkaretsky, Victor BioIn 16
Shinker, William M. 1947- St&PR 91
Shinkin Ap Shone BiDEWW
Shinkoda, Austin Tatsumi BiDrAPA 89
Shinn, Allen Mayhew 1908- WhoAm 90
Shinn, Arthur Frederick 1945- WhoEmL 91, WhoWor 91
Shinn, Bonner L 1919- BiDrAPA 89
Shinn, Clinton Wesley 1947- WhoEmL 91, WhoSSW 91, WhoWor 91
Shinn, David Hamilton 1940- WhoAm 90, WhoWor 91
Shinn, Douglas Brian 1957- St&PR 91
Shinn, Duane 1938- WhoWrEP 89
Shinn, Elliott T BiDrAPA 89
Shinn, Everett 1876-1953 WhoAmA 91N
Shinn, Frances Miller 1942- WhoAmW 91
Shinn, George BioIn 16, WhoAm 90
Shinn, George L. 1923- St&PR 91
Shinn, George Latimer 1923- WhoAm 90
Shinn, Jim BioIn 16
Shinn, Linda J. 1948- WhoAmW 91
Shinn, Michael Robert 1947- WhoEmL 91, WhoWor 91
Shinn, Richard R. 1918- St&PR 91
Shinn, Richard Randolph 1918- WhoAm 90
Shinn, Susa Jane 1940- WhoAmW 91
Shinn, Walter C. 1854- BioIn 16
Shinn, William Townsley, Jr. 1936- WhoAm 90
Shinnar, Reuel 1923- WhoAm 90
Shinners, Edward M. 1930- St&PR 91
Shinners, Jeffrey G. 1941- St&PR 91
Shinners, Stanley Marvin 1933- WhoAm 90
Shinoda, Masahiro BioIn 16
Shinoda, Masahiro 1931- WhoWor 91
Shinohara, Mutsuharu BioIn 16
Shinohara, Soichi 1945- WhoWor 91
Shinozaki, Akihiko 1927- St&PR 91
Shinozuka, Masanobu 1930- WhoAm 90, WhoWor 91
Shinpoch, Jan Willa 1953- WhoAmW 91
Shinran 1173-1263 EncJap
Shinsato, Francis G. 1951- St&PR 91
Shinto, Hisashi BioIn 16
Shinwell, Emanuel 1884-1986 BioIn 16
Shiokawa, Yoshito 1931- WhoWor 91
Shiota, Kunihiro 1937- WhoWor 91
Shiovitz, Thomas Merrill 1957- BiDrAPA 89
Shioya, Mitsuo 1929- WhoWor 91
Ship, Arthur George 1928- WhoE 91
Shipe, Don 1933- St&PR 91
Shipe, Jerry Miller 1944- St&PR 91
Shipe, Valerie A. 1943- St&PR 91
Shipko, Mary Bush 1949- WhoSSW 91
Shipko, Stuart Lee 1954- BiDrAPA 89
Shipler, David Karr 1942- WhoAm 90, WhoWrEP 89
Shiplett, June Elizabeth Lund 1930- WhoWrEP 89
Shipley, Alice Mildred 1927- WhoAmW 91
Shipley, David Elliott 1950- WhoSSW 91
Shipley, David L. BioIn 16
Shipley, Edward C BiDrAPA 89
Shipley, James R 1910-1990 WhoAmA 91N
Shipley, Joseph Twadell 1893-1988 BioIn 16
Shipley, Joyce Deborah 1956- WhoAmW 91
Shipley, Karl L. 1953- WhoE 91
Shipley, Keith 1932- St&PR 91
Shipley, L. Parks 1905- St&PR 91
Shipley, L. Parks, Jr. 1931- WhoAm 90
Shipley, Linwood Parks 1905- WhoAm 90
Shipley, Lyman Charles 1934- St&PR 91
Shipley, Margaret Rebecca Foxwell 1947- WhoSSW 91
Shipley, Nancy Louise 1950- WhoAmW 91, WhoEmL 91
Shipley, Robert Hopkins 1945- WhoWrEP 89
Shipley, Roger Douglas 1941- WhoAmA 91, WhoE 91
Shipley, Samuel Lynn 1929- WhoAm 90
Shipley, Shirley Dahl 1932- WhoAmW 91, WhoWor 91
Shipley, Thomas A. 1945- St&PR 91
Shipley, Thomas E., Jr. 1924- WhoWrEP 89
Shipley, Tony Lee 1946- WhoEmL 91
Shipley, V. Fern Wilson 1921- WhoAmW 91
Shipley, Vergil Alan 1922- WhoAm 90
Shipley, Walter Vincent 1935- St&PR 91, WhoAm 90, WhoE 91
Shipman, Charles BioIn 16
Shipman, Charles Ward BiDrAPA 89
Shipman, Charles William 1924- WhoAm 90
Shipman, David 1932- ConAu 30NR
Shipman, David Norval 1939- WhoAm 90
Shipman, Dede 1950- St&PR 91
Shipman, Ellen Biddle 1869-1950 BioIn 16
Shipman, Gregory BioIn 16
Shipman, Harry L 1948- ConAu 32NR
Shipman, J. Darrel 1948- St&PR 91
Shipman, Jack Hewitt 1937- St&PR 91
Shipman, Jean Pugh 1957- WhoAmW 91
Shipman, Jeffrey Roger 1956- WhoSSW 91
Shipman, Marcus Baldwin 1939- WhoWor 91
Shipman, Nell 1893-1970 BioIn 16
Shipman, Robert Jack 1933- St&PR 91
Shipman, Ross Lovelace 1926- WhoSSW 91
Shipman, Wanda Palmer 1950- WhoAmW 91
Shipman, William M BiDrAPA 89
Shipp, Barry Eugene 1937- WhoAm 90
Shipp, Dorothea BioIn 16
Shipp, James E. St&PR 91
Shipp, Jesse A. EarBlAP
Shipp, Jesse A 1859?-1934 DrBlPA 90
Shipp, Jimmy Ray 1961- WhoSSW 91
Shipp, Maurine Sarah Harston 1913- WhoAmW 91
Shipp, Robert L. 1928- St&PR 91
Shipp, Roger Lee 1948- St&PR 91, WhoAm 90
Shippe, Mary Lou 1942- WhoAmW 91
Shippee, Russell Robinson 1949- WhoE 91
Shippen, E Rodman 1909- BiDrAPA 89
Shippen, Katherine Binney 1892-1980 AuBYP 90
Shippen, William 1736-1808 EncCRAm
Shipper, John C BiDrAPA 89
Shippey, Frederick Alexander 1908- WhoWrEP 89
Shippey, Juanita Waters 1946- WhoWrEP 89
Shippey, William Lee 1942- St&PR 91
Shipps, Harry Woolston WhoAm 90
Shipps, Jan 1929- BioIn 16
Shiprek, Joseph Edward 1933- St&PR 91
Shipton, Geoffery Morgan 1910-1987 BioIn 16
Shipton, Harold William 1920- WhoAm 90
Shipton, Helen 1857- FemiCLE
Shipton, Oran Frederick 1933- St&PR 91
Shipton, Ursula BiDEWW
Shipule, Joseph Albert 1914- WhoE 91
Shir, Jay 1946- WhoWor 91
Shira, Gerald Dee, II 1933- WhoE 91
Shira, Robert Bruce 1910- WhoAm 90
Shirai, Akiko WhoAmA 91
Shirai, Claude Ryo 1937- St&PR 91
Shirai, Ikuma 1944- WhoWor 91
Shirai, Mitsuko 1952- IntWWM 90
Shiraki, Keizo 1936- WhoWor 91
Shirane, Gen 1924- WhoAm 90
Shiras, George 1924- ODwPR 91
Shirawi, Yousuf Ahmed 1927- WhoWor 91
Shirayamadani, Kataro PenDiDA 89
Shirbroun, Richard Elmer 1929- WhoAm 90
Shircliff, James Vanderburgh 1938- WhoWor 91
Shircliff, Robert T. 1928- St&PR 91
Shircliff, Robert Thomas 1928- WhoWor 91
Shircliff, Wayne Joseph 1949- St&PR 91
Shire, David Lee 1937- WhoAm 90
Shire, Donald Thomas 1930- St&PR 91, WhoAm 90
Shire, Harold Raymond 1910- WhoWor 91
Shire, Peter 1947- WhoAmA 91
Shire, Talia 1946- WorAlBi
Shire, Talia Rose 1946- WhoAm 90
Shirek, John Richard 1926- WhoSSW 91, WhoWor 91
Shirel, Douglas L. 1958- St&PR 91
Shirelles, The EncPR&S 89
Shirer, William L. BioIn 16, NewYTBS 90 [port]
Shirer, William L 1904- MajTwCW, WorAlBi
Shirer, William Lawrence 1904- AuBYP 90, WhoAm 90, WhoWrEP 89
Shires, Art 1907-1967 Ballpl 90
Shires, George Thomas 1925- WhoAm 90, WhoE 91, WhoWor 91
Shirey, David 1932- St&PR 91
Shirey, Pamela Sue BiDrAPA 89
Shirey, Ronald O. 1940- St&PR 91
Shirey, Wesley Don, Jr. 1950- WhoSSW 91
Shirilau, Mark Steven 1955- WhoEmL 91, WhoWor 91
Shirinsky, Sergey PenDiMP
Shirk, Annadora Vesper 1918- WhoAmW 91
Shirk, Evelyn Urban 1918- WhoAmW 91
Shirk, Everett L. 1930- St&PR 91
Shirk, Helen Z WhoAmA 91
Shirk, Jeannette Campbell 1898- AuBYP 90
Shirkey, William Dan 1951- WhoEmL 91
Shirkov, Dmitriy Vasilevich 1928- WhoWor 91
Shirley, Barbara Anne 1936- WhoAmW 91
Shirley, Bob 1954- Ballpl 90
Shirley, David Arthur 1934- WhoAm 90
Shirley, David Eugene 1952- WhoSSW 91
Shirley, Don 1926- DrBlPA 90
Shirley, Eleanor 1937- WhoAmW 91
Shirley, Elizabeth BiDEWW
Shirley, Elizabeth FemiCLE
Shirley, George 1932- PenDiMP
Shirley, George 1934- DrBlPA 90
Shirley, George Irving 1934- IntWWM 90
Shirley, George Milton, Jr. 1939- WhoSSW 91
Shirley, Glenn Dean 1916- WhoAm 90, WhoWrEP 89
Shirley, Homer Clifton, Jr. 1953- WhoE 91
Shirley, James 1596-1666 BioIn 16
Shirley, John William 1931- WhoAm 90
Shirley, Julia Linn 1956- WhoAmW 91
Shirley, Michael James 1941- St&PR 91, WhoAm 90
Shirley, Norma 1935- WhoAmW 91, WhoE 91
Shirley, Pamela Beth 1950- BiDrAPA 89
Shirley, Ralph 1865-1946 EncO&P 3
Shirley, Robert Preston 1912- WhoAm 90
Shirley, Tex 1918- Ballpl 90
Shirley, Thomas Clifton 1947- WhoEmL 91
Shirley, Virginia Lee 1936- WhoAm 90
Shirley-Quirk, John 1931- IntWWM 90, PenDiMP
Shiroma, Susan Gail 1959- WhoE 91
Shirpser, Clara 1901- WhoAm 90
Shirreff, Emily 1814-1897 FemiCLE
Shirreff, Emily Anne Eliza 1814-1897 BioIn 16
Shirreffs, Gordon D. 1914- BioIn 16
Shirreffs, Gordon Donald 1914- AuBYP 90
Shirrell, Rick D. 1957- St&PR 91
Shirriff, John Robert 1948- BiDrAPA 89
Shirtcliff, John Delzell 1948- WhoWor 91
Shirts, Morris A 1922- SmATA 63 [port]
Shirts, Randall Brent 1950- WhoEmL 91
Shirvani, Hamid 1950- WhoAm 90, WhoEmL 91, WhoWor 91
Shishido, Koichi 1936- WhoWor 91
Shishim, Francis WhoAmA 91
Shislov, Andrey PenDiMP
Shister, Joseph 1917- WhoAm 90
Shistohilis, Dimitrios Prodromos 1954- WhoWor 91
Shivack, Ian M 1930- BiDrAPA 89
Shivanandan, Sivaraman 1956- WhoWor 91
Shivapuri Baba 1826-1963 EncO&P 3
Shivas, Mark BioIn 16
Shive, Philip Augustus 1938- WhoAm 90
Shive, Richard Byron 1933- WhoE 91
Shive, T.M. 1924- St&PR 91
Shive, Thomas M. 1924- WhoAm 90
Shivek, Herbert L. 1921- St&PR 91
Shively, Daniel Charles 1938- WhoE 91
Shively, John Adrian 1922- WhoAm 90
Shively, John Terry 1943- WhoWor 91
Shively, Karl Lawrence 1956- St&PR 91
Shively, Paul A. 1943- St&PR 91
Shively, Susan 1946- BiDrAPA 89, WhoEmL 91
Shively, William Phillips 1942- WhoAm 90
Shiver, Elizabeth N. 1932- St&PR 91
Shiver, James K. St&PR 91N
Shivers, Edward Thomas 1939- St&PR 91
Shivers, Frank R., Jr. 1924- ConAu 130
Shivers, Jane 1943- WhoAmW 91
Shivers, Jay Sanford 1930- WhoE 91
Shivers, Ralph D. 1942- St&PR 91
Shivers, Ralph David 1942- WhoSSW 91
Shivers, William Frank 1945- BiDrAPA 89
Shivery, Charles W. 1945- St&PR 91
Shives, Arnold Edward 1943- WhoAmA 91
Shives, David W., Jr. 1947- St&PR 91
Shives, Ronald D. 1934- St&PR 91
Shives, Ronald Dean 1934- WhoAm 90
Shives, Thomas Clyde 1947- WhoEmL 91
Shivji, Nazimuddin Jamal A. 1955- St&PR 91
Shivler, James Fletcher, Jr. 1918- WhoAm 90, WhoSSW 91
Shivnan, Jane Caroline 1955- WhoAmW 91
Shizuta, Yutaka 1939- WhoWor 91
Shkapskaya, Mariya 1891-1952 EncCoWW
Shklanka, Roman 1932- St&PR 91
Shklar, Gerald 1924- WhoAm 90
Shklar, Judith Nisse 1928- WhoAm 90
Shklov, Mark Thomas 1950- WhoEmL 91
Shklovskii, Viktor Borisovich 1893-1984 BioIn 16
Shklyarevsky, Ludmila BiDrAPA 89
Shkolnick, Rodney 1931- WhoAm 90
Shkolnik, Sheldon BioIn 16, NewYTBS 90
Shkurkin, Ekaterina Vladimirovna 1955- WhoAmW 91
Shlapentokh, Alexandra Vladimirovna 1960- WhoE 91
Shlaudeman, Harry Walter 1926- WhoWor 91
Shleifer, Andrei BioIn 16
Shlemon, Barbara Leahy 1936- ConAu 31NR
Shlenker, Sidney L. WhoAm 90
Shlesinger, Samuel Barry 1946- St&PR 91
Shliapnikov, A. G. 1884-1943? BioIn 16
Shliapnikov, Aleksandr Gavrilovich 1884-1943? BioIn 16
Shlien, Helen S WhoAmA 91
Shlimovich, Mara BiDrAPA 89
Shlipak, Carole Rolnick 1938- WhoSSW 91
Shliselberg, Nissan BiDrAPA 89
Shlomm, Boris 1939- St&PR 91
Shlora, Raymond Bernard 1919- St&PR 91
Shmaruk, Julius 1938- St&PR 91
Shmavonian, Gerald Sergius 1945- WhoAm 90
Shmavonian, Nadya Kay 1960- WhoAmW 91
Shmelev, N. P. 1936- BioIn 16
Shmelev, Nikolai Petrovich 1936- BioIn 16
Shmelkov, Pavel Mikhailovich 1928- WhoWor 91
Shmidt, P. WhoAm 90
Shmikler, David Joel 1948- St&PR 91
Shmikler, Michael Charles 1952- St&PR 91

Shmikler, Robert Gordon 1945- *St&PR 91*
Shmoys, Jerry 1923- *WhoAm 90*
Shmukler, Stanford 1930- *WhoWor 91*
Shnaps, Yitzhak 1950- *BiDrAPA 89*
Shnayerson, Michael 1954- *ConAu 132*
Shnayerson, Robert Beahan 1925- *WhoAm 90, WhoWrEP 89*
Shneidman, Edwin S. *BioIn 16*
Shneidman, Edwin S. 1918- *WhoAm 90*
Shneidman, J. Lee 1929- *WhoAm 90*
Shnell-Hobbs, Sharon Lynn 1958- *WhoAmW 91*
Shneour, Elie Alexis 1925- *WhoAm 90*
Shnider, Ruth Wolkow 1915- *WhoAmW 91*
Shniderman, Harry Louis 1916- *WhoAm 90*
Shnier, Allan Joseph 1928- *St&PR 91*
Shnier, Cecil 1913- *St&PR 91*
Shnier, Mark Allen 1954- *St&PR 91*
Shnier, Philip 1925- *St&PR 91*
Shnitke, Alfred *PenDiMP A*
Shnitkin, David F. 1957- *St&PR 91*
Shoaf, Richard Allen 1948- *WhoSSW 91*
Shoafstall, Earl Fred 1936- *WhoWor 91*
Shoal, Dale *WhoWrEP 89*
Shoap, Kenneth Edmund 1949- *St&PR 91*
Shobe, D.W. 1925- *St&PR 91*
Shobe, Harry Rodgers 1946- *St&PR 91*
Shobe, Janet Wayne 1952- *WhoAmW 91*
Shober, John A.H. 1933- *St&PR 91*
Shober, Wharton 1927- *WhoAm 90*
Shobert, Erle Irwin, II 1913- *WhoAm 90*
Shoch, David 1918-1990 *BioIn 16*
Shoch, David Eugene 1918- *WhoAm 90*
Shochet, Bernard R 1931- *BiDrAPA 89*
Shock, Kathy Beth 1956- *WhoAmW 91*
Shock, Nathan W 1906-1989 *ConAu 130*
Shock, Nathan Wetherill 1906-1989 *BioIn 16*
Shocked, Michelle *BioIn 16*
Shocked, Michelle 1963?- *ConMus 4 [port]*
Shocker, Urban 1890-1928 *Ballpl 90 [port]*
Shocket, Everett 1925- *WhoSSW 91*
Shockey, Paul Kenneth 1923- *St&PR 91*
Shockey, Thomas Edward 1926- *WhoSSW 91, WhoWor 91*
Shockley, Alonzo Hilton, Jr. 1920- *WhoE 91*
Shockley, Ann 1927- *FemiCLE*
Shockley, Ann Allen 1927- *WhoAmW 91, WhoWrEP 89*
Shockley, Carol Frances 1948- *WhoSSW 91*
Shockley, Cynthia Waring 1950- *WhoAmW 91*
Shockley, Edward Julian 1924- *WhoAm 90, WhoSSW 91*
Shockley, Joe Thomas 1951- *St&PR 91*
Shockley, P. Norris, Jr. 1941- *St&PR 91*
Shockley, Thomas Dewey 1923- *WhoAm 90*
Shockley, Uriah B. 1925- *St&PR 91*
Shockley, W. Ray 1924- *WhoAm 90*
Shockley, Walter Gerald 1934- *St&PR 91*
Shockley, William *BioIn 16*
Shockley, William 1910-1989 *AnObit 1989, ConAu 129, WorAlBi*
Shockman, Gerald David 1925- *WhoAm 90*
Shockro, Ellen Krosney *BioIn 16*
Shoctor, Joseph Harvey 1922- *WhoAm 90*
Shoda, Katsufusa 1926- *WhoWor 91*
Shoda, Toshio 1938- *WhoWor 91*
Shoeless Joe Jackson 1887?-1951 *BioIn 16*
Shoemacher, Jeffrey Craig 1944- *St&PR 91*
Shoemake, Thomas Roark 1949- *WhoWrEP 89*
Shoemaker, Alison J. 1948- *St&PR 91*
Shoemaker, Alvin Varner 1938- *WhoE 91*
Shoemaker, Bill 1931- *BioIn 16, WhoAm 90*
Shoemaker, Cecelia M. *ODwPR 91*
Shoemaker, Clara Brink 1921- *WhoAmW 91*
Shoemaker, Craig *WhoE 91*
Shoemaker, Daniel J. 1943- *St&PR 91*
Shoemaker, David Powell 1920- *WhoAm 90*
Shoemaker, Dennis *BioIn 16*
Shoemaker, Diane Marie 1952- *WhoAmW 91*
Shoemaker, Don 1912- *WhoAm 90*
Shoemaker, Donald John 1928- *St&PR 91*
Shoemaker, Eleanor Boggs 1935- *WhoAmW 91, WhoE 91, WhoWor 91*
Shoemaker, Eugene Merle 1928- *WhoAm 90*
Shoemaker, Faith Elaine 1952- *WhoEmL 91*
Shoemaker, Frank Crawford 1922- *WhoAm 90*
Shoemaker, Gradus Lawrence 1921- *WhoAm 90*
Shoemaker, Harold Lloyd 1923- *WhoWor 91*
Shoemaker, Innis Howe *WhoAm 90*
Shoemaker, Innis Howe 1942- *WhoAmA 91*
Shoemaker, John Warren 1923- *WhoE 91*
Shoemaker, Jon Phillip 1936- *WhoSSW 91*
Shoemaker, Kent 1961- *St&PR 91*
Shoemaker, Larry Wayne 1939- *BiDrAPA 89*
Shoemaker, Linda F. 1952- *WhoAmW 91*
Shoemaker, Lynn Henry 1939- *WhoWrEP 89*
Shoemaker, Melinda Anne *WhoAmW 91*
Shoemaker, Paul Frederick 1957- *WhoEmL 91*
Shoemaker, Perry Monroe 1906- *St&PR 91*
Shoemaker, Peter 1920- *WhoAmA 91*
Shoemaker, Peter W. *WhoE 91*
Shoemaker, Phillip A. 1948- *St&PR 91*
Shoemaker, Richard W. 1944- *St&PR 91*
Shoemaker, Robert Gardner 1941- *WhoSSW 91*
Shoemaker, Robert Harold 1921- *St&PR 91*
Shoemaker, Robert Lawrence 1949- *WhoEmL 91*
Shoemaker, Robert Morin 1924- *WhoAm 90*
Shoemaker, Robert Shern 1953- *WhoEmL 91*
Shoemaker, Roger L. 1947- *St&PR 91*
Shoemaker, Sarah *ConAu 132*
Shoemaker, Sarah Ott 1939- *WhoE 91*
Shoemaker, Vaughn 1902- *WhoAmA 91*
Shoemaker, William G. 1916- *St&PR 91*
Shoemaker, Willie 1931- *BioIn 16, WorAlBi*
Shoemate, Charles R. 1939- *St&PR 91*
Shoemate, Charles Richard 1939- *WhoAm 90, WhoE 91*
Shoen, Edward J. 1949- *St&PR 91*
Shoen, Edward Joseph *WhoAm 90*
Shoen, Leonard Samuel 1916- *ConAmBL*
Shoen, Terri Lynn 1948- *WhoAmW 91*
Shoenberg, David 1911- *WhoWor 91*
Shoenfelt, Catherine Ruth 1954- *WhoAmW 91*
Shoenfelt, Joseph Franklin 1918-1968 *WhoAmA 91N*
Shoenight, Pauline Aloise Souers 1914- *WhoAmW 91*
Shoer, Louis 1928- *St&PR 91*
Shoffner, Milt 1905-1978 *Ballpl 90*
Shofstahl, Robert Maxwell 1942- *WhoSSW 91*
Shogan, Robert *WhoAm 90*
Shogren, Daniel Charles 1952- *WhoEmL 91*
Shogren, Dawn Leslie 1955- *BiDrAPA 89*
Shoham, Daniel Maxwell 1934- *St&PR 91*
Shoham, Jeffrey Alan 1954- *WhoE 91*
Shohen, Saundra *ODwPR 91*
Shohen, Saundra Anne 1934- *WhoAmW 91, WhoE 91*
Shohet, Juda Leon 1937- *WhoAm 90*
Shohet, Morris 1936- *St&PR 91*
Shohet, Norman H. 1926- *WhoWor 91*
Shohet, Stephen Byron 1934- *WhoAm 90*
Shohoji, Takao 1938- *WhoWor 91*
Shoichet, Roy P *BiDrAPA 89*
Shoji, Ichiro 1920- *WhoWor 91*
Shoji, June Midori 1957- *WhoAmW 91*
Shoji, Sadao 1931- *WhoWor 91*
Shoji, Watanabe 1932- *WhoWor 91*
Shokeir, Mohamed Hassan Kamel 1938- *WhoAm 90*
Shokler, Harry 1896- *WhoAmA 91N*
Sholakh, Marwan *St&PR 91*
Sholar, Elbert Frank *BiDrAPA 89*
Sholder, Frederic R. 1917- *St&PR 91*
Sholder, Jack *BioIn 16*
Sholder, Kevin Leonard 1963- *WhoEmL 91, WhoWor 91*
Sholem Aleichem 1859-1916 *BioIn 16*
Sholem, David Bennett 1953- *WhoEmL 91*
Sholem, Lee *BioIn 16*
Sholes, Charles Clark 1816-1867 *AmLegL*
Sholes, Christopher Warren 1953- *WhoSSW 91*
Sholes, David H. 1943- *WhoE 91*
Sholes, Ronald William 1939- *St&PR 91*
Sholevar, Bahman *BiDrAPA 89*
Sholevar, Farhad *BiDrAPA 89*
Sholevar, G Pirooz 1939- *BiDrAPA 89*
Sholiton, Marilyn Cohen 1935- *BiDrAPA 89*
Sholl, Elizabeth Neary 1945- *WhoWrEP 89*
Sholl, Jack 1941- *St&PR 91*
Sholl, Jack L. 1941- *ODwPR 91*
Shollenberger, Brian D. 1949- *St&PR 91*
Sholly, Dan *BioIn 16*
Sholokhov, Mikhail 1905-1984 *MajTwCW, WorAlBi*
Sholokhov, Mikhail A. 1905-1984 *AuBYP 90*
Sholomir, Jack *BioIn 16*
Sholomskas, Alan James 1948- *BiDrAPA 89*
Sholtes, Robert Morris *BiDrAPA 89*
Sholtis, Daniel Joseph 1935- *St&PR 91*
Shomair, Garry Y 1950- *BiDrAPA 89*
Shomaker, Gordon Alexander, Jr. 1926- *WhoWrEP 89*
Shomaker, Sharon Diane 1966- *WhoAmW 91*
Shoman, Abdul Majeed *BioIn 16*
Shomer, Enid 1944- *WhoWrEP 89*
Shomer, Tighe Paul 1947- *WhoSSW 91*
Shon, Charles M *BiDrAPA 89*
Shon, Frederick John 1926- *WhoAm 90*
Shon, Han Chul *BiDrAPA 89*
Shon, Richard *BioIn 16*
Shon, Steven Paul 1947- *BiDrAPA 89*
Shone, John R. 1962- *St&PR 91*
Shone, Patric *MajTwCW*
Shone, Phyllis B. 1929- *St&PR 91*
Shone, William E., Jr. 1926- *St&PR 91*
Shonfeld, Willard L. 1931- *St&PR 91*
Shonfield, Andrew 1917-1981 *BioIn 16*
Shonfield, Andrew Akiba 1917-1981 *DcNaB 1981*
Shonfield, Lee Jules 1943- *BiDrAPA 89*
Shongwe, Isaac *BioIn 16*
Shoniker, Fintan Raymond 1914- *WhoAm 90*
Shonk, Albert Davenport, Jr. 1932- *WhoWor 91*
Shonnard, Eugenie Frederica 1886- *BiDWomA*
Shonsui, Gorodayu-go *PenDiDA 89*
Shontz, Charles Henderson 1936- *WhoSSW 91*
Shontz, Patricia Jane 1933- *WhoAmW 91*
Shook, Don P. 1938- *St&PR 91*
Shook, Georg 1934- *WhoAmA 91*
Shook, George E. 1934- *WhoSSW 91*
Shook, Gregory Ralph 1950- *St&PR 91*
Shook, Kathleen Ann *BiDrAPA 89*
Shook, Larry *BioIn 16*
Shook, Mark Roger 1954- *St&PR 91*
Shook, Robert Louis 1938- *WhoAm 90*
Shookhoff, William S. 1948- *IntWWM 90*
Shooks, Mari-Carole 1949- *WhoAmW 91*
Shooman, Martin Lawrence 1934- *WhoAm 90*
Shooner, Pierre 1935- *St&PR 91*
Shoop, Glenn Powell 1920- *WhoSSW 91*
Shoor, Mervyn 1914- *BiDrAPA 89*
Shooter, Eric Manvers 1924- *WhoAm 90*
Shooter, Tom 1941- *WhoAmA 91*
Shope, Irvin 1900-1977 *WhoAmA 91N*
Shope, Ralph Wesley 1925- *St&PR 91*
Shope, Robert Ellis 1929- *WhoAm 90*
Shopen, Kenneth 1902-1967 *WhoAmA 91N*
Shopiro, Eleanor Marchigiani 1929- *WhoAm 90*
Shoppee, Charles William 1904- *WhoWor 91*
Shopper, Moisy 1930- *BiDrAPA 89*
Shopsin, Baron Avery *BiDrAPA 89*
Shoptaw, Marilee Sue 1937- *WhoSSW 91*
Shoquist, Joseph William 1925- *WhoAm 90*
Shor, Bernard 1904-1977 *BioIn 16*
Shor, Cynthia Lynch 1947- *WhoWrEP 89*
Shor, Edgar Leroy 1916- *WhoAm 90*
Shor, George G., Jr. 1923- *WhoAm 90*
Shor, Murray 1932- *WhoWrEP 89*
Shor, Samuel Wendell Williston 1920- *WhoAm 90*
Shor, Toots 1904-1977 *Ballpl 90, BioIn 16*
Shorb, Eugene Murray 1920- *St&PR 91, WhoAm 90*
Shorb, Mary Shaw *NewYTBS 90*
Shore, Albert Clarence 1928- *WhoSSW 91*
Shore, Albert L. *BioIn 16*
Shore, Anne *ConAu 130*
Shore, Arabella 1820?-1900? *FemiCLE*
Shore, Arnold R. *BioIn 16*
Shore, Carole Jean 1948- *WhoE 91*
Shore, Carolyn Sue 1948- *WhoSSW 91*
Shore, Cindy Brockman 1956- *WhoAmW 91*
Shore, Clare 1954- *IntWWM 90*
Shore, David *BiDrAPA 89*
Shore, Dinah 1917- *BioAmW, OxCPMus, WorAlBi*
Shore, Dinah 1920- *BioIn 16*
Shore, Dinah 1921- *WhoAm 90*
Shore, Eddie 1902-1985 *WorAlBi*
Shore, Ellis M. 1939- *St&PR 91*
Shore, Ernie 1891-1980 *Ballpl 90*
Shore, Ferdinand John 1919- *WhoAm 90*
Shore, Hannah *BiDrAPA 89*
Shore, Harvey Harris 1940- *WhoE 91*
Shore, Henrietta 1880-1963 *BiDWomA*
Shore, Herbert 1924- *WhoAm 90, WhoWrEP 89*
Shore, James H 1940- *BiDrAPA 89*
Shore, James Henry 1940- *WhoAm 90*
Shore, Janet 1951- *St&PR 91*
Shore, John 1662?-1752 *PenDiMP*
Shore, June Lewis *AuBYP 90*
Shore, Lawrence Arthur 1928- *St&PR 91*
Shore, Louisa Catherine 1824-1895 *FemiCLE*
Shore, Margaret Emily 1819-1839 *FemiCLE*
Shore, Mary 1912- *WhoAmA 91*
Shore, Matthias *PenDiMP*
Shore, Michael W 1955- *BiDrAPA 89*
Shore, Miles F 1929- *BiDrAPA 89*
Shore, Miles Frederick 1929- *WhoAm 90*
Shore, Neal Adam *BiDrAPA 89*
Shore, Richard Arnold 1946- *WhoAm 90, WhoE 91*
Shore, Richard S 1937- *BiDrAPA 89*
Shore, Samuel 1924- *WhoAm 90*
Shore, Samuel Franklin 1936- *WhoE 91*
Shore, Sherman 1931- *St&PR 91*
Shore, Shirley Walther 1931- *WhoE 91*
Shore, Stephen 1947- *WhoAm 90, WhoAmA 91*
Shore, Stephen Anthony 1945- *St&PR 91*
Shore, Thomas Spencer, Jr. 1939- *WhoAm 90*
Shore, William *PenDiMP*
Shorenstein, Louis M. 1942- *St&PR 91*
Shores, Bill 1904-1984 *Ballpl 90*
Shores, Del 1957- *ConTFT 8 [port]*
Shores, Franklin 1942- *WhoAmA 91*
Shores, Janie L. 1932- *BioIn 16*
Shores, Janie Ledlow 1932- *WhoAm 90, WhoAmW 91, WhoSSW 91*
Shores, Pearl Marie 1946- *WhoAmW 91*
Shorey, Hollis 1823-1893 *DcCanB 12*
Shorin, Abram J. *BioIn 16, NewYTBS 90*
Shorleyker, Richard *PenDiDA 89*
Shornack, Lawrence Louis 1936- *WhoSSW 91*
Shorney, George Herbert 1931- *WhoWor 91*
Shorney, Margo Kay 1930- *WhoAmA 91*
Shorr, Bernard 1928- *St&PR 91*
Shorr, Harriet *BioIn 16*
Shorr, Harriet 1939- *WhoAmA 91*
Shorr, Jay *BiDrAPA 89*
Shorr, Miriam Kronfeldt *WhoAmW 91*
Shorr, Ronald Philip 1937- *WhoWor 91*
Shorris, Earl 1936- *St&PR 91*
Shors, Clayton Marion 1925- *WhoAm 90*
Shors, Susan Debra 1954- *WhoAmW 91, WhoWor 91*
Short Bull 1845?-1915 *WhNaAH*
Short Pants *BioIn 16*
Short, Agnes E. 1930- *WhoAmW 91*
Short, Arthur William 1941- *St&PR 91*
Short, Ben 1931- *WhoSSW 91*
Short, Betty Lancaster 1942- *WhoE 91*
Short, Bill 1937- *Ballpl 90*
Short, Bobby 1924- *DrBlPA 90, WorAlBi*
Short, Bobby 1926- *OxCPMus*
Short, Brant Alison 1933- *St&PR 91*
Short, Brian Patrick 1950- *WhoEmL 91*
Short, Byron Elliott 1901- *WhoAm 90*
Short, Carol Novatnak 1945- *WhoAmW 91*
Short, Charles E. 1937- *St&PR 91*
Short, Chris 1937- *Ballpl 90*
Short, David Bruce 1953- *WhoWor 91*
Short, David Gaines 1939- *St&PR 91, WhoAm 90*
Short, Delmar Dean *BiDrAPA 89*
Short, Denis Stafford 1935- *BiDrAPA 89*
Short, Donald Ray 1944- *WhoAm 90*
Short, Earl De Gray, Jr. 1933- *BiDrAPA 89*
Short, Eugene M. 1932- *WhoSSW 91*
Short, Francis James 1927- *St&PR 91*
Short, George Ocsar, III 1957- *WhoSSW 91*
Short, Glyn David 1938- *WhoE 91*
Short, Harold Harvey 1917- *St&PR 91*
Short, Herman 1918-1989 *BioIn 16*
Short, James David 1942- *WhoE 91*
Short, James Duane 1926- *WhoAm 90*
Short, James Franklin, Jr. 1924- *WhoAm 90*
Short, James H. 1948- *St&PR 91*
Short, Jeffrey R., Jr. 1913- *St&PR 91*
Short, K. Lowell, Jr. 1956- *St&PR 91*
Short, K R M 1936- *ConAu 131*
Short, Karol Fageros *BioIn 16*
Short, Kenneth Richard MacDonald 1936- *WhoSSW 91*
Short, Laurel J. 1930- *St&PR 91*
Short, Leo N., Jr. 1926- *St&PR 91*
Short, Margaret Ann 1947- *WhoAmW 91*
Short, Marion Priscilla 1951- *WhoE 91*
Short, Martin 1951- *WhoAm 90, WorAlBi*
Short, Marvin John, II 1932- *BiDrAPA 89*
Short, Michael 1937- *IntWWM 90*
Short, Nigel *BioIn 16*
Short, Patricia Ann Reilly 1941- *WhoAmA 91*
Short, Paula Myrick 1945- *WhoAmW 91, WhoEmL 91*
Short, Peggy Carmack 1945- *WhoAmW 91*
Short, Phillip Lloyd *BiDrAPA 89*
Short, Ray Everett 1919- *WhoAm 90*
Short, Robert Allen 1927- *WhoAm 90*
Short, Robert Benton, Jr. 1930- *WhoSSW 91*
Short, Robert Henry 1924- *WhoAm 90*
Short, Robert Louis 1926- *St&PR 91*
Short, Roger John 1939- *WhoAm 90*
Short, Stephanie Doris 1956- *WhoWor 91*
Short, Thomas E. 1928- *St&PR 91*

Short, Walter J. 1918- *St&PR 91*
Short, Walter Joseph 1918- *WhoAm 90*
Short, William 1759-1849 *BioIn 16*
Short, William E. 1938- *St&PR 91*
Short, William Hosley 1924- *WhoAm 90*
Short, Winthrop Allen 1919- *WhoAm 90*
Short-Mayfield, Patricia Ahlene 1955- *WhoAmW 91*
Shortal, Helen Mary 1961- *WhoAmW 91*
Shortal, Terence Michael 1937- *WhoSSW 91, WhoWor 91*
Shorte, Dino 1947- *DrBIPA 90*
Shorten, Chick 1892-1965 *Ballpl 90*
Shorter, Alan Robert 1955- *IntWWM 90*
Shorter, Bani *AuBYP 90*
Shorter, Clement Clay 1856-1890 *AmLegL*
Shorter, Clement King 1857-1926 *BioIn 16*
Shorter, Edward Swift 1902- *WhoAmA 91N*
Shorter, Frank 1947- *WorAlBi*
Shorter, Frank C 1947- *ConAu 132*
Shorter, Kenneth James 1954- *WhoE 91*
Shorter, Walter Wyatt 1932- *St&PR 91, WhoAm 90, WhoSSW 91, WhoWor 91*
Shorter, Wayne *BioIn 16*
Shorter, Wayne 1933- *ConMus 5 [port]*
Shortess, Edwin Steevin 1920- *WhoE 91*
Shorthouse, John 1768-1828 *PenDiDA 89*
Shortley, George Melvin 1940- *St&PR 91*
Shortley, Jean Nemec 1960- *WhoAmW 91*
Shortliffe, Edward Hance 1947- *WhoAm 90*
Shortridge, Charles Emil 1941- *WhoWrEP 89*
Shortridge, Michael L. 1957- *WhoEmL 91*
Shortridge, Wayne Hall 1938- *WhoAm 90*
Shorts, Binkley Calhoun 1943- *St&PR 91*
Shortt, H. E. 1887-1987 *BioIn 16*
Shortz, Will *BioIn 16*
Shory, Carl Brian *BiDrAPA 89*
Shory, Naseeb Lein 1925- *WhoAm 90*
Shosid, Joseph Lewis 1927- *WhoAm 90*
Shosky, John Edwin 1955- *WhoE 91*
Shoss, Cynthia Renee 1950- *WhoAmW 91*
Shostack, G. Lynn *BioIn 16*
Shostak, Ed 1941- *WhoAmA 91*
Shostak, Ed Bennett 1941- *WhoE 91*
Shostak, Michael *BiDrAPA 89*
Shostak, Stanley Richard 1931- *WhoWor 91*
Shostakovich Quartet *PenDiMP*
Shostakovich, Dimitri 1906-1975 *WorAlBi*
Shostakovich, Dmitrii Dmitrievich 1906-1975 *BioIn 16*
Shostakovich, Dmitry *PenDiMP*
Shostakovich, Dmitry 1906-1975 *PenDiMP A*
Shostakovich, Maxim 1938- *IntWWM 90, PenDiMP*
Shostakovich, Maxim Dmitriyevich 1938- *WhoAm 90, WhoSSW 91, WhoWor 91*
Shot, Danny 1957- *WhoWrEP 89*
Shotlander, Sandra 1941- *FemiCLE*
Shotoku, Prince 574-622 *EncJap*
Shotoku-tenno *WomWR*
Shotola, Marilyn Edeen Wegener 1937- *IntWWM 90*
Shott, Gerald Lee 1934- *St&PR 91, WhoAm 90*
Shott, Michael John 1928- *IntWWM 90*
Shott, Robert B. 1922- *St&PR 91*
Shott, Scott 1926- *St&PR 91*
Shotton, Burt 1884-1962 *Ballpl 90*
Shotton, Burton Kent, Jr. 1937- *St&PR 91*
Shotwell, Louisa Rossiter 1902- *AuBYP 90*
Shotwell, Monica R *BiDrAPA 89*
Shotz, Linda Fleischman 1949- *WhoAmW 91*
Shotzberger, Martin Luther 1923- *WhoAm 90*
Shoub, Earle Phelps 1915- *WhoE 91, WhoWor 91*
Shoucair, Ali Mohamed 1951- *WhoWor 91*
Shoulberg, Harry 1903- *WhoAm 90, WhoAmA 91, WhoE 91*
Shoulders, John F. 1947- *St&PR 91*
Shoulvin, Daniel Robert, Jr. 1919- *St&PR 91*
Shoun, Clyde 1912-1968 *Ballpl 90*
Shoup, Andrew James, Jr. 1935- *St&PR 91, WhoAm 90*
Shoup, Carl Sumner 1902- *WhoAm 90, WhoWor 91*
Shoup, Charles S. *St&PR 91*
Shoup, Charles Samuel, Jr. 1935- *WhoAm 90*
Shoup, Charles Wilbur 1930- *St&PR 91*
Shoup, Charlotte F. 1947- *St&PR 91*
Shoup, Donald Albert 1929- *St&PR 91*
Shoup, Harold Arthur 1930- *WhoAm 90*
Shoup, Janet Blom 1943- *WhoAmW 91*
Shoup, Michael C. 1940- *WhoAm 90*
Shoup, Paul Connelly 1938- *St&PR 91*
Shoup, Richard Mahlon *BiDrAPA 89*
Shoup, Robert W. 1920- *St&PR 91*
Shoup, Walter C. 1951- *St&PR 91*
Shourd, Roy Ray 1927- *St&PR 91*
Shouse, David Sinclair 1952- *WhoEmL 91*
Shoushanian, Hrant H. 1936- *St&PR 91*
Shovald, Arlene Elizabeth 1940- *WhoWrEP 89*
Shovlin, John P 1908- *BiDrAPA 89*
Show, Eric 1956- *Ballpl 90*
Showalter, Allan Ray 1949- *BiDrAPA 89*
Showalter, Carl Robert 1938- *BiDrAPA 89*
Showalter, E. Lee *St&PR 91*
Showalter, Elaine *BioIn 16*
Showalter, English, Jr. 1935- *WhoAm 90*
Showalter, Jean *AuBYP 90*
Showalter, Jerry Newbern 1940- *WhoWor 91*
Showalter, Joan Frances 1933- *St&PR 91*
Showalter, John 1950- *St&PR 91*
Showalter, Louis Reverdy 1931- *St&PR 91*
Showalter, Madeleine Juliet 1958- *WhoAmW 91*
Showalter, Max 1917- *ConTFT 8 [port]*
Showalter, Ralph Roland 1925- *St&PR 91*
Showalter, Robert Earl 1937- *WhoAm 90*
Showalter-Keefe, Jean 1938- *WhoAmW 91*
Showanasai, Aroon 1930- *BiDrAPA 89*
Showell, Kenneth L 1939- *WhoAmA 91*
Showen, Robert 1924- *St&PR 91*
Shower, Robert Wesley 1937- *WhoAm 90*
Showering, Keith Stanley 1930-1982 *DcNaB 1981*
Showers, April *WhoWrEP 89*
Showers, James Allen 1955- *St&PR 91*
Showers, Margi *BioIn 16*
Showers, Mary *EncO&P 3*
Showers, Ralph Morris 1918- *WhoAm 90*
Showers, Rosina Mary 1857?- *EncPaPR 91*
Showers, Wayne Allen 1932- *St&PR 91*
Showes, Mrs. *FemiCLE*
Showghy, Jamshid *BiDrAPA 89*
Showich, Nicholas A. 1939- *St&PR 91*
Shown, James A 1923- *BiDrAPA 89*
Shows, Clarence Oliver 1920- *WhoSSW 91, WhoWor 91*
Shows, Thomas Byron 1938- *WhoAm 90*
Showstack, Nathaniel *BiDrAPA 89*
Shpritz, Louis Arthur 1945- *WhoE 91*
Shraberg, David 1947- *BiDrAPA 89*
Shrader, Linda Marie 1959- *WhoSSW 91*
Shrader, Marjorie A. *St&PR 91*
Shrader, Michael David *BioIn 16*
Shrady, Frederick *BioIn 16*
Shrady, Frederick 1907- *WhoAmA 91*
Shrady, Frederick Charles *NewYTBS 90*
Shrager, Daniel S 1943- *BiDrAPA 89*
Shragin, Boris *NewYTBS 90*
Shragin, Boris 1926-1990 *ConAu 132*
Shrauner, Barbara Wayne Abraham 1934- *WhoAmW 91*
Shrawder, J. Edward 1937- *St&PR 91*
Shrednick, Harvey R. 1940- *St&PR 91*
Shreeve, Daniel F *BiDrAPA 89*
Shreeve, Jean'ne Marie 1933- *WhoAm 90*
Shreffler, Donald Cecil 1933- *WhoAm 90*
Shrem, Charles J. 1930- *St&PR 91*
Shrem, Charles Joseph 1930- *WhoAm 90, WhoWor 91*
Shrem, Henry J. 1936- *St&PR 91*
Shrestha, Marich Man Singh *WhoWor 91*
Shreve, Amy *NewAgMG*
Shreve, Forrest 1878-1950 *BioIn 16*
Shreve, Henry M. 1785-1851 *WorAlBi*
Shreve, Levin Gale 1910- *SpyFic*
Shreve, Margaret Linn 1950- *WhoAmW 91*
Shreve, Norman F. 1927- *St&PR 91*
Shreve, Peg 1927- *WhoAmW 91*
Shreve, Porter Gaylord, Jr. 1939- *WhoE 91*
Shreve, Susan 1939- *AuBYP 90*
Shreve, Susan Richards *BioIn 16*
Shreve, Susan Richards 1939- *WhoAm 90, WhoAmW 91*
Shreve, William Clement 1919- *St&PR 91*
Shriber, Leon Albert 1928- *St&PR 91*
Shriber, Maurice Norden 1943- *WhoAm 90*
Shrider, Bruce J. 1952- *St&PR 91*
Shridharani, Vasant Nanalal 1937- *WhoE 91*
Shrier, Adam Louis 1938- *WhoAm 90*
Shrier, Diane K 1941- *BiDrAPA 89*
Shrier, Stefan 1942- *WhoAm 90, WhoSSW 91*
Shrieve, Michael *NewAgMG*
Shrieves, George Matthews 1935- *WhoAm 90*
Shrimpton, James Robert 1956- *WhoEmL 91*
Shriner, Herb 1918-1970 *WorAlBi*
Shriner, Wil *BioIn 16*
Shriner, William C 1937- *BiDrAPA 89*
Shriqui, Christian Lazare *BiDrAPA 89*
Shriro, Robert L 1927- *BiDrAPA 89*
Shriver, Allen 1946- *St&PR 91*
Shriver, Charles 1941- *St&PR 91*
Shriver, Denton Alfred 1923- *WhoAm 90*
Shriver, Donald Woods, Jr. 1927- *WhoAm 90*
Shriver, Duward Felix 1934- *WhoAm 90*
Shriver, Eunice Mary Kennedy *WhoAm 90, WhoAmW 91*
Shriver, Garner Edward 1912- *WhoAm 90*
Shriver, George Hite 1931- *WhoSSW 91*
Shriver, Harry Roland 1932- *St&PR 91, WhoE 91*
Shriver, Jennifer M. 1950- *St&PR 91*
Shriver, Joyce Elizabeth 1937- *WhoAmW 91*
Shriver, Kren K *BiDrAPA 89*
Shriver, Maria *BioIn 16*
Shriver, Norman 1943- *St&PR 91*
Shriver, Pamela Howard 1962- *WhoAm 90*
Shriver, Phillip Raymond 1922- *WhoAm 90*
Shriver, R. Sargent, Jr. 1915- *WorAlBi*
Shriver, Sargent 1915- *BioIn 16*
Shriver, T. Herbert *BioIn 16*
Shrock, Robert Rakes 1904- *WhoAm 90*
Shrodes, Caroline *WhoAm 90, WhoWrEP 89*
Shroeder, Janet Gregg Wallace 1902- *WhoE 91*
Shroff, Fali Jamsedji 1934- *WhoWor 91*
Shroff, Firoz Sardar 1950- *WhoWor 91*
Shroff, Srinivas Ramarao 1943- *WhoSSW 91*
Shroka, Joyce Ann 1955- *WhoAmW 91*
Shrontz, Frank Anderson 1931- *St&PR 91, WhoAm 90, WhoWor 91*
Shropshire, Donald Gray 1927- *WhoAm 90*
Shropshire, Walter, Jr. 1932- *WhoAm 90*
Shropshire, William S. 1957- *St&PR 91*
Shrosbree, Colin 1938- *ConAu 130*
Shroup, Robert Lewis 1935- *St&PR 91*
Shroyer, Georgia Ellen 1937- *WhoSSW 91*
Shroyer, Keith L. 1949- *St&PR 91*
Shroyer, Marilyn Kay 1958- *WhoSSW 91*
Shroyer, Norman Charles 1931- *St&PR 91*
Shroyer, Thomas Jerome 1952- *WhoEmL 91*
Shrum, Christine Ruth 1949- *WhoWrEP 89*
Shrut, Howard *St&PR 91*
Shryock, Burnett Henry, Sr 1904-1971 *WhoAmA 91N*
Shryock, Edwin Harold 1906- *WhoAm 90*
Shryock, Russell Webster 1917- *WhoAm 90*
Shtasel, Derri Lynn 1954- *BiDrAPA 89*
Shtohryn, Dmytro Michael 1923- *WhoAm 90*
Shtrikman, Shmuel 1930- *WhoWor 91*
Shtromas, Alexander 1931- *ConAu 132*
Shu, Chi-Wang 1957- *WhoE 91*
Shu, Pu *BiDrAPA 89*
Shu-lu shih *WomWR*
Shuard, Amy 1924-1975 *PenDiMP*
Shuart, James M. 1931- *WhoAm 90, WhoE 91*
Shub, Elizabeth *AuBYP 90*
Shub, Michael 1943- *WhoE 91*
Shuba, George 1924- *Ballpl 90*
Shube, Eugene E. 1927- *St&PR 91*
Shubert Brothers *OxCPMus*
Shubert, Beth Cohen 1941- *WhoSSW 91*
Shubert, Duane Doyle 1962- *BiDrAPA 89, WhoE 91*
Shubert, Gary Michael 1948- *WhoWor 91*
Shubert, Gustave Harry 1929- *WhoAm 90*
Shubert, Jack I. *BioIn 16*
Shubert, Jacob 1878-1963 *OxCPMus*
Shubert, Joseph Francis 1928- *WhoAm 90*
Shubert, Lee 1873-1953 *OxCPMus*
Shubert, Lee 1875-1953 *WorAlBi*
Shubert, Samuel 1876-1905 *OxCPMus*
Shubert, Thomas C., III 1946- *WhoSSW 91*
Shubin, Harry 1914- *WhoWor 91*
Shubin, Morris Jack 1920- *WhoAmA 91*
Shubin, Seymour 1921- *WhoWrEP 89*
Shubinski, Raymond 1951- *WhoAm 90*
Shubnikov, Alexei Vasilievich 1887-1970 *DcScB S2*
Shubs, Gerald Alan 1943- *BiDrAPA 89*
Shuch, Frank M. 1951- *WhoE 91*
Shuchat, Wilfred G. 1920- *BioIn 16*
Shuchman, Miriam *BiDrAPA 89*
Shuchter, Stephen Roy *BiDrAPA 89*
Shuck, Bill C. 1941- *St&PR 91*
Shuck, Emerson Clayton 1916- *WhoAm 90*
Shuck, Henrietta Hall 1817-1844 *BioIn 16*
Shuck, Jerry Mark 1934- *WhoAm 90*
Shuck, John Winfield 1940- *WhoE 91*
Shuck, Kenneth Menaugh 1921- *WhoAmA 91*
Shuck, Robert Fletcher 1937- *St&PR 91*
Shuck, Robert Fletcher, III 1937- *WhoAm 90*
Shuck, Yvonne M. *St&PR 91*
Shue, Elisabeth *BioIn 16*
Shue, Philip Michael *BiDrAPA 89*
Shue, Robert Sidney 1943- *WhoSSW 91*
Shuebrook, Ron 1943- *WhoAmA 91*
Shuebrook, Ronald Lee 1943- *WhoE 91*
Shuey, Andrea Lee *WhoWrEP 89*
Shuey, Barbara Wilson 1915- *WhoWor 91*
Shuey, Iris *BiDrAPA 89*
Shuey, Judith Lewis 1946- *WhoAmW 91*
Shuey, Sharon Rose 1947- *WhoEmL 91*
Shuey, Sidney Lee 1936- *St&PR 91*
Shufeldt, R. Charles 1950- *St&PR 91*
Shufeldt, Robert Charles 1950- *WhoAm 90*
Shufeldt, Robert Wilson 1822-1895 *BioIn 16*
Shufelt, Robert *BioIn 16*
Shuff, Lily *WhoAm 90, WhoAmA 91*
Shuffelton, Frank Charles 1940- *WhoE 91*
Shuford, A. Alex 1944- *St&PR 91*
Shuford, Calvin Howard 1927- *St&PR 91*
Shuford, Donald Lowell 1945- *WhoSSW 91*
Shuford, Harley F. 1912- *St&PR 91*
Shuford, Harley Ferguson, Jr. 1937- *WhoAm 90*
Shuford, Harry L. 1941- *St&PR 91*
Shufro, Salwyn 1905- *St&PR 91, WhoE 91*
Shugan, Steven Mark 1952- *WhoEmL 91*
Shugart, Alan F. 1930- *WhoAm 90*
Shugart, Cecil Glenn 1930- *WhoAm 90*
Shugart, Donna Lea 1948- *WhoAmW 91*
Shugart, Elizabeth Lancaster 1963- *WhoAmW 91*
Shugart, Frank 1866-1944 *Ballpl 90*
Shugart, Herman Henry 1944- *WhoAm 90*
Shugart, Howard Alan 1931- *WhoAm 90*
Shugart, Jill 1940- *WhoSSW 91*
Shugart, Margaret Ann *BiDrAPA 89*
Shugarts, Frank Harry 1866-1944 *Ballpl 90*
Shuggi, Gaby George 1947- *WhoWor 91*
Shugol, Wendy Ruth 1951- *WhoSSW 91*
Shugoll, Eugene L. *St&PR 91*
Shugrue, James Leonard 1948- *WhoWrEP 89*
Shugrue, Martin Roger, Jr. 1940- *WhoAm 90, WhoSSW 91*
Shui, Ven Hao 1943- *WhoE 91*
Shuji, Isawa 1851-1917 *BioIn 16*
Shukas, Socrates Nicholas 1931- *St&PR 91*
Shuker, Gregory Brown 1932- *WhoAm 90*
Shukert, Elfrieda Berthiaume 1948- *ConAu 129*
Shukie, John Clark 1949- *WhoE 91*
Shukla, Dhirajlal Nanalal 1930- *WhoWor 91*
Shukla, Ganesh Dutta 1948- *BiDrAPA 89*
Shukla, Jayant Harshendra 1953- *WhoE 91*
Shukla, Nilima Vikram 1958- *BiDrAPA 89*
Shukla, Rahul B. 1947- *St&PR 91*
Shukla, Sandip R 1947- *BiDrAPA 89*
Shukla, Sashi *BiDrAPA 89*
Shukla, Shailendra Shanker 1949- *WhoSSW 91*
Shukla, Sheo Bhushan 1936- *WhoWor 91*
Shukla, Vikram Rasiklal *BiDrAPA 89*
Shukman, Solomon 1927- *WhoAmA 91*
Shuko, Torii 1930- *WhoWor 91*
Shukoski, Vernon Joseph 1951- *St&PR 91*
Shukshin, Vasilii Makarovich 1929-1974 *BioIn 16*
Shula, Don 1930- *WorAlBi*
Shula, Don Francis 1930- *WhoSSW 91*
Shula, Robert Joseph 1936- *WhoAm 90*
Shulack, Norman R 1906- *BiDrAPA 89*
Shuldiner, Herbert 1929- *WhoAm 90, WhoWrEP 89*
Shuldinger, Herbert 1929- *ConAu 130*
Shulenberger, Cheryl Rene 1950- *WhoWrEP 89*
Shuler, Alan George 1947- *St&PR 91*
Shuler, Bob *BioIn 16*
Shuler, Ellie Givan, Jr. 1936- *WhoAm 90*
Shuler, Gail Karen *BiDrAPA 89*
Shuler, George Nixon, Jr. 1952- *WhoSSW 91*
Shuler, Jerry B. 1933- *St&PR 91*
Shuler, John H. 1927- *St&PR 91*
Shuler, Kurt Egon 1922- *WhoAm 90*
Shuler, Michael Louis 1947- *WhoAm 90*
Shuler, Sally Ann Smith 1934- *WhoAmW 91*
Shuler, Thomas H, Jr 1949- *WhoAmA 91*
Shulevitz, Uri 1935- *AuBYP 90, BioIn 16, WhoAm 90, WhoWrEP 89*
Shulga, Cynthia Lee 1953- *St&PR 91*
Shuliz, Robert E. *St&PR 91*
Shulkin, Anatol 1901-1961 *WhoAmA 91N*
Shulkin, David J *BiDrAPA 89*
Shulkin, David Jonathon 1959- *WhoE 91*
Shulkin, Mark Weiss 1929- *BiDrAPA 89*
Shulko, Patsy Lee 1934- *WhoAmW 91, WhoSSW 91*
Shull, Carl Edwin 1912- *WhoAmA 91*
Shull, Clifford G. 1915- *WhoAm 90*
Shull, David Scott 1946- *WhoEmL 91*
Shull, Ellen M. 1937- *WhoWrEP 89*
Shull, Harrison 1923- *WhoAm 90*
Shull, Harry Dean, Jr. *BiDrAPA 89*
Shull, James Marion 1872-1948 *WhoAmA 91N*
Shull, Leo 1913- *WhoAm 90*
Shull, Noel J. *St&PR 91*
Shull, Richard Bruce 1929- *WhoAm 90*

Shull, Willard Charles, III 1940- *St&PR 91, WhoAm 90*
Shull, William Edgar, Jr. 1947- *WhoEmL 91*
Shulman, Alfred J 1923- *BiDrAPA 89*
Shulman, Arnold 1914- *WhoAm 90*
Shulman, Bernard H 1922- *BiDrAPA 89*
Shulman, Beth 1949- *WhoE 91*
Shulman, David George 1943- *WhoE 91*
Shulman, Donald Carl 1950- *WhoSSW 91*
Shulman, Elliot Jay 1951- *WhoE 91*
Shulman, Fay Stanley *NewYTBS 90*
Shulman, Frank Joseph 1943- *ConAu 30NR*
Shulman, Irving 1913- *WhoAm 90, WhoWrEP 89*
Shulman, Kenneth Israel 1949- *BiDrAPA 89*
Shulman, Lawrence Edward 1919- *WhoAm 90*
Shulman, Lee S. *BioIn 16*
Shulman, Lenore 1934- *St&PR 91*
Shulman, Lisa 1950- *BiDrAPA 89*
Shulman, Martin 1921- *St&PR 91*
Shulman, Max 1919-1988 *BioIn 16*
Shulman, Max L. 1908- *St&PR 91, WhoAm 90*
Shulman, Melvin 1923- *BiDrAPA 89*
Shulman, Morton P. *BioIn 16*
Shulman, Morton P. 1925- *St&PR 91*
Shulman, Philip N 1931- *BiDrAPA 89*
Shulman, Richard *NewAgMG*
Shulman, Richard Elihu 1939- *WhoE 91*
Shulman, Robert Bernard *BiDrAPA 89*
Shulman, Robert Gerson 1924- *WhoAm 90*
Shulman, Robert S. 1951- *St&PR 91*
Shulman, Ronni 1953- *ODwPR 91*
Shulman, Roy M 1934- *BiDrAPA 89*
Shulman, Stephen H. 1944- *St&PR 91*
Shulman, Stephen Neal 1933- *WhoAm 90*
Shulman, Steven 1941- *St&PR 91*
Shulruff, Steven Michael *BiDrAPA 89*
Shulstad, R. Craig 1942- *ODwPR 91*
Shultis, Robert Lynn 1924- *WhoAm 90*
Shults, John R., Jr. 1926- *St&PR 91*
Shults, Robert L. 1936- *St&PR 91*
Shults, Robert Lee 1936- *WhoSSW 91, WhoWor 91*
Shults, Robert Luther, Jr. 1925- *WhoAm 90*
Shultz, Emmet L. 1934- *St&PR 91*
Shultz, George P. 1920- *WorAlBi*
Shultz, George Pratt 1920- *BiDrUSE 89, BioIn 16, WhoAm 90, WhoWor 91*
Shultz, James Michael *BiDrAPA 89*
Shultz, John David 1939- *WhoWor 91*
Shultz, Joseph Randolph 1927- *WhoAm 90*
Shultz, Leila McReynolds 1946- *WhoAmW 91*
Shultz, Lois Ann 1963- *WhoE 91*
Shultz, Martha Jane 1916- *WhoAmW 91*
Shultz, Paul Albert 1954- *St&PR 91*
Shultz, Richard Carl 1927- *WhoAm 90*
Shultz, Rick John 1952- *St&PR 91*
Shultz, Robert E. 1940- *St&PR 91*
Shum, Alex Kwok-King 1954- *IntWWM 90*
Shum, Paul P. 1929- *St&PR 91*
Shumacker, Elizabeth Wight 1912- *WhoAmA 91*
Shumacker, Harris B., Jr. 1908- *WhoAm 90*
Shumadine, William F., Jr. 1944- *St&PR 91*
Shumaker, Hugh Joseph 1914- *St&PR 91*
Shumaker, John William 1942- *WhoE 91*
Shumaker, Nita Wall *BiDrAPA 89*
Shuman, Constance *ODwPR 91*
Shuman, Deanne 1953- *WhoAmW 91*
Shuman, Hyman B. *St&PR 91*
Shuman, Irwin 1934- *WhoE 91*
Shuman, James Burrow 1932- *WhoE 91, WhoWor 91*
Shuman, Joseph O. 1944- *St&PR 91*
Shuman, Joseph Scott 1922- *BiDrAPA 89*
Shuman, Lois Anna 1952- *WhoEmL 91*
Shuman, Mark *PenDiMP*
Shuman, Mark Patrick 1952- *WhoEmL 91*
Shuman, Mark Samuel 1936- *WhoAm 90*
Shuman, Mort 1936- *OxCPMus*
Shuman, Nicholas Roman 1921- *WhoAm 90*
Shuman, Philip J. *ODwPR 91*
Shuman, Robert Baird 1929- *WhoAm 90*
Shuman, Samuel A. 1927- *St&PR 91*
Shuman, Samuel Irving 1925- *WhoAm 90*
Shuman, Sidney A. 1912- *St&PR 91*
Shuman, Willard Edward 1943- *St&PR 91*
Shumate, Anderson Everett, III 1936- *St&PR 91*
Shumate, Charles Albert 1904- *WhoWor 91*
Shumate, Gloria Jones 1927- *WhoAmW 91*
Shumate, James Bernard 1929- *St&PR 91*
Shumate, John Page 1934- *WhoE 91, WhoWor 91*
Shumate, Paul William, Jr. 1941- *WhoE 91*
Shumate, Stephen John 1948- *WhoAm 90*
Shumeyko, Theodor V. *ODwPR 91*
Shumiatskii, Boris Zakharovich 1886-1943 *BioIn 16*
Shump, Michael Eugene 1943- *St&PR 91*
Shumsky, Oscar 1917- *IntWWM 90, PenDiMP*
Shumsky, Zena *WhoWrEP 89*
Shumway, Forrest Nelson 1927- *St&PR 91*
Shumway, Jim 1939- *WhoAm 90*
Shumway, Norman D. 1934- *WhoAm 90*
Shumway, Ronald J. 1936- *St&PR 91*
Shumway, Spence A. 1955- *WhoSSW 91*
Shunney, Andrew 1921- *WhoAmA 91N*
Shunsky, Vincent 1949- *St&PR 91*
Shunta, Joseph Paul 1942- *WhoE 91*
Shupack, Harold 1936- *St&PR 91*
Shupe, Anson 1948- *ConAu 129*
Shupe, Charles B. 1933- *St&PR 91*
Shupe, David R W 1916- *BiDrAPA 89*
Shupe, John Wallace 1924- *WhoAm 90*
Shupp, David F 1926- *BiDrAPA 89*
Shupp, Franklin Richard 1934- *WhoAm 90*
Shur, Rory Craig 1957- *WhoSSW 91*
Shur, Steven Elliot 1947- *St&PR 91*
Shur, Walter 1929- *St&PR 91, WhoAm 90*
Shur, Yekutiel 1918- *IntWWM 90*
Shura, Mary Francis *WhoWrEP 89*
Shura, Mary Francis 1923- *AuBYP 90*
Shurayh, Mahmud 1952- *WhoWor 91*
Shurden, Cynthia Toles 1951- *St&PR 91*
Shure, Alan H. *BioIn 16*
Shure, Myrna Beth 1937- *WhoAmW 91*
Shure, Paul *PenDiMP*
Shurick, Edward Palmes 1912- *WhoAm 90*
Shurkin, Lorna Greene 1944- *WhoE 91*
Shurley, Jay Talmadge 1917- *BiDrAPA 89, WhoAm 90*
Shurling, Anne Marlowe 1947- *WhoAmW 91*
Shurpin, Leslie Stuart *BiDrAPA 89*
Shurrager, Phil Sheridan 1907- *WhoAm 90*
Shursky, Stanley James 1952- *WhoE 91*
Shurtleff, Edward D. 1863-1936 *AmLegL*
Shurtleff, Leonard Grant 1940- *WhoAm 90, WhoWor 91*
Shurtleff, Lynn Richard 1939- *IntWWM 90*
Shurtleff, William Roy 1941- *WhoWrEP 89*
Shurtliff, Marvin Karl 1939- *WhoAm 90*
Shustek, Leonard J. 1948- *St&PR 91*
Shuster, Addison Herbert 1952- *WhoE 91*
Shuster, Alvin 1930- *WhoAm 90*
Shuster, E. G. Bud 1932- *WhoAm 90, WhoE 91*
Shuster, Eugene 1935- *WhoE 91*
Shuster, George Whitcomb 1946- *St&PR 91*
Shuster, Herbert V. 1924- *WhoAm 90*
Shuster, Jay 1954- *St&PR 91*
Shuster, Joe 1914- *EncACom*
Shuster, John Lee 1961- *BiDrAPA 89*
Shuster, John Michael 1952- *St&PR 91*
Shuster, Lynn A. 1942- *St&PR 91*
Shuster, Moises Jacobo 1933- *BiDrAPA 89*
Shuster, Robert G. 1927- *WhoAm 90*
Shusterman, Arnold Jerome 1937- *St&PR 91*
Shusterman, Nathan 1927- *WhoSSW 91, WhoWor 91*
Shute, Ben E 1905-1986 *WhoAmA 91N*
Shute, David 1931- *WhoAm 90*
Shute, Leslie Vincent 1927- *St&PR 91*
Shute, Marcus William 1962- *WhoSSW 91*
Shute, Richard Emil 1938- *WhoAm 90*
Shute, Roberta E *WhoAmA 91*
Shuter-Dyson, Rosamund *IntWWM 90*
Shutiak, James 1932- *WhoAm 90*
Shutler, Kenneth Eugene 1938- *WhoAm 90*
Shutsky, Robert 1938- *St&PR 91*
Shutt, Edwin Holmes, Jr. 1927- *WhoAm 90, WhoE 91*
Shutt, Harry James 1932- *St&PR 91*
Shutt, Jay W. 1951- *St&PR 91*
Shutt, Steve *BioIn 16*
Shutt, Ward S., Jr. 1948- *St&PR 91*
Shuttle, Penelope 1947- *BioIn 16, FemiCLE*
Shuttlesworth, Dorothy Edwards 1907- *AuBYP 90*
Shuttleworth, Anna Lee 1927- *IntWWM 90*
Shuttleworth, Anne Margaret 1931- *BiDrAPA 89, WhoWor 91*
Shuttleworth, Carol L. 1941- *St&PR 91*
Shuttleworth, James Kay- 1804-1877 *BioIn 16*
Shutts, Kenneth Robertson 1922- *St&PR 91*
Shutts, Sharon E. 1940- *WhoAmW 91*
Shutty, Robert John 1937- *St&PR 91*
Shutz, Byron Christopher 1928- *St&PR 91, WhoAm 90*
Shutze, Philip Trammell 1890-1982 *BioIn 16*
Shuvalov, Peter A. 1827-1889 *BioIn 16*
Shuwaiky, M. Ziad *WhoWor 91*
Shuyler, Richard Harlan 1947- *St&PR 91*
Shvadron, Sholom Mordecai Hakohen 1838-1911? *BioIn 16*
Shvartsman, Leonid 1940- *BiDrAPA 89*
Shvartsman, Vladimir Antonovich 1945- *WhoSSW 91*
Shwartz, Kenneth A. 1955- *St&PR 91*
Shwartz, Martin 1923-1990 *BioIn 16*
Shwartz, Merrill D. 1922- *St&PR 91*
Shwayder, Elizabeth Yanish 1922- *WhoAmW 91*
Shwayder, Reva *BioIn 16*
Shwetz, Mary Helen *BiDrAPA 89*
Shy, Clayton Owen 1962- *WhoSSW 91*
Shy, John Willard 1931- *WhoWrEP 89*
Shy, Kathy Elaine *BiDrAPA 89*
Shy, Paul N. 1939- *St&PR 91*
Shyer, Charles 1941- *ConTFT 8*
Shyer, Herbert Paul 1930- *St&PR 91*
Shyers, Larry Edward 1948- *WhoEmL 91, WhoSSW 91, WhoWor 91*
Shyjka, Frank 1944- *St&PR 91*
Shymanski, Catherine Mary 1954- *WhoAmW 91*
Shymkus, James Lowery 1939- *WhoAm 90*
Shynn, Tae-Il 1945- *BiDrAPA 89*
Shyre, Paul *BioIn 16*
Shyre, Paul 1926- *WhoWrEP 89*
Shyre, Paul 1929?-1989 *ConAu 130*
Shyres, Mark *BioIn 16*
Shyver, Robert Burnell 1942- *WhoSSW 91*
Siack, Steven D. 1946- *St&PR 91*
Siad Barre, Mohamed 1919- *WhoWor 91*
Siahpoosh, Farideh Tamaddon 1928- *WhoAmW 91*
Siahpoosh, Sohrab 1951- *BiDrAPA 89*
Sialom, Sedat Sami 1940- *WhoWor 91*
Siamis, Janet Neal 1938- *WhoAmA 91*
Siani, Alfredo Francesco *BioIn 16*
Siano, Jerry J. *BioIn 16, WhoAm 90*
Siantz, Mary Lou deLeon 1947- *WhoAmW 91, WhoHisp 91*
Siard, Gilbert Edward 1954- *WhoWor 91*
Siardos, George C. 1938- *WhoWor 91*
Siart, William E.B. 1946- *St&PR 91*
Sias, David Kenneth, Jr. 1937- *WhoAm 90*
Sias, John *BioIn 16*
Sias, John B. 1927- *WhoAm 90, WhoE 91*
Sias, Marcia 1947- *WhoAmW 91*
Siassi, Iradj 1933- *BiDrAPA 89*
Siatos, Thomas John 1923- *WhoWrEP 89*
Siau, John Finn 1921- *WhoAm 90*
Sibal, Abner Woodruff 1921- *WhoAm 90*
Sibani, Leone 1937- *WhoWor 91*
Sibelius, Jean 1865-1957 *BioIn 16, PenDiMP A, WorAlBi*
Siberell, Anne Hicks *WhoAmA 91*
Siberry, Jane *BioIn 16*
Sibert, Ernest 1941- *WhoAm 90*
Sibert, Sharon Rogers 1959- *WhoSSW 91*
Sibert, Thomas Edwin 1949- *BiDrAPA 89*
Sibigtroth, Alan Ward 1950- *St&PR 91*
Sibigtroth, Joseph Clarence 1915- *WhoAm 90*
Sibilia, Rhonda Victor 1957- *WhoAmW 91*
Siblesz, Isabel Maria 1962- *WhoAmW 91*
Sibley, Alden Kingsland 1911- *WhoAm 90*
Sibley, Anthony Robert 1932- *WhoWor 91*
Sibley, Carol Morse 1944- *WhoAmW 91*
Sibley, Celestine *BioIn 16*
Sibley, Charles Gald 1917- *WhoAm 90*
Sibley, Charles Kenneth 1921- *WhoAmA 91*
Sibley, Charlotte Elaine 1946- *WhoAmW 91*
Sibley, David Emile 1935- *St&PR 91, WhoAm 90*
Sibley, David Sumner 1947- *WhoE 91*
Sibley, Dawn Bunnell 1939- *WhoAm 90, WhoAmW 91*
Sibley, Earl A. 1929- *St&PR 91*
Sibley, Edgar Henry 1926- *WhoSSW 91*
Sibley, Ellen *St&PR 91*
Sibley, Gerry Ogden 1937- *St&PR 91*
Sibley, Henry Hastings 1811-1891 *WhNaAH*
Sibley, Horace Holden 1939- *WhoAm 90*
Sibley, James Ashley, Jr. 1916- *WhoSSW 91*
Sibley, James Malcolm 1919- *WhoAm 90, WhoWor 91*
Sibley, Mark Anderson 1950- *WhoAm 90, WhoWor 91*
Sibley, Warren Oxsheer *BiDrAPA 89*
Sibley, William Arthur 1932- *WhoAm 90, WhoE 91*
Sibley, William Austin 1925- *WhoAm 90*
Sibley, William Francis 1947- *WhoEmL 91*
Sibley, Willis Elbridge 1930- *WhoAm 90*
Sibly, Ebenezer *EncO&P 3*
Sibmacher, Johannes *PenDiDA 89*
Sibold, Robert H. 1941- *St&PR 91*
Sibole, Richard R. 1942- *St&PR 91*
Sibolski, John Alfred, Jr. 1946- *WhoEmL 91*
Sibomana, Adrien *WhoWor 91*
Sibrack, Gerald B 1948- *BiDrAPA 89*
Sibyl 1160-1190 *WomWR*
Sibylla 1160-1190 *WomWR*
Sica 1932- *WhoAmA 91*
Sica, Mark J. 1958- *ODwPR 91*
Sica, Paolo 1935-1988 *BioIn 16*
Sicard, Jacques *PenDiDA 89*
Sicaud, Sabine 1913-1928 *EncCoWW*
Siccardi, Franco 1946- *WhoWor 91*
Siccardi, Frank John 1935- *WhoSSW 91*
Sice, Pierre Henri 1944- *St&PR 91*
Sichel, Deborah Anne *BiDrAPA 89*
Sichel, Leonard Joseph 1936- *St&PR 91*
Sichel, Peter Max Ferdinand 1922- *WhoE 91*
Sichell, Jane *BiDrAPA 89*
Sichenze, Celeste Marie 1937- *WhoAmW 91*
Sicherl, Pavle 1935- *WhoWor 91*
Sicherman, Marvin Allen 1934- *WhoAm 90*
Sichert, Paul O. 1933- *ODwPR 91, St&PR 91*
Sichewski, Vernon Roger 1942- *WhoSSW 91*
Sichi, Harry J. 1937- *St&PR 91*
Sichirollo, Livio 1928- *WhoWor 91*
Sichler, Edward H. 1935- *St&PR 91*
Sichler, Joseph E. 1941- *St&PR 91*
Sichler, Joseph Eberhardt, III. 1941- *WhoAm 90*
Sicignano, Joseph Ralph 1945- *BiDrAPA 89*
Siciliano, Enzo 1934- *WhoWor 91*
Siciliano, Rocco Carmine 1922- *St&PR 91, WhoAm 90, WhoWor 91*
Sick, Gary Gordon 1935- *WhoE 91*
Sick, William Norman, Jr. 1935- *WhoAm 90*
Sickel, Hugh V *BiDrAPA 89*
Sickels, Robert Judd 1931- *WhoAm 90*
Sickerman Hoffman, Carol Wendy 1956- *WhoAmW 91*
Sickert, Walter 1860-1942 *IntDcAA 90*
Sickinger Lins, Debra Rose 1958- *WhoAmW 91*
Sickle, Cody T. 1949- *St&PR 91, WhoAm 90*
Sickler, Francis Edgar 1928- *St&PR 91*
Sickler, John Joseph 1942- *St&PR 91*
Sickler, Michael Allan 1945- *WhoAmA 91, WhoE 91*
Sickles, Daniel E. *BioIn 16*
Sickles, Daniel James 1959- *WhoSSW 91*
Sickles, Mary *BiDrAPA 89*
Sickles, Noel 1910-1982 *EncACom*
Sicklesmith, Donna Lou 1953- *WhoAmW 91*
Sickman, Jessalee Bane 1905- *WhoAmA 91*
Sickman, Laurence 1906-1988 *AnObit 1988, BioIn 16*
Siclare, Cross R. 1955- *St&PR 91*
Sicotte, Andrew Ronald 1946- *WhoSSW 91*
Sicroff, Elan *NewAgMG*
Sicuro, Franco *BiDrAPA 89*
Sicuro, Franco 1955- *WhoE 91*
Sicuro, Natale A. *BioIn 16*
Sicuro, Natale Anthony 1934- *WhoAm 90*
Sidamon-Eristoff, Anne Phipps 1932- *WhoAm 90*
Sidamon-Eristoff, Constantine 1930- *WhoAm 90*
Sidare, Lynn Catherine 1958- *WhoE 91*
Sidarto, Amal Abadi 1937- *WhoWor 91*
Sidarweck, William John 1950- *WhoE 91*
Sidaway, Hazel Kidwell 1943- *WhoAmW 91*
Sidaway-Wolf, Daphne Mercedes 1955- *WhoWor 91*
Sidbury, James Buren 1922- *WhoAm 90*
Siddal, Elizabeth Eleanor 1829-1862 *BiDWomA*
Siddall, Elizabeth 1829-1862 *BioIn 16*
Siddall, Elizabeth Eleanor 1829-1862 *BiDWomA*
Siddappa, Doddametikurke 1936- *BiDrAPA 89*
Siddayao, Corazon Morales 1932- *WhoE 91*
Siddelley, Barbara *IntWWM 90*
Sidders, Patrick M. 1940- *St&PR 91*
Sidders, Patrick Michael 1940- *WhoAm 90*
Siddhartha Gautama *EncJap*
Siddhi Savetsila 1919- *WhoWor 91*
Siddiqi, Khurshid Alam 1943- *WhoWor 91*
Siddiqi, Mohammed Shahid 1958- *WhoWor 91*
Siddiqi, Sehba Nigar *BiDrAPA 89*
Siddique, Mohamed Nayeem *BiDrAPA 89*
Siddique, Zahida A 1940- *BiDrAPA 89*
Siddiqui, Abdur-Razzaque 1932- *BiDrAPA 89*
Siddiqui, Ather S *BiDrAPA 89*

Siddiqui, Farzana Q BiDrAPA 89
Siddon, Thomas Edward 1941- WhoAm 90, WhoE 91
Siddons, Anne Rivers BioIn 16
Siddons, Anne Rivers 1936- ConAu 33NR, MajTwCW
Siddons, Ernest George 1933- St&PR 91
Siddons, James DeWitt 1948- IntWWM 90
Siddons, Sarah 1756-1831 WorAlBi
Sidebottom, William George 1948- WhoSSW 91
Sidebottom, William Jeffrey 1947- WhoEmL 91
Sidel, Enid Ruth 1936- WhoAmW 91
Sidel, M. Kent 1950- WhoSSW 91
Sidells, Arthur F. 1907- WhoAm 90
Siden, Franklin 1922- WhoAmA 91
Sidenbladh, Erik 1946- WhoWor 91
Sider, Roger Claude 1941- BiDrAPA 89
Sideri, Anthony H. 1925- St&PR 91
Sideris, Alexander 1898-1978 WhoAmA 91N
Sideris, George J. 1926- St&PR 91
Sideris, George Nicholas John 1937- WhoSSW 91
Sideris, Michael S BiDrAPA 89
Sides, Desmond 1955- WhoSSW 91
Sides, Harold L. 1941- St&PR 91
Sides, James Ralph 1936- WhoAm 90
Sides, John Quincy 1918- St&PR 91
Sides, Kermit Franklin 1932- WhoSSW 91
Sidewater, Arthur 1914- WhoAm 90
Sidewater, Morris 1912- WhoAm 90
Sidewater, Samuel 1938- St&PR 91
Sidewater, Steven St&PR 91
Sidey, Hugh Swanson 1927- WhoAm 90
Sidey, Ian MacNaughton 1947- WhoE 91
Sidgwick, Cecily 1854-1934 FemiCLE
Sidgwick, Eleanor Mildred 1845-1936 EncPaPR 91
Sidgwick, Ethel 1877-1970 BioIn 16, FemiCLE
Sidgwick, Henry 1838-1900 BioIn 16, EncO&P 3, EncPaPR 91
Sidgwick, Henry, Mrs. 1845-1936 EncO&P 3
Sidharta, Nathanael O 1944- BiDrAPA 89
Sidhom, Mervat E BiDrAPA 89
Sidhu, Surinder K BiDrAPA 89
Sidhwa, Bapsi 1936- FemiCLE
Sidjakov, Nicholas 1924- AuBYP 90
Sidjakov, Nicolas 1924- WhoAm 90
Sidlauskas, Val 1927- St&PR 91
Sidle, Allan Charles 1940- BiDrAPA 89
Sidle, Paul Robert 1925- St&PR 91
Sidley, Nathan T BiDrAPA 89
Sidman, Arnold Brian 1940- St&PR 91
Sidman, Lawrence R. BioIn 16
Sidman, Richard Leon 1928- WhoAm 90
Sidman, Robert David WhoSSW 91
Sidnam, Caroline Northcote 1952- WhoE 91
Sidney, Ivan BioIn 16
Sidney, Margaret AuBYP 90
Sidney, Mary 1561-1621 BiDEWW
Sidney, P J DrBIPA 90
Sidney, Philip 1554-1586 BioIn 16, WorAlBi, WrPh
Sidney, Sylvia 1910- WhoAm 90, WorAlBi
Sido, Kevin Richard 1951- WhoEmL 91
Sidorowicz, Antonina 1902- BiDrAPA 89
Sidoti, Raymond 1929- IntWWM 90
Sidrak, Rafik Malak BiDrAPA 89
Sidran, Ben BioIn 16, NewAgMG
Sidran, Miriam 1920- WhoAmW 91
Sidrane, Michelle Diana 1948- WhoAm 90
Sidransky, Herschel 1925- WhoAm 90
Sidun, Nancy Marie 1955- WhoAmW 91
Sidway, Lois BioIn 16
Sidwell, Robert William 1937- WhoAm 90
Sidwell-Thompson, Doris M BiDrAPA 89
Sieban, Henry E. 1937- St&PR 91
Siebel, Franz Anton 1777-1842 PenDiDA 89
Siebel, Mathias Paul WhoAm 90
Sieben, Paul G. 1947- St&PR 91
Siebenburgen, David A. 1947- WhoAm 90
Siebenmann, Gustav 1923- WhoWor 91
Siebenmann, Nancylee Arbutus 1933- WhoAmW 91
Siebens, Harold W. BioIn 16
Siebenthal, Paul Leroy 1938- St&PR 91
Siebenthall, Curtis Alan 1929- WhoSSW 91
Sieber, Albert 1844-1907 WhNaAH
Sieber, Robert P. 1945- St&PR 91
Sieber, Roy 1923- WhoAmA 91
Siebern, Norm 1933- Ballpl 90
Siebert, Calvin D. 1934- WhoAm 90
Siebert, Charles BioIn 16
Siebert, Diane AuBYP 90
Siebert, Dick 1912-1978 Ballpl 90
Siebert, George William 1943- WhoAm 90
Siebert, Karl Joseph 1945- WhoEmL 91
Siebert, Lynn Ellen Laitman 1946- IntWWM 90
Siebert, Muriel BioIn 16, WhoAm 90, WhoAmW 91
Siebert, Muriel 1932- EncABHB 7 [port]
Siebert, Paul 1953- Ballpl 90
Siebert, Raymond Nicholas 1947- St&PR 91
Siebert, Robert J. 1920- St&PR 91
Siebert, Sonny 1937- Ballpl 90
Siebert, Stephanie Ray 1949- WhoAmW 91
Siebert, Stephen Warner 1957- BiDrAPA 89
Siebert, William McConway 1925- WhoAm 90
Sieberts, Jan Kristian 1942- St&PR 91
Siebler, Dwight 1937- Ballpl 90
Siebner, Herbert 1925- WhoAmA 91
Siebold, Bert Allen 1951- WhoSSW 91
Siebrasse, Richard William 1926- St&PR 91
Siebring, Barteld Richard 1924- WhoAm 90
Sieckman, Walter 1931- St&PR 91
Sieczkarek, Mark M. 1954- St&PR 91
Siedel, George John, III 1945- WhoEmL 91
Siedlarz, John Edward 1942- St&PR 91
Siedlecki, John W. 1938- St&PR 91
Siedlecki, Peter Anthony 1938- WhoWor 91
Siedler, Arthur James 1927- WhoAm 90
Siedlyk, Leon Lavern 1924- St&PR 91
Siedzikowski, Henry Francis 1953- WhoWor 91
Siefer, Gregor F.H. 1928- WhoWor 91
Siefers, Robert George 1945- St&PR 91, WhoAm 90
Siefert, David Michael 1951- WhoWor 91
Siefert, Robert George 1931- St&PR 91
Siefert, Tina Gilbert 1965- WhoAmW 91
Siefert-Kazanjian, Donna WhoAmW 91, WhoE 91
Sieff, John 1928- St&PR 91
Sieff, John Alexander 1923- WhoAm 90
Sieff, Marcus Joseph 1913- WhoWor 91
Sieff of Brimpton, Baron 1913- WhoWor 91
Siefkes, Dirk 1938- WhoWor 91
Siefkin, William Charles 1946- WhoE 91, WhoWor 91
Sieg, Albert Louis 1930- St&PR 91, WhoAm 90
Sieg, Dan J. 1943- St&PR 91
Sieg, Dennis A. 1932- St&PR 91
Sieg, George D., Jr. 1934- St&PR 91
Sieg, Karl Gregory 1961- BiDrAPA 89
Sieg, Robert Lawrence 1938- WhoAmA 91
Sieg, Theo Le BioIn 16
Sieg, Wilfried 1945- WhoE 91
Siegal, Alan Paul 1953- BiDrAPA 89
Siegal, Allan 1940- BioIn 16
Siegal, Allan Marshall 1940- WhoAm 90, WhoE 91
Siegal, Aranka 1930- Au&Arts 5 [port]
Siegal, Burton Lee 1931- WhoAm 90
Siegal, Charles BiDrAPA 89
Siegal, David BioIn 16
Siegal, Diana Laskin BioIn 16
Siegal, Jacob J. 1929- WhoAm 90
Siegal, John NewYTBS 90 [port]
Siegal, Lisa Aronow 1961- BiDrAPA 89
Siegal, Rita Goran 1934- WhoAm 90
Siegal, Sheppard 1909-1988 BioIn 16
Siegan, Bernard Herbert 1924- WhoAm 90
Siegbahn, Kai 1918- WorAlBi
Siegbahn, Kai Manne Borje 1918- WhoAm 90, WhoWor 91
Siegbahn, Karl M. G. 1886-1978 WorAlBi
Siegbahn, Karl Manne Georg 1886-1978 DcScB S2
Siegel, Abraham J. 1922- WhoWor 91
Siegel, Adrian 1898-1978 WhoAmA 91N
Siegel, Alan BioIn 16
Siegel, Alan 1935- WhoE 91
Siegel, Alan Michael 1938- WhoAm 90
Siegel, Allen George 1934- WhoAm 90
Siegel, Allen Martin 1940- BiDrAPA 89
Siegel, Alvan 1934- St&PR 91
Siegel, Andrew 1941- BiDrAPA 89
Siegel, Ann Musick BiDrAPA 89
Siegel, Anthony Joseph BiDrAPA 89
Siegel, Arnold 1928- St&PR 91
Siegel, Arnold 1931- St&PR 91
Siegel, Arthur 1908- WhoAm 90
Siegel, Arthur J. 1943- St&PR 91
Siegel, Barbara Zenz 1931- WhoAmW 91
Siegel, Barry 1947- BiDrAPA 89
Siegel, Benjamin Morton NewYTBS 90
Siegel, Benjamin Morton 1916-1990 BioIn 16
Siegel, Bernard S. 1932- NewAgE 90
Siegel, Bernie S. BioIn 16
Siegel, Betsy Reinman 1960- WhoSSW 91
Siegel, Betty Lentz 1931- WhoAm 90, WhoAmW 91, WhoSSW 91
Siegel, Brian Michael 1956- BiDrAPA 89
Siegel, Carl Ludwig 1896-1981 DcScB S2
Siegel, Carole 1936- WhoAmW 91
Siegel, Carolyn Lee 1951- WhoWrEP 89
Siegel, Charles 1944- WhoAm 90
Siegel, Clifford Howard 1951- BiDrAPA 89
Siegel, Cynthia Allison 1964- WhoAmW 91
Siegel, Daniel C 1917- BiDrAPA 89
Siegel, Daniel J. 1957- BiDrAPA 89
Siegel, David Donald 1931- WhoAm 90
Siegel, David J. 1948- St&PR 91
Siegel, Dean P. 1952- ODwPR 91
Siegel, Dink WhoAmA 91
Siegel, Don 1912- WhoAm 90
Siegel, Donald Bert 1935- St&PR 91
Siegel, Donald G 1924- BiDrAPA 89
Siegel, Dorothy Paula 1932- WhoWrEP 89
Siegel, Edward Allen 1939- BiDrAPA 89
Siegel, Edward J. 1944- St&PR 91
Siegel, Edward M. 1934- St&PR 91
Siegel, Eliot 1960- BioIn 16
Siegel, Eva Stern 1956- WhoAmW 91
Siegel, Everett R. 1955- BiDrAPA 89
Siegel, Fran 1960- WhoAmA 91
Siegel, Fred 1941- WhoE 91
Siegel, Frederic Richard 1932- WhoAm 90
Siegel, Gary Michael 1947- St&PR 91
Siegel, Gary Morton 1930- St&PR 91
Siegel, George Henry 1926- WhoAm 90
Siegel, Glenda June 1934- WhoAmW 91
Siegel, Glenn Ernest 1958- WhoE 91
Siegel, Glenn N BiDrAPA 89
Siegel, Harold Aryai 1931- St&PR 91
Siegel, Henry Howard BioIn 16
Siegel, Henry Winter 1946- WhoWor 91
Siegel, Herbert Bernard 1934- WhoAm 90
Siegel, Herbert J. 1928- St&PR 91
Siegel, Herbert Jay 1928- WhoAm 90, WhoE 91
Siegel, Hudie Brooke BiDrAPA 89
Siegel, Ira B. 1943- St&PR 91
Siegel, Ira Theodore 1944- WhoAm 90
Siegel, Jack Morton 1922- WhoAm 90
Siegel, Jack S. 1946- WhoAm 90
Siegel, Janis BioIn 16
Siegel, Jeffrey BioIn 16
Siegel, Jeffrey 1942- IntWWM 90, PenDiMP
Siegel, Jeffrey Stuart 1942- St&PR 91
Siegel, Jeremy James 1945- WhoE 91
Siegel, Jerome Richard 1948- WhoSSW 91
Siegel, Jerome Samuel 1944- WhoE 91
Siegel, Jerry 1914- EncACom
Siegel, Jules 1917- St&PR 91
Siegel, Kathy 1947- St&PR 91
Siegel, Larry 1935- WhoSSW 91
Siegel, Laurence 1928- WhoAm 90
Siegel, Laurence 1931- IntWWM 90
Siegel, Lawrence 1931- WhoSSW 91
Siegel, Lawrence Allen 1954- BiDrAPA 89, WhoE 91
Siegel, Leah Rothstein 1919- WhoAmW 91
Siegel, Leo Dink 1910- WhoE 91
Siegel, Leonard I. 1926- St&PR 91
Siegel, Leonard Israel 1924- BiDrAPA 89
Siegel, Lesley Pam BiDrAPA 89
Siegel, Lewis W. 1949- WhoEmL 91
Siegel, Lloyd H. 1928- WhoAm 90, WhoE 91
Siegel, Lloyd Martin BiDrAPA 89
Siegel, Louis 1902- St&PR 91
Siegel, Louis A. BioIn 16
Siegel, Louis Pendleton 1942- WhoAm 90
Siegel, Lucille Pamela 1956- WhoAmW 91
Siegel, Lucy Boswell 1950- WhoAmW 91
Siegel, Lynne Elise Moore 1957- WhoAmW 91
Siegel, M. Alden 1938- St&PR 91
Siegel, Madelyn Jane BiDrAPA 89
Siegel, Marc Monroe 1916- WhoAm 90
Siegel, Margot WomArch
Siegel, Margot, & Katherine Diamond WomArch
Siegel, Mark BiDrAPA 89
Siegel, Mark Jordan 1949- WhoEmL 91, WhoSSW 91, WhoWor 91
Siegel, Martin 1925- WhoE 91, WhoWrEP 89
Siegel, Martin David 1948- WhoEmL 91
Siegel, Martin Edward 1946- St&PR 91
Siegel, Marvin 1935- WhoAm 90
Siegel, Marvin Haas 1934- WhoSSW 91
Siegel, Max 1918-1988 BioIn 16
Siegel, Mayer 1936- WhoAm 90
Siegel, Michael D. 1937- St&PR 91
Siegel, Michael Eric 1950- WhoE 91
Siegel, Michael Ian 1942- WhoE 91
Siegel, Milt B. St&PR 91
Siegel, Milton P. 1911- WhoAm 90, WhoSSW 91, WhoWor 91
Siegel, Mo J. 1949- WhoAm 90
Siegel, Morton K. 1924- BioIn 16
Siegel, Naomi Anne 1926- WhoAmW 91
Siegel, Nathaniel Harold 1929- WhoAm 90
Siegel, Ned Lawrence 1951- WhoSSW 91
Siegel, Owen BioIn 16
Siegel, Owen R. 1919- St&PR 91
Siegel, Paul 1938- WhoWor 91
Siegel, Paul Marc 1948- St&PR 91
Siegel, Randy 1955- WhoSSW 91
Siegel, Raymond John 1947- St&PR 91
Siegel, Richard BioIn 16
Siegel, Richard Allen 1927- WhoE 91
Siegel, Richard Allen 1942- WhoE 91
Siegel, Richard David 1939- WhoAm 90
Siegel, Robert 1915- BiDrAPA 89
Siegel, Robert 1939- BioIn 16
Siegel, Robert B. 1924- St&PR 91
Siegel, Robert Harold 1939- WhoWrEP 89
Siegel, Robert James 1929- WhoSSW 91
Siegel, Robert Ted 1928- WhoAm 90
Siegel, Rubin Louis BiDrAPA 89
Siegel, Samuel 1930- St&PR 91, WhoAm 90, WhoSSW 91
Siegel, Saul M BiDrAPA 89
Siegel, Seymour 1927-1988 BioIn 16
Siegel, Seymour B 1923- BiDrAPA 89
Siegel, Seymour Louis 1933- WhoE 91
Siegel, Sheldon C. 1922- WhoAm 90
Siegel, Sheldon N 1934- BiDrAPA 89
Siegel, Sid 1927- WhoAm 90
Siegel, Stanley 1941- WhoAm 90
Siegel, Stephen B. 1944- WhoE 91
Siegel, Stuart Samuel 1926- WhoAm 90
Siegel, Susan Shins 1948- WhoSSW 91
Siegel, Thomas Joseph 1935- St&PR 91
Siegel, Thomas Louis 1939- WhoAm 90
Siegel, Wayne 1953- IntWWM 90
Siegel, William H. 1948- St&PR 91
Siegel, William Mordecai 1950- WhoWrEP 89
Siegel-Baum, Judith Ellen 1946- WhoEmL 91
Siegelaar, Herman 1941- WhoAm 90
Siegelman, Don Eugene 1946- WhoSSW 91
Siegelman, Lois Susan Dashef 1945- WhoAmW 91
Siegelman, Richard BioIn 16
Siegelman, Stanley Solomon 1932- WhoAm 90
Siegeltuch, Eric James 1947- WhoE 91
Siegenthaler, Robert BioIn 16
Siegenthaler, Walter Ernst 1923- WhoWor 91
Sieger, Charles Martin 1946- WhoAm 90
Sieger, Hermann Walter 1928- WhoWor 91
Sieger, John A. 1942- St&PR 91
Sieger, John Anthony 1942- WhoAm 90
Siegert, Barbara Marie 1935- WhoAmW 91, WhoE 91
Siegert, Marvin Giles 1948- St&PR 91
Siegfried, Bernard Albrecht 1934- WhoWor 91
Siegfried, David Lars 1949- St&PR 91
Siegfried, John Paul 1938- St&PR 91
Siegfried, Robert E. 1922- St&PR 91
Siegfried, Robert Edwin 1922- WhoE 91
Siegfried, William Lowell 1947- BiDrAPA 89
Siegfried, Willis Albert, Jr. 1944- WhoAm 90
Sieghart, Paul 1927-1988 AnObit 1988
Siegl, Theodor WhoAmA 91N
Siegl, Walter 1938- WhoWor 91
Siegle, Richard E. 1929- St&PR 91
Siegler, Howard Matthew 1932- WhoAm 90, WhoSSW 91
Siegler, Ira I. 1943- St&PR 91
Siegler, Joseph E 1957- BiDrAPA 89
Siegler, Scott Merrill 1947- St&PR 91
Siegler, Thomas E. 1934- St&PR 91
Siegler, Thomas Edmund 1934- WhoAm 90
Siegler-Lathrop, Patrick 1942- WhoWor 91
Siegman, Alfred J 1922- BiDrAPA 89
Siegman, Anthony Edward 1931- WhoAm 90
Siegman, Gita 1939- ConAu 31NR
Siegman, Henry 1930- WhoAm 90
Siegman, Marion Joyce 1933- WhoAmW 91
Siegmann, Adolf F H BiDrAPA 89
Siegmann, William Lewis 1943- WhoE 91
Siegmeister, Elie 1909- AuBYP 90, BioIn 16, EncAL, IntWWM 90, WhoAm 90
Siegmund, Richard W. 1944- St&PR 91
Siegner, Alan L. 1939- St&PR 91
Siegrist, Johannes 1943- WhoWor 91
Siegrist, Joy Helene BiDrAPA 89
Siegrist, Lundy 1925-1985 WhoAmA 91N
Siegrist, Michele Anne 1961- WhoAmW 91
Sieh, Maurine Kay 1950- WhoAmW 91
Siehl, James L. St&PR 91
Siek, Sophie 1934- St&PR 91
Siekert, Harold Richard 1928- St&PR 91
Siekert, Robert George 1924- WhoAm 90, WhoWrEP 89
Siekevitz, Philip 1918- WhoAm 90
Siekierski, Kamilla Malgorzata 1938- WhoAmW 91
Siekman, Lula Beatrice 1912- WhoAmW 91
Siekmann, Donald Charles 1938- WhoSSW 91, WhoWor 91
Siekmann, Frank H. 1925- IntWWM 90
Siel, Susan Michelle 1961- WhoAmW 91

Sielczak, Marek W. 1935- WhoSSW 91
Sieleni, Bruce Alan BiDrAPA 89
Sielicky, Theresa BioIn 16
Sieling, Gary 1952- IntWWM 90
Sielke, Eugene L BiDrAPA 89
Sielski, Gary F. 1941- St&PR 91
Sielski, Joann Elizabeth 1955- WhoAmW 91
Siembab, Kevin J. 1955- St&PR 91
Siemens, Andreas Meinhard Ernest 1921- WhoWor 91
Siemens, Charlotte Anne 1960- BiDrAPA 89
Siemens, Ernst Werner Von 1816-1892 WorAlBi
Siemens, Werner 1816-1892 BioIn 16
Siemens, William 1823-1883 BioIn 16, WorAlBi
Siemer, Deanne Clemence 1940- WhoAm 90
Siemer, Paul J. ODwPR 91
Siemer, Paul Jennings 1946- WhoAm 90
Siemer, Richard Clemens 1949- St&PR 91
Siemer, Robert Clemens 1952- St&PR 91
Siemiatycki, Jack 1946- WhoAm 90
Sieminski, Alfred Dennis NewYTBS 90
Siemon, Carl 1922- St&PR 91
Siemon, John Austin 1959- St&PR 91
Siemon, Joyce Marilyn 1944- WhoSSW 91
Siemon, Robert Lawrence 1949- St&PR 91
Siems, Margarethe 1879-1952 PenDiMP
Siena, Matteo Da 1430?-1495 BioIn 16
Siener, William Harold 1945- WhoAm 90, WhoE 91
Sienkiewicz, Henryk 1846-1916 WorAlBi
Sienkiewicz, John Casimir 1933- St&PR 91, WhoAm 90
Sienkiewicz, Julian WhoWrEP 89
Sienkiewicz, Julian M. 1929- WhoAm 90
Sienkiewicz, Stanley 1945- WhoE 91
Sienkiewicz-Mercer, Ruth BioIn 16
Siennicki, Edmund John 1920- IntWWM 90
Siepi, Cesare 1923- IntWWM 90, PenDiMP, WhoAm 90
Siepser, Ellen Hope BiDrAPA 89
Sieracki, Norbert James 1923- St&PR 91
Sierakowski, Raymond S. 1951- St&PR 91
Sierakowski, Robert Leon 1937- WhoAm 90
Sierck, Detlef 1900-1987 BioIn 16
Siering, Joel R. 1936- St&PR 91
Sierk, Arnold John 1946- WhoEmL 91
Sierles, Frederick S 1942- BiDrAPA 89
Sierles, Frederick Stephen 1942- WhoAm 90
Sierra, Debra Lynn 1962- WhoAmW 91
Sierra, Gregorio Martinez EncCoWW
Sierra, Linda Jimenez 1949- WhoWor 91
Sierra, Paul Alberto 1944- WhoHisp 91
Sierra, Ralph U 1904- EncO&P 3
Sierra, Richard Benson 1933- St&PR 91
Sierra, Roberto 1953- IntWWM 90
Sierra, Ruben 1965- Ballpl 90, WorAlBi
Sierra, Ruben Angel 1965- WhoAm 90, WhoHisp 91
Sierra, Tony M. WhoHisp 91
Sierra-Negron, Maida 1958- BiDrAPA 89
Sierro, Jean-Marc 1946- WhoWor 91
Siers, Charles Larry 1942- St&PR 91
Siers, Larry 1942- St&PR 91
Sierzant, Patricia Lucy 1948- WhoAmW 91
Sies, Helmut 1942- WhoWor 91
Siesel, Alfred J. 1929- ODwPR 91
Siess, Alfred Albert, Jr. 1935- WhoE 91, WhoWor 91
Siess, Chester Paul 1916- WhoAm 90
Siess, Elmar Alois 1939- WhoWor 91
Siess, Judith Ann 1947- WhoAmW 91
Siess, Robert D. 1943- St&PR 91
Sieubert, Antonio PenDiDA 89
Sievan, Lee BioIn 16
Sievan, Maurice 1898-1981 WhoAmA 91N
Sieveking, Lance BioIn 16
Siever, Ed 1877-1920 Ballpl 90
Siever, Larry Joseph 1947- BiDrAPA 89, WhoE 91
Siever, Raymond 1923- WhoAm 90, WhoWrEP 89
Sievering, Nelson Frederick, Jr. 1924- WhoAm 90
Sievers, Albert John, III 1933- WhoAm 90
Sievers, George Robert 1927- St&PR 91
Sievers, John N. 1952- St&PR 91
Sievers, Mark Stanley 1933- WhoSSW 91
Sievers, Michael A. 1945- St&PR 91
Sievers, Robert H. 1941- WhoAm 90
Sievers, Robert J. 1933- St&PR 91
Sievers, Roy 1926- Ballpl 90
Sievert, Dwight William 1950- BiDrAPA 89
Sievert, James Lee 1934- St&PR 91
Sievert, Michael James 1955- BiDrAPA 89
Sievert, Wayne R. 1938- St&PR 91
Sieverts, Frank Arne 1933- WhoAm 90
Siewers, Albert Bernard, Jr. 1921- BiDrAPA 89
Siewers, C. Nathaniel 1947- St&PR 91
Siewers, Christiane M F 1936- BiDrAPA 89
Siewert, Cyrill R. 1943- St&PR 91
Siewert, Edgar Allen 1927- WhoSSW 91
Siewert, Jeffrey Paul 1947- St&PR 91
Siewert, Mark S. 1953- St&PR 91
Siewert, Norman R. 1914- St&PR 91
Siewert, Robin Noelle 1956- WhoAmW 91
Siewick, Joseph Thomas 1953- WhoSSW 91
Siewicki, Brenda Joyce 1949- WhoAmW 91
Siewiorek, Daniel Paul 1946- WhoAm 90
Sieyes, Emmanuel Joseph 1748-1836 BioIn 16, WorAlBi
Siface PenDiMP
Sifers, Rodney Phillip 1954- WhoSSW 91
Siff, Elliott Justin 1930- St&PR 91
Siff, Lawrence A. 1962- St&PR 91
Siff, Marlene Ida 1936- WhoAmW 91, WhoE 91
Siff, Robert M. 1924- St&PR 91
Siffert, John Sand 1947- WhoWor 91
Siffert, Robert Spencer 1918- WhoAm 90, WhoE 91
Sifford, Darrell Charles 1931- WhoAm 90
Sifford, Marilyn Oakley 1948- WhoAmW 91
Sifneos, Peter E 1920- BiDrAPA 89
Sifneos, Peter Emanuel 1920- WhoAm 90
Sifton, Charles Proctor 1935- WhoAm 90
Sifton, David Whittier 1940- WhoAm 90, WhoE 91
Sifton, Michael Clifford 1931- St&PR 91
Sifuna, Daniel Namusonge 1944- WhoWor 91
Sigadel, Robert Douglas BiDrAPA 89
Sigal, Henry Arthur BiDrAPA 89
Sigal, Irving BioIn 16
Sigal, Roland Lee 1925- St&PR 91
Sigala, Stephanie Childs 1947- WhoAmA 91
Sigale, Barry J. 1945- ODwPR 91
Sigall, Harold Fred 1943- WhoAm 90
Sigalon, Antoine 1524?-1590 PenDiDA 89
Sigaran, Mamerto 1934- WhoHisp 91
Sigas, Ibis Dalia 1939- BiDrAPA 89
Sigaud, Eugenio de Proenca 1889-1979 ArtLatA
Sigband, Norman Bruce 1920- WhoAm 90
Sigda, Mary Elizabeth 1960- WhoAmW 91
Sigel, Efrem 1943- WhoWrEP 89
Sigel, George S 1941- BiDrAPA 89
Sigel, Louis Paul, Jr. 1921- WhoE 91
Sigel, M. Michael 1920- WhoAm 90
Sigel, Marshall Elliot 1941- WhoSSW 91
Sigel, Stanley Jordan 1920- WhoAm 90
Sigerson, Dora 1866-1918 FemiCLE
Sigerson, Marjorie Lorraine 1923- WhoAmW 91
Sigety, Charles Edward 1922- WhoAm 90, WhoSSW 91, WhoWor 91
Sigfrids, James A. 1929- St&PR 91
Sigfusson, Hannes 1922- DcScanL
Sigg, Earl Carl 1934- WhoWor 91
Siggins, Jack Arthur 1938- WhoAm 90
Siggins, Lorraine D 1937- BiDrAPA 89
Sigismund, Violet M WhoAmA 91
Siglain, Helen 1950- WhoE 91, WhoEmL 91
Sigler, Andrew Clark 1931- St&PR 91, WhoAm 90, WhoE 91, WhoWor 91
Sigler, Charlotte Lee Llewel 1926- WhoAmW 91
Sigler, Hollis 1948- WhoAmA 91
Sigler, James M. 1936- St&PR 91
Sigler, Jay Adrian 1933- WhoAm 90
Sigler, Katherine 1948- WhoAmW 91
Sigler, LeRoy Walter 1926- WhoAm 90
Sigler, Lois Oliver 1923- WhoSSW 91
Sigler, Michael Frederick 1957- WhoEmL 91
Sigler, Paul Benjamin 1934- WhoAm 90
Sigler, Richard 1945- St&PR 91
Sigler, William Franklin 1909- WhoAm 90
Sigley, Timothy Douglas 1946- WhoE 91
Sigman, Eugene M. 1928- WhoAm 90
Sigman, Helene Hannah 1946- WhoAmW 91
Sigman, Jill Karen 1955- WhoAmW 91
Sigman, John Herbert 1943- St&PR 91
Sigman, Karl 1957- WhoE 91
Sigman, Mark 1950- St&PR 91
Sigman, Melvin Monroe 1935- BiDrAPA 89
Sigman, Seymour 1925- St&PR 91
Sigmon, Anne Elizabeth 1953- WhoAmW 91
Sigmon, Daniel Ray 1949- WhoSSW 91
Sigmon, Jackson Marcus 1918- WhoE 91
Sigmon, James Edward 1948- St&PR 91
Sigmon, Scott Bart 1946- WhoEmL 91
Sigmond, Richard Brian 1944- WhoE 91, WhoWor 91
Sigmond, Robert M. 1920- WhoAm 90
Sigmund, Barbara Boggs 1939-1990 NewYTBS 90 [port], News 91-1
Sigmund, Oskar Karl Friedrich 1919- IntWWM 90
Sigmund, Paul Eugene 1929- WhoAm 90
Sigmund, Peter R. ODwPR 91
Signac, Paul 1863-1935 BioIn 16
Signell, Karl Lloyd 1933- IntWWM 90
Signer, Billie Touchstone 1930- WhoWrEP 89
Signer, Harry 1910- St&PR 91
Signer, Isador 1900-1953 BioIn 16
Signer, Robert Andrew 1942- WhoAm 90
Signer, Stephen Fortus 1956- BiDrAPA 89
Signor, Said G. 1951- St&PR 91
Signor, Sharon Smith 1943- WhoAmW 91, WhoE 91
Signora, Nabil A. 1952- St&PR 91
Signore, Carol Ann 1945- WhoE 91
Signore, Joseph A. 1934- St&PR 91
Signorelli, John Joseph 1942- St&PR 91
Signorelli, Luca 1441?-1523 BioIn 16, IntDcAA 90
Signorelli, Mark Allen 1964- WhoSSW 91
Signorelli, Suzann Marie 1960- WhoAmW 91
Signoret, Simone 1921-1985 WorAlBi
Signorile, Vincent Anthony 1959- WhoE 91, WhoWor 91
Signorini, John Ernest 1945- St&PR 91
Signorini, Telemaco 1835-1901 BioIn 16
Signorino, Charles A. 1932- St&PR 91
Signorovitch, Dennis J. 1945- ODwPR 91
Signorovitch, Dennis James 1945- WhoE 91
Sigoloff, Sanford Charles 1930- St&PR 91
Sigoni, Carlo 1524?-1584 BioIn 16
Sigourney, Andre R. ConAu 132
Sigourney, Lydia H. 1791-1865 BioAmW
Sigourney, Lydia Howard 1791-1865 FemiCLE
Sigrest, Bobby Reed 1932- St&PR 91
Sigsbee, Charles D. 1845-1923 WorAlBi
Sigsbee, H. James 1949- St&PR 91
Siguenza, Herbert 1959- WhoHisp 91
Siguenza y Gongora, Carlos de 1645-1700 BioIn 16
Siguion-Reyna, Leonardo 1921- WhoWor 91
Siguler, George William 1947- St&PR 91, WhoAm 90
Sigur, Gaston Joseph, Jr. 1924- WhoAm 90
Sigurbjornsson, Einar 1944- WhoWor 91
Sigurbjornsson, Thorkell 1938- IntWWM 90
Sigurdardottir, Johanna 1942- WhoWor 91
Sigurdson, Eric Stefan BiDrAPA 89
Sigurdson, Jon S. 1935- WhoWor 91
Sigurdson, Larry LeRoy 1950- WhoEmL 91
Sigurdson, Wilfred F 1943- BiDrAPA 89
Sigurdson, William Einar BiDrAPA 89
Sigurdsson, Haraldur 1939- WhoAm 90
Sigurdsson, Jon 1941- WhoWor 91
Sigurdsson, Jon 1946- WhoWor 91
Sigurdsson, Olafur Johann 1918- DcScanL
Sigurdsson, Stefan 1887-1933 DcScanL
Sigurdsson, Thordur Baldur 1929- WhoWor 91
Sigurjonsson, Johann 1880-1919 DcScanL
Sih, Charles John 1933- WhoAm 90
Sih, Grace Jenny 1963- WhoAmW 91
Sih, Julius Wei Wu 1922- WhoAm 90
Sihag, Neelam BiDrAPA 89
Sihanouk 1922- BioIn 16
Sihanouk, Norodom ConAu 129
Sihanouk, Norodom 1922- WhoWor 91, WorAlBi
Sihare, Laxmiprasad 1933- WhoWor 91
Sihler, Gerhard Georg 1933- WhoE 91
Sihler, William Wooding 1937- WhoAm 90
Sihvonen, Oli 1921- WhoAm 90, WhoAmA 91, WhoE 91
Siimes, Jouko 1960- WhoE 91
Siimesto, Orvo Kalervo 1943- WhoWor 91
Si'k-Okskitsis 1856?-1897 DcCanB 12
Sikand, Chander K 1923- BiDrAPA 89
Sikarskie, David Lawrence 1937- WhoAm 90
Sikelianos, Angelos 1884-1951 TwCLC 39 [port]
Siker, Ephraim S. 1926- WhoAm 90
Sikes, Alfred BioIn 16
Sikes, Cynthia BioIn 16
Sikes, David Glenn 1942- WhoWrEP 89
Sikes, James C 1945- BiDrAPA 89
Sikes, Patricia Enid 1943- WhoSSW 91
Sikes, Robert L. F. 1906- WhoAm 90
Sikes, Ruth Cox 1952- WhoSSW 91
Sikes, Shirley Ruth 1928- WhoWrEP 89
Siket, Paul 1945- St&PR 91
Siki, Bela 1923- IntWWM 90, PenDiMP
Siki'muka DcCanB 12
Sikkema, Karen A. ODwPR 91
Sikkema, Karen Ann 1946- St&PR 91
Sikkema, William D. 1949- St&PR 91
Sikman, Levent 1953- BiDrAPA 89
Sikora, Ann 1964- WhoE 91
Sikora, Eugene Stanley 1924- WhoSSW 91, WhoWor 91
Sikora, Richard Innes 1927- WhoAm 90
Sikora, Richard Paul 1931- St&PR 91
Sikora, Suzanne Marie 1952- WhoEmL 91
Sikorovsky, Eugene Frank 1927- St&PR 91, WhoAm 90
Sikorski, Barbara 1955- WhoAmW 91
Sikorski, Cynthia Rose 1947- WhoSSW 91
Sikorski, Gerry 1948- WhoAm 90
Sikorski, John B BiDrAPA 89
Sikorski, Lorena Louise 1951- WhoAmW 91
Sikorski, Wladyslaw 1881-1943 BioIn 16
Sikorsky, Igor BioIn 16
Sikorsky, Igor 1889-1972 WorAlBi
Siks, Geraldine Brain 1912- BioIn 16, NotWoAT
Sikula, John Paul 1944- WhoAm 90
Sila, Basri A 1930- BiDrAPA 89
Silag, Bill 1946- WhoWrEP 89
Silagi, Barbara Weibler 1930- WhoAmW 91
Silagi, Selma 1916- WhoAm 90
Silane, Michael Francis 1943- WhoWor 91
Silani, Vincenzo 1952- WhoWor 91
Silano, Louis Frank 1920- WhoE 91
Silantien, John Joseph 1947- IntWWM 90
Silas, His Excellency Metropolitan 1919- WhoAm 90
Silas, Cecil Jesse 1932- St&PR 91, WhoAm 90, WhoSSW 91, WhoWor 91
Silas, Darlene 1966- WhoEmL 91
Silbajoris, Frank Rimvydas 1926- WhoAm 90
Silbaugh, Preston Norwood 1918- WhoAm 90, WhoWor 91
Silber, Austin 1923- BiDrAPA 89, WhoE 91
Silber, Bernard NewYTBS 90
Silber, Earle 1925- BiDrAPA 89
Silber, James R 1923- BiDrAPA 89
Silber, Joan Karen 1945- WhoWrEP 89
Silber, John 1926- News 90 [port]
Silber, John R. BioIn 16
Silber, John Robert 1926- WhoAm 90, WhoE 91
Silber, Maurice 1922- WhoAmA 91
Silber, Norman Jules 1945- WhoSSW 91
Silber, Saul 1881-1946 BioIn 16
Silber, Terry 1940- BioIn 16
Silberberg, Donald H. 1934- WhoAm 90
Silberberg, Joel Maxim 1954- BiDrAPA 89
Silberberg-Peirce, Susan R. 1949- WhoAmW 91
Silberfarb, Peter Michael 1938- BiDrAPA 89
Silberg, Jay Eliot 1941- WhoAm 90
Silbergeld, Ellen Kovner 1945- WhoAm 90
Silbergeld, Sam 1918- BiDrAPA 89, WhoE 91
Silberger, Julius BiDrAPA 89
Silbergleid, Michael Ian 1964- WhoE 91
Silberglitt, Richard Stephen 1942- WhoE 91
Silberhartz, David Mark BiDrAPA 89
Silberhorn, Gene Michael 1938- WhoSSW 91
Silbering, Robert Howard 1947- WhoEmL 91
Silberlicht, Albert 1946- St&PR 91
Silberman, Alan Harvey 1940- WhoAm 90
Silberman, Allan David 1935- St&PR 91
Silberman, Arlin Joel 1947- BiDrAPA 89, WhoE 91
Silberman, Arnold David 1935- St&PR 91
Silberman, Arthur 1929- WhoAmA 91
Silberman, Charles Eliot 1925- WhoAm 90, WhoWrEP 89
Silberman, Charles G BiDrAPA 89
Silberman, Charles I. 1949- St&PR 91
Silberman, Corinne St&PR 91
Silberman, David B., Jr. 1920- St&PR 91
Silberman, Donald J 1915- BiDrAPA 89
Silberman, Donn Michael 1959- WhoEmL 91
Silberman, Edward Kenneth 1944- BiDrAPA 89
Silberman, Eugene Irvin 1930- St&PR 91
Silberman, Frank 1935- WhoWor 91
Silberman, Gregory Alan 1953- WhoSSW 91
Silberman, H. Lee 1919- WhoAm 90, WhoE 91
Silberman, Henry K 1914- BiDrAPA 89
Silberman, Ira J. 1936- St&PR 91
Silberman, Isaac N 1927- BiDrAPA 89
Silberman, James Henry 1927- WhoAm 90
Silberman, John Alan 1951- WhoEmL 91
Silberman, Laurence Hirsch 1935- WhoAm 90
Silberman, Lloyd Paul 1954- St&PR 91
Silberman, Lou Hackett 1914- WhoAm 90
Silberman, Murray 1921- WhoWor 91
Silberman, Peter Henry 1930- WhoAm 90
Silberman, Richard T. BioIn 16
Silberman, Shoshana Meira 1942- WhoE 91
Silbermann, Peter Thomas 1941- St&PR 91
Silbernagel, Walter 1924- St&PR 91

Silbersack, John 1954- ConAu 33NR
Silberschlag, Eisig 1903-1988 BioIn 16
Silberstein, Alan Mark 1947- WhoAm 90
Silberstein, Charles H BiDrAPA 89
Silberstein, Charles K. 1929- St&PR 91
Silberstein, Jesse BioIn 16
Silberstein, Kenneth 1920- St&PR 91
Silberstein, Lynn 1951- WhoAmW 91
Silberstein, Morton Henry 1922- BiDrAPA 89
Silberstein, N. Ronald 1927- St&PR 91, WhoAm 90
Silberstein, Stephen G 1936- BiDrAPA 89
Silberstein-Storfer, Muriel WhoE 91
Silberstein-Storfer, Muriel Rosoff WhoAmA 91
Silbert, David C BiDrAPA 89
Silbert, Howard 1950- BiDrAPA 89
Silbert, Jacqueline 1921- WhoAmW 91
Silbert, Layle WhoWrEP 89
Silbert, Marc BiDrAPA 89
Silbert, Maria EncO&P 3
Silbert, Richard Ross BiDrAPA 89
Silbert, Robert 1928- BiDrAPA 89
Silbert, Stephen David 1942- WhoAm 90
Silbert, Theodore H. 1904- WhoAm 90, WhoE 91
Silbert, William C. 1924- St&PR 91
Silberwagel, Walter Eric 1961- St&PR 91
Silbey, Joel Henry 1933- WhoAm 90
Silbey, Paula J. 1946- WhoWrEP 89
Silbiger, Jill Satzler BiDrAPA 89
Silburn, Elaine Gwendolyn 1937- WhoAmW 91
Silby, Donald Wayne 1948- St&PR 91
Silcott, George Reed 1925- St&PR 91
Silcott, William L BiDrAPA 89
Silcox, Gordon Bruce 1938- WhoE 91
Silcox, Sharon Faye 1951- St&PR 91
Silebi, Cesar Augusto 1945- WhoE 91
Silen, Deborah Anne 1953- BiDrAPA 89
Silen, Ivan 1944- BioIn 16
Silen, William 1927- WhoAm 90
Sileo, Albert J. BioIn 16
Sileo, Ann Pfeiffer 1937- WhoAmW 91
Siler, Eddie Douglas 1942- WhoWor 91
Siler, Eugene Edward, Jr. 1936- WhoAm 90, WhoSSW 91
Siler, Patrick BioIn 16
Siler, Todd 1953- WhoAmA 91
Siler, Todd Lael 1953- WhoE 91, WhoEmL 91, WhoWor 91
Siler, Walter Orlando, Jr. 1920- WhoAm 90
Siles, Hernando 1881?-1942 BioIn 16
Siles Zuazo, Hernan BioIn 16
Siles Zuazo, Hernan 1914- WhoWor 91
Silesky, Barry 1949- WhoWrEP 89
Silets, Harvey Marvin 1931- WhoAm 90
Silfen, David M. 1945- WhoAm 90
Silfen, Herman 1919- St&PR 91
Silha, Otto A. 1919- St&PR 91
Silha, Otto Adelbert 1919- WhoWor 91
Silhavy, Thomas Joseph 1948- WhoAm 90
Silhouette, Etienne De 1709-1767 WorAlBi
Siliato, Ronald J. 1959- WhoE 91
Siligmueller, Dale Scott 1949- St&PR 91
Silins, Astrida I. 1928- WhoAmW 91
Silins, Janis 1896- WhoAmA 91
Silinsh, Joan 1937- WhoAmW 91
Silitch, Clarissa MacVeagh 1930- ConAu 31NR
Silja, Anja 1940- IntWWM 90, PenDiMP
Siljak, Dragoslav D. 1933- WhoAm 90
Silk, Adam Jonathan BiDrAPA 89
Silk, Alvin John 1935- WhoAm 90
Silk, Bertram Edward 1931- St&PR 91, WhoAm 90, WhoE 91
Silk, Dennis 1928- ConAu 132
Silk, Dorothy 1883-1942 PenDiMP
Silk, Emanuel I BiDrAPA 89
Silk, Fred C. Z. 1934- WhoAm 90
Silk, Frederick C.Z. 1934- St&PR 91
Silk, George 1916- WhoAm 90
Silk, John Kevin 1938- WhoE 91
Silk, Kenneth R 1944- BiDrAPA 89
Silk, Leonard Solomon 1918- WhoAm 90
Silk, Steve BioIn 16
Silka, Van Richard 1955- BiDrAPA 89
Silke, Gary 1938- St&PR 91
Silkenat, James Robert 1947- WhoE 91
Silkes, Lawrence 1936- St&PR 91
Silkett, Robert Tillson 1929- WhoAm 90
Silkin, Lord 1918-1988 AnObit 1988
Silkin, Jon BioIn 16
Silkin, Jon 1930- WhoWor 91
Silkman-Cooper, Deb Lynn 1963- St&PR 91
Silko, Leslie 1948- FemiCLE
Silkoff, David Michael 1949- IntWWM 90
Silkotch, Mary Ellen 1911- WhoAmA 91
Silkwood, Karen 1946-1974 BioIn 16
Silkwood, Valerie Gail 1958- WhoEmL 91
Sill, Geoffrey Michael 1944- WhoE 91
Sill, Gertrude Grace WhoAmA 91
Sill, Gertrude Grace 1927- WhoE 91
Sill, Stephen E. 1945- St&PR 91
Sillanpaa, Frans Eemil 1888-1964 ConAu 129, DcScanL, MajTwCW, WorAlBi
Sillanpaa, Matti Lauri 1936- WhoWor 91
Sillari, Ralph C. 1954- St&PR 91
Sillars, David R 1949- BiDrAPA 89
Sillars, Malcolm Osgood 1928- WhoAm 90
Sillcox, John H. 1924- St&PR 91
Sillcox, Lewis Ketcham 1886-1989 BioIn 16
Sillcox, Robert Lewis 1931- St&PR 91
Silleck, Harry Garrison 1921- WhoAm 90
Sillence, David Owen 1944- WhoWor 91
Siller, Stephen I. 1949- WhoEmL 91
Sillero, Antonio 1938- WhoWor 91
Sillers, Donald A., Jr. 1926- St&PR 91
Sillery, Stephanie Felicite, Marquise de 1746-1830 BioIn 16
Silles, Victor 1940- St&PR 91
Silliman, Charles Lewis 1932- WhoSSW 91
Silliman, Elaine Joyce Rubenstein 1938- WhoAmW 91
Silliman, Leland 1906- AuBYP 90
Silliman, Richard George 1922- WhoAm 90
Silliman, Richard L. 1951- St&PR 91
Silliman, Ron 1946- WhoWrEP 89
Sillin, Lelan Flor, Jr. 1918- WhoAm 90
Silling, Cyrus Edgar, Jr. 1923- WhoE 91
Silliphant, Stirling 1918- BioIn 16
Silliphant, Stirling Dale 1918- WhoAm 90
Sillito, Kenneth PenDiMP
Sillitoe, Alan BioIn 16
Sillitoe, Alan 1928- MajTwCW, SmATA 61 [port], WhoWor 91, WorAlBi
Sillman, Colwyn Clifford 1939- IntWWM 90
Sillman, Herbert Phillip 1927- WhoAm 90
Sills, Beverly BioIn 16
Sills, Beverly 1929- ConMus 5 [port], IntWWM 90, PenDiMP, WhoAm 90, WhoAmW 91, WhoE 91, WhoWor 91, WorAlBi
Sills, David Lawrence 1920- WhoAm 90
Sills, Lawrence Ira 1939- St&PR 91
Sills, Leslie 1948- ConAu 130
Sills, Loretta 1947- St&PR 91
Sills, Lorri BiDrAPA 89
Sills, Malcolm Richard 1922- BiDrAPA 89
Sills, Myron A. 1927- St&PR 91
Sills, Philip BioIn 16
Sills, Richard Reynolds 1946- WhoE 91, WhoEmL 91
Sills, Sallie Alexander 1916- WhoAmW 91
Sills, Stephen BioIn 16
Sills, Theodore H BiDrAPA 89
Sills, Theron G 1936- BiDrAPA 89
Sills, Thomas Albert 1914- WhoAmA 91
Sills, William Henry, III 1936- WhoWor 91
Silman, James Billy 1923- WhoSSW 91
Silone, Ignazio 1900-1978 EuWr 12, MajTwCW
Silos, Irene M. 1963- WhoAmW 91
Siloti, Alexander PenDiMP
Siloti, Alexander 1863-1945 BioIn 16
Siloti, Kyriena 1895-1989 BioIn 16
Silsbury, Elizabeth Alice 1931- IntWWM 90
Silsby, Harry Dozier 1938- BiDrAPA 89
Silsby, John P., II 1955- St&PR 91
Silsby, Lucille Linda 1953- WhoAmW 91
Siltanen, John Carl 1913- WhoE 91
Siltanen, Pentti Kustaa Pietari 1926- WhoWor 91
Silton, Laura BioIn 16
Silva, Alejandro WhoHisp 91
Silva, Alvaro 1949- WhoHisp 91
Silva, Anerico Rodrigues F. 1934- WhoWor 91
Silva, Antonio C P BiDrAPA 89
Silva, Antonio Vidal 1951- WhoHisp 91
Silva, Aurelia Davila de 1946- WhoHisp 91
Silva, Beverly WhoWrEP 89
Silva, Beverly 1935- ConAu 131, HispWr 90
Silva, Carlos Alberto 1935- WhoE 91
Silva, Cesar E. 1955- WhoHisp 91
Silva, Cesar Ernestro 1955- WhoE 91
Silva, Daniel P. WhoHisp 91
Silva, David 1944- WhoHisp 91
Silva, David B. 1939- WhoHisp 91
Silva, Don 1936- WhoHisp 91
Silva, Donna Steedle 1957- WhoAmW 91
Silva, Dorothy 1948- WhoE 91
Silva, Edivaldo Oliveira 1930?-1974 EncO&P 3
Silva, Edward John 1944- WhoHisp 91
Silva, Elaine Ann 1947- WhoE 91
Silva, Elizabeth Talbot 1947- WhoAmW 91
Silva, Enrique Cimma 1918- WhoWor 91
Silva, Ernest 1948- WhoAmA 91
Silva, Felipe 1919- WhoAm 90, WhoHisp 91
Silva, Flavio J. 1946- WhoHisp 91
Silva, Francisco BiDrAPA 89
Silva, Francisco Javier 1952- WhoSSW 91
Silva, Henriquez Raul 1907- WhoWor 91
Silva, Henry 1928- ConTFT 8
Silva, Joan Yvonne WhoWrEP 89
Silva, Joe M. 1947- St&PR 91
Silva, Jose 1914- WhoHisp 91
Silva, Jose A., Jr. WhoHisp 91
Silva, Jose A., Sr. WhoHisp 91
Silva, Jose Antonio da 1909- ArtLatA
Silva, Jose Arturo 1949- BiDrAPA 89
Silva, Jose Asuncion 1865-1896 BioIn 16
Silva, Joseph Donald 1935- WhoAm 90
Silva, Joseph S. 1959- St&PR 91
Silva, Juan L. 1957- WhoHisp 91
Silva, Leonel B. 1940- WhoHisp 91
Silva, Loreina Santos 1933- BioIn 16
Silva, Mark Robert 1954- WhoE 91
Silva, Moises 1945- WhoHisp 91
Silva, Omega Logan 1936- WhoAmW 91
Silva, Pedro 1943- WhoHisp 91
Silva, Robert Russell 1928- WhoHisp 91
Silva, Rogelio A BiDrAPA 89
Silva, Rolando A. 1945- WhoHisp 91
Silva, Ruth Caridad WhoAm 90, WhoE 91
Silva, Stevan 1950- WhoE 91
Silva, Steven 1965- St&PR 91
Silva, Steven John 1954- WhoE 91
Silva, Trinidad BioIn 16
Silva, Ubirajara Da Costa E. 1921- WhoWor 91
Silva, Victor Daniel 1955- WhoHisp 91
Silva, William Posey 1859-1948 WhoAmA 91N
Silva-Corvalan, Carmen 1941- WhoHisp 91
Silva-Herzog, Jesus 1935- WhoWor 91
Silva Ortiz, Walter Ivan 1956- WhoHisp 91
Silva-Ruete, Enrique G 1939- BiDrAPA 89
Silva-Ruiz, Pedro F. 1943- WhoHisp 91
Silvaroli, Nicholas Joseph 1930- WhoAm 90
Silvas, Jose Ramon BiDrAPA 89
Silvas, Sharon Judy 1944- WhoAmW 91
Silveanu, Radu Adrian 1928- BiDrAPA 89
Silveira, Augustine, Jr. 1934- WhoAm 90
Silveira, Guiomar BiDrAPA 89
Silveira, Luiz Brandao 1951- WhoWor 91
Silveira, Milton Anthony 1929- WhoAm 90
Silveira de Queiroz, Dinah BioIn 16
Silvela y de Le Vielleuze, Francisco 1845-1905 BioIn 16
Silver, Abba Hillel 1893-1963 BioIn 16
Silver, Adele Zeidman 1932- WhoAmW 91
Silver, Alfred Sol 1920- BiDrAPA 89
Silver, Allan L. 1928- St&PR 91
Silver, Ann-Louise S 1942- BiDrAPA 89
Silver, Archie A 1917- BiDrAPA 89
Silver, Barbara Adriene 1958- BiDrAPA 89
Silver, Barnard Stewart 1933- WhoWor 91
Silver, Barry Stephen 1940- St&PR 91
Silver, Bella Wolfson 1937- WhoAmW 91
Silver, Bennett BiDrAPA 89
Silver, Bradley Scott 1956- St&PR 91
Silver, Brian David 1944- WhoAm 90
Silver, Brian Quayle 1942- WhoE 91
Silver, Carole G 1937- ConAu 132
Silver, Charles Morton 1929- WhoAm 90
Silver, Daniel Jeremy 1928-1989 BioIn 16, ConAu 130
Silver, David 1931- WhoAm 90
Silver, David Francis 1957- WhoWrEP 89
Silver, David Freeman 1949- BiDrAPA 89
Silver, David K. 1927- ODwPR 91
Silver, David Martin 1941- WhoE 91
Silver, David Mayer 1915- WhoAm 90
Silver, David P. 1940- St&PR 91
Silver, Donald 1929- WhoAm 90
Silver, Donald F 1932- BiDrAPA 89
Silver, Donna Elaine 1960- BiDrAPA 89
Silver, E. Alan BioIn 16
Silver, Elliott P. 1935- St&PR 91
Silver, Eric Aaron 1942- WhoE 91
Silver, Frank 1896-1960 OxCPMus
Silver, Gary Lee 1948- WhoWrEP 89
Silver, George A BiDrAPA 89
Silver, George Albert 1913- WhoAm 90
Silver, Gerald A 1932- ConAu 30NR
Silver, Greta B. 1934- WhoWrEP 89
Silver, H. Richard 1929- ODwPR 91
Silver, Helene Marcia 1947- WhoAmW 91
Silver, Henry K. 1918- WhoAm 90
Silver, Henry Ward 1955- WhoEmL 91
Silver, Hilary 1945- BiDrAPA 89
Silver, Horace BioIn 16
Silver, Horace 1928- OxCPMus, WorAlBi
Silver, Horace Ward Martin Tavares 1928- WhoAm 90
Silver, Howard Findlay 1930- WhoAm 90
Silver, Idora 1948- WhoAmW 91
Silver, Jacqueline WhoAmW 91
Silver, James W. 1907-1988 BioIn 16
Silver, Jean 1926- WhoAmW 91
Silver, Jeff 1942- St&PR 91
Silver, Jerry H. 1930- St&PR 91
Silver, Joan Micklin BioIn 16
Silver, Joan Micklin 1935- WhoAm 90
Silver, Joe 1922-1989 BioIn 16, ConTFT 8
Silver, John J. St&PR 91
Silver, John Joseph, Jr. 1943- WhoAm 90
Silver, Jonathan M 1953- BiDrAPA 89
Silver, Kenneth Alan 1927- WhoE 91
Silver, Larry Arnold 1947- WhoAmA 91
Silver, Larry B 1934- BiDrAPA 89
Silver, Lee Mathew 1948- WhoE 91
Silver, Malcolm David 1933- WhoAm 90
Silver, Marc Laurence 1953- WhoEmL 91
Silver, Marc S. 1951- WhoWrEP 89
Silver, Martin 1940- St&PR 91
Silver, Mary Wilcox 1941- WhoAmW 91
Silver, Max I 1922- BiDrAPA 89
Silver, Meyer 1926- WhoSSW 91
Silver, Michael Alan 1945- BiDrAPA 89
Silver, Michael Alan 1954- BiDrAPA 89
Silver, Michael Allan 1948- BiDrAPA 89
Silver, Morris ODwPR 91
Silver, Morris 1931- WhoAm 90
Silver, Nathan 1930- St&PR 91
Silver, Ned Clayton 1957- WhoSSW 91
Silver, Pat 1922- WhoAmA 91
Silver, Paul 1937- WhoAm 90
Silver, Paul Andrew 1953- BiDrAPA 89, WhoE 91
Silver, Paul Robert 1931- WhoE 91
Silver, Philip Warnock 1932- WhoAm 90
Silver, Phillip 1943- OxCCanT
Silver, R. Bruce 1923- St&PR 91
Silver, Ralph D. 1924- St&PR 91
Silver, Ralph David 1924- WhoAm 90
Silver, Rawley A WhoAmA 91
Silver, Richard 1946- BiDrAPA 89
Silver, Richard Ludwig 1920- St&PR 91
Silver, Richard Tobias 1929- WhoAm 90
Silver, Robert H. 1955- WhoAm 90
Silver, Robert S. 1913- WhoWor 91
Silver, Robert Stephen 1951- St&PR 91
Silver, Robin Candyce BiDrAPA 89
Silver, Ron 1946- BioIn 16, WhoAm 90
Silver, Ruth ConAu 31NR
Silver, Samuel Manuel 1912- WhoAm 90
Silver, Saul Zee 1925- St&PR 91
Silver, Sheila Jane 1946- IntWWM 90
Silver, Sheldon 1944- ODwPR 91
Silver, Shelly Andrea 1957- WhoAmA 91
Silver, Sidney H BiDrAPA 89
Silver, Stuart Beal 1942- BiDrAPA 89
Silver, Stuart Robert 1949- WhoE 91, WhoEmL 91
Silver, William Robert 1947- St&PR 91, WhoAm 90
Silver-Lillywhite, Eileen 1953- WhoWrEP 89
Silvera, Charlie 1924- Ballpl 90
Silvera, Frank 1914-1970 DrBlPA 90, EarBlAP
Silvera, Isaac Franklin 1937- WhoAm 90
Silvera, John EarBlAP
Silverberg, Alan Lee 1954- WhoE 91
Silverberg, Doris H BiDrAPA 89
Silverberg, Ellen Ruth 1947- WhoAmA 91
Silverberg, J William 1923- BiDrAPA 89
Silverberg, Mervin WhoAm 90
Silverberg, Robert WhoAm 90, WhoWrEP 89
Silverberg, Robert 1935- AuBYP 90, MajTwCW, RGTwCSF, WorAlBi
Silverberg, Steven Mark 1947- WhoEmL 91
Silverberg, Stuart Owen 1931- WhoAm 90, WhoWor 91
Silverblatt, Helene B BiDrAPA 89
Silvercruys, Susanne 1898-1973 WhoAmA 91N
Silverfine, Betsy Susan 1960- WhoAmW 91
Silverglat, Michael J 1943- BiDrAPA 89
Silveri, Paolo 1913- IntWWM 90, PenDiMP
Silverio, Antonio L BiDrAPA 89
Silverlight, Irwin Joseph 1924- WhoAm 90
Silverman, Al 1926- AuBYP 90, WhoAm 90, WhoWrEP 89
Silverman, Alan H. 1954- WhoEmL 91, WhoWor 91
Silverman, Albert A. 1908- St&PR 91, WhoAm 90, WhoWor 91
Silverman, Albert J 1925- BiDrAPA 89
Silverman, Albert Jack 1925- WhoAm 90
Silverman, Albert James 1906- WhoWrEP 89
Silverman, Alice Hershey BiDrAPA 89
Silverman, Alice Ruth 1922- St&PR 91
Silverman, Alvin Michaels 1912- WhoAm 90
Silverman, Anna Mae 1928- WhoAmW 91
Silverman, Arnold 1933- WhoAm 90
Silverman, Arnold Barry 1937- WhoAm 90, WhoE 91, WhoWor 91
Silverman, Barbara Gail 1937- WhoAmW 91
Silverman, Beatrice T BiDrAPA 89
Silverman, Bernard 1931- BiDrAPA 89

Silverman, Bruce Gary 1945- *WhoAm 90, WhoEmL 91*
Silverman, Burton Philip 1928- *WhoAm 90, WhoAmA 91, WhoE 91*
Silverman, Cathy Merle *BiDrAPA 89*
Silverman, Charlotte 1913- *WhoAmW 91*
Silverman, Dan *BioIn 16*
Silverman, Daniel N., III 1951- *St&PR 91*
Silverman, Daniel Nathan, Jr. 1925- *WhoSSW 91*
Silverman, David Lee 1944- *BiDrAPA 89*
Silverman, Edward *PenDiMP*
Silverman, Edward Jerome 1938- *WhoE 91*
Silverman, Elaine Roslyn 1941- *WhoAmW 91, WhoSSW 91*
Silverman, Elizabeth 1954- *WhoE 91*
Silverman, Ellen 1942- *WhoAmW 91*
Silverman, Faye-Ellen 1947- *IntWWM 90*
Silverman, Fred *BioIn 16*
Silverman, Frederic Noah 1914- *WhoAm 90*
Silverman, George Alan 1946- *WhoAm 90, WhoE 91*
Silverman, Gerard Marshal 1941- *WhoE 91*
Silverman, H Joseph *BiDrAPA 89*
Silverman, Hal *BioIn 16*
Silverman, Helene *BioIn 16*
Silverman, Henry Jacob 1934- *WhoAm 90*
Silverman, Henry Richard 1940- *WhoAm 90*
Silverman, Herbert R. 1914- *St&PR 91, WhoAm 90*
Silverman, Herschel 1926- *WhoWrEP 89*
Silverman, Hiram M. 1933- *St&PR 91*
Silverman, Hirsch Lazaar 1915- *WhoWrEP 89*
Silverman, Howard Burton 1938- *St&PR 91*
Silverman, Hugh J. 1945- *WhoAm 90*
Silverman, Ira H. 1949- *ODwPR 91*
Silverman, Ira Norton 1935- *WhoAm 90, WhoE 91*
Silverman, Jeffrey Stuart 1945- *St&PR 91, WhoAm 90, WhoE 91*
Silverman, Jerome B. 1927- *St&PR 91*
Silverman, Jerome S *BiDrAPA 89*
Silverman, Jerry T. 1928- *St&PR 91*
Silverman, Joel *BioIn 16*
Silverman, Joel 1952- *St&PR 91*
Silverman, Joel J 1943- *BiDrAPA 89*
Silverman, Jonathan *BioIn 16*
Silverman, Joseph 1922- *WhoAm 90*
Silverman, Joseph Hillel 1955- *WhoE 91*
Silverman, Joseph S 1933- *BiDrAPA 89*
Silverman, Joy *WhoAmA 91*
Silverman, Judi 1947- *ODwPR 91*
Silverman, Judith Ann *BiDrAPA 89*
Silverman, Kaja 1947- *ConAu 132*
Silverman, Kenneth Eugene 1936- *WhoAm 90, WhoWrEP 89*
Silverman, Lanny Harris 1947- *WhoAmA 91*
Silverman, Lee Harold 1933- *WhoE 91*
Silverman, Leonard M. *WhoAm 90*
Silverman, Lester 1947- *St&PR 91*
Silverman, Lester Paul 1947- *WhoE 91*
Silverman, Marc Nelson 1941- *St&PR 91*
Silverman, Mark 1952-1989 *BioIn 16*
Silverman, Mark H. 1934- *St&PR 91, WhoAm 90*
Silverman, Martin A 1935- *BiDrAPA 89*
Silverman, Marvin *BiDrAPA 89*
Silverman, Mary Delson *WhoAmW 91, WhoE 91*
Silverman, Matthew 1908-1988 *BioIn 16*
Silverman, Mel *WhoAmA 91N*
Silverman, Michael David 1946- *St&PR 91, WhoAm 90*
Silverman, Michael Harris 1949- *WhoE 91*
Silverman, Morris 1894-1972 *BioIn 16*
Silverman, Morris 1923- *St&PR 91*
Silverman, Morton Mayer 1947- *BiDrAPA 89*
Silverman, Myrna W. *ODwPR 91*
Silverman, Neil Irwin 1933- *WhoE 91, WhoWor 91*
Silverman, Pamela Sue 1958- *BiDrAPA 89*
Silverman, Paul Hyman 1924- *WhoAm 90*
Silverman, Peter Ray 1955- *WhoEmL 91*
Silverman, Raymond Mayer *BiDrAPA 89*
Silverman, Raymond Mayer 1945- *WhoEmL 91*
Silverman, Richard A. 1940- *St&PR 91*
Silverman, Richard Alan 1950- *BiDrAPA 89*
Silverman, Richard Bruce 1946- *WhoAm 90*
Silverman, Robert Alan 1947- *WhoE 91*
Silverman, Robert P. 1944- *St&PR 91*
Silverman, Ronald H 1926- *WhoAmA 91*
Silverman, Sam Mendel 1925- *WhoE 91*
Silverman, Samuel *BiDrAPA 89*
Silverman, Samuel 1912- *WhoE 91*
Silverman, Samuel Joshua 1908- *WhoAm 90*
Silverman, Samuel Morris *BiDrAPA 89*
Silverman, Sandra *ODwPR 91*
Silverman, Seth Warren 1953- *BiDrAPA 89*
Silverman, Sherley C 1909- *WhoAmA 91*
Silverman, Stacy M. 1962- *WhoAmW 91*
Silverman, Stanley W. 1947- *St&PR 91*
Silverman, Stephen Meredith 1951- *WhoE 91*
Silverman, Valerie 1962- *WhoE 91*
Silverman, Vicki Spelton 1946- *St&PR 91*
Silverman, William A. 1930- *ODwPR 91*
Silverman, William Robert 1947- *BiDrAPA 89*
Silvern, Leonard Charles 1919- *WhoWor 91*
Silvernail, Lisa Anne Phipps 1958- *WhoAmW 91*
Silvernail, Robert F. 1943- *St&PR 91*
Silvernale, Laura Gasparini 1962- *WhoAmW 91*
Silvers, David 1949- *St&PR 91, WhoAm 90*
Silvers, Frederick M *BiDrAPA 89*
Silvers, Kenneth N 1936- *BiDrAPA 89*
Silvers, Louis 1889-1954 *OxCPMus*
Silvers, Phil 1912-1985 *WorAlBi*
Silvers, Robert B. 1929- *WhoWrEP 89*
Silvers, Robert Benjamin 1929- *WhoAm 90*
Silvers, Sid 1907-1976 *OxCPMus*
Silvers, Vicki 1941- *WhoWrEP 89*
Silvers, Willys Kent 1929- *WhoAm 90*
Silversmith, Gary Jay 1956- *WhoE 91*
Silversmith, Norman 1936- *BiDrAPA 89*
Silverstein, Adolph Traub 1927- *WhoAm 90*
Silverstein, Alexander *BiDrAPA 89*
Silverstein, Alvin 1933- *AuBYP 90, WhoE 91*
Silverstein, Andrew *BioIn 16*
Silverstein, Arthur Matthew 1928- *WhoAm 90*
Silverstein, Benjamin 1925- *St&PR 91*
Silverstein, Carol Lynn 1952- *WhoAmW 91*
Silverstein, Charles M. 1951- *ODwPR 91*
Silverstein, Helma 1937- *WhoAmW 91*
Silverstein, Howard Alan 1947- *WhoAm 90*
Silverstein, Ida *WhoAmA 91*
Silverstein, Ira B 1939- *BiDrAPA 89*
Silverstein, Jacqueline *ODwPR 91*
Silverstein, Joel *BioIn 16*
Silverstein, Josef 1922- *ConAu 31NR*
Silverstein, Joseph 1932- *IntWWM 90, PenDiMP*
Silverstein, Joseph H. 1927- *St&PR 91*
Silverstein, Joseph Harry 1932- *WhoAm 90*
Silverstein, Leonard Lewis 1922- *WhoAm 90*
Silverstein, Louis 1919- *WhoAm 90, WhoE 91*
Silverstein, Marc A. 1952- *St&PR 91*
Silverstein, Ronald Terry 1945- *BiDrAPA 89*
Silverstein, Ross Stuart 1955- *BiDrAPA 89*
Silverstein, Samuel Charles 1937- *WhoAm 90*
Silverstein, Shel *BioIn 16*
Silverstein, Shelby 1932- *WhoAm 90, WhoWrEP 89*
Silverstein, Stanley Parker 1952- *St&PR 91*
Silverstein, Stephen Howard 1948- *WhoAm 90*
Silverstein, Virginia 1937- *AuBYP 90*
Silverstein, Virginia Barbara 1937- *WhoE 91*
Silverston, Bess Ellesberg 1947- *WhoEmL 91*
Silverstone, David 1932- *WhoAm 90*
Silverstone, Donald 1928- *St&PR 91*
Silverstone, Leon Martin 1939- *WhoAm 90*
Silverthorn, Robert Sterner, Jr. 1948- *WhoSSW 91*
Silverthorne, Colin Patric 1945- *WhoAm 90*
Silverthorne, Jeffrey 1963- *WhoSSW 91*
Silverthorne, Michael James 1941- *WhoAm 90*
Silverthorne, Paul *PenDiMP*
Silverton, Leigh 1956- *WhoAmW 91*
Silverton, Michael John 1935- *WhoWrEP 89*
Silvertooth, Dennis Carl 1957- *WhoAmA 91*
Silvester II, Pope *EncO&P 3*
Silvester, Bill *BioIn 16*
Silvester, Michael D. 1943- *St&PR 91*
Silvester, Peter J., Jr. 1946- *St&PR 91*
Silvester, Peter Peet 1935- *WhoAm 90, WhoWor 91*
Silvester, Victor 1900-1978 *OxCPMus*
Silvestri, Constantin 1913-1969 *PenDiMP*
Silvestri, Henry Peter 1954- *BiDrAPA 89*
Silvestri, Richard *BioIn 16*
Silvestrini, Achille 1923- *WhoWor 91*
Silvestris, Elaine Joy 1943- *WhoAmW 91*
Silvestro, Clement Mario 1924- *WhoAm 90*
Silvestro, Joy 1939- *St&PR 91*
Silvestrone, Mario 1923- *St&PR 91*
Silvestry, Lydia Mercedes 1946- *WhoAmW 91*
Silveus, Mari L. 1957- *WhoWrEP 89*
Silvey, Kathryn Ochs 1940- *St&PR 91*
Silvey, Robyn Lee 1951- *St&PR 91*
Silvi, John L. 1954- *St&PR 91*
Silvi, Laurence J., II 1956- *St&PR 91*
Silvia 1943- *WhoWor 91*
Silvia, John Edwin 1948- *St&PR 91*
Silvia, Kathleen Ford 1954- *WhoAmW 91*
Silvia, Michael Joseph 1948- *WhoE 91*
Silvia, Robert Charles 1942- *St&PR 91*
Silvija, Meznaric 1939- *WhoWor 91*
Silving, Helen *BioIn 16*
Silvio, Joseph R 1943- *BiDrAPA 89*
Silvius, Donald Joe 1932- *WhoWor 91*
Silvius, Eric L. 1951- *St&PR 91*
Silvius, Eric Lane 1951- *WhoAm 90*
Silvoso, Joseph Anton 1917- *WhoAm 90*
Silwance, Lily Asham *BiDrAPA 89*
Silwance, Wagih Bishara *BiDrAPA 89*
Silzer, Herta 1927- *BiDrAPA 89*
Sim Var 1906-1989 *BioIn 16*
Sim, Ah Tee 1944- *WhoWor 91*
Sim, Alastair 1900-1976 *BioIn 16*
Sim, Cho Boon 1935- *BiDrAPA 89*
Sim, Craig Stephen 1942- *WhoAm 90*
Sim, David G *BiDrAPA 89*
Sim, Georges *ConAu 129, MajTwCW*
Sim, Jessie *BioIn 16*
Sim, John Cameron 1911-1990 *ConAu 132*
Sim, Margaret Winnifred 1930- *IntWWM 90*
Sim, Myre *BiDrAPA 89*
Sim, Naomi 1913- *BioIn 16*
Sim, Peng Choon 1932- *WhoWor 91*
Sim, Richard G. 1944- *St&PR 91*
Sim, Richard Guild 1944- *WhoAm 90*
Sima, Al 1921- *Ballpl 90*
Sima, Horia 1906- *BioIn 16*
Simaga, Richard C. 1949- *St&PR 91*
Simaite, Ona 1899-1970 *BioIn 16*
Simak, Clifford D. 1904- *RGTwCSF*
Simak, Clifford D. 1904-1988 *AnObit 1988, BioIn 16, MajTwCW*
Simandl, Robert H. 1928- *St&PR 91*
Simangan, Preciosa *BiDrAPA 89*
Simanton, Mark Donald 1958- *St&PR 91*
Simapichaicheth, Pratak 1941- *WhoWor 91*
Simard, Michele *BiDrAPA 89*
Simard, Real 1951- *ConAu 129*
Simaskul, Sirichai 1949- *WhoWor 91*
Simbari, Nicola 1927- *AuBYP 90*
Simburg, Earl J 1915- *BiDrAPA 89*
Simchen, Giora 1939- *WhoWor 91*
Simches, Seymour Oliver 1919- *WhoAm 90*
Simcik, Luke Jacob 1962- *WhoEmL 91*
Simcoe, Annell Lacy 1941- *WhoWrEP 89*
Simcoe, Elizabeth 1762-1850 *DcLB 99 [port]*
Simcoe, Elizabeth Posthumous 1766-1851 *FemiCLE*
Simcox, Carroll E 1912- *ConAu 132*
Simcox, Craig Dennis 1939- *WhoAm 90*
Simcox, Edith J. 1844-1901 *FemiCLE*
Simcox, Edith Jemima 1844-1901 *BioIn 16*
Simcox, Flavel L. 1924- *St&PR 91*
Simcox, Glenda Beall 1939- *WhoAmW 91*
Simcox, Robert K. 1923- *St&PR 91*
Simcox, William C. 1930- *St&PR 91*
Sime, Donald Rae 1926- *WhoAm 90*
Sime, Georgina 1868-1958 *FemiCLE*
Sime, Jessie Georgina 1868-1958 *DcLB 92*
Simecka, Betty Jean 1935- *WhoAmW 91*
Simek, Joseph Ladislav 1926- *St&PR 91*
Simel, David Lee 1955- *WhoSSW 91*
Simel, Elaine *WhoAmA 91*
Simel, Elaine 1928- *WhoE 91*
Simenon, Georges 1903-1989 *AnObit 1989, BioIn 16, ConAu 129, EuWr 12, MajTwCW, TwCCr&M 91B, WorAlBi*
Simenson, Robert A *BiDrAPA 89*
Simeon, Daphne 1958- *BiDrAPA 89*
Simeon, H. Michael 1926- *St&PR 91*
Simeon, Jovan Georgi *BiDrAPA 89*
Simeon Negrin, Rosa Elena 1943- *WhoWor 91*
Simeona, Iosia 1854- *WhoWor 91*
Simeone, Edward Joseph 1959- *WhoEmL 91*
Simeone, Fiorindo Anthony 1908- *WhoAm 90*
Simeone, Robert Louis 1956- *WhoE 91*
Simer, Cheryl 1948- *WhoAmW 91*
Simer, Harvey Josef 1949- *St&PR 91*
Simeral, William Goodrich 1926- *WhoAm 90*
Simermeyer, John Lawrence 1928- *St&PR 91*
Simes, Dimitri Konstantin 1947- *WhoAm 90, WhoE 91*
Simes, E Lee 1950- *BiDrAPA 89*
Simes, Ned E. 1922- *St&PR 91*
Simes, Stephen M. 1951- *St&PR 91*
Simes, Stephen Mark 1951- *WhoEmL 91*
Simic, Charles 1938- *ConAu 33NR, DcLB 105 [port], WhoAm 90, WhoE 91, WhoWrEP 89*
Simic, Petar *BioIn 16*
Simino, Darrell W. 1942- *St&PR 91*
Siminoff, Bruce G. 1936- *St&PR 91*
Siminovitch, Louis 1920- *WhoAm 90*
Simins, Herbert J. *BioIn 16*
Simionato, Giulietta 1910- *PenDiMP*
Simionato, Giulietta 1912- *IntWWM 90*
Simionescu, Elena 1937- *IntWWM 90*
Simis, Konstantin 1919- *ConAu 130*
Simis, Theodore Luckey 1924- *WhoAm 90*
Simitis, Spiros 1934- *WhoWor 91*
Simkaitis, Helmut 1946- *WhoSSW 91*
Simkin, Penelope Payson 1938- *WhoWrEP 89*
Simkin, Peter Anthony 1935- *WhoAm 90*
Simkin, Phillips M 1944- *WhoAmA 91*
Simkin, Tom 1933- *ConAu 132*
Simkins, Dan Gene 1940- *St&PR 91*
Simkins, Leon J. 1927- *St&PR 91*
Simkins, Leon Jack 1927- *WhoAm 90*
Simkins, Modjeska Monteith 1899- *EncAL*
Simkins, Morton H. 1937- *St&PR 91*
Simko, Ilona *BiDrAPA 89*
Simko, John Stephen 1939- *St&PR 91*
Simko, Paul R. *St&PR 91*
Simko, Vincent M. 1926- *St&PR 91*
Simkowitz, Michael Abraham 1938- *WhoAm 90*
Simkowitz, Philip *BiDrAPA 89*
Simm, Anton 1799-1873 *PenDiDA 89*
Simm, David J. 1934- *St&PR 91*
Simm, Richard John 1947- *IntWWM 90*
Simmang, Arthur V *BiDrAPA 89*
Simmel, Edward C 1932- *ConAu 31NR*
Simmel, Gerhard Frederick 1930- *WhoWor 91*
Simmel, Marianne Lenore *WhoAm 90*
Simmental, David Anthony 1953- *WhoEmL 91*
Simmer, Rita Schiavino 1947- *ODwPR 91*
Simmer, William J. *BioIn 16*
Simmerman, Gary F. 1934- *St&PR 91*
Simmerman, Jim 1952- *WhoWrEP 89*
Simmermon, James Everett 1926- *WhoAm 90*
Simmers, Terry Wayne 1946- *St&PR 91, WhoAm 90*
Simmet, John L. 1927- *St&PR 91*
Simmler, Franz Josef 1942- *WhoWor 91*
Simmon, Vincent Fowler 1943- *St&PR 91*
Simmonds, Colin 1955- *WhoWor 91*
Simmonds, James Gordon 1935- *WhoAm 90*
Simmonds, Jules 1912- *St&PR 91*
Simmonds, Kennedy Alphonse 1936- *BioIn 16, WhoWor 91*
Simmonds, Martha *FemiCLE*
Simmonds, Martha 1622-1665 *BiDEWW*
Simmonds, Posy 19--?- *ChlLR 23 [port]*
Simmonds, Randy James 1951- *WhoSSW 91*
Simmonds, Ruth-Ellen Hinkley 1940- *St&PR 91, WhoE 91*
Simmons, A. J. *AmLegL*
Simmons, Abbott P *BiDrAPA 89*
Simmons, Adele Smith 1941- *WhoAm 90, WhoAmW 91*
Simmons, Al 1902-1956 *Ballpl 90 [port], WorAlBi*
Simmons, Alan Jay 1924- *WhoAm 90*
Simmons, Alan Russell 1949- *WhoEmL 91*
Simmons, Aldred John 1917- *St&PR 91*
Simmons, Almo B. 1933- *St&PR 91*
Simmons, Althea T. L. *NewYTBS 90*
Simmons, Barbara J. 1938- *WhoAmW 91*
Simmons, Barbara Jean 1946- *WhoAmW 91*
Simmons, Barry Putnam 1939- *WhoE 91*
Simmons, Barry William 1950- *WhoSSW 91*
Simmons, Belvin A 1924- *BiDrAPA 89*
Simmons, Ben D. 1950- *St&PR 91*
Simmons, Betty Jo 1936- *WhoAmW 91*
Simmons, Betty-Jo Whitaker 1939- *WhoSSW 91*
Simmons, Bradley Williams 1941- *WhoAm 90, WhoWor 91*
Simmons, Bryan A. 1933- *St&PR 91*
Simmons, Bryan John 1955- *WhoEmL 91*
Simmons, Calvin 1950-1982 *DrBlPA 90, PenDiMP*
Simmons, Carl Kenneth 1914- *WhoWor 91*
Simmons, Caroline Thompson 1910- *WhoAmW 91*
Simmons, Catherine Constance 1956- *WhoAmW 91*
Simmons, Chad Jeffrey 1953- *St&PR 91*
Simmons, Charles 1924- *WhoAm 90*
Simmons, Charles Alan 1935- *St&PR 91*
Simmons, Charles Bedford, Jr. 1956- *WhoSSW 91*
Simmons, Charles E 1927- *BiDrAPA 89*

Simmons, Charline Bayon 1948- *BiDrAPA 89*
Simmons, Chester Robert 1928- *WhoE 91*
Simmons, Clarence George 1953- *St&PR 91*
Simmons, Cleda Marie 1927- *WhoAmA 91*
Simmons, Curt 1929- *Ballpl 90*
Simmons, Cynthia J. 1957- *WhoAmW 91*
Simmons, D. Ramsay, Jr. 1931- *St&PR 91*
Simmons, Daniel Lee 1946- *WhoEmL 91*
Simmons, David Jeffrey 1961- *WhoSSW 91*
Simmons, David Ramsay, Jr. 1931- *WhoSSW 91*
Simmons, Dawn Langley *AuBYP 90*
Simmons, Dick Bedford 1937- *WhoSSW 91*
Simmons, Donald D 1930- *BiDrAPA 89*
Simmons, Donald E. 1944- *St&PR 91*
Simmons, Donna Marie 1943- *WhoAmW 91*
Simmons, Doris Jeanette 1949- *WhoAmW 91*
Simmons, Doris Yvonne 1939- *WhoAmW 91*
Simmons, Dorothea R *BiDrAPA 89*
Simmons, Dwayne Deangelo 1959- *WhoEmL 91*
Simmons, Edwin Howard 1921- *WhoAm 90, WhoE 91*
Simmons, Ellie *AuBYP 90*
Simmons, Elroy, Jr. 1928- *WhoAm 90*
Simmons, Ernest J. 1903-1972 *DcLB 103 [port]*
Simmons, Eugene 1943- *WhoE 91*
Simmons, Eugene Branson 1941- *WhoSSW 91*
Simmons, Everett B. 1902-1989 *BioIn 16*
Simmons, Everett Casey 1940- *BiDrAPA 89*
Simmons, Fielding 1939- *St&PR 91*
Simmons, Florence Maria 1958- *WhoSSW 91*
Simmons, Forrest Wiemann 1924- *St&PR 91*
Simmons, Francis Blair 1930- *WhoAm 90*
Simmons, Frederick J. 1937- *St&PR 91*
Simmons, Gene 1949- *ConTFT 8, WhoAm 90*
Simmons, Geneen Marshett 1966- *WhoAmW 91*
Simmons, George *WhoWrEP 89*
Simmons, George L. 1942- *St&PR 91*
Simmons, Glenn Reuben 1928- *WhoAm 90*
Simmons, Hardwick 1940- *St&PR 91, WhoAm 90*
Simmons, Harold C. *BioIn 16*
Simmons, Harold C. 1931- *WhoAm 90, WhoSSW 91*
Simmons, Harold Joseph 1940- *St&PR 91*
Simmons, Harris H. 1954- *St&PR 91, WhoAm 90*
Simmons, Heather Jane Edith 1960- *WhoAmW 91, WhoEmL 91*
Simmons, Helen L. 1946- *St&PR 91*
Simmons, Howard Ensign, Jr. 1929- *St&PR 91, WhoAm 90*
Simmons, Howard L. *WhoE 91*
Simmons, Howard Wilson 1918- *St&PR 91*
Simmons, Ilene White 1948- *WhoAmW 91*
Simmons, J. Gerald 1929- *WhoAm 90*
Simmons, Jake 1901-1981 *BioIn 16*
Simmons, James 1933- *WorAu 1980 [port]*
Simmons, James E 1923- *BiDrAPA 89*
Simmons, James Edwin 1923- *WhoAm 90*
Simmons, James P. 1924- *St&PR 91*
Simmons, James Pat 1949- *St&PR 91*
Simmons, James Quimby, III 1925- *BiDrAPA 89*
Simmons, James Worley Terry 1950- *WhoSSW 91*
Simmons, Jean *BioIn 16*
Simmons, Jean 1929- *WhoAm 90, WhoAmW 91, WorAlBi*
Simmons, Jean Elizabeth Margaret 1914- *WhoAm 90*
Simmons, Jerold L. 1941- *ConAu 129*
Simmons, Jerry *BioIn 16*
Simmons, Jerry Don 1943- *WhoSSW 91*
Simmons, John Derek 1931- *WhoE 91, WhoWor 91*
Simmons, John Herbert 1938- *WhoAmA 91*
Simmons, John Kaul 1938- *WhoAm 90*
Simmons, John M. 1938- *St&PR 91*
Simmons, John Stuart 1860-1944 *AmLegL*
Simmons, Joseph Edward 1941- *WhoSSW 91*
Simmons, Joseph Jacob, III 1925- *WhoAm 90*
Simmons, Judith Kay 1947- *WhoSSW 91*
Simmons, Julie Lutz *WhoAmA 91*
Simmons, Karen Ann 1948- *WhoAmW 91*
Simmons, Kenneth C. 1942- *St&PR 91*
Simmons, Kenneth Laverne, Jr. 1960- *WhoSSW 91*
Simmons, Kennett L. 1941- *St&PR 91*
Simmons, Kennett Lynn 1941- *WhoAm 90*
Simmons, L.V. 1925- *St&PR 91*
Simmons, L. Whitley 1925- *St&PR 91*
Simmons, Laurie 1949- *WhoAmA 91*
Simmons, Lee Guyton, Jr. 1938- *WhoAm 90*
Simmons, Lee Howard 1935- *WhoAm 90*
Simmons, Lee Thomas 1953- *St&PR 91*
Simmons, Marc 1937- *BioIn 16*
Simmons, Marguerite Saffold 1954- *WhoAmW 91*
Simmons, Martha *FemiCLE*
Simmons, Martha S. 1932- *St&PR 91*
Simmons, Marvin Gene 1929- *WhoAm 90*
Simmons, Merle Edwin 1918- *WhoAm 90*
Simmons, Miles Alexander, V 1958- *BiDrAPA 89*
Simmons, Miriam Quinn 1928- *WhoAmW 91*
Simmons, N. John, Jr. 1955- *WhoSSW 91*
Simmons, Obadiah Jerome Keith, Jr. 1953- *WhoSSW 91*
Simmons, Ozzie G. 1919-1988 *BioIn 16*
Simmons, Paul Allen 1921- *WhoAm 90, WhoE 91*
Simmons, Paul Barrett 1942- *WhoAm 90*
Simmons, Paul D 1936- *ConAu 31NR*
Simmons, Percy Slotsky 1906- *WhoAmA 91*
Simmons, Peter 1931- *WhoAm 90*
Simmons, Ralph Terrell 1938- *St&PR 91*
Simmons, Randon Calvin *BiDrAPA 89*
Simmons, Randy Neil 1946- *WhoWrEP 89*
Simmons, Raymond Hedelius, Jr. 1958- *WhoEmL 91*
Simmons, Rebecca Crowe *BiDrAPA 89*
Simmons, Richard 1948- *WorAlBi*
Simmons, Richard B. 1947- *St&PR 91*
Simmons, Richard De Lacey 1934- *WhoAm 90*
Simmons, Richard DeLacey 1934- *St&PR 91*
Simmons, Richard DeLacy *BioIn 16*
Simmons, Richard Milton Teagle 1948- *WhoAm 90*
Simmons, Richard Morgan, Jr. 1926- *St&PR 91*
Simmons, Richard P. 1931- *WhoAm 90*
Simmons, Richard Sheridan 1928- *St&PR 91, WhoAm 90, WhoE 91*
Simmons, Richard W. *BioIn 16*
Simmons, Robert J. 1943- *WhoAm 90*
Simmons, Robert John 1934- *BiDrAPA 89*
Simmons, Robert L. 1947- *WhoE 91*
Simmons, Robert Michael 1948- *WhoEmL 91*
Simmons, Robert Orrin, Jr. 1950- *WhoSSW 91*
Simmons, Roberta J. *ODwPR 91*
Simmons, Roy W. 1916- *St&PR 91*
Simmons, Roy William 1916- *WhoAm 90*
Simmons, Russell *BioIn 16*
Simmons, Russell D. 1943- *WhoSSW 91*
Simmons, S. Dallas 1940- *WhoAm 90*
Simmons, Sadie Vee 1929- *WhoAmW 91*
Simmons, Samuel Lee 1929- *St&PR 91, WhoAm 90*
Simmons, Samuel William 1907- *WhoWor 91*
Simmons, Seymour 1920- *St&PR 91*
Simmons, Sherry 1947- *WhoSSW 91*
Simmons, Sherwin Palmer 1931- *St&PR 91*
Simmons, Shirley J. *WhoWrEP 89*
Simmons, Sue 1944?- *DrBlPA 90*
Simmons, Suzanne *WhoWrEP 89*
Simmons, Sylvia Jeanne Quarles 1935- *WhoAmW 91*
Simmons, Ted 1949- *Ballpl 90 [port], BioIn 16*
Simmons, Ted Conrad 1916- *WhoWor 91*
Simmons, Thomas Edward 1925- *WhoSSW 91*
Simmons, Thomas Murphey 1953- *WhoSSW 91*
Simmons, Tifton 1945- *WhoE 91*
Simmons, Tillmon Lee *BiDrAPA 89*
Simmons, Vaughan Pippen 1922- *WhoAm 90*
Simmons, Virginia Anne *WhoWrEP 89*
Simmons, Virginia Ruth McConnell 1928- *WhoAmW 91*
Simmons, Walter G. 1946- *IntWWM 90*
Simmons, William 1884-1949 *WhoAmA 91N*
Simmons, William 1932- *WhoAm 90*
Simmons, William C 1940- *BiDrAPA 89*
Simmons, William Earl 1918- *WhoSSW 91*
Simmons, William J. 1849-1890 *BioIn 16*
Simmons, William Wells *BiDrAPA 89*
Simmons, Winifred J *BiDrAPA 89*
Simmons-Douglas, Rita 1933- *WhoAmW 91*
Simmons-Sixto, Camille Ann 1953- *WhoAmW 91*
Simms, Albert Egerton 1918- *WhoSSW 91*
Simms, Ami 1954- *WhoWrEP 89*
Simms, Arthur Benjamin 1921- *St&PR 91, WhoAm 90*
Simms, Charles Averill 1937- *WhoAm 90*
Simms, Frank Edward 1948- *WhoSSW 91*
Simms, Hilda 1920- *DrBlPA 90*
Simms, James Robert 1924- *WhoWor 91*
Simms, John Franklin 1933- *St&PR 91*
Simms, John Martin 1935- *WhoWor 91*
Simms, Julia J. 1931- *St&PR 91*
Simms, Karl Nigel 1961- *WhoWor 91*
Simms, Leroy Alanson 1905- *WhoAm 90*
Simms, Maria Ester 1938- *WhoAmW 91, WhoWor 91*
Simms, Mary Clay 1926- *St&PR 91*
Simms, Orville, Jr. 1934- *St&PR 91*
Simms, Phil 1955- *BioIn 16*
Simms, Phil 1956- *WorAlBi*
Simms, Phillip 1956- *WhoAm 90*
Simms, Robert Alderson, Sr. 1938- *WhoAm 90*
Simms, Robert D. 1926- *WhoAm 90*
Simms, Robert Maris *BiDrAPA 89*
Simms, Senia Julia 1931- *St&PR 91*
Simms, William Edward 1944- *St&PR 91*
Simms, William Gilmore 1806-1870 *BioIn 16, WhNaAH*
Simms-Floyd, Larita Ruth 1954- *WhoEmL 91*
Simo, Dennis Rafael 1943- *WhoWor 91*
Simoda, Mahiro 1929- *WhoWor 91*
Simoens, Mark Henri 1950- *WhoWor 91*
Simoes, Ronald Alan 1949- *St&PR 91*
Simoes Pereira, Bartolomeu *BioIn 16*
Simokaitis, Frank Joseph 1922- *WhoAm 90*
Simon and Garfunkel *EncPR&S 89*
Simon Magus *EncO&P 3*
Simon, Abbey 1920- *PenDiMP*
Simon, Abbey 1922- *IntWWM 90, WhoAm 90*
Simon, Abdallah 1922- *BioIn 16*
Simon, Albert 1924- *WhoAm 90*
Simon, Alexander *BiDrAPA 89*
Simon, Andrea Judith 1946- *St&PR 91*
Simon, Ann 1952- *ODwPR 91*
Simon, Arthur 1942- *WhoAm 90*
Simon, Arthur James 1927- *St&PR 91*
Simon, Barbara Colby 1930- *St&PR 91*
Simon, Barry Joshua *BiDrAPA 89*
Simon, Barry Philip 1942- *WhoAm 90*
Simon, Bennett 1933- *BiDrAPA 89*
Simon, Bernard 1896-1980 *WhoAmA 91N*
Simon, Bernece Kern 1914- *WhoAm 90*
Simon, Bernie *BioIn 16*
Simon, Bob *BioIn 16*
Simon, Carl Julian 1923- *St&PR 91*
Simon, Carly *BioIn 16*
Simon, Carly 1945- *ConMus 4 [port], WhoAm 90, WhoAmW 91, WorAlBi*
Simon, Caroline Klein *WhoAmW 91*
Simon, Charlie May 1897- *AuBYP 90*
Simon, Charlotte B. 1918-1989 *BioIn 16*
Simon, Cindy S. 1957- *WhoE 91*
Simon, Claude 1913- *ConAu 33NR, EuWr 13, MajTwCW, WhoWor 91, WorAlBi*
Simon, Claude Henri de Rouvroy Saint- 1760-1825 *BioIn 16*
Simon, Cyril *BioIn 16*
Simon, Daniel J. 1949- *St&PR 91*
Simon, David *BioIn 16*
Simon, David A. 1952- *St&PR 91*
Simon, David H. 1930- *ODwPR 91*
Simon, David Harold 1930- *WhoAm 90*
Simon, David J 1927- *BiDrAPA 89*
Simon, David Judah 1960- *WhoE 91*
Simon, David L. 1921- *St&PR 91*
Simon, David L 1946- *WhoAmA 91*
Simon, David S. 1941- *St&PR 91*
Simon, David Sidney 1941- *WhoAm 90*
Simon, Debra Wagner 1959- *WhoAmW 91*
Simon, Diana Lynn *BiDrAPA 89*
Simon, Dick *BioIn 16*
Simon, Dolph B.H. 1933- *St&PR 91*
Simon, Donald R. 1926- *St&PR 91*
Simon, Donald S. 1922- *St&PR 91*
Simon, Doris Marie 1932- *WhoAmW 91, WhoSSW 91*
Simon, Dorothy Elaine 1931- *WhoAmW 91*
Simon, Dorothy Martin 1919- *St&PR 91*
Simon, E. James *BioIn 16*
Simon, Eckehard 1939- *WhoAm 90*
Simon, Edward D. 1927- *St&PR 91*
Simon, Edward Dave 1927- *WhoAm 90*
Simon, Edward Herbert 1928- *St&PR 91*
Simon, Edward R., Jr. 1940- *WhoAm 90*
Simon, Elizabeth Marie 1947- *WhoAmW 91*
Simon, Elliot 1912- *WhoWor 91*
Simon, Elmer Peter 1921- *St&PR 91*
Simon, Eric Jacob 1924- *WhoAm 90*
Simon, Eric M 1892-1978 *WhoAmA 91N*
Simon, Ernest Martin 1932- *St&PR 91*
Simon, Francis Malcolm 1928- *WhoE 91*
Simon, Franklin S *BiDrAPA 89*
Simon, Gary D. 1948- *St&PR 91*
Simon, Gregory Edward 1958- *BiDrAPA 89*
Simon, H Joseph *BiDrAPA 89*
Simon, Harold 1930- *WhoAm 90*
Simon, Harold 1953- *WhoWrEP 89*
Simon, Helene *WhoAmA 91*
Simon, Hellmuth E *BiDrAPA 89*
Simon, Henry T. *St&PR 91*
Simon, Henry W. 1901-1970 *AuBYP 90*
Simon, Herbert *WhoAm 90*
Simon, Herbert Alexander 1916- *BioIn 16, WhoAm 90, WhoE 91, WhoWor 91*
Simon, Herbert Bernheimer 1927- *WhoAmA 91*
Simon, Hermann J. 1947- *WhoWor 91*
Simon, Hilda Rita 1921- *AuBYP 90*
Simon, Howard 1903-1979 *WhoAmA 91N*
Simon, Howard M. 1953- *St&PR 91*
Simon, Huey Paul 1923- *WhoAm 90, WhoSSW 91, WhoWor 91*
Simon, Ira Jonathan 1959- *St&PR 91*
Simon, J. Matthew *WhoAm 90*
Simon, Jack Aaron 1919- *WhoAm 90*
Simon, Jack William 1943- *BiDrAPA 89*
Simon, Jacqueline Albert *WhoAm 90, WhoAmW 91, WhoE 91, WhoWor 91*
Simon, Jacqueline Ann 1943- *WhoWrEP 89*
Simon, James Lowell 1944- *WhoSSW 91*
Simon, James M. 1951- *ODwPR 91*
Simon, James Michael 1951- *St&PR 91*
Simon, Jane 1942- *BiDrAPA 89*
Simon, Janos 1946- *WhoAm 90*
Simon, Jeanne *BioIn 16*
Simon, Jeffrey Scott 1955- *BiDrAPA 89*
Simon, Jerald Ira 1937- *BiDrAPA 89*
Simon, Jerome B. 1927- *St&PR 91*
Simon, Jewel Woodard 1911- *WhoAmA 91*
Simon, Jimmy Louis 1930- *WhoAm 90*
Simon, Jo Ann 1946- *WhoWrEP 89*
Simon, Joanna 1940- *WhoAm 90*
Simon, Joe *BioIn 16*
Simon, Joe 1915- *EncACom*
Simon, Joe 1941?- *DrBlPA 90*
Simon, John Bern 1942- *WhoAm 90*
Simon, John Ernest 1951- *BiDrAPA 89*
Simon, John Gerald 1928- *WhoAm 90*
Simon, John Ivan 1925- *WhoAm 90*
Simon, John L 1913- *BiDrAPA 89*
Simon, John Lewis 1947- *WhoE 91*
Simon, John Oliver 1942- *WhoWrEP 89*
Simon, John Roger 1939- *WhoAm 90*
Simon, Joseph B. 1928- *St&PR 91*
Simon, Joseph Patrick 1932- *WhoAm 90*
Simon, Jules Francois Suisse 1814-1896 *BiDFrPL*
Simon, Julian Lincoln 1932- *WhoAm 90, WhoE 91*
Simon, Julie C. *ODwPR 91*
Simon, Justin 1927- *BiDrAPA 89*
Simon, Kate *BioIn 16*
Simon, Kate 1912-1990 *ConAu 130, MajTwCW, NewYTBS 90 [port], WorAu 1980 [port]*
Simon, Keith R. 1955- *WhoSSW 91*
Simon, Kenneth D. 1918- *St&PR 91*
Simon, Kevin Charles 1956- *St&PR 91, WhoE 91*
Simon, Kurt 1913- *St&PR 91*
Simon, Lee Will 1940- *WhoAm 90*
Simon, Leonard Ronald 1936- *WhoAmA 91*
Simon, Leonard S. 1936- *St&PR 91*
Simon, Leonard Samuel 1936- *WhoAm 90*
Simon, Leslie Norman 1944- *St&PR 91*
Simon, Lois Prem 1933- *WhoE 91*
Simon, Lorena Cotts 1897- *WhoAmW 91, WhoWor 91*
Simon, Loretta L. 1948- *St&PR 91*
Simon, Lothar 1938- *WhoAm 90*
Simon, Marilyn 1941- *WhoAmW 91*
Simon, Marilyn L. *WhoAm 90*
Simon, Marilyn W. 1927- *WhoAmW 91*
Simon, Mark William 1939- *St&PR 91*
Simon, Martin *BioIn 16*
Simon, Martin S. 1926- *St&PR 91*
Simon, Martin Stanley 1926- *WhoAm 90, WhoE 91*
Simon, Martin Thomas 1950- *St&PR 91*
Simon, Marvin Kenneth 1939- *WhoAm 90*
Simon, Maurya 1950- *WhoWrEP 89*
Simon, Melvin 1926- *WhoAm 90*
Simon, Michael A 1936- *WhoAmA 91*
Simon, Michael Alexander 1936- *WhoAm 90*
Simon, Michael Andrew 1951- *WhoE 91*
Simon, Michael F. 1951- *St&PR 91*
Simon, Michael Richard 1951- *St&PR 91*
Simon, Michael Scott 1954- *WhoEmL 91*
Simon, Mike 1883-1963 *Ballpl 90*
Simon, Mina Lewiton *AuBYP 90*
Simon, Monique *BiDrAPA 89*
Simon, Mordecai 1925- *WhoAm 90*
Simon, Morton Sonny 1935- *WhoE 91*
Simon, Murray 1925- *WhoWor 91*
Simon, Nancy L. 1928- *St&PR 91*
Simon, Nancy Smith 1938- *WhoAmW 91*
Simon, Nancy Sue 1943- *WhoAmW 91*
Simon, Nat 1900-1979 *OxCPMus*
Simon, Nathan M 1926- *BiDrAPA 89*
Simon, Neil *BioIn 16*

Simon, Neil 1927- *MajTwCW, OxCPMus, WhoAm 90, WhoE 91, WorAlBi*
Simon, Netty D *WhoAmA 91*
Simon, Nicholas A 1921- *BiDrAPA 89*
Simon, Norma 1927- *AuBYP 90*
Simon, Norma Bernice 1927- *WhoAmW 91*
Simon, Norma Plavnick 1930- *WhoAmW 91*
Simon, Norton 1907- *WhoAmA 91*
Simon, Norton Winfred 1907- *ConAmBL*
Simon, Olga 1965- *WhoAmW 91*
Simon, Paul 1928- *AuBYP 90, BioIn 16, WhoAm 90, WhoWor 91, WhoWrEP 89*
Simon, Paul 1941- *OxCPMus, WhoAm 90, WorAlBi*
Simon, Paul 1942- *EncPR&S 89*
Simon, Paul Jerome 1954- *WhoWor 91*
Simon, Paul S. 1931- *St&PR 91*
Simon, Philippe Jean-Marie 1954- *WhoE 91*
Simon, Phyllis K. 1955- *St&PR 91*
Simon, Ralph 1906- *BioIn 16, WhoAm 90*
Simon, Richard A. 1938- *St&PR 91*
Simon, Richard Eric 1951- *St&PR 91*
Simon, Richard Leo 1899-1960 *WorAlBi*
Simon, Richard Michael 1942- *St&PR 91*
Simon, Richard S. 1921- *St&PR 91*
Simon, Robert Barry 1952- *WhoAmA 91, WhoE 91*
Simon, Robert G. 1927- *St&PR 91, WhoAm 90*
Simon, Robert Isaac 1934- *BiDrAPA 89*
Simon, Robert L. 1941- *WhoWrEP 89*
Simon, Robert Martin 1934- *BiDrAPA 89*
Simon, Robin *BioIn 16*
Simon, Roger L 1943- *TwCCr&M 91*
Simon, Roger Mitchell 1948- *WhoWrEP 89*
Simon, Roger Scott 1956- *St&PR 91*
Simon, Ronald I. 1938- *WhoAm 90*
Simon, Ronald Isaac 1938- *St&PR 91*
Simon, Ronald M. 1934- *St&PR 91*
Simon, Ruth Corabel 1918- *AuBYP 90*
Simon, S. Fannie *BioIn 16*
Simon, Sander *BioIn 16*
Simon, Seymour 1915- *WhoAm 90*
Simon, Seymour B. 1927- *St&PR 91*
Simon, Sheldon Weiss 1937- *WhoAm 90*
Simon, Sheridan Alan 1947- *WhoSSW 91*
Simon, Sidney 1917- *WhoAm 90, WhoAmA 91*
Simon, Stanley 1917- *St&PR 91*
Simon, Steven 1945- *St&PR 91*
Simon, Steven Cliff 1945- *St&PR 91*
Simon, Stuart B *BiDrAPA 89*
Simon, Susan C. *BioIn 16*
Simon, Susan Mindy 1957- *WhoE 91*
Simon, Ted J. 1931- *St&PR 91*
Simon, Thomas Shahean 1952- *WhoE 91*
Simon, Victoria *BioIn 16*
Simon, Walter L. 1936- *St&PR 91*
Simon, Werner 1914- *BiDrAPA 89, WhoWrEP 89*
Simon, William 1929- *WhoAm 90*
Simon, William E. 1927- *BioIn 16, WorAlBi*
Simon, William Edward 1927- *BiDrUSE 89, ConAmBL, WhoAm 90*
Simon, William George 1913- *WhoAm 90*
Simon-Cahn, Annabelle *WhoE 91*
Simon Estes, Marla 1955- *WhoWor 91*
Simon-Thomas, Frank *BiDrAPA 89*
Simonaitis, Richard Ambrose 1930- *WhoWor 91*
Simonaityte, Ieva 1897-1978 *EncCoWW*
Simonalle, Eugene 1931- *St&PR 91*
Simonard, Stephanie Harmon 1950- *WhoWor 91*
Simonds, Bruce T. 1895-1989 *BioIn 16*
Simonds, Charles Frederick 1945- *WhoAmA 91*
Simonds, John Day, Jr. 1957- *WhoSSW 91*
Simonds, John Edward 1935- *WhoAm 90*
Simonds, John F 1933- *BiDrAPA 89*
Simonds, John Ormsbee 1913- *WhoAm 90*
Simonds, Marie Celeste 1947- *WhoAmW 91*
Simonds, Marshall 1930- *WhoAm 90*
Simonds, Peter Kemble *St&PR 91N*
Simonds, Philip George 1940- *St&PR 91*
Simonds, Robert *BiDrAPA 89*
Simonds, Robert James 1924- *St&PR 91*
Simonds, William Edgar 1842-1903 *AmLegL*
Simone *WhoAmA 91*
Simone, Albert Joseph 1935- *WhoAm 90*
Simone, Ann Marie 1958- *WhoAmW 91*
Simone, Charles *BioIn 16*
Simone, Gail Elisabeth 1944- *WhoAmW 91, WhoE 91, WhoWor 91*
Simone, Gerry A. *ODwPR 91*
Simone, Johanna Francine 1963- *WhoAmW 91*
Simone, John Joseph 1941- *St&PR 91*
Simone, Joseph 1924- *WhoE 91*
Simone, Louise *BioIn 16*
Simone, Nina 1933- *DrBlPA 90, OxCPMus, WorAlBi*
Simone, Peter James 1947- *St&PR 91*
Simone, Susan Mary 1955- *WhoE 91*
Simone, Thomas B. 1942- *St&PR 91, WhoAm 90*
Simoneau, John J. 1925- *St&PR 91*
Simoneau, Leopold 1918- *IntWWM 90, PenDiMP*
Simoneau, Normand J. 1932- *WhoAm 90*
Simoneaux, Frank P. 1933- *WhoSSW 91*
Simonelli, Charles Francis 1925- *WhoAm 90*
Simonelli, Jerry 1952- *WhoEmL 91*
Simonelli, John 1946- *St&PR 91*
Simonet, Johann *PenDiDA 89*
Simonet, John Thomas 1926- *WhoAm 90*
Simonet, Sebastian 1898-1948 *WhoAmA 91N*
Simonett, John E. 1924- *WhoAm 90*
Simonetti, Azra *NewAgMG*
Simonetto, Joseph Ambrose 1943- *St&PR 91*
Simoni, Guy P. *BioIn 16*
Simoni, John Peter 1911- *WhoAm 90, WhoAmA 91*
Simonian, Judith 1945- *WhoAmA 91*
Simonian, Simon John 1932- *WhoAm 90, WhoWor 91*
Simonian, Stephan 1947- *BiDrAPA 89*
Simonich, John Charles 1951- *WhoE 91*
Simonin, Michel Gabriel 1947- *WhoWor 91*
Simonini-Fontanesi, Simona 1943- *IntWWM 90*
Simonis, Adrianus Johannes 1931- *WhoWor 91*
Simonis, John Charles 1940- *WhoSSW 91*
Simonnard, Michel A. 1933- *St&PR 91, WhoE 91*
Simonnard, Michel Andre 1933- *WhoAm 90*
Simonov, Yuri 1941- *PenDiMP*
Simonov, Yuri Ivanovich 1941- *IntWWM 90, WhoWor 91*
Simons, Albert, Jr. 1918- *WhoAm 90*
Simons, Anne Hudspeth *ODwPR 91*
Simons, Beverley 1938- *FemiCLE*
Simons, Beverley Rosen 1938- *OxCCanT*
Simons, Charles Earl, Jr. 1916- *WhoAm 90*
Simons, Charles Franklin, III 1950- *WhoSSW 91*
Simons, Charles John 1918- *St&PR 91*
Simons, Dale Edward 1931- *WhoWrEP 89*
Simons, Dennis *PenDiMP*
Simons, Dolph C. 1904-1989 *BioIn 16*
Simons, Dolph C., Jr. 1930- *St&PR 91*
Simons, Dolph Collins, Jr. 1930- *WhoAm 90*
Simons, Elizabeth Reiman 1929- *WhoAm 90, WhoAmW 91*
Simons, Elwyn LaVerne 1930- *WhoAm 90*
Simons, Francois-Marcus 1750-1828 *PenDiDA 89*
Simons, Gordon Donald, Jr. 1938- *WhoAm 90*
Simons, Henry A. *BioIn 16*
Simons, Henry Calvert 1899-1946 *BioIn 16*
Simons, Henry Mazyck, III 1948- *WhoSSW 91*
Simons, Howard *BioIn 16*
Simons, Howard 1929-1989 *AnObit 1989*
Simons, James, Jr. 1813-1879 *AmLegL*
Simons, James, Jr. 1839-1919 *AmLegL*
Simons, Jay R. 1930- *St&PR 91*
Simons, John Caldwell 1961- *WhoE 91*
Simons, John H. 1939- *WhoAm 90*
Simons, Joseph M. 1914- *St&PR 91*
Simons, Kent Cobb 1935- *WhoAm 90*
Simons, Lawrence Brook 1924- *WhoAm 90*
Simons, Leonard Norman 1904- *St&PR 91*
Simons, Leonard Norman Rashall 1904- *WhoAm 90*
Simons, Leonard R. 1928- *St&PR 91*
Simons, Lois Anne 1917- *WhoAmW 91*
Simons, Louise Bedell 1912-1977 *WhoAmA 91N*
Simons, Lynn Osborn 1934- *WhoAm 90, WhoAmW 91*
Simons, Mary Kathleen 1950- *WhoSSW 91*
Simons, Melissa Jane 1961- *WhoAmW 91*
Simons, Ray D. 1946- *WhoEmL 91*
Simons, Richard A. 1936- *St&PR 91*
Simons, Richard C *BiDrAPA 89*
Simons, Richard Duncan 1927- *WhoAm 90, WhoE 91*
Simons, Roger A. 1943- *WhoE 91*
Simons, Roland S. 1955- *St&PR 91*
Simons, Ronald C 1935- *BiDrAPA 89*
Simons, Samuel Stoney 1920- *WhoAm 90*
Simons, Shirley Ann 1937- *WhoAmW 91*
Simons, Stephen 1938- *WhoAm 90*
Simons, Steven Jay 1946- *WhoEmL 91*
Simons, Suzanne Eileen 1959- *WhoEmL 91*
Simons, Thomas C. 1928-1988 *BioIn 16*
Simons, Vicki Ann 1950- *WhoAmW 91*
Simons, William John *BiDrAPA 89*
Simonsen, Bernard Lee 1945- *St&PR 91*
Simonsen, Gregory Mark 1957- *WhoEmL 91*
Simonsen, Jeffry Scott 1953- *St&PR 91*
Simonsen, Mark Warren 1946- *St&PR 91*
Simonsen, Palle 1933- *WhoWor 91*
Simonsen, Paul Herbert 1954- *WhoSSW 91*
Simonsen, Renee *BioIn 16*
Simonsmeier, Larry Marvin 1944- *WhoWrEP 89*
Simonson, Arthur William 1924- *St&PR 91*
Simonson, David C. 1927- *WhoAm 90*
Simonson, Donna Jeanne 1947- *WhoAmW 91*
Simonson, Gerald Wallace 1930- *St&PR 91*
Simonson, John Alexander 1945- *St&PR 91, WhoAm 90*
Simonson, Lee J. 1953- *WhoE 91*
Simonson, Lee Stuart 1948- *WhoAm 90*
Simonson, Mary Kristine *BiDrAPA 89*
Simonson, Matthew Charles 1950- *WhoEmL 91*
Simonson, Melvin 1914- *BiDrAPA 89*
Simonson, Michael 1950- *WhoEmL 91*
Simonson, Miles Kevin 1950- *WhoWor 91*
Simonson, Susan Kay 1946- *WhoAmW 91, WhoWor 91*
Simonson, Teresa M. 1960- *WhoAmW 91*
Simonson, William L. 1943- *St&PR 91*
Simonsz, Huibert Jan 1951- *WhoWor 91*
Simont, Marc 1915- *AuBYP 90, WhoAm 90*
Simonte, Victor *BioIn 16*
Simonton, Ann *BioIn 16*
Simonton, Charles Henry 1829-1904 *AmLegL*
Simonton, John W. 1945- *St&PR 91*
Simonton, O. Carl *NewAgE 90*
Simonton, Robert Bennet 1933- *St&PR 91, WhoAm 90*
Simonton, Ronald Joseph 1939- *WhoSSW 91*
Simonton, Stephanie *ConAu 132*
Simony, Maggy *WhoWrEP 89*
Simonyan, Gary 1935- *St&PR 91*
Simonyi-Gindele, Steven J. 1945- *St&PR 91*
Simopoulos, Aris M *BiDrAPA 89*
Simopoulos, Artemis Panageotis 1933- *WhoAm 90*
Simor, George F *BiDrAPA 89*
Simor, Suzanna B *WhoAmA 91*
Simos, Evangelos Otto 1947- *WhoWor 91*
Simos, Miriam *NewAgE 90*
Simoson, William Eugene 1949- *WhoEmL 91*
Simpatico, Thomas A *BiDrAPA 89*
Simper, Frederick 1914- *WhoAmA 91*
Simpich, William Morris 1924- *WhoAm 90*
Simpkin, Lawrence James 1933- *WhoAm 90*
Simpkins, Anne Eddleman 1950- *WhoAmW 91*
Simpkins, Christen, Jr. 1954- *WhoSSW 91, WhoWor 91*
Simpkins, Freda 1944- *WhoWor 91*
Simpkins, Mary Nell 1956- *WhoEmL 91*
Simple Minds *EncPR&S 89*
Simplot, Jack *BioIn 16*
Simplot, John Richard 1909- *ConAmBL*
Simplot, Scott R. 1946- *WhoAm 90*
Simpson, Adele 1904- *ConDes 90*
Simpson, Adele 1908- *WhoAm 90, WhoAmW 91*
Simpson, Alan 1912- *ConAu 30NR*
Simpson, Alan K 1931- *CurBio 90 [port]*
Simpson, Alan Kooi 1931- *NewYTBS 90 [port], WhoAm 90, WhoWor 91*
Simpson, Alex Francis 1932- *St&PR 91*
Simpson, Andrea *ODwPR 91*
Simpson, Andrea Lynn 1948- *St&PR 91, WhoAmW 91, WhoEmL 91*
Simpson, Barbara L. 1947- *WhoAmW 91, WhoE 91, WhoEmL 91*
Simpson, Benjamin Franklin 1836-1916 *AmLegL*
Simpson, Bert Edward 1957- *BiDrAPA 89*
Simpson, Bradford Van 1957- *WhoSSW 91*
Simpson, Bruce C. 1939- *St&PR 91*
Simpson, Bruce Howard 1921- *WhoAm 90*
Simpson, Carol Louise 1937- *WhoAmW 91, WhoE 91, WhoWor 91*
Simpson, Cary Hatcher 1927- *WhoAm 90*
Simpson, Cathy Ann 1953- *WhoAmW 91*
Simpson, Charles A. *St&PR 91*
Simpson, Charles R., III 1945- *WhoSSW 91*
Simpson, Charles Reagan 1921- *WhoAm 90*
Simpson, Christopher Dale 1941- *WhoSSW 91*
Simpson, Cynthia Kay 1953- *WhoAmW 91*
Simpson, Dale McClure 1948- *BiDrAPA 89*
Simpson, Daniel H. 1939- *WhoWor 91*
Simpson, Daniel Reid 1927- *WhoSSW 91*
Simpson, David 1928- *WhoAmA 91*
Simpson, David Allen 1955- *WhoEmL 91*
Simpson, David Eugene 1951- *WhoEmL 91*
Simpson, David John 1946- *St&PR 91, WhoAm 90*
Simpson, David Louis, III 1936- *St&PR 91*
Simpson, David R. 1957- *St&PR 91*
Simpson, David William 1928- *WhoAm 90*
Simpson, Deanna Lynn 1956- *WhoAmW 91*
Simpson, Deborah Lynne 1962- *WhoAmW 91*
Simpson, Dennis Arden 1944- *WhoSSW 91*
Simpson, Derek *PenDiMP*
Simpson, Diane *BioIn 16*
Simpson, Diane Jeannette 1952- *WhoAmW 91*
Simpson, Dick 1940- *ConAu 30NR*
Simpson, Dick 1943- *Ballpl 90*
Simpson, Donald Bruce 1942- *WhoAm 90*
Simpson, Dorothy 1933- *ConAu 30NR, MajTwCW, TwCCr&M 91*
Simpson, Douglas Jackson 1940- *WhoAm 90*
Simpson, Dudley George 1922- *IntWWM 90*
Simpson, Edward W. 1904- *St&PR 91*
Simpson, Edwin L. 1948- *WhoWrEP 89*
Simpson, Elizabeth Alice Hilts 1921-1989 *ConAu 130*
Simpson, Elizabeth Ann 1941- *WhoAmW 91*
Simpson, Elizabeth Barlow 1954- *BiDrAPA 89*
Simpson, Ethel Chachere 1937- *WhoWrEP 89*
Simpson, Floyd Duane *BiDrAPA 89*
Simpson, Frank B, III 1936- *BiDrAPA 89*
Simpson, Frank William 1920- *St&PR 91*
Simpson, Frankie Joe 1933- *WhoAmW 91*
Simpson, Frederic Olaf 1924- *WhoWor 91*
Simpson, Frederick James 1922- *WhoAm 90*
Simpson, Gary E. 1937- *ODwPR 91*
Simpson, Gary Eldridge 1937- *St&PR 91*
Simpson, Geddes Wilson 1908- *WhoWrEP 89*
Simpson, George 1787?-1860 *WhNaAH*
Simpson, George Gaylord 1902-1984 *MajTwCW*
Simpson, George H. 1950- *ODwPR 91*
Simpson, George M *BiDrAPA 89*
Simpson, George Megahy 1926- *WhoE 91*
Simpson, Grover Benjamin 1928- *St&PR 91*
Simpson, H. Richard 1930- *WhoSSW 91, WhoWor 91*
Simpson, Harriette *MajTwCW*
Simpson, Harry 1925-1979 *Ballpl 90*
Simpson, Helen 1897-1940 *FemiCLE*
Simpson, Hilary 1954- *ConAu 131*
Simpson, Howard 1922- *St&PR 91*
Simpson, Howard Douglas 1959- *WhoE 91*
Simpson, J. Kirk 1949- *WhoAm 90*
Simpson, Jack Benjamin 1937- *WhoWor 91*
Simpson, Jack W. 1941- *St&PR 91*
Simpson, James Carroll 1931- *WhoE 91*
Simpson, James D., III 1940- *St&PR 91*
Simpson, James E. 1933- *St&PR 91*
Simpson, James Edward 1933- *WhoAm 90*
Simpson, James Lee 1924- *WhoAm 90*
Simpson, James Reid, II 1954- *WhoEmL 91*
Simpson, James Rigg 1940- *St&PR 91*
Simpson, James Roche 1946- *WhoSSW 91*
Simpson, James Young 1811-1870 *WorAlBi*
Simpson, Janet A. 1936- *St&PR 91*
Simpson, Jay A. 1947- *St&PR 91*
Simpson, Jean Marie 1927- *WhoAmW 91*
Simpson, Jess Richard 1924- *St&PR 91*
Simpson, Joanne Malkus 1923- *WhoAm 90, WhoAmW 91*
Simpson, Joe *BioIn 16*
Simpson, Joe 1951- *Ballpl 90*
Simpson, Joe B. 1949- *St&PR 91*
Simpson, Joe Leigh 1943- *WhoAm 90*
Simpson, John Alexander 1916- *WhoAm 90*
Simpson, John D. *BioIn 16*
Simpson, John Lawrence 1933- *IntWWM 90*
Simpson, John Mathes 1948- *WhoAm 90, WhoE 91*
Simpson, John Richard 1932- *WhoAm 90*
Simpson, John S. 1941- *St&PR 91*
Simpson, John Wistar 1914- *WhoAm 90*
Simpson, Joseph Anthony *BiDrAPA 89*
Simpson, Joseph Walker, III *BiDrAPA 89*

Simpson, Kathryn Jacquin 1924- *WhoAmW 91*
Simpson, Keith 1907-1985 *DcNaB 1981*
Simpson, Kenneth *IntWWM 90*
Simpson, L.W. 1916- *St&PR 91*
Simpson, Larry L. 1949- *St&PR 91*
Simpson, Larry Walker 1943- *BiDrAPA 89*
Simpson, Laura Evelyn 1917- *WhoAmW 91*
Simpson, Leatrice Harriet *BiDrAPA 89*
Simpson, Lee 1923- *WhoAmA 91*
Simpson, Lee C. 1934- *St&PR 91*
Simpson, Leslie Ainsley 1947- *WhoWor 91*
Simpson, Lillian Frances 1933- *WhoSSW 91*
Simpson, Lora Elaine 1933- *WhoAmW 91*
Simpson, Louis 1923- *MajTwCW, WorAlBi*
Simpson, Louis A. 1936- *WhoAm 90*
Simpson, Louis Allen 1936- *St&PR 91*
Simpson, Louis Aston Marantz 1923- *WhoAm 90, WhoWrEP 89*
Simpson, Lucy Picco 1940- *WhoAmW 91*
Simpson, Lyle Lee 1937- *WhoWor 91*
Simpson, Marianna Shreve 1949- *WhoAmA 91*
Simpson, Marilyn Jean *WhoAmA 91*
Simpson, Marshall 1900-1958 *WhoAmA 91N*
Simpson, Marshall A 1927- *BiDrAPA 89*
Simpson, Martin *BioIn 16*
Simpson, Martyn William 1948- *WhoSSW 91*
Simpson, Mary 1617?-1647 *BiDEWW, FemiCLE*
Simpson, Mary Elizabeth 1946- *WhoAmW 91*
Simpson, Mary Michael 1925- *WhoAmW 91*
Simpson, Maryl *BioIn 16*
Simpson, Matt 1936- *ConAu 131*
Simpson, Melancthon 1827?-1899 *DcCanB 12*
Simpson, Melvin Oren, Jr. 1926- *St&PR 91*
Simpson, Melvin V. *WhoAm 90*
Simpson, Merton D 1928- *WhoAmA 91*
Simpson, Michael 1938- *WhoAm 90*
Simpson, Michael J. 1953- *St&PR 91*
Simpson, Michael Kevin 1949- *WhoAm 90*
Simpson, Michael Marcial 1954- *WhoE 91, WhoSSW 91*
Simpson, Michael Wayne 1959- *WhoEmL 91, WhoWor 91*
Simpson, Mona *BioIn 16*
Simpson, Murray 1921- *WhoAm 90, WhoE 91, WhoWor 91*
Simpson, Murray Stephen 1962- *WhoEmL 91*
Simpson, Nancy *BioIn 16*
Simpson, Nancy Carolyn 1938- *WhoWrEP 89*
Simpson, Norman T. *BioIn 16*
Simpson, O. J. *BioIn 16*
Simpson, O J 1947- *DrBlPA 90*
Simpson, O. J. 1947- *WhoAm 90, WorAlBi*
Simpson, O. Strother 1910- *St&PR 91*
Simpson, Peggy Ann 1938- *WhoAmW 91*
Simpson, Phil 1935- *St&PR 91*
Simpson, Philip Francis 1923- *WhoWor 91*
Simpson, Ralph *PenDiDA 89*
Simpson, Ralph 1946- *ODwPR 91*
Simpson, Ralph Michael 1937- *St&PR 91*
Simpson, Reed Earl *BiDrAPA 89*
Simpson, Richard Brian 1945- *BiDrAPA 89*
Simpson, Richard Charles, Jr. 1952- *St&PR 91*
Simpson, Richard Lee 1929- *WhoAm 90*
Simpson, Robert 1834-1897 *DcCanB 12*
Simpson, Robert 1921- *IntWWM 90*
Simpson, Robert C. 1942- *St&PR 91*
Simpson, Robert Edward 1917- *WhoAm 90, WhoE 91*
Simpson, Robert Glenn 1932- *WhoAm 90*
Simpson, Robert Hope *PenDiMP*
Simpson, Robert Leatham 1915- *WhoAm 90*
Simpson, Robert Lee 1942- *WhoE 91*
Simpson, Robert Louis 1948- *IntWWM 90*
Simpson, Robert Malone 1946- *WhoSSW 91*
Simpson, Robert Smith 1906- *WhoAm 90*
Simpson, Robert Wayne 1928- *WhoE 91*
Simpson, Robert Wilfred Levick 1921- *WhoWor 91*
Simpson, Roger M., Jr. 1936- *St&PR 91*
Simpson, Ruby Laird 1910- *WhoAmW 91*
Simpson, Russell Gordon 1927- *WhoAm 90, WhoWor 91*
Simpson, Samuel Ford, Jr. 1950- *WhoE 91*
Simpson, Scott *BioIn 16, ODwPR 91*
Simpson, Shelly Anne 1959- *WhoE 91*
Simpson, Steven Drexell 1953- *WhoEmL 91*
Simpson, Susan Grace 1940- *WhoAmW 91*
Simpson, Sylvia G *BiDrAPA 89*
Simpson, Theodore Oliver 1925- *WhoWor 91*
Simpson, Thomas John 1958- *St&PR 91*
Simpson, Valerie 1946- *BioIn 16*
Simpson, Vi 1946- *WhoAmW 91*
Simpson, Vinson Raleigh 1928- *WhoAm 90*
Simpson, Virginia White 1907- *WhoAmW 91*
Simpson, Vollis 1919- *MusmAFA*
Simpson, Wade Bland 1937- *St&PR 91*
Simpson, Wallis *BioAmW*
Simpson, Wallis Warfield 1896-1986 *BioIn 16*
Simpson, Walter Willis 1925- *WhoAm 90*
Simpson, Wayne 1948- *Ballpl 90*
Simpson, Willard Kempton, Jr. 1954- *WhoSSW 91*
Simpson, William 1818-1872 *WhoAmA 91N*
Simpson, William Anderson 1941- *St&PR 91*
Simpson, William Arthur 1939- *WhoAm 90*
Simpson, William Fulton 1945- *St&PR 91*
Simpson, William Gary 1943- *WhoSSW 91*
Simpson, William H. 1941- *St&PR 91*
Simpson, William John 1936- *WhoWor 91*
Simpson, William Kelly 1928- *WhoAm 90, WhoAmA 91*
Simpson, William M., Jr. 1947- *WhoSSW 91*
Simpson, William Russell 1922- *WhoWor 91*
Simpson, William S 1924- *BiDrAPA 89*
Simpson, William Stewart 1924- *WhoAm 90*
Simpson, Winifred Rouse 1937- *WhoWrEP 89*
Simpson, Zelma Alene 1923- *WhoAm 90*
Simrall, Dorothy Van Winkle 1917- *WhoAmW 91*
Simrell, Dan *BioIn 16*
Simring, Steven S *BiDrAPA 89*
Sims, August Charles 1948- *WhoEmL 91*
Sims, Bennett Jones 1920- *WhoAm 90*
Sims, Bernard J. 1948- *St&PR 91*
Sims, Bill 1932- *WhoSSW 91*
Sims, C. Paul 1951- *St&PR 91*
Sims, Carol S. 1937- *WhoAmW 91, WhoE 91*
Sims, Carolyn Denise 1960- *WhoAmW 91*
Sims, David Suthern 1965- *WhoSSW 91*
Sims, Dean 1921- *ODwPR 91*
Sims, Duke 1941- *Ballpl 90*
Sims, Edward, Jr. *WhoSSW 91*
Sims, Edward Howell 1923- *WhoAm 90*
Sims, Edward S. 1946- *St&PR 91*
Sims, Elizabeth Ballard 1944- *WhoAmW 91*
Sims, Everett Martin 1920- *WhoAm 90*
Sims, Ezra 1928- *IntWWM 90*
Sims, Frank McNair 1932- *St&PR 91*
Sims, Fred William, Sr. 1915- *WhoSSW 91*
Sims, George 1923- *TwCCr&M 91*
Sims, George Oren, III 1955- *WhoEmL 91*
Sims, Gloria I. 1949- *St&PR 91*
Sims, Henry M *BiDrAPA 89*
Sims, Herman Christie 1960- *WhoSSW 91*
Sims, Howard *DrBlPA 90*
Sims, Idan 1947- *ODwPR 91*
Sims, Ivor Donald 1912- *WhoAm 90*
Sims, James Hylbert 1924- *WhoAm 90, WhoWrEP 89*
Sims, James M. 1934- *St&PR 91*
Sims, James Mannon 1935- *BiDrAPA 89*
Sims, James Redding 1918- *WhoAm 90*
Sims, Jethro Michael 1949- *WhoSSW 91*
Sims, Joe 1944- *WhoAm 90, WhoE 91*
Sims, John L. *BioIn 16*
Sims, John Rogers, Jr. 1924- *WhoAm 90*
Sims, John William 1917- *WhoAm 90*
Sims, Joseph S. 1932- *ODwPR 91*
Sims, Karen Jackson 1954- *WhoAmW 91*
Sims, Kathy Lou Busey 1954- *WhoAmW 91*
Sims, Kent Otway 1940- *WhoAm 90*
Sims, Lewis Burrill 1909- *WhoE 91*
Sims, Loretta James 1948- *WhoAmW 91, WhoWor 91*
Sims, Lowery Stokes 1949- *WhoAmA 91*
Sims, Lydel *AuBYP 90*
Sims, Marcy J. 1946- *WhoSSW 91*
Sims, Margaret Church 1949- *WhoAmW 91*
Sims, Marion D., III 1943- *WhoAm 90*
Sims, Michael Hall 1956- *WhoAm 90*
Sims, Micheal Hall 1956- *St&PR 91*
Sims, Norman 1948- *ConAu 132*
Sims, Patrick Mark 1966- *WhoEmL 91*
Sims, Patsy 1938- *WhoE 91*
Sims, Patterson 1947- *WhoAmA 91*
Sims, Paul Kibler 1918- *WhoAm 90*
Sims, Peter Andrew 1959- *WhoAmA 91, WhoE 91*
Sims, Peter Morris 1959- *BiDrAPA 89*
Sims, Philip Stuart 1927- *St&PR 91*
Sims, Richard Edward 1941- *St&PR 91*
Sims, Richard Lee 1929- *WhoAm 90*
Sims, Riley V. 1903- *St&PR 91, WhoAm 90*
Sims, Robert Barry 1942- *WhoAm 90*
Sims, Robert Bell 1934- *WhoAm 90*
Sims, Robert McNeill 1928- *WhoSSW 91, WhoWor 91*
Sims, Roger Lafe 1941- *WhoE 91*
Sims, Seymour E. 1914- *St&PR 91*
Sims, Sherye Lynn 1959- *WhoAmW 91*
Sims, Stephen Paul 1947- *St&PR 91*
Sims, Thaddeus Michael 1943- *WhoSSW 91*
Sims, Thomas Auburn 1925- *WhoSSW 91*
Sims, William Dale 1941- *St&PR 91*
Sims, William Marquis 1944- *St&PR 91*
Sims, William Maurice, Jr. 1937- *WhoE 91*
Sims, William Riley, Jr. 1938- *WhoAm 90*
Sims, William S. 1858-1936 *WorAlBi*
Sims, Wilson 1924- *WhoAm 90, WhoSSW 91*
Sims, Zoot *BioIn 16*
Sims, Zoot 1925-1985 *OxCPMus*
Simsek, Levent 1953- *WhoWor 91*
Simshauser, Philip Dale 1937- *St&PR 91*
Simske, Clifford J 1937- *BiDrAPA 89*
Simson, Bevlyn A 1917- *WhoAmA 91*
Simson, Jo Anne 1936- *WhoSSW 91*
Simson, Joanne 1936- *WhoWrEP 89*
Simson, Mary Turk 1951- *ODwPR 91*
Simundsson, Elva 1950- *SmATA 63*
Simunich, Mary Elizabeth Hedrick *WhoAmW 91*
Simunovic, Zlatko Josip 1931- *WhoWor 91*
Simutis, Leonard Joseph 1944- *WhoAm 90*
Sin, Jaime *BioIn 16*
Sin, Jaime Lachica 1928- *WhoWor 91*
Sina, Alejandro 1945- *WhoAmA 91*
Sinagra, Robert L. 1934- *St&PR 91*
Sinai, Allen 1939- *St&PR 91*
Sinai, Allen Leo 1939- *WhoAm 90, WhoWor 91*
Sinai, Arthur 1939- *WhoAm 90*
Sinaikin, Phillip Marc *BiDrAPA 89*
Sinaiko, Arlie 1902- *WhoAmA 91*
Sinan 1489?-1588 *BioIn 16*
Sinan, Rogelio 1902- *BioIn 16*
Sinapi, Michael Pat Anthony 1959- *WhoE 91*
Sinard, Antoinette Karabin 1909- *WhoAmW 91*
Sinate *DcCanB 12*
Sinatra, Francine *BioIn 16*
Sinatra, Frank 1915- *BioIn 16, EncPR&S 89, NewYTBS 90 [port], OxCPMus, WhoAm 90, WhoWor 91, WorAlBi*
Sinatra, Frank Paul 1949- *WhoAm 90, WhoE 91*
Sinatra, Robert S. 1938- *St&PR 91*
Sinavsky, Alexander W 1942- *BiDrAPA 89*
Sinay, Joseph 1920- *St&PR 91, WhoAm 90*
Sinbad 1956- *DrBlPA 90*
Sincaban, Virginia *BiDrAPA 89*
Sincaglia, Frank Paul 1943- *St&PR 91*
Sincerbeaux, Robert Abbott 1913- *WhoE 91*
Sinche, Robert Miller 1952- *WhoAm 90*
Sinchuayprarb, Supote 1948- *WhoWor 91*
Sinclair, Alastair James 1935- *WhoAm 90*
Sinclair, Alexander J M *BiDrAPA 89*
Sinclair, Alford C. 1930- *St&PR 91*
Sinclair, Alford Charles 1930- *WhoAm 90*
Sinclair, Andrew *BioIn 16*
Sinclair, Andrew 1935- *MajTwCW*
Sinclair, Anne Van Nuys 1924- *WhoAmW 91*
Sinclair, Bertrand William 1881-1972 *DcLB 92*
Sinclair, Bruce 1929- *WhoAm 90, WhoWrEP 89*
Sinclair, Carol Ann 1949- *WhoAmW 91*
Sinclair, Carole 1942- *WhoAm 90, WhoAmW 91*
Sinclair, Catherine 1800-1864 *BioIn 16, FemiCLE*
Sinclair, Catherine 1817-1891 *BioIn 16*
Sinclair, Catherine Norton 1817-1891 *NotWoAT*
Sinclair, Clive Marles 1940- *WhoWor 91*
Sinclair, David Cecil *WhoWor 91*
Sinclair, Duncan Gordon 1933- *WhoAm 90*
Sinclair, Edward L., Jr. 1947- *St&PR 91*
Sinclair, Emil *MajTwCW*
Sinclair, Glenn Bruce 1946- *WhoAm 90*
Sinclair, Harry F. 1876-1956 *WorAlBi*
Sinclair, Heidi 1958- *ODwPR 91*
Sinclair, Helen K. *BioIn 16*
Sinclair, Howard S. 1945- *St&PR 91*
Sinclair, Iain 1943- *ConAu 132*
Sinclair, Iain MacGregor *ConAu 132*
Sinclair, Ian D. 1913- *St&PR 91*
Sinclair, Ian David 1913- *WhoAm 90*
Sinclair, Ian McCahon 1929- *WhoWor 91*
Sinclair, James Brimmer 1947- *IntWWM 90*
Sinclair, James Garner 1952- *St&PR 91*
Sinclair, Jerry Lane 1936- *WhoSSW 91*
Sinclair, Jo 1913- *BioAmW*
Sinclair, John Alan 1948- *St&PR 91*
Sinclair, John Edward 1936- *WhoAm 90*
Sinclair, John Luther 1960- *WhoE 91*
Sinclair, John Stephen 1947- *WhoEmL 91*
Sinclair, John Taylor, Jr. 1918- *WhoAm 90*
Sinclair, Joseph Samuels 1922- *St&PR 91, WhoAm 90*
Sinclair, Judson Mark 1949- *WhoSSW 91*
Sinclair, Kenneth Richard Coates 1946- *WhoSSW 91*
Sinclair, Kenneth Roger 1927- *St&PR 91*
Sinclair, Lawrence M 1947- *BiDrAPA 89*
Sinclair, Lister 1921- *OxCCanT*
Sinclair, Lonnie Ray 1952- *WhoEmL 91*
Sinclair, Madge 1940- *DrBlPA 90*
Sinclair, Margaret Katherine 1941- *WhoAmW 91*
Sinclair, Marjorie 1913- *ConAu 132*
Sinclair, Marjorie Putnam 1913- *WhoWrEP 89*
Sinclair, Mary *BioIn 16*
Sinclair, Mary *EncPaPR 91*
Sinclair, May 1863-1946 *BioIn 16, FemiCLE*
Sinclair, Michael *ConAu 130*
Sinclair, Michael Carter 1941- *WhoE 91*
Sinclair, Michael J. *BioIn 16*
Sinclair, Nancy *EncPaPR 91*
Sinclair, Paul *EarBlAP*
Sinclair, Raymond Allen 1946- *St&PR 91*
Sinclair, Richard Carroll 1948- *WhoEmL 91, WhoWor 91*
Sinclair, Robert 1939- *WhoAmA 91*
Sinclair, Robert Ewald 1924- *WhoWor 91*
Sinclair, Robert J. *BioIn 16*
Sinclair, Robert M. *BioIn 16*
Sinclair, Rolf Malcolm 1929- *WhoAm 90*
Sinclair, Ronald 1889-1988 *AnObit 1988*
Sinclair, Steve *BioIn 16*
Sinclair, Steven Allen 1953- *WhoSSW 91*
Sinclair, Susan Jo 1949- *WhoAmW 91*
Sinclair, Thomas V. 1915-1988 *BioIn 16*
Sinclair, Upton 1878-1968 *BioIn 16, ConLC 63 [port], EncAL, EncO&P 3, EncPaPR 91, MajTwCW, WorAlBi*
Sinclair, Upton Beall 1878-1968 *AuBYP 90, SpyFic*
Sinclair, Warren Keith 1924- *WhoAm 90*
Sinclair, William Donald 1924- *WhoWor 91*
Sinclair, William H. 1832- *AmLegL*
Sincoff, Michael Z. 1943- *WhoAm 90*
Sindeband, Seymour J. 1916- *St&PR 91*
Sindelar, Joey *BioIn 16*
Sindelar, William Francis 1945- *WhoAm 90*
Sinden, Donald 1923- *ConAu 132*
Sinden, Harry 1932- *WhoAm 90, WhoE 91*
Sinder, Mike 1946- *WhoHisp 91*
Sindermann, Horst 1915-1990 *BioIn 16*
Sinderoff, Rita Joyce 1932- *WhoAmW 91*
Sinding, Richard Victor 1946- *WhoAm 90*
Sindler, Allan Paul 1928- *WhoAm 90*
Sindler, Millard S. 1918- *St&PR 91*
Sindona, Marco 1952- *WhoWor 91*
Sindorf, John C. 1949- *BiDrAPA 89*
Sindoris, Arthur Richard 1943- *WhoE 91*
Sindram, Hendrik J. 1906- *St&PR 91*
Sindt, Carol Wold 1949- *WhoAmW 91*
Sine, Jeffrey Alan 1954- *WhoE 91*
Sine, Wilbur Zinn 1947- *BiDrAPA 89*
Sinea, Diana *ODwPR 91*
Sineath, Timothy Wayne 1940- *WhoAm 90*
Sinel, Norman Mark 1941- *WhoAm 90*
Sinervo, Elvi 1912-1986 *EncCoWW*
Sines, James William 1936- *St&PR 91*
Sinesi, Harry E. 1948- *St&PR 91*
Sinewitz, Larry Steven 1954- *WhoSSW 91*
Sinex, Francis Marott 1923- *WhoAm 90*
Sinfelt, John Henry 1931- *WhoAm 90*
Sinfield, Alan 1941- *ConAu 32NR*
Sing Hoo 1908- *WhoAmA 91*
Sing, Margo 1945- *WhoAmW 91*
Sing, William Bender 1947- *WhoEmL 91*
Singal, Daniel Joseph 1944- *ConAu 129*
Singapore, Nargis *BiDrAPA 89*
Singdahlsen, Anna Maria Horner *BiDrAPA 89*
Singel, Mark Stephen 1953- *WhoAm 90, WhoE 91*
Singer, Allen Morris 1923- *WhoAm 90*
Singer, Andrew Lawrence 1942- *WhoWor 91*
Singer, Armand Edwards 1914- *WhoAm 90*
Singer, Arthur 1917-1990 *BioIn 16, SmATA 64 [port]*
Singer, Arthur A. *BioIn 16*
Singer, Arthur B. *NewYTBS 90 [port]*
Singer, Arthur B 1917-1990 *WhoAmA 91N*
Singer, Arthur Louis, Jr. 1929- *WhoAm 90*
Singer, Barry L 1928- *BiDrAPA 89*
Singer, Barry Leonard 1928- *WhoE 91*
Singer, Ben *BioIn 16*

Singer, Beth Yvonne 1965- *WhoEmL 91*
Singer, Bill 1944- *Ballpl 90*
Singer, Bradley Ray 1956- *St&PR 91*
Singer, Brent Douglas 1951- *WhoE 91*
Singer, Burton Herbert 1938- *WhoAm 90*
Singer, Carl Norman 1916- *St&PR 91*
Singer, Cecile D. *WhoAmW 91*
Singer, Charlotte *BioIn 16*
Singer, Clifford 1955- *WhoAmA 91*
Singer, Clifford Milo 1954- *BiDrAPA 89*
Singer, Clyde J 1908- *WhoAmA 91*
Singer, Colleen M. 1963- *ODwPR 91*
Singer, Craig 1947- *WhoAm 90*
Singer, Daniel Morris 1930- *WhoAm 90*
Singer, David *AuBYP 90*
Singer, David *BioIn 16*
Singer, David Michael 1957- *WhoE 91, WhoEmL 91, WhoWor 91*
Singer, David Steven 1948- *WhoSSW 91*
Singer, David V. 1955- *St&PR 91*
Singer, David Vincent 1955- *WhoAm 90*
Singer, Edwin Z. 1930- *St&PR 91*
Singer, Eleanor 1930- *WhoAm 90*
Singer, Elizabeth Rowe 1674-1737 *BiDEWW*
Singer, Elizabeth Wells 1933- *WhoAmW 91*
Singer, Elliot Roy 1940- *BiDrAPA 89*
Singer, Ellis Paul 1928- *WhoE 91*
Singer, Esther Forman *WhoAm 90, WhoE 91*
Singer, Esther Forman 1928- *WhoAmA 91*
Singer, Fred M. 1947- *St&PR 91*
Singer, Frederick Raphael 1939- *WhoAm 90*
Singer, Frieda *WhoWrEP 89*
Singer, Garold G. 1930- *St&PR 91*
Singer, Gladys Montgomery *WhoAmW 91*
Singer, Hans-Rudolf 1925- *WhoWor 91*
Singer, Hans Wolfgang 1910- *WhoWor 91*
Singer, Harvey Neil 1948- *WhoE 91*
Singer, Hedy Karen 1954- *WhoAmW 91*
Singer, Henry A. 1919- *WhoAm 90*
Singer, Herbert M. 1906- *St&PR 91*
Singer, Howard Jay 1943- *St&PR 91*
Singer, Irvin 1928- *WhoE 91*
Singer, Irving 1924- *St&PR 91*
Singer, Irving 1925- *WhoAm 90*
Singer, Irving Lewis 1922- *St&PR 91*
Singer, Irwin 1935- *St&PR 91*
Singer, Isaac *MajTwCW*
Singer, Isaac Bashevis 1904- *AuBYP 90, BioIn 16, MajTwCW, WhoAm 90, WhoE 91, WhoWor 91, WhoWrEP 89, WorAlBi, WrPh*
Singer, Isadore Manuel 1924- *WhoAm 90*
Singer, J. David 1925- *WhoAm 90*
Singer, Jack Myron *BiDrAPA 89*
Singer, Janice Gail 1947- *WhoAmW 91*
Singer, Jay 1950- *St&PR 91*
Singer, Jay Bruce 1943- *WhoWor 91*
Singer, Jeanne 1924- *WhoAmW 91*
Singer, Jeanne Walsh 1924- *IntWWM 90*
Singer, Jerome L 1924- *ConAu 132*
Singer, John J., Jr. 1921- *St&PR 91*
Singer, John Rolland *BiDrAPA 89*
Singer, Joy Daniels 1928- *WhoE 91*
Singer, Jules B. *BioIn 16*
Singer, Karam 1931- *BiDrAPA 89*
Singer, Kurt Deutsch 1911- *WhoAm 90, WhoWrEP 89*
Singer, Leslee DeLaine 1952- *WhoEmL 91*
Singer, Lewis 1934- *St&PR 91*
Singer, Linda Ellen 1948- *St&PR 91*
Singer, Malcolm John 1953- *IntWWM 90*
Singer, Marcus George 1926- *WhoAm 90, WhoWrEP 89*
Singer, Margaret Thaler 1921- *WhoAm 90*
Singer, Marilyn 1948- *AuBYP 90, BioIn 16*
Singer, Marilyn Jean 1955- *WhoAmW 91*
Singer, Markus Morton 1917- *WhoAm 90*
Singer, Matthew Ross 1961- *WhoE 91*
Singer, Max E. 1943- *St&PR 91*
Singer, Maxine Frank 1931- *WhoAm 90, WhoAmW 91, WhoWor 91*
Singer, Melvin *BiDrAPA 89*
Singer, Meriamne B *BiDrAPA 89*
Singer, Michael *BioIn 16*
Singer, Michael H 1940- *BiDrAPA 89*
Singer, Michael Howard 1941- *WhoWor 91*
Singer, Michael J 1922- *BiDrAPA 89*
Singer, Monroe S. 1927- *St&PR 91*
Singer, Nancy Barkhouse 1912- *WhoAmA 91*
Singer, Niecee *WhoAmW 91*
Singer, Niki 1937- *ODwPR 91*
Singer, Norman 1932- *WhoWrEP 89*
Singer, Norman 1941- *St&PR 91*
Singer, Paul *BiDrAPA 89*
Singer, Paul 1934- *WhoWor 91*
Singer, Paul H. 1936- *St&PR 91*
Singer, Peter 1937- *WhoWor 91*
Singer, Peter Albert David 1946- *WhoWor 91*
Singer, Phyllis 1947- *WhoAm 90, WhoAmW 91*
Singer, Raymond Marshall 1950- *WhoEmL 91*
Singer, Rhoda Ann *BiDrAPA 89*
Singer, Richard P *BiDrAPA 89*
Singer, Robert B. 1931- *St&PR 91*
Singer, Robert Norman 1936- *WhoAm 90*
Singer, Ronald 1924- *WhoAm 90*
Singer, Ronald Leonard 1944- *St&PR 91*
Singer, Sam 1916- *St&PR 91*
Singer, Samuel Loewenberg 1911- *WhoAm 90*
Singer, Sanford Robert 1930- *St&PR 91, WhoAm 90, WhoSSW 91*
Singer, Sarah Beth 1915- *WhoAm 90, WhoWrEP 89*
Singer, Scott Charles 1961- *WhoE 91*
Singer, Siegfried Fred 1924- *WhoAm 90*
Singer, Stanley Thomas, Jr. 1933- *WhoWor 91*
Singer, Steve *BioIn 16*
Singer, Steven Lloyd 1954- *BiDrAPA 89*
Singer, Susan Jennifer Rundell 1959- *WhoAmW 91*
Singer, Suzanne Fried 1935- *WhoAmW 91*
Singer, Sydnee Robin 1955- *WhoAmW 91*
Singer, Thomas D. 1952- *St&PR 91*
Singer, Thomas Eric 1926- *WhoAm 90*
Singer, Thomas Kenyon 1932- *St&PR 91, WhoAm 90*
Singer, William M 1942- *BiDrAPA 89*
Singer-Leone, Mallory Ann 1950- *WhoAmW 91*
Singer-Magdoff, Laura Joan Silver 1917- *WhoAm 90*
Singerman, Al 1932- *St&PR 91*
Singerman, Burton 1947- *BiDrAPA 89*
Singg, Sangeeta 1950- *WhoAmW 91, WhoSSW 91*
Singh, Amar Jit 1953- *BiDrAPA 89*
Singh, Amarjit 1924- *WhoAm 90*
Singh, Amrik 1938- *WhoWor 91*
Singh, Artaj 1960- *WhoWor 91*
Singh, Avtar *NewAgMG*
Singh, Chaitram 1949- *WhoSSW 91*
Singh, Charan 1902-1987 *BioIn 16*
Singh, Charanjit P 1950- *BiDrAPA 89*
Singh, Dadabhai K *BiDrAPA 89*
Singh, Gulshan *BiDrAPA 89*
Singh, Gurdial Nayar 1947- *BiDrAPA 89*
Singh, Gurucharan Kaur *BiDrAPA 89*
Singh, Gurumander *NewAgMG*
Singh, Harbhajan *BiDrAPA 89*
Singh, Hardeep 1954- *BiDrAPA 89*
Singh, Hardev 1938- *St&PR 91*
Singh, Harold Deonarine 1940- *St&PR 91*
Singh, Heminder Pal *BiDrAPA 89*
Singh, Jasbir Bhatia 1947- *BiDrAPA 89*
Singh, Jaswant 1937- *WhoAm 90*
Singh, Jyoti Shankar 1935- *WhoE 91, WhoWor 91*
Singh, Kanwar Kultar 1931- *St&PR 91*
Singh, Karan 1931- *WhoWor 91*
Singh, Kewal 1942- *WhoSSW 91*
Singh, Khushwant 1915- *WhoWor 91*
Singh, Kirpal *BiDrAPA 89*
Singh, Kirpal 1894-1974 *NewAgE 90*
Singh, Kirpal X 1942- *BiDrAPA 89*
Singh, Kripa Shankar 1932- *BiDrAPA 89*
Singh, Kuldeep Kaur *BiDrAPA 89*
Singh, Kuldip Kaur *BiDrAPA 89*
Singh, Kuljit *BiDrAPA 89*
Singh, Kulwant *NewAgMG*
Singh, Liv *NewAgMG*
Singh, Lokendra K 1944- *BiDrAPA 89*
Singh, Man Mohan 1937- *BiDrAPA 89*
Singh, Manmohan 1954- *BiDrAPA 89*
Singh, Mendhiratta S *BiDrAPA 89*
Singh, Mukhtar 1941- *WhoWor 91*
Singh, Murari Prasad 1944- *WhoE 91*
Singh, Nagendra 1914-1988 *BioIn 16*
Singh, Neena Gurpal *BiDrAPA 89*
Singh, Nirbhay Nand 1952- *WhoWor 91*
Singh, Om Nath 1935- *WhoWor 91*
Singh, Param I. 1946- *St&PR 91*
Singh, Parmjit Paul 1959- *WhoEmL 91*
Singh, Pritam *BioIn 16*
Singh, Pritam 1935- *WhoWor 91*
Singh, Raghbir *BiDrAPA 89*
Singh, Rajendra P 1958- *BiDrAPA 89*
Singh, Rajkumar R *BiDrAPA 89*
Singh, Ravi Prakash *BiDrAPA 89*
Singh, Rupendra *BiDrAPA 89*
Singh, Sardar Buta 1934- *WhoWor 91*
Singh, Sat Nam *NewAgMG*
Singh, Satrohan 1938- *WhoWor 91*
Singh, Satwant 1953- *WhoWor 91*
Singh, Shyam Pratap 1932- *WhoWor 91*
Singh, Siri Nam *NewAgMG*
Singh, Sunita 1953- *St&PR 91*
Singh, Surinder Kaur 1947- *BiDrAPA 89*
Singh, Surjit 1951- *BiDrAPA 89*
Singh, Swayam Prabha 1945- *WhoAmW 91, WhoWrEP 89*
Singh, Tejinder 1950- *WhoE 91*
Singh, V. P. *NewYTBS 90*
Singh, V P 1931- *CurBio 90 [port]*
Singh, Vikram *NewAgMG*
Singh, Vishwanath Pratap *BioIn 16*
Singh, Vishwanath Pratap 1931- *WhoWor 91*
Singh, Zail 1916- *WhoWor 91*
Singhal, Radhey Lal 1940- *WhoAm 90*
Singhal, Yatinder 1950- *BiDrAPA 89*
Singher, Martial *BioIn 16*
Singher, Martial 1904- *IntWWM 90, PenDiMP*
Singher, Martial 1904-1990 *ConAu 131, CurBio 90N, NewYTBS 90 [port]*
Singhvi, Surendra S. 1942- *St&PR 91*
Singhvi, Surendra Singh 1942- *WhoAm 90*
Singla, Om 1940- *WhoWor 91*
Single, Richard Wayne 1938- *St&PR 91*
Single, Richard Wayne, Sr. 1938- *WhoAm 90*
Singlehurst, Dona G. 1928- *St&PR 91*
Singler, John E. 1929- *St&PR 91*
Singletary, Douglas Bernard, Jr. 1952- *WhoSSW 91*
Singletary, J. Noland 1929- *St&PR 91*
Singletary, Michael 1958- *WhoAm 90*
Singletary, Michael James 1950- *WhoAmA 91, WhoE 91*
Singletary, Mike 1958- *WorAlBi*
Singletary, Otis Arnold, Jr. 1921- *WhoAm 90*
Singletary, Patricia Ann 1948- *WhoAmW 91, WhoEmL 91, WhoWor 91*
Singletary, William Marle 1946- *BiDrAPA 89*
Singleton, Albert Olin, III *BiDrAPA 89*
Singleton, Barbara Ann 1949- *WhoAmW 91*
Singleton, Donald Edward 1936- *WhoAm 90*
Singleton, Donna Marie 1960- *WhoAmW 91*
Singleton, Elmer 1918- *Ballpl 90*
Singleton, George F. 1949- *WhoSSW 91*
Singleton, George Monroe 1931- *WhoSSW 91*
Singleton, Harry Michael 1949- *WhoAm 90*
Singleton, Henry E. *BioIn 16*
Singleton, Henry Earl 1916- *ConAmBL, WhoAm 90*
Singleton, Herbert 1945- *MusmAFA*
Singleton, Joan Vietor 1951- *WhoWrEP 89*
Singleton, John Alan 1959- *WhoEmL 91*
Singleton, John Paul 1936- *St&PR 91*
Singleton, John Virgil, Jr. 1918- *WhoAm 90*
Singleton, Ken 1947- *Ballpl 90*
Singleton, Lawrence *BioIn 16*
Singleton, Linda Gail 1950- *WhoAmW 91*
Singleton, Philip Arthur 1914- *WhoAm 90*
Singleton, Richard Lynn 1944- *St&PR 91*
Singleton, Robert William 1948- *St&PR 91*
Singleton, Rupert *ConAu 129*
Singleton, Samuel Winston 1928- *WhoAm 90*
Singleton, Sara 1940- *WhoAmW 91*
Singleton, Susan Mae 1948- *WhoAmA 91*
Singleton, Teresa Eileen 1960- *St&PR 91*
Singleton, William 1941- *St&PR 91*
Singleton, William A. 1946- *St&PR 91*
Singleton, William Dean 1951- *WhoAm 90, WhoSSW 91*
Singleton, Zutty 1898-1975 *BioIn 16, OxCPMus, WorAlBi*
Singleton-Wood, Allan James 1933- *WhoAm 90*
Singley, Dale Mitchell 1952- *St&PR 91*
Singley, John Edward, Jr. 1924- *WhoAm 90*
Singley, Mark Eldridge 1921- *WhoAm 90*
Singmaster-Hernandez, Karen Amalia 1960- *WhoHisp 91*
Singstock, David John 1940- *WhoE 91*
Sington, Fred 1910- *Ballpl 90*
Sinha, Ashok Kumar 1944- *WhoWor 91*
Sinha, Atin Kumar 1948- *WhoWor 91*
Sinha, Bipin Kumar 1961- *WhoWor 91*
Sinha, Dharm B 1945- *BiDrAPA 89*
Sinha, Kumares Chandra 1939- *WhoAm 90*
Sinha, Phulgenda 1924- *ConAu 130*
Sinha, Ramesh Chandra 1934- *WhoAm 90*
Sinha, Ranjit 1931- *BiDrAPA 89*
Sinha, Rohini Pati 1932- *WhoE 91*
Sinha, Shubha P *BiDrAPA 89*
Sinha, Surya Prakash 1937- *WhoE 91*
Sinha, Tapen 1957- *WhoWor 91*
Siniawa, Daniel 1932- *WhoE 91*
Sinibaldi, Mark Robert 1947- *BiDrAPA 89*
Sinicki, Maureen T. 1952- *WhoAmW 91*
Sinicki, Sheila Jeanne 1952- *WhoAmW 91*
Sinicropi, Anthony Vincent 1931- *WhoAm 90*
Sinish, Jonathan Layton 1943- *WhoE 91*
Sinitzky, Miriam Malka 1949- *WhoAmW 91*
Sink, Alva Gordon *WhoAmW 91*
Sink, Charles Stanley 1923- *WhoAm 90*
Sink, Claire Huschka 1943- *WhoAmW 91*
Sink, Henry Ray 1934- *WhoSSW 91*
Sink, John Davis 1934- *WhoAm 90*
Sink, Joseph Steven, Jr. 1954- *St&PR 91*
Sink, Nigra Lea 1935- *WhoAmW 91*
Sink, Richard Alden 1934- *St&PR 91*
Sink, William Frederick *BiDrAPA 89*
Sinka, Arvi 1938- *IntWWM 90*
Sinkford, Jeanne Craig 1933- *WhoAm 90, WhoAmW 91, WhoWor 91*
Sinkhorn, Mary Jean 1941- *WhoAmW 91*
Sinkman, Arthur M 1946- *BiDrAPA 89, WhoE 91*
Sinkoe, Morris Benjamin 1936- *WhoSSW 91*
Sinkovic, Jelena 1924- *WhoWor 91*
Sinks, Lucius Frederick 1931- *WhoE 91*
Sinkula, William J. 1930- *St&PR 91*
Sinkwich, Frank *NewYTBS 90*
Sinn, Robert Samuel 1930- *WhoE 91*
Sinnard, Elaine 1926- *WhoAmA 91*
Sinnemaki, Ulla Ulpukka 1928- *WhoAmW 91, WhoSSW 91, WhoWor 91*
Sinner, George A. 1928- *St&PR 91*
Sinner, George Albert 1928- *WhoAm 90, WhoWor 91*
Sinnett, A P 1840-1921 *EncO&P 3*
Sinnett, Clifford H. 1919- *St&PR 91*
Sinnett, Peter Frank 1934- *WhoWor 91*
Sinnette, Elinor Des Verney 1925- *ConAu 132*
Sinno, Bassam A *BiDrAPA 89*
Sinnott, Daniel 1934- *St&PR 91*
Sinnott, Gilbert J. *BioIn 16*
Sinnott, John T. 1939- *St&PR 91*
Sinnott, John William 1938- *St&PR 91*
Sinnott, Patrick William 1952- *WhoSSW 91*
Sinnott, Richard John, III 1956- *WhoE 91*
Sinnott, Roger J. 1913- *St&PR 91*
Sinnwell, David W. *BioIn 16*
Sinopoli, Giuseppe 1946- *IntWWM 90, PenDiMP*
Sinor, Denis 1916- *WhoAm 90, WhoWor 91*
Sinowatz, Fred 1929- *WhoWor 91*
Sinquefield, Rex A. *BioIn 16*
Sinsabaugh, Art 1924-1983 *WhoAmA 91N*
Sinsheimer, Joseph G. 1928- *St&PR 91*
Sinsheimer, Lisa *BiDrAPA 89*
Sinsheimer, Warren J. 1927- *St&PR 91*
Sinsheimer, Warren Jack 1927- *WhoAm 90, WhoWor 91*
Sinsigalli, Gerald E. 1938- *St&PR 91*
Sinton, Celeste M 1948- *BiDrAPA 89*
Sinton, Nell *WhoAmA 91*
Sintz, Edward Francis 1924- *WhoAm 90, WhoSSW 91*
Sinues de Marco, Pilar de 1835-1893 *EncCoWW*
Sinyavsky, Andrei 1925- *WhoWor 91, WorAlBi*
Sinyavsky, Andrey 1925- *BioIn 16*
Sinykin, Gerald B. 1925- *St&PR 91*
Sinykin, Gordon 1910- *WhoAm 90*
Sinzer, Joseph Francis 1912- *WhoAm 90*
Siock, Robert S. 1948- *St&PR 91*
Siodmak, Kurt 1902- *BioIn 16*
Siomopoulos, Vasilis K 1938- *BiDrAPA 89*
Sion, Maurice 1928- *WhoAm 90*
Sioringas, John Nickolas 1944- *St&PR 91*
Siouffi, Gilles-Etienne 1956- *BiDrAPA 89*
Siouffi, Raja Antoine *BiDrAPA 89*
Sioukas, Jack 1936- *WhoWor 91*
Siouxsie Sioux *BioIn 16*
Sipahi, Alim 1925- *BiDrAPA 89*
Sipe, Douglas Allen 1961- *St&PR 91*
Sipe, Patricia Lilaine 1952- *WhoE 91*
Sipe, Reginald Richard 1942- *St&PR 91*
Sipe, Richard E. 1931- *St&PR 91*
Sipek, Meridith P. 1946- *St&PR 91*
Siperstein, H.B. 1923- *St&PR 91*
Sipes, J. Richard 1946- *St&PR 91*
Sipes, Jeffrey W. 1954- *WhoEmL 91*
Sipes, Lorri Dean 1950- *WhoAmW 91*
Sipes, Paul E. 1944- *St&PR 91*
Siphron, Joseph Rider 1933- *WhoAm 90*
Sipinen, Seppo Antero 1946- *WhoWor 91*
Sipiora, Leonard Paul 1934- *WhoAm 90, WhoAmA 91, WhoSSW 91*
Sipkoff, Susan Stone 1950- *WhoAmW 91*
Siple, Carl George 1936- *St&PR 91*
Sipola, Seppo Tapio 1943- *WhoWor 91*
Sipolo, Jully *FemiCLE*
Siporin, Mitchell 1910-1976 *WhoAmA 91N*
Sipp, G. Robert 1950- *WhoSSW 91*
Sippel, Wallace O. 1946- *St&PR 91*
Sippel, William Leroy 1948- *WhoEmL 91, WhoWor 91*
Sippl, James G. 1947- *St&PR 91*
Sipple, Constance S. 1962- *WhoAmW 91*
Sipple, Oliver Wellington 1941?-1989 *BioIn 16*
Sipress, David 1947- *ConAu 130*
Sipress, Jack Myron 1935- *WhoAm 90*
Sipser, Michael 1954- *WhoE 91*
Sipzener, Robert Stephen 1944- *WhoE 91*
Siqueiros, David Alfaro 1896-1974 *IntDcAA 90, WhoAmA 91N*

Siqueiros, David Alfaro 1898-1974 ArtLatA, BioIn 16
Sir Lancelot DrBlPA 90
Siracusa, Angelo John 1930- WhoWor 91
Siragusa, Gregory J. 1928- St&PR 91
Siragusa, John R. 1932- St&PR 91
Siragusa, Ross D., Jr. 1930- St&PR 91
Siranni, Joseph F., Jr. 1945- St&PR 91
Sirchio, Connie Loyce 1942- St&PR 91
Sircus, Jan Martin 1949- WhoEmL 91
Sircy, Bob Clay, Jr. 1951- St&PR 91
Siregar, Nurhayati Indra P. 1951- WhoWor 91
Siren, Jukka 1950- WhoWor 91
Siren, Katri Anna-Maija Helena 1920- WhoWor 91
Sirena WhoAmA 91
Sires, Jonathan 1955- WhoAmA 91
Sires, William O BiDrAPA 89
Siress, Donald T. 1944- St&PR 91
Sirhal, Robert James 1946- St&PR 91
Sirhan, Sirhan 1945- WorAlBi
Siri, Dena Shaw 1952- WhoAmW 91
Siri, Giuseppe 1906-1989 BioIn 16
Siri, William Emil 1919- BioIn 16, WhoAm 90
Sirianni, Fred A. 1926- St&PR 91
Sirianni, Fred Anthony 1926- WhoAm 90
Siriban, Edward C BiDrAPA 89
Sirica, John J. 1904- WhoAm 90, WorAlBi
Sirignano, William Alfonso 1938- WhoAm 90
Sirikit 1932- WomWR [port]
Sirimavo WomWR
Sirin, V. MajTwCW
Siringo, Charles A. 1855-1928 BioIn 16
Sirinyan, Aksel Manuk 1943- WhoWor 91
Siris, Burt J. BioIn 16
Siris, Michael John 1945- WhoEmL 91
Siris, Samuel G 1944- BiDrAPA 89
Sirisumpan, Tienchai 1925- WhoWor 91
Sirius ConAu 129
Sirk, Douglas 1900-1987 BioIn 16
Sirken, Irving A. 1922- WhoE 91
Sirkia, Seppo Antero 1936- WhoWor 91
Sirkis, Nancy 1936- WhoAmA 91
Sirkis, Robert Lane 1951- WhoAm 90, WhoSSW 91
Sirkus, Robert 1947- St&PR 91
Sirlin, Jerome BioIn 16
Sirman, William L. AmLegL
Sirmans, J.T. 1943- St&PR 91
Sirmay, Albert 1918-1967 OxCPMus
Sirmon, Gordon C. 1941- St&PR 91
Sirna, Anthony Alfred, III 1924- WhoAm 90
Sirocky, Michael Paul 1948- WhoAm 90
Sirof, Harriet Toby 1930- WhoWrEP 89
Sirois, Gerard 1934- WhoAm 90
Sirois, Herman Arnold 1945- WhoE 91
Sirois, L. Frank 1936- St&PR 91
Sirois, Raymond 1927- St&PR 91, WhoAm 90
Sirola, Joseph 1929- ConTFT 8 [port]
Sirota, Milton 1934- BiDrAPA 89
Sirota, Milton Stanley 1928- St&PR 91
Sirotkin, Phillip Leonard 1923- WhoAm 90
Sirotkovic, Jakov Ivo 1922- WhoWor 91
Sirovich, Lawrence 1933- WhoAm 90
Sirow, Melvin 1924- St&PR 91
Sirow, Richard Lawrence 1950- St&PR 91
Sirower, Bonnie Fox 1949- WhoAmW 91, WhoE 91
Sirrell, Tami BioIn 16
Sirtis, Marina BioIn 16
Sirugo, Sal WhoAmA 91
Sirus, Sangit NewAgMG
Sis, Peter BioIn 16
Sis, Raymond Francis 1931- WhoAm 90
Sischy, Ingrid B 1952- WhoAmA 91
Sischy, Ingrid Barbara 1952- WhoAm 90
Sisco, Alton B. 1944- WhoSSW 91
Sisco, Joseph John 1919- WhoAm 90
Sisco, Mary Elizabeth 1937- WhoAmW 91
Siscoe, George Leonard 1937- WhoAm 90
Siselman Blich, Mina WhoWor 91
Sisemore, Claudia 1937- WhoAmW 91
Sisisky, Norman 1927- WhoAm 90, WhoSSW 91
Sisisky, R.L. St&PR 91
Sisk, Daniel Arthur 1927- WhoAm 90, WhoWor 91
Sisk, Doug 1957- Ballpl 90
Sisk, Laura A. 1954- St&PR 91
Sisk, Lawrence Theodore 1950- IntWWM 90
Sisk, Paul Douglas 1950- WhoEmL 91
Sisk, Raymond M., Jr. 1940- WhoAm 90
Sisk, Robert W. BioIn 16
Sisk, Tommy 1942- Ballpl 90
Siska, Charles William, Jr. 1948- St&PR 91
Siska, Richard Stanly 1948- WhoEmL 91
Siske, Roger Charles 1944- WhoAm 90
Siskel, Gene BioIn 16
Siskel, Gene 1946- WhoAm 90
Siskin, Edward Joseph 1941- WhoAm 90
Siskind, Aaron 1903- WhoAm 90
Siskind, Donald Henry 1937- WhoAm 90, WhoE 91
Siskind, Elliott 1926- St&PR 91
Sisko, Marie Ferraris WhoAmW 91
Sisko, Wendy Lee 1957- WhoAmW 91
Sisler, Daniel G. BioIn 16
Sisler, Dave 1931- Ballpl 90
Sisler, Dick 1920- Ballpl 90, BioIn 16
Sisler, Frank BiDrAPA 89
Sisler, George 1893-1973 Ballpl 90 [port], WorAlBi
Sisler, George C 1923- BiDrAPA 89
Sisler, George Cooper 1923- WhoAm 90
Sisler, Harry Hall 1917- WhoAm 90
Sisler, Rebecca 1932- WhoAmA 91
Sisler, William Philip 1947- WhoAm 90
Sisley, Alfred 1839-1899 BioIn 16, IntDcAA 90, WorAlBi
Sisley, Becky Lynn 1939- WhoAmW 91
Sisley, G. William 1944- WhoAm 90
Sislian, Robert Jan 1938- St&PR 91
Sisman, Elaine Rochelle 1952- IntWWM 90
Sismondi, Jean Charles Leonard Simonde d 1773-1842 BioIn 16
Sismondo, Peter R. 1955- St&PR 91
Sisneros, Frederico 1894-1988 BioIn 16
Sisney, Steven Lynn 1961- WhoSSW 91
Sisodia, Ashok 1960- WhoWor 91
Sisodia, Ioni Dipti BiDrAPA 89
Sisolak, Edward R. 1951- St&PR 91
Sison, Alfredo Santos BiDrAPA 89
Sison, Gerardo P., Jr. BiDrAPA 89
Sison, Joseph Isidro BiDrAPA 89
Sison, Renato F. 1958- BiDrAPA 89
Sissel, George Allen 1936- St&PR 91, WhoAm 90
Sisselman, Murray 1930- WhoSSW 91
Sissle, Noble EarBlAP
Sissle, Noble 1889-1975 DrBlPA 90, OxCPMus
Sissom, Evelyn Janelle WhoAmA 91
Sissom, Leighton Esten 1934- WhoAm 90
Sisson, Allen Swain 1954- St&PR 91
Sisson, Betty 1934- WhoAmW 91
Sisson, Breta Cora 1935- WhoE 91
Sisson, David H. 1936- St&PR 91
Sisson, Donna Sue 1957- WhoSSW 91
Sisson, Everett A. 1920- St&PR 91
Sisson, Everett Arnold 1920- WhoAm 90, WhoWor 91
Sisson, George Allen 1920- WhoAm 90
Sisson, Jacqueline D 1925-1980 WhoAmA 91N
Sisson, Jamie Clifton 1960- WhoAmW 91
Sisson, Jerry Allan 1956- WhoEmL 91
Sisson, Jerry Tripp 1938- St&PR 91
Sisson, John Edward 1956- St&PR 91
Sisson, Laurence P 1928- WhoAmA 91
Sisson, Richard BioIn 16
Sisson, Richard Hampton 1932- St&PR 91
Sisson, Robert F. 1923- WhoAm 90
Sisson, William H 1920- BiDrAPA 89
Sisson, William Thomas 1938- WhoSSW 91
Sistar, James Leon, Jr. 1953- WhoSSW 91
Sistek, Walter J. 1940- St&PR 91
Sister Magdeleine de Jesus ConAu 130
Sister Sledge DrBlPA 90
Sisterson, Janet Margot 1940- WhoAmW 91
Sisti, Sibby 1920- Ballpl 90
Sisto, Elena 1952- WhoAmA 91, WhoE 91
Sisto, Ernest Ludwig 1904-1989 BioIn 16
Sisto, Fernando 1924- WhoAm 90, WhoE 91
Sistrunk, Catherine Eileen 1958- WhoAmW 91
Sistrunk, James Dudley 1919- WhoAm 90
Sistrunk, Max Nolen 1937- St&PR 91
Sisulu, Albertina BioIn 16
Sisulu, Walter BioIn 16
Sit, Hong Chan 1921- WhoWor 91
Sit, Meelin ODwPR 91
Sita, Michael John 1953- WhoWor 91
Sitar, Andrew A. 1928- St&PR 91
Sitar, Thomas St&PR 91
Sitarz, Anneliese Lotte 1928- WhoAmW 91
Sitarz, Daniel 1948- WhoWrEP 89
Sitarz, Paula Gaj 1955- WhoAmW 91
Sitbon, Martine BioIn 16
Sitchon, Clotilde M BiDrAPA 89
Siteman, Alvin J. 1928- St&PR 91
Siteman, Alvin Jerome 1928- WhoAm 90
Sites, Howard Fred 1938- St&PR 91
Sitka, Gregory Leo 1956- BiDrAPA 89
Sitka, Warren WhoWrEP 89
Sitkovetsky, Dmitry 1954- IntWWM 90, PenDiMP
Sitlani, Ranjit 1939- St&PR 91
Sitlinger, Leroy Edward, Jr. 1946- WhoEmL 91
Sitoe, Aline WomWR
Sitra, Joseph Anthony 1937- WhoSSW 91
Sitrick, James Baker 1935- WhoAm 90
Sitrick, Michael S. 1947- ODwPR 91, St&PR 91
Sitrick, Michael Steven 1947- WhoAm 90, WhoEmL 91
Sitsky, Larry 1934- IntWWM 90
Sittason, Charles Rex 1944- St&PR 91
Sitte, Peter 1929- WhoWor 91
Sittenfeld, Curtis Joseph 1931- St&PR 91
Sittenfield, Stephen Lee BiDrAPA 89
Sitter, Inger 1929- BiDWomA
Sitter, John E 1944- ConAu 130
Sitter, John Edward 1944- WhoAm 90
Sitter, William Hall 1939- WhoAm 90
Sitterly, Charlotte M. NewYTBS 90 [port]
Sitterly, Charlotte Moore 1898-1990 BioIn 16, CurBio 90N
Sitterly, Connie Sue 1953- WhoAmW 91
Sittig, John Joseph 1937- St&PR 91
Sitting Bear WhNaAH
Sitting Bull 1831-1890 BioIn 16, WhNaAH [port], WorAlBi
Sitting White Buffalo DcCanB 12
Sittler, Joseph BioIn 16
Sitton, Claude Fox 1925- WhoAm 90
Sitton, John M 1907- WhoAmA 91
Sitton, Myron H. 1922- St&PR 91
Sitts, Timothy M BiDrAPA 89
Sitwell, Edith 1887-1964 BioIn 16, FemiCLE, MajTwCW, WorAlBi
Sitwell, Osbert 1892-1969 DcLB 100 [port]
Sitwell, Sacheverell 1897-1988 AnObit 1988, BioIn 16
Sitzman, Everette 1951- BiDrAPA 89
Siu, Kenneth Kwong Chee 1928- WhoAm 90
Siu, Winston Wing Yan 1951- WhoWor 91
Siudela, Daniel M. 1938- St&PR 91
Siukosaari, Asko Eero Ilmari 1932- WhoWor 91
Siuru, William Dennis, Jr. 1938- WhoWrEP 89
Siv, Sichan BioIn 16
Siv, Sichan Aun 1948- WhoE 91
Siva, Albert Jean 1946- St&PR 91
Sivack, Denis 1942- WhoWrEP 89
Sivadon, Paul D BiDrAPA 89
Sivak, Andrew 1931- St&PR 91
Sivak, Robert J 1946- BiDrAPA 89
Sivakumar, Rajanga 1939- WhoWor 91
Sivali WomWR
Sivalingam, Chandrakanthi Y BiDrAPA 89
Sivalls, Charles Richard 1934- St&PR 91
Sivan, Amiran 1938- WhoWor 91
Sivananda Saraswati, Swami 1887-1963 NewAgE 90
Sivananda, Swami 1887-1963 EncO&P 3
Sivard, Robert 1914-1990 BioIn 16, NewYTBS 90
Sivard, Robert Paul 1914-1990 WhoAmA 91N
Sivasankaran, Parappurath 1944- BiDrAPA 89
Sive, David 1922- WhoAm 90
Sive, Rebecca Anne 1950- WhoAm 90
Siver, Chester A. 1912- St&PR 91
Siverd, Bonnie 1949- WhoWrEP 89
Siverd, Robert Joseph 1948- WhoEmL 91
Siverson, Randolph Martin 1940- WhoAm 90
Sivertz, Kristin Shelley 1951- BiDrAPA 89
Sivess, Pete 1913- Ballpl 90
Sivin, Nathan 1931- WhoAm 90
Sivinski, David Michael 1950- St&PR 91
Sivonen, Pekka Tapani 1955- WhoWor 91
Sivori, Camillo 1815-1894 PenDiMP
Sivright, John Avery 1929- St&PR 91, WhoAm 90
Sivulich, Kenneth George 1939- WhoE 91
Sivulich, Sandra Stroner 1941- AuBYP 90
Siwek, Reuben Mark 1919- St&PR 91
Siwertz, Per Sigfrid 1882-1970 DcScanL
Siwicki, Florian 1925- WhoWor 91
Siwinski, Dale J. 1953- St&PR 91
Six, Marvin L. 1948- St&PR 91
Sixel, Jerome A. 1933- St&PR 91
Sixto, Ramiro Ares 1935- WhoWor 91
Sizemore, Chris Costner BioIn 16
Sizemore, Dale H. 1922- St&PR 91
Sizemore, Deborah Lightfoot 1956- WhoAmW 91, WhoSSW 91, WhoWrEP 89
Sizemore, Herman Mason, Jr. 1941- WhoAm 90
Sizemore, Hiram, Jr. 1924- BiDrAPA 89
Sizemore, N.C., Jr. 1937- St&PR 91
Sizemore, Richard Ellsworth 1936- WhoWor 91
Sizemore, Robert Carlen 1951- WhoSSW 91
Sizemore, Ted 1946- Ballpl 90
Sizemore, William Christian 1938- WhoAm 90
Sizemore, William Gene 1927- WhoAm 90
Sizer, Carol ODwPR 91
Sizer, Irwin Whiting 1910- WhoAm 90
Sizer, Phillip Spelman 1926- St&PR 91, WhoAm 90
Sizer, Stephen R. ODwPR 91
Sizonenko, Pierre Claude 1932- WhoWor 91
Sizova, Alla Ivanovna 1939- WhoWor 91
Sjaastad, Anders C. 1942- WhoWor 91
Sjafruddin Prawiranegara 1911-1989 BioIn 16
Sjerven, Melvin Stanley 1921- St&PR 91
Sjiem-Fat, Paul Valentijn 1924- WhoWor 91
Sjoberg, Berndt Olof Harald 1931- WhoWor 91
Sjoberg, Birger 1885-1929 DcScanL
Sjoberg, Donald WhoAm 90
Sjoberg, Earl Dwain 1932- St&PR 91
Sjoerdsma, Albert 1924- WhoAm 90
Sjogren, Clifford Steven 1945- St&PR 91
Sjogren, Deborah Mary 1953- WhoAmW 91
Sjogren, Kenneth Andrew 1951- WhoSSW 91
Sjogren, Loriann 1960- St&PR 91
Sjogren, Merle Eugene 1923- BiDrAPA 89
Sjogren, Michael Paul 1955- WhoE 91
Sjogren, Per Jonas 1953- WhoWor 91
Sjogren, Sven Erik Gosta 1948- IntWWM 90
Sjogren, Walter R. 1928- St&PR 91
Sjoholm, Bertil Hjalmar 1947- WhoWor 91
Sjolund, Herbert E. ODwPR 91
Sjoo, Monica 1938- BiDWomA
Sjostedt, Lars Allan Vilhelm 1942- WhoWor 91
Sjostrand, Fritiof Stig 1912- WhoAm 90
Sjostrand, Per Bertil 1938- WhoWor 91
Sjostrom, Marianne Birgit Christina 1942- WhoWor 91
Sjostrom, Victor 1879-1960 BioIn 16
Sjowall, Maj 1935- WorAlBi
Skaare, Richard A. 1948- ODwPR 91
Skaaren, Warren NewYTBS 90
Skach, Lorraine Elizabeth BiDrAPA 89
Skadden, Donald Harvey 1925- WhoAm 90
Skadow, Ronald Robert 1942- St&PR 91, WhoAm 90
Skaff, Andrew Joseph 1945- WhoAm 90, WhoEmL 91
Skaff, Joseph John 1930- WhoAm 90
Skafte, Marjorie Doris 1921- WhoAmW 91, WhoWrEP 89
Skagen, James H. St&PR 91
Skagfield, Hilmar S. 1923- WhoSSW 91
Skaggs, Dave 1951- Ballpl 90
Skaggs, David E. 1943- WhoAm 90
Skaggs, Fred Aaron 1935- St&PR 91
Skaggs, Gary L. 1944- St&PR 91
Skaggs, James E. 1927- St&PR 91
Skaggs, Joey BioIn 16
Skaggs, Karen Gayle 1956- WhoSSW 91
Skaggs, Karla B. 1953- St&PR 91
Skaggs, L. Sam 1922- WhoAm 90
Skaggs, Murray C BiDrAPA 89
Skaggs, Ricky WhoAm 90
Skaggs, Ricky 1954- BioIn 16, ConMus 5 [port], WhoNeCM [port]
Skaggs, Robert E. AmLegL
Skaggs, Sanford Merle 1939- WhoAm 90
Skaggs, Wayne Gerard 1929- WhoAm 90
Skahan, Paul Laurence 1925- St&PR 91
Skahen, Thomas M. 1942- St&PR 91
Skahill, Carolyn Marie 1941- St&PR 91
Skains, Thomas E. 1956- St&PR 91
Skaja, Norbert W BiDrAPA 89
Skakle, Sybil Austin 1926- WhoAmW 91
Skala, David James 1953- St&PR 91
Skala, Gary Dennis 1946- WhoEmL 91, WhoWor 91
Skala, Mary Jane 1948- WhoWrEP 89
Skalagard, Hans 1924- WhoAmA 91
Skalak, Richard 1923- WhoAm 90
Skalbania, Nelson BioIn 16
Skaldkona, Steinunn Refsdottir EncCoWW
Skaldmaer, Jorunn EncCoWW
Skalicky, Steven S. 1948- St&PR 91
Skalka, Stanley 1939- St&PR 91
Skalko, Louise Luchetti 1938- WhoSSW 91
Skalko, Richard Gallant 1936- WhoAm 90
Skallagrimsson, Egill 910?-990? DcScanL
Skaller, Laurence D. 1932- St&PR 91
Skalova, Zuzana 1945- WhoWor 91
Skalski, Joanne Dorothy 1934- WhoAmW 91
Skamas, Demetrios C BiDrAPA 89
Skampa, Milan PenDiMP
Skan, Martin 1934- WhoWor 91
Skandalake, Eve EncCoWW
Skaniandariio 1735?-1815 EncCRAm
Skanland, Hermod 1925- WhoWor 91
Skapars, Antonina L 1933- BiDrAPA 89
Skaperdas, Wesley J. 1953- St&PR 91
Skapley, Rosemary Elaine 1937- WhoAm 90
Skaptason, Joseph Bjorn 1911-1987 BioIn 16
Skard, Sigmund 1903- WhoWor 91
Skarda, Richard Joseph 1952- WhoEmL 91, WhoWor 91
Skare, Robert Martin 1930- WhoWor 91

Skarecky, Jana Milena 1957- *IntWWM 90*
Skarmeta, Antonio *BioIn 16*
Skarmeta, Antonio 1940- *ConAu 131, HispWr 90*
Skase, Christopher *BioIn 16*
Skates, Ronald L. 1943- *St&PR 91*
Skates, Ronald Louis 1941- *WhoAm 90*
Skaugen, Morits, Jr. 1955- *WhoWor 91*
Skavlem, Steingrim 1915- *WhoWor 91*
Skea, Susan Gail *BiDrAPA 89*
Skeanendon *WhNaAH*
Skeates, William Busby 1926- *St&PR 91*
Skeath, J. Edward 1936-1990 *BioIn 16*
Skeel, Charlotte Taylor *ODwPR 91*
Skeel, Judy Ann 1957- *WhoAmW 91*
Skeen, David Ray 1942- *WhoE 91, WhoWor 91*
Skeen, Joseph Richard 1927- *WhoAm 90*
Skeen, Lyn *ODwPR 91*
Skeen, Ransom H. *BioIn 16*
Skeet, Ian 1928- *WhoWor 91*
Skeete, F. Herbert 1930- *WhoAm 90, WhoE 91*
Skeete, Monica 1920- *FemiCLE*
Skeeter, Tommy Ray 1932- *St&PR 91*
Skeggs, David Potter 1924-1973 *WhoAmA 91N*
Skei, Allen B 1935-1985 *ConAu 31NR*
Skeie, L.J. 1942- *St&PR 91*
Skein, Lilias *BiDEWW*
Skeist, Loren Richard *BiDrAPA 89*
Skeist, S. Merrill 1918- *St&PR 91*
Skellchock, Leo H. 1927- *St&PR 91*
Skellenger, Virgil V. 1923- *St&PR 91*
Skelley, Charles L. *BioIn 16*
Skelley, Gary Allen 1944- *St&PR 91*
Skelley, Robert Charles 1934- *WhoAmA 91*
Skelley, Robert D. 1948- *St&PR 91*
Skelley, Steven James 1950- *WhoWor 91*
Skellie family *BioIn 16*
Skelly, James R. *AuBYP 90*
Skelly, Janice Gaus 1928- *WhoE 91*
Skelly, Jerome Philip 1932- *WhoSSW 91*
Skelly, Joseph P. *OxCPMus*
Skelly, June Avon 1946- *WhoAmW 91*
Skelly, Richard Francis 1937- *WhoE 91*
Skelly, Thomas Francis 1934- *St&PR 91, WhoAm 90*
Skelton, Alice H. *ODwPR 91*
Skelton, Byron George 1905- *WhoAm 90*
Skelton, Don Richard 1931- *St&PR 91, WhoAm 90*
Skelton, Dorothy Geneva Simmons *WhoAmW 91, WhoSSW 91, WhoWor 91*
Skelton, Glenda Carol 1950- *WhoAmW 91*
Skelton, Glenn Edgar 1921- *St&PR 91*
Skelton, Ira Steven 1949- *WhoWrEP 89*
Skelton, Isaac Newton, IV 1931- *WhoAm 90*
Skelton, Janet McClintock 1954- *WhoAmW 91*
Skelton, Janice Kenmore 1918- *WhoAmW 91*
Skelton, John Goss, Jr. 1927- *WhoSSW 91*
Skelton, Michael D. 1947- *St&PR 91*
Skelton, Owen R 1886-1969 *EncABHB 5 [port]*
Skelton, Red 1910- *WorAlBi*
Skelton, Red 1913- *AuBYP 90, BioIn 16, ConTFT 8, WhoAm 90*
Skelton, Robert Beattie 1913- *WhoAm 90, WhoWor 91*
Skelton, Robin *BioIn 16*
Skelton, Shirley Ann 1943- *St&PR 91*
Skelton, Steven Patrick 1956- *St&PR 91*
Skelton, Thomas Allen 1947- *St&PR 91*
Skelton, Tom *BioIn 16*
Skelton, Victoria Donna *BiDrAPA 89*
Skelton, W Douglas 1938- *BiDrAPA 89*
Skemer, Arnold Marius 1946- *WhoWrEP 89*
Skemp, Robert Oliver 1910-1984 *WhoAmA 91N*
Skenadore, Nancy Cornelius 1861-1908 *BioIn 16*
Skenandoa *WhNaAH*
Skenandoa 1706?-1816 *EncCRAm*
Skenandoah *WhNaAH*
Skendi, Stavro 1906-1989 *BioIn 16*
Skene, Felicia 1821-1899 *FemiCLE*
Skene, Jeremy F. 1949- *St&PR 91*
Skenyon, John Michael 1947- *WhoEmL 91*
Skerratt, Ralph William, Jr. 1918- *St&PR 91*
Skerrett, Emma 1817-1887 *OxCCanT*
Skerrett, George 1810-1855 *OxCCanT*
Skerritt, Elizabeth 1932- *WhoAmW 91*
Skerritt, Tom 1933- *WorAlBi*
Sketch, Michael Hugh 1931- *WhoAm 90*
Skeuse, Thomas John *St&PR 91N*
Skewes, Richard Stevenson 1935- *St&PR 91*
Skewes-Cox, Bennet 1918- *WhoWor 91*
Skiba, Diane Jean 1952- *WhoAmW 91*
Skiba, Pat *BioIn 16*
Skiba, William Edward *BiDrAPA 89*
Skibinski, Arnold F. 1950- *WhoEmL 91*
Skibniewska, Halina 1921- *WhoWor 91*
Skibo, Charles Michael 1938- *St&PR 91*
Skidd, Thomas Patrick, Jr. 1936- *WhoAm 90*
Skiddell, Elliot Lewis 1951- *WhoSSW 91*
Skidmore, Arthur 1922- *St&PR 91*
Skidmore, David Theodore 1952- *WhoE 91*
Skidmore, Donald Earl 1920- *WhoWor 91*
Skidmore, Donald Earl, Jr. 1944- *WhoWor 91*
Skidmore, E. Stewart 1916- *St&PR 91*
Skidmore, Gary J. 1954- *WhoSSW 91*
Skidmore, Howard Franklyn 1917- *WhoAm 90*
Skidmore, James A., Jr. 1932- *St&PR 91*
Skidmore, James Albert, Jr. 1932- *WhoAm 90*
Skidmore, Joel A. 1929- *St&PR 91*
Skidmore, Louis 1897-1962 *WorAlBi*
Skidmore, Max Joseph 1933- *WhoAm 90*
Skidmore, Nell Burden 1931- *WhoAmW 91*
Skidmore, Paul Harold 1918- *WhoWor 91*
Skidmore, Philip M. 1940- *St&PR 91*
Skidmore, Rex Austin 1914- *WhoAm 90*
Skidmore, Sally Stephens 1960- *WhoAmW 91*
Skidmore, Thomas Elliott 1932- *WhoAm 90, WhoE 91*
Skiffington, John Joseph, III 1943- *WhoE 91*
Skiffington, Kerry Katherine 1956- *WhoAmW 91*
Skiffington-Simpson, Karen Anna 1958- *WhoWor 91*
Skigen, Jack 1928- *BiDrAPA 89*
Skigen, Patricia Sue 1942- *WhoAmW 91*
Skiles, Charles *WhoAmA 91N*
Skiles, James Jean 1928- *WhoAm 90*
Skiles, Michael L. 1946- *St&PR 91*
Skillern, Frank Lloyd, Jr. 1936- *St&PR 91*
Skillern, Paula Lynn 1949- *WhoSSW 91*
Skillin, Edward Simeon 1904- *WhoAm 90*
Skilling, David Van Diest 1933- *St&PR 91*
Skilling, John Bower 1921- *WhoAm 90*
Skilling, R.E. 1931- *St&PR 91*
Skilling, Raymond Inwood 1939- *WhoAm 90*
Skillman, Don *BioIn 16*
Skillman, Donna Lynn 1960- *WhoAmW 91*
Skillman, Ernest Edward, Jr. 1937- *WhoWor 91*
Skillman, John Harold 1927- *WhoE 91*
Skillman, Lolly *BioIn 16*
Skillman, Thomas Grant 1925- *WhoAm 90*
Skillman, William Alfred 1928- *WhoAm 90*
Skilton, Harry 1938- *WhoAm 90*
Skimin, Robert Elwayne 1929- *WhoWrEP 89*
Skinas, John Constantine *WhoAmA 91N*
Skindzier, Fran 1938- *WhoAmW 91*
Skinker, Marjorie Alyese 1928- *WhoE 91*
Skinn, Ann 1747?-1789 *FemiCLE*
Skinner, Ainslie *ConAu 30NR, TwCCr&M 91*
Skinner, Alastair 1936- *WhoAm 90*
Skinner, Alden 1945- *BioIn 16*
Skinner, Andrew Charles 1951- *WhoEmL 91*
Skinner, Anita Marier 1933- *WhoAmW 91*
Skinner, B. F. 1904- *WorAlBi*
Skinner, B F 1904-1990 *ConAu 132, CurBio 90N, MajTwCW*
Skinner, B. F. 1904-1990 *NewYTBS 90 [port], News 91-1*
Skinner, B. Franklin 1931- *WhoAm 90, WhoSSW 91, WhoWor 91*
Skinner, Bob 1931- *Ballpl 90*
Skinner, Brian John 1928- *WhoAm 90*
Skinner, Burrhus Frederic 1904- *WhoAm 90*
Skinner, C. 1920- *St&PR 91*
Skinner, Charles Gordon 1923- *WhoAm 90*
Skinner, Constance Lindsay 1877-1939 *DcLB 92 [port]*
Skinner, Cornelia Otis 1901-1979 *BioIn 16, FemiCLE, NotWoAT, WorAlBi*
Skinner, David Bernt 1935- *WhoAm 90*
Skinner, David E. *BioIn 16*
Skinner, David Edward 1920- *St&PR 91*
Skinner, David N. 1947- *St&PR 91*
Skinner, Dorothy M. 1930- *WhoAm 90*
Skinner, Edith Warman 1902?-1981 *BioIn 16, NotWoAT*
Skinner, Edward Folland 1909- *WhoSSW 91*
Skinner, George William 1925- *WhoAm 90*
Skinner, Gordon Sweetland 1924- *WhoAm 90*
Skinner, Harry Bryant 1943- *WhoAm 90*
Skinner, Helen Catherine Wild 1931- *WhoAmW 91*
Skinner, Hugh 1911-1988 *BioIn 16*
Skinner, I. G. M. 1890- *BioIn 16*
Skinner, James C *BiDrAPA 89*
Skinner, Jeffrey Thomas 1949- *WhoSSW 91*
Skinner, Joel 1961- *Ballpl 90*
Skinner, John R. 1947- *St&PR 91*
Skinner, John York 1949- *IntWWM 90*
Skinner, Judith Noella 1939- *WhoAmW 91*
Skinner, Knute 1929- *WhoWrEP 89*
Skinner, Knute Rumsey 1929- *WhoAm 90*
Skinner, Linda Walkup 1947- *WhoSSW 91*
Skinner, Marilyn M *BiDrAPA 89*
Skinner, Mary Just 1946- *WhoAmW 91*
Skinner, Maud Durbin *BioAmW*
Skinner, Maurice Edward, IV 1962- *WhoE 91*
Skinner, Mollie 1876-1955 *FemiCLE*
Skinner, Nancy Jo 1956- *WhoAmW 91*
Skinner, Ned Lloyd 1952- *WhoEmL 91*
Skinner, Odie Gary 1899- *St&PR 91*
Skinner, Orin Ensign 1892- *WhoAmA 91*
Skinner, Otis 1858-1942 *WorAlBi*
Skinner, Owen H., Jr. *St&PR 91*
Skinner, Patricia Morag 1932- *WhoAmW 91*
Skinner, Paul Elliot 1943- *WhoE 91*
Skinner, Peter Graeme 1944- *St&PR 91, WhoAm 90*
Skinner, Raymond, Jr. 1930- *WhoSSW 91*
Skinner, Rich *ODwPR 91*
Skinner, Rolland Gene 1941- *WhoWor 91*
Skinner, Samuel K. *BioIn 16*
Skinner, Samuel Knox 1938- *BiDrUSE 89, WhoAm 90, WhoE 91, WhoWor 91*
Skinner, Scott W. 1924-1990 *BioIn 16*
Skinner, Stanley Thayer 1937- *St&PR 91, WhoAm 90*
Skinner, Thomas 1934- *WhoAm 90*
Skinner, Thomas Dale 1954- *WhoE 91*
Skinner, Vicki Froelich 1948- *WhoAmW 91*
Skinner, Walter Jay 1927- *WhoAm 90*
Skinner, Wickham 1924- *WhoAm 90*
Skinner, William E. 1947- *St&PR 91*
Skinner, William Lea 1934- *St&PR 91*
Skinner, William Polk 1951- *WhoEmL 91*
Skinner, William T 1927- *BiDrAPA 89*
Skipper, Donald Bruce 1945- *WhoWrEP 89*
Skipper, Floyd Eugene 1925- *St&PR 91*
Skipper, G. C. 1939- *ODwPR 91*
Skipper, Harold Dallas, Jr. 1947- *WhoSSW 91*
Skipper, Henry T., Jr. 1924- *WhoAm 90*
Skipper, James Everett 1920- *WhoAm 90*
Skipper, Mary Carolyn 1940- *WhoAmW 91*
Skipper, Nathan Richard 1934- *St&PR 91*
Skipper, Nathan Richard, Jr. 1934- *WhoAm 90, WhoWor 91*
Skira, Albert 1904-1973 *BioIn 16, CurBio 90N*
Skirball, Richard Lewis 1951- *WhoEmL 91*
Skirboll, Bernice Weiss 1940- *WhoE 91*
Skirnick, Robert Andrew 1938- *WhoE 91*
Skirving, Catherine Seaton 1818-1897 *DcCanB 12*
Skislak, Tanis Greer 1948- *WhoAmW 91*
Skitch, Clifford H *BiDrAPA 89*
Skizas, Lou 1932- *Ballpl 90*
Skjaerstad, Ragnar 1944- *WhoWor 91*
Skjelbred, Perry Werner 1947- *St&PR 91*
Skjorten, Einar 1933- *WhoWor 91*
Skladal, Elizabeth Lee 1937- *WhoAmW 91*
Sklamberg, Joyce Elaine 1940- *WhoAmW 91*
Sklansky, Jack 1928- *WhoAm 90*
Sklansky, Morris A 1919- *BiDrAPA 89*
Sklar, Alan David 1938- *BiDrAPA 89*
Sklar, Alexander 1915- *WhoWor 91*
Sklar, Andrew Malcolm 1947- *WhoSSW 91*
Sklar, Daniel William 1953- *WhoE 91*
Sklar, Doris Roslyn 1936- *WhoAmW 91*
Sklar, Dorothy *WhoAmA 91*
Sklar, Dusty 1928- *WhoWrEP 89*
Sklar, George 1905-1968 *WhoAmA 91N*
Sklar, George 1908- *WhoWrEP 89*
Sklar, George 1908-1988 *BioIn 16*
Sklar, Holly L 1955- *WhoAmW 91*
Sklar, Joseph 1925- *BiDrAPA 89*
Sklar, Kathryn Kish 1939- *WhoAm 90, WhoAmW 91*
Sklar, Louis Selman 1939- *St&PR 91*
Sklar, Martin Daniel 1960- *WhoEmL 91*
Sklar, Marvin Allen 1937- *St&PR 91*
Sklar, Michael Glenn 1943- *WhoSSW 91*
Sklar, Morty 1935- *BioIn 16*
Sklar, Morty E. 1935- *WhoWrEP 89*
Sklar, Richard J. 1929- *WhoAm 90*
Sklar, Richard Lawrence 1930- *WhoAm 90*
Sklar, Robert Anthony 1936- *WhoAm 90, WhoWrEP 89*
Sklar, Roberta 1940- *BioIn 16, NotWoAT*
Sklar, Scott 1950- *ConAu 131, WhoSSW 91*
Sklar, Stephanie C. 1951- *ODwPR 91*
Sklar, Steve *BioIn 16*
Sklar, Steven J. 1956- *WhoEmL 91*
Sklar, William E. 1948- *ODwPR 91*
Sklar, William Edward 1918- *St&PR 91*
Sklar-Weinstein, Arlene 1931- *WhoAmA 91*
Sklare, Marshall 1921- *WhoAm 90*
Sklarew, Bruce H 1932- *BiDrAPA 89*
Sklarew, Myra 1934- *ConAu 30NR*
Sklarin, Burton S. 1932- *WhoAm 90*
Sklarin, Phillip *St&PR 91*
Sklaroff, David Mann 1912- *WhoE 91*
Sklaroff, Robert B. 1951- *WhoE 91*
Sklarow, Mark Howard 1956- *WhoSSW 91*
Sklarski, Bonnie J 1943- *WhoAmA 91*
Sklaver, Max 1930- *BiDrAPA 89*
Sklba, Richard J. 1935- *WhoAm 90*
Sklenar, Herbert Anthony 1931- *St&PR 91, WhoAm 90, WhoSSW 91*
Sklenarz, Krystyna 1933- *BiDrAPA 89*
Sklovskij, Viktor Borisovich 1893-1984 *BioIn 16*
Sklovsky, Robert Joel 1952- *WhoEmL 91, WhoWor 91*
Sklut, Josef 1928- *St&PR 91*
Skluzacek, Gayle Marie 1953- *WhoAmW 91, WhoEmL 91*
Skobba, Joseph S *BiDrAPA 89*
Skoblin, Nikolai Vasilevich *BioIn 16*
Skobtsova, Elizabeta Iur'evna *EncCoWW*
Skobtsova, Elizaveta 1891-1945 *BioIn 16*
Skochlas, John 1949- *WhoWrEP 89*
Skocpol, Theda *BioIn 16*
Skoczen, John J. 1942- *St&PR 91*
Skoczylas, Edward Joseph 1938- *St&PR 91*
Skoczynski, Stanislaw 1953- *IntWWM 90*
Skoda, Dan 1946- *St&PR 91*
Skoda, Emil Von 1839-1900 *WorAlBi*
Skodnek, Kenneth Barry *BiDrAPA 89*
Skodnek, Richard Paul 1947- *BiDrAPA 89*
Skodol, Andrew Edward, II 1945- *BiDrAPA 89*
Skodras, Vicki Herring 1958- *WhoAmW 91*
Skodwek, Richard Paul 1947- *WhoE 91*
Skoff, Gail Lynn *WhoAmA 91*
Skofield, James *AuBYP 90*
Skofronick, Bruce David 1937- *St&PR 91*
Skogerboe, Charles M. 1935- *St&PR 91*
Skogerboe, Rodney Kenneth 1931- *WhoAm 90*
Skoglund, Elizabeth Ruth 1937- *WhoAmW 91*
Skoglund, Sandra Louise 1946- *WhoAmA 91*
Skohlnik, Marten 1951- *WhoE 91*
Skok, Craig 1947- *Ballpl 90*
Skok, Martin John 1928- *St&PR 91*
Skok, Richard Arnold 1928- *WhoAm 90*
Skok, William Henry 1938- *WhoWor 91*
Skokan, Ralph J. 1943- *St&PR 91*
Skol, Armand George 1943- *WhoWor 91*
Skolan-Logue, Amanda Nicole 1954- *WhoEmL 91*
Skoler, Celia Rebecca 1931- *WhoAmW 91, WhoE 91*
Skoler, Louis 1920- *WhoAm 90, WhoWor 91*
Skoler, Steven Frederick 1959- *St&PR 91*
Skolimowski, Jerzy *BioIn 16*
Skolimowski, Jerzy 1938- *WhoWor 91*
Skolka, Jiri Vaclav 1928- *WhoWor 91*
Skolnick, Alec *BiDrAPA 89*
Skolnick, Blair Jonathan *BiDrAPA 89*
Skolnick, Blair Jonathan 1956- *WhoE 91*
Skolnick, Frances Miriam 1964- *WhoAmW 91*
Skolnick, Jeffrey S 1956- *BiDrAPA 89*
Skolnick, Lee H. *BioIn 16*
Skolnick, Malcolm Harris 1935- *WhoSSW 91*
Skolnick, Marvin Ralph *BiDrAPA 89*
Skolnik, Barnet David 1941- *WhoAm 90*
Skolnik, David Erwin 1949- *WhoEmL 91*
Skolnik, Geoffrey M. *St&PR 91*
Skolnik, Merrill I. 1927- *WhoAm 90*
Skolnik, Zalec I *BiDrAPA 89*
Skolnikoff, Alan Z 1932- *BiDrAPA 89*
Skolnikoff, Eugene B. 1928- *WhoAm 90*
Skolovsky, Zadel *WhoAm 90, WhoWor 91*
Skolovsky, Zadel 1926- *IntWWM 90*
Skolsky, Elizabeth Ellen 1943- *WhoAmW 91*
Skomal, Edward Nelson 1926- *WhoAm 90*
Skoney, Sophie Essa 1929- *WhoWor 91*
Skoog, Charles Vernon 1918- *WhoE 91*
Skoog, Donald Paul 1931- *WhoAm 90*
Skoog, Folke Karl 1908- *WhoAm 90*
Skoog, Gerald Duane 1936- *WhoAm 90*
Skoog, Joyce Eileen 1940- *WhoAmW 91*
Skoog, Ralph Edward 1929- *WhoAm 90*
Skoog, William Arthur 1925- *WhoAm 90, WhoWor 91*
Skoogfors, Olaf *WhoAmA 91N*

Skopec, H Michael *BiDrAPA 89*
Skopek, Henry A *BiDrAPA 89*
Skopic, Beverly Jane 1959- *WhoE 91*
Skopil, Otto Richard, Jr. 1919- *WhoAm 90*
Skopp, Douglas 1941- *WhoE 91*
Skora, Susan Sundman 1947- *WhoEmL 91*
Skoras, Linda Caroline 1957- *WhoAmW 91*
Skord, Jennifer Lynne 1948- *WhoEmL 91*
Skordal, Lynn M. 1949- *St&PR 91*
Skornschek, Scott Stephen 1955- *WhoSSW 91*
Skorton, David Jan 1949- *WhoAm 90*
Skorzeny, Otto 1908-1975 *BioIn 16*
Skotheim, Robert Allen 1933- *WhoAm 90*
Skotnicki, Stefan Henryk 1935- *WhoWor 91*
Skotzko, Christine Ellen *BiDrAPA 89*
Skouby, Alan Douglas 1937- *St&PR 91*
Skouge, Richard J. 1941- *St&PR 91*
Skouras, Spyros S. 1923- *St&PR 91*
Skov, Lisbeth Andersen 1949- *WhoWor 91*
Skov, Mildred Jane 1932- *WhoAmW 91*
Skove, Thomas Malcolm 1925- *WhoAm 90*
Skovron, Cecile Lawinska 1947- *WhoAmW 91*
Skovron, David A. 1939- *St&PR 91*
Skown, Bernard 1940- *St&PR 91*
Skowron, Bill 1930- *Ballpl 90*
Skowron, Donald J. 1941- *St&PR 91*
Skowronski, Mary Lynn 1965- *WhoAmW 91*
Skowronski, Thomas Edward 1942- *St&PR 91*
Skowronski, Vincent Paul 1944- *WhoAm 90*
Skoyles, John 1949- *WhoWrEP 89*
Skraba-Carr, Diane M. 1952- *WhoAmW 91*
Skrabanek, Donald W. 1951- *WhoWrEP 89*
Skrable, Russell James 1946- *St&PR 91*
Skrajewski, Dennis John 1954- *WhoE 91*
Skram, Amalie 1846-1905 *DcScanL, EncCoWW*
Skram, Knut 1937- *IntWWM 90*
Skramstad, Harold Kenneth 1941- *WhoAm 90*
Skramstad, Harold Kenneth, Jr. 1941- *St&PR 91*
Skramstad, Sherry 1942- *WhoWrEP 89*
Skratek, Sylvia Paulette 1950- *WhoAmW 91*
Skrdla, W Blake 1920- *BiDrAPA 89*
Skriner, Edward *St&PR 91*
Skripol, James Nicholas *BiDrAPA 89*
Skritek, Paul 1952- *WhoWor 91*
Skrivanek, Britt Edward 1948- *St&PR 91*
Skriver, Ansgar 1934- *WhoWor 91*
Skromme, Lawrence H. 1913- *WhoAm 90*
Skroumbelos, Nicholas George 1952- *WhoE 91, WhoEmL 91, WhoWor 91*
Skrowaczewski, Stanislaw 1923- *IntWWM 90, PenDiMP, WhoAm 90, WhoWor 91*
Skryabin, Alexander 1872-1915 *PenDiMP A*
Skrypnyk, Mstyslav Stepan 1898- *WhoAm 90*
Skrzypczak, Casimir S. 1941- *St&PR 91*
Skrzypek-Ronowska, Wieslawa 1954- *IntWWM 90*
Skubak, Bernard 1951- *St&PR 91*
Skubas, Charles E. 1944- *St&PR 91*
Skube, Michael *WhoAm 90, WhoSSW 91*
Skubic, Peter 1935- *BioIn 16*
Skubiszewski, Krzysztof 1926- *WhoWor 91*
Skuggen, Robert H. *ODwPR 91*
Skulas, Irene Michelle 1951- *WhoEmL 91*
Skulina, Thomas Raymond 1933- *WhoAm 90, WhoWor 91*
Skully, Richard Patrick 1921- *WhoAm 90*
Skup, David Alan 1952- *WhoSSW 91*
Skupinski, Bogdan Kazimierz 1942- *WhoAm 90*
Skuran, Victor 1924- *St&PR 91*
Skurdenis, Juliann Veronica 1942- *WhoAmW 91, WhoE 91*
Skurkis, Barry A 1951- *WhoAmA 91*
Skurnowicz, Elaine Marie 1953- *WhoAmW 91*
Skurnowicz, Hilary *ODwPR 91*
Skurzynski, Gloria 1930- *ConAu 30NR*
Skuse, George W. 1943- *St&PR 91*
Skutch, William G. 1924- *St&PR 91*
Skutt, Anne-Marguerite 1924- *WhoWrEP 89*
Skutt, Richard Michael 1947- *WhoEmL 91*
Skutt, Thomas James 1930- *St&PR 91, WhoAm 90*
Skutt, V.J. 1902- *St&PR 91*
Skutt, Vestor Joseph 1902- *WhoAm 90*
Skvorecky, Josef 1924- *MajTwCW*
Skvorecky, Josef Vaclav 1924- *WhoAm 90*
Skweir, Leon A 1936- *BiDrAPA 89*
Skwerer, Robert G. 1956- *BiDrAPA 89*
Skwiertz, Albert A., Jr. 1945- *St&PR 91*
Sky Chief *WhNaAH*
Sky Walker *WhNaAH*
Sky, Alison 1946- *WhoAmA 91*
Sky, Asher J. 1936- *St&PR 91*
Sky, Mickey *WhoWrEP 89*
Skye, Ione *BioIn 16*
Skyler, Denise Courshon 1948- *WhoAmW 91*
Skyllas, Drossos P. 1912-1973 *MusmAFA*
Skyllstad, Kjell Muller 1928- *IntWWM 90*
Skylstad, William S. 1934- *WhoAm 90*
Skypeck, Walter T. 1923- *St&PR 91*
Skypek, Genevieve 1945- *WhoAmW 91*
Slaaten, Doris Adele 1920- *WhoAmW 91*
Slaats, Mathew A. 1923- *WhoAm 90*
Slaats, Mathew Adrian 1923- *St&PR 91*
Slaatte, Howard A 1919- *ConAu 31NR*
Slaatte, Howard Alexander 1919- *WhoAm 90*
Slabbert, Frederik van Zyl 1940- *BioIn 16, WhoWor 91*
Slabe, James F. 1940- *St&PR 91, WhoE 91, WhoWor 91*
Slaby, Andrew Edmund 1942- *BiDrAPA 89*
Slaby, Mary Ann 1945- *WhoAmW 91*
Slack, D. Stephen 1949- *St&PR 91*
Slack, David Patrick 1952- *WhoSSW 91*
Slack, Derald Allen 1924- *WhoSSW 91*
Slack, Douglas M. 1947- *St&PR 91*
Slack, Edward Joseph 1923- *WhoAm 90*
Slack, Edward Russell 1928- *WhoSSW 91*
Slack, Fred Philip 1946- *St&PR 91*
Slack, Freddie 1910-1965 *OxCPMus*
Slack, Gary L. 1954- *ODwPR 91*
Slack, George H. 1926- *St&PR 91*
Slack, John M. 1948- *St&PR 91*
Slack, Karen Kershner 1951- *WhoSSW 91*
Slack, Lewis 1924- *WhoAm 90*
Slack, Robert George 1938- *BiDrAPA 89*
Slack, Steve D. 1946- *St&PR 91*
Slack, Vickie *WhoAmW 91*
Slade *OxCPMus*
Slade, Arthur Laird 1937- *WhoE 91*
Slade, Bernard 1930- *OxCCanT, WhoAm 90*
Slade, Caroline 1886-1975 *FemiCLE*
Slade, David Marshall 1965- *WhoE 91*
Slade, Diann Stukes 1956- *WhoAmW 91*
Slade, Doren Leslie 1945- *WhoAmW 91*
Slade, Edward Colin 1935- *WhoSSW 91*
Slade, George Kemble, Jr. 1949- *WhoEmL 91*
Slade, Gerald Jack 1919- *WhoAm 90*
Slade, Gordon 1904-1974 *Ballpl 90*
Slade, Henry *EncO&P 3, EncPaPR 91*
Slade, Hutton Davison 1912- *WhoAm 90*
Slade, Jarvis J. 1926- *St&PR 91*
Slade, Jeffrey Christopher 1946- *WhoEmL 91*
Slade, Joann Kaye 1933- *WhoAmW 91*
Slade, Julian 1930- *OxCPMus*
Slade, Julian Penkivil 1930- *IntWWM 90*
Slade, Llewellyn Eugene 1911- *WhoAm 90*
Slade, Mark J. 1959- *St&PR 91*
Slade, Norma Marie Headrick 1922- *WhoAmW 91*
Slade, Roy 1933- *WhoAm 90, WhoAmA 91*
Slade, Thomas Bog, III 1931- *WhoSSW 91*
Slade, Walter R, Jr. *BiDrAPA 89*
Slade, Walter Raleigh, Jr. 1918- *WhoE 91*
Slade-Lipkin, Heather Anne 1947- *IntWWM 90*
Sladek, John R., Jr. 1943- *WhoAm 90*
Sladek, Lyle Virgil 1923- *WhoAm 90*
Sladek, Ronald John 1926- *WhoAm 90*
Sladen, Bernard Jacob 1952- *WhoEmL 91*
Sladkevicius, Vincentas 1920- *WhoWor 91*
Sladkin, Kenneth Ray 1944- *BiDrAPA 89*
Sladkoff, Jean-Ajax 1946- *WhoWor 91*
Sladkus, John K. 1923- *St&PR 91*
Sladon, Donna J. 1957- *St&PR 91*
Sladon, Ronald B. 1929- *St&PR 91*
Sladzinski, Marianne 1942- *WhoE 91*
Slaff, Bertram 1921- *BiDrAPA 89*
Slaff, Bertram Allen 1921- *WhoE 91*
Slaff, George 1906-1989 *BioIn 16*
Slagel, Robert Clayton 1937- *WhoAm 90*
Slagle, Dodge Alan *BiDrAPA 89*
Slagle, Edward Howard *BiDrAPA 89*
Slagle, James Robert 1934- *WhoAm 90*
Slagle, James William 1955- *WhoEmL 91*
Slagle, Jimmy 1873-1956 *Ballpl 90*
Slagle, Priscilla Ann 1941- *BiDrAPA 89*
Slagle, Robert F. 1940- *St&PR 91*
Slagle, Robert Fred 1940- *WhoAm 90*
Slagle, William F. 1929- *WhoAm 90, WhoSSW 91*
Slagowitz, Martin Barry 1941- *St&PR 91*
Slaiby, Theodore George 1929- *WhoAm 90*
Slaight, Brian 1934- *St&PR 91*
Slaight, Gary John 1951- *St&PR 91*
Slain, John Joseph 1927- *WhoAm 90*
Slakas, Joseph G. *ODwPR 91*
Slakey, Linda Louise 1939- *WhoAm 90*
Slakey, Stephen Louis 1946- *WhoEmL 91*
Slamecka, Vladimir 1928- *WhoAm 90*
Slancikova, Bo'ena 1867-1951 *EncCoWW*
Slane, Ann *BiDEWW*
Slane, Charles J. 1947- *St&PR 91*
Slane, Charles Joseph 1947- *WhoAm 90*
Slane, Henry Pindell 1920- *St&PR 91*
Slaney, Mary Decker *BioIn 16*
Slansky, Jerry William 1947- *WhoAm 90*
Slansky, Paul *BioIn 16*
Slansky, Richard B. 1957- *St&PR 91*
Slap, Charles S. 1933- *WhoE 91*
Slap, Joseph W 1927- *BiDrAPA 89*
Slap, Robert *NewAgMG*
Slape, Lori Dale 1964- *St&PR 91*
Slapnicka, Cy 1886-1979 *Ballpl 90*
Slappey, Mary Mc Gowan 1914- *WhoWrEP 89*
Slappey, Mary McGowan 1914- *WhoE 91*
Slappey, Sterling Greene 1917- *WhoAm 90*
Slaske, Gerard J. *ODwPR 91*
Slatcher, Edward G. 1932- *St&PR 91*
Slate, Floyd Owen 1920- *WhoAm 90*
Slate, Joe Hutson 1930- *WhoAm 90*
Slate, John Butler 1953- *WhoAm 90, WhoEmL 91*
Slate, John R. 1955- *WhoSSW 91*
Slate, Joseph Frank 1928- *WhoAmA 91*
Slate, Sallie Y *ODwPR 91*
Slaten, Paul Edward 1933- *St&PR 91*
Slater, Alan T. 1945- *WhoE 91*
Slater, Andrea 1958- *WhoAmW 91*
Slater, Annette Sims 1951- *BiDrAPA 89*
Slater, Billy Ray 1946- *St&PR 91*
Slater, Christian *BioIn 16*
Slater, Cody *BioIn 16*
Slater, Courtenay Murphy 1933- *WhoAm 90*
Slater, Donald J. *WhoSSW 91*
Slater, Doris Ernestine Wilke *WhoWor 91*
Slater, Edward Charles 1917- *WhoWor 91*
Slater, Edward Nathan 1941- *St&PR 91*
Slater, Eliot T O *BiDrAPA 89*
Slater, Elizabeth May 1907-1988 *BioIn 16*
Slater, Frank *WhoAmA 91N*
Slater, Gary Lee 1947- *WhoAmA 91*
Slater, George R. 1924- *St&PR 91*
Slater, George Richard 1924- *WhoAm 90*
Slater, Gertrude *BiDrAPA 89*
Slater, Helene Ford Southern *WhoE 91, WhoWor 91*
Slater, Herbert 1932- *St&PR 91*
Slater, James Munro 1929- *WhoAm 90*
Slater, Jerome William, Jr. 1936- *St&PR 91*
Slater, Jim 1929- *BioIn 16*
Slater, John 1861-1932 *EncO&P 3*
Slater, John Clarke 1900-1976 *DcScB S2*
Slater, John Edmund 1922- *St&PR 91, WhoAm 90*
Slater, John Greenleaf 1935- *WhoAm 90*
Slater, John Wiley, Jr. 1948- *WhoSSW 91*
Slater, Jonathan Allen *BiDrAPA 89*
Slater, Joseph Elliott 1922- *WhoAm 90*
Slater, Karen *BiDrAPA 89*
Slater, Karen Rosenberg 1945- *WhoE 91*
Slater, Louis L. 1913- *St&PR 91*
Slater, Lydia Pasternak *BioIn 16*
Slater, Lydia Pasternak 1902-1989 *AnObit 1989*
Slater, Lynne Marie 1958- *WhoAmW 91*
Slater, Manning 1917- *WhoAm 90*
Slater, Morris Ned 1925- *WhoE 91*
Slater, Oliver Eugene 1906- *WhoAm 90*
Slater, Peggy *BioIn 16*
Slater, Ralph Evan 1948- *WhoE 91*
Slater, Richard James 1946- *St&PR 91, WhoAm 90*
Slater, Robert G 1939- *BiDrAPA 89*
Slater, Robert James 1923- *WhoAm 90*
Slater, Robert L. 1932- *ODwPR 91*
Slater, Robert R. 1934- *St&PR 91*
Slater, S. Donald 1927- *WhoWor 91*
Slater, Samuel 1768-1835 *BioIn 16, WorAlBi*
Slater, Schuyler George 1923- *WhoE 91*
Slater, Stanley L *BiDrAPA 89*
Slater, Thomas *EncO&P 3*
Slater, Thomas Glascock, Jr. 1944- *WhoAm 90*
Slater, Trevor Frank 1931- *WhoWor 91*
Slater, Victor L, Jr. 1925- *BiDrAPA 89*
Slater, William T. *BioIn 16*
Slater, William Thomas 1942- *WhoE 91*
Slater, Williams S. 1946- *St&PR 91*
Slates, Deborah Lynn 1957- *WhoE 91*
Slatford, Rodney Gerald Yorke 1944- *IntWWM 90*
Slatin, Alfred 1929- *St&PR 91*
Slatin, Yeffe Kimball 1914-1978 *WhoAmA 91N*
Slatkes, Leonard J 1930- *WhoAmA 91*
Slatkin, Burton 1920- *St&PR 91*
Slatkin, Charles E 1908-1977 *WhoAmA 91N*
Slatkin, Edward *BioIn 16*
Slatkin, Felix 1915-1963 *PenDiMP*
Slatkin, Leonard *BioIn 16*
Slatkin, Leonard 1944- *PenDiMP*
Slatkin, Leonard Edward 1944- *IntWWM 90, WhoAm 90*
Slatkin, Marcia 1943- *WhoWrEP 89*
Slatkin, Murray 1905- *St&PR 91, WhoAm 90*
Slatkin, Stephen E *BiDrAPA 89*
Slatkin, Thomas *BioIn 16*
Slatkin, Wendy 1950- *WhoAmA 91*
Slatner, Thomas Allen 1940- *WhoWor 91*
Slatoff, Walter Jacob 1922- *WhoWrEP 89*
Slaton, Brenda Dale 1962- *WhoAmW 91*
Slaton, Jim 1950- *Ballpl 90*
Slaton, John Marshall 1866-1955 *AmLegL*
Slaton, John William 1924- *St&PR 91, WhoAm 90*
Slaton, Lewis Roger 1922- *WhoSSW 91*
Slatt, Roger Malcolm 1941- *WhoSSW 91*
Slatter, Errol Mervyn 1926- *IntWWM 90*
Slatter, Sarah Piteo 1952- *St&PR 91*
Slatter, Simon *St&PR 91*
Slattery, Charles Wilbur 1937- *WhoAm 90, WhoWor 91*
Slattery, Erin Marie 1966- *WhoE 91*
Slattery, Frank P., Jr. 1937- *St&PR 91*
Slattery, James A. 1942- *St&PR 91*
Slattery, James Charles 1948- *WhoAm 90*
Slattery, James Joseph 1922- *WhoAm 90*
Slattery, Kenneth F. 1921- *WhoAm 90*
Slattery, Marcia Jean *BiDrAPA 89*
Slattery, Matthew Thomas, III 1936- *WhoWrEP 89*
Slattery, Paul Francis 1940- *WhoAm 90*
Slattery, Robert Francis 1951- *BiDrAPA 89*
Slattery, Thomas E. 1935- *WhoAm 90*
Slattery, William H. 1943- *St&PR 91*
Slaught, Don 1958- *Ballpl 90*
Slaughter, A. Walter 1860-1908 *OxCPMus*
Slaughter, Alexander Hoke 1937- *WhoAm 90*
Slaughter, Carolyn *BioIn 16*
Slaughter, Christopher Ray 1946- *St&PR 91*
Slaughter, D. French, Jr. 1925- *WhoAm 90, WhoSSW 91*
Slaughter, Deborah Jane 1954- *WhoSSW 91*
Slaughter, Edward Ratliff, Jr. 1931- *WhoAm 90*
Slaughter, Enos 1916- *Ballpl 90 [port], BioIn 16*
Slaughter, Frank Gill 1908- *WhoAm 90*
Slaughter, Freeman Cluff 1926- *WhoSSW 91*
Slaughter, Hazel Burnham 1888-1979 *WhoAmA 91N*
Slaughter, Howel William, Jr. 1947- *BiDrAPA 89*
Slaughter, James Bruce 1960- *WhoE 91*
Slaughter, James Luther, III 1944- *WhoWor 91*
Slaughter, James Richard 1946- *BiDrAPA 89*
Slaughter, Jane Mundy 1905- *WhoAmW 91*
Slaughter, Jean *AuBYP 90*
Slaughter, Jim *ConAu 31NR*
Slaughter, John B. *BioIn 16*
Slaughter, John Brooks 1934- *WhoAm 90, WhoWor 91*
Slaughter, Judy Hughes 1957- *WhoSSW 91*
Slaughter, Louise McIntosh 1929- *WhoAm 90, WhoAmW 91, WhoE 91*
Slaughter, Lurline Eddy 1919- *WhoAmA 91, WhoAmW 91*
Slaughter, M M 1940- *ConAu 131*
Slaughter, Margo Ann 1951- *WhoAmW 91*
Slaughter, Michie Paris 1941- *St&PR 91*
Slaughter, Phillip Howard 1948- *WhoSSW 91*
Slaughter, Tod 1885-1956 *BioIn 16*
Slaughter, Vernon *BioIn 16*
Slaughter, William Edward, Jr. 1908- *WhoAm 90*
Slaughter, William Gains *BiDrAPA 89*
Slaven, Mark Edward 1961- *BiDrAPA 89*
Slaven, Roy *WhoAm 90*
Slavens, Thomas Paul 1928- *WhoAm 90*
Slaveski, Elizabeth Ann 1937- *WhoAmW 91*
Slavich, Denis Michael 1940- *WhoAm 90*
Slavick, Susanne Mechtild 1956- *WhoAmA 91*
Slavicky, Milan 1947- *IntWWM 90*
Slavin, Alexandra Nadal 1943- *WhoAmW 91, WhoSSW 91*
Slavin, Arlene 1942- *WhoAmA 91*
Slavin, Daniel 1926- *St&PR 91*
Slavin, Edward Windell 1951- *WhoE 91*
Slavin, Eugene 1935- *WhoSSW 91*
Slavin, Howard Leslie 1951- *WhoEmL 91*
Slavin, Jeremy Alan 1946- *IntWWM 90*
Slavin, John Jeremiah 1921- *St&PR 91*
Slavin, Kenneth R. *ODwPR 91*
Slavin, Martin A 1934- *BiDrAPA 89*
Slavin, Neal 1941- *WhoAm 90, WhoAmA 91*

Slavin, Neil 1948- *WhoE 91*
Slavin, Patrick Lee 1950- *WhoSSW 91*
Slavin, Raymond Granam 1930- *WhoAm 90*
Slavin, Roberta Landau 1929- *WhoAmW 91*
Slavin, Simon 1916- *WhoAm 90*
Slavinska, Nonna *WhoE 91*
Slavinskas, Darius Domas 1933- *WhoE 91*
Slavit, Ann *BioIn 16*
Slavitt, David R. 1935- *BioIn 16*
Slavitt, David Rytman 1935- *WhoWrEP 89*
Slavitt, David Walton 1931- *WhoAm 90*
Slavitt, Earl Benton 1939- *WhoAm 90*
Slavney, Phillip R *BiDrAPA 89*
Slavona, Maria 1865-1931 *BiDWomA*
Slavutin, Debra Claire 1951- *WhoAmW 91*
Slavutin, Lee Jacob 1951- *WhoE 91*
Slawek, Kimberly Ann 1961- *WhoAmW 91*
Slawek, Stephen Matthew 1949- *IntWWM 90*
Slawsky, Richard Charles 1953- *BiDrAPA 89*
Slawson, Bobby Joe 1939- *WhoAm 90*
Slawson, John 1896-1989 *BioIn 16*
Slawson, Paul F 1929- *BiDrAPA 89*
Slawson, Richard Allen *BiDrAPA 89*
Slawson, Wayne A. 1932- *IntWWM 90*
Slayback, Bill 1948- *Ballpl 90*
Slaybaugh, Jon 1943- *St&PR 91*
Slayden, James Bragdon 1924- *WhoAm 90*
Slayden, Robert McLean 1943- *BiDrAPA 89*
Slaydon, Jeanne Miller *WhoSSW 91*
Slaydon, Kathleen Amelia 1951- *WhoAmW 91*
Slaymaker, Gene Arthur 1928- *WhoAm 90*
Slaymaker, H. Olav 1939- *WhoAm 90*
Slaymaker, Martha 1935- *WhoAmA 91*
Slayman, Carolyn Walch 1937- *WhoAm 90*
Slayter, Wendell Edwin 1930- *St&PR 91*
Slayton, Abigail Martha Tuckerman 1961- *WhoE 91*
Slayton, Deke 1924- *BioIn 16*
Slayton, Donald Kent 1924- *BioIn 16*, *WhoAm 90*
Slayton, Gus 1937- *WhoAm 90*
Slayton, Jeff *BioIn 16*
Slayton, Joel Charles 1948- *WhoSSW 91*
Slayton, John A. 1918- *St&PR 91*
Slayton, John Arthur 1918- *WhoAm 90*
Slayton, John Howard 1955- *WhoEmL 91*
Slayton, Lee E. 1926- *St&PR 91*
Slayton, Ransom Dunn 1917- *WhoWor 91*
Slayton, Robert Allen 1951- *WhoEmL 91*
Slayton, Robert Ira 1951- *BiDrAPA 89*
Slayton, Ronald Alfred 1910- *WhoE 91*
Slayton, Thomas Kennedy 1941- *WhoE 91*
Slayton, William Larew 1916- *WhoAm 90*
Slazinski, Darleen Marian 1938- *St&PR 91*
Sleater, Lou 1926- *Ballpl 90*
Sleath, Eleanor *FemiCLE*
Sleath, Martin David 1946- *St&PR 91*
Sleator, William *BioIn 16*
Sleator, William 1945- *Au&Arts 5 [port]*
Sleavin, F. Richard 1938- *St&PR 91*
Slechta, Robert Frank 1928- *WhoAm 90*
Sledd, James Hinton 1914- *WhoWrEP 89*
Sledge, Donald E. 1942- *St&PR 91*
Sledge, Donald Herbert 1940- *St&PR 91*
Sledge, Elizabeth Rose 1945- *WhoE 91*
Sledge, James Scott 1947- *WhoWor 91*
Sledge, Joanna *BioIn 16*
Sledge, Levin Alexander 1913- *St&PR 91*
Sledge, Reginald Leon 1954- *WhoE 91*
Sledge, Robert Watson 1932- *WhoWor 91*
Sledge, William Hurt 1945- *BiDrAPA 89*
Sledge, William Ruffin 1922- *St&PR 91*
Sledzik, William E. 1953- *ODwPR 91*
Slee, Raymond Edward 1923- *IntWWM 90*
Sleek, Harry T. 1943- *St&PR 91*
Sleek, Sewell Irwin 1936- *St&PR 91*
Sleeman, Mary 1928- *WhoAmW 91*
Sleeman, Robert John 1946- *St&PR 91*
Sleeman, Thomas Barrett 1932- *St&PR 91*, *WhoAm 90*
Sleeman, William Clifford, Jr. 1923- *WhoSSW 91*
Sleeman, William John 1935- *St&PR 91*
Sleepeck, William H., Jr. 1918- *St&PR 91*
Sleeper, David L. 1856- *AmLegL*
Sleeper, Frank Harold 1927- *WhoE 91*
Sleeper, Harold G *BiDrAPA 89*
Sleeping Preacher, The 1794- *EncO&P 3*
Sleepy Eyes 1780?-1860? *WhNaAH*
Sleet, Robert Emmett 1946- *St&PR 91*
Sleicher, Charles Albert 1924- *WhoAm 90*
Sleicher, Harry K. 1925- *St&PR 91*
Sleigh, Burrows Willcocks Arthur 1821-1869 *DcLB 99*
Sleigh, Sylvia *WhoAm 90*, *WhoAmA 91*
Sleigh, Sylvia 1935?- *BiDWomA*
Sleight, Arthur William 1939- *WhoAm 90*
Sleight, Stanley David 1951- *WhoEmL 91*
Sleisenger, Marvin Herbert 1924- *WhoAm 90*
Slemko, Morris Peter 1952- *St&PR 91*
Slemon, Gordon Richard 1924- *WhoAm 90*
Slenger, Walworth R 1914- *BiDrAPA 89*
Slepian, David 1923- *WhoAm 90*
Slepian, Don *NewAgMG*
Slepian, Jan 1921- *BioIn 16*
Slepian, Paul 1923- *WhoAm 90*, *WhoE 91*
Slepicka, Bradford Miles 1951- *St&PR 91*
Slesar, Henry 1927- *TwCCr&M 91*
Slesar, Paula Jean 1955- *WhoAmW 91*
Slesinger, Dorothy Avery *BioIn 16*
Slesinger, Earle 1919- *St&PR 91*
Slesinger, Reuben Emanuel 1916- *WhoE 91*
Slesinger, Tess 1905-1945 *DcLB 102 [port]*, *FemiCLE*
Slesnick, William Ellis 1925- *WhoAm 90*
Slessman, Donald B. 1917- *St&PR 91*
Slessor, Kenneth *BioIn 16*
Sleszynski, Raymond A *BiDrAPA 89*
Sletmo, Gunnar Kristoffer 1937- *WhoWor 91*
Slettebak, Arne 1925- *WhoAm 90*
Slettehaugh, Thomas Chester 1925- *WhoAmA 91*
Sletten, Ivan W *BiDrAPA 89*
Sletto, Verona Gwendolyn 1909- *WhoAmW 91*
Sleven, Marvin Owen 1925- *St&PR 91*
Sleven, Robert L. 1932- *WhoAm 90*
Slevin, Joseph Raymond 1918- *WhoE 91*
Slevin, Maurice Louis 1949- *WhoWor 91*
Slevin, Patrick Joseph 1951- *WhoE 91*, *WhoWor 91*
Slewitzke, Connie Lee 1931- *WhoAm 90*, *WhoAmW 91*, *WhoE 91*
Sley, Joan 1623?-1715? *BiDEWW*
Slezak, Erika Alma 1946- *WhoAm 90*
Slezak, Gary M. 1955- *St&PR 91*
Slezak, Jane Ann 1935- *WhoAmW 91*
Slezak, Karen Patricia 1950- *WhoAmW 91*
Slezak, Leo 1873-1946 *BioIn 16*, *PenDiMP*, *WorAlBi*
Slichter, Charles Pence 1924- *WhoAm 90*
Slichter, Louis Byrne 1896-1978 *DcScB S2*
Slichter, William P *NewYTBS 90 [port]*
Slichter, William Pence 1922- *WhoAm 90*
Slick, Grace 1939- *WorAlBi*
Slick, Grace Wing 1939- *WhoAm 90*
Slick, James Nelson 1901-1979 *WhoAmA 91N*
Slidell, John 1793-1871 *BioIn 16*
Slider, Dorla Dean 1929- *WhoAmA 91*
Sliepcevich, Cedomir M. 1920- *WhoAm 90*
Slifka, Alan B. 1929- *St&PR 91*
Slifkin, Lawrence Myer 1925- *WhoAm 90*
Sligar, James Leland 1952- *WhoSSW 91*
Sliger, Bernard Francis 1924- *WhoAm 90*, *WhoSSW 91*
Sligh, Charles Robert, Jr. 1906- *St&PR 91*
Sligh, Clarisa T 1939- *WhoAmA 91*
Sligh, Robert Lewis 1928- *St&PR 91*
Slight, Robert Brooks 1934- *St&PR 91*
Slightam, John David 1955- *BiDrAPA 89*
Sliker, Thomas R. 1951- *St&PR 91*
Slim, Elizabeth Middleton 1931- *WhoAmW 91*
Slim, Guitar *BioIn 16*
Slim, Memphis *WhoWrEP 89*
Slim, Memphis 1915-1988 *AnObit 1988*
Slim, William Joseph 1891-1970 *WorAlBi*
Sliman, Edward Anthony 1935- *WhoSSW 91*
Slimmer, Richard B. 1953- *St&PR 91*
Slimp, Beverly B. 1916- *St&PR 91*
Sline, Melvin Richard 1947- *WhoEmL 91*
Sliney, David Hammond 1941- *WhoE 91*
Sliney, David L. 1936- *St&PR 91*
Slingerland, Beth *BioIn 16*
Slingerman, Raymond Joseph, Jr. 1924- *St&PR 91*
Slingluff, Charles H., Jr. 1929- *St&PR 91*
Slingluff, Robert Mitchell 1953- *WhoSSW 91*
Slingsby, Ann Mary 1930- *WhoAmW 91*
Slintak, Grecia Elcilia 1937- *WhoAmW 91*
Slipman, Ronald 1939- *WhoSSW 91*
Slipp, Samuel 1924- *BiDrAPA 89*, *WhoE 91*
Slipsager, Henrik Christian 1955- *St&PR 91*
Sliski, Chester 1943- *St&PR 91*
Sliter, John E. 1937- *St&PR 91*
Sliter, John W. 1934- *WhoAm 90*
Slitor, Richard Eaton 1911- *ConAu 32NR*
Slive, Harriet Weinmann 1951- *WhoAmW 91*
Slive, Seymour 1920- *WhoAm 90*, *WhoAmA 91*
Slivinsky, Sandra Harriet 1940- *WhoAmW 91*
Slivka, David *WhoAmA 91*
Slivka, Robert Michael 1941- *WhoE 91*
Slivkin, Stanley E 1919- *BiDrAPA 89*
Slivon, F.P., Jr. 1930- *St&PR 91*
Sliwa, Curtis *BioIn 16*
Sliwinski, Marian 1932- *WhoWor 91*
Slizewski, Edward 1962- *ODwPR 91*
Sloan, A. Elizabeth 1951- *WhoAm 90*
Sloan, Albert Frazier 1929- *WhoAm 90*, *WhoSSW 91*
Sloan, Alfred P., Jr. 1875-1966 *WorAlBi*
Sloan, Alfred Pritchard, Jr. *BioIn 16*
Sloan, Alfred Pritchard, Jr. 1875-1966 *EncABHB 5 [port]*
Sloan, Anthony *ConAu 129*
Sloan, Beatrice S *BiDrAPA 89*
Sloan, Bessie Bernice 1949- *WhoAmW 91*
Sloan, Carolyn 1937- *BioIn 16*
Sloan, David Edward 1922- *St&PR 91*, *WhoAm 90*
Sloan, David Francis 1943- *St&PR 91*
Sloan, David Walter 1937- *WhoSSW 91*
Sloan, Don Alan 1952- *WhoSSW 91*
Sloan, Donald Leroy 1944-1990 *BioIn 16*
Sloan, Douglas Albert 1959- *St&PR 91*
Sloan, Edward William, III 1931- *WhoE 91*
Sloan, Frank Allen 1942- *WhoAm 90*
Sloan, Frank Blaine 1920- *WhoE 91*, *WhoWor 91*
Sloan, Frank Keenan 1921- *WhoAm 90*
Sloan, Gary Levern 1955- *WhoSSW 91*
Sloan, George Beale 1831-1904 *AmLegL*
Sloan, Gerald Eugene 1942- *WhoAm 90*
Sloan, Gerald Mark 1951- *WhoEmL 91*
Sloan, H Marjorie *BiDrAPA 89*
Sloan, Harold Stephenson *BioIn 16*
Sloan, Herbert Elias 1914- *WhoAm 90*, *WhoWor 91*
Sloan, Hiram Cooper 1929- *WhoWor 91*
Sloan, Hugh Walter, Jr. 1940- *WhoAm 90*
Sloan, Ira Harry 1942- *BiDrAPA 89*
Sloan, Jackson 1939- *St&PR 91*
Sloan, James Park 1916- *WhoSSW 91*
Sloan, James Park 1944- *WhoAm 90*, *WhoWrEP 89*
Sloan, James Richard 1943- *WhoSSW 91*
Sloan, Jeanette Pasin 1946- *WhoAm 90*, *WhoAmA 91*
Sloan, Jerry L. 1936- *ODwPR 91*
Sloan, Jody Beth 1953- *WhoAmW 91*
Sloan, John 1871-1951 *BioIn 16*, *IntDcAA 90*, *WhoAmA 91N*
Sloan, John C. 1870-1951 *EncO&P 3*
Sloan, John E. 1932- *St&PR 91*
Sloan, John Elliot, Jr. 1936- *WhoAm 90*
Sloan, John F. 1871-1951 *WorAlBi*
Sloan, Kevin Lawrence *BiDrAPA 89*
Sloan, L. Lawrence *St&PR 91*
Sloan, Lane E. 1947- *St&PR 91*
Sloan, Lane Everett 1947- *WhoAm 90*
Sloan, Lea Christy 1956- *WhoEmL 91*
Sloan, Lloyd Lawrence 1922- *WhoAm 90*
Sloan, Maceo Kennedy 1949- *WhoSSW 91*, *WhoWor 91*
Sloan, Mary Jean 1927- *WhoSSW 91*, *WhoWor 91*
Sloan, Merrill Glenn 1924- *St&PR 91*
Sloan, Michael 1946- *ConAu 130*
Sloan, Michael Dana 1960- *WhoEmL 91*, *WhoWor 91*
Sloan, Norton Q. *St&PR 91*
Sloan, Orris Temple, Jr. 1939- *St&PR 91*
Sloan, Pamela Brink 1946- *WhoAmW 91*
Sloan, Paul Lowe, III 1945- *WhoSSW 91*
Sloan, Phillip James 1961- *WhoSSW 91*
Sloan, Reece *BioIn 16*
Sloan, Richard 1935- *WhoAmA 91*
Sloan, Richard Sherman 1952- *WhoE 91*
Sloan, Robert Blake 1941- *St&PR 91*
Sloan, Robert Francis 1935- *WhoWor 91*
Sloan, Robert Hood, Jr. 1953- *WhoE 91*
Sloan, Robert Love 1947- *WhoSSW 91*
Sloan, Robert Smullyan 1915- *WhoAmA 91*
Sloan, Robert Wesley 1930- *St&PR 91*
Sloan, Ronald J 1932- *WhoAmA 91*
Sloan, Sonia Schorr 1928- *WhoAmW 91*
Sloan, Stanley 1943- *WhoAm 90*
Sloan, Stephen 1932- *WhoAm 90*
Sloan, Susan V. 1945- *WhoAmW 91*
Sloan, Suzanne Barkin 1959- *WhoAmW 91*
Sloan, Tod Stratton 1952- *WhoSSW 91*
Sloan, William David 1947- *WhoSSW 91*
Sloan, William J. 1927- *BioIn 16*
Sloan, William Patrick 1934- *St&PR 91*
Sloan-Bubrick, A. Elizabeth *ODwPR 91*
Sloane, A Baldwin 1872-1926 *OxCPMus*
Sloane, Beverly LeBov 1936- *WhoAmW 91*, *WhoWor 91*
Sloane, Bryan Jennings, Jr. 1932- *WhoSSW 91*
Sloane, Carl Stuart 1937- *WhoAm 90*
Sloane, Carolyn *AuBYP 90*
Sloane, David Jonathan 1950- *St&PR 91*
Sloane, Emilia V 1938- *BiDrAPA 89*
Sloane, Eric *BioIn 16*
Sloane, Eric 1910-1985 *WhoAmA 91N*
Sloane, Florence Adele 1873-1960 *BioIn 16*
Sloane, G. Michael 1952- *St&PR 91*
Sloane, Hans *PenDiDA 89*
Sloane, John Hunt 1933- *St&PR 91*, *WhoAm 90*
Sloane, Joseph Curtis 1909- *WhoAmA 91*
Sloane, Larry J *BiDrAPA 89*
Sloane, Marshall M. 1926- *WhoAm 90*
Sloane, Martin 1940- *ConAu 132*
Sloane, Patricia Hermine 1934- *WhoAm 90*
Sloane, Paul 1902- *BiDrAPA 89*
Sloane, Peter James 1942- *WhoWor 91*
Sloane, Phyllis Lester *WhoAmA 91*
Sloane, Robert B *BiDrAPA 89*
Sloane, Robert Lindley 1940- *WhoE 91*
Sloane, Robert Malcolm 1933- *WhoAm 90*
Sloane, Stanley Laurie *BioIn 16*
Sloane, Thomas Charles 1922- *WhoAm 90*
Sloane, Thomas O. 1929- *WhoAm 90*
Sloas, Harold Andrew, Jr. 1942- *WhoSSW 91*
Sloat, Barbara Furin 1942- *WhoAmW 91*
Sloat, Richard Joel 1945- *WhoAmA 91*, *WhoE 91*
Sloate, Daniel 1931- *ConAu 32NR*
Slobins, Jon Braden 1954- *WhoE 91*
Slobodien, Howard David 1923- *WhoE 91*, *WhoWor 91*
Slobodin, Alex 1914- *St&PR 91*
Slobodkin, Louis 1903-1975 *AuBYP 90*, *WhoAmA 91N*
Slobodkina, Esphyr 1908- *WhoAmA 91*
Slobodkina, Esphyr 1909- *AuBYP 90*
Slobodow, Jerzy *BiDrAPA 89*
Slobodskaya, Oda 1888-1970 *PenDiMP*
Slochower, Joyce Anne 1950- *WhoAmW 91*
Slocombe, Walter Becker 1941- *WhoAm 90*
Slocum, Barclay 1942- *WhoAm 90*
Slocum, Barry Yale 1943- *WhoE 91*
Slocum, Bill, Jr. 1912-1974 *Ballpl 90*
Slocum, Donald Warren *WhoWor 91*
Slocum, Elizabeth 1947- *WhoAm 90*
Slocum, Frances 1773-1847 *BioAmW*
Slocum, George Sigman 1940- *St&PR 91*, *WhoAm 90*, *WhoSSW 91*
Slocum, Hester B. 1909-1989 *BioIn 16*
Slocum, James L, Jr. 1940- *BiDrAPA 89*
Slocum, Jean B. 1920- *St&PR 91*
Slocum, John *WhNaAH*
Slocum, John Wesley, Jr. 1940- *WhoSSW 91*
Slocum, Jonathan *BiDrAPA 89*
Slocum, Richard D. 1927- *St&PR 91*
Slocum, Rosemarie Raccard 1948- *WhoAmW 91*
Slocumb, Margaret Elizabeth 1908- *WhoAmW 91*
Slodtz, Antoine-Sebastien 1695?-1754 *PenDiDA 89*
Slodtz, Paul-Amboise 1702-1758 *PenDiDA 89*
Slodtz, Rene Michel 1705-1764 *PenDiDA 89*
Slodtz, Sebastien 1655-1726 *PenDiDA 89*
Sloe, John Edward 1953- *St&PR 91*
Sloman, Charles 1808-1870 *OxCPMus*
Sloman, Leon 1929- *BiDrAPA 89*
Slomann, Aage 1891-1970 *EncO&P 3*
Slome, Michael W 1948- *BiDrAPA 89*
Slomka, Thomas W. 1965- *WhoE 91*
Slomoff, Boyd Justin 1948- *BiDrAPA 89*
Slomovitz, Carmi Malachi 1933- *WhoSSW 91*
Slomowitz, Marcia 1949- *BiDrAPA 89*
Slonaker, John R. *BioIn 16*
Slone, R. Wayne *WhoAm 90*
Slone, Sandi 1939- *WhoAmA 91*, *WhoAmW 91*
Slonecker, Charles Edward 1938- *WhoAm 90*
Sloneker, Howard L., Jr. 1919- *St&PR 91*
Sloneker, William Sauer 1953- *St&PR 91*
Slonem, Hunt 1951- *WhoAmA 91*
Sloniker, Mark *NewAgMG*
Slonim, Daphna *BiDrAPA 89*
Slonim, Gilven M. 1913- *WhoSSW 91*
Slonim, Philip Murray 1920- *St&PR 91*
Slonimsky, Nicolas 1894- *BioIn 16*, *IntWWM 90*, *PenDiMP*, *WhoAm 90*
Slonimsky, Sergey 1932- *IntWWM 90*
Slooff, Johannes Louis 1926- *WhoWor 91*
Slook, George F. 1946- *St&PR 91*
Slook, George Francis 1946- *WhoAm 90*
Slorach, Marie 1952- *IntWWM 90*
Slosar, John M. 1938- *St&PR 91*
Slosberg, Mike 1934- *WhoAm 90*
Slosberg, Myles J. 1937- *St&PR 91*
Slosberg, Robert Harvey 1930- *St&PR 91*
Slosburg-Ackerman, Jill 1948- *WhoAmA 91*
Sloshberg, Leah Phyfer 1937- *WhoAm 90*, *WhoAmA 91*, *WhoAmW 91*, *WhoE 91*
Slosman, Everett Lawrence 1935- *WhoE 91*, *WhoWrEP 89*
Slosman, Fred N. 1939- *St&PR 91*
Slosman, Frederick Norman 1939- *WhoSSW 91*
Sloss, Laurence Louis 1913- *WhoAm 90*

Slosson, Annie 1838-1926 *FemiCLE*
Slosson, Annie Trumbull 1838-1926 *WomFie*
Slot, Larry Lee 1947- *WhoE 91*
Slot, Pieter J. 1944- *WhoWor 91*
Slote, Alfred 1926- *AuBYP 90*
Slotemaker, Judy Ann 1941- *WhoWrEP 89*
Sloth, Merete Lisbet 1940- *WhoWor 91*
Slotkin, Donald *WhoAm 90*
Slotkin, Richard Sidney 1942- *WhoAm 90, WhoWrEP 89*
Slotkin, Robert Neil 1940- *BiDrAPA 89*
Slotnick, Barry Ivan *BioIn 16*
Slotnick, Barry Ivan 1939- *WhoAm 90, WhoE 91*
Slotnick, Jules B. 1931- *St&PR 91*
Slotnick, Mortimer H. 1920- *WhoAm 90, WhoAmA 91*
Slotnick, Robert 1929- *St&PR 91*
Slott, Phil *BioIn 16*
Slotte, Peter Johan 1956- *WhoWor 91*
Slotten, LeRoy Ben 1927- *St&PR 91*
Slough, John Edward 1942- *WhoSSW 91*
Slough, Marla Lynn *BiDrAPA 89*
Slough, Robert Allan 1955- *WhoSSW 91*
Slovacek, Bob Leo 1948- *WhoSSW 91*
Slovak, James P *BiDrAPA 89*
Slove, Martin L. 1936- *St&PR 91*
Sloven, David M 1952- *BiDrAPA 89*
Slover, Gail Penniman Turner 1938- *WhoAmW 91*
Sloves, Marvin 1933- *WhoAm 90, WhoE 91*
Slovic, Jack 1956- *WhoSSW 91*
Slovik, Lois Sims 1946- *BiDrAPA 89*
Slovikowski, Gerald Jude 1949- *WhoEmL 91*
Slovin, Bruce 1935- *St&PR 91, WhoAm 90, WhoSSW 91*
Slovinsky, Louis J. 1937- *ODwPR 91, St&PR 91*
Sloviter, Dolores Korman 1932- *WhoAm 90, WhoAmW 91*
Sloviter, Henry Allan 1914- *WhoAm 90*
Slovo, Gillian 1952- *TwCCr&M 91*
Slovo, Shawn *BioIn 16*
Slowacki, Juliusz 1809-1849 *BioIn 16*
Slowey, Brian Aodh 1933- *WhoWor 91*
Slowik, Barbara 1954- *WhoAmW 91*
Slowik, George William *BioIn 16*
Slowik, John R. 1937- *WhoAm 90*
Slowik, Lynn Marie 1958- *WhoE 91*
Slowik, Richard Andrew 1939- *WhoSSW 91, WhoWor 91*
Slowikowski, M. Z. Rygor 1896-1989? *ConAu 129*
Slowikowski, William Henry 1943- *St&PR 91*
Slowinski, Emil John 1922- *WhoWrEP 89*
Sloyan, Gerard Stephen 1919- *WhoAm 90*
Sloyan, James *ConTFT 8*
Sloyan, Stephanie 1918- *WhoAmW 91, WhoE 91*
Sluder, Cheryl Lynn 1960- *WhoAmW 91*
Sludikoff, Stanley Robert 1935- *St&PR 91, WhoAm 90, WhoWrEP 89*
Slugg, Ramsay Hill 1953- *WhoEmL 91*
Sluijter, Frans Willem 1936- *WhoWor 91*
Slusarz, Bernard Francis 1937- *St&PR 91, WhoAm 90, WhoE 91*
Slusher, Clinton 1923- *St&PR 91*
Slusher, Ruth Varner 1945- *WhoAmW 91*
Slusky, Joseph *BiDrAPA 89*
Slusky, Joseph 1942- *WhoAmA 91*
Slusser, Daniel E. 1938- *St&PR 91*
Slusser, Eugene A. 1922- *St&PR 91*
Slusser, Eugene Alvin 1922- *WhoE 91*
Slusser, Mark D. *St&PR 91*
Slusser, William Peter 1929- *WhoE 91*
Sluter, Claus 1340?-1405? *IntDcAA 90*
Slutsky, Eugen 1880-1948 *BioIn 16*
Slutsky, Kenneth Joel 1953- *WhoEmL 91*
Slutsky, Leonard Alan 1945- *WhoEmL 91*
Slutsky, Lorie Ann 1953- *WhoAm 90, WhoAmW 91*
Slutsky, Marc H 1946- *BiDrAPA 89*
Slutsky, Mark Sender 1947- *WhoE 91*
Slutzky, Charles B. 1944- *St&PR 91*
Slutzky, Donald S 1942- *BiDrAPA 89*
Slutzky, Gilbert 1914- *BiDrAPA 89*
Slutzky, Lorence Harley 1946- *WhoEmL 91*
Sluys, Jozef 1936- *IntWWM 90*
Sluzki, Carlos Emilio 1933- *BiDrAPA 89*
Sly and the Family Stone *EncPR&S 89*
Sly, John Eugene 1917- *WhoE 91*
Sly, Ridge Michael 1933- *WhoAm 90*
Sly, Robert F *BiDrAPA 89*
Slyder, Susan Ann 1955- *BiDrAPA 89*
Slydini, Tony *BioIn 16*
Slye, Donald M. 1951- *St&PR 91*
Slye, Leonard Franklin 1912- *BioIn 16*
Slye, Maud 1879-1954 *BioAmW*
Slye, Maude 1879-1954 *BioIn 16*
Slye, William Ronald 1934- *WhoE 91*
Slyunkov, Nikolai Nikitovich 1929- *WhoWor 91*
Smadbeck, Louis 1920- *St&PR 91*
Smadja, Alain 1943- *WhoWor 91*
Smaglick, Paul William 1932- *WhoAm 90*
Smagorinsky, Joseph 1924- *WhoAm 90*
Smaha, Joseph Philip 1938- *WhoSSW 91*
Smahelova, Helena 1910- *EncCoWW*
Smail, Richard Frank 1921- *St&PR 91*
Smaistrla, Jean Ann 1936- *WhoAmW 91, WhoSSW 91*
Smakov, Gennady *BioIn 16*
Smaldone, Edward M. 1956- *IntWWM 90*
Smale, John Gray 1927- *BioIn 16, St&PR 91, WhoAm 90, WhoWor 91*
Smales, Fred Benson 1914- *St&PR 91, WhoAm 90*
Smalis, Gregory C. 1952- *St&PR 91*
Small Faces *OxCPMus*
Small, Albert Harrison 1925- *WhoWor 91*
Small, Ambrose Joseph 1866-1919? *OxCCanT*
Small, Arthur M 1936- *BiDrAPA 89*
Small, Cleveland Leroy, Jr. 1936- *WhoSSW 91*
Small, David 1945- *BioIn 16*
Small, Donald Bridgham 1935- *WhoE 91*
Small, Elisabeth C 1934- *BiDrAPA 89*
Small, Elisabeth Chan 1934- *WhoAmW 91*
Small, Elizabeth Anne 1951- *WhoAmW 91, WhoEmL 91*
Small, Erwin 1924- *WhoAm 90*
Small, Fern Elaine *BiDrAPA 89*
Small, Gary William 1951- *BiDrAPA 89*
Small, George LeRoy 1924- *WhoAm 90*
Small, George M. 1944- *St&PR 91, WhoAm 90*
Small, George Milton 1916- *WhoAm 90*
Small, Harold S. 1945- *WhoEmL 91*
Small, Harriette R. 1930- *IntWWM 90*
Small, Harry A 1922- *BiDrAPA 89*
Small, Harvey C 1927- *BiDrAPA 89*
Small, Henry Gilbert 1941- *WhoAm 90*
Small, Iver F 1923- *BiDrAPA 89*
Small, John Grant, Jr. 1946- *St&PR 91*
Small, Jonathan Andrew 1942- *WhoAm 90*
Small, Joseph Dunnell 1941- *WhoSSW 91*
Small, Joyce G *BiDrAPA 89*
Small, Joyce Graham 1931- *WhoAmW 91*
Small, Kathy Jean 1958- *WhoAmW 91*
Small, Kenneth Lester 1957- *WhoHisp 91*
Small, Lawrence Farnsworth 1925- *WhoAm 90*
Small, Marc James 1950- *WhoEmL 91, WhoSSW 91*
Small, Marshall Lee 1927- *WhoAm 90*
Small, Marvin *BioIn 16*
Small, Melvin 1939- *ConAu 30NR, WhoAm 90*
Small, Michael J. 1957- *ODwPR 91*
Small, Natalie Settimelli 1933- *WhoAmW 91*
Small, Neal 1937- *WhoAmA 91*
Small, Pamela *BioIn 16*
Small, Parker Adams, Jr. 1932- *WhoAm 90*
Small, Peter Everett 1941- *WhoE 91*
Small, Ralph Browne, III 1942- *St&PR 91*
Small, Ralph Edward 1950- *WhoSSW 91*
Small, Ralph Milton 1917- *WhoAm 90*
Small, Rebecca Elaine 1946- *WhoAmW 91*
Small, Richard David 1945- *WhoEmL 91*
Small, Richard Donald 1929- *WhoWor 91*
Small, Robert Coleman, Jr. 1936- *WhoSSW 91*
Small, Robert Howard *BiDrAPA 89*
Small, Robert I. *BioIn 16*
Small, Robert S. 1915- *St&PR 91*
Small, Roland E. 1934- *WhoAm 90*
Small, S. Mouchly *BiDrAPA 89*
Small, Sarah Mae 1923- *WhoAmW 91, WhoE 91, WhoWor 91*
Small, Saul Mouchly 1913- *WhoE 91*
Small, Sylvia Adamson 1952- *WhoSSW 91*
Small, Takita Darnise 1959- *WhoAmW 91*
Small, Walter 1931- *St&PR 91*
Small, Wilfred Thomas 1920- *WhoWor 91*
Small, William Andrew 1914- *WhoAm 90*
Small, William Edwin, Jr. 1937- *WhoAm 90*
Small-Weil, Susan B. 1954- *WhoAmW 91*
Smallacombe, Robert J. 1933- *St&PR 91*
Smallacombe, Robert Joseph 1933- *WhoE 91*
Smallen, Hugh Jerome *BioIn 16*
Smallenberger, James Andrew 1942- *St&PR 91*
Smallenburg, Harry Russell 1942- *WhoWrEP 89*
Smallens, Alexander 1889-1972 *PenDiMP*
Smalley, Alexander 1909-1989 *BioIn 16*
Smalley, Arthur Louis, Jr. 1921- *WhoWor 91*
Smalley, Christopher Joseph 1953- *WhoE 91, WhoWor 91*
Smalley, David Allan 1940- *WhoAmA 91*
Smalley, David Vincent 1935- *WhoAm 90*
Smalley, Denis Arthur 1946- *IntWWM 90*
Smalley, Edith Renee 1960- *WhoAmW 91*
Smalley, Eugene Byron 1926- *WhoAm 90*
Smalley, George Washburn 1833-1916 *BioIn 16*
Smalley, Harold Eugene, Sr. 1921- *WhoAm 90*
Smalley, Janet 1893- *WhoAmA 91N*
Smalley, Katherine Jane *BiDrAPA 89*
Smalley, Kenneth Lee 1930- *St&PR 91*
Smalley, Larry Lee 1937- *WhoSSW 91*
Smalley, Penny Judith 1947- *WhoAmW 91*
Smalley, Philip A., Jr. 1941- *WhoAm 90*
Smalley, Philip Adam, Jr. 1941- *St&PR 91*
Smalley, Randall Steven 1949- *St&PR 91*
Smalley, Richard Errett 1943- *WhoAm 90*
Smalley, Robert Arthur 1923- *St&PR 91*
Smalley, Robert Manning 1925- *WhoAm 90, WhoWor 91*
Smalley, Roger 1943- *IntWWM 90*
Smalley, Roy, Jr. 1952- *Ballpl 90*
Smalley, Roy, Sr. 1926- *Ballpl 90*
Smalley, Scott Anthony 1953- *St&PR 91*
Smalley, Stephen Francis 1941- *WhoAmA 91*
Smalley, Webster Leroy C. 1921- *WhoSSW 91*
Smalligan, Jack Alan 1961- *WhoE 91*
Smallman, Beverley N. 1913- *WhoAm 90*
Smalls, Charlie 1943-1987 *DrBIPA 90*
Smalls, Robert 1839-1915 *BlkAmsC [port]*
Smalls, Sheila Marie *BiDrAPA 89*
Smallwood, Carol 1939- *WhoAmW 91*
Smallwood, Carol Ann 1939- *WhoWrEP 89*
Smallwood, Edmund Warren 1932- *St&PR 91*
Smallwood, Edward Louis 1950- *WhoE 91*
Smallwood, Franklin 1927- *WhoAm 90*
Smallwood, Gerald Stanley 1928- *WhoWor 91*
Smallwood, Glenn Walter, Jr. 1956- *WhoEmL 91, WhoWor 91*
Smallwood, Linda Maudell *BiDrAPA 89*
Smallwood, Norah Evelyn 1909-1984 *DcNaB 1981*
Smallwood, Robert Albian, Jr. 1946- *WhoE 91, WhoEmL 91, WhoWor 91*
Smally, Donald Jay 1922- *WhoAm 90*
Smaltz, Hugh M., II 1929- *St&PR 91*
Smara 1857-1944 *EncCoWW*
Smardon, Richard Clay 1948- *WhoE 91*
Smaridge, Norah 1903- *AuBYP 90*
Smario, Thomas Michael 1950- *WhoWrEP 89*
Smarr, Erwin R 1926- *BiDrAPA 89*
Smarr, Larry Lee 1948- *WhoAm 90*
Smart, Albert Davis 1931?-1989 *ConAu 130*
Smart, Allen Rich, II 1934- *WhoAm 90*
Smart, Ashlynn M. 1950- *WhoAmW 91*
Smart, Charles Rich 1926- *WhoAm 90*
Smart, Clifton Murray, Jr. 1933- *WhoAm 90*
Smart, Craig Stephen *BiDrAPA 89*
Smart, David Louis 1941- *WhoAm 90*
Smart, Dorothy Caroline *WhoAmW 91*
Smart, Elizabeth 1913-1986 *FemiCLE*
Smart, Gail *ODwPR 91*
Smart, Gary Lee 1953- *WhoEmL 91*
Smart, George 1776-1867 *PenDiMP*
Smart, George MacArthur 1945- *St&PR 91*
Smart, Gordon Musgrove 1929- *St&PR 91*
Smart, Harry Baird 1924- *St&PR 91, WhoAm 90*
Smart, Henry 1778-1823 *PenDiMP*
Smart, Henry 1813-1879 *PenDiMP*
Smart, Ian E.L. 1945- *St&PR 91*
Smart, Jackson W., Jr. 1930- *St&PR 91*
Smart, Jackson Wyman, Jr. 1930- *WhoAm 90*
Smart, Jacob Edward 1909- *WhoAm 90*
Smart, James D. 1932- *St&PR 91*
Smart, Jean *BioIn 16*
Smart, John Edwin 1917- *St&PR 91*
Smart, John L. *ODwPR 91*
Smart, John R. *St&PR 91*
Smart, John Robert 1942- *WhoAm 90*
Smart, L. Edwin 1923- *St&PR 91*
Smart, Larry Regan 1933- *WhoWor 91*
Smart, Louis Edwin 1923- *WhoAm 90*
Smart, Marriott Wieckhoff 1935- *WhoAmW 91*
Smart, Mary-Leigh 1917- *WhoAmA 91*
Smart, Mary-Leigh Call 1917- *WhoAmW 91, WhoE 91, WhoWor 91*
Smart, Melissa Bedor 1953- *WhoAmW 91*
Smart, Ninian 1927- *ConAu 30NR*
Smart, Paul M. 1929- *WhoAm 90*
Smart, Stephen Bruce, Jr. 1923- *WhoAm 90*
Smart, Steven Paul 1954- *St&PR 91*
Smart, Steven Tracy 1958- *WhoEmL 91*
Smart, William Buckwalter 1922- *WhoAm 90*
Smart, William Edward, Jr. 1933- *WhoWrEP 89*
Smart, William Robertson 1920- *St&PR 91*
Smart Sanchez, Barbara Ann 1948- *WhoHisp 91*
Smason, Edmund A. 1929- *ODwPR 91*
Smathers, Ben *NewYTBS 90*
Smathers, Frank, Jr. 1909- *WhoAm 90*
Smathers, James Burton 1935- *WhoAm 90*
Smathers, Scott Michael 1952- *WhoEmL 91*
Smatt, Karin *BioIn 16*
Smayling, Lyda Mozella 1923- *WhoAmW 91*
Smead, Mrs. *EncO&P 3*
Smead, Eric Michael 1947- *WhoSSW 91*
Smeal, Eleanor Cutri 1939- *WhoAm 90, WhoAmW 91*
Smeal, Frank P. 1918- *St&PR 91*
Smeallie, Peter Henry 1952- *WhoE 91*
Smeaton, Doug 1949- *St&PR 91*
Smeaton, Melvin Douglas 1949- *WhoAm 90*
Smedberg, Staffan Gunnar 1941- *WhoWor 91*
Smedegaard, Norman H. 1916- *WhoAm 90*
Smedegard, James Kenneth *BiDrAPA 89*
Smeding, Alie Van Wijhe- 1890-1938 *EncCoWW*
Smedira, Nicholas A. 1933- *St&PR 91*
Smedley, Agnes 1890-1950 *BioIn 16*
Smedley, Agnes 1892-1950 *EncAL, FemiCLE*
Smedley, Agnes 1894-1950 *BioAmW*
Smedley, Alfred B. *ODwPR 91*
Smedley, Bernard R. 1936- *St&PR 91*
Smedley, Bernard Ronald 1936- *WhoAm 90*
Smedley, Constance 1881-1941 *FemiCLE*
Smedley, Geoffrey 1927- *WhoAmA 91*
Smedley, Harold A. 1935- *St&PR 91*
Smedley, Menella Bute 1820-1877 *FemiCLE*
Smedley, Raymond William 1940- *St&PR 91*
Smedley, Robert Richard 1930- *St&PR 91*
Smedley, Will Larymore 1871- *WhoAmA 91N*
Smedman, Leif 1939- *WhoAm 90*
Smedresman, Ingeborg Freundlich 1911- *WhoAmW 91*
Smeds, Edward William 1936- *St&PR 91, WhoAm 90*
Smeds, Jarl-Erik Johannes 1945- *WhoWor 91*
Smedslund, Jan 1929- *WhoWor 91*
Smeenk, Henry 1929- *St&PR 91*
Smeeton, Donald Dean 1946- *WhoWor 91*
Smeeton, Miles 1906-1988 *BioIn 16*
Smeets, Ronald M *BiDrAPA 89*
Smejkal, Bohumil *PenDiMP*
Smejkal, Joseph Frank 1921- *St&PR 91*
Smelick, Robert Malcolm 1942- *St&PR 91, WhoWor 91*
Smelker, Edwin W *BiDrAPA 89*
Smelkinson, Lynn Marie 1955- *WhoAmW 91, WhoEmL 91*
Smelkinson, Robert N. 1929- *St&PR 91*
Smellie, Kingsley Bryce 1897-1987 *BioIn 16*
Smelser, Emmett K. 1942- *St&PR 91*
Smelser, Neil Joseph 1930- *WhoAm 90, WhoWrEP 89*
Smelser, Rebecca Forman 1961- *WhoAmW 91*
Smelson, I Harold *BiDrAPA 89*
Smelt, Ronald 1913- *WhoAm 90*
Smeltzer, David P. 1958- *St&PR 91*
Smeltzer, Debra Jean 1953- *WhoSSW 91*
Smeltzer, Mary Susan 1941- *IntWWM 90*
Smeltzer, Norman Harold 1907- *WhoAm 90*
Smeltzer, Percy J. 1918- *St&PR 91*
Smeltzer, Walter William 1924- *WhoAm 90*
Smendzianka, Regina 1924- *IntWWM 90*
Smeraldi, Florence G. Stark 1938- *WhoWrEP 89*
Smeraski, Philip John 1953- *BiDrAPA 89*
Smerge, Raymond Gene 1944- *St&PR 91*
Smerlas, Donna 1949- *WhoAmW 91*
Smerlas, Fred *BioIn 16*
Smerling, David 1933- *St&PR 91*
Smerling, Julian M. 1928- *St&PR 91*
Smerling, Julian Melvin 1928- *WhoAm 90*
Smernoff, Richard Louis 1941- *WhoAm 90*
Smestad, Russell Ray 1952- *St&PR 91*
Smetacek, Vaclav 1906-1984 *PenDiMP*
Smetana Quartet *PenDiMP*
Smetana, Bedrich 1824-1884 *PenDiMP A, WorAlBi*
Smetanin, Michael 1958- *IntWWM 90*
Smetek, John Thomas *BioIn 16*
Smethers, Lyle E. 1942- *St&PR 91*
Smethurst, Edward William, Jr. 1930- *WhoAm 90*
Smethurst, Robert Guy 1929- *WhoAm 90*
Smethurst, William J. 1946- *St&PR 91*
Smets, Loren G. *BioIn 16*
Smette, Darryl G. 1947- *St&PR 91*
Smetzer, Michael Bernie 1948- *WhoWrEP 89*
Smeyne, Fred Gary 1940- *St&PR 91*

Smialek, Robert Louis 1948- *St&PR 91*
Smialek, William 1952- *IntWWM 90*
Smibert, John 1688-1751 *EncCRAm, IntDcAA 90*
Smick, Annette M *BiDrAPA 89*
Smid, Bruno F. 1926- *St&PR 91*
Smiddy, Charles J. 1926- *St&PR 91*
Smiddy, Joseph Charles 1920- *WhoAm 90*
Smidebush, James C. 1941- *ODwPR 91*
Smidovich, Petr Germogenovich 1874-1935 *BioIn 16*
Smidt, Fred August, Jr. 1932- *WhoE 91*
Smidt, Helio *BioIn 16, NewYTBS 90*
Smidt, Seymour 1928- *WhoAm 90*
Smietanka, John Allen 1941- *WhoAm 90*
Smiga, Brian George 1954- *WhoE 91*
Smigiel, Nicole *BioIn 16*
Smigiel, Travis Christian *BioIn 16*
Smigocki, Stephen Vincent 1942- *WhoAmA 91*
Smih, Gary L. 1945- *St&PR 91*
Smil, Vaclav 1943- *ConAu 30NR*
Smiles, Samuel 1812-1904 *BioIn 16*
Smiley, Albert Keith 1828-1912 *WhNaAH*
Smiley, Albert Keith 1944- *WhoE 91*
Smiley, Billy *NewAgMG*
Smiley, D. E. *WhoAm 90*
Smiley, Daniel *BioIn 16*
Smiley, David Bruce 1942- *WhoWor 91*
Smiley, David Houston 1945- *WhoSSW 91*
Smiley, Glenn *BioIn 16*
Smiley, Irwin 1928- *WhoE 91*
Smiley, Jane 1949- *BioIn 16, ConAu 30NR, CurBio 90 [port]*
Smiley, Jane Graves 1949- *WhoAm 90*
Smiley, Jane Towler 1925- *WhoAmW 91*
Smiley, John 1965- *Ballpl 90*
Smiley, Joseph Elbert, Jr. 1922- *WhoSSW 91, WhoWor 91*
Smiley, Karen 1947- *WhoAmA 91*
Smiley, Karen Jane 1961- *WhoAmW 91, WhoEmL 91*
Smiley, Kathlyn Elaine 1958- *WhoEmL 91*
Smiley, Marilynn Jean 1932- *IntWWM 90, WhoAm 90*
Smiley, Mark David 1957- *WhoSSW 91*
Smiley, Pril 1943- *WhoAm 90*
Smiley, Reed J. 1946- *St&PR 91*
Smiley, Robert Rennslaer, III 1933- *WhoWor 91*
Smiley, Robert William 1919- *WhoAm 90*
Smiley, Robert William, Jr. 1943- *WhoAm 90*
Smiley, Robert Wilson 1921- *St&PR 91*
Smiley, Ronald Michael 1949- *WhoE 91, WhoWor 91*
Smiley, Stu *BioIn 16*
Smiley, Terah Leroy 1914- *WhoAm 90, WhoWrEP 89*
Smiley, Teresa Marlene 1951- *WhoHisp 91*
Smiley, Theresa Nix 1961- *ODwPR 91*
Smiley, Virginia Kester 1923- *WhoWrEP 89*
Smiley, Walter V. *BioIn 16*
Smiley, Walter V. 1938- *WhoAm 90*
Smilga, Ivar Tenisovich 1892-1938? *BioIn 16*
Smilie, Mollie Kay Williams 1949- *WhoAmW 91, WhoWor 91*
Smillie, Chas. M., III 1934- *St&PR 91*
Smillie, Helen V. *St&PR 91N*
Smillie, Peter *BioIn 16*
Smillie, Thomson John 1942- *IntWWM 90, WhoSSW 91*
Smilovits, Josef *PenDiMP*
Smilow, Stanford 1929- *WhoE 91*
Smins *EncCoWW*
Smiraglia, Richard Paul 1952- *IntWWM 90*
Smirl, Mitzi Lou 1961- *WhoAmW 91*
Smirni, Allan D. 1939- *St&PR 91*
Smirni, Allan Desmond 1939- *WhoAm 90*
Smirnoff, Joel *PenDiMP*
Smirnoff, Susan S. 1952- *ODwPR 91*
Smirnoff, Victor N. 1919- *BiDrAPA 89*
Smirnoff, Yakov *BioIn 16*
Smirnoff, Yakov 1951- *WorAlBi*
Smirnov, Dmitry 1882-1944 *PenDiMP*
Smirnov, Georgy *BioIn 16*
Smirnov, Ivan Nikitich 1881-1936 *BioIn 16*
Smiszko, Stephan Emil 1929- *St&PR 91*
Smit, Elmor *BiDrAPA 89*
Smit, Hans 1927- *WhoE 91*
Smit, Jacobus Wilhelmus 1930- *WhoAm 90*
Smith, A. Anthes 1920- *St&PR 91*
Smith, A O *EncABHB 4*
Smith, A. Robert 1925- *WhoWrEP 89*
Smith, Abigail Adams 1765-1813 *BioAmW*
Smith, Abram Wentworth 1843-1919 *AmLegL*
Smith, Ada 1894-1984 *OxCPMus*
Smith, Ada L. 1945- *WhoAmW 91, WhoE 91*
Smith, Adam *ConAu 31NR*
Smith, Adam 1723-1790 *BioIn 16, DcLB 104 [port], WorAlBi*
Smith, Adam 1930- *St&PR 91, WhoAm 90*
Smith, Adelaide R *BiDrAPA 89*
Smith, Adrian Devaun 1944- *WhoAm 90*
Smith, Agnes *AuBYP 90, WhoAm 90*
Smith, Agnes Monroe 1920- *WhoAmW 91*
Smith, Al 1907-1977 *Ballpl 90*
Smith, Al 1928- *Ballpl 90, BioIn 16*
Smith, Alan 1917- *BioIn 16*
Smith, Alan F. 1939- *St&PR 91*
Smith, Alan Frederick 1929- *WhoAm 90*
Smith, Alan Harvey 1920- *WhoAm 90, WhoWrEP 89*
Smith, Alan L. *ODwPR 91*
Smith, Alan McKinley 1937- *WhoAm 90*
Smith, Albert Aldous 1944- *St&PR 91*
Smith, Albert Aloysius, Jr. 1935- *WhoAm 90*
Smith, Albert Barnes, Jr. 1915- *WhoAm 90*
Smith, Albert Carl 1934- *WhoSSW 91*
Smith, Albert Charles 1906- *WhoAm 90*
Smith, Albert Delmont 1886-1962 *WhoAmA 91N*
Smith, Albert E 1929- *WhoAmA 91*
Smith, Albert E. 1932- *WhoAm 90*
Smith, Albert Edward 1935- *St&PR 91*
Smith, Albert K. 1925- *St&PR 91*
Smith, Alex Eugene 1939- *WhoSSW 91*
Smith, Alexander 1819?-1892 *DcCanB 12*
Smith, Alexander Forbes 1929- *St&PR 91*
Smith, Alexander Forbes, III 1929- *WhoAm 90*
Smith, Alexander Goudy 1919- *WhoAm 90, WhoSSW 91, WhoWor 91*
Smith, Alexander John Court 1934- *WhoAm 90, WhoE 91*
Smith, Alexander Mortimer 1818-1895 *DcCanB 12*
Smith, Alexander Wyly, Jr. 1923- *WhoAm 90*
Smith, Alexis 1921- *WhoAm 90, WorAlBi*
Smith, Alexis 1949- *WhoAmA 91*
Smith, Alfred E. 1873-1944 *WorAlBi*
Smith, Alfred Emanuel 1873-1944 *BioIn 16*
Smith, Alfred Goud 1921- *WhoAm 90*
Smith, Alfred P. 1954- *St&PR 91*
Smith, Alice Elizabeth Swilley 1948- *WhoAmW 91*
Smith, Alice Jean 1934- *WhoWrEP 89*
Smith, Alison Jann Docos 1950- *WhoAmW 91*
Smith, Allan Frederick 1911- *WhoAm 90*
Smith, Allan Laird 1937- *WhoSSW 91*
Smith, Allen Anderson 1939- *WhoSSW 91*
Smith, Allen Elmer 1932- *WhoAm 90*
Smith, Allen Harold 1925- *WhoE 91, WhoWor 91*
Smith, Allen Marion 1929- *St&PR 91*
Smith, Allen O. 1931- *St&PR 91*
Smith, Allen W. 1928- *St&PR 91*
Smith, Allie Maitland 1934- *WhoAm 90*
Smith, Allison 1969- *WorAlBi*
Smith, Alson George 1952- *St&PR 91*
Smith, Alson Jesse 1908-1965 *EncO&P 3*
Smith, Alvin A. 1938- *St&PR 91*
Smith, Amanda Berry 1837-1915 *BioAmW*
Smith, Amanda Joan Mackay 1940- *WhoSSW 91*
Smith, Amos Brittain, III 1944- *WhoAm 90*
Smith, Andre 1880-1959 *WhoAmA 91N*
Smith, Andrea Pedersen 1944- *WhoAmW 91*
Smith, Andrew Alfred, Jr. 1947- *WhoE 91*
Smith, Andrew Brian 1955- *IntWWM 90*
Smith, Andrew Leonard 1949- *WhoWor 91*
Smith, Andrew Porter 1955- *WhoAm 90, WhoWor 91*
Smith, Andrew V. 1924- *St&PR 91*
Smith, Andrew Vaughn 1924- *WhoAm 90*
Smith, Angus Frank 1941- *St&PR 91*
Smith, Anita Torres 1928- *WhoAmW 91*
Smith, Ann Elizabeth 1957- *WhoAmW 91*
Smith, Ann Marie 1960- *WhoAmW 91*
Smith, Ann Y 1950- *WhoAmA 91*
Smith, Anna 1756-1780 *FemiCLE*
Smith, Anne Bowman 1934- *WhoAmW 91*
Smith, Anne L 1958- *WhoAmA 91*
Smith, Anne Marie 1934- *WhoAmW 91*
Smith, Anne Mollegan *BioIn 16*
Smith, Anne Mollegen *WhoWrEP 89*
Smith, Anne Mollegen 1940- *WhoAm 90, WhoAmW 91*
Smith, Annette Huggins 1942- *WhoSSW 91*
Smith, Annie *WhoWrEP 89*
Smith, Anthony 1938- *BioIn 16*
Smith, Anthony Wayne *WhoAm 90, WhoE 91*
Smith, Apollo Milton Olin 1911- *WhoAm 90*
Smith, Apsley *PenDiDA 89*
Smith, Arlene J *BiDrAPA 89*
Smith, Artemis 1934- *WhoE 91*
Smith, Arthur 1917-1982 *BioIn 16*
Smith, Arthur 1921- *WhoAm 90*
Smith, Arthur E. *BioIn 16*
Smith, Arthur Hall 1929- *WhoAmA 91*
Smith, Arthur J. 1938- *St&PR 91*
Smith, Arthur John Stewart 1938- *WhoAm 90*
Smith, Arthur Kittredge, Jr. 1937- *WhoAm 90*
Smith, Arthur Ronald 1941- *St&PR 91*
Smith, Aubrey C *BiDrAPA 89*
Smith, Augustus Ledyard 1901-1985 *BioIn 16*
Smith, B J 1931- *WhoAmA 91*
Smith, Baker Armstrong 1947- *WhoAm 90*
Smith, Ballard 1821-1866 *AmLegL*
Smith, Barbara *BioIn 16*
Smith, Barbara Angela 1938- *WhoAmW 91*
Smith, Barbara Ann 1935- *WhoAmW 91*
Smith, Barbara Anne 1941- *WhoAmW 91, WhoE 91*
Smith, Barbara Barnard 1920- *WhoAm 90*
Smith, Barbara D. 1943- *WhoAmW 91*
Smith, Barbara Dail 1949- *WhoEmL 91*
Smith, Barbara Gail 1957- *WhoAmW 91, WhoWor 91*
Smith, Barbara Gallaer 1961- *WhoAmW 91*
Smith, Barbara Gosline 1909- *EncO&P 3*
Smith, Barbara Herrnstein 1932- *WhoWrEP 89*
Smith, Barbara Hollandsworth *BiDrAPA 89*
Smith, Barbara Jeanne 1939- *WhoAmW 91*
Smith, Barbara Joyce 1954- *WhoAmW 91, WhoWor 91*
Smith, Barbara Lee 1938- *WhoAmA 91*
Smith, Barbara M. *ODwPR 91*
Smith, Barbara Neff 1908-1977 *WhoAmA 91N*
Smith, Barbara Roderick 1948- *WhoAmW 91*
Smith, Barbara Turner 1931- *WhoAmA 91*
Smith, Barby Twelvetrees 1941- *St&PR 91*
Smith, Barnard Elliot 1926- *WhoAm 90*
Smith, Barry Alan 1945- *WhoSSW 91*
Smith, Barry David 1938- *WhoAm 90, WhoE 91*
Smith, Barry Hamilton 1943- *WhoWor 91*
Smith, Barton Douglas 1947- *St&PR 91*
Smith, Benita Rae 1934- *WhoWor 91*
Smith, Benjamin *PenDiDA 89*
Smith, Benjamin 1793-1850 *PenDiDA 89*
Smith, Benjamin A. 1943- *St&PR 91*
Smith, Benjamin F. 1922- *St&PR 91*
Smith, Bernard Brussel- 1914- *BioIn 16*
Smith, Bernice Driskell 1916- *WhoAmW 91*
Smith, Bernita Louise 1952- *WhoWrEP 89*
Smith, Bert Kruger 1915- *WhoAmW 91*
Smith, Bertie Reece 1913- *WhoWrEP 89*
Smith, Beryl K *WhoAmA 91*
Smith, Bessie *BioIn 16*
Smith, Bessie 1894-1937 *BioAmW, DrBlPA 90, OxCPMus, WorAlBi*
Smith, Beth Roberta 1959- *WhoAmW 91*
Smith, Betsey Clark 1957- *WhoAmW 91*
Smith, Betsy Covington 1937- *BioIn 16*
Smith, Betsy Keiser 1960- *WhoSSW 91*
Smith, Betty 1896-1972 *BioIn 16, FemiCLE*
Smith, Betty 1904-1972 *NotWoAT*
Smith, Betty 1906- *WorAlBi*
Smith, Betty Faye 1930- *WhoAm 90*
Smith, Betty Loretta 1937- *WhoAmW 91, WhoWor 91*
Smith, Betty Lou M *BiDrAPA 89*
Smith, Betty Louise 1940- *St&PR 91*
Smith, Billie M. 1933- *WhoAm 90*
Smith, Billie Nell Bryson 1933- *WhoAmW 91*
Smith, Billy 1953- *Ballpl 90*
Smith, Blake, Jr. 1912- *St&PR 91*
Smith, Bob 1898-1987 *Ballpl 90*
Smith, Bob 1917- *BioIn 16, WorAlBi*
Smith, Bob 1931- *Ballpl 90*
Smith, Bobby Gene 1934- *Ballpl 90*
Smith, Bonnie Beatrice 1948- *WhoAmW 91*
Smith, Bonnie Lou 1944- *WhoE 91*
Smith, Boylston D 1921- *BiDrAPA 89*
Smith, Bradford 1901-1988 *BioIn 16*
Smith, Bradford, III 1937- *St&PR 91*
Smith, Brenda Thompson 1944- *WhoSSW 91*
Smith, Brian *BioIn 16*
Smith, Brian C 1938- *ConAu 30NR*
Smith, Brian Christopher 1937- *WhoWor 91*
Smith, Brian Douglas 1945- *St&PR 91*
Smith, Brian Eugene 1957- *St&PR 91*
Smith, Brian J. 1944- *WhoAm 90*
Smith, Brian R. 1939- *ConAu 129*
Smith, Brian Richard 1952- *WhoEmL 91*
Smith, Brian William 1947- *WhoE 91, WhoEmL 91, WhoWor 91*
Smith, Brice Reynolds, Jr. *WhoAm 90*
Smith, Bridget Ann 1949- *WhoWrEP 89*
Smith, Bromley Keables, Jr. 1946- *WhoE 91*
Smith, Bruce *BioIn 16*
Smith, Bruce Alfred 1943- *St&PR 91*
Smith, Bruce Andrew 1940- *WhoWor 91*
Smith, Bruce D. *BioIn 16*
Smith, Bruce D. 1943- *WhoAm 90*
Smith, Bruce David 1946- *WhoAm 90*
Smith, Bruce Leonard 1946- *St&PR 91*
Smith, Bruce N. 1930- *St&PR 91*
Smith, Bruce Trago 1943- *BiDrAPA 89*
Smith, Bruce W. 1946- *St&PR 91*
Smith, Bryan E. 1897-1989 *BioIn 16*
Smith, Bryan W. 1948- *St&PR 91*
Smith, Bryn 1955- *Ballpl 90*
Smith, Bubba 1948- *DrBlPA 90*
Smith, Bunnie Othanel 1903- *WhoAm 90*
Smith, Buren Steve 1934- *BiDrAPA 89*
Smith, Byron Caplese 1908- *WhoAm 90*
Smith, Byron Owen 1916- *WhoAm 90*
Smith, C. Alan 1944- *St&PR 91*
Smith, C. Aubrey 1863-1948 *WorAlBi*
Smith, C Conway 1922- *BiDrAPA 89*
Smith, C. Earl 1922-1987 *BioIn 16*
Smith, C. Kenneth 1918- *WhoAm 90*
Smith, C.L. 1938- *St&PR 91*
Smith, C. LeMoyne 1934- *St&PR 91, WhoAm 90*
Smith, C. Paul 1951- *WhoSSW 91*
Smith, C. R. *BioIn 16*
Smith, C R 1899-1990 *CurBio 90N*
Smith, C. Ray *BioIn 16*
Smith, C. Ray 1929- *WhoWrEP 89*
Smith, C. Thomas, Jr. 1938- *WhoAm 90*
Smith, C. Wendell 1908- *St&PR 91*
Smith, Caesar *TwCCr&M 91*
Smith, Cal Joseph 1955- *WhoE 91*
Smith, Caleb Blood 1808-1864 *BiDrUSE 89*
Smith, Calvert H. *WhoAm 90*
Smith, Calvin *BioIn 16*
Smith, Calvin Bruce 1940- *WhoAm 90*
Smith, Calvin C. 1920- *St&PR 91*
Smith, Calvin J. *St&PR 91*
Smith, Carl A. 1920-1990 *BioIn 16*
Smith, Carl E. 1948- *St&PR 91*
Smith, Carl O. 1942- *St&PR 91*
Smith, Carl Richard 1933- *WhoAm 90*
Smith, Carl Roy 1927- *BiDrAPA 89*
Smith, Carl Walter, Jr. 1927- *WhoSSW 91*
Smith, Carman Sue Walker 1941- *WhoSSW 91*
Smith, Carol Ann 1941- *WhoAm 90*
Smith, Carol Ann 1949- *WhoAmW 91*
Smith, Carol Ann 1951- *WhoAmW 91, WhoEmL 91*
Smith, Carol Jean 1947- *WhoEmL 91*
Smith, Carol Sturm 1938- *WhoWrEP 89*
Smith, Carol Taylor 1935- *WhoAmW 91*
Smith, Carole J. 1949- *St&PR 91*
Smith, Carole Jean 1949- *WhoAmW 91*
Smith, Carolyn Jean *WhoAmW 91*
Smith, Carolyn Jean 1950- *WhoAmW 91*
Smith, Carolyn Louise 1960- *WhoAmW 91*
Smith, Carolyn Sue 1943- *WhoAmW 91*
Smith, Carolyn Sue 1944- *WhoAmW 91*
Smith, Cassandra Lynn 1947- *WhoAmW 91*
Smith, Catherine *FemiCLE*
Smith, Catherine Hamilton 1953- *WhoAmW 91*
Smith, Catherine Susan 1951- *WhoE 91*
Smith, Catherine W R 1912- *BiDrAPA 89*
Smith, Catherine Weinrich 1953- *St&PR 91*
Smith, Catherine Yore 1944- *WhoWrEP 89*
Smith, Cece 1944- *WhoAm 90*
Smith, Cecil Alden 1910-1984 *WhoAmA 91N*
Smith, Cedric M. *BiDrAPA 89*
Smith, Celia Marie 1944- *WhoAmW 91*
Smith, Celianne Marie 1953- *WhoAmW 91*
Smith, Charles *BioIn 16*
Smith, Charles 1947- *WhoWrEP 89*
Smith, Charles A. 1908- *St&PR 91*
Smith, Charles Alphonso 1909- *WhoAm 90*
Smith, Charles B 1923- *BiDrAPA 89*
Smith, Charles Blake 1962- *WhoSSW 91*
Smith, Charles C., Jr. 1948- *WhoSSW 91*
Smith, Charles Clyde 1926- *St&PR 91*
Smith, Charles E 1917- *BiDrAPA 89*
Smith, Charles Edward 1939- *WhoSSW 91*
Smith, Charles Edward 1940- *WhoSSW 91*
Smith, Charles Emory 1842-1908 *BiDrUSE 89, BioIn 16*
Smith, Charles F. 1940- *St&PR 91*
Smith, Charles Francis 1932- *St&PR 91*
Smith, Charles Gordon, Jr. 1942- *St&PR 91*
Smith, Charles-Gustave 1826-1896 *DcCanB 12*
Smith, Charles Haddon 1926- *WhoAm 90*
Smith, Charles Hayden 1933- *St&PR 91*
Smith, Charles Henry, Jr. 1920- *St&PR 91, WhoAm 90*

Smith, Charles Isaac 1931- *WhoAm 90*
Smith, Charles Jeremiah *EncABHB 4*
Smith, Charles Joe, Sr. 1951- *WhoEmL 91, WhoSSW 91*
Smith, Charles Kent *BiDrAPA 89*
Smith, Charles Kent 1938- *WhoAm 90*
Smith, Charles L., Jr. 1928- *St&PR 91*
Smith, Charles Madison 1948- *WhoSSW 91*
Smith, Charles Oliver 1920- *WhoAm 90*
Smith, Charles Owen, Jr. 1921- *St&PR 91*
Smith, Charles Paul 1926- *WhoAm 90*
Smith, Charles Philip 1926- *WhoAm 90*
Smith, Charles Philip 1932- *WhoAm 90*
Smith, Charles Rodney *BiDrAPA 89*
Smith, Charles Scott 1960- *WhoEmL 91*
Smith, Charles Thomas 1914- *WhoAm 90*
Smith, Charles W. *St&PR 91N*
Smith, Charles Whitley 1913- *WhoAm 90*
Smith, Charles William 1934- *WhoAm 90*
Smith, Charles Wilson, Jr. 1949- *WhoSSW 91*
Smith, Charley 1937- *Ballpl 90*
Smith, Charlie 1880-1929 *Ballpl 90*
Smith, Charlotte *BioIn 16*
Smith, Charlotte 1749-1806 *BioIn 16, FemiCLE*
Smith, Charlotte Duncan 1938- *WhoAmW 91*
Smith, Charlotte Elizabeth 1959- *WhoE 91*
Smith, Charlotte Reed 1921- *IntWWM 90, WhoAmW 91*
Smith, Charlotte Therese Wertz 1959- *WhoAmW 91*
Smith, Cheryl Lynn 1954- *WhoSSW 91*
Smith, Cheryl Lynn 1958- *WhoAmW 91*
Smith, Cheryl S. 1949- *WhoWrEP 89*
Smith, Chester *BioIn 16*
Smith, Chester 1930- *WhoWor 91*
Smith, Chester Leo 1922- *WhoAm 90, WhoWrEP 89*
Smith, Chet Joseph 1946- *WhoE 91*
Smith, Chino 1903-1932 *Ballpl 90*
Smith, Chris 1879-1949 *BioIn 16, OxCPMus*
Smith, Christina Ann 1947- *WhoWrEP 89*
Smith, Christine 1957- *BiDrAPA 89*
Smith, Christine Cosculleula 1954- *WhoSSW 91*
Smith, Christine Gay 1963- *WhoAmW 91*
Smith, Christopher Allan 1933- *WhoE 91*
Smith, Christopher Henry 1953- *WhoAm 90, WhoE 91*
Smith, Christopher Joe 1955- *St&PR 91*
Smith, Cindy Jean *BiDrAPA 89*
Smith, Claiborne T 1924- *BiDrAPA 89*
Smith, Claire M 1928- *BiDrAPA 89*
Smith, Clara 1895-1935 *BioIn 16*
Smith, Clara F. 1912- *WhoAmW 91*
Smith, Clara May Freeman 1912- *WhoWrEP 89*
Smith, Clare *BioIn 16*
Smith, Clarence Lavett 1927- *WhoAm 90*
Smith, Clark Ellis 1954- *BiDrAPA 89*
Smith, Claude Allen *WhoAm 90*
Smith, Claude D. 1925- *St&PR 91*
Smith, Claude Earle 1922-1987 *BioIn 16*
Smith, Claude T. 1932-1987 *BioIn 16*
Smith, Clement A. 1901-1988 *BioIn 16*
Smith, Cleveland John Cresswell 1963- *WhoSSW 91*
Smith, Clifford Vaughn, Jr. 1931- *WhoAm 90*
Smith, Clodus Ray 1928- *WhoAm 90*
Smith, Clyde 1932- *WhoAmA 91*
Smith, Clyde Gaylon 1945- *WhoWor 91*
Smith, Colin M 1927- *BiDrAPA 89*
Smith, Constance Babington *ConAu 131*
Smith, Constance Crouch 1946- *WhoAmW 91*
Smith, Cordwainer 1913-1966 *WorAlBi*
Smith, Corenne *BioIn 16*
Smith, Corinne Roth 1945- *WhoEmL 91*
Smith, Corlies Morgan 1929- *WhoAm 90*
Smith, Cornelius C., Jr. 1941- *St&PR 91, WhoAm 90*
Smith, Courtland Clement, Jr. 1927- *WhoE 91*
Smith, Cozee Lynn 1949- *WhoSSW 91*
Smith, Craig A 1934- *BiDrAPA 89*
Smith, Craig R. 1940- *St&PR 91*
Smith, Craig Richards 1940- *WhoAm 90*
Smith, Cullen 1925- *WhoAm 90*
Smith, Curtis Johnston 1947- *WhoAm 90*
Smith, Curtis Lee 1901- *St&PR 91*
Smith, Cynthia Lafreniere 1958- *WhoAmW 91*
Smith, Cynthia Lynn 1958- *WhoAmW 91*
Smith, Cynthia Sims 1958- *WhoSSW 91*
Smith, Cyril 1909-1974 *PenDiMP*
Smith, Cyril James 1930- *St&PR 91, WhoAm 90*
Smith, Cyrus Rowlett *BioIn 16*
Smith, Cyrus Rowlett 1899- *BiDrUSE 89*
Smith, Cyrus Rowlett 1899-1990 *NewYTBS 90*
Smith, D. Lamar 1936- *St&PR 91*
Smith, D. Michael 1938- *St&PR 91*
Smith, D. Richard 1930- *WhoAm 90*
Smith, DaCosta, Jr. 1917- *WhoAm 90*
Smith, Dale A. 1931- *WhoAm 90*
Smith, Dale B. 1944- *St&PR 91, WhoAm 90*
Smith, Dale C. 1958- *St&PR 91*
Smith, Dallas *NewAgMG*
Smith, Dana Kay 1959- *WhoAmW 91*
Smith, Daniel 1939- *IntWWM 90*
Smith, Daniel R. 1934- *St&PR 91, WhoAm 90*
Smith, Darden *BioIn 16, WhoNeCM [port]*
Smith, Darell Jene *BiDrAPA 89*
Smith, Darlene 1949- *WhoAmW 91*
Smith, Darlene 1951- *WhoSSW 91*
Smith, Darrel Ejo 1950- *St&PR 91*
Smith, Darrell Wayne 1937- *WhoWor 91*
Smith, Darwin E. *BioIn 16*
Smith, Darwin Eatna 1926- *St&PR 91, WhoAm 90, WhoSSW 91*
Smith, Daryl D. 1940- *St&PR 91*
Smith, Dasil C 1918- *BiDrAPA 89*
Smith, Datus Clifford, Jr. 1907- *WhoAm 90*
Smith, Dave 1942- *WorAu 1980 [port]*
Smith, Dave 1955- *Ballpl 90*
Smith, David *PenDiMP*
Smith, David 1906-1965 *IntDcAA 90, WhoAmA 91N, WorAlBi*
Smith, David Albert 1952- *BiDrAPA 89, WhoSSW 91*
Smith, David Alden 1956- *WhoEmL 91*
Smith, David Allen 1933- *WhoE 91*
Smith, David Arthur 1949- *WhoE 91*
Smith, David Brookman 1951- *WhoAm 90*
Smith, David Burnell 1941- *WhoWor 91*
Smith, David Byron 1936- *St&PR 91*
Smith, David Callaway 1941- *WhoAm 90*
Smith, David Charles *WhoWrEP 89*
Smith, David Charles 1944- *St&PR 91*
Smith, David Christopher 1947- *WhoE 91*
Smith, David Claiborne 1953- *WhoSSW 91*
Smith, David Clark 1937- *WhoAm 90*
Smith, David Claude 1958- *WhoE 91*
Smith, David Curtis 1949- *WhoAmA 91*
Smith, David D. 1923- *St&PR 91*
Smith, David Edmund 1934- *WhoAm 90*
Smith, David Edward 1939- *WhoSSW 91, WhoWor 91*
Smith, David Elvin 1939- *WhoWor 91*
Smith, David English 1920- *WhoAm 90*
Smith, David Gilbert 1926- *WhoAm 90*
Smith, David H *BiDrAPA 89*
Smith, David H. 1952- *WhoEmL 91*
Smith, David Harry Watrous 1938- *WhoE 91*
Smith, David Haughton 1947- *St&PR 91*
Smith, David Hector 1939- *IntWWM 90*
Smith, David Jameison 1953- *WhoE 91*
Smith, David Jeddie 1942- *WhoSSW 91, WhoWrEP 89*
Smith, David Julian 1944- *WhoE 91*
Smith, David Kingman 1928- *St&PR 91*
Smith, David Lee 1939- *WhoAm 90*
Smith, David Lionel 1940- *WhoAm 90*
Smith, David Lionel 1954- *WhoWrEP 89*
Smith, David Loeffler 1928- *WhoAmA 91, WhoE 91*
Smith, David Martin 1948- *WhoAm 90*
Smith, David Martyn 1921- *WhoAm 90*
Smith, David Odell 1951- *WhoEmL 91*
Smith, David Parkhurst *St&PR 91N*
Smith, David R. 1946- *St&PR 91*
Smith, David Richard, Jr. 1925- *St&PR 91*
Smith, David Rollins 1950- *WhoWor 91*
Smith, David Ryan 1952- *WhoSSW 91*
Smith, David Shiverick 1918- *WhoAm 90*
Smith, David Stephen 1943- *WhoSSW 91*
Smith, David Stickney 1921- *WhoE 91*
Smith, David Stuart 1946- *WhoE 91*
Smith, David Thornton 1935- *WhoAm 90*
Smith, David Todd 1953- *St&PR 91*
Smith, David Tyler 1953- *St&PR 91*
Smith, David Waldo Edward 1934- *WhoAm 90*
Smith, David Wayne 1927- *WhoAm 90*
Smith, David William Trimmer- 1937-1988 *BioIn 16*
Smith, Dean 1925- *WhoE 91, WhoWor 91*
Smith, Dean 1931- *WorAlBi*
Smith, Dean Carlton 1936- *WhoAm 90*
Smith, Dean Edwards 1931- *WhoAm 90, WhoSSW 91*
Smith, Dean R 1955- *BiDrAPA 89*
Smith, Debbi Lynn 1959- *WhoWrEP 89*
Smith, Deborah *AuBYP 90*
Smith, Deborah Bailey 1959- *WhoAmW 91*
Smith, Deborah Lynn 1951- *WhoEmL 91*
Smith, Deborah Lynn 1954- *WhoEmL 91*
Smith, Deborah Ruth 1961- *WhoAmW 91*
Smith, Delazon 1816-1860 *AmLegL*
Smith, Delbert Dudley 1940- *WhoAm 90*
Smith, Delford Michael 1930- *St&PR 91*
Smith, Denis Mack *WorAu 1980*
Smith, Denise Brewer 1959- *WhoAmW 91*
Smith, Denise Groleau 1951- *WhoAmW 91, WhoE 91, WhoEmL 91*
Smith, Denise Miller 1959- *WhoAmW 91*
Smith, Dennis 1940- *WhoAm 90*
Smith, Dennis C. 1933- *St&PR 91*
Smith, Dennis Dustin 1949- *WhoSSW 91*
Smith, Dennis E. 1947- *St&PR 91*
Smith, Dennis Edward 1945- *WhoE 91*
Smith, Dennis Harold 1933- *BiDrAPA 89*
Smith, Dennis Lee 1945- *WhoSSW 91*
Smith, Dennis Robert 1946- *WhoEmL 91*
Smith, Denny 1938- *WhoAm 90*
Smith, Derek Armand 1953- *WhoE 91*
Smith, Derek David 1959- *ConTFT 8*
Smith, Dermott A P 1924- *BiDrAPA 89*
Smith, Derrick A.M. 1931- *St&PR 91*
Smith, Derryck Harold 1947- *BiDrAPA 89*
Smith, Dewey Wayne 1953- *WhoSSW 91*
Smith, Diana *BioIn 16*
Smith, Diana 1955- *WhoAmW 91*
Smith, Diane E *BiDrAPA 89*
Smith, Diane Rapp 1946- *WhoEmL 91*
Smith, Dick *BioIn 16*
Smith, Dick King- 1922- *BioIn 16*
Smith, Dickinson M. 1933- *St&PR 91*
Smith, Dinah Maxwell 1941- *WhoAmA 91*
Smith, Dodie 1896- *FemiCLE*
Smith, Dolores Maxine Plunk 1926- *WhoWor 91*
Smith, Dolph 1933- *WhoAmA 91*
Smith, Don *AuBYP 90*
Smith, Don Harold 1948- *WhoAm 90*
Smith, Don Henry 1944- *BiDrAPA 89*
Smith, Donald C 1935- *WhoAmA 91, WhoE 91*
Smith, Donald Cameron *BiDrAPA 89*
Smith, Donald Cameron 1922- *WhoAm 90*
Smith, Donald E. 1926- *St&PR 91*
Smith, Donald Eugene 1926- *WhoAm 90*
Smith, Donald Eugene 1927- *WhoAm 90*
Smith, Donald Eugene 1934- *WhoSSW 91*
Smith, Donald G. 1927- *AuBYP 90*
Smith, Donald Gene 1941- *WhoAm 90*
Smith, Donald Kaye 1932- *St&PR 91, WhoAm 90*
Smith, Donald Kliese 1915- *WhoAm 90*
Smith, Donald L, Jr. 1921- *St&PR 91*
Smith, Donald Nickerson 1940- *WhoAm 90*
Smith, Donald Noran 1949- *WhoSSW 91*
Smith, Donald Raymond 1946- *WhoSSW 91*
Smith, Donald W. 1914- *St&PR 91*
Smith, Donald William 1933- *WhoAm 90*
Smith, Donn L. 1915- *WhoAm 90*
Smith, Donna 1954- *WhoAm 90*
Smith, Donna Emerson 1958- *WhoSSW 91*
Smith, Donna Kwall 1944- *WhoAmW 91*
Smith, Donna Lilian 1944- *WhoWor 91*
Smith, Donna S. 1957- *WhoAmW 91*
Smith, Donnetta Kay 1944- *WhoWrEP 89*
Smith, Donnie Alfred 1953- *WhoSSW 91*
Smith, Donnie Louise 1952- *WhoAmW 91*
Smith, Doris Anita 1935- *St&PR 91*
Smith, Doris Elaine 1940- *WhoE 91*
Smith, Doris Helen 1930- *WhoAmW 91*
Smith, Doris Kemp 1919- *WhoAmW 91*
Smith, Doris Reh 1944- *WhoSSW 91*
Smith, Dorland Worth 1931- *St&PR 91*
Smith, Dorothy C 1923- *BiDrAPA 89*
Smith, Dorothy Jordan 1940- *WhoAmW 91*
Smith, Dorothy Louise 1946- *WhoSSW 91*
Smith, Dorothy M. 1920- *St&PR 91*
Smith, Dorothy Ottinger 1922- *WhoWor 91*
Smith, Doug 1917-1989 *AnObit 1989*
Smith, Douglas 1940- *WhoAm 90*
Smith, Douglas C *BiDrAPA 89*
Smith, Douglas Edwin 1944- *BiDrAPA 89*
Smith, Douglas Edwin 1945- *WhoE 91*
Smith, Douglas G. 1940- *St&PR 91*
Smith, Douglas Graham *BiDrAPA 89*
Smith, Douglas Larue 1917- *WhoAm 90*
Smith, Douglas Lee 1951- *BiDrAPA 89*
Smith, Douglas Oster 1942- *St&PR 91*
Smith, Douglas R. 1915- *St&PR 91*
Smith, Douglas Sydney 1929- *WhoAm 90*
Smith, Douglas Wayne 1964- *WhoSSW 91*
Smith, Drayton Beecher, II 1949- *WhoSSW 91*
Smith, Duncan C. 1937- *St&PR 91*
Smith, Duncan Campbell 1937- *WhoAm 90*
Smith, Duncan Campbell, III 1947- *WhoE 91*
Smith, Dwight Leon 1946- *St&PR 91*
Smith, Dwight Morrell 1931- *WhoAm 90, WhoWor 91*
Smith, Dwight P. 1945- *ODwPR 91*
Smith, E. C. Bate- 1900-1989 *BioIn 16*
Smith, E. E. 1890-1965 *RGTwCSF*
Smith, E. Everett 1911- *St&PR 91*
Smith, E. Harlin 1933- *St&PR 91*
Smith, Earl *BioIn 16*
Smith, Earl 1891-1943 *Ballpl 90*
Smith, Earl 1897-1963 *Ballpl 90*
Smith, Earl Edward Tailer 1903- *BioIn 16*
Smith, Earl Pearson 1931- *WhoSSW 91*
Smith, Earl W. 1921- *St&PR 91*
Smith, Eberle Minard 1905- *WhoAm 90*
Smith, Eddie 1913- *Ballpl 90*
Smith, Eddie 1932- *WhoSSW 91*
Smith, Edgar 1857-1938 *OxCPMus*
Smith, Edgar Benton 1932- *WhoAm 90*
Smith, Edgar Eugene 1934- *WhoAm 90*
Smith, Edgar P. 1920-1989 *BioIn 16*
Smith, Edith Holden 1871-1920 *BioIn 16*
Smith, Edward A. 1918- *St&PR 91*
Smith, Edward Byron 1909- *St&PR 91*
Smith, Edward Byron, Jr. 1944- *WhoAm 90*
Smith, Edward C. 1948- *St&PR 91*
Smith, Edward Elmer 1890-1965 *WorAlBi*
Smith, Edward Herbert 1936- *WhoAm 90*
Smith, Edward Joseph 1943- *St&PR 91*
Smith, Edward K. 1922- *WhoAm 90*
Smith, Edward L. 1937- *ODwPR 91*
Smith, Edward Reaugh 1932- *WhoAm 90, WhoSSW 91*
Smith, Edward Rolph 1931- *St&PR 91*
Smith, Edward Samuel 1919- *WhoAm 90, WhoE 91*
Smith, Edwin Bradbury 1832-1914 *AmLegL*
Smith, Edwin Ely 1914- *St&PR 91*
Smith, Edwin Ide 1924- *WhoSSW 91*
Smith, Elaine Cecile Thompson 1947- *WhoAmW 91, WhoE 91, WhoWor 91*
Smith, Elaine Diana 1924- *WhoAm 90*
Smith, Elaine Janet 1939- *WhoAmW 91*
Smith, Elden Leroy 1940- *St&PR 91, WhoAm 90*
Smith, Eldred Gee 1907- *WhoAm 90*
Smith, Eldred Reid 1931- *WhoAm 90*
Smith, Eleanor Buczynski 1941- *WhoAmW 91*
Smith, Eleanor R. 1932- *St&PR 91*
Smith, Elias 1769-1846 *BioIn 16*
Smith, Elinor Bellingham 1906-1988 *AnObit 1988*
Smith, Elise Becket 1941- *WhoWor 91*
Smith, Elise Fiber 1932- *WhoAm 90*
Smith, Elizabeth *BiDEWW, FemiCLE*
Smith, Elizabeth 1776-1806 *FemiCLE*
Smith, Elizabeth 1797-1885 *BioIn 16*
Smith, Elizabeth 1943- *WhoAmA 91*
Smith, Elizabeth Ann 1958- *WhoAmW 91, WhoE 91*
Smith, Elizabeth Beth 1956- *WhoAmW 91*
Smith, Elizabeth Brooke Tyson 1818-1905 *BioIn 16*
Smith, Elizabeth M. 1951- *ODwPR 91, St&PR 91*
Smith, Elizabeth Mackey 1941- *WhoAmW 91*
Smith, Elizabeth Martinez 1943- *WhoHisp 91*
Smith, Elizabeth Oakes 1806-1893 *BioAmW*
Smith, Ellen B *BiDrAPA 89*
Smith, Ellen M. 1949- *St&PR 91*
Smith, Elliot Steven 1942- *WhoAmA 91*
Smith, Elmer 1868-1945 *Ballpl 90*
Smith, Elmer 1892-1984 *Ballpl 90*
Smith, Elmer L. 1943- *St&PR 91*
Smith, Elmer R. 1948- *WhoSSW 91*
Smith, Elouise Beard 1920- *WhoAmW 91, WhoSSW 91*
Smith, Elske Van Panhuys 1929- *WhoAmW 91*
Smith, Elvie Lawrence 1926- *WhoAm 90*
Smith, Elvin E. 1943- *St&PR 91*
Smith, Elwin Earl 1922- *WhoAm 90*
Smith, Elwood H. 1941- *BioIn 16*
Smith, Emerson Edlyn, III 1949- *WhoEmL 91*
Smith, Emerson Warfield 1922- *WhoE 91*
Smith, Emil L. 1911- *WhoAm 90*
Smith, Emily Follin 1959- *WhoAmW 91*
Smith, Emily Guthrie 1909-1987 *WhoAmA 91N*
Smith, Emma 1923- *AuBYP 90, BioIn 16*
Smith, Emma Hall 1804-1879 *BioAmW*
Smith, Ephraim Philip 1942- *WhoAm 90*
Smith, Eric Alan 1943- *WhoSSW 91*
Smith, Eric Morgan 1953- *WhoSSW 91*
Smith, Eric Parkman 1910- *WhoE 91, WhoWor 91*
Smith, Eric Wilburn, Jr. 1916- *WhoAm 90*
Smith, Ernest E. 1936- *WhoAm 90*
Smith, Ernest Frederic 1931- *WhoSSW 91*
Smith, Ernest John 1919- *WhoAmA 91*
Smith, Ernest Ketcham 1922- *WhoAm 90*
Smith, Ethel 1905- *BioIn 16*
Smith, Eugene 1918- *BiDrAPA 89*
Smith, Eugene F. 1933- *St&PR 91*
Smith, Eugene Freeman 1954- *BiDrAPA 89*
Smith, Eugene P. 1921- *WhoAm 90*
Smith, Eugene Preston 1919- *WhoAm 90*
Smith, Eugene Wilson 1930- *WhoAm 90, WhoSSW 91*
Smith, Eugenia Sewell 1922- *WhoAmW 91, WhoWor 91*
Smith, Eunice *FemiCLE*
Smith, Eva Joyce 1932- *WhoAmW 91*

Smith, James M. 1927- *St&PR 91*
Smith, James McKinley 1955- *WhoSSW 91*
Smith, James Michael *WhoAmA 91*
Smith, James Milton 1823-1890 *AmLegL*
Smith, James Morton 1919- *WhoAmA 91*
Smith, James Norman 1947- *St&PR 91*
Smith, James O. 1933- *St&PR 91*
Smith, James Oscar 1928- *WhoAm 90*
Smith, James Parker 1959- *WhoE 91*
Smith, James Payton 1950- *WhoSSW 91*
Smith, James Peyton 1956- *WhoSSW 91*
Smith, James R. 1933- *WhoAm 90*
Smith, James Richard 1947- *WhoE 91*
Smith, James Robert 1945- *St&PR 91*
Smith, James Robert 1955- *WhoE 91*
Smith, James Roy 1936- *WhoSSW 91*
Smith, James Russel 1939- *St&PR 91*
Smith, James S. 1926- *St&PR 91*
Smith, James T. *WhoAm 90*
Smith, James Thompson 1924- *St&PR 91*
Smith, James Todd *BioIn 16*
Smith, James William 1932- *St&PR 91*
Smith, Jamesetta Delorise 1942- *WhoAmW 91*
Smith, Jan *AuBYP 90*
Smith, Jane Carol 1948- *BiDrAPA 89*
Smith, Jane Davis 1949- *WhoWrEP 89*
Smith, Jane Farwell *WhoAm 90*
Smith, Jane Schneberger 1928- *WhoAmW 91*
Smith, Jane Wardell 1943- *WhoAmW 91*
Smith, Janet Marie 1957- *WhoAmW 91*
Smith, Janet Sue 1945- *WhoAmW 91, WhoE 91*
Smith, Janice Faye 1945- *WhoAmW 91*
Smith, Janice Lee *AuBYP 90*
Smith, Janice Lee 1949- *BioIn 16*
Smith, Jay D. 1940- *St&PR 91*
Smith, Jay Lawrence 1954- *WhoWor 91*
Smith, Jean Bird 1944- *WhoE 91*
Smith, Jean Chandler 1918- *WhoAm 90*
Smith, Jean G. 1946- *St&PR 91*
Smith, Jean Holthouse 1929- *WhoAmW 91*
Smith, Jean Lenora 1939- *WhoE 91*
Smith, Jean Webb *WhoAmW 91*
Smith, Jean Wheeler *BiDrAPA 89*
Smith, Jeannette M. *BioIn 16*
Smith, Jedediah Strong 1798-1831 *BioIn 16*
Smith, Jedediah Strong 1799-1831 *WhNaAH, WorAlBi*
Smith, Jeff 1958- *ConAu 132*
Smith, Jeff Allen *ConAu 132*
Smith, Jeff David 1969- *WhoWrEP 89*
Smith, Jeff P. 1950- *WhoAm 90*
Smith, Jeffery S 1945- *BiDrAPA 89*
Smith, Jeffrey *BioIn 16*
Smith, Jeffrey Bordeaux 1926- *WhoAm 90*
Smith, Jeffrey Greenwood 1921- *WhoAm 90*
Smith, Jeffrey Howard 1956- *WhoEmL 91*
Smith, Jeffrey J. 1950- *WhoEmL 91*
Smith, Jeffrey Kent 1960- *BiDrAPA 89*
Smith, Jeffrey Michael 1947- *WhoWor 91*
Smith, Jeffrey Michael 1952- *St&PR 91*
Smith, Jeffrey Peter 1956- *WhoEmL 91*
Smith, Jeffrey Robert 1961- *WhoEmL 91*
Smith, Jeffry Alan 1943- *WhoWor 91*
Smith, Jennifer *IntWWM 90*
Smith, Jennifer 1945- *PenDiMP*
Smith, Jere D. *ODwPR 91*
Smith, Jerome A 1919- *BiDrAPA 89*
Smith, Jerome A. 1943- *St&PR 91*
Smith, Jerome Hazen 1936- *WhoAm 90*
Smith, Jerry 1944-1986 *BioIn 16*
Smith, Jerry Earl *BiDrAPA 89*
Smith, Jerry Edgar 1941- *St&PR 91*
Smith, Jerry Edwin 1946- *WhoAm 90*
Smith, Jerry Lee 1943- *WhoSSW 91*
Smith, Jerry Wayne 1949- *St&PR 91*
Smith, Jesse Graham, Jr. 1928- *WhoAm 90, WhoWor 91*
Smith, Jessie Carney 1930- *WhoAm 90, WhoWrEP 89*
Smith, Jessie W. 1863-1935 *BioAmW*
Smith, Jessie Wilcox 1863-1935 *AuBYP 90*
Smith, Jessie Willcox 1863-1935 *BiDWomA*
Smith, Jim *BioIn 16*
Smith, Jim 1920- *SmATA 61*
Smith, Jim 1947- *WhoE 91*
Smith, Jim A. 1939- *St&PR 91*
Smith, Jimmy 1895-1974 *Ballpl 90*
Smith, Jimmy 1925- *BioIn 16*
Smith, Jo-An 1933- *WhoAmA 91*
Smith, Jo Anne 1930- *WhoAm 90, WhoAmW 91*
Smith, Jo Anne 1956- *WhoAmW 91*
Smith, Jo Anne Costa 1937- *WhoSSW 91*
Smith, Joachim 1929- *WhoAm 90*
Smith, Joan 1933- *BioIn 16*
Smith, Joann M *BiDrAPA 89*
Smith, Joanne J. 1939- *WhoAmW 91*
Smith, Jody Brant 1943- *WhoWor 91*
Smith, Joe 1902-1937 *WorAlBi*
Smith, Joe Dorsey, Jr. 1922- *St&PR 91, WhoAm 90*
Smith, Joe Mauk 1916- *WhoAm 90*
Smith, Joe Oscar 1925- *St&PR 91*
Smith, Joe W., Jr. 1944- *St&PR 91*
Smith, Joel 1925- *WhoAm 90*
Smith, Joel Bradley 1963- *WhoWrEP 89*
Smith, Joel F. 1942- *St&PR 91*
Smith, Joel Preston 1958- *WhoSSW 91*
Smith, John *AuBYP 90, BioIn 16*
Smith, John 1580-1631 *BioIn 16, EncCRAm [port], WhNaAH, WorAlBi*
Smith, John, Jr. 1917- *St&PR 91*
Smith, John Allen 1930- *St&PR 91*
Smith, John Brewster 1937- *WhoAm 90*
Smith, John Bundy 1939- *St&PR 91, WhoAm 90*
Smith, John Burnside 1931- *St&PR 91*
Smith, John D. 1938- *St&PR 91*
Smith, John Daniel 1926- *WhoE 91*
Smith, John David 1949- *ConAu 30NR*
Smith, John Dorrance 1951- *WhoAm 90*
Smith, John Drake, Jr. 1950- *WhoSSW 91*
Smith, John Edward 1950- *WhoE 91*
Smith, John Edwin 1921- *WhoAm 90, WhoWrEP 89*
Smith, John Ewing 1906- *St&PR 91*
Smith, John F. 1951- *St&PR 91*
Smith, John Francis 1923- *WhoAm 90*
Smith, John Francis, Jr. 1938- *WhoAm 90*
Smith, John Gelston 1923- *WhoAm 90*
Smith, John Greggory 1961- *WhoSSW 91*
Smith, John Gregory 1818-1891 *AmLegL*
Smith, John Ivor 1927- *WhoAmA 91*
Smith, John J. 1911- *St&PR 91, WhoAm 90*
Smith, John J. 1913-1988 *BioIn 16*
Smith, John Joseph 1913- *WhoAm 90*
Smith, John Kerwin 1926- *WhoWor 91*
Smith, John Lee, Jr. 1920- *WhoAm 90*
Smith, John Lewis, Jr. 1912- *WhoAm 90*
Smith, John Marsh 1818-1890 *BioIn 16*
Smith, John Martin 1949- *BiDrAPA 89*
Smith, John Matthew 1936- *St&PR 91, WhoAm 90*
Smith, John Richard 1932- *BiDrAPA 89*
Smith, John Stephen 1938- *WhoSSW 91*
Smith, John Sylvester 1914- *WhoAm 90*
Smith, John Wesley, Jr. 1946- *WhoE 91*
Smith, John Willis 1935- *WhoAm 90*
Smith, John Y. T. 1831-189-? *AmLegL*
Smith, Jonathan Riley- *BioIn 16*
Smith, Jonathan Scott 1956- *WhoEmL 91*
Smith, Jos A 1936- *WhoAmA 91*
Smith, Jose I. 1943- *St&PR 91, WhoAm 90*
Smith, Josef Riley 1926- *WhoAm 90*
Smith, Joseph 1805-1844 *BioIn 16, WorAlBi*
Smith, Joseph Benjamin 1928- *WhoAm 90*
Smith, Joseph Carruth 1941- *WhoSSW 91*
Smith, Joseph Colin 1931- *WhoWor 91*
Smith, Joseph H 1927- *BiDrAPA 89*
Smith, Joseph LeConte, Jr. 1929- *WhoAm 90*
Smith, Joseph Lorenzo 1946- *WhoE 91*
Smith, Joseph Phelan 1911- *WhoAm 90*
Smith, Joseph Robert 1927- *St&PR 91*
Smith, Joseph Roy 1927- *St&PR 91*
Smith, Joseph Showalter 1824-1884 *AmLegL*
Smith, Joseph T 1923- *BiDrAPA 89*
Smith, Joseph W. 1926- *St&PR 91*
Smith, Joseph Wilson, Jr. 1953- *WhoSSW 91*
Smith, Josephine Carroll 1884- *WhoAmW 91*
Smith, Josephine Woolley 1934- *WhoAmW 91*
Smith, Joshua L. *BioIn 16*
Smith, Joy Estelle 1915- *WhoSSW 91*
Smith, Juanita Rankin 1949- *WhoAmW 91, WhoE 91, WhoWor 91*
Smith, Judi Loy 1949- *WhoSSW 91*
Smith, Judian H. *BiDrAPA 89*
Smith, Judith Ann 1943- *WhoAmW 91*
Smith, Judith Ann 1957- *WhoAmW 91*
Smith, Judith B. *ODwPR 91*
Smith, Judith Bertenthal 1949- *WhoSSW 91*
Smith, Judith Day 1949- *WhoSSW 91*
Smith, Judith Pelham 1945- *WhoAm 90*
Smith, Judith Wilson 1941- *WhoAmW 91*
Smith, Judson 1880-1962 *WhoAmA 91N*
Smith, Jules Louis 1947- *WhoE 91*
Smith, Julia *FemiCLE*
Smith, Julia 1911-1989 *BioIn 16*
Smith, Julia Amelia 1935- *WhoAmW 91*
Smith, Julian Cleveland, Jr. 1919- *WhoAm 90*
Smith, Julian Payne 1930- *WhoAm 90, WhoE 91*
Smith, Juliann Jocelyn 1953- *WhoAmW 91*
Smith, Julie 1944- *ConAu 32NR, TwCCr&M 91*
Smith, Julie Carol 1961- *WhoSSW 91*
Smith, Julius S *BiDrAPA 89*
Smith, June Burlingame 1935- *WhoAmW 91*
Smith, Justin V 1903- *WhoAmA 91N*
Smith, K. Wayne 1938- *St&PR 91*
Smith, Kai *BioIn 16*
Smith, Karen C. 1954- *WhoAmW 91*
Smith, Karen Gail 1944- *WhoAmW 91*
Smith, Karen Jane 1935- *WhoSSW 91*
Smith, Karl Dee 1938- *WhoSSW 91*
Smith, Kate 1907-1986 *OxCPMus*
Smith, Kate 1909-1986 *WorAlBi*
Smith, Katherine E. *BioIn 16*
Smith, Katherine Eunice Young 1902- *AuBYP 90*
Smith, Katherine Virginia 1956- *WhoE 91*
Smith, Kathleen 1922- *BiDrAPA 89*
Smith, Kathleen Keer McGowan 1918- *WhoWrEP 89*
Smith, Kathleen L. 1948- *St&PR 91*
Smith, Kathleen Marie 1940- *WhoAmW 91*
Smith, Kathleen Marie 1957- *WhoAmW 91*
Smith, Kathleen Therese 1943- *WhoSSW 91*
Smith, Kathryn Ann 1955- *WhoAmW 91, WhoEmL 91*
Smith, Kathryn Baker 1946- *WhoAmW 91, WhoSSW 91*
Smith, Kathy Ann 1944- *WhoAmW 91*
Smith, Kay Nolte 1932- *TwCCr&M 91*
Smith, Keely 1935- *WorAlBi*
Smith, Keith A. 1938- *WhoAm 90, WhoAmA 91*
Smith, Keith Lewis 1922- *WhoE 91*
Smith, Kellie Michelle 1965- *WhoWrEP 89*
Smith, Kelvin 1899-1984 *BioIn 16*
Smith, Ken 1902- *Ballpl 90*
Smith, Kendon W 1935- *BiDrAPA 89*
Smith, Kennedy 1922- *St&PR 91*
Smith, Kenneth Alan 1936- *WhoAm 90*
Smith, Kenneth Blose 1926- *WhoAm 90*
Smith, Kenneth Bryant 1931- *WhoAm 90*
Smith, Kenneth Carless 1932- *WhoAm 90*
Smith, Kenneth Dudley, Jr. 1929- *WhoAm 90*
Smith, Kenneth F. *BioIn 16*
Smith, Kenneth John 1952- *WhoWor 91*
Smith, Kenneth Judson, Jr. 1930- *WhoAm 90*
Smith, Kenneth McKay 1947- *WhoEmL 91*
Smith, Kenneth Rodger 1942- *WhoAm 90*
Smith, Kenneth Warrington 1949- *WhoSSW 91*
Smith, Kent Alvin 1943- *WhoAmA 91*
Smith, Kermit Wayne 1938- *WhoAm 90*
Smith, Kerry Clark 1935- *WhoAm 90*
Smith, Kerry E. 1938- *ODwPR 91*
Smith, Kevin Anthony 1958- *WhoEmL 91*
Smith, Kevin Bryant 1959- *WhoE 91*
Smith, Kevin Hopkins 1953- *WhoE 91*
Smith, Kevin L 1955- *BiDrAPA 89*
Smith, Kevin Robert 1961- *IntWWM 90*
Smith, Kevin S. *ODwPR 91*
Smith, Kim Lee 1941- *WhoSSW 91*
Smith, Kim O'Quinn 1955- *WhoAmW 91*
Smith, Kimberly Ann *BiDrAPA 89*
Smith, Kraleen Stanfield 1958- *WhoAmW 91*
Smith, Kurtwood *ConTFT 8*
Smith, L.A., Jr. 1925- *St&PR 91*
Smith, L. Keith 1933- *WhoSSW 91*
Smith, L.L. *St&PR 91*
Smith, L. Russell 1933- *St&PR 91*
Smith, Lacey Baldwin 1922- *WhoAm 90*
Smith, Lafayette *AuBYP 90*
Smith, Lamar Seeligson 1947- *WhoAm 90, WhoSSW 91*
Smith, LaMarr *WhoSSW 91*
Smith, Lane Farr 1938- *BiDrAPA 89*
Smith, Langdon 1858-1908 *LiHiK*
Smith, Lanty L. 1942- *St&PR 91*
Smith, Lanty Lloyd 1942- *WhoAm 90*
Smith, LaPreal Monson 1920- *WhoE 91*
Smith, Larkin 1944-1989 *BioIn 16*
Smith, Larrabee M. *BioIn 16*
Smith, Larry Click 1931- *BiDrAPA 89*
Smith, Larry Dale 1938- *WhoE 91*
Smith, Larry M. 1934- *St&PR 91*
Smith, Larry R. 1943- *WhoWrEP 89*
Smith, Larry Steven 1950- *WhoSSW 91*
Smith, Larry Warren 1948- *WhoSSW 91*
Smith, Larry Wayne 1954- *WhoWrEP 89*
Smith, Laura Lee Whitely Weisbrodt 1903- *WhoAmW 91*
Smith, Laurel Diane 1953- *WhoWrEP 89*
Smith, Lauren Ashley 1924- *WhoSSW 91, WhoWor 91*
Smith, Laurence Roger 1939- *WhoE 91, WhoWor 91*
Smith, Laurie Macmillan 1960- *WhoAmW 91*
Smith, Lawrence Beall 1909- *WhoAmA 91*
Smith, Lawrence C. 1938- *St&PR 91*
Smith, Lawrence Earl, III 1919- *St&PR 91*
Smith, Lawrence Hartley 1934- *WhoAm 90*
Smith, Lawrence Jack 1941- *WhoAm 90, WhoSSW 91*
Smith, Lawrence Leighton *PenDiMP*
Smith, Lawrence Leighton 1936- *IntWWM 90, WhoAm 90, WhoSSW 91*
Smith, Lawrence M. 1921- *St&PR 91*
Smith, Lawrence M C 1902-1975 *WhoAmA 91N*
Smith, Lawrence Norfleet 1937- *St&PR 91*
Smith, Lawry 1952- *WhoAmA 91*
Smith, Lawson Wentworth 1947- *WhoAmA 91*
Smith, Le Sueur G., Jr. 1919- *St&PR 91*
Smith, Lee 1944- *FemiCLE*
Smith, Lee 1957- *Ballpl 90*
Smith, Lee Deverne 1938- *St&PR 91*
Smith, Lee Herman 1935- *WhoAm 90*
Smith, Lee L. 1936- *WhoWor 91*
Smith, Leila Hentzen 1932- *WhoAmW 91*
Smith, Leilani *ODwPR 91*
Smith, Leland D., Jr. 1931- *St&PR 91*
Smith, Lendon 1921- *SmATA 64 [port]*
Smith, Lenore *St&PR 91*
Smith, Leo C. 1932- *WhoAm 90*
Smith, Leo Gilbert 1929- *WhoAm 90*
Smith, Leon L., Sr. 1931- *WhoWrEP 89*
Smith, Leon Polk 1906- *WhoAm 90, WhoAmA 91*
Smith, Leonard B. *BioIn 16*
Smith, Leonard Bingley 1915- *WhoAm 90*
Smith, Leonard S. 1918- *St&PR 91*
Smith, LeRoi 1934- *AuBYP 90*
Smith, Leroy Harrington, Jr. 1928- *WhoAm 90*
Smith, LeRoy T. 1922- *St&PR 91*
Smith, Leslie Donald 1947- *St&PR 91*
Smith, Leslie Edward 1919- *St&PR 91, WhoWor 91*
Smith, Leslie Eugene *BiDrAPA 89*
Smith, Leslie Jack 1939- *WhoAm 90*
Smith, Leslie L. 1948- *ODwPR 91*
Smith, Leslie Roper 1928- *WhoAm 90*
Smith, Leslie Wayne 1950- *BiDrAPA 89*
Smith, Lester J. 1929- *St&PR 91*
Smith, Lester Martin 1919- *WhoAm 90*
Smith, Lewis Cass 1843-1886 *AmLegL*
Smith, Lewis Dennis 1938- *WhoAm 90*
Smith, Lewis Motter, Jr. 1932- *WhoAm 90*
Smith, Lewis O., III 1936- *St&PR 91*
Smith, Lex Burke 1922- *BiDrAPA 89*
Smith, Ley S. 1934- *WhoAm 90*
Smith, Lillian 1897-1966 *BioAmW, FemiCLE*
Smith, Lillian Eugenia 1897-1966 *BioIn 16*
Smith, Linda A. *WhoAmW 91*
Smith, Linda Ann 1951- *WhoAmW 91*
Smith, Linda Anne 1949- *WhoE 91*
Smith, Linda Lorraine 1947- *WhoAmW 91*
Smith, Linda Marlene *BiDrAPA 89*
Smith, Linda Zimbalist *BioIn 16*
Smith, Linda Zimbalist 1953- *WhoEmL 91*
Smith, Lindley Van, Jr. 1951- *WhoEmL 91*
Smith, Lindy Rae 1957- *WhoAmW 91*
Smith, Linell 1932- *AuBYP 90*
Smith, Linnea Weblemoe *BiDrAPA 89*
Smith, Lisa Elaine 1959- *WhoEmL 91*
Smith, Liz *BioIn 16, WhoAm 90, WhoWrEP 89*
Smith, Liz 1923- *WorAlBi*
Smith, Lloyd 1941- *WhoAm 90*
Smith, Lloyd A Warren *BiDrAPA 89*
Smith, Lloyd B. 1920- *St&PR 91*
Smith, Lloyd Bruce 1920- *WhoAm 90*
Smith, Lloyd Hilton 1905- *WhoAm 90, WhoWor 91*
Smith, Lloyd Hollingsworth 1924- *WhoAm 90*
Smith, Lloyd P. *BioIn 16*
Smith, Logan Pearsall 1865-1946 *DcLB 98 [port]*
Smith, Lois *ConTFT 8 [port]*
Smith, Lois Arlene 1948- *WhoAm 90*
Smith, Lois C. 1935- *WhoAm 90*
Smith, Lois Dabney- *BioIn 16*
Smith, Lois Eudora 1903- *WhoSSW 91*
Smith, Lonnie *BioIn 16*
Smith, Lonnie 1955- *Ballpl 90*
Smith, Lonnie Liston 1940- *DrBIPA 90*
Smith, Lonnie M. 1944- *St&PR 91*
Smith, Lonnie Max 1944- *WhoAm 90*
Smith, Loren Allan 1944- *WhoAm 90*
Smith, Loren Charles 1926- *WhoSSW 91*
Smith, Lori Kromis 1950- *WhoAmW 91*
Smith, Lorrie Lynn 1963- *WhoAmW 91*
Smith, Louise Hamilton 1926- *WhoWrEP 89*
Smith, Lowell Cyrus 1931- *WhoAm 90*
Smith, Lowell Ellsworth 1924- *WhoAmA 91*
Smith, Lowndes A. 1939- *St&PR 91*
Smith, Lucien T. 1913- *St&PR 91*
Smith, Lucy Toulmin 1838-1911 *FemiCLE*
Smith, Luther A 1950- *WhoAmA 91*
Smith, Lyall Carey 1942- *St&PR 91*
Smith, Lyn Wall 1909-1979 *WhoAmA 91N*
Smith, Lynda Kaye 1952- *WhoAmW 91*
Smith, Lynn Howard 1936- *WhoAm 90*
Smith, M. Brewster *BioIn 16*
Smith, M. Gregory 1947- *WhoSSW 91*

Smith, Macon Strother 1919- *WhoAm 90*
Smith, Maggie *BioIn 16, NewYTBS 90 [port]*
Smith, Maggie 1934- *WhoAm 90, WhoWor 91, WorAlBi*
Smith, Mahlon Brewster 1919- *WhoAm 90*
Smith, Malcolm B. 1923- *St&PR 91*
Smith, Malcolm Barry Estes 1939- *WhoAm 90*
Smith, Malcolm Bernard 1923- *WhoAm 90*
Smith, Malcolm N. 1921- *St&PR 91*
Smith, Malcolm Norman 1921- *WhoAm 90*
Smith, Malcolm Sommerville 1933- *IntWWM 90, WhoAm 90*
Smith, Mamie 1883-1946 *OxCPMus*
Smith, Mandy *BioIn 16*
Smith, Mara A. 1945- *WhoAmW 91*
Smith, Marcia Jean 1947- *WhoAmW 91, WhoE 91, WhoEmL 91, WhoWor 91*
Smith, Marcia Jeanne 1935- *WhoAmW 91*
Smith, Marcia Lynn Ellison 1946- *WhoSSW 91*
Smith, Marcus John 1954- *WhoE 91*
Smith, Margaret *WhoAmW 91*
Smith, Margaret 1778-1844 *FemiCLE*
Smith, Margaret Ann 1954- *BiDrAPA 89*
Smith, Margaret Chase 1897- *AuBYP 90, BioAmW, BioIn 16, WorAlBi*
Smith, Margaret Dill 1949- *WhoSSW 91*
Smith, Margaret Eleanor Jones 1921- *WhoAmW 91*
Smith, Margaret Hamilton Donald 1915- *WhoAm 90*
Smith, Margaret Mary 1912- *WhoAmW 91*
Smith, Margaret Mary 1949- *WhoAmW 91*
Smith, Margaret Phyllis 1925- *WhoAmW 91*
Smith, Margherita 1922- *WhoAmW 91*
Smith, Margie Stoy 1938- *WhoAmW 91*
Smith, Mari Lynn 1946- *WhoSSW 91*
Smith, Marianne Leigh *BiDrAPA 89*
Smith, Marie Edmonds 1927- *WhoAmW 91*
Smith, Mariel Melissa *BiDrAPA 89*
Smith, Marilyn Lynne 1944- *WhoSSW 91*
Smith, Marilyn Miller 1941- *WhoAmW 91*
Smith, Marilyn Ruedeane 1950- *WhoAmW 91*
Smith, Marilynn Ann 1950- *WhoAmW 91*
Smith, Marion Leroy 1923- *WhoAm 90*
Smith, Marion Pafford 1925- *WhoAm 90*
Smith, Mark 1952- *ODwPR 91*
Smith, Mark A. 1951- *WhoSSW 91*
Smith, Mark A 1955- *BiDrAPA 89*
Smith, Mark Alan 1934- *WhoE 91, WhoWor 91*
Smith, Mark Alan 1955- *BiDrAPA 89*
Smith, Mark Brian 1928- *WhoE 91*
Smith, Mark Eugene 1951- *WhoSSW 91*
Smith, Mark H *BiDrAPA 89*
Smith, Mark Jay 1948- *WhoSSW 91*
Smith, Mark Kuhn 1951- *WhoEmL 91*
Smith, Mark L. 1961- *St&PR 91*
Smith, Mark R. 1945- *St&PR 91*
Smith, Mark Richard 1935- *WhoWrEP 89*
Smith, Mark Richard 1955- *WhoEmL 91*
Smith, Mark Thomas 1951- *St&PR 91*
Smith, Mark Wayne 1960- *WhoSSW 91*
Smith, Markwick Kern, Jr. 1928- *WhoAm 90*
Smith, Marlan Reed 1943- *St&PR 91*
Smith, Marshall Jay 1931- *St&PR 91*
Smith, Marshall Roy, III 1947- *WhoSSW 91*
Smith, Marshall Savidge 1937- *WhoAm 90*
Smith, Marta Medaris 1933- *WhoAmW 91*
Smith, Martha Ann 1952 *WhoSSW 91*
Smith, Martin Bernhard 1930- *WhoAm 90*
Smith, Martin Brooks, Jr. 1947- *WhoSSW 91*
Smith, Martin Cruz *BioIn 16, NewYTBS 90 [port]*
Smith, Martin Cruz 1942- *CurBio 90 [port], TwCCr&M 91, WorAlBi*
Smith, Martin Henry 1921- *WhoAm 90*
Smith, Martin Jay 1942- *WhoAm 90*
Smith, Marvin *BioIn 16*
Smith, Mary *BiDEWW*
Smith, Mary *BioIn 16*
Smith, Mary Alice 1941- *WhoAmW 91*
Smith, Mary-Ann Tirone 1944- *WhoAmW 91*
Smith, Mary Anne D *BiDrAPA 89*
Smith, Mary Beth 1954- *WhoEmL 91*
Smith, Mary Faas *ODwPR 91*
Smith, Mary Frances 1927- *WhoWrEP 89*
Smith, Mary Howard Harding 1944- *WhoAmW 91*
Smith, Mary John 1943- *WhoAmW 91*
Smith, Mary Justa *EncPaPR 91*
Smith, Mary Louise 1918- *BiDrAPA 89*
Smith, Mary Louise 1935- *WhoAmW 91*
Smith, Mary R. 1920- *St&PR 91*
Smith, Mary T. 1904- *MusmAFA*
Smith, Matthew B 1949- *BiDrAPA 89*
Smith, Matthew J. 1951- *St&PR 91*
Smith, Maureen Ellen 1951- *BiDrAPA 89*
Smith, Maureen Felicity *IntWWM 90*
Smith, Maureen Jacquelene 1967- *WhoAmW 91*
Smith, Maureen Margaret 1930- *St&PR 91*
Smith, Maurice Edward 1919- *WhoAm 90*
Smith, Maurice Frederik 1908- *WhoAm 90*
Smith, Maurine Sleeper 1913- *WhoAmW 91*
Smith, Max L. 1932- *St&PR 91*
Smith, Max M *BiDrAPA 89*
Smith, Maxine *BioIn 16*
Smith, Maxwell P. 1924- *St&PR 91*
Smith, Maxwell Paul 1924- *WhoWor 91*
Smith, Mayo 1915-1977 *Ballpl 90*
Smith, Melody L. 1951- *St&PR 91*
Smith, Mendell Lafayette 1870- *AmLegL*
Smith, Merlin Gale 1928- *WhoAm 90*
Smith, Merriman 1913-1970 *BioIn 16, WorAlBi*
Smith, Merritt Roe 1940- *WhoAm 90*
Smith, Merritt Wayne 1929- *St&PR 91*
Smith, Micah P. 1916- *St&PR 91*
Smith, Micah Pearce, Jr. 1916- *WhoSSW 91, WhoWor 91*
Smith, Michael *BioIn 16*
Smith, Michael 1946- *ConAu 132*
Smith, Michael A 1942- *WhoAmA 91, WhoE 91*
Smith, Michael Alan 1954- *WhoEmL 91*
Smith, Michael Alexis 1944- *WhoAm 90*
Smith, Michael Anthony 1945- *WhoAm 90*
Smith, Michael B. 1936- *BioIn 16*
Smith, Michael Brackett 1936- *WhoE 91*
Smith, Michael C. B. 1955- *WhoAm 90*
Smith, Michael D. 1940- *St&PR 91*
Smith, Michael D. 1946- *St&PR 91*
Smith, Michael David 1945- *St&PR 91*
Smith, Michael Earl 1962- *BiDrAPA 89*
Smith, Michael F. 1961- *St&PR 91*
Smith, Michael Frank 1953- *WhoSSW 91*
Smith, Michael J. 1945-1986 *BioIn 16*
Smith, Michael James 1945- *WhoEmL 91*
Smith, Michael John 1937- *IntWWM 90*
Smith, Michael Joseph 1951- *WhoSSW 91*
Smith, Michael Judson 1949- *WhoSSW 91*
Smith, Michael L. 1948- *WhoAm 90*
Smith, Michael L. 1958- *WhoSSW 91*
Smith, Michael Louis 1947- *WhoEmL 91*
Smith, Michael Peter 1942- *WhoAm 90*
Smith, Michael R *BiDrAPA 89*
Smith, Michael R. 1938- *St&PR 91*
Smith, Michael Steven 1956- *WhoEmL 91, WhoWor 91*
Smith, Michael Timothy 1943- *St&PR 91*
Smith, Michael Townsend 1935- *WhoAm 90, WhoWrEP 89*
Smith, Michael Vincent 1957- *WhoSSW 91*
Smith, Michael Wayne 1951- *WhoSSW 91*
Smith, Michael William 1944- *WhoSSW 91*
Smith, Michele *BioIn 16*
Smith, Michele Debra 1962- *WhoE 91*
Smith, Mildred Joanne 1923- *DrBlPA 90*
Smith, Milledge Stevenson 1949- *WhoSSW 91*
Smith, Milton Lewis 1931- *WhoE 91*
Smith, Milton P *BiDrAPA 89*
Smith, Milton Ray 1935- *St&PR 91, WhoAm 90*
Smith, Miriam F *BiDrAPA 89*
Smith, Mitchell David 1961- *WhoE 91*
Smith, Moishe 1929- *WhoAm 90, WhoAmA 91*
Smith, Monte *WhoWrEP 89*
Smith, Moreland Griffith 1906-1989 *BioIn 16*
Smith, Morton 1915- *WhoAm 90*
Smith, Morton 1925- *St&PR 91*
Smith, Morton Howison 1923- *WhoAm 90*
Smith, Moyne Rice *AuBYP 90*
Smith, Muriel 1923-1985 *DcAfAmP, DrBlPA 90*
Smith, Muriel Joan 1936- *WhoWrEP 89*
Smith, Murray W. 1943- *St&PR 91*
Smith, Myron John, Jr. 1944- *WhoAm 90*
Smith, Nan S 1952- *WhoAmA 91*
Smith, Nancy Anne *BiDrAPA 89*
Smith, Nancy DuVergne 1951- *WhoAmW 91*
Smith, Nancy Elizabeth Lapple 1953- *WhoEmL 91*
Smith, Nancy Hohendorf 1943- *WhoAm 90, WhoAmW 91*
Smith, Nancy Jean 1949- *WhoE 91*
Smith, Nancy L. 1956- *WhoAmW 91*
Smith, Nancy Lynne 1947- *WhoAmW 91*
Smith, Nancy Weitman 1950- *WhoAmW 91*
Smith, Nathan 1928- *St&PR 91*
Smith, Nathan Bert 1952- *BiDrAPA 89*
Smith, Nathan McKay 1935- *WhoAm 90*
Smith, Neal Edward 1920- *WhoAm 90*
Smith, Nell Whitley 1929- *WhoAmW 91*
Smith, Nellie Ford *BioIn 16*
Smith, Nelson W. 1931- *St&PR 91*
Smith, Newman Donald 1936- *WhoWor 91*
Smith, Nico J. *BioIn 16*
Smith, Nimrod Jarrett 1838?-1893 *WhNaAH*
Smith, Nina 1955- *WhoWor 91*
Smith, Nixola Greeley- 1880-1919 *BioIn 16*
Smith, Noah, Jr. 1800-1868 *AmLegL*
Smith, Nora *BiDrAPA 89*
Smith, Nora Archibald 1859?-1924 *AuBYP 90*
Smith, Nora Lee 1959- *WhoEmL 91*
Smith, Norman Brian 1928- *WhoWor 91*
Smith, Norman Charles 1955- *WhoEmL 91*
Smith, Norman Clark 1917- *WhoAm 90*
Smith, Norman Cutler 1915- *WhoAm 90*
Smith, Norman F. 1925-1989 *BioIn 16*
Smith, Norman Obed 1914- *WhoAm 90*
Smith, Norman Raymond 1946- *WhoAm 90*
Smith, Norman Rex 1934- *WhoAm 90*
Smith, Norman T. 1935- *WhoAm 90*
Smith, Numa Lamar, Jr. 1915- *WhoAm 90*
Smith, O C 1932- *DrBlPA 90*
Smith, Obrie *ODwPR 91*
Smith, Okla Bennett 1941- *St&PR 91*
Smith, Olcott Damon 1907- *St&PR 91*
Smith, Olive Irene Perry 1924- *WhoAmW 91*
Smith, Oliver 1918- *ConDes 90, WhoAm 90*
Smith, Oliver Anderson, Jr. 1915- *WhoSSW 91, WhoWor 91*
Smith, Orin R. 1935- *St&PR 91*
Smith, Orin Robert 1935- *WhoAm 90, WhoE 91, WhoWor 91*
Smith, Orville Auverne 1927- *WhoAm 90*
Smith, Otis Milton 1922- *St&PR 91*
Smith, Ozzie *BioIn 16*
Smith, Ozzie 1954- *Ballpl 90 [port], WhoAm 90, WorAlBi*
Smith, P. Carter 1934- *St&PR 91*
Smith, Page 1917- *CurBio 90 [port]*
Smith, Paige Elaine 1963- *WhoAmW 91*
Smith, Pamela Kay 1962- *WhoAmW 91*
Smith, Pamela Kaye 1959- *WhoAmW 91*
Smith, Pat Everett 1930- *WhoSSW 91*
Smith, Patricia *WhoAmW 91*
Smith, Patricia Ann 1948- *WhoSSW 91*
Smith, Patricia Grace 1947- *WhoAmW 91*
Smith, Patricia J. 1947- *ODwPR 91*
Smith, Patricia Jacquline 1944- *WhoAmW 91*
Smith, Patricia K. 1934- *WhoAmW 91*
Smith, Patricia Lynn 1965- *WhoAmW 91*
Smith, Patricia Ruth 1932- *WhoWrEP 89*
Smith, Patricia Soret 1942- *WhoSSW 91*
Smith, Patrick A. 1953- *St&PR 91*
Smith, Patrick D. 1927- *WhoSSW 91*
Smith, Patrick Davis 1927- *WhoWrEP 89*
Smith, Patrick J. 1932- *BioIn 16*
Smith, Patsy Jane 1949- *WhoAmW 91*
Smith, Patti *BioIn 16*
Smith, Patti 1946- *EncPR&S 89, WorAlBi*
Smith, Patti Jeannean 1957- *WhoSSW 91*
Smith, Paul *BioIn 16*
Smith, Paul 1825-1912 *BioIn 16*
Smith, Paul 1931- *Ballpl 90*
Smith, Paul Abraham 1912- *WhoSSW 91*
Smith, Paul C. 1930- *St&PR 91*
Smith, Paul Daniel 1947- *WhoEmL 91*
Smith, Paul Douglas 1946- *WhoSSW 91*
Smith, Paul Edmund, Jr. 1927- *WhoSSW 91*
Smith, Paul Francis 1927- *WhoAm 90*
Smith, Paul Frederick 1919- *WhoAm 90*
Smith, Paul Gregory 1959- *WhoEmL 91*
Smith, Paul J 1931- *WhoAmA 91*
Smith, Paul J. 1932- *St&PR 91*
Smith, Paul John 1945- *WhoWor 91*
Smith, Paul L. 1918- *St&PR 91*
Smith, Paul Lester 1935- *WhoAm 90*
Smith, Paul Mapleston 1936- *WhoWor 91*
Smith, Paul T. 1938- *St&PR 91*
Smith, Paul Thomas 1938- *WhoAm 90*
Smith, Paul Traylor 1923- *WhoAm 90*
Smith, Paul V. 1924- *St&PR 91*
Smith, Paul Vergon, Jr. 1921- *WhoAm 90*
Smith, Paula Marie 1950- *WhoSSW 91*
Smith, Paula Marie 1960- *WhoAmW 91*
Smith, Pauline 1882?-1959 *FemiCLE*
Smith, Payton 1932- *WhoAm 90*
Smith, Pearce D. 1921- *St&PR 91*
Smith, Peggy Ann 1955- *WhoE 91*
Smith, Peggy Marie 1940- *WhoWor 91*
Smith, Percy Edgar 1931- *WhoSSW 91*
Smith, Pete 1966- *Ballpl 90*
Smith, Peter 1924- *WhoAm 90*
Smith, Peter 1945- *BioIn 16, WhoAm 90, WhoE 91*
Smith, Peter Bennett 1934- *WhoAm 90*
Smith, Peter C 1940- *ConAu 30NR*
Smith, Peter Garthwaite 1923- *St&PR 91, WhoAm 90*
Smith, Peter J. 1947- *St&PR 91*
Smith, Peter James 1950- *BiDrAPA 89, WhoE 91*
Smith, Peter John 1931- *WhoAm 90*
Smith, Peter Lawrence 1942- *WhoAm 90*
Smith, Peter Melville 1943- *IntWWM 90*
Smith, Peter Newhall 1932- *WhoAm 90*
Smith, Peter Robert 1956- *IntWWM 90*
Smith, Peter W. 1934- *ODwPR 91*
Smith, Peter Walker 1923- *WhoAm 90, WhoWor 91*
Smith, Peter Wilson 1938- *WhoAm 90*
Smith, Peter Windon 1934- *WhoAm 90*
Smith, Philip A. 1927- *ODwPR 91*
Smith, Philip B 1922- *BiDrAPA 89*
Smith, Philip Chadwick Foster 1939- *WhoE 91*
Smith, Philip Daniel 1933- *WhoAm 90*
Smith, Philip Edward Lake 1927- *WhoAm 90*
Smith, Philip Edwin 1947- *WhoSSW 91*
Smith, Philip George 1917- *WhoAm 90*
Smith, Philip Lawton 1933- *St&PR 91*
Smith, Philip M. 1927- *AuBYP 90*
Smith, Philip Meek 1932- *WhoAm 90, WhoE 91*
Smith, Philip Richard 1958- *IntWWM 90*
Smith, Philip S. 1936- *St&PR 91, WhoSSW 91*
Smith, Philip Swing 1926- *St&PR 91*
Smith, Philip W. 1947- *St&PR 91*
Smith, Phillip B *BiDrAPA 89*
Smith, Phillip G. 1948- *St&PR 91*
Smith, Phillip Hartley 1927- *WhoAm 90*
Smith, Phillips G. 1946- *St&PR 91*
Smith, Phillips Guy 1946- *WhoAm 90*
Smith, Phyllis Joy 1944- *WhoAmA 91*
Smith, Phyllis Mae 1935- *WhoAmW 91, WhoWor 91*
Smith, Pierce Reiland 1943- *St&PR 91, WhoAm 90*
Smith, Pine Top 1904-1929 *OxCPMus*
Smith, Pinetop 1904-1929 *WorAlBi*
Smith, Preston Gibson 1941- *WhoE 91*
Smith, Preston Leete 1930- *St&PR 91*
Smith, Quentin Ted *BiDrAPA 89*
Smith, Quentin Ted 1937- *WhoSSW 91*
Smith, Quinton Elwood 1943- *WhoSSW 91*
Smith, R. Anthony 1938- *St&PR 91*
Smith, R. K. *BioIn 16*
Smith, R. Ryrie *St&PR 91N*
Smith, R. Terry 1954- *WhoEmL 91, WhoSSW 91*
Smith, Rachel Hudson 1937- *WhoAmW 91*
Smith, Ralph 1919- *WhoSSW 91*
Smith, Ralph Alexander 1929- *WhoAm 90, WhoAmA 91*
Smith, Ralph Earl 1940- *WhoWor 91*
Smith, Ralph Ely 1944- *WhoE 91*
Smith, Ralph Lee 1927- *AuBYP 90, IntWWM 90, WhoAm 90*
Smith, Ralph Russell 1947- *WhoSSW 91*
Smith, Ralph Wayne *BiDrAPA 89*
Smith, Randall Gene 1947- *WhoWor 91*
Smith, Randall Nolen 1946- *St&PR 91*
Smith, Randall Wayne 1958- *WhoEmL 91*
Smith, Randi Sigmund 1942- *WhoAmW 91*
Smith, Randolph J. 1946- *St&PR 91*
Smith, Randy J. 1948- *St&PR 91*
Smith, Randy V. *BiDrAPA 89*
Smith, Rankin M., Jr. 1947- *WhoAm 90*
Smith, Rankin McEachern, Sr. 1925- *WhoAm 90, WhoSSW 91*
Smith, Ray Eugene 1935- *WhoSSW 91*
Smith, Ray William 1952- *WhoWor 91*
Smith, Raymond *WhoAm 90*
Smith, Raymond Dupuy, Jr. 1933- *St&PR 91*
Smith, Raymond J. 1938- *St&PR 91*
Smith, Raymond Kermit 1915- *WhoSSW 91*
Smith, Raymond Lloyd 1917- *WhoAm 90*
Smith, Raymond Thomas 1925- *WhoAm 90*
Smith, Raymond Victor 1926- *WhoAm 90*
Smith, Raymond W. 1937- *St&PR 91, WhoAm 90, WhoE 91, WhoWor 91*
Smith, Raymond Walter 1942- *WhoE 91*
Smith, Rebecca *BiDEWW*
Smith, Rebecca Anstine 1955- *WhoE 91*
Smith, Rebecca Humphries 1956- *WhoSSW 91*
Smith, Rebecca McCulloch 1928- *WhoAmW 91*
Smith, Rebecca Virtue 1953- *WhoAmW 91*
Smith, Red 1890-1966 *Ballpl 90*
Smith, Red 1905-1982 *BioIn 16*
Smith, Red 1906-1982 *Ballpl 90*
Smith, Redbird 1850-1918 *WhNaAH*
Smith, Reese Lillard, III 1948- *WhoSSW 91*
Smith, Reggie 1945- *Ballpl 90*
Smith, Reginald Brian Furness 1931- *WhoAm 90, WhoSSW 91*
Smith, Retta 1960- *WhoAmW 91*
Smith, Reuben M. 1938- *ODwPR 91*
Smith, Rex B. 1955- *St&PR 91*
Smith, Rex G. 1956- *WhoSSW 91*

Smith, Rex William 1952- *WhoAm 90*
Smith, Reynold E. 1932- *St&PR 91*
Smith, Richard 1931- *WhoWor 91*
Smith, Richard A. 1941- *St&PR 91*
Smith, Richard A. 1943- *St&PR 91*
Smith, Richard Alan 1924- *St&PR 91, WhoAm 90, WhoE 91*
Smith, Richard Anthony 1939- *WhoE 91*
Smith, Richard B. 1928- *WhoAm 90*
Smith, Richard Bowen 1938- *WhoAm 90*
Smith, Richard Brian *BiDrAPA 89*
Smith, Richard Brian 1963- *WhoE 91*
Smith, Richard C. 1949- *St&PR 91*
Smith, Richard Carl 1954- *WhoSSW 91*
Smith, Richard Carlisle 1930- *WhoAm 90*
Smith, Richard D. 1928- *WhoAm 90, WhoE 91*
Smith, Richard Edward 1948- *St&PR 91*
Smith, Richard Ellis 1948- *WhoSSW 91*
Smith, Richard Emerson 1922- *WhoAm 90, WhoWor 91*
Smith, Richard Ernest 1935- *WhoAm 90*
Smith, Richard Franklin 1946- *WhoSSW 91*
Smith, Richard Fred 1938- *WhoAm 90*
Smith, Richard Frederick 1920- *WhoE 91*
Smith, Richard Frederick 1929- *WhoAm 90*
Smith, Richard Granger 1930- *St&PR 91*
Smith, Richard Grant 1937- *WhoAm 90*
Smith, Richard H *BiDrAPA 89*
Smith, Richard Hamilton *BioIn 16*
Smith, Richard Howard 1927- *WhoAm 90*
Smith, Richard J. 1936- *St&PR 91*
Smith, Richard Jay 1930- *WhoWrEP 89*
Smith, Richard Joseph 1932- *WhoAm 90*
Smith, Richard Joseph 1950- *WhoEmL 91*
Smith, Richard Joyce 1903- *WhoAm 90*
Smith, Richard Keane 1942- *WhoWrEP 89*
Smith, Richard Kenneth 1950- *WhoSSW 91*
Smith, Richard L. *ODwPR 91*
Smith, Richard L. 1924- *St&PR 91*
Smith, Richard L. 1940- *St&PR 91*
Smith, Richard Langham 1947- *IntWWM 90*
Smith, Richard Lawrence 1933- *WhoAm 90*
Smith, Richard Lee, Jr. 1956- *WhoSSW 91*
Smith, Richard M. 1923- *St&PR 91*
Smith, Richard Mark *BiDrAPA 89*
Smith, Richard Melvyn 1940- *WhoAm 90*
Smith, Richard Mills 1946- *WhoAm 90, WhoE 91*
Smith, Richard Muldrow 1939- *WhoAm 90*
Smith, Richard N 1928- *BiDrAPA 89*
Smith, Richard N. 1937- *ODwPR 91*
Smith, Richard N. 1946- *St&PR 91*
Smith, Richard O. 1918- *St&PR 91*
Smith, Richard P. *WhoAm 90*
Smith, Richard P 1949- *ConAu 30NR*
Smith, Richard P. 1951- *St&PR 91*
Smith, Richard Pierson 1947- *St&PR 91*
Smith, Richard Robert Splaine 1955- *WhoE 91*
Smith, Richard Thomas 1925- *WhoAm 90*
Smith, Richard Wendell 1912- *WhoWor 91*
Smith, Richard Worthington 1920- *St&PR 91*
Smith, Richey 1933- *St&PR 91, WhoAm 90*
Smith, Rick Montgomery 1953- *WhoSSW 91*
Smith, Robert *BioIn 16*
Smith, Robert 1722?-1777 *EncCRAm*
Smith, Robert 1757-1842 *BiDrUSE 89, BioIn 16*
Smith, Robert, III 1939- *WhoAm 90*
Smith, Robert A. 1939- *St&PR 91*
Smith, Robert Alan 1944- *WhoE 91*
Smith, Robert Anthony 1954- *WhoEmL 91*
Smith, Robert B. 1875-1951 *OxCPMus*
Smith, Robert Bernard 1959- *WhoSSW 91*
Smith, Robert Boulware, III 1933- *WhoAm 90*
Smith, Robert Boynton 1931- *WhoSSW 91*
Smith, Robert Bruce *BiDrAPA 89*
Smith, Robert Bruce 1920- *WhoAm 90*
Smith, Robert Bruce 1937- *WhoAm 90*
Smith, Robert Burns 1929- *WhoAm 90, WhoWor 91*
Smith, Robert C *BiDrAPA 89*
Smith, Robert C 1912-1975 *WhoAmA 91N*
Smith, Robert C 1919- *BiDrAPA 89*
Smith, Robert C. 1931- *ODwPR 91*
Smith, Robert Cathcart 1914- *WhoSSW 91*
Smith, Robert Charles 1926- *WhoAmA 91*
Smith, Robert Charles 1931- *St&PR 91, WhoAm 90*
Smith, Robert Charles 1949- *St&PR 91*
Smith, Robert Charles 1953- *WhoE 91, WhoEmL 91*
Smith, Robert Clarke 1940- *WhoWrEP 89*
Smith, Robert Clinton 1941- *WhoAm 90, WhoE 91*
Smith, Robert Cornell 1948- *WhoSSW 91*
Smith, Robert Drake 1944- *WhoAm 90*
Smith, Robert E. 1927- *MusmAFA*
Smith, Robert E., Jr. 1943- *WhoWrEP 89*
Smith, Robert Earl 1923- *WhoAm 90*
Smith, Robert Edward *BiDrAPA 89*
Smith, Robert Ellis 1940- *WhoE 91, WhoWrEP 89*
Smith, Robert Ellis 1943- *WhoSSW 91*
Smith, Robert Ellsworth 1921- *WhoAm 90*
Smith, Robert Everett 1936- *WhoAm 90, WhoE 91*
Smith, Robert Forshay, Jr. 1957- *WhoSSW 91*
Smith, Robert Frederick 1958- *WhoWor 91*
Smith, Robert Freeman 1931- *WhoAm 90*
Smith, Robert H. *BioIn 16*
Smith, Robert H. 1879-1950 *WorAlBi*
Smith, Robert H. 1935- *St&PR 91*
Smith, Robert Harold 1924- *WhoAm 90*
Smith, Robert Harvey 1955- *WhoSSW 91*
Smith, Robert Henry 1937- *WhoAm 90, WhoWor 91*
Smith, Robert Houston 1931- *WhoAm 90*
Smith, Robert Howard 1935- *WhoAm 90*
Smith, Robert Imbrie 1931- *WhoAm 90, WhoWor 91*
Smith, Robert J. *NewYTBS 90*
Smith, Robert J. 1899-1989 *BioIn 16*
Smith, Robert James 1944- *WhoAm 90*
Smith, Robert John 1927- *WhoAm 90*
Smith, Robert Junius 1920- *WhoAm 90*
Smith, Robert K. 1930- *AuBYP 90*
Smith, Robert Karl *BioIn 16*
Smith, Robert Kimmel 1930- *BioIn 16*
Smith, Robert Lee 1923- *WhoAm 90*
Smith, Robert Lee, Jr. 1940- *WhoSSW 91*
Smith, Robert Leo 1925- *WhoAm 90*
Smith, Robert Letton 1928- *WhoWrEP 89*
Smith, Robert Lewis 1940- *WhoAmA 91*
Smith, Robert London 1919- *WhoAm 90*
Smith, Robert Louis 1922- *WhoAm 90*
Smith, Robert Louis 1932- *WhoAm 90*
Smith, Robert Mason 1945- *WhoEmL 91, WhoWor 91*
Smith, Robert Matthew 1961- *BiDrAPA 89*
Smith, Robert McNeil 1932- *WhoAm 90*
Smith, Robert Milton 1932- *St&PR 91*
Smith, Robert Moors 1912- *WhoAm 90*
Smith, Robert Nelson 1920- *WhoAm 90*
Smith, Robert O. 1932- *St&PR 91*
Smith, Robert P. *BioIn 16*
Smith, Robert Paul 1915-1977 *AuBYP 90, BioIn 16*
Smith, Robert Powell 1929- *WhoAm 90*
Smith, Robert Rutherford 1933- *WhoAm 90*
Smith, Robert S. 1916- *St&PR 91*
Smith, Robert Samuel 1920- *WhoAm 90*
Smith, Robert Scott 1940- *BiDrAPA 89*
Smith, Robert Sellers 1931- *WhoAm 90*
Smith, Robert Stanley 1934- *WhoAm 90*
Smith, Robert Thomas 1955- *WhoE 91*
Smith, Robert V *BiDrAPA 89*
Smith, Robert V. 1927- *St&PR 91*
Smith, Robert Victor 1942- *WhoAm 90*
Smith, Robert W. 1926- *AuBYP 90*
Smith, Robert Walter 1937- *WhoAm 90*
Smith, Robert Weston 1938- *BioIn 16, WhoAm 90*
Smith, Robert William 1923- *WhoAm 90*
Smith, Robert William 1951- *WhoSSW 91*
Smith, Roberta E. 1946- *WhoAmW 91*
Smith, Roberta Hawkins 1945- *WhoAmW 91*
Smith, Roberts Angus 1928- *WhoAm 90*
Smith, Robin Ann *BioIn 16*
Smith, Robyn Doyal 1947- *WhoSSW 91*
Smith, Roderick James Hollas 1957- *WhoWor 91*
Smith, Rodney A. 1947- *St&PR 91*
Smith, Rodney Frank 1940- *St&PR 91*
Smith, Rodney R. 1946- *St&PR 91*
Smith, Rodney T. 1948- *WhoWrEP 89*
Smith, Rodney Wike 1944- *WhoSSW 91, WhoWor 91*
Smith, Roger *BioIn 16*
Smith, Roger 1925- *News 90 [port], -90-3 [port]*
Smith, Roger 1935- *IntWWM 90*
Smith, Roger B. *BioIn 16*
Smith, Roger Bonham 1925- *ConAmBL, EncABHB 5 [port], St&PR 91, WhoAm 90, WhoWor 91*
Smith, Roger Crichton 1937- *St&PR 91*
Smith, Roger Dean 1932- *WhoAm 90*
Smith, Roger M. 1939- *ODwPR 91*
Smith, Roger Winston 1936- *WhoAm 90*
Smith, Rogers J 1920- *BiDrAPA 89*
Smith, Roland F. *St&PR 91*
Smith, Rolando Hinojosa *ConAu 131, HispWr 90*
Smith, Ronald 1922- *IntWWM 90, PenDiMP*
Smith, Ronald Arthur 1943- *St&PR 91*
Smith, Ronald Aubrey 1928- *IntWWM 90*
Smith, Ronald Earl 1942- *BiDrAPA 89*
Smith, Ronald Ehlbert 1947- *WhoSSW 91*
Smith, Ronald H. *St&PR 91*
Smith, Ronald L. 1942- *St&PR 91*
Smith, Ronald Lee 1937- *WhoAm 90*
Smith, Ronald Lynn 1940- *WhoAm 90, WhoSSW 91*
Smith, Ronald M 1926- *BiDrAPA 89*
Smith, Ronald Noel 1946- *WhoEmL 91*
Smith, Ronald Steven *BiDrAPA 89*
Smith, Ronnie L. 1936- *IntWWM 90*
Smith, Rosalie Haiblum 1933- *WhoAmW 91*
Smith, Rosamond *MajTwCW*
Smith, Rosilyn T. 1952- *BiDrAPA 89*
Smith, Rowena Marcus 1923- *WhoAmA 91*
Smith, Rowland James 1938- *WhoAm 90, WhoWrEP 89*
Smith, Roy 1961- *Ballpl 90*
Smith, Roy Emerson 1926- *WhoAm 90*
Smith, Roy Philip 1933- *WhoE 91*
Smith, Royall Brewster 1801-1849 *BioIn 16*
Smith, Ruben A. *WhoHisp 91*
Smith, Ruby Lucille 1917- *WhoAmW 91*
Smith, Rush Blackfan 1941- *St&PR 91*
Smith, Russell *WhoNeCM [port]*
Smith, Russell Bryan 1936- *WhoSSW 91*
Smith, Russell Eugene 1944- *WhoSSW 91*
Smith, Russell Evans 1908- *WhoAm 90*
Smith, Russell Francis 1944- *WhoWor 91*
Smith, Russell Lee 1924- *WhoE 91*
Smith, Russell Lynn 1933- *St&PR 91*
Smith, Russell Lynn, Jr. 1919- *WhoAm 90*
Smith, Russell Wesley 1947- *WhoE 91*
Smith, Ruth *St&PR 91*
Smith, Ruth Ann 1943- *WhoAmW 91*
Smith, Ruth Lillian Schluchter 1917- *WhoAm 90*
Smith, Ruth Reininghaus *WhoAmA 91*
Smith, S Christine *BiDrAPA 89*
Smith, S.G. 1938- *St&PR 91*
Smith, S Wayne 1914- *BiDrAPA 89*
Smith, Sally J. 1958- *St&PR 91*
Smith, Sam 1918- *WhoAmA 91*
Smith, Sam Alford 1952- *WhoSSW 91*
Smith, Sam DeVere 1936- *WhoWor 91*
Smith, Samantha *BioIn 16*
Smith, Sampson *PenDiDA 89*
Smith, Samuel Boyd 1929- *WhoAm 90*
Smith, Samuel David 1918- *WhoAm 90*
Smith, Samuel Denny 1932- *St&PR 91*
Smith, Samuel Francis 1808-1895 *BioIn 16*
Smith, Samuel Harrison 1772-1845 *BioIn 16*
Smith, Samuel Howard 1940- *WhoAm 90*
Smith, Samuel Latta 1830-1917 *EncABHB 4 [port]*
Smith, Sandford D. 1947- *St&PR 91*
Smith, Sandra Jane 1963- *WhoAmW 91*
Smith, Sandra Kay 1954- *WhoAmW 91*
Smith, Sandra Louise 1950- *WhoAmW 91*
Smith, Sandy *NewAgMG*
Smith, Sarah *BiDEWW*
Smith, Sarah 1832-1911 *BioIn 16*
Smith, Sarah Kim Huey 1952- *WhoEmL 91, WhoSSW 91*
Smith, Scott Clybourn 1950- *WhoAm 90*
Smith, Scott Lee 1926- *St&PR 91*
Smith, Scott Ormond 1948- *WhoWor 91*
Smith, Selby Robert 1933- *St&PR 91*
Smith, Selma Moidel 1919- *WhoWor 91*
Smith, Selwyn M 1942- *BiDrAPA 89*
Smith, Seymour M. 1941- *St&PR 91*
Smith, Shane *ODwPR 91*
Smith, Sharon Ann 1956- *WhoE 91*
Smith, Sharon Bennett 1953- *WhoAmW 91*
Smith, Sharon Kay 1954- *WhoWrEP 89*
Smith, Sharon Lee Chesnutt 1947- *WhoAmW 91*
Smith, Sharon Louise 1949- *WhoEmL 91*
Smith, Sharron Williams 1941- *WhoAmW 91*
Smith, Shawn T. 1963- *WhoEmL 91*
Smith, Sheila Bowman 1953- *WhoAmW 91*
Smith, Sheila Kaye- 1887-1956 *BioIn 16*
Smith, Sheldon Evard 1930- *St&PR 91*
Smith, Sheldon L. 1942- *St&PR 91*
Smith, Shelley 1912- *TwCCr&M 91*
Smith, Shelley Taylor- *BioIn 16*
Smith, Sheridan *BiDrAPA 89*
Smith, Sherman Allen 1920- *WhoAm 90*
Smith, Sherri 1943- *WhoAmA 91*
Smith, Sherri Davis 1955- *St&PR 91*
Smith, Sherry 1891-1949 *Ballpl 90*
Smith, Sherwood Draughon 1925- *WhoAm 90*
Smith, Sherwood Hubbard, Jr. 1934- *St&PR 91, WhoAm 90, WhoSSW 91*
Smith, Sheryl L. 1947- *WhoWrEP 89*
Smith, Shirley *WhoAmA 91*
Smith, Shirley 1929- *WhoE 91*
Smith, Shirley B. 1941- *St&PR 91*
Smith, Shirley Cronin 1947- *WhoSSW 91*
Smith, Shirley D. 1942- *WhoAmW 91*
Smith, Shirley Mae 1923- *WhoWrEP 89*
Smith, Shirley O'Bryan 1949- *WhoWrEP 89*
Smith, Sidney 1877-1935 *EncACom*
Smith, Sidney Kendrick, III *BiDrAPA 89*
Smith, Sidney Oslin, Jr. 1923- *WhoAm 90, WhoSSW 91*
Smith, Sidney Rufus, Jr. 1931- *WhoAm 90*
Smith, Sonny *BioIn 16*
Smith, Sophia 1796-1870 *BioAmW*
Smith, Spencer Bailey 1927- *WhoAm 90*
Smith, Stacey Ellen 1958- *WhoE 91*
Smith, Stan Vladimir 1946- *WhoAm 90, WhoEmL 91*
Smith, Stanford Lee 1935- *WhoSSW 91*
Smith, Stanford Sidney 1923- *WhoAm 90*
Smith, Stanley Doren 1944- *St&PR 91*
Smith, Stanley M. 1917- *St&PR 91*
Smith, Stanley Quinten 1954- *WhoEmL 91*
Smith, Stanley Roger 1946- *WhoAm 90*
Smith, Stanton Kinnie, Jr. 1931- *St&PR 91, WhoAm 90*
Smith, Stanton T.I. 1925- *St&PR 91*
Smith, Stephen Alexander 1957- *St&PR 91*
Smith, Stephen Atwell 1948- *WhoSSW 91*
Smith, Stephen E. 1927-1990 *NewYTBS 90 [port]*
Smith, Stephen Grant 1949- *WhoAm 90*
Smith, Stephen Keese, Jr. 1947- *WhoSSW 91*
Smith, Stephen L. *BioIn 16*
Smith, Stephen Lewis 1943- *St&PR 91*
Smith, Stephen R. 1951- *ODwPR 91*
Smith, Stephen Walter 1946- *WhoEmL 91*
Smith, Sterling T. 1918- *St&PR 91*
Smith, Steve *BioIn 16*
Smith, Steven Alden 1941- *St&PR 91*
Smith, Steven Craig 1957- *WhoWor 91*
Smith, Steven Dennis 1945- *WhoEmL 91*
Smith, Steven Harold 1954- *WhoSSW 91*
Smith, Steven Ira 1954- *WhoEmL 91*
Smith, Steven J 1946- *BiDrAPA 89*
Smith, Steven James 1945- *St&PR 91*
Smith, Steven Lee 1952- *WhoEmL 91, WhoSSW 91*
Smith, Steven Sidney 1946- *WhoEmL 91, WhoWor 91*
Smith, Steven Warren 1949- *ODwPR 91*
Smith, Stevie *MajTwCW*
Smith, Stevie 1902-1971 *BioIn 16, FemiCLE*
Smith, Stewart N. 1931- *St&PR 91*
Smith, Stewart R *BiDrAPA 89*
Smith, Stewart W., Jr. 1932- *St&PR 91*
Smith, Stewart Worland, Jr. 1932- *WhoAm 90*
Smith, Stuart A. 1941- *WhoAm 90*
Smith, Stuart H.B. 1945- *St&PR 91*
Smith, Stuart Lyon 1938- *WhoAm 90*
Smith, Stuart Seaborne 1930- *WhoAm 90*
Smith, Stuff 1909-1967 *BioIn 16, OxCPMus*
Smith, Sue Ann 1944- *WhoAmW 91*
Smith, Sue Frances 1940- *WhoAm 90, WhoWrEP 89*
Smith, Suellen Fandt 1943- *WhoAmW 91*
Smith, Sumner, Jr. 1920- *St&PR 91*
Smith, Susan *WhoAmA 91*
Smith, Susan 1960- *ODwPR 91*
Smith, Susan Carlton 1923- *WhoAmA 91*
Smith, Susan Converse 1956- *WhoAmW 91*
Smith, Susan E. 1954- *WhoAmW 91*
Smith, Susan Louise 1959- *WhoAmW 91*
Smith, Susan Patricia 1953- *BiDrAPA 89*
Smith, Susan Porter 1934- *WhoE 91*
Smith, Susan Ross 1945- *WhoWrEP 89*
Smith, Susan Saxton 1959- *WhoAmW 91*
Smith, Susan Sharp 1953- *WhoSSW 91*
Smith, Susanna 1623?-1693 *BiDEWW*
Smith, Susannah 1666?- *BiDEWW*
Smith, Susanne H. 1933- *St&PR 91*
Smith, Susy 1911- *EncO&P 3, EncPaPR 91*
Smith, Sydney David 1947- *WhoEmL 91*
Smith, Sydney G. 1938- *St&PR 91*
Smith, Sydney Strother, III 1941- *WhoSSW 91, WhoWor 91*
Smith, Sylvia Jo 1950- *WhoAmW 91*
Smith, T.J., III 1930- *St&PR 91*
Smith, T. Kent 1956- *WhoSSW 91*
Smith, Tad Randolph 1928- *WhoSSW 91, WhoWor 91*
Smith, Taggart 1939- *WhoAmW 91*
Smith, Tamara Lee *BiDrAPA 89*
Smith, Tammie Louise 1959- *WhoAmW 91*
Smith, Taylor 1953- *WhoAm 90*
Smith, Ted Jay, III 1945- *WhoSSW 91*
Smith, Templeton, Jr. 1952- *WhoEmL 91*
Smith, Terence Fitzgerald 1938- *WhoAm 90*
Smith, Teresa Ann 1963- *WhoAmW 91*
Smith, Terrence John 1931- *St&PR 91*
Smith, Terrence Lore 1942-1988 *BioIn 16*
Smith, Terri McFerrin 1954- *ConAu 129*
Smith, Thelma Marie 1936- *WhoAmW 91*
Smith, Thelma Tina Harriette 1938- *WhoAmW 91, WhoSSW 91*
Smith, Theodore Floyd 1931- *St&PR 91*

Smith, Theodore Goodwin 1934- WhoAm 90
Smith, Theodore W 1953- BiDrAPA 89
Smith, Theresa Catherine Sullivan 1924- WhoWor 91
Smith, Theresa Kalab AuBYP 90
Smith, Thom E. 1936- WhoSSW 91
Smith, Thomas 1915-1988 AnObit 1988
Smith, Thomas A BiDrAPA 89
Smith, Thomas Arthur 1954- WhoSSW 91
Smith, Thomas Clair 1925- WhoE 91, WhoWor 91
Smith, Thomas D. St&PR 91
Smith, Thomas E. 1947- St&PR 91
Smith, Thomas Earle, Jr. 1938- WhoSSW 91
Smith, Thomas Edward 1959- BiDrAPA 89
Smith, Thomas Elijah 1933- WhoE 91
Smith, Thomas Eugene 1930- WhoAm 90
Smith, Thomas Eugene 1944- WhoE 91
Smith, Thomas F. 1934- St&PR 91
Smith, Thomas George 1940- WhoAm 90
Smith, Thomas Gordon BioIn 16
Smith, Thomas Gregory 1959- WhoEmL 91, WhoWor 91
Smith, Thomas H 1926- BiDrAPA 89
Smith, Thomas H. 1948- St&PR 91
Smith, Thomas Joseph 1938- WhoAm 90
Smith, Thomas Luther, Jr. 1927- BiDrAPA 89
Smith, Thomas R. 1909- St&PR 91
Smith, Thomas Ray 1949- St&PR 91
Smith, Thomas Shore 1924- WhoWor 91
Smith, Thomas Slater 1856-1901 AmLegL
Smith, Thomas Winston 1935- WhoAm 90
Smith, Thomas Woodward 1936- WhoAm 90
Smith, Thomasina Denise 1954- WhoAmW 91
Smith, Thornton E. 1923- St&PR 91
Smith, Thorsten BiDrAPA 89
Smith, Timothy Lawrence 1924- WhoAm 90
Smith, Timothy Lynn 1957- WhoSSW 91
Smith, Tina Diane 1958- WhoSSW 91
Smith, Tom E. 1941- St&PR 91
Smith, Tom Eugene 1941- WhoAm 90, WhoSSW 91
Smith, Tom K. ODwPR 91
Smith, Tom W. 1935- St&PR 91
Smith, Toni Colette 1952- WhoAmW 91
Smith, Tony 1912- WhoAmA 91N
Smith, Toukie BioIn 16
Smith, Tracey Lee 1963- WhoAmW 91
Smith, Trefor Leslie 1948- IntWWM 90
Smith, Trixie 1895-1943 BioIn 16
Smith, Troy N., Sr. 1922- St&PR 91
Smith, Tucker 1940- BioIn 16
Smith, Twyla Jean 1955- BiDrAPA 89
Smith, Ursula 1934- BioIn 16
Smith, V Joachim 1929- WhoAmA 91
Smith, V. Kerry 1945- WhoAm 90
Smith, V. La Monte 1938- WhoWrEP 89
Smith, Valor C. 1919- St&PR 91
Smith, Van P. 1928- St&PR 91
Smith, Vangy Edith 1937- WhoAmW 91, WhoWor 91
Smith, Verity Carlisle 1922- St&PR 91
Smith, Vernon J. 1929- St&PR 91
Smith, Veronica Latta 1925- WhoAm 90
Smith, Vian 1920- AuBYP 90
Smith, Vicki Lyn 1961- WhoAmW 91
Smith, Victor Earle 1914- WhoAm 90
Smith, Victor L. 1930- St&PR 91
Smith, Victoria L BiDrAPA 89
Smith, Victoria Weilepp 1951- WhoSSW 91
Smith, Vilma J. 1927- St&PR 91
Smith, Vin 1944- WhoWor 91
Smith, Vincent D 1929- WhoAmA 91
Smith, Vincent DaCosta 1929- WhoAm 90
Smith, Vincent De Paul 1940- WhoE 91
Smith, Vincent Xavier 1923- St&PR 91
Smith, Vinnie 1916- Ballpl 90
Smith, Virginia Dodd 1911- WhoAm 90, WhoAmW 91
Smith, Vivian Hugh 1867-1956 BioIn 16
Smith, Vme 1929- WhoAmW 91
Smith, W. Alan 1949- WhoSSW 91
Smith, W. Clement 1954- St&PR 91
Smith, W. Douglass 1936- WhoAm 90
Smith, W. Eugene 1918-1978 BioIn 16
Smith, W. Griswold 1921- St&PR 91
Smith, W Harry 1875-1951 WhoAmA 91N
Smith, W. Kirk 1938- St&PR 91
Smith, W. Richard 1932- St&PR 91
Smith, W. Scott, Jr. 1924- St&PR 91
Smith, W T 1920- BiDrAPA 89
Smith, W. W. 1884-1947 EncO&P 3
Smith, Waldo Gregorius 1911- WhoWor 91
Smith, Wallace Bunnell 1929- WhoAm 90
Smith, Wallace H. 1936- St&PR 91
Smith, Wallace H, II BiDrAPA 89
Smith, Wallace Herndon 1901-1990 BioIn 16
Smith, Walt Allen 1910-1971 WhoAmA 91N
Smith, Walter Bedell 1895-1961 BioIn 16
Smith, Walter DeLos 1936- WhoWor 91
Smith, Walter Douglas 1918- WhoAm 90
Smith, Walter H. 1929- St&PR 91
Smith, Walter Hall 1920- WhoAm 90
Smith, Walter Joseph, Jr. 1936- WhoE 91
Smith, Walter S., Jr. 1940- WhoAm 90, WhoSSW 91
Smith, Walter Tilford 1907- WhoAm 90
Smith, Walter Wellesley 1905-1982 BioIn 16
Smith, Walter Wulfing 1948- St&PR 91
Smith, Wanda Janette 1952- WhoSSW 91
Smith, Wanda Jean 1949- WhoAmW 91
Smith, Ward WhoWrEP 89
Smith, Ward 1930- St&PR 91, WhoAm 90
Smith, Ward Tolbert BiDrAPA 89
Smith, Warren Allen 1921- St&PR 91, WhoWor 91
Smith, Warren E BiDrAPA 89
Smith, Warren F. St&PR 91
Smith, Warren W. 1948- St&PR 91
Smith, Watson 1897- WhoAm 90
Smith, Watson B., Jr. 1931- St&PR 91
Smith, Wayman Flynn 1940- St&PR 91
Smith, Wayman Flynn, III 1940- WhoAm 90
Smith, Wayne Calvin 1935- WhoAm 90
Smith, Wayne Cyril 1953- IntWWM 90
Smith, Wayne D. 1944- St&PR 91
Smith, Wayne David 1959- WhoEmL 91
Smith, Wayne H. 1948- St&PR 91
Smith, Wayne Henry 1941- St&PR 91
Smith, Wayne L. 1937- St&PR 91
Smith, Wayne O. St&PR 91
Smith, Wayne T. 1943- St&PR 91
Smith, Wendell M. 1935- St&PR 91
Smith, Wendell Murray 1935- WhoAm 90
Smith, Wendell Oakman 1932- WhoSSW 91
Smith, Wilber G. 1928- St&PR 91
Smith, Wilbur St&PR 91
Smith, Wilbur 1933- MajTwCW
Smith, Wilbur Burge 1931- WhoAm 90
Smith, Wilbur Cowan 1914- WhoWor 91
Smith, Wilbur S. NewYTBS 90 [port]
Smith, Wilbur Stevenson 1911- WhoAm 90, WhoWrEP 89
Smith, Wilburn Jackson, Jr. 1921- WhoAm 90
Smith, Wilburt Jackson 1922- St&PR 91
Smith, Wiley R, Jr. 1927- BiDrAPA 89
Smith, Wilfred Irvin 1919- WhoAm 90
Smith, Willi BioIn 16
Smith, William 1727-1803 EncCRAm
Smith, William 1728-1814 BioIn 16
Smith, William 1821-1897 DcCanB 12
Smith, William A., III 1927- St&PR 91
Smith, William A., Jr. 1946- St&PR 91
Smith, William Alexander DcCanB 12
Smith, William Allen 1940- WhoSSW 91
Smith, William Arthur 1918- WhoAmA 91N
Smith, William Ashley 1944- WhoAm 90
Smith, William B. 1936- St&PR 91
Smith, William Basil 1936- WhoWor 91
Smith, William Burton 1927- WhoAm 90
Smith, William Charles 1930- WhoAm 90
Smith, William Curtis 1922- WhoSSW 91
Smith, William Curtis 1946- WhoSSW 91
Smith, William Dee 1933- WhoAm 90
Smith, William E. 1824-1883 AmLegL
Smith, William E. 1912- St&PR 91
Smith, William Earl 1853?-1909 BioIn 16
Smith, William Earl 1951- WhoAm 90
Smith, William Edgar, Jr. 1940- St&PR 91
Smith, William Edward 1922- WhoAm 90
Smith, William Elliott 1951- WhoSSW 91
Smith, William Francis, Jr. 1935- WhoAm 90
Smith, William French 1917- BiDrUSE 89
Smith, William French 1917-1990 NewYTBS 90 [port]
Smith, William G. 1857- AmLegL
Smith, William Henry 1833-1896 BioIn 16
Smith, William Henry, Jr. 1942- WhoSSW 91
Smith, William Henry Preston 1924- WhoAm 90
Smith, William Hovey 1941- WhoWrEP 89
Smith, William Hulse 1939- WhoAm 90
Smith, William J BiDrAPA 89
Smith, William Jay 1918- AuBYP 90, WhoAm 90, WhoWrEP 89
Smith, William Kendall 1922- WhoAm 90
Smith, William L. 1928- St&PR 91
Smith, William Lester 1917- St&PR 91
Smith, William Lewis 1925- WhoAm 90
Smith, William Loughton 1758-1812 BioIn 16
Smith, William Lyon 1932- WhoSSW 91
Smith, William M. 1823-1886 AmLegL
Smith, William Maurice 1929- St&PR 91
Smith, William Permar 1920- St&PR 91
Smith, William R. 1929- St&PR 91
Smith, William Randolph 1928- WhoAm 90
Smith, William Ray 1925- WhoWor 91
Smith, William Reece, Jr. 1925- WhoAm 90
Smith, William Robert 1916- St&PR 91
Smith, William Robert 1926- WhoSSW 91
Smith, William Roy 1920- WhoAm 90
Smith, William Theodore 1949- WhoE 91
Smith, William U. 1940- St&PR 91
Smith, William W. 1922- St&PR 91
Smith, William Wallace 1900-1989 BioIn 16
Smith, William Young 1925- WhoAm 90
Smith, Willie 1897-1973 BioIn 16, OxCPMus, WorAlBi
Smith, Willie 1939- Ballpl 90
Smith, Willie Tesreau, Jr. 1920- WhoSSW 91, WhoWor 91
Smith, Willis Allen 1919- WhoAm 90
Smith, Wilma Janice 1926- WhoWrEP 89
Smith, Wilson Aaron, Jr. 1951- WhoSSW 91
Smith, Wilson Earl 1949- WhoSSW 91
Smith, Winfrey H. WhoSSW 91
Smith, Winthrop Davenport 1953- WhoE 91
Smith, Winthrop Hiram, Jr. 1949- WhoAm 90
Smith, Wrede H. 1921- St&PR 91
Smith, Wrede Howard, Jr. 1949- WhoEmL 91
Smith, Yvonne Carolyn 1923- WhoAmW 91
Smith, Z. Z. WhoWrEP 89
Smith, Zachary Alden 1953- WhoEmL 91
Smith, Zachary Taylor, II 1923- WhoAm 90
Smith, Zane 1960- Ballpl 90
Smith-Alexander, Melanie Sue 1959- WhoAmW 91
Smith-Blair, Gayle La Treece BiDrAPA 89
Smith Brindle, Reginald 1917- IntWWM 90
Smith-Christensen, Arild 1938- WhoWor 91
Smith-Dornan, Maggie Jo 1945- WhoAmW 91
Smith E Incas, Jaime Cornelio 1920- BiDrAPA 89
Smith-Evernden, Roberta Katherine 1931- WhoAmW 91
Smith-Holland, Elizabeth Eugenia 1960- WhoAmW 91
Smith-Pierce, Patricia A. 1939- WhoWor 91
Smith-Reardon, Janet Linda 1962- WhoAmW 91
Smith-Ryland, Robin BioIn 16
Smith-Vaniz, William Reid 1925- WhoAm 90
Smith-Vaniz, Wm. Reid 1925- St&PR 91
Smith-Wade-El, Rita Rorate 1948- WhoAmW 91
Smith-Warren, Katharine 1945- WhoAmA 91
Smith-Young, Anne Victoria 1947- WhoAmW 91, WhoE 91
Smithburg, Donald Rowan 1960- WhoEmL 91
Smithburg, William D. 1938- St&PR 91
Smithburg, William Dean 1938- WhoAm 90
Smithburton, Cynthia 1959- WhoAmW 91
Smithdeal, William Fralin 1924- St&PR 91
Smithe, Frank B. 1892-1989 BioIn 16
Smither, Edward Murray 1937- WhoAmA 91
Smither, Elizabeth 1941- FemiCLE
Smither, Howard Elbert 1925- WhoAm 90
Smither, J. Michael 1956- WhoEmL 91
Smither, Plummer Campbell, Jr. 1932- St&PR 91
Smitherman, Geneva 1940- ConAu 130
Smitherman, Gustavus Scott 1921- WhoAm 90
Smitherman, Ruth Rothmeyer 1912- WhoAmW 91
Smithers, Donald Lee 1937- WhoSSW 91
Smithers, Jane Braitmayer 1915- WhoAmW 91
Smithers, Wayne Donovan 1943- St&PR 91
Smithers, William 1927- ConTFT 8 [port]
Smithey, Jerry De Roy 1919- St&PR 91
Smithey, Sarah Elizabeth 1932- St&PR 91
Smithfield, David Alan 1945- St&PR 91
Smithfield, William Ronald 1942- St&PR 91
Smithies, Edward 1941- ConAu 132
Smithson, Alison Margaret 1928- WhoWor 91
Smithson, James 1765-1829 WorAlBi
Smithson, John Garbutt IntWWM 90
Smithson, John Wynne 1946- St&PR 91
Smithson, Luther Harris 1932- WhoAm 90
Smithson, Mike 1955- Ballpl 90
Smithson, Peter Denham 1923- WhoWor 91
Smithson, Richard Joseph 1923- St&PR 91
Smithson, Robert I 1938-1974 WhoAmA 91N
Smithwich, Jerry J. 1944- St&PR 91
Smithwick, Fred, Jr. 1934- WhoWor 91
Smitley, Barbara Anne 1956- WhoAmW 91
Smitley, Christopher K. 1952- St&PR 91
Smitrovich, Bill BioIn 16
Smitrovich, Bill 1947- ConTFT 8 [port]
Smits, Helen Lida 1936- WhoAm 90, WhoAmW 91, WhoE 91
Smits, Jimmy BioIn 16
Smits, Jimmy 1955- WhoHisp 91
Smits, Jimmy 1956- News 90 [port]
Smits, Jimmy 1958- WorAlBi
Smits, Raphaella Michaella Maria 1957- IntWWM 90
Smits, Robert L. 1943- St&PR 91
Smits, Theodore Richard 1905- WhoAm 90
Smitson, Harrison Adam, Jr. 1933- St&PR 91
Smiy, Paul R. 1923- St&PR 91
Smiy, William Charles 1927- St&PR 91
Smizinski, Linda Suzanne 1947- WhoAmW 91
Smoak, David S. 1947- WhoAm 90
Smoak, Joseph F. 1936- St&PR 91
Smoak, Neil A. 1946- St&PR 91
Smoak, Neil Arden 1946- WhoSSW 91
Smoak, Samuel D. 1933- St&PR 91
Smock, Arthur Reseau, Jr. 1920- WhoE 91
Smock, Connie Sue 1960- WhoAmW 91
Smock, James Arthur 1938- St&PR 91
Smock, Jeraldine 1943- WhoAmW 91
Smock, Joseph B. St&PR 91
Smock, Raymond William 1941- WhoAm 90
Smock, Roger P. 1942- St&PR 91
Smock, Sue WhoAm 90
Smogolski, Henry Richard 1931- St&PR 91
Smohalla 1815?-1907 WhNaAH
Smohallie 1815?-1907 WhNaAH
Smoke, Richard Edwin 1945- WhoWor 91
Smoker, Paul BioIn 16
Smokler, Jerold 1935- WhoAm 90
Smokler, Paul Edward 1951- WhoEmL 91
Smokler, Stan Barry 1944- WhoE 91
Smokler, Stanley B 1944- WhoAmA 91
Smola, Frank Albert 1949- WhoEmL 91
Smolan, Leslie BioIn 16
Smolansky, Oles M. 1930- WhoE 91
Smolarski, Joyce Amparin BiDrAPA 89
Smolen, Elwyn M BiDrAPA 89
Smolen, James Edward 1949- WhoEmL 91
Smolen, Robert S. 1931- St&PR 91
Smolen, Stan L. 1925 St&PR 91
Smolens, Joseph 1910-1988 BioIn 16
Smolenskin, Peretz 1842-1885 NinCLC 30
Smolensky, Eugene 1932- WhoAm 90
Smolensky, Jeffrey R. 1963- WhoE 91
Smolev, Barry Alan 1946- BiDrAPA 89
Smolian, Bertha BiDrAPA 89
Smolian, Joseph BiDrAPA 89
Smolich, Tom BioIn 16
Smolin, Bernard 1916- St&PR 91
Smolin, Nat 1890-1950 WhoAmA 91N
Smolin, Ronald Philip 1941- WhoAm 90
Smolinski, Edward Albert 1928- St&PR 91, WhoAm 90
Smolla, Rodney Alan 1953- WhoAm 90, WhoEmL 91
Smollen, Leonard Elliott 1930- WhoE 91
Smoller, Bruce M 1944- BiDrAPA 89
Smoller, Bruce Melvyn 1944- WhoE 91
Smoller, Howard Paul BiDrAPA 89
Smollett, Tobias 1721-1771 DcLB 104 [port], WorAlBi, WrPh
Smoltz, John 1967- Ballpl 90
Smolucha, Francine Carol 1953- WhoAmW 91
Smoluchowski, Roman 1910- WhoAm 90
Smongeski, Joseph Leon 1914- WhoAmA 91
Smook, Barbara Beatrice Lipscomb 1942- WhoSSW 91
Smook, John T. 1927- WhoSSW 91
Smook, Malcolm Andrew 1924- WhoAm 90
Smoot, Edgar G. R. 1939- WhoE 91
Smoot, Edward H. St&PR 91N
Smoot, Homer 1878-1928 Ballpl 90
Smoot, Jeanne Johannessen 1943- WhoE 91
Smoot, Joseph Grady 1932- WhoWor 91
Smoot, Leon Douglas 1934- WhoAm 90
Smoot, Leslie Allen 1953- WhoSSW 91
Smoot, Myrna L. 1945- WhoAm 90
Smoot, Oliver Reed, Jr. 1940- WhoAm 90
Smoot, Richard Leonard 1940- WhoAm 90
Smoot, Samantha Sue 1966- WhoAmW 91
Smoot, Sharene Lowery 1940- WhoAmW 91
Smoot, Wendell M., Jr. 1921- St&PR 91
Smoot, Wendell McMeans, Jr. 1921- WhoAm 90
Smoot, William Ambrose, Jr. 1951- WhoSSW 91
Smorag, Douglas John 1958- WhoEmL 91

Smorol, Albert Edward, Jr. 1940- *WhoAm 90*
Smotherman, Harold Monroe 1928- *St&PR 91*
Smotherman, Rondall D. 1938- *WhoSSW 91*
Smothers Brothers, The *WorAlBi*
Smothers, Dick *BioIn 16*
Smothers, Dick 1939- *WhoAm 90, WorAlBi*
Smothers, James Roy *BioIn 16*
Smothers, Tom *BioIn 16*
Smothers, Tom 1937- *WhoAm 90, WorAlBi*
Smothers, W.D. 1948- *St&PR 91*
Smothers, William Edgar, Jr. 1928- *St&PR 91, WhoAm 90*
Smothers, William Joseph 1919- *WhoAm 90*
Smotrich, David Isadore 1933- *WhoAm 90*
Smoulder, Blair Thomas 1942- *St&PR 91*
Smoyer, Phyllis Storm *BiDrAPA 89*
Smoyer, William P. 1942- *St&PR 91*
Smrekar, Erminio 1931- *WhoWor 91*
Smucker, Barbara Claassen 1915- *SmATA 11AS [port], WhoAm 90*
Smucker, Paul H. 1917- *St&PR 91*
Smucker, Paul Highnam 1917- *WhoAm 90*
Smuckler, Jack Dennis 1946- *WhoAm 90*
Smuckler, Mark B 1941- *BiDrAPA 89*
Smuckler, Ralph Herbert 1926- *WhoAm 90*
Smuin, Michael *BioIn 16*
Smukler, Arthur Jay 1942- *BiDrAPA 89*
Smukler, Victor 1931- *WhoE 91*
Smull, Cynthia Ann 1944- *WhoAmW 91*
Smullen, James Dennis 1916- *WhoAm 90*
Smullin, Patsy *BioIn 16*
Smullin, William B. *BioIn 16*
Smullin, William Brothers 1907- *WhoAm 90*
Smulowitz, William Joseph 1929- *St&PR 91*
Smulyan, Jeffrey *WhoAm 90*
Smurfit, Michael W. J. 1936- *WhoAm 90*
Smuskiewicz, Ted 1932- *WhoAmA 91*
Smutny, Joan Franklin *WhoAm 90*
Smutny, Peter J. 1935- *St&PR 91*
Smuts, Barbara B. *BioIn 16*
Smuts, Jan Christiaan 1870-1950 *WorAlBi*
Smuts, Mary Elizabeth 1948- *WhoAmW 91*
Smyer, Sidney William, Jr. 1928- *St&PR 91*
Smyk, Nicholas Harry 1961- *WhoSSW 91*
Smylie, Robert E. 1914- *BioIn 16*
Smyly, Barbara J. 1956- *WhoSSW 91*
Smyntek, John Eugene, Jr. 1950- *WhoAm 90, WhoEmL 91*
Smyre, Dane Ernest 1926- *St&PR 91*
Smyser, Adam A. 1920- *St&PR 91*
Smyser, Adam Albert 1920- *WhoAm 90*
Smyslovsky, Boris 1897-1988 *AnObit 1988*
Smyth, Andrew Jeffrey 1951- *WhoE 91*
Smyth, Anne 1605- *BiDEWW*
Smyth, Bernard John 1915- *WhoAm 90*
Smyth, Charles P. *NewYTBS 90*
Smyth, Charles Phelps 1895-1990 *BioIn 16*
Smyth, Craig Hugh 1915- *WhoAm 90, WhoAmA 91*
Smyth, D Edward I *ODwPR 91*
Smyth, David 1929- *WhoE 91*
Smyth, David John 1936- *WhoAm 90, WhoWor 91*
Smyth, Donald Morgan 1930- *WhoAm 90*
Smyth, Donna 1943- *FemiCLE*
Smyth, Ed 1916- *WhoAmA 91*
Smyth, Ethel 1858-1944 *FemiCLE, PenDiMP A*
Smyth, Ethel Mary 1858-1944 *BioIn 16*
Smyth, Frances Dale 1941- *WhoE 91*
Smyth, Glen Miller 1929- *WhoAm 90*
Smyth, Guy Lee *BiDrAPA 89*
Smyth, Henry Comegys, Jr. 1928- *WhoSSW 91*
Smyth, Henry DeWolf 1898-1986 *BioIn 16*
Smyth, Jeffrey J. 1940- *St&PR 91*
Smyth, Joel Douglas 1941- *WhoAm 90*
Smyth, John *BioIn 16*
Smyth, John Fletcher 1945- *WhoWor 91*
Smyth, John Henry 1844-1908 *BioIn 16*
Smyth, John M. 1915- *St&PR 91*
Smyth, Joseph Philip 1939- *St&PR 91*
Smyth, Joseph Vincent 1919- *WhoAm 90*
Smyth, Nicholas Patrick D. 1924- *WhoE 91*
Smyth, Pamela Ann 1961- *WhoAmW 91*
Smyth, Peter Hayes 1952- *WhoE 91*
Smyth, Reginald 1917- *WhoAm 90*
Smyth, Robert Edward 1947- *St&PR 91*
Smyth, Robert K. 1927- *St&PR 91*
Smyth, Whitney *ODwPR 91*
Smythe, Andrew James Hamilton 1957- *WhoWor 91*
Smythe, Marsha Susan Haller 1949- *WhoAmW 91*
Smythe, Robert C. *St&PR 91*
Smythe, Robert O. 1921- *St&PR 91*
Smythe, Russell *IntWWM 90*
Smythe, Sheila Mary 1932- *WhoAmW 91, WhoE 91*
Smythe, William Ellsworth 1861-1922 *BioIn 16*
Smythe, William Rodman 1930- *WhoAm 90*
Smythe-Haith, Mabel Murphy 1918- *WhoAm 90*
Smythe-Macaulay, Donald Charles Oguntola 1932- *WhoWor 91*
Smythies, Harriet 1813-1883 *FemiCLE*
Smythies, J R 1922- *EncO&P 3*
Smythies, John Raymond *BiDrAPA 89*
Smythies, John Raymond 1922- *EncPaPR 91*
Smythies, Susan 1721-1774? *FemiCLE*
Snape, Richard Hal 1936- *WhoWor 91*
Snaper, Alvin Allyn 1929- *St&PR 91*
Snapp, Barbara Denniston 1945- *WhoEmL 91*
Snapp, Elizabeth 1937- *WhoAmW 91, WhoSSW 91, WhoWor 91*
Snapp, Harry Franklin 1930- *WhoSSW 91*
Snapp, James A. 1935- *St&PR 91*
Snapp, Manco L. 1943- *St&PR 91*
Snapp, Robert Bruce, Jr. 1928- *St&PR 91*
Snapp, Roy Baker 1916- *WhoAm 90*
Snapper, Ernst 1913- *WhoAm 90*
Snapper, James Robert 1948- *WhoSSW 91*
Snaprud, Svein Ivar 1934- *WhoWor 91*
Snare, Carl Lawrence, Jr. 1936- *WhoWor 91*
Snare, Gary Ray 1947- *St&PR 91*
Snavely, Brant Rittenhouse 1908- *WhoAm 90*
Snavely, Cynthia Ann 1959- *WhoE 91*
Snavely, David Ashton 1946- *St&PR 91*
Snavely, Jack 1929- *IntWWM 90*
Snavely, Richard Mellinger 1931- *WhoE 91*
Snavely, William Pennington 1920- *WhoAm 90, WhoWor 91*
Snavely, William Pennington, Jr. 1948- *WhoWor 91*
Snead, Charles Budington 1928- *WhoSSW 91*
Snead, Charles D., Jr. 1932- *St&PR 91*
Snead, Edwin DeSteiguer 1929- *St&PR 91*
Snead, George Murrell, Jr. 1922- *WhoAm 90*
Snead, John L. Shaw 1912- *St&PR 91*
Snead, John Peyton, IV 1933- *BiDrAPA 89*
Snead, Richard Thomas 1951- *St&PR 91, WhoAm 90, WhoSSW 91*
Snead, Robert H. 1922- *St&PR 91*
Snead, Robert P 1940- *BiDrAPA 89*
Snead, Sam 1912- *WorAlBi*
Snead, Samuel Jackson 1912- *WhoAm 90*
Sneade, Barbara Herbert 1947- *WhoSSW 91*
Snearly, Sandra Jo 1954- *WhoAmW 91, WhoEmL 91*
Sneath, Lee 1941- *ODwPR 91*
Sneath, William Scott 1926- *St&PR 91*
Sneckenberg, William John 1946- *WhoEmL 91*
Snedaker, Catherine Raupagh *WhoAmW 91*
Snedaker, Dianne *WhoAmW 91*
Snedaker, Robert Hume, Jr. 1926- *St&PR 91*
Snedden, James Douglas 1925- *WhoAm 90*
Snedden, Louis Lyle 1913- *St&PR 91*
Snede, Donald James 1950- *St&PR 91*
Snedeker, Caroline Dale 1871- *AuBYP 90*
Snedeker, John Christian 1927- *WhoSSW 91*
Snedeker, John Haggner 1925- *WhoAm 90*
Snedeker, Joy Rowlands 1944- *WhoE 91*
Snedeker, Robert Dunbar 1943- *St&PR 91*
Sneden, George Kenneth 1932- *St&PR 91*
Snediker, Ellen 1930- *St&PR 91*
Snediker, Robert R. 1927- *St&PR 91*
Sneed, Emogene Mildred 1929- *WhoAmW 91*
Sneed, Gary Arnold 1931- *BiDrAPA 89*
Sneed, Jan *ODwPR 91*
Sneed, Jonathan Wilton *BiDrAPA 89*
Sneed, Joseph Donald 1938- *WhoAm 90*
Sneed, Joseph Tyree, III 1920- *WhoAm 90*
Sneed, Marie Eleanor Wilkey 1915- *WhoWor 91*
Sneed, Patricia M 1922- *WhoAmA 91*
Sneed, Paula Ann 1947- *WhoAmW 91*
Sneed, Spencer Craig 1951- *WhoEmL 91*
Sneeringer, Stephen Geddes 1949- *WhoEmL 91*
Snegur, Mircha Ivanovich 1940- *WhoWor 91*
Sneider, Joseph G. 1927- *St&PR 91*
Sneider, Martin Karl 1942- *St&PR 91, WhoAm 90*
Sneider, Norman Harry 1951- *WhoEmL 91*
Sneirson, Gregg Abner 1953- *WhoE 91*
Snekkestad, Tore 1958- *WhoWor 91*
Snelgrove, Gordon William *WhoAmA 91N*
Snell, Christopher Ray 1943- *St&PR 91*
Snell, Daniel Clair 1947- *WhoSSW 91*
Snell, Eric 1953- *WhoAmA 91*
Snell, Esmond Emerson 1914- *WhoAm 90*
Snell, Frank Linn 1899- *St&PR 91, WhoAm 90*
Snell, George 1903- *WorAlBi*
Snell, George D. 1909- *St&PR 91*
Snell, George Davis 1903- *WhoAm 90, WhoE 91, WhoWor 91*
Snell, Hamlin Valentine 1810-1886 *AmLegL*
Snell, Jack Eastlake 1935- *WhoAm 90*
Snell, James Laurie 1925- *WhoAm 90*
Snell, John E *BiDrAPA 89*
Snell, John Raymond 1912- *WhoAm 90*
Snell, John T. 1947- *St&PR 91*
Snell, Jonathan Getman 1962- *WhoSSW 91*
Snell, Marie Letty 1924- *WhoAmW 91*
Snell, Michael D. 1952- *St&PR 91*
Snell, Nate 1952- *Ballpl 90*
Snell, Nigel 1936- *BioIn 16*
Snell, Peter *BioIn 16*
Snell, Peter 1938- *WorAlBi*
Snell, Richard 1930- *St&PR 91, WhoAm 90*
Snell, Richard Saxon 1925- *WhoAm 90*
Snell, Robert E. 1941- *ODwPR 91*
Snell, Robert L.S. 1932- *St&PR 91*
Snell, Stephen Pedersen 1936- *St&PR 91*
Snell, V.H. 1931- *St&PR 91*
Snell, Willis Byron 1927- *WhoAm 90*
Sneller, Lee James 1940- *St&PR 91*
Snellgrove, L. E. 1928- *BioIn 16*
Snellgrove, Laurence Ernest 1928- *BioIn 16*
Snelling, Anne Morris 1935- *St&PR 91*
Snelling, Charles D. 1931- *St&PR 91*
Snelling, George Arthur 1929- *St&PR 91, WhoAm 90*
Snelling, Lee Ann 1963- *WhoAmW 91*
Snelling, Lonie Eugene, Jr. 1937- *WhoSSW 91*
Snelling, Richard Arkwright 1927- *WhoAm 90*
Snelling, Richard Kelly 1931- *St&PR 91, WhoAm 90*
Snelling, Robert O., Sr. 1932- *St&PR 91*
Snelling, Robert Orren, Sr. 1932- *WhoSSW 91*
Snelling, William Rodman 1931- *WhoE 91, WhoWor 91*
Snellman, Johan Vilhelm 1806-1881 *DcScanL*
Snelson, Donna Ayers *BioIn 16*
Snelson, Franklin Fielder, III 1964- *WhoSSW 91*
Snelson, Keith R. 1928- *St&PR 91*
Snelson, Kenneth D 1927- *WhoAmA 91*
Snelson, Kenneth Duane 1927- *WhoAm 90*
Snelson, Roy 1927- *WhoAm 90*
Snetsinger, David Clarence 1930- *WhoAm 90*
Snetzer, Michael Alan 1940- *St&PR 91, WhoAm 90*
Snezhnevskiy, Andrei V *BiDrAPA 89*
Sniadak, Gary Joseph 1948- *St&PR 91*
Snibbe, Patricia Miscall 1932- *WhoE 91, WhoWor 91*
Snibbe, Richard W. 1916- *WhoAm 90*
Snider, Albert Russell 1930- *WhoAm 90*
Snider, Basil 1927- *St&PR 91*
Snider, Bruce Alan 1946- *BiDrAPA 89*
Snider, Clifton Mark 1947- *WhoWrEP 89*
Snider, David Leslie 1957- *WhoEmL 91*
Snider, Drew 1944- *St&PR 91*
Snider, Duke 1926- *Ballpl 90 [port], BioIn 16*
Snider, Edward Malcolm 1933- *WhoE 91*
Snider, Edwin Wallace 1923- *WhoAm 90*
Snider, Eliot I. 1921- *St&PR 91*
Snider, George R., Jr. 1941- *ODwPR 91*
Snider, Gordon Lloyd 1922- *WhoAm 90*
Snider, Harlan Tanner 1926- *WhoAm 90*
Snider, Harold Wayne 1923- *WhoAm 90*
Snider, Helen Kaye 1954- *WhoEmL 91*
Snider, James Rhodes 1931- *WhoSSW 91*
Snider, Jay T. *WhoAm 90, WhoE 91*
Snider, John Joseph 1928- *WhoAm 90*
Snider, Judy K. 1945- *WhoAmW 91*
Snider, L. Britt 1945- *WhoAm 90, WhoE 91*
Snider, Lois A. Phillips 1949- *WhoAmW 91*
Snider, Marie Anna 1927- *WhoAmW 91, WhoWor 91*
Snider, Michael Robert 1953- *St&PR 91*
Snider, Paul Norman 1943- *BiDrAPA 89*
Snider, R. Larry 1932- *St&PR 91*
Snider, Robert Cusator 1924- *WhoE 91*
Snider, Robert F. 1931- *WhoAm 90*
Snider, Robert Larry 1932- *WhoAm 90*
Snider, Ronald Albert 1948- *WhoEmL 91*
Snider, Ronald Edward, Jr. 1955- *St&PR 91*
Snider, Ruth *WhoWrEP 89*
Snider, William Alan 1967- *WhoE 91*
Snider, William D. 1941- *St&PR 91*
Sniderman, Allan David 1941- *WhoAm 90*
Sniderman, Marvin 1923- *WhoE 91*
Snidow, Gordon E 1936- *WhoAmA 91*
Sniff, Mr. *AuBYP 90*
Sniffen, Michael Joseph 1949- *WhoE 91*
Sniffin, John Harrison 1942- *WhoAm 90*
Sniffin, William Charles 1946- *WhoEmL 91*
Sninchak, Faye Rita 1947- *WhoE 91*
Snipe, Valerie Brooks 1958- *WhoAmW 91*
Snipes, Barry Eugene 1953- *WhoSSW 91*
Snipes, Jackie Alice 1945- *WhoSSW 91*
Snitil, Vaclav *PenDiMP*
Snitker, Gene D. 1952- *St&PR 91*
Snitow, Charles 1907- *WhoE 91*
Snitzer, Elias 1925- *WhoAm 90*
Snitzer, Isadore 1921- *St&PR 91*
Snively, Scott Kennedy 1845-1931 *AmLegL*
Snively, William Daniel, Jr. 1911- *WhoAm 90*
Snoble, John Allen 1942- *St&PR 91*
Snoddon, Larry E. *ODwPR 91*
Snoddon, Larry E. 1945- *WhoAm 90*
Snoddy, Charles Edison, Jr. 1923- *WhoE 91*
Snoddy, James Donaldson 1837-1917 *AmLegL*
Snoddy, James Ernest 1932- *WhoAm 90*
Snoddy, Wayne Leonard 1948- *WhoSSW 91*
Snodgrass family *BioIn 16*
Snodgrass, Ann A. 1958- *WhoWrEP 89*
Snodgrass, Billie Kay 1947- *WhoWrEP 89*
Snodgrass, Donald Ray 1935- *WhoE 91*
Snodgrass, Faye Birdwell 1941- *WhoSSW 91*
Snodgrass, Fred 1887-1974 *Ballpl 90*
Snodgrass, Lanny Lloyd *BiDrAPA 89*
Snodgrass, Mary Ellen *BioIn 16*
Snodgrass, Mary Ellen 1944- *WhoAmW 91*
Snodgrass, Robert E 1930- *BiDrAPA 89*
Snodgrass, Robert William 1921- *St&PR 91*
Snodgrass, Roger E. 1927- *St&PR 91*
Snodgrass, Sheri L. 1956- *WhoAmW 91*
Snodgrass, Thomas Jefferson *AuBYP 90*
Snodgrass, Tod John 1945- *WhoWrEP 89*
Snodgrass, Virginia Harriet 1937- *St&PR 91*
Snodgrass, W. D. 1926- *BioIn 16, WhoAm 90, WhoWrEP 89, WorAlBi*
Snodgrass, William D 1926- *MajTwCW*
Snodgrass, William De Witt 1926- *BioIn 16*
Snodgrass-King, Jeanne Owens 1927- *WhoAmA 91*
Snodgres, Elizabeth Ann 1948- *WhoSSW 91*
Snoilsky, Carl 1881-1903 *DcScanL*
Snoke, George R. 1922- *St&PR 91*
Snoll, Daveed Robert 1964- *WhoSSW 91*
Snook, Herbert Edgar 1945- *WhoWrEP 89*
Snook, John Lloyd, III 1953- *WhoEmL 91*
Snook, John McClure 1917- *WhoAm 90, WhoSSW 91, WhoWor 91*
Snook, John Ramsey 1938- *WhoWor 91*
Snook, Peter *St&PR 91*
Snook, Quinton 1925- *WhoWor 91*
Snooks, Graeme Donald 1944- *WhoWor 91*
Snoozy, Robert Sherrill 1946- *St&PR 91*
Snopkowski, Daniel M. 1952- *St&PR 91*
Snorek, Randy Elgin 1951- *WhoSSW 91*
Snorf, Lowell Delford, Jr. 1919- *St&PR 91*
Snorri Hjartarson *DcScanL*
Snorri Sturluson *DcScanL*
Snortland, Howard Jerome 1912- *WhoAm 90*
Snow, Lady 1912-1981 *DcNaB 1981*
Snow, Albert Joseph 1935- *WhoE 91*
Snow, Bernard 1931- *BiDrAPA 89*
Snow, Bernard Rutherford 1953- *WhoE 91*
Snow, Bonnie 1952- *WhoWrEP 89*
Snow, C P 1905-1980 *MajTwCW*
Snow, C. P. 1905-1980 *WorAlBi*
Snow, Charles Percy 1905-1980 *DcScB S2*
Snow, Cindy 1957- *WhoAmW 91*
Snow, Claude Henry, Jr. 1954- *WhoEmL 91*
Snow, Claude Ray 1936- *St&PR 91*
Snow, Clyde *BioIn 16*
Snow, Curtis Murray 1922- *St&PR 91*
Snow, Cynthia Reeves 1907- *WhoAmA 91*
Snow, D. McKay 1937- *St&PR 91*
Snow, David Lloyd *BiDrAPA 89*
Snow, Dennis Craig 1950- *St&PR 91*
Snow, Donald Clifford *AuBYP 90*
Snow, Donald M. 1943- *WhoE 91*
Snow, Donald Ray 1931- *WhoAm 90*
Snow, Dwight L. 1933- *St&PR 91*
Snow, E. Ned 1930- *St&PR 91*
Snow, Edgar 1905-1972 *BioIn 16, EncAL*
Snow, Edward *ODwPR 91*
Snow, Edwina Feigenspan 1927- *WhoAmW 91, WhoE 91*
Snow, Elizabeth Jean 1943- *WhoAmW 91*

Snow, Emasue *BiDrAPA 89*
Snow, George Abraham 1926- *WhoAm 90*
Snow, George K. 1933- *St&PR 91*
Snow, George L. 1921- *St&PR 91*
Snow, Gordon Harold 1907- *WhoAm 90*
Snow, Hank 1914- *OxCPMus, WorAlBi*
Snow, Harold L *BiDrAPA 89*
Snow, Hugh Aldean 1924- *St&PR 91*
Snow, Jack *ODwPR 91*
Snow, James Byron, Jr. 1932- *WhoAm 90*
Snow, Jeffrey Louis 1961- *BiDrAPA 89*
Snow, John 1911- *WhoAmA 91*
Snow, John William 1939- *St&PR 91, WhoAm 90, WhoSSW 91, WhoWor 91*
Snow, Judith Rohletter 1948- *WhoAmW 91*
Snow, Karl Nelson, Jr. 1930- *WhoAm 90*
Snow, Lee Erlin 1924- *WhoAmA 91*
Snow, Lisa Renee *BiDrAPA 89*
Snow, Marie T Lane 1915- *BiDrAPA 89*
Snow, Mary R 1908- *WhoAmA 91*
Snow, Michael 1929- *BioIn 16, WhoAmA 91*
Snow, Milton Leonard 1930- *WhoE 91*
Snow, Nick 1961- *WhoWor 91*
Snow, Philip 1952- *ConAu 130*
Snow, Phoebe *BioIn 16*
Snow, Phoebe 1952- *ConMus 4 [port], EncPR&S 89*
Snow, Richard F. *BioIn 16*
Snow, Richard F. 1939- *St&PR 91*
Snow, Richard Graham, Jr. 1945- *St&PR 91*
Snow, Robert Anthony 1955- *WhoAm 90, WhoE 91*
Snow, Robert B. 1917- *St&PR 91*
Snow, Robert Brian 1953- *WhoEmL 91*
Snow, Robert Lawrence 1949- *WhoWrEP 89*
Snow, Robert W. 1931- *St&PR 91*
Snow, Sarah Turnbull 1952- *WhoAmW 91*
Snow, Stanley Steve 1951- *BiDrAPA 89*
Snow, Sue *BioIn 16*
Snow, Susan Dale *BiDrAPA 89*
Snow, Tower Charles, Jr. 1947- *WhoEmL 91*
Snow, Valaida 1900?-1956 *DrBlPA 90, OxCPMus*
Snow, William Cullum 1929- *St&PR 91*
Snow, William Hayden 1926- *St&PR 91, WhoAm 90*
Snow, William Riley *BiDrAPA 89*
Snow-Robinson, Alice 1955- *WhoE 91*
Snow-Webb, Mary Alicen 1953- *WhoAmW 91*
Snowball, Emma *BioIn 16*
Snowbarger, Vincent Keith 1949- *WhoEmL 91*
Snowbarger, Willis Edward 1921- *WhoAm 90*
Snowday, H. Terry, Jr. 1935- *St&PR 91*
Snowden, Bernice Rives 1923- *WhoAmW 91*
Snowden, Diana Emily 1947- *WhoWor 91*
Snowden, Frank Martin, Jr. 1911- *WhoAm 90*
Snowden, Gilda 1954- *WhoAmA 91*
Snowden, Guy B. 1945- *St&PR 91*
Snowden, Guy Bernhard 1945- *WhoAm 90*
Snowden, James Arthur 1948- *WhoEmL 91*
Snowden, Lawrence Fontaine 1921- *WhoAm 90*
Snowden, Muriel 1916-1988 *BioIn 16*
Snowden, Philip 1864-1937 *BioIn 16*
Snowden, Richeleen A. 1940- *WhoSSW 91*
Snowden, Robert G. 1917- *St&PR 91*
Snowden, Ruth O'Dell Gillespie 1926- *WhoAmW 91*
Snowdon, Anthony 1930- *WhoWor 91*
Snowdon, Ruth J 1896- *EncO&P 3*
Snowdon, W. Latimer, Jr. 1936- *St&PR 91*
Snowe, Olympia J. 1947- *WhoAm 90, WhoAmW 91, WhoE 91*
Snowflake *DrBlPA 90*
Snowman, Daniel 1938- *ConAu 33NR*
Snowman, Nicholas 1944- *IntWWM 90*
Snoy, Didrik 1924- *St&PR 91*
Snuggs, Graham 1955- *WhoWor 91*
Snydacker, William Fackert 1945- *St&PR 91*
Snydal, James Matthew 1949- *WhoWrEP 89*
Snyde, David Edward 1944- *St&PR 91*
Snyder, Allegra Fuller 1927- *WhoAm 90, WhoAmW 91, WhoWor 91*
Snyder, Allen Roger 1946- *WhoEmL 91*
Snyder, Alvin 1936- *WhoAm 90*
Snyder, Andrea Madeline *BiDrAPA 89*
Snyder, Andrea Madeline 1955- *WhoE 91*
Snyder, Ann Marie 1946- *BiDrAPA 89*
Snyder, Ann McNelis 1940- *WhoAmW 91*
Snyder, Anne *BioIn 16*
Snyder, Arlene 1944- *WhoAmW 91*
Snyder, Arnold Lee, Jr. 1937- *WhoE 91, WhoWor 91*
Snyder, Arthur 1925- *St&PR 91, WhoAm 90*
Snyder, Arthur, III 1955- *St&PR 91*
Snyder, Arthur Kress 1932- *WhoWor 91*
Snyder, Barbara Irene 1937- *WhoAmW 91*
Snyder, Benson R *BiDrAPA 89*
Snyder, Bernard M 1937- *BiDrAPA 89*
Snyder, Brian Keith 1963- *WhoSSW 91*
Snyder, Bruce Franklin 1938- *St&PR 91*
Snyder, Carl W., Jr. 1928- *St&PR 91*
Snyder, Charles Aubrey 1941- *WhoAm 90*
Snyder, Charles J. 1915- *St&PR 91*
Snyder, Charles Royce 1924- *WhoAm 90*
Snyder, Christine Gloria 1955- *WhoAmW 91*
Snyder, Clair A. 1921- *St&PR 91*
Snyder, Clair Allison 1921- *WhoAm 90*
Snyder, Clyde Reid *BiDrAPA 89*
Snyder, Cory 1962- *Ballpl 90*
Snyder, Dan 1948- *WhoAmA 91*
Snyder, Dana P. 1922- *WhoE 91*
Snyder, David Andrew 1949- *WhoSSW 91*
Snyder, David Lee 1954- *BiDrAPA 89*
Snyder, David Markel 1939- *WhoAm 90*
Snyder, David T. 1928- *ODwPR 91*
Snyder, Dennis Chrisman 1940- *St&PR 91*
Snyder, Diane *AuBYP 90*
Snyder, Dick *AuBYP 90*
Snyder, Dick Gene 1936- *St&PR 91*
Snyder, Diehl M 1951- *BiDrAPA 89*
Snyder, Donald Edward 1928- *WhoAm 90*
Snyder, Donald Ray 1933- *St&PR 91*
Snyder, E.H. *St&PR 91N*
Snyder, Edwin Arthur 1932- *St&PR 91*
Snyder, Elise W 1934- *BiDrAPA 89*
Snyder, Elliott Harvey 1948- *BiDrAPA 89*
Snyder, Frank 1893-1962 *Ballpl 90*
Snyder, Frank Ronald, II 1939- *St&PR 91*
Snyder, Franklin Arthur 1927- *St&PR 91*
Snyder, Franklin Farison 1910- *WhoAm 90*
Snyder, Frederick Edward 1944- *WhoE 91*
Snyder, Gary 1930- *ConAu 30NR*
Snyder, Gary Sherman 1930- *WhoAm 90, WhoWrEP 89*
Snyder, George Edward 1934- *WhoAm 90, WhoWor 91*
Snyder, George W. 1942- *St&PR 91*
Snyder, Georgie Ann 1945- *WhoAmW 91*
Snyder, Gerald 1944- *St&PR 91*
Snyder, Gerald S. 1933- *BioIn 16*
Snyder, Giles D.H. 1931- *St&PR 91*
Snyder, Giles D. H. 1931- *WhoAm 90*
Snyder, Ginger Lynne 1966- *WhoAmW 91*
Snyder, Helen Pohlabel 1916- *WhoAmW 91*
Snyder, Henry Leonard 1929- *WhoAm 90*
Snyder, Hills 1950- *WhoAmA 91*
Snyder, Hugh Robin 1936- *St&PR 91*
Snyder, Irving George, Jr. 1937- *St&PR 91, WhoAm 90*
Snyder, Jack O. 1942- *St&PR 91*
Snyder, Jack R *BiDrAPA 89*
Snyder, Jack Ralph 1940- *WhoAm 90*
Snyder, James Donald 1937- *WhoWrEP 89*
Snyder, James E 1928-1990 *ConAu 132*
Snyder, James F. 1944- *St&PR 91*
Snyder, James M. 1940- *St&PR 91*
Snyder, Jane McIntosh 1943- *ConAu 130*
Snyder, Jane Peters 1925- *WhoAmW 91, WhoE 91*
Snyder, Janet Ruth 1932- *WhoAmW 91*
Snyder, Jean Maclean 1942- *WhoAmW 91*
Snyder, Jeanne Anne 1945- *WhoAm 90*
Snyder, Jed Cobb 1955- *WhoE 91, WhoEmL 91, WhoWor 91*
Snyder, Jeff 1951- *ODwPR 91*
Snyder, Jeffery Sims 1956- *WhoSSW 91*
Snyder, Jerome 1916-1976 *ConDes 90*
Snyder, Jerry 1929- *Ballpl 90*
Snyder, Jimmy the Greek *BioIn 16*
Snyder, Joan 1940- *BiDWomA, WhoAm 90, WhoAmA 91, WhoAmW 91*
Snyder, John Bennett 1929- *St&PR 91, WhoAm 90*
Snyder, John C. *St&PR 91*
Snyder, John Field 1959- *WhoE 91*
Snyder, John Joseph 1908- *WhoWor 91*
Snyder, John Joseph 1925- *WhoAm 90, WhoSSW 91*
Snyder, John Lindsey 1933- *WhoAm 90*
Snyder, John P 1926- *ConAu 31NR*
Snyder, John S. *BioIn 16*
Snyder, John Wesley 1895-1985 *BiDrUSE 89*
Snyder, Jonathan Edvard 1958- *WhoSSW 91*
Snyder, Joseph H. 1920- *ODwPR 91*
Snyder, Joseph John 1946- *WhoEmL 91, WhoSSW 91, WhoWor 91*
Snyder, Joyce Elaine 1933- *WhoAmW 91*
Snyder, Judith B. 1947- *WhoE 91*
Snyder, Judy K *BiDrAPA 89*
Snyder, Julia Ann 1950- *WhoAmW 91, WhoEmL 91*
Snyder, Larry *NewAgMG*
Snyder, Leeann 1965- *WhoE 91*
Snyder, Leonard Michael 1948- *St&PR 91*
Snyder, Lewis Emil 1939- *WhoAm 90*
Snyder, Linda P. *ODwPR 91*
Snyder, Louis Leo 1907- *AuBYP 90, WhoAm 90*
Snyder, Luther D. *St&PR 91N*
Snyder, Lynne Ann 1958- *WhoE 91*
Snyder, Maria Lynne 1962- *WhoAmW 91*
Snyder, Marion Gene 1928- *WhoAm 90*
Snyder, Mark Alan 1942- *BiDrAPA 89*
Snyder, Mark George 1953- *WhoE 91*
Snyder, Mark Jeffrey 1947- *WhoE 91*
Snyder, Martha Jane 1953- *WhoE 91*
Snyder, Marvin 1940- *WhoAm 90*
Snyder, Michael L *BiDrAPA 89*
Snyder, Michele Manne 1952- *St&PR 91*
Snyder, Michelle Ann 1966- *WhoE 91*
Snyder, Mitch *BioIn 16*
Snyder, Mitch *NewYTBS 90 [port]*
Snyder, Mitch 1944?-1990 *News 91-1*
Snyder, Nancy Ellen 1935- *WhoWrEP 89*
Snyder, Nathan 1934- *St&PR 91, WhoAm 90*
Snyder, Norman Irwin 1945- *BiDrAPA 89*
Snyder, Oliver P. 1927- *St&PR 91*
Snyder, Pamela Spotswood 1957- *WhoE 91*
Snyder, Paul Leon 1948- *WhoEmL 91*
Snyder, Peter B. 1954- *WhoEmL 91*
Snyder, Peter Burgess 1943- *WhoE 91*
Snyder, Peter Larsen 1952- *WhoAm 90*
Snyder, Ralph Sheldon 1922- *WhoAm 90*
Snyder, Richard A. 1910- *WhoE 91*
Snyder, Richard A. 1940- *St&PR 91*
Snyder, Richard Carlton 1916- *WhoAm 90*
Snyder, Richard Donald 1931- *BiDrAPA 89*
Snyder, Richard E. 1933- *WorAlBi*
Snyder, Richard Elliot 1933- *St&PR 91, WhoAm 90, WhoE 91*
Snyder, Richard Joseph 1939- *WhoAm 90*
Snyder, Richard L. 1931- *St&PR 91*
Snyder, Richard Lee 1940- *WhoAm 90*
Snyder, Richard Lynne 1927- *WhoWrEP 89*
Snyder, Richard Wesley 1938- *WhoAm 90, WhoSSW 91*
Snyder, Robert Edgar, Jr. 1938- *WhoSSW 91*
Snyder, Robert H. 1855- *AmLegL*
Snyder, Robert Harvey 1918- *St&PR 91*
Snyder, Robert J. 1949- *St&PR 91*
Snyder, Robert Lee 1952- *WhoEmL 91*
Snyder, Robert Martin 1912- *WhoAm 90, WhoWor 91*
Snyder, Robert Martin 1940- *St&PR 91*
Snyder, Robert Raboin 1946- *WhoAm 90*
Snyder, Robin Esther 1947- *WhoAmW 91*
Snyder, Ronald R. 1944- *WhoAm 90*
Snyder, Ross L, Jr. 1931- *BiDrAPA 89*
Snyder, Russ 1934- *Ballpl 90*
Snyder, Ruth *WhoAmA 91*
Snyder, Sam A. 1930- *St&PR 91*
Snyder, Scott 1950- *BiDrAPA 89*
Snyder, Scott William 1946- *WhoSSW 91*
Snyder, Solomon H 1938- *BiDrAPA 89*
Snyder, Solomon Halbert 1938- *WhoAm 90*
Snyder, Stanley Paul 1934- *St&PR 91*
Snyder, Stephen F. 1938- *St&PR 91*
Snyder, Stephen L. 1957- *BiDrAPA 89*
Snyder, Stephen P. 1940- *St&PR 91*
Snyder, Stuart Jay 1945- *WhoEmL 91*
Snyder, Susan Brooke 1934- *WhoAm 90, WhoAmW 91, WhoWrEP 89*
Snyder, Ted 1881-1965 *BioIn 16, OxCPMus*
Snyder, Terrence B. 1951- *St&PR 91*
Snyder, Thoma Mees van'tHoff 1916- *WhoWor 91*
Snyder, Thomas Arthur 1932- *St&PR 91*
Snyder, Thomas D. 1949- *St&PR 91*
Snyder, Thomas Daniel 1925- *WhoSSW 91*
Snyder, Thomas Eugene 1948- *BiDrAPA 89*
Snyder, Thomas R. *St&PR 91*
Snyder, W.P., III 1918- *St&PR 91*
Snyder, W. Patrick *St&PR 91*
Snyder, Wanda Lorraine Webber 1944- *WhoAmW 91*
Snyder, Wesley Warren 1935- *WhoSSW 91*
Snyder, Willard A. 1936- *St&PR 91*
Snyder, Willard B. 1940- *St&PR 91*
Snyder, Willard Breidenthal 1940- *WhoWor 91*
Snyder, William B 1928- *WhoAmA 91*
Snyder, William B. 1929- *St&PR 91*
Snyder, William Burton 1929- *WhoAm 90, WhoE 91*
Snyder, William D. 1959- *WhoAm 90, WhoSSW 91*
Snyder, William E. 1914-1988 *BioIn 16*
Snyder, William Francis 1952- *WhoE 91*
Snyder, William H. 1946- *St&PR 91*
Snyder, William L. 1935- *St&PR 91*
Snyder, William Lawson 1935- *WhoAm 90, WhoE 91*
Snyder, William Penn, III 1918- *WhoAm 90*
Snyder, William Russell 1926- *St&PR 91, WhoAm 90*
Snyder, Zilpha Keatley *BioIn 16*
Snyder, Zilpha Keatley 1927- *AuBYP 90, WhoWrEP 89*
Snyder-Speak, Catherine Gail 1960- *WhoAmW 91*
Snyderman, Barbara Bloch 1932- *WhoAmW 91*
Snyderman, Perry James 1932- *WhoAm 90*
Snyderman, Ralph 1940- *WhoAm 90*
Snyderman, Reuven Kenneth 1922- *WhoAm 90*
Snyderman, Selma Eleanor 1916- *WhoAmW 91*
Snyders, Frans 1579-1657 *IntDcAA 90*
So, K. W. Andrew 1939- *WhoWor 91*
So, Rosa Rosales *BiDrAPA 89*
So, Victor Ang 1912- *WhoWor 91*
Soal, S G 1889-1975 *EncO&P 3*
Soal, Samuel George 1889-1975 *EncPaPR 91*
Soales, Madelyn Geddes 1953- *WhoEmL 91*
Soami 1455?-1525 *EncJap*
Soane, John 1753-1837 *BioIn 16*
Soar, Hank 1914- *Ballpl 90*
Soare, Robert Irving 1940- *WhoAm 90*
Soares, Eusebio Lopes 1918- *WhoWor 91*
Soares, James 1936- *BioIn 16*
Soares, Mario 1924- *WorAlBi*
Soares, Mario Alberto Nobre Lopes 1924- *WhoWor 91*
Soares, Nelson Duarte 1943- *WhoWor 91*
Soares de Mello, Adelino Jose Rodrigues 1931- *WhoWor 91*
Sobalvarro, J. Roberto 1927- *St&PR 91*
Sobczyk, James Benjamin 1957- *WhoE 91*
Sobecki, Thomas Alva 1956- *WhoEmL 91*
Sobek, David John 1962- *WhoSSW 91*
Sobel, Alan 1928- *WhoAm 90*
Sobel, Barry *BioIn 16*
Sobel, Bernard S 1943- *BiDrAPA 89*
Sobel, Bernese Panzer 1920- *WhoAmW 91*
Sobel, Burton Elias 1937- *WhoAm 90*
Sobel, Dava *BioIn 16*
Sobel, David E 1927- *BiDrAPA 89*
Sobel, Erwin 1938- *WhoWor 91*
Sobel, Howard Bernard 1929- *WhoAm 90*
Sobel, Janine M 1955- *BiDrAPA 89*
Sobel, Joan Ellen *BiDrAPA 89*
Sobel, Lawrence Jay *BiDrAPA 89*
Sobel, Lester Albert 1919- *WhoWrEP 89*
Sobel, Lori S 1958- *BiDrAPA 89*
Sobel, Morton 1917- *WorAlBi*
Sobel, Raymond *BiDrAPA 89*
Sobel, Richard M *BiDrAPA 89*
Sobel, Robert 1931- *ConAu 31NR, WhoE 91*
Sobel, Robert Neal *BiDrAPA 89*
Sobel, Stanton 1933- *St&PR 91*
Sobel, Stephen V 1956- *BiDrAPA 89*
Sobel, Walter Howard 1913- *WhoAm 90*
Soben, Robert Sidney 1947- *WhoSSW 91*
Sober, Debra E. 1953- *WhoAmW 91*
Sober, Elliott 1948- *ConAu 132*
Sober, Reva *St&PR 91*
Soberon, Presentacion Zablan 1935- *WhoAmW 91*
Soberon-Ferrer, Horacio 1954- *WhoHisp 91*
Sobey, David F. *St&PR 91*
Sobey, David F. 1931- *WhoAm 90*
Sobey, Donald Creighton Rae *WhoAm 90*
Sobey, Edwin J. C. 1948- *WhoAm 90*
Sobieraj, Jan Tarika *BiDrAPA 89*
Sobiesk, Emory John 1933- *BiDrAPA 89*
Sobieski, Carol *NewYTBS 90*
Sobieski, Carol 1939- *ConAu 129*
Sobieski, Carol 1939-1990 *ConAu 132*
Sobieski, J. Thomas 1941- *St&PR 91*
Sobieski, James Louis 1936- *St&PR 91*
Sobieski, Wanda Graham 1947- *WhoEmL 91*
Sobiloff, Myer Nathaniel 1907- *WhoAm 90*
Sobin, Anthony 1944- *WhoWrEP 89*
Sobin, Julian M 1920- *ConAu 132*
Sobin, Julian Melvin 1920- *WhoAm 90*
Sobin, Michael B. 1941- *St&PR 91*
Sobin, Morris 1913- *WhoAm 90*
Sobin, Paul Bennet *BiDrAPA 89*
Sobinov, Leonid 1872-1934 *PenDiMP*
Sobkowicz, Hanna Maria 1931- *WhoAm 90*
Soble, David S. 1943- *St&PR 91, WhoAm 90*
Soble, Stephen M. 1951- *WhoE 91, WhoEmL 91*
Sobleskie, Patricia Angela 1947- *WhoWrEP 89*
Sobol, Donald J. 1924- *AuBYP 90*
Sobol, Elizabeth 1943- *WhoAm 90*
Sobol, Harold 1930- *WhoAm 90*
Sobol, Harriet Langsam 1936- *BioIn 16*
Sobol, Joseph W. 1949- *St&PR 91*
Sobol, Joshua *BioIn 16*
Sobol, Joshua 19--?- *ConLC 60 [port]*
Sobol, Judith Ellen 1946- *WhoAmA 91, WhoE 91*

Sobol, Michael Richard 1946- *St&PR 91*
Sobol, Thomas 1932- *WhoE 91*
Soboleski, Leon 1946- *St&PR 91*
Sobolewski, Edward A *BiDrAPA 89*
Sobolewski, Timothy Richard 1951- *WhoE 91*
Sobolik, Craig Terry 1949- *WhoWrEP 89*
Sobong, Loreto Calibo 1931- *WhoSSW 91*
Sobota, Walter Louis 1946- *WhoEmL 91*
Sobotka, Dale Frank *BiDrAPA 89*
Sobotka, John Robert 1940- *BiDrAPA 89*
Sobotka, Jon Duane 1957- *BiDrAPA 89*
Sobralske, Barbara Nila 1949- *WhoAmW 91*
Sobukwe, Robert Mangaliso 1924-1978 *BioIn 16*
Soby, James Thrall 1906-1979 *WhoAmA 91N*
Sobyak, Lawrence Edward 1937- *St&PR 91*
Socarides, Charles W 1922- *BiDrAPA 89*
Socarides, Charles William 1922- *WhoE 91*
Socarras, Carlos Prio 1903-1977 *BioIn 16*
Socci, Giovanni *PenDiDA 89*
Socci, Patrick J. 1948- *St&PR 91*
Socha, Wladyslaw Wojciech 1926- *WhoAm 90*
Sochen, June 1937- *WhoAm 90, WhoAmW 91*
Socher, Karl Friedrich 1928- *WhoWor 91*
Sochet, Mary Allen 1938- *WhoAmW 91*
Sochurek, Howard James 1924- *WhoE 91*
Socie, Darrell Frederick 1948- *WhoAm 90*
Sockalexis, Lou 1871-1913 *Ballpl 90*
Sockett, Hugh Talbot 1937- *WhoSSW 91*
Sockwell, Joel Clinton 1938- *St&PR 91*
Sockwell, Oliver R., Jr. 1943- *WhoAm 90*
Socol, Howard *WhoSSW 91*
Socol, Leon S. 1926- *St&PR 91*
Socol, Leon Sheinberg 1926- *WhoSSW 91*
Socol, Sheldon Eleazer 1936- *WhoE 91*
Socolofsky, Iris Kay 1952- *WhoAmW 91, WhoEmL 91*
Socolofsky, John Edward 1946- *WhoAm 90*
Socolofsky, Jon E. 1946- *St&PR 91*
Socolofsky, Marion David 1931- *WhoSSW 91*
Socolofsky, Marth Ann *BiDrAPA 89*
Socolovsky, Alberto *BioIn 16*
Socolow, Arthur Abraham 1921- *WhoAm 90, WhoE 91*
Socolow, Elizabeth A. 1940- *WhoWrEP 89*
Socolow, Robert Harry 1937- *WhoAm 90*
Socolow, Sanford 1928- *St&PR 91*
Socrates *BioIn 16*
Socrates 469BC-399BC *EncPaPR 91*
Socrates 470?BC-399?BC *WorAlBi, WrPh P*
Sodal, Ingvar Edmund 1934- *WhoAm 90*
Sodaro, Edward R 1947- *BiDrAPA 89*
Sodaro, Edward Richard 1947- *WhoE 91*
Sodaro, Robert J. 1955- *WhoWrEP 89*
Sodd, Vincent Joseph 1934- *WhoAm 90*
Sodderland, Jan Willem 1942- *WhoWor 91*
Soddy, Frederick 1877-1956 *WorAlBi*
Sode, Lizabeth G. *St&PR 91*
Sodeman, Thomas Michael 1941- *WhoAm 90*
Sodeman, William Anthony, Sr. 1906- *WhoSSW 91*
Soden, Arlene Julie 1957- *WhoAmW 91*
Soden, Paul A. 1944- *St&PR 91*
Soden, Paul Anthony 1944- *WhoAm 90*
Sodenkamp, Andree 1906- *EncCoWW*
Soderbaum, Olof Peter Wilhelm 1937- *WhoWor 91*
Soderberg, B.W. 1931- *St&PR 91*
Soderberg, Bo Sigfrid 1939- *WhoSSW 91, WhoWor 91*
Soderberg, Dale LeRoy 1929- *WhoE 91*
Soderberg, Harold J. 1928- *St&PR 91*
Soderberg, Hjalmar 1869-1941 *DcScanL, TwCLC 39 [port]*
Soderberg, Jerry Patrick 1937- *St&PR 91*
Soderberg, Lennart Gosta 1923- *WhoWor 91*
Soderberg, Sven Per-Olof Roson 1928- *WhoWor 91*
Soderbergh, Steven *BioIn 16*
Soderbergh, Steven Andrew 1963- *WhoAm 90*
Soderblom, Nathan 1866-1931 *BioIn 16*
Soderblom, Ulf *PenDiMP*
Sodergran, Edith 1892-1923 *DcScanL*
Sodergran, Edith Irene 1892-1923 *EncCoWW*
Soderholm, Eric 1948- *Ballpl 90*
Soderholm, Lars Gustav 1924- *WhoAm 90*
Soderkvist, Jan Mats Olof 1960- *WhoWor 91*
Soderlind, Carl Robert 1933- *St&PR 91*
Soderlind, Sterling Eugene 1926- *St&PR 91, WhoAm 90*
Soderlund, John Henry 1934- *St&PR 91*
Soderlund, Robert C. 1928- *St&PR 91*
Soderlund, Stephen Charles 1944- *St&PR 91*
Soderman, Dan Jackie 1958- *WhoWor 91*
Soderman, Jackie 1927- *WhoWor 91*
Soderquist, Donald G. 1934- *St&PR 91, WhoAm 90*
Soderquist, Ellen 1945- *BioIn 16*
Soderquist, Kristina Sue 1960- *WhoAmW 91*
Soderstrom, Christian Emanuel 1938- *WhoE 91*
Soderstrom, Edward Jonathan 1954- *ConAu 30NR*
Soderstrom, Elisabeth 1927- *PenDiMP*
Soderstrom, Hans Tson 1945- *WhoWor 91*
Soderstrom, Jan *BioIn 16*
Soderstrom, Rolf 1932- *St&PR 91*
Sodhi, Jaswinder Kaur *BiDrAPA 89*
Sodin, Vlado Luis 1930- *WhoWor 91*
Sodnom, Dumaagiyn 1933- *WhoWor 91*
Sodnom, Namsrai 1923- *WhoWor 91*
Sodolski, John *BioIn 16*
Sodoma 1477-1549 *IntDcAA 90*
Sodomsky, Martin E *BiDrAPA 89*
Sodre, Roberto Costa de Abreu 1918- *WhoWor 91*
Soe, Donald Jerome 1930- *St&PR 91*
Soe, Khin Maung 1945- *BiDrAPA 89*
Soe, Thakin *BioIn 16*
Soebygaard, Henrik 1943- *WhoWor 91*
Soechtig, Jacqueline Elizabeth 1949- *WhoAmW 91*
Soederstrom, Elisabeth Anna 1927- *WhoAm 90, WhoWor 91*
Soedibjo, Roekmini Roeselowati 1925- *WhoWor 91*
Soedjatmoko *BioIn 16*
Soedjatmoko 1922-1989 *ConAu 130*
Soeharto 1921- *WhoWor 91*
Soelling, Warner M 1925- *BiDrAPA 89*
Soelter, Robert R. 1926- *WhoAm 90*
Soemantri, Nani 1927- *WhoWor 91*
Soemara, Stephen Iwan 1945- *WhoWor 91*
Soenarjo, Johanes Hardanto 1940- *WhoWor 91*
Soenen, Willy 1937- *IntWWM 90*
Soenksen, Patricia Ann 1952- *WhoAmW 91*
Soennichsen, Jean Elizabeth 1926- *WhoAmW 91*
Soens, Lawrence D. 1926- *WhoAm 90*
Soerensen, Erik *St&PR 91*
Soerensen, Svend Otto 1916- *ConAu 132*
Soerenson, Per Henrik 1947- *St&PR 91*
Soergel, Konrad Hermann 1929- *WhoAm 90*
Soergel, Richard William 1938- *St&PR 91*
Soering, Juergen 1943- *WhoWor 91*
Soeripto, Noerhajati 1932- *WhoWor 91*
Soesbee, Cynthia Lee 1965- *WhoEmL 91*
Soeteber, Ellen 1950- *WhoAm 90*
Soeya, Yoshihide 1955- *WhoWor 91*
Sofaer, Abraham David 1938- *BioIn 16, WhoAm 90, WhoE 91*
Sofair, Jane Brown *BiDrAPA 89*
Sofer, Moses 1762?-1839 *BioIn 16*
Sofer, Rena *BioIn 16*
Soffa, Albert 1920- *St&PR 91*
Soffel, Andrew J. 1930- *St&PR 91*
Soffel, Andrew Jacob 1930- *WhoAm 90*
Soffel, Doris 1948- *IntWWM 90*
Soffer, Alfred 1922- *WhoAm 90, WhoWrEP 89*
Soffer, Marvin 1930- *WhoE 91*
Soffer, Miriam Steinhardt 1926- *WhoAmW 91*
Soffer, Morton L. 1933- *St&PR 91*
Soffer, Robert M. 1947- *St&PR 91*
Soffer, Sasson 1925- *WhoAmA 91*
Soffietti, John Hubert *BiDrAPA 89*
Soffronoff, John Charles 1947- *St&PR 91*
Sofia, Theodore, Jr. 1927- *St&PR 91*
Sofia, Zuheir 1944- *WhoAm 90*
Sofia, Zuheir Zuheir 1944- *St&PR 91*
Sofianos, Leo 1941- *St&PR 91*
Sofield, Rick 1956- *Ballpl 90*
Soflin, Donna Lee Krajnik 1952- *WhoAmW 91*
Sofola, 'Zulu 1938- *FemiCLE*
Sofos, John Nikolaos 1948- *WhoEmL 91*
Sofrensson, Per Henrik 1947- *St&PR 91*
Softly, Edgar *MajTwCW*
Softly, Edward *MajTwCW*
Softness, Donald G. 1927- *ODwPR 91*
Softness, Donald Gabriel *WhoAm 90*
Softness, John 1930- *ODwPR 91, WhoAm 90*
Software *NewAgMG*
Sofya Alekseyevna 1657-1704 *WomWR*
Soga Clan *EncJap*
Soga, Tiyo 1829?-1871 *BioIn 16*
Sogg, Wilton Sherman 1935- *WhoAm 90*
Soghor, Doris S. 1931- *BiDrAPA 89*
Sogin, Harold Hyman 1920- *WhoAm 90*
Sogioka, Gene Isao *BioIn 16*
Soglin, Paul R. 1945- *WhoAm 90*
Soglo, Nicephore *WhoWor 91*
Soglow, Otto *EncACom*
Soglow, Otto 1900-1975 *WhoAmA 91N*
Sogn, Richard R *BiDrAPA 89*
Sognefest, Peter William 1941- *WhoAm 90*
Soh, A Mi 1951- *BiDrAPA 89*
Soh, Byung Hoon *BiDrAPA 89*
Soh, Chiow Teck 1951- *WhoWor 91*
Soh, Eric You Keng 1954- *WhoWor 91*
Soh, Misook Lee *BiDrAPA 89*
Sohal, Naresh 1939- *IntWWM 90*
Sohan, John Patrick 1939- *WhoSSW 91*
Sohappy, David *BioIn 16*
Soheil, Harriet *BiDrAPA 89*
Sohl, Jerry 1913- *BioIn 16, WhoWrEP 89*
Sohlenius, Gunnar H. 1935- *WhoWor 91*
Sohles, David E. 1940- *St&PR 91*
Sohm, Evan Keith 1955- *WhoE 91*
Sohm, Jacque Edward 1938- *St&PR 91*
Sohm, Lawrence Richard 1942- *St&PR 91*
Sohmer, Barbara Helene 1954- *BiDrAPA 89*
Sohmer, Bernard 1929- *WhoAm 90, WhoE 91*
Sohmers, Barbara Pearl 1930- *WhoAmW 91*
Sohn, Arthur H *BiDrAPA 89*
Sohn, Eunmee 1959- *BiDrAPA 89*
Sohn, Herbert Alvin 1929- *WhoAm 90*
Sohn, Howard A. 1929- *St&PR 91*
Sohn, Howard B. 1937-1989 *BioIn 16*
Sohn, Jeung Ho *BiDrAPA 89*
Sohn, Jong Soo 1931- *BiDrAPA 89*
Sohn, Kee Chung *BioIn 16*
Sohn, Louis Bruno 1914- *WhoAm 90*
Sohn, Stephen 1941- *St&PR 91, WhoE 91*
Sohnen, Theodore 1943- *St&PR 91*
Sohnen-Moe, Cherie Marilyn 1956- *WhoAmW 91*
Soifer, Jack 1940- *WhoWor 91*
Soifer, Lawrence M. 1927- *St&PR 91*
Soifer, Raphael 1943- *WhoE 91*
Soileau, Louis Claudmire, III 1919- *WhoAm 90*
Soileau, Marion Joseph 1944- *WhoSSW 91*
Soisson, Jean-Pierre Henri Robert 1934- *BiDFrPL*
Soja, Joseph Frank 1942- *St&PR 91*
Sojka, Gary Allan 1940- *WhoAm 90, WhoE 91*
Sojourner Truth *BioIn 16*
Sok, Robert M. 1946- *St&PR 91*
Sokal, Dina Rachel *BiDrAPA 89*
Sokal, Dina Rachel 1955- *WhoE 91*
Sokal, Joseph E. 1917-1988 *BioIn 16*
Sokal, Robert Reuven 1926- *WhoAm 90, WhoE 91*
Sokal, Yonatan *BiDrAPA 89*
Sokalski, Debra Ann 1959- *WhoAmW 91*
Sokanoff, Albert *BiDrAPA 89*
Sokas, Patrick *BiDrAPA 89*
Sokatch, John Robert 1928- *WhoAm 90*
Sokel, Walter H. 1917- *WhoAm 90*
Sokhanskaia, Nadezhda 1823-1884 *EncCoWW*
Sokil, Catherine Martha 1958- *WhoE 91*
Sokil, Ya. *ConAu 132*
Sokler, Bruce Douglas 1949- *WhoEmL 91*
Sokler, Lynn A. *ODwPR 91*
Sokmensuer, Adil 1928- *WhoAm 90*
Sokol, Anthony T. 1920- *St&PR 91*
Sokol, Barry Steven 1951- *St&PR 91*
Sokol, David Lee 1956- *St&PR 91*
Sokol, David Martin 1942- *WhoAmA 91*
Sokol, Dennis Allen 1945- *WhoEmL 91*
Sokol, Elena 1943- *WhoAmW 91*
Sokol, Eli 1912- *St&PR 91*
Sokol, Elsie 1925- *St&PR 91*
Sokol, Gerald J. *St&PR 91*
Sokol, Hilda Weyl 1928- *WhoAmW 91*
Sokol, Ivan 1937- *IntWWM 90*
Sokol, Mae Sandra *BiDrAPA 89*
Sokol, Mae Sandra 1951- *WhoE 91*
Sokol, Michael Bruce 1954- *WhoEmL 91*
Sokol, Robert J *BiDrAPA 89*
Sokol, Robert James 1941- *WhoAm 90*
Sokol, Si 1927- *St&PR 91*
Sokol, William 1923- *AuBYP 90*
Sokol, Yuri 1937- *WhoWor 91*
Sokolin, William *BioIn 16*
Sokoll, Steven *BiDrAPA 89*
Sokolnikoff, Nicholas *WhoWrEP 89*
Sokol'nikov, Grigorii Iakovlevich 1888-1939 *BioIn 16*
Sokolof, Phil *BioIn 16*
Sokoloff, Adrian Myron 1921- *St&PR 91*
Sokoloff, Louis 1921- *WhoAm 90*
Sokoloff, Shoshana Ruth *BiDrAPA 89*
Sokolofski, Edward George 1945- *St&PR 91*
Sokolov, Howard H 1940- *BiDrAPA 89*
Sokolov, Jacque J. 1954- *St&PR 91*
Sokolov, Jacque Jenning 1954- *WhoWor 91*
Sokolov, Sasha 1943- *BioIn 16*
Sokolov, Yuri Mikhailovich 1932- *WhoWor 91*
Sokolow, Al 1928- *St&PR 91*
Sokolow, Anna 1913?- *NotWoAT*
Sokolow, Anna 1915- *BioIn 16*
Sokolow, Asa D. 1919- *WhoAm 90*
Sokolow, Isobel Folb *WhoAmA 91*
Sokolow, Kenneth 1955- *WhoE 91*
Sokolow, Maurice 1911- *WhoAm 90*
Sokolow, Moshe 1947- *WhoE 91*
Sokolow, Stephen B. 1941- *St&PR 91*
Sokolower, Lester 1931- *St&PR 91*
Sokolowska, Magdalena 1922-1989 *BioIn 16*
Sokolowski, Linda Robinson 1943- *WhoAmA 91*
Sokolowski, Martin Anthony 1946- *WhoSSW 91*
Sokolowski, Peter Daniel 1928- *St&PR 91*
Sokolski, Henry David 1951- *WhoE 91*
Sokolski, Kenneth Neil *BiDrAPA 89*
Sokolsky, Robert Lawrence 1928- *WhoAm 90*
Sokolyszyn, Aleksander 1914- *ConAu 132*
Sokomanu, George Ati *WhoWor 91*
Sokurov, Alexander *BioIn 16*
Sol, Dona *EncCoWW*
Sola, Janet Elaine 1935- *WhoAmW 91*
Solaiman, Souhaila *BiDrAPA 89*
Solaini, William Reynolds 1920- *St&PR 91*
Solaita, Tony 1947- *Ballpl 90*
Solal, Jean-Louis 1928- *WhoWor 91*
Solal, Martial 1927- *ConMus 4*
Solala, Anssi Matti Tapio 1947- *WhoWor 91*
Solan, Deborah 1958- *WhoAmW 91*
Solana, Fernando Morales 1931- *WhoAm 90, WhoWor 91*
Solana, Jose L *BiDrAPA 89*
Solana, Terrel Marion 1947- *WhoSSW 91*
Soland, Norman R. 1940- *St&PR 91*
Solandt, Omond McKillop 1909- *WhoAm 90, WhoWor 91*
Solanki, Bhairon Singh 1927- *WhoWor 91*
Solano *WhNaAH*
Solano, Claudio 1926- *Ballpl 90*
Solano, Faustina Venecia 1962- *WhoHisp 91*
Solano, Henry L. 1950- *WhoHisp 91*
Solano, Juan A. 1950- *WhoHisp 91*
Solano, Julio 1960- *Ballpl 90*
Solano, Olusegum A *BiDrAPA 89*
Solano, Solita 1888-1975 *FemiCLE*
Solar, Richard L. 1939- *St&PR 91*
Solar, Richard Leon 1939- *WhoAm 90*
Solar, Xul 1887-1963 *ArtLatA*
Solares, Alberto E. 1922- *WhoHisp 91*
Solares, Andres Jose 1946- *WhoSSW 91*
Solari, Joseph G., Jr. 1945- *St&PR 91*
Solari, Larry Thomas 1942- *WhoAm 90*
Solari, Pietro Jose-Luis 1958- *WhoWor 91*
Solari, Robert M. 1951- *St&PR 91*
Solarz, Andrea Lynn 1955- *WhoAmW 91*
Solarz, Stephen Joshua 1940- *WhoAm 90, WhoE 91*
Solberg, Daniel M. 1953- *St&PR 91*
Solberg, Elizabeth *ODwPR 91*
Solberg, Elizabeth Transou 1939- *WhoAm 90, WhoAmW 91*
Solberg, James Burton 1953- *St&PR 91*
Solberg, James Joseph 1942- *WhoAm 90*
Solberg, Janet E. 1961- *ODwPR 91*
Solberg, Jeffrey M. 1952- *St&PR 91*
Solberg, Morten Edward 1935- *WhoAmA 91*
Solberg, Myron 1931- *WhoAm 90*
Solberg, Nellie Florence Coad *WhoAm 90, WhoAmW 91*
Solberg, Norman R. 1939- *St&PR 91*
Solberg, Norman Robert 1939- *WhoAm 90*
Solberg, Ronald Louis 1953- *WhoAm 90*
Solberg, Winton Udell 1922- *WhoAm 90*
Solbert, Peter Omar Abernathy 1919- *WhoE 91*
Solbrig, Ingeborg Hildegard 1923- *WhoAm 90*
Solbu, Einar 1942- *IntWWM 90*
Solcher, Gerry A. 1944- *WhoAm 90*
Soldani Benzi, Massimiliano 1658-1740 *PenDiDA 89*
Soldat, Marie 1863-1955 *PenDiMP*
Soldatos, Constantin R 1940- *BiDrAPA 89*
Soldatos, G. Eugene 1918- *St&PR 91*
Soldene, Emily 1840-1912 *OxCPMus*
Soldinger, Simon 1951- *BiDrAPA 89*
Soldner, Paul Edmund *WhoAm 90*
Soldner, Paul Edmund 1921- *WhoAmA 91*
Soldo, Beth Jean 1948- *WhoAmW 91*
Soldo, John J. 1945- *WhoWrEP 89*
Soldwedel, Kenneth J. 1947- *St&PR 91*
Sole, Carlos A. 1938- *WhoHisp 91*
Sole, Christopher John 1952- *WhoE 91*
Solecki, R. Stefan 1917- *WhoAm 90*
Solecki, Roman T *BiDrAPA 89*
Soled, Howard 1932- *St&PR 91*
Soleim, Yngve 1952- *WhoWor 91*
Solem, Dana Lyman 1946- *BiDrAPA 89*
Solem, John 1933- *WhoAmA 91*
Solem, Sigfred L. *BioIn 16*
Solender, Arthur Michael 1928- *St&PR 91*
Solender, Elsie 1928- *St&PR 91*
Solender, Mike 1928- *St&PR 91*

Solender, Robert Lawrence 1923- *St&PR 91, WhoAm 90*
Solender, Sanford 1914- *WhoAm 90*
Solender, Stephen David 1938- *WhoE 91*
Solender, Stephen L. 1951- *St&PR 91*
Solenski, Agnes Helene 1926- *WhoAmW 91*
Soler, Dona K. 1921- *WhoWrEP 89*
Soler, Dona Katherine 1921- *WhoAmW 91*
Soler, Frank *WhoHisp 91*
Soler, Gladys Pumariega 1930- *WhoHisp 91*
Soler, Julia Marie *BiDrAPA 89*
Soler, Rita *WhoHisp 91*
Soler, Terrell Diane *WhoAmW 91, WhoE 91, WhoWor 91*
Soler, Vincent Emile, Jr. 1936- *St&PR 91*
Soler-Martinez, Mercedes C. 1963- *WhoHisp 91*
Soler-Roig, Miguel 1961- *WhoWor 91*
Soleri, Paolo 1919- *BioIn 16, WhoAm 90, WhoAmA 91, WhoWor 91*
Soles, Ada Leigh 1937- *WhoAmW 91*
Soles, William *WhoAmA 91N*
Soles, William Roger 1920- *St&PR 91, WhoAm 90, WhoSSW 91*
Soletsky, Albert 1937- *WhoE 91*
Soley, Robert Lawrence 1935- *WhoE 91, WhoWor 91*
Solf, Waldemar A. *BioIn 16*
Solfisburg, Roy J., III 1943- *St&PR 91*
Solfisburg, Roy John, III 1943- *WhoAm 90*
Solfisburg Quinn, Betsy *ODwPR 91*
Solganik, Marvin 1930- *WhoAm 90*
Solganik, Marvin Joseph 1930- *St&PR 91*
Solh, Taki Eddine el- 1909-1988 *AnObit 1988*
Solh, Takieddin 1909-1988 *BioIn 16*
Solheim, James Edward 1939- *WhoE 91*
Solheim, Kaare 1928- *WhoWor 91*
Solheim, Robert Paul 1937- *St&PR 91*
Solheim, Wilhelm Gerhard, II 1924- *WhoAm 90*
Solidum, James 1925- *WhoWor 91*
Solie, Richard John 1933- *WhoAm 90*
Soliman, Ibrahim *BiDrAPA 89*
Soliman, Nabil Nazir M *BiDrAPA 89*
Soliman, Patricia Brehaut 1937- *WhoAm 90*
Soliman, Yvonne Anis *BiDrAPA 89*
Solimena, Francesco 1657-1747 *IntDcAA 90*
Solin, Darrol B. 1937- *WhoAm 90*
Solin, Dennis L. 1949- *St&PR 91*
Solin, Jean 1936- *WhoWor 91*
Solina, Franc 1955- *WhoWor 91*
Solinger, David M *WhoAmA 91*
Solinger, David Morris 1906- *WhoAm 90*
Solinger, Dorothy J 1945- *ConAu 32NR*
Solis, Alfonso 1948- *WhoHisp 91*
Solis, Alfredo 1946- *WhoSSW 91*
Solis, Arturo, Sr. 1931- *WhoHisp 91*
Solis, Carlos 1961- *WhoHisp 91*
Solis, Ernest V. *WhoHisp 91*
Solis, Gary *WhoHisp 91*
Solis, Hilda L. 1957- *WhoHisp 91*
Solis, Javier 1946- *St&PR 91*
Solis, Joel 1954- *WhoHisp 91*
Solis, Jose Alberto 1954- *WhoE 91*
Solis, Octavio 1958- *WhoHisp 91*
Solis, Rafael 1931- *BiDrAPA 89*
Solis, Richard M. 1947- *WhoAm 90*
Solis, Virgilius 1514-1562 *PenDiDA 89*
Solis, Zaragoza, III 1946- *St&PR 91*
Solis-Diaz, Javier J. 1964- *WhoEmL 91, WhoSSW 91, WhoWor 91*
Solis Garcia, Jorge 1953- *WhoWor 91*
Soliz, Joseph Guy 1954- *WhoHisp 91, WhoSSW 91*
Soliz, Juan 1949- *WhoHisp 91*
Soliz, Salvador G. 1932- *WhoHisp 91*
Solky, Charles G *BiDrAPA 89*
Solky, Hannah Joan *BiDrAPA 89*
Soll, David Benjamin 1930- *WhoE 91*
Soll, Larry 1942- *St&PR 91, WhoAm 90*
Soll, Maxwell H 1936- *BiDrAPA 89*
Soll, Richard Sigmund 1948- *WhoSSW 91*
Solla Nizzoli, Amalia 1806?-1845? *EncCoWW*
Sollami, Roseann 1935- *WhoAmW 91*
Sollano, Rosemarie 1962- *WhoAmW 91*
Sollars, E. Roe 1947- *St&PR 91*
Sollberger, Edmond 1920-1989 *ConAu 129*
Sollenberger, Harold Myers 1941- *WhoAm 90*
Sollenberger, Howard Edwin 1917- *WhoAm 90*
Sollenberger, Robert Neil 1929- *WhoE 91*
Sollender, Joel David 1926- *WhoAm 90*
Sollers, Joseph S. 1927- *St&PR 91*
Solley, Mary-Sue Pastorello 1955- *WhoAmW 91*
Solley, Thomas Treat 1924- *WhoAmA 91*
Sollid, Faye 1913- *WhoAmW 91*
Sollier, Christian 1949- *WhoWor 91*
Sollins, Susan *WhoAmW 91*
Sollitt, Bettye Herb 1911- *WhoAmW 91*
Sollitto, Ben 1923- *St&PR 91*
Sollod, H Hershey 1946- *BiDrAPA 89*
Sollov, Jacques 1935- *WhoWrEP 89*
Solloway, C. Robert 1935- *WhoAm 90*
Solloway, Charles Robert 1935- *St&PR 91*
Solloway, Erwin 1924- *St&PR 91*
Solloway, Michael Lewis 1938- *BiDrAPA 89*
Solman, Joseph 1909- *WhoAmA 91, WhoE 91*
Solmsen, Friedrich 1904-1989 *BioIn 16*
Solmssen, Kurt A. 1905-1989 *BioIn 16*
Solmssen, Peter 1931- *WhoAm 90, WhoAmA 91, WhoWor 91*
Solmundson, David L. 1941- *St&PR 91*
Solnick, Arthur Paul 1944- *WhoE 91*
Solnick, Bennett Louis 1958- *BiDrAPA 89*
Solnik, Catherine Jacqueline 1946- *WhoWor 91*
Solniker, Hyman *BioIn 16*
Solnit, Albert J 1919- *BiDrAPA 89*
Solnit, Albert Jay 1919- *WhoAm 90, WhoE 91*
Solo, Alan Jere 1933- *WhoAm 90*
Solo, Jay *MajTwCW*
Solo, Richard David 1922- *St&PR 91*
Solo, Robert Alexander 1916- *WhoAm 90*
Solochek, Sylvia *WhoAmA 91*
Solodar, Donald Jay 1942- *St&PR 91*
Solodar, Seymour Oscar *BiDrAPA 89*
Solodkin, Judith 1945- *WhoAmA 91*
Soloff, Louis Alexander 1904- *WhoAm 90*
Soloff, Paul Harris *BiDrAPA 89*
Soloff, Rav Asher 1927- *WhoE 91*
Solohub, William Robert *St&PR 91*
Solombrino, Eleucadio *PenDiDA 89*
Solomentsev, Mikhail Sergeyevich 1913- *WhoWor 91*
Solomita, Anthony Francis 1935- *St&PR 91*
Solomita, Anthony Patrick 1962- *WhoE 91*
Solomon 1902-1988 *AnObit 1988, PenDiMP*
Solomon Ibn Gabirol 1021-1058 *EncO&P 3*
Solomon, A. Malama 1951- *WhoAmW 91*
Solomon, Aaron 1908-1988 *BioIn 16*
Solomon, Albert S 1910- *BiDrAPA 89*
Solomon, Allen Lee 1956- *BiDrAPA 89*
Solomon, Andrew Wallace 1963- *WhoWor 91*
Solomon, Anthony Joseph 1932- *WhoAm 90, WhoE 91*
Solomon, Anthony Morton 1919- *WhoAm 90*
Solomon, Arthur Charles 1947- *St&PR 91, WhoEmL 91*
Solomon, Arthur Herman 1934- *St&PR 91*
Solomon, Arthur Kaskel 1912- *WhoAm 90*
Solomon, Barbara Miller 1919- *WhoAmW 91*
Solomon, Barry 1949- *St&PR 91*
Solomon, Bernard 1923- *St&PR 91*
Solomon, Bernard Alan 1946- *WhoAmA 91*
Solomon, Brenda Clorfene 1939- *BiDrAPA 89*
Solomon, Cathy Rebecca 1957- *WhoAmW 91, WhoE 91*
Solomon, Charles Francis 1932- *WhoSSW 91*
Solomon, Dan Eugene 1936- *WhoAm 90*
Solomon, David Arthur *BiDrAPA 89*
Solomon, David Eugene 1931- *St&PR 91, WhoAm 90*
Solomon, David Harris 1923- *WhoAm 90*
Solomon, David S 1938- *BiDrAPA 89*
Solomon, Dean 1951- *BiDrAPA 89*
Solomon, Deborah Antoinnette 1938- *WhoAmW 91*
Solomon, Debra J *BiDrAPA 89*
Solomon, Donald William 1944- *WhoWor 91*
Solomon, Earl G *BiDrAPA 89*
Solomon, Eddie 1951-1986 *Ballpl 90*
Solomon, Edward 1855-1895 *OxCPMus*
Solomon, Edward A. 1948- *St&PR 91*
Solomon, Edward Alfred 1948- *WhoAm 90*
Solomon, Edward B 1937- *BiDrAPA 89*
Solomon, Edward David 1931- *WhoAm 90*
Solomon, Elaine R. 1921- *St&PR 91*
Solomon, Elias Louis 1879-1956 *BioIn 16*
Solomon, Elinor Harris 1923- *WhoE 91*
Solomon, Ellen Joan 1943- *WhoAmW 91*
Solomon, Ezra 1920- *WhoAm 90*
Solomon, Frederic 1911- *WhoE 91*
Solomon, Fredric 1936- *BiDrAPA 89*
Solomon, George Freeman 1931- *BiDrAPA 89, WhoAm 90*
Solomon, George J. 1927- *St&PR 91*
Solomon, George M. 1940- *WhoAm 90*
Solomon, Gerald *WhoAmA 91*
Solomon, Gerald 1931- *St&PR 91*
Solomon, Gerald Brooks Hunt 1930- *WhoAm 90, WhoE 91*
Solomon, Henry 1926- *WhoAm 90*
Solomon, Hilda Pearl 1948- *WhoAmW 91, WhoSSW 91*
Solomon, Hollis 1934- *WhoAm 90*
Solomon, Holly *WhoAmA 91*
Solomon, Howard 1927- *St&PR 91, WhoAm 90*
Solomon, Hyde 1911- *WhoAmA 91N*
Solomon, Irwin *BiDrAPA 89*
Solomon, Jack, Jr. 1928- *St&PR 91*
Solomon, Jack Avrum 1928- *WhoAm 90*
Solomon, Jack L 1937- *BiDrAPA 89*
Solomon, James *BiDrAPA 89*
Solomon, Jeffrey Jonathan *St&PR 91*
Solomon, Jerrold M. 1951- *St&PR 91*
Solomon, Jerry I. 1924- *St&PR 91*
Solomon, Jerry L. 1917- *St&PR 91*
Solomon, Jerry Lawrence 1954- *WhoE 91*
Solomon, Joan *BioIn 16*
Solomon, Joel *BiDrAPA 89*
Solomon, John 1856-1953 *PenDiMP*
Solomon, John A. 1919- *St&PR 91*
Solomon, Jonathan G *BiDrAPA 89*
Solomon, Joseph 1904- *WhoAm 90*
Solomon, Judith Anne 1943- *WhoAmW 91*
Solomon, Kenneth *BiDrAPA 89*
Solomon, Kenneth Hadley 1945- *WhoEmL 91*
Solomon, Larry 1933- *St&PR 91*
Solomon, Louis *AuBYP 90*
Solomon, Louis 1928- *St&PR 91*
Solomon, Margaret Claire Boyle 1918- *WhoAm 90*
Solomon, Marian Audrey 1947- *WhoEmL 91*
Solomon, Marion B. 1903- *St&PR 91*
Solomon, Martin M. 1950- *WhoE 91*
Solomon, Maynard Elliott 1930- *IntWWM 90, WhoAm 90*
Solomon, Morris Jerome 1939- *WhoE 91*
Solomon, Mose 1900-1966 *Ballpl 90*
Solomon, Murry Franklin 1945- *WhoE 91*
Solomon, Nancy Anne 1947- *BiDrAPA 89*
Solomon, Paul Alan 1956- *WhoWor 91*
Solomon, Peter J. 1938- *WhoAm 90*
Solomon, Philip 1907- *BiDrAPA 89*
Solomon, Phyllis 1935- *WhoAmW 91*
Solomon, Phyllis Linda 1945- *WhoAmW 91*
Solomon, Ralph M. 1931- *St&PR 91*
Solomon, Randall Adam 1957- *BiDrAPA 89*
Solomon, Randall L *BiDrAPA 89*
Solomon, Rayman Louis 1947- *WhoEmL 91*
Solomon, Rebecca 1832-1886 *BiDWomA*
Solomon, Rebecca L *BiDrAPA 89*
Solomon, Rebecca Z *BiDrAPA 89*
Solomon, Richard Allan 1917- *WhoAm 90*
Solomon, Richard Benjamin 1942- *WhoWor 91*
Solomon, Richard H 1934- *WhoAmA 91*
Solomon, Richard L. *BioIn 16*
Solomon, Richard Lester 1918- *WhoAm 90*
Solomon, Richard Stanley *BiDrAPA 89*
Solomon, Risa Greenberg 1948- *WhoAmW 91, WhoSSW 91*
Solomon, Robert 1921- *WhoAm 90, WhoE 91*
Solomon, Robert Bailey 1930- *WhoAm 90*
Solomon, Robert C 1942- *ConAu 32NR*
Solomon, Robert Charles 1942- *WhoAm 90*
Solomon, Robert Douglas 1917- *WhoSSW 91*
Solomon, Robert Harris 1938- *WhoAm 90*
Solomon, Robert L. 1945- *St&PR 91*
Solomon, Rosalind F *WhoAmA 91*
Solomon, Ruth 1941- *WhoAmW 91*
Solomon, Samuel 1925- *WhoAm 90*
Solomon, Sanford P 1934- *BiDrAPA 89*
Solomon, Saul 1817-1892 *BioIn 16*
Solomon, Saul 1918- *St&PR 91*
Solomon, Seymour Joseph 1922- *IntWWM 90*
Solomon, Sidney 1923- *WhoAm 90*
Solomon, Sidney L Solomon, Mrs 1909- *WhoAmA 91*
Solomon, Solomon Sidney 1936- *WhoSSW 91*
Solomon, Stephen Michael 1942- *WhoAm 90*
Solomon, Susan 1956- *WhoAmW 91*
Solomon, Susan Lee 1946- *WhoAmW 91*
Solomon, Syd 1917- *WhoAm 90, WhoAmA 91*
Solomon, Vita Petrosky *WhoAmA 91*
Solomon, Vita Petrosky 1916- *WhoAm 90*
Solomon, William R. 1950- *St&PR 91*
Solomon, William Tarver 1942- *St&PR 91, WhoAm 90*
Solomon, Yonty 1938- *IntWWM 90, PenDiMP, WhoWor 91*
Solomon, Zachary Leon 1934- *WhoAm 90*
Solomon-Rice, Patti Lynn 1955- *WhoAmW 91, WhoEmL 91*
Solomons, Anthony Nathan 1930- *WhoWor 91*
Solomons, David *BioIn 16*
Solomons, Gus Martinez, Jr. *WhoAm 90*
Solomons, Mark Elliott 1946- *WhoE 91*
Solomons, William Ebenezer 1943- *WhoSSW 91*
Solomonson, Charles D. *WhoAm 90*
Solon, Daniel P. 1931- *ODwPR 91*
Solon, Daniel Peter 1931- *WhoWor 91*
Solon, Earl N 1925- *BiDrAPA 89*
Solon, Harry 1873-1958 *WhoAmA 91N*
Solon, John Thomas 1938- *St&PR 91*
Solon, Leon-Victor 1872-1957 *PenDiDA 89*
Solon, Marc-Louis-Emanuel 1835-1913 *PenDiDA 89*
Solon, Samuel 1953- *St&PR 91*
Solonche, Joel R. 1946- *WhoWrEP 89*
Solonyna, Daniel *BiDrAPA 89*
Solorzano, Carlos 1922- *HispWr 90*
Solorzano, Rosalia 1953- *WhoAmW 91, WhoSSW 91*
Soloski, Richard E. 1933- *St&PR 91*
Solot, Mary Lynn 1939- *AuBYP 90*
Solot, Robert J. 1939- *St&PR 91*
Solotaire, George *BioIn 16*
Solotaroff, Ted 1928- *WhoAm 90, WhoWrEP 89*
Solotruk, Ronald J. 1952- *St&PR 91*
Solounias, Bernadette Louise *BiDrAPA 89*
Solov, Zachary 1923- *WhoAm 90*
Solove, Alvin 1921- *St&PR 91*
Solove, Steven Daniel 1951- *St&PR 91*
Solovei, Marion 1936- *WhoAmW 91*
Soloveitchik, Joseph Baer 1903- *BioIn 16*
Solovic, Jan 1934- *WhoWor 91*
Soloviev, Yuri 1920- *ConDes 90*
Solovieva, Poliksena Sergeevna 1867-1924 *EncCoWW*
Solovjev, Vsevolod 1929- *BiDrAPA 89*
Solovovo, Count *EncO&P 3*
Solow, Charles *BiDrAPA 89*
Solow, Robert A 1925- *BiDrAPA 89*
Solow, Robert B. 1916- *St&PR 91*
Solow, Robert Irving 1922- *St&PR 91*
Solow, Robert M. *BioIn 16*
Solow, Robert M. 1924- *WorAlBi*
Solow, Robert Merton 1924- *WhoAm 90, WhoE 91, WhoWor 91*
Soloway, Albert Herman 1925- *WhoAm 90*
Soloway, Barry H. 1942- *WhoE 91*
Soloway, Elaine M. *ODwPR 91*
Soloway, Harry James *BiDrAPA 89*
Soloway, Norman Peter 1940- *WhoE 91*
Soloway, Reta Burns *WhoAmA 91*
Solowey, Ben 1901-1978 *WhoAmA 91N*
Solsby, Donald L. 1943- *St&PR 91*
Solso, Theodore Mathew 1947- *St&PR 91*
Solstad, Dag 1941- *DcScanL*
Solt, Andrew P. *NewYTBS 90*
Solt, Leo Frank 1921- *WhoAm 90*
Solt, Paul-Michael *ODwPR 91*
Solt, Walter John 1944- *St&PR 91*
Soltani, Sohrab *WhoSSW 91*
Soltanoff, Jack 1905- *WhoE 91, WhoWor 91*
Solter, Aletha Lucia 1945- *WhoWrEP 89*
Soltero, Eugene A. 1943- *St&PR 91*
Solters, Moose 1906-1975 *Ballpl 90*
Soltesz, Frank Joseph 1912-1986 *WhoAmA 91N*
Soltesz, Julius Joseph 1906-1975 *Ballpl 90*
Solti, Georg 1912- *IntWWM 90, PenDiMP, WhoAm 90, WhoWor 91, WorAlBi*
Soltis, Andrew Edward, Jr. 1939- *St&PR 91*
Soltis, Elizabeth Jean 1961- *WhoAmW 91*
Soltis, Jonas F 1931- *ConAu 31NR*
Soltis, Jonas Francis 1931- *WhoAm 90*
Soltis, Robert Alan 1955- *WhoEmL 91, WhoWor 91*
Soltis, William Thomas 1935- *St&PR 91*
Soltys, John J 1931- *BiDrAPA 89*
Soltys, Louise R. 1954- *WhoAmW 91*
Soltys, Mary Karen *BiDrAPA 89*
Soltys, Stephen Michael *BiDrAPA 89*
Soltysiak, Sandra Kantner 1948- *WhoEmL 91*
Solum, B.C. 1927- *St&PR 91*
Solum, John H. 1935- *IntWWM 90*
Solum, John Henry 1935- *WhoE 91, WhoWor 91*
Solursh, Lionel Paul *BiDrAPA 89*
Solvang, Pamela Jean 1956- *WhoAmW 91*
Solway, Carl E 1935- *WhoAmA 91*
Solway, Gordon R. 1936- *WhoAm 90*
Solway, Gordon Ridley 1936- *St&PR 91*
Solwitz, Sharon Dee 1945- *WhoWrEP 89*
Solwoska, Mara *ConAu 31NR, MajTwCW*
Solymar, George G. 1939- *St&PR 91*
Solymos, Maria B *BiDrAPA 89*
Solymossy, Joseph Martin 1945- *WhoSSW 91*
Solyom, Antal Endre *BiDrAPA 89*
Solyom, Elizabeth *BiDrAPA 89*
Solyom, Janos 1938- *IntWWM 90*
Solyom, Leslie 1921- *BiDrAPA 89*
Solyom-Nagy, Sandor 1934- *IntWWM 90*
Solzhenitsyn, Aleksandr 1918- *BioIn 16, EuWr 13*

Solzhenitsyn, Aleksandr I 1918- *MajTwCW*
Solzhenitsyn, Alexander 1918- *WhoAm 90, WhoE 91, WhoWor 91, WhoWrEP 89, WorAlBi*
Som, Max L. 1904-1990 *BioIn 16*
Som, Mihir Kumar 1943- *WhoWor 91*
Soma, Daniel *ConAu 130*
Soma, Jeffrey A. 1949- *St&PR 91*
Soma, Rose Smeraldi 1940- *WhoAmW 91*
Somach, Abraham 1931- *St&PR 91*
Somach, Beverly 1935- *IntWWM 90*
Somach, S. Dennis 1952- *WhoWor 91*
Soman, Howard 1930- *BiDrAPA 89*
Somare, Michael Thomas 1936- *WhoWor 91*
Somasundaran, Ponisseril 1939- *WhoAm 90*
Sombart, Werner 1863-1941 *BioIn 16*
Sombatsiri, Krit 1928- *WhoWor 91*
Somberg, Emilija O K 1924- *WhoAmA 91*
Somberg, Herman 1917- *WhoAmA 91*
Sombrotto, Vincent R. 1923- *WhoAm 90*
Some, Marvin Lester 1927- *St&PR 91*
Someck, Marti Belva 1937- *WhoSSW 91*
Somer, Mitchell Scott 1963- *WhoE 91*
Somerall, Leon Hanks 1919- *St&PR 91*
Somerfeld, Esther 1901- *BiDrAPA 89*
Somerfield, Neil 1953- *WhoWrEP 89*
Somerlott, Robert 1928- *SmATA 62 [port]*
Somero, George Nicholls 1940- *WhoAm 90*
Somers, Albert G. *AmLegL*
Somers, Anne Ramsay 1913- *WhoAm 90, WhoAmW 91*
Somers, Antoinette Nadezhda 1947- *WhoAm 90*
Somers, Charles W. 1869-1934 *Ballpl 90*
Somers, Clifford Louis 1940- *WhoSSW 91, WhoWor 91*
Somers, Dean Albert 1945- *St&PR 91*
Somers, Donald Louis 1931- *St&PR 91*
Somers, George Fredrick 1914- *WhoAm 90*
Somers, Ginny *ODwPR 91*
Somers, H 1922- *WhoAmA 91*
Somers, Hans Peter 1922- *WhoAm 90*
Somers, Harold Milton 1915- *WhoAm 90*
Somers, James E *BiDrAPA 89*
Somers, Jane *ConAu 33NR, MajTwCW*
Somers, Jane 1919- *BioIn 16*
Somers, John Arthur 1944- *St&PR 91, WhoAm 90*
Somers, John E. 1943- *St&PR 91*
Somers, Kendall L. 1925- *St&PR 91*
Somers, Margaret Lee 1941- *WhoWrEP 89*
Somers, Marion *WhoAmW 91, WhoE 91*
Somers, Paul *TwCCr&M 91*
Somers, Paul Preston, Jr. 1942- *WhoWrEP 89*
Somers, Robert Vance 1937- *WhoSSW 91*
Somers, Sarah Pruyn 1936- *WhoE 91*
Somers, Suzanne *BioIn 16*
Somers, Suzanne 1946- *WorAlBi*
Somerset, Dorothy Maud 1900- *OxCCanT*
Somerset, Edward Seymour, Duke of 1506?-1552 *BioIn 16*
Somerset, Elizabeth, Countess of 1666?-1722 *BiDEWW*
Somerset, Harold Richard 1935- *WhoAm 90*
Somerset, Henry Hugh Arthur Fitzroy 1900-1984 *DcNaB 1981*
Somerset, Isabel 1851-1921 *BioIn 16*
Somerset, John Scott 1953- *WhoEmL 91*
Somerset, Margaret, Countess of *BiDEWW*
Somerson, Rosanne 1954- *WhoAmA 91*
Somerto, Pekka Kaarlo 1958- *WhoWor 91*
Somerville and Ross *FemiCLE*
Somerville, A.J., Jr. 1929- *St&PR 91*
Somerville, David Tolf 1937- *WhoE 91*
Somerville, Edith Anna OEnone 1858-1949 *BioIn 16*
Somerville, Edith Oenone 1858-1949 *EncPaPR 91*
Somerville, James D. *St&PR 91*
Somerville, John Henry 1924- *St&PR 91*
Somerville, Mary 1780-1872 *BioIn 16, FemiCLE*
Somerville, Mason Harold 1941- *WhoAm 90*
Somerville, Robert Eugene *WhoAm 90*
Somerville, Romaine Stec 1930- *WhoAm 90, WhoAmA 91*
Somerville, Rosemary Elaine 1955- *WhoAmW 91*
Somerville, Theodore E. 1940- *St&PR 91*
Somerville, Theodore Elkin 1940- *WhoAm 90*
Somerville, Walter Raleigh, Jr. 1930- *WhoE 91*
Somerville, Warren Thomas 1942- *WhoE 91*
Somerville, William Nelson 1927- *St&PR 91*
Somerwil, Johannes 1926- *WhoWor 91*
Somes, Daniel Earl 1935- *St&PR 91*
Somes, Edwin 1910- *IntWWM 90*
Somfai, Laszlo 1934- *IntWWM 90*
Somigli, Alberto 1919- *WhoWor 91*
Somit, Albert 1919- *WhoAm 90*
Somjen, George Gustav 1929- *WhoAm 90*
Somlo, Peter 1948- *WhoWor 91*
Somlyo, Andrew Paul 1930- *WhoAm 90, WhoSSW 91*
Somma, Henry Jeremiah 1921- *St&PR 91*
Somma, Herman Robert 1925- *St&PR 91*
Somma, Michael Marco 1927- *St&PR 91*
Sommars, Julie *ConTFT 8 [port]*
Sommaruga, Cornelio 1932- *WhoWor 91*
Sommer, Alphonse Adam, Jr. 1924- *WhoAm 90*
Sommer, Angela *ConAu 132*
Sommer, Conrad 1905- *BiDrAPA 89*
Sommer, Elke *BioIn 16*
Sommer, Elke 1940- *WorAlBi*
Sommer, Elke 1941- *WhoAm 90*
Sommer, Elyse 1929- *AuBYP 90*
Sommer, Emil Otto, III 1947- *WhoE 91*
Sommer, Ernest Lorge 1926- *WhoE 91*
Sommer, Felix 1930- *BiDrAPA 89*
Sommer, Frank H, III 1922- *WhoAmA 91*
Sommer, Frederick 1905- *WhoAmA 91*
Sommer, Hartmut 1941- *WhoWor 91*
Sommer, Harvey Robert 1922- *St&PR 91*
Sommer, Howard Ellsworth 1918- *WhoAm 90*
Sommer, Johann Daniel 1643-1685? *PenDiDA 89*
Sommer, Johann Eberhard *PenDiDA 89*
Sommer, John A., Jr. 1933- *St&PR 91*
Sommer, Joseph T. 1941- *St&PR 91*
Sommer, Larry 1940- *St&PR 91*
Sommer, Peter R. 1938- *WhoAm 90*
Sommer, Raphael 1937- *IntWWM 90*
Sommer, Richard Arthur 1926- *St&PR 91*
Sommer, Richard Samuel 1941- *St&PR 91*
Sommer, Robert 1929- *EncO&P 3*
Sommer, Robert Eugene 1918- *St&PR 91*
Sommer, Rudolph J *BiDrAPA 89*
Sommer, Sandra Reading 1947- *WhoSSW 91*
Sommer, Theo 1930- *WhoWor 91*
Sommer, Theodore Levon 1920- *St&PR 91*
Sommer, Vilma Evelyn 1933- *WhoAmW 91*
Sommer, Wassily 1912-1979 *WhoAmA 91N*
Sommer, William G 1936- *BiDrAPA 89*
Sommer-Bodenburg, Angela 1948- *ConAu 132, SmATA 63 [port]*
Sommer-Yeager, Linda Dianne 1951- *WhoAmW 91*
Sommerburg, Miriam *WhoAmA 91N*
Sommerfeld, Jude Thomas 1936- *WhoSSW 91*
Sommerfeld, Nicholas Ulrich 1926- *WhoAm 90*
Sommerfeld, Raynard Matthias 1933- *WhoAm 90*
Sommerfeldt, John Robert 1933- *WhoAm 90, WhoSSW 91*
Sommerfeldt, Lorraine Arlene *BiDrAPA 89*
Sommerfelt, Aimee 1892- *AuBYP 90*
Sommerfelt, Kathryn Ann 1953- *BiDrAPA 89*
Sommerfelt, Soren Christian 1916- *WhoAm 90*
Sommerhalder, John Edward 1934- *WhoWor 91*
Sommerlad, Robert Edward 1937- *WhoAm 90*
Sommerness, M Duane *BiDrAPA 89*
Sommers, Albert Trumbull 1919- *WhoAm 90*
Sommers, Allen 1918- *ODwPR 91, WhoE 91*
Sommers, Bill *St&PR 91*
Sommers, Brenda Diane 1961- *WhoEmL 91*
Sommers, Dale Eugene *BiDrAPA 89*
Sommers, Dana Eugene 1953- *WhoEmL 91*
Sommers, Denny 1940- *BioIn 16*
Sommers, Elizabeth Boone 1945- *WhoEmL 91*
Sommers, Estelle Joan *WhoAmW 91*
Sommers, Herbert Myron 1925- *WhoAm 90*
Sommers, Jefferson Maurice *BiDrAPA 89*
Sommers, Lawrence Melvin 1919- *WhoAm 90*
Sommers, Margaret 1911- *BiDrAPA 89*
Sommers, Patrick Charles 1947- *St&PR 91*
Sommers, Paul Martin 1948- *WhoE 91*
Sommers, Robert Thomas 1926- *WhoAm 90*
Sommers, Shari Catherine 1950- *WhoAmW 91*
Sommers, Sharon Anne 1938- *WhoE 91*
Sommers, William Paul 1933- *WhoAm 90*
Sommerville, Frank 1952- *WhoSSW 91, WhoWor 91*
Sommerville, Kenneth William 1951- *WhoE 91*
Sommerville-O'Brien, Edith Lynn 1958- *WhoAmW 91, WhoWor 91*
Sommese, Lanny Beal 1943- *WhoAmA 91*
Sommese, Richard Alan 1954- *WhoEmL 91*
Somnolet, Michel 1940- *St&PR 91*
Somnolet, Michel Pierre 1940- *WhoAm 90, WhoWor 91*
Somodi, Joseph Michael 1917- *St&PR 91*
Somogi, Judith 1943-1988 *BioIn 16*
Somogy, Milivoj von 1928- *WhoWor 91*
Somogyi, Erwin G. 1912- *St&PR 91*
Somogyi, Jozsef 1916- *WhoWor 91*
Somolinos, Alfredo Salvador 1939- *WhoE 91*
Somoza, Anastasio 1896-1956 *BioIn 16*
Somoza, Anastasio 1925-1980 *BioIn 16*
Somoza, Eugene C *BiDrAPA 89*
Somoza-Debayle, Anastasio 1925-1980 *WorAlBi*
Somoza Debayle, Luis 1922-1967 *BioIn 16*
Somoza-Garcia, Anastasio 1896-1956 *WorAlBi*
Sompalli, Venkata Ramana *BiDrAPA 89*
Sompolinsky, David 1921- *WhoWor 91*
Somrock, J.D. 1942- *St&PR 91*
Somrock, John Douglas 1942- *WhoAm 90*
Somsen, Gus 1932- *WhoWor 91*
Son Sann 1911- *WhoWor 91*
Son Sen 1930- *WhoWor 91*
Son, Chang Hyun 1957- *WhoSSW 91*
Son, In Kyung *BiDrAPA 89*
Son, Sim *BioIn 16*
Sonafrank, Russell Eugene, II 1947- *IntWWM 90*
Sonalkar, Ashok Raghunath 1938- *WhoWor 91*
Sonberg, Michael Robert 1947- *WhoEmL 91*
Sonchik, Susan Marie 1954- *WhoAmW 91, WhoWor 91*
Soncrant, George Darrel 1949- *BiDrAPA 89*
Sondag, Rudolph 1726-1812 *PenDiDA 89*
Sondakh, Widyawati Deborah 1945- *WhoWor 91*
Sonday, Milton Franklin, Jr 1939- *WhoAmA 91*
Sonder, Carl Richard 1941- *BiDrAPA 89*
Sonderby, Susan Pierson 1947- *WhoAmW 91*
Sonderegger, John Forster 1931- *St&PR 91*
Sonderegger, Peter 1960- *IntWWM 90*
Sonderegger, Theo Brown 1925- *WhoAm 90*
Sonderen, James Bernard 1927- *St&PR 91*
Sondergaard, Jorgen 1949- *WhoWor 91*
Sondergeld, Donald Ray 1930- *WhoAm 90, WhoE 91*
Sonderleiter, Joseph P. *BiDrAPA 89*
Sondermann, Dieter Friedrich Wilhelm 1937- *WhoWor 91*
Sonders, Scott 1953- *ConAu 132*
Sondheim, Herbert 1927- *St&PR 91*
Sondheim, Stephen *BioIn 16*
Sondheim, Stephen 1930- *OxCPMus, WorAlBi*
Sondheim, Stephen Joshua 1930- *IntWWM 90, WhoAm 90, WhoE 91, WhoWor 91*
Sondheimer, Adrian Natan 1944- *BiDrAPA 89*
Sondheimer, Joseph 1918- *St&PR 91*
Sondhi, Manohar Lal 1933- *WhoWor 91*
Sondhi, Vir K. 1929- *St&PR 91*
Sondock, Ruby Kless 1926- *WhoAmW 91*
Sone, Bruce H. 1940- *St&PR 91*
Sone, Philip Geary 1949- *WhoEmL 91*
Sone, Toshio 1935- *WhoWor 91*
Sonea, Sorin I. 1920- *WhoAm 90*
Soned, Warren 1911-1966 *WhoAmA 91N*
Sonego, David Francis 1955- *BiDrAPA 89*
Sonenberg, Jack 1925- *WhoAm 90, WhoAmA 91, WhoE 91*
Sonenberg, Martin 1920- *WhoAm 90*
Sonenberg, Maya 1960- *ConAu 131, WhoWrEP 89*
Sonenklar, Neil Allen *BiDrAPA 89*
Sonenschein, David Walter 1941- *WhoWrEP 89*
Sonenshein, Nathan 1915- *WhoAm 90*
Sonenthal, I Ronald 1909- *BiDrAPA 89*
Sones, David Ethan *BiDrAPA 89*
Sones, Leon I 1928- *BiDrAPA 89*
Sonett, Charles Philip 1924- *WhoAm 90*
Sonfield, Robert Leon, Jr. 1931- *WhoAm 90*
Sonfist, Alan 1946- *WhoAmA 91*
Song *PenDiDA 89*
Song Jian 1932- *WhoWor 91*
Song Ping 1917- *WhoWor 91*
Song Renqiong 1904- *WhoWor 91*
Song, Ho Suck *BiDrAPA 89*
Song, Kenneth Kwanho 1939- *BiDrAPA 89*
Song, Nam Soo *BiDrAPA 89*
Song, Phil Woo *BiDrAPA 89*
Song, Renming 1963- *WhoSSW 91*
Song, Sae Ryoung *BiDrAPA 89*
Song, Suk Man 1945- *WhoWor 91*
Song, Young Haepark 1944- *BiDrAPA 89*
Song Ong, Roxanne Kay 1953- *WhoAmW 91*
Songayllo, Raymond Thaddeus 1930- *IntWWM 90*
Songer, Don 1899-1962 *Ballpl 90*
Songer, Frances Virginia 1957- *WhoAmW 91, WhoWor 91*
Songer, Thomas E. 1935- *St&PR 91*
Songsiridej, Vanee 1949- *WhoAmW 91*
Songstad, Steven Booth 1946- *WhoEmL 91*
Sonheim, Richard C. 1930- *St&PR 91*
Soni, Atmaram Harilal 1935- *WhoAm 90*
Soni, Bharat Keshavlal 1950- *WhoSSW 91*
Soni, Jorge 1955- *BiDrAPA 89*
Soni, Kusum Kapila 1930- *WhoAmW 91*
Soni, Pravin N *BiDrAPA 89*
Soni, Welthy H. *AuBYP 90*
Sonis, Meyer *BiDrAPA 89*
Sonis, William Allen 1948- *BiDrAPA 89*
Sonju, Norm Arnold 1938- *WhoAm 90*
Sonk, Joseph Stanley 1951- *WhoE 91*
Sonkin, Michelle Anne Eisemann 1952- *WhoAmW 91*
Sonkin, Paul Edward 1932- *St&PR 91*
Sonko, Andre 1944- *WhoWor 91*
Sonkowsky, Robert Paul 1931- *WhoAm 90*
Sonksen, Peter Henri 1936- *WhoWor 91*
Sonn, Harold Willis 1921- *St&PR 91*
Sonn, Lew 1921- *St&PR 91*
Sonn, Thomas M 1933- *BiDrAPA 89*
Sonnabend, Joan 1928- *WhoAmA 91*
Sonnabend, Lawrence C. 1943- *St&PR 91*
Sonnabend, Peter J. 1954- *St&PR 91*
Sonnabend, Roger P. 1925- *St&PR 91*
Sonnabend, Roger Philip 1925- *WhoAm 90*
Sonnabend, Stephanie 1953- *St&PR 91*
Sonne, John C 1924- *BiDrAPA 89*
Sonne, Jorgen 1925- *DcScanL*
Sonneborn, Henry, III 1918- *St&PR 91, WhoAm 90*
Sonneborn, Marcene Schnell 1954- *WhoE 91*
Sonneborn, Richard F. 1918- *St&PR 91*
Sonneborn, Tracy Morton 1905-1981 *DcScB S2*
Sonnecken, Edwin Herbert 1916- *WhoAm 90*
Sonnedecker, Glenn Allen 1917- *WhoAm 90*
Sonneman, Eve 1946- *WhoAm 90, WhoAmA 91*
Sonnemann, Harry 1924- *WhoAm 90*
Sonnenberg, Alan 1951- *St&PR 91*
Sonnenberg, Ben 1936- *WhoAm 90, WhoWrEP 89*
Sonnenberg, Frances *WhoAmA 91*
Sonnenberg, Hardy 1939- *WhoAm 90*
Sonnenberg, Jill M. 1960- *WhoE 91*
Sonnenberg, Louise Ann 1941- *BiDrAPA 89*
Sonnenberg, Nadja Salerno- *BioIn 16*
Sonnenberg, Ronnie 1956- *WhoAmW 91*
Sonnenberg, Stephen M 1940- *BiDrAPA 89*
Sonnenberg, Steven James 1955- *BiDrAPA 89*
Sonnenblick, Edmund H. 1932- *WhoWrEP 89*
Sonnenblick, Harvey Irwin 1936- *BiDrAPA 89, WhoE 91*
Sonnenfeld, Janet Marloff 1948- *WhoAmW 91*
Sonnenfeld, Joseph Hayyim 1849-1931? *BioIn 16*
Sonnenfeld, Marion 1928- *WhoAm 90*
Sonnenfeldt, Helmut 1926- *WhoAm 90, WhoE 91*
Sonnenfeldt, Marjorie Hecht *ODwPR 91*
Sonnenfeldt, Michael *BioIn 16*
Sonnenfeldt, Richard Wolfgang 1923- *WhoAm 90*
Sonnenreich, Michael Roy 1938- *WhoAm 90, WhoWor 91*
Sonnenreich, William Frederick 1932- *WhoE 91*
Sonnenschein 1917-1981 *WhoAmA 91N*
Sonnenschein, Adam 1938- *WhoAm 90*
Sonnenschein, Bonnie Jackson 1955- *WhoE 91*
Sonnenschein, Hugo Freund 1940- *WhoAm 90*
Sonnenschein, Kenneth Neal 1963- *BiDrAPA 89*
Sonnenschein, Ralph Robert 1923- *WhoAm 90*
Sonnenschein, Valentin *PenDiDA 89*
Sonnentag, Richard H. 1940- *WhoSSW 91*
Sonnerup, Bengt Ulf-Sten 1931- *WhoAm 90*
Sonneveld, A. *ConAu 131*
Sonneveld, Jan 1933- *WhoWor 91*
Sonnevi, Goran 1939- *DcScanL*
Sonneville-David, Therese de 1938-1988 *BioIn 16*
Sonnichsen, C. L. 1901- *BioIn 16*

Sonnichsen, Charles Leland 1901- *BioIn 16*
Sonnichsen, Dorothy Griffith 1942- *St&PR 91*
Sonnier, David Joseph 1939- *WhoSSW 91*
Sonnier, David W. 1959- *St&PR 91*
Sonnier, Jo-El *WhoNeCM [port]*
Sonnier, Keith 1941- *WhoAmA 91*
Sonnino, Carlo Benvenuto 1904- *WhoAm 90*
Sonnino, Roberta Elena 1952- *WhoAmW 91*
Sonntagbauer, Hans 1946- *WhoWor 91*
Sonny and Cher *EncPR&S 89*
Sonoda, Noboru 1933- *WhoWor 91*
Sonoda, Roxana Aki 1962- *WhoWor 91*
Sonogashira, Kenkichi 1931- *WhoWor 91*
Sonora, Jose de Galvez, Marquez de 1720-1787 *BioIn 16*
Sonora, Myrna 1959- *WhoHisp 91*
Sonpar, Prem Kanayalal 1935- *WhoWor 91*
Sonrel, Elizabeth 1874-1953 *BiDWomA*
Sons of the Pioneers *OxCPMus*
Sons, Linda Ruth 1939- *WhoAmW 91*
Sons, Raymond William 1926- *WhoAm 90*
Sonstelie, Richard Robert 1945- *St&PR 91, WhoAm 90, WhoEmL 91*
Sontag, Frederick Earl 1924- *WhoAm 90*
Sontag, Frederick H. 1924- *WhoAm 90*
Sontag, Henriette 1806-1854 *PenDiMP*
Sontag, James Mitchell 1939- *WhoAm 90*
Sontag, John G. 1948- *St&PR 91*
Sontag, Lester W *BiDrAPA 89*
Sontag, Peter Michael 1943- *WhoE 91*
Sontag, R.F. 1950- *St&PR 91*
Sontag, Sheldon 1938- *St&PR 91*
Sontag, Susan *WhoAm 90, WhoAmW 91*
Sontag, Susan 1933- *BioIn 16, FemiCLE, MajTwCW, NotWoAT, WorAlBi*
Sontheimer, James Albert 1926- *St&PR 91*
Sontheimer, Robert Max 1941- *St&PR 91*
Sonthineni, Sowbhagya L *BiDrAPA 89*
Soo, Kam Kwang *BiDrAPA 89*
Soo, Shao Lee 1922- *WhoAm 90*
Soo Hoo, Melvin Jay *BiDrAPA 89*
Sood, Din Dayal 1939- *WhoWor 91*
Sood, Dinesh K 1957- *BiDrAPA 89*
Sood, Rakesh K *BiDrAPA 89*
Sood, Raman Kumar 1954- *BiDrAPA 89*
Sood, Satish Chandra 1940- *WhoWor 91*
Sood, Vijay Paul 1942- *WhoWor 91*
Sooder, Karl Michael 1943- *St&PR 91*
Soofi, Jin Reynolds *BiDrAPA 89*
Sooho, Alan Moy *BiDrAPA 89*
Sooho, Alan Moy 1949- *WhoE 91*
Soohoo, Karen 1960- *WhoAmW 91*
Soohoo, Richard Dong 1950- *WhoE 91*
Soohoo-Chan, Lisa B.L. 1953- *WhoE 91*
Sooknarine, Jefferson Jaiwant 1956- *WhoWor 91*
Sookram, Atma Ram 1958- *WhoE 91*
Soong, James Chu Yul 1942- *WhoWor 91*
Soong, Tsu-Teh 1934- *WhoAm 90*
Soong, Wei-Tsuen 1945- *WhoWor 91*
Soonthornsaratoon, Chulapracha 1939- *WhoWor 91*
Soor-Melka, Marianne *BiDrAPA 89*
Soorani, Emil *BiDrAPA 89*
Soorikian, Diana Tashjian 1928- *WhoAmA 91*
Soorya, Narendir T *BiDrAPA 89*
Soos, Richard A, Jr. 1955- *WhoWrEP 89*
Soosaar, Enn 1937- *WhoWor 91*
Sooter, Edward 1934- *IntWWM 90*
Sootin, Harry *AuBYP 90*
Sooy, Charles Dalmage 1908- *St&PR 91*
Sooy, William Ray 1951- *WhoSSW 91*
Soper, Eileen A 1905-1990? *ConAu 131*
Soper, Grace 1766-1830 *FemiCLE*
Soper, Holly Spencer 1958- *WhoSSW 91*
Soper, Howard Kent 1928- *St&PR 91*
Soper, James Herbert 1916- *WhoAm 90*
Soper, James J. *ODwPR 91*
Soper, John Wayne 1944- *WhoSSW 91, WhoWor 91*
Soper, Quentin Francis 1919- *WhoAm 90*
Soper, Richard Graves 1950- *WhoSSW 91*
Soper, Richard T. *WhoAm 90*
Soper, Robert Edmund *BiDrAPA 89*
Soper, Willard *BioIn 16*
Sopher, Aaron 1905-1972 *WhoAmA 91N*
Sopher, Bernhard D 1879-1949 *WhoAmA 91N*
Sopher, Edward Orrin 1954- *WhoEmL 91*
Sopher, Vicki Elaine 1943- *WhoE 91*
Sophia *FemiCLE*
Sophia Aemilia, Queen of Denmark *BiDEWW*
Sophia Alekseevna *BioIn 16*
Sophia Alekseyevna 1657-1704 *WomWR*
Sophia, Elsa *EncCoWW*
Sophie A. *EncCoWW*
Sophie, Queen 1818-1877 *BioIn 16*
Sophocles 496?BC-406BC *WorAlBi*
Sophronius, Eusebius Hieronymus *BioIn 16*
Sophusson, Fridrik Klemenz 1943- *WhoWor 91*
Sophy, Charles Joseph *BiDrAPA 89*
Sopinka, John *BioIn 16*
Sopinka, John 1933- *WhoAm 90, WhoE 91*
Sopkin, George 1914- *WhoAm 90*
Sopko, Eugen 1949- *BioIn 16*
Sopp, Brian William 1942- *St&PR 91*
Soppelsa, George 1939- *WhoAmA 91*
Soppelsa, Jacques R. 1943- *WhoWor 91*
Soprani, Luciano *BioIn 16*
Soprani, Luciano 1946- *ConDes 90*
Sopranos, O.J. 1935- *St&PR 91*
Sopranos, Orpheus Javaras 1935- *WhoAm 90*
Sopwith, Thomas 1888-1989 *AnObit 1989, BioIn 16*
Soquel, John Albert 1928- *WhoAm 90*
Sor, Fernando 1778-1839 *PenDiMP*
Sora, Raul Juan Rodriguez *BiDrAPA 89*
Sora, Sebastian Antony 1943- *WhoE 91*
Sorabji, Cornelia 1866-1954 *FemiCLE*
Sorabji, Kaikhosru 1892-1988 *AnObit 1988*
Sorabji, Kaikhosru Shapurji *BioIn 16*
Sorabji, Kaikhosru Shapurji 1892-1988 *PenDiMP A*
Soraci, Sal A. 1952- *WhoSSW 91*
Sorauf, Francis Joseph 1928- *WhoAm 90*
Sorber, Charles Arthur 1939- *WhoAm 90*
Sorbom, Per Gunnar 1940- *WhoWor 91*
Sorby, Donald Lloyd 1933- *WhoAm 90*
Sorby, J Richard 1911- *WhoAmA 91*
Sorby, Norm *BioIn 16*
Sorce, Anthony John 1937- *WhoAmA 91, WhoE 91*
Sorce, Lawrence Roy 1945- *St&PR 91*
Sorce-Keller, Marcello 1947- *IntWWM 90*
Sordello, Enzo 1927- *IntWWM 90*
Sorden, John *AmLegL*
Sordi, Lucia 1871- *EncO&P 3*
Sordoni, Andrew J., III 1943- *St&PR 91, WhoAm 90*
Sordyl, Lenore Maureen 1958- *WhoAmW 91*
Sordylowa, Barbara Lucja 1934- *WhoWor 91*
Soreff, Helen *WhoAmA 91*
Soreff, S *WhoAmA 91*
Soreff, Stephen 1931- *WhoAmA 91*
Soreff, Stephen M 1942- *BiDrAPA 89*
Soregaroli, Arthur E. 1933- *St&PR 91*
Sorel, Bernard P. 1938- *WhoAm 90*
Sorel, Claudette Marguerite *WhoAm 90, WhoAmW 91, WhoE 91*
Sorel, Edward 1929- *BioIn 16, ConAu 33NR, WhoAm 90, WhoAmA 91*
Sorel, Eliot 1940- *BiDrAPA 89*
Sorel, Georges 1847-1922 *BiDFrPL*
Sorell, Carole Suzanne 1940- *ODwPR 91, WhoAmW 91*
Sorell, Kitty Julia 1937- *WhoAmW 91*
Sorell, Victor Alexander 1944- *WhoAmA 91*
Sorem, Alan Jay 1941- *WhoE 91*
Soren, David 1946- *WhoAm 90*
Soren, Howard 1930- *St&PR 91*
Sorensen, Allan C. 1938- *St&PR 91*
Sorensen, Bent 1958- *IntWWM 90*
Sorensen, Burton Erhard 1929- *WhoAm 90*
Sorensen, Camey 1933- *WhoAmW 91, WhoWrEP 89*
Sorensen, Candace Lynn 1960- *WhoAmW 91*
Sorensen, Charles E. 1881-1968 *EncABHB 5 [port]*
Sorensen, Charles W. *WhoAm 90*
Sorensen, Christine *WhoWrEP 89*
Sorensen, David Allen 1953- *WhoWrEP 89*
Sorensen, David E *BiDrAPA 89*
Sorensen, Debra Lynnette 1954- *WhoAmW 91*
Sorensen, Donald F. 1925- *St&PR 91*
Sorensen, Elizabeth Julia 1934- *WhoAmW 91*
Sorensen, Erik 1944- *WhoAm 90*
Sorensen, Frank C *BiDrAPA 89*
Sorensen, Gil 1935- *WhoWor 91*
Sorensen, Gladys Elaine 1922- *WhoAm 90*
Sorensen, Jacki Faye 1942- *WhoAm 90, WhoAmW 91*
Sorensen, James Kurt 1955- *WhoEmL 91*
Sorensen, Jean *WhoAmA 91*
Sorensen, John Hjelmhof 1923-1969 *WhoAmA 91N*
Sorensen, Johnny 1944- *ConDes 90*
Sorensen, Jorgen Philip 1938- *WhoWor 91*
Sorensen, Keld 1953- *WhoE 91*
Sorensen, Lary 1955- *Ballpl 90*
Sorensen, Leif Boge 1928- *WhoAm 90*
Sorensen, Mark Francis 1958- *BiDrAPA 89*
Sorensen, Meredith Jean 1940- *WhoAmW 91, WhoE 91*
Sorensen, Ove 1942- *WhoE 91*
Sorensen, Pablo Ove 1920- *WhoWor 91*
Sorensen, Philip Chaikin 1933- *WhoAm 90*
Sorensen, Robert C. 1923- *WhoAm 90, WhoE 91, WhoWor 91*
Sorensen, Robert Holm 1921- *St&PR 91, WhoAm 90*
Sorensen, Sheila 1947- *WhoAmW 91*
Sorensen, Soren Peter 1924- *St&PR 91*
Sorensen, Stuart L. 1948- *St&PR 91*
Sorensen, Svend 1950- *WhoWor 91*
Sorensen, Svend Otto *ConAu 132*
Sorensen, Svend Otto 1916- *BioIn 16*
Sorensen, Theodore Chaikin 1928- *WhoAm 90*
Sorensen, Thomas Chaikin 1926- *WhoAm 90*
Sorensen, Villy 1929- *DcScanL*
Sorensen, Virginia 1912- *AuBYP 90, WhoAm 90*
Sorenson, Brice K. 1940- *St&PR 91*
Sorenson, C.J. *St&PR 91*
Sorenson, Carol Johnson 1953- *WhoAmW 91*
Sorenson, David Paul 1955- *WhoEmL 91*
Sorenson, Dean Philip 1939- *WhoAm 90*
Sorenson, Edward Allen 1937- *BiDrAPA 89*
Sorenson, Jack 1954- *BioIn 16*
Sorenson, Jane 1926- *SmATA 63 [port]*
Sorenson, Mary Louise 1950- *WhoEmL 91*
Sorenson, Paul Victor 1955- *St&PR 91*
Sorenson, Peter Paul 1943- *WhoSSW 91*
Sorenson, Ralph Z. 1933- *St&PR 91*
Sorenson, Ralph Zellar, II 1933- *WhoAm 90*
Sorenson, Sandra Louise 1948- *WhoAmW 91, WhoEmL 91*
Sorenson, Sharon O. 1943- *WhoWrEP 89*
Sorestad, Glen 1937- *ConAu 31NR, WhoWrEP 89*
Sorett, Stephen Michael 1949- *WhoE 91*
Sorg, Francis Joseph, Jr. 1922- *St&PR 91*
Sorg, Gilbert B. 1926- *St&PR 91*
Sorg, Gilbert Bruce 1926- *WhoAm 90*
Sorg, William Darrell 1939- *St&PR 91*
Sorge, Elliott Lorenz *WhoAm 90*
Sorge, Friedrich *EncAL*
Sorge, Walter 1931- *WhoAmA 91*
Sorgenfrei, Mal Edward 1939- *St&PR 91*
Sorgenthal, Konrad von *PenDiDA 89*
Sorgenti, Harold Andrew 1934- *St&PR 91, WhoAm 90*
Sorgi, Bob 1932- *BioIn 16*
Sorgi, Paul 1955- *BiDrAPA 89*
Sorgue, Mireille 1944-1967 *EncCoWW*
Soria, Giovanni Battista 1581-1651 *PenDiDA 89*
Soria, Manuel E *BiDrAPA 89*
Soria, Martin Sebastian 1911-1961 *WhoAmA 91N*
Soriani, Paolo Ezio 1921- *WhoWor 91*
Soriano, Ernesto R *BiDrAPA 89*
Soriano, Hugo R. 1936- *WhoHisp 91*
Soriano, Louis *BioIn 16*
Soriano, Ronald Francis 1930- *WhoSSW 91*
Soriano Jara, Elena 1917- *EncCoWW*
Sorin, Arthur *BioIn 16*
Sorin, Gerald 1940- *ConAu 31NR*
Sork, Rudolf *BiDrAPA 89*
Sorkin, Aaron *BioIn 16*
Sorkin, Alan Lowell 1941- *ConAu 31NR*
Sorkin, Charles K. 1907- *WhoWor 91*
Sorkin, Emily *WhoAmA 91*
Sorkin, Gerald B. 1932- *WhoWor 91*
Sorkin, Mary Ann 1952- *St&PR 91*
Sorkin, Michael Robert 1944- *WhoE 91*
Sorkin, Steven Arthur 1937- *St&PR 91*
Sorknes, Suzanne Smith 1950- *St&PR 91*
Sorkoram, Paul Ollie 1937- *St&PR 91*
Sorkow, Eli 1923- *WhoSSW 91*
Sorley, Walker Kathrine *AuBYP 90*
Sorman, Steven 1948- *WhoAmA 91*
Sorman, Steven Robert 1948- *WhoAm 90*
Sormiou, Marie de *EncCoWW*
Sormus-Droppa, Helju *BiDrAPA 89*
Sornborger, William Edward 1926- *St&PR 91*
Sornsen, Richard C.G. *St&PR 91*
Sornstein, Anne 1915- *St&PR 91*
Sorogheye, Gabriel Eustace 1948- *WhoE 91*
Sorokin, Davis 1908-1977 *WhoAmA 91N*
Sorokin, Janet 1932- *WhoAmA 91, WhoE 91*
Sorokin, Joseph *BioIn 16*
Sorokin, Maxine Ann 1948- *WhoAmA 91, WhoE 91*
Sorokin, Pitirim Alexandrovitch 1889-1968 *EncO&P 3*
Sorokolit, Robert Joseph 1942- *WhoAm 90*
Soros, George *BioIn 16, NewYTBS 90 [port]*
Sorosky, Arthur D 1936- *BiDrAPA 89*
Sorota, Max David 1925- *St&PR 91*
Sorouri, Parviz 1929- *WhoE 91*
Sorrel, Eugene C. 1943- *St&PR 91*
Sorrel, William E *BiDrAPA 89*
Sorrel, William Edwin 1913- *WhoAm 90, WhoE 91, WhoWor 91*
Sorrell, Daniel J., Jr. 1942- *St&PR 91*
Sorrell, Furman Yates 1938- *WhoAm 90*
Sorrell, Gary Lee 1943- *WhoWor 91*
Sorrell, Martin S. *BioIn 16*
Sorrell, Martin Stuart 1945- *WhoAm 90*
Sorrell, Vic 1901-1972 *Ballpl 90*
Sorrells, Rick D. 1955- *WhoSSW 91*
Sorrells, Robert Taliaferro 1932- *WhoWrEP 89*
Sorrells, Susan *BioIn 16*
Sorrels, James E. 1933- *St&PR 91*
Sorrels, William Scott 1956- *WhoSSW 91*
Sorrentino, Charles Alan 1944- *St&PR 91*
Sorrentino, Charles L. 1928- *St&PR 91*
Sorrentino, Eleanor A 1936- *BiDrAPA 89*
Sorrentino, Franklin Edward 1940- *WhoAm 90*
Sorrentino, Gilbert 1929- *ConAu 33NR, WhoAm 90, WhoWrEP 89*
Sorrentino, Laura Ann 1959- *WhoAmW 91*
Sorrentino, Louis V 1923- *BiDrAPA 89*
Sorrentino, Renate Maria 1942- *WhoAmW 91*
Sorrentino, Richard Michael 1949- *WhoAmA 91*
Sorrier, Isabel Lane 1917- *WhoSSW 91*
Sorrow, Jerry W. 1945- *St&PR 91*
Sorrow, Ronald Thomas 1946- *St&PR 91*
Sors, Fernando 1778-1839 *PenDiMP*
Sorsa, Kalevi 1930- *WhoWor 91*
Sorsoleil, Lori Marie 1962- *WhoWrEP 89*
Sorstokke, Ellen Kathleen 1954- *WhoAmW 91*
Sorstokke, Susan Eileen 1955- *WhoAmW 91*
Sorteberg, Kenneth Warren 1945- *WhoEmL 91*
Sorter, George Hans 1927- *WhoAm 90, WhoWor 91*
Sorter, Michael Thomas *BiDrAPA 89*
Sortland, Paul Allan 1953- *WhoEmL 91*
Sortland, Trudith Ann 1940- *WhoAmW 91*
Sortor, Harold Edward 1925- *WhoAm 90*
Sortwell, Christopher T. 1957- *St&PR 91*
Sorvino, A Ronald 1933- *BiDrAPA 89*
Sorvino, Paul *WhoAm 90*
Sorvino, Paul 1939- *WorAlBi*
Sorvoja, Markku 1955- *WhoWor 91*
Sos, John 1945- *BiDrAPA 89*
Sosa, Blanca 1954- *WhoHisp 91*
Sosa, Dan 1923- *BioIn 16*
Sosa, Dan, Jr. 1923- *WhoAm 90, WhoHisp 91*
Sosa, E. J. *WhoHisp 91*
Sosa, Elias 1950- *Ballpl 90*
Sosa, Gaspar Castano De *EncCRAm*
Sosa, Juan B *BiDrAPA 89*
Sosa, Juan Jorge 1947- *WhoHisp 91*
Sosa, Lionel 1939- *WhoHisp 91*
Sosa, Mercedes *BioIn 16*
Sosa, Norma J. 1950- *WhoSSW 91*
Sosa, Pura O. 1942- *WhoHisp 91*
Sosa, Roberto 1930- *ConAu 131, HispWr 90*
Sosa, Teri 1946- *WhoHisp 91*
Sosa-Riddell, Adaljiza 1937- *WhoHisp 91*
Soshnick, Julian 1932- *St&PR 91*
Soshnik, Joseph 1920- *St&PR 91, WhoAm 90*
Sosin, David E 1935- *BiDrAPA 89*
Sosin, Sidney 1924- *St&PR 91, WhoAm 90*
Soskin, David Howell 1942- *WhoAm 90*
Soskin, Mark *BioIn 16*
Soskin, William F. 1916-1988 *BioIn 16*
Soskis, Ann K. *BioIn 16*
Soskis, David Aaron 1942- *BiDrAPA 89*
Soskis, Philip 1910-1989 *BioIn 16*
Sosland, Morton Irvin 1925- *St&PR 91*
Sosland, Neil N. 1930- *St&PR 91*
Sosman, Frederic P., III 1938- *St&PR 91*
Sosman, Herbert 1932- *St&PR 91*
Sosna, Marilyn M 1947- *BiDrAPA 89*
Sosner, Bernard 1932- *BiDrAPA 89*
Sosnoff, Martin *BioIn 16*
Sosnoff, Toni *BioIn 16*
Sosnora, Viktor Aleksandrovich *BioIn 16*
Sosnoski, Donald Raymond 1942- *St&PR 91*
Sosnovec, Milan 1946- *BiDrAPA 89*
Sosnow, Lawrence Ira 1935- *WhoAm 90*
Sosnowitz, Henry Abram 1940- *WhoAmA 91*
Sosnowski, Margaret Elizabeth 1959- *WhoAmW 91*
Sosnowski, Michael L. 1947- *St&PR 91*
Sosrodjojo, Surjanto 1939- *WhoWor 91*
Soss, Burton Jay 1944- *WhoSSW 91*
Soss, Neal M. 1949- *St&PR 91*
Soss, Neal Martin 1949- *WhoAm 90*
Sossaman, James J. 1932- *WhoAm 90*
Sossong, Anthony Terrance 1934- *St&PR 91*
Sostarich, Mark Edward 1953- *WhoEmL 91*

Sostchen, Cindy 1957- WhoWrEP 89
Sostowski, Richard Mark 1947- BiDrAPA 89
Sosville, Jerri Lynn 1944- WhoAmW 91
Sotatsu EncJap
Sotavento NewAgMG
Sotelo, Andrew 1951- WhoHisp 91
Sotelo, Antonio Andres, Jr. 1932- WhoHisp 91
Sotelo, Jose Calvo 1893-1936 BioIn 16
Sotelo, Sabino 1959- WhoHisp 91
Soter, George Nicholas 1924- WhoAm 90
Soter, Nicholas Gregory 1947- WhoEmL 91, WhoWor 91
Soteras, Solon C. 1922- St&PR 91
Soteriades, Michael Cosmas 1923- WhoE 91
Soteriou, Dido 1913?- EncCoWW
Sotero, Raymond Augustine 1953- WhoHisp 91
Soteropoulou, Erse 1953- EncCoWW
Sotheby, William 1757-1833 DcLB 93 [port]
Sotherland, Donald LeRoy 1928- WhoE 91
Sothern, Ann BioIn 16
Sothern, Ann 1909- ConTFT 8, WorAlBi
Sothern, Denny 1904-1977 Ballpl 90
Sothoron, Allen 1893-1939 Ballpl 90
Sotin, Hans 1939- IntWWM 90, PenDiMP
Sotir, Thomas Alfred 1936- WhoAm 90
Sotirhos, Michael 1928- WhoAm 90, WhoHisp 91, WhoWor 91
Sotiriadis, Sotirios 1929- WhoWor 91
Sotirios, His Grace Bishop of Toronto 1936- WhoAm 90
Soto, Aida R. 1931- WhoHisp 91
Soto, Albert Arturo 1932- BiDrAPA 89
Soto, Ana Maria BiDrAPA 89
Soto, Antonio Juan WhoHisp 91
Soto, Arlene Marie 1956- WhoAmW 91
Soto, Bernardo 1854-1931 BioIn 16
Soto, Carlos WhoHisp 91
Soto, Connie Lou 1933- St&PR 91
Soto, Gary BioIn 16
Soto, Gary 1952- HispWr 90, WhoHisp 91
Soto, Hernando de BioIn 16
Soto, Hernando de 1500?-1542 BioIn 16
Soto, Jesus Rafael 1923- ArtLatA, WhoWor 91
Soto, Jock BioIn 16
Soto, Jock 1965- WhoAm 90
Soto, John 1932- WhoHisp 91
Soto, Karen I. 1952- WhoHisp 91
Soto, Leandro P. WhoHisp 91
Soto, Louis Humberto 1912- WhoHisp 91
Soto, Lourdes Diaz WhoHisp 91
Soto, Marco Aurelio 1846-1908 BioIn 16
Soto, Maria Enid 1957- WhoHisp 91
Soto, Mario 1956- Ballpl 90
Soto, Pedro Juan 1928- BioIn 16, ConAu 131, HispWr 90
Soto, Radames Jose 1959- WhoHisp 91
Soto, Robert Louis 1949- WhoHisp 91
Soto, Roberto Fernando Eduardo 1950- WhoHisp 91
Soto, Roberto Manuel 1950- WhoHisp 91
Soto, Ronald Steven 1948- WhoHisp 91
Soto, Rosemarie WhoHisp 91
Soto, Shirlene A 1947- ConAu 131, HispWr 90
Soto, Talisa BioIn 16
Soto, Victor WhoHisp 91
Soto-Acosta, Raul BiDrAPA 89
Soto-Perrello, Jose Manuel BiDrAPA 89
Soto-Silva, Juan G BiDrAPA 89
Soto Velez, Clemente 1905- BioIn 16
Sotolongo, Alfredo WhoHisp 91
Sotolongo, Raul O. WhoHisp 91
Sotolongo, Thomas Julio 1928- WhoSSW 91
Sotomayor, Ernie WhoHisp 91
Sotomayor, Frank O. 1943- WhoHisp 91
Sotomayor, John A. 1928- WhoHisp 91
Sotomayor, Marta 1939- WhoHisp 91
Sotomayor-Rivera, Antonio BiDrAPA 89
Sotos, Hercules P. 1933- St&PR 91
Sotos, Hercules Peter 1933- WhoAm 90, WhoE 91
Sotos, Timothy S. 1948- St&PR 91
Sotsky, Raina BiDrAPA 89
Sotsky, Stuart M BiDrAPA 89
Sott, Herbert 1920- WhoAm 90
Sottarelli, Michael Ralph BiDrAPA 89
Sottile, Benjamin J. 1937- St&PR 91
Sottile, James 1913- St&PR 91, WhoAm 90, WhoSSW 91
Sottile, John H. 1947- St&PR 91
Sottile, Michael R. 1932- St&PR 91
Sottong, Philipp C 1920- BiDrAPA 89
Sottosanti, Vincent William 1936- St&PR 91, WhoAm 90
Sottsass, Ettore 1917- BioIn 16, PenDiDA 89
Sottsass, Ettore, Jr. 1917- ConDes 90
Sottung, George WhoAmA 91
Sotus-Nawar, Athena H. BiDrAPA 89
Souaid, George Joseph 1928- St&PR 91
Souaid, Robert George 1955- St&PR 91
Soublette, Carlos 1789-1870 BioIn 16
Soubliere, Jean-Pierre 1947- St&PR 91
Soubry, Kenneth W.S. 1920- St&PR 91
Souccar, Joseph Edward 1933- WhoAm 90
Souchal, Genevieve BioIn 16
Soucheray, Joe BioIn 16
Souchick, Michael Peter 1963- WhoSSW 91
Souchock, Steve 1919- Ballpl 90
Soucie, Gary Arnold 1937- WhoAm 90
Soucy, Barbara Marie 1949- WhoWrEP 89
Soucy, Gregory M. ODwPR 91
Soucy, Irene Laura 1948- St&PR 91
Soucy, Kevin Albert 1955- St&PR 91, WhoE 91
Soucy, Robert J 1933- ConAu 30NR
Souda, Robert M BiDrAPA 89
Soudeikine, Sergei 1882?-1946 BioIn 16
Souder, Charles 1948- St&PR 91
Souder, Christian L R BiDrAPA 89
Souder, Dennis E. 1945- WhoWor 91
Souder, Frances M. St&PR 91
Souder, Harvey St&PR 91
Souder, Mark Stephen 1956- WhoWrEP 89
Souder, Paul C. 1920- St&PR 91
Souder, Robert Raymond 1940- St&PR 91
Souder, Stephen Meredith 1943- St&PR 91
Souders, Bruce Chester 1920- WhoSSW 91, WhoWor 91
Souders, Thomas Lee 1946- St&PR 91
Souders, William Franklin 1928- St&PR 91, WhoAm 90
Souers, Robert T. 1943- ODwPR 91
Soufi, Hissam Edine 1935- BiDrAPA 89
Sougstad, Mike 1939- WhoAmA 91
Souham, Gerard 1928- ODwPR 91, WhoE 91, WhoWor 91
Souhami, Diana 1940- ConAu 130
Souhami, Gloria 1947- WhoAmW 91
Souhan, George G. 1929- St&PR 91
Soukup, Jane Klinkner 1958- WhoAmW 91, WhoWor 91
Soukup, Sobeslav PenDiMP
Soukupova, Vera 1932- IntWWM 90
Soul, David 1943- WorAlBi
Soul, Tom 1951- St&PR 91
Soulages, Pierre 1919- WhoWor 91
Soulati, Jayme M. 1961- ODwPR 91
Soule, Arthur B, III 1943- BiDrAPA 89
Soule, Beverly Jean 1949- WhoAmW 91
Soule, Carl BioIn 16
Soule, Charles Arthur, Jr. 1941- WhoAm 90
Soule, Charles Everett, Sr. 1934- St&PR 91
Soule, David Conder 1946- WhoE 91
Soule, Dorothy Fisher 1923- WhoAm 90
Soule, Elizabeth Sterling 1884-1972 BioIn 16
Soule, Gardner 1913- AuBYP 90
Soule, Gardner Bosworth 1913- WhoAm 90
Soule, George Melton 1952- BiDrAPA 89
Soule, Gertrude BioIn 16
Soule, James C. 1942- St&PR 91
Soule, Jeffrey Lyn 1953- WhoE 91
Soule, John Dutcher 1920- WhoAm 90
Soule, Margaret Miller 1951- WhoE 91
Soule, Minnie Meserve EncPaPR 91
Soule, Minnie Meserve EncO&P 3
Soule, Pierre 1801-1870 BioIn 16
Soule, Richard Gillette 1926- St&PR 91
Soule, Sallie Thompson 1928- WhoAmW 91
Soule, Theodate H. BioIn 16
Soule, William Stinson 1836-1908 WhNaAH
Soules, Alonso, Jr. 1933- St&PR 91
Soules, Barbara Ann 1947- WhoAmW 91
Soules, Jack Arbuthnott 1928- WhoAm 90
Soules, William Anderson WhoWor 91
Soulet, Lourdes 1953- WhoSSW 91
Souligny 1785-1864 WhNaAH
Souliotis, Barbara Anne 1942- WhoAmW 91
Souliotis, Elena 1943- IntWWM 90, PenDiMP
Soulis, Demosthenes BiDrAPA 89
Soulouque, Faustin 1785?-1867? BioIn 16
Souls, Thomas John 1930- WhoE 91
Soult, Launcelot Espy, Jr. 1928- St&PR 91
Soults, Frank B 1928- BiDrAPA 89
Soultz, Jerry Lee 1949- WhoEmL 91, WhoWor 91
Sounderarajah, Kandan BiDrAPA 89
Soupault, Philippe NewYTBS 90
Soupault, Philippe 1897-1990 BioIn 16, ConAu 131
Souphanouvong 1902- WhoWor 91
Sourbrine, Richard Don, II 1965- WhoEmL 91
Souretis, John 1938- WhoWor 91
Sourian, Peter 1933- WhoWrEP 89
Sourkes, Theodore Lionel 1919- WhoAm 90
Souroujon, Beatrice 1963- WhoAmW 91
Sourrouille, Juan Vital 1940- WhoWor 91
Sours, James Kingsley 1925- WhoAm 90
Sourwine, Kathleen Marie 1951- WhoAmW 91
Sousa, Consuelo Maria 1931- WhoAmW 91
Sousa, Joan Ann 1949- WhoE 91
Sousa, John Philip 1854-1932 OxCPMus, WorAlBi
Sousa, John Philip, III 1913- WhoAm 90
Sousa, Jose J C 1936- BiDrAPA 89
Sousa, Louis R. 1953- St&PR 91
Sousa, Maria Joao Leal de BioIn 16
Sousa, Terry 1943- St&PR 91
Sousa, William P. St&PR 91
Sousa Mendes, Aristides de 1885-1954 BioIn 16
Sousa Tavares, Sopia Andresen de 1922- EncCoWW
Soustelle, Jacques NewYTBS 90 [port]
Soustelle, Jacques 1912-1990 ConAu 132, CurBio 90N
Soustelle, Jacques Emile Yves 1912- BiDFrPL
Soustelle, Michel 1937- WhoWor 91
Souster, Raymond 1921- SmATA 63 [port], WorAu 1980 [port]
Souster, Tim Andrew James 1943- IntWWM 90
Soutar, Charles Frederick 1936- St&PR 91, WhoAm 90
Soutas-Little, Robert William 1933- WhoAm 90
Soutendijk, Dirk R. 1938- St&PR 91
Soutendijk, Dirk Rutger 1938- WhoAm 90
Souter, Camille 1929- BiDWomA
Souter, David Hackett 1939- WhoAm 90, WhoE 91
Souter, Robert Taylor 1909- WhoAm 90
South, Dudley Pritchett, Jr. 1926- St&PR 91
South, Eddie 1904-1962 DrBIPA 90
South, Edward P BiDrAPA 89
South, Elva Mae 1930- WhoWor 91
South, Frank Edwin 1924- WhoAm 90, WhoE 91
South, G.L. St&PR 91
South, Grace Devita 1957- WhoAmW 91
South, Graham Robin 1940- WhoWor 91
South, Jeffrey Lynn 1948- WhoSSW 91
South, Joe 1942- EncPR&S 89
South, Mary Ann 1933- WhoAmW 91
South, Pamela Dawn 1948- WhoAm 90
South, Richard C. 1925- St&PR 91
South, Robert Holt 1925- St&PR 91
South, William Preston 1943- St&PR 91
Southall, Ivan 1921- AuBYP 90
Southall, Ivan Francis 1921- WhoWor 91
Southam, Gordon Hamilton 1916- WhoAm 90
Southard, Curtis G BiDrAPA 89
Southard, David E. 1948- St&PR 91
Southard, David Gordon 1941- WhoE 91
Southard, Frank A. 1907-1989 BioIn 16
Southard, George William 1949- St&PR 91
Southard, Helen Elizabeth Fairbairn 1906- WhoAmW 91
Southard, Paul Raymond 1948- WhoE 91
Southard, Robert Y. 1946- St&PR 91
Southard, Samuel Lewis 1787-1842 BiDrUSE 89
Southard, Shelby Edward 1914- WhoAm 90
Southard, William 1957- ODwPR 91
Southcote, Eliza BiDEWW
Southcott, James Thomas 1824-1898 DcCanB 12
Southcott, Joanna 1750-1814 BioIn 16, EncO&P 3, FemiCLE
Southcott, Marvin Arthur 1929- WhoAm 90
Souther, George Parks 1939- St&PR 91, WhoAm 90
Souther, Glenn Michael 1957-1989 BioIn 16
Souther, Larry Alan 1952- WhoEmL 91
Souther, Richard NewAgMG
Southerington, Theresa Koogler 1950- WhoSSW 91
Southerland, Ellease 1943- FemiCLE
Southerland, Louis Feno, Jr. 1906- WhoAm 90
Southerland, Sydney Duane 1949- St&PR 91
Southern Comfort EncPR&S 89
Southern Pacific WhoNeCM [port]
Southern, Arlen D. 1933- ODwPR 91
Southern, Arlen Duane 1933- WhoE 91
Southern, Byron Scott 1946- St&PR 91
Southern, Eileen 1920- ConAu 31NR, IntWWM 90, WhoAm 90, WhoAmW 91
Southern, Hugh BioIn 16
Southern, Hugh 1932- WhoAm 90, WhoE 91
Southern, Joanne Tarabella 1949- WhoE 91
Southern, Richard 1903-1989 ConAu 129
Southern, Robert Allen 1930- WhoAm 90, WhoWor 91
Southern, Ronald Donald 1930- St&PR 91, WhoAm 90
Southey, Robert 1774-1843 BioIn 16, DcLB 93 [port]
Southey, Trevor J T 1940- WhoAmA 91
Southgate, Marie Therese 1928- WhoAm 90
Southgate, Minoo S. ConAu 132
Southgate, Richard W. 1929- WhoAm 90
Southgate, Vera BioIn 16
Southside Johnny and the Asbury Jukes EncPR&S 89
Southward, L. Leilani 1941- WhoAmW 91
Southward, Patricia Francis 1942- WhoAmW 91
Southwell, Anne 1574-1636 BiDEWW
Southwell, Caleb Azariah Paul 1913-1979 BioIn 16
Southwell, Elizabeth 1563?- BiDEWW
Southwell, Frances FemiCLE
Southwell, P.L. 1927- St&PR 91
Southwell, Raye Sumner 1950- WhoSSW 91
Southwell, Richard V. 1946- St&PR 91
Southwell, W. Wood 1955- St&PR 91
Southwell, William Joseph 1914- WhoAmA 91
Southwick, Arthur Frederick 1924- WhoAm 90
Southwick, Billy L. 1925- St&PR 91
Southwick, Charles Henry 1928- WhoAm 90
Southwick, Harry Webb 1918- WhoAm 90
Southwick, P. D. BioIn 16
Southwick, Paul 1920- WhoAm 90
Southwick, Peter D. BioIn 16
Southwick, Philip Lee 1916- WhoAm 90
Southwood, John Eugene 1929- St&PR 91
Southworth, Albert Sands 1811-1894 BioIn 16
Southworth, Anne WhoWrEP 89
Southworth, Billy 1893-1969 Ballpl 90
Southworth, David C. 1954- St&PR 91
Southworth, Douglas Belknap 1951- BiDrAPA 89
Southworth, E.D.E.N. 1819-1899 BioAmW, FemiCLE
Southworth, George Fulmer 1927- WhoE 91
Southworth, Herbert Rutledge 1908- WhoWor 91
Southworth, John David 1945- St&PR 91
Southworth, John Franklin, Jr. 1949- WhoSSW 91
Southworth, John Hayward 1927- St&PR 91
Southworth, Miles F. 1935- WhoWrEP 89
Southworth, William Dixon 1918- WhoAm 90, WhoWor 91
Soutine, Chaim 1893-1943 IntDcAA 90
Soutine, Chaim 1894-1943 BioIn 16
Souto, Jose A. WhoHisp 91
Souto Hernandez, Angel Juan WhoWor 91
Soutos, Nicolaos 1932- WhoWor 91
Soutter, Lamar 1909- WhoAm 90
Soutter, Thomas D. 1934- WhoAm 90
Soutter, Thomas Douglas 1934- St&PR 91
Soutullo, Reveriano 1884-1932 OxCPMus
Soutullo, Reveriano, and Vert, Juan OxCPMus
Souvarine, Boris 1885-1984 BiDFrPL
Souveroff, Vernon William, Jr. 1934- WhoAm 90
Souweine, Leon Edmund, Jr. 1946- WhoE 91
Souza, Adelaide-Marie-Emilie Filleul de 1761-1836 EncCoWW
Souza, Alcidio Mafra de 1925- WhoWor 91
Souza, Arthur P. 1947- St&PR 91
Souza, Ernest 1893-1963 BioIn 16
Souza, Joao da Cruz e 1861-1898 BioIn 16
Souza, Mark Richard BiDrAPA 89
Souza, Matthew F. 1957- St&PR 91
Souza, Maurene Gloria 1949- WhoAmW 91
Souza, Ralph de PenDiMP
Souza, Raymond D 1936- ConAu 30NR, HispWr 90
Souza, Ronald J. 1936- St&PR 91
Souza, Ronald Joseph 1936- WhoAm 90
Souza, Virginia A. 1946- WhoAmW 91
Souzay, Gerard 1918- IntWWM 90, PenDiMP
Sovereign, Kenneth Lester 1919- St&PR 91
Sovern, Jeff 1956- WhoEmL 91
Sovern, Michael Ira 1931- WhoAm 90, WhoE 91, WhoWor 91
Soverow, Gary Jan 1946- BiDrAPA 89
Sovey, L. Terrell, Jr. 1931- WhoAm 90, WhoSSW 91
Sovey, Terrell St&PR 91
Sovey, William Pierre 1933- WhoAm 90
Soviak, Harry 1935- WhoAmA 91N
Sovie, Margaret Doe 1934- WhoAm 90, WhoAmW 91
Soviero, Diana Barbara 1946- WhoAm 90
Sovik, Edward Anders 1918- WhoAm 90
Sovik, Ruth Johnson 1928- WhoAm 90
Sovik, William E., Jr. 1944- St&PR 91

Sovine, David L 1946- BiDrAPA 89
Sovner, Robert David 1943- BiDrAPA 89
Sovner-Ribbler, Judith W. 1947- WhoAmW 91
Sow Fall, Aminata 1941- BioIn 16
Sowa, Dorothy Rohrer 1938- WhoAmW 91
Sowada, Alphonse Augustus 1933- WhoAm 90
Sowah, Ernest Nee Pobee 1921- WhoWor 91
Sowald, Debra Kay 1951- WhoAmW 91
Sowald, Heather Gay 1954- WhoEmL 91
Sowande, Fela 1905- DrBlPA 90
Sowards, Ann Phelps 1933- St&PR 91
Sowards, Patricia Lutie 1952- WhoAmW 91
Sowatzke, James Patrick 1959- WhoSSW 91
Sowden, William B., III 1944- St&PR 91
Sowder, Elizabeth Anne 1956- WhoAmW 91
Sowder, Fred Allen 1940- WhoWor 91
Sowder, Kathleen Adams 1951- WhoWor 91
Sowder, Lynne 1948- WhoAmA 91
Sowder, Robert Robertson 1928- St&PR 91, WhoAm 90
Sowder, Tony R. 1920- St&PR 91
Sowell, Carol Ann 1946- WhoWrEP 89
Sowell, Dawn BioIn 16
Sowell, Elizabeth Lee Sledge 1938- WhoSSW 91
Sowell, James Edwin 1948- WhoAm 90
Sowell, Katye Marie Oliver 1934- WhoSSW 91
Sowell, Mayme Gust 1934- WhoSSW 91
Sowell, Mike 1948- ConAu 131
Sowell, Sam C. 1933- St&PR 91
Sowell, Thomas 1930- WhoAm 90
Sowell, W. R. 1920- WhoSSW 91, WhoWor 91
Sowell, William Hilton 1956- WhoWor 91
Sowell, William Raymond 1928- WhoWor 91
Sowerby, Desmond Chaytor 1946- WhoWor 91
Sowerby, Ronald E. 1943- St&PR 91
Sowernam, Ester BiDEWW, FemiCLE
Sowers, David Eric 1946- WhoEmL 91
Sowers, George F. 1921- St&PR 91
Sowers, George Frederick 1921- WhoAm 90
Sowers, John Phillip 1947- WhoEmL 91, WhoWor 91
Sowers, Luther BioIn 16
Sowers, Malcolm A 1921- BiDrAPA 89
Sowers, Miriam R 1922- WhoAmA 91
Sowers, Phyllis AuBYP 90
Sowers, Sandra Ann Hucke 1938- WhoE 91
Sowers, Wesley H. 1905- St&PR 91
Sowers, Wesley Hoyt 1905- WhoAm 90
Sowers, Wilma Frances 1933- WhoAmW 91
Sowersby, Lewann 1939- St&PR 91
Sowinski, Joseph Matthew 1960- WhoE 91
Sowinski, Stanislaus Joseph 1927- WhoAmA 91
Sowle, Donald Edgar 1915- WhoAm 90, WhoE 91, WhoWor 91
Sowle, Jane 1631?-1711 BiDEWW
Sowles, John Dean 1921- St&PR 91
Sowman, Harold Gene 1923- WhoAm 90
Sowokinos, Frank F. 1936- St&PR 91
Sowrenam, Ester FemiCLE
Sox, Harold Carleton, Jr. 1939- WhoAm 90
Soxx, Bob B., and the Blue Jeans EncPR&S 89
Soya, Carl Erik Martin 1896-1983 DcScanL
Soya, Kiyoshi AuBYP 90
Soyak, Ali Necip 1947- WhoWor 91
Soyak, Yusuf Edip 1951- WhoWor 91
Soyer, David PenDiMP
Soyer, David 1923- WhoAm 90
Soyer, Isaac 1902-1981 WhoAmA 91N
Soyer, Moses 1899-1974 WhoAmA 91N
Soyer, Raphael 1899-1987 BioIn 16
Soyer, Roger 1939- IntWWM 90, PenDiMP
Soyinka, Akinwande Oluwole BioIn 16
Soyinka, Wole BioIn 16
Soyinka, Wole 1934- DrBlPA 90, MajTwCW, WhoWor 91, WorAlBi
Soylemez, Sezer M. 1941- St&PR 91
Soyster, Margaret Blair 1951- WhoEmL 91
Soza, Dushan Travice Columban 1956- WhoWor 91
Soza, William 1936- WhoHisp 91
Sozen, Mete Avni 1930- WhoAm 90
Sozio, Armando WhoAmA 91N
Spa, Jacob Jan 1939- WhoWor 91
Spaak, Paul Henri 1899-1972 WorAlBi
Spaan, Cornelis Gertrudis G. 1943- WhoWor 91
Spaans, Gijsbert 1935- WhoWor 91
Spaar, Albert P., Jr. BiDrAPA 89
Spaar, Lisa Russ 1956- WhoWrEP 89
Spaarnay, Harry 1944- PenDiMP
Spaatz, Carl 1891-1974 BioIn 16, WorAlBi
Spacal, Savo BiDrAPA 89
Spaccia, Pier'Angela 1958- WhoAmW 91
Space, Theodore Maxwell 1938- WhoE 91, WhoWor 91
Spacek, Leonard Paul 1907- WhoAm 90
Spacek, Sissy BioIn 16
Spacek, Sissy 1949- WhoAm 90, WhoAmW 91, WorAlBi
Spach, Jule Christian 1923- WhoAm 90, WhoSSW 91
Spach, Madison Stockton 1926- WhoAm 90
Spache, Evelyn B 1929- ConAu 30NR
Spache, George Daniel 1909- AuBYP 90
Spacht, Jon Craige 1956- WhoEmL 91
Spackman, G. Brett 1950- St&PR 91
Spackman, John Rudolph 1829?-1885 OxCCanT
Spackman, Thomas James 1937- WhoAm 90
Spackman, W M 1905-1990 ConAu 132
Spackman, W. M. 1905-1990 NewYTBS 90
Spacks, Barry 1931- ConAu 33NR, DcLB 105 [port]
Spacks, Patricia Meyer 1929- WhoAm 90
Spada, Andrew Thomas 1962- WhoWor 91
Spada, Marietta 1943- St&PR 91
Spadafora, David Charles 1951- WhoE 91
Spadafora, Hugo BioIn 16
Spadafora, John A. St&PR 91
Spadaro, Joseph A. 1950- St&PR 91
Spade, Bob 1877-1924 Ballpl 90
Spader, Bryan D 1940- BiDrAPA 89
Spader, James BioIn 16
Spader, James 1960- News 91-2 [port]
Spadone, Charles Dubois St&PR 91
Spadone, John C. St&PR 91
Spadoni, Alex J 1935- BiDrAPA 89
Spady, Frieda Herold BiDrAPA 89
Spaeder, Roger Campbell 1943- WhoAm 90, WhoE 91
Spaeh, Winfried Heinrich 1930- WhoWor 91
Spaepen, Frans August 1948- WhoAm 90
Spaete, Richard Roger 1947- WhoEmL 91
Spaeth, Ann Barringer 1937- WhoE 91
Spaeth, Anthony Parry 1955- WhoWor 91
Spaeth, Donald Allison 1947- St&PR 91
Spaeth, Edmund Benjamin, Jr. 1920- WhoAm 90
Spaeth, Eloise O'Mara 1904- WhoAmA 91
Spaeth, George Link 1932- WhoAm 90
Spaeth, Harold J 1930- ConAu 32NR
Spaeth, Karl Henry 1929- St&PR 91, WhoAm 90
Spaeth, Melvin 1926- WhoAm 90
Spaeth, Michael E. 1941- St&PR 91
Spaeth, Nicholas John 1950- WhoAm 90
Spaeth, Otto 1897-1966 WhoAmA 91N
Spaeth, Sigmund 1885-1965 OxCPMus
Spafford, Michael Charles 1935- WhoAm 90, WhoAmA 91
Spafford, Ray P. 1943- St&PR 91
Spaggiari, Albert BioIn 16
Spagna, Gilda WhoAmW 91
Spagna, Louis Anthony 1937- St&PR 91
Spagna, Ted BioIn 16
Spagnardi, Ronald L. 1943- St&PR 91
Spagnardi, Ronald Lee 1943- WhoAm 90
Spagno, Anthony A BiDrAPA 89
Spagnoletti, Fred L. 1941- St&PR 91
Spagnoli, Nick R. 1936- St&PR 91
Spagnoli, Sharon Rosetta 1946- WhoE 91
Spagnolo, Kathleen Mary 1919- WhoAmA 91
Spagnuola, Francis Michael 1940- WhoE 91
Spahl, Gary Michael 1960- WhoWrEP 89
Spahn, Charles DeForest 1943- St&PR 91
Spahn, James Francis 1957- WhoSSW 91
Spahn, Mary Attea 1929- WhoAm 90
Spahn, Robert W. 1954- St&PR 91
Spahn, Warren 1921- Ballpl 90 [port], WorAlBi
Spahr, Christian Carson Febiger BioIn 16
Spahr, D. Lorraine 1925- St&PR 91
Spahr, Frederick Thomas 1939- WhoAm 90
Spahr, Philip M. 1951- St&PR 91
Spahr, Robert Edward St&PR 91N
Spahr, Robert N. 1938- St&PR 91
Spaid, Joseph S., Sr. 1906- St&PR 91
Spaid, Joseph Snyder 1906- WhoAm 90
Spaid, Robin Loy 1947- WhoAmW 91
Spaight, Richard Dobbs 1758-1802 BioIn 16
Spain, Clayton Jack 1938- WhoSSW 91
Spain, Jack Holland, Jr. 1939- WhoAm 90
Spain, James Dorris, Jr. 1929- WhoAm 90
Spain, James S. BioIn 16
Spain, James William 1926- WhoAm 90, WhoWor 91
Spain, John TwCCr&M 91
Spain, Johnny BioIn 16
Spain, Joseph Archie 1948- St&PR 91
Spain, Nancy 1917-1964 BioIn 16, TwCCr&M 91
Spain, Nettie Edwards 1918- WhoSSW 91, WhoWor 91
Spain, Patrick J. 1952- St&PR 91
Spain, Patrick James 1952- WhoEmL 91
Spain, Robert Hitchcock 1925- WhoAm 90
Spain, William James, Jr. 1927- St&PR 91
Spainhour, Elizabeth Anne Stroupe 1944- WhoAmW 91, WhoSSW 91
Spainhour, Kyle 1960- WhoEmL 91
Spainhour, Tremaine Howard 1924- WhoAm 90
Spainhower, Paul J. 1927- St&PR 91
Spak, Deborah Gendernalik 1963- WhoAmW 91
Spak, Donald Fivel 1948- WhoEmL 91
Spak, Lorin Mitchell 1941- St&PR 91
Spake, Ned Bernarr 1933- St&PR 91, WhoAm 90
Spake, Reuben Michael 1957- WhoSSW 91
Spalding, Albert 1850-1915 Ballpl 90 [port]
Spalding, Albert 1888-1953 BioIn 16
Spalding, Albert Dominic, Jr. 1951- WhoEmL 91
Spalding, Albert G. 1850-1915 BioIn 16
Spalding, Almut Marianne 1957- WhoAmW 91
Spalding, Amy Janette 1963- WhoAmW 91
Spalding, Charles F BiDrAPA 89
Spalding, Daniel L. 1953- St&PR 91
Spalding, Diana Jesuroga 1960- WhoAmW 91
Spalding, Donald E. 1930- St&PR 91
Spalding, Elaine R. 1940- WhoAmW 91
Spalding, Henry A. 1899- WhoWor 91
Spalding, Henry Harmon 1803-1874 WhNaAH
Spalding, Henry S. 1865-1934 LiHiK
Spalding, Jack S. 1930- St&PR 91
Spalding, James C 1921- BiDrAPA 89
Spalding, James Stuart 1934- St&PR 91, WhoAm 90
Spalding, Keith 1921- WhoAm 90
Spalding, Laura Ann BiDrAPA 89
Spalding, Mary V. Pyle BioIn 16
Spalding, Peter Edward 1927- BiDrAPA 89
Spalding, Robert George 1923- WhoE 91
Spalding, Robert T 1931- BiDrAPA 89
Spalding, Sidney P. BioIn 16
Spalla, Anne Buck WhoAmW 91
Spalla, Frank L. 1937- St&PR 91
Spallanzani, Lazzaro 1729-1799 WorAlBi
Spallholz, Julian Ernest 1943- WhoSSW 91
Spallina, James Peter 1919- St&PR 91
Spallone, Henry BioIn 16
Spallone, Henry J. WhoE 91
Spallone, Robert E. 1939- WhoE 91
Spalteholz, Robert William 1945- St&PR 91, WhoE 91
Spalter, Susan Deborah 1944- WhoSSW 91
Spalton, David John 1947- WhoWor 91
Spalty, Edward 1946- WhoEmL 91
Spampinato, Arline C. St&PR 91
Spampinato, Clemente 1912- WhoAmA 91
Spandafora, Robert William 1932- St&PR 91
Spandau Ballet EncPR&S 89
Spandorf, Lily Gabriella WhoAmA 91
Spandorfer, Merle Sue 1934- WhoAm 90, WhoAmA 91, WhoAmW 91, WhoE 91
Spang, Mark W. 1948- St&PR 91
Spang, Ralph McCurdy WhoSSW 91
Spang, Sara Crosby 1947- WhoAmW 91
Spangenberg, Dorothy Breslin 1931- WhoWor 91
Spangenberg, Edward Brindley 1935- St&PR 91
Spangenberg, Kristin L 1944- WhoAmA 91
Spangenberger, Joseph George 1933- WhoE 91
Spangfort, Erik Viggo 1923- WhoWor 91
Spangle, Clarence W. 1925- St&PR 91
Spangle, Morgan BioIn 16
Spangle, Tami Renee 1965- WhoAmW 91
Spangler, Al 1933- Ballpl 90
Spangler, Arnold E. 1948- St&PR 91
Spangler, Arnold Eugene 1948- WhoAm 90
Spangler, Arthur Stephenson, Jr. 1949- WhoE 91, WhoWor 91
Spangler, C. Gregory 1940- St&PR 91
Spangler, Clarence John 1924- St&PR 91
Spangler, Clemmie Dixon, Jr. 1932- WhoAm 90, WhoSSW 91
Spangler, Daisy Kirchoff 1913- WhoAmW 91, WhoWor 91
Spangler, David 1945- NewAgE 90
Spangler, David Robert 1940- WhoAm 90
Spangler, David Sheridan 1948- WhoEmL 91, WhoSSW 91, WhoWor 91
Spangler, Dennis Lee 1947- WhoSSW 91
Spangler, Edwin Frederic Americus 1945- WhoE 91
Spangler, J.J. PenDiDA 89
Spangler, J.L. St&PR 91
Spangler, Margaret Johnson 1951- WhoAmW 91
Spangler, Miller Brant 1923- WhoE 91
Spangler, Ronald Lee 1959- BiDrAPA 89
Spangler, Ronald Leroy 1937- WhoE 91, WhoWor 91
Spangler, Scott Michael 1938- St&PR 91, WhoAm 90
Spangler, William C. 1930- St&PR 91
Spani, Hina 1896-1969 PenDiMP
Spanidou, Irini 1946- EncCoWW
Spaniel, Frank James 1928- St&PR 91
Spaniel, Rosalie Louise Swanson WhoAmW 91
Spaniels, The EncPR&S 89
Spanier, Arthur Melvin 1948- WhoSSW 91
Spanier, Elliott J 1946- BiDrAPA 89
Spanier, Graham Basil 1948- WhoAm 90
Spanier, Maury L. 1916- St&PR 91
Spanier, Muggsy 1906-1967 OxCPMus, WorAlBi
Spanier, Muriel 1928- WhoWrEP 89
Spanier, Richard Frederick 1940- St&PR 91
Spanierman, Ira BioIn 16
Spaniol, Joseph Frederick, Jr. 1925- WhoAm 90
Spanjaard, Johannes 1938- St&PR 91
Spann, Allen Troy 1944- St&PR 91
Spann, George William 1946- WhoAm 90, WhoSSW 91, WhoWor 91
Spann, Gloria Carter NewYTBS 90
Spann, Gloria Carter 1926-1990 BioIn 16, ConAu 131
Spann, Hyman Dale, Jr. 1935- WhoWor 91
Spann, Katharine Doyle WhoWor 91
Spann, Laura Nason 1947- WhoSSW 91
Spann, Milton Graham, Jr. 1942- WhoSSW 91
Spann, Rebecca Jane 1960- WhoAmW 91
Spann, Richard Nelson 1938- St&PR 91
Spann, Ronald Thomas 1949- WhoWor 91
Spann, Stephen Allison 1941- WhoWor 91
Spann, William J BiDrAPA 89
Spano, John J. 1919- ODwPR 91
Spano, John Joseph 1919- WhoE 91
Spano, Jon Joseph 1936- WhoSSW 91
Spano, Joseph 1946- WhoAm 90
Spanos, Alexander Gus 1923- WhoAm 90
Spanos, Dean A. 1950- WhoAm 90
Spanovich, Milan 1929- St&PR 91, WhoAm 90
Spar, Carol Jean BiDrAPA 89
Spar, Edward Joel 1939- St&PR 91, WhoAm 90
Sparacio, John J. 1925- St&PR 91
Sparano, Vin T. 1934- WhoWrEP 89
Sparano, Vincent Thomas 1934- WhoAm 90
Sparatore, Maria Anna 1964- WhoAmW 91
Sparber, Margaretha Anna 1922- WhoWor 91
Sparberg, Esther B. 1922- WhoAm 90
Sparberg, Marshall Stuart 1936- WhoAm 90
Sparby, Neal 1936- St&PR 91
Spare, Austin Osmond 1889-1956 EncO&P 3
Spare, Joseph T BiDrAPA 89
Sparey, Jonathan PenDiMP
Spargo, Benjamin H. 1919- WhoAm 90
Spargo, John 1876-1966 EncAL
Spargur, Ruth Katherine BioIn 16
Sparhawk, George Roger, Jr. BiDrAPA 89
Sparing, James Byford BiDrAPA 89
Spark, Debra 1962- BioIn 16
Spark, Derek H 1924- BiDrAPA 89
Spark, Isadore 1909- BiDrAPA 89
Spark, Muriel BioIn 16
Spark, Muriel 1918- FemiCLE, MajTwCW, WorAlBi
Spark, Muriel Sarah WhoAm 90, WhoWor 91
Spark, Victor David 1898- WhoAmA 91
Sparker, William Holbrook 1925- St&PR 91
Sparkes, Catherine Adelaide 1842-1891? BiDWomA
Sparkman, Brandon Buster 1929- WhoAm 90
Sparkman, Gene, Jr 1941- WhoAmA 91
Sparkman, Gloria Ann 1954- WhoSSW 91
Sparkman, John J. 1899-1985 WorAlBi
Sparkman, Lila Gillis 1930- WhoWor 91
Sparkman, Robert Satterfield 1912- WhoAm 90
Sparkman, William ConAu 130
Sparkman, William E. 1929- St&PR 91

Sparkman, William Fraser 1947- *WhoSSW 91*
Sparks, Abbe *ODwPR 91*
Sparks, Art 1901-1984 *BioIn 16*
Sparks, Asa Howard 1937- *WhoSSW 91*
Sparks, Bertel Milas 1918- *WhoAm 90*
Sparks, Billy Schley 1923- *WhoWor 91*
Sparks, Bradley E. 1946- *St&PR 91*
Sparks, Cecil R. 1930- *St&PR 91*
Sparks, Claud Glenn 1922- *WhoAm 90*
Sparks, David Emerson 1944- *WhoE 91*
Sparks, David Stanley 1922- *WhoAm 90*
Sparks, Deane F. 1933- *St&PR 91*
Sparks, Donald James, Jr. 1960- *WhoSSW 91*
Sparks, Donna Theresa 1946- *WhoAmW 91*
Sparks, Earl Edwin 1920- *WhoAm 90*
Sparks, Edgar C. 1931- *St&PR 91*
Sparks, Garland Collins, Jr. 1937- *WhoSSW 91*
Sparks, Grant Todd 1960- *WhoSSW 91*
Sparks, Harvey Vise, Jr. 1938- *WhoAm 90*
Sparks, Hugh Cullen 1946- *WhoSSW 91*
Sparks, Jack D. 1922- *St&PR 91*
Sparks, Jack David 1922- *WhoAm 90*
Sparks, James D. 1928- *St&PR 91*
Sparks, John C 1928- *BiDrAPA 89*
Sparks, John Edward 1930- *WhoAm 90*
Sparks, John Edwin 1942- *WhoAmA 91*
Sparks, John K. 1939- *ODwPR 91*
Sparks, John Wesley 1946- *WhoEmL 91*
Sparks, Kenneth George 1935- *St&PR 91*
Sparks, Kimberly 1930- *WhoAm 90*
Sparks, Lawrence John 1942- *St&PR 91*
Sparks, Marshall F. 1940- *St&PR 91*
Sparks, Meredith Pleasant *WhoWor 91*
Sparks, Merrill 1922- *WhoWor 91, WhoWrEP 89*
Sparks, Morgan 1916- *WhoAm 90*
Sparks, Richard B. 1946- *St&PR 91*
Sparks, Richard Blaine 1946- *WhoEmL 91*
Sparks, Richard F. *BioIn 16*
Sparks, Richard Kingsley 1915- *WhoAm 90*
Sparks, Richard T. 1935- *St&PR 91*
Sparks, Robert Dean 1932- *WhoAm 90*
Sparks, Robert Edward 1930- *WhoAm 90*
Sparks, Robert Hutchen 1929- *St&PR 91*
Sparks, Robert Ronold, Jr. 1946- *WhoSSW 91*
Sparks, Robert W. 1895-1989 *BioIn 16*
Sparks, Robert William 1925- *WhoAm 90*
Sparks, Robin Dale 1940- *WhoAmW 91*
Sparks, Stephen Stone 1954- *WhoEmL 91*
Sparks, Tully 1874-1937 *Ballpl 90*
Sparks, W.A., Jr. 1935- *St&PR 91*
Sparks, Walter Chappel 1918- *WhoAm 90*
Sparks, Wilfred 1937- *WhoWor 91*
Sparks, William Barton 1945- *St&PR 91*
Sparks, Willis Breazeal, III 1934- *WhoSSW 91*
Sparler, Daniel 1917- *St&PR 91*
Sparling, George Bryant 1945- *WhoSSW 91*
Sparling, Jack 1916- *EncACom*
Sparling, Mary Christine 1928- *WhoAm 90*
Sparling, Mary Lee 1934- *WhoAmW 91*
Sparling, Peter David 1951- *WhoAm 90*
Sparling, Winston Bruce 1919- *St&PR 91*
Sparma, Joe 1942-1986 *Ballpl 90*
Sparnaay, Harry Willem 1944- *IntWWM 90*
Sparr, Betsy Carolyn 1960- *WhoAmW 91*
Sparr, Landy Ferris 1943- *BiDrAPA 89*
Sparre, Gabriel *PenDiDA 89*
Sparre, Louis *PenDiDA 89*
Sparrough, Ann Rhind 1947- *WhoE 91*
Sparrow, Barbara Jane 1935- *WhoAmW 91*
Sparrow, Ephraim Maurice 1928- *WhoAm 90*
Sparrow, Francis David *BiDrAPA 89*
Sparrow, Harry L. 1875-1920 *Ballpl 90*
Sparrow, Herbert George, III 1936- *WhoAm 90*
Sparrow, Joshua David 1955- *BiDrAPA 89*
Sparrow, Leigh W. 1956- *WhoWor 91*
Sparrow, Lissa Cadle 1964- *WhoAmW 91*
Sparrow, Lynne Orser 1939- *WhoE 91*
Sparrow, Rodney G. 1948- *St&PR 91*
Sparrow, Rory *BioIn 16*
Sparrow, Simon 1925- *MusmAFA*
Sparrow, William Holliday 1943- *St&PR 91, WhoAm 90*
Sparshott, Francis Edward 1926- *BioIn 16, WhoAm 90, WhoWrEP 89*
Sparso, Henning Hempel 1929- *WhoWor 91*
Spartacus *WorAlBi*
Spartacus, Deutero *ConAu 32NR*
Spartali, M. *BiDWomA*
Sparti, Barbara 1932- *IntWWM 90*
Sparti, Cheryl Diane 1930- *WhoAmW 91*
Spartin, David W. 1957- *St&PR 91*
Spartin, Flavia Cleo 1935- *WhoAmW 91*
Spass, Stan 1929- *St&PR 91*
Spasser, Frank B. 1929- *St&PR 91*
Spata, Kathleen Marie 1964- *WhoAmW 91*
Spatafora, J Richard *BiDrAPA 89*
Spatafora, Ron James 1951- *WhoSSW 91*
Spataro, Alan C. *St&PR 91*
Spataro, Janie Dempsey Watts 1951- *WhoAmW 91*
Spater, Herman W. *BiDrAPA 89*
Spater-Zimmerman, Susan H *BiDrAPA 89*
Spates, Thomas G. *BioIn 16*
Spath, Thomas F. 1933- *St&PR 91*
Spatt, Michael David 1957- *St&PR 91*
Spatt, Robert Edward 1956- *WhoE 91, WhoEmL 91*
Spatta, Carolyn Davis 1935- *WhoAmW 91*
Spatz, David Wayne 1959- *WhoE 91*
Spatz, Donald Dean 1944- *St&PR 91*
Spatz, Hugo David 1913- *WhoSSW 91*
Spatz, Lois Settler 1940- *WhoAmW 91*
Spatz, Ronald M. 1949- *WhoWrEP 89*
Spatz, Walter Bates 1921- *St&PR 91*
Spaude, Doris Anita Schroeder 1942- *WhoAmW 91*
Spaugh, Gerald G. 1953- *St&PR 91*
Spaulding, Douglas *ConAu 30NR, MajTwCW*
Spaulding, Douglas 1920- *SmATA X [port]*
Spaulding, Frank Henry 1932- *WhoAm 90*
Spaulding, James B *BiDrAPA 89*
Spaulding, Jean Gaillard 1947- *BiDrAPA 89*
Spaulding, Leonard *ConAu 30NR, MajTwCW*
Spaulding, Leonard 1920- *SmATA X [port]*
Spaulding, Robert Mark 1929- *WhoAm 90*
Spaulding, Susan Kay 1955- *WhoAmW 91*
Spaulding, Vanita Marie 1954- *WhoAmW 91*
Spaulding, William Rowe 1915- *WhoE 91, WhoWor 91*
Spaun, William Becker 1913- *WhoWor 91*
Spaventa, George 1918-1978 *WhoAmA 91N*
Spaventa, Luigi Aldo Maria 1934- *WhoWor 91*
Spaw, June 1925- *WhoWrEP 89*
Spaw, Louis David, Jr. 1919- *WhoAm 90*
Spaziani, JoAnn 1952- *WhoAmW 91*
Spaziani, Maria Luisa 1924- *EncCoWW*
Speace, David Dudley 1948- *WhoE 91*
Speake, Bob 1930- *Ballpl 90*
Speake, Bob C. 1930- *St&PR 91*
Speaker, Henry M. 1867-1935 *BioIn 16*
Speaker, John E. 1931- *ODwPR 91, St&PR 91*
Speaker, Richard L. 1920- *WhoSSW 91*
Speaker, Robert J. *BiDrAPA 89*
Speaker, Tris 1888-1958 *Ballpl 90 [port], WorAlBi*
Speakes, Larry Melvin *BioIn 16*
Speakes, Larry Melvin 1939- *WhoAm 90*
Speakman, Desmond Lee 1946- *WhoWor 91*
Speakman, Walter F 1919- *BiDrAPA 89*
Speakman, Willard A., III 1938- *St&PR 91*
Speaks, Donald Wesley 1921- *St&PR 91, WhoAm 90*
Speaks, Oley 1874-1948 *OxCPMus*
Speaks, Ruben Lee 1920- *WhoAm 90*
Spear, Arthur P 1879-1959 *WhoAmA 91N*
Spear, Barbara A *BiDrAPA 89*
Spear, Cecil C., Jr. 1935- *St&PR 91*
Spear, Charles Michael 1942- *St&PR 91*
Spear, Cynthia Jones 1954- *WhoEmL 91*
Spear, H Gladys *BiDrAPA 89*
Spear, Harvey M. 1922- *WhoAm 90*
Spear, Jack Byron 1918-1988 *BioIn 16*
Spear, Jean Evelyn Hinson 1944- *WhoAmW 91*
Spear, John Murray 1804?-1887 *EncO&P 3*
Spear, Kenneth Ray 1949- *St&PR 91*
Spear, Laurinda *BioIn 16*
Spear, Laurinda 1951- *WomArch [port]*
Spear, Laurinda Hope 1950- *WhoAmA 91*
Spear, Lloyd C. 1940- *St&PR 91*
Spear, Louis L. 1915- *St&PR 91*
Spear, Mark A *BiDrAPA 89*
Spear, Mary Patricia 1954- *WhoAmW 91*
Spear, Percival 1901-1982 *DcNaB 1981*
Spear, Richard Edmund 1940- *WhoAm 90, WhoAmA 91*
Spear, Robert Bruce 1931- *St&PR 91*
Spear, Robert Clinton 1939- *WhoAm 90*
Spear, Robert Douglas 1945- *St&PR 91*
Spear, Ruskin *NewYTBS 90*
Spear, Ruskin 1911-1990 *BioIn 16*
Spear, Ruth *WhoE 91*
Spear, Steven C. 1947- *St&PR 91*
Spearbecker, Kim La Rae 1957- *WhoWrEP 89*
Speare, Alden, Jr. 1939- *WhoAm 90*
Speare, Elizabeth George *BioIn 16*
Speare, Elizabeth George 1908- *AuBYP 90, SmATA 62 [port], WhoAm 90*
Speare, Eric M *BiDrAPA 89*
Speares, Scott Bruce, III 1960- *WhoSSW 91*
Spearman, Jerry C. 1943- *St&PR 91*
Spearman, Leonard H. O., Sr. 1929- *WhoAm 90, WhoWor 91*
Spearman, Lionel 1964- *WhoSSW 91*
Spearman, Maxie Ann 1942- *WhoAmW 91*
Spearman, Rawn W 1923- *DrBlPA 90*
Spears, Adrian Anthony 1910- *WhoAm 90*
Spears, Alexander White, III 1932- *St&PR 91, WhoAm 90*
Spears, C.S. 1930- *St&PR 91*
Spears, Carleton Blaise 1958- *WhoSSW 91, WhoWor 91*
Spears, Carol J. *BioIn 16*
Spears, D. Reed 1955- *WhoSSW 91*
Spears, Franklin Scott 1931- *WhoAm 90*
Spears, Howard Calvin Knox 1925- *WhoE 91*
Spears, Jae *WhoAmW 91, WhoSSW 91*
Spears, John Douglas 1948- *St&PR 91*
Spears, Joyce Ann 1939- *WhoAmW 91*
Spears, Larry Jonell 1953- *WhoEmL 91*
Spears, Marian Caddy 1921- *WhoAm 90*
Spears, Michael Eugene 1949- *WhoEmL 91*
Spears, Monroe Kirk 1916- *WhoAm 90, WhoWrEP 89*
Spears, Paul Edward 1924- *St&PR 91*
Spears, Paul Frey 1953- *WhoE 91*
Spears, R. Warren 1926- *WhoE 91*
Spears, Ralph Warren 1926- *St&PR 91*
Spears, Ronald Louis 1961- *BiDrAPA 89*
Spears, Sally 1938- *WhoAm 90*
Spears, Sandra Lee 1950- *WhoSSW 91*
Spears, Woodridge 1913- *LiHiK*
Speas, John Kelly 1946- *St&PR 91*
Speas, R. Dixon 1916- *St&PR 91*
Speas, Raymond Aaron 1925- *WhoAm 90*
Speas, Robert Dixon 1916- *WhoAm 90, WhoWor 91*
Speas, Van Reed 1940- *WhoSSW 91*
Speca, Bruce Robert 1956- *St&PR 91*
Spechalske, Phyllis Valand 1931- *WhoAmW 91*
Specht, Charles Alfred 1914- *WhoAm 90*
Specht, Diane Elizabeth 1944- *WhoAmW 91*
Specht, Donald W.J. 1939- *St&PR 91*
Specht, Friedrich 1924- *WhoWor 91*
Specht, Gordon Dean 1927- *WhoE 91*
Specht, Harry 1929- *WhoAm 90*
Specht, Lawrence H. 1931- *St&PR 91*
Specht, R. John 1937- *IntWWM 90*
Specht, Robert Gregory 1932- *WhoAm 90*
Specht, William A., III *St&PR 91*
Specht, William A., Jr. 1931- *St&PR 91*
Speciale, Richard 1945- *WhoAm 90*
Speciale, Richard E. 1945- *St&PR 91*
Specian, Rosemarie Therese 1944- *WhoAmW 91, WhoE 91*
Speck, David George 1945- *WhoSSW 91*
Speck, George 1911- *WhoWor 91*
Speck, Gerald Bennett 1923- *WhoE 91*
Speck, Hilda 1916- *WhoAmW 91, WhoWor 91*
Speck, J. Craig 1947- *St&PR 91*
Speck, Kathleen Marie 1957- *St&PR 91*
Speck, Lawrence W. 1949- *WhoAm 90*
Speck, Linda Christine *BiDrAPA 89*
Speck, Loran *BioIn 16*
Speck, Marvin Luther 1913- *WhoAm 90*
Speck, Ross V 1927- *BiDrAPA 89, WhoE 91*
Speck, Samuel Wallace, Jr. 1937- *WhoAm 90*
Specker, Sheila Ann *BiDrAPA 89*
Speckhard, Norma J. *BioIn 16*
Speckman, Carroll Duane *WhoAm 90*
Speckman, Carroll Duane 1932- *St&PR 91*
Speckman, Mark Christopher 1948- *St&PR 91*
Speckner, Georg Julius 1673- *PenDiDA 89*
Speckner, Johannes Lorenz *PenDiDA 89*
Speckner, Lorenz 1598-1669? *PenDiDA 89*
Specter, Arlen *BioIn 16*
Specter, Arlen 1930- *WhoAm 90, WhoE 91, WhoWor 91*
Specter, Richard Bruce 1952- *WhoEmL 91, WhoWor 91*
Spector, Abraham 1926- *WhoAm 90*
Spector, Barbara Holmes 1927- *WhoAmW 91*
Spector, Bernard 1923- *BiDrAPA 89*
Spector, Buzz 1948- *WhoAmA 91*
Spector, Daniel Earl 1942- *WhoSSW 91*
Spector, Dorothy J. 1918- *St&PR 91*
Spector, Earl M. 1939- *WhoAm 90*
Spector, Earl Melvin 1939- *St&PR 91*
Spector, Eleanor Ruth 1943- *WhoAm 90, WhoAmW 91*
Spector, Gail Greer 1950- *WhoAmW 91*
Spector, Gershon Jerry 1937- *WhoAm 90*
Spector, Harold 1921- *WhoWor 91*
Spector, Harold Norman 1935- *WhoAm 90*
Spector, Irwin 1916- *IntWWM 90*
Spector, Ivan Charles *BiDrAPA 89*
Spector, Jack J 1925- *WhoAmA 91*
Spector, Jeffrey S 1944- *BiDrAPA 89*
Spector, Johanna *IntWWM 90*
Spector, Johanna Lichtenberg *WhoAm 90, WhoAmW 91, WhoWor 91*
Spector, Joseph Robert 1923- *WhoAm 90*
Spector, Karen 1951- *WhoAmW 91*
Spector, Louis 1918- *WhoAm 90*
Spector, Marshall 1936- *WhoAm 90*
Spector, Martin Wolf 1938- *St&PR 91, WhoAm 90*
Spector, Melbourne Louis 1918- *WhoAm 90*
Spector, Michael Harris 1938- *WhoAm 90*
Spector, Michael Jay 1940- *WhoAm 90*
Spector, Myer 1925- *WhoE 91*
Spector, Naomi 1939- *WhoAmA 91*
Spector, Paul Joseph *BiDrAPA 89*
Spector, Paul Mitchell *BiDrAPA 89*
Spector, Phil *BioIn 16*
Spector, Phil 1940- *ConMus 4 [port], EncPR&S 89, OxCPMus, WhoAm 90, WorAlBi*
Spector, Richard Harris *BiDrAPA 89*
Spector, Robert Donald 1922- *WhoAm 90, WhoWrEP 89*
Spector, Russell 1957- *St&PR 91*
Spector, Shelley J. *ODwPR 91*
Spector, Shelley Joy Zuckerman 1953- *WhoAm 90*
Spector, Sherman David 1927- *WhoWrEP 89*
Spector, Stanley 1924- *WhoAm 90*
Spector-Zacks, Rosalind 1950- *St&PR 91*
Spectre, Jay 1929- *WhoAm 90*
Spedale, Robert Joseph 1949- *St&PR 91*
Spedden, Sewell Lee, Jr. 1938- *St&PR 91*
Spedding, Frank Donald 1929- *IntWWM 90*
Spee, Maximilian, Graf Von 1861-1914 *WorAlBi*
Speece, Richard Eugene 1933- *WhoAm 90, WhoWor 91*
Speech, Estelle Grace 1951- *WhoAmW 91*
Speed, Billie Cheney 1927- *WhoAm 90*
Speed, Carol *DrBlPA 90*
Speed, Grant 1930- *WhoAmA 91*
Speed, James 1812-1887 *BiDrUSE 89*
Speed, John S. 1927- *St&PR 91*
Speed, John Sackett 1927- *WhoAm 90*
Speed, Leland Rhymes 1932- *St&PR 91*
Speed, Shirley Adams 1937- *WhoAmW 91*
Speed, Tanya Jo Lennard 1960- *WhoAmW 91*
Speed, Thomas Hays 1951- *WhoSSW 91*
Speedie, Marilyn Kay 1947- *WhoAmW 91*
Speelman, Guy 1944- *WhoWor 91*
Speelman, Irving Arnold 1919- *WhoE 91*
Speelman, Simon *PenDiMP*
Speer, Albert 1905-1981 *BioIn 16*
Speer, Alfred Alten 1858-1935 *AmLegL*
Speer, Allen Paul, III 1951- *WhoSSW 91, WhoWrEP 89*
Speer, Betty Jean 1931- *WhoWrEP 89*
Speer, Connie Lou 1949- *BiDrAPA 89*
Speer, David J. 1927- *ODwPR 91*
Speer, David James 1927- *WhoAm 90*
Speer, Erling Dick 1940- *WhoSSW 91*
Speer, G. William 1940- *St&PR 91, WhoAm 90*
Speer, Garry Wayne 1957- *WhoWrEP 89*
Speer, Gotthard Gregor 1915- *WhoWor 91*
Speer, Iree Smith 1913- *WhoAmW 91*
Speer, Jessica Christine 1960- *WhoAmW 91*
Speer, Laurel 1940- *ConAu 132, WhoWrEP 89*
Speer, Paul *NewAgMG*
Speer, Richard Wayne *WhoSSW 91*
Speer, Robert L. 1931- *St&PR 91*
Speer, Roy M. 1932- *St&PR 91*
Speer, Thomas M. 1934- *St&PR 91*
Speer, William Thomas, Jr. 1936- *WhoAm 90, WhoWor 91*
Speers, J. Alvin 1930- *WhoWrEP 89*
Speers, J. Kent 1949- *St&PR 91*
Speers, Roland R. 1933- *St&PR 91*
Speers, Roland Root, II 1933- *WhoAm 90*
Speers, Thomas James 1954- *WhoEmL 91*
Speert, Arnold 1945- *WhoAm 90, WhoE 91*
Speert, Robert Allen 1926- *St&PR 91*
Spees, Janette Birch 1933- *WhoE 91*
Speeth, Kathleen Riordan 1937- *WhoE 91*
Speevack, Yetta *AuBYP 90*
Speght, Rachel *BioIn 16*
Speght, Rachel 1597?- *BiDEWW*
Speght, Rachel 1598?-1630? *FemiCLE*
Speicher, Betsy Mary Elizabeth 1948- *WhoAmW 91*
Speicher, Edwin W. 1931- *St&PR 91*
Speicher, Edwin Waller 1931- *WhoE 91*
Speicher, Eugene E 1883-1962 *WhoAmA 91N*
Speicher, Franklin S., Jr. 1918- *St&PR 91*
Speicher, John Albert 1940- *WhoSSW 91*
Speicher, Julia E. *BiDrAPA 89*
Speicher, Rita L. 1954- *WhoWrEP 89*

Speicher, William C. 1937- *St&PR 91*
Speicher, William Clayton 1937- *WhoAm 90*
Speidel, Benjamin Burtlin, IV 1953- *St&PR 91*
Speidel, David Harold 1938- *WhoAm 90*
Speidel, John Joseph 1937- *WhoAm 90*
Speidel, Karl-Heinz 1938- *WhoWor 91*
Speidel, Richard Eli 1933- *WhoAm 90*
Speier, Chris 1950- *Ballpl 90*
Speier, Hans *NewYTBS 90*
Speier, Hans 1905-1990 *BioIn 16, ConAu 131*
Speier, John L. 1918- *WhoAm 90*
Speier, Karen Rinardo 1947- *WhoAmW 91*
Speier, Patricia Louise *BiDrAPA 89*
Speight, Francis 1896-1989 *BioIn 16, WhoAmA 91N*
Speight, James Glassford 1940- *WhoAm 90*
Speight, Jeanette Aline 1946- *WhoE 91*
Speight, Jerry Brooks 1942- *WhoAmA 91*
Speight, Majorie L *BiDrAPA 89*
Speight, Sarah Blakeslee *WhoAmA 91*
Speights, Michael David 1951- *WhoE 91, WhoEmL 91*
Speigner, Margaret Ina 1948- *WhoEmL 91*
Speir, Betty Smith 1928- *WhoAmW 91*
Speir, Edwin G., Jr. *WhoAm 90*
Speir, Marcia Ann 1935- *WhoAmW 91*
Speirs, Derek James 1933- *WhoAm 90*
Speirs, Joseph A. 1952- *St&PR 91*
Speiser, Ambros Paul 1922- *WhoWor 91*
Speiser, E. Pat 1937- *St&PR 91*
Speiser, Elisabeth 1940- *IntWWM 90*
Speiser, Marvin M. 1925- *St&PR 91*
Speiser, Robert Douglas 1953- *St&PR 91, WhoEmL 91*
Speiser, Steven Oren 1951- *BiDrAPA 89*
Speiser, Stuart M 1923- *WhoAmA 91*
Speiser, Stuart Marshall 1923- *WhoAm 90*
Speitel, Gerald E. 1930- *St&PR 91*
Speitel, Gerald Eugene 1930- *WhoAm 90*
Speizer, Mark Adler 1943- *St&PR 91*
Spejewski, Eugene Henry 1938- *WhoAm 90*
Spek, Ron 1945- *WhoWor 91*
Speke, John 1827-1864 *WorAlBi*
Speken, Ralph Howard 1941- *BiDrAPA 89, WhoE 91*
Spelber, Leonard George 1925- *St&PR 91*
Spelce, Fannie Lou 1908- *MusmAFA*
Spelce, Neal 1936- *ODwPR 91*
Spelce, Wm. Bennett 1937- *ODwPR 91*
Spelfogel, Benjamin 1915- *BiDrAPA 89*
Spelke, Norman L. *BioIn 16*
Spelke, Richard A. 1941- *St&PR 91*
Spelker, Arnold William 1934- *WhoE 91*
Spell, Belenda Kesler 1958- *WhoSSW 91*
Spell, Ernest D. 1941- *St&PR 91*
Spell, George *DrBIPA 90*
Spell, Janyce Johnson 1953- *WhoEmL 91*
Spell, Lee Fairbanks *WhoAmW 91*
Speller, Benjamin Franklin, Jr. 1940- *WhoAm 90*
Speller, Henry 1900- *MusmAFA*
Speller, Jeffrey Lynn *BiDrAPA 89*
Speller, John Arthur Leslie 1936- *St&PR 91*
Speller, Marsha Lynn 1945- *BiDrAPA 89*
Speller, Robert Ernest Blakefield 1908- *WhoWor 91*
Speller, Thomas H. 1907- *St&PR 91*
Speller, William Thomas 1940- *WhoSSW 91*
Spellerberg, Frank 1958- *WhoWor 91*
Spelling, Aaron *BioIn 16*
Spelling, Aaron 1923- *WhoAm 90*
Spelling, Aaron 1928- *St&PR 91, WorAlBi*
Spelliscy, Peter T. 1944- *St&PR 91*
Spellman, Anthony 1929- *BiDrAPA 89*
Spellman, Eugene Paul 1930- *WhoAm 90, WhoSSW 91*
Spellman, Francis Joseph 1889-1967 *WorAlBi*
Spellman, George Geneser, Sr. 1920- *WhoAm 90*
Spellman, Gladys Noon 1918-1988 *BioIn 16*
Spellman, I. Orrin 1913- *ODwPR 91*
Spellman, Jane Ann 1930- *WhoE 91*
Spellman, John Dennis 1926- *WhoAm 90*
Spellman, John F. 1938- *WhoAm 90*
Spellman, John William, Jr. 1925- *WhoSSW 91*
Spellman, Mitchell Wright 1919- *WhoAm 90*
Spellmire, Sandra Marie 1950- *WhoAmW 91*
Spelman, Jill Sullivan 1937- *WhoAmA 91*
Spelman, Nancy Latting 1945- *WhoAmW 91*
Spelman, Philip Ohel 1923- *WhoWrEP 89*
Spelman, Risto Tapio 1946- *WhoE 91*
Spelsberg, Thomas Coonan 1940- *WhoAm 90*
Spelts, Richard E., Jr. 1919- *St&PR 91*
Spelts, Richard John 1939- *WhoAm 90*
Speltz, Stephen Eugene 1933- *St&PR 91*
Spemann, Hans 1869-1941 *WorAlBi*
Spemann, Wolf 1931- *WhoWor 91*
Spemicalawba *WhNaAH*
Spence, A. Michael 1943- *WhoAm 90*
Spence, Andrew 1947- *WhoAmA 91*
Spence, Anna Iozzo 1964- *WhoAmW 91*
Spence, Arthur *St&PR 91*
Spence, Basil 1907-1976 *ConDes 90*
Spence, Catherine Helen 1825-1910 *FemiCLE*
Spence, Clark Christian 1923- *WhoAm 90*
Spence, Craig *BioIn 16*
Spence, David Michael 1965- *WhoE 91*
Spence, Elizabeth Isabella 1768-1832 *FemiCLE*
Spence, Eugene Park 1929- *St&PR 91*
Spence, Eulalie 1894- *DrBIPA 90*
Spence, Eulalie 1894-1981 *EarBIAP, HarlReB*
Spence, Evelyn Batten 1934- *WhoAmW 91*
Spence, Floyd Davidson 1928- *WhoAm 90, WhoSSW 91*
Spence, Francis John 1926- *WhoAm 90*
Spence, George S. 1926- *St&PR 91*
Spence, Gerald Leonard 1929- *WhoAm 90, WhoWrEP 89*
Spence, Geraldine 1931- *BioIn 16*
Spence, Glen Oscar 1927- *WhoAm 90*
Spence, Harry Metcalfe 1905- *WhoAm 90*
Spence, Holly 1943- *ODwPR 91*
Spence, Howard Tee Devon 1949- *WhoEmL 91*
Spence, J. A. D. *MajTwCW*
Spence, James Robert, Jr. 1936- *WhoAm 90*
Spence, Janet Blake Conley 1915- *WhoAmW 91, WhoE 91*
Spence, Jo *BioIn 16*
Spence, John Daniel 1915- *WhoAm 90*
Spence, JohnE Joseph 1949- *WhoSSW 91*
Spence, Jonathan D. *BioIn 16*
Spence, Jonathan D 1936- *BestSel 90-4 [port], WorAu 1980 [port]*
Spence, Jonathan Dermot 1936- *WhoAm 90*
Spence, Lewis 1874-1955 *EncO&P 3*
Spence, Louis Courtney K. 1950- *WhoWor 91*
Spence, Luther B. 1929- *St&PR 91, WhoAm 90*
Spence, Mary Lee 1927- *WhoAmW 91*
Spence, Mary Stewart 1946- *WhoAm 90*
Spence, Michael Thomas 1955- *WhoSSW 91*
Spence, Norman Thomas 1934- *St&PR 91*
Spence, Paul Herbert 1923- *WhoAm 90*
Spence, Ralph 1919- *WhoSSW 91*
Spence, Ricardo *BioIn 16*
Spence, Richard Dee 1925- *St&PR 91, WhoAm 90*
Spence, Robert Dean 1917- *WhoAm 90*
Spence, Robert Leroy 1931- *WhoAm 90*
Spence, Ronald G. 1940- *St&PR 91*
Spence, Sandra 1941- *WhoAm 90*
Spence, Sarah *FemiCLE*
Spence, Sharon Lloyd 1953- *WhoAmW 91*
Spence, Shirley Harvey 1939- *WhoAmW 91*
Spence, Stan 1915-1983 *Ballpl 90*
Spence, Stevan Thomas 1947- *St&PR 91*
Spence, Susan Bateman 1947- *WhoSSW 91*
Spence, Thomas 1832-1900 *DcCanB 12*
Spence, William Rayburn 1942- *St&PR 91*
Spencer Davis Group *EncPR&S 89*
Spencer, A.J. 1922- *St&PR 91*
Spencer, Alan H. 1937- *St&PR 91*
Spencer, Anita Louise 1945- *WhoAmW 91*
Spencer, Anna Lou 1939- *WhoSSW 91*
Spencer, Anne 1882-1975 *BioAmW, FemiCLE*
Spencer, Anne Bethel Bannister Scales 1882-1976 *HarlReB [port]*
Spencer, Arthur Conover 1927- *WhoE 91*
Spencer, Barbara Joyce 1935- *WhoAmW 91*
Spencer, Billie Jane 1949- *WhoAmW 91, WhoEmL 91, WhoWor 91*
Spencer, C. Stanley 1946- *St&PR 91*
Spencer, Carl C *BiDrAPA 89*
Spencer, Carlton Wentworth 1906- *St&PR 91*
Spencer, Charles D *BiDrAPA 89*
Spencer, Charles Samuel 1920- *WhoWor 91*
Spencer, Christine *DrBIPA 90*
Spencer, Clifford Lee 1957- *WhoSSW 91*
Spencer, Cornelia *AuBYP 90*
Spencer, Dan S., Jr. 1930- *St&PR 91*
Spencer, Danielle 1965?- *DrBIPA 90*
Spencer, Daryl 1929- *Ballpl 90, BioIn 16*
Spencer, David Gelvin, Jr. 1953- *WhoWor 91*
Spencer, David S. 1940- *St&PR 91*
Spencer, David Singleton 1954- *WhoSSW 91*
Spencer, Deborah Joyce 1950- *WhoAmW 91*
Spencer, Deirdre Diane 1955- *WhoAmA 91*
Spencer, Derek Victor 1934- *BiDrAPA 89*
Spencer, Dick, III 1921- *WhoWrEP 89*
Spencer, Domina Eberle 1920- *WhoAmW 91, WhoE 91*
Spencer, Donald Clayton 1912- *WhoAm 90*
Spencer, Dwain Frank 1934- *WhoAm 90*
Spencer, Edgar Winston 1931- *WhoAm 90*
Spencer, Elaine Theresa 1949- *WhoAmW 91*
Spencer, Elizabeth *BioIn 16*
Spencer, Elizabeth 1921- *BioAmW, ConAu 32NR, FemiCLE, MajTwCW, WhoAm 90, WhoAmW 91*
Spencer, Elizabeth J. 1954- *WhoAmW 91*
Spencer, Elizabeth Kay *BiDrAPA 89*
Spencer, Foster Lewis 1932- *WhoAm 90*
Spencer, Francis Montgomery James 1943- *WhoSSW 91, WhoWor 91*
Spencer, Frank Cole 1925- *WhoAm 90*
Spencer, Frederick Gilman 1925- *WhoAm 90*
Spencer, Gale Alexandra 1951- *WhoAmW 91*
Spencer, Gayle Lynne 1960- *WhoSSW 91*
Spencer, George *BioIn 16*
Spencer, George 1926- *Ballpl 90*
Spencer, Glenn 1905-1958 *Ballpl 90*
Spencer, Harold Edwin 1920- *WhoAmA 91, WhoE 91*
Spencer, Harold Garth 1930- *WhoAm 90*
Spencer, Harry Chadwick 1905- *WhoAm 90*
Spencer, Harry Irving, Jr. 1925- *WhoAm 90*
Spencer, Henry Benning 1940- *St&PR 91, WhoAm 90*
Spencer, Herbert 1820-1903 *BioIn 16, WorAlBi, WrPh P*
Spencer, Herbert 1924- *ConDes 90*
Spencer, Howard 1946-1988 *BioIn 16*
Spencer, Howard Dalee 1950- *WhoAmA 91*
Spencer, Hugh 1887-1975 *WhoAmA 91N*
Spencer, Isabel Brannon 1940- *WhoE 91*
Spencer, Ivan Carlton 1914- *WhoAm 90*
Spencer, Ivor *BioIn 16*
Spencer, Ivor 1928- *WhoWor 91*
Spencer, James David, II 1953- *WhoE 91*
Spencer, James H, Jr. 1931- *BiDrAPA 89*
Spencer, James M. 1949- *St&PR 91*
Spencer, James Richardson *WhoWrEP 89*
Spencer, Jean W. *WhoWrEP 89*
Spencer, Jim 1946- *Ballpl 90*
Spencer, Joan 1922- *IntWWM 90*
Spencer, Joe Richard 1952- *WhoSSW 91*
Spencer, John *TwCCr&M 91*
Spencer, John Andrew 1948- *St&PR 91*
Spencer, John Canfield 1788-1855 *BiDrUSE 89*
Spencer, John Charles 1782-1845 *BioIn 16*
Spencer, John Hedley 1933- *WhoAm 90*
Spencer, John R 1923- *WhoAmA 91*
Spencer, John Richard 1923- *WhoAm 90*
Spencer, John Walter 1926- *St&PR 91*
Spencer, Joseph Frank 1939- *BiDrAPA 89*
Spencer, Judy Shifflett 1947- *WhoAmW 91*
Spencer, Julian Kaj 1946- *St&PR 91*
Spencer, Kathleen Schwartz 1961- *WhoE 91*
Spencer, Kelly Harris 1955- *St&PR 91*
Spencer, Kenneth 1913-1964 *DrBIPA 90*
Spencer, Kenneth Lee 1911-1964 *DcAfAmP*
Spencer, Kenneth W. 1935- *St&PR 91*
Spencer, Laura-Ann 1966- *WhoHisp 91*
Spencer, Leonard G *ConAu 130, MajTwCW*
Spencer, Leontine G 1882-1964 *WhoAmA 91N*
Spencer, Lewis Douglas 1917- *WhoAm 90*
Spencer, Lila *ODwPR 91*
Spencer, Lilly 1822-1902 *BiDWomA*
Spencer, Lily Martin 1822-1902 *BioIn 16*
Spencer, Linda Anne 1944- *WhoSSW 91*
Spencer, Lloyd Layton 1936- *BiDrAPA 89*
Spencer, Lloyd M. 1940- *St&PR 91*
Spencer, Mark Morris 1956- *WhoWrEP 89*
Spencer, Mary Eileen 1923- *WhoAm 90, WhoAmW 91*
Spencer, Mary Elizabeth 1955- *WhoEmL 91*
Spencer, Mary Florence 1923- *WhoWrEP 89*
Spencer, Mary Miller 1924- *WhoAmW 91, WhoWor 91*
Spencer, Max R. 1924- *St&PR 91*
Spencer, Melvin Joe 1923- *WhoAm 90*
Spencer, Michael J. *St&PR 91*
Spencer, Milton Harry 1926- *WhoAm 90*
Spencer, Murlin Bertrand 1909- *WhoAm 90*
Spencer, Niles 1893-1952 *WhoAmA 91N*
Spencer, Ouida J. 1956- *St&PR 91*
Spencer, Paula *BioIn 16*
Spencer, Raine *ConAu 132*
Spencer, Ralph D., Jr. 1923- *St&PR 91*
Spencer, Ralph Lee 1927- *WhoAm 90*
Spencer, Reid C. 1930- *St&PR 91*
Spencer, Richard A. 1928- *St&PR 91*
Spencer, Richard Beck 1948- *BiDrAPA 89*
Spencer, Richard Henry 1926- *St&PR 91*
Spencer, Richard L *BiDrAPA 89*
Spencer, Richard Paul 1929- *WhoAm 90*
Spencer, Richard Vaughn 1954- *WhoE 91*
Spencer, Robert 1932- *IntWWM 90*
Spencer, Robert C. 1920- *WhoAm 90*
Spencer, Robert Edgar 1953- *WhoSSW 91*
Spencer, Robert John 1949- *WhoWor 91*
Spencer, Roger F 1934- *BiDrAPA 89*
Spencer, Roy 1900-1973 *Ballpl 90*
Spencer, Samuel 1910- *WhoAm 90*
Spencer, Samuel C. 1937- *St&PR 91*
Spencer, Samuel Reid, Jr. 1919- *WhoAm 90*
Spencer, Sara 1908-1977 *BioIn 16, NotWoAT*
Spencer, Sharon Denise 1961- *WhoEmL 91*
Spencer, Sherwood Fredrick 1928- *WhoE 91*
Spencer, Stanley 1891-1959 *IntDcAA 90*
Spencer, Stephen Watson 1955- *WhoSSW 91*
Spencer, Stuart *BioIn 16*
Spencer, Susan Elizabeth 1954- *WhoAmA 91*
Spencer, Thomas Frederick 1943- *St&PR 91*
Spencer, Thomas Halsey 1932- *WhoE 91, WhoWor 91*
Spencer, Thomas Jellison *BiDrAPA 89*
Spencer, Thomas Watson 1929- *St&PR 91*
Spencer, Tricia Jane 1952- *WhoAmW 91, WhoEmL 91*
Spencer, Tubby 1884-1945 *Ballpl 90*
Spencer, Victor Vance 1924- *St&PR 91*
Spencer, Walter A., Jr. 1950- *St&PR 91*
Spencer, Walter Eugene 1937- *St&PR 91*
Spencer, Wayne Dennis 1940- *St&PR 91*
Spencer, William 1922- *AuBYP 90*
Spencer, William Alva 1947- *St&PR 91*
Spencer, William Courtney 1919- *WhoAm 90*
Spencer, William Edward 1941- *WhoAm 90*
Spencer, William H. 1940- *St&PR 91*
Spencer, William I. 1917- *St&PR 91*
Spencer, William Ira 1917- *WhoAm 90*
Spencer, William Micajah, III 1920- *St&PR 91*
Spencer, William Stewart 1949- *WhoE 91*
Spencer, Williametta 1931- *IntWWM 90*
Spencer-Churchill, Laura 1915-1990 *ConAu 131*
Spencer-Lemay, Carol 1957- *BiDrAPA 89*
Spencer-Wilkins, Mary Lindsey 1964- *WhoAmW 91*
Spender, Emily 1841-1922 *FemiCLE*
Spender, J A 1862-1942 *DcLB 98 [port]*
Spender, Lilian 1835-1895 *FemiCLE*
Spender, Stephen 1909- *AuBYP 90, BioIn 16, ConAu 31NR, MajTwCW, WorAlBi*
Spender, Stephen K. 1909- *WhoWor 91*
Spender, Victoria Theresa 1957- *WhoAmW 91*
Spengler, Adam *PenDiDA 89*
Spengler, Dan M. 1941- *WhoAm 90*
Spengler, John Edward 1933- *St&PR 91*
Spengler, Karen Ann 1952- *WhoEmL 91*
Spengler, Oswald 1880-1936 *WorAlBi, WrPh P*
Spengler, Silas 1930- *St&PR 91*
Spenker, Thomas J. 1915-1989 *BioIn 16*
Spenser, Edmund 1552?-1599 *WorAlBi, WrPh*
Spenser, Ian Daniel 1924- *WhoAm 90*
Spensley, James 1938- *BiDrAPA 89*
Spera, Patrice 1953- *WhoAmW 91*
Sperakis, Nicholas George 1943- *WhoAm 90, WhoAmA 91*
Sperandio, Glen Joseph 1918- *WhoAm 90*
Speranskii, Mikhail Mikhailovich 1772-1839 *BioIn 16*
Speranza 1823?-1896 *FemiCLE*
Speranza, Albert Joseph, Jr. 1962- *BiDrAPA 89*
Speranza, Ernest V. 1946- *St&PR 91*
Speranza, Pamela Lisa *St&PR 91N*
Sperber, Charlotte *St&PR 91*
Sperber, Daniel 1930- *WhoAm 90, WhoE 91, WhoWor 91*
Sperber, David Nathan *BiDrAPA 89*
Sperber, Jacob Elliott 1946- *BiDrAPA 89*
Sperber, Martin 1931- *WhoAm 90*
Sperber, Matthew Arnold 1938- *WhoSSW 91*
Sperber, Nancy B. 1953- *WhoAmW 91*
Sperber, Perry 1931- *St&PR 91, WhoE 91*
Sperber, Philip 1944- *St&PR 91*
Sperber, Sheldon Moss *BiDrAPA 89*
Sperber, William H. 1933- *St&PR 91*
Sperelakis, Nicholas 1930- *WhoAm 90, WhoWor 91*

Spergel, Steve N. 1944- *WhoSSW 91*
Sperger, Hugo 1922- *MusmAFA*
Sperger, John M. 1950- *St&PR 91*
Speriosu, Simon V 1923- *BiDrAPA 89*
Sperlich, Peter Werner 1934- *WhoAm 90*
Sperling, Allan George 1942- *WhoE 91*
Sperling, Calvin *BioIn 16*
Sperling, David Alan 1942- *BiDrAPA 89*
Sperling, Edward *BiDrAPA 89*
Sperling, Eva M Hauser *BiDrAPA 89*
Sperling, Frederick 1913- *WhoE 91*
Sperling, George *BioIn 16, WhoAm 90*
Sperling, George Elmer, Jr. 1915- *WhoAm 90*
Sperling, George Joseph 1945- *St&PR 91*
Sperling, Godfrey, Jr. 1915- *WhoAm 90*
Sperling, Jack Copeland 1940- *St&PR 91*
Sperling, James Evans 1917- *WhoAm 90*
Sperling, Lynne 1949- *WhoAm 90*
Sperling, Michael *ODwPR 91*
Sperling, Mindy Toby 1954- *WhoE 91*
Sperling, Otto E 1899- *BiDrAPA 89*
Sperling, Samuel J *BiDrAPA 89*
Spero, Craig Richard 1953- *BiDrAPA 89*
Spero, Frederick Henry 1946- *WhoE 91*
Spero, Joan E. 1944- *St&PR 91*
Spero, Joan Edelman 1944- *WhoAm 90*
Spero, Leslie W. 1926- *St&PR 91*
Spero, Leslie Wayne 1926- *WhoAm 90*
Spero, Monroe W 1926- *BiDrAPA 89*
Spero, Nancy 1926- *BiDWomA, WhoAm 90, WhoAmA 91*
Spero, Robert P. 1929- *St&PR 91*
Spero, Stanley L. 1919- *St&PR 91*
Spero, Stanley Leonard 1919- *WhoAm 90*
Speros, Jonathan Arthur 1964- *WhoE 91*
Sperr, Walter E. 1943- *ODwPR 91*
Sperrazza, Augustine J. 1941- *St&PR 91*
Sperrazza, Barbara 1949- *St&PR 91*
Sperrle, Hugo 1885-1953 *BioIn 16*
Sperry, Allen *BioIn 16*
Sperry, Armstrong W. 1897-1976 *AuBYP 90*
Sperry, Elmer A. 1860-1930 *WorAlBi*
Sperry, Elwood G. 1926- *St&PR 91*
Sperry, John Reginald 1924- *WhoAm 90*
Sperry, Len Thomas 1943- *WhoWor 91*
Sperry, Leonard Thomas 1943- *BiDrAPA 89*
Sperry, Michael Winton 1946- *St&PR 91*
Sperry, Paul 1934- *PenDiMP*
Sperry, Robert 1927- *WhoAmA 91*
Sperry, Roger W. 1913- *WorAlBi*
Sperry, Roger Wolcott 1913- *WhoAm 90, WhoWor 91, WhoWrEP 89*
Sperry, Roland *BioIn 16*
Sperry, Ronald Earl 1942- *St&PR 91*
Sperry, William Elliott 1930- *St&PR 91*
Spertus, Maurice 1902-1986 *BioIn 16*
Spertus, Philip 1934- *St&PR 91*
Sperzel, George Edward 1951- *St&PR 91*
Spessard, John Emory 1931- *WhoSSW 91*
Spessotti, Linda Bernadette 1950- *WhoE 91*
Speth, James Gustave 1942- *WhoAm 90*
Spetner, Lee Mordecai 1927- *WhoWor 91*
Spetrino, Russell John 1926- *St&PR 91, WhoAm 90*
Spett, Kenneth Mark 1952- *St&PR 91*
Spetter, Barry H. 1947- *WhoE 91*
Spetzler, Hartmut A. W. 1939- *WhoAm 90*
Spevacek, Jennifer Jeanene 1961- *WhoE 91*
Spevacek, William J. *ODwPR 91*
Spevack, Marvin 1927- *WhoAm 90*
Spevak, Irving Bertram 1917- *WhoE 91*
Spevak, Michael Bart 1940- *BiDrAPA 89*
Spevak, Robert Gerald 1932- *St&PR 91*
Spevak, Teryl A. 1951- *WhoWrEP 89*
Spewack, Bella *NewYTBS 90 [port]*
Spewack, Bella 1899- *NotWoAT*
Spewack, Bella 1899-1990 *BioIn 16, ConAu 131*
Spewack, Samuel 1899-1971 *BioIn 16*
Speyer, James 1861-1941 *EncABHB 6 [port]*
Speyer, Jason Lee 1938- *WhoAm 90*
Speyer, Jerry I. 1940- *St&PR 91*
Speyer, Nora 1922- *WhoAmA 91*
Speyr, Adrienne von 1902-1967 *EncCoWW*
Speyrer, Jude 1929- *WhoAm 90, WhoSSW 91*
Speziale, A. John 1916- *WhoAm 90*
Speziale, John Albert 1922- *WhoAm 90*
Speziale, Samuel Joseph 1928- *WhoE 91*
Spezio, Carl P. 1945- *St&PR 91*
Spezzano, Vincent Edward 1926- *WhoAm 90*
Sphar, Gail Lufkin 1946- *WhoAmW 91*
Sphar, Joe Dee 1941- *St&PR 91*
Sphar, Raymond Leslie, Jr. 1934- *WhoE 91*
Spheeris, Andrew Miltiades 1916- *St&PR 91*
Spheeris, Chris *NewAgMG*
Spheeris, Penelope *BioIn 16*
Sphire, Raymond Daniel 1927- *WhoAm 90*
Sphon, Richard J. 1937- *St&PR 91*
Spiaggia, Frank 1913- *BiDrAPA 89*
Spicak, Doris Elizabeth 1943- *WhoAmW 91*
Spice, John Overstreet 1931- *St&PR 91, WhoSSW 91*
Spicer, Alan Hugh 1940- *St&PR 91*
Spicer, Anthony J. 1929- *St&PR 91*
Spicer, Audrey Ann 1962- *WhoAmW 91*
Spicer, Bart 1918- *TwCCr&M 91*
Spicer, Carol Inglis 1907- *WhoAmW 91*
Spicer, Carolyn Marie 1947- *WhoAmW 91*
Spicer, Dorothy Gladys *AuBYP 90*
Spicer, Erik John 1926- *WhoAm 90*
Spicer, Frederick G *BiDrAPA 89*
Spicer, Holt Vandercook 1928- *WhoAm 90*
Spicer, Jean Uhl 1935- *WhoAmA 91*
Spicer, Marcella H. 1920- *WhoWrEP 89*
Spicer, Ross H. 1926- *St&PR 91*
Spicer, Ross Hugh 1926- *WhoAm 90*
Spicer, Timothy Patrick 1947- *WhoE 91*
Spicer, William Edward, III 1929- *WhoAm 90*
Spicer, William Michael Hardy 1943- *SpyFic*
Spicer-Brooks, Marianna Chase 1951- *WhoE 91*
Spicer-Simpson, Theodore 1871-1959 *WhoAmA 91N*
Spicka, George Francis 1947- *WhoE 91*
Spicka, Richard 1936- *St&PR 91*
Spicker, Stuart Francis 1937- *ConAu 30NR*
Spickerman, William Reed 1925- *WhoSSW 91*
Spicola, James R. 1930- *WhoAm 90*
Spidel, John W. 1937- *St&PR 91*
Spidell, Julia *BioIn 16*
Spidle, Harold D. 1934- *St&PR 91*
Spiech, John A. *BioIn 16*
Spiecha, Annette Joan 1939- *WhoAmW 91*
Spiegel, Abraham 1906- *WhoAm 90*
Spiegel, Barry J. *St&PR 91*
Spiegel, Bernard Herbert 1924- *St&PR 91*
Spiegel, Bobbie Carol 1940- *WhoSSW 91*
Spiegel, Burton 1944- *St&PR 91*
Spiegel, Clara *AuBYP 90*
Spiegel, David 1945- *BiDrAPA 89*
Spiegel, David A 1943- *BiDrAPA 89*
Spiegel, Edward A. *WhoAm 90*
Spiegel, Emily *BioIn 16*
Spiegel, Eugene 1941- *WhoE 91*
Spiegel, Evelyn Sclufer 1924- *WhoAmW 91*
Spiegel, Francis H. 1935- *St&PR 91*
Spiegel, Francis Herman, Jr. 1935- *WhoAm 90*
Spiegel, Frederick Michael 1939- *St&PR 91*
Spiegel, George 1924- *St&PR 91*
Spiegel, Hart Hunter 1918- *WhoAm 90*
Spiegel, Henry William 1911- *WhoE 91*
Spiegel, Herbert 1914- *BiDrAPA 89, WhoAm 90, WhoWor 91*
Spiegel, Isaiah 1906- *BioIn 16*
Spiegel, James Robert 1957- *WhoE 91*
Spiegel, Jayson Leslie 1959- *WhoE 91, WhoEmL 91, WhoWor 91*
Spiegel, Jerry *BioIn 16*
Spiegel, John E. 1929- *St&PR 91*
Spiegel, John P *BiDrAPA 89*
Spiegel, John William 1941- *St&PR 91, WhoAm 90*
Spiegel, Joseph 1928- *St&PR 91*
Spiegel, Kathleen Marie 1948- *WhoAmW 91*
Spiegel, Ladd 1952- *BiDrAPA 89*
Spiegel, Laurence Harold 1947- *WhoEmL 91*
Spiegel, Laurie 1945- *WhoAmA 91, WhoE 91*
Spiegel, Lawrence Howard 1942- *WhoAm 90*
Spiegel, Leo A *BiDrAPA 89*
Spiegel, Leonard Emile 1924- *WhoE 91*
Spiegel, Marilyn Harriet 1935- *WhoAmW 91*
Spiegel, Mark Alan 1948- *BiDrAPA 89, WhoE 91*
Spiegel, Melvin 1925- *WhoAm 90*
Spiegel, Paul 1934- *St&PR 91*
Spiegel, Phil 1917- *St&PR 91*
Spiegel, Phyllis *ODwPR 91*
Spiegel, Rene 1943- *WhoWor 91*
Spiegel, Richard Alan 1947- *ConAu 30NR*
Spiegel, Richard M 1944- *BiDrAPA 89*
Spiegel, Robert Alan 1952- *WhoEmL 91*
Spiegel, Rose *BiDrAPA 89*
Spiegel, Rosemary Fordham 1953- *WhoAmW 91*
Spiegel, S. Arthur 1920- *WhoAm 90*
Spiegel, Sam 1903-1985 *BioIn 16*
Spiegel, Shalom 1899-1984 *BioIn 16*
Spiegel, Thomas 1946- *WhoAm 90*
Spiegelberg family *BioIn 16*
Spiegelberg, Herbert 1904-1990 *ConAu 132*
Spiegelman, Art *BioIn 16*
Spiegelman, Art 1948- *EncACom*
Spiegelman, James Michael 1958- *WhoE 91*
Spiegelman, Lon Howard 1941- *WhoAmA 91*
Spiegl, Fritz 1926- *IntWWM 90*
Spiegler, Gerhard Ernst 1929- *WhoAm 90*
Spiegler, Zeva E. *BioIn 16*
Spiekerman, James Frederick 1933- *WhoAm 90*
Spiekhout, Ronald L. 1939- *St&PR 91*
Spiel, Hilde 1911- *EncCoWW*
Spiel, Walter H 1920- *BiDrAPA 89*
Spielberg, Peter 1929- *WhoWrEP 89*
Spielberg, Steven 1947- *BioIn 16, ConAu 32NR, WhoAm 90, WorAlBi*
Spieler, Francis Joseph 1943- *WhoAm 90, WhoWrEP 89*
Spielman, David Vernon 1929- *WhoSSW 91, WhoWor 91*
Spielman, Harold S. *BioIn 16*
Spielman, Olga *BiDrAPA 89*
Spielman, Patrick E. 1936- *WhoWrEP 89*
Spielman, Philip 1929- *BiDrAPA 89*
Spielman, Sheryl Beth *BiDrAPA 89*
Spielmann, Linda Gail 1955- *WhoAmW 91*
Spielmann, Marion Harry 1858-1948 *BioIn 16*
Spielmann, Zvi Hermann 1925- *WhoWor 91*
Spielmeyer, Ruth 1922- *BiDrAPA 89*
Spielvogel, Andrew Robert 1949- *St&PR 91*
Spielvogel, Bernard Franklin 1937- *WhoSSW 91*
Spielvogel, Carl *St&PR 91*
Spielvogel, Carl 1928- *WhoAm 90, WhoE 91*
Spielvogel, Sidney Meyer 1925- *WhoAm 90*
Spier, Anthony Samuel 1944- *St&PR 91*
Spier, Jerome Bertram 1928- *St&PR 91*
Spier, Luise Emma 1928- *WhoAmW 91*
Spier, Peter 1927- *BioIn 16*
Spier, Peter Edward 1927- *AuBYP 90, WhoAm 90, WhoAmA 91*
Spier, Richard Gary 1948- *WhoEmL 91*
Spier, Robert Forest Gayton 1922- *WhoAm 90*
Spier, Scott Allan 1954- *BiDrAPA 89*
Spier, William 1934- *WhoE 91*
Spierenburg, Pieter 1948- *ConAu 132*
Spierer, Charles 1953- *WhoWor 91*
Spiering, Nancy Jean 1958- *WhoAmW 91, WhoEmL 91*
Spiers, Dennis M *BiDrAPA 89*
Spiers, Donald Ellis 1948- *WhoE 91*
Spiers, Nedra Brown 1929- *WhoAmW 91*
Spiers, Ronald Ian 1925- *WhoAm 90*
Spiers, Tomas Hoskins, Jr. 1929- *WhoWor 91*
Spiers, William Thomas 1960- *WhoSSW 91*
Spies, August 1855-1887 *EncAL*
Spies, Cheri Lynn 1957- *WhoAmW 91*
Spies, Claudio 1925- *WhoAm 90*
Spies, Dennis J. 1941- *WhoSSW 91*
Spies, Emerson George 1914- *WhoAm 90*
Spies, Jacob John 1931- *WhoSSW 91*
Spies, Leon Fred 1950- *WhoEmL 91*
Spies, Philip T. 1946- *St&PR 91*
Spies, Rita R 1925- *BiDrAPA 89*
Spies, Werner Emil 1928- *WhoWor 91*
Spiess, Fred Noel 1919- *WhoAm 90*
Spiess, Gary A. 1940- *St&PR 91*
Spiess, Hans 1926- *WhoWor 91*
Spiess, Heinz 1920- *WhoWor 91*
Spiess, John Edward 1920- *St&PR 91*
Spiess, Ludovico 1938- *IntWWM 90*
Spiess, Priscilla Joice 1926- *St&PR 91*
Spiess, Robert Clayton 1921- *WhoWrEP 89*
Spiess-Ferris, Eleanor 1941- *WhoAmA 91*
Spiethoff, Arthur 1873-1957 *BioIn 16*
Spiewak, Gerald Jack 1926- *St&PR 91*
Spiewak, Martin 1931- *St&PR 91*
Spiewak, Michael I. 1951- *St&PR 91*
Spiewak, Robert Louis 1922- *St&PR 91*
Spiezia, John Anthony 1935- *St&PR 91*
Spiezio, Ed 1941- *Ballpl 90*
Spiezio, James M. 1948- *St&PR 91*
Spigai, Daniel J. 1933- *St&PR 91*
Spigai, Frances Gage 1938- *WhoAmW 91*
Spigelman, Lilian *BiDrAPA 89*
Spik, Rudolph R. *ODwPR 91*
Spike, John Thomas 1951- *WhoAmA 91*
Spiker, Duane Gerald 1946- *BiDrAPA 89*
Spiker, Thecla Marie Wagner 1948- *WhoAmW 91*
Spiker, William T. 1947- *St&PR 91*
Spikerman, Richard C. 1940- *St&PR 91*
Spikes, Benjamin F. 1888- *OxCPMus*
Spikes, Charlie 1951- *Ballpl 90*
Spikes, Dolores R. *WhoAm 90, WhoAmW 91*
Spikes, Don Lee 1939- *WhoSSW 91*
Spikes, James Louis, Jr. *BiDrAPA 89*
Spikes, John C. 1882-1955 *OxCPMus*
Spikings, Barry Peter 1939- *WhoAm 90*
Spikol, Art 1936- *WhoAm 90*
Spilbeler, Larry Neil 1954- *WhoEmL 91*
Spilerman, Seymour 1938- *WhoAm 90*
Spilfogel, Debra Kay 1953- *WhoE 91*
Spilhaus 1946- *WhoAm 90*
Spilhaus, Athelstan 1911- *ConAu 31NR, WhoAm 90*
Spilhaus, Athelstan Frederick, Jr. 1938- *WhoAm 90*
Spilka, Arnold 1917- *AuBYP 90*
Spilka, Leonard S. 1945- *St&PR 91*
Spilka, Mark 1925- *ConAu 31NR, WhoAm 90, WhoWrEP 89*
Spilker, James Julius, Jr. 1933- *St&PR 91*
Spill, Frank 1938- *St&PR 91*
Spillane, Frank Morrison 1918- *MajTwCW, SpyFic*
Spillane, L. Jerome 1949- *St&PR 91*
Spillane, Margaret A. 1958- *ODwPR 91*
Spillane, Mary Catherine 1956- *WhoAmW 91, WhoEmL 91*
Spillane, Mickey *MajTwCW, WhoWrEP 89*
Spillane, Mickey 1918- *SpyFic, TwCCr&M 91, WhoAm 90, WorAlBi*
Spillane, Richard A. 1951- *St&PR 91*
Spillane, Robert Thomas 1942- *St&PR 91*
Spillane, Sally *BioIn 16*
Spillard, E.J. 1939- *St&PR 91*
Spiller, Callie Cline, Jr. 1944- *WhoAm 90*
Spiller, Eberhard Adolf 1933- *WhoAm 90*
Spiller, Ellen Brubaker 1932- *WhoSSW 91*
Spiller, Miriam Britton 1926- *WhoAmW 91*
Spiller, Robert Ernest 1896-1988 *BioIn 16*
Spiller, Robert James 1930- *St&PR 91*
Spiller, Scott L. 1951- *St&PR 91*
Spiller, Warren Logan 1947- *St&PR 91*
Spillers, Helen Morris 1927- *St&PR 91*
Spillers, William Russell 1934- *WhoAm 90*
Spillman, Craig Warren 1960- *WhoEmL 91*
Spillman, Eugene E. *WhoSSW 91*
Spillman, John Henry 1940- *St&PR 91*
Spillman, Marjorie Rose *WhoAmW 91, WhoE 91*
Spillman, William Bert, Jr. 1946- *WhoE 91*
Spillner, Dan 1951- *Ballpl 90*
Spilman, Harry 1954- *Ballpl 90*
Spilman, Raymond 1911- *WhoAm 90*
Spilman, Richard 1946- *ConAu 132*
Spilman, Robert Henkel 1927- *St&PR 91, WhoAm 90, WhoSSW 91*
Spin, Lillian 1916- *WhoAmW 91*
Spina, Anthony *WhoAm 90*
Spina, Anthony Ferdinand 1937- *WhoWor 91*
Spina, David Anthony 1942- *St&PR 91*
Spina, Florence 1949- *WhoE 91*
Spina, Frederick Michael 1955- *WhoE 91*
Spina, George Charles 1947- *WhoE 91*
Spina, Lori Jean 1951- *WhoSSW 91*
Spina, Philip *BioIn 16*
Spinacci, Giovanni *PenDiDA 89*
Spinar, Donald E. 1948- *St&PR 91*
Spincic, Wesley James 1945- *WhoSSW 91*
Spindel, Robert Charles 1944- *WhoAm 90*
Spindel, Teresa S *BiDrAPA 89*
Spindel, William 1922- *WhoAm 90*
Spindle, Debra Osborne 1951- *WhoSSW 91*
Spindler, Albert W. 1928- *ODwPR 91*
Spindler, Alvin Curtis 1928- *BiDrAPA 89*
Spindler, Charles 1865-1938 *PenDiDA 89*
Spindler, Eunice Marie 1932- *WhoAmW 91*
Spindler, Evangeline J *BiDrAPA 89*
Spindler, G. R. *WhoSSW 91*
Spindler, George Dearborn 1920- *WhoAm 90*
Spindler, George S. 1938- *St&PR 91*
Spindler, Heinrich Wilhelm 1738-1799? *PenDiDA 89*
Spindler, Jakob 1724-1792 *PenDiDA 89*
Spindler, James W. 1939- *St&PR 91*
Spindler, Johann 1691-1770 *PenDiDA 89*
Spindler, Johann Friedrich 1726-1799? *PenDiDA 89*
Spindler, John Frederick 1929- *WhoAm 90*
Spindler, John Jay 1930- *St&PR 91*
Spindler, Paul 1931- *WhoAm 90*
Spindler, Paul R. 1931- *ODwPR 91*
Spindola-Franco, Hugo 1938- *WhoHisp 91*
Spinell, Joe *ConTFT 8*
Spinella, Joseph Carl 1925- *St&PR 91*
Spinella, Joseph Dominic 1934- *WhoE 91*
Spinella, Judy Lynn 1948- *WhoAmW 91*
Spinelli, Beatrice Ann *BiDrAPA 89*
Spinelli, Frances Markunas 1950- *WhoAmW 91, WhoE 91*
Spinelli, Frank 1930- *St&PR 91*
Spinelli, Grace Billotti *BioIn 16*
Spinelli, Jerry 1941- *BioIn 16, ConAu 30NR*
Spinelli, Luca Carlo 1955- *WhoSSW 91*

Spinelli, Margaret Gail 1947- *BiDrAPA 89*
Spinelli, Robert N 1940- *BiDrAPA 89*
Spingarn, Arthur Barnett 1878-1971 *BioIn 16*
Spingarn, Clifford Leroy 1912- *WhoE 91, WhoWor 91*
Spingarn, David Harry *BiDrAPA 89*
Spingarn, David Harry 1953- *WhoE 91*
Spingarn, Joel E. 1875-1939 *WorAlBi*
Spingarn, Lawrence Perreira 1917- *WhoWrEP 89*
Spingarn, Richard Alan 1951- *WhoE 91*
Spingola, Laura Margaret 1951- *WhoAmW 91*
Spink, Alfred H. *Ballpl 90*
Spink, Frank Henry, Jr 1935- *WhoAmA 91*
Spink, Ian 1932- *IntWWM 90*
Spink, J. G. Taylor 1888-1962 *Ballpl 90*
Spink, Walter M 1928- *WhoAmA 91*
Spink, William MacDonald 1840-1884 *Ballpl 90*
Spinka, Isadore *BiDrAPA 89*
Spinka, Ronald Barry *BiDrAPA 89*
Spinks, Alfred 1917-1982 *DcNaB 1981*
Spinks, David Wayne 1952- *WhoEmL 91*
Spinks, Jack Maples 1936- *St&PR 91*
Spinks, John Lee 1924- *WhoAm 90*
Spinks, Leon *BioIn 16*
Spinks, Mary Trimmer *BiDrAPA 89*
Spinks, Michael *BioIn 16*
Spinks, Michael 1956- *WhoAm 90*
Spinks, Nelda Hughes 1928- *WhoSSW 91, WhoWor 91*
Spinks, Paul 1922- *WhoAm 90*
Spinks, Ruthann 1959- *WhoAmW 91*
Spinks, Scipio 1947- *Ballpl 90*
Spinnato, Joseph E. 1938- *WhoE 91*
Spinner, Allan L. 1930- *St&PR 91*
Spinner, David 1758-1811 *PenDiDA 89*
Spinner, Ernest 1944- *St&PR 91*
Spinner, Kaspar Heinrich 1941- *WhoWor 91*
Spinner, Miriam Rachel *BiDrAPA 89*
Spinner, Stephanie 1943- *ConAu 32NR*
Spinners, The *OxCPMus*
Spinola, Antonio De 1910- *WorAlBi*
Spinola, Noenio Dantas Le 1938- *WhoWor 91*
Spinos, Katie 1959- *WhoE 91*
Spinosa, Gary Paul 1947- *WhoAmA 91*
Spinossimus *ConAu 31NR*
Spinoza, Baruch 1632-1677 *WorAlBi, WrPh P*
Spinoza, Benedictus de 1632-1677 *BioIn 16*
Spinrad, Bernard Israel 1924- *WhoAm 90*
Spinrad, Hyron 1934- *WhoAm 90*
Spinrad, Norman *BioIn 16*
Spinrad, Norman 1940- *RGTwCSF, WorAu 1980 [port]*
Spinrad, Richard William 1954- *WhoEmL 91, WhoSSW 91*
Spinrad, Robert Joseph 1932- *WhoAm 90*
Spinski, Victor 1940- *WhoAmA 91*
Spinweber, Steven Charles 1963- *WhoE 91*
Spiotta, Raymond Herman 1927- *WhoAm 90*
Spira, Bill 1935- *WhoAmA 91*
Spira, David Stewart 1949- *BiDrAPA 89*
Spira, Eduardo Levy- *BioIn 16*
Spira, Henry *BioIn 16*
Spira, Israel *BioIn 16*
Spira, Joel Solon 1927- *St&PR 91*
Spira, Melvin 1925- *WhoAm 90*
Spira, Neal Elliott 1951- *BiDrAPA 89*
Spira-Solomon, Darlene Joy 1959- *WhoEmL 91*
Spire, Hazel Jean 1950- *WhoWrEP 89*
Spire, Nancy Woodson 1917- *WhoAmW 91*
Spire, Robert M. 1925- *WhoAm 90*
Spirer, Gary Steven 1945- *WhoE 91*
Spirer, June Dale 1943- *WhoAmW 91*
Spirer, Peter Richman 1931- *St&PR 91*
Spires, Elizabeth 1952- *WhoWrEP 89*
Spires, R. Keith 1939- *St&PR 91*
Spires, Robert Cecil 1936- *WhoAm 90*
Spiridonova, Mariya Aleksandrovna 1884-1941 *BioIn 16*
Spirito, Kathryn Cecelia 1911- *WhoAmW 91*
Spirito, Nicholas 1950- *WhoE 91*
Spirito, Ugo 1896- *EncO&P 3*
Spirk, Terry L. *BioIn 16*
Spirko, Kenneth Stephen 1935- *St&PR 91*
Spirn, Michele Sobel 1943- *WhoAmW 91*
Spiro, Benjamin Paul 1917- *WhoAm 90, WhoWor 91*
Spiro, Carolyn S 1952- *BiDrAPA 89*
Spiro, Charles F. 1918- *St&PR 91*
Spiro, Herbert John 1924- *WhoAm 90, WhoWor 91*
Spiro, Herzl Robert 1935- *BiDrAPA 89*
Spiro, Howard Marget 1924- *WhoAm 90*
Spiro, Leslie Safford 1951- *WhoE 91*
Spiro, Lionel 1939- *St&PR 91*
Spiro, Loida Velazquez *WhoHisp 91*
Spiro, Mary Jane 1930- *WhoAmW 91*
Spiro, Melford Elliot 1920- *WhoAm 90*
Spiro, Nicholas 1936- *St&PR 91*
Spiro, Peter John 1961- *WhoE 91*
Spiro, Philip Marget 1954- *BiDrAPA 89*
Spiro, Richard I 1952- *BiDrAPA 89*
Spiro, Robert Gunter 1929- *WhoAm 90*
Spiro, Robert Harry, Jr. 1920- *WhoAm 90*
Spiro, Saul M *BiDrAPA 89*
Spiro, Terrie Gay 1956- *WhoE 91*
Spiro, Thomas George 1935- *WhoAm 90*
Spirson, Jacque Jacoby 1929- *WhoSSW 91*
Spirt, Sheri Ellen *BiDrAPA 89*
Spirtos, Nicholas George 1950- *WhoWor 91*
Spisak-Gamble, Antonina Stanislawa 1946- *WhoAmW 91, WhoWor 91*
Spital, Max 1923- *BiDrAPA 89*
Spiteri, Joseph Francis 1912- *WhoWor 91*
Spitler, Clare Blackford 1923- *WhoAmA 91*
Spitler, Richard W. 1950- *St&PR 91*
Spitsbergen, Dorothy May 1932- *WhoAmW 91*
Spitter, The *WhoWrEP 89*
Spittler, Jayne Zenaty 1948- *WhoAmW 91*
Spitulnik, Charles A. 1951- *St&PR 91*
Spitulnik, Charles Alan 1951- *WhoE 91*
Spitz, Arnold A. 1914- *St&PR 91*
Spitz, Arnoldt John 1929- *St&PR 91, WhoWor 91*
Spitz, Barbara S 1926- *WhoAmA 91*
Spitz, Barbara Salomon 1926- *WhoAm 90*
Spitz, Charles Thomas, Jr. 1921- *WhoAm 90*
Spitz, Debbie *NewAgMG*
Spitz, Deborah 1950- *BiDrAPA 89*
Spitz, Harlan *BiDrAPA 89*
Spitz, Henry Ian 1941- *BiDrAPA 89*
Spitz, Hugo Max 1927- *WhoSSW 91, WhoWor 91*
Spitz, James Robert 1940- *WhoAm 90*
Spitz, Jeff Glen 1956- *St&PR 91*
Spitz, Lewis W 1922- *ConAu 32NR*
Spitz, Lewis William 1922- *WhoAm 90*
Spitz, Louis 1936- *BiDrAPA 89*
Spitz, Margie Zepporah 1945- *WhoE 91*
Spitz, Mark *BioIn 16*
Spitz, Mark 1950- *WorAlBi*
Spitz, Randy Joseph 1958- *WhoEmL 91*
Spitz, Robert John 1947- *WhoEmL 91*
Spitz, Seymour James, Jr. 1921- *WhoAm 90*
Spitz, Steven J *BiDrAPA 89*
Spitzbart, Abraham 1915- *WhoAm 90*
Spitzberg, Irving Joseph, Jr. 1942- *WhoAm 90*
Spitzberg, Jerrold 1939- *St&PR 91*
Spitze, Hazel Taylor *BioIn 16*
Spitze, Robert George Frederick 1922- *WhoAm 90*
Spitzer, Adrian 1927- *WhoAm 90*
Spitzer, Alan Richard 1947- *WhoE 91*
Spitzer, Alexander 1946- *St&PR 91*
Spitzer, Cary Redford 1937- *WhoAm 90*
Spitzer, Frank P 1925- *BiDrAPA 89*
Spitzer, Ilene Beth *BiDrAPA 89*
Spitzer, Jack J. 1917- *WhoAm 90*
Spitzer, John Brumback 1918- *WhoAm 90*
Spitzer, John J. 1927- *WhoAm 90*
Spitzer, Karen Dawn 1957- *WhoAmW 91*
Spitzer, Lyman 1914- *WorAlBi*
Spitzer, Lyman, Jr. 1914- *WhoAm 90*
Spitzer, M. James 1911- *St&PR 91*
Spitzer, Marc Lee 1957- *WhoEmL 91*
Spitzer, Margo Fenyes 1954- *BiDrAPA 89*
Spitzer, Maureen Lynn 1961- *BiDrAPA 89*
Spitzer, Morton E. 1937- *St&PR 91*
Spitzer, Nicholas Canaday 1942- *WhoAm 90*
Spitzer, Peter George 1956- *WhoEmL 91, WhoWor 91*
Spitzer, Robert 1927- *St&PR 91*
Spitzer, Robert J 1953- *ConAu 30NR*
Spitzer, Robert L 1932- *BiDrAPA 89*
Spitzer, Robert Ralph 1922- *WhoAm 90*
Spitzer, Robert S 1926- *BiDrAPA 89*
Spitzer, Scott L. 1951- *St&PR 91*
Spitzer, Walter Oswald 1937- *WhoAm 90*
Spitzer, William George 1927- *WhoAm 90*
Spitzer-Cohn, Donald Leslie 1951- *BiDrAPA 89*
Spitzer-Hegyesi, Louis *PenDiMP*
Spitznagel, Anne Moulton Sirch 1923- *WhoAmW 91*
Spitznagel, John Keith 1923- *WhoAm 90*
Spitznagel, John Keith 1951- *WhoSSW 91*
Spivack, Edmund Sheldon 1932- *WhoE 91*
Spivack, Ellen Sue 1937- *WhoAmW 91, WhoWor 91, WhoWrEP 89*
Spivack, Gary Robert 1949- *BiDrAPA 89*
Spivack, Gordon Bernard 1929- *WhoAm 90*
Spivack, Kathleen 1938- *WhoWrEP 89*
Spivak, Alice *BioIn 16*
Spivak, Alvin A. 1927- *WhoAm 90*
Spivak, Charlie 1905-1982 *BioIn 16*
Spivak, Charlie 1906-1982 *OxCPMus*
Spivak, Gayatri 1941- *FemiCLE*
Spivak, Helayne *WhoAmW 91*
Spivak, Irwin Howard 1926- *WhoE 91*
Spivak, Jacque R. 1929- *WhoAmW 91*
Spivak, Joan Carol 1950- *WhoAmW 91*
Spivak, Jonathan M. 1928- *WhoAm 90*
Spivak, Lawrence 1900- *WorAlBi*
Spivak, Lawrence Edmund 1900- *WhoAm 90*
Spivak, Melvin Ezra 1937- *WhoWrEP 89*
Spivak, Robert Elliot 1936- *WhoE 91*
Spivak, Stanley 1940- *St&PR 91*
Spivakovsky, Jascha 1896- *PenDiMP*
Spivakovsky, Tossy 1907- *IntWWM 90, PenDiMP*
Spivey, Bruce E. 1934- *WhoAm 90*
Spivey, Cynthia *ODwPR 91*
Spivey, David R. 1948- *WhoSSW 91*
Spivey, Edward Carlyle 1932- *St&PR 91*
Spivey, Gerald Homer 1937- *St&PR 91, WhoAm 90*
Spivey, Hope *BioIn 16*
Spivey, Jim *BioIn 16*
Spivey, John Waters 1930- *St&PR 91*
Spivey, Robert Atwood 1931- *WhoAm 90, WhoSSW 91*
Spivey, Robert P. 1941- *St&PR 91*
Spivey, Shell *St&PR 91*
Spivey, Ted Ray 1927- *WhoAm 90*
Spivey, Victoria 1906-1976 *BioIn 16, OxCPMus*
Spivy, Dixon Flemon *BiDrAPA 89*
Spivy, Samuel Oscar Johnson 1952- *WhoWor 91*
Spiwak, Alana R 1956- *BiDrAPA 89*
Spizizen, Louise 1928- *IntWWM 90*
Spizzirri, Richard Dominic 1933- *WhoAm 90*
Splaine, Nancy W. 1959- *St&PR 91*
Splane, George R, III 1949- *BiDrAPA 89*
Splane, Richard Beverley 1916- *WhoAm 90*
Splaver, Sarah *WhoSSW 91*
Splaver, Sarah 1921- *AuBYP 90*
Splete, Allen Peterjohn 1938- *WhoAm 90*
Spletinckx, Christian Adelin 1944- *WhoWor 91*
Spliethoff, William Ludwig 1926- *WhoAm 90*
Splinter, Betty Ann M. 1946- *St&PR 91*
Splinter, William Eldon 1925- *WhoAm 90*
Splitstone, George Dale 1925- *WhoAm 90*
Splitt, Cody 1919- *WhoAmW 91*
Splitt, Frank George 1930- *WhoAm 90*
Splittorff, Paul 1946- *Ballpl 90*
Splittstoesser, Walter Emil 1937- *WhoAm 90*
Splude, John W. 1945- *St&PR 91*
Spock, Alexander 1929- *WhoSSW 91*
Spock, Benjamin 1903- *BioIn 16, MajTwCW*
Spock, Benjamin M. 1903- *WorAlBi*
Spock, Benjamin McLane 1903- *WhoAm 90, WhoWor 91*
Spock, Jane *BioIn 16*
Spodak, Michael K *BiDrAPA 89*
Spodak, Michael Kenneth 1944- *WhoAm 90*
Spodark, Edwina 1954- *WhoSSW 91*
Spode, Josiah 1733-1797 *PenDiDA 89*
Spode, Josiah, II 1754-1827 *PenDiDA 89*
Spodek, Bernard 1931- *WhoAm 90*
Spoegler, Christina Marie 1950- *WhoAmW 91*
Spoehel, Jerri Hoskins 1932- *WhoAmW 91*
Spoehr, Alexander 1913- *WhoAm 90*
Spoelman-Knox, Deborah Lee 1958- *WhoAmW 91*
Spoelstra, Jon *WhoAm 90*
Spoelstra, Watson *Ballpl 90*
Spoerl, Otto H 1933- *BiDrAPA 89*
Spoerlein, Kent *St&PR 91*
Spoerr, Wendy Sue 1950- *WhoAmW 91*
Spoerri, Elka Sagoroff 1924- *WhoWor 91*
Spofford, Charles Augustus 1822-1899 *AmLegL*
Spofford, Harriet 1835-1921 *FemiCLE*
Spofford, Harriet P. 1835-1921 *BioAmW*
Spofford, John S.W. 1942- *St&PR 91*
Spofford, Robert Houston 1941- *WhoAm 90*
Spofford, Sally 1929- *WhoAmA 91*
Spofford, Sally Hyslop 1929- *WhoE 91*
Spofford, William B. 1921- *WhoAm 90*
Spohler, John 1928- *St&PR 91*
Spohn, Beatrice Evelyn 1907- *WhoAmW 91*
Spohn, Brian Keith 1967- *WhoSSW 91*
Spohn, Clay 1898-1977 *WhoAmA 91N*
Spohn, Franz Frederick 1950- *WhoAmA 91*
Spohn, Herbert Emil 1923- *WhoAm 90*
Spohn, Jurgen 1934- *ConDes 90*
Spohn, Ralph Joseph 1943- *WhoE 91*
Spohn, William Gideon, Jr. 1923- *WhoE 91*
Spohr, Arnold Theodore 1927- *WhoAm 90*
Spohr, Louis 1784-1859 *PenDiMP A*
Spohrer, Al 1902-1972 *Ballpl 90*
Spokan Garry 1811-1892 *WhNaAH [port]*
Spokane Garry 1811-1892 *WhNaAH [port]*
Spokane, Earle Jay 1937- *WhoAm 90*
Spokes, Gilbert Neil 1935- *WhoSSW 91*
Spolan, Harmon S. 1935- *St&PR 91*
Spolan, Harmon Samuel 1935- *WhoAm 90*
Spolane, David A. 1954- *St&PR 91*
Spolar, Gail Teresa 1960- *WhoAmW 91*
Spolarich, Suzanne Maria 1950- *WhoEmL 91*
Spole, Kenneth M. 1931- *WhoE 91*
Spoleta, Gary P. 1943- *WhoAm 90, WhoSSW 91*
Spoliansky, Leon George Roger 1931- *WhoWor 91*
Spoliansky, Mischa 1898-1984 *OxCPMus*
Spolin, Viola Mills 1906- *BioIn 16, NotWoAT*
Spollen, Chris John 1952- *WhoE 91*
Spollen, James P. 1932- *St&PR 91*
Spoltoree, Janet Dee 1955- *WhoAmW 91*
Spolum, Robert N. 1931- *St&PR 91*
Spolum, Robert Nic 1931- *WhoAm 90*
Sponberg, Bonnie Bowsman 1945- *WhoEmL 91*
Sponenburgh, Mark 1916- *WhoAmA 91*
Spong, Douglas K. 1959- *ODwPR 91*
Spong, Douglas Kevin 1959- *St&PR 91*
Spong, John Shelby 1931- *WhoAm 90, WhoE 91*
Spong, William Belser, Jr. 1920- *WhoAm 90*
Sponholz, Joseph G. 1944- *BioIn 16, St&PR 91*
Sponholz, Joseph Gerald 1944- *WhoAm 90*
Sponseller, Mary Ann 1955- *St&PR 91, WhoSSW 91*
Sponseller, Robert W. 1933- *St&PR 91*
Sponsler, George Curtis, III 1927- *WhoAm 90*
Sponsler, James R. 1934- *St&PR 91*
Sponsler, John A 1938- *BiDrAPA 89*
Spook, H.J. 1946- *St&PR 91*
Spoon, Alan 1951- *BioIn 16*
Spoon, Alan G. 1951- *St&PR 91*
Spoon, Alan Gary 1951- *WhoAm 90*
Spoonamore, Doris Jean 1910- *WhoWor 91*
Spooner, Bernard Myrick 1934- *WhoSSW 91*
Spooner, Cecil 1888?-1953 *BioIn 16, NotWoAT*
Spooner, Edna May 1875?-1953 *BioIn 16, NotWoAT*
Spooner, Forrest Allen 1941- *St&PR 91, WhoAm 90*
Spooner, Frank Clyffurde 1924- *WhoWor 91*
Spooner, Henry Joshua 1839-1918 *AmLegL*
Spooner, Karl 1931-1984 *Ballpl 90*
Spooner, Larry Walter 1939- *St&PR 91*
Spooner, Linda Greer 1950- *WhoAmW 91, WhoE 91*
Spooner, Mary Gibbs 1853?-1940 *BioIn 16, NotWoAT*
Spooner, Thomas Clarence 1940- *WhoAm 90*
Spooner, Victoria Anne 1963- *WhoAmW 91*
Spooner, Wyman 1795-1877 *AmLegL*
Spooners, The *NotWoAT*
Spoonhour, James Michael 1946- *WhoSSW 91*
Spoont, M Lawrence 1931- *BiDrAPA 89*
Spoor, John Edward 1935- *WhoE 91*
Spoor, Thomas Richard 1934- *WhoAm 90*
Spoor, William Howard 1923- *St&PR 91, WhoAm 90*
Spoorenberg, Erna 1926- *IntWWM 90*
Spopkporn, Stanley B. *St&PR 91*
Sporborg, Henry Nathan 1905-1985 *DcNaB 1981*
Sporck, Charles E. 1928- *WhoAm 90*
Spore, Gerald Arthur 1932- *St&PR 91*
Spore, Stephanie McManus 1962- *WhoAmW 91*
Spores, Ronald Marvin 1931- *WhoAm 90*
Sporkin, Stanley *BioIn 16*
Sporkin, Stanley 1932- *WhoAm 90*
Sporn, Alexander L. *BiDrAPA 89*
Sporn, Alfred B 1926- *BiDrAPA 89*
Sporn, Alfred Bernard 1926- *WhoE 91*
Sporn, Jonathan 1958- *BiDrAPA 89*
Sporn, Stanley R. 1928- *St&PR 91*
Sporn, Stanley Robert 1928- *WhoAm 90*
Spornick, Lynna Babs 1947- *WhoAmW 91*
Sporre, Dennis John 1944- *IntWWM 90*
Sporrenberg, Jacob 1902-1952 *BioIn 16*
Sport, Bonnie Montrose 1937- *WhoAmW 91*
Sport, Haywood M. 1937- *St&PR 91*
Sportsman, Lenore May *BiDrAPA 89*
Sporty, Lawrence D *BiDrAPA 89*
Sposato, Anthony J. 1927- *St&PR 91*
Sposato, Charles Gabriel, Jr. 1927- *St&PR 91*
Sposato, Paul A. 1952- *St&PR 91*

Sposito, Garrison 1939- *WhoHisp 91*
Spota, Luis 1925-1985 *HispWr 90*
Spotnitz, Hyman 1908- *BiDrAPA 89*
Spoto, Angelo Peter, Jr. 1933- *WhoSSW 91*
Spoto, Daniel V *BiDrAPA 89*
Spoto, Donald 1941- *WhoAm 90*
Spoto, Marcia Ann Miller 1957- *WhoE 91*
Spoto, Peter J 1926- *BiDrAPA 89*
Spotswood, Alexander 1676-1740 *EncCRAm*
Spotted Tail 1833?-1881 *WhNaAH [port]*
Spotts, Bonnie Walp 1960- *WhoWrEP 89*
Spotts, Carleton Brooks 1932- *IntWWM 90*
Spotts, George R. 1922- *St&PR 91*
Spotts, Philip Gene 1950- *WhoEmL 91*
Spottsville, Deborah Denise 1955- *WhoAmW 91*
Spottswood, Maurice D *BiDrAPA 89*
Spotwood, William Edward 1929- *WhoE 91*
Sprabery, Peggy Peden 1950- *WhoAmW 91*
Spradlin, Dewey Donald 1947- *WhoEmL 91*
Spradlin, Thomas Richard 1937- *WhoE 91*
Spradlin, Wilford W 1932- *BiDrAPA 89*
Spradling, Dorris Edward 1918- *St&PR 91*
Spradling, Frank L 1885-1972 *WhoAmA 91N*
Spradling, James Barry 1934- *St&PR 91*
Spraetz, Kenneth M. 1937- *St&PR 91*
Sprafkin, Robert Peter 1940- *WhoE 91*
Spragens, Thomas Arthur 1917- *WhoAm 90*
Spragens, William Clark 1925- *WhoSSW 91*
Spragg, Howard Eugene 1917- *WhoAm 90, WhoWor 91*
Spraggins, Thomas Wayne 1937- *St&PR 91*
Spraggs, Richard William 1930- *St&PR 91*
Sprague, Amaris Jeanne 1935- *WhoAmW 91*
Sprague, B. Allan 1946- *WhoWor 91*
Sprague, Bradford M. 1951- *St&PR 91*
Sprague, Brenda Lee 1953- *WhoWrEP 89*
Sprague, Carl T. 1895- *BioIn 16*
Sprague, Carter *ConAu 131*
Sprague, Charles Cameron 1916- *WhoAm 90*
Sprague, Charles Pelton 1947- *BiDrAPA 89*
Sprague, Clifford G. 1943- *St&PR 91*
Sprague, Daniel 1908- *St&PR 91*
Sprague, David S 1933- *BiDrAPA 89*
Sprague, David White *BiDrAPA 89*
Sprague, Donald L. 1932- *St&PR 91*
Sprague, E. Russell 1915- *St&PR 91*
Sprague, Ed 1945- *Ballpl 90*
Sprague, Edward Auchincloss 1932- *WhoAm 90*
Sprague, Everett Russell 1915- *WhoAm 90*
Sprague, Forrest Raymond 1929- *St&PR 91*
Sprague, George Frederick 1902- *WhoAm 90*
Sprague, Gretchen 1926- *AuBYP 90*
Sprague, James C. 1946- *St&PR 91*
Sprague, James Darrell 1933- *WhoSSW 91*
Sprague, James Mather 1916- *WhoAm 90*
Sprague, John Louis 1930- *St&PR 91, WhoAm 90*
Sprague, Kate C. *BioAmW*
Sprague, Mark Anderson 1920- *WhoAmA 91*
Sprague, Milton Alan 1914- *WhoAm 90*
Sprague, Neil W. 1955- *ODwPR 91*
Sprague, Norman Frederick, Jr. 1914- *WhoAm 90, WhoWor 91*
Sprague, Paul Edward 1933- *WhoAmA 91*
Sprague, Peter Julian 1939- *WhoAm 90*
Sprague, Philip Allcock 1923- *WhoAm 90*
Sprague, Raymond 1947- *WhoSSW 91*
Sprague, Richard W. 1929- *ODwPR 91*
Sprague, Richard Wilder 1929- *St&PR 91*
Sprague, Robert A. *ODwPR 91*
Sprague, Robert C. 1900- *St&PR 91*
Sprague, Robert Chapman 1900- *WhoAm 90*
Sprague, Rosemary 1922- *AuBYP 90*
Sprague, Thomas H. 1928- *ODwPR 91*
Sprague, Thomas M *BiDrAPA 89*
Sprague, Thomas S. 1938- *ODwPR 91*
Sprague, Vance Glover, Jr. 1941- *WhoSSW 91*
Sprague, W.W., Jr. 1926- *St&PR 91*
Sprague, Warren Giles 1927- *WhoAm 90*
Sprague, William Leigh 1938- *WhoWrEP 89*
Sprague, William Wallace 1913- *WhoAm 90*
Sprague, William Wallace, Jr. 1926- *WhoAm 90, WhoSSW 91*
Sprague-Smith, Isabelle Dwight 1861-1951 *WhoAmA 91N*
Spralding, John Thomas, Jr. 1947- *WhoSSW 91*
Sprang, Elizabeth *WhoAmA 91*
Sprang, Harry E *BiDrAPA 89*
Sprang, Milton LeRoy 1944- *WhoAm 90*
Sprang, Pamela Sue 1953- *WhoAmW 91*
Spranger, Hanno W. 1935- *St&PR 91*
Spranger, John 1922- *EncACom*
Sprankel, Charlene Mildred 1925- *WhoAmW 91*
Sprankle, Lynn Darwin, Jr. 1936- *St&PR 91*
Sprano, Esther Johanna 1958- *WhoAmW 91*
Spratling, William 1900-1967 *BioIn 16*
Spratt, Frederick R 1927- *WhoAmA 91*
Spratt, Geoffrey Kenneth 1950- *IntWWM 90*
Spratt, John McKee, Jr. 1942- *WhoAm 90, WhoSSW 91*
Spratt, Lalla Lee 1912- *St&PR 91*
Spratt, Robin Louise 1963- *WhoAmW 91*
Sprawka, Gregory 1950- *St&PR 91*
Sprawls, Billie Jean 1938- *WhoSSW 91*
Spray of Pearls *WomWR [port]*
Spray, Paul 1921- *WhoAm 90, WhoSSW 91, WhoWor 91*
Sprayregen, Joel Jay 1934- *WhoAm 90*
Sprayregen, Morris *WhoAmA 91N*
Sprecher, David A. 1930- *WhoAm 90*
Sprecher, Gustav Ewald 1922- *WhoWor 91*
Sprecher, Paul *BioIn 16*
Sprecher, William Gunther 1924- *WhoE 91, WhoWor 91*
Sprechman, Evelyn Terry 1930- *WhoAmW 91*
Spreckels, John D. 1853-1926 *BioIn 16*
Sprehe, Daniel J 1932- *BiDrAPA 89*
Sprehn, George W 1918- *BiDrAPA 89*
Spreiregen, Paul David 1931- *WhoAm 90*
Spreiter, John Robert 1921- *WhoAm 90*
Spreitzer, Cynthia Ann 1953- *WhoAmW 91*
Spreng, Daniel Theodor 1940- *WhoWor 91*
Sprengel, Fraulein *EncO&P 3*
Sprengeler, Donald A. 1940- *St&PR 91*
Sprenger, Charles Everett 1955- *St&PR 91*
Sprenger, Jakob 1436-1495 *EncO&P 3*
Sprenger, Klaus 1946- *WhoWor 91*
Sprenger, Maurice Andrew 1950- *BiDrAPA 89*
Sprenger, Thomas Robert 1931- *WhoSSW 91*
Sprenkle, Case Middleton 1934- *WhoAm 90*
Sprenkle, John Thomas 1942- *WhoSSW 91*
Spresser, Mark A. 1950- *St&PR 91*
Sprick, Walter Antonio 1949- *WhoWor 91*
Spriegel, William B 1924- *BiDrAPA 89*
Sprieser, John R. 1947- *St&PR 91*
Spriestersbach, Duane Caryl 1916- *WhoAm 90*
Spriggs, Ann Johnson 1938- *WhoAmW 91*
Spriggs, David William 1949- *WhoEmL 91*
Spriggs, Dillard P. 1926- *St&PR 91*
Spriggs, Everett Lee 1930- *WhoAm 90, WhoWor 91*
Spriggs, George 1850-1912 *EncO&P 3, EncPaPR 91*
Spriggs, Richard Moore 1931- *WhoAm 90*
Spriggs, Robert Paul 1932- *St&PR 91*
Sprimont, Nicholas 1716?-1771 *PenDiDA 89*
Spring, Bernard Polmer 1927- *WhoAm 90*
Spring, Bonnie Joan 1949- *WhoWor 91*
Spring, Christian 1939- *IntWWM 90*
Spring, David 1918- *WhoAm 90*
Spring, Dick 1950- *WhoWor 91*
Spring, Gottfried K *BiDrAPA 89*
Spring, Jack 1933- *Ballpl 90*
Spring, John S. 1930- *St&PR 91*
Spring, Max Edward 1947- *WhoEmL 91*
Spring, Michael 1941- *WhoAm 90*
Spring, Paul 1942- *BiDrAPA 89*
Spring, Raymond Lewis 1932- *WhoAm 90*
Spring, Samuel Newton 1927- *St&PR 91*
Spring, Stanley Lloyde 1942- *WhoSSW 91*
Spring, William Donald, Jr. 1953- *BiDrAPA 89*
Springborn, Robert C. 1929- *St&PR 91*
Springborn, Rosemary Kelly 1932- *WhoAmW 91*
Springer, Allen Lawrence 1951- *WhoE 91*
Springer, Ashton, Jr. 1930- *DrBIPA 90*
Springer, Charles Edward 1928- *WhoAm 90*
Springer, Craig Tracy 1947- *WhoE 91*
Springer, David Todd 1958- *BiDrAPA 89*
Springer, Deborah R. *WhoAmW 91*
Springer, Debra Dee 1959- *WhoSSW 91*
Springer, Douglas D. 1950- *St&PR 91*
Springer, Douglas Hyde 1927- *WhoAm 90*
Springer, Edwin Kent 1912- *WhoAm 90*
Springer, George 1924- *WhoAm 90*
Springer, George C. 1932- *WhoE 91*
Springer, Hugh W. 1913- *BioIn 16*
Springer, Hugh Worrell 1913- *WhoWor 91*
Springer, Jeffrey Alan 1950- *WhoWor 91*
Springer, Jeffrey R. 1944- *St&PR 91*
Springer, Jerry M. 1932- *St&PR 91*
Springer, John Kelley 1931- *WhoAm 90*
Springer, John Lawrence 1915- *WhoE 91*
Springer, John Shipman 1916- *WhoAm 90*
Springer, Karl *BioIn 16*
Springer, Karl Josef 1935- *St&PR 91, WhoAm 90*
Springer, Kenneth S. 1953- *St&PR 91*
Springer, Leann Marie 1958- *WhoEmL 91*
Springer, Lorene 1927- *IntWWM 90*
Springer, Margaret Ann 1941- *WhoWrEP 89*
Springer, Nancy Connor 1948- *WhoWrEP 89*
Springer, Nathaniel E., Jr. 1928- *St&PR 91*
Springer, Neil A. *BioIn 16*
Springer, Neil A. 1938- *St&PR 91*
Springer, Neil Allen 1938- *WhoAm 90*
Springer, Nesha Bass 1930-1990 *ConAu 132*
Springer, Paul D. 1942- *St&PR 91*
Springer, Penny Ann 1952- *WhoAmW 91*
Springer, Philip Karl *BiDrAPA 89*
Springer, Robert Coleman, III 1945- *WhoE 91*
Springer, Robert Dale 1933- *WhoAm 90*
Springer, Sally Pearl 1947- *WhoWor 91*
Springer, Stanley G. 1927- *WhoAm 90*
Springer, Susan Mae 1953- *WhoAmW 91*
Springer, Timothy Jon 1952- *WhoEmL 91*
Springer, Wayne Gilbert 1951- *WhoEmL 91, WhoSSW 91*
Springer, William H. 1929- *WhoAm 90*
Springer, William Henry 1929- *St&PR 91*
Springer, William Lee 1909- *WhoAm 90*
Springer, Wilma Marie 1933- *WhoAmW 91*
Springfield, Dan R., III 1951- *St&PR 91*
Springfield, Dusty 1939- *OxCPMus, WorAlBi*
Springfield, James F. 1929- *St&PR 91*
Springfield, James Francis 1929- *WhoAm 90*
Springfield, Mary Susan 1944- *WhoAmW 91, WhoSSW 91*
Springfield, Rick 1949- *EncPR&S 89, WorAlBi*
Springfield, Tom 1934- *OxCPMus*
Springford, Norma 1916- *OxCCanT*
Springgate, Cynthia Letitia 1953- *WhoSSW 91*
Springgate, James E. 1927- *St&PR 91*
Springhorn, Carl 1887-1971 *WhoAmA 91N*
Springmier, Robert Samuel 1928- *St&PR 91*
Springs, John B., III *BioIn 16*
Springstead, Marty 1937- *Ballpl 90*
Springstead, Ralph E. 1925- *St&PR 91*
Springstead, Stuart Earl *BiDrAPA 89*
Springsteen, Bruce *BioIn 16*
Springsteen, Bruce 1949- *EncPR&S 89, OxCPMus, WhoAm 90, WorAlBi*
Springsteen, George Stoney, Jr. 1923- *WhoAm 90*
Springstein, Karl-August Hermann 1918- *WhoWor 91*
Springstubb, Tricia 1950- *BioIn 16*
Springweiler, Erwin Frederick 1896-1968 *WhoAmA 91N*
Sprinkel, Antoinette Miller 1945- *WhoAmW 91*
Sprinkel, Beryl Wayne 1923- *WhoAm 90*
Sprinkel, Reed 1922- *St&PR 91*
Sprinker, Michael 1950- *ConAu 129*
Sprinkle, Charles Ray 1935- *WhoAm 90*
Sprinkle, Joe, Jr. 1918- *St&PR 91*
Sprinkle, Myriam Goldsmith 1933- *St&PR 91*
Sprinkle, R. David 1944- *WhoSSW 91*
Sprinkle, Robert Shields, III 1935- *St&PR 91*
Sprinthall, Norman Arthur 1931- *WhoAm 90*
Sprinzak, Ehud Zelig 1940- *WhoWor 91*
Sprinzen, Scott 1956- *St&PR 91*
Spritzer, Ralph Simon 1917- *WhoAm 90*
Sprizzo, John Emilio 1934- *WhoAm 90*
Sproat, Christopher Townsend 1945- *WhoAmA 91, WhoE 91*
Sproat, John Gerald 1921- *WhoAm 90*
Sprock, June 1955- *WhoAmW 91*
Sprockett, Winnie *BioIn 16*
Sproge, Ralf Harold 1928- *St&PR 91*
Sproger, Charles Edmund 1933- *WhoAm 90*
Sprole, Frank Arnott 1918- *WhoAm 90*
Sprole, Robert R. 1912- *St&PR 91*
Sprong, Gerald R. 1933- *St&PR 91*
Sprong, Gerald Rudolph 1933- *WhoAm 90*
Sprott, J.M. 1925- *St&PR 91*
Sprott, Richard Lawrence 1940- *WhoAm 90*
Sproul, Ann Stephenson 1907- *WhoAmA 91*
Sproul, Dorothy G *BiDrAPA 89*
Sproul, Elmer C. 1921- *St&PR 91*
Sproul, Gordon Duane 1944- *WhoSSW 91*
Sproul, Hugh B., III 1937- *St&PR 91*
Sproul, John Allan 1924- *St&PR 91, WhoAm 90*
Sproul, Loretta Ann Schroeder 1938- *WhoSSW 91*
Sproul, Otis Jennings 1930- *WhoAm 90*
Sproul, R C 1939- *ConAu 30NR*
Sproule, Anna *AuBYP 90*
Sproule, Michael *AuBYP 90*
Sproull, Charlie 1919-1980 *Ballpl 90*
Sproull, Edward I., Jr. 1926- *St&PR 91, WhoAm 90*
Sproull, James E. 1924- *St&PR 91*
Sproull, Robert Lamb 1918- *WhoAm 90*
Sproull, Terrence R 1933- *BiDrAPA 89*
Sproull, Wayne Treber 1906- *WhoWor 91*
Sprouse, Eric Michael 1950- *WhoSSW 91*
Sprouse, Gary L. 1938- *St&PR 91*
Sprouse, James Marshall 1923- *WhoAm 90*
Sprouse, John A. 1908- *St&PR 91*
Sprouse, John Alwyn 1908- *WhoAm 90*
Sprouse, Patricia Lorraine *BiDrAPA 89*
Sprouse, Robert Allen, II 1935- *WhoAm 90*
Sprouse, Robt. A., II 1935- *St&PR 91*
Sprout, William Bradford, Jr. 1900- *WhoAm 90*
Sprout, William David 1960- *WhoE 91*
Sprow, Howard Thomas 1919- *WhoAm 90*
Sprowal, Chris *BioIn 16*
Sprowl, Charles Riggs 1910- *WhoAm 90*
Sprowl, David Charles 1940- *WhoSSW 91*
Sprowls, Robert Wayne 1946- *WhoAm 90*
Spruance, Benton 1904-1967 *WhoAmA 91N*
Spruance, Raymond A. 1886-1969 *WorAlBi*
Spruance, Raymond Ames 1886-1969 *BioIn 16*
Spruce, Everett Franklin 1908- *WhoAm 90, WhoAmA 91*
Spruce, Michelle M. 1945- *WhoAmW 91*
Spruell, Melody Anne Allen 1950- *WhoSSW 91*
Sprugel, Douglas George 1948- *WhoEmL 91*
Sprugel, George, Jr. 1919- *WhoAm 90*
Spruiell, Graham L *BiDrAPA 89*
Spruiell, Vann 1926- *BiDrAPA 89*
Spruill, David Griffin 1929- *WhoAm 90*
Spruill, Howard Vernon 1919- *WhoSSW 91, WhoWor 91*
Spruill, Louise Elam 1918- *WhoAmW 91*
Spruill, Nancy Lyon 1949- *WhoAmW 91*
Spruill, Norman Louis 1933- *St&PR 91*
Spruill, Thomas R 1958- *BiDrAPA 89*
Spruit, Johannes Emil 1937- *WhoWor 91*
Spruit, Joseph N. 1924- *St&PR 91*
Sprules, Marcia Lynn 1948- *WhoAmW 91*
Sprung, Arnold 1929- *WhoE 91*
Sprung, Guy 1947- *OxCCanT*
Sprunger, Lewis William 1944- *BiDrAPA 89*
Sprungl, Janice Marie 1960- *WhoAmW 91*
Spruyt, Michael J. 1933- *St&PR 91*
Spudich, James A. 1942- *WhoAm 90*
Spuehler, Donald Roy 1934- *WhoAm 90*
Spuhler, James Norman 1917- *WhoAm 90*
Spulber, Nicolas 1915- *WhoAm 90*
Spung, Catherine Ann 1963- *WhoEmL 91*
Spungin, Gardner Mawney 1935- *WhoAm 90*
Spungin, Joel D. 1937- *St&PR 91, WhoAm 90*
Spunt, Shepard Armin 1931- *WhoE 91, WhoWor 91*
Spurck, Fredric C. 1947- *St&PR 91*
Spurdle, John W., Jr. 1937- *WhoAm 90*
Spurgeon, Charles Haddon 1834-1892 *BioIn 16*
Spurgeon, Dennis Ray 1943- *WhoE 91*
Spurgeon, Dickie Allen 1936- *WhoWrEP 89*
Spurgeon, Edward Dutcher 1939- *WhoAm 90*
Spurgeon, Freddy 1901-1970 *Ballpl 90*
Spurgeon, Kenneth McKenzie 1925- *St&PR 91*
Spurgeon, Mark Emory 1954- *St&PR 91*
Spurgeon, Richard Dean 1953- *WhoSSW 91*
Spurgeon, Roberta Kaye 1938- *WhoAmW 91*
Spurgeon, Sarah 1903-1985 *WhoAmA 91N*
Spurgeon, Stephen 1948- *ODwPR 91*
Spurgin, John Edwin 1932- *WhoAmA 91*
Spurgin, Karen Joyce 1943- *WhoAmW 91*
Spurlin, E. Eugene 1932- *St&PR 91*
Spurling, Everett Gordon, Jr. 1923- *WhoAm 90*
Spurling, Norine M 1930- *WhoAmA 91*
Spurlock, Deborah Quirk 1944- *WhoAmW 91*
Spurlock, Delbert L., Jr. 1941- *WhoAm 90*
Spurlock, Dwight Ross 1932- *St&PR 91*
Spurlock, Edward Marshall, Jr. 1953- *WhoSSW 91*

Spurlock, Fae H *BiDrAPA 89*
Spurlock, Holly B. 1925- *St&PR 91*
Spurlock, M Jeanne 1921- *BiDrAPA 89*
Spurlock, Ted Lee 1938- *St&PR 91, WhoAm 90*
Spurlock, William Henry, II 1945- *WhoAmA 91*
Spurlock-Dahlke, Rhonda 1959- *WhoAmW 91*
Spurr, Charles Lewis 1913- *WhoAm 90*
Spurr, Gregory W., Jr. 1923- *St&PR 91*
Spurr, John H., Jr. 1946- *St&PR 91*
Spurr, Stephen H. *NewYTBS 90*
Spurrell, Roworth Adrian 1942- *WhoWor 91*
Spurrier, Hal M. 1940- *St&PR 91*
Spurrier, James Joseph 1946- *WhoEmL 91*
Spurrier, John David 1948- *WhoSSW 91*
Spute, H. William, Jr. 1941- *WhoSSW 91*
Spy 1851-1922 *BioIn 16*
Spyers-Duran, Peter 1932- *WhoAm 90*
Spyra, Michael Lee 1963- *WhoSSW 91*
Spyri, Johanna 1827-1901 *AuBYP 90, EncCoWW*
Spyropoulos, George Yorgo *WhoAmA 91*
Spyrou, George Andrew Rankin 1949- *WhoWor 91*
Squadere, Frank *St&PR 91*
Squadra, John 1932- *WhoAmA 91*
Squadron, Howard Maurice 1926- *WhoAm 90*
Squadronaires, The *OxCPMus*
Squanto *BioIn 16*
Squanto 1580?-1622 *EncCRAm, WhNaAH*
Squarciapino, Franca *BioIn 16*
Squarcy, Charlotte Van Horne 1947- *WhoAmW 91, WhoEmL 91*
Squasoni, Douglas Wade 1964- *WhoE 91*
Squassoni, Sharon Ann 1963- *WhoE 91*
Squazzo, Mildred Katherine *WhoAmW 91, WhoE 91, WhoWor 91*
Squeeze *ConMus 5 [port], EncPR&S 89*
Squeglia, Anthony D. 1942- *ODwPR 91*
Squibb, Christine Peterson 1942- *WhoAmW 91*
Squibb, Samuel Dexter 1931- *WhoAm 90*
Squibob 1823-1861 *BioIn 16*
Squiccimarro, Anne Rice *BioIn 16*
Squier, E. G., Mrs. 1836-1914 *BioIn 16*
Squier, Ephraim G. 1821-1888 *BioIn 16*
Squier, Ephraim George 1821-1888 *WhNaAH*
Squier, Florence Miriam 1836-1914 *BioIn 16*
Squier, Jack Leslie 1927- *WhoAm 90, WhoAmA 91, WhoE 91*
Squier, Leslie Hamilton 1917- *WhoAm 90*
Squier, Robert Dave 1934- *WhoAm 90*
Squiers, Carol 1948- *WhoAmA 91, WhoE 91*
Squiers, Herbert Goldsmith 1859-1911 *BioIn 16*
Squilla, Vincent D 1925- *BiDrAPA 89*
Squillace, Marques de *BioIn 16*
Squillante, F. Donald 1935- *St&PR 91*
Squillante, Judith Ann 1942- *WhoAmW 91*
Squire, Alexander 1917- *WhoAm 90*
Squire, Allan Taft *WhoAmA 91N*
Squire, Anne Marguerite 1920- *WhoAm 90*
Squire, J. R. M. *EncO&P 3*
Squire, James Robert 1922- *WhoAm 90*
Squire, Jane *FemiCLE*
Squire, Laurie Rubin 1953- *WhoAmW 91, WhoE 91*
Squire, Lisa Sharon 1953- *WhoAmW 91*
Squire, Marilyn R S *BiDrAPA 89*
Squire, Maud Hunt 1873-1955? *BiDWomA*
Squire, Molly Ann 1953- *WhoAmW 91*
Squire, Peter Hafner 1954- *WhoSSW 91*
Squire, Robert W. 1931- *St&PR 91*
Squire, Russel Nelson 1908- *WhoWor 91*
Squire, W. H. 1871-1963 *OxCPMus*
Squire, Walter Charles 1945- *WhoWor 91*
Squires, Arthur Morton 1916- *WhoAm 90*
Squires, Bonnie Stein 1940- *WhoAmW 91*
Squires, Daniel Patrick 1936- *St&PR 91*
Squires, Edwina Rachels 1942- *WhoAmW 91, WhoE 91*
Squires, Gerald Leopold 1937- *WhoAmA 91*
Squires, James Radcliffe 1917- *WhoAm 90*
Squires, James Ralph 1940- *WhoSSW 91*
Squires, James Robert 1922- *WhoWrEP 89*
Squires, John Henry 1946- *WhoEmL 91*
Squires, Kathleen Elaine 1953- *WhoE 91*
Squires, Mike 1952- *Ballpl 90*
Squires, Norma Jean *WhoAmA 91*
Squires, Patricia Eileen Coleman 1927- *WhoAmW 91, WhoE 91*
Squires, Pembroke *BioIn 16*
Squires, Radcliffe 1917- *WhoWrEP 89*
Squires, Rebecca 1945- *ODwPR 91, WhoAmW 91*
Squires, Richard Felt 1933- *WhoE 91, WhoWor 91*
Squires, William Randolph, III 1947- *WhoWor 91*
Squires-Lind, Joan A. 1941- *WhoWor 91*
Squitieri, Victor Carmine 1923- *St&PR 91*
Squyres, Janet Truitt 1961- *WhoSSW 91*
Srabstein, Jorge Carlos 1944- *BiDrAPA 89*
Sraffa, Piero 1898-1983 *BioIn 16, DcNaB 1981*
Sragow, Ellen *WhoAmA 91*
Srajer, Karen R. 1952- *WhoEmL 91*
Sramek, Alfred 1951- *IntWWM 90*
Sramek, B.B. 1933- *St&PR 91*
Sramek, Hevka 1936- *St&PR 91*
Srebnik, Herbert Harry 1923- *WhoAm 90*
Sreebny, Leo M. 1922- *WhoAm 90*
Sreekrishna, Kotikanyadanam 1953- *WhoSSW 91*
Sreenan-Auger, Melaney Kay 1955- *WhoAmW 91*
Sreenivas, Nanjappa 1945- *BiDrAPA 89*
Sreenivasan, Sudha *BiDrAPA 89*
Sreenivasan, Uma *BiDrAPA 89*
Srere, Benson M. 1928- *St&PR 91, WhoAm 90*
Srere, David Benson 1958- *WhoE 91*
Srere, Linda Jean 1955- *WhoAm 90, WhoAmW 91*
Sri-Kantha, Sachi 1953- *WhoE 91*
Sri-Vesara, Kawee 1936- *WhoWor 91*
Sri Widodo, Siti Oetarini 1934- *WhoWor 91*
Srichatrapimuk, Thirawat 1946- *WhoWor 91*
Sridhar, Mynepalli Kameswara Chandra 1942- *WhoWor 91*
Sridharan, Mahadevan 1949- *WhoWor 91*
Srigley, William R. 1941- *St&PR 91*
Srihari, Arudi *BiDrAPA 89*
Srihari, Sargur Narasimha 1950- *WhoE 91*
Srimushnam, Vittal G. 1951- *St&PR 91*
Srinarula, Pornthep *WhoWor 91*
Srinivasan, Janaki *BiDrAPA 89*
Srinivasan, Malur Ramaswamy 1930- *WhoWor 91*
Srinivasan, Mandayam Paramekanthi 1940- *WhoE 91*
Srinivasan, Samuel 1936- *WhoWor 91*
Srinivasan, Thirukodikaval Nilakanja 1933- *WhoE 91*
Srinivasan, Venkataraman 1944- *WhoAm 90*
Srinivasaraghavan, Jagannathan *BiDrAPA 89*
Sripada, Bhaskar 1949- *BiDrAPA 89*
Sripada, Prasad G M *BiDrAPA 89*
Sripada, Teresa Lupa 1951- *BiDrAPA 89*
Sriram, Pankajam M *BiDrAPA 89*
Sriranganathan, Nammalwar 1944- *WhoSSW 91*
Sriratana, Sirinan 1950- *BiDrAPA 89*
Sriskandarajah, Nalayini *BiDrAPA 89*
Srisopark, Mongkol Montri *BiDrAPA 89*
Srivastav, Ram Prasad 1934- *WhoE 91*
Srivastava, Jagdish Narain 1933- *WhoWor 91*
Srivastava, Narayan Swarup 1951- *WhoEmL 91*
Srivastava, Pratap Kumar 1943- *WhoE 91*
Srivastava, Ramesh Kumar 1931- *WhoWor 91*
Srivastava, Ramesh Kumar 1940- *WhoWor 91*
Srivastava, Saroj *BiDrAPA 89*
Srivastava, Uma *BiDrAPA 89*
Srochi, Alan B. 1932- *St&PR 91*
Sroda, George 1911- *WhoWrEP 89*
Sroge, Maxwell Harold 1927- *St&PR 91, WhoAm 90*
Sroka, Francis T. 1915- *St&PR 91*
Sroka, John Walter 1946- *WhoAm 90*
Srole, Leo 1908- *BiDrAPA 89, WhoAm 90*
Srour, Joseph Ralph 1941- *WhoAm 90, WhoWor 91*
Srubas, Robert Charles 1953- *St&PR 91*
Srybnik, Louis David 1924- *St&PR 91*
Srybnik, Simon 1918- *St&PR 91*
Ssemogerere, Paul *WhoWor 91*
Sta Maria, Thelma Pronove *BiDrAPA 89*
Staab, Gary Richard 1949- *St&PR 91*
Staab, Heinz A. 1926- *WhoWor 91*
Staab, Thomas R. 1942- *St&PR 91*
Staab, Thomas Robert 1942- *WhoAm 90*
Staab, Walter Edward 1933- *WhoAm 90*
Staack, Michael 1959- *WhoWor 91*
Staal, Baronne de 1684-1750 *EncCoWW*
Staal, Dennis R. 1948- *St&PR 91*
Staar, Richard Felix 1923- *WhoAm 90*
Staats, Dean Roy 1924- *WhoAm 90*
Staats, Elmer Boyd 1914- *WhoAm 90*
Staats, Mary Hortense 1908- *WhoAmW 91*
Staats, Norman L. 1926- *St&PR 91*
Staats, Thomas Elwyn *WhoSSW 91*
Staba, Emil John 1928- *WhoAm 90*
Stabb, Henry Hunt 1812-1892 *DcCanB 12*
Stabbe, Mitchell Howard 1955- *WhoEmL 91*
Stabej, Rudolph John 1952- *WhoEmL 91*
Stabenau, James Raymond 1930- *BiDrAPA 89, WhoAm 90, WhoWor 91*
Stabenau, Walter Frank 1942- *WhoE 91*
Stabenow, Deborah Ann 1950- *WhoAmW 91*
Stabile, Benedict Louis 1927- *WhoAm 90*
Stabile, Donald Robert 1944- *WhoE 91*
Stabile, Mariano 1888-1968 *PenDiMP*
Stabile, Rose Towne *WhoAmW 91*
Stabiner, Ronald *ODwPR 91*
Stabinsky, Harvey 1946- *BiDrAPA 89*
Stabinsky, Susan 1946- *BiDrAPA 89*
Stablein, Marilyn Estelle 1946- *WhoWrEP 89*
Stabler, Diane Eileen *BiDrAPA 89*
Stabler, Donald Billman 1908- *WhoAm 90*
Stabler, Harold 1872-1945 *PenDiDA 89*
Stabler, Ken *BioIn 16*
Stabler, Ken 1945- *WorAlBi*
Stabler, Laird A. *St&PR 91*
Stabler, Lewis Vastine, Jr. 1936- *WhoAm 90*
Stabler, Robert Eugene 1936- *WhoSSW 91*
Stabler, Robert M. 1904-1985 *BioIn 16*
Stabler, Sari Beth 1960- *WhoAmW 91*
Stabler, William L. 1925- *St&PR 91*
Stabosz, Thomas F. 1942- *St&PR 91*
Staby, Jack Bradford 1926- *WhoE 91*
Stacey Q *BioIn 16*
Stacey, Gary 1951- *WhoSSW 91*
Stacey, George Peter 1949- *WhoSSW 91*
Stacey, Kathleen Mary 1951- *WhoAmW 91*
Stacey, Nicholas Anthony Howard *WhoWor 91*
Stacey, Norma Elaine 1925- *WhoSSW 91*
Stacey, Pamela 1945- *WhoAmW 91*
Stacey, Roger Foy 1942- *WhoE 91*
Stacey, Susan Stephanie 1953- *WhoEmL 91*
Stacey, Truman 1916- *WhoSSW 91*
Stach, Erik Anthony 1961- *WhoEmL 91*
Stach, Ilse von 1879-1941 *EncCoWW*
Stach, Thomas W 1934- *BiDrAPA 89*
Stachel, John Jay 1928- *WhoAm 90*
Stachelberg, Charles G *WhoAmA 91N*
Stachiewicz, Danuta 1930- *BiDrAPA 89*
Stachler, Robert G. 1929- *WhoAm 90*
Stachler, Ronald Thomas *BiDrAPA 89*
Stacho, Zoltan A. 1930- *St&PR 91*
Stacho, Zoltan Aladar 1930- *WhoAm 90*
Stachofsky, Robert G. 1937- *St&PR 91*
Stachova, Angela 19--?- *EncCoWW*
Stachowiak, Dennis Kenneth 1943- *WhoWor 91*
Stachowski, William T. 1949- *WhoE 91*
Stachura, Bernard Morris 1963- *WhoE 91*
Stachurski, Daniel B. 1944- *St&PR 91*
Stacik, Carolyn Kaiser 1944- *WhoAmW 91*
Staciokas, Leon Joseph 1928- *St&PR 91*
Stack, Diane Virginia 1958- *WhoEmL 91*
Stack, Eddie 1887-1958 *Ballpl 90*
Stack, Edward William 1935- *WhoAm 90*
Stack, Frank Huntington 1937- *WhoAmA 91*
Stack, Gael Z 1941- *WhoAmA 91*
Stack, George Joseph *WhoAm 90*
Stack, J. William, Jr. 1918- *WhoAm 90*
Stack, Jack Michael 1938- *BiDrAPA 89*
Stack, Joan Murphy 1928- *WhoAmW 91*
Stack, Joanne Tunney 1952- *WhoEmL 91*
Stack, John P. *BioIn 16*
Stack, Kathleen Marie *BiDrAPA 89*
Stack, Mary Judith 1947- *WhoAmW 91*
Stack, Maurice Daniel 1917- *WhoAm 90*
Stack, Michael 1941- *WhoAmA 91*
Stack, Michael Leo 1958- *WhoSSW 91*
Stack, Michael P. 1949- *ODwPR 91*
Stack, Nicolete *AuBYP 90*
Stack, Paul Francis 1946- *WhoWor 91*
Stack, Philip Wayne 1946- *St&PR 91*
Stack, Raymond John, Jr. 1936- *St&PR 91*
Stack, Robert *BioIn 16*
Stack, Robert 1919- *WorAlBi*
Stack, Robert Douglas 1956- *WhoE 91, WhoEmL 91*
Stack, Robert Langford 1919- *WhoAm 90*
Stack, Stephen S. 1934- *St&PR 91, WhoAm 90*
Stack-Staikidis, William John 1933- *WhoAm 90*
Stackelberg, Constantine *BioIn 16*
Stackelberg, Olaf Patrick von 1932- *WhoAm 90*
Stackelberg, Peter Georg Johan 1946- *WhoWor 91*
Stackell, Esther Ilana 1954- *WhoAmW 91*
Stackfleth, Ellis Lee 1921- *WhoSSW 91*
Stackhouse, Marion *St&PR 91*
Stackhouse, Max L. *BioIn 16*
Stackler, Walter *BioIn 16*
Stackpole, James Allan 1932- *WhoE 91*
Stackpole, Kerry Clifford 1955- *WhoE 91*
Stackpole, Mary Patricia 1934- *WhoAmW 91*
Stackpole, Robert Dauer 1946- *WhoSSW 91*
Stacks, William Leon 1928- *WhoAmA 91*
Stacom, Matthew John 1918- *St&PR 91*
Stacy, Bill Wayne 1938- *WhoAm 90*
Stacy, Burton *BioIn 16*
Stacy, Carl J. 1929- *WhoSSW 91*
Stacy, Charles Brecknock 1924- *WhoAm 90*
Stacy, Delores *WhoWrEP 89*
Stacy, Donald *MajTwCW*
Stacy, Donald L 1925- *WhoAmA 91*
Stacy, Gardner W. 1921- *WhoAm 90*
Stacy, Jan *BioIn 16*
Stacy, Jan 1948?-1989 *ConAu 129*
Stacy, Jess 1904- *OxCPMus*
Stacy, John Russell 1919- *WhoAmA 91*
Stacy, John William 1942- *WhoSSW 91*
Stacy, Pauline French 1915- *WhoAmW 91, WhoWrEP 89*
Stacy, Ralph W. 1927- *St&PR 91*
Stacy, Richard A. 1942- *WhoAm 90*
Staddon, John Eric Rayner *WhoAm 90*
Stade, Frederica von *PenDiMP*
Stade, Frederica Von 1945- *WorAlBi*
Stade, George Gustav *WhoAm 90*
Stadelmaier, Sharon M. 1946- *WhoAmW 91*
Stadelman, Peter B. 1931- *St&PR 91*
Stadelman, Russell Carl 1913- *St&PR 91*
Stadelman, William Ralph 1919- *WhoAm 90*
Stadem, Paul David 1953- *WhoEmL 91*
Stader, Maria 1911- *PenDiMP*
Stadiem, Arthur Monroe 1952- *WhoSSW 91*
Stading, Donald Charles 1935- *St&PR 91*
Stadlen, Diane Elizabeth 1953- *WhoAmW 91*
Stadlen, Peter 1910- *IntWWM 90*
Stadler, Albert 1923- *WhoAmA 91*
Stadler, Anton 1753-1812 *PenDiMP*
Stadler, Betty 1938- *WhoAmW 91*
Stadler, Craig Robert 1953- *WhoAm 90*
Stadler, Donald Arthur 1943- *WhoSSW 91*
Stadler, Gerald P. *St&PR 91*
Stadler, Gerald P. 1937- *WhoAm 90*
Stadler, Irmgard 1937- *IntWWM 90*
Stadler, Johann 1755-1804 *PenDiMP*
Stadler, John B *BiDrAPA 89*
Stadler, Martin F. 1942- *WhoAm 90*
Stadler, Ralynn N. *BioIn 16*
Stadler, Sarah Lewis *BiDrAPA 89*
Stadlin, Walter Olaf 1929- *WhoAm 90*
Stadnick, Cyril 1946- *WhoWor 91*
Stadnyk, Vladimir Yaroslav 1952- *St&PR 91*
Stadter, Philip Austin 1936- *WhoAm 90, WhoWrEP 89*
Stadter, Richard P *BiDrAPA 89*
Stadtke, Klaus-Dietrich 1934- *WhoWor 91*
Stadtlander, Jim *BioIn 16*
Stadtlander, John K 1928- *BiDrAPA 89*
Stadtler, Beatrice Horwitz 1921- *WhoAm 90, WhoWrEP 89*
Stadtler, Walter Edward 1936- *WhoAm 90, WhoWor 91*
Stadtman, Earl Reece 1919- *WhoAm 90*
Stadtman, Thressa Campbell 1920- *WhoAm 90, WhoAmW 91*
Stadtman, Verne August 1926- *WhoAm 90*
Stadtman, Walter E. 1923- *St&PR 91*
Staeb, Rick W. 1951- *St&PR 91*
Staebler, Neil 1905- *WhoAm 90*
Staebler, Tom 1943- *St&PR 91*
Staeck, Klaus 1938- *ConDes 90*
Staed, Thomas W. *BioIn 16*
Staedel, August Wilhelm 1938- *WhoWor 91*
Staedler, Lance 1954- *BioIn 16*
Staedtler, Richard Edward 1944- *St&PR 91*
Staehelin, Lucas Andrew 1939- *WhoAm 90*
Staehelin, Martin 1937- *IntWWM 90*
Staehely, David Merle 1947- *St&PR 91*
Staehle, Albert *BioIn 16*
Staehle, Marv 1942- *Ballpl 90*
Staehle, Robert L. 1955- *WhoAm 90*
Stael, Germaine de 1766-1817 *FemiCLE, WorAlBi*
Stael, Nicolas de 1914-1955 *BioIn 16*
Stael-Holstein, Baronne de 1766-1817 *EncCoWW*
Staelens, Peter John 1940- *St&PR 91*
Staelin, Richard 1939- *WhoAm 90*
Staempfli, George W 1910- *WhoAmA 91*
Staempfli, George William 1910- *WhoAm 90*
Staff, Joel V. 1944- *St&PR 91*
Staff, La Vada Falkner 1924- *WhoWrEP 89*
Staff, Marc L. 1946- *St&PR 91*
Staff, Robert James, Jr. 1946- *WhoWor 91*
Staffel, Doris 1921- *WhoAmA 91*
Staffel, Rudolf *PenDiDA 89*
Staffel, Rudolf Harry 1911- *WhoAmA 91*
Staffelbach, Andre *BioIn 16*
Staffelbach, Andre 1939- *WhoSSW 91*
Staffeldt, Adolph Wilhelm Schack von 1769-1826 *DcScanL*

Staffier, Pamela Moorman 1942- *WhoE 91*
Stafford, Arthur Charles 1947- *WhoWor 91*
Stafford, Ashley George 1954- *IntWWM 90*
Stafford, Aubrey Lee *BiDrAPA 89*
Stafford, Betty Richardson 1949- *WhoSSW 91*
Stafford, Bill 1939- *Ballpl 90*
Stafford, Brenda Joyce 1941- *WhoSSW 91*
Stafford, Byron Donald 1946- *WhoWrEP 89*
Stafford, C. Richard 1935- *St&PR 91*
Stafford, Carlene Roussel 1952- *WhoAmW 91*
Stafford, Donald Gene 1930- *WhoAm 90*
Stafford, Ernest Kay, Jr. 1946- *St&PR 91*
Stafford, Fiona 1960- *ConAu 131*
Stafford, Frank Peter, Jr. 1940- *WhoAm 90*
Stafford, Gary Curtis 1946- *WhoWor 91*
Stafford, Gilbert Wayne 1938- *ConAu 31NR*
Stafford, Godfrey Harry 1920- *WhoWor 91*
Stafford, Helen Elizabeth Thomson 1926- *WhoAmW 91*
Stafford, J. Francis 1932- *WhoAm 90*
Stafford, James Polk, Jr. 1918- *WhoSSW 91*
Stafford, Jan 1951- *WhoWrEP 89*
Stafford, Jean 1915-1979 *BioAmW, BioIn 16, FemiCLE, MajTwCW, WorAlBi*
Stafford, Jo *WhoAm 90*
Stafford, Jo 1918- *WorAlBi*
Stafford, Jo 1920- *BioIn 16, OxCPMus*
Stafford, Joel Lindsey 1946- *WhoSSW 91*
Stafford, John Richard *BiDrAPA 89*
Stafford, John Rogers 1937- *St&PR 91, WhoAm 90, WhoE 91*
Stafford, John Warner 1932- *St&PR 91*
Stafford, Leonor Maldonado 1948- *WhoHisp 91*
Stafford, Marilyn *WhoWrEP 89*
Stafford, Nancy *BioIn 16*
Stafford, P. Gordon 1934- *St&PR 91*
Stafford, Paul Gordon 1934- *WhoAm 90*
Stafford, Rebecca 1936- *WhoAm 90, WhoAmW 91*
Stafford, Robert Mc Kinley, Jr. 1952- *WhoWrEP 89*
Stafford, Robert Neil 1940- *St&PR 91*
Stafford, Robert T. *BioIn 16*
Stafford, Robert Theodore 1913- *WhoAm 90*
Stafford, Russell Bennett 1936- *WhoWrEP 89*
Stafford, Thomas P. 1930- *WorAlBi*
Stafford, Thomas Patten 1930- *WhoAm 90*
Stafford, Will Elbert 1935- *WhoSSW 91*
Stafford, William Edgar 1914- *WhoAm 90, WhoWrEP 89*
Stafford, William Henry, Jr. 1931- *WhoAm 90, WhoSSW 91*
Stafford, William Talmadge 1924- *WhoAm 90, WhoWrEP 89*
Stafford-Clark, David 1916- *EncO&P 3*
Staffrude, Paul R. 1953- *St&PR 91*
Stafleu, Frans Antonie 1921- *WhoWor 91*
Stage Door Jimmy *ConAu 132*
Stage, Thomas B 1926- *BiDrAPA 89*
Stage, Thomas Benton 1926- *WhoAm 90*
Stage, William Syms 1947- *BiDrAPA 89*
Stagel, Elsbeth 13--?-1360? *EncCoWW*
Stagell, Daniel L. 1954- *St&PR 91*
Stagen, Mary-Patricia Healy 1955- *WhoAmW 91*
Stager, Alan N. 1949- *St&PR 91*
Stager, Lawrence E. 1943- *WhoAm 90*
Stagg, Amos Alonzo 1862-1965 *WorAlBi*
Stagg, Evelyn Wheeler 1916- *WhoAmW 91*
Stagg, Jessie A 1891-1958 *WhoAmA 91N*
Stagg, Louis Charles 1933- *WhoSSW 91*
Stagg, Tom 1923- *WhoAm 90, WhoSSW 91*
Stagg Bremm, Hazel G. *BioIn 16*
Stagge, Jonathan *TwCCr&M 91*
Staggers, Harley O., Jr. 1951- *WhoAm 90, WhoSSW 91*
Staggers, William A. Fort 1956- *St&PR 91*
Staggs, David G. 1937- *St&PR 91*
Staggs, Gary L. 1953- *St&PR 91*
Staggs, Sari *BioIn 16*
Staglin, Garen Kent 1944- *St&PR 91, WhoAm 90*
Stagman, Barry William 1946- *WhoWor 91*
Stagmeier, Terry Daniels 1948- *WhoAmW 91*
Stagmer, Holly J. 1951- *St&PR 91*
Stagnelius, Erik Johan 1793-1823 *DcScanL*
Stagner, David Lowell 1949- *BiDrAPA 89*
Stagner, John Irvin, III 1944- *WhoSSW 91*
Stagno, Susan Jorve 1954- *BiDrAPA 89*
Stagnolia, Kathi Blanton 1964- *WhoAmW 91*
Stahancyk, Jody Lee 1948- *WhoAmW 91*
Stahel, Urs 1953- *WhoWor 91*
Stahel, Walter Rudolf 1946- *WhoWor 91*
Staheli, Lana Ribble 1947- *WhoAmW 91*
Stahl, Adele Grace 1908-1983 *BioIn 16*
Stahl, Alan Glenn 1945- *WhoE 91*
Stahl, Alan M 1947- *WhoAmA 91*
Stahl, Alan Michael 1947- *WhoE 91*
Stahl, Alice S 1913- *BiDrAPA 89*
Stahl, Alice Slater 1913- *WhoE 91*
Stahl, Angelique O. *St&PR 91*
Stahl, Baruch 1949- *WhoWor 91*
Stahl, Ben 1910-1987 *BioIn 16*
Stahl, Betty Patricia 1951- *WhoEmL 91*
Stahl, Caroline Love 1943- *WhoSSW 91*
Stahl, Chester Wesley 1926- *St&PR 91*
Stahl, Chick 1873-1907 *Ballpl 90 [port]*
Stahl, David 1949- *IntWWM 90, WhoAm 90, WhoSSW 91*
Stahl, David Bohus, Sr. 1935- *St&PR 91*
Stahl, David Edward 1934- *WhoAm 90*
Stahl, David L. 1914- *St&PR 91*
Stahl, Edward T. 1947- *St&PR 91*
Stahl, Frank Ludwig 1920- *WhoAm 90*
Stahl, Fred F. 1937- *St&PR 91*
Stahl, Georg Ernst 1660-1734 *WorAlBi*
Stahl, Glenn W. 1913- *St&PR 91*
Stahl, Heinrich 1868-1942 *BioIn 16*
Stahl, Henriette Yvonne 1900- *EncCoWW*
Stahl, Henry George 1902- *WhoAm 90*
Stahl, Hilda 1938- *BioIn 16*
Stahl, Jack Leland 1934- *WhoAm 90*
Stahl, Jake 1879-1922 *Ballpl 90*
Stahl, Joe *BioIn 16*
Stahl, Joel S. 1918- *St&PR 91*
Stahl, Joel Sol 1918- *WhoWor 91*
Stahl, John Daniel 1952- *WhoSSW 91*
Stahl, Julie Beth *BiDrAPA 89*
Stahl, Kevin A *BiDrAPA 89*
Stahl, Laddie L. 1921- *WhoAm 90*
Stahl, Larry 1941- *Ballpl 90*
Stahl, Lars G. 1940- *WhoWor 91*
Stahl, Leonard 1930- *ODwPR 91*
Stahl, Lesley 1941- *WorAlBi*
Stahl, Lesley R. 1941- *WhoAm 90, WhoAmW 91, WhoE 91*
Stahl, Louis Edmund 1914- *WhoWor 91*
Stahl, Marc P. 1935- *St&PR 91*
Stahl, Oscar Glenn 1910- *WhoAm 90*
Stahl, Philip Damien 1941- *WhoAm 90*
Stahl, Philip E *BiDrAPA 89*
Stahl, Randy Dean *BiDrAPA 89*
Stahl, Ray Emerson 1917- *WhoSSW 91*
Stahl, Raymond W. 1926- *WhoAm 90*
Stahl, Richard Alan 1929- *St&PR 91*
Stahl, Richard G. C. 1934- *WhoAm 90*
Stahl, Robert 1927- *St&PR 91*
Stahl, Robert Alan 1942- *WhoE 91*
Stahl, Ronald Albert 1946- *St&PR 91*
Stahl, Rose 1870-1955 *OxCCanT*
Stahl, Roy 1952- *St&PR 91*
Stahl, Ruthanne 1939- *WhoAmW 91, WhoSSW 91*
Stahl, Stephen Michael *BiDrAPA 89*
Stahl, Theresa 1936- *WhoAmW 91*
Stahle, Donald Winslow 1935- *St&PR 91*
Stahle, Galen Wayne 1941- *BiDrAPA 89*
Stahlecker, Franz Walter 1900-1942 *BioIn 16*
Stahler, Charles *WhoWrEP 89*
Stahler, T. Richard 1941- *ODwPR 91*
Stahlfors, Ake Georg Axel 1937- *WhoWor 91*
Stahlheber, Sharon A. 1952- *ODwPR 91*
Stahlin, Paul V. 1952- *St&PR 91*
Stahlman, Mildred Thornton 1922- *WhoAm 90*
Stahlman, Sylvia 1929- *IntWWM 90*
Stahly, James A. 1940- *ODwPR 91*
Stahmann, Mark Arnold 1914- *WhoAm 90*
Stahmann, Robert F. 1939- *WhoAm 90*
Stahmer, Harold Martin, Jr. 1929- *WhoAm 90*
Stahmer, Robert T. 1924- *St&PR 91*
Stahmer, Ward Raymond 1950- *St&PR 91*
Stahr, Curtis Brent 1946- *WhoEmL 91, WhoWor 91*
Stahr, Elvis Jacob, Jr. 1916- *WhoAm 90, WhoWor 91*
Staiano, Edward Frank 1936- *St&PR 91*
Staicovici, Ianca 1947- *IntWWM 90*
Staicu, Paul 1937- *IntWWM 90*
Staiger, Bonnie Larson 1947- *WhoAmW 91*
Staiger, James Leroy *BiDrAPA 89*
Staiger, Ralph Conrad 1917- *WhoAm 90*
Staikos, Lambros Nicolaos 1941- *WhoWor 91*
Stainback, John Philip 1948- *WhoWor 91*
Stainback, Susan Bray 1947- *ConAu 31NR*
Stainback, Tuck 1910- *Ballpl 90*
Stainback, William 1943- *ConAu 31NR*
Stainbrook, Edward *BiDrAPA 89*
Staine, Ross 1924- *WhoAm 90*
Stainer, John 1840-1901 *BioIn 16*
Staines, David McKenzie 1946- *WhoAm 90*
Staines, Laura Catherine 1953- *WhoAmW 91*
Staines, Trevor *MajTwCW*
Stair, Charles William 1940- *WhoAm 90*
Stair, Frederick Rogers 1918- *WhoAm 90*
Stair, Gobin 1912- *WhoAm 90*
Stair, Randel Nelson 1950- *St&PR 91*
Stairs, Denis Winfield 1939- *WhoAm 90*
Stairs, Gerald *WhoAm 90*
Stairway *NewAgMG*
Stajduhar, Peter P *BiDrAPA 89*
Stajner, Karlo 1902- *BioIn 16*
Stake, Robert Eric 1950- *BiDrAPA 89*
Stakelin, William L. *BioIn 16*
Staker, Robert Jackson 1925- *WhoAm 90, WhoSSW 91*
Stakes, Richard Stewart 1923- *WhoAm 90*
Stakgold, Ivar 1925- *WhoAm 90*
Stalberg, John M *BiDrAPA 89*
Stalberg, Zachary 1947- *St&PR 91*
Stalcup, Joe Alan 1931- *WhoAm 90*
Stalder, Florence Lucille 1920- *WhoAmW 91*
Stalder, Hans Rudolf 1930- *IntWWM 90*
Staley, Allen Percival Green 1935- *WhoAm 90*
Staley, Augustus Eugene, III 1928- *WhoAm 90*
Staley, Charles Ralls 1938- *WhoAm 90*
Staley, Christopher 1954- *BioIn 16*
Staley, Christopher P 1954- *WhoAmA 91*
Staley, Delbert C. 1924- *St&PR 91, WhoAm 90, WhoE 91*
Staley, Elaine Mary 1943- *WhoAmW 91*
Staley, Eugene Alvah 1906-1989 *BioIn 16*
Staley, Gerry 1920- *Ballpl 90*
Staley, Henry Mueller 1932- *WhoAm 90*
Staley, Kenneth Bernard 1948- *WhoE 91*
Staley, Oren Lee 1923-1988 *BioIn 16*
Staley, Paul L. 1930- *St&PR 91*
Staley, Paul R. 1929- *St&PR 91*
Staley, Robert Eric 1947- *WhoSSW 91*
Staley, Robert W *BiDrAPA 89*
Staley, Robert W. 1935- *WhoAm 90*
Staley, Robert Wayne 1935- *St&PR 91*
Staley, Robin Cheryl 1954- *St&PR 91*
Staley, Thomas F 1935- *ConAu 30NR*
Staley, Thomas Fabian 1935- *WhoAm 90*
Stalfort, John Alfred, II 1946- *WhoSSW 91*
Stalfort, John Arthur 1951- *WhoEmL 91*
Stalin, Joseph 1879-1953 *BioIn 16, WorAlBi*
Stalker, Alfred Joseph 1906- *WhoAm 90*
Stalker, Jacqueline D'Aoust 1933- *WhoAmW 91*
Stalker, John *BioIn 16*
Stalker, John, and Parker, George *PenDiDA 89*
Stalker, Suzy Wooster 1948- *WhoAmW 91*
Stalkup, Fred Irving, Jr. 1936- *WhoAm 90*
Stall, Alan David 1951- *WhoEmL 91, WhoWor 91*
Stall, Dorothy *AuBYP 90*
Stall, Richard *BiDrAPA 89*
Stallaerts, Robert 1947- *WhoWor 91*
Stallard, Carl Eldon 1929- *St&PR 91*
Stallard, Glenn E. 1922- *St&PR 91*
Stallard, Hugh R. 1937- *WhoAm 90, WhoSSW 91*
Stallard, Richard Elgin 1934- *WhoWor 91*
Stallard, Tracy 1937- *Ballpl 90*
Stallard, Troy Francis 1944- *St&PR 91*
Stallcup, Virgil 1922- *Ballpl 90*
Stallcup, William Blackburn, Jr. 1920- *WhoAm 90*
Staller, Eric P 1947- *WhoAmA 91*
Staller, Jud Adam 1951- *BiDrAPA 89*
Stalling, Gustav H., III 1930- *St&PR 91*
Stallings, Charles Edgar 1941- *BiDrAPA 89*
Stallings, Charles Henry 1941- *St&PR 91*
Stallings, Frank, Jr. 1954- *WhoSSW 91*
Stallings, Gene Clifton 1935- *WhoAm 90*
Stallings, George 1867-1929 *Ballpl 90 [port]*
Stallings, George A., Jr. *BioIn 16*
Stallings, George A., Jr. 1948- *News 90 [port]*
Stallings, James H. *NewYTBS 90*
Stallings, Jesse Daniel 1915- *WhoSSW 91*
Stallings, Jimmy Ellwood 1944- *WhoSSW 91*
Stallings, Jo Alessi 1934- *St&PR 91*
Stallings, Jody W., Jr. 1957- *WhoSSW 91*
Stallings, Larry Joseph 1941- *St&PR 91*
Stallings, Laurence 1894- *WorAlBi*
Stallings, Norman 1914- *WhoAm 90*
Stallings, Richard Howard 1940- *WhoAm 90*
Stallings, Ronald Denis 1943- *WhoAm 90*
Stallings, Sandra Petersen 1948- *WhoSSW 91*
Stallings-Dorsett, Mary Ellen 1941- *WhoAmW 91*
Stallkamp, James Hubert 1936- *St&PR 91*
Stallman, Alvin 1929- *St&PR 91*
Stallman, Emma S 1888-1959 *WhoAmA 91N*
Stallman, Robert Wooster, Jr. 1946- *IntWWM 90*
Stallmeyer, James Edward 1926- *WhoAm 90*
Stallone, Jacqueline *BioIn 16*
Stallone, Susan Beth 1961- *WhoAmW 91*
Stallone, Sylvester *BioIn 16*
Stallone, Sylvester 1946- *ConTFT 8 [port], WorAlBi*
Stallone, Sylvester Enzio 1946- *WhoAm 90*
Stallwitz, Carolyn 1936- *WhoAmA 91*
Stallworth, Alma Grace *WhoAmW 91*
Stallworth, Doris A. Carter 1932- *WhoAmW 91*
Stallworth, John *BioIn 16*
Stallworth, Nicholas Jack 1920- *St&PR 91*
Stallworth, Nicholas R *BiDrAPA 89*
Stallworth, Terresa *BiDrAPA 89*
Stallworthy, Jon Howie 1935- *WhoWrEP 89*
Stalmack, Lawrence S. 1948- *St&PR 91*
Stalman, Roger Claude 1927- *IntWWM 90*
Stalnaker, Armand C. 1916- *St&PR 91*
Stalnaker, Armand Carl 1916- *WhoAm 90*
Stalnaker, John M. *NewYTBS 90*
Stalnaker, John M 1903-1990 *CurBio 90N*
Stalnaker, John Marshall 1903- *WhoAm 90*
Stalnaker, Judith Ann 1942- *WhoAmW 91*
Stalnecker, Mark E. 1951- *St&PR 91*
Stalnecker, Mark Eric 1951- *WhoAm 90*
Staloch, James Edward, Jr. 1946- *WhoEmL 91*
Staloff, Arnold Fred 1944- *WhoAm 90*
Stalon, Charles Gary 1929- *WhoE 91*
Stalowicz, Bruce Thomas 1953- *WhoE 91*
Stalsberg, Geraldine McEwen 1936- *WhoAmW 91*
Staluppi, John *BioIn 16*
Stalvey, Harold D *BiDrAPA 89*
Stalzer, David 1914- *WhoWrEP 89*
Stalzer, Richard Francis 1936- *WhoE 91*
Stalzer, Robert Joseph 1942- *St&PR 91*
Stalzer, Susan Marie 1958- *BiDrAPA 89*
Stam, Barbara H. 1942- *WhoSSW 91*
Stam, David Harry 1935- *WhoAm 90*
Stam, Hendrikus Gerardus 1922- *IntWWM 90*
Stam, Mart 1899-1986 *PenDiDA 89*
Stam, Medeleine *BiDrAPA 89*
Stamas, Stephen 1931- *St&PR 91, WhoAm 90*
Stamatakis, Carol Marie 1960- *WhoAmW 91*
Stamato, Philomena M. 1958- *WhoEmL 91*
Stamatovich, Constantine 1924- *BiDrAPA 89*
Stamats, Peter Owen 1929- *St&PR 91, WhoAmA 91*
Stamaty, Mark Alan 1947- *EncACom, WhoAm 90*
Stamaty, Stanley 1916-1979 *WhoAmA 91N*
Stambaugh, Armstrong A., Jr. 1920- *WhoAm 90*
Stambaugh, Charles Lee 1945- *St&PR 91*
Stambaugh, Curvin Donald 1939- *WhoE 91*
Stambaugh, John E. *BioIn 16*
Stambaugh, John Edgar 1940- *WhoE 91*
Stambaugh, Perry Allen 1960- *WhoWrEP 89*
Stambaugh, Reginald Jack 1930- *WhoSSW 91, WhoWor 91*
Stamberg, Arthur Jay 1934- *St&PR 91*
Stamberg, Susan Levitt 1938- *WhoAm 90*
Stamberger, Edwin Henry 1916- *WhoWor 91*
Stambler, Irwin 1924- *AuBYP 90, WhoWrEP 89*
Stambler, Morris J L 1943- *BiDrAPA 89*
Stambler, Peter Lane 1944- *WhoWrEP 89*
Stambone, Lisa Marie 1964- *WhoE 91*
Stamboulian, Marcia Ann 1951- *WhoAmW 91*
Stamell, Benjamin B 1911- *BiDrAPA 89*
Stamelman, Richard Howard 1942- *WhoAm 90*
Stamelos, Electra Georgia Mousmoules *WhoAmA 91*
Stamenova, Galina 1958- *IntWWM 90*
Stamenova, Tsvetanha T *BiDrAPA 89*
Stamer, Howard 1929- *St&PR 91*
Stamey, William Gregg, Jr. 1962- *WhoSSW 91*
Stamler, Jeremiah 1919- *WhoAm 90*
Stamler, John H. 1938-1990 *BioIn 16*
Stamler, William Raymond 1934- *St&PR 91*
Stamm, Alan 1931- *WhoAm 90*
Stamm, Geoffrey Eaton 1943- *WhoAmA 91*
Stamm, Harald 1938- *IntWWM 90*
Stamm, Henry Otto 1919- *WhoWor 91*
Stamm, John Robert *BiDrAPA 89*
Stamm, Julian L 1916- *BiDrAPA 89*
Stamm, Patricia Jane 1948- *BiDrAPA 89*
Stamm, Robert Calvin 1925- *WhoSSW 91*
Stamm, Robert J. 1921- *St&PR 91*

Stamm, Robert Jenne 1921- WhoAm 90
Stamm, Russell 1915-1969 EncACom
Stammer, Roger Wilbert 1938- St&PR 91
Stamminger, Gudrun Mathilde 1943- WhoWor 91
Stamoolis, Gus 1940- St&PR 91
Stamos, John BioIn 16
Stamos, John James 1924- WhoAm 90
Stamos, M. 1932- St&PR 91
Stamos, Theodoros 1922- WhoAm 90, WhoAmA 91
Stamp, Frederick Pfarr, Jr. 1934- St&PR 91
Stamp, Neal Roger 1918- WhoAm 90
Stamp, Terence 1939- WorAlBi
Stamp, Terence 1940- BioIn 16
Stamp, Terence Henry 1938- WhoWor 91
Stamp, Warren Gene 1926- WhoAm 90
Stamp, Zack BioIn 16
Stampa, Gaspara 1524?-1554 EncCoWW
Stamper, Dave 1883-1963 OxCPMus
Stamper, David Harold 1954- WhoSSW 91
Stamper, James Henri 1954- WhoSSW 91
Stamper, James Walter 1932- St&PR 91
Stamper, Joe Allen 1914- WhoAm 90
Stamper, Lori 1959- WhoWrEP 89
Stamper, Malcolm T. 1925- St&PR 91
Stamper, Malcolm Theodore 1925- WhoAm 90
Stamper, Wilson Young 1912-1988 WhoAmA 91N
Stamperius, Hannemieke EncCoWW
Stampfer, Meir Jonathan 1950- WhoE 91
Stampfl, Rudolf Alois 1926- WhoAm 90
Stampfle, Felice 1912- WhoAmA 91
Stampfli, Jakob 1934- IntWWM 90
Stampley, Jan Orkney 1947- BiDrAPA 89
Stampley, Norris Lochlen 1920- WhoAm 90
Stampp, Kenneth Milton 1912- WhoAm 90
Stamps, E. Roe, IV 1946- St&PR 91
Stamps, George Moreland 1924- WhoWor 91
Stamps, Thomas Paty 1952- WhoEmL 91, WhoSSW 91, WhoWor 91
Stams, Frank BioIn 16
Stamsta, Jean 1936- WhoAmA 91
Stan, Patricia 1952- WhoEmL 91
Stanage, Oscar 1883-1964 Ballpl 90
Stanaland, Sandra Lee 1946- WhoAmW 91
Stanaland, William Whit, Jr. 1930- WhoSSW 91, WhoWor 91
Stanard, H. Michael 1945- WhoEmL 91
Stanard, James Northrup 1948- WhoE 91
Stanat, Donald F. 1937- WhoAm 90
Stanat, Ruth Ellen 1947- WhoE 91
Stanaway, Anne 1931- WhoE 91
Stanback, Fred St&PR 91
Stanberry, Mark Chauncy BiDrAPA 89
Stanberry, Robert Mitchell 1940- St&PR 91
Stanbery, Henry 1803-1881 BiDrUSE 89
Stanbridge, Harry Andrew 1943- WhoAmA 91
Stanbridge, Roger P. 1941- St&PR 91
Stanbury, H. Norman 1911- St&PR 91
Stanbury, John Bruton 1915- WhoAm 90
Stanbury, Robert Douglas George 1929- WhoAm 90
Stancel, Charles John 1935- St&PR 91
Stanch, James Michael BiDrAPA 89
Stanchi, Edward Francis BiDrAPA 89
Stancil, John Luther 1946- WhoSSW 91
Stancill, James McNeill 1932- WhoAm 90
Stancliffe, Floyd S 1916- BiDrAPA 89
Stanculescu, Victor Atanasie WhoWor 91
Stanczak, Julian 1928- WhoAm 90, WhoAmA 91
Stanczyk, Ann Maria 1948- IntWWM 90
Standaert, Frank George 1929- WhoAm 90
Standaert, James Victor 1938- St&PR 91
Standage, Simon 1941- IntWWM 90
Standard, Elizabeth Newton 1963- WhoAmW 91
Standard, James Noel 1940- WhoAm 90
Standard, Mary Russell 1926- WhoAmW 91
Standard, Raymond Linwood 1925- WhoAm 90
Standberry, Herman Lee 1945- WhoEmL 91, WhoWor 91
Standbridge, Peter Thomas 1934- WhoAm 90
Standefer, Betty Jean Albury 1951- WhoAmW 91
Standel, Richard Reynold, Jr. 1936- St&PR 91, WhoAm 90
Standen, Edith Appleton 1905- WhoAmA 91, WhoE 91
Standen, John Francis 1948- WhoWor 91
Standen, Michael Alan 1937- St&PR 91
Standen, Nika BioIn 16
Standen, Richard IntWWM 90
Stander, Joseph William 1928- WhoAm 90
Stander, Richard Wright 1922- WhoAm 90
Stander, Siegfried 1935- WorAu 1980 [port]
Stander, Stephen F. 1943- St&PR 91
Standerford, Marilyn Sue 1957- WhoAmW 91
Standfast, Susan Jane 1935- WhoAmW 91
Standford, Patric 1939- IntWWM 90
Standifer, John James 1928- BiDrAPA 89
Standifer, Noah Orval 1950- WhoSSW 91
Standiford, Lester Alan 1945- WhoSSW 91
Standig, Harold 1921- St&PR 91
Standing Bear 1829?-1908 WhNaAH
Standing Buffalo, Chief 1833?-1871 BioIn 16
Standing, Sue 1952- WhoWrEP 89
Standing Bear, Zugguelgeres Galafach 1941- WhoSSW 91
Standish, Buck ConAu 31NR
Standish, Burt L. 1866-1945 Ballpl 90
Standish, Carole ConAu 30NR
Standish, Craig Peter 1953- WhoWrEP 89
Standish, J. Spencer 1925- St&PR 91
Standish, John Spencer 1925- WhoAm 90
Standish, Linda S. 1952- St&PR 91
Standish, Linda Sue 1952- WhoAmW 91
Standish, Miles 1584?-1656 EncCRAm, WhNaAH, WorAlBi
Standish, Samuel Miles 1923- WhoAm 90
Standish, Victor J. 1936- St&PR 91
Standish, William Lloyd 1930- WhoE 91, WhoWor 91
Standlee, Joe Ann 1935- WhoSSW 91
Standley, Doc 1845-1908 BioIn 16
Standley, Gilbert Danfield 1959- WhoEmL 91
Standley, Jayne Marsh 1944- WhoSSW 91
Standley, Jeremiah BioIn 16
Standley, William Harrison 1872-1963 BioIn 16
Standow, Hans W 1920- BiDrAPA 89
Standridge, George M. 1937- St&PR 91
Standridge, Kim Diane 1957- WhoEmL 91, WhoSSW 91, WhoWor 91
Standring, James Douglas 1951- WhoWor 91
Standwill, Nancy Anne 1965- WhoE 91
Staneff, K Steven BiDrAPA 89
Stanek, Alan Edward 1939- IntWWM 90, WhoAm 90
Stanek, Lou Willett 1931- SmATA 63 [port]
Stanek, Martha L. 1946- WhoSSW 91
Stanek, Vladimir 1939- WhoWor 91
Stanev, Emilian 1907-1979 AuBYP 90
Stanfield, Clyde E 1915- BiDrAPA 89
Stanfield, Elizabeth Poplin 1930- WhoSSW 91
Stanfield, F. Thomas 1943- St&PR 91
Stanfield, Jack Gordon 1942- WhoSSW 91
Stanfield, John Richard 1931- St&PR 91
Stanfield, Myres Tarry 1946- WhoSSW 91
Stanfield, Rebecca Jo 1954- WhoSSW 91
Stanfield, Robert Lorne 1914- BioIn 16
Stanfield, Sally Fite 1956- WhoEmL 91
Stanfill, Dennis C. 1927- St&PR 91
Stanfill, Dennis Carothers 1927- WhoAm 90
Stanford, A. Leland 1824-1893 WorAlBi
Stanford, Ann 1916-1987 ConAu 32NR, FemiCLE
Stanford, Charles Villiers 1852-1924 BioIn 16, PenDiMP A
Stanford, Daniel William 1954- St&PR 91
Stanford, Dennis Joe 1943- WhoAm 90
Stanford, Donald Elwin 1913- WhoAm 90, WhoWrEP 89
Stanford, Donald Harvey BiDrAPA 89
Stanford, Eddie BiDrAPA 89
Stanford, G.K., Jr. BiDrAPA 89
Stanford, George A 1909- BiDrAPA 89
Stanford, Ginny C 1950- WhoAmA 91
Stanford, Henry King 1916- WhoAm 90
Stanford, Jack Arthur 1947- WhoEmL 91
Stanford, James M. WhoAm 90
Stanford, Jamie Farrell 1952- WhoSSW 91
Stanford, Jane Lathrop 1828-1905 BioAmW
Stanford, John Leonard 1935- WhoAm 90
Stanford, Kenneth Charles 1955- WhoEmL 91
Stanford, Kenneth L. 1947- WhoSSW 91
Stanford, Kimberley Alice 1954- WhoAmW 91
Stanford, Linda Oliphant 1946- WhoAmA 91
Stanford, Lydia Ann 1958- WhoEmL 91
Stanford, Melvin Joseph 1932- WhoAm 90, WhoWor 91
Stanford, Peter 1927- WhoE 91
Stanford, Ray 1938- EncPaPR 91
Stanford, Rex G 1938- EncO&P 3, EncPaPR 91
Stanford, Rose Mary 1942- WhoAmW 91
Stanford, Thomas Welton 1832-1918 EncPaPR 91
Stanforth, Melvin Sidney 1937- WhoAmA 91
Stang, Ivan 1949- ConAu 129
Stang, John H. 1944- St&PR 91
Stang, Judy Ann 1963- WhoAmW 91
Stang, Patrick William 1961- BiDrAPA 89
Stang, Richard 1925- WhoWrEP 89
Stang, Sondra J. 1928- ConAu 131
Stanga, Buckli Marlu 1967- WhoAmW 91
Stange, Dennis Earle 1952- WhoEmL 91
Stange, Lee 1936- Ballpl 90
Stange, Luise Magdalene Christine 1926- WhoWor 91
Stange, Richard Thomas 1947- St&PR 91
Stangeland, Arlan Inghart 1930- WhoAm 90
Stangeland, Ludvig Bernhard 1923- WhoWor 91
Stangeland, Ole Ingvaldson 1903- WhoWor 91
Stangeland, Roger E. 1929- St&PR 91
Stangeland, Roger Earl 1929- WhoAm 90
Stanger, Abraham M. 1921- WhoAm 90
Stanger, David N. 1926- WhoAm 90
Stanger, Douglas Scott 1956- WhoEmL 91
Stanger, Ila 1940- WhoAm 90, WhoWrEP 89
Stanger, John W. 1923- St&PR 91
Stanger, John William 1923- WhoAm 90
Stanger, Melvin 1935- BiDrAPA 89
Stanger, Paul Norman 1944- St&PR 91
Stanger, Robert H 1937- BiDrAPA 89
Stanger, Robert Henry 1937- WhoE 91
Stanger, Wesley A., Jr. 1909- St&PR 91
Stangerup, Helle 1939- ConAu 132
Stangl, Franz 1908-1971 BioIn 16
Stangl, Peter 1936- WhoAm 90
Stangle, James F. 1948- St&PR 91
Stangler, Ferdinand 1928- WhoWor 91
Stangler, Greg Frank 1960- WhoEmL 91
Stangler, Kevin John 1948- St&PR 91
Stangler, Ronnie Sue 1946- BiDrAPA 89
Stangos, Nicolas 1936- WhoWor 91
Stanhagen, William H. 1928- St&PR 91
Stanhaus, James Steven 1945- WhoEmL 91
Stanhope, David 1952- IntWWM 90
Stanhope, E. Raymond 1932- St&PR 91
Stanhope, Eugenia 1730?-1786 FemiCLE
Stanhope, Hester 1776-1839 FemiCLE
Stanhope, Hester Lucy 1776-1839 BioIn 16
Stanhope, Louisa Sidney FemiCLE
Stanhope, Russell C. BioIn 16
Stanhouse, Don 1951- Ballpl 90
Staniar, Burton B. 1942- St&PR 91, WhoAm 90
Staniar, Linda B. ODwPR 91
Stanich, Stephen E. 1952- St&PR 91
Stanig, Gerald Joseph 1944- WhoE 91
Stanis, Bernnadette 1953- DrBlPA 90
Stanisci, Thomas William 1928- WhoE 91
Stanisic, Milomir Mirkov 1914- WhoAm 90
Stanislao, Joseph 1928- WhoAm 90
Stanislaus WhNaAH
Stanislaus, Lamuel Arnold 1921- WhoWor 91
Stanislavsky, Konstantin 1863-1938 BioIn 16, WorAlBi
Stanislaw, Richard K. 1949- St&PR 91
Stanislawa, P. EncO&P 3
Stanislawska, Anna 1651?-1701? EncCoWW
Stanistreet, Grace M. 1902-1984 BioIn 16, NotWoAT
Stanitsky, N. EncCoWW
Stank, Gerald J. 1947- St&PR 91, WhoAm 90
Stanka, Joe BioIn 16
Stankaitis, Joseph Alfonsas 1952- WhoE 91
Stankard, Francis Xavier 1932- WhoAm 90
Stanke, Howard Joseph 1948- St&PR 91
Stankey, Suzanne M. 1951- WhoAm 90, WhoAmW 91
Stankiewicz, Richard Peter 1922-1983 WhoAmA 91N
Stankiewicz, Wladyslaw Jozef 1922- WhoAm 90
Stanklus, Gary L. St&PR 91
Stanko, Kenneth Mark 1949- BiDrAPA 89, WhoE 91
Stankovic, Milorad Dragutin 1928- WhoWor 91
Stankowski, Anton 1906- ConDes 90
Stankus-Saulaitis, Algirdas 1950- WhoE 91
Stanky, Eddie 1916- Ballpl 90
Stankye, C.M., Jr. 1933- St&PR 91
Stanlake, George Frederick 1919- WhoWor 91
Stanley, Alfred M BiDrAPA 89
Stanley, Arthur Jehu, Jr. 1901- WhoAm 90
Stanley, Bennett TwCCr&M 91
Stanley, Bob 1932- WhoAm 90, WhoAmA 91
Stanley, Bob 1954- Ballpl 90
Stanley, Brian Keith 1950- WhoEmL 91
Stanley, Carl M. 1935- St&PR 91
Stanley, Catherine 1792-1862 FemiCLE
Stanley, Charles J. 1943- WhoWrEP 89
Stanley, Clifford W. 1946- St&PR 91
Stanley, D. FemiCLE
Stanley, Daniel Calvin, Jr 1948- WhoEmL 91
Stanley, Daniel Jean 1934- WhoAm 90, WhoE 91
Stanley, David 1935- St&PR 91, WhoAm 90
Stanley, Dean Peter 1935- St&PR 91
Stanley, Deborah Alexander 1952- WhoAmW 91
Stanley, Diane 1943- BioIn 16, ConAu 32NR
Stanley, Edmund A., Jr. 1924- St&PR 91
Stanley, Edmund Allport, Jr. 1924- WhoAm 90
Stanley, Edward BioIn 16
Stanley, Edward Alexander 1929- WhoAm 90, WhoWor 91
Stanley, Edward L. 1916- St&PR 91
Stanley, Elizabeth FemiCLE
Stanley, Ellis Early 1926- St&PR 91
Stanley, Ernest James 1938- BiDrAPA 89
Stanley, Francis E 1849-1918 EncABHB 4 [port], WorAlBi
Stanley, Fred 1947- Ballpl 90
Stanley, Freelan O 1849-1940 EncABHB 4 [port], WorAlBi
Stanley, Furman K., Jr. 1942- St&PR 91
Stanley, George Edward 1942- BioIn 16
Stanley, George F. 1929- St&PR 91
Stanley, George Taylor 1950- WhoSSW 91
Stanley, Harold Watkins 1950- WhoE 91
Stanley, Harriett Lari 1950- St&PR 91
Stanley, Harry Eugene 1941- WhoAm 90, WhoWor 91
Stanley, Helen Camille 1930- IntWWM 90
Stanley, Henry M. 1841-1904 BioIn 16, WorAlBi
Stanley, Henry Morton 1841-1904 EncPaPR 91
Stanley, Henry T., Jr. 1936- ODwPR 91
Stanley, Hugh Monroe, Jr. 1944- WhoAm 90
Stanley, J. Wayne 1946- St&PR 91
Stanley, James Alan 1952- St&PR 91
Stanley, James Gordon 1925- WhoSSW 91
Stanley, James Paul 1915- WhoAm 90
Stanley, James R. 1931- St&PR 91
Stanley, James Richard 1931- WhoAm 90
Stanley, Jamie BioIn 16
Stanley, Jean Agatha Fuller 1951- WhoAmW 91
Stanley, Jean Cooper 1953- WhoAmW 91
Stanley, Joel Francis 1934- WhoSSW 91
Stanley, John 1914- EncACom
Stanley, John Harlan 1936- BiDrAPA 89
Stanley, John Jacob 1929- WhoAmA 91
Stanley, John Maxwell 1936- St&PR 91
Stanley, John Mix 1814-1872 WhNaAH
Stanley, John R. 1939- WhoAm 90
Stanley, John W. 1940- WhoWrEP 89
Stanley, John Walker 1906- St&PR 91
Stanley, Julian Cecil, Jr. 1918- WhoAm 90
Stanley, Justin Armstrong 1911- WhoAm 90, WhoWor 91
Stanley, Kendra Eunice 1936- WhoAmW 91
Stanley, Kim 1925- BioIn 16, NotWoAT, WhoAmW 91, WorAlBi
Stanley, LaNett Lorraine 1962- WhoAmW 91
Stanley, Lawrence 1947- St&PR 91
Stanley, LeAnn 1952- WhoSSW 91
Stanley, Lisa Ann 1965- WhoAmW 91
Stanley, Lisa Marie 1960- WhoAmW 91
Stanley, Louise BioIn 16
Stanley, M Louise 1942- WhoAmA 91
Stanley, Malchan Craig 1948- WhoEmL 91
Stanley, Margaret Dureta Sexton 1931- WhoWor 91
Stanley, Margaret King 1929- WhoAmW 91
Stanley, Mark BioIn 16
Stanley, Mark James 1955- WhoE 91
Stanley, Marlyse Reed 1934- WhoWor 91
Stanley, Mary 1919-1980 FemiCLE
Stanley, Mickey 1942- Ballpl 90
Stanley, Mike 1963- Ballpl 90
Stanley, Pamela Mary 1947- WhoAmW 91
Stanley, Patricia Mary 1948- WhoAmW 91
Stanley, Peter William 1940- WhoAm 90
Stanley, Ralph 1927- ConMus 5, WhoAm 90
Stanley, Richard Eugene 1947- St&PR 91
Stanley, Richard H. 1932- St&PR 91
Stanley, Richard Holt 1932- WhoAm 90
Stanley, Richard P. 1944- WhoE 91
Stanley, Robert Warren 1941- WhoAm 90
Stanley, Ron 1947- St&PR 91
Stanley, Scott, Jr. 1938- WhoAm 90
Stanley, Steven Mitchell 1941- WhoAm 90
Stanley, Terry L. 1951- St&PR 91
Stanley, Thomas A. 1917-1989 BioIn 16
Stanley, Thomas Bahnson, Jr. 1927- WhoAm 90

Stanley, Timothy Wadsworth 1927- WhoAm 90, WhoWor 91
Stanley, Vance Neal 1959- WhoSSW 91
Stanley, Wendell M. 1904-1971 WorAlBi
Stanley, Wendell Meredith 1904-1971 DcScB S2
Stanley, William, Jr. 1919- WhoAm 90
Stanley, Wilmer Austin 1907- St&PR 91
Stanley Gilbert, Janice Gail 1940- St&PR 91
Stanley Wrench, Margaret 1916-1974 FemiCLE
Stanley Wrench, Mollie 1880-1966 FemiCLE
Stannard, Carole Christine 1956- WhoAmW 91
Stannard, Derek C. 1927- St&PR 91
Stannard, Eloise Harriet 1828-1915 BiDWomA
Stannard, Emily 1803-1885 BiDWomA
Stannard, Henrietta Eliza Vaughn Palmer 1856-1911 BioIn 16
Stannard, Janet Hilary BiDrAPA 89
Stannard, Richard L. St&PR 91
Stanners, Jerry K. 1935- St&PR 91
Stannett, Vivian Thomas 1917- WhoAm 90
Stannus, Gordon 1902-1989 ConAu 129
Stanny, Gary 1953- WhoEmL 91
Stanovich, Betty Jo 1954- BioIn 16
Stanovnik, Branko 1938- WhoWor 91
Stanowick, Daniel G. 1951- ODwPR 91
Stans, Maurice H. 1908- WorAlBi
Stans, Maurice Hubert 1908- BiDrUSE 89, WhoAm 90
Stansberry, Domenic Joseph 1952- WhoWrEP 89
Stansberry, James Wesley 1927- WhoAm 90
Stansberry, Jennifer R. ODwPR 91
Stansbury, Philip Roger 1931- WhoAm 90
Stansell, James Lewis 1953- WhoSSW 91, WhoWor 91
Stansell, Ronald Bruce 1945- WhoEmL 91, WhoWor 91
Stansifer, Charles Lee 1930- WhoAm 90
Stansky, Peter David Lyman 1932- WhoAm 90
Stanton, Alexander 1953- ODwPR 91, WhoAm 90
Stanton, Ambrose P. 1834-1912 AmLegL
Stanton, Bruce Clifton 1947- BiDrAPA 89
Stanton, David Bert 1941- St&PR 91
Stanton, Donald S. 1932- St&PR 91
Stanton, Donald Sheldon 1932- WhoAm 90
Stanton, Edmund C. BioIn 16
Stanton, Edward M. 1921- ODwPR 91, WhoAm 90
Stanton, Edwin M. 1814-1869 WorAlBi
Stanton, Edwin McMasters 1814-1869 BiDrUSE 89
Stanton, Elizabeth 1815-1902 FemiCLE
Stanton, Elizabeth Cady 1815-1902 BioAmW, BioIn 16, WorAlBi
Stanton, Elizabeth McCool 1947- WhoAmW 91
Stanton, Elizabeth Shirley BiDrAPA 89
Stanton, Florence Feaster 1946- WhoEmL 91, WhoSSW 91
Stanton, Frank 1908- BioIn 16, WhoAm 90
Stanton, Frank 1929- WhoAm 90
Stanton, Frank Anthony 1939- BiDrAPA 89
Stanton, Frank N. 1908- St&PR 91
Stanton, Frank Nichols 1908- WorAlBi
Stanton, Geoffrey Theodore 1956- IntWWM 90
Stanton, George T BiDrAPA 89
Stanton, Gerald Elroy 1922- WhoAm 90
Stanton, Gregory Howard 1946- WhoSSW 91
Stanton, Harriet L 1924- WhoAmA 91
Stanton, Henry T. 1834-1898 LiHiK
Stanton, Ivens V. ODwPR 91
Stanton, Ivens V. 1929- WhoE 91
Stanton, James E. 1945- St&PR 91
Stanton, Jane Graham 1922- WhoAmW 91
Stanton, Jeanne Frances 1920- WhoAmW 91, WhoWor 91
Stanton, Joanne 1944- WhoAmW 91
Stanton, John P. 1936- St&PR 91
Stanton, John Pinckney 1936- WhoWor 91
Stanton, Leroy 1946- Ballpl 90
Stanton, Louis Lee 1927- WhoAm 90
Stanton, Margaret Elizabeth 1948- WhoAmW 91
Stanton, Martha 1935- WhoE 91
Stanton, Maura 1946- WhoWrEP 89
Stanton, Maurice David 1940- WhoWor 91
Stanton, Mike 1952- Ballpl 90
Stanton, Morris Rachell 1959- WhoSSW 91
Stanton, Peter Harrison 1922- St&PR 91
Stanton, Peter V. ODwPR 91
Stanton, Peter W. 1938- St&PR 91
Stanton, Philip Ackley 1868-1945 AmLegL
Stanton, Philip H. 1930- St&PR 91
Stanton, Priscilla Anne 1953- WhoWrEP 89
Stanton, Robert 1963- ConTFT 8
Stanton, Robert James, Jr. 1931- WhoAm 90
Stanton, Robert John 1913- WhoSSW 91
Stanton, Robert Otto 1946- WhoE 91
Stanton, Robert W 1935- BiDrAPA 89
Stanton, Roger 1928- WhoAm 90
Stanton, Roger D. 1938- WhoAm 90
Stanton, Rosamond AuBYP 90
Stanton, Sky ODwPR 91
Stanton, Stuart Lawrence 1938- WhoWor 91
Stanton, Thomas Cousar 1929- WhoAm 90
Stanton, Thomas J. 1941- WhoAm 90
Stanton, Thomas Joyce, Jr. 1928- St&PR 91, WhoAm 90
Stanton, Thomas Mitchell 1922- WhoAm 90
Stanton, Tom-Eric 1947- WhoAmA 91
Stanton, Vance TwCCr&M 91
Stanton, Vincent A. 1926- St&PR 91
Stanton, Walter Oliver 1914- WhoWor 91
Stanton, William John, Jr. 1919- WhoAm 90, WhoWor 91
Stanton, William K. 1942- St&PR 91
Stanton, William Taylor 1926- WhoWor 91
Stanton-Kelleher, Carol 1961- WhoAmW 91
Stanuszek, Mark Edward 1948- WhoWor 91
Stanwick, Kathy Ann 1950- WhoAmW 91
Stanwick, Tad 1916- WhoAm 90
Stanwood, Cordelia 1865-1958 WomFie [port]
Stanworth, R. Howard St&PR 91, WhoSSW 91
Stanwyck, Barbara BioIn 16
Stanwyck, Barbara 1907- BioAmW
Stanwyck, Barbara 1907-1990 ConTFT 8 [port], CurBio 90N, NewYTBS 90 [port], WorAlBi
Stanwyck, Gary Dean 1949- BiDrAPA 89
Stanziano, Gary Joseph BiDrAPA 89
Stanzione, Daniel C. 1945- St&PR 91
Stanzione, Dominick Michael 1952- WhoE 91
Stap, Donald L. 1949- WhoWrEP 89
Stapel, Paul Frederick 1940- WhoAm 90
Stapells, Richard Bredin 1925- St&PR 91
Stapely, Sue 1946- WhoWor 91
Stapen, Joseph Ira BiDrAPA 89
Stapen, Nancy 1950- WhoAmA 91
Stapf, Kristin Marie 1966- WhoAmW 91
Staph, C. C. ConAu 129
Staph, Jack Alan 1945- St&PR 91
Stapier, Michael J. 1935- St&PR 91
Staple, Harvey Scott 1956- WhoE 91
Stapledon, William Olaf 1886-1950 RGTwCSF
Stapleford, John Edward 1946- WhoE 91
Stapleford, R.H. 1952- St&PR 91
Stapleman, Ronald C 1938- St&PR 91
Staples, Donald Paul 1959- WhoEmL 91
Staples, Eugene Leo 1926- WhoAm 90
Staples, Herman D 1918- BiDrAPA 89
Staples, Herman David 1918- WhoE 91
Staples, Ian Laurence 1946- WhoWor 91
Staples, James R. WhoAm 90
Staples, Judith Linwood 1947- WhoAmW 91
Staples, Lyle Newton 1945- WhoEmL 91
Staples, Mark Andrew 1954- WhoE 91
Staples, Norman Hamilton 1948- WhoSSW 91
Staples, O. Sherwin 1908- WhoAm 90
Staples, Richard Farnsworth 1919- WhoAm 90
Staples, Robert Taylor 1931- St&PR 91
Staples, Roy Harvard 1905-1958 WhoAmA 91N
Staples, Suzanne Fisher 1945- ConAu 132
Stapleton, Claudia Ann 1947- WhoAmW 91
Stapleton, Dave 1954- Ballpl 90
Stapleton, Harvey James 1934- WhoAm 90
Stapleton, James Alford 1916- St&PR 91
Stapleton, James Francis 1932- WhoAm 90
Stapleton, James Hall 1931- WhoAm 90
Stapleton, Jean WhoAm 90, WhoAmW 91
Stapleton, Jean 1923- WorAlBi
Stapleton, Joan WhoAmW 91
Stapleton, John Owen 1951- WhoEmL 91, WhoSSW 91
Stapleton, Joseph F 1921- WhoAmA 91
Stapleton, Katharine Hall 1919- WhoAmW 91
Stapleton, Katharine Laurence 1911- WhoAm 90, WhoWrEP 89
Stapleton, Katherine TwCCr&M 91
Stapleton, Kathleen Mary 1938- St&PR 91
Stapleton, Margaret M. 1936- St&PR 91
Stapleton, Maureen 1925- BioIn 16, NotWoAT, WhoAm 90, WhoAmW 91, WorAlBi
Stapleton, Patrick Dennis 1951- WhoSSW 91
Stapleton, Raymond D. 1939- St&PR 91
Stapleton, Ruth 1929-1983 WorAlBi
Stapleton, Ruth Carter EncO&P 3
Stapleton, Sharon Marie 1957- WhoAmW 91
Stapleton, Thomas David 1912- WhoE 91, WhoWor 91
Stapleton, Thomas F. 1939- St&PR 91
Stapleton, Thomas Robert 1940- BiDrAPA 89
Stapleton, Walter King 1934- WhoAm 90
Stapleton, William 1886-1950 WorAlBi
Stapp, Arthur Donald 1906-1972 AuBYP 90
Stapp, Bruce B. 1933- St&PR 91
Stapp, Bruce Michael 1944- WhoWor 91
Stapp, Dan Ernest 1934- St&PR 91, WhoAm 90
Stapp, Emily Joyce 1948- BiDrAPA 89
Stapp, Gregory Lee 1954- IntWWM 90
Stapp, John Barr 1962- St&PR 91
Stapp, Mary E. 1909- St&PR 91
Stapp, Miriam Dow 1953- WhoAmW 91
Stapp, Olivia 1940- IntWWM 90
Stapp, Olivia Brewer 1940- WhoAm 90
Stapp, Ray Veryl 1913- WhoAmA 91
Stapp, William F 1945- WhoAmA 91
Staprans, Raimonds 1926- WhoAmA 91
Staprans, Theodore BiDrAPA 89
Staprans, Vija BiDrAPA 89
Star, Anne Marie 1947- WhoAmW 91
Star, Ely 1847-1942 EncO&P 3
Star, Richard William 1934- St&PR 91
Starbird, Kaye 1916- AuBYP 90
Starbranch, Eileen K BiDrAPA 89
Starbuck, Helen L BiDrAPA 89
Starbuck, Mary Coffyn 1644-1717 EncCRAm
Starcevic, Joseph Francis 1956- WhoEmL 91
Starck, Christian Walter 1937- WhoWor 91
Starck, Louis P. 1923- St&PR 91
Starck, Philippe 1949- ConDes 90, PenDiDA 89
Starck, Philippe 1950?- BioIn 16
Starcke, Edgar Nolte, Jr. 1938- WhoWor 91
Stare, Fredrick J 1910- ConAu 132
Stare, Fredrick John 1910- WhoAm 90, WhoE 91
Starek, Jiri 1928- IntWWM 90
Starer, David 1955- WhoE 91
Starer, Robert 1924- IntWWM 90, WhoAm 90
Staresmore, Sabine BiDEWW
Starfield, Barbara Helen 1932- WhoAm 90, WhoAmW 91
Starfin, Victor Ballpl 90
Starford, Markus Jay 1952- WhoSSW 91
Stargell, Willie BioIn 16
Stargell, Willie 1940- Ballpl 90 [port]
Stargell, Willie 1941- WorAlBi
Starhawk 1951- NewAgE 90
Staring, Graydon Shaw 1923- WhoAm 90, WhoWor 91
Starita, Joseph 1922- St&PR 91
Stark, Abe 1894-1972 Ballpl 90
Stark, Agnes Louise 1929- WhoAmW 91
Stark, Allen Lytton 1949- BiDrAPA 89
Stark, Amy Louise 1954- WhoAmW 91
Stark, Antony Albert 1953- WhoE 91
Stark, Arthur Alan 1935- St&PR 91
Stark, Betty Ruth 1935- WhoAmW 91
Stark, Beverly Roff 1959- WhoSSW 91
Stark, Bruce Gunsten 1933- WhoAm 90, WhoAmA 91
Stark, Carol L R 1948- BiDrAPA 89
Stark, Caroline WhoSSW 91
Stark, Charles Alan 1951- WhoE 91
Stark, Daniel Ernest 1927- St&PR 91
Stark, David Callum Carmichael 1927- WhoAm 90
Stark, David Charles 1936- WhoAm 90
Stark, David Charles 1953- WhoEmL 91
Stark, David Keith 1937- St&PR 91
Stark, Dennis Edwin 1937- WhoAm 90
Stark, Diana ODwPR 91
Stark, Dolly Ballpl 90
Stark, Donald Gerald 1926- St&PR 91, WhoAm 90
Stark, Douglas Derwood 1925- St&PR 91
Stark, Edward J. 1938- St&PR 91
Stark, Edward Joseph 1938- WhoAm 90
Stark, Eliot Richard 1952- St&PR 91
Stark, Fortney Hillman 1931- WhoAm 90
Stark, Francis C., Jr. 1919- WhoAm 90
Stark, Freya BioIn 16
Stark, Freya 1893- FemiCLE
Stark, George King 1923- WhoAmA 91
Stark, George Luther BiDrAPA 89
Stark, Harold Walter 1932- St&PR 91
Stark, Harry Faber 1923- WhoE 91
Stark, Herbert H. 1922- WhoAm 90
Stark, Jack Everett 1931- WhoAm 90
Stark, Jack Fenwick 1926- St&PR 91
Stark, Jack Gage 1882-1950 WhoAmA 91N
Stark, Jack Lee 1934- WhoAm 90
Stark, James AuBYP 90
Stark, James Michael 1952- WhoE 91
Stark, Jaroslav Frantisek 1934- WhoWor 91
Stark, Joan Scism 1937- WhoAm 90, WhoAmW 91
Stark, John 1728-1822 BioIn 16, EncCRAm, WorAlBi
Stark, John 1841-1927 BioIn 16
Stark, John Edwin 1916- WhoAm 90
Stark, John Everett 1918- WhoAm 90
Stark, John Thomas 1926- WhoSSW 91
Stark, Karen WhoAm 90
Stark, Kelly Shira 1942- WhoAmW 91
Stark, Lawrence 1926- WhoAm 90
Stark, Martha C 1947- BiDrAPA 89
Stark, Marvin 1921- St&PR 91
Stark, Marvin L. 1937- St&PR 91
Stark, Mary Barbara 1920- WhoAmW 91
Stark, Maurice Gene 1935- St&PR 91, WhoAm 90
Stark, Michael Wayne 1951- WhoE 91
Stark, Milton Dale 1932- WhoWor 91
Stark, Nathan Julius 1920- WhoAm 90
Stark, Nellie May 1933- WhoAmW 91
Stark, Patricia Ann 1937- WhoAmW 91, WhoWor 91
Stark, Philip Herald 1936- St&PR 91
Stark, Richard TwCCr&M 91
Stark, Richard Alvin 1921- WhoAm 90
Stark, Richard Boies 1915- WhoAm 90
Stark, Richard J. 1943- ODwPR 91
Stark, Robert 1939- WhoAmA 91
Stark, Robert Alfred 1934- St&PR 91
Stark, Robert Martin 1930- WhoAm 90
Stark, Robin Caryl 1953- WhoAmW 91
Stark, Roger N. 1922- St&PR 91
Stark, Sherman D 1935- BiDrAPA 89
Stark, Stanley 1948- St&PR 91, WhoE 91
Stark, Stephen Douglas 1949- WhoEmL 91
Stark, Steven 1943- WhoE 91
Stark, Steven Z. 1946- WhoE 91
Stark, Theodore E., Jr. 1930- St&PR 91
Stark, Vivienne Rose 1926- WhoE 91
Stark, W.P., Jr. 1927- St&PR 91
Stark, Wendy Patricia 1954- WhoAm 90
Stark, Werner E. 1921- St&PR 91, WhoAm 90
Stark, William 1919- BiDrAPA 89
Stark, William Richard 1945- WhoSSW 91
Stark-Veltel, Gerd 1956- WhoWor 91
Stark Walsh, Lisa Catherine 1955- WhoAmW 91
Starke, Chester Norman 1943- WhoSSW 91
Starke, Edgar Arlin, Jr. 1936- WhoAm 90
Starke, Linda WhoWrEP 89
Starke, Mariana 1762?-1838 FemiCLE
Starke, Mary Celnik 1947- WhoAmW 91
Starke, Sandra 1959- WhoAmW 91
Starken, George Mathew 1934- WhoE 91
Starker, Janos 1924- IntWWM 90, PenDiMP, WhoAm 90
Starkey, James Henry, III 1940- WhoAm 90
Starkey, John Frederick 1926- WhoSSW 91
Starkey, Kevin Don 1960- WhoSSW 91
Starkey, Patrick E. 1933- St&PR 91
Starkey, Richard WhoWor 91
Starkey, Richard L. 1952- St&PR 91
Starkey, Robert Lyman 1899- WhoAm 90
Starkey, Russell Bruce, Jr. 1942- WhoSSW 91
Starkey, Thomas 1499?-1538 BioIn 16
Starkey, William E. 1935- St&PR 91
Starkey, William Edward 1935- WhoAm 90, WhoSSW 91
Starkie, Enid 1897-1970 BioIn 16
Starklint, Jan Faber 1945- WhoWor 91
Starkman, Barry Steven 1956- WhoE 91
Starkman, Betty Provizer 1929- WhoAmW 91
Starkman, Edward Jay 1958- WhoE 91
Starkman, Monica Naomi 1938- BiDrAPA 89
Starkoff, Bernard Julius 1917- WhoAm 90, WhoSSW 91
Starks, Fred William 1921- WhoAm 90
Starks, Hamlin A BiDrAPA 89
Starkweather, Frederick Thomas 1933- WhoWor 91
Starkweather, William E B 1879-1969 WhoAmA 91N
Starkweather-Nelson, Cynthia Louise 1950- WhoAmA 91
Starling, Ernest Henry 1866-1927 WorAlBi
Starling, Jade BioIn 16
Starling, James Lyne 1930- WhoAm 90
Starling, Thomas WhoWrEP 89
Starman, Marvin L BiDrAPA 89

Starmann, George H., III 1943- *St&PR 91*
Starmann, R. G. 1945- *ODwPR 91*
Starn Twins 1961- *WhoAmA 91*
Starn, Doug *BioIn 16*
Starn, Douglas *WhoAmA 91*
Starn, Mike *BioIn 16*
Starn, Mike P *WhoAmA 91*
Starn, Randolph 1939- *ConAu 32NR*
Starner, Bradley W. 1964- *St&PR 91*
Starnes, Earl Maxwell 1926- *WhoAm 90*
Starnes, Edward Clinton 1950- *WhoE 91*
Starnes, Henry 1816-1896 *DcCanB 12*
Starnes, James Wright 1933- *WhoAm 90, WhoWor 91*
Starnes, Kenneth Deen 1942- *WhoSSW 91*
Starnes, Vearl Porter 1929- *WhoAm 90*
Starnes, William Herbert, Jr. 1934- *WhoAm 90, WhoSSW 91*
Starnes, William Love 1919- *WhoAm 90*
Starobin, David Nathan 1951- *IntWWM 90*
Starobinski, Jean 1920- *ConAu 131*
Starobinski, Jean Isaac 1920- *WhoWor 91*
Starosel'skaja, V. *EncCoWW*
Starostovic, Edward Joseph, Jr. 1933- *WhoWor 91*
Starowieyski, Franciszek 1930- *ConDes 90*
Starr, Alice M. 1949- *WhoSSW 91*
Starr, Anne *ConAu 130*
Starr, Bart 1934- *WorAlBi*
Starr, Belle 1848-1889 *BioIn 16, WorAlBi*
Starr, Bill 1911- *BioIn 16*
Starr, Blaze *BioIn 16*
Starr, Brenda K. *BioIn 16*
Starr, Bruce 1952- *WhoE 91*
Starr, Carol Weinberg *BiDrAPA 89*
Starr, Chauncey 1912- *WhoAm 90*
Starr, Chester 1914- *WhoWrEP 89*
Starr, Chester G. 1914- *WhoAm 90*
Starr, Danforth White 1939- *St&PR 91*
Starr, David 1922- *WhoAm 90, WhoE 91*
Starr, David Zalman 1945- *BiDrAPA 89*
Starr, Dick 1906-1963 *Ballpl 90*
Starr, Dorothy A 1922- *BiDrAPA 89*
Starr, Dorothy Anne 1922- *WhoE 91*
Starr, Duane Edwin 1942- *St&PR 91*
Starr, Edward 1926- *ODwPR 91*
Starr, Ellen Gates 1859-1910 *BioIn 16*
Starr, Frank O. 1922- *St&PR 91*
Starr, Frederick Brown 1932- *WhoSSW 91*
Starr, Gary 1955- *St&PR 91*
Starr, Harold Page 1932- *WhoE 91*
Starr, Harvey 1946- *WhoSSW 91*
Starr, Ila Mae 1917- *WhoAmW 91*
Starr, Irene 1939- *WhoE 91*
Starr, Isaac 1895-1989 *BioIn 16*
Starr, Ivar Miles 1950- *WhoEmL 91*
Starr, James 1904?-1990 *ConAu 132*
Starr, Jan *WhoWrEP 89*
Starr, Jimmy *ConAu 132*
Starr, John C. 1939- *WhoAm 90*
Starr, John Robert 1927- *WhoAm 90, WhoSSW 91*
Starr, Jonathan Andrew 1951- *St&PR 91*
Starr, Joyce Ives 1932- *WhoE 91*
Starr, Kenneth W. 1946- *BioIn 16*
Starr, Kenneth Winston 1946- *NewYTBS 90 [port], WhoAm 90*
Starr, Kimberly Gail 1960- *WhoAmW 91*
Starr, Leon 1937- *St&PR 91, WhoAm 90*
Starr, Leonard 1925- *EncACom*
Starr, Louisa 1845-1909 *BiDWomA*
Starr, Lowell Edmond 1935- *WhoAm 90*
Starr, M. Philip 1945- *St&PR 91*
Starr, Malcolm White 1943- *St&PR 91*
Starr, Martha Patricia 1950- *WhoEmL 91*
Starr, Martin Kenneth 1927- *WhoAm 90*
Starr, Maurice Kenneth 1922- *WhoAm 90*
Starr, Melvin *St&PR 91N*
Starr, Melvin *BioIn 16*
Starr, Miriam Carolyn 1951- *WhoAmW 91*
Starr, Nancy Hamburger 1958- *WhoAmW 91*
Starr, Nina Kennedy 1942- *WhoAmW 91*
Starr, Pamela Thomae 1966- *WhoAmW 91*
Starr, Paul Elliot 1949- *WhoAm 90*
Starr, Pearl 1867-1925 *BioAmW*
Starr, Phillip Henry *BiDrAPA 89*
Starr, Ray 1906-1963 *Ballpl 90*
Starr, Richard Cawthon 1924- *WhoAm 90*
Starr, Richard Dean 1944- *St&PR 91*
Starr, Richard Marc 1951- *WhoEmL 91*
Starr, Richard Spencer 1961- *WhoE 91*
Starr, Ringo *BioIn 16*
Starr, Ringo 1940- *EncPR&S 89, OxCPMus, WhoAm 90, WhoWor 91, WorAlBi*
Starr, Robert Alan 1942- *St&PR 91*
Starr, Robert M. 1928- *St&PR 91*
Starr, Robert Morton 1928- *WhoAm 90*
Starr, Roger Samuel 1918- *WhoE 91*
Starr, Roger W. 1946- *St&PR 91*
Starr, Ross Marc 1945- *WhoAm 90*
Starr, Shirley 1848-1889 *BioAmW*
Starr, Stephen D *BiDrAPA 89*
Starr, Stephen Frederick 1940- *WhoAm 90*
Starr, Steve Marshall 1946- *WhoEmL 91*
Starr, Steven Dawson 1944- *WhoAm 90*
Starr, Tama *St&PR 91*
Starr, Toni Jolene *BiDrAPA 89*
Starr, V. Hale 1936- *WhoAm 90*
Starr, Walter Douglas 1944- *St&PR 91*
Starr, Walter Douglas, Jr. 1944- *WhoAm 90*
Starr, Warren David 1939- *WhoE 91, WhoWor 91*
Starr, William J. 1923- *WhoWrEP 89*
Starr-White, Debi *WhoWrEP 89*
Starratt, Patricia Elizabeth 1943- *WhoAmW 91*
Starrels, James 1926- *BiDrAPA 89*
Starrels, Sidney H 1924- *BiDrAPA 89*
Starrett, Agnes Lynch *BioIn 16*
Starrett, Cam 1949- *WhoAm 90, WhoAmW 91, WhoE 91*
Starrett, David 1926- *BiDrAPA 89*
Starrett, Kemp 1890-1952 *EncACom*
Starrett, Loyd Milford 1933- *WhoWor 91*
Starrett, Vincent 1886-1974 *AuBYP 90, ConAu 31NR, TwCCr&M 91*
Starrett, William 1959- *WhoSSW 91*
Starron, Robert Edward 1935- *St&PR 91*
Starrs, Elizabeth Anne 1954- *WhoAmW 91*
Starrs, Mildred *WhoAmA 91N*
Starry, Donn Albert 1925- *WhoAm 90*
Stars, William Kenneth 1921-1985 *WhoAmA 91N*
Start, Henry R. 1845-1905 *AmLegL*
Start, Joanne E. *St&PR 91*
Start, Joe 1842-1927 *Ballpl 90*
Startup, Charles Harry 1914- *WhoAm 90*
Startzman, Shirley Kayleen 1946- *WhoAmW 91*
Staryk, Steven S. 1932- *IntWWM 90, WhoAm 90*
Starzak, Michael Edward 1942- *WhoWrEP 89*
Starzinger, Vincent Evans 1929- *WhoAm 90*
Starzl, Thomas E. 1926- *BioIn 16*
Starzl, Thomas Earl 1926- *WhoAm 90*
Stasack, Edward Armen 1929- *WhoAm 90, WhoAmA 91*
Stasch, Jeffrey John 1958- *WhoEmL 91*
Stasco, Daphne Jo 1942- *WhoAmW 91*
Staser, Betty Jo 1921- *WhoAmW 91*
Stasey, Michael J. 1946- *St&PR 91*
Stashower, Daniel 1960- *ConAu 131*
Stashower, David L. 1929- *St&PR 91*
Stashower, Gloria *ODwPR 91*
Stashower, Michael David 1926- *WhoAm 90*
Stasi, Linda 1947- *WhoAm 90, WhoAmW 91*
Stasiak, Krystyna *BioIn 16*
Stasik, Andrew J 1932- *WhoAmA 91*
Stasik, Walter William 1946- *St&PR 91*
Stasio, Marilyn *BioIn 16*
Stasio, Marilyn 1939?- *NotWoAT*
Staska, Erich 1942- *WhoWor 91*
Stasko, Robert S 1953- *BiDrAPA 89*
Stasney, Ted Joseph 1947- *WhoSSW 91*
Stasov, V. V. 1824-1906 *BioIn 16*
Stasov, Vladimir Vasil'evich *BioIn 16*
Stassen, Harold E. 1907- *WorAlBi*
Stassen, Jacques Marcel 1911- *WhoWor 91*
Stassinopoulos, Arianna *BioIn 16, ConAu 129*
Stasson, Shelley Andrea 1953- *WhoEmL 91*
Stasz, Peter J. 1947- *St&PR 91*
Staszesky, Francis Myron 1918- *WhoAm 90*
Stata, Ray 1934- *St&PR 91*
Staten, Stephen Earl *BiDrAPA 89*
Staten, Willie Clark 1950- *WhoSSW 91*
Stater, Stanley Frank, III 1950- *WhoSSW 91*
States, Carl Leroy 1945- *WhoE 91*
Statezny, Judith Mary 1946- *WhoWrEP 89*
Statham, Bill R. 1934- *WhoSSW 91*
Statham, Peter B. 1936- *St&PR 91*
Stathis, Nicholas John 1924- *WhoE 91, WhoWor 91*
Stathopoulos, Theodore George 1947- *WhoWor 91*
Stathos, Margaret Allen Moreland 1925- *IntWWM 90*
Statius van Eps, Lodewijk Wilhelm 1926- *WhoWor 91*
Statler, Irving Carl 1923- *WhoAm 90*
Statman, Andy *NewAgMG*
Statman, Jan B *WhoAmA 91*
Statman, Jerome M 1931- *BiDrAPA 89*
Staton, Dakota 1932- *DrBIPA 90*
Staton, David Michael 1940- *WhoE 91*
Staton, Johanna Bilbo 1939- *WhoWrEP 89*
Staton, Robert Emmett 1946- *St&PR 91*
Staton, Robert Lafayette 1942- *WhoSSW 91*
Statten, Taylor 1915- *BiDrAPA 89*
Statter, Edward F. 1934- *St&PR 91*
Stattin, Eric Laurentius 1933- *WhoAm 90*
Statton, Philip James 1944- *St&PR 91*
Statton, Robert A. 1919- *St&PR 91*
Status Quo *OxCPMus*
Statz, Jigger 1897-1988 *Ballpl 90*
Staub, Anita 1947- *WhoAmW 91*
Staub, August William 1931- *WhoAm 90*
Staub, Barry Alan *St&PR 91N*
Staub, James Dunn 1933- *WhoAm 90*
Staub, Jerry Davis 1936- *WhoSSW 91*
Staub, Mario Otto 1931- *WhoE 91*
Staub, Michael Joseph 1952- *St&PR 91*
Staub, Molly Belle 1937- *WhoWrEP 89*
Staub, Randy Craig 1947- *St&PR 91*
Staub, Ronald J. 1930- *ODwPR 91, St&PR 91*
Staub, Rudolf 1890-1961 *DcScB S2*
Staub, Rusty 1944- *Ballpl 90 [port], BioIn 16*
Staub, Travis Edwin 1933- *St&PR 91*
Staub, W. Arthur 1923- *WhoAm 90*
Staubach, John Francis 1925- *St&PR 91*
Staubach, Roger 1942- *BioIn 16, WorAlBi*
Staubach, Roger Thomas 1942- *WhoAm 90*
Stauber, Leah Joyce 1957- *WhoAmW 91*
Stauber, Patricia Marron 1923- *WhoAmW 91*
Stauber, Robb *BioIn 16*
Stauber, Ronald J. 1940- *St&PR 91*
Staubitz, Arthur Frederick 1939- *St&PR 91, WhoAm 90*
Stauble, Antonio Ernesto 1933- *WhoWor 91*
Stauble, William J 1927- *BiDrAPA 89*
Staublin, Judith Ann 1936- *WhoAmW 91, WhoSSW 91, WhoWor 91*
Staubus, George Joseph 1926- *WhoAm 90*
Stauch, Victor Daniel 1932- *St&PR 91*
Staudenmaier, Mary Louise 1938- *WhoAmW 91*
Staudenmayer, Ralph *WhoSSW 91*
Staudenmeier, James Joseph, Jr. *BiDrAPA 89*
Staudenmeier, James Joseph, Jr. 1963- *WhoEmL 91*
Staudenmier, Karen Louise 1959- *WhoEmL 91*
Stauder, James N. 1927- *St&PR 91*
Stauder, William Vincent 1922- *WhoAm 90*
Stauderman, Bruce Ford 1919- *WhoAm 90, WhoWor 91*
Staudigl, Joseph 1807-1861 *PenDiMP*
Staudt, Calvin Charles, Jr. 1954- *WhoSSW 91*
Staudt, Erich Erwin 1941- *WhoWor 91*
Staudt, John Eugene 1948- *St&PR 91*
Stauffacher, C.F., Jr. 1921- *St&PR 91*
Stauffacher, Charles B. 1916- *WhoAm 90*
Stauffacher, David George 1931- *St&PR 91*
Stauffenberg, Klaus Philipp Schenk von 1907-1944 *BioIn 16*
Stauffer, Charles Henry 1913- *WhoAm 90*
Stauffer, Clay Wallace 1954- *WhoEmL 91*
Stauffer, Delmar J. *WhoAm 90*
Stauffer, Dietrich 1943- *WhoWor 91*
Stauffer, Dorothy Hubbell 1905- *WhoWrEP 89*
Stauffer, Dwight G. *AuBYP 90*
Stauffer, Edna Pennypacker 1887-1956 *WhoAmA 91N*
Stauffer, George Boyer 1947- *IntWWM 90*
Stauffer, Helen Winter 1922- *ConAu 30NR*
Stauffer, Joanne Rogan 1956- *WhoAmW 91*
Stauffer, Lawrence B. *ODwPR 91*
Stauffer, Leonard Joseph 1936- *WhoE 91*
Stauffer, Louise Lee 1915- *WhoAmW 91*
Stauffer, Peggy 1944- *WhoAmW 91*
Stauffer, Richard L 1932- *WhoAmA 91*
Stauffer, Robert Allen 1920- *WhoAm 90*
Stauffer, Sarah Ann 1915- *WhoAm 90*
Stauffer, Shelby Alvina 1958- *St&PR 91*
Stauffer, Stanley H. 1920- *St&PR 91*
Stauffer, Stanley Howard 1920- *WhoAm 90*
Stauffer, Thomas George 1932- *St&PR 91, WhoAm 90*
Stauffer, Thomas Michael 1941- *WhoAm 90, WhoSSW 91*
Stauffer, Tom G *BiDrAPA 89*
Stauffer, William Albert 1930- *WhoAm 90*
Stauffer, Zane Richard 1932- *St&PR 91*
Stauffer-Cole, Patricia Irene 1957- *WhoEmL 91*
Staughton, William 1770-1829 *BioIn 16*
Staum, Sonja 1959- *WhoAmA 91*
Staunton, Charles E *BiDrAPA 89*
Staunton, Mary Ursula *BiDrAPA 89*
Staunton, Patrick R 1928- *BiDrAPA 89*
Staunton, Schuyler *MajTwCW*
Staupers, Mabel Keaton 1890-1989 *BioIn 16, ConAu 129*
Staur, Martin John 1933- *WhoWor 91*
Staus, Frank A. 1915- *St&PR 91*
Stauss, Hans Josef 1956- *WhoWor 91*
Stautberg, Susan Schiffer 1945- *ODwPR 91, WhoAmW 91*
Stavans, Ilan 1961- *WhoHisp 91*
Stavans, Isaac 1931- *WhoAmA 91*
Stavaridis, Pat 1942- *WhoAmA 91*
Stavchansky, Ilan 1961- *WhoHisp 91*
Staveacre, Tony 1942- *ConAu 130*
Staveacre, Victoria *ODwPR 91*
Staveley-O'Carroll, Maud 1927- *BiDrAPA 89*
Stavely, Richard William 1927- *St&PR 91*
Staven, Leland Carroll 1933- *WhoAmA 91*
Stavenhagen, Joseph 1930- *St&PR 91*
Stavenhagen, Sandi 1958- *WhoAmW 91*
Stavenitz, Alexander Raqul 1901-1960 *WhoAmA 91N*
Staver, Leroy Baldwin 1908- *WhoAm 90*
Staver, Mathew Duane 1956- *WhoSSW 91*
Staves, Susan 1942- *WhoAm 90*
Stavig, Mark Luther 1935- *WhoAm 90*
Stavin, Robert 1937- *St&PR 91*
Stavinoha, Marcus J. 1933- *St&PR 91*
Stavisky, Alexandre Sacha 1886-1934 *BiDFrPL*
Stavitsky, Abram Benjamin 1919- *WhoAm 90*
Stavola, John Joseph 1929- *WhoWor 91*
Stavrinos, George *NewYTBS 90*
Stavrinos, George Philip 1948- *WhoAmA 91*
Stavropoulos, D. John 1933- *St&PR 91*
Stavropoulos, Dionysos John 1933- *WhoAm 90*
Stavropoulos, George 1920- *BioIn 16*
Stavropoulos, George Peter *NewYTBS 90 [port]*
Stavropoulos, Nickolas 1958- *St&PR 91*
Stavropoulos, William S. *BioIn 16*
Stavropoulos, William S. 1939- *St&PR 91, WhoAm 90*
Stavros, Gus A. 1925- *St&PR 91*
Stavrou, Nikolaos Athanasios 1935- *WhoAm 90*
Stavrou, Tatiana 1898- *EncCoWW*
Stavroudis, Orestes Nicholas 1923- *WhoE 91*
Staw, Barry Martin 1945- *WhoAm 90*
Staw, Harold 1917- *WhoAm 90*
Stawasz, Cherie 1946- *WhoAm 90*
Stawicki, Robert James 1953- *WhoE 91*
Stawowy, Ludomira 1937- *IntWWM 90*
Stay, Barbara 1926- *WhoAmW 91*
Stayduhar, John J. 1935- *St&PR 91*
Stayer, Lawrence F. *BioIn 16*
Stayer, Loraine Edith 1946- *WhoE 91*
Stayman, Samuel M. 1909- *WhoAm 90*
Stayner, Kay *BioIn 16*
Stayner, Steven *BioIn 16*
Stayton, Janet *WhoE 91*
Stayton, Janet 1939- *WhoAmA 91*
Stazewski, Henryk 1894-1988 *AnObit 1988*
Stazoni, Ray *St&PR 91*
Stea, Cesare 1893-1960 *WhoAmA 91N*
Stea, David 1936- *WhoAm 90*
Stead, Bette Ann 1935- *WhoSSW 91*
Stead, Christina 1902-1983 *BioIn 16, ConAu 33NR, FemiCLE, MajTwCW*
Stead, Eugene Anson, Jr. 1908- *WhoAm 90*
Stead, George 1928- *WhoE 91*
Stead, Ivan Ward 1928- *St&PR 91*
Stead, James Joseph, Jr. 1930- *WhoAm 90, WhoWor 91*
Stead, Jerre L. *BioIn 16*
Stead, Jerre L. 1943- *WhoAm 90*
Stead, Rexford Arthur 1923- *WhoAmA 91N*
Stead, Robert J C 1880-1959 *DcLB 92*
Stead, Ronald 1935- *WhoWor 91*
Stead, William T 1849-1912 *EncO&P 3*
Stead, William Thomas 1849-1912 *BioIn 16, EncPaPR 91*
Stead, William White 1919- *WhoAm 90*
Steadham, Charles Victor, Jr. 1944- *WhoSSW 91*
Steadman, Bevan Ellis 1943- *BiDrAPA 89*
Steadman, Charles Walters 1914- *WhoAm 90*
Steadman, David R.A. *St&PR 91*
Steadman, David Rosslyn Ayton 1937- *WhoAm 90*
Steadman, David Wilton 1936- *WhoAm 90, WhoAmA 91*
Steadman, Douglas 1926- *WhoSSW 91*
Steadman, Jack W. 1928- *WhoAm 90*
Steadman, John 1927- *Ballpl 90*
Steadman, John Daniel 1935- *St&PR 91*
Steadman, John Marcellus, III 1918- *WhoAm 90, WhoWrEP 89*
Steadman, John Montague 1930- *WhoAm 90, WhoE 91*
Steadman, Lanette Pittard 1955- *WhoE 91*
Steadman, Lydia Duff 1934- *WhoAmW 91*
Steadman, Mark S. 1930- *WhoWrEP 89*
Steadman, Ralph *BioIn 16*
Steadman, Richard Anderson, Jr. 1954- *WhoEmL 91*
Steadman, Richard Cooke 1932- *WhoSSW 91*

Steadman, Robert Frederick 1965- IntWWM 90
Steadman, Sue Ann 1931- St&PR 91
Steafel, Sheila 1935- ConTFT 8 [port]
Steagall, Henry Bascom, II 1922- WhoAm 90
Steahly, Lance Preston 1944- WhoAm 90
Steakley, Marvin L. St&PR 91
Steakley, Zollie Coffer, Jr. 1908- WhoAm 90
Stealey, James Francis 1948- St&PR 91
Stealey, Patricia Ann Terrill 1942- WhoSSW 91
Steamer, Robert Julius 1920- WhoAm 90
Steane, James H., II 1944- St&PR 91
Stear, Edwin Byron 1932- WhoAm 90
Stearley, Mildred Sutcliffe Volandt 1905- WhoAmW 91, WhoSSW 91, WhoWor 91
Stearley, Robert Jay 1929- WhoAm 90
Stearman, Ralph Wayne 1937- WhoSSW 91
Stearnes, Turkey 1901-1979 Ballpl 90
Stearns, Betty Jane ODwPR 91, WhoAm 90, WhoAmW 91
Stearns, Carol Zisowitz 1943- BiDrAPA 89, WhoE 91
Stearns, Cliff 1941- BioIn 16
Stearns, Clifford Bundy 1941- WhoAm 90, WhoSSW 91
Stearns, Dennis Gale 1957- WhoSSW 91
Stearns, E. Norris AmLegL
Stearns, Elizabeth Carolyn 1928- WhoAmW 91
Stearns, Frank B 1878-1955 EncABHB 4
Stearns, James Gerry 1922- WhoAm 90
Stearns, Jay Gregory 1948- BiDrAPA 89
Stearns, John 1951- Ballpl 90
Stearns, Jon Rod 1958- WhoWrEP 89
Stearns, Linda WhoAm 90
Stearns, Lloyd Worthington 1910- WhoWor 91
Stearns, Marcellus Lovejoy 1839-1891 AmLegL
Stearns, Mary Beth 1925- BioIn 16
Stearns, Michael NewAgMG
Stearns, Milton S., Jr. 1923- St&PR 91
Stearns, Milton Sprague, Jr. 1923- WhoAm 90
Stearns, Monroe 1913-1987 BioIn 16
Stearns, Monroe Mather 1913- AuBYP 90
Stearns, Monteagle 1924- WhoE 91
Stearns, Peter Nathaniel 1936- WhoAm 90
Stearns, Peter Ogden 1937- WhoAm 90
Stearns, Robert 1947- WhoAmA 91
Stearns, Robert B. 1952- St&PR 91
Stearns, Robert Breuer 1952- WhoE 91
Stearns, Robert John 1931- WhoE 91
Stearns, Robert Leo 1926- WhoAm 90
Stearns, Robert Paul 1937- St&PR 91
Stearns, Sheldon E BiDrAPA 89
Stearns, Shubal 1706-1771 BioIn 16
Stearns, Stephen Russell 1915- WhoAm 90
Stearns, Stewart Warren 1947- WhoSSW 91, WhoWor 91
Stearns, Suzanne Anderson 1944- WhoSSW 91
Stearns, Thomas Robert 1936- WhoAmA 91
Stearns, William Allen 1937- WhoAm 90
Stebbings, Robert Yeo 1942- WhoE 91
Stebbins, Arthur P 1912- BiDrAPA 89
Stebbins, Edward Clinton 1930- St&PR 91
Stebbins, Emma 1815-1882 BiDWomA
Stebbins, Esther Signe 1947- WhoWrEP 89
Stebbins, George Ledyard 1906- WhoAm 90
Stebbins, George McKinley 1957- WhoEmL 91
Stebbins, Gregory Kellogg 1951- WhoEmL 91, WhoWor 91
Stebbins, H. Lyman 1911-1989 BioIn 16
Stebbins, Henry Blanchard 1951- WhoEmL 91
Stebbins, John Marvin 1942- WhoSSW 91
Stebbins, Lou Hirsch 1930- WhoSSW 91
Stebbins, Marilyn Mason WhoAmW 91
Stebbins, Nancy K 1960- BiDrAPA 89
Stebbins, Richard Henderson 1938- WhoSSW 91
Stebbins, Robert A 1938- ConAu 30NR
Stebbins, Robert Alan 1938- WhoAm 90
Stebbins, Sheryl Beth 1953- WhoAmW 91
Stebbins, Stuart John 1916- St&PR 91
Stebbins, Theodore Ellis, Jr. 1938- WhoAm 90, WhoAmA 91
Stebbins, Theodore Leon 1941- St&PR 91
Stebbins, William Cooper 1929- WhoAm 90
Steben, Raymond Henry, Jr. 1938- St&PR 91, WhoAm 90
Steber, Eleanor 1914- WhoAm 90
Steber, Eleanor 1914-1990 NewYTBS 90 [port]
Steber, Eleanor 1916- IntWWM 90, PenDiMP
Steblay, Ralph E. 1921- St&PR 91
Stebleton, Brian C. 1942- St&PR 91
Stec, John Z. 1925- St&PR 91
Stec, John Zygment 1925- WhoAm 90
Stec, Ronald Joseph 1946- St&PR 91
Stecewycz, Kathleen Ann 1958- WhoAmW 91
Stech, David BioIn 16
Stecher, Brian Mark 1946- WhoEmL 91
Stecher, Cheryl Chadurgian 1950- WhoAmW 91
Stecher, Donald A. St&PR 91
Stecher, Emma Dietz 1905- WhoAmW 91
Stecher, Kenneth William 1946- St&PR 91
Stecher, Renate 1950- BioIn 16
Stechmesser, Gary R. ODwPR 91
Stechow, Wolfgang 1896-1975 WhoAmA 91N
Steck, Amy 1963- WhoAmW 91
Steck, Carol R. 1954- WhoWrEP 89
Steck, Lynn A. 1953- WhoE 91
Steck, Theodore Lyle 1939- WhoAm 90
Steckel, Anita WhoAmA 91, WhoE 91
Steckel, Barbara Jean 1939- WhoAm 90, WhoAmW 91
Steckel, Richard J. 1936- WhoAm 90
Stecker, Bonnie Yanky 1958- WhoAmW 91
Stecker, Debra Ann 1958- WhoAmW 91
Stecker, Harold 1926- St&PR 91
Stecklein, Jonette Marie 1962- WhoAmW 91
Stecklein, Leonard F. 1946- St&PR 91
Steckler, Eric Alan 1947- BiDrAPA 89
Steckler, Larry 1933- WhoAm 90
Steckler, Phyllis Betty WhoAm 90, WhoAmW 91
Steckler, Stuart Jay 1931- WhoAmA 91
Steckler, William Elwood 1913- WhoAm 90
Steckline, Larry E. 1941- WhoAm 90
Steckling, Adrienne WhoAm 90, WhoAmW 91
Steckman, Walter Gerald 1940- St&PR 91
Steczynski, John Myron 1936- WhoAmA 91
Stedem, Anthony F., Jr. 1920- BiDrAPA 89
Stedham, Austin W. 1928- St&PR 91
Stedham, Brenda Smith 1954- WhoEmL 91
Steding, Thomas Lyne 1944- WhoAm 90
Stedman, Edmund Clarence 1833-1908 BioIn 16
Stedman, John Branch 1924- WhoAm 90
Stedman, John Gabriel 1744-1797 BioIn 16
Stedman, Mary Louise BiDrAPA 89
Stedman, Murray Salisbury, Jr. 1917- WhoAm 90
Stedman, Richard Ralph 1936- WhoAm 90
Stedman, Robert William 1941- St&PR 91
Stedman, Wilfred Henry 1892-1950 WhoAmA 91N
Stedman Jones, Gareth 1942- ConAu 31NR
Stedmond, John Mitchell 1916- WhoAm 90
Stedronsky, Frank 1935- St&PR 91, WhoWor 91
Steeby, Patty Jeanne 1955- WhoAmW 91
Steed, Diane K. BioIn 16
Steed, Ethel Laverna Williams 1920- WhoSSW 91
Steed, Graham 1913- IntWWM 90
Steed, James Larry 1939- WhoSSW 91
Steed, Joseph Mark 1951- WhoE 91
Steed, Robert Lee 1936- WhoAm 90
Steed, Virgil 1901- LiHiK
Steed, W David BiDrAPA 89
Steed, William Franklin 1920- St&PR 91
Steede, David W. 1943- St&PR 91
Steedle, Joseph Richard 1952- WhoSSW 91
Steedly, James E., Jr. 1938- St&PR 91
Steedman, Donald L. 1945- St&PR 91
Steedman, Doria Lynne Silberberg 1936- WhoAmW 91
Steedman, Marguerite Couturier 1908- AuBYP 90
Steedman, Ralph Bruce 1944- St&PR 91
Steefel, Lawrence D., Jr. 1926- WhoAm 90
Steeg, Carl Nathan 1937- WhoE 91
Steeg, Helga 1927- WhoWor 91
Steeg, James Howe 1950- WhoE 91
Steeg, Melba Law 1923- WhoSSW 91
Steeg, Moise S., Jr. 1916- WhoWor 91
Steeg, Rose Mary 1958- WhoAmW 91
Steeg, Theodore Jules Joseph 1868-1950 BiDFrPL
Steege, Deborah Anderson 1946- WhoAmW 91
Steeger, Henry, III NewYTBS 90
Steeger, William Paul 1945- WhoSSW 91
Steegmann, Albert Theodore, Jr. 1936- WhoAm 90
Steegmuller, Beatrice Stein WhoAmA 91N
Steegmuller, Francis 1906- WhoAm 90
Steel, Alan Richard 1945- St&PR 91
Steel, Ann Elizabeth BiDrAPA 89
Steel, Burton B 1923- BiDrAPA 89
Steel, C. Eugene 1934- St&PR 91
Steel, Charles Lowndes 1924- St&PR 91
Steel, Charles Lowndes, III 1924- WhoAm 90
Steel, Christopher Charles 1939- IntWWM 90
Steel, Claudia Williamson 1918- WhoAmW 91
Steel, Danielle BestSel 90-4 [port], BioIn 16
Steel, Danielle 1947- MajTwCW, WorAlBi
Steel, Danielle Fernande 1947- WhoAm 90, WhoAmW 91, WhoWrEP 89
Steel, Dawn BioIn 16
Steel, Dawn 1946- News 90 [port], WhoAm 90, WhoAmW 91
Steel, Dean E. ODwPR 91
Steel, Ewing T BiDrAPA 89
Steel, Flora Annie 1847-1929 FemiCLE
Steel, Flora Annie Webster 1847-1929 BioIn 16
Steel, Geoffrey A. 1926- St&PR 91
Steel, Geoffrey Arthur 1926- WhoAm 90
Steel, Howard Haldeman 1921- WhoAm 90
Steel, Joan E. 1953- St&PR 91
Steel, Johannes BioIn 16
Steel, Keith William 1917- WhoWor 91
Steel, Kurt 1904-1946 TwCCr&M 91
Steel, Richard W. 1932- St&PR 91
Steel, Robert Howard 1929- WhoAm 90
Steel, Roger K. 1937- St&PR 91
Steel, Ronald 1931- WorAu 1980 [port]
Steel, Ronald Lewis 1931- WhoAm 90
Steel, Tex ConAu 32NR
Steel, Virginia Oberlin 1950- WhoAmA 91
Steelberg, Elsie Enns 1934- BiDrAPA 89
Steele, Addison, II 1935- SmATA X
Steele, Alfred Nu 1901-1959 ConAmBL
Steele, Ana Mercedes 1939- WhoAmW 91
Steele, Anna 1840-1914? FemiCLE
Steele, Anne 1717-1778 FemiCLE
Steele, Benjamin Charles 1917- WhoAmA 91
Steele, Betty Louise 1920- WhoAm 90
Steele, Beverly Louise 1944- WhoAmW 91
Steele, Bill 1885-1949 Ballpl 90
Steele, Bill F. 1928- St&PR 91
Steele, Bob 1894-1962 Ballpl 90
Steele, Bob 1906-1988 BioIn 16
Steele, Brandt F 1907- BiDrAPA 89
Steele, Carolyn Ann 1946- WhoAmW 91
Steele, Carolyn Skinner 1928- St&PR 91
Steele, Catherine Anne Gallant BiDrAPA 89
Steele, Charles Glen 1925- WhoAm 90
Steele, Curtis A 1933- BiDrAPA 89
Steele, Davis Tillou 1923- WhoSSW 91
Steele, Derwent TwCCr&M 91
Steele, Diana Marie 1960- WhoE 91
Steele, Donald Ernest 1923- St&PR 91
Steele, Douglas Walter 1942- WhoSSW 91
Steele, Earl Larsen 1923- WhoAm 90
Steele, Edwin PenDiDA 89
Steele, Ellen Lively 1936- WhoAmW 91
Steele, Elmer 1884-1966 Ballpl 90
Steele, Ernest Clyde 1925- St&PR 91, WhoAm 90
Steele, Evelyn Jane 1911- WhoAmW 91
Steele, Fletcher 1885-1971 BioIn 16
Steele, Frank Pettus 1935- WhoWrEP 89
Steele, Frederic R. 1953- St&PR 91
Steele, George Peabody 1924- WhoE 91, WhoWor 91
Steele, Harry Gerard 1942- WhoAm 90
Steele, Herbert David, Jr. 1954- WhoSSW 91
Steele, Hilda Hodgson 1911- WhoAmW 91
Steele, Horatio PenDiDA 89
Steele, Howard Loucks 1929- WhoE 91, WhoWor 91
Steele, J Michael 1941- BiDrAPA 89
Steele, James B. WhoAm 90, WhoE 91
Steele, James Lewis, Jr. 1954- WhoSSW 91
Steele, Jan 1950- IntWWM 90
Steele, John 1764-1815 BioIn 16
Steele, John F. 1924- St&PR 91
Steele, John Hyslop 1926- WhoAm 90
Steele, John Lawrence 1917- WhoAm 90
Steele, Joseph Raymond 1932- St&PR 91
Steele, Kathleen Frances 1960- WhoAmW 91
Steele, Kathryn Ann 1949- WhoAmW 91
Steele, Kenneth Franklin, Jr. 1944- WhoSSW 91
Steele, Laura BioIn 16
Steele, Lendell Eugene 1928- WhoAm 90
Steele, Lewis McKinnie 1911- St&PR 91
Steele, Loren Dean 1940- WhoAm 90
Steele, Margaret Mary BiDrAPA 89
Steele, Martin Carl 1919- WhoAm 90
Steele, Mary M. 1936- WhoAmW 91
Steele, Mary Q. 1922- BioIn 16
Steele, Mary Quintard 1922- AuBYP 90
Steele, Matthew R. 1956- St&PR 91
Steele, Michael 1951- IntWWM 90
Steele, Mildred Romedahl 1924- WhoAmW 91
Steele, Oliver 1928- WhoAm 90
Steele, Pamela Busher 1962- WhoAmW 91
Steele, Patricia Kay 1958- WhoAmW 91
Steele, Patrick Scott 1949- St&PR 91
Steele, Richard 1672-1729 DcLB 101 [port], WorAlBi
Steele, Richard Allen 1927- St&PR 91
Steele, Richard C. 1917- St&PR 91
Steele, Richard Charles 1917- WhoAm 90, WhoE 91
Steele, Richard J. 1925- WhoE 91
Steele, Richard Lewis 1929- WhoSSW 91
Steele, Robert Bainum, Jr. 1937- WhoWrEP 89
Steele, Robert Carl 1953- St&PR 91
Steele, Robert Edward 1954- St&PR 91
Steele, Robert G 1926- BiDrAPA 89
Steele, Rose Marie 1949- WhoAmW 91
Steele, Samuel S. 1916- St&PR 91
Steele, Shelby NewYTBS 90
Steele, Shelby 1946- News 91-2 [port]
Steele, Terri Sue BiDrAPA 89
Steele, Thomas 1772-1850 PenDiDA 89
Steele, Thomas A., III 1940- St&PR 91
Steele, Thomas Elrod 1937- BiDrAPA 89
Steele, Timothy Reid 1948- WhoWrEP 89
Steele, Tommy ConAu 129
Steele, Tommy 1936- IntWWM 90, OxCPMus
Steele, Vernon H. 1925- St&PR 91
Steele, W. Perrin 1924- St&PR 91
Steele, Walter Albert 1937- WhoWor 91
Steele, William A. 1900-1989 BioIn 16
Steele, William Owen 1917- BioIn 16
Steele, William Owen 1917-1979 AuBYP 90
Steele, Yvonne Potts 1957- WhoAmW 91
Steele-Herman, Lisa Michelle 1964- WhoAmW 91
Steele-Perkins, Chris 1947- BioIn 16
Steele-Williams, Rhea L. 1958- WhoAmW 91
Steeley, Charles B. 1931- St&PR 91
Steeleye Span EncPR&S 89
Steelhammer, Carl Goode 1911- St&PR 91
Steelman, Bennett Loften 1954- WhoSSW 91
Steelman, Charles William 1941- St&PR 91, WhoAm 90
Steelman, Jacob DeHart 1946- WhoEmL 91
Steelman, John Knight 1952- WhoSSW 91
Steelman, John S. 1946- St&PR 91
Steelman-Bragato, Susan Jean 1957- WhoWor 91
Steelsmith, Rick BioIn 16
Steely Dan ConMus 5 [port], EncPR&S 89
Steely-Brown, Diane Marie 1961- WhoE 91
Steen, A.B. 1929- St&PR 91
Steen, Bill 1887-1979 Ballpl 90
Steen, Carl Bertil 1938- WhoWor 91
Steen, Carlton Duane 1932- WhoAm 90
Steen, Carol J 1943- WhoAmA 91
Steen, Donald Mariner 1924- WhoWor 91
Steen, Douglas 1925- EncO&P 3
Steen, Gordon E., Jr. 1941- St&PR 91
Steen, Jan 1626-1679? IntDcAA 90
Steen, John Thomas, Jr. 1949- WhoAm 90, WhoEmL 91, WhoSSW 91, WhoWor 91
Steen, Lowell Harrison 1923- WhoAm 90
Steen, Marguerite 1894-1975 BioIn 16
Steen, Maria van der 1906- EncCoWW
Steen, Melvin Clifford 1907- WhoAm 90, WhoE 91, WhoWor 91
Steen, Norman Frank 1933- WhoAm 90
Steen, Paul Joseph 1932- WhoAm 90
Steen, Reiulf 1933- WhoWor 91
Steen, Ronald Ardis 1954- WhoEmL 91
Steenbeke, James Henry, Jr. 1939- St&PR 91
Steenberg, Borje Karl 1912- WhoWor 91
Steenblik, Joseph F. 1904- St&PR 91
Steenbock, Harry 1886-1967 DcScB S2
Steenburgen, Mary BioIn 16
Steenburgen, Mary 1953- WhoAm 90, WhoAmW 91, WorAlBi
Steene, William 1888-1965 WhoAmA 91N
Steeneck, Lee Robert 1948- St&PR 91
Steeneck, Regina A. WhoAmW 91
Steenhagen, Robert Lewis 1922- WhoAm 90
Steenland, Thomas 1950- IntWWM 90
Steensland, Ronald Paul 1946- WhoAm 90, WhoSSW 91
Steensma, Robert Charles 1930- WhoAm 90
Steenson, Delos Vernal 1934- St&PR 91
Steenson, Teddy Jay 1943- WhoWor 91
Steeples, Douglas Wayne 1935- WhoAm 90
Steeples, James Duane 1949- St&PR 91
Steer, Alfred Gilbert, Jr. 1913- WhoAm 90
Steer, Charles M. 1913-1990 BioIn 16
Steer, Mike 1946- IntWWM 90
Steer, Wilson 1860-1942 IntDcAA 90
Steere, Allen Caruthers, Jr. 1943- WhoAm 90

Steere, Bruce 1918- *St&PR 91*
Steere, Douglas Van 1901- *WhoAm 90*
Steere, Norman M. 1931- *St&PR 91*
Steere, Ralph Edward 1925- *St&PR 91*
Steere, Terry 1949- *St&PR 91*
Steere, Thomas, Jr. 1819-1897 *AmLegL*
Steere, William C. 1936- *St&PR 91*
Steere, William Campbell 1907-1989 *BioIn 16*
Steers, Newton Ivan, Jr. 1917- *WhoAm 90*
Stees, Timothy Lynn 1957- *WhoSSW 91*
Steese, Ruth Junia 1907- *WhoAmW 91*
Steetle, David Ross 1930- *St&PR 91*
Steeves, Lynne Mary 1922- *WhoE 91*
Steeves, Robert Francis 1938- *WhoE 91*
Steeves, Sherri Lee 1960- *WhoEmL 91*
Stefan fra Hvitadal *DcScanL*
Stefan Hordur Grimsson *DcScanL*
Stefan Sigurdsson *DcScanL*
Stefan, Jillian Marie 1965- *WhoAmW 91*
Stefan, Joseph *WhoAm 90*
Stefan, Joseph P. 1953- *St&PR 91*
Stefan, Paul 1929- *St&PR 91*
Stefan, Ross 1934- *BioIn 16, WhoAmA 91*
Stefan, Steve A. 1937- *WhoAm 90*
Stefan, Verena 1947- *EncCoWW*
Stefanelli, Joe 1921- *WhoAmA 91*
Stefanelli, Joseph James 1921- *WhoAm 90*
Stefanescu-Barnea, Georgeta 1934- *IntWWM 90*
Stefani, Fritz Heinrich 1941- *WhoWor 91*
Stefaniak, Norbert John 1921- *WhoAm 90*
Stefanic, David W. 1950- *St&PR 91*
Stefanick, Patti Ann 1957- *WhoAmW 91*
Stefanick, Tom Alan 1956- *WhoSSW 91*
Stefanik, Alfred T. 1939- *BioIn 16*
Stefanis, Costas N *BiDrAPA 89*
Stefaniuk, Robert Michael 1955- *St&PR 91*
Stefanko, Leona Evans 1945- *WhoAmW 91*
Stefanko, Robert Allen 1943- *St&PR 91, WhoAm 90*
Stefano, Giuseppe di *PenDiMP*
Stefano, Joseph William 1922- *WhoAm 90*
Stefano, R.L. 1923- *St&PR 91*
Stefanou, John 1962- *WhoE 91*
Stefanowicz, A. Richard 1939- *St&PR 91*
Stefans, Vikki Ann 1957- *WhoSSW 91*
Stefanschi, Sergiu 1941- *WhoAm 90*
Stefanska-Lukowicz, Elzbieta *PenDiMP*
Stefanssen, Stephanie *ODwPR 91*
Stefansson, David 1895-1964 *DcScanL*
Stefansson, Evelyn Baird 1913- *AuBYP 90*
Stefansson, Vilhjalmur 1879-1962 *BioIn 16, WorAlBi*
Steffan, Freda Reininga 1911- *WhoAmW 91*
Steffan, Frederick V. 1948- *St&PR 91*
Steffe, Cynthia *BioIn 16*
Steffek, Hanny 1927- *IntWWM 90*
Steffek, Mark Charles 1959- *WhoSSW 91*
Steffek, Marvin C. 1930- *St&PR 91*
Steffel, Sheila Gorman 1959- *WhoAmW 91*
Steffel, Vern John, Jr. 1950- *WhoEmL 91*
Steffen, Christopher James 1942- *St&PR 91*
Steffen, David Joseph 1938- *St&PR 91*
Steffen, Patricia *BiDrAPA 89*
Steffen, Patrick Mathew 1949- *St&PR 91*
Steffen, Thomas Lee 1930- *WhoAm 90*
Steffen, Tina Marie 1958- *WhoAmW 91*
Steffens, David Carl *BiDrAPA 89*
Steffens, Dorothy R. 1921- *WhoAm 90*
Steffens, Jeffrey Edward 1953- *WhoE 91*
Steffens, John L. 1941- *St&PR 91*
Steffens, John Laundon 1941- *WhoAm 90*
Steffens, Lincoln 1866-1936 *BioIn 16, WorAlBi*
Steffens, Robert S. 1946- *St&PR 91*
Steffensen, Dwight A. 1943- *St&PR 91, WhoAm 90*
Steffenson, Carol Elizabeth *BiDrAPA 89*
Stefferud, Alfred Daniel 1903- *AuBYP 90*
Steffes, Arnold M., Jr. 1931- *St&PR 91*
Steffey, Lela 1928- *WhoAmW 91*
Steffke, Glenn T. 1938- *WhoSSW 91*
Steffler, Alva W 1934- *WhoAmA 91*
Steffler, Christel 1930- *WhoWor 91*
Steffler, John 1947- *ConAu 33NR*
Steffy, James Barton 1934- *WhoE 91*
Stefoff, James E. 1928- *St&PR 91*
Stefoff, James Edward 1938- *WhoAm 90*
Stefopoulos, Athanasios D 1941- *BiDrAPA 89*
Steg, James Anthony 1954- *BiDrAPA 89*
Steg, James Louis *WhoAmA 91*
Steg, James Louis 1922- *WhoAm 90*
Steg, John Paul 1944- *BiDrAPA 89*
Steg, Joseph 1928- *BiDrAPA 89*
Steg, Leo 1922- *WhoAm 90, WhoE 91*
Stegall, H Frederick 1934- *BiDrAPA 89*
Stegall, Joel Ringgold 1939- *WhoSSW 91*
Stegall, Pauline M. 1923- *WhoWrEP 89*
Stegall, Rodney B. 1933- *St&PR 91*
Stegall, Wendy Lee 1961- *WhoAmW 91*
Stege, George Henry 1947- *St&PR 91*
Stegeman, Charles 1924- *WhoAmA 91*
Stegeman, Janet A. 1923- *BioIn 16*
Stegeman, Thomas Albert 1948- *WhoE 91*
Stegeman, William H. 1914- *WhoWrEP 89*
Stegemann, Otto *St&PR 91*
Stegemeier, Richard J. 1928- *St&PR 91*
Stegemeier, Richard Joseph 1928- *WhoAm 90*
Stegemier, Edward J. 1939- *St&PR 91*
Stegemoeller, Susan Warner 1956- *WhoEmL 91*
Stegemoller, Donald L. 1938- *St&PR 91*
Stegenga, Preston Jay 1924- *WhoAm 90*
Steger, Charles William 1947- *WhoAm 90*
Steger, Evan Evans, III 1937- *WhoAm 90*
Steger, Hugo 1929- *WhoWor 91*
Steger, Joseph A. *WhoAm 90*
Steger, Melvin Edward 1930- *WhoSSW 91*
Steger, Meritt Homer 1906- *WhoAm 90*
Steger, Ron E. 1945- *St&PR 91*
Steger, Will *BioIn 16*
Steger, Will 1945?- *News 90 [port]*
Steger, William Merritt 1920- *WhoAm 90*
Steger-Gratz, Christine 1942- *WhoAmW 91*
Steggall, Stuart Norris 1937- *St&PR 91*
Steggell, Sandra Sue 1944- *WhoAmW 91*
Steggles, John Charles 1919- *WhoAm 90*
Stegina, Michael Eugene 1950- *St&PR 91*
Steglich, W G 1921- *ConAu 30NR*
Steglich, Winfred George 1921- *WhoAm 90*
Steglitz, Marc H. 1942- *WhoAm 90*
Steglitz, Mark H. 1942- *St&PR 91*
Stegman, Charles Alexander 1959- *WhoWor 91*
Stegman, Gary L. 1949- *St&PR 91*
Stegman, Margery Jane 1952- *WhoE 91*
Stegman, Patricia 1929- *WhoAmA 91*
Stegmann, Eugene C. 1931- *St&PR 91*
Stegmann, Hartmut Bernhard 1931- *WhoWor 91*
Stegmann, Thomas Joseph 1946- *WhoWor 91*
Stegmar, Pamela Anderson 1959- *WhoAmW 91*
Stegmayer, Joseph H. 1951- *St&PR 91*
Stegmayer, Joseph Henry 1951- *WhoAm 90*
Stegner, Douglas Dewitt 1928- *St&PR 91*
Stegner, Phyllis Yaws 1958- *WhoAmW 91*
Stegner, Robert D. 1931- *St&PR 91*
Stegner, Stuart Page 1937- *WhoWrEP 89*
Stegner, Wallace 1909- *BestSel 90-3 [port], MajTwCW, WorAlBi*
Stegner, Wallace Earle 1909- *BioIn 16, WhoAm 90, WhoWrEP 89*
Steh, Beth Ann *BiDrAPA 89*
Stehle, Edward Raymond 1942- *WhoE 91*
Stehli, Francis Greenough 1924- *WhoAm 90*
Stehlin, John Sebastian, Jr. 1923- *WhoAm 90*
Stehling, Kurt Richard 1919- *WhoAm 90*
Stehman, Betty Kohls 1952- *WhoEmL 91*
Stehman, Burnell Ray 1931- *St&PR 91*
Stehr, Donald Edgar 1934- *WhoSSW 91*
Stehr, Hermann 1864-1940 *BioIn 16*
Steibelt, Daniel 1765-1823 *BioIn 16, PenDiMP*
Steibly, Robert Lewis 1946- *WhoE 91*
Steichen, Edward 1879-1973 *BioIn 16, WorAlBi*
Steichen, Edward 1879-1979 *WhoAmA 91N*
Steichen, James Matthew 1947- *WhoEmL 91*
Steichen, Joanna T 1933- *ConAu 132*
Steichen, Joanna Taub 1933- *WhoE 91*
Steichen, Lillian 1883-1977 *BioAmW*
Steidel, Robert Francis, Jr. 1926- *WhoAm 90*
Steider, Doris 1924- *WhoAmA 91*
Steidley, Roy Burke 1937- *WhoE 91*
Steier, Rodney Dean 1949- *WhoWrEP 89*
Steiert, Jerry Carl *BiDrAPA 89*
Steif, Jeffrey Edward 1960- *WhoE 91*
Steifel, S. Gray, Jr. 1938- *St&PR 91*
Steig, Arthur *BioIn 16*
Steig, William 1907- *BioIn 16, WhoAm 90*
Steig, William H. 1907- *AuBYP 90*
Steigelman, Steven L. 1941- *St&PR 91*
Steiger, Anna 1960- *IntWWM 90*
Steiger, Bettie Alexander 1934- *WhoAmW 91*
Steiger, Brad 1936- *EncO&P 3, NewAgE 90*
Steiger, Dale Arlen 1928- *WhoE 91, WhoWor 91*
Steiger, Frederic *WhoAmA 91*
Steiger, Frederic 1905-1990 *WhoAm 90, WhoE 91, WhoWor 91*
Steiger, Fredric Adams 1945- *BiDrAPA 89, WhoEmL 91*
Steiger, Gus 1897-1988 *Ballpl 90*
Steiger, Heidi Schwarzbauer 1953- *WhoE 91*
Steiger, Janet Dempsey 1939- *WhoAm 90, WhoAmW 91*
Steiger, Otto Martin Karl 1938- *WhoWor 91*
Steiger, Paul Ernest 1942- *WhoAm 90*
Steiger, Robert Wayne 1928- *St&PR 91*
Steiger, Rod 1925- *WhoAm 90, WorAlBi*
Steigerwald, Carl Jacob, II 1939- *St&PR 91*
Steigerwald, Louis John, III 1953- *St&PR 91*
Steigerwald, Robert Joseph 1939- *St&PR 91*
Steigerwaldt, Donna Wolf 1929- *WhoAm 90, WhoAmW 91*
Steighner, Richard Lee 1957- *WhoEmL 91*
Steigler, Sarah Ann 1955- *WhoE 91*
Steigman, Andrew L. 1933- *WhoE 91*
Steigman, Arnold Leonard 1932- *WhoE 91*
Steigman, Margot *WhoAmA 91*
Steigrod, Alan August 1937- *WhoSSW 91*
Steijn, Ton Nicolaas 1944- *WhoWor 91*
Steil, George Kenneth, Sr. 1924- *WhoAm 90*
Steil, Gordon E. 1920- *St&PR 91*
Steil, Robert A. 1925- *St&PR 91*
Steiman, Alexander 1926- *St&PR 91*
Steiman, Leon A 1909- *BiDrAPA 89*
Steimatzky, Eri Mordechai 1942- *WhoWor 91*
Steimel, Raymond Joseph 1924- *WhoAm 90*
Steimer, Mollie 1897-1980 *BioIn 16*
Steimle, Bruce E. 1953- *ODwPR 91*
Steimle, Raoul Henri 1922- *WhoWor 91*
Stein, Aaron Marc 1906-1985 *TwCCr&M 91*
Stein, Abraham Oscar 1914- *BiDrAPA 89*
Stein, Adlyn Robinson 1908- *WhoAmW 91*
Stein, Alan Harvey 1947- *WhoE 91*
Stein, Alan L. 1948- *WhoE 91*
Stein, Alfred Joseph 1933- *St&PR 91*
Stein, Allan Mark 1951- *WhoEmL 91*
Stein, Allen A. 1934-1988 *BioIn 16*
Stein, Alvin Maurice 1924- *WhoAm 90*
Stein, Andrew *BioIn 16*
Stein, Arnold 1915- *WhoAm 90*
Stein, Arthur Harold 1940- *BiDrAPA 89, WhoE 91*
Stein, Arthur William 1953- *WhoAm 90*
Stein, Barbara Ann *BiDrAPA 89*
Stein, Barbara Lambert 1945- *WhoAmW 91*
Stein, Benjamin 1944- *BioIn 16*
Stein, Bennett Mueller 1931- *WhoAm 90*
Stein, Bernard 1913- *St&PR 91, WhoAm 90*
Stein, Bernard Alvin 1923- *WhoAm 90*
Stein, Besty Ann *BiDrAPA 89*
Stein, Beth Ellen 1952- *WhoAmW 91*
Stein, Bill 1947- *Ballpl 90*
Stein, Bob 1920- *St&PR 91*
Stein, Carey M. 1947- *St&PR 91, WhoAm 90*
Stein, Carl 1943- *WhoAm 90*
Stein, Carolyn Kerner *WhoSSW 91*
Stein, Charles 1912- *WhoAm 90*
Stein, Charlotte Albertine Ernestine von 1742-1827 *EncCoWW*
Stein, Cheryl Denise 1953- *WhoAmW 91*
Stein, Christine K. 1946- *St&PR 91*
Stein, Claire A 1923- *WhoAmA 91*
Stein, Dale Franklin 1935- *WhoAm 90*
Stein, Dan Joseph *BiDrAPA 89*
Stein, Daniel Stephen 1947- *WhoSSW 91*
Stein, David F. 1940- *St&PR 91*
Stein, Diane C 1943- *BiDrAPA 89*
Stein, Dieter 1934- *WhoAm 90, WhoE 91*
Stein, Donald Gerald 1939- *WhoAm 90*
Stein, Donald Gilbert 1941- *St&PR 91*
Stein, Donald Jay 1931- *St&PR 91*
Stein, Donald L. 1934- *St&PR 91*
Stein, Donald U 1938- *BiDrAPA 89*
Stein, Donna Michele 1942- *WhoAmA 91*
Stein, Douglas J. 1947- *St&PR 91*
Stein, Edith 1891-1942 *EncCoWW*
Stein, Edward B. 1917- *St&PR 91*
Stein, Edward Dalton *WhoWrEP 89*
Stein, Edward E. 1937- *St&PR 91*
Stein, Edward H 1936- *BiDrAPA 89*
Stein, Edward William 1928- *St&PR 91*
Stein, Eleanor Bankoff 1923- *WhoAmW 91, WhoWor 91*
Stein, Elias M. 1931- *WhoAm 90*
Stein, Ellen Gail 1951- *WhoEmL 91*
Stein, Elliot H. 1918- *St&PR 91, WhoAm 90*
Stein, Elliott M *BiDrAPA 89*
Stein, Eric 1913- *WhoAm 90*
Stein, Eric A. 1952- *WhoSSW 91*
Stein, Eric Sedwick 1930- *WhoSSW 91*
Stein, Florence C 1901- *BiDrAPA 89*
Stein, Frances Patiky *BioIn 16*
Stein, Fritz Henry 1932- *WhoAmA 91, WhoE 91*
Stein, Gary S. 1933- *WhoAm 90, WhoE 91*
Stein, George Henry 1934- *WhoAm 90, WhoWrEP 89*
Stein, Gerald 1937- *St&PR 91*
Stein, Gerald S 1943- *BiDrAPA 89*
Stein, Gertrude 1874-1946 *BioAmW, ConAu 132, FemiCLE, MajTwCW, NotWoAT, WorAlBi*
Stein, Gertrude Emilie *WhoAmW 91*
Stein, Gertude 1874-1946 *BioIn 16*
Stein, Gilbert Taylor 1928- *St&PR 91*
Stein, H Thomas 1931- *BiDrAPA 89*
Stein, Harry *BioIn 16*
Stein, Harve 1904- *WhoAmA 91*
Stein, Helen D 1931- *BiDrAPA 89*
Stein, Herb 1917- *BioIn 16*
Stein, Herbert *St&PR 91*
Stein, Herbert 1916- *BioIn 16, WhoAm 90*
Stein, Herbert H 1945- *BiDrAPA 89*
Stein, Herman D 1917- *ConAu 30NR*
Stein, Herman David 1917- *WhoAm 90, WhoWrEP 89*
Stein, Horst 1928- *IntWWM 90, PenDiMP*
Stein, Howard *BioIn 16*
Stein, Howard 1926- *WhoAm 90*
Stein, Howard 1929- *WhoAm 90*
Stein, Howard S. 1939- *WhoAm 90*
Stein, Ira *NewAgMG*
Stein, Irvin 1906- *WhoAm 90*
Stein, Irwin Daniel 1907-1988 *BioIn 16*
Stein, Isaac 1946- *WhoAm 90*
Stein, J. Dieter *BioIn 16*
Stein, Janet Ellen 1955- *WhoAmW 91*
Stein, Jay M. 1946- *WhoAm 90*
Stein, Jeff 1947- *St&PR 91*
Stein, Jeff M. 1940- *St&PR 91*
Stein, Jerome Leon 1928- *WhoAm 90*
Stein, Jess 1914- *WhoWrEP 89*
Stein, Joan *BiDrAPA 89*
Stein, Jodi Lynn 1959- *WhoAmW 91*
Stein, Joel Mitchel 1931- *BiDrAPA 89*
Stein, John Frederick 1951- *St&PR 91*
Stein, Josef Dieter 1934- *St&PR 91*
Stein, Joseph *WhoAm 90*
Stein, Joseph 1912- *ConAu 31NR, WhoWrEP 89*
Stein, Judith Ellen 1943- *WhoAmA 91*
Stein, Julia A. 1946- *WhoWrEP 89*
Stein, Julian S., Jr. 1918- *ODwPR 91*
Stein, Julian U. *BioIn 16*
Stein, Karl Ulrich *BioIn 16*
Stein, Karl-Ulrich 1936- *WhoWor 91*
Stein, Kirk Lawson 1961- *WhoSSW 91*
Stein, Leon *NewYTBS 90*
Stein, Leon 1910- *IntWWM 90, WhoAm 90*
Stein, Leon 1912-1990 *BioIn 16, ConAu 130*
Stein, Leonard *ODwPR 91*
Stein, Leonard 1916- *IntWWM 90*
Stein, Leonard I 1929- *BiDrAPA 89*
Stein, Leslie Ellen 1956- *WhoEmL 91*
Stein, Leslie Reicin 1946- *WhoEmL 91*
Stein, Lewis *WhoAmA 91*
Stein, Lewis 1937- *St&PR 91*
Stein, Linda Ann 1955- *WhoWrEP 89*
Stein, Linda Joan 1958- *WhoAmW 91*
Stein, Lorrayne H *BiDrAPA 89*
Stein, Lotte C. 1926- *WhoSSW 91*
Stein, Louis Philip *BiDrAPA 89*
Stein, Ludwig 1938- *WhoAmA 91*
Stein, Marius *EncCoWW*
Stein, Mark Andrew 1958- *WhoE 91*
Stein, Mark Brian 1961- *WhoE 91*
Stein, Mark Rodger 1943- *WhoSSW 91*
Stein, Mark S. 1950- *WhoEmL 91*
Stein, Marshall Jay 1946- *BiDrAPA 89*
Stein, Martin E. 1922- *St&PR 91*
Stein, Martin H *BiDrAPA 89*
Stein, Martin Howard 1913- *BiDrAPA 89*
Stein, Marvin 1923- *BiDrAPA 89, WhoAm 90*
Stein, Marvin Leonard 1924- *WhoAm 90*
Stein, Mary 1959- *WhoAmW 91*
Stein, Mary Katherine 1944- *WhoAmW 91*
Stein, Meyer Lewis 1920- *AuBYP 90*
Stein, Michael *BioIn 16*
Stein, Michael B. 1940- *ConAu 32NR*
Stein, Milton Michael 1936- *WhoE 91, WhoWor 91*
Stein, Mina Benedicte 1933- *WhoAmW 91*
Stein, Mitchel Jules 1941- *BiDrAPA 89*
Stein, Morris J. 1905-1988 *BioIn 16*
Stein, Murray Brent *BiDrAPA 89*
Stein, Murray Walter 1943- *WhoWrEP 89*
Stein, Myron 1925- *WhoAm 90*
Stein, Myron L 1928- *BiDrAPA 89*
Stein, Nelson *BioIn 16*
Stein, Otto Ludwig 1925- *WhoAm 90*
Stein, Paul Arthur 1937- *WhoE 91*
Stein, Paul David 1934- *WhoAm 90, WhoWor 91*
Stein, Paul G *BiDrAPA 89*
Stein, Paula Barton 1929- *WhoAmW 91, WhoWor 91*
Stein, Peter 1937- *BioIn 16*
Stein, Peter Adalbert 1927- *WhoWor 91*
Stein, Peter Jay *BiDrAPA 89*
Stein, Philip 1930- *St&PR 91*
Stein, Philip M 1932- *BiDrAPA 89*
Stein, Phillip L *BiDrAPA 89*
Stein, Phoebe Hockstader *BioIn 16*

Stein, Phyllis Rosenstein 1941- WhoAmW 91
Stein, Randy 1953- Ballpl 90
Stein, Richard Alan 1959- St&PR 91
Stein, Richard Arno 1945- St&PR 91
Stein, Richard G. NewYTBS 90 [port]
Stein, Richard George 1916-1990 BioIn 16
Stein, Richard H BiDrAPA 89
Stein, Richard Henry 1950- BiDrAPA 89
Stein, Richard M. 1948- St&PR 91
Stein, Richard P. 1925- St&PR 91
Stein, Richard Paul 1925- WhoAm 90
Stein, Richard Stephen 1925- WhoAm 90
Stein, Robert St&PR 91
Stein, Robert Alan 1930- WhoAm 90
Stein, Robert Allen 1938- WhoAm 90
Stein, Robert Benjamin 1950- WhoEmL 91
Stein, Robert J BiDrAPA 89
Stein, Robert M BiDrAPA 89
Stein, Robert Michael 1961- WhoWor 91
Stein, Roberta Katchen 1941- WhoWrEP 89
Stein, Roger Breed 1932- WhoAmA 91
Stein, Ronald Jay 1930- WhoAm 90, WhoAmA 91
Stein, Ronald Marc 1951- WhoSSW 91
Stein, Roy Mendel BiDrAPA 89
Stein, Samuel 1937- BiDrAPA 89
Stein, Sanders Martin 1951- BiDrAPA 89
Stein, Sandra Lou 1942- WhoAmW 91
Stein, Sanford W 1933- BiDrAPA 89
Stein, Seena Deborah 1941- WhoE 91
Stein, Seymour 1928- WhoAm 90
Stein, Seymour 1930- WhoE 91
Stein, Sharon Carol 1961- WhoE 91
Stein, Simon 1896-1989 BioIn 16
Stein, Sol 1926- WhoAm 90, WhoWor 91
Stein, Stanley J. 1920- WhoAm 90
Stein, Stefan P BiDrAPA 89
Stein, Steven B. 1948- St&PR 91
Stein, Stuart Leonard 1946- WhoEmL 91
Stein, Susan Alyson 1956- WhoE 91
Stein, Terry S BiDrAPA 89
Stein, Vilja Kreek 1937- BiDrAPA 89
Stein, Wilfred Donald 1931- WhoWor 91
Stein, William H. 1911-1980 WorAlBi
Stein, William Howard 1911-1980 DcScB S2
Stein, William Warner 1921- WhoAm 90
Steinacker, Ronald Alan 1940- St&PR 91
Steinarr, Steinn 1908-1958 DcScanL
Steinau, Bernard M BiDrAPA 89
Steinbach, Alice WhoAm 90, WhoAmW 91
Steinbach, Charles Albert 1951- WhoEmL 91
Steinbach, Elaine Thielke 1946- WhoAmW 91
Steinbach, Haim BioIn 16
Steinbach, Haim 1944- WhoAmA 91
Steinbach, Harold 1956- WhoE 91, WhoEmL 91
Steinbach, Kenneth Alan 1953- BiDrAPA 89
Steinbach, L. Rawls 1953- St&PR 91
Steinbach, Lynne Susan 1953- WhoAmW 91
Steinbach, Meredith Lynn 1949- WhoWrEP 89
Steinbach, Meyer BiDrAPA 89
Steinbach, Sandra 1936- BiDrAPA 89
Steinbach, Sandra Joy 1950- WhoAmW 91
Steinbach, Terry 1962- Ballpl 90
Steinbaugh, Robert P. 1927- WhoAm 90, WhoWor 91
Steinbaum, Bernice 1941- WhoAmA 91
Steinbaum, Harlan 1932- St&PR 91
Steinbeck, Hans David 1925- IntWWM 90
Steinbeck, John 1902-1968 AuBYP 90, BioIn 16, MajTwCW, WorAlBi
Steinberg, Alan Lloyd BiDrAPA 89
Steinberg, Alfred 1917- AuBYP 90
Steinberg, Alvin M. 1921- St&PR 91
Steinberg, Andrew David 1957- WhoE 91
Steinberg, Annie G BiDrAPA 89
Steinberg, Arthur Gerald 1912- WhoAm 90
Steinberg, Arthur Irwin 1935- WhoE 91
Steinberg, Barry Charles 1952- St&PR 91
Steinberg, Ben 1930- IntWWM 90
Steinberg, Bernard D. 1924- St&PR 91
Steinberg, Bernard David 1924- WhoAm 90
Steinberg, Bernhard Evanbar 1900- WhoWrEP 89
Steinberg, Bruce Richard BiDrAPA 89
Steinberg, Burt 1945- St&PR 91
Steinberg, Charles 1943- St&PR 91
Steinberg, Charles A. BioIn 16, WhoE 91
Steinberg, Charles Allan 1934- WhoAm 90, WhoE 91
Steinberg, Daniel BioIn 16
Steinberg, Daniel 1922- WhoAm 90
Steinberg, David 1942- WhoAm 90
Steinberg, David 1944- WhoWrEP 89
Steinberg, David Isaac 1928- WhoE 91
Steinberg, David Joel 1937- WhoAm 90, WhoE 91
Steinberg, David Joseph 1934- St&PR 91
Steinberg, Elana BioIn 16
Steinberg, Eugene Barry 1953- WhoSSW 91
Steinberg, Fran C BiDrAPA 89
Steinberg, Gilbert 1931- St&PR 91
Steinberg, Harry 1925- BiDrAPA 89
Steinberg, Harvey 1937- BiDrAPA 89
Steinberg, Herbert J BiDrAPA 89
Steinberg, Herbert Joseph 1929- WhoE 91
Steinberg, Herman Joseph 1911- St&PR 91
Steinberg, Howard 1926- St&PR 91, WhoAm 90
Steinberg, Howard E. 1944- WhoAm 90
Steinberg, Ilse L 1908- BiDrAPA 89
Steinberg, Ira Bruce 1963- BiDrAPA 89
Steinberg, Irwin Ira 1926- St&PR 91
Steinberg, Jack 1915- WhoWor 91
Steinberg, Jack 1926- ODwPR 91
Steinberg, Janet DeBerry 1940- WhoWor 91
Steinberg, Janet Eckstein 1932- WhoAmW 91
Steinberg, Jill 1962- St&PR 91
Steinberg, Jill Enid 1955- WhoAmW 91
Steinberg, Joel BioIn 16
Steinberg, Joel Larry 1948- BiDrAPA 89
Steinberg, Joel Stuart BiDrAPA 89
Steinberg, Jorge 1936- BiDrAPA 89
Steinberg, Joseph S. 1944- St&PR 91
Steinberg, Joseph Saul 1944- WhoAm 90
Steinberg, Lance Bradley BiDrAPA 89
Steinberg, Lawrence E. 1935- St&PR 91
Steinberg, Lawrence Edward 1935- WhoAm 90
Steinberg, Lawrence William 1942- St&PR 91
Steinberg, Leigh BioIn 16
Steinberg, Leo 1920- WhoAm 90, WhoAmA 91
Steinberg, Lilli BioIn 16
Steinberg, Lisa BioIn 16
Steinberg, M Robert 1925- BiDrAPA 89
Steinberg, Malcolm Saul 1930- WhoAm 90
Steinberg, Marcia Irene 1944- WhoAmW 91
Steinberg, Margot ODwPR 91
Steinberg, Mark Stephen 1941- WhoSSW 91
Steinberg, Marlene BiDrAPA 89
Steinberg, Marshall 1932- St&PR 91, WhoAm 90
Steinberg, Martha Jean BioIn 16
Steinberg, Maurice David 1938- BiDrAPA 89
Steinberg, Melvin Allen 1933- WhoAm 90, WhoE 91
Steinberg, Meyer 1924- WhoAm 90
Steinberg, Michael WhoSSW 91
Steinberg, Michael 1928- WhoAm 90
Steinberg, Michael Alan 1952- WhoE 91
Steinberg, Milton 1903-1950 BioIn 16
Steinberg, Milton, Mrs 1910-1970 WhoAmA 91N
Steinberg, Morris Albert 1920- WhoAm 90
Steinberg, Morton 1928- St&PR 91
Steinberg, Paul Jay 1948- BiDrAPA 89, WhoE 91
Steinberg, Richard Maurice 1928- St&PR 91
Steinberg, Robert Alan 1946- WhoSSW 91
Steinberg, Robert Lee BiDrAPA 89
Steinberg, Robert M. 1942- St&PR 91, WhoAm 90, WhoE 91
Steinberg, Rolf 1929- ConAu 132
Steinberg, Rubin 1934- WhoAmA 91
Steinberg, S. Ty 1928- St&PR 91
Steinberg, Saul 1914- WhoAm 90, WhoAmA 91
Steinberg, Saul 1939- St&PR 91
Steinberg, Saul Phillip 1939- ConAmBL, WhoAm 90, WhoE 91
Steinberg, Selwyn F. 1934- St&PR 91
Steinberg, Sherwin L. 1936- St&PR 91
Steinberg, Sherwin Lewis 1936- WhoAm 90
Steinberg, Stanford Mark 1936- BiDrAPA 89
Steinberg, Stanley Alvin 1923- BiDrAPA 89
Steinberg, Steven BioIn 16
Steinberg, Susan 1949- WhoE 91
Steinberg, Wallace Herbert 1934- WhoE 91
Steinberg, Warren Linnington 1924- WhoWor 91
Steinberg, William 1899-1978 PenDiMP
Steinberger, Jack BioIn 16
Steinberger, Jack 1921- WhoAm 90, WhoWor 91, WorAlBi
Steinberger, Jeffrey Wayne 1947- WhoEmL 91
Steinberger, Richard L. 1939- St&PR 91
Steinbock, Bonnie 1947- WhoE 91
Steinbock, John T. 1937- WhoAm 90
Steinbock, Robert Ted 1952- WhoSSW 91
Steinbook, Richard Mark 1940- BiDrAPA 89
Steinborn, Leonard 1946- WhoWor 91
Steinbrecker, John E. 1950- St&PR 91
Steinbreder, H. John BioIn 16
Steinbrenner, George 1930- Ballpl 90 [port], News 91-1 [port], WorAlBi
Steinbrenner, George Edward 1947- WhoEmL 91
Steinbrenner, George M. 1930- BioIn 16
Steinbrenner, George M., III 1930- St&PR 91
Steinbrenner, George Michael, III 1930- WhoAm 90, WhoE 91
Steinbrenner, Paul A. BioIn 16
Steinbrink, Jerold C. 1953- WhoWrEP 89
Steinbronn, Richard Eugene 1941- WhoAm 90
Steinbruckner, Bruno Friedrich 1941- WhoAm 90
Steinbruegge, Robert Wallace 1947- St&PR 91
Steinbuchel, Carla Faye 1949- WhoEmL 91
Steindler, Walter G. 1927- WhoE 91
Steinebach, Josef Gerhard 1949- WhoWor 91
Steinecke, Hartmut 1940- WhoWor 91
Steineger, Margaret Leisy 1926- WhoAmW 91
Steineker, Virginia Caldwell 1923- WhoSSW 91
Steinem, Gloria BioIn 16
Steinem, Gloria 1934- ConLC 63 [port], FemiCLE, MajTwCW, WhoAm 90, WhoAmW 91, WorAlBi
Steiner, Alan Burton 1941- St&PR 91
Steiner, Alberto 1913-1974 ConDes 90
Steiner, Andrew D. 1942- St&PR 91
Steiner, Barbara A 1934- ConAu 30NR
Steiner, Barbara Annette 1934- AuBYP 90, WhoWrEP 89
Steiner, Betty W 1919- BiDrAPA 89
Steiner, Bruce Alan 1955- WhoEmL 91
Steiner, Bruce Edwin 1960- WhoEmL 91
Steiner, Charles L. 1936- St&PR 91
Steiner, Charlotte 1900-1981 AuBYP 90
Steiner, Clarence H. 1958- St&PR 91
Steiner, David Andrew BiDrAPA 89
Steiner, Donald Frederick 1930- WhoAm 90
Steiner, Edward L. 1944- St&PR 91
Steiner, Elisabeth 1935- IntWWM 90
Steiner, Eric 1946- OxCCanT
Steiner, Frederick Karl, Jr. 1927- WhoAm 90
Steiner, George 1929- BioIn 16, ConAu 31NR, MajTwCW, SmATA 62 [port], WhoAm 90
Steiner, Gilbert Yale 1924- WhoAm 90
Steiner, Gitta Hana 1932- IntWWM 90, WhoAm 90
Steiner, Gloria Litwin 1922- WhoAmW 91
Steiner, Hans 1946- BiDrAPA 89
Steiner, Hans-Ueli 1936- BiDrAPA 89
Steiner, Henry 1934- ConDes 90
Steiner, Henry Jacob 1930- WhoAm 90
Steiner, Herbert Max 1927- WhoAm 90
Steiner, Howard 1946- ODwPR 91
Steiner, Jacque 1929- WhoAmW 91
Steiner, Jane Laura 1953- BiDrAPA 89
Steiner, Jeanne Laura 1954- BiDrAPA 89
Steiner, Jeffrey Josef 1937- WhoAm 90
Steiner, Jerome 1929- BiDrAPA 89
Steiner, John Victor 1944- WhoSSW 91
Steiner, Joyce Janene 1952- BiDrAPA 89
Steiner, Kenneth Donald 1936- WhoAm 90
Steiner, Kurt 1912- WhoAm 90
Steiner, Lawrence Frederick 1947- St&PR 91
Steiner, Lee Rabinowitz 1901- WhoAm 90
Steiner, Lisa Amelia 1933- WhoAm 90
Steiner, Martin 1919- BiDrAPA 89
Steiner, Max 1888-1971 OxCPMus, WorAlBi
Steiner, Meir BiDrAPA 89
Steiner, Mel 1920- Ballpl 90
Steiner, Michael 1945- WhoAmA 91
Steiner, Michael Steven 1950- WhoE 91
Steiner, Paul WhoAmA 91, WhoE 91
Steiner, Paul 1913- WhoAm 90
Steiner, Paul Andrew 1929- St&PR 91
Steiner, Peter Otto 1922- WhoAm 90
Steiner, Phillip G. 1901- St&PR 91
Steiner, R.L. 1926- St&PR 91
Steiner, Ralph 1899-1986 WhoAmA 91N
Steiner, Raymond George 1931- St&PR 91
Steiner, Richard R. 1923- St&PR 91
Steiner, Richard Russell 1923- WhoAm 90
Steiner, Robert Frank 1926- WhoAm 90, WhoE 91, WhoWor 91
Steiner, Robert Lisle 1921- WhoAm 90
Steiner, Roger J 1924- ConAu 32NR
Steiner, Rudolf 1861-1925 EncO&P 3, EncPaPR 91, NewAgE 90
Steiner, Stan BioIn 16
Steiner, Stuart 1937- WhoAm 90
Steiner, Sylvia R BiDrAPA 89
Steiner, Thomas A. 1936- St&PR 91
Steiner, Timothy John 1946- WhoWor 91
Steiner, Warren 1959- BiDrAPA 89
Steiner, Wilfred Alfred, Jr. 1940- WhoAm 90
Steiner, Wilfred Joseph 1916- WhoAm 90
Steiner, William 1913- WhoE 91
Steiner, Zara S 1928- ConAu 129
Steiner-Scott, Geoffrey 1948- WhoWor 91
Steinerman, Debora Andrews 1961- WhoEmL 91
Steinert, Alan, Jr. 1936- St&PR 91, WhoAm 90
Steines, S. John 1947- St&PR 91
Steinetz, Bernard George 1927- WhoE 91
Steinfals, Christian Werner 1933- WhoAm 90
Steinfeld, Jeffrey Irwin 1940- WhoAm 90
Steinfeld, Manfred 1924- St&PR 91, WhoAm 90
Steinfeld, Thomas Albert 1917- WhoAm 90, WhoE 91
Steinfeldt, Harry 1877-1914 Ballpl 90
Steinfels, Margaret O'Brien BioIn 16, WhoAmW 91
Steinfels, Melville P 1910- WhoAmA 91
Steinfels, Peter Francis 1941- WhoAm 90
Steinfield, Carl F. 1931- St&PR 91
Steinfink, Dan Elliot BiDrAPA 89
Steinfink, Hugo 1924- WhoAm 90
Steinfink, Murray 1940- WhoWor 91
Steinfort, Charles Roy 1921- WhoAm 90, WhoE 91
Steinfort, Robert E. 1918- St&PR 91
Steinfort, Rosemary G. 1917- St&PR 91
Steinforth, Alex W. 1924- St&PR 91
Steingard, Ronald Jay BiDrAPA 89
Steingard, Sandra 1955- BiDrAPA 89, WhoE 91
Steingard, Sharon K 1960- BiDrAPA 89
Steingass, David Herbert 1940- WhoWrEP 89
Steinglass, Peter J 1939- BiDrAPA 89
Steinglass, Peter Joseph 1939- WhoE 91
Steingold, Fred Saul 1936- WhoAm 90
Steingold, Rose G BiDrAPA 89
Steingold, Stuart Geoffrey 1945- WhoEmL 91
Steingraber, Fred George 1938- St&PR 91
Steingraber, Frederick George 1938- WhoAm 90
Steingrimur Thorsteinsson DcScanL
Steingut, Stanley 1920-1989 BioIn 16
Steinhagen, Frederick Houston 1948- St&PR 91
Steinhardt, Alice 1950- WhoAmA 91
Steinhardt, Arnold PenDiMP
Steinhardt, David St&PR 91
Steinhardt, Henry 1920- WhoAm 90
Steinhardt, Laurence Adolph 1892-1950 BioIn 16
Steinhardt, Michael BioIn 16
Steinhardt, Milton Jacob 1909- IntWWM 90
Steinhardt, Milton Joseph BiDrAPA 89
Steinhardt, Paul Joseph 1952- WhoAm 90
Steinhardt, Ralph Gustav, Jr. 1918- WhoAm 90
Steinhardt, Robert F. St&PR 91
Steinhart, Albert B. 1930- St&PR 91
Steinhart, Albert Benny 1930- WhoAm 90
Steinhart, Carol 1935- WhoAmW 91
Steinhart, Gary 1955- St&PR 91
Steinhart, Kathy Sue 1952- WhoAmW 91
Steinhart, Melvin J 1936- BiDrAPA 89
Steinhart, Ronald G. 1940- WhoAm 90
Steinhart, Ronald Glen 1940- St&PR 91
Steinhauer, F. Chuck 1952- St&PR 91
Steinhauer, Gillian 1938- WhoAmW 91, WhoWor 91
Steinhauer, John Robert 1946- WhoEmL 91
Steinhauer, W.R. 1941- St&PR 91
Steinhaus, John Edward 1917- WhoAm 90
Steinhaus, Randall Brian BiDrAPA 89
Steinhaus, Richard Z. 1927-1989 BioIn 16
Steinhausen, Theodore Behn, Jr. 1942- WhoE 91
Steinhauser, Fredric Robert 1918- WhoAm 90
Steinhauser, J. Chris 1959- St&PR 91
Steinhauser, Janice Maureen 1935- WhoAmW 91
Steinhauser, John 1958- St&PR 91
Steinhauser, John W. 1924- St&PR 91
Steinhauser, Sheldon Eli 1930- WhoWor 91
Steinheimer, Judy Morales 1941- WhoHisp 91
Steinherz, Laurel Judith 1947- WhoAmW 91
Steinhilber, Ernest John, III BiDrAPA 89
Steinhilber, George 1930- St&PR 91
Steinhilber, Richard M 1921- BiDrAPA 89
Steinhoff, Edward 1934- St&PR 91, WhoAm 90
Steinhoff, Harold William 1919- WhoAm 90
Steinhoff, Kenneth Wayne BiDrAPA 89
Steinhoff, Monika 1941- WhoAmA 91

Steinhoff, William Richard 1914- *WhoAm 90, WhoWrEP 89*
Steinhorn, Irwin Harry 1940- *WhoAm 90, WhoWor 91*
Steinhouse, Carl Lewis 1931- *WhoAm 90*
Steinhouse, Clarence Leroy 1920- *St&PR 91*
Steinhouse, Clarence Leroy, III 1950- *St&PR 91*
Steinhouse, James Welch 1956- *St&PR 91*
Steinhouse, John Thomas 1953- *St&PR 91*
Steinhouse, Kenneth Martin 1939- *WhoE 91*
Steinhouse, Lurene Richardson 1921- *St&PR 91*
Steinhouse, Roy 1943- *BiDrAPA 89*
Steinhouse, Tobie *WhoAmA 91*
Steinig, Stephen N. 1945- *St&PR 91*
Steinig, Stephen Nelson 1945- *WhoAm 90*
Steinitz, Bernard *BioIn 16*
Steinitz, Kate Trauman 1893- *WhoAmA 91N*
Steinitz, Paul 1909-1988 *AnObit 1988, BioIn 16, PenDiMP*
Steinkamp, J. Alan *St&PR 91*
Steinke, Ann E 1946- *ConAu 32NR*
Steinke, Bettina 1913- *WhoAmA 91*
Steinke, Greg A. 1942- *IntWWM 90*
Steinke, Hans-Dieter Rolf 1941- *WhoE 91*
Steinke, Herbert Albert, Jr. 1927- *WhoAm 90*
Steinke, Klaus Dieter Helmut 1942- *WhoWor 91*
Steinke, Ralph G. *BioIn 16*
Steinke, Robert F. 1936- *St&PR 91*
Steinke, Terry 1951- *BioIn 16*
Steinlage, Paul Nicholas 1941- *St&PR 91*
Steinle, John G 1916-1990 *ConAu 132*
Steinle, John Gerard 1916- *WhoWor 91*
Steinle, Paul Michael 1939- *WhoAm 90*
Steinle, Russell Joseph 1950- *WhoE 91*
Steinman, Helen *BioIn 16*
Steinman, Ira Michael *BiDrAPA 89*
Steinman, John F 1916- *BiDrAPA 89*
Steinman, Lisa Malinowski 1950- *WhoAmW 91, WhoWrEP 89*
Steinman, Richard H. 1945- *St&PR 91*
Steinman, Robert Cleeton 1931- *WhoAm 90*
Steinmanis, Karl Sven 1948- *WhoEmL 91*
Steinmann, Matthias Friedrich 1942- *WhoWor 91*
Steinmetz, Charles P. 1865-1923 *WorAlBi*
Steinmetz, David Curtis 1936- *WhoAm 90*
Steinmetz, Donald Walter 1924- *WhoAm 90*
Steinmetz, Grace Ernst Titus *WhoAmA 91*
Steinmetz, Mary Darlene 1959- *WhoAmW 91*
Steinmetz, Richard Bird, Jr. 1929- *WhoAm 90, WhoWor 91*
Steinmetz, Wayne Edward 1945- *WhoEmL 91*
Steinmetz, William Richard 1948- *St&PR 91*
Steinmeyer, Kilian Paul 1942- *WhoE 91*
Steinmiller, Frank Neal 1931- *St&PR 91*
Steinmiller, John F. *WhoAm 90*
Steinmuller, Robert Isaac *BiDrAPA 89*
Steinmuller, Warren Jay 1955- *BiDrAPA 89*
Steinn Steinarr *DcScanL*
Steinohrt, William John 1937- *IntWWM 90*
Steinrauf, Jean Hamilton 1938- *WhoAmW 91*
Steinruck, Charles Francis, Jr. 1908- *WhoAm 90*
Steins, Jean C 1928- *BiDrAPA 89*
Steinsaltz, Adin *BioIn 16*
Steinschneider, Heinrich *EncO&P 3*
Steinsholt, Kjell 1929- *WhoWor 91*
Steinthal, A. John, Jr. 1936- *St&PR 91*
Steinthal, Kenneth L. 1952- *WhoEmL 91*
Steinthal, Nicholas 1931- *St&PR 91*
Steinwandel, A. Charles 1941- *St&PR 91*
Steinway, Henry E. 1797-1871 *WorAlBi*
Steinway, John Howland *BioIn 16*
Steinway, William 1835-1896 *WorAlBi*
Steinworth, Skip *BioIn 16*
Steiny, John Olerich 1922- *St&PR 91*
Steip, Richard Henry 1947- *BiDrAPA 89*
Steir, Pat 1940- *BiDWomA, WhoAmA 91*
Steisel, Jerald *BiDrAPA 89*
Steitz, Edward *BioIn 16, NewYTBS 90 [port]*
Steitz, Edward S 1920-1990 *ConAu 131*
Steitz, Joan Argetsinger 1941- *WhoAm 90, WhoAmW 91*
Steitz, Simon Heinrich *PenDiDA 89*
Steitz, William N. 1933- *St&PR 91*
Steizel, Walter Tell 1940- *St&PR 91*
Steketee, Jakob Abraham 1927- *WhoWor 91*
Steketee, Richard Walton 1924- *St&PR 91*
Stelck, Charles Richard 1917- *WhoAm 90*
Stelian, Judith 1937- *St&PR 91*
Stelios, Jean J. 1925- *St&PR 91*
Stelk, Marianne Boyd 1930- *WhoAmW 91*
Stell, Bernard S 1910- *BiDrAPA 89*
Stell, H Kenyon 1910- *WhoAmA 91*
Stella C. *EncO&P 3, EncPaPR 91*
Stella, Albert A.M. 1942- *WhoWrEP 89*
Stella, Antonietta 1929- *IntWWM 90*
Stella, Carl C. 1938- *St&PR 91*
Stella, Daniel Francis 1943- *WhoWor 91*
Stella, Frank *BioIn 16*
Stella, Frank 1936- *WhoAmA 91, WorAlBi*
Stella, Frank Daniel 1919- *St&PR 91*
Stella, Frank Dante 1919- *WhoAm 90*
Stella, Frank Philip 1936- *WhoAm 90*
Stella, Guido Maria Balsamo 1882-1942 *PenDiDA 89*
Stella, John Anthony 1938- *WhoAm 90*
Stella, Joseph 1877-1946 *BioIn 16, IntDcAA 90*
Stella, Joseph Henry 1953- *BiDrAPA 89*
Stellar, Eliot 1919- *WhoAm 90*
Stelle, Kellogg Sheffield 1948- *WhoWor 91*
Stelle, Lynn Douglas 1949- *WhoE 91*
Steller, Arthur Wayne 1947- *WhoAm 90, WhoWor 91*
Steller, Karel-Bram Ferdinand 1947- *WhoWor 91*
Steller, L.A. 1935- *St&PR 91*
Steller, Mitchell Edward 1948- *WhoAm 90*
Stellick, Gordon *WhoE 91*
Stellinger, Thomas S. 1948- *St&PR 91*
Stellmacher, Karl Ludwig 1909- *WhoE 91*
Stellmacher, Virginia Mae *BiDrAPA 89*
Stellman, L. Mandy 1922- *WhoAmW 91*
Stellman, Leslie Robert 1951- *WhoE 91*
Stellman, Martin *BioIn 16*
Stellman, Roberta Elise *BiDrAPA 89*
Stellman, Samuel David 1918- *WhoAm 90*
Stello, Dick 1934-1987 *Ballpl 90*
Stellwagen, Robert Harwood 1941- *WhoAm 90*
Stellwagen, Walter R. 1929- *St&PR 91*
Stelly, Matthias 1916- *WhoAm 90*
Stelly, Noelie Marie *WhoSSW 91*
Stelmach, Leigh 1939- *WhoSSW 91*
Stelmack, Joan 1948- *WhoAmW 91*
Steloff, Frances *BioIn 16*
Steloff, Frances 1887-1989 *AnObit 1989*
Stelow, Alice M. 1905- *St&PR 91*
Stelsel, Linda Hope 1948- *WhoAmW 91*
Stelting-Schultz, Kathleen M. 1942- *St&PR 91*
Steltmann, Harry Frederick 1943- *St&PR 91*
Steltz, Marie Ann *BiDrAPA 89*
Steltzlen, Janelle Hicks 1937- *WhoAmW 91, WhoWor 91*
Stelzel, Walter Tell, Jr. 1940- *WhoAm 90*
Stelzer, Irwin Mark 1932- *WhoE 91, WhoWor 91*
Stelzer, Joan *ODwPR 91*
Stelzer, Michael Norman 1938- *WhoAmA 91*
Stelzer, Winfried 1942- *WhoWor 91*
Stelzl, Ingeborg 1944- *WhoWor 91*
Stelzner, Charles Anthony 1943- *WhoSSW 91*
Stem, Carl Herbert 1935- *WhoAm 90*
Steman, Pamela Wheeler 1956- *WhoSSW 91*
Stemberg, Thomas G. 1949- *St&PR 91*
Stemberg, Thomas George 1949- *WhoE 91*
Stembridge, Vernie Albert 1924- *WhoAm 90*
Stemen, Noel L. E. 1946- *WhoAmW 91*
Stemer, Ross *ODwPR 91*
Stemme, Fred George 1939- *WhoWrEP 89*
Stemmer, Jay John 1939- *WhoWor 91*
Stemmer, Wayne J. 1942- *St&PR 91, WhoAm 90*
Stemmerman, Jane Elizabeth *St&PR 91*
Stemmler, Edward Joseph 1929- *WhoAm 90, WhoE 91*
Stemmler, Guin 1929- *St&PR 91*
Stemmy, Thomas Joseph 1938- *WhoWor 91*
Stemp, Ruth 1955- *BiDrAPA 89*
Stempel, Edward M *BiDrAPA 89*
Stempel, Ernest Edward 1916- *St&PR 91, WhoAm 90*
Stempel, Guido Hermann, III 1928- *WhoAm 90*
Stempel, Rina 1936- *WhoAmW 91*
Stempel, Robert C. *BioIn 16*
Stempel, Robert C. 1933- *WhoAm 90, WhoWor 91*
Stemper, John A 1919- *BiDrAPA 89*
Stemper, Mary Elaine 1964- *WhoAmW 91*
Stemper, William Herman, Jr. *WhoAm 90, WhoWor 91*
Stempien, William P. 1925- *ODwPR 91*
Stemple, Jane H. *BioIn 16*
Stemple, Joel Gilbert 1942- *WhoE 91*
Stempler, Allan Ivan 1942- *BiDrAPA 89, WhoE 91*
Stempler, Carrie Beth 1957- *WhoSSW 91*
Stempler, Jack Leon 1920- *WhoAm 90*
Stenander, Sylvia Larson 1947- *WhoAmW 91*
Stenback, Asser I 1913- *BiDrAPA 89*
Stenback, Guy Olof 1924- *WhoWor 91*
Stenberg, Abraham B. 1935- *St&PR 91*
Stenberg, Carl Waldamer, III 1943- *WhoAm 90*
Stenberg, Kjell Goran 1952- *WhoWor 91*
Stenberg, Robert T *BiDrAPA 89*
Stenberg, Sheldon LeRoy 1957- *WhoEmL 91*
Stenberg, William J. 1932- *St&PR 91*
Stenchever, Morton Albert 1931- *WhoAm 90*
Stendahl 1783-1842 *WorAlBi*
Stendahl, Krister 1921- *WhoAm 90, WhoWor 91*
Stendel, David 1927- *St&PR 91*
Steneck, Lawrence 1947- *St&PR 91*
Stenehjem, Leland Manford 1918- *WhoAm 90*
Stenehjem, Wayne Kevin 1953- *WhoEmL 91*
Stengel, Casey *BioIn 16*
Stengel, Casey 1889-1975 *Ballpl 90 [port]*
Stengel, Casey 1890-1975 *WorAlBi*
Stengel, David M 1947- *BiDrAPA 89*
Stengel, James Lamont 1956- *WhoEmL 91*
Stengel, James Lowell 1926- *St&PR 91*
Stengel, Jerome 1936- *St&PR 91*
Stengel, John J. 1936- *St&PR 91*
Stengel, Robert Frank 1938- *WhoAm 90, WhoE 91*
Stengel, Robert H. *St&PR 91*
Stenger, Amelia 1948- *WhoSSW 91*
Stenger, Leslie Ann 1961- *WhoAmW 91*
Stenger, Scott Charles 1967- *WhoE 91*
Stengert, Krzysztof B. *BioIn 16*
Stenholm, Anne *WhoWrEP 89*
Stenholm, Charles W. 1938- *WhoAm 90, WhoSSW 91*
Stenhouse, Dave 1933- *Ballpl 90*
Stenius, Goran Erik 1909- *DcScanL*
Stenkvist, Bjorn Gunnar 1934- *WhoWor 91*
Stenlake, Rodney Lee 1957- *WhoE 91*
Stenley, Stella B *BiDrAPA 89*
Stenmark, Ingemar 1956- *WorAlBi*
Stenmark, Jean Kerr 1922- *WhoAmW 91*
Stenner, Jerome M. 1919- *St&PR 91*
Stennes, Herbert J. 1932- *St&PR 91*
Stennett, Rennie 1951- *Ballpl 90*
Stennett, Steve Marshall 1951- *WhoE 91, WhoWor 91*
Stennett, William Mitchell 1948- *WhoSSW 91*
Stennis, John C. 1901- *WorAlBi*
Stennis, John Cornelius 1901- *WhoAm 90*
Stennis, William 1930- *BiDrAPA 89*
Stenquist, Connie Underwood 1949- *WhoAmW 91*
Stenquist, Donald Ray 1929- *St&PR 91*
Stenram, Robert 1941- *WhoWor 91*
Stenson, James T. 1954- *St&PR 91*
Stenson, Randall Lee 1947- *BiDrAPA 89*
Stenson, Richard Marshall 1935- *St&PR 91, WhoAm 90*
Stenson, Sherman David 1958- *WhoEmL 91*
Stenstrop, Ernest 1927- *WhoSSW 91*
Stent, Gunther Siegmund 1924- *WhoAm 90, WhoWrEP 89*
Stent, Keith Geoffrey 1934- *IntWWM 90*
Stentz, Patricia Hodder 1936- *WhoE 91*
Stenvall, Aleksis *DcScanL*
Stenvall, Kurt Arnold 1932- *WhoWor 91*
Stenzel, Alvin Milton, Jr. 1951- *St&PR 91*
Stenzel, Howard E. 1932- *St&PR 91*
Stenzel, Jeffrey Rheinhold *BiDrAPA 89*
Stenzel, Karen Louise 1951- *WhoAmW 91*
Stenzel, Kurt Hodgson 1932- *WhoAm 90*
Stenzel, Larry G. 1949- *WhoWrEP 89*
Stenzel, Pallie Jean 1928- *St&PR 91*
Stenzel, William A. 1923- *St&PR 91, WhoAm 90*
Stenzl, Jurg Thomas 1942- *IntWWM 90*
Steodle, Laurence J. 1947- *St&PR 91*
Steorts, Nancy Harvey 1936- *WhoAm 90, WhoAmW 91*
Step, Eugene L. 1929- *St&PR 91*
Step, Eugene Lee 1929- *WhoAm 90*
Stepan, Adolf Arnold 1942- *WhoWor 91*
Stepan, Alfred C. 1936- *WhoAm 90*
Stepan, F. Quinn 1937- *St&PR 91*
Stepan, Frank Quinn 1937- *WhoAm 90*
Stepan, Margaret Jean 1947- *WhoEmL 91*
Stepanchev, Stephen 1915- *WhoAm 90*
Stepanek, Anton G. 1924- *St&PR 91*
Stepanek, Jan 1937- *WhoWor 91*
Stepanek, Joseph Edward 1917- *WhoWor 91*
Stepanek, Pavel *EncPaPR 91*
Stepanian, Ira 1936- *St&PR 91, WhoAm 90*
Stepanik, Dennis S. 1944- *St&PR 91*
Stepanov, Aleksandr Vasil'evich 1908-1972 *DcScB S2*
Stepanova, Varara Feodorovna 1894-1958 *BiDWomA*
Stepanski, Anthony Francis 1942- *St&PR 91*
Stepanski, Anthony Francis, Jr. 1941- *WhoAm 90*
Stephan G. Stephansson *DcScanL*
Stephan, Alexander 1946- *WhoWor 91*
Stephan, Alexander H. 1946- *WhoAm 90*
Stephan, Bodo 1939- *WhoWor 91*
Stephan, Charles Robert 1911- *WhoSSW 91*
Stephan, Dan Sanders 1936- *St&PR 91*
Stephan, Edmund A. 1911- *St&PR 91*
Stephan, Edmund Anton 1911- *WhoAm 90*
Stephan, Edward Clark *NewYTBS 90*
Stephan, Edwin Bernard 1937- *St&PR 91*
Stephan, George Peter 1933- *St&PR 91, WhoAm 90, WhoE 91*
Stephan, John Jason 1941- *WhoAm 90, WhoWor 91*
Stephan, Karl *WhoWor 91*
Stephan, Pierre *PenDiDA 89*
Stephan, Richard C. 1940- *St&PR 91*
Stephan, Rita F. 1937- *St&PR 91*
Stephan, Robert A. 1932- *St&PR 91*
Stephan, Robert Conrad 1952- *WhoE 91*
Stephan, Robert Joseph, Jr. 1947- *WhoEmL 91*
Stephan, Robert M. 1942- *St&PR 91*
Stephan, Robert Taft 1933- *WhoAm 90*
Stephan, Ulrich 1929- *WhoWor 91*
Stephani, Michael James 1944- *St&PR 91*
Stephanie *EncCoWW*
Stephanie, Princess of Monaco *BioIn 16*
Stephanites, Conrad R. 1940- *St&PR 91*
Stephano, Stephen L. 1953- *St&PR 91*
Stephanoff, Kathryn 1929- *WhoE 91*
Stephanopoulos, Gregory 1950- *WhoAm 90*
Stephanos II *WhoWor 91*
Stephanou, Lydia 1927- *EncCoWW*
Stephanova, Lilyana 1929- *EncCoWW*
Stephans, William Jacob, Jr. 1926- *WhoAm 90*
Stephans, William W.T. 1942- *St&PR 91*
Stephans, William Walter Thomas 1942- *WhoAm 90*
Stephanson, Loraine Ann 1950- *WhoAmA 91*
Stephansson, Stephan G. 1853-1927 *DcScanL*
Stephany, Edward George, Jr. 1944- *WhoE 91*
Stephany, Jaromir 1930- *WhoAmA 91*
Stephen, King of England 1097?-1154 *BioIn 16*
Stephen, Adam *BioIn 16*
Stephen, Alexander M. *WhNaAH*
Stephen, Benjamin 1934- *BiDrAPA 89*
Stephen, Donald Alexander 1935- *St&PR 91*
Stephen, Francis B 1916- *WhoAmA 91*
Stephen, James Fitzjames 1829-1894 *BioIn 16*
Stephen, John Erle 1918- *WhoAm 90, WhoWor 91*
Stephen, Leslie 1832-1904 *BioIn 16, WorAlBi*
Stephen, Michael A. 1929- *WhoAm 90*
Stephen, Ninian Martin 1923- *WhoWor 91*
Stephen, Patrice 1927- *St&PR 91*
Stephen, Richard Joseph 1945- *WhoEmL 91, WhoWor 91*
Stephen, Robert Joseph *BiDrAPA 89*
Stephen, Samuel Jeyaraja 1929- *WhoWor 91*
Stephen, Virginia *ConAu 130, MajTwCW*
Stephens, Adele 1949- *WhoWrEP 89*
Stephens, Albert B 1925- *BiDrAPA 89*
Stephens, Alexander H. 1812-1883 *WorAlBi*
Stephens, Alexander Hamilton 1812-1883 *BioIn 16*
Stephens, Alice 1858-1932 *BiDWomA*
Stephens, Alice Elizabeth 1926- *WhoAmW 91*
Stephens, Alison Amy 1949- *WhoAmW 91*
Stephens, Ann Katherine Hamilton 1958- *WhoE 91*
Stephens, Ann Sophia 1810-1886 *FemiCLE*
Stephens, Bart Nelson 1922- *WhoAm 90*
Stephens, Bernard *BioIn 16, NewYTBS 90*
Stephens, Bobby Gene 1935- *WhoAm 90*
Stephens, Brad 1951- *WhoAm 90*
Stephens, Bruce 1924- *St&PR 91*
Stephens, Bryan 1920- *Ballpl 90*
Stephens, C. Michael 1949- *WhoSSW 91*
Stephens, Catherine 1794-1882 *PenDiMP*
Stephens, Charles Howard 1937- *St&PR 91*
Stephens, Charles William 1930- *WhoAm 90, WhoWor 91*
Stephens, Christopher P. *WhoWrEP 89*
Stephens, Curtis 1932- *WhoAmA 91*
Stephens, Deborah Haines 1960- *WhoAmW 91*
Stephens, Denny 1932- *WhoAm 90*
Stephens, Donald Joseph 1918- *WhoAm 90*

Stephens, Duncan C BiDrAPA 89
Stephens, Dwight F. 1913-1989 BioIn 16
Stephens, E. Barrie WhoSSW 91
Stephens, Edward B. 1947- St&PR 91
Stephens, Edward Carl 1924- WhoAm 90, WhoE 91, WhoWor 91, WhoWrEP 89
Stephens, Edward Martin 1937- BiDrAPA 89
Stephens, Elton B. 1911- St&PR 91
Stephens, Elton Bryson 1911- WhoAm 90
Stephens, Frank BioIn 16
Stephens, Frank Pearson 1944- WhoSSW 91
Stephens, Frederick Howard, Jr. 1931- St&PR 91
Stephens, Gay 1951- WhoAmW 91
Stephens, Gene 1933- Ballpl 90
Stephens, George Charles 1941- WhoSSW 91
Stephens, George Edward, Jr. 1936- WhoAm 90
Stephens, George Vincent BiDrAPA 89
Stephens, Gerald D. 1932- WhoAm 90
Stephens, Gerald Dean 1932- St&PR 91
Stephens, Gertrude W. 1910- St&PR 91
Stephens, Glenn Arthur 1926- WhoWrEP 89
Stephens, Harold 1954- WhoEmL 91
Stephens, J.T. 1923- St&PR 91
Stephens, Jack Edward, Jr. 1955- WhoE 91
Stephens, Jack Thomas, Jr. 1947- WhoAm 90, WhoSSW 91
Stephens, Jackson Thomas 1923- WhoAm 90, WhoSSW 91
Stephens, Jacqueline Griffith 1962- WhoSSW 91
Stephens, James 1882-1950 AuBYP 90
Stephens, James Haley 1951- WhoSSW 91
Stephens, James M. 1946- WhoAm 90
Stephens, James T. 1939- WhoAm 90
Stephens, Jay BioIn 16
Stephens, Jay B. 1946- WhoAm 90
Stephens, Jerry Wayne 1949- WhoAm 90
Stephens, Jim 1883-1965 Ballpl 90
Stephens, John F. 1916- St&PR 91
Stephens, John F. 1949- WhoAm 90, WhoE 91
Stephens, John F., Jr. 1948- WhoEmL 91
Stephens, John Joseph 1928- St&PR 91
Stephens, John Lloyd BioIn 16
Stephens, John P. 1941- St&PR 91
Stephens, John Robert 1944- BiDrAPA 89
Stephens, John S. 1943- St&PR 91
Stephens, John Wellington 1934- WhoE 91
Stephens, Jonathan Paul 1951- IntWWM 90
Stephens, Joseph H 1927- BiDrAPA 89
Stephens, Kate 1853-1938 BioAmW
Stephens, Laura Lynne 1958- WhoAmW 91
Stephens, Leonora 1951- BiDrAPA 89
Stephens, Lester D 1933- ConAu 32NR
Stephens, Lester John 1943- St&PR 91
Stephens, Lester John, Jr. 1943- WhoAm 90
Stephens, Lisa Ann 1959- WhoAmW 91
Stephens, Marlin Gerard 1946- WhoEmL 91
Stephens, Martha 1927- BiDrAPA 89
Stephens, Martha Anne 1939- BiDrAPA 89
Stephens, Martha T. 1937- WhoWrEP 89
Stephens, Mary Elizabeth 1949- WhoAmW 91
Stephens, Milton E. 1927- St&PR 91
Stephens, Mitchell Smart, II BiDrAPA 89
Stephens, Norma J. 1928- WhoAmW 91
Stephens, Norval Blair, Jr. 1928- WhoAm 90
Stephens, Olin James, II 1908- WhoAm 90
Stephens, Pamela Mitchell 1955- WhoAmW 91
Stephens, Paul Andrew, Jr. 1950- WhoSSW 91
Stephens, Peggy AuBYP 90
Stephens, Peggy Sue 1956- BiDrAPA 89
Stephens, Perrin Stanford 1941- WhoSSW 91
Stephens, Peter James 1957- WhoE 91
Stephens, Peter John AuBYP 90
Stephens, Ralph E. 1906- St&PR 91
Stephens, Reed WhoWrEP 89
Stephens, Richard Bernard 1934- St&PR 91, WhoAm 90
Stephens, Richard M. 1825-1887 AmLegL
Stephens, Robert 1931- WhoWor 91
Stephens, Robert Allan 1937- WhoAm 90, WhoE 91
Stephens, Robert David 1949- WhoSSW 91
Stephens, Robert F. 1927- WhoAm 90, WhoSSW 91
Stephens, Robert F. 1948- St&PR 91
Stephens, Robert Grier, III 1943- BiDrAPA 89
Stephens, Robert J. BioIn 16
Stephens, Robert J. 1917- St&PR 91
Stephens, Robert Newton 1945- St&PR 91
Stephens, Robert W. 1939- St&PR 91
Stephens, Ronald Carlyle 1941- WhoSSW 91
Stephens, Scott Mitchell 1955- WhoE 91
Stephens, Sheryl Lynne 1949- WhoAmW 91
Stephens, Sidney Dee 1945- WhoEmL 91, WhoSSW 91
Stephens, Solomon William 1949- WhoSSW 91
Stephens, Stanley Graham 1929- WhoAm 90
Stephens, Susan Kay 1954- WhoAmW 91
Stephens, Suzanne 1949- SmATA X [port]
Stephens, Thomas B. 1944- St&PR 91
Stephens, Thomas Edwin 1903-1988 BioIn 16
Stephens, Thomas M. 1931- WhoWrEP 89
Stephens, Thomas Maron 1931- WhoAm 90
Stephens, Thomas Michael 1941- WhoAmA 91
Stephens, Vern 1920-1965 Ballpl 90
Stephens, Vernon 1920-1968 BioIn 16
Stephens, Victoria Lynn 1960- WhoAmW 91
Stephens, Vincent Joseph 1943- BiDrAPA 89
Stephens, W. Thomas BioIn 16
Stephens, Wade Carroll BioIn 16
Stephens, Wanda J BiDrAPA 89
Stephens, Warren A. WhoSSW 91
Stephens, Wheeler Ralph 1926- St&PR 91
Stephens, William Blakely 1930- WhoAmA 91
Stephens, William Harold, III 1949- St&PR 91
Stephens, William Henry 1948- WhoE 91
Stephens, William Leonard 1929- WhoAm 90
Stephens, William M. 1925- AuBYP 90
Stephens, William Richard 1932- WhoAm 90
Stephens, William Ronald 1944- WhoWrEP 89
Stephens, William T. 1922- St&PR 91
Stephens, William Theodore 1922- WhoAm 90
Stephens, William Thomas WhoAm 90
Stephens, Woodford Cefis 1913- WhoAm 90
Stephens, Wray M. 1948- St&PR 91
Stephensen, Jens Severin 1941- WhoWor 91
Stephensen, Magnus 1903- ConDes 90
Stephenson, Amy Marie 1960- WhoAmW 91
Stephenson, Anthony 1937- WhoWrEP 89
Stephenson, Arthur Emmet, Jr. 1945- St&PR 91, WhoAm 90, WhoEmL 91, WhoWor 91
Stephenson, Bette M. 1924- WhoAmW 91
Stephenson, Blair Y. 1947- WhoSSW 91
Stephenson, Bryan W. 1950- St&PR 91
Stephenson, Calvin P. 1924- St&PR 91
Stephenson, D H BiDrAPA 89
Stephenson, Daryl R BiDrAPA 89
Stephenson, David Curtis 1891-1966 BioIn 16
Stephenson, Deborah Mae 1946- WhoAmW 91
Stephenson, Donald Gray 1956- WhoSSW 91
Stephenson, Donald Grier, Jr. 1942- WhoE 91
Stephenson, Donald James 1947- IntWWM 90
Stephenson, Donnan 1919- WhoAm 90
Stephenson, Dorothy Belcher 1930- St&PR 91
Stephenson, Dorothy Esther 1944- WhoWor 91
Stephenson, Dorothy Griffith 1949- WhoEmL 91
Stephenson, Dwight 1957- WhoAm 90
Stephenson, Earl 1947- Ballpl 90
Stephenson, Everett Southward 1923- St&PR 91
Stephenson, Gary 1944- St&PR 91
Stephenson, Garylee 1968- WhoEmL 91
Stephenson, George 1781-1848 BioIn 16, WorAlBi
Stephenson, George M. St&PR 91
Stephenson, H. Howard 1929- BioIn 16, St&PR 91
Stephenson, Harold F. 1915- WhoAm 90
Stephenson, Herman Howard 1929- WhoAm 90
Stephenson, Hugh Edward, Jr. 1922- WhoAm 90
Stephenson, Irene Hamlen 1923- WhoAmW 91, WhoWor 91
Stephenson, J. Phil, Jr. 1941- St&PR 91
Stephenson, James M., Jr. 1936- St&PR 91
Stephenson, Jan Lynn 1951- WhoAm 90, WhoAmW 91
Stephenson, Jeffrey Scott BiDrAPA 89
Stephenson, Jerry 1943- Ballpl 90
Stephenson, Joe 1921- Ballpl 90
Stephenson, John Bell 1937- WhoAm 90
Stephenson, John H. 1929- BioIn 16, WhoAmA 91
Stephenson, John Phillip 1951- WhoSSW 91
Stephenson, Johnny 1941- Ballpl 90
Stephenson, Joseph E. 1933- St&PR 91
Stephenson, Junius Winfield 1922- St&PR 91
Stephenson, Kathryn Lyle 1912- WhoWrEP 89
Stephenson, Kent R. 1949- St&PR 91
Stephenson, Linda F. ODwPR 91
Stephenson, Linda Jean 1952- WhoAmW 91
Stephenson, Linda Sue 1939- WhoAmW 91
Stephenson, Lisa G. 1955- WhoAmW 91
Stephenson, Lois Carpenter 1929- WhoSSW 91
Stephenson, Louise Scott 1921- St&PR 91
Stephenson, Marjory 1885-1948 DcScB S2
Stephenson, Mark Ray 1949- WhoEmL 91
Stephenson, Mary Rita 1917- WhoAm 90, WhoAmW 91
Stephenson, Michael James 1945- St&PR 91
Stephenson, Ned Eldon 1957- WhoEmL 91
Stephenson, Nelson L. 1952- St&PR 91
Stephenson, Peter St&PR 91
Stephenson, Phil 1941- St&PR 91
Stephenson, R.H., III 1922- St&PR 91
Stephenson, Rebecca Lynn 1963- WhoEmL 91
Stephenson, Richard Ismert 1937- WhoWor 91
Stephenson, Richard Keith 1925- St&PR 91
Stephenson, Riggs 1898-1985 Ballpl 90
Stephenson, Robert 1803-1859 BioIn 16
Stephenson, Robert Allan 1934- WhoE 91
Stephenson, Robert Harper, III 1922- WhoSSW 91
Stephenson, Roscoe Bolar, Jr. 1922- WhoAm 90, WhoSSW 91
Stephenson, Russell L. 1915- St&PR 91
Stephenson, Samuel Edward, Jr. 1926- WhoAm 90, WhoSSW 91
Stephenson, Sarah 1738-1802 FemiCLE
Stephenson, Shelby 1938- WhoWrEP 89
Stephenson, Susanne 1935- BioIn 16
Stephenson, Susanne G 1935- WhoAmA 91
Stephenson, Sylvia Alexandra 1945- WhoSSW 91
Stephenson, Thomas N BiDrAPA 89
Stephenson, Toni Edwards 1945- WhoAm 90, WhoAmW 91, WhoEmL 91, WhoWor 91
Stephenson, Violet BiDrAPA 89
Stephenson, W. David 1945- ODwPR 91
Stephenson, William 1896-1989 AnObit 1989
Stephenson, William 1902-1989 BioIn 16
Stephenson, William E. 1942- St&PR 91
Stephenson, William Edward 1934- WhoE 91
Stephenson, William Samuel 1896-1989 BioIn 16
Stepkoski, Robert John 1933- WhoSSW 91
Stepler, Paul Stoneham 1949- St&PR 91
Stepner, Laraine E. Adler 1943- WhoAmW 91
Stepnick, Donna Lynne 1963- WhoSSW 91
Stepp, Ann AuBYP 90
Stepp, George Allan, Jr. 1922- WhoWor 91
Stepp, James Michael 1944- WhoAm 90
Stepp, John R. 1941- WhoAm 90
Stepp Bejarano, Linda Sue 1950- WhoHisp 91
Steppacher, Robert Clarke 1930- BiDrAPA 89
Steppat, Leo Ludwig 1910-1964 WhoAmA 91N
Steppe, Donald Joseph 1942- St&PR 91
Steppenwolf EncPR&S 89
Steppler, Howard Alvey 1918- WhoAm 90
Stepro, B.J. 1929- St&PR 91
Stept, Michael BiDrAPA 89
Stept, Sammy H. 1897-1964 OxCPMus
Stepto, Michele 1946- SmATA 61
Stepto, Robert Charles 1920- WhoAm 90
Steptoe, John 1950- AuBYP 90
Steptoe, John 1950-1989 AnObit 1989, BioIn 16, ConAu 129, SmATA 63 [port]
Steptoe, Lydia MajTwCW
Steptoe, Patrick 1913-1988 AnObit 1988, BioIn 16
Steptoe, Roger Guy 1953- IntWWM 90
Ster, John W. 1937- St&PR 91
Ster, Thomas Dale 1952- WhoEmL 91
Steranko, James 1938- EncACom
Sterba, Richard F. 1898-1989 BioIn 16
Sterban, Richard Anthony 1943- WhoAm 90
Sterchi, Robert Perin 1938- St&PR 91
Steremberg, Susan BiDrAPA 89
Stergios, Jerry 1917- St&PR 91
Stergiou, Angeline BiDrAPA 89
Sterian, Margareta 1897- EncCoWW
Sterken, R. PenDiDA 89
Sterling, A. Mary Fackler 1955- WhoAm 90, WhoAmW 91, WhoEmL 91
Sterling, Alan Louis 1946- BiDrAPA 89
Sterling, Antoinette 1850-1904 PenDiMP
Sterling, Bonnie K. ODwPR 91
Sterling, Brett 1920- SmATA X [port]
Sterling, Donald Justus, Jr. 1927- WhoAm 90
Sterling, Donald R. 1936- St&PR 91
Sterling, Donald T. WhoAm 90
Sterling, Dorothy 1913- AuBYP 90
Sterling, Dorothy Anne 1963- WhoAmW 91
Sterling, Frank 1945- St&PR 91
Sterling, Gary Campbell 1941- WhoWrEP 89
Sterling, George 1869-1926 BioIn 16
Sterling, Harold G. 1925- WhoE 91
Sterling, Harry BiDrAPA 89
Sterling, Harry, Jr. 1943- St&PR 91
Sterling, Helen AuBYP 90, ConAu 131
Sterling, Jack 1915-1990 NewYTBS 90 [port]
Sterling, Jan 1923- WorAlBi
Sterling, Jeffrey 1934- WhoWor 91
Sterling, John BioIn 16
Sterling, John Robert 1945- St&PR 91
Sterling, Keir Brooks 1934- WhoAm 90, WhoE 91, WhoWor 91
Sterling, Kenneth 1920- WhoAm 90
Sterling, Patricia Ann 1947- WhoSSW 91
Sterling, Philip 1907-1989 BioIn 16, ConAu 129, SmATA 63
Sterling, Robert H. St&PR 91
Sterling, Robert Lee, Jr. 1933- WhoE 91, WhoWor 91
Sterling, Shirley Frampton 1920- WhoSSW 91
Sterling, Steven ODwPR 91
Sterling, Stewart 1895- TwCCr&M 91
Sterling, Thomas William, III 1947- St&PR 91
Stermac, Anthony George 1921- WhoAm 90
Sterman, Betsy AuBYP 90
Sterman, Irvin 1929- WhoAm 90
Sterman, Samuel AuBYP 90
Stermer, Dugald Robert 1936- WhoAm 90, WhoAmA 91, WhoWor 91
Stern, Aaron BiDrAPA 89
Stern, Aaron 1918- WhoAm 90, WhoWrEP 89
Stern, Alan I. 1934- St&PR 91
Stern, Alan Isaac 1948- WhoE 91
Stern, Alan Robert 1957- WhoE 91
Stern, Alfred Phillip 1933- WhoAm 90
Stern, Alice H. 1953- WhoE 91
Stern, Allan D.R. 1932- St&PR 91
Stern, Andrew M. ODwPR 91
Stern, Andrew Milton 1949- WhoEmL 91
Stern, Ann C. 1952- St&PR 91
Stern, Annie Ward 1944- WhoE 91
Stern, Anthony John BiDrAPA 89
Stern, Arlene Helen 1950- WhoAmW 91
Stern, Arthur Cecil 1909- WhoAm 90
Stern, Arthur Charles 1957- WhoEmL 91, WhoWrEP 89
Stern, Arthur I 1950- WhoAmA 91
Stern, Arthur Lewis 1911- WhoAmA 91N
Stern, Arthur Lewis, Mrs 1913- WhoAmA 91N
Stern, Arthur Paul 1925- St&PR 91, WhoAm 90, WhoWor 91
Stern, Barry John 1944- St&PR 91
Stern, Carl Leonard 1937- WhoAm 90
Stern, Catherine 1894-1973 AuBYP 90
Stern, Celia Ellen 1954- WhoE 91
Stern, Charles 1920- St&PR 91, WhoAm 90
Stern, Charles Bertram 1915- St&PR 91
Stern, Charles M. 1943- WhoAm 90
Stern, Charlotte Cohen 1926- BiDrAPA 89
Stern, Chester Martin 1923- St&PR 91
Stern, Clarence Ames 1913- WhoAm 90
Stern, Curt 1902-1981 DcScB S2
Stern, Daniel EncCoWW
Stern, Daniel 1928- WhoAm 90
Stern, Darryl Roland 1942- BiDrAPA 89
Stern, David Harold 1935- WhoWor 91
Stern, David Joel 1942- WhoAm 90, WhoE 91
Stern, David Michael 1956- WhoE 91
Stern, Dennis M. 1941- St&PR 91
Stern, Dennis M. 1947- WhoAm 90
Stern, Douglas Donald 1939- WhoSSW 91
Stern, Edgar B., Jr. 1922- St&PR 91
Stern, Edward Mayer 1946- WhoEmL 91
Stern, Edward R. 1914- St&PR 91
Stern, Elaine 1961- ODwPR 91
Stern, Elizabeth 1889-1954 FemiCLE
Stern, Ernest 1920- St&PR 91
Stern, Ernest 1928- WhoAm 90
Stern, Eugene E BiDrAPA 89
Stern, Frank 1928- WhoAm 90

Stern, Fred 1927- *BiDrAPA 89*
Stern, Frederick H. 1953- *ODwPR 91*
Stern, Frederick M. *St&PR 91N*
Stern, Frederick M. *BioIn 16*
Stern, Fritz Richard 1926- *WhoAm 90*
Stern, G. B. 1890-1973 *BioIn 16, FemiCLE*
Stern, Gary Hilton 1944- *St&PR 91*
Stern, Gary Peter 1943- *St&PR 91*
Stern, Geoffrey 1942- *WhoAm 90*
Stern, Geoffrey Adlai 1955- *WhoAm 90*
Stern, George 1924- *St&PR 91*
Stern, George M *BiDrAPA 89*
Stern, Gerald 1925- *DcLB 105 [port]*
Stern, Gerald Daniel 1933- *WhoAm 90*
Stern, Gerald Joseph 1925- *WhoAm 90*
Stern, Gerald M. 1937- *St&PR 91, WhoAm 90*
Stern, Gladys Bronwyn 1890-1973 *BioIn 16*
Stern, Gloria Jean *BiDrAPA 89*
Stern, Grace Mary 1925- *WhoAmW 91*
Stern, Guy 1922- *WhoAm 90*
Stern, H. H. 1913-1987 *BioIn 16*
Stern, H Peter *WhoAmA 91*
Stern, Hans Heinrich 1913-1987 *BioIn 16*
Stern, Hans L. 1929- *St&PR 91*
Stern, Harold Phillip 1922-1977 *WhoAmA 91N*
Stern, Harriet Carol *BiDrAPA 89*
Stern, Harris I. 1928- *St&PR 91*
Stern, Harvey B. 1939- *St&PR 91*
Stern, Henry L. 1924- *St&PR 91*
Stern, Henry Louis 1924- *WhoAm 90*
Stern, Herbert B. 1937- *St&PR 91*
Stern, Herbert Jay 1936- *WhoAm 90*
Stern, Hersh Leon 1950- *WhoE 91*
Stern, Howard *BioIn 16*
Stern, Howard S. 1931- *St&PR 91*
Stern, Irene Monat 1932- *WhoAmA 91*
Stern, Isaac *BioIn 16*
Stern, Isaac 1920- *IntWWM 90, PenDiMP, WhoAm 90, WhoWor 91, WorAlBi*
Stern, J Edward *BiDrAPA 89*
Stern, James A. 1950- *St&PR 91*
Stern, James Max 1955- *WhoEmL 91*
Stern, Jan Peter 1926- *WhoAm 90, WhoAmA 91*
Stern, Jean 1946- *WhoAmA 91*
Stern, Jerry J 1933- *BiDrAPA 89*
Stern, Joel Mark 1941- *WhoAm 90*
Stern, John 1926- *WhoE 91*
Stern, John Jules 1955- *WhoEmL 91*
Stern, John Peter 1944- *WhoWor 91*
Stern, Jonathan H. 1944- *St&PR 91*
Stern, Jonathan Michael 1959- *WhoE 91*
Stern, Joseph Smith, Jr. 1918- *WhoAm 90*
Stern, Julian N. 1924- *St&PR 91*
Stern, Kathleen Elizabeth *BiDrAPA 89*
Stern, Kenneth B 1937- *BiDrAPA 89*
Stern, Larry N. 1949- *St&PR 91*
Stern, Lee Edward 1936- *ODwPR 91*
Stern, Leo 1862-1904 *PenDiMP*
Stern, Leon 1947- *BiDrAPA 89*
Stern, Leon M. 1930- *St&PR 91*
Stern, Leonard *BioIn 16*
Stern, Leonard 1938- *ConAmBL*
Stern, Leonard Bernard 1923- *WhoAm 90*
Stern, Leonard Norman 1938- *WhoAm 90*
Stern, Leonard Wayne 1952- *BiDrAPA 89*
Stern, Lewis Arthur 1934- *WhoAm 90*
Stern, Lilian Sarah 1958- *WhoE 91*
Stern, Lloyd G *BiDrAPA 89*
Stern, Louis 1945- *WhoAmA 91*
Stern, Louis William 1935- *WhoAm 90*
Stern, Louise 1921- *WhoAmA 91*
Stern, Madeleine 1912- *AuBYP 90*
Stern, Madeleine Bettina 1912- *WhoAm 90, WhoWrEP 89*
Stern, Marc Irwin 1944- *WhoAm 90, WhoWor 91*
Stern, Marianne 1950- *WhoAmW 91, WhoE 91, WhoWor 91*
Stern, Martha Dodd *NewYTBS 90 [port]*
Stern, Martha Eccles Dodd 1908-1990 *ConAu 132*
Stern, Marvin 1916- *BiDrAPA 89, WhoAm 90*
Stern, Marvin 1923- *WhoAm 90*
Stern, Maurice L *BiDrAPA 89*
Stern, Melissa 1986- *BioIn 16*
Stern, Melvin Joseph 1940- *BiDrAPA 89*
Stern, Merle Naomi *BiDrAPA 89*
Stern, Michael 1910- *WhoWor 91*
Stern, Michael D. 1949- *St&PR 91*
Stern, Michael Lawrence 1948- *WhoE 91, WhoEmL 91*
Stern, Michele Suchard 1943- *WhoAmW 91*
Stern, Milton *BioIn 16*
Stern, Milton 1927- *WhoAm 90*
Stern, Mortimer Phillip 1926- *WhoAm 90*
Stern, Nancy Ann 1944- *WhoAmW 91*
Stern, Nancy Fortgang 1944- *WhoAmW 91*
Stern, Neal M. 1951- *St&PR 91*
Stern, Ned *St&PR 91*
Stern, Nicholas Herbert 1946- *WhoWor 91*
Stern, Norman Stanley 1947- *WhoEmL 91*
Stern, Otto 1888-1969 *WorAlBi*
Stern, Paul *BioIn 16*
Stern, Paul G. *WhoAm 90*
Stern, Paula 1945- *WhoAm 90*
Stern, Peter R. 1947- *WhoE 91*
Stern, Philip Maurice 1926- *WhoWrEP 89*
Stern, Philip VanDoren 1900-1984 *AuBYP 90*
Stern, Richard David 1936- *WhoAm 90*
Stern, Richard G. 1928- *BioIn 16*
Stern, Richard Gustave 1928- *WhoAm 90, WhoWrEP 89*
Stern, Richard J. 1913- *St&PR 91*
Stern, Richard James 1922- *WhoAm 90*
Stern, Richard Martin 1915- *TwCCr&M 91, WhoWrEP 89*
Stern, Robert *BiDrAPA 89*
Stern, Robert 1936- *WhoAm 90*
Stern, Robert A. M. 1939- *BioIn 16*
Stern, Robert Arthur Morton 1939- *WhoAm 90*
Stern, Robert D. 1929- *St&PR 91*
Stern, Robert Joel 1939- *BiDrAPA 89*
Stern, Robert Louis 1908- *WhoAm 90*
Stern, Robert M *BiDrAPA 89*
Stern, Robert Morris 1937- *WhoAm 90*
Stern, Ronald J. 1931- *St&PR 91*
Stern, Ronald Norman *BioIn 16*
Stern, Roslyne Paige 1926- *WhoAm 90, WhoAmW 91*
Stern, Roy *BiDrAPA 89*
Stern, Roy D. 1943- *St&PR 91*
Stern, Russell T., Jr. 1927- *St&PR 91*
Stern, Ruth 1929- *WhoAmW 91*
Stern, Samu 1874-1947 *BioIn 16*
Stern, Samuel Alan 1929- *WhoAm 90*
Stern, Sandra Smolnicky 1960- *WhoE 91*
Stern, Stanley *BiDrAPA 89*
Stern, Stephen L 1946- *BiDrAPA 89*
Stern, Steve 1947- *ConAu 132*
Stern, Steven A. 1943- *St&PR 91*
Stern, Stuart *TwCCr&M 91*
Stern, Susan 1953- *ODwPR 91*
Stern, Sydney S. *BioIn 16*
Stern, T. Noel 1913- *WhoAm 90*
Stern, Theodore 1929- *WhoAm 90, WhoE 91*
Stern, Theodore A 1949- *BiDrAPA 89*
Stern, Theodore Allan 1949- *WhoE 91*
Stern, Tracy 1953- *ConAu 129*
Stern, Walter Eugene 1920- *WhoAm 90*
Stern, Walter P. 1928- *St&PR 91*
Stern, Walter Phillips 1928- *WhoAm 90, WhoE 91*
Stern, Walter S. 1925- *St&PR 91*
Stern, Warren Charles 1944- *St&PR 91*
Stern, Wayne Brian 1948- *WhoSSW 91*
Stern, Wilhelm Z. V. 1927-1989 *BioIn 16*
Stern, William Howard 1930- *WhoE 91*
Stern, William Louis 1926- *WhoAm 90*
Stern Bellowe, Jacqueline 1958- *WhoAmW 91*
Stern-Chaves, Elidieth I. 1960- *WhoHisp 91*
Sternad, Susan Marie 1957- *WhoAmW 91*
Sternal, Sandra Gaunt 1946- *WhoAmW 91*
Sternbach, Abraham *BiDrAPA 89*
Sternbach, Anna 1912- *BiDrAPA 89*
Sternbach, Harvey 1924- *St&PR 91*
Sternbach, Harvey Allen 1951- *BiDrAPA 89*
Sternbach, Leo Henryk 1908- *WhoAm 90*
Sternbach, Seymour Bernard 1928- *St&PR 91*
Sternbach, Sidney M., Jr. 1909- *St&PR 91*
Sternbach, Stephen Eric *BiDrAPA 89*
Sternberg, Arthur 1936- *BiDrAPA 89*
Sternberg, Arthur M 1926- *BiDrAPA 89*
Sternberg, Charles Paul *BiDrAPA 89*
Sternberg, Daniel Arie 1913- *WhoAm 90*
Sternberg, David Edward 1946- *BiDrAPA 89*
Sternberg, David J. 1948- *WhoEmL 91*
Sternberg, David Joel 1962- *WhoEmL 91*
Sternberg, Donna Udin 1951- *WhoAmW 91*
Sternberg, Harry 1904- *WhoAm 90, WhoAmA 91*
Sternberg, Hilgard O'Reilly 1917- *WhoAm 90*
Sternberg, Jonathon 1919- *IntWWM 90*
Sternberg, Judi Ann 1941- *WhoE 91*
Sternberg, Marvin Edward 1934- *St&PR 91*
Sternberg, Michael R. *BiDrAPA 89*
Sternberg, Patricia 1930- *BioIn 16*
Sternberg, Patricia Ann Sikes 1930- *NotWoAT*
Sternberg, Paul 1918- *WhoAm 90*
Sternberg, Paul Edward, Sr 1934- *WhoAmA 91, WhoSSW 91*
Sternberg, Paul J. 1933- *WhoAm 90*
Sternberg, Richard Ira 1948- *WhoE 91*
Sternberg, Robert Jeffrey 1949- *WhoE 91*
Sternberg, Ronald I. *St&PR 91*
Sternberg, Saul *BioIn 16*
Sternberg, Sigmund 1921- *WhoWor 91*
Sternberg, Stephen Stanley 1920- *WhoE 91*
Sternberger, Ludwig Amadeus 1921- *WhoAm 90*
Sternberger, Stephen Jeffrey 1949- *St&PR 91*
Sternbuch, Recha 1905-1971 *BioIn 16*
Sterndale-Bennett, Barry Monkhouse 1939- *IntWWM 90*
Sterne, Bobbie Lynn 1919- *WhoAmW 91*
Sterne, Harold E. 1926- *St&PR 91*
Sterne, Hedda 1916- *BiDWomA, WhoAmA 91*
Sterne, Joseph Robert Livingston 1928- *WhoAm 90*
Sterne, Laurence 1713-1768 *WorAlBi*
Sterne, Lawrence Jon 1949- *WhoE 91, WhoWor 91*
Sterne, Maurice 1878-1957 *WhoAmA 91N*
Sterne, Michael Lyon 1936- *WhoAm 90*
Sterne, Richard Joseph, Jr. 1943- *St&PR 91*
Sterner, Charles Gene 1926- *St&PR 91*
Sterner, Douglas Wyatt 1945- *WhoE 91*
Sterner, Frank Maurice 1935- *St&PR 91, WhoAm 90*
Sterner, Gene Edward 1940- *St&PR 91*
Sterner, James Hervi 1904- *WhoAm 90*
Sterner, Jerry *BioIn 16*
Sterner, Jerry Joseph 1938- *WhoAm 90*
Sterner, John 1912- *St&PR 91*
Sterner, Judy Murtz 1953- *WhoAmW 91*
Sterner, Katherine Schmidt *EncO&P 3*
Sterner, Michael Edmund 1928- *WhoAm 90*
Sterner, Robert Warner 1958- *WhoSSW 91*
Sternfield, Frederick William 1914- *IntWWM 90*
Sternfield, Scott Frederic 1940- *St&PR 91*
Sternglass, Lila M. 1934- *WhoAm 90*
Sternhagen, Frances 1930- *ConTFT 8*
Sternheim, Carl 1878-1942 *BioIn 16*
Sternheim, Maria Anna Antonia *EncCoWW*
Sternheim, William Adolf Carl 1878-1942 *BioIn 16*
Sternheimer, Mark Aiden 1929- *St&PR 91*
Sterni, John 1938- *St&PR 91*
Sternklar, Avraham 1930- *IntWWM 90*
Sternlicht, Harold C 1960- *BiDrAPA 89*
Sternlicht, Manny 1932- *WhoAm 90*
Sternlicht, Sanford 1931- *WhoAm 90*
Sternlieb, Barry F. 1947- *WhoWrEP 89*
Sternlieb, George 1928- *WhoE 91*
Sternlight, Peter Donn 1928- *WhoAm 90*
Sterns, Joel Henry 1934- *WhoAm 90*
Sterns, Patricia Margaret 1952- *WhoEmL 91*
Sternschein, Irving 1919- *BiDrAPA 89*
Sternson, Larry Allen 1946- *WhoE 91*
Sternstein, Alan Barry 1950- *WhoEmL 91*
Sternstein, Gerson Marc *BiDrAPA 89*
Sterrenberg, Elsie Wright 1928- *IntWWM 90*
Sterrett, Cliff *EncACom*
Sterrett, Cliff 1883-1964 *WhoAmA 91N*
Sterrett, James Edward 1931- *St&PR 91*
Sterrett, Joel A. 1936- *St&PR 91*
Sterrett, Malcolm McCurdy Burdett 1942- *WhoAm 90*
Sterrett, Samuel Black 1922- *WhoAm 90, WhoWor 91*
Sterritt, Coleen 1953- *WhoAmA 91*
Sterry, Barbara Reed 1943- *WhoAmW 91*
Sterud, Eugene LeRoy 1933- *WhoAm 90*
Sterzel, Fredrik Albert Christian 1934- *WhoWor 91*
Sterzer, Fred 1929- *WhoAm 90*
Steslow, John Jacob 1932- *WhoE 91*
Stessin, Herbert *BioIn 16*
Stessin, Nancy *BioIn 16*
Steszewski, Jan Maria 1929- *IntWWM 90*
Stethem, Robert Dean 1961-1985 *BioIn 16*
Stetkiewych, Roman 1936- *WhoE 91*
Stetler, C. Joseph 1917- *WhoAm 90*
Stetler, Deborah Jo *BiDrAPA 89*
Stetler, Larry D. 1934- *St&PR 91, WhoAm 90*
Stetler, Marvin M. *WhoSSW 91*
Stetler, Russell Dearnley, Jr. 1945- *WhoAm 90, WhoWrEP 89*
Stets, Debra Kay 1958- *WhoAmW 91*
Stetser, Dana George 1921- *St&PR 91*
Stetson, Daniel Everett 1956- *WhoAm 90*
Stetson, Eugene William, III 1951- *WhoE 91, WhoWor 91*
Stetson, Isaiah Kidder 1858-1940 *AmLegL*
Stetson, John B. 1936- *St&PR 91*
Stetson, John Benjamin Blank 1927- *WhoAm 90, WhoWor 91*
Stetson, John Charles 1920- *WhoAm 90, WhoWor 91*
Stetson, Nancy E. 1936- *WhoAmW 91*
Stetson, Richard Brian 1928- *St&PR 91*
Stetson, Robert *St&PR 91*
Stetson, Sean Randolph 1960- *BiDrAPA 89*
Stetson, William Wallace 1941- *St&PR 91*
Stetten, DeWitt, Jr. *NewYTBS 90 [port]*
Stettenheim, Peter Rich 1928- *WhoE 91*
Stettheimer, Florine 1871-1944 *BiDWomA, BioAmW*
Stetting, Lauge 1925- *WhoWor 91*
Stettinius, Edward R., Jr. 1900-1949 *WorAlBi*
Stettinius, Edward Reilley, Jr. 1900-1949 *BiDrUSE 89*
Stettinius, Edward Reilly 1900-1949 *BioIn 16*
Stettinius, Joseph 1933- *WhoSSW 91*
Stettinius, Wallace 1933- *St&PR 91, WhoAm 90, WhoSSW 91*
Stettler, Carla Rice 1947- *WhoAmW 91*
Stettner, Louis 1922- *WhoAmA 91, WhoE 91*
Stettner, Shelly Ann *BiDrAPA 89*
Stetz, Frederick W. 1927- *St&PR 91*
Steuart, James 1712-1780 *BioIn 16*
Steuart, Sybil Jean 1954- *WhoAmW 91*
Steuben, Friedrich 1730-1794 *WorAlBi*
Steuben, Friedrich Wilhelm, Baron Von 1730-1794 *EncCRAm*
Steuben, Norton Leslie 1936- *WhoAm 90*
Steude, Philip G 1945- *BiDrAPA 89*
Steudtner, Michelle Rother 1965- *WhoAmW 91*
Steuer, Erwin 1928- *St&PR 91*
Steuer, Joanne *WhoAmW 91*
Steuer, Richard Marc 1948- *WhoE 91*
Steuerle, C. Eugene 1946- *WhoAm 90*
Steuerman, Jean Louis C. 1949- *IntWWM 90*
Steuermann, Eduard 1892-1964 *PenDiMP*
Steuert, D. Michael 1948- *St&PR 91*
Steuert, Douglas Michael 1948- *WhoAm 90*
Steuerwald, David A. 1940- *St&PR 91*
Steurer, Joseph Frederick 1936- *St&PR 91*
Steury, Rudy 1939- *St&PR 91*
Steury, Steven R *BiDrAPA 89*
Stevanov, Zoran 1945- *WhoAmA 91*
Stevanovic, Militza *BiDrAPA 89*
Stevans, Ernest *BiDrAPA 89*
Steven, James Michael 1938- *WhoAmA 91*
Steven, Ranald James Maclaren 1920- *WhoE 91*
Stevens Family *ConAmBL*
Stevens, Alan Douglas 1926- *WhoAm 90*
Stevens, Alden Gifford 1886- *AuBYP 90*
Stevens, Alfred 1817-1875 *PenDiDA 89*
Stevens, Allyssa Elizabeth 1961- *WhoE 91*
Stevens, Amelia Lou *BiDrAPA 89*
Stevens, Andrew 1955- *WhoAm 90*
Stevens, Andrew L. 1936- *WhoWrEP 89*
Stevens, Anita *BiDrAPA 89*
Stevens, Ann Robinson 1951- *WhoAmW 91*
Stevens, Anne Hawley 1956- *WhoAmW 91*
Stevens, April 1957- *WhoAmW 91*
Stevens, Art 1935- *ODwPR 91, WhoAm 90, WhoE 91*
Stevens, Arthur J. 1934- *St&PR 91*
Stevens, Arthur Wilber, Jr. 1921- *WhoAm 90, WhoWrEP 89*
Stevens, Barbara Constance 1924- *WhoWrEP 89*
Stevens, Barbara Joan 1947- *WhoE 91*
Stevens, Benjamin 1915- *St&PR 91*
Stevens, Bette Anne 1947- *WhoE 91*
Stevens, Betty Nevels 1941- *WhoAmW 91*
Stevens, Bradford Lee 1951- *WhoEmL 91*
Stevens, Bruce 1935- *St&PR 91*
Stevens, Bryan James *BiDrAPA 89*
Stevens, C. Glenn 1941- *WhoWor 91*
Stevens, C. J. 1927- *WhoWrEP 89*
Stevens, Carl *BioIn 16, WhoWrEP 89*
Stevens, Carla 1928- *AuBYP 90*
Stevens, Carole Borden 1949- *WhoE 91*
Stevens, Cat *BioIn 16*
Stevens, Cat 1948- *EncPR&S 89, WorAlBi*
Stevens, Charles Harry 1923- *St&PR 91*
Stevens, Charles Roy *BiDrAPA 89*
Stevens, Chester Wayne 1925- *WhoWor 91*
Stevens, Chris Anne 1939- *WhoAmW 91*
Stevens, Christine Hyde 1926- *WhoWrEP 89*
Stevens, Chuck 1918- *Ballpl 90*
Stevens, Clark V. 1933- *St&PR 91*
Stevens, Clark Valentine 1933- *WhoWor 91*
Stevens, Connie *BioIn 16*
Stevens, Connie 1938- *WhoAm 90, WorAlBi*
Stevens, Cornelia Rockwell 1953- *WhoAmW 91*
Stevens, Craig Stewart 1947- *St&PR 91*
Stevens, Cynthia Brown 1948- *BiDrAPA 89*
Stevens, Dale Marvin 1955- *WhoSSW 91*
Stevens, Dalton *BioIn 16*
Stevens, Daniel David Dean 1935- *WhoE 91*
Stevens, Daniel Josephus 1946- *WhoE 91*
Stevens, David 1926- *WhoAm 90*
Stevens, David J. *BioIn 16*
Stevens, David Lee *BioIn 16*

Stevens, Denis William 1922- *IntWWM 90, WhoAm 90*
Stevens, Dennis Max 1944- *WhoSSW 91*
Stevens, Donald *WhoSSW 91*
Stevens, Donald King 1920- *WhoSSW 91, WhoWor 91*
Stevens, Doris 1888-1963 *BioIn 16*
Stevens, Dorothy Emma 1923- *WhoE 91*
Stevens, Douglas N. 1935- *St&PR 91*
Stevens, Duane Arthur 1948- *St&PR 91*
Stevens, Duke William 1953- *WhoSSW 91*
Stevens, Dwight Marlyn 1933- *WhoAm 90*
Stevens, Earl Patrick 1925- *WhoSSW 91*
Stevens, Ed 1925- *Ballpl 90*
Stevens, Edith S. *BioIn 16*
Stevens, Edmund 1910- *BioIn 16*
Stevens, Edmund William 1910- *WhoAm 90, WhoWor 91*
Stevens, Edward John, Jr 1923-1988 *WhoAmA 91N*
Stevens, Edward M. 1941- *ODwPR 91*
Stevens, Eileen *BioIn 16*
Stevens, Elisabeth 1929- *WhoWrEP 89*
Stevens, Elisabeth Goss 1929- *WhoAm 90, WhoAmA 91, WhoAmW 91, WhoE 91*
Stevens, Elliot Leslie 1948- *WhoAm 90*
Stevens, Forrest Wayne 1928- *St&PR 91*
Stevens, Frances A. 1930- *WhoAmW 91*
Stevens, Frank Dana 1932- *St&PR 91*
Stevens, Frank W 1917- *BiDrAPA 89*
Stevens, Frank Wilson, Jr. 1947- *BiDrAPA 89*
Stevens, Frederick M. 1936- *WhoAm 90*
Stevens, Garth, Jr. 1953- *WhoSSW 91*
Stevens, George 1904-1975 *WorAlBi*
Stevens, George, Jr. 1932- *WhoAm 90*
Stevens, George C *BiDrAPA 89*
Stevens, George Richard 1932- *WhoAm 90*
Stevens, Georgianna Ann 1943- *WhoAmW 91*
Stevens, Gladstone Taylor, Jr. 1930- *WhoAm 90*
Stevens, Glen Roy *St&PR 91*
Stevens, Greg Peter 1946- *WhoWor 91*
Stevens, Halsey 1908- *IntWWM 90*
Stevens, Harold 1911- *BiDrAPA 89, WhoE 91*
Stevens, Harold A. 1907-1990 *NewYTBS 90*
Stevens, Harold Russell 1930- *WhoAm 90*
Stevens, Harold Sanford 1950- *WhoEmL 91*
Stevens, Harry M. 1856-1934 *Ballpl 90*
Stevens, Helen Jean 1934- *WhoAmW 91*
Stevens, Herbert Francis 1948- *WhoEmL 91*
Stevens, Holly 1924- *WhoAm 90, WhoWrEP 89*
Stevens, Inger 1934?-1970 *BioIn 16*
Stevens, Isaac H. *WhoE 91*
Stevens, Isaac Ingalls 1818-1862 *WhNaAH*
Stevens, J. Paul 1942- *WhoWor 91*
Stevens, Jacquie 1949- *WhoAmA 91*
Stevens, James Harris 1939- *WhoE 91*
Stevens, James Walter 1932- *WhoE 91*
Stevens, James William 1936- *St&PR 91, WhoAm 90*
Stevens, Jane Alden 1952- *WhoAmA 91*
Stevens, Jane E. *BioIn 16*
Stevens, Jane Sexton 1947- *WhoAmW 91*
Stevens, Janet *BioIn 16*
Stevens, Jeffrey L. 1948- *St&PR 91*
Stevens, Jill Winifred *WhoAmW 91*
Stevens, Joan Evans 1950- *WhoAmW 91*
Stevens, Joann *ODwPR 91*
Stevens, John 1912-1981 *Ballpl 90*
Stevens, John Alan 1951- *WhoE 91*
Stevens, John Christopher 1918- *WhoAm 90*
Stevens, John Flournoy 1914- *WhoSSW 91*
Stevens, John Galen 1943- *WhoE 91*
Stevens, John Levitt 1820-1895 *BioIn 16*
Stevens, John M, Jr. *BiDrAPA 89*
Stevens, John Michael 1940- *St&PR 91*
Stevens, John P. 1929- *St&PR 91*
Stevens, John Paul 1920- *WhoAm 90, WhoE 91, WorAlBi*
Stevens, John Peters, Jr. 1897?-1976 *ConAmBL*
Stevens, John R. *St&PR 91*
Stevens, Jonathan A. 1951- *St&PR 91*
Stevens, Jonathan Buell 1948- *WhoEmL 91*
Stevens, Jonathan Lee 1948- *WhoEmL 91*
Stevens, Joseph B., Jr. 1916- *St&PR 91, WhoAm 90*
Stevens, Joseph Charles 1929- *WhoAm 90*
Stevens, Joseph Edward, Jr. 1928- *WhoAm 90*
Stevens, Kathleen 1936- *BioIn 16*
Stevens, Kenneth Noble 1924- *WhoAm 90*
Stevens, Kent Allen 1948- *WhoEmL 91*
Stevens, Laurie Ann *BiDrAPA 89*
Stevens, Lawrence Tenny 1896-1972 *WhoAmA 91N*
Stevens, Lee 1930-1989 *BioIn 16*
Stevens, Lee 1949- *BiDrAPA 89*
Stevens, Leith 1909-1970 *OxCPMus*
Stevens, Leota Mae 1921- *WhoAmW 91*
Stevens, Linda 1954?- *BioIn 16*
Stevens, Linda Lee 1942- *WhoAmA 91*
Stevens, Lisa Helton *BiDrAPA 89*
Stevens, Lucile V. 1899- *BioIn 16*
Stevens, Lydia Hastings 1918- *WhoAmW 91*
Stevens, Lynn 1953- *WhoAmW 91*
Stevens, Marilyn Ruth 1943- *St&PR 91, WhoAmW 91*
Stevens, Mark *WhoWrEP 89*
Stevens, Mark 1947- *St&PR 91, WhoAm 90*
Stevens, Mark L. 1941- *St&PR 91*
Stevens, Martin 1927- *WhoAm 90*
Stevens, Martin Brian 1957- *WhoE 91*
Stevens, Mary Louise 1945- *WhoEmL 91*
Stevens, May 1924- *BiDWomA, WhoAm 90, WhoAmA 91, WhoE 91*
Stevens, Michael Cooper 1947- *BiDrAPA 89*
Stevens, Michael Dale 1958- *WhoSSW 91*
Stevens, Michael Keith 1945- *WhoAmA 91*
Stevens, Michael Ray 1957- *St&PR 91*
Stevens, Milton Lewis, Jr. 1942- *WhoAm 90*
Stevens, Missy *BioIn 16*
Stevens, Montague *BioIn 16*
Stevens, Nelson L 1938- *WhoAmA 91*
Stevens, Nettie Maria 1861-1912 *DcScB S2*
Stevens, Nina *BioIn 16*
Stevens, Norman 1937-1988 *AnObit 1988*
Stevens, Norman Dennison 1932- *WhoE 91*
Stevens, Patricia Ann 1946- *WhoAmW 91*
Stevens, Paul Edward 1916- *WhoAm 90*
Stevens, Paul I. 1915- *St&PR 91*
Stevens, Paul Irving 1915- *WhoAm 90*
Stevens, Paul K. 1946- *St&PR 91*
Stevens, Paul Richard 1953- *WhoWor 91*
Stevens, Paul Schott 1952- *WhoE 91*
Stevens, Peter B. 1937- *St&PR 91*
Stevens, Philip Ashworth 1934- *St&PR 91*
Stevens, Philip L. 1940- *St&PR 91*
Stevens, Phyliss Elizabeth 1953- *WhoAmW 91*
Stevens, R.A. 1928- *St&PR 91*
Stevens, R. L. *TwCCr&M 91, WhoWrEP 89*
Stevens, Raymond D., Jr. 1927- *St&PR 91*
Stevens, Raymond Donald, Jr. 1927- *WhoAm 90*
Stevens, Richard 1924- *ConDes 90*
Stevens, Richard Yates 1948- *WhoSSW 91*
Stevens, Rise 1913- *BioIn 16, IntWWM 90, PenDiMP, WorAlBi*
Stevens, Robert Bocking 1933- *WhoAm 90*
Stevens, Robert David 1921- *WhoAm 90*
Stevens, Robert Duane 1940- *St&PR 91*
Stevens, Robert Edwin 1927- *WhoAm 90*
Stevens, Robert Gene 1930- *WhoAm 90, WhoE 91*
Stevens, Robert Jay 1945- *WhoAm 90, WhoWrEP 89*
Stevens, Robert L. 1932- *St&PR 91*
Stevens, Robert L. 1947- *St&PR 91*
Stevens, Robert Lewis 1937- *WhoE 91*
Stevens, Robert Ten Broeck 1899-1983 *ConAmBL*
Stevens, Roberta L. 1948- *WhoAmW 91*
Stevens, Robin *BioIn 16*
Stevens, Roger L. 1910- *WhoAm 90*
Stevens, Roger R. 1949- *St&PR 91*
Stevens, Rolland Elwell 1915- *WhoAm 90*
Stevens, Ron A. 1945- *WhoAm 90, WhoEmL 91*
Stevens, Rosemary Anne *WhoAm 90, WhoAmW 91*
Stevens, Roy W. 1924- *St&PR 91, WhoAm 90*
Stevens, Rutherford B 1911- *BiDrAPA 89*
Stevens, Sally Ann 1944- *WhoAmW 91*
Stevens, Sally Wallace 1949- *WhoSSW 91*
Stevens, Scooter 1973- *ConTFT 8 [port]*
Stevens, Shadoe *BioIn 16*
Stevens, Shakin' 1948- *OxCPMus*
Stevens, Shakin' 1950?- *EncPR&S 89*
Stevens, Shelley Salem 1956- *WhoSSW 91*
Stevens, Siaka 1905-1988 *AnObit 1988*
Stevens, Siaka Probyn 1905-1988 *BioIn 16*
Stevens, Sinclair McKnight 1927- *WhoAm 90*
Stevens, Stanley Smith 1906-1973 *DcScB S2*
Stevens, Stella *BioIn 16*
Stevens, Stella 1936- *WorAlBi*
Stevens, Susan Virginia 1955- *WhoAmW 91*
Stevens, Suzanne *WhoWrEP 89*
Stevens, Ted *BioIn 16*
Stevens, Thaddeus 1792-1868 *BioIn 16*
Stevens, Thelma K 1932- *WhoAmA 91*
Stevens, Thelma Kaplan 1932- *WhoE 91*
Stevens, Theodore F. 1923- *WorAlBi*
Stevens, Theodore Fulton 1923- *WhoAm 90, WhoWor 91*
Stevens, Thomas *PenDiDA 89*
Stevens, Thomas 1855- *BioIn 16*
Stevens, Thomas Jeffrey *BiDrAPA 89*
Stevens, Thomas Terry Hoar 1911-1990 *ConAu 130*
Stevens, Victor Louis 1952- *BiDrAPA 89*
Stevens, Violet Bernice 1940- *WhoAmW 91*
Stevens, Wallace 1879-1955 *BioIn 16, MajTwCW, WorAlBi, WrPh*
Stevens, Walter C. 1867- *AmLegL*
Stevens, Walter Hollis 1927-1980 *WhoAmA 91N*
Stevens, Warren 1919- *WhoAm 90*
Stevens, Wendell Claire 1931- *WhoAm 90*
Stevens, Whitney 1926- *ConAmBL, St&PR 91*
Stevens, Willem Frans Casimir 1938- *WhoWor 91*
Stevens, William Ansel, Sr 1919- *WhoAmA 91*
Stevens, William David 1934- *WhoAm 90, WhoSSW 91*
Stevens, William Dollard 1918- *WhoAm 90*
Stevens, William H. 1929- *St&PR 91*
Stevens, William H., Jr. 1918- *St&PR 91*
Stevens, William J *BiDrAPA 89*
Stevens, William John 1915- *WhoSSW 91, WhoWor 91*
Stevens, William Kenneth 1917- *WhoAm 90*
Stevens, William Louis 1932- *WhoAm 90*
Stevens, William Oliver 1878- *AuBYP 90*
Stevens, William Oliver 1878-1955 *EncO&P 3*
Stevens-Silver, Emily Fabella 1928- *WhoAmW 91*
Stevenson, A. Brockie 1919- *WhoAm 90*
Stevenson, A Brockie 1919- *WhoAmA 91*
Stevenson, Adlai E. 1835-1914 *WorAlBi*
Stevenson, Adlai E. 1900-1965 *BioIn 16*
Stevenson, Adlai E., II 1900-1965 *WorAlBi*
Stevenson, Adlai E., III 1930- *WorAlBi*
Stevenson, Adlai Ewing 1835-1914 *BiDrUSE 89*
Stevenson, Adlai Ewing, III 1930- *WhoAm 90*
Stevenson, Alan B. 1943- *St&PR 91*
Stevenson, Alexandra *BioIn 16*
Stevenson, Andrew 1784-1857 *BioIn 16*
Stevenson, Anne 1933- *BioIn 16, ConAu 33NR, FemiCLE, MajTwCW*
Stevenson, Augusta 1869?-1976 *AuBYP 90*
Stevenson, Ben 1936- *WhoAm 90*
Stevenson, Beulah *WhoAmA 91N*
Stevenson, Charles Philip *BiDrAPA 89*
Stevenson, Coke R. 1888-1975 *BioIn 16*
Stevenson, Dave Carl 1951- *St&PR 91*
Stevenson, David R. 1949- *St&PR 91*
Stevenson, David Ralph 1958- *WhoSSW 91*
Stevenson, Denise L. 1946- *WhoAmW 91, WhoEmL 91*
Stevenson, Dennis Elliott 1943- *WhoSSW 91*
Stevenson, Dewie O. 1926- *St&PR 91*
Stevenson, Donald V *BiDrAPA 89*
Stevenson, Donald Williams 1912- *St&PR 91*
Stevenson, Douglas 1953- *WhoWrEP 89*
Stevenson, Drew 1947- *SmATA 60 [port]*
Stevenson, Dwight Eshelman 1906- *WhoWrEP 89*
Stevenson, Earl, Jr. 1921- *WhoWor 91*
Stevenson, Edward Augustus 1831-1896 *AmLegL*
Stevenson, Edward D 1905- *BiDrAPA 89*
Stevenson, Edward Irenaeus Prime- 1868-1942 *BioIn 16*
Stevenson, Edward Kent 1941- *BiDrAPA 89*
Stevenson, Elizabeth 1919- *WhoAm 90*
Stevenson, Elmer Clark 1915- *WhoAm 90*
Stevenson, Eric Van Cortlandt 1926- *WhoAm 90*
Stevenson, Ernest Vail 1922- *WhoAm 90*
Stevenson, Frances Grace 1921- *WhoAmW 91*
Stevenson, Frances Kellogg *WhoAmW 91*
Stevenson, Frank John 1938- *St&PR 91, WhoAm 90*
Stevenson, Gary Lyn 1945- *WhoSSW 91*
Stevenson, George Franklin 1922- *WhoAm 90*
Stevenson, Gerald L. 1937- *St&PR 91*
Stevenson, Grace Hope 1904- *WhoAmW 91*
Stevenson, Harold 1929- *WhoAmA 91*
Stevenson, Harold William 1924- *WhoAm 90*
Stevenson, Helen Elizabeth 1955- *WhoAmW 91*
Stevenson, Henry S. 1924- *St&PR 91*
Stevenson, Howard Higginbotham 1941- *WhoAm 90*
Stevenson, Ian 1918- *BiDrAPA 89, EncO&P 3, WhoAm 90*
Stevenson, James 1813-1894 *DcCanB 12*
Stevenson, James 1929- *AuBYP 90*
Stevenson, James 1934- *WhoWor 91*
Stevenson, James David 1925- *WhoAm 90*
Stevenson, James Harold 1933- *WhoAm 90*
Stevenson, James M, II *BiDrAPA 89*
Stevenson, James R. 1940- *St&PR 91*
Stevenson, James Rufus 1925- *WhoAm 90*
Stevenson, Janet 1913- *AuBYP 90*
Stevenson, Jo Ann C. 1942- *WhoAmW 91*
Stevenson, JoAnne 1935- *WhoSSW 91*
Stevenson, John Edward 1952- *WhoWrEP 89*
Stevenson, John Landee 1927- *St&PR 91*
Stevenson, John P. *St&PR 91*
Stevenson, John Pevey 1926- *St&PR 91*
Stevenson, John Reese 1921- *WhoAm 90, WhoE 91, WhoWor 91*
Stevenson, John S. 1950- *St&PR 91*
Stevenson, Josiah, IV 1935- *WhoE 91*
Stevenson, Judy G. 1937- *St&PR 91*
Stevenson, Karl William 1940- *BiDrAPA 89*
Stevenson, Kenneth Lee 1939- *WhoAm 90*
Stevenson, Langdon Riddle 1935- *St&PR 91, WhoAm 90*
Stevenson, Marilyn Esther 1933- *WhoAmW 91*
Stevenson, Matilda Coxe 1850?-1915 *WhNaAH*
Stevenson, Maybelle Ida 1933- *WhoAmW 91*
Stevenson, Monica *BioIn 16*
Stevenson, Orlando John 1869- *AuBYP 90*
Stevenson, Paul E. 1928- *St&PR 91*
Stevenson, Philip Davis 1936- *WhoAm 90*
Stevenson, Ralph Charles 1931- *WhoSSW 91*
Stevenson, Richard Albert 1947- *WhoSSW 91*
Stevenson, Robert 1951- *St&PR 91*
Stevenson, Robert B *BiDrAPA 89*
Stevenson, Robert Benjamin, III 1950- *WhoEmL 91*
Stevenson, Robert Edwin 1926- *WhoAm 90*
Stevenson, Robert H. 1942- *St&PR 91*
Stevenson, Robert L. 1952- *WhoE 91*
Stevenson, Robert Louis 1850-1894 *AuBYP 90, BioIn 16, EncPaPR 91, WorAlBi*
Stevenson, Robert Murrell 1916- *IntWWM 90, WhoAm 90, WhoWor 91*
Stevenson, Robert Neal 1949- *BiDrAPA 89*
Stevenson, Robert W. 1939- *St&PR 91*
Stevenson, Ronald 1928- *IntWWM 90, PenDiMP*
Stevenson, Ronald J. 1951- *St&PR 91*
Stevenson, Ruth Carter 1923- *WhoAmA 91, WhoAmW 91*
Stevenson, Ruth Rolston 1897- *WhoAmA 91*
Stevenson, Sandra Jean 1949- *WhoAmW 91*
Stevenson, Sucie *AuBYP 90*
Stevenson, Sybil Jordan 1944- *BioIn 16*
Stevenson, Thomas Herbert 1951- *WhoEmL 91, WhoWor 91*
Stevenson, W. P. Fred *ODwPR 91*
Stevenson, Wayne L. 1945- *WhoEmL 91*
Stevenson, Wilf *BioIn 16*
Stevenson, William Francis 1861- *AmLegL*
Stevenson, William Henri 1924- *WhoAm 90, WhoWrEP 89*
Stevenson, William John, III 1948- *St&PR 91*
Stevenson, William T. 1928- *St&PR 91*
Steventon, Robert Wesley 1948- *WhoSSW 91*
Stever, Horton Guyford 1916- *WhoAm 90, WhoWor 91*
Stever, Margo Taft 1950- *WhoAmW 91, WhoWrEP 89*
Steverman, Walter 1926- *St&PR 91*
Steves, Edward G. 1952- *St&PR 91*
Steves, Edward Mickel 1953- *WhoEmL 91*
Steves, Marshall T. 1923- *St&PR 91*
Steves, Sonja Lee 1938- *St&PR 91*
Steves, William Arthur 1946- *St&PR 91*
Stevich-Larson, Alison Joy 1952- *WhoAmW 91*
Stevick, Philip T. 1930- *ConAu 132*
Stevin, Simon 1548-1620 *BioIn 16*
Stevinus, Simon 1548-1620 *WorAlBi*
Stevovich, Andrew Vlastimir 1948- *WhoAmA 91*
Steward, Ann 1898- *LiHiK*
Steward, Bette Ann 1949- *WhoAmW 91*
Steward, Carlos Warren 1950- *WhoEmL 91, WhoSSW 91*
Steward, Charles Robert 1935- *WhoWor 91*
Steward, D.E. 1936- *WhoWrEP 89*
Steward, Donn Horatio 1921-1986 *WhoAmA 91N*
Steward, George H. 1829- *AmLegL*
Steward, H. Leighton 1934- *WhoSSW 91*
Steward, Hal David 1918- *WhoWrEP 89*
Steward, Hugh Leighton 1934- *St&PR 91*
Steward, John R. 1931- *St&PR 91*

Steward, Linda Susan 1956- WhoWor 91
Steward, Nanncy Jean 1953- WhoWrEP 89
Steward, Oswald 1948- WhoAm 90
Steward, Patricia Ann Rupert 1945- WhoAmW 91
Steward, Weldon Cecil 1934- WhoAm 90
Stewart, A. C. AuBYP 90
Stewart, A. William 1940- ODwPR 91
Stewart, Alan R. 1954- St&PR 91
Stewart, Alana BioIn 16
Stewart, Albert 1914- LiHiK
Stewart, Albert Elisha 1927- WhoAm 90
Stewart, Alec Thompson 1925- WhoAm 90
Stewart, Alexander Doig 1926- WhoAm 90
Stewart, Alexandra 1939- ConTFT 8
Stewart, Alice Jean 1958- WhoAmW 91
Stewart, Alice Martha BioIn 16
Stewart, Allan H 1921- BiDrAPA 89
Stewart, Altha Jeanne BiDrAPA 89
Stewart, Ann Harleman WhoAmW 91, WhoWrEP 89
Stewart, Anna Bird AuBYP 90
Stewart, Arlene Jean Golden 1943- WhoAmW 91, WhoE 91, WhoWor 91
Stewart, Arthur 1915- WhoAmA 91
Stewart, Arthur Irving, III 1958- WhoE 91, WhoEmL 91
Stewart, B. A. 1932- BioIn 16
Stewart, Balfour 1828-1887 EncO&P 3, EncPaPR 91
Stewart, Barbara Elizabeth 1923- WhoAmW 91
Stewart, Barbara Vee Jenkins 1944- WhoSSW 91
Stewart, Bennett McVey 1912-1988 BlkAmsC [port]
Stewart, Betty Greene BiDrAPA 89
Stewart, Bill 1895-1964 Ballpl 90
Stewart, Bill 1941- WhoAmA 91
Stewart, Bob BioIn 16
Stewart, Bob 1915- Ballpl 90
Stewart, Bobby Alton 1932- BioIn 16
Stewart, Bud 1916- Ballpl 90
Stewart, Bunky 1931- Ballpl 90
Stewart, Burton Gloyden, Jr. 1933- St&PR 91, WhoAm 90
Stewart, Byran James 1956- WhoEmL 91, WhoWor 91
Stewart, Carleton M. 1921- WhoAm 90
Stewart, Carol Hardwick 1953- WhoEmL 91
Stewart, Carol Johnson 1949- WhoAmW 91
Stewart, Catherine Anne 1959- WhoAmW 91
Stewart, Charles 1778-1869 WorAlBi
Stewart, Charles C. 1925- St&PR 91
Stewart, Charles David 1910- WhoAm 90
Stewart, Charles E. 1935- WhoAm 90
Stewart, Charles Edward, Jr. 1916- WhoAm 90
Stewart, Charles Evan 1952- WhoE 91
Stewart, Charles Everett 1935- St&PR 91
Stewart, Charles Haines 1958- WhoE 91
Stewart, Charles Henry 1929- St&PR 91
Stewart, Charles Henry, Jr. 1929- WhoSSW 91
Stewart, Charles Leslie 1919- WhoAm 90
Stewart, Charles P, Jr. BiDrAPA 89
Stewart, Charles T 1926- BiDrAPA 89
Stewart, Charles Wayne 1955- WhoSSW 91
Stewart, Charmaine Marcia 1954- WhoAmW 91
Stewart, Chere Lynn 1955- WhoWrEP 89
Stewart, Cherie Anita 1945- WhoAmW 91, WhoSSW 91
Stewart, Christine Susan 1941- WhoAmW 91
Stewart, Clara Woodard 1952- WhoAmW 91, WhoWor 91
Stewart, Colston R, III BiDrAPA 89
Stewart, Connie Ward 1938- WhoSSW 91
Stewart, Cornelius James, II 1925- St&PR 91, WhoAm 90
Stewart, Cornelius Van Leuven 1936- WhoAm 90
Stewart, Cynthia Anne 1952- WhoSSW 91
Stewart, Daniel Robert 1938- WhoAm 90
Stewart, Dave BioIn 16
Stewart, Dave 1957- Ballpl 90, News 91-1 [port], WorAlBi
Stewart, David Dickson 1949- WhoEmL 91
Stewart, David Edward 1945- St&PR 91
Stewart, David H.M. 1918- St&PR 91
Stewart, David Howat 1945- WhoWor 91
Stewart, David Hugh 1926- WhoAm 90
Stewart, David L 1923- BiDrAPA 89
Stewart, David Marshall 1916- WhoAm 90
Stewart, David Wayne 1951- WhoEmL 91, WhoWor 91
Stewart, David Wood 1929- WhoE 91
Stewart, Deborah Ruth 1954- WhoAmW 91
Stewart, Derek Kenneth Bernard 1948- WhoSSW 91
Stewart, Desmond 1924-1981 ConAu 30NR
Stewart, Diane BioIn 16
Stewart, Diane Basnett 1955- WhoAmW 91
Stewart, Diane Marie BiDrAPA 89
Stewart, Dolores Ann 1947- WhoAmW 91
Stewart, Don M. 1937- St&PR 91
Stewart, Donald Alan 1954- WhoE 91
Stewart, Donald Alexander 1851-1897 DcCanB 12
Stewart, Donald Bruce 1935- WhoAm 90
Stewart, Donald C. 1930- WhoWrEP 89
Stewart, Donald Edwin 1927- WhoAm 90
Stewart, Donald George 1935- IntWWM 90
Stewart, Donald James 1952- St&PR 91
Stewart, Donald M. 1938- WhoAm 90
Stewart, Donna Eileen BiDrAPA 89
Stewart, Donna Ludwig 1945- WhoSSW 91
Stewart, Donna Ruth 1947- WhoAmW 91
Stewart, Donovan Patrick 1958- WhoSSW 91
Stewart, Dorothy Anne 1937- WhoAmW 91, WhoSSW 91
Stewart, Doris Mae 1927- WhoAmW 91
Stewart, Dorothy S WhoAmA 91
Stewart, Dorothy S. 1922- WhoE 91
Stewart, Douglas A. 1940- St&PR 91
Stewart, Dudley Marcus, Jr. 1941- BiDrAPA 89
Stewart, Duncan E 1940- WhoAmA 91
Stewart, Duncan James 1939- St&PR 91, WhoAm 90
Stewart, Earl Douglas 1940- St&PR 91
Stewart, Edgar Allen 1909- WhoAm 90
Stewart, Edward 1938- BioIn 16
Stewart, Edward William 1931- WhoAm 90
Stewart, Eileen Rose 1942- WhoAmW 91
Stewart, Elaine Thelma 1952- WhoAmW 91
Stewart, Eleanor May Guggenheim Castle 1898- BioIn 16
Stewart, Elinore Pruitt 1878- BioIn 16
Stewart, Elizabeth 1943- WhoAmW 91
Stewart, Elizabeth Laing 1907- AuBYP 90
Stewart, Ellen BioIn 16, DrBIPA 90
Stewart, Ellen 1920?- NotWoAT
Stewart, Ellen Smith 1945- WhoAmW 91
Stewart, Elmer Roy, Jr. 1950- WhoSSW 91
Stewart, Eugene Joel 1960- WhoWrEP 89
Stewart, Eugene Lawrence 1920- WhoAm 90, WhoE 91, WhoWor 91
Stewart, F Clark 1942- WhoAmA 91
Stewart, Frances Irene 1955- BiDrAPA 89
Stewart, Frank Maurice 1939- WhoAm 90
Stewart, Frederick Henry 1916- WhoWor 91
Stewart, Frederick Neal 1931- WhoSSW 91
Stewart, G. Cope, III 1941- WhoE 91
Stewart, Gary WhoNeCM [port]
Stewart, Gary L. 1953- WhoE 91
Stewart, Gayle K BiDrAPA 89
Stewart, George, Jr. 1848-1906 DcLB 99 [port]
Stewart, George David 1938- WhoSSW 91
Stewart, George E. 1929- St&PR 91
Stewart, George H. 1931- St&PR 91
Stewart, George Hoague BiDrAPA 89
Stewart, George O.M. 1935- St&PR 91
Stewart, George Ray 1944- WhoAm 90, WhoSSW 91
Stewart, George Taylor 1924- St&PR 91, WhoAm 90, WhoWor 91
Stewart, Gilbert Wright 1940- WhoAm 90
Stewart, Glen Jay 1949- WhoEmL 91
Stewart, Gloria EncPaPR 91
Stewart, Gordon 1943- ODwPR 91
Stewart, Gordon C. 1942- St&PR 91
Stewart, Greg NewAgMG
Stewart, Gregory K. 1956- St&PR 91
Stewart, Guy Harry 1924- WhoAm 90
Stewart, Harold Brown 1921- WhoAm 90
Stewart, Harold Leroy 1899- WhoAm 90
Stewart, Harris Bates, Jr. 1922- WhoAm 90
Stewart, Harry A 1936- BiDrAPA 89
Stewart, Helen G. 1948- St&PR 91
Stewart, Homer Joseph 1915- WhoAm 90
Stewart, Howard H., III ODwPR 91
Stewart, Howard James 1925- St&PR 91
Stewart, Ian Nicholas 1945- WhoWor 91
Stewart, Inez 1956- WhoHisp 91
Stewart, Ireland J. 1934- St&PR 91
Stewart, Iris Parsons 1926- St&PR 91, WhoAm 90
Stewart, Irvin NewYTBS 90
Stewart, Isaac Daniel, Jr. 1932- WhoAm 90, WhoWor 91
Stewart, Isaac Mitton 1904- WhoAm 90
Stewart, Isabel Maitland 1878-1963 BioIn 16
Stewart, J Douglas 1934- WhoAmA 91
Stewart, J. I. M. TwCCr&M 91
Stewart, J. I. M. 1906- BioIn 16
Stewart, J I M 1906- MajTwCW
Stewart, J. Vernon 1939- St&PR 91
Stewart, Jack 1926- WhoAmA 91
Stewart, Jack Lauren 1924- WhoAm 90
Stewart, Jackie BioIn 16
Stewart, Jackie 1939- WorAlBi
Stewart, James BioIn 16, ConTFT 8
Stewart, James 1908- NewYTBS 90 [port], WorAlBi
Stewart, James 1912- St&PR 91, WhoAm 90
Stewart, James, III 1926- St&PR 91
Stewart, James Alden 1946- WhoEmL 91
Stewart, James Andrew 1936- BiDrAPA 89
Stewart, James B. WhoE 91
Stewart, James Brewer 1940- ConAu 32NR, WhoAm 90
Stewart, James Burke 1949- WhoAm 90
Stewart, James Charles, II 1952- WhoSSW 91
Stewart, James E. BioIn 16, WhoAm 90
Stewart, James F.C. 1946- St&PR 91
Stewart, James Gathings 1942- St&PR 91, WhoAm 90
Stewart, James Hunter BiDrAPA 89
Stewart, James M. 1943- WhoAm 90
Stewart, James Maitland 1908- WhoAm 90, WhoWor 91
Stewart, James Montgomery 1939- St&PR 91, WhoAm 90
Stewart, James Pentland 1906- WhoAm 90
Stewart, James S 1896-1990 ConAu 132
Stewart, James Vernon 1939- WhoAm 90
Stewart, James William 1926- WhoWor 91
Stewart, Janelle Haraughty 1953- WhoAmW 91
Stewart, Jarvis Anthony 1914-1981 WhoAmA 91N
Stewart, Jay TwCCr&M 91
Stewart, Jay BioIn 16
Stewart, Jean ConAu 31NR
Stewart, Jean Catherine 1948- WhoAmW 91
Stewart, Jeff 1939- WhoWor 91
Stewart, Jeffrey 1947- WhoAmA 91
Stewart, Jeffrey Bayrd 1952- WhoEmL 91
Stewart, Jeffrey Wayne 1950- WhoSSW 91
Stewart, Jennifer 1940- WhoAm 90
Stewart, Jimmy BioIn 16
Stewart, Jimmy 1939- Ballpl 90
Stewart, JoAnne 1944- WhoAmW 91
Stewart, Joe J. 1938- St&PR 91
Stewart, John 1812-1891 DcCanB 12
Stewart, John 1945- WhoAmA 91
Stewart, John Antenen 1920- WhoWor 91
Stewart, John Cameron 1943- WhoE 91, WhoWor 91
Stewart, John Charles BiDrAPA 89
Stewart, John D. 1915- St&PR 91
Stewart, John Daugherty 1915- WhoAm 90
Stewart, John F. 1925- St&PR 91
Stewart, John H., Jr. 1929- St&PR 91
Stewart, John Harger WhoAm 90
Stewart, John Innes Mackintosh 1906- BioIn 16
Stewart, John K. 1905- St&PR 91
Stewart, John Lincoln 1917- WhoAm 90, WhoAmA 91
Stewart, John MacDonald 1945- WhoE 91
Stewart, John Mathews 1920- WhoAm 90
Stewart, John P 1945- WhoAmA 91
Stewart, John Richard 1947- St&PR 91
Stewart, John T., III 1936- St&PR 91
Stewart, John Thomas, Jr. 1928- WhoE 91
Stewart, John W. WhoAm 90
Stewart, John Wolcott 1825-1915 AmLegL
Stewart, John Woods, II 1942- WhoE 91
Stewart, Jonathan Taylor 1956- BiDrAPA 89
Stewart, Jonathan W 1946- BiDrAPA 89
Stewart, Joseph Allen 1949- WhoE 91
Stewart, Joseph Lester 1915- WhoAm 90
Stewart, Joseph M. 1942- St&PR 91
Stewart, Joseph Turner, Jr. 1929- St&PR 91, WhoAm 90, WhoWor 91
Stewart, Judith ConAu 129
Stewart, Judith Underwood 1955- WhoAmW 91, WhoE 91, WhoWor 91
Stewart, June 1931- WhoAmW 91
Stewart, June Gary 1931- WhoWrEP 89
Stewart, Karen M. 1954- ODwPR 91
Stewart, Kendall L 1950- BiDrAPA 89
Stewart, Kendall Leuomon 1950- WhoEmL 91
Stewart, Kenneth Malcolm 1916- EncO&P 3
Stewart, Kent Kallam 1934- WhoAm 90
Stewart, Kim Kristine 1952- WhoAmW 91
Stewart, Kimberly Kay 1964- WhoAmW 91
Stewart, Kirk T. 1951- ODwPR 91
Stewart, Kyle Leslie 1948- BiDrAPA 89
Stewart, Larry Lee BiDrAPA 89
Stewart, Lefty 1900-1974 Ballpl 90
Stewart, Leon Otto 1929- WhoAm 90
Stewart, Lewis Moore 1935- WhoSSW 91
Stewart, Lewis R. 1899-1988 BioIn 16
Stewart, Luther Leroy 1947- WhoSSW 91
Stewart, Madison W. AmLegL
Stewart, Margaret Jensen 1950- WhoAmW 91
Stewart, Margaret McBride 1927- WhoAm 90, WhoE 91
Stewart, Maria W. 1803-1879 FemiCLE
Stewart, Marianne J. 1943- ODwPR 91
Stewart, Mark BioIn 16
Stewart, Mark A 1929- BiDrAPA 89
Stewart, Mark Armstrong 1929- WhoAm 90
Stewart, Mark Carroll 1947- WhoAm 90
Stewart, Mark Steven 1950- WhoSSW 91
Stewart, Mark Thomas 1948- WhoE 91
Stewart, Martha BioIn 16
Stewart, Mary 1916- BioIn 16, FemiCLE, TwCCr&M 91, WorAlBi
Stewart, Mary Agnes 1899- WhoAmW 91, WhoWor 91
Stewart, Mary Catherine WhoAmW 91, WhoWor 91
Stewart, Mary Elinore Pruitt 1878- BioIn 16
Stewart, Mary Florence Elinor 1916- WhoAm 90, WhoWrEP 89
Stewart, Mary Leeuw 1929- WhoAmW 91
Stewart, Mary Lou 1927- WhoAmW 91
Stewart, Maxwell S. BioIn 16, NewYTBS 90
Stewart, Maxwell S 1900-1990 ConAu 131
Stewart, Mel DrBIPA 90
Stewart, Melbourne George, Jr. 1927- WhoAm 90
Stewart, Melvin BioIn 16
Stewart, Mervin S 1927- BiDrAPA 89
Stewart, Michael 1906-1990 BioIn 16, ConAu 131, CurBio 90N, NewYTBS 90 [port]
Stewart, Michael James 1951- St&PR 91
Stewart, Michael Jerome 1948- WhoE 91
Stewart, Michael McFadden 1938- WhoSSW 91
Stewart, Michael Steven 1956- WhoSSW 91
Stewart, Michele A BiDrAPA 89
Stewart, Mildred Simpson 1940- WhoAmW 91
Stewart, Millie Andrea 1946- WhoSSW 91
Stewart, Murray Baker 1931- WhoSSW 91
Stewart, Neville 1932- St&PR 91
Stewart, Norm BioIn 16
Stewart, Norman 1947- WhoAmA 91
Stewart, Norman J. 1948- St&PR 91
Stewart, Norman L. 1942- St&PR 91
Stewart, Norman Lawrence 1942- WhoAm 90
Stewart, Ora Marie 1927- WhoAmW 91
Stewart, Oro Rozella 1917- WhoAmW 91
Stewart, Pamela Tabor 1958- WhoAmW 91
Stewart, Pangle 1915- St&PR 91
Stewart, Patrice Lafferty 1933- WhoAmW 91
Stewart, Patricia BioIn 16
Stewart, Patricia Ann 1953- WhoAmW 91
Stewart, Patricia Carry 1928- WhoAm 90, WhoAmW 91
Stewart, Patricia Leslie 1956- WhoAmW 91
Stewart, Patricia Maria 1952- WhoAmW 91
Stewart, Paul 1925- BioIn 16
Stewart, Paul Leroy 1928- WhoAmA 91
Stewart, Paul Norfleet BiDrAPA 89
Stewart, Paul Richard 1934- St&PR 91
Stewart, Paula Ward 1949- WhoAmW 91
Stewart, Payne BioIn 16
Stewart, Perry Franklin 1955- WhoSSW 91
Stewart, Peter Beaufort 1923- WhoAm 90
Stewart, Peter Pauls 1920- WhoWor 91
Stewart, Potter 1915-1985 WorAlBi
Stewart, Priscilla Ann Mabie 1926- WhoSSW 91
Stewart, Ralph P. 1940- St&PR 91
Stewart, Randall 1896-1964 DcLB 103 [port]
Stewart, Rege Szuts 1941- BiDrAPA 89
Stewart, Rex 1907-1967 OxCPMus
Stewart, Rex William 1907-1967 BioIn 16
Stewart, Richard BioIn 16
Stewart, Richard Alfred 1945- WhoAm 90
Stewart, Richard Burleson 1940- WhoAm 90
Stewart, Richard Edwin 1933- WhoAm 90, WhoE 91, WhoWor 91
Stewart, Richard More 1910- WhoAm 90
Stewart, Richard R. 1930- St&PR 91
Stewart, Richard W. 1943- St&PR 91
Stewart, Richard Warren 1951- WhoEmL 91
Stewart, Robert, Jr. 1919- WhoAm 90
Stewart, Robert Andrew 1928- WhoAm 90
Stewart, Robert Bruce 1896-1988 BioIn 16
Stewart, Robert C. 1932- St&PR 91
Stewart, Robert Charles 1950- WhoEmL 91
Stewart, Robert Eugene, Jr. 1950- WhoSSW 91
Stewart, Robert F. 1927- St&PR 91

Stewart, Robert Forrest, Jr. 1943- *WhoAm 90*
Stewart, Robert G. 1956- *St&PR 91*
Stewart, Robert Gordon 1931- *WhoAm 90, WhoAmA 91*
Stewart, Robert H *BiDrAPA 89*
Stewart, Robert H., III 1925- *St&PR 91*
Stewart, Robert J. 1944- *WhoE 91*
Stewart, Robert L 1919- *BiDrAPA 89*
Stewart, Robert Lee 1942- *WhoAm 90*
Stewart, Robert Morrison 1922- *St&PR 91*
Stewart, Robert N. 1917- *St&PR 91*
Stewart, Robert William 1948- *WhoAm 90*
Stewart, Rod *BioIn 16*
Stewart, Rod 1945- *EncPR&S 89, OxCPMus, WorAlBi*
Stewart, Roderick David 1945- *WhoAm 90*
Stewart, Rollen *BioIn 16*
Stewart, Ronald Mark *BiDrAPA 89*
Stewart, Ronald Vernon 1949- *St&PR 91*
Stewart, Rosalind Landis 1941- *WhoAmW 91*
Stewart, Roy Herbert 1928- *WhoE 91*
Stewart, Roy Joseph 1938- *BioIn 16*
Stewart, Ruth Ann 1942- *WhoAm 90*
Stewart, Ruth F. 1928- *WhoSSW 91*
Stewart, S. Jay 1938- *WhoAm 90*
Stewart, Sam 1915- *WhoAm 90*
Stewart, Sammy 1954- *Ballpl 90*
Stewart, Samuel B. 1908- *WhoAm 90*
Stewart, Sandra Gowers 1962- *WhoAmW 91*
Stewart, Sandy Brown 1938- *WhoE 91*
Stewart, Sarah Emily 1923- *BiDrAPA 89*
Stewart, Scottye Griffin 1939- *WhoSSW 91*
Stewart, Sharon Diane 1951- *WhoEmL 91, WhoWrEP 89*
Stewart, Sheila L *WhoAmA 91*
Stewart, Sheila Marie 1960- *WhoAmW 91*
Stewart, Sherwood *BioIn 16*
Stewart, Shirley Anne 1957- *WhoE 91*
Stewart, Sidney Andrew, Jr. 1926- *St&PR 91*
Stewart, Slam 1914-1987 *BioIn 16, DrBIPA 90*
Stewart, Stephanie 1961- *WhoAmW 91*
Stewart, Stephen Thompson 1954- *St&PR 91*
Stewart, Sue Stern 1942- *WhoAmW 91*
Stewart, Susan 1953- *WomArch*
Stewart, Susan Cochran 1954- *WhoAmW 91*
Stewart, Susan F. 1946- *St&PR 91*
Stewart, Suzanne Florence 1939- *WhoAmW 91*
Stewart, Suzanne Leigh 1963- *WhoAmW 91*
Stewart, Terence Harry 1938- *WhoWor 91*
Stewart, Terry *WhoE 91*
Stewart, Thomas 1926- *IntWWM 90, PenDiMP*
Stewart, Thomas C. 1945- *St&PR 91*
Stewart, Thomas David 1942- *BiDrAPA 89, WhoE 91*
Stewart, Thomas James, Jr. 1928- *WhoAm 90*
Stewart, Thomas Kerr 1930- *WhoSSW 91*
Stewart, Thomas Penney 1927- *WhoAm 90*
Stewart, Thomas S. 1938- *St&PR 91*
Stewart, Timothy Michael 1950- *WhoE 91*
Stewart, Tod Ernest 1958- *WhoSSW 91*
Stewart, Trevor Richard 1946- *WhoAm 90*
Stewart, Vernon Edwin 1938- *WhoSSW 91*
Stewart, W C 1936- *EncO&P 3*
Stewart, W. Neill, Jr. *St&PR 91N*
Stewart, W. P. 1924- *BioIn 16*
Stewart, W. Roderick 1916- *WhoWor 91*
Stewart, Walter *BioIn 16*
Stewart, Walter 1931- *ConAu 129*
Stewart, Walter P. 1924- *BioIn 16*
Stewart, Warren Earl 1924- *WhoAm 90*
Stewart, Wellington *AmLegL*
Stewart, Whitney 1959- *WhoAmW 91, WhoE 91*
Stewart, William *WhoSSW 91*
Stewart, William 1938- *WhoAmA 91*
Stewart, William Alexander 1825-1892 *AmLegL*
Stewart, William C. 1929- *St&PR 91*
Stewart, William Charles 1926- *WhoAm 90*
Stewart, William Charles 1955- *WhoSSW 91*
Stewart, William Clayton 1928- *St&PR 91*
Stewart, William Donald 1920- *WhoAm 90*
Stewart, William Glen 1941- *St&PR 91*
Stewart, William H. 1942- *St&PR 91*
Stewart, William Histaspas 1939- *WhoSSW 91*
Stewart, William James 1939- *WhoE 91*
Stewart, William P. 1934- *ODwPR 91*
Stewart, William Payne 1957- *WhoAm 90*
Stewart, William Robert 1941- *WhoE 91*
Stewart, Winburn Earl 1917- *St&PR 91*
Stewart, Zeph 1921- *WhoAm 90*
Stewart-Clarke, John Ernest 1928- *WhoWor 91*
Stewart-Frank, Jean Hood 1956- *WhoAmW 91*
Stewart-Morris, Malcolm 1936- *BiDrAPA 89*
Stewart-Newman, Chere Lynn 1955- *WhoAmW 91*
Stewart of Fulham, Robert Michael M 1906-1990 *BioIn 16*
Stewart-Payne, Geraldine *BiDrAPA 89*
Stewart-Pinkham, Sandra Morral 1942- *WhoAmW 91*
Stewart-Smith, David Allen 1952- *WhoEmL 91*
Stewart-Smith, Marilyn 1941- *BiDrAPA 89*
Stewig, John Warren 1937- *ConAu 32NR*
Steyer, Hume Richmond 1953- *WhoEmL 91*
Steyer, Roy Henry 1918- *WhoAm 90, WhoE 91, WhoWor 91*
Steyert, William A. *BioIn 16*
Steyn, Rolf William 1928- *BiDrAPA 89*
Steytler, Alan L.S. 1947- *St&PR 91*
Steytler, Carolyn Sue 1957- *WhoEmL 91*
Stiadle, Thomas Albert, Jr. 1966- *WhoEmL 91*
Stibal, Marcia Raye 1948- *WhoSSW 91*
Stibich, Donald Clinton 1931- *St&PR 91*
Stibich, Peter G. 1956- *St&PR 91*
Stibitz, George Robert 1904- *WhoAm 90*
Stibler, Mary G *BiDrAPA 89*
Stice, James Edward 1928- *WhoAm 90*
Stice, Richard Beil *BiDrAPA 89*
Stice, Susan E. 1956- *BiDrAPA 89*
Stich, Hans Franz 1927- *WhoAm 90*
Stich, Otto 1927- *WhoWor 91*
Stich-Randall, Teresa 1927- *IntWWM 90, PenDiMP*
Stichman, Robert W. 1948- *St&PR 91*
Stichmann, Wilfried 1934- *WhoWor 91*
Sticht, Douglas John 1945- *WhoEmL 91*
Sticht, J. Paul 1917- *St&PR 91, WhoAm 90, WhoSSW 91*
Stick, Thomas Howard Fitchett 1938- *WhoE 91*
Stickel, Fred A. 1921- *St&PR 91*
Stickel, Frederick A. 1921- *WhoAm 90*
Stickel, Tom C. 1949- *St&PR 91*
Stickeler, Carl Ann Louise 1930- *WhoSSW 91*
Stickeler, Stephan 1960- *WhoWor 91*
Stickell, Vance 1925-1987 *BioIn 16*
Sticker, Robert Edward 1922- *WhoAmA 91*
Stickle, Charles Edward 1941- *WhoWrEP 89*
Stickler, Alfons Maria 1910- *WhoWor 91*
Stickler, Daniel Lee 1938- *WhoAm 90, WhoSSW 91*
Stickler, Fred Charles 1931- *WhoAm 90*
Stickler, Gunnar Brynolf 1925- *WhoAm 90*
Stickler, Mitchell Gene 1934- *WhoE 91*
Stickler, Peter Bleier 1952- *St&PR 91*
Stickles, Wayne Arthur 1945- *St&PR 91*
Stickley, Carlisle Martin 1933 *WhoAm 90*
Stickley, Gustav 1857-1942 *PenDiDA 89*
Stickley, Gustav 1858-1942 *BioIn 16*
Stickley, J.G. *PenDiDA 89*
Stickley, Kim Arthur 1950- *St&PR 91*
Stickley, L. *PenDiDA 89*
Stickney, Charles E., Jr. 1922- *St&PR 91*
Stickney, Jessica 1929- *WhoAmW 91*
Stickney, Walt Christopher 1944- *WhoWrEP 89*
Stickney, William Wallace 1853-1932 *AmLegL*
Stidham, Shaler, Jr. 1941- *WhoSSW 91*
Stidvent, Thomas Wesley 1943- *BiDrAPA 89*
Stidworthy, John 1943- *SmATA 63 [port]*
Stieb, Dave 1957- *Ballpl 90*
Stieb, David Andrew 1957- *WhoAm 90*
Stieb, Ronald Peter 1939- *St&PR 91*
Stiebel, Eric 1911- *WhoAmA 91*
Stiebel, Gerald Gustave 1944- *WhoAmA 91, WhoE 91*
Stiebel, Penelope Hunter *WhoAmA 91*
Stiebel, Victor Gordon 1958- *BiDrAPA 89*
Stiebeling, Hazel K. *BioIn 16*
Stiedry, Fritz 1883-1968 *PenDiMP*
Stief, Louis John 1933- *WhoAm 90*
Stiefel, David 1957- *ODwPR 91*
Stiefel, Janice J. 1936- *WhoWrEP 89*
Stiefel, John T. *BioIn 16, NewYTBS 90*
Stiefel, Roger H. 1949- *St&PR 91*
Stieff, Charles C. 1922- *St&PR 91*
Stieff, Rodney Gilbert 1925- *St&PR 91*
Stiegel, Henry William 1729-1785 *EncCRAm, PenDiDA 89*
Stiegelmeyer, Norman Earl 1937- *WhoAmA 91N*
Stiegler, Karl Drago 1919- *WhoWor 91*
Stiegler, Paul W., Jr. 1939- *St&PR 91*
Stiegler, Theodore Donald 1934- *WhoSSW 91*
Stieglitz, Alfred 1864-1946 *BioIn 16, WorAlBi*
Stieglitz, John Franklin 1953- *WhoEmL 91*
Stieglitz, Leonard 1929- *St&PR 91*
Stieglitz, Perry Jesse 1920- *WhoE 91*
Stiehl, Charles William 1924- *WhoWor 91*
Stiehl, Robert J. 1935- *St&PR 91*
Stiehm, E. Richard 1933- *WhoAm 90*
Stiehm, Judith Hicks 1935- *WhoAm 90*
Stieler, Kathryn Lee 1956- *St&PR 91*
Stielow-Leach, Fay Ann 1939- *WhoAmW 91*
Stienmier, Saundra Kay Young 1938- *WhoAmW 91*
Stier, Serena Deborah 1939- *WhoE 91*
Stierhoff, Harold F. 1933- *St&PR 91*
Stierle, Walter O.F. 1949- *WhoWor 91*
Stierle, Wolf F. 1937- *St&PR 91*
Stierlin, Helm 1926- *BiDrAPA 89, WhoWor 91*
Stiernhielm, Georg 1598-1672 *DcScanL*
Stiers, David Ogden 1942- *WhoAm 90*
Stievater, James Edward 1934- *St&PR 91*
Stifel, Frederick Benton 1940- *WhoWor 91*
Stiff, Henry C. 1859- *AmLegL*
Stiff, John Sterling 1921- *WhoAm 90*
Stiff, Robert M 1931- *ConAu 132*
Stiff, Robert Martin 1931- *WhoAm 90, WhoWrEP 89*
Stiffler, David B. 1948- *St&PR 91*
Stiffler, Jack Justin 1934- *WhoAm 90*
Stiffler, LaVonne Marie 1936- *WhoSSW 91*
Stiffler, Marjorie Larue 1935- *St&PR 91*
Stifler, Richard Bond 1939- *BiDrAPA 89*
Stifter, Francis J. 1930- *St&PR 91*
Stigall, Ray 1932- *St&PR 91*
Stigen, Terje 1922- *DcScanL*
Stigers, Nancy B. *ODwPR 91*
Stigler, George J. 1911- *WorAlBi*
Stigler, George Joseph 1911- *BioIn 16, WhoAm 90, WhoWor 91*
Stigliani, Wiliam Michael 1945- *WhoWor 91*
Stiglitz, Beatrice 1945- *WhoSSW 91*
Stiglitz, Douglas E. 1953- *St&PR 91*
Stiglitz, Martin Richard 1920- *WhoE 91, WhoWor 91*
Stigman, Dick 1936- *Ballpl 90*
Stignani, Ebe 1903-1974 *PenDiMP*
Stigson, Stig *EncCoWW*
Stigwood, Robert Colin 1934- *WhoAm 90*
Stiha, Vladan 1908- *BioIn 16*
Stiles, Curtis F. 1942- *St&PR 91*
Stiles, Donald George 1926- *St&PR 91*
Stiles, Ezra 1727-1795 *EncCRAm*
Stiles, Frank 1924- *IntWWM 90*
Stiles, G.E.R. 1932- *St&PR 91*
Stiles, G. E. R. 1932- *WhoAm 90*
Stiles, Helen *WhoAmA 91, WhoAmW 91, WhoE 91*
Stiles, John Barry 1951- *St&PR 91*
Stiles, John S. 1913- *St&PR 91*
Stiles, John Stephen 1913- *WhoAm 90*
Stiles, Joseph D. *EncO&P 3*
Stiles, Kevin Patrick 1949- *WhoAm 90*
Stiles, Kristine 1947- *WhoAmA 91*
Stiles, Linford E. 1937- *St&PR 91*
Stiles, Marshall F, III 1945- *BiDrAPA 89*
Stiles, Martha Bennett *WhoWrEP 89*
Stiles, Martha Bennett 1933- *LiHiK*
Stiles, Mary Ann 1944- *WhoAmW 91, WhoSSW 91*
Stiles, Phillip John 1934- *WhoAm 90*
Stiles, Rebecca Ann 1951- *WhoAmW 91*
Stiles, Rollie 1906- *Ballpl 90*
Stiles, Stephen Lee 1946- *St&PR 91*
Stiles, Stuart L. 1915- *St&PR 91*
Stiles, Stuart Lee 1915- *WhoAm 90*
Stiles, Thomas B. 1940- *St&PR 91*
Stiles, Thomas Beveridge, II 1940- *WhoAm 90*
Stiles, Thomas Edward 1934- *St&PR 91, WhoAm 90*
Stiles, William Henry 1810-1864 *AmLegL*
Stilgenbauer, Nancy Kieffer 1934- *WhoAmW 91*
Still, Andrew Taylor 1828-1917 *NewAgE 90*
Still, Bayrd 1906- *WhoAm 90*
Still, Charles Herbert 1963- *WhoSSW 91*
Still, Clifford 1904- *WorAlBi*
Still, Clyfford 1904-1981 *WhoAmA 91N*
Still, David Barnes 1949- *WhoAm 90*
Still, Edgar *ConAu 132*
Still, Ellen Perry *ODwPR 91*
Still, Eugene Fontaine, II 1937- *WhoSSW 91*
Still, James 1906- *AuBYP 90, LiHiK*
Still, John Taylor, III 1947- *St&PR 91*
Still, Judith Anne 1942- *IntWWM 90*
Still, Mark Douglas 1955- *WhoSSW 91*
Still, Mary Jane 1940- *WhoSSW 91*
Still, Ray 1920- *WhoAm 90*
Still, Richard Ralph 1921- *WhoAm 90*
Still, Ronald Bruce 1957- *WhoSSW 91*
Still, Stephen Allen 1919- *WhoAm 90*
Still, William Clark, Jr. 1946- *WhoAm 90*
Still, William Grant 1895-1978 *DcAfAmP, DrBIPA 90*
Stille, Dexter L. 1951- *St&PR 91*
Stille, Marvin A. 1941- *St&PR 91*
Stiller, Andrew Philip 1946- *IntWWM 90*
Stiller, Ben *BioIn 16*
Stiller, Jennifer Anne 1948- *WhoEmL 91*
Stiller, Jerry *WhoAm 90*
Stiller, Jerry 1929- *WorAlBi*
Stiller, Peter Frederick 1951- *WhoE 91*
Stiller, Rochus 1909- *BiDrAPA 89*
Stiller, Shale David 1935- *WhoAm 90*
Stiller, Sharon Paula 1951- *WhoEmL 91*
Stillerman, Bernard *BiDrAPA 89*
Stillerman, Lottie 1906-1989 *BioIn 16*
Stilley, Deborah A. 1964- *St&PR 91*
Stilley, Frank Wood 1954- *St&PR 91*
Stilley, Walter A., III 1930- *St&PR 91*
Stillinger, Frank Henry 1934- *WhoAm 90*
Stillinger, Jack Clifford 1931- *WhoAm 90*
Stillings, Frank Stuart 1921- *WhoAm 90*
Stillings, Irene Cordiner 1918- *WhoAmW 91, WhoE 91*
Stillings, Wayne Andrew *BiDrAPA 89*
Stillman, Alfred William, Jr. 1942- *WhoWor 91*
Stillman, Anne Walker 1951- *WhoAmW 91, WhoEmL 91*
Stillman, Chauncey 1907-1989 *BioIn 16*
Stillman, Damie 1933- *WhoAmA 91, WhoE 91*
Stillman, E Clark 1907- *WhoAmA 91*
Stillman, Elinor Hadley 1938- *WhoAmW 91*
Stillman, G. Patrick 1940- *St&PR 91*
Stillman, George 1921- *WhoAmA 91*
Stillman, Irving Mayer *BiDrAPA 89*
Stillman, Isadore W *BiDrAPA 89*
Stillman, James 1850-1918 *EncABHB 6 [port]*
Stillman, Larry Barr 1941- *WhoWor 91*
Stillman, Leo *BioIn 16*
Stillman, Lucille T *WhoAmA 91*
Stillman, Maria 1844-1927 *BiDWomA*
Stillman, Marie Spartali 1844-1927 *BioIn 16*
Stillman, Martha 1924- *WhoAmW 91*
Stillman, Mary Elizabeth 1929- *WhoAmW 91*
Stillman, Myra Stephens 1915- *AuBYP 90*
Stillman, Paul Oster 1933- *St&PR 91*
Stillman, Robert D. 1929- *St&PR 91*
Stillman, Stephanie Matusz 1946- *WhoAmW 91*
Stillman, W. Paul *St&PR 91*
Stillman, W. Paul 1897-1989 *BioIn 16*
Stillman, William Everett 1952- *WhoWrEP 89*
Stillman, William Lavalla Heyl 1942- *St&PR 91*
Stillman, William M., Jr. 1939- *St&PR 91*
Stillner, Verner 1940- *BiDrAPA 89*
Stillpass, John Edward 1956- *WhoEmL 91*
Stills, Gracie Wiggins *WhoAmW 91*
Stills, Stephen 1945- *ConMus 5 [port], EncPR&S 89, WorAlBi*
Stillwagon, James R. *St&PR 91*
Stillwagon, Wesley William 1940- *WhoE 91*
Stillwater, Maloah *NewAgMG*
Stillwater, Michael *NewAgMG*
Stillwell, Frank Leslie 1888-1963 *DcScB S2*
Stillwell, George Keith 1918- *WhoAm 90*
Stillwell, James Todd 1965- *WhoSSW 91*
Stillwell, Kurt 1965- *Ballpl 90*
Stillwell, Mary Kathryn 1944- *WhoWrEP 89*
Stillwell, Ralph Berry 1945- *WhoSSW 91*
Stillwell, Naemi *BiDrAPA 89*
Stilson, Christie Carol 1952- *WhoAmW 91*
Stilson, Suzanne L. *St&PR 91*
Stilson, Walter Leslie 1908- *WhoWor 91*
Stiltner, Gary L. 1940- *St&PR 91*
Stilwell, James Edward 1947- *St&PR 91*
Stilwell, Jeane Kay 1954- *WhoSSW 91*
Stilwell, Joseph W. 1883-1946 *WorAlBi*
Stilwell, Kathy *BioIn 16*
Stilwell, R Bronson 1951- *BiDrAPA 89*
Stilwell, Richard 1942- *IntWWM 90, PenDiMP*
Stilwell, Richard Dale 1942- *WhoAm 90*
Stilwell, Richard Giles 1917- *WhoAm 90*
Stilwell, Richard William 1936- *St&PR 91*
Stilwell, Ronald E. 1948- *St&PR 91*
Stilwell, Susan Farmer 1946- *WhoSSW 91*
Stilwell, Wilbur Moore 1908-1974 *WhoAmA 91N*
Stilz, Gerhard 1940- *WhoWor 91*
Stimac, Gary Allen 1951- *St&PR 91*
Stimler, Michael Kevin 1959- *WhoE 91*
Stimmel, Barry 1939- *WhoAm 90*
Stimmel, David Craig 1954- *WhoSSW 91*
Stimpert, Michael Alan 1944- *St&PR 91, WhoAm 90*
Stimpson, Catharine R. *BioIn 16*
Stimpson, Catharine R. 1936- *FemiCLE*
Stimpson, Catharine Roslyn 1936- *WhoAm 90, WhoAmW 91*

Stimpson, J.R. 1949- *St&PR 91*
Stimpson, James Wilbert, Sr. 1934- *WhoAm 90*
Stimpson, John Hallowell 1926- *WhoAm 90*
Stimson, Dorothy 1890-1988 *BioIn 16*
Stimson, Frederick Sparks 1919- *WhoAm 90*
Stimson, Henry L. 1867-1950 *WorAlBi*
Stimson, Henry Lewis 1867-1950 *BiDrUSE 89, BioIn 16*
Stimson, Janice A. 1956- *St&PR 91*
Stimson, Judith Ann 1957- *WhoEmL 91*
Stimson, Julia Catherine 1881-1948 *BioIn 16*
Stimson, Paul R *BiDrAPA 89*
Stimson, Robert Frederick 1939- *WhoWor 91*
Stincer, Carlos E 1948- *BiDrAPA 89*
Stinchcomb, Carl J. 1938- *St&PR 91*
Stinchcomb, Carl Joseph 1938- *WhoAm 90, WhoE 91*
Stinchcomb, James Delwin *WhoSSW 91*
Stinchfield, John Edward 1947- *St&PR 91, WhoE 91, WhoEmL 91*
Stine, Anna Mae 1938- *WhoAmW 91*
Stine, Clifford R. 1906-1986 *BioIn 16*
Stine, Deborah Diane 1960- *WhoAmW 91*
Stine, Earle John, Jr. 1932- *WhoSSW 91*
Stine, G Harry 1928- *ConAu 30NR*
Stine, George Harry 1928- *AuBYP 90, WhoAm 90*
Stine, Gordan Bernard 1924- *WhoWor 91*
Stine, Jack William 1924- *St&PR 91, WhoAm 90*
Stine, John Jacob 1938- *BiDrAPA 89*
Stine, Joseph Evans 1937- *St&PR 91*
Stine, Larry Wayne 1941- *St&PR 91*
Stine, Linda France 1956- *WhoAmW 91*
Stine, R. L. 1943- *WhoWrEP 89*
Stine, Richard Dengler 1926- *WhoAm 90*
Stine, Robert John *BiDrAPA 89*
Stine, Susan Marie *BiDrAPA 89*
Stine, Susan Marie 1949- *WhoE 91*
Stinebring, Warren Richard 1924- *WhoAm 90*
Stinecipher, Mary Margaret 1940- *WhoAmW 91*
Stinehart, Roger Ray 1945- *WhoWor 91*
Stiner, Frederic Matthew, Jr. 1946- *WhoE 91*
Stines, Fred, Jr. 1925- *WhoAm 90*
Sting *BioIn 16*
Sting 1951- *WhoAm 90, WorAlBi*
Sting 1952?- *EncPR&S 89*
Stingel, Donald Eugene 1920- *WhoAm 90, WhoWor 91*
Stingel, Russell E. 1930- *St&PR 91*
Stingelin, Valentin 1933- *WhoAm 90*
Stinger, Keith W. 1935- *WhoE 91*
Stingle, Sandra Fromer 1946- *WhoAmW 91*
Stini, William Arthur 1930- *WhoAm 90*
Stinnett, Charles Edgar, Jr. 1934- *St&PR 91*
Stinnett, Glenn Harold 1925- *St&PR 91*
Stinnett, Hester A 1956- *WhoAmA 91*
Stinnett, Hester Ann 1956- *WhoE 91*
Stinnett, James Le Baron 1938- *BiDrAPA 89*
Stinnett, James T, III 1941- *BiDrAPA 89*
Stinnett, Lee Houston 1939- *WhoAm 90*
Stinnett, Mark Allan 1955- *WhoEmL 91, WhoSSW 91*
Stinnett, Wayne D., Jr. 1951- *St&PR 91*
Stinsen, Clara Gottier 1910- *WhoWrEP 89*
Stinsmuehlen-Amend, Susan *WhoAmA 91*
Stinsmuehlen-Amend, Susan 1948- *WhoAmA 91*
Stinson, Andrea *BioIn 16*
Stinson, Benoni 1798-1869 *BioIn 16*
Stinson, Bob 1945- *Ballpl 90*
Stinson, Charles B. 1930- *St&PR 91*
Stinson, Daniel T 1936- *BiDrAPA 89*
Stinson, David Leo 1957- *WhoWrEP 89*
Stinson, Deane Brian 1930- *WhoWor 91*
Stinson, Dilys Ann 1949- *BiDWomA*
Stinson, Edward Brad 1938- *WhoAm 90*
Stinson, George A. 1915- *St&PR 91*
Stinson, George Arthur 1915- *WhoAm 90*
Stinson, Joseph McLester 1939- *WhoAm 90*
Stinson, Katharine 1917- *WhoAmW 91*
Stinson, Lawrence 1906- *MusmAFA*
Stinson, Louis, Jr. 1943- *St&PR 91*
Stinson, Richard James 1929- *WhoAm 90*
Stinson, Robert C. 1946- *St&PR 91*
Stinson, Stanley Thomas 1961- *WhoEmL 91, WhoSSW 91*
Stinson, Steven Arthur 1946- *WhoSSW 91*
Stinson, William W. 1933- *WhoAm 90, WhoWor 91*
Stinson, William Wade 1933- *St&PR 91*
Stipak, James Paul 1950- *WhoEmL 91*
Stipanowich, Joseph Jean 1921- *WhoAm 90*
Stipanowich, Thomas Joseph 1952- *WhoEmL 91*
Stipe, Gene 1926- *WhoSSW 91*
Stipes, Albert Henry 1942- *BiDrAPA 89*
Stipp, John Edgar 1914- *WhoAm 90*
Stipp, John S. 1925- *St&PR 91*
Stipp, Norman J. 1947- *St&PR 91*
Stipp, Scott Lee 1951- *St&PR 91*
Stirba, Anne Melinda Morr 1951- *WhoEmL 91*
Stirbois, Jean-Pierre *BioIn 16*
Stirbois, Jean-Pierre 1945-1988 *BiDFrPL*
Stirbu, Constantin-Teofanescu 1944- *WhoWor 91*
Stires, Barbara Bonham 1936- *WhoE 91*
Stires, David Warfield 1933- *WhoAm 90*
Stires, William Dennis 1939- *WhoE 91*
Stirewalt, Glenn M. 1935- *WhoAm 90*
Stirewalt, John Newman 1931- *WhoWor 91*
Stiritz, William P. 1934- *WhoAm 90*
Stiritz, William Paul 1934- *St&PR 91*
Stirling, Arthur *MajTwCW*
Stirling, Dale Alexander 1956- *WhoWrEP 89*
Stirling, David *NewYTBS 90*
Stirling, Edwin Murdoch 1940- *WhoSSW 91*
Stirling, Geoffrey William 1925- *WhoAm 90*
Stirling, James 1926- *WhoWor 91*
Stirling, James Frazer *BioIn 16*
Stirling, James Paulman 1941- *WhoAm 90*
Stirling, Lilla 1902- *AuBYP 90*
Stirling, Mary, Countess of *FemiCLE*
Stirling, Mary Alexander, Countess of *BiDEWW*
Stirling, Monica 1916-1983 *AuBYP 90*
Stirling, Nora Bramley 1900- *AuBYP 90*
Stirling, Roger Ludington 1951- *WhoWor 91*
Stirm, Eugene Robert 1945- *WhoWor 91*
Stirn, Jack Joseph 1927- *St&PR 91*
Stirnemann, S. A. *WhoWrEP 89*
Stirnweis, Shannon 1931- *WhoAmA 91*
Stirnweiss, Snuffy 1918-1958 *Ballpl 90*
Stirrat, William Albert 1919- *WhoE 91*
Stirredge, Elizabeth 1634-1706 *BiDEWW, FemiCLE*
Stirrett, David Douglass, Jr. 1958- *WhoE 91*
Stishan, Peter Michael 1949- *WhoE 91*
Stitch, Malcolm Lane 1923- *WhoAm 90*
Stitelman, Michael 1940- *BiDrAPA 89*
Stites, C. Thomas 1942- *WhoAm 90*
Stites, Larry L. 1941- *St&PR 91*
Stites, Raymond Sommers 1899-1974 *WhoAmA 91N*
Stites, Thomas *ODwPR 91*
Stith, Daniel Carroll 1956- *WhoSSW 91*
Stith, David L. 1941- *St&PR 91*
Stith, Deborah Prothrow- *BioIn 16*
Stith, Forest C. 1934- *WhoAm 90*
Stith, Henry Hammond, Jr. 1936- *WhoSSW 91*
Stith, John Edward 1947- *WhoEmL 91*
Stith, John Stephen 1939- *WhoAm 90*
Stith, Joseph 1962- *WhoEmL 91*
Stith, Marice W. *WhoE 91*
Stith, Reginald B. 1953- *St&PR 91*
Stith, Richard Taylor, Jr. 1919- *WhoAm 90*
Stitham, Mark Dillen 1950- *BiDrAPA 89*
Stitt, Gerald Earl 1932- *St&PR 91*
Stitt, Howard Stephen 1931- *WhoSSW 91*
Stitt, John Brenneman 1947- *WhoSSW 91*
Stitt, Richard Payne 1926- *St&PR 91*
Stitt, Sonny 1924- *WorAlBi*
Stitt, Sonny 1924-1982 *BioIn 16, DrBlPA 90*
Stitt, Susan 1942- *WhoAmA 91*
Stitt, Susan Margaret 1942- *WhoAm 90*
Stitzer, H. Todd 1952- *St&PR 91*
Stitziel, George L. *St&PR 91N*
Stivell, Alan *NewAgMG*
Stiven, Alan Ernest 1935- *WhoAm 90*
Stivender, David *BioIn 16*
Stivender, David 1933-1990 *NewYTBS 90*
Stivender, Donald Lewis 1932- *WhoAm 90, WhoWor 91*
Stivender, Edward David 1933- *WhoAm 90*
Stiver, Inezetta Orel Eliason 1916- *WhoAmW 91*
Stiver, William Earl 1921- *WhoE 91, WhoWor 91*
Stivers, David Neil 1967- *WhoSSW 91*
Stivers, Roger Neil 1936- *St&PR 91*
Stivers, William Charles 1938- *St&PR 91, WhoAm 90*
Stives, J. Jeffrey 1942- *ODwPR 91*
Stivetts, Jack 1868-1930 *Ballpl 90*
Stivison, David Vaughn 1946- *WhoE 91, WhoEmL 91, WhoWor 91*
Stix, Christopher Terry 1955- *WhoE 91*
Stix, Gerulf 1935- *WhoWor 91*
Stix, Regine Kronacker 1895-1988 *BioIn 16*
Stix, Robert Dryer 1928- *St&PR 91*
Stix, Thomas Howard 1924- *WhoAm 90*
Stjernquist, Berta Ingeborg 1918- *WhoWor 91*
Stjernschantz, Beda Maria 1867-1910 *BiDWomA*
Stob, Martin 1926- *WhoAm 90*
Stob, Warren Keith 1938- *St&PR 91*
Stobart, St. Clair, Mrs. *EncO&P 3*
Stobaugh, Robert Blair 1927- *WhoAm 90*
Stobb, Margaret Anne 1937- *WhoAmW 91*
Stobbe, Alfred Fritz 1924- *WhoWor 91*
Stobbe, Victor John 1941- *St&PR 91*
Stobbs, Chuck 1929- *Ballpl 90*
Stober, Mark *ODwPR 91*
Stober, Quentin Jerome 1938- *WhoSSW 91*
Stober, William John, II 1933- *WhoAm 90*
Stobie, Charles 1845-1931 *WhNaAH*
Stobo, John David 1941- *WhoAm 90*
Stobwasser, Johann Heinrich 1740-1829 *PenDiDA 89*
Stoch, Mavis Belle 1929- *BiDrAPA 89*
Stock, Ann S. *ODwPR 91*
Stock, Carl William 1945- *WhoSSW 91*
Stock, Charles Chester 1910- *WhoAm 90*
Stock, David Frederick 1939- *IntWWM 90*
Stock, Elyse Gail *BiDrAPA 89*
Stock, Frederick 1872-1942 *PenDiMP*
Stock, Gregg Francis 1925- *WhoAm 90*
Stock, Gregory *BioIn 16*
Stock, Howard F 1937- *BiDrAPA 89*
Stock, Jan Hendrik 1931- *WhoWor 91*
Stock, John Alan 1945- *WhoSSW 91*
Stock, Leon Milo 1930- *WhoAm 90*
Stock, Leroy A. 1942- *St&PR 91*
Stock, Margot Therese 1936- *WhoAmW 91*
Stock, Milt 1893-1977 *Ballpl 90*
Stock, Mitchell B. *BioIn 16*
Stock, Naomi Ferguson 1932- *WhoAmW 91*
Stock, Norman 1940- *WhoWrEP 89*
Stock, Otto F., Jr. 1935- *St&PR 91*
Stock, Peggy Ann 1936- *WhoAm 90, WhoAmW 91, WhoE 91*
Stock, Rodney Clifford 1929- *WhoWor 91*
Stock, Simon S., Jr. 1927- *St&PR 91*
Stock, Sybil Allyson *BiDrAPA 89*
Stock, Wes 1934- *Ballpl 90*
Stock, Wolfgang Rudolf 1959- *WhoWor 91*
Stockamer, Balthazar *PenDiDA 89*
Stockard, James Alfred 1935- *WhoAm 90*
Stockbauer, Roger Lewis 1944- *WhoSSW 91*
Stockberger, Warner W. *BioIn 16*
Stockbridge, John Jason 1943- *St&PR 91*
Stockdale, Gayle Sue 1955- *WhoAmW 91*
Stockdale, George William 1932- *WhoWor 91*
Stockdale, Harold James 1931- *WhoAm 90*
Stockdale, James Bond 1923- *WhoAm 90*
Stockdale, John A D 1936- *WhoAmA 91*
Stockdale, Mary 1769- *FemiCLE*
Stockdale, Ronald Allen 1934- *St&PR 91, WhoAm 90*
Stockel, Ernst Franz 1941- *WhoE 91*
Stockel, Joseph 1743-1800 *PenDiDA 89*
Stocker, Arthur Frederick 1914- *WhoAm 90*
Stocker, Frederick, Jr. *BiDrAPA 89*
Stocker, John Edward 1924- *WhoSSW 91*
Stocker, Jule E. 1906- *St&PR 91*
Stocker, Jule Elias 1906- *WhoAm 90*
Stocker, Karl Josef 1929- *WhoWor 91*
Stocker, Kurt P. 1937- *ODwPR 91*
Stocker, Mark 1956- *ConAu 131*
Stocker, Markus 1945- *IntWWM 90*
Stocker, Peter C. *BioIn 16*
Stocker, Ronald John 1934- *St&PR 91*
Stocker, Wilhelm 1940- *WhoWor 91*
Stockert, Thomas R. 1941- *St&PR 91*
Stockfisch, Robert Thomas *BiDrAPA 89*
Stockford, David M 1938- *BiDrAPA 89*
Stockglausner, William George 1950- *WhoEmL 91*
Stockham, Pamela 1952- *WhoE 91*
Stockham, Peter 1928- *BioIn 16*
Stockham, Thomas Greenway, Jr. 1933- *WhoAm 90*
Stockhammer, Jacques 1931- *WhoWor 91*
Stockhausen, Hans Gottfried von 1920- *PenDiDA 89*
Stockhausen, Karlheinz 1928- *IntWWM 90, PenDiMP A, WhoWor 91*
Stockhausen, Sharron Renee 1948- *WhoAmW 91*
Stockholm, Charles M. 1933- *St&PR 91*
Stockholm, Donald Dean 1925- *St&PR 91*
Stocking, Charles Albert 1950- *WhoE 91*
Stocking, Clifford Ralph 1913- *WhoAm 90*
Stocking, George Ward, Jr. 1928- *WhoAm 90*
Stocking, Marion Kingston 1922- *WhoWrEP 89*
Stocking, Myron R 1930- *BiDrAPA 89*
Stockinger, Leopold 1919- *WhoWor 91*
Stockl, Marie-Claude 1951- *ODwPR 91*
Stocklan, Martin B. 1941- *St&PR 91*
Stocklin, Alma Katherine 1926- *WhoAmW 91, WhoE 91*
Stockmal, Henry F., Jr. 1942- *WhoE 91*
Stockman, Gordon 1929- *St&PR 91*
Stockman, Jennifer Blei 1954- *WhoE 91*
Stockman, Kenneth B. 1940- *St&PR 91*
Stockman, Pamela Ybarguen 1945- *WhoAmW 91*
Stockman, Richard Owen 1930- *St&PR 91*
Stockman, Tommy Eugene 1938- *WhoSSW 91*
Stockmar, Ted P. 1921- *WhoAm 90*
Stockmayer, Walter Hugo 1914- *WhoAm 90*
Stockmeyer, C.B., Jr. 1939- *St&PR 91*
Stockner, Robert David 1958- *WhoEmL 91, WhoSSW 91*
Stocks, Chester Lee, Jr. 1928- *WhoAm 90*
Stocks, Gerald Richard 1932- *WhoWor 91*
Stocks, John Anthony *BiDrAPA 89*
Stocks, Kenneth Duane 1934- *St&PR 91, WhoAm 90*
Stocks, Rundell Kingsley 1925- *WhoWor 91*
Stocksdale, Bob 1913- *BioIn 16*
Stockton, Earl of 1943- *WhoWor 91*
Stockton, Anne *BiDrAPA 89*
Stockton, Annis 1736-1801 *FemiCLE*
Stockton, Billy G. 1944- *WhoSSW 91*
Stockton, Brenda Evelyn 1949- *WhoAmW 91*
Stockton, Christine Mary 1947- *WhoWor 91*
Stockton, David Knapp 1941- *WhoAm 90*
Stockton, David Louis 1933- *WhoE 91*
Stockton, Dick 1942- *WhoAm 90*
Stockton, Francis Richard *AuBYP 90*
Stockton, Frank Richard 1834-1902 *AuBYP 90*
Stockton, J. Roy *Ballpl 90*
Stockton, John *BioIn 16*
Stockton, John 1962- *WorAlBi*
Stockton, Kenton L. 1928- *St&PR 91*
Stockton, Michael Alan 1951- *BiDrAPA 89*
Stockton, Ralph Madison, Jr. 1927- *WhoAm 90*
Stockton, Richard 1730-1781 *EncCRAm*
Stockton, Robert Field 1795-1866 *BioIn 16*
Stockton, Robert Louis 1932- *WhoSSW 91*
Stockton, Robert Standeford 1939- *WhoSSW 91*
Stockton, Roberta Susan 1954- *WhoAmW 91*
Stockton, Sandra Lee Kearse 1949- *WhoAmW 91*
Stockton, Stephen F. 1947- *St&PR 91*
Stockton, Stephen Finch 1947- *WhoEmL 91*
Stockton, Thomas B. 1930- *WhoAm 90, WhoSSW 91*
Stockton, Virginia 1964- *WhoAmW 91*
Stockton, William J *BiDrAPA 89*
Stockton, William James 1929- *WhoE 91*
Stockwell, Amy Carol 1953- *WhoAmW 91*
Stockwell, Christopher Edmund Vigurs 1956- *WhoE 91*
Stockwell, David Hunt, Jr. 1940- *WhoE 91*
Stockwell, Dean 1935- *BioIn 16*
Stockwell, Dean 1936- *WhoAm 90*
Stockwell, Ernest Farnham 1923- *St&PR 91*
Stockwell, Ernest Farnham, Jr. 1923- *WhoAm 90*
Stockwell, Evangelina Ramirez *WhoHisp 91*
Stockwell, George Lewis 1928- *St&PR 91*
Stockwell, Oliver Perkins 1907- *WhoAm 90, WhoSSW 91, WhoWor 91*
Stockwell, Richard E. 1917- *WhoAm 90*
Stockwell, Robert Paul 1925- *WhoAm 90*
Stockwell, Shelley Lessin 1945- *WhoWrEP 89*
Stockwell, Sherwood Beach 1926- *WhoAm 90*
Stockwell, Wayne Verne 1950- *WhoEmL 91*
Stoddard, Alexandra 1941- *WhoWor 91*
Stoddard, Bob 1957- *Ballpl 90*
Stoddard, Brandon *BioIn 16*
Stoddard, Brandon 1937- *WhoAm 90*
Stoddard, Charles Hatch 1912- *WhoAm 90*
Stoddard, Charles Warren 1843-1909 *BioIn 16*
Stoddard, Donald A. *BioIn 16*
Stoddard, Edward G. 1923- *AuBYP 90*
Stoddard, Elizabeth Drew 1823-1902 *FemiCLE*
Stoddard, Ellwyn R. 1927- *WhoSSW 91*
Stoddard, Forrest Shaffer 1944- *WhoE 91, WhoWor 91*
Stoddard, Frances Ellen 1941- *WhoWrEP 89*
Stoddard, Fred R 1943- *BiDrAPA 89*
Stoddard, Frederick J, Jr. 1942- *BiDrAPA 89*
Stoddard, George Earl 1917- *WhoAm 90*
Stoddard, George Edward 1921- *WhoAm 90*
Stoddard, Gerard 1934- *ODwPR 91*
Stoddard, Gerard F. 1934- *St&PR 91*
Stoddard, Hope 1900- *AuBYP 90*

Stoddard, Laurence Ralph, Jr. 1936- *WhoAm 90*
Stoddard, Linda Gandrud 1944- *WhoAmW 91*
Stoddard, Patrick Clare 1941- *WhoE 91*
Stoddard, Richard Ethridge 1950- *WhoAm 90*
Stoddard, Richard Henry 1825-1903 *BioIn 16*
Stoddard, Roger Eliot 1935- *WhoAm 90*
Stoddard, Sandol *AuBYP 90*
Stoddard, Sandol 1927- *WhoAmW 91*
Stoddard, Stephen Davidson 1925- *WhoAm 90*
Stoddard, Susan 1942- *WhoAmW 91*
Stoddard, Tim 1953- *Ballpl 90*
Stoddard, William Bert, Jr. 1926- *WhoE 91, WhoWor 91*
Stoddart, Alfred 1941- *St&PR 91*
Stoddart, George A. 1933- *St&PR 91*
Stoddart, George Anderson 1933- *WhoAm 90*
Stoddart, Jack Elliott 1916- *WhoAm 90*
Stodder, John Wesley 1923- *St&PR 91, WhoAm 90*
Stoddert, Benjamin 1751-1813 *BiDrUSE 89*
Stodnick, Gregory John 1942- *St&PR 91*
Stodola, Gerald William 1951- *St&PR 91*
Stodola, Kenneth G. 1926- *St&PR 91*
Stodola, Randall Joseph 1953- *St&PR 91*
Stoebermann, Marina Nicole 1963- *WhoAmW 91*
Stoecker, David Thomas 1939- *WhoAm 90*
Stoecker, Leo Joseph 1919- *WhoAm 90*
Stoecker, Steven O. 1948- *St&PR 91*
Stoeckl, Ernst G. *BioIn 16*
Stoeckl, Ernst G. 1944- *St&PR 91*
Stoeckl, Shelley Joan 1951- *WhoAmW 91*
Stoeckle, M.L. 1931- *St&PR 91*
Stoeckley, John Bolton 1943- *St&PR 91*
Stoefen, Gary E. 1939- *St&PR 91*
Stoeffhaas, W.H. *St&PR 91*
Stoehr, Charles Michael 1946- *St&PR 91, WhoAm 90*
Stoehr, James Harkness 1929- *St&PR 91*
Stoehr, Richard J. 1927- *St&PR 91*
Stoeltje, Beverly June 1940- *WhoAmW 91*
Stoelzle-Midden, Karen Lynn 1952- *WhoAmW 91*
Stoepel, Theodore Robert 1924- *St&PR 91*
Stoeppelwerth, Sydney A. *BioIn 16*
Stoesen, Alexander Rudolph 1932- *WhoSSW 91*
Stoessel, Henry Kurt 1909- *WhoAmA 91N*
Stoessel, Walter J. 1920-1986 *BioIn 16*
Stoett, Herman Pieter 1930- *WhoAm 90*
Stoetzel, Jean 1910-1987 *BioIn 16*
Stoetzner, Eric W. *NewYTBS 90*
Stoetzner, Eric Woldemar 1901- *WhoE 91, WhoWor 91*
Stoeveken, Anthony Charles 1938- *WhoAmA 91*
Stoeveken, Christel E *WhoAmA 91*
Stoewe, Judith Kay *BiDrAPA 89*
Stofer, Kermit Lea 1943- *WhoE 91*
Stoffa, Michael *WhoAmA 91*
Stoffa, Paul L. 1948- *WhoAm 90*
Stoffel, Jack O 1924- *BiDrAPA 89*
Stoffel, Klaus Peter 1957- *WhoE 91, WhoEmL 91, WhoWor 91*
Stoffer, James Myron, Jr. 1952- *WhoSSW 91*
Stoffer, Terry James 1946- *WhoEmL 91*
Stofferahn, Bruce Eugene 1951- *WhoE 91*
Stofferson, Terry Lee 1957- *WhoEmL 91, WhoWor 91*
Stofflet, Mary 1942- *WhoAmA 91*
Stofflet, Ty *BioIn 16*
Stofka, David Andrew 1936- *St&PR 91*
Stofko, Karl Peter 1938- *WhoE 91*
Stoft, Delmar Duane 1917- *St&PR 91*
Stogner, Jennifer Dawn 1961- *WhoAmW 91*
Stogner, William Louis 1957- *WhoSSW 91*
Stohl, Bob *NewAgMG*
Stohl, Stephen A. 1945- *St&PR 91*
Stohler, Michael Joe 1956- *WhoWor 91*
Stohlman, Robert Stuart 1929- *St&PR 91*
Stohlquist, Roger Harold 1925- *St&PR 91*
Stoianov, Carmen Antoaneta 1950- *IntWWM 90*
Stoianovich, Marcelle *WhoAmA 91*
Stoica, Susana 1946- *WhoAmW 91, WhoWor 91*
Stoicheff, Boris Peter 1924- *WhoAm 90*
Stoik, John Lentis 1920- *St&PR 91, WhoAm 90*
Stoikos, Nicolas Paul 1959- *WhoWor 91*
Stoikov, Judith Hirsch 1941- *WhoE 91*
Stojak, James Richard 1946- *WhoE 91*
Stojanovich, Kosta *BiDrAPA 89*
Stojoa, Michael 1963- *WhoE 91*
Stojowski, Sigismund 1869-1946 *PenDiMP*
Stok, T. *ConAu 131*
Stokely, Alfred J. 1916- *St&PR 91*
Stokely, Craig Ranford 1945- *St&PR 91*
Stokely, Edith Margaret Dawley 1922- *WhoAmW 91*
Stokely, Hugh Lawson 1933- *WhoAm 90*
Stokely, John Edwin 1952- *St&PR 91*
Stokely, Mary Curry 1950- *WhoE 91*
Stoker, Austin *DrBlPA 90*
Stoker, Bram 1847-1912 *BioIn 16, EncO&P 3, WorAlBi*
Stoker, David Larry *BiDrAPA 89*
Stoker, James Rienewerf 1935- *St&PR 91, WhoAm 90*
Stoker, Jim *BioIn 16*
Stoker, Jim 1935- *BioIn 16*
Stoker, Michael George Parke 1918- *WhoWor 91*
Stoker, Richard 1938- *IntWWM 90*
Stoker, Warren Cady 1912- *WhoAm 90*
Stoker, Warren Lance *BiDrAPA 89*
Stokes, Arch Yow 1946- *WhoWor 91*
Stokes, Arnold Paul 1932- *WhoAm 90*
Stokes, B. R. 1924- *WhoAm 90*
Stokes, Barbara S. *WhoAm 90*
Stokes, Bruce 1948- *ConAu 130*
Stokes, Bruce Edward 1948- *WhoE 91*
Stokes, Carl Burton 1927- *WhoAm 90*
Stokes, Charles Junius 1922- *WhoAm 90, WhoE 91*
Stokes, David Kershaw, Jr. 1927- *WhoSSW 91*
Stokes, Donald Elkinton 1927- *WhoAm 90*
Stokes, Donald Gresham 1914- *WhoAm 90*
Stokes, Donald W. 1947- *ConAu 132*
Stokes, Doris *BioIn 16*
Stokes, Doris 1920-1987 *EncO&P 3*
Stokes, Douglas Leon 1951- *WhoEmL 91*
Stokes, Douglas Miller 1947- *WhoE 91*
Stokes, Edmond Harold 1940- *WhoAm 90*
Stokes, Elizabeth Hendon 1922- *WhoAmW 91*
Stokes, Eric Godfrey 1949- *WhoE 91*
Stokes, Frances Clarity 1957- *WhoWor 91*
Stokes, George Alwin 1920- *WhoAm 90*
Stokes, George Gabriel 1819-1903 *BioIn 16*
Stokes, Hugh Gregorie *BiDrAPA 89*
Stokes, James Sewell 1944- *WhoAm 90*
Stokes, Jeffrey Ralph 1960- *WhoSSW 91*
Stokes, John Emmett 1947- *St&PR 91*
Stokes, John Lemacks, II 1908- *WhoAm 90*
Stokes, Jordan 1817-1886 *AmLegL*
Stokes, Joseph 1924-1989 *BioIn 16*
Stokes, Joseph C., Jr. 1947- *St&PR 91*
Stokes, Joseph Clement, Jr. 1947- *WhoAm 90*
Stokes, Joseph Powell 1946- *WhoEmL 91*
Stokes, Katharine M. 1906-1989 *BioIn 16*
Stokes, Linda Kay 1948- *St&PR 91*
Stokes, Linda P. 1947- *WhoAmW 91*
Stokes, Louis *BioIn 16*
Stokes, Louis 1925- *BlkAmsC [port], WhoAm 90*
Stokes, Louis 1941- *WhoAmA 91*
Stokes, Mack Boyd 1911- *WhoAm 90*
Stokes, Marianne 1855-1927 *BiDWomA*
Stokes, Oliver Charles 1939- *WhoSSW 91*
Stokes, Patrick 1942- *St&PR 91*
Stokes, Patrick T. 1942- *WhoAm 90*
Stokes, Paul Allen 1927- *WhoAm 90*
Stokes, Penelope June 1950- *WhoWrEP 89*
Stokes, Peter Edwin *BiDrAPA 89*
Stokes, Robert Allan 1942- *WhoAm 90*
Stokes, Ron 1950- *WhoE 91*
Stokes, Ronald Edward 1927- *BiDrAPA 89*
Stokes, Ronald Wayne 1951- *WhoSSW 91*
Stokes, Rose Pastor 1879-1933 *EncAL*
Stokes, Sara Margaret 1945- *WhoAmW 91*
Stokes, Sim E., III 1944- *WhoSSW 91*
Stokes, Terry 1943- *WhoWrEP 89*
Stokes, Terry Craig 1956- *WhoSSW 91*
Stokes, Theodore Frederick 1938- *St&PR 91*
Stokes, Theresa Emma 1943- *WhoAmW 91, WhoE 91, WhoWor 91*
Stokes, Walter R *BiDrAPA 89*
Stokes, Wayne *WhoSSW 91*
Stokes, William Finley, Jr. 1938- *WhoSSW 91*
Stokes, William Forest 1931- *WhoWrEP 89*
Stokes, William Forrest 1931- *WhoAm 90*
Stokes, William James Nicks 1940- *IntWWM 90*
Stokes-Elias, Janice Elaine 1952- *WhoAmW 91*
Stokesbury, Leon 1945- *WhoWrEP 89*
Stokholm, Gunnar Kuur 1949- *WhoWor 91*
Stokke, Diane Rees 1951- *WhoEmL 91*
Stokke, Leif 1942- *WhoWor 91*
Stokke, Milo B. 1926- *St&PR 91*
Stokke, Per Rudolf 1943- *WhoWor 91*
Stokkelien, Vigdis 1934- *EncCoWW*
Stokl, Stephen Bernard 1952- *BiDrAPA 89*
Stokley, Robert Willson 1918- *WhoAm 90*
Stokoe, Kenneth H., II *WhoAm 90*
Stokoe, Norman Leslie 1923- *WhoWor 91*
Stokowski, Leopold 1882-1977 *BioIn 16, PenDiMP, WorAlBi*
Stokstad, Marilyn 1929- *WhoAmA 91*
Stokstad, Marilyn Jane 1929- *WhoAm 90*
Stokvis, Jack Raphael 1944- *WhoAm 90*
Stolar, Abe 1911- *BioIn 16*
Stolar, Henry S. 1939- *St&PR 91*
Stolar, Henry Samuel 1939- *WhoAm 90*
Stolar, Marc Howard 1954- *BiDrAPA 89*
Stolar, Neal Myles *BiDrAPA 89*
Stolarik, M. Mark 1943- *WhoAm 90, WhoE 91*
Stolba, K. Marie 1919- *IntWWM 90*
Stolber, Dean C. 1944- *WhoAm 90*
Stolber, Dean Charles 1944- *St&PR 91*
Stolberg, Christian, Graf zu 1748-1821 *DcLB 94 [port]*
Stolberg, Friedrich Leopold, Graf zu 1750-1819 *DcLB 94 [port]*
Stolberg, Irving J. 1936- *WhoAm 90*
Stolberg, Sheryl Gay 1961- *WhoAmW 91*
Stolberg, William H., Jr. *ODwPR 91*
Stolberg-Acosta, Robert A *BiDrAPA 89*
Stolbun, Martin Alan *BiDrAPA 89*
Stolee, Michael Joseph 1930- *WhoWor 91*
Stolen, Joanne Siu 1943- *WhoAmW 91*
Stoler, Peter *BioIn 16*
Stoler, Shirley 1929- *ConTFT 8*
Stolier, Louis 1907- *St&PR 91*
Stoline, Anne Marie 1961- *WhoE 91*
Stolk, Anthonie 1916- *ConAu 131*
Stoll, Barbara J. *WhoAmW 91*
Stoll, Berry Vincent, Mrs 1906- *WhoAmA 91*
Stoll, Charles Buckner 1923- *WhoAm 90*
Stoll, Clifford *BioIn 16*
Stoll, Clifford 1950- *BestSel 90-3 [port]*
Stoll, Elizabeth Pinney 1947- *IntWWM 90*
Stoll, Eric D. 1938- *WhoE 91*
Stoll, Forrest Duane 1921- *WhoAm 90*
Stoll, Hans Heinrich 1926- *WhoWor 91*
Stoll, Hans Reiner 1939- *WhoAm 90*
Stoll, Howard Lester, Jr. 1928- *WhoAm 90*
Stoll, Karl-Heinz 1942- *WhoWor 91*
Stoll, Kathleen H. 1936- *WhoAmW 91*
Stoll, Linus M. 1927- *WhoAm 90*
Stoll, Richard Edmund 1927- *St&PR 91, WhoAm 90, WhoWor 91*
Stoll, Richard Giles 1946- *WhoE 91*
Stoll, Rod Ray 1951- *WhoE 91*
Stoll, Rosanna *WhoHisp 91*
Stoll, Toni 1922- *WhoAmA 91*
Stoll, Wilhelm 1923- *WhoAm 90*
Stolla, Daniel Paul 1944- *WhoWor 91*
Stollenwerk, James Henry 1930- *St&PR 91*
Stollenwerk, John Joseph 1940- *St&PR 91*
Stoller, Alan *BiDrAPA 89*
Stoller, Alyce 1955- *WhoAmW 91*
Stoller, Claude 1921- *WhoAm 90*
Stoller, Ezra 1915- *WhoAm 90*
Stoller, Gary 1953- *St&PR 91*
Stoller, Herbert E. 1942- *St&PR 91*
Stoller, Jerry Joe 1936- *BiDrAPA 89*
Stoller, John Chapman 1940- *WhoAmA 91*
Stoller, Lillian Misle 1951- *BiDrAPA 89*
Stoller, Manning *BioIn 16*
Stoller, Michael Jay 1931- *WhoAm 90*
Stoller, Mike 1933- *BioIn 16*
Stoller, Robert Jesse 1924- *BiDrAPA 89, WhoAm 90*
Stoller, William J. *ODwPR 91*
Stollerman, Gene Howard 1920- *WhoAm 90*
Stollerman, Ray 1931- *WhoAm 90*
Stollery, Robert 1924- *WhoAm 90*
Stolley, Alexander 1922- *St&PR 91, WhoAm 90*
Stolley, Paul David 1937- *WhoAm 90*
Stolley, Richard Brockway 1928- *WhoAm 90*
Stollman, Israel 1923- *WhoAm 90*
Stollmeyer, Charles Victor Humphrey 1947- *WhoWor 91*
Stollmeyer, Jeffrey 1921-1989 *AnObit 1989*
Stollsteimer, John F. 1932- *WhoAm 90*
Stolmeier, Robert C. 1944- *St&PR 91*
Stolnitz, George Joseph 1920- *WhoAm 90*
Stoloff, Carolyn *WhoAmA 91*
Stoloff, Carolyn 1927- *WhoWrEP 89*
Stolove, Lorraine P. 1942- *WhoAmW 91*
Stolp, Lauren Elbert 1921- *WhoAm 90*
Stolpe, Daniel Owen 1939- *WhoAmA 91*
Stolpe, George W., Jr. *ODwPR 91*
Stolpe, Herman 1904- *WhoWor 91*
Stolper, Antonie *BioIn 16*
Stolper, Carolyn Louise 1953- *WhoAmW 91, WhoEmL 91*
Stolper, Pinchas Aryeh 1931- *WhoAm 90*
Stolper, Wolfgang Friedrich 1912- *WhoAm 90*
Stolte, Dieter 1934- *WhoWor 91*
Stolte, Larry Gene 1945- *St&PR 91, WhoEmL 91, WhoWor 91*
Stoltenberg, Carl Henry 1924- *WhoAm 90*
Stoltenberg, Donald Hugo 1927- *WhoAmA 91*
Stoltenberg, Gerhard *BioIn 16*
Stoltenberg, Gerhard 1928- *WhoWor 91*
Stoltenberg, Thorvald 1931- *WhoWor 91*
Stoltenberg, Wendy Fain 1949- *BiDrAPA 89*
Stoltz, Charles Edward 1936- *St&PR 91*
Stoltz, Deane H. 1929- *St&PR 91*
Stoltz, Eric *BioIn 16*
Stoltz, Johan Louis 1940- *WhoSSW 91*
Stoltz, Jon T. 1946- *St&PR 91*
Stoltz, Merton P. 1913-1989 *BioIn 16*
Stoltz, Robert C 1921- *BiDrAPA 89*
Stoltz, Rosine 1815-1903 *PenDiMP*
Stoltz, Sabina E. *BiDrAPA 89*
Stoltze, John R. 1895- *St&PR 91*
Stoltzfus, Victor Ezra 1934- *WhoAm 90*
Stoltzman, Richard Leslie 1942- *IntWWM 90, WhoAm 90*
Stoltzman, Roger Kenneth 1951- *BiDrAPA 89*
Stolwijk, Jan Adrianus Jozef 1927- *WhoAm 90*
Stolz, Benjamin Armond 1934- *WhoAm 90*
Stolz, John William 1931- *St&PR 91*
Stolz, Mary 1920- *AuBYP 90, BioIn 16*
Stolz, Neil N. 1935- *St&PR 91*
Stolz, Robert 1880-1975 *OxCPMus*
Stolz, Stephanie Balog 1938- *WhoWor 91*
Stolz, Teresa 1834-1902 *PenDiMP*
Stolz, Walter Sargent 1938- *WhoAm 90*
Stolzberg, Mark Elliott 1944- *WhoE 91*
Stolze, Gerhard 1926-1979 *PenDiMP*
Stolzel, Samuel *PenDiDA 89*
Stolzenberg, Alan Mitchell 1954- *WhoSSW 91*
Stolzenberg, Bessie *BioIn 16*
Stolzenberg, Hans Wilhelm 1939- *WhoWor 91*
Stolzenberg, Pearl 1946- *WhoAmW 91*
Stolzer, Herbert G. 1925- *St&PR 91*
Stolzer, Leo William 1934- *WhoAm 90*
Stolzheise, Ralph M *BiDrAPA 89*
Stolzman, Robert I. 1961- *WhoE 91*
Stomber, Stephen John 1949- *WhoSSW 91*
Stommel, Henry Melson 1920- *WhoAm 90*
Stomps, Walter E, Jr 1929- *WhoAmA 91*
Stonaker, Frances Benson *AuBYP 90*
Stone Calf *WhNaAH*
Stone, A. Harris *AuBYP 90*
Stone, A Howard *BiDrAPA 89*
Stone, Alan 1928- *St&PR 91, WhoAm 90*
Stone, Alan A 1929- *BiDrAPA 89*
Stone, Alan James 1944- *WhoAm 90*
Stone, Alan Jay 1942- *WhoAm 90*
Stone, Alan John 1940- *WhoE 91*
Stone, Alison Jo 1964- *WhoWrEP 89*
Stone, Amasa 1818-1883 *WorAlBi*
Stone, Andrea Bein *BiDrAPA 89*
Stone, Andrew L. 1915- *St&PR 91*
Stone, Andrew Michael *BiDrAPA 89*
Stone, Anna B 1874-1949 *WhoAmA 91N*
Stone, Arnold Joseph 1923- *BiDrAPA 89*
Stone, Arthur Harold 1916- *WhoAm 90, WhoE 91*
Stone, Arthur J. 1929- *WhoE 91*
Stone, Barry Michael 1944- *BiDrAPA 89*
Stone, Beatrice 1900-1962 *WhoAmA 91N*
Stone, Ben M. 1914- *St&PR 91*
Stone, Beth 1940- *WhoAmW 91*
Stone, Bonnie Carol 1945- *WhoAmW 91*
Stone, Bradford W. *BioIn 16*
Stone, Bradley H. 1946- *St&PR 91*
Stone, Bradley Hayes 1946- *WhoE 91*
Stone, Brenda Hemphill 1944- *WhoAmW 91*
Stone, Caroline Fleming 1936- *WhoAmW 91*
Stone, Cassandra Reeve 1941- *WhoE 91*
Stone, Catherine Louise 1956- *WhoAmW 91*
Stone, Charles B *BiDrAPA 89*
Stone, Charles R. 1932- *St&PR 91*
Stone, Charles Rivers 1936- *WhoAm 90*
Stone, Chester B., Jr. 1935- *St&PR 91, WhoAm 90*
Stone, Clarence N 1935- *ConAu 30NR*
Stone, Curtis J. 1930- *St&PR 91*
Stone, Cynthia Hutchinson 1940- *WhoAmW 91*
Stone, Daciano W. 1927- *St&PR 91*
Stone, Daniel Jonathan 1950- *WhoEmL 91*
Stone, David B. 1927- *St&PR 91*
Stone, David Barnes 1927- *WhoAm 90*
Stone, David Brian 1933- *WhoAm 90*
Stone, David Elphinstone 1922- *IntWWM 90*
Stone, David Kendall 1942- *St&PR 91, WhoE 91*
Stone, David Shelton 1942- *St&PR 91*
Stone, Dean 1930- *Ballpl 90*
Stone, Deborah Lee 1956- *WhoAmW 91*
Stone, Diane Lipson *BiDrAPA 89*
Stone, Dianne S. 1964- *WhoAmW 91*
Stone, Don 1929- *WhoAmA 91*
Stone, Donald Crawford 1903- *WhoAm 90*
Stone, Donald D. 1924- *WhoWor 91*
Stone, Donald E. *BioIn 16, St&PR 91*
Stone, Donald James 1929- *WhoSSW 91*

Stone, Donald L. 1934- *St&PR 91*
Stone, Donald Raymond 1938- *WhoAm 90*
Stone, Donald Wayne 1931- *St&PR 91*
Stone, Dorothy Maharam 1917- *WhoAm 90, WhoE 91*
Stone, Douglas H. 1941- *St&PR 91*
Stone, Ed *NewYTBS 90 [port]*
Stone, Edmund Crispen, III 1942- *WhoAm 90*
Stone, Edward Arthur 1941- *WhoSSW 91*
Stone, Edward C. *BioIn 16*
Stone, Edward C 1936- *CurBio 90 [port]*
Stone, Edward Carroll, Jr. 1936- *WhoAm 90*
Stone, Edward Durell 1902-1978 *WhoAmA 91N, WorAlBi*
Stone, Edward Durell, Jr. 1932- *WhoAm 90*
Stone, Edward Harris, II 1933- *WhoAm 90*
Stone, Edward Luke 1937- *WhoE 91*
Stone, Elizabeth 1803- *FemiCLE*
Stone, Elizabeth 1803-1858? *BioIn 16*
Stone, Elizabeth Caecilia 1949- *WhoAmW 91*
Stone, Elizabeth Campbell 1957- *WhoEmL 91*
Stone, Elizabeth Hean 1927- *WhoE 91*
Stone, Elizabeth Wenger 1918- *WhoAm 90, WhoAmW 91, WhoWor 91*
Stone, Elsa Louise 1943- *WhoAmW 91*
Stone, Erik Jon 1953- *St&PR 91*
Stone, Evelyn M *BiDrAPA 89*
Stone, Ezra Chaim 1917- *WhoAm 90*
Stone, Ferdinand F. 1908-1989 *BioIn 16*
Stone, Ferdinand Fairfax 1908-1989 *ConAu 129*
Stone, Frances 1923- *WhoE 91*
Stone, Frank Sandler 1952- *WhoE 91*
Stone, Franklin Martin *WhoAm 90*
Stone, Franz Theodore 1907- *WhoAm 90, WhoWor 91*
Stone, Fred 1873-1959 *OxCPMus*
Stone, Fred A. 1916- *St&PR 91*
Stone, Fred J 1919- *WhoAmA 91*
Stone, Fred Michael 1943- *WhoAm 90*
Stone, Frederick Anderson 1943- *St&PR 91*
Stone, Frederick H. 1921- *St&PR 91*
Stone, Frederick William 1930- *WhoWor 91*
Stone, Gail Hetzel 1950- *WhoAmW 91*
Stone, Garold L. 1956- *St&PR 91*
Stone, Gary H. 1953- *St&PR 91*
Stone, Gary Leon 1941- *St&PR 91*
Stone, Geoffrey Richard 1946- *WhoAm 90*
Stone, George 1877-1945 *Ballpl 90*
Stone, George 1946- *Ballpl 90*
Stone, George E. 1934- *St&PR 91*
Stone, George Eliot 1934- *WhoSSW 91*
Stone, George Ernest 1951- *WhoE 91*
Stone, George K. *AuBYP 90*
Stone, George Milton 1929- *St&PR 91*
Stone, Gerald Paul 1918- *WhoAm 90*
Stone, Gilbert Rodney *BioIn 16*
Stone, Gloria C *BiDrAPA 89*
Stone, Gregory Michael 1959- *WhoEmL 91, WhoWor 91*
Stone, Gwen 1913- *WhoAmA 91*
Stone, Hampton *TwCCr&M 91*
Stone, Harlan Fiske 1872-1946 *BiDrUSE 89, WorAlBi*
Stone, Harold C. 1924- *St&PR 91*
Stone, Harold Stuart 1938- *WhoAm 90*
Stone, Harriett Abramson 1941- *St&PR 91*
Stone, Harry 1926- *ConAu 130*
Stone, Harry H. 1917- *WhoAm 90*
Stone, Henry 1852- *AmLegL*
Stone, Henry P. 1933- *St&PR 91*
Stone, Herbert 1919- *ODwPR 91*
Stone, Howard Ernest *BiDrAPA 89*
Stone, Howard Francis 1931- *WhoAm 90*
Stone, Howard Lawrence 1941- *WhoWor 91*
Stone, Hubert Dean 1924- *WhoSSW 91, WhoWor 91*
Stone, I. F. 1907-1989 *AnObit 1989, BioIn 16*
Stone, I F 1907-1989 *ConAu 129*
Stone, I. F. 1907-1989 *EncAL*
Stone, I F 1907-1989 *News 90*
Stone, I. F. 1907-1989 *WorAlBi*
Stone, Irving 1903-1989 *AnObit 1989, BioIn 16, ConAu 129, MajTwCW, News 90, SmATA 64, WorAlBi*
Stone, Irving Charles, Jr. 1930- *WhoSSW 91*
Stone, Irving I. 1909- *St&PR 91, WhoAm 90*
Stone, Isidor Feinstein 1907-1989 *BioIn 16*
Stone, Jack I. 1920- *WhoE 91*
Stone, Jack Wayne, Jr. 1934- *St&PR 91*
Stone, James A. 1947- *ODwPR 91*
Stone, James Allen 1945- *WhoSSW 91*
Stone, James Byron 1954- *BiDrAPA 89*
Stone, James H. 1922- *St&PR 91*
Stone, James Herbert 1918- *WhoAm 90*
Stone, James Howard 1939- *WhoWor 91*
Stone, James J. 1947- *WhoAm 90*
Stone, James Lester 1940- *WhoE 91*
Stone, James M. 1826- *AmLegL*
Stone, James Merrill 1952- *WhoEmL 91*
Stone, James Munroe 1817- *AmLegL*
Stone, James Robert 1948- *WhoWor 91*
Stone, James Thomas 1948- *St&PR 91*
Stone, James William 1917- *St&PR 91*
Stone, Jan *ODwPR 91*
Stone, Jane Buffington 1942- *WhoAmW 91*
Stone, Jeff 1960- *Ballpl 90*
Stone, Jeffrey 1946- *IntWWM 90*
Stone, Jeffrey Ingram 1945- *WhoAmA 91*
Stone, Jennifer 1933- *WhoWrEP 89*
Stone, Jeremy 1957- *WhoAmA 91*
Stone, Jeremy Judah 1935- *WhoAm 90*
Stone, Jerome H. 1913- *St&PR 91*
Stone, Jerry Broadwell 1923- *WhoSSW 91*
Stone, Jim 1947- *WhoAmA 91*
Stone, Joan Elizabeth *WhoWrEP 89*
Stone, Joe Allan 1948- *WhoAm 90*
Stone, John 1905-1955 *Ballpl 90*
Stone, John 1936- *WhoWrEP 89*
Stone, John Mc Williams, Jr. 1927- *St&PR 91*
Stone, John R. 1938- *St&PR 91*
Stone, John T. 1933- *St&PR 91*
Stone, John Timothy, Jr. 1933- *WhoWor 91*
Stone, John Young 1843-1928 *AmLegL*
Stone, Joseph 1920- *WhoAm 90*
Stone, Joseph E. 1961- *St&PR 91*
Stone, Julie Lynn 1959- *WhoWrEP 89*
Stone, Katherine *BiDEWW*
Stone, Kathleen Patricia 1955- *WhoAmW 91*
Stone, Kathryn Dolores 1929- *WhoAmW 91*
Stone, Kay Crockette 1940- *WhoSSW 91*
Stone, Kenneth Michael 1942- *WhoWrEP 89*
Stone, Kirk Haskin 1914- *WhoAm 90*
Stone, Kurt 1911-1989 *BioIn 16*
Stone, L. Mark 1957- *WhoE 91*
Stone, Larry R. 1935- *St&PR 91*
Stone, Laurence M. 1925- *St&PR 91*
Stone, Lawrence 1919- *WhoAm 90, WorAu 1980 [port]*
Stone, Lawrence A 1933- *BiDrAPA 89*
Stone, Lawrence Anderson 1933- *WhoSSW 91*
Stone, Lawrence Maurice 1931- *WhoAm 90*
Stone, Leo *BiDrAPA 89*
Stone, Leon 1914- *St&PR 91, WhoAm 90*
Stone, LeRoy Allen 1931- *WhoE 91*
Stone, Lesley *TwCCr&M 91*
Stone, Lew 1898-1969 *OxCPMus*
Stone, Lewis Bart 1938- *WhoAm 90*
Stone, Lewis M. 1927- *St&PR 91*
Stone, Linda Lee 1942- *WhoAmW 91*
Stone, Lisa Jane 1944- *WhoAmW 91*
Stone, Lloyd Evan 1962- *WhoSSW 91*
Stone, Lucinda H. 1814-1900 *BioAmW*
Stone, Lucius Harold 1940- *WhoAm 90*
Stone, Lucy 1818-1893 *BioAmW, BioIn 16, FemiCLE, WorAlBi*
Stone, Lynn M. *AuBYP 90*
Stone, M Lee 1937- *WhoAmA 91*
Stone, M.S. 1911- *St&PR 91*
Stone, Margaret 1959- *ODwPR 91*
Stone, Margaret N. *ConAu 132*
Stone, Marguerite Beverley 1916- *WhoAm 90*
Stone, Marie Kirchner *WhoWrEP 89*
Stone, Mark *BioIn 16*
Stone, Mark Hartman 1954- *BiDrAPA 89*
Stone, Mark L *BiDrAPA 89*
Stone, Marshall H. 1903-1989 *AnObit 1989*
Stone, Marshall Harvey 1903-1989 *BioIn 16*
Stone, Martha Janette Staff 1953- *WhoAmW 91*
Stone, Martin 1915- *WhoAm 90*
Stone, Martin 1928- *St&PR 91*
Stone, Marvin Allen 1942- *BiDrAPA 89*
Stone, Marvin Jules 1937- *WhoAm 90, WhoSSW 91, WhoWor 91*
Stone, Marvin Lawrence 1924- *WhoAm 90*
Stone, Maurine Rainer 1940- *WhoAmW 91*
Stone, Melville 1848-1929 *BioIn 16*
Stone, Melville E. *BioIn 16*
Stone, Melvin *BioIn 16*
Stone, Michael E 1938- *ConAu 132*
Stone, Michael H 1933- *BiDrAPA 89*
Stone, Michael Horace 1939- *WhoAm 90*
Stone, Michael Howard 1933- *WhoE 91*
Stone, Michael Reeves 1958- *St&PR 91*
Stone, Michael Robert 1951- *WhoWrEP 89*
Stone, Mildred Mary-Anne *WhoAmW 91*
Stone, Morris S. 1911-1989 *BioIn 16*
Stone, Morton B. 1929- *ODwPR 91*
Stone, Nancy J. 1957- *St&PR 91*
Stone, Nancy W *BiDrAPA 89*
Stone, Naomi *BioIn 16*
Stone, Nelson 1923- *St&PR 91, WhoAm 90*
Stone, Nelwyn Louise 1950- *WhoSSW 91*
Stone, Nicholas 1587?-1647 *BioIn 16*
Stone, Oliver *BioIn 16*
Stone, Oliver 1946- *News 90 [port], WhoAm 90, WorAlBi*
Stone, Paula S. *WhoAmW 91*
Stone, Peter 1930- *WhoAm 90*
Stone, Peter George 1937- *St&PR 91, WhoAm 90*
Stone, Ralph Kenny 1952- *WhoEmL 91*
Stone, Randolph 1890-1981 *NewAgE 90*
Stone, Raymond William 1945- *WhoSSW 91*
Stone, Raymond William, III 1950- *WhoE 91*
Stone, Reynolds 1909-1979 *ConDes 90*
Stone, Richard 1913- *WhoWor 91, WorAlBi*
Stone, Richard Cole, Jr. 1959- *WhoSSW 91*
Stone, Richard L. 1963- *WhoWor 91*
Stone, Rob *BioIn 16*
Stone, Robert 1937- *BioIn 16, MajTwCW*
Stone, Robert Alan 1935- *WhoAm 90*
Stone, Robert Anthony 1937- *WhoAm 90, WhoWrEP 89*
Stone, Robert B 1916- *ConAu 31NR*
Stone, Robert G., Jr. 1923- *St&PR 91*
Stone, Robert J. 1920- *ODwPR 91*
Stone, Robert K *BiDrAPA 89*
Stone, Robert Ryrie 1943- *WhoAm 90*
Stone, Robert Samuel 1922- *WhoAm 90*
Stone, Robin Dominic Alexander *IntWWM 90*
Stone, Roger *BioIn 16*
Stone, Roger Warren 1935- *St&PR 91, WhoAm 90*
Stone, Ron 1942- *Ballpl 90*
Stone, Rosetta *ConAu 32NR, MajTwCW*
Stone, Russell A. 1944- *WhoAm 90, WhoE 91*
Stone, Ruth 1915- *DcLB 105 [port], FemiCLE*
Stone, Ruth Marie 1945- *IntWWM 90*
Stone, Samuel 1913-1989 *BioIn 16*
Stone, Samuel Spencer 1947- *WhoEmL 91*
Stone, Sarah *FemiCLE*
Stone, Scott *BioIn 16*
Stone, Shepard *NewYTBS 90 [port]*
Stone, Shepard 1908-1990 *BioIn 16, ConAu 131*
Stone, Sly *BioIn 16*
Stone, Sly 1944- *DrBlPA 90, WorAlBi*
Stone, Stephen A. 1917- *St&PR 91*
Stone, Steve *BioIn 16*
Stone, Steve 1947- *Ballpl 90*
Stone, Steven David 1952- *WhoEmL 91*
Stone, Steven Michael 1947- *WhoAm 90*
Stone, Steven Michael 1951- *WhoE 91*
Stone, Sumner *BiDrAPA 89*
Stone, Susan Gail 1957- *WhoWrEP 89*
Stone, Sylvia 1928- *BiDWomA, WhoAmA 91*
Stone, Sylvia Iris 1928- *WhoAm 90*
Stone, Tammy Ann 1963- *WhoAmW 91*
Stone, Teena Marie 1948- *WhoAmW 91*
Stone, Thomas 1743-1787 *EncCRAm*
Stone, Thomas 1852-1897 *DcCanB 12*
Stone, Thomas Edward 1948- *WhoE 91*
Stone, Thomas L *BiDrAPA 89*
Stone, Thomas Richardson 1939- *WhoE 91*
Stone, Thomas S. 1909- *WhoAm 90*
Stone, Todd Alan 1961- *WhoSSW 91*
Stone, Tony *BioIn 16*
Stone, Virginia McIntyre 1947- *WhoSSW 91*
Stone, W. Arthur 1940- *ODwPR 91*
Stone, W. Clement 1902- *St&PR 91, WhoAm 90*
Stone, Walter B. 1941- *St&PR 91*
Stone, Walter N 1931- *BiDrAPA 89*
Stone, Ward *BioIn 16*
Stone, Warren R. *St&PR 91*
Stone, Willard John 1913- *WhoAm 90*
Stone, William A. 1936- *St&PR 91*
Stone, William Bruhn 1929- *WhoWor 91*
Stone, William C. *WhoAm 90*
Stone, William Earl 1925- *BiDrAPA 89*
Stone, William Edward 1945- *WhoAm 90, WhoEmL 91*
Stone, William Gene 1931- *BiDrAPA 89*
Stone, William Harold 1924- *WhoAm 90*
Stone, William Johnson 1841-1923 *AmLegL*
Stone, William Ross 1947- *WhoEmL 91*
Stone, William Samuel 1923- *WhoSSW 91*
Stone, Williard Everard 1910- *WhoAm 90*
Stone, Zachary *ConAu 33NR, MajTwCW, TwCCr&M 91*
Stone, Zachary 1949- *BioIn 16*
Stoneback, James W. 1930- *St&PR 91*
Stoneback, W. Keith 1953- *St&PR 91*
Stonebarger, Virginia 1926- *WhoAmA 91*
Stonebraker, Barbara J. 1944- *St&PR 91*
Stonebreaker, Michael *BioIn 16*
Stonecipher, David Allen 1941- *St&PR 91*
Stonecipher, Harland C. 1938- *St&PR 91*
Stonecipher, Harry C. *WhoAm 90*
Stonefield, Liz Topete 1955- *WhoHisp 91*
Stoneham, Charles 1878-1936 *BioIn 16*
Stoneham, Edward Bryant 1946- *WhoEmL 91*
Stoneham, Horace 1903-1990 *BioIn 16*
Stoneham, Horace C *NewYTBS 90 [port]*
Stoneham, John 1929- *WhoAmA 91*
Stonehill, Anna-Lisa B. *BiDrAPA 89*
Stonehill, Mary 1900-1951 *WhoAmA 91N*
Stonehill, Robert Berrell 1921- *WhoAm 90*
Stonehouse, James Adam 1937- *WhoWor 91*
Stonehouse, John 1925-1988 *AnObit 1988, BioIn 16*
Stoneking, Carole Lynne 1937- *WhoAmW 91*
Stoneking, Lillian Stanford 1951- *WhoAmW 91*
Stoneman, Bill 1944- *Ballpl 90*
Stoneman, Douglas Grayson 1931- *WhoAm 90*
Stoneman, Richard 1951- *ConAu 130*
Stoneman, Samuel Sidney 1911- *WhoAm 90*
Stoneman, William, III 1927- *WhoAm 90*
Stoneman, William H. 1904-1987 *BioIn 16*
Stoneman, William Hambly, III 1944- *WhoAm 90, WhoE 91*
Stoner, Edmund Clifton 1899-1968 *DcScB S2*
Stoner, Elaine Blatt 1939- *WhoAmW 91*
Stoner, Emerson A. *BioIn 16*
Stoner, Frances Wynette 1943- *WhoAmW 91*
Stoner, Graham Alexander 1929- *WhoSSW 91*
Stoner, Harold E 1924- *BiDrAPA 89*
Stoner, James Lloyd 1920- *WhoAm 90*
Stoner, Jeffrey Wayne 1953- *WhoE 91*
Stoner, John David 1935- *St&PR 91*
Stoner, John Richard 1958- *WhoAm 90*
Stoner, Joyce H. 1946- *WhoE 91*
Stoner, Joyce Hill 1946- *WhoAmA 91*
Stoner, Leonard Dudley 1950- *WhoEmL 91, WhoWor 91*
Stoner, Lil 1899-1966 *Ballpl 90*
Stoner, Nora Leszczynski 1960- *WhoE 91*
Stoner, Richard Burkett 1920- *St&PR 91, WhoAm 90*
Stoner, Richard Burkett, Jr. 1946- *St&PR 91*
Stoner, Robert Franklin 1933- *St&PR 91*
Stoner, Sue 1942- *WhoAmW 91*
Stoner, Virgil Ray 1923- *St&PR 91*
Stones, Dwight 1953- *WorAlBi*
Stones, Edward Lionel Gregory 1914-1987 *BioIn 16*
Stones, Margaret Alison 1942- *WhoAmA 91*
Stonesifer, Richard James 1922- *WhoAm 90*
Stonestreet, Charles 1940- *St&PR 91*
Stonestreet, Dana Lawton 1953- *St&PR 91*
Stoney, Alfred Bedle 1842-1907 *AmLegL*
Stoney, Janice D. 1940- *St&PR 91, WhoAm 90*
Stong, Philip Duffield 1899-1957 *AuBYP 90*
Stong, Stephen J. *St&PR 91*
Stonich, Timothy W. 1947- *St&PR 91*
Stonich, Timothy Whitman 1947- *WhoAm 90*
Stonier, Daryle L. *WhoAm 90*
Stonier, Kenneth Brian 1932- *WhoWor 91*
Stonnington, Cynthia M *BiDrAPA 89*
Stonnington, Henry Herbert 1927- *WhoSSW 91*
Stoodley, Dale G. 1939- *St&PR 91*
Stoodt, Barbara Dern 1934- *WhoAmW 91, WhoSSW 91*
Stooges, The *EncPR&S 89*
Stookesberry, James J. 1940- *St&PR 91*
Stookey, George Kenneth 1935- *WhoAm 90*
Stookey, John Hoyt 1930- *St&PR 91, WhoAm 90, WhoE 91*
Stookey, Laurence Hull 1937- *WhoAm 90, WhoWor 91*
Stookey, Noel Paul 1937- *WhoAm 90*
Stookey, Paul 1937- *WorAlBi*
Stookey, Stanley Donald 1915- *WhoAm 90*
Stooksberry, Stanley Dwight 1934- *St&PR 91*
Stoop, Bert Emile Louis 1928- *WhoWor 91*
Stoop, Michael David 1959- *St&PR 91*
Stoop, Norma McLain 1910- *WhoAmW 91, WhoE 91, WhoWor 91, WhoWrEP 89*
Stoopler, Mark Benjamin 1950- *WhoE 91*
Stoops, Denzel D. 1946- *St&PR 91*
Stoops, Herbert M 1887-1948 *WhoAmA 91N*
Stoops, Reginald *BioIn 16*
Stopek, Susan Ellen 1951- *BiDrAPA 89*
Stopes, Charlotte 1841-1929 *FemiCLE*
Stopes, Marie 1880-1950 *FemiCLE*

Stopes, Marie Charlotte Carmichael 1880-1958 *BioIn 16*
Stopford, John Morton 1939- *WhoWor 91*
Stoph, Willi 1914- *WhoWor 91*
Stopher, Robert Estes 1952- *WhoEmL 91*
Stopher, Ronald Lee 1957- *St&PR 91*
Stopka, Christine Boyd *BioIn 16*
Stopkey, Linda Johanna 1960- *WhoAmW 91*
Stopp, Jacklin Bolton 1926- *IntWWM 90*
Stoppani, Andres Oscar Manuel 1915- *WhoWor 91*
Stoppard, Tom 1937- *ConLC 63 [port], MajTwCW, WhoAm 90, WhoWor 91, WorAlBi*
Stoppert, Mary Kay 1941- *WhoAmA 91*
Stoppino, Giotto 1926- *ConDes 90*
Storace, Nancy 1765-1817 *PenDiMP*
Storace, Stephen 1762-1796 *PenDiMP A*
Storandt, Martha 1938- *WhoAm 90*
Storaro, Vittorio 1940- *BioIn 16, ConTFT 8, WhoAm 90*
Storb, Ursula Beate 1936- *WhoAmW 91*
Storch, Anne B. *AuBYP 90*
Storch, Arthur 1925- *WhoAm 90*
Storch, Daniel David *BiDrAPA 89*
Storch, Donald J. 1934- *ODwPR 91*
Storch, Marcus 1942- *WhoWor 91*
Storchio, Rosina 1876-1945 *PenDiMP*
Storchschnabel, Georg 1932- *WhoWor 91*
Storck, Dorothy deVerdery 1934- *WhoAm 90*
Storck, Herbert Evan 1954- *WhoE 91*
Storck, Michael Guy *BiDrAPA 89*
Stordahl, Larry D. 1942- *St&PR 91*
Stordy, Mary *BiDEWW*
Storek, Ben 1930- *St&PR 91*
Storer, Charles D., Jr. *ODwPR 91*
Storer, Dean James 1955- *BiDrAPA 89*
Storer, Donald Edgar 1939- *St&PR 91*
Storer, Frances Nell 1917- *WhoAmA 91*
Storer, Inez Mary 1933- *WhoAmA 91*
Storer, Morris Brewster 1904- *WhoAm 90*
Storer, Norman William 1930- *WhoAm 90*
Storer, Robert L. 1923- *St&PR 91*
Storer, Rosemarie 1956- *WhoAmW 91*
Storey, Benjamin B *BiDrAPA 89*
Storey, Benjamin M., Jr. 1915- *St&PR 91*
Storey, Beverly Lu 1953- *WhoSSW 91*
Storey, Charles Porter 1922- *WhoAm 90*
Storey, Chompunut *WhoAmW 91*
Storey, David 1933- *MajTwCW*
Storey, David Malcolm 1933- *WhoWor 91*
Storey, Edward J. 1901-1988 *BioIn 16*
Storey, Frank H. 1933- *St&PR 91*
Storey, Gregory D. 1950- *ODwPR 91*
Storey, Isabel Nagy 1955- *WhoAmW 91*
Storey, James Moorfield 1931- *WhoAm 90*
Storey, Jay R. 1928- *St&PR 91*
Storey, M. John 1943- *St&PR 91*
Storey, Scott Alfred 1954- *WhoEmL 91*
Storey, Tammy Jo 1961- *WhoAmW 91*
Storey, Thomas J. 1922- *St&PR 91*
Storey, Wilbur Fisk 1819-1884 *BioIn 16*
Storey, Will Miller 1931- *St&PR 91, WhoAm 90*
Storey, Woodrow Wilson 1912- *WhoAm 90*
Storhoff, Donald C. 1935- *WhoAm 90*
Storin, Edward Michael 1929- *WhoAm 90*
Storin, Matthew Victor 1942- *WhoAm 90*
Storing, Paul Edward 1929- *WhoAm 90*
Storjohann, Darlys William 1959- *WhoEmL 91, WhoWor 91*
Storjohann, Helmut 1920- *IntWWM 90*
Stork, Diana *NewAgMG*
Stork, Donald Arthur 1939- *WhoAm 90*
Stork, Gilbert 1921- *WhoAm 90*
Stork, Karl 1935- *St&PR 91*
Stork, Walter Wilhelm 1935- *WhoWor 91*
Storkan, Margaret Ann 1919- *BiDrAPA 89*
Storke, William Frederick Joseph 1922- *WhoAm 90*
Storlie, David Charles 1949- *St&PR 91*
Storm, Bobby Dale 1949- *WhoEmL 91*
Storm, Colton 1908-1988 *BioIn 16*
Storm, Gale 1922- *WorAlBi*
Storm, George 1893-1976 *EncACom*
Storm, Howard 1946- *WhoAmA 91*
Storm, Jonathan Morris *WhoAm 90*
Storm, June Gleason 1918- *St&PR 91*
Storm, Larue *WhoAmA 91*
Storm, Lesley 1898-1975 *FemiCLE*
Storm, Mark 1911- *WhoAmA 91*
Storm, Richard Frederick 1943- *WhoSSW 91*
Storm, Theodor 1817-1888 *AuBYP 90*
Storm, William George 1826-1892 *DcCanB 12*
Storm, William J. 1925- *St&PR 91*
Stormare, Peter *BioIn 16*
Storme, Marcel Leon 1930- *WhoWor 91*
Storme, Peter *AuBYP 90*
Stormer, Barbara Jean 1935- *WhoSSW 91*
Stormer, Horst Ludwig 1949- *WhoAm 90*
Stormer, John Charles, Jr. 1941- *WhoAm 90*
Stormes, Ben F. 1922- *St&PR 91*
Stormont, Richard Mansfield 1936- *WhoAm 90, WhoSSW 91*
Storms, Clifford Beekman 1932- *St&PR 91, WhoAm 90, WhoWor 91*
Storms, Kate 1954- *WhoEmL 91*
Storms, Lowell Hanson 1928- *WhoAm 90*
Storni, Alfonsina 1892-1938 *BioIn 16, ConAu 131, HispWr 90, WorAlBi*
Storper, Dan *BioIn 16*
Storper, Henry Michael 1944- *BiDrAPA 89*
Storr, Catherine 1913- *AuBYP 90*
Storr, Hans George 1931- *BioIn 16, St&PR 91*
Storr, John Frederick 1915- *WhoWrEP 89*
Storr, Paul 1771-1844 *PenDiDA 89*
Storrie-Lombardi, Michael C. *BiDrAPA 89*
Storrier, Tim 1949- *BioIn 16*
Storrow, Hugh A 1926- *BiDrAPA 89*
Storrow, James J. 1864-1926 *EncABHB 4 [port]*
Storrs, David *NewAgMG*
Storrs, Eleanor *BioIn 16*
Storrs, Eleanor Emerett 1926- *WhoAm 90*
Storrs, John 1885-1956 *WhoAmA 91N*
Storrs, Norman B. 1934- *St&PR 91*
Storrs, Thomas I. 1918- *St&PR 91*
Storrs, Val B. 1931- *St&PR 91*
Storry, Junis Oliver 1920- *WhoAm 90*
Storry, Richard 1913-1982 *DcNaB 1981*
Storseth, Jeannie Pearce 1948- *WhoAmW 91*
Storseth, Marjorie *St&PR 91*
Storseth, S.L. 1927- *St&PR 91*
Storsteen, Linda Lee 1948- *WhoAmW 91*
Storto, Allison *ODwPR 91*
Storto, Kimberly *ODwPR 91*
Stortz, John Dixon 1935- *WhoAm 90*
Stortz, Lisa Ann 1958- *WhoAmW 91*
Stortz, Nanette Esther 1944- *WhoAmW 91*
Storvick, Clara Amanda 1906- *WhoAmW 91*
Storvick, Truman Sophus 1928- *WhoAm 90*
Story, Anne Winthrop 1914- *WhoAmW 91*
Story, Benjamin Sprague, III 1945- *St&PR 91*
Story, Charles S. 1946- *St&PR 91*
Story, Edward T., Jr. 1943- *WhoSSW 91*
Story, George Morley 1927- *WhoAm 90, WhoWrEP 89*
Story, George Philliskirk 1853-1894 *DcCanB 12*
Story, Gertrude 1929- *ConAu 129*
Story, Jim Lewis 1931- *WhoAm 90*
Story, John Townsend 1940- *St&PR 91*
Story, Joseph 1779-1845 *WorAlBi*
Story, Liz *BioIn 16, NewAgMG*
Story, Mona Dee 1945- *WhoAmW 91, WhoSSW 91*
Story, Patience *BiDEWW*
Story, Richard P. 1952- *St&PR 91*
Story, Thomas Lane 1947- *WhoEmL 91*
Story, Tim *NewAgMG*
Story, William Easton 1925- *WhoAmA 91*
Story Wilson, Martha Redy 1947- *WhoAmA 91*
Storz, Ferdinand 1930- *WhoWor 91*
Storz, John 1926- *St&PR 91*
Stoss, Viet 1440?-1533 *IntDcAA 90*
Stossinger, Verena 1951- *EncCoWW*
Stoterau, Suzanne *BiDrAPA 89*
Stothard, James Vincent 1943- *St&PR 91*
Stothart, Herbert 1885-1949 *OxCPMus*
Stothers, John B. 1931- *WhoAm 90*
Stotland, Nada Logan 1943- *BiDrAPA 89*
Stotlar, Cynthia Byrd 1953- *WhoAmW 91*
Stotlar, David W. 1948- *St&PR 91*
Stotler, Alicemarie H. 1942- *WhoAm 90, WhoAmW 91*
Stotler, Diana G. *ODwPR 91*
Stotler, Jacob 1833- *AmLegL*
Stotler, John Leonard 1938- *St&PR 91, WhoAm 90*
Stotler, Patricia S. 1941- *WhoAmW 91*
Stoto, Michael Anthony 1954- *WhoE 91*
Stotsky, Bernard A 1926- *BiDrAPA 89*
Stott, Barbara Paxton 1925- *WhoAmW 91, WhoSSW 91*
Stott, Brian 1941- *WhoAm 90*
Stott, Deborah 1942- *WhoAmA 91*
Stott, Donald B. 1939- *St&PR 91*
Stott, Donald Franklin 1928- *WhoAm 90*
Stott, Grady Bernell 1921- *WhoAm 90*
Stott, Kathryn Linda 1958- *IntWWM 90*
Stott, Mary 1907- *FemiCLE*
Stott, Mary Roelofs 1918- *WhoWrEP 89*
Stott, Richard Keith 1943- *WhoWor 91*
Stott, Thomas Edward, Jr. 1923- *WhoAm 90*
Stott, William Ross, Jr. 1935- *WhoAm 90*
Stotter, David W. 1904- *WhoAm 90*
Stotter, Harry Shelton 1928- *WhoAm 90*
Stotter, Lawrence Henry 1929- *WhoAm 90*
Stotter, Ruth 1936- *WhoAmW 91*
Stottlemyer, David Lee 1935- *WhoAm 90*
Stottlemyre, Mel 1941- *Ballpl 90*
Stottlemyre, Todd 1965- *Ballpl 90*
Stottrup, Vagn 1925- *WhoWor 91*
Stotts, Edwin Keith 1933- *WhoSSW 91*
Stotts, Paul Alan 1943- *St&PR 91*
Stotz, June Ellen *BiDrAPA 89*
Stotz, Natalie Hamer 1921- *WhoAmW 91*
Stotzer, Beatriz Olvera *ODwPR 91*
Stotzer, Beatriz Olvera 1950- *WhoHisp 91*
Stotzfus, Ben Frank 1927- *WhoWrEP 89*
Stotzky, Guenther 1931- *WhoE 91*
Stoudemire, G. Alan 1950- *BiDrAPA 89*
Stoudemire, Sterling Aubrey 1902- *WhoSSW 91*
Stouder, John Albert 1933- *WhoWor 91*
Stouder, Leo Benjamin, Jr. 1956- *WhoSSW 91*
Stoudt, Marilyn Ann 1934- *WhoAmW 91*
Stoudt, Richard Mayo 1929- *St&PR 91*
Stouffer, Daniel Henry, Jr 1937- *WhoAmA 91*
Stouffer, Kelly *BioIn 16*
Stouffer, Larry Lee 1942- *St&PR 91*
Stouffer, Nancy Kathleen 1951- *WhoAmW 91, WhoE 91*
Stoufflet, Paul Eric 1962- *BiDrAPA 89*
Stouge, Niels Sandbergh 1907- *WhoWor 91*
Stough, Charles Daniel 1914- *WhoWor 91*
Stough, Furman Charles 1928- *WhoAm 90*
Stough, Robert Clarence 1948- *WhoSSW 91*
Stough, Sellers 1923- *St&PR 91, WhoAm 90*
Stoughton, Beverly Foss 1932- *WhoWrEP 89*
Stoughton, Cecil *BioIn 16*
Stoughton, Richard Baker 1923- *WhoAm 90*
Stoughton, Richard E. 1920- *St&PR 91*
Stoughton, W. Vickery 1946- *WhoAm 90*
Stoumen, Lou 1917- *WhoAmA 91*
Stoup, Arthur Harry 1925- *WhoAm 90, WhoWor 91*
Stout, Alan 1932- *IntWWM 90*
Stout, Alan C. 1947- *St&PR 91*
Stout, Allyn 1904-1974 *Ballpl 90*
Stout, Anthony Carder 1939- *WhoAm 90, WhoWor 91*
Stout, Arthur Wendel, III 1949- *WhoEmL 91, WhoSSW 91*
Stout, Bill A. 1932- *WhoAm 90*
Stout, Byron Gray 1829-1896 *AmLegL*
Stout, Carl Frederick 1942- *WhoSSW 91*
Stout, Carter Louis 1960- *WhoSSW 91*
Stout, Clare Kellogg *BioIn 16*
Stout, D.R. 1937- *St&PR 91*
Stout, David Lee *BiDrAPA 89*
Stout, Don B. 1936- *St&PR 91*
Stout, Donald Everett 1926- *St&PR 91, WhoWor 91*
Stout, Edward L., Jr. 1925- *WhoAm 90*
Stout, Frank J 1926- *WhoAmA 91*
Stout, Gail Bielby 1946- *WhoAmW 91*
Stout, Gene Edwin 1933- *St&PR 91*
Stout, George Leslie 1897-1978 *WhoAmA 91N*
Stout, Glenn Emanuel 1920- *WhoAm 90*
Stout, Gregory Stansbury 1915- *WhoAm 90, WhoWor 91*
Stout, Harry Lee 1947- *St&PR 91*
Stout, Hosea 1810-1889 *AmLegL*
Stout, James C. 1936- *St&PR 91*
Stout, John Frederick 1925- *St&PR 91*
Stout, John T. 1923- *WhoAm 90*
Stout, John Thomas, Jr. 1954- *St&PR 91*
Stout, Juanita Kidd *BioIn 16*
Stout, Juanita Kidd 1919- *WhoAmW 91, WhoE 91*
Stout, Karen Lee 1959- *WhoAmW 91*
Stout, Kate 1949- *WhoWrEP 89*
Stout, Linda Elaine 1951- *WhoAmW 91*
Stout, Lonnie James, II 1947- *St&PR 91*
Stout, Madalyn Joanne 1954- *WhoWrEP 89*
Stout, Marguerite Annette *WhoAmW 91*
Stout, Mary 1627?-1707 *BiDEWW*
Stout, Nathaniel Meigs 1952- *WhoE 91*
Stout, Patricia Joan 1932- *WhoAmW 91*
Stout, Rex 1886-1975 *TwCCr&M 91, WorAlBi*
Stout, Richard E *BiDrAPA 89*
Stout, Richard Gordon 1934- *WhoAmA 91*
Stout, Robert Daniel 1915- *WhoAm 90*
Stout, Robert L. *St&PR 91*
Stout, Robert N. 1924- *St&PR 91*
Stout, Rodney Jan 1936- *BiDrAPA 89*
Stout, Samuel Darrel 1943- *WhoAm 90*
Stout, Thomas Calvin 1939- *St&PR 91*
Stout, Thomas James 1964- *WhoWrEP 89*
Stout, Thomas Milton 1915- *St&PR 91*
Stout, Victoria *BiDrAPA 89*
Stout, Virgil Loomis 1921- *WhoAm 90*
Stout, Virginia Falk 1932- *WhoAmW 91*
Stout, William Jewell 1914- *WhoAm 90*
Stout, William M. 1941- *St&PR 91*
Stout-Pierce, Susan 1954- *WhoAmW 91*
Stoutamore, James B. 1931- *St&PR 91*
Stoutenburg, Adrien 1916- *AuBYP 90*
Stoutt, Hamilton Lewity 1929- *BioIn 16*
Stovall, David Calvin 1941- *WhoSSW 91*
Stovall, David D. 1956- *St&PR 91*
Stovall, George 1878-1951 *Ballpl 90*
Stovall, James Truman, III 1937- *WhoWor 91*
Stovall, Jeffrey Gress 1958- *BiDrAPA 89*
Stovall, Jerry 1936- *WhoAm 90, WhoSSW 91*
Stovall, Jerry C. 1936- *St&PR 91*
Stovall, Jesse 1875-1955 *Ballpl 90*
Stovall, Luther McKinley 1937- *WhoAmA 91*
Stovall, Queena 1887-1980 *MusmAFA*
Stovall, Robert Henry 1926- *WhoAm 90*
Stovall, Sheryl Ann 1951- *WhoAmW 91*
Stovall, Warren Scott 1942- *WhoSSW 91*
Stoveken, James Edwin, Jr. 1939- *St&PR 91*
Stover, Barbara M. *St&PR 91*
Stover, Brian Allan 1947- *WhoSSW 91*
Stover, Carl Frederick 1930- *WhoAm 90, WhoE 91*
Stover, Donald Lewis 1943- *WhoAmA 91*
Stover, Ellen Simon 1950- *WhoAmW 91*
Stover, F. Gary 1945- *St&PR 91*
Stover, Harry M. 1926- *WhoAm 90*
Stover, Harry Manning 1926- *St&PR 91*
Stover, James Howard 1911- *WhoAm 90*
Stover, James Robert 1927- *St&PR 91, WhoAm 90*
Stover, John Ford 1912- *WhoAm 90*
Stover, Leon 1929- *WhoAm 90*
Stover, Marjorie Filley 1914- *ConAu 31NR*
Stover, Matthew J. 1955- *ODwPR 91*
Stover, Matthew Joseph 1955- *WhoE 91*
Stover, Phil Sheridan, Jr. 1926- *WhoAm 90*
Stover, Richard Louis 1942- *St&PR 91*
Stover, W. Robert 1921- *St&PR 91*
Stover, William James 1945- *WhoEmL 91*
Stover, William K. *WhoSSW 91*
Stover, William R. 1922- *St&PR 91*
Stover, William Reitzel 1906- *WhoSSW 91*
Stover, William Ruffner 1922- *WhoAm 90*
Stover-Pock, Robin Jo 1955- *WhoAmW 91*
Stovey, George *Ballpl 90*
Stovey, Harry 1856-1937 *Ballpl 90 [port]*
Stovin, Cornelius 1830-1921 *BioIn 16*
Stow, Baron 1801-1869 *BioIn 16*
Stow, Randolph 1935- *ConAu 33NR, MajTwCW*
Stow, William W. 1824?-1895 *AmLegL*
Stowasser, Friedrich 1928- *WhoWor 91*
Stowe, Allen Howard 1937- *St&PR 91*
Stowe, Arthur Wilkinson 1951- *WhoE 91*
Stowe, Bernie *BioIn 16*
Stowe, David Henry 1910- *WhoAm 90*
Stowe, David Henry, Jr. 1936- *St&PR 91, WhoAm 90*
Stowe, David Metz 1919- *WhoAm 90*
Stowe, Harold Crosby 1946- *WhoAm 90*
Stowe, Harriet 1811-1896 *FemiCLE*
Stowe, Harriet Beecher 1811-1896 *AuBYP 90, BioAmW, BioIn 16, EncPaPR 91, LiHiK, WorAlBi*
Stowe, Harry Duffield 1856-1937 *Ballpl 90 [port]*
Stowe, Jacqueline 1936- *WhoSSW 91*
Stowe, Leland 1899- *BioIn 16, SmATA 60 [port], WhoAm 90*
Stowe, Michael William 1953- *WhoEmL 91*
Stowe, Nonnie *St&PR 91*
Stowe, Phineas 1812-1868 *BioIn 16*
Stowe, Robert Lee, III 1954- *WhoSSW 91*
Stowe, Ronald Floyd 1945- *WhoE 91*
Stowe, Suzanne Marie 1952- *WhoAmW 91*
Stowell, Calvin S. 1950- *St&PR 91*
Stowell, Charles Raymond, Jr. 1927- *WhoAm 90*
Stowell, Christopher Eldon 1943- *WhoSSW 91*
Stowell, Deanna Marion 1938- *WhoAmW 91*
Stowell, Jeremy Averill *BiDrAPA 89*
Stowell, Jett E. 1942- *St&PR 91*
Stowell, Kent *BioIn 16*
Stowell, Kent 1939- *WhoAm 90*
Stowell, Kerry Hart 1932- *WhoE 91*
Stowell, Ronald S. *St&PR 91*
Stowell, Warren David 1952- *WhoSSW 91*
Stowers, Carlton 1942- *ConAu 31NR*
Stowers, Carlton Eugene 1942- *WhoAm 90*
Stowers, Harry E., Jr. 1926- *WhoAm 90*
Stowers, Mark Alan 1957- *WhoSSW 91*
Stowes, Patricia Anne 1948- *WhoAmW 91*
Stoy, Jay *St&PR 91*
Stoy, Patrick James 1949- *WhoEmL 91*
Stoykovich, Christine Anne 1949- *WhoAmW 91*
Stoynoff, R.D. 1946- *St&PR 91*
Stoytshev, Luben 1932- *WhoWor 91*
Straat, Kent Leon 1934- *WhoE 91*
Straatman, Maria G. 1948- *St&PR 91*
Straatsma, Bradley Ralph 1927- *WhoAm 90*
Strabel, Heidi Ann 1963- *WhoAmW 91*

Strabo 63?BC-23?AD *WorAlBi*
Strach, Michael William 1930- *St&PR 91*
Strachan, Andrew Crichton 1951- *St&PR 91*
Strachan, Donald M. 1923- *WhoAm 90*
Strachan, Michael Francis 1919- *WhoWor 91*
Strachan, Patricia Harting 1948- *WhoWrEP 89*
Stracher, Alfred 1930- *WhoAm 90*
Stracher, Dorothy Altman 1934- *WhoAmW 91, WhoE 91*
Strachey, Jack 1894-1972 *OxCPMus*
Strachey, Julia 1901-1979 *FemiCLE*
Strachey, Lytton 1880-1932 *WorAlBi*
Strachey, Ray 1887-1940 *FemiCLE*
Strachman, Howard Lewis 1944- *St&PR 91*
Strachwitz, Chris *BioIn 16*
Strack, Dean Arthur 1934- *St&PR 91*
Strack, Harold Arthur 1923- *WhoAm 90*
Strack, William Richard 1936- *St&PR 91, WhoAm 90, WhoWor 91*
Strada, Anna Maria *PenDiMP*
Strada, Christina Bryson 1925- *WhoAmW 91*
Strada, Michael Anthony 1944- *WhoSSW 91*
Strada del Po, Anna Maria *PenDiMP*
Strade, Terry Lynn 1954- *WhoEmL 91*
Stradella, Charles Gillet 1898-1989 *BioIn 16*
Strader, Ann Wallace 1940- *WhoAmW 91*
Strader, Haywood 1935- *St&PR 91*
Strader, Jacqueline W. 1946- *WhoAmW 91*
Strader, Theodore J. 1953- *St&PR 91*
Stradiot, James E. 1959- *St&PR 91*
Stradley, David Cowan 1922- *WhoAm 90*
Stradley, William Jackson 1939- *WhoSSW 91, WhoWor 91*
Stradley, William Lamar 1940- *WhoSSW 91*
Stradling, Harry, Jr. 1925- *ConTFT 8*
Stradtner, James Bernard 1935- *WhoAm 90*
Stradwick, John Conway 1930- *St&PR 91*
Straehley, Clifford John, III 1945- *BiDrAPA 89*
Straetmans, John Patrick *BiDrAPA 89*
Straetz, Muriel R 1920- *BiDrAPA 89*
Straetz, Robert P. 1921- *St&PR 91, WhoAm 90*
Straface, Frank J. *BioIn 16*
Straffon, Ralph Atwood 1928- *WhoAm 90*
Strafford, Thomas Wentworth, Earl of 1593-1641 *BioIn 16, WorAlBi*
Strafford, William Francis 1944- *St&PR 91, WhoAm 90*
Strahan, Alene P *BiDrAPA 89*
Strahan, Bradley R. 1937- *WhoWrEP 89*
Strahan, Charles 1921- *WhoE 91*
Strahan, Charles, Jr. 1921- *BiDrAPA 89*
Strahan, Julia Celestine 1938- *WhoAmW 91*
Strahan, Ronald 1922- *WhoWor 91*
Strahan, Susan Thomson *BiDrAPA 89*
Strahilevitz, Aharona *BiDrAPA 89*
Strahilevitz, Meir *BiDrAPA 89*
Strahine, Pamela Kay 1957- *WhoAmW 91*
Strahl, Margaret O 1917- *BiDrAPA 89*
Strahl, Nathan R *BiDrAPA 89*
Strahl-Bolstorff, Donna Myrtle 1940- *WhoAmW 91*
Strahle, Julia Ann 1946- *WhoAmW 91*
Strahle, Warren Charles 1938- *WhoAm 90*
Strahler, Arthur Newell 1918- *WhoAm 90*
Strahler, Mike 1947- *Ballpl 90*
Strahler, Patricia L. 1959- *ODwPR 91*
Strahm, Samuel Edward 1936- *WhoAm 90*
Strahm, Waymer John *BiDrAPA 89*
Straight, Beatrice 1918- *WorAlBi*
Straight, Beatrice Whitney 1918- *WhoAm 90, WhoE 91, WhoWor 91*
Straight, Belinda *BiDrAPA 89*
Straight, Dorothy W. *BioAmW*
Straight, Elsie H *WhoAmA 91*
Straight, H. Stephen 1943- *WhoE 91*
Straight, Willard *BioIn 16*
Strain, Boyd Ray 1935- *WhoSSW 91*
Strain, David L. 1921- *St&PR 91*
Strain, Douglas C. 1919- *St&PR 91*
Strain, Douglas Campbell 1919- *WhoAm 90, WhoWor 91*
Strain, Edward Richard 1925- *WhoWor 91*
Strain, Gladys Witt 1934- *WhoAmW 91*
Strain, Herbert Arthur, III 1954- *WhoEmL 91*
Strain, James Ellsworth 1923- *WhoAm 90*
Strain, James J 1933- *BiDrAPA 89*
Strain, Joe 1954- *Ballpl 90*
Strain, John J. 1939- *St&PR 91*
Strain, Richard Allen 1942- *St&PR 91*
Strain, Ronald Reid 1935- *St&PR 91*
Strait, A. Marvin *BioIn 16*
Strait, Bradley Justus 1932- *WhoAm 90*
Strait, Charles McIver 1931- *St&PR 91*
Strait, George *WhoNeCM [port]*
Strait, George 1952- *ConMus 5 [port], WhoAm 90*
Strait, Loraine Hall 1944- *St&PR 91*
Strait, Margaret Jean 1945- *WhoAmW 91*
Strait, Peggy Tang 1933- *WhoE 91*
Strait, Rick E. 1947- *St&PR 91*
Straite, James Richard 1928- *St&PR 91*
Straiton, Archie Waugh 1907- *WhoAm 90*
Straiton, Thomas Harmon, Jr. 1941- *WhoSSW 91*
Straitz, John Frederick 1946- *St&PR 91*
Straka, Laszlo 1934- *St&PR 91*
Straka, Laszlo Richard 1934- *WhoAm 90, WhoE 91, WhoWor 91*
Straka, Randolph J. 1952- *St&PR 91*
Straka, Ronald Albert 1937- *WhoAm 90*
Strake, D.A. 1940- *St&PR 91*
Straker, Anita *BioIn 16*
Straker, Edward Albert, Sr. 1937- *St&PR 91*
Straker, J F 1904- *TwCCr&M 91*
Straker, J.W. 1921- *St&PR 91*
Straker, Les 1959- *Ballpl 90*
Straker, Manuel 1916- *BiDrAPA 89*
Straker, Norman Lewis 1941- *BiDrAPA 89*
Strakhov, Nikolai Mikhailovich 1900-1978 *DcScB S2*
Strakosch, Katherine Wenton 1933- *WhoAmW 91*
Stral, Lee Philip *ODwPR 91*
Stralem, Donald S 1903-1976 *WhoAmA 91N*
Stralem, Pierre 1909- *WhoAm 90*
Straley, Joanetta Sue 1950- *WhoAmW 91*
Straley, Keith L. 1940- *St&PR 91*
Straling, Phillip Francis 1933- *WhoAm 90*
Stralo, F. Jay 1954- *St&PR 91*
Stram, Hank Louis 1923- *WhoAm 90*
Stranahan, Marion 1899- *BiDrAPA 89*
Stranahan, Robert A., Jr. 1915- *St&PR 91*
Stranahan, Robert Paul, Jr. 1929- *WhoAm 90*
Stranberg, Wynne Lee 1948- *WhoAmW 91*
Strand, Curt Robert 1920- *WhoAm 90*
Strand, David Axel 1935- *WhoAm 90*
Strand, Gerald C. 1938- *St&PR 91*
Strand, Glenn T 1925- *BiDrAPA 89*
Strand, Jens Alvin 1946- *WhoEmL 91*
Strand, Kenneth T. 1931- *WhoAm 90*
Strand, Marion Delores 1927- *WhoAmW 91*
Strand, Mark 1934- *WhoAm 90, WhoWrEP 89*
Strand, Mary *ODwPR 91*
Strand, Nancy Marie 1926- *WhoAmW 91*
Strand, Paul 1890-1976 *BioIn 16*
Strand, Paul 1893-1974 *Ballpl 90*
Strand, Ray Walter 1924- *St&PR 91*
Strand, Richard A. 1935- *St&PR 91*
Strand, Roger Gordon 1934- *WhoAm 90*
Strand, Sally 1954- *BioIn 16*
Strand, Theodore L. 1943- *WhoSSW 91*
Strand, William Keith 1931- *St&PR 91*
Strandberg, James B. 1935- *ODwPR 91*
Strandberg, Keith William 1957- *WhoWrEP 89*
Strandberg, Malcom Woodrow Pershing 1919- *WhoAm 90*
Strandberg, Newton Dwight 1921- *WhoSSW 91*
Strandberg, Rebecca Newman 1951- *WhoEmL 91*
Strandberg, Sven Ake 1927- *WhoWor 91*
Strandenes, Siri Pettersen 1949- *WhoWor 91*
Strandgaard, Charlotte 1943- *EncCoWW*
Strandhagen, Adolf Gustav 1914- *WhoWor 91*
Strandhoy, Jack Willard 1944- *WhoSSW 91*
Strandjord, Mary Jeannine 1945- *St&PR 91*
Strandjord, Paul Edphil 1931- *WhoAm 90*
Strandness, Donald Eugene, Jr. 1928- *WhoAm 90*
Strandwitz, Norman C. 1933- *St&PR 91*
Straney, Ellen Carmen 1947- *WhoE 91*
Strang, Allen Louis 1951- *St&PR 91*
Strang, Butler B. 1829-1884 *AmLegL*
Strang, Charles D. 1921- *St&PR 91*
Strang, Charles Daniel 1921- *WhoAm 90*
Strang, Edward E. 1943- *St&PR 91*
Strang, George Ellis 1939- *St&PR 91*
Strang, James Jesse 1813-1856 *BioIn 16*
Strang, John Robert 1946- *WhoE 91*
Strang, Jonathan Peter *BiDrAPA 89*
Strang, Marian Boundy 1918- *WhoAm 90*
Strang, Richard N. 1929- *St&PR 91*
Strang, Roger Andrew 1945- *St&PR 91*
Strang, Ruth Hancock 1923- *WhoAm 90*
Strang, Sammy 1876-1932 *Ballpl 90*
Strang, Sandra Lee 1936- *WhoAmW 91*
Strang, Stephen Edward 1951- *WhoAm 90*
Strang, William C *BiDrAPA 89*
Strang, William Gilbert 1934- *WhoAm 90, WhoE 91*
Strange, Alan 1909- *Ballpl 90*
Strange, Ben W. 1929- *ODwPR 91*
Strange, Curtis *BioIn 16, NewYTBS 90 [port]*
Strange, Curtis 1955- *WorAlBi*
Strange, Curtis Northrop 1955- *WhoAm 90*
Strange, Donald Ernest 1944- *WhoAm 90, WhoE 91, WhoWor 91*
Strange, Elwin *TwCCr&M 91*
Strange, J. Leland 1941- *WhoAm 90*
Strange, James Leland 1941- *St&PR 91*
Strange, John Robert 1950- *WhoSSW 91*
Strange, John Stephen 1896- *TwCCr&M 91*
Strange, Marty *BioIn 16*
Strange, Richard Eugene 1928- *IntWWM 90*
Strange, Robert E 1933- *BiDrAPA 89*
Strange, Steven Alger 1952- *WhoSSW 91*
Strange, T. Bland 1831-1925 *BioIn 16*
Strange, Thomas Bland 1831-1925 *BioIn 16*
Stranger, Hannah *BiDEWW*
Stranger, Peter 1949- *WhoAm 90*
Strangfeld, James E. 1946- *St&PR 91*
Strangi, Thomas Carl 1957- *St&PR 91*
Strangway, David William 1934- *WhoAm 90, WhoWor 91*
Strasberg, Andy *BioIn 16*
Strasberg, John *BioIn 16*
Strasberg, Lee 1901- *WorAlBi*
Strasberg, Susan 1938- *WhoAm 90, WorAlBi*
Strasburger, Joseph Julius 1913- *WhoAm 90*
Strasburger, Larry H 1935- *BiDrAPA 89*
Strasburger, Laurie *ODwPR 91*
Strasen, Barbara Elaine 1942- *WhoAmA 91*
Strasen, Kenneth Richard 1945- *St&PR 91*
Strasfogel, Ian 1940- *WhoAm 90*
Strasfogel, Ignace 1909- *WhoAm 90*
Strasheim, Gene A. 1940- *St&PR 91*
Strasma, John Drinan 1932- *WhoAm 90*
Strasma, Norman Edward 1932- *St&PR 91*
Strass, Georges Frederic 1701-1773 *PenDiDA 89*
Strass, Hermann Heinrich 1938- *WhoWor 91*
Strass, John J. 1956- *St&PR 91*
Strass, Stephanie A. 1947- *ODwPR 91*
Strassberg, Merri *St&PR 91*
Strassberg, Roy I 1950- *WhoAmA 91*
Strassberg, Stanley 1932- *St&PR 91*
Strassberger, James Carroll 1947- *WhoE 91*
Strassburger, Gustav Alfred 1939- *WhoSSW 91*
Strasser, Alfred Anthony 1927- *WhoE 91*
Strasser, Bruce Elliott 1925- *St&PR 91*
Strasser, Elmer E. 1912- *St&PR 91*
Strasser, Elvira Rapaport 1913- *WhoE 91*
Strasser, Gabor 1929- *WhoAm 90, WhoWor 91*
Strasser, Gerhard Friedrich 1940- *WhoWor 91*
Strasser, Harold A. 1907- *St&PR 91*
Strasser, Hermann 1941- *WhoWor 91*
Strasser, Jack C. 1934- *WhoSSW 91*
Strasser, Joel A. 1938- *ODwPR 91, WhoE 91, WhoWor 91*
Strasser, Judith Louise 1944- *WhoAmW 91*
Strasser, Louis A. 1934- *St&PR 91*
Strasser, Nancy Sowers 1947- *WhoAmW 91*
Strasser, Peter R. 1938- *St&PR 91*
Strasser, Richard J., Jr. 1947 *St&PR 91*
Strasser, Robin *BioIn 16*
Strasser, Robin 1945- *WhoAm 90*
Strasser, Scott *BioIn 16*
Strasser, Todd 1950- *BioIn 16, WhoWrEP 89*
Strasser, William Carl, Jr. 1930- *WhoAm 90*
Strassler, Gerald N. 1927- *St&PR 91*
Strassman, Charles Robert 1941- *St&PR 91*
Strassman, Harvey D 1922- *BiDrAPA 89*
Strassman, John Michael 1953- *St&PR 91*
Strassman, Rick Jan 1952- *BiDrAPA 89*
Strassmann, Friedrich Wilhelm 1902-1980 *DcScB S2*
Strassmann, Paul A. *BioIn 16*
Strassmann, W. Paul 1926- *WhoAm 90*
Strassmeyer, Mary 1929- *WhoAm 90*
Strassner, Kenneth Allen 1946- *WhoEmL 91*
Strassner, Laurence M. 1941- *St&PR 91*
Straszak, Irena Marta *BiDrAPA 89*
Stratakis, Anastasi 1938- *PenDiMP*
Stratas, Nicholas E 1932- *BiDrAPA 89*
Stratas, Teresa *BioIn 16, NewYTBS 90 [port]*
Stratas, Teresa 1938- *IntWWM 90, PenDiMP, WhoAm 90, WhoWor 91*
Strate, Robert A. 1944- *St&PR 91*
Stratemeyer, Edward 1862-1930 *Ballpl 90, WorAlBi*
Strater, Henry 1896-1987 *WhoAmA 91N*
Stratford, Brian Reginald 1931- *WhoWor 91*
Stratford, Carol Ann Deering 1946- *WhoAmW 91*
Stratford, Philip 1927- *BioIn 16*
Stratford, William David, Jr. *BiDrAPA 89*
Strathairn, David *ConTFT 8*
Strathearn, Richard Alan 1955- *WhoEmL 91*
Strathmann, William D 1938- *BiDrAPA 89*
Strathmeyer, Michael 1953- *St&PR 91*
Strathmore, Mary Eleanor Bowes 1749-1800 *FemiCLE*
Strathy, Janette Hansen 1956- *WhoAmW 91*
Stratigos, James Alvin, Jr. 1952- *WhoEmL 91*
Stratkos, Steve John 1954- *WhoAmA 91*
Stratman, Joseph Lee 1924- *WhoAm 90*
Stratman, Orlando John 1951- *St&PR 91*
Straton, John Charles, Jr. 1932- *WhoAm 90*
Stratoudakis, James Peter 1949- *WhoE 91*
Stratt, Randy Allen 1956- *St&PR 91*
Strattan, Byron Doan 1930- *St&PR 91*
Stratten, Dorothy 1960-1980 *BioIn 16*
Strattner, Lawrence J. *St&PR 91*
Strattner, Lawrence Wenz, Jr. 1917- *WhoAm 90*
Stratton Quartet *PenDiMP*
Stratton, Allan 1951- *OxCCanT*
Stratton, Carson G. 1930- *St&PR 91*
Stratton, Charles Lynn 1944- *St&PR 91*
Stratton, Debra J. *ODwPR 91*
Stratton, Dorothy 1908- *WhoAmA 91*
Stratton, Eugene 1861-1918 *OxCPMus*
Stratton, F J M 1881-1960 *EncO&P 3*
Stratton, Frederick Prescott, Jr. 1939- *St&PR 91, WhoAm 90*
Stratton, Hal 1950- *WhoAm 90*
Stratton, Harold Duane 1924- *WhoAm 90*
Stratton, James W. 1936- *St&PR 91*
Stratton, Joanne M. *ODwPR 91*
Stratton, John E. 1929- *St&PR 91*
Stratton, Julius Adams 1901- *WhoAm 90*
Stratton, Lois Jean 1927- *WhoAmW 91*
Stratton, Lowell Alan *BiDrAPA 89*
Stratton, Lucille *AuBYP 90*
Stratton, Mary Chase Perry 1868-1961 *BioIn 16*
Stratton, Monty 1912-1982 *Ballpl 90*
Stratton, Norma Jean 1936- *WhoAmW 91*
Stratton, Owen Tully 1868-1950 *BioIn 16*
Stratton, Robert 1928- *WhoAm 90*
Stratton, Robert R. *St&PR 91N*
Stratton, Samuel S. *NewYTBS 90 [port]*
Stratton, Samuel Studdiford 1916- *WhoAm 90*
Stratton, Samuel Wesley 1861-1931 *DcScB S2*
Stratton, Stacia A. 1946- *St&PR 91*
Stratton, Suzanne L 1943- *WhoAmA 91*
Stratton, Thomas *AuBYP 90*
Stratton, Thomas Oliver 1930- *WhoAm 90*
Stratton, Thomas William 1946- *WhoWrEP 89*
Stratton, Walter Love 1926- *WhoAm 90*
Stratton, William Crapo 1826-1898 *AmLegL*
Stratton, William David 1896- *AuBYP 90*
Stratton, William Grant 1914- *St&PR 91*
Stratton, William Morris 1947- *WhoSSW 91*
Stratton, William R. 1934- *St&PR 91*
Stratton, William Richard 1934- *WhoAm 90*
Stratton-Crooke, Thomas Edward 1933- *WhoAm 90*
Stratton-Porter, Gene 1863-1924 *BioAmW, FemiCLE*
Straty, Stephen M. 1955- *St&PR 91*
Straub, Carole Louise Boyce 1943- *WhoE 91*
Straub, Chester J. 1937- *St&PR 91*
Straub, Chester John 1937- *WhoAm 90*
Straub, Denise Margaret 1959- *WhoAmW 91*
Straub, F. Bruno 1914- *BioIn 16, WhoWor 91*
Straub, Frank G. 1932- *St&PR 91*
Straub, Gerard Donald 1945- *St&PR 91*
Straub, J. Vanderbilt 1907- *St&PR 91*
Straub, Jean-Marie *BioIn 16*
Straub, Jennifer 1959- *St&PR 91*
Straub, John W. 1926- *St&PR 91*
Straub, Leonard R 1918- *BiDrAPA 89*
Straub, Melvin J. 1930- *St&PR 91*
Straub, Peter *BioIn 16*
Straub, Peter 1943- *MajTwCW*
Straub, Peter Francis 1943- *WhoAm 90, WhoWrEP 89*
Straub, Peter Thornton 1939- *WhoAm 90*
Straub, William D. 1928- *St&PR 91*
Straube, Ann *BioIn 16*
Straube, Harald Heinz 1926- *WhoWor 91*

Straube, Win *St&PR 91*
Straubel, James Henderson 1915- *WhoAm 90*
Strauber, Donald I. 1936- *WhoAm 90*
Straubing, Charles Robert 1921- *St&PR 91*
Strauch, Charles S. 1935- *St&PR 91*
Strauch, Gary J. 1941- *St&PR 91*
Strauch, Gerald Neal 1958- *WhoSSW 91*
Strauch, Gerald Otto 1932- *WhoAm 90*
Strauch, Inge H 1932- *EncO&P 3*
Strauch, John L. 1939- *WhoAm 90*
Strauch, Karl 1922- *WhoAm 90, WhoE 91*
Strauch, Patricia *St&PR 91*
Strauch, Ralph E. 1937- *WhoWrEP 89*
Strauch, Richard George 1934- *WhoAm 90*
Strauf, Hubert Heinr 1904- *WhoWor 91*
Straughan, Carol Annette 1935- *WhoAmW 91*
Straughn, Claire Valencia Lee 1953- *WhoAmW 91*
Straumanis, John Janis, Jr. 1935- *BiDrAPA 89, WhoAm 90*
Straumann, Bruno *PenDiMP*
Straumfjord, Agnar 1928- *BiDrAPA 89*
Straumfjord, Marianne 1944- *BiDrAPA 89*
Straus, Austin Guy 1939- *WhoWrEP 89*
Straus, David J. 1923- *St&PR 91*
Straus, Dennis *WhoWrEP 89*
Straus, Donald Blun 1916- *WhoAm 90*
Straus, Ellen Sulzberger 1925- *WhoAm 90, WhoAmW 91*
Straus, Gladys Guggenheim 1895-1980 *BioIn 16*
Straus, Helen Lorna Puttkammer 1933- *WhoAmW 91*
Straus, Helen Sachs *NewYTBS 90*
Straus, Irving L. 1921- *ODwPR 91*
Straus, Irving Lehman 1921- *WhoAm 90*
Straus, Isidor 1845-1912 *WorAlBi*
Straus, Jack Isidor 1900-1985 *WorAlBi*
Straus, Jacqueline Harris *AuBYP 90*
Straus, Jesse Isidor 1872-1936 *BioIn 16, WorAlBi*
Straus, Joseph 1938- *WhoWor 91*
Straus, Joseph Pennington 1911- *WhoAm 90*
Straus, Kathleen Nagler 1923- *WhoAmW 91*
Straus, Kenneth Hollister 1925- *WhoAm 90*
Straus, Leonard H. 1914- *WhoAm 90*
Straus, Ludwig *PenDiMP*
Straus, Nathan 1848-1931 *WorAlBi*
Straus, Oscar 1870-1954 *OxCPMus, PenDiMP A*
Straus, Oscar S. 1914- *St&PR 91*
Straus, Oscar S., II 1914- *WhoAm 90, WhoWor 91*
Straus, Oscar Solomon 1850-1926 *BioIn 16*
Straus, Oscar Solomon 1850-1931 *BiDrUSE 89*
Straus, Percy Selden 1876-1944 *WorAlBi*
Straus, Peter *St&PR 91*
Straus, R. Peter 1923- *WhoAm 90*
Straus, Robert 1923- *WhoAm 90*
Straus, Robert Ware 1909- *WhoE 91*
Straus, Roger W. *BioIn 16*
Straus, Roger W., Jr. 1917- *WhoAm 90, WorAlBi*
Straus, Sandy 1938- *WhoAmA 91*
Straus, William Marc 1956- *WhoEmL 91*
Strausbaugh, Melvin Roy 1936- *WhoE 91*
Strausbaugh, Teresa Elaine 1964- *WhoAmW 91*
Strausborger, David Edwin 1948- *St&PR 91*
Strausburg, William Wayne 1939- *St&PR 91*
Strause, Glynis Holm 1952- *WhoAmW 91*
Strauser, Sterling Boyd 1907- *WhoAmA 91*
Strauser, Walter William *BiDrAPA 89*
Strauss, Abbey 1947- *BiDrAPA 89*
Strauss, Albrecht Benno 1921- *WhoAm 90*
Strauss, Alfred C. 1932- *St&PR 91*
Strauss, Alfred Johann *BiDrAPA 89*
Strauss, Andrew Alexander 1953- *St&PR 91, WhoE 91*
Strauss, Andrew Leopold 1958- *WhoE 91*
Strauss, Annette 1924- *WhoAm 90, WhoAmW 91, WhoSSW 91*
Strauss, Arthur J L 1933- *BiDrAPA 89*
Strauss, Bernard Marvin 1946- *WhoE 91*
Strauss, Bernard S. 1927- *WhoAm 90*
Strauss, Bill *BioIn 16*
Strauss, Botho 1944- *WhoAu 1980 [port]*
Strauss, Bruno 1926- *St&PR 91*
Strauss, Burton M. *BioIn 16*
Strauss, Carol Kahn 1944- *WhoAmW 91, WhoE 91*
Strauss, Catherine B. 1947- *St&PR 91*
Strauss, Charles Bernhard 1943- *St&PR 91*
Strauss, Charles Bernhard, Jr. 1943- *WhoAm 90*
Strauss, Christopher 1943- *St&PR 91*
Strauss, David Levi 1953- *WhoWrEP 89*
Strauss, David Sheldon 1932- *St&PR 91*
Strauss, Diane Carol Wheeler 1943- *WhoSSW 91*
Strauss, Dorothy Brandfon *WhoAmW 91, WhoE 91, WhoWor 91*
Strauss, Eduard 1835-1916 *OxCPMus*
Strauss, Eduard 1853-1916 *BioIn 16*
Strauss, Edward Robert 1942- *WhoE 91*
Strauss, Elliott Bowman 1903- *WhoAm 90*
Strauss, Eugene Milton 1919- *St&PR 91*
Strauss, Franz Josef 1915-1988 *AnObit 1988, BioIn 16*
Strauss, Gerald 1922- *ConAu 33NR*
Strauss, Gordon Darrow 1947- *BiDrAPA 89*
Strauss, Harlee Sue 1950- *WhoAmW 91*
Strauss, Harold Lloyd 1931- *St&PR 91*
Strauss, Harvey S 1940- *BiDrAPA 89*
Strauss, Herbert Leopold 1936- *WhoAm 90*
Strauss, Howard E. 1933- *St&PR 91*
Strauss, Jack S. 1900- *St&PR 91*
Strauss, Jean *BioIn 16*
Strauss, Jean Anne Sacconaghi 1955- *WhoAmW 91*
Strauss, Jeanne H. 1928- *WhoSSW 91, WhoWor 91*
Strauss, Jennifer 1933- *FemiCLE*
Strauss, Jerome Manfred 1934- *WhoAm 90*
Strauss, Johann 1804-1849 *BioIn 16, OxCPMus*
Strauss, Johann 1825-1899 *BioIn 16, PenDiMP A, WorAlBi*
Strauss, Johann, II 1825-1899 *OxCPMus*
Strauss, John *ODwPR 91*
Strauss, John S 1932- *BiDrAPA 89*
Strauss, John Steaven 1932- *WhoE 91*
Strauss, John Steinert 1926- *WhoAm 90*
Strauss, Jon Calvert 1940- *WhoAm 90, WhoE 91*
Strauss, Jonathan 1954- *St&PR 91*
Strauss, Jose 1930- *WhoAm 90*
Strauss, Josef 1827-1870 *BioIn 16, OxCPMus*
Strauss, Joyce 1936- *BioIn 16*
Strauss, Judith Feigin 1942- *WhoAmW 91*
Strauss, Justin J. 1933- *St&PR 91*
Strauss, Karl Martin 1912- *WhoAm 90*
Strauss, Kathy Jane 1953- *WhoE 91*
Strauss, Leo H. 1911- *St&PR 91*
Strauss, Leon 1928- *BioIn 16*
Strauss, Levi 1829-1902 *BioIn 16, WorAlBi*
Strauss, Lewis Lichtenstein 1896- *BiDrUSE 89*
Strauss, Lindy *BioIn 16*
Strauss, Michael E. 1943- *WhoE 91*
Strauss, Michael Ernest 1943- *St&PR 91*
Strauss, Molly Meyers 1953- *BiDrAPA 89*
Strauss, Norman, Jr. 1937- *St&PR 91*
Strauss, Paul U 1928- *BiDrAPA 89*
Strauss, Peter 1947- *WhoAm 90, WorAlBi*
Strauss, Phyllis R. 1943- *WhoAmW 91*
Strauss, Raymond Bernard 1930- *WhoE 91*
Strauss, Richard 1864-1949 *BioIn 16, PenDiMP A, WorAlBi*
Strauss, Robert C. 1941- *St&PR 91*
Strauss, Robert David 1951- *WhoSSW 91*
Strauss, Robert Philip *WhoAm 90, WhoE 91*
Strauss, Robert S. 1918- *WorAlBi*
Strauss, Robert Schwarz 1918- *WhoAm 90*
Strauss, Rodolfo *WhoHisp 91*
Strauss, Sally 1925- *WhoWrEP 89*
Strauss, Sidney R. 1923- *St&PR 91*
Strauss, Simon David 1911- *WhoAm 90*
Strauss, Stanley Carroll 1935- *St&PR 91*
Strauss, Stanley Robert 1915- *WhoAm 90*
Strauss, Susan Louise 1946- *WhoAmW 91*
Strauss, Thomas W. *St&PR 91*
Strauss, Thomas W. 1942- *WhoAm 90, WhoE 91*
Strauss, Ulrich Paul 1920- *WhoAm 90*
Strauss, W.A. 1922- *St&PR 91*
Strauss, Walter Adolf 1923- *WhoAm 90*
Strauss, Walter Leopold 1932-1988 *WhoAmA 91N*
Strauss, William David 1949- *St&PR 91*
Strauss und Torney, Lulu von 1873-1956 *EncCoWW*
Strausz-Hupe, Robert 1903- *WhoAm 90, WhoWor 91*
Strautin, Mary Perkins 1956- *WhoE 91*
Strautmanis, Edvins 1933- *WhoAmA 91*
Stravinski, Steven John 1945- *St&PR 91*
Stravinsky, Igor 1882-1971 *BioIn 16, PenDiMP A, WorAlBi*
Straw, Erwin T. 1929- *St&PR 91*
Straw, Gary Robert 1951- *WhoWor 91*
Straw, Gregory Martin 1950- *BiDrAPA 89*
Straw, Jack 1946- *BioIn 16*
Straw, John Whitaker *BioIn 16*
Straw, Michelle Marie 1958- *WhoAmW 91*
Straw, Syd *BioIn 16*
Strawberry, Darryl *BioIn 16*
Strawberry, Darryl 1962- *Ballpl 90, WhoAm 90, WorAlBi*
Strawbridge, Francis Reeves, III 1937- *St&PR 91, WhoAm 90*
Strawbridge, G. Stockton 1913- *WhoAm 90*
Strawbridge, George *BioIn 16*
Strawbridge, Herbert Edward 1918- *St&PR 91*
Strawbridge, Peter S. 1938- *St&PR 91, WhoAm 90, WhoE 91*
Strawbridge, Steven Lowry 1943- *St&PR 91, WhoAm 90*
Strawderman, Virginia 1949- *WhoAmW 91*
Strawinsky, Elizabeth R 1925- *BiDrAPA 89*
Strawn, Bernice I *WhoAmA 91*
Strawn, David Updegraff 1936- *WhoWor 91*
Strawn, Frances Freeland 1946- *WhoAmW 91, WhoSSW 91*
Strawn, Jarrett W 1943- *WhoAmA 91*
Strawn, Judy C. 1950- *WhoAmW 91*
Strawn, Kirk Bradley *BiDrAPA 89*
Strawn, Melvin Nicholas 1929- *WhoAmA 91*
Strawn, Steven Kirk 1956- *BiDrAPA 89*
Strawn-Hamilton, Frank 1934- *WhoAm 90*
Strawser, Robert Dale 1924- *St&PR 91*
Strawsma, Ronald Keith 1937- *WhoSSW 91*
Strawther, William W., Jr. 1926- *St&PR 91*
Strax, Philip 1909- *WhoAm 90, WhoE 91*
Strax, Selig 1913- *WhoE 91*
Strayer, Barry Lee 1932- *WhoE 91*
Strayer, Gene Paul 1942- *IntWWM 90*
Strayer, Joseph Reese 1904-1987 *BioIn 16*
Strayer, Marilynn Ann 1938- *BiDrAPA 89*
Strayhorn, Billy 1915-1967 *DrBIPA 90, OxCPMus*
Strayhorn, Earlene E *BiDrAPA 89*
Strayhorn, Joseph M *BiDrAPA 89*
Strayhorn, Ralph Nichols, Jr. 1923- *WhoAm 90*
Strayton, Robert G. 1935- *ODwPR 91*
Strayton, Robert Gerard 1935- *WhoAm 90*
Strazdon, Maureen Elaine 1948- *WhoAmW 91*
Straznickas, John R *BiDrAPA 89*
Strazzella, James Anthony 1939- *WhoE 91*
Stream, Arnold Crager 1918- *WhoAm 90*
Stream, Jay Wilson 1921- *WhoAm 90, WhoWor 91*
Strean, Bernard M. 1910- *WhoAm 90, WhoWor 91*
Strean, Bernard Max, Jr. 1936- *WhoE 91*
Strear, Joseph D. 1933- *ODwPR 91, WhoAm 90*
Streatfeild, David Anthony 1945- *St&PR 91*
Streatfeild, Mary Noel 1895-1986 *BioIn 16*
Streatfeild, Noel 1895?-1986 *AuBYP 90, BioIn 16, ConAu 31NR, FemiCLE*
Streator, Edward James 1930- *WhoAm 90*
Streator, George *EarBIAP*
Streb, David Alan 1959- *WhoE 91*
Streb, Jack Martin 1931- *WhoE 91*
Streb, Joseph Edward 1931- *St&PR 91*
Strebeigh, Barbara 1902- *WhoAmW 91*
Strebel, Hans 1943- *St&PR 91*
Strebel, Heinz 1939- *WhoWor 91*
Streber, Barbara Kovacs 1939- *WhoAmW 91*
Strebig, Mary Catherine 1948- *WhoAmW 91*
Streblow, James Bruce 1951- *St&PR 91*
Strecansky, James Frank 1940- *St&PR 91*
Strechay, Robert J. *St&PR 91*
Streck, Ludwig A. 1945- *St&PR 91*
Streckeisen, Albert Ludwig 1901- *WhoWor 91*
Strecker, David Eugene 1950- *WhoSSW 91*
Strecker, Georg Ewald 1929- *WhoWor 91*
Strecker, Ignatius J. 1917- *WhoAm 90*
Strecker, Ivo Andreas 1940- *WhoWor 91*
Strecker, Mark N. *BiDrAPA 89*
Strecker, Richard L. 1944- *St&PR 91*
Streckfuss, Michelle Adrienne 1964- *WhoAmW 91*
Stredde, Sharon 1946- *WhoAmW 91*
Streeb, Gordon Lee 1935- *WhoAm 90*
Streed, Donna 1923- *St&PR 91*
Streelman, Peter H. 1940- *St&PR 91*
Streep, Meryl *BioIn 16*
Streep, Meryl 1949- *ConTFT 8 [port], News 90 [port], WhoAm 90, WhoAmW 91, WhoWor 91, WorAlBi*
Street, Dana Morris 1910- *WhoAm 90*
Street, David Hargett 1943- *St&PR 91, WhoAm 90, WhoWor 91*
Street, Deborah Daisey 1957- *WhoEmL 91*
Street, Edward Robert *St&PR 91N*
Street, Emmet *BioIn 16*
Street, Gabby 1882-1951 *Ballpl 90*
Street, George Edmund 1824-1881 *BioIn 16*
Street, Gordon P., Jr. 1938- *WhoAm 90, WhoSSW 91*
Street, Gordon Parkhurst, Jr. 1938- *St&PR 91*
Street, Hugh McQueen *AmLegL*
Street, J. C. 1906-1989 *BioIn 16*
Street, Jabez 1906-1989 *AnObit 1989*
Street, Jabez Curry 1906-1989 *BioIn 16*
Street, James H. 1915-1988 *BioIn 16*
Street, James Richard 1937- *St&PR 91, WhoAm 90*
Street, John Arthur 1954- *WhoSSW 91*
Street, John Charles 1930- *WhoAm 90*
Street, Julia Montgomery 1898- *WhoWrEP 89*
Street, Kathryn Carol 1960- *WhoAmW 91*
Street, Lairold Maurice 1951- *WhoE 91*
Street, Linda Kaye 1958- *WhoAmW 91*
Street, Patricia Lynn 1940- *WhoAmW 91, WhoE 91*
Street, Richard Arnold 1951- *WhoE 91*
Street, Robert 1920- *WhoWor 91*
Street, Robert Lynnwood 1934- *WhoAm 90*
Street, Shelby Bennett 1940- *WhoAmW 91*
Street, Tison 1943- *IntWWM 90*
Street, William D. 1850?-1911 *AmLegL*
Street, William May 1938- *St&PR 91, WhoAm 90, WhoSSW 91*
Street, William Sherman 1904- *WhoAm 90*
Street-Porter, Janet *BioIn 16*
Streeter, Anne Paul 1926- *WhoAmW 91*
Streeter, David *BioIn 16*
Streeter, David Louis 1941- *St&PR 91*
Streeter, George A 1916- *BiDrAPA 89*
Streeter, George William 1947- *St&PR 91*
Streeter, Henry Schofield 1920- *WhoAm 90*
Streeter, Myron 1926- *St&PR 91*
Streeter, Richard Edward 1934- *WhoAm 90*
Streeter, Rienzi 1838- *AmLegL*
Streeter, Ruth Cheney *NewYTBS 90*
Streeter, Sam 1900- *Ballpl 90*
Streeter, Tal 1934- *WhoAm 90, WhoAmA 91*
Streeter, Tom 1948- *WhoEmL 91*
Streeter, William J. 1938- *St&PR 91*
Streetman, Ben Garland 1939- *WhoAm 90*
Streetman, John William, III 1941- *WhoAm 90, WhoAmA 91*
Streetman, Nancy Katherine 1933- *WhoAmW 91*
Streeton, Jacqui 1943- *WhoSSW 91*
Streets, Gerald Martin *BiDrAPA 89*
Streets, John 1928- *IntWWM 90*
Streett, Alexander Graham 1939- *WhoAm 90*
Streett, Donald Howard 1934- *St&PR 91*
Streett, Tylden Westcott 1922- *WhoAmA 91*
Streett, William Bernard 1932- *WhoAm 90*
Strefling, John Louis 1927- *BiDrAPA 89*
Strehblow, Hans-Henning Steffen 1939- *WhoWor 91*
Strehle, Wilfried *PenDiMP*
Strehlke, Carl Brandon 1955- *WhoWor 91*
Strehlow, Roger Albert 1925- *WhoAm 90*
Streibich, Harold Cecil 1928- *WhoAm 90*
Streich, Eric 1959- *WhoE 91*
Streich, Peter Wakely 1931- *St&PR 91*
Streich, Rita 1920-1987 *PenDiMP*
Streichenwein, Suzan M 1944- *BiDrAPA 89*
Streicher, Fred W. 1948- *ODwPR 91*
Streicher, James Franklin 1940- *WhoAm 90, WhoWor 91*
Streicher, Julius 1885-1946 *BioIn 16*
Streichler, Jerry 1929- *WhoAm 90*
Streicker, Richard Daniel 1952- *WhoEmL 91*
Streifer, Philip Alan 1949- *WhoE 91*
Streifer, William 1936- *WhoAm 90*
Streiff, Katrina 1945- *BiDrAPA 89*
Streim, Joel E *BiDrAPA 89*
Streips, Laimonis V. 1931- *St&PR 91*
Streisand, Barbara *BioIn 16*
Streisand, Barbra 1942- *BioAmW, EncPR&S 89, OxCPMus, WorAlBi*
Streisand, Barbra Joan 1942- *WhoAm 90, WhoAmW 91*
Streissler, Erich Wolfgang 1933- *WhoWor 91*
Streit, Clarence K. 1896-1986 *BioIn 16*
Streit, Ruth A. 1947- *St&PR 91*
Streitel, Walter P *BiDrAPA 89*
Streitfeld, Jane Cole 1933- *WhoSSW 91*
Streitfeld, Nina *ODwPR 91*
Streitfeld, Stephen Victor *BiDrAPA 89*
Streitwieser, Andrew, Jr. 1927- *WhoAm 90*
Streitwieser, Franz Xaver 1939- *WhoE 91*
Strelau, Conrad A. 1931- *WhoE 91*
Strelerte, Veronika 1912- *EncCoWW*
Streletzky, Kathryn Diane 1957- *WhoE 91*
Streller, Richard 1943- *St&PR 91*
Streltzer, Jon Mark 1944- *BiDrAPA 89*
Strelzer, Martin 1925- *WhoAm 90*
Strem, Michael E. 1936- *St&PR 91*

Strembitsky, Michael Alexander 1935- *WhoWor 91*
Stremler, Ferrel G. 1933- *WhoAm 90*
Stremsterfer, John G. 1947- *St&PR 91*
Streng, William Paul 1937- *WhoAm 90*
Strenger, Christian H. 1943- *WhoAm 90*
Strength, Janis Grace 1934- *WhoAmW 91*
Strength, Robert Samuel 1929- *WhoSSW 91*
Strenski, James B. 1930- *ODwPR 91, WhoAm 90*
Strepponi, Giuseppina 1815-1897 *PenDiMP*
Stresemann, Erwin 1889-1972 *DcScB S2*
Stresemann, Gustav 1878-1929 *BioIn 16, WorAlBi*
Stresov, Alexander 1935- *WhoWor 91*
Stretch, John Joseph 1935- *WhoAm 90*
Stretch, Shirley Marie 1949- *WhoAmW 91*
Stretch, Thomas G. 1939- *St&PR 91*
Stretton, Frederic Leighton *BioIn 16*
Stretton, Hesba 1832-1911 *BioIn 16, FemiCLE*
Stretton, Julia 1812-1878 *FemiCLE*
Stretton, Ross *WhoAm 90*
Streusand, William Charles *BiDrAPA 89*
Strevell, Robert Stuart 1945- *St&PR 91, WhoSSW 91*
Strevey, Guy Donald 1932- *WhoWor 91*
Strevinsky, Christine Maria 1932- *WhoWrEP 89*
Strey, Fred L. 1937- *St&PR 91*
Striar, Bernard *BioIn 16*
Stribling, Cherry Davis 1930- *St&PR 91*
Stribling, T S 1881-1965 *TwCCr&M 91*
Strich, Michel Henry 1937- *WhoWor 91*
Strich-Mougenot, Christel Marie Yvonne 1939- *WhoWor 91*
Strichman, George A. 1916-1989 *BioIn 16*
Strick, Joseph 1923- *BioIn 16, WhoAm 90*
Strick, Sadie Elaine 1929- *WhoAmW 91*
Stricker, Augie E. 1929- *St&PR 91*
Stricker, Irwin J. 1932- *St&PR 91*
Stricker, James Albert 1940- *WhoSSW 91*
Strickholm, Karen *ODwPR 91*
Strickholm, Karen 1958- *WhoAmW 91*
Strickland, A.J., III 1928- *St&PR 91*
Strickland, Agnes 1796-1874 *BioIn 16, FemiCLE*
Strickland, Anita Maurine 1923- *WhoSSW 91*
Strickland, Arney Lee 1930- *WhoSSW 91*
Strickland, Arvarh Eunice 1930- *WhoAm 90*
Strickland, B.L. 1940- *St&PR 91*
Strickland, Bill *WhoSSW 91*
Strickland, Bonnie Ruth 1936- *WhoAm 90*
Strickland, Brad 1947- *ConAu 130*
Strickland, Carol A. 1949- *St&PR 91*
Strickland, Catharine Parr 1802-1899 *DcCanB 12*
Strickland, Cheryl Ann 1951- *WhoAmW 91*
Strickland, Clinton Vernal 1950- *WhoEmL 91*
Strickland, Daniel S. 1931- *WhoSSW 91*
Strickland, David Gordon 1946- *St&PR 91*
Strickland, David Miles 1948- *St&PR 91*
Strickland, Dudley W. *St&PR 91N*
Strickland, Elizabeth 1794-1875 *FemiCLE*
Strickland, Eugene Lee 1917- *WhoWor 91*
Strickland, Frances Melvina 1957- *WhoAmW 91*
Strickland, Frank 1928- *WhoWor 91*
Strickland, Frank Dallas 1946- *WhoSSW 91*
Strickland, Fred William, Jr. *BiDrAPA 89*
Strickland, George 1926- *Ballpl 90*
Strickland, George Thomas, Jr. 1934- *WhoAm 90*
Strickland, Hugh Alfred 1931- *WhoAm 90*
Strickland, James Allan 1924- *St&PR 91*
Strickland, James Mell, Jr. 1929- *St&PR 91*
Strickland, John David 1956- *WhoWrEP 89*
Strickland, Jon Chace 1936- *WhoSSW 91*
Strickland, Judy Evelyn 1947- *WhoWrEP 89*
Strickland, Julia Allison 1963- *WhoAmW 91*
Strickland, Keith *BioIn 16*
Strickland, Mabel 1899-1988 *AnObit 1988*
Strickland, Mark Clayton 1953- *BiDrAPA 89*
Strickland, Mary Opal 1933- *St&PR 91*
Strickland, Nellie B. 1932- *WhoAm 90*
Strickland, Norma Jean 1942- *WhoSSW 91*
Strickland, R. Michael 1950- *WhoSSW 91*
Strickland, Richard 1922- *St&PR 91*
Strickland, Robert 1927- *St&PR 91, WhoAm 90*
Strickland, Robert Louis 1931- *St&PR 91, WhoAm 90, WhoSSW 91, WhoWor 91*
Strickland, Rose Mary Namee 1935- *WhoAmW 91*
Strickland, Samuel 1804-1867 *DcLB 99 [port]*
Strickland, Samuel Ray 1950- *St&PR 91*
Strickland, Shirley 1925- *BioIn 16*
Strickland, Sidney C 1934- *BiDrAPA 89*
Strickland, Silas Allen 1831?-1878 *AmLegL*
Strickland, Stephen Parks 1933- *WhoE 91*
Strickland, Tamara Gunsard 1939- *WhoE 91*
Strickland, Ted L. 1932- *WhoAm 90*
Strickland, Thomas J 1932- *WhoAmA 91*
Strickland, Thomas Joseph 1932- *WhoAm 90, WhoSSW 91, WhoWor 91*
Strickland, Vernon Brantley 1925- *St&PR 91*
Strickland, William Bradley 1947- *WhoWrEP 89*
Strickler, Frank A *BiDrAPA 89*
Strickler, Frank H. 1920- *St&PR 91*
Strickler, Howard Martin 1950- *WhoSSW 91*
Strickler, Ivan K. 1921- *WhoAm 90*
Strickler, Janis Jean 1951- *BiDrAPA 89*
Strickler, Susan Elizabeth 1952- *WhoAmA 91*
Stricklett, Elmer 1876-1964 *Ballpl 90*
Stricklin, Alice Carolyn 1959- *WhoAmW 91*
Stricklin, Carl Spencer 1917- *WhoE 91*
Stricklin, James Thomas, II 1947- *WhoSSW 91*
Stricklin, Robert Curtis 1943- *St&PR 91*
Stricklin, W.C. 1936- *St&PR 91*
Strickling, James Henry 1865?-1934 *AmLegL*
Strickman, Arthur Edwin 1924- *St&PR 91, WhoAm 90*
Strickman, Stephen E. 1938- *St&PR 91*
Stricoff, R. Scott 1949- *St&PR 91*
Stride, Richard J. 1927- *St&PR 91*
Strider, Marjorie Virginia *WhoAm 90, WhoAmA 91*
Strider, Marjorie Virginia 1939- *BiDWomA*
Stridsberg, Albert Borden 1929- *WhoE 91, WhoWor 91*
Striebel, John H. *EncACom*
Strieber, Louis Whitley 1945- *WhoE 91*
Strieber, Whitley 1945- *EncO&P 3*
Strieder, John William 1901- *WhoAm 90*
Strieder, Peter 1913- *ConAu 131*
Striefsky, Linda Ann 1952- *WhoAmW 91*
Striefsy, Linda Ann 1952- *WhoEmL 91*
Striegel, Lawrence William 1957- *WhoE 91*
Striegel, Peggy Simsarian 1941- *WhoAmW 91*
Striem, Kaarl Javier 1961- *WhoWor 91*
Strife, Mary Louise 1959- *WhoAmW 91*
Striffler, David Frank 1922- *WhoAm 90*
Striffolino, Robert 1950- *BioIn 16*
Striganov, Vasilii Mikhailovich 1920-1985 *BioIn 16*
Stright, I. Leonard 1916- *WhoAm 90*
Strigl, Dennis Francis 1946- *St&PR 91*
Strigle, Richard Bush 1939- *St&PR 91*
Strik, Hajo Pieter 1947- *WhoWor 91*
Strika, Gerda Hartl 1942- *BiDrAPA 89*
Strike, Anthony Young 1955- *WhoEmL 91*
Strike, George L. 1930- *St&PR 91*
Striker, Cecil L 1932- *WhoAmA 91*
Striker, Cecil Leopold 1932- *WhoAm 90*
Striker, Gary E. 1934- *WhoAm 90*
Striker, Sandra Darlene *WhoAmW 91*
Striker, Susan 1942- *SmATA 63 [port]*
Strimbu, Victor, Jr. 1932- *WhoAm 90, WhoWor 91*
Strin-Gold, Laurie Michelle 1961- *WhoAmW 91*
Strincevich, Nick 1915- *Ballpl 90*
Strindberg, August 1849-1912 *BioIn 16, WorAlBi, WrPh*
Strindberg, Johan August 1849-1912 *DcScanL*
Strindberg, Madeleine *BioIn 16*
Strindberg, Madeleine 1955- *BiDWomA*
Striner, Herbert Edward 1922- *WhoAm 90*
String, John F. 1946- *WhoAm 90*
Stringer, A. Wendell 1942- *WhoSSW 91*
Stringer, Ann *NewYTBS 90*
Stringer, Ann 1918-1990 *BioIn 16*
Stringer, Arthur 1874-1950 *DcLB 92 [port], TwCLC 37 [port]*
Stringer, David Walter 1961- *St&PR 91*
Stringer, Earl Dwayne 1942- *St&PR 91*
Stringer, Howard *BioIn 16*
Stringer, Howard 1942- *St&PR 91, WhoAm 90, WhoWor 91*
Stringer, Loren Frank 1925- *WhoAm 90*
Stringer, Lou 1917- *Ballpl 90*
Stringer, Mary Evelyn 1921- *WhoAm 90, WhoAmA 91*
Stringer, Terrance Lee 1941- *St&PR 91*
Stringfellow, John 1779-1883 *BioIn 16*
Stringfellow, John Henry 1819-1905 *AmLegL*
Stringfellow, Tom Lynn 1953- *WhoSSW 91*
Stringfellow, William George 1952- *WhoSSW 91*
Stringfield, Charles David 1939- *WhoAm 90, WhoSSW 91*
Stringfield, Clarence 1903-1976 *MusmAFA*
Stringfield, Hezz, Jr. 1921- *WhoAm 90*
Stringham, Jack Fred, II 1946- *St&PR 91, WhoAm 90*
Stringham, James A 1907- *BiDrAPA 89*
Stringham, James H. 1937- *St&PR 91*
Stringham, Luther Winters 1915- *WhoAm 90*
Stripe, James T 1932- *BiDrAPA 89*
Stripling, Hortense M. 1950- *WhoHisp 91*
Stripling, Robert O. 1915- *BioIn 16*
Stripling, Rosanne 1944- *WhoSSW 91*
Stripp, Alan 1924- *IntWWM 90*
Stripp, Joe 1903- *Ballpl 90*
Strippelhoff, Henry August 1910- *St&PR 91*
Strisik, Paul 1918- *WhoAm 90, WhoAmA 91*
Stritch, Clifford Francis, Jr. 1947- *St&PR 91*
Stritch, Elaine *BioIn 16*
Stritch, Elaine 1926- *WhoAm 90, WorAlBi*
Strite, Joseph O 1925- *BiDrAPA 89*
Strite, L. Gerald *St&PR 91*
Strite, Lewis Edgar 1920- *St&PR 91*
Strittmater, Richard Christian 1955- *WhoE 91*
Strittmater, Victoria Moulton 1954- *WhoE 91*
Strittmatter, Cornelius Frederick, IV 1926- *WhoAm 90, WhoSSW 91*
Strittmatter, Eva 1930- *EncCoWW*
Strittmatter, Peter Albert 1939- *WhoAm 90*
Strittmatter, Walter Edward 1921- *St&PR 91*
Strizic, Mark 1928- *WhoWor 91*
Stro, Mary Anne 1943- *WhoAmW 91*
Strobach, Lothar 1940- *WhoWor 91*
Strobel, Charles F, III *BiDrAPA 89*
Strobel, David Allen 1942- *WhoAm 90*
Strobel, Edward Henry 1855-1908 *BioIn 16*
Strobel, Eric Cameron *WhoAm 90*
Strobel, Fredric Andrew 1935- *WhoAm 90*
Strobel, Howard Austin 1920- *WhoAm 90*
Strobel, John Robert 1927- *St&PR 91*
Strobel, Martin Jack 1940- *St&PR 91, WhoAm 90*
Strobel, Norman Stewart 1944- *St&PR 91*
Strobel, Roddy Marlene *BiDrAPA 89*
Strobel, Shirley Holcomb 1929- *WhoAmW 91*
Strobel, Thomas Richard *BiDrAPA 89*
Strobell, Ella *BioIn 16*
Strober, Lisa Raymon *BiDrAPA 89*
Strober, Samuel 1940- *WhoAm 90*
Strober, Warren 1937- *WhoAm 90*
Strobl, Bernd Karl 1953- *WhoWor 91*
Strobl, Reiner Maria 1942- *WhoWor 91*
Stroble, Colette Mary Houle 1947- *WhoAmW 91*
Stroble, Francis Anthony 1930- *St&PR 91, WhoAm 90*
Stroble, Willie Lee, Jr. 1958- *WhoSSW 91*
Strobos, Semon Gerard 1949- *WhoSSW 91*
Strobos, Tina B 1920- *BiDrAPA 89*
Strocchia-Rivera, Lenore 1959- *WhoAmW 91*
Strock, Henry 1925- *St&PR 91*
Strock, Herbert L. 1918- *BioIn 16*
Strock, Herbert Leonard 1918- *WhoAm 90*
Strock, James Martin 1956- *WhoAm 90, WhoWor 91*
Strode, Jan M 1951- *ODwPR 91*
Strode, Joseph Arlin 1946- *WhoWor 91*
Strode, Steven Wayne 1949- *WhoSSW 91*
Strode, W Stevens *BiDrAPA 89*
Strode, William Hall, III 1937- *WhoAm 90*
Strode, Woody 1914- *DrBlPA 90*
Strodel, Adrienne Macatee 1962- *WhoAmW 91*
Strodel, Robert Carl 1930- *WhoAm 90*
Stroebel, Richard H. 1929- *St&PR 91*
Stroebele, Wolfgang Johann 1948- *WhoWor 91*
Stroecker, William G. 1920- *St&PR 91*
Stroeckx, August 1953- *WhoWor 91*
Stroeher, Roy Edgar 1929- *St&PR 91*
Stroesenreuther, George Dale 1954- *WhoWor 91*
Stroessner, Alfredo *BioIn 16*
Stroessner, Alfredo 1912- *WhoWor 91*
Stroessner, Robert Joseph 1942- *WhoAmA 91*
Stroetmann, Karl Antonius 1944- *WhoWor 91*
Strogoff, Alfred 1928- *St&PR 91, WhoAm 90*
Stroh, Charles 1943- *WhoAmA 91*
Stroh, John W. *St&PR 91*
Stroh, Oscar Henry 1908- *WhoWor 91*
Strohan, James Michael 1946- *St&PR 91*
Strohbehn, John Walter 1936- *WhoAm 90*
Strohecker, Ethel 1913- *St&PR 91*
Strohecker, H. Ross 1913- *St&PR 91*
Strohecker, James W. 1957- *ODwPR 91*
Strohl, James A. 1937- *St&PR 91*
Strohl, Lowell K. 1937- *St&PR 91*
Strohm, David L. 1951- *St&PR 91*
Strohm, Michael D. 1951- *St&PR 91*
Strohm, Paul Holzworth, Jr. 1938- *WhoAm 90*
Strohm, Robert Dean 1945- *WhoSSW 91*
Strohm, Thomas Gregory 1949- *St&PR 91*
Strohmayer, John 1946- *Ballpl 90*
Strohmeyer, John 1924- *WhoAm 90*
Strohschneider-Kohrs, Ingrid 1922- *WhoWor 91*
Stroik, E.R. 1928- *St&PR 91*
Strojny, Mariano 1906- *WhoWor 91*
Stroke, George Wilhelm 1924- *WhoWor 91*
Stroke, Hinko Henry 1927- *WhoAm 90*
Stroker, Claire 1951- *BiDrAPA 89*
Stroker, Elisabeth 1928- *WhoWor 91*
Strom, Brent 1948- *Ballpl 90*
Strom, David Hugh 1913- *WhoAm 90*
Strom, Elizabeth Ann 1965- *WhoAmW 91*
Strom, Frederick W. 1939- *St&PR 91*
Strom, Gordon H. 1914-1989 *BioIn 16*
Strom, Gunnar Olof Fredrik 1922- *WhoWor 91*
Strom, John Christoph 1931- *St&PR 91*
Strom, Julie Kay 1947- *WhoAmW 91*
Strom, Lyle Elmer 1925- *WhoAm 90*
Strom, Mark Neal 1947- *WhoSSW 91*
Strom, Shirley Longeteig 1931- *WhoAmW 91*
Strom, Stephen Eric 1942- *WhoAm 90*
Strom-Paikin, Joyce Elizabeth 1946- *WhoAmW 91, WhoWrEP 89*
Stroman, Carolyn A. 1945- *WhoE 91*
Stroman, Patricia Ann Harris 1953- *WhoAmW 91*
Stromberg, Andrew Melvin *BiDrAPA 89*
Stromberg, Anne B. *WhoAmW 91*
Stromberg, Arthur H. 1928- *St&PR 91*
Stromberg, Arthur Harold 1928- *WhoAm 90*
Stromberg, Asta *PenDiDA 89*
Stromberg, Edvard 1872-1946 *PenDiDA 89*
Stromberg, Eric *PenDiDA 89*
Stromberg, Gerda Helga Elisabeth 1879-1960 *PenDiDA 89*
Stromberg, Gregory 1948- *WhoEmL 91, WhoWor 91*
Stromberg, Gustaf 1882-1962 *EncO&P 3*
Stromberg, John 1853-1902 *OxCPMus*
Stromberg, Juhani Rikhard 1953- *WhoWor 91*
Stromberg, Patricia Roberts 1932- *WhoAmW 91*
Stromberg, Roland Nelson 1916- *WhoAm 90*
Stromberger, Theodore Leo 1905- *WhoWrEP 89*
Strome, Charles Bowman, Jr. 1928- *St&PR 91, WhoAm 90*
Strome, Stephen 1945- *St&PR 91, WhoAm 90*
Stromgren, Bengt Georg Daniel 1908-1987 *BioIn 16*
Stromgren, Erik 1909- *BiDrAPA 89*
Stromholm, Stig Fredrik 1931- *WhoWor 91*
Strommen, Linda 1957- *IntWWM 90*
Stromnes, Frode Jens 1937- *WhoWor 91*
Stromquist, Walter Rees 1949- *WhoE 91*
Stromsness, John E. 1932- *St&PR 91*
Stromsoe, Erik 1943- *WhoWor 91*
Stromstedt, Bo Eugen 1929- *WhoWor 91*
Stronach, Frank *BioIn 16, WhoAm 90*
Stronberg, Michael David 1942- *St&PR 91*
Stronczer, John J. 1937- *St&PR 91*
Strone, Michael Jonathan 1953- *WhoE 91*
Strong, Alda 1911- *WhoAmW 91*
Strong, Anna L. 1885-1970 *BioAmW*
Strong, Anna Louise 1885-1970 *FemiCLE*
Strong, Anthony John 1941- *WhoWor 91*
Strong, Arturo Carrillo 1930- *WhoHisp 91*
Strong, Augustus 1836-1921 *BioIn 16*
Strong, Barbara Irene 1935- *WhoAmW 91*
Strong, Benjamin 1872-1928 *EncABHB 7 [port]*
Strong, Bethany J. 1906- *WhoWrEP 89*
Strong, Bethany June 1906- *WhoAmW 91, WhoWor 91*
Strong, Beverly Jean 1927- *WhoAmA 91*
Strong, C.W., Jr. 1929- *St&PR 91*
Strong, Caleb 1745-1819 *BioIn 16*
Strong, Carolyn Jean 1947- *WhoAmW 91*
Strong, Carolyn Ray 1951- *WhoAmW 91*
Strong, Charles *AuBYP 90*
Strong, Charles Ralph 1938- *WhoAmA 91*
Strong, Charles Stanley 1906- *AuBYP 90*
Strong, Cornelia L. Van R. *BioIn 16*
Strong, Damaris *BiDEWW, FemiCLE*
Strong, Donald Russell 1931- *WhoSSW 91*
Strong, Earl Poe 1910- *WhoWor 91*

Strong, Edward W. *NewYTBS 90*
Strong, Edward W. 1901-1990 *BioIn 16*
Strong, Gary Eugene 1944- *WhoAm 90*
Strong, Gay 1930- *WhoAmW 91*
Strong, George Gordon 1947- *St&PR 91*
Strong, George Gordon, Jr. 1947- *WhoEmL 91, WhoWor 91*
Strong, George Hotham 1926- *St&PR 91*
Strong, George Templeton 1820-1875 *BioIn 16*
Strong, Geri *BioIn 16*
Strong, Harry M. 1918- *St&PR 91*
Strong, Henry 1923- *WhoAm 90*
Strong, Henry K. 1798-1860 *AmLegL*
Strong, Jack Perry 1928- *WhoAm 90*
Strong, Janet Konhaus *WhoWrEP 89*
Strong, Joan 1951- *WhoAmW 91*
Strong, John David 1936- *St&PR 91, WhoAm 90*
Strong, John Van Rensselaer 1912- *WhoE 91*
Strong, John William 1935- *WhoAm 90*
Strong, Josiah 1847-1916 *BioIn 16*
Strong, Julia Helen 1954- *WhoSSW 91*
Strong, Ken 1906-1979 *Ballpl 90*
Strong, Kenneth William Dobson 1900-1982 *DcNaB 1981*
Strong, Laura Marie 1963- *WhoAmW 91*
Strong, Lawrence Franklin 1940- *St&PR 91*
Strong, Leonard V. *BioIn 16*
Strong, Leslie 1953- *WhoAmA 91*
Strong, Louise Connally 1944- *WhoAmW 91*
Strong, Maggie *BioIn 16*
Strong, Marcella Lee 1954- *WhoAmW 91*
Strong, Maurice F. *BioIn 16*
Strong, Mervyn Stuart 1924- *WhoAm 90*
Strong, Moses McCure 1810-1894 *AmLegL*
Strong, Pat *AuBYP 90*
Strong, Patience *ConAu 132*
Strong, Paul Joseph 1947- *St&PR 91*
Strong, Peter Thomas *BiDrAPA 89*
Strong, Robert George 1916- *WhoWor 91*
Strong, Robert S. 1949- *St&PR 91, WhoAm 90*
Strong, Roy Colin 1935- *WhoWor 91*
Strong, Susan Clancey 1939- *WhoAmW 91*
Strong, Ted *Ballpl 90*
Strong, Warren Robert 1933- *WhoAm 90*
Strong, Wendi *ODwPR 91*
Strong, William *BioIn 16*
Strong, William James 1934- *WhoAm 90*
Strong, William L. *St&PR 91*
Strong, Willis A 1902- *BiDrAPA 89*
Strong-Cuevas, Elizabeth 1929- *WhoAmW 91, WhoE 91*
Strong-Tidman, Virginia Adele 1947- *WhoAmW 91, WhoSSW 91*
Stronge, William James, Jr. 1937- *WhoWor 91*
Stronghilos, Carol *WhoAmA 91*
Strongin, Ira Scott *BiDrAPA 89*
Strongin, Theodore 1918- *WhoAm 90*
Strongin-Katz, Martha *PenDiMP*
Strongrich, Andrew L. 1928- *St&PR 91*
Stronska, Anna 1931- *EncCoWW*
Stronski, Victor 1932- *WhoAm 90*
Stronz, Michelle Marie 1957- *WhoAmW 91*
Stroo, Hans H *BiDrAPA 89*
Stroock, Daniel Wyler 1940- *WhoAm 90*
Stroock, Mark Edwin, II 1922- *WhoAm 90*
Stroock, Thomas Frank 1925- *WhoAm 90, WhoWor 91*
Stroomer, Kathryn Paulette 1949- *WhoAmW 91*
Stroop, Joseph E. *ODwPR 91*
Stroop, Jurgen 1895-1951 *BioIn 16*
Strople, Peter W. *St&PR 91*
Strosahl, William 1910- *WhoAmA 91*
Strosahl, William Austin 1910- *WhoAm 90*
Stroscio, Michael Anthony 1949- *WhoAm 90*
Strosnider, Lloyd N. 1936- *St&PR 91*
Stross, Howard Francis 1948- *WhoEmL 91*
Stross, Jeoffrey Knight 1941- *WhoAm 90*
Stross, Raymond 1916-1988 *BioIn 16*
Strother, Arnold F 1933- *BiDrAPA 89*
Strother, Arnold Franklin 1933- *WhoSSW 91*
Strother, Barbara Jacobs 1935- *WhoSSW 91*
Strother, Joseph Willis 1933- *WhoAmA 91*
Strother, Lane Howard 1945- *WhoEmL 91*
Strother, Lester James 1925- *WhoWrEP 89*
Strother, Pat Wallace 1929- *WhoAmW 91*
Strother, Virginia Vaughn 1920- *WhoAmA 91*
Strothman, Eleanor Shawfield Jacobs 1940- *WhoAmW 91*
Strothman, James Edward 1939- *WhoAm 90*
Strothman, Wendy Jo 1950- *WhoAm 90, WhoAmW 91*
Strothmann, Fred 1880-1958 *WhoAmA 91N*
Strotman, Stanley W. 1922- *St&PR 91*
Strottman, Robert Edward 1932- *St&PR 91*
Strotz, Robert H. 1922- *St&PR 91*
Strotz, Robert Henry 1922- *WhoAm 90*
Strouce, Richard Arnold 1933- *WhoAm 90*
Strouch, Stanley I. 1940- *St&PR 91*
Stroud, Bill *BioIn 16*
Stroud, Cassandra India 1960- *WhoAmW 91, WhoSSW 91*
Stroud, Drew McCord 1944- *WhoWrEP 89*
Stroud, Ed 1939- *Ballpl 90*
Stroud, J. B., Jr. 1944- *WhoSSW 91*
Stroud, James Stanley 1915- *WhoAm 90*
Stroud, Joe Hinton 1936- *St&PR 91, WhoAm 90*
Stroud, John A 1921- *BiDrAPA 89*
Stroud, John Fred, Jr. 1931- *WhoAm 90*
Stroud, Joseph E., Jr. 1951- *WhoEmL 91*
Stroud, Junius Brutus, III 1929- *WhoSSW 91*
Stroud, Mary E T 1927- *BiDrAPA 89*
Stroud, Meg Danielson 1955- *WhoAmW 91*
Stroud, Morris W. 1913-1990 *BioIn 16*
Stroud, Peter Anthony 1921- *WhoAm 90, WhoAmA 91*
Stroud, Richard Hamilton 1918- *WhoAm 90*
Stroud, Robert Edward 1934- *WhoAm 90*
Stroud, Sailor 1885-1970 *Ballpl 90*
Stroud, Sally Dawley 1947- *WhoSSW 91*
Stroud, William A. 1920- *St&PR 91*
Stroud, William Harvey 1942- *WhoAm 90*
Strougal, Lubomir 1924- *WhoWor 91*
Strougal, Patricia Greganti 1939- *WhoSSW 91*
Strougo, Robert 1943- *WhoE 91*
Stroup, Elizabeth Faye 1939- *WhoAm 90, WhoAmW 91*
Stroup, Kala Mays *WhoAm 90, WhoAmW 91*
Stroup, Larry Dale 1942- *St&PR 91*
Stroup, Margaret Ann 1939- *WhoAmW 91*
Stroup, Ray Bernard 1942- *St&PR 91*
Stroup, Richard Lyndell 1943- *WhoAm 90*
Stroup, Stanley S. 1944- *St&PR 91*
Stroup, Stanley Stephenson 1944- *WhoAm 90*
Stroupe, Henry Smith 1914- *WhoAm 90*
Stroupe, William Edward 1943- *WhoWrEP 89*
Strouse, Carol Louise Kirchman 1947- *WhoAmW 91*
Strouse, Charles 1928- *OxCPMus, WhoAm 90, WorAlBi*
Strouse, Dorothy 1901-1989 *BioIn 16*
Strouse, Joseph George 1945- *St&PR 91*
Strouse, Thomas Benjamin 1958- *BiDrAPA 89*
Strout, Arthur Edwards 1935- *WhoE 91*
Strout, Richard L 1898-1990 *ConAu 132, CurBio 90N, NewYTBS 90 [port]*
Strout, Richard Lee 1898-1990 *BioIn 16*
Strout, Richard Robert 1932- *WhoSSW 91*
Strout, Sewall Cushing, Jr. 1923- *WhoAm 90*
Strout, Steven Brian 1957- *WhoSSW 91*
Strover, Russell G. 1937- *St&PR 91*
Strow-Piccolo, Lynne 1947- *IntWWM 90*
Strowger, Almon Brown 1839-1902 *BioIn 16*
Strowger, Wade *St&PR 91*
Stroyd, Arthur Heister, Jr. 1945- *WhoEmL 91*
Stroyman, Roland L. 1924- *St&PR 91*
Stroynowski, Juliusz 1919- *ConAu 132*
Strozdas, Jerome Mark 1953- *WhoEmL 91*
Strozeski, Charles 1962- *WhoWrEP 89*
Strozier, Robert Edward 1934- *WhoSSW 91*
Strozzi, Alessandra di Filippo Macinghi 1407-1471 *EncCoWW*
Strozzi, Barbara 1619- *BioIn 16*
Strozzi, Bernardo 1581-1644 *IntDcAA 90*
Strozzi, Lorenza 1514-1591 *EncCoWW*
Strub, Armin A. 1937- *WhoWor 91*
Strub, Christopher Michael 1959- *WhoSSW 91*
Strubbe, John Lewis 1921- *WhoAm 90*
Strubbe, Thomas R. 1940- *St&PR 91, WhoAm 90*
Strubel, Ella Doyle 1940- *WhoAmW 91*
Strubel, Richard Perry 1939- *WhoAm 90*
Strubelt, Wendelin 1943- *WhoWor 91*
Struble, George R. 1836- *AmLegL*
Struble, Steve *AuBYP 90*
Struble, Sue Ann Rudolph *WhoAmW 91*
Struchen, J. Maurice 1920- *St&PR 91*
Struck, Ann Marie 1955- *WhoEmL 91*
Struck, David Carl 1937- *St&PR 91*
Struck, Hermann 1876-1944 *BioIn 16*
Struck, Karin 1947- *EncCoWW*
Struck, Norma Johansen *WhoAmA 91*
Struck, Norma Johansen 1929- *WhoE 91*
Struck-by-the-Ree 1804-1888 *WhNaAH*
Struckmeyer, Frederick Christian, Jr. 1912- *WhoAm 90*
Strudler, Robert J. 1942- *St&PR 91*
Strudler, Robert Jacob 1942- *WhoAm 90, WhoSSW 91*
Strudwick, Dorothy J. 1918- *WhoWrEP 89*
Struebing, Robert Virgil 1919- *WhoAm 90*
Struelens, Michel Maurice Joseph Georges 1928- *WhoAm 90*
Strugatch, Ellen 1962- *WhoSSW 91*
Strugatsky, Arkady 1925- *RGTwCSF*
Strugatsky, Boris 1933- *RGTwCSF*
Struggles, John E. 1913- *St&PR 91*
Struick, Thomas Wynand 1939- *WhoWor 91*
Struik, Dirk Jan 1894- *BioIn 16, WhoE 91*
Strukoff, Rudolf Stephen 1935- *WhoWor 91*
Strul, Gene M. 1927- *WhoSSW 91, WhoWor 91*
Strull, Gene 1929- *WhoAm 90*
Strull, Steven H. *St&PR 91*
Strull, Wm. 1916- *St&PR 91*
Strulowitz, Jack Joel 1942- *WhoWor 91*
Strum, Jay Gerson 1938- *WhoAm 90*
Strum, Judy May 1938- *WhoE 91*
Strum, Lonny Robert 1952- *WhoAm 90*
Strum, Marvin Kent 1943- *WhoAm 90*
Strumingher, Laura Sharon 1945- *WhoAm 90*
Strumpf, Andrea J *BiDrAPA 89*
Strung, Robert Daniel 1950- *BiDrAPA 89*
Strunk, Amos 1889-1979 *Ballpl 90*
Strunk, Carl A. 1938- *St&PR 91*
Strunk, Gary Arnold 1940- *St&PR 91*
Strunk, Herbert Julian 1891- *WhoAmA 91N*
Strunk, Marvin R. 1923- *St&PR 91*
Strunk, Michael Joseph 1949- *St&PR 91*
Strunk, Orlo C. *WhoWrEP 89*
Strunk, Orlo Christopher, Jr. 1925- *WhoAm 90*
Strunk, Robert Keen, II 1951- *WhoE 91*
Strunk, Rosemary 1959- *WhoAmW 91*
Strunk, Steven 1943- *IntWWM 90*
Strunz, Jorge *NewAgMG*
Strupp, David John 1938- *WhoAm 90*
Strupp, Hans H. *BioIn 16*
Strupp, Hans Hermann 1921- *WhoAm 90*
Strupp, Jacqueline Virginia 1963- *WhoAmW 91*
Struppeck, Jules 1915- *WhoAmA 91*
Struss, Andrea Lydia *BiDrAPA 89*
Struther, Jan 1901-1953 *BioIn 16, FemiCLE*
Struthers, Alan M., Jr. 1947- *ODwPR 91*
Struthers, Archibald Gold 1928- *St&PR 91*
Struthers, Barbara Joan 1940- *WhoAmW 91*
Struthers, Deborah Mary 1952- *WhoAmW 91*
Struthers, John Joseph 1953- *WhoWor 91*
Struthers, Sally 1948- *WorAlBi*
Struthers, Sally Anne 1948- *WhoAm 90*
Strutner, Raymond James 1934- *St&PR 91*
Strutt, Arthur Charles 1878-1973 *EncO&P 3*
Strutt, Elizabeth *FemiCLE*
Strutt, John William 1842-1919 *EncO&P 3, EncPaPR 91*
Strutt, Robert John 1875-1947 *EncO&P 3, EncPaPR 91*
Strutton, Larry D. 1940- *WhoAm 90*
Strutton, Larry Dean 1940- *St&PR 91*
Strutton, Robert James 1948- *WhoWor 91*
Strutz, George Arthur 1932- *St&PR 91, WhoAm 90*
Strutz, William Charles 1945- *WhoEmL 91*
Struve, Friedrich G. W. Von 1793-1864 *WorAlBi*
Struve, Friedrich Georg Wilhelm von 1793-1864 *BioIn 16*
Struve, Guy Miller 1943- *WhoAm 90, WhoWor 91*
Struve, O. W. 1819-1905 *BioIn 16*
Struve, Otto von 1897-1963 *BioIn 16*
Struve, Otto W. 1819-1905 *BioIn 16*
Struve, Walter 1935- *WhoWor 91*
Struve, William Walter 1936- *WhoAmA 91*
Struyk, Raymond Jay 1944- *WhoAm 90, WhoE 91*
Struyk, Robert John 1932- *WhoAm 90*
Struys, Wally Ronald 1942- *WhoWor 91*
Struzinski, Allan David 1954- *St&PR 91*
Strychalski, Irene Dorothea 1948- *WhoAmW 91*
Stryckers, Jos Marie Theodore 1921- *WhoWor 91*
Stryer, Lubert 1938- *WhoAm 90*
Strygler, Harry Sam 1918- *St&PR 91*
Stryjkowski, Julian 1905- *ConAu 30NR*
Stryker, Charles William 1947- *WhoAm 90*
Stryker, Derek Jan 1940- *St&PR 91*
Stryker, John E. 1923- *St&PR 91*
Stryker, Richard Ripley, Jr. 1948- *WhoAm 90*
Stryker, Sheldon 1924- *WhoAm 90*
Stryker, Steven C. 1944- *St&PR 91*
Stryker, Steven Charles 1944- *WhoAm 90*
Stryker, William H. 1925- *ODwPR 91*
Stryker, William I 1929- *BiDrAPA 89*
Stryker-Rodda, Kenn 1903-1990 *ConAu 132*
Stuard, James E. 1934- *St&PR 91*
Stuart, Alexander Hugh Holmes 1807-1891 *BiDrUSE 89*
Stuart, Alice Melissa 1957- *WhoAmW 91, WhoE 91, WhoEmL 91, WhoWor 91*
Stuart, Andrew 1812-1891 *DcCanB 12*
Stuart, Andrew B *BiDrAPA 89*
Stuart, Andrew Woodson 1965- *WhoE 91*
Stuart, Anne Elizabeth 1956- *WhoAmW 91, WhoWrEP 89*
Stuart, Arbella 1576-1615 *FemiCLE*
Stuart, Augusta Amelia *FemiCLE*
Stuart, Beverly Ann 1937- *WhoAmW 91*
Stuart, Bruce L. 1938- *St&PR 91*
Stuart, C E 1907-1947 *EncO&P 3*
Stuart, Carol *BioIn 16*
Stuart, Carole 1941- *St&PR 91*
Stuart, Charles *BioIn 16*
Stuart, Charles E. 1907-1947 *EncPaPR 91*
Stuart, Charles Edward 1720-1788 *BioIn 16*
Stuart, Charles Edward 1850-1889 *AmLegL*
Stuart, D. Riley 1927- *St&PR 91*
Stuart, Dabney 1937- *DcLB 105 [port], WhoAm 90, WhoWrEP 89*
Stuart, David *AuBYP 90, BioIn 16, WhoAmA 91*
Stuart, David B. 1929- *St&PR 91*
Stuart, Derald Archie 1925- *WhoAm 90*
Stuart, Diana *WhoWrEP 89*
Stuart, Dick 1932- *Ballpl 90*
Stuart, Don A. *MajTwCW*
Stuart, Donald *TwCCr&M 91*
Stuart, Donald Alexander 1944- *WhoAmA 91*
Stuart, Donald E. 1925- *St&PR 91*
Stuart, Dorothy Mae 1933- *WhoAmW 91*
Stuart, Edwin J. 1936- *St&PR 91*
Stuart, Elbridge A. 1856-1944 *WorAlBi*
Stuart, Eleanor 1901-1977 *OxCCanT*
Stuart, Elizabeth *BiDEWW*
Stuart, Esme 1851-1934 *FemiCLE*
Stuart, Gary Miller 1940- *WhoAm 90*
Stuart, Gene *AuBYP 90*
Stuart, George E. *AuBYP 90*
Stuart, Gerard William, Jr. 1939- *WhoWor 91*
Stuart, Gilbert 1755-1828 *IntDcAA 90, WorAlBi*
Stuart, Gloria 1909?- *BioIn 16*
Stuart, Granville 1834-1918 *WhNaAH*
Stuart, H James 1930- *BiDrAPA 89*
Stuart, Harold C. 1912- *St&PR 91*
Stuart, Harold Cutliff 1912- *WhoAm 90*
Stuart, Ian *AuBYP 90, MajTwCW, TwCCr&M 91*
Stuart, Ian 1922-1987 *BioIn 16*
Stuart, Ian 1927- *ConAu 30NR, TwCCr&M 91*
Stuart, J. E. B. 1833-1864 *WorAlBi*
Stuart, James 1713-1788 *PenDiDA 89*
Stuart, James Alexander 1925- *St&PR 91*
Stuart, James Fortier 1928- *WhoAm 90*
Stuart, Jane 1942- *ConAu 31NR, LiHiK*
Stuart, Jesse 1906-1984 *ConAu 31NR, DcLB 102 [port]*
Stuart, Jesse 1907-1984 *LiHiK*
Stuart, Jesse Hilton 1907-1984 *AuBYP 90*
Stuart, Joan Martha 1945- *WhoAmW 91, WhoEmL 91*
Stuart, John 1718-1784 *WhNaAH*
Stuart, John 1936- *St&PR 91*
Stuart, John James, Jr. 1939- *St&PR 91*
Stuart, John Leighton 1876-1962 *BioIn 16*
Stuart, John M. 1927- *WhoAm 90, WhoWor 91*
Stuart, John McHugh, Jr. 1916- *WhoAm 90*
Stuart, Johnny 1901-1970 *Ballpl 90*
Stuart, Joseph Martin 1932- *WhoAm 90, WhoAmA 91*
Stuart, Julia Davis 1910-1990 *BioIn 16*
Stuart, Kenneth James *WhoAmA 91*
Stuart, Kenneth James 1905- *WhoAm 90*
Stuart, Kiel 1951- *WhoWrEP 89*
Stuart, Lance Bivens 1952- *WhoWor 91*
Stuart, Leonard A. *St&PR 91*
Stuart, Leslie 1864-1928 *OxCPMus*
Stuart, Louisa 1757-1851 *BioIn 16, FemiCLE*
Stuart, Lyle 1922- *WhoAm 90*
Stuart, Margaret *ConAu 31NR*
Stuart, Marie *EncCoWW*
Stuart, Marie Jean 1943- *WhoE 91*
Stuart, Marilynn Rae 1950- *BiDrAPA 89*
Stuart, Marjorie Louise 1926- *WhoAmW 91, WhoE 91, WhoWor 91*
Stuart, Marlin 1918- *Ballpl 90*
Stuart, Marty *WhoNeCM [port]*
Stuart, Mary *WhoAm 90*
Stuart, Michelle 1935?- *BiDWomA*

Stuart, Michelle 1940- *WhoAmA 91*
Stuart, Michelle Rae 1940- *WhoE 91*
Stuart, Murray 1933- *WhoWor 91*
Stuart, Norton A. 1935- *St&PR 91*
Stuart, Pamela Bruce 1949- *WhoE 91, WhoEmL 91*
Stuart, Pamela Elizabeth 1956- *WhoAmW 91*
Stuart, Peter 1924- *WhoWor 91*
Stuart, Preston Alan 1952- *WhoE 91*
Stuart, Robert 1921- *St&PR 91, WhoAm 90*
Stuart, Robert Crampton 1938- *WhoAm 90*
Stuart, Robert Douglas, Jr. 1916- *WhoAm 90, WhoWor 91*
Stuart, Roy O. 1914- *St&PR 91*
Stuart, Ruth McEnery 1849-1917 *BioAmW*
Stuart, Sally Elizabeth 1940- *WhoWrEP 89*
Stuart, Sandra Joyce 1950- *WhoAmW 91, WhoEmL 91, WhoWor 91*
Stuart, Scott Philip 1961- *BiDrAPA 89*
Stuart, Sidney *TwCCr&M 91*
Stuart, Signe Nelson *WhoAmA 91*
Stuart, Spencer R. 1922- *St&PR 91*
Stuart, Suzanne Marie 1949- *WhoE 91, WhoSSW 91*
Stuart, Thomas B. *AmLegL*
Stuart, Thomas R. 1944- *St&PR 91*
Stuart, Valerie Ann 1957- *WhoE 91*
Stuart, Virginia Elaine 1953- *WhoWrEP 89*
Stuart, Walter Bynum 1922- *St&PR 91*
Stuart, Walter Bynum, III 1922- *WhoAm 90*
Stuart, Walter Bynum, IV 1946- *WhoWor 91*
Stuart, William Corwin 1920- *WhoAm 90*
Stuart, William David 1932- *WhoE 91, WhoWor 91*
Stuart, William J. 1951- *St&PR 91*
Stuart-Buttle, Carol Monica Ann 1955- *WhoE 91*
Stuart-DeCrane, Karen *BioIn 16*
Stuart-Stubbs, Basil Frederick 1930- *WhoAm 90*
Stub, Ambrosius 1705-1758 *DcScanL*
Stubbart, Wanda Estelle 1930- *WhoAmW 91*
Stubbe, Dorothy Ella *BiDrAPA 89*
Stubbe, JoAnne *WhoAm 90*
Stubben, Dolus Jane 1951- *WhoEmL 91*
Stubbins, George Edward, Sr. 1940- *St&PR 91*
Stubbins, Hugh 1912- *BioIn 16*
Stubbins, Hugh A., Jr. 1912- *WhoAm 90*
Stubblebine, James H. 1920-1987 *BioIn 16*
Stubblebine, James Harvey 1920- *WhoAmA 91*
Stubblebine, James Malcolm 1920- *BiDrAPA 89*
Stubblebine, William Craig 1936- *WhoAm 90*
Stubblefield, Austin Peay 1926- *St&PR 91*
Stubblefield, David E. 1937- *St&PR 91*
Stubblefield, David Edward 1937- *WhoAm 90*
Stubblefield, Dewey Austin 1937- *St&PR 91*
Stubblefield, Hal S. 1932- *St&PR 91*
Stubblefield, Harold Wayne 1934- *WhoSSW 91*
Stubblefield, Jerry Wayne 1948- *St&PR 91*
Stubblefield, P.K. 1914- *St&PR 91*
Stubblefield, Page Kindred 1914- *WhoAm 90*
Stubblefield, Robert L *BiDrAPA 89*
Stubblefield, Robert LeRoy 1918- *WhoSSW 91*
Stubbs, Daniel Gaie 1940- *WhoWor 91*
Stubbs, Donald Francis 1930- *St&PR 91*
Stubbs, Franklin 1960- *Ballpl 90*
Stubbs, George 1724-1806 *IntDcAA 90, WorAlBi*
Stubbs, Glenn R. 1947- *St&PR 91*
Stubbs, Harold LeRoy 1918- *WhoAm 90*
Stubbs, J. Eugene 1939- *St&PR 91*
Stubbs, James Carlton 1924- *WhoAm 90*
Stubbs, Jan Didra 1937- *WhoAmW 91*
Stubbs, Jean 1926- *TwCCr&M 91*
Stubbs, Joanna 1940- *BioIn 16*
Stubbs, Kendon Lee 1938- *WhoAm 90*
Stubbs, Kerry *BioIn 16*
Stubbs, Linwood L., Jr. 1956- *St&PR 91*
Stubbs, Louise *DrBlPA 90*
Stubbs, Lu 1925- *WhoAmA 91*
Stubbs, Nelson Day 1931- *WhoE 91*
Stubbs, Steven Howard 1938- *St&PR 91*
Stubbs, Timothy John 1960- *WhoE 91*
Stubbs, Walter Roscoe 1858-1929 *AmLegL*
Stubbs, William *BioIn 16*
Stubenhaus, Jay H 1923- *BiDrAPA 89*
Stubenhaus, Jay Hackel 1923- *WhoE 91*
Stubenrauch, Robert *AuBYP 90*
Stuber, Charles William 1931- *WhoAm 90*
Stuber, James William 1947- *St&PR 91*
Stuber, Margaret Lois 1953- *BiDrAPA 89*
Stuber, Marilyn Martha Cook 1930- *WhoSSW 91*
Stuber, William G. 1864-1959 *WorAlBi*
Stuberfield, William 1909- *St&PR 91*
Stubert, Harald Gunnar 1948- *WhoWor 91*
Stubi, Pascal Andre 1954- *WhoWor 91*
Stubing, Peter R 1930- *BiDrAPA 89*
Stubits, Eva Sylvia 1953- *WhoAmW 91*
Stubits, Joseph Stephen 1943- *St&PR 91*
Stuby, Camela 1963- *ODwPR 91*
Stuchins, Carol Mayberry 1946- *WhoAmW 91*
Stuchka, P. L. 1865-1932 *BioIn 16*
Stuchlik, Ludwig 1935- *St&PR 91*
Stuck, Bart William 1946- *WhoE 91*
Stuck, David T. 1924- *St&PR 91*
Stuck, Nelda Marian 1937- *WhoAmW 91*
Stuckart, Wilhelm 1902-1953 *BioIn 16*
Stucke, John F. 1924- *St&PR 91*
Stucke, Kenneth Joseph 1948- *St&PR 91*
Stuckelman, Robert 1932- *St&PR 91*
Stuckeman, H. Campbell 1914- *St&PR 91*
Stuckeman, Herman Campbell 1914- *WhoAm 90*
Stucken, Frank van der *PenDiMP*
Stuckenschmidt, H. H. 1901-1988 *AnObit 1988*
Stucker, Darren Michael 1947- *WhoEmL 91*
Stucker, Gilles A.E. 1947- *St&PR 91*
Stucker, Gilles Alfred Eugene 1947- *WhoAm 90*
Stuckey, Bruce D. 1946- *St&PR 91*
Stuckey, Elma 1907-1988 *BioIn 16*
Stuckey, Helen S. 1959- *WhoAmW 91*
Stuckey, James H. *St&PR 91*
Stuckey, Lindalee Irene 1952- *WhoAmW 91*
Stuckey, Ray David 1959- *St&PR 91*
Stuckey, Robert F 1930- *BiDrAPA 89*
Stuckey, Sheila Costner 1954- *WhoAmW 91, WhoEmL 91*
Stuckey, Walter Jackson 1927- *WhoAm 90*
Stuckey, Williamson Sylvester, III 1958- *WhoSSW 91*
Stucki, Jorg Werner 1942- *WhoWor 91*
Stuckman, Bruce Edward 1959- *WhoSSW 91*
Stuckwisch, Clarence George 1916- *WhoAm 90*
Stucky, James B. 1945- *St&PR 91*
Stucky, Marvin Wayne 1932- *St&PR 91*
Stucky, R Christopher 1942- *BiDrAPA 89*
Stucky, Rolf Andreas 1942- *WhoWor 91*
Stucynski, Susan Moen 1950- *WhoAmW 91*
Studdert-Kennedy, Gerald 1933- *ConAu 131*
Studds, Gerry Eastman 1937- *WhoAm 90, WhoE 91*
Stude, Everett Wilson, Jr. 1939- *WhoAm 90*
Studebaker, Clement 1831-1901 *WorAlBi*
Studebaker, J. W. *ConAu 129*
Studebaker, John M *EncABHB 4 [port]*
Studebaker, John W 1887-1989 *ConAu 129*
Studebaker, John Ward 1887-1989 *BioIn 16*
Studebaker, Joseph Elizah, III 1956- *WhoWrEP 89*
Studebaker, Michael John 1949- *WhoWrEP 89*
Studebaker, Sandra Sue 1952- *WhoAmW 91*
Studebaker, William Vern 1947- *WhoWrEP 89*
Studenski, Eugene Robert *BiDrAPA 89*
Studer, Bruce Allen 1948- *St&PR 91*
Studer, Cheryl 1957- *IntWWM 90*
Studer, Constance Elaine 1942- *WhoWrEP 89*
Studer, Dennis Paul 1948- *St&PR 91*
Studer, Gregory N. 1947- *St&PR 91*
Studer, Richard T. 1927- *St&PR 91*
Studer, Robert *St&PR 91*
Studer, William Joseph 1936- *WhoAm 90*
Studer-Johnson, Marian Kaye 1954- *WhoWrEP 89*
Studier, Eugene Herbert 1940- *WhoAm 90*
Studier, Frederick William 1936- *WhoAm 90*
Studinski, Wendy Lee 1955- *WhoAmW 91*
Studley, Helen Ormson 1937- *WhoAmW 91, WhoWor 91*
Studley, John Edward 1852-1924 *AmLegL*
Studley, Mark J. 1947- *St&PR 91*
Studley, Michael H. 1946- *St&PR 91*
Studner, Alan 1933- *BiDrAPA 89*
Studner, Michael S. 1936- *St&PR 91*
Studness, Charles Michael 1935- *WhoE 91*
Studnicki, Peter 1946- *St&PR 91*
Studstill, Felecia Gayle 1964- *WhoAmW 91*
Studstill, Pamela 1957- *WhoAmA 91*
Studstill, Zack Daniel 1938- *WhoSSW 91*
Studt, Timothy *BioIn 16*
Study, Mary Margaret 1945- *WhoAmW 91*
Study, Robert Smith 1921- *BiDrAPA 89*
Studzinski, Edward Alfred 1949- *St&PR 91*
Stueart, Robert D. *WhoAm 90*
Stuebe, David Charles 1940- *St&PR 91*
Stuebe, John Walter 1949- *St&PR 91*
Stueber, Gustav 1909- *WhoE 91, WhoWor 91*
Stuebgen, William J. 1947- *St&PR 91*
Stueck, Clifford Joseph 1932- *St&PR 91*
Stueck, Lois Elaine 1936- *WhoAmW 91*
Stuecker, Phillip James 1951- *St&PR 91*
Stueland, Dean Theodore 1950- *WhoAm 90*
Stuen, Marcus R *BiDrAPA 89*
Stuermer, Daryl *BioIn 16*
Stuerner, Lienhard 1938- *WhoAm 90*
Stuessi, Keith Allan 1944- *St&PR 91*
Stuessy, Clarence Joseph, Jr. 1943- *WhoSSW 91*
Stuessy, Tod Falor 1943- *WhoAm 90*
Stuewe, Paul 1943- *ConAu 130*
Stufflebean, John Howard 1918- *WhoAm 90*
Stufft, Maynard Ray 1939- *St&PR 91*
Stuhl, Harold Maxwell 1934- *St&PR 91*
Stuhl, Michelle 1957- *WhoAmA 91*
Stuhl, Oskar Paul 1949- *WhoWor 91*
Stuhl, Robert C. *St&PR 91*
Stuhldreher, Donald J. 1935- *St&PR 91*
Stuhlfire, Thomas Albert 1935- *St&PR 91*
Stuhlinger, Ernst 1913- *WhoAm 90*
Stuhlman, Daniel D. 1950- *WhoWrEP 89*
Stuhlmann, Dean Michael 1959- *WhoSSW 91*
Stuhlreyer, Paul A., Jr. 1924- *St&PR 91*
Stuhlreyer, Paul Augustus, III 1952- *WhoAm 90*
Stuhr, David Paul 1938- *WhoAm 90*
Stuhr, Edward Phillip 1905- *WhoAm 90*
Stuhr, Walter M. 1932- *WhoAm 90*
Stuiber, Heinz Werner 1940- *WhoWor 91*
Stuida, William 1877-1959 *WhoAmA 91N*
Stuiver, Minze 1929- *WhoAm 90*
Stukel, James Joseph 1937- *WhoAm 90*
Stukenbroeker, Berthold Karl-Heinz 1945- *WhoWor 91*
Stukes, Donald Alvin 1958- *WhoE 91*
Stukey, Virginia *WhoAmA 91*
Stula, Michael James 1914- *WhoE 91*
Stulberg, Bernard Nathan 1948- *WhoEmL 91*
Stulberg, Burton 1919- *BiDrAPA 89*
Stulberg, Michael V 1944- *BiDrAPA 89*
Stulberg, Neal 1954- *IntWWM 90*
Stulberg, Neal Howard 1954- *WhoAm 90*
Stulce, L. Jefferson 1925- *St&PR 91*
Stuler, Jack 1932- *WhoAmA 91*
Stull, Donald LeRoy 1937- *WhoAm 90*
Stull, G. Alan 1933- *WhoAm 90*
Stull, James L. 1948- *St&PR 91*
Stull, Jean Himrod 1929- *WhoAmA 91*
Stull, Lonnie N. 1939- *St&PR 91*
Stull, Robert J 1935- *WhoAmA 91*
Stull, Sylvia Joyce 1939- *WhoAmW 91*
Stulp, Fred *BiDrAPA 89*
Stulpnagel, Karl Heinrich von 1886-1944 *BioIn 16*
Stults, Dennis Wayne 1942- *WhoAm 90*
Stults, Harold Leland 1905-1990 *BioIn 16*
Stults, Theodore McConnell, II 1937- *St&PR 91*
Stults, Walter Black 1921- *WhoAm 90*
Stultz, John L. 1930- *St&PR 91*
Stultz, Newell Maynard 1933- *WhoAm 90*
Stultz, Richard Thomas 1944- *St&PR 91*
Stum, Kenneth Eugene 1939- *St&PR 91*
Stumbaugh, Everette Don 1937- *WhoAm 90*
Stumbling Bear 1832-1903 *WhNaAH*
Stumbo, Anita Yvonne 1948- *WhoAmW 91*
Stumbo, Gregory D. 1951- *WhoSSW 91*
Stumbo, Helen Luce 1947- *WhoAmW 91*
Stumbo, Richard William, Jr. 1933- *WhoAm 90*
Stumbras, Jerome M. 1933- *St&PR 91*
Stumler, David James 1954- *St&PR 91*
Stump, Bob 1927- *WhoAm 90*
Stump, C. Jeffrey 1956- *St&PR 91*
Stump, Cary Johanson 1948- *WhoEmL 91*
Stump, Charles H. 1925- *St&PR 91*
Stump, Gail Alden 1951- *WhoWrEP 89*
Stump, Jacob E 1923- *BiDrAPA 89*
Stump, John Edward 1934- *WhoAm 90*
Stump, John Sutton 1929- *WhoAm 90*
Stump, M Pamela 1928- *WhoAmA 91*
Stump, Roger Vincent 1946- *St&PR 91*
Stump, Ronald K. *BioIn 16*
Stump, Troy Elwood 1954- *WhoAm 90*
Stump, Weldon Frederick 1915- *St&PR 91*
Stumpe, Warren Robert 1925- *St&PR 91, WhoAm 90*
Stumpf, Bill *PenDiDA 89*
Stumpf, Helmut 1934- *WhoWor 91*
Stumpf, J. *BiDWomA*
Stumpf, John Anthony 1952- *St&PR 91*
Stumpf, Joseph George 1938- *WhoAm 90*
Stumpf, Lowell Clinton 1917- *WhoWor 91*
Stumpf, Michael Howard 1952- *BiDrAPA 89*
Stumpf, Paul Karl 1919- *WhoAm 90*
Stumpf, Robert Marion, II 1947- *WhoEmL 91*
Stumpf, Samuel Enoch 1918- *WhoAm 90*
Stumpf, Suzanne Elizabeth 1958- *IntWWM 90*
Stumpf, William 1936- *ConDes 90*
Stumpo, Carmine DeRogatis 1963- *WhoWrEP 89*
Stumpo, Patrick P. 1954- *BiDrAPA 89*
Stumpp, Charles Frederick 1931- *St&PR 91*
Stundza, Thomas John 1948- *WhoAm 90*
Stunkard, Albert J 1922- *BiDrAPA 89*
Stunkard, Horace W. 1889-1989 *BioIn 16*
Stuntz, Edgar C 1929- *BiDrAPA 89*
Stuntz, Reid Pendleton Fitzhugh 1952- *WhoEmL 91*
Stuntz, Richard Clark 1921- *BiDrAPA 89*
Stup, Janet Anita 1945- *WhoAmW 91*
Stuper, John 1957- *Ballpl 90*
Stupin, Susan Lee 1954- *WhoAmW 91, WhoE 91, WhoEmL 91, WhoWor 91*
Stupp, Robert P. 1930- *St&PR 91*
Stupple, Donna-Marie Kathleen 1945- *WhoWrEP 89*
Sturchio, Jeffrey Louis 1952- *WhoE 91*
Sturdevant, Charles O 1907- *BiDrAPA 89*
Sturdevant, Wayne Alan 1946- *WhoSSW 91*
Sturdevant, William D 1922- *EncO&P 3*
Sturdivant, Frederick David 1937- *WhoWrEP 89*
Sturdivant, Kelly Kemp 1957- *WhoAmW 91*
Sturdivant, Roddy Stephen 1941- *WhoSSW 91*
Sturdivant, Susan 1944- *WhoAmW 91*
Sturdivant, Tom 1930- *Ballpl 90*
Sturge, Michael Dudley 1931- *WhoAm 90*
Sturgeon, Anna Louise 1951- *WhoAmW 91*
Sturgeon, Bobby 1919- *Ballpl 90*
Sturgeon, Charles E. 1928- *St&PR 91*
Sturgeon, Charles Edwin 1928- *WhoAm 90*
Sturgeon, John A. 1940- *St&PR 91*
Sturgeon, John Floyd 1946- *WhoAmA 91*
Sturgeon, Mary C 1943- *WhoAmA 91*
Sturgeon, Theodore 1918- *WorAlBi*
Sturgeon, Theodore 1918-1985 *ConAu 32NR, MajTwCW, RGTwCSF*
Sturges, Darcy Jean 1956- *WhoAmW 91*
Sturges, Hollister *WhoAmA 91*
Sturges, Hollister, III 1939- *WhoAm 90*
Sturges, Jeffrey Robert, Sr. 1947- *St&PR 91*
Sturges, John Eliot 1910- *WhoAm 90*
Sturges, John Siebrand 1939- *WhoAm 90*
Sturges, Michael S 1937- *BiDrAPA 89*
Sturges, Preston *BioIn 16*
Sturges, Stanley G 1929- *BiDrAPA 89*
Sturges, Stephen P 1945- *BiDrAPA 89*
Sturges, Tom *BioIn 16*
Sturges, Wilton, III 1935- *WhoAm 90*
Sturgess, Jeffrey Charles 1948- *St&PR 91*
Sturgess, Thomas W. 1950- *St&PR 91*
Sturgis, Bruce Thomas 1959- *St&PR 91*
Sturgis, Joan *BiDrAPA 89*
Sturgis, Laura Marie 1955- *WhoAmW 91*
Sturgis, Mack Edwin *BiDrAPA 89*
Sturgis, Robert Shaw 1922- *WhoAm 90*
Sturgis, Stokeley *BioIn 16*
Sturgis, William Beaufort 1934- *St&PR 91, WhoAm 90*
Sturgulewski, Arliss 1927- *WhoAmW 91*
Sturhahn, Betty J. 1933- *WhoAmW 91*
Sturkie, Roy D. *St&PR 91*
Sturluson, Snorri 1178-1241 *DcScanL*
Sturm, Angelica 1955- *WhoAmW 91*
Sturm, Donald L. 1932- *WhoAm 90*
Sturm, Douglas Earl 1929- *WhoAm 90*
Sturm, Edith S. 1947- *WhoAmW 91*
Sturm, Frank Conrad 1930- *St&PR 91*
Sturm, George 1930- *IntWWM 90*
Sturm, Glen Mark 1956- *St&PR 91*
Sturm, Hertha 1925- *WhoWor 91*
Sturm, J. C. 1927- *FemiCLE*
Sturm, Johannes Von 1507-1589 *WorAlBi*
Sturm, Lora Rose 1956- *WhoAmW 91*
Sturm, Maxine Shirlee 1934- *WhoAmW 91*
Sturm, Michael Richard 1930- *St&PR 91*
Sturm, Omer O. 1922- *St&PR 91*
Sturm, Ruth Foster 1911- *WhoAmW 91*
Sturman, Eugene 1945- *WhoAmA 91*
Sturman, Eugene Goch 1945- *WhoEmL 91*
Sturman, Jonathan Mark 1943- *St&PR 91*
Sturman, Joseph Benjamin 1937- *St&PR 91*
Sturman, Joseph Howard 1931- *WhoAm 90*
Sturman, Neal Sanford 1944- *WhoE 91*
Sturman, Paul 1943- *IntWWM 90*
Sturman, Reuben *BioIn 16*
Sturman, Robert Harries 1923- *WhoAm 90, WhoWor 91*

Sturms, Arnolds Fricis 1912- *IntWWM 90*
Sturmthal, Adolf Fox *BioIn 16*
Sturner, Michael 1962- *St&PR 91*
Sturnick, Judith Ann 1939- *WhoAm 90, WhoAmW 91, WhoE 91*
Sturrock, Jeremy 1908- *TwCCr&M 91*
Sturrock, Thomas Tracy 1921- *WhoAm 90*
Sturt, George 1863-1927 *BioIn 16*
Sturtevant, Brereton 1921- *WhoAm 90*
Sturtevant, Julian Munson 1908- *WhoAm 90*
Sturtevant, Richard Pearce 1943- *WhoE 91*
Sturtevant, Rolland Lee *BiDrAPA 89*
Sturtevant, William Curtis 1926- *WhoAm 90*
Sturtz, Donald Lee 1933- *WhoSSW 91*
Sturtz, George Stephen 1924- *WhoE 91*
Sturtz, Laura G. 1955- *ODwPR 91*
Sturtz, Theodore Samuel 1958- *St&PR 91*
Sturtz-Davis, Shirley Zampelli 1937- *WhoE 91*
Sturtzel, Jane L. *AuBYP 90*
Sturup, George K *BiDrAPA 89*
Sturza-Scheianu, Constantin 1797-1877 *BioIn 16*
Sturzenacker, Linda M. 1947- *WhoAmW 91*
Sturzenegger, Otto *NewYTBS 90*
Sturzenegger, Otto 1926-1990 *BioIn 16*
Stuscavage, Debora J. 1962- *WhoE 91*
Stusek, Anton 1932- *WhoWor 91*
Stusnick, Madeline Seidelle 1943- *WhoAmW 91*
Stussman, Howard B. *BioIn 16*
Stussy, Maxine Kim 1923- *WhoAmA 91*
Stussy, Peggy J. 1957- *WhoAmW 91*
Stuteville, Elizabeth *BiDEWW*
Stutheit, Lynn Sheryl 1958- *WhoAmW 91*
Stutman, Leonard Jay 1928- *WhoE 91*
Stutman, Nancy 1938- *WhoAmW 91*
Stutsman, Enos 1826-1874 *AmLegL*
Stutt, William C. 1927- *St&PR 91*
Stutt, William Chapman 1927- *WhoAm 90*
Stutts, Elbert Harrison 1947- *WhoWor 91*
Stutts, Terrell E. 1929- *St&PR 91*
Stutz, Eleanor E 1947- *BiDrAPA 89*
Stutz, George L. 1921- *St&PR 91*
Stutz, Geraldine *BioIn 16*
Stutz, Harry C *EncABHB 5*
Stutz, Philip Alan 1947- *BiDrAPA 89*
Stutz, Rolf 1949- *St&PR 91*
Stutz, Roy L. 1930- *St&PR 91*
Stutz, Sandra Lee 1948- *WhoAmW 91*
Stutzman, Anita 1934- *St&PR 91*
Stutzman, Daniel *BioIn 16*
Stutzman, Eli *BioIn 16*
Stutzman, Frederic M. 1949- *St&PR 91*
Stutzman, Rebecca Lynn 1953- *WhoAmW 91*
Stutzman, Sandra Louise 1953- *WhoAmW 91*
Stutzman, Thomas Chase, Sr 1950- *WhoWor 91*
Stutzman, Thomas Michael 1953- *WhoSSW 91*
Stutzman, Warren Lee 1941- *WhoSSW 91*
Stuver, Francis Edward 1912- *WhoAm 90*
Stuvinski, B. C. 1953- *WhoEmL 91*
Stux, Stefan Victor 1942- *WhoAmA 91*
Stuyt, Jan Jacobes 1949- *WhoWor 91*
Stuyvesant, Peter 1592?-1672 *WorAlBi*
Stuyvesant, Peter 1610?-1672 *EncCRAm, WhNaAH*
Stuzin, Charles Bryan 1942- *St&PR 91, WhoSSW 91*
Stwalley, William Calvin 1942- *WhoAm 90*
Styan, John Louis 1923- *WhoAm 90, WhoWor 91*
Styblova, Valja 1922- *EncCoWW*
Stycos, Joseph Mayone 1927- *WhoAm 90*
Styer, Robert Alan 1955- *WhoE 91*
Styers, Carolyn Jeanette 1939- *WhoAmW 91*
Styka, Adam 1890-1959 *WhoAmA 91N*
Styles, Beverly 1923- *WhoAmW 91, WhoWor 91*
Styles, Ellen Sanders 1955- *WhoAmW 91*
Styles, George William 1887-1949 *WhoAmA 91N*
Styles, John Henry 1937- *St&PR 91*
Styles, Margretta Madden 1930- *WhoAmW 91*
Styles, Richard Geoffrey Pentland 1930- *WhoAm 90*
Styles, Ronald Arthur 1917- *IntWWM 90*
Styles, Showell *TwCCr&M 91*
Styles, Showell 1908- *AuBYP 90*
Styles, Teresa Jo 1950- *WhoAmW 91, WhoWrEP 89*
Stylistics, The *EncPR&S 89*
Stymiest, Andrew Robert James 1949- *WhoE 91*
Styne, Jule 1905- *BioIn 16, OxCPMus, WhoAm 90, WorAlBi*
Stynes, Barbara Bilello 1951- *WhoAmW 91, WhoWor 91*
Stynes, Stanley Kenneth 1932- *WhoAm 90*
Stypinski, Anthony 1947- *St&PR 91*
Styra, Rima *BiDrAPA 89*
Styron, Clarence *BioIn 16*
Styron, Patty *BioIn 16*
Styron, William 1925- *BestSel 90-4 [port], BioIn 16, ConAu 33NR, ConLC 60 [port], MajTwCW, WhoAm 90, WhoE 91, WhoWor 91, WhoWrEP 89, WorAlBi, WrPh*
Styron, William Durwood, Jr. 1950- *WhoSSW 91*
Styrt, Jerome 1919- *BiDrAPA 89, WhoE 91*
Stys, Rudolph Donald 1935- *St&PR 91*
Styslinger, Lee Joseph, Jr. 1933- *St&PR 91, WhoAm 90, WhoWor 91*
Styx *EncPR&S 89*
Su Cong *BioIn 16*
Su, Diana T *BiDrAPA 89*
Su, Helen Chien-fan 1922- *WhoAmW 91, WhoSSW 91*
Su, Judy Ya Hwa Lin 1938- *WhoAmW 91*
Su, Kendall Ling-Chiao 1926- *WhoAm 90*
Su, Nan-Yao 1951- *WhoSSW 91*
Su, Stephen Y. H. 1938- *WhoAm 90*
Su, Tsung-Chow Joe 1947- *WhoSSW 91*
Su, Tung-Ping *BiDrAPA 89*
Suadlenak, Loree Dean 1931- *St&PR 91*
Sual, Reinhard Hendrik 1961- *WhoWor 91*
Suansilppongse, Aroon 1949- *BiDrAPA 89*
Suarez, Adolfo 1932- *BioIn 16*
Suarez, Adrian 1954- *WhoHisp 91*
Suarez, Amado Francisco *BiDrAPA 89*
Suarez, Angel Antonio *BiDrAPA 89*
Suarez, Celia Cristina 1943- *WhoHisp 91*
Suarez, Diego *WhoHisp 91*
Suarez, Diego A. 1928- *WhoHisp 91*
Suarez, Hugo Banzer *BioIn 16*
Suarez, Jaime *BiDrAPA 89*
Suarez, James A. 1944- *St&PR 91*
Suarez, Jesus *WhoHisp 91*
Suarez, John M 1934- *BiDrAPA 89*
Suarez, Jorge Alberto 1948- *BiDrAPA 89*
Suarez, Jorge Mario 1932- *WhoHisp 91*
Suarez, Jose Ignacio 1951- *WhoHisp 91*
Suarez, Jose Manuel *BiDrAPA 89*
Suarez, Ken 1943- *Ballpl 90*
Suarez, Leo 1957- *WhoHisp 91*
Suarez, Lionel *WhoHisp 91*
Suarez, Luis 1934- *WhoHisp 91*
Suarez, Manuel, Jr. 1930- *WhoHisp 91*
Suarez, Marcos N. 1949- *WhoHisp 91*
Suarez, Margarita M. W. 1957- *WhoHisp 91*
Suarez, Mariano Arroyo 1910- *WhoHisp 91*
Suarez, Michael Anthony 1948- *WhoEmL 91*
Suarez, Miguel 1952- *Ballpl 90*
Suarez, Modesto Jose *BiDrAPA 89*
Suarez, Omero 1947- *WhoHisp 91*
Suarez, R. A. *WhoHisp 91*
Suarez, Rafael Angel, Jr. 1957- *WhoHisp 91*
Suarez, Raleigh Anthony, Jr. 1925- *WhoAm 90*
Suarez, Ricardo 1930- *WhoSSW 91*
Suarez, Robert P. 1949- *ODwPR 91*
Suarez, Roberto *St&PR 91*
Suarez, Roberto 1928- *WhoHisp 91*
Suarez, Roberto J. 1928- *St&PR 91*
Suarez, Ruben Dario 1925- *WhoHisp 91*
Suarez, Sally Ann Tevis 1944- *WhoAmW 91*
Suarez, Tem *WhoHisp 91*
Suarez, Victor Omar 1934- *WhoHisp 91*
Suarez, Virgil 1962- *ConAu 131, HispWr 90*
Suarez, Xavier L. 1949- *WhoHisp 91*
Suarez, Xavier Louis 1949- *WhoAm 90, WhoSSW 91*
Suarez-Burguet, Celestino 1955- *WhoWor 91*
Suarez de Deza, Maria Aurelia 1920- *EncCoWW*
Suarez Gonzales, Adolfo 1932- *WorAlBi*
Suarez Gonzalez, Adolfo 1932- *WhoWor 91*
Suarez Lynch, B. *ConAu 33NR, HispWr 90, MajTwCW*
Suarez Mason, Carlos Guillermo *BioIn 16*
Suarez-Murias, Edward L *BiDrAPA 89*
Suarez-Murias, Marguerite C. 1921- *WhoAm 90, WhoWor 91*
Suarez Rivera, Adolfo Antonio 1927- *WhoAm 90*
Suarez-Rivero, Eliana 1940- *WhoHisp 91*
Suarez-Solar, Pedro Luis *BiDrAPA 89*
Suarez Torres, Humberto *BiDrAPA 89*
Suart, Richard Martin 1951- *IntWWM 90*
Suassuna, Ariano Vilar *BioIn 16*
Suau, Anthony 1956- *WhoAm 90*
Suba, Antonio Ronquillo 1927- *WhoAm 90*
Suba, Steven Antonio 1957- *WhoSSW 91*
Suba, Susanne *WhoAmA 91*
Subach, Albert John 1943- *St&PR 91*
Subach, James Alan 1948- *WhoWor 91*
Subak, John Thomas 1929- *St&PR 91, WhoAm 90*
Subak, Maria Elina *BiDrAPA 89*
Subak-Sharpe, Genell J 1936- *ConAu 31NR*
Subak-Sharpe, Genell Jackson *WhoAmW 91, WhoE 91*
Subak-Sharpe, Gerald Emil 1925- *WhoAm 90, WhoE 91, WhoWor 91*
Subari, Maria Theresia Sulasmi 1917- *WhoWor 91*
Subbarao, Bollepalli *BiDrAPA 89*
Subejano, Ramon Simpas *BioIn 16*
Suben, Joel Eric 1946- *IntWWM 90*
Suber, Donald Byron 1935- *St&PR 91*
Suberri, Keren Chansky 1957- *WhoAmW 91*
Subhas Chandra Bose 1897-1945 *BioIn 16*
Subias, Eusebio *BiDrAPA 89*
Subich, Linda Mezydlo 1956- *WhoEmL 91*
Subkowsky, Elizabeth 1949- *WhoAmW 91*
Subler, Edward Pierre 1927- *WhoAm 90*
Sublett, Carl C 1919- *WhoAmA 91*
Sublett, Carl Cecil 1919- *WhoAm 90*
Sublett, Henry Lee, Jr. 1926- *WhoAm 90*
Sublette, William Lewis 1799-1845 *WhNaAH*
Subotky, Norman A. 1941- *St&PR 91*
Subotnick, Morton 1933- *IntWWM 90, WhoAm 90*
Subotnick, Stuart 1942- *St&PR 91*
Subramaniam, Shivan Sivaswamy 1949- *St&PR 91, WhoAm 90*
Subramanian, Bala 1940- *WhoWor 91*
Subramanian, Nurani Venkatakrishnan 1939- *WhoWor 91*
Subramanian, Sundaram 1934- *WhoWor 91*
Subrin, Mayer 1928- *BiDrAPA 89*
Subrin, Renee Kluger 1931- *ODwPR 91*
Subroto 1928- *WhoWor 91*
Subuh, Muhammad 1901- *EncO&P 3*
Such, Mary Jane 1942- *WhoAmW 91*
Such, Peter 1939- *BioIn 16*
Suchan, Hans Georg 1925- *WhoWor 91*
Suchanek, Leonard Joseph 1937- *WhoAm 90*
Suchecki, Jim 1927- *Ballpl 90*
Sucher, Cynthia Clayton Crumb 1943- *WhoAmW 91*
Suchik, Martin 1945- *St&PR 91*
Suchil, Sally 1951- *St&PR 91, WhoAm 90*
Suchinsky, Richard T 1930- *BiDrAPA 89*
Suchinsky, Richard Theodore 1930- *WhoE 91*
Suchla, David F. 1947- *St&PR 91*
Suchlicki, Jaime 1939- *WhoHisp 91*
Suchodolski, Stanley Edward, Jr. 1949- *WhoE 91*
Sucholeiki, Moises 1929- *BiDrAPA 89*
Suchomel, James M. 1950- *St&PR 91*
Suchomel, Jeffrey Raymond 1956- *WhoWor 91*
Suchon, Eugen 1908- *IntWWM 90*
Suchowiecky, David *BiDrAPA 89*
Suchy, Jiri Jan 1931- *WhoWor 91*
Suchy, Susanne N. 1945- *WhoAmW 91*
Suchy-Pilalis, Jessica Ray 1954- *IntWWM 90*
Sucich, Diana Catherine 1948- *WhoE 91*
Sucke, John Howard, III 1942- *WhoE 91*
Suckiel, Ellen Kappy 1943- *WhoAm 90*
Suckling, John 1609-1642 *BioIn 16*
Suckno, Lee Jeffrey 1953- *BiDrAPA 89*
Suckow, George Robert, Jr. 1934- *BiDrAPA 89*
Suckow, Ruth 1892-1960 *BioAmW, DcLB 102 [port], FemiCLE*
Sucksdorff, Harry Christoffer 1936- *WhoWor 91*
Sucre, Antonio Jose de 1795-1830 *BioIn 16*
Sucre, Guillermo 1933- *HispWr 90*
Sucsy, Leonard Graham 1939- *WhoE 91*
Suczek, Alexander 1928- *St&PR 91*
Suda, Debra Ann *BiDrAPA 89*
Suda, Zdenek 1920- *ConAu 31NR*
Sudak, Howard S 1932- *BiDrAPA 89*
Sudakis, Bill 1946- *Ballpl 90*
Sudakoff, Marlene Mitchell Mooers 1935- *WhoAmW 91*
Sudan, Ranjan 1958- *BiDrAPA 89*
Sudan, Ravindra Nath 1931- *WhoAm 90*
Sudanowicz, Elaine Marie 1956- *WhoAmW 91*
Sudarkasa, Niara *BioIn 16*
Sudarkasa, Niara 1938- *WhoAm 90, WhoAmW 91*
Sudarshan, George 1931- *WhoSSW 91*
Sudarsky, Daniel 1927- *St&PR 91*
Sudarsky, Jerry M. 1918- *WhoAm 90, WhoWor 91*
Sudarsky, Michael 1924- *St&PR 91*
Sudarsono, Budiman 1952- *WhoWor 91*
Sudbrink, Jane Marie 1942- *WhoAmW 91*
Sudbury, Charles Steven 1954- *WhoSSW 91*
Sudbury, David Marshall 1945- *St&PR 91, WhoAm 90*
Sudbury, John Dean 1925- *WhoAm 90*
Suddarth, Roscoe Seldon 1935- *WhoAm 90, WhoWor 91*
Suddath, Richard Lee 1952- *BiDrAPA 89*
Sudderth, Robert J., Jr. 1942- *WhoSSW 91*
Sudderth, Robert Jamison, Jr. 1942- *St&PR 91*
Suddick, Patrick Joseph 1923- *WhoAm 90*
Suddick, Richard Phillips 1934- *WhoAm 90*
Suddock, Frances Suter Thorson 1914- *WhoAmW 91*
Sudds, Richard Huyette, Jr. 1927- *WhoAm 90*
Sudduth, David Lloyd 1944- *BiDrAPA 89*
Sudduth, Jimmy Lee 1910- *MusmAFA [port]*
Sudduth, Stephen Hugh 1953- *BiDrAPA 89*
Sudduth, William McLean 1945- *WhoAm 90, WhoSSW 91*
Sudeikin, Sergei 1882?-1946 *BioIn 16*
Suder, Pete 1916- *Ballpl 90*
Sudeten German Quartet *PenDiMP*
Sudhalter, David Louis 1927- *WhoE 91*
Sudharmono 1927- *WhoWor 91*
Sudhoff, Robert J. 1955- *St&PR 91*
Sudhoff, Willie 1874-1917 *Ballpl 90*
Sudindranath, Usha *BiDrAPA 89*
Sudler, Barbara Welch 1925- *WhoAm 90, WhoAmW 91*
Sudler, Louis Courtenay 1903- *WhoAm 90*
Sudler, N. Anika 1949- *WhoE 91*
Sudlow, Robert Evans 1933- *WhoE 91*
Sudlow, Robert N 1920- *WhoAmA 91*
Sudnick, Edward L. 1939- *St&PR 91*
Sudo, Toshio 1950- *WhoWor 91*
Sudol, Casimer Stanley, Jr. 1946- *WhoE 91*
Sudol, Ed 1920- *Ballpl 90*
Sudol, Rita A. 1949- *WhoHisp 91*
Sudol, Walter Edward 1942- *St&PR 91*
Sudrann, Jean 1919- *WhoAm 90*
Sudre, Rene 1880- *EncO&P 3, EncPaPR 91*
Sue, Alan Kwai Keong 1946- *WhoWor 91*
Sue, Kil Sook *BiDrAPA 89*
Sue, Louis 1875-1968 *PenDiDA 89*
Sue, Samuel S *BiDrAPA 89*
Suebsaeng, Apinya 1951- *St&PR 91*
Suedfeld, Peter 1935- *WhoAm 90*
Suedhoff, Carl John, Jr. 1925- *WhoAm 90*
Suehs, Derrick Jourdain 1954- *WhoEmL 91*
Sueksdorf, William Donald *BiDrAPA 89*
Suelflow, August Robert 1922- *WhoAm 90*
Sueltenfuss, Elizabeth Anne 1921- *WhoAm 90, WhoAmW 91, WhoSSW 91*
Suematsu, Hiroyuki 1935- *WhoWor 91*
Suematsu, Ken-ichi *BioIn 16*
Suen, James Yee 1940- *WhoAm 90*
Suenens, Leo Joseph 1904- *WhoWor 91*
Suenholz, Herman H. 1924- *St&PR 91*
Suenholz, Herman Harry 1924- *WhoAm 90*
Suenos, Carlos 1952- *WhoAmA 91*
Suescum, Alfredo T *BiDrAPA 89*
Suess, Gene G. 1941- *St&PR 91*
Suess, Lawrence Edward *BiDrAPA 89*
Suesse, Dana 1909- *OxCPMus*
Suesse, Dana 1911-1987 *BioIn 16*
Suetin, Nikolai *PenDiDA 89*
Suetonius 69?-140? *WorAlBi*
Suey, David P. 1932- *St&PR 91*
Sueyoshi, Akiko 1942- *ConAu 132*
Suffet, Irwin 1939- *WhoAm 90*
Suffin, Stephen Chester *BiDrAPA 89*
Suffolk, Charles Brandon, Duke of *BioIn 16*
Suffolk, Henrietta, Countess of 1681-1767 *BiDEWW*
Suffolk, Henrietta Howard, Countess of 1681-1767 *BioIn 16*
Suffolk, John Arnold 1946- *WhoWor 91*
Suffolk, Katherine, Duchess of 1520-1580 *FemiCLE*
Suffredini, Kathleen Deery 1951- *WhoAmW 91*
Suffredini Sassetti, Ann Maria 1932- *WhoAmW 91*
Suflas, Steven William 1951- *WhoEmL 91*
Sufrin, Howard Leon 1930- *St&PR 91*
Sufrin, Marcel *BiDrAPA 89*
Sufrin, Sidney Charles 1910- *WhoE 91*
Suga, Takayuki 1930- *WhoWor 91*
Suga, Yusuke *NewYTBS 90*
Sugahara, Kay *BioIn 16*
Sugahara, Tsutomu 1921- *WhoWor 91*
Sugandha *WomWR*
Sugandhi, Sanjay D *BiDrAPA 89*
Sugano, Shigeru 1924- *WhoWor 91*
Sugar, Alan Mark 1952- *WhoE 91*
Sugar, Bert Randolph 1937- *WhoWrEP 89*
Sugar, Carl 1904- *BiDrAPA 89*
Sugar, Jeffrey A. *BiDrAPA 89*
Sugar, Jonathan A 1953- *BiDrAPA 89*
Sugar, Jonathan Akiba 1953- *WhoE 91*
Sugar, Lawrence D. 1945- *St&PR 91*
Sugar, Maurice 1891-1974 *EncAL*

Sugar, Max 1925- *BiDrAPA 89*
Sugar, Oscar 1914- *WhoAm 90*
Sugar, Peter Charles 1932- *WhoE 91*
Sugar, Peter Frigyes 1919- *WhoAm 90*
Sugar, Sandra Lee 1942- *WhoAmW 91*
Sugarman, Abraham Perry *BiDrAPA 89*
Sugarman, Alan William 1924- *WhoAm 90*
Sugarman, Barry 1944- *BiDrAPA 89*
Sugarman, Burt *ConTFT 8*
Sugarman, Charles Jules 1949- *WhoSSW 91*
Sugarman, Elias E. *BioIn 16*
Sugarman, George 1912- *WhoAm 90, WhoAmA 91*
Sugarman, Joan G. 1917- *SmATA 64*
Sugarman, Jule M. 1927- *WhoAm 90*
Sugarman, Leonard *St&PR 91*
Sugarman, Muriel M 1936- *BiDrAPA 89*
Sugarman, Nathan 1917- *WhoAm 90*
Sugarman, Paul Ronald 1931- *WhoAm 90*
Sugarman, Paul William 1947- *WhoEmL 91*
Sugarman, Robert Gary 1939- *WhoAm 90*
Sugarman, Robert Jay 1938- *WhoAm 90*
Sugarman, Samuel Louis 1927- *WhoAm 90*
Sugarman, Stuart Ronald 1948- *BiDrAPA 89*
Sugars, Thomas W *BiDrAPA 89*
Sugawara no Michizane 845-903 *EncJap*
Sugay, Elena R *BiDrAPA 89*
Sugden, George W. 1924- *St&PR 91*
Sugden, Joe 1870-1959 *Ballpl 90*
Sugden, Mark 1902-1990 *ConAu 130*
Sugden, Morris 1919-1984 *DcNaB 1981*
Sugden, Richard Lee 1959- *WhoEmL 91, WhoWor 91*
Sugerman, A Arthur 1929- *BiDrAPA 89*
Sugerman, Abraham Arthur 1929- *WhoAm 90*
Sugerman, Barry Martin 1948- *BiDrAPA 89*
Sugerman, Dale Stephen 1952- *WhoSSW 91*
Sugerman, Daniel *BioIn 16*
Sugerman, Lewis 1927- *St&PR 91*
Sugerman, Peter Allen *BiDrAPA 89*
Sugg, B. Alan *WhoAm 90*
Sugg, John Logan 1914- *WhoAm 90*
Sugg, Joyce 1926- *ConAu 131*
Sugg, Reed Waller 1952- *WhoEmL 91*
Sugg, Richard P 1941- *ConAu 131*
Sugg, Richard Peter 1941- *WhoSSW 91*
Sugg, Robert Perkins 1916- *WhoAm 90*
Suggia, Guilhermina 1888-1950 *PenDiMP*
Suggs, George 1883-1949 *Ballpl 90*
Suggs, Harold Vincent 1948- *WhoE 91*
Suggs, Marion Jack 1924- *WhoAm 90*
Suggs, Patricia Kaylor 1952- *WhoAmW 91*
Suggs, Robert Carl 1932- *AuBYP 90*
Suggs, Robert Leslie *St&PR 91N*
Sughrue, Karen Marie 1951- *WhoAmW 91*
Sughrue, Kathryn Eileen 1913- *WhoAmW 91*
Sugie, Ei-Ichi 1929- *WhoWor 91*
Sugihara, Hajime 1939- *WhoWor 91*
Sugihara, James Masanobu 1918- *WhoAm 90*
Sugihara, Kenzi 1940- *WhoAm 90*
Sugihara, Sempo 1900-1986 *BioIn 16*
Sugihara, Teruo 1949- *WhoWor 91*
Sugihara, Thomas Tamotsu 1924- *WhoAm 90*
Sugiki, Shigemi 1936- *WhoWor 91*
Sugimoto, Kinya 1952- *WhoWor 91*
Sugimoto, Yoshio 1939- *ConAu 130*
Sugimura, Hiromichi 1952- *WhoWor 91*
Sugimura, Takashi 1926- *WhoWor 91*
Sugimura, Yukio 1931- *WhoWor 91*
Sugino, Hiromu 1940- *WhoWor 91*
Sugioka, Kenneth 1920- *WhoAm 90*
Sugisaki, Mitsuyo Kawase 1929- *WhoWor 91*
Sugiura, Kohei 1932- *ConDes 90*
Sugiura, Masahisa 1925- *WhoWor 91*
Sugiura, Tadoshi 1935- *Ballpl 90*
Sugiyama, Meiko 1934- *WhoWor 91*
Sugiyama, Shinya 1949- *ConAu 132*
Sugiyama, Toku Mary 1921- *WhoAmW 91, WhoE 91, WhoWor 91*
Sugiyama, Yoko 1930- *WhoWor 91*
Suglia, Anthony F. 1926- *WhoAm 90*
Sugrue, Denis Francis 1951- *WhoWor 91*
Suguitan, Manuel Guzman *BiDrAPA 89*
Suguro, Osamu 1931- *St&PR 91*
Suh, Chang Sam *BiDrAPA 89*
Suh, Hwi Yol 1936- *BiDrAPA 89*
Suh, Matthew C K 1931- *BiDrAPA 89*
Suh, Nam Pyo 1936- *WhoAm 90*
Suh, Ome Sun *BioIn 16*
Suhag, Sunil 1958- *St&PR 91*
Suhaka, Walter Frederick 1947- *WhoE 91*
Suhandron, Ingrid 1938- *WhoAmW 91*
Suhany, Mark Vincent *BiDrAPA 89*
Suhardiman, Hendrik 1955- *WhoWor 91*
Suharto 1921- *WhoWor 91, WorAlBi*
Suhl, Harry 1922- *WhoAm 90*
Suhl, Yuri 1908- *AuBYP 90*
Suhl, Yuri 1908-1986 *BioIn 16*
Suhler, John Stuart 1943- *WhoAm 90*
Suhowatsky, Stephen J. 1939- *St&PR 91*
Suhowatsky, Stephen Joseph 1939- *WhoAm 90*
Suhr, Gregory Kelley 1947- *WhoEmL 91, WhoSSW 91*
Suhr, Gus 1906- *Ballpl 90*
Suhr, J. Nicholas 1942- *WhoE 91*
Suhr, L. Gene 1934- *St&PR 91*
Suhr, Melanie Ann 1951- *BiDrAPA 89*
Suhr, Meredith L. 1943- *St&PR 91*
Suhr, Peter John 1927- *St&PR 91*
Suhre, Fred Harold, Jr. 1940- *St&PR 91*
Suhre, Joanne Osman 1944- *St&PR 91*
Suhre, Walter Anthony, Jr. 1933- *St&PR 91, WhoAm 90*
Suhrheinrich, Richard F. 1936- *WhoAm 90*
Suhrholm, Ole 1932- *WhoWor 91*
Sui Sin Far 1867-1914 *FemiCLE*
Sui Wen Ti 541-604 *WorAlBi*
Suid, Murray 1942- *ConAu 30NR*
Suiko, Empress 554-628 *EncJap*
Suiko-tenno 554-628 *WomWR*
Suinn, Richard Michael 1933- *WhoAm 90*
Suisala, Emoni Tesese 1948- *WhoWor 91*
Suisman, Michael 1928- *St&PR 91*
Suit, John McCeney, II 1944- *St&PR 91*
Suite, Winston Herbert Edward 1940- *WhoWor 91*
Suiter, Clarence 1923- *St&PR 91*
Suiter, John William 1926- *WhoWor 91*
Suiter, Sheary Sue 1951- *WhoWrEP 89*
Suitner, Otmar 1922- *IntWWM 90, PenDiMP, WhoWor 91*
Suitor, M. Lee 1942- *IntWWM 90*
Suits, Bernard Herbert 1925- *WhoAm 90, WhoWrEP 89*
Suits, Chauncey Guy 1905- *WhoAm 90*
Suits, Daniel Burbidge 1918- *WhoAm 90*
Suits, Valerie Faye 1957- *WhoAmW 91*
Suitt, Thomas Howard 1926- *St&PR 91*
Sujack, Edwin Thomas 1927- *WhoAm 90*
Sujo, Clara Diament *WhoAmA 91*
Suk, Josef *PenDiMP*
Suk, Josef 1929- *IntWWM 90, PenDiMP, WhoWor 91*
Sukarno 1901-1970 *WorAlBi*
Sukawatana, Sompotch *BiDrAPA 89*
Sukay *NewAgMG*
Sukeforth, Clyde 1901- *Ballpl 90*
Sukel, Arthur 1937- *St&PR 91, WhoAm 90*
Sukenick, Martin 1917- *St&PR 91*
Sukenick, Ronald *BioIn 16*
Sukenick, Ronald 1932- *ConAu 32NR, WorAu 1980 [port]*
Sukert, Bruce S. 1960- *WhoSSW 91*
Suket, Judith Ann 1942- *WhoAmW 91*
Sukhanov, N. N. 1882-1940 *BioIn 16*
Sukhanov, Nikolai Nikolaevich 1882-1940 *BioIn 16*
Sukhanova, Yulia *BioIn 16*
Sukharev, Aleksandr *BioIn 16*
Sukhatme, Shashikala Balkrishna 1932- *WhoAmW 91*
Sukhdeo, Hardat A S *BiDrAPA 89*
Sukin, Peter Jay 1952- *BiDrAPA 89*
Suknow, Irving 1920- *St&PR 91*
Sukow, Russell L. 1943- *St&PR 91*
Sukowa, Barbara *BioIn 16*
Sukriket, Parichote 1946- *WhoWor 91*
Sukumaran, Pandaraparambil 1943- *BiDrAPA 89*
Sukun, Kamil Mehmet 1948- *WhoWor 91*
Sukun, Ziya 1958- *WhoE 91*
Sukup, Eugene George 1929- *WhoWor 91*
Sulaiman, Richani 1942- *WhoWor 91*
Sulcer, Frederick Durham 1932- *WhoAm 90*
Sule, Olufemi Shafih 1936- *WhoWor 91*
Suleiman, Mahmoud A 1944- *BiDrAPA 89*
Suleiman, William Wassif *BiDrAPA 89*
Suleimanov, Naim *BioIn 16*
Suleman, Farid 1951- *St&PR 91*
Suleski, Scott D. 1959- *St&PR 91*
Suleymanoglu, Naim *BioIn 16*
Sulfaro, Joyce A. 1948- *WhoAmW 91, WhoSSW 91*
Sulg, Madis 1943- *WhoAm 90*
Sulik, Edwin 1957- *WhoSSW 91, WhoWor 91*
Sulimirski, Witold Stanislaw 1933- *St&PR 91, WhoAm 90*
Suliotis, Elena *PenDiMP*
Suliotis, Elena 1943- *WhoWor 91*
Sulis, William Herbert 1955- *WhoWor 91*
Sulkin, Howard Allen 1941- *WhoAm 90*
Sulkin, Sidney 1918- *WhoAm 90, WhoWrEP 89*
Sulkin, Valery *BiDrAPA 89*
Sulkowicz, Kerry Jeff *BiDrAPA 89*
Sulkowski, Toni Jean 1953- *WhoE 91*
Sullam, Sara Copia 1588-1641 *EncCoWW*
Sullavan, Margaret 1896-1960 *BioAmW*
Sullavan, Margaret 1911-1960 *BioIn 16, WorAlBi*
Sullavan, Margaret Brooke 1911-1960 *NotWoAT*
Sullender, J.E. 1930- *St&PR 91*
Suller, Debra Jane 1948- *WhoAmW 91*
Sullins, Jill Packales 1945- *WhoAmW 91*
Sullins, Katherine Pendleton 1959- *WhoSSW 91*
Sullins, Robert M 1926- *WhoAmA 91*
Sullins, Robert Michael 1926- *WhoE 91*
Sullivan, Ada *BioIn 16*
Sullivan, Adele Woodhouse *WhoAm 90*
Sullivan, Al *BioIn 16*
Sullivan, Alan 1868-1947 *DcLB 92 [port]*
Sullivan, Albert W *BiDrAPA 89*
Sullivan, Allen Trousdale 1927- *WhoAm 90*
Sullivan, Alma Jean 1945- *WhoAmW 91*
Sullivan, Ann Marie T 1948- *BiDrAPA 89*
Sullivan, Anna Shaw 1960- *WhoSSW 91*
Sullivan, Anne *BioAmW*
Sullivan, Anne Dorothy Hevner 1929- *WhoAmA 91*
Sullivan, Anne Elizabeth 1942- *WhoAm 90*
Sullivan, Arthur 1842-1900 *BioIn 16, OxCPMus, PenDiMP A, WorAlBi*
Sullivan, Arthur Philip 1943- *WhoE 91*
Sullivan, Arthur Seymour 1842-1900 *AuBYP 90*
Sullivan, Austin P., Jr. 1940- *St&PR 91*
Sullivan, Austin Padraic, Jr. 1940- *WhoAm 90*
Sullivan, Barbara Boyle 1937- *WhoAm 90*
Sullivan, Barbara Kathryn 1948- *WhoEmL 91*
Sullivan, Barry *ConAu 132*
Sullivan, Barry 1949- *WhoEmL 91*
Sullivan, Barry F. 1930- *BioIn 16, St&PR 91, WhoAm 90*
Sullivan, Barry M. 1945- *St&PR 91*
Sullivan, Benjamin Joseph 1918- *St&PR 91*
Sullivan, Bernice Dekko 1927- *St&PR 91*
Sullivan, Betty Julia 1902- *WhoAmW 91*
Sullivan, Betty Louise 1953- *WhoE 91*
Sullivan, Beverly Martin 1954- *WhoWor 91*
Sullivan, Bill 1942- *BioIn 16, WhoAmA 91*
Sullivan, Billy 1875-1965 *Ballpl 90*
Sullivan, Billy 1910- *Ballpl 90*
Sullivan, Brian 1924- *WhoAm 90*
Sullivan, Brian S 1955- *BiDrAPA 89*
Sullivan, C. W., III 1944- *WhoSSW 91*
Sullivan, Carl Rollynn, Jr. 1926- *WhoAm 90*
Sullivan, Charles A. *WhoAm 90*
Sullivan, Charles Edward, Jr. 1933- *WhoE 91*
Sullivan, Charles Irving 1918- *WhoE 91*
Sullivan, Charles J. 1939- *St&PR 91*
Sullivan, Charlie 1903-1935 *Ballpl 90*
Sullivan, Claire Ferguson 1937- *WhoAmW 91, WhoWor 91*
Sullivan, Colleen Driscoll 1937- *WhoE 91*
Sullivan, Connie Castleberry 1934- *WhoAmW 91, WhoWor 91*
Sullivan, Cornelius Wayne 1943- *WhoAm 90*
Sullivan, Dan *BioIn 16*
Sullivan, Daniel A. 1951- *St&PR 91*
Sullivan, Daniel Carl 1945- *BiDrAPA 89*
Sullivan, Daniel Edmond 1946- *WhoSSW 91*
Sullivan, Daniel F. 1935- *St&PR 91*
Sullivan, Daniel Joseph 1935- *WhoAm 90*
Sullivan, Daniel Joseph 1940- *St&PR 91, WhoAm 90*
Sullivan, Daniel M. 1924- *St&PR 91*
Sullivan, Daniel Richard 1951- *WhoE 91*
Sullivan, David Francis 1941- *WhoAmA 91*
Sullivan, David Ignatius 1951- *St&PR 91*
Sullivan, David J., Jr. 1931- *St&PR 91*
Sullivan, David Michael *BiDrAPA 89*
Sullivan, Dennis F. 1943- *WhoAm 90*
Sullivan, Dennis Francis 1943- *St&PR 91*
Sullivan, Dennis J., Jr. 1932- *St&PR 91*
Sullivan, Dennis James, Jr. 1932- *WhoAm 90*
Sullivan, Dennis W. 1938- *St&PR 91, WhoAm 90*
Sullivan, Don *BioIn 16*
Sullivan, Donald *BioIn 16*
Sullivan, Donald 1930- *WhoAm 90, WhoE 91*
Sullivan, Donald 1942?-1989 *ConAu 130*
Sullivan, Donald G. 1941- *St&PR 91*
Sullivan, Dorothy Louise 1938- *WhoE 91*
Sullivan, Dorothy Rona 1941- *WhoE 91, WhoWor 91*
Sullivan, Douglas Robert 1933- *St&PR 91*
Sullivan, Earl Iseman 1923- *WhoSSW 91*
Sullivan, Ed 1902-1974 *BioIn 16, WorAlBi*
Sullivan, Edward 1832-1899 *DcCanB 12*
Sullivan, Edward Cuyler 1906- *WhoAm 90*
Sullivan, Edward Holden, Jr. 1941- *WhoWor 91*
Sullivan, Edward J. 1929- *St&PR 91*
Sullivan, Edward Joseph 1915- *WhoWor 91*
Sullivan, Edward M. 1947- *St&PR 91*
Sullivan, Edward Myles 1948- *WhoSSW 91*
Sullivan, Eleanor Regis 1928- *WhoAm 90, WhoAmW 91*
Sullivan, Ellen 1951- *BioIn 16*
Sullivan, Ellen F. 1956- *St&PR 91*
Sullivan, Eugene J. 1920- *St&PR 91*
Sullivan, Eugene John Joseph 1920- *WhoAm 90*
Sullivan, Eugene Joseph 1943- *WhoAm 90*
Sullivan, Eugene R. 1903-1989 *BioIn 16*
Sullivan, Eugene Raymond 1941- *WhoAm 90*
Sullivan, Francis Charles 1927- *WhoAm 90*
Sullivan, Francis Edward 1941- *WhoAm 90*
Sullivan, Francoise *BioIn 16*
Sullivan, Francoise 1925- *WhoAmA 91*
Sullivan, Frank 1930- *Ballpl 90*
Sullivan, Frank E. 1923- *WhoAm 90*
Sullivan, Frank Larry 1947- *WhoSSW 91*
Sullivan, Frank W 1935- *BiDrAPA 89*
Sullivan, Fred G. *BioIn 16*
Sullivan, Fred R. 1914- *St&PR 91, WhoAm 90*
Sullivan, Frederick William 1928- *St&PR 91, WhoAm 90*
Sullivan, Garrett 1945- *St&PR 91*
Sullivan, Gary *ODwPR 91*
Sullivan, George Anderson *WhoWor 91*
Sullivan, George Edmund 1932- *WhoAm 90*
Sullivan, George Edward 1927- *AuBYP 90, WhoAm 90*
Sullivan, George Murray 1922- *WhoAm 90, WhoWor 91*
Sullivan, Gerald Clayton 1930- *St&PR 91*
Sullivan, Gerald Daniel 1932- *WhoAm 90*
Sullivan, Gerard Francis 1944- *St&PR 91*
Sullivan, Gladys Ann 1931- *WhoWrEP 89*
Sullivan, Gregory B. *BiDrAPA 89*
Sullivan, Gregory Benen 1960- *WhoEmL 91*
Sullivan, Harold E., III 1959- *St&PR 91*
Sullivan, Harry Truman 1952- *WhoSSW 91*
Sullivan, Haywood 1930- *Ballpl 90*
Sullivan, Haywood Cooper 1930- *WhoAm 90, WhoE 91*
Sullivan, Herbert Patrick 1932- *WhoAm 90*
Sullivan, Howard A. 1921-1989 *BioIn 16*
Sullivan, Hugh D. 1958- *St&PR 91*
Sullivan, Irene Agatha 1928- *WhoE 91*
Sullivan, J. Langdon 1903- *St&PR 91*
Sullivan, J. Langdon, Mrs. *WhoE 91*
Sullivan, James Anderson 1925- *WhoWor 91*
Sullivan, James Ash 1946- *WhoE 91*
Sullivan, James Benjamin 1941- *WhoSSW 91*
Sullivan, James C. 1934- *St&PR 91*
Sullivan, James Dwight 1942- *St&PR 91*
Sullivan, James Edward 1928- *WhoWrEP 89*
Sullivan, James Edward, Jr. 1937- *WhoE 91*
Sullivan, James F. 1926- *St&PR 91*
Sullivan, James Francis 1930- *WhoAm 90*
Sullivan, James Hall 1918- *WhoAm 90*
Sullivan, James Joseph 1922- *WhoE 91*
Sullivan, James Kirk 1935- *WhoAm 90, WhoWor 91*
Sullivan, James Lenox 1910- *WhoAm 90*
Sullivan, James Leo 1925- *WhoAm 90, WhoE 91*
Sullivan, James N. 1937- *WhoAm 90*
Sullivan, James Norman 1937- *St&PR 91*
Sullivan, James Richard 1930- *WhoE 91*
Sullivan, James Stephen 1929- *WhoAm 90*
Sullivan, Jan Greer *BiDrAPA 89*
Sullivan, Janet Spring 1944- *WhoAmW 91*
Sullivan, Janet Wright 1926- *WhoWrEP 89*
Sullivan, Janice Calhoun 1953- *WhoWrEP 89*
Sullivan, Jay Michael 1936- *WhoAm 90*
Sullivan, Jeremiah Stephen 1920- *WhoAm 90*
Sullivan, Jerry Ford 1944- *St&PR 91*
Sullivan, Jerry Stephen 1945- *WhoSSW 91*
Sullivan, Jerry Warner 1942- *WhoSSW 91*
Sullivan, Jerry Wayne 1933- *BiDrAPA 89*
Sullivan, Jim 1939- *WhoAm 90, WhoAmA 91*
Sullivan, Joan *BioIn 16*
Sullivan, Joe 1906-1971 *OxCPMus*
Sullivan, Joe 1910-1985 *Ballpl 90*
Sullivan, John 1740-1795 *EncCRAm, WhNaAH*
Sullivan, John 1920- *Ballpl 90, St&PR 91*
Sullivan, John Arthur, Jr. 1945- *WhoAm 90*
Sullivan, John Daniel 1924- *WhoWor 91*
Sullivan, John Fox 1943- *WhoAm 90*
Sullivan, John Francis 1920- *WhoE 91*

Sullivan, John Greenfelder 1936- *WhoSSW 91*
Sullivan, John Henry 1935- *St&PR 91*
Sullivan, John J, Jr. 1929- *BiDrAPA 89*
Sullivan, John James, Jr. 1938- *WhoSSW 91*
Sullivan, John Joseph 1920- *WhoAm 90*
Sullivan, John L *BiDrAPA 89*
Sullivan, John L. 1858-1918 *BioIn 16, WorAlBi*
Sullivan, John Louis, Jr. 1928- *WhoAm 90*
Sullivan, John Magruder 1959- *WhoSSW 91*
Sullivan, John Mark 1935- *St&PR 91*
Sullivan, John Matthew 1963- *WhoEmL 91*
Sullivan, John Patrick 1930- *WhoAm 90, WhoWrEP 89*
Sullivan, John Paul *BiDrAPA 89*
Sullivan, John Paul 1926- *St&PR 91*
Sullivan, John W. 1934- *WhoAm 90*
Sullivan, Joseph *BioIn 16*
Sullivan, Joseph A. 1923- *WhoE 91*
Sullivan, Joseph Deuel 1913- *BiDrAPA 89*
Sullivan, Joseph Deuel 1917- *WhoE 91*
Sullivan, Joseph Edward 1934- *St&PR 91*
Sullivan, Joseph M. 1930- *WhoAm 90*
Sullivan, Joseph Michael 1939- *St&PR 91*
Sullivan, Joseph Robert 1931- *St&PR 91, WhoAm 90*
Sullivan, Joseph T. P. 1895-1989 *BioIn 16*
Sullivan, Julia Benitez 1957- *WhoHisp 91*
Sullivan, Justin L. 1939- *St&PR 91*
Sullivan, Kathleen *BioIn 16*
Sullivan, Kathleen Mary 1953- *WhoAm 90*
Sullivan, Kathryn Ann 1954- *WhoAmW 91*
Sullivan, Kathryn D. 1951- *WhoAmW 91*
Sullivan, Kathryn D. 1953- *BioIn 16*
Sullivan, Kathryn Meara 1942- *WhoAmW 91*
Sullivan, Kenneth W. 1943- *St&PR 91*
Sullivan, Larry Michael 1948- *WhoWrEP 89*
Sullivan, Laura P. 1947- *St&PR 91*
Sullivan, Laura Patricia 1947- *WhoAm 90, WhoAmW 91*
Sullivan, Leon Howard 1922- *WhoAm 90*
Sullivan, Leonor K. 1902-1988 *BioIn 16*
Sullivan, Linda Susan 1952- *WhoAmA 91*
Sullivan, Louis 1933- *News 90 [port]*
Sullivan, Louis H. 1856-1924 *BioIn 16*
Sullivan, Louis Henry 1856-1924 *PenDiDA 89, WorAlBi*
Sullivan, Louis W. *BioIn 16*
Sullivan, Louis W. 1934- *BiDrUSE 89*
Sullivan, Louis Wade 1933- *WhoAm 90, WhoE 91, WhoWor 91*
Sullivan, Marcia M. 1952- *St&PR 91*
Sullivan, Marcia Waite 1950- *WhoEmL 91*
Sullivan, Margaret E 1919- *BiDrAPA 89*
Sullivan, Margaret Murphy 1944- *WhoSSW 91*
Sullivan, Margaret Patricia 1922- *WhoAm 90*
Sullivan, Margaret Wolan 1952- *WhoAmW 91*
Sullivan, Marie Celeste 1929- *WhoAm 90, WhoAmW 91, WhoSSW 91*
Sullivan, Marilyn Dill 1939- *St&PR 91*
Sullivan, Marjorie Ann 1931- *WhoAmW 91*
Sullivan, Mark Daniel *BiDrAPA 89*
Sullivan, Martin E. 1944- *WhoAm 90*
Sullivan, Mary Ann 1954- *SmATA 63 [port]*
Sullivan, Mary Anna 1953- *BiDrAPA 89*
Sullivan, Mary E. 1956- *St&PR 91*
Sullivan, Mary Jane Leahy 1939- *WhoAmW 91*
Sullivan, Mary Lou 1945- *WhoAmW 91*
Sullivan, Mary Maureen 1950- *WhoAmW 91*
Sullivan, Mary Rose 1931- *WhoAm 90*
Sullivan, Matthew Barry 1915- *ConAu 132*
Sullivan, Maureen Patricia 1946- *WhoAmW 91*
Sullivan, Max William 1909- *WhoAm 90*
Sullivan, Maxine 1911-1987 *DrBlPA 90, OxCPMus*
Sullivan, Melanie-Prejean 1953- *WhoAm 90*
Sullivan, Michael 1948- *WhoSSW 91*
Sullivan, Michael C. 1940- *St&PR 91*
Sullivan, Michael David 1938- *WhoSSW 91*
Sullivan, Michael Evan 1940- *WhoWor 91*
Sullivan, Michael F. 1935- *St&PR 91*
Sullivan, Michael J. *BioIn 16*
Sullivan, Michael J. 1939- *WhoAm 90, WhoWor 91*
Sullivan, Michael Joseph 1941- *WhoE 91*
Sullivan, Michael Lee 1945- *St&PR 91*
Sullivan, Michael P. 1948- *St&PR 91*
Sullivan, Michael Patrick 1934- *St&PR 91, WhoAm 90*
Sullivan, Michael Tipton 1949- *WhoSSW 91*
Sullivan, Michael V. *ODwPR 91*
Sullivan, Nancy Jean 1957- *WhoAmW 91, WhoSSW 91*
Sullivan, Neil Maxwell 1942- *WhoSSW 91, WhoWor 91*
Sullivan, Neil Samuel 1942- *WhoWor 91*
Sullivan, Nicholas G. 1927- *WhoAm 90, WhoE 91*
Sullivan, P. Lance 1950- *WhoWrEP 89*
Sullivan, Pamela Mardones *BiDrAPA 89*
Sullivan, Patricia Ann 1956- *WhoAmW 91*
Sullivan, Patricia Bowe 1937- *WhoE 91*
Sullivan, Patricia Clare 1928- *WhoAmW 91*
Sullivan, Patricia Lance 1950- *WhoAmW 91*
Sullivan, Patricia Sue 1956- *WhoAmW 91*
Sullivan, Patricia W. 1936- *WhoAmW 91*
Sullivan, Patrick *WhoAm 90, WhoE 91*
Sullivan, Patrick 1894-1967 *MusmAFA*
Sullivan, Patrick J. 1948- *St&PR 91*
Sullivan, Patrick James 1943- *WhoWor 91*
Sullivan, Paul A., Jr. 1934- *St&PR 91*
Sullivan, Paul D 1928- *BiDrAPA 89*
Sullivan, Paul Joseph 1947- *WhoE 91*
Sullivan, Paul Richard 1940- *St&PR 91*
Sullivan, Paul William 1939- *WhoSSW 91*
Sullivan, Peggy 1929- *WhoAm 90*
Sullivan, Philip *BiDrAPA 89*
Sullivan, Philip G. 1932- *St&PR 91*
Sullivan, Philip Joseph 1952- *WhoE 91*
Sullivan, Philip Wright *BiDrAPA 89*
Sullivan, Phillip Anthony 1951- *WhoSSW 91*
Sullivan, Potter Charles 1823-1883 *AmLegL*
Sullivan, R 1939- *WhoAmA 91*
Sullivan, Ralph M. 1936- *St&PR 91*
Sullivan, Randall Gene *BiDrAPA 89*
Sullivan, Raymond Peter 1954- *WhoE 91*
Sullivan, Richard C. 1928- *St&PR 91*
Sullivan, Richard Cyril 1928- *WhoAm 90*
Sullivan, Richard J. 1949- *ODwPR 91*
Sullivan, Richard John 1949- *WhoAm 90*
Sullivan, Richard Leo 1953- *WhoSSW 91*
Sullivan, Richard Morrissey 1942- *WhoSSW 91*
Sullivan, Richard T. 1955- *St&PR 91*
Sullivan, Rick 1964- *ODwPR 91*
Sullivan, Robert 1949- *BiDrAPA 89*
Sullivan, Robert B 1917- *BiDrAPA 89*
Sullivan, Robert Bryan 1960- *WhoE 91*
Sullivan, Robert Edward 1936- *WhoAm 90*
Sullivan, Robert Edwin 1917- *WhoAm 90*
Sullivan, Robert Emmet, Jr. 1955- *WhoWor 91*
Sullivan, Robert J. 1936- *St&PR 91*
Sullivan, Robert K. 1947- *St&PR 91*
Sullivan, Robert T. *ODwPR 91*
Sullivan, Roger Charles, Jr. 1946- *WhoEmL 91*
Sullivan, Roger J. 1928- *ConAu 132*
Sullivan, Roger John 1921- *St&PR 91*
Sullivan, Roger Winthrop 1929- *WhoAm 90*
Sullivan, Ronald Dee 1939- *WhoSSW 91*
Sullivan, Ronald Frederick 1930- *WhoAm 90*
Sullivan, Ronald Lee 1946- *WhoSSW 91*
Sullivan, Ruth Wilkins 1926- *WhoAmA 91*
Sullivan, Sandra Jones 1948- *WhoAmW 91, WhoEmL 91*
Sullivan, Sandy *ODwPR 91*
Sullivan, Sarah Louise 1954- *WhoAmW 91*
Sullivan, Scott A 1947- *WhoAmA 91*
Sullivan, Sean 1923-1985 *OxCCanT*
Sullivan, Sean Mei *WhoWrEP 89*
Sullivan, Selby William 1934- *WhoAm 90, WhoSSW 91*
Sullivan, Sharon 1947- *WhoAmW 91*
Sullivan, Sherry E. 1961- *WhoAmW 91*
Sullivan, Stephen Gene *BiDrAPA 89*
Sullivan, Stephen Gene 1947- *WhoE 91*
Sullivan, Stephen J. *St&PR 91*
Sullivan, Stephen Joseph 1955- *WhoEmL 91*
Sullivan, Stephen Wentworth 1946- *WhoAm 90*
Sullivan, Susan *BioIn 16*
Sullivan, Susan Carol 1942- *WhoAmW 91*
Sullivan, Terrence M. 1938- *St&PR 91*
Sullivan, Terry *BioIn 16*
Sullivan, Thomas *BioIn 16*
Sullivan, Thomas C. 1937- *St&PR 91*
Sullivan, Thomas Christopher 1937- *WhoAm 90*
Sullivan, Thomas J. 1935- *St&PR 91*
Sullivan, Thomas John 1935- *WhoAm 90*
Sullivan, Thomas M 1933- *BiDrAPA 89*
Sullivan, Thomas M. 1942- *St&PR 91*
Sullivan, Thomas P. 1936- *St&PR 91*
Sullivan, Thomas Patrick 1930- *WhoAm 90*
Sullivan, Timothy Bernard *BiDrAPA 89*
Sullivan, Timothy Burns 1940- *St&PR 91*
Sullivan, Timothy Jackson 1944- *WhoAm 90*
Sullivan, Timothy James *BiDrAPA 89*
Sullivan, Timothy John 1943- *St&PR 91*
Sullivan, Timothy Patrick 1942- *St&PR 91*
Sullivan, Timothy Patrick 1958- *WhoEmL 91, WhoWor 91*
Sullivan, Walter *BioIn 16*
Sullivan, Walter Francis 1928- *WhoAm 90, WhoSSW 91*
Sullivan, Walter H., Jr. 1917- *St&PR 91*
Sullivan, Walter Laurence 1924- *WhoSSW 91*
Sullivan, Walter Seager 1918- *WhoAm 90, WhoWrEP 89*
Sullivan, Walter T. 1940- *St&PR 91*
Sullivan, William Alan 1951- *St&PR 91*
Sullivan, William Beaumont 1945- *WhoE 91, WhoEmL 91*
Sullivan, William Butler 1934- *St&PR 91*
Sullivan, William C. 1928- *St&PR 91*
Sullivan, William C 1937- *BiDrAPA 89*
Sullivan, William Courtney 1928- *WhoAm 90*
Sullivan, William Francis 1952- *WhoEmL 91*
Sullivan, William Francis 1957- *WhoEmL 91*
Sullivan, William Hallisey, Jr. 1915- *WhoAm 90*
Sullivan, William J. 1919- *St&PR 91*
Sullivan, William James 1919- *WhoAm 90*
Sullivan, William James 1930- *WhoAm 90*
Sullivan, William Joseph 1931- *WhoWrEP 89*
Sullivan, William L. 1935- *ODwPR 91*
Sullivan, William Lescalette, Jr. 1935- *St&PR 91*
Sullivan, William Michael 1946- *BiDrAPA 89*
Sullivan, William Patrick 1952- *WhoE 91*
Sullivan, William Robert, II 1962- *BiDrAPA 89*
Sullivan, Willie 1937- *WhoSSW 91*
Sullivan-Hanley, Carol 1956- *WhoAmW 91*
Sullivant, Robert Scott 1925- *WhoAm 90*
Sullo, Joseph Anthony 1921- *WhoAmA 91*
Sullum, Daniel Shimon 1954- *BiDrAPA 89*
Sullwold, Arthur F 1942- *BiDrAPA 89*
Sullwold, Corliss Kay 1946- *WhoAmW 91*
Sully Prudhomme 1839-1907 *WorAlBi*
Sully, Alfred 1821-1879 *WhNaAH*
Sully, Francois 1927-1971 *AuBYP 90*
Sully, Thomas 1783-1872 *WorAlBi*
Sulman, Charles 1942- *WhoWor 91*
Sulpicia *EncCoWW*
Sulsona, Michael *WhoHisp 91*
Sult, Charles W, Jr. *BiDrAPA 89*
Sultan bin Muhammad Al-Qasimi, Sheikh 1939- *WhoWor 91*
Sultan Ibn Abdulaziz, Prince 1924- *WhoWor 91*
Sultan, Abd-El-Rahman Ahmed 1947- *WhoWor 91*
Sultan, Altoon 1948- *WhoAmA 91*
Sultan, Donald K. 1951- *BioIn 16, WhoAmA 91*
Sultan, Donald Keith 1951- *WhoAm 90*
Sultan, Joseph A *BiDrAPA 89*
Sultan, Larry A 1946- *WhoAmA 91*
Sultan, Richard Gabriel 1940- *WhoE 91*
Sultan, Sady R *BiDrAPA 89*
Sultan, Shahid 1952- *WhoE 91*
Sultan, Stanley 1928- *WhoWrEP 89*
Sultan-Galiev, M. S. 1880?-1940? *BioIn 16*
Sultan-Galiev, Mir Said 1880?-1940? *BioIn 16*
Sultana, Joseph Angelo 1946- *WhoWor 91*
Sultana, Najma *BiDrAPA 89*
Sultana, Najma 1948- *WhoAmW 91, WhoEmL 91*
Sultanof, Jeffrey Brad 1954- *WhoE 91, WhoEmL 91, WhoWor 91*
Sulte, Benjamin 1841-1923 *DcLB 99 [port]*
Sulter, Maud 1960- *FemiCLE*
Sulton, Anne Thomas 1952- *WhoAmW 91*
Sulton, John Dennis 1912- *WhoAm 90*
Sultzbaugh, C. Tom 1917- *St&PR 91*
Sultzer, David L. *BiDrAPA 89*
Sultzer, Randy Thomas 1964- *WhoE 91*
Sulvetta, Anthony J. 1939- *St&PR 91*
Sulyk, Stephen 1924- *WhoAm 90, WhoE 91*
Sulzbach, Daniel Scott 1949- *WhoEmL 91*
Sulzberger, Arthur Hays 1891-1968 *BioIn 16*
Sulzberger, Arthur O., Jr. *BioIn 16*
Sulzberger, Arthur Ochs 1926- *BioIn 16, WorAlBi*
Sulzberger, Arthur Ochs, Jr. 1951- *WhoE 91*
Sulzberger, Arthur Ochs, Sr. 1926- *WhoAm 90, WhoE 91*
Sulzberger, Cyrus Leo 1912- *WhoAm 90*
Sulzberger, Edward *BioIn 16*
Sulzberger, Iphigene Ochs 1892-1990 *BioIn 16, ConAu 131, NewYTBS 90 [port]*
Sulzer, Georg 1844-1929 *EncPaPR 91*
Sulzer, Joseph Paul 1947- *WhoEmL 91*
Sulzer, William 1863-1941 *AmLegL*
Suma, Kozo 1932- *WhoWor 91*
Sumac, Yma 1922- *OxCPMus*
Sumac, Yma 1927- *PenDiMP*
Sumanth, David Jonnakoty 1946- *WhoSSW 91*
Sumarno, Ishak 1943- *WhoWor 91*
Sumas, James 1933- *St&PR 91*
Sumaya, Ciro Valent 1941- *WhoHisp 91*
Sumbel, Leah 1759?-1821? *FemiCLE*
Sumer, Cengiz M 1927- *BiDrAPA 89*
Sumer, Emel Aktan 1933- *BiDrAPA 89*
Sumerlin, Katherine Marie 1920- *WhoAmW 91*
Sumichrast, Jozef 1948- *WhoAm 90*
Sumichrast, Michael *BioIn 16*
Sumida, Gerald Aquinas 1944- *WhoWor 91*
Sumien, Lola *BioIn 16*
Sumita, Yoichi 1924- *ConDes 90, WhoWor 91*
Sumizawa, Takashi 1934- *St&PR 91*
Sumlin, Roger Lewis 1942- *WhoSSW 91*
Summ, Helmut 1908- *WhoAmA 91*
Summa, Don Joseph 1926- *WhoAm 90*
Summa, Homer 1898-1966 *Ballpl 90*
Summanen, Paula Anneli 1952- *WhoWor 91*
Summar, Alvin Jonah 1935- *BiDrAPA 89*
Summar, Dwayne *BioIn 16*
Summar, Dwayne 1939- *ODwPR 91*
Summer, Alexander, Jr. 1938- *St&PR 91*
Summer, Charles Edgar 1923- *WhoAm 90*
Summer, Cree *BioIn 16*
Summer, Donna 1948- *DrBlPA 90, EncPR&S 89, OxCPMus, WhoAm 90, WhoAmW 91, WorAlBi*
Summer, Eugenia 1923- *WhoAmA 91*
Summer, Henry Lee *BioIn 16*
Summer, Lloyd Langston, Jr. 1923- *St&PR 91*
Summer, Loraine 1953- *WhoAmW 91*
Summer, V.C. 1920- *St&PR 91*
Summerall, Pat *WhoAm 90*
Summerfield, Arthur E., Jr. 1922- *St&PR 91*
Summerfield, Arthur Ellsworth 1899-1972 *BiDrUSE 89*
Summerfield, Joanne 1940- *WhoAmW 91*
Summerfield, John Robert 1917- *WhoAm 90*
Summerfield, Lin 1952- *ConAu 132*
Summerfield, Martin 1916- *WhoAm 90, WhoE 91*
Summerfield, Paddy 1947- *BioIn 16*
Summerfield, Thomas Warren 1947- *St&PR 91*
Summerford, Ben Long 1924- *WhoAm 90*
Summerford, Harold C. 1936- *St&PR 91*
Summerford, R. Michael 1948- *St&PR 91*
Summerford, Sherry R. 1948- *WhoAmW 91, WhoSSW 91*
Summergrad, Paul *BiDrAPA 89*
Summergrad, Paul 1949- *WhoE 91*
Summerhayes, Martha 1846-1911 *BioIn 16*
Summerhays, Charles Callis 1932- *St&PR 91*
Summerlin, Glenn Wood 1934- *St&PR 91*
Summerlin, Kristin Lee 1961- *WhoAmW 91*
Summerlin, Roy C. 1923- *St&PR 91*
Summerlin, Sam 1928- *WhoWrEP 89*
Summerour, Robert Brooke *BiDrAPA 89*
Summers, Alan Lee *BiDrAPA 89*
Summers, Albert E. 183-?- *AmLegL*
Summers, Alfred Lawrence, Jr. 1950- *WhoEmL 91*
Summers, Alphonsus Joseph Mary Augustus 1880-1948 *BioIn 16, EncO&P 3*
Summers, Andy *BioIn 16*
Summers, Anita Arrow 1925- *WhoAm 90, WhoE 91*
Summers, Anne 1945- *BioIn 16, News 90 [port]*
Summers, Anne Fairhurst 1945- *WhoAmW 91, WhoE 91*
Summers, Anthony J. 1953- *WhoWrEP 89*
Summers, Augustus Montague 1880-1948 *BioIn 16*
Summers, Bessie Eva 1937- *WhoAmW 91*
Summers, Bill 1895-1966 *Ballpl 90*
Summers, Carol 1925- *WhoAm 90, WhoAmA 91*
Summers, Champ 1946- *Ballpl 90*
Summers, Clarke C *BiDrAPA 89*
Summers, Clyde Wilson 1918- *WhoAm 90*
Summers, Dale Edwards 1949- *WhoE 91*
Summers, David C *BiDrAPA 89*
Summers, Denise Ottinger 1951- *WhoAmW 91*
Summers, Donald Bruce *BiDrAPA 89*
Summers, Dudley Gloyne 1892-1975 *WhoAmA 91N*
Summers, E. Hardy 1933- *WhoAm 90*
Summers, Ed 1884-1953 *Ballpl 90*
Summers, Edward Lee 1937- *WhoAm 90*
Summers, Ellen Sidelle 1932- *WhoAmW 91*
Summers, Frances Phaye 1938- *WhoAmW 91*

Summers, Frank William 1933- *WhoAm 90*
Summers, Frederick J 1948- *BiDrAPA 89*
Summers, Gene 1939- *WhoWor 91*
Summers, George H 1865-1941 *OxCCanT*
Summers, Glenda Jeanne 1956- *WhoSSW 91*
Summers, H. Meade, Jr. 1936- *WhoAm 90*
Summers, Hollis 1916-1987 *LiHiK*
Summers, Hugh Bloomer, Jr. 1921- *WhoSSW 91*
Summers, James 1910- *AuBYP 90*
Summers, James Irvin 1921- *WhoAm 90*
Summers, James L. 1910-1973 *BioIn 16*
Summers, James Richard 1962- *WhoWor 91*
Summers, Janie I. *WhoAmW 91*
Summers, John David 1941- *WhoAm 90*
Summers, John L. *BioIn 16*
Summers, Jonathan *IntWWM 90*
Summers, Joseph Frank 1914- *WhoSSW 91, WhoWor 91*
Summers, Joseph Holmes 1920- *WhoAm 90*
Summers, Kermit Leon 1935- *WhoE 91*
Summers, Lawrence H. *BioIn 16*
Summers, Lorraine Dey Schaeffer 1946- *WhoAmW 91*
Summers, Mary Ellen 1949- *St&PR 91*
Summers, Max Duane 1938- *WhoAm 90*
Summers, Merna 1933- *ConAu 131*
Summers, Montague 1880-1948 *BioIn 16*
Summers, Richard Fredric 1956- *BiDrAPA 89, WhoE 91*
Summers, Robert 1922- *WhoAm 90, WhoE 91*
Summers, Robert Samuel 1933- *WhoWrEP 89*
Summers, Ronald Dean *BiDrAPA 89*
Summers, Stephanie Horanszki 1944- *WhoSSW 91*
Summers, Terry J. 1942- *St&PR 91*
Summers, Thomas Morgan 1946- *WhoSSW 91*
Summers, Timothy *BiDrAPA 89*
Summers, Vernon Lloyd 1922- *BiDrAPA 89*
Summers, William Cofield 1939- *WhoAm 90*
Summers, William John 1945- *IntWWM 90*
Summers, William Lawrence 1942- *WhoAm 90*
Summersby, Edmund Kirkwood 1931- *St&PR 91*
Summersell, Charles Grayson 1908- *WhoWrEP 89*
Summersell, Frances Sharpley *WhoAmW 91, WhoSSW 91, WhoWor 91*
Summerskill, John *BioIn 16, NewYTBS 90*
Summerskill, Shirley Catherine W. 1931- *WhoWor 91*
Summerville, James 1947- *WhoWrEP 89*
Summerville, Jessica Diana 1950- *WhoAmW 91*
Summey, Steven Michael 1946- *WhoSSW 91*
Summit, Pamela Honey 1959- *BiDrAPA 89*
Summit, Roger K. *BioIn 16*
Summit, Roger Kent 1930- *WhoAm 90*
Summitt, Pat Head *BioIn 16*
Summitt, Robert 1935- *WhoAm 90*
Summitt, Robert Layman 1932- *WhoAm 90, WhoSSW 91*
Summy, Anne Tunis 1912-1986 *WhoAmA 91N*
Sumner, Anthony, *BioIn 16*
Sumner, Billy Taylor 1923- *WhoAm 90*
Sumner, Calvin Russell 1949- *BiDrAPA 89*
Sumner, Charles 1811-1874 *BioIn 16, WorAlBi*
Sumner, Charles Hanson 1928- *WhoE 91*
Sumner, Edwin Vose 1797-1863 *WhNaAH*
Sumner, Eric Eden 1924- *WhoAm 90*
Sumner, George 1940- *WhoAmA 91*
Sumner, Gordon *BioIn 16*
Sumner, James B. 1887-1955 *WorAlBi*
Sumner, Michael G *BiDrAPA 89*
Sumner, Randall Clay 1949- *St&PR 91*
Sumner, Stanley J. 1902- *St&PR 91*
Sumner, Stephen I. 1941- *WhoWrEP 89*
Sumner, Stephen Isaac *WhoE 91*
Sumner, William Evans, Jr. 1948- *WhoSSW 91*
Sumner, William Graham 1840-1910 *EncABHB 6 [port]*
Sumner, William Marvin 1928- *WhoAm 90*
Sumners, William Glenn, Jr. 1928- *WhoWor 91*
Sumney, Roland L. 1933- *St&PR 91*
Sumnicht, June E. 1936- *St&PR 91*
Sumowski, Werner 1931- *WhoWor 91*
Sumpter, James Hardee, III 1950- *WhoSSW 91*
Sumrall, Lester Frank 1913- *WhoAm 90*
Sumrall, Oliphant Malcolm 1932- *St&PR 91*
Sumray, Monty 1918- *WhoWor 91*
Sumrell, Gene 1919- *WhoSSW 91, WhoWor 91*
Sumrow, Kathie 1947- *IntWWM 90*
Sumsion, Herbert Whitton 1899- *IntWWM 90*
Sumsion, Owen Willis 1927- *St&PR 91*
Sumter, Thomas 1734-1832 *BioIn 16, EncCRAm*
Sumwalt, Robert Llewellyn, Jr. 1927- *WhoSSW 91*
Sun Bear 1929- *NewAgE 90*
Sun Li-jen *NewYTBS 90*
Sun Myung Moon *BioIn 16*
Sun Old Man *DcCanB 12*
Sun Ra *BioIn 16, DrBIPA 90, WhoAm 90*
Sun Ra 1914- *ConMus 5, OxCPMus*
Sun Yat-Sen 1866-1925 *WorAlBi*
Sun, Chieh 1943- *St&PR 91, WhoAm 90*
Sun, Christopher I-Chum 1953- *WhoWor 91*
Sun, Congting 1962- *WhoEmL 91*
Sun, David *NewAgMG*
Sun, Linda Christine 1943- *WhoAmW 91, WhoSSW 91*
Sun, Patricia 1941- *NewAgE 90*
Sun, Richard Alan 1950- *St&PR 91*
Sun, Robert Zu Jei 1948- *WhoE 91, WhoEmL 91, WhoWor 91*
Sun, Shan C. 1939- *WhoSSW 91*
Sun, Zuxun 1937- *WhoWor 91*
Sunahara, Yoshifumi 1927- *WhoWor 91*
Sunatrio, Sun 1945- *WhoWor 91*
Sunazaki, Tomoko *NewAgMG*
Sund, Eldon Harold 1930- *WhoSSW 91*
Sund, Horst 1926- *WhoWor 91*
Sund, Jerome Louis 1943- *St&PR 91*
Sund, Rick *WhoAm 90*
Sundaram, Kalpathy Balakrishnan 1950- *WhoSSW 91*
Sundaram, Narayanan 1939- *WhoWor 91*
Sundaram, Savitri *BiDrAPA 89*
Sundaram, T. R. 1937- *WhoE 91*
Sundaresan, Mosur Kalyanaraman 1929- *WhoAm 90*
Sundari, T A 1934- *EncO&P 3*
Sunday, Billy 1862-1935 *Ballpl 90 [port]*
Sunday, John 1796?-1855? *WhNaAH*
Sunday, William 1862-1935 *WorAlBi*
Sundberg, Alan Carl 1933- *WhoAm 90, WhoSSW 91*
Sundberg, Carl Gustave 1928- *WhoAmA 91, WhoE 91*
Sundberg, Edward August 1947- *WhoEmL 91*
Sundberg, Frederick Michael 1942- *St&PR 91*
Sundberg, Jim 1951- *Ballpl 90*
Sundberg, Johan Emil Fredrik 1936- *IntWWM 90*
Sundberg, John Edwin 1947- *WhoEmL 91*
Sundberg, Mark William 1957- *WhoE 91*
Sundberg, Norma Jean 1933- *WhoWrEP 89*
Sundberg, R. Dorothy 1915- *WhoAm 90*
Sundberg, Richard 1927- *St&PR 91*
Sundberg, Richard Jay 1938- *WhoAm 90*
Sundberg, Rolf Theodor 1940- *WhoWor 91*
Sundberg, Wilda 1930- *WhoAmA 91*
Sundby, Harold C., Jr. 1942- *St&PR 91*
Sunde, Arnold J. 1940- *St&PR 91*
Sunde, David Alan *BiDrAPA 89*
Sunde, Elizabeth Read *BiDrAPA 89*
Sunde, Roger Allan 1950- *WhoEmL 91*
Sundeen, John E. 1936- *St&PR 91*
Sundel, Claire 1907- *St&PR 91*
Sundel, Jack 1905- *St&PR 91*
Sundel, Martin 1940- *WhoAm 90*
Sundell, Abner *AuBYP 90*
Sundell, Duane J. 1931- *St&PR 91*
Sundell, Seymour Zane *BiDrAPA 89*
Sundem, Gary Lewis 1944- *WhoWor 91*
Sunder, Shyam 1944- *WhoE 91*
Sunderhaft, Eugene R. 1948- *St&PR 91*
Sunderland, Dale W 1921- *BiDrAPA 89*
Sunderland, David Kendall 1930- *WhoWor 91*
Sunderland, Dorothy, Countess Dowager of 1620?-1715 *BiDEWW*
Sunderland, Dorothy, Countess of 1617-1684 *FemiCLE*
Sunderland, Harry D. 1935- *WhoAm 90*
Sunderland, Harry David 1935- *St&PR 91*
Sunderland, James P. 1928- *St&PR 91*
Sunderland, La Roy 1804-1885 *EncO&P 3*
Sunderland, Nita Kathleen 1927- *WhoAmA 91*
Sunderland, Ray, Jr. 1913- *WhoAm 90*
Sunderland, Riley 1917- *WhoSSW 91*
Sunderland, Robert 1921- *St&PR 91, WhoAm 90*
Sunderland, Susan 1819-1905 *PenDiMP*
Sunderland, Thomas Elbert 1907- *WhoAm 90*
Sunderland, Trey 1951- *BiDrAPA 89*
Sunderman, Deborah Ann 1955- *WhoAmW 91*
Sunderman, Duane Neuman 1928- *St&PR 91*
Sunderman, Frederick William 1898- *WhoAm 90, WhoWor 91*
Sunderman, Martha-Lee 1934- *WhoAmW 91, WhoWor 91*
Sundermann, Edward Harry 1942- *St&PR 91*
Sundermann, Justus Daniel 1934- *WhoAm 90*
Sundermann, Richard H. 1953- *BiDrAPA 89*
Sundermann, Richard Henry 1925- *BiDrAPA 89*
Sundgaard, Arnold Olaf 1909- *WhoWor 91*
Sundheim, Suzanne T *BiDrAPA 89*
Sundholm, Micaela *BioIn 16*
Sundin, Adelaide Toombs 1915- *WhoAmA 91*
Sundin, Karen Marie 1951- *WhoEmL 91*
Sundin, Kjell 1937- *WhoWor 91*
Sundin, Lennart Karl 1935- *St&PR 91*
Sundin, Nils-Goran 1951- *IntWWM 90*
Sundin, Ted Tryggve 1956- *BiDrAPA 89*
Sundius, Robert Edwin 1930- *St&PR 91*
Sundlun, Bruce 1920- *St&PR 91*
Sundlun, Bruce George 1920- *WhoAm 90*
Sundmacher, Robley W. *ODwPR 91*
Sundman, John E. 1926- *St&PR 91*
Sundman, Per Olof 1922- *DcScanL*
Sundman, Ulf Johan 1929- *IntWWM 90*
Sundnes, Gunnar 1926- *WhoWor 91*
Sundquist, Dean Allan 1960- *St&PR 91*
Sundquist, Donald Kenneth 1936- *WhoAm 90, WhoSSW 91*
Sundquist, Eric J. 1952- *ConAu 129*
Sundquist, Helge Erik 1930- *WhoWor 91*
Sundquist, James Lloyd 1915- *WhoAm 90*
Sundquist, Martha Carolyn 1937- *WhoE 91*
Sundquist, Wesley Burton 1927- *WhoAm 90*
Sundra, Steve 1910-1952 *Ballpl 90*
Sundry, Arthur P. *WhoAm 90*
Sundstrom, Alan C. 1934- *St&PR 91*
Sundstrom, Charles 1930- *St&PR 91*
Sundstrom, John Christer 1943- *WhoWor 91*
Sundstrom, Katherine A 1949- *BiDrAPA 89*
Sundstrom, V. Glenn 1928- *St&PR 91*
Sundstrom, Virgil Glenn 1928- *WhoAm 90*
Sundt, H. Wilson 1932- *St&PR 91*
Sundt, Harry Wilson 1932- *WhoAm 90, WhoWor 91*
Sundt, Robert Stout 1926- *St&PR 91, WhoAm 90*
Sundt, Thoralf Mauritz, Jr. 1930- *WhoAm 90*
Sundukov, Alex 1952- *BioIn 16*
Sunell, Robert John 1929- *WhoAm 90*
Suner, Ramon Serrano 1901- *BioIn 16*
Sunergren, Mary Anne 1942- *WhoAmW 91*
Suneson, Scott *St&PR 91*
Sung *WomWR*
Sung, Alfred 1948- *WhoAm 90*
Sung, Eunsook *BiDrAPA 89*
Sung, Kihong 1933- *St&PR 91*
Sung, Nak-Ho 1940- *WhoAm 90*
Sung, Sui-Kwong 1949- *BiDrAPA 89*
Sung, Yuan-Ming 1930- *WhoWrEP 89*
Sunguroglu, Sabahattin 1919- *WhoWor 91*
Sunier, Katherine Johnson 1952- *WhoAmW 91*
Sunil, Saigal 1957- *WhoE 91*
Sunkavalli, Prasad T *BiDrAPA 89*
Sunkel, Robert C 1933- *WhoAmA 91*
Sunkel, Robert Jacob 1926- *St&PR 91*
Sunkel, Tom 1912- *Ballpl 90*
Sunkin, Howard H. *ODwPR 91*
Sunley, Emil McKee 1942- *WhoAm 90*
Sunlight, Carole *WhoAmW 91*
Sunn, Laura *BiDrAPA 89*
Sunne, Randall Henry 1950- *WhoEmL 91*
Sunnen, Gerard Vitold 1942- *BiDrAPA 89*
Sunol, Celia 1899- *EncCoWW*
Sunshine, Adrian *IntWWM 90*
Sunshine, Eugene Samuel 1950- *WhoAm 90, WhoWor 91*
Sunshine, Leonard *BioIn 16*
Sunshine, Morton 1915-1990 *BioIn 16*
Sunstein, Carolyn *BioIn 16*
Sununu, John *BioIn 16*
Sununu, John H. 1939- *WhoAm 90, WhoE 91*
Sununu, John M. *NewYTBS 90 [port]*
Suojanen, Waino W. 1920- *WhoAm 90*
Suojanen, Wayne William 1950- *WhoEmL 91, WhoWor 91*
Suomala, Richard Michael 1947- *St&PR 91*
Suomalainen, Mikko Antero 1955- *WhoWor 91*
Suomi, Heikki Ilmari 1944- *WhoWor 91*
Suomi, Verner Edward 1915- *WhoAm 90*
Suonio, Aino *DcScanL*
Suosalmi, Kerttu-Kaarina 1921- *EncCoWW*
Suotmaa, Juha Olavi 1963- *WhoWor 91*
Suovaniemi, Osmo Antero 1943- *WhoWor 91*
Suozzo, Frank Vincent 1928- *WhoAm 90*
Sup, Stuart Allen 1943- *WhoE 91, WhoWor 91*
Supan, Angelina A 1941- *BiDrAPA 89*
Super Barrio *BioIn 16*
Super, Donald E. 1910- *WhoAm 90*
Super, Robert Henry 1914- *WhoAm 90*
Super, William Alan 1953- *WhoEmL 91*
Super, William C *BiDrAPA 89*
Supervia, Conchita 1895-1936 *PenDiMP*
Supey, Robert Andrew 1941- *St&PR 91*
Supino, David J. 1933- *St&PR 91*
Supinski, Dawn Jacqueline 1961- *WhoAmW 91*
Supinsky, Kathy Lee 1948- *WhoEmL 91*
Suplee, Carol Janet Cunningham 1934- *WhoWrEP 89*
Suppan, Wolfgang 1933- *IntWWM 90*
Suppe, Francis J. 1940- *St&PR 91*
Suppe, Franz von 1819-1895 *OxCPMus*
Suppe, John *WhoAm 90*
Suppes, Patricia 1951- *BiDrAPA 89*
Suppes, Patrick 1922- *WhoAm 90*
Supple, Diane Marie 1956- *WhoAmW 91*
Supple, Jerome H. 1936- *WhoAm 90*
Supplee, James E. 1946- *St&PR 91*
Suppon, Charles *BioIn 16*
Supremes, The *EncPR&S 89, OxCPMus*
Suprenant, Thomas Terry 1942- *WhoAm 90*
Supriano, Susan Jean 1938- *WhoAmW 91*
Suput, Ray Radoslav 1922- *WhoAm 90*
Suquet, Jose S. 1956- *WhoHisp 91*
Suquia Goicoechea, Angel 1916- *WhoWor 91*
Sura, Ashwin Bachubha *BiDrAPA 89*
Sura, Peter Erich 1941- *St&PR 91*
Sura-Thomson, Wendy 1950- *WhoEmL 91*
Suraci, Charles Xavier, Jr. 1933- *WhoAm 90*
Suraci, Henry A. 1932- *St&PR 91*
Surana, Hem Raj 1945- *WhoWor 91*
Surany, Anico *AuBYP 90*
Suranyi-Unger, Theodore, Jr. 1930- *WhoAm 90*
Surapaneni, Bujji Babu *BiDrAPA 89*
Surapaneni, Purna Rao *BiDrAPA 89*
Suratt, Theodore P *BiDrAPA 89*
Surawicz, Borys 1917- *WhoAm 90*
Surawicz, Frida Gerarda *BiDrAPA 89*
Surbeck, Leighton Homer 1902- *WhoAm 90, WhoWor 91*
Surber, David Francis 1940- *WhoSSW 91, WhoWor 91*
Surchin, Harold P 1923- *BiDrAPA 89*
Surdam, John L. 1916- *St&PR 91*
Surdam, John Lewis 1915- *WhoAm 90*
Surdam, Robert McClellan 1917- *WhoAm 90*
Surdick, Robert F. 1934- *St&PR 91*
Surdoval, Donald James 1932- *WhoAm 90*
Surdoval, Lawrence Anthony, Jr. 1930- *WhoE 91, WhoWor 91*
Surdovel, Catherine Patricia 1939- *WhoE 91*
Sure, Al B. *BioIn 16*
Surendran-Nair, Kodakkatu G 1936- *BiDrAPA 89*
Sures, Jack 1934- *WhoAmA 91*
Suresh, Bindinganavle Raghavan 1953- *WhoEmL 91*
Suresh, Philbert Joseph 1948- *WhoWor 91*
Surface, Joseph Robert 1952- *WhoEmL 91*
Surface, Stephen Walter 1943- *WhoWor 91*
Surfus, Sandra Sue 1941- *WhoAmW 91*
Surgalski, Patrick J 1953- *WhoAmA 91*
Surgenor, Daniel Delaney 1945- *St&PR 91*
Surgi, Elizabeth Benson 1955- *WhoAmW 91*
Surguy, Maria Teresa 1922- *WhoSSW 91*
Surhoff, B.J. 1964- *Ballpl 90*
Suri, Jagdish C *BiDrAPA 89*
Suri, Kamlaish Marc 1942- *WhoWor 91*
Suri, Vinod *BiDrAPA 89*
Suria, Tomas De *WhNaAH*
Suria, Violeta Lopez *HispWr 90*
Suria-Colon, Jorge L. *BiDrAPA 89*
Surinach Carreras, Ricardo Antonio 1928- *WhoAm 90, WhoWor 91*
Surkin, Elliot Mark 1942- *WhoAm 90*
Surkin, Martin 1920- *St&PR 91*
Surkont, Max 1922-1986 *Ballpl 90*
Surks, Martin I. 1934- *WhoAm 90*
Surlaker, Samir Manohar 1953- *WhoWor 91*
Surles, Glen Craig 1947- *WhoE 91*
Surles, Kathryn Douglas 1936- *WhoSSW 91*
Surles, Walter Wayne 1946- *WhoE 91*
Surls, James *BioIn 16*
Surls, James 1943- *WhoAmA 91*
Surma, Ronald F. 1936- *St&PR 91*

Surman, Owen Stanley 1943- *BiDrAPA 89, WhoE 91*
Surman, William Robert 1926- *WhoAm 90*
Surmeli, Suphi 1931- *BiDrAPA 89, WhoE 91*
Surmeyan, Hazaros Artur 1943- *WhoAm 90*
Surmonte, Hugo N. 1908- *St&PR 91*
Surnamer, Shulamith *WhoWrEP 89*
Suro, Dario 1917- *WhoWor 91*
Suro, David Guillermo 1961- *WhoHisp 91*
Suro-Bredie, Carmen Cecilia 1947- *WhoE 91*
Surowiec, Stanley Albert 1943- *St&PR 91*
Surplus, Robert W. 1923- *WhoSSW 91*
Surprenant, Mark Christopher 1951- *WhoEmL 91*
Surprise, Juanee 1944- *WhoAmW 91*
Surr, John Vernon 1937- *WhoE 91*
Surratt, Charles Finch 1936- *St&PR 91*
Surratt, John H. 1844-1916 *WorAlBi*
Surratt, Kelly Allen 1959- *WhoEmL 91*
Surratt, Mary E. 1820-1865 *BioAmW, WorAlBi*
Surratt, Nancy Abercrombie 1957- *WhoSSW 91*
Surrency, Erwin Campbell 1924- *WhoAm 90*
Surrey, Berne 1915- *BiDrAPA 89*
Surrey, Milt 1922- *WhoAm 90, WhoAmA 91, WhoE 91*
Surrey, Philip Henry 1910- *WhoAm 90*
Surrey, Philip Henry 1910-1990 *WhoAmA 91N*
Surridge, Stephen Zehring 1940- *WhoAm 90*
Sursa, Charles David 1925- *WhoAm 90*
Sursa, David 1925- *St&PR 91*
Surtees, Bruce *ConTFT 8*
Surtees, John *BioIn 16*
Surtees, Robert E. 1933- *St&PR 91*
Surti, Bhadresh V *BiDrAPA 89*
Surtshin, Stephen J 1952- *BiDrAPA 89*
Surwillo, Walter W. 1926- *WhoSSW 91*
Sury, Earl 1937- *St&PR 91*
Surya, Gundlapalli *BiDrAPA 89*
Suryadevara, Raveendra Babu *BiDrAPA 89*
Suryani, Luh Ketut *BiDrAPA 89*
Suryavanshi, O.P.S. 1961- *WhoWor 91*
Suryodipuro, Budi Aswinto 1949- *WhoWor 91*
Susa, Conrad 1935- *WhoAm 90*
Susag, Millins Philip 1921- *WhoE 91*
Susann, Jacqueline 1921-1974 *BioAmW, MajTwCW*
Susanne of Bourbon 1491-1521 *WomWR [port]*
Susce, George 1931- *Ballpl 90*
Susco, David Michael *BiDrAPA 89*
Susco, Michael C *BiDrAPA 89*
Susco, Michael J. 1943- *St&PR 91*
Susens, Millicent Milanovich *WhoAmW 91*
Susi, Mart Sven 1955- *WhoEmL 91*
Susie *WhoWrEP 89*
Susie, Sharon Kay 1951- *WhoAmW 91*
Susin, Alfredo 1928 *WhoWor 91*
Suske, Joe E. 1931- *St&PR 91*
Suskin, Douglas Sidney 1920- *St&PR 91*
Suskind, Davis Alan 1947- *BiDrAPA 89*
Suskind, Dennis A. 1942- *WhoAm 90*
Suskind, Lieselotte *BiDrAPA 89*
Suskind, Raymond Robert 1913- *WhoAm 90*
Suskind, Sigmund Richard 1926- *WhoAm 90*
Suslak, Howard Robinson 1920- *WhoAm 90, WhoWor 91*
Suslak, Howard Robinson 1922- *St&PR 91*
Suslov, Mikhail Andreevich 1902-1982 *BioIn 16*
Susman, Karen Lee 1942- *WhoAmW 91*
Susman, Margarete 1874-1966 *EncCoWW*
Susman, Millard 1934- *WhoAm 90*
Susman, Morton Lee 1934- *WhoWor 91*
Susman, Stephen D. *BioIn 16*
Susman, Stephen Daily 1941- *WhoAm 90*
Susman, Virginia L 1949- *BiDrAPA 89*
Susman, Virginia Lehmann 1949- *WhoAmW 91*
Susmarski, Ronald James 1954- *WhoEmL 91*
Susnjara, Gary *BioIn 16*
Susnjara, Gary M. 1939- *WhoAm 90, WhoE 91*
Susnjara, Ken *BioIn 16*
Susnjara, Kenneth John 1947- *St&PR 91*
Susong, Walter Lynn, Jr. 1941- *WhoSSW 91*
Susor, Dorothy Marie Alma Leffel 1922- *WhoAmW 91*
Suss, Lester J. 1913- *St&PR 91*
Sussan, Nancy Frederick 1949- *WhoAmW 91*
Susselman, Samuel 1906- *BiDrAPA 89*
Sussen, Daniel Charles 1928- *St&PR 91*
Sussen, Joseph J. 1925- *St&PR 91*
Sussenbach, John Samuel 1938- *WhoWor 91*
Sussenguth, Edward Henry 1932- *WhoAm 90*
Susser, Cynthia Rose 1956- *WhoAmW 91*
Susser, Ezra Saul 1952- *WhoE 91*
Sussex, James N 1917- *BiDrAPA 89*
Sussex, James Neil 1917- *WhoAm 90*
Susskind, Charles *WhoAm 90*
Susskind, David 1920-1987 *BioIn 16, WorAlBi*
Susskind, Harriet *WhoWrEP 89*
Susskind, Herbert 1929- *WhoAm 90*
Susskind, J. Wallace 1924- *St&PR 91*
Susskind, Lawrence Elliott 1947- *WhoAm 90*
Susskind, Nathan 1898-1989 *BioIn 16*
Susskind, Siegfried 1919- *WhoAm 90*
Susskind, Teresa Gabriel 1921- *WhoAm 90*
Susskind, Walter 1913-1980 *PenDiMP*
Sussler, Betsy Ruth 1952- *WhoWrEP 89*
Sussman, Alfred Sheppard 1919- *WhoAm 90*
Sussman, Andrew David 1951- *St&PR 91*
Sussman, Arthur 1927- *WhoAmA 91*
Sussman, Barbara Helen J. 1955- *WhoE 91*
Sussman, Barbara J 1955- *WhoAmA 91*
Sussman, Barry 1934- *WhoAm 90*
Sussman, Barry 1939- *St&PR 91*
Sussman, Bernard Jules 1926- *WhoAm 90*
Sussman, Bonnie K *WhoAmA 91*
Sussman, Cornelia *BioIn 16*
Sussman, Daniel L. 1957- *BiDrAPA 89*
Sussman, Deborah Evelyn 1931- *WhoAmW 91, WhoWor 91*
Sussman, Elisabeth Sacks 1939- *WhoAmA 91*
Sussman, Gary Lawrence 1952- *WhoAmA 91*
Sussman, Gary Mark 1954- *WhoEmL 91*
Sussman, Gerald 1933-1989 *BioIn 16, ConAu 130*
Sussman, Gerald 1934- *St&PR 91, WhoAm 90*
Sussman, Gertrude 1933- *WhoAmW 91*
Sussman, Harry 1912- *St&PR 91*
Sussman, I. Harvey 1939- *St&PR 91*
Sussman, Irving 1908- *BioIn 16*
Sussman, Joel Fredric 1948- *St&PR 91*
Sussman, Leon Nathaniel 1907- *WhoE 91*
Sussman, Leonard Richard 1920- *WhoAm 90, WhoE 91*
Sussman, M. Hal *WhoWrEP 89*
Sussman, Martin Victor *WhoAm 90*
Sussman, Marvin 1927- *WhoAm 90*
Sussman, Marvin Lawrence 1948- *WhoSSW 91*
Sussman, Marvin S. 1947- *St&PR 91*
Sussman, Norma J. *St&PR 91*
Sussman, Norman *BiDrAPA 89*
Sussman, Ocie Jones 1935- *WhoWrEP 89*
Sussman, Peter 1958- *ConTFT 8*
Sussman, Raquel Rotman 1921- *WhoAmW 91*
Sussman, Richard N 1908-1971 *WhoAmA 91N*
Sussman, Robert 1932- *WhoE 91*
Sussman, Robert B *BiDrAPA 89*
Sussman, S. Donald *BioIn 16*
Sussman, Sally *BioIn 16*
Sussman, Stephen P. 1945- *St&PR 91*
Sussman, Susan *WhoWrEP 89*
Sussman, Susan 1942- *BioIn 16, ConAu 30NR*
Sussman, Wendy 1949- *WhoAmA 91*
Sussman-Walla, Jill 1954- *WhoAmA 91*
Sussmann, Leila Aline 1922- *WhoAm 90*
Sussmann, M Hal *WhoAmA 91*
Sussna, Edward 1926- *WhoAm 90, WhoWor 91*
Sussna, Marshall 1935- *St&PR 91*
Sustendal, Diane Marie 1944- *WhoE 91*
Sutcliff, Rosemary 1920- *AuBYP 90, BioIn 16*
Sutcliffe, Alice *BiDEWW, FemiCLE*
Sutcliffe, Eric 1909- *WhoAm 90, WhoWor 91*
Sutcliffe, James Helme 1929- *WhoWor 91*
Sutcliffe, Rick 1956- *Ballpl 90*
Sutcliffe, Sidney Clement 1918- *IntWWM 90*
Sutcliffe, William H., Jr. 1923- *WhoSSW 91*
Sutema, Liune 1927- *EncCoWW*
Suter, Albert E. 1935- *BioIn 16*
Suter, Albert Edward 1935- *St&PR 91, WhoAm 90*
Suter, Bruce H. 1921- *St&PR 91*
Suter, Carol Joan 1949- *WhoEmL 91*
Suter, David *BioIn 16*
Suter, David Thomas 1927- *St&PR 91*
Suter, George August 1934- *WhoSSW 91, WhoWor 91*
Suter, Johan August 1803-1880 *WhNaAH*
Suter, Jon Michael 1941- *WhoSSW 91*
Suter, Kathryn Ann *BiDrAPA 89*
Suter, Sherwood Eugene 1928- *WhoAmA 91, WhoSSW 91*
Suter, Suzanne *St&PR 91*
Suter, Vane Edward 1929- *St&PR 91*
Suter, William Kent 1937- *WhoAm 90*
Sutera, Salvatore Philip 1933- *WhoAm 90*
Sutermeister, Heinrich 1910- *IntWWM 90, PenDiMP A*
Suthaus, Ludwig 1906-1971 *BioIn 16, PenDiMP*
Sutherin, Sharna J. *BioIn 16*
Sutherland, Alan Roy 1944- *WhoE 91*
Sutherland, Alasdair *ODwPR 91*
Sutherland, Allan T 1950- *ConAu 132*
Sutherland, Amanda *BiDrAPA 89*
Sutherland, Bruce *IntWWM 90, WhoWor 91*
Sutherland, Bruce Taylor 1930- *St&PR 91*
Sutherland, Darrell 1941- *Ballpl 90*
Sutherland, David Russell 1945- *WhoEmL 91*
Sutherland, Donald 1934- *BioIn 16, OxCCanT, WorAlBi*
Sutherland, Donald 1935- *WhoAm 90*
Sutherland, Donald Eugene 1947- *WhoSSW 91*
Sutherland, Donald Gray 1929- *WhoAm 90*
Sutherland, Donald James 1931- *St&PR 91, WhoAm 90*
Sutherland, Earl W., Jr. 1915-1974 *WorAlBi*
Sutherland, Efua 1924- *FemiCLE*
Sutherland, Efua Theodora 1924- *BioIn 16*
Sutherland, Gail Russell 1923- *WhoAm 90*
Sutherland, Gary 1944- *Ballpl 90*
Sutherland, Gary Edward 1941- *St&PR 91*
Sutherland, George Leslie 1922- *WhoAm 90*
Sutherland, Graham 1903-1980 *IntDcAA 90*
Sutherland, Ivan E. 1938- *BioIn 16*
Sutherland, Jack L. 1943- *St&PR 91*
Sutherland, Jeffrey Victor 1941- *WhoE 91*
Sutherland, Joan 1890-1947 *FemiCLE*
Sutherland, Joan 1926- *BioIn 16, IntWWM 90, PenDiMP, WhoAm 90, WhoWor 91, WorAlBi*
Sutherland, Joe Allen 1934- *WhoAm 90*
Sutherland, John Beattie 1932- *WhoAm 90*
Sutherland, John Carlyn 1928- *WhoE 91*
Sutherland, John M., Jr. 1923- *St&PR 91*
Sutherland, Jon Nicholas 1941-1977 *ConAu 32NR*
Sutherland, Joseph Edward *BiDrAPA 89*
Sutherland, Julia K. 1956- *ODwPR 91*
Sutherland, Kiefer *BioIn 16, WorAlBi*
Sutherland, Lewis Frederick 1952- *St&PR 91, WhoAm 90, WhoEmL 91*
Sutherland, Lowell Francis 1939- *WhoWor 91*
Sutherland, Lynn Sparks 1958- *WhoSSW 91*
Sutherland, Malcolm Read, Jr. 1916- *WhoAm 90*
Sutherland, Marcia Elizabeth *WhoAmW 91*
Sutherland, Margaret 1941- *FemiCLE*
Sutherland, Monika Lea 1955- *WhoAmW 91*
Sutherland, Pamela 1943- *IntWWM 90*
Sutherland, Peter 1956- *St&PR 91*
Sutherland, Peter Denis 1946- *WhoWor 91*
Sutherland, Ralph M. 1943- *St&PR 91*
Sutherland, Randolph Clarence 1947- *St&PR 91*
Sutherland, Raymond Carter 1917- *WhoAm 90, WhoWrEP 89*
Sutherland, Raymond E. 1937- *St&PR 91*
Sutherland, Rhoda Clarke 1908?-1989 *BioIn 16*
Sutherland, Robert Alec 1945- *WhoE 91*
Sutherland, Robert D. 1937- *WhoWrEP 89*
Sutherland, Robert Louis 1916- *WhoAm 90*
Sutherland, Sandy 1902- *WhoAmA 91N*
Sutherland, Scott McKellan 1951- *WhoE 91*
Sutherland, Steven Michael *BiDrAPA 89*
Sutherland, Suzanne M *BiDrAPA 89*
Sutherland, Thomas Lee, Jr. 1938- *WhoAm 90*
Sutherland, Veronica *WhoWor 91*
Sutherland, William Owen Sheppard 1921- *WhoAm 90, WhoWrEP 89*
Sutherland, William Paul 1941- *WhoAm 90*
Sutherland, Wm. G., Jr. 1915- *St&PR 91*
Sutherland, Zena 1915- *AuBYP 90*
Sutherland-Brown, Malcolm Corsan 1917- *WhoAm 90*
Sutherlund, David Arvid 1929- *WhoAm 90, WhoWor 91*
Suthers, John William 1951- *WhoEmL 91*
Suthikant, Deja 1941- *BiDrAPA 89*
Suthren, Victor J. H. 1942- *WhoAm 90*
Sutin, Norman *WhoAm 90*
Sutin, Paul *NewAgMG*
Sutker, Lawrence H 1948- *BiDrAPA 89*
Sutley, Kaye Walker 1948- *WhoSSW 91*
Sutley, Robert M. 1925- *St&PR 91*
Sutliff, Diane Louise Peek 1948- *WhoAmW 91*
Sutlin, Vivian *WhoAmW 91, WhoWor 91*
Sutman, Francis Xavier 1927- *WhoAm 90*
Sutnick, Alton Ivan 1928- *WhoAm 90*
Suto, Carla Marie 1959- *WhoAmW 91*
Sutowski, Thor Brian 1945- *WhoSSW 91*
Sutphen, Dick 1937- *NewAgE 90*
Sutphen, Harold Amerman, Jr. 1926- *WhoAm 90*
Sutphin, Lester Insley, Jr. 1956- *WhoSSW 91*
Sutphin, Winfield Blair *BioIn 16, NewYTBS 90*
Sutphin, Winfield Blair 1919?-1990 *ConAu 131*
Sutphin, Wyn Blair *ConAu 131*
Sutresna, Nana S. 1933- *WhoWor 91*
Sutro, Frederick Charles, Jr. 1920- *St&PR 91*
Sutro, John Alfred 1905- *WhoAm 90*
Suttenfield, Diana 1944- *WhoAmA 91*
Suttenfield, Virginia 1917- *BiDrAPA 89*
Sutter, Bruce 1953- *Ballpl 90 [port]*
Sutter, Dale Merle 1934- *St&PR 91*
Sutter, David L. 1953- *St&PR 91*
Sutter, Diane 1950- *BioIn 16, WhoSSW 91*
Sutter, Elizabeth Henby 1912- *WhoAmW 91*
Sutter, Emily May Geeseman 1939- *WhoAmW 91*
Sutter, Harvey Mack 1906- *WhoWor 91*
Sutter, James Francis 1937- *WhoAm 90*
Sutter, James Stewart 1940- *WhoAmA 91*
Sutter, James T 1917- *BiDrAPA 89*
Sutter, John Augustus 1803-1880 *WhNaAH, WorAlBi*
Sutter, John Ben 1953- *WhoSSW 91*
Sutter, John R. 1937- *St&PR 91*
Sutter, Joseph F. 1921- *WhoAm 90*
Sutter, Leslie Strong *WhoAmA 91*
Sutter, Madeline Ann 1941- *St&PR 91*
Sutter, Margaret Moffett 1953- *WhoAmW 91*
Sutter, Martin Paul 1955- *WhoSSW 91, WhoWor 91*
Sutter, Morley Carman 1933- *WhoAm 90*
Sutter, Richard Anthony 1909- *WhoAm 90*
Sutter, Sandy Coffee 1942- *WhoSSW 91*
Sutter, William Franklin 1938- *St&PR 91*
Sutter, William Paul 1924- *WhoAm 90*
Sutterer, M. Glennon 1954- *WhoE 91*
Sutterfield, Thomas Wayne 1949- *WhoSSW 91*
Sutterley, Edward Carter 1932- *WhoE 91*
Sutthoff, Jack 1873-1942 *Ballpl 90*
Suttin, Doris Beth 1940- *WhoAmW 91*
Suttle, Dorwin Wallace 1906- *WhoAm 90, WhoSSW 91*
Suttle, Jimmie Ray 1932- *WhoAm 90*
Suttle, Stephen Hungate 1940- *WhoWor 91*
Suttles, David Clyde 1948- *WhoEmL 91*
Suttles, Larry 1950- *St&PR 91*
Suttles, Mule 1901-1968 *Ballpl 90*
Suttles, Shirley Janet 1922- *WhoWrEP 89*
Suttles, Virginia Grant 1931- *WhoAmW 91*
Suttles, William Maurrelle 1920- *WhoAm 90, WhoSSW 91*
Suttman, Paul 1933- *WhoAmA 91*
Suttner, Berta von 1843-1914 *EncCoWW*
Suttner, Lee J. *BioIn 16*
Sutton, Barbara Jean 1949- *WhoAmW 91*
Sutton, Barrett Boulware 1927- *WhoAm 90*
Sutton, Berrien Daniel 1926- *WhoAm 90*
Sutton, Beverley Ann 1939- *WhoAmW 91*
Sutton, Beverly J 1932- *BiDrAPA 89*
Sutton, Bruce Morris *BiDrAPA 89*
Sutton, Carol 1945- *WhoAmA 91*
Sutton, Daniel John *BiDrAPA 89*
Sutton, David B. 1939- *WhoAm 90*
Sutton, Don *BioIn 16*
Sutton, Don 1945- *Ballpl 90 [port], WorAlBi*
Sutton, Donald Raymond 1926- *St&PR 91*
Sutton, Dorothy Moseley 1938- *WhoWrEP 89*
Sutton, Ezra 1850-1907 *Ballpl 90*
Sutton, Felix 1910?- *AuBYP 90*
Sutton, Frances Hammer 1941- *WhoAmW 91*
Sutton, Francis Xavier 1917- *WhoAm 90*
Sutton, Frank T. 1946- *St&PR 91*
Sutton, Fred Milton, Jr. 1952- *WhoSSW 91*
Sutton, Frederick Isler, Jr. 1916- *WhoSSW 91, WhoWor 91*
Sutton, Gary Scott 1954- *WhoEmL 91*
Sutton, Geoffrey William 1950- *WhoEmL 91*
Sutton, George Douglas 1949- *St&PR 91*
Sutton, George Louis 1930- *St&PR 91*

Sutton, George Miksch 1898-1982 *WhoAmA 91N*
Sutton, George Walter 1927- *WhoAm 90*
Sutton, Gerald Winfred 1943- *St&PR 91*
Sutton, Hal *BioIn 16*
Sutton, Harold L *BiDrAPA 89*
Sutton, Harry Eldon 1927- *WhoAm 90*
Sutton, Henry *WhoWrEP 89*
Sutton, Hirst 1911- *WhoSSW 91*
Sutton, Homer Bates 1949- *WhoSSW 91*
Sutton, Horace Ashley 1919- *WhoAm 90*
Sutton, Howard George 1950- *St&PR 91*
Sutton, James Andrew 1934- *St&PR 91, WhoAm 90, WhoE 91*
Sutton, James Edgar 1945- *St&PR 91*
Sutton, James Kenneth 1936- *St&PR 91*
Sutton, Jane 1950- *BioIn 16*
Sutton, Jean *AuBYP 90*
Sutton, Jeff 1913-1979 *AuBYP 90*
Sutton, Jeffrey Paul *BiDrAPA 89*
Sutton, Jeffrey Paul 1958- *WhoE 91*
Sutton, John B., Jr. 1918- *St&PR 91*
Sutton, John E. 1947- *St&PR 91*
Sutton, John Ewing 1950- *WhoSSW 91, WhoWor 91*
Sutton, John F., Jr. 1918- *WhoAm 90, WhoWor 91*
Sutton, John Paul 1934- *WhoAm 90*
Sutton, Jonathan Stone 1944- *WhoAm 90*
Sutton, Joseph Thomas 1922- *WhoAm 90*
Sutton, Joyce Elaine 1946- *WhoAmW 91*
Sutton, Judith Kay 1947- *WhoAmW 91*
Sutton, Judith Louise 1941- *WhoWrEP 89*
Sutton, Julia Sumberg 1928- *IntWWM 90, WhoAm 90*
Sutton, Katherine *BiDEWW, FemiCLE*
Sutton, Kelso Furbush 1939- *St&PR 91, WhoAm 90, WhoE 91*
Sutton, Larry 1858-1944 *Ballpl 90*
Sutton, Leonard von Bibra 1914- *WhoWor 91*
Sutton, Lester Earl 1937- *WhoAm 90*
Sutton, Lewis Richard *BiDrAPA 89*
Sutton, Loree Kimberly 1959- *BiDrAPA 89*
Sutton, M. W. 1848-1918 *BioIn 16*
Sutton, Marcella French 1946- *WhoAmW 91*
Sutton, Margaret Beebe 1903- *AuBYP 90*
Sutton, Mary Ellen 1940- *IntWWM 90*
Sutton, Michael Westernhouse 1848-1918 *BioIn 16*
Sutton, Milton 1914- *WhoE 91*
Sutton, Myron Daniel 1925- *AuBYP 90*
Sutton, Myron Daniel, and Ann Sutton *AuBYP 90*
Sutton, Pat 1941- *WhoAmA 91*
Sutton, Pat Lipsky 1941- *WhoAm 90*
Sutton, Paul J. 1939- *WhoWor 91*
Sutton, Peter Alfred 1934- *WhoAm 90*
Sutton, Peter C. 1949- *ConAu 132, WhoAmA 91*
Sutton, Peter Campbell 1949- *WhoAm 90*
Sutton, Philip John 1928- *WhoWor 91*
Sutton, Pierre 1947- *DrBlPA 90*
Sutton, R. Anderson 1949- *IntWWM 90*
Sutton, Ralph 1922- *OxCPMus*
Sutton, Ray Sandy 1937- *St&PR 91*
Sutton, Reginald Miller 1899-1989 *BioIn 16*
Sutton, Renee Colette 1958- *WhoAmW 91*
Sutton, Richard Donald 1925- *WhoAm 90*
Sutton, Richard Lauder 1935- *WhoAm 90*
Sutton, Robert Mize 1915- *WhoAm 90*
Sutton, Ronald Gene 1941- *St&PR 91*
Sutton, Ruth Haviland 1898-1960 *WhoAmA 91N*
Sutton, Selden W. *ODwPR 91*
Sutton, Sharyn Mallamad *ODwPR 91*
Sutton, Sherill Marie 1954- *WhoE 91*
Sutton, Thomas C. 1942- *WhoAm 90*
Sutton, Thomas Carl 1921- *St&PR 91*
Sutton, Tony Wayne 1955- *WhoWor 91*
Sutton, Walter 1916- *WhoAm 90*
Sutton, William Alexander 1943- *WhoSSW 91*
Sutton, William Michael 1940- *St&PR 91*
Sutton, Willis Anderson, Jr. 1917- *WhoAm 90*
Sutton-Salley, Virginia B. *WhoAmW 91*
Sutton-Straus, Joan M. 1932- *WhoAm 90*
Sutzkever, Abraham *BioIn 16*
Suu Kyi *BioIn 16*
Suud, Khaled Abu *BioIn 16*
Suurmond, Dirk 1926- *WhoWor 91*
Suva, Suzanne 1947- *WhoAmW 91*
Suval, Marcia *BiDrAPA 89*
Suvanashiep, Sujarit *BiDrAPA 89*
Suvar, Stipe 1936- *WhoWor 91*
Suvarnakar, Smita J. 1948- *WhoE 91*
Suvorov, Aleksandr 1729-1800 *WorAlBi*
Suwa, Kanenori 1928- *WhoWor 91*
Suwa, Nozomi 1912- *BiDrAPA 89*
Suwak, Lawrence M. 1940- *St&PR 91*
Suwansathien, Bhasna 1936- *WhoWor 91*
Suwarno, Harijono 1952- *WhoWor 91*
Suwinski, Jan H. 1941- *St&PR 91*
Suwinsky, Pam Pokorney 1954- *WhoAmW 91*
Suy, Erik 1933- *WhoWor 91*
Suydam, Eunice M. *St&PR 91*
Suyematsu, Toshiro 1918- *WhoAm 90*
Suyetsugu, Grace Tamiko 1957- *WhoEmL 91*
Suykens, Fernand Lucie Hubert 1927- *WhoWor 91*
Suzanne of Bourbon 1491-1521 *WomWR [port]*
Suzanne, Jamie 1943- *SmATA X [port]*
Suzanne, Jamie 1952- *SmATA X [port]*
Suze, Comtesse de La 1618-1673 *EncCoWW*
Suzen 1946- *WhoAmA 91*
Suziedelis, Vytautas A. 1930- *WhoAm 90*
Suzman, Helen *BioIn 16*
Suzman, Richard Michael 1942- *WhoE 91*
Suzuki Daisetz Teitaro 1870-1966 *EncJap*
Suzuki Kantaro 1867-1948 *EncJap*
Suzuki Shin'ichi 1898- *EncJap*
Suzuki Zenko 1911- *EncJap*
Suzuki, Barnabas Tatsuya 1938- *WhoWor 91*
Suzuki, D T *MajTwCW*
Suzuki, Daisetz T. *MajTwCW*
Suzuki, Daisetz Teitaro 1870-1966 *MajTwCW*
Suzuki, Daniel Thomas *BiDrAPA 89*
Suzuki, David T. 1936- *BioIn 16*
Suzuki, Fujio 1933- *WhoWor 91*
Suzuki, Gengo 1904- *WhoSSW 91, WhoWor 91*
Suzuki, Hidetaro 1937- *IntWWM 90, WhoAm 90*
Suzuki, Howard Kazuro 1927- *WhoAm 90*
Suzuki, Isamu 1930- *WhoAm 90*
Suzuki, James Hiroshi 1933- *WhoAmA 91*
Suzuki, Jon Byron 1946- *WhoE 91, WhoWor 91*
Suzuki, Katsko *WhoAmA 91*
Suzuki, Kazunobu 1936- *WhoWor 91*
Suzuki, Kei 1920- *WhoWor 91*
Suzuki, Kunihiko 1932 *WhoAm 90*
Suzuki, Michio 1926- *WhoAm 90*
Suzuki, Norihisa 1935- *WhoWor 91*
Suzuki, Sakari *WhoAmA 91*
Suzuki, Shin'ichi 1898- *PenDiMP*
Suzuki, Taira 1918- *WhoWor 91*
Suzuki, Takashi 1967- *WhoSSW 91*
Suzuki, Takuya 1935- *St&PR 91, WhoAm 90*
Suzuki, Taro 1953- *WhoAmA 91*
Suzuki, Tateyuki 1945- *WhoWor 91*
Suzuki, Teiichi 1888-1989 *BioIn 16*
Suzuki, Teitaro *MajTwCW*
Suzuki, Toshio 1926- *WhoWor 91*
Suzuki, Yoshio *NewAgMG*
Suzuki, Zenko 1911- *WhoWor 91*
Suzuri, Hiroaki 1942- *WhoAm 90*
Suzy *BioIn 16*
Svadlenak, Jean Hayden 1955- *WhoAm 90, WhoAmW 91, WhoEmL 91*
Svadlenak, Loree Dean 1932- *St&PR 91*
Svahn, John Alfred 1943- *WhoAm 90, WhoWor 91*
Svan, Gunde *BioIn 16*
Svanda, Peter L. 1934- *St&PR 91*
Svanholm, Bert-Olof 1935- *WhoWor 91*
Svanholm, Karl Viktor *BioIn 16*
Svanholm, Set 1904-1964 *BioIn 16, PenDiMP*
Svare, A.O. 1927- *St&PR 91*
Svare, J. Christopher 1946- *ODwPR 91*
Svarzman, Norberto Luis 1937- *WhoHisp 91*
Svava Jakobsdottir *DcScanL*
Svebak, Sven Egil 1941- *WhoWor 91*
Svec, Charles H. 1941- *St&PR 91*
Svec, Cynthia Lillian 1941- *WhoAmW 91*
Svec, Frederick Joseph 1937- *WhoAm 90*
Svec, Harry John 1918- *WhoAm 90*
Svec, Janice Lynn 1948- *WhoAmW 91*
Svec, Susan Marie 1945- *WhoAmW 91, WhoEmL 91*
Sved, Margery 1952- *BiDrAPA 89*
Sveda, Michael 1912- *WhoAm 90, WhoWor 91*
Sveda, Sally Anne *BiDrAPA 89*
Svedberg, Bjorn Magnus Ivar 1937- *WhoWor 91*
Svedberg, Sune Ingvar 1932- *WhoWor 91*
Svedberg, Theodor H. E. 1884-1971 *WorAlBi*
Svedlow, Andrew Jay 1955- *WhoE 91*
Svee, Gary Duane 1943- *WhoAm 90*
Sveen, Donald Earl 1932- *St&PR 91*
Sveen, Karin 1948- *EncCoWW*
Svehla, John John 1946- *WhoWrEP 89*
Svehla, William Joseph 1928- *St&PR 91*
Sveinar, Sverre 1934- *WhoWor 91*
Sveinsson, Johannes 1912- *WhoWor 91*
Sveinsson, Linda Rodgers 1938- *WhoAmW 91*
Svejkovsky, Mark E. 1958- *St&PR 91*
Svend Otto S. 1916- *BioIn 16*
Svendsbye, Lloyd August 1930- *WhoAm 90*
Svendsen, Dale Phillip *BiDrAPA 89*
Svendsen, Eline Marguerite 1924- *WhoAmW 91*
Svendsen, Joyce Rose 1948- *WhoAmW 91*
Svendsen, Knud Erik 1926- *WhoWor 91*
Svendsen, Lars Bo 1949- *WhoWor 91*
Svendsen, Louise Averill 1915- *WhoAmA 91*
Svendsen, Sven B. 1921- *St&PR 91*
Svengalis, Kendall Frayne 1947- *WhoEmL 91*
Svensen-Smith, Carol Alyce 1947- *WhoAmW 91*
Svensk, Thomas Bengt 1953- *WhoWor 91*
Svenson, Charles Oscar 1939- *WhoAm 90, WhoWor 91*
Svenson, Ernest O 1923- *BiDrAPA 89*
Svenson, John Edward 1923- *WhoAmA 91*
Svensson, Inez 1932- *ConDes 90*
Svensson, Jean Harald Yngve 1917- *WhoWor 91*
Svensson, Sven-Ingvar 1932- *St&PR 91*
Sverd, Jeffrey 1943- *BiDrAPA 89*
Sverdlin, Hannah Grad *BioIn 16*
Sverdlov, Yakov *BioIn 16*
Sverdlove, Zolita 1936- *WhoAmA 91*
Svete, Tomaz 1956- *IntWWM 90*
Svetla, Karolina 1830-1899 *EncCoWW*
Svetlanov, Evgeny Fyodorovich 1928- *IntWWM 90*
Svetlanov, Yevgeny 1928- *PenDiMP*
Svetlova, Marina 1922- *WhoAm 90, WhoAmW 91*
Sveum, Dale 1963- *Ballpl 90*
Svevo, Italo *MajTwCW*
Svezia, Vera Tisheff 1937- *WhoAmW 91*
Svich, Caridad 1963- *WhoHisp 91*
Svigals, Morton P *BiDrAPA 89*
Svigel, Carrie Ann 1948- *WhoEmL 91*
Svihus, Richard Harold *BiDrAPA 89*
Svikhart, Clifford Miles 1926- *St&PR 91*
Svikhart, Edwin G. 1930- *St&PR 91*
Svingen, Peder *BiDrAPA 89*
Svirsky, Alla 1939- *WhoAmW 91*
Svirsky, Zin 1935- *WhoWor 91*
Svob, Vladimir 1939- *WhoWor 91*
Svoboda, Elizabeth Jane 1944- *WhoAmW 91*
Svoboda, Glenn Richard 1930- *St&PR 91*
Svoboda, Joanne Dzitko 1948- *WhoEmL 91*
Svoboda, Josef 1920- *ConDes 90, IntWWM 90*
Svoboda, Tomas 1939- *IntWWM 90*
Svoboda, Vincent A 1877-1961 *WhoAmA 91N*
Svobodova, Ru'ena 1868-1920 *EncCoWW*
Svokos, Steve G. 1934- *St&PR 91*
Svoren, Velimir 1942- *BiDrAPA 89*
Svoronos, Spyros Artchariyavivit 1954- *WhoSSW 91*
Svrcek, Leonard Edward, Jr. 1954- *St&PR 91*
Swaab, Dick Frans 1944- *WhoWor 91*
Swaback, Dwight Oran 1938- *BiDrAPA 89*
Swabash, Kirk Paul *BiDrAPA 89*
Swacina, Harry 1881-1944 *Ballpl 90*
Swack, Irwin 1916- *IntWWM 90*
Swacker, Frank Warren 1922- *WhoSSW 91*
Swackhamer, Gene L. 1938- *St&PR 91*
Swaddling, David Curtis 1946- *St&PR 91*
Swader, Claude W., Jr. 1931- *St&PR 91*
Swados, Elizabeth A. 1951- *WhoAmW 91*
Swados, Harvey 1920-1972 *AuBYP 90, EncAL*
Swados, Robert O. *WhoE 91*
Swadosh, Robert E. *ODwPR 91*
Swaffer, Hannen 1879-1962 *EncO&P 3*
Swafford, Douglas Richard, Sr. 1951- *WhoSSW 91*
Swafford, Earl L. 1943- *St&PR 91*
Swafford, Jan Johnson 1946- *IntWWM 90*
Swafford, Joseph Lee 1954- *WhoSSW 91*
Swafford, William Milam Andrew 1956- *IntWWM 90*
Swager, James R. 1943- *St&PR 91*
Swaggart, Jimmy 1935- *WorAlBi*
Swaggart, Jimmy Lee *BioIn 16*
Swaggart, Paul E. 1941- *St&PR 91*
Swaim, Alice Mackenzie 1911- *WhoWrEP 89*
Swaim, Bob 1943- *ConTFT 8*
Swaim, Charles Hall 1939- *WhoAm 90*
Swaim, David Dee 1947- *WhoAm 90*
Swaim, David W. 1956- *St&PR 91*
Swaim, James C. 1952- *St&PR 91*
Swaim, Joe Terry 1937- *St&PR 91*
Swaim, John Franklin 1935- *WhoWor 91*
Swaim, Joseph Carter, Jr. 1934- *WhoAm 90*
Swaim, Lloyd B. 1936- *St&PR 91*
Swaim, Mary Lou *WhoSSW 91*
Swaim, Robert Kurt 1950- *WhoEmL 91*
Swaim, Wilborn Sink 1916- *St&PR 91*
Swaiman, Kenneth Fred 1931- *WhoAm 90, WhoWor 91*
Swain, Clara A. 1834-1910 *BioAmW*
Swain, Daniel Mack 1939- *St&PR 91*
Swain, David Philip 1953- *WhoSSW 91*
Swain, Donald Christie 1931- *WhoAm 90, WhoSSW 91*
Swain, Dorothy Joy 1933- *WhoAmW 91*
Swain, Edward B 1926- *BiDrAPA 89*
Swain, Edward Parsons, Jr. 1935- *WhoAm 90*
Swain, James C. 1933- *St&PR 91*
Swain, James G. *St&PR 91*
Swain, Joe Oliver 1931- *St&PR 91*
Swain, John J. 1922-1987 *BioIn 16*
Swain, Joyce *BioIn 16*
Swain, Kenneth Robert 1943- *WhoE 91*
Swain, Marcia M. 1819-1900 *EncO&P 3*
Swain, Mark *ConAu 129*
Swain, Michael Eugene *BiDrAPA 89*
Swain, Mike *BioIn 16*
Swain, Nancy Jane Cox 1901- *WhoAmW 91*
Swain, Nancy Jo 1957- *WhoEmL 91*
Swain, Nola V. 1942- *WhoAmW 91*
Swain, Philip Raymond 1929- *WhoE 91*
Swain, Ray Filmore 1922- *St&PR 91*
Swain, Robert 1940- *WhoAm 90, WhoAmA 91*
Swain, Robert Cuthbertson 1907-1989 *BioIn 16*
Swain, Robert Francis 1942- *WhoAm 90, WhoAmA 91, WhoE 91*
Swain, Robert J. 1934- *St&PR 91*
Swain, Roger 1924- *St&PR 91*
Swain, Scott C. 1946- *St&PR 91*
Swain, Stephen James 1949- *WhoE 91*
Swain, Susan Elaine 1950- *WhoAmW 91*
Swain, Susan Marie 1954- *WhoE 91*
Swain, Tony 1922-1987 *BioIn 16*
Swain, Wilburn Darl 1944- *WhoSSW 91*
Swain, William A. 1937- *St&PR 91*
Swainson, Donald 1938- *ConAu 30NR*
Swainson, Sharon C. *BioIn 16*
Swaisgood, Harold Everett 1936- *WhoAm 90*
Swales, William Edward 1925- *St&PR 91, WhoAm 90, WhoE 91*
Swalin, Benjamin Franklin 1901- *IntWWM 90*
Swalin, Richard Arthur 1929- *WhoAm 90*
Swall, Charles *BioIn 16*
Swallow, Elizabeth Charlotte 1937- *WhoSSW 91*
Swallow, Ellen H. 1842-1911 *BioAmW*
Swallow, LaLee L. 1952- *WhoHisp 91*
Swallow, Stanford Bennett 1940- *WhoAm 90*
Swalm, Thomas Sterling 1931- *WhoAm 90, WhoWor 91*
Swaminarayan, Shree 1781-1830 *EncO&P 3*
Swaminathan, Jagdish 1928- *WhoWor 91*
Swaminathan, Monkombu Sambasivan 1925- *WhoWor 91*
Swaminathan, Shastri *BiDrAPA 89*
Swaminathan, Viswanathan *BiDrAPA 89*
Swamy, Manjula S *BiDrAPA 89*
Swamy, Sivappa S *BiDrAPA 89*
Swan, Annie S. 1859-1943 *FemiCLE*
Swan, Barbara 1922- *WhoAm 90, WhoAmA 91*
Swan, Bradford F 1907-1976 *WhoAmA 91N*
Swan, Carl Wayne 1925- *St&PR 91*
Swan, Charles E. 1935- *WhoE 91*
Swan, Clara Lincoln 1912- *WhoAm 90*
Swan, Craig *BioIn 16*
Swan, Craig 1950- *Ballpl 90*
Swan, David Michael *BiDrAPA 89*
Swan, Ezra D. 1839- *BioIn 16*
Swan, Frances Adele 1919- *WhoWrEP 89*
Swan, George Lorenzo 1959- *WhoE 91*
Swan, George Steven 1948- *WhoEmL 91, WhoWor 91*
Swan, Gladys 1934- *WhoWrEP 89*
Swan, Harry David 1926- *WhoSSW 91, WhoWor 91*
Swan, James Ellery 1937- *WhoE 91*
Swan, James G. 1818-1900 *WhNaAH*
Swan, Janet Elizabeth 1944- *WhoAmW 91*
Swan, John 1935- *WhoWor 91*
Swan, Joseph Wilson 1828-1914 *WorAlBi*
Swan, Joyce Ann 1964- *WhoAmW 91*
Swan, Kenneth Carl 1912- *WhoAm 90*
Swan, Marshall Wilbur Stephen 1917- *WhoE 91*
Swan, Martha Louise 1912- *WhoAmW 91, WhoWrEP 89*
Swan, Peter Lawrence 1944- *WhoWor 91*
Swan, Ralph Edward 1946- *WhoE 91*
Swan, Richard Gordon 1933- *WhoAm 90*
Swan, Roberta J. 1942- *St&PR 91*
Swan, Roy Craig 1920- *WhoAm 90*
Swan, Sandra Sanderson 1942- *WhoAmW 91, WhoE 91*
Swan, Sara *BioIn 16*
Swan, Stuart Bulkley 1957- *St&PR 91*
Swanbeck, Gunnar Poutos Emanuel 1934- *WhoWor 91*
Swanberg, Carol Jean 1961- *WhoAmW 91*
Swanberg, Edmund R. 1921- *St&PR 91*
Swanberg, Edmund Raymond 1921- *WhoAm 90*

Swanberg, Ingrid 1947- *WhoWrEP 89*
Swanberg, W. A. 1907- *BioIn 16, ConAu 13AS [port], DcLB 103 [port]*
Swanberg, William Andrew 1907- *WhoAm 90*
Swanborn, Peter Gustaaf 1935- *WhoWor 91*
Swanek, Richard E. *St&PR 91*
Swaner, Paula Margetts 1927- *WhoWor 91*
Swaney, Cynthia Ann 1959- *WhoAmW 91*
Swaney, William Chinnick 1938- *WhoAm 90*
Swanger, Christina Letitia 1963- *WhoAmW 91*
Swanger, David 1940- *WhoWrEP 89*
Swanger, Lee Allen 1946- *WhoSSW 91*
Swanger, Sterling Orville 1922- *WhoAm 90*
Swango, Billy Joe 1928- *St&PR 91*
Swank, Emory Coblentz 1922- *WhoAm 90*
Swank, Robert Roy, Jr. 1939- *WhoSSW 91*
Swank, Roy Laver 1909- *WhoAm 90*
Swank, Thaddeus W. 1925- *St&PR 91*
Swank, William A. *WhoAm 90*
Swanke, Albert Homer 1909- *WhoAm 90*
Swanke, Albert Homer, Jr. 1942- *WhoE 91*
Swanke, William Roy 1939- *BiDrAPA 89*
Swankin, David Arnold 1934- *WhoAm 90*
Swann, Alan Craig 1946- *BiDrAPA 89*
Swann, Brian 1940- *ConAu 31NR, WhoAm 90, WhoWrEP 89*
Swann, Donald 1923- *OxCPMus*
Swann, Donald Ibrahim 1923- *IntWWM 90*
Swann, Elizabeth Anne *BiDrAPA 89*
Swann, Elizabeth Hayden 1927- *IntWWM 90*
Swann, Erwin 1906-1973 *WhoAmA 91N*
Swann, Frederick 1931- *IntWWM 90*
Swann, Frederick Lewis 1931- *WhoAm 90*
Swann, Harold S. 1942- *St&PR 91*
Swann, Harry Kirk, Jr. 1946- *WhoE 91*
Swann, Ingo 1933- *EncO&P 3, EncPaPR 91*
Swann, Jerre Bailey 1939- *WhoAm 90*
Swann, John William 1937- *St&PR 91*
Swann, Lois 1944- *WhoWrEP 89*
Swann, Lynn 1952- *WorAlBi*
Swann, Lynn Curtis 1952- *WhoAm 90*
Swann, Madeline Bruce 1951- *WhoAmW 91*
Swann, Marjorie *BioIn 16*
Swann, Patricia Lambert 1951- *WhoAmW 91*
Swann, Richard Rockwell 1940- *WhoAm 90*
Swann, Roberta 1947- *WhoWrEP 89*
Swann, Roberta 1948- *WhoAmW 91*
Swann, Stephen Lucas 1946- *WhoSSW 91*
Swann, Thomas Weston 1925- *St&PR 91*
Swann, Wayne Lamont 1954- *WhoE 91*
Swann, William F G 1884-1962 *EncO&P 3*
Swansen, Samuel Theodore 1937- *WhoAm 90*
Swansiger, Rosalind Elaine Windsor 1945- *WhoAmW 91*
Swanson, Angela Karen 1963- *WhoWrEP 89*
Swanson, Anne *AuBYP 90*
Swanson, Arlene Collyer 1913- *AuBYP 90*
Swanson, Armour 1932- *St&PR 91*
Swanson, Arnold Arthur 1923- *WhoSSW 91*
Swanson, August George 1925- *WhoAm 90*
Swanson, Bernet Steven 1921- *WhoAm 90*
Swanson, Bert Elmer 1924- *WhoAm 90*
Swanson, Beverly Jane 1949- *WhoAmW 91*
Swanson, Byron Ernest *BioIn 16*
Swanson, Carl Sylvester 1924- *WhoE 91*
Swanson, Charles Andrew 1929- *WhoAm 90*
Swanson, Charles Howard 1935- *WhoSSW 91*
Swanson, Charles Otto, II 1931- *St&PR 91*
Swanson, Charles Richard 1953- *WhoWor 91*
Swanson, Claude Augustus 1862-1939 *BiDrUSE 89*
Swanson, Coy E 1935- *BiDrAPA 89*
Swanson, Cynthia Stump 1953- *WhoSSW 91*
Swanson, Dale Charles 1927- *St&PR 91*
Swanson, Darlene Marie Carlson 1925- *WhoAmW 91*
Swanson, David *BioIn 16*
Swanson, David Arvid 1964- *WhoE 91*
Swanson, David Dean 1951- *St&PR 91*
Swanson, David H. *St&PR 91*
Swanson, David Heath 1942- *WhoAm 90, WhoWor 91*
Swanson, David W 1930- *BiDrAPA 89*
Swanson, David Warren 1932- *WhoAm 90*
Swanson, Don Richard 1924- *WhoAm 90*
Swanson, Don Wallace 1934- *St&PR 91*
Swanson, Donald Alan 1938- *WhoAm 90*
Swanson, Donald Angus 1939- *BiDrAPA 89*
Swanson, Donald D. 1959- *St&PR 91*
Swanson, Donald Frederick 1927- *WhoAm 90*
Swanson, Donald Lee 1947- *St&PR 91*
Swanson, Donald Max 1946- *WhoEmL 91*
Swanson, Douglas E. 1938- *St&PR 91*
Swanson, Duane Richard 1939- *St&PR 91*
Swanson, Edward Benjamin 1953- *St&PR 91*
Swanson, Edwin Leroy 1938- *St&PR 91*
Swanson, Eleanora 1916- *WhoWrEP 89*
Swanson, Esther Marie 1954- *St&PR 91*
Swanson, Evar 1902-1973 *Ballpl 90*
Swanson, Fern Rose *WhoAmW 91*
Swanson, George E. 1934- *St&PR 91*
Swanson, Gerald Craig 1946- *WhoEmL 91*
Swanson, Gerald R. 1937- *St&PR 91*
Swanson, Gladys Irene 1922- *WhoWrEP 89*
Swanson, Gloria 1898-1983 *BioAmW, BioIn 16*
Swanson, Gloria 1899-1983 *WorAlBi*
Swanson, Gordon Merle 1930- *WhoAm 90*
Swanson, Guy Edwin 1922- *WhoAm 90*
Swanson, H N 1899- *ConAu 132*
Swanson, Harry Frederick 1931- *WhoE 91*
Swanson, Howard 1907-1978 *DcAfAmP, DrBlPA 90*
Swanson, J N 1927- *WhoAmA 91*
Swanson, James T. 1949- *St&PR 91*
Swanson, Joel O. 1921- *St&PR 91*
Swanson, John Stewart *BiDrAPA 89*
Swanson, Johnny Mack 1930- *St&PR 91*
Swanson, Joseph Mark 1938- *WhoSSW 91*
Swanson, Judith Ann 1957- *WhoE 91*
Swanson, Karin 1942- *WhoAmW 91*
Swanson, Karl Thor Waldemar 1922- *WhoAm 90*
Swanson, Kent Alan 1960- *St&PR 91*
Swanson, Laurence Albert 1941- *WhoWrEP 89*
Swanson, Levi William *BioIn 16*
Swanson, Linda L. 1948- *St&PR 91*
Swanson, Lloyd Oscar 1913- *WhoAm 90*
Swanson, Lowell N. 1926- *St&PR 91*
Swanson, Marilyn Ann 1945- *WhoAmW 91*
Swanson, Mark Douglas 1951- *WhoEmL 91*
Swanson, Marsha Kristin 1953- *WhoAmW 91*
Swanson, Martha Madden 1944- *WhoAmW 91*
Swanson, Murray L. 1941- *St&PR 91*
Swanson, Murray Luverne 1941- *WhoAm 90*
Swanson, Neil Harmon 1896-1983 *AuBYP 90*
Swanson, Norma Frances 1923- *WhoE 91*
Swanson, Norma Lee 1934- *WhoWor 91*
Swanson, Norman E. 1926- *St&PR 91*
Swanson, Patricia K. 1940- *WhoAm 90, WhoAmW 91*
Swanson, Patricia Louise 1948- *WhoAmW 91*
Swanson, Patrick Gale *BiDrAPA 89*
Swanson, Peggy Eubanks 1936- *WhoSSW 91*
Swanson, Peter Hyde *BiDrAPA 89*
Swanson, Phillip Dean 1932- *WhoAm 90*
Swanson, Ralph William *WhoSSW 91*
Swanson, Ray V 1937- *WhoAmA 91*
Swanson, Raynold A. 1920- *WhoWor 91*
Swanson, Reuel Clarion 1938- *St&PR 91*
Swanson, Rhonda Wojahn 1955- *WhoAmW 91*
Swanson, Ric *NewAgMG*
Swanson, Richard Paul 1955- *WhoEmL 91*
Swanson, Robert A. *BioIn 16*
Swanson, Robert Draper 1915- *WhoAm 90*
Swanson, Robert Hilton 1954- *WhoSSW 91*
Swanson, Robert J. *St&PR 91*
Swanson, Robert Killen 1932- *WhoAm 90*
Swanson, Roy Arthur 1925- *WhoAm 90, WhoWor 91, WhoWrEP 89*
Swanson, Rune E. 1919- *WhoAm 90*
Swanson, Sandra *ODwPR 91*
Swanson, Scott *BioIn 16*
Swanson, Stephen Olney 1932- *WhoWrEP 89*
Swanson, Steven Richard 1956- *WhoEmL 91*
Swanson, Thomas R 1941- *BiDrAPA 89*
Swanson, Thomas Richard 1954- *WhoEmL 91, WhoWor 91*
Swanson, Thomas Willard 1943- *WhoAm 90*
Swanson, Vern Grosvenor 1945- *WhoAmA 91*
Swanson, W. Clarke *BioIn 16*
Swanson, Wallace Martin 1941- *WhoAm 90*
Swanson, Wayne 1951- *ConAu 130*
Swanson, William Fredin, Jr. 1928- *WhoAm 90*
Swanson, William Henry 1949- *WhoAm 90*
Swanson, Wyman Peter 1942- *St&PR 91*
Swanson, Zana Burkart *BiDrAPA 89*
Swanston, David C. 1942- *ODwPR 91*
Swanston, Roderick Brian 1948- *IntWWM 90*
Swanston, Thomas Robinson 1931- *St&PR 91*
Swanstrom, John Oakley 1937- *St&PR 91*
Swanstrom, Thomas Evan 1939- *WhoAm 90*
Swantak, Judy L. 1955- *St&PR 91*
Swantek, John F. *WhoAm 90*
Swanton, Robert 1957- *St&PR 91*
Swanton, Robert Howard 1944- *WhoWor 91*
Swanwick, Anna 1813-1899 *FemiCLE*
Swanwick, Betty 1915- *BiDWomA*
Swanwick, Keith 1937- *IntWWM 90*
Swanzey, Robert Joseph 1935- *St&PR 91, WhoAm 90*
Swanzy, Mary 1882-1978 *BiDWomA*
Swap, Walter Charles 1943- *WhoE 91*
Swapp, Charles Henry Chippendale 1955- *WhoWor 91*
Swarc, Christopher *BioIn 16*
Sward, Edward Lawrence, Jr. 1933- *WhoSSW 91*
Sward, Jeffrey Edwin 1953- *WhoEmL 91*
Sward, Robert 1933- *ConAu 13AS [port]*
Sward, Robert S 1933- *WhoAmA 91, WhoWrEP 89*
Swardson, Mary Anne 1928- *WhoAmW 91*
Swaringen, Nathan Kenneth 1933- *WhoSSW 91*
Swaroop, Naresh 1944- *St&PR 91*
Swarowsky, Hans 1899-1975 *PenDiMP*
Swart, Marvin Dale 1934- *WhoSSW 91*
Swart, Michael 1941- *WhoAm 90*
Swart, Wayne Andrew *BiDrAPA 89*
Swartburg, B Robert 1895-1975 *WhoAmA 91N*
Swarth, Helena 1859-1941 *EncCoWW*
Swarthout, Gladys 1900-1969 *PenDiMP*
Swarthout, Glendon 1918- *AuBYP 90*
Swarthout, Glendon Fred 1918- *WhoAm 90, WhoWrEP 89*
Swarthout, Herbert Marion 1900- *WhoAm 90*
Swarthout, Kathryn 1919- *AuBYP 90*
Swartley, David Warren 1950- *WhoWrEP 89*
Swarton, Hannah *FemiCLE, WhNaAH*
Swartout, Jean Ann 1945- *WhoAmW 91*
Swarts, Richard R. 1938- *St&PR 91*
Swartwood, Ed 1859-1924 *Ballpl 90*
Swartwood, T. Marshall 1933- *St&PR 91*
Swartwout, Joseph Rodolph 1925- *WhoAm 90, WhoWor 91*
Swartwout, Paul Richard *BiDrAPA 89*
Swartz, Adelaide *BioIn 16*
Swartz, Alan Jay 1957- *WhoEmL 91*
Swartz, Allen 1924- *St&PR 91*
Swartz, Ann Lamontagne 1966- *WhoAmW 91*
Swartz, Benjamin Kinsell, Jr. 1931- *WhoAm 90*
Swartz, Beth Ames 1936- *WhoAmA 91*
Swartz, Burton Eugene 1934- *WhoWrEP 89*
Swartz, Carl Axel Richard 1945- *WhoWor 91*
Swartz, Christian LeFevre 1915- *WhoSSW 91*
Swartz, Conrad Melton 1946- *BiDrAPA 89*
Swartz, Dan R. 1951- *St&PR 91*
Swartz, Dennis Alan 1949- *St&PR 91*
Swartz, Donald Edward, Jr. 1934- *St&PR 91*
Swartz, Donald Everett 1916- *WhoAm 90*
Swartz, Donald Percy 1921- *WhoAm 90*
Swartz, Duane E. 1942- *St&PR 91*
Swartz, Edward M. 1934- *BioIn 16*
Swartz, Glenn I. 1940- *St&PR 91*
Swartz, Helga Maria *DcScanL*
Swartz, Jack Ernest 1931- *St&PR 91*
Swartz, James Franklin, Jr. 1930- *St&PR 91*
Swartz, James Richard 1942- *WhoE 91, WhoWor 91*
Swartz, John *BioIn 16*
Swartz, John Michael 1936- *WhoAm 90*
Swartz, Jon David 1934- *WhoAm 90*
Swartz, Leonard Norman 1937- *St&PR 91*
Swartz, Leonard S. 1932- *St&PR 91*
Swartz, Linda 1950- *WhoAmA 91*
Swartz, Lorna Kay 1938- *BiDrAPA 89*
Swartz, Malcolm Gilbert 1931- *WhoAm 90*
Swartz, Maria Christina 1960- *WhoAmW 91, WhoE 91*
Swartz, Marvin Stanley 1950- *BiDrAPA 89*
Swartz, Morton Norman 1923- *WhoAm 90*
Swartz, Phillip Scott 1936- *WhoAmA 91*
Swartz, Randall Wolfe 1946- *WhoE 91*
Swartz, Renee Becker 1935- *WhoAmW 91*
Swartz, Robert Gilleran 1927- *WhoE 91, WhoWor 91*
Swartz, Robert Mark 1952- *St&PR 91*
Swartz, Stephen Arthur 1941- *St&PR 91, WhoAm 90*
Swartz, Steven *ODwPR 91*
Swartz, Thomas B. 1932- *St&PR 91*
Swartz, William John 1934- *WhoAm 90*
Swartz-Buckley, Rita Bryna 1955- *WhoAmW 91*
Swartzbaugh, Marc L. 1937- *WhoAm 90*
Swartzell, Ann Garling 1955- *WhoAmW 91*
Swartzendruber, Dale 1925- *WhoAm 90*
Swartzendruber, Harlan L. 1922- *St&PR 91*
Swartzfager, Cynthia Anne 1961- *WhoSSW 91*
Swartzlander, Earl Eugene, Jr. 1945- *WhoAm 90*
Swartzman, Roslyn 1931- *WhoAmA 91*
Swartzwelder, John Joseph 1949- *WhoWor 91*
Swarz, Sahl 1912- *WhoAm 90*
Swarzenski, Georg 1876-1957 *WhoAmA 91N*
Swasey, Chester Clinton 1943- *WhoE 91*
Swasey, Steve 1957- *ODwPR 91*
Swatek, Frank Edward 1929- *WhoAm 90*
Swathirajan, Hema *BiDrAPA 89*
Swaty, Joe *BioIn 16*
Swatzell, Marilyn 1942- *WhoAmW 91*
Sway, Albert 1913- *WhoAmA 91*
Sway, Marlene 1950- *ConAu 129*
Swayne, Giles 1946- *IntWWM 90*
Swayne, Gregory M. *BioIn 16*
Swayne, Keith Dauer 1940- *St&PR 91*
Swayne, Sam 1907- *BioIn 16*
Swayne, Thompson M. *BioIn 16*
Swayne, Thompson M. 1951- *St&PR 91*
Swayne, Zoa 1905- *BioIn 16*
Swayze, Frances Goehring 1901- *WhoAmW 91*
Swayze, John Cameron, Sr. 1906- *WhoAm 90, WorAlBi*
Swayze, Patrick *BioIn 16*
Swayze, Patrick 1954- *WhoAm 90, WorAlBi*
Swazey, Judith Pound 1939- *WhoAm 90, WhoAmW 91*
Swazo 1924-1974 *WhoAmA 91N*
Swe, Nini *BiDrAPA 89*
Sweaney, Robert Eugene 1930- *St&PR 91*
Swearengen, Jack Clayton, II 1940- *WhoE 91*
Swearengen, Mark T. 1912- *St&PR 91*
Swearer, Donald Keeney 1934- *WhoAm 90*
Swearer, Howard Robert 1932- *WhoAm 90*
Swearingen, Barbara Joan *BiDrAPA 89*
Swearingen, Charles W 1942- *BiDrAPA 89*
Swearingen, John Eldred 1918- *WhoAm 90*
Swearingen, Johnnie 1908- *MusmAFA*
Swearingen, Judson Sterling 1907- *WhoAm 90, WhoWor 91*
Swearingen, Marjorie Eileen 1939- *WhoAmW 91*
Swearingen, Wayne E. 1924- *St&PR 91*
Swasy, Joyce Elizabeth 1948- *WhoAmW 91*
Sweat, George *WhoSSW 91*
Sweat, Keith *BioIn 16*
Sweat, Lynn 1934- *BioIn 16*
Sweat, Margaret 1823- *FemiCLE*
Sweat, Robert Warren 1946- *WhoEmL 91, WhoSSW 91*
Sweat, William T. 1931- *St&PR 91*
Sweatman, Alan Travers 1946- *St&PR 91*
Sweatman, Phillip J. 1955- *St&PR 91*
Sweatman, Phillip Jay 1955- *WhoEmL 91, WhoWor 91*
Sweatman, Wilbur C. 1882-1961 *BioIn 16, OxCPMus*
Sweatt, Walt 1941- *St&PR 91*
Sweatt, William David 1947- *St&PR 91, WhoAm 90*
Swec, Diane Marie 1959- *WhoAmW 91*
Swecker, John *St&PR 91*
Sweda, Gerald J. 1942- *ODwPR 91, St&PR 91*
Swedback, James M. 1935- *WhoWor 91*
Swedback, James Miller 1935- *St&PR 91*
Swedberg, Robert Mitchell 1950- *WhoE 91*
Swedborg, Emanuel 1688-1772 *EncPaPR 91*
Swede, George 1940- *ConAu 32NR*
Swedenborg, Emanuel 1688-1772 *BioIn 16, DcScanL, EncO&P 3, EncPaPR 91, WorAlBi, WrPh P*
Swedenborg, Samuel W *BiDrAPA 89*
Sweebe, Richard Dale 1951- *WhoEmL 91*
Sweed, Phyllis 1931- *St&PR 91*
Sweedler, Barry Martin 1937- *WhoAm 90*
Sweedler, Charles W. 1916- *St&PR 91*
Sweel, Alexander 1922- *BiDrAPA 89*
Sween, Terri Lynn 1963- *WhoAmW 91*
Sweeney, Anne 1942- *ODwPR 91*
Sweeney, Anthony John 1929- *St&PR 91*
Sweeney, Arthur Hamilton, Jr. 1920- *WhoAm 90*

Sweeney, Asher William 1920- *WhoAm 90*
Sweeney, Bernard Thomas, Jr. 1946- *WhoE 91*
Sweeney, Bill 1858-1908 *Ballpl 90*
Sweeney, Bill 1886-1948 *Ballpl 90*
Sweeney, Bill 1904-1957 *Ballpl 90*
Sweeney, Brian J. 1952- *ODwPR 91*
Sweeney, Charles H., Jr. 1916- *St&PR 91*
Sweeney, Charlie 1863-1902 *Ballpl 90*
Sweeney, Christee A. 1950- *WhoEmL 91*
Sweeney, Clayton Anthony 1931- *St&PR 91, WhoAm 90*
Sweeney, D. B. *BioIn 16*
Sweeney, Daniel P. A. *BioIn 16*
Sweeney, Daniel Thomas 1929- *WhoAm 90*
Sweeney, David Michael 1948- *St&PR 91*
Sweeney, Donald R 1937- *BiDrAPA 89*
Sweeney, Dorothy Anne 1927- *WhoAmW 91*
Sweeney, Earl Martin 1937- *WhoE 91*
Sweeney, Edward J. *ODwPR 91*
Sweeney, Edward J. 1931- *St&PR 91*
Sweeney, Eileen Cecilia 1952- *WhoEmL 91*
Sweeney, Elizabeth Ann 1946- *WhoAmW 91*
Sweeney, Ellen Kate 1947- *ODwPR 91*
Sweeney, Ermengarde Collins 1922- *WhoWor 91*
Sweeney, Francis Joseph, Jr. 1925- *WhoAm 90*
Sweeney, Frank B. 1938- *St&PR 91*
Sweeney, George Bernard, Jr. 1933- *WhoSSW 91, WhoWor 91*
Sweeney, George F. *ODwPR 91*
Sweeney, George H 1930- *BiDrAPA 89*
Sweeney, Gerald Bingham 1946- *WhoEmL 91*
Sweeney, J Gray 1943- *WhoAmA 91*
Sweeney, James Edward William 1933- *WhoSSW 91*
Sweeney, James F. *BioIn 16*
Sweeney, James F., Jr. 1922- *St&PR 91*
Sweeney, James Johnson 1900-1986 *BioIn 16*
Sweeney, James L. 1951- *St&PR 91*
Sweeney, James Patrick 1952- *WhoWor 91*
Sweeney, James Raymond 1928- *WhoAm 90*
Sweeney, Jeff 1888- *Ballpl 90*
Sweeney, John Dean 1948- *St&PR 91*
Sweeney, Joy Elaine 1937- *St&PR 91*
Sweeney, Julia 1927- *WhoAmW 91*
Sweeney, Karen A. 1959- *WhoAmW 91*
Sweeney, Kevin M. 1929- *St&PR 91*
Sweeney, Kevin Michael 1956- *WhoEmL 91*
Sweeney, Kristine Kinna 1960- *WhoEmL 91*
Sweeney, Lawrence E. 1942- *St&PR 91*
Sweeney, Leo 1918- *WhoAm 90*
Sweeney, Linda 1934- *St&PR 91*
Sweeney, Lisa Anne 1962- *WhoAmW 91*
Sweeney, Margaret Mary 1921- *WhoAmW 91*
Sweeney, Maria *ODwPR 91*
Sweeney, Mark O. 1942- *St&PR 91*
Sweeney, Mark Owen 1942- *WhoAm 90*
Sweeney, Martin B. *BioIn 16*
Sweeney, Mary Francis 1938- *WhoAmW 91*
Sweeney, Mary Margaret 1957- *WhoAmW 91*
Sweeney, Matthew Joseph, Jr. 1915- *WhoE 91*
Sweeney, Maureen Rose 1963- *WhoAmW 91*
Sweeney, Michael Andrew 1948- *WhoE 91*
Sweeney, Michael G. 1938- *St&PR 91*
Sweeney, Ned Francis 1955- *WhoSSW 91*
Sweeney, Oliver *BioIn 16*
Sweeney, Paul R. 1942- *St&PR 91*
Sweeney, Peter Alan 1950- *IntWWM 90*
Sweeney, Randall James *St&PR 91*
Sweeney, Richard James 1944- *WhoAm 90, WhoE 91*
Sweeney, Robert E. 1932- *St&PR 91*
Sweeney, Robert H. 1929- *St&PR 91*
Sweeney, Robert Joseph, Jr. 1927- *WhoAm 90*
Sweeney, Roger Damien 1942- *St&PR 91*
Sweeney, Scott *ODwPR 91*
Sweeney, Stender Edward 1939- *St&PR 91*
Sweeney, Stephen Joseph 1928- *St&PR 91, WhoAm 90, WhoE 91*
Sweeney, Stephen Michael 1936- *St&PR 91*
Sweeney, Thomas *BioIn 16*
Sweeney, Thomas Bell, III 1936- *St&PR 91*
Sweeney, Thomas Carl 1959- *WhoE 91*
Sweeney, Thomas Joseph, Jr. 1923- *WhoAm 90*
Sweeney, Vincent C *BiDrAPA 89*
Sweeney, William Edward 1933- *St&PR 91*
Sweeney, William J. 1898-1988 *BioIn 16*
Sweeney, William J., III 1922- *ConAu 33NR*
Sweeney, William Jones, Jr. 1947- *WhoEmL 91*
Sweeney, William S. 1944- *St&PR 91*
Sweeny, Bradley Patterson 1940- *WhoE 91*
Sweeny, Charles David 1936- *WhoE 91*
Sweeny, Henry Ware Allen 1934- *WhoAm 90*
Sweeny, Kenneth S. 1948- *WhoE 91*
Sweet, Alexander Edwin 1841-1901 *BioIn 16*
Sweet, Bernard 1923- *St&PR 91*
Sweet, Beryle Gregory 1928- *WhoE 91*
Sweet, Charles Wheeler 1943- *St&PR 91*
Sweet, Cody *WhoAm 90*
Sweet, Dee 1913- *WhoAmW 91*
Sweet, Donald C. 1944- *St&PR 91*
Sweet, Harold 1929- *St&PR 91*
Sweet, James Brooks 1934- *WhoSSW 91*
Sweet, James W. 1918- *WhoSSW 91*
Sweet, John H Kerr 1942- *BiDrAPA 89*
Sweet, John Howard 1907-1988 *BioIn 16*
Sweet, Lawrence Lester 1938- *WhoAm 90*
Sweet, Lynn Adams 1960- *WhoSSW 91*
Sweet, Marge Jean 1947- *WhoAmW 91*
Sweet, Mary 1937- *WhoAmA 91*
Sweet, Michael Lloyd 1944- *St&PR 91*
Sweet, Neale E. 1943- *St&PR 91*
Sweet, Norbert H. 1930- *St&PR 91*
Sweet, Ozzie 1918- *BioIn 16*
Sweet, Patrick Henry 1938- *St&PR 91*
Sweet, Pauline *BiDrAPA 89*
Sweet, Richard G. *BioIn 16*
Sweet, Rick *BioIn 16*
Sweet, Rick 1952- *Ballpl 90*
Sweet, Robert *BiDrAPA 89, BioIn 16*
Sweet, Robert T. 1938- *St&PR 91*
Sweet, Robert Workman 1922- *WhoE 91*
Sweet, Roger 1946- *WhoAmA 91*
Sweet, Stedman Glenn 1936- *St&PR 91*
Sweet, Steve 1952- *WhoAmA 91*
Sweet, Steve Mark 1952- *WhoAm 90*
Sweet, Susan Cooke 1944- *WhoAmW 91*
Sweet-Escott, Bickham Aldred Cowan 1907-1981 *DcNaB 1981*
Sweethearts Of The Rodeo *WhoNeCM [port]*
Sweeting, George 1924- *BioIn 16, WhoAm 90*
Sweeting, Linda Marie 1941- *WhoAmW 91*
Sweetland, Gayle Morris *ODwPR 91*
Sweetland, Les 1901-1974 *Ballpl 90*
Sweetland, Nancy A. *BioIn 16*
Sweetman, Brian Jack 1936- *WhoSSW 91*
Sweetman, Jack 1940- *WhoE 91*
Sweetman, James Edward, Jr. 1937- *St&PR 91*
Sweetman, William Edward 1925- *St&PR 91*
Sweets, Clarence Atlee 1928- *St&PR 91*
Sweetser, Alan 1928- *St&PR 91*
Sweetser, Albert Gibby 1915- *WhoAm 90*
Sweetser, Elliott H 1917- *BiDrAPA 89*
Sweetser, Jesse W. 1902-1989 *BioIn 16*
Sweetser, Peter J. 1946- *St&PR 91*
Sweetser, Richard Stuart 1950- *WhoE 91*
Sweezey, Robert L. 1957- *WhoSSW 91*
Sweezy, Paul *EncAL*
Sweezy, Paul Marlor 1910- *WhoAm 90*
Sweger, Glenda Lee 1946- *WhoAmW 91*
Sweger, John Bouldin 1919- *WhoAm 90*
Sweigart, Anne Brossman 1914- *St&PR 91*
Sweigart, Frederick Charles 1952- *St&PR 91*
Sweigart, Terry Joe 1952- *WhoSSW 91*
Sweisgood, John Peter *BioIn 16*
Sweitzer, Charles Leroy 1939- *WhoAmA 91*
Sweitzer, James M. 1947- *St&PR 91*
Sweitzer, Karol M. 1959- *WhoAmW 91*
Sweitzer, Thomas Cummins 1929- *St&PR 91*
Swenby, Sandra Mae *BiDrAPA 89*
Swencicki, Robert Edward 1935- *St&PR 91*
Swencki, Steven J. 1943- *St&PR 91*
Swendrowski, John 1948- *St&PR 91*
Swenka, Arthur J. 1937- *St&PR 91*
Swenka, Arthur John 1937- *WhoAm 90*
Swenn, Gaylene Louise 1953- *WhoAmW 91, WhoSSW 91*
Swensen, Clifford Henrik, Jr. 1926- *WhoAm 90*
Swensen, J Mary Jeanette Hamilton 1910- *WhoAmA 91*
Swensen, Timothy K *BiDrAPA 89*
Swenson, Al *BioIn 16*
Swenson, Anne *WhoAmA 91*
Swenson, Barbara A. 1947- *WhoAmW 91*
Swenson, Brian Robert 1953- *BiDrAPA 89*
Swenson, Charles Robert 1949- *BiDrAPA 89*
Swenson, Clayton A. 1923- *WhoAm 90*
Swenson, Courtland Sevander 1936- *WhoAm 90*
Swenson, Craig S. 1946- *St&PR 91*
Swenson, Curtis R. 1939- *ODwPR 91*
Swenson, Daniel Lee 1928- *WhoAm 90, WhoE 91*
Swenson, David Dean *BiDrAPA 89*
Swenson, Edward 1939- *St&PR 91*
Swenson, Eric Pierson 1918- *St&PR 91, WhoAm 90*
Swenson, Erick Noak 1926- *WhoWor 91*
Swenson, Gary L. 1937- *St&PR 91*
Swenson, George Warner, Jr. 1922- *WhoAm 90*
Swenson, George Wendell 1926- *St&PR 91*
Swenson, Grace Stageberg *WhoWrEP 89*
Swenson, Harold Francis 1915- *WhoWor 91*
Swenson, Howard William 1901-1960 *WhoAmA 91N*
Swenson, James Duane 1935- *BiDrAPA 89*
Swenson, James Warren 1932- *St&PR 91*
Swenson, John Robert *BiDrAPA 89*
Swenson, Karen 1936- *ConAu 13AS [port], WhoAm 90, WhoWrEP 89*
Swenson, Kari *BioIn 16*
Swenson, Kathleen Susan 1938- *WhoAmW 91*
Swenson, Kenneth Burdette 1945- *WhoSSW 91*
Swenson, Kurt McFarland 1945- *St&PR 91*
Swenson, Lawrence Paul 1931- *St&PR 91*
Swenson, Leland H. 1947- *St&PR 91*
Swenson, Lloyd A. 1924- *St&PR 91*
Swenson, Mark Gregory 1949- *WhoEmL 91*
Swenson, May 1919- *AuBYP 90, FemiCLE, WhoWrEP 89*
Swenson, May 1919-1989 *AnObit 1989, BioIn 16, ConAu 130, ConLC 61 [port], MajTwCW*
Swenson, Melvin John 1917- *WhoAm 90*
Swenson, Michael *ODwPR 91*
Swenson, Orvar 1909- *WhoAm 90*
Swenson, Roderic Burwell *BioIn 16*
Swenson, Ronald J. 1930- *St&PR 91*
Swenson, Ruth Ann *WhoAm 90*
Swenson, Victoria Sue 1956- *WhoAmW 91*
Swensson, Earl Simcox 1930- *WhoAm 90*
Swensson, Evelyn Dickenson 1928- *IntWWM 90*
Swensson, Jonas 1828-1873 *BioIn 16*
Swepston, Jack Herbert 1928- *WhoSSW 91*
Swepston, Stephen McGee 1950- *WhoEmL 91*
Swerdlick, Peter *BiDrAPA 89*
Swerdloff, David Alan 1948- *WhoEmL 91*
Swerdlove, Dorothy Louise 1928- *WhoAm 90*
Swerdlow, Amy 1923- *WhoAmW 91*
Swerdlow, Martin Abraham 1923- *WhoAm 90*
Swergold, Marcelle M 1927- *WhoAmA 91*
Swergold, Marcelle Miriam 1927- *WhoAmW 91, WhoE 91*
Swerling, Gerald *ODwPR 91*
Swerling, Jack Bruce 1946- *WhoSSW 91, WhoWor 91*
Swersky, Phyllis Sherry *WhoE 91*
Swert, Robert Edward 1925- *St&PR 91*
Swertlow, Frank *BioIn 16*
Swet, Charles Jacob 1922- *WhoE 91, WhoWor 91*
Swetcharnik, Sara Morris 1955- *WhoAmA 91, WhoAmW 91*
Swetcharnik, William Norton 1951- *WhoAmA 91, WhoEmL 91*
Swetland, Rosemary 1945- *IntWWM 90*
Swetlik, William Philip 1950- *WhoWor 91*
Swetman, Glenn Robert 1936- *WhoSSW 91, WhoWor 91*
Swetmon, Sharon Thompson 1957- *WhoAmW 91*
Swetmon, Stephen Craig 1956- *WhoSSW 91*
Swetnam, Monte Newton 1936- *St&PR 91, WhoAm 90*
Swetonic, Steve 1903-1974 *Ballpl 90*
Swets, John Arthur 1928- *WhoAm 90*
Swets, Paul William 1941- *WhoWrEP 89*
Swett, Albert Hersey 1923- *WhoAm 90*
Swett, Chester P., Jr. 1939- *BiDrAPA 89*
Swett, Chester Parker, Jr. 1939- *WhoE 91*
Swett, Daniel Robert 1936- *WhoAm 90*
Swett, Richard Williams 1939- *St&PR 91*
Swett, Russell Jackson 1933- *WhoE 91*
Swett, Stephen Frederick, Jr. 1935- *WhoE 91, WhoWor 91*
Swett, Wilbra H. 1860- *AmLegL*
Swetz, Ken *BioIn 16*
Swetz, Ken J. 1942- *St&PR 91*
Swezey, Charles Mason 1935- *WhoSSW 91*
Swhier, Robert Dewain, Jr. 1949- *WhoEmL 91*
Swiatkowski, Cheryl L. 1951- *St&PR 91*
Swibel, Steven Warren 1946- *WhoEmL 91*
Swichkow, Louis Judah 1912- *BioIn 16*
Swick, James Robert 1950- *WhoE 91*
Swick, Joseph Morris 1928- *St&PR 91*
Swick, Larry Marvin 1932- *WhoWor 91*
Swick, Linda Ann 1948- *WhoAmA 91*
Swick, Norman H. 1949- *St&PR 91*
Swicord, Earl L. 1930- *St&PR 91*
Swid, Stephen Claar *BioIn 16*
Swid, Stephen Claar 1940- *WhoAm 90*
Swidler, Ann 1944- *ConAu 132*
Swidler, Joseph Charles 1907- *WhoAm 90*
Swidler, S. Zachary 1917-1990 *BioIn 16*
Swidler, Thomas Alan 1936- *St&PR 91*
Swiener, Rita *BioIn 16*
Swierad, Otto Walter 1933- *WhoSSW 91*
Swierk, Alan Edward 1945- *St&PR 91*
Swiers, Peter Bird 1938- *WhoE 91*
Swiers, Richard Howard 1929- *St&PR 91*
Swierzy, Waldemar 1931- *ConDes 90*
Swietek, Richard Michael 1962- *WhoE 91*
Swift, Al 1935- *WhoAm 90*
Swift, Aubrey Earl 1933- *St&PR 91, WhoWor 91*
Swift, Augustus *MajTwCW*
Swift, Bill 1908-1969 *Ballpl 90*
Swift, Bill 1961- *Ballpl 90*
Swift, Bob 1915-1966 *Ballpl 90*
Swift, Calvin Thomas 1937- *WhoAm 90*
Swift, Charles R 1919- *BiDrAPA 89*
Swift, Clive 1936- *ConAu 129*
Swift, Clive, Mrs. *WhoWor 91*
Swift, David Bearce 1936- *BiDrAPA 89*
Swift, David L. 1936- *St&PR 91, WhoAm 90*
Swift, Dolores M. 1936- *ODwPR 91*
Swift, Dolores Monica Marcinkevich 1936- *WhoAm 90*
Swift, E. Kent, Jr. 1924- *St&PR 91*
Swift, Edward Foster 1923- *St&PR 91*
Swift, Edward Foster, III 1923- *WhoAm 90*
Swift, Elizabeth *WhoWrEP 89*
Swift, Evangeline Wilson 1939- *WhoAm 90, WhoAmW 91*
Swift, Frank Meador 1911- *WhoAm 90*
Swift, George P., Jr. 1919- *St&PR 91, WhoAm 90, WhoSSW 91*
Swift, Graham 1949- *WorAu 1980 [port]*
Swift, Gustavus F. 1839-1903 *WorAlBi*
Swift, Helen Miller 1914- *AuBYP 90*
Swift, Henry 1848-1891 *DcCanB 12*
Swift, Hewson Hoyt 1920- *WhoAm 90*
Swift, Hildegarde 1890?-1977 *AuBYP 90*
Swift, Humphrey H. 1915- *St&PR 91*
Swift, Jay James *BioIn 16*
Swift, John Francis 1935- *WhoAm 90*
Swift, John Franklin 1829-1891 *BioIn 16*
Swift, John Goulding 1955- *WhoEmL 91*
Swift, John Staples, III 1952- *St&PR 91*
Swift, Jonathan 1667-1745 *BioIn 16, DcLB 101 [port], -95 [port], WorAlBi, WrPh*
Swift, Jonathan 1932- *IntWWM 90, WhoWor 91*
Swift, Kenneth Rod 1930- *St&PR 91*
Swift, Margaret 1939- *BioIn 16*
Swift, Mary Howard Davidson 1926- *WhoWrEP 89*
Swift, Mathews Dismuke 1947- *St&PR 91*
Swift, Merlin *AuBYP 90*
Swift, Michael Ronald 1935- *WhoAm 90*
Swift, Paul 1942- *WhoE 91*
Swift, Richard 1927- *IntWWM 90*
Swift, Richard Gene 1927- *WhoAm 90*
Swift, Robert Frederic 1940- *WhoE 91*
Swift, Robert Michael 1951- *BiDrAPA 89*
Swift, Robert Walter 1956- *WhoEmL 91*
Swift, Ronnie Gorman 1948- *BiDrAPA 89*
Swift, Stephen Jensen 1943- *WhoAm 90*
Swift, Theodore J. *ODwPR 91*
Swift, Theodore John 1935- *St&PR 91*
Swift, Virgil Neil 1928- *St&PR 91*
Swig, Charlotte Mailliard *BioIn 16*
Swig, Roselyne Chroman 1930- *WhoAm 90*
Swigart, Edmund Kearsley 1931- *WhoE 91*
Swigart, John W. *St&PR 91N*
Swigart, Lynn S 1930- *WhoAmA 91*
Swigart, Richard P. *ODwPR 91*
Swigart, Rob 1941- *WhoWrEP 89*
Swigart, Theodore Earl 1895- *WhoAm 90*
Swiger, Elinor Porter 1927- *AuBYP 90, WhoAmW 91*
Swiger, Elizabeth Davis 1926- *WhoAmW 91*
Swigert, Donna Lee 1939- *WhoAmW 91*
Swigert, James Mack 1907- *WhoAm 90*
Swiggett, Hal 1921- *WhoSSW 91, WhoWor 91*
Swiggett, Jean Donald 1910- *WhoAmA 91*
Swiggett, Robert Lewis 1921- *St&PR 91*
Swihart, Fred Jacob 1919- *WhoWor 91*
Swihart, Jean Ogden 1945- *BiDrAPA 89*
Swihart, John Marion 1923- *WhoAm 90*
Swihart, Lynne Andrews 1961- *WhoSSW 91, WhoWor 91*
Swihart, Patricia Pearl 1932- *WhoAmW 91*
Swikard, Janet L. 1949- *St&PR 91*
Swilik, Robert Charles 1934- *St&PR 91*
Swiller, Helen E *BiDrAPA 89*
Swiller, Hillel Isaiah 1939- *BiDrAPA 89, WhoE 91*
Swilling, Annelle W. 1937- *St&PR 91*
Swinarton, Robert Wallace 1926- *WhoAm 90*
Swinburn, Charles 1942- *WhoAm 90*
Swinburne, Algernon Charles 1837-1909 *BioIn 16, WorAlBi*

Swinburne, Herbert Hillhouse 1912- *WhoAm 90*
Swindale, Leslie Denis 1928- *WhoWor 91*
Swindall, Ernest Harry 1929- *St&PR 91*
Swindall, Sarah Earlene 1941- *WhoAmW 91*
Swindell, Archie Calhoun, Jr. 1936- *WhoAm 90*
Swindell, Bertha 1874-1951 *WhoAmA 91N*
Swindell, Brennon Ray 1933- *St&PR 91*
Swindell, Calvin M. 1923- *St&PR 91*
Swindell, Greg 1965- *Ballpl 90*
Swindells, Janice Elizabeth 1963- *WhoE 91*
Swindells, Robert E. 1939- *BioIn 16*
Swindells, Susan Peters 1952- *WhoAmW 91*
Swindle, Albert Brintwood, Jr. 1949- *WhoEmL 91*
Swindle, Jonathan Cameron 1942- *St&PR 91*
Swindler, Sherry Horton 1957- *WhoSSW 91*
Swindoll, Charles R. *BioIn 16*
Swinea, Robert Wayne 1950- *WhoWrEP 89*
Swinehart, Frank Jeffrey 1949- *BiDrAPA 89*
Swinehart, Philip Ross 1945- *WhoAm 90*
Swinehart, Robert Dane 1937- *St&PR 91*
Swinerton, William Arthur 1917- *WhoAm 90*
Swinford, Betty 1927- *BioIn 16*
Swinford, John Walker 1909- *WhoSSW 91*
Swing, Bruce H. 1941- *St&PR 91*
Swing, John Temple 1929- *WhoAm 90*
Swing, Peter Gram 1922- *IntWWM 90, WhoAm 90*
Swing, Raymond 1887-1968 *BioIn 16*
Swing, Roger Neil 1945- *St&PR 91*
Swing, William Edwin 1936- *WhoAm 90*
Swing, William Lacy 1934- *WhoAm 90, WhoWor 91*
Swingen, Daniel Lock 1960- *St&PR 91*
Swingen, Lowell James 1929- *St&PR 91*
Swingle, Richard Steven 1945- *St&PR 91, WhoE 91*
Swingle, Ward Lamar 1927- *IntWWM 90*
Swings, Andre Arnold Louise 1933- *WhoWor 91*
Swink, David Blair 1944- *WhoSSW 91*
Swink, Larry Dwaine 1966- *WhoSSW 91*
Swink, Mark Edgar *WhoSSW 91*
Swinkels, Henri 1927- *WhoWor 91*
Swinnerton, A. R. 1912- *AuBYP 90*
Swinnerton, Edna Huestis *WhoAmA 91N*
Swinnerton, Frank Arthur 1884-1982 *DcNaB 1981*
Swinnerton, James 1875-1974 *WhoAmA 91N*
Swinnerton, Jimmy 1875-1974 *EncACom*
Swinnerton-Dyer, Peter *BioIn 16*
Swinnerton-Dyer, Peter 1927- *WhoWor 91*
Swinney, Harry Leonard 1939- *WhoAm 90*
Swinsky, Bruce Clayton 1946- *St&PR 91*
Swinson, Cindy Marie 1957- *St&PR 91*
Swint, Thomas Lloyd 1933- *St&PR 91*
Swinton, R. Timothy 1946- *St&PR 91*
Swinton, William Elgin 1900- *AuBYP 90, WhoAm 90*
Swintosky, Joseph Vincent 1921- *WhoAm 90*
Swinyard, Chester Allan 1906- *WhoAm 90*
Swinyard, Ewart Ainslie 1909- *WhoAm 90*
Swire, Edith Wypler 1943- *WhoAmW 91*
Swire, Willard 1910- *WhoAm 90*
Swirsky, Benjamin *WhoAm 90*
Swirsky, Judith Perlman 1928- *WhoAmW 91*
Swirszczynska, Anna 1909-1984 *EncCoWW*
Swisher, Daniel N. 1932- *St&PR 91*
Swisher, Gloria Agnes Wilson 1935- *IntWWM 90*
Swisher, James Edwin 1933- *St&PR 91*
Swisher, Leonard 1947- *St&PR 91*
Swisher, Lloyd K. *St&PR 91*
Swisher, Ronald Dale 1936- *WhoSSW 91*
Swisher, Scott Neil 1918- *WhoAm 90*
Swisher, Steve 1951- *Ballpl 90*
Swisher, Thane 1956- *St&PR 91*
Swisher, Thane Allison 1956- *WhoAm 90*
Swisher, Viola Hegyi 1904?-1990 *ConAu 131*
Swisshelm, Beverly Ann 1949- *St&PR 91*
Swisshelm, Jane Grey Cannon 1815-1884 *BioIn 16*
Swistak, Irena 1964- *WhoAmW 91*
Swit, Loretta 1937- *WhoAm 90, WhoAmW 91, WorAlBi*
Switala, William John 1939- *WhoE 91*
Switalski, Joyce Dooley 1947- *WhoAmW 91*
Swithen, John *ConAu 30NR, MajTwCW*
Swithinbank, Charles Winthrop 1926- *WhoWor 91*
Switlik, Richard 1918- *St&PR 91*
Switten, Margaret Louise *WhoAm 90, WhoAmW 91*
Switz, Mary Ann 1944- *WhoAmW 91*
Switz, Paul F. *BioIn 16*
Switz, Robert E. 1946- *St&PR 91*
Switz, Thomas Richard 1957- *WhoE 91*
Switzer, Ellen Eichenwald 1923- *BioIn 16*
Switzer, Hugh Kent 1938- *St&PR 91*
Switzer, Jon Rex 1937- *WhoWor 91*
Switzer, Lisle J. 1929- *St&PR 91*
Switzer, Paul Kent *BiDrAPA 89*
Switzer, Ralph Joseph, Jr. 1930- *St&PR 91, WhoAm 90*
Switzer, Rebecca Shinn 1888-1988 *BioIn 16*
Switzer, Robert E *BiDrAPA 89*
Switzer, Robert Earl 1929- *WhoSSW 91*
Switzer, Robert Lee 1940- *WhoAm 90*
Switzer, Ronald H. 1938- *St&PR 91*
Switzer, Thomas W. 1945- *St&PR 91*
Switzer, Vernon J. 1930- *St&PR 91*
Switzer, William Paul 1927- *WhoAm 90*
Switzman, Fred Stanley 1932- *WhoE 91*
Swoap, David Bruce 1937- *WhoAm 90*
Swoboda, Peter 1937- *WhoWor 91*
Swoboda, Ralph S. 1948- *St&PR 91*
Swoboda, Ralph Sande 1948- *WhoAm 90*
Swoboda, Ron 1944- *Ballpl 90, BioIn 16*
Swofford, Donald Anthony 1947- *WhoAm 90*
Swofford, Hugh de Guille *ODwPR 91*
Swoger, Marcia Kay 1951- *WhoAmW 91*
Swogger, Glenn, Jr. 1935- *BiDrAPA 89*
Swogger, Kurt W. 1950- *St&PR 91*
Swomley, James Anthony 1929- *WhoAm 90*
Swon, Cassandra Ann *St&PR 91*
Swon, James Ellis 1946- *St&PR 91*
Swonger, Alvin Kent 1943- *WhoAm 90*
Swope, Charles Evans 1930- *WhoAm 90, WhoWor 91*
Swope, David Kent *BiDrAPA 89*
Swope, Donald Downey 1926- *WhoAm 90*
Swope, Elaine Helen 1947- *WhoAmW 91*
Swope, Garnet Howard 1960- *WhoSSW 91*
Swope, George Wendell 1916- *WhoWor 91*
Swope, Herbert Bayard 1882-1958 *BioIn 16, WorAlBi*
Swope, Hunter 1927- *St&PR 91*
Swope, Janice K *BiDrAPA 89*
Swope, Jeffrey Lynn 1950- *WhoSSW 91*
Swope, John Franklin 1938- *St&PR 91, WhoAm 90, WhoE 91*
Swope, Joseph John 1958- *WhoWrEP 89*
Swope, Ken *BioIn 16*
Swope, Samuel David 1949- *St&PR 91*
Swope, Tom 1888-1969 *Ballpl 90*
Swope, William Richards 1920- *WhoSSW 91*
Sword, Carl Harry 1947- *WhoEmL 91*
Sword, Christopher Patrick 1928- *WhoAm 90*
Sword, Richard O *BiDrAPA 89*
Swords, Charles Raymond 1935- *St&PR 91*
Swords, Gary A. 1947- *St&PR 91*
Swords, Maurice J. 1929- *St&PR 91*
Swords, Robert Francis 1940- *BiDrAPA 89*
Swormstedt, J.R. 1934- *St&PR 91*
Swoyer, Kenneth G., Jr. *ODwPR 91*
Swoyer, Thomas M. *St&PR 91N*
Swoyer, Vincent Harry 1932- *St&PR 91, WhoAm 90*
Swyer, Lewis A. *BioIn 16*
Swygert, H. Patrick 1943- *WhoAm 90*
Swygert, Ronnie Marvin 1951- *WhoSSW 91*
Swynnerton, Annie Louisa 1844-1933 *BiDWomA*
Swystun-Rives, Bohdana Alexandra 1925- *WhoAmW 91, WhoWor 91*
Sy, Francisco Santos 1949- *WhoSSW 91*
Sy, Teofilo Santos 1935- *BiDrAPA 89*
Sy-Quenel, Claude-Germaine 1944- *WhoWor 91*
Syalee, Sangat S 1920- *BiDrAPA 89*
Syamour, Marguerite 1861- *BiDWomA*
Syberberg, Hans Jurgen 1935- *BioIn 16*
Sybesma, Christiaan 1928- *WhoWor 91*
Sybesma, Jetske 1940- *SmATA X [port]*
Sybilla 1963- *BioIn 16*
Syblik, Detlev Adolf 1943- *WhoWor 91*
Sychev, Vyacheslav Vladimirovich 1933- *WhoWor 91*
Sychterz, Teresa Anne 1952- *WhoE 91*
Sycip, George Edwin 1956- *St&PR 91*
Sycks, Richard A. 1931- *St&PR 91*
Syde, Harvey 1927- *St&PR 91*
Sydenstricker, Charles Michael 1939- *WhoSSW 91*
Sydney, Albert David *BiDrAPA 89*
Sydney, Allan William 1928- *St&PR 91*
Sydney, Doris S. 1934- *WhoAmW 91*
Sydney, Sydelle Marian 1935- *St&PR 91*
Sydnor, Ashby Kendall, Jr. 1943- *St&PR 91*
Sydnor, Charles F. 1958- *St&PR 91*
Sydnor, Earl L. *BioIn 16*
Sydnor, Edythe Lois 1920- *WhoAmW 91, WhoE 91*
Sydnor, John Terry 1928- *St&PR 91*
Sydnor, Rebecca *BioIn 16*
Sydor, Daniel J. 1939- *St&PR 91*
Sydor, Edward J. 1923- *St&PR 91*
Sydow, Bo John Olof 1946- *WhoWor 91*
Sydow, Max von 1929- *BioIn 16*
Syed Putra Ibni Al-Marhum Syed Hassan J 1920- *WhoWor 91*
Syed, Abu Nasir 1952- *BiDrAPA 89*
Syed, Ahmed N 1941- *BiDrAPA 89*
Syed, Ibrahim Bijli 1939- *WhoWor 91*
Syed, Jainullabdin *BiDrAPA 89*
Syed, Muhammad H 1938- *BiDrAPA 89*
Syed, Riaz Sibtain 1948- *BiDrAPA 89*
Syer, Warren Bertram 1923- *WhoAm 90*
Syiek, Joseph Alexander 1951- *WhoE 91*
Syjalon, Antoine *PenDiDA 89*
Sykas, Peter William 1928- *St&PR 91*
Sykes, Bob 1954- *Ballpl 90*
Sykes, Bobbi 1943- *FemiCLE*
Sykes, Brenda 1949?- *DrBlPA 90*
Sykes, Brian Douglas 1943- *WhoAm 90*
Sykes, Charles 1905-1982 *DcNaB 1981*
Sykes, Christopher Simon 1948- *BioIn 16*
Sykes, David B. 1918- *St&PR 91*
Sykes, David Michael 1954- *WhoWor 91*
Sykes, David Terrence 1937- *WhoAm 90*
Sykes, Gresham M'Cready 1922- *WhoAm 90*
Sykes, Henrietta 1766-1823 *FemiCLE*
Sykes, Homer *BioIn 16*
Sykes, Jo *AuBYP 90*
Sykes, Joseph Stuart 1923- *St&PR 91*
Sykes, Lynn Ray 1937- *WhoAm 90*
Sykes, Maltby 1911- *WhoAmA 91*
Sykes, Martha Moore *ODwPR 91*
Sykes, Melvin Julius 1924- *WhoAm 90*
Sykes, Pamela *AuBYP 90*
Sykes, Richard M. 1940- *St&PR 91*
Sykes, Robert F. 1924- *St&PR 91*
Sykes, Robert H. 1927- *WhoWrEP 89*
Sykes, Roy Arnold, Jr. 1948- *St&PR 91*
Sykes, Thomas Dale 1954- *WhoEmL 91*
Sykes, Vivian M. *BioIn 16*
Sykes, Wilbert R *BiDrAPA 89*
Sykes, William M 1944- *BiDrAPA 89*
Sykes, William Maltby 1911- *WhoAm 90*
Sykora, Adolf *PenDiMP*
Sykora, Donald D. 1930- *St&PR 91*
Sykora, Harold James 1939- *WhoAm 90*
Sykora, Richard J. 1940- *St&PR 91*
Sykora, Sandra Lynn 1954- *WhoAmW 91*
Sylbert, Richard *BioIn 16*
Sylbert, Richard 1928- *ConDes 90*
Sylk, Harry Stanley 1903- *WhoAm 90*
Sylk, Leonard Allen 1941- *WhoE 91*
Sylvan, Melvin M 1915- *BiDrAPA 89*
Sylvan, Rita M 1928- *WhoAmA 91*
Sylvander, Yvette *BioIn 16*
Sylvander, Yvonne *BioIn 16*
Sylvanowicz, Wayne Thomas 1952- *WhoE 91*
Sylvest, Harold Maynard, Jr. 1941- *St&PR 91*
Sylvester *BioIn 16*
Sylvester 1946-1988 *DrBlPA 90*
Sylvester, A. J. 1889-1989 *AnObit 1989*
Sylvester, Emmy *BiDrAPA 89*
Sylvester, George Howard 1927- *WhoAm 90*
Sylvester, Harold *ConTFT 8, DrBlPA 90*
Sylvester, Janet 1950- *WhoWrEP 89*
Sylvester, John 1935- *St&PR 91*
Sylvester, Johnny *BioIn 16, NewYTBS 90 [port]*
Sylvester, Leonard 1933- *St&PR 91*
Sylvester, Lucille 1909- *WhoAmA 91N*
Sylvestre, Guy 1918- *WhoAmA 91*
Sylvestre, Jean Guy 1918- *WhoAm 90*
Sylvestri, Mario Frank 1948- *WhoEmL 91*
Sylvia *BiDEWW, MajTwCW*
Sylvia, B. Ralph 1940- *St&PR 91*
Sylvia, Benjamin Ralph 1940- *WhoAm 90*
Sylvian, David *BioIn 16*
Symank, Oleta Marlene 1957- *WhoAmW 91*
Symanski, Robert A. 1946- *St&PR 91*
Symanski, Robert Anthony 1946- *WhoAm 90, WhoE 91*
Symansky, Gary K. 1950- *St&PR 91*
Syme, Daniel B. *BioIn 16*
Syme, Daniel Bailey 1946- *WhoE 91*
Syme, Robert P. 1934- *St&PR 91*
Syme, Ronald 1903-1989 *AnObit 1989, BioIn 16, ConAu 129*
Syme, Ronald 1913- *AuBYP 90*
Syme, Sherman Leonard 1932- *WhoAm 90*
Symes, Dilwyn Edward *BiDrAPA 89*
Symes, Robin James 1939- *WhoWor 91*
Syming *WhoWrEP 89*
Symington, Stuart 1901-1988 *AnObit 1988, BioIn 16, WorAlBi*
Symm, Robert Edwin 1957- *WhoSSW 91*
Symmers, William Garth 1910- *WhoAm 90*
Symmes, Daniel Leslie 1949- *WhoEmL 91*
Symmes, Deborah Jean 1959- *WhoE 91*
Symmes, John Cleves 1780-1829 *EncO&P 3*
Symmes, Lee Richardson 1941- *WhoAm 90*
Symmes, Robert Edward *MajTwCW*
Symmmes, William Daniel 1938- *WhoWor 91*
Symmonds, Richard Earl 1922- *WhoAm 90*
Symms, Steven Douglas 1938- *WhoAm 90, WhoWor 91*
Symon, Lindsay 1929- *WhoWor 91*
Symon, Robert J. 1931- *St&PR 91*
Symonds, Alexandra 1918- *BiDrAPA 89, WhoE 91*
Symonds, Arlene R. 1932- *St&PR 91*
Symonds, Carl Joseph 1920- *St&PR 91*
Symonds, Glen Regan 1950- *WhoEmL 91*
Symonds, John 1914- *EncO&P 3*
Symonds, John Addington 1840-1893 *BioIn 16*
Symonds, Johnnie Pirkle 1900- *WhoAmW 91, WhoE 91, WhoWor 91*
Symonds, Martin *BiDrAPA 89*
Symonds, Paul Southworth 1916- *WhoAm 90*
Symonds, Raymond Paul 1948- *WhoWor 91*
Symonette, Craig Roland 1951- *WhoWor 91*
Symons, Arthur 1865-1945 *BioIn 16*
Symons, Edward Leonard, Jr. 1941- *WhoAm 90*
Symons, Harry Clay 1922- *WhoE 91*
Symons, Irving Joseph 1907- *St&PR 91*
Symons, J. Keith 1932- *WhoAm 90, WhoSSW 91*
Symons, James Martin 1931- *WhoAm 90*
Symons, John 1930- *WhoAm 90*
Symons, Julian 1912- *ConAu 33NR, MajTwCW, TwCCr&M 91, WorAlBi*
Symons, Julian Gustave 1912- *WhoAm 90*
Symons, Robert Spencer 1925- *WhoAm 90*
Symons, Thomas H. B. 1929- *WhoAm 90, WhoE 91*
Symons, Walter Vaughan 1930- *St&PR 91*
Syms, Sy 1926- *St&PR 91*
Symuleski, Richard Aloysius 1947- *WhoEmL 91*
Synan, Edward Aloysius, Jr. 1918- *WhoAm 90*
Synar, Michael Lynn 1950- *WhoAm 90, WhoSSW 91*
Synchestra *NewAgMG*
Synder, Jane W. 1928- *St&PR 91*
Synder, Robert B. 1941- *St&PR 91*
Synek, M. 1930- *WhoWor 91*
Synenko, Nicholas *St&PR 91*
Synergy *NewAgMG*
Syng, Philip 1703-1789 *PenDiDA 89*
Synge, John Lighton 1897- *WhoAm 90*
Synge, John Millington 1871-1909 *TwCLC 37 [port], WorAlBi*
Synge, Richard L. M. 1914- *WorAlBi*
Synge, Richard Laurence Millington 1914- *WhoWor 91*
Synnett, Robert John 1958- *St&PR 91*
Synnott, William Raymond 1929- *St&PR 91, WhoAm 90*
Synodinos, John Anthony 1934- *WhoAm 90*
Synowiec, Ewa Krystyna 1942- *IntWWM 90*
Syozi, Itiro 1920- *WhoWor 91*
Sypek, Donald William 1936- *St&PR 91*
Sypek, Janice Mary *BiDrAPA 89*
Sypert, George Walter 1941- *WhoAm 90*
Syphax, John Lesesne *BiDrAPA 89*
Sypherd, Paul Starr 1936- *WhoAm 90*
Syphers, Grant 1940- *BiDrAPA 89*
Sypitkowski, James R. 1946- *St&PR 91*
Syquia, Enrique Pineda 1930- *WhoWor 91*
Syracuse, Paul F 1926- *BiDrAPA 89*
Syreeta *DrBlPA 90*
Syrek, Richard William 1947- *St&PR 91, WhoE 91*
Syren, Kurt Ingemar 1931- *WhoWor 91*
Syrkin, Marie 1900-1989 *BioIn 16*
Syron, Martin Bernard 1936- *WhoAm 90*
Syron, Richard F. 1943- *St&PR 91*
Syron, Richard Francis 1943- *WhoAm 90*
Syrop, Mitchell 1953- *WhoAmA 91*
Syrquin, Moshe 1944- *WhoWor 91*
Syruc, J. *MajTwCW*
Syse, Glenna Marie Lowes *WhoAm 90*
Syse, Jan P. 1930- *WhoWor 91*
Sytsema, Gerald D. 1938- *St&PR 91*
Sytsma, Frederick Ray 1939- *St&PR 91*
Sytsma, John *BiDrAPA 89*
Sytsma, Karen L. 1964- *WhoAmW 91*
Syvertsen, Edwin T., Jr. 1923- *St&PR 91*
Syvertson, Clarence Alfred 1926- *WhoAm 90*
Sywolski, Robert John 1938- *St&PR 91*
Sywottek, Arnold Erich 1942- *WhoWor 91*
Syz, Hans C 1894- *BiDrAPA 89*
Szabad, George Michael 1917- *WhoAm 90*
Szabados, Georgy 1939- *IntWWM 90*

Szablak, Laura Rosemary 1957- *WhoAmW 91*
Szablowski, Jerzy Jan 1906- *WhoWor 91*
Szablya, John Francis 1924- *WhoAm 90*
Szabo, Albert 1925- *WhoAm 90*
Szabo, Barna Aladar 1935- *WhoAm 90*
Szabo, Daniel 1933- *WhoAm 90*
Szabo, Denis 1929- *WhoAm 90*
Szabo, Denise Zarotney 1953- *WhoAmW 91, WhoE 91*
Szabo, Francis Michael 1948- *WhoSSW 91*
Szabo, Frank Charles 1952- *St&PR 91*
Szabo, George 1928- *WhoAm 90*
Szabo, Helga 1933- *IntWWM 90*
Szabo, Istvan *BioIn 16*
Szabo, Istvan 1938- *ConTFT 8, WhoWor 91*
Szabo, Joseph George 1950- *WhoAmA 91, WhoE 91*
Szabo, Lynn Christine 1951- *WhoE 91*
Szabo, Magda 1917- *EncCoWW, WhoWor 91, WorAu 1980 [port]*
Szabo, Miklos *WhoWrEP 89*
Szabo, Paul *PenDiMP*
Szabo, Richard Wayne 1956- *WhoE 91*
Szabo, Robert Morris 1952- *WhoEmL 91*
Szabo, Stephen J 1940- *BiDrAPA 89*
Szabo, Stephen Lee 1940- *WhoAmA 91*
Szabo, Zoltan 1928- *BioIn 16*
Szabo, Zoltan 1943- *WhoWor 91*
Szabo, Zoltan 1959- *WhoE 91*
Szabolcsi, Miklos 1921- *WhoWor 91*
Szadkowski, Sylwester A 1939- *BiDrAPA 89*
Szafraniec, Ewa 1949- *BiDrAPA 89*
Szafranski, John George 1935- *St&PR 91*
Szajna, Jozef *BioIn 16*
Szajna, Jozef 1922- *ConDes 90, WhoWor 91*
Szalasi, Ferenc 1897-1946 *BioIn 16*
Szalay, Carolyn Ruth O'Connor 1943- *WhoAmW 91*
Szalinski, Ellen 1963- *ODwPR 91*
Szalita-Pemow, Alberta B 1910- *BiDrAPA 89*
Szalkowski, Charles Conrad 1948- *WhoEmL 91*
Szalkowski, Mary B. 1951- *WhoAmW 91*
Szalonek, Witold Jozef 1927- *IntWWM 90*
Szamek, Pierre Ervin *WhoAm 90*
Szamuely, Laszlo 1936- *WhoWor 91*
Szanti, Richard J. 1939- *St&PR 91*
Szanto, George 1940- *WhoAm 90*
Szanto, Louis P 1889-1965 *WhoAmA 91N*
Szanto, Paul 1904-1989 *BioIn 16*
Szapocznik, Jose 1947- *WhoHisp 91*
Szarama, Judith Layne 1940- *WhoAmA 91*
Szarek, Walter Anthony 1938- *WhoAm 90*
Szarka, Sandor I. 1937- *St&PR 91*
Szarkowski, John *BioIn 16*
Szarkowski, Thaddeus John *BioIn 16*
Szaro, Judith Salomea 1952- *WhoAmW 91, WhoEmL 91*
Szaro, Richard Stanley 1942- *St&PR 91*
Szasz, Frank V 1925- *WhoAmA 91*
Szasz, Suzanne Shorr 1915- *AuBYP 90*
Szasz, Thomas 1920- *BiDrAPA 89*
Szasz, Thomas Stephen 1920- *WhoAm 90, WhoE 91*
Szathmary, Ivan K. 1936- *St&PR 91*
Szathmary, Louis Istvan, II 1919- *WhoWor 91*
Szatmari, Marianne 1931- *WhoWor 91*
Szczarba, Robert Henry 1932- *WhoAm 90*
Szczepanik, Edward Franciszek 1915- *WhoWor 91*
Szczepanski, Jan 1913- *WhoWor 91*
Szczepkowski, Albert Z. 1924- *St&PR 91*
Szczesiul, Walter 1928- *St&PR 91*
Szczesniak, Alina Surmacka 1925- *WhoAmW 91*
Szczesniak, Edward Stanley 1948- *WhoSSW 91*
Szczesny, Frances Evelyn 1951- *WhoAmW 91*
Szczesny, Ronald William 1940- *WhoWor 91*
Szczucka, Zofia Kossak- 1890-1968 *BioIn 16*
Szczucki, Denise 1962- *BiDrAPA 89*
Sze, Andy Hok Fan 1951- *St&PR 91, WhoAm 90*
Sze, Celestina K. 1938- *St&PR 91*
Sze, Mai-Mai *AuBYP 90*
Sze, Tsung Wei 1922- *WhoAm 90*
Szebehely, Victor G. 1921- *WhoAm 90*
Szebenyi, Doletha Marian Evans 1947- *WhoAmW 91*
Szechi, Daniel 1956- *WhoSSW 91*
Szecsi, Margit 1928- *EncCoWW*
Szecsody, Imre G M 1928- *BiDrAPA 89*
Szeeley, Pamela 1953- *BiDrAPA 89*
Szefler, Stanley James 1948- *WhoAm 90*
Szegedi, Erno 1911- *IntWWM 90*
Szegedy-Maszak, Aladar *BioIn 16*
Szeglin, Arthur Ronald 1934- *St&PR 91*
Szego, Clara Marian 1916- *WhoAm 90, WhoAmW 91*
Szekany, Andreas 1945- *WhoWor 91*
Szekely, Clara J *BiDrAPA 89*
Szekely, Edmond Bordeaux 19--?-1980 *NewAgE 90*
Szekely, Julian 1934- *WhoAm 90*
Szekely, Zoltan 1903- *PenDiMP*
Szekeres, Cyndy 1933- *SmATA 60 [port]*
Szekfu, Julius 1883-1955 *BioIn 16*
Szelachowski, Tadeusz 1932- *WhoWor 91*
Szelburg-Zarembina, Ewa 1899-1986 *BioIn 16, EncCoWW*
Szelecsenyi, Ferenc 1957- *WhoWor 91*
Szell, George 1897-1970 *PenDiMP, WorAlBi*
Szemes, Stephen Paul 1937- *St&PR 91*
Szenberg, Michael 1934- *WhoAm 90*
Szendrey, Thomas Laszlo 1941- *WhoE 91*
Szenes, Hannah 1921-1944 *BioIn 16*
Szent-Gyorgyi, Albert 1893-1986 *BioIn 16, WorAlBi*
Szentirmai, George 1928- *WhoAm 90*
Szep, Paul Michael 1941- *WhoAm 90*
Szeps-Zuckerkandl, Bertha 1893-1945 *EncCoWW*
Szeptycki, Andreas 1865-1944 *BioIn 16*
Szer, Wlodzimierz 1924- *WhoAm 90*
Szeransky, Peter *PenDiMP*
Szeremany, Richard J. 1931- *IntWWM 90*
Szeremeta-Browar, Taisa Lydia 1957- *WhoAmW 91*
Szeri, Andras Zoltan 1934- *WhoAm 90*
Szerlip, Barbara L. 1949- *WhoWrEP 89*
Szerlip, William Alan 1949- *St&PR 91*
Szeryng, Henryk *BioIn 16*
Szeryng, Henryk 1918-1988 *AnObit 1988, PenDiMP*
Szesko, Deborah Pulda 1958- *WhoAmW 91*
Szesko, Judith Clarann *WhoAmA 91*
Szesko, Lenore Rundle 1933- *WhoAm 90, WhoAmA 91*
Szesny, Terry Lee 1946- *St&PR 91*
Szetela, Brian R *BiDrAPA 89*
Szeto, Alexander Koon Ping 1940- *WhoE 91*
Szeto, Elaine Gee 1949- *WhoEmL 91*
Szeto, Onward *BiDrAPA 89*
Szewalski, Robert 1903- *WhoWor 91*
Szewczyk, Albin Anthony 1935- *WhoAm 90*
Szewinska, Irena 1946- *BioIn 16*
Szigethy, Attila 1932- *St&PR 91*
Szigeti, Joseph 1892-1973 *PenDiMP*
Szilagyi, Desiderius Emerick 1910- *WhoAm 90, WhoWor 91*
Szilagyi, John Alex 1940- *WhoE 91*
Szilard, Leo *BioIn 16*
Szilard, Leo 1898-1964 *WorAlBi*
Szilvasy, Linda Markuly 1940- *WhoAmA 91*
Szilvay, Geza 1943- *IntWWM 90*
Szink, David A. 1935- *St&PR 91*
Szirmai, Endre Anreas Franz 1922- *WhoWor 91*
Szirmay, Marte 1946- *BioIn 16*
Szlabowicz, Jerzy Wieslaw 1943- *BiDrAPA 89*
Szladits, Lola L. *BioIn 16, NewYTBS 90 [port]*
Szladits, Lola Leontin 1923- *WhoWrEP 89*
Szlazak, Anita Christina 1943- *WhoAm 90*
Szlengel, Wladyslaw *BioIn 16*
Szlyk, John Joseph 1947- *BiDrAPA 89*
Szlyk, Patricia Carol 1952- *WhoAmW 91, WhoE 91*
Szmant, Alina Margarita 1946- *WhoAm 90*
Szmant, Herman Harry 1918- *WhoSSW 91*
Szmarag, Ruth *BiDrAPA 89*
Szmit, Frederick A. 1938- *St&PR 91*
Szmuilowicz, Julio 1949- *BiDrAPA 89*
Szmurlo, Piotr Andrzej 1956- *BiDrAPA 89*
Szmyt, Davena D. 1939- *WhoAmW 91*
Sznajderman, Marius S 1926- *WhoAmA 91*
Sznewajs, Robert David 1946- *St&PR 91*
Szobotka, Tibor, Mrs. 1917- *WhoWor 91*
Szogyi, Alex 1929- *WhoWrEP 89*
Szoka, Edmund Casimir 1927- *WhoAm 90, WhoWor 91*
Szoke, David Frank *BiDrAPA 89*
Szoke, John *WhoAmA 91*
Szoke, John 1943- *WhoE 91*
Szoke, Joseph Louis 1947- *WhoEmL 91*
Szokolay, Sandor 1931- *IntWWM 90, PenDiMP A, WhoWor 91*
Szold, Henrietta 1860-1945 *BioAmW, BioIn 16, WorAlBi*
Szollosy, Andras 1921- *IntWWM 90*
Szomjas-Schiffert, Gyorgy 1910- *IntWWM 90*
Szoradi, Charles 1923- *WhoWor 91*
Szorenyi, Suzana 1929- *IntWWM 90*
Szostak, John S. 1952- *St&PR 91*
Szostak, Lorri Lewis 1957- *WhoE 91*
Szpak, Anthony M. 1954- *St&PR 91*
Szporn, Renee Marla 1956- *WhoE 91*
Sztehlo, Gabor 1909-1974 *BioIn 16*
Szteinbaum, Edward M. *BiDrAPA 89*
Sztojay, Dome 1883-1946 *BioIn 16*
Sztrik, Janos 1953- *WhoWor 91*
Szuba, Martin Peter *BiDrAPA 89*
Szubski, James 1941- *ODwPR 91*
Szuch, Stephanie 1936- *WhoAmW 91*
Szucs, Andrew Eric 1946- *WhoWrEP 89*
Szucs, H. *St&PR 91*
Szudek, Agnes *BioIn 16*
Szuets, Judie Elizabeth 1956- *WhoAmW 91*
Szugda, Bernard W. 1923- *St&PR 91*
Szuhay, Joseph Alexander 1925- *WhoAm 90*
Szujewski, Phillip Andrew 1948- *WhoE 91*
Szulc, Joseph 1875-1956 *OxCPMus*
Szulc, Tad 1926- *SpyFic, WhoAm 90, WhoWrEP 89*
Szulecki, John S. 1932- *St&PR 91*
Szumigalski, Anne 1922- *FemiCLE*
Szumylo, Helen Barbara 1946- *WhoAmW 91*
Szurek, Stanislaus A 1907- *BiDrAPA 89*
Szurszewski, Joseph Henry 1940- *WhoAm 90*
Szuster, Julja Isabel 1946- *IntWWM 90*
Szuster, Richard R. *BiDrAPA 89*
Szwajgier, Olga 1944- *IntWWM 90*
Szwalbenest, Benedykt Jan 1955- *WhoEmL 91*
Szwech, Susan Nancy 1964- *WhoSSW 91*
Szybala, Renee Leslie 1952- *WhoEmL 91*
Szybalski, Waclaw 1921- *WhoAm 90*
Szydlowski, Mary Frances *WhoWrEP 89*
Szyk, Arthur 1894-1951 *BioIn 16, WhoAmA 91N*
Szykowny, Lee S 1958- *BiDrAPA 89*
Szymanowski, Karol 1882-1987 *PenDiMP A*
Szymanski, Andrzej Antoni 1947- *WhoE 91*
Szymanski, David J. *ODwPR 91*
Szymanski, David Mark 1957- *WhoEmL 91*
Szymanski, Frank Stanislaus, Jr. 1952- *WhoEmL 91*
Szymanski, George M. 1920- *St&PR 91*
Szymanski, Herman V *BiDrAPA 89*
Szymanski, Herman Vincent 1951- *WhoE 91*
Szymanski, Jerome F *BiDrAPA 89*
Szymanski, Joseph Leonard 1935- *St&PR 91*
Szymanski, Karen Ann 1951- *WhoAmW 91*
Szymanski, Ludwik S *BiDrAPA 89*
Szymanski, Sally Rose *BiDrAPA 89*
Szymanski, Waclaw A. 1949- *WhoE 91*
Szymanski Ramirez, Arturo 1922- *WhoAm 90*
Szymborska, Wislawa 1923- *EncCoWW, WorAu 1980*
Szymoniak, Elaine Eisfelder 1920- *WhoAmW 91*
Szynkiewicz, Matthew L. 1946- *St&PR 91*
Szyrynski, Victor *BiDrAPA 89*
Szyszkeiwicz, Regina F. 1962- *WhoAmW 91*

T

T, Mr. BioIn 16
T, Mr. 1952- WorAlBi
T. Rex EncPR&S 89
T-Bone Slim 188-?-1942 EncAL
't Hart, Lenie BioIn 16
't Hart, Maarten 1944- ConAu 129
Ta-pu-yen WomWR
Taaffe, James Griffith 1932- WhoAm 90
Taagepera, Rein 1933- WhoAm 90
Taalas, Jaakko Adolf 1939- WhoWor 91
Taam, Ronald Everett 1948- WhoAm 90
Taapken, Albertus 1916- St&PR 91
Tabachnick, Anne 1937- WhoAmA 91, WhoE 91
Tabachnick, Norman D BiDrAPA 89
Tabachnick, Theodore M 1935- BiDrAPA 89
Tabachnik, Bernard 1933- WhoE 91
Tabachnik, Douglas T. 1955- WhoEmL 91
Tabachnik, Michel 1942- IntWWM 90, PenDiMP
Tabachuk, Emelia 1926- WhoAmW 91
Taback, Harry 1945- St&PR 91
Taback, Simms 1932- WhoAmA 91
Tabai, Ieremia 1950- WhoWor 91
Tabak, Chaim 1946- WhoAmA 91
Tabak, Marvin BioIn 16
Tabak, Michael L. 1946- WhoEmL 91
Tabak, S. Charles 1932- St&PR 91, WhoAm 90
Tabaka, Maija 1939- BioIn 16
Tabakin, Burnley M. 1926- St&PR 91
Tabakin, Gary Alan 1955- St&PR 91
Tabakin, Loraine Smith 1940- WhoAmW 91
Tabakin, Mark H. 1946- St&PR 91
Tabakoff, Widen 1919- WhoAm 90
Tabaksblat, Israel Severin 1953- WhoE 91
Tabalujan, Hans Gerard 1952- WhoWor 91
Tabano, Luis 1941- St&PR 91
Tabas, Daniel M. 1923- St&PR 91
Tabasco, Evangeline WhoAmA 91
Tabata, Shigeaki 1948- WhoWor 91
Tabata, Yukio 1948- WhoEmL 91, WhoWor 91
Tabatabai, Hamid 1948- BiDrAPA 89
Tabatchnick, Meryl S. 1950- WhoAmW 91
Tabatoni, Pierre 1923- WhoWor 91
Tabatznik, Bernard 1927- WhoAm 90
Tabau, Robert Louis 1928- WhoWor 91
Tabb, Charles Jordan 1955- WhoEmL 91
Tabb, J.H. 1908- St&PR 91
Tabb, Sharon Lynn 1951- WhoSSW 91
Tabba, Mohammad Myassar 1946- WhoWor 91
Tabbat, Samuel F BiDrAPA 89
Tabbert, Rondi Jo 1953- WhoAmW 91
Tabei, Junko 1940- WorAlBi
Tabell, Anthony 1931- WhoAm 90
Taben, Charles L. 1961- WhoE 91
Tabenkin, Lev 1952- BioIn 16
Taber, Carol A. WhoAm 90, WhoAmW 91
Taber, Elsie 1915- WhoAmW 91
Taber, James Lester 1921- St&PR 91
Taber, Linda 1941- ODwPR 91
Taber, Linda Perrin 1941- WhoAmW 91
Taber, Margaret Ruth 1935- WhoAm 90
Taber, Robert Clinton 1917- WhoAm 90
Taber, Steve 1924- BioIn 16
Taber, Steve 1963- WhoSSW 91
Tabickman, Maurice Louis 1944- St&PR 91
Tabin, Janet Hale 1946- WhoWrEP 89
Tabin, Julius 1919- WhoAm 90
Tabin, Morton S 1929- BiDrAPA 89
Tabio, Martha S. 1948- St&PR 91
Tabisz, George Conrad 1939- WhoWor 91
Tabiszewski, Edward Kazimierz 1927- WhoWor 91
Tablada, Jose Juan 1871-1945 BioIn 16
Tableman, Betty BioIn 16
Tabler, J Boswell 1949- BiDrAPA 89
Tabler, Levi Earl, Jr. 1927- WhoAm 90
Tabler, Pat BioIn 16
Tabler, Pat 1958- Ballpl 90
Tabler, William Benjamin 1914- WhoAm 90
Tabner, Mary Frances 1918- WhoAmW 91, WhoE 91, WhoWor 91
Taboada, Viola Ybanez 1940- BiDrAPA 89
Tabone, Vincent 1913- WhoWor 91
Tabor, Baby Doe BioIn 16
Tabor, David 1913- WhoWor 91
Tabor, Doris Dee 1918- WhoAm 90
Tabor, Eliza 1835-1914 FemiCLE
Tabor, Elizabeth 1854-1935 BioAmW
Tabor, Ellen Beth 1957- BiDrAPA 89
Tabor, Franklin Claire 1919- WhoWrEP 89
Tabor, Horace 1830-1899 BioIn 16
Tabor, Jack BioIn 16
Tabor, James Daniel 1946- WhoSSW 91
Tabor, Jim 1913-1953 Ballpl 90
Tabor, John Kaye 1921- WhoAm 90
Tabor, Jon Kenneth 1933- St&PR 91
Tabor, Leslie A. 1932- St&PR 91
Tabor, Marvin, Jr. 1938- WhoSSW 91
Tabor, Ray Alfred, Sr. 1940- WhoSSW 91
Tabor, Robert Jay 1944- WhoE 91
Tabor, Sandra L. 1954- St&PR 91
Tabor, Shirley BioIn 16
Tabor, Steven Allen 1952- St&PR 91
Tabor, Virginia S 1926- WhoAmA 91
Tabora, Cristina 1944- St&PR 91
Taborda, Carlos A. 1942- St&PR 91
Tabori, Paul 1908-1974 EncO&P 3
Taborsky, Carol Jeanne 1947- WhoAmW 91
Tabouis, Genevieve Rapatel 1892-1985 BiDFrPL
Tabrar, Joseph 1857-1931 OxCPMus
Tabris, Michael D. 1937- ODwPR 91
Tabrisky, Joseph 1931- WhoWor 91
Tabrizi, Firooz N 1932- BiDrAPA 89
Tabroff, Norman Richard BiDrAPA 89
Tabuchi, Koichi 1946- Ballpl 90
Tabuchi, Mamoru 1924- WhoAm 90, WhoWor 91
Taccone, Bonnie Krier 1953- WhoSSW 91
Tacey, Ronald William 1949- St&PR 91
Tacha, Athena 1936- BiDWomA, WhoAmA 91
Tacha, Deanell Reece 1946- WhoAm 90, WhoAmW 91
Tache, Alexandre-Antonin 1823-1894 DcCanB 12
Tache, Joseph-Charles 1820-1894 DcCanB 12, DcLB 99 [port]
Tache, Josephine-Eleonore DcCanB 12
Tache, Yvette France 1945- WhoEmL 91
Tachi, Ryuichiro 1921- WhoWor 91
Tachibana Clan EncJap
Tachibana, Sei 1923- WhoWor 91
Tachick, Robert Daniel 1948- St&PR 91
Tachmindji, Alexander John 1928- WhoAm 90, WhoWor 91
Tacitus, Cornelius 56?-120? WorAlBi
Tacka, Walter Francis 1927- St&PR 91
Tackaberry, Robert R. 1939- St&PR 91
Tackel, Ira S. 1954- WhoE 91
Tacker, Edgar Carroll 1935- WhoAm 90
Tackett, Ben Dahlman, Jr. 1962- WhoSSW 91
Tackett, Kathleen Coleman 1961- WhoSSW 91
Tackett-Nelson, Steven Charles BiDrAPA 89
Tacki, Bernadette Susan 1913- WhoAmW 91
Tackovich, Jo Ann 1938- WhoAmW 91
Tacuchian, Ricardo 1939- IntWWM 90
Tadano, Kota 1934- St&PR 91
Tadavarthy, Jyothi Pavani 1957- BiDrAPA 89
Taddei, Armando 1926- St&PR 91
Taddei, Giuseppe WhoAm 90
Taddei, Giuseppe 1916- BioIn 16, IntWWM 90, PenDiMP
Taddei, Mirian Hunter 1930- St&PR 91
Taddei, Tiziano 1934- WhoWor 91
Taddeo, John August 1955- WhoE 91
Taddeo, Ronald James 1942- BiDrAPA 89
Tade, George Thomas 1923- WhoAm 90
Tadema, Laurence Alma 1864?-1940 FemiCLE
Tadic, Marko 1953- WhoWor 91
Tadjpour, Seyed Ali BiDrAPA 89
Tadlip, Marilou Palicte 1946- WhoWor 91
Tadlock, Paul BioIn 16
Tadokoro, Masayuki 1956- WhoWor 91
Tadolini, Eugenia 1809-1850? PenDiMP
Tadros, Gamal Habib 1953- WhoE 91
Tadros, Richard 1945- WhoWor 91
Tadross, Emmanuel Habib 1940- BiDrAPA 89
Tadry, Raymond Stephen 1934- St&PR 91
Taeffner, John H 1904- BiDrAPA 89
Taenzer, Hans J. 1932- St&PR 91
Taeschler, Debra Ann 1953- WhoAmW 91, WhoE 91, WhoWor 91
Taets, James E. 1955- St&PR 91
Taetzsch, Robert Leonard 1931- EncO&P 3
Taeuber, Conrad 1906- WhoAm 90
Taeuber, Karl Ernst 1936- WhoAm 90
Tafari Makonnen 1891-1975 BioIn 16
Tafel, Edgar 1912- WhoAm 90
Tafero, Jessie Joseph BioIn 16
Taff, Warren Russell 1947- BiDrAPA 89
Taffer, Deborah Batts 1954- WhoAmW 91
Taffet, Elizabeth Rose 1934- WhoAmW 91
Taffner, Don BioIn 16
Tafl, Zdenek Emil 1927- WhoWor 91
Tafolla, Carmen 1951- ConAu 131, HispWr 90, WhoHisp 91
Tafoya, Alfonso WhoHisp 91N
Tafoya, Cathy Jo 1953- WhoWrEP 89
Tafoya, Charles P. WhoHisp 91
Tafoya, Roman L. 1945- St&PR 91
Tafrui, Nancy 1946- AuBYP 90
Taft, Alphonso 1810-1891 BiDrUSE 89, BioIn 16
Taft, Charles Kirkland 1928- WhoAm 90
Taft, David Dakin 1938- WhoAm 90
Taft, Donald Allen 1951- St&PR 91
Taft, Earl Jay 1931- WhoE 91
Taft, Frances Prindle 1921- WhoAmA 91
Taft, Frederick Irving 1945- WhoEmL 91
Taft, Helen Herron 1861-1943 BioIn 16
Taft, James W. 1945- St&PR 91
Taft, Jessie 1882-1960 BioAmW
Taft, Nathaniel Belmont 1919- WhoE 91, WhoWor 91
Taft, Richard George 1913- WhoAm 90
Taft, Robert, Jr. 1917- WhoAm 90
Taft, Robert A. BioIn 16
Taft, Robert A. 1889-1953 WorAlBi
Taft, Robert W. 1937- ODwPR 91
Taft, Seth Chase 1922- WhoAm 90
Taft, Sheldon Ashley 1937- WhoAm 90
Taft, Steven David BiDrAPA 89
Taft, William H. 1857-1930 BioIn 16
Taft, William Howard 1857-1930 Ballpl 90, BiDrUSE 89, WorAlBi
Taft, William Howard 1915- WhoAm 90
Taft, William Wilson 1932- WhoAm 90
Tafur, Albert 1917- BiDrAPA 89
Tafur, Mario Humberto 1940- BiDrAPA 89
Tafuri, Nancy BioIn 16
Tafuri, Spencer Andrew 1952- WhoWor 91
Tagatz, George Elmo 1935- WhoAm 90
Tager, Benjamin N BiDrAPA 89
Tager, Jack 1936- WhoAm 90
Tager, William Samuel 1928- St&PR 91
Tagg, John BioIn 16
Tagg, Philip D. 1944- IntWWM 90
Taggard, Genevieve 1894-1948 FemiCLE
Taggares, Kathy BioIn 16
Taggart, Austin Dale, II 1952- WhoSSW 91
Taggart, David Peter 1954- WhoE 91
Taggart, Ganson Powers 1918- WhoAm 90, WhoE 91, WhoWor 91
Taggart, James Knox 1937- WhoAm 90
Taggart, John P. 1942- WhoWrEP 89
Taggart, Leslie Davidson 1910- St&PR 91, WhoAm 90, WhoE 91, WhoWor 91
Taggart, Maureen Anne Wetherbee 1960- WhoE 91
Taggart, Philip 1930- ODwPR 91
Taggart, Philip W. 1930- St&PR 91
Taggart, Rita ConTFT 8 [port]
Taggart, Robert Wallace 1937- St&PR 91
Taggart, Sondra 1934- WhoAmW 91
Taggart, William John 1940- WhoAmA 91
Tagger, Ziona 1900-1988 BioIn 16
Taggie, Benjamin Fredrick 1938- WhoAm 90
Taghavy, Ebrahim BiDrAPA 89
Taghizadeh, Fereidoon BiDrAPA 89
Tagiuri, Renato 1919- WhoWrEP 89
Tagle, Hilda Gloria 1946- WhoHisp 91
Taglia, R. Victor St&PR 91
Tagliabue, Charles J. 1931- St&PR 91
Tagliabue, John 1923- WhoWrEP 89
Tagliabue, Paul BioIn 16
Tagliabue, Paul 1940- News 90 [port]
Tagliabue, Paul John 1940- WhoAm 90, WhoE 91
Tagliaferri, Lee Gene 1931- WhoE 91, WhoWor 91
Tagliaferro, John Anthony BioIn 16
Tagliaferro, John Anthony 1944- WhoAm 90
Tagliaferro, Magda 1893- PenDiMP
Tagliapetra, Giovanni PenDiMP
Tagliarino, Peggy BioIn 16
Tagliarino, Scott A. ODwPR 91

Tagliavini, Ferruccio 1913- IntWWM 90, PenDiMP
Tagliavini, Franco 1934- IntWWM 90
Tagliavini, Luigi 1929- PenDiMP
Tagliavini, Luigi Ferdinando 1929- IntWWM 90
Tagliolini, Filippo PenDiDA 89
Taglioni, Marie 1804-1884 WorAlBi
Tagore, Rabindranath 1861-1941 BioIn 16, MajTwCW, WorAlBi
Taguchi, Tadao 1929- St&PR 91
Tague, Barry Elwert 1938- WhoAm 90
Tague, Charles F. 1924- St&PR 91
Tague, Charles Francis 1924- WhoAm 90
Tague, Karl Raymond 1946- WhoAm 90, WhoSSW 91
Tahan, William Nicholas 1924- St&PR 91
Tahara, Stanley Makoto 1952- WhoEmL 91
Tahchee 1790?- WhNaAH
Tahedl, Ernestine 1940- WhoAmA 91
Taheri, Amanollah 1933- BiDrAPA 89
Tahir, Abe M, Jr 1931- WhoAmA 91
Tahir, Bassam Mahmoud 1962- WhoWor 91
Tahir, Kishwar Ara 1954- BiDrAPA 89
Tahir, M. Elizabeth 1933- St&PR 91
Tahmoush, Albert Joseph 1921- St&PR 91
Tahourdin, Peter 1928- IntWWM 90
Tahzib, Nezamuddin 1933- WhoWor 91
Tai, Chen-To 1915- WhoAm 90
Tai, Chong-Soo Stephen 1940- WhoSSW 91
Tai, Douglas Leung-Tak 1940- WhoSSW 91
Tai, Heng-Ming 1957- WhoSSW 91
Tai, Jane S 1944- WhoAmA 91
Tai, Julia Chow 1935- WhoAmW 91
Tai, Rafique 1943- BiDrAPA 89
Taibleson, Mitchell Herbert 1929- WhoAm 90
Taibo, Paco Ignacio, II 1949- ConAu 131, HispWr 90
Taicher, Richard 1929- BioIn 16
Taichert, Louise Cecile BiDrAPA 89
Taichman, Norton Stanley 1936- WhoAm 90
Tailleferre, Germaine 1892-1983 PenDiMP A
Taillibert, Rene Roger 1926- WhoWor 91
Taillon, Jocelyn 1941- IntWWM 90
Taillon, Roger DeBoucherville 1946- St&PR 91
Taima 1790?-1830? WhNaAH
Taimah 1790?-1830? WhNaAH
Taimuty, Samuel Isaac 1917- WhoWor 91
Taine, Hippolyte Adolphe 1828-1893 WorAlBi
Taintor, Zebulo Charles 1940- WhoE 91
Taintor, Zebulon C 1940- BiDrAPA 89
Taiomah 1790?-1830? WhNaAH
Taira Clan EncJap
Taira, Frances Snow 1935- WhoAmW 91, WhoWor 91
Taira, Masa Morioka 1923- WhoAmA 91
Taishin WhoWrEP 89
Taishoff, Lawrence B. 1933- St&PR 91
Taishoff, Lawrence Bruce 1933- WhoAm 90, WhoWor 91
Taishoff, Sol Joseph 1904-1982 BioIn 16
Tait, Agnes 1894-1981 BiDWomA
Tait, Avis Rodness 1934- WhoE 91
Tait, C Downing, Jr. BiDrAPA 89
Tait, Elizabeth Leeds 1906- WhoWrEP 89
Tait, Harold R. 1912- St&PR 91
Tait, Irene Grayson 1918- WhoWrEP 89
Tait, J.W. 1915- St&PR 91
Tait, Jack BioIn 16
Tait, John Charles 1945- WhoAm 90
Tait, John Edwin 1932- St&PR 91, WhoAm 90, WhoE 91
Tait, John Reid 1946- WhoWor 91
Tait, Katharine Lamb 1895-1981 WhoAmA 91N
Tait, Malcolm John 1933- WhoAm 90
Tait, Nancy Louise 1947- St&PR 91
Tait, Robert Ed 1946- WhoEmL 91
Tait, Stewart R. 1945- St&PR 91
Tait, Thomas John 1948- WhoWor 91
Tait, Will H 1942- WhoAmA 91
Taitelbaum, Ben 1939- BiDrAPA 89
Taitt, Doug 1902-1970 Ballpl 90
Taittinger, Pierre-Charles 1887-1967 BiDFrPL
Taitu WomWR
Taitz, Marshall Michael 1944- WhoWor 91
Taitz, Steven Carter 1956- WhoEmL 91
Tajani, Hadi R BiDrAPA 89
Tajima, Yutaka 1940- WhoWor 91
Tajiri, Kaneo 1931- WhoWor 91
Tajiri, Shinkichi 1923- WhoAmA 91
Tajo, Italo 1915- IntWWM 90, PenDiMP
Tajon, Encarnacion Fontecha 1920- WhoAmW 91, WhoWor 91
Tak, Peter Johan 1944- WhoWor 91
Takach, Joe BioIn 16
Takach, Mary H WhoAmA 91
Takach, Mary Jo Ann 1945- WhoAmW 91
Takach, Patrick Bernard 1950- WhoEmL 91
Takacs Quartet PenDiMP
Takacs, Andrew J. 1933- ODwPR 91, St&PR 91
Takacs, Michael Joseph 1940- WhoE 91, WhoWor 91
Takacs, Richard Steven 1957- WhoE 91
Takacs, Wendy Emery 1947- WhoE 91
Takacs-Nagy, Gabor PenDiMP
Takada Kenzo EncJap
Takado, Kenzo WhoWor 91
Takafuji, June 1942- WhoE 91
Takagi, Haruo 1949- WhoWor 91
Takagi, Hiroshi 1924- WhoWor 91
Takagi, Seizo 1933- St&PR 91, WhoAm 90
Takagi, Teiji 1875-1960 DcScB S2
Takahama, Yasuhide 1928- WhoWor 91
Takahara, Paul Osamu 1937- WhoWor 91
Takahashi, Akihiro BioIn 16
Takahashi, Harunori BioIn 16
Takahashi, Hisashi 1927- WhoWor 91
Takahashi, Ken 1946- WhoWor 91
Takahashi, Masanori NewAgMG
Takahashi, Masayoshi 1926- WhoWor 91
Takahashi, Megumi 1929- WhoWor 91
Takahashi, Michio 1925- WhoWor 91
Takahashi, Shigeharu 1921- WhoE 91
Takahashi, Shotaro 1920- WhoWor 91
Takahashi, Shozo 1932- WhoWor 91
Takahashi, Teney Kunio 1938- St&PR 91
Takahashi, Tomoko 1955- WhoAmW 91
Takahashi, Toshio 1938- IntWWM 90
Takahashi, Yasuo BiDrAPA 89
Takahashi, Yasuo 1925- WhoE 91
Takahashi, Yoriko 1937- IntWWM 90
Takahashi, Yoshindo 1931- WhoWor 91
Takahashi, Yuzo 1948- WhoWor 91
Takaki, Carol 1930- BioIn 16
Takaki, Hideaki 1933- WhoWor 91
Takaki, Ronald T. 1939- BioIn 16
Takaki, Ryuji 1940- WhoWor 91
Takakjian, Munjig J BiDrAPA 89
Takakura, Hideo 1936- WhoWor 91
Takakura, Ken 1931- WhoWor 91
Takakuwa, Yasuo 1929- WhoWor 91
Takal, Peter 1905- WhoAm 90, WhoAmA 91
Takala, Jukka Antero 1953- WhoWor 91
Takamori, Akio 1950- WhoAmA 91
Takamori, Yoichiro 1930- WhoWor 91
Takamune, Robert Katsutoshi 1929- WhoWor 91
Takamura Kotaro 1883-1956 WorAu 1980 [port]
Takanashi, Katsuya BioIn 16
Takane, Evelyn Sachie 1954- WhoAmW 91
Takano, Etsuko 1929- BioIn 16
Takano, Masaharu 1935- WhoAm 90
Takano, Takeo BiDrAPA 89
Takano-tenno WomWR
Takao, Hama 1931- WhoWor 91
Takasaki, Etsuji 1929- WhoWor 91
Takase, Fumiko 1927- WhoWor 91
Takase, Mitsuo 1954- WhoWor 91
Takashi, Ogawa 1915- WhoWor 91
Takashima, Hideo 1919- WhoE 91
Takashima, Shizuye Violet 1928- WhoAmA 91
Takasugi, Nao 1922- WhoAm 90
Takasugi, Noboru 1927- WhoWor 91
Takasugi, Robert Mitsuhiro 1930- WhoAm 90
Takata, Marcel Ray 1923- St&PR 91
Takata, Richard T. 1949- St&PR 91
Takatera, Sadao 1929- WhoWor 91
Takatsukasa, Kazuko 1929-1989 BioIn 16
Takawira, John 1938-1989 BioIn 16
Takaya, Akio 1939- St&PR 91
Takayama, Akira WhoAm 90
Takayama, Ken Hideshi 1951- WhoEmL 91
Takayanagi, Kenjiro BioIn 16
Takayanagi, Shunichi Hubert 1932- WhoWor 91
Takazawa, Robert S., Jr. 1951- St&PR 91
Takbhate, Dilip Pandurang 1948- WhoWor 91
Takeda, Eiji 1934- WhoWor 91
Takeda, Tsuneo 1925- WhoWor 91
Takehara, Dan E. 1922- St&PR 91
Takei, George BioIn 16
Takei, Kei 1946- News 90 [port]
Takei, Toshihisa 1931- WhoWor 91
Takemae, Eiji 1930- WhoWor 91
Takemitsu, Toru 1930- IntWWM 90, PenDiMP A
Takemoto, Henry Tadaaki 1930- WhoAmA 91
Takemoto, Hideharu WhoE 91
Taken, Richard Lee 1944- St&PR 91
Takenouchi, Osamu 1925- WhoWor 91
Takeshi, Masuda 1944- BioIn 16
Takeshita Noboru 1924- EncJap
Takeshita, John BioIn 16
Takeshita, Junji BiDrAPA 89
Takeshita, Noboru BioIn 16
Takeshita, Noboru 1924- WhoWor 91
Taketomo, Yasuhiko BiDrAPA 89
Taketomo, Yasuhiko 1921- WhoE 91
Takeuchi, Hiroyuki 1932- WhoWor 91
Takeuchi, Shokoh Akira 1920- WhoWor 91
Takeuchi, Yoshinori 1913- ConAu 132
Takhar, Harinder S. 1951- St&PR 91
Taki ConAu 129
Taki, Amir 1932- St&PR 91
Takil, Tayfun 1958- WhoWor 91
Takino, Masuichi 1905- WhoWor 91
Takis, Nicholas 1903-1965 WhoAmA 91N
Takishita, Yoshihiro BioIn 16
Takkabutr, Chen 1940- WhoWor 91
Takkunen, Candyce Sue 1947- WhoAmW 91
Takla, Nader Kamel 1946- BiDrAPA 89
Tako, Anthony St&PR 91
Takrani, Lal Bikhchand 1935- BiDrAPA 89
Taktsis, Costas 1927-1988 AnObit 1988
Taku, Michael Arong 1949- WhoSSW 91
Takvam, Marie 1926- DcScanL
Tal, Jacob 1945- WhoSSW 91
Tal, Josef 1910- IntWWM 90, PenDiMP A, WhoWor 91
Talaba, L 1943- WhoAmA 91
Talag, Trinidad Santos 1932- WhoAmW 91
Talagrand, Noel Charles 1938- WhoWor 91
Talal, Marilynn Carole Glick WhoWrEP 89
Talalakina, Ol'ga Ivanovna 1924-1985 BioIn 16
Talalay, Paul 1923- WhoAm 90
Talamantes, Frank 1943- WhoHisp 91
Talamantez, Connie Juarez 1947- WhoHisp 91
Talamo, Sal 1941- St&PR 91
Talan, Jamie Lynn 1956- WhoWrEP 89
Talan, Kenneth H 1942- BiDrAPA 89
Talard, Jean-Pierre 1942- WhoWor 91
Talarek, Walter Glenn 1946- WhoEmL 91
Talarico, Maria Theresa 1960- WhoEmL 91
Talarico, Rita 1941- IntWWM 90
Talasila, Hema Nalini BiDrAPA 89
Talasila, Venkateswara B BiDrAPA 89
Talati, Amita N 1957- BiDrAPA 89
Talavera, Sandra 1956- WhoHisp 91
Talbert, Ansel Edward McLaurine 1915- AuBYP 90
Talbert, Bruce James 1831-1881 PenDiDA 89
Talbert, Charles H 1934- ConAu 31NR
Talbert, Florence Cole 1890-1961 BioIn 16
Talbert, Harold Judson, Jr. 1937- St&PR 91
Talbert, J. Michael 1947- WhoAm 90
Talbert, James Lewis 1931- WhoAm 90
Talbert, John Berry, Jr. 1939- St&PR 91
Talbert, Leslie D. 1937- St&PR 91
Talbert, Luther Marcus 1926- WhoAm 90
Talbert, Richard Harrison 1957- WhoAmA 91
Talbert, Roy, Jr. 1943- WhoSSW 91
Talbo, Norma Borja 1944- BiDrAPA 89
Talbo, Ralph Edward BiDrAPA 89
Talbot, Barbara H. BioIn 16
Talbot, Bernard 1937- WhoAm 90
Talbot, Carol Lynn 1952- WhoAmW 91
Talbot, Catherine 1721-1770 BioIn 16, FemiCLE
Talbot, Charlene Joy 1928- AuBYP 90
Talbot, Desiree Ruth 1926- IntWWM 90
Talbot, Donald Roy 1931- WhoAm 90
Talbot, Elizabeth BiDEWW
Talbot, Emile Joseph 1941- WhoAm 90
Talbot, Frances May 1934- WhoSSW 91
Talbot, Frank Hamilton 1930- WhoAm 90, WhoE 91
Talbot, Fred 1941- Ballpl 90
Talbot, Howard 1865-1928 OxCPMus
Talbot, Howard Chase, Jr. 1925- WhoAm 90, WhoE 91
Talbot, Hugh BioIn 16
Talbot, James E. 1939- ODwPR 91
Talbot, James Thomas 1935- WhoAm 90
Talbot, Jarold Dean 1907- WhoAmA 91
Talbot, John Coffin, Jr. 1816-1900 AmLegL
Talbot, John George 1933- WhoE 91
Talbot, John J. 1956- St&PR 91
Talbot, John Mayo 1913- WhoAm 90
Talbot, John Michael NewAgMG
Talbot, Jonathan 1939- WhoAmA 91
Talbot, Lee Merriam 1930- WhoAm 90
Talbot, Mary Jane 1934- WhoSSW 91
Talbot, Mary Lee 1953- WhoE 91
Talbot, Matthew J. 1937- WhoAm 90
Talbot, Michael Owen 1943- IntWWM 90
Talbot, Nita 1930- ConTFT 8
Talbot, Pamela 1946- ODwPR 91, WhoAm 90, WhoAmW 91
Talbot, Phillips 1915- WhoAm 90, WhoWor 91
Talbot, Richard Burritt 1933- WhoAm 90
Talbot, Richard Joseph 1932- WhoAm 90
Talbot, Timothy R. 1916-1988 BioIn 16
Talbot, Toby 1928- AuBYP 90
Talbot, William 1918-1980 WhoAmA 91N
Talbot, William Henry Fox 1800-1877 BioIn 16
Talbott, Audrey Sharpe 1918- St&PR 91
Talbott, Fenton R. 1941- WhoAm 90
Talbott, Frank, III 1929- WhoAm 90
Talbott, Gloria BioIn 16
Talbott, John Andrew 1935- BiDrAPA 89
Talbott, John Harold NewYTBS 90
Talbott, Nelson S. 1920- St&PR 91
Talbott, Orwin Clark 1918- WhoAm 90
Talbott, Strobe BioIn 16
Talbott, Susan Ellen 1962- WhoAmW 91
Talbott, Yvonne Chatelain 1942- WhoAmW 91
Talcott, James Austin 1951- WhoE 91
Talenti, Pier F. 1925- St&PR 91
Talero, Luis Alberto 1926- St&PR 91
Talese, Gay BioIn 16
Talese, Gay 1932- MajTwCW, WhoAm 90, WhoWrEP 89
Talese, Nan Ahearn 1933- WhoAm 90, WhoAmW 91
Talesnick, Alan Lee 1945- WhoEmL 91
Talesnick, Isadore BiDrAPA 89
Talevi, Melissa Ann Marie 1959- WhoAmW 91
Talge, Henry Stephen 1937- St&PR 91
Taliadoros, Constantin 1920- WhoWor 91
Taliaferro, Al EncACom
Taliaferro, E. Lenwood, Jr. 1938- ODwPR 91
Taliaferro, Edwin Turner 1849-1919 AmLegL
Taliaferro, Elizabeth Ann 1953- WhoEmL 91
Taliaferro, James Hubert, Jr. 1924- WhoE 91
Taliaferro, Lawrence 1794-1871 WhNaAH
Taliaferro, Robert BioIn 16
Taliaferro, Wellons Caulk 1938- WhoSSW 91
Talich, Vaclav 1883-1961 PenDiMP
Talingdan, Arsenio Preza 1930- WhoE 91
Talion, Robert W. St&PR 91
Talking Heads EncPR&S 89, OxCPMus
Talkington, Jane BioIn 16
Talkington, Perry C 1909- BiDrAPA 89
Talkington, Robert Van 1929- WhoAm 90
Talkington, Robin Jean 1956- WhoE 91
Tall Bull 1815?-1869 WhNaAH
Tall, Deborah 1951- WhoWrEP 89
Tall, Franklin David 1944- WhoAm 90
Tallackson, Harvey 1925- St&PR 91
Tallackson, Jeffrey S. 1943- St&PR 91
Tallackson, Jeffrey Stephen 1943- WhoAm 90
Tallal, Lisa BiDrAPA 89
Tallamy, Bertram Dalley 1901-1989 BioIn 16
Tallamy, Lawrence Norbert 1949- WhoE 91
Tallant, David, Jr. 1931- WhoAm 90, WhoWor 91
Tallant, Robert 1909-1957 AuBYP 90
Tallchief, Maria BioIn 16
Tallchief, Maria 1925- BioAmW, WhoAm 90, WhoAmW 91
Tallent, Robert Glenn 1954- WhoSSW 91
Tallent, Stephen Edison 1937- WhoAm 90
Tallent, William Hugh 1928- WhoAm 90
Tallett, Elizabeth Edith 1949- WhoAmW 91
Talleur, John Joseph 1925- WhoAm 90
Talley, Andre Leon BioIn 16
Talley, Bob Eugene 1935- St&PR 91
Talley, Bruce Gordon 1932- St&PR 91
Talley, Carol Lee 1937- WhoAm 90, WhoAmW 91
Talley, Charles Peter 1941- WhoE 91
Talley, Charles Richmond 1925- WhoAm 90
Talley, Dan R 1951- WhoAmA 91
Talley, David Robert BiDrAPA 89
Talley, Dennis R. 1947- WhoSSW 91
Talley, Don Charles 1944- WhoSSW 91
Talley, Dorsey Jim 1934- WhoAm 90
Talley, James Arthur 1942- St&PR 91
Talley, Jody Elizabeth 1958- WhoAmW 91
Talley, John E 1904- BiDrAPA 89
Talley, John Edward BiDrAPA 89
Talley, Madelon DeVoe BioIn 16
Talley, Richard Bates 1947- WhoWor 91
Talley, Richard Woodrow 1941- WhoSSW 91
Talley, Robert Cochran 1936- WhoAm 90
Talley, Robert Morrell 1924- WhoAm 90
Talley, Ronda Carol 1951- WhoAmW 91
Talley, Truman Macdonald 1925- WhoAm 90
Talley, Warren Dennis Rick 1934- WhoAm 90
Talley, William Giles, Jr. 1939- St&PR 91, WhoSSW 91
Talley, Wilson Kinter 1935- WhoWor 91

Talley-Morris, Neva Bennett 1909- *WhoAm 90*
Talley-Schmidt, Eugene 1932- *IntWWM 90*
Talleyrand-Perigord, Charles Maurice De 1754-1838 *WorAlBi*
Tallgren, John H. 1929- *St&PR 91*
Tallgren, Leif Gustav 1928- *WhoWor 91*
Tallgren, R. 1935- *St&PR 91*
Tallgren, Robert Waldemar 1935- *WhoAm 90*
Tallichet, Jan Bowen 1936- *WhoSSW 91*
Tallichet, Leon Edgar 1925- *WhoAm 90*
Tallini, Fiory Anthony 1962- *WhoE 91*
Tallis, Alan L. 1946- *St&PR 91*
Tallis, Alan Louis 1946- *WhoAm 90*
Tallmadge, Nathaniel Pitcher 1795-1864 *EncO&P 3*
Tallmadge, William Henry 1916- *IntWWM 90*
Tallman, Daniel Culler 1925- *St&PR 91*
Tallman, Edward R *BiDrAPA 89*
Tallman, Francine R. 1966- *WhoAmW 91*
Tallman, Gerald Morris 1931- *St&PR 91*
Tallman, Johanna Eleonore 1914- *WhoAm 90, WhoWor 91*
Tallman, Karen Ramsey 1951- *WhoAmW 91*
Tallman, Kenneth L. 1925- *WhoSSW 91*
Tallman, Robert O. 1935- *St&PR 91*
Tallman, Ronald Duea 1941- *WhoAm 90*
Tallman, Ruth Marchak 1929- *WhoWor 91*
Tallman, Samuel Vose, Jr. 1947- *St&PR 91*
Tallman, Steven Charles 1955- *St&PR 91*
Tallman, William Chester 1920- *WhoAm 90*
Tallmer, Margot 1925- *WhoAm 90*
Tallon, Robert 1935- *AuBYP 90*
Tallon, Robert Eugene 1926- *WhoAm 90, WhoSSW 91*
Tallon, Robert M., Jr. 1946- *WhoAm 90, WhoSSW 91*
Tallon, Roger 1929- *ConDes 90*
Tallon, Ronald 1927- *WhoWor 91*
Tallon, Stephen William 1942- *St&PR 91*
Tallon, Wesley Carlisle 1950- *WhoSSW 91*
Tallone, Eugene F. 1939- *St&PR 91*
Tally, Lura Self 1921- *WhoAmW 91, WhoSSW 91*
Tallyn, Robert Douglas 1939- *St&PR 91*
Talma, Louise J. 1906- *WhoAmW 91*
Talmadge, Alexander Zakariah, Jr. 1959- *WhoE 91*
Talmadge, Constance 1900-1973 *BioAmW*
Talmadge, Herman E. *BioIn 16*
Talmadge, Herman E. 1913- *WorAlBi*
Talmadge, Jeffrey D. 1953- *WhoWrEP 89*
Talmadge, Jeffrey David 1953- *WhoEmL 91*
Talmadge, John Mills, Jr. 1946- *BiDrAPA 89*
Talmadge, Marian *AuBYP 90*
Talmadge, Marion L. 1923- *St&PR 91*
Talmadge, Marion Lyman 1923- *WhoAm 90*
Talmadge, Mary Christine 1940- *WhoAmW 91, WhoWor 91*
Talmadge, Natalie 1899-1969 *BioAmW*
Talmadge, Norma 1893-1957 *WorAlBi*
Talmadge, Norma 1897-1957 *BioAmW*
Talmadge, Robert Louis *BioIn 16*
Talmadge, Sharon Sue 1950- *WhoAmW 91, WhoE 91*
Talmage, David Wilson 1919- *WhoAm 90*
Talmage, John H. *WhoAm 90*
Talmage, Kenneth Kellogg 1946- *WhoWor 91*
Talmage, Oliver Arthur 1923- *St&PR 91*
Talmage, Ralph William 1948- *St&PR 91*
Talman, Rachel B 1917- *BiDrAPA 89*
Talmi, Igal 1925- *WhoWor 91*
Talmi, Yoav 1943- *IntWWM 90, WhoWor 91*
Talner, Norman Stanley 1925- *WhoAm 90*
Talon, Neil Stuart 1950- *BiDrAPA 89*
Talon-Lesperance *DcCanB 12*
Talone, Rosalie Murray 1900- *WhoE 91*
Talonen, Markku Juhani 1946- *WhoWor 91*
Talpalar, Jose 1925- *St&PR 91*
Talsania, Bharat Himatlal 1948- *WhoWor 91*
Talty, Lorraine Caguioa 1957- *WhoAmW 91, WhoEmL 91, WhoWor 91*
Talucci, Samuel James 1929- *St&PR 91, WhoAm 90*
Talvacchia, John L. 1950- *St&PR 91*
Talvela, Martti 1935-1989 *AnObit 1989, BioIn 16, PenDiMP*
Talvi, Ilkka Ilari 1948- *IntWWM 90, WhoAm 90*
Talvi, Jussi 1920- *WhoWor 91*
Talvio, Maila 1871-1951 *EncCoWW*
Talvj 1797-1870 *BioIn 16*
Talwani, Manik 1933- *WhoAm 90*
Talwar, Nandini *BiDrAPA 89*
Talwar, Vinod K. 1953- *St&PR 91*
Talyzin, Nikolai Vladimirovich 1929- *WhoWor 91*
Talz, F.J. 1944- *St&PR 91*
Tam, Alfred Yat-Cheung 1953- *WhoWor 91*
Tam, Christopher K. W. 1939- *WhoSSW 91*
Tam, Colin Shiutung 1948- *WhoE 91, WhoWor 91*
Tam, Paul Kwong Hang 1952- *WhoWor 91*
Tam, Reuben 1916- *WhoAm 90, WhoAmA 91*
Tam, Thomas 1946- *WhoE 91*
Tam, Tsun Yam 1949- *WhoE 91*
Tamagni, John Searle 1935- *St&PR 91, WhoAm 90*
Tamagno, Francesco 1850-1905 *PenDiMP*
Tamaha 1775-1860 *WhNaAH*
Tamahaw 1775-1860 *WhNaAH*
Tamaki, Henry S. 1924- *St&PR 91*
Tamaklo, Wilberforce 1948- *BiDrAPA 89*
Tamamura, Kentaro 1928- *WhoWor 91*
Taman, Mahmoud S 1933- *BiDrAPA 89*
Tamanend 1625?-1701? *WhNaAH*
Tamang, Parizat *BioIn 16*
Tamaque *WhNaAH*
Tamar *EncCoWW*
Tamar, Erika 1934- *SmATA 62 [port]*
Tamara 1156?-1212 *WomWR*
Tamara, Queen of Georgia 1160-1212 *BioIn 16*
Tamarelli, A. Wayne 1941- *St&PR 91*
Tamarelli, Alan Wayne 1941- *WhoAm 90*
Tamarin, Lillian G *BiDrAPA 89*
Tamarin, Sidney L *BiDrAPA 89*
Tamarindi, Enrico 1943- *WhoWor 91*
Tamarkin, Jerry Paul 1931- *St&PR 91*
Tamarkin, Norman Ross *BiDrAPA 89*
Tamarkin, Robert Allen 1937- *WhoAm 90*
Tamashiro, Lynn Yoshiko 1967- *WhoAmW 91*
Tamasi, Michael 1961- *St&PR 91*
Tamayo, Carlos *WhoHisp 91*
Tamayo, James Anthony 1949- *WhoHisp 91*
Tamayo, Mario Alejandro *WhoHisp 91*
Tamayo, Raymond Thomas 1953- *St&PR 91*
Tamayo, Reve *WhoWrEP 89*
Tamayo, Rufino *NewYTBS 90 [port]*
Tamayo, Rufino 1899- *ArtLatA, IntDcAA 90, WhoAmA 91*
Tamberlik, Enrico 1820-1889 *PenDiMP*
Tambiah, Stanley Jeyarajah 1929- *WhoAm 90*
Tamblyn, Ken C. 1943- *St&PR 91*
Tamblyn, Wayne I. 1932- *St&PR 91*
Tamblyn, Wayne Irvin 1932- *WhoAm 90*
Tamborlane, Rebecca L. 1966- *St&PR 91*
Tambs, Lewis Arthur 1927- *WhoAm 90, WhoWor 91*
Tamburine, Jean 1930- *AuBYP 90, WhoAmA 91*
Tamburine, Jean Helen 1930- *WhoWor 91*
Tamburini, Antonio 1800-1876 *PenDiMP*
Tamburino, John Vincent 1957- *IntWWM 90*
Tamburo, Constance Dolores 1940- *WhoAmW 91*
Tamburo, Linda 1957- *ODwPR 91*
Tamburo, Vincent A. 1934- *St&PR 91*
Tamburrino, Marijo B *BiDrAPA 89*
Tamburro, Harold C. *St&PR 91*
Tambuzi, Jitu *WhoWrEP 89*
Tambyraja, Samuel M 1942- *BiDrAPA 89*
Tamen, Harriet 1947- *WhoAmW 91*
Tamenend 1625?-1701? *WhNaAH*
Tamer, Robert Steven 1935- *St&PR 91*
Tamerin, John S 1937- *BiDrAPA 89*
Tamez, Eloisa G. 1935- *WhoHisp 91*
Tamez, George N. *WhoHisp 91*
Tamez, Gilberto A. 1951- *WhoHisp 91*
Tamietti, Carlo *PenDiDA 89*
Tamimi, Raid R *BiDrAPA 89*
Taminy 1625?-1701? *WhNaAH*
Tamir, Alexander *PenDiMP*
Tamir, Mordechay V 1927- *BiDrAPA 89*
Tamir, Theodor 1927- *WhoAm 90*
Tamiris, Helen 1902?-1966 *NotWoAT*
Tamiris, Helen 1905-1966 *BioIn 16*
Tamiroff, Akim 1899-1972 *WorAlBi*
Tamisiea, Bruce 1955- *WhoEmL 91*
Tamisiea, Leo John 1922- *St&PR 91*
Tamiso, Stephen 1931- *WhoE 91*
Tamke, George William 1947- *WhoAm 90*
Tamkeen-Alvi, Sharif Ahmed Kaiser 1938- *WhoWor 91*
Tamkin, S. Jerome 1926- *WhoAm 90*
Tamlin, Sarah *EncO&P 3*
Tamm, Geraldine Kurcz 1932- *WhoAmW 91*
Tamm, Igor 1895-1971 *WorAlBi*
Tamm, Igor 1922- *WhoAm 90*
Tamm, Igor Evgenievich 1895-1971 *BioIn 16*
Tamm, Johanna M *BiDrAPA 89*
Tamm, Mary Anne DeCamp 1949- *WhoE 91*
Tammany 1625?-1701? *EncCRAm, WhNaAH*
Tammany, Saint 1625?-1701? *WhNaAH*
Tammany, Albert Squire, III 1946- *WhoWor 91*
Tammen, Harry Heye 1856-1924 *BioIn 16*
Tammero, Robert *WhoAm 90*
Tammeus, William David 1945- *WhoAm 90*
Tamminen, Kalevi Reino 1928- *WhoWor 91*
Tammuz, Benjamin 1919-1989 *BioIn 16, ConAu 129, SmATA 63*
Tamola, Pacita De Sagun 1940- *BiDrAPA 89*
Tamondong-Helin, Susan Daet 1957- *WhoAmW 91*
Tamparong, Casimiro Roy, Jr. 1926- *WhoWor 91*
Tamposi, Elizabeth Marian 1955- *WhoAm 90*
Tampow, Don 1942- *St&PR 91*
Tamres, Herbert J. 1940- *St&PR 91*
Tamres, Milton 1922- *WhoAm 90*
Tams, Gerald Raymond 1939- *WhoWor 91*
Tamsberg, William Templeton 1945- *St&PR 91*
Tam'si, Tchicaya U *ConAu 129*
Tamu *DrBlPA 90*
Tamulevich, Janet A. 1948- *St&PR 91*
Tamulevich, Kevin Paul 1949- *St&PR 91*
Tamulevich, Peter Dominic 1947- *BiDrAPA 89*
Tamulis, Vito 1911-1974 *Ballpl 90*
Tamura, Clayton Toshihiro *BiDrAPA 89*
Tamura, Imao 1923- *WhoWor 91*
Tamura, Kenji 1933- *WhoWor 91*
Tamura, Taro 1923-1988 *BioIn 16*
Tan Guidicelli 1934- *ConDes 90*
Tan Zheng *BioIn 16*
Tan, Alexis Sebastian 1944- *WhoAm 90*
Tan, Allen Li 1947- *WhoWor 91*
Tan, Amy *BioIn 16*
Tan, Amy 1952- *ConLC 59 [port]*
Tan, Arjun 1943- *WhoSSW 91*
Tan, Chee Keong 1960- *WhoWor 91*
Tan, Daniel T *BiDrAPA 89*
Tan, Edwin Ladja 1944- *BiDrAPA 89*
Tan, Ek-Sheng *BiDrAPA 89*
Tan, Eng Kock Chan *BiDrAPA 89*
Tan, Eng Meng 1926- *WhoAm 90*
Tan, Eng-Seong 1934- *BiDrAPA 89*
Tan, Frank Marden 1952- *BiDrAPA 89*
Tan, Fred *BioIn 16, NewYTBS 90*
Tan, Fred 1955?-1990 *ConAu 131*
Tan, Hock 1954- *WhoWor 91*
Tan, John K. 1934- *WhoWor 91*
Tan, Kiat W. 1943- *WhoWor 91*
Tan, Kim Leong 1936- *WhoWor 91*
Tan, Kong Yam 1955- *WhoWor 91*
Tan, Lamberto Alpay *BiDrAPA 89*
Tan, Lourdes Rabara *BiDrAPA 89*
Tan, Melvyn 1956- *IntWWM 90*
Tan, Oon Tian 1945- *WhoE 91*
Tan, Poly 1944- *BiDrAPA 89*
Tan, Ramon K *BiDrAPA 89*
Tan, Rizalina Brusas *BiDrAPA 89*
Tan, Sam Boon Yeow 1945- *WhoWor 91*
Tan, Terry R. 1942- *St&PR 91*
Tan, Tjiauw-Ling 1935- *BiDrAPA 89, WhoE 91, WhoWor 91*
Tan, Tom Yong Tian 1931- *WhoWor 91*
Tan, Victor Gotamco 1939- *St&PR 91*
Tan, Wai H. *BioIn 16, NewYTBS 90*
Tan, Yew-oo 1945- *WhoWor 91*
Tan-Chi, Ernesto, Jr. 1947- *WhoWor 91*
Tan-Lachica, Nieves I 1938- *BiDrAPA 89*
Tan-Wong, Lily 1947- *WhoAmW 91*
Tana, Patti 1945- *WhoWrEP 89*
Tanacharison *WhNaAH*
Tanagras, Angelos 1875- *EncO&P 3*
Tanagras, Angelos 1875-1970? *EncPaPR 91*
Tanaka Kakuei 1918- *EncJap*
Tanaka Kinuyo 1910-1977 *EncJap*
Tanaka, Hideyuki 1940- *ConAu 132*
Tanaka, Hiroshi 1939- *WhoWor 91*
Tanaka, Hisao 1924- *WhoWor 91*
Tanaka, Ikko 1930- *ConDes 90*
Tanaka, Janet M. Cullen 1936- *WhoWrEP 89*
Tanaka, Junji 1929- *WhoWor 91*
Tanaka, Kakuei 1918- *WorAlBi*
Tanaka, Kengo 1920- *BiDrAPA 89*
Tanaka, Kouichi Robert 1926- *WhoAm 90*
Tanaka, Leila Chiyako 1954- *WhoAmW 91, WhoEmL 91, WhoWor 91*
Tanaka, Manabu 1947- *WhoWor 91*
Tanaka, Masaaki 1931- *ConDes 90*
Tanaka, Masao 1947- *St&PR 91*
Tanaka, Motoharu 1926- *WhoWor 91*
Tanaka, Nobuyuki 1936- *St&PR 91*
Tanaka, Norihito 1937- *WhoWor 91*
Tanaka, Richard I. 1928- *St&PR 91, WhoAm 90, WhoWor 91*
Tanaka, Soji George 1934- *WhoWor 91*
Tanaka, Stanley Katsuki 1932- *WhoWor 91*
Tanaka, Takashi 1923- *WhoWor 91*
Tanaka, Tsuneo 1935- *St&PR 91*
Tanaka, William Hiroshi 1925- *WhoWor 91*
Tanaka, Yoshinobu 1944- *WhoWor 91*
Tanakadate, Aikitsu 1856-1952 *DcScB S2*
Tanana, Frank 1953- *Ballpl 90*
Tananbaum, Steven Andrew 1965- *WhoE 91*
Tanarro, Fernando Manuel 1933- *WhoWor 91*
Tanas, Khalil Saliba 1944- *BiDrAPA 89*
Tanasie, Petre 1927- *WhoWor 91*
Tanay, Emanuel 1928- *BiDrAPA 89*
Tanchev, Peter Zhelev 1920- *WhoWor 91*
Tanck, James Robert 1944- *WhoSSW 91*
Tancock, John Leon 1942- *WhoAmA 91*
Tancredi, Laurence R 1940- *BiDrAPA 89*
Tancredi, Laurence Richard 1940- *WhoSSW 91*
Tancrell, Joseph E. 1932- *St&PR 91*
Tancreti, Cheryl Ann 1960- *WhoAmW 91*
Tancs, Linda Ann 1963- *WhoAmW 91, WhoE 91*
Tancu, Andrei 1938- *WhoWor 91*
Tanczak-Dycio, Mary 1922- *WhoAmW 91*
Tand, David 1923- *St&PR 91*
Tandler, Bernard 1933- *WhoAm 90*
Tandlich, Steve Eric 1952- *St&PR 91*
Tandon, Rajiv 1956- *BiDrAPA 89*
Tandon, Usha Kiran *BiDrAPA 89*
Tandourjian, Rebecca Ellen Donzanti 1957- *WhoAmW 91*
Tandowsky, Ralph Myron 1929- *St&PR 91*
Tandy, Charles C. *BioIn 16*
Tandy, Charles C. 1929- *WhoSSW 91*
Tandy, Charles David 1918-1978 *ConAmBL*
Tandy, James Bruce 1953- *BiDrAPA 89*
Tandy, Jessica *BioIn 16, NewYTBS 90 [port]*
Tandy, Jessica 1909- *News 90 [port], NotWoAT, WhoAm 90, WhoAmW 91, WhoE 91, WorAlBi*
Tane, Irwin R. 1923- *St&PR 91*
Tanen, Michael William 1944- *WhoE 91*
Tanen, Ned Stone 1931- *BioIn 16, WhoAm 90*
Tanen, Ted M. G. 1926- *WhoE 91*
Tanenbaum, Basil Samuel 1934- *WhoAm 90*
Tanenbaum, Bernard Jerome, Jr. 1934- *WhoAm 90*
Tanenbaum, Elias 1924- *WhoAm 90*
Tanenbaum, Gerald Stephen 1945- *WhoE 91*
Tanenbaum, Jill Nancy 1954- *WhoE 91*
Tanenbaum, Morris 1928- *St&PR 91, WhoAm 90, WhoE 91*
Tanenbaum, Susan G. *WhoAmW 91*
Tanenbaum, Warren *BiDrAPA 89*
Tanenbaum, Wil J *BiDrAPA 89*
Tanenhaus, Herbert M 1941- *BiDrAPA 89*
Taney, Charles R. 1946- *St&PR 91*
Taney, J. Charles *WhoAm 90*
Taney, Roger B. 1777-1864 *WorAlBi*
Taney, Roger Brooke 1777-1864 *BiDrUSE 89*
Tanfield, Dorothy 1921- *St&PR 91*
Tanford, Charles 1921- *WhoAm 90*
Tang *PenDiDA 89, -89*
Tang Yungmei 1940- *ConAu 129*
Tang Zhaoyou *BioIn 16*
Tang, Anthony Matthew 1924- *WhoAm 90*
Tang, Dalin 1955- *WhoE 91*
Tang, Donald T. 1932- *WhoAm 90*
Tang, Esther Don 1917- *WhoAmW 91*
Tang, James Yue-Tak 1941- *St&PR 91*
Tang, Jordan Cho-Tung 1948- *IntWWM 90*
Tang, Laura Anne 1959- *BiDrAPA 89*
Tang, Muhai 1949- *IntWWM 90*
Tang, Stephen Shun-Chien 1960- *WhoE 91*
Tang, Thomas 1922- *WhoAm 90*
Tang, Tom T. 1931- *St&PR 91*
Tang, Tom Y.C. 1918- *St&PR 91*
Tang, Wilson Hon-chung 1943- *WhoAm 90*
Tang, You-shan 1946- *BioIn 16*
Tang, Yun-Teh *BiDrAPA 89*
Tange, Kenzo *BioIn 16*
Tange, Kenzo 1913- *WhoWor 91*
Tanger, Alexander *BioIn 16*
Tanger, Douglas *BioIn 16*
Tanger, Howard *BioIn 16*
Tanger, Susanna 1942- *WhoAmA 91*
Tangney, Eugene M. 1928- *St&PR 91*
Tangney, Eugene Michael 1928- *WhoAm 90*
Tangney, Joseph G. 1944- *St&PR 91*
Tangney, June Price 1958- *WhoAmW 91*
Tangney, Michael J. 1945- *St&PR 91*
Tangney, Scott *ODwPR 91*
Tangora, Albert L. 1937- *St&PR 91*
Tangredi, Vincent 1950- *WhoAmA 91*

Tanguay, Anita Walburga 1936- WhoAmW 91, WhoE 91
Tanguay, Eva 1878-1947 BioIn 16, NotWoAT
Tanguay, Eva 1878-1948 OxCPMus
Tanguay, George R. 1932- WhoSSW 91
Tanguay, Marcel M. 1940- St&PR 91
Tanguay, Peter E 1935- BiDrAPA 89
Tanguma, Baldemar WhoHisp 91
Tanguy, Charles Reed 1921- WhoAm 90
Tanguy, Henri Jean 1930- WhoWor 91
Tanguy, Yves 1900-1955 IntDcAA 90, WhoAmA 91N
Tangvald, Thor, IV BiDrAPA 89
Tanham, George Kilpatrick 1922- WhoAm 90
Tanhehco, Meliton Li BiDrAPA 89
Tani, Andrew Emmanuel B. 1955- WhoWor 91
Tanick, Marshall Howard 1947- WhoEmL 91
Taniguchi, Diane Kimi Tambara 1955- WhoEmL 91
Taniguchi, Elsie Leilani 1936- WhoAmW 91
Taniguchi, Izumi 1926- WhoAm 90
Taniguchi, Tokuso 1915- WhoWor 91
Tanikawa Shuntaro 1931- WorAu 1980 [port]
Tanimoto, George 1926- WhoWor 91
Tanis, James Robert 1928- WhoAm 90
Tanis, John J. 1926- St&PR 91
Tanis, John Jacob 1926- WhoAm 90
Tanis, Nicholas George 1952- WhoE 91
Tanis, Norman Earl 1929- WhoAm 90, WhoWor 91
Tanisha, Ta DrBIPA 90
Tanizaki Junichiro 1886-1965 EncJap
Tanizaki, Jun'ichiro 1886-1965 BioIn 16
Tanjeloff, Julio 1916-1988 BioIn 16
Tanjutco, Paul Saldana 1946- WhoWor 91
Tank, Carolyn S BiDrAPA 89
Tank, Earl A. St&PR 91
Tankard, Elaine Fuller 1947- WhoWrEP 89
Tankard, Perry Elroy 1957- WhoSSW 91
Tankeh, Victoria A. 1955- BiDrAPA 89
Tankersley, Charles W. AmLegL
Tankersley, George Jackson 1921- St&PR 91, WhoAm 90
Tankersley, James I. 1942- St&PR 91
Tankersley, Kevin Joseph 1961- WhoE 91
Tankersley, Michael Wayne 1956- WhoEmL 91
Tankersley, Michele Ann 1966- WhoAmW 91
Tankersley, Stephen Maurice 1955- BiDrAPA 89
Tankersley, Thomas Channing 1949- WhoEmL 91
Tankin, Richard Samuel 1924- WhoAm 90
Tanko, Calvin James 1941- St&PR 91
Tankoos, Sandra Maxine 1936- WhoAmW 91, WhoE 91, WhoWor 91
Tanksley, Ann 1934- WhoAmA 91
Tanksley, Barbara Diane 1957- WhoSSW 91
Tanler, Ronald F. WhoAm 90
Tanna, Suresh J BiDrAPA 89
Tanna, Vasantkumar L 1936- BiDrAPA 89
Tannaes, Marie Katherine Helene 1854-1939 BiDWomA
Tannahill, Mary Harvey 1863-1951 BiDWomA
Tannebaum, Edward Jay 1948- St&PR 91
Tannebaum, Samuel Hugo 1933- WhoSSW 91, WhoWor 91
Tannehill, Bobby Edward 1952- WhoE 91
Tannehill, Elaine B. 1934- St&PR 91
Tannehill, Ivan Ray 1890- AuBYP 90
Tannehill, Jesse 1874-1956 Ballpl 90 [port]
Tannehill, Kenneth L. 1917- St&PR 91
Tannehill, Lee 1880-1938 Ballpl 90
Tannehill, Steven James 1956- St&PR 91
Tannen, Charles Ian 1941- WhoAm 90
Tannen, Leonard P. 1937- St&PR 91
Tannen, Stephen Daniel 1946- WhoE 91
Tannenbaum, Arthur J. 1931- St&PR 91
Tannenbaum, Barbara Lee 1952- WhoAmA 91
Tannenbaum, Beulah Goldstein 1916- AuBYP 90
Tannenbaum, Frank 1893-1969 BioIn 16
Tannenbaum, Harvey 1923- WhoE 91
Tannenbaum, Henry BioIn 16
Tannenbaum, Judith E 1944- WhoAmA 91
Tannenbaum, Judith Nettie 1947- WhoWrEP 89
Tannenbaum, Leonard H. 1933- St&PR 91
Tannenbaum, Michael David 1934- WhoE 91
Tannenbaum, Samuel Victor 1942- WhoSSW 91
Tannenbaum, Steven Robert 1937- WhoAm 90
Tannenbaum, Ted M. 1947- St&PR 91
Tannenberg, Dieter E.A. 1932- St&PR 91
Tannenwald, Leslie Keiter 1949- WhoAmW 91
Tannenwald, Theodore, Jr. 1916- WhoAm 90
Tanner, Alain BioIn 16
Tanner, Alain 1929- ConTFT 8, CurBio 90 [port]
Tanner, Alexandra 1951- WhoAmW 91
Tanner, Champ Bean 1920- WhoAm 90
Tanner, Chuck 1929- Ballpl 90
Tanner, Courtenay Tyler 1948- WhoAmW 91
Tanner, Daniel 1926- WhoAm 90, WhoWor 91
Tanner, Debra McDonald 1964- WhoSSW 91
Tanner, Frank Edward 1949- WhoSSW 91
Tanner, Frederick C., Jr. 1917- St&PR 91
Tanner, H. Max 1926- St&PR 91
Tanner, Harold 1932- WhoAm 90, WhoE 91
Tanner, Harry Max 1926- WhoAm 90
Tanner, Helen Hornbeck 1916- WhoAm 90, WhoAmW 91
Tanner, Henry Ossawa 1859-1937 WhoAmA 91N
Tanner, Jack Gene 1940- WhoSSW 91
Tanner, Jacqui Dian 1946- WhoE 91
Tanner, James L 1941- WhoAmA 91
Tanner, Jimmie Eugene 1933- WhoAm 90
Tanner, John WhoWrEP 89
Tanner, John 1780?-1846? WhNaAH
Tanner, John 1944- BioIn 16
Tanner, John Douglas, Jr. 1943- WhoWor 91
Tanner, John S. 1944- WhoAm 90, WhoSSW 91
Tanner, Judith BiDrAPA 89
Tanner, Kylan Inger 1952- WhoWor 91
Tanner, L. Gene 1932- St&PR 91
Tanner, Laurel Nan 1929- WhoAm 90, WhoWor 91
Tanner, Laurence Aram 1946- WhoE 91
Tanner, Louise AuBYP 90
Tanner, Martha M. 1934- St&PR 91
Tanner, Mary Catherine 1951- St&PR 91
Tanner, Mauri Uuno Ensio 1930- WhoWor 91
Tanner, Nancy Makepeace BioIn 16
Tanner, Nancy Makepeace 1933-1989 ConAu 129
Tanner, Obert C. 1904- St&PR 91
Tanner, Ray U. 1931- St&PR 91
Tanner, Richard Stephen 1940- St&PR 91
Tanner, Robert Hugh 1915- WhoSSW 91
Tanner, Robert J. WhoSSW 91
Tanner, Robert Stanley 1928- St&PR 91
Tanner, Robin 1904-1988 BioIn 16
Tanner, Roger Ian 1933- WhoWor 91
Tanner, Scott Lee 1961- WhoSSW 91
Tanner, Stephen B. 1953- St&PR 91
Tanner, Stephen Leetham 1942- St&PR 91
Tanner, Terry Finley 1926- St&PR 91
Tanner, Thomas William 1952- WhoEmL 91
Tanner, Vernon W. 1934- St&PR 91
Tanner, Walter Rhett 1938- WhoAm 90
Tanner, Warren 1942- WhoAmA 91N
Tanner, William MajTwCW
Tanner, William George 1939- St&PR 91
Tanner, William H. EarBlAP
Tanner-Inman, Lynne E. BiDrAPA 89
Tannert, Charles W. 1938- St&PR 91
Tanney, Allen D. NewYTBS 90
Tanney, Allen D. 1911-1990 BioIn 16
Tannian, Francis Xavier 1933- WhoAm 90
Tannian, Joy 1932-1988 BioIn 16
Tannich, Johann Samuel Friedrich 1728-1785? PenDiDA 89
Tanning, Dorothea 1910?- BiDWomA
Tanning, Dorothea 1913- BioIn 16
Tanno, Setsu 1902- BioIn 16
Tannor, Herman 1925- BiDrAPA 89
Tanny, Gerald Brian 1945- St&PR 91
Tanoos, Ann 1940- WhoAmW 91
Tanous, Alex EncPaPR 91
Tanous, Helen Nicol 1917- AuBYP 90
Tanous, Helene Mary 1939- WhoAmW 91, WhoSSW 91
Tanous, James C BiDrAPA 89
Tanous, Peter Joseph 1938- WhoWor 91
Tanouye, Elyse Toshie 1955- WhoWrEP 89
Tanphaichitr, Kongsak 1946- WhoEmL 91
Tanquary, Fred T. 1943- St&PR 91
Tanquary, John Frank 1956- BiDrAPA 89
Tanqueray, Anne PenDiDA 89
Tanqueray, David PenDiDA 89
Tanselle, Donald William 1924- St&PR 91
Tanselle, George Thomas 1934- WhoAm 90
Tansey, Edward Nelson 1944- WhoE 91
Tansey, Joseph A. St&PR 91
Tansi, Theodore Thomas 1931- St&PR 91
Tansill, Frederick Joseph 1948- WhoEmL 91
Tansill, Frederick Riker 1914- WhoAm 90
Tansill, Mel 1954- WhoWrEP 89
Tansing, Robert W. 1950- St&PR 91
Tanski, James Michael 1946- WhoEmL 91
Tansky, Burton 1938- WhoAm 90, WhoE 91
Tansor, Robert Henry 1935- St&PR 91, WhoAm 90
Tantia, Shyam BiDrAPA 89
Tantillo, James Michael 1938- St&PR 91
Tantillo, Joseph George, Jr. 1952- WhoE 91
Tantillo, Thomas Joseph 1923- St&PR 91
Tantri, K'tut BioIn 16
Tanur, Judith Mark 1935- WhoAmW 91
Tanz, Frederick J BiDrAPA 89
Tanzer, Charles 1912- WhoWor 91
Tanzer, Jed Samuel 1947- WhoWor 91
Tanzer, Lester 1929- WhoAm 90
Tanzer, Martin E. 1933- St&PR 91
Tanzer, Stephen Thomas 1948- IntWWM 90
Tanzman, Linn 1957- ODwPR 91
Tanzola, Anthony James 1939- St&PR 91
Tanzola, Frank John 1931- St&PR 91
Tanzosh, Erma Carolyn 1936- WhoAmW 91
Tao Lao ConAu 131, HispWr 90
Tao, Jie 1936- WhoWor 91
Taofinu'u, Pio 1923- WhoWor 91
Taor, Sean Richard 1965- WhoWor 91
Tape, Gerald Frederick 1915- WhoAm 90
Tapellini, Donna Lynn 1955- WhoWrEP 89
Taper, Geri 1929- WhoAmA 91, WhoE 91
Taperell, Geoffrey Quentin 1943- WhoWor 91
Tapia, Don WhoHisp 91
Tapia, Farzana Moiez 1943- WhoSSW 91
Tapia, Fernando 1922- BiDrAPA 89
Tapia, Lorenzo E. 1931- WhoHisp 91
Tapia, Luis 1950- MusmAFA
Tapia, Mario E. 1947- WhoHisp 91
Tapia, Richard Alfred 1939- WhoHisp 91
Tapia-Videla, Jorge WhoHisp 91
Tapie, Pierre Edmond 1931- WhoWor 91
Tapies, Antoni 1923- BioIn 16
Tapio, Eeva 1927- WhoWor 91
Tapiovaara, Ilmari 1914- ConDes 90, PenDiDA 89
Taplett, Lloyd Melvin 1924- WhoAm 90
Taplett, Lynn Craven WhoAmW 91
Tapley, Byron Dean 1933- WhoAm 90
Tapley, Caroline AuBYP 90
Tapley, Daisy Robinson 1870?-1925 DcAfAmP
Tapley, David A. 1931- St&PR 91
Tapley, Donald Fraser 1927- WhoAm 90
Tapley, Earl Mays 1913- WhoSSW 91
Tapley, Harold Louis BiDrAPA 89
Tapley, James Leroy 1923- WhoAm 90
Tapley, John Mark 1929- St&PR 91
Tapley, Lance E. 1944- WhoWrEP 89
Taplin, Frank E. 1915- WhoAm 90
Taplin, Jonathan Trumbull 1947- WhoAm 90
Taplin, Ronald E. 1949- WhoSSW 91
Tapp, Anthony Clement 1934- IntWWM 90
Tapp, John Cecil 1940- WhoSSW 91, WhoWor 91
Tapp, June Louin WhoAmW 91
Tapp, Kathy Kennedy 1949- AuBYP 90, BioIn 16
Tapp, Lawrence G. 1937- St&PR 91, WhoAm 90
Tapp, Mara Anne 1956- WhoAmW 91
Tapp, Ronald Gene 1941- WhoWor 91
Tapp, Shelley Raye 1953- WhoAmW 91
Tapp, William F., Jr. 1927- St&PR 91
Tappa, Richard Joseph 1932- IntWWM 90
Tappan, David S., Jr. 1922- WhoAm 90
Tappan, David Stanton, Jr. 1922- St&PR 91
Tappan, James Alexander, Jr. 1952- WhoSSW 91
Tappan, James Camp 1825-1906 AmLegL
Tappan, Ronald P. 1934- St&PR 91
Tappan, Samuel F. WhNaAH
Tappan, Sandra Hazen 1940- WhoWor 91
Tappe, Albert Anthony 1928- WhoAm 90, WhoE 91
Tappeiner, Gottfried 1955- WhoWor 91
Tappen, Edgar W., Jr. 1928- St&PR 91
Tappen, Mary Lou WhoE 91
Tapper, David Alfred 1928- WhoE 91
Tapper, F Bruce 1946- BiDrAPA 89
Tapper, Joan Judith 1947- WhoAm 90, WhoWrEP 89
Tappin, Anthony Gerald 1925- St&PR 91
Tapping, Roger PenDiMP
Tapply, William G. 1940- TwCCr&M 91
Tapply, William George 1940- WhoWrEP 89
Tappy, Eric 1931- IntWWM 90
Tapscott, Horace BioIn 16
Tapscott, Robert Carl 1951- St&PR 91
Tapsell, Peter 1930- WhoWor 91
Taqqu, Murad Salman 1942- WhoE 91
Taquey, Charles Henri WhoAm 90
Taquey, Charles Henri 1912- WhoWrEP 89
Taraba, Tibor WhoE 91
Tarabishi, Farida Nasr 1944- BiDrAPA 89
Taraborelli, David A. 1936- St&PR 91
Tarabotti, Arcangela 1604-1652 EncCoWW
Tarabulski, Noelle Leocadia 1959- WhoE 91
Tarachow, Michael 1954- WhoWrEP 89
Taracido, Esteban WhoHisp 91
Taradash, Meryl 1953- WhoAmA 91
Tarakji, Nael M BiDrAPA 89
Tarallo, Angelo N. 1940- St&PR 91
Tarallo, Angelo Nicholas 1940- WhoAm 90
Taran, Carole WhoAmW 91
Taran, Leonardo 1933- WhoAm 90
Tarango, Yolanda 1948- WhoHisp 91
Taranik, James Vladimir 1940- WhoAm 90
Taranovsky, Kiril 1911- WhoAm 90
Taranta, Angelo 1927- WhoAm 90
Tarantino, Frank N. 1935- St&PR 91
Tarantino, Louis Gerald 1934- WhoE 91
Tarantino, Robert Vincent 1943- St&PR 91
Tarantino, Rocco J. 1933- St&PR 91
Taranto, Kenneth Francis 1953- WhoE 91
Tarantolo, Joseph 1943- BiDrAPA 89
Tarar, Ahmad Khan BiDrAPA 89
Taras, John 1919- WhoAm 90
Taras, Paul 1941- WhoAm 90
Tarascio, Vincent Joseph 1930- WhoSSW 91
Tarascon-Auriol, Regine Ginette 1957- WhoAmW 91
Tarasin, Pichai 1945- WhoE 91
Tarasoff, Koozma John 1932- WhoWrEP 89
Tarasovic, Nicholas J. 1952- St&PR 91
Tarassoff, Lev ConAu 33NR, MajTwCW
Tarassuk, Leonid NewYTBS 90
Tarassuk, Leonid 1925- ConAu 130
Tarassuk, Leonid 1925-1990 ConAu 132
Tarasti, Eero Aarne Pekka 1948- IntWWM 90
Taraszka, Anthony John 1935- St&PR 91
Taraszkiewicz, Waldemar 1936- WhoWor 91
Taratoot, Bradly Marshall 1963- WhoSSW 91
Taratoot, Louis J. 1923- St&PR 91
Taravell, Hans Reinhardt PenDiDA 89
Taraz, Afshin 1948- WhoWor 91
Tarbell, Dean Stanley 1913- WhoAm 90
Tarbell, Ida 1857-1944 TwCLC 40 [port], WorAlBi
Tarbell, Ida M. BioIn 16
Tarbell, Ida M. 1857-1944 BioAmW
Tarbell, James 1949- WhoWrEP 89
Tarbell, Roberta Kupfrian 1944- WhoAmA 91, WhoE 91
Tarbet, Ted N. 1953- St&PR 91
Tarbet, Urania Christy BioIn 16
Tarbox, Frank Kolbe 1923- St&PR 91, WhoAm 90
Tarbox, Gurdon Lucius, Jr 1927- WhoAmA 91, WhoSSW 91, WhoWor 91
Tarbox, John William 1921- St&PR 91
Tarbox, Katharine R. 1948- ODwPR 91
Tarbox, Katharine Riggs 1948- WhoAmW 91
Tarbox, Richard J. 1920- St&PR 91
Tarbutton, Lloyd Tilghman 1932- WhoAm 90
Tarchoff, Nicolas 1871-1930 BioIn 16
Tarde, Jerry 1956- St&PR 91
Tardieu, Andre Pierre Gabriel Amedee 1876-1945 BiDFrPL
Tardif, Monique Bernatchez 1936- WhoAmW 91
Tardiff, Kenneth J 1944- BiDrAPA 89
Tardiff, Kenneth Joseph 1944- WhoE 91
Tardiff, Richard C. 1944- St&PR 91
Tardio, Robert F. 1929- St&PR 91
Tardits, Richard BioIn 16
Tardivel, Jules-Paul 1851-1905 DcLB 99 [port]
Tardivo, Giuseppe 1948- WhoWor 91
Tardo, Rodulfo 1919- WhoAmA 91
Tarella, Douglas Francis 1952- WhoE 91
Tarello, John Alexander 1931- St&PR 91
Taren, James Arthur 1924- WhoAm 90
Tarenzi, Sergio 1926- WhoE 91
Targ, Elisabeth Fischer BiDrAPA 89
Targ, Russell 1934- EncO&P 3, EncPaPR 91
Targ, William 1907- WhoAm 90
Targan, Judy 1931- WhoAmA 91
Targan, Larry E. 1947- St&PR 91
Targan, Lynnda Lewis 1948- WhoAmW 91
Targe, David M. BioIn 16
Targoff, Matthew S 1949- BiDrAPA 89
Targoff, Michael B. 1944- St&PR 91
Targonski, Paul Victor 1965- WhoEmL 91
Targownik, Karl K BiDrAPA 89
Targowski, Andrew Stanislaw 1937- WhoWor 91
Targum, Steven David 1948- BiDrAPA 89

Tarhe 1742-1818 WhNaAH
Tarigo, Enrique E. 1927- WhoWor 91
Tarila, B. Sophia 1938- WhoWrEP 89
Tarin, Gilberto A 1943- WhoAmA 91
Tariot, Alice M BiDrAPA 89
Tarjan, George 1912- BiDrAPA 89
Tarjan, Robert Endre 1948- WhoAm 90, WhoE 91
Tarjanne, Pekka Johannes 1937- WhoWor 91
Tarkanian, Jerry 1930- BioIn 16, News 90 [port]
Tarkenton, Fran 1940- WorAlBi
Tarkhoff, Nicolas 1871-1930 BioIn 16
Tarkiainen, Maria DcScanL
Tarkington, Booth 1869-1946 BioIn 16, DcLB 102 [port], WorAlBi
Tarkington, Rockne DrBlPA 90
Tarkka, Jaakko Toivo 1938- WhoWor 91
Tarkovsky, Andrei BioIn 16
Tarlau, Milton 1910- BiDrAPA 89
Tarle, Marc E 1953- BiDrAPA 89
Tarleton, Banastre 1754-1833 EncCRAm
Tarleton, Bennett 1943- WhoSSW 91
Tarleton, George Wilson 1924- St&PR 91
Tarleton, K.F. 1940- St&PR 91
Tarlov, Alvin Richard 1929- WhoAm 90
Tarlow, Dick BioIn 16
Tarlow, Karen Anne 1947- IntWWM 90
Tarlow, Lawrence E. 1924- St&PR 91
Tarlow, Richard N. 1923- St&PR 91
Tarlow, Rose BioIn 16
Tarlton, Peter W. 1940- St&PR 91
Tarman, Charles William 1923- St&PR 91
Tarman, Paul Bernard St&PR 91
Tarn, Nathaniel 1928- ConAu 30NR, WhoAm 90, WhoWrEP 89
Tarn, Pauline Mary EncCoWW
Tarnacki, Duane L. 1953- WhoEmL 91
Tarnay, Dennis B. 1952- St&PR 91
Tarney, Julie ODwPR 91
Tarnoff, Gerald Mark 1948- BiDrAPA 89
Tarnoff, Peter 1937- WhoAm 90
Tarnopol, Gregoire 1891-1979 WhoAmA 91N
Tarnopol, Michael L. 1936- WhoAm 90, WhoWor 91
Tarnopolsky, Rafael 1922- WhoWrEP 89
Tarnopolsky, Walter Surma 1932- WhoAm 90
Tarnoski, Lori M. 1940- WhoAm 90, WhoAmW 91
Tarnove, Elizabeth Joy 1955- WhoAmW 91
Tarnow, Jay Dennis 1947- BiDrAPA 89
Tarnow, Robert L. 1924- WhoAm 90
Tarnow, Robert Laurence 1924- St&PR 91
Tarnower, Samuel M BiDrAPA 89
Tarnower, William BiDrAPA 89
Tarnowski, John Robert 1940- St&PR 91
Tarone, Gregory John 1950- WhoSSW 91
Taroni, Tony Christopher 1942- St&PR 91
Tarpirian, Gregory 1956- St&PR 91
Tarpley, Brenda Mae 1944- WhoAmW 91
Tarpley, Fred Anderson WhoWrEP 89
Tarpley, James Douglas 1946- WhoEmL 91, WhoSSW 91, WhoWor 91
Tarpley, James Merrell 1934- St&PR 91, WhoSSW 91
Tarpley, Jim BioIn 16
Tarpley, Robert W. 1940- St&PR 91
Tarpley, Timothy Norman 1943- St&PR 91
Tarpy, Martin L. 1913- St&PR 91
Tarpy, Martin Lyster 1913- WhoE 91
Tarpy, Thomas Lynn 1951- WhoEmL 91
Tarquini, Achille 1928- WhoWor 91
Tarr, Charles Edwin 1940- WhoAm 90, WhoWor 91
Tarr, Curtis W. 1924- WhoAm 90, WhoWrEP 89
Tarr, Curtis William 1924- St&PR 91
Tarr, David William 1931- WhoAm 90
Tarr, Edward 1936- PenDiMP
Tarr, Herbert BioIn 16
Tarr, Hugh Lewis Aubrey 1905- WhoAm 90
Tarr, Joel Arthur 1934- WhoAm 90, WhoWrEP 89
Tarr, John Robert 1949- BiDrAPA 89
Tarr, Judith 1955- SmATA 64 [port]
Tarr, Kenneth Jay 1945- WhoE 91, WhoWor 91
Tarr, Murray 1928- St&PR 91
Tarr, Paul Cresson, III 1933- St&PR 91
Tarr, Ralph William 1948- WhoAm 90
Tarr, Richard Robert 1948- WhoEmL 91
Tarr, Robert J., Jr. 1943- St&PR 91
Tarr, Robert Joseph, Jr. 1943- WhoAm 90, WhoE 91
Tarr, William Lewis 1930- St&PR 91
Tarradellas, Josep BioIn 16
Tarragano, Morris 1929- ODwPR 91
Tarrance, Vernon Lance, Jr. 1940- WhoAm 90
Tarrant, Dick BioIn 16
Tarrant, Doris M. 1927- St&PR 91
Tarrant, Eddie Faye Battee 1942- WhoSSW 91
Tarrant, J.E. St&PR 91N
Tarrant, James Richard 1936- WhoWor 91
Tarrant, John TwCCr&M 91
Tarrant, John Edward 1898- WhoAm 90, WhoWor 91
Tarrant, Kathleen McGrath 1954- St&PR 91
Tarrant, Mae Cross 1923- WhoWrEP 89
Tarrant, Margaret Joan 1935- St&PR 91
Tarrant, Mary Theresa 1966- WhoWrEP 89
Tarrant, Richard John 1945- WhoAm 90
Tarrants, William Eugene 1927- WhoAm 90
Tarras, Dave BioIn 16
Tarras-Wahlberg, Bo Casper Andreas 1934- WhoWor 91
Tarrega, Francisco 1852-1909 PenDiMP
Tarrega y Eixea, Francisco 1852-1909 PenDiMP
Tarres, Enriqueta 1934- IntWWM 90
Tarring, Faith Nelle WhoE 91
Tarro, Giulio 1938- WhoWor 91
Tarrow, Sidney G. WhoAm 90
Tarry, Ellen 1906- AuBYP 90, BioIn 16, HarlReB [port]
Tarry, Sam 1918- WhoSSW 91
Tarsell, Thomasine Missouri 1941- WhoAmW 91
Tarses, Jay BioIn 16
Tarshis, Barry AuBYP 90
Tarshis, Jerome 1936- WhoAmA 91
Tarsila ArtLatA
Tarsitano, Betty Jeanne 1930- WhoAmW 91
Tarski, Alfred 1901-1983 DcScB S2
Tarsky, Sue 1946- ConAu 31NR
Tarsoly, Balazs Kolozsvary 1923- WhoE 91
Tarson, Herbert Harvey 1910- WhoAm 90, WhoWor 91
Tart, Charles T 1937- EncO&P 3, EncPaPR 91
Tart, Marueen B. 1955- St&PR 91
Tartabull, Danny 1962- Ballpl 90, WhoHisp 91
Tartabull, Jose 1938- Ballpl 90
Tartaglia, Charles R BiDrAPA 89
Tartaglia, Louis Anthony 1949- BiDrAPA 89
Tartaglino, Francis J BiDrAPA 89
Tartaglione, Michael Albert 1957- WhoE 91
Tartakow, Dennis Jeffrey 1942- WhoSSW 91
Tartalia, Clifford L 1934- BiDrAPA 89
Tarte, Bernard J., Jr. 1948- St&PR 91
Tartell, Robert Morris 1926- WhoE 91
Tarter, C. Bruce 1939- WhoAm 90
Tarter, Fred Barry 1943- WhoAm 90, WhoE 91
Tarter, Robert Richmond 1948- St&PR 91
Tarter, Robert Richmond, Jr. 1948- WhoE 91
Tarter, Samuel BiDrAPA 89
Tarthang Tulku EncO&P 3
Tartikoff, Brandon BioIn 16, NewYTBS 90 [port]
Tartikoff, Brandon 1949- WhoAm 90
Tartikoff, Peter Allen 1941- St&PR 91
Tartt, Blake 1929- WhoAm 90
Tartt, Ruby Pickens 1880-1974 BioAmW
Tartter, Vivien Carol 1952- WhoAmW 91
Taruffi, Piero BioIn 16
Taruffi, Piero 1906-1988 AnObit 1988
Tarui, Seiichiro 1927- WhoWor 91
Tarulli, Beverly Ann 1954- WhoAmW 91
Tarver, David J. 1951- WhoSSW 91
Tarver, David Paul 1951- WhoWrEP 89
Tarver, Jackson Williams 1917- WhoAm 90
Tarver, Michael Keith 1941- WhoAm 90
Tarvin, Susan Kay 1951- WhoEmL 91
Tarzian, Mary WhoAm 90
Tarzik, Jack 1946- WhoWrEP 89
Tarzwell, Clarence Matthew 1907- WhoAm 90
Tas, Richard Francis WhoSSW 91
Tasa, Kendall Sherwood 1947- WhoSSW 91
Tasby, Willie 1933- Ballpl 90
Tascaluca WhNaAH
Tascalusa WhNaAH
Tasch, Bruce Jeffrey BiDrAPA 89
Tasch, Gail Ann 1957- BiDrAPA 89
Taschereau, Elzear-Alexandre 1820-1898 DcCanB 12
Taschereau, Jean-Thomas 1814-1893 DcCanB 12
Tasco, Frank J. 1927- St&PR 91
Tasco, Frank John 1927- WhoAm 90, WhoE 91
Tascona, Antonio Tony 1926- WhoAmA 91
Tasende, Jose Maria 1932- WhoAmA 91
Tash, Joy Alene 1943- WhoAmA 91
Tash, Martin E. 1941- St&PR 91
Tash, Martin Elias 1941- WhoAm 90
Tashjian, Charmian B. 1950- IntWWM 90
Tashjian, Gail Marie 1963- WhoSSW 91
Tashjian, Joy Marie 1958- WhoAmW 91
Tashjian, Julia Zakarian 1938- WhoAm 90, WhoAmW 91, WhoE 91
Tashjian, Levon Donald 1934- BiDrAPA 89
Tashjian, Raffi 1950- BiDrAPA 89
Tashjian, Richard Herach 1926- WhoE 91
Tashjian, Virginia A. 1921- AuBYP 90
Tashlin, Frank 1913-1972 BioIn 16
Tashman, Philip N. 1924- St&PR 91
Tasini, Miriam Finder 1936- BiDrAPA 89
Taska, Ronald Joe BiDrAPA 89
Tasker, Joe 1948-1982 ConAu 129
Tasker, John 1942- St&PR 91
Tasker, John Baker 1933- WhoAm 90
Taskova, Slavka 1940- IntWWM 90
Tasma 1848-1897 FemiCLE
Tasman, Allan BiDrAPA 89
Tasman, Paul BioIn 16
Tasony, Theodore A BiDrAPA 89
Tasovac, Ivan 1966- IntWWM 90
Tassani, Sally Marie 1948- WhoAmW 91
Tasse, Joseph 1848-1895 DcCanB 12
Tasse, M Jeanne WhoAmA 91
Tasse, Roger 1931- St&PR 91
Tasse, Yvon Roma 1910- WhoWor 91
Tassello, Ronald J. 1957- St&PR 91
Tassi, Franco BioIn 16
Tassin, Maurice Francis, Jr. 1940- WhoSSW 91
Tassin, Raymond Jean 1926- WhoSSW 91
Tassinari, Audrey Knight 1938- St&PR 91
Tassinari, Robin Baker 1945- BiDrAPA 89, WhoE 91
Tassinari, Silvio John 1922- WhoE 91, WhoWor 91
Tasso, Maria Geralyn 1958- WhoAmW 91
Tasso, Pierre Charif 1959- WhoWor 91
Tasso, Richard Michael 1925- St&PR 91
Tasso, Torquato 1544-1595 WorAlBi
Tassone, Bruce Anthony 1960- WhoE 91
Tassone, Gelsomina 1944- WhoAmW 91, WhoE 91
Tassone, Timothy L. 1946- St&PR 91
Tassopoulos, Timothy Paul 1959- WhoSSW 91
Tassotti, Teresa 1957- WhoAmW 91
Tassy, Eugenio BiDrAPA 89
Tastaluca WhNaAH
Tastu, Sabine-Casimir-Amable Voiart 1798-1885 EncCoWW
Taswell, Carl 1956- BiDrAPA 89
Taswell, Eric BiDrAPA 89
Taswell, Howard Filmore 1928- WhoAm 90
Taszaluza WhNaAH
Tat, Peter Kiet 1947- WhoSSW 91
Tata, Giovanni 1954- WhoWor 91
Tata, Ratan Naval 1937- WhoWor 91
Tata, Sam Bejan 1911- WhoAmA 91
Tata, Terry 1940- Ballpl 90
Tatanene Manata 1946- WhoWor 91
Tatanga Mani 1871-1967 WhNaAH
Tatangelo, Aldo 1913- WhoHisp 91
Tatar, Harold R BiDrAPA 89
Tatar, Tilly 1926- St&PR 91
Tatarczuk, Anthony J. 1947- St&PR 91
Tatarewicz, Joseph Nicholas 1950- WhoE 91
Tatarian, Hrach Roger 1916- WhoAm 90
Tatay, Rafael 1947- BiDrAPA 89
Tate, Allen 1899-1979 BioIn 16, ConAu 32NR, LiHiK, MajTwCW, WorAlBi
Tate, Arthur William 1940- St&PR 91
Tate, Bennie 1901-1973 Ballpl 90
Tate, Blair 1952- WhoAmA 91
Tate, Carey K. 1944- St&PR 91
Tate, Charlotte Anne 1944- WhoAmW 91
Tate, David Kirk 1939- WhoWor 91
Tate, Edward ConAu 30NR
Tate, Eleanora E. 1948- BioIn 16
Tate, Elizabeth AuBYP 90
Tate, Ellienne Todd 1940- WhoAmW 91
Tate, Ernest D. 1926- St&PR 91
Tate, Evelyn Ruth 1914- WhoAmW 91
Tate, Fran M. 1929- WhoAmW 91
Tate, Fred U BiDrAPA 89
Tate, Frederick George 1925- WhoAm 90
Tate, Fredericka C BiDrAPA 89
Tate, Gayle Blair 1944- WhoAmA 91
Tate, Gene M. 1948- St&PR 91
Tate, George 1932- BioIn 16
Tate, Geraldine Williams 1954- WhoAmW 91
Tate, Grover Cleveland, Jr. 1922- WhoWrEP 89
Tate, Guy Morris, III 1944- St&PR 91
Tate, Harold Simmons, Jr. 1930- WhoAm 90
Tate, J. Robert 1936- St&PR 91
Tate, James 1943- WhoWrEP 89
Tate, James, IV 1934- WhoE 91
Tate, James Fletcher 1922- St&PR 91
Tate, James Preston 1953- WhoSSW 91
Tate, James Scott 1966- WhoEmL 91
Tate, James W. 1875-1922 OxCPMus
Tate, Jeffrey BioIn 16
Tate, Jeffrey 1943- IntWWM 90, PenDiMP
Tate, Jeffrey Lewis 1953- BiDrAPA 89
Tate, Jo Osborne WhoAmW 91
Tate, John E. 1919- St&PR 91
Tate, John E. 1920- WhoSSW 91
Tate, Loretta Ann 1936- WhoSSW 91
Tate, Manley Sidney 1919- WhoSSW 91
Tate, Merze 1905- WhoAmW 91
Tate, Octava Louise 1940- WhoAmW 91
Tate, Orren Roy 1938- St&PR 91
Tate, Patricia Marshall BioIn 16
Tate, Paul Hamilton 1951- St&PR 91, WhoAm 90
Tate, Peter J. 1946- St&PR 91
Tate, Raymond Grant 1935- WhoE 91
Tate, Robert L. 1924- St&PR 91
Tate, Robin ConAu 32NR
Tate, Sharon BioIn 16
Tate, Sheila Burke 1942- ODwPR 91, WhoAm 90, WhoAmW 91
Tate, Sherman E. 1945- St&PR 91
Tate, Shirley Ann 1943- WhoSSW 91
Tate, Stonewall Shepherd 1917- WhoAm 90
Tate, Thaddeus Wilbur, Jr. 1924- WhoAm 90
Tate, Thomas Jefferson, Jr. 1932- WhoSSW 91
Tate, William Arnold 1930- WhoSSW 91
Tate, Willis McDonald 1911-1989 BioIn 16
Tatebe, Hiroko 1950- St&PR 91
Tatelbaum, Brenda Loew 1951- WhoWrEP 89
Tatelman, Herbert 1919- St&PR 91
Tatem, Nancy Gauer 1942- WhoAmW 91
Tatemy 1690?-1761? WhNaAH
Tateossian, Robert Tateos 1962- WhoWor 91
Tateum, William Aldrich 1858- AmLegL
Tatgenhorst, Robert 1918- WhoAm 90
Tatham, Campbell AuBYP 90
Tatham, Charles Heathcote 1772-1842 PenDiDA 89
Tatham, Charles Heathcote 1937- St&PR 91
Tatham, David Frederic 1932- WhoAm 90, WhoAmA 91
Tatham, George 1907-1987 BioIn 16
Tatham, Julie Campbell 1908- WhoAmW 91, WhoWor 91
Tatham, Robert Haines 1943- WhoSSW 91
Tatham, Thomas 1763-1817 PenDiDA 89
Tati, Jacques 1907-1982 BioIn 16
Tatibouet, Andre Stephan 1941- WhoAm 90
Tatineni, Kameswara Rao 1948- BiDrAPA 89
Tatineni, Radha Sundari 1957- BiDrAPA 89
Tatistcheff, Alexis B. NewYTBS 90
Tatistcheff, Peter Alexis 1938- WhoAmA 91
Tatlin, Vladimir 1885-1953 IntDcAA 90
Tatlin, Vladimir Evgrafovic 1885-1953 PenDiDA 89
Tatlin, Vladimir Evgrafovich 1885-1953 BioIn 16
Tatliyev, Suleyman Bayram ogly WhoWor 91
Tatlock, Anne M. 1939- St&PR 91, WhoAmW 91
Tatlock, Eleanor FemiCLE
Tatlock, Thomas Ward BiDrAPA 89
Tatlonghari, Rafael M BiDrAPA 89
Tatlow, Marilyn Rose 1940- WhoWrEP 89
Tatlow, Mark 1955- IntWWM 90
Tatlow, Richard H., III 1906- St&PR 91
Tatlow, Richard H., IV 1939- St&PR 91
Tatlow, Ruth Mary 1956- IntWWM 90
Tatman, Gil D. 1934- St&PR 91
Tatman, Richard W. 1943- St&PR 91
Tatnall, Robert Paul 1951- St&PR 91
Tatoian, John Avidis 1961- WhoE 91
Tatom, James Francis 1927- St&PR 91
Tatom, James Rodgers, Jr. 1963- WhoSSW 91
Tatom, Kenneth Duke 1949- WhoSSW 91
Tatomer, William R 1945- BiDrAPA 89
Tatooles, Constantine John 1936- WhoAm 90
Tatossian, Armand 1948- WhoAmA 91
Tatrai Quartet PenDiMP
Tatrai, Vilmos PenDiMP
Tatro, Dwight W. 1950- St&PR 91
Tatro, Paul E. 1938- St&PR 91
Tatro, Peter Richard 1936- St&PR 91
Tatro, Ronald Edward 1943- WhoAmA 91
Tatsis, George Peter 1958- WhoSSW 91
Tatsumi, Keigo 1927- WhoWor 91
Tatsumi, Takayuki 1955- WhoWor 91
Tatta, John Louis 1920- WhoAm 90
Tattam, Timothy Mark 1958- St&PR 91
Tattema 1690?-1761? WhNaAH
Tatter, George Carl 1940- St&PR 91

Tatter, Jordan Bradley 1937- *St&PR 91*
Tattermuschova, Helena 1933- *IntWWM 90*
Tattersall, Alan Peter 1943- *St&PR 91*
Tattersall, Hargreaves Victor, III 1943- *St&PR 91*
Tattersall, Norman 1924- *IntWWM 90*
Tattersall, Paul Arnold 1934- *WhoAm 90*
Tattersall, William James 1932- *WhoWor 91*
Tattersfield, Brian 1936- *ConDes 90*
Tattershall, Susan 1949- *IntWWM 90*
Tatterson, George Howe, Jr. 1943- *WhoSSW 91*
Tatti, Benedict Michael 1917- *WhoAmA 91*
Tattle-well, Mary, & Joane Hit-him-home *FemiCLE*
Tattlewell, Mary *BiDEWW*
Tattooed Serpent *WhNaAH*
Tatum, Allyn Carr 1942- *WhoWor 91*
Tatum, Art 1909-1956 *OxCPMus*
Tatum, Art 1910-1956 *BioIn 16, DrBlPA 90, WorAlBi*
Tatum, David 1953- *St&PR 91*
Tatum, David Rowe 1956- *WhoSSW 91*
Tatum, Deborah Elaine 1952- *WhoAmW 91*
Tatum, Donn Benjamin 1913- *WhoAm 90*
Tatum, Edward L. 1909-1975 *WorAlBi*
Tatum, Frank Donovan, Jr. 1920- *WhoAm 90*
Tatum, Frank M., Jr. 1919- *St&PR 91*
Tatum, Fred Menefee, Jr. 1927- *WhoSSW 91*
Tatum, H. Michael 1928- *St&PR 91*
Tatum, Joe F. 1925- *St&PR 91*
Tatum, John Allen, Jr. 1936- *St&PR 91*
Tatum, John Benjamin 1968- *WhoWor 91*
Tatum, John Merl, Jr. 1951- *St&PR 91*
Tatum, John Michael 1948- *BiDrAPA 89*
Tatum, Ken 1944- *Ballpl 90*
Tatum, Lawrie 1822- *WhNaAH*
Tatum, Nancy 1934- *IntWWM 90*
Tatum, Rita 1948- *WhoAm 90*
Tatum, Stephanie Lynne 1962- *WhoEmL 91*
Tatum, Thomas Walter 1937- *St&PR 91*
Tatyrek, Alfred Frank 1930- *WhoE 91, WhoWor 91*
Tatz, Paul H. 1935- *St&PR 91, WhoAm 90*
Taub, Abraham 1901-1990 *BioIn 16*
Taub, Albert Hiram 1935- *BiDrAPA 89*
Taub, Chaim *PenDiMP*
Taub, Edward 1931- *WhoSSW 91*
Taub, Henry 1927- *WhoAm 90*
Taub, Jay *BioIn 16*
Taub, Jesse 1923- *St&PR 91*
Taub, Jesse J. 1927- *WhoAm 90*
Taub, Larry 1945- *WhoSSW 91*
Taub, Larry Steven 1952- *WhoE 91*
Taub, Marcia Jean 1957- *WhoAmW 91*
Taub, Mel *BioIn 16*
Taub, Norman 1915- *BiDrAPA 89*
Taub, Patricia Gail 1954- *WhoAmW 91*
Taub, Richard Paul 1937- *WhoAm 90*
Taub, Robert Allan 1923- *WhoAm 90*
Taub, Robert David 1955- *IntWWM 90*
Taub, Robert Jay 1952- *WhoE 91*
Taub, Ronald H. 1929- *WhoWor 91*
Taub, Roy N. 1948- *St&PR 91*
Taub, Sherry 1958- *BiDrAPA 89*
Taub-Katz, Julia Elana *BiDrAPA 89*
Taube, Carl Arvid 1939-1989 *BioIn 16*
Taube, Henry 1915- *WhoAm 90, WhoWor 91, WorAlBi*
Taube, Irvin *BiDrAPA 89*
Taube, Lester S. 1920- *WhoWrEP 89*
Taube, Steven L *BiDrAPA 89*
Taube, Thomas N. 1928- *St&PR 91*
Taubel, David E *BiDrAPA 89*
Taubeneck, Ted D. 1926- *St&PR 91*
Taubenfeld, Harry Samuel 1929- *WhoE 91*
Tauber, Alfred Imre 1947- *WhoAm 90*
Tauber, Charles Paul 1936- *BiDrAPA 89*
Tauber, Joel David 1935- *WhoAm 90*
Tauber, Kathleen Grisanti 1949- *WhoAmW 91*
Tauber, Richard 1891-1948 *PenDiMP, -A*
Tauber, Richard 1892-1948 *OxCPMus*
Tauber, Ronald Steven 1944- *WhoAm 90*
Tauber, Sophie Henriette 1889-1942 *BiDWomA*
Tauber, Stuart Paul 1940- *WhoE 91*
Tauber, Thomas Ernst 1939- *St&PR 91*
Tauber-Arp, Sophie Henriette 1889-1942 *BiDWomA*
Taubes, Frederic 1900-1981 *WhoAmA 91N*
Taubes, Timothy Evan 1955- *WhoAmA 91, WhoE 91*
Taubitz, Fredricka 1944- *WhoAm 90, WhoAmW 91, WhoWor 91*
Taubkin, Irvin S. *BioIn 16*
Taubkin, Irvin S. 1906- *ODwPR 91*
Taubman, A. Alfred 1925- *WhoAm 90*
Taubman, Dorothy *BioIn 16*
Taubman, Glenn Matthew 1956- *WhoEmL 91*
Taubman, Jane A. 1942- *ConAu 130*
Taubman, Jane Andelman 1942- *WhoAmW 91*
Taubman, Martin Arnold 1940- *WhoAm 90*
Taubman, Paul James 1939- *WhoAm 90*
Taubman, Robert E *BiDrAPA 89*
Taubman, Robert S. 1953- *WhoAm 90*
Taubman, William Chase 1941- *WhoAm 90*
Taubner, Valentine J., III 1966- *St&PR 91*
Tauc, Jan 1922- *WhoAm 90*
Tauch, Waldine Amanda 1892-1986 *WhoAmA 91N*
Tauchert, Theodore Richmond *WhoAm 90*
Tauer, John Anthony 1941- *St&PR 91*
Taufa'ahau, Tupou, IV 1918- *WhoWor 91*
Taufer, Veno 1933- *WhoWor 91*
Taufiq, Farook 1940- *WhoWor 91*
Taugen, Denis Roger 1939- *St&PR 91*
Tauke, Beverly Hubble *BioIn 16*
Tauke, Beverly Hubble 1949- *WhoWrEP 89*
Tauke, Thomas J. *BioIn 16*
Tauke, Thomas Joseph 1950- *WhoAm 90*
Taulbee, Carl D. 1928- *St&PR 91*
Taunton, Kathryn Jayne 1953- *WhoAmW 91*
Taunton-Rigby, Alison 1944- *WhoAmW 91*
Taupin, Bernie *EncPR&S 89*
Taureau, Edgard 1948- *St&PR 91*
Taurel, Sidney A. 1949- *St&PR 91*
Tauro, Joseph Louis 1931- *WhoAm 90, WhoE 91*
Taus, Kathryn G. 1948- *ODwPR 91*
Taus, Robert Leo 1938- *WhoSSW 91*
Tausch, Gerry Margaret 1930- *WhoWrEP 89*
Tausch, Gilbert H. 1926- *St&PR 91*
Tausch, Susan Diane 1955- *WhoWrEP 89*
Tausch, William Joseph 1930- *St&PR 91*
Tauscher, John Walter 1929- *WhoAm 90*
Tausert *WomWR*
Tausig, Carl 1841-1871 *PenDiMP*
Tausig, Hans Eric 1931- *IntWWM 90*
Tausig, Karl 1841-1871 *BioIn 16*
Tausky, Curt 1933- *WhoE 91*
Tausky, Vilem 1910- *IntWWM 90, PenDiMP*
Taussig, Andrew Richard 1951- *St&PR 91, WhoAm 90*
Taussig, Helen Brooke 1898-1986 *BioIn 16*
Taussig, Hugo 1921- *BiDrAPA 89*
Taussig, Joseph Knefler, III 1945- *St&PR 91*
Taussig, Joseph Knefler, Jr. 1920- *WhoAm 90*
Tautkus, Richard *BioIn 16*
Tautphoeus, Jemima, Baroness von 1807-1893 *FemiCLE*
Tautu, Cornelia 1938- *IntWWM 90*
Tauzin, Wilbert J., II 1943- *WhoAm 90, WhoSSW 91*
Tavani, Carol A 1946- *BiDrAPA 89*
Tavani, Carol Ann *WhoE 91*
Tavares *EncPR&S 89*
Tavares, Almir R, Jr. 1954- *BiDrAPA 89*
Tavares, Antone 1960?- *EncPR&S 89*
Tavares, Arthur 1948?- *EncPR&S 89*
Tavares, Feliciano 1951?- *EncPR&S 89*
Tavares, Joan Christine 1941- *WhoAmW 91*
Tavares, Joseph 1945- *WhoSSW 91*
Tavares, Perry Lee 1953?- *EncPR&S 89*
Tavares, Rafael *BioIn 16*
Tavares, Ralph Vierra 1947?- *EncPR&S 89*
Tavaststjerna, Karl August 1860-1898 *DcScanL*
Tavcar, Lawrence R. 1936- *ODwPR 91*
Tave, Stuart Malcolm 1923- *WhoAm 90*
Taveggia, Thomas Charles 1943- *WhoAm 90*
Tavel, Diana M. 1941- *WhoAmW 91*
Tavel, Mark Kivey 1945- *St&PR 91, WhoAm 90*
Tavel, Morton Allen 1939- *WhoAm 90*
Tavel, Ronald *WhoWrEP 89*
Tavel, Ronald 1940- *ConAu 33NR*
Tavella, Elise Shannon 1950- *WhoEmL 91*
Tavenas, Francois 1942- *WhoAm 90*
Tavener, Jackie 1897-1969 *Ballpl 90*
Tavener, John 1944- *IntWWM 90, PenDiMP A*
Tavener, Roy H 1926- *BiDrAPA 89*
Tavenner, John Stephen *BiDrAPA 89*
Tavenner, Patricia *WhoAmA 91*
Tavens, Albert L. 1927- *St&PR 91*
Tavens, Lester 1931- *St&PR 91*
Taveras, Frank 1950- *Ballpl 90*
Taveras, Juan Manuel 1919- *WhoAm 90*
Taverna, Americo John 1913- *St&PR 91*
Taverne, Aart Alexander Richard 1945- *WhoWor 91*
Taverne, Dick 1928- *St&PR 91*
Taverne-Peteri, Maryke Elisabeth H. 1948- *WhoWor 91*
Tavernier, Albert 1854-1929 *OxCCanT [port]*
Tavernier, Bertrand *BioIn 16*
Tavernier, Bertrand Rene Maurice 1941- *WhoWor 91*
Tavernier, Jules 1844-1889 *WhNaAH*
Tavernier, Rene G. 1917- *WhoWor 91*
Tavernini, Lucio 1943- *WhoSSW 91*
Taves, Donald R 1926- *BiDrAPA 89*
Taviani, Paolo 1931- *BioIn 16*
Taviani, Vittorio 1929- *BioIn 16*
Tavibo 1810?-1870 *WhNaAH*
Tavino, Ralph Rohlfing 1952- *St&PR 91*
Tavis, Lee A. *WhoAm 90*
Tavitian, Henry O *BiDrAPA 89*
Tavlan-Dogan, Kutas 1932- *BiDrAPA 89*
Tavlin, Michael J. 1946- *St&PR 91*
Tavo, Gus *AuBYP 90*
Tavoulareas, William P. 1919- *St&PR 91*
Tavoularis, Dean 1932- *ConDes 90*
Tavoularis, Marjorie O *BiDrAPA 89*
Tavrow, Richard Lawrence 1935- *St&PR 91, WhoAm 90*
Taw, Dudley Joseph 1916- *WhoAm 90*
Tawa, Nicholas Edward 1923- *IntWWM 90*
Tawarayu Sotatsu *EncJap*
Taweewatanasan, Piya 1950- *WhoWor 91*
Tawfik, Sayed *NewYTBS 90*
Tawil, Henry 1942- *St&PR 91*
Tawil, Joseph E. 1913- *WhoAm 90, WhoE 91*
Tawil, Moise 1934- *St&PR 91*
Tawney, Aruni *BiDrAPA 89*
Tawney, Cyril 1930- *OxCPMus*
Tawney, Lenore *PenDiDA 89, WhoAmA 91*
Tawney, Lenore 1925- *BiDWomA*
Tax, Meredith *FemiCLE*
Tax, Sol 1907- *WhoAm 90*
Taxe, Howard A. 1953- *St&PR 91*
Taxil, Leo *EncO&P 3*
Taxin, Ira 1950- *IntWWM 90*
Taxis, Gloria Thurn und *BioIn 16*
Taxis, Johannes Thurn Und *BioIn 16*
Tay, Ah Kee *BioIn 16*
Taya, Maaouya Ould Sid Ahmed 1943- *WhoWor 91*
Tayback, Vic *NewYTBS 90 [port]*
Tayback, Vic 1929?-1990 *BioIn 16*
Taye, John *BioIn 16*
Tayler, David Leonard 1937- *St&PR 91*
Tayloe, Edward Dickinson, II 1942- *WhoSSW 91*
Taylor, A J P 1906- *MajTwCW*
Taylor, A J P 1906-1990 *ConAu 132, -32NR, CurBio 90N*
Taylor, A. Paul, Jr. *ODwPR 91*
Taylor, Adele Chatfield- *BioIn 16*
Taylor, Al C 1948- *WhoAmA 91*
Taylor, Alan John Percivale 1906-1990 *NewYTBS 90 [port]*
Taylor, Alec Clifton- 1907-1985 *DcNaB 1981*
Taylor, Alexander Douglas 1931- *WhoWrEP 89*
Taylor, Alfred Hendricks, Jr. 1930- *WhoAm 90*
Taylor, Alfred Swaine 1806-1880 *BioIn 16*
Taylor, Alison Jean 1952- *WhoAmW 91*
Taylor, Allan R. 1932- *St&PR 91*
Taylor, Allan Richard 1932- *WhoAm 90*
Taylor, Allan Ross 1931- *WhoAm 90*
Taylor, Alton Lee 1936- *WhoSSW 91*
Taylor, Andrew 1951- *TwCCr&M 91*
Taylor, Andrew Clayton 1957- *WhoEmL 91*
Taylor, Ann 1782-1866 *BioIn 16*
Taylor, Ann 1941- *WhoAmA 91*
Taylor, Ann Leslie *BiDrAPA 89*
Taylor, Ann Louise 1937- *WhoAmW 91*
Taylor, Ann Marie *BiDrAPA 89*
Taylor, Anna Diggs 1932- *WhoAm 90, WhoAmW 91*
Taylor, Anna Heyward 1879-1956 *WhoAmA 91N*
Taylor, Annie Edson 1838-1921 *BioIn 16*
Taylor, Arthur *AuBYP 90*
Taylor, Arthur H. 1960- *St&PR 91*
Taylor, Arthur Robert 1935- *WhoAm 90*
Taylor, Aubrey Elmo 1933- *WhoWor 91*
Taylor, Audilee Boyd 1931- *BioIn 16*
Taylor, Austin Randall 1954- *WhoSSW 91*
Taylor, Barbara A. *ODwPR 91*
Taylor, Barbara A. 1943- *St&PR 91*
Taylor, Barbara Alden 1943- *WhoAmW 91*
Taylor, Barbara Ann 1944- *WhoAmW 91*
Taylor, Barbara Jo Anne Harris 1936- *WhoAm 90, WhoAmW 91, WhoE 91, WhoWor 91*
Taylor, Barbara Lynn 1933- *BiDrAPA 89*
Taylor, Barbara Q. 1940- *St&PR 91*
Taylor, Barry 1945- *WhoE 91*
Taylor, Barry Norman 1936- *WhoAm 90*
Taylor, Bayard 1825-1878 *BioIn 16*
Taylor, Ben 1888- *Ballpl 90*
Taylor, Benedict 1960- *BioIn 16*
Taylor, Bernard J., II 1925- *St&PR 91*
Taylor, Beth 1953- *BiDrAPA 89*
Taylor, Bev 1924- *St&PR 91*
Taylor, Beverly 1947- *ConAu 132*
Taylor, Beverly W. 1941- *WhoAmW 91*
Taylor, Bill 1926- *WhoAmA 91*
Taylor, Bill G. 1925- *WhoAm 90*
Taylor, Billy 1921- *BioIn 16, DrBlPA 90, OxCPMus, WorAlBi*
Taylor, Bob *ODwPR 91*
Taylor, Boyd D. 1932- *St&PR 91, WhoSSW 91*
Taylor, Brent Douglas 1957- *WhoEmL 91*
Taylor, Brian D. 1941- *St&PR 91*
Taylor, Brian James 1948- *WhoAm 90*
Taylor, Brie 1923- *WhoAmA 91*
Taylor, Bruce *WhoWrEP 89*
Taylor, Bruce R. 1945- *WhoE 91*
Taylor, Bruce Terry 1950- *BiDrAPA 89, WhoE 91*
Taylor, Byron David 1943- *WhoSSW 91*
Taylor, Byron L. 1930- *St&PR 91*
Taylor, C. I. 1875-1922 *Ballpl 90*
Taylor, Camilla *BioIn 16*
Taylor, Candy Jim 1884-1948 *Ballpl 90*
Taylor, Carl 1937- *AuBYP 90*
Taylor, Carl 1944- *Ballpl 90*
Taylor, Carl Ernest 1916- *WhoAm 90*
Taylor, Carmela Mae 1962- *WhoAmW 91*
Taylor, Carol Rose 1950- *WhoAmW 91*
Taylor, Carolyn Sue 1936- *WhoAmW 91*
Taylor, Carson William 1942- *WhoAm 90*
Taylor, Catherine A *BiDrAPA 89*
Taylor, Cecil *BioIn 16*
Taylor, Cecil 1933- *DrBlPA 90, OxCPMus*
Taylor, Cecil Percival 1933- *WhoAm 90*
Taylor, Celianna I. *WhoAm 90, WhoWor 91*
Taylor, Charles 1931- *WorAu 1980*
Taylor, Charles Andrew 1950- *WhoEmL 91*
Taylor, Charles Bruce 1949- *WhoWrEP 89*
Taylor, Charles Durwood 1946- *WhoEmL 91*
Taylor, Charles E. *BioIn 16*
Taylor, Charles Edwin 1924- *WhoAm 90*
Taylor, Charles F. 1946- *St&PR 91*
Taylor, Charles F., Jr. 1948- *St&PR 91*
Taylor, Charles Henry 1928- *WhoAm 90*
Taylor, Charles McArthur *BioIn 16*
Taylor, Charles R. 1941- *St&PR 91*
Taylor, Charles Richard 1939- *WhoAm 90*
Taylor, Christopher Andrew 1947- *WhoE 91*
Taylor, Christopher Joseph 1950- *St&PR 91*
Taylor, Chuck 1942- *Ballpl 90*
Taylor, Clarice *BioIn 16, DrBlPA 90*
Taylor, Clarke *BioIn 16*
Taylor, Claude I. 1925- *WhoAm 90*
Taylor, Claudia Ann 1946- *WhoAmW 91*
Taylor, Clayton Charles 1952- *WhoSSW 91*
Taylor, Clementia 1818-1908 *BioIn 16*
Taylor, Clifford Aubrey 1952- *BiDrAPA 89, WhoE 91*
Taylor, Clive Roy 1944- *WhoAm 90*
Taylor, Cloyd Veron, Jr. 1952- *WhoE 91*
Taylor, Clyde Calvin, Jr. 1936- *WhoAm 90*
Taylor, Clyde Willis 1904-1988 *BioIn 16*
Taylor, Colleen C. *BioIn 16*
Taylor, Conciere Marlana 1950- *WhoWrEP 89*
Taylor, Cora 1936- *SmATA 64*
Taylor, Cora Hodge 1942- *WhoAmW 91*
Taylor, Cora Howarth Stewart 1868-1910 *BioIn 16*
Taylor, Creed Richmond 1955- *WhoSSW 91*
Taylor, Cynthia Ann 1949- *BiDrAPA 89*
Taylor, Cynthia Roberts 1958- *WhoAmW 91*
Taylor, D. Edgar 1958- *WhoSSW 91*
Taylor, Dalmas Arnold 1933- *WhoAm 90*
Taylor, Dan 1738-1816 *BioIn 16*
Taylor, Daniel J. 1906- *St&PR 91*
Taylor, Daniel Robert 1962- *WhoE 91*
Taylor, Daniel William 1946- *WhoAm 90*
Taylor, Danny 1900-1972 *Ballpl 90*
Taylor, Darl Coder 1913- *WhoAm 90*
Taylor, Dave *BioIn 16*
Taylor, David Blakely 1955- *WhoSSW 91*
Taylor, David Brooke 1942- *WhoE 91, WhoWor 91*
Taylor, David Edward 1951- *WhoSSW 91*
Taylor, David George 1929- *WhoAm 90, WhoE 91*
Taylor, David John 1943- *WhoE 91*
Taylor, David Victor 1936- *WhoWor 91*
Taylor, David Watson 1864-1940 *BioIn 16*
Taylor, David Wyatt Aiken 1925- *WhoAm 90*
Taylor, Davidson 1907-1979 *WhoAmA 91N*
Taylor, Deborah Lynn 1953- *WhoAmW 91*
Taylor, Della Mae 1932- *WhoAmW 91*
Taylor, Dennis Lee, Sr. 1946- *WhoSSW 91*
Taylor, Derek Noel 1929- *IntWWM 90*
Taylor, Dermot Brownrigg 1915- *WhoAm 90*

Taylor, Diana Lynn 1957- *WhoAmW 91*
Taylor, Dib *BioIn 16*
Taylor, Don L. 1932- *St&PR 91*
Taylor, Donald *BioIn 16, NewYTBS 90 [port]*
Taylor, Donald 1927- *WhoAm 90*
Taylor, Donald Arthur 1923- *WhoAm 90*
Taylor, Donald C. 1921- *St&PR 91*
Taylor, Donald Christopher 1948- *WhoWor 91*
Taylor, Donald D. 1932- *St&PR 91*
Taylor, Donald E *BiDrAPA 89*
Taylor, Donald Eldridge, III 1953- *WhoEmL 91*
Taylor, Donald Harry *BiDrAPA 89*
Taylor, Donald J. *WhoAm 90*
Taylor, Donald M. 1932- *St&PR 91*
Taylor, Donald R., Jr. 1958- *BiDrAPA 89*
Taylor, Donna Bloyd 1958- *WhoAmW 91*
Taylor, Donna Brooks *ODwPR 91*
Taylor, Donna Marie 1960- *WhoAmW 91*
Taylor, Doris Denice 1955- *WhoAmW 91*
Taylor, Dorothy Harlow 1932- *St&PR 91*
Taylor, Dorothy Harris 1931- *WhoAmW 91, WhoE 91, WhoWor 91*
Taylor, Dorothy Jane *WhoAmW 91*
Taylor, Dorothy Jean 1950- *WhoWrEP 89*
Taylor, Douglas Jennings 1917- *WhoSSW 91*
Taylor, Dowie George 1937- *IntWWM 90*
Taylor, Dummy 1875-1958 *Ballpl 90*
Taylor, Durran H. 1959- *WhoSSW 91, WhoWor 91*
Taylor, E. J. 1934- *WhoAmW 91*
Taylor, Earl Chip 1950- *WhoE 91*
Taylor, Edith S *BiDrAPA 89*
Taylor, Edmond Lapierre 1908- *BioIn 16*
Taylor, Edmund Dryer 1920- *St&PR 91*
Taylor, Edward Arnold 1942- *St&PR 91*
Taylor, Edward Curtis 1923- *WhoAm 90*
Taylor, Edward Michael 1947- *WhoE 91*
Taylor, Edward Plunket *BioIn 16*
Taylor, Edward Stewart 1911- *WhoAm 90*
Taylor, Eldon Donivan 1929- *WhoAm 90*
Taylor, Eleanor Ashworth 1847-1912 *FemiCLE*
Taylor, Elisabeth Coler 1942- *WhoAmW 91*
Taylor, Elizabeth *BiDEWW*
Taylor, Elizabeth *BiDEWW, FemiCLE*
Taylor, Elizabeth *BiDEWW*
Taylor, Elizabeth 1912-1975 *BioIn 16, FemiCLE, MajTwCW*
Taylor, Elizabeth 1932- *BioAmW, BioIn 16, WhoAm 90, WhoAmW 91, WhoWor 91, WorAlBi*
Taylor, Elizabeth Ann *BiDrAPA 89*
Taylor, Elizabeth Jane 1941- *WhoAmW 91, WhoSSW 91, WhoWor 91*
Taylor, Ellen Borden Broadhurst 1913- *WhoAmW 91, WhoWor 91*
Taylor, Elmer Louis, Jr. 1926- *St&PR 91*
Taylor, Emily 1860-1952 *WhoAmA 91N*
Taylor, Eric *WhoNeCM [port]*
Taylor, Ernest Lee 1949- *WhoSSW 91*
Taylor, Estelle Wormley 1924- *WhoAm 90*
Taylor, Eugene Charles 1914- *WhoAm 90*
Taylor, Eugene E 1921- *BiDrAPA 89*
Taylor, Eulon Ross *BiDrAPA 89*
Taylor, Euphemia Jane 1874-1970 *BioIn 16*
Taylor, Eva *WhoWor 91*
Taylor, Eva Marietta *WhoAmW 91*
Taylor, Evelyn D. *ODwPR 91*
Taylor, Foster Jay 1923- *WhoAm 90*
Taylor, Frances *BiDEWW*
Taylor, Frances *BiDEWW*
Taylor, Frances Marie 1942- *WhoAmW 91*
Taylor, Francine Marie Conat 1937- *WhoAmW 91*
Taylor, Francis Henry 1903-1957 *WhoAmA 91N*
Taylor, Frank Gordon 1940- *St&PR 91*
Taylor, Franklin 1843-1919 *PenDiMP*
Taylor, Fred J. *WhoSSW 91*
Taylor, Fred J. 1929- *St&PR 91*
Taylor, Frederick B. 1941- *St&PR 91*
Taylor, Frederick Bourchier 1906- *WhoAmA 91N*
Taylor, Frederick W. 1856-1915 *BioIn 16, WorAlBi*
Taylor, Frederick William, Jr. 1933- *WhoWor 91*
Taylor, Frederick Winslow 1856-1915 *EncABHB 4 [port]*
Taylor, Gary Lee 1953- *WhoWor 91*
Taylor, Gayland Wayne 1958- *WhoEmL 91*
Taylor, Gene 1928- *WhoAm 90*
Taylor, Gene 1953- *BioIn 16, WhoAm 90*
Taylor, Geoffrey Ingram 1886-1975 *DcScB S2*
Taylor, George 1716-1781 *EncCRAm*
Taylor, George 1904- *WhoWor 91*
Taylor, George Allen 1906- *WhoAm 90*
Taylor, George F. *BioIn 16*
Taylor, George F. 1932- *St&PR 91*
Taylor, George Farrell 1932- *WhoAm 90*
Taylor, George Frederick 1928- *WhoAm 90*
Taylor, George H. 1943- *St&PR 91*
Taylor, George Keith 1942- *IntWWM 90*
Taylor, George Kimbrough, Jr. 1939- *WhoAm 90*
Taylor, George Malcolm, III 1953- *WhoEmL 91*
Taylor, George Simpson 1940- *St&PR 91, WhoAm 90*
Taylor, George William 1934- *WhoWor 91*
Taylor, Gerald 1935- *IntWWM 90*
Taylor, Gerald Dale 1943- *BiDrAPA 89*
Taylor, Gerald J *BiDrAPA 89*
Taylor, Gerald R. 1940- *St&PR 91*
Taylor, Geraldine *BioIn 16*
Taylor, Gloria A *BiDrAPA 89*
Taylor, Gordon Rattray 1911-1981 *EncO&P 3*
Taylor, Grace Elizabeth Woodall 1926- *WhoAmW 91*
Taylor, Grace Martin *WhoAmA 91*
Taylor, Graeme John 1940- *BiDrAPA 89*
Taylor, Graham 1851-1938 *WorAlBi*
Taylor, Graham Daniel Stewart 1945- *WhoWor 91*
Taylor, Grantley Walder *BiDrAPA 89*
Taylor, Gregory Lee 1951- *St&PR 91, WhoEmL 91*
Taylor, Grover Durwood 1937- *WhoSSW 91*
Taylor, Guy Watson 1919- *WhoAm 90*
Taylor, H. Baldwin *TwCCr&M 91*
Taylor, H. Lyndon 1931- *WhoSSW 91*
Taylor, Hal Winslow 1940- *WhoAm 90*
Taylor, Hannah *BiDEWW*
Taylor, Hannah 1774-1812 *FemiCLE*
Taylor, Hannis 1851-1922 *BioIn 16*
Taylor, Harold 1914- *WhoAm 90*
Taylor, Harold 1925- *IntWWM 90*
Taylor, Harold Allen, Jr. 1936- *WhoE 91*
Taylor, Harold Landes *BiDrAPA 89*
Taylor, Harriet 1807-1858 *FemiCLE*
Taylor, Harriet George 1948- *WhoSSW 91*
Taylor, Harrison *AmLegL*
Taylor, Harry 1919- *Ballpl 90*
Taylor, Harry Danner 1944- *St&PR 91*
Taylor, Harry George 1918- *WhoAmA 91*
Taylor, Harry William 1925- *WhoAm 90*
Taylor, Harry Winfield 1921- *WhoE 91*
Taylor, Hawk 1939- *Ballpl 90*
Taylor, Helen 1831-1907 *FemiCLE*
Taylor, Henry 1841-1893 *DcCanB 12*
Taylor, Henry 1942- *BioIn 16, ConAu 31NR, WorAu 1980 [port]*
Taylor, Henry L. 1952- *St&PR 91*
Taylor, Henry Merle, Jr. 1928- *WhoSSW 91*
Taylor, Henry Milton 1903- *WhoWor 91*
Taylor, Henry Roth 1940- *WhoE 91*
Taylor, Henry Splawn 1942- *WhoAm 90, WhoWrEP 89*
Taylor, Herb 1942-1987 *BioIn 16*
Taylor, Herbert Cecil, Jr. 1924- *WhoAm 90*
Taylor, Hershel L. 1914- *St&PR 91*
Taylor, Hillary 1950- *WhoAmW 91*
Taylor, Hollis 1935- *St&PR 91*
Taylor, Howard Francis 1939- *WhoAm 90*
Taylor, Howard R. 1923- *St&PR 91*
Taylor, Hugh Holloway 1941- *WhoAmA 91*
Taylor, Hugh Pettingill, Jr. 1932- *WhoAm 90*
Taylor, Hugh Stott 1890-1974 *DcScB S2*
Taylor, I. *PenDiDA 89*
Taylor, Ida Ashworth 1850-1929 *FemiCLE*
Taylor, Ira Mooney 1935- *WhoAmA 91*
Taylor, Irving J *BiDrAPA 89*
Taylor, Irving J. 1919- *St&PR 91*
Taylor, J. *PenDiDA 89*
Taylor, J. Allyn 1907- *St&PR 91*
Taylor, J.F. Reeh 1924- *St&PR 91*
Taylor, Jack 1874-1938 *Ballpl 90*
Taylor, Jack Arthur 1935- *IntWWM 90, WhoSSW 91*
Taylor, Jacqueline Diane 1934- *WhoAmW 91*
Taylor, James 1948- *EncPR&S 89, OxCPMus, WorAlBi*
Taylor, James A *BiDrAPA 89*
Taylor, James Bayard 1825-1878 *BioIn 16*
Taylor, James D., Jr. 1910- *St&PR 91*
Taylor, James Danforth 1954- *WhoEmL 91*
Taylor, James Daniel 1928- *WhoSSW 91*
Taylor, James Daniel 1941- *WhoE 91*
Taylor, James E 1921- *BiDrAPA 89*
Taylor, James Francis 1951- *WhoSSW 91*
Taylor, James Francis Nuttall 1938- *WhoWor 91*
Taylor, James Harold 1945- *WhoAm 90*
Taylor, James Harry, II 1951- *WhoWor 91*
Taylor, James Herbert 1916- *WhoAm 90*
Taylor, James Howard 1947- *WhoAm 90*
Taylor, James Hutchings 1930- *WhoAm 90*
Taylor, James I. 1939- *St&PR 91*
Taylor, James Leon 1948- *WhoE 91*
Taylor, James Marion, II 1926- *St&PR 91*
Taylor, James Robert, III 1950- *WhoWrEP 89*
Taylor, James Stover 1947- *WhoEmL 91*
Taylor, James Vernon 1948- *WhoAm 90*
Taylor, James W. 1918- *St&PR 91*
Taylor, James Wagner 1925- *St&PR 91*
Taylor, James Walter 1933- *WhoWor 91*
Taylor, James Wickes 1819-1893 *DcCanB 12*
Taylor, Jan *ODwPR 91*
Taylor, Jan Hudson 1949- *WhoAmW 91*
Taylor, Jana *BioIn 16*
Taylor, Jane 1783-1824 *BioIn 16, FemiCLE*
Taylor, Janelle Diane Williams 1944- *WhoSSW 91*
Taylor, Janet R 1941- *WhoAmA 91*
Taylor, Janine *BioIn 16*
Taylor, Jay Eugene 1918- *WhoAm 90*
Taylor, Jay G. 1947- *St&PR 91*
Taylor, Jean *St&PR 91*
Taylor, Jean Grove 1927- *St&PR 91*
Taylor, Jeanine Marie 1960- *WhoSSW 91*
Taylor, Jeremy 1943- *BioIn 16*
Taylor, Jerry Duncan 1938- *BioIn 16, WhoSSW 91*
Taylor, Jerry Lynn 1947- *WhoAmW 91*
Taylor, Jesse Douglas Allen- *BioIn 16*
Taylor, Joan Koslosky 1929- *WhoAmW 91*
Taylor, Joanna Wanda 1942- *WhoAmW 91, WhoWor 91*
Taylor, Job, III 1942- *WhoWor 91*
Taylor, Jocelyn Mary 1931- *WhoAm 90, WhoAmW 91*
Taylor, Jody Lockhart 1931- *WhoE 91*
Taylor, Joe Clinton 1942- *WhoAm 90*
Taylor, Joe Franklin 1942- *WhoSSW 91*
Taylor, John *BioIn 16, PenDiDA 89*
Taylor, John 1753-1824 *EncCRAm*
Taylor, John 1808-1887 *AmLegL*
Taylor, John 1897-1983 *WhoAmA 91N*
Taylor, John 1931- *EncO&P 3, EncPaPR 91*
Taylor, John Andrew 1953- *WhoE 91*
Taylor, John Anthony 1954- *WhoE 91*
Taylor, John B. *ODwPR 91*
Taylor, John B. 1946- *BioIn 16*
Taylor, John Brian 1946- *WhoAm 90*
Taylor, John C E 1902-1985 *WhoAmA 91N*
Taylor, John Chestnut, III 1928- *WhoAm 90*
Taylor, John Curtis 1951- *WhoSSW 91*
Taylor, John D. 1933- *ODwPR 91*
Taylor, John Earl 1935- *WhoSSW 91*
Taylor, John Howard 1913- *WhoAm 90*
Taylor, John I 1958- *ODwPR 91*
Taylor, John Jackson 1931- *WhoAm 90*
Taylor, John Joseph 1922- *WhoAm 90*
Taylor, John L. *WhoAm 90*
Taylor, John Lee 1933- *WhoSSW 91*
Taylor, John Lloyd 1935- *WhoAmA 91N*
Taylor, John Lockhart 1927- *WhoAm 90*
Taylor, John Pickens 1936- *BiDrAPA 89*
Taylor, John R. 1939- *BioIn 16*
Taylor, John Randolph 1929- *WhoAm 90*
Taylor, John Richard 1945- *WhoSSW 91*
Taylor, John Robert *BiDrAPA 89*
Taylor, John Robert 1952- *WhoWrEP 89*
Taylor, John Russell 1935- *WhoWor 91*
Taylor, John Russell 1964- *WhoEmL 91*
Taylor, John Sherrod 1947- *WhoSSW 91*
Taylor, John Whitfield 1914- *WhoE 91*
Taylor, John Wilkinson 1906- *WhoAm 90, WhoWor 91*
Taylor, Jonathan Francis 1935- *WhoAm 90*
Taylor, Joseph F. 1950- *St&PR 91*
Taylor, Joseph H. 1927- *St&PR 91*
Taylor, Joseph Hooton, Jr. 1941- *WhoAm 90*
Taylor, Joseph N. 1822-1864 *AmLegL*
Taylor, Joseph Richard 1907- *WhoAmA 91*
Taylor, Joseph Thomas 1913- *WhoAm 90*
Taylor, Joseph William 1953- *WhoSSW 91*
Taylor, Josephine Lister *BioIn 16*
Taylor, Joshua Charles 1917-1981 *WhoAmA 91N*
Taylor, Joycelynn W. 1931- *St&PR 91*
Taylor, Juanita Lynn 1954- *BiDrAPA 89*
Taylor, Judy 1932- *BioIn 16, SmATA X [port]*
Taylor, Julia W. *WhoAmW 91*
Taylor, Kathleen 1942- *WhoAm 90*
Taylor, Kathleen Mary 1964- *WhoAmW 91*
Taylor, Kathryn Evans 1929- *WhoAmW 91*
Taylor, Keith 1952- *WhoWrEP 89*
Taylor, Keith Breden 1924- *WhoAm 90*
Taylor, Kendall Frances *WhoAmA 91, WhoAmW 91*
Taylor, Kendrick Jay 1914- *WhoWor 91*
Taylor, Kenneth D. *St&PR 91*
Taylor, Kenneth Douglas 1942- *WhoE 91*
Taylor, Kenneth Grant 1936- *WhoAm 90*
Taylor, Kenneth John W. 1939- *WhoAm 90*
Taylor, Kenneth Lapham 1941- *WhoSSW 91*
Taylor, Kenneth Macdonald 1947- *WhoWor 91*
Taylor, Kenneth Nathaniel 1917- *WhoAm 90*
Taylor, Kent 1954- *WhoE 91*
Taylor, Kent Gregory 1941- *WhoE 91*
Taylor, Kristin Clark 1959- *WhoAm 90, WhoAmW 91*
Taylor, L A 1939- *ConAu 30NR*
Taylor, Lance Jerome 1940- *WhoAm 90*
Taylor, Larry R *BiDrAPA 89*
Taylor, Laurette 1884-1946 *BioAmW, BioIn 16*
Taylor, Laurette Cooney 1884-1946 *NotWoAT*
Taylor, Laurie *ConAu 30NR*
Taylor, Lauriston Sale 1902- *WhoAm 90*
Taylor, Lawrence *BioIn 16*
Taylor, Lawrence 1959- *CurBio 90 [port], WorAlBi*
Taylor, Lawrence W *BiDrAPA 89*
Taylor, Leigh H. 1941- *WhoAm 90*
Taylor, Leonard Bernard 1955- *WhoE 91*
Taylor, Leonard E. 1897- *St&PR 91*
Taylor, Leonard Stuart 1928- *WhoE 91*
Taylor, Lesli Ann 1953- *WhoAmW 91*
Taylor, Leslie G. 1922- *St&PR 91*
Taylor, Leslie George 1922- *WhoWor 91*
Taylor, Lester B., Jr. 1932- *ODwPR 91*
Taylor, Libby *DrBlPA 90*
Taylor, Linda Lee 1948- *WhoAmW 91*
Taylor, Linda Marianne 1948- *WhoSSW 91*
Taylor, Linda Rathbun 1946- *WhoAmW 91*
Taylor, Lindajean Thorton 1942- *WhoWor 91*
Taylor, Lindsay David, Jr. 1945- *WhoAm 90*
Taylor, Lisa 1933- *WhoAm 90, WhoAmA 91*
Taylor, Lisa Marlene 1933- *WhoAmW 91*
Taylor, Louise Todd 1939- *BioIn 16, WhoSSW 91*
Taylor, Lucille Marie 1939- *WhoAmW 91*
Taylor, Lyle Dewey 1934- *WhoAm 90*
Taylor, Lynn Boggess 1945- *WhoAmW 91*
Taylor, Lynn Ramona 1962- *WhoE 91*
Taylor, M.D.K. 1818-1897 *AmLegL*
Taylor, M. Hal *St&PR 91*
Taylor, M. Hillsman 1884-1948? *AmLegL*
Taylor, Mallie C *BiDrAPA 89*
Taylor, Marcia 1919- *St&PR 91*
Taylor, Marcus James 1957- *WhoEmL 91*
Taylor, Margaret 1917- *AuBYP 90*
Taylor, Margaret Lee 1949- *WhoAmW 91*
Taylor, Margaret Smith 1788-1852 *BioIn 16*
Taylor, Margaret Turner 1944- *WhoAmW 91, WhoE 91*
Taylor, Margaret Uhrich 1952- *WhoAmW 91, WhoEmL 91*
Taylor, Margaret W. 1920- *WhoAmW 91*
Taylor, Maria Centofanti 1963- *WhoSSW 91*
Taylor, Maria Del Pico *IntWWM 90*
Taylor, Maria Dyer 1837-1870 *BioAmW*
Taylor, Mark *AuBYP 90*
Taylor, Mark Cooper 1945- *WhoAm 90*
Taylor, Marshall W. 1878- *BioIn 16*
Taylor, Mary *BiDEWW*
Taylor, Mary 1670?- *BiDEWW*
Taylor, Mary 1817-1893 *FemiCLE*
Taylor, Mary A. 1948- *WhoAmW 91*
Taylor, Mary Cazort *WhoAmA 91*
Taylor, Mary Cutis Smith 1937- *WhoAmW 91*
Taylor, Mary D. 1936- *WhoAmW 91*
Taylor, Mary Elizabeth 1933- *WhoAmW 91*
Taylor, Mary Joan 1926- *WhoAmW 91*
Taylor, Mary Scott 1752?-1793 *BioIn 16*
Taylor, Maurice D. 1927- *St&PR 91*
Taylor, Maurice Derrick 1927- *WhoAm 90*
Taylor, Maurine Pacenta 1944- *ODwPR 91*
Taylor, Maxwell D. 1901-1987 *BioIn 16, WorAlBi*
Taylor, Merrily Ellen 1945- *WhoAm 90, WhoAmW 91*
Taylor, Meshach *BioIn 16, ConTFT 8*
Taylor, Michael 1944- *WhoAmA 91*
Taylor, Michael Alan 1940- *BiDrAPA 89, WhoAm 90*
Taylor, Michael Conrad 1955- *WhoEmL 91*
Taylor, Michael Estes 1944- *WhoE 91*
Taylor, Michael John 1945- *BiDrAPA 89*
Taylor, Michael L. 1944- *St&PR 91*
Taylor, Michael William 1947- *WhoEmL 91*
Taylor, Mildred D. *AuBYP 90, BioIn 16*
Taylor, Mildred Juanita 1947- *WhoAmW 91*

Taylor, Millard Benjamin 1913- *WhoAm 90*
Taylor, Minna 1947- *WhoAmW 91*
Taylor, Monifa *BioIn 16*
Taylor, Morris 1956- *WhoWrEP 89*
Taylor, Moses 1806-1882 *EncABHB 6 [port]*
Taylor, Muriel King 1936- *BiDrAPA 89*
Taylor, Nancy Elizabeth 1953- *WhoAmW 91*
Taylor, Nancy Stirling 1960- *WhoAmW 91*
Taylor, Nathalee Britton 1941- *WhoAmW 91*
Taylor, Nathan C. D. 1810-1887 *AmLegL*
Taylor, Nelson Ferebee 1921- *WhoAm 90*
Taylor, Nicholas C. 1937- *St&PR 91*
Taylor, Noel C. 1924- *WhoSSW 91*
Taylor, Noel Ellen 1954- *BiDrAPA 89*
Taylor, Norman William 1923- *WhoAm 90, WhoE 91*
Taylor, Norton Warren 1922- *St&PR 91*
Taylor, Oliver B. 1931- *St&PR 91*
Taylor, Osborne K. *BioIn 16*
Taylor, Pamela Jane *BiDrAPA 89*
Taylor, Patricia May 1919- *WhoAmW 91*
Taylor, Patrick Franklin 1937- *WhoSSW 91*
Taylor, Patrick Robinson 1927- *WhoSSW 91*
Taylor, Paul 1930- *WhoWor 91, WorAlBi*
Taylor, Paul 1958- *WhoAmA 91*
Taylor, Paul Albert 1943- *WhoAm 90*
Taylor, Paul Daniel 1939- *WhoAm 90*
Taylor, Paul J. 1946- *WhoWrEP 89*
Taylor, Paul Kent 1940- *WhoWrEP 89*
Taylor, Paula 1942- *BioIn 16*
Taylor, Pearlie Beatrice *WhoAmW 91*
Taylor, Peggy Louise 1946- *WhoAmW 91*
Taylor, Peter 1917- *MajTwCW, WorAlBi*
Taylor, Peter Hillsman 1917- *WhoWrEP 89*
Taylor, Peter V. 1934- *ODwPR 91*
Taylor, Peter van Voorhees 1934- *WhoWor 91*
Taylor, Phillip Seyfang 1921- *WhoAm 90*
Taylor, Phoebe Atwood 1909-1976 *FemiCLE, TwCCr&M 91*
Taylor, Prentiss 1907- *WhoAmA 91*
Taylor, Prentiss Hottel 1907- *WhoAm 90*
Taylor, Priscilla W. 1941- *WhoAmW 91*
Taylor, Quintard, Jr. 1948- *WhoEmL 91*
Taylor, R.L., II 1941- *St&PR 91*
Taylor, R. Lee, II 1941- *WhoSSW 91*
Taylor, R. William *BioIn 16*
Taylor, Ralph C. 1941- *St&PR 91*
Taylor, Ralph Orien, Jr. 1919- *WhoWor 91*
Taylor, Ramona G. 1930- *St&PR 91*
Taylor, Ramona Garrett 1930- *WhoAm 90, WhoAmW 91*
Taylor, Randall William 1948- *WhoEmL 91*
Taylor, Reese Hale, Jr. 1928- *WhoAm 90*
Taylor, Reeves 1946- *WhoEmL 91*
Taylor, Reeves Ramsey 1929- *WhoSSW 91*
Taylor, Reid Sampson *BiDrAPA 89*
Taylor, Rene Claude 1916- *WhoAmA 91*
Taylor, Rex Payne 1931- *St&PR 91*
Taylor, Richard *ODwPR 91*
Taylor, Richard 1919- *WhoAm 90, WhoWrEP 89*
Taylor, Richard 1941- *LiHiK*
Taylor, Richard 1946- *ODwPR 91*
Taylor, Richard Alan 1950- *WhoSSW 91*
Taylor, Richard Bertrom 1951- *WhoSSW 91*
Taylor, Richard Bingham 1944- *WhoWor 91*
Taylor, Richard Breckinridge 1930- *St&PR 91*
Taylor, Richard Douglas, Sr. 1931- *WhoSSW 91*
Taylor, Richard Edward 1929- *WhoAm 90*
Taylor, Richard F. 1933- *St&PR 91*
Taylor, Richard Fred, Jr. 1933- *WhoAm 90*
Taylor, Richard Green 1922- *St&PR 91*
Taylor, Richard John *BioIn 16*
Taylor, Richard L. 1944- *St&PR 91*
Taylor, Richard Leroy, Jr. 1935- *WhoAm 90*
Taylor, Richard Martin *BiDrAPA 89*
Taylor, Richard Powell 1928- *WhoAm 90, WhoE 91*
Taylor, Richard Trelore 1917- *WhoAm 90*
Taylor, Richard W. *WhoAm 90*
Taylor, Richard W 1923- *BiDrAPA 89*
Taylor, Richard W. 1926- *St&PR 91*
Taylor, Richard William 1926- *WhoAm 90*
Taylor, Richard Wirth 1923- *WhoAm 90*
Taylor, Rick Joseph 1956- *WhoE 91, WhoEmL 91, WhoWor 91*
Taylor, Robbie Louise 1947- *WhoSSW 91*
Taylor, Robbie R. 1947- *WhoAmW 91*
Taylor, Robbins 1925- *St&PR 91*
Taylor, Robbins 1956- *St&PR 91*
Taylor, Robert 1911-1969 *WorAlBi*
Taylor, Robert 1925- *WhoAmA 91*
Taylor, Robert Brown 1936- *WhoAm 90*
Taylor, Robert Chatfield- *BioIn 16*
Taylor, Robert Edward 1931- *WhoSSW 91*
Taylor, Robert G. 1943- *St&PR 91*
Taylor, Robert John 1935- *St&PR 91*
Taylor, Robert K. 1928- *St&PR 91*
Taylor, Robert L. 1949- *St&PR 91*
Taylor, Robert L., Jr. 1932- *St&PR 91*
Taylor, Robert Lee 1944- *WhoAm 90*
Taylor, Robert Lewis 1912- *WhoWrEP 89*
Taylor, Robert Lewis 1939- *WhoAm 90*
Taylor, Robert Love 1914- *WhoWor 91*
Taylor, Robert Love, Jr. 1941- *WhoWrEP 89*
Taylor, Robert M. 1942- *St&PR 91*
Taylor, Robert Morgan 1941- *WhoAm 90*
Taylor, Robert Richard, Jr. 1939- *WhoSSW 91*
Taylor, Robert S. 1929- *St&PR 91*
Taylor, Robert Sundling 1925- *WhoAm 90*
Taylor, Robert William 1929- *WhoAm 90*
Taylor, Robert William 1934- *WhoSSW 91*
Taylor, Rod 1929- *WorAlBi*
Taylor, Rod 1930- *WhoAm 90*
Taylor, Roger K. 1948- *St&PR 91*
Taylor, Roger Scott 1946- *WhoSSW 91*
Taylor, Romey A. 1934- *St&PR 91*
Taylor, Ron 1937- *Ballpl 90*
Taylor, Ronald Dean 1948- *WhoEmL 91*
Taylor, Ronald Joseph 1944- *BiDrAPA 89, WhoE 91*
Taylor, Rosanne Cappiello 1945- *WhoAmW 91*
Taylor, Rosemary *WhoAmA 91, WhoAmW 91, WhoE 91*
Taylor, Roy G. 1918- *WhoWrEP 89*
Taylor, Roy Lewis 1932- *WhoAm 90*
Taylor, Rush Walker, Jr. 1934- *WhoAm 90, WhoWor 91*
Taylor, Russel Reid 1917- *WhoWor 91*
Taylor, Sally Edith 1958- *BiDrAPA 89*
Taylor, Sally Jane 1948- *WhoAmW 91*
Taylor, Sammy 1933- *Ballpl 90*
Taylor, Samuel A.L., Jr. 1935- *St&PR 91*
Taylor, Samuel Albert 1912- *WhoAm 90*
Taylor, Samuel Douglas 1924- *BiDrAPA 89*
Taylor, Samuel J. 1939- *St&PR 91*
Taylor, Samuel James 1929- *WhoAm 90*
Taylor, Samuel L. *BioIn 16*
Taylor, Sandra Lynn 1962- *WhoAmW 91*
Taylor, Sandra Ortiz 1936- *WhoAmA 91*
Taylor, Sarah Louisa 1942- *WhoAmW 91*
Taylor, Sarah Mary 1916- *MusmAFA*
Taylor, Sarah Wightman 1956- *WhoAmW 91*
Taylor, Scott Maxfield 1953- *St&PR 91, WhoEmL 91*
Taylor, Scott Robert 1948- *WhoSSW 91*
Taylor, Scott Thomas 1955- *WhoSSW 91*
Taylor, Shahane Richardson, Jr. 1928- *WhoSSW 91, WhoWor 91*
Taylor, Sharon K. 1945- *ODwPR 91*
Taylor, Sherril Wightman 1924- *WhoAm 90*
Taylor, Shirley Ann 1948- *WhoAmW 91*
Taylor, Sidney 1934- *WhoWor 91*
Taylor, Stanford E. 1927- *St&PR 91*
Taylor, Stephen Dale 1936- *St&PR 91*
Taylor, Stephen Earle 1946- *WhoSSW 91*
Taylor, Stephen John 1954- *WhoSSW 91*
Taylor, Steve Martin *BiDrAPA 89*
Taylor, Steven James 1946- *WhoSSW 91*
Taylor, Stratton 1956- *WhoSSW 91*
Taylor, Stuart Symington 1913- *WhoAm 90*
Taylor, Susan Eleanor 1959- *WhoE 91*
Taylor, Susanne Gregory 1946- *WhoAmW 91*
Taylor, Susie King 1848-1912 *FemiCLE*
Taylor, Sussiana 1955- *WhoWor 91*
Taylor, Sydney Brenner 1904-1978 *AuBYP 90*
Taylor, T. G. 1919-1987 *BioIn 16*
Taylor, Ted 1940- *WhoSSW 91*
Taylor, Telford 1908- *MajTwCW, WhoAm 90, WhoWrEP 89*
Taylor, Terrence N 1927- *BiDrAPA 89*
Taylor, Tessa Jane 1964- *WhoAmW 91*
Taylor, Theodore 1921?- *BioIn 16*
Taylor, Theodore 1924- *AuBYP 90*
Taylor, Theodore Brewster 1925- *WhoAm 90*
Taylor, Theodore Langhans *WhoWrEP 89*
Taylor, Theodore Langhans 1921- *WhoAm 90*
Taylor, Theophilus Mills 1909-1989 *BioIn 16*
Taylor, Thomas 1820-1910 *BioIn 16*
Taylor, Thomas A. 1942- *St&PR 91*
Taylor, Thomas Alexander, III 1930- *WhoAm 90, WhoSSW 91*
Taylor, Thomas Ancel 1940- *WhoSSW 91*
Taylor, Thomas Edward 1946- *St&PR 91*
Taylor, Thomas Franklin 1951- *St&PR 91*
Taylor, Thomas Fuller 1937- *WhoWor 91*
Taylor, Thomas H., Jr. 1935- *St&PR 91*
Taylor, Thomas Hewitt, Jr. 1935- *WhoAm 90*
Taylor, Thomas Hudson, Jr. 1920- *WhoSSW 91, WhoWor 91*
Taylor, Thomas James 1931- *St&PR 91, WhoAm 90*
Taylor, Thomas L. *St&PR 91*
Taylor, Thomas Perry 1958- *St&PR 91*
Taylor, Thomas Roger 1945- *WhoWor 91*
Taylor, Timothy Gilbert 1951- *WhoSSW 91*
Taylor, Timothy Robert *BiDrAPA 89*
Taylor, Toby Teret 1945- *WhoAmW 91*
Taylor, Tom 1817-1880 *BioIn 16*
Taylor, Tony 1935- *Ballpl 90, WhoHisp 91*
Taylor, Una Ashworth 1857-1922 *FemiCLE*
Taylor, Valerie 1902-1988 *AnObit 1988, ConTFT 8*
Taylor, Vernon F., III 1947- *St&PR 91*
Taylor, Volney 1939- *St&PR 91*
Taylor, W. Howson 1876-1935 *PenDiDA 89*
Taylor, W. Royce 1926- *St&PR 91*
Taylor, Walter Willard 1913- *WhoWor 91*
Taylor, Wanda Anita *BiDrAPA 89*
Taylor, Warren Fredrick 1925- *St&PR 91*
Taylor, Warren G. 1940- *St&PR 91*
Taylor, Watson Robbins 1925- *St&PR 91*
Taylor, Watson Robbins, Jr. 1956- *WhoSSW 91*
Taylor, Wayne Fletcher 1943- *WhoAm 90*
Taylor, Wesley B. 1944- *BioIn 16*
Taylor, Wilbur Spencer 1928- *WhoE 91*
Taylor, William 1930- *WhoWor 91*
Taylor, William A., Jr. 1931- *St&PR 91*
Taylor, William Al 1938- *WhoSSW 91, WhoWor 91*
Taylor, William Brooks, II 1910- *WhoAm 90*
Taylor, William Davis 1908- *St&PR 91, WhoAm 90*
Taylor, William Desmond 1877-1922 *BioIn 16*
Taylor, William Edward 1921- *BioIn 16*
Taylor, William Halstead 1924- *WhoWor 91*
Taylor, William James 1948- *WhoAm 90*
Taylor, William Jape 1924- *WhoAm 90*
Taylor, William Jesse, Jr. 1933- *WhoAm 90*
Taylor, William M *BiDrAPA 89*
Taylor, William M. 1944- *St&PR 91*
Taylor, William Menke, Jr. 1946- *WhoEmL 91*
Taylor, William O. 1932- *BioIn 16, St&PR 91*
Taylor, William Osgood 1932- *WhoAm 90*
Taylor, William R 1933- *BiDrAPA 89*
Taylor, William S. 1795-1858 *AmLegL*
Taylor, William S. 1938- *St&PR 91*
Taylor, William Stokes *BiDrAPA 89*
Taylor, William Thomas 1958- *WhoSSW 91*
Taylor, William Warren 1951- *St&PR 91*
Taylor, Wilma Lee 1948- *WhoEmL 91*
Taylor, Wilson H. *WhoAm 90, WhoE 91*
Taylor, Yvonne S M 1939- *BiDrAPA 89*
Taylor, Zachary 1784-1850 *BiDrUSE 89, BioIn 16, WhNaAH, WorAlBi*
Taylor, Zachary, III 1951- *WhoEmL 91*
Taylor, Zachary L. 1954- *St&PR 91*
Taylor, Zack 1898-1974 *Ballpl 90*
Taylor Clark, Andrea 1952- *WhoAmW 91*
Taylor-Hunt, Mary Bernis Buchanan 1904- *WhoAmW 91*
Taylor-Little, Carol Joyce 1941- *WhoAmW 91*
Taylor Lucien, Deborah J. *ODwPR 91*
Taylor Mc Daniel, Lu Anne *BiDrAPA 89*
Taylor-Payne, Mary Lee 1931- *WhoSSW 91*
Taylor-Smith, Cheminne 1963- *WhoAmW 91*
Taylor-Smith, Shelley *BioIn 16*
Taylor-Sneddon, Phyllis Arlene 1955- *IntWWM 90*
Taylor Williams, Teresa Katherine 1957- *WhoAmW 91*
Taymor, Julie *BioIn 16*
Taymor, Julie 1952- *NotWoAT*
Taysi, Engin *BiDrAPA 89*
Taysom, Wayne Pendelton 1925- *WhoAmA 91*
Taza *WhNaAH*
Tazuma, Laurie Midori *BiDrAPA 89*
Tazzini, Rinaldo 1942- *IntWWM 90*
Tchaikovsky, Peter Ilich 1840-1893 *BioIn 16*
Tchaikovsky, Peter Ilyich 1840-1893 *WorAlBi*
Tchaikovsky, Pyotr Ilyich 1840-1893 *PenDiMP A*
Tchaikowsky, Andre 1935-1982 *PenDiMP, -A*
Tchakalian, Sam 1929- *WhoAmA 91*
Tchakarov, Emil 1948- *PenDiMP*
Tchalla, Pitang 1954- *WhoWor 91*
Tchelistcheff, Victor 1929- *WhoSSW 91*
Tchen, Andre Han Ting 1948- *WhoE 91*
Tchen, Peter *BiDrAPA 89*
Tcherepnin, Alexander 1899-1977 *BioIn 16*
Tcherkassky, Marianna Alexsavena 1952- *WhoAmW 91*
Tcherneshoff, Lyndon Mark 1956- *WhoSSW 91*
Tchetchet, Tatiana *WhoAmA 91*
Tchicaya, Gerald Felix 1931-1988 *ConAu 129*
Tchinnis, John F. *St&PR 91*
Tchitcherov, Alexander Ivanovitch 1932- *WhoWor 91*
Tchobanoglous, George 1935- *WhoAm 90*
Tchon, Wallace Edward 1944- *St&PR 91*
Tchoryk, Robert Charles 1956- *WhoEmL 91, WhoSSW 91, WhoWor 91*
Tchudi, Stephen N. *AuBYP 90*
Tchudi, Stephen N. 1942- *BioIn 16*
Tchudi, Susan J. *AuBYP 90*
Tea Banh *WhoWor 91*
Tea, Charles Lewis, Jr. 1934- *St&PR 91*
Teach, Carole A. 1944- *St&PR 91*
Teach, Robert *EncCRAm*
Teachout, Bud 1904-1985 *Ballpl 90*
Teadt, Michael L. 1946- *ODwPR 91*
Teaford, Jane Brown 1935- *WhoAmW 91*
Teaford, John Harry 1947- *St&PR 91*
Teagan, J. Gerard 1947- *St&PR 91*
Teagan, John Gerard 1947- *WhoAm 90*
Teagan, Mark Tilden 1945- *WhoWrEP 89*
Teagarden, Jack *BioIn 16*
Teagarden, Jack 1905-1964 *OxCPMus, WorAlBi*
Teagle, Madeline Louise 1924- *WhoAmW 91*
Teagno, Herman J. 1937- *BiDrAPA 89*
Teague, Barry Elvin 1944- *WhoAm 90*
Teague, Bernice Rita 1957- *WhoE 91*
Teague, Bob 1929- *BioIn 16, DrBlPA 90*
Teague, Bruce Williams 1947- *WhoEmL 91*
Teague, Burton William 1912- *WhoWrEP 89*
Teague, Donald 1897- *WhoAm 90, WhoAmA 91*
Teague, Edward H *WhoAmA 91*
Teague, Frank Dean *BioIn 16*
Teague, Henry H. 1936- *St&PR 91*
Teague, Hyman Faris 1916- *WhoAm 90*
Teague, James W 1938- *BiDrAPA 89*
Teague, Jane Taran 1956- *WhoE 91*
Teague, Larry Gene 1954- *WhoAm 90*
Teague, Lavette Cox, Jr. 1934- *WhoWor 91*
Teague, Michael Allen 1946- *WhoSSW 91, WhoWor 91*
Teague, Peyton Clark 1915- *WhoAm 90, WhoSSW 91, WhoWor 91*
Teague, Richalyn Elaine 1941- *WhoAmW 91*
Teague, Robert *AuBYP 90*
Teague, S.W., Jr. 1927- *St&PR 91*
Teague, Sam Fuller 1918- *WhoAm 90*
Teague, Stuart Alan 1946- *St&PR 91*
Teague, W. Dorwin 1910- *WhoE 91*
Teague, Walter Dorwin 1883-1960 *PenDiDA 89*
Teague, Walter Dorwin 1884-1960 *WhoAmA 91N*
Teague, Walter Dorwin, Jr. *PenDiDA 89*
Teague, Wayne 1927- *WhoAm 90, WhoSSW 91*
Teahan, Frederick H. *ODwPR 91*
Teal, Ernest David 1946- *St&PR 91*
Teal, Gordon Kidd 1907- *WhoAm 90, WhoWor 91*
Teal, Ramona Rose 1937- *WhoSSW 91*
Teal, Robert James 1947- *WhoSSW 91*
Teal, Stewart E 1939- *BiDrAPA 89*
Teale, Alan Arthur 1931- *WhoSSW 91*
Teale, Edwin Way 1899-1980 *AuBYP 90*
Teale, William Herbert 1947- *WhoSSW 91*
Teall, Robert Wayne 1941- *St&PR 91*
Teaney, Myron Rex, II 1943- *St&PR 91*
Teannaki, Teatao *WhoWor 91*
Tear, Robert 1939- *IntWWM 90, PenDiMP*
Teare, George William, Jr. 1930- *St&PR 91*
Teare, Gregory L. 1954- *St&PR 91*
Teare, Max Eugene 1928- *BiDrAPA 89*
Tearney, Michael Gautier 1942- *WhoSSW 91*
Teas, Gregory Alan 1948- *BiDrAPA 89*
Teas, John Frederick 1934- *WhoSSW 91*
Teas, Kathie B. 1955- *St&PR 91*
Teas, Thomas Scattergood 1941- *WhoSSW 91*
Teaschner, Patricia Ann 1943- *WhoAmW 91*
Teasdale, Russell Edward 1931- *St&PR 91*
Teasdale, Sara 1884-1933 *BioAmW, BioIn 16, FemiCLE, WorAlBi*
Teasdale, Thomas Hennings 1933- *WhoAm 90*
Tease, James Edward 1939- *WhoAm 90*

Teasley, Anna Delores 1949- *WhoAmW 91*
Teasley, Edgar William 1912- *WhoWor 91*
Teasley, Harry E., Jr. 1937- *St&PR 91*
Teasley, Larkin 1936- *St&PR 91*
Teasley, Melanie *BiDrAPA 89*
Teasley, Merrily Austin 1943- *WhoSSW 91*
Teater, Joseph B 1915- *BiDrAPA 89*
Teates, Charles David 1936- *WhoAm 90*
Tebaldi, Renata 1922- *PenDiMP, WhoAm 90, WorAlBi*
Tebay, James Elwood 1930- *WhoAm 90*
Tebbe, Horst 1940- *St&PR 91*
Tebbel, John 1912- *WhoAm 90, WhoWrEP 89*
Tebbetts, Birdie 1912- *Ballpl 90, BioIn 16*
Tebbit, Norman *BioIn 16*
Tebbitt, Barbara Volk *WhoAmW 91*
Tebbs, Edward David B. 1938- *WhoWor 91*
Tebeau, Patsy 1864-1918 *Ballpl 90*
Tebedo, Mary Anne *WhoAmW 91*
Teberg, Mary H *BiDrAPA 89*
Tebet, David William 1920- *WhoAm 90, WhoWor 91*
Teblum, Gary Ira 1955- *WhoEmL 91*
Tebo, Mr. *PenDiDA 89*
Tebo, Stephen Dwane 1944- *WhoWor 91*
Tebor, Douglas Alan 1949- *BiDrAPA 89*
Teboul, Albert 1936- *WhoWor 91*
Teboul, Eric Alex *BiDrAPA 89*
Tec, Leon *BiDrAPA 89*
Tec, Leon 1919- *WhoE 91*
Tecce, Susan Marilyn 1961- *WhoAmW 91*
Tecco, Betsy Dru 1960- *WhoWrEP 89*
Tecco, Romuald Gilbert Louis Joseph 1941- *WhoAm 90*
Tece, Sungur 1934- *BiDrAPA 89*
Tece, Sungur Alp 1934- *WhoE 91*
Technotronic *ConMus 5*
Techter, David 1932- *EncO&P 3*
Tecklenburg, Harry 1927- *St&PR 91, WhoAm 90*
Tecumseh 1768-1813 *BioIn 16, WhNaAH [port], WorAlBi*
Tecumtha 1768?-1813 *WhNaAH [port]*
Teczar, Steven W 1948- *WhoAmA 91*
Tedder, Arthur William 1890-1967 *WorAlBi*
Tedder, Dewey Ray 1937- *St&PR 91*
Tedder, S. Russell 1935- *St&PR 91*
Teddy Bears, The *EncPR&S 89*
Tedeschi, John Alfred 1931- *WhoAm 90*
Tedeschi, Michael A. 1946- *St&PR 91*
Tedesco, Beth Boston 1960- *WhoEmL 91*
Tedesco, Francis Joseph 1944- *WhoAm 90*
Tedesco, Kristine J. 1961- *WhoAmW 91*
Tedesco, Shelby Ann 1965- *WhoAmW 91*
Tedesco, Susan Mary 1954- *WhoAmW 91*
Tedesko, Anton 1903- *WhoAm 90*
Tedeuscung 1700-1763 *WhNaAH*
Tedford, Jack Nowlan, III 1943- *WhoWor 91*
Tedford, William Howard, Jr. 1936- *WhoAm 90*
Tedford, William L. 1939- *St&PR 91*
Tedin, Delia Marie 1942- *WhoWor 91*
Tediuscung 1700-1763 *WhNaAH*
Tediuskung 1700-1763 *WhNaAH*
Tedlock, Dennis 1939- *WhoAm 90*
Tedone, David A. 1953- *ConAu 132*
Tedrick, Richard Newman 1931- *WhoE 91*
Tedros, Theodore Zaki 1910- *WhoSSW 91, WhoWor 91*
Tedrow, Eugene Leroy 1950- *St&PR 91*
Tedrow, Jack L *BiDrAPA 89*
Tedrow, John Charles Fremont 1917- *WhoAm 90*
Tedrow, Lynn Edward 1949- *WhoSSW 91*
Tedyuscung 1700-1763 *WhNaAH*
Tedyuskung 1700-1763 *WhNaAH*
Tee, John *ConAu 130*
Tee-Van, Helen Damrosch 1893-1976 *WhoAmA 91N*
Teed, C. Cason 1941- *WhoAmW 91*
Teed, Cason 1941- *WhoWrEP 89*
Teed, David Samuel 1954- *WhoAm 90*
Teed, Raymond L. *St&PR 91*
Teed, Roy Norman 1928- *IntWWM 90*
Teedjouskon 1700-1763 *WhNaAH*
Teedyuscung 1700-1763 *WhNaAH*
Teedyuskung 1705?-1763 *EncCRAm*
Teegarden, James W. 1936- *St&PR 91*
Teegarden, Kenneth Leroy 1921- *WhoAm 90*
Teegen, Evelyn Irene Hoopes 1931- *WhoAm 90, WhoAmW 91, WhoWor 91*
Teeger, John L. 1943- *St&PR 91*
Teeguarden, Dennis Earl 1931- *WhoAm 90*
Teehankee, Claudio *BioIn 16*
Teel, Bertha L. 1918- *St&PR 91*
Teel, Dale 1925- *WhoAm 90*
Teel, Edwin Alfred 1911- *St&PR 91*
Teel, John David 1947- *WhoSSW 91*
Teel, Olivia Ann 1946- *WhoSSW 91*
Teel, Sandra Louise 1944- *WhoAmW 91*
Teel, Theodore Trevanian, Jr. 1928- *WhoSSW 91*
Teele, Arthur Earle, Sr. 1910- *WhoAm 90*
Teele, Gerald Allen 1944- *St&PR 91*
Teelen, Gina *EncCoWW*
Teem, John McCorkle 1925- *WhoAm 90*
Teem, Paul Lloyd, Jr. 1948- *WhoEmL 91, WhoSSW 91, WhoWor 91*
Teena Marie 1957- *EncPR&S 89*
Teenagers, The *EncPR&S 89*
Teepen, Thomas Henry 1935- *WhoAm 90*
Teeple, Charles E. 1928- *ODwPR 91*
Teeple, Howard Merle 1911- *BioIn 16, WhoWor 91*
Teeple, Richard Duane 1942- *St&PR 91, WhoAm 90*
Teer, Barbara Ann 1937- *DrBlPA 90*
Teer, Harold Benton, Jr. 1945- *WhoEmL 91*
Teerlink, Richard F. *St&PR 91*
Teerlink, Richard Francis 1936- *WhoAm 90*
Teerman, John H. 1948- *St&PR 91*
Tees, Richard Chisholm 1940- *WhoAm 90*
Teesing, H P H 1907- *EncO&P 3*
Teeter, Dwight Leland, Jr. 1935- *WhoAm 90*
Teeter, Karl van Duyn 1929- *WhoAm 90*
Teeter, Martha Mary 1944- *WhoAmW 91*
Teeter, Robert *BioIn 16*
Teeter, Robert M. 1939- *WhoAm 90*
Teeters, Bruce William 1945- *St&PR 91*
Teeters, Nancy H. 1930- *St&PR 91*
Teeters, Nancy Hays 1930- *WhoAm 90, WhoAmW 91*
Teetor, Judith Lynn 1943- *WhoE 91*
Teets, Charles Edward 1947- *St&PR 91*
Teets, Frank David 1936- *St&PR 91*
Teets, Frank David, Jr. 1959- *WhoSSW 91*
Teets, John Phillip 1948- *ConAu 132*
Teets, John W. 1933- *St&PR 91*
Teets, Joyce Marie 1952- *WhoSSW 91*
Teets, Linda Barrett *BioIn 16*
Teetzen, Merle Lee 1947- *WhoEmL 91*
Teevan, Richard Collier 1919- *WhoAm 90*
Tefet, Charles Eugene 1874- *WhoAmA 91N*
Tefferteller, Ruth S. *BioIn 16*
Tefft, Elden Cecil 1919- *WhoAmA 91*
Tefft, Melvin 1932- *WhoAm 90*
Teft, Elizabeth 1723- *FemiCLE*
Tegarden, LoRetta Tudor 1940- *WhoSSW 91*
Tegeler, Dorothy 1950- *WhoWrEP 89*
Tegerdine, Maria *ConAu 132*
Tegeris, Andrew Stanley 1929- *WhoAm 90*
Teggin, Margaret Louise 1946- *IntWWM 90*
Tegholm, Karl Bo Allan 1926- *WhoWor 91*
Teghtmeyer, Edward Lee 1943- *St&PR 91*
Tegmeyer, Marlene M. 1932- *St&PR 91*
Tegner, Bruce 1928-1985 *SmATA 62 [port]*
Tegner, Esaias 1782-1846 *DcScanL*
Tegtmeier, Patricia Mae Read 1937- *WhoWrEP 89*
Tegtmeier, Richard Lewis 1946- *WhoEmL 91*
Tegtmeyer, Charles John 1939- *WhoSSW 91, WhoWor 91*
Tehan, Arline Boucher 1930- *ConAu 130*
Tehoragwanegen 1758?-1849 *WhNaAH*
Tehoragwarregen 1758?-1849 *WhNaAH*
Tehrani, Abolghasem 1941- *BiDrAPA 89*
Tehrani, Hossein Ebadi *BiDrAPA 89*
Tehrani, Julliette S. 1946- *St&PR 91*
Tei, Takuri 1924- *WhoWor 91*
Teich, Albert Harris 1942- *WhoE 91*
Teich, Daniel B. 1947- *St&PR 91*
Teich, Erwin Richard 1923- *St&PR 91*
Teich, Irwin 1937- *St&PR 91*
Teich, Jeffrey C 1945- *BiDrAPA 89*
Teich, Malvin Carl 1939- *WhoAm 90*
Teich, Mark Andrew 1951- *WhoE 91*
Teich, Richard E. 1942- *St&PR 91*
Teich, Robert Scott 1939- *WhoSSW 91*
Teich, Stephen S 1941- *BiDrAPA 89*
Teich, Theresa Marie 1948- *WhoAmW 91*
Teicher, Arthur Mace 1946- *WhoE 91*
Teicher, Joseph D 1912- *BiDrAPA 89*
Teicher, Marcia Harriet 1947- *WhoWor 91*
Teicher, Mark L. 1956- *WhoEmL 91*
Teicher, Martin 1945- *WhoEmL 91*
Teicher, Martin Hersch 1951- *BiDrAPA 89, WhoE 91*
Teicher, Morton Irving 1920- *WhoAm 90*
Teichert, Curt 1905- *WhoAm 90*
Teichert, Minerva Kohlhepp 1889-1976 *BioIn 16*
Teichgraeber, Richard Koenig 1928- *St&PR 91*
Teichler, Ulrich Christian 1942- *WhoWor 91*
Teichman, Carl F. 1956- *St&PR 91*
Teichman, David *BioIn 16*
Teichman, Evelyn 1929- *WhoAmW 91*
Teichman, Jeb Stuart 1953- *WhoSSW 91*
Teichman, Mary Melinda 1954- *WhoAmA 91*
Teichman, Sabina *WhoAmA 91N*
Teichmuller, Paul Julius Oswald 1913-1943? *DcScB S2*
Teichner, Lester 1944- *WhoAm 90*
Teichroew, Daniel 1925- *WhoAm 90*
Teig, Gerald Carlyle 1947- *St&PR 91*
Teig, Marlowe G. 1938- *St&PR 91*
Teiger, David 1929- *WhoAm 90*
Teikari, Veikko Olavi 1943- *WhoWor 91*
Teil, Kurt Henry 1923- *WhoWor 91*
Teilhard de Chardin, Pierre *BioIn 16*
Teilhard De Chardin, Pierre 1881-1955 *WorAlBi, WrPh P*
Teilhet, Hildegarde Tolman 1906- *WhoWor 91*
Teilhet-Fisk, Jehanne Hildegarde 1939- *WhoAmA 91*
Teillac, Jean 1920- *WhoWor 91*
Teiman, James Edward 1947- *St&PR 91*
Teisler, David 1953- *WhoE 91*
Teisler, David A. 1953- *WhoWrEP 89*
Teismann, Kevin P. 1945- *St&PR 91*
Teison, Herbert J. 1927- *WhoWrEP 89*
Teison, Herbert Jerome 1927- *WhoE 91*
Teissier, Georges 1900-1972 *DcScB S2*
Teitcher, Norman Gideon 1944- *WhoE 91*
Teitel, Bernard A 1921- *BiDrAPA 89*
Teitel, Jeffrey Hale 1943- *WhoE 91*
Teitel, Simon 1928- *WhoE 91*
Teitelbaum, Alan Michael *BiDrAPA 89*
Teitelbaum, David *BioIn 16, NewYTBS 90*
Teitelbaum, David 1906- *WhoAm 90*
Teitelbaum, David Richard 1964- *WhoSSW 91*
Teitelbaum, Harry Allen *BiDrAPA 89*
Teitelbaum, Hubert 1915- *WhoAm 90*
Teitelbaum, Louis K 1958- *BiDrAPA 89*
Teitelbaum, Mark Lewis 1941- *BiDrAPA 89*
Teitelbaum, Michael 1953- *BioIn 16*
Teitelbaum, Michael Stewart 1944- *WhoE 91*
Teitelbaum, Myron Morton 1936- *BiDrAPA 89*
Teitelbaum, Naftali 1934- *St&PR 91*
Teitelbaum, Paula Irene *BiDrAPA 89*
Teitelbaum, Philip 1928- *WhoAm 90*
Teitelbaum, Richard Lowe 1939- *IntWWM 90*
Teitelbaum, Seymour 1927- *WhoE 91*
Teitelbaum, Steven Lazarus 1938- *WhoAm 90*
Teitell, Conrad Laurence 1932- *WhoAm 90*
Teitelman, Edward A 1937- *BiDrAPA 89*
Teitelman, Michael Louis *BiDrAPA 89*
Teitgen, John R. 1945- *WhoAm 90*
Teitgen, Pierre-Henri 1908- *BiDFrPL*
Teitsworth, Robert Allan *St&PR 91*
Teitz, Michael B. 1935- *WhoAm 90*
Teiwes, William Manfred 1941- *St&PR 91*
Teixeira, Cathy Ann 1956- *WhoAmW 91, WhoE 91*
Teixeira, Fernando Manuel Da Silva 1948- *WhoWor 91*
Teixeira, MaryAnn C. 1948- *WhoAmW 91*
Teja, Jagdish S 1937- *BiDrAPA 89*
Tejada, Sebastian Lerdo de 1823-1889 *BioIn 16*
Tejada, Victor Manuel *BiDrAPA 89*
Tejada-Flores, Lito *BioIn 16*
Tejeda, Frank M. 1945- *WhoHisp 91*
Tejeda, Hector M *BiDrAPA 89*
Tejeda, Rennie *WhoHisp 91*
Tejera, Carlos Alberto *BiDrAPA 89*
Tejera Paris, Enrique 1919- *WhoWor 91*
Tejidor, Roberto A. 1942- *WhoHisp 91*
Tejima, Keizaburo *AuBYP 90*
Tek, Arthur D. 1949- *St&PR 91*
Tekakwitha, Catherine 1656-1680 *EncCRAm*
Tekakwitha, Kateri 1656-1680 *BioAmW, WhNaAH*
Te Kanawa, Kiri 1944- *IntWWM 90, PenDiMP, WhoAm 90, WhoWor 91, WorAlBi*
Tekben, Erdogan *BiDrAPA 89*
Tekelioglu, Meral 1936- *WhoWor 91*
Tekell, Janet L *BiDrAPA 89*
Tekere, Edgar *BioIn 16*
Te Kolste, Dale 1920- *St&PR 91, WhoAm 90*
Tekulve, Kent 1947- *Ballpl 90*
Tel Aviv Quartet *PenDiMP*
Te Laake, Heinz 1925- *BioIn 16*
Telaranta, Teuvo Antero 1949- *WhoWor 91*
Telban, Sharon Grace 1944- *WhoAmW 91*
Telberg, Val 1910- *WhoAmA 91*
Teleki, Jane King 1943- *WhoSSW 91*
Telemann, Georg Philipp 1681-1767 *WorAlBi*
Telepchak, M.J. 1947- *St&PR 91*
Teles de Oliveira, Geraldo 1913- *ArtLatA*
Telesca, Francis Eugene 1921- *WhoAm 90*
Telesca, Michael Anthony 1929- *WhoE 91*
Telesca, Thomas Louis 1936- *St&PR 91*
Telesetsky, Walter 1938- *WhoE 91, WhoWor 91*
Telesha, Meredith Carol 1948- *WhoAmW 91*
Telesilla *EncCoWW*
Telesmanic, Anthony Stephen 1952- *WhoSSW 91*
Teletzke, Gary Francis 1956- *WhoSSW 91*
Telew, Nicholas W *BiDrAPA 89*
Telfair, Richard *TwCCr&M 91*
Telfer, James Stuart 1932- *WhoAm 90*
Telford, Ira Rockwood 1907- *WhoAm 90*
Telford, Robert Lee *St&PR 91N*
TeLinde, Richard Wesley 1894-1989 *BioIn 16*
Telingator, Richard H 1927- *BiDrAPA 89*
Telionis, Demetri Pyrros 1941- *WhoSSW 91*
Telitz, Gary Lee 1947- *St&PR 91*
Telkamp, Wilhelmus Anthonius 1927- *WhoWor 91*
Tell, A. Charles 1937- *WhoAm 90*
Tell, Ronald J. 1934- *St&PR 91, WhoAm 90*
Tell, William Kirn, Jr. 1934- *St&PR 91, WhoAm 90*
Telle, Jim *ODwPR 91*
Telleen, John Martin 1922- *WhoAm 90*
Tellefsen, Arve *IntWWM 90*
Tellefsen, Christiane *BiDrAPA 89*
Tellefsen, Gerald 1938- *WhoE 91*
Tellem, Susan Mary 1945- *WhoAm 90, WhoAmW 91, WhoEmL 91*
Tellep, Daniel Michael 1931- *BioIn 16, St&PR 91, WhoAm 90*
Teller *BioIn 16*
Teller, Aaron Joseph 1921- *WhoAm 90*
Teller, Al *BioIn 16*
Teller, Alvin Norman 1944- *WhoAm 90*
Teller, Andrew Szanto 1938- *WhoE 91*
Teller, Barbara Gorely 1920- *WhoAmW 91, WhoE 91*
Teller, Benjamin E *BiDrAPA 89*
Teller, David Norton 1936- *WhoAm 90*
Teller, Davida Young 1938- *WhoAmW 91*
Teller, Dean G. 1932- *St&PR 91*
Teller, Donna Elaine 1959- *WhoSSW 91*
Teller, Douglas H 1933- *WhoAmA 91*
Teller, Edward 1908- *BioIn 16, ConAu 33NR, MajTwCW, WhoAm 90, WorAlBi*
Teller, Gayl Florene 1946- *WhoWrEP 89*
Teller, Griffith H. *BioIn 16*
Teller, Henry Moore 1830-1914 *BiDrUSE 89, BioIn 16*
Teller, Jane *WhoAmA 91*
Teller, Judith L. 1949- *WhoAmW 91*
Teller, Mary Margaret 1945- *WhoAmW 91*
Telleria, Anthony F. 1938- *WhoWor 91*
Tellers, John Gregory 1947- *BiDrAPA 89*
Telles, Lygia Fagundes 1923- *BioIn 16*
Telles, Raymond L. 1915- *BioIn 16*
Tellesbo, Marsha Louise 1948- *WhoAmW 91*
Tellez, Gorki C. *WhoHisp 91*
Tellez, Isabelle Ogaz 1924- *WhoHisp 91*
Tellez, Theresa Pino 1929- *WhoAm 90*
Tellian, Frank Frederick 1955- *BiDrAPA 89*
Tellier, Diane Angela 1953- *WhoAmW 91, WhoE 91*
Tellier, Genevieve 1956- *BiDrAPA 89*
Tellier, Henri 1918- *WhoAm 90*
Tellier, Paul M. 1939- *WhoWor 91*
Tellier, Richard Dale 1933- *WhoE 91*
Tellier, Richard Davis 1942- *WhoAm 90*
Telling, Edward Riggs 1919- *St&PR 91, WhoAm 90*
Tellis, Richard 1930- *ODwPR 91*
Tellman, Robert C. 1935- *St&PR 91*
Tellman, Tom 1954- *Ballpl 90*
Tello, Donna 1955- *WhoAmW 91*
Tellor, M.D. 1951- *St&PR 91*
Tellson, J. Richard 1923- *St&PR 91*
Telma, Robert Joseph 1946- *St&PR 91*
Telmanyi, Emil 1892-1988 *PenDiMP*
Telmer, Frederick H. 1937- *St&PR 91*
Telmosse, Robert Dennis 1941- *WhoAm 90*
Telnack, John J. *BioIn 16*
Telot, Gabriel J 1928- *BiDrAPA 89*
Telser, Lester Greenspan 1931- *WhoAm 90, WhoWrEP 89*
Telshaw, H.L., Jr. 1925- *St&PR 91*
Telson, Bob *BioIn 16*
Telson, Howard Warren 1955- *BiDrAPA 89*
Teltsch, Kathleen *AuBYP 90*
Teltscher, Henry Otto *WhoE 91*
Telzrow, Dennis Lee 1945- *WhoSSW 91*
Tema-Lyn, Laurie 1951- *WhoAmW 91*
Tembreull, Michael A. *BioIn 16*
Tembreull, Mike *St&PR 91*
Temby, Fred C. *St&PR 91*
Temby, William D 1925- *BiDrAPA 89*
Temeles, Lawrence *BiDrAPA 89*
Temeles, Margaret S *BiDrAPA 89*
Temelkoff, Vonda Lee 1937- *WhoAmW 91*
Temeraire, Charles 1433-1477 *EncO&P 3*

Temerlin, Liener 1928- St&PR 91, WhoAm 90
Temerson, Leon 1904-1988 BioIn 16
Temes, Gabor Charles 1929- WhoAm 90
Temes, Mort 1928- WhoAmA 91
Temes, Mortimer Robert 1928- WhoE 91
Temesvari, Andrea BioIn 16
Temianka, Henri 1906- PenDiMP, WhoAm 90
Temin, Davia B. ODwPR 91
Temin, Howard M. 1934- WorAlBi
Temin, Howard Martin 1934- WhoAm 90, WhoWor 91
Temin, Michael Lehman 1933- WhoAm 90
Temin, Peter 1937- WhoAm 90, WhoE 91
Temirkanov, Yuri 1938- IntWWM 90, PenDiMP
Temirkanov, Yuri Khatuevich 1938- WhoWor 91
Temkin, Mairlyn Lisa 1954- WhoAmW 91
Temkin, Mira Hymen 1951- WhoEmL 91
Temkin, Penelope Catherine 1947- WhoAmW 91
Temkin, Robert Harvey 1943- WhoAm 90, WhoE 91
Temkin, Sara Anne Schlossberg 1913- AuBYP 90
Temkin, Steven Mark 1957- St&PR 91
Temko, Allan Bernard 1924- WhoAm 90
Temko, Florence AuBYP 90
Temko, Stanley Leonard 1920- WhoAm 90
Temling, W. Peter 1947- WhoSSW 91
Temmen, Robert P. 1925- St&PR 91
Temmerman, John Francis 1955- WhoEmL 91
Tempel, Jean C. WhoAmW 91
Tempel, Paul F BiDrAPA 89
Tempelis, Constantine Harry 1927- WhoAm 90
Temperance Seven OxCPMus
Tempereau, Clinton E 1924- BiDrAPA 89
Temperley, Harold William Vazeille 1879-1939 BioIn 16
Temperley, Nicholas 1932- IntWWM 90
Temperly, Deborah Snella 1954- WhoEmL 91
Tempero, Kenneth Floyd 1939- St&PR 91, WhoAm 90
Tempest, Gerard Francis 1918- WhoAmA 91
Tempest, Joey BioIn 16
Tempest, Marie 1864-1942 OxCPMus
Tempest, Theresa AuBYP 90
Tempey, Fred W., Jr. BiDrAPA 89
Templar, George 1904-1988 BioIn 16
Templar Smith, Joan 1927- IntWWM 90
Temple, Anne 1709?-1777 FemiCLE
Temple, Arthur 1920- WhoAm 90, WhoSSW 91
Temple, Arthur, Jr. 1920- St&PR 91
Temple, Barry James 1946- WhoAm 90
Temple, Charles St&PR 91
Temple, Danny Ray 1952- WhoSSW 91
Temple, David John 1945- WhoWor 91
Temple, Donald 1933- WhoAm 90
Temple, Donald Edward 1946- WhoE 91
Temple, Dorothy Osborne 1627-1694 BioIn 16
Temple, George 1801? AmLegL
Temple, Johnny 1928- Ballpl 90
Temple, Joseph G., Jr. 1929- St&PR 91
Temple, Joseph George, Jr. 1929- WhoAm 90
Temple, Julien BioIn 16
Temple, Laura Sophia 1763-1820? FemiCLE
Temple, Paul NewAgMG, TwCCr&M 91
Temple, Paul N., Jr. 1923- St&PR 91
Temple, Paul Nathaniel 1923- WhoWor 91
Temple, Penelope Denver WhoWrEP 89
Temple, Phillip Aaron 1940- WhoAm 90
Temple, Richard 1847-1912 OxCPMus
Temple, Robert 1941- WhoAm 90
Temple, Robert Jay 1942- BiDrAPA 89
Temple, Robert Kyle Grenville 1945- WhoWor 91
Temple, Robert Michael 1952- WhoSSW 91
Temple, Robert Winfield 1934- WhoSSW 91, WhoWor 91
Temple, Shirley 1928- BioAmW, BioIn 16, OxCPMus, WorAlBi
Temple, Stephen David 1954- St&PR 91
Temple, Wayne Calhoun 1924- WhoAm 90
Temple, Wick 1937- WhoAm 90
Temple, William 1628-1699 BioIn 16, DcLB 101 [port]
Temple, William Norman 1932- St&PR 91
Temple Lang, John 1936- WhoWor 91
Temple-Troya, Jose Carlos 1947- WhoHisp 91
Templeman, Eleanor Lee 1906-1990 ConAu 131
Templeman, Kristine Hofgren 1947- WhoWrEP 89
Templeman, Wilfred 1908- WhoAm 90
Templer, Jeffrey Arnold 1947- St&PR 91
Templer, John Arthur 1928- WhoAm 90
Temples, Dent L., Jr. 1946- St&PR 91
Temples, Dent Larkin, Jr. 1946- WhoAm 90
Templeton, Alan Robert 1947- WhoEmL 91
Templeton, Alec 1909-1963 OxCPMus
Templeton, Arthur William St&PR 91N
Templeton, Benjamin D BiDrAPA 89
Templeton, Benjamin John 1936- WhoAm 90
Templeton, Bryce 1932- BiDrAPA 89
Templeton, Christina J BiDrAPA 89
Templeton, Cornelia Van Rensselaer King BioIn 16
Templeton, Darrel Lloyd 1943- St&PR 91
Templeton, Edith 1916- FemiCLE
Templeton, Fay 1865-1939 OxCPMus
Templeton, Fiona Anne 1951- WhoWrEP 89
Templeton, Floyd L BiDrAPA 89
Templeton, Garry 1956- Ballpl 90
Templeton, Hilda B BiDrAPA 89
Templeton, Ian Malcolm 1929- WhoAm 90
Templeton, J. Earl 1915- St&PR 91
Templeton, John 1912- BioIn 16
Templeton, John Marks 1912- WhoAm 90
Templeton, John Marks, Jr. 1940- St&PR 91
Templeton, Randall Keith 1957- WhoSSW 91
Templeton, Richard Allan 1922- St&PR 91
Templeton, Richard Kron 1948- BiDrAPA 89
Templeton, Robert Clark 1929- WhoAmA 91, WhoE 91
Templeton, Robert Earl 1931- WhoAm 90
Templier, Raymond PenDiDA 89
Templin, Howard Paul 1932- St&PR 91
Templin, Kenneth Elwood 1927- WhoAm 90
Templin, Mildred BioIn 16
Temptations, The EncPR&S 89, OxCPMus, WorAlBi
Temske, Arthur John, Jr. 1935- St&PR 91
Ten 1930- WhoAmA 91
Ten Bears 1792-1872 WhNaAH
Ten cc OxCPMus
Ten Years After EncPR&S 89
Tenace, Gene 1946- Ballpl 90
Tenaglia, John Franc 1935- WhoAm 90, WhoWor 91
Tenaglia, Nicholas C BiDrAPA 89
Tenaille, Jean 1882-1962 EncO&P 3
Tenaya WhNaAH
Tenayuca, Emma 1916- BioIn 16
TenBrink-Wyngarden, Helen Dorothea 1921- WhoAmW 91
Ten Broeke, Jan WhoAmA 91
Tenbrook, Don M. 1932- St&PR 91
Ten Cate, Arnold Richard 1933- WhoAm 90
Tenchavez, Paulino S 1936- BiDrAPA 89
Tencin, Madame de 1682-1749 EncCoWW
Tencza, Jack P. 1946- St&PR 91
Tencza, Patricia Ann 1962- WhoAmW 91
Tendero, Emmanuel M 1937- BiDrAPA 89
Tendler, David 1938- WhoAm 90
Tendler, Jacob BiDrAPA 89
Tendler, Jonathan M. 1946- St&PR 91
Tendler, Paul Marc 1943- WhoE 91, WhoWor 91
Tendler, Ruth BioIn 16
Tendoi 1834?-1907 WhNaAH
Tendoy 1834?-1907 WhNaAH
Tenducci, Giusto Ferdinando 1735?-1790 PenDiMP
Teneback, Anders Helmer 1946- St&PR 91
Tenenbaum, Arthur Sorrel 1942- BiDrAPA 89
Tenenbaum, Bernard Hirsh 1954- WhoE 91, WhoEmL 91
Tenenbaum, Harvey 1933- St&PR 91
Tenenbaum, Henry Lawrence 1946- WhoE 91
Tenenbaum, Jeffrey Mark 1945- WhoE 91
Tenenbaum, Louis 1922- WhoAm 90
Tenenbaum, Michael 1913- WhoAm 90
Tenenbaum, Mordechai 1916-1943 BioIn 16
Tenenblatt, Sarah Shtoffer 1920- BiDrAPA 89
Tener, Constance Trevor 1948- WhoE 91
Tener, John 1863-1946 Ballpl 90
Tener, Robert L. 1924- WhoWrEP 89
Tenerelli, L. Donald 1948- St&PR 91
Tenewitz, Maryrose Clark 1952- WhoAmW 91
Ten Eyck, Catryna 1931- WhoAmA 91
Ten Eyck, Charles Scott 1948- St&PR 91
Ten Eyck, Ernest Lauder 1944- WhoAm 90
Ten Eyck, Mary Elizabeth 1953- WhoAmW 91
Teng WomWR
Teng Hsiao-Ping 1904- WorAlBi
Teng, Hsiao-p'ing 1904- BioIn 16
Teng, Max Sioe-Hong 1933- BiDrAPA 89
Teng, Ssu-yu 1906-1988 BioIn 16
Tengbom, Anders 1911- WhoWor 91
Tengdin, Robert C. 1930- St&PR 91
Tenges, Robert Eugene 1942- St&PR 91
Tenges, Tom Alan 1949- WhoE 91
Tenggren, Gustav Adolf 1896-1970 WhoAmA 91N
Tengonciang, Hermes Camacho BiDrAPA 89
Tengroth, Mirra WhoAmA 91
Tenhaeff, W H C 1894-1981 EncO&P 3
Tenhaeff, Wilhelm Heinrich Carl 1894-1981 EncPaPR 91
Ten Hoopen, Carl A., Jr. 1927- St&PR 91
Ten Hoor, Foppe 1927- WhoWor 91
Ten Hove, Paul August 1932- WhoWor 91
Tenhundfeld, A.H., Jr. 1947- St&PR 91
Tenhundfeld, Lynda A BiDrAPA 89
Teniers, David 1610-1690 IntDcAA 90
Teninga, Walter Henry 1928- St&PR 91, WhoAm 90
Tenison, Robert B. 1924- St&PR 91
Tenkiller, Louis WhoWrEP 89
Tenkotte, Paul Allen 1960- WhoSSW 91
Tenn, William 1920- RGTwCSF
Tennant, Colin BioIn 16
Tennant, Donna Kay 1949- WhoAmA 91
Tennant, Dorothy 1855-1926 BiDWomA
Tennant, Emma 1937- BioIn 16, FemiCLE, WorAu 1980 [port]
Tennant, Geraldine B. 1922- WhoAmW 91
Tennant, James Browder 1954- WhoSSW 91
Tennant, John Randall 1940- WhoAm 90
Tennant, Kylie AuBYP 90, MajTwCW
Tennant, Kylie 1912-1988 AnObit 1988, BioIn 16, FemiCLE
Tennant, Mary Jo 1938- WhoAmW 91
Tennant, Neil BioIn 16
Tennant, Otto Addison 1918- WhoAm 90
Tennant, Samuel M. St&PR 91
Tennant, Samuel McKibben 1928- WhoAm 90
Tennant, Steven Craig 1959- WhoEmL 91
Tennant, Veronica 1946- BioIn 16
Tennant, Victoria BioIn 16
Tenne, Abraham Isaak 1947- WhoWor 91
Tennen, Leslie Irwin 1952- WhoWor 91
Tennenbaum, Michael Ernest 1935- St&PR 91, WhoAm 90
Tennent, Frank Dewey 1926- St&PR 91
Tennent, Gilbert 1703-1764 EncCRAm [port]
Tennent, Thomas Gavin 1937- BiDrAPA 89
Tennent, William 1673-1746 EncCRAm
Tenner, Eugene Arthur 1947- WhoEmL 91
Tennesen, Paul Robert 1937- WhoE 91
Tenneshaw, S. M. ConAu 130, MajTwCW
Tenneson, Joyce BioIn 16
Tennessen, Carol 1938- WhoAmW 91
Tenney, Charles Daniel 1857-1930 BioIn 16
Tenney, Charles H., II 1918- St&PR 91
Tenney, Charles Henry 1911- WhoAm 90
Tenney, Daniel Gleason, Jr. 1913- WhoAm 90
Tenney, Del 1930- BioIn 16
Tenney, Della Wooton 1930- WhoAmW 91
Tenney, Dudley Bradstreet 1918- WhoAm 90
Tenney, Frank Putnam 1937- WhoE 91
Tenney, Fred 1859-1952 Ballpl 90 [port]
Tenney, Irene 1941- WhoHisp 91
Tenney, Mark William 1936- WhoWor 91
Tenney, Paul Anthony 1928- WhoAm 90
Tenney, Stephen Marsh 1922- WhoAm 90
Tenney, Tabitha 1763-1837 FemiCLE
Tenney, Tom Fred 1933- WhoSSW 91
Tenney, William Frank 1946- WhoEmL 91, WhoWor 91
Tennfjord, Oddbjorn 1941- IntWWM 90
Tenniel, John 1820-1914 BioIn 16
Tennill, William Robert 1927- St&PR 91
Tennille, Toni 1943- WorAlBi
Tennis, Calvin Cabell WhoAm 90
Tennis, Douglas D. 1947- St&PR 91
Tennis, Jane Suzanne 1948- WhoAmW 91
Tennison, Clifton Raymond, Jr. 1949- BiDrAPA 89
Tennison, Deborah C. 1950- ODwPR 91
Tennstedt, Dominique 1950- WhoWor 91
Tennstedt, Klaus 1926- IntWWM 90, PenDiMP, WhoAm 90, WhoWor 91
Tenny, Francis Briggs 1920- WhoAm 90
Tennyson, Alfred 1809-1892 AuBYP 90, BioIn 16, EncPaPR 91, NinCLC 30 [port], WorAlBi
Tennyson, Brian 1928-1988 BioIn 16
Tennyson, Edward 1814-1890 BioIn 16
Tenofsky-Ealy, Deanna V. 1956- WhoAmW 91
Tenold, Robert Gordon 1942- St&PR 91
Tenopyr, Mary Louise Welsh 1929- WhoAmW 91, WhoE 91, WhoWor 91
Tenore, Marilynn Joyce 1948- WhoAmW 91
Tenorio, Pedro Pangelinan 1934- WhoWor 91
Tenorth, Heinz-Elmar 1944- WhoWor 91
Tenover, Fred Carron 1954- WhoEmL 91
Tenpas, Kathleen Mason 1952- WhoWrEP 89
Tenpas, Kevin S. 1957- St&PR 91
Tenreiro, Alfred 1935- St&PR 91
Tenscher, Alan Clement 1955- St&PR 91
Tensen, Ruth Marjorie AuBYP 90
Tenskwatawa 1778?-1837 WhNaAH
Tenskwautawaw 1778?-1837 WhNaAH
Tentler, Robert Edward 1935- St&PR 91
Tentoni, Stuart Charles 1949- WhoEmL 91
Tentser, Evelina BiDrAPA 89
Tenuta, Jean Louise 1958- WhoAmW 91, WhoWrEP 89
Tenuta, Judy BioIn 16
Tenuta, Luigia 1954- WhoEmL 91, WhoWor 91
Tenzel, Richard Ruvin 1929- WhoAm 90
Tenzer, Benjamin Ellis BioIn 16
Tenzer, Joel 1924- St&PR 91
Tenzer, Jonathan A 1940- WhoAmA 91
Tenzer, Jonathan A, Mrs WhoAmA 91
Tenzer, Michael L. 1930- St&PR 91, WhoWor 91
Tenzing Norgay 1914-1986 BioIn 16
Teo Eng Seng BioIn 16
Teo, Kian Seng 1952- IntWWM 90
Teo, Kim-See 1948- WhoWor 91
Teodoru, Constantin Valeriu 1915- WhoE 91, WhoWor 91
Teodosiu, Nicholas Ioan 1940- WhoE 91
Teoh, George Min-Loke 1941- WhoSSW 91
Teoli, Emery William 1934- WhoE 91
Teonge, Henry 1621-1690 BioIn 16
Te Pas, Theodore E 1929- BiDrAPA 89
TePaske, John Jay 1929- WhoSSW 91
Tepedino, Frank 1947- Ballpl 90
Tephly, Thomas Robert 1936- WhoAm 90
Tepley, Norman 1935- WhoAm 90
Teplick, Ellen 1949- WhoWrEP 89
Teplick, Joseph George 1911- WhoE 91
Teplin, Daniel BiDrAPA 89
Teplin, Ervin 1923- BiDrAPA 89
Teplitz, Saul I. 1921- BioIn 16
Teplitz, Terry Alan 1949- BiDrAPA 89
Teplitz, Zelda BiDrAPA 89
Teplova, Nadezhda 1814-1848 EncCoWW
Teplow, Theodore H. 1928- St&PR 91
Teplow, Theodore Herzl 1928- WhoAm 90
Teply, Karleen Ingrid 1944- WhoE 91
TePoel, Donna Lee Fuller 1942- WhoAmW 91
Tepper, Albert 1921- IntWWM 90
Tepper, Donald Edward 1951- ODwPR 91
Tepper, Eric Alan 1957- WhoEmL 91
Tepper, Frederick 1934- St&PR 91
Tepper, Harold Max 1930- St&PR 91
Tepper, Lisa Dickson 1960- WhoAmW 91
Tepper, Lynn Marsha 1946- WhoE 91
Tepper, Nancy Boxley 1933- WhoAmW 91
Tepper, Natalie Arras 1895-1950 WhoAmA 91N
Tepper, Neal Gary 1951- WhoWor 91
Tepperman, Lynda BioIn 16
Teppo EncCoWW
Terada, Kazuo 1928-1987 BioIn 16
Teranchi, Erik Iraj 1945- St&PR 91
Terao, Toshio 1930- WhoWor 91
Teraoka, Masami 1936- BioIn 16, WhoAmA 91
Ter-Arutunian, Rouben 1920- ConDes 90
Terasawa, Kuniko BioIn 16
Teraskiewicz, Edward Arnold 1946- WhoE 91
Terasmae, Jaan 1926- WhoAm 90
Terauds, Vita Anda 1962- WhoSSW 91
Terban, Marvin AuBYP 90, BioIn 16
Ter Beek, Aurelus Louis 1944- WhoWor 91
Terbell, Joseph B. 1906-1988 BioIn 16
Terbell, Thomas Green, Jr. 1938- WhoWor 91
Ter Borch, Gerard 1617-1681 IntDcAA 90
Terborch, Gerard 1617-1681 WorAlBi
Terborg-Penn, Rosalyn Marian 1941- WhoAmW 91
Terborgh, Bert 1945- WhoAm 90
Terbrugghen, Hendrick 1588-1629 IntDcAA 90
Terc, Alexander WhoHisp 91
Terc, Miguel Angel, Jr. 1968- WhoHisp 91
Terc, Sigrid Roslyn 1962- WhoHisp 91
Terchi, Bartolommeo 1691-1753? PenDiDA 89
Terdiman, Allen M 1933- BiDrAPA 89
Terebilov, Vladimir Ivanovich 1916- WhoWor 91
Terek, A. EncCoWW
Terekh, Kondrat Zigmundovich 1935- WhoWor 91
Terekhov, Miguel R. 1928- WhoSSW 91
Terence 195?BC-159?BC WorAlBi
Terenzio, Joseph Vincent 1918- WhoAm 90
Terenzio, Peter Bernard 1916- WhoAm 90
Teresa Cepeda y Ahumada 1515-1582 EncPaPR 91

Teresa, Mother 1910- *BioIn 16, WhoWor 91, WorAlBi*
Teresa, of Avila 1515-1582 *BioIn 16*
Teresa of Avila, Saint 1515-1582 *EncPaPR 91, WorAlBi*
Teresa of Castile *WomWR*
Teresa, Vincent *BioIn 16, NewYTBS 90*
Tereshkova, Valentina *BioIn 16*
Tereshkova, Valentina 1937- *WorAlBi*
Teresi, Joseph 1941- *WhoAm 90, WhoWor 91*
Teret, Stephen Paul 1945- *WhoEmL 91*
Terey-Smith, Mary *IntWWM 90*
Terfera, Raymond Anthony 1929- *St&PR 91, WhoAm 90*
Terfloth, Klaus 1929- *WhoWor 91*
Terfruchte, James J. 1957- *BiDrAPA 89*
Terhaar, Ann *WhoAmW 91*
ter Haar, Otto 1929- *WhoAm 90*
Ter Heege Mim, Willemieke Lydia 1957- *WhoWor 91*
Terhes, Joyce Lyons 1940- *WhoE 91*
terHorst, Jerald Franklin 1922- *WhoAm 90*
Terhorst, Paul *BioIn 16*
Terhorst, Paul Byrne 1914- *WhoAm 90*
Terhune, Albert Payson 1872-1942 *AuBYP 90, WorAlBi*
Terhune, Stanley Banks 1925- *St&PR 91*
Terk, Jeffrey Elliot 1941- *St&PR 91*
Terkel, Lawrence Arthur 1947- *St&PR 91*
Terkel, Louis 1912- *BioIn 16, MajTwCW*
Terkel, Studs *MajTwCW*
Terkel, Studs 1912- *BioIn 16, WhoAm 90, WorAlBi*
Terkel, Studs Louis 1912- *WhoWrEP 89*
Terkel, Susan Neiburg 1948- *BioIn 16*
Terkelsen, Kenneth G *BiDrAPA 89*
Terken, John 1912- *WhoAmA 91*
Terkhorn, Henry K. 1930- *WhoAm 90*
Terkhorn, Robert Eugene 1936- *St&PR 91*
Terkla, David Gabriel 1953- *WhoE 91*
Terkla, Louis Gabriel 1925- *WhoAm 90*
Terlecki, Tymon Tadeusz J 1905- *ConAu 132*
Terlini, Marcello 1937- *WhoWor 91*
Terlizzi, Daniel Edward, Jr. 1951- *WhoE 91*
Terlizzi, Garth J. 1949- *St&PR 91*
Terman, David M 1935- *BiDrAPA 89*
Terman, Lewis Madison 1877-1956 *BioIn 16*
Terman, Lewis Madison 1935- *WhoAm 90*
Terman, Stanley A *BiDrAPA 89*
Termeer, Henri Adrianus 1946- *St&PR 91*
Termeer, Louis Petrus 1951- *WhoWor 91*
Termes 1941- *WhoAmA 91*
Termini, Christine 1947- *WhoAmA 91*
Termini, Deanne Lanoix 1943- *WhoWor 91*
Termini, Olga Ascher 1930- *IntWWM 90*
Termini, Roseann Bridget 1953- *WhoEmL 91*
Ternberg, Jessie Lamoin 1924- *WhoAm 90, WhoAmW 91*
Ternbo, Gosta Verner Ingemar 1927- *WhoWor 91*
Ternent, Billy 1899-1977 *OxCPMus*
Terner, Felix *BiDrAPA 89*
Ternes, Alan Paul 1931- *WhoAm 90*
Ternina, Milka 1863-1941 *PenDiMP*
Ternullo, Karen Marie 1965- *WhoAmW 91*
Teroerde, Friedrich 1944- *St&PR 91*
Te Ronde, Allan William 1941- *St&PR 91*
Ter-Ovanesyan, Igor *BioIn 16*
Terpak, John B. 1912- *St&PR 91*
Terpeluk, Diane Guglielmino 1957- *WhoAmW 91*
Terpening, Virginia Ann 1917- *WhoAmW 91, WhoWor 91*
Terpning, Howard 1927- *BioIn 16*
Terr, Lenore C 1936- *BiDrAPA 89*
Terra, Daniel J. 1911- *St&PR 91, WhoAmA 91*
Terra, Daniel James 1911- *WhoAm 90*
Terra, Gabriel 1873-1942 *BioIn 16*
Terracciano, Anthony Patrick 1938- *WhoE 91*
Terracciano, Dominic Peter 1935- *WhoE 91*
Terracina, Laura 1519-1577 *EncCoWW*
Terracina, Roy David 1946- *WhoAm 90, WhoEmL 91*
Terragno, Paul James 1938- *WhoAm 90, WhoSSW 91*
Terraine, John Alfred 1921- *WhoWor 91*
Terral, Thomas Forrest 1942- *St&PR 91*
Terral, Thomas Jefferson 1884-1946 *BioIn 16*
Terrana, Judith Anne Hahn 1942- *WhoAmW 91*
Terranova, Paul 1919- *St&PR 91*
Terranova, Terese-Marie Christine 1958- *WhoAmW 91*
Terras, Audrey Anne 1942- *WhoAmW 91*
Terras, Victor 1921- *WhoAm 90*
Terrazano, Maureen Cathy *BiDrAPA 89*
Terrazas, Eduardo 1936- *ConDes 90*
Terrazas de la Pena, Eduardo 1936- *ConDes 90*
Terrazzano, Jeann Russo 1945- *WhoE 91*
Terrebonne, Annie Marie 1932- *WhoAmW 91, WhoSSW 91, WhoWor 91*
Terrebonne, Ray Antoine 1945- *WhoSSW 91*
Terrel, Ronald Lee 1936- *WhoAm 90*
Terrell, Antoinette Yvonne 1963- *WhoAmW 91*
Terrell, Charles Leroy 1941- *St&PR 91*
Terrell, Charles William 1927- *WhoAm 90*
Terrell, Clark D. *BiDrAPA 89*
Terrell, Edgar A., Jr. 1920- *St&PR 91*
Terrell, Edgar Allen, Jr. 1920- *WhoSSW 91*
Terrell, Edwin Holland 1848-1910 *BioIn 16*
Terrell, Howard Bruce *BiDrAPA 89*
Terrell, Howard Bruce 1952- *WhoEmL 91, WhoWor 91*
Terrell, James *BioIn 16*
Terrell, James 1923- *WhoAm 90*
Terrell, James Franklin, Jr. 1920- *St&PR 91*
Terrell, Jerry 1946- *Ballpl 90*
Terrell, John Canada *DrBlPA 90*
Terrell, John Upton 1900- *AuBYP 90*
Terrell, John Upton 1900-1988 *BioIn 16, SmATA 60*
Terrell, Leonetta Eloise 1956- *WhoSSW 91*
Terrell, Mary Church 1863-1954 *WorAlBi*
Terrell, Mary Eliza Church 1863-1954 *HarlReB [port]*
Terrell, Norman Edwards 1933- *WhoAm 90*
Terrell, Randolph Querbes 1951- *St&PR 91*
Terrell, Tammi 1946-1970 *DrBlPA 90*
Terrell, Timothy Prater 1949- *WhoEmL 91*
Terrell, Todd Allan 1960- *WhoSSW 91*
Terrell, W. Glenn 1920- *WhoAm 90*
Terrell, Walt 1958- *Ballpl 90*
Terrell, William Pace 1937- *St&PR 91*
Terrence, Christopher F *BiDrAPA 89*
Terrenzi, John Thomas 1946- *St&PR 91*
Terreri, Malinda Ann 1964- *WhoAmW 91*
Terres, Edward A. *BioIn 16*
Terretta, Paul 1916- *St&PR 91*
Terribile, Deborah Anne 1959- *WhoSSW 91*
Terrill, Clair Elman 1910- *WhoAm 90, WhoE 91*
Terrill, Daryl Thomas 1939- *WhoSSW 91*
Terrill, Delbert Ray, Jr. 1947- *WhoE 91*
Terrill, Edward Berkshire, Jr. 1912- *St&PR 91*
Terrill, James E. 1944- *WhoAm 90*
Terrill, Richard Dean 1954- *St&PR 91*
Terrill, Robert Carl 1927- *WhoAm 90*
Terrill, Ross Gladwin *WhoAm 90, WhoWrEP 89*
Terris, Albert 1916- *WhoAmA 91*
Terris, Lillian Dick 1914- *WhoAmW 91*
Terris, Milton 1915- *WhoAm 90*
Terris, Norma *BioIn 16*
Terris, Norma 1904-1989 *AnObit 1989*
Terris, Susan 1937- *WhoWrEP 89*
Terris, Virginia Rinaldy 1917- *WhoWrEP 89*
Terris, William 1937- *St&PR 91*
Terriss, Ellaline 1871-1971 *OxCPMus*
Terroir, Patrick 1948- *WhoWor 91*
Terrone, Maria 1951- *WhoAmW 91*
Terroni, Raphael 1945- *IntWWM 90*
Terry, Adonis 1864-1915 *Ballpl 90*
Terry, Alfred Howe 1827-1890 *WhNaAH*
Terry, Bill 1896-1989 *Ballpl 90 [port]*
Terry, Bill 1898-1989 *AnObit 1989, BioIn 16*
Terry, Billy Eugene 1939- *WhoSSW 91*
Terry, Bobbye Rucker 1953- *WhoWrEP 89*
Terry, Carol Dee 1955- *WhoEmL 91*
Terry, Charles P. 1935- *St&PR 91*
Terry, Clark *BioIn 16*
Terry, Clark 1920- *OxCPMus, WhoAm 90*
Terry, Clifford Lewis 1937- *WhoAm 90*
Terry, Dian L. 1946- *ODwPR 91*
Terry, Dixon *BioIn 16*
Terry, Duncan Niles 1901-1989 *BioIn 16*
Terry, Duncan Niles 1909-1989 *WhoAmA 91N*
Terry, Elizabeth Ann *BiDrAPA 89*
Terry, Ellen 1847-1928 *WorAlBi*
Terry, Ellen 1848-1928 *BioIn 16*
Terry, Eugene 1934- *St&PR 91*
Terry, Fernando Belaunde 1912- *BioIn 16*
Terry, Frank Reilly 1928- *St&PR 91*
Terry, Frederick Arthur, Jr. 1932- *WhoAm 90*
Terry, Gary A. 1935- *WhoAm 90*
Terry, Georgena *BioIn 16*
Terry, Hilda 1914- *WhoAmA 91*
Terry, Howard L. *WhoAm 90*
Terry, James Joseph, Jr. 1952- *WhoEmL 91*
Terry, James M. 1931- *St&PR 91*
Terry, Jane Brower *BiDrAPA 89*
Terry, Janet Nicholson 1959- *WhoSSW 91*
Terry, Jay Dean 1931- *WhoSSW 91*
Terry, John Alfred 1933- *WhoAm 90, WhoE 91*
Terry, John Hart 1924- *WhoAm 90*
Terry, John Joseph 1937- *WhoAm 90*
Terry, John Timothy 1933- *WhoAm 90*
Terry, Kay Adell 1939- *WhoAmW 91*
Terry, Kibrel S. 1938- *St&PR 91*
Terry, LaDene C 1934- *BiDrAPA 89*
Terry, Laurie N. *ODwPR 91*
Terry, Leon Cass 1940- *WhoAm 90*
Terry, Louisa Ward *BioAmW*
Terry, Lucy 1730?-1821 *FemiCLE*
Terry, Margaret *ConAu 31NR*
Terry, Marshall Northway, Jr. 1931- *WhoAm 90*
Terry, Mary Sue 1947- *WhoAmW 91, WhoSSW 91*
Terry, Megan 1932- *BioIn 16, FemiCLE, NotWoAT, WhoAm 90*
Terry, Michael Durham 1946- *St&PR 91*
Terry, Michael Joseph 1957- *WhoEmL 91*
Terry, Michael Patrick 1940- *St&PR 91*
Terry, Nancy A. 1940- *WhoSSW 91*
Terry, Nicole 1934- *St&PR 91*
Terry, Nigel 1945- *ConTFT 8*
Terry, Peter 1926- *WhoWor 91*
Terry, Quinlan 1937- *BioIn 16*
Terry, R.M. 1918- *St&PR 91*
Terry, Ralph 1936- *Ballpl 90*
Terry, Randall *BioIn 16*
Terry, Randall B., Jr. 1934- *St&PR 91*
Terry, Richard Allan 1920- *WhoAm 90*
Terry, Richard Edward 1937- *St&PR 91, WhoAm 90*
Terry, Ricky Don 1957- *WhoSSW 91*
Terry, Robert Davis 1924- *WhoAm 90*
Terry, Robert J. *WhoAm 90*
Terry, Roger Harold 1925- *WhoWor 91*
Terry, Roland 1917- *BioIn 16, WhoAm 90*
Terry, Ronald A. 1930- *St&PR 91*
Terry, Ronald Anderson 1930- *WhoAm 90, WhoSSW 91*
Terry, Sarah Meiklejohn 1937- *WhoE 91*
Terry, Scott 1959- *Ballpl 90*
Terry, Sean M. 1959- *WhoAmW 91*
Terry, Sonny 1911-1986 *DrBlPA 90, OxCPMus*
Terry, Stephanie Ann 1947- *WhoAmW 91*
Terry, Stephen C. *ODwPR 91*
Terry, Stephen C. 1942- *St&PR 91*
Terry, Steven Craig 1950- *WhoSSW 91*
Terry, Susan K. *BioIn 16*
Terry, Thomas E. 1937- *St&PR 91*
Terry, Thomas Edward 1937- *WhoAm 90*
Terry, Victor Taylor 1910- *St&PR 91*
Terry, Walter 1913-1982 *AuBYP 90*
Terry, Wanda Kay *BiDrAPA 89*
Terry, William D. 1933- *St&PR 91*
Terry, William F. 1941- *St&PR 91*
Terry, William Henry 1836-1913 *EncPaPR 91*
Terry, William Hutchinson 1951- *WhoSSW 91*
Terry, William T *BiDrAPA 89*
Terry, Yank 1911-1979 *Ballpl 90*
Terry, Zeb 1891- *Ballpl 90*
Terry-Thomas *ConAu 130*
Terry-Thomas 1911-1990 *BioIn 16, CurBio 90N, NewYTBS 90 [port], WorAlBi*
Tersalvi, Antonio 1956- *WhoWor 91*
Terschluse, Marilyn Ann 1956- *WhoWrEP 89*
Tershakovec, Andrew 1921- *BiDrAPA 89*
Tersmeden, Gerard Arend Herman Benjamin *WhoWor 91*
Terstiege, Heinz 1934- *WhoWor 91*
Tertis, Lionel 1876-1975 *PenDiMP*
Tertocha, Jean-Paul Richard 1955- *WhoEmL 91*
Tertz, Abram 1925- *BioIn 16, WhoWor 91*
Teruel, Javier G. *WhoHisp 91*
Tervapaa, Juhani *DcScanL, EncCoWW*
Tervo, Timo Martti 1950- *WhoWor 91*
Terwillger, Dennis Thomas 1948- *St&PR 91*
Terwilliger, Elizabeth *BioIn 16*
Terwilliger, Herbert Lee 1914- *WhoAm 90*
Terwilliger, John William 1927- *WhoE 91*
Terwilliger, Wayne 1925- *Ballpl 90*
Terwood, James A. 1947- *St&PR 91*
Terzian, Carl R. 1935- *ODwPR 91*
Terzian, James P. 1915- *AuBYP 90*
Terzian, Karnig Yervant 1928- *WhoE 91, WhoWor 91*
Terzian, Mary 1932- *WhoAmW 91*
Terzian, Richard H. 1937- *St&PR 91*
Terzian, Yervant 1939- *WhoAm 90*
Tesar, Delbert 1935- *WhoAm 90*
Tesar, George Emil 1950- *BiDrAPA 89*
Tesar, Jenny Elizabeth 1937- *WhoAmW 91*
Tesar, Milo Benjamin 1920- *WhoAm 90*
Tesarek, Dennis George 1935- *WhoSSW 91*
Tesauro, Lorraine Helen 1957- *WhoE 91*
Tesauro, Thomas Samuel 1959- *WhoE 91*
Tescee, Ian *NewAgMG*
Tesch, Emmanuel Camille Georges Victor 1920- *WhoWor 91*
Tesch, Julia 1956- *WhoAmW 91*
Tesch, Lorraine Barbara 1948- *WhoE 91*
Teschemacher, Frank 1906-1932 *BioIn 16, OxCPMus*
Teschemacher, Margarete 1903-1959 *PenDiMP*
Teschendorf, Alan David 1957- *WhoEmL 91*
Tescher, John P. 1938- *St&PR 91*
Teschner, Anne Farrar 1956- *WhoAmW 91*
Teschner, Douglass Paul 1949- *WhoE 91*
Teschner, Manfred George 1935- *WhoE 91*
Teschner, Richard Rewa 1908- *WhoAm 90*
Teschner, Thomas Martin 1956- *St&PR 91*
Te Selle, Grace H. 1928- *WhoWrEP 89*
Tesfagiorgis, Freida 1946- *WhoAmA 91*
Tesfaye, Dinka *WhoWor 91*
Tesh, John *BioIn 16*
Tesh, Samuel Lee, III 1937- *WhoSSW 91*
Teshoian, Nishan 1941- *WhoAm 90*
Tesich, Steve 1942- *WhoAm 90*
Tesio, Vittorio 1940- *WhoWor 91*
Teske, Edmund Rudolph 1911- *WhoAmA 91*
Teske, Elnathan Edward 1933- *St&PR 91*
Teske, Gerald Peter 1934- *St&PR 91*
Teske, John Alfred 1953- *WhoE 91*
Teske, John Arthur 1925- *St&PR 91*
Teske, Patricia Loos 1921- *WhoAmW 91*
Teskey, Adeline Margaret 185-?-1924 *FemiCLE*
Tesla, Nikola 1856-1943 *BioIn 16, EncO&P 3, WorAlBi*
Tesler, Lawrence Gordon 1945- *St&PR 91*
Tesler, Ruth Ellen *BiDrAPA 89*
Tesluk, Catherine Emily 1955- *BiDrAPA 89*
Tesone, Judy 1943- *WhoAmW 91*
Tesoriero, Albert 1939- *St&PR 91*
Tesoriero, Anthony Ronald 1943- *St&PR 91*
Tesoriero, Lisa Monica 1958- *St&PR 91*
Tesoriero, Philip James 1942- *WhoE 91*
Tesoro, Giuliana Cavaglieri 1921- *WhoAmW 91*
Tesreau, Jeff 1889-1946 *Ballpl 90, BioIn 16*
Tess-Mattner, Kent A. 1954- *WhoEmL 91*
Tessa, Marian Lorraine 1950- *WhoAmW 91, WhoE 91, WhoWor 91*
Tessarowicz, M.H. 1944- *St&PR 91*
Tesse, Frederick Halstead 1823-1894 *AmLegL*
Tesselschade, Maria 1594-1649 *EncCoWW*
Tessendorf, K. C. *AuBYP 90*
Tesser, Sheldon *BiDrAPA 89*
Tesseur, Yvan W. H. 1946- *WhoWor 91*
Tessier, Charles *PenDiMP*
Tessier, Gaston 1887-1960 *BiDFrPL*
Tessier, Jean-Michel 1941- *St&PR 91, WhoAm 90*
Tessier, Jocelyne 1958- *BiDrAPA 89*
Tessier, Karen Patricia 1943- *WhoAmW 91*
Tessier, Oliver 1947- *WhoE 91*
Tessier, Ulric-Joseph 1817-1892 *DcCanB 12*
Tessier-Lavigne, Marc Trevor 1959- *WhoE 91*
Tessler, Aaron Neil *BiDrAPA 89*
Tessler, Allan Roger 1936- *WhoAm 90*
Tessler, Barnett 1942- *St&PR 91*
Tessler, Julia Ann 1959- *WhoAmW 91*
Tessler, Stephanie Gordon 1940- *SmATA 64*
Tessman, Irwin 1929- *WhoAm 90*
Tessmer, Craig Robert 1952- *WhoEmL 91*
Tesson, Alan Ray 1947- *BiDrAPA 89*
Testa, Armando 1917- *BioIn 16, ConDes 90*
Testa, Douglas 1944- *St&PR 91*
Testa, Jack Anthony 1927- *St&PR 91*
Testa, John William 1936- *St&PR 91*
Testa, Joseph 1925- *St&PR 91*
Testa, Michael Harold 1939- *WhoAm 90*
Testa, Nicholas Michael 1940- *St&PR 91*
Testa, Richard J. 1939- *St&PR 91*
Testa, Richard Joseph 1939- *WhoE 91*
Testa, Sharon Anne 1948- *WhoAmW 91*
Testa, Stephen Michael 1951- *WhoWor 91*
Testa-Feliciano, Leonor L *BiDrAPA 89*
Testanero, Nick 1950- *St&PR 91*
Testaverde, R. Salve *BioIn 16*
Testaverde, Vinny *BioIn 16*
Teste, Richard *PenDiDA 89*
Tester, John Robert 1929- *WhoAm 90*
Tester, Sylvia Root 1939- *SmATA 64*
Testerman, Jean Leighton 1923- *WhoWrEP 89*
Testut, Richard Stanton 1910- *St&PR 91*
Testwuide, Thomas R. 1945- *St&PR 91*
Tetard, John Peter 1722-1787 *BioIn 16*
Tetelman, Alice Fran 1941- *WhoE 91*
Tetenbaum, Sidney 1922- *WhoSSW 91*

Teter, George Heber 1944- *BiDrAPA 89*
Teter, Gordon F. *WhoAm 90*
Teter, James A. *St&PR 91*
Teter, John S. 1930- *St&PR 91*
Teter, Lenore 1949- *BiDrAPA 89*
Teteris, Nicholas John 1929- *WhoAm 90*
Teters, J Charlene 1952- *WhoAmA 91*
Teterycz, Barbara Ann 1952- *WhoAmW 91, WhoWor 91*
Tetherow, C. Joseph *ODwPR 91*
Tetherow, Michael 1942- *WhoAmA 91*
Teti, Alfred L. 1935- *WhoAm 90*
Tetirick, Daniel Hartman *BiDrAPA 89*
Tetkowski, Neil 1956?- *BioIn 16*
Tetley, Arthur Russell 1930- *WhoWrEP 89*
Tetley, Glen 1926- *WhoAm 90*
Tetlow, Edwin 1905- *WhoAm 90, WhoWrEP 89*
Tetlow, Norman 1899-1982 *DcNaB 1981*
Tetlow, William Lloyd 1938- *WhoWor 91*
Tetrazzini, Eva 1862-1948 *PenDiMP*
Tetrazzini, Luisa 1871-1940 *PenDiMP, WorAlBi*
Tetreault, Joseph Paul 1953- *WhoE 91*
Tetreault, Pierre L J *BiDrAPA 89*
Tetreault, Wilfred F. 1927- *WhoWrEP 89*
Tetrick, Elbert Lain 1923- *WhoAm 90*
Tetro, John M. 1946- *St&PR 91*
Tettambel, Melicien Ann 1951- *WhoEmL 91*
Tettleton, Mickey *BioIn 16*
Tettleton, Mickey 1960- *Ballpl 90*
Tettleton, Robert Lynn 1929- *WhoAmA 91*
Tetu, Cleophee 1824-1891 *DcCanB 12*
Tetzeli, Frederick Edward 1930- *WhoAm 90*
Tetzlaff, Charles David 1954- *St&PR 91*
Tetzner, Gerti 1936- *EncCoWW*
Tetzner, Ruth 1917- *WhoWor 91*
Teu, Sanfjord Brogdyne, III 1943- *St&PR 91*
Teubal, Savina J. 1926- *ConAu 132*
Teubner, Ferdinand C. 1921- *St&PR 91*
Teubner, Ferdinand Cary, Jr. 1921- *WhoAm 90*
Teubner-Rhodes, Donn M 1950- *BiDrAPA 89*
Teufel, Dolores Enid Arlene 1921- *WhoWrEP 89*
Teufel, Tim 1958- *Ballpl 90*
Teuscher, Enrique Jorge 1943- *BiDrAPA 89*
Teuscher, George William 1908- *WhoAm 90*
Teusink, J Paul 1941- *BiDrAPA 89*
Teutsch, Walter 1909- *IntWWM 90*
Tevebaugh, Charles Richard 1935- *St&PR 91*
Teverbaugh, Kerry Dean 1954- *WhoWor 91*
Tevere, Margaret 1922- *St&PR 91*
Teves, Thomas William 1947- *WhoE 91*
Tevington, Kathryn Macye *BiDrAPA 89*
Tevis, D Kinne 1934- *BiDrAPA 89*
Tevis, G. Phillip 1942- *St&PR 91*
Tevis, George Phillip 1942- *WhoSSW 91*
Tevis, Walter 1928-1984 *LiHiK*
Tevlin, Lois Penketh 1935- *WhoAmW 91*
Tevlin, Michael F. 1953- *WhoWrEP 89*
Tevor-Roper, Patrick Dacre 1916- *WhoWor 91*
Tevrizian, Dickran M., Jr. 1940- *WhoAm 90*
Tew, E. James, Jr. 1933- *WhoSSW 91, WhoWor 91*
Tew, Stephen Alter 1949- *BiDrAPA 89*
Tewari, Prayag Dutta 1935- *WhoWor 91*
Tewell, Joseph Robert, Jr. 1934- *WhoAm 90*
Tewes, Robin J 1950- *WhoAmA 91, WhoE 91*
Tewi, Thea *WhoAm 90, WhoAmA 91*
Te Winkel, Mattheus Johannes 1938- *WhoWor 91*
Tewkesbury, Joan F. 1936- *WhoAm 90*
Tewksbury, Bob 1960- *Ballpl 90*
Tewolde Berhan, Gebre Egziabher 1949- *WhoWor 91*
Tews, William L. 1936- *St&PR 91*
Tews-Yocum, Eve Lynn 1956- *WhoAmW 91*
Tewson, Vincent 1898-1981 *DcNaB 1981*
Tex, Joe 1933-1982 *EncPR&S 89, OxCPMus*
Texada, Davidson H, Jr. *BiDrAPA 89*
Texidor, Greville 1902-1964 *FemiCLE*
Texter, Elmer Clinton, Jr. 1923- *WhoAm 90, WhoWor 91*
Textor, Robert Bayard 1923- *WhoAm 90*
Tey, Josephine 1896-1952 *BioIn 16, FemiCLE, WorAlBi*
Tey, Josephine 1897-1952 *TwCCr&M 91*
Tey, Wei-Ming 1952- *WhoWor 91*
Teyral, John 1912- *WhoAmA 91*
Teyssandier, Marie-Jose 1931- *WhoWor 91*
Teyssieras, Anne 1945- *EncCoWW*
Teyte, Maggie 1888-1976 *PenDiMP*
Tezak, Paul 1954- *St&PR 91*
Tezel, Ahmet 1943- *WhoE 91*
Tezla, Albert 1915- *ConAu 31NR*
Tezza, Angel 1951- *WhoWor 91*
Thabolingam, Kathiravelu *BiDrAPA 89*
Thach, Andrew B, Jr. *BiDrAPA 89*
Thacher, Anita 1936- *WhoAmA 91*
Thacher, John H., Jr. 1944- *St&PR 91*
Thacher, Russell 1919?-1990 *ConAu 132*
Thackara, James 1944- *ConAu 129*
Thacker, John E. 1944- *St&PR 91*
Thacker, Michael M. 1936- *St&PR 91*
Thacker, William Ivanhoe 1955- *WhoSSW 91*
Thackeray, Anne Isabella 1837-1919 *BioIn 16*
Thackeray, James William 1957- *WhoE 91*
Thackeray, Jonathan E. 1936- *WhoAm 90*
Thackeray, William Makepeace 1811-1863 *BioIn 16, EncO&P 3, WorAlBi*
Thackeray, William Makepiece 1811-1863 *EncPaPR 91*
Thackray, Arnold Wilfrid 1939- *WhoAm 90*
Thackray, James Carden 1924- *St&PR 91, WhoAm 90*
Thackray, Richard Irving 1927- *WhoAm 90*
Thackrey, Ted, Jr. 1918- *ConAu 132*
Thackston, Edward Lee 1937- *WhoSSW 91*
Thacore, Vinod Rai *BiDrAPA 89*
Thadani, Narendra Mulchand 1949- *WhoE 91*
Thadden, Eberhard von 1909-1964 *BioIn 16*
Thaddeus, Patrick 1932- *WhoAm 90*
Thaddeus, Thomas Edward 1961- *WhoSSW 91*
Thaden, Edward Carl 1922- *WhoAm 90*
Thaden, James Thomas 1952- *St&PR 91*
Thadhani, Suresh 1939- *St&PR 91*
Thaete, Larry Gene 1947- *WhoEmL 91*
Thagard, Norman E. 1943- *WhoAm 90*
Thaggard, Sherry L 1958- *BiDrAPA 89*
Thaine, Francisco Prada 1948- *WhoE 91*
Thakar, David Hari, Jr. 1956- *WhoE 91*
Thakker, Ashok Bhagwanday 1947- *WhoSSW 91*
Thakker, Mangal G 1942- *BiDrAPA 89*
Thakker, Promila M 1945- *BiDrAPA 89*
Thakor, Haren Bhaskerrao 1938- *St&PR 91, WhoAm 90*
Thakor, Sushen J 1927- *BiDrAPA 89*
Thakral, R.P. 1949- *St&PR 91*
Thakur, Arvind 1941- *WhoWor 91*
Thakur, Hemant Krishna *BiDrAPA 89*
Thakur, Prithviraj S *BiDrAPA 89*
Thal, Jeffrey *BioIn 16*
Thal, Russell K. 1934- *St&PR 91*
Thal, Samuel 1903- *WhoAmA 91N*
Thalacker, Arbie Otto 1907- *St&PR 91*
Thalacker, Arbie Robert 1935- *WhoAm 90*
Thalacker, Donald William 1939-1987 *WhoAmA 91N*
Thalanany, Thomas Sebastian 1954- *WhoSSW 91*
Thalben-Ball, George 1896-1987 *PenDiMP*
Thalberg, Irving 1899-1936 *WorAlBi*
Thalberg, Irving Grant 1899-1936 *BioIn 16*
Thalberg, Sigismond 1812-1871 *BioIn 16, PenDiMP*
Thalbourne, Michael 1955- *EncPaPR 91*
Thalden, Barry R. 1942- *WhoWor 91*
Thale, Thomas 1915- *BiDrAPA 89*
Thalenfeld, David 1919- *St&PR 91*
Thaler, Donald Bruce 1947- *St&PR 91*
Thaler, Gail Benet *BiDrAPA 89*
Thaler, James D. 1929- *St&PR 91*
Thaler, Martin S. 1932- *WhoAm 90*
Thaler, Mike *AuBYP 90*
Thaler, Mike 1936- *BioIn 16*
Thaler, Otto F 1923- *BiDrAPA 89*
Thaler, Richard H. 1945- *WhoAm 90*
Thaler, Richard Winston, Jr. 1951- *WhoE 91, WhoWor 91*
Thaler, Robert Lee 1931- *WhoAm 90*
Thaler, Wendell L. 1934- *St&PR 91*
Thales 624?BC-546?BC *WorAlBi*
Thales 1952- *BioIn 16*
Thalheim, David T. 1954- *St&PR 91*
Thalheimer, Louis B. 1944- *WhoE 91*
Thalheimer, Richard Hastings 1940- *St&PR 91*
Thalhimer, William B., Jr. 1914- *St&PR 91*
Thaliath, Lizy Joseph *BiDrAPA 89*
Thall, Burnett Murray 1922- *WhoAm 90*
Thall, Letty Derman 1947- *WhoAmW 91*
Thall, Mark Richard *BiDrAPA 89*
Thall, Neil 1946- *WhoSSW 91*
Thall, Richard Vincent 1940- *WhoWor 91*
Thaller, Thomas Victor 1941- *St&PR 91*
Thalmann, Joan Louise 1952- *WhoAmW 91*
Tham, Hilary *WhoWrEP 89*
Tham, Seong Chee 1932- *WhoWor 91*
Thaman, Konai Helu *FemiCLE*
Thaman, Michael Edwards 1949- *St&PR 91, WhoAm 90*
Thamar 1160-1212 *BioIn 16*
Thambidurai, Lilian *BiDrAPA 89*
Thames, C. A. *TwCCr&M 91*
Thames, C. H. *AuBYP 90*
Thames, Emmitt Eugene 1933- *WhoAmA 91*
Thames, George Wesley 1946- *St&PR 91*
Thames, J.A. 1935- *St&PR 91*
Thames, Redden Jefferson 1932- *WhoWor 91*
Thames, William Gordon, Jr. 1960- *WhoSSW 91*
Thamm, Erik Gerhardt 1950- *St&PR 91*
Thampi, Mohan Varghese 1960- *WhoEmL 91, WhoSSW 91, WhoWor 91*
Thampy, Kishore J 1947- *BiDrAPA 89*
Than, Karoly 1834-1908 *BioIn 16*
Than, Tin Myo *BiDrAPA 89*
Thanaphum, Sritham 1936- *BiDrAPA 89*
Thane, Adele 1904- *AuBYP 90*
Thanel, Christopher J *BiDrAPA 89*
Thanepohn, Donald A. 1925- *St&PR 91*
Thanet, Neil *ConAu 32NR*
Thanet, Octave 1850-1934 *BioAmW*
Thani, Abdul Aziz bin Khalifa Al 1948- *WhoWor 91*
Thani, Hamad Bin Khalifa Al 1949- *WhoWor 91*
Thani, Khalifa bin Hamad Al 1932- *WhoWor 91*
Thankappan, Kunjathan 1938- *BiDrAPA 89*
Thant, U 1909-1974 *WorAlBi*
Thapar, Renu Kapur 1942- *BiDrAPA 89*
Thar, Ferdinand August 1940- *WhoWor 91*
Tharakan, Mathew Parayil Kochupappu 1935- *WhoWor 91*
Thariani, Azad Hasan 1940- *WhoWor 91*
Tharin, Frank *NewYTBS 90*
Tharin, Frank 1910-1990 *BioIn 16*
Tharp, B. Carroll, Jr. 1919- *WhoAm 90*
Tharp, Charlotte S. 1943- *ODwPR 91*
Tharp, David Minton 1948- *WhoSSW 91*
Tharp, David T 1950- *BiDrAPA 89*
Tharp, Joseph B. 1934- *St&PR 91*
Tharp, Louis Clay 1951- *ODwPR 91*
Tharp, Louise Hall 1898- *AuBYP 90, ConAu 33NR*
Tharp, Marye Charlese 1947- *WhoSSW 91*
Tharp, Twyla *BioIn 16*
Tharp, Twyla 1941- *NotWoAT, WhoAmW 91, WhoE 91, WorAlBi*
Tharpe, Byron 1953- *WhoSSW 91*
Tharpe, Frazier Eugene 1941- *WhoAm 90*
Tharpe, Rosetta 1915-1973 *DrBlPA 90*
Tharpe, Sister Rosetta 1915-1973 *OxCPMus*
Thase, Michael Edward 1952- *BiDrAPA 89*
Thatcher, Beverly Rose 1965- *WhoAmW 91*
Thatcher, Blythe Darlyn 1947- *WhoWrEP 89*
Thatcher, Bruce *BioIn 16*
Thatcher, Denis *BioIn 16*
Thatcher, Grant William *BiDrAPA 89*
Thatcher, J.R. 1940- *St&PR 91*
Thatcher, Kristine Marie 1950- *WhoAmW 91*
Thatcher, Margaret *BioIn 16*
Thatcher, Margaret 1925- *WomWR [port], WorAlBi*
Thatcher, Margaret Hilda 1925- *WhoWor 91*
Thatcher, Paul R. 1935- *St&PR 91*
Thatcher, Rex Howard 1932- *WhoAm 90*
Thau, Claude 1948- *St&PR 91*
Thau, Rosemarie Brigitte 1936- *WhoAmW 91*
Thau, William Albert, Jr. 1940- *WhoAm 90, WhoSSW 91*
Thauli, Gulraj *BiDrAPA 89*
Thaw, Barbara Cooley 1958- *St&PR 91*
Thaw, Clare *BioIn 16*
Thaw, David *PenDiMP*
Thaw, Eugene Victor *BioIn 16*
Thaw, Eugene Victor 1927- *WhoAmA 91*
Thaw, Harry K. 1871-1947 *WorAlBi*
Thaw, Murray Charles 1915- *St&PR 91*
Thaw, Robert M. 1953- *St&PR 91*
Thaw, Wayne Howard 1957- *St&PR 91*
Thawerbhoy, Nazim G. 1947- *St&PR 91*
Thawley, Mary Nancy 1947- *WhoAmW 91*
Thaxter, Celia 1835-1894 *FemiCLE*
Thaxter, Celia L. 1835-1894 *BioAmW*
Thaxter, Celia Laighton 1835-1894 *BioIn 16*
Thaxton, Carlton James 1935- *WhoAm 90*
Thaxton, Cecil R. 1925- *St&PR 91*
Thaxton, Everette Frederick 1938- *WhoSSW 91, WhoWor 91*
Thaxton, Linda Nell 1945- *WhoWrEP 89*
Thaxton, Mary Lynwood 1944- *WhoSSW 91*
Thayendanegea *WhNaAH*
Thayer, Abbott Handerson *BioIn 16*
Thayer, Artemas Bronson 1939- *WhoAm 90*
Thayer, Barbara Zaring *BioIn 16*
Thayer, Carlyle Alan 1945- *WhoWor 91*
Thayer, Caroline Matilda 1787?-1844 *FemiCLE*
Thayer, Charles James 1944- *WhoAm 90*
Thayer, Christine *ODwPR 91*
Thayer, Edna Louise 1936- *WhoAmW 91*
Thayer, Edwin Cabot 1935- *WhoAm 90*
Thayer, Ernest L. *Ballpl 90*
Thayer, Ernest Lawrence 1863-1940 *AuBYP 90, SmATA 60 [port]*
Thayer, Gerald Campbell 1943- *St&PR 91, WhoAm 90*
Thayer, Graydon Allan 1931- *St&PR 91*
Thayer, James Norris 1926- *WhoAm 90*
Thayer, Jane *AuBYP 90*
Thayer, Jane 1904- *WhoAm 90, WhoAmW 91*
Thayer, Jane Hillis 1930- *WhoAmW 91*
Thayer, Lee 1874-1973 *TwCCr&M 91*
Thayer, Lee 1927- *WhoAm 90*
Thayer, Louis M. *BioIn 16*
Thayer, M B *EncO&P 3*
Thayer, Nina Nichols 1945- *WhoAmW 91*
Thayer, Paul Arthur 1940- *WhoAm 90*
Thayer, Robert E. 1931- *St&PR 91*
Thayer, Russell, III 1922- *WhoAm 90*
Thayer, Stephen C. 1939- *St&PR 91*
Thayer, Stuart Wallace 1924- *St&PR 91*
Thayer, Stuart Wilson Walker 1926- *WhoAm 90*
Thayer, Sylvanius 1785-1872 *WorAlBi*
Thayer, Walter 1910-1989 *AnObit 1989*
Thayer, Walter Nelson 1910-1989 *BioIn 16*
Thayer, Walter Stephen, III 1946- *WhoE 91*
Thayer, Wanda E. 1943- *WhoAmW 91*
Thayer, William E. 1925- *St&PR 91*
Thayne, Emma Lou Warner 1924- *WhoWrEP 89*
Thayne, Richard Grant 1930- *WhoWor 91*
The Prophet *ConAu 132*
The, Victor 1942- *WhoWor 91*
Thea, Carolee B 1942- *WhoAmA 91*
Theall, Donald Francis 1928- *WhoAm 90*
Thebaud, Adely *BiDrAPA 89*
Thebaud, E F 1936- *BiDrAPA 89*
Theberge, Josee *BiDrAPA 89*
Theberge, Pierre Georges 1942- *WhoAm 90*
Thebom, Blanche 1918- *IntWWM 90, PenDiMP*
Thecla *WomWR*
Thedinger, Robert Scott 1949- *St&PR 91*
Theen, John Frederick 1952- *St&PR 91*
Theen, Rolf Heinz-Wilhelm 1937- *WhoAm 90*
Theesfeld, Carole Ann 1943- *WhoAmW 91*
Theesfeld, Harold L. 1935- *St&PR 91*
Theeuwes, Felix 1937- *St&PR 91*
Theibert, Philip Reed 1952- *WhoWrEP 89*
Theil, Henri 1924- *WhoAm 90*
Theil, Leon S. 1915- *ODwPR 91*
Theiler, Hans 1937- *WhoWor 91*
Theiler, Thomas Carl 1931- *St&PR 91*
Theiller, George J. 1950- *St&PR 91*
Theimer, Axel Knut 1946- *IntWWM 90*
Theimer, Charles Patrick, Sr. 1942- *WhoSSW 91*
Thein, Edmund 1934- *WhoWor 91*
Thein, Jack Lee 1945- *St&PR 91*
Thein, Peter Joseph, Jr. 1938- *St&PR 91*
Theiner, George *BioIn 16*
Theis, Adolf 1933- *WhoWor 91*
Theis, Francis William 1920- *WhoAm 90*
Theis, Frank Gordon 1911- *WhoAm 90*
Theis, Henry E. 1933- *St&PR 91*
Theis, Paul Anthony 1923- *WhoE 91*
Theis, Robert Jean Paul 1947- *WhoWor 91*
Theis, Ronald L. 1937- *ODwPR 91*
Theis, Steven Thomas 1959- *WhoE 91*
Theis, William Harold 1945- *WhoEmL 91*
Theisen, Clifford Richard 1951- *St&PR 91*
Theisen, Edwin M. 1930- *St&PR 91*
Theisen, George I. 1926- *St&PR 91*
Theisen, George Ingild 1926- *WhoSSW 91*
Theisen, Virgil J. 1942- *St&PR 91*
Theismann, Joe *BioIn 16*
Theiss, Chester B, Jr. *BiDrAPA 89*
Theiss, Clifford Anthony 1941- *WhoE 91*
Theiss, Lewis Edwin *AuBYP 90*
Theiss, Louis Leonard, Jr. 1925- *WhoE 91*
Theiss, Robert Mitchell 1959- *WhoE 91*
Theiss, Sally Ann 1950- *WhoAmW 91*
Thek, Paul 1933-1988 *BioIn 16*
Thekkekara, Jack 1949- *St&PR 91*
Thekla *EncCoWW*
Thelander, Harald *BioIn 16*
Thelander, Kristin Pederson 1954- *IntWWM 90*
Thelen, Edmund 1913- *WhoE 91*

Thelen, Jodi *BioIn 16*
Thelen, Jodi 1962- *ConTFT 8*
Thelen, John Frederick 1949- *St&PR 91*
Thelen, Max, Jr. 1919- *WhoAm 90*
Thelen, Robert Frederick 1950- *WhoSSW 91*
Thelen, Wolfgang Hermann 1931- *WhoWor 91*
Thelian, Lorraine 1948- *WhoAmW 91*
Thelin, Valfred P 1934- *WhoAmA 91*
Thellman, Fred 1933- *St&PR 91*
Thelot, Johann Andreas 1655-1734 *PenDiDA 89*
Thelwall, John 1764-1834 *DcLB 93 [port]*
Them *EncPR&S 89*
Themal, Henry Gunther 1926- *St&PR 91*
Themerson, Stefan 1910-1988 *AnObit 1988*
Themis, John *NewAgMG*
Themistocles 524?BC-460?BC *WorAlBi*
Themstrup, Bendt 1941- *St&PR 91*
Then, George J. 1942- *St&PR 91*
Theobald, Dale Eugene 1947- *BiDrAPA 89*
Theobald, Edward Robert 1947- *WhoEmL 91, WhoWor 91*
Theobald, Gillian Lee 1944- *WhoAmA 91*
Theobald, Harold L., Jr. 1961- *WhoSSW 91*
Theobald, Jean Ann 1958- *WhoAmW 91*
Theobald, Jon A. 1945- *St&PR 91*
Theobald, Jurgen Peter 1933- *WhoWor 91*
Theobald, Lewis, Jr. *MajTwCW*
Theobald, Morell 1828-1908 *EncO&P 3*
Theobald, Robert 1929- *WhoWrEP 89*
Theobald, Ron 1944- *Ballpl 90*
Theobald, Sharon A 1942- *WhoAmA 91*
Theobald, Thomas Charles 1937- *St&PR 91, WhoAm 90*
Theobald, William Louis 1936- *WhoAm 90*
Theocritus 310?BC-250?BC *WorAlBi*
Theodelinda *WomWR*
Theodolinda *WomWR*
Theodora *WomWR*
Theodora *WomWR*
Theodora 981?-1056 *WomWR*
Theodoracopulos, Taki 1937- *ConAu 129*
Theodorakis, Mikis 1925- *BioIn 16, OxCPMus, WhoWor 91*
Theodore, Ares Nicholas 1933- *WhoWor 91*
Theodore, Eustace D. 1941- *WhoAm 90*
Theodore, George T. 1940- *WhoWor 91*
Theodore, Nick Andrew 1928- *WhoSSW 91*
Theodore, Samuel Serban 1952- *WhoE 91*
Theodores, Theodore Peter 1935- *WhoE 91*
Theodorescu, Radu Amza Serban 1933- *WhoAm 90*
Theodoridis, Dimitrios *BiDrAPA 89*
Theodoro, Graciela M *BiDrAPA 89*
Theodoro, Leonidas 1940- *BiDrAPA 89*
Theodoros, Patricia *ODwPR 91*
Theodorou, Jerry 1959- *WhoE 91*
Theodorou, Victoria 1926?- *EncCoWW*
Theodosius, Metropolitan *WhoAm 90*
Theodosius I, the Great 347-395 *BioIn 16*
Theodoulou, Othon Leonidou 1950- *WhoWor 91*
Theodule, Adele Maginot 1812-1886 *EncPaPR 91*
Theofiles, George 1947- *WhoAmA 91*
Theogaraj, Janakibai *BiDrAPA 89*
Theoharides, Theoharis Constantin 1950- *WhoWor 91*
Theoharis, Athan G 1936- *ConAu 30NR*
Theologitis, John Michael 1956- *WhoWor 91*
Theon, John Speridon 1934- *WhoAm 90*
Theophano *WomWR*
Theophilus *PenDiDA 89*
Theoret, France 1942- *FemiCLE*
Theosebeia *EncCoWW*
Theosebia Chemica *EncCoWW*
Theosobia *EncCoWW*
Theotokis, Spyros 1908-1988 *BioIn 16*
Theotokopoulos, Domenikos 1541-1614 *BioIn 16*
Therese de Jesus 1824-1891 *DcCanB 12*
Therese, de Lisieux 1873-1897 *BioIn 16*
Theriault, Levite 1837-1896 *DcCanB 12*
Theriault, Omer Courtland 1922- *St&PR 91*
Theriault, Yves 1915-1983 *OxCCanT*
Therio, Adrien 1925- *WhoWrEP 89*
Theriot, Rosemary 1954- *WhoAmW 91*
Thermansen, Peter H. 1955- *St&PR 91*
Thernstrom, Stephan Albert 1934- *WhoAm 90, WhoE 91, WhoWrEP 89*
Theros, Christina Marie 1962- *WhoAmW 91*
Theros, Elias George 1919- *WhoAm 90*
Theroux, Paul *BioIn 16*
Theroux, Paul 1941- *MajTwCW, WorAlBi*
Theroux, Paul Edward 1941- *WhoAm 90*
Theroux, Peter 1956- *ConAu 132*
Theroux, William Gerard 1959- *WhoE 91*
Therre, John Patrick 1951- *St&PR 91*
Therrien, Francois Xavier, Jr. 1928- *WhoSSW 91, WhoWor 91*
Therrien, Rene A. 1945- *St&PR 91*
Therrien, Robert Wilfrid 1929- *St&PR 91*
Therrien, Valerie Monica 1951- *WhoEmL 91*
Therrien, Wally C. 1950- *WhoE 91*
Thesen, Arne 1943- *WhoAm 90*
Thesen, Sharon 1946- *FemiCLE*
Thesiger, Wilfred 1910- *BioIn 16*
Thesing, William B 1947- *ConAu 32NR*
Thesleff, Ellen 1869-1954 *BiDWomA [port]*
Thesleff, Stephen Wilhelm 1924- *WhoWor 91*
Thespis *WorAlBi*
Thestrup, Per 1935- *WhoWor 91*
Theuer, Paul John 1936- *St&PR 91*
Theuer, Richard C. 1939- *St&PR 91*
Theuner, Douglas Edwin 1938- *WhoAm 90, WhoE 91*
Theunissen, Lydia Marie 1959- *WhoSSW 91*
Theunissen, Michael 1932- *ConAu 132*
Theunissen, Michael Heinrich 1932- *WhoWor 91*
Theurer, Byron W. 1939- *WhoWor 91*
Theus, Jeremiah 1719?-1774 *EncCRAm*
Theut, Clarence Peter 1938- *WhoWor 91*
Theut, Susan Katherine *BiDrAPA 89*
Thevenet, Susanne Dorothy 1947- *WhoE 91*
Thevenin, Denis *MajTwCW*
Thevenot, Maude Travis 1914- *WhoAmW 91*
Thevenote, William J. 1934- *St&PR 91*
Thevenow, Anna Victoria 1954- *WhoAmW 91*
Thevenow, Tommy 1903-1957 *Ballpl 90*
Thevoz, Michel 1936- *ConAu 132*
Thew, Lisbet 1920- *IntWWM 90*
Thews, William B. 1849-1910 *AmLegL*
T'hezan, Helia 1934- *IntWWM 90*
Thiagaraj, Henry *BioIn 16*
Thiagarajan, Kumaraswami 1950- *WhoWor 91*
Thiandoum, Hyacinthe 1921- *WhoWor 91*
Thibaud, Jacques 1880-1953 *PenDiMP*
Thibaudeau, Isidore 1819-1893 *DcCanB 12*
Thibaudeau, Jon R. 1960- *WhoSSW 91*
Thibaudeau, May Murphy 1908- *ConAu 131*
Thibaudet, Jean-Yves 1961- *IntWWM 90*
Thibault, Claude 1948- *WhoAmA 91*
Thibault, Jacques Anatole Francois 1844-1924 *MajTwCW*
Thibault, Ronald Martin 1943- *St&PR 91*
Thibaut, Charest deLauzon, Jr. 1922- *WhoAm 90*
Thibaut, Howard Woodrow 1938- *St&PR 91*
Thibaut, Monique *WhoWor 91*
Thibeault, Dale Wilkins 1938- *WhoAmW 91*
Thibert, Patrick A 1943- *WhoAmA 91*
Thibert, Roger Joseph 1929- *WhoAm 90*
Thibodeau, David Michael 1940- *St&PR 91*
Thibodeau, Gary Arthur 1938- *WhoAm 90*
Thibodeau, Gilles 1935- *St&PR 91*
Thibodeau, Nicole *BiDrAPA 89*
Thibodeau, Paul E. 1946- *St&PR 91*
Thibodeaux, Julius P. 1929- *St&PR 91*
Thibodeaux, Lynne W. 1946- *WhoAmW 91*
Thibodeaux, Michael Jay 1948- *St&PR 91*
Thibodeaux, Walter Joseph 1922- *WhoSSW 91*
Thibos, Charles Ray 1947- *St&PR 91*
Thicke, Alan *BioIn 16*
Thicke, Alan 1947- *WorAlBi*
Thickins, Graeme Richard 1946- *WhoEmL 91*
Thicknesse, Ann 1737-1824 *FemiCLE*
Thickstun, James T 1918- *BiDrAPA 89*
Thickstun, Timothy Lee 1950- *St&PR 91*
Thiebaud, Jean-Marie Andre Marcel 1944- *WhoWor 91*
Thiebaud, Wayne 1920- *News 91-1, WhoAmA 91*
Thiebauth, Bruce Edward 1947- *WhoEmL 91*
Thiede, James F. 1938- *St&PR 91*
Thiede, Jorn 1941- *WhoWor 91*
Thieffry, Augustin Bernard 1953- *St&PR 91*
Thiel, Bernardo Augusto 1850-1901? *BioIn 16*
Thiel, Douglas J. 1942- *St&PR 91*
Thiel, Frank A. 1928- *WhoAm 90*
Thiel, Frank Anthony 1928- *St&PR 91*
Thiel, George A. 1925- *St&PR 91*
Thiel, Gregory Robert 1939- *St&PR 91*
Thiel, James Richard 1946- *BiDrAPA 89*
Thiel, John Charles 1945- *WhoAm 90, WhoEmL 91*
Thiel, John Thomas 1945- *BiDrAPA 89*
Thiel, Lisa *NewAgMG*
Thiel, Philip 1920- *WhoAm 90*
Thiel, Sandra Schoofs 1956- *WhoAmW 91*
Thiel, Susan *WhoAmW 91*
Thiel, Wilbert A. 1937- *St&PR 91*
Thiel, Winfried Werner 1940- *WhoWor 91*
Thielbar, Frances Charlotte 1908-1962 *BioIn 16*
Thiele, Bob 1922- *OxCPMus*
Thiele, David A 1919- *BiDrAPA 89*
Thiele, Edward Earl 1940- *St&PR 91*
Thiele, Gloria Day 1931- *WhoAmW 91*
Thiele, Herbert William Albert 1953- *WhoEmL 91, WhoSSW 91, WhoWor 91*
Thiele, Howard Nellis, Jr. 1930- *WhoAm 90*
Thiele, Irma E. 1918- *WhoAmW 91*
Thiele, Jeffrey Robert *BiDrAPA 89*
Thiele, Paul Frederick 1914- *St&PR 91*
Thiele, Ronald Lewis 1925- *WhoAm 90*
Thiele, William Edward 1942- *St&PR 91, WhoAm 90, WhoE 91*
Thielemans, Johan Valentine 1939- *WhoWor 91*
Thielemans, Toots 1922- *BioIn 16*
Thielen *DcCanB 12*
Thielen, Benedict 1903-1965 *DcLB 102 [port]*
Thielen, Greg Glen 1940- *WhoAmA 91*
Thieler, Peter 1943- *WhoWor 91*
Thielke, Michael Murray 1953- *WhoEmL 91*
Thielman, Jake 1879-1928 *Ballpl 90*
Thielman, Samuel Barnett 1955- *BiDrAPA 89*
Thielman, William Albert 1915- *St&PR 91*
Thielsch, Deborah L. *St&PR 91*
Thielsch, Helmut John 1922- *WhoAm 90*
Thieman, Alice Anne 1941- *WhoAmW 91*
Thieman, Ralph 1932- *St&PR 91*
Thieman, Thomas G *BiDrAPA 89*
Thiemann, Bernd 1943- *WhoWor 91*
Thiemann, Charles Lee 1937- *WhoAm 90*
Thiemann, Jeffrey J. 1957- *St&PR 91*
Thiemann, Paul P. 1927- *St&PR 91*
Thiemann, Ronald Frank 1946- *WhoAm 90*
Thieme, Allan Roy 1937- *St&PR 91*
Thieme, Beth L. 1955- *St&PR 91*
Thieme, Jerzy Krzysztof 1947- *WhoE 91*
Thieme, R. B., Jr. *BioIn 16*
Thieme, Ulrich 1950- *IntWWM 90*
Thiemeyer, Fleur *BioIn 16*
Thienemann, Margo L *BiDrAPA 89*
Thienhaus, Ole J. 1953- *BiDrAPA 89*
Thier, Herbert David 1932- *WhoAm 90*
Thier, J. Jay 1952- *St&PR 91*
Thier, Mike Louis 1956- *St&PR 91*
Thier, Norman S. 1930- *St&PR 91*
Thier, Samuel Osiah 1937- *WhoAm 90, WhoE 91*
Thierack, Otto 1889-1946 *BioIn 16*
Thierfelder, Hans 1858-1930 *DcScB S2*
Thierfelder, Vivian *BioIn 16*
Thierfelder, William Richard, III *WhoE 91*
Thieriot, Charles H. 1914- *St&PR 91*
Thierry, John Adams 1913- *WhoAm 90*
Thierry, Robert Charles 1938- *WhoWor 91*
Thiers, Eugene Andres 1941- *WhoHisp 91, WhoWor 91*
Thiers, George Frederick 1921- *WhoE 91*
Thiers, Louis-Adolphe 1797-1877 *BiDFrPL, WorAlBi*
Thiery, Marthe 1902-1979 *OxCCanT*
Thies, Austin Cole 1921- *WhoAm 90, WhoWor 91*
Thies, Charles Herman 1940- *WhoAmA 91*
Thies, David Charles 1955- *WhoEmL 91*
Thies, Frank R. 1929- *St&PR 91*
Thies, Jake 1926- *Ballpl 90*
Thies, Richard Henry 1941- *St&PR 91*
Thies, Roger Elliot 1933- *WhoSSW 91*
Thiesenhusen, William Charles 1936- *WhoAm 90*
Thiessen, Cornie R. 1910- *WhoAm 90*
Thiessen, Delbert Duane 1932- *WhoAm 90*
Thiessen, G.G. 1938- *St&PR 91*
Thiessen, Peter-Adolf 1899-1990 *BioIn 16*
Thiessen, Tiffani-Amber *BioIn 16*
Thiewes, Rachelle R 1952- *WhoAmA 91*
Thigpen, Alton Hill 1927- *WhoAm 90*
Thigpen, Bobby 1963- *Ballpl 90*
Thigpen, Corbett H *BiDrAPA 89*
Thigpen, Ed *BioIn 16*
Thigpen, Helen 192-?- *DcAfAmP*
Thigpen, James C. 1949- *St&PR 91*
Thigpen, James Tate 1944- *WhoWor 91*
Thigpen, James W. 1937- *St&PR 91*
Thigpen, Lynne *ConTFT 8, DrBlPA 90*
Thigpen, Marsha Evette 1956- *WhoSSW 91*
Thigpen, Morris Lee, Sr. 1939- *WhoSSW 91*
Thigpen, Norma Jean 1957- *WhoAmW 91*
Thigpen, Peter Lee 1939- *St&PR 91*
Thigpen, Richard E., Jr. 1930- *WhoSSW 91*
Thigpenn, Anthony *BioIn 16*
Thiher, Allen 1941- *ConAu 31NR*
Thijsse, Wilhelmus Hermanus 1916- *IntWWM 90*
Thijssen, Johan Maria 1939- *WhoWor 91*
Thil, Jeanne 1887-1938? *BiDWomA*
Thill, Georges 1897-1984 *PenDiMP*
Thill, James Francis 1939- *St&PR 91*
Thill, John Peter 1912- *St&PR 91*
Thill, John Val 1953- *WhoEmL 91*
Thillmann, John Horst 1946- *WhoE 91*
Thimann, Kenneth Vivian 1904- *WhoAm 90*
Thimelby, Catherine *BiDEWW*
Thimelby, Eliza *BiDEWW*
Thimelby, Gertrude 1617?-1668 *FemiCLE*
Thimelby, Winefrid 1618-1690 *FemiCLE*
Thimelby, Winefrid 1619-1690 *BiDEWW*
Thimm, Alfred Louis 1923- *WhoAm 90*
Thimm, Heinz Ulrich 1927- *WhoWor 91*
Thimmaiah, Manavattira B *BiDrAPA 89*
Thin Lizzy *EncPR&S 89*
Thiollier, Eliane 1926- *BiDWomA*
Thiounn, Prasith 1930- *WhoWor 91*
Third World *EncPR&S 89*
Thirkell, Angela 1890-1961 *BioIn 16, FemiCLE*
Thirkell, Gary J. 1944- *St&PR 91*
Thirkell, Thomas James 1960- *St&PR 91*
Thirlwall, Anthony Philip 1941- *WhoWor 91*
Thirty-Eight Special *EncPR&S 89*
Thiruvathukal, Teresa 1948- *WhoEmL 91*
Thiry, Paul 1904- *WhoAm 90, WhoAmA 91, WhoWor 91*
Thistlethwaite, Mark Edward 1948- *WhoAmA 91*
Thliveris, Elizabeth Hope 1939- *WhoWrEP 89*
Thobae, Charles Peter 1930- *WhoSSW 91*
Thoburn, Tina *AuBYP 90*
Thocaven, Pierre Jean 1941- *WhoWor 91*
Thode, Edward Frederick 1921- *WhoAm 90*
Thoden Van Velzen, Syo Kornelius 1934- *WhoWor 91*
Thodos, Constantine N. 1926- *St&PR 91*
Thoele-Ryan, Sylvia Kathleen 1949- *WhoAmW 91*
Thoemke, Kris Walter 1951- *WhoSSW 91*
Thoene, Carl Louis 1927- *St&PR 91*
Thoenes, Wolfgang Carl 1929- *WhoWor 91*
Thoeni, Erich 1946- *WhoWor 91*
Thoeni, Gustavo 1951- *WorAlBi*
Thoet, Carolyn D. 1943- *St&PR 91*
Thoke, Ann Elisabeth 1952- *St&PR 91*
Thole, Jerome Louis 1930- *WhoSSW 91*
Thole, Rodney G. 1939- *St&PR 91*
Tholen, Nellie 1903- *IntWWM 90*
Tholey, James Michael 1952- *St&PR 91*
Tholey, Paul 1937- *WhoWor 91*
Thollander, Earl 1922- *WhoAmA 91*
Tholstrup, Lars Mogens Henrik 1927- *WhoWor 91*
Thom, Clifford 1948- *St&PR 91*
Thom, Darrow Jay *BiDrAPA 89*
Thom, Douglas A. 1939- *St&PR 91*
Thom, Douglas Andrew 1939- *WhoAm 90*
Thom, Drummond Robert 1936- *WhoSSW 91*
Thom, James Alexander 1933- *WhoWrEP 89*
Thom, John 1940- *ODwPR 91*
Thom, Joseph M. 1919- *WhoAm 90*
Thom, Joseph Pembroke 1828-1899 *AmLegL*
Thom, Julia S 1904- *BiDrAPA 89*
Thom, Ronald James 1923- *WhoWor 91*
Thoma, Carl Dee 1948- *WhoAm 90*
Thoma, Edward W. 1945- *St&PR 91*
Thoma, Kurt Michael 1946- *WhoWor 91*
Thoma, Ludwig 1867-1921 *BioIn 16*
Thoma, Russell James 1936- *WhoSSW 91*
Thomadakis, Panagiotis Evangelos 1941- *WhoWor 91*
Thomalske, R.E. Gunther 1925- *WhoWor 91*
Thoman, George M. 1926- *St&PR 91*
Thoman, Joseph Karol, Jr. 1947- *WhoE 91*
Thoman, Mark 1935- *WhoAm 90*
Thoman, Mark Edward 1936- *WhoAm 90*
Thomaneck, J. K. A. 1941- *ConAu 132*
Thomarios, Paul Nick 1947- *St&PR 91*
Thomas A Becket 1118?-1170 *WorAlBi*
Thomas A Kempis 1379?-1471 *WorAlBi*
Thomas, a Kempis 1380-1471 *BioIn 16*
Thomas, Aquinas 1225?-1274 *BioIn 16*
Thomas Aquinas, Saint 1224?-1274 *WorAlBi*
Thomas, of Villanova 1488-1555 *BioIn 16*
Thomas the Rhymer 1220?-1297? *EncO&P 3*
Thomas, Aelamkalam C 1936- *BiDrAPA 89*
Thomas, Alan 1923- *WhoWor 91*
Thomas, Alan Richard 1942- *WhoAm 90*
Thomas, Albert Aristide 1878-1932 *BiDFrPL*

Thomas, Albert Fisher 1935- *WhoSSW 91*
Thomas, Albert G *BiDrAPA 89*
Thomas, Alexander 1914- *BiDrAPA 89, WhoAm 90*
Thomas, Allen Leonard 1941- *WhoSSW 91*
Thomas, Allen Lloyd 1939- *WhoE 91, WhoWor 91*
Thomas, Alma Woodsey 1891-1978 *BiDWomA, WhoAmA 91N*
Thomas, Alva Lee 1929- *WhoAmW 91*
Thomas, Amanda Jane 1961- *IntWWM 90*
Thomas, Ambroise 1811-1896 *PenDiMP A*
Thomas, Andra Carol 1948- *WhoAmW 91*
Thomas, Andrea *AuBYP 90*
Thomas, Andres 1963- *Ballpl 90*
Thomas, Andrew Houston 1935- *WhoE 91*
Thomas, Ann *BioIn 16*
Thomas, Ann Louise 1930- *WhoAmW 91*
Thomas, Ann Van Wynen 1919- *WhoAm 90*
Thomas, Anne Elizabeth 1920- *WhoAmW 91*
Thomas, Annie 1838-1918 *FemiCLE*
Thomas, Anthony 1947- *St&PR 91*
Thomas, Archibald Johns, III 1952- *WhoSSW 91, WhoWor 91*
Thomas, Arline 1913-1989 *BioIn 16*
Thomas, Art 1952- *BioIn 16*
Thomas, Arthur E. *WhoAm 90*
Thomas, Arthur Ellis 1938- *St&PR 91*
Thomas, Arthur Goring 1850-1892 *PenDiMP A*
Thomas, Arthur L. 1947- *St&PR 91*
Thomas, Arthur Lawrence 1931- *WhoAm 90*
Thomas, Arthur Lawrence 1952- *WhoEmL 91, WhoWrEP 89*
Thomas, Aubrey Stephen, Jr. 1933- *WhoE 91*
Thomas, Audrey 1935- *FemiCLE, MajTwCW*
Thomas, Audrey Callahan *BioIn 16*
Thomas, Augusta Wales *BioIn 16*
Thomas, Babu 1950- *WhoSSW 91*
Thomas, Bailey Alfred *WhoAm 90, WhoE 91*
Thomas, Barbara *BioIn 16*
Thomas, Barbara Ann 1935- *WhoWor 91*
Thomas, Barbara Ann Porte- *BioIn 16*
Thomas, Barbara Lowry 1951- *BiDrAPA 89*
Thomas, Barbara Singer 1946- *WhoAm 90, WhoAmW 91, WhoE 91, WhoWor 91*
Thomas, Benjamin Platt 1902-1956 *AuBYP 90*
Thomas, Bertha 1845-1918 *FemiCLE*
Thomas, Berthold 1910- *WhoWor 91*
Thomas, Beth Eileen Wood 1916- *WhoAm 90, WhoAmW 91*
Thomas, Betty *WhoAm 90, WhoAmW 91*
Thomas, Beverly Phyllis 1938- *WhoAmW 91, WhoWrEP 89*
Thomas, Bide L. 1935- *St&PR 91*
Thomas, Bide Lakin 1935- *WhoAm 90*
Thomas, Billy 1920- *WhoE 91, WhoWor 91*
Thomas, Billy Joe 1942- *WhoAm 90*
Thomas, Bob *ODwPR 91*
Thomas, Bob Gene 1947- *WhoSSW 91*
Thomas, Bonnie Lou 1942- *WhoAmW 91*
Thomas, Brantley D., Jr. 1933- *St&PR 91*
Thomas, Brenda E. 1957- *WhoAmW 91*
Thomas, Brian G. 1934- *St&PR 91*
Thomas, Brooks 1931- *WhoAm 90*
Thomas, Bruce *ConAu 31NR*
Thomas, Bruce Gregory, Sr. 1946- *WhoSSW 91*
Thomas, Brunhilde S. 1911- *St&PR 91*
Thomas, Bud 1910- *Ballpl 90*
Thomas, Byron 1902-1978 *WhoAmA 91N*
Thomas, C David 1946- *WhoAmA 91*
Thomas, C Drayton 1867-1953 *EncO&P 3*
Thomas, C.S. 1939- *St&PR 91*
Thomas, Calvert 1916- *WhoAm 90*
Thomas, Carey 1857-1935 *BioAmW*
Thomas, Carla *BioIn 16*
Thomas, Carla 1942- *EncPR&S 89*
Thomas, Carol 1965- *WhoWrEP 89*
Thomas, Carol Todd 1952- *WhoAmW 91*
Thomas, Carolyn Elise 1943- *WhoAmW 91*
Thomas, Carrie *ODwPR 91*
Thomas, Caryl 1958- *IntWWM 90*
Thomas, Charles Alan *BiDrAPA 89*
Thomas, Charles Brosius 1935- *St&PR 91*
Thomas, Charles Davis 1928- *WhoWrEP 89*
Thomas, Charles Drayton *EncPaPR 91*
Thomas, Charles F. *WhoAm 90*
Thomas, Charles Henry 1920- *BiDrAPA 89*
Thomas, Charles Howard, II 1934- *WhoAm 90*
Thomas, Charles William 1937- *WhoAm 90*
Thomas, Charles William, II 1926- *WhoAm 90*
Thomas, Christina Joan *WhoAmW 91*
Thomas, Christopher R. 1948- *St&PR 91*
Thomas, Christopher Yancey, III 1923- *WhoAm 90*
Thomas, Christopher Yancey, IV 1948- *WhoSSW 91*
Thomas, Clara McCandless 1919- *WhoAm 90, WhoAmW 91, WhoWrEP 89*
Thomas, Claude Gibson 1926- *St&PR 91*
Thomas, Claudewell Sidney 1932- *BiDrAPA 89*
Thomas, Claudia *BiDrAPA 89*
Thomas, Clint 1896- *Ballpl 90*
Thomas, Coleen Suzanne 1965- *WhoSSW 91*
Thomas, Colin Gordon, Jr. 1918- *WhoAm 90*
Thomas, Craig 1933- *WhoAm 90*
Thomas, Cyrus H. 1925- *St&PR 91*
Thomas, D A 1917- *BiDrAPA 89*
Thomas, D. M. *BioIn 16*
Thomas, D M 1935- *MajTwCW*
Thomas, Damon Jay 1962- *WhoSSW 91*
Thomas, Dan Anderson 1922- *WhoAm 90*
Thomas, Daniel B. *WhoWrEP 89*
Thomas, Daniel Foley 1950- *St&PR 91, WhoAm 90, WhoE 91*
Thomas, Daniel Holcombe 1906- *WhoAm 90*
Thomas, Danny 1914- *WorAlBi*
Thomas, Danny 1914-1991 *WhoAm 90*
Thomas, Dave *BioIn 16*
Thomas, David *BioIn 16*
Thomas, David 1943- *IntWWM 90, PenDiMP*
Thomas, David A. 1958- *St&PR 91*
Thomas, David A., Jr. 1936- *St&PR 91*
Thomas, David Allen 1939- *WhoSSW 91*
Thomas, David Ansell 1917- *WhoAm 90, WhoWor 91*
Thomas, David Craig Owen 1942- *SpyFic*
Thomas, David Earl 1948- *BiDrAPA 89*
Thomas, David Earl, III 1945- *St&PR 91*
Thomas, David Geoffrey 1954- *IntWWM 90*
Thomas, David Gilbert 1928- *WhoAm 90*
Thomas, David Glyndor Treharne 1941- *WhoWor 91*
Thomas, David Hudson 1942- *St&PR 91*
Thomas, David Hurst 1945- *WhoAm 90*
Thomas, David John 1924- *WhoWor 91*
Thomas, David L., Jr. 1949- *WhoEmL 91*
Thomas, David Lloyd 1942- *WhoSSW 91*
Thomas, David Michael 1960- *BiDrAPA 89*
Thomas, David Northcutt 1934- *WhoSSW 91*
Thomas, David Phillip 1918- *WhoAm 90*
Thomas, David Raymond 1946- *WhoSSW 91*
Thomas, David Robert 1954- *WhoE 91, WhoWor 91*
Thomas, David St. John 1929- *ConAu 30NR*
Thomas, David Walter, Jr. 1938- *WhoAm 90, WhoSSW 91*
Thomas, David William 1947- *WhoE 91*
Thomas, Davis 1928- *WhoAm 90*
Thomas, Dawn C. *BioIn 16*
Thomas, Debi *BioIn 16*
Thomas, Debi 1967- *WhoAmW 91*
Thomas, Deborah Anne 1957- *WhoAmW 91*
Thomas, Deborah Brooks 1951- *WhoAmW 91*
Thomas, Deborah Rochelle 1960- *WhoE 91*
Thomas, Deroy C. 1926- *St&PR 91, WhoAm 90, WhoE 91*
Thomas, Derrel 1951- *Ballpl 90*
Thomas, Donald Arnett 1933- *St&PR 91*
Thomas, Donald Charles 1935- *WhoAm 90*
Thomas, Donald Gene, Jr. 1963- *WhoSSW 91*
Thomas, Donald L. *BioIn 16*
Thomas, Douglas Alan, Sr. 1952- *WhoSSW 91*
Thomas, Douglas Mackubin 1952- *WhoE 91*
Thomas, Douglas W 1921- *BiDrAPA 89*
Thomas, Duane 1947- *BioIn 16*
Thomas, Dudley Jerome 1940- *WhoE 91*
Thomas, Dwight Erric 1953- *WhoE 91*
Thomas, Dylan 1914-1953 *BioIn 16, MajTwCW, PoeCrit 2 [port], SmATA 60 [port], WorAlBi*
Thomas, E. Parry 1921- *WhoAm 90*
Thomas, Eapen 1939- *WhoAm 90*
Thomas, Ed *BioIn 16*
Thomas, Edward 1878-1917 *BioIn 16, DcLB 98 [port]*
Thomas, Edward Donnall 1920- *WhoAm 90*
Thomas, Edward Francis, Jr. 1937- *WhoAm 90*
Thomas, Edwin John 1927- *WhoAm 90*
Thomas, Edwin Ross 1850- *EncABHB 4*
Thomas, Elaine Freeman 1923- *WhoAmA 91*
Thomas, Elean 1947- *FemiCLE*
Thomas, Elizabeth 1675-1731 *BiDEWW, FemiCLE*
Thomas, Elizabeth 1771- *FemiCLE*
Thomas, Elizabeth Anne 1959- *WhoAmW 91*
Thomas, Elizabeth Frances 1716-1779 *FemiCLE*
Thomas, Elizabeth Ruth, II 1964- *WhoE 91*
Thomas, Ellen Dillon 1958- *WhoAmW 91*
Thomas, Ellen McVeigh 1952- *WhoAmW 91*
Thomas, Elmer *BioIn 16*
Thomas, Emmett Nicholson 1855- *AmLegL*
Thomas, Esther Merlene 1945- *WhoAmW 91, WhoEmL 91, WhoWor 91*
Thomas, Ethel Colvin Nichols 1913- *WhoAmW 91, WhoE 91*
Thomas, Eugene Anthony 1930- *St&PR 91*
Thomas, Evelyn F. 1922- *WhoWrEP 89*
Thomas, Ewart A. C. *WhoAm 90*
Thomas, F. Richard 1940- *WhoWrEP 89*
Thomas, Fay 1904- *Ballpl 90*
Thomas, Fillmore 1916- *St&PR 91*
Thomas, Florence Kathleen 1945- *WhoAmW 91*
Thomas, Frances 1943- *ConAu 130*
Thomas, Francis Lamar 1941- *WhoSSW 91*
Thomas, Francis Thornton 1939- *WhoSSW 91*
Thomas, Frank 1929- *Ballpl 90, BioIn 16*
Thomas, Frank Howard 1929- *St&PR 91*
Thomas, Frank Joseph 1943- *St&PR 91*
Thomas, Franklin A. 1934- *BioIn 16*
Thomas, Franklin Augustine 1934- *WhoAm 90*
Thomas, Fred C. *BioIn 16*
Thomas, Frederic Joseph 1929- *WhoE 91*
Thomas, Frederick Elmer 1945- *WhoSSW 91*
Thomas, G June *BiDrAPA 89*
Thomas, Gareth 1932- *WhoAm 90*
Thomas, Gareth Jacob 1930- *St&PR 91*
Thomas, Garnett Jett 1920- *WhoSSW 91, WhoWor 91*
Thomas, Garth Johnson 1916- *WhoAm 90*
Thomas, Gary Allen 1956- *WhoEmL 91*
Thomas, Gary Lynn 1942- *WhoAm 90, WhoE 91*
Thomas, George 1937- *Ballpl 90*
Thomas, George H. 1816-1870 *WorAlBi*
Thomas, George Leicester, III 1934- *St&PR 91*
Thomas, George Martin 1941- *WhoSSW 91*
Thomas, George Stanley 1942- *St&PR 91*
Thomas, George T. 1856- *AmLegL*
Thomas, Georgia Mae 1939- *WhoAmW 91*
Thomas, Georgie A. *WhoAmW 91, WhoE 91*
Thomas, Gerald Everett 1935- *St&PR 91*
Thomas, Gerard 1925- *St&PR 91*
Thomas, Gerard P. 1930- *St&PR 91*
Thomas, Germain *PenDiDA 89*
Thomas, Gladys 1935- *FemiCLE*
Thomas, Gladys Roberts *WhoAmW 91*
Thomas, Glenn Gilmore 1925- *WhoAm 90*
Thomas, Gloria *NewAgMG*
Thomas, Gordon C G 1919- *BiDrAPA 89*
Thomas, Gorman 1950- *Ballpl 90*
Thomas, Grace F *BiDrAPA 89*
Thomas, Gregory C. 1947- *St&PR 91*
Thomas, Gregory E. 1949- *WhoWrEP 89*
Thomas, Guy Richard 1950- *WhoSSW 91*
Thomas, Gwyn 1913-1981 *DcNaB 1981*
Thomas, H. C. *AuBYP 90*
Thomas, H. Emerson 1902- *St&PR 91*
Thomas, H. Landon *BioIn 16*
Thomas, H Reynolds 1927- *WhoAmA 91*
Thomas, Harold *BioIn 16*
Thomas, Harold Allen, Jr. 1913- *WhoAm 90*
Thomas, Harold George 1948- *WhoSSW 91*
Thomas, Harry *BioIn 16*
Thomas, Harry Reynolds 1927- *WhoE 91*
Thomas, Hazel Foster 1923- *WhoWrEP 89*
Thomas, Hazel Louise 1947- *WhoE 91*
Thomas, Heather Fletcher 1961- *WhoE 91*
Thomas, Helen *WhoAmA 91*
Thomas, Helen 1871-1956 *BioAmW*
Thomas, Helen 1920- *WorAlBi*
Thomas, Helen A. 1920- *WhoAm 90, WhoAmW 91*
Thomas, Henri 1912- *WhoWor 91*
Thomas, Henry *BioIn 16*
Thomas, Herbert E 1928- *BiDrAPA 89*
Thomas, Hilary Bryn 1943- *WhoE 91*
Thomas, Horace H. 1831-1904 *AmLegL*
Thomas, Hugh Swynnerton 1931- *WhoWor 91*
Thomas, Ianthe 1951- *BioIn 16*
Thomas, Ira 1881-1958 *Ballpl 90*
Thomas, Irene 1957- *WhoSSW 91*
Thomas, Irma *BioIn 16*
Thomas, Isaiah 1750-1831 *BioIn 16*
Thomas, Isiah *BioIn 16*
Thomas, Isiah 1962- *WorAlBi*
Thomas, Isiah Lord 1961- *WhoAm 90*
Thomas, J D 1910- *ConAu 31NR*
Thomas, J. Earl 1918- *WhoAm 90*
Thomas, J. Edward, Jr. 1923- *St&PR 91*
Thomas, J. Kerry 1934- *WhoAm 90*
Thomas, J. Randall 1906- *St&PR 91*
Thomas, Jack Anthony 1940- *WhoSSW 91*
Thomas, Jack Boyd 1944- *St&PR 91*
Thomas, Jack Eugene 1910- *WhoE 91*
Thomas, Jack Lyndon 1944- *St&PR 91*
Thomas, Jack Robert 1937- *St&PR 91*
Thomas, Jackie L. 1941- *St&PR 91*
Thomas, Jacqueline *PenDiMP*
Thomas, Jacquelyn May 1932- *WhoAmW 91*
Thomas, Jacques Henri 1933- *BiDrAPA 89*
Thomas, James Bert, Jr. 1935- *WhoAm 90*
Thomas, James Blake 1930- *BiDrAPA 89*
Thomas, James Edward 1944- *WhoE 91*
Thomas, James H *BiDrAPA 89*
Thomas, James Harold *BiDrAPA 89*
Thomas, James Henry 1926- *MusmAFA*
Thomas, James Lloyd 1943- *BiDrAPA 89*
Thomas, James Phillip 1959- *WhoEmL 91*
Thomas, James Raymond 1947- *WhoSSW 91*
Thomas, James Robert 1948- *WhoEmL 91*
Thomas, James Russell, Jr. 1941- *WhoSSW 91*
Thomas, James Talbert, IV 1951- *WhoSSW 91*
Thomas, Jane Resh 1936- *AuBYP 90*
Thomas, Janet Marie *WhoE 91*
Thomas, Janice Sandlin 1939- *WhoSSW 91*
Thomas, Jarrett Neil 1935- *St&PR 91*
Thomas, Jean *WhoWor 91*
Thomas, Jean-Jacques Robert 1948- *WhoSSW 91*
Thomas, Jean W. 1928- *IntWWM 90*
Thomas, Jeanette Mae 1946- *WhoAmW 91*
Thomas, Jeanne Monique Patin 1929- *WhoWor 91*
Thomas, Jeremy 1949- *BioIn 16*
Thomas, Jess 1927- *BioIn 16, IntWWM 90, PenDiMP, WhoAm 90*
Thomas, Jesse James 1933- *WhoWrEP 89*
Thomas, Jimmy Lynn 1941- *St&PR 91, WhoAm 90, WhoSSW 91*
Thomas, Joab Langston 1933- *WhoAm 90*
Thomas, Joan *BiDEWW*
Thomas, Joan Gale *AuBYP 90*
Thomas, Joe Carroll 1931- *WhoAm 90*
Thomas, John 1826-1913 *PenDiMP*
Thomas, John 1927- *WhoAmA 91*
Thomas, John 1946- *WhoEmL 91*
Thomas, John B 1920- *BiDrAPA 89*
Thomas, John Bowman 1925- *WhoAm 90*
Thomas, John C. *BioIn 16*
Thomas, John C. 1928- *St&PR 91*
Thomas, John Charles 1891-1960 *PenDiMP*
Thomas, John Charles 1950- *St&PR 91, WhoAm 90*
Thomas, John Charles 1959- *WhoSSW 91*
Thomas, John David 1947- *WhoAm 90*
Thomas, John David 1951- *WhoWor 91*
Thomas, John Earl 1943- *WhoAm 90*
Thomas, John Edward 1947- *WhoAm 90*
Thomas, John Edwin 1931- *WhoAm 90, WhoSSW 91*
Thomas, John F 1874-1940 *EncO&P 3*
Thomas, John Frederick 1874-1940 *EncPaPR 91*
Thomas, John Griffith, III 1948- *WhoE 91*
Thomas, John Howard 1941- *WhoAm 90*
Thomas, John K 1924- *BiDrAPA 89*
Thomas, John Melvin 1933- *WhoAm 90, WhoWor 91*
Thomas, John Meurig 1932- *WhoWor 91*
Thomas, John Paul 1940- *WhoAm 90*
Thomas, John R. 1917- *St&PR 91*
Thomas, John Thieme 1935- *St&PR 91, WhoAm 90*
Thomas, John W *BiDrAPA 89*
Thomas, John Wesley 1932- *WhoE 91*
Thomas, John Willard, Jr. 1927- *St&PR 91*
Thomas, John William 1937- *WhoAm 90*
Thomas, John Wix *BiDrAPA 89*
Thomas, Jon Roger 1946- *WhoAm 90*
Thomas, Jonathan Wesley 1963- *WhoEmL 91*
Thomas, Jorge A. 1946- *WhoHisp 91*
Thomas, Joseph Allan 1929- *St&PR 91, WhoAm 90*
Thomas, Joseph Deer, Jr. 1953- *WhoSSW 91*
Thomas, Joseph Fleshman 1915- *WhoAm 90*
Thomas, Joseph Paul 1947- *BiDrAPA 89*
Thomas, Joseph S *BiDrAPA 89*
Thomas, Joseph Wesley 1955- *WhoEmL 91*

Thomas, Joyce Carol *BioIn 16*
Thomas, Joyce Carol 1938- *FemiCLE, MajTwCW, WhoWrEP 89*
Thomas, Judith C. 1944- *IntWWM 90*
Thomas, Judy Michele 1954- *WhoSSW 91*
Thomas, Julia Ann *BiDrAPA 89*
Thomas, Karen *BiDrAPA 89*
Thomas, Karen M. 1949- *WhoAmW 91*
Thomas, Karl 1883-1969 *DcScB S2*
Thomas, Katherine *BioIn 16*
Thomas, Katherine Hitchcock 1952- *BiDrAPA 89*
Thomas, Kathleen *AuBYP 90*
Thomas, Kathleen K 1940- *WhoAmA 91, WhoE 91*
Thomas, Kay Lee 1942- *WhoAmW 91*
Thomas, Keith Vern 1946- *WhoEmL 91*
Thomas, Kenneth Glyndwr 1944- *St&PR 91*
Thomas, Konrad Boyd *BiDrAPA 89*
Thomas, Kuruvilla 1956- *BiDrAPA 89*
Thomas, L.B. 1936- *St&PR 91*
Thomas, Landon *St&PR 91*
Thomas, Langley C. 1953- *St&PR 91*
Thomas, Larry W 1943- *WhoAmA 91*
Thomas, Laura Marlene 1936- *WhoAmW 91, WhoWor 91*
Thomas, Laurence W. 1927- *WhoWrEP 89*
Thomas, Lawrason Dale 1934- *WhoAm 90*
Thomas, Lawrence R. 1935- *St&PR 91*
Thomas, Lee *BioIn 16*
Thomas, Lee 1936- *Ballpl 90*
Thomas, Lee B., Jr. 1926- *St&PR 91*
Thomas, Lee Muller 1944- *WhoAm 90*
Thomas, Leo 1947- *WhoEmL 91, WhoWor 91*
Thomas, Leo John 1936- *St&PR 91*
Thomas, Leona Marlene 1933- *WhoAmW 91, WhoWor 91*
Thomas, Lewis 1913- *BioIn 16, MajTwCW, WhoAm 90, WhoWor 91, WorAlBi*
Thomas, Lewis Jones, Jr. 1930- *WhoAm 90*
Thomas, Lillo *DrBlPA 90*
Thomas, Linda B. 1946- *WhoAmW 91*
Thomas, Lindsey Kay, Jr. 1931- *WhoWor 91*
Thomas, Llewellyn Hilleth 1903- *WhoAm 90*
Thomas, Lori Rae 1954- *WhoAmW 91*
Thomas, Lothar 1941- *WhoWor 91*
Thomas, Louis Godfrey Lee 1896- *WhoAm 90*
Thomas, Lowell 1892-1981 *BioIn 16, WorAlBi*
Thomas, Lowell, Jr. 1923- *WhoAm 90*
Thomas, Lowell Jackson 1892-1981 *AuBYP 90*
Thomas, Lowell Jackson, Jr. 1923- *AuBYP 90*
Thomas, Lowell S., Jr. 1931- *St&PR 91*
Thomas, Loyd A. 1933- *St&PR 91*
Thomas, Lucille Cole 1921- *WhoAmW 91*
Thomas, Lyn Ellen 1958- *WhoAmW 91*
Thomas, M. Donald 1926- *WhoAm 90*
Thomas, Mable *BioIn 16*
Thomas, Mable 1957- *WhoAmW 91*
Thomas, Malayilmelathethil 1932- *WhoSSW 91*
Thomas, Margaret Ann 1945- *WhoAmW 91, WhoEmL 91*
Thomas, Margaret Jean 1943- *WhoAm 90, WhoAmW 91*
Thomas, Maria *ConAu 129*
Thomas, Maria 1941-1989 *BioIn 16*
Thomas, Maria De Fatima *BiDrAPA 89*
Thomas, Marie *DrBlPA 90*
Thomas, Marion G *BiDrAPA 89*
Thomas, Marjorie Bekaert 1947- *WhoAmW 91, WhoSSW 91*
Thomas, Marjorie Oliviene *WhoAmW 91*
Thomas, Mark Ellis 1955- *WhoWrEP 89*
Thomas, Mark Roads 1957- *WhoSSW 91*
Thomas, Mark Stanton 1931- *IntWWM 90, WhoAm 90*
Thomas, Marlin Uluess 1942- *WhoE 91*
Thomas, Marlo 1943- *WhoAm 90, WhoAmW 91, WorAlBi*
Thomas, Marsha L. 1947- *WhoAmW 91*
Thomas, Marshall R 1954- *BiDrAPA 89*
Thomas, Martha Carey 1857-1953 *WorAlBi*
Thomas, Martha Janice 1949- *WhoAmW 91*
Thomas, Martha Wetterhall 1949- *WhoAmW 91*
Thomas, Mary *BioIn 16*
Thomas, Mary 1932- *PenDiMP*
Thomas, Mary Barton 1954- *WhoSSW 91*
Thomas, Mary Jo *BiDrAPA 89*
Thomas, Mary Leath 1905-1959 *WhoAmA 91N*
Thomas, Mary Louise 1927- *WhoWrEP 89*
Thomas, Mary M. 1946- *St&PR 91*
Thomas, Mary Martin 1961- *WhoEmL 91*
Thomas, Matt *BioIn 16*
Thomas, Matthew Henderson, Jr. 1948- *WhoWrEP 89*
Thomas, Michael *ODwPR 91, PenDiMP*
Thomas, Michael 1943- *IntWWM 90*
Thomas, Michael A. 1949- *St&PR 91*
Thomas, Michael Allan 1957- *WhoSSW 91*
Thomas, Michael Duane 1948- *WhoSSW 91*
Thomas, Michael Leo 1953- *WhoE 91*
Thomas, Michael M. 1936- *SpyFic*
Thomas, Michael R. *BioIn 16*
Thomas, Michael Tilson 1944- *BioIn 16, IntWWM 90, News 90 [port], -90-3 [port], PenDiMP, WhoAm 90, WhoWor 91, WorAlBi*
Thomas, Michel *BioIn 16*
Thomas, Michele Karin 1948- *WhoSSW 91*
Thomas, Michelle Rochon 1962- *WhoAmW 91*
Thomas, Mildred 1930- *St&PR 91*
Thomas, Milton Carter, II 1946- *WhoWor 91*
Thomas, Minnie *BioIn 16*
Thomas, Minor Wine, Jr. 1917- *WhoAm 90*
Thomas, Miriam Higgins 1920- *WhoAmW 91*
Thomas, Mitchell, Jr. 1936- *WhoAm 90*
Thomas, Mivart G W *BiDrAPA 89*
Thomas, Monica G. 1939- *WhoAmW 91*
Thomas, Myles 1897-1963 *Ballpl 90*
Thomas, Niles Buchanan 1945- *WhoSSW 91*
Thomas, Norman 1884-1968 *EncAL*
Thomas, Norman Carl 1932- *WhoAm 90, WhoWrEP 89*
Thomas, Norman M. 1884-1968 *WorAlBi*
Thomas, Norvin Eugene 1945- *WhoEmL 91*
Thomas, Norwood Anderson, Jr. 1932- *St&PR 91*
Thomas, Oomman 1950- *WhoSSW 91*
Thomas, Orville C. 1915- *WhoAm 90*
Thomas, Owen Clark 1922- *WhoAm 90*
Thomas, Patricia 1934- *AuBYP 90*
Thomas, Patricia Anne 1927- *WhoAmW 91*
Thomas, Patricia Grafton 1921- *WhoAmW 91*
Thomas, Patricia J. 1934- *BioIn 16*
Thomas, Patrick E. 1954- *St&PR 91*
Thomas, Patrick Herbert 1942- *WhoAm 90*
Thomas, Paul *MajTwCW*
Thomas, Paul Anthony 1956- *WhoSSW 91*
Thomas, Paul Bert 1925- *St&PR 91*
Thomas, Paul Emery 1927- *WhoAm 90*
Thomas, Paul G. 1955- *St&PR 91*
Thomas, Paul Gregory 1958- *WhoWor 91*
Thomas, Paul Jones 1914- *WhoAm 90*
Thomas, Paula Dugas 1960- *WhoSSW 91*
Thomas, Payne Edward Lloyd 1919- *WhoAm 90*
Thomas, Peggy Lee 1948- *WhoEmL 91*
Thomas, Pendleton Emmett, III 1929- *WhoSSW 91*
Thomas, Penelope Jane 1949- *WhoAmW 91*
Thomas, Peter D. 1928- *WhoWrEP 89*
Thomas, Peter M. 1950- *St&PR 91*
Thomas, Philip 1949- *DrBlPA 90*
Thomas, Philip Francis 1810-1890 *BiDrUSE 89*
Thomas, Philip L 1935- *ODwPR 91*
Thomas, Philip Michael *BioIn 16*
Thomas, Philip Robinson 1934- *WhoWor 91*
Thomas, Philip Stanley 1928- *WhoAm 90*
Thomas, Pinch 1888-1953 *Ballpl 90*
Thomas, Piri 1928- *BioIn 16, HispWr 90*
Thomas, Powys 1926-1977 *OxCCanT*
Thomas, R Buckland 1931- *BiDrAPA 89*
Thomas, R. David *BioIn 16*
Thomas, R. David 1932- *St&PR 91*
Thomas, R S 1913- *ConAu 30NR, MajTwCW*
Thomas, Ralph Edward 1928- *St&PR 91*
Thomas, Ralph Upton 1942- *WhoSSW 91*
Thomas, Rand T. 1950- *ODwPR 91*
Thomas, Ranota Delores *BiDrAPA 89*
Thomas, Raymond Lamar 1943- *St&PR 91*
Thomas, Reba Tucker 1935- *WhoSSW 91*
Thomas, Richard 1917-1988 *BioIn 16*
Thomas, Richard 1951- *WhoAm 90, WhoE 91, WorAlBi*
Thomas, Richard C. *WhoAm 90*
Thomas, Richard Emery 1929- *WhoE 91, WhoWor 91*
Thomas, Richard L. 1931- *St&PR 91*
Thomas, Richard Lee 1931- *WhoAm 90*
Thomas, Richard Llewellyn 1947- *WhoE 91*
Thomas, Richard Nathan 1947- *WhoE 91*
Thomas, Richard Stephen 1949- *WhoEmL 91*
Thomas, Richard Suner 1945- *WhoE 91*
Thomas, Robert Allen 1946- *WhoSSW 91*
Thomas, Robert Chester 1924-1987 *WhoAmA 91N*
Thomas, Robert D. *BioIn 16*
Thomas, Robert D. 1933- *St&PR 91*
Thomas, Robert Dean 1933- *WhoAm 90, WhoE 91*
Thomas, Robert Dickinson 1945- *WhoAm 90, WhoWrEP 89*
Thomas, Robert E *BiDrAPA 89*
Thomas, Robert Eggleston 1914- *WhoAm 90*
Thomas, Robert Knoll 1933- *WhoAm 90*
Thomas, Robert Lee 1938- *WhoSSW 91*
Thomas, Robert Lindsay 1943- *WhoAm 90, WhoSSW 91*
Thomas, Robert Lloyd 1941- *WhoSSW 91, WhoWor 91*
Thomas, Robert Murray 1921- *WhoAm 90*
Thomas, Robert Ray 1926- *WhoSSW 91, WhoWor 91*
Thomas, Robert Stanley 1947- *St&PR 91*
Thomas, Robert W. 1921- *St&PR 91*
Thomas, Robert Wilburn 1937- *WhoAm 90*
Thomas, Robert William 1944- *WhoE 91*
Thomas, Robin Elliott 1953- *WhoE 91*
Thomas, Roderick Edward 1957- *WhoE 91*
Thomas, Roger Humphrey 1942- *St&PR 91*
Thomas, Roger Meriwether 1930- *WhoAm 90*
Thomas, Roger Parry 1951- *WhoWor 91*
Thomas, Roger Warren 1937- *WhoAm 90*
Thomas, Roland Jay 1900-1967 *EncABHB 5 [port]*
Thomas, Ronald Carson 1944- *WhoE 91*
Thomas, Rosalind 1959- *ConAu 132, WhoWor 91*
Thomas, Rose 1952- *St&PR 91*
Thomas, Ross 1926- *TwCCr&M 91*
Thomas, Ross Elmore 1926- *SpyFic, WhoAm 90*
Thomas, Roy 1874-1959 *Ballpl 90*
Thomas, Roy 1953- *Ballpl 90*
Thomas, Roy Edward 1929- *BiDrAPA 89*
Thomas, Roy Weldon 1929- *St&PR 91*
Thomas, Rufus 1917?- *EncPR&S 89*
Thomas, Rufus 1920- *BioIn 16*
Thomas, Russell Alvin 1939- *St&PR 91*
Thomas, Ruth *AuBYP 90*
Thomas, Sally Smith 1938- *St&PR 91*
Thomas, Samuel Dee 1930- *WhoE 91*
Thomas, Samuel F 1913- *BiDrAPA 89*
Thomas, Samuel F. 1913-1989 *BioIn 16*
Thomas, Sandra Paul 1940- *WhoAmW 91*
Thomas, Sarah Beth 1957- *WhoAmW 91*
Thomas, Scott E. 1953- *WhoAm 90*
Thomas, Sharla Marie 1950- *WhoEmL 91*
Thomas, Sheryl Elaine 1950- *WhoAmW 91*
Thomas, Shirley *WhoAmW 91*
Thomas, Sidney 1915- *WhoAm 90*
Thomas, Stan 1949- *Ballpl 90*
Thomas, Steffen Wolfgang 1906-1990 *WhoAmA 91N*
Thomas, Stephen Allen 1950- *WhoEmL 91*
Thomas, Stephen Paul 1938- *WhoAm 90*
Thomas, Steven Murray 1946- *IntWWM 90*
Thomas, Susan A. 1956- *ODwPR 91*
Thomas, Susan Kay 1959- *WhoSSW 91*
Thomas, Tamara B *WhoAmA 91*
Thomas, Tammy Jean 1962- *WhoE 91*
Thomas, Ted LaRue 1935- *WhoSSW 91*
Thomas, Terence Michael 1952- *WhoEmL 91*
Thomas, Teresa Ann 1939- *WhoAmW 91*
Thomas, Thalia Ann Marie 1935- *WhoAmA 91*
Thomas, Theodore *BioIn 16*
Thomas, Theodore 1835-1905 *PenDiMP*
Thomas, Tommy 1899- *Ballpl 90*
Thomas, Tony *BioIn 16*
Thomas, Tori Winkler *BioIn 16*
Thomas, Tracy Richard 1934- *St&PR 91*
Thomas, V Jose 1937- *BiDrAPA 89*
Thomas, Valerie Michelle 1963- *WhoAmW 91*
Thomas, Valmy 1928- *Ballpl 90*
Thomas, Vanessa Elaine 1965- *WhoEmL 91*
Thomas, Vera Marline 1953- *WhoAmW 91*
Thomas, Vernon 1934- *BioIn 16*
Thomas, Vickie Martin 1951- *WhoAmW 91*
Thomas, Violeta de los Angeles 1949- *WhoAmW 91, WhoEmL 91, WhoWor 91*
Thomas, Virginia Lee 1916- *WhoAmW 91, WhoWor 91*
Thomas, Vivien T. 1910-1985 *BioIn 16*
Thomas, W. Bruce 1926- *St&PR 91*
Thomas, W. Dennis 1943- *WhoAm 90*
Thomas, Ward F. 1906- *WhoSSW 91*
Thomas, Warren Deane 1930- *WhoAm 90*
Thomas, Warren G. 1921- *St&PR 91*
Thomas, Warren Hafford 1933- *WhoAm 90*
Thomas, Wayne D. 1949- *St&PR 91*
Thomas, Wilbur Arlen 1930- *St&PR 91*
Thomas, William 1905- *Ballpl 90*
Thomas, William 1931?-1980 *DrBlPA 90*
Thomas, William Andrew 1962- *WhoWor 91*
Thomas, William B. *St&PR 91*
Thomas, William Bruce 1926- *WhoAm 90*
Thomas, William Charles 1926- *WhoAm 90*
Thomas, William Culwell 1928- *St&PR 91*
Thomas, William F. 1924- *BioIn 16*
Thomas, William Harry 1949- *WhoSSW 91*
Thomas, William Henry 1934- *WhoSSW 91*
Thomas, William Holland 1805-1893 *WhNaAH*
Thomas, William J 1933- *BiDrAPA 89*
Thomas, William LeRoy 1920- *WhoAm 90*
Thomas, William Marshall 1941- *WhoAm 90*
Thomas, William Neal 1927- *WhoSSW 91*
Thomas, William Orvill, Jr. 1914- *WhoAm 90*
Thomas, William Richard 1920- *WhoAm 90*
Thomas, William Scott 1949- *WhoEmL 91*
Thomas, William Stewart *BioIn 16*
Thomas, William T. 1935- *St&PR 91*
Thomas, William Widgery 1839-1927 *BioIn 16*
Thomas, William Widgery, Jr. 1839-1927 *AmLegL*
Thomas, Yvonne *WhoAmA 91*
Thomas, Yvonne 1960- *WhoE 91*
Thomas-Buckle, Suzann Remington 1945- *WhoAmW 91*
Thomas-Cote, Nancy Denece 1959- *WhoAmW 91*
Thomas-Phillips, Linda 1940- *St&PR 91*
Thomas-Ringley, Cathy J. 1958- *WhoAmW 91*
Thomaschke, Thomas 1943- *IntWWM 90*
Thomasen, Ole 1934 *WhoWor 91*
Thomases, Robert *BioIn 16*
Thomasey, James F. 1954- *St&PR 91*
Thomashow, Peter M 1953- *BiDrAPA 89*
Thomashow, Stanley Melvin 1943- *St&PR 91*
Thomason, Ann Wenninger 1934- *WhoAmW 91*
Thomason, Edward *PenDiDA 89*
Thomason, Fred Godwin *BiDrAPA 89*
Thomason, Harry Jack Lee, Jr. 1953- *WhoWor 91*
Thomason, Hubert H 1921- *St&PR 91*
Thomason, Hubert Hiram, Jr. 1950- *BiDrAPA 89*
Thomason, Janice Martechia 1945- *WhoAmW 91*
Thomason, Jessica L. 1950- *WhoEmL 91*
Thomason, Ken 1954- *St&PR 91*
Thomason, Michael Vincent 1942- *WhoAmA 91*
Thomason, Robert Earl 1932- *WhoWor 91*
Thomason, Tom William 1934- *WhoAmA 91*
Thomass, Chantal 1947- *ConDes 90*
Thomasson, Dan King 1933- *WhoAm 90, WhoE 91*
Thomasson, Donald Louis 1939- *BiDrAPA 89*
Thomasson, Gary 1951- *Ballpl 90*
Thomasson, Karen Raburn *BiDrAPA 89*
Thomasson, Sharon Biddle 1943- *WhoSSW 91*
Thombre, Melanie Susan 1953- *BiDrAPA 89*
Thomchick, Gerard M. 1955- *St&PR 91*
Thome, Diane 1942- *IntWWM 90*
Thome, John R. 1943- *St&PR 91*
Thomerson, Tim *ConTFT 8*
Thomes, Howard M. 1941- *St&PR 91*
Thometz, Kurt *BioIn 16*
Thometz, Nick *BioIn 16*
Thomford, Arline Gesine 1932- *WhoWrEP 89*
Thomford, Neil Roger 1931- *WhoAm 90*
Thominet, Maurice J. 1928- *WhoAm 90*
Thomire, Pierre-Philippe 1751-1843 *PenDiDA 89*
Thomlinson, Ralph 1925- *WhoAm 90*
Thomlison, Ray J. 1943- *WhoAm 90*
Thomlison, Terry Dean 1945- *WhoEmL 91*
Thomma, Mark Steven 1950- *BiDrAPA 89*
Thommen, Lynn 1954- *WhoE 91*
Thomopulos, Gregs G. 1942- *St&PR 91, WhoAm 90*
Thompkins, Gayle Lynette 1960- *WhoAmW 91*
Thompkins, Stephen R. 1944- *St&PR 91*
Thompsen, Joyce A. 1946- *St&PR 91*
Thompsen, Joyce Ann 1946- *WhoAmW 91, WhoEmL 91*
Thompson Family *ConAmBL*
Thompson Twins, The *EncPR&S 89*
Thompson, A. Frederick 1941- *St&PR 91*
Thompson, Adrian *IntWWM 90*
Thompson, Alan Eric 1924- *WhoWor 91*

Thompson, Alan Simon Halford 1945- *WhoWor 91*
Thompson, Albert Riley 1879-1947 *BioIn 16*
Thompson, Alden Lloyd 1943- *WhoAm 90*
Thompson, Allen Joseph 1937- *WhoSSW 91*
Thompson, Almose Alphonse 1942- *WhoSSW 91*
Thompson, Alvin J. 1924- *WhoAm 90*
Thompson, Amanda S. 1952- *St&PR 91*
Thompson, Ann Elizabeth 1937- *BiDrAPA 89*
Thompson, Anna Kathryn 1954- *WhoSSW 91*
Thompson, Anna Sue 1930- *WhoSSW 91*
Thompson, Anne Elise 1934- *WhoAmW 91, WhoE 91*
Thompson, Anne Marguerite *BiDrAPA 89*
Thompson, Anne Marie 1920- *WhoAmW 91*
Thompson, Annie Figueroa 1941- *WhoAm 90*
Thompson, Annie Laura 1937- *WhoSSW 91*
Thompson, Anthony Wayne 1940- *WhoAm 90*
Thompson, Arthur Charles 1942- *DrBlPA 90*
Thompson, Arthur Leonard Bell 1917-1975 *SpyFic*
Thompson, Arthur Raymond 1938- *WhoSSW 91*
Thompson, Baird McKee 1950- *St&PR 91*
Thompson, Barbara Anna 1889-1973 *BioIn 16*
Thompson, Barbara Storck 1924- *WhoAm 90*
Thompson, Benjamin 1918- *WhoAm 90*
Thompson, Benjy *BioIn 16*
Thompson, Bernadine L. 1936- *WhoSSW 91*
Thompson, Bert Allen 1930- *WhoAm 90*
Thompson, Bette Lee 1935- *WhoWrEP 89*
Thompson, Betty Lou 1927- *St&PR 91*
Thompson, Betty Lucille 1943- *WhoAmW 91*
Thompson, Bill Lawrence 1950- *WhoEmL 91*
Thompson, Bill M. 1932- *WhoSSW 91*
Thompson, Bill M. 1934- *St&PR 91*
Thompson, Bjorn J. 1934- *St&PR 91, WhoAm 90*
Thompson, Blair H. 1925- *St&PR 91*
Thompson, Blair Harris 1925- *WhoAm 90*
Thompson, Blanche Jennings 1887- *AuBYP 90*
Thompson, Blanche Lee 1958- *WhoAmW 91*
Thompson, Bob *WhoAmA 91N*
Thompson, Bobby 1912-1988 *AnObit 1988*
Thompson, Bobby Jack 1930- *WhoAm 90*
Thompson, Boyd 1921- *WhoAm 90*
Thompson, Bradbury 1911- *BioIn 16, ConDes 90, WhoAm 90, WhoAmA 91, WhoWor 91*
Thompson, Brenda Clare 1961- *WhoAmW 91*
Thompson, Brett F. 1949- *St&PR 91*
Thompson, Brian Edward 1955- *WhoE 91*
Thompson, Brian John 1932- *WhoAm 90*
Thompson, Bruce Alfred 1937- *IntWWM 90*
Thompson, Bruce Ashton 1958- *WhoEmL 91*
Thompson, Bruce Edward, Jr. 1949- *WhoAm 90, WhoEmL 91*
Thompson, Bruce Rutherford 1911- *WhoAm 90*
Thompson, Bryan Earnest 1922- *St&PR 91*
Thompson, Buck *ConAu 31NR*
Thompson, C.H., Jr. 1927- *St&PR 91*
Thompson, Caleb C. 1846-1909 *AmLegL*
Thompson, Carla Jo Horn 1951- *WhoSSW 91*
Thompson, Carmi Alderman 1870-1942 *AmLegL*
Thompson, Carol Belita 1951- *WhoE 91*
Thompson, Carol Lewis 1918- *WhoAm 90, WhoWrEP 89*
Thompson, Carolyn *BioIn 16*
Thompson, Carson R. 1939- *St&PR 91*
Thompson, Caryn Elizabeth 1954- *WhoAmW 91*
Thompson, Cedric Fitz-Oswald *BioIn 16*
Thompson, Charlene Brown 1940- *WhoE 91*
Thompson, Charles Edward 1929- *WhoAm 90*
Thompson, Charles Edwin 1938- *WhoAm 90*
Thompson, Charles Glover 1928- *WhoSSW 91*
Thompson, Charles I. 1950- *St&PR 91*
Thompson, Charles Kerry 1943- *WhoSSW 91*
Thompson, Charles Murray 1942- *WhoAm 90*
Thompson, Charles Otis 1942- *WhoSSW 91*
Thompson, Charles R. 1949- *St&PR 91*
Thompson, Cheryl L. 1950- *St&PR 91*
Thompson, Chester C. 1921- *St&PR 91*
Thompson, China *TwCCr&M 91*
Thompson, China 1907-1988 *SmATA X*
Thompson, Chris R. 1940- *St&PR 91*
Thompson, Christine Epps 1940- *WhoAmW 91*
Thompson, Christine Klena 1960- *WhoAmW 91*
Thompson, Clara Ann 1869?-1949 *FemiCLE, HarlReB*
Thompson, Clarence Miles 1929- *St&PR 91*
Thompson, Clarence Miles, Jr. 1929- *WhoAm 90*
Thompson, Clarissa Minnie *FemiCLE*
Thompson, Claude 1931?- *DrBlPA 90*
Thompson, Cleon F., Jr. *WhoAm 90*
Thompson, Cliff F. 1934- *WhoAm 90*
Thompson, Clifton C. 1939- *WhoAm 90*
Thompson, Clive *BioIn 16, DrBlPA 90*
Thompson, Clyde Douglas 1947- *WhoSSW 91*
Thompson, Courtney Ralph 1955- *WhoSSW 91*
Thompson, Craig Ringwalt 1911- *WhoAm 90*
Thompson, Craig S. 1932- *ODwPR 91*
Thompson, Craig Snover 1932- *WhoAm 90*
Thompson, Curtis Arthur 1951- *WhoE 91, WhoEmL 91*
Thompson, Curtis Brooks 1930- *WhoAm 90*
Thompson, Dale Gilbert, Jr. 1951- *WhoSSW 91*
Thompson, Dale Moore 1897- *WhoAm 90*
Thompson, Daley *BioIn 16*
Thompson, Daniel Joseph 1940- *St&PR 91*
Thompson, Daniel Joseph 1947- *WhoE 91*
Thompson, Danny 1947- *Ballpl 90*
Thompson, Darrell Theodore 1929- *St&PR 91*
Thompson, David 1770-1857 *DcLB 99 [port], WhNaAH, WorAlBi*
Thompson, David A. 1941- *St&PR 91*
Thompson, David Alfred 1929- *WhoAm 90*
Thompson, David Andrew *BiDrAPA 89*
Thompson, David Anthony 1939- *WhoAm 90*
Thompson, David C. 1945- *WhoAm 90*
Thompson, David Duvall 1922- *WhoAm 90*
Thompson, David Edmund 1925- *WhoE 91*
Thompson, David Elbridge *WhoAmA 91*
Thompson, David James 1945- *WhoWrEP 89*
Thompson, David Jerome 1937- *WhoAm 90*
Thompson, David R. 1955- *St&PR 91*
Thompson, David William 1914- *WhoAm 90, WhoWor 91*
Thompson, Dean Allan 1934- *WhoSSW 91, WhoWor 91*
Thompson, Deborah Colussy 1954- *WhoWrEP 89*
Thompson, Deborah Kemp 1947- *WhoAmW 91*
Thompson, Debra Jean 1954- *WhoAmW 91*
Thompson, Denman 1893- *Ballpl 90*
Thompson, Dennis Frank 1940- *WhoAm 90*
Thompson, Dennis Peters 1937- *WhoAm 90, WhoWor 91*
Thompson, Dennis Roy 1939- *WhoWor 91*
Thompson, Dennis Scott 1943- *BiDrAPA 89*
Thompson, Diane Janelle 1950- *WhoAmW 91*
Thompson, Didi Castle 1918- *WhoAmW 91*
Thompson, Diedra *St&PR 91*
Thompson, Don Clinton 1933- *St&PR 91*
Thompson, Donald Bycroft 1923- *St&PR 91*
Thompson, Donald Charles 1930- *WhoAm 90*
Thompson, Donald Edward 1930- *St&PR 91*
Thompson, Donald Prosser 1928- *IntWWM 90*
Thompson, Donald Roy 1936- *WhoAmA 91*
Thompson, Donna Byrd 1947- *WhoSSW 91*
Thompson, Donna Marie 1956- *WhoAmW 91*
Thompson, Donnis 1928- *AuBYP 90*
Thompson, Dora Elizabeth 1876-1954 *BioIn 16*
Thompson, Dora Jean 1929- *WhoSSW 91*
Thompson, Doris Leone Ardolf 1958- *WhoAmW 91*
Thompson, Dorothy *BioIn 16*
Thompson, Dorothy 1894-1961 *BioAmW, WorAlBi*
Thompson, Dorothy Brown 1896- *WhoAmW 91*
Thompson, Dorothy Burr *BioIn 16*
Thompson, Dorothy Burr 1900- *WhoAmA 91*
Thompson, Douglas *PenDiMP*
Thompson, Douglas Maison 1929- *WhoAm 90*
Thompson, E. *BiDWomA*
Thompson, E. Joyce 1943- *WhoAmW 91, WhoSSW 91*
Thompson, E P 1924- *WorAu 1980 [port]*
Thompson, Earl Albert 1938- *WhoAm 90*
Thompson, Earl Ryan 1939- *St&PR 91*
Thompson, Earlene 1942- *WhoAmW 91*
Thompson, Edith Maureen 1938- *WhoAmW 91*
Thompson, Edward *DrBlPA 90*
Thompson, Edward Francis 1938- *St&PR 91*
Thompson, Edward George 1936- *St&PR 91*
Thompson, Edward Kramer 1907- *WhoAm 90*
Thompson, Edward P. *St&PR 91*
Thompson, Edward Thorwald 1928- *WhoAm 90, WhoWrEP 89*
Thompson, Edwin R. 1949- *St&PR 91*
Thompson, Egberth E. 1883-1927 *BioIn 16*
Thompson, Eileen 1920- *AuBYP 90, BioIn 16*
Thompson, Eldon D. 1934- *St&PR 91*
Thompson, Eldon Dale 1934- *WhoAm 90*
Thompson, Eleanor Dumont 1935- *WhoAmW 91*
Thompson, Elizabeth Abrams 1954- *WhoAmW 91*
Thompson, Elizabeth C. 1924- *St&PR 91*
Thompson, Elizabeth Jane 1927- *WhoAmW 91*
Thompson, Elizabeth Southerden 1850-1933 *BioIn 16*
Thompson, Ellen Kubacki 1950- *WhoE 91*
Thompson, Ellen N *BiDrAPA 89*
Thompson, Eloise 1878-1928 *FemiCLE*
Thompson, Eloise Alberta Veronica Bibb 1878-1928 *HarlReB*
Thompson, Eloise Bibb 1878-1928 *EarBlAP*
Thompson, Era Bell 1906-1986 *HarlReB [port]*
Thompson, Ernest B. 1936- *St&PR 91*
Thompson, Ernest L. 1938- *St&PR 91*
Thompson, Ernest Thorne *WhoAmA 91*
Thompson, Ernest Thorne 1897- *WhoAm 90*
Thompson, Ernest Thorne, Jr 1928- *WhoAmA 91, WhoE 91*
Thompson, Ervin Magnus *BiDrAPA 89*
Thompson, Eve Lloyd 1934- *WhoAmW 91*
Thompson, Ezra Enwood 1916- *St&PR 91*
Thompson, Flora 1876-1947 *FemiCLE, WorAu 1980 [port]*
Thompson, Flora 1877-1947 *BioIn 16*
Thompson, Frances Ann 1945- *WhoAmW 91*
Thompson, Frances Hoene 1954- *WhoEmL 91*
Thompson, Francesca *BioIn 16*
Thompson, Francesca Morosani *BioIn 16*
Thompson, Francis 1859-1907 *BioIn 16*
Thompson, Francis Clegg *MajTwCW*
Thompson, Frank 1918-1989 *BioIn 16*
Thompson, Frank Edward 1943- *WhoSSW 91*
Thompson, Frank French 1946- *BiDrAPA 89*
Thompson, Frank Joseph 1944- *WhoAm 90*
Thompson, Fred *BioIn 16*
Thompson, Fred 1884-1949 *OxCPMus*
Thompson, Fred Clayton 1928- *St&PR 91, WhoAm 90*
Thompson, Fred D. 1915-1988 *BioIn 16*
Thompson, Fred T. 1940- *St&PR 91*
Thompson, Frederic Louis 1868- *EncPaPR 91*
Thompson, Frederick 1904-1956 *WhoAmA 91N*
Thompson, Frederick G. 1946- *ODwPR 91*
Thompson, Fresco 1902-1968 *Ballpl 90*
Thompson, Garland Lee 1938- *DrBlPA 90*
Thompson, Gary Allen 1951- *WhoWrEP 89*
Thompson, Gary Arthur 1953- *WhoEmL 91*
Thompson, Gary Harold 1940- *St&PR 91*
Thompson, Gary S. 1944- *St&PR 91*
Thompson, Gary W. 1947- *ODwPR 91*
Thompson, Gary William 1947- *St&PR 91*
Thompson, Geneva Florence 1915- *WhoAmW 91*
Thompson, Geoffrey A. 1940- *St&PR 91*
Thompson, Geoffrey Acheson 1940- *WhoAm 90*
Thompson, George *BioIn 16*
Thompson, George Albert 1919- *WhoAm 90*
Thompson, George Clifford 1920- *WhoAm 90*
Thompson, George Francis 1939- *St&PR 91*
Thompson, George Lee 1933- *WhoAm 90, WhoE 91, WhoWor 91*
Thompson, George Leroy 1952- *WhoSSW 91*
Thompson, George Louis 1913-1981 *WhoAmA 91N*
Thompson, George Mersereau 1939- *WhoSSW 91*
Thompson, George N 1909- *BiDrAPA 89*
Thompson, George Selden 1929-1989 *AuBYP 90, ConAu 130, SmATA 63*
Thompson, Georgiana Stroh *St&PR 91*
Thompson, Gerald E. 1947- *WhoAm 90*
Thompson, Gerald Luther 1923- *WhoAm 90, WhoWrEP 89*
Thompson, Gerald P. 1959- *ODwPR 91*
Thompson, Gertrude Caton- 1888-1985 *DcNaB 1981*
Thompson, Glenn Arthur William 1959- *WhoE 91*
Thompson, Glenn Judean 1936- *WhoAm 90*
Thompson, Gordon, Jr. 1929- *WhoAm 90*
Thompson, Gordon Ellef 1933- *WhoE 91*
Thompson, Gordon William 1940- *WhoAm 90*
Thompson, Granville Berry 1929- *WhoSSW 91*
Thompson, Greg Ross *BiDrAPA 89*
Thompson, Guy Bryan 1940- *WhoAm 90*
Thompson, Guy Thomas 1942- *WhoSSW 91*
Thompson, H. Brian 1939- *WhoAm 90*
Thompson, H. Neill 1942- *St&PR 91*
Thompson, Hank 1925-1969 *Ballpl 90*
Thompson, Harlan 1894-1987 *BioIn 16*
Thompson, Harlan H. 1894- *AuBYP 90*
Thompson, Harold Jerome 1947- *WhoSSW 91*
Thompson, Harold Lee 1945- *WhoEmL 91*
Thompson, Harold Warris 1908-1983 *DcNaB 1981*
Thompson, Harry Hyman 1939- *BiDrAPA 89*
Thompson, Helen Virginia 1941- *WhoAmW 91*
Thompson, Henrietta Spotts 1920- *WhoAmW 91*
Thompson, Henry Denman 1833-1911 *OxCCanT*
Thompson, Henry L. 1935- *St&PR 91*
Thompson, Henry L., Jr. 1915- *St&PR 91*
Thompson, Herbert Ernest 1923- *WhoWor 91*
Thompson, Herbert Stanley 1932- *WhoAm 90*
Thompson, Herbert Walter 1915- *WhoE 91*
Thompson, Hilary 1943- *BioIn 16*
Thompson, Hildegard 1901- *AuBYP 90*
Thompson, Horace Edwards 1921- *WhoAm 90*
Thompson, Howard Elliott 1934- *WhoAm 90*
Thompson, Howard H. 1924- *St&PR 91*
Thompson, Hugh Allison 1935- *WhoAm 90*
Thompson, Hugh Currie 1906- *WhoAm 90*
Thompson, Hugh Lee 1934- *WhoAm 90*
Thompson, Hunter 1939- *LiHiK*
Thompson, Hunter S. *BioIn 16*
Thompson, Hunter S 1939- *MajTwCW, WorAu 1980 [port]*
Thompson, Hunter Stockton 1939- *WhoAm 90, WhoWrEP 89*
Thompson, Inga *BioIn 16*
Thompson, Irving Benard, Jr. 1948- *WhoSSW 91*
Thompson, J.A. 1934- *St&PR 91*
Thompson, J. Robert *BioIn 16*
Thompson, J. Stark 1941- *WhoAm 90*
Thompson, J. Walter 1847-1928 *WorAlBi*
Thompson, Jack Edward 1924- *WhoAm 90*
Thompson, Jacob 1810-1885 *BiDrUSE 89*
Thompson, Jacqueline 1945- *WhoWrEP 89*
Thompson, Jacqueline Anne 1948- *WhoE 91*
Thompson, James 1931- *WhoSSW 91*
Thompson, James B. 1929- *WhoSSW 91*
Thompson, James Burleigh, Jr. 1921- *WhoAm 90*
Thompson, James C. 1939- *St&PR 91*
Thompson, James Charles 1928- *WhoAm 90*
Thompson, James Dan 1935- *St&PR 91*
Thompson, James David 1945- *WhoAm 90*
Thompson, James Edward 1941- *St&PR 91*
Thompson, James Edwin 1903-1989 *BioIn 16*
Thompson, James Gordon 1934- *St&PR 91*
Thompson, James Guyton 1944- *St&PR 91*

Thompson, James Howard 1934- WhoAm 90
Thompson, James Mace 1941- St&PR 91
Thompson, James N. 1931- St&PR 91
Thompson, James Patrick 1946- St&PR 91
Thompson, James R. 1906- St&PR 91
Thompson, James R. 1936- BioIn 16, WorAlBi
Thompson, James Richard 1933- WhoSSW 91
Thompson, James Richard 1951- WhoSSW 91
Thompson, James Robert 1936- WhoAm 90, WhoWor 91
Thompson, James Robert, Jr. 1936- WhoAm 90
Thompson, James Ronald 1947- WhoSSW 91
Thompson, James S., III 1947- St&PR 91
Thompson, James Wade 1960- St&PR 91
Thompson, James William 1939- St&PR 91, WhoAm 90
Thompson, James William 1944- BiDrAPA 89
Thompson, Jane WomArch
Thompson, Jane Johnson 1951- WhoAmW 91
Thompson, Janet Keith 1929- WhoAmW 91
Thompson, Janice 1955- WhoAmW 91
Thompson, Jarrett BioIn 16
Thompson, Jason 1954- Ballpl 90
Thompson, Jay 1931- IntWWM 90
Thompson, Jean Blake 1919- St&PR 91
Thompson, Jean Danforth 1933- WhoAmA 91
Thompson, Jean Dunivant 1927- WhoAmW 91
Thompson, Jean Tanner 1929- WhoAm 90
Thompson, Jeanne Coombs 1949- St&PR 91
Thompson, Jeffery D. 1947- ODwPR 91
Thompson, Jeffrey Dodd BiDrAPA 89
Thompson, Jeffrey Nelson 1951- WhoE 91
Thompson, Jere William 1932- ConAmBL, WhoAm 90, WhoSSW 91
Thompson, Jerry A. 1934- St&PR 91
Thompson, Jerry Andrew 1948- WhoSSW 91
Thompson, Jesse Eldon 1919- WhoAm 90
Thompson, Jill Ellen 1951- WhoAmW 91
Thompson, Jim 1906-1967? BioIn 16
Thompson, Jim 1906-1977 TwCCr&M 91
Thompson, Joan Kathryn 1956- WhoAmW 91, WhoWor 91
Thompson, Joe C., Jr. 1901-1961 ConAmBL
Thompson, Joe O. 1915- St&PR 91
Thompson, John BioIn 16
Thompson, John 1938-1976 BioIn 16
Thompson, John 1941- WhoAm 90, WorAlBi
Thompson, John Albert, Jr. 1942- WhoSSW 91
Thompson, John Archibald 1934- WhoAm 90
Thompson, John Brown 1929- WhoAm 90
Thompson, John C. 1926- St&PR 91
Thompson, John Daniel 1927- WhoAm 90
Thompson, John Douglas 1934- St&PR 91, WhoAm 90
Thompson, John E., Jr. 1923- St&PR 91
Thompson, John Frederick, Jr. 1951- St&PR 91
Thompson, John G. 1940- St&PR 91
Thompson, John Henry 1938- St&PR 91
Thompson, John Larkin 1930- WhoE 91
Thompson, John Lester 1926- WhoAm 90
Thompson, John M. 1843-1882 AmLegL
Thompson, John M 1926- ConAu 129
Thompson, John P. 1925- ConAmBL
Thompson, John Richard 1946- WhoSSW 91
Thompson, John Robert BiDrAPA 89
Thompson, John Sparrow David 1845-1894 DcCanB 12
Thompson, John Theodore 1917- WhoAm 90
Thompson, John Thomas 1947- WhoE 91
Thompson, John W. 1926- St&PR 91
Thompson, John Walter, Jr. 1924- St&PR 91
Thompson, John Wilson, Jr. 1946- WhoEmL 91
Thompson, Johnny W. 1952- ODwPR 91
Thompson, Jon Brent 1943- WhoSSW 91
Thompson, Joseph Edward 1940- St&PR 91
Thompson, Joseph F. 1944- St&PR 91
Thompson, Joseph Mark 1949- BiDrAPA 89
Thompson, Joseph V. 1942- St&PR 91
Thompson, Josh BioIn 16
Thompson, Josiah BioIn 16
Thompson, Joyce Elizabeth 1951- WhoAmW 91
Thompson, Joyce Lurine 1931- WhoAmW 91
Thompson, Judith 1954- OxCCanT
Thompson, Judith Curfman 1942- WhoAmW 91
Thompson, Judy L. 1948- WhoEmL 91
Thompson, Julia Ann 1943- WhoAmW 91
Thompson, Julia Charlotte 1907-1972 BioIn 16
Thompson, Julian F. 1927- BioIn 16, ConAu 30NR
Thompson, Juliet H WhoAmA 91N
Thompson, Junior 1917- Ballpl 90
Thompson, Juul Harold 1945- WhoEmL 91
Thompson, Karen Elaine 1958- WhoAmW 91
Thompson, Katherine Genevieve 1945- WhoEmL 91
Thompson, Kay AuBYP 90, WorAlBi
Thompson, Kay 1912?- ChlLR 22 [port]
Thompson, Kay Francis WhoE 91
Thompson, Keith Bruce 1932- WhoWor 91
Thompson, Kelly Rhea 1959- WhoSSW 91
Thompson, Kenneth A. 1936- St&PR 91
Thompson, Kenneth C 1935- BiDrAPA 89
Thompson, Kenneth Webster 1907- WhoAmA 91
Thompson, Kenneth Winfred 1921- WhoAm 90
Thompson, Kid 1871-1925 BioIn 16
Thompson, Kirk 1953- St&PR 91
Thompson, Kyla T. ODwPR 91
Thompson, Lance Eric 1956- St&PR 91
Thompson, Larry Angelo 1944- WhoAm 90, WhoWor 91
Thompson, Larry Cole, Sr. 1939- WhoSSW 91
Thompson, Larry Dean 1945- WhoAm 90
Thompson, Larry Flack 1944- WhoAm 90
Thompson, Laverne Elizabeth Thomas 1945- WhoAmW 91, WhoWor 91
Thompson, Lawrance 1906-1973 DcLB 103 [port]
Thompson, Lawrence Franklin, Jr. 1941- WhoWor 91
Thompson, Leah Denise 1952- WhoE 91
Thompson, Lee Bennett 1902- WhoAm 90, WhoSSW 91, WhoWor 91
Thompson, Leonard Monteath 1916- WhoE 91
Thompson, Leonti H 1929- BiDrAPA 89
Thompson, LeRoy, Jr. 1913- WhoSSW 91, WhoWor 91
Thompson, Leslie Melvin 1936- WhoAm 90
Thompson, Leslie P 1880-1963 WhoAmA 91N
Thompson, Lester Eugene 1938- St&PR 91
Thompson, Lillian Hurlburt 1947- WhoAmW 91, WhoE 91
Thompson, Lincoln, Jr. 1928- St&PR 91
Thompson, Linda Barrow 1948- WhoSSW 91
Thompson, Linda Joy 1959- WhoSSW 91
Thompson, Linda Lee 1940- WhoAmW 91
Thompson, Linda Ruth 1941- BiDrAPA 89
Thompson, Llewellyn E. 1904-1972 BioIn 16
Thompson, Lockwood 1901- WhoAmA 91
Thompson, Lohren Matthew 1926- WhoAm 90, WhoWor 91
Thompson, Lois Jean Ore 1933- WhoAmW 91
Thompson, Lola May 1931- WhoAmW 91
Thompson, Loring Moore 1918- WhoAm 90
Thompson, Lou Ann 1953- WhoWrEP 89
Thompson, Louis Milton 1914- WhoAm 90, WhoWor 91
Thompson, Louise Marie 1945- WhoWrEP 89
Thompson, Louise Saari 1943- WhoWrEP 89
Thompson, Lucky 1925- BioIn 16
Thompson, Lynn P 1922- WhoAmA 91
Thompson, Mack Eugene 1921- WhoAm 90
Thompson, Malcolm Barton 1916- WhoAmA 91
Thompson, Malcolm Francis 1921- WhoWor 91
Thompson, Marcia Lynn 1956- WhoAmW 91
Thompson, Margaret Douglas 1947- WhoAmW 91
Thompson, Margaret M. 1921- WhoAm 90
Thompson, Marguerite Myrtle Graming 1912- WhoAmW 91, WhoSSW 91
Thompson, Maria Markham 1958- WhoE 91
Thompson, Marian Kaye BiDrAPA 89
Thompson, Mark BioIn 16
Thompson, Mark L WhoAmA 91
Thompson, Martin Christian 1938- WhoAm 90
Thompson, Mary 1886- AuBYP 90
Thompson, Mary E. WhoAmW 91
Thompson, Mary Eileen 1928- WhoAmW 91
Thompson, Mary Jean 1935- WhoWor 91
Thompson, Mary Koleta 1938- WhoAmW 91, WhoSSW 91
Thompson, Maureen Fielder 1951- WhoAmW 91
Thompson, Maurice BioIn 16
Thompson, Mavis Sarah 1927- WhoAmW 91
Thompson, Melvin John 1933- WhoE 91
Thompson, Michael David 1929- St&PR 91
Thompson, Michael E. ODwPR 91
Thompson, Michael George 1940- BiDrAPA 89
Thompson, Michael James 1939- WhoSSW 91
Thompson, Mickey BioIn 16
Thompson, Mike 1949- Ballpl 90
Thompson, Milt 1959- Ballpl 90
Thompson, Milton Orville 1926- WhoAm 90
Thompson, Mimi BioIn 16
Thompson, Mollie Sue 1939- WhoAmW 91
Thompson, Morley P. 1927- St&PR 91
Thompson, Morley Punshon 1927- WhoAm 90
Thompson, Mozelle Willmont 1954- WhoE 91
Thompson, N. WhoSSW 91
Thompson, N. David 1934- WhoAm 90
Thompson, Nainoa BioIn 16
Thompson, Nancy Ethelyn 1925- WhoAmW 91, WhoWor 91
Thompson, Nancy Kunkle 1941- WhoAmA 91
Thompson, Nancy Lynn 1956- WhoAmW 91
Thompson, Neil E. 1932- St&PR 91
Thompson, Nicolas de la Mare 1928- WhoWor 91
Thompson, Noel BioIn 16
Thompson, Noel 1927- St&PR 91
Thompson, Norman Winslow 1932- WhoAm 90
Thompson, Olivia WhoAmW 91
Thompson, Orval N. 1914- St&PR 91
Thompson, Orval Nathan 1914- WhoWor 91
Thompson, Ott, II 1924- St&PR 91
Thompson, Pamela Ashley 1954- WhoAmW 91
Thompson, Pamela Kay 1951- WhoAmW 91
Thompson, Patreece May BiDrAPA 89
Thompson, Patrick Alan 1949- WhoEmL 91
Thompson, Paul 1940- OxCCanT
Thompson, Paul 1943- ConAu 32NR
Thompson, Paul Banks 1951- WhoSSW 91
Thompson, Paul Jan David 1957- WhoWor 91
Thompson, Paul Joseph 1954- WhoSSW 91
Thompson, Paul Michael 1935- WhoAm 90
Thompson, Peter Campbell 1933- St&PR 91
Thompson, Peter Mannering 1946- St&PR 91
Thompson, Phebe Kirsten 1897- WhoAmW 91, WhoWor 91
Thompson, Phil DeWayne 1954- WhoSSW 91
Thompson, Philip Andrew 1928- WhoAm 90
Thompson, Phillip Wayne 1949- St&PR 91
Thompson, Phyllis Hoge 1926- ConAu 30NR, WhoWrEP 89
Thompson, Prescott W BiDrAPA 89
Thompson, Priscilla Jane 1871-1942 FemiCLE, HarlReB
Thompson, R.S. St&PR 91
Thompson, R. Stanley St&PR 91
Thompson, Ralph Gordon 1934- WhoAm 90, WhoSSW 91
Thompson, Ralph LaSalle 1929- St&PR 91
Thompson, Ralph Newell 1918- WhoAm 90, WhoWor 91
Thompson, Randi ODwPR 91
Thompson, Randi Eileen 1952- WhoAm 90, WhoAmW 91
Thompson, Randy Earl 1951- WhoE 91
Thompson, Randy Lane 1950- BiDrAPA 89
Thompson, Ray 1905-1982 EncACom
Thompson, Ray Fern 1936- St&PR 91
Thompson, Raymond Harris 1924- WhoAm 90
Thompson, Rebecca WhoWrEP 89
Thompson, Rebecca Agatha DcCanB 12
Thompson, Rena 1950- WhoAmA 91
Thompson, Renold Durant 1926- St&PR 91, WhoAm 90
Thompson, Richard Arlen 1930- WhoSSW 91
Thompson, Richard Arlyn 1946- WhoEmL 91
Thompson, Richard Craig 1945- WhoAmA 91
Thompson, Richard E, Jr 1939- WhoAmA 91
Thompson, Richard Earl, Sr 1914- WhoAmA 91
Thompson, Richard Ford 1938- WhoSSW 91
Thompson, Richard Frederick 1930- WhoAm 90
Thompson, Richard Ives 1947- St&PR 91
Thompson, Richard Stephen 1931- WhoAm 90
Thompson, Richard Victor, Jr. 1951- WhoSSW 91
Thompson, Richard Wigginton 1809-1900 BiDrUSE 89
Thompson, Robby 1962- Ballpl 90
Thompson, Robert Allan 1937- WhoE 91
Thompson, Robert Charles 1923- WhoAm 90
Thompson, Robert Charles 1936- WhoAmA 91, WhoSSW 91
Thompson, Robert Charles 1942- WhoAm 90
Thompson, Robert Clay 1949- WhoE 91
Thompson, Robert Earl 1947- WhoSSW 91
Thompson, Robert Elliott 1921- WhoAm 90
Thompson, Robert Eugene 1942- St&PR 91, WhoAm 90
Thompson, Robert F. 1926- St&PR 91
Thompson, Robert Grainger Ker 1916- BioIn 16
Thompson, Robert Howard 1929- St&PR 91
Thompson, Robert Ian 1943- IntWWM 90
Thompson, Robert J. NewYTBS 90 [port]
Thompson, Robert J. 1940- St&PR 91
Thompson, Robert L., Jr. 1937- ODwPR 91, St&PR 91
Thompson, Robert Lee 1945- WhoAm 90, WhoEmL 91
Thompson, Robert M. 1928- St&PR 91
Thompson, Robert McBroom 1928- WhoAm 90
Thompson, Robert P. 1924- ODwPR 91
Thompson, Robert Thomas 1930- WhoAm 90
Thompson, Robert Thomas, Jr. 1951- WhoSSW 91
Thompson, Robert W. 1939- St&PR 91
Thompson, Roby Calvin, Jr. 1934- WhoAm 90
Thompson, Roger Dennis 1950- WhoSSW 91
Thompson, Roger Kennedy 1929- St&PR 91
Thompson, Rolanda G. 1950- WhoAmW 91
Thompson, Ronald 1947- WhoSSW 91
Thompson, Ronald Edward 1931- WhoAm 90
Thompson, Ronald F. 1945- WhoSSW 91
Thompson, Ronald O. BioIn 16
Thompson, Ronald Russell 1942- WhoE 91
Thompson, Ronald Wesley 1937- WhoSSW 91
Thompson, Rosalie 1868- EncPaPR 91
Thompson, Roscoe Eugene 1926- St&PR 91
Thompson, Roscoe Treeve Fawcett 1907-1984 DcNaB 1981
Thompson, Rosina 1868- EncO&P 3
Thompson, Rufus E. 1943- WhoAm 90
Thompson, Russ ConAu 31NR
Thompson, Russell Glenwood 1929- WhoSSW 91
Thompson, Ruth Lyn ODwPR 91
Thompson, S. C. 1898-1967 Ballpl 90
Thompson, S. Mark 1947- BioIn 16
Thompson, Sada 1929- BioIn 16, NotWoAT, WorAlBi
Thompson, Sally WhoAmW 91
Thompson, Sally Wright BiDrAPA 89
Thompson, Sam 1860-1922 Ballpl 90 [port]
Thompson, Sandra Jean 1943- WhoWrEP 89
Thompson, Sandra Romaine 1938- WhoE 91
Thompson, Scot 1955- Ballpl 90
Thompson, Scot Bycroft St&PR 91
Thompson, Scott Gallatin 1944- St&PR 91
Thompson, Sharon Andrea 1948- WhoAmW 91
Thompson, Sharon Pearl 1949- WhoE 91
Thompson, Sheldon Lee 1938- WhoAm 90
Thompson, Sherwood 1952- WhoE 91
Thompson, Smith 1768-1843 BiDrUSE 89
Thompson, Stacy Jo 1958- WhoAmW 91
Thompson, Stanley Jay 1960- WhoEmL 91
Thompson, Starley BioIn 16
Thompson, Stephen M. 1935- St&PR 91
Thompson, Stith 1885-1976 BioIn 16
Thompson, Sue Ellen 1948- WhoWrEP 89
Thompson, Susan 1946- ConAu 132
Thompson, Susan Arnetas Conklin 1956- WhoWrEP 89
Thompson, Susan Lynne 1950- WhoAmW 91

Thompson, Sylvia Taylor 1946- *WhoSSW 91*
Thompson, Tamara 1935- *WhoAmA 91*
Thompson, Tara Denise 1962- *WhoAmW 91*
Thompson, Terence James 1928- *IntWWM 90*
Thompson, Terence William 1952- *WhoEmL 91, WhoWor 91*
Thompson, Terrance Michael 1947- *St&PR 91*
Thompson, Terry J. 1941- *ODwPR 91*
Thompson, Theodore Kvale 1944- *WhoAm 90*
Thompson, Theodore Robert 1943- *WhoAm 90*
Thompson, Thomas 1913- *BioIn 16*
Thompson, Thomas Dean 1944- *St&PR 91*
Thompson, Thomas Dwight 1945- *WhoWrEP 89*
Thompson, Thomas Henry 1924- *WhoAm 90*
Thompson, Thomas Martin 1943- *WhoAm 90*
Thompson, Thomas Phillips 1843-1933 *DcLB 99*
Thompson, Thomas Read *BiDrAPA 89*
Thompson, Thomas Sanford 1916- *WhoAm 90*
Thompson, Thomas W. *BioIn 16*
Thompson, Tim 1924- *Ballpl 90*
Thompson, Tina Diane 1950- *WhoAmW 91*
Thompson, Tom G. 1929- *ODwPR 91*
Thompson, Tommy 1910-1971 *Ballpl 90*
Thompson, Tommy George 1941- *WhoAm 90, WhoWor 91*
Thompson, Tommy R. 1952- *St&PR 91*
Thompson, Tracy Kathleen 1961- *WhoAmW 91*
Thompson, Treva Levi 1951- *WhoSSW 91*
Thompson, Troy L, II 1946- *BiDrAPA 89*
Thompson, Truet Bradford 1917- *WhoAm 90*
Thompson, Tyler 1915- *WhoAm 90*
Thompson, U.S. Slow Kid 1888?- *DrBlPA 90*
Thompson, Verona Cooper 1932- *St&PR 91*
Thompson, Victor Alexander 1912- *WhoAm 90*
Thompson, Victor Montgomery, Jr. 1924- *WhoAm 90*
Thompson, Virginia *ConAu 130*
Thompson, Virginia McLean 1903-1990 *BioIn 16*
Thompson, Virginia Williams 1938- *WhoAmW 91*
Thompson, Vivian Laubach 1911- *AuBYP 90*
Thompson, Vivian Opal 1925- *WhoAmW 91*
Thompson, W. Blair *BioIn 16*
Thompson, W. Blair 1928- *St&PR 91*
Thompson, W. Reid 1924- *St&PR 91, WhoE 91*
Thompson, Waddy 1798-1868 *BioIn 16*
Thompson, Wade 1946- *WhoAmA 91*
Thompson, Wade Francis Bruce 1940- *WhoAm 90, WhoWor 91*
Thompson, Walker 1909- *BiDrAPA 89*
Thompson, Wallace Brown 1938- *WhoSSW 91*
Thompson, Walter E *BiDrAPA 89*
Thompson, Walter Earl, Jr. 1946- *WhoEmL 91*
Thompson, Walter Whitcomb 1882-1948 *WhoAmA 91N*
Thompson, Wayne Edwin 1927- *WhoAm 90*
Thompson, Wayne Wray 1945- *WhoE 91, WhoEmL 91, WhoWor 91*
Thompson, Wendy Lynn 1952- *BiDrAPA 89*
Thompson, Wesley D. 1926- *St&PR 91*
Thompson, Wesley Duncan 1926- *WhoAm 90*
Thompson, Wesley Ernest 1939- *St&PR 91*
Thompson, Wiley 1781-1835 *WhNaAH*
Thompson, Willard Linn 1914- *WhoAm 90*
Thompson, William 1920- *St&PR 91*
Thompson, William, Jr. 1936- *WhoAm 90*
Thompson, William Allen 1953- *WhoSSW 91*
Thompson, William Bell 1922- *WhoAm 90*
Thompson, William Bonner, Jr. 1956- *St&PR 91*
Thompson, William C 1918- *BiDrAPA 89*
Thompson, William Cannon, Jr. 1938- *WhoAm 90*
Thompson, William Carey, III 1951- *WhoE 91*
Thompson, William D. *St&PR 91*
Thompson, William David 1921- *WhoAm 90*
Thompson, William David 1929- *WhoAm 90*
Thompson, William Edwin 1950- *WhoEmL 91*
Thompson, William F *BiDrAPA 89*
Thompson, William Francis 1947- *St&PR 91*
Thompson, William Grant 1925- *WhoE 91*
Thompson, William Grant 1943- *St&PR 91*
Thompson, William Irwin 1938- *EncO&P 3, WhoAm 90, WhoWrEP 89*
Thompson, William Joseph 1926- *WhoAmA 91*
Thompson, William Joseph 1934- *St&PR 91*
Thompson, William Magill, Jr. 1926- *WhoE 91*
Thompson, William Moreau 1943- *WhoAm 90*
Thompson, William Neil 1920- *WhoAm 90*
Thompson, William Reid 1924- *WhoAm 90*
Thompson, William Richey 1956- *WhoEmL 91*
Thompson, William Taliaferro, Jr. 1913- *WhoAm 90, WhoWor 91*
Thompson, Wilmer Leigh 1938- *WhoAm 90*
Thompson, Winfred Lee 1945- *WhoAm 90, WhoSSW 91*
Thompson, Winston 1940- *WhoWor 91*
Thompson, Winston E. 1933- *WhoE 91*
Thompson, Wynelle Doggett 1914- *WhoAmW 91*
Thompson, Yaakov 1954- *WhoE 91*
Thompson, Yvonne Elizabeth 1948- *WhoAmW 91*
Thompson-Benike, Kimberley *ODwPR 91*
Thompson Lyons, Kelton Rae 1959- *WhoEmL 91*
Thoms, Adah B. *BioIn 16*
Thoms, Robert A. *St&PR 91*
Thoms, Thomas Hill 1909-1987 *BioIn 16*
Thomsen, Carl A. 1945- *St&PR 91*
Thomsen, Charles B. 1932- *St&PR 91*
Thomsen, Charles Burton 1932- *WhoAm 90*
Thomsen, Christian *PenDiDA 89*
Thomsen, Christopher Jay 1957- *WhoSSW 91*
Thomsen, Dietrick E. *BioIn 16*
Thomsen, Donald Laurence, Jr. 1921- *WhoAm 90*
Thomsen, Grimur 1820-1896 *DcScanL*
Thomsen, Henning 1952- *WhoWor 91*
Thomsen, Ib Scheel 1944- *WhoWor 91*
Thomsen, John G. 1921- *WhoAm 90*
Thomsen, Louis C. 1895-1988 *BioIn 16*
Thomsen, Marcia Rozen 1958- *WhoAmW 91*
Thomsen, Michelle Fluckey 1950- *WhoAmW 91*
Thomsen, Oscar William, Jr. 1922- *BiDrAPA 89*
Thomsen, Peter Karl 1942- *St&PR 91*
Thomsen, Steuart Hill 1954- *WhoE 91*
Thomsen, Theron 1923- *St&PR 91*
Thomsen, Thomas Richard 1935- *WhoE 91*
Thomsen, William Howard, Jr. 1946- *St&PR 91*
Thomsen-Hall, Kathleen Ann 1955- *BiDrAPA 89*
Thomson, Alan Craft 1931- *WhoE 91*
Thomson, Albert W. 1915- *St&PR 91*
Thomson, Alexander Bennett, Jr. 1954- *WhoE 91, WhoEmL 91, WhoSSW 91, WhoWor 91*
Thomson, Alexander McDonald 1822-1898 *AmLegL*
Thomson, Barbara Jeanne 1929- *WhoAmW 91*
Thomson, Basil 1861-1939 *TwCCr&M 91*
Thomson, Basil Henry, Jr. 1945- *WhoSSW 91*
Thomson, Belinda Collings 1950- *WhoSSW 91*
Thomson, Bobby 1923- *Ballpl 90 [port], BioIn 16*
Thomson, Bryden 1928- *IntWWM 90, PenDiMP*
Thomson, Captane Peter 1930- *BiDrAPA 89*
Thomson, Carl L 1913- *WhoAmA 91*
Thomson, Carl Louis 1913- *WhoE 91*
Thomson, Cesar 1857-1931 *PenDiMP*
Thomson, Charles 1729-1824 *BioIn 16, EncCRAm*
Thomson, Chris *WhoWrEP 89*
Thomson, Clare Julia 1964- *WhoWor 91*
Thomson, Dale Cairns 1923- *WhoAm 90*
Thomson, David 1914-1988 *BioIn 16*
Thomson, Donald Spencer 1935- *WhoE 91*
Thomson, Edward H., III 1953- *St&PR 91*
Thomson, Edward William 1849-1924 *DcLB 92 [port]*
Thomson, Edward Wilson 1931- *St&PR 91*
Thomson, Elizabeth Louise 1948- *WhoWor 91*
Thomson, Frederick Clifton 1890-1928 *BioIn 16*
Thomson, George P. 1892-1975 *WorAlBi*
Thomson, George Paget 1892-1975 *DcScB S2*
Thomson, George Ronald 1959- *WhoEmL 91, WhoWor 91*
Thomson, Gerald Edmund 1932- *WhoAm 90, WhoWor 91*
Thomson, Gordon 1951- *ConTFT 8*
Thomson, Grace Marie 1932- *WhoAmW 91, WhoWor 91*
Thomson, Harriet *FemiCLE*
Thomson, Heather 1940- *IntWWM 90*
Thomson, J. S. 1949- *WhoSSW 91*
Thomson, Jack *BioIn 16*
Thomson, James 1700-1748 *BioIn 16, DcLB 95 [port]*
Thomson, James Alan 1945- *WhoAm 90*
Thomson, James Anderson, Jr. 1948- *BiDrAPA 89*
Thomson, James C, Jr. 1931- *ConAu 32NR*
Thomson, James Miln 1921- *WhoWor 91*
Thomson, James Robert, Jr. 1926- *WhoAm 90*
Thomson, Joe *BioIn 16*
Thomson, John A F 1934- *ConAu 132*
Thomson, John H. *BioIn 16*
Thomson, John W. 1928- *St&PR 91*
Thomson, Joseph J. 1856-1940 *WorAlBi*
Thomson, June 1930- *TwCCr&M 91*
Thomson, Karen S. 1943- *St&PR 91*
Thomson, Kathleen Ruth 1934- *WhoAmW 91*
Thomson, Keith Stewart 1938- *WhoAm 90, WhoE 91*
Thomson, Kenneth *BioIn 16*
Thomson, Kenneth Roy 1923- *St&PR 91*
Thomson, Larry Elwood 1944- *St&PR 91*
Thomson, Mabel Amelia 1910- *WhoAmW 91*
Thomson, Margaret Faith 1941- *WhoAmW 91*
Thomson, Mary Otten 1940- *WhoAmW 91*
Thomson, Michael J C *BiDrAPA 89*
Thomson, Pat *AuBYP 90*
Thomson, Paul Rice, Jr. 1941- *WhoAm 90*
Thomson, Peggy 1922- *BioIn 16*
Thomson, Peter 1913- *AuBYP 90*
Thomson, R H 1947- *OxCCanT*
Thomson, Richard James 1932- *WhoAm 90*
Thomson, Richard M. 1933- *St&PR 91*
Thomson, Richard Murray 1933- *WhoAm 90, WhoWor 91*
Thomson, Robert H. 1933- *St&PR 91*
Thomson, Robert Hennessey 1933- *WhoAm 90*
Thomson, Robert James 1927- *St&PR 91, WhoAm 90*
Thomson, Robert M. *St&PR 91*
Thomson, Robert Stephen 1955- *WhoAm 90*
Thomson, Robert William 1934- *WhoAm 90, WhoE 91*
Thomson, Roger Farley 1949- *St&PR 91*
Thomson, Sandra Stavac 1950- *St&PR 91*
Thomson, Sarah Elizabeth 1906- *WhoWrEP 89*
Thomson, Shirley Lavinia 1930- *WhoAm 90, WhoE 91*
Thomson, Steven Dean 1957- *BiDrAPA 89*
Thomson, Susan Marie 1951- *WhoAmW 91*
Thomson, Thomas D. 1936- *St&PR 91*
Thomson, Thomas Harold 1935- *St&PR 91, WhoAm 90*
Thomson, Thyra Godfrey 1916- *WhoAm 90, WhoAmW 91*
Thomson, Todd Stuart 1961- *WhoE 91*
Thomson, Vernon C. 1924- *St&PR 91*
Thomson, Vernon Wallace 1905-1988 *BioIn 16*
Thomson, Virgil 1896- *IntWWM 90*
Thomson, Virgil 1896-1989 *AnObit 1989, BioIn 16, ConAu 129, PenDiMP A, WorAlBi*
Thomson, Virginia Winbourn 1930- *WhoAmW 91, WhoWrEP 89*
Thomson, Warren Milton 1935- *IntWWM 90*
Thomson, William Barry 1952- *St&PR 91, WhoAm 90*
Thomson, William Donald 1931- *WhoWor 91*
Thomson, William Gregory 1948- *St&PR 91*
Thomson, William Joseph 1939- *WhoAm 90*
Thomson of Fleet, Roy Herbert 1894-1976 *WorAlBi*
Thon, Dickie 1958- *Ballpl 90*
Thon, William 1906- *WhoAm 90, WhoAmA 91*
Thondukolam, Krishnan R. 1951- *WhoE 91*
Thonet, John A. 1950- *WhoE 91, WhoEmL 91*
Thonet, Michael 1796-1871 *PenDiDA 89*
Thong, Denny 1940- *BiDrAPA 89*
Thong-Horton, Julietta Khanteya 1960- *WhoAmW 91*
Thoolen, Johannes Gerardus H. 1947- *WhoWor 91*
Thor Vilhjalmsson *DcScanL*
Thor, Edward C. 1950- *St&PR 91*
Thor, Linda M. 1950- *WhoAmW 91*
Thorarensen, Bjarni 1787-1841 *DcScanL*
Thorarinsson, Hjalti 1920- *WhoWor 91*
Thorbeck, John Shepard 1952- *St&PR 91*
Thorbecke, Erik 1929- *WhoAm 90*
Thorbecke, Willem Henry 1924- *WhoE 91, WhoWor 91*
Thorbergur Thordarson *DcScanL*
Thorborg, Kerstin 1896-1970 *PenDiMP*
Thorbun, Allan K *BiDrAPA 89*
Thorburn, Alexander Gillan 1836-1894 *DcCanB 12*
Thorburn, David 1940- *WhoAm 90*
Thorburn, James Alexander 1923- *WhoSSW 91, WhoWor 91*
Thorburn, John 1903-1987 *BioIn 16*
Thordarson, Agnar 1917- *DcScanL*
Thordarson, Thorbergur 1889-1974 *DcScanL*
Thore, Sten Anders 1930- *WhoSSW 91*
Thoreau, Henry David 1817-1862 *BioIn 16, WorAlBi, WrPh*
Thorelli, Hans Birger *WhoAm 90*
Thoren, Lars Olof 1921- *WhoWor 91*
Thoren, Marja Christine 1938- *WhoWor 91*
Thoren, Thomas *DcScanL*
Thorens, Justin 1931- *WhoWor 91*
Thoresen, Asa Clifford 1930- *WhoAm 90*
Thoreson, Richard M. 1935- *St&PR 91*
Thorez, Maurice 1900-1964 *BiDFrPL*
Thorfinn, Karlsefni *EncCRAm*
Thorfinn, Karlsefni 980?- *WorAlBi*
Thorgeirsson, Gudmundur 1946- *WhoWor 91*
Thorgrimsson, Grimur Thomsen *DcScanL*
Thorild, Thomas 1759-1808 *DcScanL*
Thorington, Robert Dinning 1932- *WhoAm 90*
Thorkelsdottor, Mist Barbara 1960- *IntWWM 90*
Thorkelson, Willmar 1918- *WhoAm 90*
Thorkilsen, Harold *NewYTBS 90*
Thorlakson, Rosemary Ahearn 1947- *WhoAmW 91*
Thormahlen, Hank 1896-1955 *Ballpl 90*
Thormahlen, Stephen Clinton 1952- *WhoSSW 91*
Thorman, Richard 1924- *WhoWrEP 89*
Thormann, Wolfgang E. 1924- *WhoAm 90*
Thormodsgard, Paul 1953- *Ballpl 90*
Thorn, Arline Roush 1946- *WhoSSW 91*
Thorn, Barbara *ConAu 31NR*
Thorn, Ben K. 1829-1905 *BioIn 16*
Thorn, Brian Earl 1955- *WhoEmL 91*
Thorn, George Widmer 1906- *WhoAm 90*
Thorn, John 1947- *Ballpl 90, BioIn 16*
Thorn, Kenneth Hunter 1948- *St&PR 91*
Thorn, Robert Nicol 1924- *WhoAm 90*
Thorn, Susan Howe 1941- *WhoAmW 91*
Thorn, Thomas Leonard 1943- *St&PR 91*
Thornber, Judy Paulene 1941- *WhoAmW 91*
Thornberry, James William 1944- *WhoSSW 91*
Thornberry, Susan L. 1944- *WhoAmW 91*
Thornberry, Terence Patrick 1945- *WhoAm 90*
Thornbrook, Bill *ConAu 31NR*
Thornburg, Donald Delwin 1937- *St&PR 91*
Thornburg, Frederick F. 1940- *St&PR 91*
Thornburg, Frederick Fletcher 1940- *WhoAm 90*
Thornburg, Lacy Herman 1929- *WhoAm 90, WhoSSW 91*
Thornburg, Larry Steve 1953- *WhoE 91*
Thornburg, Mary Lou *BioIn 16*
Thornburg, Newton 1930- *TwCCr&M 91*
Thornburgh, Dick *BioIn 16*
Thornburgh, Dick 1932- *NewYTBS 90, WhoAm 90, WhoE 91, WhoWor 91*
Thornburgh, George 1847- *AmLegL*
Thornburgh, James Thomas *BiDrAPA 89*
Thornburgh, Richard 1932- *WorAlBi*
Thornburgh, Richard Edward 1952- *St&PR 91*
Thornburgh, Richard Lewis 1932- *BiDrUSE 89*
Thornburgh, Robert Phillip 1949- *WhoWor 91*
Thornburgh, Thomas T. 1843?-1879 *WhNaAH*
Thornbury, John Rousseau 1929- *WhoAm 90*
Thornbury, P.L. *St&PR 91N*
Thornbury, Thomas Glidden 1931- *St&PR 91, WhoE 91*
Thornbury, William Mitchell 1944- *WhoWor 91*
Thorndal, Herbert Louis 1929- *WhoAm 90*

Thorndike, Daniel Carl 1955- *WhoEmL 91*
Thorndike, Edward Harmon 1934- *WhoAm 90*
Thorndike, John Lowell 1926- *St&PR 91*
Thorndike, Joseph Jacobs, Jr. 1913- *WhoAm 90*
Thorndike, Richard King 1913- *WhoAm 90*
Thorndike, Robert Ladd *NewYTBS 90*
Thorndike, Robert Ladd 1910-1990 *ConAu 132*
Thorndike, Sybil 1882-1976 *WorAlBi*
Thorndike, William D. 1923- *St&PR 91*
Thorndike, William D., Jr. 1953- *St&PR 91*
Thorndyke, Lloyd Milton 1927- *WhoAm 90*
Thorne, Charles H. 1934- *ODwPR 91*
Thorne, David Hoadley 1944- *WhoE 91*
Thorne, Francis 1922- *WhoAm 90*
Thorne, Frank 1930- *EncACom*
Thorne, Frederick G.P. 1935- *St&PR 91*
Thorne, Gerald M. 1938- *St&PR 91*
Thorne, Gerald Mortenson 1938- *WhoAm 90*
Thorne, James G. 1941- *St&PR 91*
Thorne, Jean D. 1925- *St&PR 91*
Thorne, John C. 1930- *St&PR 91*
Thorne, John Reinecke 1926- *WhoAm 90, WhoE 91*
Thorne, John Watson, III 1934- *WhoAm 90*
Thorne, Kip Stephen 1940- *WhoAm 90*
Thorne, Norman Alan 1933- *BiDrAPA 89*
Thorne, Oakleigh Blakeman 1932- *St&PR 91*
Thorne, Richard Mansergh 1942- *WhoAm 90*
Thorne, Samuel, Jr. 1929- *St&PR 91, WhoE 91*
Thorne, William Wain, III 1946- *WhoSSW 91*
Thorne-Thomsen, Fletcher, Jr. 1948- *St&PR 91*
Thorne-Thomsen, Ruth T 1943- *WhoAmA 91*
Thornell, Jack Randolph 1939- *WhoAm 90*
Thorneloe, William Frank 1951- *BiDrAPA 89*
Thorner, Brooke Joann 1952- *BiDrAPA 89*
Thorner, Michael Oliver 1945- *WhoAm 90*
Thorner, Paul M. 1921- *St&PR 91*
Thorner, Peter 1943- *St&PR 91, WhoAm 90*
Thorner, Prudence Maria 1944- *WhoAmW 91*
Thorneycroft, Peter 1909- *WhoWor 91*
Thornhill, Arthur Horace, Jr. 1924- *WhoAm 90*
Thornhill, Claude 1909-1965 *BioIn 16, OxCPMus*
Thornhill, French W. 1804-1892 *AmLegL*
Thornhill, Gabriel Felder, III 1928- *WhoSSW 91*
Thornhill, Glenn 1946- *St&PR 91*
Thornhill, James 1675?-1734 *IntDcAA 90*
Thornhill, Kenneth J. *BioIn 16*
Thornhill, Lois 1945- *WhoAmW 91*
Thornhill, Robert Jean 1925- *St&PR 91*
Thornhill, Russell A. 1921- *St&PR 91*
Thornley, David George 1950- *St&PR 91*
Thornley, Denis Glyn *BioIn 16*
Thornley, Wendy Ann 1948- *WhoAmA 91*
Thornlow, Carolyn 1954- *WhoAmW 91, WhoEmL 91*
Thornock, David Eugene 1962- *WhoE 91*
Thorns, John Cyril, Jr 1926- *WhoAmA 91*
Thornsley, Susan Lynn *BiDrAPA 89*
Thornton, Alice 1626-1707 *FemiCLE*
Thornton, Alice 1627-1707 *BiDEWW*
Thornton, Alice Wandesford 1627-1707 *BioIn 16*
Thornton, Andre *BioIn 16*
Thornton, Andre 1949- *Ballpl 90*
Thornton, Ann Murphy 1920- *WhoAmW 91*
Thornton, Barbara Johnson 1947- *WhoSSW 91*
Thornton, Bernard Terry 1942- *WhoSSW 91*
Thornton, Big Mama 1926-1984 *EncPR&S 89*
Thornton, Bruce H. 1936- *St&PR 91*
Thornton, Charles Victor 1915- *St&PR 91, WhoAm 90, WhoWor 91*
Thornton, Christopher Gordon 1955- *WhoSSW 91*
Thornton, Clarence Gould 1925- *WhoAm 90*
Thornton, D.M., Jr. 1920- *St&PR 91*
Thornton, Dean Dickson 1929- *St&PR 91, WhoAm 90*
Thornton, Donald Norman 1933- *St&PR 91*
Thornton, Donald Ray 1936- *WhoWrEP 89*
Thornton, Edmund Arwin, Sr. 1924- *WhoSSW 91*
Thornton, Edmund B. 1930- *WhoWor 91*
Thornton, Edward Ralph 1935- *WhoAm 90*
Thornton, Elizabeth Dee Kaplan 1940- *WhoAmW 91*
Thornton, Elizabeth Sharon Eckart 1960- *WhoAmW 91*
Thornton, Frank 1921- *ConTFT 8 [port]*
Thornton, George Whiteley 1936- *WhoAm 90*
Thornton, Gerald D. 1924- *St&PR 91*
Thornton, Gerard Francis 1947- *St&PR 91*
Thornton, Hall *MajTwCW*
Thornton, Henry 1760-1815 *BioIn 16*
Thornton, J. Edward 1907- *WhoAm 90*
Thornton, J. Ronald 1939- *WhoSSW 91*
Thornton, Jack Nelson 1932- *St&PR 91, WhoAm 90*
Thornton, James 1861-1938 *BioIn 16, OxCPMus*
Thornton, James Bruce 1951- *WhoSSW 91*
Thornton, James E. 1925- *St&PR 91*
Thornton, James Ivan, Jr. 1944- *WhoAm 90*
Thornton, Jeanette F *BiDrAPA 89*
Thornton, Jim 1937- *WhoAmA 91*
Thornton, John *BioIn 16*
Thornton, John A. 1933-1987 *BioIn 16*
Thornton, John H. *BioIn 16*
Thornton, John T. 1937- *St&PR 91, WhoAm 90*
Thornton, John Vincent 1924- *St&PR 91, WhoAm 90*
Thornton, John W., Sr. 1928- *WhoSSW 91*
Thornton, John William 1921- *WhoAm 90*
Thornton, John William, Jr. 1948- *WhoSSW 91*
Thornton, Joseph Keith 1931- *WhoSSW 91*
Thornton, Joseph Scott 1936- *WhoAm 90, WhoWor 91*
Thornton, Kathryn C. 1952- *WhoAmW 91*
Thornton, Kathy Elizabeth 1955- *WhoAmW 91*
Thornton, Larry Lee 1937- *WhoSSW 91*
Thornton, Lawrence 1937- *ConAu 132*
Thornton, Linda Wierman 1942- *St&PR 91, WhoAmW 91*
Thornton, Mary Jane 1923- *WhoWrEP 89*
Thornton, Mary Janice *WhoAmW 91*
Thornton, Matthew 1714-1803 *EncCRAm*
Thornton, Michael Joseph 1947- *WhoE 91*
Thornton, Neil Robert 1930- *St&PR 91*
Thornton, Ralph 1922?-1989 *ConAu 129*
Thornton, Ralph J. 1943- *St&PR 91*
Thornton, Ray 1928- *WhoSSW 91*
Thornton, Rebecca Ruth *BiDrAPA 89*
Thornton, Richard Leon 1949- *WhoSSW 91*
Thornton, Richard Samuel 1934- *WhoAmA 91, WhoE 91*
Thornton, Rita *ODwPR 91*
Thornton, Robert Dale 1959- *WhoSSW 91*
Thornton, Robert James, Sr. 1943- *WhoE 91*
Thornton, Robert R. 1926- *St&PR 91*
Thornton, Robert Richard 1926- *WhoAm 90*
Thornton, Sandi Tokoa 1953- *WhoSSW 91*
Thornton, Spencer P. 1929- *WhoAm 90, WhoWor 91*
Thornton, Sue Bonner *WhoAm 90*
Thornton, Ted Douglas 1958- *BiDrAPA 89*
Thornton, Theodore Kean 1949- *St&PR 91, WhoAm 90*
Thornton, Thomas Noel 1950- *WhoAm 90*
Thornton, Walter *BioIn 16, NewYTBS 90*
Thornton, Wayne Allen 1952- *WhoE 91, WhoEmL 91*
Thornton, William G. 1914- *St&PR 91*
Thornton, William James 1919- *IntWWM 90*
Thornton, William James, Jr. 1919- *WhoAm 90*
Thornton, William Lewis 1923- *WhoSSW 91, WhoWor 91*
Thornton, Winfred L. 1928- *St&PR 91*
Thornton, Winfred Lamotte 1928- *WhoSSW 91*
Thornwell, Allison, Jr. *St&PR 91*
Thornycroft, Alyce Mary 1844-1906 *BiDWomA*
Thornycroft, Ann 1944- *WhoAmA 91*
Thornycroft, Helen 1848-1937 *BiDWomA*
Thornycroft, Mary 1809-1895 *BiDWomA*
Thornycroft, Theresa Georgiana 1853-1947 *BiDWomA*
Thorogood, Brackett K 1881- *EncO&P 3*
Thorogood, George 1951- *EncPR&S 89*
Thorp, Benjamin A., III 1938- *WhoAm 90*
Thorp, Earl Norwell *WhoAmA 91N*
Thorp, Edward O. *BioIn 16*
Thorp, Jack L *BiDrAPA 89*
Thorp, Kenneth Edward 1926- *WhoAm 90*
Thorp, Willard *NewYTBS 90*
Thorp, Willard 1899-1990 *BioIn 16, ConAu 130*
Thorp, Willard Long 1899- *WhoE 91*
Thorpe, Adam 1956- *ConAu 129*
Thorpe, Betsy Tucker 1956- *WhoAmW 91*
Thorpe, Carole *BioIn 16*
Thorpe, D. R. 1943- *ConAu 129*
Thorpe, Deborah Lee Moorehead 1948- *WhoWor 91*
Thorpe, Dina *BioIn 16*
Thorpe, Elliott R. 1897-1989 *BioIn 16, ConAu 129*
Thorpe, Gary Stephen 1951- *WhoEmL 91*
Thorpe, Hilda 1919- *WhoAmA 91*
Thorpe, James 1888-1953 *WorAlBi*
Thorpe, James 1915- *WhoAm 90, WhoWrEP 89*
Thorpe, James, III 1942- *WhoAm 90*
Thorpe, James A. 1929- *St&PR 91*
Thorpe, James Alfred 1929- *WhoAm 90*
Thorpe, James George 1951- *WhoAmA 91*
Thorpe, Janet Claire 1953- *St&PR 91*
Thorpe, Jim 1887-1953 *Ballpl 90*
Thorpe, Jim 1888-1953 *BioIn 16*
Thorpe, John Alden 1936- *WhoE 91*
Thorpe, Joseph B. 1930- *St&PR 91*
Thorpe, Kenneth Earl 1956- *WhoE 91*
Thorpe, Marion *IntWWM 90*
Thorpe, Martha Campbell 1922- *WhoAmW 91*
Thorpe, Merle, Jr. 1917- *WhoAm 90*
Thorpe, Stephen J. 1944- *WhoWrEP 89*
Thorpe, Susan M. 1956- *WhoAmW 91*
Thorpe, Trebor *ConAu 32NR*
Thorpe, Trevor *ConAu 32NR*
Thorpy, Frank Thomas 1919- *WhoWor 91*
Thors, J. Emerson *BioIn 16*
Thorse, David S. 1957- *WhoSSW 91*
Thorsen, Arthur Carl 1934- *WhoAm 90*
Thorsen, Carolyn Crawford Chesnutt 1933- *WhoWor 91*
Thorsen, James Hugh 1943- *WhoWor 91*
Thorsen, Jan Vilhelm Mainz 1963- *WhoWor 91*
Thorsen, Nancy Dain 1944- *WhoAmW 91, WhoWor 91*
Thorsen, Roy T. 1930- *St&PR 91*
Thorsen, Thomas Oliver 1931- *St&PR 91*
Thorshov, Roy Norman 1905- *WhoAm 90*
Thorson, Alice R 1953- *WhoAmA 91*
Thorson, Barbara Ann 1949- *WhoAmW 91*
Thorson, Connie Capers 1940- *WhoAmW 91*
Thorson, David Morris 1950- *WhoEmL 91*
Thorson, Diane Rae 1953- *WhoAmW 91*
Thorson, Gretchen 1957- *WhoAmW 91*
Thorson, James Donald 1933- *St&PR 91*
Thorson, John Eric 1946- *WhoEmL 91*
Thorson, John Martin, Jr. 1929- *WhoAm 90*
Thorson, Larry Jonathan 1951- *WhoEmL 91*
Thorson, Marcelyn Marie 1927- *WhoAmW 91, WhoSSW 91*
Thorson, Milton Z. 1902- *St&PR 91*
Thorson, Oswald Hagen 1912- *WhoAm 90*
Thorson, Robert Mark 1951- *WhoWrEP 89*
Thorson, Stuart J. 1946- *WhoAm 90*
Thorson, Thomas Bertel 1917- *WhoAm 90*
Thorsson, Inga Margrette 1915- *WhoWor 91*
Thorstad, Bruce 1946- *WhoWrEP 89*
Thorstad, Linda E. 1954- *St&PR 91*
Thorstad, Willis Myron *BiDrAPA 89*
Thorstein, Eric *MajTwCW*
Thorsteinn Erlingsson *DcScanL*
Thorsteinn fra Hamri 1938- *DcScanL*
Thorsteinn Jonsson *DcScanL*
Thorsteinsson, Indridi G. 1926- *DcScanL*
Thorsteinsson, Raymond 1921- *WhoAm 90*
Thorsteinsson, Steingrimur 1831-1913 *DcScanL*
Thorstenberg, Laurence 1925- *WhoAm 90*
Thorstrom, Borje Henrik 1941- *WhoWor 91*
Thorud, Gary Dennis 1939- *WhoSSW 91*
Thorup, Jesper 1952- *IntWWM 90*
Thorup, Kirsten 1942- *DcScanL*
Thorvaldsen, Bertel 1768-1844 *IntDcAA 90*
Thorward, Sul Ross Olen 1947- *BiDrAPA 89*
Thostenson, Donald K. 1934- *St&PR 91*
Thostrup, Nils 1936- *WhoWor 91*
Thottam, Johnson John 1947- *WhoEmL 91*
Thottappilly, George 1941- *WhoWor 91*
Thouless, David James 1934- *WhoAm 90*
Thouless, Robert Henry 1894-1984 *EncO&P 3, EncPaPR 91*
Thouret, Nikolaus Friedrich von 1766-1845 *PenDiDA 89*
Thow, George Bruce 1930- *WhoAm 90*
Thraenhardt, Dietrich Joachim 1941- *WhoWor 91*
Thrailkill, Francis Marie 1937- *WhoAm 90, WhoAmW 91*
Thrakopoula *EncCoWW*
Thrall, Arthur 1926- *WhoAmA 91*
Thrall, Arthur Alvin 1926- *WhoAm 90*
Thrall, Bart 1944- *WhoAmA 91*
Thrall, Donald Stuart 1918- *WhoAm 90, WhoWor 91*
Thrall, Edwin Fiske, Jr. 1936- *WhoE 91*
Thrall, James Hunter 1943- *WhoAm 90*
Thrall, Robert McDowell 1914- *WhoAm 90*
Thrane, Marcus 1817-1890 *BioIn 16*
Thrash, Bobby Floyd 1956- *WhoSSW 91*
Thrash, Cecil *ODwPR 91*
Thrash, Edsel E. 1925- *WhoAm 90*
Thrash, James Lee 1949- *St&PR 91*
Thrash, Melvin Lawrence *BiDrAPA 89*
Thrash, Melvin Lawrence 1940- *WhoE 91*
Thrash, Patricia Ann 1929- *WhoAm 90*
Thrash, Purvis James, Sr. 1927- *St&PR 91, WhoAm 90*
Thrasher, Bessie G. *WhoAmW 91*
Thrasher, Crystal 1921- *BioIn 16*
Thrasher, Henry Grady, III 1942- *WhoSSW 91*
Thrasher, Hugh 1941- *St&PR 91*
Thrasher, James Parker 1932- *WhoWor 91*
Thrasher, James W, Jr. *BiDrAPA 89*
Thrasher, John M. 1952- *St&PR 91*
Thrasher, Kenneth 1949- *St&PR 91*
Thrasher, Lee-Hope 1954- *WhoEmL 91*
Thrasher, Patrick D 1947- *BiDrAPA 89*
Thrasher, Paul McNeel, III 1950- *WhoE 91*
Thrasher, Randell Hue 1955- *WhoSSW 91*
Thrasher, Robert H *BiDrAPA 89*
Thrasher, Thais Verdelle 1930- *BiDrAPA 89*
Threadcraft, Hal Law, III 1952- *WhoEmL 91, WhoSSW 91*
Threadgill, Henry *BioIn 16*
Threadgill, Walter Leonard 1945- *St&PR 91*
Threadgold, Michael Andrew 1950- *WhoAm 90*
Threatt, Ned Leon, Sr. 1922- *WhoAm 90*
Threatte, Leslie L., Jr. 1943- *WhoAm 90*
Thredgold, Jeff K. 1951- *St&PR 91*
Three Dog Night *ConMus 5 [port], EncPR&S 89*
Threefoot, Sam Abraham 1921- *WhoAm 90*
Threet, Jack Curtis 1928- *WhoAm 90*
Threinen, David T. 1934- *St&PR 91*
Threlkeld, Dale 1944- *WhoAmA 91*
Threlkeld, Dennis John 1942- *St&PR 91*
Threlkeld, Richard Davis 1937- *WhoAm 90, WhoE 91*
Threlkeld, William A, Jr. 1933- *BiDrAPA 89*
Thribb, E. J. *ConAu 129*
Thrift, Syd 1929- *Ballpl 90*
Thrift, Syd, Jr. *BioIn 16*
Thring, M W 1915- *ConAu 130*
Throckmorton, Elizabeth *BiDEWW*
Throckmorton, John *St&PR 91*
Throckmorton, John Ford 1941- *St&PR 91*
Throckmorton, Peter *NewYTBS 90*
Throckmorton, Peter 1928- *AuBYP 90*
Throckmorton, Peter 1928-1990 *BioIn 16, ConAu 131*
Throckmorton, Robert Bentley 1915- *WhoAm 90*
Throckmorton, William Robert, Sr. 1923- *WhoE 91*
Throdahl, Monte Corden 1919- *WhoAm 90*
Throgmorton, Richard Leon 1940- *St&PR 91*
Throne, John M. *WhoAm 90*
Throne, Malachi *ConTFT 8*
Throne, Marilyn Elizabeth 1939- *WhoAmW 91, WhoWrEP 89*
Throne, Robin M. 1954- *WhoAmW 91*
Throneberry, Faye 1931- *Ballpl 90*
Throneberry, Marv 1933- *Ballpl 90*
Throneburg, James *AuBYP 90*
Throner, Guy Charles, Jr. 1919- *WhoAm 90*
Thronson, Leah *BiDrAPA 89*
Throop, Allen Eaton 1900-1989 *BioIn 16*
Thrower, Norman Joseph William 1919- *WhoAm 90*
Thrower, Percy 1913-1988 *AnObit 1988*
Thrower, Richard 1947- *WhoSSW 91*
Thruelsen, Richard 1908-1989 *ConAu 129*
Thruelsen, Richard D. *BioIn 16*
Thryft, Ann R. 1950- *WhoAmW 91*
Thubthom, Boonsakdi 1947- *WhoWor 91*
Thucydides *BioIn 16*
Thucydides 455?BC-400?BC *WorAlBi*
Thue, Anniken 1944- *WhoWor 91*
Thueme, William Harold 1945- *WhoEmL 91, WhoWor 91*
Thuer, Gerhard 1941- *WhoWor 91*
Thuering, George Lewis 1919- *WhoAm 90*
Thuermer, Karen Elaine 1955- *WhoAmW 91*
Thuesen, Gerald Jorgen 1938- *WhoAm 90, WhoSSW 91*
Thuestad, Lori Lynn 1957- *WhoAmW 91*
Thul, Frederick Warren 1921- *St&PR 91*
Thul, Nicholas R. 1950- *St&PR 91*

Thulasi, Srinivasa Seetharama 1957- *WhoWor 91*
Thulean, Donald Myron 1929- *WhoAm 90*
Thulin, Ingrid 1929- *WhoWor 91, WorAlBi*
Thulin, Walter Willis 1929- *WhoAm 90*
Thullen, Manfred 1938- *WhoHisp 91*
Thum, Lawrence C *BiDrAPA 89*
Thum, Marcella *AuBYP 90*
Thum, Melvin Joseph 1932- *St&PR 91*
Thuma, Nathan H 1957- *BiDrAPA 89*
Thumann, Albert 1942- *WhoAm 90*
Thumbtzen, Tatiana *BioIn 16*
Thumim, Roberta 1945- *ODwPR 91*
Thumm, Micheal Walter 1953- *WhoE 91*
Thummel, Moritz August von 1738-1817 *DcLB 97*
Thummler, Fritz Ernst 1924- *WhoWor 91*
Thums, Charles William 1945- *WhoEmL 91, WhoWor 91*
Thun, Matteo *PenDiDA 89*
Thun, Matteo 1952- *BioIn 16*
Thunborg, Anders Ingemar 1934- *WhoWor 91*
Thundiyil, Grace Muricken *BiDrAPA 89*
Thunen, Johann Heinrich von 1783-1850 *BioIn 16*
Thunfors, Lyman C. *BioIn 16*
Thunholm, Lars-Erik 1914- *WhoWor 91*
Thunman, Nils Ronald 1932- *WhoAm 90*
Thuraisingham, Bhavani Marienne 1954- *WhoAmW 91*
Thurber, Cleveland, Jr. 1925- *WhoAm 90*
Thurber, Davis P. 1925- *St&PR 91*
Thurber, Davis Peabody 1925- *WhoAm 90*
Thurber, Deborah L. 1961- *BiDrAPA 89*
Thurber, Donald MacDonald Dickinson 1918- *WhoAm 90, WhoWor 91*
Thurber, Gerrie *BioIn 16*
Thurber, James 1894-1961 *AuBYP 90, Ballpl 90, BioIn 16, DcLB 102 [port], MajTwCW, WorAlBi*
Thurber, James Perry, Jr. 1928- *WhoE 91*
Thurber, Jefferson Gage 1807-1857 *AmLegL*
Thurber, John Alexander 1939- *WhoAm 90*
Thurber, John Newton *BioIn 16*
Thurber, Peter Palms 1928- *WhoAm 90*
Thurber, Robert E. 1940- *St&PR 91, WhoAm 90*
Thurber, Robert Eugene 1932- *WhoAm 90, WhoSSW 91*
Thurer, Daniel Georg 1945- *WhoWor 91*
Thurer, Richard Jerome 1936- *WhoSSW 91*
Thurian, Max 1921- *ConAu 129*
Thurin, Jan 1955- *WhoE 91*
Thurlbeck, William Michael 1929- *WhoAm 90*
Thurlimann, Bruno 1923- *WhoWor 91*
Thurloe, John 1616-1668 *BioIn 16*
Thurlow, Alan John 1947- *IntWWM 90*
Thurlow, Fearn Cutler 1924-1982 *WhoAmA 91N*
Thurlow, Willard Rowand 1918- *WhoAm 90*
Thurm, Ulrich 1931- *WhoWor 91*
Thurman, Addison Eugene, Jr. 1943- *WhoSSW 91*
Thurman, Andrew Edward 1954- *WhoE 91, WhoEmL 91, WhoWor 91*
Thurman, Bob 1917- *Ballpl 90*
Thurman, Christa Charlotte Mayer 1934- *WhoAmA 91*
Thurman, David Michael 1947- *St&PR 91*
Thurman, Harold Curtis, Jr. *BiDrAPA 89*
Thurman, Henry Louis, Jr. 1927- *WhoAm 90*
Thurman, Howard 1899-1981 *BioIn 16*
Thurman, Janet Louise 1957- *WhoAmW 91*
Thurman, Jerry W. 1947- *St&PR 91*
Thurman, Joyce Evelyn 1953- *WhoE 91*
Thurman, Judith 1946- *BioIn 16*
Thurman, Karen 1951- *WhoAmW 91*
Thurman, Mark 1948- *ConAu 131, SmATA 63 [port]*
Thurman, Maxwell R. 1931- *WhoAm 90*
Thurman, Oliver 1935- *St&PR 91*
Thurman, Ralph H. 1949- *St&PR 91*
Thurman, Ralph Holloway 1949- *WhoWor 91*
Thurman, Samuel David 1913- *WhoAm 90*
Thurman, Tracey *BioIn 16*
Thurman, Uma *BioIn 16*
Thurman, Wallace 1902-1934 *DrBlPA 90, EarBlAP*
Thurman, William Gentry 1928- *WhoAm 90*
Thurmann, Hollis 1946- *WhoWrEP 89*
Thurmeier, Edward F. 1948- *St&PR 91*
Thurmond, Charles J. 1910- *St&PR 91*
Thurmond, George Murat 1930- *WhoSSW 91*
Thurmond, Jimmie Victor, Jr. 1934- *St&PR 91*
Thurmond, Mark 1956- *Ballpl 90*
Thurmond, Nancy Moore 1946- *ConAu 132*
Thurmond, Sandra Barker 1961- *WhoAmW 91*
Thurmond, Strom 1902- *WhoAm 90, WhoSSW 91, WhoWor 91, WorAlBi*
Thurn und Taxis, Gloria *BioIn 16*
Thurn und Taxis, Johannes, Furst von *BioIn 16*
Thurn und Taxis, Johannes von 1926- *WhoWor 91*
Thurn-Valsassina, Isabelle von *BioIn 16*
Thurnblad, Robert J 1933- *BiDrAPA 89*
Thurow, Lester C 1938- *CurBio 90 [port]*
Thurow, Mattias *NewAgMG*
Thurrell, Marian 1960- *WhoAmW 91*
Thurrell, Richard J 1929- *BiDrAPA 89*
Thursby, Emma C. 1845-1931 *BioAmW*
Thursby, Gene Robert 1939- *WhoSSW 91*
Thursby, Peter Michael 1945- *WhoWor 91*
Thursfield, Maurice *PenDiDA 89*
Thurston, Alice Janet 1916- *WhoAm 90*
Thurston, Anne Elizabeth 1957- *WhoAmW 91*
Thurston, Barry 1942- *BioIn 16*
Thurston, Benjamin Francis 1829-1890 *AmLegL*
Thurston, Charles R. 1933- *St&PR 91*
Thurston, Charles W. 1960- *St&PR 91*
Thurston, Charlie A. 1939- *St&PR 91*
Thurston, David E. 1957- *WhoE 91*
Thurston, Donald Allen 1930- *WhoAm 90*
Thurston, Doris 1929- *WhoAmW 91*
Thurston, Ella Isabelle 1925- *WhoAmW 91*
Thurston, Ethel Holbrooke 1911- *IntWWM 90*
Thurston, Fred Stone 1931- *St&PR 91*
Thurston, Frederick 1901-1953 *PenDiMP*
Thurston, Fuzzy 1933- *BioIn 16*
Thurston, George Butte 1924- *WhoAm 90*
Thurston, Gilbert L. *BioIn 16*
Thurston, Harry 1950- *ConAu 32NR*
Thurston, Herbert 1856-1939 *EncPaPR 91*
Thurston, Herbert Henry Charles 1856-1939 *EncO&P 3*
Thurston, Howard 1869-1936 *BioIn 16*
Thurston, Jacqueline Beverly 1939- *WhoAmA 91*
Thurston, John A. 1951- *St&PR 91*
Thurston, John Kent 1946- *WhoSSW 91*
Thurston, John Thomas 1948- *WhoE 91*
Thurston, Kenneth P. 1945- *St&PR 91*
Thurston, Lawrence 1952- *WhoE 91*
Thurston, Maryjane B. 1927- *WhoSSW 91*
Thurston, Richard Maurice Joseph 1949- *WhoE 91*
Thurston, Robert N. 1932- *St&PR 91*
Thurston, Ronald C 1939- *BiDrAPA 89*
Thurston, Russell Charles 1939- *St&PR 91*
Thurston, Sloppy 1899-1973 *Ballpl 90*
Thurstone, Fredrick Louis 1932- *WhoAm 90*
Thurstone, Thelma Gwinn *BioIn 16*
Thursz, Daniel 1929- *WhoAm 90*
Thurtell, John 1794-1824 *BioIn 16*
Thury, Marc 1822-1905 *EncO&P 3*
Thuy, Thu Le *BioIn 16*
Thwaites, Charles Winstanley 1904- *WhoAmA 91*
Thwaites, Penelope Mary 1944- *IntWWM 90*
Thweatt, Charley *NewAgMG*
Thweatt, Rayford W 1944- *BiDrAPA 89*
Thwing, R.C. 1921- *St&PR 91*
Thyberg, Kenneth Robert 1948- *St&PR 91*
Thyen, Herbert Edward 1912- *St&PR 91, WhoAm 90*
Thyen, James C. 1943- *WhoAm 90*
Thyen, James Conrad 1943- *St&PR 91*
Thyen, John T. *WhoAm 90*
Thyen, Ronald J. 1937- *WhoAm 90*
Thyen, Ronald Joseph 1937- *St&PR 91*
Thyfault, Michel Daniel 1947- *St&PR 91*
Thygerson, Kenneth J. 1945- *St&PR 91*
Thygesen, Rud 1932- *ConDes 90*
Thym, Jurgen 1943- *IntWWM 90*
Thynell, Stefan 1954- *WhoE 91*
Thynn, Alexander 1932- *ConAu 132*
Thynne, Alexander *ConAu 132*
Thynne, Harriet Frances 1816-1881 *FemiCLE*
Thynne, Joan 1558-1612 *BiDEWW, FemiCLE*
Thynne, Maria 1578?-1611 *BiDEWW, FemiCLE*
Thyra *EncCoWW*
Thyrre, Kristina Karen 1959- *WhoWor 91*
Thys, Thierry N. 1931- *St&PR 91*
Thyssen, Fritz 1873-1951 *WorAlBi*
Thyssen-Bornemisza, Hans Heinrich 1921- *BioIn 16*
Thyssen-Bornemisza, Tita *BioIn 16*
Tian *EncCoWW*
Tian Jiyun 1929- *WhoWor 91*
Tian, Zhaowu 1927- *WhoWor 91*
Tiangco, Elito 1940- *WhoE 91*
Tiano, J. Richard 1944- *St&PR 91*
Tiant, Luis 1940- *WorAlBi*
Tiant, Luis, Jr. 1940- *Ballpl 90 [port]*
Tiant, Luis, Sr. 1906- *Ballpl 90*
Tibaek, Poul 1920- *WhoWor 91*
Tibbalds, Francis Eric 1941- *WhoWor 91*
Tibbals, David Lester 1945- *WhoSSW 91*
Tibbats, Rodney B. 1939- *St&PR 91*
Tibbels, Nancy Ann 1963- *WhoAmW 91*
Tibbet, Lawrence 1896-1960 *PenDiMP*
Tibbets, Albert B. 1888- *AuBYP 90*
Tibbets, Paul W. *BioIn 16*
Tibbets, Robin Frank 1924- *WhoWor 91*
Tibbett, Lawrence 1896-1960 *PenDiMP*
Tibbetts, Cathy D. 1954- *WhoAmW 91*
Tibbetts, Douglas *BioIn 16*
Tibbetts, George C. 1925- *St&PR 91*
Tibbetts, H.M. 1924- *St&PR 91*
Tibbetts, Larry Newton 1934- *WhoAm 90*
Tibbits, John Arnold 1844-1893 *AmLegL*
Tibbitts, Kent D. 1937- *WhoWor 91*
Tibbitts, Samuel John 1924- *WhoAm 90, WhoWor 91*
Tibbles, Percy Thomas *BioIn 16*
Tibbles, Thomas Henry 1840-1928 *WhNaAH*
Tibbs, Casey 1929?-1990 *BioIn 16*
Tibbs, Harry Edward 1933- *IntWWM 90*
Tibbs, Jay 1962- *Ballpl 90*
Tibbs, Martha Jane Pullen 1932- *WhoSSW 91*
Tibbs, Thomas S 1917- *WhoAmA 91*
Tibensky, James Walter 1948- *WhoEmL 91*
Tiber, Elliot 1935- *ConAu 129*
Tiberend, Gregory Quinn 1962- *ODwPR 91*
Tibergien, Mark C. 1952- *St&PR 91*
Tiberi-Smolenski, Sandra Josephine 1964- *WhoAmW 91*
Tiberio, Faith Kuhrt 1926- *WhoE 91*
Tiberius 42BC-37AD *WorAlBi*
Tibi, Bassam 1944- *ConAu 130*
Tibler, Lee Walter 1952- *WhoSSW 91*
Tibon, Gutierre 1905- *EncPaPR 91*
Tibors 12--?- *EncCoWW*
Tiburzi, Anita M. *ODwPR 91*
Tiburzi, Anita Marie 1944- *WhoAmW 91*
Tice, Carol Hoff 1931- *WhoAmW 91*
Tice, Carolyn Kay 1945- *WhoAmW 91*
Tice, Charles L. 1934- *St&PR 91*
Tice, Charles Raymond 1937- *St&PR 91*
Tice, David Allan 1952- *WhoSSW 91*
Tice, George Andrew 1938- *WhoAm 90, WhoAmA 91*
Tice, John Norman, Jr. 1946- *St&PR 91*
Tice, Kirk Clifford 1954- *WhoE 91*
Tice, Linwood Franklin 1909- *WhoAm 90*
Tice, Mark H. 1915- *St&PR 91*
Tice, Mark Randolph 1941- *St&PR 91*
Tice, Patricia Kaye 1953- *WhoAmW 91*
Tice, Raphael Dean 1927- *WhoAm 90*
Tice, Robert Galen 1956- *WhoEmL 91*
Tice, Timothy Vernley *BiDrAPA 89*
Ticha, Hans 1940- *BioIn 16*
Tichatschek, Joseph 1807-1886 *BioIn 16*
Tichelaar, Freerk Jans *PenDiDA 89*
Tichener, Edward Bradford 1867-1927 *BioIn 16*
Tichenor, Arthur G. 1913- *St&PR 91*
Tichenor, Charles Beckham 1926- *St&PR 91*
Tichenor, Donald Keith 1937- *WhoAm 90*
Tichenor, Fred Cooper, Jr. 1932- *WhoSSW 91*
Tichenor, Stanley Hume 1926- *St&PR 91*
Tichenor, Tom 1923- *AuBYP 90*
Tichenor, Trebor Jay 1940- *IntWWM 90*
Tichik, Evelyn Kay 1942- *WhoAmW 91*
Ticho, Gabriel Chaim 1960- *BiDrAPA 89*
Ticho, Gertrude R *BiDrAPA 89*
Ticho, Harold Klein 1921- *WhoAm 90*
Tichy, Franz Hermann 1921- *WhoWor 91*
Tichy, Georg 1944- *IntWWM 90*
Tichy, Paul 1933- *St&PR 91*
Tichy, Susan Elizabeth 1952- *WhoWrEP 89*
Tick, Judith 1943- *IntWWM 90*
Tickell, Crispin 1930- *WhoWor 91*
Tickell, Dorothy *BiDEWW*
Tickett, Deborah L. 1951- *WhoAmW 91*
Tickey, Lynda Callahan 1950- *St&PR 91*
Tickle, Phyllis Alexander 1934- *WhoWrEP 89*
Ticknor, Arthur W. 1934- *St&PR 91*
Ticknor, Christopher B 1956- *BiDrAPA 89*
Ticknor, George 1791-1871 *BioIn 16*
Ticknor, Howard Malcolm 1936- *St&PR 91*
Ticknor, William Davis, III 1932- *WhoAm 90*
Ticotin, Rachel 1958- *WhoHisp 91*
Tidball, Charles Stanley 1928- *WhoAm 90*
Tidball, Lewis C. 1848-1917 *AmLegL*
Tidball, M. Elizabeth Peters 1929- *WhoAm 90, WhoAmW 91*
Tidball, Robert N. 1939- *St&PR 91*
Tidball, Robert Nial 1939- *WhoAm 90*
Tidd, Cynthia Ann 1956- *WhoWrEP 89*
Tidd, Margaret E 1951- *BiDrAPA 89*
Tiddens, Mark E. 1951- *St&PR 91*
Tideman, Christopher Charles 1941- *WhoWor 91*
Tidick-Ulveling, Marie-Louise 1892-1989 *EncCoWW*
Tidmore, Terri Lacey 1955- *WhoAmW 91*
Tidrick, Cheryl Latham 1946- *WhoSSW 91*
Tidrick, Larry James 1939- *St&PR 91*
Tidrow, Dick 1947- *Ballpl 90*
Tidus, David Bernard 1923- *St&PR 91*
Tidwell, Ardis M. 1932- *St&PR 91*
Tidwell, Drew Virgil, III 1948- *WhoEmL 91*
Tidwell, Frank Morris 1942- *WhoSSW 91*
Tidwell, Joey Samuel 1957- *WhoSSW 91*
Tidwell, John Lewis 1937- *WhoSSW 91*
Tidwell, Moody R. 1939- *WhoAm 90*
Tidwell, Robert 1934- *St&PR 91*
Tidwell, Thomas Tinsley 1939- *WhoAm 90*
Tidwell, Trudy 1948- *WhoAmW 91*
Tidwell, W.T. 1937- *St&PR 91*
Tidwell, W. Ted 1937- *ODwPR 91*
Tidyman, Ernest 1928-1984 *TwCCr&M 91*
Tiecke, Richard William 1917- *WhoAm 90*
Tiede, Patricia Lee 1937- *WhoAmW 91*
Tiede, Tom Robert 1937- *WhoAm 90, WhoWor 91*
Tiedeken, Kathleen Helen 1945- *WhoAmW 91*
Tiedeman, David Valentine 1919- *WhoAm 90*
Tiedeman, Edward D. 1944- *St&PR 91*
Tiedeman, George Ralph 1946- *WhoSSW 91*
Tiedemann, Albert William, Jr. 1924- *WhoSSW 91, WhoWor 91*
Tiedemann, Arthur Everett 1921- *WhoAm 90*
Tiedemann, Carl Hans 1926- *St&PR 91*
Tiedemann, Edward Eric 1954- *WhoWor 91*
Tiedemann, H. Frank 1948- *WhoEmL 91*
Tiedemann, Hermann Otto 1821-1891 *DcCanB 12*
Tiedemann, John H. *BioIn 16*
Tiedemann, Margaret Mary 1920- *St&PR 91*
Tiedemann, Waldemar 1937- *St&PR 91*
Tiedemann, William Harold 1943- *WhoAm 90*
Tiedge, Laura Renwick 1961- *WhoE 91*
Tiedtke, John Meyer 1907- *WhoSSW 91*
Tiefel, Virginia May 1926- *WhoAm 90*
Tiefel, William Reginald 1934- *St&PR 91, WhoAm 90*
Tiefenauer, Bobby 1929- *Ballpl 90*
Tiefenbach, E.J. 1941- *St&PR 91*
Tiefenbrun, Susan 1943- *WhoE 91*
Tiefenthal, Marguerite Aurand 1919- *WhoAmW 91*
Tiefenthaler, Carlyn Jones 1928- *WhoE 91*
Tiegen, Elaine Malin 1944- *WhoAmW 91*
Tieger, Carolyn *ODwPR 91*
Tieger, Jeff *St&PR 91*
Tiegreen, Alan F 1935- *WhoAmA 91*
Tiegs, Cheryl *BioIn 16, WhoAm 90, WhoAmW 91*
Tiel, Vicky *BioIn 16*
Tielen, Jean 1824-1897 *DcCanB 12*
Tielke, James Clemens 1931- *WhoAm 90*
Tielsch, Ilse 1929- *EncCoWW*
Tieman, Nathan 1943- *St&PR 91*
Tieman, Suzannah Bliss 1945- *WhoAmW 91*
Tiemann, Norbert Theodore 1924- *WhoAm 90*
Tiemann, Robert E 1936- *WhoAmA 91*
Tien, Allen Y 1954- *BiDrAPA 89*
Tien, Chang Lin 1935- *WhoAm 90, WhoWor 91*
Tien, H. Ti 1928- *WhoAm 90*
Tien, Hsin Chen *BiDrAPA 89*
Tien, Ping King 1919- *WhoAm 90*
Tienari, Pekka J 1931- *BiDrAPA 89*
Tienda, Marta *WhoAmW 91*
Tienda, Marta 1950- *WhoHisp 91*
Tienken, Arthur T. 1922- *WhoAm 90*
Tiensch, Charles John 1941- *St&PR 91*
Tiepolo, Giovanni Battista 1696-1770 *IntDcAA 90, WorAlBi*
Tiernan, Frances 1846-1920 *FemiCLE*
Tiernan, Julie Fletcher 1952- *WhoAmW 91*
Tiernan, Mike 1867-1918 *Ballpl 90*
Tierney, Brian 1922- *WhoAm 90*
Tierney, Brian P. 1957- *ODwPR 91*
Tierney, Brian Patrick 1957- *WhoAm 90, WhoE 91*
Tierney, Colleen Blick 1946- *WhoE 91*
Tierney, Cotton 1894-1953 *Ballpl 90*
Tierney, David Bernard 1949- *St&PR 91*
Tierney, David John 1962- *WhoE 91*
Tierney, Frank M. 1930- *BioIn 16*
Tierney, Gene 1920- *WorAlBi*
Tierney, Harry 1890-1965 *OxCPMus*
Tierney, Howard Sherwood 1918-1990 *BioIn 16*

Tierney, James Edward 1947- WhoAm 90, WhoE 91
Tierney, James T. 1942- St&PR 91
Tierney, John Gregory, II BiDrAPA 89
Tierney, John Mark 1924- WhoE 91
Tierney, John Patrick 1931- St&PR 91, WhoAm 90
Tierney, John William 1923- WhoAm 90
Tierney, Kevin Joseph 1951- St&PR 91
Tierney, Mary E. St&PR 91
Tierney, Mary Elisabeth 1942- WhoE 91
Tierney, Michael Peter 1947- St&PR 91
Tierney, Patrick Lennox 1914- WhoAmA 91
Tierney, T. E. WhoAm 90
Tierney, Theodore James 1940- WhoAm 90
Tierno, Philip Mario, Jr. 1943- WhoE 91, WhoWor 91
Tierno Galvan, Enrique 1918-1986 BioIn 16
Tiernon, Carlos H. 1930- St&PR 91
Tiernon, Carlos Herschel 1930- WhoAm 90
Tiernon, John Luke 1840?- AmLegL
Tiesenga, Donald 1944- St&PR 91
Tieszen, Stuart Carl BiDrAPA 89
Tietavainen, Algot DcScanL
Tietavainen-Untola, Algot DcScanL
Tietgens, Edward R. 1938- St&PR 91
Tietje, Gerda Alice 1929- WhoAmW 91
Tietje, Les 1911- Ballpl 90
Tietjen, John Henry 1940- WhoAm 90
Tietjen, Karl Heinz 1911- WhoE 91
Tietjen, Mildred Campbell 1940- WhoAm 90
Tietjens, Eunice 1884-1944 BioAmW, FemiCLE
Tietjens, Therese 1831-1877 PenDiMP
Tietke, Wilhelm 1938- WhoSSW 91, WhoWor 91
Tietz, Gerald R. 1944- St&PR 91
Tietz, J. B. 1900-1988 BioIn 16
Tietz, Jean Paul 1938- St&PR 91
Tietz, Norbert Wolfgang 1926- WhoAm 90
Tietz, Walter 1927- BiDrAPA 89
Tietze, Heinrich Franz Friedrich 1880-1964 DcScB S2
Tietze, Lutz Friedjan 1942- WhoWor 91
Tiezzi, Enzo 1938- WhoWor 91
Tiffany BioIn 16
Tiffany 1972- ConMus 4 [port]
Tiffany, Arthur L. 1933- St&PR 91
Tiffany, C. Hunton 1939- St&PR 91
Tiffany, Charles L. 1812-1902 WorAlBi
Tiffany, Charles Louis 1812-1902 PenDiDA 89
Tiffany, Louis Comfort 1848-1933 BioIn 16, PenDiDA 89, WorAlBi
Tiffany, Marsha Belmont 1954- WhoAmW 91
Tiffany, Mary Margaret 1947- WhoAmW 91
Tiffany, Verne 1933- St&PR 91
Tiffany, William J, Jr. 1919- BiDrAPA 89
Tiffeau, Jacques 1928-1988 BioIn 16
Tiffen, Ira A. 1951- St&PR 91
Tiffen, Nathan 1925- St&PR 91
Tiffen, Steven D. 1960- St&PR 91
Tiffin, Jay H. 1928- St&PR 91
Tiffin, Pamela 1942- BioIn 16
Tifft, Ellen WhoWrEP 89
Tift, Mary Louise 1913- WhoAm 90, WhoAmA 91, WhoAmW 91
Tift, Thomas W., Jr. 1927- St&PR 91
Tigar, Kenneth 1942- ConTFT 8
Tigay, Alan Merrill 1947- WhoAm 90
Tigel, Phillip David BiDrAPA 89
Tiger, Derry MajTwCW
Tiger, Ira Paul 1936- WhoAm 90
Tiger, John ConAu 33NR
Tiger, Lionel 1937- WhoAm 90
Tiger, Lynne Forrester 1938- WhoAmW 91
Tiger, Madeline Joan 1934- WhoWrEP 89
Tigerman, Stanley 1930- BioIn 16, WhoAm 90, WhoAmA 91
Tigges, John Thomas 1932- WhoWrEP 89
Tigges, Kenneth Edwin 1927- WhoAm 90
Tighe, Joseph J. 1944- St&PR 91
Tighe, Mary 1772-1810 FemiCLE
Tighe, Michael J. 1931- St&PR 91
Tighe, Patti Jayne BiDrAPA 89
Tighe, Peggy Jo 1949- WhoAmW 91
Tighe, Sonia 1957- WhoAmW 91
Tighe, Spencer Alan 1957- BiDrAPA 89
Tighe, Thomas J. WhoAm 90
Tight, Dexter Corwin 1924- St&PR 91, WhoAm 90
Tignanelli, A. Andrew 1925- St&PR 91
Tigner, Brooks K. 1953- WhoWor 91
Tihany, Adam D. 1948?- BioIn 16
Tiilikainen, Anja Salli Kaarina 1934- WhoWor 91
Tijerina, Antonio A., Jr. 1950- WhoHisp 91
Tijerina, Felix 1915?- BioIn 16
Tijerina, Reies Lopez 1926- BioIn 16
Tijerino Lesher, Carmenza 1917- WhoAmW 91
Tijou, Jean PenDiDA 89
Tikaram, Tanita BioIn 16
Tikare, Sneha BiDrAPA 89
Tikhonov, Valentin ConAu 31NR
Tikka, Kari Juhani 1946- IntWWM 90
Tikkanen, George D. 1934- St&PR 91
Tikkanen, Henrik 1924-1984 DcScanL
Tikkanen, Marta 1935- DcScanL
Tikkanen, Marta Eleonora 1935- EncCoWW
Tiktin, Carl 1930- WhoWrEP 89
Tiktopoulos, Alexandros 1934- WhoWor 91
Tilahun, Yonas 1947- WhoWor 91
Tilbury, Dorothy Elizabeth 1946- IntWWM 90
Tilbury, Roger Graydon 1925- WhoAm 90
Tilden, Charles R. 1953- St&PR 91
Tilden, Charles Ripley ODwPR 91
Tilden, Samuel J. 1814-1886 WorAlBi
Tilden, William 1893-1953 WorAlBi
Tiley, Sharon Kay 1952- WhoWrEP 89
Tilg, Howard A. 1914- St&PR 91
Tilger, Justine Tharp 1931- WhoAmW 91
Tilghman, Michelle Lynn 1957- WhoAmW 91
Tilghman, Richard Albert, Jr. 1945- St&PR 91
Tilghman, Richard Granville 1940- St&PR 91, WhoAm 90, WhoSSW 91
Tilghman, Shirley Marie WhoAm 90
Tilipko, Laura 1953- WhoAmW 91
Tilis, Jerome S. WhoAm 90
Tilker, Marvin Joel 1936- St&PR 91, WhoAm 90
Tilkin, Jeffrey M BiDrAPA 89
Till, D. Allen 1951- St&PR 91
Till, Geoffrey 1945- ConAu 132
Till, George G. 1929- St&PR 91
Till, James Edgar 1931- WhoAm 90
Till, Larry Percy 1944- St&PR 91
Till, Paul H. 1929- St&PR 91
Tillage, Granville Christian 1936- St&PR 91
Tillander, Thomas 1938- St&PR 91
Tillberg, Bjorn Tomas 1944- WhoWor 91
Tillem, Ivan L. 1956-1989 BioIn 16
Tillenius, Clarence 1913- WhoAmA 91
Tiller, Carl William 1915- WhoAm 90, WhoE 91, WhoWor 91
Tiller, Joseph Patrick 1953- WhoSSW 91
Tiller, Kathleen Blanche 1925- WhoAmW 91
Tiller, Martha R. ODwPR 91
Tiller, Ronald Roy 1947- St&PR 91
Tiller, Ted BioIn 16
Tillery, Bill W. 1938- WhoAm 90, WhoWor 91
Tillery, Linda Ann 1951- WhoEmL 91
Tilles, Gilbert NewYTBS 90 [port]
Tilles, Jerome 1934- BiDrAPA 89
Tilleskjor, Darrell Erwin 1936- St&PR 91
Tilley, C. Ronald 1935- WhoAm 90
Tilley, Carolyn Bittner 1947- WhoAm 90
Tilley, Cecil Edgar 1894-1973 DcScB S2
Tilley, Frank William 1945- WhoSSW 91
Tilley, John Leonard 1928- WhoSSW 91
Tilley, Larry Lamar 1950- WhoSSW 91
Tilley, Lewis Lee 1921- WhoAmA 91
Tilley, Norwood Carlton, Jr. WhoAm 90
Tilley, Samuel Leonard 1818-1896 DcCanB 12
Tilley, Terrence William 1947- WhoSSW 91
Tilley, Thomas Alfred 1938- St&PR 91
Tilley, Thomas G. 1946- St&PR 91
Tilley, Vesta BioIn 16
Tilley, Vesta 1864-1952 OxCPMus
Tilley, William Jesse 1908- WhoAm 90
Tilley, William Jesse, Jr. 1932- St&PR 91
Tilliard, Jean-Baptiste 1685-1766 PenDiDA 89
Tillich, Hannah 1896- WhoWrEP 89
Tillich, Hannah 1896-1988 BioIn 16
Tillich, Paul 1886-1965 ConAu 33NR, MajTwCW, WorAlBi
Tillim, David 1906- BiDrAPA 89
Tillim, Sidney 1925- BioIn 16, WhoAmA 91
Tillinger, Arnold Jules 1938- BiDrAPA 89
Tillinghast, Charles C. 1936- St&PR 91
Tillinghast, Charles Carpenter, III 1936- WhoAm 90
Tillinghast, Charles Carpenter, Jr. 1911- WhoAm 90
Tillinghast, David Rollhaus 1930- WhoAm 90, WhoE 91
Tillinghast, John A. 1927- St&PR 91
Tillinghast, John Avery 1927- WhoAm 90
Tillinghast, Mary BiDEWW
Tillinghast, Meta Ione WhoAmW 91
Tillinghast, Pardon Elisha 1920- WhoAm 90
Tillinghast, Richard Williford 1940- WhoWrEP 89
Tillinghast, Walter C. 1929- St&PR 91
Tillis, David Roger 1955- WhoSSW 91
Tillis, Frederick 1930- DrBlPA 90
Tillis, Mel BioIn 16
Tillis, Rosalyn Brantley 1932- WhoAmW 91
Tillison, Jim ODwPR 91
Tillitski, Stephan William 1951- WhoSSW 91
Tillius, Sven-Gunnar Carl 1937- WhoWor 91
Tillman, Barrett 1948- ConAu 132
Tillman, Bob 1937- Ballpl 90
Tillman, Douglas Leon 1948- WhoEmL 91
Tillman, Frank Aubrey 1937- WhoAm 90
Tillman, Jacqueline 1944- WhoHisp 91
Tillman, June Torrison 1917- IntWWM 90
Tillman, Katherine Davis EarBlAP
Tillman, Kay Heidt 1945- WhoAmW 91
Tillman, Kayla Linn 1962- WhoWrEP 89
Tillman, Mary Anne Tuggle 1935- WhoAmW 91
Tillman, Mary Norman 1926- WhoAmW 91
Tillman, Raymond St&PR 91
Tillman, Robert Erwin 1937- WhoE 91
Tillman, Rollie, Jr. 1933- WhoAm 90, WhoSSW 91
Tillman, Vickie A. 1951- St&PR 91
Tillmann, George Lloyd 1931- WhoAm 90
Tillmann, William A BiDrAPA 89
Tillmes, Sandra Jean 1956- WhoEmL 91
Tillo, Zosimo Garay BiDrAPA 89
Tillon, Charles Joseph 1897- BiDFrPL
Tillotson, Henry Barber 1921- St&PR 91
Tillotson, James Edward 1929- St&PR 91
Tillotson, Thad 1940- Ballpl 90
Tillstrom, Burr 1917- WorAlBi
Tilly, Lola Cremeans 1898- WhoAmW 91
Tilly, Louise Audino 1930- WhoAmW 91
Tilly, Meg BioIn 16
Tilly, Nancy 1935- SmATA 62 [port]
Tillyard, R J 1881-1937 EncO&P 3
Tillyard, Robin John 1881-1937 EncPaPR 91
Tilokaikt WhNaAH
Tiloukaikt WhNaAH
Tilsa ArtLatA
Tilschova, Anna Maria 1873-1957 EncCoWW
Tilson, Donn J. 1950- ODwPR 91
Tilson, Hugh Hanna 1940- WhoAm 90
Tilson, Joe Charles 1928- WhoWor 91
Tilson, John Quillin 1866-1958 AmLegL
Tilson, John Quillin 1911- WhoAm 90
Tilson, Katherine Anne 1951- WhoAmW 91
Tilson, Philip A. 1930- St&PR 91
Tilt, Charles Arthur 1877-1956 EncABHB 4 [port]
Tilton, Alice TwCCr&M 91
Tilton, Bernice Sheppard WhoAmW 91
Tilton, Charlene BioIn 16
Tilton, Charlene 1958- ConTFT 8 [port]
Tilton, David L. 1926- St&PR 91
Tilton, David Lloyd 1926- WhoAm 90
Tilton, George Robert 1923- WhoAm 90
Tilton, James D. 1960- WhoSSW 91
Tilton, James Floyd 1937- WhoAm 90
Tilton, John Elvin 1939- WhoAm 90
Tilton, Kenneth L. 1940- WhoAm 90
Tilton, Kenneth Lee 1940- St&PR 91
Tilton, Rafael 1929- WhoWrEP 89
Tilton, Stanley R. 1947- St&PR 91
Tilton, Tanya Tylene 1960- WhoAmW 91
Tilton, Webster, Jr. 1922- WhoE 91
Tilyou, George C. 1862-1914 WorAlBi
Tilzer, Ira L. 1914-1988 BioIn 16
Tilzer, James A. 1939- St&PR 91
Tilzer, Seth A 1954- BiDrAPA 89
Timaeus of Locri EncO&P 3
Timakata, Fred 1936- WhoWor 91
Timanus, Debra Dunston 1953- WhoAmW 91
Timar, Tibor 1953- WhoWor 91
Timban, Teresita Sunga BiDrAPA 89
Timberg, Sigmund 1911- WhoAm 90
Timberg, Thomas Arnold 1942- WhoE 91
Timberlake, Charles Edward 1935- WhoAm 90
Timberlake, E. Wrenne 1925- ODwPR 91
Timberlake, Stephen Grant 1958- WhoSSW 91
Timberlin, Beverly Jean 1935- WhoWor 91
Timbers, Michael J. 1941- St&PR 91
Timbers, Stephen B. 1944- St&PR 91
Timbers, William Homer 1915- WhoAm 90
Timblin, Carol Lowe 1940- WhoSSW 91
Timblin, Stanley Walter 1937- WhoWor 91
Timboe, Harold L. 1946- BioIn 16
Timbrell, Charles 1942- IntWWM 90
Timbrell, Clayton BioIn 16
Timbury, Jane 1749?- FemiCLE
Time, Fred 1935- WhoAm 90
Timens, Lawrence J BiDrAPA 89
Timerman, Jacobo 1923- ConAu 32NR, HispWr 90
Timinski, Robert WhoAm 90
Timio, Mario 1938- WhoWor 91
Timken, Harold A., Jr. 1922- WhoE 91
Timken, Henry H. 1831-1909 EncABHB 4 [port]
Timken, Kenneth R 1927- BiDrAPA 89
Timken, W. Robert, Jr. 1938- WhoAm 90
Timken, William Robert, Jr. 1938- St&PR 91
Timko, Barbara Jean 1959- WhoE 91
Timko, John, Jr. 1923- St&PR 91
Timlake, William P. BioIn 16
Timlen, Thomas M., Jr. 1928- St&PR 91
Timlen, Thomas Michael 1928- WhoAm 90
Timlin, James Clifford 1927- WhoE 91
Timm, Jerry Roger 1942- St&PR 91
Timm, Marianna 1947- WhoAmW 91
Timm, Ralph Fulton 1921- WhoAm 90
Timm, Reginald Claude 1928- WhoWor 91
Timm, Tammy Marie 1959- St&PR 91
Timm, Ulrich 1938- EncPaPR 91
Timm, Uwe 1940- ConAu 130
Timm, Volker 1941- WhoWor 91
Timm, William 1930- St&PR 91
Timma, M.C. St&PR 91
Timmas, Osvald 1919- WhoAmA 91
Timmer, Charles Peter 1941- WhoAm 90
Timmer, William Charles 1952- WhoE 91
Timmerhaus, Klaus Dieter 1924- WhoAm 90
Timmerman, George Bell, Jr. 1912- WhoAm 90
Timmerman, Iva Marie 1956- BiDrAPA 89
Timmerman, Leon Bernard 1924- WhoE 91
Timmerman, Tom 1940- Ballpl 90
Timmerman, William B. 1946- WhoAm 90
Timmermann, Barbara Nawalany 1947- WhoAmW 91
Timmermann, Leni 1901- IntWWM 90
Timmermans, Lia 1920- EncCoWW
Timmermans, Pieter B. BioIn 16
Timmers, Jacob 1938- St&PR 91
Timmes, Charles J NewYTBS 90
Timmes, John Francis 1935- St&PR 91
Timmins, Edward Patrick 1955- WhoEmL 91, WhoWor 91
Timmins, James Donald 1955- WhoWor 91
Timmins, John Michael 1937- St&PR 91
Timmins, John Thomas 1931- St&PR 91
Timmins, Lois Fahs 1914- WhoWrEP 89
Timmins, Michael Joseph 1953- St&PR 91
Timmins, Patrick Anthony 1932- St&PR 91
Timmons, Alfreda Joyce 1956- WhoAmW 91
Timmons, Anita Abbott 1938- WhoAmW 91
Timmons, Curtis Lee 1951- WhoSSW 91
Timmons, Dale L. 1950- ODwPR 91
Timmons, Edwin O'Neal 1928- WhoAm 90
Timmons, Evelyn Deering 1926- WhoAmW 91
Timmons, Gerald Dean 1931- WhoAm 90, WhoWor 91
Timmons, Glen Robert 1939- St&PR 91
Timmons, Gordon David 1919- WhoSSW 91, WhoWor 91
Timmons, Jay 1927- St&PR 91
Timmons, Joseph Dean 1948- WhoAm 90
Timmons, Mary Ann Mikkelson 1950- WhoEmL 91
Timmons, Richard Brendan 1938- WhoAm 90
Timmons, Steve BioIn 16
Timmons, Thomas Cyril 1940- WhoE 91
Timmons, Thomas Ray 1947- St&PR 91
Timmons, William E. 1924- St&PR 91
Timmons, William Evan 1930- WhoAm 90
Timmons, William R., Jr. 1924- St&PR 91
Timmreck, Thomas C. 1946- WhoEmL 91, WhoWor 91
Timms, Donald 1927- St&PR 91
Timms, Leonard Joseph, Jr. 1936- St&PR 91, WhoAm 90, WhoSSW 91
Timms, Peter Rowland 1942- WhoAm 90, WhoAmA 91
Timms, Rex A. 1932- St&PR 91
Timofeeff-Ressovsky, Nikolai V 1900-1981 DcScB S2
Timol, Mamoojee Essop 1937- WhoWor 91
Timon, Clay Scott 1943- St&PR 91
Timon, Lawrence Joseph 1927- St&PR 91
Timoney, John Henry 1933- St&PR 91
Timoschuk, Walter J., III WhoSSW 91
Timoshenko, Semyon 1895-1970 WorAlBi
Timoshenko, Stepan Prokof'evich 1878-1972 DcScB S2
Timothy WhNaAH
Timothy, Bishop 1928- WhoAm 90
Timothy, Ann Donovan 1727-1792 BioIn 16
Timothy, David H. 1928- WhoAm 90
Timothy, Elizabeth 1700?-1757 BioIn 16
Timothy, Grover WhoAmA 91
Timothy, Peter BioIn 16
Timothy, Robert Keller 1918- WhoAm 90
Timour, John Arnold 1926- WhoAm 90

Timpane, Philip Michael 1934- WhoAm 90, WhoE 91
Timpano, Anne 1950- WhoAm 90, WhoSSW 91
Timpany, Robert Daniel 1919- WhoSSW 91
Timpson, Robert Clermont Livingston 1908-1988 BioIn 16
Timpte, Shannon Talbert 1942- WhoWor 91
Timrava EncCoWW
Timrud, David Hugh BiDrAPA 89
Tims, Michael Wayne WhoAmA 91
Tims, Robert Austin 1942- WhoSSW 91
Timtiman, Rizalina N BiDrAPA 89
Timyan, Steve J. 1955- St&PR 91
Tin Star WhoNeCM [port]
Tin, Saw 1938- WhoWor 91
Tina EncCoWW
Tinajero, Josefina Villamil 1949- WhoHisp 91
Tinari, Anthony Philip 1952- WhoEmL 91
Tinbergen, Jan 1903- WhoAm 90, WhoWor 91
Tinbergen, Niko 1907-1988 BioIn 16, SmATA 60
Tinbergen, Nikolaas 1907-1988 AnObit 1988, WorAlBi
Tincher, Charlotte Leggitt 1943- WhoSSW 91
Tincker, Mary 1831-1907 FemiCLE
Tincup, Ben 1890-1980 Ballpl 90
Tindal Family BioIn 16
Tindal, Henrietta Euphemia 1818?-1879 FemiCLE
Tindale, Lawrence Victor Dolman 1921- WhoWor 91
Tindale, Patricia 1926- WomArch
Tindall, Alphonso Eugene, Jr. 1955- WhoE 91
Tindall, George Brown 1921- WhoAm 90
Tindall, George Taylor 1928- WhoAm 90
Tindall, Gillian BioIn 16
Tindall, Gillian 1938- WorAu 1980 [port]
Tindall, James Robert 1945- WhoAm 90
Tindall, Jill Denise 1958- WhoAmW 91
Tindall, John William 1948- WhoEmL 91
Tindall, Marilyn BioIn 16
Tindall, Monica Elaine 1953- WhoAmW 91
Tindall, Robert E. 1932- St&PR 91
Tindell, William Norman 1921- WhoSSW 91
Tindemans, Leo 1922- WhoWor 91
Tinder, John Everett 1939- St&PR 91
Tinder, Sue 1953- WhoWrEP 89
Tinder, Wallace Winfrey, Jr. 1925- St&PR 91
Tindle, Charles Dwight Wood 1950- WhoWor 91
Tine, Michael P. 1945- St&PR 91
Tinebra, Carl Peter 1934- WhoAm 90
Tinelli, Eugene Thomas 1943- BiDrAPA 89
Tiner, Donna Townsend 1947- WhoAmW 91
Tiner, Elza Cheryl 1952- WhoSSW 91
Tiner, Stanley Ray 1942- WhoAm 90
Ting ConAu 129
Ting, Albert Chia 1950- WhoAm 90
Ting, Chong 1956- WhoSSW 91
Ting, Jan Y BiDrAPA 89
Ting, Kwun-Lon 1948- WhoSSW 91
Ting, Samuel C. C. 1936- WorAlBi
Ting, Samuel Chao Chung 1936- WhoAm 90, WhoE 91, WhoWor 91
Ting, Walasse 1929- WhoAmA 91
Tingay, Lance 1915-1990 ConAu 131
Tingelstad, Jon Bunde 1935- WhoAm 90, WhoSSW 91
Tingey, Carol 1933- WhoAmW 91, WhoWor 91
Tinggren, Carl Jurgen 1958- St&PR 91
Tinghitella, Stephen 1915- WhoAm 90, WhoWrEP 89
Tingir, Raffi Nurhan 1954- WhoE 91
Tingle, Aubrey James 1943- WhoAm 90
Tingle, David 1929- BiDrAPA 89
Tingle, James O'Malley 1928- WhoAm 90
Tingleff, John Burnier 1935- St&PR 91
Tingleff, Thomas Alan 1946- WhoAm 90
Tingley, Charles E. 1939- St&PR 91
Tingley, Floyd Warren 1933- WhoAm 90
Tingley, Katherine 1847-1929 BioIn 16, EncO&P 3
Tingley, Kenneth Elliott 1932- St&PR 91
Tingley, Merle R 1921- ConAu 129
Tingstad, Eric NewAgMG
Tingstad, Mark BioIn 16
Tinic, Seha Mehmet 1941- WhoAm 90
Tinio, Caridad G BiDrAPA 89
Tinio, Florante Interior BiDrAPA 89
Tinker, Beamish TwCCr&M 91
Tinker, Christopher Geoffrey 1950- IntWWM 90
Tinker, Cynthia Aloma 1953- WhoAmW 91
Tinker, Debra Ann 1951- WhoAmW 91, WhoSSW 91
Tinker, Grant BioIn 16
Tinker, Grant A. 1926- WhoAm 90, WorAlBi
Tinker, Jack 1938- ConAu 132
Tinker, Joe 1880-1948 Ballpl 90 [port]
Tinker, John Heath 1941- WhoAm 90
Tinker, Richard William 1929- St&PR 91
Tinkham, Ace ConAu 132
Tinkham, Barbara Hopper 1935- St&PR 91
Tinkham, David R. 1955- St&PR 91
Tinkham, Gary L. 1935- St&PR 91
Tinkham, Harley 1923-1990 ConAu 132
Tinkham, Michael 1928- WhoAm 90
Tinkle, F. Lorain 1913- WhoAmW 91
Tinklenberg, Jared Ray BiDrAPA 89
Tinkler, Barrie Keith 1935- WhoAmA 91
Tinkoff, Florence 1937- St&PR 91
Tinkoff, Jay 1956- St&PR 91
Tinley, H.L. 1917- St&PR 91
Tinling, Ted 1910-1990 ConAu 131, NewYTBS 90 [port]
Tinling, Teddy BioIn 16, ConAu 131
Tinnel Matheny, Betty Jennette 1937- WhoSSW 91
Tinnell, Al 1949- WhoWrEP 89
Tinnell, Carol Ann 1959- WhoAmW 91
Tinnes, Eric Lorain 1944- WhoSSW 91
Tinney, Hugh 1958- IntWWM 90
Tinney, J.F. 1937- St&PR 91
Tinney, James S. BioIn 16
Tinney, M.E. 1944- St&PR 91
Tinney, William Frank 1921- WhoAm 90
Tinnin, David Bruce 1930- WhoWor 91
Tinnin, Louis W 1932- BiDrAPA 89
Tinning, Bud 1906-1961 Ballpl 90
Tinning, Fred C. 1936- WhoAm 90
Tinning, George Campbell 1910- WhoAmA 91
Tinning, Marybeth BioIn 16
Tinniswood, Peter Maurice 1951- WhoWor 91
Tinoco, Federico 1870-1931 BioIn 16
Tinsley, Adrian 1937- WhoAm 90, WhoE 91
Tinsley, Annie 1808-1885 FemiCLE
Tinsley, Barry 1942- WhoAmA 91
Tinsley, Harry Lee, III 1947- WhoSSW 91
Tinsley, Jackson Bennett 1934- St&PR 91, WhoAm 90, WhoSSW 91
Tinsley, Joyce Ann BiDrAPA 89
Tinsley, Pauline 1928- IntWWM 90, PenDiMP
Tinsley, Robert 1949- St&PR 91
Tinsley, Shelia C. 1955- WhoAmW 91
Tinsley, Thomas Aloysius 1924- WhoAm 90
Tinsley, Walton Eugene 1921- WhoAm 90
Tinsley-Dalton, Inez Maria BiDrAPA 89
Tinsman, Margaret Neir 1936- WhoAmW 91
Tinsman, Sue St&PR 91
Tinstman, Dale 1919- St&PR 91
Tinstman, Robert A. WhoAm 90
Tinterow, Gary BioIn 16
Tintes, Philip H. 1945- St&PR 91
Tintinalli, Judith Ellen 1943- WhoAm 90
Tintl, Richard NewAgMG
Tintle, Carmel J. 1924- ODwPR 91
Tintner, Georg Bernhard 1917- IntWWM 90
Tintoretto 1518-1594 IntDcAA 90, WorAlBi
Tinucci, Georgia Mae 1930- WhoAmW 91
Tinworth, George 1843-1913 PenDiDA 89
Tinz, Bernhard Harald 1945- WhoWor 91
Tio, Aurelio 1907- HispWr 90
Tio y Nazario de Figueroa, Aurelio 1907- HispWr 90
Tioleco, Ruby Pido BiDrAPA 89
Tiomkin, Dimitri 1894-1979 OxCPMus
Tiona, Jim 1934- St&PR 91
Tiong, Domingo Chua WhoWor 91
Tiongco, Dionisio Ciria Cruz 1910- WhoWor 91
Tiongco, Dolores D BiDrAPA 89
Tiongco, Dolores Donato 1949- WhoAmW 91
Tipei, Sever 1943- IntWWM 90
Tipermas, Alan BiDrAPA 89
Tipler, Frank Jennings, III 1947- WhoSSW 91
Tippens, Jack Kelvin 1939- WhoSSW 91
Tipper, Elizabeth BiDEWW, FemiCLE
Tipper, Harry, III 1949- WhoEmL 91
Tippet, Clark BioIn 16
Tippet, Karl Mathie 1928- WhoAm 90
Tippets, Dennis Wilcock 1938- St&PR 91, WhoAm 90
Tippets, Dianne Barkley 1939- St&PR 91
Tippett, Charles Allen 1929- St&PR 91
Tippett, Donn L BiDrAPA 89
Tippett, Michael 1905- BioIn 16, IntWWM 90, PenDiMP A
Tippett, Michael Kemp 1905- WhoWor 91
Tippett, Virginia Monroe 1901- WhoWrEP 89
Tippett, Willis Paul, Jr. 1932- WhoAm 90
Tippie, Henry B. 1927- St&PR 91, WhoAm 90
Tipping, William Malcolm 1931- WhoSSW 91
Tippit, John Harlow 1916- WhoAm 90
Tipple, Colin John 1942- IntWWM 90
Tipple, H. D. WhoAm 90
Tipple, Henry Albert 1925- WhoWor 91
Tippo, Oswald 1911- BioIn 16, WhoAm 90
Tipps, Tina J. 1962- WhoAmW 91
Tipson, Lynn Baird 1943- WhoAm 90
Tipton, Bernard J. 1943- St&PR 91
Tipton, Billy 1914-1989 BioIn 16
Tipton, Carl Belt 1957- St&PR 91
Tipton, Carolyn Louise 1950- WhoWrEP 89
Tipton, Clyde Raymond, Jr. 1921- WhoAm 90
Tipton, Donald Lloyd 1931- St&PR 91
Tipton, Eric 1915- Ballpl 90
Tipton, Gary Lee 1941- WhoWor 91
Tipton, Hiram Gardner 1943- St&PR 91
Tipton, James McCall 1948- WhoSSW 91
Tipton, James W. 1943- St&PR 91
Tipton, Jennifer BioIn 16
Tipton, Jennifer 1937- NotWoAT, WhoAmW 91
Tipton, Joe 1923- Ballpl 90
Tipton, John Applewhite 1858-1925 AmLegL
Tipton, John Howard 1965- WhoSSW 91
Tipton, Marilyn Oglesby 1944- WhoAmW 91
Tipton, Mary Davison 1947- WhoAmW 91, WhoEmL 91, WhoWor 91
Tipton, Paul S. WhoAm 90
Tipton, Steven Michael 1956- WhoSSW 91
Tipton, Thomas 1926- IntWWM 90
Tipton, Thomas J. 1926- St&PR 91
Tiptree, James, Jr. MajTwCW
Tiptree, James, Jr. 1915-1987 RGTwCSF
Tirado, Olga Luz 1960- WhoHisp 91
Tirado, Othon M BiDrAPA 89
Tirakis, Judith Angelina 1938- WhoAmW 91
Tirana, Bardyl Rifat 1937- WhoAm 90
Tirandaz, Houshmand BiDrAPA 89
Tirard, Paul-Emmanuel 1837-1893 BiDFrPL
Tiras, Herbert Gerald 1924- WhoWor 91
Tirimo, Martino 1942- IntWWM 90, PenDiMP
Tirino, Philip Joseph 1940- WhoE 91
Tirlemont, Eric Pierre 1964- WhoWor 91
Tirole, Jean BioIn 16
Tiroler, Zoltan 1914- WhoWor 91
Tirone, Robert J. 1945- WhoE 91
Tirozzi, Gerald N. WhoE 91
Tirpitz, Alfred Von 1849-1930 WorAlBi
Tirrell, Edward Leo, Jr. 1917- St&PR 91
Tirrell, Genevieve M BiDrAPA 89
Tirrell, Jane Marie Rutter 1924- WhoAmW 91
Tirrell, Janet Anthony 1938- WhoAmW 91
Tirrell, John Albert 1934- WhoAm 90
Tirrell, William Barclay, Sr. 1946- WhoSSW 91
Tirrill, Nancy Taylor 1936- WhoSSW 91
Tirro, Frank P. 1935- IntWWM 90
Tirro, Frank Pascale 1935- WhoAm 90
Tirtoff, Romain de 1892-1990 BioIn 16
Tiryakian, Edward Ashod 1929- WhoAm 90
Tisbe, Michael 1922- BiDrAPA 89
Tisch, Andrew BioIn 16
Tisch, Andrew Herbert 1949- St&PR 91, WhoAm 90
Tisch, Frank C. 1935- St&PR 91
Tisch, James S. 1953- WhoAm 90
Tisch, Jonathan Mark 1953- WhoAm 90
Tisch, Laurence A. BioIn 16
Tisch, Laurence A. 1923- St&PR 91, WorAlBi
Tisch, Laurence Alan 1923- ConAmBL, WhoAm 90, WhoE 91, WhoWor 91
Tisch, Preston Robert 1926- ConAmBL, St&PR 91, WhoAm 90, WhoE 91
Tisch, Ronald Irwin 1944- WhoAm 90
Tischer, Carolyn Lois 1943- WhoE 91
Tischer, Donald 1944- St&PR 91
Tischler, Barbara Leonora 1949- IntWWM 90
Tischler, Gary Lowell 1935- BiDrAPA 89, WhoAm 90
Tischler, Hans 1915- IntWWM 90
Tischler, Herbert 1924- WhoAm 90
Tischler, Louis 1915- St&PR 91
Tischler, Monte Maurice 1931- WhoWrEP 89
Tischler, Victor 1890-1951 WhoAmA 91N
Tischner, Rudolf 1879-1961 EncO&P 3, EncPaPR 91
Tisci, Michael Anthony 1960- WhoEmL 91
Tiscornia, James Waldo 1944- St&PR 91
Tiscornia, Lester 1910- St&PR 91
Tiscornia, Lester Clinton 1910- WhoAm 90
Tisdale, Bruce R. 1948- St&PR 91
Tisdale, Douglas Michael 1949- WhoEmL 91, WhoWor 91
Tisdale, Patricia Claire 1951- WhoEmL 91
Tisdale, Patrick David WhoSSW 91
Tisdale, Robert Clayton 1958- WhoSSW 91
Tisdale, Stuart Williams 1928- St&PR 91, WhoAm 90
Tisdel, Donald L. 1934- St&PR 91
Tise, Larry Edward 1942- WhoAm 90, WhoE 91
Tishchenko, Boris 1939- IntWWM 90
Tisher, Paul Winslow BiDrAPA 89
Tishkin, Nancy Ann 1959- WhoAmW 91
Tishler, Kenneth S BiDrAPA 89
Tishler, Louis B., Jr. 1933- St&PR 91
Tishler, Max 1907-1989 BioIn 16
Tishler, William H. 1937- BioIn 16
Tishler, William Henry 1936- WhoAm 90
Tishman, Alan V. 1917- St&PR 91
Tishman, Edward S. 1923- WhoE 91
Tishman, Henry 1931- St&PR 91
Tishman, Jack A WhoAmA 91N
Tishman, John L. 1926- WhoAm 90
Tishman, Judith Rothenberg BioIn 16
Tishue, Gary Alan 1954- WhoE 91
Tisinger, Catherine Anne 1936- WhoAm 90, WhoAmW 91, WhoE 91
Tislow, Richard F 1906- BiDrAPA 89
Tisnado, Rodo 1940- WhoWor 91
Tiso, Barbara June 1945- WhoE 91
Tiso, Joseph 1887-1947 BioIn 16
Tison, Benjamin T., III 1930- St&PR 91
Tison, Gary Gene 1935-1978 BioIn 16
Tison, Joseph Southwood 1943- WhoE 91
Tison, William Henry Heywood 1822-1882 AmLegL
Tison-Braun, Micheline Lucie 1913- WhoAm 90
Tisquantum WhNaAH
Tisquantum BioIn 16
Tissenbaum, Morris Joseph BiDrAPA 89
Tisser, Doron Moshe 1955- WhoEmL 91
Tissi, Rosmarie 1937- ConDes 90
Tissian, Norman R. 1930- ODwPR 91
Tissot, James Jacques Joseph 1836-1902 BioIn 16
Tissot, James Joseph Jacques 1836-1902 EncO&P 3
Tisza, Veronica B BiDrAPA 89
Tisza, Veronica Benedek 1912- WhoAmW 91
Titchell, Haskell C. 1927- St&PR 91
Titchener, James L 1922- BiDrAPA 89
Titcomb, Bonnie L. WhoAmW 91
Titcomb, Caldwell 1926- WhoAm 90
Titcomb, Woodbury Cole 1923- WhoAm 90
Titheridge, John Edward 1932- WhoWor 91
Titherington, Jeanne AuBYP 90
Titherington, Jeanne 1951- BioIn 16
Titian 148-?-1576 IntDcAA 90
Titian 1487?-1576 WorAlBi
Titica, Jean BiDrAPA 89
Titiens, Therese PenDiMP
Titland, Martin Nils 1938- WhoAm 90
Title, Gary William 1964- WhoE 91
Titler, Dale Milton 1926- AuBYP 90
Titlow, Larry Wayne 1945- WhoSSW 91
Titman, Lionel George 1931- WhoWor 91
Tito 1892-1980 WorAlBi
Tito, Josip Broz 1892-1980 BioIn 16
Tito, Kostag St&PR 91
Tito, Richard Joseph 1947- St&PR 91
Titon, Jeff Todd 1943- IntWWM 90
Titone, Vito BioIn 16
Titone, Vito Joseph 1929- WhoAm 90, WhoE 91
Tittensor, Ruth Margaret 1945- WhoWor 91
Titterington, David Michael 1958- IntWWM 90
Titterton, Judith Leslie 1951- WhoAmW 91
Tittle, Carole Jean 1959- WhoAmW 91
Tittle, Y. A. 1926- WorAlBi
Titulaer, Urbaan Maria 1941- WhoWor 91
Titus, Alan 1945- IntWWM 90, PenDiMP
Titus, Alice Cestandina 1950- WhoAmW 91
Titus, Arthur Leroy 1944- St&PR 91
Titus, Barbara WhoAmW 91
Titus, Charles C 1933- BiDrAPA 89
Titus, Christina Maria 1950- St&PR 91, WhoEmL 91
Titus, Curtis Vest 1933- WhoE 91
Titus, David Anson 1934- WhoAm 90
Titus, Edward D 1931- BiDrAPA 89
Titus, Edward William 1870-1952 BioIn 16
Titus, Eve 1922- AuBYP 90, ConAu 30NR
Titus, Gerald M. 1928- St&PR 91
Titus, Graham 1949- IntWWM 90
Titus, Jack L. 1926- WhoAm 90

Titus, James Fairbanks, Jr. 1961- *St&PR 91*
Titus, James G. 1910- *St&PR 91*
Titus, James Paul 1933- *WhoE 91*
Titus, John 1876-1943 *Ballpl 90*
Titus, John P 1936- *BiDrAPA 89*
Titus, John Samuel 1940- *St&PR 91*
Titus, Jon Alan 1955- *WhoEmL 91*
Titus, Lowell Dean 1926- *St&PR 91*
Titus, Myer L. *WhoAm 90*
Titus, Pamela Louise 1953- *WhoAmW 91, WhoWor 91*
Titus, Randolph Joe 1950- *WhoSSW 91*
Titus, Roy Valentine *BioIn 16*
Titus, Shirley Carew 1892-1967 *BioIn 16*
Titz, Peter JosefJohannes 1953- *WhoWor 91*
Titze, Ingo Roland 1941- *WhoAm 90*
Tiu-Tanedo, Rosalind Enage *BiDrAPA 89*
Tiusanen, Bertil 1949- *WhoAm 90*
Tivnan, Robert W. 1920- *St&PR 91*
Tixier, Maurice Pierre 1913- *WhoSSW 91*
Tixier-Vignancour 1907-1989 *BiDFrPL*
Tixier-Vignancour, Jean-Louis 1907-1989 *AnObit 1989*
Tiy *WomWR*
Tizard, Robert James 1924- *WhoWor 91*
Tiziani, Joseph J 1935- *BiDrAPA 89*
Tizoc *WhoWrEP 89*
Tizol, Juan 1900-1984 *OxCPMus*
Tizzio, Thomas R. 1938- *St&PR 91*
Tizzio, Thomas Ralph 1938- *WhoAm 90*
Tjader, Cal 1925-1982 *BioIn 16*
Tjakrasudjatma, Sugana 1926- *WhoWor 91*
Tjekalia, Hiesmantajaya 1954- *WhoWor 91*
Tjeknavorian, Loris-Zare 1937- *WhoWor 91*
Tjelmeland, M. Katherine 1937- *St&PR 91*
Tjernstrom, Bjorn Harald 1949- *WhoWor 91*
Tjibaou, Jean-Marie *BioIn 16*
Tjiptoherijanto, Prijono 1948- *WhoWor 91*
Tjoa, Liong B 1932- *BiDrAPA 89*
Tjoflat, Gerald Bard 1929- *WhoAm 90*
Tjortjevits, Tjortj 1945- *WhoWor 91*
Tjossem, Theodore D. 1918-1989 *BioIn 16*
Tkach, David John 1959- *WhoEmL 91*
Tkach, Walter Robert 1917-1989 *BioIn 16*
Tlali, Miriam 1933- *FemiCLE*
Tlalka, Dorota *BioIn 16*
Tlalka, Jacek 1937- *WhoSSW 91*
Tlalka, Malgorzata *BioIn 16*
Tlass, Mustafa Abdul-Kader 1932- *WhoWor 91*
Toal, James Francis 1932- *WhoAm 90*
Toal, Jean Hoefer 1943- *WhoAmW 91*
Toan, Charles S. 1919- *St&PR 91*
Tobach, Ethel 1921- *WhoAmW 91*
Toback, James *BioIn 16*
Tobak, Mark 1951- *BiDrAPA 89*
Tobar, Lea Martinez 1942- *WhoHisp 91*
Tobe, Edward H 1946- *BiDrAPA 89*
Tobe, John E. 1940- *WhoSSW 91*
Tobe, Susan Bring 1949- *WhoAmW 91, WhoEmL 91*
Tobeason, Peter Ferdinand 1960- *WhoE 91*
Tobel, Paul Von 1940- *St&PR 91*
Tober, Barbara D. 1934- *WhoAmW 91*
Tober, Gary Paul 1950- *WhoEmL 91*
Tober, Lester Victor 1916- *St&PR 91, WhoAm 90*
Tober, Stephen Lloyd 1949- *WhoEmL 91*
Tobes, Edwin S *BiDrAPA 89*
Tobey, Alton S 1914- *WhoAmA 91*
Tobey, Alton Stanley 1914- *WhoE 91*
Tobey, B. 1906-1989 *BioIn 16*
Tobey, Barney 1906-1989 *BioIn 16*
Tobey, Carl Wadsworth 1923- *WhoAm 90*
Tobey, Charles 1831-1888 *PenDiDA 89*
Tobey, Edward David 1939- *St&PR 91*
Tobey, Francis Bassett 1833-1913 *PenDiDA 89*
Tobey, James Ashley 1958- *WhoE 91*
Tobey, Jean Carla 1952- *WhoEmL 91*
Tobey, Joel Nye 1929- *St&PR 91*
Tobey, Mark 1890-1976 *IntDcAA 90, WhoAmA 91N*
Tobey, Robert F. 1945- *St&PR 91*
Tobey, Timothy A. 1949- *St&PR 91*
Tobia, Blaise Joseph 1953- *WhoAmA 91*
Tobias, Abraham Joel 1913- *WhoAmA 91*
Tobias, Andrew Previn 1947- *WhoAm 90, WhoWrEP 89*
Tobias, Barbara Bowman *BiDrAPA 89*
Tobias, Carmelita R *BiDrAPA 89*
Tobias, Charles 1898-1970 *OxCPMus*
Tobias, Charles Harrison, Jr. 1921- *WhoAm 90*
Tobias, Charles William 1920- *WhoAm 90*
Tobias, Donald E. 1928- *St&PR 91*
Tobias, Henry 1905- *BioIn 16*
Tobias, Jeffrey 1956- *WhoEmL 91*
Tobias, John L.M. 1921- *St&PR 91*
Tobias, Judy *WhoAmW 91*
Tobias, Julius 1915- *WhoAm 90, WhoAmA 91*
Tobias, Kathy J 1953- *BiDrAPA 89*
Tobias, Lester Lee 1946- *WhoE 91, WhoWor 91*
Tobias, Paul Henry 1930- *WhoAm 90*
Tobias, Phillip Vallentine 1925- *WhoWor 91*
Tobias, Richard 1952- *WhoAmA 91*
Tobias, Robert M., Jr. 1954- *WhoHisp 91*
Tobias, Robert Max 1943- *WhoAm 90*
Tobias, Robert Paul 1933- *WhoAmA 91*
Tobias, Ronald Benjamin 1946- *WhoWrEP 89*
Tobias, Sheila 1935- *WhoAmW 91*
Tobias, Thomas J 1906-1970 *WhoAmA 91N*
Tobias-Jones, Brian 1936- *WhoWor 91*
Tobiasen, Carl G. 1955- *St&PR 91*
Tobiasz, Robert Brian 1945- *St&PR 91, WhoAm 90*
Tobik, Dave 1953- *Ballpl 90*
Tobin, Alexander 1927- *WhoE 91*
Tobin, Arnold D 1928- *BiDrAPA 89*
Tobin, Avis Ann 1920- *WhoAmW 91*
Tobin, Bruce Daniel 1934- *WhoAm 90*
Tobin, Calvin Jay 1927- *WhoAm 90, WhoWor 91*
Tobin, Carol R. 1948- *WhoE 91*
Tobin, Daniel J. 1875-1955 *WorAlBi*
Tobin, Dennis Michael 1948- *WhoEmL 91, WhoWor 91*
Tobin, Donald 1939- *St&PR 91*
Tobin, Gerald J. 1935- *WhoSSW 91, WhoWor 91*
Tobin, H Wayne *BiDrAPA 89*
Tobin, Harold William 1922- *WhoWor 91*
Tobin, Ilona Lines 1943- *WhoAmW 91*
Tobin, Jack 1892-1969 *Ballpl 90*
Tobin, James 1918- *WhoAm 90, WhoE 91, WhoWor 91, WorAlBi*
Tobin, James Michael 1948- *WhoAm 90*
Tobin, James Robert 1944- *WhoAm 90*
Tobin, Jean Holloway *BioIn 16*
Tobin, Jean Holloway 1917?-1989 *ConAu 130*
Tobin, Jim 1912-1969 *Ballpl 90*
Tobin, John Everard 1923- *WhoAm 90*
Tobin, John Henry, Jr. 1930- *St&PR 91*
Tobin, Joseph M *BiDrAPA 89*
Tobin, Katrin *BioIn 16*
Tobin, Margaret Batts *BioIn 16*
Tobin, Maurice Joseph 1901-1953 *BiDrUSE 89*
Tobin, Michael Alan 1952- *WhoEmL 91*
Tobin, Michael E. 1926- *St&PR 91*
Tobin, Michael Edward 1926- *WhoAm 90*
Tobin, Nancy 1943- *WhoAmA 91*
Tobin, Peter J. 1944- *St&PR 91*
Tobin, Philip D. 1942-1989 *BioIn 16*
Tobin, Richard George 1943- *WhoE 91*
Tobin, Richard J. 1934- *WhoAm 90*
Tobin, Robert G. 1938- *St&PR 91*
Tobin, Robert Timothy 1957- *WhoWrEP 89*
Tobin, Ronald William 1936- *WhoAm 90*
Tobin, Shirley Ann 1953- *WhoSSW 91*
Tobin, Steven Michael 1940- *St&PR 91*
Tobin, Wayne Ernest 1934- *WhoSSW 91*
Tobin, William James 1929- *St&PR 91*
Tobin, William Joseph 1944- *St&PR 91*
Tobin, William Thomas 1931- *St&PR 91, WhoAm 90*
Tobing, Alexander *BiDrAPA 89*
Tobis, Jerome Sanford 1915- *WhoAm 90*
Tobita, Shigeo 1927- *WhoWor 91*
Tobkin, Christine Anderson 1952- *WhoAm 90*
Tobler, D. Lee 1933- *St&PR 91, WhoAm 90*
Tobler, George P. 1917- *WhoSSW 91*
Tobler, Waldo Rudolph 1930- *WhoAm 90*
Tobolowsky, David Martone 1953- *BiDrAPA 89*
Tobolowsky, Sarah *WhoAmW 91*
Tobon, Hector 1934- *WhoHisp 91*
Toborowsky, Robert M 1938- *BiDrAPA 89*
Tobriner, M.W. 1939- *St&PR 91*
Toburen, Lawrence Richter 1915- *WhoAm 90*
Toby, Jackson 1925- *WhoAm 90*
Toca, Vivian Tabares 1934- *WhoSSW 91*
Tocci, Salvatore *AuBYP 90*
Tocco, James 1943- *WhoAm 90*
Toce, Dominic R. 1931- *St&PR 91*
Toch, Ernst 1887-1964 *PenDiMP A*
Tocher, Gordon James MacLaren 1957- *IntWWM 90*
Tochigi, Yoshitada 1935- *WhoWor 91*
Tochner, Max 1938- *WhoSSW 91*
Tochter Anna, Hans Owens *EncCoWW*
Tock, Elizabeth W *BiDrAPA 89*
Tock, Joseph 1954- *WhoWor 91*
Tocklin, Adrian Martha 1951- *St&PR 91, WhoAmW 91, WhoE 91, WhoEmL 91*
Tocque, Philip 1814-1899 *DcCanB 12*
Tocquet, Robert 1898- *EncO&P 3*
Tocqueville, Alexis de *BioIn 16*
Tocqueville, Alexis De 1805-1859 *WhNaAH, WorAlBi*
Toczek, Peter Martin 1931- *St&PR 91*
Toczyska, Stefania *BioIn 16*
Toczyska, Stefania 1943- *IntWWM 90*
Tod, Martha Ann 1927- *WhoAmW 91*
Tod, Osma Gallinger *WhoAmA 91N*
Toda, August Albert 1934- *WhoE 91*
Toda, Fujio 1934- *WhoWor 91*
Toda, Kunio 1915- *IntWWM 90*
Toda, Shusaku 1938- *St&PR 91*
Toda, Tadasumi 1946- *WhoWor 91*
Todaro, F. Keith 1956- *WhoSSW 91*
Todaro, George Joseph 1937- *WhoAm 90*
Todaro, John *AuBYP 90*
Todaro, Laura Jean 1956- *WhoAmW 91, WhoEmL 91*
Todaro, Ralph 1950- *St&PR 91*
Todaro, Raphaele Ann 1952- *WhoAmW 91*
Todd, Al 1902-1985 *Ballpl 90*
Todd, Alexander Calhoun, Jr. 1912- *WhoAm 90*
Todd, Alexander R. 1907- *WorAlBi*
Todd, Alexander Robertus 1907- *WhoAm 90, WhoWor 91*
Todd, Ann 1909- *ConAu 129*
Todd, Anna C *BiDrAPA 89*
Todd, Anne Ophelia *AuBYP 90*
Todd, Barbara Ann 1954- *WhoAmW 91, WhoSSW 91*
Todd, Beverly 1946- *ConTFT 8, DrBlPA 90*
Todd, Charles Byron 1934- *WhoSSW 91*
Todd, Charles Payson 1958- *WhoSSW 91*
Todd, Christina Adrian Tamburo 1943- *WhoE 91*
Todd, David Arnold, II 1932- *St&PR 91, WhoAm 90*
Todd, David B. 1925- *WhoE 91*
Todd, David F. M. 1915- *BioIn 16*
Todd, David Fenton Michie 1915- *WhoAm 90*
Todd, David Keith 1923- *WhoAm 90*
Todd, David L. *ODwPR 91*
Todd, Deborah J. 1951- *WhoAmW 91*
Todd, Duby D. 1934- *WhoSSW 91*
Todd, Edward Francis, Jr. 1956- *WhoE 91*
Todd, Elizabeth *WhoWrEP 89*
Todd, Elizabeth 1918- *IntWWM 90*
Todd, Gilbert H. 1927- *St&PR 91*
Todd, Glenn Daniel 1952- *WhoSSW 91*
Todd, Glenn William 1927- *WhoAm 90*
Todd, Grant Edward 1939- *St&PR 91*
Todd, Harold Wade 1938- *WhoAm 90*
Todd, Harry Williams 1922- *St&PR 91, WhoAm 90*
Todd, Henry C. 1913- *St&PR 91*
Todd, Henry Reynolds, Jr. 1951- *WhoEmL 91*
Todd, Herbert Eatton 1908-1988 *ConAu 30NR*
Todd, Hollis Elbert *WhoSSW 91*
Todd, Ian A 1941- *ConAu 31NR*
Todd, J. Donald *St&PR 91*
Todd, Jackie Steele 1950- *WhoAmW 91*
Todd, Jackson 1951- *Ballpl 90*
Todd, Jacob Hunter 1827-1899 *DcCanB 12*
Todd, James A., Jr. 1928- *St&PR 91*
Todd, James Averill, Jr. 1928- *WhoAm 90*
Todd, James Dale 1943- *WhoAm 90, WhoSSW 91*
Todd, James Marion 1929- *WhoSSW 91*
Todd, James Martin *BiDrAPA 89*
Todd, James William 1946- *St&PR 91*
Todd, Jessie A. 1946- *WhoAmW 91*
Todd, Jim 1947- *Ballpl 90*
Todd, John 1911- *WhoAm 90*
Todd, John 1939- *BioIn 16*
Todd, John Blair Smith 1814-1872 *AmLegL*
Todd, John C *BiDrAPA 89*
Todd, John Dickerson, Jr. 1912- *WhoAm 90*
Todd, John Duncan 1914- *St&PR 91*
Todd, John Joseph 1927- *WhoAm 90*
Todd, John Odell 1902- *WhoWor 91*
Todd, John Robert 1946- *WhoEmL 91*
Todd, John Thomas 1940- *WhoSSW 91*
Todd, John Thomas, III 1943- *WhoE 91*
Todd, Joyce Anderson 1940- *WhoAmW 91*
Todd, Kenneth S., Jr. 1936- *WhoAm 90*
Todd, Kristin Korf 1956- *WhoAmW 91*
Todd, Kyle Eugene 1950- *WhoSSW 91*
Todd, L. Kay 1941- *St&PR 91*
Todd, Mabel 1856-1932 *FemiCLE*
Todd, Malcolm Clifford 1913- *WhoAm 90*
Todd, Malcolm F.W. *St&PR 91*
Todd, Margaret 1859-1918 *FemiCLE*
Todd, Mary Fidelis *AuBYP 90*
Todd, Michael 1909-1958 *WorAlBi*
Todd, Michael Cullen 1935- *WhoAm 90, WhoAmA 91*
Todd, Norma Jean Ross 1920- *WhoAmW 91, WhoE 91*
Todd, Patricia 1946- *WhoAmW 91*
Todd, Paul Clark *BiDrAPA 89*
Todd, Paul Rodney 1952- *IntWWM 90*
Todd, R. Campbell 1927- *St&PR 91*
Todd, Renate Kloppinger *WhoAmW 91*
Todd, Richard Henry 1906- *WhoE 91*
Todd, Robert Anthony *BiDrAPA 89*
Todd, Robert H.O. 1962- *St&PR 91*
Todd, Robert Lee 1953- *WhoSSW 91, WhoWor 91*
Todd, Robert Royce 1937- *St&PR 91*
Todd, Rodney Dale 1944- *WhoSSW 91*
Todd, Ruthven 1914- *AuBYP 90*
Todd, Samuel Richard, Jr. 1940- *WhoWrEP 89*
Todd, Shirley Ann 1935- *WhoAmW 91, WhoSSW 91, WhoWor 91*
Todd, Stephen Michael 1961- *WhoEmL 91*
Todd, Sudol 1946- *WhoE 91*
Todd, T.W. 1928- *St&PR 91*
Todd, Thomas Abbott 1928- *WhoAm 90*
Todd, Virgil Holcomb 1921- *WhoAm 90*
Todd, Walter Bradford 1948- *WhoAm 90*
Todd, Webb 1929- *St&PR 91*
Todd, Webster B. 1899-1989 *BioIn 16*
Todd, William Burton 1919- *WhoAm 90, WhoWrEP 89*
Todd, William E 1922- *BiDrAPA 89*
Todd, William Russell 1928- *WhoAm 90*
Todd, Zane Grey 1924- *St&PR 91, WhoAm 90, WhoWor 91*
Todd Copley, Judith Ann 1950- *WhoAmW 91, WhoEmL 91*
Toder, Eric J. 1944- *WhoWor 91*
Todman, Terence A. *BioIn 16*
Todman, Terence A. 1926- *WhoAm 90, WhoWor 91*
Todman, Terence Alphonso, Jr. 1953- *WhoEmL 91*
Todorov, Nikolai 1921- *ConAu 132*
Todorov, Stanko 1920- *WhoWor 91*
Todorov, Tzvetan 1939- *WorAu 1980 [port]*
Todorovic, Radmilo Antonije 1927- *WhoWor 91*
Todorovich, Boris J. 1913-1984 *BioIn 16*
Todreas, Neil Emmanuel 1935- *WhoAm 90*
Todryk, Alan A. 1946- *St&PR 91*
Todsen, Dana Rognar 1947- *WhoEmL 91*
Todsicher, J Edgar 1926- *ConAu 31NR*
Todt, Malcolm S. 1945- *WhoAm 90*
Todt, Malcolm Spenker 1945- *St&PR 91*
Todt, Michael Arthur 1947- *WhoSSW 91*
Todt, Phil 1901-1973 *Ballpl 90*
Toedte, Sharon Lynn Simon 1957- *WhoAmW 91*
Toedtman, James Smith 1941- *WhoAm 90*
Toefield, Alfred *BioIn 16*
Toegemann, Alfred Conrad 1928- *St&PR 91*
Toelle, Ronald Warren 1926- *St&PR 91*
Toenjes, Wayne Arthur 1950- *St&PR 91*
Toenniessen, Linda M 1947- *BiDrAPA 89*
Toensing, Victoria 1941- *WhoAm 90, WhoAmW 91*
Toepel, Steven E. *St&PR 91*
Toepfer, Heinrich Alfred 1930- *WhoWor 91*
Toepfer, Robert Adolph 1920- *WhoAm 90*
Toepfer, Susan Jill 1948- *WhoAmW 91*
Toepke, Barry K. *ODwPR 91*
Toeplitz, Gideon 1944- *WhoE 91*
Toepp, Lisa Marie 1959- *BiDrAPA 89*
Toer, Pramoedya Ananta 1925- *BioIn 16*
Toews, John Allan *BiDrAPA 89*
Tofalli, Christopher G. 1956- *ODwPR 91*
Tofani, Henry *WhoWor 91*
Tofani, Loretta A. 1953- *WhoAm 90, WhoAmW 91*
Tofani, Michael *BiDrAPA 89*
Tofel, Jennings 1892-1959 *WhoAmA 91N*
Toff, Howard David 1947- *BiDrAPA 89*
Toff, Nancy Ellen 1955- *WhoE 91*
Toffel, Alvin Eugene 1935- *WhoAm 90*
Toffey, H. James 1930- *St&PR 91*
Toffler, Alvin 1928- *MajTwCW, WhoWrEP 89*
Toffolo, Luigi J. 1929- *St&PR 91*
Tofias, Allan 1930- *WhoE 91, WhoWor 91*
Toft, Carolyn Hewes *BioIn 16*
Toft, Charles 1832-1909 *PenDiDA 89*
Toft, James *PenDiDA 89*
Toft, Ralph *PenDiDA 89*
Toft, Richard Paul 1936- *St&PR 91*
Toft, Thomas *PenDiDA 89*
Tofteland, Curt L. 1952- *WhoSSW 91*
Toftner, Richard O. 1935- *St&PR 91*
Toftner, Richard Orville 1935- *WhoAm 90*
Toftness, Cecil Gillman 1920- *WhoWor 91*
Togasaki, Shinobu 1932- *WhoWor 91*
Togashi, Karen 1962- *IntWWM 90*
Togawa, Masako 1933- *TwCCr&M 91B*
Togliatti, Palmiro 1893-1964 *WorAlBi*
Tognacci, Eugene 1929- *WhoSSW 91*
Tognazzi, Ugo 1922-1990 *NewYTBS 90 [port]*
Togneri, Enrico Natale 1946- *WhoEmL 91*
Tognozzi, Olando 1927- *IntWWM 90*
Togo Heihachiro 1848-1934 *EncJap*
Togo, Heihachiro 1848-1934 *WorAlBi*
Togo, Yasar 1936- *WhoWor 91*
Togo, Yukiyasu 1924- *WhoAm 90*
Tohak, Victor J. 1959- *WhoE 91*
Tohen, Mauricio 1951- *BiDrAPA 89, WhoE 91*

Tohgi, Hideo 1937- *WhoWor 91*
Toia, Margaret Elizabeth 1962- *WhoAmW 91*
Toigo, Daniel Joseph 1912- *WhoAmA 91*
Toigo-D'Angeli, Miriam *BioIn 16, NewYTBS 90 [port]*
Toikka, Oiva 1931- *ConDes 90*
Toinet, Marie-France 1942- *WhoWor 91*
Tointon, Robert G. 1933- *WhoAm 90*
Toirac, Margarita 1935- *WhoHisp 91*
Toivanen, Erkki Jalmari 1927- *WhoWor 91*
Toivola, Yrjo Ilmari 1927- *WhoWor 91*
Toja, Peter Michael 1943- *St&PR 91*
Tojo Hideki 1884-1948 *EncJap, WorAlBi*
Tokaji, Ted Jinichiro *BiDrAPA 89*
Tokar, John T *BiDrAPA 89*
Tokar, Maureen Tansey 1931- *WhoAmW 91*
Tokareva, Viktoriia 1937- *EncCoWW*
Tokarz, Kenneth J. *ODwPR 91*
Toker, Eugene *BiDrAPA 89*
Toker, Franklin 1944- *WhoAmA 91*
Toker, Franklin K. 1944- *WhoAm 90, WhoE 91*
Toker, Leona 1950- *WhoWor 91*
Tokes, Laszlo *BioIn 16*
Tokes, Rudolf L. *BioIn 16*
Tokhie, Sarabjit Singh 1950- *BiDrAPA 89*
Tokioka, Franklin Makoto 1936- *St&PR 91*
Toklas, Alice B. *BioIn 16*
Toklas, Alice B. 1877-1967 *BioAmW, FemiCLE*
Tokofsky, Jerry Herbert 1936- *WhoAm 90*
Tokoli, John Francis *BiDrAPA 89*
Tokoly, Mary Andree 1940- *WhoAmW 91, WhoSSW 91*
Tokoro, Masaaki 1929- *WhoWor 91*
Tokowitz, Harold I. 1929- *St&PR 91*
Tokubo, Cathleen C. 1958- *WhoAmW 91*
Tokugawa Iemitsu 1605-1651 *EncJap*
Tokugawa Ieyasu 1543-1616 *EncJap*
Tokugawa Yoshinobu *EncJap*
Tokumitsu, Yoshito 1936- *St&PR 91*
Tokyo Quartet *PenDiMP*
Tokyo Rose *EncJap*
Tokyo Rose 1916- *WorAlBi*
Tolan, Alfred Norman 1928- *St&PR 91*
Tolan, Bobby 1945- *Ballpl 90*
Tolan, Cornelius R. 1921- *St&PR 91*
Tolan, David Joseph 1933- *St&PR 91, WhoAm 90, WhoE 91*
Tolan, James F. *ODwPR 91*
Tolan, James Francis 1934- *WhoAm 90*
Tolan, John William 1947- *WhoE 91*
Tolan, Stephanie S. 1942- *BioIn 16*
Toland, Alain Daniel 1953- *WhoSSW 91*
Toland, Clyde William 1947- *WhoEmL 91*
Toland, Gregory John 1966- *WhoEmL 91*
Toland, John 1912- *MajTwCW*
Toland, John Willard 1912- *WhoAm 90, WhoWor 91, WhoWrEP 89*
Toland, Joy E. 1965- *WhoAmW 91*
Tolar, Billy Joe 1948- *WhoSSW 91*
Tolar, Carroll T. 1929- *St&PR 91*
Tolar, Thomas Ray, Jr. 1948- *St&PR 91*
Tolba, Mostafa Kamal 1922- *WhoWor 91*
Tolbecque, Auguste 1830-1919 *PenDiMP*
Tolbecque, Jean-Baptiste-Joseph 1797-1869 *OxCPMus*
Tolbert, Amy Sue Schroeder 1964- *WhoAmW 91*
Tolbert, Berlinda 1949- *DrBlPA 90*
Tolbert, Bert Mills 1921- *WhoAm 90*
Tolbert, Charles Madden 1922- *WhoAm 90*
Tolbert, Charles Ray 1936- *WhoSSW 91*
Tolbert, Cledith Cassidy 1922- *WhoWrEP 89*
Tolbert, Herman Andre 1948- *BiDrAPA 89, WhoEmL 91*
Tolbert, James R. 1935- *St&PR 91*
Tolbert, James R., III 1935- *WhoAm 90*
Tolbert, John T. 1913- *St&PR 91*
Tolbert, Nathan Edward 1919- *WhoAm 90*
Tolbert, Richard Martin 1939- *WhoAm 90*
Tolbert, William R. 1942- *St&PR 91*
Tolces, Stephen B. 1934- *St&PR 91*
Tolchin, Joan Gubin *BiDrAPA 89*
Tolchin, Martin 1928- *WhoAm 90, WhoWrEP 89*
Tolchin, Matthew A 1937- *BiDrAPA 89*
Tolchin, Susan Jane 1941- *WhoAmW 91*
Tolchinsky, Valery *BiDrAPA 89*
Toledano, John O.H. 1931- *St&PR 91*
Toledano, Ralph de 1916- *ConAu 31NR, WhoAm 90, WhoWrEP 89*
Toledano, Raul G. 1939- *WhoSSW 91*
Toledano, Vicente Lombardo 1894-1968 *BioIn 16*
Toledo, Amanda A. 1955- *BiDrAPA 89*
Toledo, Angel D. *WhoHisp 91*
Toledo, Angeles 1958- *WhoAmA 91*
Toledo, Bridget Marie 1959- *WhoAm 90*
Toledo, Francisco 1940- *ArtLatA, WhoAmA 91*
Toledo, Jesefino Chino 1959- *WhoWor 91*
Toledo, Josefino Chino Javier 1959- *IntWWM 90*
Toledo, Robert A. 1942- *St&PR 91*
Toledo, Robert Anthony 1942- *WhoHisp 91*
Toledo-Pereyra, Luis Horacio 1943- *WhoWrEP 89*
Toledo Ugarte, Pedro *BioIn 16*
Tolentino, Edgardo B 1942- *BiDrAPA 89*
Tolentino, Paulino Defante 1926- *WhoWor 91*
Tolentino-Mirasol, Isabel M 1949- *BiDrAPA 89*
Toler, James E. 1931- *St&PR 91*
Toler, James Larkin 1935- *WhoAm 90*
Toler, Melissa Ann 1953- *WhoAmW 91, WhoEmL 91*
Toler, Penny *BioIn 16*
Tolerton, Robert H. 1926- *St&PR 91*
Toles, Edward Bernard 1909- *WhoAm 90*
Toles, Mary Jo 1951- *BioIn 16*
Toles, Thomas Gregory 1951- *WhoAm 90, WhoE 91*
Toles, Tom 1951- *BioIn 16*
Toletana, Luisa Sigea *EncCoWW*
Tolete-Velcek, Francisca Agatep 1943- *WhoAmW 91*
Tolford, George K. 1938- *St&PR 91*
Tolgesy, Victor 1928-1980 *WhoAmA 91N*
Tolhurst, Desmond 1933- *WhoE 91*
Tolhurst, Judith Elaine *BiDrAPA 89*
Tolia, Bhupendra Manilal 1936- *WhoE 91*
Tolin, Donald Lee 1953- *WhoWor 91*
Toliver, Fred 1961- *Ballpl 90*
Toliver, O. Graham *BiDrAPA 89*
Tolk, Charles 1940- *BiDrAPA 89*
Tolk, Jeffrey M. 1939- *St&PR 91*
Tolk, Roy 1916- *St&PR 91*
Tolkan, James 1931- *ConTFT 8*
Tolkien, J. R. R. 1892-1973 *BioIn 16*
Tolkien, J R R 1892-1973 *MajTwCW*
Tolkien, J. R. R. 1892-1973 *WorAlBi*
Tolkien, John R. R. 1892-1973 *AuBYP 90*
Tolkien, John Ronald Reuel 1892-1973 *BioIn 16*
Tolkin, Michael *BioIn 16*
Tolkunov, Lev N. 1919-1989 *BioIn 16*
Toll, Barbara Elizabeth 1945- *WhoAmA 91*
Toll, Bruce E. *BioIn 16*
Toll, Bruce E. 1943- *St&PR 91*
Toll, Charles Hansen, Jr. *St&PR 91N*
Toll, Daniel Roger 1927- *St&PR 91, WhoAm 90*
Toll, Gordon L. 1947- *St&PR 91*
Toll, Jack Benjamin 1925- *WhoAm 90*
Toll, John Sampson 1923- *WhoAm 90, WhoWor 91*
Toll, Maynard Joy, Jr. 1942- *WhoAm 90, WhoE 91*
Toll, Norma Spear *BiDrAPA 89*
Toll, Robert I. *BioIn 16*
Toll, Robert Irwin 1940- *St&PR 91*
Toll, Roberta Darlene 1944- *WhoAmW 91, WhoWor 91*
Toll, Sheldon Samuel 1940- *WhoAm 90*
Toll-Crossman, Jacqueline Joy 1947- *WhoAmW 91*
Tolle, Donald James 1918- *WhoAm 90*
Tolle, Henning 1932- *WhoWor 91*
Tollefson, Arthur Ralph 1942- *IntWWM 90*
Tollefson, Gary Dennis 1951- *BiDrAPA 89*
Tollefson, John Oliver 1937- *WhoAm 90*
Tollefson, Linda 1949- *WhoE 91*
Tollefson, Steve K. 1960- *St&PR 91*
Tollefson, William Brantley 1950- *WhoSSW 91*
Tollenaere, Lawrence R. 1922- *St&PR 91*
Tollenaere, Lawrence Robert 1922- *WhoAm 90*
Toller, Larry Allan 1953- *WhoSSW 91*
Toller, William R. 1930- *St&PR 91*
Toller, William Robert 1930- *WhoAm 90, WhoE 91*
Tolleris, Morton R. 1908-1990 *BioIn 16*
Tollers, Vincent Louis 1939- *WhoE 91*
Tolles, Bryant Franklin, Jr. 1939- *WhoAm 90, WhoAmA 91, WhoE 91*
Tolles, E. Leroy 1922- *WhoAm 90*
Tolles, Martha *WhoWrEP 89*
Tolles, Walter Edwin 1916- *WhoAm 90*
Tolleson, Evangeline W. *WhoWrEP 89*
Tolleson, Laurie A. 1949- *ODwPR 91*
Tolleson, Wayne 1955- *Ballpl 90*
Tollestrup, Alvin Virgil 1924- *WhoAm 90*
Tollet, Elizabeth 1694-1754 *DcLB 95, FemiCLE*
Tollett, Glenna Belle 1913- *WhoAmW 91*
Tollett, Leland Edward 1937- *WhoAm 90, WhoSSW 91*
Tolley, A Granville *BiDrAPA 89*
Tolley, Aubrey Granville 1924- *WhoAm 90*
Tolley, Carolyn Jackson 1953- *WhoAmW 91*
Tolley, Gary Maurice 1935- *WhoSSW 91, WhoWor 91*
Tolley, James L. 1930- *ODwPR 91*
Tolley, James Little 1930- *WhoAm 90*
Tolley, Jerry Russell 1942- *WhoAm 90*
Tolley, John Patrick 1941- *WhoWor 91*
Tolley, Randall Blake 1961- *WhoSSW 91*
Tolley, Richard *BioIn 16*
Tolley, Richard Earl 1933- *WhoSSW 91*
Tolley, Tresa Gail 1946- *WhoWrEP 89*
Tolley, William Pearson 1900- *BioIn 16, WhoAm 90*
Tollison, Peggy S. 1953- *ODwPR 91*
Tolliver, Don L. 1938- *WhoAm 90*
Tolliver, Dorothy Olivia *WhoAmW 91, WhoWor 91*
Tolliver, Harold J. 1919- *St&PR 91*
Tolliver, Jack D. 1924- *St&PR 91*
Tolliver, Melba 1939- *DrBlPA 90*
Tolliver, Mose 1919- *MusmAFA*
Tolliver, Norris L. *St&PR 91*
Tolliver, Ruby C. 1922- *BioIn 16*
Tolliver, William Mack 1951- *WhoSSW 91*
Tolly, David Hayes 1950- *St&PR 91*
Tolman, Gareth Wells 1938- *St&PR 91*
Tolman, K. Wade 1948- *St&PR 91*
Tolmatchov, Youri Alexandrovitch 1945- *WhoWor 91*
Tolmie, Donald McEachern 1928- *St&PR 91, WhoAm 90*
Tolmie, Kenneth Donald 1941- *WhoAm 90, WhoAmA 91*
Tolo, Marc Thorpe 1949- *WhoE 91*
Tolone, Thomas Allen 1952- *St&PR 91*
Tolor, Alexander 1928- *WhoAm 90*
Tolosko, Karen Lynn 1965- *WhoAmW 91*
Tolpa, John Michael 1944- *St&PR 91*
Tolpin, Marian 1925- *BiDrAPA 89*
Tolpin, Paul H 1926- *BiDrAPA 89*
Tolpo, Carolyn Lee 1940- *WhoAmA 91*
Tolpo, Vincent Cary 1950- *WhoAmA 91*
Tolsdorf, Frank Frederick 1936- *St&PR 91*
Tolsma, Dennis Dwayne 1939- *WhoAm 90, WhoSSW 91*
Tolson, Dean *BioIn 16*
Tolson, Donald Lee 1958- *MusmAFA*
Tolson, Edgar 1904-1984 *MusmAFA*
Tolson, Jay Henry 1935- *St&PR 91, WhoAm 90*
Tolson, John J. 1948- *WhoAm 90*
Tolson, Julius Henry *St&PR 91N*
Tolson, Melvin B. 1900-1966 *EarBlAP*
Tolson, Sharon Grace 1947- *WhoAmW 91*
Tolstaia, Tat'iana 1951- *EncCoWW*
Tolstaya, Tatyana 1951- *ConAu 130*
Tolstoshey, Paul 1947- *WhoE 91*
Tolstoy, Alexandra 1884-1979 *EncCoWW*
Tolstoy, Alexandra 1947- *WhoE 91*
Tolstoy, Leo 1828-1910 *BioIn 16, WorAlBi, WrPh*
Tolstoy, Serge *AuBYP 90*
Tolstrup, Rex W. 1939- *St&PR 91*
Tolstrup, Tor 1938- *WhoWor 91*
Tolton, Stephen P. 1946- *St&PR 91*
Toltzis, Robert Joshua 1949- *WhoEmL 91*
Tolwin, Michael Hirsch 1954- *BiDrAPA 89*
Tom Tom Club *EncPR&S 89*
Tom, C. F. Joseph 1922- *WhoE 91*
Tom, Chung Ping *BioIn 16*
Tom, Creighton Harvey 1944- *WhoWrEP 89*
Tom, Eliza 1963- *WhoAmW 91*
Tom, Jack Mung 1950- *WhoE 91*
Tom, James Robert 1939- *WhoSSW 91*
Tom, Lawrence 1950- *WhoEmL 91, WhoWor 91*
Tom, Sanford S 1930- *BiDrAPA 89*
Tom, Willard Ken 1952- *WhoEmL 91*
Toma, George *BioIn 16*
Toma, Jeanne Broemmelsick 1950- *WhoAmW 91*
Tomah 1752?-1817 *WhNaAH*
Tomain, Robert F. 1941- *St&PR 91*
Tomaino, Michael Thomas 1937- *WhoAm 90*
Tomaino, William N. 1954- *St&PR 91*
Tomajko, Kathy Gillespie 1948- *WhoSSW 91*
Tomakin, John M. *ODwPR 91*
Tomalia, Donald Andrew 1938- *WhoAm 90*
Tomalin, Ruth *FemiCLE*
Toman, Michael Allen 1954- *WhoE 91*
Toman, Stephen E. *WhoAm 90*
Toman, Walter Karl 1920- *WhoWor 91*
Tomandl, Theodor 1933- *WhoWor 91*
Tomanek, Dick 1931- *Ballpl 90*
Tomao, Doreen Elizabeth 1949- *WhoAmW 91*
Tomara, Sonia 1897-1982 *BioIn 16*
Tomarin, Harry P. 1916- *St&PR 91*
Tomarin, Seymour Aaron 1948- *St&PR 91*
Tomas Gudmundsson *DcScanL*
Tomas, Carlos Maria 1926- *WhoWor 91*
Tomas, Jerold F.V. *WhoAm 90*
Tomasch, Maria Christine 1964- *WhoAmW 91*
Tomaschewsky, Michaela Maria 1947- *WhoAmW 91*
Tomasek, Frantisek 1899- *WhoWor 91*
Tomasek, Robert Dennis 1928- *WhoAm 90*
Tomasetti, Perry Joseph 1963- *WhoSSW 91*
Tomash, Erwin 1921- *St&PR 91, WhoAm 90*
Tomasi, Thomas B. 1927- *WhoAm 90*
Tomasi Di Lampedusa, Giuseppe 1896-1957 *BioIn 16*
Tomasini, David Richard *BiDrAPA 89*
Tomasini, Wallace J 1926- *WhoAmA 91*
Tomasini, Wallace John 1926- *WhoAm 90*
Tomasko, Mark Daniel 1948- *St&PR 91, WhoAm 90*
Tomasko, Michael, IV 1942- *St&PR 91*
Tomasko, Robert Michael 1948- *WhoE 91*
Tomassi, Joseph J. *BioIn 16*
Tomassi, Ralph Vincent 1954- *WhoEmL 91*
Tomassini, Lawrence Anthony 1945- *WhoAm 90*
Tomasson, Helgi 1942- *WhoAm 90*
Tomasson, Verna 1932- *WhoWrEP 89*
Tomasulo, Virginia Merrills 1919- *WhoAm 90*
Tomaszek, Thomas Richard 1952- *WhoE 91*
Tomaszewicz, Elizabeth Eleonora 1946- *St&PR 91, WhoAmW 91*
Tomaszewski, Carlos Alberto 1930- *St&PR 91*
Tomaszewski, Henryk 1914- *ConDes 90*
Tomau 1752?-1817 *WhNaAH*
Tomazi, George Donald 1935- *WhoWor 91*
Tomazinis, Anthony Rodoflos 1929- *WhoAm 90, WhoWor 91*
Tomb, Paul David 1929- *WhoAm 90*
Tomb, Richard Clyde 1950- *BiDrAPA 89*
Tomba, Alberto *BioIn 16*
Tombaugh, Clyde 1906- *BioIn 16*
Tombaugh, Clyde William 1906- *WhoAm 90*
Tomberlin, George E., Jr. 1949- *WhoEmL 91*
Tomberlin, Joseph Aaron 1937- *WhoSSW 91*
Tomberlin, W.J. 1944- *St&PR 91*
Tombet, Andre 1927- *WhoWor 91*
Tomblinson, James Edmond 1927- *WhoAm 90*
Tombrello, Thomas Anthony, Jr. 1936- *WhoAm 90*
Tombrink, Richard, Jr. 1950- *WhoEmL 91*
Tombros, Peter George 1942- *WhoAm 90*
Tombuloglu, Serafettin *BiDrAPA 89*
Tomchick, D.H. 1931- *St&PR 91*
Tomchuk, Marjorie 1933- *WhoAmA 91, WhoE 91*
Tomcik, Andrew Michael 1938- *WhoAmA 91*
Tomczak, Nancy Jean 1938- *WhoAmW 91*
Tomczak, Robert F. 1935- *St&PR 91*
Tomczyk, Rebecca Bloomfield 1942- *WhoAmW 91*
Tomczyk, Ronald J. 1954- *ODwPR 91*
Tomczyk, Stanislawa *EncO&P 3, EncPaPR 91*
Tomei, Lawrence 1909-1989 *BioIn 16*
Tomei, Marisa *BioIn 16*
Tomek, William Goodrich 1932- *WhoAm 90*
Tomelleri, Carlos Julio *BiDrAPA 89*
Tomenko, Mary A. 1952- *ODwPR 91*
Tomer, Herman Deemar 1949- *WhoWor 91*
Tomerlin, John *AuBYP 90*
Tomes, Margot 1917- *BioIn 16*
Tomes, Margot Ladd *WhoAmA 91*
Tomes, Preshias Gittel 1962- *WhoSSW 91*
Tomeu, Enrique J. *WhoHisp 91*
Tomeychee 1650?-1739 *WhNaAH*
Tomfohrde, Heinn F., III *WhoAm 90*
Tomfohrde, Heinn Frederic, III 1933- *St&PR 91*
Tomic, Biljana Jelesije 1940- *WhoWor 91*
Tomich, Lillian 1935- *WhoWor 91*
Tomich, Nancy Ellen 1945- *WhoAmW 91, WhoWrEP 89*
Tomich, Susan Myserian 1957- *WhoE 91*
Tomich, Terry T. 1940- *St&PR 91*
Tomimoto, Kenkichi 1886-1963 *PenDiDA 89*
Tominovich, A. Robert 1935- *St&PR 91*
Tomiska, Cora Lorena 1928- *WhoAmW 91*
Tomita, Isao *NewAgMG*
Tomita, Tadanori 1945- *WhoEmL 91*
Tomita, Tsuneo 1908- *WhoWor 91*
Tomiyasu, Kiyo 1919- *WhoAm 90*
Tomkiel, Judith Irene 1949- *WhoAmW 91, WhoWrEP 89*
Tomkiewicz, Michael John 1961- *WhoSSW 91*
Tomkiewicz, Ralph E *BiDrAPA 89*
Tomkin, Michael 1948- *St&PR 91*
Tomkins, Alexander C., Jr. 1933- *St&PR 91*
Tomkins, Bruce Allen 1951- *WhoWor 91*

Tomkins, Calvin 1925- *WhoAm 90, WhoAmA 91, WhoWrEP 89, WorAu 1980 [port]*
Tomkins, David 1940- *St&PR 91*
Tomkins, Frank Sargent 1915- *WhoAm 90*
Tomkins, Jasper 1946- *BioIn 16*
Tomkins, Louise Collums 1943- *BiDrAPA 89*
Tomkinson, Robert Charles 1941- *WhoWor 91*
Tomko, George Peter 1936- *WhoAmA 91*
Tomko, Jozef 1924- *WhoWor 91*
Tomko, Martha Louise 1947- *WhoE 91*
Tomlin, Bradley Walker 1899-1953 *WhoAmA 91N*
Tomlin, Dave 1949- *Ballpl 90*
Tomlin, Eugene B. 1933- *St&PR 91*
Tomlin, J. Bert 1944- *St&PR 91*
Tomlin, Lily *BioIn 16*
Tomlin, Lily 1939- *WhoAm 90, WhoAmW 91, WorAlBi*
Tomlin, Robert Michael 1945- *St&PR 91, WhoWor 91*
Tomlin, Tom *ODwPR 91*
Tomlins, Elizabeth Sophia 1763-1828 *FemiCLE*
Tomlinson, A. Robert, III 1934- *St&PR 91*
Tomlinson, Alexander Cooper 1922- *WhoAm 90*
Tomlinson, Betty S. 1948- *ODwPR 91*
Tomlinson, Charles 1927- *ConAu 33NR*
Tomlinson, Charles Wesley, Jr. 1947- *WhoAm 90*
Tomlinson, David 1940- *WhoWor 91*
Tomlinson, David R. 1928- *St&PR 91*
Tomlinson, Dorothy Montgomery 1946- *WhoWor 91*
Tomlinson, Elizabeth F. *BiDrAPA 89*
Tomlinson, George Herbert 1912- *WhoAm 90*
Tomlinson, Gerald 1933- *WhoWrEP 89*
Tomlinson, Gerald Arthur 1933- *WhoE 91*
Tomlinson, Gus 1933- *WhoAm 90*
Tomlinson, H M 1873-1958 *DcLB 100 [port]*
Tomlinson, J. Richard 1930- *WhoAm 90, WhoWor 91*
Tomlinson, James Christopher 1958- *WhoEmL 91*
Tomlinson, James F. 1925- *St&PR 91*
Tomlinson, James Francis 1925- *WhoAm 90*
Tomlinson, Jan Howard 1954- *WhoSSW 91*
Tomlinson, Janet Fox 1944- *WhoWrEP 89*
Tomlinson, Janice Meyer 1950- *WhoAmW 91*
Tomlinson, John 1946- *IntWWM 90, PenDiMP*
Tomlinson, Joseph Ernest 1939- *WhoAm 90*
Tomlinson, Karl E 1927- *BiDrAPA 89*
Tomlinson, Kenneth Y. 1944- *St&PR 91*
Tomlinson, Margaret Lynch 1929- *WhoE 91*
Tomlinson, Mark *BioIn 16*
Tomlinson, Michael *NewAgMG*
Tomlinson, Richard Warren 1949- *WhoE 91*
Tomlinson, Robert John 1936- *St&PR 91, WhoAm 90, WhoWor 91*
Tomlinson, Stephenson Anthony 1950- *WhoWor 91*
Tomlinson, Thomas Stanley 1937- *WhoSSW 91*
Tomlinson, Thomas William 1946- *WhoEmL 91*
Tomlinson, Wallace Kuehn 1936- *BiDrAPA 89*
Tomlinson, Warren Leon 1930- *WhoAm 90*
Tomlinson, William Holmes 1922- *WhoSSW 91, WhoWor 91*
Tomlinson-Keasey, Carol Ann 1942- *WhoAmW 91*
Tommaso, Anne Kathryn 1960- *WhoAmW 91*
Tomme, John Carlin 1930- *WhoWrEP 89*
Tommeraasen, Miles 1923- *WhoAm 90*
Tommerdahl, James B. 1926- *St&PR 91*
Tommey, Belinda Stokes 1957- *WhoAmW 91*
Tomney, T Richard 1922- *St&PR 91*
Tomo Chachi Mico 1650?-1739 *WhNaAH*
Tomo-chee-chee 1650?-1739 *WhNaAH*
Tomochachi 1650?-1739 *WhNaAH*
Tomochichi *EncCRAm*
Tomochichi 1650?-1739 *WhNaAH*
Tomonaga, Sin-Itiro 1906-1979 *DcScB S2, WorAlBi*
Tomowa-Sintow, Anna 1941- *IntWWM 90, PenDiMP, WhoAm 90*
Tompalski, Sherry Lynn 1955- *BiDrAPA 89*
Tompert, Ann 1918- *BioIn 16*
Tompetrini, Kenneth Frank 1943- *WhoE 91*
Tompkins, A. Kathleen Kelly 1903- *WhoAmW 91*
Tompkins, Alan 1907- *WhoAmA 91, WhoE 91*
Tompkins, Angel *ConTFT 8*
Tompkins, Betty 1945- *WhoAmA 91*
Tompkins, Curtis Johnston 1942- *WhoAm 90, WhoWor 91*
Tompkins, Daniel D. 1774-1825 *BiDrUSE 89*
Tompkins, Donna Ellen 1959- *WhoAmW 91*
Tompkins, Douglas R. *WhoAm 90*
Tompkins, Edgar M. 1938- *WhoE 91*
Tompkins, Edward Eugene 1936- *St&PR 91*
Tompkins, Francine Maria 1947- *WhoE 91*
Tompkins, J Richard 1938- *St&PR 91*
Tompkins, James Arthur 1946- *WhoAm 90*
Tompkins, James Haviland 1923- *St&PR 91*
Tompkins, James McLane 1913- *WhoAm 90*
Tompkins, Jane 1898- *AuBYP 90*
Tompkins, Joseph Buford, Jr. 1950- *WhoWor 91*
Tompkins, Keith R. 1942- *St&PR 91*
Tompkins, Mark Allen 1949- *WhoEmL 91*
Tompkins, Mary Moulton 1951- *WhoAmW 91*
Tompkins, Michael 1955- *WhoAmA 91*
Tompkins, Pamela Sue 1955- *WhoAmW 91*
Tompkins, Ralph Joel 1919- *WhoWrEP 89*
Tompkins, Richard Allison 1935- *WhoE 91*
Tompkins, Robert George 1923- *WhoAm 90, WhoWor 91*
Tompkins, Ronald K. 1934- *WhoAm 90*
Tompkins, Sally Louisa 1833-1916 *BioIn 16*
Tompkins, Seldon T. 1943- *St&PR 91*
Tompkins, Stuart Ramsay 1886- *BioIn 16*
Tompkins, Susie *BioIn 16, WhoAm 90*
Tompkins, Thomas MacGregor 1952- *IntWWM 90*
Tompkins, Walker Allison 1909- *AuBYP 90*
Tompkins, William F. 1913-1989 *BioIn 16*
Tompsett, Margaret E 1942- *BiDrAPA 89*
Tompsett, Michael Francis 1939- *WhoAm 90*
Tompsett, Ralph 1913- *WhoAm 90*
Tompson, Marian Leonard 1929- *WhoAm 90*
Toms, Bate Carpenter, Jr. 1918- *WhoSSW 91*
Toms, Bonnie Bayer 1954- *WhoEmL 91*
Toms, Carl 1927- *ConDes 90*
Toms, Carlton Ralph 1937- *St&PR 91*
Toms, Kathleen Moore 1943- *WhoAmW 91, WhoWor 91*
Tomsett, Janet Moffat 1943- *WhoAmW 91*
Tomsic, Joseph Andrew Michael 1949- *WhoEmL 91, WhoWor 91*
Tomsich, Rosa Basilia *BiDrAPA 89*
Tomsky, Judy 1959- *WhoEmL 91*
Tomson, William Coburn 1935- *WhoE 91*
Tomsovic, Edward J. 1922- *WhoAm 90*
Tomsyck, Rebecca Reinovsky *BiDrAPA 89*
Tomter, Gary Lynn 1950- *St&PR 91*
Tomyris *WomWR*
Tona, Andrew Joseph 1951- *St&PR 91*
Tondeur, Jean-Philippe 1957- *WhoWor 91*
Tondeur, Philippe Maurice 1932- *WhoAm 90*
Tondkar, Rasoul Habib *WhoSSW 91*
Tondury, Barblina Fiammetta 1956- *IntWWM 90*
Tone, Franchot 1905-1968 *WorAlBi*
Tone, Kenneth Edward 1930- *WhoAm 90*
Tone, Philip Willis 1923- *WhoAm 90*
Tone, Theobald Wolfe 1763-1798 *BioIn 16*
Tone-Loc *BioIn 16*
Tone-Loc 1966- *News 90 [port], -90-3 [port]*
Tonegawa, Susumu 1939- *WhoAm 90, WhoE 91, WhoWor 91, WorAlBi*
Tonelli, Edith Ann 1949- *WhoAm 90, WhoAmA 91, WhoAmW 91*
Tonelli, Giovanna Marie 1951- *WhoAmW 91*
Tonelli, James D. R. 1949- *WhoSSW 91*
Tonello-Stuart, Enrica Maria 1926- *WhoAm 90, WhoWor 91*
Tonelson, Jack Martin 1930- *St&PR 91, WhoAm 90*
Toner, Edward Joseph 1921- *St&PR 91*
Toner, Frederick Littleton 1948- *WhoSSW 91*
Toner, Tommie Carr 1942- *WhoSSW 91*
Toney, Anthony 1913- *WhoAm 90, WhoAmA 91*
Toney, Edna 1914- *WhoAmW 91*
Toney, Ellis E *BiDrAPA 89*
Toney, Fred 1888-1953 *Ballpl 90*
Toney, George B. 1927- *St&PR 91*
Toney, Glen O. *St&PR 91*
Toney, James Wayne 1939- *St&PR 91*
Toney, Kelly Lynne Smith 1959- *WhoSSW 91*
Toney, Mark *BioIn 16*
Toney, Robert L. 1934- *WhoAm 90*
Toney, Sam D. *BiDrAPA 89*
Toney, Thomas Clifford 1958- *WhoSSW 91*
Tong, Edward *BiDrAPA 89*
Tong, Hing 1922- *WhoAm 90*
Tong, Lowell D *BiDrAPA 89*
Tong, Shiu Yu F 1911- *BiDrAPA 89*
Tong, Siu Wing 1950- *WhoEmL 91*
Tong, Theody Mongaya 1955- *WhoWor 91*
Tong, Winton 1927- *WhoAm 90*
Tongate, Darrel Edwin 1943- *WhoSSW 91*
Tonge, Muriel Smith 1926- *WhoAmW 91*
Tongour, Michael Alexander 1956- *WhoEmL 91*
Tongue, Paul Graham 1932- *St&PR 91, WhoAm 90*
Tongue, William Walter 1915- *WhoAm 90*
Tonha, Pedro Maria *WhoWor 91*
Toni, Bernard S. 1943- *St&PR 91*
Toni, Domenic Louis 1950- *WhoWor 91*
Toni, Eugene Joseph 1949- *WhoE 91*
Tonielli, Richard B. 1939- *St&PR 91*
Tonini, Carrie Beal 1950- *WhoAmW 91*
Tonino, Robert Henry Anthony 1944- *St&PR 91*
Tonissen, Dan Norman 1950- *St&PR 91*
Tonk, Robert 1947- *St&PR 91*
Tonkin, Dean G. 1940- *St&PR 91*
Tonkin, Humphrey Richard 1939- *WhoAm 90, WhoWor 91*
Tonkin, Leo Sampson 1937- *WhoAm 90*
Tonkin, Terry Michael 1942- *St&PR 91*
Tonkovich, Robert Steven 1945- *St&PR 91*
Tonks, Robert Stanley *WhoAm 90*
Tonks, Rosemary 1932- *BioIn 16*
Tonkyn, Richard George 1927- *St&PR 91, WhoAm 90*
Tonn, Melissa Dawn 1959- *WhoSSW 91*
Tonna, Arthur J. 1927- *St&PR 91, WhoAm 90*
Tonna, Charlotte Elizabeth 1790-1846 *BioIn 16, FemiCLE*
Tonna, Edgar Anthony 1928- *WhoAm 90*
Tonndorf, Juergen 1914-1989 *BioIn 16*
Tonnessen, Diana *BioIn 16*
Tonogbanua, Gabino Conwi *BiDrAPA 89*
Tonoyan, S.K. *WhoWor 91*
Tonsend, Teryl 1938- *WhoAmA 91*
Tonsing, Carol E. *WhoWrEP 89*
Tonsing, Robert Elton 1958- *BiDrAPA 89*
Tonsmeire, Arthur *St&PR 91*
Tonti, Henri De 1650?-1704 *WhNaAH*
Tonti, Rita Rose 1943- *WhoWrEP 89*
Tonty, Henri de 1649?-1704 *EncCRAm*
Tonty, Henri de 1650?-1704 *WhNaAH*
Tontz, Jay Logan 1938- *WhoAm 90*
Tonucci, Elizabeth Fox 1944- *WhoAmW 91*
Tood, Troy W. 1928- *St&PR 91*
Toodle, Brenda Elaine 1940- *WhoAmW 91*
Toogood, Granville Newbold 1943- *WhoE 91*
Tooher, James Marshall 1931- *St&PR 91, WhoE 91*
Toohey, Edward Joseph 1930- *St&PR 91, WhoE 91, WhoWor 91*
Toohey, Richard 1929- *St&PR 91*
Toohey, William D., Jr. 1952- *ODwPR 91*
Toohig, Michael Francis 1924- *St&PR 91*
Toohill, Carol Marie 1961- *WhoAmW 91*
Toohill, Vivian Elaine 1943- *WhoAmW 91*
Toohoolhoolzote 1810?-1877 *WhNaAH*
Toohulhulsote 1810?-1877 *WhNaAH*
Took, Kevin John 1959- *BiDrAPA 89*
Tooke, Thomas 1774-1858 *BioIn 16*
Tooker, Carl E. 1947- *St&PR 91, WhoAm 90*
Tooker, Gary Lamarr 1939- *WhoAm 90*
Tooker, George 1920- *WhoAmA 91*
Tooker, Laura Lee 1952- *WhoE 91*
Tookes, James Nelson 1934- *WhoSSW 91*
Tool, Brian John 1945- *WhoEmL 91*
Tool, Dennis Casler 1948- *WhoWrEP 89*
Tool, Marc R. *BioIn 16*
Toolan, Dennis Michael 1946- *St&PR 91, WhoAm 90*
Toolan, James 1922- *BiDrAPA 89*
Toole, Albert J. 1937- *St&PR 91*
Toole, Allan H. 1920- *WhoAm 90*
Toole, Arthur Fulkerson, III 1940- *WhoSSW 91*
Toole, Edward D. *St&PR 91*
Toole, James Francis 1925- *WhoAm 90, WhoWor 91*
Toole, John Edward 1934- *WhoE 91*
Toole, John Kennedy 1937-1969 *ConLC 64 [port], WorAlBi*
Toole, John William 1924- *WhoE 91*
Toole, Timothy O. 1953- *WhoAm 90*
Toole, Wm. K., II 1926- *St&PR 91*
Tooley, Charles Frederick 1947- *WhoEmL 91*
Tooley, John 1924- *IntWWM 90*
Tooley, Lowell James 1923- *WhoE 91*
Tooley, Michael James 1941- *WhoWor 91*
Tooley, Terry Lee 1948- *St&PR 91, WhoEmL 91*
Toolson, Kay L. 1944- *St&PR 91*
Toombs, Jane Ellen 1926- *WhoWrEP 89*
Toombs, Kenneth Eldridge 1928- *WhoAm 90*
Toombs, Robert Augustus 1810-1885 *BioIn 16*
Toombs, Russ William 1951- *WhoE 91*
Toomer, Cynthia Yvonne 1947- *WhoE 91*
Toomer, Jean 1894-1967 *EarBlAP, MajTwCW*
Toomer, Ron 1930- *News 90 [port]*
Toomer, Ronald *BioIn 16*
Toomey, David Charles 1938- *WhoAm 90*
Toomey, Jeanne Elizabeth *WhoWrEP 89*
Toomey, Jim *BioIn 16*
Toomey, John Boyne 1924- *St&PR 91*
Toomey, John Edward 1952- *St&PR 91*
Toomey, Kent E. 1935- *St&PR 91*
Toomey, Stephen J. 1959- *St&PR 91*
Toomey, T Murray 1923- *St&PR 91*
Toomey, Thomas Murray 1923- *WhoAm 90*
Toomre, Alar 1937- *WhoAm 90*
Toon, Al 1963- *WorAlBi*
Toon, John Graham 1931- *WhoWor 91*
Toon, Malcolm 1916- *BioIn 16, WhoAm 90*
Toon, Peter 1939- *ConAu 30NR*
Toon, Steven Bates 1948- *St&PR 91*
Toone, Bill *BioIn 16*
Toone, Elam Cooksey, Jr. 1908- *WhoAm 90*
Toones, Fred *DrBlPA 90*
Tooney, Nancy Marion 1939- *WhoE 91*
Toops, Thorndike C *BiDrAPA 89*
Toor, Helen Mary 1956- *WhoE 91*
Toorup, Charley 1891-1955 *BiDWomA*
Toos, A.J. *WhoWrEP 89*
Toot, Joseph F., Jr. 1935- *WhoAm 90*
Toot, Joseph Frederick, Jr. 1935- *St&PR 91*
Toote, Gloria E. A. *WhoAm 90, WhoAmW 91*
Toothman, John William 1954- *WhoEmL 91*
Tootle, Milton, Jr. 1943- *St&PR 91*
Toots & the Maytals *EncPR&S 89*
Toovey, Rebeckah, Jr. 1704-1714 *BiDEWW*
Toovey, Rebeckah, Sr. 1664-1734 *BiDEWW*
Tooze, Ruth 1892- *AuBYP 90*
Top, Franklin Henry, Jr. 1936- *WhoAm 90*
Topakoglu, Huseyin Cavit 1925- *WhoSSW 91*
Topaz, William N. 1947- *St&PR 91, WhoEmL 91*
Topazio, Virgil William 1915- *WhoAm 90*
Topchevsky, Morris 1899- *WhoAmA 91N*
Topel, David Glen 1937- *WhoAm 90*
Topelius, Zacharias 1818-1898 *DcScanL*
Topenebee *WhNaAH*
Topenibe *WhNaAH*
Toperoff, Sam 1933- *ConAu 30NR*
Toperzer, Thomas Raymond 1939- *WhoAm 90, WhoAmA 91, WhoSSW 91*
Topete Stonefield, Liz 1955- *WhoHisp 91*
Topfer, Morton Louis 1936- *St&PR 91, WhoAm 90*
Topham, Douglas William *WhoWor 91*
Topham, John G. *St&PR 91*
Topham, Margaret Ann 1950- *WhoAmW 91*
Topham, Murray Herbert 1937- *St&PR 91*
Topham, Verl Reed 1934- *St&PR 91*
Topholm, Ib Le Roy 1935- *WhoWor 91*
Topinibe *WhNaAH*
Topinka, Judy Baar 1944- *WhoAmW 91*
Topino, Charles *PenDiDA 89*
Topirceanu, G. *EncCoWW*
Topjian, Mena Rose 1936- *WhoAmW 91*
Topjon, Gary Malcolm 1940- *St&PR 91*
Topkins, Katharine 1927- *WhoWrEP 89*
Topliss, Harry, Jr. 1923- *WhoAm 90*
Toplitz, George Nathan 1936- *WhoWor 91*
Toplyn, Elaine Cynthia 1959- *WhoE 91*
Toplyn, Sherryl Judd 1952- *WhoE 91*
Topnibe *WhNaAH*
Topol, Chaim 1935- *WhoWor 91*
Topol, Eric Jeffrey 1954- *WhoAm 90*
Topol, Robert Martin 1925- *St&PR 91, WhoAm 90, WhoAmA 91*
Topol, Sidney 1924- *St&PR 91, WhoSSW 91*
Topoleski, Sally Caroline 1933- *WhoE 91*
Topolosky, Sanford 1924- *St&PR 91*
Topolski, Feliks 1907-1989 *AnObit 1989, BioIn 16*
Topolski, Jerzy 1928- *WhoWor 91*
Topolsky, Sharon-Faye 1952- *BiDrAPA 89*
Topor, Thomas Karl 1952- *WhoSSW 91*
Toporcer, Specs 1899- *Ballpl 90*
Toporcer, Specs 1899-1989 *BioIn 16*
Topp, Barbara Harrison 1937- *WhoAmW 91*
Topp, Elliott 1930- *St&PR 91*
Topp, Erik Davis 1932- *WhoE 91*

Topp, Robert George 1937- St&PR 91
Topp, Stephen William 1955- WhoAm 90
Toppan, Clara Ann Raab 1910- WhoAmW 91
Toppe, Richard Spencer 1949- WhoSSW 91
Toppel, Harold 1924- St&PR 91
Toppel, Milton 1919- WhoAm 90
Toppen, John T BiDrAPA 89
Topper, Barbara MacNeal Blake 1942- WhoE 91
Topper, David R 1943- WhoAmA 91
Topper, Hertha 1924- IntWWM 90
Topper, J Ray 1928- St&PR 91
Topper, Paul Quinn 1925- WhoSSW 91
Topper, Philip D., Sr. 1942- St&PR 91
Topping, Brian B. 1934- St&PR 91
Topping, Brian Barclay 1934- WhoAm 90
Topping, James 1879-1949 WhoAmA 91N
Topping, James Francis 1931- St&PR 91
Topping, John Carruthers, Jr. 1943- WhoE 91
Topping, John Thomas 1934- St&PR 91
Topping, Karin Dianne 1942- ODwPR 91
Topping, Linda BiDrAPA 89
Topping, Nancy Grace 1934- WhoAmW 91
Topping, Norman Hawkins 1908- WhoAm 90
Topping, Peter 1916- WhoAm 90
Topping, Peter Alan 1953- WhoSSW 91
Topping, Robert Stephen 1963- WhoEmL 91
Topping, T. Edward 1923- WhoAm 90
Topping, Thomas Edwin 1933- St&PR 91
Toppins, Sarah Elizabeth 1952- WhoAmW 91
Topsacalian, Harutiun 1961- WhoE 91
Topsch, Wilhelm 1941- WhoWor 91
Topuzes, Thomas 1947- WhoHisp 91
Tor, Regina AuBYP 90
Toradze, Alexander BioIn 16
Toradze, Alexander 1952- WhoAm 90
Toragana WomWR
Toragina WomWR
Toran, Daniel James 1948- WhoAm 90
Toran, Stacy 1961-1989 BioIn 16
Toran, Yancie Antoinette 1962- WhoAmW 91
Torano, Francisco Jose 1944- WhoHisp 91
Torano-Pantin, Maria Elena 1938- WhoHisp 91
Toraskar, Jayashree 1938- WhoE 91
Toraty, Surya B BiDrAPA 89
Torban, Richard I BiDrAPA 89
Torbert, Carl A., Jr. 1935- St&PR 91
Torbert, Carl Allen, Jr. 1935- WhoAm 90
Torbert, Clement Clay, Jr. 1929- WhoAm 90
Torbert, Donald Robert 1910-1985 WhoAmA 91N
Torbert, Frank Duke 1936- WhoSSW 91
Torbert, Stephanie Birch 1945- WhoAmA 91
Torbet, Oliver Brooks 1827-1864 AmLegL
Torbet, Sylvia Lily 1930- WhoSSW 91
Torborg, Jeff 1941- Ballpl 90
Torborg, Jeffrey Allen 1941- WhoAm 90
Torch, Evan Malcolm 1950- BiDrAPA 89
Torchiana, Donald Thornhill 1923- WhoAm 90, WhoWrEP 89
Torchin, Robert Paul 1941- BiDrAPA 89
Torchinsky, Abe 1920- IntWWM 90, WhoAm 90
Torchinsky, Alberto 1944- WhoHisp 91
Torchinsky, Benjamin B. 1926- St&PR 91
Torcivia, Benedict J. 1929- St&PR 91
Torcivia, Benedict J., Sr. 1929- WhoAm 90, WhoWor 91
Torcivia, Benedict Joseph, Jr. 1957- WhoAm 90
Torcivia, Joseph Arthur 1959- WhoAm 90
Torcoletti, Enzo 1943- WhoAmA 91
Torda, Clara BiDrAPA 89
Torda, T. Paul 1911- WhoE 91
Tordjman, Jean Daniel 1944- WhoE 91
Tordjmann, Fabien BioIn 16
Tordoff, Harrison Bruce 1923- WhoAm 90
Tordoir, Peter Paul 1952- St&PR 91
Toregene WomWR
Torell, John Raymond, III 1939- St&PR 91
Torem, Moshe BiDrAPA 89
Toren, David Arend 1929- WhoE 91
Toren, Mark 1950- WhoE 91
Toren, Robert 1915- WhoWor 91
Torentinos, Anthony 1948- WhoAm 90
Toresco, Donald M. 1939- St&PR 91
Toretti, Christine Jack 1957- WhoAmW 91
Torf, Lois Beurman 1926- WhoAmA 91
Torfason, Kristjan Gudmundur 1953- WhoWor 91
Torffield, Marvin 1943- WhoAmA 91
Torfs, Jozef Edouard 1924- WhoWor 91
Torg, Joseph Steven 1934- WhoAm 90
Torgersen, Don Arthur 1934- BioIn 16
Torgersen, Paul Ernest 1931- WhoAm 90
Torgersen, Torwald Harold 1929- WhoAm 90
Torgerson, Arthur Dennis 1929- St&PR 91
Torgerson, Larry Keith 1935- WhoWor 91
Torgerson, Paul E. 1947- St&PR 91
Torgeson, Earl 1924- Ballpl 90
Torgow, Eugene N. 1925- WhoAm 90
Torgusen, Robert Guy 1935- St&PR 91
Toribara, Taft Yutaka 1917- WhoAm 90
Torii, Shizuo 1931- WhoWor 91
Torii, Tetsuya 1918- WhoWor 91
Torimiro, Frederic Belle 1957- WhoSSW 91
Torinus, John B., Jr. 1937- St&PR 91
Torio, Lydia M BiDrAPA 89
Torisky, Donald David 1938- St&PR 91, WhoAm 90
Torkan, Akbar WhoWor 91
Torke, Hans Joachim 1938- WhoWor 91
Torke, Michael 1961- IntWWM 90
Torkelson, Dean J. 1944- St&PR 91
Torkelson, Lucile Emma 1915- WhoAmW 91
Torki, Mostafa Ahmad 1940- WhoWor 91
Torlakson, James Daniel 1951- WhoAmA 91
Torlen, Michael Arnold 1940- WhoAmA 91
Torley, John Frederic 1911- St&PR 91, WhoAm 90
Torley, Luke MajTwCW
Tormay, Cecile 1876-1937 EncCoWW
Torme, Margaret A. 1943- ODwPR 91
Torme, Mel 1925- BioIn 16, ConMus 4 [port], OxCPMus, WhoAm 90, WorAlBi
Tormey, Terrence O'Brien 1954- St&PR 91
Tormey, Thomas James 1925- WhoAm 90
Torn, Jerry 1933- WhoAmA 91
Torn, Lawrence J. 1926- St&PR 91
Torn, Rip 1931- WhoAm 90, WorAlBi
Tornabene, Russell C. 1923- WhoAm 90
Tornabene, Thomas Guy 1937- WhoAm 90
Tornabuoni, Lucrezia 1425-1482 EncCoWW
Tornatore, Janice Firlit 1954- St&PR 91
Tornberg, Edward Wilmer 1934- St&PR 91
Tornblom, Bjorn 1918- WhoWor 91
Tornborg, Rita 1926- EncCoWW
Tornborg, Rita 1930- DcScanL
Torneden, Roger Lee 1944- WhoWor 91
Tornheim, Norman 1942- WhoAmA 91
Tornimparte, Alessandra EncCoWW
Tornquist, Harold Everett 1918- WhoAm 90
Tornquist, Perry Lee 1938- St&PR 91
Tornstrom, Robert Ernest 1946- WhoEmL 91
Toro, Carlos H. 1943- St&PR 91
Toro, Carlos Hans 1943- WhoHisp 91
Toro, Emilio 1947- WhoSSW 91
Toro, Felix R 1956- BiDrAPA 89
Toro, Frank Louis 1928- St&PR 91
Toro, Jean-Bernard-Honore 1672-1731 PenDiDA 89
Toro, Joe WhoHisp 91
Toro, Manuel A. 1937- WhoHisp 91
Toro, Ricardo J BiDrAPA 89
Toro, Robert 1942- BiDrAPA 89
Toro-Leyton, Claudio E 1939- BiDrAPA 89
Toroean, Mangiring L. 1944- WhoWor 91
Torok, Arthur F. 1928- St&PR 91
Torok, Istvan 1939- WhoWor 91
Torok, Margaret Louise 1922- WhoAmW 91
Torok, Sophie 1895-1955 EncCoWW
Torop, Paul 1940- BiDrAPA 89
Torosian, Jeanne Wylie 1913- WhoWrEP 89
Torp, Lisbet 1949- IntWWM 90
Torpie, Barbara Ann BiDrAPA 89
Torpy, Joseph L. St&PR 91
Torquemada, Tomas De 1420-1498 WorAlBi
Torrance, Carol Louise 1936- WhoAmW 91
Torrance, Ellis Paul 1915- WhoAm 90
Torrance, Gregory Scott 1946- St&PR 91
Torrance, Philip Mitchell, II 1936- BiDrAPA 89
Torrance, Walter F., Jr. 1927- St&PR 91
Torrando, Francisco WhoHisp 91
Torras, Cesar A BiDrAPA 89
Torras, Joseph Hill 1924- St&PR 91, WhoAm 90, WhoE 91
Torras, Silke 1935- BiDrAPA 89
Torre, Carlos 1951- WhoHisp 91
Torre, Douglas Paul 1919- WhoAm 90
Torre, Elizabeth Lassiter 1931- WhoAmW 91
Torre, Frank 1931- Ballpl 90
Torre, Joe 1940- Ballpl 90 [port], WorAlBi
Torre, Josefina de la 1907?- EncCoWW
Torre, Lisa A. 1964- ODwPR 91
Torre, Raoul della MajTwCW
Torre, Susana 1944- WomArch [port]
Torre, Victor Raul Haya de la BioIn 16
Torre Nilsson, Leopoldo 1924-1978 BioIn 16
Torrealba, Pablo 1948- Ballpl 90
Torreano, John Francis 1941- WhoAmA 91
Torregrossa, Richard 1947- St&PR 91
Torrella, Carlos Rudolph 1943- WhoAm 90
Torrellas, Carlos BiDrAPA 89
Torrellas, Marianne BioIn 16
Torrence, David J. St&PR 91
Torrence, Gwen BioIn 16
Torrence, Margaret Ann 1946- WhoAmW 91
Torrence, Richard 1936- WhoAm 90
Torrens, Duncan ConAu 130
Torrens, Frank J. 1938- St&PR 91
Torrens, John K 1920- BiDrAPA 89
Torrens, Robert 1780-1864 BioIn 16
Torrente Ballester, Gonzalo 1910- IntvSpW [port]
Torrenzano, Richard WhoE 91
Torrenzano, Richard 1950- ODwPR 91, St&PR 91
Torres, Adeline WhoHisp 91
Torres, Anthony R. 1959- St&PR 91
Torres, Art 1946- WhoHisp 91
Torres, Arturo A BiDrAPA 89
Torres, Arturo D. WhoHisp 91
Torres, Arturo G. WhoHisp 91
Torres, Arturo Lopez 1948- WhoHisp 91
Torres, Baldomero Chapa 1935- WhoHisp 91
Torres, Celia Margaret 1936- WhoHisp 91
Torres, Christine Marie 1962- WhoAmW 91
Torres, Cynthia Ann 1958- WhoAmW 91, WhoWor 91
Torres, David 1934- WhoHisp 91, WhoSSW 91
Torres, David P., Jr. WhoHisp 91
Torres, David R 1960- BiDrAPA 89
Torres, Edwin BioIn 16, WhoHisp 91
Torres, Elizabeth 1947- WhoHisp 91
Torres, Erika Vogel 1939- WhoWor 91
Torres, Esteban E. 1930- WhoHisp 91
Torres, Esteban Edward 1930- BioIn 16, WhoAm 90
Torres, Esther A. 1949- WhoHisp 91
Torres, Eugenio 1950- WhoEmL 91, WhoWor 91
Torres, Felix 1932- Ballpl 90
Torres, Fernando 1924- WhoAm 90
Torres, Francesc 1948- WhoAmA 91
Torres, Frank 1928- WhoHisp 91
Torres, Fred WhoHisp 91
Torres, Gerald 1952- WhoHisp 91
Torres, Geronimo S 1928- BiDrAPA 89
Torres, Gil 1915-1983 Ballpl 90
Torres, Gladys 1938- WhoHisp 91
Torres, Guillermo M. WhoHisp 91
Torres, Hector NewYTBS 90
Torres, Hector 1945- Ballpl 90
Torres, Helen Rosemarie WhoAmW 91
Torres, Horacio 1924-1976 WhoAmA 91N
Torres, Humberto A 1921- BiDrAPA 89
Torres, Israel 1934- WhoSSW 91, WhoWor 91
Torres, J. Antonio 1949- WhoHisp 91
Torres, Jake WhoHisp 91
Torres, Jane Allen 1947- WhoSSW 91
Torres, Jess G. WhoHisp 91
Torres, John, Jr. 1939- WhoSSW 91
Torres, John R. 1959- WhoHisp 91
Torres, Jose Acosta 1925- ConAu 32NR, HispWr 90
Torres, Jose B. 1946- WhoHisp 91
Torres, Jose Manuel 1935- WhoHisp 91
Torres, Joseph James 1950- WhoHisp 91
Torres, Joseph L. 1927- WhoHisp 91
Torres, Juan Fremiot WhoAm 90
Torres, Julio WhoHisp 91
Torres, Lawrence E. 1927- WhoHisp 91
Torres, Lawrence J. 1946- WhoHisp 91
Torres, Leida I. 1949- WhoHisp 91
Torres, Leonard 1926- WhoHisp 91
Torres, Leyda Luz 1955- WhoHisp 91
Torres, Linda Marie WhoHisp 91
Torres, Liz BioIn 16
Torres, Lois Ann 1954- WhoAmW 91
Torres, Loretta Ruby 1946- WhoWor 91
Torres, Lucille WhoHisp 91
Torres, Luis 1943- WhoHisp 91
Torres, Luis A. 1922- WhoHisp 91
Torres, Luis A., Jr. WhoHisp 91
Torres, Luis Llorens 1876-1944 BioIn 16
Torres, Luis Ruben 1950- WhoHisp 91
Torres, Magdalena 1930- WhoHisp 91
Torres, Manuel 1963- WhoE 91
Torres, Maruja 194-?- EncCoWW
Torres, Milton J. 1940- WhoHisp 91
Torres, Nelson 1947- WhoSSW 91
Torres, Niceto Alcala Zamora y 1877-1949 BioIn 16
Torres, Noe Acosta 1956- WhoHisp 91
Torres, Omar 1945- BioIn 16
Torres, Oscar WhoHisp 91
Torres, Oscar L., Sr. WhoHisp 91
Torres, Oscar M., Jr. 1945- St&PR 91
Torres, Oscar Modesto, Jr. 1945- WhoHisp 91
Torres, Paul 1952- WhoHisp 91
Torres, Penny NewAgE 90
Torres, Penny 1960- EncPaPR 91
Torres, Raymond 1957- WhoHisp 91
Torres, Refugio R. 1925- WhoHisp 91
Torres, Rene Clemente 1945- WhoE 91
Torres, Ricardo WhoHisp 91
Torres, Richard Roy 1961- WhoHisp 91
Torres, Rosario WhoHisp 91
Torres, Rusty 1948- Ballpl 90, BioIn 16
Torres, Sally WhoHisp 91
Torres, Salvio 1932- WhoHisp 91
Torres, Sara 1942- WhoHisp 91
Torres, Vera Trinchero 1938- St&PR 91
Torres, Xiomara WhoHisp 91
Torres, Yolanda 1936- WhoAmW 91
Torres-Aguiar, Luis 1921- BiDrAPA 89
Torres-Aguiar, Manuel A 1920- BiDrAPA 89
Torres Bodet, Jaime 1902-1974 BioIn 16, ConAu 32NR, HispWr 90, MajTwCW
Torres Cortez, Hernan BioIn 16
Torres-Garcia, Joaquin 1874-1949 ArtLatA
Torres-Geary, Miriam Beatriz 1956- WhoHisp 91
Torres-Gil, Fernando 1948- WhoHisp 91
Torres Gonzales, Juan Jose 1921?-1976 BioIn 16
Torres-Horwitt, C. Aida WhoHisp 91
Torres-Labawld, Jose D. 1932- WhoHisp 91
Torres-Lisboa, Patricio 1941- BiDrAPA 89
Torres-Melendez, Elaine 1957- WhoHisp 91
Torres Moore, Dominga WhoHisp 91
Torres-Nieves, Hector L BiDrAPA 89
Torres-Parra, Manuel 1934- WhoWor 91
Torres-Reaves, Carmen Nellie 1954- WhoAmW 91
Torres Rivademar, Luis De 1929- WhoWor 91
Torres Rivera, Lina M. 1953- WhoHisp 91
Torres-Rivera, Rebeca 1931- WhoHisp 91
Torres-Santiago, Jose Manuel 1940- WhoHisp 91
Torres-Santos, Raymond 1958- IntWWM 90
Torres-Ullauri, Maria Isabel WhoAmW 91
Torres-Velez, Felix L. 1939- WhoHisp 91
Torrese, Dante Michael 1949- WhoE 91
Torreson, Michael Wayne 1955- WhoEmL 91
Torresy, Frank Louis 1921- WhoWor 91
Torrey, Alice BioIn 16
Torrey, Benjamin Harvey, Jr. 1958- WhoSSW 91
Torrey, Charles Wray 1947- BiDrAPA 89
Torrey, David L. 1931- St&PR 91
Torrey, David Leonard 1931- WhoAm 90
Torrey, Jay L. AmLegL
Torrey, John Gordon 1921- WhoAm 90
Torrey, R. A. 1856-1928 BioIn 16
Torrey, Reuben Archer 1856-1928 BioIn 16
Torrey, Richard Frank 1926- St&PR 91, WhoAm 90, WhoE 91
Torrey, William Arthur 1934- WhoE 91
Torrey, William Chandler BiDrAPA 89
Torrez, Ervin E. 1935- WhoHisp 91
Torrez, Mike 1946- Ballpl 90
Torriani-Gorini, Annamaria 1918- WhoAm 90
Torricella, Roland A. 1924- St&PR 91
Torricelli, Evangelista 1608-1647 WorAlBi
Torricelli, Robert G. 1951- WhoAm 90, WhoE 91
Torrie, Malcolm TwCCr&M 91
Torrie, R. Elaine 1961- WhoAmW 91
Torriente, Christobel 1895-1948 Ballpl 90
Torrieri, Joan Maria 1950- WhoAmW 91
Torriero, Dolores Frances 1957- WhoAmW 91
Torrijos-Herrera, Omar 1929-1979 WorAlBi
Torrijos Herrera, Omar 1929-1981 BioIn 16
Torrington, Arthur Edward 1940- WhoE 91
Torrington, John Byng, Viscount 1742?-1813 BioIn 16
Torrio, John 1882-1970 BioIn 16
Torro, Pel ConAu 32NR
Torroba, Federico Moreno 1891-1982 OxCPMus
Torsekar, Pratap Govind BiDrAPA 89
Torsello, Marino Sanuto BioIn 16
Torshell, Elizabeth BiDEWW
Torsleff, Carl Richard 1938- WhoSSW 91
Torson, Victor J. 1930- St&PR 91
Torstenson, Lennart 1603-1651 WorAlBi
Torsvan, Ben Traven MajTwCW
Torsvan, Benno Traven MajTwCW
Torsvan, Berick Traven MajTwCW
Torsvan, Berwick Traven MajTwCW
Torsvan, Bruno Traven MajTwCW
Torsvan, Traven BioIn 16, MajTwCW

Tortelier, Paul 1914- BioIn 16, IntWWM 90, PenDiMP
Tortelier, Paul 1914-1990 NewYTBS 90 [port]
Tortelier, Yan Pascal 1947- IntWWM 90, PenDiMP
Torter, Robert E. 1945- St&PR 91
Torti, Henry J. 1925- St&PR 91
Torto, Raymond Gerald 1941- WhoE 91
Tortolano, James Vincent 1949- WhoEmL 91
Tortora, Richard Robert 1948- WhoE 91
Tortorella, Albert J. ODwPR 91
Tortorella, Robert Anthony 1939- WhoE 91
Tortorello, MaryEllen Bridget 1959- WhoE 91
Tortorello, Nicholas John 1948- WhoE 91
Tortorello, Robert Joseph 1949- St&PR 91
Tortoric, B. K. WhoWrEP 89
Tortorice, Michael J. 1945- St&PR 91
Tortorici, Anthony J. ODwPR 91
Tortorici, John 1942- St&PR 91
Tortorici, Linda Reese 1947- St&PR 91
Tortoriello, Robert Laurence 1950- WhoEmL 91
Tortosa-Nacher, Rafael Manuel BiDrAPA 89
Toru, Matsunaga 1929- WhoWor 91
Torvi, Kai Antero 1954- WhoWor 91
Tory, Anthony David 1942- St&PR 91
Torza, John 1944- St&PR 91
Tosato, Massimo 1954- WhoWor 91
Tosawai WhNaAH
Tosawi WhNaAH
Toscani, Dominic Paul 1928- St&PR 91
Toscanini, Arturo 1867-1957 BioIn 16, PenDiMP, WorAlBi
Toscanini, Wally BioIn 16
Toscano, Dee BioIn 16
Toscano, Eamon F. 1946- St&PR 91
Toscano, James Vincent 1937- WhoAm 90
Toscano, Maria Guadalupe 1965- WhoHisp 91
Toscano, Sergio 1935- BiDrAPA 89
Toschik, Larry 1922- WhoAmA 91
Tosh, Juanita Prillaman 1930- WhoAmW 91
Tosh, Nancy Peckham 1932- WhoAm 90, WhoAmW 91
Tosh, Peter 1944-1987 BioIn 16, DrBlPA 90, EncPR&S 89
Toshav, Nina Lorraine BiDrAPA 89
Toshaway WhNaAH
Tosheff, Julij G BiDrAPA 89
Toshihiro, Katauama 1928- WhoAmA 91
Toshiko 1929- BioIn 16
Toshiro PenDiDA 89
Toshua WhNaAH
Tosi, Laurence A., Jr. 1935- St&PR 91
Tosi, Oscar I. 1929- WhoAm 90
Tosi, Pier Francesco 1653?-1732 PenDiMP
Tosic, Silvana Cecelia 1961- WhoAmW 91
Tosk, Nadine D. 1955- ODwPR 91
Toskos, Elizabeth Ann 1941- WhoAmW 91
Tosky, Julian 1925- BiDrAPA 89
Tossberg, Frederick B. St&PR 91
Tossell, Julia Weinstein BiDrAPA 89
Tossizza, Evangelos Averoff- 1910-1990 BioIn 16
Tostado, Maria Elena 1940- WhoHisp 91
Tostanoski, John E. 1953- WhoAm 90, WhoEmL 91
Tosteson, Daniel Charles 1925- WhoAm 90
Tosteson, Heather 1950- WhoWrEP 89
Tostevin, Lola Lemire 1937- FemiCLE
Tosti-Vasey, Joanne Louise 1953- WhoAmW 91
Tostrup, Jacob 1806-1890 PenDiDA 89
Tosunlar, Akif Zafer 1950- WhoWor 91
Totaro, David J. 1947- St&PR 91
Totaro, J Burt St&PR 91
Totaro, James M. 1956- St&PR 91
Totels, Darlene 1958- WhoAmW 91
Totenberg, Amy Mil 1950- WhoEmL 91
Totenberg, Jill 1947- ODwPR 91
Totenberg, Roman 1911- IntWWM 90, PenDiMP, WhoAm 90
Toter, Benjamin 1940- St&PR 91
Toter, Kimberly Mrowiec 1956- WhoAmW 91, WhoEmL 91, WhoWor 91
Totero, Nestor John 1907- BiDrAPA 89
Totero, Nestor John 1907-1989 BioIn 16
Totfalusi Kis, Miklos 1650-1702 BioIn 16
Toth, Aladar PenDiMP
Toth, Alex 1928- EncACom
Toth, Anne Patten 1947- WhoAmW 91
Toth, Anthony Wayne 1949- WhoEmL 91
Toth, Bruce Anthony 1965- WhoE 91
Toth, Carl 1947- WhoAmA 91
Toth, Christina Ann 1947- WhoEmL 91
Toth, Claire E. 1958- WhoEmL 91
Toth, Elizabeth Levay WhoAmW 91
Toth, Erzsebet 1951- EncCoWW
Toth, Gabor Andras 1954- WhoE 91
Toth, Georgina Gy 1932- WhoAmA 91
Toth, Gwendolyn Joyce 1955- WhoAmW 91
Toth, Imre Abraham 1921- WhoWor 91
Toth, Judit 1936- EncCoWW
Toth, Laura Anne 1949- WhoAmW 91
Toth, Michele K BiDrAPA 89
Toth, Paul 1935- Ballpl 90
Toth, Peter Wolf BioIn 16
Toth, Richard J. 1947- ODwPR 91
Toth, Robert Charles 1928- WhoAm 90
Toth, Stephen Michael 1946- WhoSSW 91
Toth, Susan Allen BioIn 16
Toth, Susan Erickson Allen 1940- WhoWrEP 89
Toth, William J. 1936- St&PR 91
Totis, Tony Floriano 1948- WhoSSW 91
Totman, Conrad Davis 1934- WhoAm 90
Totman, Patrick Steven 1944- St&PR 91, WhoAm 90
Toto EncPR&S 89
Totopotomoi WhNaAH
Totopotomoy WhNaAH
Totten, Dwight L. 1944- St&PR 91
Totten, George Oakley, III 1922- WhoAm 90
Totten, Vicken Yuriko 1953- WhoEmL 91
Totter, Audrey 1918- BioIn 16
Totter, John Randolph 1914- WhoAm 90
Tottle, John AuBYP 90
Tottopottomoi WhNaAH
Totty, Shirley Jean 1937- WhoSSW 91
Tou Hsien WomWR
Tou, Jen-sie Hsu 1936- WhoAmW 91
Tou, Julius T. 1926- WhoAm 90
Toubon, Jacques 1941- BiDFrPL, WhoWor 91
Touborg, Margaret Earley Bowers 1941- WhoE 91
Touby, Kathleen A. BioIn 16
Touby, Kathleen Anita 1943- WhoSSW 91
Toucey, Isaac 1796-1869 BiDrUSE 89
Touchard, Jacques Jean Henry 1921- WhoWor 91
Touchet, Eleanor BiDEWW
Touchett, John Louis 1933- St&PR 91
Touchin, Colin Michael 1953- IntWWM 90
Touchstone, Billie L. WhoWrEP 89
Touchstone, Martha Jones 1948- WhoAmW 91
Touchstone, W. Joseph WhoE 91
Touchstone, William J 1948- BiDrAPA 89
Touchton, Robert Allen 1952- WhoSSW 91
Touffaire, Pierre Julien 1933- WhoWor 91
Tougas, Roger C. 1936- St&PR 91
Touger, Judy B. 1942- St&PR 91
Tough, Allen Mac Neill 1936- WhoWor 91
Tough, Dave BioIn 16
Touliatos, Diane Helen 1949- IntWWM 90
Toulios, Vassiliki BiDrAPA 89
Toulis, Vasilios 1931- WhoAmA 91
Toulmin, Peter Noyes 1927- St&PR 91
Toulmin, Priestley, III 1930- WhoAm 90
Toulmin, Stephen 1922- WorAu 1980 [port]
Toulmin, Stephen Edelston 1922- WhoAm 90
Toulouse, Robert Bartell 1918- WhoAm 90
Toulouse-Lautrec, Henri 1864-1901 IntDcAA 90
Toulouse-Lautrec, Henri de 1864-1901 BioIn 16, WorAlBi
Toulson, Shirley 1924- FemiCLE
Touma, Elie Fawzi 1949- WhoWor 91
Toumey, Hubert John WhoAm 90
Toupin, Arthur Vernon 1921- St&PR 91
Toupin, Harold Ovid 1927- WhoAm 90
Toupin, Paul 1918- OxCCanT
Toups, John M. 1926- St&PR 91
Toups, Kathleen M 1959- BiDrAPA 89
Tour, Robert Louis 1918- WhoWor 91
Tourangeau, Adolphe 1831-1894 DcCanB 12
Tourangeau, David Matthew 1939- St&PR 91
Tourassis, Vassilios Dimitrios 1958- WhoWor 91
Touray, Njogu 1959- BioIn 16
Tourel, Jennie 1899-1973 PenDiMP
Touretz, Lillian Carole Conrad 1923- WhoAmW 91
Touretz, William 1915- St&PR 91
Tourgeman, Eli A. 1945- WhoHisp 91
Tourigny-Rivard, Marie-France BiDrAPA 89
Tourjman, Smadar Valerie BiDrAPA 89
Tourkow, Frederick R. 1918- St&PR 91
Tourkow, Lawrence P BiDrAPA 89
Tourlentes, Thomas T 1922- BiDrAPA 89
Tourlentes, Thomas Theodore 1922- WhoAm 90
Tournachon, Gaspard Felix 1820-1910 BioIn 16
Tourneur, Cyril 1575?-1626 BioIn 16
Tourneur, Maurice 1876-1961 BioIn 16
Tourney, Garfield 1927- BiDrAPA 89
Tournier, Michel BioIn 16
Tournier, Michel 1924- CurBio 90 [port], MajTwCW, WhoWor 91
Tournillon, Nicholas Brady 1933- St&PR 91, WhoAm 90
Tournimparte, Alessandra ConAu 33NR, MajTwCW
Touron-Martin, Edilberto BiDrAPA 89
Tours, Frank E. 1877-1963 OxCPMus
Tourtelier, Michel Francois 1937- WhoWor 91
Tourtellot, Robert C. 1939- St&PR 91
Tourtellotte, Charles Dee 1931- WhoAm 90
Tourtellotte, Mills Charlton 1922- WhoWor 91
Tourtet, Christiane Andree 1945- WhoAmW 91
Tourville, Charles Arthur 1941- St&PR 91
Tous de Torres, Luz M. 1944- WhoSSW 91
Touscany, William J. 1918- St&PR 91
Tousey, Richard 1908- WhoAm 90
Tousey, Sanford AuBYP 90
Tousignant, Claude 1932- WhoAmA 91
Tousignant, Jacques 1948- St&PR 91
Tousley, J. C. AmLegL
Tousley, Martha Merritt 1943- WhoAmW 91
Toussaint Louverture 1743?-1803 BioIn 16
Toussaint, Allen 1938- OxCPMus
Toussaint, Francois-Xavier 1821-1895 DcCanB 12
Toussaint, Frederick John 1936- St&PR 91
Toussaint, Jeanne Isabella 1964- WhoAmW 91
Toussaint, Rose Marie 1956- WhoAmW 91
Toussaint, Wayne E. 1918- WhoAm 90
Toussaint du Wast, Nicole BioIn 16
Toussaint L'Ouverture, Francois 1743-1803 WorAlBi
Toussieng, Povl W 1918- BiDrAPA 89
Tousson, Maurice WhoAm 90
Touster, Irwin AuBYP 90
Touster, Saul 1925- WhoAm 90
Toutant, Claire BiDrAPA 89
Toutant, William 1948- IntWWM 90
Toutin, Jean PenDiDA 89
Toutz, James Otto 1932- St&PR 91
Touvier, Paul BioIn 16
Touyz, Stephen William 1950- WhoWor 91
Tovar, Cesar 1940- Ballpl 90
Tovar, Dora Olivia 1963- WhoAmW 91
Tovar, Getulio V 1948- BiDrAPA 89
Tovar, Lorenzo 1942- WhoHisp 91
Tovish, Harold 1921- WhoAm 90, WhoAmA 91, WhoE 91
Tovstonogov, Georgi 1915-1989 AnObit 1989, BioIn 16
Tow, Charles W, Jr. BiDrAPA 89
Tow, Marc Raymond 1951- WhoEmL 91
Tow, Suzanne 1950- WhoAmW 91
Towar, Jeanne C. St&PR 91
Towater, Ronnie Andrew 1953- WhoSSW 91
Towbin, Abraham Robert 1935- WhoAm 90
Towbin, Belmont 1910- St&PR 91
Towbin, Carl 1924- BiDrAPA 89
Towbin, Kenneth Evan BiDrAPA 89
Towbin, Richard Bruce 1948- WhoEmL 91
Towe, Nancy Ellen Carpenter 1941- WhoAmW 91
Towe, Rolf Harvy 1938- St&PR 91
Towell, Linda Ladd 1948- WhoSSW 91
Towell, S Gilmer 1928- St&PR 91
Towell, Thomas 1941- St&PR 91
Towell, Timothy Lathrop 1934- WhoAm 90, WhoE 91, WhoWor 91
Towell, William Earnest 1916- WhoAm 90
Tower, Burton Harry 1909- WhoE 91
Tower, Charlemagne 1848-1923 BioIn 16
Tower, David C BiDrAPA 89
Tower, Ensley Anthony 1938- St&PR 91
Tower, H. L. 1932- St&PR 91
Tower, Horace Linwood, III 1932- WhoAm 90
Tower, James 1919-1988 BioIn 16
Tower, James 1945- St&PR 91
Tower, Janet May 1925- WhoAmW 91
Tower, Joan 1938- IntWWM 90
Tower, Joan Peabody 1938- WhoAm 90, WhoAmW 91
Tower, John BioIn 16
Tower, John G. NewYTBS 90 [port]
Tower, John Goodwin 1925- WhoAm 90, WorAlBi
Tower, Lucia E BiDrAPA 89
Tower, Ray J. 1918- St&PR 91
Tower, Raymond C. 1925- St&PR 91
Tower, Roni Beth 1943- WhoAmW 91
Towers, Bernard Leonard 1922- WhoAm 90
Towers, Graham F. 1897-1975 BioIn 16
Towers, Irwin BioIn 16
Towers, John 1921- St&PR 91, WhoAm 90
Towers, John Henry 1885-1955 BioIn 16
Towers, June Crozier 1922- WhoAmW 91
Towers, Lawrence Alan 1952- WhoEmL 91
Towers, Regina ConAu 130
Towers, Robert 1923- ConAu 132
Towers, Robert, Jr. 1923- WhoAm 90
Towers, Thomas W. ODwPR 91
Towery, Curtis Kent 1954- WhoEmL 91, WhoSSW 91, WhoWor 91
Towery, Matthew Allen, Sr. 1959- WhoSSW 91
Towery, O.B., III 1945- BiDrAPA 89
Towey, Anne Patricia 1945- WhoE 91
Towey, J. Desmond 1937- ODwPR 91
Towey, Marie Elizabeth 1934- WhoAmW 91, WhoWor 91
Towill, John Bell 1907- St&PR 91
Towl, E. Clinton NewYTBS 90 [port]
Towl, E. Clinton 1905-1990 BioIn 16
Towle, Dean Leon 1927- BiDrAPA 89
Towle, Edwin Sargent 1843-1931 AmLegL
Towle, Leland Hill 1931- WhoAm 90
Towle, Nadine Valery 1947- WhoAmW 91
Towlen, Gary BioIn 16
Towler, John Orchard 1937- WhoWrEP 89
Towler, Martin L BiDrAPA 89
Towles, Donald Blackburn 1927- St&PR 91, WhoAm 90
Towles, Louis Palmer, Jr. 1943- WhoSSW 91
Towles, Nat 1905-1963 BioIn 16
Towles, Stokley Porter 1935- St&PR 91, WhoAm 90
Town, Harold Barling 1924- WhoAm 90, WhoAmA 91
Town, Joe R. 1943- St&PR 91
Town, Joe Ray 1943- WhoAm 90
Town, Stephen Joe 1952- IntWWM 90
Town, Susan Barbara 1947- WhoAmW 91
Town, William Richard 1942- WhoE 91
Towne, Bonnie AuBYP 90
Towne, Claudia Ciacco 1945- WhoE 91
Towne, Edward S. 1933- St&PR 91
Towne, Gary Spaulding 1950- IntWWM 90
Towne, Lockwood 1915- BiDrAPA 89
Towne, Mary 1934- AuBYP 90
Towne, Richard Peale 1935- St&PR 91
Towne, Robert 1936- BioIn 16, ConTFT 8
Towne, Ross C. 1944- WhoAm 90
Towne, Ruth Warner 1917- WhoAmW 91
Towne, Stuart TwCCr&M 91
Towner, George Rutherford 1933- WhoWrEP 89
Towner, Lawrence William 1921- WhoAm 90, WhoWor 91
Towner, Mark Andrew WhoAmA 91
Towner, Naomi Whiting 1940- WhoAmW 91
Towner, Ralph BioIn 16
Townes, Bobby Joe 1932- WhoSSW 91
Townes, Charles H. 1915- BioIn 16, WorAlBi
Townes, Charles Hard 1915- WhoAm 90, WhoWor 91
Townes, Edgar Eggleston, Jr. 1906- WhoSSW 91, WhoWor 91
Townes, Philip Leonard 1927- WhoAm 90
Townes, Stephen Douglas 1952- St&PR 91
Townesend, Frances Eliza Hodgson Burnett 1849-1924 BioIn 16
Townhill, Dennis William 1925- IntWWM 90
Townley, Hugh 1923- WhoAmA 91
Townley, John Mark 1932- WhoAm 90, WhoWrEP 89
Townley, Kathy Joy 1956- BiDrAPA 89
Townley, Lawrence Earl 1933- St&PR 91
Townley, Linda Rose 1947- WhoAmW 91
Townley, Merlin C 1927- BiDrAPA 89
Townley, Preston BioIn 16
Townley, Preston 1939- St&PR 91, WhoAm 90
Towns, Edolphus 1934- BlkAmsC [port], WhoAm 90, WhoE 91
Towns, George A 1870-1961 EarBlAP
Towns-Spencer, Gina Anita 1965- WhoAmW 91
Townsend, A Paul, Jr. 1905- St&PR 91
Townsend, Alair Ane 1942- WhoAmW 91
Townsend, Anna Stofflet 1899- WhoAmW 91
Townsend, Arthur Thomas 1957- WhoSSW 91
Townsend, Betty Jean 1934- WhoSSW 91
Townsend, Charles Coe 1917- WhoAm 90
Townsend, Charles Edward 1932- WhoAm 90
Townsend, Cheryl Ann 1957- WhoWrEP 89
Townsend, David D. 1927- St&PR 91
Townsend, David Dallam 1927- WhoSSW 91
Townsend, David Lee 1954- St&PR 91
Townsend, Don 1908- St&PR 91
Townsend, Douglas 1921- IntWWM 90
Townsend, Earl Cunningham, Jr. 1914- WhoAm 90, WhoWor 91
Townsend, Edward Allen 1942- WhoAm 90
Townsend, Edward Thomas 1910- WhoAm 90
Townsend, Eleanor M BiDrAPA 89
Townsend, Francis E. 1867-1960 WorAlBi

Townsend, Frank Marion 1914- *WhoAm 90, WhoSSW 91, WhoWor 91*
Townsend, Gavin Edward 1956- *WhoAmA 91*
Townsend, Harold Guyon, Jr. 1924- *WhoAm 90*
Townsend, Irene Fogleman 1932- *WhoAmW 91, WhoE 91, WhoSSW 91, WhoWor 91*
Townsend, J Benjamin 1918- *WhoAmA 91*
Townsend, Jack 1879-1963 *Ballpl 90*
Townsend, Jacqueline Ariza 1961- *WhoAmW 91*
Townsend, James Douglas 1959- *WhoEmL 91, WhoWor 91*
Townsend, Jane Kaltenbach 1922- *WhoAmW 91*
Townsend, Janet *AuBYP 90*
Townsend, Jean 1921- *WhoAmA 91*
Townsend, Jennifer Elizabeth 1967- *WhoAmW 91*
Townsend, Jerry L. 1947- *St&PR 91*
Townsend, Job 1699-1765 *PenDiDA 89*
Townsend, John 1819-1892 *DcCanB 12, OxCCanT*
Townsend, John F *WhoAmA 91*
Townsend, John Ford 1936- *WhoAm 90*
Townsend, John Holt 1947- *WhoEmL 91*
Townsend, John Michael 1947- *WhoEmL 91*
Townsend, John Rowe *BioIn 16*
Townsend, John Rowe 1922- *AuBYP 90*
Townsend, John William 1949- *WhoSSW 91*
Townsend, John William, Jr. 1924- *WhoAm 90*
Townsend, Josephine Catherine 1960- *WhoAmW 91*
Townsend, Katherine Irwin 1952- *BiDrAPA 89*
Townsend, Kathleen *BioIn 16*
Townsend, Kim Renuart 1955- *WhoSSW 91*
Townsend, Lee 1895-1965 *WhoAmA 91N*
Townsend, Leroy B. 1933- *WhoAm 90*
Townsend, Linda Louise 1952- *WhoSSW 91*
Townsend, Lisa Camille 1965- *WhoAmW 91*
Townsend, Lynn Alfred 1919- *EncABHB 5 [port]*
Townsend, M. Wilbur 1912- *WhoAm 90*
Townsend, Margaret Elizabeth 1947- *WhoSSW 91*
Townsend, Marjorie Rhodes 1930- *WhoAm 90, WhoAmW 91*
Townsend, Mark Harold *BiDrAPA 89*
Townsend, Marvin J 1915- *WhoAmA 91*
Townsend, Mary 1832-1901 *FemiCLE*
Townsend, Maurice Karlen 1926- *WhoAm 90, WhoWor 91*
Townsend, Melvin C. 1927- *St&PR 91*
Townsend, Miles Averill 1935- *WhoAm 90*
Townsend, Neal 1934- *WhoAmA 91*
Townsend, Okey 1929- *WhoSSW 91*
Townsend, P Coleman, Jr. 1945- *St&PR 91*
Townsend, Pamela Gwin 1945- *WhoEmL 91*
Townsend, Patricia Lee 1955- *WhoAmW 91*
Townsend, Paul Brorstrom 1919- *WhoE 91*
Townsend, Phinn William 1927- *St&PR 91*
Townsend, Preston Coleman 1945- *WhoAm 90*
Townsend, Ralph N. 1931- *St&PR 91*
Townsend, Rhonda Joyce 1960- *WhoAmW 91*
Townsend, Richard Kennard 1939- *St&PR 91*
Townsend, Robert *BioIn 16*
Townsend, Robert 1956- *DrBlPA 90*
Townsend, Robert Glenn, Jr. 1929- *WhoSSW 91*
Townsend, Robert Wilton 1924- *St&PR 91*
Townsend, Storm D 1937- *WhoAmA 91*
Townsend, Sue *BioIn 16*
Townsend, Sue 1945- *FemiCLE*
Townsend, Sue 1946- *ConLC 61 [port], MajTwCW*
Townsend, Susan Elaine 1946- *WhoAmW 91, WhoWor 91*
Townsend, Terry *WhoAm 90*
Townsend, Terry 1920- *ODwPR 91, St&PR 91, WhoAmW 91, WhoE 91*
Townsend, Teryl Archer 1938- *WhoAmW 91, WhoE 91*
Townsend, Thatcher L., Jr. 1932- *St&PR 91*
Townsend, Theophila *FemiCLE*
Townsend, Theophila 1656-1692 *BiDEWW*
Townsend, Thomas Gerald 1941- *WhoSSW 91*
Townsend, Thomas P., Jr. 1937- *St&PR 91*
Townsend, Thomas Perkins 1917- *WhoAm 90*
Townsend, Tom 1944- *BioIn 16*
Townsend, Tom David 1952- *WhoSSW 91*
Townsend, Vera B 1923- *WhoAmA 91*
Townsend, Walter R 1927- *BiDrAPA 89*
Townsend, Willa A. *EarBlAP*
Townsend, Willard 1895-1957 *WorAlBi*
Townsend Ezcurra, Andres 1915- *BioIn 16*
Townsend-Parchman, W.R. 1953- *BiDrAPA 89*
Townshend, Charles 1725-1767 *EncCRAm*
Townshend, Peter *EncPR&S 89*
Townshend, Peter 1945- *WhoAm 90, WorAlBi*
Townshend, Peter Dennis Blandford 1945- *IntWWM 90*
Townsley, Mary Elizabeth 1930- *WhoSSW 91*
Towsend, Richard Craig 1945- *WhoEmL 91*
Towsley, John E. 1950- *St&PR 91*
Towson, Sheldon K., Jr. 1927- *St&PR 91*
Toxey, Andrew F. 1927- *St&PR 91*
Toy, Arthur Dock Fon 1915- *WhoAm 90*
Toy, Atala Dorothy 1941- *WhoE 91*
Toy, Charles M *BiDrAPA 89*
Toy, Crawford Howell 1836-1919 *BioIn 16*
Toy, F. C. 1892-1988 *BioIn 16*
Toy, Jana M 1949- *BiDrAPA 89*
Toy, Karen W. 1962- *WhoAmW 91*
Toy, Madeline Shen 1926- *WhoAmW 91*
Toy, Malcolm Delano 1934- *WhoWor 91*
Toy, Theresa Maureen 1947- *WhoAmW 91*
Toy, Wing Noon 1926- *WhoAm 90*
Toyah 1958- *BioIn 16*
Toye, Geoffrey 1889-1942 *PenDiMP*
Toye, Wendy 1917- *WhoWor 91*
Toyen 1902-1980 *BiDWomA*
Toynbee, Arnold 1889-1975 *WorAlBi*
Toynbee, Arnold Joseph 1889-1975 *BioIn 16*
Toynbee, Philip *BioIn 16*
Toynbee, Philip 1916-1981 *DcNaB 1981*
Toyne, Marguerite Castles 1942- *WhoAmW 91*
Toyoda, Eiji *BioIn 16*
Toyoda, Eiji 1913- *WhoWor 91*
Toyoda, Shoichiro 1925- *WhoWor 91*
Toyomura, Dennis Takeshi 1926- *WhoAm 90, WhoWor 91*
Toyotomi Hideyori *EncJap*
Toyotomi Hideyoshi 1536-1598 *EncJap*
Toyozawa, Yutaka 1926- *WhoWor 91*
Toypurina *WhNaAH*
Toyser, Francine 1946- *WhoAmW 91*
Tozawa, Kenji 1949- *WhoWor 91*
Tozawa, Yasuhisa 1923- *WhoWor 91*
Tozer, Charles W. 1832- *AmLegL*
Tozer, Forrest Leigh 1922- *WhoAm 90*
Tozer, George Knowlton 1926- *St&PR 91*
Tozer, Theodore William 1957- *WhoEmL 91, WhoWor 91*
Tozer, W James, Jr. 1941- *St&PR 91*
Tozer, W. James, Jr. 1941- *WhoAm 90*
Tozer, William Thomas 1934- *St&PR 91*
Tozier, Allen J. 1942- *St&PR 91*
Tozman, Seymour 1938- *BiDrAPA 89*
Tozzer, Charles Phillip 1953- *WhoWor 91*
Tozzi, Giorgio 1923- *IntWWM 90, PenDiMP*
Trabal, Jose Francisco 1941- *WhoSSW 91*
Traber, Jim 1961- *Ballpl 90*
Trabert, Greg *BioIn 16*
Trabocco, Ronald Edward 1939- *WhoE 91*
Trabucco, John Edward 1946- *St&PR 91*
Trabulus, Norman *BiDrAPA 89*
Trac, F. *PenDiDA 89*
Trace, Eileene Cecelia 1958- *WhoE 91*
Tracer, Irving H 1932- *BiDrAPA 89*
Tracewski, Dick 1935- *Ballpl 90*
Tracey, Edward John 1931- *WhoAm 90*
Tracey, Jay Walter, Jr. 1925- *WhoAm 90*
Tracey, John M 1926- *BiDrAPA 89*
Tracey, Kenneth Louis 1946- *WhoSSW 91*
Tracey, Margaret *BioIn 16*
Trach, Robert John 1954- *WhoE 91*
Trachman, Susan B *BiDrAPA 89*
Trachman, Susan Bildner 1955- *WhoE 91*
Trachsel, Myrtle Jamison *AuBYP 90*
Trachsel, William Henry 1943- *St&PR 91, WhoAm 90*
Trachtenberg, Alexander *EncAL*
Trachtenberg, Bruce S. 1952- *ODwPR 91*
Trachtenberg, David 1935- *BiDrAPA 89*
Trachtenberg, Gloria P *WhoAmA 91*
Trachtenberg, Jacob *BiDrAPA 89*
Trachtenberg, Joan Ruth *BiDrAPA 89*
Trachtenberg, Lawrence 1956- *St&PR 91*
Trachtenberg, Marvin Lawrence 1939- *WhoAm 90*
Trachtenberg, Matthew J. 1953- *WhoAm 90, WhoE 91, WhoEmL 91, WhoWor 91*
Trachtenberg, Stephen Joel 1937- *WhoAm 90, WhoE 91*
Trachtman, Arnold S 1930- *WhoAmA 91*
Trachtman, Arnold Sheldon 1930- *WhoAm 90*
Trachtman, Leslie Stuart 1955- *WhoSSW 91*
Track, F. *PenDiDA 89*
Track, Gerhard 1934- *IntWWM 90*
Track, Micaela Maihart 1937- *IntWWM 90*
Tract, Harold M. 1926- *WhoAm 90*
Tractenberg, Paul L. 1938- *WhoE 91*
Tracton, Syndi Robin 1961- *WhoAmW 91*
Tracy, Alan Thomas 1947- *WhoAm 90*
Tracy, Aloise 1914- *WhoAmW 91*
Tracy, Barbara Marie 1945- *WhoAmW 91, WhoEmL 91, WhoSSW 91*
Tracy, Benjamin Franklin 1830-1915 *BiDrUSE 89*
Tracy, Berry Bryson 1933-1984 *WhoAmA 91N*
Tracy, Carley Dean 1923- *WhoAmW 91*
Tracy, Craig Arnold 1945- *WhoAm 90*
Tracy, Daniel LeRoy 1946- *WhoSSW 91*
Tracy, David 1939- *WhoAm 90*
Tracy, David M. 1924- *WhoAm 90*
Tracy, Dorothy Shea 1920- *WhoAmW 91*
Tracy, Elizabeth *WhoAmA 91*
Tracy, Else B P *BiDrAPA 89*
Tracy, Eugene Arthur 1927- *St&PR 91, WhoAm 90*
Tracy, Harry P. 1913- *St&PR 91*
Tracy, Honor Lilbush Wingfield 1913-1989 *BioIn 16*
Tracy, James Donald 1938- *WhoAm 90, WhoWrEP 89*
Tracy, Jean C. 1930- *St&PR 91*
Tracy, John Michael, III 1949- *WhoEmL 91*
Tracy, Karen Ann 1963- *WhoAmW 91*
Tracy, Lee 1898-1968 *WorAlBi*
Tracy, Lois Bartlett 1901- *WhoAmA 91*
Tracy, Lorna 1934- *ConAu 132*
Tracy, Marsha 1947- *BiDrAPA 89*
Tracy, Mary Elizabeth 1922- *WhoAmW 91*
Tracy, Michael 1943- *WhoAmA 91*
Tracy, Michael Cameron 1952- *WhoAm 90*
Tracy, Neal Thomas 1952- *IntWWM 90*
Tracy, Philip R. 1942- *St&PR 91*
Tracy, Richard E. 1934- *WhoSSW 91*
Tracy, Robert 1928- *WhoAm 90*
Tracy, Spencer 1900-1967 *BioIn 16, WorAlBi*
Tracy, Stephen V. 1941- *WhoWrEP 89*
Tracy, Stephen Victor 1941- *WhoAm 90*
Tracy, Thomas Kit 1938- *WhoAm 90*
Tracy, Thomas Miles 1936- *WhoAm 90*
Tracy, William Lee 1947- *St&PR 91*
Trader Vic *AuBYP 90*
Trader, David Walter *BiDrAPA 89*
Trader, Ella King Newsom 1838-1919 *BioIn 16*
Trader, Herbert Frederick 1937- *WhoAm 90*
Trader, Joseph Edgar 1946- *WhoAm 90, WhoEmL 91*
Trader, Mary Elizabeth 1936- *WhoAmW 91*
Trado, Charles E *BiDrAPA 89*
Tradup, Allison *BioIn 16*
Tradup, Janetta Freeman 1951- *WhoAmW 91*
Traeger, Charles Henry, III 1942- *WhoAm 90*
Traeger, Jules 1920- *WhoWor 91*
Traeger, Norman Lewis 1939- *St&PR 91*
Traendly, Wallace F. 1910-1989 *BioIn 16*
Traenkle, Jeffrey William 1934- *St&PR 91*
Traerup, Birthe 1930- *IntWWM 90*
Traerup Sark, Einar 1921- *IntWWM 90*
Trafas, Nan 1960- *WhoAmW 91*
Traffas, Wayne H. 1936- *St&PR 91*
Traffic *EncPR&S 89, OxCPMus*
Trafford, Lord 1932-1989 *AnObit 1989*
Trafford, Edmund 1948- *IntWWM 90*
Trafford, Rebeckah *BiDEWW*
Trafford of Falmer, Baron of 1932-1989 *BioIn 16*
Traficant, James A., Jr. 1941- *WhoAm 90*
Traficant, Ronald Edward *BiDrAPA 89*
Traficante, Daniel Dominick 1933- *WhoWor 91*
Trafton, Edwin Burnham 1853-1922 *BioIn 16*
Trafton, Jack R. 1948- *St&PR 91*
Trafton, Kipp *BioIn 16*
Trafton, R. M. *St&PR 91*
Tragakiss, Michael J. 1932- *St&PR 91*
Tragarz, Nancy D. 1943- *St&PR 91*
Trager, Bernard H. 1906- *WhoE 91*
Trager, David G. 1937- *WhoAm 90*
Trager, Eugene Peretz 1933- *BiDrAPA 89*
Trager, Neil C *WhoAmA 91*
Trager, Neil Charles 1947- *WhoE 91*
Trager, Neil Jay 1939- *St&PR 91*
Trager, Philip 1935- *WhoAm 90, WhoAmA 91*
Trager, William 1910- *WhoAm 90*
Tragert, Joseph Paul 1964- *WhoE 91*
Trageser, Raymond Mattern, Jr. 1934- *WhoE 91, WhoWor 91*
Tragesser, Charles W. 1938- *St&PR 91*
Tragle, William H *BiDrAPA 89*
Tragos, George Euripedes 1949- *WhoWor 91*
Tragos, William George 1934- *WhoAm 90*
Trahan, Ellen Vauneil 1941- *WhoAmW 91*
Trahan, James Ray *BiDrAPA 89*
Trahan, Loralice Anne 1955- *WhoSSW 91*
Trahan, Margaret Fritchey 1934- *WhoWor 91*
Trahanovsky-Orletsky, Ann Elizabeth 1926- *WhoSSW 91*
Trahern, Joseph Baxter, Jr. 1937- *WhoAm 90*
Traherne, Michael *ConAu 132*
Trahey, Nancy Marie 1941- *WhoE 91*
Trahms, George D *BiDrAPA 89*
Traicoff, Ellen Braden *WhoWor 91*
Traicoff, George 1932- *WhoAm 90*
Traicoff, Sandra M. 1944- *WhoAm 90*
Traigis, Mary Elizabeth 1963- *WhoAmW 91*
Trail, George Arthur, III 1936- *WhoAm 90, WhoWor 91*
Trail, Jack R. 1931- *St&PR 91*
Traill, Catharine Parr *DcCanB 12*
Traill, Catharine Parr 1802-1899 *DcLB 99 [port], FemiCLE*
Trailovic, Mira *BioIn 16*
Trails, Mayette *WhoWrEP 89*
Train, Arthur 1875-1945 *TwCCr&M 91*
Train, David 1935- *St&PR 91*
Train, George J 1907- *BiDrAPA 89*
Train, Harry Depue, II 1927- *WhoAm 90*
Train, Jack Durkee 1922- *WhoAm 90*
Train, John 1928- *ConAu 30NR, WhoAm 90, WhoWor 91, WhoWrEP 89*
Train, John B 1913- *BiDrAPA 89*
Traina, Albert Salvatore 1927- *WhoAm 90*
Traina, Gale Ann 1941- *WhoE 91*
Traina, Richard Paul 1937- *WhoAm 90, WhoE 91*
Trainer, Ellen McCart 1922- *St&PR 91*
Trainer, Orvel Leroy 1925- *WhoWrEP 89*
Trainer, Raymond Edward 1947- *St&PR 91*
Trainer, William Francis 1939- *St&PR 91*
Traini, Francesco *IntDcAA 90*
Trainor, Bernard Edmund 1928- *WhoAm 90*
Trainor, Bernard Michael 1954- *St&PR 91*
Trainor, Charles 1953- *BioIn 16*
Trainor, Charles J. 1937- *St&PR 91*
Trainor, Francis Rice 1929- *WhoE 91*
Trainor, Howard Edgar 1943- *St&PR 91*
Trainor, Jean Ann, Sr. 1938- *WhoE 91*
Trainor, Ken *BioIn 16*
Trainor, Lillian 1936- *WhoAmW 91, WhoE 91*
Traisman, Howard Sevin 1923- *WhoAm 90*
Trajan 53-117 *WorAlBi*
Trakas, Demetrius A *BiDrAPA 89*
Trakas, Deno 1952- *WhoWrEP 89*
Trakas, George 1944- *WhoAmA 91*
Trakis, Louis 1927- *WhoAmA 91*
Trakofler, Carl J. 1936- *St&PR 91*
Trakselis, John Joseph 1945- *St&PR 91*
Traldi, Pietro 1948- *WhoWor 91*
Trama, Ugo 1932- *IntWWM 90*
Tramaglini, Salvatore L., Jr. 1941- *St&PR 91*
Trambley, Estela Portillo 1936- *BioIn 16, WhoHisp 91*
Tramburg, Robert Steven 1947- *St&PR 91*
Tramel, Gregory Lee 1960- *WhoSSW 91*
Tramel, Thomas Milton 1959- *WhoSSW 91*
Tramiel, Jack *BioIn 16*
Tramiel, Jack 1928- *WhoAm 90*
Tramiel, Sam 1950- *St&PR 91*
Tramier, Henry Jean Louis 1938- *WhoWor 91*
Trammell, Alan *BioIn 16*
Trammell, Alan 1958- *Ballpl 90, WorAlBi*
Trammell, Dennis C. 1940- *St&PR 91*
Trammell, Dennis L. 1947- *St&PR 91*
Trammell, Herbert Eugene 1927- *WhoAm 90*
Trammell, Homer Conrad 1937- *WhoWor 91*
Trammell, Jeffrey *ODwPR 91*
Trammell, Philip Wilton 1954- *WhoSSW 91*
Trammell, Robert Joel 1941- *WhoSSW 91*
Trammer, Monte Irvin 1951- *WhoE 91*
Trammps, The *EncPR&S 89*
Tramontano, Anthony Richard 1933- *St&PR 91*
Tramonte, Barbara Paturick 1946- *WhoAmW 91*
Trampler, Walter 1915- *PenDiMP*
Trampler, Walter 1925- *IntWWM 90*
Tramuta, Gregory J *BiDrAPA 89*
Tramuto, James Arnold 1948- *St&PR 91*
Tran, Alan R., Jr. 1945- *St&PR 91*
Tran, Christine Thien-Huong 1958- *WhoSSW 91*
Tran, Dao Xuanthi *BiDrAPA 89*
Tran, Dung Phuoc 1949- *BiDrAPA 89, WhoE 91*
Tran, Henry Bang Q. 1952- *WhoEmL 91*
Tran, Hien Tien 1951- *BiDrAPA 89*

Tran, John Kim-Son Tan 1945- *WhoE 91, WhoWor 91*
Tran, Long Trieu 1956- *WhoSSW 91*
Tran, Minh Son 1938- *WhoWor 91*
Tran, Nang Tri 1948- *WhoWor 91*
Tran, Nhung Thihong *BiDrAPA 89*
Tran, Pamela Vinh *BiDrAPA 89*
Tran, Phuong My *BiDrAPA 89*
Tran, Pierre Van *BiDrAPA 89*
Tran, Quang Hai 1944- *WhoWor 91*
Tran, Tim 1950- *St&PR 91*
Tran, Tuong Quang 1957- *BiDrAPA 89*
Tran Trung, Hien 1962- *WhoWor 91*
Tran-Viet, Tu 1949- *WhoWor 91*
Tranbarger, Ossie Elmo 1914- *WhoWrEP 89*
Tranchell, Peter Andrew 1922- *IntWWM 90*
Tranchina, Thomas J. *St&PR 91*
Tranchitella, Vincent Edward 1938- *WhoE 91*
Trandel, Richard Samuel 1937- *WhoSSW 91*
Trane, Fredrick Charles 1950- *WhoSSW 91*
Traner, Donna Marie 1958- *WhoAmW 91*
Tranfaglia, Michael Robert *BiDrAPA 89*
Trang, John Milton 1950- *WhoSSW 91*
Tranggono, Retno Iswari 1939- *WhoWor 91*
Trangkasombat, Umaporn Sriprasidh 1955- *WhoE 91*
Trangle, Michael Arno *BiDrAPA 89*
Trank, Douglas Monty 1944- *WhoAm 90*
Trank, Lynn Edgar 1918- *WhoAmA 91*
Tranquada, Robert Ernest 1930- *WhoAm 90*
Tranquillo, Mary Dora 1943- *WhoSSW 91*
Transou, Lynda Lew 1949- *WhoAmW 91*
Transou, Thomas Bowie 1935- *St&PR 91*
Transtroemer, Tomas 1931- *ConAu 129*
Transtromer, Tomas 1931- *DcScanL*
Transue, Seward M 1910- *BiDrAPA 89*
Transue, William Reagle 1914- *WhoE 91*
Tranter, John 1948- *IntWWM 90*
Tranter, Nigel 1909- *AuBYP 90*
Trantham, William Eugene 1929- *WhoAm 90*
Trantowski, Kenneth G. 1948- *ODwPR 91*
Traore, Jean *WhoWor 91*
Traore, Moussa 1936- *WhoWor 91*
Traore, Ngolo *WhoWor 91*
Trap, M. *WhoWrEP 89*
Trapaga, Rene David Michel- 1942- *BioIn 16*
Trapani, Frank *BioIn 16*
Trapasso, Patricia M. 1932- *St&PR 91*
Trapasso, Victor G. *BioIn 16*
Trapasso, Victor Gerard 1935- *WhoSSW 91*
Traphagan, Kathleen E. 1958- *WhoAmW 91*
Traphagan, Tracy Lynne 1964- *WhoAmW 91*
Traphagen, Ethel 1882-1963 *WhoAmA 91N*
Traphagen, Ross Edwin, Jr. 1923- *St&PR 91*
Trapido, Michael Mark 1945- *BiDrAPA 89*
Trapier, Pierre Pinckney Alston 1897-1957 *WhoAmA 91N*
Trapl, Herbert F *BiDrAPA 89*
Trapnel, Anna *FemiCLE*
Trapnel, Anna 1622?- *BiDEWW*
Trapnell, Richard H 1928- *BiDrAPA 89*
Trapold, Milton Alvin 1936- *WhoAm 90*
Trapolin, Frank Winter 1913- *WhoSSW 91, WhoWor 91*
Trapp, Adeline *BioIn 16*
Trapp, Carl E *BiDrAPA 89*
Trapp, Erich 1942- *WhoWor 91*
Trapp, Frank Anderson 1922- *WhoAm 90, WhoAmA 91, WhoE 91*
Trapp, Fritz C E *BiDrAPA 89*
Trapp, George A 1933- *BiDrAPA 89*
Trapp, George J. *ODwPR 91*
Trapp, George Joseph 1947- *St&PR 91*
Trapp, Gerald Bernard 1932- *WhoAm 90*
Trapp, Henry, Jr. 1924- *WhoE 91*
Trapp, Kathryn Anne 1957- *WhoAmW 91*
Trapp, Maria von *BioIn 16*
Trapp, Marvin D. 1929- *St&PR 91*
Trapp, Peter Jarl Rudolf 1945- *WhoE 91*
Trapp, Peter Paul 1944- *St&PR 91*
Trapp, Walter Franklin 1950- *WhoAm 90*
Trappe, James Martin 1931- *WhoAm 90*
Trappler, Brian 1951- *BiDrAPA 89*
Trask, Betty M. 1928- *WhoAmW 91*
Trask, Betty May 1928- *WhoWrEP 89*
Trask, Blair Dwayne 1933- *St&PR 91*
Trask, Brad *ODwPR 91*
Trask, Charles Reese, Jr. 1946- *WhoSSW 91*
Trask, David Frederic 1929- *WhoAm 90*
Trask, George W., Jr. 1947- *St&PR 91*
Trask, Jonathan *ConAu 31NR*
Trask, Tallman Harlow, Jr. 1918- *St&PR 91*
Trasvina, John D. 1958- *WhoHisp 91*
Tratnik, Lek 1932- *BiDrAPA 89, WhoSSW 91*
Trattner, Robert E *BiDrAPA 89*
Traub, Charles *WhoE 91*
Traub, Charles H 1945- *WhoAmA 91*
Traub, Ella B 1911- *BiDrAPA 89*
Traub, George Michael 1958- *WhoSSW 91*
Traub, Joseph Frederick 1932- *WhoAm 90*
Traub, Leo M *BiDrAPA 89*
Traub, Marvin S. *BioIn 16*
Traub, Marvin S. 1925- *St&PR 91*
Traub, Marvin Stuart 1925- *WhoAm 90*
Traub, Todd Steven 1952- *WhoE 91*
Trauba, Thomas Kent *BiDrAPA 89*
Traube, Sylvia 1909-1989 *BioIn 16*
Traube, Sylvia G *BiDrAPA 89*
Traubel, Helen 1899-1972 *PenDiMP, WorAlBi*
Trauber, A Anthony 1939- *St&PR 91*
Trauerman, Margy Ann *WhoAmA 91*
Trauger, Donald Byron 1920- *WhoAm 90*
Traughber, Sam Hendley 1935- *WhoSSW 91*
Traugott, Arthur R 1940- *BiDrAPA 89*
Traugott, Elizabeth Closs 1939- *WhoAm 90, WhoWrEP 89*
Traugott, Fritz A. 1928- *WhoE 91*
Traulsen, Harry *BioIn 16*
Traulsen, Harry, Sr. *NewYTBS 90*
Traum, Jerome S. 1935- *WhoAm 90*
Traum, Zeev *BioIn 16*
Trauner, Alexandre 1906- *ConDes 90*
Traurig, Leona 1934- *WhoAmW 91*
Trausch, Paul Joseph 1941- *St&PR 91, WhoAm 90*
Trausch, Thomas V 1943- *WhoAmA 91*
Trauscht, Donald Charles 1933- *St&PR 91*
Trausti, Jon *DcScanL*
Traut, Carol Enola *BiDrAPA 89*
Traut, Donald Louis 1932- *St&PR 91*
Traut, John D. 1926- *St&PR 91*
Traut, Walther 1934- *WhoWor 91*
Trautlein, Donald Henry 1926- *St&PR 91*
Trautman, Beverly John 1937- *St&PR 91*
Trautman, Donald Theodore 1924- *WhoAm 90*
Trautman, Donald W. 1936- *WhoAm 90*
Trautman, Gerald H. 1912- *St&PR 91*
Trautman, Paul Douglas 1949- *BiDrAPA 89*
Trautman, Richard P *BiDrAPA 89*
Trautman, Wayne B. 1953- *St&PR 91*
Trautmann, Frederic 1936- *ConAu 132*
Trautmann, Les Raymond 1918- *WhoAm 90*
Trautmann, Thomas R 1940- *ConAu 131*
Trautmann, Thomas Roger 1940- *WhoAm 90*
Trautner, Rick Jeffrey *BiDrAPA 89*
Trautwein, Betty Baldwin 1947- *WhoAm 90*
Trautwein, Betty Boldwin 1947- *St&PR 91*
Trautwein, George 1927- *IntWWM 90*
Trautwein, George William 1927- *WhoAm 90*
Trautwein, James William 1935- *St&PR 91, WhoWor 91*
Travaglini, A. F. 1923- *St&PR 91*
Travaille, Hubert Duane 1939- *St&PR 91*
Travanti, Daniel J. 1940- *WorAlBi*
Travanti, Daniel John *WhoAm 90*
Travanti, Leon Emidio 1936- *WhoAmA 91*
Travelstead, Chester Coleman 1911- *WhoAm 90*
Traven, B. *BioIn 16*
Traven, B *MajTwCW*
Traver, Donald 1957- *WhoAmA 91*
Traver, Noel Allen 1959- *WhoWor 91*
Traver, Phyllis Anne 1952- *WhoAmW 91*
Traver, Robert William, Sr. 1930- *WhoE 91*
Travers, Ann 1628?-1689 *BiDEWW*
Travers, Bill 1952- *Ballpl 90*
Travers, Curt Whitney 1954- *WhoE 91*
Travers, David Morris William 1943- *WhoE 91*
Travers, George F. 1928- *St&PR 91*
Travers, Gwyneth Mabel 1911-1982 *WhoAmA 91N*
Travers, Harvey Charles 1923- *WhoE 91*
Travers, James Francis 1923- *St&PR 91*
Travers, John 1878-1959 *FemiCLE*
Travers, Judith Lynnette 1950- *WhoAmW 91*
Travers, Linus 1936- *WhoE 91*
Travers, Lorraine A. 1943- *WhoAmW 91*
Travers, Mary 1936- *WorAlBi*
Travers, Noel Jeffrey 1930- *IntWWM 90*
Travers, Oliver S., Jr. 1926- *WhoAm 90, WhoE 91*
Travers, Oliver Slater, Jr. 1926- *St&PR 91*
Travers, P. L. 1906- *BioIn 16*
Travers, P L 1906- *ConAu 30NR*
Travers, P. L. 1906- *FemiCLE*
Travers, Pamela 1906- *AuBYP 90*
Travers, Pamela L. 1906- *BioIn 16*
Travers, Rebecca 1609?-1688 *FemiCLE*
Travers, Rebeckah 1609-1688 *BiDEWW*
Travers, Rose Elaine 1056- *WhoAmW 91*
Travers, Scott Andrew 1961- *WhoE 91, WhoEmL 91, WhoWor 91*
Travers, W. Lawrence 1943- *WhoWor 91*
Travers, William H. *AmLegL*
Travers-Smith, Brian John 1931- *WhoAmA 91*
Traverse, Alfred 1925- *WhoAm 90*
Traverso, Frederick Patrick 1947- *WhoE 91*
Traverso, Joseph L *BiDrAPA 89*
Travilla, Bill *NewYTBS 90*
Travillian-Vonesh, Ami Lynn 1961- *WhoSSW 91*
Travin, Sheldon *BiDrAPA 89*
Travis, Andrew D. 1944- *St&PR 91*
Travis, Andrew David 1944- *WhoAm 90*
Travis, Anita Hartman 1944- *WhoAmW 91*
Travis, Aubrey Lawrence 1927- *WhoSSW 91*
Travis, Cecil 1913- *Ballpl 90, BioIn 16*
Travis, David B. 1948- *WhoAm 90, WhoAmA 91*
Travis, Dempsey Jerome 1920- *WhoAm 90*
Travis, Erin Jane 1969- *WhoAmW 91*
Travis, Harold 1929- *St&PR 91*
Travis, J. A. 1919- *St&PR 91*
Travis, Jack Beryl 1944- *St&PR 91*
Travis, Julius C 1914- *BiDrAPA 89*
Travis, Karen Anne 1965- *WhoAmW 91*
Travis, Kathryne Hail 1894-1972 *WhoAmA 91N*
Travis, Lawrence Allan 1942- *WhoWor 91*
Travis, Lee Edward 1896-1987 *BioIn 16*
Travis, Linda Diane 1943- *BiDrAPA 89*
Travis, Marlene O. *WhoWor 91*
Travis, Martin Bice 1917- *WhoAm 90*
Travis, Merle 1917-1983 *OxCPMus*
Travis, Nancy 1936- *WhoAmW 91, WhoSSW 91*
Travis, Olin 1888-1975 *WhoAmA 91N*
Travis, R. L. *WhoWrEP 89*
Travis, Randy *BioIn 16, WhoNeCM [port]*
Travis, Randy 1959- *WorAlBi*
Travis, Randy Bruce 1959- *WhoAm 90*
Travis, Robin 1949- *WhoE 91, WhoEmL 91*
Travis, Susan Kathryn 1940- *WhoAmW 91*
Travis, Susan Topper 1951- *WhoEmL 91*
Travis, Terry Arthur 1937- *BiDrAPA 89*
Travis, Vance Kenneth 1926- *WhoAm 90*
Travis, William Barret 1809-1836 *BioIn 16, WorAlBi*
Travisano, Ron *BioIn 16*
Traviss, Donald Parthen 1944- *St&PR 91*
Travnicek, Jiri *PenDiMP*
Travolta, John *BioIn 16*
Travolta, John 1954- *WhoAm 90, WorAlBi*
Trawick, Jack Durward 1932- *St&PR 91*
Trawin, Nancy Lynn 1947- *WhoAmW 91*
Traxler, Bob *BioIn 16*
Traxler, Bob 1931- *WhoAm 90*
Traxler, Rita Arianoutsos 1957- *WhoAmW 91*
Trayler, Alfred Glenn 1935- *WhoSSW 91*
Trayling, Karen Jeannette 1950- *WhoEmL 91*
Traylor, Angelika 1942- *WhoAmA 91*
Traylor, Bill 1854-1947 *MusmAFA*
Traylor, Cherie Lee 1944- *WhoAmW 91*
Traylor, Claire Guthrie 1931- *WhoAmW 91*
Traylor, Frank Allen 1929- *WhoAm 90*
Traylor, Joan Sadler *WhoSSW 91*
Traylor, John Austin 1941- *BiDrAPA 89*
Traylor, Judy Gaut 1951- *WhoSSW 91*
Traylor, Orba Forest 1910- *WhoAm 90*
Traylor, William Robert 1921- *WhoWor 91*
Traynham, James Gibson 1925- *WhoAm 90*
Traynor, Anne *BiDrAPA 89*
Traynor, Harry Sheehy 1911- *WhoAm 90*
Traynor, J. Michael 1934- *WhoAm 90*
Traynor, James Edmund 1949- *St&PR 91*
Traynor, Mary E M 1930- *BiDrAPA 89*
Traynor, Michael H. 1940- *St&PR 91*
Traynor, Pie 1899-1972 *Ballpl 90 [port]*
Traynor, Sara E. *ODwPR 91*
Traywick, Joseph B. 1945- *St&PR 91*
Trazkovich, Laszlo Richard *BiDrAPA 89*
Trazkovich, Laszlo Richard 1959- *WhoE 91*
Trazkovich, Michele Klein *BiDrAPA 89*
TRB *ConAu 132*
Trbovich, Mike 1921- *St&PR 91*
Trbovich, Robert 1937- *St&PR 91*
Treace, James T. 1946- *St&PR 91*
Treacher, Arthur 1894-1975 *WorAlBi*
Treacy, Gerald Bernard 1951- *WhoEmL 91*
Treacy, James Bernard 1921- *St&PR 91*
Treacy, James Joseph, Jr. 1958- *WhoE 91*
Treacy, Richard F. 1945- *St&PR 91*
Treacy, Sandra Joanne Pratt 1934- *WhoAmW 91, WhoSSW 91, WhoWor 91*
Treacy, Susan 1946- *IntWWM 90*
Treadgold, Donald Warren 1922- *WhoAm 90*
Treadgold, Mary 1910- *BioIn 16*
Treadway, Antoinette *WhoAmW 91*
Treadway, C. Richard F. 1939- *BiDrAPA 89*
Treadway, Douglas Morse 1942- *WhoAm 90*
Treadway, James C. 1943- *WhoAm 90*
Treadway, Jeff 1963- *Ballpl 90*
Treadway, John David 1950- *WhoSSW 91*
Treadway, Ruby Peeples *AuBYP 90*
Treadway, Stephen Joseph 1947- *WhoAm 90*
Treadway, Susan Marie 1951- *WhoAmW 91, WhoSSW 91, WhoWor 91*
Treadway, William Murray 1946- *WhoSSW 91*
Treadwell, Ann 1957- *WhoAmW 91*
Treadwell, Barry Lincoln 1942- *St&PR 91*
Treadwell, Debbie J. 1963- *WhoAmW 91*
Treadwell, George 1919- *DrBIPA 90*
Treadwell, Hugh Wilson 1921- *WhoAm 90*
Treadwell, Sophie 1885?-1970 *NotWoAT*
Treadwell, Sophie 1890-1970 *BioIn 16, FemiCLE*
Treadwell-Deering, Diane E *BiDrAPA 89*
Treanor, Betty McKee 1938- *WhoSSW 91*
Treanor, Charles Edward 1924- *St&PR 91, WhoAm 90*
Treanor, Gerard Francis, Jr. 1943- *WhoAm 90*
Treanor, John J. 1931- *WhoE 91*
Treanor, John James 1931- *BiDrAPA 89*
Treanor, Robert V. 1948- *St&PR 91*
Trease, Geoffrey 1909- *AuBYP 90, SmATA 60 [port]*
Treaster, Richard A 1932- *WhoAmA 91*
Treasure, John Albert Penberthy 1924- *WhoAm 90*
Treat, Amos Sherman 1816-1886 *AmLegL*
Treat, Asher Eugene 1907- *WhoE 91*
Treat, John Elting 1946- *WhoAm 90*
Treat, Lawrence 1903- *BioIn 16, TwCCr&M 91, WhoAm 90, WhoWrEP 89*
Treat, Mary 1830-1923 *WomFie [port]*
Treat, Robert S 1939- *BiDrAPA 89*
Treat, Roger L. *AuBYP 90*
Treat, William Wardwell 1918- *WhoAm 90*
Trebby, James Paul 1949- *WhoEmL 91*
Trebek, Alex 1940- *WhoAm 90*
Trebelhorn, Thomas Lynn 1948- *WhoAm 90*
Trebelhorn, Tom 1948- *Ballpl 90*
Trebelli, Zelia 1834-1892 *PenDiMP*
Trebesch, Karsten 1941- *WhoWor 91*
Trebilcock, Charles Edward 1926- *St&PR 91*
Trebilcock, Dorothy Warner 1926- *WhoWrEP 89*
Trebilcot, Joyce 1933- *WhoAmW 91*
Trebilcott, James Joseph 1917- *WhoAm 90*
Trebing, Harry M 1926- *ConAu 31NR*
Trebino, Stephen G. 1953- *St&PR 91*
Trebitsch-Lincoln, Ignatius Timothy 1879-1943 *BioIn 16*
Trebon, Lawrence Alan 1949- *WhoEmL 91*
Trebour, Burton Charles 1942- *St&PR 91*
Trechsel, Gail Andrews 1953- *WhoAmA 91*
Trechsel, Stefan 1937- *WhoWor 91*
Treckelo, Richard M. 1926- *WhoAm 90*
Trecker, Janice Law 1941- *WhoWrEP 89*
Trecker, Stan Matthew 1944- *WhoE 91*
Trecker, Stanley Matthew 1944- *WhoAmA 91*
Treco-Jones, Sheryl Lynn 1948- *WhoAmW 91*
Tredennick, Dorothy W 1914- *WhoAmA 91*
Tredez, Denise 1930- *BioIn 16*
Tredinnick, Frank A., Jr. 1921- *St&PR 91*
Tredway, John Thomas 1935- *WhoAm 90*
Tree, David L. *WhoAm 90*
Tree, Gregory *TwCCr&M 91*
Tree, Herbert 1853-1917 *WorAlBi*
Tree, Herbert Beerbohm 1852-1917 *BioIn 16*
Tree, Iris 1897-1968 *FemiCLE*
Tree, Marietta Peabody *WhoAmW 91*
Tree, Michael *PenDiMP*
Tree, Michael 1934- *IntWWM 90, WhoAm 90*
Tree, Viola 1884-1938 *FemiCLE*
Treece, Eleanor Mae 1921- *WhoAmW 91*
Treece, Henry 1911-1966 *AuBYP 90*
Treece, Malra Clifft 1923- *WhoAmW 91*
Treece, Patricia 1938- *WhoWrEP 89*
Treece, Wen-Hsuan *BiDrAPA 89*
Treen, David Conner 1928- *WhoSSW 91*
Treen, Mary 1907-1989 *BioIn 16*
Trees, Candice D. 1953- *WhoAmW 91*
Trees, Clyde C 1885-1960 *WhoAmA 91N*
Trees, George S. 1916- *St&PR 91*
Trees, Joe C. 1869-1943 *WorAlBi*

Trees, John Simmons 1932- WhoAm 90
Treese, William R 1932- WhoAmA 91
Trefas, Gyorgy 1931- IntWWM 90
Trefethen, Florence 1921- WhoWrEP 89
Trefethen, Lloyd MacGregor 1919- WhoAm 90
Trefethen, Lloyd Nicholas 1955- WhoE 91
Treffers, Adriaan Johan 1932- WhoWor 91
Treffert, Darold A 1933- BiDrAPA 89, ConAu 131
Treffert, Darold Allen 1933- WhoAm 90
Treffinger, Donald John 1941- WhoE 91
Trefftzs, Kenneth Lewis 1911- St&PR 91, WhoAm 90
Trefonas, Louis Marco 1931- WhoAm 90, WhoSSW 91
Trefouel, Jacques Gustave Marie 1897-1977 DcScB S2
Trefsgar, Theodore Webster, Jr. 1961- WhoE 91
Treft, Richard V. St&PR 91
Trefusis, Elizabeth 1763?-1808 FemiCLE
Trefusis, Violet 1894-1972 FemiCLE
Trefusis, Violet Keppel 1894-1972 BioIn 16
Trefzger, Elizabeth Carol BiDrAPA 89
Tregaskis, Richard William 1916-1973 AuBYP 90
Tregenza, Norman Hughson 1937- WhoE 91
Treger, Robert 1945- WhoE 91
Treglia, Michael WhoE 91
Treglown, Jeremy Dickinson 1946- WhoWor 91
Tregoe, Benjamin Bainbridge 1927- WhoAm 90
Tregurtha, Paul Richard 1935- St&PR 91, WhoAm 90
Trehan, Rajeev Ratan 1955- BiDrAPA 89
Trehan, Rajender 1952- WhoSSW 91
Treherne, John 1929-1989 AnObit 1989
Trehy, Joan Ellen 1942- WhoAmW 91
Trei, Alan 1932- WhoE 91
Trei, Alice Rosalie 1909- WhoAmW 91, WhoE 91
Treibergs, Juris Egils BiDrAPA 89
Treichel, Jeanie Nieri 1931- WhoAmW 91
Treichel, Jurgen Klaus 1937- WhoWor 91
Treichel, Paul Morgan, Jr. 1936- WhoAm 90
Treichel, William F BiDrAPA 89
Treichler, Francis Norman 1928- WhoE 91
Treichler, Jessie 1906?-1972 AuBYP 90
Treichler, Ray 1907- WhoE 91
Treiger, Irwin Louis 1934- WhoAm 90
Treigle, Norman 1923-1975 PenDiMP
Treiki, Ali A. 1938- WhoWor 91
Treiman, Joyce 1922- BiDWomA
Treiman, Joyce Wahl 1922- WhoAm 90, WhoAmA 91, WhoAmW 91
Treiman, Sam Bard 1925- WhoAm 90
Treimer, Wilbert M. 1911- St&PR 91
Treinavicz, Kathryn Mary 1957- WhoAmW 91, WhoEmL 91
Treinen, David C. 1939- St&PR 91
Treinkman, Leonard 1928- St&PR 91
Treint, Albert Edmund 1889-1971 BiDFrPL
Treirat, Eduard 1912- WhoE 91
Treisman, Glenn J BiDrAPA 89
Treister, George Marvin 1923- WhoAm 90
Treister, Kenneth 1930- WhoAmA 91
Treitel, David Henry 1954- St&PR 91
Treitel, Rudolf 1938- St&PR 91
Treitel, Sven 1929- WhoAm 90
Treitel, Theodore 1933- St&PR 91
Treitler, Leo 1931- IntWWM 90
Treitschke, Heinrich Von 1834-1896 WorAlBi
Trejo, Arnulfo D 1922- ConAu 32NR, HispWr 90
Trejo, Arnulfo Duenes 1922- WhoHisp 91
Trejo, Jose Diaz 1948- WhoWor 91
Trejo, Jose Humberto 1942- WhoHisp 91
Trelawney, Elizabeth 1617-1668? BiDEWW
Trelease, Allen W. 1928- AuBYP 90
Trelease, Allen William 1928- WhoAm 90
Trelease, Jim BioIn 16
Trelease, Stephen W. 1934- St&PR 91
Treleaven, John Waterloo 1922- WhoWrEP 89
Treleaven, Joseph H BiDrAPA 89
Treleaven, Phillips Albert 1928- WhoAm 90, WhoWor 91
Trelfa, Richard Thomas 1918- WhoAm 90
Trelford, Donald Gilchrist 1937- WhoWor 91
Trell, Erik Yngvar 1939- WhoWor 91
Trella, Anthony 1939- St&PR 91
Trellis, Emil S 1929- BiDrAPA 89
Treloar, Leslie Ronald George 1906-1985 BioIn 16
Treloar, Ronald C. 1933- WhoAm 90
Tremaglio, Angelo F. 1926- St&PR 91
Tremaglio, Caesar D. 1929- St&PR 91
Tremaglio, Neil L. 1924- St&PR 91
Tremain, Alan BioIn 16
Tremain, Edward W.H. 1935- St&PR 91
Tremain, Lyman 1819-1878 AmLegL
Tremain, Ronald 1923- IntWWM 90
Tremain, Rose 1943- FemiCLE
Tremaine, B. G., Jr. 1922- St&PR 91
Tremaine, Frank 1914- WhoAm 90
Tremayne, Bertram William, Jr. 1914- WhoAm 90
Tremayne, William A 1864-1939 OxCCanT
Tremayne, William H. ODwPR 91
Tremayne, William H. 1935- St&PR 91
Tremayne, William Howard 1935- WhoAm 90
Trembath, Peter H. 1952- St&PR 91
Tremblay, Andre Gabriel 1937- WhoAm 90
Tremblay, Anthony Michael 1945- WhoE 91
Tremblay, Charles N. 1930- St&PR 91
Tremblay, Clifford William 1933- WhoSSW 91
Tremblay, Lambert 1938- BiDrAPA 89
Tremblay, Madeleine D BiDrAPA 89
Tremblay, Marc Adelard 1922- WhoAm 90
Tremblay, Marcel J. 1941- St&PR 91
Tremblay, Michel 1942- BioIn 16, MajTwCW, OxCCanT [port]
Tremblay, Pierre 1959- BiDrAPA 89
Tremblay, Rodrigue 1939- WhoAm 90
Tremblay, William Andrew 1940- WhoWrEP 89
Tremblay-Jolicoeur, Claudine BiDrAPA 89
Tremble, Edward C. 1913- St&PR 91
Tremble, Rita Mae 1916- St&PR 91
Trembly, Ara C. 1950- ODwPR 91
Treml, Raymond Francis 1940- St&PR 91
Treml, Vladimir Guy 1929- WhoAm 90
Tremlett, George 1939- WhoWor 91
Tremmel, Robert Arnold 1948- WhoWrEP 89
Tremols, Guillermo Antonio 1937- WhoHisp 91
Tremonti, John C. 1937- St&PR 91
Tremot, Francis Raymond 1943- WhoWor 91
Trempe, Nance Joan WhoAmW 91
Tremper, Kimberly Ann 1963- WhoAmW 91
Tremulis, Joanne C. ODwPR 91
Trenary, Jill BioIn 16
Trench, Brinsley Le Poer 1911- EncO&P 3
Trench, David 1915-1988 AnObit 1988
Trench, David Clive Crosbie 1915-1988 BioIn 16
Trench, James M 1923- BiDrAPA 89
Trench, James McKechan 1923- WhoE 91
Trench, John 1920- TwCCr&M 91
Trench, Melesina 1768-1827 FemiCLE
Trench, William Frederick 1931- WhoAm 90
Trenchard, Hugh Montague 1873-1956 WorAlBi
Trend, Steven Richard 1959- WhoE 91
Trendelenburg, Ullrich Georg 1922- WhoWor 91
Trendov, Oscar 1920- St&PR 91
Trenet, Charles 1913- BioIn 16, OxCPMus
Trenhaile, John 1949- TwCCr&M 91
Trenhaile, John Stevens 1949- SpyFic
Trenholm, K Richard 1929- St&PR 91
Trenholm, Thomas David 1955- WhoE 91
Trenk, Lawrence Ira 1954- WhoE 91
Trenker, Alois Franz 1892-1990 ConAu 131
Trenker, Luis ConAu 131
Trenker, Luis 1892-1990 NewYTBS 90
Trenker, Luis 1893-1990 BioIn 16
Trenkler, Gerhard 1929- WhoWor 91
Trenkler, Tamera Sue 1957- WhoE 91
Trenkmann, Richard S. 1942- St&PR 91
Trennel, Lawrence William 1955- WhoEmL 91
Trennepohl, Gary Lee 1946- WhoAm 90, WhoEmL 91
Trent, A. G. 1789-1850 EncO&P 3
Trent, Bertram James 1918- WhoE 91
Trent, Chester L BiDrAPA 89
Trent, Darrell M. 1938- St&PR 91, WhoAm 90
Trent, Jacquelyn C BiDrAPA 89
Trent, James Alfred 1946- WhoE 91
Trent, John Thomas, Jr. 1954- WhoEmL 91, WhoSSW 91
Trent, Joyce Miller 1946- WhoAmW 91
Trent, Olaf ConAu 32NR
Trent, Robbie 1894- AuBYP 90
Trent, Robert Harold 1933- WhoAm 90, WhoSSW 91
Trent, Rose Marie 1943- WhoAmW 91
Trent, Ted 1905-1944 Ballpl 90
Trent, William Bret, Jr. 1947- St&PR 91
Trentham, Barbara Newton 1939- WhoAmW 91
Trentham, Gary Lynn 1939- WhoAmA 91
Trentham, Jimmy Keith 1950- WhoSSW 91
Trenton, Patricia Jean WhoAmA 91
Trepanowski, Judith Mary 1948- WhoAmW 91
Trepka, William James 1933- WhoSSW 91
Trepo, Georges Xavier 1942- WhoWor 91
Trepp, Gian 1947- WhoWor 91
Trepp, L Ronald 1938- St&PR 91
Trepper, Leopold 1904-1982 BioIn 16
Treppler, Irene Esther 1926- WhoAmW 91
Treppunti, Philip J. 1930- St&PR 91
Tresalti, Emilio 1935- WhoWor 91
Tresca, Carlo 1879-1943 BioIn 16, EncAL
Treschitta, Domenick Phillip 1941- St&PR 91
Trescot, William Henry 1822-1898 BioIn 16
Trescott, Paul Barton 1925- WhoWrEP 89
Trese, Thomas Joseph 1950- WhoEmL 91, WhoSSW 91
Tresh, Mike 1914-1966 Ballpl 90
Tresh, Tom 1937- Ballpl 90
Treshow, Marilyn BioIn 16
Tresmontan, Olympia Davis 1925- WhoAmW 91
Tresnowski, Bernard Richard 1932- WhoAm 90
Tress, Mitchell 1942- St&PR 91
Tresselt, Alvin R. 1916- AuBYP 90
Tresser, Norman S 1930- BiDrAPA 89
Tressler, Clyde L. 1937- St&PR 91
Trest, Fred Alan BiDrAPA 89
Trester, Joseph Edward 1952- WhoEmL 91
Trestman, Frank D. 1934- St&PR 91, WhoAm 90
Trestman, Robert Lee 1953- BiDrAPA 89, WhoE 91
Tretheway, Barton Glenn 1945- WhoEmL 91
Trethewey, James Alger 1937- WhoAm 90
Trethowan, William Henry BiDrAPA 89
Tretter, Ann Daly 1945- ODwPR 91
Tretter, James Ray 1933- St&PR 91, WhoAm 90, WhoE 91
Tretter, Vincent Joseph, Jr. 1940- WhoSSW 91
Trettin, Clifford F. 1924- St&PR 91
Tretyakov, Viktor 1946- PenDiMP
Treu, Dennis L. 1947- St&PR 91
Treu, Jesse Isaiah 1947- WhoE 91
Treuhold, Charles Richard 1930- St&PR 91
Treuhold, Robert Charles 1957- WhoE 91
Treumann, William Borgen 1916- WhoAm 90
Treurnicht, Andries Petrus 1921- WhoWor 91
Treutel, Lucile Veronica WhoWrEP 89
Trevanian 1925- SpyFic
Trevanian 1931- TwCCr&M 91
Trevarrow, David St&PR 91
Trevaskis, G K N 1915-1990 ConAu 131
Trevaskis, Kennedy ConAu 131
Trevaskis, Richard White, Jr. BiDrAPA 89
Trevathan, Robert Duncan 1918- BiDrAPA 89
Treveiler, A. R. 1927- St&PR 91
Trevelyan, George NewAgE 90
Trevelyan, George 1906- EncO&P 3
Trevelyan, George Macaulay 1876-1962 WorAlBi
Trevelyan, Humphrey 1905-1985 DcNaB 1981
Trevelyan, Julian 1910-1988 AnObit 1988
Treves, Alain Ilan BiDrAPA 89
Treves, Samuel Blain 1925- WhoAm 90
Trevett, Barbara ODwPR 91
Trevifio, Elizabeth Borton de 1904- BioIn 16
Trevillian, Wallace Dabney 1918- WhoAm 90, WhoSSW 91
Trevino, A. L. WhoHisp 91
Trevino, Alex 1957- Ballpl 90
Trevino, Armando Lozano 1941- St&PR 91
Trevino, Baldomero 1956- WhoSSW 91
Trevino, Carlos B. 1935- EncPaPR 91
Trevino, Daniel Louis 1943- WhoHisp 91
Trevino, Elizabeth de 1904- AuBYP 90
Trevino, Fernando Manuel 1949- WhoHisp 91
Trevino, Jesse WhoHisp 91
Trevino, Jesse 1947- WhoHisp 91
Trevino, Joe A. 1951- WhoSSW 91
Trevino, Joseph J 1926- BiDrAPA 89
Trevino, Justin James BiDrAPA 89
Trevino, Lee BioIn 16
Trevino, Lee 1939- WhoHisp 91, WorAlBi
Trevino, Lee Buck 1939- WhoAm 90
Trevino, Linda Klebe 1949- WhoE 91
Trevino, Marcela Gomezharper de 1936- EncPaPR 91
Trevino, Mario 1952- WhoHisp 91
Trevino, Teresa Roque 1960- WhoHisp 91
Trevino Diaz, Josue 1959- WhoWor 91
Trevisan, Bernard of 1406-1490 EncO&P 3
Trevisan, Nello R. 1947- St&PR 91
Trevithick, Earl F. 1933- St&PR 91
Trevithick, Richard 1771-1833 WorAlBi
Trevor, Alexander B. 1945- St&PR 91
Trevor, Alexander Bruen 1945- WhoAm 90
Trevor, Bronson 1910- WhoE 91, WhoWor 91
Trevor, Claire 1909- WorAlBi
Trevor, Elleston TwCCr&M 91
Trevor, Elleston 1920- SpyFic
Trevor, Kirk David Niell 1952- WhoAm 90
Trevor, Leigh Barry 1934- WhoAm 90
Trevor, Steve BioIn 16
Trevor, William MajTwCW
Trevor, William 1928- WhoWor 91
Trevor-Roper, Hugh Redwald 1914- WhoWor 91
Trevorrow, David Edward 1953- WhoE 91
Trew, John Labatt 1939- WhoWor 91
Trew, Michael NewAgMG
Trewartha, Glenn Thomas 1896-1984 BioIn 16
Trewartha, Mark BiDrAPA 89
Trewhella, Raymond M. 1935- St&PR 91
Trewhella, Stephen W. 1926- St&PR 91
Trewin, J C 1908-1990 ConAu 131
Trewitt, George Woodrow 1936- WhoSSW 91
Treworgy, Scott W 1954- BiDrAPA 89
Trexler, Edgar Ray 1937- WhoAm 90
Trexler, Henry Flowe 1922- WhoSSW 91
Trexler, James N. 1932- St&PR 91
Treybig, Edwina Hall 1949- WhoAmW 91
Treyz, Joseph Henry 1926- WhoAm 90
Treyz, Russell 1940- ConAu 132
Trez, Denise 1930- BioIn 16
Trezek, George James 1937- WhoAm 90
Trezevant, John Gray 1923 WhoAm 90
Trezise, Percy 1923- ConAu 132
Trezise, Philip Harold 1912- WhoAm 90
Trezza, Alphonse Fiore 1920- WhoAm 90
Trezza, William Robert 1946- St&PR 91
Trezzo, Jacopo da 1514-1589 PenDiDA 89
Tri Atma NewAgMG
Triana, Estrella WhoHisp 91
Triana, Gisela Maria BiDrAPA 89
Triana, Jose 1932?- ConAu 131, HispWr 90
Triana, Jose 1933- BioIn 16
Triandis, Harry Charalambos 1926- WhoAm 90
Triandos, Gus 1930- Ballpl 90
Triano, Anthony Thomas 1928- WhoAmA 91
Triano, Michael Anthony 1960- St&PR 91
Triano, Nicholas D. 1931- St&PR 91
Triantaphilides, Constantin 1951- WhoSSW 91
Trias, Jose Enrique 1944- WhoAm 90
Trias-Monge, Jose 1920- WhoAm 90
Tribbe, Frank C. 1914- EncPaPR 91
Tribbey, John A 1931- BiDrAPA 89
Tribble, B. Jodie 1932- WhoAmW 91
Tribble, Harriett Gee 1944- WhoAmW 91
Tribble, James E. 1931- St&PR 91
Tribby, Richard Louis Calvin, Jr. 1948- WhoEmL 91
Tribe, Laurence H. BioIn 16
Tribe, Laurence Henry 1941- WhoAm 90, WhoE 91
Tribhuvana WomWR
Trible, Paul Seward, Jr. 1946- WhoAm 90
Tribull, Christoph 1941- St&PR 91
Tribus, Myron 1921- St&PR 91
Tricarico, James A., Jr. 1952- WhoAm 90
Tricarico, Joel Francis 1939- BiDrAPA 89
Tricarico, Linda Marie 1961- WhoAmW 91, WhoE 91
Trice, Bob 1928- Ballpl 90
Trice, J Clarence BiDrAPA 89
Trice, Jack BioIn 16
Trice, Robert Glenn 1957- WhoSSW 91
Trice, William H. 1933- St&PR 91
Trice, William Henry 1933- WhoAm 90
Trice-Daughdrill, Ann Morton 1932- WhoAmW 91
Trick, O Lee 1931- BiDrAPA 89
Trick, Thomas Lee 1947- WhoSSW 91
Trick, Timothy N. 1939- WhoAm 90
Trickle, Kathleen A. 1955- WhoSSW 91
Tricoles, Gus Peter 1931- WhoAm 90
Tricou, Betty Jo Line 1930- BiDrAPA 89
Tridle, David Russeel 1950- St&PR 91
Triebel, William A BiDrAPA 89
Triebwasser, Jonah Ignatius 1950- WhoEmL 91
Triebwasser, Sol 1921- WhoAm 90
Trieff, Richard P. 1940- St&PR 91
Trieff, Selina 1934- BiDWomA, WhoAmA 91
Trier, Herbert P 1927- BiDrAPA 89
Trier, Jerry Steven 1933- WhoAm 90
Trier, Stephen Luke 1930- IntWWM 90
Trier Morch, Dea 1941- DcScanL
Trieschmann, James Shipp 1944- WhoSSW 91
Triest, Willard Gustav BioIn 16
Trieu Au 222- WomWR
Triffin, Robert 1911- WhoAm 90
Triffleman, Elisa BiDrAPA 89

Trifoli, Laura Catherine 1958- WhoAmW 91
Trifon, Harriette WhoAmA 91N
Trifone, Carol A. 1953- WhoAmW 91
Trifonidis, Beverly Ann 1947- WhoAm 90, WhoAmW 91
Trifonov, Yuri 1925-1981 MajTwCW
Trigari, Giancarlo 1945- WhoWor 91
Trigere, Pauline BioIn 16
Trigere, Pauline 1912- ConDes 90, WhoAmW 91
Trigg, Harold L BiDrAPA 89
Trigg, Jack Walden, Jr. 1932- WhoSSW 91
Trigg, John Herbert 1940- WhoSSW 91
Trigg, Karen Ann 1947- WhoAmW 91
Trigg, Paul R., Jr. 1913- St&PR 91
Trigg, Shari Jenell 1957- WhoEmL 91
Trigger, Bruce Graham 1937- WhoAm 90
Triggle, David John 1935- WhoAm 90
Triggs, Jonna Frances 1950- WhoAmW 91
Triggs, Lee Otis, Jr. 1947- St&PR 91
Triglione-Weiner, Janice 1956- WhoAmW 91
Trigos, Edmundo Javier 1949- WhoSSW 91
Triguboff, Michael P. 1955- WhoE 91
Trigueros, Raul C. 1944- WhoHisp 91
Trihas, Maria 1942- WhoAmW 91
Trikilis, E. M. 1916- St&PR 91
Trillas Ruiz, Enrique 1940- WhoWor 91
Trillat, Albert 1910-1988 BioIn 16
Trillaud, Fabienne 1958- WhoWor 91
Trillin, Calvin BioIn 16
Trillin, Calvin 1935- CurBio 90 [port], MajTwCW, WorAlBi
Trillin, Calvin Marshall 1935- WhoAm 90, WhoWrEP 89
Trilling, Diana BioIn 16
Trilling, Diana 1905- MajTwCW, WhoAm 90
Trilling, George Henry 1930- WhoAm 90
Trilling, Helen Regina 1950- WhoEmL 91
Trilling, Leon 1924- WhoAm 90
Trilling, Lionel 1905-1975 BioIn 16, MajTwCW, WorAlBi
Trilling, Morton 1929- St&PR 91
Trillo, Manny 1950- Ballpl 90, WhoHisp 91
Trimarchi, Carmen N. St&PR 91
Trimarchi, Domenico 1940- IntWWM 90
Trimarchi, Eugene James 1922- St&PR 91
Trimbach, Martha 1941- WhoSSW 91
Trimball, W. H. MajTwCW
Trimble, Alfred James 1936- St&PR 91
Trimble, Arch Edward, III 1953- WhoSSW 91
Trimble, Barbara Margaret 1921- ConAu 132
Trimble, Barbara White 1955- St&PR 91
Trimble, Celia Denise 1953- WhoAmW 91
Trimble, Cesar WhoHisp 91
Trimble, Dale Lee 1954- WhoSSW 91
Trimble, George Simpson 1915- WhoAm 90, WhoWor 91
Trimble, James Whitman 1925- St&PR 91
Trimble, Joe AuBYP 90
Trimble, Joyce Ann 1947- St&PR 91
Trimble, Lora Nelle Garretson 1935- WhoAmW 91
Trimble, Marian Alice 1933- WhoAm 90
Trimble, Marian Eddy 1933- St&PR 91
Trimble, Michael Robert 1946- BiDrAPA 89
Trimble, P Joseph 1930- St&PR 91
Trimble, Paul Joseph 1930- WhoAm 90
Trimble, Preston Albert 1930- WhoAm 90
Trimble, Richard Wade 1948- St&PR 91
Trimble, Rose Marie 1956- WhoAmW 91
Trimble, South 1864-1946 AmLegL
Trimble, Thomas J. 1931- St&PR 91
Trimble, Thomas James 1931- WhoAm 90, WhoWor 91
Trimble, Vance Henry 1913- WhoAm 90
Trimble, Virginia Louise 1943- WhoAm 90
Trimble, Wanda Jean 1947- WhoSSW 91
Trimble, William Cattell, Jr. 1935- WhoAm 90
Trimble, William Fraser, Jr. 1948- WhoSSW 91
Trimbur, William 1951- St&PR 91
Trimby, Elisa 1948- BioIn 16
Trimby, Madeline Jean 1943- WhoAmW 91
Trimm, Adon 1895-1959 WhoAmA 91N
Trimm, H Wayne 1922- WhoAmA 91
Trimm, Kathleen A. 1932- St&PR 91
Trimm, Maureen Patricia 1948- WhoEmL 91
Trimm, Wendelyn Barbara 1948- WhoE 91
Trimmer, Harold S., Jr. 1938- St&PR 91
Trimmer, Harold Sharp, Jr. 1938- WhoAm 90
Trimmer, Larry Lee 1936- WhoAm 90
Trimmer, Sarah 1741-1810 FemiCLE
Trimmer, Sarah Kirby 1741-1810 BioIn 16
Trimmer, William Christian, Jr. 1954- WhoSSW 91
Trimmer-Smith, David William 1937- WhoAm 90
Trimmer-Smith, David William 1937-1988 BioIn 16
Trimmier, Roscoe, Jr. 1944- WhoWor 91
Trinchero, Louis 1936- St&PR 91
Trinchieri, Oreste BioIn 16
Trinder, Tommy 1909-1989 AnObit 1989, BioIn 16
Tring, A Stephen 1899-1989 SmATA X
Tringale, Anthony Rosario 1942- WhoSSW 91, WhoWor 91
Tringali, John Cameron 1964- WhoSSW 91
Trinh Van Can 1921-1990 NewYTBS 90
Trinh, Phuong Duc 1955- WhoE 91
Trinh, Quang Binh 1944- St&PR 91
Trinh Van Can, Joseph Marie 1921-1990 BioIn 16
Trinidad, Antolin Canlas BiDrAPA 89
Trinidad, David Allen 1953- WhoWrEP 89
Trinidad, Ruben WhoHisp 91
Trinkaus, Charles Edward, Jr. 1911- WhoAm 90
Trinkaus, John Philip 1918- WhoAm 90
Trinkaus-Randall, Gregor 1946- WhoE 91
Trinkaus-Randall, Vickery 1953- WhoAmW 91
Trinkle, David B 1961- BiDrAPA 89
Trinkle, Ken 1919-1976 Ballpl 90
Trinkley, Jane Wilroy 1955- WhoEmL 91
Trinkley, Karla WhoAmA 91
Trinsey, Anna Michels 1902- WhoWor 91
Trintignant, Jean-Louis BioIn 16
Trintignant, Jean-Louis 1930- WhoWor 91
Trintzius, Rene 1898-1953 EncO&P 3
Triola, Tony J. 1947- St&PR 91
Triolo, Peter 1927- WhoAm 90
Trion, Richard Fales 1928- St&PR 91
Tripathi, Amitabha 1961- WhoE 91
Tripathi, Anang K. 1948- WhoWor 91
Tripathi, Brenda Jennifer 1946- WhoAmW 91
Tripathi, Gaya-Charan 1939- WhoWor 91
Tripathi, Prabha R 1942- BiDrAPA 89
Tripathi, Ramesh Chandra 1936- WhoAm 90, WhoWor 91
Tripathi, Usha BiDrAPA 89
Triplehorn, Charles A 1927- ConAu 130, WhoAm 90
Triplett, Arlene Ann 1942- WhoAm 90
Triplett, Coaker 1911- Ballpl 90
Triplett, Gayle Kathleen 1952- BiDrAPA 89
Triplett, Jane Dinsmoor 1918- BioIn 16, NotWoAT
Triplett, Jerry Ray 1943- St&PR 91
Triplett, Rosalynd ODwPR 91
Triplett, Thomas McIntyre 1940- WhoAm 90
Triplett, William E., III 1953- St&PR 91
Tripodi, Louis A. 1931- ODwPR 91
Tripodi, Louis Anthony 1930- St&PR 91
Tripodi, Louis Anthony 1931- WhoAm 90
Tripodi, Richard F. 1945- St&PR 91
Tripoli, Louis Anthony 1931- WhoAm 90
Tripolitis, Antonia WhoAmW 91
Tripp, David L. 1941- St&PR 91
Tripp, Dorothy 1922- WhoAmW 91
Tripp, Gilbert Allen, Jr. 1943- WhoSSW 91
Tripp, Gordon A 1935- BiDrAPA 89
Tripp, John Peter 1947- WhoE 91
Tripp, L Joseph St&PR 91
Tripp, Larry E 1935- BiDrAPA 89
Tripp, Linda Lynn 1946- WhoSSW 91
Tripp, Margaret H BiDrAPA 89
Tripp, Marian B. 1921- ODwPR 91
Tripp, Miles 1923- TwCCr&M 91
Tripp, Montie Udell 1946- St&PR 91
Tripp, Patricia Marie 1948- WhoAmW 91
Tripp, Paul 1911- AuBYP 90
Tripp, Paul 1916- WhoAm 90
Tripp, Randy L. 1956- St&PR 91
Tripp, Susan Gerwe 1945- WhoAmA 91, WhoE 91
Tripp, Thomas Neal 1942- WhoWor 91
Trippe, Charles White 1935- WhoE 91, WhoWor 91
Trippe, J. T. 1899-1981 BioIn 16
Trippe, Juan 1899-1981 WorAlBi
Trippe, Juan Terry 1899-1981 BioIn 16
Trippe, Kenneth Alvin Battershill 1933- WhoAm 90, WhoSSW 91
Trippe, W. D. 1903- St&PR 91
Trippeer, Richard Allen 1939- St&PR 91
Trippett, Peter 1934- St&PR 91
Tripuraneni, Bhaskara Rao BiDrAPA 89
Trischetta, Elaine Anne 1951- WhoAmW 91
Trischler, W Ronald 1936- St&PR 91
Trisco, Robert Frederick 1929- WhoAm 90
Triska, Jan Francis 1922- WhoAm 90
Trisler, Henry Franklin, Jr. 1937- WhoWrEP 89
Trissel, James Nevin 1930- WhoAmA 91
Trissel, Sandra Lynne 1941- WhoAmW 91
Trist, Margaret 1914-1986 FemiCLE
Trist, Nicholas Philip 1800-1874 BioIn 16
Tristan HispWr 90
Tristan, Flora Celestine Therese H 1803-1844 EncCoWW
Tristan, Flore EncCoWW
Tristan-Morcoso, Flore EncCoWW
Tristano, Lennie 1919-1978 OxCPMus
Tristano, Leonard Joseph 1919-1978 BioIn 16
Tristine, Martin P. 1944- St&PR 91
Tristram MajTwCW
Trites, Beatrice Virginia 1917- WhoAmW 91
Trites, Donald George 1941- WhoE 91
Trithemius 1462-1519 EncO&P 3
Tritico, Frank Edward 1930- WhoSSW 91
Tritsch, Len BioIn 16
Tritsch, Robert Grant 1926- St&PR 91
Tritt, Clyde Edward 1920- WhoAm 90
Tritt, Herman 1913- BiDrAPA 89
Tritter, Richard Paul 1945- WhoE 91
Trittinger, John George 1945- WhoEmL 91
Triumph EncPR&S 89
Trivas, Irene AuBYP 90
Trivedi, Bal C. 1943- WhoWor 91
Trivedi, Daksha Hemant BiDrAPA 89
Trivedi, Dushyant G 1946- BiDrAPA 89
Trivedi, Hasumati B BiDrAPA 89
Trivedi, Madhukar H BiDrAPA 89
Trivedi, Narendra K 1943- BiDrAPA 89
Trivedi, Pankaj 1940- WhoSSW 91
Trivedi, Rajendra M 1941- BiDrAPA 89, WhoE 91
Trivedi, Sandhya 1958- BiDrAPA 89
Trivelpiece, Alvin William 1931- St&PR 91, WhoAm 90
Trivelpiece, Laurel 1926- BioIn 16
Trivigno, Pat 1922- WhoAmA 91
Trivison, Margaret Ann 1942- WhoAmW 91
Trivisonno, Nicholas Louis 1947- WhoAm 90
Trivitt, Roxanna S. 1962- WhoAmW 91
Trivus, Robert H 1935- BiDrAPA 89
Troast, John G. 1931- St&PR 91
Troast, Paul L., Jr. 1921- St&PR 91
Troast, William C. 1904- St&PR 91
Troch, Etienne 1925- WhoWor 91
Troche, E Gunter 1909-1971 WhoAmA 91N
Trockel, Rosemarie 1952- BiDWomA
Trockman, Gordon James 1945- BiDrAPA 89
Troedel, Lowell Jean 1937- WhoSSW 91
Troedson, Rich 1950- Ballpl 90
Troedsson, Tryggve 1923- WhoWor 91
Troeger, Curtis Ralph 1931- St&PR 91
Troeger, Richard Walter 1953- IntWWM 90
Troell, Jan BioIn 16
Troell, Jan 1931- ConTFT 8
Troeller, Linda ODwPR 91
Troeller, Linda 1949- WhoAmW 91
Troelstra, Arne 1935- WhoAm 90
Troen, Philip 1925- WhoAm 90
Troester, Carl A. BioIn 16
Troester, Carl Augustus, Jr. 1916- WhoAm 90
Trofatter, Kenneth Frank 1951- WhoSSW 91
Troffkin, Walter H 1937- BiDrAPA 89
Trofimenkoff, Susan Mann 1941- WhoAmW 91
Trogan, John Frederick 1937- St&PR 91
Trogden, Zelbie 1936- St&PR 91
Trogdon, Dewey Leonard 1932- St&PR 91
Trogdon, Dewey Leonard, Jr. 1932- WhoAm 90, WhoSSW 91
Trohan, Walter 1903- WhoAm 90, WhoWor 91
Trohatos, Peter John 1924- St&PR 91
Troiani, Daniela 1956- IntWWM 90
Troiano, Carl E. 1952- St&PR 91
Troiano, Gabriel 1934- BiDrAPA 89
Troiano, Gabriele John 1941- St&PR 91
Troiano, John Paul 1961- WhoE 91
Troiano, Lawrence St&PR 91
Troiano, Paul Francis 1937- St&PR 91
Troiano, Theresa Marie 1963- WhoAmW 91
Troiano, Thomas A BiDrAPA 89
Troidl, Richard John 1944- St&PR 91, WhoAm 90
Troike, Gero 1945- ConDes 90
Troilo, Joseph Carmen 1934- St&PR 91, WhoAm 90
Troise, Fred 1937- WhoWrEP 89
Troise, Fred L. 1937- St&PR 91
Troisi, Barbara Davies 1937- WhoE 91
Troisi, Lawrence Anthony 1952- St&PR 91
Troitino, Carmen 1918- EncCoWW
Trojan, Judith 1947- ConAu 131
Trojan, Vera Maria 1960- WhoE 91
Trojanowicz, John M ConAu 31NR
Trojanowicz, Robert C 1941- ConAu 31NR
Trolan, Karen Lynn Weinman 1958- WhoAmW 91
Trolander, Hardy W. 1921- St&PR 91
Trolinger, Jane Catherine 1952- WhoAmW 91
Trolinger, Mildred Sue 1947- WhoEmL 91
Trolio, Andrew Edmond 1929- St&PR 91
Trolio, William Michael 1947- WhoE 91
Troller, Fred 1930- WhoAm 90
Trollope, Anthony 1815-1882 BioIn 16, WorAlBi, WrPh
Trollope, Frances 1780-1863 FemiCLE, NinCLC 30 [port]
Trollope, Frances Eleanor 1834-1913 FemiCLE
Trollope, Frances Milton 1780-1863 BioIn 16
Trollope, Thomas Adolphus 1810-1892 EncO&P 3
Tromanhauser, Roger Karl 1936- St&PR 91
Tromberg, Robert H. 1944- ODwPR 91
Trombetta, R Nick 1925- St&PR 91
Trombetta, Victoria 1961- WhoAmW 91
Trombino, Roger A. 1939- WhoAm 90
Trombka, Jacob Israel 1930- WhoE 91
Trombka, Lawrence Henry BiDrAPA 89
Trombley, Stephen 1954- ConAu 129
Trombley, William Holden 1929- WhoAm 90
Trombold, Walter S. 1910- St&PR 91
Trommer, Joseph Abraham 1925- St&PR 91
Trommer, Robert 1952- WhoSSW 91
Tromp, S W 1909-1983 EncO&P 3
Tron, Dionn M. 1951- ODwPR 91
Tron, Giorgio 1884-1963 EncO&P 3
Troncale, Frank Thomas 1941- WhoAmA 91
Troncin, James Edward 1934- St&PR 91
Troncone, Reginald C. 1932- St&PR 91
Trone, Donald Burnell 1954- WhoE 91
Tronson, Keith Frederick 1943- WhoAm 90
Trook, Jackie Lee 1942- St&PR 91, WhoAm 90
Troost, Carol Marie 1945- WhoE 91
Trop, Jeffrey Lee BiDrAPA 89
Trop, Sandra WhoAmA 91, WhoE 91
Tropauer, Alan 1933- BiDrAPA 89
Trope, Jack Frederick 1955- WhoEmL 91
Tropea, Orland 1919- WhoAm 90
Tropeano, Elio 1953- St&PR 91
Tropf, Cheryl Griffiths 1946- WhoAmW 91
Tropiano, Marie Joyce 1942- WhoAmW 91
Tropnas, Jean B BiDrAPA 89
Tropovskii, Lev Naumovich 1885-1944 BioIn 16
Tropp, James B. 1956- St&PR 91
Tropp, Louise Constance Velardi 1942- WhoAmW 91
Tropp, Robert Lloyd 1947- WhoEmL 91
Tropper, Joel M. BioIn 16
Troppito, Charles C., Jr. 1947- WhoEmL 91
Tropsa, John Joseph 1928- St&PR 91
Trosch, Joel S. 1939- St&PR 91
Troshinsky, Charles H 1932- BiDrAPA 89
Troshinsky, Charles Hilary 1932- WhoE 91
Trosin, Walter R. 1933- St&PR 91
Trosino, Vincent Joseph 1940- St&PR 91, WhoAm 90
Troske, Robert L BiDrAPA 89
Trosky, Hal 1912- Ballpl 90
Trosky, Helene Roth WhoAmA 91
Trosman, Harry 1924- BiDrAPA 89
Trosper, Mary Sue 1953- WhoAmW 91
Trossen, Margaret Anne 1952- WhoAmW 91, WhoE 91
Trost, Barry Martin 1941- WhoAm 90
Trost, Carlisle A. H. 1930- BioIn 16
Trost, Carlisle Albert Herman 1930- WhoAm 90
Trost, Dennis Keith 1949- BiDrAPA 89
Trost, Donald Craig 1951- WhoE 91
Trost, J. Ronald 1932- WhoAm 90
Trostel, Michael Frederick 1931- WhoAm 90
Trostel, Otto Paul 1944- St&PR 91
Trosten, Leonard Morse 1932- WhoAm 90
Trotere, Henry 1855-1912 OxCPMus
Trotman, Alexander J. 1933- WhoAm 90
Trotman, Bob 1947- WhoAmA 91
Trotman, Jack H ConAu 129
Trotman-Dickenson, Aubrey Fiennes 1926- WhoWor 91
Trotman-Freeburn, Elizabeth Cordelia 1953- WhoE 91
Trotot, Pierre Marcel 1942- WhoWor 91
Trotsky BioIn 16
Trotsky, Leon 1879-1940 BioIn 16, WorAlBi
Trott, Dennis Charles 1946- WhoWor 91
Trott, Helen 1936- WhoAmA 91
Trott, John E. 1944- St&PR 91
Trott, Millard Clinton BiDrAPA 89
Trott, Sabert Scott, II 1941- St&PR 91, WhoAm 90
Trott, Stephen Spangler 1939- WhoAm 90

Trott, Thomas F 1938- BiDrAPA 89
Trott, William Macnider 1946- WhoSSW 91
Trotta, Anna Marie 1937- WhoWrEP 89
Trotta, Frank Paul, Jr. 1955- WhoEmL 91
Trotta, George Benedict 1930- St&PR 91, WhoAm 90
Trotta, Liz BioIn 16
Trotta, Margarethe von BioIn 16
Trotte, Gennaro E. 1932- St&PR 91
Trottenberg, Arthur Donald 1917- WhoAm 90, WhoE 91
Trotter, Betty Lou 1925- WhoAmW 91
Trotter, Bill 1908-1984 Ballpl 90
Trotter, Catharine 1679-1749 BioIn 16, FemiCLE
Trotter, Catherine BiDEWW
Trotter, Debra Mills 1953- WhoAmW 91
Trotter, Frederick Thomas 1926- WhoAm 90
Trotter, Grace Violet 1900- AuBYP 90
Trotter, Ide 1932- WhoSSW 91
Trotter, John J. 1935- St&PR 91
Trotter, John Thomas 1951- WhoSSW 91
Trotter, Johnny Ray 1950- WhoWor 91
Trotter, Nancy H. 1951- St&PR 91
Trotter, Ronald 1927- WhoWor 91
Trotter, Thomas Andrew 1957- IntWWM 90
Trotter, Thomas Robert 1949- WhoEmL 91
Trotter, William C. 1934- St&PR 91
Trotter, William E., II 1936- WhoSSW 91
Trotter, William Harry 1925- WhoSSW 91
Trotter, William Monroe 1872-1934 BioIn 16
Trotti, John Boone 1935- WhoAm 90
Trottier, Bryan 1956- WorAlBi
Trottier, Bryan John 1956- WhoAm 90
Trottier, Maurice Edmond 1917- WhoWrEP 89
Trottier, Michel 1952- St&PR 91
Trottier, Pierre 1925- BioIn 16
Trotzig, Birgitta 1929- DcScanL, EncCoWW
Trou, Henri-Charles PenDiDA 89
Troubetzkoy, Amelie 1863-1945 FemiCLE
Troubetzkoy, Dorothy Ulrich WhoWrEP 89
Trouche, Perry Edwin BiDrAPA 89
Troup, Diana Claire 1942- WhoAm 90
Troup, Frank W. 1921- St&PR 91
Troup, James S. 1945- St&PR 91
Troup, Malcolm 1930- IntWWM 90
Troup, Thomas James 1923- WhoAm 90
Troupe, Joseph E. 1945- St&PR 91
Troupe, Lee Wayne 1946- WhoSSW 91
Troupe, Quincy BioIn 16
Troupe, Terry Lee 1947- St&PR 91, WhoAm 90, WhoEmL 91
Trouppe, Quincy 1912- Ballpl 90
Trousdale, Julius Augustus AmLegL
Trout, Arthur Roger 1917- St&PR 91, WhoAm 90
Trout, Charles Hathaway 1935- WhoAm 90
Trout, Dizzy 1915-1972 Ballpl 90 [port]
Trout, Douglas Graham 1931- WhoE 91
Trout, G. Malcolm NewYTBS 90
Trout, Kilgore WhoWrEP 89
Trout, Margie Marie Mueller 1923- WhoAmW 91
Trout, Maurice Elmore 1917- WhoAm 90
Trout, Monroe Eugene 1931- St&PR 91, WhoAm 90, WhoWor 91
Trout, Robert BioIn 16
Trout, Roscoe Marshall, Jr. 1944- WhoSSW 91
Trout, Steve 1957- Ballpl 90, BioIn 16
Troutman, Courtland Warren 1929- WhoAm 90
Troutman, E. Mac 1915- WhoAm 90
Troutman, Edward L. 1943- St&PR 91
Troutman, Gerald Stevenson 1933- WhoAm 90
Troutman, James Voight 1946- St&PR 91
Troutman, Martha C BiDrAPA 89
Troutman, Toby Ray 1959- WhoSSW 91
Troutman, W Wilson 1954- St&PR 91
Troutman, William M. 1940- WhoAm 90
Troutner, Joanne Johnson 1952- WhoAmW 91
Troutner, Leonard P. 1951- St&PR 91
Troutt, William Earl 1949- WhoAm 90
Troutwine-Braun, Charlotte Temperley 1906- WhoAmW 91, WhoWor 91
Trova, Ernest Tino 1927- WhoAm 90, WhoAmA 91
Trovata, Aldo BiDrAPA 89
Trovato, Anthony John 1947- St&PR 91
Trovato, Frank Douglas 1948- St&PR 91
Trovato, Frank Nick BiDrAPA 89
Trover, Ellen Lloyd 1947- WhoAmW 91
Trovero, Leonard J. St&PR 91
Trow, Jo Anne Johnson 1931- WhoAmW 91
Trowbridge, Alexander Buel 1929- BiDrUSE 89, WhoWor 91
Trowbridge, Alexander Buel, Jr. 1929- WhoAm 90
Trowbridge, Bob 1930-1980 Ballpl 90
Trowbridge, Douglas NewAgMG
Trowbridge, Edmund 1709-1793 EncCRAm
Trowbridge, Edward Kenneth 1928- St&PR 91, WhoAm 90
Trowbridge, Ellsworth H, Jr. BiDrAPA 89
Trowbridge, John Parks 1947- WhoSSW 91
Trowbridge, Leslie W. 1920- AuBYP 90
Trowbridge, Martin E. 1925- St&PR 91
Trowbridge, Vicki Jane 1950- WhoAmW 91
Trowbridge, William L. 1941- WhoWrEP 89
Trowell, Brian Lewis 1931- IntWWM 90
Trower, Robin 1945- EncPR&S 89
Troxel, James Paul 1946- WhoEmL 91
Troxell, Deborah Anne 1950- WhoAmW 91
Troxell, Jane Lee 1963- WhoAmW 91
Troxell, Raymond Robert, Jr. 1932- WhoSSW 91
Troxell, Rebecca Lynne 1959- WhoAmW 91
Troxler, Niklaus 1947- ConDes 90
Troy, Ann BioIn 16
Troy, B. Theodore 1932- WhoAm 90
Troy, Dale Winokur 1958- WhoAmW 91
Troy, Henry EarBIAP
Troy, Jack 1938- BioIn 16
Troy, Janet E. ODwPR 91
Troy, Joseph Freed 1938- WhoAm 90, WhoWor 91
Troy, Mary Delphine 1948- WhoWrEP 89
Troy, Michael A St&PR 91
Troy, Richard E BiDrAPA 89
Troy, Shaung Sharon 1940- BiDrAPA 89
Troy, Simon TwCCr&M 91
Troy, Steven M. 1948- St&PR 91
Troy, William C. 1932- St&PR 91
Troya, Ilion 1947- WhoHisp 91
Troya, Rafael 1845-1920 ArtLatA
Troyan, George William 1932- St&PR 91
Troyanek, Richard L. 1932- St&PR 91
Troyanos, Tatiana 1938- IntWWM 90, PenDiMP
Troyanovich, John M 1936- ConAu 31NR
Troyanovsky, Oleg Alexandrovich 1919- WhoWor 91
Troyansky, David George 1955- WhoSSW 91
Troyat, Henri 1911- ConAu 33NR, MajTwCW
Troyer, Alvah Forrest 1929- WhoAm 90
Troyer, John David 1953-1981 BioIn 16
Troyer, Paul St&PR 91
Troyer, Thomas Alfred 1933- WhoE 91
Troyka, Jay St&PR 91
Trozelle, Valerie BioIn 16
Trozzolo, Anthony Marion 1930- WhoAm 90, WhoWor 91
Trpis, Milan 1930- WhoAm 90
Truan, Carlos F. 1935- WhoHisp 91
Truan, Susan Carol 1952- WhoAmW 91
Truax, A. Brad BioIn 16
Truax, Bonnie M. 1945- WhoAmW 91
Truax, Dennis Dale 1953- WhoSSW 91, WhoWor 91
Truax, James Francis 1948- WhoSSW 91
Truax, Richard Allan 1936- BiDrAPA 89
Truax, Valerie W. 1957- WhoSSW 91
Trub, Aaron D. 1935- St&PR 91
Trub, Richard Gibson 1930- St&PR 91
Trubeck, William Lewis 1946- WhoAm 90
Trubee, Suzanne Kathleen 1959- St&PR 91
Trubek, Josephine Susan 1942- WhoAm 90
Trubestein, Gustav Klaus 1939- WhoWor 91
Trubin, John 1917- WhoAm 90
Trubitt, Allen R. 1931- IntWWM 90
Trubner, Henry 1920- WhoAmA 91
Trubo, Herbert Alan 1948- WhoEmL 91
Trubow, Howard Bruce 1951- WhoSSW 91
Trubow, Patricia A. ODwPR 91
Trubowitz, Mark Brian BiDrAPA 89
Truby, Betsy Kirby 1926- WhoAmA 91
Truby, Charles L. 1928- St&PR 91
Truby, John Louis 1933- WhoAm 90
Truby, Michael Clark 1944- WhoSSW 91
Truce, William Everett 1917- WhoAm 90
Truchinski, Jerome Ray 1952- WhoSSW 91
Truck, James L. 1945- St&PR 91
Truckee WhNaAH
Truckee, Captain WhNaAH
Truckenbrod, Phillip 1941- IntWWM 90
Truckenbrodt, Charles David 1939- St&PR 91
Trucks, Virgil 1919- Ballpl 90
Trucksess, A William St&PR 91
Trucksess, H. A., III 1949- St&PR 91
Trudeau, G B 1948- ConAu 31NR
Trudeau, Garry 1948- EncACom, News 91-2 [port], WorAlBi
Trudeau, Garry B ConAu 31NR
Trudeau, Garry B. 1948- WhoAm 90, WhoAmA 91, WhoE 91, WhoWrEP 89
Trudeau, James O. 1916- ODwPR 91
Trudeau, Jane Pauley BioIn 16
Trudeau, Kevin Mark 1963- WhoE 91
Trudeau, Michele ODwPR 91
Trudeau, Noah Andre 1949- ConAu 132
Trudeau, Patricia Margaret 1931- WhoWrEP 89
Trudeau, Pierre Elliott 1919- WhoAm 90, WhoE 91, WhoWor 91, WorAlBi
Trudeau, Toussaint 1826-1893 DcCanB 12
Trudeau, Yves 1930- WhoAmA 91
Trudel, Marc J. WhoAm 90
Trudel, Mary WhoAmW 91
Trudel, Mary R. 1946- ODwPR 91
Trudel, Terry 1943- BiDrAPA 89
Trudell, Sharon WhoWrEP 89
Trudinger, John Philip 1943- St&PR 91
Trudnak, Stephen Joseph 1947- WhoSSW 91
Trudo, Jerry Norman 1944- St&PR 91
True, A Curtis 1929- St&PR 91
True, Charles Wesley, Jr. 1916- WhoSSW 91
True, Claudia 1948- WhoAmW 91
True, Edward B. 1840-1913 AmLegL
True, Edward Keene 1915- WhoAm 90
True, Henry Alfonso, Jr. 1915- WhoAm 90
True, James David BiDrAPA 89
True, Jean Durland 1915- WhoAmW 91, WhoWor 91
True, June Audrey 1927- WhoWrEP 89
True, Louis Poole, Jr. 1943- WhoAm 90
True, Marion 1948- WhoAm 90
True, Nelita BioIn 16
True, Randall Lee BiDrAPA 89
True, Roy Joe 1938- WhoAm 90
True, Wendell Cleon 1934- St&PR 91, WhoAm 90, WhoWor 91
Trueb, Kurt 1926- St&PR 91
Trueba, Fernando 1955- WhoWor 91
Trueba-Zamanillo, Araceli 1928- BiDrAPA 89
Trueblood, Alan Stubbs 1917- WhoAm 90
Trueblood, Cecil Ross 1933- WhoE 91
Trueblood, David Elton 1900- WhoAm 90
Trueblood, Emily Herrick BioIn 16
Trueblood, Gene E. 1951- St&PR 91
Trueblood, Harry A., Jr. 1925- St&PR 91
Trueblood, Harry Albert, Jr. 1925- WhoAm 90
Trueblood, Kenneth Nyitray 1920- WhoAm 90
Trueblood, Paul Graham 1905- WhoAm 90
Trueblood, Samuel E 1923- BiDrAPA 89
Trued, Micheal Eugene 1945- WhoE 91
Trueheart, William E. 1942- WhoAm 90
Truehill, Marshall, Jr. 1948- WhoSSW 91
Truelove, Angelyn Y. 1951- WhoSSW 91
Truelove, C Keith 1949- St&PR 91
Truelove, C. Keith 1949- WhoEmL 91
Truelove, James 1942- St&PR 91
Trueman, Terry Earl 1947- WhoWrEP 89
Trueman, W Hazen 1936- St&PR 91
Trueman, Walter 1928- WhoAm 90
Trueman, William Peter Main 1934- WhoAm 90
Truemper, John James, Jr. 1924- WhoAm 90
Trueschler, Bernard C. 1923- St&PR 91
Truesdale, C W 1929- ConAu 30NR
Truesdale, John Cushman 1921- WhoAm 90
Truesdell, Carolyn Gilmour 1939- WhoAmW 91
Truesdell, Clifford Ambrose, III 1919- WhoAm 90, WhoE 91, WhoWrEP 89
Truesdell, James E., Jr. 1930- St&PR 91
Truesdell, James Leslie 1949- St&PR 91
Truesdell, Jerry William 1940- St&PR 91
Truesdell, Lillian W. 1917- St&PR 91
Truesdell, Wesley E. 1927- ODwPR 91, St&PR 91
Truesdell, Wesley Edwin 1927- WhoAm 90
Truett, Bob 1932- WhoSSW 91
Truett, Casey 1944- WhoSSW 91
Truett, George Washington 1867-1944 BioIn 16
Truett, Harold Joseph, III 1946- WhoEmL 91
Truett, Lila Flory 1947- WhoSSW 91
Truettner, W James 1931- St&PR 91
Truettner, William WhoAmA 91
Truex, Dorothy Adine 1915- WhoAm 90
Truex, Duane Philip, III 1947- WhoAmA 91
Truex, Frances Beach 1938- WhoSSW 91
Truex, Van Day 1904- WhoAmA 91N
Trufelman, Lloyd P. ODwPR 91
Truffaut, Francois 1932-1984 BioIn 16, WorAlBi
Truffelman, Joanne 1943- WhoAmW 91
Trugly, Edith S BiDrAPA 89
Truhlar, Donald Gene 1944- WhoAm 90
Truhlsen, Stanley Marshall 1920- WhoAm 90
Truhol, Eric Horst 1930- St&PR 91
Truillier-Lacombe, Joseph-Patrice 1807-1863 DcLB 99
Truitt, Anne 1921- BiDWomA, WhoAmA 91
Truitt, Anne Dean 1921- WhoAm 90
Truitt, Bryant David 1942- WhoSSW 91
Truitt, Evelyn Mack 1931- WhoAmW 91
Truitt, Gloria A 1939- ConAu 30NR
Truitt, James W. 1937- St&PR 91
Truitt, Kendall L. BioIn 16
Truitt, Phyllis Lynn 1945- WhoAmW 91
Truitt, Richard H. 1932- ODwPR 91
Truitt, Richard Hunt 1932- WhoAm 90
Truitt, Robert Flournoy, Jr. 1949- BiDrAPA 89
Truitt, Robert Ralph, Jr. 1948- WhoEmL 91, WhoSSW 91
Truitt, Thomas Hulen 1935- WhoAm 90
Truitt, Victoria Mize 1949- WhoAmW 91
Trujillo, Anthony J. 1933- WhoHisp 91
Trujillo, Arnold Paul 1951- WhoHisp 91
Trujillo, Candelario, Jr. 1932- WhoHisp 91
Trujillo, Carlos Alberto 1957- WhoHisp 91
Trujillo, Edward M. 1947- WhoHisp 91
Trujillo, Jaime 1941- BiDrAPA 89
Trujillo, Jake Antonio 1944- WhoHisp 91
Trujillo, Joe D. 1940- WhoHisp 91
Trujillo, Larry E. WhoHisp 91
Trujillo, Lionel Gil WhoHisp 91
Trujillo, Luis WhoHisp 91
Trujillo, Manuel 1945- BiDrAPA 89
Trujillo, Michael Joseph 1939- WhoHisp 91
Trujillo, Mike 1960- Ballpl 90
Trujillo, Paul Edward 1952- WhoWrEP 89
Trujillo, Roberto Gabriel 1951- WhoHisp 91
Trujillo, Rudolpho Andres 1939- WhoHisp 91
Trujillo, Solomon D. 1951- WhoHisp 91
Trujillo, Tony A., Jr. ODwPR 91
Trujillo, Veda Arlene Spriggs 1924- St&PR 91
Trujillo-Maestas, Abby WhoHisp 91
Trujillo Molina, Rafael L. 1891-1961 WorAlBi
Trujillo Molina, Rafael Leonidas 1891-1961 BioIn 16
Trukenbrod, William Sellery 1939- WhoAm 90
Trull, Francine Sue 1950- WhoAm 90
Trull, J Larry 1940- St&PR 91
Trulove, Harry David 1927- WhoSSW 91
Trulove, Paul Chappell 1961- WhoE 91
Truluck, Jefferson Ray 1922- St&PR 91
Truly, Richard H. 1937- WhoAm 90
Truman, Bess W. 1885-1982 BioAmW
Truman, Bess Wallace 1885-1982 BioIn 16
Truman, Edwin Malcolm 1941- WhoE 91
Truman, Gary Tucker 1950- WhoSSW 91, WhoWor 91
Truman, Harry S 1884-1972 BiDrUSE 89, BioIn 16, WorAlBi
Truman, Margaret 1924- MajTwCW, WhoAm 90, WhoAmW 91
Trumbauer, Frankie 1901-1956 OxCPMus
Trumble, Melvin Joseph, II 1940- WhoAm 90
Trumble, Robert Roy 1940- WhoAm 90
Trumble, Thomas E. 1953- St&PR 91
Trumbo, Cynthia L. 1955- WhoSSW 91
Trumbo, Dalton 1905-1976 BioIn 16
Trumbull, Dianne Welch BiDrAPA 89
Trumbull, John 1750-1831 EncCRAm, NinCLC 30 [port]
Trumbull, John 1756-1843 EncCRAm, IntDcAA 90, WorAlBi
Trumbull, Jonathan 1710-1785 EncCRAm, WorAlBi
Trumbull, Jonathan 1740-1809 BioIn 16
Trumbull, Jonathan, Jr. 1740-1809 EncCRAm
Trumbull, Joseph 1737-1778 EncCRAm
Trumbull, Richard 1916- WhoAm 90
Trumbull, Robert 1912- WhoAm 90
Trumbull, Ronald Eugene 1931- WhoSSW 91
Trumbull, Stephen Michael 1954- WhoEmL 91
Trumbull, Suzanne Sydney 1939- WhoWor 91
Trumley, Richard L. St&PR 91
Trumm, Paulette C. BiDrAPA 89
Trump, Becky Ann 1955- WhoAmW 91, WhoE 91
Trump, Benjamin Franklin 1932- WhoAm 90
Trump, Clifford WhoAm 90
Trump, Donald J. BioIn 16
Trump, Donald J 1946- ConAu 130, WorAlBi
Trump, Donald John 1946- ConAmBL, WhoAm 90, WhoE 91, WhoSSW 91
Trump, Ivana BioIn 16
Trump, Virginia Lucille 1945- St&PR 91
Trumpler, Paul Robert 1914- WhoAm 90

Trumpy, Hermann Jakob 1936- *WhoWor 91*
Trumpy, R. C. 1928- *St&PR 91*
Trumpy, Thomas Benbow 1938- *WhoWor 91*
Trundle, W Scott 1939- *St&PR 91*
Trundle, Winfield Scott 1939- *WhoAm 90*
Trundlett, Helen B. *MajTwCW*
Trundt, Linda Kay 1955- *WhoSSW 91*
Trung Nhi *WomWR [port]*
Trung Trac *WomWR [port]*
Trungpa Rinpoche, Chogyam 1939-1987 *NewAgE 90*
Trunk, Georg Karl 1961- *WhoWor 91*
Trunnell, Eugene E 1925- *BiDrAPA 89*
Trunnell, Thomas L *BiDrAPA 89*
Trunsky, Ronald E 1931- *BiDrAPA 89*
Trunzo, Nicholas Peter 1928- *St&PR 91*
Truog, W Randle 1912- *St&PR 91*
Truog, William R. 1945- *St&PR 91*
Truong Chinh 1907-1988 *AnObit 1988*
Truong, Chinh 1907-1988 *BioIn 16*
Truong, Hang *BioIn 16*
Truong, Hieu Trong *BiDrAPA 89*
Trupp, Barbara Lee 1950- *WhoAmA 91*
Trupp, Michael S 1933- *BiDrAPA 89*
Trupp, Robin Jean 1953- *WhoWor 91*
Truppin, Ada *BiDrAPA 89*
Truran, James Wellington, Jr. 1940- *WhoAm 90*
Truran, William R. 1951- *WhoE 91, WhoWor 91*
Truschel, Timothy L *BiDrAPA 89*
Truscio, James, Jr. 1942- *WhoE 91*
Trusdell, Mary Louise Cantrell 1921- *WhoWor 91*
Trusheim, H. Edwin 1927- *WhoAm 90*
Trusler, Suzanne Small 1949- *WhoAmW 91*
Truslow, Robert Gurdon 1936- *St&PR 91*
Trussel, Harold Junior 1936- *WhoWor 91*
Trussell, Charles Tait 1925- *WhoAm 90*
Trussell, Robert Stephen 1952- *WhoE 91*
Trusselle, Gar Delano 1946- *WhoE 91*
Trussler, Phyllis Ann 1936- *WhoAmW 91*
Trustman, Benjamin Arthur 1902- *WhoAm 90*
Trusty, Arline Lois 1950- *WhoAmW 91*
Trusty, James Clanton, Sr. 1936- *WhoSSW 91*
Trusty, Mickey Joe 1951- *WhoSSW 91*
Trusty, Roy Lee 1924- *WhoAm 90*
Truswell, Jane 1663-1721? *BiDEWW*
Truta, Joseph M. 1944- *St&PR 91*
Truta, Marianne Patricia 1951- *WhoAmW 91*
Trutanic, Richard Stanley 1952- *WhoE 91*
Truth, Sojourner *BioIn 16*
Truth, Sojourner 1797-1883 *BioAmW, FemiCLE, WorAlBi*
Trutt, Simon Michael 1944- *BiDrAPA 89*
Trutter, John T. *ODwPR 91*
Trutter, John Thomas 1920- *St&PR 91, WhoAm 90, WhoWor 91*
Trutty-Coohill, Patricia *WhoAmA 91*
Truver, Scott Curtis 1950- *WhoE 91*
Truxell, James 1914- *St&PR 91*
Truzinski, Charles G. 1934- *St&PR 91*
Truzzi, Marcello 1935- *EncO&P 3, EncPaPR 91*
Trybula, Walter Joseph 1940- *WhoSSW 91*
Trye, Mary *BiDEWW, FemiCLE*
Trygg, I. A. 1925- *St&PR 91*
Trygg, John L. *ODwPR 91*
Trygstad, Lawrence Benson 1937- *WhoAm 90*
Tryhane, Gerald Aubrey Lisle 1929- *St&PR 91*
Trynin, Nathan Kalman 1930- *St&PR 91*
Tryon, Edward Polk 1940- *WhoAm 90*
Tryon, Georgiana Shick 1945- *WhoAmW 91*
Tryon, Richard R. 1932- *St&PR 91*
Tryon, Rolla Milton, Jr. 1916- *WhoAm 90*
Tryon, Thomas 1926- *ConAu 32NR, MajTwCW, WhoAm 90*
Tryon, Tom *ConAu 32NR, MajTwCW*
Tryon, W S 1901-1989 *ConAu 129*
Tryon, Warren S. 1901-1989 *BioIn 16*
Tryon, William 1729-1788 *EncCRAm*
Tryon, William S. 1931- *St&PR 91*
Trythall, Gil 1930- *IntWWM 90*
Trythall, Harry Gilbert 1930- *WhoAm 90*
Trythall, Richard Aaker 1939- *IntWWM 90*
Trzasko, Joseph Anthony 1946- *WhoE 91, WhoEmL 91, WhoWor 91*
Trzcinski, Ronald E. 1944- *WhoAm 90*
Trzebiatowski, Gregory L. 1937- *WhoAm 90*
Trzepacz, Paula Terese 1952- *BiDrAPA 89, WhoAmW 91*
Trznadel, Frank Dwight 1942- *St&PR 91*
Trznadel, Frank Dwight, Jr. 1942- *WhoAm 90*
Tsafrir, Judy Reis 1956- *BiDrAPA 89*
Tsai Lun 50?-118? *WorAlBi*
Tsai, Chun Ching 1942- *BiDrAPA 89*
Tsai, Gerald, Jr. *BioIn 16*
Tsai, Gerald, Jr. 1928- *St&PR 91*
Tsai, Gerald, Jr. 1929- *WhoE 91*
Tsai, Hsiao Hsia *WhoAmA 91*
Tsai, John W. *WhoE 91*
Tsai, Luke Yihchou 1945- *BiDrAPA 89*
Tsai, Shuenn Jeou 1920- *BiDrAPA 89*
Tsai, Thomas T F 1913- *BiDrAPA 89*
Tsai, Thomas T L *BiDrAPA 89*
Tsai, Wen-Ying 1928- *WhoAm 90, WhoAmA 91*
Tsakalos, Stratos Vasilios 1948- *WhoWor 91*
Tsakanikas, Konstantinos T. 1933- *St&PR 91*
Tsakiridis, Christos L. 1941- *St&PR 91*
Tsakonas, George 1937- *WhoWor 91*
Tsali *WhNaAH*
Tsaloumas, Dimitris 1921- *WorAu 1980 [port]*
Tsaltas, Margaret Owen 1922- *BiDrAPA 89*
Tsambis, Elias *BiDrAPA 89*
Tsang, Carl T. 1947- *St&PR 91*
Tsang, Linda Hansford 1946- *WhoEmL 91*
Tsang, Philip Chung-Tak 1949- *St&PR 91*
Ts'ao Yu *WorAu 1980*
Tsao, Daniel *BiDrAPA 89*
Tsao, Hai Cheng *BiDrAPA 89*
Tsao, Thomas K S 1941- *BiDrAPA 89*
Tsapogas, Makis J. 1926- *WhoAm 90, WhoWor 91*
Tsaruk, Oles Volodymyr 1962- *WhoWor 91*
Tsatsos, Constantine Adam 1963- *WhoE 91*
Tsbouchi, Kazuhiro 1929- *WhoWor 91*
Tschacbasov, Nahum 1899-1984 *WhoAmA 91N*
Tschacher, Klaus Herbert 1942- *WhoSSW 91*
Tschaikov, Basil Nichols 1925- *IntWWM 90*
Tschannen, Robert Albert 1922- *St&PR 91*
Tschantz, Bruce Allen 1938- *WhoAm 90*
Tschappat, Douglas Wilson 1927- *St&PR 91, WhoAm 90*
Tscherny, George 1924- *BioIn 16, ConDes 90, WhoAm 90*
Tschichold, Jan 1902-1974 *ConDes 90*
Tschiedel, Hans Jurgen 1941- *WhoWor 91*
Tschinkel, Sheila Lerner 1940- *WhoAm 90, WhoAmW 91, WhoSSW 91*
Tschinkel, Victoria Jean 1947- *WhoAmW 91*
Tschirky, Oscar 1866-1950 *WorAlBi*
Tschirnhausen, Ehrenfried Walther von *PenDiDA 89*
Tschoepe, Thomas 1915- *WhoAm 90, WhoSSW 91*
Tschopp, Bernard 1952- *WhoWor 91*
Tschudi, Theo 1941- *WhoWor 91*
Tse, Charlene Kit-Yu 1958- *WhoAmW 91*
Tse, John Wai-Kwong 1951- *WhoWor 91*
Tse, Mary Mo-Yung 1949- *WhoE 91*
Tse, Stephen 1938- *WhoAmA 91*
Tse, Stephen Y.N. 1931- *St&PR 91*
Tse, Stephen Yung Nien 1931- *WhoAm 90, WhoWor 91*
Tse, Tenny Ping-Hang 1948- *WhoSSW 91*
Tseckares, Charles Nicholas 1936- *WhoAm 90*
Tsederbaum, Iurii Osipovich 1873-1923 *BioIn 16*
Tselos, Dimitri Theodore 1900- *WhoAmA 91*
Tseng Yu-Ho 1924- *WhoAmA 91*
Tseng, Ampere An-Pei 1946- *WhoWor 91*
Tseng, Evelin Meichih 1938- *WhoSSW 91*
Tseng, Howard Shih Chang 1935- *WhoSSW 91, WhoWor 91*
Tseng, Jack H.N. 1950- *St&PR 91*
Tseng, Joan Liu 1939- *WhoAmW 91*
Tseng, Kwo-Hwa 1937- *BiDrAPA 89*
Tseng, Kwong-chi 1950-1990 *BioIn 16*
Tseng, Ling-Yuan 1948- *WhoWor 91*
Tseng, Wen-Shing 1935- *BiDrAPA 89*
Tsenin, Ksenia 1947- *WhoEmL 91*
Tsereteli, Irakil Georgievich 1882-1959 *BioIn 16*
Tsering, Dawa 1935- *WhoWor 91*
Tseu, Lawrence Kum Wing 1932- *WhoWor 91*
Tshombe, Moise K. 1919-1969 *WorAlBi*
Tshusick *WhNaAH*
Tsiapera, Maria 1935- *WhoAm 90*
Tsien, Richard Winyu 1945- *WhoAm 90*
Tsiganov, Dmitry *PenDiMP*
Tsigdinos, Karl Andrew 1954- *WhoWor 91*
Tsikis, Eugene K. 1958- *WhoSSW 91*
Tsilivakos, Dimitrios 1959- *WhoWor 91*
Tsimboukis, Demetrios George 1946- *WhoWor 91*
Tsinisizelis, Michael 1955- *WhoWor 91*
Tsiolas, Stelios 1955- *IntWWM 90*
Tsiolkovskii, Konstantin 1857-1935 *BioIn 16*
Tsiolkovsky, Konstantin 1857-1935 *WorAlBi*
Tsiouris, John A 1942- *BiDrAPA 89*
Tsipis, Kosta Michael 1934- *WhoE 91*
Tsirilaki, Katerina *BiDrAPA 89*
Tsitos, Tony A 1935- *BiDrAPA 89*
Tsitouris, John 1936- *Ballpl 90*
Tsivitse, Peter J. 1930- *St&PR 91*
Tso, Faye 1933- *MusmAFA*
Ts'o, Paul On-Pong 1929- *WhoAm 90*
Tso, Thomasze Chung Mou 1949- *WhoSSW 91*
Tso, Tien Chioh 1917- *WhoAm 90*
Ts'O, Timothy On To *BiDrAPA 89*
Tsoi, Viktor *NewYTBS 90*
Ts'ong, Fou *PenDiMP*
Tsongas, Paul Efthemios 1941- *WhoAm 90*
Tsou, Jung-Kwang 1936- *WhoWor 91*
Tsou, Tang 1918- *WhoAm 90*
Tsoucalas, Nicholas 1926- *WhoAm 90*
Tsoulfanidis, Nicholas 1938- *WhoAm 90*
T'Souvas, Robert *BioIn 16*
Tsu, John B. 1924- *WhoAm 90*
Tsuang, Debby Wen *BiDrAPA 89*
Tsuang, Ming Tso 1931- *BiDrAPA 89, WhoAm 90*
Tsuboi, Hirotsugu 1933- *BiDrAPA 89*
Tsubouchi, Daniel T. *St&PR 91*
Tsuchida, Kiyomasa 1947- *WhoWor 91*
Tsuchiya, Arthur S. 1945- *St&PR 91*
Tsuchiya, Suma 1924- *WhoWor 91*
Tsuchiya, Tilsa 1932-1984 *ArtLatA*
Tsuda, Hideo 1918- *WhoWor 91*
Tsuda, Kazuichi 1935- *WhoWor 91*
Tsuda, Michiko 1949- *IntWWM 90*
Tsuda, Nobuo 1936- *WhoWor 91*
Tsue, John Masaichi 1949- *WhoWor 91*
Tsuge, Shin 1939- *WhoWor 91*
Tsui, Daisy *BioIn 16*
Tsui, Hark *BioIn 16*
Tsui, Lap-Chee *BioIn 16*
Tsui, Lap-Chee 1950- *WhoE 91*
Tsuji, Shojiro 1927- *WhoWor 91*
Tsujimoto, Trude A. 1953- *St&PR 91*
Tsujioka, Katsuhiko 1947- *WhoWor 91*
Tsukada, Kenichi 1950- *IntWWM 90*
Tsukada, Osamu 1929- *WhoWor 91*
Tsukamoto, Mary *BioIn 16*
Tsukamoto, Naoki 1940- *WhoWor 91*
Tsukazaki, Seiki 1911- *WhoWor 91*
Tsukerman, Vladislav 1939- *WhoWor 91*
Tsukioka, Mitsuko 1940- *WhoWor 91*
Tsumi *NewAgMG*
Tsunashima, Kunio 1949- *WhoWor 91*
Tsunehiko, Tani 1938- *WhoE 91*
Tsuneishi, Warren Michio 1921- *WhoE 91*
Tsung, Der-Cheng 1937- *BiDrAPA 89*
Tsuno, Yukindo 1930- *WhoWor 91*
Tsurtani, Taketsugu 1935- *WhoAm 90*
Tsuruno, Shiro 1946- *WhoWor 91*
Tsuruta, Kuniaki 1936- *St&PR 91*
Tsushima, Nobuko 1937- *WhoWor 91*
Tsushima, Yukio 1941- *WhoWor 91*
Tsushima, Yuko 1947- *WhoWor 91*
Tsusue, Akio 1928- *WhoWor 91*
Tsutakawa, George 1910- *WhoAmA 91*
Tsutani, Motohiro 1935- *WhoWor 91*
Tsutsui, Yoriko 1945- *ConAu 132*
Tsutsumi, Seiji *BioIn 16*
Tsutsumi, Tsuyoshi 1942- *IntWWM 90*
Tsutsumi, Yoshiaki *BioIn 16, WhoWor 91*
Tsuyoshi, Nakamura 1926- *WhoWor 91*
Tsuzaki, Koichi 1953- *WhoE 91*
Tsvetaeva, Marina 1882-1941 *EncCoWW*
Tsvetaeva, Marina 1892-1941 *MajTwCW*
Tsvetaeva, Marina Ivanovna 1892-1941 *BioIn 16*
Tsvetayeva, Marina 1892-1941 *FemiCLE*
Tsvett, Mikhail 1872-1919 *WorAlBi*
Tswett, Mikhail 1872-1919 *BioIn 16*
Tsynman, Alexander 1939- *BiDrAPA 89*
Tsypin, George *BioIn 16*
Tu Fu 712-770 *WorAlBi*
Tu, Loring Wuliang 1952- *WhoE 91*
Tu, Wei-Ming 1940- *WhoAm 90*
Tua, Teresina 1867-1955 *PenDiMP*
Tuan, Chung-Hao *BiDrAPA 89*
Tuan, Debbie Fu-Tai 1930- *WhoAmW 91*
Tuan, Paul 1944- *St&PR 91*
Tuan, San Fu 1932- *WhoAm 90*
Tuason, Amenra Formoso 1956- *BiDrAPA 89*
Tuason, Vicente B 1930- *BiDrAPA 89*
Tubb, Carrie 1876-1976 *PenDiMP*
Tubb, Ernest *WhoNeCM C*
Tubb, Ernest 1914-1984 *ConMus 4 [port], OxCPMus*
Tubb, James Clarence *WhoAm 90*
Tubbert, Margaret A. *WhoAmW 91*
Tubbs, Billy *BioIn 16*
Tubbs, Clifford Lee 1948- *WhoSSW 91*
Tubbs, David Eugene 1948- *WhoSSW 91*
Tubbs, LeVester 1938- *WhoSSW 91*
Tubbs, Linda Marie 1947- *St&PR 91*
Tubbs, Richard Holmes, Jr. 1946- *St&PR 91, WhoEmL 91*
Tubbs, Vincent *BioIn 16*
Tubbs, Vincent 1959- *DrBlPA 90*
Tubby, Gertrude Ogden 1878- *EncO&P 3*
Tubby, Josiah Thomas 1875-1958 *WhoAmA 91N*
Tubby, Roger Wellington 1910- *WhoAm 90, WhoWor 91*
Tuberville, W. P. *St&PR 91*
Tubiana, Raoul Leon 1915- *WhoWor 91*
Tubis, Seymour 1919- *WhoAm 90, WhoAmA 91*
Tubis, Stuart Harvey *BiDrAPA 89*
Tublitz, Evan 1952- *WhoE 91*
Tubman, Harriet 1815?-1913 *BioIn 16*
Tubman, Harriet 1820?-1913 *WorAlBi*
Tubman, Harriet Ross 1826-1913 *BioAmW*
Tubman, William Charles 1932- *WhoAm 90*
Tuby, Robert 1907-1989 *BioIn 16*
Tucapsky, Antonin 1928- *IntWWM 90*
Tucceri, Clive Knowles 1953- *WhoAmW 91, WhoE 91, WhoEmL 91, WhoWor 91*
Tucci, Carolyn *WhoAmW 91*
Tucci, Daniel Patrick 1943- *St&PR 91*
Tucci, Gabriella 1929- *IntWWM 90*
Tucci, Gerald F. 1926- *St&PR 91*
Tucci, Gerald Frank 1926- *WhoE 91*
Tucci, John Vincent 1949- *WhoE 91*
Tucci, Mark A. 1950- *WhoE 91, WhoEmL 91*
Tucci, Nicholas 1936- *WhoE 91*
Tucci, Tony 1935- *St&PR 91*
Tuccillo, Anthony J. 1938- *St&PR 91*
Tuch, Richard H *BiDrAPA 89*
Tuchi, Ben Joseph 1936- *WhoSSW 91*
Tuchin, Terry Allen 1942- *BiDrAPA 89*
Tuchman, Avraham 1935- *WhoAm 90*
Tuchman, Barbara 1912-1989 *AnObit 1989, WorAlBi*
Tuchman, Barbara W 1912-1989 *MajTwCW*
Tuchman, Barbara Wertheim *BioIn 16*
Tuchman, Maurice 1936- *WhoAmA 91*
Tuchman, Michael M *BiDrAPA 89*
Tuchman, Phyllis 1947- *WhoAmA 91*
Tuchman, Sidney 1924- *WhoWor 91*
Tuchman, Steven Leslie 1946- *WhoEmL 91*
Tuchman, Thomas Earl 1945- *WhoE 91*
Tuchman, Walter W 1929- *BiDrAPA 89*
Tucholke, Christel-Anthony 1941- *WhoAmA 91*
Tucholsky, Kurt 1890-1935 *BioIn 16*
Tuck, Alan W. 1948- *St&PR 91*
Tuck, April Elizabeth 1956- *WhoAmW 91*
Tuck, Dennis R. 1943- *St&PR 91*
Tuck, Donald Richard 1935- *WhoSSW 91*
Tuck, Edward Hallam 1927- *WhoAm 90*
Tuck, Grayson Edwin 1927- *WhoAm 90*
Tuck, Hugh Macauley 1945- *St&PR 91*
Tuck, John 1945- *WhoAm 90*
Tuck, Lynne 1938- *WhoAmW 91*
Tuck, Michael R. 1941- *St&PR 91*
Tuck, Michael Ray 1941- *WhoAm 90*
Tuck, Murray 1920- *WhoE 91, WhoWor 91*
Tuck, N Barton 1938- *St&PR 91*
Tuck, Robert Mell 1921- *St&PR 91*
Tuck, Russell R., Jr. 1934- *WhoAm 90*
Tuck, William Richard, Jr. 1922- *WhoWor 91*
Tucker, Alan Curtiss 1943- *WhoAm 90*
Tucker, Alan David 1936- *WhoAm 90*
Tucker, Allan 1921- *WhoAm 90*
Tucker, Allen Brown, Jr. 1942- *WhoAm 90*
Tucker, Allen Phillip 1936- *St&PR 91*
Tucker, Anne Wilkes 1945- *BioIn 16, WhoAm 90, WhoAmA 91*
Tucker, Annette La Verne *WhoAmW 91*
Tucker, Annette Veree 1925- *WhoE 91*
Tucker, Anthony 1924- *WhoWor 91*
Tucker, Arthur Farrar 1948- *St&PR 91*
Tucker, Arthur V. 1949- *St&PR 91*
Tucker, Aubrey Stephen 1945- *WhoSSW 91*
Tucker, Avis Green 1915- *WhoAm 90*
Tucker, Barbara Hartman 1942- *WhoAmW 91*
Tucker, Benjamin R. 1854-1939 *EncAL*
Tucker, Benjamin Ricketson 1854-1939 *BioIn 16*
Tucker, Beverly Sowers 1936- *WhoAmW 91*
Tucker, Bob 1932- *BioIn 16*
Tucker, Carll 1951- *St&PR 91*
Tucker, Caroline *AuBYP 90*
Tucker, Charles B. 1920- *St&PR 91*
Tucker, Charles Christopher 1950- *WhoWrEP 89*
Tucker, Charles Clement 1913- *WhoAmA 91*
Tucker, Charles Ray 1950- *WhoSSW 91, WhoWor 91*
Tucker, Charlie Alexander *BioIn 16*
Tucker, Charlotte Maria 1821-1893 *BioIn 16, FemiCLE*
Tucker, Clifton A. 1948- *St&PR 91*
Tucker, Cora Lee *BioIn 16*
Tucker, Curtis 1939- *WhoAmA 91*
Tucker, Cynthia Delores Nottage 1927- *WhoAm 90*
Tucker, D Weston 1938- *St&PR 91*

Tucker, Dale D. 1940- *St&PR 91*
Tucker, Daniel M *BiDrAPA 89*
Tucker, David Milton 1937- *WhoSSW 91*
Tucker, Deborah Diane 1952- *WhoAmW 91*
Tucker, Deborah M. 1952- *St&PR 91*
Tucker, Don Eugene 1928- *St&PR 91, WhoAm 90*
Tucker, Donald M. 1922- *St&PR 91*
Tucker, Douglas Eliot 1958- *BiDrAPA 89*
Tucker, Earl *St&PR 91*
Tucker, Edith McMillan 1938- *WhoAmW 91*
Tucker, Edward Llewellyn 1921- *WhoSSW 91*
Tucker, Elizabeth M *BiDrAPA 89*
Tucker, Elmer Dean 1927- *WhoAm 90*
Tucker, Ernest Edward 1916-1969 *AuBYP 90*
Tucker, Forrest 1919-1986 *BioIn 16, WorAlBi*
Tucker, Frances Laughridge 1916- *WhoAmW 91*
Tucker, Frank T. 1949- *St&PR 91*
Tucker, Fred C., Jr. 1918- *WhoAm 90*
Tucker, Frederick C 1946- *BiDrAPA 89*
Tucker, Frederick Thomas 1940- *WhoAm 90*
Tucker, Gardiner Luttrell 1925- *WhoAm 90*
Tucker, Garland Scott, III 1947- *St&PR 91, WhoE 91*
Tucker, Gary Francis 1936- *St&PR 91*
Tucker, Gary Jay 1934- *BiDrAPA 89, WhoAm 90*
Tucker, Geoffrey A *BiDrAPA 89*
Tucker, George 1775-1861 *EncABHB 6 [port]*
Tucker, George Maxwell, Sr. 1950- *WhoEmL 91*
Tucker, George McKinney, Jr. 1934- *St&PR 91*
Tucker, Glenn Allan 1948- *St&PR 91*
Tucker, Glenn Gorham 1928- *WhoSSW 91*
Tucker, Gordon Michael 1955- *St&PR 91*
Tucker, H. Richard 1936- *WhoAm 90*
Tucker, Harlan Winthrop 1923- *WhoSSW 91*
Tucker, Harry Jackson, Jr. 1928- *WhoE 91*
Tucker, Harvey Michael 1938- *WhoAm 90*
Tucker, Helen W. 1926- *WhoWrEP 89*
Tucker, Herbert J. 1934- *St&PR 91*
Tucker, Howard McKeldin 1930- *WhoE 91, WhoWor 91*
Tucker, James David 1937- *St&PR 91*
Tucker, James Drew 1957- *BiDrAPA 89*
Tucker, James E. 1943- *St&PR 91*
Tucker, James Ewing 1930- *WhoAmA 91*
Tucker, James F. 1924- *St&PR 91*
Tucker, Janee Michelle 1946- *WhoAmW 91*
Tucker, Janet Lynn 1956- *WhoAmW 91*
Tucker, Janet Lynn 1961- *WhoEmL 91*
Tucker, Jay Scott 1957- *St&PR 91*
Tucker, Jeffrey Allen 1947- *St&PR 91*
Tucker, Jeffrey Thornton 1950- *WhoEmL 91*
Tucker, Jennifer Beth *BiDrAPA 89*
Tucker, Jerry *BioIn 16*
Tucker, Jim Boyce *BiDrAPA 89*
Tucker, John Avery 1924- *WhoE 91*
Tucker, John D. 1943- *ODwPR 91*
Tucker, John Pierce, Jr. 1943- *WhoSSW 91*
Tucker, John Stanley 1940- *WhoE 91*
Tucker, Joyce Elaine 1948- *WhoAmW 91*
Tucker, Judy Carolyn *BiDrAPA 89*
Tucker, Julius Lafayette *BioIn 16*
Tucker, Katharine 1885-1957 *BioIn 16*
Tucker, Kay Hartman 1957- *WhoWrEP 89*
Tucker, Keith A. 1945- *St&PR 91, WhoAm 90*
Tucker, Keith A. 1962- *WhoSSW 91*
Tucker, Keith E. 1933- *WhoAm 90*
Tucker, Kenneth F *BiDrAPA 89*
Tucker, Landrum S, Jr. 1939- *BiDrAPA 89*
Tucker, Laurey Dan 1936- *WhoAm 90, WhoSSW 91*
Tucker, Leatrice Yvonne *WhoAmA 91*
Tucker, Ledyard R. *BioIn 16*
Tucker, Lem 1938- *DrBIPA 90, WhoAm 90*
Tucker, Linda Wise 1955- *WhoAmW 91*
Tucker, Lorenzo 1907-1986 *BioIn 16, DrBIPA 90*
Tucker, Louis Leonard 1927- *WhoAm 90, WhoE 91*
Tucker, Lucy C *BiDrAPA 89*
Tucker, Lynn Weddington *ODwPR 91*
Tucker, Marcia 1940- *WhoAm 90, WhoAmA 91*
Tucker, Margaret Ruth *IntWWM 90*
Tucker, Marshall D. 1932- *St&PR 91*
Tucker, Martin 1928- *WhoE 91, WhoWrEP 89*
Tucker, Mary Louise 1945- *WhoAmW 91*
Tucker, Melody Sue 1947- *WhoAmW 91*
Tucker, Melvin Jay 1931- *WhoWrEP 89*
Tucker, Michael *BioIn 16*
Tucker, Michael Brian 1948- *St&PR 91*
Tucker, Michael Corhitt 1958- *WhoSSW 91*
Tucker, Morrison G. 1911- *St&PR 91*
Tucker, Morrison Graham 1911- *WhoAm 90, WhoSSW 91*
Tucker, Myrna Blanca *BiDrAPA 89*
Tucker, N George 1920- *St&PR 91*
Tucker, Nancy Meredith 1946- *WhoWrEP 89*
Tucker, Neil Thomas 1949- *WhoSSW 91*
Tucker, Nicholas J. 1951- *St&PR 91*
Tucker, Nimrod Holt, III 1947- *WhoSSW 91*
Tucker, Pama Lee 1953- *WhoAmW 91*
Tucker, Patricia S. 1944- *WhoAmW 91*
Tucker, Paul Andrew 1939- *St&PR 91*
Tucker, Paul Hayes 1950- *WhoE 91*
Tucker, Paul William 1921- *WhoAm 90*
Tucker, Peri 1911- *WhoAmA 91*
Tucker, Phebe Mary 1949- *BiDrAPA 89*
Tucker, Preston 1901-1956 *BioIn 16*
Tucker, Preston Thomas 1903-1956 *EncABHB 5 [port]*
Tucker, Randall 1931- *ODwPR 91*
Tucker, Randolph Wadsworth 1949- *WhoAm 90*
Tucker, Ray Moss *WhoSSW 91*
Tucker, Richard 1913-1975 *PenDiMP*
Tucker, Richard 1914-1975 *WorAlBi*
Tucker, Richard 1938- *WhoAm 90*
Tucker, Richard Frank 1926- *WhoAm 90*
Tucker, Richard Lee 1935- *WhoAm 90*
Tucker, Richard Lee 1940- *St&PR 91, WhoAm 90*
Tucker, Robert A. 1926- *St&PR 91*
Tucker, Robert D. 1933- *St&PR 91*
Tucker, Robert Dennard 1933- *WhoAm 90, WhoWor 91*
Tucker, Robert Macom 1959- *WhoSSW 91*
Tucker, Robert Warren 1924- *WhoAm 90*
Tucker, Royster M., Jr. 1931- *St&PR 91*
Tucker, Samuel Brian 1953- *BiDrAPA 89*
Tucker, Sara S 1933- *BiDrAPA 89*
Tucker, Sheridan G 1950- *BiDrAPA 89*
Tucker, Sheridan Gregory 1950- *WhoWor 91*
Tucker, Shirley Lois 1927- *WhoAm 90*
Tucker, Sophie 1884-1966 *BioAmW, BioIn 16, OxCPMus, WorAlBi*
Tucker, Spencer Coakley 1937- *WhoSSW 91*
Tucker, Stefan Franklin 1938- *WhoAm 90*
Tucker, Susan 1950- *ConAu 130*
Tucker, Susan Carol 1944- *WhoAmW 91*
Tucker, Susan Rona *BiDrAPA 89*
Tucker, Suzanne Marie 1945- *WhoEmL 91*
Tucker, Tanya 1958- *BioIn 16, WhoNeCM [port], WorAlBi*
Tucker, Tanya Denise 1958- *WhoAm 90*
Tucker, Terry Lee 1948- *WhoSSW 91*
Tucker, Theresa Peterson 1946- *WhoAmW 91*
Tucker, Thomas 1812-1890 *PenDiDA 89*
Tucker, Thomas Andrew 1937- *BiDrAPA 89*
Tucker, Thomas James 1929- *St&PR 91, WhoAm 90*
Tucker, Thomas S., Jr. 1948- *St&PR 91*
Tucker, Thomas Tudor 1745-1828 *BioIn 16*
Tucker, Thomas William 1945- *WhoE 91*
Tucker, Thurman 1917- *Ballpl 90*
Tucker, Todd Stephan 1942- *St&PR 91*
Tucker, Tommy 1863-1935 *Ballpl 90*
Tucker, Tommy 1903-1989 *BioIn 16*
Tucker, Tracy J. 1948- *St&PR 91*
Tucker, Walter I 1911- *BiDrAPA 89*
Tucker, Wanda Hall 1921- *WhoAmW 91*
Tucker, Weir M *BiDrAPA 89*
Tucker, William E. 1937- *WhoWor 91*
Tucker, William Edward 1932- *WhoAm 90, WhoSSW 91*
Tucker, William Ellis *PenDiDA 89*
Tucker, William G 1935- *WhoAmA 91*
Tucker, William M 1941- *BiDrAPA 89*
Tucker, William Vincent 1934- *WhoAm 90*
Tucker, Willis Carleton 1907- *WhoAm 90*
Tucker, Wilson 1914- *RGTwCSF*
Tucker-Diggs, Francine Marie 1949- *WhoAmW 91*
Tucker-Griffith, Gail Susan 1945- *WhoAmW 91*
Tucker-Parrish, Florence Denslow *WhoAmW 91, WhoSSW 91*
Tucker-Pickens, Mary Olive 1947- *WhoWrEP 89*
Tuckerman, Henry Theodore 1813-1871 *BioIn 16*
Tuckerman, Jane Bayard 1947- *WhoAmA 91, WhoE 91*
Tuckett, Alan *BioIn 16*
Tuckett, George Elias 1835-1900 *DcCanB 12*
Tuckett, Gordon 1928- *WhoWor 91*
Tuckett, Rhona Bennett 1947- *WhoAmW 91*
Tuckey, Bruce M. 1957- *St&PR 91*
Tuckman, Alan Joel 1938- *BiDrAPA 89*
Tuckman, Bruce Wayne 1938- *WhoAm 90*
Tuckman, Howard Paul 1941- *WhoAm 90*
Tuckman, Marvin Alfred 1925- *WhoAm 90*
Tuckman, Toby Burke 1937- *WhoE 91*
Tuckwell, Barry 1931- *BioIn 16, PenDiMP*
Tuckwell, Barry Emmanuel 1931- *WhoAm 90*
Tuculescu, Radu 1949- *IntWWM 90*
Tuddenham, Read Duncan 1915- *WhoAm 90*
Tuder, Edward Neal 1944- *BiDrAPA 89*
Tudisco, Jasper Thomas 1917- *WhoE 91*
Tudor, Antony 1909-1987 *BioIn 16, WorAlBi*
Tudor, Bethany *AuBYP 90*
Tudor, David 1926- *BioIn 16, PenDiMP*
Tudor, Edward C. 1920- *St&PR 91*
Tudor, Guy *BioIn 16*
Tudor, Ina Pollack 1955- *WhoAmW 91*
Tudor, James Cameron 1918- *WhoWor 91*
Tudor, Jim Patrick 1946- *WhoWrEP 89*
Tudor, John 1954- *Ballpl 90 [port]*
Tudor, John Colin 1941- *WhoWor 91*
Tudor, Ray Gerald 1940- *WhoSSW 91*
Tudor, Robert Beall, Jr. 1935- *St&PR 91*
Tudor, Rosamond 1878-1949 *WhoAmA 91N*
Tudor, Tasha 1915- *AuBYP 90*
Tudryn, Joyce Marie 1959- *WhoE 91*
Tudy, Mildred *BioIn 16*
Tudzynski, Paul 1951- *WhoWor 91*
Tuegel, Michele A 1952- *WhoAmA 91*
Tuemmler, William B. *St&PR 91N*
Tuempel, Christian Ludwig 1937- *WhoWor 91*
Tuerff, James Rodrick 1941- *St&PR 91, WhoAm 90, WhoSSW 91*
Tuerk, Isadore *BiDrAPA 89*
Tuerk, James R. 1953- *St&PR 91*
Tuerk, Jonathan D 1939- *BiDrAPA 89*
Tuerk, Jonathan David 1939- *WhoE 91*
Tuerk, Richard Carl 1941- *WhoSSW 91*
Tuesday, David Sheffield 1956- *WhoEmL 91*
Tueting, William Francis 1942- *WhoAm 90*
Tufano, Manuela 1957- *WhoAmW 91, WhoE 91*
Tufariello, Joseph James 1935- *WhoAm 90*
Tufaro, Richard Chase 1944- *WhoE 91*
Tufeld, Howard L. 1935- *St&PR 91*
Tuff, Timothy C. *WhoAm 90*
Tuffley, Francis Douglas 1946- *WhoEmL 91*
Tuffy, John C. 1938- *ODwPR 91*
Tufly, Elvin G. 1939- *St&PR 91*
Tufo, Robert Peter 1942- *BiDrAPA 89*
Tuft, Jerold H. 1929- *St&PR 91*
Tuft, Jerold Herbert 1929- *WhoAm 90*
Tuft, Mary Ann 1934- *WhoAm 90*
Tufte, Edward Rolf 1942- *WhoAm 90, WhoWrEP 89*
Tufte, Obert Norman 1932- *WhoAm 90*
Tufton, Elizabeth *BiDEWW*
Tufts, Anne *AuBYP 90*
Tufts, Arthur James 1914- *WhoE 91*
Tufts, David Albert, Jr. 1945- *WhoAm 90, WhoE 91*
Tufts, Eleanor M *WhoAmA 91*
Tufts, Eleanor May 1927- *WhoAm 90, WhoSSW 91*
Tufts, Georgia *AuBYP 90*
Tufts, James 1829-1884 *AmLegL*
Tufts, John 1689-1752 *EncCRAm*
Tufts, Warren 1925-1982 *EncACom*
Tufts, Warren G. 1917- *St&PR 91*
Tufty, Barbara Jean 1923- *WhoE 91*
Tufty, Esther Van Wagoner 1896-1986 *BioIn 16*
Tufty, Harold Guilford 1922- *WhoE 91*
Tugcu, Nejat 1945- *WhoWor 91*
Tugend, Harry 1898-1989 *BioIn 16, ConAu 129*
Tugendhat, Christopher 1937- *St&PR 91*
Tuggle, Francis Douglas 1943- *WhoAm 90*
Tuggle, Judy Gail 1946- *WhoAmW 91*
Tuggle, Ralph E. 1937- *St&PR 91*
Tuggle, Richard Brittain *NewYTBS 90*
Tuggle, William Orrie 1841-1885 *WhNaAH*
Tugman, John Charles 1949- *St&PR 91*
Tugman, Stuart Grady 1937- *St&PR 91*
Tugwell, Cynthia Kay 1954- *WhoAmW 91*
Tugwell, Rexford G. 1891-1979 *BioIn 16*
Tuhkio, Kari Juhani 1948- *WhoWor 91*
Tuholski, Elizabeth Murray 1956- *WhoAmW 91*
Tuholski, James Martin 1924- *WhoAm 90*
Tuhy, Marie Ruth 1961- *WhoAmW 91*
Tuhy, Philip Radmir 1930- *WhoE 91*
Tuinstra, Robert Jacob 1925- *St&PR 91*
Tu'ipelehake, Fatafehi 1922- *WhoWor 91*
Tuita, Siosaia Aleamotu'a Laufilitonga 1920- *WhoWor 91*
Tuite, Eliza Dorothea 1764-1850 *FemiCLE*
Tuite, John Francis 1927- *WhoAm 90*
Tuite, John J., III 1944- *St&PR 91*
Tuite, Joseph Patrick 1914- *WhoAm 90*
Tuite, Michael Leon 1943- *WhoWor 91*
Tuitt, Ron S. 1958- *WhoWrEP 89*
Tujague, Arthur William 1913- *St&PR 91*
Tuka, Vojtech 1880-1946 *BioIn 16*
Tuke, Anthony Favill 1920- *St&PR 91*
Tukes, Sammuel Lee 1947- *WhoSSW 91*
Tukey, Brad R. 1946- *St&PR 91*
Tukey, Harold Bradford, Jr. 1934- *WhoAm 90*
Tukey, Loren Davenport 1921- *WhoAm 90*
Tukhachevsky, Mikhail N. 1893-1937 *BioIn 16*
Tukuafu, Rose A. 1954- *WhoAmW 91*
Tuley, B. B. 1936- *St&PR 91*
Tuley, John L. 1922- *St&PR 91*
Tuley, Margaret *WhoAmW 91*
Tuley, Richard William 1942- *St&PR 91*
Tuley, Thomas W. 1940- *St&PR 91*
Tuley, Thomas Wayne 1940- *WhoAm 90*
Tuli, Felix *EncCoWW*
Tulin, George A *BiDrAPA 89*
Tulin, James Edward 1951- *St&PR 91*
Tulin, Marshall 1918- *St&PR 91*
Tulin, Shale Leon 1915- *WhoE 91*
Tulipan, Alan B 1920- *BiDrAPA 89*
Tulis, Jeffrey K 1950- *ConAu 30NR*
Tulk, Alfred James 1899- *WhoAmA 91*
Tull, Ann Hinds 1938- *WhoE 91*
Tull, Donald Stanley 1924- *WhoAm 90*
Tull, Fisher Aubrey 1934- *IntWWM 90*
Tull, Patrick 1941- *ConTFT 8 [port]*
Tull, Renee Martin 1950- *WhoAmW 91*
Tull, Robert Lewis 1926- *St&PR 91*
Tull, Theresa Anne 1936- *WhoAmW 91, WhoWor 91*
Tull, William G. 1928- *St&PR 91*
Tull, Willis Clayton, Jr. 1931- *WhoE 91, WhoWor 91*
Tulledge, Robert Eugene 1929- *St&PR 91*
Tullidge, Edward William 1829-1894 *BioIn 16*
Tullin, Harvey 1938- *BiDrAPA 89*
Tullio, Douglas J. 1943- *St&PR 91*
Tullio, Louis J. 1917-1990 *BioIn 16*
Tullis, Bill 1953- *WhoSSW 91*
Tullis, Edward Lewis 1917- *WhoAm 90, WhoWor 91*
Tullis, Garner H 1939- *WhoAmA 91*
Tullis, James Luther Lyman 1947- *WhoAm 90, WhoE 91*
Tullis, John Ledbetter 1911- *WhoAm 90*
Tullis, Kenneth Frank 1944- *BiDrAPA 89*
Tullis, Lucy Meryl 1906- *WhoAmW 91*
Tullis, William H *BiDrAPA 89*
Tulliu, Sybilla 1927- *BiDrAPA 89*
Tullman, Arthur S. 1917- *St&PR 91*
Tullman, Glen Edward 1959- *St&PR 91*
Tullman, Howard A. 1945- *St&PR 91*
Tulloch, George S. 1932- *St&PR 91*
Tulloch, George Sherlock, Jr. 1932- *WhoAm 90, WhoWor 91*
Tulloch, John R. 1947- *St&PR 91*
Tulloch, Rodney William 1939- *WhoSSW 91*
Tulloch, William W. 1954- *St&PR 91*
Tulloch, William W., Jr. 1930- *St&PR 91*
Tullock, Gordon 1922- *WhoAm 90*
Tullos, Allen 1950- *ConAu 132*
Tullos, Hugh Simpson 1935- *WhoAm 90*
Tullos, John Baxter 1915- *St&PR 91, WhoAm 90*
Tullsen, Rex 1907- *WhoAmA 91*
Tully, Albert Julian 1911- *WhoAm 90*
Tully, Alice 1902- *BioIn 16*
Tully, Andrew Frederick, Jr. 1914- *WhoAm 90, WhoWrEP 89*
Tully, Carol Thorpe 1946- *WhoAmW 91*
Tully, Christopher Carl 1913- *WhoSSW 91*
Tully, Daniel Patrick 1932- *WhoAm 90, WhoE 91*
Tully, Darrow 1932- *WhoAm 90*
Tully, Elizabeth M 1954- *BiDrAPA 89*
Tully, James K. 1921- *St&PR 91*
Tully, John Edward 1920- *WhoSSW 91*
Tully, Judd 1947- *WhoAmA 91, WhoE 91*
Tully, Paul C. 1917- *St&PR 91*
Tully, Richard Lowden 1911- *WhoAm 90*
Tully, Robert Gerard 1955- *WhoEmL 91*
Tully, Ronald 1960- *WhoWor 91*
Tully, Suzan M. 1944- *St&PR 91*
Tully, Thomas Alois 1940- *St&PR 91, WhoAm 90*
Tully, William P. 1940- *WhoAm 90*
Tulp, Gaye G.K. 1947- *WhoAmW 91*
Tulsky, Alex Sol 1911- *WhoAm 90*
Tulsky, Fredric Neal 1950- *WhoAm 90*
Tulumello, Peter M 1954- *WhoAmA 91*
Tulving, Endel 1927- *WhoAm 90*
Tulving, Ruth *WhoAmA 91*
Tumanyan, Barseg 1958- *IntWWM 90*
Tumarkin, Bernard 1916- *BiDrAPA 89*
Tumarkin, Louise *BiDrAPA 89*
Tumbali, Alfredo J 1951- *BiDrAPA 89*
Tumbleson, Arthur Louis 1934- *WhoSSW 91*

Tumbleson, Treva Rose 1927- *WhoAmW 91*
Tumbocon, Lolito Sta. Maria 1924- *WhoWor 91*
Tumelson, Betsy Martin 1943- *WhoAmW 91*
Tumelty, Joe 1905- *Ballpl 90*
Tumi, Christian Wiyghan 1930- *WhoWor 91*
Tumin, Melvin Marvin 1919- *WhoAm 90*
Tuminello, William Joseph 1920- *WhoE 91, WhoWor 91*
Tummala, Rao Koteswara 1931- *WhoWor 91*
Tummers, Gerard Joseph 1937- *St&PR 91*
Tumminello, Stephen C. 1936- *St&PR 91*
Tumola, Thomas Joseph 1941- *WhoE 91*
Tumpane, John D. 1922- *WhoWrEP 89*
Tumperi, Linda Brown 1962- *WhoSSW 91*
Tumpson, Albert Joseph 1953- *WhoEmL 91*
Tumulty, Philip A. 1921-1989 *BioIn 16*
Tumuluru, Rameshwari V 1958- *BiDrAPA 89*
Tun Tan Siew Sin 1916-1988 *AnObit 1988*
Tun Tin *WhoWor 91*
Tunbridge, Joseph 1886-1961 *OxCPMus*
Tundermann, John Hayes 1940- *St&PR 91*
Tune, Larry Evans 1949- *BiDrAPA 89*
Tune, Ruth Anne 1947- *WhoSSW 91*
Tune, Tommy 1939- *WhoAm 90, WhoE 91, WorAlBi*
Tung, David Hsi Hsin 1923- *WhoAm 90*
Tung, Po-Nan 1949- *WhoE 91*
Tung, Rosalie Lam 1948- *WhoAmW 91, WhoEmL 91*
Tung, Theodore H. 1934- *St&PR 91*
Tung, Theodore Hschum 1934- *WhoAm 90*
Tung, Tran Minh 1930- *BiDrAPA 89*
Tung, William Ling 1907- *WhoE 91*
Tungol, Ma Dinah V *BiDrAPA 89*
Tungpalan, Eloise Yamashita 1945- *WhoAmW 91*
Tungsvik, Mary Elizabeth 1932- *WhoAmW 91*
Tunheim, Jerald Arden 1940- *WhoAm 90*
Tunheim, Kathryn H. 1956- *ODwPR 91*
Tunick, Archibald H. *BioIn 16, NewYTBS 90*
Tunick, Barry *BioIn 16*
Tunick, David 1943- *WhoAmA 91*
Tunick, Richard David 1946- *St&PR 91, WhoE 91*
Tunick, Stanley Block 1900-1988 *BioIn 16*
Tunis, Edwin 1897-1973 *WhoAmA 91N*
Tunis, Edwin Burdett 1897-1973 *AuBYP 90*
Tunis, John Robert 1889-1975 *AuBYP 90*
Tunis, Roslyn *WhoAmA 91*
Tunison, James H. 1938- *St&PR 91*
Tunison, Larry Ronald 1947- *WhoSSW 91*
Tunkieicz, Mary Ursula 1937- *WhoAmW 91*
Tunley, David Evatt 1930- *IntWWM 90*
Tunley, Roul 1912- *WhoAm 90*
Tunnadine, Prudence 1928- *ConAu 129*
Tunnell, Clida Diane 1946- *WhoAmW 91*
Tunnell, Ira Earl *BiDrAPA 89*
Tunnell, John *PenDiMP*
Tunnell, Kenneth Welch 1929- *St&PR 91*
Tunnell, Lee 1960- *Ballpl 90*
Tunnell, William Newton, Jr. 1945- *WhoSSW 91*
Tunner, William Sams 1933- *WhoSSW 91*
Tunnessen, Arthur Michael 1950- *WhoE 91*
Tunney, Francis R. 1947- *St&PR 91*
Tunney, Gene 1898-1978 *WorAlBi*
Tunney, Jim *BioIn 16*
Tunnicliffe, C F 1901-1979 *SmATA 62 [port]*
Tunnicliffe, William Warren 1922- *WhoE 91, WhoWor 91*
Tunno, Robert 1946- *St&PR 91*
Tunstall, Alfred Moore 1863- *AmLegL*
Tunstall, Sharon Sue 1949- *WhoAmW 91*
Tunstall-Pedoe, Hugh David 1939- *WhoWor 91*
Tunstrom, Goran 1937- *DcScanL*
Tunusluoglu, Mustafa Kemal 1929- *WhoWor 91*
Tuohey, Susan Krumholz 1945- *WhoAmW 91*
Tuohy, John Joseph 1926- *St&PR 91*
Tuohy, William 1926- *WhoAm 90*
Tuomala, Pertti Kalevi 1931- *WhoWor 91*
Tuomilehto, Jaakko Olavi 1946- *WhoWor 91*
Tuominen, Francis William 1943- *WhoAm 90*
Tuominen, Mirjam Irene 1913-1967 *EncCoWW*
Tuomioja, Erkki Sakari 1946- *WhoWor 91*
Tupin, Joe P 1934- *BiDrAPA 89*
Tupitza, Thomas Anton 1957- *WhoEmL 91*
Tupler, Harriett Gloria 1935- *WhoAmW 91*
Tupoumoheofo *BioIn 16*
Tupouto'a, Prince 1948- *WhoWor 91*
Tupper, Alexander Garfield *WhoAmA 91N*
Tupper, Charles John 1920- *WhoAm 90*
Tupper, Charles John, Jr. 1955- *BiDrAPA 89*
Tupper, Loretta Clemens *NewYTBS 90*
Tupurkovksi, Vasil 1951- *WhoWor 91*
Tur, Evgeniia *EncCoWW*
Tura, Cosme 1430?-1495 *IntDcAA 90*
Tura, Tessi *WhoWrEP 89*
Turaj, Frank 1934- *WhoAm 90, WhoWor 91*
Turak, August Francis 1952- *St&PR 91*
Turak, Maryann *BiDrAPA 89*
Turan, Kenneth 1946- *ConAu 132*
Turan, Paul 1910-1976 *DcScB S2*
Turanciol, Nihat O. 1934- *St&PR 91*
Turano, Adolfo 1935- *WhoWor 91*
Turano, Don 1930- *WhoAmA 91*
Turano, Emanuel Nicolas 1917- *WhoAm 90*
Turato, Marianne K 1960- *BiDrAPA 89*
Turbak, Edward F. 1961- *St&PR 91*
Turbayne, Colin Murray 1916- *WhoAm 90*
Turben, Susan Hanrahan 1936- *WhoAmW 91*
Turberg, Phillip A. 1928- *St&PR 91*
Turbergue, Henri Jean Marie 1951- *WhoWor 91*
Turbeville, Ann Cook *BiDrAPA 89*
Turbeville, Becky Luann 1964- *WhoAmW 91*
Turbeville, George 1914-1983 *Ballpl 90*
Turbeville, Gus 1923- *WhoAm 90*
Turbeville, James Clyde 1932- *St&PR 91*
Turbeville, William Jackson, Jr. 1915- *WhoAm 90*
Turbidy, John Berry 1928- *WhoAm 90*
Turbina, Nika *BioIn 16*
Turbiville, J. F. 1928- *St&PR 91*
Turbyfill, John R. 1931- *St&PR 91*
Turchetti, Anthony J *BiDrAPA 89*
Turchyn, William, Jr. 1945- *WhoAm 90, WhoWor 91*
Turcic, Lawrence *BioIn 16*
Turck, Joseph Neil 1944- *St&PR 91*
Turco, El *WhNaAH*
Turco, Alfred, Jr. 1940- *WhoAm 90*
Turco, Alfred John 1929- *St&PR 91*
Turco, Jenifer 1950- *WhoAmW 91*
Turco, Lewis 1934- *ConLC 63 [port]*
Turco, Lewis Putnam 1934- *WhoWrEP 89*
Turco, Richard Peter 1943- *WhoAm 90*
Turconi, Sue Kinder 1939- *WhoAmA 91*
Turconi, Susan Kinder 1939- *WhoE 91*
Turconi, Teri Lynn 1962- *WhoAmW 91*
Turcot, Marguerite Hogan 1934- *WhoAmW 91*
Turcott, Richard D *BiDrAPA 89*
Turcott, Robert George 1944- *St&PR 91*
Turcotte, Denise Marie 1966- *WhoSSW 91*
Turcotte, Donald Lawson 1932- *WhoAm 90*
Turcotte, Guy N *BiDrAPA 89*
Turcotte, Jean-Claude 1936- *WhoAm 90*
Turcotte, Jeremiah George 1933- *WhoAm 90*
Turcotte, Margaret Jane 1927- *WhoAmW 91*
Turcotte, Maurice Emile 1938- *WhoSSW 91*
Turcotte, Ron *BioIn 16*
Turcq, Dominique Florimond 1950- *WhoWor 91*
Turczyn-Toles, Doreen Marie 1958- *WhoAmW 91*
Ture, Norman Bernard 1923- *WhoAm 90*
Tureck, Rosalyn 1914- *IntWWM 90, PenDiMP, WhoAm 90, WhoAmW 91*
Turecki, Stanley K *BiDrAPA 89*
Turek, Ibrahim Sait 1930- *BiDrAPA 89*
Turek, Mark Edward 1949- *WhoEmL 91*
Turek, Michael Allen 1940- *BiDrAPA 89*
Turekian, Karl Karekin 1927- *WhoAm 90*
Turel, Anthony Paul, Jr. 1941- *WhoE 91*
Turell, Jane 1708-1735 *FemiCLE*
Turell, Jane Colman 1708-1735 *EncCRAm*
Turell, Robert 1902-1990 *BioIn 16*
Turenne, Henri De La Tour D, Vicomte De 1611-1675 *WorAlBi*
Turer, Richard Bruce 1943- *WhoE 91*
Turesson, Gote Wilhelm 1892-1970 *DcScB S2*
Turetsky, Judith 1944- *WhoAmW 91*
Turetsky, Samuel Harvey 1946- *St&PR 91*
Turett, Nancy Mensch 1959- *ODwPR 91*
Turey, Maureen *BiDrAPA 89*
Turgenev, Ivan 1818-1883 *ShSCr 7 [port], WorAlBi*
Turgenev, Ivan Sergeevich 1818-1883 *BioIn 16*
Turgeon, Alfred Joseph 1943- *WhoAm 90*
Turgeon, Christine Patricia 1962- *WhoE 91*
Turgeon, Edgar Lynn 1920- *WhoE 91*
Turgeon, Guy 1942- *St&PR 91*
Turgeon, Leo 1928- *St&PR 91*
Turgeon, Pierre *BioIn 16*
Turgot, Anne Robert Jacques 1727-1781 *BioIn 16*
Turiace, Eleanor Marie 1939- *WhoAmW 91*
Turiano, Vincent Charles 1950- *St&PR 91*
Turiel, Maurizio 1948- *WhoWor 91*
Turillo, Michael Joseph, Jr. 1947- *WhoAm 90, WhoEmL 91, WhoWor 91*
Turin, George Lewis 1930- *WhoAm 90*
Turina, Marko Ivan 1937- *WhoWor 91*
Turing, Penelope 1925- *ConAu 132*
Turino, Gerard Michael 1924- *WhoAm 90*
Turinsky, Paul Josef 1944- *WhoAm 90, WhoSSW 91*
Turissini, Robert 1930- *WhoAm 90*
Turits, Philip D. 1933- *St&PR 91*
Turk *WhNaAH*
Turk, A Elaine 1948- *St&PR 91*
Turk, Catherine H. *WhoAmW 91*
Turk, Charles E 1936- *BiDrAPA 89*
Turk, Cynthia Cohen 1953- *WhoAmW 91*
Turk, Elaine Elizabeth 1946- *WhoAmW 91*
Turk, Harold 1915-1988 *BioIn 16*
Turk, Herman 1924- *WhoAm 90*
Turk, Jack L. 1931- *St&PR 91, WhoAm 90*
Turk, James Clinton 1923- *WhoAm 90, WhoSSW 91*
Turk, James Clinton, Jr. 1956- *WhoEmL 91, WhoSSW 91*
Turk, Joseph E. 1943- *St&PR 91*
Turk, Melissa Jane 1953- *WhoE 91*
Turk, Richard E 1925- *BiDrAPA 89*
Turk, Rudy H 1927- *WhoAmA 91*
Turk, Rudy Henry 1927- *WhoAm 90*
Turk, S Maynard 1925- *St&PR 91*
Turk, S. Maynard 1925- *WhoAm 90*
Turk, Stanley Martin 1934- *WhoAm 90*
Turk, Thomas Liebig 1936- *WhoSSW 91*
Turk-Dieker, Paula Ann 1956- *WhoSSW 91*
Turkal, Mark James 1952- *St&PR 91*
Turke, Walter 1930- *BiDrAPA 89*
Turkel, Ann Ruth 1928- *BiDrAPA 89*
Turkel, Harris A. 1945- *St&PR 91*
Turkel, Stanley 1920- *BiDrAPA 89*
Turkel, Stuart Simon 1929- *BiDrAPA 89*
Turkel, Susan Beckwitt 1946- *BiDrAPA 89*
Turkevich, Anthony Leonid 1916- *WhoAm 90*
Turki, Fawzi Gasem 1951- *WhoWor 91*
Turkiewicz, Witold Wladyslaw 1930- *WhoSSW 91*
Turkin, Marshall William 1926- *WhoAm 90*
Turkington, Gregg McPatrick 1967- *WhoWrEP 89*
Turkleson, Don Alan 1954- *WhoSSW 91*
Turko, John Walter 1944- *St&PR 91*
Turkoly-Joczik, Robert Louis 1931- *WhoE 91*
Turkovic, Michael James 1932- *St&PR 91*
Turkstra, Carl John 1936- *WhoAm 90*
Turkus, Joan Adele *BiDrAPA 89*
Turley, Bob 1930- *Ballpl 90*
Turley, Brian Christian 1936- *St&PR 91*
Turley, Fred 1895-1981 *BioIn 16*
Turley, James Anthony, Jr. 1918- *WhoAm 90, WhoE 91, WhoWor 91*
Turley, Jeffrey Martin *BiDrAPA 89*
Turley, John N. 1945- *St&PR 91*
Turley, Joseph Francis 1925- *St&PR 91*
Turley, June Williams 1929- *WhoAmW 91*
Turley, Keith L. 1923- *St&PR 91*
Turley, Mark William 1954- *St&PR 91*
Turley, Robert Joe 1926- *WhoWor 91*
Turley, Robert Joseph 1938- *WhoSSW 91*
Turley, Robert Walters 1939- *St&PR 91*
Turley, Sara Jean *WhoAmW 91*
Turley, Stephen John 1966- *WhoE 91*
Turley, Stewart 1934- *St&PR 91, WhoAm 90, WhoSSW 91*
Turley, William Blaine 1924- *St&PR 91*
Turley, William Harrison 1930- *St&PR 91*
Turley, Windle 1939- *WhoAm 90*
Turlington, Bayly 1919-1977 *BioIn 16*
Turlington, Christy *BioIn 16*
Turlington, Phyllis Nibe 1944- *WhoSSW 91*
Turman, George 1928- *WhoAm 90*
Turman, Glynn 1947- *DrBlPA 90*
Turman, Michael H. 1948- *St&PR 91*
Turmel, Antoine 1918- *St&PR 91*
Turmel, Jean 1944- *St&PR 91*
Turmel, Jean Bernard 1944- *WhoAm 90*
Turmelle, Michael Conrad 1959- *St&PR 91*
Turnage, Donna-Marie 1964- *WhoE 91*
Turnage, Fred Douglas 1920- *WhoAm 90*
Turnage, Jean A. 1926- *WhoAm 90*
Turnage, Mark Anthony 1960- *IntWWM 90, PenDiMP A*
Turnage, Wayne Jackson *NewYTBS 90*
Turnbaugh, Douglas Blair 1934- *WhoAm 90*
Turnbaugh, William A 1948- *ConAu 31NR*
Turnberg, Martha Ann *BiDrAPA 89*
Turnbole, Kathleen McCombe 1951- *WhoAmW 91*
Turnbough, David R. *St&PR 91*
Turnbow, Walter 1924- *St&PR 91*
Turnbull, A *BiDWomA*
Turnbull, Adam Michael Gordon 1935- *WhoAm 90*
Turnbull, Agnes Sligh 1888-1982 *AuBYP 90*
Turnbull, Andrew 1921-1970 *DcLB 103 [port]*
Turnbull, Anthony Robert 1944- *WhoWor 91*
Turnbull, Augustus Bacon, III 1940- *WhoAm 90*
Turnbull, Benjamin H. 1938- *St&PR 91*
Turnbull, Benjamin Huntley 1938- *WhoAm 90, WhoSSW 91*
Turnbull, Benjamin Walton 1920- *WhoAm 90*
Turnbull, Betty 1924- *WhoAmA 91*
Turnbull, Charles Vincent 1933- *WhoAm 90*
Turnbull, Cheryl Lankard 1960- *WhoAmW 91*
Turnbull, David 1915- *WhoAm 90*
Turnbull, Doreen Joyce 1938- *WhoAmW 91*
Turnbull, Fiona Mary 1954- *WhoAmW 91*
Turnbull, George Henry 1926- *WhoWor 91*
Turnbull, Gordon Keith 1935- *WhoAm 90*
Turnbull, Grace Hill 1880-1976 *WhoAmA 91N*
Turnbull, James B 1906-1976 *WhoAmA 91N*
Turnbull, James M 1938- *BiDrAPA 89*
Turnbull, John Arlie 1950- *WhoSSW 91*
Turnbull, John Cameron 1923- *WhoAm 90*
Turnbull, Joseph Francis 1942- *WhoE 91*
Turnbull, Keith 1944- *OxCCanT*
Turnbull, Lucy *WhoAmA 91*
Turnbull, Michael F. *ODwPR 91*
Turnbull, Norman A. 1949- *St&PR 91*
Turnbull, Peter 1950- *ConAu 130, TwCCr&M 91*
Turnbull, Robert John 1924- *St&PR 91*
Turnbull, Robert Mosby 1950- *WhoSSW 91*
Turnbull, Robert Scott 1929- *St&PR 91, WhoAm 90*
Turnbull, Vernona Harmsen 1916- *WhoAmW 91*
Turnbull, Wendy *BioIn 16*
Turnbull, William, Jr. 1935- *WhoAm 90*
Turnbull, William W. 1919-1987 *BioIn 16*
Turnbull, William Wallace 1828-1899 *DcCanB 12*
Turndorf, Herman 1930- *WhoAm 90*
Turner, A Richard 1932- *WhoAmA 91*
Turner, Alan *BioIn 16*
Turner, Alan 1943- *WhoAmA 91*
Turner, Alan Forbes 1929- *WhoAm 90*
Turner, Alberta T. 1919- *WhoWrEP 89*
Turner, Almon Richard 1932- *WhoAm 90, WhoE 91*
Turner, Amos 1926- *St&PR 91*
Turner, Angela Marie *BiDrAPA 89*
Turner, Ann *EncO&P 3*
Turner, Ann Coffeen 1930- *WhoAmW 91*
Turner, Ann Marie P 1942- *BiDrAPA 89*
Turner, Ann W 1945- *ConAu 31NR*
Turner, Ann Warren *BioIn 16*
Turner, Ann Warren 1945- *AuBYP 90*
Turner, Anne *BiDEWW*
Turner, Anne Halligan 1941- *WhoAmW 91*
Turner, Arlin 1909-1980 *DcLB 103 [port]*
Turner, Arthur 1940- *WhoAmA 91*
Turner, Arthur Campbell 1918- *WhoAm 90*
Turner, Arthur Edward 1931- *WhoAm 90, WhoWor 91*
Turner, Benjamin Sterling 1825-1894 *BlkAmsC [port]*
Turner, Big Joe 1911- *WorAlBi*
Turner, Big Joe 1911-1985 *BioIn 16, OxCPMus*
Turner, Billie Lee 1925- *WhoAm 90, WhoSSW 91*
Turner, Billy Joe 1945- *WhoSSW 91*
Turner, Bonese Collins *WhoAmA 91*
Turner, Bradwell *BioIn 16*
Turner, Bruce 1922- *ConAu 132*
Turner, Bruce Backman 1941- *WhoAmA 91*
Turner, Burnett Coburn 1902- *WhoAm 90*
Turner, C. Denise Yarbrough 1956- *WhoAmW 91*
Turner, C Phillip 1940- *St&PR 91*
Turner, Cal, Jr. *WhoAm 90, WhoSSW 91*
Turner, Cal, Jr. 1940- *St&PR 91*
Turner, Cal, Sr. *WhoSSW 91*
Turner, Cal, Sr. 1915- *St&PR 91*
Turner, Caren Z. *ODwPR 91*
Turner, Carl Jeane 1933- *WhoE 91, WhoSSW 91, WhoWor 91*
Turner, Carl Joseph 1931- *St&PR 91*

Turner, Carolyn Ann 1949- *WhoWrEP 89*
Turner, Charles Dean 1938- *St&PR 91*
Turner, Charles Lloyd 1948- *IntWWM 90*
Turner, Charles W 1916- *ConAu 30NR*
Turner, Cheri Anne 1949- *WhoAmW 91*
Turner, Christopher John 1933- *WhoWor 91*
Turner, Claramae 1920- *IntWWM 90*
Turner, Claudia Marjorie 1939- *WhoAmW 91*
Turner, Clinton Adlai 1952- *WhoSSW 91*
Turner, Clorinda Matto de 1852-1909 *BioIn 16*
Turner, Clyde T. 1937- *WhoAm 90*
Turner, Corbett H 1928- *BiDrAPA 89*
Turner, Cornelius P. *NewYTBS 90*
Turner, Curtis L. 1939- *St&PR 91*
Turner, Cynthia Jeanne 1957- *WhoSSW 91*
Turner, Dana Joan 1956- *WhoAmW 91*
Turner, Daniel F. 1947-1990 *BioIn 16*
Turner, Daniel L. 1947- *St&PR 91*
Turner, Daniel Shelton 1945- *WhoSSW 91*
Turner, Darwin Theodore Troy 1931- *WhoAm 90*
Turner, David 1948- *WhoAmA 91*
Turner, David Avery 1940- *BiDrAPA 89*
Turner, David Kay 1942- *St&PR 91*
Turner, David Reuben 1915- *WhoAm 90*
Turner, Debbye *BioIn 16*
Turner, Denise Dunn 1947- *WhoEmL 91*
Turner, Denise Michelle 1951- *WhoAmW 91*
Turner, Dennis C *BiDrAPA 89*
Turner, Dennis Roy 1947- *St&PR 91, WhoE 91*
Turner, Don L. 1953- *St&PR 91*
Turner, Don Lee 1953- *WhoSSW 91*
Turner, Don W 1935- *BiDrAPA 89*
Turner, Donald Frank 1921- *WhoAm 90*
Turner, Donald Hedley 1956- *WhoEmL 91*
Turner, Donald Hunter 1933- *WhoWor 91*
Turner, Donald M. 1947- *St&PR 91*
Turner, Doris Sewell 1925- *WhoAmW 91*
Turner, Dorothy Bremer *WhoAmW 91*
Turner, Douglas Keith 1948- *WhoEmL 91*
Turner, E. Deane 1928- *WhoAm 90*
Turner, E. Victoria 1946- *WhoAmW 91*
Turner, Edith Litton 1919- *St&PR 91*
Turner, Edward T., Jr. 1925- *St&PR 91*
Turner, Edward W. *AmLegL*
Turner, Eldridge John, Jr. 1947- *WhoSSW 91*
Turner, Elizabeth Adams Noble 1931- *WhoAm 90, WhoAmW 91, WhoSSW 91, WhoWor 91*
Turner, Eloise Fain 1906- *AuBYP 90*
Turner, Elsie Lewis *BiDrAPA 89*
Turner, Erick Howard *BiDrAPA 89*
Turner, Ethel 1872-1958 *FemiCLE*
Turner, Eugene Andrew 1928- *WhoAm 90*
Turner, Eugene Lauderdale, Jr. 1918- *St&PR 91*
Turner, Eva 1892- *IntWWM 90, PenDiMP*
Turner, Eva 1892-1990 *NewYTBS 90*
Turner, Evan Hopkins 1927- *WhoAm 90, WhoAmA 91, WhoWor 91*
Turner, Fitzhugh *BioIn 16*
Turner, Francis Joseph 1929- *WhoWrEP 89*
Turner, Frank K. 1939- *St&PR 91*
Turner, Frank Miller 1944- *WhoAm 90*
Turner, Fred 1943- *WorAu 1980 [port]*
Turner, Fred L. *BioIn 16*
Turner, Fred L. 1933- *St&PR 91*
Turner, Fred Lamar 1949- *WhoEmL 91*
Turner, Frederick 1943- *ConAu 30NR*
Turner, Frederick Cortez 1926- *St&PR 91*
Turner, Fredrick W *BiDrAPA 89*
Turner, George Bonham 1943- *St&PR 91*
Turner, George P., Jr. 1928- *BiDrAPA 89*
Turner, George Pearce 1915- *WhoAm 90*
Turner, Gerald Rufus 1950- *WhoSSW 91*
Turner, Gerry *AuBYP 90*
Turner, Girard Hart 1943- *WhoSSW 91*
Turner, Gloria Townsend Burke 1938- *WhoAmW 91*
Turner, Grenville 1936- *WhoWor 91*
Turner, Gwenda 1947- *BioIn 16*
Turner, H. Allen 1952- *St&PR 91*
Turner, H. E. 1929- *St&PR 91*
Turner, Halcott Mebane 1930- *WhoE 91*
Turner, Harold 1925- *St&PR 91*
Turner, Harold Edward 1921- *WhoAm 90*
Turner, Harold W. 1949- *St&PR 91*
Turner, Harriet French *WhoAmA 91N*
Turner, Harry Edward 1927- *WhoAm 90*
Turner, Harry M. 1903- *St&PR 91*
Turner, Harry Woodruff 1939- *WhoE 91*
Turner, Harvey S. *ODwPR 91*
Turner, Harvey Stewart 1930- *WhoE 91*
Turner, Henry A., Jr. 1919- *WhoAm 90*
Turner, Henry Brown 1936- *WhoAm 90, WhoWor 91*
Turner, Henry McNeal 1834-1915 *WorAlBi*
Turner, Hester Hill 1917- *WhoAm 90*
Turner, Homer, Jr. 1940- *BiDrAPA 89*
Turner, Howard Sinclair 1911- *WhoAm 90*
Turner, Ike 1929- *DrBlPA 90*
Turner, Ike 1931- *OxCPMus, WorAlBi*
Turner, Ike 1933?- *EncPR&S 89*
Turner, Ike, and Tina 1939?- *EncPR&S 89*
Turner, Iris Evelyn 1927- *WhoWrEP 89*
Turner, J. M. W. 1775-1851 *BioIn 16*
Turner, J M W 1775-1851 *IntDcAA 90*
Turner, J. M. W. 1775-1851 *WorAlBi*
Turner, J. P., Jr. 1924- *St&PR 91*
Turner, Jacquie *BioIn 16*
Turner, James G. 1938- *St&PR 91*
Turner, James Herbert *BiDrAPA 89*
Turner, James Herschel 1947- *WhoSSW 91*
Turner, James Hilton 1918- *WhoE 91*
Turner, James Milton 1840-1915 *BioIn 16*
Turner, James P. 1930- *WhoAm 90*
Turner, James R. 1928- *St&PR 91*
Turner, James Taft 1931- *WhoAm 90*
Turner, James Thomas, Sr 1933- *WhoAmA 91*
Turner, Jane *BiDEWW, FemiCLE*
Turner, Jane 1960- *IntWWM 90*
Turner, Janet E 1914-1988 *WhoAmA 91N*
Turner, Janet Sullivan 1935- *WhoAmA 91, WhoAmW 91, WhoE 91*
Turner, Janice Maria 1951- *WhoAmW 91*
Turner, Jean-Rae 1920- *WhoWrEP 89*
Turner, Jennie A *BiDrAPA 89*
Turner, Jenny Lee 1954- *WhoAmW 91*
Turner, Jerome 1942- *WhoAm 90, WhoSSW 91*
Turner, Jerry 1954- *Ballpl 90*
Turner, Jim 1903- *Ballpl 90, BioIn 16*
Turner, Jim L. 1945- *St&PR 91*
Turner, Joanna 1732-1784 *FemiCLE*
Turner, Joe 1907-1990 *NewYTBS 90*
Turner, Joe 1911-1985 *BioIn 16, DrBlPA 90, EncPR&S 89*
Turner, Joe Stewart 1909- *WhoSSW 91, WhoWor 91*
Turner, John *BioIn 16, PenDiDA 89*
Turner, John *PenDiDA 89*
Turner, John A 1917- *BiDrAPA 89*
Turner, John Bunyan 1916- *WhoSSW 91*
Turner, John D. 1946- *St&PR 91*
Turner, John Freeland 1942- *WhoAm 90*
Turner, John G. 1931- *St&PR 91*
Turner, John Gosney 1939- *St&PR 91*
Turner, John L. 1924- *St&PR 91*
Turner, John Sidney, Jr. 1930- *WhoAm 90, WhoWor 91*
Turner, John W. 1923- *St&PR 91*
Turner, John Walter 1923- *WhoAm 90*
Turner, Jonathan H. 1942- *ConAu 32NR*
Turner, Joseph 1892-1973 *WhoAmA 91N*
Turner, Joseph 1934- *St&PR 91*
Turner, Joseph Crawford 1955- *WhoEmL 91*
Turner, Joseph Mallord William 1775-1851 *BioIn 16*
Turner, Justin G 1898-1976 *ConAu 32NR*
Turner, Justin Leroy 1915- *WhoSSW 91*
Turner, Karen M. 1954- *WhoAmW 91*
Turner, Kathleen *BioIn 16*
Turner, Kathleen 1954- *WhoAm 90, WhoAmW 91*
Turner, Keith Stanley 1929- *WhoAm 90*
Turner, Kirby Van Cleve 1947- *BiDrAPA 89*
Turner, L. Aldora 1939- *WhoAmW 91*
Turner, L. S., Jr. 1926- *WhoAm 90*
Turner, Lana 1920- *BioAmW, BioIn 16, WorAlBi*
Turner, Landon *BioIn 16*
Turner, Laura Smith 1955- *WhoAmW 91*
Turner, LaWalta Dean 1941- *WhoAmW 91*
Turner, Lawrence Anthony 1927- *St&PR 91*
Turner, Lawrence Oliver, Jr. 1940- *St&PR 91*
Turner, Leonard 1921- *St&PR 91*
Turner, Leslie 1899-1988 *EncACom*
Turner, Lester Liggett 1925- *St&PR 91*
Turner, Lillian Erna 1918- *WhoAmW 91*
Turner, Lisa Phillips 1951- *WhoAmW 91, WhoEmL 91, WhoSSW 91*
Turner, Lisa Suzanne 1962- *WhoAmW 91*
Turner, Louisa Aline 1953- *WhoAmW 91*
Turner, Loyd Leonard 1917- *St&PR 91, WhoAm 90, WhoSSW 91*
Turner, Lucy M. *EarBlAP*
Turner, Lucy Mae 1884- *HarlReB*
Turner, Lynne 1943- *WhoAmW 91*
Turner, Lynne Alison 1941- *WhoAm 90*
Turner, M E 1929- *EncO&P 3*
Turner, Malcolm Elijah, Jr. 1929- *WhoAm 90*
Turner, Marguerite Rose Cowles 1941- *WhoSSW 91, WhoWor 91*
Turner, Marshall Ross 1941- *St&PR 91*
Turner, Marta Dawn 1954- *WhoAmW 91*
Turner, Martha 1941- *BiDrAPA 89*
Turner, Mary Louise 1954- *WhoAmW 91, WhoSSW 91*
Turner, Melanie Ann 1957- *WhoAmW 91*
Turner, Michael Griswold 1925- *WhoAm 90*
Turner, Michael Hugh 1947- *WhoSSW 91*
Turner, Michael Thomas 1944-1987 *BioIn 16*
Turner, Morrie 1923- *EncACom*
Turner, Myles 1921-1984 *BioIn 16*
Turner, Nancy DeLane 1956- *WhoSSW 91*
Turner, Nancy Elizabeth 1955- *WhoAmW 91*
Turner, Nat 1800?-1831 *BioIn 16, WorAlBi*
Turner, Neville Keith 1935- *IntWWM 90*
Turner, Norman Huntington 1939- *WhoAmA 91*
Turner, Pamela Walker 1943- *WhoAmW 91*
Turner, Patricia Busby Whitney 1923- *WhoAmW 91*
Turner, Paul *BioIn 16*
Turner, Paul 1929- *ODwPR 91*
Turner, Pete 1934- *WhoAm 90*
Turner, Peter Merrick 1931- *St&PR 91*
Turner, Peter Merrick 1931- *WhoAm 90*
Turner, Philip Michael 1948- *WhoAm 90*
Turner, Phyllis Irene 1935- *WhoAmW 91*
Turner, R. E. 1921- *St&PR 91*
Turner, R Edward 1926- *BiDrAPA 89*
Turner, Ralph Herbert 1919- *WhoAm 90*
Turner, Ralph James 1935- *WhoAmA 91*
Turner, Randall Mead 1949- *WhoSSW 91*
Turner, Raymond 1903-1985 *WhoAmA 91N*
Turner, Raymond Joseph 1929- *WhoAm 90*
Turner, Richard E. 1924- *St&PR 91*
Turner, Richard Nichols 1952- *BiDrAPA 89*
Turner, Rick Dale 1955- *BiDrAPA 89*
Turner, Robert A. 1937- *BioIn 16*
Turner, Robert C *BiDrAPA 89*
Turner, Robert Carlton 1952- *WhoSSW 91, WhoWor 91*
Turner, Robert Chapman 1913- *WhoAmA 91*
Turner, Robert Comrie 1920- *WhoAm 90*
Turner, Robert Edward 1926- *WhoAm 90*
Turner, Robert Edward 1938- *ConAmBL, WhoAm 90*
Turner, Robert F 1944- *ConAu 30NR*
Turner, Robert Foster 1944- *WhoAm 90*
Turner, Robert Gerald 1945- *WhoAm 90, WhoSSW 91*
Turner, Robert Harrison 1952- *St&PR 91*
Turner, Robert Lee 1940- *WhoAm 90*
Turner, Roderick L. 1931- *St&PR 91, WhoAm 90*
Turner, Ronald D.V. 1936- *St&PR 91*
Turner, Ronald Gary 1936- *St&PR 91*
Turner, Rosa F. *BiDrAPA 89*
Turner, Ross J. 1930- *St&PR 91*
Turner, Ross James 1930- *WhoAm 90*
Turner, Ruth Elaine 1922- *WhoAmW 91*
Turner, Sally Ann 1934- *WhoAmW 91*
Turner, Sandra *BiDrAPA 89*
Turner, Sandra Stephens 1945- *WhoAmW 91*
Turner, Sheila Gaye 1949- *WhoAmW 91*
Turner, Sherri *BioIn 16*
Turner, Sherrod E. 1939- *St&PR 91*
Turner, Sophia *BioIn 16*
Turner, Stansfield 1923- *WhoAm 90, WorAlBi*
Turner, Stephen Miller 1939- *WhoAm 90*
Turner, Steven Wilson 1959- *WhoEmL 91*
Turner, Stuart *St&PR 91*
Turner, Sylvia Joyce *BiDrAPA 89*
Turner, Tamara Adele 1940- *WhoAmW 91*
Turner, Ted 1938- *Ballpl 90, BioIn 16, WhoAm 90, WhoSSW 91, WorAlBi*
Turner, Terri Lynn 1956- *WhoEmL 91*
Turner, Terry 1881-1960 *Ballpl 90 [port]*
Turner, Theodore Roy 1922- *WhoAmA 91*
Turner, Thomas *PenDiDA 89*
Turner, Thomas 1729-1793 *BioIn 16*
Turner, Thomas Edwin 1939- *WhoSSW 91*
Turner, Thomas Gerald 1930- *St&PR 91*
Turner, Thomas Johnston 1815-1874 *AmLegL*
Turner, Thomas Marshall 1951- *WhoE 91*
Turner, Thomas R *BiDrAPA 89*
Turner, Thomas W. 1925- *St&PR 91*
Turner, Tina *BioIn 16*
Turner, Tina 1939- *DrBlPA 90, EncPR&S 89, OxCPMus, WhoAm 90, WhoAmW 91, WorAlBi*
Turner, Tuck 1873-1945 *Ballpl 90*
Turner, Victor Paul 1953- *WhoSSW 91*
Turner, Violet Bender 1902?-1990 *ConAu 130*
Turner, Virgil L. 1938- *St&PR 91*
Turner, Virgil Luther, Jr. 1938- *WhoE 91*
Turner, Virginia 1946- *St&PR 91*
Turner, Wallace L. 1921- *WhoAm 90*
Turner, Wallace R. 1906- *St&PR 91*
Turner, Walter Emery 1927- *St&PR 91*
Turner, Warren Austin 1926- *WhoWor 91*
Turner, Wayne Connelly 1942- *WhoAm 90, WhoSSW 91*
Turner, Wesley Dale 1952- *WhoEmL 91*
Turner, William *PenDiDA 89*
Turner, William Cochrane 1929- *St&PR 91, WhoAm 90, WhoWor 91*
Turner, William Ervin, III 1948- *St&PR 91*
Turner, William Eugene 1928- *WhoAmA 91*
Turner, William F. *BioIn 16*
Turner, William F. 1936?-1989 *ConAu 130*
Turner, William Frederick, Jr. 1959- *WhoWor 91*
Turner, William Ian MacKenzie, Jr. 1929- *WhoAm 90, WhoWor 91*
Turner, William J 1907- *BiDrAPA 89*
Turner, William J. 1944- *WhoE 91*
Turner, William Joseph 1907- *WhoE 91*
Turner, William Kay 1933- *WhoAm 90*
Turner, William R. 1943- *St&PR 91*
Turner, William Smith *BiDrAPA 89*
Turner, William T., Jr. 1928- *St&PR 91*
Turner, William Thomas, Jr. 1928- *WhoAm 90*
Turner, William Wilson 1916- *WhoAm 90*
Turner, Winifred 1903-1983 *BiDWomA*
Turner, Zephaniah, Jr. 1812-1876 *AmLegL*
Turner-Graham, Cynthia 1954- *BiDrAPA 89*
Turner-Maybank, Vanessa *BioIn 16*
Turnes, George Keeler 1947- *WhoE 91*
Turney, Catherine 1906- *FemiCLE*
Turney, Charles 1930- *WhoAm 90*
Turney, Emma Lee Preslar 1928- *WhoSSW 91, WhoWor 91*
Turney, Kenneth Wayne 1952- *WhoEmL 91*
Turney, Terence William 1947- *WhoWor 91*
Turngren, Annette 1902?-1980 *AuBYP 90*
Turngren, Ellen *AuBYP 90*
Turnheim, Palmer 1921- *WhoAm 90*
Turnik *WhoWrEP 89*
Turnipseed, Pamela Jean 1947- *WhoAmW 91*
Turnipseed, Patsy Ruth 1935- *St&PR 91*
Turnipseed, Tina Marie 1958- *WhoSSW 91*
Turnlund, Judith Rae 1936- *WhoAmW 91*
Turnock, Bernard John, Jr. 1947- *WhoAm 90*
Turnovsky, Martin 1928- *IntWWM 90, PenDiMP*
Turnow, Rolland 1929- *St&PR 91*
Turnquest, Jean Marie *BiDrAPA 89*
Turnquist, Kevin Neil 1953- *BiDrAPA 89*
Turns, Calvin N 1929- *BiDrAPA 89*
Turns, Danielle M 1936- *BiDrAPA 89*
Turnure, James Harvey 1924- *WhoAm 90, WhoAmA 91*
Turock, Betty J *ConAu 30NR*
Turock, Betty Jane *WhoAmW 91*
Turock, Jane Parsick 1947- *WhoAmW 91*
Turoff, Carole Ruth 1937- *WhoWor 91*
Turoff, Deborah Dryden 1944- *WhoAmW 91*
Turofsky, Charles Sheldon 1942- *WhoE 91*
Turok, Paul Harris 1929- *IntWWM 90, WhoAm 90*
Turow, E Alan 1935- *BiDrAPA 89*
Turow, Irving Louis 1909- *BiDrAPA 89*
Turow, Joseph G 1950- *ConAu 30NR*
Turow, Scott *BioIn 16*
Turow, Scott 1949- *BestSel 90-3 [port], TwCCr&M 91*
Turow, Scott F. 1949- *WhoAm 90*
Turowicz, Andrzej *BioIn 16*
Turpen, Michael Craig 1949- *WhoAm 90*
Turpie, David 1829-1909 *AmLegL*
Turpin, Ben 1869-1940 *WorAlBi*
Turpin, Charles David 1943- *WhoSSW 91*
Turpin, Gerard Christian 1939- *WhoWor 91*
Turpin, James Shafter 1953- *WhoSSW 91*
Turpin, John Timothy 1945- *WhoWor 91*
Turpin, Luci *BioIn 16*
Turpin, Mark 1963- *WhoE 91*
Turpin, Tom 1873-1922 *OxCPMus*
Turpin, Waters E. 1910-1968 *EarBlAP*
Turpin, William H. 1929- *St&PR 91*
Turrant, Mary *BiDEWW*
Turrell, Clifford John 1944- *St&PR 91*
Turrell, Eugene S 1919- *BiDrAPA 89*
Turrell, James Archie 1943- *WhoAmA 91*
Turrell, Julia Brown 1951- *WhoAm 90*
Turrell, Richard H. 1925- *St&PR 91*
Turrell, Richard Horton, Sr. 1925- *WhoE 91, WhoWor 91*
Turrell, Terry N. 1946- *MusmAFA*
Turrens, Julio Francisco 1953- *WhoSSW 91*
Turrentine, Howard Boyd 1914- *WhoAm 90*
Turrentine, Robert E. 1927- *St&PR 91*
Turrentine, Stanley William 1934- *WhoAm 90*
Turriff, Thomas J. 1946- *St&PR 91*
Turrin, Joseph 1947- *IntWWM 90*
Turrin, Joseph Egidio 1947- *WhoEmL 91*
Turro, Nicholas John 1938- *WhoAm 90*
Turry, Bruce 1939- *WhoSSW 91*

Tursi, Carl Thomas 1941- St&PR 91, WhoAm 90
Turska, Joanna Lucja 1958- IntWWM 90
Tursky, Andrea ODwPR 91
Turso, Vito Anthony 1948- WhoE 91
Turtil, Lawrence C 1951- BiDrAPA 89
Turtil, Lawrence Charles 1951- WhoE 91
Turtles, The EncPR&S 89
Turtola, Risto Pekka 1934- WhoWor 91
Turton, Robert Lawrence BiDrAPA 89
Turunen, Denise Ellen 1958- WhoSSW 91
Turunku Bakwa WomWR
Turunku Bazao WomWR
Turvey, Vincent Newton 1873-1912 EncO&P 3
Turzo, Joseph A. St&PR 91
Tusa, Joseph, Jr. 1942- St&PR 91, WhoAm 90
Tusa, Kathryn Smith 1958- WhoAmW 91
Tusel, Donald J BiDrAPA 89
Tuseo, Norbert Joseph John 1950- WhoSSW 91
Tusher, Alan Lewis 1950- BiDrAPA 89
Tusher, Thomas William 1941- St&PR 91, WhoAm 90
Tushingham, Douglas 1914- WhoAm 90
Tushingham, Rita 1940- WorAlBi
Tushinsky, Joseph S. BioIn 16
Tusiani, Joseph 1924- AuBYP 90, WhoWrEP 89
Tusing, James C. 1926- WhoSSW 91
Tuska, George 1916- EncACom
Tuskan, Maria Krocker BiDrAPA 89
Tuskegee Institute Singers DcAfAmP
Tusken, Roger Anthony 1929- WhoAm 90
Tusquets, Esther 1936- EncCoWW
Tussaud, Marie 1761-1850 BioIn 16
Tussing, Whitney Baldwin 1960- WhoEmL 91
Tustin, Richard Don 1948- WhoWor 91
Tusty, James Robert 1949- WhoEmL 91
Tuszynski, Daniel J., Jr. 1947- WhoSSW 91, WhoWor 91
Tut-Ankh-Amen EncPaPR 91
Tutag, Robert S. 1941- St&PR 91
Tutak, Victoria Mary 1955- WhoAmW 91
Tutankhamen WorAlBi
Tutankhamun EncO&P 3
Tutcher, Larry Clifford 1945- WhoSSW 91
Tute, Sophia Lucinda Jane 1960- WhoWor 91
Tute, Warren Stanley 1914- SpyFic
Tutela, Domenic V. 1938- St&PR 91
Tutelian, Mary Jean St&PR 91
Tutelman, Jacki Deena 1954- WhoAmW 91
Tuten, Robert Barry 1959- WhoSSW 91
Tuteur, Franz B. 1923-1988 BioIn 16
Tuteur, Werner 1911- BiDrAPA 89
Tuthill, Allen Floyd 1961- St&PR 91
Tuthill, Edward Wilmar 1940- BiDrAPA 89
Tuthill, Harry J. 1886-1957 EncACom
Tuthill, James G. 1926- St&PR 91
Tuthill, James Gates, Jr. 1953- St&PR 91
Tuthill, John Wills 1910- WhoAm 90
Tuthill, Oliver W. 1906- St&PR 91
Tuthill, Robert E. 1928- St&PR 91
Tuthill, Walter Warren 1941- WhoAm 90
Tuthill, William Edgar 1934- St&PR 91
Tutin, Dorothy 1930- WhoWor 91
Tutino, Rosalie Jacqueline 1937- WhoAmW 91, WhoE 91
Tutins, Antons 1933- WhoWor 91
Tutnauer, Steven Irving 1950- BiDrAPA 89
Tutolo, Leonard J. 1931- St&PR 91
Tutrone, Joseph A. 1951- St&PR 91
Tutt, Charles Leaming, Jr. 1911- WhoAm 90, WhoWor 91
Tutt, Fred David 1946- WhoSSW 91
Tutt, Gloria J. Rutherford 1945- WhoAmW 91, WhoSSW 91
Tutt, J. Homer EarBlAP
Tutt, Kay Cunningham AuBYP 90
Tutt, Russell Thayer 1913- St&PR 91, WhoAm 90, WhoWor 91
Tutt, Sylvia Irene Maud WhoWor 91
Tutt, William Bullard 1941- St&PR 91
Tuttle, Bill 1929- Ballpl 90
Tuttle, Brian John 1950- St&PR 91
Tuttle, Charles E. EncJap
Tuttle, Clifford Horace, Jr. 1930- St&PR 91
Tuttle, Dale Blakeslee 1959- WhoEmL 91
Tuttle, Dave G. 1961- WhoEmL 91
Tuttle, David Bauman 1948- WhoE 91
Tuttle, Donna Frame BioIn 16
Tuttle, Donna Frame 1947- WhoAm 90, WhoAmW 91
Tuttle, Dorothy Edith Lorne 1916- WhoAmW 91
Tuttle, Edward E. 1907- St&PR 91
Tuttle, Edwin E. 1927- St&PR 91
Tuttle, Edwin Ellsworth 1927- WhoAm 90, WhoE 91
Tuttle, Elbert Parr 1897- WhoAm 90
Tuttle, F. M. 1932- St&PR 91
Tuttle, Frank Day BioIn 16
Tuttle, Frank James 1941- St&PR 91
Tuttle, Frank M., Jr. BioIn 16
Tuttle, Gedney 1926- St&PR 91
Tuttle, George Palliser 1933- WhoE 91
Tuttle, Holmes P. 1905-1989 BioIn 16
Tuttle, Hudson 1836-1910 EncO&P 3
Tuttle, Hugh A. 1937- St&PR 91
Tuttle, James N., Jr. 1929- St&PR 91
Tuttle, Jay F BiDrAPA 89
Tuttle, John Hull, Jr. 1946- IntWWM 90
Tuttle, Judith Aurre 1942- WhoWrEP 89
Tuttle, June WhoE 91
Tuttle, L. Ray BioIn 16
Tuttle, Lawrence Emerson 1925- WhoE 91
Tuttle, Linda Suzanne 1953- WhoAmW 91
Tuttle, Lisa 1951- WhoAmA 91
Tuttle, Lynda Lee 1947- WhoAmW 91
Tuttle, Margaret Diane 1945- WhoAmW 91
Tuttle, Margaret Goss 1958- WhoAmW 91
Tuttle, Mark Gerald 1947- St&PR 91
Tuttle, Merlin D. BioIn 16
Tuttle, Phyllis Faye 1947- WhoAmW 91
Tuttle, Richard 1941- WhoAmA 91
Tuttle, Robert D. 1925- St&PR 91, WhoAm 90
Tuttle, Robert H. 1944- WhoAm 90
Tuttle, Rose Mary Guerra 1920- WhoAmW 91
Tuttle, Samuel Joseph 1959- WhoSSW 91
Tuttle, Toni Brodax 1952- WhoEmL 91
Tuttle, Wilbur Fisk 1841- AmLegL
Tuttle, Will NewAgMG
Tuttle, William Gilbert Townsend, Jr. 1935- WhoAm 90
Tuttle, William McCullough, Jr. 1937- WhoAm 90
Tuttle, William R. 1939- St&PR 91
Tuttle, Wylie F.L. 1922- St&PR 91
Tuttleton, James Wesley 1934- WhoAm 90
Tuttman, Saul 1926- BiDrAPA 89
Tutton, James Wilfred 1939- St&PR 91
Tutton, Joseph Corydon BiDrAPA 89
Tutton, Rebecca Sue 1950- WhoAmW 91, WhoSSW 91
Tutu, Desmond BioIn 16
Tutu, Desmond Mpilo 1931- WhoWor 91
Tutu, Mpho BioIn 16
Tutun, Edward H. 1924- WhoAm 90
Tutunjian, John Peter BioIn 16
Tutunjian, John Peter 1936- St&PR 91, WhoE 91
Tutuola, Amos 1920- MajTwCW, WhoWor 91
Tutwiler, Margaret D. BioIn 16
Tutwiler, Margaret DeBardeleben 1950- WhoAm 90, WhoAmW 91
Tuuri, Matti Olavi 1931- WhoWor 91
Tuutti, Heikki 1946- WhoWor 91
Tuve, Merle A. BioIn 16
Tuve, Merle Antony 1901-1982 DcScB S2
Tuxbury, William F. 1942- St&PR 91
Tuxen, Erik 1902-1957 PenDiMP
Tuzio, Mary Patricia 1961- WhoE 91
Tuzla, Kemal 1943- WhoAm 90
Tuzzio, Margaret 1962- WhoAmW 91
Tuzzo, Salvatore R BiDrAPA 89
Tuzzolino, Cara Maria 1966- WhoE 91
T'Vault, William G. AmLegL
Tveitaraas, Randi Anne 1959- WhoAmW 91
Tversky, Amos 1937- WhoAm 90
Twa, Inez Louisa Arbuthnot 1905- WhoAmW 91
Twaddell, John Scott, III 1957- WhoE 91
Twaddell, W F 1906-1982 ConAu 32NR
Twaddell, William H. 1941- WhoAm 90, WhoWor 91
Twaddle, Andrew C. 1938- WhoAm 90
Twaddle, Joan Botham 1927- WhoAmW 91
Twaddle, Randy 1957- WhoAmA 91
Twain, Mark AuBYP 90
Twain, Mark 1835-1910 EncPaPR 91, ShSCr 6 [port], WorAlBi
Twamley, John Paul 1940- St&PR 91
Twardowicz, Stanley Jan 1917- WhoAm 90, WhoAmA 91
Twardowski, Romuald 1930- IntWWM 90
Twardy, Stanley Albert, Jr. 1951- WhoAm 90
Twardzik, George B. 1941- WhoE 91
Twardzik, Timothy F. 1959- St&PR 91
Twarogowski, Leroy Andrew 1937- WhoAmA 91
Tway, Patricia 1931- WhoWrEP 89
Tweddell, Rick BioIn 16
Tweddle, John Matthew 1931- WhoSSW 91
Tweed, Andre Reynold BiDrAPA 89
Tweed, David G. 1944- WhoAm 90
Tweed, George R. BioIn 16
Tweed, John Louis 1947- WhoEmL 91
Tweed, Lindsey BiDrAPA 89
Tweed, Paul Basset 1913- WhoSSW 91
Tweed, Tommy 1908-1971 OxCCanT
Tweed, William J. 1923- St&PR 91
Tweed, William Marcy 1823-1878 BioIn 16, WorAlBi
Tweedale, Charles L EncO&P 3
Tweedale, Douglas 1958?-1990 ConAu 132
Tweedale, Violet 1862-1936 EncO&P 3
Tweeddale, Violet 1862-1936 FemiCLE
Tweedie, Adelbert Thomas 1931- WhoE 91
Tweedie, Carol E. 1942- WhoAmW 91
Tweedie, St. Clair J. 1937- ODwPR 91
Tweedley, John M., Jr. 1945- St&PR 91
Tweedsmuir, Susan 1882-1977 FemiCLE
Tweedy, David Alan 1953- WhoE 91
Tweedy, Isabella G. 1915- WhoAmW 91
Tweedy, John Bayard 1921- St&PR 91
Tweedy, John R. 1929- St&PR 91
Tweedy, Rackham WhoWrEP 89
Tweedy, Robert James 1942- St&PR 91
Tweel, Nicholas J. 1916- WhoE 91
Tweito, Eleanor Marie 1909- WhoAmW 91
Twells, Thomas R. 1934- St&PR 91
Twemlow, Stuart West BiDrAPA 89
Twente, Elmer W 1929- BiDrAPA 89
Twente, George Edward, II 1945- BiDrAPA 89
Twente, Michael Edwin 1950- BiDrAPA 89
Twentyman, Scott Sheldon 1956- BiDrAPA 89
Twerdahl, James S. 1942- St&PR 91
Twerdochlib, Michael 1942- WhoSSW 91
Twersky, Meyer St&PR 91N
Twersky, Victor 1923- WhoAm 90
Tweton, D. Jerome 1933- BioIn 16
Twian, Mark 1835-1910 BioIn 16
Twichell, Chase 1950- WhoWrEP 89
Twichell, Treadwill 1864-1937 AmLegL
Twidale, Charles Rowland 1930- WhoWor 91
Twietmeyer, Don Henry 1954- WhoE 91, WhoEmL 91
Twiford, H. Hunter, III 1949- WhoSSW 91
Twigg, David 1956- IntWWM 90
Twigg, Dennis Thomas BiDrAPA 89
Twigg, Ena 1914- EncO&P 3
Twigg, Ena 1914-198-? EncPaPR 91
Twigg, Rebecca BioIn 16
Twigg-Smith, Thurston 1921- St&PR 91, WhoAm 90
Twiggs, Leo Franklin 1934- WhoAmA 91
Twiggs, Russell Gould 1898- WhoAmA 91
Twinam, Joseph Wright 1934- WhoAm 90
Twiname, John Dean 1931- WhoAm 90
Twine, Linda DrBlPA 90
Twining, Louisa 1820-1911 BioIn 16
Twining, Lynne Dianne 1951- WhoAmW 91
Twining, Marilyn J. 1939- WhoAmW 91
Twining, Nathan Farragut 1897-1982 WorAlBi
Twisdale, Harold Winfred 1933- WhoAm 90
Twiss, Page Charles 1929- WhoAm 90
Twiss, Wanda May 1934- WhoAmW 91
Twiste, Walter Leroy 1945- St&PR 91
Twisted Sister EncPR&S 89
Twitchell, E Eugene 1932- St&PR 91
Twitchell, H. Kenaston BioIn 16
Twitchell, H Mead 1927- St&PR 91
Twitchell, Karen A. 1955- St&PR 91
Twitchell, Paul 1908?-1971 ConAu 132, EncO&P 3
Twitchell, Wayne 1948- Ballpl 90
Twitchett, Denis Crispin 1925- WhoAm 90
Twito, Timothy J 1957- BiDrAPA 89
Twitty, Conway 1933- BioIn 16, OxCPMus, WorAlBi
Twitty, H. R. 1941- WhoSSW 91
Twitty, Howard Allen 1909- WhoAm 90
Twitty, James W 1916- WhoAmA 91
Twitty, James Watson 1916- WhoAm 90
Twitty, Roy L. ODwPR 91
Twitty, William Bradley 1920- WhoWrEP 89
Two Crows 1826?-1894 WhNaAH
Two Leggings 1845?-1923 WhNaAH [port]
Two Moon WhNaAH
Two Moon 1847-1917 WhNaAH
Two Moons WhNaAH
Two Moons 1847-1917 WhNaAH
Twohig, Elizabeth Shee 1946- ConAu 132
Twohy, Robert TwCCr&M 91
Twombly, Cy 1928- BioIn 16, WhoAmA 91
Twombly, Florence Adele Vanderbilt 1853-1952 BioIn 16
Twombly, Gray Huntington 1905- WhoAm 90
Twombly, Harriet E BiDrAPA 89
Twombly, Mary Field BioIn 16
Twombly, Stephen Doane 1953- WhoAm 90, WhoWor 91
Twombly, Wells 1936-1977 Ballpl 90
Twomey, Elizabeth Ann 1965- WhoAmW 91
Twomey, Janet Louise Wilkov 1952- WhoAmW 91
Twomey, John Joseph 1934- St&PR 91
Twomey, Joseph Gerald 1926- St&PR 91, WhoAm 90
Twomey, Kevin Mitchell 1947- St&PR 91, WhoAm 90
Twomey, Mary Regina 1941- WhoAmW 91
Twomey, Robert Denis 1947- St&PR 91
Twomey, Seamus BioIn 16
Twomey, Thomas Aloysius, Jr. 1945- WhoE 91
Twomey, William P. 1942- St&PR 91
Twomey, William Peter 1942- WhoAm 90
Tworkov, Jack 1900-1982 BioIn 16, WhoAmA 91N
Tworoger, Peter C. 1940- WhoSSW 91
Twosret WomWR
Twyman, Carl R. St&PR 91
Twyman, J. Paschal 1933-1989 BioIn 16
Twyman, Jack 1934- WhoAm 90
Twyman, Terena BioIn 16
Twyner, Alexis Cheryle 1946- WhoAmW 91
Twyon, Jane BioIn 16
Twysden, Isabella 1605-1657 BiDEWW, FemiCLE
Ty, James, Jr. BiDrAPA 89
Ty, Mary Ann 1957- BiDrAPA 89
Tyack, George Gary 1946- WhoEmL 91
Tyagi, Krishana Gopal 1942- WhoWor 91
Tyano, Shmuel 1939- WhoWor 91
Tyau, Gaylore Choy Yen 1934- WhoAmW 91
Tybjerg, Lars 1939- WhoWor 91
Tybring, Gilbert B BiDrAPA 89
Tyburczy, Edward 1949- St&PR 91
Tyce, Francis A J BiDrAPA 89
Tyce, Francis Anthony 1917- WhoAm 90
Tychowski, Christopher Roman 1937- WhoWor 91
Tyde, Eddie ConAu 130
Tydings, Joseph Davies 1928- WhoAm 90
Tydings, Millard E. 1890-1961 WorAlBi
Tye, Alan 1933- ConDes 90
Tye, Henry, Jr. 1962- WhoWrEP 89
Tye, William Roy 1939- WhoAmA 91
Tyer, Edward L. 1939- St&PR 91
Tyer, Travis Earl 1930- WhoAm 90
Tyerman, David M. 1906- St&PR 91
Tyerman, Donald 1908-1981 DcNaB 1981
Tyers, Geddes Frank Owen 1935- WhoAm 90
Tyers, Kathy 1952- WhoWrEP 89
Tygiel, Jules 1949- ConAu 132
Tygrett, Howard Volney, Jr. 1940- WhoAm 90
Tyhurst, James S BiDrAPA 89
Tyirin, William C. 1905- St&PR 91
Tykeson, Donald Erwin 1927- WhoAm 90
Tykie 1932- WhoAmA 91
Tykot, Howard Benson 1937- WhoE 91
Tyl, Noel 1936- IntWWM 90
Tyl, Noel Jan 1936- WhoAm 90
Tylak, Daniel Joseph 1950- WhoSSW 91
Tylczak, Lynn BioIn 16
Tyle, Robert M. 1937- St&PR 91
Tylecote, R F 1916-1990 ConAu 132
Tyler, Alan James 1948- WhoSSW 91
Tyler, Alton Thomas 1921- St&PR 91
Tyler, Andrew R. BioIn 16
Tyler, Anne 1931- WorAlBi
Tyler, Anne 1941- BioIn 16, ConAu 33NR, ConLC 59 [port], FemiCLE, MajTwCW, WhoAm 90, WhoAmW 91, WhoWrEP 89
Tyler, Carl Walter, Jr. 1933- WhoAm 90
Tyler, Charles M BiDrAPA 89
Tyler, David Earl 1928- WhoAm 90
Tyler, David Lendon BiDrAPA 89
Tyler, Ewen William John 1928- WhoWor 91
Tyler, Gail Madeleine 1953- WhoAmW 91, WhoWor 91
Tyler, Gus 1911- ConAu 130
Tyler, H. Richard 1927- WhoAm 90
Tyler, Harold Russell, Jr. 1922- WhoAm 90, WhoWor 91
Tyler, James 1940- PenDiMP
Tyler, James B. 1938- St&PR 91
Tyler, James Henry 1940- IntWWM 90
Tyler, Jean B. 1929- WhoAmW 91
Tyler, Joe Earle 1917- BiDrAPA 89
Tyler, John 1790-1826 BiDrUSE 89
Tyler, John 1790-1862 BioIn 16, WorAlBi
Tyler, John Keith 1941- WhoSSW 91
Tyler, John Randolph, Jr. 1934- WhoAm 90
Tyler, Julia G. 1820-1889 BioAmW
Tyler, Julia Gardiner 1820-1889 BioIn 16
Tyler, Kenneth Scott, Jr. 1940- St&PR 91
Tyler, Lefty 1889-1953 Ballpl 90
Tyler, Leon John 1902-1988 BioIn 16
Tyler, Leslie Bradley 1952- WhoE 91
Tyler, Leslie J. 1919- WhoAm 90
Tyler, Letitia Christian 1790-1842 BioIn 16
Tyler, Lloyd John 1924- WhoAm 90
Tyler, Margaret BioIn 16, FemiCLE
Tyler, Margo Hills 1921- WhoE 91
Tyler, Marie O. 1959- WhoAmW 91
Tyler, Marilyn 1928- IntWWM 90
Tyler, Mary 1775-1866 FemiCLE
Tyler, Moses Coit 1835-1900 BioIn 16
Tyler, Patricia Aileen BiDrAPA 89

Tyler, Paul Edward 1930- *WhoE 91*
Tyler, Priscilla C. 1816-1889 *BioAmW*
Tyler, Ralph Sargent, III 1947- *WhoEmL 91*
Tyler, Ralph Winfred 1902- *BioIn 16*
Tyler, Richard D., Jr. 1944- *St&PR 91*
Tyler, Richard Dale, Jr. 1944- *WhoAm 90*
Tyler, Richard R. *ODwPR 91*
Tyler, Richard Sidney 1951- *WhoEmL 91*
Tyler, Robert L. 1922- *WhoWrEP 89*
Tyler, Robert L. 1935- *St&PR 91*
Tyler, Robert Norton 1921- *St&PR 91*
Tyler, Ron C 1941- *WhoAmA 91*
Tyler, Ronnie Curtis 1941- *WhoAm 90*
Tyler, Royall 1757-1826 *BioIn 16*
Tyler, Royall 1757-1862 *EncCRAm*
Tyler, Shirley Kay 1947- *WhoEmL 91*
Tyler, Sidney F., Jr. 1932- *St&PR 91, WhoAm 90*
Tyler, Terry Glenn 1952- *WhoSSW 91*
Tyler, Thomas Lee 1933- *St&PR 91*
Tyler, Todd Kent 1952- *St&PR 91*
Tyler, Valton 1944- *WhoAmA 91*
Tyler, Varro Eugene 1926- *WhoAm 90*
Tyler, Vicki 1952- *SmATA 64*
Tyler, William *BioIn 16*
Tyler, William Ed 1952- *WhoAm 90*
Tyler, William Howard, Jr. 1932- *WhoAm 90, WhoWor 91*
Tyler, William Jefferson 1945- *WhoWor 91*
Tyler, William King 1944- *St&PR 91, WhoAm 90*
Tyler, Willie *DrBlPA 90*
Tyler, Wynell Baxter 1934- *WhoE 91*
Tyler-Slaughter, Cecil Lord 1958- *WhoWor 91*
Tylka, Lawrence M. 1958- *WhoSSW 91*
Tyll, Al *AuBYP 90*
Tyllton, Mary *BiDEWW*
Tylor, Edward Burnett 1832-1917 *BioIn 16*
Tylston, Katharine 1665-1747 *BiDEWW*
Tymeson, Martha Ellen 1959- *BiDrAPA 89*
Tymn, Gregory Anthony 1949- *St&PR 91*
Tymochko, Joseph *BiDrAPA 89*
Tymon, Leo F., Jr. 1942- *WhoAm 90*
Tymon, Leo Francis, Jr. 1942- *St&PR 91*
Tynan, John Patrick 1945- *St&PR 91*
Tynan, Katharine 1861-1931 *BioIn 16, FemiCLE*
Tynan, Kathleen *BioIn 16*
Tynan, Kenneth 1927-1980 *BioIn 16, MajTwCW*
Tynan, Kevin 1947- *ODwPR 91*
Tynan, Laurie Francine 1951- *WhoAmW 91*
Tynan, Patricia Tynan 1927- *St&PR 91*
Tynberg, Katherine *ODwPR 91*
Tyndale-Biscoe, James 1940- *WhoWor 91*
Tyndall, David Gordon 1919- *WhoAm 90*
Tyndall, Donald Alton 1951- *WhoSSW 91*
Tyndall, Gene Ramon 1939- *WhoE 91, WhoWor 91*
Tyndall, James B. 1950- *St&PR 91*
Tyndall, John 1820-1893 *WorAlBi*
Tyndall, Marshall Clay, Jr. 1943- *WhoAm 90*
Tyndall, Rommie Winfred, Jr. 1952- *WhoSSW 91*
Tyndel, Milo 1911- *BiDrAPA 89*
Tynell, Lars Victor 1923- *WhoWor 91*
Tyner, Charles 1925- *ConTFT 8*
Tyner, Earl L. 1918- *WhoSSW 91*
Tyner, George S. 1916- *WhoAm 90*
Tyner, Howard A. 1943- *WhoAm 90*
Tyner, James Howard 1940- *WhoSSW 91*
Tyner, James Noble 1826-1904 *BiDrUSE 89*
Tyner, John Hill *BioIn 16*
Tyner, Larry 1940- *ODwPR 91*
Tyner, Lee Reichelderfer 1946- *WhoAmW 91*
Tyner, McCoy *BioIn 16*
Tyner, Neal Edward 1930- *St&PR 91, WhoAm 90*
Tynes, Bayard Shields 1929- *WhoSSW 91*
Tynes, Margaret 1929- *BioIn 16, DrBlPA 90, IntWWM 90*
Tynes, Sheryl Renee 1957- *WhoSSW 91*
Tynes, William Donnie 1953- *St&PR 91*
Tyng, Anne Griswold *WomArch*
Tyng, Anne Griswold 1920- *WhoAm 90, WhoAmW 91*
Tynni, Aale 1913- *EncCoWW*
Typermass, Arthur G. 1937- *St&PR 91, WhoAm 90*
Typermass, Carl 1906-1988 *BioIn 16*
Typhoid Mary *BioIn 16*
Tyr, Guillaume de 1130?-1190? *BioIn 16*
Tyra, Kenneth Thomas 1957- *WhoEmL 91*
Tyra, Thomas 1933- *IntWWM 90*
Tyre, Milton S. *St&PR 91*
Tyre, Nedra *TwCCr&M 91*
Tyre, Norman Ronald 1910- *WhoAm 90*
Tyree, Alan Dean 1929- *WhoAm 90*
Tyree, Donald Andrew 1930- *WhoAm 90*
Tyree, Earl Garland 1921- *WhoWor 91*
Tyree, Lewis, Jr. 1922- *WhoAm 90*
Tyren, Arne 1928- *IntWWM 90*
Tyrer, John Lloyd 1928- *WhoAm 90*
Tyrie, James Campbell 1938- *St&PR 91*
Tyring, Nels Andrew 1931- *WhoE 91*
Tyrl, Paul 1951- *WhoEmL 91*
Tyrnauer, Isaac M.Z. 1949- *St&PR 91*
Tyrrel, Robert E. 1920- *St&PR 91*
Tyrrel, Thomas B. *St&PR 91*
Tyrrell, Albert Ray 1919- *WhoE 91*
Tyrrell, Calvin E. *WhoWrEP 89*
Tyrrell, Eleanore Day 1938- *WhoAmW 91*
Tyrrell, G N M 1879-1952 *EncO&P 3*
Tyrrell, George Nugent Merle 1879-1952 *EncPaPR 91*
Tyrrell, James 1931- *St&PR 91*
Tyrrell, James William 1954- *WhoE 91*
Tyrrell, Joseph P. 1925- *St&PR 91*
Tyrrell, Thomas Neal 1945- *St&PR 91*
Tyrrell, Thomas Neil 1945- *WhoEmL 91*
Tyrwhit, Elizabeth *BiDEWW*
Tyrwhit, Elizabeth *FemiCLE*
Tysall, John Robert 1938- *St&PR 91, WhoAm 90*
Tyser, Patricia Ellen 1952- *WhoAmA 91*
Tysiac, Lawrence Leon 1953- *St&PR 91*
Tyson, Alan 1926- *IntWWM 90*
Tyson, Anne Guerci 1954- *BiDrAPA 89*
Tyson, Carl Newton 1949- *St&PR 91*
Tyson, Cathy 1966?- *DrBlPA 90*
Tyson, Charlotte Rose 1954- *WhoAmW 91*
Tyson, Cicely *BioIn 16, WhoAm 90, WhoAmW 91*
Tyson, Cicely 1933- *NotWoAT, WorAlBi*
Tyson, Cicely 1939- *DrBlPA 90*
Tyson, Cynthia Haldenby 1937- *WhoAmW 91*
Tyson, Dara *ODwPR 91*
Tyson, Don *BioIn 16*
Tyson, Don 1930- *St&PR 91*
Tyson, Donald John 1930- *WhoAm 90, WhoSSW 91*
Tyson, Edwin L. 1888-1968 *Ballpl 90*
Tyson, Graham 1923- *St&PR 91*
Tyson, Greta England 1933- *WhoAmW 91*
Tyson, Gretchel Hathaway 1957- *WhoE 91*
Tyson, H Michael 1938- *St&PR 91*
Tyson, H. Michael 1938- *WhoAm 90*
Tyson, Helen Flynn 1913- *WhoAmW 91*
Tyson, Ian 1933- *BioIn 16*
Tyson, James Edward, Jr. 1941- *WhoE 91*
Tyson, Jane 1952- *WhoSSW 91*
Tyson, Jeff 1948- *St&PR 91*
Tyson, Jesse E. 1926- *St&PR 91*
Tyson, John D. *ODwPR 91*
Tyson, John E. 1942- *St&PR 91*
Tyson, John Marsh 1953- *WhoEmL 91, WhoSSW 91*
Tyson, Karen Elaine 1945- *WhoAmW 91*
Tyson, Kenneth Robert Thomas 1936- *WhoAm 90*
Tyson, Lawrence Davis 1861-1929 *AmLegL*
Tyson, Luther E. 1922- *St&PR 91*
Tyson, Mary 1909- *WhoAmA 91*
Tyson, Matthews Stanley 1954- *IntWWM 90*
Tyson, Mike *BioIn 16*
Tyson, Mike 1950- *Ballpl 90*
Tyson, Mike 1966- *WorAlBi*
Tyson, Mike G. 1966- *WhoAm 90*
Tyson, Nathan N. 1914- *St&PR 91*
Tyson, Patti Birge *WhoAm 90, WhoAmW 91*
Tyson, Phoebe Whatley 1926- *WhoAmW 91*
Tyson, Remer 1934- *ConAu 131*
Tyson, Richard *BioIn 16*
Tyson, Robert L 1929- *BiDrAPA 89*
Tyson, Shirley Ann 1934- *WhoAmW 91*
Tyson, Wayne Lewis 1933- *WhoE 91*
Tytell, John 1939- *WhoAm 90, WhoWrEP 89*
Tytell, Louis 1913- *WhoAmA 91*
Tytler, Harriet 1828-1907 *FemiCLE*
Tytler, Linda Jean 1947- *WhoAmW 91*
Tytler, Sarah 1826?-1914 *FemiCLE*
Tyus, Wyomia 1945- *BioIn 16, WorAlBi*
Tyzack, Michael 1933- *WhoAmA 91*
Tyznik, William *BioIn 16*
Tzagournis, Manuel *WhoAm 90*
Tzallas, Niove 1938- *WhoWor 91*
Tzamaras, George Paul 1960- *ODwPR 91*
Tzannetakis, Tzannis 1927- *WhoWor 91*
Tzara, Tristan 1896-1963 *WorAlBi*
Tzavaras, Anastasia *WhoAmW 91*
Tzelios, Christos George 1934- *WhoWor 91*
Tzetzo, Hillary Earl *BiDrAPA 89*
Tzimas, Nicholas Achilles 1928- *WhoAm 90*
Tzimet, Naftali *WhoWrEP 89*
Tzipine, Georges 1907- *PenDiMP*
Tzonis, Alexander 1937- *WhoWor 91*
Tzou, Horn-Sen 1952- *WhoSSW 91*
Tz'u Hsi *WomWR*
Tz'u-an *WomWR*
Tzvetin, Angela Danadjieva *BioIn 16*
Tzveych, Biserka *PenDiMP*
Tzvieli, Dvora 1948- *WhoE 91*

U

U.E.V. *EncCoWW*
U Tam'si, Gerald Felix Tchicaya *ConAu 129*
U Tam'si, Tchicaya *ConAu 129*
U2 *EncPR&S 89, OxCPMus*
Uauy, Richard Dagach 1948- *WhoSSW 91*
Uazzano, Janice Demicco 1948- *WhoAmW 91*
UB40 *ConMus 4 [port], EncPR&S 89*
Uba, Jude Ebere 1960- *WhoSSW 91, WhoWor 91*
Ubach, Anthony Domenic *BioIn 16*
Ubaghs, Georges Charles 1916- *WhoWor 91*
Ubans, Juris K 1938- *WhoAmA 91*
Ubarry, Grizel 1953- *WhoHisp 91*
Ubben, Donald Thomas 1946- *WhoE 91*
Ubelaker, Douglas Henry 1946- *WhoE 91*
Ubell, Earl 1926- *WhoAm 90, WhoWrEP 89*
Ubell, Robert Neil 1938- *WhoAm 90, WhoWrEP 89*
Uber, David A. 1921- *IntWWM 90*
Uberall, Herbert Michael Stefan 1931- *WhoAm 90*
Uberoi, Mahinder Singh 1924- *WhoAm 90, WhoWor 91*
Ubico, Jorge 1878-1946 *BioIn 16*
Ubl, Walter William 1941- *St&PR 91*
Ubogy, Jo 1940- *WhoAmA 91*
Ubuka, Toshihiko 1934- *WhoWor 91*
Uccello, Paolo 1397?-1475 *IntDcAA 90, WorAlBi*
Uccello, Vincenza Agatha *WhoAmA 91*
Uccello, Vincenza Agatha 1921- *WhoAm 90*
Ucci, Donald Richard 1948- *WhoEmL 91*
Ucciardi, Frank J. 1930- *WhoAm 90*
Uceda, Julia 1925- *EncCoWW*
Ucer, Erol 1931- *BiDrAPA 89*
Uceta, Acacia 1927- *EncCoWW*
Uchendu, Innocent Chukwuemeka 1939- *WhoWor 91*
Uchibayashi, Masao 1930- *WhoWor 91*
Uchida, Hiroshi Bob 1945- *St&PR 91*
Uchida, Irene Ayako 1917- *WhoAm 90*
Uchida, Mitsuko *BioIn 16*
Uchida, Mitsuko 1948- *IntWWM 90, PenDiMP*
Uchida, Prentiss Susumu 1940- *WhoWor 91*
Uchida, Ruriko 1920- *IntWWM 90*
Uchida, Shigeru 1932- *BiDrAPA 89*
Uchida, Takahiro 1929- *WhoWor 91*
Uchida, Yoshiko *BioIn 16*
Uchida, Yoshiko 1921- *AuBYP 90, MajTwCW*
Uchill, Ida Libert 1917- *WhoWrEP 89*
Uchima, Ansei 1921- *WhoAmA 91*
Uchima, Toshiko *WhoAmA 91*
Uchimoto, Dennis Den 1945- *St&PR 91*
Uchimura, Yushi *BiDrAPA 89*
Uchitelle, Louis 1932- *WhoAm 90*
Ucko, Felix A 1919- *BiDrAPA 89*
Ucko, Gisela Hedwig *BiDrAPA 89*
Uda, Fumio 1941- *WhoWor 91*
Udagawa, Hideko *IntWWM 90*
Udall, Calvin Hunt 1923- *WhoAm 90*
Udall, Ella Royston *BioIn 16*
Udall, Lynn 1870-1963 *OxCPMus*
Udall, Morris K. *BioIn 16*
Udall, Morris K. 1922- *WorAlBi*
Udall, Morris King 1922- *WhoAm 90*
Udall, Nicholas 1505-1556 *BioIn 16*
Udall, Stewart L. 1920- *WorAlBi*
Udall, Stewart Lee 1920- *BiDrUSE 89*
Udaltsova, Nadiejda Andreyevna 1886-1961 *BiDWomA*
Udcoff, George J. 1946- *St&PR 91*
Uddenberg, A Keith 1915- *St&PR 91*
Uddenberg, Thomas W. 1936- *St&PR 91*
Uddin, Khutb M *BiDrAPA 89*
Ude, Wayne Richard 1946- *WhoWrEP 89*
Udel, Melvin M 1924- *BiDrAPA 89*
Udell, John G. 1956- *WhoE 91*
Udell, Richard 1932- *St&PR 91, WhoAm 90*
Udell, William Nathan 1921- *WhoSSW 91*
Udelman, Harold D *BiDrAPA 89*
Uden, Grant *AuBYP 90*
Uden, Janice Lynn 1958- *WhoAmW 91*
Udenfriend, Sidney 1918- *WhoAm 90*
Udet, Ernst 1896-1941 *BioIn 16*
Udevitz, Norman 1929- *WhoAm 90*
Udham Bai *WomWR*
Uding, George 1932- *St&PR 91*
Udink, John Ray 1947- *St&PR 91*
Udinotti, Agnese 1940- *WhoAmA 91*
Udouj, Richard John 1936- *St&PR 91*
Udovich, William Richard 1938- *St&PR 91*
Udovitch, Abraham Labe 1933- *WhoAm 90, WhoWrEP 89*
Udow, Rosalyn Long 1926- *WhoAmW 91*
Udry, Janice 1928- *AuBYP 90*
Udvardy, John Warren *WhoAmA 91*
Udwadia, Firdaus Erach 1947- *WhoEmL 91, WhoWor 91*
Udy, Lex Lynn 1933- *St&PR 91*
Udziela, Loretta Ann 1933- *WhoAmW 91*
Ueberhorst, Reinhard Ernst 1948- *WhoWor 91*
Ueberroth, Peter *BioIn 16*
Ueberroth, Peter 1937- *Ballpl 90, WorAlBi*
Uecker, Bob 1935- *Ballpl 90, WhoAm 90, WorAlBi*
Uecker, Jonathan Charles *BiDrAPA 89*
Uecker, Wilfred Charles 1944- *WhoAm 90, WhoSSW 91*
Ueda, Denmei 1933- *WhoWor 91*
Ueda, Kenichi 1927- *WhoWor 91*
Ueda, Masao 1918- *WhoWor 91*
Ueda, Takeshi 1941- *WhoWor 91*
Ueda, Yukio 1932- *WhoWor 91*
Uehara, Kazuma 1916- *WhoWor 91*
Uehlein, Edward Carl, Jr. 1941- *WhoE 91*
Uehlin, Stephen L. 1947- *St&PR 91*
Uehling, Barbara Staner 1932- *WhoAm 90, WhoAmW 91, WhoWor 91*
Uehling, Gordon Alexander, Jr. 1939- *St&PR 91*
Uehlinger, John Clark 1929- *WhoAm 90*
Uek, Robert William 1941- *WhoE 91*
Uekusa, Masu 1937- *WhoWor 91*
Ueland, P. Craig 1958- *WhoEmL 91*
Ueland, Sigurd, Jr. 1937- *St&PR 91, WhoAm 90*
Uelner, Roy Walter 1935- *St&PR 91*
Uelsmann, Jerry 1934- *WhoAmA 91*
Uelsmann, Jerry Norman 1934- *WhoAm 90*
Ueltschi, Albert L. 1917- *St&PR 91*
Uematsu, Keiji 1947- *WhoWor 91*
Uematsu, Minoru 1920- *WhoWor 91*
Uematsu, Tadashi 1941- *WhoWor 91*
Uemoto, Karen Toshie 1942- *St&PR 91*
Uemura, Ken Takashi 1948- *St&PR 91*
Uemura, Masaru 1930- *WhoWor 91*
Uemura, Teruki 1944- *WhoE 91*
Ueng, Tzuu-Huei 1947- *WhoWor 91*
Ueno, Akira 1937- *WhoWor 91*
Ueno, Hiroshi 1941- *WhoE 91*
Ueno, Hisanori 1919- *WhoWor 91*
Ueno, Keihei 1920- *WhoWor 91*
Ueno, Noriko *AuBYP 90*
Ueno, Noriko 1940- *BioIn 16*
Ueno, Tomiko F. 1930- *WhoWor 91*
Uenohara, Michiyuki *BioIn 16*
Ufema, John William 1946- *WhoEmL 91*
Uffelman, Malcolm Rucj 1935- *WhoAm 90*
Uffen, Robert James 1923- *WhoAm 90, WhoWor 91*
Uffner, Gary Harold 1954- *St&PR 91*
Uffner, William M 1947- *BiDrAPA 89*
Ufford, Charles Wilbur, Jr. 1931- *WhoAm 90*
Ufford, Elizabeth 1909- *WhoAmW 91*
Ufford, Kimberly 1954- *St&PR 91*
Ufheil, John Lloyd 1933- *St&PR 91, WhoAm 90*
Ugarte, Augusto Pinochet *BioIn 16*
Ugarte, Nydia Enid 1946- *WhoSSW 91*
Ugarte, Pedro Toledo *BioIn 16*
Ugarteche, Manuel Prado 1889-1967 *BioIn 16*
Uggams, Leslie 1943- *DrBIPA 90, WhoAm 90, WorAlBi*
Uggerud, Ward Lee 1949- *WhoEmL 91*
Ughetta, Henry L. 1926-1989 *BioIn 16*
Ughetta, William C. 1933- *St&PR 91*
Ughetta, William Casper 1933- *WhoAm 90*
Ughi, Uto 1944- *IntWWM 90*
Ugino, Richard Peter 1949- *WhoE 91*
Ugiss, Carolyn *BioIn 16*
Ugiss-Altieri, Carolyn 1947- *WhoAmW 91*
Uglow, Alan 1941- *WhoAmA 91*
Ugolini, Richard P. *St&PR 91*
Ugolino di Vieri *PenDiDA 89*
Ugolyn, Victor 1947- *St&PR 91*
Ugresic, Dubravka 1950- *EncCoWW*
Ugrin, Bela 1928- *WhoAm 90, WhoWor 91*
Uh, David Keun 1935- *WhoE 91*
Uhde, George Irvin 1912- *WhoAm 90*
Uhde, Hermann 1914-1965 *PenDiMP*
Uhde, Larry Jackson 1939- *WhoWor 91*
Uhde, Thomas W *BiDrAPA 89*
Uhen, James Richard 1933- *St&PR 91*
Uher, William John 1950- *WhoEmL 91*
Uhl, Diana Lois 1941- *WhoAmW 91, WhoSSW 91*
Uhl, Donald P. 1936- *St&PR 91*
Uhl, Edwin Fuller 1841-1901 *BioIn 16*
Uhl, Fritz 1928- *IntWWM 90*
Uhl, George David 1934- *St&PR 91, WhoAm 90*
Uhl, Jack Earle 1934- *WhoAm 90*
Uhl, Joseph A. 1906- *St&PR 91*
Uhl, Philip Edward 1949- *WhoEmL 91, WhoWor 91*
Uhl, Scott Mark 1950- *WhoE 91*
Uhl, Vincent William 1917- *WhoAm 90*
Uhlaender, Ted 1940- *Ballpl 90*
Uhlan, Edward *BioIn 16*
Uhland, Ludwig 1787-1862 *EncO&P 3*
Uhle, George 1898-1985 *Ballpl 90 [port]*
Uhlein, John Wyatt, III 1957- *WhoE 91*
Uhlenbeck, Eugenius Marius 1913- *WhoWor 91*
Uhlenbeck, George 1900-1988 *AnObit 1988*
Uhlenbeck, George Eugene 1900-1988 *BioIn 16*
Uhlenbeck, Karen Keskulla 1942- *WhoAm 90, WhoAmW 91*
Uhlenburg, Donald G. 1934- *St&PR 91*
Uhlenburg, Donald George 1934- *WhoE 91*
Uhlenhaut, Rudolf *BioIn 16*
Uhlenhuth, Eberhard H 1927- *BiDrAPA 89*
Uhlenhuth, Eberhard Henry 1927- *WhoAm 90*
Uhler, Michael David 1956- *WhoEmL 91*
Uhler, Ruth Pershing 1898- *WhoAmA 91N*
Uhler, Walter Charles 1948- *WhoE 91*
Uhlig, Barney Uve 1939- *St&PR 91*
Uhlig, Gregory Edward 1955- *St&PR 91*
Uhlir, Arthur, Jr. 1926- *WhoAm 90*
Uhlir, Golby Cleigh 1932- *WhoWor 91*
Uhlir, Paul Francis 1954- *WhoE 91*
Uhlmann, Frederick Godfrey 1929- *WhoAm 90*
Uhlmann, Paul, III 1950- *St&PR 91*
Uhlmann, Paul, Jr. 1920- *St&PR 91*
Uhlmann, R. H. 1916- *St&PR 91*
Uhlmann, Richard F 1898-1989 *CurBio 90N*
Uhlmann, Richard Frederick 1898-1989 *BioIn 16*
Uhnak, Dorothy 1933- *FemiCLE, TwCCr&M 91*
Uhr, Jonathan W. 1927- *WhoAm 90*
Uhr, Sarita 1956- *BiDrAPA 89*
Uhr, Stanley A. 1946- *St&PR 91*
Uhrich, Carole J. 1943- *St&PR 91*
Uhrich, Karen Elizabeth 1960- *WhoSSW 91*
Uhrich, Richard Beckley 1932- *WhoAm 90*
Uhrich, Susan Elizabeth *BiDrAPA 89*
Uhrig, Ira John 1957- *WhoEmL 91*
Uhrig, Robert Eugene 1928- *WhoAm 90, WhoSSW 91*
Uhrik, Steven Brian 1949- *WhoEmL 91, WhoWor 91*
Uhrman, Celia 1927- *WhoAmA 91, WhoAmW 91, WhoE 91*
Uhrman, Esther 1921- *WhoAmA 91, WhoE 91, WhoWrEP 89*
Uhry, Alfred *BioIn 16*
Uhry, Alfred Fox 1936- *WhoAm 90, WhoWor 91*
Ui, Jun 1932- *WhoWor 91*
Uible, John D. 1936- *St&PR 91*
Uicab, Maria *WomWR*
Uicker, Jospeh Bernard 1940- *St&PR 91*
Uihlein, Stephen Ellis 1953- *St&PR 91*
Uilkema, Gayle Burns 1938- *WhoAmW 91*
Uitermark, Helen Joan 1941- *WhoAmW 91*
Uitti, Karl David 1933- *WhoAm 90, WhoWrEP 89*
Ujdur, Jerry 1957- *Ballpl 90*
Ujhely, Richard J. 1941- *St&PR 91*
Ujiiee, Hiroshi 1931- *WhoWor 91*
Ujvary, Liesl 1939- *EncCoWW*
Ukeles, Mierle 1939- *BiDWomA*

Ukeles, Mierle Laderman 1939- *WhoAmA 91*
Ukeles, Ravenna 1926- *WhoE 91*
Ukhueduan, Michael Edd 1962- *WhoE 91*
Ukkonen, Keijo Allan 1951- *WhoWor 91*
Ukrajinka, Lesja *EncCoWW*
Ukropina, James Robert 1937- *St&PR 91, WhoAm 90*
Ulaki, Shirley Jane 1936- *WhoSSW 91*
Ulam, Adam B. 1922- *WhoAm 90*
Ulam, Stanislaw M. *BioIn 16*
Ulan, Martin Sylvester 1912- *WhoE 91*
Ulane, Karen *BioIn 16*
Ulane, Kenneth *BioIn 16*
Ulanhu 1904-1988 *AnObit 1988*
Ulanhu 1906-1988 *BioIn 16*
Ulanov, Barry 1918- *WhoAm 90, WhoWrEP 89*
Ulanov, Nicholas Augustine 1956- *WhoE 91*
Ulanova, Galina 1910- *WorAlBi*
Ulansey, Vivienne K. 1922- *WhoAmW 91*
Ulasi, Adaora Lily 1932- *FemiCLE*
Ulate Blanco, Otilio 1891?-1973 *BioIn 16*
Ulbert, Tilo 1939- *WhoWor 91*
Ulbrecht, Jaromir Josef 1928- *WhoAm 90*
Ulbrich, Carlton W. 1932- *WhoSSW 91*
Ulbrich, Fred, Jr. 1930- *St&PR 91*
Ulbrich, Richard J. 1934- *St&PR 91*
Ulbricht, John 1926- *WhoAm 90*
Ulbricht, Robert E. 1930- *St&PR 91*
Ulbricht, Walter 1893-1973 *WorAlBi*
Ulchaker, Stanley L. 1938- *ODwPR 91*
Ulehla, Boris *BiDrAPA 89*
Ulene, Art 1936- *ConAu 30NR*
Ulerich, William Keener 1910- *St&PR 91, WhoAm 90*
Ulery, Byron Wayne 1940- *St&PR 91*
Ulery, Dana Lynn 1938- *WhoWor 91*
Ulett, George A 1918- *BiDrAPA 89*
Ulett, Pearl C 1920- *BiDrAPA 89*
Ulevich, Janis M. 1952- *ODwPR 91*
Ulevich, Neal Hirsh 1946- *WhoAm 90*
Ulf, Franklin E. 1931- *St&PR 91*
Ulf, John R. 1928- *ODwPR 91*
Ulfelder, Howard *NewYTBS 90 [port]*
Ulfelder, Howard 1911-1990 *BioIn 16*
Ulfeldt, Leonora Christina 1621-1698 *EncCoWW*
Ulferts, T. A. 1928- *St&PR 91*
Ulfung, Ragnar 1927- *IntWWM 90, PenDiMP*
Ulgur, Ulku *BiDrAPA 89*
Ulguray, Metin 1940- *WhoWor 91*
Ulibarri, Eduardo Rene 1952- *WhoWor 91*
Ulibarri, John E. 1939- *WhoHisp 91*
Ulibarri, Sabine R. 1919- *BioIn 16, ConAu 131, HispWr 90, WhoHisp 91*
Ulich, Waltraud Gisela *BiDrAPA 89*
Ulichny, Barbara L. 1947- *WhoAmW 91*
Ulicny, Patricia Ann 1951- *WhoSSW 91*
Ulisse, Peter James 1944- *WhoWrEP 89*
Ulker, Murat 1959- *WhoWor 91*
Ull, Eugenio 1932- *WhoWor 91*
Ulland, James E. 1942- *ODwPR 91*
Ullberg, Kent 1945- *BioIn 16, WhoAmA 91*
Ullberg, Kent Jean 1945- *WhoAm 90*
Ulle, Albin Edward 1938- *St&PR 91*
Ullensvang, Leon P. 1933- *St&PR 91*
Ullerich, Fritz-Helmut 1933- *WhoWor 91*
Ullery, Donald E., Jr. 1935- *St&PR 91*
Ullery, Judith Ann 1945- *WhoAmW 91*
Ullery, Laurie Vanderbilt 1948- *WhoE 91*
Ullestad, Merwin Allan 1949- *WhoSSW 91*
Ullman, Albert D. 1918- *St&PR 91*
Ullman, Daniel Howard 1958- *WhoE 91*
Ullman, Edwin Fisher 1930- *WhoAm 90*
Ullman, George W, Mrs *WhoAmA 91*
Ullman, Gerald W., Jr. 1961- *St&PR 91*
Ullman, Harlan Kenneth 1941- *WhoE 91*
Ullman, Harold P 1899- *WhoAmA 91N*
Ullman, James Ramsey 1907-1971 *AuBYP 90*
Ullman, Jane F 1908- *WhoAmA 91*
Ullman, Jeffrey David 1942- *WhoAm 90*
Ullman, Joan Connelly 1929- *WhoAm 90*
Ullman, Kenneth C 1941- *BiDrAPA 89*
Ullman, Leo Solomon 1939- *WhoAm 90*
Ullman, Louis Jay 1931- *St&PR 91, WhoAm 90*
Ullman, Marie 1914- *WhoAmW 91, WhoWor 91*
Ullman, Montague 1916- *BiDrAPA 89, EncO&P 3, EncPaPR 91*
Ullman, Myron E. 1946- *St&PR 91*
Ullman, Myron Edward, III 1946- *WhoAm 90*
Ullman, Nelly Szabo 1925- *WhoAmW 91*
Ullman, Richard Henry 1933- *WhoAm 90*
Ullman, Tracey *BioIn 16*
Ullman, Tracey 1959- *WhoAm 90, WhoAmW 91, WhoWor 91*
Ullman, Virginia Melody *WhoWor 91*
Ullmann, Andrew E. 1926-1989 *BioIn 16*
Ullmann, Klaus 1937- *St&PR 91*
Ullmann, Liv *BioIn 16*
Ullmann, Liv 1938- *WhoAm 90, WhoWor 91, WorAlBi*
Ullmann, Regina 1884-1961 *EncCoWW*
Ullmer, John 1932- *WhoSSW 91*
Ulloa, Antonio De 1716-1795 *EncCRAm*
Ulloa, Justo Celso 1942- *WhoSSW 91*
Ulloa-Garcia, Ricardo 1957- *WhoSSW 91*
Ullrey, Richard Dee 1951- *WhoEmL 91*
Ullrich, Bruce 1938- *WhoWor 91*
Ullrich, Daniel Joseph 1964- *WhoEmL 91*
Ullrich, George Jackson *BiDrAPA 89*
Ullrich, Helen Elizabeth *BiDrAPA 89*
Ullrich, John Frederick 1940- *St&PR 91, WhoAm 90*
Ullrich, Mary *ODwPR 91*
Ullrich, Robert Charles 1949- *WhoE 91*
Ullring, Sven Bang 1935- *WhoWor 91*
Ullstein, Hans L. 1930- *St&PR 91*
Ulm, Ernest H. 1916- *St&PR 91*
Ulman, Alan B. 1960- *ODwPR 91*
Ulman, Elinor *BioIn 16*
Ulmann, Elisabeth von 1929- *EncCoWW*
Ulmer, Alfred Conrad 1916- *WhoAm 90*
Ulmer, Evonne Gail 1947- *WhoAmW 91*
Ulmer, Gordon I. *BioIn 16*
Ulmer, Gordon I. 1932- *St&PR 91, WhoAm 90, WhoE 91*
Ulmer, Harriet Glass 1940- *WhoAmW 91*
Ulmer, John Christopher 1945- *WhoSSW 91*
Ulmer, Louise 1943- *BioIn 16*
Ulmer, Melville Jack 1911- *WhoAm 90, WhoE 91*
Ulmer, Melville Paul 1943- *WhoAm 90*
Ulmer, Nicolas Courtland 1952- *WhoEmL 91*
Ulmer, Owen McKendry, Jr. 1939- *WhoSSW 91*
Ulmer, Shirley Sidney 1923- *WhoAm 90, WhoWor 91*
Ulmer, Thomas L. 1938- *St&PR 91*
Ulmer, Walter F., Jr. 1929- *WhoAm 90*
Ulmschneider, Rene J. 1952- *WhoSSW 91*
Ulmstedt, Rolf Reinhold Georg 1928- *WhoWor 91*
Ulon, Robert Joseph 1935- *St&PR 91*
Ulosevich, Steven Nils 1947- *WhoWor 91*
Ulp, Clifford McCormick 1885-1957 *WhoAmA 91N*
Ulreich, Nura Woodson *WhoAmA 91N*
Ulrey, Dale Conner *EncACom*
Ulrica Eleanora 1688-1741 *WomWR*
Ulrich, Ann Carol 1952- *WhoWrEP 89*
Ulrich, Carolyn F. 1880-1969 *BioIn 16*
Ulrich, David Alan 1950- *WhoAmA 91*
Ulrich, David Mark 1956- *St&PR 91*
Ulrich, Donald R. *NewYTBS 90*
Ulrich, Donna M. 1944- *St&PR 91*
Ulrich, Dutch 1899-1929 *Ballpl 90*
Ulrich, Edwin Abel 1897- *WhoAmA 91, WhoE 91*
Ulrich, Elizabeth *ODwPR 91*
Ulrich, Emery E 1927- *BiDrAPA 89*
Ulrich, Eugene C. 1942- *St&PR 91*
Ulrich, Harold Charles, Jr. 1929- *St&PR 91*
Ulrich, Henri 1925- *WhoAm 90*
Ulrich, Homer 1906- *AuBYP 90*
Ulrich, Jurgen 1939- *IntWWM 90*
Ulrich, Lawrence P. 1947- *St&PR 91*
Ulrich, Max M. 1925- *St&PR 91*
Ulrich, Max Marsh 1925- *WhoAm 90, WhoE 91*
Ulrich, Norbert M. 1922- *St&PR 91*
Ulrich, Paul Graham 1938- *WhoAm 90, WhoWor 91*
Ulrich, Paul Stanley 1944- *WhoWor 91*
Ulrich, Peter Henry 1922- *WhoAm 90*
Ulrich, Richard Kevin 1955- *WhoSSW 91*
Ulrich, Richard William 1950- *St&PR 91, WhoSSW 91*
Ulrich, Robert Gardner 1935- *St&PR 91, WhoAm 90*
Ulrich, Robert Gene 1941- *WhoAm 90*
Ulrich, Robert L. 1933- *WhoSSW 91*
Ulrich, Robert Michael 1953- *WhoSSW 91*
Ulrich, Theodore Albert 1943- *WhoE 91*
Ulrich, Timothy W. 1948- *St&PR 91*
Ulrich, Werner 1931- *WhoAm 90*
Ulrich, Wesley A. 1950- *St&PR 91*
Ulrika Eleonora, Queen of Sweden 1688-1741 *BioIn 16*
Ulsamer, Andrew George 1941- *WhoAm 90*
Ulsh, Keith Allen 1961- *St&PR 91*
Ultan, Lloyd 1929- *WhoAm 90*
Ultan, Lloyd 1938- *WhoE 91, WhoWor 91*
Ultmann, John Ernest 1925- *WhoAm 90*
Ultra Violet *BioIn 16*
Ulunay, Ergin Adnan 1948- *WhoWor 91*
Ulus, Ahmet *BiDrAPA 89*
Ulus, Mehmet Fuat 1943- *BiDrAPA 89*
Ulverstad, Larry 1941- *St&PR 91*
Ulvila, Jacob Walter 1950- *WhoSSW 91*
Ulvund, Stein Erik 1952- *WhoWor 91*
Ulwelling, William P 1945- *BiDrAPA 89*
Ulyanov, Mikhail 1927- *BioIn 16*
Ulyshen, Michael 1922- *WhoAm 90*
Um, Christine Lee *BiDrAPA 89*
Umakanthan, Jeremiah *BiDrAPA 89*
Umana, Mario A. *WhoE 91*
Umanah, Imeh Samson 1943- *WhoWor 91*
Umans, Al R. 1927- *St&PR 91*
Umans, Alvin Robert 1927- *WhoAm 90*
Umansky, David J 1942- *ODwPR 91*
Umansky, Raphael Douglas 1950- *WhoSSW 91*
Umar, Muftah al-Usta 1935- *WhoWor 91*
Umashankar, Shantala *BiDrAPA 89*
Umbach, Clayton August, Jr. 1930- *St&PR 91, WhoSSW 91*
Umbarger, Jim 1953- *Ballpl 90*
Umbdenstock, Judy Jean 1952- *WhoAmW 91, WhoWor 91*
Umber, Steven Howard 1955- *WhoSSW 91*
Umberfield, Sherry Ann 1954- *St&PR 91*
Umbert, Pablo 1942- *WhoWor 91*
Umbhau, Jurgen 1943- *St&PR 91*
Umbral, Francisco 1935- *IntvSpW [port]*
Umbreit, Wayne William 1913- *WhoAm 90*
Umegaki, Haruki 1951- *WhoWor 91*
Umemoto, Takao 1921- *WhoWor 91*
Umen, Samuel 1917?-1990 *ConAu 132*
Umezawa, Hiroomi 1924- *WhoAm 90*
Umhoefer, Ivo Anton 1911- *St&PR 91*
Umhoefer, Lois 1936- *St&PR 91*
Umhoefer, Paul 1935- *St&PR 91*
Umiker-Sebeok, Jean 1946- *WhoEmL 91*
Umilta of Faenza 1226-1310 *EncCoWW*
Umlauf, Charles 1911- *WhoAmA 91*
Umlauf, Charles W *BiDrAPA 89*
Umlauf, Ignaz 1746-1796 *PenDiMP*
Umlauf, Karl A 1939- *WhoAmA 91*
Umlauf, Lynn 1942- *WhoAmA 91*
Umlauf, Mary Grace 1949- *WhoAmW 91*
Umlauf, Michael 1781-1842 *PenDiMP*
Umlauff, Michael 1781-1842 *PenDiMP*
Umminger, Bruce Lynn 1941- *WhoAm 90, WhoE 91, WhoWor 91*
Umont, Frank 1918- *Ballpl 90*
Umov, Nikolai Alexeevich 1846-1915 *DcScB S2*
Umphenour, Jillian Darrelyn 1957- *WhoWrEP 89*
Umphers, Lucretia Snelling 1912- *WhoAmW 91*
Umphlett, Lonnie *BioIn 16*
Umphlett, Tommy 1930- *Ballpl 90*
Umphred, William James 1928- *St&PR 91*
Umphress, Agnes Ellen 1925- *WhoAmW 91*
Umpierre, Anthony Henry *BiDrAPA 89*
Umpierre, Gustavo 1931- *WhoHisp 91*
Umpierre, Luz Maria 1947- *HispWr 90, WhoHisp 91*
Umpierre-Herrera, Luzma 1947- *WhoHisp 91*
Umstead, Deborah 1951- *BiDrAPA 89*
Umstead, William Lee 1921- *WhoAm 90*
Umthun, Virgil Louis 1930- *St&PR 91*
Un *WhoWrEP 89*
Un femme chrestienne de Tornay *EncCoWW*
Un marchand de Geneve *EncCoWW*
Un, Chong Hyok 1925- *BiDrAPA 89*
Un, Hyong 1954- *BiDrAPA 89*
Unaduti *WhNaAH*
Unakar, Nalin Jayantilal 1935- *WhoAm 90*
Unamuno, Miguel de 1864-1936 *BioIn 16, ConAu 131, HispWr 90, MajTwCW, WorAlBi, WrPh*
Unamuno, Pedro De *EncCRAm*
Unamuno y Jugo, Miguel de 1864-1936 *HispWr 90, MajTwCW, WorAlBi*
Unanue, Frank *WhoHisp 91*
Unanue, Joseph A. 1926- *WhoHisp 91*
Unanue, Joseph F. 1957- *WhoHisp 91*
Unanue, Mary Ann 1962- *WhoHisp 91*
Unbekant, Donald E. 1932- *St&PR 91*
Uncapher, Ivan T. 1924- *WhoAm 90*
Uncapher, Mark Elson 1926- *St&PR 91*
Uncapher, Mark Elson 1953- *WhoE 91*
Uncas 1588?-1683? *WorAlBi*
Uncas 1606?-1682? *EncCRAm, WhNaAH*
Undavia, Suresh V 1944- *BiDrAPA 89*
Under, Marie 1883-1980 *EncCoWW*
Underberg, Mark A. 1955- *St&PR 91*
Underberg, Neil 1928- *WhoAm 90*
Underdown, David Edward 1925- *WhoAm 90*
Underdown, Joy 1935- *WhoAmW 91*
Underhill, Anne Barbara 1920- *WhoAm 90, WhoAmW 91*
Underhill, Charles *ConAu 32NR*
Underhill, Chip *ODwPR 91*
Underhill, David, Mrs. *EncO&P 3*
Underhill, Evelyn 1875-1941 *BioIn 16, FemiCLE*
Underhill, Henry Willets *BioIn 16*
Underhill, Jacob Berry, III 1926- *WhoAm 90, WhoWor 91*
Underhill, James Felton 1955- *St&PR 91*
Underhill, John 1597?-1672 *WhNaAH*
Underhill, Liz 1948- *BioIn 16*
Underhill, Martha Jean 1948- *WhoAmW 91*
Underhill, Phil Eugene 1945- *St&PR 91*
Underhill, Phyllis Louise Jaynes 1928- *WhoAmW 91*
Underhill, Robert Louis 1953- *St&PR 91*
Underhill, Robert S 1931- *BiDrAPA 89*
Underhill, Stephen Michael 1951- *WhoEmL 91*
Underhill, William 1933- *WhoAmA 91*
Underkofler, James R. 1923- *St&PR 91*
Underweiser, Irwin Philip 1929- *WhoAm 90, WhoE 91, WhoWor 91*
Underwood, Allen Joseph 1941- *WhoE 91*
Underwood, Anthony Alla 1957- *WhoSSW 91*
Underwood, Arthur Louis, Jr. 1924- *WhoAm 90*
Underwood, Benjamin Hayes 1942- *WhoSSW 91*
Underwood, Benton J. 1915- *BioIn 16*
Underwood, Betty 1921- *AuBYP 90*
Underwood, Blair *BioIn 16*
Underwood, Blair 1964- *DrBlPA 90*
Underwood, Cecil H. 1922- *WhoAm 90*
Underwood, David W. 1946- *St&PR 91*
Underwood, David William 1946- *WhoEmL 91*
Underwood, Edwin Hill 1920- *WhoWor 91*
Underwood, Elisabeth 1896-1976 *WhoAmA 91N*
Underwood, Ellen Franklin 1955- *WhoAmW 91*
Underwood, Evelyn Notman 1898-1983 *WhoAmA 91N*
Underwood, George C., II *St&PR 91*
Underwood, George Claude Leon 1890-1975 *BioIn 16*
Underwood, Harry Burnham, II 1943- *St&PR 91, WhoAm 90*
Underwood, Harvey Cockrell *WhoSSW 91*
Underwood, Jack L 1928- *BiDrAPA 89*
Underwood, Jack Lawrence 1928- *WhoE 91*
Underwood, James Martin 1909- *WhoAm 90*
Underwood, Jane Hainline Hammons 1931- *WhoAm 90*
Underwood, Joanna DeHaven 1940- *WhoAm 90*
Underwood, John William Henderson 1816-1888 *AmLegL*
Underwood, Karon M. 1945- *WhoAmW 91*
Underwood, Laura 1963- *ConAu 129*
Underwood, Leon 1890-1975 *BioIn 16*
Underwood, Marvin List, Jr. 1950- *WhoAm 90*
Underwood, Marylyn Joyce 1939- *WhoWrEP 89*
Underwood, McLean Rodney 1951- *WhoWor 91*
Underwood, Michael 1916- *TwCCr&M 91*
Underwood, Pat 1957- *Ballpl 90*
Underwood, Paul 1940- *WhoAm 90*
Underwood, Paul Benjamin 1934- *WhoAm 90*
Underwood, Peter 1923- *EncO&P 3*
Underwood, Peter John 1957- *IntWWM 90*
Underwood, Ralph Edward 1947- *WhoEmL 91, WhoWor 91*
Underwood, Richard Allan 1933- *WhoSSW 91*
Underwood, Richard Folson 1927- *WhoWor 91*
Underwood, Robert K. 1917- *St&PR 91*
Underwood, Shirley Ann 1958- *WhoAmW 91*
Underwood, Stephen G 1947- *BiDrAPA 89*
Underwood, Thomas Carroll 1936- *St&PR 91*
Underwood, Tom 1953- *Ballpl 90*
Underwood, Virgie Dunman 1951- *WhoAmW 91*
Undesser, Cynthia Lufkin 1951- *BiDrAPA 89*
Undesser, Eric Karl 1953- *WhoSSW 91*
Undine, P F *ConAu 31NR*
Undlin, Charles Thomas 1928- *WhoAm 90*
Undset, Sigrid 1882-1949 *AuBYP 90, ConAu 129, DcScanL, EncCoWW, MajTwCW, WorAlBi*
Uner, Randall Steven 1943- *WhoE 91*
Unetich, Robert M. 1946- *St&PR 91*
Unfried, Gregory James 1960- *BiDrAPA 89*
Unfried, Stephen Mitchell 1943- *St&PR 91, WhoAm 90*
Unfried, W Thomas 1926- *St&PR 91*
Unfried, Walter Thomas 1926- *WhoSSW 91*
Ung, Chinary 1942- *BioIn 16*
Ungar, Emanuel 1933- *St&PR 91*
Ungar, Eric Edward 1926- *WhoE 91*
Ungar, Frederick *BioIn 16*
Ungar, Irwin Allan 1934- *WhoAm 90*
Ungar, Keith Stephan 1959- *WhoWor 91*
Ungar, Manya Shayon 1928- *WhoAm 90*
Ungaro, Emanuel *BioIn 16*
Ungaro, Emanuel 1933- *ConDes 90*
Ungaro, Emanuel Matteotti 1933- *WhoWor 91*

Ungaro, Joseph Michael 1930- WhoAm 90
Ungarsohn, Lori Sue 1956- WhoAmW 91
Unger, Arthur Charles 1943- St&PR 91
Unger, Barbara Frankel 1932- WhoAmW 91
Unger, Burton 1939- WhoWrEP 89
Unger, Burton M. 1939- WhoE 91
Unger, David 1934- St&PR 91
Unger, David 1950- HispWr 90, WhoHisp 91
Unger, Donna Jean 1951- WhoE 91
Unger, Douglas 1952- ConAu 130
Unger, Douglas Arthur 1952- WhoWrEP 89
Unger, Elizabeth Betty 1936- WhoAmW 91
Unger, Emerson V. 1946- St&PR 91
Unger, Frederick Branson 1940- St&PR 91
Unger, Friederike Helene 1741?-1813 DcLB 94 [port]
Unger, Georg 1837-1887 PenDiMP
Unger, Gerald Franz 1950- St&PR 91
Unger, Gerhard 1916- PenDiMP
Unger, H Thomas 1934- BiDrAPA 89
Unger, Hans-Georg 1926- WhoWor 91
Unger, Heinz 1895-1965 PenDiMP
Unger, Howard Albert 1944- WhoAm 90, WhoE 91, WhoWor 91
Unger, Irwin 1927- WhoAm 90
Unger, James J. 1942- WhoE 91
Unger, James Joseph 1948- WhoAm 90
Unger, Jim BioIn 16
Unger, Jochem Hans Emil 1944- WhoWor 91
Unger, John F. 1939- St&PR 91
Unger, Karoline 1803-1877 PenDiMP
Unger, Kathleen Bell 1944- BiDrAPA 89
Unger, Larry D. 1948- St&PR 91
Unger, Leonard Howard 1916- WhoAm 90
Unger, Lonny F. 1956- ODwPR 91
Unger, Lonny Frederick 1956- WhoE 91
Unger, Marianne Louise 1957- WhoAmW 91
Unger, Mary Ann WhoE 91
Unger, Mary Ann 1945- WhoAmA 91
Unger, Max BiDrAPA 89
Unger, Neil R. St&PR 91
Unger, Nell Avery BioIn 16
Unger, Paul A. 1914- St&PR 91, WhoWor 91
Unger, Paul R. 1902- St&PR 91
Unger, Peter Kenneth 1942- WhoE 91
Unger, Richard Watson 1942- WhoAm 90
Unger, Robert James 1951- WhoSSW 91
Unger, Robert Martin 1954- WhoE 91
Unger, Roger Harold 1924- WhoAm 90
Unger, Ronald Lawrence 1930- WhoAm 90
Unger, Sherry Louise 1942- WhoE 91
Unger, Sonja Franz 1921- St&PR 91
Unger, Stefan Howard 1944- WhoAm 90
Unger, Stephen Alan 1946- St&PR 91
Unger, Stephen Herbert 1931- WhoAm 90
Unger, Walter Scott 1928- St&PR 91
Unger, William L 1920- BiDrAPA 89
Unger-Smith, David Lloyd 1951- WhoE 91
Ungerboeck, Gottfried BioIn 16
Ungerbuehler, Richard Arthur 1941- St&PR 91
Ungerer, Herbert BioIn 16
Ungerer, Jean Tomi 1931- WhoWrEP 89
Ungerer, Roland H BiDrAPA 89
Ungerer, Tomi 1931- AuBYP 90, BioIn 16
Ungerer, Werner 1927- WhoWor 91
Ungericht, Rhonda Diane 1949- WhoAmW 91
Ungerleider, Harry Eduarde BioIn 16
Ungerleider, John Thomas 1931- BiDrAPA 89
Ungerman, Robert T. 1943- St&PR 91
Ungers, Oswald M. 1926- WhoAm 90
Ungers, Oswald Mathias 1926- BioIn 16
Ungher, Karoline 1803-1877 PenDiMP
Unglaub, Bob 1881-1916 Ballpl 90
Unglesbee, Steven W. 1955- ODwPR 91
Unglesby, Lewis O. 1949- WhoSSW 91
Ungricht, Yvette Scharffs 1960- IntWWM 90
Ungvary, Tamas 1936- IntWWM 90
Unholz, Stefan Paul 1953- WhoWor 91
Unik, Pierre 1909-1945 BioIn 16
Uninsky, Alexander 1910-1972 PenDiMP
Unipan, John T. 1943- St&PR 91
Unis, Alan Stephen 1950- BiDrAPA 89
Unis, Max Jay 1914- St&PR 91
Unitan, Larry D. 1946- St&PR 91
Unitas, Eileen Marie 1959- WhoE 91
Unitas, John 1933- WorAlBi
Unitas, John Constantine 1933- WhoAm 90
Unitas, Johnny 1933- BioIn 16
Unithan, Dolly 1940- WhoAmA 91
Unkefer, Barbara B. 1939- St&PR 91
Unkefer, Barbara Morgan Baxter 1939- WhoAmW 91
Unkefer, Ronald A. 1944- St&PR 91
Unkelbach, Kurt 1913- AuBYP 90
Unklesbay, Athel Glyde 1914- WhoAm 90
Unkovic, Dennis 1948- WhoEmL 91
Unna, Warren W. 1923- WhoAm 90
Unnerstad, Edith 1900- AuBYP 90
Unni, Chandra Sheila 1940- BiDrAPA 89
Unnikrishnan, Parayil 1926- WhoWor 91
Uno Sosuke 1922- EncJap
Uno, Chiyo 1897- BioIn 16
Uno, Koji 1925- IntWWM 90
Uno, Sosuke BioIn 16
Unrue, Bill 1959- St&PR 91
Unruh, Elizabeth Lee 1943- WhoAm 90
Unruh, Fritz von 1885-1970 BioIn 16
Unruh, Gary Lee 1941- IntWWM 90
Unruh, James A. 1941- St&PR 91
Unruh, James Arlen 1941- WhoAm 90
Unruh, Robert John 1946- St&PR 91
Unruh, William G. 1945- WhoAm 90
Unseld, Wes BioIn 16
Unseld, Wes 1946- WorAlBi
Unseld, Westley Sissel 1946- WhoAm 90, WhoE 91
Unsell, Lloyd Neal 1922- WhoAm 90
Unser, Al 1939- WorAlBi
Unser, Al, Jr. BioIn 16
Unser, Bobby 1934- WhoAm 90, WorAlBi
Unser, Del 1944- Ballpl 90
Unsoeld, Jolene 1931- BioIn 16, WhoAm 90, WhoAmW 91
Unstead, R. J. BioIn 16
Unstead, R. J. 1915-1988 AnObit 1988
Unstead, Robert John BioIn 16
Unsworth, Barry 1930- ConAu 30NR
Unsworth, Richard Preston 1927- WhoAm 90, WhoE 91
Unterberg, Mark Paul BiDrAPA 89
Unterberg, Thomas I. 1931- St&PR 91
Unterberger, Betty Miller 1923- WhoAm 90, WhoAmW 91, WhoWrEP 89
Unterecker, John 1922- AuBYP 90
Unterecker, John Eugene 1922- WhoWrEP 89
Unterecker, John Eugene 1922-1989 BioIn 16
Unterkoefler, Ernest L. 1917- WhoSSW 91
Unterman, Eugene Rex 1953- WhoEmL 91
Unterman, Israel BioIn 16
Untermann, Jurgen 1928- WhoWor 91
Untermeyer, Bryna Ivens 1909- ConAu 31NR
Untermeyer, Bryna Ivens 1909-1985 SmATA 61
Untermeyer, Charles G. 1946- WhoAm 90
Untermeyer, Jean 1886-1970 FemiCLE
Untermeyer, Louis 1885-1977 AuBYP 90, ConAu 31NR, WorAlBi
Untermeyer, Salle Podos 1938- WhoAmW 91
Unterreiner, Karen Ann 1959- WhoAmW 91
Unterseher, Chris Christian 1943- WhoAmA 91
Unthank, Tessa WhoSSW 91
Unti, Sharon Marsha 1957- WhoAmW 91
Unti, Walter John 1942- St&PR 91
Untiedt, Klaus 1934- WhoWor 91
Unverfehrt, Carl A. 1954- St&PR 91
Unverferth, Donald V. BioIn 16
Unverzagt, John Gerald 1939- WhoSSW 91
Unwin, David Storr 1918- AuBYP 90
Unwin, Nora Spicer WhoAmA 91N
Unwin, Nora Spicer 1907-1982 AuBYP 90, BioIn 16
Unz, Richard Frederick 1935- WhoAm 90
Unzaga de la Vega, Oscar 1916-1959 BioIn 16
Unzer, Johanna Charlotte 1724-1782 EncCoWW
Unzicker, Rae Engles 1948- WhoAmW 91
Unzueta, Manuel 1949- BioIn 16, WhoHisp 91
Uotila, Urho Antti Kalevi 1923- WhoAm 90
Uotinen, Veijo Johannes 1945- WhoWor 91
Upadhya, Gopalakrishna K BiDrAPA 89
Upadhyay, Yogendra Nath BiDrAPA 89
Upadhyay, Yogendra Nath 1938- WhoE 91
Upadhyaya, Belle Raghavendra 1943- WhoSSW 91
Upadhyaya, Krishna Kumar 1941- WhoWor 91
Upadhyaya, Shailendra Kumar 1929- WhoWor 91
Upadhyaya, Shrinivasa Kumbhashi 1950- WhoEmL 91
Upadrashta, Kameswara Rao WhoWor 91
Upbin, Hal J. 1939- St&PR 91
Upbin, Hal Jay 1939- WhoAm 90
Upbin, Shari Dolors Kiesler WhoAm 90, WhoAmW 91
Upchurch, Samuel Earl, Jr. 1952- St&PR 91
Updegraff, Fred M. 1934- St&PR 91
Updegraff, Jan Peter 1943- St&PR 91
Updegraff, W. W. AmLegL
Updegrove, Andrew Scott 1953- WhoEmL 91
Updegrove, Kimberly Kay 1963- WhoAmW 91
Updike, Caesar A. 1824-1877 AmLegL
Updike, Elizabeth Ann 1961- WhoSSW 91
Updike, Helen Hill 1941- WhoAm 90, WhoAmW 91
Updike, John BioIn 16
Updike, John 1932- AuBYP 90, ConAu 33NR, MajTwCW, WorAlBi, WrPh
Updike, John Hoyer 1932- WhoAm 90, WhoE 91, WhoWor 91, WhoWrEP 89
Updike, Malon S. 1951- St&PR 91
Updike, Robert Stanley 1940- St&PR 91
Upfield, Arthur W. 1888-1964 BioIn 16, TwCCr&M 91
Upgren, Arthur Reinhold, Jr. 1933- WhoAm 90
Uphoff, James Kent 1937- WhoAm 90
Uphoff, Joseph Anthony, Jr. 1950- WhoWrEP 89
Uphoff, Walter 1913- EncO&P 3
Uphoff, Walter H. 1913- EncPaPR 91
Uphold, Marge Broadwater 1948- WhoAmW 91
Upington, Marion AuBYP 90
Upjohn, Everard Miller 1903-1978 WhoAmA 91N
Upjohn, Mary Kirby 1949- WhoAmW 91
Upjohn, Richard 1802-1878 WorAlBi
Uplinger, Robert Jaqua 1912- WhoAm 90
Uppaluri, Subbarao V. 1949- St&PR 91
Uppdal, Kristofer 1878-1961 DcScanL
Uppenkamp, Glenn Charles 1956- St&PR 91
Upperco, John Jesse, Jr. 1954- WhoSSW 91
Uppleger, Ruth Simpson 1943- WhoAmW 91
Uppman, Theodor 1920- IntWWM 90, PenDiMP, WhoAm 90
Uppuluri, Sudha BiDrAPA 89
Upright, Diane BioIn 16
Upright, Diane W WhoAmA 91
Upright, Diane Warner WhoAmW 91
Upshaw, Cecil 1942- Ballpl 90
Upshaw, Dawn BioIn 16
Upshaw, Dawn 1960- CurBio 90 [port], News 91-2 [port]
Upshaw, Gene 1945- WhoAm 90, WorAlBi
Upshaw, Harry Stephan 1926- WhoAm 90
Upshaw, Lisa Gaye 1959- WhoAmW 91, WhoEmL 91, WhoSSW 91, WhoWor 91
Upshaw, Lynn Benjamin 1947- St&PR 91
Upshaw, Margaret Mitchell MajTwCW
Upshaw, Marge LaVerne Harper WhoAmW 91
Upshaw, Martha G. 1936- St&PR 91
Upshaw, Willie 1957- Ballpl 90
Upshaw-McClenny, Louise Adams 1953- WhoAmW 91
Upshur, Abel Parker 1790-1844 BiDrUSE 89, BioIn 16
Upshur, Carole Christofk 1948- WhoAmW 91, WhoEmL 91
Upshur, Doris Nash 1921- WhoAm 90
Upshur, George M., Jr. 1847-1924 AmLegL
Upson, Donald V. 1934- WhoAm 90
Upson, James Frederick 1928- WhoE 91
Upson, Stuart Barnard 1925- WhoAm 90, WhoE 91
Upson, Thomas Fisher 1941- WhoE 91
Upston, John Edwin 1935- WhoAm 90, WhoWor 91
Upthegrove, Franklin John 1921- WhoE 91, WhoWor 91
Upton, Arthur Canfield 1923- WhoAm 90
Upton, Arvin Edward 1914- WhoAm 90
Upton, Catharine FemiCLE
Upton, Catherine Ann 1951- WhoEmL 91
Upton, David Leslie BiDrAPA 89
Upton, Edward F. 1950- St&PR 91
Upton, Frederick Stephen 1953- WhoAm 90
Upton, Hiram Duncan 1859-1900 AmLegL
Upton, Howard B., Jr. 1922- WhoAm 90
Upton, John Cowherd 1957- WhoSSW 91
Upton, John David 1932- WhoAmA 91
Upton, Lee 1953- WhoWrEP 89
Upton, Letitia Graydon BiDrAPA 89
Upton, Mark ConAu 33NR
Upton, Mark 1957- St&PR 91
Upton, Mary Davis 1942- WhoAmW 91
Upton, Richard Alvin 1929- St&PR 91
Upton, Richard F. 1914- WhoAm 90
Upton, Richard T. 1953- WhoSSW 91
Upton, Richard Thomas WhoAmA 91
Upton, Richard Thomas 1931- WhoAm 90
Upton, Robert Chapman, Jr. 1935- WhoWrEP 89
Upton, Robert Glenn 1932- St&PR 91
Upton, Robert J. 1934- WhoWrEP 89
Upton, Stephen E. 1924- St&PR 91
Upton, Susan Hollis 1950- WhoAmW 91
Upton, Theodore Alexander 1959- WhoSSW 91
Upton, Tom 1926- Ballpl 90
Upton, Wade E. 1945- St&PR 91
Urabe, Masao 1947- WhoWor 91
Uragoda, Christopher Gunapala 1928- WhoWor 91
Uram, Lauren Michelle 1957- WhoAmA 91
Uram, Louise Susan 1961- WhoE 91
Uram, Shelley 1953- BiDrAPA 89
Uranga, Jose N. 1946- WhoHisp 91
Uranga, Rima BioIn 16
Uranga McKane, Steven 1952- WhoHisp 91
Uranitsch, Gustav 1926- WhoWor 91
Uras, Tevfik Gungor 1933- WhoWor 91
Urash, Robert N.M. 1923- St&PR 91
Urato, Barbra Casale 1941- WhoAmW 91
Urba, Vytautas V 1924- BiDrAPA 89
Urbach, Frederick 1922- WhoAm 90
Urbach, Herbert J 1920- BiDrAPA 89
Urbach, John Richard 1952- BiDrAPA 89
Urbach, Phyllis Ann Rose 1936- WhoAmW 91
Urbach, Susan Kay 1956- WhoAmW 91
Urbaitis, Barbara BioIn 16
Urbaitis, Elena WhoAmA 91
Urbaitis, John Chapman 1941- BiDrAPA 89
Urban II 1035?-1099 WorAlBi
Urban, Albert 1909-1959 WhoAmA 91N
Urban, Anne Holmes 1954- WhoAmW 91
Urban, Bohumil 1934- WhoWor 91
Urban, Carlyle Woodrow 1914- WhoAm 90
Urban, Edward Louis BiDrAPA 89
Urban, Frank Elmer BiDrAPA 89
Urban, Frank J. 1937- St&PR 91
Urban, Gilbert William 1928- WhoAm 90
Urban, Henry Zeller 1920- WhoAm 90
Urban, Horst Werner 1936- WhoWor 91
Urban, Hubert Josef 1904- EncO&P 3
Urban, Jack 1928- Ballpl 90
Urban, James Arthur 1927- WhoAm 90, WhoSSW 91
Urban, Jeanne Marie 1950- WhoAmW 91
Urban, Jerome Andrew 1914- WhoAm 90
Urban, John Carl, Jr. 1942- WhoWor 91
Urban, Joseph 1871-1933 PenDiDA 89
Urban, Joseph 1872-1933 BioIn 16
Urban, Joseph Jaroslav 1922- WhoWor 91
Urban, Laszlo Andrew 1951- WhoSSW 91
Urban, Lee Donald 1946- WhoEmL 91
Urban, Mary Helen 1942- WhoAmW 91
Urban, Reva 1925-1987 WhoAmA 91N
Urban, Robert C. BioIn 16
Urban, Sharon Kay WhoAmW 91
Urban, Stanley B. 1928- St&PR 91
Urban, Theodore W. 1950- St&PR 91
Urban, Timothy Lou 1956- WhoSSW 91
Urban, Vladimir T 1952- WhoAmA 91
Urbanek, Fred Francis 1935- St&PR 91
Urbanek, James Frank 1925- WhoAm 90
Urbani, Anthony, II 1953- WhoEmL 91
Urbaniak, George Carl 1947- WhoWrEP 89
Urbaniak, Janine ODwPR 91
Urbaniak, Michal BioIn 16
Urbanick, Burton Alfred 1929- St&PR 91
Urbaniec, Maciej 1925- ConDes 90
Urbanik, Allan Francis, Sr. 1949- WhoSSW 91
Urbanik, Thomas, II 1946- WhoSSW 91
Urbankova, Jarmila 1911- EncCoWW
Urbano, Maria Rosina BiDrAPA 89
Urbanowicz, Lynne Jennifer 1965- WhoAmW 91
Urbanowski, Frank 1936- WhoAm 90
Urbanski, Bill 1903-1973 Ballpl 90
Urbanski, James F. 1927- St&PR 91
Urbanski, Leon 1926- ConDes 90
Urbanski, Mary Margaret 1948- WhoE 91
Urbantke, Hugh Edmund 1922- WhoAm 90
Urbauer, Kristine Joanne 1964- WhoAmW 91
Urben, Fredrick E. 1941- St&PR 91
Urbigkit, Walter C., Jr. 1927- WhoAm 90
Urbik, Jerome Anthony 1929- WhoWor 91
Urbina, Eduardo 1948- WhoHisp 91
Urbina, Jeffrey Alan 1955- WhoHisp 91
Urbina, Manuel, II 1939- WhoHisp 91
Urbina, Marlene Victoria 1958- WhoHisp 91
Urbina, Ricardo Manuel 1946- WhoHisp 91
Urbom, David Ward 1952- WhoEmL 91
Urbom, Warren Keith 1925- WhoAm 90
Urch, Daisy Dean 1876-1952 BioIn 16
Urciolo, John Raphael, II 1947- WhoE 91
Urciuoli, J. Arthur 1937- WhoAm 90, WhoWor 91
Urciuoli, Patrick Joseph 1942- WhoE 91
Urcuyo, Leonel BiDrAPA 89
Urda, Michael William 1954- St&PR 91
Urda, Richard Bernard, Jr. 1950- WhoEmL 91
Urdan, James Alan 1931- WhoAm 90

Urdaneta, Leonel A BiDrAPA 89
Urdaneta, Luis Fernando 1936- WhoHisp 91
Urdaneta, Maria-Luisa 1931- WhoHisp 91
Urdaneta, Rafael 1788-1845 BioIn 16
Urdang, Alexandra 1956- WhoAm 90
Urdang, Elliott B BiDrAPA 89
Urdang, Laurence 1927- WhoAm 90
Ure, Barbara Ann BiDrAPA 89
Ure, Barbara Ann 1928- IntWWM 90, WhoE 91
Ure, Jean AuBYP 90, BioIn 16
Ure, John Burns WhoWor 91
Urechia, Alexander Gregor Georg 1938- IntWWM 90
Ureel, Patricia Lois 1923- WhoAmW 91
Uremovich, Michael Elliott 1943- St&PR 91
Uren, Howard Angus, Jr. 1935- St&PR 91
U'Ren, Richard C 1939- BiDrAPA 89
Urena, Pedro Henriquez BioIn 16
Urenovitch, Joseph Victor 1937- St&PR 91, WhoAm 90
Uretz, Robert Benjamin 1924- WhoAm 90
Urey, Harold C. 1893-1981 WorAlBi
Urey, Harold Clayton 1893-1981 DcScB S2
Urfer, Bonnie BioIn 16
Urfirer, Michael J. 1959- St&PR 91
Urhan, Chretien 1790-1845 PenDiMP
Uri, George Wolfsohn 1920- WhoAm 90
Uria, Miguel 1937- WhoHisp 91
Uriah Heep EncPR&S 89
Uriarte Rebaudi, Lia Noemi 1925- WhoWor 91
Urias-Islas, Martha Alicia 1960- WhoHisp 91
Uribe, Charles 1937- WhoAm 90, WhoHisp 91, WhoWor 91
Uribe, Ernesto 1937- WhoHisp 91
Uribe, Hector R. 1946- WhoHisp 91
Uribe, Javier Miguel 1941- WhoSSW 91
Uribe, Javier R. WhoHisp 91
Uribe, Jose 1952- Ballpl 90
Uribe, Jose Alta 1959- WhoHisp 91
Uribe, Juan Camilo 1945- ArtLatA
Uribe, Victor M 1936- BiDrAPA 89
Uribe Villegas, Oscar 1928- WhoWor 91
Urich, Andrew Louis 1960- WhoSSW 91
Urich, Robert BioIn 16, WhoAm 90
Urich, Robert 1946- WorAlBi
Uricho, Robert, Jr. 1915- St&PR 91
Urick, Robert J. 1915- BioIn 16
Urie, John James 1920- WhoAm 90, WhoE 91
Urie, Murray G 1916- BiDrAPA 89
Urion, David Kimball 1954- WhoE 91
Urioste, Mary Louise 1947- WhoAmW 91
Urioste, Pat L. WhoWrEP 89
Uris, Leon 1924- BioIn 16, MajTwCW, SpyFic, WhoWrEP 89, WorAlBi
Urist, Joseph J. 1934- St&PR 91
Urist, Marshall Raymond 1914- WhoAm 90
Urista, Alberto H. 1947- ConAu 32NR, HispWr 90
Urista-Heredia, Alberto Baltazar 1947- WhoAm 90
Uritsky, Moisei Solomonovich 1873-1918 BioIn 16
Urkowitz, Harry 1921- WhoAm 90
Urkowitz, Michael 1943- St&PR 91, WhoAm 90
Urlacher, Gordon F. 1943- WhoE 91
Urland, Alice Irene 1934- St&PR 91
Urland, Robert S. 1941- St&PR 91
Urlocker, Robert J. St&PR 91
Urman, Mark ODwPR 91
Urmer, Diane Hedda 1934- WhoAmW 91, WhoWor 91
Urness, Cindy Lynn 1963- WhoAmW 91
Urofsky, Melvin I 1939- ConAu 31NR
Urofsky, Melvin Irving 1939- WhoAm 90, WhoSSW 91, WhoWrEP 89
Urowsky, Richard J. 1946- WhoEmL 91
Urquhart, Alexander W. 1924- St&PR 91
Urquhart, Andrew Willard 1939- WhoAm 90
Urquhart, Brian E. BioIn 16
Urquhart, Henry Oliver, Jr. 1945- WhoSSW 91
Urquhart, Jane 1949- ConAu 32NR
Urquhart, Jennifer Mack 1947- St&PR 91
Urquhart, John 1934- St&PR 91, WhoAm 90
Urquhart, John Alexander 1928- St&PR 91, WhoAm 90
Urquhart, Margaret M. 1949- St&PR 91
Urquhart, Robert 1901-1988 AnObit 1988
Urquhart, Robert E. 1901-1988 BioIn 16
Urquhart, Stephen E. 1949- WhoE 91, WhoEmL 91, WhoWor 91
Urquhart, Tony 1934- WhoAm 90, WhoAmA 91
Urquiza, Justo Jose de 1800?-1870 BioIn 16
Urrabazo, Rosendo 1952- WhoHisp 91
Urraca 1081?- WomWR
Urrea, John 1955- Ballpl 90
Urrea, Oscar 1944- BiDrAPA 89
Urrea, Teresa 1873-1906 BioIn 16
Urrechaga, Jose L. WhoHisp 91
Urrows, David Francis 1957- IntWWM 90
Urrutia, Alejandro M 1938- BiDrAPA 89
Urrutia, Guillermo 1932- BiDrAPA 89
Urrutia, Lupe G. 1943- WhoHisp 91
Urrutia-Cardenas, Hernan 1940- WhoWor 91
Urry, Dan W. BioIn 16
Urry, Dan Wesley 1935- WhoAm 90
Urry, Grant Wayne 1926- WhoAm 90
Urry, Vern William 1931- WhoE 91
Ursache, Victorin 1912- WhoAm 90
Ursano, James Joseph 1921- WhoAm 90
Ursano, Robert Joseph 1947- BiDrAPA 89, WhoE 91
Urschel, Harold C, III 1958- BiDrAPA 89
Urschel, Joe Richard 1913- St&PR 91
Urshan, Nathaniel A. 1920- WhoAm 90
Ursi, Corrado 1908- WhoWor 91
Ursic, Srebrenka Radulovic 1947- WhoWor 91
Ursin, Bjorn 1943- WhoWor 91
Ursines, Princesse des 1642-1722 EncCoWW
Ursino, Joseph St&PR 91
Urso, Josette Marie 1959- WhoAmA 91
Urstadt, Charles Deane 1959- WhoE 91, WhoEmL 91, WhoWor 91
Urstadt, Charles J. 1928- St&PR 91
Ursuleac, Viorica 1894-1985 PenDiMP
Urteaga, Mario 1875-1957 ArtLatA
Urushibara, Keiji 1940- WhoWor 91
Urwick, Alan BioIn 16
Ury, Bernard E. 1929- ODwPR 91
Ury, Perry S. 1925- WhoAm 90
Ury, Perry Saul 1925- St&PR 91
Usabel, Gaizka Salvador 1933- WhoHisp 91
Usakligil, Emine 1944- WhoWor 91
Usandizaga, Jose Maria 1887-1915 OxCPMus
Usategui, Lydia Maria BiDrAPA 89
Usategui, Ramon 1925- WhoHisp 91
Uschuk, Pamela Marie 1948- WhoWrEP 89
Usdan, James Morris 1949- WhoSSW 91
Usdin, Gene L 1922- BiDrAPA 89
Usdin, Gene Leonard 1922- WhoAm 90
Usdin, Ted Bjorn BiDrAPA 89
Useem, John Hearld 1910- WhoAm 90
Useem, Ruth Hill 1915- WhoAm 90
Uselding, Paul John 1938- WhoAm 90
Uselton, James Clayton 1939- St&PR 91, WhoAm 90
Uselton, Kenneth Wayne 1943- St&PR 91
Usen, Irving BioIn 16
Usera, John Joseph 1941- WhoWor 91
Usera, Joseph Andrew 1949- WhoE 91
Usery, Willie J., Jr. 1923- BiDrUSE 89
Usher, Bob 1925- Ballpl 90
Usher, David 1939- WhoAmA 91
Usher, David Preston 1939- WhoE 91
Usher, Elizabeth Reuter WhoAm 90, WhoAmA 91
Usher, Frederick Barrie 1942- WhoAm 90
Usher, John Palmer 1816-1889 BiDrUSE 89
Usher, Jonell Adair 1947- WhoAmW 91
Usher, Juan Oscar 1928- WhoWor 91
Usher, Julia 1945- IntWWM 90
Usher, Leonard Gray 1907- WhoAm 90, WhoWor 91
Usher, Margo Scegge AuBYP 90
Usher, Ruby Walker 1889-1957 WhoAmA 91N
Usher-Johen, Brian Ernest 1946- St&PR 91
Usher-Kerr, Marva Dianne 1955- WhoAmW 91
Ushijima, Carol M. 1958- WhoAmW 91
Ushijima, Jean Miyoko 1933- WhoAmW 91
Ushijima, John Takeji 1924- WhoAm 90
Ushkow, Charmaine Marie 1955- WhoAmW 91
Usiak, Ronald Henry 1936- BiDrAPA 89
Usigli, Rodolfo 1905-1979 BioIn 16, ConAu 131, HispWr 90
Usinger, Jane Elizabeth 1951- WhoAmW 91
Usinger, Martha Putnam 1912- WhoAmW 91, WhoWor 91
Uskokovic, Moira Sanvila BiDrAPA 89
Uslan, Michael Elliot 1951- WhoWor 91
Uslar Pietri, Arturo 1906- BioIn 16, HispWr 90, WhoWor 91
Usner, Arthur BioIn 16
Usoskin, Michael Neil 1956- St&PR 91
Usoskin, Robert N. 1920- St&PR 91
Uspensky, Alex 1944- BiDrAPA 89
Usrey, Euleta Gustava 1956- WhoAmW 91, WhoSSW 91, WhoWrEP 89
Usrey, Martin William 1911- St&PR 91
Usry, George Howard 1938- St&PR 91
Usry, Milton Franklin 1931- WhoAm 90
Ussachevsky, Vladimir 1911-1990 NewYTBS 90
Ussachevsky, Vladimir A. 1911-1990 BioIn 16
Ussery, Albert Travis 1928- WhoAm 90
Ussery, Luanne 1938- WhoAm 90
Ussery, Michael 1951- WhoWor 91
Ussery, William L. 1961- ODwPR 91
Ustick, Maryann Intermont 1947- WhoAmW 91
Ustinov, Peter BioIn 16
Ustinov, Peter 1921- ConTFT 8 [port], WorAlBi
Ustinov, Peter Alexander 1921- WhoAm 90, WhoWor 91
Usui, Kiichi 1931- WhoAmA 91
Usui, Leslie Raymond 1946- WhoEmL 91, WhoWor 91
Usui, Masao 1953- WhoWor 91
Usui, Noriyuki 1940- WhoWor 91
Utada, Beth Brown 1953- WhoWrEP 89
Utada, Katsuhiro 1925- WhoWor 91
Utamaro 1753-1806 EncJap
Utans, Paul P. 1932- St&PR 91
Utaski, James Richard 1939- WhoAm 90
Utayba, Mani ibn Said Al- 1946- WhoWor 91
Utegaard, Rolf W. 1929- ODwPR 91
Utell, Henry BioIn 16
Utesch, Dorothy Marie 1923- WhoAmW 91
Utevsky, David 1951- WhoEmL 91
Utgoff, Kathleen Platt 1948- WhoAm 90, WhoAmW 91
Uthoff, Michael 1943- WhoAm 90
Utica Jubilee Singers DcAfAmP
Utidjian, Michael Dikran 1931- WhoE 91
Utiger, Robert David 1931- WhoAm 90, WhoWrEP 89
Utinsky, Margaret Doolin 1900- BioIn 16
Utku, Senol 1931- WhoAm 90, WhoSSW 91
Utlaut, William Frederick 1922- WhoAm 90
Utley, Anne Clark 1939- BiDrAPA 89
Utley, Cheryl Anita 1952- WhoSSW 91
Utley, Clarence W. 1941- St&PR 91
Utley, Clifton Garrick 1939- WhoAm 90
Utley, Clifton Maxwell 1904-1978 BioIn 16
Utley, Donna Lavelle 1948- WhoAmW 91
Utley, Edd L. 1926- St&PR 91
Utley, Garrick WhoE 91
Utley, John Dement BiDrAPA 89
Utley, John Eddy 1941- WhoAm 90
Utley, Jonathan G. 1942- ConAu 129
Utley, Peter BioIn 16
Utley, Robert Marshall 1929- BioIn 16
Utley, Susan G. 1957- WhoAmW 91
Utley, T. E. BioIn 16
Utley, T. E. 1921-1988 AnObit 1988
Utomo, Rudy Tjipto 1935- WhoWor 91
Utrillo, Maurice 1883-1955 BioIn 16
Utsinger, Carl Devlin BiDrAPA 89
Utsumi, Junichi 1942- St&PR 91
Utt, Glenn S., Jr. 1926- WhoAm 90
Uttal, William Reichenstein 1931- WhoAm 90
Uttaro, Angela E. 1959- St&PR 91
Uttech, Thomas Martin 1942- WhoAmA 91
Utter, Charles H. 1838- BioIn 16
Utter, Charles W. 1917- St&PR 91
Utter, Charles Wilbar 1917- WhoE 91
Utter, Colorado Charley 1838- BioIn 16
Utter, George H. 1922- St&PR 91
Utter, George Herbert 1854-1912 AmLegL
Utter, Helen St&PR 91
Utter, Howard M. 1909- St&PR 91
Utter, Nicholas Charles 1948- St&PR 91
Utter, Robert French 1930- WhoAm 90
Utterback, Betty Harris 1927- WhoE 91
Utterback, Will Hay, Jr. 1947- WhoSSW 91
Uttley, Alice Jane AuBYP 90
Uttley, Alison 1884-1976 AuBYP 90, BioIn 16, FemiCLE
Uttley, David 1934- WhoWor 91
Uttley, Thomas Eugene 1956- BiDrAPA 89
Utz, Deborah E. 1961- WhoAmW 91
Utz, Edward Joseph 1918- WhoAm 90
Utz, John Philip 1922- WhoAm 90
Utz, Lois 1932-1986 BioIn 16
Utz, Sarah Winifred 1921- WhoAmW 91
Utz, Thornton 1914- WhoAmA 91
Utzinger, David Ray 1947- St&PR 91
Utzinger, Pauline Rose 1925- WhoAmW 91
Utzschneider, Paul PenDiDA 89
Uusitalo, Jyrki Juha 1950- WhoWor 91
Uussaar, Ingemar Evert 1945- St&PR 91
Uvarov, Boris Petrovitch 1889-1970 BioIn 16
Uveges, George 1948- St&PR 91
Uvena, Frank John 1934- WhoAm 90
Uviller, H. Richard 1929- ConAu 129
Uwah, Daniel N 1931- BiDrAPA 89
Uy, Eduardo Santero 1953- WhoSSW 91
Uy, Romualdo O BiDrAPA 89
Uy, William C. 1940- WhoE 91
Uyeda, Marianne Yoko BiDrAPA 89
Uyehara, Lisa Ann Yoshi BiDrAPA 89
Uyemura, Dennis G. St&PR 91
Uyenishi, Roy I. 1932- St&PR 91
Uyeno, Frank I BiDrAPA 89
Uygur, Vural 1929- St&PR 91
Uymatiao, Catherine Lim 1953- BiDrAPA 89
Uyterhoeven, Hugo Emil Robert 1931- WhoAm 90
Uyttebroek, Michael NewAgMG
Uyttenbroeck, Frans J. 1921- WhoWor 91
Uyttenhove, Yolande 1925- IntWWM 90
Uz, Johann Peter 1720-1796 DcLB 97 [port]
Uzawa, Hirofumi 1928- WhoWor 91
Uzcategui, Luis Jose BiDrAPA 89
Uzee, Edward P 1933- BiDrAPA 89
Uzenda, Jara Carlow 1946- WhoAmW 91, WhoEmL 91
Uzes, Marie Anne Clementine D' 1847-1933 BiDFrPL
Uzielli, Philip Albert 1931- St&PR 91
Uzilevsky, Marcus WhoAmA 91
Uzl, Ralph R. 1933- St&PR 91
Uzman, Betty Geren 1922- WhoAm 90
Uzun, Galip Ergul 1947- WhoWor 91
Uzzell, John Douglas 1937- WhoSSW 91
Uzzle, Burk 1938- WhoAm 90

V

V 1801-1873 *BioIn 16*
V. V-an *EncCoWW*
V., Octavio I. Romano- 1932- *BioIn 16*
V.S. *EncCoWW*
Vaa, Aslaug 1889-1965 *DcScanL, EncCoWW*
Vaadia, Boaz *WhoAmA 91*
Vaagen, Wayne Alvin 1955- *St&PR 91*
Vaarandi, Debora 1916- *EncCoWW*
Vaca, Anthony M *BiDrAPA 89*
Vacanti, Alfred Charles, Jr. 1951- *WhoEmL 91*
Vacca, John Joseph, Jr. 1922- *WhoAm 90*
Vaccare, Carmel John 1950- *WhoSSW 91*
Vaccarino, Flora Maria *BiDrAPA 89*
Vaccarino, Robin 1928- *WhoAmA 91*
Vaccaro, Brenda 1939- *WhoAm 90*
Vaccaro, Christopher Mark 1959- *WhoWor 91*
Vaccaro, Donato 1957- *WhoE 91*
Vaccaro, Francis G. 1936- *St&PR 91*
Vaccaro, Jerome Vincent 1955- *BiDrAPA 89*
Vaccaro, Louis Charles 1930- *WhoAm 90*
Vaccaro, Luella Grace 1934- *WhoAmA 91*
Vaccaro, Nick Dante 1931- *WhoAmA 91*
Vaccaro, Nunzio J. *St&PR 91*
Vaccaro, Patrick Frank *WhoAmA 91*
Vaccaro, Ralph Francis 1919- *WhoAm 90*
Vaccaro, Richard Francis 1949- *WhoE 91*
Vaccaro, Robin Colleen 1950- *WhoEmL 91*
Vaccaro, Sonny *BioIn 16*
Vaccaro, V Michael 1929- *BiDrAPA 89*
Vacchelli, Robert Francis 1951- *WhoE 91*
Vacchiano, Carla Marie 1964- *WhoE 91*
Vacek, Miroslav *WhoWor 91*
Vache', Claude Charles 1926- *WhoAm 90, WhoSSW 91*
Vache, Marilyn Jean *BiDrAPA 89*
Vache, Warren Webster 1914- *WhoWrEP 89*
Vachek, Josef 1909- *ConAu 132*
Vacher-Morris, Elizabeth Michele 1963- *WhoAmW 91*
Vachha, Michel Rumy 1955- *IntWWM 90*
Vachher, Prehlad S 1933- *BiDrAPA 89*
Vachher, Prehlad Singh 1933- *WhoWor 91*
Vachon, Brian 1941- *St&PR 91*
Vachon, Jean Francois *BiDrAPA 89*
Vachon, John 1914-1975 *BioIn 16*
Vachon, Louis 1932- *BiDrAPA 89*
Vachon, Louis-Albert 1912- *WhoAm 90, WhoWor 91*
Vachon, Marilyn Ann 1924- *WhoAm 90*
Vachon, Reginald Irenee 1937- *WhoSSW 91*
Vachon, Rogatien Rosaire 1945- *WhoAm 90*
Vachon, Serge Jean 1939- *WhoAm 90*
Vachss, Andrew 1942- *TwCCr&M 91*
Vachss, Andrew H. *BioIn 16*
Vachula, Miles Thomas 1950- *BiDrAPA 89*
Vacik, James Paul 1931- *WhoSSW 91*
Vacketta, Carl Lee 1941- *WhoAm 90*
Vaculik, Ludvik *BioIn 16*
Vad, Lata Bal *BiDrAPA 89*
Vadakin, Charles Edward, II 1941- *St&PR 91*
Vadasz, Christine 1946- *WomArch [port]*
Vadasz, Csaba 1946- *WhoE 91*
Vaddadi, Lalitha *BiDrAPA 89*
Vadehra, Dave Kumar 1941- *WhoE 91, WhoWor 91*
Vadeika, Edward A *BiDrAPA 89*
Vadgama, Virji Karabhai 1924- *WhoWor 91*
Vadia, Rafael 1950- *WhoAmA 91*
Vadim, Roger *BioIn 16*
Vadim, Roger Plemiannikov 1928- *WhoWor 91*
Vadim, Vanessa *BioIn 16*
Vadkerti-Gavornikova, Lydia 1932 *EncCoWW*
Vadlamudi, Babu R P *BiDrAPA 89*
Vadman, David R. *St&PR 91*
Vadnais, Alfred William 1935- *WhoAm 90*
Vadnal, Robert E 1948- *BiDrAPA 89*
Vadney, Laura LeClair 1945- *WhoAmW 91*
Vadovicky, Paul J. 1952- *St&PR 91*
Vadus, Gloria A. *WhoE 91*
Vaekehu *WomWR*
Vaes, Alain *BioIn 16*
Vaeth, George Bernard 1928- *St&PR 91*
Vaeth, Joseph Gordon 1921- *WhoAm 90*
Vaeth, Werner Karl 1945- *WhoWor 91*
Vafakos, William Paul 1927- *WhoAm 90*
Vafi, Houshang 1936- *BiDrAPA 89*
Vagell, Peter Michael 1948- *St&PR 91*
Vagell, Theodore Peter 1934- *St&PR 91*
Vagelos, P. Roy 1929- *St&PR 91*
Vagelos, Pindaros Roy 1929- *WhoAm 90, WhoE 91*
Vagenakis, Apostolos George 1938- *WhoWor 91*
Vaget, Hans Rudolf 1938- *WhoAm 90*
Vaggione, Horacio 1943- *IntWWM 90*
Vagin, Vladimir Vasil'evich 1937- *BioIn 16*
Vagis, Polygnotis 1894-1965 *WhoAmA 91N*
Vagley, Robert Everett 1940- *WhoAm 90*
Vagliano, Alexander Marino 1927- *WhoAm 90*
Vaglio, Nicholas P. 1950- *ODwPR 91*
Vaglio-Laurin, Roberto 1929- *WhoAm 90*
Vagnarelli, Joseph *St&PR 91*
Vagneur, Kathryn Otto 1946- *WhoAmW 91, WhoWor 91*
Vagnini, Kenneth L. 1947- *St&PR 91*
Vago, Luis Nick 1925- *St&PR 91*
Vago, Pierre 1910- *WhoWor 91*
Vagramian-Nishanian, Violet *WhoSSW 91*
Vagshenian, Gregory Simon 1947- *BiDrAPA 89*
Vagts, Detlev Frederick 1929- *WhoAm 90*
Vague, Jean Marie 1911- *WhoWor 91*
Vahan, Richard 1927- *WhoAm 90*
Vahaviolos, Sotirios John 1946- *WhoAm 90*
Vahey, Daniel A. 1945- *St&PR 91*
Vahia, Nalinkant S 1916- *BiDrAPA 89*
Vahia, Vihang Nalinkant 1950- *BiDrAPA 89*
Vahl, Richard James 1940- *WhoSSW 91*
Vahlteich, Hans W. 1896-1989 *BioIn 16*
Vahora, Shiraj 1953- *BiDrAPA 89*
Vahsholtz, Robert John 1935- *St&PR 91, WhoAm 90*
Vai, Steve 1961- *ConMus 5 [port]*
Vaicaitis, Rimas 1941- *WhoWor 91*
Vaiciunaite, Judita 1937- *EncCoWW*
Vaidya, Alzira Francisca 1949- *BiDrAPA 89*
Vaidya, Kirit Rameshchandra 1937- *WhoE 91*
Vaidya, Vic 1935- *St&PR 91*
Vail, Aaron 1796-1878 *BioIn 16*
Vail, Beth H. 1932- *WhoE 91*
Vail, Beverly Oliva 1949- *WhoSSW 91*
Vail, Charles Daniel 1936- *WhoAm 90*
Vail, Charles Rowe 1915- *WhoAm 90*
Vail, Dennis 1951- *St&PR 91*
Vail, Eleanor *St&PR 91*
Vail, Frederick Scott 1944- *WhoSSW 91*
Vail, George A. 1933- *St&PR 91*
Vail, Iris Jennings 1928- *WhoAmW 91, WhoWor 91*
Vail, James L. 1937- *St&PR 91*
Vail, Laurence 1857-1968 *WhoAmA 91N*
Vail, Mike 1951- *Ballpl 90*
Vail, Richard C. 1930- *St&PR 91*
Vail, Richard T. 1938- *WhoE 91*
Vail, Theodore N. 1845-1920 *WorAlBi*
Vail, Thomas V.H. 1926- *St&PR 91*
Vail, Thomas Van Husen 1926- *WhoAm 90*
Vail, Van Horn 1934- *WhoAm 90, WhoE 91*
Vail, Warren Hetherington, Jr. 1931- *St&PR 91*
Vaile, Jean Elizabeth 1938- *WhoAmW 91*
Vaill, Peter Brown 1936- *WhoAm 90*
Vaill, Timothy L. 1941- *St&PR 91*
Vaillancourt, Armand 1929- *WhoAmA 91*
Vaillancourt, Daniel Gilbert 1947- *WhoEmL 91, WhoWrEP 89*
Vaillancourt, Donald Charles 1943- *St&PR 91, WhoWor 91*
Vaillancourt, Jean-Guy 1937- *WhoAm 90*
Vaillancourt, Louise B. 1926- *St&PR 91*
Vaillant, George E 1934- *BiDrAPA 89*
Vaillant, George Eman 1934- *WhoAm 90*
Vaillant, Jean-Marie 1927- *WhoWor 91*
Vaillant, Marie-Edouard 1840-1915 *BiDFrPL*
Vails, Nelson *BioIn 16*
Vainstein, Gustavo Alfredo 1949- *WhoWor 91*
Vainstein, Rose 1920- *WhoAm 90*
Vaintola, Raimo Kalervo 1951- *WhoWor 91*
Vaio, Bruce A. 1960- *St&PR 91*
Vaira, Peter Francis 1937- *WhoAm 90*
Vairo, Philip Dominic 1933- *WhoAm 90*
Vairo, Robert John 1930- *St&PR 91, WhoAm 90*
Vais, Mario Nunes 1856-1932 *BioIn 16*
Vaisanen, Raimo A 1938- *BiDrAPA 89*
Vaishnavi, Vijay Kumar 1948- *WhoSSW 91*
Vaisman, Meyer 1960- *WhoAmA 91*
Vaisman, Naum G *BiDrAPA 89*
Vaithiyanathan, Sivalingam 1957- *WhoWor 91*
Vaitkus, V. Anthony 1932- *St&PR 91*
Vaivods, Julijans 1895- *WhoWor 91*
Vaizey, John Ernest 1929-1984 *DcNaB 1981*
Vajda, Deborah Louise 1956- *WhoAmW 91*
Vajda, Igor Joseph Milan 1935- *IntWWM 90*
Vajdos, Vanessa Ellen 1951- *WhoAmW 91*
Vajeeprasee Thongsak, Thomas 1935- *WhoE 91*
Vajk, Hugo 1928- *WhoAm 90, WhoWor 91*
Vakalo, Eleni *EncCoWW*
Vakalo, Helene 1921- *EncCoWW*
Vakhitov, Mulla-Nur 1855-1918 *BioIn 16*
Vakil, Hassan Charharsough 1934- *WhoE 91, WhoWor 91*
Vakil, Sadegh Meissami 1935- *WhoWor 91*
Vakiparta, Jorma Juhani 1945- *WhoWor 91*
Vaks, Jeffrey Elias 1935- *WhoE 91*
Vaky, Viron Peter 1925- *WhoAm 90*
Val, Eduardo R 1938- *BiDrAPA 89*
Val, Vito V. 1933- *St&PR 91*
Val Baker, Denys *AuBYP 90*
Vala, Katri 1901-1944 *DcScanL, EncCoWW*
Valade, Robert C. 1926- *St&PR 91*
Valadez, Gustavo 1952- *WhoHisp 91*
Valadez, John 1951- *WhoAmA 91*
Valadez, Stanley David 1924- *WhoHisp 91*
Valadier, Andrea 1695-1759 *PenDiDA 89*
Valadier, Filippo 1770- *PenDiDA 89*
Valadier, Giovanni 1732-1805 *PenDiDA 89*
Valadier, Giuseppe 1762-1839 *PenDiDA 89*
Valadier, Luigi 1726-1785 *PenDiDA 89*
Valadier, Luigi, II 1781- *PenDiDA 89*
Valadier, Tommaso 1772- *PenDiDA 89*
Valadon, Suzanne 1865-1938 *BiDWomA*
Valagussa, Roberto Paolo 1952- *WhoWor 91*
Valaika, George A. 1943- *St&PR 91*
Valan, Michael N *BiDrAPA 89*
Valance, Marsha Jeanne 1946- *WhoAmW 91, WhoWor 91*
Valanty, Burton John 1949- *WhoEmL 91*
Valaskovic, David William 1961- *WhoWor 91*
Valasquez, Joseph Louis 1955- *WhoEmL 91, WhoSSW 91, WhoWor 91*
Valavanis, Tasso George 1928- *IntWWM 90*
Valbrun, Leon P. *BiDrAPA 89*
Valbuena-Briones, Angel Julian 1928- *WhoAm 90*
Valcarcel, Edgar 1932- *IntWWM 90*
Valcarcel, Emilio Diaz *HispWr 90*
Valcarcel, Marta Iris 1931- *WhoAm 90*
Valcavi, Umberto 1928- *WhoWor 91*
Valcic, Susan Joan 1956- *WhoAmW 91*
Valcour, Francis Leo 1938- *BiDrAPA 89*
Valcourt, Bernard 1952- *WhoE 91*
Valdemarin, Livio 1944- *WhoWor 91*
Valdengo, Giuseppe 1914- *IntWWM 90, PenDiMP*
Valdepenas, Vicente Babaran 1937- *WhoWor 91*
Valder, Hans 1813-1899 *BioIn 16*
Valderrama, Pilar de 1892-1979 *EncCoWW*
Valdes, Albert Charles 1907- *WhoHisp 91*
Valdes, Alberto 1935- *WhoE 91*
Valdes, Berardo A. 1943- *WhoHisp 91*
Valdes, Carlos Leonardo 1951- *WhoHisp 91*
Valdes, Daniel T. 1918- *BioIn 16*
Valdes, Dario 1938- *WhoHisp 91*
Valdes, Gilberto *WhoHisp 91*

Valdes, Gonzalo Fernandez de Oviedo 1478-1557 *BioIn 16*
Valdes, Humberto, Jr. 1949- *BiDrAPA 89*
Valdes, James John 1951- *WhoHisp 91*
Valdes, Jorge E. 1940- *WhoHisp 91*
Valdes, Juan Jose 1953- *WhoHisp 91*
Valdes, Julius 1948- *WhoE 91*
Valdes, Luis G 1933- *BiDrAPA 89*
Valdes, Maria L *BiDrAPA 89*
Valdes, Mario James 1934- *WhoWor 91*
Valdes, Maximiano *WhoAm 90*
Valdes, Pedro Hilario, Jr. 1945- *WhoHisp 91*
Valdes, Teresa A. 1938- *WhoHisp 91*
Valdes, Victor A., Sr. 1936- *WhoHisp 91*
Valdes-Castillo, Esteban 1932- *BiDrAPA 89*
Valdes-Castillo, Juan *BiDrAPA 89*
Valdes-Dapena, Marie Agnes 1921- *WhoAm 90, WhoAmW 91*
Valdes-Fauli, Jose Javier 1951- *WhoSSW 91*
Valdes-Fauli, Raul Jacinto 1943- *WhoHisp 91*
Valdes Leal, Juan de 1622-1691 *IntDcAA 90*
Valdes-Valle, Nancy Zaida 1938- *WhoAmW 91*
Valdespino, Sandy 1939- *Ballpl 90*
Valdez, Abelardo 1942- *BioIn 16*
Valdez, Abelardo L. 1942- *WhoHisp 91*
Valdez, Arnold 1954- *WhoWor 91*
Valdez, Bernard R. 1931- *WhoHisp 91*
Valdez, Bert *WhoHisp 91*
Valdez, Celedonio 1817?-1884 *AmLegL*
Valdez, David 1949- *WhoHisp 91*
Valdez, Elizabeth O. de 1945- *WhoHisp 91*
Valdez, Filiberto 1946-1967 *BioIn 16*
Valdez, Guillermo Bernardo 1928- *BiDrAPA 89*
Valdez, Horacio 1929- *MusmAFA*
Valdez, Joel D. 1934- *WhoHisp 91*
Valdez, Joel David 1934- *WhoAm 90*
Valdez, Joseph Thomas 1950- *WhoHisp 91*
Valdez, Linda L. 1952- *WhoHisp 91*
Valdez, Luis *BioIn 16*
Valdez, Luis 1940- *ConAu 32NR, HispWr 90*
Valdez, Maria del Rosario 1955- *WhoSSW 91*
Valdez, Mary Alejandra 1950- *WhoHisp 91*
Valdez, Miguel Aleman 1903-1983 *BioIn 16*
Valdez, Oscar Jesus 1960- *WhoHisp 91*
Valdez, Pedro Antonio 1825-1884 *AmLegL*
Valdez, Pete, Jr. 1945- *WhoHisp 91*
Valdez, Raul Anguiano 1915- *BioIn 16*
Valdez, Rebecca Katharine 1954- *WhoHisp 91*
Valdez, Ted, Sr. 1928- *WhoHisp 91*
Valdez, Troy Harold 1938- *WhoHisp 91*
Valdez, Valdamar Eluid 1929- *WhoHisp 91*
Valdez, Victor Raul 1962- *WhoHisp 91*
Valdez, Vincent E 1940- *WhoAmA 91*
Valdez, William Marcos 1912- *WhoWor 91*
Valdiserri, Edwin Vincent *BiDrAPA 89*
Valdivia, Fernando Joseph 1930- *WhoE 91*
Valdivia, Jose F., Jr. 1932- *St&PR 91*
Valdivia, Jose Maria, Jr. 1949- *BiDrAPA 89*
Valdivia, Oscar *BiDrAPA 89*
Valdivielso, Jose 1934- *Ballpl 90, BioIn 16*
Valdivielso, Jose Martinez 1934- *WhoHisp 91*
Valdivieso, Rafael 1942- *WhoHisp 91*
Valdiya, Prem Singh 1944- *BiDrAPA 89*
Valdman, Albert 1931- *WhoAm 90*
Valdonio, Giulio Cesare 1937- *WhoWor 91*
Valdovinos, J. Lauro 1938- *WhoHisp 91*
Valdre, Ugo 1926- *WhoWor 91*
Vale, James W. 1916- *St&PR 91*
Vale, Juliet 1952- *ConAu 132*
Vale, Marie *BioIn 16, NewYTBS 90*
Vale, Norman 1930- *St&PR 91, WhoAm 90*
Vale, Sydney 1931- *IntWWM 90*
Valeani, Bernard Marie 1945- *WhoWor 91*
Valen, Felice *AuBYP 90*
Valen, Robert John 1947- *WhoSSW 91*
Valena, Maria A 1960- *BiDrAPA 89*
Valencia, Amalia 1943- *WhoHisp 91*
Valencia, Carmen 1962- *WhoHisp 91*
Valencia, Guillermo 1873-1943 *BioIn 16*
Valencia, Guillermo 1927- *St&PR 91*
Valencia, Henry 1942- *WhoHisp 91*
Valencia, Jesus Maria 1950- *WhoE 91*
Valencia, Lydia J. 1942- *WhoHisp 91*
Valencia, Manuel S *BiDrAPA 89*
Valencia, Rogelio Pasco 1939- *WhoWor 91*
Valencia, Valerie J. 1951- *WhoHisp 91*
Valenciano, Anna Elizabeth 1958- *WhoWor 91*
Valenciano, Randal Grant Bolosan 1958- *WhoEmL 91, WhoWor 91*
Valency, Maurice 1903- *WhoAm 90*
Valens, Evans G. 1920- *AuBYP 90*
Valens, Evans Gladstone 1920- *WhoAm 90*
Valens, Ritchie 1942-1959 *EncPR&S 89*
Valensi, Paul Elie 1953- *WhoWor 91*
Valenstein, Alice 1904- *WhoAmA 91*
Valenstein, Arthur F 1914- *BiDrAPA 89, WhoE 91*
Valenstein, Elliot S 1923- *ConAu 132*
Valenstein, Elliot Spiro 1923- *WhoAm 90*
Valenstein, Marcia Thacker 1955- *BiDrAPA 89*
Valenstein, Suzanne Gebhart 1928- *WhoAm 90, WhoAmA 91*
Valent, Michele D. 1965- *WhoAmW 91*
Valenta, Marie 1944- *WhoSSW 91*
Valenta, Zdenek 1927- *WhoAm 90*
Valente, Benita *BioIn 16, IntWWM 90, WhoAm 90*
Valente, John Anthony 1950- *WhoE 91*
Valente, Louis P. 1930- *St&PR 91*
Valente, Louis Patrick 1930- *WhoAm 90*
Valente, Malangatana Gowenha 1936- *BioIn 16*
Valente, Patricia Lucille 1940- *WhoAmW 91*
Valente, Sandra Debra 1940- *WhoAmW 91*
Valentekovich, Marija Nikoletic 1932- *WhoAmW 91*
Valenti, Carl Michael 1938- *St&PR 91*
Valenti, Dan 1951- *WhoWrEP 89*
Valenti, Fernando *NewYTBS 90*
Valenti, Helena 1940- *EncCoWW*
Valenti, Jack *BioIn 16*
Valenti, Jack Joseph 1921- *WhoAm 90*
Valenti, JoAnn Myer 1945- *WhoSSW 91*
Valenti, Leo Frank 1925- *WhoE 91*
Valenti, Peter Carl 1943- *WhoSSW 91*
Valenti, Samuel 1946- *St&PR 91*
Valentien, Albert R. *PenDiDA 89*
Valentien, Anne Marie *PenDiDA 89*
Valentin, Angel Luis 1955- *WhoHisp 91*
Valentin, Ann Margaret 1936- *WhoAmW 91*
Valentin, Jean-Pierre 1949- *WhoAmA 91*
Valentin, Nilda 1950- *WhoAmW 91*
Valentina *BioIn 16*
Valentina 1899-1989 *AnObit 1989*
Valentine, Al 1931- *St&PR 91*
Valentine, Alan Darrell 1958- *IntWWM 90, WhoSSW 91*
Valentine, Basil *EncO&P 3*
Valentine, Bobby 1950- *Ballpl 90*
Valentine, Brunhilde E. 1929- *St&PR 91*
Valentine, Carol Ann 1942- *WhoAmW 91*
Valentine, Charles Francis 1934- *WhoE 91*
Valentine, Clifton Carnell 1945- *WhoSSW 91*
Valentine, Corky 1929- *Ballpl 90*
Valentine, Daniel Thomas 1946- *WhoE 91*
Valentine, De Wain 1936- *WhoAm 90*
Valentine, Dewain 1936- *WhoAmA 91*
Valentine, Dickie 1929-1971 *OxCPMus*
Valentine, Don *BioIn 16*
Valentine, Dorris Lynn 1906- *WhoAm 90*
Valentine, Douglas *TwCCr&M 91*
Valentine, Ellis 1954- *Ballpl 90*
Valentine, Eugene R *BiDrAPA 89*
Valentine, Foy Dan 1923- *WhoAm 90*
Valentine, Fred 1935- *Ballpl 90*
Valentine, George Edward 1942- *WhoE 91*
Valentine, George Gordon 1919- *WhoAm 90*
Valentine, Helen 1893-1986 *BioIn 16*
Valentine, Henry *BioIn 16*
Valentine, Herman Edward 1937- *St&PR 91, WhoAm 90*
Valentine, I.T., Jr. 1926- *WhoAm 90, WhoSSW 91*
Valentine, Inge 1927- *St&PR 91*
Valentine, James William 1926- *WhoAm 90*
Valentine, Jeffrey 1945- *WhoAm 90, WhoEmL 91*
Valentine, Jimmie Lloyd 1940- *WhoSSW 91*
Valentine, Jo *TwCCr&M 91*
Valentine, John Howard 1941- *BiDrAPA 89*
Valentine, Judith L. 1938- *St&PR 91*
Valentine, Malcolm K T *BiDrAPA 89*
Valentine, Maryann 1935- *WhoAmW 91*
Valentine, Max G 1918- *BiDrAPA 89*
Valentine, Melinda Stauffer 1954- *WhoAmW 91*
Valentine, Ralph Schuyler 1932- *WhoAm 90*
Valentine, Richard Lawson 1955- *WhoSSW 91*
Valentine, Robert John 1950- *WhoSSW 91*
Valentine, Steven Richards 1956- *WhoAm 90*
Valentine, William Edson 1937- *WhoAm 90*
Valentine, William Newton 1917- *WhoAm 90*
Valentine, William Terry 1932- *WhoSSW 91*
Valentine-Thon, Eliza Anne 1948- *WhoWor 91*
Valentiner, William Reinhold 1880-1958 *WhoAmA 91N*
Valentinetti, Vito 1928- *Ballpl 90*
Valentini, Susan Marie 1963- *WhoAmW 91*
Valentini-Terrani, Lucia 1946- *IntWWM 90*
Valentino *BioIn 16*
Valentino 1932- *ConDes 90, WhoWor 91*
Valentino, Frank 1907- *IntWWM 90*
Valentino, Harry 1944- *St&PR 91*
Valentino, John 1940- *St&PR 91*
Valentino, Paul 1902- *BioIn 16*
Valentino, Rene X. 1961- *WhoAmW 91*
Valentino, Rudolph 1895-1926 *BioIn 16, WorAlBi*
Valentino, Tina 1959- *WhoWrEP 89*
Valentis, John Stephen 1945- *WhoE 91*
Valenza, Elaine Dawn 1938- *St&PR 91*
Valenza, Ricci Anthony 1960- *WhoE 91*
Valenza, S. W. 1935- *St&PR 91*
Valenzuela, Amadeo T, Jr. *BiDrAPA 89*
Valenzuela, Edward 1935- *WhoHisp 91*
Valenzuela, Fernando *BioIn 16*
Valenzuela, Fernando 1960- *Ballpl 90 [port], WhoAm 90, WhoHisp 91, WorAlBi*
Valenzuela, Luisa 1938- *BioIn 16, ConAu 32NR, HispWr 90*
Valenzuela, Luisa 1944- *WorAu 1980 [port]*
Valenzuela, Manuel Anthony, Jr. 1955- *WhoWor 91*
Valenzuela, Pablo Detarso 1941- *St&PR 91*
Valenzuela, Patrick 1962- *WhoHisp 91*
Valenzuela, Rafael L. *WhoHisp 91*
Valenzuela Fernandez, Jaime 1953- *WhoWor 91*
Valera-Padayhag, Elisa *BiDrAPA 89*
Valerdi, Jorge 1944- *St&PR 91*
Valeri, Martin 1917- *St&PR 91*
Valeriani, Richard Gerard 1932- *WhoAm 90*
Valerio, Dennis C. 1947- *St&PR 91*
Valerio, Helen Josephine 1938- *WhoAmW 91*
Valerio, James Robert 1938- *WhoAmA 91*
Valerio, Louis J. 1949- *St&PR 91*
Valerio, Michael Anthony 1953- *WhoAm 90*
Valerius, M. Mark 1929- *St&PR 91*
Valero, Rene Arnold 1930- *WhoHisp 91*
Valero, Roberto 1955- *WhoHisp 91*
Valeros, Jose A *BiDrAPA 89*
Valery, Lenore Dorothy 1947- *WhoAmW 91*
Valery, Paul 1871-1945 *MajTwCW, WorAlBi*
Vales, Alina E *BiDrAPA 89*
Vales, Ramon John 1939- *St&PR 91*
Valesano, Robert D. 1929- *St&PR 91*
Valesco, Frances 1941- *WhoAmA 91*
Valesio, Paolo 1939- *WhoAm 90*
Valeskie-Hamner, Gail Yvonne 1953- *WhoAmW 91*
Valetta 1940- *WhoAmA 91*
Valette, Jean Paul 1937- *WhoE 91*
Valette, Marguerite *EncCoWW*
Valette, Rebecca Marianne 1938- *WhoAm 90, WhoAmW 91*
Valeur, Bent Andreas Heidicke 1929- *WhoWor 91*
Valgardson, W. D. 1939- *BioIn 16*
Valgemae, Allan Heino 1951- *BiDrAPA 89*
Valiant, Leslie Gabriel 1949- *WhoAm 90*
Valiantine, George 1874?- *EncO&P 3, EncPaPR 91*
Valice, Debra Diane 1956- *St&PR 91*
Valicenti, Albert Biagio *BiDrAPA 89*
Valicenti, Mitchel J. 1909- *St&PR 91*
Valicenti, Mitchel Joseph 1909- *WhoAm 90*
Valicenti, Rick *BioIn 16*
Valido, Damaso 1924- *WhoSSW 91*
Valimahomed, Salim Akbarali 1948- *WhoWor 91*
Valin, Jonathan 1948- *TwCCr&M 91*
Valin, Pierre-Vincent 1827-1897 *DcCanB 12*
Valinakis, Yannis George 1955- *WhoWor 91*
Valine, Joseph *BioIn 16*
Valines, A. Irene 1958- *WhoEmL 91*
Valins, Eugene *BiDrAPA 89*
Valinski, Dennis John 1946-1979 *WhoAmA 91N*
Valinski, Jack 1954- *WhoSSW 91*
Valiquette, E. Charlene 1951- *St&PR 91*
Valiquette, Jean Guy 1938- *BiDrAPA 89*
Valjakka, Taru 1938- *IntWWM 90*
Valk, Henry Snowden 1929- *WhoAm 90, WhoSSW 91*
Valk, Jerome E. 1935- *St&PR 91*
Valk, Lisa *BioIn 16*
Valk, Neil Anthony 1952- *WhoSSW 91*
Valk, Robert Earl 1914- *WhoAm 90, WhoWor 91*
Valk, Shirley Rounelle 1948- *WhoAmW 91*
Valk, Thomas Heyward 1947- *BiDrAPA 89*
Valkhoff, Marius 1905- *EncO&P 3*
Valko, Tim Robert *BiDrAPA 89*
Valkovic, Vlado 1939- *WhoWor 91*
Valkovic, Zvonimir 1941- *WhoWor 91*
Valla, Pierre 1947- *St&PR 91*
Valla, Rebecca Suzanne *BiDrAPA 89*
Valla, Thomas John 1933- *St&PR 91*
Vallabhaneni, Rao Rama C *BiDrAPA 89*
Vallach, Glenn *ODwPR 91*
Vallan, Ronald Louis 1946- *St&PR 91*
Vallandigham, Clement L. 1820-1871 *WorAlBi*
Vallano, Gary *BiDrAPA 89*
Vallar, William H., Jr. 1931- *St&PR 91*
Vallarino, Joaquin J., Jr. 1921- *St&PR 91*
Vallarta, Ray 1927- *St&PR 91*
Vallat, Xavier 1891-1972 *BioIn 16*
Vallat, Xavier Joseph 1891-1972 *BiDFrPL*
Vallayer-Coster, Anne 1744-1818 *BioIn 16*
Vallbona, R. Nuri 1957- *WhoHisp 91*
Vallbona, Rima de 1931- *BioIn 16, WhoWrEP 89*
Vallbona, Rima-Gretel Rothe 1931- *WhoAmW 91*
Valle, Dave 1960- *Ballpl 90*
Valle, Delia 1934- *St&PR 91*
Valle, Georgette Wald 1924- *WhoAmW 91*
Valle, Hector Jose *BiDrAPA 89*
Valle, Jose B., Jr. 1947- *WhoHisp 91*
Valle, Jose Cecilio del 1777-1834 *BioIn 16*
Valle, Mark *WhoHisp 91*
Valle, Rafael Heliodoro 1891-1959 *BioIn 16*
Valle-Clemente, Carlos Felipe *BiDrAPA 89*
Valle-Inclan, Ramon del 1870-1936 *BioIn 16*
Valle-Jones, Peter Anthony 1950- *WhoWor 91*
Valle y Caviedes, Juan del *BioIn 16*
Valleau, Emily *BioIn 16*
Valleau, Norma Kathryn Sass 1933- *WhoAmW 91*
Valledor, Leo 1936-1989 *BioIn 16*
Vallee, Bert Lester 1919- *WhoAm 90*
Vallee, Francine 1949- *WhoAm 90*
Vallee, Jacques F. 1939- *EncO&P 3*
Vallee, Jacques Fabrice 1939- *WhoWor 91*
Vallee, Jacques Laurent 1939- *St&PR 91*
Vallee, Lisa M. 1959- *ODwPR 91*
Vallee, Martha Ruth 1942- *WhoAmW 91*
Vallee, Pierre-Gabriel 1941- *WhoWor 91*
Vallee, Pierre M. 1941- *WhoAm 90*
Vallee, Rudy 1901-1986 *BioIn 16, OxCPMus, WorAlBi*
Vallee, William Oscar 1934- *WhoAmA 91*
Vallees, Marie des 1590-1656 *EncCoWW*
Vallejo, Antonio Buero *HispWr 90, MajTwCW*
Vallejo, Cesar 1892-1938 *HispWr 90, WorAlBi*
Vallejo, Cesar Abraham 1892-1938 *BioIn 16*
Vallejo, Lisa Elena 1965- *WhoHisp 91*
Vallejo, Mariano Guadalupe 1808-1890 *BioIn 16, WhNaAH*
Vallejo, Marmaduke Grove 1879-1954 *BioIn 16*
Vallejos, Ricardo Paul 1959- *WhoHisp 91*
Vallejos, Roberta F. 1944- *WhoAmW 91*
Vallem, Bradley S. 1953- *St&PR 91*
Vallender, Charles Francis, III 1939- *WhoE 91*
Valler, Rachel 1929- *IntWWM 90*
Vallerand, Patricia Ann 1951- *WhoEmL 91*
Vallery, Janet Alane 1948- *WhoAmW 91, WhoWor 91*
Valles, Evelyn 1953- *WhoHisp 91*
Valles, Jean Paul 1936- *St&PR 91*
Valles, Jules 1832-1885 *BiDFrPL*
Vallet, M *BiDWomA*
Vallet, Odoardo *PenDiDA 89*
Vallett, Walter Irving, Jr. 1923- *St&PR 91*
Valletti, Cesare 1921- *IntWWM 90*
Valletutti, Angelo *BiDrAPA 89*
Valley, Bruce L. 1944- *WhoE 91*
Valley, George Edward, Jr. 1913- *WhoAm 90*
Valley, Mary Margaret 1947- *WhoEmL 91*
Vallgreen, Ville 1855-1940 *BioIn 16*
Valli, Frankie *EncPR&S 89*
Valli, Frankie 1937- *WorAlBi*
Valli, Louis A. 1932- *St&PR 91*
Valli, Peter Constantine 1927- *St&PR 91, WhoAm 90*
Vallien, Bertil 1938- *ConDes 90*
Vallila, Marja R 1950- *WhoAmA 91*
Vallin, Eugene 1856-1922 *PenDiDA 89*
Vallin, Ninon 1886-1961 *PenDiMP*
Vallis, Alberta Y 1930- *BiDrAPA 89*
Vallois, Robert *BioIn 16*

Vallon, Michael L. *BioIn 16*
Vallone, Norman J. 1949- *St&PR 91*
Vallone, Pam 1953- *St&PR 91*
Vallone, Ralph, Jr. 1947- *WhoSSW 91*
Vallort, Ronald Peter 1942- *St&PR 91*
Valls, Joaquin Cassado *PenDiMP*
Valluri, Jagannath Venkatsai 1961- *WhoSSW 91*
Vallury, Sivachandra M *BiDrAPA 89*
Valo, Carolyn Rose 1952- *WhoAmW 91*
Valo, Elmer 1921- *Ballpl 90, BioIn 16*
Valo, Martha Ann 1938- *WhoAmW 91*
Valo, Thomas Scott 1952- *WhoEmL 91*
Valois 1878-1945 *BiDFrPL*
Valois, Marguerite de 1553-1615 *EncCoWW*
Valois, Renee Marie 1958- *WhoAmW 91*
Valone, Thomas Francis 1951- *WhoWrEP 89*
Valoon, Patricia Louise 1936- *WhoAmW 91*
Valor, Jack 1944- *WhoHisp 91*
Valore, Kenneth Joseph 1941- *St&PR 91, WhoAm 90*
Valore, Richard Howard 1931- *St&PR 91*
Valsamis, Marius Peter 1932- *WhoE 91*
Valsassina, Isabelle von Thurn- *BioIn 16*
Valtasaari, Jukka Robert 1940- *WhoWor 91*
Valtierra, Cesar A 1930- *BiDrAPA 89*
Valtin, Donald Edward 1936- *St&PR 91*
Valtman, Edmund 1914- *WhoAmA 91, WhoE 91*
Valuchek, Andrew J. 1911- *WhoWrEP 89*
Valukas, Anton *BioIn 16*
Valuska, Kenneth W. 1948- *St&PR 91*
Valvano, James Thomas 1946- *WhoAm 90*
Valvano, Jim *BioIn 16*
Valvassori, Giovanni Andrea *PenDiDA 89*
Valverde, Joaquin 1846-1910 *OxCPMus*
Valverde, Joe A. 1935- *WhoHisp 91*
Valverde, Leonard A. 1943- *WhoHisp 91*
Valverde, Manuel Mora 1908- *BioIn 16*
Valverde, Sylvia Ann 1956- *WhoHisp 91*
Valverde, William Mark 1947- *BiDrAPA 89*
Valverde-Ward, Deborah Louise 1957- *WhoAmW 91*
Valys, Monika Vainius 1954- *WhoE 91*
Valys, Susan Patricia 1962- *WhoWrEP 89*
Vambery, Arminius 1832-1913 *EncO&P 3*
Van Cliburn *PenDiMP*
Van, George Paul 1940- *WhoAm 90*
Van, Peter 1936- *WhoE 91, WhoWor 91*
Vana, Josef *BiDrAPA 89*
Van Aalst, Ron 1944- *St&PR 91*
Van Aalten, Jacques 1907- *WhoAmA 91*
Van Acker, Juliaan Charles Arthur 1940- *WhoWor 91*
Van Ackere, Jules-Emile 1914- *IntWWM 90*
Van Ackeren, Maurice Edward 1911- *WhoAm 90*
Vanacore, Frederick 1927- *ODwPR 91*
Van Aeken, Alexander Louis 1957- *IntWWM 90*
Van Agtmael, Antoine Willem 1944- *WhoE 91*
Van Aken, Joan Ernst 1942- *WhoWor 91*
van Aken, John Henry 1922- *WhoSSW 91*
Van Aken, Valentina Petrone 1963- *WhoE 91*
Vanall, Emilie *AuBYP 90*
Van Allan, Richard 1935- *IntWWM 90, PenDiMP*
Van Allen, Barbara Martz *ODwPR 91*
Van Allen, David N. 1934- *St&PR 91*
Van Allen, James A. 1914- *WorAlBi*
Van Allen, James Alfred 1914- *BioIn 16, WhoAm 90*
Van Allen, John Bevier 1911- *St&PR 91*
Van Allen, William K. 1914- *St&PR 91*
Van Allen, William Kent 1914- *WhoAm 90, WhoSSW 91*
Van Allsburg, Chris *BioIn 16*
Van Allsburg, Chris 1949- *AuBYP 90, WhoAm 90*
Van Allsburg, Jon Aaron 1955- *WhoEmL 91*
Van Alphen, H. August M. 1934- *WhoWor 91*
Van Alstine, John Richard 1952- *WhoAmA 91*
Van Alstine, Susana Lopez- *BiDrAPA 89*
Van Alstyne, Egbert 1882-1951 *BioIn 16, OxCPMus*
Van Alstyne, Frances *BioAmW*
Van Alstyne, Judith Sturges 1934- *WhoAmW 91*
Van Alstyne, Vance Brownell 1924- *WhoE 91, WhoWor 91*
Van Alstyne, W. Scott, Jr. 1922- *WhoAm 90, WhoWor 91*
Van Alstyne, William Warner 1934- *WhoAm 90*
Van Altena, William Foster 1939- *WhoAm 90*
Vanaman, David C. 1954- *St&PR 91*
Vanaman, Linda Bell 1941- *WhoAmW 91*
Van Amberg, Robert Joseph 1913- *BiDrAPA 89*
Van Ameringen, Michael *BiDrAPA 89*
Van Amringe, Jon Eric 1948- *St&PR 91*
Van Anda, Allen David 1929- *St&PR 91*
Van Anda, Carr Vattel 1864-1945 *BioIn 16*
Van Andel, Betty Jean 1921- *WhoAmW 91*
Van Andel, Carol Cox *BiDrAPA 89*
Van Andel, Hendrikus 1926- *WhoWor 91*
Van Andel, Jay 1924- *ConAmBL, St&PR 91, WhoAm 90*
Van Andel, Nan 1953- *St&PR 91*
Van Andel-Gaby, Barbara A. 1962- *WhoAmW 91*
Van Anden, Anne Linda 1945- *WhoAmW 91*
Van Anden, Charles R. 1927- *St&PR 91*
Van Anrooy, Sara 1960- *BiDrAPA 89*
Van Antwerp, James Dillier, Jr. *BiDrAPA 89*
Van Antwerp, Rosemary D. 1946- *St&PR 91*
Van Antwerpen, Franklin Stuart 1941- *WhoAm 90, WhoE 91, WhoWor 91*
Van Antwerpen, Regina Lane 1939- *WhoAmW 91*
Van Apeldoorn, Douglas Keith 1952- *St&PR 91*
Van Appeldoorn, Henk 1937- *St&PR 91*
Van Appledorn, Mary Jeanne 1927- *IntWWM 90*
Vanaria, Robert John 1945- *St&PR 91*
Van Ark, Joan *BioIn 16, WhoAm 90, WhoAmW 91*
Van Ark, Joan 1943- *WorAlBi*
Van Arnam, Barbara June 1946- *WhoAmW 91*
Van Arnem, Harold L. 1940- *St&PR 91*
Van Arsdale, Dick 1943- *WhoAm 90*
Van Arsdale, Nancy P. 1957- *WhoAmW 91*
Van Arsdall, Robert Armes 1925- *WhoAm 90*
Van Arsdell, Paul Marion 1905- *WhoAm 90*
Van Arsdol, Maurice Donald, Jr. 1928- *WhoAm 90*
Van Artevelde, Jacob 1290?-1345 *BioIn 16*
Van Artevelde, Philip 1340?-1382 *BioIn 16*
Van Artsdalen, Ervin Robert 1913- *WhoAm 90*
Vanasco-Knudsen, Darlene Marie 1964- *WhoE 91*
Vanasek, James George 1944- *St&PR 91*
Vanaskie, William F. 1947- *WhoE 91*
Van Assche, Pierre 1936- *WhoAm 90, WhoWor 91*
Vanasse, Louis Raymond 1931- *WhoAmA 91*
Vanat, Laurent-Raymond 1961- *WhoWor 91*
Vanatta, Chester B. 1935- *WhoAm 90*
Vanatta, John Crothers, III 1919- *WhoAm 90*
Van Atta, Ralph Edward 1933- *WhoSSW 91*
Van Atta, Robert Ernest 1924- *WhoAm 90*
Van Atta, Russ 1906-1986 *Ballpl 90*
Van Auken, Richard A. 1934- *St&PR 91*
Van Auken, Robert Danforth 1915- *WhoSSW 91, WhoWor 91*
Vanbalen, A. *ConAu 131*
Van Balen, Cissy 1941- *WhoAmW 91*
Van Bark, Bella S *BiDrAPA 89*
VanBarriger, Carol Lynne 1941- *WhoAmW 91*
Van Barthold, Kenneth 1927- *IntWWM 90*
Van Basten, Marco *NewYTBS 90 [port]*
Van Bavel, Peter Cornelius 1948- *WhoSSW 91*
Van Becelaere, Robert Morris 1941- *St&PR 91*
Van Beek, Gus Willard 1922- *WhoAm 90*
Van Beijeren, Henk 1943- *WhoWor 91*
Van Beinum, Eduard 1901-1959 *PenDiMP*
Van Bellingham, Heidi 1956- *BiDrAPA 89*
Van Bellinghen, Jean-Paul 1925- *WhoWor 91*
Van Bendegem, Jean Paul 1953- *WhoWor 91*
Van Benschoten, L.D., Jr. 1916- *St&PR 91*
Van Benthuysen, Walter G. 1939- *St&PR 91*
Van Berg, Jack 1936- *BioIn 16*
Van Bergen, Frederick Hall 1914- *WhoAm 90*
van Bergen, Johannes Frans A. 1942- *WhoE 91*
Van Bergen, Marilyn Anne *WhoAmW 91*
Van Bergh, Dick 1960- *St&PR 91*
Van Bergh, Rick *St&PR 91*
Van Berkel, Thomas R. 1926- *St&PR 91*
Van Besien, Maurice J *BiDrAPA 89*
Van Beuzekom, Dirk Herman 1955- *WhoWor 91*
Van Biber, John Charles *BiDrAPA 89*
Van Bladel, Jean Georges 1922- *WhoWor 91*
Van Blarcom, Carolyn Conant 1879-1960 *BioIn 16*
Van Blarcom, Peter Payne 1932- *St&PR 91*
Vanblaricom, Barry *St&PR 91*
Van Blenis, Grace *St&PR 91*
Van Blerk, Gerardus J. M. 1924- *IntWWM 90*
Van Boer, Bertil Herman, Jr. 1952- *IntWWM 90*
Van Bokkelen, Jacobus Jan Hogerworth 1816-1889 *AmLegL*
Van Booven, Judy Lee 1952- *WhoAmW 91*
Van Bortel, Francis J. 1921-1989 *BioIn 16*
Van Bosstraeten, Philip 1939- *WhoWor 91*
Van Branteghem, Luc 1910- *IntWWM 90*
Van Bree, Cornelis 1932- *WhoWor 91*
Van-Breemen, Bertram 1919- *WhoWor 91*
Van Bridge, Tony 1917- *OxCCanT*
Van Briggle, Artus 1869-1904 *PenDiDA 89*
Van Brocklin, Norm 1926-1983 *WorAlBi*
VanBrode, Derrick Brent, IV 1940- *WhoAm 90*
van Bruchem, Jan 1929- *WhoAm 90*
Van Bruggen, Robert Earl *BiDrAPA 89*
Vanbrugh, John 1664-1726 *BioIn 16*
Van Bruhesen, Peter *EncO&P 3*
Van Brunt, Albert Daniel 1920- *WhoAm 90*
Van Brunt, Edwin, Jr. 1932- *WhoAm 90*
Van Brunt, Marcia Adele 1937- *WhoAmW 91*
Van Brunt, Philip G 1935- *WhoAmA 91*
Van Brunt, Philip Grant 1935- *WhoE 91*
Van Brunt, Rinaldo 1901-1989 *BioIn 16*
Van Brunt, William Albert 1944- *St&PR 91*
Van Bruwaene, Raymond T. 1938- *WhoAm 90*
Van Bulck, Hendrikus Eugenius 1950- *WhoSSW 91*
van Bulck, Margaret West 1955- *WhoAmW 91*
Van Buren, Abigail 1918- *BioAmW, BioIn 16, WhoAm 90, WorAlBi*
Van Buren, Angelica Singleton 1817-1878 *BioIn 16*
Van Buren, Hannah Hoes 1783-1819 *BioIn 16*
Van Buren, John *BioIn 16*
Van Buren, John B. 1943- *St&PR 91*
Van Buren, Karen Lynn 1957- *WhoWrEP 89*
Van Buren, Kurt Edwin 1957- *WhoEmL 91*
Van Buren, Linda Jeanne 1946- *WhoWor 91*
Van Buren, Maarten 1941- *St&PR 91*
Van Buren, Martin 1782-1862 *BiDrUSE 89, BioIn 16, WorAlBi*
Van Buren, Paul Matthews 1924- *WhoAm 90*
Van Buren, Phyllis Eileen 1947- *WhoAmW 91*
Van Buren, Raeburn 1891-1987 *EncACom, WhoAmA 91N*
Van Buren, Robert 1925- *St&PR 91, WhoAm 90, WhoE 91*
Van Buren, William Benjamin, III 1922- *WhoAm 90*
Van Buren, William Ralph, Jr. 1914- *St&PR 91*
VanBurkalow, Anastasia 1911- *WhoAmW 91, WhoE 91*
Van Buskirk, David 1932- *BiDrAPA 89*
VanBuskirk, John *BioIn 16*
Van Busschbach, J G 1896-1974 *EncO&P 3*
Van Busschbach, John George 1896-1974 *EncPaPR 91*
Van Caenegem, Raoul Charles 1927- *WhoWor 91*
Van Camp, Brian Ralph 1940- *WhoAm 90*
Van Camp, Gilbert C. 1817-1900 *WorAlBi*
VanCamp, Jean 1937- *WhoSSW 91*
Van Campen, Karl *MajTwCW*
Van Campen, M. Joannes 1937- *St&PR 91*
Van Caspel, Venita Walker *WhoAm 90, WhoAmW 91*
Vance, Alfred 1839-1888 *OxCPMus*
Vance, Anita Paine *BiDrAPA 89*
Vance, Carol Stoner 1933- *WhoAm 90*
Vance, Courtney 1960- *ConTFT 8*
Vance, Courtney B. *BioIn 16*
Vance, Courtney B 1960?- *DrBlPA 90*
Vance, Cyrus R. 1917- *BioIn 16, WorAlBi*
Vance, Cyrus Roberts 1917- *BiDrUSE 89, WhoAm 90, WhoE 91*
Vance, Danitra *DrBlPA 90*
Vance, Dazzy 1891-1961 *Ballpl 90 [port]*
Vance, Dennis Edward 1942- *WhoAm 90*
Vance, Don Kelvin 1935- *WhoAm 90*
Vance, Donald *ODwPR 91*
Vance, Dorothy Saunders 1944- *WhoAmW 91*
Vance, Elbridge Putnam 1915- *WhoAm 90*
Vance, Gary Craig 1952- *WhoEmL 91*
Vance, Gary R. 1935- *St&PR 91*
Vance, Gerald *ConAu 130, MajTwCW*
Vance, Graham Alexander 1919- *WhoAm 90*
Vance, Harold Sines 1890-1959 *EncABHB 5 [port]*
Vance, Herbert A. 1901- *St&PR 91*
Vance, Jack *MajTwCW*
Vance, Jack 1920- *RGTwCSF*
Vance, James 1930- *WhoAm 90, WhoWor 91*
Vance, James Harrison 1941- *WhoE 91*
Vance, James Richard 1957- *WhoEmL 91*
Vance, John Burton 1944- *WhoSSW 91*
Vance, John Eric 1959- *BiDrAPA 89*
Vance, John Holbrook *WhoWrEP 89*
Vance, John Holbrook 1916- *MajTwCW, TwCCr&M 91*
Vance, Kenneth E. 1917- *WhoAm 90*
Vance, Lee 1907- *WhoAm 90, WhoWor 91*
Vance, Leland S. 1929- *St&PR 91*
Vance, Louis Joseph 1879-1933 *TwCCr&M 91*
Vance, Marguerite 1889-1965 *AuBYP 90*
Vance, Martin J. 1917- *St&PR 91*
Vance, Nina 1914-1980 *BioIn 16, NotWoAT*
Vance, Richard Moon 1938- *WhoE 91*
Vance, Robert Mercer 1916- *St&PR 91, WhoAm 90*
Vance, Robert Raschig, Jr. 1927- *WhoE 91*
Vance, Robert S. 1931-1989 *BioIn 16*
Vance, Ronald Jay 1952- *St&PR 91*
Vance, Roy Newton 1921- *WhoAm 90*
Vance, Sandy 1947- *Ballpl 90*
Vance, Sheldon Baird 1917- *WhoAm 90*
Vance, Stanley Charles 1915- *WhoAm 90*
Vance, Stephen Glenn *BiDrAPA 89*
Vance, Stephen Marvin 1956- *WhoEmL 91*
Vance, Verne Widney, Jr. 1932- *WhoAm 90*
Vance, Vivian 1911-1979 *WorAlBi*
Vance, William Colekin 1947- *St&PR 91*
Vance, William L 1934- *ConAu 132*
Vance, Zinna Barth 1917- *WhoAmW 91, WhoSSW 91*
Vanceburg, Martha *WhoWrEP 89*
Vancisin, Joseph Richard 1922- *WhoAm 90*
Van Citters, Robert Lee 1926- *WhoAm 90*
Van Cleave, J.M.S. *AmLegL*
van Cleave, Kirstin Dean 1940- *WhoSSW 91*
Van Cleave, William Robert 1935- *WhoAm 90*
Van Cleef, Lee 1925-1989 *AnObit 1989, BioIn 16, ConTFT 8, WorAlBi*
Van Cleve, John Vickrey 1947- *WhoAm 90*
Van Cleve, Ruth Gill 1925- *WhoAm 90*
Van Cleve, William Moore 1929- *WhoAm 90*
Vanco, John Leroy 1945- *WhoAmA 91*
Van Coetsem, Frans Camille Cornelis 1919- *WhoAm 90*
Van Coevering, Jack 1900- *AuBYP 90*
Van Coevering, Jan Adrian *AuBYP 90*
Van Coevering, Russell James, II 1951- *WhoE 91*
van Compernolle, Rene 1923- *WhoWor 91*
Van Cortland, Ida 1854-1924 *OxCCanT [port]*
Van Cortlandt Family *EncCRAm*
Van Cortlandt, Oloff 1600-1684 *EncCRAm*
Van Cortlandt, Philip 1749-1831 *EncCRAm*
Van Cortlandt, Pierre 1721-1814 *EncCRAm*
Van Cortlandt, Stephanus 1643-1700 *EncCRAm*
Van Cott, Alan W. 1949- *WhoE 91*
Van Cott, Margaret N. 1830-1914 *BioAmW*
Vancouver, George 1757-1798 *WorAlBi*
Van Culin, Samuel 1930- *WhoAm 90*
Van Cuyk, Chris 1927- *Ballpl 90*
Vanda, Charles *BioIn 16*
Van Daele, Alexander L *BiDrAPA 89*
Van daele, Henk 1930- *WhoWor 91*
Vandaele, Walter Henri Alfons 1945- *WhoE 91*
van Dalen, Dirk J. 1927- *WhoSSW 91*
van Dalen, Pieter Adriaan 1942- *WhoWor 91*
Van Daley, Donald Phillip 1928- *St&PR 91*
Vandall, Allan Lee 1942- *St&PR 91*
van Dam, Andries 1938- *WhoAm 90*
Van Dam, Brian Mathys, Sr. 1959- *WhoE 91*
van Dam, Bruce Edward 1950- *WhoE 91*
Van Dam, Forrest R *BiDrAPA 89*
van Dam, Heiman 1920- *WhoAm 90*
Van Dam, Jose 1940- *IntWWM 90, PenDiMP*
Van Dam, R. Paul *WhoAm 90*
Van Dam, Wils 1941- *St&PR 91*
Vandament, William Eugene 1931- *WhoAm 90*

Van Damme, Johannes Martinus G. 1937- *WhoWor 91*
Vandaveer, Linda Irene 1944- *WhoAmW 91*
Van Davelaar, Mary Jo *BiDrAPA 89*
van de Beek, Abraham 1946- *WhoWor 91*
Vande Berg, Ed 1958- *Ballpl 90*
Van De Bovenkamp, Hans 1938- *WhoAmA 91*
Van de Bovenkamp, Sue Erpf 1938- *WhoAmW 91, WhoWor 91*
van de Bunt, Dirk Wouter 1957- *WhoEmL 91*
Van De Car, Diana Lee 1952- *WhoAmW 91, WhoEmL 91*
VanDeCasteele, Jeffrey James 1960- *WhoEmL 91*
Van de Castle, Robert L 1927- *EncO&P 3*
Van de Castle, Robert Leon 1927- *EncPaPR 91*
Vandecruys, Eduard 1949- *WhoWor 91*
Van De Graaf, Jacobus John 1938- *St&PR 91*
Vandegrift, Alexander A. 1887-1973 *WorAlBi*
Vandegrift, Alfred Eugene 1937- *WhoAm 90*
Vandegrift, Barbara Price 1941- *WhoE 91*
Vande Hey, James Michael 1916- *WhoAm 90*
van de Kaa, Dirk Jan 1933- *WhoWor 91*
Van de Kamp, John K. *NewYTBS 90 [port]*
Van de Kamp, John Kalar 1936- *WhoAm 90*
Van De Kreeke, Gerald Richard, Sr. 1946- *WhoEmL 91*
Vandeleur, Joe 1903-1988 *AnObit 1988*
Vande Linde, Vernon David 1942- *WhoAm 90*
Vandell, Deborah Lowe 1949- *WhoAmW 91*
VanDell, Sharon Lynn 1960- *WhoE 91*
Van de Maele, Albert Camille Louis 1914- *WhoAm 90*
VanDemark, James *BioIn 16*
Van De Mark, Julie Ann 1957- *WhoEmL 91*
Van Demark, Robert Eugene 1913- *WhoAm 90, WhoWor 91*
Vandemark, Robert Goodyear 1921- *WhoAm 90*
Van Demark, Ruth Elaine 1944- *WhoAmW 91*
Van Den Akker, Koos 1939- *ConDes 90*
Vandenakker, Martin *BiDrAPA 89*
van den Ban, Anne Willem 1928- *WhoWor 91*
Van den Beld, Clare E. 1948- *WhoWor 91*
Vandenbelt, Russell Albert *BiDrAPA 89*
Vandenberg, Arthur H. 1884-1951 *BioIn 16, WorAlBi*
Vandenberg, Diana 1923- *BiDWomA*
Vandenberg, Hoyt Sanford 1899-1954 *BioIn 16*
Vandenberg, Hy 1907- *Ballpl 90*
Van Den Berg, Jan B. 1930- *St&PR 91*
Van Den Berg, John Howard 1956- *WhoEmL 91*
Vanden Berg, Les D. 1948- *St&PR 91*
Vandenberg, Patricia Clasina 1948- *WhoAmW 91*
Vandenberg, Peter, Jr. 1955- *St&PR 91*
Vandenberg, Roger A. 1947- *St&PR 91*
Vandenberg, Russell Clayton 1933- *St&PR 91*
Vanden Berge, Peter Willem 1935- *WhoAmA 91*
Vandenbergh, Richard L *BiDrAPA 89*
van den Bergh, Sidney 1929- *WhoAm 90*
Van Den Berghe, Herman 1933- *WhoWor 91*
Van den Berghe, Pierre L. *BioIn 16*
van den Berghe, Pierre Louis 1933- *WhoAm 90*
Van DenBerghe, Roland A. F. 1943- *WhoWor 91*
van den Blink, Nelson Mooers 1934- *St&PR 91*
Van Den Boom, Esperanza 1953- *WhoAmW 91*
Vandenbos, Gary Roger 1943- *WhoAm 90, WhoE 91*
Vanden Bosch, Henry *St&PR 91*
Van Den Bosch, Wallace R 1920- *BiDrAPA 89*
Vanden Bout, Paul Adrian 1939- *WhoAm 90*
Vandenbroeck, Paul Rosa 1953- *WhoWor 91*
Van Den Bulcke, Daniel Gustaaf 1939- *WhoWor 91*
VanDenburg, Arland Franklin 1920- *St&PR 91*
Vandenburg, Howard 1918- *IntWWM 90*
Vandenburg, Mary Lou 1943- *WhoAmW 91*
Vandenburg, Robin Cordary 1964- *WhoAmW 91*
Vandenburgh, Edward Clinton, III 1915- *WhoAm 90, WhoWor 91*
Vandenburgh, Jane *ConLC 59 [port]*
Van Den Essen, Louis 1939- *WhoHisp 91*
Van den Eynde, Jean Jules 1953- *WhoWor 91*
van den Haag, Ernest 1914- *WhoE 91*
Van Den Hende, Jan Henri 1934- *WhoE 91*
VandenHeuvel, Dirk J., Jr. *ODwPR 91*
Vanden Heuvel, Thomas John 1949- *WhoEmL 91*
van den Hurk, Johannes G. 1942- *WhoWor 91*
van-den-Noort, Stanley 1930- *WhoAm 90*
Van Den Schrieck, Henry-George 1925- *WhoWor 91*
Van den Wijngaerde, Paul 1937- *WhoWor 91*
van de Paverd, Petrus Aloysius 1931- *WhoWor 91*
Vandepitte, Daniel C. C. 1922- *WhoWor 91*
Vandeplassche, Marcel-Marie 1914- *WhoWor 91*
Van De Polder, Jean Ann 1942- *BiDrAPA 89*
Van de Poll, Klaas Willem 1942- *WhoWor 91*
Van de Putte, Marc Emile 1926- *WhoWor 91*
Van De Putte, Robert Alexander 1950- *WhoWor 91*
Van Der, Erik Hans 1940- *St&PR 91*
Vandera, Alonso Carrio de la *BioIn 16*
van der Avoird, Ad 1943- *WhoWor 91*
Vanderbank, John *PenDiDA 89*
Van Der Beek, Edward Stanley 1927-1984 *WhoAmA 91N*
Vanderbeek, Hattie Borman 1920- *WhoE 91*
VanderBeek, Helen Free 1944- *WhoAmW 91*
Vanderbeek, Robert Easton 1928- *WhoWor 91*
Vanderbei, Robert Joseph 1955- *WhoE 91*
van der Bent, Ans J 1924- *ConAu 131*
Vanderberg, James Leonard 1943- *St&PR 91*
Vanderberry, James Greer 1932- *St&PR 91*
Vanderbilt, Alfred G., Jr. 1949- *ODwPR 91*
Vanderbilt, Alice Claypoole Gwynne 1843-1899 *BioIn 16*
Vanderbilt, Amy 1908-1974 *WorAlBi*
Vanderbilt, Arthur T., II 1950- *WhoE 91, WhoEmL 91*
Vanderbilt, Consuelo *BioAmW*
Vanderbilt, Consuelo 1877-1964 *BioIn 16*
Vanderbilt, Corneel 1830-1882 *BioIn 16*
Vanderbilt, Cornelius 1794-1877 *BioIn 16, WorAlBi*
Vanderbilt, Cornelius 1843-1899 *BioIn 16*
Vanderbilt, Cornelius 1873-1942 *BioIn 16*
Vanderbilt, Cornelius 1898-1974 *BioIn 16*
Vanderbilt, Cornelius Jeremiah 1830-1882 *BioIn 16*
Vanderbilt, Frank Crawford 1839-1885 *BioIn 16*
Vanderbilt, Frankie 1839-1885 *BioIn 16*
Vanderbilt, George O. 1844- *AmLegL*
Vanderbilt, George Washington *BioIn 16*
Vanderbilt, Gertrude Whitney *BioIn 16*
Vanderbilt, Gloria 1924- *BioIn 16*
Vanderbilt, Gloria M. 1924- *BioAmW*
Vanderbilt, Gloria Morgan 1904-1965 *BioIn 16*
Vanderbilt, Gloria Morgan 1924- *WhoAmW 91*
Vanderbilt, Grace Wilson 1870-1953 *BioAmW, BioIn 16*
Vanderbilt, Hugh Bedford 1921- *St&PR 91*
Vanderbilt, Hugh Bedford, Sr. 1921- *WhoAm 90*
Vanderbilt, Kermit 1925- *WhoAm 90*
Vanderbilt, Oliver DeG 1914- *St&PR 91*
Vanderbilt, Reginald Claypoole 1880-1925 *BioIn 16*
Vanderbilt, William H. 1821-1885 *BioIn 16, WorAlBi*
Vanderbilt, William K. 1849-1920 *WorAlBi*
Vanderbilt, William Kissam 1849-1920 *BioIn 16*
Vander Boom, Mae M. *AuBYP 90*
Vanderbosch, James E 1926- *BiDrAPA 89*
Vanderburg, Kathleen 1951- *WhoAmW 91*
Vanderburg, Paul Stacey 1941- *WhoSSW 91*
Van Der Burght, Gregorius 1944- *WhoWor 91*
Vanderbylt, Whiteford *WhoWrEP 89*
Vander Clute, Howard Edmund, Jr. 1929- *WhoAm 90*
Vander Clute, Norman Roland 1932- *WhoAm 90*
Vanderclute, Robert Charles 1945- *WhoE 91*
Vandercook, Margaret Womack 1868-1936 *LiHiK*
Vandercruse, Roger *PenDiDA 89*
van der Does, Ton 1933- *WhoWor 91*
Vander Dussen, Neil Richard 1931- *WhoAm 90*
Van der Eb, Alex Jan 1934- *WhoWor 91*
Van der Eb, Henry Gerard 1918- *WhoAm 90*
Vander Els, Betty 1936- *BioIn 16, SmATA 63 [port]*
Van Der Erve, Marc 1947- *WhoWor 91*
Vanderflugt, Gary Daryl 1948- *St&PR 91*
Vandergarde, Alfred Frederik 1948- *WhoWor 91*
Van Der Goes, Hugo 1440?-1482 *IntDcAA 90*
Vandergriff, Jerry Dodson 1943- *WhoWor 91*
Van Der Haas, Henrietta *AuBYP 90*
Van Der Heide, Charles J *BiDrAPA 89*
Van Der Heide, Douglas John 1949- *BiDrAPA 89*
Vander Heide, G. Peter 1947- *WhoEmL 91*
Van der Heyden, Frans 1949- *BioIn 16*
Vanderheyden, Jan F. 1903-1987 *BioIn 16*
Vander Heyden, W.H. 1936- *St&PR 91*
Vanderhill, Charles Warren 1937- *WhoAm 90*
Vanderhoef, Eunice Taylor *BioIn 16*
Vanderhoef, Larry Neil 1941- *WhoAm 90*
Vanderhoef, Peter C. 1940- *St&PR 91*
Vanderhoof, Irwin T. 1927- *St&PR 91*
Vanderhoof, Irwin Thomas 1927- *WhoAm 90*
Vander Horst, Donald J. 1924- *St&PR 91*
Van Der Horst, Ellen G. 1956- *St&PR 91*
Vander Horst, Frank Davis 1954- *WhoSSW 91*
Vander Houwen, Boyd A. 1946- *WhoEmL 91*
Vanderjagt, Arie Johan 1948- *WhoWor 91*
Vander Jagt, Guy 1931- *WhoAm 90*
Van Der Kelen, Gustraaf 1928- *WhoWor 91*
Van der Kloot, William George 1927- *WhoAm 90*
Van Der Kolk, Bessel Anton 1943- *BiDrAPA 89*
Vander Kolk, Kenneth Jay 1928- *WhoAm 90*
van der Kroef, Justus Maria 1925- *WhoAm 90, WhoWor 91*
Van Der Laan, Paul 1937- *WhoWor 91*
van der Laan, Paul 1952- *WhoWor 91*
Van Der Laan, Piet Cornelis Tobias 1935- *WhoWor 91*
Vanderlaan, Richard B. 1931- *WhoWor 91*
VanderLaan, Robert D. 1952- *WhoWor 91*
Vanderlans, Rudy *BioIn 16*
van der Leun, Jan Cornelis 1928- *WhoWor 91*
Vanderlinde, Derek E. 1946- *St&PR 91*
Vander Linde, Leonard C, III *BiDrAPA 89*
Vanderlinde, Raymond Edward 1924- *WhoAm 90*
Vanderlinde, Susan Kay 1951- *WhoAmW 91*
VanderLinden, Camilla Denice Dunn 1950- *WhoAmW 91*
Vanderlinden, Robert E. 1932- *St&PR 91*
Vanderlip, Dianne Perry 1941- *WhoAmA 91*
Vanderlip, Frank Arthur 1864-1937 *EncABHB 6 [port]*
Vanderlippe, Richard Hampton 1932- *St&PR 91*
van der Marck, Jan 1929- *WhoAm 90*
Van Der Mast, Karel Diederick 1948- *WhoWor 91*
Vandermate, Elda 1930- *St&PR 91*
Vandermause, Richard Lee 1948- *St&PR 91*
Van Der Meer, Herman Kurt *BiDrAPA 89*
Van der Meer, Jan 1632-1675 *BioIn 16*
Vander Meer, Johnny 1914- *Ballpl 90 [port]*
van der Meer, Simon 1925- *WhoWor 91, WorAlBi*
Vandermeersssche, Gaston *BioIn 16*
van der Merwe, Nikolaas Johannes 1940- *WhoAm 90*
Van Der Meulen, Barry 1937- *St&PR 91*
Vander Meulen, Conrad 1925- *St&PR 91*
Van Der Meulen, Jan 1929- *WhoAmA 91*
Van Der Meulen, Joseph Pierre 1929- *WhoAm 90, WhoWor 91*
Vanderminden, Henry J.W., III 1925- *St&PR 91*
Vanderminden, Henry J.W., Jr. 1896- *St&PR 91*
Vandermolen, Mimi *BioIn 16*
Vander Molen, Robert L. 1947- *WhoWrEP 89*
Vander Myde, Paul Arthur 1937- *St&PR 91, WhoAm 90*
Van Dernoot, Peter R. *ODwPR 91*
Van Dernoot, Richard Norman 1945- *St&PR 91*
Vanderplank, James Edward 1908- *BioIn 16*
Vander Pluym, Todd *BioIn 16*
van der Poel, Pieter Willem 1931- *WhoWor 91*
Vander Pol, Daryl Lee 1944- *St&PR 91*
Van Der Pol, Denise Marie 1955- *WhoAmW 91*
Vanderpol, Maurice 1922- *BiDrAPA 89*
Vanderpool, Beverly J *BiDrAPA 89*
Vanderpool, Eugene 1906-1989 *BioIn 16*
Van Der Pool, James Grote 1903-1979 *WhoAmA 91N*
Vanderpool, John P *BiDrAPA 89*
Van Derpool, Karen 1946- *WhoAmA 91*
Vanderpool, Ramon A *BiDrAPA 89*
Vanderpool, Robert Lee, Jr. 1918- *St&PR 91*
Vanderpool, Ward Melvin 1917- *WhoWor 91*
Vander Poorte, Ida Cornelia 1948- *St&PR 91*
Van der Post, Laurens *BioIn 16*
Vander Putten, Leroy Andrew 1934- *St&PR 91*
Van Der Rhoer, Edward 1917- *WhoWor 91*
Van Der Rohe, Ludwig M *WhoAmA 91N*
Van Der Roost, Jan Frans Joseph 1956- *IntWWM 90*
Vanderryn, Jack 1930- *WhoAm 90*
Van Dersal, William R 1907-1990 *ConAu 131*
Vandersall, Amy L 1933- *WhoAmA 91*
Vandersall, John Henry 1928- *WhoAm 90*
Vandersall, Thornton A 1928- *BiDrAPA 89*
Vander Schaaf, Rachelle *BioIn 16*
Vander Schraaf, Anna H 1928- *BiDrAPA 89*
Vander Schraaf, Anna Henriette 1928- *WhoE 91*
Vanderscoff, David Paul 1944- *St&PR 91*
Vandersee, Charles Andrew 1938- *WhoWrEP 89*
Vanderselt, Robert Lee 1946- *St&PR 91*
Vanderslice, Joseph Thomas 1927- *WhoAm 90*
Vanderslice, Thomas Aquinas *BioIn 16*
Vanderslice, Thomas Aquinas 1932- *St&PR 91, WhoAm 90, WhoE 91*
Van Der Slik, Jack R 1936- *ConAu 30NR*
Vandersloot, Valda Ilze 1947- *WhoAmW 91*
Vander Sluis, George J 1915-1984 *WhoAmA 91N*
Vandersluis, Kenneth Carl 1941- *St&PR 91*
Vanderstappen, Harrie Albert 1921- *WhoAm 90*
Vanderstappen, Victor Donald 1944- *WhoWor 91*
Vanderstar, John 1933- *WhoAm 90*
Vander Starre, Adrian 1932- *St&PR 91*
Vandersteel, William 1919- *St&PR 91, WhoE 91*
Vanderstelt, Mark J. 1946- *St&PR 91*
Vander Stoep, Evert 1932- *BiDrAPA 89*
Van der Stucken, Frank 1858-1929 *PenDiMP*
Vandersypen, Rita DeBona 1953- *WhoAmW 91*
Vander Tuig, Jane Marie 1951- *WhoAmW 91*
Van der Tuin, Jan *BioIn 16*
Vandertuin, Victoria Elva 1933- *WhoWrEP 89*
Van der Tuuk, Terry 1941- *St&PR 91*
Van der Vaeren, Charles Julien 1930- *WhoWor 91*
Van Der Veen, Eddy 1922- *WhoWor 91*
Vanderveen, John M. 1924- *St&PR 91*
Vander Veen, Marvin William 1930- *St&PR 91*
Vanderveen, Peter 1931- *WhoAm 90*
Van der Veen, Ruud Gerard 1941- *WhoWor 91*
Van Der Veen, Teunis *BiDrAPA 89*
Vander Veer, John Rutgert 1925- *BiDrAPA 89*
Vanderveer, Peter James 1947- *BiDrAPA 89*
Van der Veken, Luc Alexis 1944- *WhoWor 91*
Vanderveld, John, Jr. 1926- *WhoAm 90*
Vanderveld, Richard L. 1925- *ODwPR 91*
Vandervelde, Ann Elizabeth 1946- *WhoAmW 91*
Van Der Velde, Christiaan D 1924- *BiDrAPA 89*
Vander Velde, David Dirk 1952- *BiDrAPA 89*
Van der Velde, Jan *PenDiMP*
Vander Velde, John Christian 1930- *WhoAm 90*
Vander Velde, Wallace Earl 1929- *WhoAm 90, WhoE 91*
Van Der Velden, Renier 1910- *IntWWM 90*

Van Der Veldt, James A. 1893?-1977 *AuBYP 90*
Vander Vennet, George William, Jr. 1937- *St&PR 91*
Van der Vinne, Leonardo *PenDiDA 89*
Vander Vliet, David William *BiDrAPA 89*
Van der Voo, Rob 1940- *WhoAm 90*
Van Der Voort, Amanda Venelia *WhoAmA 91N*
Vander Voort, Dale Gilbert 1924- *WhoAm 90, WhoWor 91*
Vander Voort, George Frederic 1944- *WhoE 91*
Van der Voort, Hanna *BioIn 16*
Vandervoort, Peter 1929- *St&PR 91, WhoAm 90*
Vandervoort, Robert Benton 1921- *St&PR 91*
Vandervoort, Thomas J. *ODwPR 91*
Van Der Voort, Warren G. 1944- *St&PR 91*
Vander Vorst, Andre Sylvain Joseph 1935- *WhoWor 91*
Vandervort, Lowell Miller 1922- *WhoAm 90*
Vander Waal, Deborah Kay 1952- *WhoAmW 91*
van der Waals, J. H. 1920- *WhoWor 91*
Van Der Waals, Johannes D. 1837-1923 *WorAlBi*
Van Der Walde, Peter Horst 1933- *BiDrAPA 89*
van der Walt, Dawid Hermanus 1934- *WhoWor 91*
Van Der Walt, Deon 1958- *IntWWM 90*
Vanderwarker, Carlton Edward, Jr. 1943- *WhoAm 90*
Van Der Wateren, Jan Floris 1940- *WhoWor 91*
VanDerway, Richard E. 1937- *St&PR 91*
Vanderweide, Harry 1944- *WhoWrEP 89*
Van Der Weide, Thomas Gerald 1940- *St&PR 91*
Vanderweil, Raimund Gerhard, Jr. 1940- *St&PR 91, WhoAm 90*
VanderWerf, Calvin A. 1917-1988 *BioIn 16*
Vanderwerf, David Andrew 1944- *WhoE 91*
Vander Werf, Lester S. 1910-1990 *BioIn 16*
Vander Werf, Rod Wayne 1956- *WhoEmL 91*
Van der Werff, Ivo-Jan *PenDiMP*
Van Der Werff, Jacob A *BiDrAPA 89*
Vanderwerken, Karen Baurle 1947- *WhoSSW 91*
Van Der Weyden, Rogier 1399?-1464 *IntDcAA 90*
Vanderwicken, Peter *ODwPR 91*
VanderWiel-Schleenvoigt, Carole Jean 1950- *WhoAmW 91*
Vander Wilt, Carl Eugene 1942- *St&PR 91, WhoAm 90*
van der Worp, Ton 1935- *WhoWor 91*
Van der Woude, Edward Charles 1950- *St&PR 91*
Van Der Woude, Mary Elizabeth 1939- *WhoAmW 91, WhoWor 91*
Vander Zalm, William *BioIn 16*
Vander Zalm, William Nick 1934- *WhoAm 90*
van der Zee, John 1936- *ConAu 32NR*
Van Derzee, Pieter Sayles 1943- *WhoE 91*
Van der Ziel, Aldert 1910- *WhoAm 90*
Vandett, Nancy McInnis 1945- *WhoSSW 91*
Van Deursen, Arie Theodorus 1931- *WhoWor 91*
VanDeusen, Bruce Dudley 1931- *WhoAm 90*
Van Deusen, Donald T. 1929- *ODwPR 91*
VanDeusen, Roger W. 1943- *St&PR 91*
Van De Vall, Mark 1923- *ConAu 30NR*
Van Devanter, Susan Earling 1960- *WhoAmW 91, WhoE 91*
Van de Vate, Nancy Hayes 1930- *BioIn 16, IntWWM 90*
Vande Velde, Carl 1951- *St&PR 91*
Van de Velde, Henry 1863-1957 *PenDiDA 89*
Vande Velde, Vivian 1951- *SmATA 62*
Van De Velde, Willem 1633- *IntDcAA 90*
Van De Ven, Richard A. *ODwPR 91*
Vandevender, Barbara Jewell 1929- *WhoAmW 91*
Vandevender, Robert Lee, II 1958- *WhoEmL 91, WhoWor 91*
Vandeventer, Algeron F. 1862- *AmLegL*
Vandeventer, Braden 1921- *WhoAm 90*
Van Deventer, Donald Robert 1951- *WhoWor 91*
Van Deventer, Frank G 1936- *BiDrAPA 89*
Van Deventer, Ruby Steele 1892-1974 *BioIn 16*
Vandever, William Dirk 1949- *WhoEmL 91, WhoWor 91*
Van Devere, Chris Allen 1939- *BiDrAPA 89*
Vandevert, Alan P. 1928- *St&PR 91*
Vandevier, J. E. 1948- *St&PR 91*
Van De Visser, Larry William 1936- *St&PR 91*
Van de Voort, Leonadrus Petaw Francisus 1958- *WhoWor 91*
Van de Vyver, Mary Francilene 1941- *WhoAmW 91*
Van de Wall, Willem 1887-1953 *BioIn 16*
Vandewalle, Michael Bernard *BiDrAPA 89*
Van de Walle, Rudy Julien 1953- *WhoWor 91*
Van De Water, John Ward 1913- *WhoWrEP 89*
Van De Weghe, Raymond Francis 1934- *St&PR 91*
van de Wetering, Janwillem 1931- *TwCCr&M 91*
Van de Wetering, John Edward 1927- *WhoAm 90, WhoE 91*
Van de Wetering, Richard Lee 1928- *WhoAm 90*
Van De Wetering, Robert John 1923- *BiDrAPA 89*
Van de Winckel, Eddy A. 1941- *WhoWor 91*
Van de Workeen, Priscilla Townsend 1946- *WhoAmW 91*
Vande Woude, George Franklin 1935- *WhoAm 90*
Vande Zande, Orlin Kent 1938- *St&PR 91*
Van Dieren, Bernard 1887-1936 *BioIn 16*
Van Dijk, Meine Pieter 1949- *WhoWor 91*
van Dijk, Pieter 1943- *WhoWor 91*
Van Dine, Alan Charles 1933- *WhoE 91*
Van Dine, Harold Forster, Jr. 1930- *WhoAm 90*
VanDine, MaryAnn Elizabeth 1953- *WhoAmW 91*
Van Dine, Robert 1938- *WhoAm 90*
Van Dine, S. S. 1888-1939 *TwCCr&M 91, WorAlBi*
Van Dine, Vance 1925- *WhoAm 90, WhoE 91, WhoWor 91*
Van Dinter, Robert Lawrence 1927- *St&PR 91*
Vandiver, Frank Everson 1925- *WhoAm 90, WhoSSW 91, WhoWor 91*
Vandiver, Harry Schultz 1882-1973 *DcScB S2*
Vandiver, J. Murray 1845-1916 *AmLegL*
Vandiver, John *BioIn 16*
Vandiver, Robert E. 1928- *St&PR 91*
Vandiver, Robert F. 1955- *BiDrAPA 89*
Vandiver, Thomas Crymes 1907- *WhoAm 90*
Vandiver, William F. 1942- *St&PR 91*
Vandivier, Blair Robert 1955- *WhoEmL 91*
Vandivier, Frances Finnell *BioIn 16*
Van Domelen, John E 1935- *ConAu 130*
Van Dommelen, David B 1929- *WhoAmA 91, WhoE 91*
Van Dongen, James Charles 1951- *WhoE 91*
van Donkelaar, Eduard Christiaan 1954- *WhoE 91*
van Donkelaar, Pieter 1927- *WhoWor 91*
Van Dooren, Hugo *BiDrAPA 89*
Van Doorn, Donald William 1921- *St&PR 91*
Vandor, Ivan 1932- *IntWWM 90*
Van Doren, Carl 1885-1950 *WorAlBi*
Van Doren, Charles 1926- *WhoAm 90*
VanDoren, Charles 1926- *WhoWrEP 89*
Van Doren, Glenn Henry 1927- *WhoAm 90*
Van Doren, Harold 1895-1957 *PenDiDA 89*
Van Doren, Harold Livingston 1896-1957 *WhoAmA 91N*
Van Doren, Mamie 1933- *WorAlBi*
Van Doren, Mark 1894-1972 *MajTwCW, WorAlBi*
Van Doren, Thomas H 1945- *BiDrAPA 89*
Vandover, Terry *BioIn 16*
Van Drasek, Dean Scott 1960- *WhoWor 91*
Vandrepol, Francois 1929- *WhoWor 91*
Van Dreser, Merton Lawrence 1929- *WhoAm 90*
Van Dresser, William 1871-1950 *WhoAmA 91N*
Van Driessche, Hugo 1953- *WhoWor 91*
Vandross, Luther *BioIn 16*
Vandross, Luther 1951?- *DrBIPA 90, EncPR&S 89*
Van Druten, William A 1932- *BiDrAPA 89*
Van Duinwyk, George Paul 1941- *WhoAmA 91*
Van Dunem, Afonso *WhoWor 91*
Van Dusen, Albert Clarence 1915- *WhoAm 90*
Van Dusen, Betsy Anne 1932- *WhoE 91*
Van Dusen, Bruce Buick 1930- *WhoAm 90*
Van Dusen, Francis Lund 1912- *WhoAm 90*
Van Dusen, Henry Hugh 1934- *WhoAm 90, WhoWrEP 89*
Van Dusen, Lewis H. 1910- *St&PR 91*
Van Dusen, Richard C. 1925- *St&PR 91*
Van Dusen, Richard Campbell 1925- *WhoAm 90*
Van Duyn, Mona *BioIn 16*
Van Duyn, Mona 1921- *ConLC 63 [port], FemiCLE*
Van Duyn, Mona Jane 1921- *WhoAm 90, WhoAmW 91, WhoWrEP 89*
Van Duyne, Harrison 1845-1914 *AmLegL*
Van Duyne, William V *BiDrAPA 89*
Van Duzer, Clarence Dunn 1866-1947 *AmLegL*
Vanduzer, M. Keith 1946- *St&PR 91*
Vandy, Edgar 1895?-1933 *EncPaPR 91*
Van Dyck, Anthonie 1599-1641 *BioIn 16*
Van Dyck, Anthony 1599-1641 *IntDcAA 90, WorAlBi*
Van Dyck, Dawn Cornelia 1962- *WhoAmW 91*
Van Dyck, Ernest 1861-1923 *PenDiMP*
Van Dyck, Michael 1949- *WhoWor 91*
van Dyck, Nicholas Booraem 1933- *WhoAm 90*
Van Dyck, Robert G. 1935- *St&PR 91*
Van Dyck, Timothy Kurt *BiDrAPA 89*
Van Dyk, Frederick Theodore 1934- *WhoAm 90*
Van Dyk, Jere *ConAu 131*
Van Dyk, Thomas William 1943- *BiDrAPA 89*
Van Dyk, Wilmer Jerald 1945- *ConAu 131*
Van Dyke, Ann Elizabeth 1954- *BiDrAPA 89*
Van Dyke, Clifford Craig 1929- *WhoAm 90*
Van Dyke, David Allyn 1948- *BiDrAPA 89*
Van Dyke, Dick 1925- *BioIn 16, OxCPMus, WhoAm 90, WorAlBi*
Van Dyke, Gene 1926- *WhoWor 91*
Van Dyke, Henry 1928- *WhoWrEP 89*
Van Dyke, Jacob 1920- *St&PR 91*
Van Dyke, Jean Anita 1953- *WhoAmW 91*
Van Dyke, Jerry *BioIn 16*
VanDyke, Jill 1954- *WhoAmW 91, WhoEmL 91*
Van Dyke, John Wm. 1939- *St&PR 91*
Van Dyke, Joseph Gary Owen 1939- *WhoE 91*
Van Dyke, Milton Denman 1922- *WhoAm 90*
Van Dyke, Roger William 1938- *St&PR 91*
Van Dyke, Susan Carol 1945- *WhoAmW 91*
Van Dyke, Thomas W. 1938- *St&PR 91*
Van Dyke, William Duncan, III 1931- *WhoAm 90*
Van Dyke, William Grant 1945- *St&PR 91*
Van Dyke-Cooper, Anny Marion 1928- *WhoAmW 91*
Van Dyne, Edith *AuBYP 90, MajTwCW*
Van Dyne, Michele Miley 1959- *WhoAmW 91*
Vane, John R. 1927- *WorAlBi*
Vane, John Robert 1927- *WhoAm 90, WhoWor 91*
Vane, Julia R. 1918-1988 *BioIn 16*
Vane, Mary Kathleen 1951- *WhoAmW 91*
Vane, Nigel *TwCCr&M 91*
Vane, Sylvia Brakke 1918- *WhoAmW 91*
VanEaton, Earl Neal 1940- *WhoAm 90*
Vanecek, Michael Thomas 1942- *WhoSSW 91*
Van Eck, John C. 1915- *St&PR 91*
Van Eck, Linda Marie 1962- *WhoEmL 91*
Vanecko, Andrea D. 1957- *St&PR 91*
Van Eeckhoutte, Paul Marcel Joseph 1922- *WhoWor 91*
Van Eeden, Frederik 1860-1932 *EncO&P 3*
Van Eerden, William Ellis 1941- *BiDrAPA 89*
Van Eerdewegh, Michele Marie 1945- *BiDrAPA 89*
Van Eesteren, Cornelis 1897-1988 *BioIn 16*
Van Eetvelt, Francois 1946- *IntWWM 90*
Vaneev, Anatolii Nikolaevich *BioIn 16*
Vanegas, Guillermo J. *WhoHisp 91*
Van Egmond, John 1950- *St&PR 91*
Van Egmond, Max 1936- *PenDiMP*
Vanek, Anne Elizabeth Tayloe 1959- *WhoE 91*
Vanek, Barbara S. 1957- *WhoAmW 91*
Vanek, Eugenia Poporad 1949- *WhoEmL 91*
Vanek, Jaroslav 1930- *WhoAm 90*
Van Ekeren, Philip Theodore 1931- *St&PR 91*
Vanel, Charles 1892-1989 *AnObit 1989, BioIn 16*
Van Elzakker, Anton Hendrik Marie 1935- *WhoWor 91*
Van Eperen, David Gerard 1961- *St&PR 91*
Van Epp, Murray 1949- *St&PR 91*
Van Erden, Donald Henry 1948- *St&PR 91*
Van Eron, Kevin J. 1957- *WhoEmL 91, WhoWor 91*
Van Erp, Dirk 1859-1933 *BioIn 16, PenDiDA 89*
Van Ert, Barbara Marie 1943- *WhoAmW 91*
Van Ert, Robert M. 1951- *St&PR 91*
Van Eschen, Paula J. 1949- *WhoWrEP 89*
Van Eseltine, William Parker 1924- *WhoAm 90*
Vaness, Carol *BioIn 16*
Vaness, Carol 1952- *IntWWM 90, PenDiMP, WhoAm 90*
Vaness, Margaret Helen 1919- *WhoAmA 91, WhoAmW 91*
Van Esselstyn, Sherman T. *BioIn 16*
Van Essen, Calvin J. 1956- *St&PR 91*
Vanet, Judith Ann 1951- *WhoAmW 91*
Vanetsky, Myron N. 1943- *St&PR 91*
Van Evera, Emily *PenDiMP*
Van Evera, Mary Patricia 1920- *WhoAmW 91*
Van Eyck, Jan 1390?-1441? *IntDcAA 90*
van Eys, Jan 1929- *WhoAm 90*
Vaneysinga, Frans W. 1940- *WhoAm 90, WhoWor 91*
Van Fenema, Greta H 1907- *BiDrAPA 89*
Van Ferney, Shirley May *BiDrAPA 89*
Van Fleet, George Allan 1953- *WhoEmL 91*
Van Fleet, William V *BiDrAPA 89*
Van Fossan, Neal Everett 1919- *St&PR 91*
Van Fossan, Robert V. 1926- *St&PR 91*
Van Fossan, Robert V. 1926-1989 *BioIn 16*
Van Fossen, L. Jack 1937- *St&PR 91*
Van Fossen, Larry Jack 1937- *WhoAm 90*
Van Fossen, Thomas Frederick 1943- *St&PR 91*
Van Fossen Bravo, Ruiess Yvonne 1940- *WhoWor 91*
Vang, Ole 1944- *IntWWM 90*
Van Gaasbeck, Harry Robert 1919- *WhoAm 90*
Vangalen, Jan Carel 1937- *St&PR 91*
Van Geel, Tyll R. 1940- *WhoAm 90*
Van Geem, Virginia 1950- *St&PR 91*
van Geert, Paul 1950- *ConAu 132*
Van Gelder, Dora 1904- *EncO&P 3*
van Gelder, Irvin J. 1925- *WhoWor 91*
Van Gelder, John M. 1942- *St&PR 91*
Van Gelder, Nick Maurice 1914- *St&PR 91*
Van Gelder, Richard G. *AuBYP 90*
Van Gelder, Richard George 1928- *WhoAm 90*
Vangelis *NewAgMG*
Vangelisti, Paul 1945- *ConAu 31NR*
Vangelisti, Paul Louis 1945- *WhoWrEP 89*
Vangell, Thomas 1935- *St&PR 91*
Vangellow, John S. 1938- *St&PR 91*
Van Gennep, Adrian Theodore G. 1937- *WhoWor 91*
Van Gennep, Arnold 1873-1957 *BioIn 16*
Van Genuchten, Martinus Theodorus 1945- *WhoAm 90*
Vanger, Milton Isadore 1925- *WhoAm 90*
van Gestel, Allan 1935- *WhoAm 90*
Vanghel, Ruth Margaret 1950- *WhoAmW 91*
Van Gilder, Barbara Jane Dixon 1933- *WhoAmW 91, WhoWor 91*
Van Gilder, Caron Howell 1947- *WhoAmW 91*
Van Gilder, Derek Robert 1950- *WhoEmL 91, WhoSSW 91, WhoWor 91*
Vangilder, Elam 1896-1977 *Ballpl 90*
Van Gilder, John Corley 1935- *WhoAm 90*
Van Gils, Gilbert Jan 1938- *WhoWor 91*
Van Ginkel, Blanche Lemco *WhoAmA 91*
van Ginkel, Blanche Lemco 1923- *WhoAm 90*
van Ginkel, Johannes Auguste 1940- *WhoWor 91*
Van Gogh, Theo 1857-1891 *BioIn 16*
Van Gogh, Vincent 1853-1890 *BioIn 16, IntDcAA 90*
Van Gool, August Peter 1939- *WhoWor 91*
Vangorden, Claude Dewayne 1930- *St&PR 91*
Van Gorder, Barbara Ellen 1958- *WhoAmW 91*
Van Gordon, Donald James *BiDrAPA 89*
Van Gorkom, Jerome William 1917- *WhoAm 90*
Van Gorp, Gary Wayne 1953- *WhoWor 91*
Van Graafeiland, Ellsworth Alfred 1915- *WhoAm 90*
Van Grack, Steven 1948- *WhoEmL 91*
Van Greenaway, Peter 1929-1988 *TwCCr&M 91*
Van Grouw, Margaret Ellen 1935- *WhoAmW 91*
Vangrov, Ronald Steven 1957- *WhoSSW 91*
Vangsgard, Gerald Eugene 1928- *BiDrAPA 89*
Van Guilder, Stephen A. 1906- *St&PR 91*
van Gulik, Robert H 1910-1967 *TwCCr&M 91B*

Van Gundy, Gregory Frank 1945- *St&PR 91, WhoAm 90*
Van Gundy, James Justin 1939- *WhoSSW 91*
Van Haaften, Egbert *BioIn 16*
Van Haaften, Julia 1946- *WhoAmA 91*
Van Haastrecht, John Peter 1943- *WhoAm 90*
Van Haersolte, Roelof Arent V. 1919- *WhoWor 91*
Van Hagey, Connie W. 1946- *WhoAmW 91*
Van Hal, Mary Phyllis 1948- *WhoE 91*
Van Halen *EncPR&S 89*
Van Halen, Alex 1955- *EncPR&S 89*
Van Halen, Eddie 1957- *EncPR&S 89, WhoAm 90, WorAlBi*
Van Halm, Renee 1949- *WhoAmA 91*
Van Haltren, George 1866-1945 *Ballpl 90 [port]*
Van Hamel, Martine 1945- *WhoAmW 91*
Van Hamersveld, John 1941- *BioIn 16*
VanHandel, Ralph Anthony 1919- *WhoAm 90*
Van Hare, George Frederick, Jr. 1923- *WhoWor 91*
Van Haren, James Adrian 1954- *BiDrAPA 89*
Van Harlingen, Jean 1947- *WhoAmA 91*
VanHarn, Gordon Lee 1935- *WhoAm 90*
van Hartesveldt, Fred Raymond 1945- *WhoSSW 91*
Van Hassel, Henry John 1933- *WhoAm 90*
Van Hauer, Robert 1910- *WhoAm 90*
Van Hecke, Madeleine Louise 1943- *WhoAmW 91*
Van Hee, Kees Max 1946- *WhoWor 91*
Van Helmont, Jean Baptiste 1577-1644 *EncO&P 3*
Van Hemert, Judy 1947- *WhoAmW 91*
Van Hemmen, Hendrik Fokko 1960- *WhoE 91*
Van Hengel, Maarten 1927- *St&PR 91, WhoAm 90*
Van Herik, Judith 1947- *WhoAmW 91*
Van Herk, Aritha 1954- *FemiCLE*
Van Herpe, Leo Bryant 1929- *WhoE 91*
van Heteren, Louis Hubertus Joannes 1927- *WhoWor 91*
Van Heusen, James 1913-1990 *CurBio 90N, OxCPMus*
Van Heusen, Jimmy *NewYTBS 90 [port]*
Van Heusen, Jimmy 1913-1990 *BioIn 16, WorAlBi*
Van Heyningen, Robert 1957- *St&PR 91*
Van Heyningen, Roger Steven 1927- *WhoAm 90*
VanHoebrouck, Jules 1950- *WhoWor 91*
Van Hoecke, Robert George 1962- *WhoSSW 91*
Van Hoesen, Beth 1926- *WhoAmA 91*
Van Hoesen, Beth Marie 1926- *WhoAm 90*
Van Hoeven, James W. *BioIn 16*
Van Hoeven, L. C., Jr. 1936- *WhoAm 90*
van Hoften, James Dougal Adrianus 1944- *WhoAm 90*
Van Holde, Kensal Edward 1928- *WhoAm 90*
VanHole, William Remi 1948- *WhoAm 90*
Van Hollebeke, Richard P. 1927- *St&PR 91*
Van Holsbeke, Martha *BioIn 16*
Van Homrigh, Clay M. R. *AuBYP 90*
Vanhomrigh, Esther 1687?-1723 *FemiCLE*
van Hooff, Jan A.R.A.M. 1936- *WhoWor 91*
Van Hook, Beverly Hennen *AuBYP 90*
Van Hook, David H 1923-1986 *WhoAmA 91N*
Van Hook, Donald 1945- *WhoE 91*
Van Hook, George *BioIn 16*
Vanhook, Marvin Randall 1945- *St&PR 91*
Van Hoorde, Ernest Eugene 1922- *WhoWor 91*
Van Hooser, David G. 1946- *St&PR 91*
Van Hooser, Russell Earl 1938- *St&PR 91*
Van Horn, Dana Carl 1950- *WhoAmA 91*
Van Horn, Gail 1951- *WhoWrEP 89*
Van Horn, Grace *AuBYP 90*
Van Horn, James Robert 1956- *WhoAm 90*
Van Horn, Joanne Marie 1953- *WhoAmW 91*
Van Horn, Karl *BioIn 16*
Van Horn, Lecia Joseph 1963- *WhoAmW 91, WhoSSW 91*
Van Horn, Margaret R 1930- *BiDrAPA 89*
Van Horn, R. Charles 1941- *St&PR 91*
Van Horn, Rebecca Ann 1957- *WhoAmW 91*
Van Horn, Richard Linley 1932- *WhoAm 90, WhoSSW 91*
Van Horn, V.H. 1938- *St&PR 91*
Van Horn, Verne Hile, III 1938- *WhoAm 90, WhoSSW 91*
Van Horne, James Carter 1935- *WhoAm 90*
Van Horne, Keith *BioIn 16*
Van Horne, R. Richard 1931- *WhoAm 90*
Van House, Nancy Anita 1950- *WhoAm 90*
Van Housen, Edward I. 1922- *St&PR 91*
Van Housen, Edward Irvin 1922- *WhoAm 90*
Van Hout, Lucien *PenDiMP*
Van Houten, Beth 1945- *ODwPR 91*
Van Houten, Donald Roger 1936- *WhoAm 90*
Van Houten, Elizabeth Ann 1945- *St&PR 91, WhoAmW 91*
Van Houten, Franklyn Bosworth 1914- *WhoAm 90*
Van Houten, Leonard Erskine 1924- *WhoAm 90*
Van Houten, Lois M. 1918- *WhoWrEP 89*
Van Houten, Olivia Lee 1955- *WhoAmW 91*
Van Houten, Pamela 1965- *ODwPR 91*
VanHouten, Rebecca Jane 1952- *WhoSSW 91*
Van Houten, Wiecher H 1931- *BiDrAPA 89*
van Houtte, Albert Marcel 1941- *WhoWor 91*
Van Houtte, Raymond A. 1924- *WhoAm 90*
van Houtum, Diana Chang 1945- *WhoE 91*
Van Houweling, Douglas Edward 1943- *WhoAm 90*
Van Hove, Alex 1933- *WhoWor 91*
Van Hove, Fred 1937- *IntWWM 90*
Van Hove, Hansa *BiDrAPA 89*
Van Hoven, Frank 1886-1929 *BioIn 16*
Van Howe, Annette Evelyn 1921- *WhoAmW 91, WhoWor 91*
Van Hoy, William V. 1940- *St&PR 91*
van Huffelen, Gerrit Gijsbert 1944- *WhoWor 91*
Vanhulst, Jan Jozef 1932- *WhoWor 91*
Van Hulten, Michel Henricus 1930- *WhoWor 91*
Vanicek, Catherine 1946- *WhoWrEP 89*
Vanicek, Petr 1935- *WhoAm 90*
Vanier, Claude 1954- *BiDrAPA 89*
Vanier, Denis Kieran 1942- *St&PR 91*
Vanier, Jacques 1934- *WhoAm 90*
Vanier, Kieran Francis 1914- *WhoAm 90*
van Iersel, Bastiaan Martinus 1924- *WhoWor 91*
Vaniman, Jean Ann 1960- *WhoAmW 91*
van Imhoff, Evert 1959- *WhoWor 91*
Van Impe, Lucien *BioIn 16*
Vanin, John R *BiDrAPA 89*
Vanini, Francesca *PenDiMP*
van Innis, Philippe Xavier 1949- *WhoWor 91*
van Inwagen, Peter Jan 1942- *WhoAm 90*
Van Itallie, Hugo F. 1908- *St&PR 91*
van Itallie, Jean-Claude 1936- *WhoAm 90, WhoWrEP 89*
Van Itallie, Theodore Bertus 1919- *WhoAm 90*
Vanity *BioIn 16*
Vanity 1958- *DrBlPA 90*
van Kammen, Daniel P. 1943- *WhoE 91*
Van Kammen, Evert 1941- *WhoWor 91*
Van Kampen, Robert D. *BioIn 16*
Van Kampen, Russell 1926- *St&PR 91*
Van Kampen, Vlasta 1943- *BioIn 16*
Van Kanegan, Roy W., Jr. 1947- *St&PR 91*
Van Kempen, Paul *PenDiMP*
Van Keppel, Gerald William, Jr. 1935- *St&PR 91*
Van Kersen, Christopher Philip Ashley 1954- *St&PR 91*
Van Kessel, John J. 1930- *St&PR 91*
Van Keyk, Daniel *PenDiDA 89*
Van Kinsbergen, Jan Elliot 1937- *St&PR 91*
Van Kirk, Cheryl Ann 1964- *WhoAmW 91*
Van Kirk, John H. 1924- *St&PR 91*
Vankirk, Marsha Lauterbach 1949- *WhoAmW 91*
Vankirk, Robert A. *St&PR 91*
Van Kleeck, Donald Wilbur 1928- *St&PR 91*
Van Kleeck, Kenneth D. 1937- *St&PR 91*
Van Kleek, R. John 1924- *St&PR 91*
Vanko, Mary Frances 1952- *WhoEmL 91*
Van Kooy, Cornelia 1885-1945 *BioIn 16*
van Kralingen, Roland Maurits 1946- *WhoWor 91*
Van Kregten, Anthony Gerard Lodewyk, Jr. 1906- *WhoWor 91*
van Kreveld, David 1937- *WhoWor 91*
Van Kuyk, Jan 1950- *WhoWor 91*
Van La, Dat 1954- *St&PR 91*
Van Laan, Thomas Franklyn 1931- *WhoAm 90*
Van Laar, Timothy 1951- *WhoAmA 91*
Vanlandingham, James Patteson 1949- *St&PR 91*
Van Landingham, John Henry, Jr. 1922- *St&PR 91*
Van Landingham, Leander Shelton, Jr. 1925- *WhoE 91, WhoSSW 91, WhoWor 91*
Vanlandingham, Stanly Phillip 1945- *St&PR 91*
Van Lanen, James L. 1945- *St&PR 91*
Van Lanen, William H. 1927- *St&PR 91*
Van Lawick, Hugo *AuBYP 90*
van Lawick-Goodall, Jane *MajTwCW*
Van Leckwijck, William 1902-1975 *DcScB S2*
Van Leer, Elizabeth Sanford 1905- *WhoAmA 91*
Vanleer, Jay *ConAu 131*
Van Leer, W Leicester 1905- *WhoAmA 91N*
Van Leeuwen, Cornelis 1924- *WhoWor 91*
Van Leeuwen, Eugene Joseph *BiDrAPA 89*
Van Leeuwen, Gerard 1929- *WhoAm 90*
Van Leeuwen, Jean *AuBYP 90*
Van Leeuwen, Kato *BiDrAPA 89*
VanLeeuwen, Liz Susan 1925- *WhoAmW 91*
Van Leeuwen, Patricia Ann Szczepanik 1939- *WhoAmW 91*
Van Leight-Frank, Margit *BioIn 16*
Van Lengen, Karen 1951- *WhoAmW 91*
van Lent, Henri J.E.J. 1945- *WhoWor 91*
Van Lenten, Howard 1939- *ODwPR 91*
Van Lenten, Liz *ODwPR 91*
Van Leunen, Alice Louise 1943- *WhoAmA 91*
Van Leunen, Johannes Antonie J. 1941- *WhoWor 91*
Van Leuven, Arthur Edwin 1925- *St&PR 91*
Van Leuven, Holly Goodhue 1935- *WhoAmW 91*
Van Leuven, Norman Eric 1952- *BiDrAPA 89*
Van Leuven, Robert Joseph 1931- *WhoAm 90*
Van Lew, J.H. 1934- *St&PR 91*
Van Leyden, Ernst Oscar Mauritz *BioIn 16*
Van Lhin, Erik *MajTwCW*
Van Lieu, Ron *BioIn 16*
Van Liew, David A 1935- *BiDrAPA 89*
van Lingen, Gabriele 1944- *WhoAmW 91*
Van Lint, Victor Anton Jacobus 1928- *WhoAm 90*
Van Lint, Wenceslaus Joseph 1948- *WhoWor 91*
Van Loan, Charles C. 1947- *St&PR 91*
Van Loan, Charles E. 1876-1919 *Ballpl 90*
Van Loan, Mary Kirkwood 1934- *WhoAmW 91*
Van Loen, Alfred 1924- *WhoAmA 91*
Van Lohuizen-DeLeeuw, Johanna Engelberta 1919-1983 *BioIn 16*
Van Lone, Janet Anne 1963- *WhoEmL 91*
Van Loo, J. Roger 1948- *St&PR 91*
Van Loon, Hendrik Willem 1882-1944 *AuBYP 90*
Van Loon, Paul Johannes Josephus M. 1947- *WhoWor 91*
Van Looy, Walter Rene 1958- *WhoWor 91*
Van Lopik, Jack Richard 1929- *WhoAm 90*
VanLuvanee, Donald Robert 1944- *WhoAm 90*
Vanluven, Gary Alvin 1937- *St&PR 91*
Van Luven, William Robert 1931- *St&PR 91*
Van Lynn, Edwin B. 1934- *St&PR 91*
Van Mander, Karel 1610-1670 *BioIn 16*
Vanmarcke, Erik Hector 1941- *WhoAm 90, WhoWor 91*
Van Marter, Neal Dahl 1927- *WhoSSW 91*
Van Mater, Paul Rapelye, Jr. 1925- *WhoWor 91*
Van Meer, Mary Ann *WhoWrEP 89*
VanMeer, Mary Ann 1947- *WhoWor 91*
van Merkensteijn, Eric Cornelis 1946- *WhoEmL 91*
Van Meter, A.D. 1922- *St&PR 91*
Van Meter, Abram DeBois 1922- *WhoAm 90*
Van Meter, James A. 1938- *St&PR 91*
Van Meter, James C. 1938- *St&PR 91*
Van Meter, James Combs 1938- *WhoAm 90*
Van Meter, Jan R. 1941- *ODwPR 91*
Van Meter, John David 1951- *WhoSSW 91*
Van Meter, Linda Lieselotte 1950- *WhoAmW 91*
Van Meter, Theodore 1921- *St&PR 91*
van Michaels, Christopher 1924- *WhoWor 91*
Van Middlesworth, Lester 1919- *WhoAm 90*
Van Mol, Gordon K. 1949- *ODwPR 91*
Van Mol, John 1943- *ODwPR 91*
Van Mol, Louis John, Jr. 1943- *WhoAm 90*
Van Mols, Brian 1931- *WhoAm 90*
Van Montagu, Marc Charles 1933- *WhoWor 91*
Van Mourik, Dan 1948- *WhoWrEP 89*
Van Munching, Leo *BioIn 16, NewYTBS 90*
Van Musscher, Michiel 1645-1705 *BioIn 16*
Vann, Allan Stewart 1946- *WhoE 91*
Vann, Elizabeth R *BiDrAPA 89*
Vann, Frank Simms 1947- *St&PR 91*
Vann, James A., Jr. 1931- *St&PR 91*
Vann, James Murdock 1928- *St&PR 91*
Vann, John Paul *BioIn 16*
Vann, Joseph Mc Alpin 1937- *WhoE 91*
Vann, Loli 1913- *WhoAmA 91*
Vann, Lora Jane *WhoAmW 91*
Vann, Robert Lee *BioIn 16*
Vann, Robin Iris 1952- *WhoAmW 91*
Vann, Samuel Le Roy 1952- *WhoAmA 91*
Vann, Sun Heng 1944- *WhoWor 91*
Vann, Thomas Phillips 1939- *St&PR 91*
Vann, Wendy Yvonne 1966- *WhoEmL 91*
Vann, William Stanley 1910- *IntWWM 90*
Van Name, Esmond Austin *BioIn 16*
Van Name, Judith Ann 1945- *WhoAmW 91*
Van Natta, John Wayne 1944- *BiDrAPA 89*
Vanneck, Richard Bourne- *BioIn 16*
Van Nek, Cornelis 1942- *WhoWor 91*
Van Nelson, Nicholas L. 1942- *St&PR 91*
Van Nelson, Nicholas Lloyd 1942- *WhoAm 90*
Vanneman, Edgar, Jr. 1919- *WhoAm 90*
Vannerberg, Nils-Gosta 1930- *WhoWor 91*
Van Ness, Albert Lyle 1926- *St&PR 91*
Van Ness, C. Charles 1920- *St&PR 91*
Van Ness, Edward Harry 1929- *WhoAm 90*
Van Ness, Hendrick Charles 1924- *WhoAm 90*
Van Ness, James Edward 1926- *WhoAm 90*
Van Ness, John Ralph 1939- *WhoE 91*
Van Ness, Lottye Gray 1925- *WhoSSW 91*
Van Ness, Marjorie Schuyler *BioIn 16, NewYTBS 90*
Van Ness, Patricia Catheline 1951- *WhoAmW 91*
Vanngard, Tore Ingemar 1932- *WhoWor 91*
Vanni-Marcoux *PenDiMP*
Van Niel, Maureen Sayres *BiDrAPA 89*
Vannier, Theresa Marie 1955- *WhoAmW 91*
Van Nimwegen, Nico 1949- *WhoWor 91*
Van Noord, Andrew 1922- *St&PR 91*
Van Norden, Langdon 1915- *WhoAm 90*
Van Norman, Daniel L. *St&PR 91*
Van Norman, Peggy Shinn 1951- *WhoAmW 91*
Van Norman, Willis Roger 1938- *WhoWor 91*
Van Norstrand, R. E. 1937- *WhoAm 90*
Van Nort, Alan Delos 1943- *WhoSSW 91*
Van Nortwick, Barbara Louise 1940- *WhoAmW 91*
Van Nortwick, Terry Biehl 1948- *WhoWrEP 89*
Van Nost, John *BioIn 16*
Van Nostrand, Bruce F. 1944- *St&PR 91*
Van Nostrand, Catharine Marie Herr 1937- *WhoAmW 91*
Van Nostrand, Diane Eve 1948- *WhoSSW 91*
Van Nostrand, Leslie *BiDrAPA 89*
Van Nostrand, M. Abbott 1911- *St&PR 91*
Van Nostrand, Morris Abbott, Jr. 1911- *WhoAm 90*
Vannoy, Charles Franklin 1940- *WhoSSW 91*
Van Noy, Christine Ann 1948- *WhoAmW 91*
Van Noy, Elene Meury 1943- *WhoAmW 91*
Van Noy, Richard L. *BioIn 16*
Vannoy, Robert Glenn, III 1956- *St&PR 91*
Van Noy, Terry Willard 1947- *St&PR 91*
Vannoy, Walter Monroe, Jr. 1928- *WhoSSW 91*
Vannucci, Giorgio 1931- *St&PR 91*
Vannucci, Pasquale 1946- *WhoE 91, WhoEmL 91*
van Nuffel, Jeannette Therese W. 1932- *WhoAmW 91*
Van Oeveren, Edward Lanier 1954- *WhoSSW 91*
Van Ommen, Joke 1948-1988 *BioIn 16*
Vanoni, Vito August 1904- *WhoAm 90*
van Ooijen, David Adrianus Th. 1939- *WhoWor 91*
Van Oordt, Peter 1903-1988 *WhoAmA 91N*
van Oort, Jan 1921- *ConAu 31NR*
Van Oosbree, Charlyne Selma Nelson 1930- *WhoAmW 91*
Van Ooteghem, Stephen Andrew 1950- *WhoSSW 91*
van Ootmarsum, Harry Robert 1941- *WhoWor 91*
Van Opdorp, Albert Frederik Reinout 1932- *WhoWor 91*
Van Oppen, Peter Henry 1952- *St&PR 91*

Van Orden, Frank 1938- *BiDrAPA 89*
Van Orden, Herbert George 1912- *St&PR 91*
Van Orden, Lucas S., III 1928- *BiDrAPA 89*
Van Orden, M. D. 1921- *AuBYP 90*
Van Orden, Stuart Copeland 1918- *WhoSSW 91*
Van Orden, William *BioIn 16*
Van Orden, William *NewYTBS 90*
Van Order, Robert Albert 1945- *WhoE 91*
Vanore, Michael John 1945- *St&PR 91*
Van Orman, Chandler L. 1941- *WhoAm 90*
Van Orman, Jeanne 1939- *WhoAmW 91, WhoE 91*
Van Ornum, Harry Delbert 1946- *St&PR 91*
Vanorsdale, David William, Jr. 1965- *WhoE 91*
Van Os, Leo Willem 1940- *WhoWor 91*
Van Osdel, Lewis A, III 1946- *BiDrAPA 89*
Van Osdol, Donovan H. 1942- *St&PR 91*
Van Oss, Elizabeth *BiDrAPA 89*
Van Otterloo, John N. 1941- *St&PR 91*
Van Otterloo, Willem 1907-1978 *PenDiMP*
Van Oudenhover, Frank J.M. 1935- *St&PR 91*
Van Overstraeten, Frank J. 1932- *St&PR 91*
Van Overstraeten, Roger Joseph 1937- *WhoWor 91*
Vanoy, Juanita *BioIn 16*
Van Pamel, Duane 1943- *St&PR 91*
Van Patten, Dick 1928- *WorAlBi*
Van Patten, James Jeffers 1925- *WhoSSW 91, WhoWor 91*
Vanpatten, Robert M. 1945- *St&PR 91*
Van Peebles, Mario *BioIn 16*
Van Peebles, Mario 1960?- *DrBIPA 90*
Van Peebles, Melvin 1932- *BioIn 16, DrBIPA 90*
Van Pelt, Frances Evelyn 1937- *WhoAmW 91*
Van Pelt, Jack Franklin 1938- *St&PR 91*
Van Pelt, Janet Ruth 1948- *WhoAmW 91*
Van Pelt, John Robert, Jr. *WhoAm 90*
Van Pelt, Lloyd Franklin 1930- *WhoWor 91*
Van Pelt, Louise Ellen 1940- *St&PR 91*
Van Pelt, Peter J. 1937- *St&PR 91*
Van Pelt, Robert Irving 1931- *WhoWor 91*
Van Pelt, Thomas E. 1939- *St&PR 91*
Van Pelt, Wesley R. 1943- *WhoE 91*
Van Peursen, C A 1920- *EncO&P 3*
Van Poole, Thomas Bennett 1921- *WhoAm 90*
Van Poppelen, Joseph *BioIn 16*
Van Poucke, Peter Guy Camille 1960- *IntWWM 90*
Van Praag, Herman M 1929- *BiDrAPA 89*
Van Praag, Herman Meir 1929- *WhoAm 90, WhoE 91*
Van Praagh, Margaret 1910-1990 *BioIn 16, ConAu 130*
Van Praagh, Peggy *ConAu 130*
Van Praagh, Peggy 1910-1990 *BioIn 16*
Van Putten, Robert Alan 1952- *BiDrAPA 89*
Van Putten, Theodore 1938- *BiDrAPA 89*
van Raalte, John A 1938- *WhoAm 90*
Van Raalte, Polly Ann 1951- *WhoAmW 91, WhoE 91, WhoEmL 91*
Van Raden, David Frederick 1949- *St&PR 91*
Van Raden, Toya Ann 1936- *WhoAmW 91*
Van Ravenswaay, Charles *BioIn 16*
van Ravenswaay, Charles *NewYTBS 90*
Van Ravenswaay, Paul Alexander 1952- *BiDrAPA 89*
Van Reekum, Robert 1958- *BiDrAPA 89*
vanReken, Mary K. 1947- *WhoSSW 91*
Van Remoortel, Edouard 1926-1977 *PenDiMP*
van Remoortere, Francois Petrus 1943- *WhoAm 90*
Van Rensler, Barry Wilson 1947- *WhoE 91*
Van Rensselaer, Alexander 1892-1962 *AuBYP 90*
Van Rensselaer, Kiliaen 1580-1643 *EncCRAm*
Van Rensselaer, Maria Van Cortlandt 1645-1689 *EncCRAm*
Van Rensselaer, Stephen 1905- *WhoAm 90*
Van Rheenen, Fredric J *BiDrAPA 89*
van Rhyn, Constance Carey 1960- *WhoAmW 91*
Vanriet, Jan 1948- *WhoAmA 91*
Van Riper, Guernsey 1909- *AuBYP 90*
Van Riper, Jeffrey L. 1956- *St&PR 91*
Van Riper, Paul P 1916- *ConAu 31NR*
Van Riper, Paul Pritchard 1916- *WhoAm 90*
Van Riper, Peter 1942- *WhoAmA 91*
Van Riper, Robert 1921- *ODwPR 91*
Van Riper, Robert Austin 1921- *WhoE 91*
Van Riper, Steven L *BiDrAPA 89*
Van Robays, Maurice 1914-1965 *Ballpl 90*
Van Roden, Donald 1924- *St&PR 91*
Van Roijen, Robert Dudley 1939- *St&PR 91*
Van Rompuy, Paul Frans 1940- *WhoWor 91*
Van Roosen, Donald Collett 1923- *WhoE 91*
Van Rooy, Anton 1870-1932 *PenDiMP*
Van Rooyen, Edward Van 1952- *St&PR 91*
Van Rooyen, Philip 1923- *St&PR 91*
Van Rosen, Robert E 1904-1966 *WhoAmA 91N*
Van Rosmalen, Jan W.G. 1920- *WhoWor 91*
van Rossum, Jacques Marie 1930- *WhoWor 91*
Van Royen, Oliver Henri Aurel 1930- *WhoWor 91*
Van Ryn, Paul Franklin 1954- *WhoE 91*
Van Rysselberge, Charles H. 1945- *WhoSSW 91*
Van Sandick, Leonard Hendrik Willem 1933- *WhoWor 91*
VanSant, Joanne Frances 1924- *WhoAmW 91*
Van Sant, Robert M. 1922- *St&PR 91*
Van Sant, Robert William 1938- *St&PR 91, WhoAm 90, WhoSSW 91*
Van Sant, Samuel Rinnah 1844-1936 *AmLegL*
Van Sant, Tom R 1931- *WhoAmA 91*
Van Sant, Vernon, Jr. 1921- *St&PR 91*
Van Santvoord, Alice Dresel Beal *BioIn 16*
Van Saun, Richard W. 1937- *St&PR 91*
Van Schaack, Eric 1931- *WhoAm 90, WhoAmA 91, WhoE 91*
Van Schaick, Anthony Gerard 1945- *St&PR 91, WhoAm 90*
Vanschaick, Francis G. 1942- *St&PR 91*
Van Schaick, Mary Jane 1958- *WhoAmW 91*
Van Schaik, Jan Cornelius 1953- *BiDrAPA 89*
Van Schaik, Peter *BioIn 16*
Van Schilfgaarde, Jan 1929- *WhoAm 90*
VanSchoiack, Dean Allen 1958- *WhoEmL 91*
Van Schoik, Milton L. 1928- *St&PR 91*
Van Schoonenberg, Robert G. 1946- *St&PR 91, WhoAm 90, WhoEmL 91*
Van Schuyver, Connie Jo 1951- *WhoAmW 91*
Van Schyndel, Mitzi Dorton 1954- *WhoSSW 91*
Van Sciver, Warner *St&PR 91*
Van Scott, Glory *DrBIPA 90*
Van Scotter, Donald Eugene 1930- *WhoWrEP 89*
Van Scoy, H Virginia *BiDrAPA 89*
Van Scoyk, Susan Mary 1950- *BiDrAPA 89*
Van Scyoc, Sydney J. 1939- *ConAu 33NR*
Van See, John *MajTwCW*
Vanselow, Neal Arthur 1932- *WhoAm 90*
Van Seters, John 1935- *WhoAm 90, WhoWrEP 89*
Van Seters, Virginia Ann 1947- *WhoAmW 91, WhoWor 91*
van Seventer, Christiaan Willem 1941- *WhoWor 91*
Van Shelton, Ricky *BioIn 16, WhoNeCM [port]*
Van Shelton, Ricky 1952?- *ConMus 5 [port], WhoAm 90*
Van Sickel, Edward Lincoln 1929- *St&PR 91*
Van Sickels, Martin J. 1942- *St&PR 91*
Vansickle, Barbara Jean 1948- *WhoAmW 91*
Van Sickle, Bruce Marion 1917- *WhoAm 90*
Vansickle, Charles D. 1941- *St&PR 91*
Van Sickle, David Clark 1934- *WhoAm 90*
Van Sickle, Donald Ritchie 1932- *St&PR 91*
Van Sickle, John Babcock 1936- *WhoWrEP 89*
Van Sickle, Paul B. 1939- *St&PR 91*
VanSickler, Carole Marie 1955- *WhoE 91*
Van Sinderen, Alfred White 1924- *WhoAm 90*
Van Singel, Willard J. 1918- *St&PR 91*
Vansittart, Peter 1920- *WhoAm 90*
VanSittert, Carol Ann 1936- *WhoAmW 91*
Van Slett, Karen Ann 1950- *WhoAmW 91*
Van Slobig, Robert Charles 1942- *St&PR 91*
Vanslot, Lowell S. 1942- *St&PR 91*
Van Sloun, Leon H. 1926- *St&PR 91*
Van Slyck, Philip 1920- *WhoE 91*
Van Slyke, Andy *BioIn 16*
Van Slyke, Andy 1960- *Ballpl 90*
Van Slyke, Leonard DuBose, Jr. 1944- *WhoE 91, WhoWor 91*
Van Soelen, Theodore 1890-1964 *WhoAmA 91N*
Van Soest, Robert David 1927- *St&PR 91*
Vansova, Terezia 1857-1942 *EncCoWW*
Van Spanckeren, Kathryn 1945- *WhoSSW 91, WhoWrEP 89*
Van Stavoren, William David 1936- *WhoAm 90*
Van Stee, Donn C. 1927- *St&PR 91*
Van Stee, Robert Clay, Jr. 1946- *WhoEmL 91*
Van Stee, Scott A. 1959- *St&PR 91*
Vansteelandt, Rene J. 1938- *St&PR 91*
Van Steenberge, Kevin Paul 1957- *St&PR 91*
Van Steenberge, Vickie 1928- *St&PR 91*
Van Steenberghen, Fernand 1904- *ConAu 130*
Van Steenburgh, Barbara Jean 1927- *WhoWrEP 89*
Van Steenkiste, Dwight P. 1951- *St&PR 91*
Van Steenkiste, Julian Charles 1924- *St&PR 91*
Van Steenwyk, Elizabeth 1928- *AuBYP 90*
Van Stockum, Hilda 1908- *AuBYP 90*
Vanston, Diarine 1903- *BiDWomA*
Van Stone, Donald L. 1942- *St&PR 91*
Van Stone, Jack 1930- *St&PR 91*
Van Stone, William W *BiDrAPA 89*
Van Straten, Clyde Kenneth 1935- *St&PR 91*
Vanstreels, Rene L. 1925- *IntWWM 90*
Van Strien, Pieter Johannes 1928- *WhoWor 91*
Vanstrum, Paul Ross 1920- *WhoAm 90*
Vanstry, Robert Francis 1950- *St&PR 91*
Van Suchtelen, Adrian 1941- *WhoAmA 91*
Van Susteren, Lise Conway *BiDrAPA 89*
van Swol, Noel Warren 1941- *WhoE 91, WhoWor 91*
VanSyckel, Thomas Sanford 1940- *WhoE 91*
Van't Hoff, Jacobus H. 1852-1911 *WorAlBi*
van't Hoff, Winfried C. J. 1928- *WhoAm 90*
Van 'T Zelfde, Pieter 1941- *WhoWor 91*
van Tamelen, Eugene Earle 1925- *WhoAm 90*
Van Tassel, Daniel R. 1941- *ODwPR 91*
Van Tassel, George W. 1910-1978 *EncO&P 3*
Van Tassel, James Henry 1929- *WhoAm 90*
Van Tassel, Katrina 1921- *WhoWrEP 89*
Van Tassell, John Frank 1926- *WhoSSW 91*
Van Tassell, Robert E. 1935- *St&PR 91*
Vanterpool, Eleanor Loretta 1955- *WhoAmW 91*
van Thal, Herbert 1904-1983 *ConAu 30NR*
Van Til, William *BioIn 16*
Van Til, William 1911- *WhoAm 90*
van Tilborg, Andre Marcel 1953- *WhoSSW 91*
Van Tilburg, Jaap J. 1950- *WhoWor 91*
Van Tilburg, Johan Justus G. Ch. 1934- *WhoWor 91*
Van Tonder, William Thabo 1946- *WhoE 91*
Van Tongeren, Herk 1943-1988 *WhoAmA 91N*
van Tongeren, Philip Edward 1950- *WhoE 91*
Vantrease, Alice Twiggs 1943- *WhoAmW 91, WhoSSW 91*
Van Treese, Glenn Joseph 1929- *WhoSSW 91*
Van Troeyen, Bernard 1939- *WhoWor 91*
Van Trump, James Edmond 1943- *WhoE 91*
Van Trump, Joseph W. 1933- *St&PR 91*
Van Tuinen, Craig Rooke *BiDrAPA 89*
Vantus, Istvan 1935- *IntWWM 90*
Van Tuyl, Andrew Heuer 1922- *WhoE 91*
Van Tuyl, Kathryn Ursula Leach 1909- *WhoAmW 91*
Van Tyne, Natalie Christine T. 1952- *WhoAmW 91*
Van Uitert, LeGrand Gerard 1922- *WhoAm 90*
Van Ummersen, Claire Ann 1935- *WhoAm 90, WhoAmW 91, WhoE 91*
van Urk, J. Blan 1902- *WhoAm 90*
Van Valen, Leigh Maiorana 1935- *WhoAm 90*
Van Valin, Clyde Emory 1929- *WhoAm 90*
Van Valin, Sharon F. 1939- *WhoAmW 91*
Van Valkenburg, Charles Mac *BiDrAPA 89*
Van Valkenburg, Edgar Walter 1953- *WhoEmL 91*
Van Valkenburg, Mac Elwyn 1921- *WhoAm 90*
Van Valkenburg, Ronald Jack *BiDrAPA 89*
Van Varick, H.L. 1939- *St&PR 91*
Van Varick, H. L. 1939- *WhoAm 90*
Van Vechten, Carl 1880-1964 *BioIn 16*
Van Vechten, Jay H. 1944- *ODwPR 91*
Van Vechten, Schuyler 1923-1988 *BioIn 16*
Van Veen, Andre Gerard 1903-1986 *BioIn 16*
Van Veen, Frederick Thomas 1930- *St&PR 91*
Van Veen, Kathleen Louise 1947- *WhoAmW 91*
Van Veen, Stuyvesant 1910-1988 *BioIn 16*
Van Veen, William J 1935- *BiDrAPA 89*
Van Veghel, Lawrence Adrian 1947- *WhoWrEP 89*
Van Velzer, Verna Jean 1929- *WhoAmW 91*
Van Vinkenroye du Waysaeck, Fedia M G 1932- *WhoWor 91*
Van Vlack, Lawrence Hall 1920- *WhoAm 90*
Van Vleck, James 1930- *St&PR 91, WhoAm 90*
Van Vleck, John H. 1899-1980 *WorAlBi*
Van Vleck, John Hasbrouck 1899-1980 *DcScB S2*
Van Vleck, Pamela Kay 1951- *WhoAmW 91*
Van Vleet, K. Troy 1952- *St&PR 91*
Van Vliet, Carolyne Marina 1929- *WhoAm 90*
Van Vliet, Claire 1933- *WhoAm 90, WhoAmA 91*
Van Vliet, Richard Alan 1935- *WhoSSW 91*
Van Vogt, A. E. 1912- *RGTwCSF*
Van Vogt, Alfred 1912- *WorAlBi*
van Vogt, Alfred Elton 1912- *WhoAm 90*
Van Voorhis, Dale W. 1941- *St&PR 91*
Van Voorhis, John Albright 1939- *St&PR 91*
Van Voorhis, Linda Lyon *BioIn 16*
Van Voorhis, Linda Lyon 1902-1989 *ConAu 129*
Van Voorst, John 1804-1898 *BioIn 16*
Van Voorthuysen, Jan 1911- *IntWWM 90*
Van Vorhes, Nelson Holmes 1822-1882 *AmLegL*
Van Voris, Peter *BioIn 16*
Van Vorst Family *BioIn 16*
Van Vort, Walter Burton 1947- *BiDrAPA 89*
Van Vranken, David Lee 1965- *WhoEmL 91*
Van Vranken, J. Frederick, Jr. 1935- *St&PR 91*
Van Vranken, John Frederick, Jr. 1935- *WhoAm 90*
Van Vranken, Nadine 1958- *WhoEmL 91*
Van Vranken, Rose 1919- *WhoAmA 91*
Van Wachem, L.C. *St&PR 91*
Van Wachem, Lodewijk Christiaan 1931- *WhoAm 90, WhoSSW 91*
Van Wagenen, Paul G. 1946- *St&PR 91*
Van Wageninge, June 1942- *WhoE 91*
Van Wageninge, Robert 1953- *WhoE 91*
Van Wagner, Bruce 1925- *St&PR 91*
Van Wagner, George Herbert 1938- *WhoAm 90*
Van Wagner, Judy Collischan 1940- *WhoAmA 91*
Van Wagner, Nancy Lee 1938- *WhoAmW 91*
Van Walleghen, Michael J. 1938- *WhoWrEP 89*
Van Wallendael, Lori Robinson 1960- *WhoSSW 91*
van Walt van Praag, Michael Christian 1951- *WhoE 91*
Van Wart, Gay Ann 1937- *WhoAmW 91*
Van Waters, Miriam 1887-1974 *BioAmW*
Van Weelden, Richard Thomas 1931- *IntWWM 90*
Van Werkhooven, Anthony John 1945- *St&PR 91*
Van Westerborg, Edward *BioIn 16*
van Wezel, Jan Adrianus Maria 1938- *WhoWor 91*
Van Why, Rebecca Rivera 1932- *WhoAmW 91*
Van Wie, David Michael 1958- *WhoE 91*
Van Wie, Steven Howard 1950- *St&PR 91*
Van Wijk, Theo 1916- *WhoWor 91*
Van Winckel, Nance 1951- *ConAu 131*
Van Winkelen, Barbara *WhoAmA 91*
Van Winkle, Edgar Walling 1913- *WhoWor 91*
Van Winkle, Lester G 1944- *WhoAmA 91*
Van Winkle, Nickie Joan 1938- *WhoAmW 91*
Van Winkle, Richard A. 1913- *St&PR 91*
Van Winkle, Thomas Leo 1922-1988 *BioIn 16*
van Wissen, Gerardus Wilhelmus Johannes 1941- *WhoWor 91*
Vanwittenberghe, Robert J *BiDrAPA 89*
Van Woerkom, Dorothy 1924- *AuBYP 90*
Van Woerkom, Dorothy O'Brien 1924- *WhoAm 90, WhoWrEP 89*
Van Wolf, Henry 1898-1982 *WhoAmA 91N*
Van Wouwe, Jacobus Pieter 1950- *WhoWor 91*

Van Wyck, George Richard 1928- *WhoAm 90*
Van Wye, Benjamin David 1941- *IntWWM 90*
Van Wyk, Brooke 1941- *St&PR 91*
Van Wyk, Helen *WhoAmA 91*
Van Wyk, James Adrian 1936- *WhoE 91*
Van Wyk, James Lavern 1932- *St&PR 91*
Van Wyk, Judson John 1921- *WhoAm 90, WhoSSW 91*
Van Wyk, Marinus 1909- *St&PR 91*
Van Wyk, Roger L. 1931- *St&PR 91*
Van Wylen, Gordon John 1920- *WhoAm 90*
Van Wylen, Margaret E D 1924- *BiDrAPA 89*
Van Young, Oscar *WhoAmA 91*
Van Young, Oscar 1906- *WhoAm 90*
Van Yperen, Cathy 1952- *St&PR 91*
Vanyur, John Martin 1956- *WhoE 91*
Van Zandt, Charles Collins 1830-1894 *AmLegL*
Van Zandt, Clough M., Sr. 1917- *St&PR 91*
Van Zandt, Deborah Susan 1954- *WhoE 91*
Van Zandt, Elaine Marian 1945- *WhoAmW 91*
Van Zandt, Gloria Jean *WhoAmW 91*
Van Zandt, J. Parker *NewYTBS 90*
Van Zandt, J. Parker 1894-1990 *BioIn 16*
Van Zandt, Jeffrey R. 1942- *St&PR 91*
Van Zandt, Marie 1861-1919 *PenDiMP*
Van Zandt, Steve *EncPR&S 89*
Van Zandt, Townes *WhoNeCM [port]*
Van Zandt, William Chamblee 1939- *St&PR 91*
Van Zandt, William Frank 1953- *WhoSSW 91*
Van Zant, Carlos Ray 1939- *St&PR 91*
Vanzant, Iyanla *BioIn 16*
Van Zant, John L. 1901- *ODwPR 91*
Vanzant, Rebecca L 1957- *BiDrAPA 89*
Van Zante, Shirley Mae *WhoAm 90*
Van Zanten, Arnold 1912- *St&PR 91*
Van Zanten, Dorothy June 1934- *WhoAmW 91*
Van Zanten, Frank Veldhuyzen 1932- *WhoAm 90*
Van Zelst, Theodore David 1963- *WhoEmL 91*
Van Zelst, Theodore W. 1923- *St&PR 91*
Van Zelst, Theodore William 1923- *WhoAm 90*
Vanzetti, Bartolomeo 1888-1927 *BioIn 16, WorAlBi*
Van Zile, Philip Taylor, III 1945- *WhoE 91*
Van Zile-Stabins, Christine Helen 1958- *WhoAmW 91*
Vanzo, Alain 1928- *IntWWM 90*
Van Zoeren, Charles Andrew 1931- *St&PR 91*
Van Zoeren, Jay 1924- *BiDrAPA 89*
Van Zoeren, Joan Carol 1931- *St&PR 91*
Van Zoeren, John Burr 1926- *St&PR 91*
Van Zyl Slabbert, Frederik 1940- *BioIn 16*
Vaporciyan, Harutun 1929- *St&PR 91*
Vappi, C. Vincent 1926- *St&PR 91*
Vaquer, Frederick 1938- *BiDrAPA 89*
Vaquera, Steve *WhoHisp 91*
Vaquero Sanchez, Antonio 1938- *WhoWor 91*
Vara, John Robert 1953- *BiDrAPA 89*
Varacalli, Claire 1930- *St&PR 91*
Varacalli, Joseph A. 1961- *St&PR 91*
Varadhan, Srinivasa S. R. 1940- *WhoAm 90*
Varady, Julia 1941- *IntWWM 90, PenDiMP*
Varagona, Alan Joseph 1956- *WhoSSW 91*
Varaklis, Tass 1934- *St&PR 91*
Varalli, E.R. 1931- *St&PR 91*
Varalli, Ernest Ralph 1931- *WhoAm 90*
Varanelli, Thomas Michael 1926- *WhoE 91*
Varanka, Teresa Maria *BiDrAPA 89*
Varas, Antonio 1817-1886 *BioIn 16*
Varas, Barbara Guadalupe 1953- *WhoE 91*
Varas, Hector Osvaldo *BiDrAPA 89*
Varas, Manny *WhoHisp 91*
Varasteh, Sassan 1960- *WhoWor 91*
Varawa, Joana McIntyre *BioIn 16*
Varawa, Male *BioIn 16*
Varble, Rachel M. 1893-1976 *LiHiK*
Varblow, Roger L. 1953- *St&PR 91*
Varchmin, Thomas Edward 1947- *WhoAm 90*
Varco, Richard Lynn 1912- *WhoAm 90*
Varcoe, Christopher Stephen 1949- *IntWWM 90*
Varcoe, Jonathan Philip 1941- *IntWWM 90*
Varda, Agnes *BioIn 16*
Varda, Agnes 1926- *WhoWor 91*
Varda, Agnes 1928- *ConTFT 8*
Vardaman, James Kimble 1861-1930 *AmLegL*
Vardaro, Joseph E. 1949- *St&PR 91*
Vardavas, Stephanie *BioIn 16*
Vardeman, Jan Michael 1936- *St&PR 91*
Varderi, Alejandro 1960- *HispWr 90*
Vardill, Anna Jane 1781-1852 *FemiCLE*
Vardill, John 1749-1811 *EncCRAm*
Vardinoyannis, Yannis V. 1962- *WhoWor 91*
Vardon, James Lewes 1941- *St&PR 91, WhoAm 90*
Vardopoulos, Constantine B *BiDrAPA 89*
Vardre, Leslie *TwCCr&M 91*
Vardy, Agnes Huszar *WhoWrEP 89*
Vardy, John *PenDiDA 89*
Vardy, Peter 1930- *St&PR 91*
Vardy, Steven Bela 1936- *WhoE 91*
Vare, Glenda 1903-1989 *WorAlBi*
Vare, Glenna Collett 1903-1989 *BioIn 16*
Vareilles, Yves 1928- *WhoWor 91*
Varela, Alberto M 1942- *BiDrAPA 89*
Varela, George Gilbert 1947- *WhoEmL 91*
Varela, Julio A. 1959- *WhoHisp 91*
Varela, Luciano *WhoHisp 91*
Varela, Maria *BioIn 16*
Varela, Melvin 1949- *WhoHisp 91*
Varellas, Sandra Motte 1946- *WhoAmW 91*
Varenne, Andre Georges 1926- *WhoWor 91*
Varenne, Gaston *BiDrAPA 89*
Vareschi, Susan Luigs 1951- *WhoAmW 91*
Varese, Edgard 1883-1965 *PenDiMP A*
Varese, Louise 1890-1989 *BioIn 16, ConAu 129*
Varet, Michael A. 1942- *WhoE 91, WhoWor 91*
Varg, Paul Albert 1912- *WhoAm 90*
Varga, Andras 1947- *WhoWor 91*
Varga, Balint Andras 1941- *ConAu 132, IntWWM 90*
Varga, Ervin 1925- *BiDrAPA 89*
Varga, Ferenc *WhoAmA 91*
Varga, Frances Andrea Irma 1956- *WhoAmW 91*
Varga, George 1936- *WhoWor 91*
Varga, Gilbert 1952- *PenDiMP*
Varga, Gilbert Anthony 1952- *IntWWM 90*
Varga, Janos 1927- *WhoWor 91*
Varga, John Henry 1955- *WhoWor 91*
Varga, Joseph 1941- *ODwPR 91*
Varga, L. Elizabeth 1922- *WhoAmW 91*
Varga, Laszlo 1920- *BiDrAPA 89*
Varga, Louis Stephen, Jr. 1947- *WhoSSW 91*
Varga, Margit 1908- *WhoAmA 91*
Varga, Richard Steven 1928- *WhoAm 90*
Varga, Steven Carl 1952- *WhoEmL 91*
Varga, Tamas *BioIn 16*
Varga, Tibor 1921- *PenDiMP*
Varga, Vera *BiDrAPA 89*
Varga-Biro, Edith 1927-1986 *BioIn 16*
Varga-Golovcsenko, Steven 1944- *BiDrAPA 89*
Vargas, Allen H. 1944- *WhoHisp 91*
Vargas, Arnulfo *WhoHisp 91*
Vargas, Clifford E. *BioIn 16*
Vargas, Eduardo 1944- *St&PR 91, WhoAm 90, WhoWor 91*
Vargas, Edward Anthony 1951- *WhoHisp 91*
Vargas, Edwin, Jr. 1949- *WhoHisp 91*
Vargas, Fernando Rodolfo *St&PR 91N*
Vargas, Fiameta R *BiDrAPA 89*
Vargas, Francisco *EncCRAm*
Vargas, George 1939- *WhoHisp 91*
Vargas, Getulio 1883-1954 *BioIn 16*
Vargas, Getulio Dorneles 1883-1954 *WorAlBi*
Vargas, Gloria M. 1926- *WhoHisp 91*
Vargas, Hernan 1957- *St&PR 91*
Vargas, Jaime *BiDrAPA 89*
Vargas, Jimmy 1939- *BiDrAPA 89*
Vargas, Joe Flores 1940- *WhoSSW 91*
Vargas, John David 1947- *WhoE 91*
Vargas, Jorge A. 1937- *WhoHisp 91*
Vargas, Jorge Justin 1960- *BiDrAPA 89*
Vargas, Jose *BioIn 16*
Vargas, Josephine 1946- *WhoAmA 91*
Vargas, Kathy 1950- *WhoHisp 91*
Vargas, Laura Dennison 1945- *WhoWrEP 89*
Vargas, Lena Bessette 1922- *WhoAmW 91, WhoWor 91*
Vargas, Lourdes Hernandez 1963- *WhoHisp 91*
Vargas, M James 1930- *BiDrAPA 89*
Vargas, Margarita 1956- *WhoHisp 91*
Vargas, Pedro 1904-1989 *BioIn 16*
Vargas, Pilar 1944- *BiDrAPA 89*
Vargas, Ray M. *WhoHisp 91*
Vargas, Rosa 1962- *BiDrAPA 89*
Vargas, Virgilio Barco *BioIn 16*
Vargas, William 1946- *WhoHisp 91*
Vargas, William J 1928- *BiDrAPA 89*
Vargas-Carreno, D. Edmundo 1937- *WhoE 91*
Vargas Llosa, Mario *NewYTBS 90*
Vargas Llosa, Mario 1936- *BioIn 16, ConAu 32NR, HispWr 90, MajTwCW, WhoWor 91*
Vargas Zapata Y Lujan Ponce De Leon, D 1643?-1704 *WhNaAH*
Varges, Gabe Shawn 1957- *WhoE 91*
Varghese, K Thomas *BiDrAPA 89*
Varghese, Praymol 1939- *BiDrAPA 89*
Vargo, Ed *Ballpl 90*
Vargo, Edward Paul 1935- *WhoWor 91*
Vargo, George Francis, Jr. 1942- *St&PR 91*
Vargo, George James, Jr. 1956- *WhoE 91*
Vargo, James Dennis *BiDrAPA 89*
Vargo, John 1929- *WhoAmA 91*
Vargo, Ronald Paul 1954- *WhoAm 90*
Vargyas, Lajos Karoly 1914- *IntWWM 90*
Varhegyi, Patricia Ilona 1960- *WhoAmW 91*
Varholak, Dorothy Malisek 1939- *WhoAmW 91*
Vari, S. Stephen 1963- *WhoE 91*
Varia, Indira Mahesh *BiDrAPA 89*
Varia, Mahesh Amratlal 1943- *WhoSSW 91*
Variag *EncCoWW*
Varian, Charles Stetson 1846-1922 *AmLegL*
Varian, Hal Ronald 1947- *WhoAm 90*
Varian, Russell Harrison 1898-1959 *BioIn 16*
Varias, Rodolfo R 1929- *BiDrAPA 89*
Varigos, Andrew John 1915- *WhoWor 91*
Varilla, Mary *BioIn 16*
Varin, Edward C.H. 1957- *St&PR 91*
Varin, Roger Robert 1925- *WhoSSW 91*
Varion, Giovanni Pietro *PenDiDA 89*
Varis, Martti Jouko Henrik 1945- *WhoWor 91*
Varjabedian, Anthony *BiDrAPA 89*
Varkonyi, Peter 1931- *WhoWor 91*
Varlamova, Inna 1922?- *EncCoWW*
Varley, Andrew 1934- *St&PR 91*
Varley, Cromwell 1828-1883 *EncPaPR 91*
Varley, Cromwell Fleetwood 1828-1883 *EncO&P 3*
Varley, Frederick H *WhoAmA 91N*
Varley, Herbert Paul 1931- *WhoAm 90*
Varley, John 1947- *RGTwCSF*
Varley, John Herbert 1947- *WhoWrEP 89*
Varley, John J. 1929- *St&PR 91*
Varley, Joseph David 1960- *BiDrAPA 89*
Varley, Susan 1961- *SmATA 63*
Varley, Thomas Arthur 1950- *St&PR 91*
Varma, Arvind 1947- *WhoAm 90*
Varma, Asha 1942- *WhoAmW 91*
Varma, Ashoka 1952- *WhoE 91*
Varma, Devendra P. 1923- *EncO&P 3*
Varma, Gurbachan K 1943- *BiDrAPA 89*
Varma, Himanshu 1955- *WhoSSW 91*
Varma, Lakshman P 1915- *BiDrAPA 89*
Varma, Rajender Singh 1951- *WhoSSW 91*
Varma, Satish C 1936- *BiDrAPA 89*
Varma, Vijoy Kumar 1937- *BiDrAPA 89*
Varma, Vish 1948- *St&PR 91*
Varmecky, Betty Jo 1927- *WhoAmW 91*
Varmus, Harold E. 1939- *WorAlBi*
Varmus, Harold Eliot 1939- *WhoAm 90, WhoWor 91*
Varnai, Peter Pal 1922- *IntWWM 90*
Varnai, Zseni 1890-1981 *EncCoWW*
Varnau, Mark A. 1934- *St&PR 91*
Varnay, Astrid 1918- *IntWWM 90, PenDiMP*
Varnay Jones, Theodora 1942- *WhoAmA 91*
Varnedoe, Barbara Spohr 1941- *WhoSSW 91*
Varnedoe, Heeth, III 1937- *WhoSSW 91*
Varnedoe, John Kirk Train 1946- *WhoAm 90, WhoAmA 91*
Varnedoe, Kirk 1946- *BioIn 16, NewYTBS 90 [port]*
Varnelis, Kazys 1917- *WhoAmA 91*
Varner, Barton Douglas 1920- *WhoAm 90, WhoWor 91*
Varner, Charleen LaVerne McClanahan 1931- *WhoAmW 91, WhoWor 91*
Varner, David Eugene 1937- *St&PR 91, WhoAm 90*
Varner, David M. *ODwPR 91*
Varner, Harold Richard 1935- *WhoAm 90*
Varner, Jeannette J. *ConAu 132*
Varner, Jeannette Johnson 1909- *ConAu 132*
Varner, John W *BiDrAPA 89*
Varner, Joseph Elmer 1921- *WhoAm 90*
Varner, Joyce Ehrhardt 1938- *WhoAmW 91*
Varner, Nellie Mae 1935- *WhoAmW 91*
Varner, Robert Bernard 1930- *WhoWor 91*
Varner, Robert Edward 1921- *WhoAm 90*
Varner, Roy V 1936- *BiDrAPA 89*
Varner, Sterling V. 1919- *St&PR 91*
Varner, Sterling Verl 1919- *WhoAm 90*
Varner, Theodore R. 1936- *St&PR 91*
Varner, Thomas L. 1957- *IntWWM 90*
Varner, Vernon Paul *BiDrAPA 89*
Varnerin, Lawrence John, Jr. 1923- *WhoAm 90*
Varney, Carleton Bates, Jr. 1937- *WhoAm 90, WhoWor 91*
Varney, Charles W., Jr. 1912- *St&PR 91*
Varney, David Donald 1930- *St&PR 91*
Varney, Edwin 1944- *WhoAmA 91*
Varney, Hewitt I 1912- *BiDrAPA 89*
Varney, Louis 1844-1908 *OxCPMus*
Varney, Robert Charles 1944- *WhoSSW 91*
Varney, Suzanne Glaab 1951- *WhoAmW 91*
Varnum, Bruce H. 1945- *St&PR 91*
Varnum, James William 1940- *WhoAm 90*
Varnum, Joseph Bradley, Jr. 1818-1874 *AmLegL*
Varnum, Laurent Kimball 1895- *WhoAm 90*
Varnum-Gallant, Billie Mae 1951- *WhoWrEP 89*
Varo, Remedios *BioIn 16*
Varo, Remedios 1908-1963 *ArtLatA*
Varo, Remedios 1913-1963 *BiDWomA*
Varoglu, Mary 1960- *WhoAmW 91*
Varol, Adnan Osman 1927- *BiDrAPA 89*
Varon, Dan G. 1948- *St&PR 91*
Varon, Michael Nathan 1950- *WhoEmL 91*
Varon, Stuart Russell *BiDrAPA 89*
Varone, Antonio 1952- *WhoWor 91*
Varrenti, Adam, Jr. 1949- *WhoE 91*
Varriale, Wanda 1927- *WhoAmA 91*
Varro, Barbara Joan 1938- *WhoAm 90*
Varro, Charles Louis 1920- *St&PR 91*
Varrone, Angelo Robert 1947- *WhoAm 90, WhoSSW 91*
Varshnei, Subhas Chandra 1942- *WhoWor 91*
Varshney, Anil Kumar 1948- *WhoWor 91*
Varshni, Yatendra Pal 1932- *WhoAm 90*
Vartan, Vartanig Garabed 1923-1988 *BioIn 16*
Vartanian, Aram 1922- *WhoAm 90*
Vartanian, Elsie Virginia 1930- *WhoAmW 91*
Vartiainen, Osmo Oiva 1926- *WhoWor 91*
Vartio, Marja-Liisa 1924-1966 *DcScanL, EncCoWW*
Vartnaw, William R. 1949- *WhoWrEP 89*
Vartorella, William Frederick 1949- *WhoSSW 91*
Varty, Duncan Price 1944- *St&PR 91*
Varvias, Spiridon 1923- *WhoWor 91*
Varvil, Candace Joan 1950- *WhoAmW 91*
Varviso, Silvio 1924- *IntWWM 90, PenDiMP*
Varvitsiotis, Ioannis Miltiadis 1933- *WhoWor 91*
Vary, Marshall G *BiDrAPA 89*
Varzally, Michael Alan 1947- *St&PR 91*
Vas, Istvan 1910- *WhoWor 91*
Vasa 1933- *WhoAmA 91*
Vasa, Robin Leah 1953- *WhoAmW 91*
Vasalis 1909- *EncCoWW*
Vasallo, Pedro E. *WhoHisp 91*
Vasan, Srini S. 1938- *St&PR 91*
Vasarely, Victor 1908- *IntDcAA 90*
Vasari, Giorgio 1511-1574 *IntDcAA 90, WorAlBi*
Vasary, Tamas 1933- *IntWWM 90, PenDiMP, WhoWor 91*
Vasavada, Nishendu M 1950- *BiDrAPA 89*
Vascik, Steven C. 1942- *St&PR 91*
Vasconcellos, John 1932- *WhoHisp 91*
Vasconcellos, Muriel 1933- *WhoAmW 91*
Vasconcelos, Jose 1882-1959 *BioIn 16*
Vasconcelos, Olga 1944- *WhoWor 91*
Vase, Gillan 1841-1921 *FemiCLE*
Vaseff, James Richard 1947- *WhoSSW 91*
Vasek, Richard Jim 1935- *WhoAm 90*
Vasey, Robert C. 1937- *St&PR 91*
Vasholz, Lothar A. 1930- *St&PR 91, WhoAm 90*
Vasil, Vimla 1932- *WhoAmW 91*
Vasilchuk, Vasily *BioIn 16*
Vasile, Gennaro James 1946- *WhoAm 90*
Vasile, Russell George *BiDrAPA 89*
Vasilescu, Alexandru Anghel 1926- *WhoWor 91*
Vasili, Paul *EncCoWW*
Vasiliades, Mary *ODwPR 91*
Vasiliauskas, Al 1945- *St&PR 91*
Vasilieff, Nicholas 1892-1970 *WhoAmA 91N*
Vasiliev, Leonid Leonidovich 1891-1966 *EncO&P 3*
Vasiliev, Leonid Leonidovitch 1891-1966 *EncPaPR 91*
Vasiliev, Vladimir 1940- *BioIn 16*
Vasils, Albert 1915- *WhoAmA 91N*
Vasily, Michael William 1944- *St&PR 91*
Vasington, Frank Daniel 1928- *WhoAm 90*
Vasireddy, Prasad S R K 1946- *BiDrAPA 89*
Vaslef, Irene 1934- *WhoAm 90*
Vaslef, Nicholas P. 1930- *WhoAm 90*
Vasquez, Arturo *WhoHisp 91*
Vasquez, Cesar Luis 1935- *WhoHisp 91*
Vasquez, Ernesto 1941- *BiDrAPA 89*
Vasquez, Francis A *BiDrAPA 89*
Vasquez, Gabriel Marcus 1960- *WhoHisp 91*
Vasquez, Gaddi Holguin 1955- *WhoHisp 91*

Vasquez, Gilbert Reynaldo 1939- *WhoHisp 91*
Vasquez, Hector Rey 1952- *WhoHisp 91*
Vasquez, Horacio 1860- *BioIn 16*
Vasquez, Irene Sosa 1950- *WhoHisp 91*
Vasquez, James Alan 1932- *WhoHisp 91*
Vasquez, Joseph Anthony, Jr. 1950- *WhoHisp 91*
Vasquez, Joseph J. 1927- *WhoHisp 91*
Vasquez, Juanita Sylvia 1919- *WhoHisp 91*
Vasquez, Julio *BiDrAPA 89*
Vasquez, Kevin R. 1956- *St&PR 91*
Vasquez, Marden E. 1934- *WhoWor 91*
Vasquez, Paul 1933- *WhoE 91*
Vasquez, Paul 1952- *WhoHisp 91*
Vasquez, Philip Daniel 1955- *WhoHisp 91*
Vasquez, Raul 1954- *WhoHisp 91*
Vasquez, Raul Herrera, Jr. 1949- *WhoHisp 91*
Vasquez, Richard *BioIn 16*
Vasquez, Richard 1928- *ConAu 131, HispWr 90, WhoHisp 91*
Vasquez, Robert J. 1931- *WhoHisp 91*
Vasquez, Susan Dolores 1946- *St&PR 91*
Vasquez, Tiburcio 1835-1875 *BioIn 16*
Vasquez, William Leroy 1944- *WhoSSW 91*
Vasquez Amaral, Jose 1913-1987 *HispWr 90*
Vasquez de Mella y Fanjul, Juan 1861-1928 *BioIn 16*
Vasquez Garcia, Isaac *BioIn 16*
Vasquez Jimenez, Alberto *BioIn 16*
Vass, David T. 1946- *St&PR 91*
Vass, George 1927- *BioIn 16*
Vass, Joan *BioIn 16*
Vass, Joan 1925- *WhoAmW 91*
Vass, Lisa Taylor 1953- *WhoAmW 91*
Vassall, Robert Fitzgerald *BiDrAPA 89*
Vassallo, Enrique Mario *BiDrAPA 89*
Vassallo, Jo Ann 1960- *WhoAmW 91*
Vassallo, Nicolo 1946- *WhoWor 91*
Vassallo, Paul 1937- *WhoE 91*
Vassar, John Dixie, Jr. 1953- *WhoE 91*
Vassar, Thomas Paul 1943- *St&PR 91*
Vassar, Tina Marrie 1956- *WhoAmW 91*
Vassberg, David E 1936- *ConAu 131*
Vassberg, David Erland 1936- *WhoSSW 91*
Vassberg, Stephen M. 1945- *WhoSSW 91*
Vasse, Christiane M Piot 1922- *EncO&P 3*
Vasse, Francois-Antoine 1681-1736 *PenDiDA 89*
Vasse, Paul M 1910- *EncO&P 3*
Vassell, Gregory S. 1921- *WhoAm 90*
Vasser, Lynn Tracy 1961- *WhoAmW 91*
Vasseur, Roger 1944- *WhoWor 91*
Vassi, Frank 1950- *St&PR 91*
Vassil, Pamela 1943- *WhoAm 90*
Vassilev, Rosa Tusa *WhoSSW 91*
Vassiliades, Elias Demetrios 1946- *WhoWor 91*
Vassilieff, Marie 1884-1957 *BiDWomA*
Vassiliou, George A *BiDrAPA 89*
Vassiliou, George Vassos 1931- *WhoWor 91*
Vassos, John 1898-1985 *ConDes 90*
Vasta, Bruno Morreale 1933- *WhoAm 90*
Vasta, Edward 1928- *WhoWrEP 89*
Vasta, Vincent Joseph, Jr. 1944- *WhoE 91*
Vastardis, Anthony George 1949- *St&PR 91*
Vasters, Reinhold 1827-1909 *PenDiDA 89*
Vastine, John R. 1942- *WhoSSW 91*
Vastine, John Robert, Jr. 1937- *WhoE 91*
Vasu, Ronald James 1939- *BiDrAPA 89*
Vasudevan, Ambalapetta K 1937- *BiDrAPA 89*
Vasudevan, S M *BiDrAPA 89*
Vasudevan, Vasumathy *BiDrAPA 89*
Vasuki, Nuggehalli Chokkanna 1939- *WhoE 91*
Vasuta, Lorinda 1955- *WhoAmW 91*
Vaswani, Mithoo Ajit 1946- *WhoEmL 91*
Vaswani, Nari P *BiDrAPA 89*
Vaswani, Rajan Chatur 1948- *WhoWor 91*
Vatandoost, Nossi Malek 1935- *WhoSSW 91*
Vatanen, J. I. *DcScanL*
Vatel, Veta *BiDrAPA 89*
Vater, Heinz 1932- *WhoWor 91*
Vater, Mark F. 1952- *St&PR 91*
Vater, Regina *BioIn 16*
Vater, Regina 1943- *WhoAmA 91*
Vater Lundberg, Regina 1943- *WhoAmA 91*
Vath, Edwin Raymond 1930- *St&PR 91, WhoAm 90*
Vath, Elizabeth Marie 1951- *WhoAmW 91*
Vath, James E. 1940- *St&PR 91*
Vath, Raymond Eugene 1931- *BiDrAPA 89*
Vath, Thomas George 1933- *St&PR 91*
Vatter, Paul August 1924- *WhoAm 90*
Vattilana, Joseph William 1928- *WhoE 91*
Vatz, Jack A *BiDrAPA 89*
Vatza, Edward J. 1949- *St&PR 91*
Vauban, Sebastien Le Prestre De 1633-1707 *WorAlBi*
Vauclain, Samuel M. 1856-1940 *WorAlBi*
Vauclair, Marguerite Renee 1945- *WhoEmL 91, WhoWor 91*
Vaucouleurs, Antoinette de *BioIn 16*
Vaudreuil-Cavagnial, Marquis de 1698-1778 *EncCRAm*
Vaugeois, Henri 1864-1916 *BiDFrPL*
Vaughan, Alan 1936- *EncO&P 3, EncPaPR 91*
Vaughan, Alice Felicie 1937- *WhoSSW 91*
Vaughan, Ann H. *ODwPR 91*
Vaughan, Arky 1912-1952 *Ballpl 90 [port]*
Vaughan, Bernard Joseph 1955- *WhoE 91*
Vaughan, Brigid Louise *BiDrAPA 89*
Vaughan, Brigid Louise 1963- *WhoE 91*
Vaughan, Bruce A. 1935- *St&PR 91*
Vaughan, Carter A 1914-1988 *SmATA X*
Vaughan, Charles K. 1937- *St&PR 91*
Vaughan, Clefton Durell 1941- *WhoSSW 91*
Vaughan, Curtis T., III 1951- *St&PR 91*
Vaughan, Curtis T., Jr. 1927- *St&PR 91*
Vaughan, Curtis Torrey, III 1951- *WhoSSW 91*
Vaughan, David Allen *St&PR 91*
Vaughan, David John 1924- *WhoWor 91*
Vaughan, David Lisle 1922- *WhoAm 90*
Vaughan, David Ross 1931- *WhoSSW 91*
Vaughan, Denis 1926- *PenDiMP*
Vaughan, Denis Edward 1926- *IntWWM 90*
Vaughan, Donald Ray 1952- *WhoEmL 91*
Vaughan, Donna Ann 1945- *BiDrAPA 89*
Vaughan, Douglas Stanwood 1946- *WhoSSW 91*
Vaughan, Earle Russell 1912- *WhoSSW 91*
Vaughan, Edwin Campion 1897-1931 *BioIn 16*
Vaughan, Edwin Darracott, Jr. 1939- *WhoAm 90*
Vaughan, Elizabeth 1936- *PenDiMP*
Vaughan, Elizabeth 1937- *IntWWM 90*
Vaughan, Elizabeth Ardrey 1963- *WhoAmW 91, WhoEmL 91*
Vaughan, Emmett John 1934- *WhoAm 90*
Vaughan, Frances Elizabeth 1935- *WhoAmW 91*
Vaughan, Frankie 1928- *OxCPMus*
Vaughan, George Christopher 1957- *St&PR 91*
Vaughan, Hal Weston 1928- *WhoE 91*
Vaughan, Harry A. 1911- *St&PR 91*
Vaughan, Herbert Alfred 1832-1903 *BioIn 16*
Vaughan, Herbert Wiley 1920- *WhoAm 90, WhoE 91, WhoWor 91*
Vaughan, Hines S. 1936- *St&PR 91*
Vaughan, Irving 1888- *Ballpl 90*
Vaughan, J. Bryan 1914- *St&PR 91*
Vaughan, Jack Chapline 1912- *WhoSSW 91, WhoWor 91*
Vaughan, Jack Chapline, Jr. 1943- *WhoSSW 91*
Vaughan, James H. *BioIn 16*
Vaughan, James Herbert 1927- *WhoAm 90*
Vaughan, James Rodney Mitchell 1921- *WhoAm 90*
Vaughan, Jeff *BioIn 16*
Vaughan, Jerry Lynn 1939- *WhoWrEP 89*
Vaughan, John Charles 1934- *St&PR 91*
Vaughan, John Charles, III 1934- *WhoAm 90*
Vaughan, John Nolen 1941- *WhoSSW 91*
Vaughan, John Thomas 1932- *WhoAm 90*
Vaughan, John Willis 1925- *St&PR 91*
Vaughan, Joseph Bryan 1914- *WhoAm 90*
Vaughan, Joseph Lee 1905- *WhoAm 90*
Vaughan, Joseph Lee, Jr. 1942- *WhoSSW 91*
Vaughan, Joseph Robert 1916- *St&PR 91, WhoAm 90*
Vaughan, Karen Newton 1943- *St&PR 91*
Vaughan, Keith 1912-1977 *BioIn 16*
Vaughan, Kirk William 1943- *WhoAm 90*
Vaughan, Marcia 1951- *SmATA 60 [port]*
Vaughan, Margaret Evelyn 1948- *WhoAmW 91*
Vaughan, Margery 1927- *IntWWM 90*
Vaughan, Martha 1926- *WhoAm 90, WhoAmW 91*
Vaughan, Mary Kathleen 1943- *WhoAmW 91*
Vaughan, Meg *BioIn 16*
Vaughan, Millicent *BiDEWW*
Vaughan, Mittie Kathleen 1950- *WhoAmW 91*
Vaughan, Nancy E. 1948- *ODwPR 91*
Vaughan, Odie Frank 1936- *St&PR 91*
Vaughan, Peggy Thorpe 1942- *WhoAmW 91*
Vaughan, Philip Alfred 1923- *St&PR 91*
Vaughan, Ray 1961- *WhoSSW 91*
Vaughan, Richard Dugger 1926- *WhoSSW 91*
Vaughan, Richard Patrick 1919- *WhoAm 90*
Vaughan, Robert Lamar 1937- *WhoSSW 91*
Vaughan, Rowland *BioIn 16*
Vaughan, Samuel S. 1928- *St&PR 91*
Vaughan, Samuel Snell 1928- *WhoAm 90, WhoWrEP 89*
Vaughan, Sara C. 1908- *St&PR 91*
Vaughan, Sarah 1924- *DrBlPA 90*
Vaughan, Sarah 1924-1990 *BioIn 16, CurBio 90N, NewYTBS 90 [port], News 90, -90-3, OxCPMus, WorAlBi*
Vaughan, Steve *BioIn 16*
Vaughan, Stevie Ray *NewYTBS 90*
Vaughan, Stevie Ray 1955?- *EncPR&S 89*
Vaughan, Stevie Ray 1956?-1990 *News 91-1*
Vaughan, Thomas 1622-1666 *EncO&P 3*
Vaughan, Thomas 1924- *BioIn 16*
Vaughan, Thomas James Gregory 1924- *WhoAm 90*
Vaughan, Thomas Martin 1946- *WhoE 91*
Vaughan, Tom Brooks, Jr. 1942- *BiDrAPA 89*
Vaughan, Victor Clarence, III 1919- *WhoAm 90*
Vaughan, Warren Taylor, Jr. 1920- *BiDrAPA 89*
Vaughan, Wayland Edward 1934- *WhoE 91, WhoWor 91*
Vaughan, William Conway 1909- *St&PR 91*
Vaughan, William H, Jr. 1941- *BiDrAPA 89*
Vaughan, William Walton 1930- *WhoAm 90*
Vaughan, Worth Edward 1936- *WhoAm 90*
Vaughan-Thomas, Wynford 1908-1987 *ConAu 130*
Vaughan Williams, Ralph 1872-1958 *BioIn 16, PenDiMP A*
Vaughan Williams, Ursula 1911- *IntWWM 90*
Vaughey, John Cowman 1939- *St&PR 91*
Vaughin, John C. 1946- *St&PR 91*
Vaughn, Alease Juet 1945- *WhoAmW 91*
Vaughn, Alexandra Jean 1940- *St&PR 91*
Vaughn, Alvin 1939- *WhoE 91*
Vaughn, Bonnie Jean 1921- *WhoWrEP 89*
Vaughn, Charlie Frederick 1928- *St&PR 91*
Vaughn, Cindy Gail 1953- *WhoAmW 91*
Vaughn, Donald Charles 1936- *St&PR 91, WhoAm 90, WhoSSW 91*
Vaughn, Donald G. 1941- *St&PR 91*
Vaughn, Donna Jean *BiDrAPA 89*
Vaughn, Dorris Weldon 1909- *WhoAm 90*
Vaughn, Eleanor 1922- *WhoAmW 91*
Vaughn, Elizabeth Marie 1958- *WhoAmW 91*
Vaughn, Emmet P. 1905- *St&PR 91*
Vaughn, Emmet P., Jr. 1937- *St&PR 91*
Vaughn, Frank E. 1929- *St&PR 91*
Vaughn, Frank Edward, Jr. 1929- *WhoAm 90*
Vaughn, Garold Forrest 1919- *WhoSSW 91*
Vaughn, George A. 1897-1989 *BioIn 16*
Vaughn, Gerald E. 1942- *St&PR 91*
Vaughn, Glenn, Jr. 1929- *St&PR 91*
Vaughn, Hippo 1888-1966 *Ballpl 90 [port]*
Vaughn, Jack Hood 1920- *BioIn 16*
Vaughn, James Hurd 1927- *St&PR 91*
Vaughn, James Michael 1939- *WhoWrEP 89*
Vaughn, James W 1923- *BiDrAPA 89*
Vaughn, John Rolland 1938- *WhoAm 90*
Vaughn, John V. 1909- *St&PR 91*
Vaughn, John Vernon 1909- *WhoAm 90, WhoWor 91*
Vaughn, Joyce Elaine 1946- *WhoAmW 91*
Vaughn, Karen Iversen 1944- *WhoAm 90*
Vaughn, Lauralyn 1953- *WhoE 91*
Vaughn, Lowry D. 1944- *St&PR 91*
Vaughn, Mary 1930- *WhoAmW 91*
Vaughn, Mary Ann 1947- *WhoAmW 91*
Vaughn, Michael O'Connor 1947- *St&PR 91*
Vaughn, Phoebe Juanita 1939- *WhoWrEP 89*
Vaughn, Regis *BioIn 16*
Vaughn, Richard Van W. 1929- *St&PR 91*
Vaughn, Robert 1932- *WhoAm 90, WorAlBi*
Vaughn, Robert Lockard 1922- *WhoAm 90*
Vaughn, Ronald H. 1936- *St&PR 91*
Vaughn, Rufus Mahlon 1924- *WhoAm 90*
Vaughn, Stephanie 19--?- *ConLC 62 [port]*
Vaughn, Stuart F. 1935- *St&PR 91*
Vaughn, Virginia A. 1956- *WhoAmW 91*
Vaughn, Wallace R. 1929- *St&PR 91*
Vaughn, William, Jr. 1951- *WhoSSW 91*
Vaughn, William John 1931- *WhoSSW 91*
Vaughn, William Preston 1933- *WhoAm 90*
Vaughn, William T. 1947- *St&PR 91*
Vaughn, William Weaver 1930- *WhoAm 90*
Vaughn Williams, Ralph 1872-1958 *WorAlBi*
Vaught, Carl G. 1939- *WhoAm 90*
Vaught, Darrel Mandel 1943- *WhoSSW 91*
Vaught, Donald Ray 1938- *St&PR 91*
Vaught, Janet Maureen Burger 1952- *WhoAmW 91*
Vaught, Wilma L. 1930- *WhoAm 90*
Vaumont, Jean *PenDiDA 89*
Vaupel, Douglas Lee *BiDrAPA 89*
Vaupel, Jane Kathryn 1963- *WhoAmW 91*
Vaupel, Louis *PenDiDA 89*
Vaupel, Michael Christian 1936- *St&PR 91*
Vaupen, Burton 1930- *St&PR 91*
Vaurabourg, Andree 1894-1980 *PenDiMP*
Vause, Edwin Hamilton 1923- *WhoAm 90*
Vause, Karen Lee *BiDrAPA 89*
Vautier, Alice Forsha 1940- *WhoAmW 91*
Vautier, Ghislaine 1932- *BioIn 16*
Vautin, William C. *St&PR 91*
Vaux, Dora Louise 1922- *WhoAmW 91, WhoWor 91*
Vaux, Henry James 1912- *WhoAm 90*
Vaux, Richard 1940- *WhoAmA 91, WhoE 91*
Vaux, Sandra Marie *WhoAmA 91*
Vavala, Domenic Anthony 1925- *WhoAm 90*
Vavalidis, Stefanos 1946- *WhoWor 91*
Vavilov, N. I. 1887-1943 *BioIn 16*
Vavilov, Nikolai Ivanovich 1887-1943 *BioIn 16*
Vavoudis, Arthur Plato 1959- *WhoWrEP 89*
Vavrick, Ellan Finman 1943- *WhoAmW 91*
Vavrinecz, Bela 1925- *IntWWM 90*
Vawter, Gordon Fuller *NewYTBS 90*
Vawter, Gordon Fuller 1923-1990 *BioIn 16*
Vawter, Jay 1934- *WhoE 91*
Vawter, Kathy Floyd 1951- *WhoSSW 91*
Vawter, Mary H Murray 1871- *WhoAmA 91N*
Vax, John Joseph 1929- *St&PR 91*
Vay, Adelma 1840-1924 *EncO&P 3*
Vayer, Paul Stephen 1946- *WhoE 91*
Vaynberg, Dina *BiDrAPA 89*
Vaynberg, Moisei 1919- *PenDiMP A*
Vayrynen, Paavo Matti 1946- *WhoWor 91*
Vayrynen, Timo Matti Sakari 1957- *WhoWor 91*
Vaz, Daniel E. 1951- *St&PR 91*
Vaz, Kim Marie 1960- *WhoAmW 91*
Vazak, P.H. *ConTFT 8*
Vazakas, Byron *WhoWrEP 89*
Vazirani, Suresh Hassanand 1950- *WhoWor 91*
Vaziri, Fakhri Fay 1929- *WhoAmW 91, WhoE 91*
Vaziri, Habib *BiDrAPA 89*
Vazquez, Albert 1947- *WhoHisp 91*
Vazquez, Amalia 1956- *WhoHisp 91*
Vazquez, Anna T. 1918- *WhoHisp 91*
Vazquez, Carmen Inoa 1942- *WhoAmW 91*
Vazquez, Eduardo D 1944- *BiDrAPA 89*
Vazquez, Eloy 1935- *WhoHisp 91*
Vazquez, Emil C. 1947- *WhoHisp 91*
Vazquez, Gilbert Falcon 1952- *WhoEmL 91*
Vazquez, Heriberto 1927- *BiDrAPA 89*
Vazquez, Ileana 1955- *BiDrAPA 89*
Vazquez, John David 1935- *WhoHisp 91*
Vazquez, Jorge *BioIn 16*
Vazquez, Jose A *BiDrAPA 89*
Vazquez, Jose Salvador *BiDrAPA 89*
Vazquez, Juan J 1929- *BiDrAPA 89*
Vazquez, Maria Blanca *BiDrAPA 89*
Vazquez, Maria Laudelina 1951- *St&PR 91*
Vazquez, Martha Elisa 1954- *WhoHisp 91*
Vazquez, Paul 1933- *WhoAmA 91*
Vazquez, Raul A. 1939- *WhoHisp 91*
Vazquez, Rebecca C. 1957- *WhoHisp 91*
Vazquez, Roberto 1923- *WhoHisp 91*
Vazquez, Siro *BioIn 16*
Vazquez, Siro 1910-1990 *WhoHisp 91N*
Vazquez Garcia, J. Angel 1944- *WhoWor 91*
Vazquez Montalban, Manuel 1939- *IntvSpW [port]*
Vazquez-Rana, Mario 1932- *WhoAm 90, WhoHisp 91, WhoWor 91*
Vazquez-Sotomayor, Jose *BiDrAPA 89*
Vazsonyi, Andrew 1916- *WhoAm 90*
Vazsonyi, Balint 1936- *PenDiMP*
Vazuka, Jean Tierney *BiDrAPA 89*
Vazzano, Andrew Anthony 1948- *St&PR 91*
Veach, Bobby 1888-1945 *Ballpl 90*
Veader, Dorothy Phyllis 1937- *WhoE 91*
Veal, Charlotte Kelly *ODwPR 91*
Veal, Coot 1932- *Ballpl 90*
Veal, John E. 1959- *WhoE 91*
Veal, Rex R. 1956- *WhoE 91, WhoEmL 91*
Veal, Steven L. 1958- *St&PR 91*
Veal, Tracey Yvonne 1962- *WhoAmW 91*
Veale, Angela M. 1948- *WhoAmW 91*
Veale, Bob 1935- *Ballpl 90*

Veale, Erwin Olin 1930- St&PR 91
Veale, John 1922- IntWWM 90
Veale, John Edmond 1954- WhoEmL 91, WhoWor 91
Veale, Tinkham, II 1914- St&PR 91
Veasey, E. Norman 1933- St&PR 91
Veasey, Josephine 1930- IntWWM 90, PenDiMP
Veatch, Donald Hugh 1928- BiDrAPA 89
Veatch, John William 1923- WhoWor 91
Veatch, Julian Lamar, Jr. 1949- WhoSSW 91
Veatch, Robert Marlin 1939- WhoAm 90
Veazey, John Hobson 1901- WhoSSW 91, WhoWor 91
Veazey, Mary Virginia 1943- WhoWrEP 89
Veber, Gayle L. 1939- St&PR 91
Veblen, Thomas Clayton 1929- WhoE 91
Veblen, Thorstein 1857-1929 BioIn 16
Veblen, Thorstein B. 1857-1929 WorAlBi
Vecchia, Eugene F. 1925- St&PR 91
Vecchiarelli, Panfilo Guido 1937- WhoE 91
Vecchietta 1412-1480 BioIn 16
Vecchio, Robert Peter 1950- WhoAm 90, WhoWor 91
Vecchione, Alfred Thomas 1931- WhoAm 90
Vecchione, John E. 1915- St&PR 91
Vecchione, Joseph A. 1931- ODwPR 91
Vecellio, C. PenDiDA 89
Vecellio, Leo 1915- St&PR 91
Vecellio, Leo Arthur, Jr. 1946- WhoAm 90
Vechte, Antoine 1800-1868 PenDiDA 89
Veciana-Suarez, Ana 1956- WhoHisp 91
Vecino, Francisco 1945- WhoWor 91
Vecker, Lawrence 1929- St&PR 91
Vecoli, Rudolph John 1927- WhoAm 90, WhoWrEP 89
Vecozols, Aivests L 1919- BiDrAPA 89
Vecsey, Esther Barbara 1944- WhoAmA 91
Vecsey, Ferenc 1893-1935 PenDiMP
Vecsey, George BioIn 16
Vecsey, George Spencer 1939- WhoAm 90
Vedak, Chandragupta S 1953- BiDrAPA 89
Vedam, Kuppuswamy 1926- WhoAm 90
Vedder, Byron Charles 1910- WhoAm 90
Vedder, John K. TwCCr&M 91
Veder, Slava J. WhoAm 90
Vedernikov, Alexander 1927- PenDiMP
Vedra, Joseph John 1946- St&PR 91
Vedros, Jamsel Joseph 1948- St&PR 91
Vedros, Julian Barry 1934- St&PR 91
Vedros, Neylan Anthony 1929- WhoAm 90
Vedung, Evert Oskar 1938- WhoWor 91
Vee, Bobby 1943- EncPR&S 89
Veech, Alex B., III 1949- St&PR 91
Veech, Loren M. 1925- St&PR 91
Veeck, Bill BioIn 16
Veeck, Bill 1914-1987 Ballpl 90 [port]
Veeck, Richard Irvin 1947- St&PR 91
Veeck, William Ballpl 90
Veeder, Raymond 1919- BiDrAPA 89
Veelenturf, John 1928- St&PR 91
Veelken, Ludger 1938- WhoWor 91
Veeman, Frank Charles 1946- WhoEmL 91
Veen, Andre Gerard Van 1903-1986 BioIn 16
Veen, James Cornelius, Jr. 1923- St&PR 91
Veen, John P. 1928- St&PR 91
Veenhuis, Philip E 1935- BiDrAPA 89
Veenker, Claude Harold 1919- WhoAm 90
Veenker, Ronald Allen 1937- WhoSSW 91
Veenstra, Mark Allen 1956- WhoSSW 91
Veeramasuneni, Raghu Ramaiah 1947- BiDrAPA 89
Veerjee, Rudy 1958- St&PR 91
Veerkamp, Patrick Burke 1943- WhoAmA 91
Veesenmayer, Edmund 1904- BioIn 16
Veevers, Kirby 1958- ODwPR 91
Vega, Antonio M. 1959- St&PR 91
Vega, Benjamin Urbizo 1916- WhoWor 91
Vega, Beth Susan 1950- WhoAmW 91
Vega, Celestino 1960- WhoSSW 91
Vega, Ed BioIn 16
Vega, Edward 1938- WhoAmA 91
Vega, Edward J. 1947- St&PR 91
Vega, Flavio 1943- WhoHisp 91
Vega, Garcilaso de la 1539-1616 BioIn 16
Vega, Herman 1954- WhoSSW 91
Vega, J. William 1931- WhoAm 90
Vega, Lazaro Nava, III 1960- WhoHisp 91
Vega, Lope De 1562-1635 WorAlBi
Vega, Marylois Purdy 1914- WhoAm 90
Vega, Matias Alfonso 1952- WhoEmL 91
Vega, Milo C. St&PR 91
Vega, Moises Giroldi BioIn 16
Vega, Oscar Unzaga de la 1916-1959 BioIn 16
Vega, Rafael Evaristo, Jr. 1934- WhoHisp 91
Vega, Rosa Elia 1952- WhoAmW 91, WhoHisp 91
Vega, Rufino A. WhoHisp 91
Vega-Bonilla, Carlos V BiDrAPA 89
Vega-Garcia, Edna Rosa 1950- WhoHisp 91
Vega Jacome, Rafael 1944- WhoHisp 91
Vegard, Lars 1880-1963 DcScB S2
Vegas, Victor Pitre 1956- St&PR 91
Vegh Quartet PenDiMP
Vegh, Sandor 1905- PenDiMP
Veghte, Richard 1932- St&PR 91
Veglahn, Nancy Crary 1937- AuBYP 90
Vehar, Nila A. 1940- WhoAmW 91
Vehar, Persis Anne 1937- IntWWM 90
VeHaun, Marshall Jerry 1943- WhoSSW 91
Vehe, Richard Karl 1958- WhoEmL 91
Vehlewald, Steven John 1956- St&PR 91
Vehlhaber, Don Robert 1947- WhoSSW 91
Vehr, Bill BioIn 16
Veich, Joseph BiDrAPA 89
Veicopoulos, Nicholas 1920- WhoWor 91
Veidenheimer, Malcolm Charles 1928- WhoAm 90
Veiga, Jose J. 1915- ConAu 33NR
Veigel, Jon Michael 1938- WhoSSW 91
Veihmeyer, Carol Anne 1957- WhoAmW 91
Veil, Simone 1927- BioIn 16, WhoWor 91
Veil, Simone Annie 1927- BiDFrPL
Veillette, William Paul 1960- WhoE 91
Veilleux, Gerard 1942- WhoAm 90
Veilleux, Kimberley Anne 1958- WhoE 91
Veilleux, Richard Ernest 1948- WhoSSW 91
Veilleux, Ronald B. 1941- St&PR 91
Veino, Jens 1949- WhoWor 91
Veinott, Cyril George 1905- WhoAm 90
Veit, Christine Maria 1959- WhoAmW 91
Veit, Fritz 1907- WhoAm 90
Veit, Henry BiDrAPA 89
Veit, Herman C. 1934- St&PR 91
Veit, Kenneth Phillip 1938- WhoE 91
Veit, Werner 1929- St&PR 91
Veitch, Boyer Lewis 1930- St&PR 91, WhoWor 91
Veitch, E. Barbara 1932- St&PR 91
Veitch, Marion BiDEWW
Veitch, Marion 1638?-1722 FemiCLE
Veitch, Patrick Lee 1944- IntWWM 90, WhoWor 91
Veitch, Sophie 183-?-1921? FemiCLE
Veitch, Stephen William 1927- WhoAm 90
Veitenheimer, Michael Joseph 1956- St&PR 91
Veith, Anthony James 1957- WhoSSW 91
Veith, Ilza BiDrAPA 89, BioIn 16
Veith, Ilza 1915- WhoAm 90
Veith, Richard Charles 1947- BiDrAPA 89
Veith, Richard Lee 1940- WhoAm 90
Veits, Harold R 1945- BiDrAPA 89
Veizer, Jan 1941- WhoAm 90
Vejar, Rudolph Lawrence 1933- WhoHisp 91
Vejlupek, Fred James 1924- St&PR 91
Vejvoda, Jaromir BioIn 16
Vejzovic, Dunja 1943- IntWWM 90
Vekas, Mary Kelly 1961- St&PR 91
Vekovic, Marinko 1954- WhoWor 91
Vela, Filemon B. 1935- WhoAm 90
Vela, Gerard Roland 1927- WhoSSW 91
Vela, Ricardo M 1947- BiDrAPA 89, WhoE 91
Vela, Ricardo Rene 1956- WhoHisp 91
Vela, William Paul 1953- WhoEmL 91
Vela-Bueno, Antonio 1945- BiDrAPA 89
Velarde, Carlos E. 1929- WhoHisp 91
Velarde, Luis Alfonso, Jr. 1936- WhoHisp 91
Velarde, Manuel Garcia 1941- WhoWor 91
Velarde, Ramon Lopez 1888-1921 BioIn 16
Velarde, Robert M. 1950- WhoWor 91
Velardo, Joseph Thomas 1923- WhoAm 90, WhoWor 91
Velas, Carlos Manly BiDrAPA 89
Velasco, Agustin C. WhoHisp 91
Velasco, Alfredo Frank 1944- WhoHisp 91
Velasco, Alvarado 1910-1977 BioIn 16
Velasco, Carlos I. 1837-1914 BioIn 16
Velasco, Fe Aquino BiDrAPA 89
Velasco, Frank E. 1948- WhoHisp 91
Velasco, J.A. 1954- St&PR 91
Velasco, Jose Maria 1840-1912 ArtLatA
Velasco, Joseph Eugene 1931- WhoSSW 91
Velasco, Kathy Lynn 1956- WhoWrEP 89
Velasco Ibarra, Jose Maria 1893-1979 BioIn 16
Velasco-Mills, John Anthony 1945- WhoE 91
Velasco-Suarez, Manuel BiDrAPA 89
Velasquez, Ana Maria 1947- WhoWor 91
Velasquez, Angelo WhoHisp 91
Velasquez, Arthur Raymond 1938- WhoHisp 91
Velasquez, Baldemar 1947- WhoHisp 91
Velasquez, Geraldine Khaner 1943- WhoAmW 91
Velasquez, Oscar 1945- WhoAmA 91
Velasquez, Patti A. 1955- WhoEmL 91
Velasquez, William C. BioIn 16
Velasquez, William C., III WhoHisp 91N
Velasquez Giacarini, Julio WhoWor 91
Velasquez-Walsh, Kellie Elaine 1961- WhoAmW 91
Velayati, Ali Akbar 1945- WhoWor 91
Velazco, Jorge 1942- IntWWM 90
Velazquez, Anabel 1958- WhoAmW 91
Velazquez, Diego 1599-1660 BioIn 16, IntDcAA 90, WorAlBi
Velazquez, Hector WhoHisp 91
Velde, Jacoba van 1913-1985 EncCoWW
Velde, Jan van der PenDiMP
Velde, John Ernest, Jr. 1917- WhoAm 90, WhoWor 91
Veldekens, Bertrand Frederic 1961- WhoWor 91
Veldkamp, Gerald W. 1937- St&PR 91
Veldman, Donald John 1931- WhoAm 90
Veldman, Ilja Maria 1944- WhoWor 91
Veldman, Vicki Lynn 1963- WhoAmW 91
Veleda EncO&P 3
Velek, Miroslav BiDrAPA 89
Velella, Guy J. 1944- WhoE 91
Veler, Kevin Michael 1957- WhoSSW 91
Velett, Laurie C. 1953- ODwPR 91
Veley, Hugh J. 1926- St&PR 91
Veley, Margaret 1843-1887 FemiCLE
Velez, Anita 1922- WhoHisp 91
Velez, Carlos 1927- WhoWor 91
Velez, Carmelo WhoHisp 91
Velez, Clemente Soto 1905- BioIn 16
Velez, Edin 1951- WhoAmA 91
Velez, Francisco S. 1935- WhoSSW 91
Velez, Ismael A. WhoHisp 91
Velez, Jose WhoHisp 91
Velez, Lisa BioIn 16
Velez, Luis 1955- WhoHisp 91
Velez, Maria Lourdes C BiDrAPA 89
Velez, Mario Isaac BiDrAPA 89
Velez, Otto 1950- Ballpl 90
Velez, Theresa Lynn 1967- WhoHisp 91
Velez, Tony 1946- WhoHisp 91
Velez, William 1950- WhoHisp 91
Velez-Ibanez, Carlos G 1936- HispWr 90, WhoHisp 91
Velez-Mitchell, Anita 1922- WhoHisp 91
Velge, Sophie 1956- WhoWor 91
Velgouse, Michael 1940- St&PR 91
Velicangil, Omer 1952- WhoWor 91
Velicer, Leland Frank 1939- WhoAm 90
Velichko, Vladimir Makarovich 1937- WhoWor 91
Velicina, Neznama EncCoWW
Velick, Bruce 1949- WhoAmA 91
Velick, Paul WhoAmA 91
Velick, Sidney Frederick 1913- WhoAm 90
Velie, Lester 1907- WhoAm 90
Veligdan, Robert George 1949- WhoE 91
Velikhov, Yevgeny P. BioIn 16
Velikovsky, Immanuel 1895-1979 EncO&P 3, WorAlBi
Velimirovic, Milos M. 1922- WhoAm 90
Veliotes, Nicholas Alexander 1928- WhoAm 90
Velisetty, Asha 1952- BiDrAPA 89
Veliz, Claudio 1930- WhoWor 91
Veliz-Cruz, Jorge Raul 1953- BiDrAPA 89, WhoE 91
Veljohnson, Reginald BioIn 16
Velk, Robert James 1938- WhoWor 91
Velker, Hugo BiDrAPA 89
Velkov, Wes BioIn 16
Vella, David Charles 1954- WhoE 91
Vellacott, Elizabeth 1905- BiDWomA
Vellekoop, Pieter 1947- WhoWor 91
Vellenga, Kathleen Osborne 1938- WhoAmW 91
Vellenoweth, Carole Leland 1941- WhoAmW 91
Veller, Margaret Paxton 1925- WhoAmW 91
Vellert, Dirick PenDiDA 89
Velluti, Giovanni Battista 1781-1861 PenDiMP
Velmans, Loet Abraham 1923- WhoAm 90
Velmere, Lolita BiDrAPA 89
Veloric, Gary 1960- St&PR 91
Velosa, Luis H 1942- BiDrAPA 89
Veloz, Bradley, Jr. 1948- WhoHisp 91
Veloz, George A. 1947- WhoHisp 91
Veloz Maggiolo, Marcio E. 1936- HispWr 90
Velsey, Seth M 1903-1967 WhoAmA 91N
Velsink, Willem Bernhard 1938- WhoAm 90
Velte, Hansjoachim 1947- BioIn 16
Velten, Kathleen Ann 1950- WhoWrEP 89
Velthuijs, Max 1923- BioIn 16
Veltman, Arthur P. BioIn 16
Veltman, C.A. 1929- St&PR 91
Veltman, Jamie Dawn 1958- WhoAmW 91
Veltman, Martinus J. WhoAm 90
Veltman, Peter 1917- WhoAm 90
Vel'tman, Vera EncCoWW, MajTwCW
Veltmann, Christopher P. 1954- St&PR 91
Veltri, Michelangelo 1940- IntWWM 90
Veluswamy, Angammal N BiDrAPA 89
Veluswamy, Varudeyam P 1939- BiDrAPA 89
Velvet Underground OxCPMus
Velvet Underground, The EncPR&S 89
Velvikis, Claire BioIn 16
Velz, John William 1930- WhoAm 90
Velzy, Charles O. 1930- WhoAm 90, WhoE 91
Vemuri, Lalitha Y BiDrAPA 89
Vemuri, Ramesh Babu 1948- BiDrAPA 89
Vemuri, Sarma Lakshminarayana 1928- WhoSSW 91
Vena, Dante 1930- WhoAmA 91
Venable, Charles H. 1932- St&PR 91
Venable, Demetrius Dante 1947- WhoSSW 91
Venable, Frank Fornshell 1937- WhoAm 90
Venable, Max 1957- Ballpl 90
Venable, Patricia Lengel 1930- WhoAmW 91, WhoE 91
Venable, Phillip W. St&PR 91
Venable, Susan C 1944- WhoAmA 91
Venables, Elizabeth BiDEWW
Venables, Terry TwCCr&M 91
Venables, Thomas Russell 1955- St&PR 91
Venaleck, Howard Joseph 1940- St&PR 91
Venard, Elisabeth-Celeste EncCoWW
Venard, Neil Alden BiDrAPA 89
Venard, Steve 1824-1891 BioIn 16
Venard, Theophane 1829-1861 BioIn 16
Vencer, Agustin Baldonasa 1946- WhoWor 91
Vencer, Jun BioIn 16
Vencill, Gay T. 1944- WhoAmW 91
Venckus, Ronald Bernard 1934- St&PR 91
Vencovsky, Eugen Josef WhoWor 91
Venderhei, George Lloyd 1921- St&PR 91
Venderhoof, Lina May 1938- St&PR 91
Vendetti, Mildred Mae 1931- WhoSSW 91
Vendetti, Randall Peter 1953- WhoE 91
Vendice, William 1948- IntWWM 90
Venditto, James Joseph 1951- WhoEmL 91, WhoSSW 91, WhoWor 91
Venditto, Joseph BioIn 16
Vendler, Helen 1933- MajTwCW
Vendler, Helen Hennessy 1933- WhoAm 90, WhoAmW 91, WhoWrEP 89
Vendrell, John Donald Oromi 1934- WhoWor 91
Venegas, Emilio J. 1928- St&PR 91
Venegas, Haydee E 1950- WhoAmA 91
Venegas, Joseph M. WhoHisp 91
Venegas-Avila, Haydee E. 1950- WhoHisp 91
Veneman, Gerard E. 1920- St&PR 91
Veneman, Gerard Earl 1920- WhoAm 90
Veneruso, Ciro 1929- BiDrAPA 89
Venet, Bernar P 1941- WhoAmA 91
Venet, Michelle WhoWrEP 89
Venetis, Nicholas G. 1950- St&PR 91
Veneto, A. Joseph 1941- WhoE 91
Venetsanopoulos, Anastasios Nicolaos 1941- WhoAm 90
Venetta, Anne Marie 1959- WhoE 91
Veney, Anderson 1845?-1894 DcCanB 12
Venezia, Joyce Ann 1960- WhoAmW 91, WhoE 91
Venezia, Linda Crista 1961- WhoE 91
Venezia, Mary Ann BiDrAPA 89
Venezia, Michael 1935- WhoAmA 91
Venezia, Mike BioIn 16
Venezia, Morris St&PR 91
Veneziani, Jole BioIn 16
Veneziano, Agostino PenDiDA 89
Veneziano, Patricia Joan Morse 1931- WhoAmW 91
Venezio, August 1930- St&PR 91
Venezky, Richard Lawrence 1938- WhoAm 90, WhoWrEP 89
Vengerova, Isabella 1877-1956 PenDiMP
Vengerova, Zinaida 1867-1941 EncCoWW
Veniamin, Maria EncCoWW
Veniaminoff, Ioann 1797-1879 WhNaAH
Veniaminov, Ivan 1797-1879 WhNaAH
Venice, Frank Paul 1940- St&PR 91
Venick, Robert Benjamin WhoAm 90
Venincasa, Mark Anthony 1961- WhoSSW 91
Veninga, James Frank 1944- WhoWrEP 89
Veninga, Karen Ann 1944- WhoAmW 91
Veninga, Louise Ann 1948- WhoAmW 91, WhoEmL 91, WhoWor 91
Veninga, Robert Louis 1941- WhoWrEP 89
Venini, Paolo 1895-1959 PenDiDA 89
Venino, Thomas M. 1928- St&PR 91
Venison, Alfred MajTwCW
Venissat, Wade Louis, Jr. 1944- WhoSSW 91
Venizelos, Eleftherios 1864-1936 BioIn 16
Venizelos, Eleutherios 1864-1936 WorAlBi
Venkataraman, Balakrishnan 1945- St&PR 91

Venkataraman, Krishnamurthy 1946- *WhoWor 91*
Venkataraman, Krishnaswamy 1935- *WhoWor 91*
Venkataraman, Ramaswamy 1910- *BioIn 16, WhoWor 91*
Venkataraman, Shanmuga S 1960- *BiDrAPA 89*
Venkatesh, Eswarahalli Sundararajan 1949- *WhoE 91*
Venkatram, Veena P *BiDrAPA 89*
Venken, Raf 1958- *WhoWor 91*
Venker, Marty *BioIn 16*
Venn, Anne *FemiCLE*
Venn, Anne 1626?-1654 *BiDEWW*
Venn, George Andrew 1943- *WhoWrEP 89*
Venn, John Jeffrey 1949- *WhoSSW 91*
Venn, Mary Eleanor 1908- *AuBYP 90*
Venn, Paul Adrian 1943- *IntWWM 90*
Venn-Watson, Patricia C 1944- *BiDrAPA 89*
Vennam, Padmaja *BiDrAPA 89*
Vennard, David Leigh 1945- *WhoE 91*
Vennberg, Karl Gunnar 1910- *DcScanL*
Vennel, Charles Reed 1933- *St&PR 91*
Venner, George A. 1929- *St&PR 91*
Vennesland, Birgit 1913- *WhoAmW 91*
Vennik, Roelof Klaas 1954- *WhoWor 91*
Venning, Michael *TwCCr&M 91*
Veno, Glen Corey 1951- *WhoEmL 91*
Venrick, Naomi B. 1938- *St&PR 91*
Vensel, Clarence R. 1939- *St&PR 91*
Vent, Richard H. 1941- *St&PR 91*
Venta, Mario 1945- *WhoEmL 91*
Venter, Josiah B. 1945- *St&PR 91*
Venter, Pieter Jacobus 1933- *WhoWor 91*
Venters, Daniel Joseph 1950- *WhoSSW 91*
Ventiere, David Eric 1950- *WhoSSW 91*
Ventimiglia, John Thomas 1943- *WhoAmA 91*
Ventimiglia, Katharine Jane Garver 1949- *WhoAmW 91*
Ventline, Joseph S. 1944- *St&PR 91*
Vento, Bruce F. *BioIn 16*
Vento, Bruce Frank 1940- *WhoAm 90*
Vento, Richard Patrick 1948- *St&PR 91*
Ventola, Dean Samuel 1958- *WhoE 91*
Ventre, Francis Thomas 1937- *WhoAm 90*
Ventre, Martin A. 1945- *St&PR 91*
Ventres, Judith Martin 1943- *WhoAmW 91, WhoWor 91*
Ventres, Romeo J. 1924- *St&PR 91*
Ventres, Romeo John 1924- *WhoAm 90, WhoE 91, WhoWor 91*
Ventresca, Deborah Anne 1948- *WhoAmW 91*
Ventresca, Louis N. 1944- *St&PR 91*
Ventress, William T., Jr. 1956- *St&PR 91*
Ventriglia, Franco-Basso 1927- *IntWWM 90*
Ventrilio, James J. 1949- *ODwPR 91*
Ventrone, Penny James 1960- *WhoAmW 91*
Ventry, Catherine Valerie 1949- *WhoAmW 91, WhoE 91, WhoWor 91*
Ventry, Paul Guerin 1934- *WhoE 91, WhoWor 91*
Ventsel, Elena 1907- *EncCoWW*
Ventulett, Thomas Walker, III 1935- *WhoAm 90*
Ventura, Anthony 1927- *WhoAmA 91*
Ventura, Judy 1951- *WhoAmW 91*
Ventura, Jules C. 1925- *St&PR 91*
Ventura, Piero 1937- *SmATA 61 [port]*
Ventura, Ray 1908-1979 *OxCPMus*
Ventura, Sergio 1935- *WhoWor 91*
Ventura i Sala, Josep 1957- *WhoWor 91*
Venturanza, Lucille E *BiDrAPA 89*
Venturello, John *BioIn 16*
Ventures, The *EncPR&S 89*
Venturi, Franco 1914- *ConAu 130*
Venturi, Robert 1925- *PenDiDA 89, WhoAm 90, WhoAmA 91*
Venturini, Martin John 1948- *St&PR 91*
Venturo, Betty Lou Baker *AuBYP 90*
Venuti, Dennis P. 1943- *St&PR 91*
Venuti, Joe 1900?-1978 *BioIn 16*
Venuti, Joe 1903-1978 *OxCPMus*
Venuti, Lawrence M. 1953- *WhoWrEP 89*
Venuti, Michael H. 1940- *St&PR 91*
Venuto, Joseph L., II 1944- *WhoE 91*
Venuto, T. 1954- *St&PR 91*
Venutolo, Felix J 1928- *BiDrAPA 89*
Venz, David C. *ODwPR 91*
Venz, Donald Ray 1938- *WhoSSW 91*
Venza, Jac 1926- *WhoAm 90*
Venzago, Mario 1948- *IntWWM 90*
Venzon, Tony 1915-1971 *Ballpl 90*
Veon, Dorothy Helene 1914- *WhoAmW 91, WhoWor 91*
Vepa, Narayana Murty 1946- *WhoWor 91*
Vepraskas, Nancy Murphy 1950- *WhoAmW 91*
Vera, Enrique 1939- *BiDrAPA 89*
Vera, Francisco Luis 1947- *WhoE 91*
Vera, Marcelo 1957- *WhoHisp 91*
Vera, Moises Giroldi *BioIn 16*
Vera, Nancy 1961- *BiDrAPA 89*
Vera, Reinaldo *BiDrAPA 89*
Verage, Thomas Joseph 1941- *St&PR 91*
Verani, Daniela Elda 1955- *WhoAmW 91*
Verano, Anthony Frank 1931- *WhoAm 90*
Verardi, Peter Louis 1945- *St&PR 91*
Verati, Laura Maria Caterina Bassi 1711-1778 *EncCoWW*
Verba, Sidney 1932- *WhoAm 90*
Verban, Emil 1915- *Ballpl 90*
Verban, Emil 1915-1989 *BioIn 16*
Verbanic, Joe 1943- *Ballpl 90*
Ver Becke, W. Edwin 1913- *WhoWrEP 89*
Verbeek, Paul 1925- *WhoWor 91*
Verbeke, Gerard 1910- *ConAu 131*
Verbeke, Karen Ann 1948- *WhoE 91*
Verberckt, Jacques 1704-1771 *PenDiDA 89*
Verbik, Robert Charles 1950- *WhoEmL 91*
Verbinnen, Paul *ODwPR 91*
Verbitskaia, Anastasia 1861-1928 *EncCoWW*
Verbitsky, Bernardo 1907- *HispWr 90*
Verbraeken, Carl Gustav 1950- *IntWWM 90*
Verbraeken, Joseph Constant 1940- *St&PR 91*
Verbrugge, Betty Lou 1927- *WhoWor 91*
Verbruggen, Marion 1950- *IntWWM 90*
Verbrugghen, Henri 1873-1934 *PenDiMP*
Verbryke, Louis Eugene 1926- *St&PR 91*
Verburg, David Lee 1950- *BiDrAPA 89*
Verburg, Edwin Arnold 1945- *WhoE 91, WhoWor 91*
Verby, Jane Crawford 1923- *WhoWrEP 89*
Vercammen, Hugo 1946- *WhoWor 91*
Verches, Dan 1956- *WhoHisp 91*
Verciglio, Tina Maria 1955- *WhoAmW 91*
Vercio, Raymond A *BiDrAPA 89*
Vercoe, Elizabeth 1941- *IntWWM 90, WhoE 91*
Vercollone, Richard Walter 1947- *St&PR 91*
Vercruysse, Jozef Pieter 1950- *WhoWor 91*
Vercz, Carol Ann 1946- *WhoWrEP 89*
Verdaasdonk, Hugo Jeroen 1945- *WhoWor 91*
Verdan, Amanda *BioIn 16*
Verdeaux, Cyrille *NewAgMG*
Verderame, Maria Giovanna *BiDrAPA 89*
Verderame, Philip Joseph 1950- *BiDrAPA 89*
Verderber, Joseph Anthony 1938- *St&PR 91, WhoAm 90*
Verdery, Ben *NewAgMG*
Verdery, Katherine Maureen 1948- *WhoE 91*
Verdeyen, Guido 1938- *WhoWor 91*
Verdi, Barry E. 1937- *WhoHisp 91*
Verdi, Giuseppe 1813-1901 *BioIn 16, PenDiMPA, WorAlBi*
Verdi, Marie de *MajTwCW*
Verdi, Nejat Hasan 1913- *WhoWor 91*
Verdi, Philip Paul 1940- *WhoAm 90*
Verdi, Robert William 1946- *WhoAm 90*
Verdier, Philippe Maurice 1912- *WhoAm 90*
Verdier, Quentin Roosevelt 1921- *WhoWor 91*
Verdile, Silvio R. 1941- *St&PR 91*
Verdile, Vincent Paul 1955- *WhoE 91*
Verdon, Gwen 1925- *BioIn 16, WhoAm 90, WorAlBi*
Verdon, Gwen 1926- *NotWoAT, OxCPMus*
Verdon, John Joseph, Jr. 1939- *BiDrAPA 89, WhoE 91*
Verdon, Joseph Michael 1941- *WhoE 91*
Verdoorn, Frans 1906-1984 *BioIn 16*
Verdoorn, Robert James 1934- *St&PR 91*
Verdu, Matilde *ConAu 32NR, HispWr 90, MajTwCW*
Ver Dught, ElGene Clark 1951- *WhoEmL 91*
Verdugo, Jose Miguel Carrera 1785-1821 *BioIn 16*
Verduin, Bert M. 1947- *WhoAmW 91*
Verduin, Claire Leone 1932- *WhoAmW 91, WhoWor 91*
Verduin, Jacob 1913- *WhoAm 90*
Verdun, Michel *EncO&P 3*
Vere, Cora Eliza 1919- *WhoWrEP 89*
Vere, Robert de 1362-1392 *BioIn 16*
Vereb, Michael Joseph 1931- *WhoE 91*
Vereb, Teresa B 1941- *BiDrAPA 89*
Verebay, Leonard Jay 1944- *WhoAm 90*
Verebelyi, Ernest Raymond 1947- *WhoEmL 91*
Verebes, Thomas Edward *BiDrAPA 89*
Vered, Ruth 1940- *WhoAmW 91*
Vereen, Ben *BioIn 16*
Vereen, Ben 1946- *ConTFT 8 [port], DrBlPA 90, WhoAm 90, WorAlBi*
Vereen, D.G. 1939- *St&PR 91*
Vereen, Donald Ray, Jr. 1958- *BiDrAPA 89*
Vereen, Eugene M. 1920- *St&PR 91*
Vereen, Harvey Bunn 1945- *St&PR 91*
Vereen, Robert Charles 1924- *WhoAm 90*
Vereen, Ronald Lloyd *BiDrAPA 89*
Vereen, William Jerome 1940- *St&PR 91, WhoAm 90, WhoWor 91*
Vereketis, Constantin Kimon 1908- *WhoWor 91*
Verendrye, Sieur De La 1685-1749 *WhNaAH*
Verendrye, Pierre Gaultier, Sieur De La 1685-1749 *WorAlBi*
Vereskov, Nikolai Ivanovich 1931- *WhoWor 91*
Veress, Frank *BiDrAPA 89*
Veress, Sandor 1907- *IntWWM 90*
Verey, Rosemary 1918- *ConAu 130*
Verfasser der Alme *EncCoWW*
Verfasser des Walther von Montbarry *EncCoWW*
Verga, Giovanni 1840-1922 *WorAlBi*
Vergamini, Jerome C 1939- *BiDrAPA 89*
Vergara, Alejandro F 1934- *BiDrAPA 89*
Vergara, Alfonso Ignacio 1931- *WhoHisp 91*
Vergara, Felix M, Jr. *BiDrAPA 89*
Vergara, Herman 1931- *BiDrAPA 89*
Vergara, Luis Ernesto *BiDrAPA 89*
Vergara, Virgil Panti 1941- *WhoSSW 91*
Vergara-Vives, Alfonso 1931- *WhoHisp 91*
Vergare, Michael J 1945- *BiDrAPA 89*
Vergari, Edward Louis 1947- *St&PR 91*
Verge, George David 1942- *St&PR 91*
Verge, Pierre 1936- *WhoAm 90*
Verger, Don Marshall 1926- *WhoAm 90*
Verger, Lynn Rosel *BiDrAPA 89*
Verger, Morris David 1915- *WhoAm 90*
Vergeront, Susan Bowers 1945- *WhoAmW 91*
Vergeront, Thomas Allan 1955- *WhoEmL 91*
Verges, Lisa Blount 1955- *BiDrAPA 89*
Vergez, Johnny 1906- *Ballpl 90*
Vergin, Timothy Lynn 1962- *WhoWor 91*
Vergith, Douglas Wayne 1948- *St&PR 91*
Vergne, Marie-Madeleine, Pioche de la 1634-1693 *EncCoWW*
Vergne-Marini, Pedro Juan 1942- *WhoAm 90*
Vergnes, Michel Noel 1932- *WhoWor 91*
Vergon, James F. 1948- *St&PR 91*
Vergona, Kathleen Dobrosielski 1948- *WhoAmW 91*
Vergoni, Paul R. 1947- *St&PR 91*
Verhaegen, Georges Marie Alexis 1937- *WhoWor 91*
Verhaeghe, George Arthur 1918- *St&PR 91*
Verhaert, Piet Edmond 1924- *WhoWor 91*
Verhage, David James 1950- *St&PR 91*
Verhage, Paul Alan 1938- *St&PR 91*
Ver Hagen, Jan Karol 1937- *St&PR 91, WhoAm 90*
Verhagen, Patrick 1947- *WhoWor 91*
Verhagen, Timothy James 1946- *St&PR 91*
Verhalen, Robert Donald 1935- *WhoAm 90*
Verhey, Joseph W 1928- *BiDrAPA 89*
Verheyen, Egon 1936- *WhoAm 90*
Verhines, Jack 1932- *St&PR 91*
Verhoek, Susan Elizabeth 1942- *WhoAmW 91*
Ver Hoeve, Raymond Warren 1925- *St&PR 91*
Verhoeven, John 1953- *Ballpl 90*
Verhoeven, Paul 1940- *ConTFT 8*
Verhoogen, John 1912- *WhoAm 90*
Verhulst, Adrian Edward 1929- *WhoWor 91*
Verhulst, Johan M F 1938- *BiDrAPA 89*
Verhulst, Johannes 1816-1891 *PenDiMP*
Verillo, Josmar 1952- *WhoWor 91*
Verin, Donald W 1934- *BiDrAPA 89*
Vering, John Albert 1951- *WhoEmL 91*
Veringa, Frans Theodore Hubert 1925- *WhoWor 91*
Verini, Gregory A. 1952- *St&PR 91*
Verink, Ellis Daniel, Jr. 1920- *WhoAm 90*
Verissimo, Erico 1905-1975 *BioIn 16*
Verity, C William, Jr. 1917- *BiDrUSE 89*
Verity, Calvin William *BioIn 16*
Verity, George Luther 1914- *WhoAm 90*
Verity, James Edward 1947- *WhoE 91*
Verity, Maurice Anthony 1931- *WhoAm 90*
Verity, Simon *BioIn 16*
Verkaart, Isabelle McDonough 1915- *WhoSSW 91*
Verkerk, Gerard C. 1943- *St&PR 91*
Verkler, Richard Lee 1936- *WhoAm 90*
Verkoeyen, Jos *PenDiMP*
Verkuil, Paul Robert 1939- *WhoAm 90, WhoSSW 91*
Verlaine, Paul 1844-1896 *PoeCrit 2 [port], WorAlBi*
Verlaine, Tom 1949- *EncPR&S 89*
Verlander, W. Ashley 1920- *St&PR 91*
Verlander, William Ashley 1920- *WhoAm 90*
Verlanic, Kenneth Joseph 1953- *St&PR 91*
Verlaque, Robert 1955- *ConTFT 8 [port]*
Verlet, Pierre 1908-1987 *BioIn 16*
Verley, Roy E. 1950- *ODwPR 91*
Verlich, Jean E. *ODwPR 91*
Verlich, Jean Elaine 1950- *WhoAmW 91*
Verma, Arun Kumar 1942- *WhoSSW 91*
Verma, Bipin Bihari 1929- *BiDrAPA 89*
Verma, Ghasi Ram 1927- *WhoE 91*
Verma, Krishna Murari 1948- *BiDrAPA 89*
Verma, Mahadeo Prasad 1929- *WhoE 91*
Verma, Neelam *BiDrAPA 89*
Verma, Serge Lal 1940- *WhoSSW 91*
Verma, Sumer 1940- *BiDrAPA 89*
Vermann, C. Peter 1937- *St&PR 91*
Vermeer, Arnold 1921- *St&PR 91*
Vermeer, Jackie *AuBYP 90*
Vermeer, Jan 1632-1675 *BioIn 16, IntDcAA 90, WorAlBi*
Vermeer, Johannes 1632-1675 *BioIn 16*
Vermeer, Maureen Dorothy 1945- *WhoAmW 91*
Vermeer, Richard Douglas 1938- *WhoAm 90*
Vermeersch, B. C. 1943- *IntWWM 90*
Vermeersch, Jef 1928- *IntWWM 90*
Vermeersch, Julie 1910- *BiDFrPL*
Vermeersch, Pierre Marie 1938- *WhoWor 91*
Vermes, Hal G. *AuBYP 90*
Vermes, Jean Campbell Pattison 1907- *AuBYP 90*
Vermes, Jules 1828-1905 *AuBYP 90*
Vermeule, Cornelius Clarkson, III 1925- *WhoAm 90, WhoAmA 91, WhoE 91, WhoWor 91*
Vermeule, Emily Townsend 1928- *WhoAm 90, WhoAmW 91*
Vermeulen, Carl William 1939- *WhoSSW 91*
Vermeulen, John H *BiDrAPA 89*
Vermeulen-Cranch, Doreen Mary 1915- *WhoWor 91*
Vermiglio-Smith, Janice Anna 1948- *WhoAmW 91*
Vermillion, Joe Ann 1943- *WhoSSW 91*
Vermillion, Mark Edward, Sr. 1957- *WhoSSW 91*
Vermillion, Richard D. 1920- *St&PR 91*
Vermillion, Stephen Dorsey, III 1960- *WhoE 91*
Vermillion, William C. 1945- *St&PR 91*
Vermilya, Claire 1919- *WhoWrEP 89*
Vermilya, Dale Nelson 1959- *WhoEmL 91*
Vermilye, Henry Rowland 1936- *St&PR 91*
Vermilye, Peter Hoagland 1920- *WhoAm 90*
Vermilyea, Ross Orrin 1945- *WhoWor 91*
Vermylen, Paul A. 1919- *St&PR 91*
Vermylen, Paul A., Jr. 1946- *St&PR 91*
Vermylen, Paul Anthony, Jr. 1946- *WhoAm 90*
Vermylen, Robert Arthur 1954- *St&PR 91*
Verna, Barbara 1942- *WhoAmW 91*
Verna, Mario 1937- *WhoE 91*
Verna, Peter J., Jr. 1926- *St&PR 91*
Vernadskii, Vladimir Ivanovich 1863-1945 *BioIn 16*
Vernberg, Frank John 1925- *WhoAm 90*
Verne, Adela 1877-1952 *PenDiMP*
Verne, Alice 1868-1958 *PenDiMP*
Verne, Jules 1828-1905 *ConAu 131, WorAlBi*
Verne, Mathilde 1865-1936 *PenDiMP*
Verner, Betty Smith 1930- *WhoSSW 91*
Verner, Elizabeth O'Neill 1883-1979 *WhoAmA 91N*
Verner, Gerald 1896-1980 *TwCCr&M 91*
Verner, James Melton 1915- *WhoAm 90*
Verner, Jules L. 1925- *St&PR 91*
Verner, Oliver A., Jr. 1929- *St&PR 91*
Verner-Loehr, Dean G. 1952- *St&PR 91*
Vernerder, Gloria Jean 1930- *WhoAmW 91*
Verney, Ernest Basil 1894-1967 *DcScB S2*
Verney, John 1913- *AuBYP 90*
Verney, Richard Greville 1946- *St&PR 91, WhoE 91*
Verni, Ernest Aurelio, Jr. 1949- *WhoEmL 91*
Verni, Ralph Francis 1943- *St&PR 91, WhoAm 90*
Vernick, Ruth 1934- *St&PR 91*
Vernicos-Eugenides, Nicolas Michel 1920- *WhoWor 91*
Vernier, Richard 1929- *WhoAm 90*
Vernier, Robert Lawrence 1924- *WhoAm 90*
Verniere, Daniel Georges 1941- *WhoWor 91*
Verniero, Robert 1926- *St&PR 91*
Vernon 1948- *WhoAmA 91*
Vernon, Barbara 1916-1978 *FemiCLE*
Vernon, Brian Elliot 1953- *St&PR 91*
Vernon, Carl Atlee, Jr. 1926- *WhoAm 90*
Vernon, Charles R 1926- *BiDrAPA 89*
Vernon, Charles Robertson 1926- *WhoSSW 91*
Vernon, Darryl Mitchell 1956- *WhoEmL 91, WhoWor 91*

Vernon, David Harvey 1925- *WhoAm 90, WhoWrEP 89*
Vernon, David Michael Jude 1960- *WhoE 91*
Vernon, Elizabeth 1580?-1655? *BiDEWW*
Vernon, Faye Marie 1959- *WhoAmW 91*
Vernon, Gerald B. 1941- *St&PR 91*
Vernon, Harriet Dorothy 1914- *WhoWrEP 89*
Vernon, J Taylor 1921- *BiDrAPA 89*
Vernon, Jack Allen 1922- *WhoAm 90*
Vernon, Jack Hayward 1930- *WhoE 91*
Vernon, Joyce Ann 1947- *WhoAmW 91*
Vernon, Lacy Sinkford 1931- *St&PR 91*
Vernon, Lawrence Gordon 1937- *WhoWor 91*
Vernon, Leo Preston 1925- *WhoAm 90*
Vernon, Lillian *BioIn 16, WhoAm 90, WhoAmW 91*
Vernon, Mickey 1918- *Ballpl 90 [port]*
Vernon, Philip Ewart *BioIn 16*
Vernon, Raymond 1913- *WhoAm 90, WhoWrEP 89*
Vernon, Richard 1950- *IntWWM 90*
Vernon, Robert *BioIn 16*
Vernon, Shirley Jane 1930- *WhoAm 90*
Vernon, Sidney 1906- *WhoWor 91, WhoWrEP 89*
Vernon, Suzanne Marie 1960- *WhoSSW 91*
Vernon, Thomas Martin, Jr. 1939- *WhoAm 90*
Vernon, Weston, III 1931- *WhoAm 90, WhoE 91*
Vernon, William F., Jr. 1931- *St&PR 91*
Vernone, Michael Jerome 1962- *WhoSSW 91*
Vernor, Bruce 1930- *WhoE 91*
Vernov, Sergei Nikolaevich 1910-1982 *DcScB S2*
Verny, Thomas R 1936- *BiDrAPA 89*
Vero, Radu 1926- *WhoE 91*
Veron, Earl Ernest 1922- *WhoAm 90*
Veron, J. Michael 1950- *WhoEmL 91, WhoSSW 91*
Veron, James D. 1930- *St&PR 91*
Verona, Ante Fedor Maria 1941- *WhoWor 91*
Verona, David Alan 1954- *WhoSSW 91*
Verona, Liberale da 1445-1526? *BioIn 16*
Verona, Pasquale A. 1936- *St&PR 91*
Verona, Paula 1950- *WhoAmA 91*
Veronda, Antica *BiDrAPA 89*
Veronese 1528-1588 *BioIn 16*
Veronese, Angela 1779-1847 *EncCoWW*
Veronese, Paolo 1528-1588 *IntDcAA 90, WorAlBi*
Veronesi, Judith M. 1946- *St&PR 91*
Veronis, Peter 1923- *WhoAm 90*
Verostko, Roman Joseph 1929- *WhoAmA 91*
Verosub, Kenneth Lee 1944- *WhoAm 90*
Verpent, Gregory 1947- *St&PR 91*
Verplanck, Gulian Crommelin 1786-1870 *BioIn 16*
Verplanck, William Samuel 1916- *WhoAm 90*
Verplank, Scott *BioIn 16*
Verplanke, Anna Louise 1935- *WhoAmW 91*
Verral, Charles Spain *NewYTBS 90*
Verral, Charles Spain 1904- *AuBYP 90, WhoWor 91*
Verral, Charles Spain 1904-1990 *BioIn 16, ConAu 131*
Verrall, Arthur Woollgar 1851-1912 *EncO&P 3*
Verrall, Margaret de Gaudrion Merrifield 1859-1916 *EncO&P 3, EncPaPR 91*
Verrant, James J. 1938- *St&PR 91*
Verrazano, Giovanni da 1485?-1527 *BioIn 16*
Verrazano, Giovanni Da 1485?-1528? *EncCRAm, WhNaAH, WorAlBi*
Verrazzano, Giovanni da 1485?-1528? *WhNaAH*
Verreault, Richard *BiDrAPA 89*
Verrecchia, Alfred J. 1943- *St&PR 91, WhoAm 90*
Verrecchia, Robert Ernest 1949- *WhoAm 90*
Verret, Joseph Marc 1953- *BiDrAPA 89, WhoE 91*
Verret, Steve *BioIn 16*
Verrett, Shirley *BioIn 16*
Verrett, Shirley 1931- *DrBlPA 90, IntWWM 90, PenDiMP, WhoAm 90, WhoWor 91*
Verrette, Joyce 1939- *ConAu 129*
Verrette, Louise Madeleine 1949- *WhoWrEP 89*
Verri, Carlo *BioIn 16*
Verrier, John J. 1935- *St&PR 91*
Verrill, Addison H. *St&PR 91N*
Verrill, Charles Owen, Jr. 1937- *WhoAm 90, WhoE 91*
Verrill, Dana C. *St&PR 91*
Verrill, David C. 1943- *St&PR 91*
Verrill, F. Glenn 1923- *WhoAm 90, WhoWor 91*
Verrill, W. David 1928- *St&PR 91*
Verrocchio, Andrea del 1435-1488 *IntDcAA 90*
Verroust, Denis 1958- *IntWWM 90*
Verry, James Edward 1953- *WhoE 91*
Verry, William Robert 1933- *WhoWor 91*
Versacci, Alfred C. 1942- *St&PR 91*
Versace, Gianni 1946- *BioIn 16, ConDes 90, WhoWor 91*
Versace, Richard 1940- *WhoAm 90*
Versage, Linda Marie 1956- *WhoAmW 91*
Versales, Gilda R D R *BiDrAPA 89*
Versalie, Robert M. 1931- *St&PR 91*
Versalles, Zoilo 1939- *Ballpl 90*
Verschoor, Curtis Carl 1931- *WhoAm 90*
Verschraegen, Herman Elie Bertha 1936- *IntWWM 90*
Vershbow, Arthur *St&PR 91*
Versmold, Hans Theodor 1937- *WhoWor 91*
Versnel, Hendrik Simon 1936- *WhoWor 91*
Verson, Karol Ruth 1939- *WhoAmW 91*
Verst, Paul Thomas 1957- *St&PR 91*
Verst, William G. 1931- *St&PR 91*
Verstandig, Lee Lovely 1937- *WhoE 91*
Ver Steeg, Clarence Lester 1922- *WhoAm 90, WhoWor 91, WhoWrEP 89*
Ver Steeg, Donna Lorraine Frank 1929- *WhoAmW 91*
Versteeg, Frans Anton 1954- *WhoWor 91*
Verstringhe, Marc Emile Sidonie 1934- *WhoWor 91*
Vert, Paul 1933- *WhoWor 91*
Verter, Mini 1949- *BiDrAPA 89*
Vertes, Marcel 1895-1961 *WhoAmA 91N*
Vertes, Victor 1927- *WhoAm 90*
Vertin, Thomas *St&PR 91*
Vertlieb, Steve 1945- *WhoWrEP 89*
Vertopoulos, Stefanos *St&PR 91*
Vertreace, Martha Modena 1945- *WhoWrEP 89*
Verts, Lita Jeanne 1935- *WhoAmW 91*
Vertucci, Frank L. 1914- *St&PR 91*
Vertuel, Monique Meryse 1950- *WhoWor 91*
Vervaet, Jozef Florent 1948- *WhoWor 91*
Vervier, Joseph John 1940- *WhoE 91*
Verville, Anne-Lee *BioIn 16*
Verville, Anne-Lee 1945- *WhoE 91*
Vervliet, E.M. *EncCoWW*
Vervoordeldonk, Rene 1952- *WhoWor 91*
Verweyen, Theodor 1937- *WhoWor 91*
Verwoerd, Hendrik F. 1901-1966 *WorAlBi*
Verwoerd, Hendrik Frensch 1901-1966 *BioIn 16*
Verwoerdt, Adriaan *BiDrAPA 89*
Verwoerdt, Adriaan 1927- *WhoAm 90*
Verwys, Bonnie 1934- *WhoAmW 91*
Verwys, David Allen 1948- *St&PR 91*
Verwys, Phillip Marvin 1952- *St&PR 91*
Veryzer, Tom 1953- *Ballpl 90*
Verzar, Christine B 1940- *WhoAmA 91*
Verzelini, Giacomo 1522-1606 *PenDiDA 89*
Verzone, Ronald Dickens 1947- *WhoE 91*
Verzosa, Purificacion Lahoz 1914- *WhoWor 91*
Verzosa, Rogelio Cueto *BiDrAPA 89*
Verzyl, June Carol 1928- *WhoAmA 91*
Verzyl, Kenneth H 1922- *WhoAmA 91*
Vesaas, Halldis Moren 1907- *DcScanL, EncCoWW*
Vesaas, Tarjei 1897-1970 *DcScanL*
Vesak, Norbert *NewYTBS 90*
Vesak, Norbert Franklin 1936- *WhoAm 90, WhoWor 91*
Vesalius, Andreas 1514-1564 *BioIn 16, WorAlBi*
Vesce, James J 1950- *BiDrAPA 89*
Vescovi, Ricardo 1948- *WhoWor 91*
Vescovo, Giorgio 1941- *St&PR 91*
Veselitskaya, Lidia Ivanovna 1857-1936 *EncCoWW*
Vesely, Alexander 1926- *WhoAm 90, WhoWor 91*
Vesely, Donald V. 1929- *St&PR 91*
Vesely, Kenneth Donald 1936- *St&PR 91*
Vesen'ev, Iv. *EncCoWW*
Vesey, A 1939- *SmATA 62*
Vesey, Elizabeth 1715?-1791 *FemiCLE*
Vesey, Elizabeth Handcock 1715?-1791 *BioIn 16*
Vesey, Gary Lee 1928- *St&PR 91*
Vesich, Julie *BioIn 16*
Veski, Erik 1952- *WhoE 91*
Vesnaver, Donna Marie 1964- *WhoE 91*
Vespa, Ned Angelo 1942- *WhoAm 90*
Vesper, Bruce Eugene 1951- *WhoE 91*
Vesper, Gerald Wallace 1932- *WhoAm 90*
Vesperi, Maria Davoren 1951- *WhoAmW 91*
Vespo, Jo Ellen 1956- *WhoAmW 91*
Vespucci, Amerigo 1451-1512 *BioIn 16*
Vespucci, Amerigo 1454-1512 *EncCRAm, WorAlBi*
Vespucci, Richard Joseph 1952- *WhoE 91*
Vessey, John William, Jr. 1922- *WhoAm 90*
Vessey, Judith Ann 1951- *WhoAmW 91*
Vessot, Robert Frederick Charles 1930- *WhoAm 90*
Vest, Charles Marstiller 1941- *WhoAm 90, WhoE 91, WhoWor 91*
Vest, Frank Harris, Jr. 1936- *WhoSSW 91*
Vest, George B. 1895-1989 *BioIn 16*
Vest, George Graham 1930- *WhoAm 90*
Vest, George Southall 1918- *WhoAm 90*
Vest, Hyrum Grant, Jr. 1935- *WhoAm 90*
Vest, John Charles 1949- *WhoSSW 91*
Vest, Jon Phillip 1949- *St&PR 91*
Vest, Marlyn Marie 1947- *WhoAmW 91*
Vest, Marvin Lewis 1906- *WhoAm 90*
Vest, Mary Elizabeth 1954- *WhoAmW 91*
Vest, Randy Johnson 1949- *St&PR 91*
Vest, Robert Wilson 1930- *WhoAm 90*
Vestal, Addison Alexander 1905- *WhoWor 91*
Vestal, David 1924- *WhoAmA 91*
Vestal, George A. 1927- *St&PR 91*
Vestal, George Alexander 1927- *WhoAm 90*
Vestal, Jeanne Marie Goodspeed 1930- *WhoAm 90, WhoAmW 91*
Vestal, John Harrison 1951- *WhoSSW 91*
Vestal, Kirk R. 1957- *BiDrAPA 89*
Vestal, Lucian LaRoe 1925- *WhoAm 90*
Vestal, Robert 1933- *ODwPR 91*
Vestal, Tommy Ray 1939- *WhoWor 91*
Vestergaard-Jensen, Svend 1941- *WhoWor 91*
Vestergren, Hakan 1930- *WhoWor 91*
Vestmar, Brigel Johannes Ahlmann 1937- *WhoWor 91*
Vestris, Lucia Elizabeth 1797-1856 *PenDiMP*
Vestris, Lucia Elizabeth Bartolozzi 1797-1856 *BioIn 16*
Vetere, Colleen Marie 1957- *WhoAmW 91, WhoSSW 91*
Vetere, Robert Louis 1949- *WhoEmL 91*
Veteri, Paul A. 1941- *St&PR 91*
Vetog, Edwin Joseph 1921- *St&PR 91, WhoAm 90*
Vetrano, Anthony Philip 1946- *St&PR 91*
Vetrano, Joseph S 1945- *BiDrAPA 89*
Vetrano Tiberge, J. Bea 1956- *WhoAmW 91*
Vetri, Peter Joseph 1955- *St&PR 91*
Vets, Jean-Pierre 1950- *WhoWor 91*
Vetsch, Gordon Joseph 1954- *WhoEmL 91*
Vett, Carl Christian 1871-1956 *EncO&P 3*
Vette, John Lyle, III 1937- *St&PR 91*
Vette, John R. 1935- *St&PR 91*
Vetter, Betty M. *BioIn 16*
Vetter, Betty McGee 1924- *WhoAm 90*
Vetter, Charles Richard 1927- *St&PR 91*
Vetter, Edward Oswald 1920- *WhoSSW 91*
Vetter, Emily Durso 1950- *WhoAmW 91*
Vetter, Frank William 1936- *St&PR 91*
Vetter, Herbert 1920- *WhoAm 90*
Vetter, James George, Jr. 1934- *WhoAm 90, WhoSSW 91*
Vetter, John Joseph *BiDrAPA 89*
Vetter, Mary Margaret 1945- *WhoAmW 91*
Vetter, Philip L. 1954- *St&PR 91*
Vetter, Robert Steven 1956- *WhoSSW 91*
Vetter, Udo Johannes 1954- *WhoE 91*
Vettorazzi, Gaston 1928- *WhoWor 91*
Vettori, Ernst *BioIn 16*
Vetulani, Jerzy Adam 1936- *WhoWor 91*
Veuhoff, Heinz 1933- *WhoWrEP 89*
Veuthey, Pierre Louis 1931- *BiDrAPA 89*
Veuve, Michael L. *St&PR 91*
Vever, Henri 1854-1942 *PenDiDA 89*
Vever, Paul 1851-1915 *PenDiDA 89*
Veverica, Henry William 1927- *St&PR 91*
Veveris, Ieva *BiDrAPA 89*
Veverka, George F. 1927- *St&PR 91*
Vevers, Gwynne 1916-1988 *BioIn 16*
Vevers, Henry Gwynne 1916-1988 *BioIn 16*
Vevers, Tony 1926- *WhoAmA 91*
Vevier, Charles 1924- *WhoAm 90*
Vevoda, Ernest 1927- *St&PR 91*
Vey, Edward L. 1942- *St&PR 91*
Veysey, Arthur Ernest 1914- *WhoAm 90*
Vezeau, Jeannette Eva 1913- *WhoAm 90*
Vezelay, Paule 1892- *BiDWomA*
Vezer, Arpad 1957- *WhoWor 91*
Vezeridis, Michael Panagiotis 1943- *WhoE 91*
Vezin, Jean 1933- *WhoWor 91*
Vezina, George Robert 1935- *WhoAm 90*
Vezina, Martin 1962- *BiDrAPA 89*
Vezina, Monique 1935- *WhoAm 90, WhoAmW 91, WhoE 91*
Veziroglu, Turhan Nejat 1924- *WhoAm 90*
Vezys, Gintautas 1926- *WhoAmA 91*
Vezzetti, Thomas *BioIn 16*
Vezzi, Francesco 1651-1740 *PenDiDA 89*
Vgontzas, Alexandros 1953- *BiDrAPA 89*
Via, Sara Stephenson 1942- *WhoAmW 91*
Via, Susan R. 1951- *WhoAmW 91*
Viacava, Lillian D. *WhoAmW 91*
Viada, Raul Manuel *BiDrAPA 89*
Vial, Pedro 1746?-1814 *WhNaAH*
Vialardi, Enzo Joseph 1936- *St&PR 91*
Vialis, Gaston *ConAu 129, MajTwCW*
Viall, Paul G., Jr. 1946- *St&PR 91*
Viall, Richmond 1920- *WhoE 91*
Vialle, Karen *WhoAmW 91*
Viamontes, Jorge A 1923- *BiDrAPA 89*
Vian, Orfeo 1924-1989 *WhoAmA 91N*
Viana, Javier de 1868-1926 *HispWr 90*
Vianen, Adam 1569?-1627 *PenDiDA 89*
Vianen, Bea 1935- *EncCoWW*
Vianen, Christiaen 1600?-1667 *PenDiDA 89*
Vianen, Paulus van 1570?-1613 *PenDiDA 89*
Viani, James L. 1932- *WhoAm 90*
Vianney, Jean Baptiste Marie 1786-1859 *BioIn 16*
Viano, David Charles 1946- *WhoAm 90*
Viano, Fernando 1933- *BiDrAPA 89*
Viardot, Louise Pauline Marie Heritte- 1841-1919 *BioIn 16*
Viardot, Pauline Garcia 1821-1910 *BioIn 16*
Viardot-Garcia, Pauline 1821-1910 *PenDiMP*
Viart, Guy Pascal 1957- *WhoEmL 91, WhoWor 91*
Viat, Marijane 1939- *WhoAmW 91*
Viator, Ray 1952- *ODwPR 91*
Viau, Charles-Theodore 1843-1898 *DcCanB 12*
Vibat, Edison Munar 1931- *WhoWor 91*
Vibber, Foster Lane 1906- *BiDrAPA 89*
Vibe, Kjeld 1927- *WhoWor 91*
Vibet, Claude Yves Maurice 1942- *WhoWor 91*
Vibia Perpetua, Saint *BioIn 16*
Vicar, Henry *AuBYP 90*
Vicars, Richard John 1940- *St&PR 91*
Vicary, Thomas C. 1941- *St&PR 91*
Vicary, William Tice 1943- *BiDrAPA 89*
Viccajee, Victor Framjee 1903- *IntWWM 90*
Viccellio, Charles Steele 1960- *WhoSSW 91*
Viccellio, Nancy Blair 1914- *WhoSSW 91*
Vice, LaVonna Lee 1952- *WhoAmW 91, WhoE 91, WhoWor 91*
Vice, Royden T. *St&PR 91*
Vicente, Esteban *BioIn 16*
Vicente, Esteban 1903- *WhoAmA 91*
Vicente, Gil *PenDiDA 89*
Vicente, Jose Alberto 1954- *WhoHisp 91*
Vicente, Traci Elizabeth 1963- *WhoAmW 91*
Vici, Andrea Busiri 1903-1989 *BioIn 16*
Vicioso, Enrique E 1922- *BiDrAPA 89*
Vick, Alfred 1925- *St&PR 91*
Vick, Connie R 1947- *WhoAmA 91*
Vick, John Braxton, Jr. 1952- *WhoAm 90*
Vick, Judith Anola 1939- *WhoAmW 91*
Vick, Marie 1922- *WhoAm 90*
Vick, Randol Johnson 1959- *WhoSSW 91*
Vick, Robert Louis 1946- *St&PR 91*
Vick, William Edward, Jr. 1958- *WhoWrEP 89*
Vickar, Garry Martin 1946- *BiDrAPA 89*
Vicker, Angus *AuBYP 90*
Vicker, John *PenDiDA 89*
Vicker, Ray 1917- *WhoAm 90, WhoWor 91, WhoWrEP 89*
Vickerman, Keith 1933- *WhoWor 91*
Vickers, Allen Douglas, Jr. 1949- *WhoAm 90*
Vickers, Claude Leon 1943- *WhoSSW 91*
Vickers, Clinton John 1941- *WhoE 91*
Vickers, David Leroy 1942- *St&PR 91, WhoWor 91*
Vickers, Edward Davin 1945- *WhoWrEP 89*
Vickers, Geoffrey 1894-1982 *DcNaB 1981*
Vickers, Hugo *BioIn 16*
Vickers, James Hudson 1930- *WhoAm 90, WhoWor 91*
Vickers, Jon 1926- *BioIn 16, IntWWM 90, PenDiMP, WorAlBi*
Vickers, Montez Moser 1953- *WhoAmW 91*
Vickers, Naomi R. 1917- *WhoAmW 91*
Vickers, Raymond *BiDrAPA 89*
Vickers, Roger Spencer 1937- *WhoAm 90*
Vickers, Roy C 1888?-1965 *TwCCr&M 91*
Vickers, Rube 1878-1958 *Ballpl 90*
Vickers, Russ 1923- *WhoAmA 91*
Vickers, Thomas H. *St&PR 91*
Vickers, Thomas Joseph 1939- *WhoSSW 91*
Vickers, Thomas Wesley 1945- *WhoSSW 91*
Vickery, Byrdean Eyvonne Hughes 1928- *WhoAmW 91*
Vickery, Charles Bridgeman 1913- *WhoAmA 91*
Vickery, Clement C 1922- *BiDrAPA 89*
Vickery, Diane M *BiDrAPA 89*
Vickery, Eugene Livingstone 1913- *WhoWor 91*

Vickery, Harold Kirby, Jr. 1941- WhoWor 91
Vickery, Hubert Bradford 1893-1978 DcScB S2
Vickery, James Alexander 1931- St&PR 91
Vickery, Jim Dale 1951- WhoWrEP 89
Vickery, Loyd Thomas, Jr. 1943- WhoSSW 91
Vickery, Sukey 1779-1821 FemiCLE
Vicknair, Tommy J. 1943- St&PR 91
Vickrey, Barry Roland 1950- WhoEmL 91
Vickrey, Herta Miller WhoAmW 91
Vickrey, Robert Remsen 1926- WhoAm 90, WhoAmA 91
Vickrey, Roy L. 1937- St&PR 91
Vicky 1913-1966 BioIn 16
Vico, Enea 1520?-1567 PenDiDA 89
Vico, Paul 1946- WhoE 91
Victor Emmanuel II, King of Italy 1820-1878 BioIn 16
Victor, A. Paul 1938- WhoAm 90
Victor, Bruce Scott BiDrAPA 89
Victor, David BioIn 16
Victor, David 1910?-1989 ConAu 130
Victor, David Gregory 1954- WhoE 91
Victor, Ed BioIn 16
Victor, Ernesto Rodrigues 1931- WhoWor 91
Victor, Frances 1826-1902 FemiCLE
Victor, Frances Fuller 1826-1902 WhNaAH
Victor, Janet Marshall 1914- WhoAm 90
Victor, Mario T. 1913- St&PR 91
Victor, Mary O'Neill 1924- WhoAmA 91
Victor, Metta 1831-1885 FemiCLE
Victor, Michael T. 1961- St&PR 91
Victor, Richard Michael 1929- WhoAm 90
Victor, Richard Steven 1949- WhoEmL 91, WhoWor 91
Victor, Robert E. 1929- St&PR 91
Victor, Robert Eugene 1929- WhoAm 90
Victor, Ronald Joseph, Jr. 1964- WhoE 91
Victor, Sherri Beth 1959- WhoAmW 91
Victor, Simon L BiDrAPA 89
Victor, Thomas BioIn 16
Victor, William W. 1924- St&PR 91
Victor, William Weir 1924- WhoAm 90
Victoria 1819-1901 EncPaPR 91, WomWR [port], WorAlBi
Victoria, Queen 1819-1901 EncO&P 3, FemiCLE
Victoria, Queen of Great Britain 1819-1901 BioIn 16
Victoria, Anthony BioIn 16
Victoria, Guadalupe 1789?-1843 BioIn 16
Victoria, Vesta 1874-1951 OxCPMus
Victoria-Franken, Bonnie Gay 1958- WhoEmL 91
Victorio 1825?-1880 WhNaAH
Victoroff, Jeffrey Ivan BiDrAPA 89
Victoroff, Victor M 1918- BiDrAPA 89
Victory, A. Michael 1934- St&PR 91
Victory, Antony Michael 1934- WhoAm 90
Victory, Gerard 1921- IntWWM 90
Victory-Hannisian, Kathleen Mary 1961- WhoAmW 91
Vicuna, Patricio Ricardo 1953- WhoHisp 91
Vicuna Mackenna, Benjamin 1831-1886 BioIn 16
Vida, Judith Ellen 1943- BiDrAPA 89
Vida, Stephen BiDrAPA 89
Vidal, Eduardo Rene 1957- WhoE 91
Vidal, Francisco Fernandez 1946- WhoAmA 91
Vidal, Gore TwCCr&M 91
Vidal, Gore 1925- BioIn 16, MajTwCW, WhoAm 90, WhoWrEP 89, WorAlBi
Vidal, Hahn 1919- WhoAmA 91
Vidal, Jacques Georges 1928- WhoWor 91
Vidal, K.J. 1943- St&PR 91
Vidal, Marcos Antonio 1937- WhoSSW 91
Vidal, Mary 1815-1869 FemiCLE
Vidal, Ricardo 1931- WhoWor 91
Vidal, Robert Emile 1927- St&PR 91
Vidal, Ulises WhoHisp 91
Vidal, Yves BioIn 16
Vidali, Roberto 1953- WhoWor 91
Vidalin, Robert BioIn 16
Vidalis, Orestis Efthimios 1917- WhoWor 91
Vidanagama, Bandupriya P 1939- BiDrAPA 89
Vidas, Scott Quinn 1953- WhoEmL 91
Vidaud-Bobes, Cibeles E BiDrAPA 89
Vidaurri, Alfredo Garcia 1930- WhoHisp 91
Vidaver, Robert M BiDrAPA 89
Videan, Ann Narcisian 1959- WhoAmW 91, WhoEmL 91
Videla, Felipe G 1937- BiDrAPA 89
Videla, Gabriel Gonzalez 1898-1980 BioIn 16
Videla, Jorge Rafael 1925- BioIn 16
Viderman, Linda Jean 1957- WhoSSW 91
Videtti, Nicholas A. 1957- BiDrAPA 89
Videtti, Nicholas F BiDrAPA 89
Vidic, Branislav 1934- WhoE 91
Vidmar, J Ted, III 1939- BiDrAPA 89
Vidor, King 1895-1982 BioIn 16
Vidor, Robert BiDrAPA 89
Vidov, Oleg BioIn 16
Vidovic, Agnes Ann 1929- WhoAmW 91
Vidovszky, Laszlo 1944- IntWWM 90
Vidueira, Joe R. 1963- WhoHisp 91
Vie, Richard C. 1937- St&PR 91
Vie, Richard Carl 1937- WhoAm 90
Viebig, Clara 1860-1952 BioIn 16
Viederman, Milton 1930- BiDrAPA 89, WhoE 91
Viederman, Stephen 1935- WhoE 91
Viedt, Conrad 1893-1943 WorAlBi
Viegas, Francis J. 1929- St&PR 91
Viegas, Kenneth Dell 1931- WhoHisp 91
Viegas, Louis Paul 1940- WhoE 91
Viegbesie, Anthony O'Chuko 1955- WhoSSW 91
Viehe, John S. 1937- St&PR 91
Viehl, Steven L. 1951- St&PR 91
Viehman, John W. 1929- St&PR 91
Viehman, John William 1929- WhoAm 90
Viehman, Russel R. 1928- St&PR 91
Vieillard-Baron, Bertrand Louis 1940- WhoWor 91
Vieira, Asia BioIn 16
Vieira, Carlos Jose 1937- WhoWor 91
Vieira, David John 1950- WhoEmL 91
Vieira, Joao Bernardo 1939- WhoWor 91
Vieira, Meredith BioIn 16
Vieira, Michael John 1953- WhoWrEP 89
Vieira, N.J. 1934- St&PR 91
Vieira Da Silva, Maria Elena 1908- BiDWomA
Viele, Arnout Cornelissen 1640-1704? EncCRAm
Viele, George Brookins 1932- WhoSSW 91
Viele, William A BiDrAPA 89
Vielehr, William Ralph 1945- WhoAmA 91
Vieley, Jill Marie 1964- WhoEmL 91
Vielhauer, Michelle Renee 1964- WhoAmW 91
Vielman-Tejeda, Liza Maria 1955- WhoWor 91
Vielstich, Johann Christian PenDiDA 89
Viemeister, Tucker L. 1948- WhoE 91
Viene, Lawrence Edward 1948- WhoEmL 91
Viener, John David 1939- WhoAm 90
Viener, Seymour J 1932- BiDrAPA 89
Vienot, Marc BioIn 16
Vienot, Marc Andre 1928- WhoWor 91
Viens, Kenneth P. 1951- St&PR 91
Viens, Nancy Fitz-Gerald 1932- WhoWrEP 89
Viera, Antonio Torres 1962- WhoHisp 91
Viera, Charles David 1950- WhoAmA 91
Viera, James Joseph 1940- St&PR 91, WhoAm 90
Viera, John Joseph 1932- St&PR 91, WhoAm 90
Viera, Ricardo 1945- WhoAmA 91
Vierbuchen, Richard C. 1927- St&PR 91
Vierck, Charles John, Jr. 1936- WhoAm 90
Viereck, Ellen 1928- AuBYP 90
Viereck, Peter 1916- WhoAm 90, WhoWrEP 89
Viereck, Phillip R. 1925- AuBYP 90
Vieregg, James Robert 1950- St&PR 91
Vierleger, Barnaert PenDiDA 89
Viermetz, Kurt F. 1939- WhoAm 90
Vierny, Dina 1919?- BioIn 16
Vierra, Fred A. 1931- St&PR 91
Viers, Johnny Frank 1942- WhoSSW 91
Viertel, Joseph 1915- St&PR 91
Viertel, Thomas M. 1941- St&PR 91
Vierthaler, Alan William 1948- St&PR 91
Vierthaler, Bonnie WhoAmA 91
Vieru, Anatol 1926- IntWWM 90
Vieser, Milford August 1903- WhoAm 90
Vieser, Richard W. 1927- St&PR 91
Vieser, Richard William 1927- WhoAm 90, WhoE 91
Viesselman, John O 1941- BiDrAPA 89
Viest, Ivan Miroslav 1922- WhoAm 90
Viesulas, Romas 1918- WhoAmA 91N
Vieta, Franciscus 1540-1603 WorAlBi
Viete, Francois 1540-1603 BioIn 16
Vieth, Charles A 1920- BiDrAPA 89
Vieth, G. Duane 1923- WhoAm 90
Vieth, George W., Jr. 1955- St&PR 91
Vieth, John C. 1942- St&PR 91
Vieth, Wolf Randolph 1934- WhoAm 90
Vietor, Harold Duane 1931- WhoAm 90
Vietor, Marjorie C. BioIn 16
Vietoris, Leopold 1891- WhoWor 91
Viets, Hermann 1943- WhoAm 90
Viets, Karen Joyce 1963- WhoAmW 91
Viets, Marina Woroniecka BioIn 16
Viets, Robert O. 1943- WhoAm 90
Viets, Robert Oscar 1943- St&PR 91
Viets, Roger 1738-1811 DcLB 99
Vieu, Louis-Charles, Mme EncCoWW
Vieuxtemps, Henry 1820-1881 PenDiMP
Vieweg, W Victor R 1934- BiDrAPA 89
Vig, Peter R. 1940- St&PR 91
Vig, Pradeep Kumar 1954- WhoSSW 91
Vig, Vernon Edward 1937- WhoAm 90
Vigay, Denis 1926- IntWWM 90
Vigdor, Irving 1929- St&PR 91
Vigdor, Moshe 1947- WhoWor 91
Vigdor, Robert C 1947- BiDrAPA 89
Vigdorova, Frida 1915-1965 EncCoWW
Vigee-Le Brun, Elisabeth 1755-1842 IntDcAA 90
Vigee-Lebrun, Louise-Elisabeth 1755-1842 BioIn 16
Vigerstad, Alice Emily Frost 1907- WhoAmW 91
Vigfusson, Bjarni DcScanL
Viggiano, Victor A. 1925- St&PR 91
Vigier, Marc-Noel 1935- WhoWor 91
Vigil, Allan R. 1947- WhoHisp 91
Vigil, Arthur 1955- MusmAFA
Vigil, Arthur Margarito 1942- WhoHisp 91
Vigil, Charles S. 1912- WhoAm 90, WhoWor 91
Vigil, Daniel A. 1947- WhoHisp 91
Vigil, David Charles 1944- WhoWor 91
Vigil, Diego ConAu 130
Vigil, Donaciano 1802-1877 BioIn 16
Vigil, James Diego 1938- ConAu 130
Vigil, John Carlos 1939- WhoHisp 91
Vigil, Manuel 1900- MusmAFA
Vigil, Martina 1856-1916 BioIn 16
Vigil, Ralph H. 1932- BioIn 16, WhoHisp 91
Vigil, Samuel F., Jr. WhoHisp 91
Vigil, Veloy Joseph 1931- WhoAmA 91
Vigil-Giron, Rebecca 1954- WhoHisp 91
Vigil-Giron, Rebecca D. 1954- WhoAm 90, WhoAmW 91
Vigil-Perez, Angie WhoHisp 91
Vigil-Pinon, Evangelina WhoHisp 91
Vigilante, Joseph Louis 1925- WhoAm 90
Vigilante, Rose-Anne BioIn 16
Vigler, Mildred Sceiford 1914- WhoAmW 91
Viglianco, Marsha Louise 1956- WhoAmW 91
Vigliatore, Leonard James 1954- WhoE 91
Viglienzone, James 1953- St&PR 91
Vigmo, Josef 1922- WhoWor 91
Vigna, Angelo Albert 1941- St&PR 91
Vigna, Gerald S. ODwPR 91
Vigna, Judith 1936- AuBYP 90
Vignal, Philippe 1951- WhoWor 91
Vignali, Carl Louis 1934- WhoSSW 91
Vignat, Jean-Pierre 1940- WhoWor 91
Vignaud, Henry 1830-1922 BioIn 16
Vignaud, J. L. 1943- WhoWor 91
Vigneau, Nance Jean 1952- WhoAmW 91
Vigneault, Gilles 1928- BioIn 16
Vigneault, Lucien St&PR 91
Vigneault, Nelson 1951- ConDes 90
Vignelli, Lella BioIn 16
Vignelli, Lella 1936- ConDes 90
Vignelli, Lella Elena WhoAm 90
Vignelli, Massimo BioIn 16
Vignelli, Massimo 1931- ConDes 90, WhoAm 90
Vigneri, Joseph William 1956- WhoEmL 91
Vignes, Michelle Marie WhoAmA 91
Vignier, Michel Robert 1948- WhoWor 91
Vignocchi, Madalena Joan 1952- WhoAmW 91
Vignola, Anthony J., Jr. 1946- WhoAm 90
Vignoles, Roger 1945- PenDiMP
Vignoles, Roger Hutton 1945- IntWWM 90
Vignolo, Biagio N. 1947- St&PR 91
Vignolo, Biagio Nickolas, Jr. 1947- WhoAm 90
Vignone, Ronald John 1941- WhoAm 90
Vignos, Janice A. St&PR 91
Vignos, Lawrence R. St&PR 91
Vignos, Susan Louise 1958- WhoAmW 91
Vigny, Alfred Victor, Comte De 1797-1863 WorAlBi
Vigny, Anne de la 1634-1684 EncCoWW
Vigo, Joseph Maria Francisco 1747-1836 EncCRAm
Vigoda, Abe 1921- BioIn 16, WorAlBi
Vigon, Larry BioIn 16
Vigor, Mrs. 1699-1783 FemiCLE
Vigor-Zierk, Carey 1952- BiDrAPA 89
Vigoreaux, Jose Ramon BiDrAPA 89
Vigran, Thomas Samuel 1950- BiDrAPA 89
Vigren, Suzanne Jo 1965- WhoAmW 91, WhoE 91
Vigtel, Gudmund 1925- WhoAm 90, WhoAmA 91, WhoSSW 91
Viguera, Laurel M. 1961- WhoAmW 91
Viguers, Ruth 1903-1971 AuBYP 90
Vihavainen, Timo Juhani 1947- WhoWor 91
Vihon, Charles F. 1937- WhoAm 90
Viidikas, Vicki 1948- FemiCLE
Viita, Lauri Arvi 1916-1965 DcScanL
Vijapura, Amit 1958- BiDrAPA 89
Vijapura, Ashit Kanaiyalal 1956- BiDrAPA 89
Vijapura, Dhvanit K 1961- BiDrAPA 89
Vijay, Gambhir Indo-Aryan 1946- WhoE 91
Vijayakumar, Sarojini 1944- BiDrAPA 89
Vijayakumaran, P G 1947- BiDrAPA 89
Vijayvargiya, Indira BiDrAPA 89
Vijh, Ashok Kumar 1938- WhoAm 90
Vik, Bjorg 1935- DcScanL, EncCoWW
Vik, Stanley Merle 1941- St&PR 91
Vikan, Gary Kent 1946- WhoE 91
Vikander, Richard A. 1927- St&PR 91
Vikar, Laszlo 1929- IntWWM 90
Vikas, Suniti BiDrAPA 89
Viker, Dacques 1965- WhoSSW 91
Viking, Nancy Lee 1943- WhoAmW 91
Vikis-Freibergs, Vaira 1937- WhoAm 90
Viklund, William Edwin 1940- St&PR 91, WhoAm 90
Vikova-Kuneticka, Bo'ena 1862- EncCoWW
Vikram, Revathi Kandarpa BiDrAPA 89
Viksnins, George Juris 1937- WhoE 91
Viksten, Albert 1889- AuBYP 90
Vila, Adis Maria 1953- WhoAm 90, WhoHisp 91
Vila, Aracelia 1942- ODwPR 91
Vila, Bob BioIn 16
Vila, Bob 1946- WhoHisp 91
Vila, Joe Ballpl 90
Vila, Joseph Spencer 1866-1934 BioIn 16
Vila, Robert Joseph 1946- WhoAm 90
Vila-Mascarell, Emilio 1937- WhoWor 91
Viladesau, Richard R., Jr. 1944- WhoHisp 91
Vilakazi, Benedict Wallet 1906-1947 TwCLC 37 [port]
Vilanova, Jose M BiDrAPA 89
Vilaplana, Jose M. 1927- WhoHisp 91
Vilar, Antonio 1944- St&PR 91
Vilar, Antonio Luis 1950- WhoWor 91
Vilardi, Ted, Jr. 1933- WhoE 91
Vilardo, Lawrence Joseph 1955- WhoEmL 91
Vilarino, Idea 1920- HispWr 90
Vilaro-Colon, Miguel A BiDrAPA 89
Vilas NewAgMG
Vilas, Guillermo BioIn 16
Vilas, William Freeman 1840-1908 BiDrUSE 89
Vilasuso, Adolfo Manuel BiDrAPA 89
Vilcek, Jan Tomas 1933- WhoAm 90
Vilches-O'Bourke, Octavio Augusto 1923- WhoSSW 91
Vilchez, Blanca Rosa 1957- WhoHisp 91
Vile, William 1700?-1767 PenDiDA 89
Vilen, Erik Olavi 1933- St&PR 91
Vilenskaya, Larissa 1948- EncPaPR 91
Viles, Daniel F. 1912- St&PR 91
Viles, Nicholas John 1962- WhoWor 91
Vilhjalmsson, Thor 1925- DcScanL
Vilim, Nancy Catherine 1952- WhoAmW 91
Vilinsky, Debra Fran 1955- BiDrAPA 89
Viljakainen, Raili 1954- IntWWM 90
Vilkin, Morris I 1922- BiDrAPA 89
Vilko, Naomi 1952- BiDrAPA 89
Vilko, Naomi Rella 1952- WhoE 91
Villa, Alvaro J. 1940- WhoHisp 91
Villa, Carlos WhoAmA 91
Villa, Carlos Cesar 1941- WhoHisp 91
Villa, Francisco 1878-1923 WorAlBi
Villa, John Joseph 1917- WhoHisp 91
Villa, Jose E 1926- BiDrAPA 89
Villa, Mario BioIn 16
Villa, Mario 1956- WhoAmA 91
Villa, Pancho 1878-1923 BioIn 16
Villa, Rita C. 1954- St&PR 91
Villa, Russell Steven 1957- St&PR 91
Villa, Theodore B 1936- WhoAmA 91
Villa-Flores, Adalberto 1955- WhoSSW 91
Villa-Komaroff, Lydia 1947- WhoAmW 91, WhoHisp 91
Villa-Lobos, Heitor BioIn 16
Villa-Lobos, Heitor 1887-1959 PenDiMP A, WorAlBi
Villablanca, Jaime Rolando 1929- WhoAm 90
Villaca, Lucio F M BiDrAPA 89
Villadsen, Villads 1945- WhoWor 91
Villafana, Manuel A. 1940- WhoHisp 91
Villafane, Angel De EncCRAm
Villafane, Helen 1944- WhoE 91
Villafane, Robert 1941- WhoHisp 91
Villafranca, Joseph J. 1944- WhoAm 90
Villafranca, Manuel V BiDrAPA 89
Villafuerte, Pablo Dandoy 1940- BiDrAPA 89
Villagonzalo, Amparo De la Cerna 1939- WhoAmW 91
Villagran Rodriguez, Dolores 1954- WhoHisp 91
Villalba, Abdon Enrique 1929- BiDrAPA 89
Villalba, Jorge Julian 1955- BiDrAPA 89
Villalba, Jovito 1908- BioIn 16
Villali, Jorge 1944- WhoE 91
Villalobos, Ruben L., Jr. 1946- WhoHisp 91
Villalobos Padilla, Francisco 1921- WhoAm 90

Villalon, Dalisay Manuel 1941- WhoAmW 91
Villalon, Ivan Orlando BiDrAPA 89
Villalon, Silvia Duran 1941- WhoAmW 91
Villalpando, Catalina V. 1940- BioIn 16
Villalpando, Catalina Vasquez WhoAm 90, WhoAmW 91
Villalpando, Catalina Vasquez 1940- WhoHisp 91
Villamanan, Manuel WhoHisp 91
Villamarin, Juan A. 1939- WhoHisp 91
Villamena, Anthony Francis 1944- BiDrAPA 89
Villamil, Jose Antonio 1946- WhoHisp 91
Villamil, Richard J. 1942- WhoE 91
Villamor, Catherine WhoHisp 91
Villandon, Marie-Jeanne L'Heritier de 1664-1734 EncCoWW
Villani, G. Joseph 1937- St&PR 91
Villani, Jim 1948- WhoWrEP 89
Villani, Kevin Emil 1948- WhoAm 90
Villani, Virginia S BiDrAPA 89
Villano, Joseph 1939-1990 BioIn 16
Villano, William N. 1943- St&PR 91
Villanueva, Alma Luz 1944- ConAu 131, HispWr 90, WhoHisp 91
Villanueva, Armando 1915- BioIn 16
Villanueva, Daniel 1937- BioIn 16
Villanueva, Dario 1950- WhoWor 91
Villanueva, David Jardio BiDrAPA 89
Villanueva, Edward 1935- St&PR 91
Villanueva, Edward Anthony 1946- WhoHisp 91
Villanueva, Jose Antonio WhoHisp 91
Villanueva, Jose E BiDrAPA 89
Villanueva, Ludovico S BiDrAPA 89
Villanueva, Miriam T BiDrAPA 89
Villanueva, Miriam Tankiang 1950- WhoE 91
Villanueva, Tino 1941- BioIn 16, HispWr 90, WhoHisp 91
Villapalos, Gustavo Salas 1949- WhoWor 91
Villar, Arturo Ignacio 1933- WhoHisp 91
Villar, Isabel Elsa 1948- WhoE 91
Villar, James Walter 1930- St&PR 91
Villar, Ofelia T BiDrAPA 89
Villar Mir, Juan-Miguel 1931- WhoWor 91
Villara, Joseph John BiDrAPA 89
Villard, de Honnecourt BioIn 16
Villard, Dimitri Serrano 1943- St&PR 91
Villard, Henry 1835-1900 BioIn 16, WorAlBi
Villard, Oswald Garrison 1872-1949 BioIn 16, WorAlBi
Villari, Linda 1836-1915 FemiCLE
Villarin, Adrian V BiDrAPA 89
Villarini, Pedro WhoHisp 91
Villarreal, Carlos Castaneda 1924- BioIn 16, WhoAm 90, WhoWor 91
Villarreal, David 1958- WhoHisp 91
Villarreal, Diana 1954- BiDrAPA 89
Villarreal, Fernando M. 1956- WhoHisp 91
Villarreal, G. Claude 1930- St&PR 91
Villarreal, Gloria Guerrero 1954- WhoEmL 91
Villarreal, Homer Anthony 1932- WhoHisp 91
Villarreal, Homero Atenogenes 1946- WhoAm 90
Villarreal, Humberto 1940- WhoHisp 91
Villarreal, Jesse M. 1939- St&PR 91
Villarreal, Jose Antonio BioIn 16
Villarreal, Jose Antonio 1924- HispWr 90
Villarreal, Martha Ellen 1942- WhoHisp 91
Villarreal, Richard 1929- BiDrAPA 89
Villarreal, Robert P. 1951- WhoHisp 91
Villarreal, Roberto E. WhoHisp 91
Villarreal, Romeo Manuel 1936- WhoHisp 91
Villarreal, Rosalva 1957- WhoHisp 91
Villarroel Lopez, Gualberto 1908-1946 BioIn 16
Villarrubia, Carolyn T 1937- BiDrAPA 89
Villarrubia, Jan 1948- WhoWrEP 89
Villars, Felix Marc Hermann 1921- WhoAm 90
Villasenor, Edmund ConAu 32NR, HispWr 90
Villasenor, Ranol F BiDrAPA 89
Villasenor, Victor ConAu 32NR, HispWr 90
Villasenor, Victor E 1940- ConAu 32NR, HispWr 90
Villasur, Pedro EncCRAm
Villaurrutia, Xavier 1903-1950 BioIn 16, HispWr 90
Villavecchia, Roberta Lee Griffin 1938- WhoAmW 91
Villaverde, Cirilo 1812-1894 BioIn 16
Villeda Morales, Ramon 1908-1971 BioIn 16
Villedieu, Madame de 1640?-1683 EncCoWW
Villee, Claude Alvin, Jr. 1917- WhoAm 90
Villegas, Carmen Milagros 1954- WhoHisp 91
Villegas, Daniel Cosio 1898-1976 BioIn 16
Villegas, Emilio 1943- WhoHisp 91
Villegas, J. Frank WhoHisp 91
Villella, Edward BioIn 16
Villella, Edward 1936- WorAlBi
Villella, Edward Joseph 1936- WhoAm 90, WhoSSW 91, WhoWor 91
Villemaire, Roland 1937- St&PR 91
Villemaire, Yolande 1949- BioIn 16
Villena, Milagros S BiDrAPA 89
Villeneuve, dame de 1695?-1755 EncCoWW
Villeneuve, Andre 1932- BiDrAPA 89
Villeneuve, Jocelyne 1941- ConAu 132
Villeneuve, Jocelyne Marie 1941- WhoWrEP 89
Villeneuve, Timothy 1966- St&PR 91
Villeponteaux, Virginia Anne 1959- BiDrAPA 89
Villeroy, Madame de EncCoWW
Villers, Philippe 1935- WhoAm 90
Villessot, Daniel Georges 1944- WhoWor 91
Villforth, John Carl 1930- WhoAm 90
Villiard, Paul 1910-1974 AuBYP 90, BioIn 16
Villiers, Alan John 1903- AuBYP 90
Villiers, George William Frederick 1800-1870 BioIn 16
Villines, Debianne 1955- WhoAmW 91
Villinski, Paul 1960- WhoAmA 91
Villion, Jean-Francois St&PR 91
Villoch, Kelly Carney 1950- WhoAmW 91
Villon, Francois 1431-1463? WorAlBi
Villon, Vladimar 1905-1976 WhoAmA 91N
Villone, Maryann 1951- WhoAmW 91
Villum, K DcScanL
Villwock, George F. 1928- St&PR 91
Viloria, Rosalinda C BiDrAPA 89
Vilpo, Juhani Antero 1945- WhoWor 91
Vilt, James Joseph BiDrAPA 89
Vilter, Richard William 1911- WhoAm 90
Vilzak, Anatole 1898- BioIn 16
Vimal, Richard NewAgMG
Vimalananda, Meenakshi 1948- BiDrAPA 89
Vimalananda, Samson G 1948- BiDrAPA 89
Vinacke, W. Edgar 1917- WhoWrEP 89
Vinao, Alejandro 1951- IntWWM 90
Vinarub, Murray E. 1934- St&PR 91
Vinas, D. HispWr 90
Vinas, David 1929?- HispWr 90
Vinatieri, John David 1942- WhoE 91
Vinay, Ramon 1912- IntWWM 90, PenDiMP
Vinazzer, Helmut Albert 1923- WhoWor 91
Vince, Clinton Andrew 1949- WhoE 91
Vince, Mary BiDrAPA 89
Vince, Michael Alexander 1935- WhoE 91
Vince, Terry 1929- St&PR 91
Vincel, Donald George 1940- St&PR 91
Vincelette, Muril D. 1931- St&PR 91
Vincelli, Mary Nicholas 1927- WhoAmW 91, WhoSSW 91
Vincens, Louis-Francois 1939- WhoWor 91
Vincent de Paul, Saint 1581-1660 BioIn 16, EncPaPR 91
Vincent, Anthony M. 1946- St&PR 91
Vincent, Bruce Havird 1947- WhoSSW 91, WhoWor 91
Vincent, Burton J. 1925- St&PR 91
Vincent, Charles Eagar, Jr. 1940- WhoAm 90
Vincent, Charles M. 1938- St&PR 91
Vincent, Claire ConAu 30NR
Vincent, Clare 1935- WhoAmA 91
Vincent, Clark Edward 1923- WhoAm 90
Vincent, Conway 1931- WhoAm 90
Vincent, David Eddy 1948- BiDrAPA 89
Vincent, David Paul 1943- St&PR 91
Vincent, David Ridgely 1941- WhoAm 90, WhoWor 91
Vincent, E. Duke 1932- St&PR 91
Vincent, Edward 1920- WhoAm 90
Vincent, Fay BioIn 16
Vincent, Fay 1938- Ballpl 90, NewYTBS 90 [port], News 90 [port]
Vincent, Fernand 1934- WhoWor 91
Vincent, Francis T., Jr. BioIn 16
Vincent, Francis Thomas, Jr. 1938- WhoAm 90, WhoE 91
Vincent, Frederick Michael 1948- WhoEmL 91, WhoWor 91
Vincent, Gabrielle BioIn 16, SmATA 61 [port]
Vincent, Gene 1935-1971 EncPR&S 89, OxCPMus
Vincent, Geoffrey Alan 1941- WhoWor 91
Vincent, H Bartlett, Jr. 1935- BiDrAPA 89
Vincent, Hal Wellman 1927- WhoAm 90
Vincent, Helen WhoWrEP 89
Vincent, James BiDrAPA 89
Vincent, James Louis 1939- St&PR 91, WhoAm 90, WhoWor 91
Vincent, Jan-Michael 1944- WorAlBi
Vincent, Jennifer G. 1956- BiDrAPA 89
Vincent, Joe Michael 1956- WhoSSW 91
Vincent, John Carter 1900-1972 BioIn 16
Vincent, John Heyl 1832-1920 WorAlBi
Vincent, Kay P. ODwPR 91
Vincent, Kenneth C. 1940- St&PR 91
Vincent, Leslie Joan 1959- WhoSSW 91
Vincent, Lloyd Drexell 1924- WhoAm 90, WhoSSW 91
Vincent, Margaret BiDrAPA 89
Vincent, Mary BioIn 16
Vincent, Michael Paul 1950- WhoE 91
Vincent, Nicholas F 1907- BiDrAPA 89
Vincent, Norman Fuller 1930- WhoAm 90
Vincent, Norman L. 1933- WhoAm 90
Vincent, Raymond 1928- St&PR 91
Vincent, Roger Bracher 1945- St&PR 91
Vincent, Ronald 1960- St&PR 91
Vincent, Sarah Anne 1833-1898 DcCanB 12
Vincent, Stenio 1874-1959 BioIn 16
Vincent, Thomas James 1934- WhoAm 90
Vincent, Tony 1946- WhoE 91
Vincent, Victor James 1958- WhoSSW 91
Vincent, Woody Durward 1934- St&PR 91
Vincent-Rodriguez, Kelli Ann 1961- WhoAmW 91
Vincenti, John Richard 1946- WhoE 91
Vincenti, Walter Guido 1917- WhoAm 90
Vincenti Mareri, Ippolito 1935- WhoWor 91
Vinchon, Jean 1884- EncO&P 3
Vinci, John Nicholas 1937- WhoAm 90
Vinci, Leonardo da 1452-1519 BioIn 16
Vinci, Vincent ODwPR 91
Vinciguerra, Ralph D. 1951- St&PR 91
Vinciguerra, Salvatore J. 1938- St&PR 91
Vinciguerra, Salvatore Joseph 1938- WhoAm 90
Vinciolo, F. PenDiDA 89
Vinciquerra, Anthony J, II 1950- BiDrAPA 89
Vinck, William Charles 1947- WhoEmL 91
Vinco, Ivo 1927- IntWWM 90
Vincola, Lyman David 1941- St&PR 91
Vincoli, Jeffrey Wayne 1959- WhoSSW 91
Vincow, Gershon 1935- WhoAm 90
Vind, Karl Damkjaer 1933- WhoWor 91
Vine, Allyn Collins 1914- BioIn 16, WhoAm 90
Vine, Barbara BioIn 16, ConAu 32NR, MajTwCW, TwCCr&M 91, WorAu 1980
Vine, Barbara 1930- BestSel 90-4 [port]
Vine, David 1943- IntWWM 90
Vine, David 1951- ODwPR 91
Vine, David Alexander 1951- WhoE 91, WhoEmL 91
Vine, Dorothy Goldberg 1943- St&PR 91
Vine, Janet Diana 1937- WhoWrEP 89
Vine, Phyllis 1945- ConAu 130
Vineberg, Arthur Martin 1903-1988 BioIn 16
Vineburgh, James Hollander 1943- WhoAm 90
Vinecour, Howard Mort BiDrAPA 89
Vinekar, Shreekumar S BiDrAPA 89
Vinella, Ray 1933- WhoAmA 91
Viner, Arthur William 1922- St&PR 91, WhoAm 90
Viner, Frank Lincoln 1937- WhoAmA 91
Viner, Jeanne ODwPR 91
Viner, Jesse 1951- BiDrAPA 89
Vines, Benito BioIn 16
Vines, Deborah Kaye 1961- WhoAmW 91
Vines, Dwight Delbert 1931- WhoSSW 91
Vines, Martha Timberlake 1951- WhoSSW 91
Vines, Pamela Lynn Dyson 1955- WhoAmW 91, WhoEmL 91, WhoWor 91
Vines, Ricardo 1875-1943 PenDiMP
Vines, William Joshua 1916- WhoWor 91
Vineyard, Bonney Jay 1939- WhoSSW 91
Vineyard, Mary Owens 1808-1877 BioAmW
Vineyard, Michael Gene 1944- St&PR 91
Vineyard, Phillis Smith 1924- St&PR 91
Vinge, Joan D. 1948- RGTwCSF
Vingo, James Ray 1938- St&PR 91, WhoAm 90
Vinha, Luiz Augusto Nogueira 1926- WhoWor 91
Vinick, Philip Brod 1951- WhoEmL 91
Vinik, Hymie Ronald 1932- WhoAm 90
Vining, Elizabeth Gray AuBYP 90
Vining, Elizabeth Gray 1902- EncJap, WhoAm 90
Vining, Glen W., Jr. 1939- St&PR 91
Vining, John Wiley 1942- St&PR 91
Vining, Joseph 1938- WhoAm 90
Vining, Leo Charles 1925- WhoAm 90
Vining, Michael Paul 1949- WhoE 91
Vining, Pamelia Sarah 1826-1897 DcCanB 12
Vining, Peggy Sue 1929- WhoWrEP 89
Vining, Robert Luke, Jr. 1931- WhoAm 90
Vinje, Aasmund Olavsson 1818-1870 DcScanL
Vinje-Morpurgo, Anselm 1934- WhoE 91
Vink, Frans 1918- WhoWor 91
Vinke, James Paul 1940- St&PR 91
Vinken, Pierre Jacques 1927- WhoWor 91
Vinne, Leonard van der PenDiDA 89
Vinney, Les C. 1948- St&PR 91
Vinocur, Edward William 1951- WhoEmL 91
Vinocur, M. Richard 1934- WhoAm 90
Vinocur, Patricia Ana 1961- WhoAmW 91
Vinod, Hrishikesh Dhundiraj 1939- WhoE 91
Vinograd, Jerome Ruben 1913-1976 DcScB S2
Vinogradoff, Anna Patricia WhoAmW 91
Vinogradov, Anatolii Kornelievich 1888-1946 BioIn 16
Vinogradov, Oleg BioIn 16
Vinogradov, Sophia 1958- BiDrAPA 89
Vinolus, Anastazy 1932- BiDrAPA 89
Vinolus, Elaine Ann BiDrAPA 89
Vinolus, Evelyn Marie 1956- BiDrAPA 89
Vinovich, Steve 1945- ConTFT 8 [port]
Vinson, B. Finley 1914- St&PR 91
Vinson, Bernard L. 1919- WhoE 91, WhoWor 91
Vinson, C. Roger 1940- WhoSSW 91
Vinson, Chuck BioIn 16
Vinson, Craig Olin 1950- WhoSSW 91
Vinson, Eddie BioIn 16
Vinson, Eddie 1917-1988 AnObit 1988
Vinson, Fred A BiDrAPA 89
Vinson, Frederick M. 1890-1953 WorAlBi
Vinson, Frederick Moore 1890-1953 BiDrUSE 89
Vinson, Jack Roger 1929- WhoE 91
Vinson, James A. 1945- WhoAm 90
Vinson, James Anthony 1945- St&PR 91
Vinson, James Spangler 1941- WhoAm 90
Vinson, Leila Terry Walker 1928- WhoAmW 91
Vinson, S. Bradleigh 1938- WhoSSW 91
Vinson, Sandra Tipton 1951- WhoAmW 91
Vinson, Shelly Garland 1954- WhoSSW 91
Vinson, Thomas Glenn 1923- St&PR 91
Vinson-Nieves, Anne Hartman 1959- WhoAmW 91
Vint, Karalee 1943- St&PR 91
Vint, Robert J. 1934- St&PR 91
Vint, Thelma Kineer BioIn 16
Vintas, Gustavo H 1948- BiDrAPA 89
Vintem, Antonio Feliciano Bento 1945- WhoWor 91
Vinter, Gilbert 1909-1969 OxCPMus
Vintiadis, Polyvios Constantine 1935- St&PR 91
Vinton, Bobby 1935- EncPR&S 89, WorAlBi
Vinton, Doris BioIn 16
Vinton, Iris AuBYP 90, BioIn 16
Vinton, John 1937- IntWWM 90
Vintras, Eugene 1807-1875 EncO&P 3
Vinueza, Tirso L 1926- BiDrAPA 89
Vinyard, Clarence Dale 1932- WhoAm 90
Vinz, Mark 1942- WhoWrEP 89
Vinzant, William Randall 1963- WhoSSW 91
Vinzing, Ute 1945- IntWWM 90
Viola EncCoWW
Viola, Bill 1951- WhoAmA 91
Viola, Frank 1960- Ballpl 90, BioIn 16, WorAlBi
Viola, Frank John, Jr. 1960- WhoAm 90
Viola, Herman Joseph 1938- WhoAm 90
Viola, Paul Richard BiDrAPA 89
Viola, Ronald James 1943- St&PR 91
Violand, Carol Ann 1954- WhoAmW 91
Violante, Joseph Anthony 1950- WhoEmL 91
Violet, Arlene BioIn 16
Violette, Daniel Markus 1951- St&PR 91
Violette, Diane Marie 1958- WhoAmW 91
Violette, E Jeffrey 1955- BiDrAPA 89
Violette, Edmond Jeffrey 1955- WhoE 91
Violette, Janice Freed BiDrAPA 89
Violi, D. William BioIn 16
Violi, Paul Randolph 1944- WhoWrEP 89
Violis, G. ConAu 129, MajTwCW
Viollet-le-Duc, Eugene-Emanuel 1814-1879 PenDiDA 89
Vionnet, Madeleine 1876-1975 ConDes 90
Viorst, Judith AuBYP 90, BioIn 16
Viorst, Judith Stahl 1931- WhoAm 90, WhoWrEP 89
Viorst, Milton 1930- WhoAm 90, WhoWrEP 89
Viosky, George Thomas 1935- St&PR 91
Viotti, Givanni Battista 1755-1824 PenDiMP
Viotti, Marcello 1954- IntWWM 90
Viox, Jim 1890-1969 Ballpl 90
Vip AuBYP 90
Vipond, Arthur 1832-1889 BioIn 16
Vipont, Elfrida 1902- BioIn 16
Vipperman, Joseph H. 1940- St&PR 91

Viquez, Cleto Gonzalez 1858-1937 *BioIn 16*
Vira, Naren R. 1949- *WhoE 91*
Virahsawmy, Dev 1942- *WhoWor 91*
Viramontes, Arnold 1948- *St&PR 91*
Viramontes, Julio Cesar *WhoHisp 91*
Virata, Cesar 1930- *WhoWor 91*
Virata, Maria Luisa Alfonso 1965- *WhoEmL 91*
Virato, Swami 1938- *WhoWrEP 89*
Viravaidya, Marisa *BioIn 16*
Virchow, Rudolf Ludwig Karl 1821-1902 *BioIn 16*
Virchow, Rudolph 1821-1902 *WorAlBi*
Virdon, Bill 1931- *Ballpl 90*
Viret, Margaret Mary 1913- *WhoAmA 91*
Virey, Maselle Gaerlan 1953- *BiDrAPA 89*
Virga, Karen Faye 1951- *WhoAmW 91*
Virgalitte, Anthony David 1949- *St&PR 91*
Virgil 70BC-19BC *WorAlBi*
Virgil, Ozzie 1933- *Ballpl 90, WhoHisp 91*
Virgil, Ozzie 1956- *Ballpl 90, WhoHisp 91*
Virgil, Richard *BiDrAPA 89*
Virgili, Marianne Kathleen 1948- *WhoAmW 91*
Virgilio, Abramo 1925- *St&PR 91*
Virgilio, Nick 1928-1989 *BioIn 16*
Virgillio, Lucien Joseph 1927- *WhoSSW 91*
Virgin Mary *BioIn 16*
Virgin, Cheri Lyn 1959- *WhoAmW 91*
Virgintino, Michael R. 1957- *ODwPR 91*
Virgo, John Michael 1943- *WhoWor 91*
Virgo, Julie Anne Carroll 1944- *WhoAm 90*
Virgo, Katherine Sue 1959- *WhoAmW 91*
Virgona, Hank 1929- *WhoAmA 91*
Virgona, Henry Peter 1929- *WhoE 91*
Virgous, Felix 1948- *MusmAFA*
Virkhaus, Taavo 1934- *IntWWM 90*
Virnig, Jerry T. 1932- *St&PR 91*
Virsaladze, Eliso 1942- *IntWWM 90*
Virsaladze, Simon 1909-1989 *BioIn 16*
Virshup, Edward Marc 1945- *St&PR 91*
Virtue, Joyce Swain 1936- *WhoAmW 91*
Virtue, Noel 1947- *ConAu 130*
Viry, Francois, I 1614-1689 *PenDiDA 89*
Viry, Francois, II 1659-1697 *PenDiDA 89*
Viry, Gaspard 1668-1720 *PenDiDA 89*
Viry, Jean-Baptiste, I 1671-1726 *PenDiDA 89*
Viry, Jean-Baptiste, II 1698-1750 *PenDiDA 89*
Viry, Joseph 1709-1759 *PenDiDA 89*
Virzi, Joseph A *BiDrAPA 89*
Virzi, Richard A. 1927- *St&PR 91*
Vis, Pieter 1949- *IntWWM 90*
Visa, Baba *EncCoWW*
Visanescu, Janet Winkler 1952- *WhoAmW 91*
Visca, Arturo Sergio 1917- *WhoWor 91*
Viscardi, Christopher James 1946- *WhoSSW 91*
Viscardi, Peter G. 1947- *WhoE 91*
Viscardi, Robert Thomas 1947- *WhoEmL 91*
Visceglia, Frank 1914- *St&PR 91*
Visceglia, Frank Diego *WhoE 91*
Visceglia, Frank Diego 1942- *St&PR 91*
Visceglia, Vincent 1905- *St&PR 91*
Viscelli, Therese Rauth 1955- *WhoAmW 91*
Vischer, Harold Harry 1914- *WhoAm 90*
Vischer, Lukas 1926- *ConAu 131*
Viscio, Donald P. 1934- *St&PR 91*
Visclosky, Peter John 1949- *WhoAm 90*
Visco, Anthony Salvatore 1948- *WhoAmA 91*
Visco, Denise Marie 1957- *WhoAmW 91*
Visco, Giuseppe 1927- *WhoWor 91*
Visco, Susan Josephine 1938- *WhoAmW 91*
Visconti, Janna Pearl 1952- *WhoAmW 91*
Visconti, Julius Arthur 1931- *St&PR 91*
Visconti, Luchino 1906-1976 *WorAlBi*
Visconti, Verde *BioIn 16*
Viscosi, Donna Lucia 1965- *WhoE 91*
Viscusi, Anthony 1932- *St&PR 91*
Viscusi, William G. Kip 1949- *WhoSSW 91, WhoWor 91*
Vise, Harry 1921- *St&PR 91*
Visee, Robert de 1660?-1725? *PenDiMP*
Visek, Willard James 1922- *WhoAm 90*
Visetti, Alberto 1846-1928 *PenDiMP*
Visha, Carla Antonette *BiDrAPA 89*
Visher, John S 1921- *BiDrAPA 89*
Vishnevskaya, Galina 1926- *IntWWM 90, PenDiMP*
Vishnevskaya, Galina Pavlovna 1926- *WhoAm 90*
Vishnevsky, Valentina Michailovna *WhoAmW 91*
Vishniac, Ethan Tecumseh 1955- *WhoSSW 91*
Vishniac, Roman *BioIn 16*
Vishniac, Roman 1897-1990 *CurBio 90N, NewYTBS 90 [port]*
Vishnisky, Morris Irving 1941- *WhoWrEP 89*
Vishnudevananda, Swami 1927- *EncO&P 3*
Visich, Dennis Frank 1948- *WhoAm 90*
Visich, Marian, Jr. 1930- *WhoAm 90*
Visintin, Arnaldo 1954- *WhoSSW 91*
Visintin, Otto *BiDrAPA 89*
Visintine, Elizabeth Anne 1938- *WhoSSW 91*
Viskanta, Raymond 1931- *WhoAm 90*
Vislocky, Joseph M. 1943- *St&PR 91*
Vislosky, George, Jr. 1933- *St&PR 91*
Visner, Cynthia *BiDrAPA 89*
Visocki, Nancy Gayle 1952- *WhoAmW 91*
Visotsky, Harold M 1924- *BiDrAPA 89*
Visotsky, Harold Meryle 1924- *WhoAm 90*
Vispo, Raul H *BiDrAPA 89*
Visscher, Anna 1583-1651 *PenDiDA 89*
Visscher, Helga Bjornson 1946- *WhoAmW 91*
Visscher, Hubert Bartlett 1914- *St&PR 91*
Visscher, Maria Tesselschade Roemers 1595-1649 *PenDiDA 89*
Visser, Greg D. 1957- *St&PR 91*
Visser, John Evert 1920- *WhoAm 90*
Visser, Leo *BioIn 16*
Visser, Lieuwe 1940- *IntWWM 90*
Visser, Lodewijk Ernst 1871-1942 *BioIn 16*
Visser, Theofilus Johannes 1949- *WhoWor 91*
Visser't Hooft, Martha 1906- *WhoAmA 91*
Vissicchio, Andrew John, Jr. 1941- *WhoSSW 91*
Viste, Arlen Ellard 1936- *WhoWor 91*
Visvesvaraya, M. 1861-1962 *BioIn 16*
Visvesvaraya, Mokshgundam 1861-1962 *BioIn 16*
Viswanath, Rampur Sakala 1940- *WhoSSW 91*
Viswanathan, Chand Ram 1929- *WhoAm 90*
Viswanathan, Ramaswamy 1949- *BiDrAPA 89, WhoE 91, WhoEmL 91, WhoWor 91*
Viswanathan, S 1933- *ConAu 132*
Vita, Diana 1955- *WhoAmW 91*
Vita, Giulio 1926- *WhoAm 90*
Vitagliano, Halyna Lobay *BiDrAPA 89*
Vital, Claude Bernard 1932- *WhoWor 91*
Vital, David *BioIn 16*
Vital-Herne, Jacques *BiDrAPA 89*
Vital-Herne, Marc *BiDrAPA 89*
Vitale, Alberto *BioIn 16*
Vitale, Alberto Aldo 1933- *WhoAm 90*
Vitale, Anna M. 1942- *WhoAmW 91*
Vitale, David 1946- *St&PR 91*
Vitale, Dick *BioIn 16*
Vitale, Francis X. 1944- *St&PR 91*
Vitale, Francis X., Jr. 1944- *ODwPR 91*
Vitale, Gerald Lee 1950- *WhoEmL 91, WhoWor 91*
Vitale, John Vincent 1958- *WhoEmL 91*
Vitale, Louis 1902- *St&PR 91*
Vitale, Louis J *BiDrAPA 89*
Vitale, Magda *WhoAmA 91*
Vitale, Nick 1948- *BioIn 16*
Vitale, Richard A. 1944- *WhoE 91*
Vitale, Robert J. 1930- *St&PR 91*
Vitale, Salvatore John, Jr. 1939- *St&PR 91*
Vitale, Stefano *BioIn 16*
Vitale, Tamaam 1948- *WhoE 91*
Vitale, Thomas George *WhoSSW 91*
Vitale, Vincent 1947- *WhoAmA 91*
Vitali, Julius Michael 1952- *WhoE 91*
Vitaliano, Charles Joseph 1910- *WhoAm 90*
Vitaliano, Dorothy Brauneck 1916- *WhoAmW 91*
Vitalie, Carl Lynn 1937- *St&PR 91, WhoWor 91*
Vitalino, Mestre 1909-1963 *ArtLatA*
Vitalos, Robert Francis 1947- *WhoWrEP 89*
Vitamante, Robert J. 1945- *St&PR 91*
Vitanza, Lorraine Lucy Istre 1938- *WhoSSW 91*
Vite, Mark Steven 1956- *WhoEmL 91*
Vitek, Donna *ConAu 131*
Vitek, Donna Kimel 1947- *ConAu 131*
Vitek, James Allen 1958- *WhoWor 91*
Vitek, Jan 1928- *WhoWor 91*
Vitek, Kenn E. 1926- *St&PR 91*
Vitek, Vaclav 1940- *WhoAm 90*
Viteles, Morris S. 1898- *BioIn 16*
Vitell, Goran Erik 1945- *WhoWor 91*
Vitenas, Birute Kazlauskas 1949- *WhoAmW 91*
Viterbi, Andrew James 1935- *WhoAm 90*
Viteri, Osealdo 1931- *ArtLatA*
Vitez, Antoine 1930-1990 *BioIn 16, NewYTBS 90 [port]*
Vitger, John Rolf 1927- *WhoWor 91*
Vitiello, Benedetto *BiDrAPA 89*
Vitiello, Justin 1941- *WhoWrEP 89*
Vitier, Cintio *HispWr 90*
Vitier, Cynthio 1921- *HispWr 90*
Vitier y Bolanos, Cynthio 1921- *HispWr 90*
Vititoe, William P. 1938- *St&PR 91*
Vititoe, William Paul 1938- *WhoAm 90*
Vitkowsky, Vincent Joseph 1955- *WhoE 91, WhoEmL 91, WhoWor 91*
Vitkus, Richard F. 1939- *WhoAm 90*
Vito, Gioconda de *PenDiMP*
Vito, Steven M. 1954- *St&PR 91*
Vitola, Jack Joseph 1931- *St&PR 91*
Vitole, Nicholas M. 1937- *St&PR 91*
Vitolo, Arlene Gayle 1945- *St&PR 91*
Vitolo, Joseph Glen *BiDrAPA 89*
Vitols, Edite T *BiDrAPA 89*
Vitols, Mintauts M 1921- *BiDrAPA 89*
Vitrey, Daniele Roure 1940- *WhoWor 91*
Vitsky, Brian Howard 1939- *WhoSSW 91*
Vitt, David Aaron 1938- *WhoAm 90, WhoWor 91*
Vitt, David Arron 1938- *St&PR 91*
Vitt, Ossie 1890-1963 *Ballpl 90*
Vitt, Sam B. 1926- *St&PR 91, WhoAm 90, WhoE 91, WhoWor 91*
Vitt-Maucher, Gisela Maria 1934- *WhoAm 90*
Vittadini, Adrienne *WhoAm 90, WhoAmW 91*
Vittands, Jekabs Paulis 1936- *St&PR 91*
Vitte, Ray 1949-1983 *DrBlPA 90*
Vittengl, Morgan John 1928- *AuBYP 90*
Vitter, Patricia Butler 1951- *WhoAmW 91*
Vitters, Alan George 1946- *WhoSSW 91*
Vittetoe, Marie Clare 1927- *WhoAmW 91*
Vitton, Patricia Eva 1953- *WhoEmL 91*
Vittone, Bernard John 1951- *BiDrAPA 89, WhoE 91*
Vittor, Kenneth M. 1949- *St&PR 91*
Vittore, Nicholas A. 1935- *St&PR 91*
Vittoria *WomWR*
Vittoria, Alessandro 1525-1608 *IntDcAA 90*
Vittoria, Joseph V. 1935- *WhoAm 90*
Vittorini, Carlo 1929- *St&PR 91, WhoAm 90*
Vittorini, Elio 1908-1966 *EuWr 12*
Vittorino Da Feltre 1378-1446 *WorAlBi*
Vittorio, Joseph Anthony *BiDrAPA 89*
Vitug, Fausto R *BiDrAPA 89*
Vitulli, Clark J. *BioIn 16*
Vitulli, William Joseph 1918- *St&PR 91*
Vivaldi, Antonio 1678-1741 *BioIn 16, WorAlBi*
Vivante, Arturo 1923- *ConAu 12AS [port], WhoWrEP 89*
Vivanti, Annie 1868-1942 *EncCoWW*
Vivar, Rodrigo Diaz de 1043?-1099 *BioIn 16*
Vivar, Zenaida Loza *BiDrAPA 89*
Vivek, Seeth 1951- *WhoE 91*
Vivek, Seetharaman 1951- *BiDrAPA 89*
Vivekananda, Swami 1863-1902 *EncO&P 3, NewAgE 90*
Vivelo, Jackie 1943- *SmATA X [port]*
Vivelo, Jacqueline J. 1943- *SmATA 63 [port]*
Vivelo, Jacqueline Jean 1943- *WhoE 91*
Vivera, Arsenio Bondoc 1931- *WhoE 91, WhoWor 91*
Vivero, Fernando Leon de 1906- *BioIn 16*
Vives, Amadeo 1871-1932 *OxCPMus*
Vives, Juan Luis 1492-1540 *BioIn 16*
Vives, Xavier 1955- *WhoWor 91*
Vivian, Beverly Meece 1949- *WhoSSW 91*
Vivian, Daisy *WhoWrEP 89*
Vivian, David James 1941- *St&PR 91*
Vivian, Frederick *AuBYP 90*
Vivian, Johnson Edward 1913- *WhoAm 90*
Vivian, Linda Bradt 1945- *WhoAmW 91*
Vivian, Rodney Elgar *BiDrAPA 89*
Viviani, Rene Jean Raphael Adrien 1863-1925 *BiDFrPL*
Viviani, Vincenzo 1622-1703 *BioIn 16*
Viviano, Joseph P. 1938- *St&PR 91*
Vivien, Renee 1877-1909 *BioIn 16, EncCoWW, FemiCLE*
Vivier, Roger *BioIn 16*
Viville, Charles 1929- *WhoWor 91*
Vivion, Della Maier 1925- *WhoAmW 91*
Vivo, Paquita *WhoHisp 91*
Vivolo, John 1886-1987 *MusmAFA*
Vivona, John Anthony 1952- *WhoE 91*
Vivoni, Armando 1924- *St&PR 91*
Vivonne, Heliette de 1560?-1625 *EncCoWW*
Vivot, Lea *WhoAmA 91*
Vizcaino, Federico *BiDrAPA 89*
Vizcaino, Sebastian 1550?-1628 *BioIn 16, EncCRAm*
Vizner, Nikola 1945- *WhoAmA 91*
Vizner, Tatjana 1944- *BiDrAPA 89*
Vizquel, Omar 1967- *WhoHisp 91*
Vizueto, Carmen Carrillo 1960- *WhoHisp 91*
Vizy, Kalman Nicholas 1940- *WhoE 91*
Vizza, Robert Francis 1933- *WhoAm 90*
Vlach Quartet *PenDiMP*
Vlach, Jiri 1922- *WhoAm 90*
Vlach, Josef *PenDiMP*
Vlachos, Nicholas Spyro 1943- *WhoSSW 91*
Vlad II, Dracul 1431-1476 *BioIn 16*
Vlad, Marina Marta 1949- *IntWWM 90*
Vlad, Roman 1919- *IntWWM 90*
Vlad, Ulpiu 1945- *IntWWM 90*
Vladeck, Bruce Charney 1949- *WhoAm 90*
Vladeck, Judith *BioIn 16*
Vladeck, Judith Pomarlen 1923- *WhoE 91*
Vladi, Farhad *BioIn 16*
Vladimir II 1053-1125 *WorAlBi*
Vladimirov, Vasilii Sergeevich 1923- *WhoWor 91*
Vladimirskii, Mikhail Fedorovich 1874-1951 *BioIn 16*
Vlahac, Mary Ann Rita 1954- *WhoWor 91*
Vlahakis, George John, Jr. 1944- *BiDrAPA 89*
Vlahokosta, Frideriki Y. *WhoAmW 91*
Vlajkovic, Radovan 1922- *WhoWor 91*
Vlame, Eva 1914-1974 *EncCoWW*
Vlami, Eva *EncCoWW*
Vlaminck, Maurice de 1876-1958 *IntDcAA 90*
Vlasak, Walter Raymond 1938- *WhoWor 91*
Vlaschiha, Ekkerhard 1938- *IntWWM 90*
Vlasho, Louis 1937- *St&PR 91*
Vlasic, R. J. *St&PR 91*
Vlasic, Robert Joseph 1926- *WhoAm 90*
Vlaskamp, Peter Leslie 1932- *St&PR 91*
Vlasnik, Lincoln A. 1914- *St&PR 91*
Vlasov, Aleksandr V. 1932- *BioIn 16*
Vlasov, Aleksandr Vladimirovich 1932- *WhoWor 91*
Vlasov, Andrei Andreevich 1900-1946 *BioIn 16*
Vlasto, James S. *ODwPR 91*
Vlastos, Carol Jo 1941- *WhoAmW 91*
Vlastos, Gregory 1907- *ConAu 130*
Vlaun, Lawrence S. *ODwPR 91*
Vlavianos, George J *BiDrAPA 89*
Vlavianos, John G. 1933- *WhoE 91*
Vlazny, John George 1937- *WhoAm 90*
Vlcek, Donald Joseph, Jr. 1949- *WhoWor 91*
Vlcek, Jan Benes 1943- *WhoAm 90, WhoE 91*
Vleggeert, Arend 1937- *St&PR 91*
Vlerick, Philippe M. *WhoWor 91*
Vlerk, Isaak Martinus Van Der 1892-1974 *DcScB S2*
Vlick, Robert P. 1938- *St&PR 91*
Vliet, Elizabeth Lee *BiDrAPA 89*
Vliet, Gary Clark 1933- *WhoAm 90*
Vliet, R.G. 1929-1984 *WorAu 1980 [port]*
Vlock, Jay Irwin 1926- *WhoE 91*
Vnuk, John Andrew 1934- *St&PR 91*
Vo Chi Cong 1913- *WhoWor 91*
Vo Nguyen Giap 1911- *NewYTBS 90 [port]*
Vo, Nguyen Giap 1912- *BioIn 16*
Vo-Dinh, Mai 1933- *WhoAmA 91*
Voaden, Herman 1903- *OxCCanT*
Voake, Charlotte *AuBYP 90*
Voake, Richard Charles 1940- *St&PR 91, WhoWor 91*
Vobel, Friedrich Wilhelm 1936- *WhoWor 91*
Vocalan, Leopoldo U 1943- *BiDrAPA 89*
Voce, William 1909-1984 *DcNaB 1981*
Vocht, Michelle Elise 1956- *WhoAmW 91, WhoWor 91*
Voci, Frank Anthony 1936- *St&PR 91*
Vocke, Louis J. 1924- *St&PR 91*
Vockel, Richard L. 1920- *St&PR 91*
Vocker, Robert *St&PR 91*
Voda, Rudolph Stephen 1930- *St&PR 91*
Vodak, James W. 1943- *St&PR 91*
Vodden, Lisa A. 1966- *St&PR 91*
Vodegel, Richard D *BiDrAPA 89*
Voderberg, Kurt Ernest 1921- *St&PR 91*
Vodicka, Ruth Kessler *WhoAmA 91*
Vodovnik, Raymond Frank 1935- *St&PR 91*
Vodyanoy, Vitaly Jacob 1941- *WhoSSW 91*
Voecks, Daniel Michael 1934- *St&PR 91*
Voegele, George E *BiDrAPA 89*
Voegelein, Glenn E. 1912- *St&PR 91*
Voegeli, Victor Jacque 1934- *WhoAm 90*
Voegelin, Charles Frederick 1906-1986 *BioIn 16*
Voegelin, Eric 1901-1985 *BioIn 16, ConAu 132*
Voeks, Dean W. 1942- *St&PR 91*
Voelckers, Gwenn 1954- *WhoEmL 91*
Voelkening, Burkhard W *BiDrAPA 89*
Voelker, Elizabeth 1931- *WhoAmA 91*
Voelker, Gerald Milton 1955- *WhoEmL 91*
Voelker, Gottfried Eberhard 1939- *WhoWor 91*
Voelker, John *WhoAmA 91*
Voelker, Larry 1933- *St&PR 91, WhoAm 90*
Voelker-Corby, Catherine Angela 1957- *WhoE 91*
Voell, James Wells *BiDrAPA 89*
Voell, Richard Allen 1933- *WhoAm 90*

Voelpel, Lawrence W. 1950- St&PR 91
Voepel, Karl H. 1931- St&PR 91
Voepel, Karl Heinz 1931- WhoAm 90
Voet, Paul C. 1946- St&PR 91, WhoAm 90
Vogan, Edwina BioIn 16
Vogan, Sara 1947- WhoWrEP 89
Vogds, Daniel E. 1948- St&PR 91
Voge, Jean Paul 1921- WhoWor 91
Voge-Black, Victoria Mae 1943- WhoE 91
Vogel, Albert Vance 1941- BiDrAPA 89
Vogel, Alfred 1927- St&PR 91
Vogel, Arthur Anton 1924- WhoAm 90
Vogel, B Frank 1909- BiDrAPA 89
Vogel, Benjamin 1945- IntWWM 90
Vogel, Candace Klampert 1943- WhoE 91
Vogel, Cedric Wakelee 1946- WhoWor 91
Vogel, Charles A., Jr. 1925- WhoAm 90
Vogel, Charles Stimmel 1932- WhoAm 90
Vogel, Daniel James 1960- St&PR 91
Vogel, David Jay 1947- WhoAm 90
Vogel, Diane Dorothy 1944- WhoAmW 91
Vogel, Donald Bruce 1941- BiDrAPA 89
Vogel, Donald S 1917- WhoAmA 91
Vogel, Donna Lee 1950- WhoE 91
Vogel, Edith 1912- IntWWM 90
Vogel, Edwin Chester 1883-1973 WhoAmA 91N
Vogel, Elton Richard 1941- St&PR 91
Vogel, Eugene L. 1931- WhoAm 90
Vogel, Ezra F 1930- ConAu 30NR, WhoAm 90
Vogel, Frank Edward 1949- WhoE 91
Vogel, George Becker 1926- St&PR 91
Vogel, George Sigmund 1912- WhoE 91
Vogel, Gerald Leon 1952- St&PR 91, WhoEmL 91
Vogel, Gerald W BiDrAPA 89
Vogel, H. Victoria WhoE 91, WhoWor 91
Vogel, Hans-Jochen 1926- WhoWor 91
Vogel, Harold L. 1946- BioIn 16
Vogel, Harold Ray 1936- St&PR 91
Vogel, Harold T. 1910-1990 BioIn 16
Vogel, Heinz G 1926- BiDrAPA 89
Vogel, Henry Elliott 1925- WhoAm 90
Vogel, Herbert 1922- WhoAmA 91
Vogel, Herbert, Mrs 1935- WhoAmA 91
Vogel, Herman L. 1923- St&PR 91
Vogel, Howard Levi 1933- IntWWM 90
Vogel, Howard Stanley 1934- WhoE 91, WhoWor 91
Vogel, Hunter Bertram August 1903-1990 ConAu 131
Vogel, Irene Susan WhoAmW 91
Vogel, J Leslie, Jr. 1919- St&PR 91
Vogel, Jack 1936- ODwPR 91
Vogel, John Denning 1946- WhoEmL 91
Vogel, John H. 1917- WhoAm 90
Vogel, John Michael 1945- WhoE 91
Vogel, John Walter 1948- WhoE 91, WhoEmL 91
Vogel, Joseph 1911- WhoAmA 91
Vogel, Joseph Otto 1936- WhoAm 90
Vogel, Julius 1924- St&PR 91, WhoAm 90
Vogel, June Elaine 1940- St&PR 91
Vogel, Klaus WhoWor 91
Vogel, Laura Beth BiDrAPA 89
Vogel, Lawrence F. ODwPR 91
Vogel, Lawrence Mark 1953- WhoEmL 91
Vogel, Leonard Bernard 1924- St&PR 91
Vogel, Malvina Graff 1932- WhoAmW 91
Vogel, Manfred Henry 1930- WhoAm 90
Vogel, Martin 1923- WhoWor 91
Vogel, Mary Stalgaitis 1949- WhoAmW 91
Vogel, Michael John 1935- St&PR 91
Vogel, Michael W. 1962- St&PR 91
Vogel, Nancy Louise BiDrAPA 89
Vogel, Paul Mark 1968- WhoWrEP 89
Vogel, Ray AuBYP 90
Vogel, Raymond John 1940- WhoAm 90
Vogel, Richard Hunter 1930- WhoAm 90
Vogel, Robert 1918- WhoAm 90
Vogel, Robert 1919- WhoWor 91
Vogel, Robert Henry 1946- St&PR 91
Vogel, Robert Lee 1934- WhoAm 90
Vogel, Roger Craig 1947- IntWWM 90
Vogel, Sheldon A. 1920-1989 BioIn 16
Vogel, Siegfried 1937- IntWWM 90
Vogel, Stanley W. BioIn 16
Vogel, Steve 1946- ConAu 132
Vogel, Theodore John 1952- WhoEmL 91
Vogel, Val G., Jr. 1955- WhoSSW 91
Vogel, Willa Hope 1929- WhoAmW 91, WhoWor 91
Vogelberger, Peter John, Jr. 1932- St&PR 91
Vogelfanger, Roger Bruce BiDrAPA 89
Vogelgesang, Sandra Louise 1942- WhoAmW 91
Vogelhuber, William W. 1933- St&PR 91
Vogelman, Carol BioIn 16
Vogelman, Joseph Herbert 1920- WhoAm 90
Vogelsang, Carl Richard 1946- St&PR 91
Vogelsang, Charee Francis 1946- St&PR 91
Vogelsang, Johanna 1929- WhoAmW 91
Vogelsgesang, Wolfgang Maria 1932- WhoWor 91
Vogelstein, John L. 1934- St&PR 91
Vogely, William Arthur 1924- WhoAm 90
Voggel, Gerhard 1935- St&PR 91
Vogian, Peter John 1931- St&PR 91
Vogl, Alexander J. 1926- St&PR 91
Vogl, Don George 1929- WhoAmA 91
Vogl, Heinrich 1845-1900 PenDiMP
Vogl, Johann Michael 1768-1840 PenDiMP
Vogl, Otto 1927- WhoAm 90
Vogl, Therese 1845-1921 PenDiMP
Vogl, Thomas Paul 1929- WhoE 91
Vogler, Charles D BiDrAPA 89
Vogler, David Leonard 1962- WhoE 91
Vogler, Dennis Joseph 1950- WhoEmL 91
Vogler, Donald Charles 1924- St&PR 91
Vogler, Frederick Wright 1931- WhoAm 90
Vogler, Harry William 1925- St&PR 91
Vogler, Herbert BioIn 16
Vogler, Jan 1964- IntWWM 90
Vogler, Jody Louise 1960- WhoAmW 91
Vogt, Birdie May 1876-1989 BioIn 16
Vogt, Erich Wolfgang 1929- WhoAm 90
Vogt, Evon Zartman, Jr. 1918- WhoAm 90, WhoWrEP 89
Vogt, Ferd August 1935- St&PR 91
Vogt, Gerard Robert 1942- St&PR 91
Vogt, Hans 1903-1986 BioIn 16
Vogt, Hans 1911- IntWWM 90
Vogt, Hartmut 1923- WhoWor 91
Vogt, Helmut Joachim 1936- WhoWor 91
Vogt, Hermann Josef 1932- WhoWor 91
Vogt, James Wayne 1950- WhoEmL 91
Vogt, Joel Alan BiDrAPA 89
Vogt, John Henry 1918- WhoAm 90
Vogt, Larry Gene WhoAm 90
Vogt, Mathias Theodor 1959- IntWWM 90
Vogt, Molly Thomas 1939- WhoAmW 91
Vogt, Rochus E. 1929- St&PR 91
Vogt, Rochus Eugen 1929- WhoAm 90
Vogt, Ronald Charles 1942- St&PR 91
Vogt, Thomas Robert 1957- WhoEmL 91
Vogt, Walter W 1924- BiDrAPA 89
Vogt, Wess Richard 1939- BiDrAPA 89
Vogt, William Handley 1940- St&PR 91
Vogtsberger, Kenneth N 1950- BiDrAPA 89
Vogtsberger, Martin Henry 1947- St&PR 91
Vogue, Adalbert de 1924- WhoWor 91
Vohra, Ranbir 1928- WhoAm 90
Vohra, Sudershan Lal 1936- St&PR 91
Vohs, James Arthur 1928- WhoAm 90
Vohs, Thomas Raymond 1920- WhoAm 90
Voiculescu, Dan 1940- IntWWM 90
Voiculescu, Dan Dumitru 1946- WhoWor 91
Voight, Charles A. 1887-1947 EncACom
Voight, David 1926- Ballpl 90
Voight, Elizabeth Anne 1944- WhoAmW 91
Voight, Jon 1938- WhoAm 90, WorAlBi
Voight, K. W. 1946- St&PR 91
Voight, Virginia Frances 1909- AuBYP 90
Voigt, Adolf Frank 1914- WhoAm 90
Voigt, Alfred E 1927- BiDrAPA 89
Voigt, Cynthia BioIn 16
Voigt, Cynthia 1942- AuBYP 90, WhoAmW 91, WhoWrEP 89
Voigt, David Quentin 1926- ConAu 32NR
Voigt, Ehrhard 1905- WhoWor 91
Voigt, Ellen Bryant 1943- WhoWrEP 89
Voigt, Garth K. 1923- WhoAm 90
Voigt, Hans-Heinrich 1921- WhoWor 91
Voigt, Harry Holmes 1931- WhoAm 90
Voigt, Jane Ellen 1945- WhoAmW 91
Voigt, John Jacob 1942- WhoE 91, WhoWor 91
Voigt, Lieselotte E. Kurth 1923- BioIn 16
Voigt, Mark A. 1951- St&PR 91
Voigt, Paul Warren 1940- WhoAm 90
Voigt, Robert D. 1951- St&PR 91
Voigt, Robert Louis 1918- St&PR 91
Voigt, Ruediger 1941- WhoWor 91
Voigtlander, Ted 1913-1988 BioIn 16
Voigtschmidt, Joep PenDiMP
Voilquin, Suzanne 1801-1876? EncCoWW
Voils, Georgia Elizabeth 1947- WhoWrEP 89
Voinea, Radu Policarp 1923- WhoWor 91
Voineskos, George BiDrAPA 89
Voinovich, Vladimir 1932- ConAu 33NR, ConAu 12AS [port], MajTwCW
Voinovich, Vladimir Nikolayevich 1932- WhoWor 91
Voiselle, Bill 1919- Ballpl 90
Voisin, Russell L. 1932- St&PR 91
Voisin, William R. 1935- St&PR 91
Voisinet, James Raymond 1931- St&PR 91, WhoAm 90, WhoWor 91
Voissem, Marvin C. St&PR 91
Voit, Franz Johann, Jr. 1932- WhoWor 91
Voith, Charles J. St&PR 91
Voitle, Robert Allen 1938- WhoAm 90
Voivodas, Gita Kedar 1942- WhoAmW 91
Vojir, Norman John 1960- WhoE 91
Vojta, George J. 1935- WhoAm 90
Vojtasko, Stephen Francis 1941- WhoE 91
Vokac, David Roland 1940- WhoWrEP 89
Vokes, Howard Dean WhoE 91
Voketaitis, Arnold Mathew 1930- WhoAm 90
Vokins, Elizabeth BiDEWW
Vokins, Joan BiDEWW, FemiCLE
Vokouma, Prosper WhoWor 91
Volavka, Jan 1934- BiDrAPA 89
Volberding, Noel Keith 1935- BiDrAPA 89
Volcker, Paul A. BioIn 16
Volcker, Paul A 1927- ConAu 129, EncABHB 7 [port], WhoWor 91, WorAlBi
Volckhausen, William A. 1937- St&PR 91
Volckhausen, William Alexander 1937- WhoAm 90
Vold, Bjorn 1933- WhoWor 91
Vold, Jan Erik 1939- DcScanL
Vold, Raymond S. 1933- St&PR 91
Vold, Robert Dale 1930- St&PR 91
Voldemaras, Augustinas 1883-1942 BioIn 16
Volding, M. J. 1923- St&PR 91
Voldman, Steven Howard 1957- WhoE 91, WhoEmL 91, WhoWor 91
Voldseth, Beverly Ann 1935- WhoWrEP 89
Voldseth, Edward Victor 1922- WhoAm 90
Voldseth, John Eric 1949- St&PR 91
Vole, Zenobia N. ConAu 129
Voles, Roger 1930- WhoWor 91
Volet, William B. BioIn 16
Volguine, Alexandre EncO&P 3
Volgy, Thomas John 1946- WhoAm 90
Volianskaia, Galina Evgenievna 1911-1963 EncCoWW
Volid, Ruth WhoAmA 91
Volin 1882-1945 BioIn 16
Volinsky, Simon 1931- St&PR 91
Volio, Jorge 1882-1955 BioIn 16
Volk, David Lawrence 1947- WhoAm 90
Volk, Eugene John 1931- St&PR 91
Volk, Harry J. 1905- WhoAm 90
Volk, Hermann 1903-1988 BioIn 16
Volk, Jan WhoAm 90, WhoE 91
Volk, John 1945- ODwPR 91
Volk, John Louis 1943- St&PR 91
Volk, Patricia Gay 1943- WhoAmW 91
Volk, Peter 1949- St&PR 91
Volk, Richard Whitcomb 1936- St&PR 91
Volk, Spencer BioIn 16
Volk, Spencer J. 1934- St&PR 91
Volk, Timothy R. ODwPR 91
Volkan, Vamik D 1932- BiDrAPA 89
Volkart, Edmund Howell 1919- WhoWrEP 89
Volkema, Kay Summers 1951- WhoAmW 91
Volkenant, Allen J. 1930- St&PR 91
Volkening, Debra Lynn 1962- WhoAmW 91
Volker, Dale Martin 1940- WhoE 91
Volkerding, Laura 1939- WhoAmA 91
Volkering, Mary Joe 1936- WhoAmW 91
Volkert, Evelyn C. BioIn 16
Volkhardt, John Malcolm 1917- WhoAm 90
Volkin, Hilda Appel 1933- WhoAmA 91
Volkman, Alvin 1926- WhoSSW 91
Volkman, Edward A BiDrAPA 89
Volkman, Ellen M BiDrAPA 89
Volkman, Ernest 1940- ConAu 132
Volkman, P. E., Jr. 1931- St&PR 91
Volkman, Sage BioIn 16
Volkmann, Bodo 1929- WhoWor 91
Volkmann, Daniel George, Jr. 1924- WhoAm 90
Volkmann, Frances Cooper 1935- WhoAm 90, WhoAmW 91
Volkmann, Heiko Willy 1944- WhoSSW 91
Volkmann, Helmuth BioIn 16
Volkmar, Charles 1841-1914 PenDiDA 89
Volkmar, Fred Robert 1950- BiDrAPA 89
Volkmar, Leon 1879-1959 PenDiDA 89, WhoAmA 91N
Volkmer, Harold L. 1931- WhoAm 90
Volkoff, George Michael 1914- WhoAm 90
Volkov, Aleksandr BioIn 16
Volkow, Nora Dolores BiDrAPA 89
Voll, John O 1936- ConAu 129
Voll, John Obert 1936- WhoAm 90
Voll, Sarah Potts 1942- WhoE 91
Voll, William Holland 1925- St&PR 91
Vollack, Anthony F. 1929- WhoAm 90
Volland, Carol Tascher 1935- WhoAmW 91
Volland, Richard K. 1938- St&PR 91
Volland, Robert S. 1941- St&PR 91
Vollaro, John D. 1944- St&PR 91
Vollbrecht, Edward Alan 1941- WhoE 91
Volldal, Olav 1950- WhoWor 91
Volle, Robert Leon 1930- WhoAm 90
Vollebergh, Jos J. A. 1925- WhoWor 91
Vollen, Robert Jay 1940- WhoAm 90
Vollenweider, Andreas NewAgMG
Vollenweider, Emmett J. 1956- St&PR 91
Vollenweider, Richard Henry 1942- St&PR 91
Voller, Kathleen Grignon 1952- WhoE 91
Vollhardt, Bodo Richard BiDrAPA 89
Vollhardt, Kurt Peter Christian 1946- WhoEmL 91
Vollhardt, Maria EncO&P 3
Vollman, Rita Rae 1942- WhoAmW 91
Vollmar, Gary Lee 1951- St&PR 91
Vollmar, John Raymond 1929- WhoAm 90
Vollmar, Jorg-Friedrich 1923- WhoWor 91
Vollmar, Michael B. BiDrAPA 89
Vollmar, Michael Bruce 1953- WhoE 91
Vollmar, Roland 1939- WhoWor 91
Vollmar, Warren ODwPR 91
Vollmayer, Gloria Breckenridge ODwPR 91
Vollmer, Clyde 1921- Ballpl 90
Vollmer, Helen ODwPR 91
Vollmer, James 1924- WhoAm 90, WhoWor 91
Vollmer, Lula 1898?-1955 BioIn 16
Vollmer, Lulu 1898?-1955 NotWoAT
Vollmer, Matthew S. St&PR 91
Vollmer, Richard Henry 1931- St&PR 91
Vollmer, Ruth WhoAmA 91N
Vollmer, Ruth 1899- BiDWomA
Vollmer, Shirah Adah 1961- BiDrAPA 89
Vollmerhausen, Joseph W 1917- BiDrAPA 89
Vollmuth, Lloyd William 1955- WhoEmL 91
Vollrath, Carl Paul 1931- IntWWM 90
Vollrath, Marilyn A. 1949- ODwPR 91
Vollrath, Philip K. 1942- ODwPR 91
Vollrath, Walter J. 1955- St&PR 91
Vollstedt, Steve 1951- St&PR 91
Vollum, Robert Boone 1933- WhoE 91, WhoWor 91
Volmat, Robert 1920- BiDrAPA 89
Volmer, Everett Anton 1946- WhoE 91
Volny, Peter Ivan 1946- St&PR 91
Volodarskii, V. 1891-1918 BioIn 16
Volovic, Robert C. 1936- St&PR 91
Volow, George BiDrAPA 89
Volpato, Giovanni 1733-1803 PenDiDA 89
Volpe, Angelo Anthony 1938- WhoAm 90, WhoSSW 91
Volpe, Angelo John 1956- WhoE 91
Volpe, Edmond Loris 1922- WhoAm 90
Volpe, Ellen Marie 1949- WhoE 91
Volpe, Erminio Peter 1927- WhoAm 90
Volpe, Harold James 1939- WhoE 91
Volpe, John Anthony 1908- BiDrUSE 89
Volpe, Joseph B., Jr. 1931- St&PR 91
Volpe, Joseph John 1938- WhoAm 90
Volpe, Michael John 1952- ODwPR 91
Volpe, Peter Anthony 1936- WhoAm 90
Volpe, Peter Eugene BiDrAPA 89
Volpe, Ralph C. 1924- St&PR 91
Volpe, Ralph Pasquale 1936- WhoE 91
Volpe, Robert 1926- WhoAm 90, WhoE 91, WhoWor 91
Volpe, Robert 1942- WhoAmA 91
Volpe, Thomas J. 1935- WhoAm 90
Volpe, Thomas James 1935- St&PR 91
Volpert, Barry Stuart 1959- WhoE 91
Volpert, Howard Alan 1934- WhoWor 91
Volpert, Richard Sidney 1935- WhoAm 90
Volpi, Walter Mark 1946- WhoAm 90
Volpicelli, Joseph Robert 1953- BiDrAPA 89
Volpp, Louis Donovan 1929- WhoAm 90
Volstead, Andrew J. 1860-1947 WorAlBi
Volta, Alessandro Giuseppe Antonio A. 1745-1827 WorAlBi
Voltaggio, Vic 1941- Ballpl 90
Voltaire 1694-1778 LitC 14 [port], WorAlBi, WrPh P
Voltes, Pedro 1926- WhoWor 91
Voltolina, Eugene Joseph BiDrAPA 89
Voltz, David L. 1953- St&PR 91
Voltz, Gunnar Charles 1945- St&PR 91
Voltz, Jeanne Appleton 1920- WhoAmW 91, WhoSSW 91
Voluck, Allan S. WhoE 91
Voluck, Allan Stuart 1924- St&PR 91
Volymer, Yuriy Mikhaylovich 1933- WhoWor 91
Volz, Berneta Kay 1955- WhoEmL 91
Volz, Charles Harvie, Jr. 1925- WhoAm 90
Volz, Jim 1953- WhoSSW 91
Volz, Joe BioIn 16
Volz, John Phillip 1935- WhoAm 90
Volz, John Richard 1948- WhoSSW 91
Volz, Marlin Milton 1917- WhoAm 90, WhoWor 91
Volz, Michael George 1945- WhoEmL 91
Volz, Nedra ConTFT 8
Volz, Robert George 1932- WhoAm 90
Volz, William Harry 1946- WhoAm 90
vom Baur, Francis Trowbridge 1908- WhoAm 90, WhoWor 91
Vom Brocke, Hans Heinrich 1941- BiDrAPA 89
Vomacka, David H. 1943- St&PR 91
Von, Michael H. 1937- St&PR 91

Vona, Carmine 1938- *WhoAm 90*
Vona, Donna Jean 1959- *WhoE 91*
Vona, Joseph *St&PR 91*
Vona Evans, Gail Margaret 1954- *WhoE 91*
von Ah, Josef Florentin 1928- *WhoWor 91*
von Albertini, Rudolf 1923- *ConAu 131*
von Ammon, Philip Ernst 1915- *WhoAm 90*
Von Appen, Karl 1900-1981 *ConDes 90*
von Arnauld de la Periere, Angelique 1940- *WhoAmW 91*
Von Arnim, Bettina 1785-1859 *BioIn 16*
Von Arnim, Elizabeth 1866-1941 *BioIn 16, FemiCLE*
Von Arx, Dolph William 1934- *St&PR 91, WhoAm 90, WhoSSW 91*
Vonarx, Mark 1950- *St&PR 91*
Von Arx, Victoria *ODwPR 91*
Von Auersperg, Alexander *BioIn 16*
Von Auersperg Kneissl, Ala *BioIn 16*
von Balthasar, Hans U. *ConAu 130*
Von Balthasar, Hans Urs 1905-1988 *BioIn 16, ConAu 130*
von Barandy, Richard Dwight 1935- *St&PR 91*
Von Barghan, Barbara 1949- *WhoAmA 91*
Von Bauer, Eric Ernst 1942- *St&PR 91*
Von Behren, Ruth Lechner 1933- *WhoAmW 91*
Von Bennigsen-Foerder, Rudolf 1926-1989 *BioIn 16*
Von Berg, Horst Rudiger 1941- *St&PR 91, WhoE 91*
Von Bergen, Drew 1940- *ODwPR 91*
Von Bergen, John Axel 1939- *WhoAmA 91*
von Bernuth, Carl 1944- *St&PR 91*
Von Beroldingen, Paul 1944- *ODwPR 91*
von Beyme, Klaus 1934- *WhoWor 91*
Von Blanckenhagen, Peter Heinrich 1909-1990 *BioIn 16*
Von Blomberg, Werner 1878-1946 *BioIn 16*
Von Blon, Philip 1921- *St&PR 91*
Von Bohlen und Halbach, Gustav Krupp 1870-1950 *BioIn 16*
Von Bohm-Bawerk, Eugen 1851-1914 *BioIn 16*
von Bonin, Wibke Anna 1936- *WhoWor 91*
Von Bortkiewicz, Ladislaus 1868-1931 *BioIn 16*
Von Brauchitsch, Hans Konrad 1931- *BiDrAPA 89*
von Braun, Peter Carl Moore Stewart 1940- *WhoE 91, WhoWor 91*
Von Braun, Wernher 1912-1977 *BioIn 16*
Von Braun-Janssen, Claudia 1954- *WhoWor 91*
Von Brentano, Bernard 1901-1964 *BioIn 16*
von Briesen, Dorothy Alice 1912- *WhoAmW 91*
von Brock, A. Raymond 1922- *WhoAm 90*
Von Bruenchenhein, Eugene 1910-1983 *MusmAFA*
Von Bulow, Claus *BioIn 16*
Von Bulow, Hans 1830-1894 *BioIn 16*
Von Bulow, Martha *BioIn 16*
von Bun, Friedrich Otto 1925- *WhoE 91*
von Bunau, Gunther 1930- *WhoWor 91*
Von Buttlar, Norman *BiDrAPA 89*
Voncanon, Robert Dale 1933- *St&PR 91*
Von Carolsfeld, Ludwig Schnorr 1836-1865 *BioIn 16*
Von Chielanski-Lallinger, Manuela *BioIn 16*
Vonck, Irene *PenDiDA 89*
Vonckx, Paul Nelson, Jr. 1938- *St&PR 91*
von Clemm, Michael 1935- *WhoAm 90*
von Craigh, Bertha Theresa 1939- *WhoE 91*
Von Culin, Raymond Pearson 1913- *St&PR 91*
Von Dalmata, Kurt Franz Paul 1950- *WhoWor 91*
Von Damm, Helene 1938- *BioIn 16*
Von Daniken, Erich 1935- *AuBYP 90, EncO&P 3*
Von Dassanowsky, Elfriede 1924- *IntWWM 90*
Von Dem Bussche, Wolf *WhoAmA 91*
Vonderach, Stephen H. 1934- *St&PR 91*
von der Ahe, Chris 1851-1913 *Ballpl 90*
Von der Ahe, Christian Frederick Wilhelm 1851-1913 *BioIn 16*
von der Dunk, Hermann Walther 1928- *WhoWor 91*
Von der Embse, Marie Annette 1947- *WhoEmL 91*
von der Esch, Hans Ulrik 1928- *WhoWor 91*
Von Der Golz, Jan *WhoAmA 91*
VonderHaar, William Purcell 1930- *WhoAm 90*
VonderHeide, Heidi Tauscher 1960- *WhoAmW 91*
Vonderheide, Susan Gwen 1957- *WhoAmW 91*
von der Heyden, Ingolf Mueller 1936- *WhoAm 90*
Von Der Heyden, Karl M. 1936- *St&PR 91*
von der Heydt, James Arnold 1919- *WhoAm 90*
von der Heydte, Friedrich August 1907- *WhoWor 91*
Von Der Lancken, Frank 1872-1950 *WhoAmA 91N*
Von der Lippe, Edward Joseph 1934- *WhoSSW 91*
von der Mehden, Fred R. 1927- *WhoAm 90*
Von Der Mosel, Valentina *BiDrAPA 89*
Von Der Osten, Harold R. 1929- *St&PR 91*
Von Der Portern, Peter G. 1946- *St&PR 91*
von der Schulenburg, J. Matthias 1950- *WhoWor 91*
Vondersmith, Bernard Joseph 1943- *WhoE 91*
von Dewitz, Victor Botho Jobst 1942- *WhoWor 91*
Von Doenhoff, Laura Jean 1948- *WhoE 91*
Von Doepp, Christian 1936- *BiDrAPA 89*
von Dohlen, Robert John 1928- *WhoAm 90*
Von Dohnanyi, Christoph *BioIn 16, PenDiMP*
von Dohnanyi, Christoph 1929- *WhoAm 90, WhoWor 91*
Vondran, Janet Elise *BiDrAPA 89*
Vondrasek, Frank Charles 1928- *St&PR 91*
Vondrasek, Frank Charles, Jr. 1928- *WhoAm 90*
Von Drehle, Ramon Arnold 1930- *St&PR 91, WhoAm 90*
Vondrell, James Henry, Sr. 1950- *WhoEmL 91*
Vondrich, Yari Vaclav 1931- *St&PR 91*
Vondy, David Ray 1927- *WhoWrEP 89*
Von Eckardt, Wolf 1918- *WhoAm 90*
von Egidy, Till 1933- *WhoWor 91*
von Eiff, August Wilhelm 1921- *WhoWor 91*
von Elbe, Joachim 1902- *ConAu 132*
Von Ende, Carl H. 1942- *WhoAm 90*
von Erichsen, Lothar Carl 1915- *WhoWor 91*
Von Eschen, Kenneth B. 1948- *St&PR 91*
Vonesh, Raymond James 1916- *WhoAm 90*
von Essen, Dean R. 1958- *WhoE 91*
Von Eye, Rochelle Kay 1949- *WhoAmW 91*
Von Feldt, Elmer 1919- *WhoAm 90*
von Fieandt, Dorrit Margareta 1927- *WhoWor 91*
von Friedeburg, Friedrich 1926- *WhoWor 91*
Von Fritsch, Gunther *BioIn 16*
Von Fuehrer, Ottmar F *WhoAmA 91N*
von Fuerer-Haimendorf, Christoph 1909- *ConAu 131*
von Furstenberg, Betsy 1931- *WhoAm 90*
Von Furstenberg, Diane *BioIn 16*
Von Furstenberg, Diane Simone Michelle 1946- *WhoAm 90, WhoAmW 91*
von Furstenberg, George Michael 1941- *WhoAm 90*
Von Galen, Clemens August 1878-1946 *BioIn 16*
Vongas, Gregory Sotrimos 1953- *WhoE 91*
Von Gierke, Henning Edgar 1917- *WhoAm 90*
Von Gruben, Brian Gerard 1948- *St&PR 91*
Von Gunten, Robert L *BiDrAPA 89*
Von Haam, Emmerich 1903-1988 *BioIn 16*
Von Hafften, Alexander H *BiDrAPA 89*
Von Hagen, Christine *AuBYP 90*
Von Hagen, Karl O 1905- *BiDrAPA 89*
Von Hagen, Victor Wolfgang 1908- *AuBYP 90*
von Hahn, Walther 1942- *WhoWor 91*
von Hake, Margaret Joan 1933- *WhoE 91*
von Hamm, M. Kent 1937- *WhoAm 90*
von Harz, James Lyons 1915- *WhoAm 90*
Von Hassel, George A. 1929- *St&PR 91*
Von Hassel, William R. 1929- *St&PR 91*
Von Hassell, Fey *BioIn 16*
Von Hassell, Ulrich 1881-1944 *BioIn 16*
Von Hayek, Friedrich A. 1899- *BioIn 16*
von Hayek, Friedrich August *MajTwCW*
Von Henselt, Adolf 1814-1889 *BioIn 16*
Von Herkomer, Hubert 1849-1914 *BioIn 16*
vonHernried Ritter vonWasel-Waldingau, P *WhoAm 90*
Von Herrmann, Denise Keefer 1962- *WhoAmW 91*
Von Herzen, Bruce A *BiDrAPA 89*
Von Herzen, Richard Pierre 1930- *WhoAm 90*
Von Hess, Jovak *WhoWrEP 89*
Vonheyn, William A. 1922- *St&PR 91*
Von Hindenburg, Paul 1847-1934 *BioIn 16*
Von Hippel, Frank Niels 1937- *WhoAm 90*
Von Hippel, Gertrud *AuBYP 90*
Von Hippel, Josephine B R 1929- *BiDrAPA 89*
von Hippel, Peter Hans 1931- *WhoAm 90*
Von Hoelscher, Russel 1942- *WhoWrEP 89*
von Hofe, Harold 1912- *WhoAm 90*
von Hoffman, Nicholas 1929- *WhoAm 90, WhoE 91*
Von Holden, Martin Harvey 1942- *WhoAm 90, WhoE 91*
Von Hollen, James 1925- *St&PR 91*
Von Holt, Lael Powers 1927- *WhoAmW 91*
Von Huene, Friedrich Alexander 1929- *IntWWM 90*
Vonic, Nancy 1938- *WhoE 91*
Von Ins, James A. 1932- *St&PR 91*
Von Ins, James Alfred 1932- *WhoAm 90*
Von Jost, Alexander 1889-1968 *WhoAmA 91N*
Vonk, Christiaan 1931- *WhoWor 91*
Vonk, Hans 1942- *IntWWM 90, PenDiMP*
von Kalinowski, Julian Onesime 1916- *WhoAm 90*
von Kann, Clifton Ferdinand 1915- *WhoAm 90, WhoE 91*
Von Karajan, Herbert *BioIn 16*
von Keviczky, Colman Stephen 1909- *WhoE 91*
Von Keyserling, Eduard 1855-1918 *BioIn 16*
Von Killinger, Manfred 1886-1944 *BioIn 16*
Von Kirschbaum, Charlotte 1899-1975 *BioIn 16*
von Klemperer, Klemens 1916- *WhoAm 90*
Von Klemperer, Lily *BioIn 16*
Von Klopp, Vahrah *AuBYP 90*
von Knorring, Anne-Liis 1945- *WhoWor 91*
von Knorring, Hans Otto Theodor 1938- *WhoWor 91*
Von Kohorn, Ralph 1919- *St&PR 91*
von Kohorn, Ralph Steven 1919- *WhoWor 91*
von Krockow, Graf Matthias Henning D. 1949- *WhoWor 91*
Von Kurowsky, Agnes *BioIn 16*
von Kutzleben, Siegfried Edwin 1920- *WhoE 91, WhoWor 91*
von Lang, Frederick William 1929- *WhoAm 90*
Von Laue, Theodore Herman 1916- *WhoAm 90, WhoWrEP 89*
von Leden, Hans Victor 1918- *WhoAm 90*
von le Fort, Gertrud *ConAu 31NR*
Von Lehman, John I. 1952- *St&PR 91*
Von Liebig, William J. 1923- *St&PR 91*
von Liebig, William John 1923- *WhoAm 90, WhoE 91*
Von Lilienfeld, Georg 1912-1989 *BioIn 16*
Von Losch, Maria Magdalena 1904- *WhoAm 90, WhoWor 91*
Von Mangoldt, Hans Karl Emil 1824-1868 *BioIn 16*
Von Manstein, Erich 1887-1973 *BioIn 16*
von Matt, Peter 1937- *WhoWor 91*
Von Maur, J. R. 1919- *St&PR 91*
von Mehren, Arthur Taylor 1922- *WhoAm 90*
von Mehren, Robert Brandt 1922- *WhoAm 90*
Von Mendelssohn, Felix 1918- *BiDrAPA 89*
von Mering, Otto Oswald 1922- *WhoAm 90*
von Minckwitz, Bernhard 1944- *WhoWor 91*
Von Mises, Ludwig 1881-1973 *BioIn 16*
Von Morpurgo, Henry 1909- *WhoWrEP 89*
Von Muehlen, Lutz H 1929- *BiDrAPA 89*
Vonnegut, Kurt 1922- *Au&Arts 6 [port], BestSel 90-4 [port], BioIn 16*
Vonnegut, Kurt, Jr. 1922- *ConLC 60 [port], MajTwCW, RGTwCSF, SpyFic, WhoAm 90, WhoE 91, WhoWor 91, WhoWrEP 89, WorAlBi*
Von Neumann, John 1903-1957 *BioIn 16*
Vonnoh, Bessie Onahotema 1872-1955 *BiDWomA*
von Notenberg, Genrikhovna 1877-1913 *EncCoWW*
Von Oder, Emily *BioIn 16*
von Ohain, Hans Joachim 1911- *WhoAm 90*
Von Ohlen, Dave 1958- *Ballpl 90*
Von Oldenburg, Albert A 1930- *BiDrAPA 89*
von Oldenburg, Albert Elimar 1930- *WhoE 91*
von Palko, David Michael 1953- *WhoSSW 91*
Von Papen, Franz 1878-1969 *BioIn 16*
Von Paradis, Maria Theresia 1759-1824 *BioIn 16*
Von Paris, George H. 1924- *St&PR 91*
von Post, Olle Ernst Olof 1945- *WhoWor 91*
von Raffay, Anita Sophia 1922- *WhoWor 91*
von Raffler-Engel, Walburga 1920- *WhoAm 90, WhoAmW 91, WhoSSW 91, WhoWor 91*
von Rannenberg, Barbara Ann 1959- *WhoE 91*
Von Reich, Momoe Malietoa *FemiCLE*
Von Reichenau, Walter 1884-1942 *BioIn 16*
Von Reichenberg, Audre Auge Ellen 1958- *WhoE 91*
von Reviczky, Stephan Karl Julius 1936- *WhoWor 91*
Von Rhein, John Richard 1945- *WhoAm 90*
Von Ribbentrop, Joachim 1893-1946 *BioIn 16*
Von Ringelheim, Paul Helmut *WhoAm 90, WhoAmA 91*
von Roemer, Beatrice 1929- *WhoAmW 91*
Von Roenn, Kelvin Alexander 1949- *WhoEmL 91*
Von Roenn, Kenneth F 1924- *BiDrAPA 89*
Von Rohr, Jerry S. 1945- *St&PR 91*
Von Rosen, Ulric Eugene 1944- *St&PR 91*
Von Rosenberg, Arthur James 1936- *St&PR 91*
von Rosenberg, Marjorie Taylor 1932- *WhoAmW 91*
Von Rosenstiel, Martha E. 1950- *WhoE 91*
Von Rydingsvard, Ursula 1942- *BioIn 16, WhoAmA 91*
Von Schack, Wesley W. 1944- *St&PR 91, WhoAm 90*
Von Schirach, Baldur 1907-1974 *BioIn 16*
Von Schlegel, Friedrich 1772-1829 *BioIn 16*
Von Schlegell, David 1920- *WhoAmA 91*
Von Schlichten, Alexander P 1931- *BiDrAPA 89*
Von Schmidt, Eric 1931- *AuBYP 90, BioIn 16, WhoAmA 91*
Von Schmoller, Gustav 1838-1917 *BioIn 16*
Von Schomberg, Frederick Hermann 1615-1690 *BioIn 16*
von Schubert, Andreas 1922- *WhoWor 91*
Von Scotti, Harald 1940- *BiDrAPA 89*
von Seidlein, Peter C. 1925- *WhoWor 91*
Von Seldeneck, G Clay 1941- *St&PR 91*
von Seldeneck, Judith Metcalfe 1940- *WhoAmW 91, WhoE 91*
Von Senger und Etterlin, Frido 1891- *BioIn 16*
Von Seyss-Inquart, Artur 1892-1946 *BioIn 16*
Von Simson, Paula 1923- *BiDrAPA 89*
Von Spreckelsen, Henry H. *ODwPR 91*
Von Stade, Frederica *BioIn 16*
Von Stade, Frederica 1945- *IntWWM 90, PenDiMP, WhoAm 90, WhoAmW 91*
von Stark, G *ConAu 31NR*
Von Stauffenberg, Klaus Philipp Schenk 1907-1944 *BioIn 16*
Von Stein, Alfred 1930- *St&PR 91*
Von Stroheim, Erich 1885-1957 *WorAlBi*
Von Struve, Friedrich Georg Wilhelm 1793-1864 *BioIn 16*
Von Struve, Otto 1897-1963 *BioIn 16*
Von Stulpnagel, Karl Heinrich 1886-1944 *BioIn 16*
von Summer, Alexander Carl, Jr. 1938- *WhoAm 90*
Von Sydow, Max 1929- *BioIn 16, WhoAm 90, WhoWor 91, WorAlBi*
Von Tauber, Olga Maria 1911- *BiDrAPA 89, WhoAmW 91*
Von Tavel, Hans Christoph 1935- *WhoWor 91*
Von Tersch, Lawrence Wayne 1923- *WhoAm 90*
Von Thadden, Eberhard 1909-1964 *BioIn 16*
Von Thunen, Johann Heinrich 1783-1850 *BioIn 16*
von Thurn und Taxis, Johannes *NewYTBS 90*
Von Thurn-Valsassina, Isabelle *BioIn 16*
von Tiesenhausen, Georg H.P., Jr. 1945- *WhoSSW 91*
Von Tilzer, Albert 1878-1956 *BioIn 16, OxCPMus*
Von Tilzer, Harry 1872-1946 *BioIn 16, OxCPMus, WorAlBi*
Vontobel, Paul *WhoAm 90*
Von Trapp, George Edward 1948- *St&PR 91*
Von Trapp, Johannes Georg 1939- *St&PR 91*
Von Trapp, Maria *BioIn 16*
Von Trotta, Margarethe *BioIn 16*
von Tungeln, George Robert 1931- *WhoAm 90*
von Uhlit, Ruth Raeder 1911- *WhoAmW 91*
Von Unruh, Fritz 1885-1970 *BioIn 16*
Von Urff, Charles A. 1934- *St&PR 91*

Von Valtier, William Franz 1936- BiDrAPA 89
Von Wacker, Alexander WhoWrEP 89
Von Wald, Richard B. St&PR 91
VonWallenstein, Albrecht Wenzel Eusebius 1583-1634 BioIn 16
Von Weber, Carl Maria 1786-1826 BioIn 16
Von Weise, Wenda Fraker 1941- WhoAmA 91N
Von Weizsacker, Ernst Heinrich 1882-1951 BioIn 16
Von Weizsacker, Richard 1920- WhoWor 91
Von Westenholz, Piers BioIn 16
Von Westernhagen, Thilo, and Band NewAgMG
von Wettengell, Willi William 1933- WhoE 91
Von Wicht, John 1888-1970 WhoAmA 91N
Von Wiegand, Charmion 1898-1983 WhoAmA 91N
Von Wiesenthal, Peter BioIn 16, NewYTBS 90
Von Wieser, Friedrich 1851-1926 BioIn 16
von Winckler, Beverly Ann Purnell 1935- WhoAmW 91
Von Witzleben, Henry D BiDrAPA 89
Von Wright, Georg Henrik 1916- WhoWor 91
Von Wyss, Marc R. 1931- St&PR 91
von Wyss, Marc Robert 1931- WhoAm 90
von Zallinger, Ursula 1939- WhoWor 91
Von Zemenszky, Elisabeth BiDrAPA 89
Von Ziegesar, Franz 1924- St&PR 91, WhoAm 90
von Zinkernagel, Eric Irwin 1952- WhoEmL 91
Von Zur Muehlen, Bernis Susan 1942- WhoAmA 91
Von Zur Muehlen, Peter 1939- WhoAmA 91
Von Zur Muhlen, Alexander 1936- WhoWor 91
Von zur Muhlen, Raimund PenDiMP
Von Zwehl, Joanne 1959- WhoAmW 91
Voobus, Arthur 1909-1988 BioIn 16
Vooijs, Gijsbert Peter 1937- WhoWor 91
Vook, Frederick Ludwig 1931- WhoAm 90
Voorhees, Donald 1903-1989 BioIn 16
Voorhees, Donald Edward 1926- WhoAmA 91
Voorhees, Donald S. 1916-1989 BioIn 16
Voorhees, James Dayton, Jr. 1917- WhoAm 90
Voorhees, Jerry Lee 1939- WhoSSW 91
Voorhees, John Henry 1936- WhoAm 90
Voorhees, John James 1938- WhoAm 90
Voorhees, John Schenck 1923- WhoAm 90
Voorhees, Josephine Palmer 1894-1989 BioIn 16
Voorhees, Richard Lesley 1941- WhoAm 90
Voorhees, William Wolverton, Jr. 1946- WhoE 91
Voorheis, Marion Marascio 1946- WhoAmW 91, WhoE 91
Voorheis, T. S. 1914- St&PR 91
Voorhess, Mary Louise 1926- WhoAmW 91
Voorhies, Alice Joyce 1940- WhoAmW 91, WhoSSW 91
Voorhies, Archie C. 1908- St&PR 91
Voorhies, Barbara WhoAmW 91
Voorman, Gary John BiDrAPA 89
Voorneveld, Richard Burke 1949- WhoSSW 91
Voorsanger, Bartholomew 1937- WhoAm 90, WhoWor 91
Voorst, John van 1804-1898 BioIn 16
Voorst Vader, Pieter Cornelis 1946- WhoWor 91
Voort, Hannavan der BioIn 16
Voortman, John J. 1931- WhoAm 90
Voos, James St&PR 91
Voos, William John 1930- WhoAm 90, WhoAmA 91
Voparil, Kurt Franz 1942- WhoAm 90
Vopicka, Charles J. 1857-1935 BioIn 16
Vopnford, David Thor, Sr. 1942- St&PR 91
Vor, Jon ur DcScanL
Vor Broker, Robert Stuart 1946- St&PR 91
Vora, Ashok 1947- WhoAm 90
Vora, Chandan Sheskaran 1945- WhoE 91
Vora, Chintamani Raju BiDrAPA 89
Vora, Dipak Venilal 1943- WhoSSW 91
Vora, Nikhil K. 1956- BiDrAPA 89
Vora, S. B. 1946- St&PR 91
Vorachek, Mitzi M. 1944- WhoSSW 91
Vorbach, Renee R. 1946- WhoWrEP 89
Vorbrich, Lynn Karl 1939- St&PR 91, WhoAm 90
Vorce, Betsy 1954- ODwPR 91
Vorchheimer, Neal P. St&PR 91
Vorder-Bruegge, Frederick Mark, Jr. 1953- WhoSSW 91
Vordoni, Teresa Albarelli 1788-1870 EncCoWW
Vore, Mary Edith 1947- WhoAmW 91
Voreis, Marilyn Louise 1941- WhoWor 91
Vorenberg, F. Frank BioIn 16
Vorenberg, James 1928- WhoAm 90
Vorenberg, John 1926- BiDrAPA 89
Vorhauer, Delia Villegas 1940- WhoHisp 91
Vorhauer, George Franklin, Jr. 1941- WhoE 91
Vorhies, Mahlon Wesley 1937- WhoAm 90
Vorhoff, Gilbert Harold 1919- St&PR 91
Voris, Albert T BiDrAPA 89
Voris, D. Thomas 1940- St&PR 91
Voris, Mark 1907-1974 WhoAmA 91N
Voris, William 1924- WhoAm 90, WhoWor 91
Vorisek, Richard J. BioIn 16
Vorkas, Andreas Pavlou 1940- WhoWor 91
Vorkoper, Joan Hammett 1938- WhoSSW 91
Voroblevskii, Vasilii Grigor'evich 1730-1797 BioIn 16
Voron, Diane Pasternak 1955- WhoE 91
Voronin, Lev Alekseyevich 1928- WhoWor 91
Voros, Gerald J. 1930- ODwPR 91
Voros, Gerald John 1930- St&PR 91, WhoAm 90
Voroshilov, Kliment 1881-1969 WorAlBi
Voroshilov, Kliment Efremovich 1881-1969 BioIn 16
Vorotnikov, Vitaliy Ivanovich 1926- WhoWor 91
Vorpahl, Jerry ODwPR 91
Vorsanger, Fred S. 1928- WhoAm 90
Vorse, Mary 1874-1966 FemiCLE
Vorse, Mary Heaton 1874-1966 BioIn 16, EncAL
Vorselman, Torsten Gerrit 1942- WhoWor 91
Vorspan, Max 1916- BioIn 16
Vorster, Balthazar Johannes 1915-1983 WorAlBi
Vorster, Dewet S 1928- BiDrAPA 89
Vorwald, Alan AuBYP 90
Vorwerk, E Charlsie 1934- WhoAmA 91
Vorys, Arthur Isaiah 1923- WhoAm 90
Vos, Frank 1919- WhoAm 90
Vos, Hubert Daniel 1933- St&PR 91, WhoAm 90
Vos, Thomas J. 1947- St&PR 91
Vos Savant, Marilyn 1946- WhoE 91
Vos Savant, Marilyn Mach BioIn 16
Vosbeck, Robert Randall 1930- WhoAm 90
Vosbein, Eleanor Edna 1935- WhoAmW 91, WhoSSW 91
Vosburg, Robert L 1926- BiDrAPA 89
Vosburgh, Frederick George 1904- WhoAm 90
Vosburgh, Kenneth Vernon 1933- WhoE 91
Vosburgh, Lisa Gayle BiDrAPA 89
Vosburgh, Peter G. 1930- St&PR 91
Vosburgh, Thomas Birdsall BiDrAPA 89
Vosburgh, Victoria Lynn 1965- WhoAmW 91
Vosce, Trudie MajTwCW
Vose, Barbara Workman 1944- WhoSSW 91
Vose, David A. WhoAm 90
Vose, Robert C 1873-1965 WhoAmA 91N
Vose, Robert Churchill, Jr. 1911- WhoAm 90, WhoAmA 91
Vosefski, Edith King 1930- WhoAmW 91
Vosgerau, Hans Jurgen 1931- WhoWor 91
Vosika, Marijana K. 1956- BiDrAPA 89
Voska, William A. 1932- St&PR 91
Voskanyan, Grant Mushegovich 1924- WhoWor 91
Vosler, David M. 1951- St&PR 91
Vosmik, Joe 1910-1962 Ballpl 90
Voso, Deborah Elizabeth 1950- WhoAmW 91, WhoEmL 91
Vosotas, Paula J. 1942- St&PR 91
Vosotas, Peter L. 1941- St&PR 91
Vosper, Robert Gordon 1913- WhoAm 90
Voss, Alain Jean-Marie 1959- WhoSSW 91
Voss, Angela Mary 1957- WhoWor 91
Voss, Arthur E. 1897-1988 BioIn 16
Voss, August Eduardovich 1916- WhoWor 91
Voss, Bernd 1942- WhoWor 91
Voss, Bill 1943- Ballpl 90
Voss, Carl Hermann 1910- WhoAm 90
Voss, Carlyle B 1940- BiDrAPA 89
Voss, Claus Manfred 1932- WhoWor 91
Voss, Edward E. 1916-1989 BioIn 16
Voss, Edward William, Jr. 1933- WhoAm 90
Voss, Edwin Price 1936- St&PR 91
Voss, Friedrich 1930- IntWWM 90
Voss, Frithjof 1937- WhoWor 91
Voss, Gerhard Ernst PenDiMP
Voss, Gilbert L. BioIn 16
Voss, Harlan F. 1925- St&PR 91
Voss, Harry F. 1937- St&PR 91
Voss, Helen Harris 1933- WhoAmW 91
Voss, Hermann PenDiMP
Voss, Jack D. 1921- St&PR 91
Voss, Jack Donald 1921- WhoAm 90
Voss, James Frederick 1930- WhoAm 90
Voss, Jay W. 1957- St&PR 91
Voss, Jeffrey M. 1958- St&PR 91
Voss, Jerrold Richard 1932- WhoAm 90
Voss, John 1917- WhoAm 90
Voss, Katherine Evelyn 1957- WhoAmW 91
Voss, Ken BioIn 16
Voss, Lawrence Richard 1953- WhoEmL 91
Voss, Mary Louise 1950- WhoAmW 91
Voss, Ned Aus 1936- St&PR 91
Voss, Omer Gerald 1916- WhoAm 90
Voss, Philip, Jr. 1941- WhoAm 90
Voss, Thomas Gorman 1938- WhoSSW 91
Voss, Werner Konrad Karl 1935- WhoWor 91
Voss, William Charles 1937- St&PR 91, WhoAm 90
Voss, William R. 1951- WhoSSW 91
Voss-Jones, Rosemary 1946- WhoAmW 91
Vossbein, Reinhard 1934- WhoWor 91
Vossberg, Carl A., III 1948- St&PR 91
Vossberg, Carl August 1918- St&PR 91
Vossers, Gerrit 1926- WhoWor 91
Vosteen, William Earle 1952- WhoE 91
Vota, John Philip 1939- St&PR 91
Votano, Paul A. 1929- ODwPR 91
Votano, Paul Anthony 1929- WhoWrEP 89
Votapek, Ralph James 1939- WhoAm 90
Votava, Cari Lynn 1957- WhoE 91
Votava, Kathryn McCabe 1954- WhoAmW 91
Votaw, Carmen Delgado WhoHisp 91
Voteur, Ferdinand EarBlAP
Voth, Harold M 1922- BiDrAPA 89
Voth, Melvin Harvey 1932- WhoAm 90
Votik, Barbara Meier 1944- WhoAmW 91
Votto, Antonino 1896-1985 PenDiMP
Vouet, Simon 1590?-1649 IntDcAA 90
Vought, Kenneth Dean 1926- St&PR 91
Voulkos, Peter 1924- PenDiDA 89, WhoAm 90, WhoAmA 91
Voultsos-Vourtzis, Pericles 1910- WhoAm 90, WhoWor 91
Vourlekis, Alkinoos 1930- BiDrAPA 89
Vourvoulias, Joyce Bush WhoAmA 91
Voute, William J. St&PR 91
Voute, William Joseph 1938- WhoAm 90
Voutsas, Alexander Matthew 1923- WhoWor 91
Voves, Joseph Anthony 1922- St&PR 91
Vowell, Evelene C. 1940- WhoAmW 91
Vowell, Jeff D. 1952- WhoE 91
Vowell, Larry Kay 1944- WhoSSW 91
Vowels, Eleanor Elaine 1937- WhoAmW 91
Vowels, Marty 1949- WhoSSW 91
Vowinckel, Andreas Gottlieb 1940- WhoWor 91
Vowles, Richard Beckman 1917- WhoAm 90
Voxman, Himie 1912- WhoAm 90
Voyager, Alyn 1950- WhoE 91, WhoWor 91
Voyez, John PenDiDA 89
Voyle, Kim Marcia Kempton 1958- WhoAmW 91
Voyle, Mary AuBYP 90
Voyles, J. Bruce 1953- WhoWrEP 89
Voyles, James Wesley 1931- St&PR 91
Voyles, Lin Perry 1943- WhoSSW 91
Voyles, Robb Lawrence 1957- WhoEmL 91
Voynich, E. L. 1864-1960 BioIn 16
Voynich, Ethel Lilian 1864-1960 FemiCLE
Voynich, Ethel Lillian 1864-1960 BioIn 16
Voypick, Joseph A. 1935- St&PR 91
Voysey, Charles Francis Annesley 1857-1941 PenDiDA 89
Vozdvizhensky, N. EncCoWW
Vozick, David 1940- St&PR 91
Voznesensky, Andrei 1933- MajTwCW, WhoWor 91, WorAlBi
Vozza, Nestor Claudio BiDrAPA 89
Vrabel, Marilynn Patricia 1948- WhoAmW 91, WhoE 91
Vrablik, Edward Robert 1932- WhoAm 90
Vradenburg, Beatrice White 1922- WhoAmW 91
Vradenburg, George A., III 1943- St&PR 91
Vradenburgh, Merry Christine 1963- WhoWrEP 89
Vrana, Barbara Brown 1955- WhoSSW 91
Vrana, Peter 1957- WhoE 91
Vrangel', Petr Nikolaevich 1878-1928 BioIn 16
Vranitzky, Franz BioIn 16
Vranitzky, Franz 1937- WhoWor 91
Vratsinas, Gus Michael 1944- St&PR 91
Vrba, Frederick John 1949- WhoEmL 91
Vrbancic, John Emerick 1955- WhoEmL 91, WhoWor 91
Vrbka, Stephen Louis 1949- WhoWor 91
Vrbova, Alena 1919- EncCoWW
Vredenbregt, Jeffrey Carl 1953- St&PR 91
Vredenburg, Dwight Charles 1914- St&PR 91
Vredenburg, Jo Ann 1940- WhoAmW 91
Vredevoe, Donna Lou 1938- WhoAm 90
Vreede, Henny de 1936- EncCoWW
Vreede, Mischa de EncCoWW
Vreeland, David Linden 1954- WhoEmL 91
Vreeland, Diana BioIn 16
Vreeland, Diana WorAlBi
Vreeland, Diana 1903?-1989 AnObit 1989, ConAu 129, News 90
Vreeland, Ellwyne Mae 1909-1971 BioIn 16
Vreeland, Herbert Henry 1948- St&PR 91
Vreeland, Russell Glenn 1960- WhoE 91
Vrenios, Anastasios Nicholas 1940- WhoAm 90
Vrentas, James S. WhoAm 90
Vretblad, Maud 1942- WomArch [port]
Vrhovec, Josip 1926- WhoWor 91
Vriend, Jan 1938- IntWWM 90
Vries, Adriaen de 1545-1626 IntDcAA 90
Vries, Hans Vredeman de 1527-1604 PenDiDA 89
Vries, Hugo Marie de 1848-1935 BioIn 16
Vries, Leonard de 1919- AuBYP 90
Vries, Paul 1567- PenDiDA 89
Vrieze, David J. 1945- St&PR 91
Vrla, Libbie M. 1932- St&PR 91
Vroman, Adam Clark 1856-1916 WhNaAH
Vroman, Barbara Fitz WhoWrEP 89
Vroman, Karen Lyn 1963- WhoAmW 91
Vronsky, Vitya 1909- PenDiMP
Vroom, Victor Harold 1932- WhoAm 90
Vrooman, Erwin Ray 1943- St&PR 91
Vrugt, Johanna Petronella 1905-1960 EncCoWW
Vrydagh, P. Andre 1943- WhoWor 91
Vryonis, Speros, Jr. 1928- WhoAm 90
Vu, Bach Thien 1949-1987 BioIn 16
Vu, David Hien 1948- BiDrAPA 89
Vu, Jean-Pierre 1934- WhoWor 91
Vu, Oanh Ngoc 1936- BiDrAPA 89
Vucanovich, Barbara Farrell 1921- WhoAm 90, WhoAmW 91
Vucenich, Momchilo 1945- St&PR 91
Vuchelen, Joseph 1947- WhoWor 91
Vucicevic, Anna R. 1966- ODwPR 91
Vuckovic, Alexander 1955- BiDrAPA 89
Vuckovich, Carol Yetso 1940- WhoAmW 91, WhoE 91, WhoWor 91
Vuckovich, Dragomir Michael 1927- WhoAm 90
Vuckovich, Pete 1952- Ballpl 90
Vugia, Holly Danforth 1957- WhoEmL 91
Vugman, Il'ia Semenovich 1890-1962 BioIn 16
Vugteveen, Verna Aardema AuBYP 90
Vuich, Rose Ann WhoAmW 91
Vuiet, Caroline EncCoWW
Vuillard, Edouard 1868-1940 BioIn 16, IntDcAA 90, WorAlBi
Vuillemenot, Fred A 1890-1952 WhoAmA 91N
Vuillemot, Lynne BioIn 16
Vuillemot, Patricia Maretta 1953- WhoAmW 91
Vuillet, Didier 1953- St&PR 91
Vuitton, Henry-Louis 1911- WhoAm 90
Vujan, Alexander S BiDrAPA 89
Vujovich, Christine M. 1951- WhoAmW 91
Vukasin, John Peter, Jr. 1928- WhoAm 90
Vukcevich, Vjera BiDrAPA 89
Vukhac, Dung 1944- St&PR 91
Vukich, Susan Claypool 1926- WhoAmW 91
Vukin, Gerri Patricia 1939- WhoAmW 91
Vukosav-Sepic, Ljiljana BiDrAPA 89
Vukov, Judith Ann BiDrAPA 89
Vukovic, Drago Vuko 1934- WhoWor 91
Vukovich, George 1956- Ballpl 90
Vukovich, John 1947- Ballpl 90
Vukovich, Robert Anthony 1943- WhoE 91
Vukovich, Sheryl Jan 1952- WhoAmW 91
Vuksinick, Louis Martin 1934- BiDrAPA 89
Vukson, John Thomas 1954- St&PR 91
Vulakh, Leonid Ya 1940- WhoE 91
Vuletic, Zivko ConAu 130
Vulgamore, Melvin L. 1935- WhoAm 90
Vulis, Dimitri 1964- WhoEmL 91
Vulpescu, Ileana 1932- EncCoWW
Vultaggio, Gasper D. 1948- St&PR 91
Vumbacco, Joseph Vincent 1945- St&PR 91
Vumbaco, Brenda J. 1941- WhoAmW 91
Vuncannon, Scott Branson 1959- WhoSSW 91
Vunibobo, Berenado 1932- WhoWor 91

Vunkannon, Charles Raymond 1931- *IntWWM 90*
Vuolo, Mark Dean 1953- *BiDrAPA 89*
Vuolo, Timothy John 1960- *St&PR 91*
Vuolvinius *PenDiDA 89*
Vuong, Lynette 1938- *SmATA 60 [port]*
Vuong, Lynette Dryer 1938- *WhoWrEP 89*
Vuono, Carl E. 1934- *WhoAm 90*
Vuorensola, Risto Juhani 1944- *WhoWor 91*
Vuori, Pekka 1935- *ConDes 90*
Vuorinen, Lasse Reino 1952- *WhoWor 91*
Vuoristo, Osmo Jalmari 1929- *WhoWor 91*
Vuran, Arif Ates 1944- *WhoWor 91*
Vuturo, Anthony Francis 1940- *WhoAm 90*
Vuurde, Willem van 1909- *EncPaPR 91*
Vuyk, Beb 1905- *EncCoWW*
Vxxx, Mme. de *EncCoWW*
Vyas, Bal Kishan *BiDrAPA 89*
Vyas, Chand B. 1944- *St&PR 91*
Vyas, Chetan M. *BiDrAPA 89*
Vyas, Dilip S. 1948- *St&PR 91*
Vyas, Girish Narmadashankar 1933- *WhoAm 90*
Vyas, Hasmukh A 1953- *BiDrAPA 89*
Vyas, Jagdish N 1939- *BiDrAPA 89*
Vyas, Mahendra Nath 1956- *WhoWor 91*
Vyas, Udaykumar Dayalal 1940- *WhoSSW 91*
Vybiral, Bretislav *PenDiMP*
Vychodil, Ladislav 1920- *ConDes 90*
Vydas, Saulius J *BiDrAPA 89*
Vye, John Quentin 1942- *St&PR 91,* *WhoAm 90*
Vyent, Louise *BioIn 16*
Vygotskii, L. S. 1896-1934 *BioIn 16*
Vygotskii, Lev Semenovich 1896-1934 *BioIn 16*
Vykukal, Eugene Lawrence 1929- *WhoAm 90*
Vymetal, Jan Karel 1941- *WhoWor 91*
Vynne, Nora 1870?-1914 *FemiCLE*
Vyroubal, Vlasta *BiDrAPA 89*
Vysotsky, Vladimir *BioIn 16*
Vytlacil, Vaclav 1892- *WhoAmA 91N*
Vyverman, Jules 1900- *IntWWM 90*
Vyvyan, Jennifer 1925-1974 *PenDiMP*
Vyzandis *EncCoWW*

W

W, Ez *BiDEWW*
W, M *BiDEWW*
wa Kinyatti, Maina 1944- *ConAu 132*
Waage, Donn Lester 1948- *WhoEmL 91*
Waage, Frederick Oswin 1943- *WhoSSW 91*
Waage, Mervin Bernard 1944- *WhoSSW 91*
Waak, Richard Walter 1946- *WhoSSW 91*
Waaland, James Brearley, II 1953- *WhoAmA 91*
Waalen, Annmarie 1960- *WhoAmW 91*
Waaler, Bjarne Arentz 1925- *WhoWor 91*
Waalkes, Jay Wendell 1947- *WhoEmL 91*
Waals, Jacqueline E. van der 1868-1922 *EncCoWW*
Waanders, Frederik Marcus Johannes 1945- *WhoWor 91*
Waanders, Wilhelmus 1931- *St&PR 91*
Waano-Gano, Joe 1906-1982 *WhoAmA 91N*
Waard, Elly de 1940- *EncCoWW*
Waart, Edo de *PenDiMP*
Waart, Edo de 1941- *BioIn 16*
Waban 1604?-1677? *WhNaAH*
Wabasha *WhNaAH*
Wabasha 1718-1799? *WhNaAH*
Wabasha, Joseph *WhNaAH*
Wabaunsee *WhNaAH*
Waber, Bernard *BioIn 16*
Waber, Bernard 1924- *AuBYP 90*
Wabler, Robert Charles, II 1948- *WhoSSW 91, WhoWor 91*
Wabokieshek *WhNaAH*
Wabrek, Carl W. 1925- *St&PR 91*
Wach, Roger 1929- *St&PR 91*
Wachal, David E. 1939- *WhoAm 90*
Wachal, Robert Stanley 1929- *WhoAm 90*
Wachenfeld, Johann Heinrich 1694-1725 *PenDiDA 89*
Wachenfeld, William Thomas 1926- *WhoAm 90*
Wachman, Harold Yehuda 1927- *WhoAm 90*
Wachman, Marvin 1917- *WhoAm 90*
Wachman, Murray 1931- *WhoE 91*
Wachner, Brian Gary 1945- *St&PR 91*
Wachner, Linda Joy 1946- *WhoAm 90, WhoAmW 91, WhoE 91*
Wachner, Linda Joy 1949- *ConAmBL*
Wachniak, Lana Jane 1952- *WhoAmW 91*
Wacholtz, Mary Catherine 1947- *WhoAmW 91*
Wachowiak, Frank *BioIn 16*
Wachowitz, Walter J., Jr. 1921- *St&PR 91*
Wachs, David V. 1926- *St&PR 91*
Wachs, Ethel 1923- *WhoAmA 91*
Wachs, Jay S. 1930- *St&PR 91*
Wachs, Kate Mary *WhoAmW 91*
Wachs, Martin 1941- *WhoAm 90*
Wachs, Moses 1913- *WhoAm 90*
Wachs, Robert M. 1923- *St&PR 91*
Wachs, Saul P 1931- *ConAu 30NR*
Wachsberger, Ken 1949- *WhoWrEP 89*
Wachsler, Robert Alan 1934- *WhoAm 90*
Wachsman, Harvey Frederick 1936- *WhoAm 90, WhoWor 91*
Wachsman, Kathryn Mary 1949- *WhoAmW 91*
Wachsman, Phyllis Geri 1947- *WhoAmW 91*
Wachsman, Richard M *BiDrAPA 89*
Wachspress, Morton 1924- *BiDrAPA 89*
Wachstein, Joan Martha 1941- *WhoE 91*
Wachsteter, George 1911- *WhoAmA 91*
Wacht, Jules L. *BioIn 16*
Wachtel, Alan B 1946- *BiDrAPA 89*
Wachtel, Arthur A 1926- *BiDrAPA 89*
Wachtel, Daniel Leonard 1937- *WhoE 91*
Wachtel, Eli 1951- *WhoAm 90*
Wachtel, George S. 1943- *ODwPR 91*
Wachtel, Harry H. 1917- *WhoAm 90*
Wachtel, Philip B. 1851-1913 *AmLegL*
Wachtel, Theodor 1823-1893 *PenDiMP*
Wachtell, Esther 1935- *WhoAmW 91*
Wachtell, Richard Lloyd 1920- *WhoAm 90*
Wachter, Eileen Renee *BiDrAPA 89*
Wachter, Joseph Edward 1933- *St&PR 91*
Wachter, Louise D. Noga 1942- *WhoE 91*
Wachter, Oralee *BioIn 16*
Wachter, Oralee 1935- *SmATA 61*
Wachter, Paul I *BiDrAPA 89*
Wachter, Paul J. 1931- *St&PR 91*
Wachter, Paul Sidney 1946- *St&PR 91*
Wachter, Stuart *BiDrAPA 89*
Wachter, William B. 1946- *St&PR 91*
Wachterman, Richard 1947- *St&PR 91*
Wachters, Laurentius Hendricus 1934- *WhoWor 91*
Wachtler, Sol 1930- *WhoAm 90, WhoE 91*
Wachtmeister, Wilhelm H. F. 1923- *WhoAm 90, WhoWor 91*
Wachtveitl, Kurt 1937- *WhoWor 91*
Waciuma, Charity *FemiCLE*
Wackenhut, Fred *NewAgMG*
Wackenhut, George R. 1919- *St&PR 91*
Wackenhut, George Russell 1919- *WhoAm 90*
Wackenhut, Richard Russell 1947- *St&PR 91, WhoAm 90, WhoSSW 91*
Wackenhut, Ruth J. 1922- *St&PR 91*
Wacker, Carl J 1932- *BiDrAPA 89*
Wacker, Charles H. *AuBYP 90*
Wacker, Ernest A *BiDrAPA 89*
Wacker, Frederick G., III 1960- *St&PR 91*
Wacker, Frederick Glade, Jr. 1918- *WhoAm 90*
Wacker, John Lee 1934- *WhoAm 90*
Wacker, Margaret Morrissey 1951- *WhoAmW 91, WhoEmL 91, WhoWor 91*
Wacker, Peter Oscar 1936- *WhoAm 90*
Wacker, Warren Ernest Clyde 1924- *WhoAm 90, WhoWor 91*
Wackerle, Hilmar *BioIn 16*
Wackerle, Joseph 1880-1959 *PenDiDA 89*
Wackers, Frans Jozef 1939- *WhoE 91*
Wackley, Sharon Marie 1941- *St&PR 91*
Wacks, Jerry H. 1938- *BiDrAPA 89*
Wacynski, Richard J. 1922- *St&PR 91*
Wada, Harry Nobuyoshi 1919- *WhoAm 90*
Wada, Osamu 1948- *WhoEmL 91*
Wada, Sadami 1932- *WhoAm 90*
Wada, Takao 1930- *WhoWor 91*
Waddell, Alfred Moore, Jr. 1939- *WhoAm 90*
Waddell, Daniel James 1950- *St&PR 91*
Waddell, David Robert 1951- *WhoWor 91*
Waddell, Dennis William 1954- *WhoSSW 91*
Waddell, Douglas M. 1954- *St&PR 91*
Waddell, Harry Lee 1912- *WhoAm 90*
Waddell, Helen 1889-1965 *FemiCLE*
Waddell, Helen Jane 1889-1965 *BioIn 16*
Waddell, Herbert 1903-1988 *AnObit 1988*
Waddell, Jimmy Carroll 1946- *St&PR 91*
Waddell, John Comer 1937- *St&PR 91, WhoAm 90*
Waddell, John Henry 1921- *WhoAmA 91*
Waddell, John Kenneth 1962- *WhoSSW 91*
Waddell, Lisa Bird 1960- *St&PR 91*
Waddell, M Keith 1957- *St&PR 91*
Waddell, Oliver W. 1930- *WhoAm 90*
Waddell, Oliver Wendell 1930- *St&PR 91*
Waddell, Phillip Dean 1948- *WhoSSW 91*
Waddell, Richard Dennis 1947- *WhoE 91*
Waddell, Richard H *WhoAmA 91N*
Waddell, Robert Fowler 1926- *St&PR 91*
Waddell, Rube 1876-1914 *Ballpl 90 [port], BioIn 16*
Waddell, Sandra Sue 1940- *WhoAmW 91*
Waddell, Stewart Douglas *BiDrAPA 89*
Waddell, Theodore 1941- *WhoAmA 91*
Waddell, Tom 1958- *Ballpl 90*
Waddell, William Joseph 1929- *WhoAm 90*
Waddell, William L. 1931- *St&PR 91*
Wadden, Richard Albert 1936- *WhoAm 90*
Wadden, Thomas Antony 1952- *WhoE 91*
Waddill, Graham Walker 1927- *St&PR 91*
Waddill, Graham Walker 1931- *WhoAm 90*
Waddingham, John Alfred 1915- *WhoAm 90, WhoAmA 91*
Waddington, Bette Hope *WhoAmW 91*
Waddington, Henry Richard 1939- *WhoSSW 91*
Waddington, Miriam 1917- *ConAu 30NR, FemiCLE*
Waddington, Raymond Bruce, Jr. 1935- *WhoAm 90*
Waddington, William Henry 1826-1894 *BiDFrPL*
Waddle, James E. 1949- *St&PR 91*
Waddle, Jeffrey R. *WhoWrEP 89*
Waddle, John Frederick 1927- *WhoAm 90, WhoWor 91*
Wadds, Jean Casselman 1920- *WhoAm 90*
Waddy, John Lane 1925- *WhoWor 91*
Wade, Adam 1935- *DrBIPA 90*
Wade, Alan *MajTwCW, TwCCr&M 91*
Wade, Ben 1922- *Ballpl 90*
Wade, Ben Frank 1935- *WhoAm 90*
Wade, Bill 1948- *WhoSSW 91*
Wade, Bonnie Claire 1941- *WhoAm 90*
Wade, Bryan 1950- *OxCCanT*
Wade, Byron 1947- *St&PR 91*
Wade, Carole *St&PR 91*
Wade, Charles D. 1946- *St&PR 91*
Wade, Cheryl Marie 1948- *WhoWrEP 89*
Wade, Clare *ODwPR 91*
Wade, David 1910- *BiDrAPA 89*
Wade, Deborah Ann 1954- *WhoSSW 91*
Wade, Dennis Michael 1958- *WhoSSW 91*
Wade, Dudley Freeman 1918- *St&PR 91*
Wade, Edwin Lee 1932- *St&PR 91, WhoAm 90*
Wade, Elmo B. 1925- *St&PR 91*
Wade, Ernestine *DrBIPA 90*
Wade, Evelyn C *BiDrAPA 89*
Wade, George Joseph 1938- *WhoAm 90*
Wade, George Sinclair 1926- *St&PR 91*
Wade, Glen 1921- *WhoAm 90*
Wade, Henry 1887-1969 *TwCCr&M 91*
Wade, Hubert Claude 1936- *St&PR 91*
Wade, Ingrid Sletten 1954- *WhoAmW 91*
Wade, Jack Warren, Jr. 1948- *ConAu 131*
Wade, Jake 1912- *Ballpl 90*
Wade, James M. 1943- *St&PR 91*
Wade, James Michael 1943- *WhoAm 90*
Wade, James O'Shea 1940- *WhoAm 90*
Wade, Jane 1925- *WhoAmA 91*
Wade, Jarrel Blake 1943- *WhoSSW 91*
Wade, Jeptha H. 1924- *St&PR 91*
Wade, Jeptha Homer, III 1924- *WhoAm 90*
Wade, Jimmie L. 1954- *St&PR 91*
Wade, John Stevens *WhoWrEP 89*
Wade, John Webster 1911- *WhoWor 91*
Wade, John William 1925- *WhoAm 90*
Wade, Judith Anne 1963- *WhoEmL 91*
Wade, Larry Allen *BiDrAPA 89*
Wade, Lawrence 1949?-1990 *ConAu 131*
Wade, Levi Clifford 1843-1891 *AmLegL*
Wade, Lowell Earle 1932- *WhoSSW 91*
Wade, Margaret Gaston 1948- *WhoSSW 91*
Wade, Mary Carroll 1909- *WhoAmW 91, WhoSSW 91*
Wade, Merry Gayle 1937- *WhoAmW 91*
Wade, Michael Daniel 1961- *WhoSSW 91*
Wade, Michael James 1954- *St&PR 91*
Wade, Michael R.A. 1945- *St&PR 91*
Wade, Ormand Joseph 1939- *St&PR 91, WhoAm 90, WhoWor 91*
Wade, Patricia Joan 1949- *WhoAmW 91*
Wade, Patricia Lynne 1950- *WhoAmW 91*
Wade, Richard Archer 1930- *WhoAm 90*
Wade, Robert *TwCCr&M 91*
Wade, Robert 1943- *BioIn 16*
Wade, Robert Hirsch Beard 1916- *WhoAm 90*
Wade, Robert Patrick 1947- *St&PR 91*
Wade, Robert Paul 1936- *WhoAm 90*
Wade, Robert Schrope 1943- *WhoAmA 91*
Wade, Rodger Grant 1945- *WhoWor 91*
Wade, Ronald J. 1936- *St&PR 91*
Wade, Rosalind *BioIn 16*
Wade, Rosalind 1909-1989 *FemiCLE*
Wade, Seth 1928- *WhoWrEP 89*
Wade, Susie Ann 1955- *WhoAmW 91*
Wade, Suzanne 1938- *WhoAmW 91, WhoWor 91*
Wade, Theodore Everett, Jr 1936- *WhoWrEP 89*
Wade, Thomas Edward 1943- *WhoAm 90*
Wade, Timothy Andrew 1958- *WhoWrEP 89*
Wade, Tom W. 1933- *St&PR 91*
Wade, Tom Wilton, Jr. 1933- *WhoSSW 91*
Wade, Vicki Lynne 1953- *WhoAmW 91*
Wade, Virginia 1945- *ConAu 132, WhoWor 91*
Wade, Warren Thomas 1935- *WhoWor 91*
Wade, William Edward, Jr. 1942- *WhoAm 90*
Wadell, Inga Maj-Brit 1931- *WhoWor 91*
Wadensten, Ted S. 1931- *St&PR 91*
Wadenstrom, Karin Alice *DcScanL*
Wadeson, Ralph W, Jr. 1924- *BiDrAPA 89*
Wadhawan, Jag Mohan *BiDrAPA 89*
Wadhwa, Gulshan R. 1931- *St&PR 91*
Wadhwa, Jasvinder Kaur *BiDrAPA 89*
Wadia, Behram Hormusji 1927- *WhoWor 91*
Wadier, Max *WhoWrEP 89*
Wadle, Charles Vincent 1955- *BiDrAPA 89*
Wadleigh, Richard Stanley 1944- *WhoE 91*

Wadler, Allen B. 1933- *St&PR 91*
Wadler, Allen Bernard 1933- *WhoAm 90*
Wadler, Arnold L. 1943- *St&PR 91, WhoAm 90*
Wadler, Sanford *St&PR 91*
Wadley, Harlan Dean 1947- *BiDrAPA 89*
Wadley, M. Richard 1942- *WhoAm 90, WhoWor 91*
Wadley, Susan Snow 1943- *WhoAmW 91*
Wadlin, George Knowlton, Jr. 1923- *WhoAm 90*
Wadlin, Martha Stedman 1937- *WhoWor 91*
Wadlington, Walter James 1931- *WhoAm 90*
Wadlington, Warwick Paul 1938- *WhoAm 90*
Wadlow, Joan Krueger 1932- *WhoAm 90*
Wadman, Beth E 1952- *BiDrAPA 89*
Wadman, Bruce William 1931- *St&PR 91*
Wadman, Walter J. 1935- *St&PR 91, WhoAm 90*
Wadman, Wesley Woodrow 1937- *St&PR 91*
Wadman, William Wood, III 1936- *WhoWor 91*
Wadowicz, Karen Ann 1964- *WhoAmW 91*
Wadsworth, Brenton H. 1929- *St&PR 91*
Wadsworth, Charles William 1929- *WhoAm 90*
Wadsworth, David A. 1949- *St&PR 91*
Wadsworth, Dyer Seymour 1936- *St&PR 91, WhoAm 90, WhoWor 91*
Wadsworth, Frank Whittemore 1919- *WhoAm 90*
Wadsworth, Frederick John 1933- *St&PR 91*
Wadsworth, George Leland *BiDrAPA 89*
Wadsworth, Homer Clark 1913- *WhoAm 90*
Wadsworth, Howard C. 1944- *St&PR 91*
Wadsworth, James Inge 1938- *WhoSSW 91*
Wadsworth, James Wolcott, Jr. 1877-1952 *AmLegL*
Wadsworth, Jeremiah 1743-1804 *BioIn 16*
Wadsworth, Joel Stuart 1946- *WhoEmL 91*
Wadsworth, John Murray 1937- *BiDrAPA 89*
Wadsworth, John Spencer, Jr. 1939- *WhoAm 90*
Wadsworth, Lee A. 1946- *St&PR 91*
Wadsworth, Maurice Arden 1929- *St&PR 91*
Wadsworth, Melissa *ODwPR 91*
Wadsworth, Milton Elliot 1922- *WhoAm 90*
Wadsworth, Morton L *BiDrAPA 89*
Wadsworth, Robert Arthur 1949- *St&PR 91*
Wadsworth, Robert David 1942- *St&PR 91, WhoAm 90*
Wadsworth, Robertson Lee 1927- *WhoSSW 91*
Wadsworth, Susan Linda Popkin 1936- *IntWWM 90*
Wadsworth, William Whitney 1934- *St&PR 91*
Wadud, Abdul *BiDrAPA 89*
Wadya, Hubert 1953- *St&PR 91*
Waechter, Antoine 1949- *BiDFrPL*
Waechter, Arthur Joseph, Jr. 1913- *WhoAm 90*
Waechter, Eberhard 1929- *IntWWM 90, PenDiMP*
Waechter, Eleanor Horwood Morrison 1939- *WhoAmW 91, WhoE 91*
Waechter, Friedrich Karl *BioIn 16*
Waechter, Julie Marie 1958- *WhoAmW 91*
Waechter, William F. 1938- *WhoAm 90*
Waeger, Robert W. 1946- *St&PR 91*
Waeger, Robert Wright 1946- *WhoE 91*
Waehner, Ralph Livingston 1935- *WhoAm 90*
Waelde, Thomas Walther 1949- *WhoE 91*
Waelsch, Salome Gluecksohn 1907- *WhoAm 90, WhoAmW 91*
Waelty, Beatryce Ann 1938- *WhoAmW 91*
Waesche, Richard Henley Woodward 1930- *WhoSSW 91*
Waetjen, Herman Charles 1929- *WhoAm 90*
Waetjen, Walter Bernhard 1920- *WhoAm 90*
Waffen, Bruce 1942- *ODwPR 91*
Waffle, David Ross 1950- *WhoEmL 91*
Wafford, James 1806-1896 *WhNaAH*
Wagaman, Jeffrey Scott 1963- *WhoEmL 91*
Waganheim, Arthur Brian 1959- *WhoEmL 91*
Wagar, Bruce Clayton 1947- *WhoSSW 91*
Wagar, James Lee 1934- *St&PR 91*
Wagemaker, Herbert 1929- *BiDrAPA 89*
Wageman, Thomas J. *WhoSSW 91*
Wageman, Tom *BioIn 16*
Wagenaar, Jan 1931- *WhoWor 91*
Wagenaar, Larry John 1962- *WhoEmL 91*
Wagenbrenner, William J *BiDrAPA 89*
Wagener, Donna Lynn 1959- *WhoWor 91*
Wagener, James Wilbur 1930- *WhoAm 90, WhoSSW 91*
Wagener, Johann Heinrich *PenDiDA 89*
Wagener, Marguerite Mary 1954- *WhoAmW 91*
Wagenet, Robert Jeffrey 1950- *WhoAm 90*
Wagenfeld, Wilhelm 1900- *ConDes 90, PenDiDA 89*
Wagenheim, Charles 1946- *WhoWor 91*
Wagenheim, Elliot C 1947- *BiDrAPA 89*
Wagenheim, Harry H 1918- *BiDrAPA 89*
Wagenheim, Helen Stochen 1919- *BiDrAPA 89*
Wagenheim, Laura Robin 1965- *WhoAmW 91*
Wagenheim, Susan Debra 1955- *BiDrAPA 89*
Wagenknecht, Edward 1900- *DcLB 103 [port], WhoAm 90*
Wagenmann, William David, Jr. 1943- *St&PR 91*
Wager, David W. *BioIn 16*
Wager, James Joseph 1937- *St&PR 91*
Wager, Laurence Rickard 1904-1965 *DcScB S2*
Wager, Richard Kenneth 1939- *WhoAm 90*
Wager, Ross Gaylord 1939- *St&PR 91*
Wager, Steven Gary *BiDrAPA 89*
Wager, Walter H. 1924- *ConAu 33NR*
Wager, Walter Herman 1924- *SpyFic, WhoAm 90*
Wagers, Robert Shelby 1943- *WhoAm 90*
Wages, Raymond B. 1932- *St&PR 91*
Wagg, Timothy John 1934- *WhoAm 90*
Waggener, Karl J *BiDrAPA 89*
Waggener, Ronald Edgar 1926- *WhoAm 90*
Waggle, Doyle Hans 1939- *WhoAm 90*
Waggoner, D. E. 1935- *St&PR 91*
Waggoner, David Carroll 1943- *BiDrAPA 89*
Waggoner, Hyatt Howe 1913-1988 *BioIn 16*
Waggoner, James Norman 1925- *WhoAm 90*
Waggoner, James Virgil 1927- *St&PR 91*
Waggoner, Keith *BioIn 16*
Waggoner, Leland Tate 1916- *WhoAm 90*
Waggoner, Margaret Ann 1926- *WhoAm 90*
Waggoner, Nancy 1924-1989 *BioIn 16*
Waggoner, Paul Edward 1923- *WhoAm 90*
Waggoner, Paulette Amburgey 1945- *WhoAmW 91*
Waggoner, Raymond W, Jr. 1934- *BiDrAPA 89*
Waggoner, Raymond W, Sr. 1901- *BiDrAPA 89*
Waggoner, Raymond Walter 1901- *WhoAm 90*
Waggoner, Samuel Lee 1930- *St&PR 91*
Waggoner, Thomas Jefferson, III 1934- *St&PR 91*
Waggoner, Thomas R. *AmLegL*
Waggoner, Thomas S. 1951- *St&PR 91*
Waggoner, Timothy Edward 1961- *WhoWrEP 89*
Waggoner, William Albert 1936- *St&PR 91*
Waggoner, William Johnson 1928- *WhoSSW 91*
Wagle, Sharad D 1949- *BiDrAPA 89*
Wagley, John Raible 1931- *WhoE 91*
Wagman, Albert David 1928- *BiDrAPA 89*
Wagman, Frederick Herbert 1912- *WhoAm 90*
Wagman, Gerald Howard 1926- *WhoE 91, WhoWor 91*
Wagman, John F. 1955- *St&PR 91*
Wagman, Robert John 1942- *WhoAm 90, WhoWor 91*
Wagman, Sheldon Paul 1937- *BiDrAPA 89*
Wagner, Alan Cyril 1931- *WhoAm 90, WhoE 91*
Wagner, Albert Charles 1932- *St&PR 91*
Wagner, Allan Ray 1934- *WhoAm 90*
Wagner, Allison Jean 1960- *WhoAmW 91*
Wagner, Ann Karlen 1944- *WhoAmW 91*
Wagner, Anne Marie 1951- *WhoEmL 91*
Wagner, Arthur Ward, Jr. 1930- *WhoSSW 91*
Wagner, Aubrey Joseph 1912- *St&PR 91, WhoAm 90*
Wagner, Barbara Christy 1937- *WhoWrEP 89*
Wagner, Barry J. 1940- *St&PR 91*
Wagner, Bart Jay 1937- *St&PR 91*
Wagner, Bertram 1937- *St&PR 91*
Wagner, Blanche Collet 1873- *WhoAmA 91N*
Wagner, Brett *BioIn 16*
Wagner, Bruce Stanley 1943- *St&PR 91, WhoAm 90*
Wagner, Burton Allan 1941- *WhoAm 90*
Wagner, Carl 1799-1841 *PenDiDA 89*
Wagner, Carl J. 1933- *St&PR 91*
Wagner, Carol Anne 1942- *WhoAmW 91*
Wagner, Carruth John 1916- *WhoAm 90*
Wagner, Catherine 1953- *WhoAmA 91*
Wagner, Charlene Brook *WhoAmW 91*
Wagner, Charles Abraham 1901- *WhoWrEP 89*
Wagner, Charles H *WhoAmA 91*
Wagner, Charles Leonard 1925- *WhoAm 90*
Wagner, Charlie 1912- *Ballpl 90*
Wagner, Christian Nikolaus Johann 1927- *WhoAm 90*
Wagner, Cindy Louise 1962- *WhoAmW 91*
Wagner, Clark Leslie 1932- *St&PR 91*
Wagner, Clifford Henry 1946- *WhoE 91*
Wagner, Curtis Lee, Jr. 1928- *WhoAm 90*
Wagner, Cynthia Kaye 1957- *WhoAmW 91*
Wagner, Dan *BioIn 16*
Wagner, David Edward 1938- *WhoE 91*
Wagner, David J *WhoAmA 91*
Wagner, David J. 1952- *WhoAm 90*
Wagner, David J. 1954- *St&PR 91*
Wagner, David James 1954- *WhoAm 90*
Wagner, David Lee 1955- *BiDrAPA 89*
Wagner, David Lynn 1943- *WhoE 91*
Wagner, David W. 1954- *WhoE 91*
Wagner, Debi L. 1955- *WhoEmL 91*
Wagner, Dennis Larry 1940- *WhoE 91*
Wagner, Donald Bert 1930- *WhoAm 90*
Wagner, Donald Roger 1926- *WhoSSW 91*
Wagner, Donna Mae 1939- *WhoAmW 91*
Wagner, Dorothy Marie 1924- *WhoAmW 91, WhoWor 91*
Wagner, Dottie *BiDrAPA 89*
Wagner, Douglas A. 1945- *St&PR 91*
Wagner, Douglas Edward 1952- *IntWWM 90*
Wagner, Douglas W.E. 1938- *WhoWrEP 89*
Wagner, Douglas Walker Ellyson 1938- *WhoAm 90*
Wagner, Durrett 1929- *WhoAm 90*
Wagner, Earl T. 1908-1990 *BioIn 16*
Wagner, Edmund F. 1898-1989 *BioIn 16*
Wagner, Edward A. 1906- *EncO&P 3*
Wagner, Edward Kurt 1936- *WhoAm 90*
Wagner, Edyth Elizabeth 1916- *IntWWM 90*
Wagner, Elin 1882-1949 *DcScanL*
Wagner, Elizabeth Ann 1934- *WhoAmW 91*
Wagner, Elizabeth L. *ODwPR 91*
Wagner, Elmer Lenhart 1931- *St&PR 91*
Wagner, Eric Armin 1941- *WhoWor 91*
Wagner, Ewald 1927- *WhoWor 91*
Wagner, Florence Signaigo 1919- *WhoAmW 91*
Wagner, Florent Wm. 1937- *St&PR 91*
Wagner, Frank A., Jr. 1932- *WhoE 91*
Wagner, Fred John, Jr. 1929- *WhoSSW 91*
Wagner, Frederick 1928- *AuBYP 90*
Wagner, Frederick Reese 1928- *WhoAm 90*
Wagner, Frederick William 1933- *WhoAm 90*
Wagner, G Keith 1929- *St&PR 91*
Wagner, G Noble 1907- *WhoAmA 91*
Wagner, Gary 1940- *Ballpl 90*
Wagner, Gary Wayne 1946- *WhoSSW 91*
Wagner, George Hoyt 1914- *WhoSSW 91*
Wagner, George Phillip 1946- *St&PR 91*
Wagner, Glenn A. *AuBYP 90*
Wagner, Gordon Parsons 1915-1987 *WhoAmA 91N*
Wagner, Grace Carson 1924- *WhoSSW 91*
Wagner, Grant Hulse 1936- *BiDrAPA 89*
Wagner, Hal 1915-1979 *Ballpl 90*
Wagner, Harbart J. 1937- *St&PR 91*
Wagner, Harvey Alan 1941- *St&PR 91*
Wagner, Harvey Arthur 1905- *WhoAm 90*
Wagner, Heinie 1881-1943 *Ballpl 90*
Wagner, Heinrich Leopold 1747-1779 *DcLB 94*
Wagner, Helmut Michael 1951- *WhoWor 91*
Wagner, Henry Carrh, III 1942- *WhoSSW 91*
Wagner, Henry Nicholas, Jr. 1927- *WhoAm 90*
Wagner, Honus 1874-1955 *Ballpl 90 [port], WorAlBi*
Wagner, Horst 1906-1977 *BioIn 16*
Wagner, I. J. 1915- *St&PR 91*
Wagner, Inez *BioIn 16*
Wagner, Irene *BioIn 16*
Wagner, J Richard 1928- *St&PR 91*
Wagner, Jack Andrew, Jr. 1949- *WhoSSW 91*
Wagner, Jack E. *St&PR 91*
Wagner, James Arthur 1945- *WhoSSW 91*
Wagner, James D. 1930- *St&PR 91*
Wagner, James Howe 1958- *WhoE 91*
Wagner, James Theodore 1837-1896 *DcCanB 12*
Wagner, James W. 1922- *St&PR 91*
Wagner, Jane *AuBYP 90*
Wagner, Jochen Bernhard 1950- *WhoWor 91*
Wagner, Johanna 1826-1894 *PenDiMP*
Wagner, John 1955- *WhoWrEP 89*
Wagner, John A. 1930- *St&PR 91*
Wagner, John Edward, Sr. 1931- *St&PR 91*
Wagner, John G. *St&PR 91*
Wagner, John Garnet 1921- *WhoAm 90*
Wagner, John Leo 1954- *WhoEmL 91*
Wagner, John Robert 1949- *WhoE 91*
Wagner, John Thomas 1933- *St&PR 91*
Wagner, Jolyn Welsh 1954- *BiDrAPA 89*
Wagner, Jonathan William 1942- *WhoAm 90*
Wagner, Joseph Edward 1938- *WhoAm 90*
Wagner, Judith A. *St&PR 91*
Wagner, Judith B. 1943- *St&PR 91*
Wagner, Judith Buck 1943- *WhoAm 90, WhoAmW 91*
Wagner, Julia Anne 1924- *WhoAm 90*
Wagner, Karen Dineen *BiDrAPA 89*
Wagner, Karen Sheila 1946- *WhoAmW 91*
Wagner, Kathleen Ann 1947- *WhoAmW 91*
Wagner, Katie *BioIn 16*
Wagner, Kaye Marie 1951- *WhoAmW 91*
Wagner, Keith Anthony 1932- *WhoAm 90*
Wagner, Kenneth C. 1928- *St&PR 91*
Wagner, Kenneth John 1951- *St&PR 91*
Wagner, Kenneth Ray 1940- *WhoSSW 91*
Wagner, Lavern John 1925- *IntWWM 90*
Wagner, Leon 1934- *Ballpl 90*
Wagner, Leslie 1953- *WhoAmW 91, WhoEmL 91*
Wagner, Lindsay *NewAgE 90*
Wagner, Lindsay 1949- *WorAlBi*
Wagner, Lindsay J. 1949- *WhoAm 90*
Wagner, Louis Carson, Jr. 1932- *WhoAm 90*
Wagner, Louise H.B. 1937- *St&PR 91*
Wagner, Louise Hemingway Benton 1937- *WhoAm 90, WhoAmW 91, WhoWor 91*
Wagner, Lynn Edward 1941- *WhoSSW 91*
Wagner, Mahlon Whitney 1935- *WhoE 91*
Wagner, Marjorie Coogan Downing 1917- *WhoAm 90*
Wagner, Mark 1954- *Ballpl 90*
Wagner, Mary Anthony 1916- *WhoAmW 91*
Wagner, Mary Innes 1947- *WhoAmW 91*
Wagner, Mary Kathryn 1932- *WhoAmW 91*
Wagner, Maryfrances Cusumano 1947- *WhoWrEP 89*
Wagner, Matthew George *BiDrAPA 89*
Wagner, Merrill 1935- *WhoAmA 91*
Wagner, Michael Duane 1948- *WhoEmL 91*
Wagner, Morton Jules 1925- *St&PR 91*
Wagner, Nancy Esther 1947- *WhoAmW 91*
Wagner, Nancy Lynn 1955- *WhoAmW 91*
Wagner, Norbert 1935- *St&PR 91*
Wagner, Norman Paul 1924- *St&PR 91, WhoAm 90*
Wagner, Otto Koloman 1841-1918 *PenDiDA 89*
Wagner, Pam Jean 1946- *WhoSSW 91*
Wagner, Patricia A. 1947- *WhoAmW 91*
Wagner, Paul A., III 1946- *ODwPR 91*
Wagner, Paul Alexander, III 1946- *WhoWor 91*
Wagner, Paul Anthony, Jr. 1947- *WhoEmL 91*
Wagner, Paul F. 1917- *ODwPR 91*
Wagner, Peter Ewing 1929- *WhoAm 90*
Wagner, Philip Marshall 1904- *WhoAm 90*
Wagner, Philip S *BiDrAPA 89*
Wagner, Ralph B. 1933- *WhoAm 90*
Wagner, Randy 1948- *ODwPR 91*
Wagner, Raymond C. 1926- *St&PR 91*
Wagner, Raymond Lee 1946- *WhoEmL 91*
Wagner, Richard 1813-1883 *BioIn 16, PenDiMP A, WorAlBi*
Wagner, Richard 1927- *WhoAm 90, WhoE 91, WhoWor 91*
Wagner, Richard Carl 1941- *WhoE 91*
Wagner, Richard Charles 1931- *St&PR 91*
Wagner, Richard Ellis 1923- *WhoAmA 91*
Wagner, Richard J. *ODwPR 91*
Wagner, Richard S *BiDrAPA 89*
Wagner, Richard W. *ODwPR 91*
Wagner, Robert *BioIn 16*
Wagner, Robert 1930- *WhoAm 90, WorAlBi*
Wagner, Robert Allan 1951- *St&PR 91*
Wagner, Robert C. 1927- *St&PR 91*
Wagner, Robert Deuane 1960- *WhoEmL 91*
Wagner, Robert Earl 1921- *WhoAm 90, WhoSSW 91*
Wagner, Robert F. 1877-1953 *WorAlBi*
Wagner, Robert F. 1910- *WhoAm 90*
Wagner, Robert F., Jr. 1910- *WorAlBi*
Wagner, Robert Ferdinand, Jr. 1944- *WhoAm 90*
Wagner, Robert G. 1957- *ODwPR 91*
Wagner, Robert K. 1931- *St&PR 91*

Wagner, Robert L. 1932- *St&PR 91*
Wagner, Robert Owen 1935- *WhoAm 90*
Wagner, Robert Roderick 1923- *WhoAm 90*
Wagner, Robert S. 1908- *St&PR 91*
Wagner, Robert Todd 1932- *WhoAm 90*
Wagner, Robert Wayne 1926- *WhoAm 90*
Wagner, Robert Wayne 1956- *WhoSSW 91*
Wagner, Roberta Anne *BiDrAPA 89*
Wagner, Robin 1933- *ConDes 90*
Wagner, Robin Samuel Anton 1933- *WhoAm 90*
Wagner, Roger 1914- *PenDiMP*
Wagner, Ronald Francis Vincent 1952- *WhoE 91*
Wagner, Roy *BioIn 16*
Wagner, Roy 1938- *WhoAm 90*
Wagner, Roy S 1930- *BiDrAPA 89*
Wagner, Samuel Albin Mar 1942- *WhoWor 91*
Wagner, Sara Bailey 1921- *WhoAmW 91*
Wagner, Seymour *BiDrAPA 89*
Wagner, Siegfried 1869-1930 *PenDiMP*
Wagner, Sieglinde 1921- *IntWWM 90*
Wagner, Sigrid 1942- *WhoSSW 91*
Wagner, Sigurd *WhoAm 90*
Wagner, Stephen Anthony 1953- *WhoAm 90*
Wagner, Sterling Robacker 1904- *WhoE 91*
Wagner, Sue Ellen 1940- *WhoAmW 91*
Wagner, Susan Jane *WhoAmW 91, WhoE 91*
Wagner, Suzanne Elizabeth 1958- *WhoAmW 91*
Wagner, Sylvia R. 1949- *St&PR 91*
Wagner, Terri Lee 1953- *WhoAmW 91*
Wagner, Thomas Alfred 1953- *WhoWor 91*
Wagner, Thomas Edward 1956- *WhoSSW 91*
Wagner, Thomas John 1938- *St&PR 91, WhoAm 90*
Wagner, Thomas Joseph 1939- *WhoAm 90*
Wagner, Timothy Charles 1959- *WhoE 91*
Wagner, Timothy W. 1942- *St&PR 91*
Wagner, Virgil D. 1935- *St&PR 91*
Wagner, Walter 1944- *BioIn 16*
Wagner, Warren Herbert, Jr. 1920- *WhoAm 90*
Wagner, Wayne Elwell 1938- *WhoE 91*
Wagner, William Burdette 1941- *WhoAm 90*
Wagner, William Charles 1932- *WhoAm 90*
Wagner, William Gerard 1936- *WhoAm 90*
Wagner, William Lowell 1931- *St&PR 91*
Wagner, William O. 1931- *St&PR 91*
Wagner, Wolfgang 1919- *IntWWM 90*
Wagner, Wolfgang E. 1925- *WhoWor 91*
Wagner Dahl, Margaret Gilman 1956- *WhoAmW 91*
Wagner-Egelhaaf, Martina Gabriele 1957- *WhoWor 91*
Wagner-Marmaluk, Diana 1965- *WhoAmW 91*
Wagner-Stevens, Tina Marie 1957- *WhoWrEP 89*
Wagner-Westbrook, Bonnie Joan 1953- *WhoAmW 91*
Wagnitz, John Gabriel 1942- *BiDrAPA 89*
Wagnon, John Cornelius 1926- *St&PR 91*
Wagoneers, The *WhoNeCM [port]*
Wagoner, David Everett 1928- *WhoAm 90, WhoWor 91*
Wagoner, David Russell 1926- *WhoAm 90, WhoWrEP 89*
Wagoner, John *WhoAm 90*
Wagoner, Porter 1927- *WhoAm 90, WorAlBi*
Wagoner, Ralph Howard 1938- *WhoAm 90*
Wagoner, Randy 1951- *St&PR 91*
Wagoner, Richard K. 1937- *St&PR 91*
Wagoner, Robert B 1928- *WhoAmA 91*
Wagoner, Robert Vernon 1938- *WhoAm 90*
Wagoner, W Ray 1935- *St&PR 91*
Wagoner, William Douglas 1947- *WhoEmL 91, WhoWor 91*
Wagoner, William Hampton 1927- *WhoAm 90, WhoSSW 91*
Wagonfeld, Samuel 1931- *BiDrAPA 89*
Wagonseller, James Myrl 1920- *WhoAm 90*
Wagstaff, Joan Kay 1951- *WhoAmW 91*
Wagstaff, Lula Virginia 1935- *WhoSSW 91*
Wagstaff, Marguerite Falkenburg *NewYTBS 90*
Wagstaff, Robert Rhamy, Jr. 1942- *WhoE 91*
Wagstaff, Robert Wilson 1909- *St&PR 91, WhoAm 90*
Wagstaff, Sam *BioIn 16*
Wagstaff, Suzanne 1941- *WhoAmW 91*
Wagstaff, Thomas Walton 1946- *St&PR 91*
Wah, Fred 1939- *BioIn 16*
Waha, Eric *BioIn 16*
Wahab, Abdul 1936- *WhoWor 91*
Wahab, Abdul 1956- *WhoWor 91*
Wahba, Grace *WhoAm 90*
Wahba, Leon M. *St&PR 91*
Wahba, M Safwat A *BiDrAPA 89*
Wahba, Mahmoud Mohamed 1955- *BiDrAPA 89*
Wahby, Samir Cecil 1935- *BiDrAPA 89*
Wahdan, Josephine Barrios 1937- *WhoHisp 91*
Wahl, Albert J. 1908- *St&PR 91*
Wahl, C Richard 1937- *St&PR 91*
Wahl, Charles William 1923- *BiDrAPA 89*
Wahl, David Samuel 1949- *BiDrAPA 89*
Wahl, Floyd Michael 1931- *WhoAm 90*
Wahl, Jacques Henri 1932- *St&PR 91*
Wahl, Jan 1933- *AuBYP 90*
Wahl, Jan Boyer 1933- *WhoAm 90*
Wahl, Jeff *BiDrAPA 89*
Wahl, Joan Constance 1921- *WhoAmW 91, WhoWor 91*
Wahl, Joan Lydia 1935- *WhoAmW 91*
Wahl, Jonathan Michael 1945- *WhoSSW 91*
Wahl, Kermit 1922- *Ballpl 90*
Wahl, Margaret Derby 1911- *St&PR 91*
Wahl, Martha Stoessel 1916- *WhoAmW 91*
Wahl, Paul 1922- *WhoAm 90, WhoWor 91*
Wahl, Raymond 1948- *St&PR 91*
Wahl, Roger A. 1942- *St&PR 91*
Wahl, Rosalie E. 1924- *WhoAm 90, WhoAmW 91*
Wahl, William Bryan 1963- *WhoSSW 91*
Wahlberg, Allen H. 1933- *St&PR 91*
Wahlberg, Allen Henry 1933- *WhoAm 90*
Wahlberg, Henrik 1944- *BiDrAPA 89*
Wahlberg, Philip Lawrence 1924- *WhoAm 90*
Wahlberg, Stanley L. 1936- *St&PR 91*
Wahlberg, Thomas Bertil 1943- *WhoWor 91*
Wahle, F. Keith 1947- *WhoWrEP 89*
Wahle, James L. 1936- *St&PR 91*
Wahlen, Edwin Alfred 1919- *WhoAm 90*
Wahlen, Edwin Alfred, Jr. 1947- *WhoSSW 91*
Wahlert, Robert Henry 1939- *St&PR 91*
Wahlgren, Erick 1911- *WhoWrEP 89*
Wahlgren, Erik 1911- *WhoAm 90*
Wahling, Jon B 1938- *WhoAmA 91*
Wahlke, John Charles 1917- *WhoAm 90*
Wahlman, Mark M. 1948- *St&PR 91*
Wahlman, Maude Southwell *WhoAmA 91*
Wahlmeier, Mark Anthony 1955- *St&PR 91*
Wahloo, Per 1926-1975 *TwCCr&M 91B, WorAlBi*
Wahloo, Per, and Maj Sjowall *TwCCr&M 91B*
Wahlquist, Jack Rainard 1933- *St&PR 91*
Wahlstrom, Bertil 1943- *WhoWor 91*
Wahlstrom, Carl M, Jr. *BiDrAPA 89*
Wahlstrom, Ernest Eugene 1909- *WhoAm 90*
Wahnfried, Richard *NewAgMG*
Wahoske, Michael James 1953- *WhoEmL 91*
Wahunsonacock *WhNaAH*
Wai, Grace Ming-Yee *BioIn 16*
Wai, Logan L. 1947- *St&PR 91*
Wai, Samuel Siu Ming 1953- *WhoAm 90*
Waid, Allen G. 1946- *St&PR 91*
Waid, Jim 1942- *WhoAmA 91*
Waid, Richard File 1928- *St&PR 91*
Waid, Stephen Hamilton 1948- *WhoWrEP 89*
Waide, Michael J. 1947- *St&PR 91*
Waide, Patrick Joseph, Jr. 1937- *WhoAm 90*
Waide Beuchemin, Mary Marie 1946- *WhoEmL 91*
Waigand, Ann Hutchinson 1954- *WhoWrEP 89*
Waigel, Theodor 1939- *WhoWor 91*
Waihee, John David, III 1946- *WhoAm 90, WhoWor 91*
Wailand, Adele R. 1949- *St&PR 91*
Wailand, Adele Rosen 1949- *WhoAmW 91*
Wailes, Isabel *BiDEWW*
Wain, Edward *ConTFT 8*
Wain, John 1925- *MajTwCW*
Wain, John Barrington 1925- *WhoWor 91*
Wain, Louis 1860-1939 *BioIn 16*
Wainberg, Alan 1937- *WhoAm 90*
Wainberg, Jacob M. 1906- *St&PR 91*
Wainer, Dorothy *BioIn 16*
Wainer, Herbert Alan 1941- *St&PR 91*
Wainer, Sandra N *BiDrAPA 89*
Wainer, Stanley A. 1926- *St&PR 91*
Wainerdi, Richard Elliott 1931- *WhoAm 90, WhoSSW 91*
Wainess, Marcia Watson 1949- *WhoAmW 91, WhoEmL 91, WhoWor 91*
Wainger, Allen Jay 1953- *WhoE 91*
Wainger, Gail Dubiel 1943- *BiDrAPA 89*
Wainger, Robert Alan *BiDrAPA 89*
Wainick, Daniel 1929- *St&PR 91*
Wainio, Mark Ernest 1953- *WhoEmL 91, WhoWor 91*
Wainright, Sharon Anne 1950- *BiDrAPA 89*
Wainscott, John Milton 1910-1981 *BioIn 16*
Wainscott, Ronald H 1948- *ConAu 131*
Wainston, Michael 1925- *BiDrAPA 89*
Wainwright, Carol Ann 1948- *WhoAmW 91*
Wainwright, Carroll Livingston, Jr. 1925- *WhoAm 90*
Wainwright, Charles Anthony 1933- *WhoAm 90*
Wainwright, Hilary 1949- *ConAu 131*
Wainwright, Hilda Alexander 1925- *WhoAmW 91, WhoE 91*
Wainwright, John 1921- *TwCCr&M 91*
Wainwright, Jonathan M. 1883-1953 *WorAlBi*
Wainwright, Loudon *BioIn 16*
Wainwright, Loudon, III *BioIn 16*
Wainwright, Mary Katherine 1942- *WhoSSW 91*
Wainwright, Nicholas Biddle 1914-1986 *BioIn 16*
Wainwright, Paul Edward Blech 1917- *WhoAm 90*
Wainwright, Robert Barry 1935- *WhoAmA 91*
Wainwright, Roy H *BiDrAPA 89*
Wainwright, Stephen A. 1931- *WhoAm 90*
Wainwright, Stuyvesant, II 1921- *WhoAm 90*
Wainwright, Susan Linda 1954- *BiDrAPA 89*
Wainwright, William H *BiDrAPA 89*
Wair, Donald *BiDrAPA 89*
Wait, Benjamin 1813-1895 *DcCanB 12*
Wait, Charles Valentine 1951- *WhoE 91, WhoWor 91*
Wait, Cheryl J. *ODwPR 91*
Wait, David Bryan 1961- *BiDrAPA 89*
Wait, James Richard 1924- *WhoAm 90*
Wait, John Turner 1811-1899 *AmLegL*
Wait, Mark 1947- *IntWWM 90*
Wait, Samuel Charles, Jr. 1932- *WhoE 91*
Wait, Samuel Kimball 1930- *St&PR 91*
Wait, Susan B *BiDrAPA 89*
Wait, Tynan Arthur 1949- *WhoEmL 91*
Waite, Arthur Edward 1857-1942 *EncO&P 3*
Waite, Benjamin 1813-1895 *DcCanB 12*
Waite, Charles Morrison 1932- *WhoAm 90*
Waite, Clark Greene 1932- *St&PR 91*
Waite, Daniel Elmer 1926- *WhoAm 90*
Waite, Darvin Danny *WhoWor 91*
Waite, Dennis V. *ODwPR 91*
Waite, Edward J. 1947- *St&PR 91*
Waite, Ellen Jane 1951- *WhoAmW 91*
Waite, Henry Chester 1949- *BiDrAPA 89*
Waite, James Lewis 1947- *St&PR 91*
Waite, John Graham 1943- *BiDrAPA 89*
Waite, Lawrence Wesley 1951- *WhoWor 91*
Waite, Louis E. 1926- *St&PR 91*
Waite, Mary *FemiCLE*
Waite, Mary *BiDEWW*
Waite, Norman, Jr. 1936- *WhoAm 90*
Waite, P B 1922- *SmATA 64*
Waite, Peter Arthur 1951- *WhoE 91*
Waite, Ralph 1928- *ConTFT 8*
Waite, Ralph 1929- *WhoAm 90, WorAlBi*
Waite, Robert George Leeson 1919- *WhoAm 90, WhoWrEP 89*
Waite, Robert Nelson 1945- *WhoE 91*
Waite, Stephen Holden 1936- *WhoAm 90*
Waite-Smith, Cicely 1913- *FemiCLE*
Waiter, Joseph J. 1951- *St&PR 91*
Waiter, Serge-Albert *WhoAm 90, WhoWor 91*
Waites, Althea Mitchell 1939- *IntWWM 90*
Waites, Candy Yaghjian 1943- *WhoAmW 91*
Waites, Lucius *BioIn 16*
Waites, William Ernest 1934- *WhoSSW 91*
Waithe, Mary Rebecca 1934- *WhoWor 91*
Waitkus, Eddie 1919-1972 *Ballpl 90*
Waitman, B. A. 1946- *WhoEmL 91, WhoWor 91*
Waiton, Rudolph O. 1922- *WhoWor 91*
Waits, Freddie *BioIn 16*
Waits, Rick 1952- *Ballpl 90*
Waits, S John 1948- *St&PR 91*
Waits, Thomas Alan 1949- *WhoAm 90*
Waits, Tom 1949- *BioIn 16, EncPR&S 89, WorAlBi*
Waitzkin, Evelyn Davis *BiDrAPA 89*
Waitzkin, Evelyn Davis 1918- *WhoE 91*
Waitzkin, Fred *BioIn 16*
Waitzkin, Josh *BioIn 16*
Waitzkin, Stella *WhoAmA 91*
Waizero *WomWR*
Wajda, Andrzej 1926- *BioIn 16, ConTFT 8, WhoWor 91*
Wajenberg, Arnold Sherman 1929- *WhoAm 90*
Wajer, Roman R. 1919- *St&PR 91*
Wajnert, Thomas C. 1943- *WhoAm 90*
Wakabayishi, Bozo *Ballpl 90*
Wakahara, Yasuyuki 1926- *WhoWor 91*
Wakamatu, Nobuyuki 1949- *WhoWor 91*
Wakao, Noriaki 1930- *WhoWor 91*
Wakara 1808?-1855 *WhNaAH*
Wakasugi, Hiroshi 1935- *IntWWM 90, PenDiMP*
Wakatsuki, James H. 1929- *WhoAm 90*
Wake, David Burton 1936- *WhoAm 90*
Wake, J Byron 1940- *St&PR 91*
Wake, Marvalee Hendricks 1939- *WhoAm 90, WhoAmW 91*
Wake, Thomas H. 1905- *St&PR 91*
Wakefield, Allan Gale 1941- *St&PR 91*
Wakefield, Benton McMillin, Jr. 1920- *WhoAm 90*
Wakefield, Beverly 1938- *ODwPR 91*
Wakefield, Dan *BioIn 16*
Wakefield, Dan 1932- *WhoAm 90, WhoWrEP 89*
Wakefield, David Dean 1930- *WhoAm 90*
Wakefield, Dean Matthews 1931- *WhoE 91*
Wakefield, Dick 1921-1985 *Ballpl 90*
Wakefield, Edward Gibbon 1796-1862 *BioIn 16*
Wakefield, Gerald T. 1956- *WhoSSW 91*
Wakefield, Hannah *TwCCr&M 91*
Wakefield, Harold R *BiDrAPA 89*
Wakefield, James Beach 1828-1910 *AmLegL*
Wakefield, John 1936- *IntWWM 90*
Wakefield, Joseph Sefton, Jr. 1941- *BiDrAPA 89*
Wakefield, Kim Stoeckle 1953- *WhoWrEP 89*
Wakefield, Lyman E., Jr. 1911- *St&PR 91*
Wakefield, Mary 1853-1910 *PenDiMP*
Wakefield, Meri Kelline 1962- *WhoWrEP 89*
Wakefield, P Lynn 1944- *BiDrAPA 89*
Wakefield, Priscilla 1750-1832 *BioIn 16*
Wakefield, Priscilla 1751-1832 *FemiCLE*
Wakefield, Robert Harmon 1936- *St&PR 91*
Wakefield, Stanley M. 1948- *St&PR 91*
Wakefield, Stephen Alan 1940- *WhoAm 90*
Wakefield, Wavell 1898-1983 *DcNaB 1981*
Wakeham, Helmut Richard Rae 1916- *WhoAm 90*
Wakeham, John 1932- *WhoWor 91*
Wakelee, Adah Mae 1935- *WhoAmW 91*
Wakelin, David Shattuck 1947- *WhoE 91*
Wakelin, James H. 1911-1990 *NewYTBS 90 [port]*
Wakelin, James Henry, Jr. 1911- *WhoAm 90*
Wakely, Jimmy 1914-1982 *OxCPMus*
Wakeman, Fred Joseph 1928- *St&PR 91, WhoAm 90*
Wakeman, Frederic Evans, Jr. 1937- *WhoAm 90*
Wakeman, Harold Max, Jr. 1928- *St&PR 91*
Wakeman, Mary Lalley 1955- *WhoAmW 91, WhoSSW 91*
Wakeman, Olivia *ODwPR 91*
Wakeman, Rick *EncPR&S 89, WhoAm 90*
Wakeman, Rick 1949- *OxCPMus*
Wakeman, Timothy Roy 1946- *WhoWor 91*
Wakeman-Linn, John Kenneth 1958- *WhoE 91*
Wakenhut, Roland 1944- *WhoWor 91*
Wakerlin, George Earle 1901- *WhoWor 91*
Wakid, Shukri *BioIn 16*
Wakil, Abdul 1945- *WhoWor 91*
Wakil, Salih Jawad 1927- *WhoAm 90*
Wakin, Edward 1927- *WhoWrEP 89*
Wakin, Frances Battipaglia *WhoAmW 91*
Wakita, Naoe *BioIn 16*
Wakoski, Diane 1937- *FemiCLE, WhoAm 90, WhoWrEP 89*
Waks, Dennis Stanford 1949- *WhoEmL 91*
Waksberg, Naomi 1947- *WhoAmA 91*
Waksman, Byron Halsted 1919- *WhoAm 90*
Waksman, Selman A. 1888-1973 *WorAlBi*
Waksman, Selman Abraham 1888-1973 *DcScB S2*
Walaszek, Edward Joseph 1927- *WhoAm 90*
Walatka, Pamela Portugal 1942- *WhoWrEP 89*
Walb, William Richard 1949- *WhoE 91*
Walbank, Jeremy Simon 1958- *IntWWM 90*

Walbaum, Matthaus 1554-1632 PenDiDA 89
Walberg, Herbert John 1937- WhoAm 90, WhoWor 91
Walberg, Rube 1896-1978 Ballpl 90
Walbert, David Frank 1945- WhoSSW 91
Walborsky, Harry M. 1923- WhoAm 90
Walbrecker, Ernest 1928- WhoE 91
Walbridge, Haydee 1936- WhoAmW 91
Walbridge, Irene E. 1942- St&PR 91
Walbridge, John T. 1950- St&PR 91
Walbridge, John T., Jr. 1925- St&PR 91
Walbridge, Willard E. 1913- St&PR 91
Walbridge, Willard Eugene 1913- WhoAm 90
Walbridge, William C. 1933- St&PR 91
Walbrun, Steven Carl 1961- WhoEmL 91
Walburg, Gerald 1936- WhoAmA 91
Walburg, James Brenner 1953- St&PR 91
Walby, Thomas Francis 1940- WhoWor 91
Walch, John James BiDrAPA 89
Walch, John Leo 1918- WhoAmA 91
Walch, Klaus 1938- WhoWor 91
Walch, Peter Sanborn 1940- WhoAm 90
Walch, Tina Jamnback BiDrAPA 89
Walcha, Helmut 1907- IntWWM 90, PenDiMP
Walcher, Alan Ernest 1949- WhoWor 91
Walcher, Dwain Newton 1915- WhoWor 91
Walcott, Ardell Williams 1945- WhoSSW 91
Walcott, Bruce Lanier 1959- WhoSSW 91
Walcott, Delbert Lee 1930- St&PR 91, WhoSSW 91
Walcott, Derek BioIn 16
Walcott, Derek 1930- DrBIPA 90, MajTwCW
Walcott, Derek Alton 1930- WhoWor 91
Walcott, Eustis ODwPR 91
Walcott, Frank Leslie 1916- BioIn 16
Walcott, Jersey Joe 1914- WorAlBi
Walcott, John Andrew 1947- WhoE 91
Walcott, Samuel Alexander 1902- BiDrAPA 89
Walcutt, Charles C. 1908-1989 BioIn 16
Walczak, Karl St&PR 91
Walczak, Lee 1946- WhoE 91
Walczak, Zbigniew Kazimierz 1932- WhoSSW 91
Walczynski, Ann BiDrAPA 89
Wald, Alan M 1946- ConAu 129
Wald, Bernard Joseph 1932- WhoE 91, WhoWor 91
Wald, Carol 1935- WhoAmA 91
Wald, Elfriede WhoWrEP 89
Wald, Francine Joy Weintraub 1938- WhoAmW 91, WhoE 91, WhoWor 91
Wald, George 1906- WhoAm 90, WhoE 91, WhoWor 91, WorAlBi
Wald, Grover 1936- BiDrAPA 89
Wald, Jeff 1944- St&PR 91
Wald, Jerome 1911-1962 WorAlBi
Wald, Jonathan Stuart BiDrAPA 89
Wald, Kenneth D. 1949- ConAu 129
Wald, Lillian D. 1867-1940 BioAmW, BioIn 16, WorAlBi
Wald, Marla Frances BiDrAPA 89
Wald, Marla Frances 1961- WhoE 91
Wald, Marlena Malmstedt 1950- WhoSSW 91
Wald, Martin 1934- WhoAm 90
Wald, Mary S. 1943- WhoAmW 91
Wald, Michael 1911- St&PR 91
Wald, Michael H. 1953- WhoEmL 91
Wald, Niel 1925- WhoAm 90
Wald, Palmer B 1930-1988 WhoAmA 91N
Wald, Palmer Bernard 1930-1988 BioIn 16
Wald, Patricia McGowan 1928- WhoAm 90, WhoAmW 91, WhoE 91
Wald, Richard Charles WhoAm 90
Wald, Robert D 1924- BiDrAPA 89
Wald, Robert J 1941- BiDrAPA 89
Wald, Sylvia WhoAmA 91
Wald, Sylvia 1915- WhoAm 90, WhoAmW 91
Wald, William G. 1927- St&PR 91
Waldau, Helen Frances 1925- WhoAmW 91, WhoE 91
Waldauer, Charles 1935- WhoE 91
Waldbauer, Gilbert Peter 1928- WhoAm 90
Waldbaum, Ira 1927- WhoAm 90
Waldbaum, Jane Cohn 1940- WhoAmW 91
Waldbaum, Ruth BiDrAPA 89
Waldberg, Isabelle 1911- BiDWomA
Waldbillig, Charles Craig 1926- St&PR 91
Walde, William L. BioIn 16
Waldeck, Dennis J. 1940- St&PR 91
Waldeck, Glen BioIn 16
Waldeck, Jacqueline Ashton WhoAmW 91, WhoSSW 91, WhoWor 91
Waldeck, John Walter, Jr. 1949- WhoEmL 91, WhoWor 91
Waldeck, Kenneth Theodore 1942- WhoSSW 91
Waldeck, Kenneth Theodore, Jr. 1942- St&PR 91
Waldeck, Lewis 1935- IntWWM 90
Waldeck, Steve P. 1951- St&PR 91
Waldeck, Theodore J. 1894- AuBYP 90
Waldeck-Rousseau, Pierre-Marie Rene E. 1846-1904 BiDFrPL
Waldecker, Thomas Raymond 1950- WhoEmL 91
Waldegrave, James 1715-1763 BioIn 16
Waldegrave, William 1946- BioIn 16
Waldemar, Jose Ovidio C 1947- BiDrAPA 89
Waldemar, Shirley Elise 1944- WhoAmW 91
Walden, Alfred S. 1941- St&PR 91
Walden, Amelia Elizabeth WhoAm 90
Walden, Amelia Elizabeth 1909- AuBYP 90
Walden, Barbara ODwPR 91
Walden, Charles W 1938- BiDrAPA 89
Walden, Daniel 1922- WhoAm 90
Walden, James William 1936- WhoWor 91
Walden, Joseph Lawrence 1956- WhoSSW 91
Walden, Lea Ann 1964- WhoWrEP 89
Walden, Marion Patrick 1939- St&PR 91
Walden, Mickey Joe 1953- WhoEmL 91
Walden, Nelson Ewing 1924- St&PR 91
Walden, Philip Michael 1940- WhoAm 90
Walden, Richard Henry 1913- WhoWor 91
Walden, Richard Keith 1913- WhoWor 91
Walden, Robert 1943- WhoAm 90
Walden, Robert E BiDrAPA 89
Walden, Royce B. 1928- St&PR 91
Walden, Stanley Eugene 1932- IntWWM 90, WhoAm 90
Walden, Sue Cole 1947- WhoAmW 91
Walden, Thomas, III 1940- St&PR 91
Walden, Thomas Alfred 1949- WhoSSW 91
Waldenberg, Leopold Mark 1941- WhoSSW 91
Waldenborg, Torsten 1925- WhoWor 91
Waldenfels, Bernhard 1934- WhoWor 91
Waldenfels, Hans 1931- ConAu 131
Waldenstrom, Martin M. 1948- St&PR 91
Walder, Phileas EncO&P 3
Walder, Robert Alan 1953- WhoEmL 91
Walder, Russell NewAgMG
Waldera, Katherine Ann 1956- WhoAmW 91
Waldeyer, Heinrich W. G. Von 1836-1921 WorAlBi
Waldfogel, Morton Sumner 1922- St&PR 91, WhoAm 90
Waldfogel, Peter Douglas 1951- St&PR 91
Waldfogel, Shimon BiDrAPA 89
Waldhauer, Fred Donald 1927- WhoAm 90
Waldhausen, John Anton 1929- WhoAm 90
Waldhauser, Cathy H. 1949- St&PR 91
Waldhauser, Cathy Howard 1949- WhoAmW 91
Waldheim, Betty Jean 1947- WhoAmW 91
Waldheim, Franklin 1896-1990 BioIn 16
Waldheim, Hugo, Jr. BiDrAPA 89
Waldheim, Kurt BioIn 16
Waldheim, Kurt 1918- WhoWor 91, WorAlBi
Waldinger, Martin Harris 1938- St&PR 91
Waldinger, Robert Jon 1951- BiDrAPA 89, WhoE 91
Waldkirch, Dale E. St&PR 91
Waldman, A.J. 1954- BiDrAPA 89
Waldman, A. M. 1926- St&PR 91
Waldman, Abraham L BiDrAPA 89
Waldman, Albert Louis BiDrAPA 89
Waldman, Anne Lesley 1945- WhoAm 90, WhoWrEP 89
Waldman, Barry Jerome 1940- St&PR 91
Waldman, Bart 1948- WhoEmL 91
Waldman, Bernard 1913-1986 BioIn 16
Waldman, Diane 1936- WhoAm 90
Waldman, Edward BioIn 16
Waldman, Frank 1919- AuBYP 90
Waldman, George Dewey 1932- WhoE 91
Waldman, Harry 1942- St&PR 91
Waldman, Jay Carl 1944- WhoAm 90
Waldman, Jeffrey 1941- WhoE 91
Waldman, Judith L. 1942- WhoAmW 91
Waldman, Jules Lloyd 1912- WhoAm 90, WhoWor 91
Waldman, Maria 1842-1920 PenDiMP
Waldman, Martin Jay 1934- St&PR 91
Waldman, Maurice 1926- BiDrAPA 89
Waldman, Neil 1947- BioIn 16
Waldman, Paul 1936- WhoAmA 91, WhoE 91
Waldman, Robert Allan 1952- WhoEmL 91
Waldman, Robert Hart 1938- WhoAm 90
Waldman, Robert Irwin 1948- WhoEmL 91
Waldman, Roy David BiDrAPA 89
Waldman, Sanford 1929- BiDrAPA 89
Waldman, Saul J. 1931- ODwPR 91
Waldman, Saul Joseph 1931- St&PR 91
Waldman, Stanley St&PR 91
Waldman, Susie Berg BioIn 16
Waldman-Schwartz, Myra Susan 1942- WhoE 91
Waldmann, Thomas Alexander 1930- WhoAm 90
Waldmeir, Peter Nielsen 1931- WhoAm 90
Waldmuller, Ferdinand Georg 1793-1865 IntDcAA 90
Waldo, Carolyn BioIn 16
Waldo, Dwight 1913- WhoAm 90
Waldo, E. Hunter ConAu 32NR, MajTwCW
Waldo, Edward Hamilton ConAu 32NR, MajTwCW
Waldo, Joseph Thomas 1950- WhoEmL 91
Waldo, Judy BiDrAPA 89
Waldo, Robert Carl, Jr. 1954- WhoE 91
Waldo, Robert Leland 1923- WhoAm 90
Waldo, Suzanne Tracey 1953- WhoE 91
Waldo, Willard H. 1912- St&PR 91
Waldoch, Donna Mae 1951- WhoAmW 91
Waldock, Humphrey 1904-1981 DcNaB 1981
Waldoff, Milton 1931- St&PR 91
Waldoks, Phillip Harry 1952- St&PR 91, WhoEmL 91
Waldon, Alton Ronald, Jr. 1936- BlkAmsC [port]
Waldor, Melanie 1796-1871 EncCoWW
Waldorf, Dolores BioIn 16
Waldorf, James A. 1938- St&PR 91
Waldrep, Jack Marion, Jr. 1952- WhoSSW 91
Waldrep, Kent BioIn 16
Waldrep, Phil 1960- WhoWrEP 89
Waldrip, Bryan 1939- BioIn 16
Waldron, Ann Marie 1957- BiDrAPA 89
Waldron, Anthony James 1924- WhoE 91
Waldron, Arthur Nelson 1948- WhoE 91
Waldron, Carol Waters 1942- WhoAmW 91
Waldron, Charles F. 1920- St&PR 91
Waldron, Deloris Meta 1949- WhoAmW 91
Waldron, Ellis Leigh 1915- WhoAm 90
Waldron, Eric L. St&PR 91
Waldron, Gail 1936- BiDrAPA 89
Waldron, Hicks Benjamin BioIn 16
Waldron, Hicks Benjamin 1923- St&PR 91, WhoAm 90
Waldron, Ingrid Lore 1939- WhoAmW 91
Waldron, James MacKeilar 1909-1974 WhoAmA 91N
Waldron, Maggie ODwPR 91
Waldron, Margaret Ann 1927- WhoAmW 91
Waldron, Reuben Howard 1920- St&PR 91
Waldron, Robert E. St&PR 91
Waldron, Robert Leroy, II 1936- WhoSSW 91
Waldron, Rodney K. 1919- WhoAm 90
Waldron, Sharon Elaine 1941- WhoE 91
Waldron, Sherwood, Jr. 1936- BiDrAPA 89
Waldron, Stuart Edward 1953- WhoSSW 91
Waldron, Theodore Charles 1946- WhoEmL 91
Waldron, William Augustus 1913- WhoAm 90
Waldrop, Bernard Keith 1932- WhoAm 90
Waldrop, Charles Wesley 1933- WhoSSW 91
Waldrop, Don R. 1945- St&PR 91
Waldrop, F Neil BiDrAPA 89
Waldrop, Francis Neil 1926- WhoAm 90
Waldrop, Gideon William 1919- WhoAm 90
Waldrop, Gideon William, Jr. 1919- IntWWM 90
Waldrop, Howard Leon 1948- WhoEmL 91
Waldrop, Robert Louis 1937- St&PR 91
Waldrop, Rosmarie 1935- WhoWrEP 89
Waldrop, S. M. 1930- St&PR 91
Waldrop, William McGuire BiDrAPA 89
Waldschmidt, Paul Edward 1920- WhoAm 90
Waldstein, Sheldon Saul 1924- WhoAm 90
Waldstein, Susan M. 1947- WhoAmW 91
Waldteufel, Emile 1837-1915 OxCPMus
Waldy, Donald Michael 1949- WhoE 91
Wale, Norman Edward 1947- WhoAm 90
Walek, Thomas 1957- ODwPR 91
Walen, Harry Leonard 1915- WhoAm 90, WhoWor 91
Walen, Kimball F. 1945- WhoE 91
Walendowski, George Jerry 1947- WhoEmL 91
Walenta, Albert Heinrich 1943- WhoWor 91
Walentia, John R. St&PR 91
Wales, Gwynne Huntington 1933- WhoAm 90
Wales, Harold Webster 1928- WhoAm 90
Wales, Hugh Gregory 1910- WhoAm 90
Wales, Richard P. 1933- St&PR 91
Wales, Walter D. 1933- WhoAm 90
Walesa, Lech 1943- BioIn 16, News 91-2 [port], WhoWor 91, WorAlBi
Walesa, Slawek BioIn 16
Waletzky, Jeremy Peter 1943- BiDrAPA 89
Waletzky, Lucy R 1941- BiDrAPA 89
Walewander, Jim BioIn 16
Waley, Arthur David 1889-1966 EncJap
Walford, E John 1945- WhoAmA 91
Walford, Harvie Dyke 1927- St&PR 91
Walford, Leslie Nicholl 1927- WhoWor 91
Walford, Lucy 1845-1915 FemiCLE
Walford, Lucy Bethia 1845-1915 BioIn 16
Walfred, Hugo Anderson 1925- WhoAm 90
Walgreen, Charles R., III BioIn 16
Walgreen, Charles R., III 1935- St&PR 91
Walgreen, Charles Rudolph, III 1935- WhoAm 90
Walgreen, John Arthur 1938- WhoE 91
Walgren, Bette Jo Weber 1942- WhoAmW 91
Walgren, Doug 1940- WhoAm 90, WhoE 91
Walheim, John Eugene 1927- WhoE 91
Walhout, Justine Simon 1930- WhoAmW 91
Wali, Kameshwar 1927- WhoAm 90
Wali, Mohan Kishen 1937- WhoAm 90
Wali, Sima 1951- WhoE 91
Waligora, James 1954- WhoEmL 91
Waligurski, Raymond J. 1940- St&PR 91
Walinska, Anna 1916- WhoAmA 91
Walinski, Nicholas Joseph 1920- WhoAm 90
Walinsky, Adam 1937- WhoWor 91
Walinsky, Louis Joseph 1908- WhoAm 90
Walish, Geralyn Rose 1956- WhoE 91
Walk, Bob 1956- Ballpl 90
Walk, Donald R 1933- BiDrAPA 89
Walk, Donald Willard 1951- WhoEmL 91
Walk, Richard David 1920- WhoAm 90, WhoWor 91
Walk, Thomas Preston 1956- WhoEmL 91
Walk-in-the-Water 1775?-1825? WhNaAH
Walkara 1808?-1855 WhNaAH
Walke, David 1954- ODwPR 91
Walke, David Michael 1954- WhoAm 90
Walke, Jean Holland 1950- WhoAmW 91
Walke, Julia Annette 1908- WhoWrEP 89
Walken, Christopher 1943- CurBio 90 [port], WhoAm 90, WorAlBi
Walkenhorst, Stewart R. 1953- St&PR 91
Walker 1808?-1855 WhNaAH
Walker, Ada Overton 1880-1914 DrBIPA 90
Walker, Adrian David WhoE 91
Walker, Alan 1930- IntWWM 90
Walker, Alan 1949- ConAu 129
Walker, Alexander M BiDrAPA 89
Walker, Alexander Muir 1948- WhoE 91
Walker, Alice 1944- BioIn 16, FemiCLE, MajTwCW, WorAlBi
Walker, Alice Malsenior 1944- WhoAm 90, WhoAmW 91, WhoWrEP 89
Walker, Amasa 1799-1875 EncABHB 6 [port]
Walker, Anita L. 1936- St&PR 91
Walker, Annie Louisa 1836-1907 FemiCLE
Walker, Arleen Denise 1957- WhoEmL 91
Walker, Arthur Dennis 1932- IntWWM 90
Walker, Arthur Lonzo 1926- WhoSSW 91
Walker, Audley Lawson 1935- WhoWor 91
Walker, B. D. 1937- WhoSSW 91
Walker, B. J. 1919- St&PR 91
Walker, Barbara BioIn 16
Walker, Barbara Muhs 1928- BioIn 16
Walker, Barry J. 1936- WhoE 91
Walker, Benjamin H. 1921- St&PR 91
Walker, Bernadette Marie 1960- WhoAmW 91
Walker, Bert H. 1923- St&PR 91
Walker, Berta WhoAmA 91
Walker, Betsy Ellen 1953- St&PR 91, WhoAm 90
Walker, Bill DrBIPA 90
Walker, Bill 1903-1966 Ballpl 90
Walker, Billie Rae 1944- WhoAmW 91
Walker, Billy Kenneth 1946- WhoSSW 91
Walker, Bree BioIn 16
Walker, Bridgett 1958- St&PR 91
Walker, Brigitte Maria 1934- WhoSSW 91
Walker, Brooks, Jr. 1928- St&PR 91, WhoAm 90
Walker, Bruce Edward 1926- WhoAm 90
Walker, Bruce M. 1923- WhoAm 90
Walker, C. Alan 1944- WhoE 91
Walker, C. Eugene 1939- WhoSSW 91
Walker, C. J., Madame 1867-1919 BioIn 16
Walker, Calvin Cecil 1952- BiDrAPA 89
Walker, Candace Lea BiDrAPA 89

Walker, Carol Ann 1937- WhoAmW 91
Walker, Carol Ellen Burton 1934- WhoSSW 91
Walker, Carol Lee 1957- WhoAmW 91
Walker, Carolyn WhoAmW 91
Walker, Carolyn Peyton 1942- WhoAmW 91
Walker, Carrie Ramsey 1948- WhoEmL 91
Walker, Catherine BioIn 16
Walker, Cecil L. BioIn 16
Walker, Cecil L. 1923- St&PR 91
Walker, Cedric Frank 1950- WhoSSW 91
Walker, Ceil Ann 1952- WhoAmW 91
Walker, Ceil Thomas 1952- ODwPR 91
Walker, Charles A. 1935- WhoAm 90
Walker, Charles Allen 1914- WhoAm 90
Walker, Charles Arthur 1944- St&PR 91
Walker, Charles B. 1939- St&PR 91
Walker, Charles Edward, Jr. 1957- WhoSSW 91
Walker, Charles G 1935- BiDrAPA 89
Walker, Charles Leland 1926- St&PR 91, WhoAm 90
Walker, Charles Montgomery 1915- WhoAm 90
Walker, Charles Norman 1923- WhoAm 90
Walker, Charles R., III 1930- WhoAm 90
Walker, Charles Simonton 1934- St&PR 91
Walker, Charles Urmston 1931- WhoAm 90
Walker, Charlotte F BiDrAPA 89
Walker, Charlotte Geraldine 1944- WhoAmW 91
Walker, Charls Edward 1923- WhoAm 90
Walker, Clarence Wesley 1931- WhoAm 90
Walker, Coleman Carter BioIn 16
Walker, Constance Maxfield 1949- WhoAmW 91
Walker, Cora Thomesina 1926- WhoAm 90
Walker, Corliss Powers 1853-1942 OxCCanT [port]
Walker, Craig J. BioIn 16
Walker, Craig James 1940- St&PR 91
Walker, Craig Michael 1947- WhoE 91
Walker, Curt 1896-1955 Ballpl 90
Walker, D. A. 1946- St&PR 91
Walker, D. P. BioIn 16
Walker, Dale L. BioIn 16
Walker, Dale N. 1952- St&PR 91
Walker, Dale Rush 1943- WhoAm 90
Walker, Daniel Gordon BiDrAPA 89
Walker, Daniel Pickering BioIn 16
Walker, Darcy Lynn 1949- WhoAmW 91
Walker, David Alan 1941- WhoE 91
Walker, David Bradstreet 1927- WhoE 91
Walker, David G 1926- SmATA 60
Walker, David Harry 1911- WhoAm 90
Walker, David James 1905- BioIn 16
Walker, David M. BioIn 16
Walker, David Michael 1951- WhoAm 90, WhoEmL 91
Walker, David Parker 1950- BiDrAPA 89
Walker, David Todd 1937- St&PR 91, WhoAm 90
Walker, David Wild 1941- WhoAm 90
Walker, David William 1955- WhoSSW 91
Walker, Deborah Colleen Rose 1959- WhoAmW 91
Walker, Deborah Lou 1958- WhoAmW 91
Walker, Debra May 1956- WhoAmW 91
Walker, Deloss 1931- WhoSSW 91
Walker, Dennis William 1948- WhoSSW 91
Walker, Deward Edgar, Jr. 1935- WhoWor 91
Walker, Diana 1925- AuBYP 90
Walker, Dixie 1887-1965 Ballpl 90
Walker, Dixie 1910-1982 Ballpl 90 [port]
Walker, Doak 1927- BioIn 16
Walker, Don 1907-1989 BioIn 16
Walker, Don T. 1942- St&PR 91
Walker, Donald Anthony WhoAm 90
Walker, Donald Ezzell 1921- WhoAm 90
Walker, Donald S. 1901- St&PR 91
Walker, Donna Henry 1954- WhoEmL 91
Walker, Dorothy Mae BioIn 16
Walker, Douglas Dunning 1940- St&PR 91, WhoAm 90
Walker, Duane 1957- Ballpl 90
Walker, Duard Lee 1921- WhoAm 90
Walker, Duncan Roy 1942- WhoWor 91
Walker, E Cardon 1916- St&PR 91
Walker, Eben T. 1948- St&PR 91
Walker, Edmund F BiDrAPA 89
Walker, Edward Anthony 1951- BiDrAPA 89
Walker, Edward D 1946- WhoAmA 91
Walker, Edward John, III 1944- St&PR 91
Walker, Edward Keith, Jr. 1933- WhoAm 90
Walker, Edward S., Jr. 1940- WhoAm 90, WhoWor 91
Walker, Edwin O BiDrAPA 89
Walker, Edyth 1867-1950 PenDiMP
Walker, Elaine Nogay 1951- WhoAmW 91
Walker, Elizabeth 1623-1690 BiDEWW, FemiCLE
Walker, Elizabeth Ann Eyer 1954- IntWWM 90
Walker, Elizabeth Anne 1959- WhoAmW 91
Walker, Elizabeth Sue 1948- WhoAmW 91
Walker, Eljana M. du Vall 1924- WhoAmW 91, WhoWor 91
Walker, Elva Mae Dawson 1914- WhoWor 91
Walker, Emery 1851-1933 BioIn 16
Walker, Eric Arthur 1910- WhoAm 90
Walker, Ernest Winfield 1917- WhoAm 90
Walker, Esper Lafayette, Jr. 1930- WhoSSW 91
Walker, Ethel 1861-1951 BiDWomA
Walker, Eunice Miriam Arnaud WhoWor 91
Walker, Evelyn WhoAmW 91, WhoSSW 91, WhoWor 91
Walker, Everett WhoAmA 91N
Walker, Ewell Doak 1927- St&PR 91
Walker, F. Ann 1940- WhoAmW 91
Walker, Fergus Joseph, Jr. 1934- WhoAm 90
Walker, Fleet 1856-1924 Ballpl 90
Walker, Florence Ann 1939- WhoSSW 91
Walker, Frances Ola 1939- WhoAmW 91
Walker, Francis Amasa 1840-1897 EncABHB 6 [port]
Walker, Francis G. 1928- St&PR 91
Walker, Francis Joseph 1922- WhoWor 91
Walker, Francis Roach 1944- WhoSSW 91
Walker, Frank Banghart 1931- WhoAm 90, WhoWor 91
Walker, Frank Comerford 1886-1959 BiDrUSE 89
Walker, Frank D. 1934- St&PR 91
Walker, Frank Dilling 1934- WhoAm 90
Walker, Franklin D BiDrAPA 89
Walker, Fred Collins 1921- WhoAm 90
Walker, Fred Elmer 1931- WhoAm 90
Walker, Fred Wyeth 1942- WhoWrEP 89
Walker, Frederic Rockwell 1933- WhoSSW 91
Walker, Frederick 1840-1875 BioIn 16
Walker, Gabriel F. 1950- St&PR 91
Walker, Gail Flanagan 1946- WhoAmW 91
Walker, Gail Juanice 1937- WhoAmW 91
Walker, Gail Russell 1954- St&PR 91
Walker, Gary Bainbridge 1941- WhoE 91
Walker, Gary Lamar 1949- WhoSSW 91
Walker, Gary Lee 1941- St&PR 91
Walker, Gay Hunner Parsons 1939- WhoAm 90
Walker, Gayle Jean 1947- WhoAmW 91
Walker, Gee 1908-1981 Ballpl 90
Walker, Geoffrey de Q 1940- ConAu 131
Walker, George 1873-1911 BioIn 16
Walker, George A. St&PR 91
Walker, George F. BioIn 16
Walker, George F. 1927- St&PR 91
Walker, George F 1947- ConLC 61 [port], OxCCanT [port]
Walker, George Herbert, III 1931- WhoAm 90
Walker, George Kontz 1938- WhoAm 90, WhoSSW 91, WhoWor 91
Walker, George Lee 1944- WhoSSW 91
Walker, George R. 1915- St&PR 91
Walker, George Theophilus 1922- DrBlPA 90, IntWWM 90
Walker, George Theophilus, Jr. 1922- WhoAm 90
Walker, George W 1873-1911 DrBlPA 90
Walker, George William, III 1944- WhoE 91
Walker, Gerri Hendricks 1944- WhoAmW 91
Walker, Gladys Lorraine 1927- WhoWrEP 89
Walker, Glen Dale 1934- WhoSSW 91
Walker, Gordon Arlon 1928- St&PR 91
Walker, Gordon Davies 1944- WhoAm 90, WhoWor 91
Walker, Gordon R. 1904- St&PR 91
Walker, Greg BioIn 16
Walker, Greg 1959- Ballpl 90
Walker, Gus A. 1899- St&PR 91, WhoAm 90
Walker, Gwyneth Van Anden 1947- IntWWM 90
Walker, Harold Allen 1945- WhoSSW 91
Walker, Harold Blake 1904- WhoAm 90
Walker, Harold Emmett 1932- WhoSSW 91
Walker, Harold Osmonde 1928- WhoAm 90
Walker, Harriette Ish BioIn 16
Walker, Harry TwCCr&M 91
Walker, Harry 1918- Ballpl 90, BioIn 16
Walker, Harry Grey 1924- WhoAm 90
Walker, Harry Webster, II 1921- WhoSSW 91
Walker, Hay 1931- St&PR 91
Walker, Helen BioIn 16
Walker, Helen 1950- IntWWM 90
Walker, Helen Smith 1917- WhoSSW 91
Walker, Henry A., Jr. 1922- St&PR 91
Walker, Henry Alexander, Jr. 1922- WhoAm 90
Walker, Henry Babcock, Jr 1885-1966 WhoAmA 91N
Walker, Henry Gary 1921- WhoSSW 91
Walker, Henry Gilbert 1947- WhoAm 90
Walker, Herbert Brooks 1927- WhoAmA 91
Walker, Herbert I 1929- BiDrAPA 89
Walker, Herbert Leslie, Jr. 1918- WhoAm 90
Walker, Herschel BioIn 16
Walker, Herschel 1962- WorAlBi
Walker, Herschel Carey WhoAmA 91N
Walker, Hiram 1816-1899 DcCanB 12
Walker, Howard Allen 1932- St&PR 91
Walker, Howard Kent 1935- WhoAm 90
Walker, Howard Oldham 1923- St&PR 91
Walker, Hub 1906-1982 Ballpl 90
Walker, Hudson D 1907-1976 WhoAmA 91N
Walker, Hyral Berwyn, Jr. 1963- WhoSSW 91
Walker, Inez Nathaniel 1911-1990 MusmAFA
Walker, Jack Leroy 1925- WhoAm 90
Walker, James Adams 1921-1987 WhoAmA 91N
Walker, James Alvin, Jr. 1946- St&PR 91
Walker, James Arthur 1948- WhoEmL 91
Walker, James Carroll 1931- BiDrAPA 89
Walker, James Cornelius 1953- WhoSSW 91
Walker, James Elliot Cabot 1926- WhoAm 90
Walker, James George 1958- WhoE 91
Walker, James J. 1881-1946 WorAlBi
Walker, James Kenneth 1936- WhoAm 90
Walker, James Lynwood WhoAm 90
Walker, James Roy 1937- WhoAm 90
Walker, James Silas 1933- WhoAm 90
Walker, James W., Jr. 1927- St&PR 91
Walker, James Whittenburg 1935- WhoSSW 91
Walker, James Willard 1943- WhoAm 90
Walker, James William, Jr. 1927- WhoAm 90, WhoE 91
Walker, Jane Beck 1933- WhoAmW 91
Walker, Jeanne Murray 1944- WhoWrEP 89
Walker, Jeffrey Clemens 1955- WhoE 91
Walker, Jerald Carter 1938- WhoAm 90
Walker, Jerry 1939- Ballpl 90
Walker, Jerry Vanzant 1925- WhoAm 90
Walker, Jessie WhoWor 91
Walker, Jewett Lynius 1930- WhoSSW 91, WhoWor 91
Walker, Jimmie 1947- DrBlPA 90
Walker, Joe Louis BioIn 16
Walker, Joe Robert 1932- St&PR 91
Walker, John ODwPR 91
Walker, John 1939- BioIn 16
Walker, John 1952- BioIn 16
Walker, John Andrew 1939- WhoAm 90
Walker, John Anthony BioIn 16
Walker, John Denley 1921- WhoAm 90
Walker, John Edwin Blake 1956- WhoWor 91
Walker, John Ernst 1938- St&PR 91
Walker, John Hanson 1843?-1933 BioIn 16
Walker, John Ingram 1944- BiDrAPA 89
Walker, John M NewYTBS 90
Walker, John Mercer, Jr. 1940- WhoAm 90
Walker, John Michael 1942- WhoSSW 91
Walker, John Neal 1930- WhoAm 90
Walker, John Sumpter, Jr. 1921- WhoWor 91
Walker, John Thomas BioIn 16
Walker, John U., Jr. 1919- St&PR 91
Walker, Johnny Del 1947- WhoSSW 91
Walker, Jonathan Lee 1948- WhoEmL 91
Walker, Joseph 1865-1941 AmLegL
Walker, Joseph 1922- WhoAm 90
Walker, Joseph A 1935- DrBlPA 90
Walker, Joseph Lawrence, III 1946- WhoE 91
Walker, Joseph P. 1946- St&PR 91
Walker, Joseph Reddeford 1798-1876 WhNaAH
Walker, Jr. 1942?- EncPR&S 89
Walker, Jr., & the All Stars EncPR&S 89
Walker, Juanita Fay 1959- WhoAmW 91
Walker, Julian Wilson, Jr. 1934- St&PR 91
Walker, K. Grahame BioIn 16
Walker, K. Grahame 1937- WhoAm 90
Walker, Karen 1935- WhoAmW 91
Walker, Kate 1942- BiDWomA
Walker, Kathleen Mae 1947- WhoAmW 91
Walker, Kathrine Sorley AuBYP 90
Walker, Keith Grahame 1937- St&PR 91
Walker, Kelley Denise BiDrAPA 89
Walker, Kenneth A. 1949- St&PR 91
Walker, Kenneth Adley 1949- WhoE 91
Walker, Kenneth Edward 1956- WhoSSW 91
Walker, Kenneth Henry 1940- WhoAm 90
Walker, Kenneth Lane 1936- WhoWor 91
Walker, Kenneth Lynn 1948- WhoEmL 91
Walker, Kenneth Macfarlane 1882-1966 EncO&P 3
Walker, Kenneth R. BioIn 16
Walker, Kenneth Richard 1931-1989 ConAu 129
Walker, Kenton Blair 1952- WhoWor 91
Walker, Kimberly Louise 1964- WhoAmW 91
Walker, L. Harrall 1925- WhoSSW 91
Walker, Larry 1935- WhoAmA 91
Walker, Larry 1952- WhoAmA 91
Walker, Larry Moore 1935- WhoSSW 91
Walker, Laura 1960- BioIn 16
Walker, Leland Jasper 1923- WhoAm 90
Walker, Leland Max 1940- St&PR 91
Walker, Lenore E. BioIn 16
Walker, Leroy Tashreau 1918- WhoAm 90
Walker, Leslie D. 1930- St&PR 91
Walker, Lois Virginia 1929- WhoAmW 91, WhoWrEP 89
Walker, Loren Haines 1936- WhoAm 90
Walker, Lorene 1911- WhoAmW 91
Walker, Lou Ann BioIn 16
Walker, Lou Ann 1952- WhoWrEP 89
Walker, Luke 1943- Ballpl 90
Walker, Lydia Le Baron 1869-1958 WhoAmA 91N
Walker, Lynda Jean 1944- WhoAmW 91
Walker, M. Lucius, Jr. 1936- WhoAm 90
Walker, Maggie L. 1867-1934 EncABHB 7 [port]
Walker, Maggie Lena BioIn 16
Walker, Mallory 1939- WhoAm 90
Walker, Mallory Elton 1935- WhoAm 90
Walker, Margaret 1915- BioIn 16, FemiCLE, MajTwCW, WorAu 1980 [port]
Walker, Margaret Abigail Alexander 1915- HarlReB [port]
Walker, Margaret Elizabeth 1955- WhoAmW 91
Walker, Marie Sheehy 1952- WhoAmA 91
Walker, Mark Christopher 1952- BiDrAPA 89
Walker, Mark Edward 1958- St&PR 91
Walker, Mark Steven 1952- WhoAmA 91
Walker, Marsha Church 1955- WhoE 91
Walker, Marshall 1941- St&PR 91
Walker, Martin Alan 1947- WhoE 91
Walker, Martin Dean 1932- St&PR 91
Walker, Mary BiDEWW
Walker, Mary 1832-1919 WorAlBi
Walker, Mary Alexander 1927- SmATA 61 [port]
Walker, Mary Ann 1953- WhoAmW 91, WhoEmL 91
Walker, Mary B. 1892-1974 BioIn 16
Walker, Mary Bright 1932- WhoSSW 91
Walker, Mary Carolyn 1938- WhoAmA 91, WhoE 91
Walker, Mary Chase BioIn 16
Walker, Mary Christine BioIn 16
Walker, Mary Cunningham 1944- WhoAmW 91
Walker, Mary Edwards 1832-1919 BioAmW
Walker, Mary L. 1948- WhoAm 90, WhoAmW 91, WhoEmL 91
Walker, Mary Richardson 1811-1897 BioAmW
Walker, Mary Yvonne 1958- WhoAmW 91
Walker, Max N. 1936- St&PR 91
Walker, Maynard Bartram 1930- St&PR 91
Walker, Michael Claude 1940- WhoAm 90, WhoWor 91
Walker, Michael John 1932-1989? ConAu 129
Walker, Michael John 1946- WhoE 91
Walker, Michael K. ODwPR 91
Walker, Michael Robert, Sr. 1942- WhoSSW 91
Walker, Mike 1947- ODwPR 91
Walker, Moira Kaye 1940- WhoAmW 91
Walker, Mort BioIn 16
Walker, Mort 1923- EncACom, WhoAm 90, WhoAmA 91
Walker, Moses Fleetwood 1857-1924 BioIn 16
Walker, N Gene 1926- St&PR 91
Walker, Nancy 1921- OxCPMus, WorAlBi
Walker, Norman S. 1925- St&PR 91
Walker, Pamela 1948- WhoWrEP 89
Walker, Pamela Arnold 1935- WhoSSW 91
Walker, Parks Warren 1925- BiDrAPA 89
Walker, Patricia Lillian 1943- WhoAmW 91
Walker, Patrick Barrington 1946- WhoWor 91
Walker, Paul Dean 1937- WhoSSW 91
Walker, Paul Norvell 1948- WhoE 91

Walker, Peggy Jean 1940- *WhoAmW 91*
Walker, Penelope 1956- *IntWWM 90*
Walker, Percival Duane 1931- *WhoWor 91*
Walker, Peter Edward 1932- *WhoWor 91*
Walker, Philip C. 1944- *St&PR 91*
Walker, Philip Mitchell 1943- *St&PR 91*
Walker, Philip Smith 1933- *WhoAm 90*
Walker, Preston A 1930- *BiDrAPA 89*
Walker, Ralph P. 1914- *St&PR 91*
Walker, Ralph Waldo 1928- *BiDrAPA 89, WhoSSW 91, WhoWor 91*
Walker, Randolph Clive 1950- *WhoE 91*
Walker, Ray Carter 1933- *BiDrAPA 89, WhoE 91*
Walker, Ray Starkey 1912- *St&PR 91*
Walker, Raymond Francis 1914- *WhoWor 91*
Walker, Renee Kelley 1961- *WhoAmW 91*
Walker, Richard 1952- *ConAu 132*
Walker, Richard Bruce 1948- *WhoEmL 91*
Walker, Richard David 1931- *WhoAm 90*
Walker, Richard G. 1935- *St&PR 91*
Walker, Richard H. 1950- *St&PR 91*
Walker, Richard Harold 1928- *WhoAm 90*
Walker, Richard Louis 1922- *WhoAm 90*
Walker, Richard Oren, Jr. *BiDrAPA 89*
Walker, Richard Wilde 1823-1874 *AmLegL*
Walker, Richard Willard 1946- *WhoE 91*
Walker, Robert 1914-1951 *WorAlBi*
Walker, Robert Alander 1912- *WhoAm 90*
Walker, Robert Bruce 1923- *WhoAm 90*
Walker, Robert Dixon, III 1936- *WhoAm 90*
Walker, Robert Gerald 1925- *St&PR 91*
Walker, Robert Harris 1924- *WhoAm 90*
Walker, Robert Hugh 1935- *WhoAm 90*
Walker, Robert James 1801-1869 *BiDrUSE 89*
Walker, Robert Jerome 1944- *WhoE 91*
Walker, Robert Matthew 1946- *IntWWM 90*
Walker, Robert Mowbray 1929- *WhoAm 90*
Walker, Robert Ross 1954- *WhoEmL 91*
Walker, Robert Smith 1942- *WhoAm 90, WhoE 91*
Walker, Robert Wayne 1948- *WhoWrEP 89*
Walker, Robert Zabriski, Jr. 1952- *WhoSSW 91*
Walker, Roger Dale 1945- *BiDrAPA 89*
Walker, Roger Geoffrey 1939- *WhoAm 90*
Walker, Roger Raymond 1935- *St&PR 91*
Walker, Roland 1907- *EncO&P 3*
Walker, Ronald Dean 1952- *WhoSSW 91*
Walker, Ronald Edward 1935- *WhoAm 90*
Walker, Ronald Eugene 1942- *St&PR 91*
Walker, Ronald F. 1938- *WhoAm 90*
Walker, Ronald Frederick 1938- *St&PR 91*
Walker, Ronald Hugh 1937- *WhoAm 90, WhoWor 91*
Walker, Ronald M. 1938- *St&PR 91*
Walker, Ronald R. 1934- *WhoSSW 91, WhoWor 91*
Walker, Roy 1893-1962 *Ballpl 90*
Walker, Roy W. 1935- *ODwPR 91*
Walker, Rozelle Jenee *BiDrAPA 89*
Walker, Rube 1926- *Ballpl 90*
Walker, Rufus Flanders, Jr. 1946- *WhoSSW 91*
Walker, Russell Craig 1946- *WhoSSW 91*
Walker, Ruth Ann 1954- *WhoAmW 91*
Walker, Ruth Ferguson 1922- *WhoAmW 91*
Walker, Sally Barbara 1921- *WhoAmW 91, WhoE 91, WhoWor 91*
Walker, Sally Jo 1946- *WhoWrEP 89*
Walker, Sally Warden 1929- *WhoAmW 91*
Walker, Sam Sims 1925- *WhoAm 90*
Walker, Samuel Craig, Jr. 1924- *St&PR 91*
Walker, Samuel Sloan, Jr. 1926- *WhoAm 90*
Walker, Sandra 1946- *WhoAm 90*
Walker, Sandra Jean 1957- *WhoSSW 91*
Walker, Sandra Radcliffe 1937- *WhoAmA 91*
Walker, Sarah *IntWWM 90*
Walker, Sarah 1943- *PenDiMP*
Walker, Scott R 1958- *BiDrAPA 89*
Walker, Scott William 1962- *WhoSSW 91*
Walker, Sebastian 1942- *WhoWor 91*
Walker, Sherri 1953- *St&PR 91*
Walker, Sherry *ODwPR 91*
Walker, Shirley Dawn Kincaid 1935- *WhoAmW 91*
Walker, Stanley 1935- *St&PR 91*
Walker, Stephanie Jo 1968- *WhoEmL 91*
Walker, Stephen 1941- *ConAu 131*
Walker, Steven C. 1949- *St&PR 91*
Walker, Steven G. 1949- *St&PR 91*
Walker, Stuart 1888-1941 *LiHiK*
Walker, Suanne Stephens 1937- *St&PR 91*
Walker, Sue *BioIn 16*
Walker, Sue Brannan *WhoWrEP 89*
Walker, Sue Brannan 1940- *WhoAmW 91*
Walker, T-Bone 1910-1975 *ConMus 5, OxCPMus*
Walker, Ted A. 1955- *St&PR 91*
Walker, Tennyson A. 1927- *St&PR 91, WhoAm 90*
Walker, Teresa Beth *BiDrAPA 89*
Walker, Teresa Lee 1943- *WhoAmW 91*
Walker, Terry W. 1947- *St&PR 91*
Walker, Thane 1890?- *EncO&P 3*
Walker, Theodore Delbert 1933- *WhoAm 90*
Walker, Theodore Roscoe 1921- *WhoAm 90*
Walker, Thomas 1715-1794 *EncCRAm*
Walker, Thomas 1936- *IntWWM 90*
Walker, Thomas Cole 1929- *WhoAm 90*
Walker, Thomas J. 1920- *St&PR 91*
Walker, Thomas Michael 1947- *WhoWor 91*
Walker, Thomas N. 1946- *St&PR 91*
Walker, Tilly 1887-1959 *Ballpl 90*
Walker, Timothy Blake 1940- *WhoAm 90*
Walker, Timothy Craig 1945- *WhoE 91, WhoEmL 91, WhoWor 91*
Walker, Tom 1881-1944 *Ballpl 90*
Walker, Tom 1948- *Ballpl 90*
Walker, Tommie *BioIn 16*
Walker, Vanessa Jane 1962- *WhoAmW 91*
Walker, Vern Robert 1945- *WhoEmL 91*
Walker, Vincent Henry 1915- *WhoAm 90*
Walker, Virginia May 1957- *WhoE 91*
Walker, Waldo Sylvester 1931- *WhoAm 90*
Walker, Walter G. 1911- *St&PR 91*
Walker, Walter Herbert, III 1949- *WhoEmL 91*
Walker, Walton H. 1899-1950 *WorAlBi*
Walker, Warren H 1922- *BiDrAPA 89*
Walker, Warren Stanley 1921- *WhoAm 90*
Walker, Wendell Kirshman 1908- *WhoE 91*
Walker, Wendy 1951- *ConAu 131*
Walker, Wendy Diana Knight 1961- *WhoAmW 91*
Walker, Wendy Joy 1949- *WhoAm 90*
Walker, Wesley M. 1915- *WhoAm 90*
Walker, Wilbert Lee 1925- *WhoWrEP 89*
Walker, Willard Brewer 1926- *WhoAm 90*
Walker, William *EncO&P 3*
Walker, William 1800-1874 *WhNaAH*
Walker, William 1824-1860 *BioIn 16*
Walker, William 1840-1864 *BioIn 16*
Walker, William Baker 1942- *St&PR 91*
Walker, William Bond 1930- *WhoAm 90, WhoAmA 91*
Walker, William Delany 1923- *WhoAm 90*
Walker, William Earl 1929- *WhoAm 90*
Walker, William Easton 1945- *WhoAm 90*
Walker, William Frank 1939- *St&PR 91*
Walker, William George 1942- *WhoWor 91*
Walker, William Graham 1935- *WhoAm 90, WhoWor 91*
Walker, William H., III 1940- *St&PR 91*
Walker, William Homer, III 1940- *WhoAm 90*
Walker, William James 1935- *WhoSSW 91*
Walker, William Laurens 1937- *WhoAm 90*
Walker, William Ray 1923- *WhoAm 90*
Walker, William Ray 1940- *BiDrAPA 89*
Walker, William Ross 1934- *WhoAm 90*
Walker, William Tidd, Jr. 1931- *WhoAm 90*
Walker, William W, Jr. *BiDrAPA 89*
Walker, Winston Wakefield 1943- *St&PR 91*
Walker, Winston Wakefield, Jr. 1943- *WhoAm 90, WhoSSW 91*
Walker, Woodrow Wilson 1919- *WhoSSW 91, WhoWor 91*
Walker-Gras, Norma Elizabeth Peden 1921- *WhoAm 90*
Walker-Harrison, Alice M. 1962- *WhoAmW 91*
Walker-McCarthy, Jeri Ann *BiDrAPA 89*
Walker-Nelson, Colleen Mae 1944- *WhoAmW 91*
Walker-Ratliff, Joan Charlene 1957- *WhoAmW 91*
Walker-Smith, Angelique Keturah 1958- *WhoAmW 91, WhoE 91*
Walkerdine, Ken Martin 1946- *St&PR 91*
Walkey, Frederick P 1922- *WhoAmA 91*
Walkey, John R. 1938- *WhoAm 90*
Walkingstick, Kay 1935- *WhoAmA 91, WhoE 91*
Walkington, Ethlyn Lindley 1895- *WhoWrEP 89*
Walkland, S. A. *BioIn 16*
Walklet, John James, Jr. 1922- *WhoAm 90*
Walkosak, William J. *St&PR 91*
Walkovitz, D Neil 1944- *St&PR 91*
Walkowicz, Chris J. 1943- *WhoWrEP 89*
Walkowitz, Abraham 1880-1965 *WhoAmA 91N*
Walkowitz, Daniel J. 1942- *WhoE 91*
Walkowski, Kevin Michael 1964- *WhoE 91*
Walkup, Bruce 1914- *WhoAm 90*
Walkup, Glenn Frederick 1928- *St&PR 91*
Walkup, Homer Allen 1917- *WhoSSW 91*
Walkup, Jim 1909- *Ballpl 90*
Walkup, John Frank 1941- *WhoAm 90*
Walkup, John Timothy 1951- *BiDrAPA 89*
Walkup, William Bryan 1961- *WhoE 91*
Walkush, Margaret Ann 1963- *WhoAmW 91*
Wall, Ann *FemiCLE*
Wall, Barron Stephan 1951- *WhoE 91*
Wall, Bennett Harrison 1914- *WhoAm 90*
Wall, Betty Jane 1936- *WhoAmW 91*
Wall, Brian 1931- *WhoAmA 91*
Wall, Brian Arthur 1931- *WhoAm 90*
Wall, Bruce C 1954- *WhoAmA 91*
Wall, C. R. *WhoSSW 91*
Wall, Carol F. *BioIn 16*
Wall, Carolyn Raimondi 1942- *WhoAmW 91*
Wall, Carroll Edward 1942- *WhoAm 90*
Wall, Constance Mary 1945- *WhoEmL 91*
Wall, David Royal *BiDrAPA 89*
Wall, Donna Durno 1937- *WhoE 91*
Wall, Dorothy Celeste 1948- *WhoAmW 91*
Wall, Edward A. *WhoAm 90*
Wall, Edward Millard 1929- *WhoWor 91*
Wall, Eleanor Ann 1932- *WhoAmW 91*
Wall, Ellen Turmo 1945- *WhoSSW 91*
Wall, F L, III 1947- *WhoAmA 91*
Wall, Fletcher H., Jr. 1925- *St&PR 91*
Wall, Florence E. 1893-1988 *BioIn 16*
Wall, Frank Bennett, Jr. 1930- *WhoSSW 91*
Wall, Fred G. 1934- *St&PR 91*
Wall, Fred Graham 1934- *WhoAm 90*
Wall, Frederick Theodore 1912- *WhoAm 90*
Wall, Garrett Buckner, III 1932- *St&PR 91*
Wall, George Edward 1919- *St&PR 91*
Wall, Gertrude Wallace *AuBYP 90*
Wall, Howard Elden 1929- *St&PR 91, WhoAm 90*
Wall, Howard Milton, Jr. 1945- *St&PR 91*
Wall, Isaac B. *AmLegL*
Wall, Isabelle Louise Wood 1909- *WhoWrEP 89*
Wall, James Edward 1947- *St&PR 91, WhoAm 90*
Wall, James H *BiDrAPA 89*
Wall, James M. *BioIn 16*
Wall, James McKendree 1928- *WhoAm 90*
Wall, Jean Marie 1936- *WhoAmW 91*
Wall, Jerry Leon 1942- *WhoSSW 91, WhoWor 91*
Wall, Jerry S. 1926- *WhoWrEP 89*
Wall, John 1708-1776 *PenDiDA 89*
Wall, John B. 1905- *St&PR 91*
Wall, John Edmund 1926- *St&PR 91*
Wall, John Murray 1930- *St&PR 91*
Wall, John Patrick 1928- *St&PR 91*
Wall, John Winthrop 1924- *St&PR 91*
Wall, Joseph Frazier 1920- *WhoAm 90, WhoWor 91*
Wall, Lloyd L. 1936- *WhoWor 91*
Wall, M. Danny *BioIn 16, WhoAm 90*
Wall, Macy 1945- *St&PR 91*
Wall, Margaret V 1895-1958 *WhoAmA 91N*
Wall, Mark Emanuel 1937- *WhoE 91*
Wall, Max 1908-1990 *BioIn 16, NewYTBS 90*
Wall, Mervyn 1908- *ConAu 129*
Wall, Michael B. 1952- *WhoEmL 91*
Wall, Murray 1926-1971 *Ballpl 90*
Wall, O Edward 1934- *St&PR 91*
Wall, O. Edward 1934- *WhoAm 90*
Wall, Patrick D. *BioIn 16*
Wall, Patrick Lawson 1947- *St&PR 91*
Wall, Ralph Alan 1932- *WhoAmA 91*
Wall, Ralph J. 1930- *St&PR 91*
Wall, Rhonda 1956- *WhoAmA 91*
Wall, Robert *BioIn 16*
Wall, Robert Emmet 1937- *WhoAm 90, WhoWrEP 89*
Wall, Robert Joseph 1932- *St&PR 91*
Wall, Robert Wilson, Jr. 1916- *WhoAm 90*
Wall, Sheila Teresa 1952- *BiDrAPA 89*
Wall, Shelley Marie 1949- *WhoAmW 91*
Wall, Sigrid H. *St&PR 91*
Wall, Sonja Eloise 1938- *WhoAmW 91, WhoWor 91*
Wall, Stephen E. 1942- *St&PR 91*
Wall, Stephen Everett 1942- *WhoAm 90*
Wall, Sue 1950- *WhoAmA 91*
Wall, Thomas J. 1958- *WhoWrEP 89*
Wall, Vernon Antonio 1959- *WhoSSW 91*
Wall, William E. 1928- *St&PR 91*
Wall, William Herbert 1943- *WhoSSW 91*
Wall, William Lloyd 1946- *St&PR 91*
Wall-Angelides, Phyllis 1957- *WhoAmW 91*
Wallace, Alfred C. 1935- *St&PR 91*
Wallace, Alfred Leon 1931- *WhoWrEP 89*
Wallace, Alfred R. 1823-1913 *WorAlBi*
Wallace, Alfred Russel 1823-1913 *BioIn 16, EncO&P 3, EncPaPR 91*
Wallace, Allen 1953- *WhoEmL 91*
Wallace, Amy Elizabeth *BiDrAPA 89*
Wallace, Andrew Grover 1935- *WhoAm 90*
Wallace, Ann E. *ODwPR 91*
Wallace, Annette 1958- *WhoAmW 91*
Wallace, Anthony Francis Clarke 1923- *WhoAm 90*
Wallace, Arlie N. *BiDrAPA 89*
Wallace, Arnold Delaney, Sr. 1932- *WhoE 91*
Wallace, Arthur 1939- *St&PR 91*
Wallace, Arthur, Jr. 1939- *WhoAm 90*
Wallace, Barbara Brooks 1922- *BioIn 16*
Wallace, Barbara Faith 1952- *WhoAmW 91*
Wallace, Barbara Livingstone 1941- *WhoAmW 91*
Wallace, Barton Brinker, Jr. 1925- *WhoSSW 91*
Wallace, Betty Ann Woolard 1954- *WhoAmW 91*
Wallace, Betty Frances Abernathy 1926- *WhoWrEP 89*
Wallace, Betty Jean 1927- *WhoAmW 91*
Wallace, Big-Foot 1817-1899 *BioIn 16*
Wallace, Bill 1947- *BioIn 16*
Wallace, Bobby 1873-1960 *Ballpl 90 [port]*
Wallace, Bonnie Ann 1951- *WhoAmW 91*
Wallace, Brian S. 1946- *St&PR 91*
Wallace, Bridget Kelly 1962- *WhoAmW 91*
Wallace, Bronwen 1945-1989 *FemiCLE*
Wallace, Bruce Jay 1947- *St&PR 91*
Wallace, Charles Allen 1917- *WhoSSW 91*
Wallace, Charles Dixon, Sr. 1933- *BiDrAPA 89*
Wallace, Charles Edward 1929- *WhoAm 90*
Wallace, Charles Leslie 1945- *WhoAm 90, WhoEmL 91*
Wallace, Christopher 1947- *WhoAm 90*
Wallace, Christopher Baird 1953- *WhoEmL 91*
Wallace, Clifford Noble, III 1947- *WhoEmL 91, WhoSSW 91*
Wallace, Craig Kesting 1928- *WhoAm 90*
Wallace, Cynthia Day 1942- *WhoE 91*
Wallace, Daniel A *BiDrAPA 89*
Wallace, Daniel Philip 1910- *WhoE 91*
Wallace, Darrell R. 1951- *St&PR 91*
Wallace, David Foster 1962- *ConAu 132*
Wallace, David Francis 1923- *St&PR 91*
Wallace, David Harold 1936- *St&PR 91*
Wallace, David Rains 1945- *ConAu 31NR*
Wallace, David W. 1924- *St&PR 91*
Wallace, David William 1924- *WhoAm 90, WhoE 91*
Wallace, Dee *BioIn 16*
Wallace, Derrick Donnell 1953- *WhoSSW 91*
Wallace, DeWitt 1889-1981 *BioIn 16, WorAlBi*
Wallace, Dexter *MajTwCW*
Wallace, Don *BioIn 16*
Wallace, Don, Jr. 1932- *WhoAm 90*
Wallace, Donald John, III 1941- *WhoSSW 91*
Wallace, Donald Querk 1931- *WhoAm 90*
Wallace, Donald Sheridan 1915- *WhoAm 90*
Wallace, Doreen 1897- *FemiCLE*
Wallace, Doris Blumenthal 1928- *WhoWor 91*
Wallace, Duncan S 1937- *BiDrAPA 89*
Wallace, Dwane L. 1911- *ConAmBL*
Wallace, Dwane L. 1911-1989 *BioIn 16*
Wallace, Edgar 1875-1932 *TwCCr&M 91, WorAlBi*
Wallace, Edward M. 1918- *St&PR 91*
Wallace, Edwin Ruthven, IV 1950- *BiDrAPA 89*
Wallace, Eglinton *FemiCLE*
Wallace, Elaine Maria 1954- *WhoEmL 91*
Wallace, Elizabeth Ann *BiDrAPA 89*
Wallace, Elizabeth M. 1954- *WhoAmW 91*
Wallace, Elizabeth Marie *BiDrAPA 89*
Wallace, Elizabeth S *WhoAmA 91*
Wallace, Ellen 1815?-1894 *FemiCLE*
Wallace, Fitzhugh Lee, Jr. 1928- *St&PR 91*
Wallace, Floyd 1921- *St&PR 91*
Wallace, Fran *BioIn 16*
Wallace, Frederick E 1893-1958 *WhoAmA 91N*
Wallace, Gael Lynn 1941- *WhoAmA 91*
Wallace, George *DrBIPA 90*
Wallace, George C. *BioIn 16*
Wallace, George C. 1919- *WorAlBi*
Wallace, George C., Jr. 1951- *WhoSSW 91*
Wallace, George Corley 1919- *BioIn 16, WhoAm 90, WhoSSW 91*
Wallace, George Wilson 1914- *WhoE 91*
Wallace, Gladys Baldwin 1923- *WhoSSW 91, WhoWor 91*
Wallace, Gordon 1909- *WhoWrEP 89*
Wallace, Harold James, Jr. 1930- *WhoAm 90*
Wallace, Harold Lew 1932- *WhoAm 90*
Wallace, Harry Leland 1927- *WhoAm 90*
Wallace, Helen *FemiCLE*

Wallace, Helen Margaret 1913- WhoAm 90, WhoAmW 91
Wallace, Henry EncAL
Wallace, Henry A. 1888-1965 WorAlBi
Wallace, Henry Agard 1888-1965 BiDrUSE 89, BioIn 16
Wallace, Henry Cantwell 1866-1924 BiDrUSE 89
Wallace, Herbert Norman 1937- WhoWor 91
Wallace, Herbert William 1930- WhoAm 90
Wallace, Holly Salop 1956- WhoAmW 91
Wallace, Hugh Campbell 1863-1931 BioIn 16
Wallace, Ian 1919- PenDiMP
Wallace, Ian 1950- BioIn 16
Wallace, Ian Bryce 1919- IntWWM 90
Wallace, Irving NewYTBS 90 [port]
Wallace, Irving 1916- WhoWrEP 89
Wallace, Irving 1916-1990 BioIn 16, ConAu 132, CurBio 90N, MajTwCW, News 91-1, WorAlBi
Wallace, J. Anthony 1946- WhoAm 90
Wallace, J. Clifford 1928- WhoAm 90
Wallace, Jack Harold 1950- WhoEmL 91
Wallace, James A BiDrAPA 89
Wallace, James J. 1939- ODwPR 91, St&PR 91
Wallace, James J, III 1947- BiDrAPA 89
Wallace, James M BiDrAPA 89
Wallace, James Magee 1903-1990 BioIn 16
Wallace, James Martin 1939- WhoAm 90
Wallace, James O. BioIn 16
Wallace, James P. 1928- WhoSSW 91
Wallace, James Wendell 1930- WhoAm 90
Wallace, James William Scott 1957- BiDrAPA 89
Wallace, Jane House 1926- WhoE 91
Wallace, Jane Young 1933- WhoAm 90, WhoAmW 91
Wallace, Janice Lee 1943- WhoSSW 91
Wallace, Jay S. 1931- St&PR 91
Wallace, Jean NewYTBS 90
Wallace, Jean 1923-1990 BioIn 16
Wallace, Jerry McLain 1935- WhoAm 90
Wallace, Joan S. 1930- WhoAm 90, WhoAmW 91
Wallace, Jody Marie 1954- WhoWrEP 89
Wallace, John 1929- WhoAmA 91
Wallace, John 1949- PenDiMP
Wallace, John Adam 1915- AuBYP 90
Wallace, John Clements 1920- St&PR 91, WhoAm 90, WhoWor 91
Wallace, John Douglas 1951- WhoE 91
Wallace, John Duncan 1933- St&PR 91, WhoAm 90
Wallace, John Edwin 1913- WhoAm 90
Wallace, John G 1931- BiDrAPA 89
Wallace, John H. 1906-1989 BioIn 16
Wallace, John Kennard 1903- WhoAm 90
Wallace, John Loys 1941- St&PR 91, WhoAm 90, WhoSSW 91
Wallace, John Mack 1956- WhoSSW 91
Wallace, John Malcolm 1928- WhoAm 90
Wallace, John Melvin 1942- St&PR 91
Wallace, John Powell 1923- St&PR 91
Wallace, John R. 1913- WhoAm 90
Wallace, Karen Elaine 1952- WhoEmL 91, WhoSSW 91
Wallace, Kathleen Dawn 1963- WhoAmW 91
Wallace, Kathryn L. 1945- WhoAmW 91
Wallace, Keith G. 1926- St&PR 91, WhoAm 90
Wallace, Kenneth Donald 1918- WhoAm 90, WhoWor 91
Wallace, Kenneth William 1945- WhoAmA 91
Wallace, Kirk 1944- St&PR 91
Wallace, Leigh Allen, Jr. 1927- WhoAm 90
Wallace, Len 1940- St&PR 91
Wallace, Leon 1925- BiDrAPA 89
Wallace, Lew 1827-1905 BioIn 16
Wallace, Lew Gerald 1946- WhoWrEP 89
Wallace, Lila Norma WhoAmA 91
Wallace, Linn Alfred 1938- St&PR 91
Wallace, Lucille PenDiMP
Wallace, Malcolm Vincent Timothy 1915- WhoAm 90
Wallace, Marcia 1942- ConTFT 8
Wallace, Marilyn 1941- TwCCr&M 91
Wallace, Mark Allen 1953- WhoAm 90, WhoSSW 91
Wallace, Mark E 1955- BiDrAPA 89
Wallace, Mark Edward 1955- WhoE 91
Wallace, Martha Redfield 1927-1989 BioIn 16
Wallace, Mary Ann 1939- WhoAmW 91, WhoWor 91
Wallace, Mary Ann 1944- WhoAmW 91
Wallace, Mary Elaine WhoAm 90, WhoSSW 91
Wallace, Mary Hardwick 1924- WhoWrEP 89
Wallace, Mary Hunter BioIn 16
Wallace, Matthew Walker 1924- St&PR 91
Wallace, May Nickerson 1902- AuBYP 90
Wallace, Michael Arthur 1951- WhoEmL 91, WhoWor 91
Wallace, Michael John 1948- St&PR 91
Wallace, Mike 1918- WhoAm 90, WhoE 91, WorAlBi
Wallace, Mike 1951- Ballpl 90
Wallace, Miles Jay 1957- WhoE 91
Wallace, Milton J. 1935- St&PR 91
Wallace, Minor Gordon, Jr. 1936- WhoSSW 91
Wallace, Mona Sue 1937- St&PR 91
Wallace, Mozelle BioIn 16
Wallace, Nellie 1870-1948 OxCPMus
Wallace, Ottilie 1875-1947 BiDWomA
Wallace, Patrick ODwPR 91
Wallace, Patty A 1957- WhoAmA 91
Wallace, Paul Harvey 1944- WhoWor 91
Wallace, Paul Joseph 1946- St&PR 91
Wallace, Paula Kathleen 1951- WhoAmW 91
Wallace, Paula Yvette 1965- WhoSSW 91
Wallace, Peatsa Christina 1956- WhoSSW 91
Wallace, Philip Russell 1915- WhoAm 90
Wallace, Phyllis Ann WhoAm 90, WhoE 91
Wallace, Priscilla Corwin Jack 1951- WhoEmL 91
Wallace, R Duncan BiDrAPA 89
Wallace, Ralph Howes 1916- WhoAm 90
Wallace, Ralph Stuart, Jr. 1944- WhoE 91
Wallace, Raymond Paul WhoE 91, WhoWor 91
Wallace, Reginald James 1919- WhoWor 91
Wallace, Richard S. 1934- WhoAm 90
Wallace, Richard William 1933- WhoAmA 91
Wallace, Roanne 1949- WhoAmW 91, WhoSSW 91, WhoWor 91
Wallace, Robert TwCCr&M 91
Wallace, Robert 1932- BioIn 16, WhoWrEP 89
Wallace, Robert Ash WhoAm 90
Wallace, Robert Bruce 1931- WhoAm 90
Wallace, Robert Bruce 1937- WhoE 91
Wallace, Robert Bruce 1944- WhoE 91
Wallace, Robert C. 1837-1928 BioIn 16
Wallace, Robert Dan 1923- WhoAmA 91
Wallace, Robert E. 1903-1989 BioIn 16
Wallace, Robert Earl 1916- WhoAm 90
Wallace, Robert George 1928- WhoAm 90
Wallace, Robert Glenn 1926- St&PR 91, WhoAm 90
Wallace, Robert H. 1932- St&PR 91
Wallace, Robert Keith 1938- WhoSSW 91
Wallace, Robert Kimball 1944- WhoSSW 91
Wallace, Rodney Sanford 1924- St&PR 91
Wallace, Roger ConAu 31NR
Wallace, Ron WhoE 91
Wallace, Ronald E. 1946- St&PR 91
Wallace, Ronald K. 1935- St&PR 91
Wallace, Ronald Lynn 1945- WhoWrEP 89
Wallace, Ronald W. 1945- WhoWrEP 89
Wallace, Ronald Wesley 1934- St&PR 91
Wallace, Roy 1938- ODwPR 91
Wallace, Royce 1923?- DrBlPA 90
Wallace, Rusty BioIn 16
Wallace, Ruth Ann 1932- WhoAm 90
Wallace, Samuel Taylor 1943- WhoAm 90
Wallace, Sandy 1950- WhoEmL 91
Wallace, Sherwood Lee 1940- ODwPR 91
Wallace, Sippie 1898-1986 BioIn 16
Wallace, Soni 1931- WhoAmA 91
Wallace, Spencer Miller, Jr. 1923- WhoAm 90
Wallace, Stanford Aubrey St&PR 91N
Wallace, Stanley F BiDrAPA 89
Wallace, Stanley L. 1923-1989 BioIn 16
Wallace, Steven Charles 1953- WhoSSW 91, WhoWor 91
Wallace, Sue Mitchell 1944- IntWWM 90
Wallace, Susan C. 1947- WhoAmW 91
Wallace, Susan J. 1931- FemiCLE
Wallace, Teddy P 1929- BiDrAPA 89
Wallace, Thomas C. 1933- WhoWrEP 89
Wallace, Thomas Christopher 1933- WhoAm 90
Wallace, Thomas Clyde 1951- BiDrAPA 89
Wallace, Thomas Llewellyn, Jr. 1952- WhoSSW 91
Wallace, Thomas Patrick 1935- WhoAm 90
Wallace, Thomas R. ODwPR 91
Wallace, Volney St&PR 91
Wallace, W. Bradley WhoE 91
Wallace, W. R. 1923- St&PR 91
Wallace, Walter C. 1924- WhoAm 90
Wallace, Walter L. 1927- WhoAm 90
Wallace, William BioIn 16
Wallace, William 1933- IntWWM 90
Wallace, William, III 1926- WhoAm 90
Wallace, William Alan 1935- WhoAm 90
Wallace, William Augustine 1918- WhoAm 90
Wallace, William Edward 1917- WhoAm 90
Wallace, William Hall 1933- WhoAm 90
Wallace, William Henry 1827-1901 AmLegL
Wallace, William L. 1934- St&PR 91
Wallace, William Ray 1923- WhoAm 90, WhoSSW 91
Wallace, William Sheldon 1915- WhoE 91
Wallace, Wilton Lawrence 1949- WhoAm 90
Wallace, Wm Dean 1946- St&PR 91
Wallace-Brodeur, Ruth 1941- BioIn 16
Wallace-Hadrill, Michael 1916-1985 DcNaB 1981
Wallace-Whitfield, Cecil 1930-1990 BioIn 16
Wallach, Alan 1942- WhoAmA 91
Wallach, Allan Henry 1927- WhoAm 90
Wallach, Anne Jackson WhoAm 90, WhoAmW 91
Wallach, Beth Kakerbeck 1934- WhoAmW 91
Wallach, E. Robert 1934- BioIn 16
Wallach, Edward Eliot 1933- WhoAm 90
Wallach, Eli 1915- WhoAm 90, WorAlBi
Wallach, Evan Jonathan 1949- WhoWor 91
Wallach, Hans 1904- WhoAm 90
Wallach, Hans Gert Peter 1938- WhoE 91
Wallach, Howard F 1923- BiDrAPA 89
Wallach, Ira 1913- WhoAm 90, WhoWrEP 89
Wallach, Ira D. 1909- St&PR 91
Wallach, Ira David 1909- WhoAm 90
Wallach, Janet Lee 1942- WhoE 91
Wallach, Joelle 1946- IntWWM 90
Wallach, John Paul 1943- WhoE 91
Wallach, John Sidney 1939- WhoAm 90
Wallach, Magdalena Falkenberg WhoAmW 91
Wallach, Otto 1847-1931 WorAlBi
Wallach, Philip 1928- WhoAm 90
Wallach, Philip C. 1912- St&PR 91
Wallach, Philip Charles 1914- WhoAm 90, WhoWor 91
Wallach, Robert Charles 1935- WhoAm 90
Wallach, Rochelle Lamm 1948- WhoAmW 91
Wallach, Ronald Michael 1937- St&PR 91
Wallach, Stephen Martin 1942- WhoSSW 91
Wallach, Steven J. 1945- WhoAm 90
Wallach, Tim 1957- Ballpl 90
Wallach, Tom Harlan 1950- BiDrAPA 89
Wallack, Erwin N BiDrAPA 89
Wallack, Joel Jeffrey 1946- BiDrAPA 89
Wallack, Rina Evelyn 1949- WhoAmW 91
Walladah bint al-Mustakfi 994-1077? EncCoWW
Wallaesa, Jack 1919-1986 Ballpl 90
Wallance, Don NewYTBS 90
Wallance, Don 1909- ConDes 90
Wallance, Don 1909-1990 BioIn 16
Wallander, Jan Rickard 1920- WhoWor 91
Wallant, Edward Lewis 1926-1962 MajTwCW
Wallas, Charles H. 1938- WhoSSW 91
Wallas, Graham 1858-1932 BioIn 16
Wallbaum PenDiDA 89
Wallbridge, Lewis C. 1943- St&PR 91
Walle, James Paul 1956- WhoEmL 91
Walle, Sheldon Ernest 1950- St&PR 91
Walleen, Hans Axel 1902-1978 WhoAmA 91N
Walleigh, Robert Shuler 1915- WhoAm 90
Wallek, Lee 1908- WhoWrEP 89
Wallen, Burr 1941- WhoAmA 91
Wallen, Mark Charles 1949- BiDrAPA 89, WhoE 91
Wallen, Martti 1948- IntWWM 90
Wallenberg, Peter 1926- St&PR 91, WhoWor 91
Wallenberg, Raoul BioIn 16
Wallenborn, Janice Rae 1938- WhoAmW 91
Wallenborn, White McKenzie 1929- WhoSSW 91
Wallenbrock, Angela Bell 1947- BiDrAPA 89, WhoEmL 91
Wallender, Alf PenDiDA 89
Wallens, Donald E 1938- BiDrAPA 89
Wallens, Laura Beth 1953- WhoAmW 91
Wallenstein, Albrecht Wenzel Eusebius v 1583-1634 BioIn 16
Wallenstein, Albrecht Wenzel Von 1583-1634 WorAlBi
Wallenstein, Alfred 1898-1983 PenDiMP
Wallenstein, James Harry 1942- WhoAm 90, WhoSSW 91
Wallenstein, Sandra L. 1951- WhoAmW 91
Wallensten, Richard Theodor 1945- WhoWor 91
Waller, Aaron Bret 1935- WhoAmA 91
Waller, Aaron Bret, III 1935- WhoAm 90
Waller, Alan Vernon 1944- WhoWor 91
Waller, Anne BioIn 16
Waller, Anne FemiCLE
Waller, Barbara C 1944- BiDrAPA 89
Waller, Bob D. 1928- St&PR 91
Waller, Charles E. 1849- AmLegL
Waller, Charlotte Reid 1936- WhoSSW 91
Waller, David Allan 1942- BiDrAPA 89
Waller, David Barclay 1948- St&PR 91, WhoAm 90
Waller, Donald Fredrick 1928- WhoE 91
Waller, Doris L. 1909- St&PR 91
Waller, Edmund Meredith, Jr. 1931- WhoWor 91
Waller, Fats 1904-1943 BioIn 16, DrBlPA 90, OxCPMus, WorAlBi
Waller, Frederic 1886-1954 WorAlBi
Waller, G F 1944- ConAu 31NR
Waller, Gary ConAu 31NR
Waller, Gary F. 1944- WhoWrEP 89
Waller, Gary Fredric 1944- WhoAm 90
Waller, George Macgregor 1919- WhoAm 90
Waller, Harold Myron 1940- WhoAm 90
Waller, Helen BioIn 16
Waller, Henry Buford 1944- WhoSSW 91
Waller, J. Garland 1950- WhoAmW 91
Waller, Jack 1885-1957 OxCPMus
Waller, James Edward 1937- St&PR 91
Waller, Jane 1944- ConAu 132
Waller, John 1741-1802 BioIn 16
Waller, John Henry 1923- WhoWor 91
Waller, John Oscar 1916- WhoAm 90
Waller, Judith Cary 1889-1973 BioIn 16
Waller, Julia Reva 1950- WhoEmL 91
Waller, Larry Gene 1948- WhoWor 91
Waller, Leslie 1923- AuBYP 90
Waller, Marlene Waite 1933- WhoSSW 91
Waller, Mary Ella 1855-1938 FemiCLE
Waller, Pamela Rawn 1947- WhoAmW 91
Waller, Paul H., Jr. 1933- St&PR 91
Waller, Philip BioIn 16
Waller, Robert A. 1928- St&PR 91
Waller, Robert A. 1931- WhoSSW 91
Waller, Robert Edward 1936- St&PR 91
Waller, Robert Morris 1944- WhoWor 91
Waller, Robert Rex 1937- WhoAm 90, WhoWor 91
Waller, Rodney L. St&PR 91
Waller, Sandra Kay 1943- WhoAmW 91
Waller, Saul 1916- St&PR 91
Waller, Seth 1933- St&PR 91
Waller, Stephen Kenneth 1959- WhoE 91
Waller, Thomas MacDonald 1840-1924 AmLegL
Waller, Thomas Mercer BioIn 16
Waller, Wilhelmine Kirby 1914- WhoAm 90, WhoAmW 91
Waller, William 1597?-1668 BioIn 16
Wallerstedt, Robert W. 1928- St&PR 91
Wallerstedt-Wehrle, JoAnna Katherine 1944- WhoAmW 91, WhoWrEP 89
Wallerstein, David B. 1905- St&PR 91, WhoAm 90
Wallerstein, Edward Manley 1925- BiDrAPA 89, WhoE 91
Wallerstein, Immanuel 1930- EncAL
Wallerstein, Judith S. BioIn 16
Wallerstein, Lawrence Bernard 1919- St&PR 91
Wallerstein, Leibert Benet 1922- WhoE 91
Wallerstein, Lothar 1882-1949 PenDiMP
Wallerstein, Ralph Oliver 1922- WhoAm 90
Wallerstein, Robert S 1921- BiDrAPA 89
Wallerstein, Robert Solomon 1921- WhoAm 90
Wallerstein, Seth Michael 1960- WhoE 91
Wallerstein, Sheldon M. 1931- WhoE 91
Walles, James A. 1933- St&PR 91
Walles, Willem Egbert 1960- WhoEmL 91
Wallestad, Philip Weston 1922- WhoWor 91
Walley, Byron 1951- WhoAm 90
Walley, Craig D. 1943- St&PR 91
Walley, David Gordon 1945- WhoE 91
Walley, Deborah BioIn 16
Walley, George L. 1925- St&PR 91
Walley, James M., Jr. 1947- WhoSSW 91
Wallfisch, Lory 1922- IntWWM 90
Wallfisch, Peter 1924- IntWWM 90, PenDiMP
Wallfisch, Raphael 1953- IntWWM 90, PenDiMP
Wallgren, Anita BioIn 16
Wallgren, Georg Rabbe 1920- WhoWor 91
Wallgren, Sven Einar 1929- WhoAm 90
Wallhauser, George Marvin 1900- WhoAm 90
Wallhauser, Henry T. ODwPR 91
Wallich, Henry Christopher 1914-1988 BioIn 16
Wallich, Hermann 1833-1928 BioIn 16
Wallich, Paul 1882-1938 BioIn 16
Wallick, Robert Daniel 1926- WhoAm 90
Wallick, Ruth BioIn 16
Wallin, Ann Lewis 1937- WhoE 91
Wallin, Brian L. 1943- WhoE 91
Wallin, Daniel Neil 1947- St&PR 91
Wallin, David Allen 1945- St&PR 91
Wallin, Fanny Mae 1943- WhoAmW 91

Wallin, Franklin Whittelsey 1925- *WhoAm 90*
Wallin, Jack Robb 1915- *WhoAm 90*
Wallin, Judith Kerstin 1938- *WhoAmW 91, WhoE 91, WhoWor 91*
Wallin, Lawrence Bier 1944- *WhoAmA 91*
Wallin, Leland Dean 1942- *WhoAmA 91*
Wallin, Luke 1943- *ConAu 130*
Wallin, Nils Lennart 1924- *WhoWor 91*
Wallin, Norman Elroy 1914- *St&PR 91*
Wallin, Robert M. 1923- *St&PR 91*
Wallin, Winston Roger 1926- *St&PR 91, WhoAm 90, WhoWor 91*
Walling, Cheves T. 1916- *WhoAm 90*
Walling, Dana McNeil 1950- *WhoWrEP 89*
Walling, David Percy 1932- *WhoAm 90*
Walling, Denny 1954- *Ballpl 90*
Walling, Derald Dee 1937- *WhoSSW 91*
Walling, Georgia 1940- *WhoAmW 91, WhoE 91, WhoWor 91*
Walling, M. L. 1944- *St&PR 91*
Walling, Russell G *BiDrAPA 89*
Walling, Susan Eileen Femrite 1944- *WhoAmW 91*
Walling, Vernon Ray, II 1953- *BiDrAPA 89*
Walling, William English 1877-1936 *EncAL*
Walling, William Russell 1959- *WhoSSW 91*
Wallinger, George Arthur 1930- *St&PR 91*
Wallinger, Mark *ODwPR 91*
Wallinger, Ralph Scott 1939- *St&PR 91*
Wallingford, Logan Wilson 1932- *WhoAm 90*
Wallington, Dale James *BiDrAPA 89*
Wallington, Maria Joanne 1946- *WhoAmW 91*
Wallington, Patricia M. *BioIn 16*
Wallington, Patricia McDevitt 1940- *WhoE 91*
Wallington-Nijenkamp, Kristy 1961- *ODwPR 91*
Wallis, Bernard Joseph 1910- *St&PR 91*
Wallis, Carlton Lamar 1915- *WhoAm 90*
Wallis, Delia 1944- *IntWWM 90*
Wallis, Delmas Edward 1924- *WhoSSW 91*
Wallis, Diana Lynn 1946- *WhoAm 90*
Wallis, E. W. 1848-1914 *EncO&P 3*
Wallis, Elizabeth Susan 1953- *WhoAmW 91*
Wallis, Ellen Mae 1953- *WhoAmW 91*
Wallis, Ernest Martin 1921- *WhoWor 91*
Wallis, Glenn Philip 1950- *BiDrAPA 89*
Wallis, Graham Blair 1936- *WhoAm 90*
Wallis, H Dann 1930- *St&PR 91*
Wallis, Hal B. 1898?-1986 *BioIn 16, WorAlBi*
Wallis, James Rees 1948- *St&PR 91*
Wallis, Joe 1952- *Ballpl 90*
Wallis, John 1616-1703 *BioIn 16*
Wallis, Lynn *BioIn 16*
Wallis, Michael 1945- *ODwPR 91*
Wallis, Provo William Parry 1791-1892 *DcCanB 12*
Wallis, Richard Fisher 1924- *WhoAm 90, WhoWor 91*
Wallis, Robert Charles 1921-1989 *BioIn 16*
Wallis, Robert Ray 1927- *WhoAm 90*
Wallis, Sandra Rhodes 1945- *WhoE 91*
Wallis, W Merle 1941- *BiDrAPA 89*
Wallis, William Budge 1940- *St&PR 91*
Wallis, William George 1946- *WhoWrEP 89*
Wallis, William Robert 1931- *WhoE 91*
Wallis, Wilson Allen 1912- *WhoAm 90, WhoE 91*
Walliser, Maria *BioIn 16*
Walliser, Otto Heinrich 1928- *WhoWor 91*
Wallison, Frieda K. 1943- *WhoAmW 91*
Wallison, Peter J. 1941- *WhoAm 90*
Wallman, Bernard H. 1926- *St&PR 91*
Wallman, David Thees 1949- *St&PR 91*
Wallman, George 1917- *WhoAm 90*
Wallman, Judy Clingan 1952- *WhoSSW 91*
Wallman, Stephen Jay 1942- *WhoWor 91*
Wallmann, Jeffrey M. 1941- *BioIn 16*
Wallmann, Jeffrey Miner 1941- *WhoWor 91*
Wallmark, John Torkel 1919- *WhoWor 91*
Wallnau, Carl N., Jr. 1920- *St&PR 91*
Wallner, Alexandra 1946- *BioIn 16*
Wallner, John C. *BioIn 16*
Wallner, Julius M *BiDrAPA 89*
Wallner, Mats Erik Vilhelm 1948- *WhoWor 91*
Wallner, Richard Alan 1945- *WhoEmL 91*
Wallo, Phyllis Bryan *BiDrAPA 89*
Walloch, Antone S *BiDrAPA 89*
Walloch, Betsy Oglesby 1934- *BiDrAPA 89*
Walloch, Esther Coto 1938- *WhoHisp 91*
Wallop, Douglas *Ballpl 90*
Wallop, Malcolm 1933- *WhoAm 90, WhoWor 91*
Wallot, Hubert Antoine 1945- *BiDrAPA 89*
Wallot, Jean-Pierre 1935- *WhoAm 90, WhoE 91, WhoWrEP 89*
Wallower, Lucille 1910- *AuBYP 90*
Wallrapp, Yustin 1932- *ODwPR 91*
Wallrath, Janet Frances 1945- *WhoSSW 91*
Wallrock, John 1922- *WhoWor 91*
Walls, Carmage 1908- *WhoAm 90, WhoWor 91*
Walls, Clyde Wayne 1939- *St&PR 91*
Walls, Donald W. *St&PR 91*
Walls, Dwayne Estes 1932- *WhoAm 90, WhoWrEP 89*
Walls, Edward Franklin 1929- *WhoSSW 91*
Walls, Gary Lee 1949- *WhoSSW 91*
Walls, George Rodney 1945- *WhoAm 90*
Walls, Glenn Truman, III 1954- *WhoSSW 91*
Walls, Heather Elaine 1951- *WhoE 91*
Walls, Henry Briggs 1906- *St&PR 91*
Walls, John William 1927- *St&PR 91*
Walls, Josiah Thomas 1842-1905 *BlkAmsC [port]*
Walls, Lee 1933- *Ballpl 90*
Walls, Martha Ann Williams 1927- *WhoAm 90, WhoWor 91*
Walls, Nettie Katherine 1907- *St&PR 91*
Walls, Patricia Rae 1936- *WhoWrEP 89*
Walls, Philip D 1942- *BiDrAPA 89*
Walls, Robert Boen 1910- *IntWWM 90*
Walls, Robert C. 1950- *St&PR 91*
Walls, T. S. *WhoSSW 91*
Walls, Tina A. *ODwPR 91*
Walls, Vicki L. 1946- *WhoAmW 91*
Walls, William L 1934- *BiDrAPA 89*
Walls, William Thomas 1914- *IntWWM 90*
Walls, William Walton, Jr. 1932- *WhoE 91*
Wallsh, Rita 1933-1990 *BioIn 16*
Wallskog, Alan George 1940- *St&PR 91*
Wallskog, Joyce Marie 1942- *WhoAmW 91*
Wallsom, Richard Ernest 1935- *WhoSSW 91*
Wallstab, Kurt 1920- *PenDiDA 89*
Wallston, Barbara Strudler *BioIn 16*
Wallstrom, Wesley Donald 1929- *WhoWor 91*
Wallwork, Alan *BioIn 16*
Wallwork, William Wilson, Jr. 1922- *St&PR 91*
Wally, Josef 1939- *St&PR 91*
Wally, Walter Edward 1929- *St&PR 91*
Walman, Jerome 1937- *WhoE 91, WhoWor 91*
Walmer, Edwin Fitch 1930- *WhoAm 90*
Walmer, James L. 1948- *WhoEmL 91*
Walmer, John D 1917- *BiDrAPA 89*
Walmisley, Douglas M. *ODwPR 91*
Walmsley, Arthur Edward 1928- *WhoAm 90, WhoE 91*
Walmsley, Judith Abrams 1936- *WhoAmW 91*
Walmsley, Tom 1948- *OxCCanT*
Walmsley, William Aubrey 1923- *WhoAmA 91*
Walmsley-Clark, Penelope *IntWWM 90*
Waln, Jack R. 1929- *ODwPR 91*
Walner, Robert Joel 1946- *WhoAm 90, WhoEmL 91*
Walnes, Jack Robert 1947- *St&PR 91*
Walode, Scott 1958- *St&PR 91*
Walpin, Gerald 1931- *WhoAm 90, WhoE 91, WhoWor 91*
Walpole, Forrest 1941- *St&PR 91*
Walpole, Horace 1717-1797 *DcLB 104 [port], WorAlBi*
Walpole, Robert 1676-1745 *WorAlBi*
Walpole, Ronald N. 1903-1986 *BioIn 16*
Walras, Leon 1834-1910 *BioIn 16*
Walras, Marie Esprit Leon *BioIn 16*
Walrath, Harry Rienzi 1926- *WhoWor 91*
Walravens, Guy Baudouin 1943- *WhoWor 91*
Walrod, David James 1946- *St&PR 91, WhoAm 90*
Walrond, Errol Ricardo 1936- *WhoWor 91*
Walsch, Nellie Lee 1920- *WhoAmW 91*
Walser, Donald 1940- *St&PR 91*
Walser, John T., Jr. 1939- *St&PR 91*
Walser, Mackenzie 1924- *WhoAm 90*
Walser, Martin 1927- *WhoWor 91*
Walser, Robert 1878-1956 *BioIn 16*
Walser, Robert Otto 1878-1956 *WorAu 1980*
Walser, William Duke 1918- *St&PR 91*
Walser, Zeb Vance 1863- *AmLegL*
Walsh, Abigail Margaret 1935- *WhoWrEP 89*
Walsh, Ann 1942- *SmATA 62 [port]*
Walsh, Anne Huddleston 1949- *St&PR 91*
Walsh, Annmarie Hauck 1938- *WhoAm 90, WhoAmW 91*
Walsh, Anthony Francis 1930- *WhoSSW 91*
Walsh, Arthur C *BiDrAPA 89*
Walsh, Arthur William 1945- *St&PR 91*
Walsh, B Timothy *BiDrAPA 89*
Walsh, Beatrice Metcalfe Passage 1917- *WhoAmW 91*
Walsh, Betty Jane 1931- *St&PR 91*
Walsh, Bill 1931- *BioIn 16, WorAlBi*
Walsh, Bryan *BioIn 16*
Walsh, Catherine A. 1953- *WhoAmW 91*
Walsh, Charles Richard 1939- *WhoE 91*
Walsh, Charles Stratton *BioIn 16*
Walsh, Christina Lee 1961- *WhoAmW 91*
Walsh, Christy 1871-1955 *Ballpl 90*
Walsh, Colin Stephen 1955- *IntWWM 90*
Walsh, Cornelius Stephen 1907- *St&PR 91, WhoAm 90*
Walsh, Daniel Francis 1937- *WhoAm 90*
Walsh, David G. 1950- *St&PR 91*
Walsh, David James 1936- *St&PR 91*
Walsh, David Kevin 1952- *WhoSSW 91*
Walsh, Deborah Quintman 1959- *WhoAmW 91*
Walsh, Debra *ODwPR 91*
Walsh, Deleon 1905- *St&PR 91*
Walsh, Denis Edward 1941- *BiDrAPA 89*
Walsh, Denny Jay 1935- *WhoAm 90*
Walsh, Diane 1950- *WhoAmW 91*
Walsh, Don 1931- *WhoAm 90*
Walsh, Donald Francis 1932- *St&PR 91, WhoAm 90, WhoSSW 91*
Walsh, Donald James 1949- *WhoWrEP 89*
Walsh, Donald Peter 1930- *St&PR 91, WhoAm 90*
Walsh, Donnie *WhoAm 90*
Walsh, Doris Montague Huntley *WhoWrEP 89*
Walsh, Ed 1881-1959 *Ballpl 90 [port]*
Walsh, Ed 1905-1937 *Ballpl 90*
Walsh, Edward Joseph 1932- *St&PR 91, WhoAm 90*
Walsh, Edward Patrick 1924- *WhoAm 90*
Walsh, Eileen Cecile 1914- *WhoWrEP 89*
Walsh, Eileen Frances 1943- *WhoAmW 91*
Walsh, Eleanor Lucille 1962- *WhoAmW 91*
Walsh, Ellen Stoll 1942- *BioIn 16*
Walsh, Eva Barnett 1929- *WhoAmW 91*
Walsh, F. Howard 1913- *WhoAm 90, WhoSSW 91*
Walsh, Florence *BioIn 16*
Walsh, Frances Waggener *AuBYP 90*
Walsh, Francis Damien 1948- *WhoE 91*
Walsh, Francis Michael 1923- *St&PR 91*
Walsh, Frank J. 1920- *St&PR 91*
Walsh, Gary James 1958- *WhoSSW 91*
Walsh, Gene H. 1933- *ODwPR 91*
Walsh, George B. 1946-1989 *BioIn 16*
Walsh, George H. 1845-1913 *AmLegL*
Walsh, George Johnston 1889-1981 *BioIn 16*
Walsh, George William 1923- *WhoAm 90*
Walsh, George William 1931- *WhoWrEP 89*
Walsh, Gordon R. 1944- *St&PR 91*
Walsh, Harry 1918-1987 *BioIn 16*
Walsh, Howard Edmund 1929- *St&PR 91*
Walsh, J Michael 1953- *WhoAmA 91*
Walsh, James 1954- *WhoAmA 91*
Walsh, James Andrew 1957 *WhoE 91*
Walsh, James David 1947- *WhoEmL 91, WhoWor 91*
Walsh, James Hamilton 1947- *WhoEmL 91, WhoSSW 91*
Walsh, James Jerome 1924- *WhoAm 90*
Walsh, James Louis 1909- *WhoAm 90*
Walsh, James Michael 1947- *St&PR 91, WhoWor 91*
Walsh, James Morrow 1840-1905 *WhNaAH*
Walsh, James P. 1913- *St&PR 91*
Walsh, James Patrick 1954- *St&PR 91, WhoSSW 91*
Walsh, James Patrick, Jr. 1910- *WhoAm 90, WhoWor 91*
Walsh, James Starrak 1933- *St&PR 91*
Walsh, James T. 1947- *BioIn 16*
Walsh, James Thomas 1947- *WhoAm 90, WhoE 91*
Walsh, James William 1923- *St&PR 91*
Walsh, Jane Ellen McCann 1941- *WhoAmW 91*
Walsh, Janet Barbara 1939- *WhoAmA 91*
Walsh, Janet Laurentia 1954- *WhoAmW 91, WhoWor 91*
Walsh, Jeanne 1924- *WhoAmW 91*
Walsh, Jeni Lee 1944- *WhoE 91*
Walsh, Jennette 1948- *WhoEmL 91*
Walsh, Jill Paton 1937- *BioIn 16*
Walsh, Jill Paton 1939- *AuBYP 90*
Walsh, Jimmy 1885-1962 *Ballpl 90*
Walsh, Jimmy 1886-1947 *Ballpl 90*
Walsh, Joe 1947- *ConMus 5 [port]*
Walsh, John *BioIn 16*
Walsh, John 1830-1898 *DcCanB 12*
Walsh, John 1937- *WhoAm 90, WhoAmA 91, WhoWor 91*
Walsh, John Breffni 1927- *WhoAm 90*
Walsh, John Bronson 1927- *WhoE 91, WhoWor 91*
Walsh, John Charles 1924- *WhoAm 90*
Walsh, John E., Jr. 1927- *WhoAm 90*
Walsh, John Flewellen 1928- *WhoE 91*
Walsh, John Harley 1938- *WhoAm 90*
Walsh, John Joseph 1924- *WhoAm 90*
Walsh, John Patrick *BioIn 16*
Walsh, John Patrick 1905-1989 *BioIn 16*
Walsh, John Robert 1930- *St&PR 91, WhoAm 90*
Walsh, John Walter 1918- *WhoAm 90*
Walsh, Joseph Michael 1943- *St&PR 91, WhoAm 90*
Walsh, Joseph Thomas 1930- *WhoAm 90, WhoE 91*
Walsh, Joy 1935- *WhoWrEP 89*
Walsh, Julia Montgomery 1923- *WhoAm 90, WhoAmW 91*
Walsh, Junior 1919- *Ballpl 90*
Walsh, Karren Louise *WhoE 91*
Walsh, Kathleen Huberta 1929- *St&PR 91*
Walsh, Kevin M. 1950- *St&PR 91*
Walsh, Lawrence A. 1930- *St&PR 91*
Walsh, Lawrence Edward 1912- *WhoAm 90, WhoWor 91*
Walsh, Lawrence R. *ODwPR 91*
Walsh, Leo Marcellus 1931- *WhoAm 90*
Walsh, Loren M. 1927- *St&PR 91*
Walsh, Loren Melford 1927- *WhoAm 90, WhoWrEP 89*
Walsh, Louise 1962- *BiDWomA*
Walsh, Margaret Ellen Walsh 1923- *WhoAm 90*
Walsh, Marianne Lyda 1942- *WhoE 91*
Walsh, Marie Leclerc 1928- *WhoAmW 91*
Walsh, Marie Therese 1935- *WhoAm 90*
Walsh, Marilyn 1929- *St&PR 91*
Walsh, Martha Bosse *WhoE 91*
Walsh, Martin J. *BioIn 16*
Walsh, Martin Raymond 1952- *St&PR 91*
Walsh, Mary D. Fleming 1913- *WhoAmW 91, WhoSSW 91, WhoWor 91*
Walsh, Mary Ellen *BiDrAPA 89*
Walsh, Mary Ellen Budge 1950- *WhoE 91*
Walsh, Mary Frances *WhoAmW 91*
Walsh, Mary Williams 1955- *WhoWor 91*
Walsh, Mason 1912- *WhoAm 90*
Walsh, Mason, Jr. 1935- *St&PR 91*
Walsh, Matthew Myles, Jr. *St&PR 91*
Walsh, Maureen Marie 1949- *WhoAmW 91*
Walsh, Maurice David, Jr. 1924- *WhoAm 90*
Walsh, Maurice N *BiDrAPA 89*
Walsh, Michael 1949- *IntWWM 90*
Walsh, Michael Brendan 1967- *WhoE 91*
Walsh, Michael Elliott 1966- *WhoEmL 91*
Walsh, Michael F. *St&PR 91*
Walsh, Michael Harries 1942- *WhoAm 90*
Walsh, Michael J. 1932- *WhoAm 90*
Walsh, Michael Joseph, Jr. 1939- *St&PR 91*
Walsh, Michiyo Shiota 1953- *WhoE 91*
Walsh, Mike 1955- *WhoWrEP 89*
Walsh, Monica Mary *ODwPR 91*
Walsh, Patricia Ruth *WhoAmA 91*
Walsh, Patrick M *BiDrAPA 89*
Walsh, Patrick Robert 1948- *WhoEmL 91*
Walsh, Patrick W. 1939- *St&PR 91*
Walsh, Paul F. *St&PR 91*
Walsh, Peter Joseph 1929- *WhoAm 90*
Walsh, Philip Cornelius 1921- *St&PR 91, WhoAm 90*
Walsh, Philip Joseph, III 1951- *WhoSSW 91*
Walsh, R. F. 1930- *St&PR 91*
Walsh, Ralph Edward 1923- *WhoE 91*
Walsh, Raoul 1887-1980 *BioIn 16*
Walsh, Raymond J. 1949- *St&PR 91*
Walsh, Raymond M. 1919- *St&PR 91*
Walsh, Richard George 1930- *WhoAm 90*
Walsh, Richard John 1886-1960 *AuBYP 90*
Walsh, Richard Troy 1935- *St&PR 91, WhoAm 90*
Walsh, Robert 1784-1859 *BioIn 16*
Walsh, Robert Anthony 1938- *WhoWor 91*
Walsh, Robert C. 1938- *St&PR 91*
Walsh, Robert Charles 1938- *WhoAm 90*
Walsh, Robert Joseph 1944- *WhoE 91*
Walsh, Rodger John 1924- *St&PR 91, WhoAm 90*
Walsh, Ruth Laird *WhoE 91*
Walsh, Sandra Jo 1956- *WhoE 91*
Walsh, Semmes Guest 1926- *WhoAm 90*
Walsh, Sheila 1956- *BioIn 16*
Walsh, Stephen John 1938- *BiDrAPA 89*
Walsh, T Kevin 1941- *St&PR 91*
Walsh, Teresa Gladys 1954- *BiDrAPA 89*
Walsh, Thomas 1908-1984 *TwCCr&M 91*
Walsh, Thomas Charles 1940- *WhoAm 90*
Walsh, Thomas E. 1949- *St&PR 91*
Walsh, Thomas Gerald 1949- *WhoE 91*
Walsh, Thomas Gerard 1942- *St&PR 91, WhoAm 90*
Walsh, Thomas Joseph 1931- *WhoAm 90, WhoE 91, WhoWor 91*
Walsh, Thomas K. 1946- *St&PR 91*

Walsh, Thomas Lawrence 1946- *BiDrAPA 89*
Walsh, Thomas Patrick 1953- *WhoE 91*
Walsh, Timothy J. 1927- *WhoE 91*
Walsh, Timothy John 1949- *WhoSSW 91*
Walsh, Tom 1911-1988 *AnObit 1988*
Walsh, Walter J. 1929- *ODwPR 91*
Walsh, Walter Joseph 1929- *St&PR 91*
Walsh, William A. 1932- *St&PR 91*
Walsh, William Albert 1933- *WhoAm 90*
Walsh, William B. 1920- *AuBYP 90*
Walsh, William Bertalan *BioIn 16*
Walsh, William Bertalan 1920- *WhoAm 90*
Walsh, William Desmond 1930- *St&PR 91, WhoAm 90*
Walsh, William Egan 1948- *St&PR 91*
Walsh, William Egan, Jr. 1948- *WhoE 91*
Walsh, William F. 1938- *St&PR 91*
Walsh, William I. *BioIn 16, NewYTBS 90*
Walsh, William Joseph, III 1945- *St&PR 91*
Walsh, William Marshall 1936- *St&PR 91*
Walsh, William V *BiDrAPA 89*
Walshak, Henry T. *ODwPR 91*
Walshak, Rebecca Whyte 1963- *WhoSSW 91*
Walshe, Peter 1934- *ConAu 130*
Walsingham, Frances 1560?-1603? *BiDEWW*
Walske, Max Carl, Jr. 1922- *WhoAm 90*
Walstad, Dennis Carlton 1942- *St&PR 91*
Walstam, Rune Ellert 1923- *WhoWor 91*
Walston, Carl Frederick 1939- *WhoAm 90*
Walston, Claude Ellsworth 1926- *WhoAm 90*
Walston, Lola Inge 1943- *WhoWor 91*
Walston, Lynn Mauryne 1956- *WhoAmW 91*
Walston, Ray 1924- *WhoAm 90, WorAlBi*
Walston, Roderick Eugene 1935- *WhoAm 90, WhoWor 91*
Walsworth, James Frank 1927- *St&PR 91*
Walsworth, Ronald Lee 1935- *WhoAm 90*
Walt, Alexander Jeffrey 1923- *WhoAm 90*
Walt, Deon Van Der 1958- *IntWWM 90*
Walt, Dick K. 1935- *WhoAm 90, WhoWrEP 89*
Walt, Harold Richard 1923- *WhoAm 90*
Walt, Lewis W. 1913-1989 *BioIn 16*
Walt, Martin 1926- *WhoAm 90*
Walt, Melanie Gay Miller 1947- *WhoAmW 91*
Walt, Robert William 1956- *ODwPR 91*
Walt, Sherman 1923-1989 *BioIn 16*
Walt, Sherman Abbott 1923- *WhoAm 90*
Walta, Jaring Douwe 1941- *IntWWM 90*
Waltari, Mika Toimi 1908-1979 *DcScanL*
Waltcher, Milton *BioIn 16*
Waltemeyer, Robert Victor 1934- *St&PR 91, WhoAm 90*
Walter, Alfred Anthony 1932- *St&PR 91*
Walter, Almeric 1859-1942 *PenDiDA 89*
Walter, Anita R. 1949- *WhoAmW 91*
Walter, Barbara 1931- *WorAlBi*
Walter, Beverly Toney 1946- *WhoAmW 91*
Walter, Bruno 1876-1962 *PenDiMP, WorAlBi*
Walter, Carl Waldemar 1905- *WhoE 91*
Walter, Carole A. 1947- *St&PR 91*
Walter, Chrysandra Lou 1947- *WhoAmW 91*
Walter, David 1913- *IntWWM 90*
Walter, David E. 1950- *St&PR 91*
Walter, David K. 1944- *St&PR 91*
Walter, Dennis John 1944- *St&PR 91*
Walter, Devon Sloan 1948- *WhoAmW 91*
Walter, Donald Ellsworth 1936- *WhoAm 90*
Walter, Dorothy Lee 1926- *WhoSSW 91*
Walter, Elizabeth Mitchell 1936- *WhoAmA 91*
Walter, Elizabeth Thomas 1958- *WhoAmW 91*
Walter, Eugene Julian, Jr. 1932- *WhoAm 90*
Walter, Evelyn Seide *BioIn 16*
Walter, Frank Sherman 1926- *WhoAm 90*
Walter, Gary Steven 1949- *WhoSSW 91*
Walter, Gene 1960- *Ballpl 90*
Walter, George *PenDiMP*
Walter, George Herbert *BioIn 16*
Walter, Heather Jean 1950- *BiDrAPA 89, WhoE 91*
Walter, Helen Joy 1938- *WhoAmW 91*
Walter, Horst 1931- *IntWWM 90*
Walter, Ingo 1940- *WhoAm 90*
Walter, J. Jackson 1940- *WhoAm 90, WhoE 91*
Walter, J. W. 1922- *St&PR 91*
Walter, James Arnot 1949- *WhoWor 91*
Walter, James Rodney 1939- *St&PR 91*
Walter, James W. 1922- *WhoAm 90, WhoSSW 91*
Walter, Jessica 1944- *WhoAm 90, WorAlBi*
Walter, Johannes *NewAgMG*
Walter, John Grant 1932- *St&PR 91*
Walter, John Robert 1947- *WhoAm 90*
Walter, Judith *EncCoWW*
Walter, Kenneth D. 1929- *St&PR 91*
Walter, Linda Jo 1959- *WhoAmW 91*
Walter, Lloyd Guy, Jr. 1934- *WhoSSW 91*
Walter, Marie-Therese *BioIn 16*
Walter, Marion *AuBYP 90*
Walter, Mark M, Jr. 1924- *BiDrAPA 89*
Walter, Martha 1875-1976 *WhoAmA 91N*
Walter, May E *WhoAmA 91*
Walter, May Elizabeth 1935- *WhoAmW 91*
Walter, Michael Charles 1956- *WhoEmL 91*
Walter, Mildred Pitts *AuBYP 90*
Walter, Mildred Pitts 1922- *BioIn 16, SmATA 12AS [port]*
Walter, Miriam Gully 1940- *WhoAmW 91*
Walter, Norma *ODwPR 91*
Walter, Paul F. 1935- *St&PR 91, WhoAmA 91*
Walter, Paul Ryder 1937- *WhoSSW 91*
Walter, Peter *BioIn 16*
Walter, Richard Lawrence 1933- *WhoAm 90*
Walter, Robert C. 1918- *St&PR 91*
Walter, Robert D. 1945- *WhoAm 90*
Walter, Robert Irving 1920- *WhoAm 90*
Walter, Robert John 1948- *WhoWor 91*
Walter, Robert L. 1928- *St&PR 91*
Walter, Rolf Wilhelm 1937- *WhoWor 91*
Walter, Rudolf 1918- *IntWWM 90*
Walter, Sandra *BioIn 16*
Walter, Stephen 1912- *St&PR 91*
Walter, Thomas 1696-1725 *EncCRAm*
Walter, Thomas G. 1941- *St&PR 91*
Walter, Thomas Ustick 1804-1887 *BioIn 16*
Walter, Virginia Lee 1937- *WhoAm 90*
Walter, W.G.E. *EncCoWW*
Walter, W Grey 1910-1977 *EncO&P 3*
Walter, William Arnold, Jr. 1922- *WhoAm 90*
Walter, William F 1904-1977 *WhoAmA 91N*
Walter, William R. 1938- *St&PR 91*
Walter, William Roy 1948- *WhoE 91*
Walterhouse, George Francis 1937- *St&PR 91*
Walters, Adale Marie *BiDrAPA 89*
Walters, Alan Arthur 1926- *WhoWor 91*
Walters, Alan Stanley 1941- *WhoE 91*
Walters, Alton Joseph 1949- *WhoEmL 91*
Walters, Anna Lee 1946- *WhoAmW 91*
Walters, Barbara 1931- *BioIn 16, WhoAm 90, WhoAmW 91, WhoWor 91*
Walters, Bernard 1948- *IntWWM 90*
Walters, Bette Jean 1946- *WhoAm 90*
Walters, Billie 1927- *WhoAmA 91*
Walters, Bradford Blair 1952- *WhoEmL 91*
Walters, Bruce Wilson 1950- *BiDrAPA 89*
Walters, Bucky 1909- *Ballpl 90 [port]*
Walters, C Thomas 1934- *St&PR 91*
Walters, Carol Price 1941- *WhoAmW 91*
Walters, Celesta Scott 1906- *WhoAmW 91*
Walters, Charles Joseph 1945- *WhoE 91*
Walters, Charles Lee 1945- *BiDrAPA 89*
Walters, Clarence Ronald 1932- *WhoAm 90*
Walters, Cornelius J *BiDrAPA 89*
Walters, D. Wynn *ODwPR 91*
Walters, David Brian 1964- *WhoSSW 91*
Walters, David D. 1932- *St&PR 91*
Walters, David George 1939- *St&PR 91*
Walters, David McLean 1917- *WhoAm 90, WhoWor 91*
Walters, David R *BiDrAPA 89*
Walters, Deborah 1955- *WhoAmW 91*
Walters, Deborah Kaye Wright 1951- *WhoAmW 91*
Walters, Dennis R. 1946- *WhoE 91*
Walters, Denny W 1934- *BiDrAPA 89*
Walters, Diane *BioIn 16*
Walters, Donald E. *NewYTBS 90*
Walters, Dottie *BioIn 16*
Walters, Ernest 1927- *WhoAmA 91*
Walters, Ernest Edward 1927- *WhoE 91*
Walters, Everett 1915- *WhoAm 90*
Walters, Ewart James 1950- *ConTFT 8 [port]*
Walters, Floyd G. 1926- *St&PR 91*
Walters, G. Scott 1962- *WhoSSW 91*
Walters, Gene *BioIn 16*
Walters, Geoffrey King 1931- *WhoAm 90*
Walters, Glen Robert 1943- *WhoAm 90*
Walters, Guy M 1900- *BiDrAPA 89*
Walters, Harolene *BioIn 16*
Walters, Harry N. 1936- *WhoAm 90, WhoE 91*
Walters, Helen B. *BioIn 16*
Walters, Henry 1848-1931 *BioIn 16*
Walters, Hugh 1910- *AuBYP 90*
Walters, J. Donald 1926- *ConAu 132*
Walters, Jack Henry 1925- *WhoE 91*
Walters, James Michael 1947- *WhoE 91*
Walters, Janet Lee *BiDrAPA 89*
Walters, Jay B. 1946- *St&PR 91, WhoAm 90*
Walters, Jayne E. 1957- *St&PR 91*
Walters, Jefferson Brooks 1922- *WhoWor 91*
Walters, Jerry 1931- *WhoE 91*
Walters, Jesse Marvin 1940- *St&PR 91*
Walters, Joe A. 1920- *St&PR 91*
Walters, John Edward 1925- *St&PR 91*
Walters, John Paul *BiDrAPA 89*
Walters, John Sherwood 1917- *WhoAm 90*
Walters, Johnnie McKeiver 1919- *WhoAm 90*
Walters, Judith Richmond 1944- *WhoAmW 91*
Walters, Ken 1933- *Ballpl 90*
Walters, Kenn David 1957- *WhoWor 91*
Walters, Kenneth D. 1941- *ConAu 132*
Walters, Leigh Beaulieu 1961- *WhoSSW 91*
Walters, Leonard M. 1922- *St&PR 91*
Walters, Leslie 1902- *IntWWM 90*
Walters, Marguerite *AuBYP 90*
Walters, Martha Bernadine 1947- *WhoAmW 91*
Walters, Mary Coon 1922- *WhoAmW 91*
Walters, Mary Dawson 1923- *WhoWrEP 89*
Walters, Milt Kirkland 1940- *St&PR 91*
Walters, Milton James 1942- *St&PR 91, WhoAm 90*
Walters, Nancy Ethel 1953- *WhoAmW 91*
Walters, Nancy Lu 1938- *WhoAmW 91*
Walters, Nancy R. 1944- *ODwPR 91*
Walters, Patricia Diane 1961- *WhoAmW 91*
Walters, Paul A, Jr. 1927- *BiDrAPA 89*
Walters, Peter Ingram 1931- *WhoWor 91*
Walters, Ratus William 1932- *St&PR 91*
Walters, Raymond, Jr. 1912- *WhoAm 90, WhoWrEP 89*
Walters, Raymond L. 1949- *St&PR 91*
Walters, Rebecca Ellis 1955- *WhoSSW 91*
Walters, Rebecca Russell Yarborough 1951- *WhoAmW 91*
Walters, Robert Stephen 1941- *WhoE 91*
Walters, Robert Willis 1953- *WhoSSW 91*
Walters, Ronald E. *St&PR 91*
Walters, Ronald Ogden 1939- *St&PR 91, WhoAm 90*
Walters, Roxy 1892-1956 *Ballpl 90*
Walters, Sharon Beverly 1948- *WhoAmW 91*
Walters, Stephen R *BiDrAPA 89*
Walters, Sue Fox 1941- *WhoSSW 91*
Walters, Sylvia A. 1951- *ODwPR 91*
Walters, Sylvia Solochek 1938- *WhoAmA 91*
Walters, Teresa *IntWWM 90*
Walters, Vernon A. *BioIn 16*
Walters, Vernon Anthony 1917- *WhoAm 90, WhoWor 91*
Walters, Wilfred Nelson, Jr. 1942- *WhoSSW 91*
Walters, William 1819-1894 *BioIn 16*
Walters, William Armand 1944- *St&PR 91*
Walters, William Burnette, III 1952- *WhoE 91*
Walters, William Gary 1942- *BiDrAPA 89*
Walters, William Lee 1946- *WhoSSW 91*
Walters, William LeRoy 1932- *WhoAm 90*
Walters, William Peter 1943- *WhoSSW 91*
Walters-Jones, Beth 1949- *BiDrAPA 89*
Walters-Lucy, Jean 1941- *WhoWrEP 89*
Walters-Scherrer, Barbara Ann 1952- *BiDrAPA 89*
Waltersdorf, John Galt 1954- *St&PR 91*
Waltersdorf, John Maurice 1926- *St&PR 91*
Waltersdorf, Margaret Stott 1929- *St&PR 91*
Walthall, Gary David 1942- *St&PR 91*
Walthall, Lee Wade 1953- *WhoAm 90*
Walthall, Wilson Jones, Jr. 1918- *WhoAm 90*
Walther, Clemens Paul *PenDiDA 89*
Walther, Franz Erhard 1939- *WhoWor 91*
Walther, Fritz R 1921- *ConAu 132*
Walther, Gerda 1897- *EncO&P 3*
Walther, Gerda 1898-1977 *EncPaPR 91*
Walther, Gotfried Friedrich 1933- *WhoWor 91*
Walther, Gregory Louis 1954- *WhoWor 91*
Walther, Johannes 1860-1937 *DcScB S2*
Walther, John H. 1935- *St&PR 91*
Walther, John Henry 1935- *WhoAm 90*
Walther, Joseph Edward 1912- *WhoAm 90*
Walther, Judith *EncCoWW*
Walther, Ralph 1951- *St&PR 91*
Walther, Robert Thomas 1958- *WhoE 91*
Walther, Thomas Evans 1938- *St&PR 91*
Walther, Zerita 1927- *WhoAmW 91*
Walthers, B. J. 1919- *St&PR 91*
Walthers, J Philip 1948- *St&PR 91*
Walti, Kenneth John 1947- *St&PR 91*
Waltman, Lynne Marie 1952- *WhoSSW 91*
Waltman, Paul Elvis 1931- *WhoSSW 91*
Waltmann, Harry Franklin 1871-1951 *WhoAmA 91N*
Waltner, Beverly Ruland *WhoAmA 91, WhoSSW 91*
Waltner, Charles 1908- *BiDrAPA 89*
Waltner, Elma 1912- *AuBYP 90*
Waltner, G. H. 1918- *St&PR 91*
Waltner, Harry George, Jr. 1906- *WhoWor 91*
Waltner, Willard 1909- *AuBYP 90*
Walton, Alan George 1936- *St&PR 91, WhoAm 90*
Walton, Alice *BioIn 16*
Walton, Amanda Loretta 1941- *WhoAmW 91, WhoE 91*
Walton, Anthony *BioIn 16*
Walton, Anthony John 1934- *WhoWor 91*
Walton, Barbara Gayle 1955- *WhoEmL 91*
Walton, Bill 1952- *WorAlBi*
Walton, Booker T., Jr. 1950- *WhoSSW 91*
Walton, Carmelita Noreen 1926- *WhoAmW 91*
Walton, Cecile 1891-1956 *BiDWomA*
Walton, Charles *BiDrAPA 89*
Walton, Charles Michael 1941- *WhoAm 90*
Walton, Chelle Koster 1954- *WhoWrEP 89*
Walton, Chester Lee, Jr. 1926- *WhoSSW 91*
Walton, Clarence 1915- *WhoAm 90, WhoWrEP 89*
Walton, Clyde Cameron 1925- *WhoAm 90, WhoWrEP 89*
Walton, Conrad Gordon, Sr. 1928- *WhoSSW 91*
Walton, Corinne Hemeter 1925- *WhoSSW 91*
Walton, Daniel 1941- *St&PR 91*
Walton, Danny 1947- *Ballpl 90, BioIn 16*
Walton, Donald William *WhoAmA 91*
Walton, Ernest T. S. 1903- *WorAlBi*
Walton, Ernest Thomas Sinton 1903- *WhoWor 91*
Walton, Francis Ray 1910- *WhoAm 90*
Walton, Francis Xavier 1937- *WhoSSW 91*
Walton, Frank E. 1909- *WhoWrEP 89*
Walton, Frank Emulous 1909- *WhoAm 90*
Walton, Frank H. 1933- *St&PR 91*
Walton, Franklin J. 1951- *ODwPR 91*
Walton, Gary M. 1941- *WhoAm 90*
Walton, George 1750-1804 *EncCRAm*
Walton, George 1867-1933 *PenDiDA 89*
Walton, Gerald Wayne 1934- *WhoAm 90*
Walton, Gorman Wilber, Jr. 1946- *WhoSSW 91*
Walton, Grant *BioIn 16*
Walton, Guy E 1935- *WhoAmA 91*
Walton, Harold Vincent 1921- *WhoAm 90*
Walton, Harry A, Jr 1918- *WhoAmA 91*
Walton, Henry Foster 1858-1921 *AmLegL*
Walton, Isaac 1593-1683 *BioIn 16*
Walton, Izaak 1593-1683 *BioIn 16, WorAlBi*
Walton, J. H. 1933- *St&PR 91*
Walton, James Dana 1946- *BiDrAPA 89*
Walton, James M. 1930- *WhoAm 90*
Walton, James Stephen 1946- *WhoEmL 91*
Walton, Jean B. *WhoAm 90*
Walton, Jerome 1965- *Ballpl 90*
Walton, Jess *BioIn 16*
Walton, Joan 1939- *WhoAm 90*
Walton, Joe *BioIn 16*
Walton, John *PenDiDA 89*
Walton, John H. 1939- *St&PR 91*
Walton, John Sheppard 1930- *WhoAm 90*
Walton, Jon David 1942- *WhoAm 90*
Walton, Jonathan Taylor 1930- *St&PR 91, WhoAm 90*
Walton, Joseph A. 1935- *St&PR 91*
Walton, Joseph Carroll 1955- *WhoEmL 91*
Walton, Joseph M. 1926- *St&PR 91*
Walton, Judith D *BiDrAPA 89*
Walton, Karen Kay 1944- *WhoAmW 91*
Walton, Larry E. 1947- *WhoSSW 91*
Walton, Linda *BioIn 16*
Walton, Lorraine Hopson 1934- *WhoAmW 91*
Walton, M Douglas 1942- *WhoAmA 91*
Walton, Marion 1899- *WhoAmA 91*
Walton, Mark Alan 1955- *WhoE 91*
Walton, Matt Savage 1915- *WhoAm 90*
Walton, Meredith 1936- *WhoAm 90*
Walton, Morgan Lauck, III 1932- *WhoAm 90, WhoE 91, WhoWor 91*
Walton, Ned Ephram 1941- *WhoSSW 91*
Walton, Nigel David 1944- *IntWWM 90*
Walton, Paul Talmage 1914- *St&PR 91*
Walton, Ralph Gerald 1942- *BiDrAPA 89*
Walton, Richard Eugene 1931- *WhoAm 90, WhoWrEP 89*
Walton, Robert Cutler 1932- *WhoWor 91*
Walton, Robert Edward 1923- *WhoAm 90, WhoWor 91*
Walton, Robert Owen 1927- *WhoAm 90*
Walton, Robert Wheeler 1919- *WhoAm 90*
Walton, Rodney Earl 1947- *WhoEmL 91*
Walton, Roland Jerome 1934- *St&PR 91*
Walton, Sam M. *BioIn 16*
Walton, Sam Moore 1920- *WhoAm 90, WhoSSW 91, WhoWor 91*
Walton, Samuel Moore 1918- *ConAmBL*

Walton, Sandra Stevenson 1949- *WhoAmW 91*
Walton, Valli Yvonne 1950- *WhoAmW 91*
Walton, William 1902-1983 *BioIn 16, PenDiMP A*
Walton, William B. 1945- *St&PR 91*
Walton, William Buford 1942- *WhoSSW 91*
Walton, William C. 1924- *WhoAm 90*
Walton, William Robert 1949- *WhoEmL 91*
Walton, William Turner 1902-1983 *DcNaB 1981*
Waltos, David Lawrence *BiDrAPA 89*
Waltrip, Darrell Lee 1947- *WhoAm 90*
Waltrip, Robert L. *BioIn 16*
Waltrip, Robert L. 1931- *WhoSSW 91*
Waltrip, Royce W, II 1954- *BiDrAPA 89*
Waltrip, Travis W *BiDrAPA 89*
Walts, Charles F. 1948- *St&PR 91*
Walts, Jack C. 1919- *St&PR 91*
Walts, Loren W. 1940- *St&PR 91*
Walts, Robert Warren 1921- *WhoAm 90, WhoWrEP 89*
Waltz, Elizabeth Cherry 1866-1903 *LiHiK*
Waltz, Gary 1952- *BiDrAPA 89*
Waltz, Gerald Donn 1939- *St&PR 91, WhoAm 90*
Waltz, Gustavus *PenDiMP*
Waltz, J Mark 1943- *St&PR 91*
Waltz, Jon Richard 1929- *WhoAm 90, WhoWrEP 89*
Waltz, Joseph McKendree 1931- *WhoAm 90, WhoWor 91*
Waltz, Kenneth Neal 1924- *WhoAm 90*
Waltz, Thomas M. 1933- *St&PR 91*
Waltz, Thomas William 1940- *WhoE 91*
Waltzer, Herbert 1925- *BiDrAPA 89*
Waltzer, Herbert 1930- *WhoAm 90*
Waltzer, Stewart Paul 1948- *WhoAmA 91*
Waltzman, Allan Joel *BiDrAPA 89*
Waltzman, Stuart Alan 1936- *BiDrAPA 89*
Waluk, Stanley Peter 1943- *WhoE 91*
Walvoord, Edgar A. 1936- *St&PR 91*
Walvoord, John Flipse 1910- *WhoAm 90*
Walwer, Frank Kurt 1930- *WhoAm 90*
Walwicz, Ania 1951- *FemiCLE*
Walworth, Arthur 1903- *WhoAm 90*
Walworth, Charles Arthur 1931- *WhoAm 90*
Walworth, Edward Henry, Jr. 1915- *WhoAm 90*
Walworth, Jeannette 1837-1918 *FemiCLE*
Walwyn, Mary *BiDEWW*
Walz, Barbra *NewYTBS 90 [port]*
Walz, James Eric 1951- *St&PR 91*
Walz, John Robert *St&PR 91N*
Walz, Mary Kathryn 1951- *WhoAmW 91*
Walz, Mona Langguth 1931- *WhoAmW 91*
Walz, Robert DeHaven 1944- *WhoWor 91*
Walz, Royce Clifton *BiDrAPA 89*
Walz, Stewart Chaussee 1951- *WhoEmL 91*
Walz, Tommy 1945- *WhoWrEP 89*
Walzak, Edward J. 1945- *St&PR 91*
Walzer, Ann Elaine 1957- *WhoAmW 91*
Walzer, David Mark 1949- *BiDrAPA 89*
Walzer, Judith Borodovko 1935- *WhoAm 90*
Walzer, Michael Laban 1935- *WhoAm 90*
Walzer, Robert S *BiDrAPA 89*
Walzer, Robert Steven 1932- *WhoE 91*
Walzer, Stanley *BiDrAPA 89*
Walzer, William Charles 1912- *WhoAm 90*
Walzog, Nancy Lee 1963- *WhoAmW 91*
Wamaling, Mark Hunter 1959- *WhoWrEP 89*
Wambaugh, Joseph 1937- *MajTwCW, TwCCr&M 91, WhoAm 90, WorAlBi*
Wambaugh, Sarah 1882-1955 *BioIn 16*
Wamble, Clara 1947- *St&PR 91*
Wamble, John Lee 1942- *BiDrAPA 89*
Wambles, Lynda England 1937- *WhoAmW 91*
Wambold, Ali E. 1954- *St&PR 91*
Wambold, Karen J. 1961- *WhoAmW 91*
Wambold, Richard Lawrence 1952- *WhoAm 90*
Wamboldt, Donald G. 1932- *St&PR 91*
Wamboldt, Donald George 1932- *WhoAm 90*
Wamboldt, Frederick S *BiDrAPA 89*
Wamboldt, Marianne *BiDrAPA 89*
Wambolt, Ronald Ralph 1934- *St&PR 91, WhoAm 90*
Wambsganss, Bill 1894-1985 *Ballpl 90 [port]*
Wambsganss, Jacob Roy 1950- *WhoEmL 91*
Wambsganss, Richard E. 1940- *St&PR 91*
Wambuzi, Samuel William Wako 1931- *WhoWor 91*
Wamhoff, Heinrich Franz J. 1937- *WhoWor 91*
Wampler, Barbara Bedford 1932- *WhoAmW 91, WhoWor 91*
Wampler, Bernard Campbell 1931- *St&PR 91*
Wampler, Charles Edwin 1908- *WhoAm 90*
Wampler, Jack Lon 1946- *WhoSSW 91*
Wampler, James Allen 1944- *WhoAm 90*
Wampler, Lloyd Charles 1920- *WhoAm 90*
Wampler, Patricia Shannon 1957- *WhoSSW 91*
Wampler, Thornton Garland 1925- *St&PR 91*
Wampold, Charles Henry, Jr. 1925- *WhoAm 90*
Wamsley, Alice Mary 1922- *IntWWM 90*
Wamsutta *WhNaAH*
Wan Li *BioIn 16*
Wan Li 1917- *WhoWor 91*
Wan Li, Emperor 1573-1620 *PenDiDA 89*
Wan Nik *BioIn 16*
Wan Runnan *BioIn 16*
Wan, Chin Chin Yip 1945- *WhoWor 91*
Wan, Frederic Yui-Ming 1936- *WhoAm 90*
Wan, Lawrence A. *St&PR 91*
Wan, Paul A. 1945- *St&PR 91*
Wan, Shao-Hong 1946- *WhoE 91*
Wan, Sul Te 1873-1959 *DrBlPA 90*
Wanamaker, Archie Cook 1962- *WhoSSW 91*
Wanamaker, John 1838-1922 *BiDrUSE 89, WorAlBi*
Wanamaker, Robert Joseph 1924- *WhoAm 90*
Wanamaker, Sam 1919- *WorAlBi*
Wanat, Nancy Anne 1953- *WhoAmW 91*
Wanata 1795?-1848 *WhNaAH*
Wanberg, Geneve Christensen 1952- *WhoAmW 91*
Wanberg, Scott *BioIn 16*
Wanchisn, James Peter 1951- *WhoSSW 91*
Wancier, Zisalo *BiDrAPA 89*
Wanck, Bick 1951- *BiDrAPA 89*
Wanck, Bick Nicholas 1951- *WhoE 91*
Wand, Gunter 1912- *BioIn 16, IntWWM 90, PenDiMP*
Wand, Marilyn Maxine 1951- *WhoAmW 91*
Wand, Martin Austin 1953- *WhoSSW 91*
Wand, Richard Thomas 1938- *WhoSSW 91*
Wand, Richard Walton 1939- *St&PR 91, WhoAm 90*
Wand, Steven M. 1955- *St&PR 91*
Wandasiewicz, Stefania 1948- *WhoE 91*
Wandel, Lee Palmer 1954- *WhoAmW 91*
Wandel Cruse, Elise *BioIn 16*
Wandell, Linda Ann 1947- *WhoEmL 91*
Wander, Elyse Gay 1948- *St&PR 91, WhoAm 90*
Wander, Herbert Stanton 1935- *WhoAm 90*
Wander, Maxie 1933-1977 *EncCoWW*
Wander, Philip 1922- *WhoAm 90*
Wander, Philip 1923- *St&PR 91*
Wander, Waif 1833?-1909? *FemiCLE*
Wanderer, Kenneth Herbert 1923- *WhoAm 90*
Wanderley, Dalva Marli Valerio 1949- *WhoWor 91*
Wanderman, Susan Mae 1947- *WhoEmL 91*
Wanders, Hans W. 1925- *St&PR 91*
Wanders, Hans Walter 1925- *WhoAm 90*
Wandesford, Lady *BiDEWW*
Wandesford, Elizabeth *BiDEWW*
Wandler, Kevin Richard *BiDrAPA 89*
Wandler, Leslie Roy 1945- *St&PR 91, WhoAm 90*
Wandmacher, Cornelius 1911- *WhoAm 90*
Wandor, Mary Ann 1961- *WhoEmL 91*
Wandor, Michelene 1940- *FemiCLE*
Wandrisco, John L. 1925- *St&PR 91*
Wands, Alfred James 1904- *WhoAm 90, WhoAmA 91*
Wands, Robert James 1939- *WhoAmA 91*
Wandschneider, John Frederick 1943- *St&PR 91*
Wandycz, Piotr Stefan 1923- *WhoAm 90*
Waner, Lloyd 1906-1982 *Ballpl 90 [port]*
Waner, Paul 1903-1965 *Ballpl 90 [port]*
Wanerman, Leon Ralph *BiDrAPA 89*
Waneta 1795?-1848 *WhNaAH*
Wanfalt, George B. 1930- *St&PR 91*
Wang Bingqian 1925- *WhoWor 91*
Wang Cheng-Chung *WomWR*
Wang Dan *BioIn 16*
Wang Danfeng *BioIn 16*
Wang Fang *WhoWor 91*
Wang Mang, Emperor of China 33BC-23AD *BioIn 16*
Wang Meng *BioIn 16*
Wang Meng 1934- *WorAu 1980 [port]*
Wang Shixiang 1914- *BioIn 16*
Wang Zhen 1908- *WhoWor 91*
Wang, Amy Chi-Wen 1928- *WhoAmW 91*
Wang, An *BioIn 16*
Wang, An *St&PR 91N*
Wang, An 1920- *ConAmBL*
Wang, An 1920-1990 *ConAu 132, CurBio 90N, NewYTBS 90 [port], News 90, -90-3*
Wang, Andrew Chun-Lih *BiDrAPA 89*
Wang, Arthur Woods 1918- *WhoAm 90, WhoWrEP 89*
Wang, C C 1907- *WhoAmA 91*
Wang, Calvin Chih-Ping 1951- *WhoWor 91*
Wang, Cecil Kwei-Heng 1947- *WhoWor 91*
Wang, Cecilia Chu 1947- *IntWWM 90*
Wang, Chang Yi 1951- *WhoE 91, WhoEmL 91*
Wang, Chao-Cheng 1938- *WhoAm 90*
Wang, Charles *BioIn 16*
Wang, Chen Chi 1932- *WhoWor 91*
Wang, Cheng-Teh 1940- *WhoWor 91*
Wang, Chi-Sun 1942- *WhoSSW 91*
Wang, Chia-Gee 1936- *St&PR 91*
Wang, Chia Ping *WhoAm 90, WhoE 91, WhoWor 91*
Wang, Chung Yu 1880-1958 *EncO&P 3*
Wang, Clark John *BiDrAPA 89*
Wang, Daniel I-Chyau 1936- *WhoAm 90*
Wang, David I.J. 1932- *St&PR 91*
Wang, David I. J. 1932- *WhoAm 90*
Wang, Dennis 1954- *WhoE 91*
Wang, Deyan 1931- *WhoWor 91*
Wang, Eddy An Di 1923- *WhoWor 91*
Wang, Edwin James 1962- *WhoE 91*
Wang, Eva King *BiDrAPA 89*
Wang, Fusheng 1945- *WhoSSW 91*
Wang, Gar *WhoAmA 91*
Wang, George Shih Chang 1933- *WhoWor 91*
Wang, George Y 1941- *BiDrAPA 89*
Wang, Ging-Long 1938- *BiDrAPA 89*
Wang, Gung H. 1909- *WhoWor 91*
Wang, Hao 1921- *WhoAm 90*
Wang, Harry Carl 1950- *BiDrAPA 89*
Wang, Howard Wai-Ko 1954- *WhoWor 91*
Wang, Hsien Chung 1918-1978 *DcScB S2*
Wang, Hsioh-Shan 1928- *BiDrAPA 89*
Wang, Hubert K W *BiDrAPA 89*
Wang, James Chia-Fang 1926- *WhoAm 90*
Wang, James Chuo 1936- *WhoAm 90*
Wang, Jaw-Kai 1932- *WhoAm 90*
Wang, Jui Hsin 1921- *WhoAm 90*
Wang, Julie C. *ODwPR 91*
Wang, Knut W. 1937- *WhoWor 91*
Wang, Kuk-Kei Kenneth 1947- *WhoWor 91*
Wang, Kung-Lee 1925- *WhoE 91*
Wang, L. Edwin 1919- *WhoAm 90*
Wang, Leon Ru-Liang 1932- *WhoSSW 91*
Wang, Lin 1929- *WhoWor 91*
Wang, Ling 1918- *WhoWor 91*
Wang, Michael *BioIn 16*
Wang, Pearl Yun 1949- *WhoAmW 91*
Wang, Peter Ju-Pao 1945- *St&PR 91*
Wang, Richard Tienyunn 1944- *St&PR 91*
Wang, Robert Li Hsueh 1949- *WhoE 91*
Wang, Ruby Hwa 1933- *WhoE 91*
Wang, Rui Cong 1919- *WhoWor 91*
Wang, Ruqu 1965- *WhoE 91*
Wang, Sam 1939- *WhoAmA 91*
Wang, Shih C. 1910- *WhoAm 90*
Wang, Shih-Ho 1944- *WhoAm 90*
Wang, Shih-hsiang 1914- *BioIn 16*
Wang, Sing-wu 1920- *WhoWor 91*
Wang, Stanley *BiDrAPA 89*
Wang, Stephen 1947- *WhoWor 91*
Wang, Sue Hwa 1948- *WhoAmW 91*
Wang, Taylor Gunjin 1940- *WhoAm 90*
Wang, Tih-wu *BioIn 16*
Wang, Tsanshao 1952- *WhoSSW 91*
Wang, Tsing-Shih Peter 1952- *WhoWor 91*
Wang, Tso-Ren 1943- *WhoWor 91*
Wang, William Kai-Sheng 1946- *WhoAm 90*
Wang, William Shi-Yuan 1933- *WhoAm 90*
Wang, Xiao Lu 1954- *WhoE 91*
Wang, Xingwu 1953- *WhoWor 91*
Wang, Ya Ko 1956- *WhoWor 91*
Wang, Yahui 1930- *WhoWor 91*
Wang, Yao Chun *BiDrAPA 89*
Wang, Yao Chun 1938- *WhoE 91*
Wang, Zhongde 1937- *WhoWor 91*
Wang, Zuoliang 1916- *WhoWor 91*
Wang-Birnbaum, Ruth Deborah 1961- *WhoE 91*
Wangaard, Arthur Carl, Jr. 1927- *St&PR 91*
Wangaard, Clark F. 1950- *St&PR 91*
Wangberg, Mark Thomas 1952- *WhoWrEP 89*
Wangbichler, Robert James 1938- *St&PR 91*
Wangchuck, Jigme Singye 1955- *WhoWor 91*
Wangchuck, Sonam Chhoden 1953- *WhoWor 91*
Wangelin, Robert Lester 1945- *BiDrAPA 89*
Wangenheim, Volker 1928- *IntWWM 90, PenDiMP*
Wangensteen, Stephen Lightner 1933- *WhoSSW 91*
Wanger, Barry David 1946- *WhoE 91*
Wanger, Ralph *BioIn 16*
Wanger, Shelley Antonia 1948- *WhoAmW 91*
Wanger, Walter 1894-1968 *WorAlBi*
Wangermann, Jochen Rolf 1939- *WhoWor 91*
Wangford, Hank *WhoNeCM B [port]*
Wangh, Martin 1911- *BiDrAPA 89*
Wangh, Mitchell W 1947- *BiDrAPA 89*
Wangler, Francis D. 1941- *IntWWM 90*
Wangler, Gary William 1946- *WhoEmL 91*
Wangler, John G, Jr. 1937- *BiDrAPA 89*
Wangler, Kenneth John 1948- *WhoE 91*
Wangler, William Clarence 1929- *St&PR 91, WhoAm 90*
Wangsgard, Robert Louis 1915- *WhoAm 90*
Wangsness, Roald Klinkenberg 1922- *WhoAm 90*
Wanguri, Deloris McGee 1949- *WhoSSW 91*
Waniek, Marilyn 1946- *SmATA 60 [port]*
Waniek, Marilyn Nelson 1946- *WhoWrEP 89*
Waniewski, Eugene C. 1946- *St&PR 91*
Wank, Gerald Sidney 1925- *WhoAm 90*
Wank, Rolf 1943- *WhoWor 91*
Wanke, Henry Hans 1925- *St&PR 91*
Wanke, Klaus 1933- *WhoWor 91*
Wankel, Charlotte 1888-1956? *BiDWomA*
Wankel, Felix 1902-1988 *AnObit 1988, BioIn 16*
Wankelman, Willard Fred 1916- *WhoAm 90*
Wanland, Ruby Evelyn 1937- *WhoAmW 91*
Wanlass, Stanley Glen 1941- *WhoAmA 91*
Wanman, Agnes White 1945- *WhoAmW 91*
Wann, Albert B. 1941- *ODwPR 91*
Wann, Andrew Jackson 1919- *WhoAm 90*
Wann, David L. 1949- *WhoWrEP 89*
Wann, Laymond Doyle 1924- *WhoWor 91*
Wann, Patsy Gordon 1952- *WhoAmW 91*
Wannall, Walter Raymond, III 1944- *WhoE 91*
Wannemacher, Thomas Lee 1947- *WhoEmL 91*
Wannen, Herbert Richmond 1946- *WhoEmL 91*
Wanner, Albert Louis *BiDrAPA 89*
Wanner, Eric 1942- *WhoE 91*
Wanner, George Lewis, III 1958- *WhoE 91*
Wanner, James E. 1930- *St&PR 91*
Wanninger, Paul 1902-1981 *Ballpl 90*
Wanotan 1795?-1848 *WhNaAH*
Wanrooy, Willem Frederik 1925- *WhoWrEP 89*
Wansbrough, J. Christopher C. 1932- *St&PR 91*
Wansbrough-Jones, Owen Haddon 1905-1982 *DcNaB 1981*
Wansing, Alvin Daniel 1947- *WhoEmL 91*
Wansley, Larry *BioIn 16*
Wansley, William Dunn 1962- *WhoSSW 91*
Wanta, Debra Ann 1964- *WhoAmW 91*
Wanthal, Theodore Ray 1937- *St&PR 91*
Wantland, Evelyn Kendrick 1917- *WhoAmW 91*
Wantland, William Charles 1934- *WhoAm 90*
Wantz, George Edward 1923- *WhoE 91*
Wanvig, James Louis 1921- *WhoAm 90*
Wanwig, J Daniel 1945- *BiDrAPA 89*
Wanzek, Joseph M., Jr. 1951- *WhoEmL 91*
Wanzer, Richard Mott 1818?-1900 *DcCanB 12*
Wanzo, Cassandra Lee *BiDrAPA 89*
Wapana 1787-1842 *WhNaAH*
Wapella 1787-1842 *WhNaAH*
Wapello 1787-1842 *WhNaAH*
Wapiennik, Carl Francis 1926- *WhoAm 90*
Wapler, Vincent 1947- *WhoWor 91*
Waples, John Christopher 1940- *St&PR 91*
Wapner, Frederick *BioIn 16*
Wapner, Joseph A. *BioIn 16*
Wapner, Joseph A. 1919- *WhoAm 90*
Wapner, Peggy Ann 1950- *WhoAmW 91*
Wapner, Seymour 1917- *WhoAm 90*
Wapp, Edward 1943- *IntWWM 90*
Wappaus, Herbert Edward 1939- *St&PR 91*
Waquie, Al *BioIn 16*
War *EncPR&S 89*
War Eagle 1785?-1851 *WhNaAH*
War, Thomas L. 1914- *St&PR 91*
Warakomski, Alphonse Walter Joseph, Jr. 1943- *WhoWor 91*
Warashina, M Patricia *WhoAmA 91*
Warbel, Samuel 1930- *St&PR 91*
Warbinton, Douglas L. 1952- *St&PR 91*
Warbritton, Patricia Ann 1949- *WhoAmW 91*
Warbritton, Scott 1951- *St&PR 91*
Warburg, Aby 1866-1929 *BioIn 16*
Warburg, Bettina *BiDrAPA 89*
Warburg, Eric M. 1900-1990 *NewYTBS 90 [port]*

Warburg, Felix M. 1871-1937 WorAlBi
Warburg, Gerald F. ODwPR 91
Warburg, James P. 1896-1969 WorAlBi
Warburg, Jeremy BioIn 16
Warburg, Max Moritz 1867-1946 BioIn 16
Warburg, Otto Heinrich 1883-1970 WorAlBi
Warburg, Paul M. 1868-1932 EncABHB 7 [port]
Warburg, Sandol Stoddard 1927- AuBYP 90
Warburg, Siegmund George 1902-1982 DcNaB 1981
Warburg, Stephanie Wenner 1941- WhoAmA 91
Warburton, Clark A. 1896-1979 EncABHB 7
Warburton, Ralph Joseph 1935- WhoAm 90, WhoSSW 91, WhoWor 91
Warburton, William 1698-1779 DcLB 104 [port]
Warch, Richard 1939- WhoAm 90
Warchaizer, Edward Stanley 1937- WhoE 91
Warchal, Bohdan 1930- IntWWM 90
Warcollier, Rene 1881-1962 EncO&P 3, EncPaPR 91
Warcup, Howard J. 1932- St&PR 91
Ward, A Almon 1933- BiDrAPA 89
Ward, Aaron 1896-1961 Ballpl 90
Ward, Alan S. 1931- WhoAm 90
Ward, Alex 1944- WhoAm 90
Ward, Andino BioIn 16
Ward, Ann Curtin BiDrAPA 89
Ward, Annie 1824-1895 BioAmW
Ward, Anthony John 1931- WhoWor 91
Ward, Arch 1901-1956 Ballpl 90
Ward, Artemas 1727-1800 EncCRAm
Ward, Artemus 1834-1867 BioIn 16
Ward, Arthur Henry 1883-1959 EncO&P 3
Ward, Arthur Wesley, Jr. BiDrAPA 89
Ward, Barbara 1914- BioIn 16
Ward, Barbara 1914-1981 WorAlBi
Ward, Barbara Conner 1940- WhoAmW 91
Ward, Barbara Mary 1914-1981 DcNaB 1981
Ward, Benjamin BioIn 16
Ward, Benjamin 1926- WhoAm 90, WhoE 91
Ward, Benjamin D. 1929- St&PR 91
Ward, Benjamin Porter 1897- WhoSSW 91
Ward, Bethea 1924- WhoAmW 91
Ward, Billy EncPR&S 89
Ward, Bradford James 1945- WhoE 91
Ward, Brendan Noel 1947- ConAu 129
Ward, Brooke BioIn 16
Ward, Burt BioIn 16
Ward, Carl Donald 1950- WhoEmL 91
Ward, Carl Edward 1948- WhoEmL 91
Ward, Carol Lee BiDrAPA 89
Ward, Catherine George 1787- FemiCLE
Ward, Cecil 1929- WhoWor 91
Ward, Charles Douglas 1941- WhoAm 90
Ward, Charles Eugene 1937- WhoSSW 91
Ward, Charles Stuart 1939- WhoSSW 91
Ward, Chester Lawrence 1932- WhoAm 90
Ward, Chester Virgil 1949- WhoEmL 91
Ward, Christopher James 1937- St&PR 91
Ward, Chuck 1894-1969 Ballpl 90
Ward, Clara 1924-1973 DrBIPA 90
Ward, Claude 1930- St&PR 91
Ward, Claudia Faye 1951- WhoSSW 91
Ward, Cranley Thomas 1966- WhoSSW 91
Ward, Cynthia Vaune 1958- WhoAmW 91
Ward, Daniel P. 1918- WhoAm 90
Ward, David ODwPR 91
Ward, David 1929-1983 PenDiMP
Ward, David Allen 1933- WhoAm 90
Ward, David E. 1939- WhoSSW 91
Ward, David Ernest 1947- WhoWor 91
Ward, David Harris 1933- WhoAm 90
Ward, David Lynn 1957- WhoSSW 91
Ward, David Schad 1947- WhoAm 90
Ward, David W. B. 1942- IntWWM 90
Ward, Deborah 1960- ODwPR 91
Ward, Denise Pagano 1959- WhoE 91
Ward, Deva Jean 1953- WhoAmW 91
Ward, Diane A. 1946- WhoEmL 91
Ward, Diane Korosy 1939- WhoAmW 91
Ward, Donald Butler 1919- WhoAm 90
Ward, Donald Roger 1938- WhoE 91
Ward, Doris Elizabeth 1935- WhoAmW 91, WhoE 91, WhoWor 91
Ward, Douglas Turner 1930- DrBIPA 90
Ward, Duane 1964- Ballpl 90
Ward, Dudley Avery 1922- St&PR 91
Ward, E D ConAu 30NR
Ward, Elaine 1929- WhoAmA 91
Ward, Elizabeth C. 1958- WhoE 91
Ward, Emma Payne 1944- WhoAmW 91
Ward, Evan, Jr. 1942- WhoWor 91
Ward, Evelyn Svec WhoAmA 91N
Ward, Francis 1920- IntWWM 90
Ward, Frank Jay 1934- St&PR 91
Ward, G William 1931- St&PR 91
Ward, Gary 1953- Ballpl 90
Ward, Gary Ardus 1950- WhoEmL 91
Ward, Gary Lee, Jr. 1952- WhoSSW 91
Ward, Genevieve 1838-1922 BioIn 16
Ward, Geoffrey Champion 1940- WhoAm 90, WhoWrEP 89
Ward, George B.P., Jr. 1935- St&PR 91
Ward, George Truman 1927- WhoSSW 91
Ward, Gerald Wayne Richmond 1949- WhoE 91
Ward, Grace Anne 1951- WhoSSW 91
Ward, H. Bailey 1940- WhoSSW 91
Ward, Harold Anson, III 1933- WhoSSW 91
Ward, Harry Merrill WhoSSW 91
Ward, Harry P. 1876?- AmLegL
Ward, Harry Pfeffer 1933- WhoAm 90
Ward, Haskell George 1940- WhoE 91
Ward, Henrietta Mary Ada 1832-1924 BiDWomA
Ward, Henry P 1926- BiDrAPA 89
Ward, Herbert Eugene BiDrAPA 89
Ward, Hilary Margaret 1957- WhoAmW 91
Ward, Hiley Henry 1929- WhoAm 90, WhoWrEP 89
Ward, Hiram Hamilton 1923- WhoAm 90, WhoSSW 91
Ward, Horace Taliaferro 1927- WhoAm 90, WhoSSW 91
Ward, Humphry, Mrs. 1851-1920 BioIn 16
Ward, J Dexter 1948- St&PR 91
Ward, J Richard 1933- St&PR 91
Ward, Jack D. 1952- WhoEmL 91
Ward, Jack Francis 1921- WhoWor 91
Ward, Jack L BiDrAPA 89
Ward, James 1833?-1891 DcCanB 12
Ward, James K 1917- BiDrAPA 89
Ward, James Michael 1953- WhoWor 91
Ward, James S BiDrAPA 89
Ward, James William 1953- WhoSSW 91
Ward, Jane Abercrombie 1930- WhoAmW 91
Ward, Jane Pamela 1948- WhoAmW 91
Ward, Jasper Dudley, III 1921- WhoAm 90
Ward, Jay BioIn 16
Ward, Jay 1920-1989 AnObit 1989, ConTFT 8, SmATA 63
Ward, Jean Marie 1954- WhoAmW 91
Ward, Jeanne Patricia 1945- WhoAmW 91
Ward, Jeannette Poole 1932- WhoAmW 91
Ward, Jerry Leroy 1945- WhoE 91
Ward, Jerry Mack 1943- WhoE 91
Ward, John Brooks 1946- St&PR 91
Ward, John D. 1945- St&PR 91
Ward, John Elliott 1814-1902 AmLegL
Ward, John Lawrence 1938- WhoAmA 91
Ward, John Milton 1917- WhoAm 90
Ward, John Montgomery 1860-1925 Ballpl 90 [port], BioIn 16
Ward, John N. ODwPR 91
Ward, John Owen 1919- IntWWM 90
Ward, John P. 1930- St&PR 91
Ward, John Paul 1930- WhoAm 90
Ward, John Robert 1923- WhoAm 90
Ward, John Thomas 1925- WhoE 91
Ward, John Wesley 1925- WhoAm 90
Ward, Joseph 1942- IntWWM 90
Ward, Joseph Marshall 1922- WhoAmA 91
Ward, Joseph Simeon 1925- WhoAm 90
Ward, Josephine 1864-1932 FemiCLE
Ward, Judy Kitchen 1940- WhoAmW 91
Ward, Karin 1936- St&PR 91
Ward, Kathy Ann 1956- WhoAmW 91
Ward, Kenneth Gray 1946- St&PR 91
Ward, Kenneth Joseph 1954- St&PR 91
Ward, Kent Miles 1956- BiDrAPA 89
Ward, L. E. 1944- WhoWrEP 89
Ward, Lauriston 1883-1960 WhoAmA 91N
Ward, Leonard George 1930- WhoSSW 91
Ward, Leslie 1851-1922 BioIn 16
Ward, Leslie Allyson 1946- WhoAmW 91
Ward, Lester Lowe, Jr. 1930- WhoAm 90
Ward, Lewis Burt 1931- BiDrAPA 89
Ward, Lewis W. 1940- St&PR 91
Ward, Linda Elaine 1949- WhoAmW 91
Ward, Llewellyn Orcutt, III 1930- WhoSSW 91, WhoWor 91
Ward, Lloyd Arthur 1927- St&PR 91
Ward, Louis Emmerson 1918- WhoAm 90
Ward, Louis L. 1919- St&PR 91
Ward, Louis Larrick 1920- WhoAm 90
Ward, Louisa 1823-1897 BioAmW
Ward, Lyle Edward 1922- WhoAmA 91
Ward, Lynd 1905-1985 WhoAmA 91N
Ward, Lynd Kendall 1905-1985 AuBYP 90
Ward, Maisie 1889-1975 BioIn 16
Ward, Margaret Anne 1944- WhoAmW 91
Ward, Maria Frances 1949- WhoAmW 91
Ward, Marilyn Sue BiDrAPA 89
Ward, Mark Lee, Sr. 1958- WhoWrEP 89
Ward, Mary BiDEWW
Ward, Mary 1585-1645 BiDEWW, FemiCLE
Ward, Mary Augusta 1851-1920 FemiCLE
Ward, Mary Augusta Arnold 1851-1920 BioIn 16
Ward, Matthew NewYTBS 90
Ward, Matthew 1951?-1990 ConAu 132
Ward, Max BioIn 16
Ward, Michael BioIn 16
Ward, Michael 1957- WhoAmA 91
Ward, Michael Moses BioIn 16
Ward, Michael W. 1950- WhoEmL 91
Ward, Michelle Annette 1961- WhoAmW 91
Ward, Milton Hawkins 1932- St&PR 91, WhoAm 90, WhoSSW 91
Ward, Montgomery 1843-1913 WorAlBi
Ward, Nancy 1738?-1824? EncCRAm, WhNaAH
Ward, Nancy Elizabeth 1942- WhoAmW 91
Ward, Nancy Elizabeth 1946- WhoAmW 91
Ward, Nancy Joan 1939- WhoWrEP 89
Ward, Nanda Weedon 1932- AuBYP 90
Ward, Nelson 1941- St&PR 91
Ward, Nicholas Donnell 1941- WhoAm 90
Ward, Nicholas G 1947- BiDrAPA 89
Ward, Norman 1918- WhoAm 90
Ward, Olivia DrBIPA 90
Ward, Patricia Ellen 1927- WhoE 91
Ward, Paul Clarendon 1918- IntWWM 90
Ward, Paul Herbert, Jr. 1948- WhoEmL 91
Ward, Paul Hutchins 1928- WhoAm 90
Ward, Paul Jerald 1949- WhoSSW 91
Ward, Paulette Clemma 1945- WhoAmW 91
Ward, Pauline 1898- WhoAm 90, WhoAmW 91, WhoE 91, WhoWor 91
Ward, Penny L. 1961- WhoWrEP 89
Ward, Perry William 1939- WhoSSW 91
Ward, Pete 1939- Ballpl 90
Ward, Peter Allan 1934- WhoAm 90
Ward, Peter Garnet 1928- IntWWM 90
Ward, Peter Minton 1924- WhoAm 90
Ward, Philip 1938- ConAu 30NR
Ward, Philip 1951- WhoSSW 91
Ward, Philip Stewart 1944- St&PR 91
Ward, Phillip A 1927- WhoAmA 91
Ward, Phillip Wayne 1935- WhoSSW 91
Ward, Preston 1927- Ballpl 90
Ward, Rachel BioIn 16
Ward, Rachel 1957- WhoAmW 91
Ward, Rebecca BiDEWW
Ward, Richard 1915-1979 DrBIPA 90
Ward, Richard H. 1932- St&PR 91
Ward, Richard Hurley 1939- WhoWor 91
Ward, Richard John 1953- WhoE 91
Ward, Richard Joseph 1921- WhoAm 90
Ward, Richard S 1920- BiDrAPA 89
Ward, Richard S. 1940- St&PR 91
Ward, Richard Vance, Jr. 1929- WhoAm 90
Ward, Robert 1917- IntWWM 90, WhoAm 90
Ward, Robert B. Ballpl 90
Ward, Robert Edward 1916- WhoAm 90
Ward, Robert Foster BiDrAPA 89
Ward, Robert Franklin 1949- WhoAm 90
Ward, Robert James 1926- St&PR 91
Ward, Robert Joseph 1926- WhoAm 90
Ward, Robert K BiDrAPA 89
Ward, Robert Ross 1943- WhoWrEP 89
Ward, Robertson BioIn 16
Ward, Robertson, Jr. 1922- WhoAm 90
Ward, Rodman, Jr. 1934- WhoAm 90
Ward, Roger Coursen 1922- WhoAm 90
Ward, Roger Harrison 1959- WhoE 91
Ward, Roscoe Fredrick 1930- WhoAm 90
Ward, Russell 1924- WhoE 91
Ward, S. Joseph 1928- ODwPR 91
Ward, S Joseph 1928- St&PR 91
Ward, Sally Ann 1938- WhoE 91
Ward, Sharon Lynne 1942- WhoAmW 91
Ward, Sheila Daneen 1935- WhoAmW 91
Ward, Sidney Charles 1929- WhoSSW 91, WhoWor 91
Ward, Simon Barrington- 1930- BioIn 16
Ward, Spencer A 1936- BiDrAPA 89
Ward, Stephanie A BiDrAPA 89
Ward, Stephen Beecher 1955- WhoE 91
Ward, Stephen D 1925- BiDrAPA 89
Ward, Stephen William 1955- WhoSSW 91
Ward, Susan ODwPR 91
Ward, Susan Bayer 1944- WhoWrEP 89
Ward, Susan Marie 1954- WhoAmW 91
Ward, Suzanne Mary 1956- WhoAmW 91
Ward, Sylvan Donald 1909- WhoAm 90
Ward, Terry BioIn 16
Ward, Theodore 1902-1983 DrBIPA 90, EarBlAP
Ward, Thomas Francis 1934- St&PR 91
Ward, Thomas Howard, Jr. 1929- St&PR 91
Ward, Thomas Jerome 1936- St&PR 91, WhoAm 90
Ward, Thomas Leon 1930- WhoAm 90
Ward, Thomas P 1931- St&PR 91
Ward, Thomas Richard 1940- St&PR 91
Ward, Thomas W 1934- St&PR 91
Ward, Thomas Wren 1786-1858 EncABHB 6 [port]
Ward, Velox 1901- MusmAFA
Ward, Virginia Lee 1944- WhoAmW 91
Ward, Wallace Dixon 1924- WhoAm 90
Ward, Walter Bernard, Jr. 1927- St&PR 91
Ward, Willard B. 1914- BioIn 16
Ward, William 1911-1984 MusmAFA
Ward, William Binnington 1917- WhoAm 90
Ward, William Carroll 1930- WhoSSW 91
Ward, William David 1943- St&PR 91
Ward, William Edward 1922- WhoAmA 91
Ward, William Forrest, Jr. 1945- St&PR 91
Ward, William Francis 1951- WhoEmL 91
Ward, William Francis, Jr. 1928- WhoAm 90
Ward, William Harrison 1946- WhoSSW 91
Ward, William Herbert 1931- St&PR 91
Ward, William J. BioIn 16
Ward, William J. 1852-1938 AmLegL
Ward, William J., III 1939- WhoAm 90
Ward, William Joseph 1928- WhoSSW 91
Ward, William R., Jr. 1928- St&PR 91
Ward, William Ralph 1908-1988 BioIn 16
Ward, William Reed 1918- WhoAm 90
Ward, William Roy St&PR 91N
Ward, Windsor Earl 1939- St&PR 91
Ward, Winifred 1884-1975 NotWoAT
Ward, Winifred Louise 1884-1975 BioIn 16
Ward, Wm. Michael 1957- WhoWrEP 89
Ward, Yvette Hennig 1910- WhoAm 90
Ward-Hunt, David NewAgMG
Ward-Jackson, Adrian Alexander 1950- WhoWor 91
Ward Jones, Peter Arthur 1944- IntWWM 90
Ward-McLemore, Ethel 1908- WhoAmW 91, WhoSSW 91, WhoWor 91
Ward of Witley, Viscount 1907-1988 AnObit 1988
Ward-Perkins, John Bryan 1912-1981 DcNaB 1981
Ward-Racy, Elizabeth Ann BiDrAPA 89
Ward Russell, Gillian Ann 1953- IntWWM 90
Ward-Shaw, Sheila Theresa 1951- WhoAmW 91
Ward-Steinman, David 1936- IntWWM 90, WhoAm 90
Ward-Steinman, Irving 1905- WhoSSW 91
Warda, Mark 1952- WhoWrEP 89
Warde, Alan 1949- ConAu 31NR
Warde, Charles R. 1917- St&PR 91
Warde, Frances 1810-1884 BioAmW
Warde, George Andres 1921- WhoAm 90
Wardell, Charles Willard Bennett, III 1945- St&PR 91, WhoAm 90
Wardell, David Joseph 1956- WhoEmL 91
Wardell, Doris Erway 1939- WhoE 91
Wardell, Joe Russell, Jr. 1929- WhoE 91
Wardell, John Watson 1929- WhoWor 91
Wardell, Martin Bernard 1951- WhoWor 91
Wardell, Ricky Ray 1949- WhoSSW 91
Wardell, Robert BioIn 16
Wardell, Virginia Simonson 1943- WhoAmW 91
Warden, Deborah Lee 1952- BiDrAPA 89
Warden, Florence 1857-1929 FemiCLE
Warden, Gail Lee 1938- WhoAm 90
Warden, Gary Russell 1950- WhoE 91, WhoWor 91
Warden, Hays R. 1942- St&PR 91
Warden, Jack 1920- ConTFT 8 [port], WhoAm 90, WorAlBi
Warden, James Bryce 1937- St&PR 91
Warden, Karen Eleanor 1959- WhoE 91
Warden, Michael L. 1950- St&PR 91
Warden, Richard Dana 1931- WhoAm 90
Warder, Charles A. 1933- St&PR 91
Warder, Lee Oran 1949- St&PR 91
Warder, Margaret A. 1940- ODwPR 91
Warder, Richard Currey, Jr. 1936- WhoAm 90
Warder, William 1920- WhoAmA 91
Wardlaw, Anita Louise WhoWrEP 89
Wardlaw, Barbara Anne 1958- St&PR 91
Wardlaw, Elizabeth 1677-1727 BiDEWW, FemiCLE
Wardlaw, Frank Harper 1913-1989 BioIn 16
Wardlaw, George Melvin 1927- WhoAmA 91
Wardle, Curt 1960- Ballpl 90
Wardle, Eric Peter 1947- WhoE 91
Wardle, Ralph 1909-1988 DcLB 103 [port]
Wardle, Rhea Rose 1951- WhoAmW 91
Wardlow, Bill 1921- WhoAm 90
Wardropper, Bruce Wear 1919- WhoAm 90
Wardwell, Allen 1935- WhoAm 90, WhoAmA 91, WhoE 91
Wardwell, William Francis 1944- St&PR 91
Wardynski, Edmund St&PR 91
Wardynski, Raymond Francis 1921- St&PR 91

Wardzinski, Georgean M. 1954- St&PR 91
Ware, Abbot K. 1914- St&PR 91
Ware, Alton Douglas 1943- St&PR 91
Ware, Barbara BioIn 16
Ware, Brendan John 1932- WhoAm 90
Ware, Caroline F. 1899-1990 ConAu 131
Ware, Clifton, Jr. 1937- WhoAm 90
Ware, Constance Everett 1931-1989 BioIn 16
Ware, D. Clifton 1937- IntWWM 90
Ware, E. Frank 1944- St&PR 91
Ware, Edward W., III ODwPR 91
Ware, Edward Winslow 1919- St&PR 91
Ware, Elias, Jr. AmLegL
Ware, Eugene Harry 1940- WhoE 91
Ware, Gary Wayne 1942- St&PR 91
Ware, George 1829-1895 OxCPMus
Ware, Guilford Dudley 1925- St&PR 91
Ware, James Edwin 1925- WhoAm 90
Ware, James Gareth 1929- WhoSSW 91
Ware, James Patrick 1947- BiDrAPA 89
Ware, James T. 1926- WhoSSW 91
Ware, Jennifer Peyton 1955- WhoE 91
Ware, Joan K. 1958- WhoSSW 91
Ware, Joe Day 1952- WhoSSW 91
Ware, John David 1947- WhoSSW 91
Ware, John Manning 1944- IntWWM 90
Ware, John Rosswork 1922- WhoAm 90
Ware, Judith Lee 1939- WhoAmW 91
Ware, Karl E. 1926- St&PR 91
Ware, Kenneth Dale 1935- WhoSSW 91
Ware, Leon Vernon 1909-1976 AuBYP 90
Ware, Lucile Mahieu 1929- BiDrAPA 89
Ware, Marcus John 1904- WhoAm 90
Ware, Margaret Isabel Rose 1915- WhoAmW 91
Ware, Mary Blanton 1964- WhoAmW 91
Ware, Mary Catherine 1945- WhoEmL 91
Ware, Michael Raymond 1952- BiDrAPA 89
Ware, Mitchell 1933- WhoAm 90, WhoWor 91
Ware, Paul Dean BiDrAPA 89
Ware, Paul W. 1946- St&PR 91
Ware, Randolph Wayne 1951- WhoSSW 91
Ware, Richard Anderson 1919- WhoAm 90
Ware, Robert Basil 1931- WhoE 91
Ware, Roger B. 1934- St&PR 91
Ware, Sandra Cole 1935- WhoE 91
Ware, Thaddeus Van 1935- WhoAm 90
Ware, Wallace Peyton, Jr. 1941- WhoSSW 91
Ware, Willis Howard 1920- WhoAm 90
Ware-Campbell, Louise WhoWrEP 89
Warehall, William Donald 1942- WhoAmA 91
Wareham, Julie Gay BiDrAPA 89
Wareing, Carol 1950- WhoAmW 91
Wareing, Deryck John Highfield 1944- IntWWM 90
Wareing, Lavere Hansen 1924- St&PR 91
Wareing, Peter Staub 1951- St&PR 91
Waren, Allan David 1935- WhoWor 91
Waren, Jack L. 1936- St&PR 91
Waren, Stanley A. 1919- WhoAm 90
Warf, James Curren 1917- WhoAm 90
Warfel, Daniel L. 1947- St&PR 91
Warfel, Floretta Emma 1916- MusmAFA
Warfel, Kay 1955- WhoE 91
Warfield, Catherine Ann 1816-1877 FemiCLE
Warfield, Donald Herman 1934- St&PR 91
Warfield, Edwin, III 1924- St&PR 91
Warfield, Frank 1895-1932 Ballpl 90
Warfield, George 1919- WhoAm 90
Warfield, Gerald Alexander 1940- WhoAm 90
Warfield, Janet Smith 1936- WhoAmW 91
Warfield, John Nelson 1925- WhoAm 90
Warfield, Marlene 1941- DrBIPA 90
Warfield, Marsha BioIn 16, DrBIPA 90
Warfield, Penny 1946- WhoEmL 91
Warfield, Sandra PenDiMP
Warfield, Sandra 1929- IntWWM 90
Warfield, Wallis 1896-1986 BioIn 16, WorAlBi
Warfield, William 1920- DrBIPA 90, IntWWM 90, PenDiMP, WorAlBi
Warfield, William Caesar BioIn 16
Warfield, William Caesar 1920- DcAfAmP, WhoAm 90
Warford, Walton R BiDrAPA 89
Warga, Jack 1922- WhoAm 90
Wargetz, Georgia Lynn Rance 1959- WhoSSW 91
Wargo, Chris A. 1948- St&PR 91
Wargo, Peter 1922- St&PR 91
Wargo, William D. BioIn 16
Wargo, William Denis 1956- WhoE 91
Wargotz, Eric Samuel 1956- WhoE 91
Warhaftig, Zorah 1906- BioIn 16
Warhol, Andy 1928?-1987 BioIn 16, IntDcAA 90 [port], WorAlBi
Warhola, Paul BioIn 16
Warhop, Jack 1884-1960 Ballpl 90
Warhover, Stephen H. 1944- St&PR 91
Warick, Lawrence H 1936- BiDrAPA 89
Warin, Oliver N. 1931- St&PR 91
Wariner, Steve 1954- WhoNeCM [port]
Waring, Alan George 1929- WhoWor 91
Waring, Anna Laetitia 1823-1910 FemiCLE
Waring, Charles Douglas 1923- St&PR 91
Waring, Edward Graham, Jr. 1924- WhoAm 90
Waring, Fred 1900-1984 OxCPMus, WorAlBi
Waring, Glenn Howell 1948- St&PR 91
Waring, John Alfred 1913- WhoSSW 91, WhoWor 91
Waring, Kate 1953- IntWWM 90
Waring, Laura 1887-1948 BiDWomA
Waring, Laura Wheeler WhoAmA 91N
Waring, Milton George 1948- BiDrAPA 89
Waring, Richard Babcock 1955- WhoWrEP 89
Waring, Thomas A. 1947- St&PR 91
Waring, Thomas R. 1907- St&PR 91
Waring, Virginia 1915- St&PR 91, WhoAmW 91
Waring, Virginia Clotfelter 1915- IntWWM 90
Waring, Walter Weyler 1917- WhoAm 90
Waring, William Winburn 1923- WhoAm 90
Warioba, Joseph Sinde 1940- WhoWor 91
Waris, Michael, Jr. 1921- WhoAm 90
Wark, Robert Rodger 1924- WhoAm 90, WhoAmA 91
Wark, Sherrill Christine 1944- WhoWrEP 89
Wark, Thomas Edison 1934- WhoAm 90
Warkenthien, John Frank 1956- WhoSSW 91
Warkentin, Harold J BiDrAPA 89
Warkentin, John BioIn 16
Warkov, Esther 1941- WhoAmA 91
Warland, Betsy 1946- FemiCLE
Warley, Carlin BioIn 16
Warley, Jason BioIn 16
Warlick, Robert Patterson 1924- WhoAm 90
Warlitner, Todd Jeffrey 1962- WhoSSW 91
Warlock, Billy BioIn 16
Warlock, Peter 1894-1930 BioIn 16
Warm, Hermann 1889-1976 ConDes 90
Warm, Stephen F. St&PR 91
Warm, Theodore R 1931- BiDrAPA 89
Warman, C. Dale 1929- St&PR 91
Warmann, Christine Louise BiDrAPA 89
Warmath, John Thomas, Jr. 1929- St&PR 91
Warmbold, Ted 1943-1989 BioIn 16
Warmbrod, James Robert 1929- WhoAm 90
Warmenhoven, Daniel John 1950- WhoAm 90
Warmer, Richard Craig 1936- WhoAm 90
Warming, Per 1943- IntWWM 90
Warmond, Ellen 1930- EncCoWW
Warn, Emily 1953- WhoWrEP 89
Warn, Michael Thurston 1952- St&PR 91
Warnath, Maxine Ammer 1928- WhoAmW 91
Warne, Colston E. 1900-1987 BioIn 16
Warne, David W. 1940- St&PR 91
Warne, Katharine 1923- IntWWM 90
Warne, Richard Arthur 1932- St&PR 91
Warne, William Elmo 1905- WhoAm 90, WhoWor 91
Warneke, Heinz 1895-1983 WhoAmA 91N
Warneke, Lon 1909-1976 Ballpl 90
Warnell, Ronald Lee 1946- BiDrAPA 89
Warnemunde, Bradley L. 1933- St&PR 91
Warnemunde, Bradley Lee 1933- WhoAm 90, WhoWor 91
Warner, Abby EncO&P 3
Warner, Adolphe Joseph 1917- WhoE 91
Warner, Albert 1884-1967 WorAlBi
Warner, Allan M 1929- BiDrAPA 89
Warner, Allen 1933- BiDrAPA 89
Warner, Andrew James 1948- WhoEmL 91
Warner, Ann Marie 1944- WhoAmW 91
Warner, Anna B. 1827-1915 BioAmW
Warner, Anne 1869-1913 FemiCLE
Warner, Anne R. ODwPR 91
Warner, Arthur E. 1922- WhoAm 90
Warner, Barbara Ann 1949- BiDrAPA 89
Warner, Bonny BioIn 16
Warner, Bradford Arnold 1910- WhoAm 90
Warner, Brainard H. 1959- St&PR 91
Warner, Brainard Henry, III 1925- WhoE 91
Warner, Bruce E. 1912- St&PR 91
Warner, Carol Joyce 1959- WhoAmW 91
Warner, Carolyn 1930- WhoAmW 91
Warner, Cecil Randolph, Jr. 1929- St&PR 91, WhoAm 90, WhoSSW 91
Warner, Charles A. 1928- St&PR 91
Warner, Charles Arthur 1928- WhoAm 90
Warner, Charles Dudley 1829-1900 BioIn 16
Warner, Charles Schoen 1963- St&PR 91
Warner, Darrell G. WhoAm 90
Warner, David 1941- WhoWor 91
Warner, David K. 1950- St&PR 91
Warner, David T. 1930- St&PR 91
Warner, Dennis Allan 1940- WhoAm 90
Warner, Don Lee 1934- WhoAm 90
Warner, Donald Francis 1931- WhoAm 90, WhoE 91, WhoWor 91
Warner, Douglas Alexander, III 1946- WhoAm 90, WhoE 91, WhoEmL 91
Warner, Douglas Warfield 1930- WhoAmA 91
Warner, Edith 1891?-1951 BioAmW
Warner, Elizabeth Ann BiDrAPA 89
Warner, Elliott Bruce BiDrAPA 89
Warner, Everett Longley 1877-1963 WhoAmA 91N
Warner, Francis J BiDrAPA 89
Warner, Gertrude Chandler 1890-1979 AuBYP 90
Warner, Glen W. 1940- St&PR 91
Warner, Guy Edward, Jr. 1919- St&PR 91
Warner, H. B. 1876-1958 WorAlBi
Warner, H. Colin 1927- St&PR 91
Warner, H Waldo PenDiMP
Warner, Harland W. ODwPR 91
Warner, Harland Walter 1931- WhoE 91
Warner, Harold Clay 1939- St&PR 91
Warner, Harold Clay, Jr. 1939- WhoAm 90
Warner, Harold G. 1908-1990 BioIn 16
Warner, Harold Jerome 1910- WhoE 91
Warner, Harry Hathaway 1935- WhoAm 90
Warner, Herbert James 1926- St&PR 91, WhoAm 90
Warner, Herbert Kelii, Jr 1943- WhoAmA 91
Warner, Howard Wayne 1931- St&PR 91, WhoE 91
Warner, Jack 1872-1943 Ballpl 90
Warner, Jack 1895-1981 DcNaB 1981
Warner, Jack 1903-1986 Ballpl 90
Warner, Jack, Jr. 1916- WhoAm 90
Warner, Jack B. 1931- St&PR 91
Warner, Jack L. 1892-1978 WorAlBi
Warner, Jacquelyn Smith 1950- WhoSSW 91
Warner, James J. 1942- St&PR 91
Warner, Jerry A. 1947- St&PR 91
Warner, Jo 1931- WhoAmA 91
Warner, John 1942- St&PR 91
Warner, John Andrew 1924- St&PR 91, WhoAm 90
Warner, John Christian 1897-1989 BioIn 16
Warner, John Edward 1936- WhoAm 90
Warner, John Hilliard, Jr. 1941- WhoAm 90, WhoWor 91
Warner, John W. BioIn 16
Warner, John W. 1927- WorAlBi
Warner, John William 1927- WhoAm 90, WhoSSW 91, WhoWor 91
Warner, John William 1936- WhoAm 90
Warner, Jonathan W., Sr. 1917- St&PR 91
Warner, Judith Ebright 1940- WhoAmW 91
Warner, Kenneth E. 1947- WhoAm 90
Warner, Kenneth Wilson, Jr. 1928- WhoAm 90
Warner, Laverne 1941- WhoAmW 91, WhoSSW 91
Warner, Lawrence Askew 1933- St&PR 91
Warner, Lee Marlene 1942- WhoSSW 91
Warner, Leigh 1955- WhoE 91
Warner, Lesley Rae 1940- WhoWor 91
Warner, Louise Oman 1930- WhoAmW 91
Warner, Lucien 1900- EncO&P 3
Warner, Lucy Ann BioIn 16
Warner, M. Richard 1951- WhoAm 90
Warner, Malcolm 1937- WhoWor 91
Warner, Malcolm-Jamal BioIn 16
Warner, Malcolm-Jamal 1970- DrBIPA 90
Warner, Marina 1946- ConLC 59 [port], FemiCLE
Warner, Marina Sarah 1946- WhoAmA 91
Warner, Marvin Leon 1919- WhoAm 90
Warner, Matt 1922- AuBYP 90
Warner, Michael Alan 1954- WhoSSW 91
Warner, Mickey BioIn 16
Warner, Miner Hill 1942- WhoAm 90
Warner, Nancy Elizabeth 1923- WhoAm 90, WhoWor 91
Warner, Nathaniel BiDrAPA 89
Warner, Pamela BioIn 16
Warner, Pascal D'Angelis 1822-1910 AmLegL
Warner, Paul M. 1930- St&PR 91
Warner, Peter David 1942- WhoAm 90
Warner, Phillip 1947-1987 BioIn 16
Warner, Rawleigh, Jr. 1921- St&PR 91, WhoAm 90
Warner, Rebecca H 1953- BiDrAPA 89
Warner, Richard 1943- BiDrAPA 89
Warner, Richard A. 1936- ODwPR 91
Warner, Richard Alan 1936- St&PR 91, WhoAm 90
Warner, Richard B 1945- BiDrAPA 89
Warner, Richard Patrick 1951- WhoSSW 91
Warner, Richard Vance 1929- St&PR 91
Warner, Robert Anio 1966- WhoE 91
Warner, Robert E. 1934- St&PR 91
Warner, Robert Mark 1927- WhoAm 90
Warner, Robert S. 1907- WhoAm 90
Warner, Rodney Harold 1956- WhoSSW 91
Warner, Rollin Miles, Jr. 1930- WhoWor 91
Warner, Ronald Douglass 1946- WhoSSW 91
Warner, Russell Stuart 1924- St&PR 91
Warner, Sam Bass, Jr. 1928- WhoAm 90
Warner, Seth L. 1927- WhoAm 90, WhoSSW 91
Warner, Sidney R. 1935- St&PR 91
Warner, Sidney Taylor 1934- St&PR 91
Warner, Silas L 1924- BiDrAPA 89
Warner, Susan 1940- WhoAmW 91
Warner, Susan B. 1819-1885 BioAmW
Warner, Susan Bogert 1819-1885 FemiCLE
Warner, Sylvia Ashton MajTwCW
Warner, Sylvia Ashton- 1908-1984 BioIn 16
Warner, Sylvia Townsend 1893-1978 BioIn 16, FemiCLE, MajTwCW
Warner, Theodore Kugler, Jr. 1909- WhoAm 90
Warner, Thomas S. 1949- St&PR 91
Warner, Thomas William 1919- WhoAm 90
Warner, Tucker H. 1932- St&PR 91
Warner, Val 1946- FemiCLE
Warner, Valerie ODwPR 91
Warner, Vanessa Anne 1953- WhoAmW 91
Warner, W. Lloyd 1898-1970 BioIn 16
Warner, Walter Duke 1952- WhoEmL 91
Warner, Warren Edward 1936- WhoSSW 91
Warner, Wellman Joel 1897- WhoAm 90
Warner, William Diaz 1929- WhoAm 90
Warner, William Eaton 1954- WhoWrEP 89
Warner, William H. 1944- St&PR 91
Warner, William Hamer 1929- WhoAm 90
Warner, William Lloyd 1898-1970 BioIn 16
Warner, William Millard 1946- WhoEmL 91
Warner, William S. 1924- St&PR 91
Warner, Willis Lee 1930- WhoWor 91
Warner, Wyannette 1943- WhoAmW 91
Warner-Allen, George 1916-1988 AnObit 1988
Warnes, Hector 1936- BiDrAPA 89
Warnick, Charles Terry 1943- WhoWor 91
Warnick, Edward Eugene 1927- WhoE 91
Warnick, John Peter 1946- St&PR 91
Warnick, Kenneth L. 1944- St&PR 91
Warnick, Terry Lee 1947- WhoEmL 91
Warnke, Frank J. 1925-1988 BioIn 16
Warnke, Martin 1937- WhoWor 91
Warnke, Paul C. 1920- BioIn 16, WorAlBi
Warnke, Paul Culliton 1920- WhoAm 90, WhoE 91
Warnken, Douglas Richard 1930- WhoAm 90
Warnken, Virginia Muriel Thompson 1927- WhoAmW 91
Warnock, Benny Wyman 1943- WhoSSW 91
Warnock, Curtlon Lee 1954- WhoEmL 91, WhoWor 91
Warnock, Fred William 1940- St&PR 91
Warnock, Inez Elizabeth 1934- St&PR 91
Warnock, John Edward 1932- WhoAm 90
Warnock, John William 1951- WhoSSW 91
Warnock, Julia K BiDrAPA 89
Warnock, Paul Franklin 1942- St&PR 91
Warnock, William K. BioIn 16
Warns, Raymond H. 1920- WhoAm 90
Waronka, Joseph Martin 1941- St&PR 91
Warp, Harold 1903- St&PR 91
Warr, Susan Naomi 1960- WhoAmW 91
Warrack, Guy PenDiMP
Warrack, John 1928- IntWWM 90
Warrack, Maria Perini 1931- WhoE 91
Warre-Cornish, Blanche 1847?-1914 FemiCLE
Warrell, Lincoln A. 1931- St&PR 91
Warren, Adrienne Rochelle 1957- WhoAmW 91
Warren, Alex McLean, Jr. 1940- WhoAm 90
Warren, Alfred J BiDrAPA 89
Warren, Alfred S., Jr. 1926- WhoAm 90
Warren, Andrea Jean 1946- WhoWrEP 89
Warren, Anne Elizabeth 1952- BiDrAPA 89
Warren, Anthony J. 1945- St&PR 91
Warren, Barbara C. ODwPR 91

Warren, Barbara Kathleen 1943- WhoAmW 91
Warren, Barbara Leonard 1943- WhoWrEP 89
Warren, Barbara Stone 1950- WhoSSW 91
Warren, Bennie 1912- Ballpl 90
Warren, Bertram 1932- BiDrAPA 89
Warren, Beth Imogene 1938- WhoAmW 91
Warren, Betty WhoAmA 91
Warren, Billy AuBYP 90
Warren, Bruce Alfred 1937- WhoE 91
Warren, Bruce H 1927- BiDrAPA 89
Warren, Bruce Willard 1949- WhoEmL 91
Warren, Bryan Pope, Jr. 1925- BiDrAPA 89
Warren, Callie WhoAmA 91N
Warren, Carlos Scott 1936- WhoSSW 91
Warren, Cathy AuBYP 90
Warren, Cathy 1951- SmATA 62 [port]
Warren, Charles David 1944- WhoAm 90
Warren, Charles M. NewYTBS 90
Warren, Charles Marquis WhoAm 90
Warren, Charles Marquis 1913?-1990 ConAu 132
Warren, Charles P. 1921-1987 BioIn 16
Warren, Charles Robert 1948- St&PR 91
Warren, Cornelia Lyman 1857-1921 BioIn 16
Warren, Craig Bishop 1939- WhoAm 90
Warren, David Boardman 1937- WhoAm 90, WhoAmA 91
Warren, David Chipley 1954- WhoSSW 91
Warren, David Grant 1936- WhoAm 90
Warren, David Hardy 1943- WhoAm 90
Warren, David Liles 1943- WhoAm 90
Warren, David Stephen 1949- WhoSSW 91
Warren, Debra Lynn 1960- WhoAmW 91
Warren, Dennis R. 1943- St&PR 91
Warren, Diana Lynn 1946- WhoAmW 91
Warren, Doane Herring 1924- St&PR 91
Warren, Donald William 1935- WhoAm 90
Warren, Douglas Edgar 1955- WhoSSW 91
Warren, Earl 1891-1974 BioIn 16, WorAlBi
Warren, Earl Francis 1933- WhoAm 90
Warren, Edgar W BiDrAPA 89
Warren, Edus Houston, Jr. 1923- St&PR 91, WhoAm 90
Warren, Edward L. 1952- ODwPR 91
Warren, Edward Perry 1860-1928 BioIn 16
Warren, Edward Willard 1929- WhoAm 90
Warren, Elizabeth BiDEWW, FemiCLE
Warren, Eric Alonzo 1959- WhoSSW 91
Warren, Ferdinand Earl 1899-1981 WhoAmA 91N
Warren, Fiske 1862-1938 BioIn 16
Warren, Frank Z BiDrAPA 89
Warren, Fred AuBYP 90
Warren, Frederick J. 1939- St&PR 91
Warren, George Henry, Mrs 1897-1976 WhoAmA 91N
Warren, George Lewis 1940- BiDrAPA 89
Warren, Gerald Edward 1924- WhoAm 90
Warren, Gerri ODwPR 91
Warren, H. David 1937- St&PR 91
Warren, Harris Gaylord 1906-1988 BioIn 16
Warren, Harry 1893-1981 BioIn 16, OxCPMus
Warren, Harry Verney 1904- WhoAm 90
Warren, Helen Billett 1932- WhoAmW 91
Warren, Henry Clarke 1854-1899 BioIn 16
Warren, Henry L. 1940- St&PR 91
Warren, Henry W. 1838- AmLegL
Warren, Howell Rudolph, Jr. BiDrAPA 89
Warren, Ira Marshall 1950- St&PR 91
Warren, J. Benedict 1930- WhoAm 90
Warren, Jack Hamilton 1921- WhoAm 90
Warren, Jack Keith 1934- St&PR 91
Warren, Jacqueline Louise 1946- WhoAmA 91
Warren, James 1726-1808 EncCRAm
Warren, James C. St&PR 91
Warren, James Caldwell 1930- WhoAm 90
Warren, James Edward 1931- St&PR 91
Warren, James Edward, Jr. 1908- WhoWrEP 89
Warren, James Ronald 1925- WhoAm 90
Warren, James V. 1915-1990 BioIn 16
Warren, James Vaughn NewYTBS 90
Warren, James Vaughn 1915-1990 ConAu 130
Warren, James Walter, Jr. 1944- WhoAm 90
Warren, Jean A 1933- BiDrAPA 89
Warren, Jerry BioIn 16
Warren, Jesse Francis 1944- WhoE 91
Warren, Joe G., Jr. 1945- St&PR 91
Warren, John 1753-1815 EncCRAm
Warren, John A. 1925- WhoSSW 91
Warren, John Charles 1945- St&PR 91
Warren, John H., III 1948- St&PR 91
Warren, John Hertz, III 1946- WhoSSW 91
Warren, John M. 1944- St&PR 91
Warren, Johnny Wilmer 1946- WhoWrEP 89
Warren, Jon M. 1937- St&PR 91
Warren, Joseph 1741-1775 EncCRAm, WorAlBi
Warren, Joseph F 1925- BiDrAPA 89
Warren, Julianne Bussert Baker 1916- WhoAmA 91
Warren, Katherine Virginia 1948- WhoAmW 91
Warren, Kathleen Janine 1942- WhoWrEP 89
Warren, Kelcy L. 1955- St&PR 91
Warren, Kenneth 1931- WhoWor 91
Warren, Kenneth S. 1929- WhoAm 90
Warren, L. D. 1906- WhoAm 90
Warren, L D 1906- WhoAmA 91
Warren, Larry K. 1946- St&PR 91
Warren, Leonard 1911-1960 PenDiMP, WorAlBi
Warren, Lesley Ann BioIn 16
Warren, Lesley Ann 1946- WhoAm 90, WorAlBi
Warren, Lisa S. ODwPR 91
Warren, Lisbeth Ann 1953- WhoEmL 91
Warren, Lucian C. 1913-1988 BioIn 16
Warren, Lynne 1952- WhoAmA 91
Warren, M. Robert 1921- St&PR 91
Warren, Manning Gilbert, III 1948- WhoEmL 91
Warren, Margaret Lucille 1912- WhoWrEP 89
Warren, Maria Adelina Emelia Otero- 1882-1965 BioIn 16
Warren, Mark 1938- DrBlPA 90
Warren, Mark 1963- WhoSSW 91
Warren, Mark Jay 1953- BiDrAPA 89
Warren, Mark Taylor 1951- WhoSSW 91
Warren, Mary Phraner 1929- AuBYP 90
Warren, Mary Sigman 1961- WhoAmW 91
Warren, Matthew 1918- WhoAm 90
Warren, Max 1919- BiDrAPA 89
Warren, Mercy 1728-1814 FemiCLE
Warren, Mercy Otis 1728-1814 BioAmW, BioIn 16, EncCRAm, NotWoAT, WorAlBi
Warren, Michael 1946- DrBlPA 90, WhoAm 90
Warren, Mike 1961- Ballpl 90
Warren, Minnie Mae 1945- WhoAmW 91
Warren, Ned 1860-1928 BioIn 16
Warren, Norman O., Jr. 1962- St&PR 91
Warren, Paul Lansing 1950- WhoE 91
Warren, Peggy Ellen BiDrAPA 89
Warren, Peter 1943- WhoE 91
Warren, Peter Gigstad 1958- WhoSSW 91
Warren, Peter Whitson WhoAmA 91
Warren, Philip Hamilton, III 1945- WhoE 91
Warren, Ralph J BiDrAPA 89
Warren, Raymond Joseph 1957- WhoEmL 91
Warren, Raymond McLeod, Jr. 1931- WhoSSW 91
Warren, Renee Elaine 1965- WhoAmW 91
Warren, Richard 1938- WhoWor 91
Warren, Richard Allen 1932- St&PR 91
Warren, Richard Ernest 1942- WhoSSW 91
Warren, Richard Jordan 1945- WhoAm 90
Warren, Richard K. 1920- St&PR 91
Warren, Richard Kearney 1920- WhoAm 90
Warren, Richard M. 1925- WhoAm 90
Warren, Richard Wayne 1935- WhoWor 91
Warren, Rita Simpson 1949- WhoAmW 91
Warren, Robert C. 1918- St&PR 91
Warren, Robert Carlton 1918- WhoAm 90
Warren, Robert Franklin BioIn 16
Warren, Robert Kenneth 1948- WhoSSW 91
Warren, Robert Penn 1905- LiHiK, WhoWrEP 89
Warren, Robert Penn 1905-1989 AnObit 1989, BioIn 16, ConAu 129, ConLC 59 [port], MajTwCW, News 90, SmATA 63, WorAlBi, WrPh
Warren, Robert Willis 1925- WhoAm 90
Warren, Roger Frederick 1941- St&PR 91
Warren, Ronald Allen 1954- WhoSSW 91
Warren, Ronald L. 1940- St&PR 91
Warren, Rupert 1908- St&PR 91
Warren, Russ 1951- WhoAmA 91
Warren, Russell Glen 1942- WhoAm 90
Warren, Russell James 1938- WhoWor 91
Warren, Sally Ann 1943- WhoAmW 91
Warren, Samuel Dennis 1817-1888 BioIn 16
Warren, Samuel Dennis 1852-1910 BioIn 16
Warren, Sara Ann BiDrAPA 89
Warren, Sharon Jones 1949- BiDrAPA 89
Warren, Susan Cornelia Clarke BioIn 16
Warren, Susan Lisa BiDrAPA 89
Warren, Tanja Eikenboom 1957- WhoAmW 91
Warren, Theodore Ray 1947- St&PR 91
Warren, Thomas S. 1903- St&PR 91
Warren, Tony Davis 1944- WhoSSW 91
Warren, Tony Edwin 1952- WhoSSW 91
Warren, Virginia Lee 1907- BioIn 16
Warren, Wendy Kaye 1957- WhoAmW 91
Warren, Whitney 1864-1943 WorAlBi
Warren, Wilfrid BiDrAPA 89
Warren, William Bradford 1934- WhoAm 90
Warren, William Clements 1909- WhoAm 90, WhoE 91, WhoWor 91
Warren, William David 1924- WhoAm 90
Warren, William Gerald 1930- WhoAm 90
Warren, William Herbert 1924- WhoAm 90
Warren, William Michael 1947- St&PR 91
Warren, William Michael, Jr. 1947- WhoAm 90, WhoSSW 91
Warren, William Robinson 1931- WhoAm 90
Warren, William Stanford 1955- St&PR 91
Warren, William Stephen 1882-1968 AuBYP 90
Warren, William Whipple 1825-1853 WhNaAH
Warren, Win 1914- WhoAmA 91
Warren-Green, Christopher 1955- IntWWM 90
Warrender, Glenda Kay 1949- WhoSSW 91
Warrender, Jonathan BioIn 16
Warrener, John Joseph 1952- IntWWM 90
Warrener, Richard Carlton 1944- St&PR 91
Warrener, Vincent Anthony 1930- IntWWM 90
Warrenfeltz, Sylvia Annette 1948- WhoE 91
Warrens, Robert A. BioIn 16
Warrenski, Joan 1955- BiDrAPA 89
Warres, Neil Eric 1950- BiDrAPA 89
Warres, Stephen Elliot BiDrAPA 89
Warrick, Bennie Mervin 1953- St&PR 91
Warrick, Harley BioIn 16
Warrick, James C. 1938- St&PR 91
Warrick, James Craig 1938- WhoAm 90
Warrick, James Gordon 1953- WhoWrEP 89
Warrick, Martha Haltom 1939- BiDrAPA 89
Warrick, Merv St&PR 91
Warrick, Mildred Lorine 1917- WhoAmW 91
Warrick, Ruth BioIn 16
Warrick, Ruth 1916- WhoAm 90
Warrick, Stuart C., Jr. 1937- St&PR 91
Warrick, William Wiley 1940- St&PR 91
Warrick, Woodward A. 1922- St&PR 91
Warrilow, Clive 1938- St&PR 91
Warriner, Frederic Freeman 1916- WhoAm 90
Warriner, John E. BioIn 16
Warriner, Laura B 1943- WhoAmA 91
Warriner, Thurman TwCCr&M 91
Warrington, Frank J. 1943- St&PR 91
Warrington, John Wesley 1914- WhoAm 90
Warrington, Pauline BioIn 16
Warrington, Willard Glade 1920- WhoAm 90
Warrior, Kathryn Ann 1939- WhoAmW 91
Warsaski, Abraham 1926- BiDrAPA 89
Warsaw, Charles Edward, II 1946- St&PR 91
Warsaw, Ernest E. 1920- St&PR 91
Warsaw, Irene 1908- WhoWrEP 89
Warsaw, Stanley 1922- St&PR 91
Warsawer, Harold Newton WhoE 91
Warschauer, Bonnie ODwPR 91
Warschefsky, Thomas Lee 1951- WhoEmL 91
Warshauer, Marshall A. 1930- St&PR 91
Warshavsky, Eli Samuel 1930- WhoWor 91
Warshaw, Alexandra Anne 1940- WhoE 91
Warshaw, Allen Charles 1948- WhoE 91
Warshaw, Bruce J. 1947- St&PR 91
Warshaw, Carole L BiDrAPA 89
Warshaw, Eileen Reilly 1948- WhoAmW 91
Warshaw, Elaine N 1924- WhoAmA 91
Warshaw, Howard 1920- WhoAmA 91N
Warshaw, Jerome BioIn 16
Warshaw, Joseph Bennett 1936- WhoAm 90
Warshaw, Larry 1936- WhoAmA 91
Warshaw, Leon J. 1917- WhoAm 90
Warshaw, Martin Richard 1924- WhoAm 90
Warshaw, Saul L. 1931- ODwPR 91
Warshaw, Stanley 1929- WhoWrEP 89
Warshaw, Stanley Irving 1931- WhoAm 90
Warshawsky, Abel George 1884-1962 WhoAmA 91N
Warshawsky, Mark Joel 1958- WhoE 91
Warshawsky, Rebecca Jon 1952- WhoAmW 91
Warshawsky, Stanford S. 1937- St&PR 91
Warshof, Richard Stephen 1948- St&PR 91
Warshofsky, Isaac MajTwCW
Warsick, Mary Katrina 1956- WhoSSW 91
Warsinske, Norman George 1929- WhoAmA 91
Warsinske, Robyn ODwPR 91
Warson, Samuel R 1909- BiDrAPA 89
Warstadt, Gary Michael 1959- BiDrAPA 89, WhoE 91
Warstler, Rabbit 1903-1964 Ballpl 90
Wartell, Roger Martin 1945- WhoSSW 91
Wartelle, Barbara Louisa 1954- WhoEmL 91
Wartels, Nat 1902-1990 BioIn 16, ConAu 130, NewYTBS 90 [port]
Wartenbee, D.R. 1949- St&PR 91
Warter, Gregg D. 1954- St&PR 91
Warth, Robert Douglas 1921- WhoAm 90, WhoSSW 91
Warthen, Dan 1952- Ballpl 90
Wartik, Thomas 1921- WhoAm 90
Wartluft, David Jonathan 1938- WhoAm 90, WhoWrEP 89
Wartman, Carl H. St&PR 91
Warton, Jane 1724-1809 FemiCLE
Warton, Joseph 1722-1800 DcLB 104 [port]
Warton, Thomas 1728-1790 DcLB 104 [port], LitC 15 [port]
Wartski, James Zygmunt 1959- WhoSSW 91
Wartski, Maureen Crane 1940- BioIn 16
Waruk, Kona MajTwCW
Warvarovsky, Carl Michels BiDrAPA 89
Warwick, Arthur Mark 1944- BiDrAPA 89
Warwick, Carl 1937- Ballpl 90
Warwick, Cathy BioIn 16
Warwick, David Andrew 1958- IntWWM 90
Warwick, Dee Dee DrBlPA 90
Warwick, Dionne BioIn 16
Warwick, Dionne 1940- DrBlPA 90, EncPR&S 89, OxCPMus
Warwick, Dionne 1941- WhoAmW 91, WorAlBi
Warwick, Frances E Greville, Countess of 1861-1933 BioIn 16
Warwick, Jarvis ConAu 31NR
Warwick, John Benjamin 1948- WhoWor 91
Warwick, John S. 1930- St&PR 91
Warwick, Margaret Ann 1931- WhoE 91
Warwick, Mary BiDEWW
Warwick, Mary Rich, Countess of 1624-1678 FemiCLE
Warwick, William J. WhoAm 90
Warwick, William James 1934- St&PR 91
Warwick, William O. 1932- St&PR 91
Warwick-Evans, C PenDiMP
Warwicke, Dionne 1940- EncPR&S 89
Warzak, Barry Frank 1954- St&PR 91
Warzak, Frank J. 1925- St&PR 91
Warzak, Lavera A. 1926- St&PR 91
Warzala, Richard S. 1953- St&PR 91
Warzecha, Ladislaus William 1929- WhoE 91
Warzel, Ronald J. 1933- St&PR 91
Wasacz, Michael S. WhoAm 90
Wasan, Darsh Tilakchand 1938- WhoAm 90, WhoWor 91
Wasch, Monroe Sylvan 1941- WhoE 91
Wascou, Ellen Fern 1950- WhoAmW 91
Wasdell, Jimmy 1914-1983 Ballpl 90
Wasegoboah, Charles WhoWrEP 89
Waser, Maria 1878-1939 EncCoWW
Waserman, Jack 1951- BiDrAPA 89
Wasescha, Paul John 1926- WhoWor 91
Wasey, Jane 1912- WhoAmA 91
Wasfi, Annis Abraham BiDrAPA 89
Wash, Allan J. 1915- ODwPR 91
Wash, Marilyn Johnson 1954- WhoAmW 91
Wash, Thomas O. 1923- St&PR 91
Washakie 1804?-1900 WhNaAH
Washawanny, William J. 1954- St&PR 91
Washbourne, Mona 1903-1988 AnObit 1988, ConTFT 8
Washburn, A. Michael 1940- WhoE 91
Washburn, Abbott McConnell 1915- WhoAm 90
Washburn, Albert Henry 1866-1930 BioIn 16
Washburn, Albert Lincoln 1911- WhoAm 90
Washburn, Cadwallader 1866-1965 WhoAmA 91N
Washburn, Carver Lorenz 1932- St&PR 91
Washburn, David Thacher 1930- WhoAm 90
Washburn, Donald Arthur 1944- St&PR 91, WhoAm 90
Washburn, Gordon Bailey 1904- WhoAmA 91N
Washburn, H.B. 1946- St&PR 91

Washburn, Henry Bradford, Jr. 1910- *WhoAm 90*
Washburn, Jack 1921- *WhoAm 90*
Washburn, Jan 1926- *SmATA 63 [port]*
Washburn, Joan T 1929- *WhoAmA 91*
Washburn, Joan Thomas 1929- *WhoE 91*
Washburn, John E. *BioIn 16*
Washburn, John Merrow, Jr. 1927- *St&PR 91*
Washburn, Keith Edward 1944- *WhoE 91*
Washburn, Lawrence L, Jr. *BiDrAPA 89*
Washburn, Louese B 1875-1959 *WhoAmA 91N*
Washburn, Louis George 1933- *St&PR 91*
Washburn, Mary Wilson 1957- *WhoAmW 91*
Washburn, Patricia Jane 1965- *WhoAmW 91*
Washburn, Paul *BioIn 16*
Washburn, Ray 1938- *Ballpl 90*
Washburn, Robert Brooks 1928- *IntWWM 90, WhoAm 90*
Washburn, Robert Douglas 1935- *St&PR 91*
Washburn, Robert Michael 1955- *WhoEmL 91*
Washburn, Stan 1943- *BioIn 16, WhoAm 90, WhoAmA 91*
Washburn, Stephen L 1925- *BiDrAPA 89*
Washburn, Stewart Putnam 1929- *St&PR 91*
Washburn, Thomas Dale 1947- *St&PR 91*
Washburn, Wilcomb Edward 1925- *WhoAm 90, WhoWrEP 89*
Washburn, William D. 1831-1912 *WorAlBi*
Washburne, Carleton W. 1889-1968 *BioIn 16*
Washburne, Elihu Benjamin 1816-1887 *BiDrUSE 89, BioIn 16*
Washburne, Heluiz Chandler 1892-1970 *AuBYP 90*
Washburne, Joe 1904-1974 *OxCPMus*
Washington, Alvin C. *St&PR 91*
Washington, Angela Yvette 1961- *WhoAmW 91*
Washington, Barbara Jean Wright 1946- *WhoAmW 91*
Washington, Bennetta Bullock 1918- *WhoAm 90*
Washington, Beverly Diana 1956- *WhoAmW 91*
Washington, Booker T. 1856-1915 *BioIn 16, WorAlBi*
Washington, Bruce Edward 1951- *WhoSSW 91*
Washington, C.J. 1957- *WhoAmW 91*
Washington, Caesar G. *EarBlAP*
Washington, Catherine Elizabeth Mahrt 1962- *WhoAmW 91*
Washington, Charles Joseph 1938- *St&PR 91, WhoAm 90*
Washington, Clarence Edward, Jr. 1953- *WhoE 91*
Washington, Claudell 1954- *Ballpl 90*
Washington, Clotee Woodruff 1947- *WhoEmL 91*
Washington, Craig A. 1941- *WhoAm 90, WhoSSW 91*
Washington, Craig Anthony 1941- *BlkAmsC [port]*
Washington, Dawn Carter 1970- *WhoAmW 91*
Washington, Deborah Kaye 1958- *WhoAmW 91*
Washington, Denzel *BioIn 16, WhoAm 90*
Washington, Denzel 1954- *DrBlPA 90*
Washington, Diane *BiDrAPA 89*
Washington, Dinah 1924-1963 *BioAmW, BioIn 16, ConMus 5 [port], DrBlPA 90, EncPR&S 89, OxCPMus, WorAlBi*
Washington, Earl S. *BioIn 16*
Washington, Evelyn Burrell 1961- *WhoAmW 91*
Washington, Ford Lee 1903-1955 *DrBlPA 90*
Washington, Fredi 1903- *DrBlPA 90*
Washington, George 1732-1799 *BiDrUSE 89, BioIn 16, EncCRAm [port], WhNaAH, WorAlBi*
Washington, George Toe 1928- *WhoWor 91*
Washington, Gregory Keith 1952- *WhoEmL 91*
Washington, Grover, Jr. 1943- *ConMus 5 [port], DrBlPA 90, EncPR&S 89, WhoAm 90*
Washington, Harold *BioIn 16*
Washington, Harold 1922-1987 *BlkAmsC [port]*
Washington, Herb 1951- *Ballpl 90*
Washington, James W, Jr *WhoAmA 91*
Washington, James Winston, Jr. 1909- *WhoAm 90*
Washington, Jean B. 1926- *WhoAmW 91*
Washington, John 1632?- *BioIn 16*
Washington, Johnny *BioIn 16*
Washington, Kenny 1918-1971 *DrBlPA 90*
Washington, Kermit *BioIn 16*
Washington, Lamont 1944?-1968 *DrBlPA 90*
Washington, Lawrence *BioIn 16*
Washington, Linda Little 1950- *WhoAmW 91*
Washington, Lionel Joseph 1950- *St&PR 91*
Washington, Luis 1869-1957 *BioIn 16*
Washington, Margaret 1935- *WhoAmW 91*
Washington, Martha 1731-1802 *BioIn 16*
Washington, Martha 1732-1802 *BioAmW*
Washington, Martha Custis 1731-1804 *EncCRAm*
Washington, Mary Ball 1708-1789 *BioAmW*
Washington, Mary Helen *BioIn 16*
Washington, Napoleon, Jr. 1948- *WhoWor 91*
Washington, Ned 1901-1976 *OxCPMus*
Washington, Paolo 1932- *IntWWM 90*
Washington, Patricia Leatreal 1947- *WhoEmL 91*
Washington, Reginald Louis 1949- *WhoWor 91*
Washington, Robert Benjamin, Jr. 1942- *WhoE 91*
Washington, Robert Everett 1938- *WhoAm 90*
Washington, Robert Orlanda 1935- *WhoAm 90*
Washington, Ron 1952- *Ballpl 90*
Washington, Ruth V. *BioIn 16*
Washington, Ruth V. *NewYTBS 90*
Washington, Shelley Lynne 1954- *WhoAm 90*
Washington, Tom F. 1949- *WhoWrEP 89*
Washington, U.L. 1953- *Ballpl 90*
Washington, Valdemar Luther 1952- *WhoEmL 91*
Washington, Valora 1953- *WhoAmW 91*
Washington, Vivian Edwards 1914- *WhoAmW 91*
Washington, Walter 1923- *WhoAm 90, WhoSSW 91*
Washington, Walter Edward 1915- *WhoAm 90, WhoE 91*
Washington, Warren Morton 1936- *WhoAm 90*
Washington, William 1752-1810 *EncCRAm*
Washington, Willis *WhoWrEP 89*
Washington, Wilma J. 1949- *WhoAmW 91*
Washlow, Robert J. 1944- *St&PR 91*
Washo, Gabriel A. 1944- *St&PR 91*
Washow, Lawrence E. 1953- *St&PR 91*
Washow, Paula Burnette 1948- *WhoAmW 91*
Washuettl, Josef Rudolf 1941- *WhoWor 91*
Wasicki, James C. 1942- *St&PR 91*
Wasiele, Harry W., Jr. 1926- *WhoAm 90*
Wasieleski, David Thomas 1968- *WhoWrEP 89*
Wasieleski, John Charles 1947- *St&PR 91*
Wasik, John Francis 1957- *WhoAm 90*
Wasik, Robert A. 1938- *St&PR 91*
Wasik, Vincent A. 1944- *WhoAm 90*
Wasilewski, Edward John 1950- *St&PR 91*
Wasilewski, Hope Thompson 1930- *WhoE 91*
Wasilewski, Vincent Thomas 1922- *WhoAm 90*
Wasinger, Virginia Lee 1932- *WhoAmW 91*
Wasiolek, Edward 1924- *WhoAm 90*
Waskiewicz, R. W. 1952- *St&PR 91*
Wasko, Cassie Horton 1949- *WhoAmW 91*
Wasko, Lawrence Dennis 1932- *WhoE 91*
Wasko, Melody Ann 1948- *WhoAmW 91*
Wasko-Flood, Sandra Jean 1943- *WhoAmA 91, WhoAmW 91*
Waskom, Michael A. 1940- *St&PR 91*
Waskow, Arthur Ocean 1933- *WhoAm 90*
Waslewski, Gary 1941- *Ballpl 90*
Waslien, Glenn Selmer 1943- *WhoSSW 91*
Wasmund, Suzanne 1936- *WhoAmW 91, WhoWor 91*
Wasmundt, Suzanne Marie Bayer 1950- *WhoAmW 91*
Wasmuth, Carl Erwin 1916- *WhoAm 90*
Wasmuth, Edmund M. 1927- *St&PR 91*
Wason, Elizabeth 1912- *BioIn 16*
Wason, Robert A. 1951- *St&PR 91*
Wasow, Oliver *BioIn 16*
Waspe, Robert A. 1952- *St&PR 91*
Waspe, Robert Alan 1952- *WhoE 91*
Wass, Hannelore Lina 1926- *WhoAm 90, WhoAmW 91*
Wass, Herbert Franklin 1932- *St&PR 91*
Wass, Wallace Milton 1929- *WhoAm 90*
Wassaja *WhNaAH*
Wassef, Adel A *BiDrAPA 89*
Wassell, Ben Bohdan *BiDrAPA 89*
Wassell, Loren W. 1948- *WhoEmL 91*
Wassenaar, Ella *EncCoWW*
Wassenar, Catherine Lynn 1957- *WhoEmL 91*
Wassenberg, Evelyn M. 1933- *WhoAmW 91*
Wasser, David A 1925- *BiDrAPA 89*
Wasser, Henry 1919- *WhoAm 90, WhoWor 91*
Wasser, Lawrence Jay 1948- *WhoSSW 91*
Wasser, Sidney 1929- *St&PR 91*
Wasserburg, Gerald Joseph 1927- *WhoAm 90*
Wasserlein, John H. 1941- *St&PR 91*
Wasserlein, John Henry 1941- *WhoAm 90*
Wasserman, Abby Louis *BiDrAPA 89*
Wasserman, Albert 1920- *WhoAmA 91, WhoE 91*
Wasserman, Albert 1921- *WhoAm 90*
Wasserman, Albert Julian 1928- *WhoSSW 91*
Wasserman, Andrew Philip *BiDrAPA 89*
Wasserman, Arnold Saul 1934- *WhoE 91*
Wasserman, August Von 1866-1925 *WorAlBi*
Wasserman, Barbara Albis 1948- *WhoAm 90*
Wasserman, Barry Lee 1935- *WhoAm 90*
Wasserman, Bernard 1925- *WhoE 91*
Wasserman, Bert W. *WhoE 91*
Wasserman, Burton 1929- *WhoAmA 91, WhoE 91*
Wasserman, Cary 1939- *WhoAmA 91*
Wasserman, Charles 1929- *St&PR 91*
Wasserman, Charles Irwin 1945- *BiDrAPA 89*
Wasserman, Dale 1917- *WhoAm 90*
Wasserman, David Sherman 1942- *St&PR 91*
Wasserman, Debra *WhoWrEP 89*
Wasserman, Dora 1920- *OxCCanT*
Wasserman, Edel 1932- *WhoAm 90*
Wasserman, Edward Arnold 1946- *WhoAm 90*
Wasserman, Edward M 1928- *BiDrAPA 89*
Wasserman, Gerhard Dietrich 1919- *EncO&P 3*
Wasserman, Harry Hershal 1920- *WhoAm 90*
Wasserman, Harvey Franklin 1945- *WhoEmL 91*
Wasserman, Harvey R *BiDrAPA 89*
Wasserman, Harvey S. 1943- *St&PR 91*
Wasserman, Herbert 1916- *St&PR 91*
Wasserman, J. Donald 1930- *St&PR 91*
Wasserman, Jack 1921- *WhoAmA 91*
Wasserman, James Michael 1941- *BiDrAPA 89*
Wasserman, Jeffrey 1946- *WhoAmA 91*
Wasserman, Jerry 1931- *St&PR 91*
Wasserman, Krystyna 1937- *WhoE 91*
Wasserman, Kurt Jonah 1921- *St&PR 91*
Wasserman, Larry Alan 1959- *WhoE 91*
Wasserman, Lawrence Alan 1942- *St&PR 91*
Wasserman, Leonard M. 1931- *St&PR 91*
Wasserman, Lew R. 1913- *BioIn 16, St&PR 91*
Wasserman, Louis Robert 1910- *WhoAm 90*
Wasserman, Marlie Parker 1947- *WhoAmW 91*
Wasserman, Martin S 1938- *BiDrAPA 89*
Wasserman, Marvin David 1942- *BiDrAPA 89*
Wasserman, Michael Gary 1946- *WhoEmL 91*
Wasserman, Myron Beau 1947- *WhoE 91*
Wasserman, Paul 1924- *WhoAm 90*
Wasserman, Paul Zachary 1943- *WhoE 91*
Wasserman, Rhonda Sharon 1958- *WhoE 91*
Wasserman, Richard Leo 1948- *WhoEmL 91*
Wasserman, Robert Harold 1926- *WhoAm 90*
Wasserman, Saul 1942- *BiDrAPA 89*
Wasserman, Steve 1952- *WhoAm 90*
Wasserman, Sy *St&PR 91*
Wasserman, Theodore Wolf 1936- *BiDrAPA 89*
Wasserman-Arthur, Lorraine Jean 1938- *St&PR 91*
Wassermann, Franz W 1920- *BiDrAPA 89*
Wassermann, Jakob 1873-1934 *BioIn 16*
Wasserspring, Arthur J. 1941- *WhoE 91*
Wasserstein, Bernard Mano Julius 1948- *WhoAm 90*
Wasserstein, Bruce *BioIn 16, NewYTBS 90 [port]*
Wasserstein, Bruce 1947- *St&PR 91, WhoAm 90*
Wasserstein, Wendy *BioIn 16*
Wasserstein, Wendy 1950- *ConAu 129, ConLC 59 [port], ConTFT 8, FemiCLE, NotWoAT, WhoAm 90, WhoAmW 91, WhoE 91, WorAu 1980 [port]*
Wasserstrum, Harriet Sue 1948- *St&PR 91*
Wassersug, Joseph David 1912- *AuBYP 90*
Wasserthal, Elfriede 1911- *IntWWM 90*
Wasshausen, Dieter Carl 1938- *WhoAm 90*
Wassil, Michael J. 1951- *St&PR 91*
Wassinger, Marion *St&PR 91*
Wassler, Alfred Richard 1944- *St&PR 91, WhoAm 90*
Wassman, James A. 1941- *St&PR 91*
Wassmo, Herbjorg 1942- *EncCoWW*
Wassmus, Henri-Leonard *PenDiDA 89*
Wassmus, Jean-Henri-Chretien *PenDiDA 89*
Wassmus, Jean-Henri-Christophe *PenDiDA 89*
Wassner, Steven Joel 1946- *WhoAm 90*
Wassom, Allan Wayne 1933- *St&PR 91*
Wassom, Herbert M. *BioIn 16*
Wasson, Barbara Hickam 1918- *IntWWM 90, WhoAmW 91, WhoWor 91*
Wasson, Catherine Church 1948- *WhoAmW 91*
Wasson, Craig 1954- *ConTFT 8 [port]*
Wasson, D. DeWitt 1921- *IntWWM 90*
Wasson, Eleanor Walsh 1908- *WhoAmW 91*
Wasson, John Calvin 1931- *St&PR 91*
Wasson, Lila Elizabeth 1924- *WhoAmW 91*
Wasson, Margaret 1908- *WhoAmW 91*
Wasson, R.G. 1945- *St&PR 91*
Wasson, R. Gordon 1898-1986 *BioIn 16*
Wasson, R Gordon 1898-1986 *EncO&P 3*
Wasson, Robert Doane 1935- *BiDrAPA 89*
Wasson, Samuel Brown 1936- *St&PR 91*
Wasson, Samuel C., Jr. 1939- *St&PR 91*
Wasson, Steven D. *St&PR 91*
Wassong, Dan Karol 1930- *St&PR 91*
Wassong, Joseph Francis, Jr. 1938- *WhoE 91*
Wast, Nicole Toussaint Du *BioIn 16*
Wastberg, Olle M. 1945- *WhoWor 91*
Wastberg, Per 1933- *DcScanL*
Wasylenki, Donald Alexande 1946- *BiDrAPA 89*
Waszkiewicz, Janice Lynn Vitale 1955- *WhoAmW 91*
Waszkiewicz, Joan E. 1927- *St&PR 91*
Waszkiewicz, John Chester, III 1953- *St&PR 91*
Waszkiewicz, John Chester, Jr. 1927- *St&PR 91*
Wat, Aleksander *BioIn 16*
Watanabe, Akeo 1919- *IntWWM 90, PenDiMP*
Watanabe, August Masaru 1941- *WhoAm 90*
Watanabe, Fukutaro 1924- *WhoWor 91*
Watanabe, Gary Yoichi 1945- *St&PR 91*
Watanabe, Henry K 1934- *BiDrAPA 89*
Watanabe, Hiroshi 1927- *WhoWor 91*
Watanabe, Hiroshi 1929- *WhoWor 91*
Watanabe, Hirosuko *WhoAm 90*
Watanabe, Jiro 1931- *WhoWor 91*
Watanabe, Joanne Ellen Steen 1955- *WhoAmW 91*
Watanabe, Kazutami 1932- *WhoWor 91*
Watanabe, Kazuyuki 1932- *WhoWor 91*
Watanabe, Kenji 1930- *WhoWor 91*
Watanabe, Kouichi 1942- *WhoWor 91*
Watanabe, Mamoru 1933- *WhoAm 90*
Watanabe, Mark David 1955- *WhoWor 91*
Watanabe, Meiji 1935- *WhoWor 91*
Watanabe, Roy Noboru 1947- *WhoEmL 91*
Watanabe, Ruth Taiko 1916- *WhoAm 90, WhoAmW 91, WhoE 91, WhoWor 91*
Watanabe, Ryojiro 1936- *WhoWor 91*
Watanabe, Shigeo 1928- *BioIn 16*
Watanabe, Takao 1940- *WhoWor 91*
Watanabe, Takashi 1926- *WhoWor 91*
Watanabe, Tokuji 1934- *ConDes 90*
Watanabe, Tsuneo 1926- *WhoWor 91*
Watanabe, Yoichi 1954- *WhoSSW 91*
Watanabe, Yoko 1956- *IntWWM 90*
Watchorn, William E. 1943- *St&PR 91*
Watchorn, William Ernest 1943- *WhoAm 90*
Waterbury, Marcia W 1945- *BiDrAPA 89*
Waterbury, Theodore Robinson 1928- *WhoSSW 91*
Waterfall, Cornelia E. Lien 1929- *WhoE 91*
Waterfield, Harry Lee, II 1943- *St&PR 91*
Waterfield, Robert Lee 1924- *WhoSSW 91*
Waterfield, William, Jr. 1930- *BiDrAPA 89*
Waterford, Cheri Denise 1960- *WhoAmW 91*
Waterford, Louisa Ann 1818-1891 *BiDWomA*
Waterford, Van *WhoWrEP 89*
Waterhouse, Alfred 1830-1905 *BioIn 16*
Waterhouse, Charles Horatio 1814-1892 *DcCanB 12*
Waterhouse, Charles Howard 1924- *WhoAmA 91*
Waterhouse, Edwin *BioIn 16*
Waterhouse, Ellis Kirkham 1905-1985 *DcNaB 1981*

Waterhouse, Ernest Lewis, III 1952- *WhoSSW 91*
Waterhouse, John Percival 1920- *WhoAm 90*
Waterhouse, Keith 1929- *MajTwCW*
Waterhouse, Mona Elisabeth 1942- *WhoAmW 91*
Waterhouse, Ralph *BioIn 16*
Waterhouse, Roger 1940- *ConAu 129*
Waterhouse, Russell Rutledge 1928- *WhoAmA 91*
Waterhouse, Stephen Lee 1943- *WhoE 91, WhoWor 91*
Waterhouse, William 1931- *IntWWM 90*
Waterhouse, William Charles 1941- *WhoE 91*
Waterhouse, William James 1917- *WhoAm 90*
Waterlow, Simon Gordon 1941- *St&PR 91, WhoAm 90*
Waterman, Andrew 1940- *ConAu 31NR*
Waterman, Asa 1940- *St&PR 91*
Waterman, Daniel 1927- *WhoAm 90, WhoE 91*
Waterman, David *PenDiMP*
Waterman, David Allen Woodrow 1950- *IntWWM 90*
Waterman, Donald Calvin 1928-1979 *WhoAmA 91N*
Waterman, Douglas Lloyd 1945- *St&PR 91*
Waterman, Fanny 1920- *IntWWM 90, PenDiMP*
Waterman, G. Scott 1956- *BiDrAPA 89*
Waterman, George Walter, III 1949- *WhoE 91*
Waterman, Guy *BioIn 16*
Waterman, Helen Anne 1940- *WhoAmW 91*
Waterman, John Thomas 1918- *WhoAm 90*
Waterman, Joseph Francis 1951- *St&PR 91*
Waterman, Laura *BioIn 16*
Waterman, Michael Spencer 1942- *WhoAm 90*
Waterman, Robert William 1952- *BiDrAPA 89*
Waterman, Ruth Anna 1947- *IntWWM 90*
Waterman, Thomas Chadbourne 1937- *WhoAm 90*
Waterman, Waldo Dean 1894-1976 *BioIn 16*
Waterman, William E 1931- *BiDrAPA 89*
Watermann, C Eugene 1929- *BiDrAPA 89*
Waterous, Charles Horatio 1814-1892 *DcCanB 12*
Waterreus, Willem 1939- *WhoWor 91*
Waters *TwCCr&M 91A*
Waters, Aaron Clement 1905- *WhoAm 90*
Waters, Alice *BioIn 16*
Waters, Barbara Krumsieg 1942- *WhoAmW 91*
Waters, Bernard J. *St&PR 91*
Waters, Betty Lou 1943- *WhoAmW 91, WhoSSW 91*
Waters, Bob *BioIn 16*
Waters, Brent Geoffrey 1948- *BiDrAPA 89*
Waters, Charlotte Ann 1947- *WhoAm 90*
Waters, Chocolate 1949- *WhoWrEP 89*
Waters, Clarence Pharo 1923- *St&PR 91*
Waters, Claude J., Jr. 1939- *St&PR 91*
Waters, David M. 1942- *St&PR 91*
Waters, David Rogers 1932- *St&PR 91, WhoAm 90*
Waters, Donald Henry 1937- *WhoWor 91*
Waters, Donald Joseph 1952- *WhoAm 90*
Waters, Donald Samuel B. 1916- *St&PR 91*
Waters, Donovan W. 1928- *WhoAm 90*
Waters, Ellen Maureen 1938- *WhoAmW 91*
Waters, Ethel 1896-1977 *BioIn 16, DrBlPA 90, OxCPMus*
Waters, Ethel 1900?-1976 *NotWoAT*
Waters, Ethel 1900-1977 *BioAmW, WorAlBi*
Waters, Frank 1902- *BioIn 16, ConAu 13AS [port]*
Waters, George Bausch 1920- *WhoAm 90*
Waters, George Fite 1894-1961 *WhoAmA 91N*
Waters, George Wilbur 1916- *WhoAm 90*
Waters, H. Franklin 1932- *WhoSSW 91*
Waters, Helen Eugenia 1917- *WhoWrEP 89*
Waters, Herbert 1903- *WhoAmA 91*
Waters, Horace John 1895-1981 *DcNaB 1981*
Waters, Jack 1954- *WhoAmA 91*
Waters, James F., Jr. 1929- *WhoAm 90*
Waters, James Lee 1953- *WhoSSW 91*
Waters, James Logan 1925- *St&PR 91, WhoAm 90*
Waters, John 1946- *BioIn 16, ConAu 130, CurBio 90 [port]*
Waters, John B. 1929- *WhoSSW 91*
Waters, John F. 1930- *AuBYP 90*
Waters, John Ingersoll 1958- *BiDrAPA 89*
Waters, John Knight 1906-1989 *BioIn 16*
Waters, John L *BiDrAPA 89*
Waters, Louis Albert 1938- *St&PR 91*
Waters, Margaret *BiDEWW*
Waters, Martha *ODwPR 91*
Waters, Martha Elizabeth 1959- *WhoAmW 91*
Waters, Maxine *BioIn 16*
Waters, Maxine 1938- *WhoAmW 91*
Waters, Michael 1949- *WhoWrEP 89*
Waters, Michael George 1952- *WhoE 91*
Waters, Muddy 1915-1983 *BioIn 16, ConMus 4 [port], DrBlPA 90, EncPR&S 89, OxCPMus*
Waters, Ray 1931- *ODwPR 91*
Waters, Reita Olita Clifton 1930- *WhoWrEP 89*
Waters, Richard 1926- *St&PR 91, WhoAm 90*
Waters, Richard George 1936- *St&PR 91*
Waters, Robert Leslie 1934- *St&PR 91*
Waters, Rodney Lewis 1936- *WhoWor 91*
Waters, Rollie Odell 1942- *WhoSSW 91, WhoWor 91*
Waters, Ruth Loene 1949- *WhoSSW 91*
Waters, Scott Hamilton 1953- *WhoE 91*
Waters, Sheila Marie 1961- *WhoAmW 91*
Waters, Shirley B. 1921- *St&PR 91*
Waters, Susan Catherine 1823-1900 *BiDWomA*
Waters, Sylvia *WhoAm 90*
Waters, Wayne Arthur 1929- *WhoWor 91*
Waters, William Alexander 1903-1985 *DcNaB 1981*
Waters, William Alfred 1912- *WhoSSW 91*
Waters, William Ernest 1928- *WhoWor 91*
Waters, William Leroy 1936- *WhoE 91*
Waters, Willie Anthony *BioIn 16*
Waters, Willie Anthony 1951- *WhoAm 90, WhoHisp 91, WhoSSW 91*
Waterston, Harry Clement 1909- *WhoAmA 91*
Waterston, James R. 1941- *St&PR 91*
Waterston, James Rufus *WhoAm 90*
Waterston, Rebecca Lynn 1950- *WhoAmW 91*
Waterston, Sam 1940- *WorAlBi*
Waterston, William King 1937- *WhoE 91*
Waterstreet, Ken 1940- *WhoAmA 91*
Waterton, Eric 1943- *WhoAm 90*
Waterwash, James Samuel 1938- *St&PR 91*
Waterworth, Donald Lyle, Sr. 1927- *WhoSSW 91*
Wates, Neil Edward 1932-1985 *DcNaB 1981*
Watford, George Franklin 1921- *St&PR 91*
Watford, Jamie Denise 1955- *WhoAmW 91*
Watford, Paula Sargent 1954- *WhoAmW 91*
Wathall, Bettie Geraldine *WhoAmA 91*
Wathan, John 1949- *Ballpl 90*
Wathen, Daniel Everett 1939- *WhoAm 90, WhoE 91*
Wathen, Dave *BioIn 16*
Wathey, Andrew Brian 1958- *IntWWM 90*
Watia, Tarmo 1938- *WhoAmA 91*
Watie, Stand 1806-1871 *WhNaAH*
Watkin, David 1925- *WhoWor 91*
Watkin, Virginia Guild 1925- *WhoAm 90*
Watkin, Virginia Ruth 1955- *WhoEmL 91*
Watkin, William Ward, Jr. 1919- *WhoE 91*
Watkins, Armitage *BioIn 16*
Watkins, Bill *St&PR 91*
Watkins, Carlton Gunter 1919- *WhoAm 90*
Watkins, Carol E 1956- *BiDrAPA 89*
Watkins, Charles Booker, Jr. 1942- *WhoAm 90, WhoE 91*
Watkins, Clifton Edward, Jr. 1954- *WhoSSW 91*
Watkins, Clyde Ater, Jr. 1946- *BiDrAPA 89*
Watkins, Daniel J. 1923- *St&PR 91*
Watkins, Daniel Joseph 1923- *WhoAm 90*
Watkins, David J., II 1959- *St&PR 91*
Watkins, David Kerry 1946- *St&PR 91*
Watkins, David Ogden 1862-1938 *AmLegL*
Watkins, Dean A. 1922- *St&PR 91*
Watkins, Dean Allen 1922- *WhoAm 90*
Watkins, Diane Margaret Otto 1955- *WhoAmW 91*
Watkins, Don L. 1952- *St&PR 91*
Watkins, Edwin H. 1924- *St&PR 91*
Watkins, Eileen Frances 1950- *WhoAmA 91*
Watkins, Eugene Leonard 1918- *WhoE 91*
Watkins, Evan Scott 1961- *WhoWrEP 89*
Watkins, F. Scott 1946- *St&PR 91*
Watkins, Felix Scott 1946- *WhoEmL 91*
Watkins, Floyd C. 1920- *WhoSSW 91*
Watkins, Franklin Chenault 1894-1972 *WhoAmA 91N*
Watkins, Geoffrey 1896-1981 *EncO&P 3*
Watkins, George 1902-1970 *Ballpl 90*
Watkins, George Daniels 1924- *WhoAm 90*
Watkins, Gerald Ray 1946- *BiDrAPA 89*
Watkins, Gilbert Kim 1952- *WhoE 91*
Watkins, Glenn 1927- *IntWWM 90*
Watkins, Glenn Elson 1927- *WhoAm 90*
Watkins, Glenn G. 1951- *WhoSSW 91*
Watkins, Guy Lewis, Jr. 1953- *WhoSSW 91*
Watkins, H. Griffin 1929- *ODwPR 91*
Watkins, Hays T. 1926- *St&PR 91*
Watkins, Hays Thomas 1926- *WhoAm 90, WhoSSW 91, WhoWor 91*
Watkins, J. David 1948- *IntWWM 90*
Watkins, James D. *BioIn 16*
Watkins, James D. 1927- *BiDrUSE 89*
Watkins, James David 1927- *WhoAm 90, WhoE 91, WhoWor 91*
Watkins, Jane Aileen 1948- *WhoEmL 91*
Watkins, Jerry West 1931- *St&PR 91, WhoAm 90, WhoSSW 91*
Watkins, Joe 1947- *St&PR 91*
Watkins, John 1950- *WhoWor 91*
Watkins, John Arden 1939- *WhoSSW 91*
Watkins, John C.A. 1912- *St&PR 91*
Watkins, John Chester Anderson 1912- *WhoAm 90*
Watkins, John F. 1925- *St&PR 91*
Watkins, John Goodrich 1913- *WhoAm 90*
Watkins, John Lear 1931- *WhoE 91*
Watkins, John M. 1940- *WhoAm 90*
Watkins, John Michael 1946- *WhoE 91*
Watkins, Julia M. 1941- *WhoAmW 91*
Watkins, Julia M. 1942- *WhoSSW 91*
Watkins, June *BioIn 16*
Watkins, Levi *BioIn 16*
Watkins, Lewis 1945- *WhoAmA 91*
Watkins, Lewis Boone 1945- *WhoSSW 91, WhoWor 91*
Watkins, Lloyd Irion 1928- *WhoAm 90*
Watkins, Lovelace 1938- *DrBlPA 90*
Watkins, Mary *NewAgMG*
Watkins, Michael Blake 1948- *IntWWM 90*
Watkins, Nathaniel W. 1796-1876 *AmLegL*
Watkins, Norma Lea 1923- *St&PR 91*
Watkins, Paul 1964- *ConAu 132*
Watkins, Paul Barnett 1949- *WhoEmL 91*
Watkins, Paul Lindsay 1947- *WhoWor 91*
Watkins, Peter 1935- *ConTFT 8*
Watkins, Pia Marie 1964- *WhoAmW 91*
Watkins, Ragland Tolk 1948- *WhoAmA 91*
Watkins, Raymond Louis 1941- *WhoE 91*
Watkins, Richard D *BiDrAPA 89*
Watkins, Robert Camp *BiDrAPA 89*
Watkins, Robert Fred 1927- *WhoWor 91*
Watkins, Robert Todd, Sr. 1929- *St&PR 91, WhoAm 90*
Watkins, Roland H.W. 1932- *St&PR 91*
Watkins, Ronald J. *BioIn 16*
Watkins, Rosalind Jeannette 1942- *WhoAmW 91, WhoSSW 91*
Watkins, Sallie A. *BioIn 16*
Watkins, Sally Marie 1954- *WhoAmW 91*
Watkins, Samuel Rayburn 1923- *WhoWor 91*
Watkins, Sara Van Horn 1945- *IntWWM 90*
Watkins, Scott D. 1949- *St&PR 91*
Watkins, Stephen Edward 1922- *WhoAm 90*
Watkins, T H 1936- *ConAu 31NR*
Watkins, Taylor Jackson, III 1952- *WhoE 91*
Watkins, Vincent Gates 1945- *WhoSSW 91, WhoWor 91*
Watkins, Wallace Holmes 1936- *St&PR 91*
Watkins, Walter David 1943- *WhoAm 90*
Watkins, Warren Hyde 1953- *WhoEmL 91*
Watkins, Wendell Lynn 1932- *St&PR 91*
Watkins, Wesley Lee 1953- *WhoSSW 91*
Watkins, Wesley Wade 1938- *WhoAm 90, WhoSSW 91*
Watkins, William, Jr. 1932- *St&PR 91*
Watkins, William John 1942- *WhoWrEP 89*
Watkins, William Law 1910- *WhoAm 90*
Watkins-Pitchford, Denys James 1905-1990 *ConAu 132*
Watkinson, Alan Harold 1958- *St&PR 91*
Watkinson, Andrew *PenDiMP*
Watkinson, Carolyn 1949- *IntWWM 90*
Watkinson, Fabian Nicholas Velentine 1954- *IntWWM 90*
Watkinson, Patricia Grieve 1946- *WhoAmA 91*
Watkinson, Thomas Guy 1931- *St&PR 91*
Watlack, Linda Ann 1959- *WhoAmW 91*
Watley, Jody *BioIn 16*
Watley, Martha Jones 1936- *WhoAmW 91, WhoSSW 91*
Watlington, John Francis, Jr. 1911- *WhoAm 90*
Watlington, Phillip B. 1944- *St&PR 91*
Watlington, Rosalind Thayer 1925- *IntWWM 90*
Watlington-Cox, Adrian Denise 1954- *WhoE 91*
Watman, Carolyn Prescott 1944- *WhoAmW 91*
Watman, William A. 1949- *St&PR 91*
Watmough, David 1926- *ConAu 33NR, OxCCanT*
Watney-Klass, Lynne Mountford 1953- *WhoWor 91*
Watniss, Wendy 1943- *WhoAmA 91*
Watomika 1823-1889 *BioIn 16*
Watrel, Albert A. *WhoAm 90*
Watrelot, Antoine-Andre 1952- *WhoWor 91*
Watrous, Bill *BioIn 16*
Watrous, James Scales 1908- *WhoAmA 91*
Watrous, Joan Cheevers *WhoAmW 91*
Watrous, John S. *AmLegL*
Watrous, P.J. 1933- *St&PR 91*
Watrous, William Russell 1939- *WhoAm 90*
Watsa, V. Prem 1950- *St&PR 91*
Watsky, Sheldon R 1918- *BiDrAPA 89*
Watson, Abbie I. 1905- *WhoWor 91*
Watson, Ada Louise Mitchell 1951- *WhoAmW 91*
Watson, Alan E. 1956- *St&PR 91*
Watson, Albert MacKenzie 1942- *WhoE 91*
Watson, Aldren A 1917- *WhoAmA 91*
Watson, Alexander Fletcher 1939- *WhoAm 90, WhoWor 91*
Watson, Alfred N. *St&PR 91N*
Watson, Allen C. 1917- *St&PR 91*
Watson, Alonzo Wallace, Jr. 1922- *WhoAm 90*
Watson, Andrew Orr 1946- *WhoAm 90*
Watson, Andrew S 1920- *BiDrAPA 89*
Watson, Ann McWhinney 1925- *WhoAmW 91*
Watson, Anthony I. 1926-1990 *ConAu 132*
Watson, Anthony J. *BioIn 16*
Watson, Arthur Dennis 1950- *WhoAm 90, WhoEmL 91*
Watson, Arthur Kittredge 1919-1974 *BioIn 16*
Watson, Arthur Richard 1915- *WhoE 91*
Watson, Barry Lee 1963- *WhoSSW 91*
Watson, Ben Charles 1944- *WhoAm 90*
Watson, Bernard Charles *WhoAm 90, WhoE 91, WhoWor 91*
Watson, Betty Ann 1942- *WhoSSW 91*
Watson, Beverly Ann 1948- *WhoAmW 91*
Watson, Bob 1946- *Ballpl 90*
Watson, Bruce Dunstan 1928- *WhoWor 91*
Watson, Bruce W. 1926- *St&PR 91*
Watson, Carl 1922- *WhoAm 90, WhoSSW 91*
Watson, Carlos Ronaldo 1951- *WhoWor 91*
Watson, Carol 1957- *WhoAmW 91*
Watson, Carol Ann 1948- *WhoAmW 91*
Watson, Carolyn Garrett 1941- *WhoSSW 91*
Watson, Catherine Elaine 1944- *WhoAm 90, WhoAmW 91*
Watson, Charles Bruce 1928- *St&PR 91*
Watson, Charles H. 1937- *St&PR 91*
Watson, Charlotte Allene 1953- *WhoAmW 91*
Watson, Charlotte Bushnell 1943- *WhoE 91*
Watson, Christine Donna 1958- *WhoAmW 91*
Watson, Christopher S. 1946- *St&PR 91*
Watson, Claire 1927-1986 *PenDiMP*
Watson, Claire 1936- *WhoAmW 91*
Watson, Clarissa Alden *WhoE 91*
Watson, Clarissa H *WhoAmA 91*
Watson, Clyde Dingman 1947- *AuBYP 90*
Watson, Colin 1920-1982 *TwCCr&M 91*
Watson, Connia Henry, Jr. 1936- *St&PR 91*
Watson, Curtis S. 1810- *AmLegL*
Watson, Cynthia Lou 1952- *WhoAmW 91*
Watson, D. J. *BioIn 16*
Watson, Dale Alan 1955- *WhoEmL 91*
Watson, Darlene McFadden 1956- *WhoSSW 91*
Watson, Darliene Keeney 1929- *WhoAmA 91*
Watson, David 1943- *St&PR 91*
Watson, David 1946- *WhoSSW 91*
Watson, David Colquitt 1936- *WhoWor 91*
Watson, Dennis *DrBlPA 90*
Watson, Dennis Wallace 1914- *WhoAm 90*
Watson, Derek 1948- *ConAu 129*
Watson, Diane Edith 1933- *WhoAmW 91*
Watson, D'Jaris Hinton 1928-1989 *BioIn 16*
Watson, Doc 1885-1949 *Ballpl 90*
Watson, Doc 1923- *BioIn 16, WhoAm 90*
Watson, Don *BioIn 16*
Watson, Donald Charles 1945- *WhoWor 91*
Watson, Donald Ralph 1937- *WhoAm 90, WhoWrEP 89*
Watson, Douglas 1916- *St&PR 91*
Watson, Douglas George 1945- *WhoAm 90*

Watson, Douglass 1921-1989 *BioIn 16, ConTFT 8*
Watson, Edward Albert 1945- *St&PR 91*
Watson, Edwin C. *ODwPR 91*
Watson, Elaine 1921- *WhoWrEP 89*
Watson, Elbert 1926- *St&PR 91*
Watson, Elizabeth *IntWWM 90, ODwPR 91*
Watson, Elizabeth 1949- *News 91-2 [port]*
Watson, Eric George 1926- *IntWWM 90*
Watson, Evelyn Egner 1928- *WhoAmW 91*
Watson, Felicia 1962- *WhoAmW 91*
Watson, Fletcher D. 1922- *St&PR 91*
Watson, Forrest Albert 1951- *WhoEmL 91, WhoSSW 91, WhoWor 91*
Watson, Forrest I. 1926- *St&PR 91*
Watson, Frank Burton, Jr. 1921- *WhoSSW 91*
Watson, Frank Daniel 1952- *WhoE 91*
Watson, Gary Hunter 1951- *WhoSSW 91*
Watson, George Henry, Jr. 1936- *WhoAm 90, WhoWor 91*
Watson, Georgia Brown *WhoAmW 91, WhoWor 91*
Watson, Georgianna 1949- *WhoAmW 91, WhoEmL 91*
Watson, Gerald Glenn 1945- *WhoEmL 91*
Watson, Glenn R. 1917- *WhoWor 91*
Watson, Grace 1668-1688 *BiDEWW*
Watson, H. Mitchell, Jr. *WhoAm 90*
Watson, Harold George 1931- *WhoAm 90*
Watson, Helen Orr 1892-1978 *AuBYP 90*
Watson, Helen Richter 1926- *WhoAmA 91*
Watson, Henry Knox, III 1951- *St&PR 91*
Watson, Hildegarde Lasell *WhoAmA 91N*
Watson, Howard N 1929- *WhoAmA 91*
Watson, Hugh Seton- 1916-1984 *DcNaB 1981*
Watson, Ian Allen 1954- *WhoE 91*
Watson, Irving S. *MajTwCW*
Watson, Irwin C 1934- *DrBlPA 90*
Watson, J. Hugh 1917- *St&PR 91*
Watson, J. Robert *St&PR 91*
Watson, J Wreford 1915-1990 *ConAu 132*
Watson, Jack Crozier 1928- *WhoAm 90*
Watson, Jack H., Jr. 1938- *WhoAm 90*
Watson, Jack McLaurin 1908- *IntWWM 90*
Watson, Jackie Rieves 1945- *WhoEmL 91*
Watson, James 1928- *CurBio 90 [port]*
Watson, James A., Jr. *DrBlPA 90*
Watson, James Alexander 1821-1869 *BioIn 16*
Watson, James D. 1928- *BioIn 16, WorAlBi*
Watson, James Dewey 1928- *WhoAm 90, WhoE 91, WhoWor 91*
Watson, James Lopez 1922- *WhoAm 90*
Watson, James R. 1920- *St&PR 91*
Watson, James Ray, Jr. 1935- *WhoSSW 91*
Watson, Jan Carole 1942- *WhoAmW 91*
Watson, Jane 1915- *AuBYP 90*
Watson, Jane Elizabeth *BiDrAPA 89*
Watson, Jane Werner 1915- *BioIn 16*
Watson, Janet Lee Cox 1940- *WhoAmW 91*
Watson, Janet Vida 1923-1985 *DcNaB 1981*
Watson, Jean 1933- *FemiCLE*
Watson, Jennifer *BioIn 16*
Watson, Jennifer Darrow 1960- *WhoE 91*
Watson, Jerome Richard 1938- *WhoAm 90*
Watson, Jerry Allan 1935- *WhoSSW 91*
Watson, Jerry Carroll 1943- *WhoE 91, WhoSSW 91, WhoWor 91*
Watson, Jerry Franklin 1936- *WhoSSW 91*
Watson, Jill *BioIn 16*
Watson, Jim Albert 1939- *WhoSSW 91*
Watson, Joan Sutton 1931- *WhoSSW 91*
Watson, John B. 1878-1958 *WorAlBi*
Watson, John Broadus 1878-1958 *BioIn 16*
Watson, John C. 1850-1916 *AmLegL*
Watson, John Christopher 1950- *WhoSSW 91*
Watson, John D. 1937- *St&PR 91*
Watson, John H. 1940- *St&PR 91*
Watson, John King, Jr. 1926- *WhoAm 90*
Watson, John Lawrence, III 1932- *St&PR 91, WhoAm 90, WhoE 91*
Watson, John Mark 1945- *WhoSSW 91*
Watson, John Milton 1945- *WhoEmL 91*
Watson, John R. 1922- *WhoAm 90*
Watson, John Slater 1952- *WhoEmL 91*
Watson, John W. 1858- *AmLegL*
Watson, John William 1930- *WhoSSW 91*
Watson, Julian 1918- *WhoAm 90*
Watson, Kate J. 1936- *WhoAmW 91*
Watson, Katharine Johnson 1942- *WhoAm 90, WhoAmA 91, WhoAmW 91, WhoE 91*
Watson, Keith Dewey 1957- *St&PR 91*
Watson, Keith Stuart 1942- *WhoAm 90*
Watson, Kenneth Harrison *St&PR 91*
Watson, Kenneth Marshall 1921- *WhoAm 90*
Watson, Kenneth W. 1942- *St&PR 91*
Watson, Kenneth William 1942- *WhoAm 90*
Watson, Kerr Francis 1944- *WhoSSW 91*
Watson, Kittie Wells 1953- *WhoAmW 91*
Watson, Kurt Douglas 1952- *St&PR 91*
Watson, Larry Paul 1948- *St&PR 91*
Watson, Laura Humphreys 1954- *WhoSSW 91*
Watson, Leland H. 1926-1989 *BioIn 16*
Watson, Leland Hale 1926- *WhoAm 90, WhoWor 91*
Watson, Leland Hale 1926-1989 *ConAu 130*
Watson, Lillian 1947- *IntWWM 90*
Watson, Linda R. 1943- *St&PR 91*
Watson, Louis H. 1938- *St&PR 91*
Watson, Lucile 1879-1962 *BioIn 16, NotWoAT*
Watson, Lyall 1939- *EncO&P 3*
Watson, M. Douglas, Jr. 1946- *St&PR 91*
Watson, Marian Etoile *DrBlPA 90*
Watson, Marilyn Fern 1934- *WhoWrEP 89*
Watson, Marsha Jean 1957- *WhoAmW 91, WhoWrEP 89*
Watson, Mary *BiDEWW*
Watson, Mary Anne *WhoAmA 91*
Watson, Mary Spencer 1913- *BiDWomA*
Watson, Mary Stone 1909- *WhoAmW 91*
Watson, Milt 1890-1962 *Ballpl 90*
Watson, Mule 1896-1949 *Ballpl 90*
Watson, Muriel Anita Ellis 1951- *WhoAmW 91*
Watson, Nancy Dingman *AuBYP 90*
Watson, Nancy Louise 1948- *WhoAmW 91*
Watson, Pat *BioIn 16*
Watson, Patricia Kay *BiDrAPA 89*
Watson, Patricia L. 1939- *WhoSSW 91*
Watson, Patricia Leonard 1945- *WhoAmW 91*
Watson, Patrick *BioIn 16*
Watson, Patty Jo 1932- *WhoAm 90, WhoAmW 91*
Watson, Paul Louis 1923- *BiDrAPA 89*
Watson, Paula D. 1945- *WhoAm 90*
Watson, Peter Dekker 1924- *WhoE 91*
Watson, Phil 1933- *WhoSSW 91*
Watson, Ralph Edward 1948- *WhoWor 91*
Watson, Raymond Leslie 1926- *WhoAm 90*
Watson, Richard Allan 1931- *WhoAm 90, WhoWrEP 89*
Watson, Richard F. *MajTwCW*
Watson, Richard Jesse 1951- *SmATA 62 [port]*
Watson, Richard Paul 1937- *St&PR 91*
Watson, Robert Atlas, III 1949- *WhoSSW 91*
Watson, Robert Bruce 1931- *WhoE 91*
Watson, Robert Eugene *BiDrAPA 89*
Watson, Robert G. 1935- *St&PR 91*
Watson, Robert Joseph 1931- *WhoAm 90*
Watson, Robert N., Jr. 1942- *St&PR 91*
Watson, Robert R. 1963- *WhoWrEP 89*
Watson, Robert Tanner 1922- *WhoAm 90*
Watson, Robert William 1949- *St&PR 91*
Watson, Robert Winthrop 1925- *WhoAm 90, WhoWrEP 89*
Watson, Roberta Casper 1949- *WhoAmW 91, WhoEmL 91*
Watson, Roger 1955- *WhoWor 91*
Watson, Roger Elton 1944- *WhoSSW 91*
Watson, Roland L. 1927- *St&PR 91*
Watson, Ronald G 1941- *WhoAmA 91*
Watson, Ross 1934- *WhoAmA 91*
Watson, Sally 1924- *AuBYP 90*
Watson, Sandra Stiles 1944- *WhoAmW 91, WhoE 91*
Watson, Sara Ruth 1907- *AuBYP 90*
Watson, Sara Ruth, and Emily Watson *AuBYP 90*
Watson, Scott MacAlpin 1951- *WhoE 91*
Watson, Sharee Leigh 1951- *WhoAmW 91*
Watson, Sharon Gitin 1943- *WhoAm 90, WhoAmW 91*
Watson, Sheila *BioIn 16*
Watson, Sheila 1909- *FemiCLE*
Watson, Solomon Brown, IV 1944- *St&PR 91, WhoAm 90*
Watson, Stanley Jack, Jr. 1943- *BiDrAPA 89*
Watson, Stella Marie 1953- *WhoAmW 91*
Watson, Sterl Arthur, Jr. 1942- *WhoAm 90*
Watson, Stewart Charles 1922- *WhoAm 90*
Watson, Stuart D. 1916- *St&PR 91*
Watson, Susan Elizabeth 1960- *WhoAmW 91*
Watson, Sydney 1903- *IntWWM 90*
Watson, T. A. G. 1947- *ODwPR 91*
Watson, Thomas *PenDiDA 89*
Watson, Thomas Allan, Jr. 1950- *WhoSSW 91*
Watson, Thomas Campbell 1931- *WhoAm 90, WhoSSW 91*
Watson, Thomas Coile 1924- *WhoSSW 91*
Watson, Thomas J. 1874-1956 *BioIn 16, WorAlBi*
Watson, Thomas J. 1914- *BioIn 16*
Watson, Thomas J., Jr. *NewYTBS 90 [port]*
Watson, Thomas J., Jr. 1914- *BestSel 90-4 [port], WhoAm 90, WorAlBi*
Watson, Thomas Riley 1947- *WhoEmL 91*
Watson, Thomas Sturges 1949- *WhoAm 90*
Watson, Tom 1949- *WorAlBi*
Watson, Valerie M. 1947- *St&PR 91*
Watson, Wallace Robert 1943- *WhoSSW 91*
Watson, Warren Edward 1925- *WhoE 91*
Watson, Wilfred 1911- *BioIn 16, OxCCanT*
Watson, William 1917- *WhoAm 90*
Watson, William A. J. 1933- *WhoAm 90*
Watson, William Calvin, Jr. 1938- *WhoE 91*
Watson, William Clarance 1924- *WhoSSW 91*
Watson, William Downing, Jr. 1938- *WhoWor 91*
Watson, William G. 1949- *St&PR 91*
Watson, William Hughes 1950- *WhoE 91*
Watson, William Keith Ross 1930- *WhoWor 91*
Watson, William Marvin, Jr. 1924- *BiDrUSE 89*
Watson, William Noel 1947- *BiDrAPA 89*
Watson, William V. 1939- *St&PR 91*
Watson-Brodnax, Shirley Jean *WhoAmW 91, WhoWor 91*
Watson-Johnson, Vernee *DrBlPA 90*
Watson-Lee, Debra Ann 1956- *WhoAmW 91*
Watson-Sutkowski, Susan Ellen 1957- *WhoE 91*
Watson-Watt, Robert 1892-1973 *WorAlBi*
Watson-Watt, Robert Alexander 1892-1973 *DcScB S2*
Watson-Williams, M. *BiDWomA*
Watsone, Sarah *BiDEWW*
Watstein, George Joseph 1938- *BiDrAPA 89*
Watt, Alexander Stuart 1892-1985 *DcNaB 1981*
Watt, Alison 1965- *BiDWomA*
Watt, Andrew J. 1916- *WhoAm 90*
Watt, Andrew Matthew 1954- *WhoE 91*
Watt, Arthur Dwight, Jr. 1955- *WhoSSW 91*
Watt, Barbara Ann 1939- *St&PR 91*
Watt, Charles Vance 1934- *WhoE 91, WhoWor 91*
Watt, Dean Day 1917- *WhoAm 90*
Watt, Diana Lynn 1956- *WhoEmL 91*
Watt, Donald J 1931- *BiDrAPA 89*
Watt, Douglas 1914- *WhoAm 90*
Watt, Eddie 1942- *Ballpl 90*
Watt, Frederick B. 1901- *ConAu 129*
Watt, Gary Wayne 1947- *WhoWor 91*
Watt, Graham Wend 1926- *WhoAm 90*
Watt, Ian Pierre 1917- *WhoAm 90*
Watt, J.R. 1927- *St&PR 91*
Watt, Jaimie Jacobs 1943- *WhoAmW 91*
Watt, James 1736-1819 *WorAlBi*
Watt, James Gaius 1938- *BiDrUSE 89, WhoAm 90*
Watt, James Henderson 1943- *WhoE 91*
Watt, James Walker 1936- *St&PR 91*
Watt, John A 1938- *BiDrAPA 89*
Watt, John Everett *BiDrAPA 89*
Watt, John H. 1927- *WhoAm 90*
Watt, Leslie Allen 1913- *St&PR 91*
Watt, Molly Lynn 1938- *WhoE 91*
Watt, Richard Martin 1930- *St&PR 91*
Watt, Robert Douglas 1945- *WhoAm 90*
Watt, Ronald W. 1943- *ODwPR 91*
Watt, Ronald William 1943- *WhoAm 90, WhoWor 91*
Watt, Stuart George 1934- *WhoAm 90*
Watt, Thomas Christian 1936- *St&PR 91*
Watt, Thomas Joseph 1939- *St&PR 91*
Watt, Tim 1939- *St&PR 91*
Watt, William Buell 1919- *St&PR 91*
Watt, William G. 1934- *St&PR 91*
Watt, William John 1943- *WhoE 91*
Watt, William Joseph 1925- *WhoAm 90, WhoSSW 91*
Watt-Evans, Lawrence *ConAu 32NR*
Watteau, Antoine 1684-1721 *IntDcAA 90, WorAlBi*
Watteau, Jean-Antoine 1684-1721 *PenDiDA 89*
Wattel, Harold Louis 1921- *WhoAm 90*
Wattelet, Benny J. 1936- *St&PR 91*
Wattenberg, Albert 1917- *WhoAm 90*
Wattenberg, Ben J. 1933- *ConAu 33NR, WhoAm 90, WhoWrEP 89*
Wattenberg, Carl August, Jr. 1938- *St&PR 91*
Wattenberg, Martin Paul 1956- *WhoEmL 91*
Wattenmaker, Bernard M *BiDrAPA 89*
Wattenmaker, Richard J 1941- *WhoAmA 91*
Wattenmaker, Richard Joel 1941- *WhoAm 90*
Watters, Bud 1923- *WhoWrEP 89*
Watters, Charles Kenneth 1929- *St&PR 91*
Watters, Cynthia Ellen 1944- *WhoAmW 91, WhoSSW 91*
Watters, Earl G., Sr. 1915- *St&PR 91*
Watters, Ginger Perkins 1952- *WhoSSW 91*
Watters, Laura Lynn 1961- *WhoAmW 91*
Watters, Lu 1911-1989 *AnObit 1989, OxCPMus*
Watters, Patricia Anne 1948- *WhoAmW 91*
Watters, Raymond Wendell 1948- *WhoEmL 91, WhoSSW 91, WhoWor 91*
Watterson, Bill *BioIn 16, WhoAm 90*
Watterson, Bill 1958- *EncACom, News 90, -90-3*
Watterson, Donald J 1912- *BiDrAPA 89*
Watterson, Henry 1840-1921 *BioIn 16*
Watterson, Joan Cook 1931- *WhoAmW 91*
Watterson, Martha V. *ODwPR 91*
Watterworth, Darlene Mary 1965- *WhoE 91*
Wattleton, Faye *BioIn 16*
Wattleton, Faye 1943- *CurBio 90 [port], WhoAm 90, WhoAmW 91*
Watts, Al F. *EarBlAP*
Watts, Alan 1915-1973 *ConAu 32NR, EncO&P 3*
Watts, Alan Witson 1915-1973 *WorAlBi*
Watts, Andre 1946- *BioIn 16, DrBlPA 90, IntWWM 90, PenDiMP, WorAlBi*
Watts, Anna Mary Howitt 1824-1884 *BioIn 16*
Watts, Anthony Lee 1947- *WhoEmL 91, WhoSSW 91*
Watts, Bernadette 1942- *ConAu 31NR*
Watts, Carlton Bedford, Mrs. 1941- *WhoWor 91*
Watts, Charles DeWitt 1917- *WhoAm 90*
Watts, Charles H., II 1926- *St&PR 91*
Watts, Charles Henry, II 1926- *WhoAm 90*
Watts, Charles Phillip 1938- *WhoE 91*
Watts, Claudius Elmer, III 1936- *WhoAm 90*
Watts, Daniel Jay 1943- *WhoE 91*
Watts, Daniel Thomas 1916- *WhoAm 90*
Watts, Dave Henry 1932- *St&PR 91, WhoAm 90*
Watts, David Eide 1921- *WhoAm 90*
Watts, David L. 1943- *St&PR 91*
Watts, Deborah Clark *BiDrAPA 89*
Watts, Dennis Lester 1947- *WhoSSW 91*
Watts, Dey Wadsworth 1923- *WhoAm 90*
Watts, Doris Earlene 1923- *WhoAmW 91*
Watts, Dorothy Burt 1892-1977 *WhoAmA 91N*
Watts, Edward Quentin 1936- *IntWWM 90*
Watts, Emily Stipes 1936- *WhoAm 90, WhoAmW 91*
Watts, Ernest Francis 1937- *WhoAm 90*
Watts, Fredric *BiDrAPA 89*
Watts, George Frederick 1817-1904 *BioIn 16*
Watts, Glenn Ellis 1920- *WhoAm 90*
Watts, Glenn Richard 1929- *St&PR 91*
Watts, Gordon Edward 1945- *WhoEmL 91*
Watts, Hal 1935- *WhoSSW 91*
Watts, Harold Ross 1944- *WhoAm 90, WhoWor 91*
Watts, Harold Wesley 1932- *WhoAm 90*
Watts, Heather 1953- *WhoAm 90, WhoAmW 91*
Watts, Helen 1927- *IntWWM 90, PenDiMP*
Watts, Helen L. Hoke 1903-1990 *ConAu 131*
Watts, Helena Roselle 1921- *WhoAmW 91, WhoSSW 91, WhoWor 91*
Watts, Henry Miller, Jr. 1904- *WhoAm 90*
Watts, Hugh M. 1926- *St&PR 91*
Watts, Irene N. 1931- *BioIn 16*
Watts, Isaac 1674-1748 *BioIn 16, DcLB 95 [port]*
Watts, James 1955- *BioIn 16*
Watts, James Foster, Jr. 1936- *St&PR 91*
Watts, Jeffrey Alan 1950- *St&PR 91*
Watts, John M., Jr. 1941- *WhoWrEP 89*
Watts, John McCleave 1933- *St&PR 91, WhoAm 90*
Watts, John R. 1926- *St&PR 91*
Watts, Joyce Lannom 1942- *WhoAmW 91*
Watts, K. G. O. *AuBYP 90*
Watts, Katherine 1949- *WhoAmW 91*
Watts, Kathryn M.S. 1948- *WhoEmL 91*
Watts, Lloyd E 1905- *BiDrAPA 89*
Watts, Mabel Pizzey 1906- *AuBYP 90*
Watts, Malcolm Stuart McNeal 1915- *WhoAm 90*
Watts, Mary *BiDrAPA 89*
Watts, Mary 1868-1958 *FemiCLE*
Watts, Mary Ann 1927- *WhoAmW 91, WhoE 91*
Watts, Maurice A 1918- *BiDrAPA 89*
Watts, Michael P. 1937- *St&PR 91*

Watts, Michael Wayne 1950- WhoEmL 91
Watts, Nigel 1957- ConAu 130
Watts, Oliver Edward 1939- WhoAm 90
Watts, Patsy Jeanne 1943- WhoAmW 91, WhoWor 91
Watts, R Michael 1951- WhoAmA 91
Watts, Ralph Charles 1944- St&PR 91
Watts, Reginald John 1931- ConAu 30NR
Watts, Richard Eugene 1956- WhoSSW 91
Watts, Robert 1923-1988 BioIn 16
Watts, Robert B., Jr. 1930- St&PR 91
Watts, Robert Christian 1939- St&PR 91
Watts, Robert Glenn 1933- WhoSSW 91
Watts, Robert William 1948- WhoWor 91
Watts, Rolanda DrBlPA 90
Watts, Ronald Lester 1934- WhoAm 90
Watts, Ross Leslie 1942- WhoE 91
Watts, Sandra Jean BiDrAPA 89
Watts, Sewell S., III 1932- St&PR 91
Watts, Steven C. 1951- St&PR 91
Watts, Steven Richard 1955- WhoEmL 91
Watts, Susanna 1768-1842 FemiCLE
Watts, Thomas Lee 1938- WhoAm 90
Watts, Valeria Kay 1929- WhoAmW 91
Watts, Valerie Robbin 1953- WhoAmW 91
Watts, Vinita Sinha 1958- BiDrAPA 89
Watts, Wendy Burch 1955- St&PR 91
Watts, William Courtney 1830-1897 LiHiK
Watts, William David 1938- WhoSSW 91
Watts, William E. 1952- St&PR 91
Watts, William Edward 1952- WhoAm 90
Watts, William F., Jr. 1939- WhoSSW 91
Watts, William Park 1916- WhoSSW 91
Watwood, Cliff 1905-1980 Ballpl 90
Watz, Martin Charles 1938- WhoWor 91
Watzman, Barry Alan 1949- WhoEmL 91
Wauchope, Dorothy Thomson 1912- WhoAmW 91
Wauchope, Keith L. 1941- WhoWor 91
Waud, Alfred Rodolph 1828-1891 BioIn 16
Waud, Morrison 1910- St&PR 91
Waud, Roger Neil 1938- WhoAm 90
Waufle, Alan Duane 1951- WhoAmA 91
Waugaman, Richard Merle 1949- BiDrAPA 89, WhoE 91
Waugh, A. Bruce 1949- St&PR 91
Waugh, Alec 1898- WorAlBi
Waugh, Alexander Raban 1898-1981 DcNaB 1981
Waugh, Auberon BioIn 16
Waugh, Auberon 1939- CurBio 90 [port]
Waugh, Auberon Alexander 1939- WhoWor 91
Waugh, Butler Huggins 1934- WhoAm 90
Waugh, Carol-Lynn Rossel 1947- WhoAmW 91
Waugh, Coulton 1896-1973 EncACom, WhoAmA 91N
Waugh, Dorothy 1636?- BiDEWW
Waugh, Douglas Oliver William 1918- WhoAm 90
Waugh, Eric Stanley BiDrAPA 89
Waugh, Evelyn 1903-1966 BioIn 16, MajTwCW, WorAlBi
Waugh, George St&PR 91
Waugh, Greg 1953- WhoSSW 91
Waugh, Hillary 1920- TwCCr&M 91
Waugh, James Stephen 1947- St&PR 91
Waugh, Jane BiDEWW
Waugh, Jennie Suiter 1930- WhoAmW 91
Waugh, Jim 1933- Ballpl 90
Waugh, John David 1932- WhoAm 90
Waugh, John Stewart 1929- WhoAm 90
Waugh, Lyndon Dale 1945- BiDrAPA 89
Waugh, Richard Earl 1947- WhoE 91
Waugh, Robert J L BiDrAPA 89
Waugh, Robert James 1934- St&PR 91
Waugh, Sidney PenDiDA 89
Waugh, Sidney B 1904-1963 WhoAmA 91N
Waugh, Theodore Rogers 1926- WhoAm 90
Waughtal, Perry McAllister 1935- St&PR 91
Wauhop, Iles William 1934- St&PR 91
Wauquier, Albert 1940- WhoWor 91
Waurishuk, James M., Jr. 1954- WhoWor 91
Wauters, Luc 1926- St&PR 91
Wauters, Michel PenDiDA 89
Wauters, Philippe PenDiDA 89
Wauters, Pierre PenDiDA 89
Wauters, Ronald John 1959- BiDrAPA 89
Wautier, Jean Luc 1942- WhoWor 91
Wavell, Archibald Percival 1883-1950 WorAlBi
Wavestar NewAgMG
Wawrose, Frederick E 1929- BiDrAPA 89
Wawrose, Frederick Eugene 1929- WhoE 91
Wawrzyniak, Stephen David 1949- St&PR 91, WhoWor 91
Wax, Bernard 1930- WhoAm 90, WhoE 91
Wax, David 1939- St&PR 91
Wax, David M. WhoSSW 91
Wax, Edward L. BioIn 16
Wax, Edward L. 1937- WhoAm 90, WhoE 91
Wax, George Louis 1928- WhoSSW 91
Wax, Irving N. BioIn 16
Wax, John M 1948- WhoAmA 91
Wax, Morton 1932- ODwPR 91
Wax, Nadine Virginia 1927- St&PR 91, WhoAmW 91
Wax, Ray Van 1944- WhoWor 91
Wax, Rosalie Hankey 1911- WhoAm 90
Wax, Stanley H. 1941- St&PR 91
Wax, William Edward 1956- WhoAm 90
Waxberg, Joseph D 1922- BiDrAPA 89
Waxberg, Myron D. 1933- St&PR 91
Waxenberg, Alan M. 1935- WhoAm 90, WhoE 91
Waxenberger, Gabriele Maria 1956- WhoWor 91
Waxlax, Lorne R. 1933- WhoAm 90
Waxlax, Lorne Rudolph 1933- St&PR 91
Waxler, Robert Phillip 1944- WhoE 91
Waxman, Albert Samuel 1935- WhoAm 90
Waxman, Armond 1938- St&PR 91
Waxman, Avrom S. 1930- St&PR 91
Waxman, David 1918- WhoAm 90
Waxman, Franz 1906-1967 OxCPMus
Waxman, Henry Arnold BioIn 16
Waxman, Henry Arnold 1939- WhoAm 90
Waxman, Herbert J. 1913- WhoWrEP 89
Waxman, Joanne 1934- WhoAmW 91
Waxman, Judith Leslie 1953- BiDrAPA 89
Waxman, Louis E. St&PR 91N
Waxman, Melvin 1934- St&PR 91
Waxman, Mordecai 1917- BioIn 16
Waxman, Stephen George 1945- WhoAm 90
Way, Alva Otis 1929- WhoAm 90
Way, Alva Otis, III 1929- St&PR 91
Way, Carol Jane 1940- WhoAmW 91
Way, Charles D. 1953- St&PR 91
Way, Darryl NewAgMG
Way, Edward Leong 1916- WhoAm 90
Way, George Erwin 1946- WhoEmL 91
Way, Jacob Edson, III 1947- WhoAm 90
Way, James L. 1926- WhoSSW 91
Way, Jeffrey Ivan 1962- WhoE 91
Way, Paul H. 1937- St&PR 91
Way, Richard D. 1941- St&PR 91
Way, Robert E. 1919- St&PR 91
Way, Robert L. 1941- ODwPR 91
Way, Walter Lee 1931- WhoAm 90
Way, Wilson Spencer 1910- WhoSSW 91
Wayans, Keenen BioIn 16
Wayans, Keenen Ivory 1958?- News 91-1 [port]
Waybourn, Marilu M. 1931- WhoWrEP 89
Waybright, George Warren St&PR 91
Wayburn, Ned 1874-1942 OxCPMus
Waydo, George J. 1943- WhoAm 90
Wayenberg, Daniel 1929- IntWWM 90, PenDiMP
Waygood, Ernest Roy 1918- WhoAm 90
Waylan, C.J. 1941- St&PR 91
Waylan, Mildred WhoWrEP 89
Wayland, April Halprin AuBYP 90
Wayland, Bill BioIn 16
Wayland, David M. 1943- St&PR 91
Wayland, Francis 1796-1865 BioIn 16
Wayland, J. A. EncAL
Wayland, James Harold 1909- WhoAm 90
Wayland, Janice Rhea 1949- WhoE 91
Wayland, Joan T 1940- BiDrAPA 89
Wayland, Julius Augustus BioIn 16
Wayland, L. C. Newton 1909- WhoWor 91
Wayland, Newton Hart 1940- IntWWM 90, WhoAm 90
Wayland, Russell Gibson, Jr. 1913- WhoAm 90
Wayland, William F. 1935- St&PR 91
Waylor, Cheryl Watson 1943- WhoAmW 91
Wayman, C. Marvin 1930- WhoAm 90
Wayman, David Anthony 1950- WhoEmL 91, WhoWor 91
Wayman, Morris 1915- WhoAm 90
Wayman, Patrick Arthur 1927- WhoWor 91
Wayman, Richard E. 1934- St&PR 91
Wayman, Russell 1945- St&PR 91
Waymire, Donald Marion 1928- WhoSSW 91
Waymire, Jimmy D. 1944- St&PR 91
Waymon, Sam DrBlPA 90
Waymouth, Charity 1915- WhoAmW 91
Waymouth, John Francis 1926- WhoE 91
Wayne, Aissa BioIn 16
Wayne, Alan B. 1939- ODwPR 91
Wayne, Anthony 1745-1796 BioIn 16, EncCRAm, WhNaAH, WorAlBi
Wayne, Barry 1941- St&PR 91
Wayne, Bill Tom 1946- WhoSSW 91
Wayne, David 1914- WorAlBi
Wayne, Dennis Owen 1943- BiDrAPA 89
Wayne, Donald 1913- WhoAm 90
Wayne, Elsie Eleanore 1932- WhoAmW 91, WhoE 91
Wayne, Frances 1870-1951 BioIn 16
Wayne, George J 1914- BiDrAPA 89
Wayne, Hal WhoWrEP 89
Wayne, Henriette L BiDrAPA 89
Wayne, Herbert Monteith 1932- St&PR 91
Wayne, Jane O. 1938- WhoWrEP 89
Wayne, John 1907-1979 BioIn 16, WorAlBi
Wayne, Johnny 1918-1990 NewYTBS 90
Wayne, June WhoAmA 91
Wayne, June Claire 1918- BiDWomA
Wayne, Justine Washington 1945- WhoAmW 91
Wayne, Kyra Petrovskaya 1918- WhoAmW 91
Wayne, Mabel 1904- OxCPMus
Wayne, Martin S BiDrAPA 89
Wayne, Marvin BioIn 16
Wayne, Michael 1944- St&PR 91
Wayne, Norman Murray 1941- St&PR 91
Wayne, Richard AuBYP 90
Wayne, Robert Andrew 1938- WhoWor 91
Wayne, Robert Jonathan 1951- WhoEmL 91
Wayne, Victor Samuel 1953- WhoWor 91
Waynick, Roger Scott St&PR 91
Waynick, William Thomas 1922- St&PR 91
Waynik, Cyril 1928- BiDrAPA 89, WhoE 91
Waynik, Mark 1953- BiDrAPA 89
Wayrick, Isobel 1937- St&PR 91
Ways, C. R. MajTwCW
Ways, John A. 1942- St&PR 91
Wayte, Alan 1936- WhoAm 90, WhoWor 91
Waytena, Gary Albert 1942- St&PR 91
Waz, Joseph Walter, Jr. 1953- WhoEmL 91
Wazeter, Francis X. 1925- St&PR 91
Wazeter, Mary BioIn 16
Wazir, Khalil al- BioIn 16
Waziri, Rafiq BiDrAPA 89
Wazzan, Ahmed Rassem Frank 1935- WhoAm 90
Wdowiak, John S. 1963- WhoE 91
Wdowinski, David 1895-1970 BioIn 16
Weadock, Daniel Peter 1939- WhoAm 90, WhoE 91, WhoWor 91
Weadock, Edward E. 1932- St&PR 91
Weadon, David Allan 1956- IntWWM 90
Weadon, Donald Alford, Jr. 1945- WhoWor 91
Weadon, William Randolph 1926- St&PR 91
Weagant, William Daniel 1929- St&PR 91
Weagly, W. Richard BioIn 16
Weagraff, John Duane 1928- WhoAm 90
Weakland, Kevin L. 1963- WhoE 91
Weakley, Clare George, Jr. 1928- WhoSSW 91, WhoWor 91
Weaks, Dan 1952- BioIn 16
Weaks, Nathan E. 1956- St&PR 91
Weale, Malcolm Angus 1947- IntWWM 90
Weale, Mary Jo 1924- WhoAmA 91
Weales, Randall S. WhoAm 90
Wealleans, Jon 1946- ConDes 90
Weamys, Anna BiDEWW, FemiCLE
Wean, John David BiDrAPA 89
Wean, Raymond John, Jr. 1921- St&PR 91
Wear, Donald D., Jr. BioIn 16
Wear, Donald D., Sr. BioIn 16
Wear, Kenneth Willard 1932- WhoSSW 91
Wear, Robert Joseph 1917- WhoE 91
Weare, Ashley 1927- St&PR 91
Weare, Mary E 1948- BiDrAPA 89
Weare, Shane 1936- WhoAmA 91
Wearin, Otha D. 1903-1990 BioIn 16, ConAu 131
Wearly, William Levi 1915- WhoAm 90
Wearn, Jonathan Richard 1943- WhoWor 91
Wearn, Wilson Cannon 1919- WhoAm 90, WhoSSW 91
Wearne, Michael Collin 1942- IntWWM 90
Weart, Carole Ege BioIn 16
Weart, Edith Lucie 1898?-1977 AuBYP 90
Weart, Spencer Richard 1942- WhoE 91
Weart, William 1872-1917 Ballpl 90
Weary, Daniel Croft 1927- St&PR 91
Weary, Marianne 1929- St&PR 91
Weary, Marlys Elaine 1939- WhoAmW 91
Weary, Ogdred ConAu 30NR
Weary, Peyton Edwin 1930- WhoAm 90
Weary, Thomas Squires 1925- WhoE 91, WhoWor 91
Weasler, Anthony B. 1905- St&PR 91
Weasler, Paul Anthony 1943- St&PR 91
Weather Report OxCPMus
Weatherbee, Artemus Edwin 1918- WhoAm 90
Weatherbee, Donald Emery 1932- WhoAm 90
Weatherbee, Ellen Gene Elliott 1939- WhoAmW 91
Weatherbee, Linda 1956- WhoAmW 91
Weatherbie, John Torrance 1939- WhoSSW 91
Weatherby, Buc 1939- St&PR 91
Weatherby, Eugene James 1943- WhoE 91
Weatherby, Gregg L. 1950- WhoWrEP 89
Weatherby, Susan Moormann 1950- WhoAmW 91
Weatherford, Elizabeth Ann BiDrAPA 89
Weatherford, J McIver ConAu 30NR
Weatherford, Jack ConAu 30NR
Weatherford, Jack McIver 1946- ConAu 30NR
Weatherford, Jack Ozburn 1924- St&PR 91, WhoSSW 91
Weatherford, James K. 1850- AmLegL
Weatherford, Ken M., Jr. 1951- St&PR 91
Weatherford, Marion BioIn 16
Weatherford, Teddy 1903-1945 OxCPMus, WorAlBi
Weatherford, William 1780?-1824 WhNaAH
Weatherford, Willis Duke, Jr. 1916- WhoAm 90
Weathergill, Anne BioIn 16
Weatherhead, Albert John 1925- St&PR 91
Weatherhead, Arthur Dixon 1921- BiDrAPA 89
Weatherhead, Bernard Anthony 1946- WhoWor 91
Weatherhead, Leslie 1893-1976 EncO&P 3
Weatherhead, Leslie D. 1893-1976 EncPaPR 91
Weatherholtz, Karen D. 1950- St&PR 91
Weatherly, Fred E. 1848-1929 OxCPMus
Weatherly, Haldon Lee 1933- St&PR 91
Weatherly, John Stephen 1952- St&PR 91
Weatherly, Margaret Hiscock 1926- WhoE 91
Weatherly, Phyllis Norrington 1957- WhoSSW 91
Weatherly, Robert Stone, Jr. 1929- WhoAm 90
Weatherly, Roy 1915- Ballpl 90
Weatherly, Thomas Burdett 1914- WhoAm 90
Weatherly, Toby Lane 1953- WhoSSW 91
Weatherly, William Kingsley, Jr. 1933- BiDrAPA 89
Weatherred, Thurman W. 1932- St&PR 91
Weathers, Carl BioIn 16
Weathers, Carl 1948- DrBlPA 90
Weathers, Felicia 1937- BioIn 16, IntWWM 90, PenDiMP
Weathers, Lawrence Martin 1924- WhoSSW 91
Weathersby, Cecil Jerry 1952- WhoSSW 91
Weathersby, George Byron 1944- St&PR 91, WhoAm 90, WhoWrEP 89
Weathersby, William Cecil 1941- WhoAm 90
Weatherseed, Joan BioIn 16
Weatherston, George Douglas, Jr. 1952- WhoSSW 91
Weatherstone, Dennis 1930- WhoAm 90, WhoE 91
Weatherup, Wendy Gaines 1952- WhoAmW 91, WhoWor 91
Weatherwax, Clara FemiCLE
Weatherwax, David E. 1930- St&PR 91
Weaver, Albert Bruce 1917- WhoAm 90
Weaver, Alvin BioIn 16
Weaver, Amanda Louise 1948- WhoAmW 91
Weaver, Andrew Bennett 1946- WhoSSW 91
Weaver, Andrew Dudley 1929- St&PR 91
Weaver, Arthur Gordon 1915- WhoAm 90
Weaver, Arthur Lawrence 1936- WhoWor 91
Weaver, Barbara Frances 1927- WhoAm 90, WhoAmW 91
Weaver, Betty Louise 1929- St&PR 91
Weaver, Bill Thomas 1925- WhoWor 91
Weaver, Bobby Joe 1934- WhoSSW 91
Weaver, Buck 1890-1956 Ballpl 90 [port]
Weaver, Carlton Davis 1921- WhoAm 90
Weaver, Carrie Etta 1935- WhoSSW 91
Weaver, Charles Henry 1914- WhoAm 90
Weaver, Charles Horace 1927- WhoSSW 91
Weaver, Charles Lyndell, Jr. 1945- WhoEmL 91, WhoWor 91
Weaver, Charles Richard 1928- WhoAm 90
Weaver, Charles S. 1932- St&PR 91
Weaver, Charles Stanley 1922- WhoSSW 91
Weaver, Charles Steele 1918- WhoAm 90
Weaver, Clarence Lahr 1904- WhoWrEP 89
Weaver, Clark E. 1940- St&PR 91
Weaver, Connie Marie 1950- WhoAmW 91
Weaver, David Hugh 1946- WhoAm 90
Weaver, Dawn Lerene 1948- WhoAmW 91
Weaver, Debbie Lakin BiDrAPA 89
Weaver, Dennis NewAgE 90
Weaver, Dennis 1924- WhoAm 90, WorAlBi
Weaver, Donna B. 1950- ODwPR 91
Weaver, Donna Rae 1945- WhoAmW 91, WhoEmL 91, WhoWor 91

Weaver, Doodles 1911-1983 *BioIn 16*
Weaver, Earl *BioIn 16*
Weaver, Earl 1930- *Ballpl 90 [port], WorAlBi*
Weaver, Earl W. 1908- *St&PR 91*
Weaver, Edward H 1947- *BiDrAPA 89*
Weaver, Edward Myers 1927- *St&PR 91*
Weaver, Edward T. 1931- *WhoAm 90*
Weaver, Elissa Barbara 1940- *WhoAmW 91*
Weaver, Eric James 1938- *WhoE 91*
Weaver, Floyd *BioIn 16*
Weaver, Floyd 1941- *Ballpl 90*
Weaver, Francis Joseph, Jr. 1945- *WhoWor 91*
Weaver, Franklin Thomas 1932- *WhoAm 90*
Weaver, Fritz 1926- *ConTFT 8, WorAlBi*
Weaver, Galen Roy 1931- *BiDrAPA 89*
Weaver, George S. 1934- *St&PR 91*
Weaver, Glenn M 1921- *BiDrAPA 89*
Weaver, Gordon Allison 1937- *WhoWrEP 89*
Weaver, Howard Cecil 1950- *WhoAm 90*
Weaver, Jacqueline Lang 1947- *WhoEmL 91*
Weaver, James 1937- *IntWWM 90*
Weaver, James Elmer 1947- *WhoEmL 91*
Weaver, James P. 1929- *St&PR 91*
Weaver, James Richard 1953- *WhoEmL 91*
Weaver, Jerry Kent 1941- *St&PR 91*
Weaver, Jim 1903-1983 *Ballpl 90*
Weaver, John Barney 1920- *WhoAmA 91*
Weaver, John Borland 1937- *WhoAm 90*
Weaver, John Boyd 1925- *St&PR 91*
Weaver, John Carrier 1915- *WhoAm 90*
Weaver, John Clark 1933- *WhoAm 90*
Weaver, John Downing 1912- *AuBYP 90*
Weaver, John H. 1915- *St&PR 91*
Weaver, John L. 1936- *St&PR 91*
Weaver, John Lockerbie 1936- *WhoAm 90, WhoSSW 91*
Weaver, John Whiteside 1929- *WhoSSW 91*
Weaver, Karl E.C. 1950- *BiDrAPA 89*
Weaver, Katherine Bell 1954- *BiDrAPA 89*
Weaver, Kennard R. 1940- *St&PR 91*
Weaver, Kenneth Newcomer 1927- *WhoAm 90*
Weaver, Lawrence Clayton 1924- *WhoAm 90*
Weaver, Lee A. 1932- *St&PR 91*
Weaver, Linda M. 1946- *WhoAmW 91*
Weaver, Linda Susan 1965- *WhoAmW 91*
Weaver, Lloyd *BioIn 16*
Weaver, Lynn Edward 1930- *WhoAm 90, WhoSSW 91*
Weaver, Marguerite McKinnie 1925- *WhoAmW 91, WhoSSW 91, WhoWor 91*
Weaver, Marianne Carol Gruhn 1942- *IntWWM 90*
Weaver, Marita V. 1924- *BiDrAPA 89*
Weaver, Mark R. 1961- *ODwPR 91*
Weaver, Marshall Gueringer 1954- *WhoSSW 91*
Weaver, Martha Louise 1926- *WhoAmW 91*
Weaver, Melissa Ellen 1961- *WhoEmL 91*
Weaver, Michael James 1946- *WhoWor 91*
Weaver, Mollie Little 1934- *WhoAmW 91*
Weaver, Monte 1906- *Ballpl 90*
Weaver, Pamela Ann 1947- *WhoAmW 91*
Weaver, Pat *BioIn 16*
Weaver, Paul David 1943- *St&PR 91, WhoAm 90*
Weaver, Paulino *WhNaAH*
Weaver, Richard L., II 1941- *WhoAm 90, WhoWrEP 89*
Weaver, Richard M. 1910-1963 *BioIn 16*
Weaver, Richard R. 1935- *St&PR 91*
Weaver, Rita Margaret 1925- *WhoAmW 91*
Weaver, Robert B. 1939- *St&PR 91*
Weaver, Robert C. 1907- *WorAlBi*
Weaver, Robert Clifton 1907- *BiDrUSE 89, WhoAm 90*
Weaver, Sharon Tamargo 1947- *WhoAmW 91, WhoSSW 91*
Weaver, Sigourney *BioIn 16*
Weaver, Sigourney 1949- *WhoAm 90, WhoAmW 91, WorAlBi*
Weaver, Susan M. 1948- *WhoEmL 91*
Weaver, Sylvester *BioIn 16*
Weaver, Sylvester Laflin, Jr. 1908- *WhoAm 90*
Weaver, Terry Royce 1951- *WhoEmL 91*
Weaver, Thomas 1929- *WhoWrEP 89*
Weaver, Thomas Harwell 1950- *WhoSSW 91*
Weaver, Troy *BioIn 16*
Weaver, Vey Oden 1954- *WhoSSW 91*
Weaver, Vicky Lynn 1950- *WhoAmW 91*
Weaver, Virginia D. *ODwPR 91*
Weaver, Virginia Dove *WhoAmW 91*
Weaver, Ward *AuBYP 90*
Weaver, Warren, Jr. 1923- *WhoAm 90, WhoE 91*
Weaver, Warren Eldred 1921- *WhoAm 90*
Weaver, William 1923- *BioIn 16*
Weaver, William Bruce 1946- *WhoEmL 91*
Weaver, William Charles 1941- *WhoAm 90*
Weaver, William Clair, Jr. 1936- *WhoWor 91*
Weaver, William Edward 1931- *St&PR 91*
Weaver, William Merritt, Jr. 1912- *St&PR 91, WhoAm 90*
Weavers, The *OxCPMus*
Weavil, David C. 1951- *St&PR 91*
Weavil, David Carlton 1951- *WhoAm 90*
Weaving, John Weymouth 1936- *IntWWM 90*
Weawa *WhNaAH*
Weawea *WhNaAH*
Webb, Adrian Leslie 1956- *BiDrAPA 89*
Webb, Aileen Osborn 1892-1979 *WhoAmA 91N*
Webb, Alan Whitney 1939- *WhoAm 90*
Webb, Alexander Dwight 1952- *WhoAmA 91*
Webb, Alyce Elizabeth 1935- *DrBlPA 90*
Webb, Andrew 1961- *BioIn 16*
Webb, Anthony Allan 1943- *WhoAm 90*
Webb, Arthur Philip 1945- *St&PR 91*
Webb, Beatrice 1858-1943 *FemiCLE, WorAlBi*
Webb, Beatrice Potter 1858-1943 *BioIn 16*
Webb, Bernice Larson *WhoWrEP 89*
Webb, Billie Jean 1952- *WhoSSW 91*
Webb, Boyd 1947- *BioIn 16*
Webb, Brainard Troutman, Jr. 1943- *St&PR 91, WhoAm 90*
Webb, Brian Lockwood 1949- *WhoSSW 91, WhoWor 91*
Webb, Bruce *BioIn 16*
Webb, Carlos Swan 1951- *WhoSSW 91*
Webb, Carmen Thurston 1961- *BiDrAPA 89*
Webb, Cecil S. *AuBYP 90*
Webb, Charles *PenDiDA 89*
Webb, Charles Albert 1917- *WhoAm 90*
Webb, Charles Allen, Jr. 1916- *St&PR 91*
Webb, Charles Haizlip 1933- *IntWWM 90*
Webb, Charles Haizlip, Jr. 1933- *WhoAm 90*
Webb, Charles Harry 1953- *WhoSSW 91*
Webb, Charles Richard 1919- *WhoAm 90*
Webb, Charles Richard 1939- *BioIn 16*
Webb, Chick 1907-1939 *DrBlPA 90*
Webb, Chick 1909-1939 *BioIn 16, OxCPMus, WorAlBi*
Webb, Chloe *BioIn 16, ConTFT 8*
Webb, Chris *BioIn 16*
Webb, Clarence H. 1902- *BioIn 16*
Webb, Clifford Cyril 1895-1972 *AuBYP 90*
Webb, Clifton 1891-1966 *OxCPMus*
Webb, Clifton 1896-1966 *WorAlBi*
Webb, Cyrus E. 1930- *St&PR 91*
Webb, Dana Luanne 1952- *WhoAmW 91*
Webb, David Allardice 1912- *WhoWor 91*
Webb, David F. 1930- *St&PR 91*
Webb, Deleno H, III 1939- *BiDrAPA 89*
Webb, Donald Arthur 1926- *WhoAm 90*
Webb, Donna Louise 1929- *WhoAmW 91*
Webb, Douglas A. 1942- *St&PR 91*
Webb, Earl 1898-1965 *Ballpl 90*
Webb, Edmund Fuller 1835-1898 *AmLegL*
Webb, Electra *BioIn 16*
Webb, Eliza Osgood Vanderbilt 1860-1936 *BioIn 16*
Webb, Elizabeth 1663?-1726? *FemiCLE*
Webb, Elizabeth S 1943- *BiDrAPA 89*
Webb, Esther *BioIn 16*
Webb, Eugene 1938- *WhoAm 90*
Webb, Faye Rappold 1941- *WhoSSW 91*
Webb, Frank 1927- *WhoAmA 91*
Webb, Frank McConville 1954- *WhoSSW 91*
Webb, George 1917- *OxCPMus*
Webb, George H. 1920- *St&PR 91*
Webb, George Henry 1920- *WhoAm 90*
Webb, Gilson Shaw *BiDrAPA 89*
Webb, Glenda Jefferson 1954- *WhoSSW 91*
Webb, Gloria O. 1931- *WhoAmW 91, WhoSSW 91*
Webb, Guy Edmund, Jr. 1931- *WhoAm 90*
Webb, Hank 1950- *Ballpl 90*
Webb, Helene B. 1951- *WhoAmW 91*
Webb, Henry Calhoun, Jr. 1939- *WhoSSW 91*
Webb, Horace S. 1940- *ODwPR 91*
Webb, Howard E. 1940- *St&PR 91*
Webb, Howard William, Jr. 1925- *WhoAm 90*
Webb, Igor Michael 1941- *WhoAm 90*
Webb, Ivan Wayne 1951- *St&PR 91*
Webb, J.S. 1919- *St&PR 91*
Webb, Jack *TwCCr&M 91*
Webb, Jack 1920-1982 *WorAlBi*
Webb, Jack M. 1936- *WhoAm 90*
Webb, James 1946-1980 *EncO&P 3*
Webb, James B. 1945- *St&PR 91*
Webb, James Edward 1928- *WhoWrEP 89*
Webb, James H. *BioIn 16*
Webb, James Hammond 1820-1896 *AmLegL*
Webb, James Louis, Jr. 1955- *WhoEmL 91*
Webb, James Okrum, Jr. 1931- *WhoAm 90*
Webb, James Robert 1954- *WhoSSW 91*
Webb, James Robert, III 1943- *WhoSSW 91*
Webb, James T. *BioIn 16*
Webb, James Wallace 1938- *WhoSSW 91*
Webb, James Watson 1802-1884 *BioIn 16*
Webb, Jennifer *BioIn 16*
Webb, Jere M. 1944- *WhoAm 90*
Webb, Jerry Edward 1945- *WhoSSW 91*
Webb, Jervis Campbell 1915- *St&PR 91*
Webb, Jilla Rose 1923- *WhoAmW 91*
Webb, Jimmy 1946- *EncPR&S 89, OxCPMus*
Webb, Joan L *BiDrAPA 89*
Webb, Joe Steve 1932- *St&PR 91*
Webb, John 1926- *WhoAm 90*
Webb, John Clayton, Jr. 1937- *WhoSSW 91*
Webb, John Day, III 1949- *WhoEmL 91*
Webb, John Patten, Jr. 1939- *WhoSSW 91*
Webb, Joseph S. *St&PR 91*
Webb, Judith E. 1952- *ODwPR 91*
Webb, Julian 1911- *WhoAm 90, WhoWor 91*
Webb, Julian H. 1902-1988 *BioIn 16*
Webb, Kaye 1914- *SmATA 60 [port]*
Webb, Kenneth B. 1928- *St&PR 91*
Webb, Kristi Chambers 1946- *WhoAmW 91*
Webb, Lamar Thaxter 1928- *WhoSSW 91*
Webb, Lance 1909- *WhoAm 90*
Webb, Leon, Jr. 1943- *St&PR 91*
Webb, Lise McClendon 1952- *WhoAmW 91*
Webb, Lorrayne Beth 1925- *WhoAm 90*
Webb, Lynne McGovern 1951- *WhoAmW 91*
Webb, Margaret Taylor 1928- *WhoAmW 91*
Webb, Marianne 1936- *IntWWM 90*
Webb, Mark Chatman 1959- *BiDrAPA 89*
Webb, Martha Jeanne 1947- *WhoAmW 91*
Webb, Martin E. 1946- *St&PR 91*
Webb, Marvin LeRoy 1946- *WhoEmL 91*
Webb, Mary 1617-1697 *BiDEWW*
Webb, Mary 1779-1861 *BioIn 16*
Webb, Mary 1881-1927 *FemiCLE*
Webb, Mary Gladys Meredith 1881-1927 *BioIn 16*
Webb, Melody 1946- *WhoWrEP 89*
Webb, Michael D *BiDrAPA 89*
Webb, Michael Steven 1954- *WhoEmL 91*
Webb, Murrell Lee 1938- *St&PR 91*
Webb, Norene Elizabeth 1948- *St&PR 91*
Webb, Omri Kenneth, Jr. 1926- *WhoAm 90*
Webb, Orville Lynn 1931- *WhoSSW 91*
Webb, Patricia Ruth Jarvis 1938- *WhoSSW 91*
Webb, Patrick 1955- *WhoAmA 91*
Webb, Paul D. 1935- *St&PR 91*
Webb, Paula Stephania 1961- *WhoWrEP 89*
Webb, Peggy Sue Ezzell 1958- *WhoAmW 91*
Webb, Peter 1945- *ODwPR 91*
Webb, Philip 1831-1915 *PenDiDA 89*
Webb, Philip John, Sr. 1934- *WhoSSW 91*
Webb, Phyllis 1927- *FemiCLE*
Webb, R.G. 1926- *St&PR 91*
Webb, Ralph 1951- *WhoSSW 91*
Webb, Ralph Lee 1934- *WhoAm 90*
Webb, Rebecca Keith 1952- *WhoE 91*
Webb, Rex Livingston, Jr. 1940- *WhoSSW 91*
Webb, Richard C. 1915- *WhoAm 90*
Webb, Richard Duarte 1937- *WhoWor 91*
Webb, Richard Gilbert 1932- *WhoAm 90*
Webb, Richard Marshall *BiDrAPA 89*
Webb, Richard Olin 1938- *St&PR 91*
Webb, Richard Pierce 1941- *St&PR 91*
Webb, Richard Wilson *TwCCr&M 91*
Webb, Robert Kiefer 1922- *WhoAm 90*
Webb, Robert Lee 1926- *WhoAm 90*
Webb, Robert Mark *BiDrAPA 89*
Webb, Robert Mark 1953- *WhoE 91*
Webb, Robert N. *AuBYP 90*
Webb, Robert P. 1948- *St&PR 91*
Webb, Robert W 1906- *BiDrAPA 89*
Webb, Roger Stuart 1950- *WhoSSW 91*
Webb, Ronald Duane 1949- *WhoWor 91*
Webb, Rubin W. 1926- *WhoSSW 91*
Webb, Samuel F. 1853-1920 *AmLegL*
Webb, Sarah A 1948- *WhoAmA 91*
Webb, Sawney David 1936- *WhoAm 90*
Webb, Schuyler Cleveland 1951- *WhoSSW 91*
Webb, Sharon 1936- *ConAu 32NR*
Webb, Sharon Lynn 1936- *WhoWrEP 89*
Webb, Sidney 1859-1947 *BioIn 16*
Webb, Sidney James 1859-1947 *WorAlBi*
Webb, Skeeter 1909-1986 *Ballpl 90*
Webb, Spud *BioIn 16*
Webb, Theodore Stratton 1930- *St&PR 91*
Webb, Theodore Stratton, Jr. 1930- *WhoAm 90*
Webb, Thomas *PenDiDA 89*
Webb, Thomas C. 1934- *St&PR 91*
Webb, Thomas Evan 1932- *WhoAm 90*
Webb, Thomas Irwin, Jr. 1948- *WhoEmL 91, WhoWor 91*
Webb, Thomas Wilkes *PenDiDA 89*
Webb, Todd 1905- *WhoAm 90, WhoAmA 91*
Webb, Virginia 1920- *BioIn 16*
Webb, W. Roger 1941- *WhoSSW 91*
Webb, Walter Prescott 1888-1963 *BioIn 16*
Webb, Watt Wetmore 1927- *WhoAm 90*
Webb, Watts Rankin 1922- *WhoAm 90*
Webb, Wilfred T. 1865?- *AmLegL*
Webb, William Duncan 1930- *WhoAm 90*
Webb, William Hess 1905- *WhoAm 90*
Webb, William John 1922- *WhoE 91, WhoWor 91*
Webb, William L, Jr. 1930- *BiDrAPA 89*
Webb, William Larry 1946- *WhoEmL 91, WhoSSW 91*
Webb, William Loyd, Jr. 1925- *WhoAm 90*
Webb, William Y. 1935- *WhoAm 90*
Webb, Yvonne 1954- *St&PR 91*
Webbe, Frank Michael 1947- *WhoSSW 91*
Webbe, Gale D. *BioIn 16*
Webbe, Scotson 1917- *St&PR 91*
Webber, Andrew Lloyd 1948- *BioIn 16*
Webber, Charles Owen 1926- *BiDrAPA 89*
Webber, Charles Wilkins 1819-1856 *LiHiK*
Webber, David Anthony 1929- *WhoAm 90, WhoE 91*
Webber, Diana L. 1960- *WhoAmW 91*
Webber, Donald E. 1945- *St&PR 91*
Webber, E. Leland *NewYTBS 90*
Webber, E. Leland 1920-1990 *BioIn 16*
Webber, Edythe Marie 1954- *WhoAmW 91*
Webber, Frederick N 1934- *BiDrAPA 89*
Webber, George Ethen *BiDrAPA 89*
Webber, H Price 1845-1927 *OxCCanT [port]*
Webber, Helen *WhoAmA 91*
Webber, Howard Rodney 1933- *WhoAm 90*
Webber, Janet Dee 1958- *WhoAmW 91*
Webber, Janet Ellen 1963- *WhoAmW 91*
Webber, Joel *BioIn 16*
Webber, John 1949- *IntWWM 90*
Webber, John A. 1912- *St&PR 91*
Webber, John Bentley 1941- *WhoAm 90, WhoWor 91*
Webber, John E. 1751-1793 *WhNaAH*
Webber, Julian Lloyd *PenDiMP*
Webber, Les 1915-1987 *Ballpl 90*
Webber, Lisa Marie 1964- *WhoAmW 91*
Webber, Lynne Josephine 1956- *IntWWM 90*
Webber, Michael David 1940- *WhoWor 91*
Webber, Mildred *BioIn 16*
Webber, Mildred 1956- *WhoAmW 91*
Webber, Pamela Bayliss 1954- *WhoSSW 91*
Webber, Ralph G. 1923- *St&PR 91*
Webber, Randall M. 1942- *St&PR 91*
Webber, Robert 1924-1989 *BioIn 16*
Webber, Robert Ernest 1947- *WhoE 91*
Webber, Robert F. 1946- *St&PR 91*
Webber, Thomas Raymond 1943- *WhoAm 90*
Webber, William Alexander 1934- *WhoAm 90*
Webber, William Francis 1943- *WhoE 91*
Webby, George J. 1929-1989 *BioIn 16*
Webeck, Alfred Stanley 1913- *St&PR 91*
Webel, James Buell 1923- *St&PR 91*
Webel, Lewis A. 1934- *ODwPR 91*
Webel, Richard Karl *WhoAm 90*
Weber & Fields *OxCPMus*
Weber, Adolf Otto Albert 1922- *WhoWor 91*
Weber, Alan J. 1949- *St&PR 91*
Weber, Alan Jay 1949- *WhoAm 90*
Weber, Albert Jacob 1919- *WhoAmA 91*
Weber, Alexander 1921- *St&PR 91*
Weber, Alfred 1868-1958 *BioIn 16*
Weber, Alfred Herman 1906- *WhoAm 90*
Weber, Aloysia 1759?-1839 *PenDiMP*
Weber, Amy L. *EarBlAP*
Weber, Anthony Clemens 1952- *St&PR 91*
Weber, Arnold R. 1929- *WhoAm 90, WhoWor 91*
Weber, Arthur 1926- *WhoAm 90*
Weber, Barbara M. 1945- *WhoAmW 91, WhoWor 91*
Weber, Barrie R. 1940- *St&PR 91*
Weber, Beverly Joy 1932- *WhoWrEP 89*
Weber, Bob 1934- *EncACom*
Weber, Bradley Paul 1961- *WhoSSW 91*
Weber, Brom 1917- *WhoAm 90, WhoWrEP 89*
Weber, Carl Maria von 1786-1826 *BioIn 16, PenDiMP A, WorAlBi*
Weber, Carol A. 1940- *WhoAmW 91*

Weber, Charlene Lydia 1943- *WhoAmW 91*
Weber, Charles Edward 1924- *WhoWrEP 89*
Weber, Charles Edward 1930- *WhoAm 90*
Weber, Clarence Adam 1903- *WhoE 91, WhoWor 91*
Weber, Cynthia Green 1962- *WhoSSW 91*
Weber, Daniel J *BiDrAPA 89*
Weber, Daniel Joseph *BiDrAPA 89*
Weber, Daniel R. *St&PR 91*
Weber, David Carter 1924- *WhoAm 90*
Weber, David Harold *BiDrAPA 89*
Weber, David Malcolm 1948- *St&PR 91, WhoEmL 91*
Weber, David Paul 1945- *St&PR 91*
Weber, Debora 1955- *BioIn 16*
Weber, Debra Rose 1952- *WhoEmL 91*
Weber, Donald Joseph 1950- *WhoSSW 91*
Weber, Donald Otto 1953- *St&PR 91*
Weber, Donald W. 1936- *St&PR 91, WhoAm 90, WhoSSW 91*
Weber, Donna Lyn 1948- *WhoSSW 91*
Weber, Donna Marie *BiDrAPA 89*
Weber, Douglas Jay 1952- *St&PR 91*
Weber, Elizabeth Ann 1950- *WhoWrEP 89*
Weber, Emile S *BiDrAPA 89*
Weber, Enid W. *WhoAmW 91*
Weber, Ernest Theodore 1938- *WhoAm 90*
Weber, Ernesto Juan 1930- *WhoWor 91*
Weber, Ernst 1901- *WhoAm 90*
Weber, Ernst Friedrich Albrecht 1945- *WhoWor 91*
Weber, Ernst Heinrich 1795-1878 *WorAlBi*
Weber, Eugen 1925- *WhoAm 90*
Weber, Eugene E. 1942- *St&PR 91*
Weber, Eva L 1929- *BiDrAPA 89*
Weber, Evelyn Joyce 1928- *WhoAmW 91*
Weber, Fred I. *BioIn 16*
Weber, Fred J. 1919- *WhoAm 90*
Weber, Fred Warner 1922- *BiDrAPA 89*
Weber, Frederick Theodore 1883-1956 *WhoAmA 91N*
Weber, Gail E. 1943- *St&PR 91*
Weber, George 1922- *WhoAm 90*
Weber, George R 1919- *BiDrAPA 89*
Weber, George Richard 1929- *WhoWor 91*
Weber, George Russell 1911- *WhoWor 91*
Weber, George Thomas, Jr. 1947- *WhoE 91*
Weber, Gerald J. 1914-1989 *BioIn 16*
Weber, Gerald Joseph 1914- *WhoE 91*
Weber, Glenn Allan 1945- *BiDrAPA 89*
Weber, Gordon J. 1947- *St&PR 91*
Weber, Gustav Friedrich, Jr. 1916- *WhoAm 90*
Weber, H. Patrick 1949- *WhoEmL 91*
Weber, Hans Hermann Julius Wilhelm 1896-1974 *DcScB S2*
Weber, Harm Allen 1926- *WhoAm 90*
Weber, Henry A. 1915- *St&PR 91*
Weber, Herbert G. 1941- *St&PR 91*
Weber, Herman *BioIn 16*
Weber, Herman Jacob 1927- *WhoAm 90*
Weber, Hugo 1918-1971 *WhoAmA 91N*
Weber, I. 1920- *St&PR 91*
Weber, Idelle *WhoAmA 91*
Weber, Idelle Lois 1932- *WhoAm 90*
Weber, Jack E., Jr. 1937- *St&PR 91*
Weber, James A. 1932- *ODwPR 91*
Weber, James Stuart 1947- *WhoEmL 91*
Weber, Jan *WhoAmA 91*
Weber, Janet M. 1936- *WhoAm 90, WhoAmW 91*
Weber, Jean M 1933- *WhoAmA 91*
Weber, Jean MacPhail 1933- *WhoAm 90*
Weber, Jeff *BioIn 16*
Weber, Jeffery Allen 1953- *St&PR 91*
Weber, Jeffrey Eric 1950- *WhoE 91*
Weber, Jerome Charles 1938- *WhoAm 90*
Weber, Joe 1867-1942 *OxCPMus*
Weber, John *WhoAmA 91*
Weber, John Bertram 1930- *WhoWor 91*
Weber, John Fisher 1956- *WhoSSW 91*
Weber, John J. 1941- *St&PR 91*
Weber, John Joseph *BiDrAPA 89*
Weber, John Pitman 1942- *WhoAmA 91*
Weber, John R. 1946- *St&PR 91*
Weber, Joseph 1920- *St&PR 91*
Weber, Joseph A., Jr. 1932- *St&PR 91*
Weber, Joseph H. 1930- *WhoAm 90*
Weber, Joseph R. *BioIn 16*
Weber, Josepha 1758?-1819 *PenDiMP*
Weber, Judith E 1938- *SmATA 64 [port]*
Weber, Julian L. 1929- *St&PR 91, WhoAm 90*
Weber, Karen *WhoAmA 91*
Weber, Karin Michele 1965- *WhoAmW 91*
Weber, Karl A. *NewYTBS 90*
Weber, Karl William 1953- *WhoAm 90*
Weber, Katharine *BioIn 16*
Weber, Kathleen Susan 1954- *WhoAmW 91*
Weber, Kem 1889-1963 *PenDiDA 89*
Weber, Lawrence James 1941- *St&PR 91*
Weber, Lenora 1895-1971 *AuBYP 90*
Weber, Leo L. 1929- *St&PR 91, WhoAm 90*
Weber, Linda Ficklin 1926- *WhoAmW 91*
Weber, Lois 1882-1939 *BioIn 16*
Weber, Louis M. *BioIn 16*
Weber, Ludwig 1899-1974 *PenDiMP*
Weber, Margaret Laura Jane 1933- *WhoAmW 91*
Weber, Margrit 1924- *PenDiMP*
Weber, Marilyn Ann Minch 1934- *WhoAmW 91*
Weber, Mark Alan 1953- *WhoEmL 91*
Weber, Mary Aquinas 1923- *WhoAm 90*
Weber, Mary Carol *BiDrAPA 89*
Weber, Mary Nord *ODwPR 91*
Weber, Marysia *BiDrAPA 89*
Weber, Max 1864-1920 *BioIn 16, WorAlBi*
Weber, Max 1881-1961 *WhoAmA 91N*
Weber, Max O. 1929- *WhoAm 90*
Weber, Max Otis 1929- *St&PR 91*
Weber, Miles L 1934- *BiDrAPA 89*
Weber, Mili *BioIn 16*
Weber, Molly Smith 1957- *WhoAmW 91, WhoEmL 91, WhoWor 91*
Weber, Morton M. 1922- *WhoAm 90*
Weber, Nanci Trivers 1935- *WhoAmW 91*
Weber, Nancy Dworkin 1951- *WhoAmW 91*
Weber, Nicholas Fox 1947- *BioIn 16*
Weber, Nicholas Noyes 1936- *St&PR 91*
Weber, Owen 1946- *WhoAm 90*
Weber, Patricia Frances *WhoAmW 91*
Weber, Paul J. 1937- *St&PR 91*
Weber, Perry James 1945- *St&PR 91*
Weber, Pete *BioIn 16*
Weber, Peter *St&PR 91*
Weber, Peter W. 1955- *ODwPR 91*
Weber, Philip, Jr. 1935- *St&PR 91*
Weber, Philip Joseph 1909- *WhoAm 90*
Weber, R. Christopher 1955- *St&PR 91*
Weber, Ralph L. 1913- *St&PR 91*
Weber, Read *BioIn 16*
Weber, Rebecca Cecile 1959- *WhoAmW 91*
Weber, Richard Albert 1948- *WhoSSW 91*
Weber, Richard Frank 1931- *St&PR 91*
Weber, Richard K. 1934- *St&PR 91*
Weber, Robert Carl 1950- *WhoEmL 91*
Weber, Robert Donald 1936- *St&PR 91*
Weber, Robert Mathias 1939- *St&PR 91*
Weber, Robert Maxwell 1924- *WhoAm 90*
Weber, Ronald E. *ODwPR 91*
Weber, Ronald Gilbert 1916- *WhoAm 90*
Weber, Roy Edwin 1928- *WhoAm 90*
Weber, Samuel 1926- *WhoAm 90, WhoWrEP 89*
Weber, Shirley Anne 1928- *WhoWrEP 89*
Weber, Sol 1933- *WhoWrEP 89*
Weber, Stephen Lewis 1942- *WhoAm 90, WhoE 91*
Weber, Steven Allen 1945- *St&PR 91*
Weber, Susan Lee 1948- *WhoAmW 91*
Weber, Sybilla Mittell 1892-1957 *WhoAmA 91N*
Weber, Thomas William 1930- *WhoAm 90*
Weber, Vernon William 1949- *St&PR 91*
Weber, Vin 1952- *BioIn 16, WhoAm 90*
Weber, Walter Jacob, Jr. 1934- *WhoAm 90*
Weber, Warren G. 1938- *St&PR 91*
Weber, Warren Mark 1950- *WhoE 91*
Weber, Wendell William 1925- *WhoAm 90*
Weber, Wilford Alexander 1939- *WhoSSW 91*
Weber, William F 1937- *BiDrAPA 89*
Weber, William Frank 1927- *BiDrAPA 89*
Weber, William H. 1915- *St&PR 91*
Weber, William John 1928- *IntWWM 90*
Weber, William John 1949- *WhoEmL 91*
Weber, William P. 1940- *WhoAm 90, WhoSSW 91*
Weber-Kellermann, Ingeborg 1918- *EncCoWW*
Weber-Ries, Susan Ann 1956- *WhoAmW 91*
Weber-Toler, Wendy Diane 1951- *WhoAm 90*
Weberg, Lynn H. 1958- *St&PR 91*
Weberling, Ernest A. 1916- *St&PR 91*
Weberling, Patricia Kay 1959- *WhoAmW 91*
Webern, Anton 1883-1945 *PenDiMP A*
Webern, Anton Von 1883-1945 *WorAlBi*
Weberyd, Curt Allan 1926- *WhoWor 91*
Webling, Lucy 187-?- *FemiCLE*
Webling, Peggy 1870?- *FemiCLE*
Webne-Behrman, Harry Michael 1954- *WhoEmL 91*
Webster, Albert Knickerbocker 1937- *WhoAm 90, WhoE 91*
Webster, Arthur Gordon 1863-1923 *DcScB S2*
Webster, Augusta 1837-1894 *BioIn 16, FemiCLE*
Webster, Barbara D. *BioIn 16*
Webster, Ben 1909- *DrBIPA 90*
Webster, Ben 1909-1973 *BioIn 16, OxCPMus*
Webster, Bethuel M. 1900-1989 *BioIn 16*
Webster, Beveridge 1908- *IntWWM 90*
Webster, Bruce Charles 1957- *WhoEmL 91*
Webster, Burnice Hoyle 1910- *WhoSSW 91, WhoWor 91*
Webster, Charles Linsley 1930- *St&PR 91*
Webster, Charles M. 1918- *St&PR 91*
Webster, Christopher White 1953- *WhoEmL 91*
Webster, Daniel 1782-1852 *BiDrUSE 89, BioIn 16, WorAlBi*
Webster, Daniel J., Jr. 1947- *St&PR 91*
Webster, David *BioIn 16*
Webster, David 1930- *AuBYP 90*
Webster, David Arthur 1937- *WhoAm 90*
Webster, David Clark 1927- *WhoE 91*
Webster, David Deane 1939- *St&PR 91*
Webster, David Locke 1888-1976 *DcScB S2*
Webster, David Logan 1951- *WhoEmL 91*
Webster, David Newton 1934- *WhoE 91*
Webster, Dean K. 1929- *St&PR 91*
Webster, Derek 1934- *MusmAFA*
Webster, Diane Lynn 1954- *WhoWrEP 89*
Webster, Donald Frederick 1926- *IntWWM 90*
Webster, Donald Jordan 1946- *St&PR 91*
Webster, Ed *BioIn 16*
Webster, Edgar Lewis 1941- *WhoSSW 91*
Webster, Edward William 1922- *WhoAm 90*
Webster, Edwin Henry 1918- *WhoAm 90*
Webster, Eleanor Rudd 1920- *WhoAm 90*
Webster, Elroy *WhoAm 90*
Webster, Ernest 1923- *ConAu 132*
Webster, Francis Sinclair, III 1945- *St&PR 91*
Webster, Frank Craig *BiDrAPA 89*
Webster, Frederick Elmer, Jr. 1937- *WhoAm 90*
Webster, George Calvin 1924- *WhoWrEP 89*
Webster, George Drury 1921- *WhoAm 90*
Webster, Gerald Best 1944- *IntWWM 90*
Webster, Gladys *St&PR 91*
Webster, Guy Noble 1933- *St&PR 91*
Webster, H. Max 1931- *WhoAm 90*
Webster, H T 1885-1952 *WhoAmA 91N*
Webster, H. T. 1885-1953 *EncACom*
Webster, Harold A. *BioIn 16*
Webster, Harold S. 1935- *ODwPR 91, St&PR 91*
Webster, Helen Kay 1947- *WhoAmW 91*
Webster, Henry deForest 1927- *WhoAm 90, WhoE 91, WhoWor 91*
Webster, Jack *BioIn 16*
Webster, James A. 1952- *St&PR 91*
Webster, James Carmody 1938- *WhoE 91*
Webster, James E. 1919- *St&PR 91*
Webster, James Randolph, Jr. 1931- *WhoAm 90*
Webster, Jani Johe *WhoWrEP 89*
Webster, Jeffrey Leon 1941- *WhoWor 91*
Webster, Joe *AuBYP 90*
Webster, John 1575?-1634? *WorAlBi*
Webster, John 1580?-1625? *BioIn 16*
Webster, John Goodwin 1932- *WhoAm 90*
Webster, John K. 1928- *St&PR 91*
Webster, John Kimball 1934- *WhoAm 90*
Webster, John Richard 1845-1909 *AmLegL*
Webster, Joseph Curley *BiDrAPA 89*
Webster, Lamont 1928- *St&PR 91*
Webster, Larry 1930- *WhoAmA 91*
Webster, Larry Russell 1930- *WhoAm 90*
Webster, Lee 1948- *WhoWrEP 89*
Webster, Lee D. 1923- *St&PR 91*
Webster, Lee Davis 1923- *WhoAm 90*
Webster, Leslie Tillotson, Jr. 1926- *WhoAm 90*
Webster, Linda Mae 1941- *WhoAmW 91*
Webster, Lois Shand 1929- *WhoAmW 91*
Webster, Margaret 1905-1972 *BioIn 16, NotWoAT*
Webster, Mark K. 1954- *St&PR 91*
Webster, Marsha Elveria 1955- *WhoE 91*
Webster, Mary Patrice 1958- *BiDrAPA 89*
Webster, Mel *ODwPR 91*
Webster, Michael Lee 1949- *WhoE 91*
Webster, Mitch 1959- *Ballpl 90*
Webster, Moses 1792-1870 *PenDiDA 89*
Webster, Nell *BioIn 16, NewYTBS 90*
Webster, Noah *TwCCr&M 91*
Webster, Noah 1758-1843 *BioIn 16, EncCRAm [port], NinCLC 30 [port], WorAlBi*
Webster, Norman Eric 1941- *WhoE 91*
Webster, Paul T. 1924- *St&PR 91*
Webster, Peter Davies 1940- *St&PR 91*
Webster, Philip J. 1939- *ODwPR 91*
Webster, Philip Jonathan 1939- *St&PR 91, WhoE 91*
Webster, Ralph Leroy 1940- *St&PR 91*
Webster, Ramon 1942- *Ballpl 90*
Webster, Reginald Howard 1910- *St&PR 91*
Webster, Richard Bradford 1927- *WhoWor 91*
Webster, Robert Byron 1932- *WhoWor 91*
Webster, Robert David 1938- *WhoAm 90*
Webster, Robert R. 1928- *St&PR 91*
Webster, Robert W. 1925- *St&PR 91*
Webster, Ronald David 1949- *St&PR 91*
Webster, Ronald Lee 1937- *WhoAm 90*
Webster, Ruth Ann 1949- *WhoAmW 91*
Webster, Sally 1938- *WhoAmA 91*
Webster, Samuel William, Jr. 1939- *WhoSSW 91*
Webster, Sharon B. 1937- *WhoE 91*
Webster, Shelley Rose 1952- *WhoAmW 91*
Webster, Steven Alan 1951- *WhoSSW 91*
Webster, Stokely 1912- *WhoAmA 91, WhoWor 91*
Webster, Thomas Edward 1944- *WhoSSW 91*
Webster, Thomas G *BiDrAPA 89*
Webster, Thomas Glenn 1924- *WhoAm 90*
Webster, Thomas Nathan 1920- *St&PR 91*
Webster, Vera R. *AuBYP 90*
Webster, Victor Alexander 1934- *St&PR 91*
Webster, Warnie Louise 1949- *BiDrAPA 89*
Webster, William Charles 1935- *WhoE 91*
Webster, William H. *BioIn 16*
Webster, William H. 1924- *WorAlBi*
Webster, William Hedgcock 1924- *WhoAm 90*
Webster, William John 1927- *St&PR 91*
Webster, William Lawrence 1953- *WhoAm 90*
Webster, William M. 1918- *St&PR 91*
Wechman, Robert Joseph 1939- *WhoE 91*
Wechsier, Herman J 1904-1976 *WhoAmA 91N*
Wechsler, Alfred Elliot 1934- *St&PR 91, WhoAm 90*
Wechsler, Andrew Robert 1946- *WhoWor 91*
Wechsler, Andrew Stephen 1939- *WhoAm 90*
Wechsler, Bert 1933- *IntWWM 90*
Wechsler, Gil 1942- *WhoE 91, WhoWor 91*
Wechsler, Henry 1932- *WhoAm 90*
Wechsler, Herbert 1909- *WhoAm 90*
Wechsler, Jessica 1943- *WhoAmW 91*
Wechsler, Jill 1946- *WhoWrEP 89*
Wechsler, Judith Glatzer 1940- *WhoAmA 91, WhoE 91*
Wechsler, Marlene E. 1934- *WhoE 91*
Wechsler, Marlene Edith 1934- *WhoAmW 91*
Wechsler, Raymond H. 1945- *St&PR 91*
Wechsler, Richard Lance 1946- *WhoE 91*
Wechsler, Robert Frank 1954- *WhoE 91*
Wechsler, Sergio 1944- *WhoWor 91*
Wechsler, Susan 1943- *WhoAmA 91*
Wecht, Cyril Harrison 1931- *WhoE 91*
Wechte, Antoine *PenDiDA 89*
Wechter, Clari Ann 1953- *WhoAmW 91*
Wechter, Georg 1526?-1586 *PenDiDA 89*
Wechter, Nell Wise 1913- *SmATA 60 [port]*
Wechter, Norman Robert 1926- *WhoWor 91*
Wechter, Vivienne Thaul *WhoAm 90, WhoAmA 91*
Weck, Kristin Willa 1959- *WhoAmW 91*
Weck, Thomas L 1942- *SmATA 62 [port]*
Wecke, Friedrich Christian Claude J. 1921- *IntWWM 90*
Weckenbrock, James R. 1947- *St&PR 91*
Wecker, Myron Sydney *WhoE 91*
Wecker, Stu *BioIn 16*
Weckerle, Katherine Elizabeth 1952- *WhoAmW 91*
Weckerle, Lawrence Franklin 1954- *St&PR 91*
Weckesser, Ernest Prosper, Jr. 1933- *WhoAm 90*
Weckesser, Paul Maurice 1933- *WhoE 91*
Weckesser, Sandra Weaver 1944- *WhoE 91*
Wecksell, Josef Julius 1838-1907 *DcScanL*
Wecksler, Becky Lynn 1951- *BioIn 16*
Weckstein, Marvin S 1929- *BiDrAPA 89*
Weckstein, Naomi Gail *BiDrAPA 89*
Weckstein, Richard Selig 1924- *WhoAm 90, WhoE 91*
Weckstein, Sander Michael *BiDrAPA 89*
Weckstrom, Bjorn 1935- *ConDes 90*
Weckstrom, Lasse 1941- *WhoWor 91*
Weclew, Robert George 1911- *WhoAm 90*
Weclew, Thaddeus Victor 1906- *WhoAm 90*
Weclew, Victor T. 1916- *WhoAm 90*
Wedbush, Edward W. 1932- *St&PR 91*
Wedd, Kate *ConAu 131*
Weddell, Mrs. *FemiCLE*
Weddell, Alexander Wilbourne 1876-1948 *BioIn 16*
Weddell, James 1787-1834 *WorAlBi*
Weddepohl, Hubertus Nicolaus 1937- *WhoWor 91*
Wedderburn, Kenneth William 1927- *WhoWor 91*
Weddig, Lee John 1935- *WhoAm 90, WhoE 91*

Weddige, Emil 1907- *WhoAmA 91*
Weddige, Richard L 1939- *BiDrAPA 89*
Wedding, Charles Randolph 1934- *WhoAm 90*
Wedding, Walter Joseph 1952- *WhoAmA 91*
Weddington, Elizabeth Gardner 1932- *WhoE 91*
Weddington, Patricia Diane 1950- *WhoAmW 91, WhoEmL 91*
Weddington, Sarah Ragle 1945- *WhoAm 90*
Weddington, William W, Jr. *BiDrAPA 89*
Weddle, Ethel Harshbarger 1897- *AuBYP 90*
Weddle, Robert Bruce, Jr. 1940- *St&PR 91*
Weddle, Stephen Shields 1938- *St&PR 91*
Wedeen, Marvin Meyer 1926- *WhoE 91*
Wedeen, Robert Samson 1926- *WhoE 91*
Wedekind, Carl L., Jr. 1926- *St&PR 91*
Wedel, Janine 1957- *ConAu 132*
Wedel, Millie Redmond 1939- *WhoWor 91*
Wedel, Paul George 1927- *WhoAm 90*
Wedel, Waldo Rudolph 1908- *WhoAm 90*
Wedeman, Sara Capen 1956- *WhoAmW 91*
Wedemeyer, Albert *BioIn 16*
Wedemeyer, Albert C. 1897-1989 *AnObit 1989, ConAu 130, CurBio 90N*
Wedemeyer, Charlie *BioIn 16*
Wedemeyer, Lucy *BioIn 16*
Wedepohl, Leonhard M. 1933- *WhoAm 90*
Weder, Janet M. 1951- *St&PR 91*
Weder, Ricardo Alberto 1948- *WhoWor 91*
Wedge, Dorothy Ann 1935- *WhoAmW 91*
Wedge, George Francis, III 1927- *WhoWrEP 89*
Wedge, Will 1889-1951 *Ballpl 90*
Wedgeworth, Phillip Wayne 1951- *WhoSSW 91*
Wedgeworth, Robert 1937- *WhoAm 90, WhoWor 91*
Wedgle, Richard Jay 1951- *WhoEmL 91*
Wedgwood, C. V. 1910- *BioIn 16*
Wedgwood, C V 1910- *MajTwCW*
Wedgwood, Cicely Veronica 1910- *BioIn 16*
Wedgwood, Josiah 1730-1795 *PenDiDA 89, WorAlBi*
Wedgwood, Julia 1833-1913 *FemiCLE*
Wedgwood, Ralph Josiah Patrick 1924- *WhoAm 90*
Wedgwood, Ruth 1949- *WhoE 91*
Wedgwood, William Darwin 1922- *St&PR 91*
Wedgworth, Ruth Springer 1903- *WhoAmW 91*
Wedick, John Lawrence, Jr. 1930- *WhoE 91*
Wedinger, Robert Scott 1957- *WhoSSW 91*
Wedlake, Gary Douglas 1944- *WhoSSW 91*
Wedow, David Walter 1953- *WhoSSW 91*
Wedow, Rudy 1906-1965 *WhoAmA 91N*
Wedrow, Earl M 1924- *BiDrAPA 89*
Wedrow, Earl Manuel 1924- *WhoE 91*
Wee Kim Wee 1915- *WhoWor 91*
Wee, Elena I *BiDrAPA 89*
Weeber, Claire Joanne 1936- *WhoAmW 91*
Weeber, Dieter Karl 1934- *St&PR 91*
Weeber, Gretchen *WhoAmA 91N*
Weech, Alexander A, Jr. 1933- *BiDrAPA 89*
Weed, Cheryl Anne 1947- *WhoWrEP 89*
Weed, Edward R. 1940- *St&PR 91*
Weed, Frederic Augustus 1918- *WhoAm 90*
Weed, Herbert M. 1921-1989 *BioIn 16*
Weed, Ithamar Dryden 1914- *WhoAm 90*
Weed, Joe Keith 1936- *St&PR 91*
Weed, Lois Lorraine Hora 1949- *WhoEmL 91*
Weed, Maurice James 1912- *WhoAm 90*
Weed, Roger Oven 1944- *WhoSSW 91*
Weed, Sherryle Matthew 1954- *WhoSSW 91*
Weed, Thurlow 1797-1882 *BioIn 16*
Weeda, Kryn 1946- *WhoWor 91*
Weeda, Wouter Cornelus 1946- *WhoWor 91*
Weeden, Donald E. 1930- *St&PR 91*
Weeden, Jeffrey Blane 1956- *St&PR 91, WhoEmL 91*
Weeden, Lula Lowe 1918- *HarlReB*
Weeden, Mary Ann 1948- *WhoAmW 91*
Weeder, Richard S. *BioIn 16*
Weedman, Kenneth Russell 1939- *WhoAmA 91*
Weedon, Daniel Reid, Jr. 1919- *St&PR 91*
Weedon, Douglas Lee 1935- *St&PR 91*
Weege, William *WhoAmA 91*
Weekes, Leroy Randolph 1913- *WhoAm 90*
Weekes, Shirley Marie 1917- *WhoAmA 91*
Weekley, Anne Nichols 1947- *WhoAmW 91*
Weekley, Frederick Clay, Jr. 1939- *WhoAm 90*
Weekley, Larry *ODwPR 91*
Weekley, Mary E. 1956- *WhoAmW 91*
Weekley, Terri Fisher *BioIn 16*
Weekly, James Keith 1933- *WhoSSW 91*
Weekly, John William 1931- *St&PR 91, WhoAm 90*
Weekly, Richard J. 1945- *WhoWrEP 89*
Weeks, Albert Loren 1923- *WhoAm 90, WhoE 91, WhoWor 91, WhoWrEP 89*
Weeks, Andi Emerson 1932- *WhoE 91*
Weeks, Arthur Andrew 1914- *WhoAm 90, WhoWor 91*
Weeks, Brian Francis 1953- *WhoE 91*
Weeks, Brigitte 1943- *ConAu 132, WhoAm 90, WhoAmW 91, WhoE 91*
Weeks, Charles, Jr. 1919- *WhoSSW 91*
Weeks, Charles Carson 1914- *WhoAm 90*
Weeks, Charles R. 1934- *WhoAm 90*
Weeks, Charles Richard 1934- *St&PR 91*
Weeks, David Anthony 1933- *WhoE 91*
Weeks, David Frank 1926- *WhoAm 90*
Weeks, David Lee 1930- *WhoAm 90*
Weeks, David Leonard 1935- *St&PR 91*
Weeks, Donna Dorman 1958- *WhoSSW 91*
Weeks, Dorothy W. *NewYTBS 90*
Weeks, Dorothy W. 1893-1990 *BioIn 16*
Weeks, E. Wayne, Jr. *WhoAm 90*
Weeks, Edward 1898-1989 *BioIn 16*
Weeks, Edward A. 1898-1989 *AnObit 1989*
Weeks, Edward F *WhoAmA 91*
Weeks, Edward John 1927- *St&PR 91*
Weeks, Elinor Eastman 1937- *BiDrAPA 89*
Weeks, Francis William 1916- *WhoAm 90*
Weeks, Fred L. 1920- *St&PR 91*
Weeks, George 1921- *BioIn 16*
Weeks, George Elias 1839- *AmLegL*
Weeks, George Granville 1860-1923 *AmLegL*
Weeks, Gerald 1941- *WhoAm 90*
Weeks, Gwendolen Brannon 1943- *WhoAmW 91*
Weeks, James 1922- *WhoAmA 91*
Weeks, James R. *ODwPR 91*
Weeks, James W. 1937- *St&PR 91*
Weeks, Jane L. 1938- *BioIn 16*
Weeks, Jane Sutherland 1924- *WhoWrEP 89*
Weeks, Janet Healy 1932- *WhoAm 90, WhoAmW 91*
Weeks, Jeffrey 1945- *WhoWor 91*
Weeks, John David 1943- *WhoAm 90*
Weeks, John Robert 1944- *WhoAm 90*
Weeks, John Wingate 1860-1926 *BiDrUSE 89*
Weeks, John Wingate 1920- *WhoAm 90*
Weeks, Karren Gentle 1951- *WhoAmW 91*
Weeks, Leo Rosco 1903-1977 *WhoAmA 91N*
Weeks, Martha G. 1950- *WhoAmW 91*
Weeks, Otto Schwartz 1830-1892 *DcCanB 12*
Weeks, Patsy Ann Landry 1930- *WhoAmW 91, WhoWor 91*
Weeks, Paul Martin 1932- *WhoAm 90*
Weeks, Richard Elvin 1924- *WhoAm 90*
Weeks, Richard Ralph 1932- *WhoAm 90, WhoWor 91*
Weeks, Robert Andrew 1924- *WhoAm 90*
Weeks, Robert Earl 1925- *WhoWor 91*
Weeks, Robert Gray 1936- *WhoAm 90*
Weeks, Robert Lewis 1924- *WhoWrEP 89*
Weeks, Robert W. 1926- *St&PR 91*
Weeks, Robert Walker 1926- *WhoAm 90*
Weeks, Robin Allan 1942- *St&PR 91*
Weeks, Roland, Jr. 1936- *WhoAm 90*
Weeks, Ross, Jr. 1936- *ODwPR 91*
Weeks, Ruth B 1925- *BiDrAPA 89*
Weeks, Sheldon G 1931- *ConAu 30NR*
Weeks, Sherry Lee Cranford 1944- *WhoSSW 91*
Weeks, Sinclair 1893-1972 *BiDrUSE 89*
Weeks, Sinclair, Jr. 1923- *St&PR 91*
Weeks, Terry *BioIn 16*
Weeks, Virginia Lynn 1952- *WhoAmW 91*
Weeks, Walter LeRoy 1923- *WhoAm 90*
Weeks, Wilford Frank 1929- *WhoAm 90*
Weeks, William Brinson *BiDrAPA 89*
Weeks, William Clayton 1936- *St&PR 91*
Weeks, William Isaac 1962- *WhoSSW 91*
Weeks-Shaw, Clara S. 1856-1940 *BioIn 16*
Weems, Clara C. 1933- *WhoAmW 91*
Weems, Frank Taylor 1924- *St&PR 91*
Weems, George S. 1940- *St&PR 91*
Weems, John Edgar 1932- *WhoAm 90*
Weems, John Edward 1924- *WhoSSW 91, WhoWor 91*
Weems, Katharine Lane *BioIn 16*
Weems, Katherine Lane 1899- *WhoAmA 91N*
Weems, Katherine Ward 1899- *BiDWomA*
Weems, M. L. 1759-1825 *BioIn 16*
Weems, Mason Locke 1759-1825 *BioIn 16*
Weems, Renita *BioIn 16*
Weems, Robert Cicero 1910- *WhoAm 90*
Weems, Rodger Cary 1952- *WhoSSW 91*
Weems, Ted 1901-1963 *OxCPMus*
Weening, Richard William, Jr. 1945- *WhoAm 90*
Weenix, Jan 1642-1719? *IntDcAA 90*
Weepie, Charles Martin 1932- *St&PR 91*
Weerasekera, Priyanthy *BiDrAPA 89*
Weerasinghe, Chandra Margret 1943- *BiDrAPA 89*
Weertman, Johannes 1925- *WhoAm 90*
Weertman, Julia Randall 1926- *WhoAm 90, WhoAmW 91*
Weerts, Richard Kenneth 1928- *WhoWor 91*
Wees, Frances 1902-1982 *FemiCLE*
Wees, Frances Shelley 1902- *AuBYP 90*
Wees, Frances Shelley 1902-1982 *BioIn 16*
Weese, Benjamin Horace 1929- *WhoAm 90*
Weese, Cynthia Rogers 1940- *WhoAm 90, WhoAmW 91*
Weese, Harry Mohr 1915- *WhoAm 90*
Weese, John Augustus 1933- *WhoSSW 91*
Weesner, Thomas E. 1929- *St&PR 91*
Weetman, Robert Ray 1937- *WhoWrEP 89*
Weeton, Ellen 1775-1844? *FemiCLE*
Weevers, Peter *BioIn 16*
Wefald, Jon 1937- *WhoWor 91*
Weffenstette, Bruce Everett 1951- *BiDrAPA 89*
Weg, Howard Jay 1954- *WhoEmL 91*
Weg, John Gerard 1934- *WhoAm 90, WhoWor 91*
Wege, Peter M. *WhoAm 90*
Wegeforth, Harry Milton 1882-1941 *BioIn 16*
Wegelin, Arthur Willem 1908- *IntWWM 90*
Wegely, Wilhelm Kaspar *PenDiDA 89*
Wegener, Barry *ODwPR 91*
Wegener, Charles William 1921- *WhoAm 90*
Wegener, Dietrich Burckhardt 1939- *WhoWor 91*
Wegener, Larry Edward 1946- *WhoWrEP 89*
Wegener, Mark Douglas 1948- *WhoEmL 91*
Wegener, Mike 1946- *Ballpl 90*
Wegener Sleeswyk, Andre 1927- *WhoWor 91*
Weger, Joseph G. 1931- *St&PR 91*
Wegg, S. James 1952- *IntWWM 90*
Wegge, Leon Louis Francois 1933- *WhoAm 90*
Weggel, John Richard 1941- *WhoE 91*
Weggel, William James *BiDrAPA 89*
Weghorst, Margaret Lynn 1948- *WhoAmW 91*
Wegiel, Glenn Alan 1948- *WhoSSW 91*
Weglarz, Edward Miljon 1941- *WhoSSW 91*
Weglarz, Jan 1947- *WhoWor 91*
Weglarz, Terri Marie 1965- *WhoWrEP 89*
Wegman, Bill 1962- *Ballpl 90*
Wegman, David Howe 1940- *WhoE 91*
Wegman, Harold Hugh 1916- *WhoAm 90*
Wegman, Myron Ezra 1908- *WhoAm 90*
Wegman, Steven Michael 1953- *WhoEmL 91*
Wegman, William *BioIn 16*
Wegman, William 1942?- *News 91-1 [port]*
Wegman, William 1943- *WhoAmA 91*
Wegman, William George 1943- *WhoAm 90*
Wegmann, Cynthia Anne 1949- *WhoSSW 91*
Wegmann, Karen 1944- *WhoAmW 91*
Wegmann, Paul Francis 1941- *St&PR 91*
Wegmann, Robert Gene 1938- *WhoSSW 91*
Wegmiller, Donald Charles 1938- *WhoAm 90*
Wegner, Arthur Eduard 1937- *WhoAm 90*
Wegner, E. Donald 1929- *St&PR 91*
Wegner, Gary Alan 1944- *WhoAm 90*
Wegner, Gary Louis 1936- *St&PR 91*
Wegner, Hans 1914- *PenDiDA 89*
Wegner, Hans J 1914- *ConDes 90*
Wegner, Helmuth Adalbert 1917- *WhoAm 90*
Wegner, Karl Heinrich 1930- *WhoAm 90*
Wegner, Mary Michelle *BiDrAPA 89*
Wegner, Nadene R 1950- *WhoAmA 91*
Wegner, Ronald A. *St&PR 91*
Wegrzynek, Raymond Frank 1934- *WhoE 91*
Wehage, Robert Arthur 1940- *St&PR 91*
Wehausen, John Vrooman 1913- *WhoAm 90*
Wehdorn, Manfred 1942- *WhoWor 91*
Wehe, David Carl 1949- *WhoE 91*
Wehe, Diana Joycelyn 1943- *WhoAmW 91*
Wehe, Fred Gustave 1929- *St&PR 91*
Wehe, Herbert W. 1928- *St&PR 91*
Wehe, Homer A. 1931- *St&PR 91*
Weheba, Abdulsalam Mohamad 1930- *WhoWor 91*
Wehen, Joy De Weese 1926- *AuBYP 90*
Wehl, Brandon L. 1953- *St&PR 91*
Wehl, Glenn Eugene 1926- *St&PR 91*
Wehlage, David Francis 1939- *BiDrAPA 89*
Wehle, Bob *BioIn 16*
Wehle, John L. 1916- *St&PR 91*
Wehle, John Louis 1916- *WhoAm 90*
Wehle, Richard J. *St&PR 91N*
Wehling, Jeffrey T. 1954- *ODwPR 91*
Wehling, Ralph Joseph 1914- *St&PR 91*
Wehlitz, Annie Louise *WhoWrEP 89*
Wehman, Adele 1916- *WhoAmW 91, WhoE 91, WhoWor 91*
Wehman, Henry Joseph *BiDrAPA 89*
Wehmeier, Herm 1927-1973 *Ballpl 90*
Wehmer, Edward Joseph 1954- *St&PR 91*
Wehner, Alfred Peter 1926- *WhoAm 90*
Wehner, Donald Clifford 1929- *WhoSSW 91*
Wehner, Edward Adam *WhoSSW 91*
Wehner, Herbert 1906-1990 *BioIn 16, NewYTBS 90*
Wehner, Richard Karl 1957- *WhoEmL 91*
Wehner, Thomas J. 1950- *St&PR 91*
Wehr, Allan Gordon 1931- *WhoSSW 91*
Wehr, Cullie Robert, Jr. 1925- *St&PR 91*
Wehr, David August 1934- *IntWWM 90*
Wehr, Paul Adam 1914-1973 *WhoAmA 91N*
Wehr, Roberta S. *St&PR 91*
Wehr, Thomas A 1941- *BiDrAPA 89*
Wehr, Wesley Conrad 1929- *WhoAmA 91*
Wehrenberg, Donald Otto 1938- *St&PR 91*
Wehrenberg, James Harvey *BiDrAPA 89*
Wehrenberg, Kathleen Ann 1960- *WhoAmW 91*
Wehrenberg, Kim Allen 1951- *St&PR 91*
Wehrheim, Carol Ann 1940- *WhoAmW 91*
Wehrheim, Hans K *BiDrAPA 89*
Wehring, Bernard William 1937- *WhoAm 90*
Wehrle, Gary L. 1942- *St&PR 91*
Wehrle, Henry B., Jr. 1922- *St&PR 91, WhoAm 90*
Wehrle, Leroy Snyder 1932- *WhoAm 90*
Wehrle, Martha Gaines 1925- *WhoAm 90, WhoAmW 91*
Wehrle, Thomas Edward 1934- *St&PR 91*
Wehrlen, Deborah Trub 1954- *WhoE 91*
Wehrli, Robert Louis 1922- *WhoAm 90*
Wehrlin, Gerald Thomas 1938- *St&PR 91*
Wehrman, Stephanie Ann 1959- *WhoAmW 91, WhoEmL 91*
Wehrmeister, Dave 1952- *Ballpl 90*
Wehrwein, Austin Carl 1916- *WhoAm 90*
Wehry, Susan Marie *BiDrAPA 89*
Wei Jingsheng *BioIn 16*
Wei, Benjamin Min 1930- *WhoSSW 91*
Wei, Fu-Shang 1948- *WhoE 91*
Wei, I-Chiang 1952- *WhoWor 91*
Wei, James 1930- *WhoAm 90*
Wei, Tingcheng 1926- *WhoWor 91*
Wei, Victor Mark *BiDrAPA 89*
Weiant, C W 1897- *EncO&P 3*
Weiant, Elizabeth Abbott 1913- *WhoE 91*
Weibel, Charles Alexander 1950- *WhoE 91*
Weible, Robert L. 1938- *St&PR 91*
Weibull, Claes Peter Walter 1921- *WhoWor 91*
Weibye, Bjarne 1931- *WhoWor 91*
Weich, Martin J *BiDrAPA 89*
Weich, Mervyn D. 1938- *St&PR 91*
Weich, Patricia Gallant 1945- *WhoWrEP 89*
Weich-Shahak, Susana 1939- *IntWWM 90*
Weichbrodt, Gary Dean 1957- *BiDrAPA 89*
Weichel, Kenneth 1946- *WhoWrEP 89*
Weicher, John C. 1938- *WhoAm 90*
Weichsel, Manfred 1903-1989 *BioIn 16*
Weichsel, Richard Henry 1928- *St&PR 91*
Weick, George Paul 1951- *WhoSSW 91*
Weickel, Robert W., Jr. 1938- *WhoSSW 91*
Weicker, D.E. *St&PR 91*
Weicker, Lowell P., Jr. *NewYTBS 90*
Weicker, Lowell P., Jr. 1931- *WorAlBi*
Weicker, Lowell Palmer, Jr. 1931- *WhoE 91*
Weickgenant, Peter D. 1928- *St&PR 91*
Weickhardt, George Davis 1915- *BiDrAPA 89*
Weida, George A.F. 1936- *St&PR 91*
Weida, Lewis Dixon 1924- *WhoWor 91*
Weidacher, Alois Sebastian 1941- *WhoWor 91*
Weide, William W. 1923- *St&PR 91*
Weide, William Wolfe 1923- *WhoAm 90*
Weidel, Herbert Benjamin 1931- *St&PR 91*
Weidel, Lynne Catherine 1946- *WhoAmW 91*
Weidell, Carolyn L. 1955- *WhoAmW 91*
Weidemann, Anton Fredrick 1917- *WhoWrEP 89*
Weidemann, Celia Jean 1942- *WhoAm 90, WhoAmW 91, WhoE 91, WhoWor 91*

Weidemann, Julia Clark 1937- *WhoAmW 91*
Weidemeyer, Carleton Lloyd 1933- *IntWWM 90, WhoSSW 91*
Weiden, Peter 1955- *BiDrAPA 89*
Weidenaar, Reynold Henry 1915-1985 *WhoAmA 91N*
Weidenaar, Reynold Henry 1945- *IntWWM 90*
Weidenbaum, Murray Lew 1927- *WhoAm 90*
Weidenbruch, Anna Mae 1926- *WhoAmW 91*
Weidenfeld, Edward Lee 1943- *WhoAm 90*
Weidenfeld, Sheila Rabb 1943- *WhoAmW 91, WhoE 91*
Weidenfeller, Geraldine Carney 1933- *WhoAmW 91*
Weidenhamer, John *BioIn 16*
Weidenhammer, Robert Houston 1937- *St&PR 91*
Weidenthal, Maurice David 1925- *WhoAm 90*
Weider, Jerome D. 1941- *St&PR 91*
Weider, John *NewAgMG*
Weider, John Richard 1946- *WhoEmL 91*
Weider, Larry 1950- *St&PR 91*
Weidhorn, Manfred 1931- *SmATA 60 [port]*
Weidinger, Anton 1767-1852 *PenDiMP*
Weidinger, Christine *IntWWM 90*
Weidler, Ralph A. 1954- *WhoEmL 91*
Weidlinger, Paul 1914- *WhoAm 90, WhoE 91*
Weidman, Hazel Hitson 1923- *WhoAm 90*
Weidman, James, III 1930- *ODwPR 91*
Weidman, Jeffrey 1945- *WhoAmA 91*
Weidman, Jerome 1913- *WhoAm 90, WhoWrEP 89*
Weidman, Marsha Claman 1949- *St&PR 91*
Weidmann, Eric R. 1949- *St&PR 91*
Weidmann, Victor Hugo 1926- *WhoAm 90*
Weidner, Edward William 1921- *WhoAm 90*
Weidner, Gary *BioIn 16*
Weidner, Gary Richard 1948- *WhoEmL 91*
Weidner, Marilyn Kemp 1928- *WhoAmA 91*
Weidner, Mary Elizabeth 1950- *WhoAmA 91*
Weidner, Matthew Wilbert 1947- *WhoE 91*
Weidner, Richard Tilghman 1921- *WhoAm 90*
Weidner, Roswell Theodore 1911- *WhoAm 90, WhoAmA 91*
Weidner, Wayne Russell 1942- *St&PR 91*
Weidtman, Victor Joseph 1919- *WhoWor 91*
Weier, T. Elliott 1903- *WhoAm 90*
Weier, Thomas Edward 1939- *BiDrAPA 89*
Weier, Winfried 1934- *WhoWor 91*
Weierman, Robert Joseph 1942- *WhoE 91*
Weigand, Herbert Michael 1951- *WhoAmA 91*
Weigand, James Gary 1935- *St&PR 91, WhoAm 90*
Weigand, Philip Clayton 1937- *WhoAm 90*
Weigand, William Keith 1937- *WhoAm 90*
Weigel, Alice M. 1909- *WhoWrEP 89*
Weigel, Barbara Broback 1935- *WhoAmW 91*
Weigel, C. Philip 1933- *St&PR 91*
Weigel, Carl E. 1932- *St&PR 91*
Weigel, Donald A. 1943- *St&PR 91*
Weigel, Elsie Diven 1948- *WhoAmW 91, WhoE 91*
Weigel, Gerald Edward 1943- *St&PR 91*
Weigel, Joseph H *BiDrAPA 89*
Weigel, Nancy Lynn 1946- *WhoSSW 91*
Weigel, Raymond A. 1917- *St&PR 91*
Weigel, Richard David 1945- *WhoSSW 91*
Weigel, Stanley Alexander 1905- *WhoAm 90*
Weigel, William Frederick 1923- *WhoAm 90*
Weigelt, Horst Erich 1934- *WhoWor 91*
Weigen, Stanley 1931- *St&PR 91*
Weigend, Guido Gustav 1920- *WhoAm 90*
Weiger, John George 1933- *WhoAm 90*
Weigert, Wolfgang O *BiDrAPA 89*
Weigert, Wolfgang U *BiDrAPA 89*
Weighmann, Richard A. 1951- *St&PR 91*
Weightman, Judy Mae 1941- *WhoAmW 91, WhoWor 91*
Weigl, Bruce 1949- *ConAu 30NR*
Weigle, Debbie Kay 1954- *WhoSSW 91*
Weigle, Joerg-Peter 1953- *WhoWor 91*
Weigle, Marta *WhoAmW 91*
Weigle, Richard Daniel 1912- *WhoAm 90*
Weigle, William Oliver 1927- *WhoAm 90*
Weigold, Calvin C. 1926- *St&PR 91*
Weigold, Franklin 1939- *St&PR 91*
Weihaupt, John George 1930- *WhoAm 90*
Weihe, James Howard 1950- *BiDrAPA 89*
Weiher, Claudine Jackson 1941- *WhoAm 90*
Weihofen, Henry *BiDrAPA 89*
Weihrich, Heinz *WhoAm 90, WhoWor 91*
Weihs, Daniel 1942- *WhoWor 91*
Weihs, Erika 1917- *WhoAmA 91*
Weihs, John *BiDrAPA 89*
Weihs, John Stephen 1952- *WhoE 91*
Weihs, Karen L *BiDrAPA 89*
Weik, Dick 1927- *Ballpl 90*
Weik, Martin Herman 1922- *WhoSSW 91*
Weik, Mary Hays 1878-1979 *AuBYP 90*
Weikart, H.N. 1935- *St&PR 91*
Weikart, Lynne Alkire 1943- *WhoE 91*
Weikel, Dana Rose 1943- *WhoWrEP 89*
Weikel, M.K. 1938- *St&PR 91*
Weikel, Robin R. 1953- *St&PR 91*
Weikert, Ralf 1940- *WhoWor 91*
Weikert, Rolf 1940- *PenDiMP*
Weikert, Roy J. 1913- *St&PR 91*
Weikl, Bernd 1942- *PenDiMP*
Weikl, Bernhard 1942- *IntWWM 90*
Weikle, William Henry 1938- *St&PR 91*
Weiksner, George Bernard 1944- *St&PR 91*
Weiksner, George Bernard, Jr. 1944- *WhoAm 90*
Weil, Albert M. 1907- *St&PR 91*
Weil, Andrew 1942- *NewAgE 90*
Weil, Andrew Thomas 1942- *BiDrAPA 89*
Weil, Annemarie P 1909- *BiDrAPA 89*
Weil, Barbara 1933- *WhoWor 91*
Weil, Ben Lee 1939- *WhoSSW 91*
Weil, Bert 1951- *St&PR 91*
Weil, Cass Sargent 1946- *WhoEmL 91*
Weil, Charles Donald 1944- *St&PR 91*
Weil, Daniel Simon 1957- *WhoE 91*
Weil, David S. 1925- *St&PR 91, WhoAm 90*
Weil, Donald 1944- *St&PR 91*
Weil, Donald Wallace 1923- *WhoAm 90*
Weil, Ernst *WhoAm 90*
Weil, Frank A. 1931- *WhoAm 90*
Weil, Gary A. 1954- *BiDrAPA 89*
Weil, Gertrude L. 1922- *St&PR 91*
Weil, Gilbert Harry 1912- *WhoAm 90*
Weil, Herman 1905- *WhoAm 90*
Weil, Inga Frenkel 1914- *BiDrAPA 89*
Weil, Irwin 1928- *WhoAm 90*
Weil, Jack A. 1901- *St&PR 91*
Weil, Jerry Morris 1957- *WhoSSW 91*
Weil, John *WhoAm 90*
Weil, John Ashley 1929- *WhoAm 90*
Weil, John David 1947- *St&PR 91, WhoAm 90*
Weil, John L 1920- *BiDrAPA 89*
Weil, John William 1928- *WhoAm 90*
Weil, Joseph *BioIn 16*
Weil, Kenneth Spencer 1948- *WhoAm 90*
Weil, Leon Jerome 1927- *WhoAm 90*
Weil, Leonard 1922- *WhoAm 90*
Weil, Lise 1950- *WhoWrEP 89*
Weil, Lisl *WhoAmA 91, WhoE 91*
Weil, Louis A., III *BioIn 16*
Weil, M. Harvey 1916- *WhoSSW 91*
Weil, Marjorie *BioIn 16, NewYTBS 90*
Weil, Myron 1918- *WhoAm 90*
Weil, Nancy Hecht 1936- *WhoAmW 91*
Weil, Paul P. 1936- *WhoAm 90*
Weil, Peter Henry 1933- *WhoAm 90, WhoE 91*
Weil, Richard A. 1925- *St&PR 91*
Weil, Richard K. 1924- *St&PR 91*
Weil, Rolf Alfred 1921- *WhoAm 90, WhoWor 91*
Weil, Roman Lee 1940- *WhoAm 90*
Weil, Ronald David 1948- *St&PR 91*
Weil, Roswell J. 1916- *St&PR 91*
Weil, Simone 1909-1943 *BioIn 16, EncCoWW, EuWr 12, WorAlBi*
Weil, Stephen E 1928- *WhoAmA 91*
Weil, Stephen Edward 1928- *WhoAm 90*
Weil, Suzanne S. Fern 1933- *WhoAm 90, WhoAmW 91*
Weil, Thomas Eliot 1906- *WhoE 91*
Weil, Thomas P. 1932- *WhoSSW 91*
Weil, Tibor V. 1942- *IntWWM 90*
Weil, William Bachrach, Jr. 1924- *WhoAm 90*
Weil-Garris Brandt, Kathleen 1934- *WhoE 91*
Weiland, Bob 1905- *Ballpl 90*
Weiland, Charles Hankes 1921- *WhoAm 90*
Weiland, Frederik Christoffel 1933- *IntWWM 90*
Weiland, Gustave J *BiDrAPA 89*
Weiland, Irvin Hyman 1921- *BiDrAPA 89*
Weiland, Mark 1956- *St&PR 91*
Weiland, Robert Michael 1948- *St&PR 91*
Weilbacher, William Manning 1928- *WhoAm 90*
Weilbacker, Kristine 1961- *WhoAmW 91*
Weilburg, Donald Karl 1936- *WhoE 91*
Weilburg, Jeffrey B 1952- *BiDrAPA 89*
Weilenmann, Carl Woolworth 1889-1924 *Ballpl 90*
Weiler, A.R. 1936- *St&PR 91*
Weiler, Benny Berthold 1955- *WhoWor 91*
Weiler, Edgar D. 1930- *St&PR 91*
Weiler, Joseph Ashby 1946- *WhoAm 90*
Weiler, Joseph Flack 1943- *WhoAmA 91*
Weiler, Martin Andrew 1950- *BiDrAPA 89*
Weiler, Martin E *BiDrAPA 89*
Weiler, Melody M 1947- *WhoAmA 91*
Weiler, Murray N *BiDrAPA 89*
Weiler, Robert E. 1932- *St&PR 91*
Weiler, Robert Pape 1952- *WhoE 91*
Weiler, Stephen James 1946- *BiDrAPA 89*
Weilerstein, Donald *PenDiMP*
Weiling, Franz Joseph Bernard 1909- *WhoWor 91*
Weill, Alan 1937- *St&PR 91*
Weill, David P. 1941-1988 *BioIn 16*
Weill, Erna *WhoAmA 91, WhoE 91*
Weill, Georges Gustave 1926- *WhoAm 90*
Weill, Hans 1933- *WhoAm 90*
Weill, Joseph 1902-1988 *BioIn 16*
Weill, Kurt 1900-1950 *BioIn 16, OxCPMus, PenDiMP A, WorAlBi*
Weill, Samuel, Jr. 1916- *WhoWor 91*
Weill, Sandy 1933- *News 90 [port]*
Weill, Sanford I. *BioIn 16*
Weill, Sanford I. 1933- *WhoAm 90, WhoE 91*
Weill, Sheldon Dennis 1943- *St&PR 91*
Weill, Terry Lister *BiDrAPA 89*
Weiller, Paul Annik 1933- *WhoWor 91*
Weilman, Carl 1889-1924 *Ballpl 90*
Weilminster, Anne Elizabeth 1948- *WhoAmW 91*
Weiman, Stephen L. 1958- *St&PR 91*
Weimann, Christopher 1946-1988 *BioIn 16*
Weimar, Robert 1932- *WhoWor 91*
Weimer, Gerald A. 1945- *St&PR 91*
Weimer, Jake 1873-1928 *Ballpl 90*
Weimer, Michael John 1945- *WhoWor 91*
Weimer, Paul Kessler 1914- *WhoAm 90*
Weimer, Peter Dwight 1938- *WhoSSW 91, WhoWor 91*
Weimer, Peter Thomas 1945- *WhoEmL 91*
Weimer, Robert Jay 1926- *WhoAm 90*
Weimer, Sanford Roy *BiDrAPA 89*
Weimer, Stephen J. 1955- *WhoSSW 91*
Weimer, Vaughn H. 1953- *St&PR 91*
Wein, Alan Jerome 1941- *WhoAm 90, WhoE 91*
Wein, Albert W 1915- *WhoAmA 91*
Wein, Cynthia Ellen 1957- *WhoAmW 91*
Wein, Esther Pearl *BiDrAPA 89*
Wein, Hermann Franz Randolph 1953- *WhoWor 91*
Wein, Joseph Alexander 1931- *WhoAm 90*
Wein, Margaret Ruth *BiDrAPA 89*
Wein, Steven Jay 1953- *BiDrAPA 89*
Weinauer, Heribert F *BiDrAPA 89*
Weinbach, Arthur F. 1943- *St&PR 91*
Weinbach, Arthur Frederic 1943- *WhoAm 90*
Weinbach, Lawrence Allen 1940- *WhoAm 90*
Weinbaum, Claire M. 1925- *St&PR 91*
Weinbaum, Eleanor Perlstein *WhoSSW 91, WhoWrEP 89*
Weinbaum, Jean 1926- *WhoAmA 91*
Weinbaum, Marc 1949- *BiDrAPA 89*
Weinbaum, Martin Paul 1947- *WhoE 91*
Weinbaum, Morris J. 1924- *St&PR 91*
Weinbaum, Raquel *HispWr 90*
Weinbaum, Wiktor 1915- *IntWWM 90*
Weinberg, Abraham *BiDrAPA 89*
Weinberg, Alan 1952- *WhoSSW 91*
Weinberg, Alan Marc 1955- *BiDrAPA 89*
Weinberg, Alex E. 1944-1989 *BioIn 16*
Weinberg, Alvin Martin 1915- *WhoAm 90*
Weinberg, Bella Hass 1949- *WhoWrEP 89*
Weinberg, Bella Rebecca 1912- *WhoAmA 91*
Weinberg, Carroll A 1928- *BiDrAPA 89*
Weinberg, Edward 1918- *WhoAm 90*
Weinberg, Edward Herbert 1920- *St&PR 91*
Weinberg, Elbert 1928- *WhoAm 90, WhoAmA 91*
Weinberg, Ellen Laura 1954- *BiDrAPA 89, WhoE 91*
Weinberg, Ephraim 1938- *WhoAmA 91*
Weinberg, Eugene David 1922- *WhoAm 90*
Weinberg, Felix Jiri 1928- *WhoWor 91*
Weinberg, Francine Arrow 1939- *WhoE 91*
Weinberg, Gerhard Ludwig 1928- *WhoAm 90, WhoWrEP 89*
Weinberg, H Barbara *WhoAmA 91*
Weinberg, Harold P. 1925- *St&PR 91*
Weinberg, Harry 1908-1990 *NewYTBS 90 [port]*
Weinberg, Harry Bernard 1913- *WhoAm 90*
Weinberg, Harvey 1937- *St&PR 91*
Weinberg, Harvey A. 1937- *WhoAm 90*
Weinberg, Hazel Joan 1934- *BiDrAPA 89*
Weinberg, Herschel Mayer 1927- *WhoAm 90*
Weinberg, Howard 1949- *St&PR 91*
Weinberg, Howard J *BiDrAPA 89*
Weinberg, Irwin Robert 1928- *WhoAm 90*
Weinberg, James L. 1922- *St&PR 91*
Weinberg, Jane Ruth *BiDrAPA 89*
Weinberg, Jeffrey Mark 1949- *BiDrAPA 89*
Weinberg, John L. 1925- *St&PR 91*
Weinberg, John Livingston 1925- *WhoAm 90*
Weinberg, Jonathan David 1967- *WhoWrEP 89*
Weinberg, Larry *BioIn 16*
Weinberg, Leon 1925- *St&PR 91*
Weinberg, Leonard Burton 1939- *WhoAm 90*
Weinberg, Lila Shaffer *WhoAm 90, WhoAmW 91, WhoWrEP 89*
Weinberg, Louis 1918- *WhoAmA 91N*
Weinberg, Louise *WhoSSW 91*
Weinberg, Mark *BioIn 16*
Weinberg, Mark 1945- *WhoSSW 91*
Weinberg, Marshall Maslansky 1929- *St&PR 91*
Weinberg, Martin H *BiDrAPA 89*
Weinberg, Martin Herbert 1923- *WhoAm 90*
Weinberg, Martin J. 1952- *St&PR 91*
Weinberg, Matt M. 1957- *WhoE 91*
Weinberg, Meyer 1920- *WhoAm 90*
Weinberg, Michael, Jr. 1925- *WhoAm 90*
Weinberg, Mikel Day 1947- *BiDrAPA 89*
Weinberg, Mortimer 1922- *St&PR 91*
Weinberg, Ofra 1949- *WhoEmL 91*
Weinberg, Raymond *BioIn 16*
Weinberg, Richard L. 1922- *St&PR 91*
Weinberg, Robert Allan 1942- *WhoAm 90*
Weinberg, Robert Leonard 1923- *WhoAm 90*
Weinberg, Robert Stephen 1945- *WhoAm 90*
Weinberg, Robert W. 1936- *St&PR 91*
Weinberg, Ronald E. 1941- *St&PR 91*
Weinberg, Sarah Kibbee 1940- *WhoAmW 91*
Weinberg, Saul A 1925- *BiDrAPA 89*
Weinberg, Saul Abram 1925- *WhoE 91*
Weinberg, Sidney J., Jr. 1923- *St&PR 91*
Weinberg, Stephen Lee 1947- *WhoE 91*
Weinberg, Steven 1933- *WhoAm 90, WhoSSW 91, WhoWor 91, WorAlBi*
Weinberg, Susan Clare 1959- *WhoWrEP 89*
Weinberg, Sydney Stahl 1938- *WhoAmW 91*
Weinberg, Sylvan Lee 1923- *WhoAm 90*
Weinberger, Alan D. 1945- *St&PR 91*
Weinberger, Alan David 1945- *WhoAm 90, WhoWor 91*
Weinberger, Arnold 1924- *WhoAm 90*
Weinberger, Caspar W. *BioIn 16*
Weinberger, Caspar W. 1917- *WorAlBi*
Weinberger, Caspar Willard 1917- *BiDrUSE 89, WhoAm 90, WhoE 91, WhoWor 91*
Weinberger, Daniel Roy *BiDrAPA 89*
Weinberger, David S *BiDrAPA 89*
Weinberger, Donald C. 1942- *ODwPR 91*
Weinberger, Doreen Anne 1954- *WhoAmW 91*
Weinberger, Eric 1916- *WhoSSW 91*
Weinberger, Ernest 1955- *WhoE 91*
Weinberger, George Martin 1947- *WhoSSW 91*
Weinberger, Hans Felix 1928- *WhoAm 90*
Weinberger, Jaromir 1896-1967 *BioIn 16, PenDiMP A*
Weinberger, Jerome L *BiDrAPA 89*
Weinberger, Julius 1893- *EncO&P 3*
Weinberger, Leon Joseph 1931- *St&PR 91, WhoAm 90*
Weinberger, Marie 1946- *BiDrAPA 89*
Weinberger, Martin *WhoAmA 91N*
Weinberger, Miles M. 1938- *WhoAm 90*
Weinberger, Myron Hilmar 1937- *WhoAm 90*
Weinberger, Steven 1953- *WhoEmL 91*
Weinblatt, Bernard 1929- *St&PR 91*
Weinblatt, Margaret Didi 1943- *WhoE 91*
Weinblatt, Myron Benjamin 1929- *WhoAm 90*
Weinblatt, Richard B. 1962- *WhoE 91*
Weinblatt, Seymour Solomon 1922- *WhoE 91*
Weinbrenner, George Ryan 1917- *WhoSSW 91*
Weinbrot, Howard David 1936- *WhoAm 90, WhoWrEP 89*
Weindruch, Ronald L. 1947- *WhoSSW 91*
Weiner, Aaron D *BiDrAPA 89*
Weiner, Abe 1917- *WhoAmA 91*
Weiner, Alison *BiDrAPA 89*
Weiner, Annette B. 1933- *WhoAm 90, WhoAmW 91*
Weiner, Arnold Lawrence 1937- *St&PR 91*
Weiner, Barry M. 1951- *St&PR 91*
Weiner, Benjamin H. 1922- *St&PR 91*
Weiner, Beryl 1918- *St&PR 91*
Weiner, Betsy Platt 1920- *BiDrAPA 89*
Weiner, Brian Lewis 1945- *WhoE 91*
Weiner, Carl Dorian 1934- *WhoAm 90*
Weiner, Carl Phillip 1951- *WhoEmL 91*
Weiner, Carolyn Judith 1932- *WhoAmW 91*

Weiner, Charles 1923- *St&PR 91*
Weiner, Charles 1931- *WhoAm 90*
Weiner, Charles R. 1922- *WhoAm 90, WhoE 91*
Weiner, Claire Muriel 1951- *WhoAmW 91, WhoE 91*
Weiner, David Iver 1952- *St&PR 91*
Weiner, Debra H. 1952- *EncPaPR 91*
Weiner, Earl David 1939- *WhoAm 90, WhoE 91, WhoWor 91*
Weiner, Edward 1941- *WhoE 91*
Weiner, Ellen Lustbader 1947- *WhoEmL 91*
Weiner, Eugene L. 1931- *St&PR 91*
Weiner, Gerry 1933- *WhoE 91*
Weiner, Gloria 1925- *WhoE 91*
Weiner, Hannah A. 1928- *WhoWrEP 89*
Weiner, Harold M. 1937- *WhoE 91*
Weiner, Herbert B. 1949- *St&PR 91*
Weiner, Herbert M 1921- *BiDrAPA 89*
Weiner, Herman L. 1914- *St&PR 91*
Weiner, Howard A 1933- *BiDrAPA 89*
Weiner, Howard Lee 1944- *WhoAm 90*
Weiner, Ira Lewis 1946- *BiDrAPA 89*
Weiner, Irving Bernard 1933- *WhoAm 90*
Weiner, Irving J. 1920- *St&PR 91*
Weiner, Irwin M. 1930- *WhoAm 90*
Weiner, Jan Davis *ODwPR 91*
Weiner, Jay H. 1925- *St&PR 91*
Weiner, Jeffrey Robert 1949- *BiDrAPA 89*
Weiner, Jerome Harris 1923- *WhoAm 90*
Weiner, Joel David 1936- *WhoAm 90*
Weiner, Jonathan J *BiDrAPA 89*
Weiner, Karen Lynn 1943- *WhoAmW 91*
Weiner, Katherine Shephard 1964- *WhoAmW 91*
Weiner, Kenneth L *BiDrAPA 89*
Weiner, Laurie Beth 1950- *WhoSSW 91*
Weiner, Lawrence Charles 1942- *WhoAmA 91*
Weiner, Lawrence G *BiDrAPA 89*
Weiner, Lawrence Ian *BiDrAPA 89*
Weiner, Lili Ruth 1951- *WhoSSW 91*
Weiner, Lynn Joy 1959- *WhoAmW 91, WhoE 91*
Weiner, Margaret B *BiDrAPA 89*
Weiner, Marian Murphy 1954- *WhoAmW 91*
Weiner, Mark 1955- *ODwPR 91*
Weiner, Martin Norman 1943- *BiDrAPA 89*
Weiner, Martin S. 1938- *St&PR 91*
Weiner, Marvin 1925- *St&PR 91*
Weiner, Max 1926- *WhoAm 90*
Weiner, Mervyn 1935- *WhoE 91*
Weiner, Mervyn Lester 1922- *WhoE 91*
Weiner, Michael J. 1947- *WhoAm 90*
Weiner, Michael Lewis 1954- *WhoEmL 91*
Weiner, Morton David 1922- *WhoAm 90*
Weiner, Murray 1934- *WhoE 91*
Weiner, Myron 1931- *WhoAm 90, WhoWrEP 89*
Weiner, Myron F 1934- *BiDrAPA 89*
Weiner, Neil Allen *BiDrAPA 89*
Weiner, Paul 1941- *St&PR 91*
Weiner, Richard 1927- *ODwPR 91, St&PR 91, WhoAm 90*
Weiner, Richard B 1953- *BiDrAPA 89*
Weiner, Richard David 1945- *BiDrAPA 89*
Weiner, Richard Max 1930- *WhoWor 91*
Weiner, Robert L. *BioIn 16*
Weiner, Robert M 1931- *BiDrAPA 89*
Weiner, Robert Neil 1952- *WhoEmL 91*
Weiner, Robert Stephen 1947- *WhoE 91*
Weiner, Ronald Gary 1945- *WhoEmL 91*
Weiner, Sandra 1922- *AuBYP 90*
Weiner, Seymour W. *BioIn 16*
Weiner, Sharon R. 1944- *ODwPR 91*
Weiner, Sheldon 1938- *BiDrAPA 89*
Weiner, Stephen Arthur 1933- *WhoAm 90*
Weiner, Stuart 1942- *WhoE 91*
Weiner, Susan Beth *WhoAmW 91*
Weiner, Sy 1949- *WhoSSW 91*
Weiner, Ted 1911-1979 *WhoAmA 91N*
Weiner, Tess Manilla *WhoAmA 91*
Weiner, Theodore Jeffrey 1947- *WhoE 91*
Weiner, Thomas Edgar 1949- *St&PR 91*
Weiner, Timothy Emlyn 1956- *WhoAm 90, WhoE 91*
Weiner, Walter H. 1930- *St&PR 91*
Weiner, Walter Herman 1930- *WhoAm 90, WhoE 91*
Weiner, Warren 1943- *St&PR 91, WhoAm 90*
Weiner-Alexander, Sandra Samuel 1947- *WhoEmL 91*
Weinerman, Rivian *BiDrAPA 89*
Weinert, Carl R. 1923- *St&PR 91*
Weinert, Carl Robert 1923- *WhoAm 90*
Weinert, Donald Gregory 1930- *WhoAm 90*
Weinert, Fritzie Johanna 1933- *WhoAmW 91*
Weinert, Jack M. 1943- *St&PR 91*
Weinert, Lefty 1901-1973 *Ballpl 90*
Weinfeld, Lewis Arthur 1943- *St&PR 91*
Weinfeld, Morris 1898-1988 *BioIn 16*
Weingaertner, Hans 1896-1970 *WhoAmA 91N*
Weingard, Joseph D. 1945- *St&PR 91*
Weingard, Joseph David 1945- *WhoAm 90*
Weingard, Marvin Allen 1934- *St&PR 91*
Weingart, Wolfgang 1941- *ConDes 90*
Weingarten, Henry *EncO&P 3*
Weingarten, Herbert N. 1927- *WhoAm 90*
Weingarten, Hilde *WhoAm 90, WhoAmA 91*
Weingarten, Judith Careyn 1951- *BiDrAPA 89*
Weingarten, Kathy 1947- *WhoAmW 91*
Weingarten, Max 1914- *St&PR 91*
Weingarten, Morey Abram 1941- *BiDrAPA 89*
Weingarten, Murray 1925- *St&PR 91, WhoAm 90*
Weingarten, R 1942- *BiDrAPA 89*
Weingarten, Robert I. 1941- *St&PR 91*
Weingarten, Sol 1925- *BiDrAPA 89*
Weingarten, William Andrew 1936- *WhoE 91*
Weingartner, Felix 1863-1942 *PenDiMP*
Weingartner, Hans Martin 1929- *WhoAm 90*
Weingartner, Pedro 1853-1929 *ArtLatA*
Weingartner, Rudolph Herbert 1927- *WhoAm 90*
Weingast, David Elliott 1912- *AuBYP 90*
Weingeist, Thomas Alan 1940- *WhoAm 90*
Weingold, Allan B. 1930- *WhoAm 90*
Weingold, Peter Joshua 1950- *BiDrAPA 89*
Weingrod, Carol Eve *BiDrAPA 89*
Weingrow, Howard L. 1922- *WhoAm 90*
Weinhardt, Carl 1922- *WhoAmA 91N*
Weinhauer, William Gillette 1924- *WhoSSW 91*
Weinhaus, Robert Stanley 1922- *BiDrAPA 89*
Weinheim, Donna L. 1951- *WhoAmW 91*
Weinhold, Donald Leroy, Jr. 1946- *WhoEmL 91*
Weinhold, Kerry Lee 1942- *WhoE 91*
Weinhold, Kurt *BioIn 16, NewYTBS 90*
Weinhold, Otto 1854-1912 *PenDiDA 89*
Weinhold, Virginia Beamer 1932- *WhoAm 90, WhoWor 91*
Weinholt, Francis Edward, Jr. *BiDrAPA 89*
Weinhouse, Sidney 1909- *WhoAm 90*
Weinig, Robert Walter 1930- *St&PR 91, WhoAm 90, WhoE 91*
Weinig, Sheldon 1928- *St&PR 91, WhoAm 90*
Weiniger, Salomon *PenDiDA 89*
Weininger, Janet *BioIn 16*
Weininger, Jean 1945- *WhoEmL 91*
Weinitschke, Hubertus Josef 1929- *WhoWor 91*
Weinkam, John W. 1951- *St&PR 91*
Weinkauf, Mary Louise S. 1938- *WhoWrEP 89*
Weinkauf, Mary Louise Stanley 1938- *WhoAmW 91*
Weinklam, Walter J. 1915- *St&PR 91*
Weinland, George C 1923- *BiDrAPA 89*
Weinman, Adolph Alexander 1870-1952 *WhoAmA 91N*
Weinman, Connie G. 1943- *St&PR 91*
Weinman, Connie Germann 1943- *WhoAmW 91*
Weinman, Ellen Shelton 1951- *WhoEmL 91*
Weinman, Glenn Alan 1955- *WhoEmL 91*
Weinman, Joel B. 1937- *WhoE 91*
Weinman, Robert Alexander 1915- *WhoAm 90, WhoAmA 91*
Weinman, Roberta Sue 1945- *WhoEmL 91*
Weinmann, Bert Millicent Landes 1924- *WhoE 91*
Weinmann, Donald Eugene 1934- *St&PR 91*
Weinmann, Gerald Albert 1930- *St&PR 91*
Weinmann, John Giffen 1928- *WhoAm 90, WhoSSW 91, WhoWor 91*
Weinpel, Marc John 1949- *WhoEmL 91*
Weinraub, Michael N. 1943- *St&PR 91*
Weinreb, Efrem 1921- *St&PR 91*
Weinreb, Joseph 1908- *BiDrAPA 89*
Weinreich, Agnes 1873-1946 *BiDWomA*
Weinreich, Beatrice Silverman 1928- *ConAu 129*
Weinreich, Gabriel 1928- *WhoAm 90*
Weinreich, Howard B. 1942- *St&PR 91*
Weinrib, Sidney 1919- *WhoAm 90*
Weinrich, Brian Erwin 1952- *WhoE 91*
Weinrich, Harald 1927- *WhoWor 91*
Weinrod, Emanuel 1929- *St&PR 91*
Weinroth, Abe 1912- *WhoE 91*
Weinroth, Leonard A *BiDrAPA 89*
Weinroth, Robert Stuart 1952- *WhoE 91*
Weinroth, Stephen D. *WhoAm 90*
Weins, Leo Matthew 1912- *WhoAm 90*
Weinschel, Bruno Oscar 1919- *WhoAm 90, WhoE 91, WhoWor 91*
Weinschelbaum, Emilio 1935- *WhoWor 91*
Weinshank, Herbert S *BiDrAPA 89*
Weinsheimer, Alfred J. 1936- *St&PR 91*
Weinsheimer, William Cyrus 1941- *WhoAm 90*
Weinshel, Edward M 1919- *BiDrAPA 89*
Weinshenker, Naomi Joyce *BiDrAPA 89*
Weinshienk, Zita Leeson 1933- *WhoAm 90, WhoAmW 91*
Weinstein, Abraham Hyman 1912- *St&PR 91*
Weinstein, Alan I. 1943- *St&PR 91*
Weinstein, Alfred Bernard 1917- *WhoE 91*
Weinstein, Alice *BioIn 16*
Weinstein, Allan M. 1945- *WhoAm 90*
Weinstein, Barry Gerald 1942- *BiDrAPA 89*
Weinstein, Bernard 1920- *St&PR 91*
Weinstein, Beryl J. 1928- *St&PR 91*
Weinstein, Carol Barbara 1937- *WhoE 91*
Weinstein, Carol Wendy *BiDrAPA 89*
Weinstein, Carol Wendy 1958- *WhoE 91*
Weinstein, Charles David 1953- *WhoEmL 91*
Weinstein, David B 1939- *BiDrAPA 89*
Weinstein, Deena *BioIn 16*
Weinstein, Diane Gilbert 1947- *WhoAmW 91*
Weinstein, Dorothy Oshlag 1933- *WhoSSW 91*
Weinstein, Elliott 1934- *St&PR 91*
Weinstein, Erica *BiDrAPA 89*
Weinstein, Frederic 1944- *BiDrAPA 89*
Weinstein, Gary Stephen *BiDrAPA 89*
Weinstein, George 1924- *St&PR 91*
Weinstein, George 1927- *WhoE 91*
Weinstein, George William 1935- *WhoAm 90, WhoWor 91*
Weinstein, Gerald Edwin 1929- *BiDrAPA 89*
Weinstein, Gerald Saul 1931- *WhoAm 90*
Weinstein, Harris *WhoE 91, WhoWor 91*
Weinstein, Harvey Marvin 1942- *BiDrAPA 89*
Weinstein, Henry C *BiDrAPA 89*
Weinstein, Henry T. *WhoAm 90*
Weinstein, Herbert 1933- *WhoAm 90*
Weinstein, I. Bernard 1930- *WhoAm 90*
Weinstein, Ira Phillip 1919- *WhoAm 90*
Weinstein, Irwin Marshall 1926- *WhoAm 90*
Weinstein, Jack H *BiDrAPA 89*
Weinstein, James Gerald 1948- *WhoEmL 91*
Weinstein, Jay A. 1942- *WhoAm 90*
Weinstein, Jeffrey A. 1951- *St&PR 91*
Weinstein, Jeffrey Allen 1951- *WhoAm 90*
Weinstein, Jerome J. 1924- *St&PR 91*
Weinstein, Jerry L. 1936- *St&PR 91*
Weinstein, Joyce 1931- *WhoAmA 91, WhoAmW 91*
Weinstein, Leo 1921- *WhoAm 90*
Weinstein, Leo Steven *BiDrAPA 89*
Weinstein, Leonard Harlan 1926- *WhoE 91*
Weinstein, Lewis H. 1905- *WhoAm 90, WhoWor 91*
Weinstein, Lewis M. 1940- *St&PR 91*
Weinstein, Louis 1909- *WhoAm 90*
Weinstein, M Howard 1941- *BiDrAPA 89*
Weinstein, Marion Louis 1944- *WhoSSW 91*
Weinstein, Mark Michael 1942- *WhoAm 90*
Weinstein, Martin 1936- *St&PR 91, WhoAm 90*
Weinstein, Martin 1940- *BiDrAPA 89*
Weinstein, Martin Paul 1952- *WhoEmL 91*
Weinstein, Marvin M. 1943- *St&PR 91*
Weinstein, May *BiDrAPA 89*
Weinstein, Michael *BioIn 16*
Weinstein, Michael A 1942- *ConAu 129*
Weinstein, Michael Alan 1942- *WhoAm 90*
Weinstein, Michael Magen 1948- *WhoE 91*
Weinstein, Milton Charles 1949- *WhoAm 90*
Weinstein, Monte M 1933- *BiDrAPA 89*
Weinstein, Morris 1931- *St&PR 91*
Weinstein, Nadine Barbara 1942- *WhoE 91*
Weinstein, Nancy Anne 1925- *WhoAmW 91*
Weinstein, Nathan *MajTwCW*
Weinstein, Nathan Von Wallenstein *MajTwCW*
Weinstein, Norman 1948- *WhoWrEP 89*
Weinstein, Norman Charles 1948- *ConAu 31NR*
Weinstein, Norman Warren *BiDrAPA 89*
Weinstein, Paul Allen 1933- *WhoE 91*
Weinstein, Peter M. 1947- *WhoSSW 91*
Weinstein, Richard Neal 1948- *WhoSSW 91*
Weinstein, Richard S. *WhoAm 90*
Weinstein, Robert Harvey 1942- *BiDrAPA 89*
Weinstein, Robert J. 1945- *St&PR 91*
Weinstein, Rocio Aitania 1943- *WhoWrEP 89*
Weinstein, Ronald B 1932- *BiDrAPA 89*
Weinstein, Ronald S. 1938- *WhoAm 90*
Weinstein, Roy 1927- *WhoAm 90, WhoSSW 91, WhoWor 91*
Weinstein, Ruth Joseph 1933- *WhoAm 90*
Weinstein, Sharon Ruth 1950- *BiDrAPA 89, WhoE 91*
Weinstein, Sharon Schlein 1942- *ODwPR 91*
Weinstein, Sidney 1920- *WhoAm 90*
Weinstein, Sidney 1922- *WhoAm 90*
Weinstein, Stanley 1926- *WhoE 91*
Weinstein, Stanley 1929- *WhoAm 90*
Weinstein, Stanley Howard 1948- *St&PR 91*
Weinstein, Stephen Brant 1938- *WhoAm 90*
Weinstein, Stephen Saul 1939- *WhoWor 91*
Weinstein, Steven David 1946- *WhoEmL 91*
Weinstein, Steven H *BiDrAPA 89*
Weinstein, Wendy M. 1962- *WhoE 91*
Weinstein, William Joseph 1917- *WhoWor 91*
Weinstein-Bacal, Stuart Allen 1948- *WhoWor 91*
Weinstock, Lord 1924- *WhoWor 91*
Weinstock, Adolph 1913- *BiDrAPA 89*
Weinstock, Benjamin 1953- *WhoEmL 91*
Weinstock, Charles 1930- *BiDrAPA 89*
Weinstock, Eleanor 1929- *WhoAmW 91*
Weinstock, George David 1937- *WhoE 91*
Weinstock, Grace Evangeline 1904- *WhoAmW 91*
Weinstock, Harold 1925- *WhoAm 90*
Weinstock, Herbert 1905-1971 *AuBYP 90*
Weinstock, Herbert Frank 1913- *WhoAm 90*
Weinstock, Jerrold *BiDrAPA 89*
Weinstock, Joseph Saul *BiDrAPA 89*
Weinstock, Leonard 1935- *WhoAm 90*
Weinstock, Lotus *BioIn 16*
Weinstock, M D 1922- *ConAu 131*
Weinstock, Marya 1928- *WhoAmW 91*
Weinstock, Robert 1919- *WhoWor 91*
Weinstock, Robert 1941- *BiDrAPA 89*
Weinstock, Rose *WhoAmA 91*
Weinstock, Walter Wolfe 1925- *WhoAm 90*
Weintraub, Abner Edward 1954- *WhoSSW 91*
Weintraub, Amy 1951- *WhoAmW 91*
Weintraub, Annette 1946- *WhoAmA 91*
Weintraub, Arden Loren 1949- *BiDrAPA 89*
Weintraub, Daniel Ralph 1939- *WhoE 91*
Weintraub, Edward Alan 1947- *St&PR 91*
Weintraub, Eliot Roy 1943- *WhoAm 90*
Weintraub, Ellen Ruth 1949- *WhoE 91*
Weintraub, Eric *BiDrAPA 89*
Weintraub, Fred 1928- *ConTFT 8*
Weintraub, Gershon Henry 1957- *St&PR 91*
Weintraub, Harvey 1937- *BiDrAPA 89*
Weintraub, Harvey B 1929- *BiDrAPA 89*
Weintraub, Henry 1937- *WhoAm 90*
Weintraub, Herbert 1933- *St&PR 91*
Weintraub, Howard 1929- *BiDrAPA 89*
Weintraub, Hyman L. 1914- *St&PR 91*
Weintraub, Jacob D *WhoAmA 91*
Weintraub, Jane Ann 1954- *WhoEmL 91, WhoSSW 91*
Weintraub, Joseph 1904- *St&PR 91*
Weintraub, Joseph 1945- *WhoWrEP 89*
Weintraub, Linda 1942- *WhoAmA 91*
Weintraub, Louis *ODwPR 91*
Weintraub, Michael 1938- *St&PR 91*
Weintraub, Michael Ira 1940- *WhoAm 90*
Weintraub, Phil 1907- *Ballpl 90*
Weintraub, Phil 1907-1987 *BioIn 16*
Weintraub, Philippe *BiDrAPA 89*
Weintraub, Richard J 1944- *BiDrAPA 89*
Weintraub, Robert M 1935- *ODwPR 91*
Weintraub, Robert Martin 1938- *BiDrAPA 89*
Weintraub, Russell Jay 1929- *WhoAm 90*
Weintraub, Ruth G. 1909- *WhoAm 90*
Weintraub, Sam, Jr. 1915- *St&PR 91*
Weintraub, Sidney 1922- *WhoAm 90*
Weintraub, Stan J. 1935- *St&PR 91*
Weintraub, Stanley 1905- *St&PR 91*
Weintraub, Stanley 1929- *WhoAm 90, WhoWrEP 89*
Weintraub, Thomas E. 1922- *St&PR 91*
Weintraub, Walter *BiDrAPA 89*
Weintraub, Wiktor 1908-1988 *BioIn 16*
Weintraub, Zachery Allan 1951- *St&PR 91*
Weintrob, Alex 1935- *BiDrAPA 89, WhoE 91*
Weintz, Caroline Giles 1952- *WhoAmW 91, WhoE 91, WhoEmL 91*
Weintz, J. Fred, Jr. 1926- *St&PR 91*
Weintz, Jacob Frederick, Jr. 1926- *WhoAm 90*
Weiny, George Azem 1933- *WhoWor 91*
Weinzapfel, Connie A 1956- *WhoAmA 91*
Weinzieher, Sana *EncCoWW*
Weinzierl, Erika 1925- *WhoWor 91*
Weippl, Gerald Theodor 1927- *WhoWor 91*

Weir, Alexander, Jr. 1922- *WhoAm 90*
Weir, Anthony 1936- *St&PR 91*
Weir, Benjamin *BioIn 16*
Weir, Carol *BioIn 16*
Weir, Charles Dudley 1935- *St&PR 91*
Weir, David Stewart 1932- *WhoAm 90*
Weir, Don Clair 1912- *WhoAm 90*
Weir, Felix Fowler 1884-1978 *DcAfAmP*
Weir, Gavin 1931- *St&PR 91*
Weir, Gillian 1941- *PenDiMP*
Weir, Gillian Constance 1941- *IntWWM 90, WhoWor 91*
Weir, Gloria Jane 1921- *WhoAmW 91, WhoSSW 91*
Weir, Irene 1862-1944 *BiDWomA*
Weir, James 1821-1906 *LiHiK*
Weir, Joan 1928- *ConAu 31NR*
Weir, Judith 1954- *IntWWM 90, PenDiMP A*
Weir, Kenneth Wynn 1930- *WhoAm 90*
Weir, Linda Katherine *BiDrAPA 89*
Weir, Mary Avis *BiDrAPA 89*
Weir, Morton Webster 1934- *WhoAm 90, WhoWor 91*
Weir, Paul Carlson 1951- *BiDrAPA 89*
Weir, Paul Joseph 1923- *St&PR 91, WhoAm 90*
Weir, Peter 1944- *BioIn 16*
Weir, Peter Frank 1933- *WhoAm 90*
Weir, Peter Lindsay 1944- *WhoWor 91*
Weir, Rayner 1930- *St&PR 91*
Weir, Robert McColloch 1933- *WhoSSW 91*
Weir, Rosemary 1905- *AuBYP 90*
Weir, Stephen James 1940- *WhoAm 90*
Weir, Stephen Lynn 1949- *WhoAm 90*
Weir, Theresa Ann 1954- *WhoWrEP 89*
Weir, Thomas Charles 1933- *WhoAm 90*
Weir, Thomas Henry 1934- *St&PR 91*
Weir, Todd Michael 1953- *WhoEmL 91*
Weir, Virginia Leigh 1958- *WhoWrEP 89*
Weir, Walter, Jr. 1947- *WhoEmL 91*
Weir, William C. 1937- *St&PR 91*
Weir, William C., III 1937- *WhoAm 90, WhoSSW 91*
Weir, William Wilbur *NewYTBS 90*
Weirauch, Anna Elisabet 1887-1970 *EncCoWW*
Weirich, Richard D. 1944- *St&PR 91*
Weirick, William Newton 1952- *WhoSSW 91*
Weirman, Krista A. *ODwPR 91*
Weis, Al 1938- *Ballpl 90*
Weis, Arthur M. 1925- *St&PR 91*
Weis, David H. 1931- *St&PR 91*
Weis, Dierk Joachim 1925- *WhoWor 91*
Weis, Henry B., III 1940- *St&PR 91*
Weis, Joseph Francis, Jr. 1923- *WhoAm 90, WhoE 91*
Weis, Judith Shulman 1941- *WhoAmW 91, WhoE 91*
Weis, Konrad M. 1928- *St&PR 91*
Weis, Konrad Max 1928- *WhoAm 90, WhoE 91*
Weis, Marcia Rae 1955- *WhoEmL 91*
Weis, Margaret Edith 1948- *WhoEmL 91*
Weis, Michael Thomas 1945- *St&PR 91*
Weis, Robert F. 1919- *St&PR 91*
Weis, Sigfried 1916- *WhoE 91*
Weis, Thomas Bernard 1942- *St&PR 91*
Weis, Walter Robert 1941- *St&PR 91*
Weisbach, Theodore Lowell 1953- *St&PR 91*
Weisbard, Dena M. *ODwPR 91*
Weisbard, James Joseph *BiDrAPA 89*
Weisbard, James Joseph 1953- *WhoE 91*
Weisbard, Samuel 1922- *WhoAm 90*
Weisbecker, Clement *WhoAmA 91N*
Weisbecker, Frank D. 1934- *St&PR 91*
Weisbecker, Norman C. 1923- *WhoAm 90*
Weisberg, Alfred Mhyron 1926- *WhoAm 90*
Weisberg, Alma Raynes 1927- *WhoE 91*
Weisberg, Arthur 1931- *IntWWM 90*
Weisberg, Arthur Barry *BiDrAPA 89*
Weisberg, David Herman 1950- *St&PR 91*
Weisberg, Gabriel P 1942- *WhoAmA 91*
Weisberg, Harry M. 1932- *WhoAm 90*
Weisberg, Herbert Frank 1941- *WhoAm 90*
Weisberg, Ira 1949- *St&PR 91*
Weisberg, Jay Gilbert *BiDrAPA 89*
Weisberg, Jonathan M. 1943- *ODwPR 91*
Weisberg, Jonathan Mark 1943- *WhoAm 90*
Weisberg, Joseph S. *AuBYP 90*
Weisberg, Leonard R. 1929- *WhoAm 90*
Weisberg, Louis W 1949- *BiDrAPA 89*
Weisberg, Lynne W *BiDrAPA 89*
Weisberg, Lynne W. 1948- *WhoE 91*
Weisberg, Michael S. *BioIn 16*
Weisberg, Morris L. 1921- *WhoAm 90*
Weisberg, Paul S 1932- *BiDrAPA 89*
Weisberg, Ruth *WhoAmW 91*
Weisberg, Ruth Ellen 1942- *WhoAmA 91*
Weisberg, Ruth Maxine 1956- *WhoAmW 91*
Weisberg, Stuart Elliot 1949- *WhoE 91*
Weisberg, Tim *NewAgMG*
Weisberger, Barbara 1926- *WhoAm 90, WhoAmW 91*
Weisberger, Gerald L. 1932- *St&PR 91*
Weisberger, Joseph Robert 1920- *WhoAm 90, WhoE 91, WhoWor 91*
Weisberrg, Alfred P. 1926- *St&PR 91*
Weisblat, Howard Alan 1935- *St&PR 91*
Weisblatt, Sanford Aaron 1929- *BiDrAPA 89*
Weisblatt, Steven A 1958- *BiDrAPA 89*
Weisbrod, Annette 1937- *IntWWM 90*
Weisbrod, Burton Allen 1931- *WhoWrEP 89*
Weisbrod, Harold 1921- *St&PR 91*
Weisbrod, Marcy Helfand 1954- *WhoEmL 91*
Weisbrot, Deborah Marcia *BiDrAPA 89*
Weisbrot, Robert 1951- *ConAu 131*
Weisbruch, William Douglas 1935- *St&PR 91*
Weisbuch, Robert Alan 1946- *WhoAm 90*
Weisburd, Arthur Mark 1948- *WhoSSW 91*
Weisburd, Steven I. 1949- *WhoEmL 91*
Weisburger, Elizabeth Kreiser 1924- *WhoAm 90, WhoAmW 91*
Weisburger, John Hans 1921- *WhoAm 90*
Weischenberg, Peter H. 1938- *St&PR 91*
Weisdorf, William 1910- *BiDrAPA 89*
Weise, Charles C 1929- *BiDrAPA 89*
Weise, Charles Martin 1926- *WhoAm 90*
Weise, Joan Carolyn 1939- *WhoAmW 91*
Weise, Richard H. 1935- *St&PR 91*
Weisel, Deborah Delp *WhoAmA 91N*
Weisel, Walter K. 1940- *St&PR 91*
Weisenberger, Anthony J 1944- *BiDrAPA 89*
Weisenberger, Janet Ann *BiDrAPA 89*
Weisenberger, Scott 1955- *WhoE 91*
Weisenburger, Theodore M. 1930- *WhoWor 91*
Weisend, C. Frederick 1926- *St&PR 91*
Weisenfluh, Frederick Allen 1934- *St&PR 91*
Weisenfreund, Jochanan M 1938- *BiDrAPA 89*
Weiser, Conrad 1696-1760 *WhNaAH*
Weiser, David Joseph 1945- *BiDrAPA 89*
Weiser, Donna Louise 1963- *WhoE 91*
Weiser, Elsie Lievens 1930- *WhoAmW 91*
Weiser, Frank Alan 1953- *WhoEmL 91, WhoWor 91*
Weiser, Irving 1947- *St&PR 91, WhoAm 90*
Weiser, Johann Conrad 1696-1760 *EncCRAm*
Weiser, John Wolfgang 1932- *St&PR 91*
Weiser, Marjorie Phillis Katz *AuBYP 90*
Weiser, Michael L. 1952- *ODwPR 91*
Weiser, Neil 1952- *BiDrAPA 89*
Weiser, Norman Sidney 1919- *WhoAm 90, WhoE 91, WhoWor 91*
Weiser, Paul David 1936- *St&PR 91, WhoAm 90*
Weiser, Peter Michael 1943- *BiDrAPA 89*
Weiser, Robert C. 1946- *St&PR 91*
Weiser, Ronald S. 1943- *WhoSSW 91*
Weiser, Sherwood Manuel 1931- *WhoAm 90, WhoSSW 91*
Weiser, Steven F. 1946- *WhoSSW 91*
Weiser, Terry L. 1954- *St&PR 91*
Weiser, Terry Lee 1954- *WhoWor 91*
Weisert, Kent Albert Frederick 1949- *WhoE 91, WhoWor 91*
Weisfeld, Lewis Bernard 1929- *St&PR 91, WhoE 91*
Weisfeld, Sheldon 1946- *WhoEmL 91*
Weisfeldt, Myron Lee 1940- *WhoAm 90*
Weisfelner, Marion *BioIn 16*
Weisfogel, Jerry *BiDrAPA 89*
Weisgal, Jeanne Nancy 1925- *WhoE 91*
Weisgall, Hugo 1912- *IntWWM 90*
Weisgall, Hugo David 1912- *WhoAm 90*
Weisgall, Jonathan Michael 1949- *WhoEmL 91*
Weisgarber, Elliot 1919- *IntWWM 90*
Weisgard, Leonard Joseph 1916- *AuBYP 90*
Weisgerber, David Wendelin 1938- *WhoAm 90, WhoWrEP 89*
Weisgerber, George Ronald 1933- *St&PR 91*
Weisgerber, Jean 1924- *WhoWor 91*
Weishaar, Sandra J. 1947- *WhoAmW 91*
Weishar, Beverly Norman 1931- *ODwPR 91*
Weishaus, James 1919- *BiDrAPA 89*
Weishaus, Joel 1939- *WhoWrEP 89*
Weisheit, Lawrence Ernest 1938- *St&PR 91*
Weisiger, Edward Innes 1931- *St&PR 91, WhoAm 90*
Weisiger, Kathleen Wendell 1949- *WhoE 91*
Weisiger, Richard A. 1946- *WhoEmL 91*
Weisinger, Ronald Jay 1946- *WhoEmL 91, WhoSSW 91, WhoWor 91*
Weiskel, Catherine Lacny 1950- *WhoAm 90, WhoAmW 91*
Weiskittel, Ralph Joseph 1924- *WhoAm 90*
Weiskopf, Paul D. 1929- *St&PR 91*
Weisl, Edwin L., Jr. 1929- *WhoWor 91*
Weisler, Bob 1930- *Ballpl 90*
Weisler, Jacob M 1928- *BiDrAPA 89*
Weisler, Richard Harry *BiDrAPA 89*
Weislogel, Lee David 1937- *St&PR 91*
Weisman, Abner I. *NewYTBS 90*
Weisman, Adele *BioIn 16*
Weisman, Ann E. 1948- *WhoWrEP 89*
Weisman, Avery Danto 1913- *BiDrAPA 89, WhoE 91*
Weisman, Barbara 1954- *WhoAmW 91*
Weisman, Charles Leon 1952- *BiDrAPA 89*
Weisman, Daniel Otto 1956- *WhoEmL 91*
Weisman, Edward Bernard 1924- *BiDrAPA 89*
Weisman, Ezra 1940- *St&PR 91*
Weisman, Gilbert K 1936- *BiDrAPA 89*
Weisman, Henry *St&PR 91*
Weisman, Henry W J 1951- *BiDrAPA 89*
Weisman, Howard Jay 1940- *BiDrAPA 89*
Weisman, Irving 1918- *WhoAm 90*
Weisman, Joel 1928- *WhoAm 90*
Weisman, John *BioIn 16*
Weisman, John 1942- *WhoE 91*
Weisman, Kenneth E 1930- *EncO&P 3*
Weisman, Leslie Helen 1953- *WhoAmW 91*
Weisman, Lorenzo David 1945- *St&PR 91*
Weisman, Maxwell N 1912- *BiDrAPA 89*
Weisman, Maxwell Napier 1912- *WhoE 91*
Weisman, Michael Henry 1929- *St&PR 91*
Weisman, Mike *BioIn 16*
Weisman, Walter L. 1935- *WhoAm 90*
Weismann, Donald Leroy 1914- *WhoAm 90, WhoAmA 91*
Weismantel, Gregory N. 1940- *St&PR 91*
Weismantle, John Arthur 1942- *St&PR 91*
Weismeyer, Leonard 1936- *WhoSSW 91*
Weismiller, David R. 1943- *WhoAm 90*
Weismiller, Edward Ronald 1915- *SpyFic, WhoAm 90, WhoWrEP 89*
Weisner, Jeffrey T. 1947- *St&PR 91*
Weisner, Lynnette Brant 1958- *WhoAmW 91*
Weisner, Maurice Franklin 1917- *WhoAm 90*
Weisner, Ronald Alan 1947- *BiDrAPA 89*
Weisner, Wayne Michael 1923- *BiDrAPA 89*
Weiss, Alarich 1925- *WhoWor 91*
Weiss, Allan Joseph 1932- *WhoAm 90*
Weiss, Allen 1918- *WhoE 91*
Weiss, Allen C *BiDrAPA 89*
Weiss, Allen Charles 1945- *WhoE 91*
Weiss, Alvin Harvey 1928- *WhoAm 90*
Weiss, Amalie *PenDiMP*
Weiss, Andre *BiDrAPA 89*
Weiss, Andre 1926- *WhoE 91*
Weiss, Andrea Joy *BiDrAPA 89*
Weiss, Andrea Mendes 1955- *St&PR 91*
Weiss, Ann 1949- *WhoAmW 91, WhoE 91, WhoEmL 91, WhoWor 91*
Weiss, Ann E. 1943- *BioIn 16*
Weiss, Anthony O. *ODwPR 91*
Weiss, Armand Berl 1931- *WhoAm 90, WhoSSW 91, WhoWor 91*
Weiss, Arthur J. 1925- *WhoE 91*
Weiss, Bettejane 1947- *WhoAmW 91*
Weiss, Bob *WhoAm 90*
Weiss, Brian 1945- *WhoE 91*
Weiss, Brian Leslie 1944- *BiDrAPA 89*
Weiss, Burton 1947- *BiDrAPA 89*
Weiss, Carl 1938- *St&PR 91*
Weiss, Carl Otto 1941- *WhoWor 91*
Weiss, Carol J. 1957- *BiDrAPA 89*
Weiss, Carol Juliet 1957- *WhoE 91*
Weiss, Charles F. 1939- *St&PR 91*
Weiss, Charles Manuel 1918- *WhoAm 90*
Weiss, Charles S. 1952- *St&PR 91*
Weiss, Charles Zwi 1934- *BiDrAPA 89*
Weiss, Charlotte C 1927- *BiDrAPA 89*
Weiss, Clifford L. 1937- *St&PR 91*
Weiss, Daniel Leigh 1923- *WhoSSW 91*
Weiss, Daniel M 1917- *BiDrAPA 89, WhoE 91*
Weiss, David *BioIn 16*
Weiss, David 1928- *WhoAm 90*
Weiss, David Ansel 1909- *AuBYP 90*
Weiss, David Martin 1943- *WhoE 91*
Weiss, David Murry *BiDrAPA 89*
Weiss, David S. 1943- *St&PR 91*
Weiss, Debra S. 1953- *WhoAmW 91*
Weiss, Dennis S 1939- *BiDrAPA 89*
Weiss, Dennis V 1953- *BiDrAPA 89*
Weiss, Diane Judith 1954- *BiDrAPA 89*
Weiss, Donald J. 1943- *St&PR 91*
Weiss, Donald Logan 1926- *WhoAm 90*
Weiss, Dudley A. 1912- *St&PR 91*
Weiss, Dudley Albert 1912- *WhoE 91*
Weiss, Earle Burton 1932- *WhoAm 90*
Weiss, Edgar Jay *BiDrAPA 89*
Weiss, Edmund Charles, Jr. 1943- *St&PR 91*
Weiss, Edna *AuBYP 90*
Weiss, Edward 1929- *St&PR 91, WhoE 91*
Weiss, Edward Craig 1924- *WhoSSW 91*
Weiss, Edward G. *BioIn 16*
Weiss, Edward J 1911- *BiDrAPA 89*
Weiss, Edward J. 1918- *St&PR 91*
Weiss, Edwin 1927- *WhoAm 90*
Weiss, Edwin T. 1901- *St&PR 91*
Weiss, Egon Arthur 1919- *WhoAm 90*
Weiss, Elaine Landsberg *WhoAmW 91, WhoE 91*
Weiss, Emilio 1918- *WhoE 91*
Weiss, Eric Joshua 1953- *WhoE 91*
Weiss, Erwin 1924- *St&PR 91*
Weiss, Ferdinand 1933- *IntWWM 90*
Weiss, Fred Geoffrey 1941- *St&PR 91*
Weiss, Gene J. 1952- *BiDrAPA 89*
Weiss, Georg Veit *PenDiDA 89*
Weiss, George 1894-1972 *Ballpl 90 [port]*
Weiss, George 1895-1972 *BioIn 16*
Weiss, George Arthur 1921- *WhoE 91*
Weiss, Gerhard Hans 1926- *WhoAm 90*
Weiss, Gerson 1939- *WhoAm 90*
Weiss, Harlan Lee 1941- *WhoE 91*
Weiss, Harold Peter 1951- *WhoE 91*
Weiss, Harry Joseph 1923- *WhoAm 90*
Weiss, Harvey 1922- *AuBYP 90, WhoAmA 91, WhoE 91*
Weiss, Helen L. 1925- *St&PR 91*
Weiss, Herbert D. 1929- *St&PR 91*
Weiss, Herbert J 1919- *BiDrAPA 89*
Weiss, Herbert Klemm 1917- *WhoAm 90, WhoWor 91*
Weiss, Hermann 1940- *WhoWor 91*
Weiss, Howard A. *IntWWM 90, WhoAm 90*
Weiss, Howard Rich 1924- *St&PR 91*
Weiss, Howard Seth *BiDrAPA 89*
Weiss, Ira Francis 1909- *WhoAm 90*
Weiss, Irving 1921- *WhoWrEP 89*
Weiss, Irving I. 1927- *St&PR 91*
Weiss, James M A *BiDrAPA 89*
Weiss, James Michael 1946- *WhoAm 90*
Weiss, James Moses Aaron 1921- *WhoAm 90, WhoWrEP 89*
Weiss, James Richard 1947- *BiDrAPA 89*
Weiss, James Robert 1953- *St&PR 91*
Weiss, James William 1940- *WhoSSW 91*
Weiss, Janet Lois 1946- *WhoE 91*
Weiss, Jeffrey Allan 1943- *WhoE 91*
Weiss, Jeffrey G. 1942- *St&PR 91*
Weiss, Jeffrey Paul 1957- *WhoE 91*
Weiss, Jerome Nathan 1959- *WhoAmA 91*
Weiss, Jerome Paul 1934- *St&PR 91, WhoAm 90*
Weiss, Joan R. 1937- *WhoAmW 91*
Weiss, Joan Wyzkoski 1949- *WhoE 91*
Weiss, Joel J. *WhoSSW 91*
Weiss, Joel Joseph 1931- *St&PR 91*
Weiss, Joel Marvin 1932- *WhoE 91*
Weiss, John Carroll, III 1948- *WhoE 91*
Weiss, John Joseph 1941- *WhoAmA 91*
Weiss, Jonathan Arthur 1939- *WhoE 91*
Weiss, Jonathan Samuel *BiDrAPA 89*
Weiss, Jordan Paul *BiDrAPA 89*
Weiss, Joseph 1924- *BiDrAPA 89*
Weiss, Joseph Joel 1931- *WhoAm 90*
Weiss, Joseph Walton *BiDrAPA 89*
Weiss, Judith Kelner 1950- *WhoAmW 91*
Weiss, Jules M 1928- *BiDrAPA 89*
Weiss, Kenneth Jay 1948- *BiDrAPA 89*
Weiss, Kim Elizabeth 1954- *WhoSSW 91*
Weiss, Laurence B *BiDrAPA 89*
Weiss, Lawrence James 1939- *St&PR 91*
Weiss, Leatie 1928- *BioIn 16*
Weiss, Lee 1928- *WhoAmA 91*
Weiss, Lee David *BiDrAPA 89*
Weiss, Leon P. 1925- *WhoAm 90*
Weiss, Leonard 1918- *WhoAm 90*
Weiss, Leonard 1934- *WhoAm 90*
Weiss, Leonard Aaron 1946- *St&PR 91*
Weiss, Leonard R. 1927- *St&PR 91*
Weiss, Leslie 1947- *WhoE 91*
Weiss, Lester 1957- *WhoE 91*
Weiss, Lionel Edward 1927- *WhoAm 90*
Weiss, Louis 1950- *St&PR 91*
Weiss, Louise 1893-1983 *BiDFrPL*
Weiss, Lucinda 1950- *WhoAmW 91*
Weiss, Mabel Louise 1897- *WhoAmW 91*
Weiss, Maria Cristina Rodriguez 1949- *WhoAmW 91*
Weiss, Marilyn Magaliff 1932- *WhoAmW 91*
Weiss, Marjorie 1954- *WhoAmW 91*
Weiss, Mark 1950- *ODwPR 91*
Weiss, Mark 1960- *St&PR 91*
Weiss, Mark Anschel 1937- *WhoAm 90*
Weiss, Mark Lawrence 1945- *WhoAm 90*
Weiss, Martin Harvey 1939- *WhoAm 90*
Weiss, Marvin 1929- *WhoE 91*
Weiss, Marvin Arnold 1924- *WhoWor 91*
Weiss, Mary Alice 1957- *WhoAmW 91*
Weiss, Matthew 1951- *WhoE 91*
Weiss, Max Leslie 1933- *WhoAm 90*
Weiss, Max Tibor 1922- *WhoAm 90*
Weiss, Michael Armin 1948- *St&PR 91*
Weiss, Michael David 1942- *WhoE 91*
Weiss, Milton 1912- *WhoAmA 91, WhoE 91*
Weiss, Mitchell G 1947- *BiDrAPA 89*
Weiss, Morris 1924- *BiDrAPA 89*

Weiss, Morry 1940- St&PR 91, WhoAm 90
Weiss, Murray C. BioIn 16
Weiss, Myrna Colitz 1941- BiDrAPA 89
Weiss, Myrna Grace 1939- WhoAm 90, WhoAmW 91
Weiss, Nathan 1922- WhoE 91
Weiss, Neil Morton 1941- BiDrAPA 89
Weiss, Nicholas Albert 1929- St&PR 91
Weiss, Nicki 1951- BioIn 16
Weiss, Noel S. 1943- WhoAm 90
Weiss, Norman 1935- BiDrAPA 89
Weiss, Norman Jay 1942- WhoE 91
Weiss, Paul ConAu 129
Weiss, Paul 1898-1989 AnObit 1989
Weiss, Paul 1901- ConAu 12AS [port], WhoAm 90
Weiss, Paul A. 1898-1989 BioIn 16, ConAu 129
Weiss, Paul Irving BiDrAPA 89
Weiss, Paul Thomas 1944- WhoAm 90
Weiss, Pauline Edith BiDrAPA 89
Weiss, Peter 1916-1982 AuBYP 90, WorAlBi
Weiss, Peter, and Carol Weiss AuBYP 90
Weiss, Peter Jacques 1938- WhoWor 91
Weiss, Rachel 1954- WhoAmA 91, WhoE 91
Weiss, Raymond Otto, Jr. 1952- WhoE 91
Weiss, Renee 1923- AuBYP 90
Weiss, Rhett Louis 1961- WhoEmL 91, WhoSSW 91, WhoWor 91
Weiss, Rhoda Elaine 1949- WhoEmL 91
Weiss, Richard A. ODwPR 91
Weiss, Richard B 1954- BiDrAPA 89
Weiss, Richard T. St&PR 91
Weiss, Richard W 1944- BiDrAPA 89
Weiss, Richard William 1944- WhoE 91
Weiss, Rita S. 1935- WhoAmW 91
Weiss, Robert A. 1948- St&PR 91
Weiss, Robert Francis 1924- WhoAm 90
Weiss, Robert G. 1931- St&PR 91
Weiss, Robert H. 1931- ODwPR 91
Weiss, Robert J 1917- BiDrAPA 89
Weiss, Robert Jerome 1917- WhoAm 90
Weiss, Robert M. 1936- WhoAm 90
Weiss, Robert Michael 1940- WhoE 91
Weiss, Robert Orr 1926- WhoAm 90
Weiss, Robert S BiDrAPA 89
Weiss, Robert S. 1946- St&PR 91
Weiss, Robert Stephen 1946- WhoAm 90
Weiss, Roger Douglas 1951- BiDrAPA 89, WhoAm 90, WhoE 91
Weiss, Roger Eliot BiDrAPA 89
Weiss, Roger M. 1930- St&PR 91
Weiss, Ronald 1942- St&PR 91
Weiss, Ronald Phillip 1947- WhoE 91, WhoWor 91
Weiss, Ronald Whitman 1939- WhoAm 90
Weiss, Russell L. 1930- St&PR 91
Weiss, Russell Leonard 1930- WhoAm 90
Weiss, Ruth 1928- WhoWrEP 89
Weiss, Samson Raphael BioIn 16
Weiss, Samson Raphael 1910- WhoAm 90
Weiss, Samual 1924- St&PR 91, WhoWor 91
Weiss, Samuel BioIn 16
Weiss, Samuel 1923- BiDrAPA 89
Weiss, Samuel Scott 1954- WhoE 91
Weiss, Seymour 1925- WhoAm 90
Weiss, Seymour 1930- St&PR 91
Weiss, Shirley F. 1921- WhoAm 90, WhoAmW 91, WhoSSW 91
Weiss, Shmuel 1934- WhoWor 91
Weiss, Sidney WhoAm 90
Weiss, Sigmund WhoWrEP 89
Weiss, Stanford L. 1927- St&PR 91
Weiss, Stanley Alan 1926- WhoE 91
Weiss, Stanley C. 1929- St&PR 91
Weiss, Stanley I. 1925- St&PR 91
Weiss, Stanley Irwin 1925- WhoAm 90
Weiss, Stanley S 1925- BiDrAPA 89
Weiss, Stephen Edward 1953- WhoE 91
Weiss, Stephen Gary 1946- WhoE 91
Weiss, Stephen Henry 1935- WhoAm 90
Weiss, Stephen Joel 1938- WhoAm 90
Weiss, Susan Forscher 1944- IntWWM 90
Weiss, Theodore 1939- BiDrAPA 89
Weiss, Theodore Russell 1916- WhoAm 90, WhoWrEP 89
Weiss, Theodore S. 1927- WhoAm 90, WhoE 91
Weiss, Theresa Dominguez 1950- WhoAmW 91
Weiss, Thomas Edward 1916- WhoAm 90
Weiss, Thomas Keith 1947- WhoE 91
Weiss, Vickey Evelyn 1938- WhoAmW 91
Weiss, Victor J, Jr. 1929- BiDrAPA 89
Weiss, Volker 1930- WhoAm 90
Weiss, Walt BioIn 16
Weiss, Walt 1963- Ballpl 90
Weiss, Walter Stanley 1929- WhoAm 90
Weiss, William BioIn 16
Weiss, William L. 1929- St&PR 91
Weiss, William Lee 1929- WhoAm 90, WhoWor 91
Weiss, Yitzhak Yaakov BioIn 16
Weiss Geline, Deborah Lynn 1951- WhoAmW 91
Weiss-Schwartz, Sandra M BiDrAPA 89
Weissbach, Herbert 1932- WhoAm 90, WhoE 91
Weissbard, Samuel Held 1947- WhoE 91, WhoWor 91
Weissberg, Gary Alan 1949- BiDrAPA 89
Weissberg, Josef H 1928- BiDrAPA 89
Weissberg, Josef Herbert 1928- WhoE 91
Weissberg, Laura H 1959- BiDrAPA 89
Weissberg, Lawrence 1921- St&PR 91, WhoAm 90
Weissberg, Michael Peter 1942- BiDrAPA 89
Weissbourd, Bernice BioIn 16
Weissbuch, Oscar WhoAmA 91N
Weissburg, Estelle Doris 1932- WhoE 91
Weisse, Allen Barry 1929- WhoE 91
Weisse, Christian Felix 1726-1804 DcLB 97 [port]
Weisse, Guenter 1935- St&PR 91
Weissel, William St&PR 91
Weisselberger, David BiDrAPA 89
Weissen, Andre M. 1949- WhoWor 91
Weissenberg, Alexis 1929- IntWWM 90, PenDiMP, WhoWor 91
Weissenberg, Catherine Anne 1960- WhoAmW 91
Weissenborn, Sheridan Kendall 1948- WhoEmL 91
Weissenborn, Stanton F. 1925- St&PR 91
Weissenburger, Susan Kaye 1946- WhoWrEP 89
Weissenstein, Herbert 1945- WhoE 91
Weissensteiner, Raimund 1905- IntWWM 90
Weisser, John Dietmar 1933- WhoWor 91
Weisser, Thomas G. 1957- St&PR 91
Weisser, William James 1948- WhoSSW 91
Weisshaar, Kenneth R. 1950- St&PR 91
Weisskopf, Bernard 1929- WhoAm 90, WhoWor 91
Weisskopf, Thomas E. 1940- ConAu 130
Weisskopf, Victor Frederick 1908- WhoAm 90
Weisskopf-Joelson, Edith 1910-1983 BioIn 16
Weissler, Arnold Mervin 1927- WhoAm 90
Weissman, Alan M. 1944- St&PR 91
Weissman, Barry Jay 1938- St&PR 91
Weissman, Barry Leigh 1948- WhoWor 91
Weissman, Carol Sacker 1944- WhoAmW 91
Weissman, Edward 1927- St&PR 91
Weissman, Edward Joseph Herling 1943- WhoE 91
Weissman, Ellen Marcie 1960- BiDrAPA 89
Weissman, Eugene Yehuda 1931- WhoAm 90
Weissman, George 1919- BioIn 16, St&PR 91, WhoAm 90
Weissman, Ira J. 1931- St&PR 91
Weissman, Jack 1921- WhoAm 90
Weissman, Jack Burton BioIn 16
Weissman, Jerrold A. 1936- St&PR 91
Weissman, Joseph 1926- WhoAm 90
Weissman, Julian Paul 1943- WhoAmA 91
Weissman, Leon 1920- St&PR 91
Weissman, Maurice B. 1915- St&PR 91
Weissman, Michael Lewis 1934- WhoAm 90
Weissman, Norman 1925- ODwPR 91, WhoAm 90
Weissman, Paul Marshall 1931- WhoAm 90
Weissman, Robert Evan 1940- St&PR 91, WhoAm 90, WhoE 91
Weissman, Ronee Freeman 1951- WhoAmW 91
Weissman, Rozanne ODwPR 91
Weissman, Seymour P BiDrAPA 89
Weissman, Sidney Herman 1939- BiDrAPA 89
Weissman, Stephen M 1937- BiDrAPA 89
Weissman, Susan 1938- WhoE 91
Weissman, Walter 1947- WhoAmA 91
Weissman, William R. 1940- WhoAm 90
Weissmandel, Michael Dov 1903-1956 BioIn 16
Weissmann, Ben 1925- St&PR 91
Weissmann, Charles 1931- WhoWor 91
Weissmann, Gerald 1930- WhoAm 90
Weissmann, Heidi Seitelblum 1951- WhoAmW 91, WhoE 91, WhoEmL 91, WhoWor 91
Weissmuller, Johnny 1904-1984 BioIn 16, WorAlBi
Weisstein, Ulrich Werner 1925- WhoAm 90
Weisstub, Eli Bernard 1943- BiDrAPA 89
Weist, Dwight 1910- ConAu 132
Weist, Robert D., Sr. 1939- St&PR 91
Weistrop, Donna Etta 1944- WhoAmW 91
Weiswasser, Stephen Anthony 1940- St&PR 91, WhoAm 90
Weisweiler, Adam 1744-1820 PenDiDA 89
Weisweiler, Jean PenDiDA 89
Weisz, Louis Max 1941- St&PR 91
Weisz, Paul Burg 1919- WhoAm 90
Weisz, Stephen 1902- BiDrAPA 89
Weisz, Stephen Ranken 1940- WhoSSW 91
Weisz, Victor 1913-1966 BioIn 16
Weisz, William J. 1927- St&PR 91
Weisz, William Julius 1927- WhoAm 90
Weitekamper, Hans 1934- St&PR 91
Weiter, Eduard 1889-1945 BioIn 16
Weith, Jerrie Kay 1956- WhoAmW 91
Weith, John Robert 1949- St&PR 91
Weithas, William V. 1929- St&PR 91
Weithas, William Vincent 1929- WhoAm 90, WhoE 91
Weithers, John Gregory 1933- St&PR 91
Weithorn, Stanley Stephen 1924- WhoAm 90
Weitkamp, James George 1945- WhoE 91
Weitman, Robert M. 1905-1989 BioIn 16
Weitz, Bruce 1943- WhoAm 90
Weitz, Frederick William 1929- St&PR 91, WhoAm 90
Weitz, Jeanne Stewart 1920- WhoSSW 91
Weitz, John 1923- ConDes 90, WhoAm 90, WhoWor 91
Weitz, Leonard 1929- St&PR 91
Weitz, Martin Mishli 1909- WhoAm 90
Weitz, Michael Neal 1939- St&PR 91
Weitz, Wayne Paul 1966- WhoSSW 91
Weitzel, Harry John, Jr. 1938- St&PR 91, WhoAm 90
Weitzel, J.A. 1945- St&PR 91
Weitzel, James Winfield 1942- St&PR 91
Weitzel, John Anthony 1945- WhoEmL 91
Weitzel, John F., Jr. 1930- St&PR 91
Weitzel, John Patterson 1923- WhoAm 90
Weitzel, John Quinn 1928- WhoAm 90
Weitzel, Lori Louderback 1960- WhoAmW 91
Weitzel, Paul Edward, Jr. 1958- St&PR 91
Weitzel, Paul J. 1937- St&PR 91
Weitzel, Robert Allan BiDrAPA 89
Weitzel, Vernon Craig 1947- WhoWor 91
Weitzel, William Conrad, Jr. 1935- WhoAm 90
Weitzel, William David 1942- BiDrAPA 89, WhoSSW 91
Weitzen, Edward H. 1920- St&PR 91
Weitzen, Frederick BioIn 16
Weitzen, Hyman G 1914- BiDrAPA 89
Weitzenfeld, Marvin L. 1938- St&PR 91
Weitzenhoffer, A Max 1939- WhoAmA 91
Weitzenhoffer, Aaron Max, Jr. 1939- WhoE 91, WhoWor 91
Weitzer, Bernard 1929- St&PR 91, WhoAm 90
Weitzman, Arthur Joshua 1933- WhoAm 90
Weitzman, Marilyn 1950- WhoAmW 91
Weitzman, Martin L. 1942- WhoAm 90
Weitzman, Mary C. 1914- WhoE 91
Weitzman, Patricia Walsh BiDrAPA 89
Weitzman, Robert Harold 1937- WhoAm 90
Weitzman, Ronald 1945- IntWWM 90
Weitzman, Sarah Brown 1935- WhoE 91, WhoWrEP 89
Weitzmann, Kurt 1904- WhoAm 90, WhoAmA 91
Weitzner, Eric BiDrAPA 89
Weitzner, Harold 1933- WhoAm 90
Weitzner, Martin 1934- ODwPR 91
Weitzner, Michael Alfred BiDrAPA 89
Weix, Joseph B. 1927- St&PR 91
Weix, Joseph B., Jr. 1927- WhoAm 90
Weixel, Annetta Esther 1951- WhoEmL 91
Weixler, Robert Henry, Jr. 1943- St&PR 91
Weixlmann, Joseph Norman 1946- WhoWrEP 89
Weizman, Savine Gross 1929- ConAu 131
Weizmann, Chaim 1874-1952 BioIn 16, PolLCME, WorAlBi
Weizner, Denise Cecile 1962- WhoAmW 91
Weizsacker, Carl Friedrich, Freiherr Von 1912- WorAlBi
Weizsacker, Carl-Friedrich von 1912- WhoWor 91
Weizsacker, Ernst Heinrich von 1882-1951 BioIn 16
Weizsacker, Richard von 1920- WhoWor 91
Wejchert, Alexandra 1920- BiDWomA
Wejchert, Andrzej 1937- WhoWor 91
Wejdling, Sven Otto 1930- WhoWor 91
Weker, Jonathan Lloyd 1954- BiDrAPA 89
Welaj, Johnny 1914- Ballpl 90
Welbaum, Daniel Louis 1952- WhoSSW 91
Welber, Herbert 1935- St&PR 91
Welber, Robert AuBYP 90
Welborn, Elsie Elender Jenkins 1937- WhoAmW 91
Welborn, Ernest W., Jr. 1922- St&PR 91
Welborn, Randy Clyde 1957- WhoSSW 91
Welborn, Reich Lee 1945- WhoEmL 91
Welborn, Sarah 1943- WhoAmW 91
Welburn, Ron 1944- WhoWrEP 89
Welby, Amelia 1819-1852 FemiCLE
Welby, Amelia B. 1819-1852 LiHiK
Welch, Arnold DeMerritt 1908- WhoAm 90
Welch, Arthur W. 1935- St&PR 91
Welch, Ashley James 1933- WhoAm 90
Welch, Betty Leonora 1961- WhoAmW 91, WhoEmL 91
Welch, Bob 1956- Ballpl 90, BioIn 16
Welch, Brian Craig 1941- St&PR 91
Welch, Byron Eugene 1928- WhoAm 90
Welch, C. William 1941- ODwPR 91
Welch, Calvert Joel 1957- WhoSSW 91
Welch, Carol Ann 1938- WhoAm 90
Welch, Carol Mae 1947- WhoAmW 91
Welch, Charles Alfred BiDrAPA 89
Welch, Charles D 1948- WhoAmA 91
Welch, Cindy BioIn 16
Welch, Claude E., Jr. 1939- ConAu 32NR
Welch, Claude Emerson 1906- WhoAm 90
Welch, Claude Emerson, Jr. 1939- WhoAm 90
Welch, Claude Raymond 1922- WhoAm 90
Welch, David 1950- ConAu 130
Welch, David William 1941- WhoWor 91
Welch, Dawn Renee 1965- WhoAmW 91
Welch, Denton BioIn 16
Welch, Donald Andrew 1939- St&PR 91
Welch, Douglas F. St&PR 91
Welch, Earl E. NewYTBS 90
Welch, Earl E. 1901-1990 BioIn 16
Welch, Edwin Hugh 1944- WhoAm 90
Welch, Elisabeth 1908- OxCPMus
Welch, Elisabeth 1909- BioIn 16, DrBlPA 90
Welch, Elizabeth Ann 1950- WhoAmW 91
Welch, Frank 1897-1957 Ballpl 90
Welch, Frederick Arthur 1949- St&PR 91
Welch, Garth Larry 1937- WhoAm 90
Welch, Gary William 1943- WhoAm 90
Welch, Gerald Martin BiDrAPA 89
Welch, Glenn Charles 1948- WhoSSW 91
Welch, Harry J. 1921- ODwPR 91
Welch, Harry Scoville 1923- WhoAm 90
Welch, James 1940- WorAu 1980
Welch, James Allen 1950- St&PR 91
Welch, James E 1924- BiDrAPA 89
Welch, James O. St&PR 91
Welch, James S. WhoAm 90
Welch, James Weldon BiDrAPA 89
Welch, James Weldon 1954- WhoE 91
Welch, James Wymore 1928- WhoAmA 91
Welch, Jeanie Maxine 1946- WhoAmW 91
Welch, Jeffrey Dean 1954- St&PR 91
Welch, Jerry 1963- WhoSSW 91
Welch, Joan Kathleen 1950- WhoAmW 91, WhoE 91, WhoEmL 91, WhoWor 91
Welch, John David 1936- BiDrAPA 89
Welch, John F., Jr. BioIn 16
Welch, John F., Jr. 1935- WorAlBi
Welch, John Francis 1935- St&PR 91
Welch, John Francis, Jr. 1935- WhoAm 90, WhoE 91, WhoWor 91
Welch, John Greer BiDrAPA 89
Welch, John J., Jr. WhoAm 90
Welch, John Stanley 1920- WhoAm 90
Welch, Johnny 1906-1940 Ballpl 90
Welch, K. M. A. WhoAm 90
Welch, Kathy Jane 1952- WhoAmW 91
Welch, Keith L. 1956- WhoEmL 91
Welch, L. Dean 1928- St&PR 91, WhoAm 90
Welch, Larry Deane 1934- WhoAm 90
Welch, Lawrence H. 1930- St&PR 91
Welch, Lee 1940- WhoAm 90
Welch, Linda Ogden 1958- WhoAmW 91
Welch, Livingston 1901-1976 WhoAmA 91N
Welch, Lloyd Richard 1927- WhoAm 90
Welch, Louie 1918- WhoAm 90
Welch, Mabel R WhoAmA 91N
Welch, Martha G 1944- BiDrAPA 89
Welch, Mary Eddison 1917- WhoAmW 91
Welch, Mary Frances 1938- WhoAmW 91, WhoSSW 91
Welch, Mary-Scott 1919- WhoAmW 91, WhoE 91
Welch, Mary Therese 1958- WhoEmL 91
Welch, Michael John 1939- WhoAm 90
Welch, Michelle Leslie 1953- WhoAmW 91
Welch, Mickey 1859-1941 Ballpl 90 [port]
Welch, Neal William 1908- WhoAm 90
Welch, Noble 1930- St&PR 91
Welch, Noreen O'Hara 1938- WhoE 91
Welch, O. J. 1929- WhoSSW 91
Welch, Olga Michele 1948- WhoSSW 91
Welch, Patrick Errett 1925- WhoAm 90
Welch, Pauline AuBYP 90
Welch, Priscilla BioIn 16
Welch, R. Dewey 1928- St&PR 91

Welch, Raquel 1940- *BioIn 16, WhoHisp 91, WorAlBi*
Welch, Richard E. *BioIn 16*
Welch, Richard Edwin, Jr. 1924- *WhoWrEP 89*
Welch, Richard W. *BioIn 16*
Welch, Robert 1929- *ConDes 90*
Welch, Robert Bennett 1935- *IntWWM 90*
Welch, Robert Bond 1927- *WhoAm 90*
Welch, Robert G 1915- *WhoAmA 91*
Welch, Robert G, Mrs *WhoAmA 91*
Welch, Robert Gibson 1915- *WhoAm 90*
Welch, Robert James *BiDrAPA 89*
Welch, Robert Morrow, Jr. 1927- *WhoAm 90*
Welch, Robert Thomas 1958- *WhoEmL 91*
Welch, Robin B. 1940- *St&PR 91*
Welch, Robin Bilyeaux 1940- *WhoAm 90*
Welch, Roger 1946- *WhoAmA 91*
Welch, Ronald *BiDrAPA 89*
Welch, Ronald J. 1945- *WhoAm 90*
Welch, Ronald Jay 1945- *St&PR 91*
Welch, Ross Maynard 1943- *WhoAm 90*
Welch, Stephen Anthony 1942- *WhoAm 90*
Welch, Stuart Cary 1928- *WhoAmA 91*
Welch, Stuart E. 1945- *St&PR 91*
Welch, Tahnee *BioIn 16*
Welch, Theodore Franklyn 1933- *WhoAm 90*
Welch, Thomas *EncCRAm*
Welch, Thomas C. 1926- *St&PR 91, WhoWor 91*
Welch, Thomas Kenyon 1944- *WhoAm 90*
Welch, Tillmin Gene 1951- *WhoEmL 91*
Welch, Van Allen 1955- *WhoSSW 91*
Welch, Victor C 1924- *BiDrAPA 89*
Welch, Walter Andrew, Jr. *WhoWor 91*
Welch, Wayne Willard 1934- *WhoAm 90*
Welch, William B. 1922- *St&PR 91*
Welch, William Claude, Jr. *BiDrAPA 89*
Welch, William Henry 1929- *WhoAm 90*
Welch, William M. 1842- *AmLegL*
Welch, William Roger 1946- *WhoE 91*
Welcher, Gilbert Glenn 1944- *WhoE 91*
Welcher, Stephanie Denise 1961- *WhoAmW 91*
Welchman, Gordon 1906-1985 *DcNaB 1981*
Welchman, Harry 1886-1966 *OxCPMus*
Welcome, John 1914- *TwCCr&M 91*
Welcome, Verda Freeman *BioIn 16*
Weld, Jonathan Minot 1941- *WhoAm 90*
Weld, Roger Bowen 1953- *WhoEmL 91, WhoWor 91*
Weld, Tuesday *BioIn 16*
Weld, Tuesday 1943- *WorAlBi*
Weld, Tuesday Ker 1943- *WhoAm 90, WhoAmW 91*
Weld, William 1824-1891 *DcCanB 12*
Weld, William F. *NewYTBS 90 [port]*
Weld, William Floyd *BioIn 16*
Weld, William George, Jr. 1929- *St&PR 91*
Welden, Arthur Luna 1927- *WhoAm 90*
Welden, Daniel W 1941- *WhoAmA 91*
Welder, Thomas 1940- *WhoAm 90, WhoAmW 91*
Weldon, Barbara M. *BioIn 16*
Weldon, Barbara Maltby *WhoAmA 91*
Weldon, Daniel Patrick 1950- *WhoE 91*
Weldon, David Black 1925- *WhoAm 90*
Weldon, Doris May 1925- *WhoAmW 91*
Weldon, Elaine Joyce *WhoAmW 91*
Weldon, Eunice Bertha 1941- *WhoAmW 91*
Weldon, Fay *BioIn 16*
Weldon, Fay 1931?- *CurBio 90 [port], FemiCLE*
Weldon, Fay 1933- *ConLC 59 [port], MajTwCW*
Weldon, George 1906-1963 *PenDiMP*
Weldon, Georgina 1837-1914 *PenDiMP*
Weldon, Harry *Ballpl 90*
Weldon, Irene I. 1938- *IntWWM 90*
Weldon, James E. 1934- *St&PR 91*
Weldon, James Ernest 1934- *WhoAm 90*
Weldon, Karla Elaine Hart 1935- *WhoAmW 91*
Weldon, L Dennis 1934- *BiDrAPA 89*
Weldon, Martin 1913- *AuBYP 90*
Weldon, Norman Ross 1934- *WhoAm 90*
Weldon, Robert William 1934- *St&PR 91*
Weldon, Susanna Lucy Anne *DcCanB 12*
Weldon, Thomas A *BiDrAPA 89*
Weldon, Virginia V. 1935- *WhoAm 90, WhoAmW 91*
Weldon, Wayne Curtis 1947- *WhoAm 90, WhoE 91*
Weldon, William H. 1932- *St&PR 91*
Weldt, Cristina S 1943- *BiDrAPA 89*
Weldy, Art *BioIn 16*
Weldy, Dennis Kay 1948- *St&PR 91*
Weldy, Norma Jean 1929- *WhoAmW 91*
Welfens, Paul J. J. 1957- *WhoWor 91*
Welfer, Nancy 1920- *St&PR 91*
Welfer, Thomas, Jr. 1936- *St&PR 91, WhoAm 90*
Welffens, Peter 1924- *IntWWM 90*
Welford, George Seymour 1933- *St&PR 91*
Welford, John Mack 1939- *WhoSSW 91*
Welge, Donald 1935- *St&PR 91*
Welge, Donald Edward 1935- *WhoAm 90*
Welham, George *ODwPR 91*
Welhaven, Johann Sebastian Cammermeyer 1807-1873 *DcScanL*
Welikson, Jeffrey A. 1957- *St&PR 91*
Welikson, Jeffrey Alan 1957- *WhoE 91*
Welin, Walter 1908- *WhoWor 91*
Welitsch, Ljuba 1913- *PenDiMP*
Welitsch, Luba 1913- *IntWWM 90*
Weliver, Delmer E. 1939- *IntWWM 90*
Weliver, Howard Ray, Sr. 1942- *WhoSSW 91*
Welk, Katherine D *BiDrAPA 89*
Welk, Lawrence 1903- *OxCPMus, WorAlBi*
Welka, Eugene August 1945- *WhoE 91*
Welke, Bernadine Maryanna 1946- *WhoE 91*
Welke, Elton *ODwPR 91*
Welke, James William 1936- *WhoSSW 91*
Welker, Edward Philip 1932- *WhoE 91*
Welker, Hartmut 1941- *IntWWM 90*
Welker, Jerome L. 1933- *St&PR 91*
Welker, Juanita Margaret 1941- *St&PR 91*
Welker, Wallace Irving 1926- *WhoAm 90*
Welker, William G. 1930- *St&PR 91*
Welkowitz, Joan *WhoAm 90*
Well, Julie O'Rourke *ODwPR 91*
Welland, Mark F. *BioIn 16*
Wellard, Charles L. 1924- *St&PR 91*
Wellbaum, Edgar Winston 1927- *St&PR 91*
Wellborn, Charles I. 1941- *WhoWor 91*
Wellborn, J D 1943- *WhoAmA 91*
Wellborn, Stanley Nickell 1944- *WhoE 91*
Wellborn, Walter Horry, Jr. 1922- *BiDrAPA 89*
Wellehan, Daniel Joseph, Jr. 1933- *St&PR 91*
Wellejus, Henning 1919- *IntWWM 90*
Wellek, Jeffrey A. 1961- *St&PR 91*
Wellek, Mark Alan 1937- *BiDrAPA 89*
Wellek, Rene *BioIn 16*
Wellek, Richard Lee 1938- *St&PR 91, WhoAm 90*
Wellenkotter, Harry W. 1929- *St&PR 91*
Weller, Albert Hermann 1922- *WhoWor 91*
Weller, Allen Stuart 1907- *WhoAmA 91*
Weller, Andrew Michael *WhoAm 90*
Weller, Ann Louise 1954- *WhoE 91*
Weller, Barton L. 1916- *St&PR 91*
Weller, Barton L. 1916-1990 *BioIn 16*
Weller, Berthold Leysaht 1932- *St&PR 91*
Weller, Carl William 1934- *St&PR 91*
Weller, Conrad P 1937- *BiDrAPA 89*
Weller, Dieter 1937- *IntWWM 90*
Weller, Don Mighell 1937- *WhoAmA 91*
Weller, Edgar O. 1917- *St&PR 91*
Weller, Elizabeth B 1949- *BiDrAPA 89*
Weller, Frank Harlow, Jr. 1938- *WhoAm 90*
Weller, Gunter Ernst 1934- *WhoAm 90*
Weller, James Patrick 1948- *St&PR 91*
Weller, Janis Ferguson 1950- *IntWWM 90*
Weller, John Sidney 1928-1981 *WhoAmA 91N*
Weller, John William, Jr. 1935- *WhoE 91*
Weller, Joseph C. 1939- *St&PR 91*
Weller, Kenneth Jay 1925- *WhoAm 90*
Weller, Kenneth Roy 1948- *St&PR 91*
Weller, Laurie June 1953- *WhoAmA 91*
Weller, Malcolm Philip Isadore 1935- *WhoWor 91*
Weller, Michael *BioIn 16*
Weller, Michael 1942- *WhoAm 90*
Weller, Paul 1912- *WhoAmA 91*
Weller, Paul Franklin 1935- *WhoAm 90, WhoE 91*
Weller, Paul S., Jr. 1938- *ODwPR 91*
Weller, Penny Sue 1948- *WhoAmW 91*
Weller, Ralph Albert 1921- *WhoAm 90*
Weller, Robert Norman 1939- *WhoAm 90*
Weller, Rodger Norman 1946- *WhoSSW 91*
Weller, Ronald Alan 1948- *BiDrAPA 89*
Weller, Samuel A. 1851-1925 *PenDiDA 89*
Weller, Sheila 1945- *WhoWrEP 89*
Weller, Sol William 1918- *WhoAm 90*
Weller, Thomas H. 1915- *WorAlBi*
Weller, Thomas Huckle 1915- *WhoAm 90, WhoE 91, WhoWor 91*
Weller, Tom *WhoAm 90*
Weller, Walter 1939- *IntWWM 90, PenDiMP, WhoWor 91*
Wellershoff, Dieter 1925- *BioIn 16, WhoWor 91*
Welles, Charles Hopkins 1907- *St&PR 91*
Welles, Cynthia M. *BioIn 16*
Welles, David Keith, Jr. 1952- *WhoAm 90, WhoEmL 91*
Welles, David Wilder 1938- *WhoAm 90*
Welles, Edward Randolph 1907- *WhoAm 90*
Welles, Ferne Bingham Malcolm 1921- *WhoAmW 91*
Welles, Gideon 1802-1878 *BiDrUSE 89*
Welles, James Bell, Jr. 1918- *WhoAm 90*
Welles, Marilyn Teeter 1935- *WhoAmW 91*
Welles, Mel *BioIn 16*
Welles, Melinda Fassett 1943- *WhoAmW 91, WhoWor 91*
Welles, Orson 1915-1985 *BioIn 16, WorAlBi*
Welles, Sumner 1892-1961 *BioIn 16, WorAlBi*
Welles, Virginia Chrisman 1954- *WhoE 91*
Wellesley, Arthur 1769-1852 *BioIn 16*
Wellesley, Charles 1816-1855 *BioIn 16*
Wellesley, Dorothy 1889-1956 *FemiCLE*
Wellford, Harry Walker 1924- *WhoAm 90*
Wellhouse, James L 1926- *BiDrAPA 89*
Wellikoff, Alan Gabriel 1946- *WhoWrEP 89*
Wellin, Julia Ann 1947- *BiDrAPA 89*
Wellin, Keith Sears 1926- *WhoAm 90*
Welling, Douglas Steven 1952- *WhoEmL 91*
Welling, James *BioIn 16*
Welling, James 1951- *WhoAmA 91*
Welling, Juha Olavi 1961- *WhoWor 91*
Welling, Katharine Hutchins 1948- *WhoE 91*
Welling, Kathryn Marie 1952- *WhoAmW 91*
Welling, W. Lambert 1932- *WhoE 91*
Wellington, Arthur Wellesley, Duke of 1769-1852 *BioIn 16, WorAlBi*
Wellington, Christopher Ramsay 1930- *IntWWM 90*
Wellington, Duke 1896-1987 *WhoAmA 91N*
Wellington, Gail Patricia 1940- *WhoE 91*
Wellington, Harry Hillel 1926- *WhoAm 90*
Wellington, James Ellis 1921- *WhoAm 90*
Wellington, John Stanley 1916- *WhoAm 90*
Wellington, P.S. 1940- *St&PR 91*
Wellington, Robert Hall 1922- *St&PR 91, WhoAm 90*
Wellington, Roger Dewitt 1927- *St&PR 91*
Wellington, Roger U., Jr. 1941- *St&PR 91*
Wellington, Sheila W. 1932- *WhoAm 90*
Wellington, Thomas Dutton 1921- *St&PR 91*
Wellington, William George 1920- *WhoAm 90*
Wellington-Johnson, Sharon L. 1957- *WhoAmW 91*
Wellins, Sheldon Gary 1944- *WhoWor 91*
Wellish, Carl S 1934- *BiDrAPA 89*
Welliver, Neil 1929- *WhoE 91*
Welliver, Neil G 1929- *WhoAmA 91*
Welliver, Rick E. 1955- *St&PR 91*
Welliver, Warren Dee 1920- *WhoAm 90*
Welljams-Dorof, Eugene B *BiDrAPA 89*
Wellman, Abby 1958- *BiDrAPA 89*
Wellman, Adele *EncO&P 3*
Wellman, Alice 1900-1984 *BioIn 16*
Wellman, Anthony Donald Emerson 1955- *WhoE 91*
Wellman, Brad 1959- *Ballpl 90*
Wellman, Carl Pierce 1926- *WhoAm 90*
Wellman, David B. 1850- *AmLegL*
Wellman, Dawn Elizabeth 1949- *WhoAmW 91*
Wellman, Donald 1944- *WhoWrEP 89*
Wellman, Harvey R. 1916-1988 *BioIn 16*
Wellman, Howard Stolte 1939- *WhoE 91*
Wellman, Iona V *BiDrAPA 89*
Wellman, Manly Wade 1903-1986 *BioIn 16*
Wellman, Manly Wade 1905-1986 *AuBYP 90*
Wellman, Mark *BioIn 16*
Wellman, Paul Iselin 1898-1966 *AuBYP 90*
Wellman, Richard Vance 1922- *WhoAm 90*
Wellman, Timothy Wayne 1953- *St&PR 91*
Wellman, W. Arvid 1918- *WhoAm 90*
Wellman, William 1896-1975 *WorAlBi*
Wellman, William Augustus 1896-1975 *BioIn 16*
Wellner, Alfred M. *BioIn 16*
Wellner, Marcel Nahum 1930- *WhoAm 90*
Wellner, Robert Francis 1928- *WhoE 91*
Wellnitz, Barbara Louise 1945- *WhoAmW 91*
Wellnitz, Barbara W. *ODwPR 91*
Wells, Albert Philip 1922- *WhoAm 90*
Wells, Allan Bernard 1935- *BiDrAPA 89*
Wells, Andrew Norman 1953- *WhoEmL 91*
Wells, Arthur Stanton 1931- *St&PR 91, WhoAm 90*
Wells, Barbara D. 1944- *WhoSSW 91*
Wells, Barry Holland 1962- *WhoSSW 91*
Wells, Basil Eugene 1912- *WhoWrEP 89*
Wells, Ben Harris 1906- *WhoAm 90, WhoWor 91*
Wells, Bernadette Nickle 1951- *WhoAmW 91*
Wells, Bernard *BiDrAPA 89*
Wells, Berri Ann 1963- *WhoAmW 91*
Wells, Betty Childs 1926- *WhoAmA 91*
Wells, Betty Ruth 1927- *WhoAmW 91, WhoWor 91*
Wells, Bill *BioIn 16*
Wells, Bill 1956- *St&PR 91*
Wells, Bill Charles 1956- *WhoEmL 91*
Wells, Brian Scott 1963- *WhoSSW 91*
Wells, Cady 1904-1954 *WhoAmA 91N*
Wells, Calvin B. 1936- *St&PR 91*
Wells, Carolyn 1869-1942 *TwCCr&M 91*
Wells, Cecil Harold, Jr. 1927- *WhoAm 90*
Wells, Charles Edmon 1929- *BiDrAPA 89*
Wells, Charles Joseph 1948- *WhoE 91*
Wells, Charles Marion 1905- *WhoAm 90*
Wells, Charles R. 1939- *St&PR 91*
Wells, Charles W. 1934- *St&PR 91*
Wells, Charles William 1934- *WhoAm 90*
Wells, Christopher Brian 1948- *WhoEmL 91*
Wells, Clifford Eugene 1927- *St&PR 91*
Wells, Clyde Kirby 1937- *WhoAm 90, WhoE 91*
Wells, Crosby 1922- *St&PR 91, WhoAm 90*
Wells, Dale Kent 1930- *St&PR 91*
Wells, Damon, Jr. 1937- *WhoSSW 91, WhoWor 91*
Wells, David *BioIn 16*
Wells, David 1963- *Ballpl 90*
Wells, David John 1949- *WhoE 91*
Wells, David T *BiDrAPA 89*
Wells, Dawn *BioIn 16*
Wells, Deborah Linn 1954- *WhoEmL 91*
Wells, Deborah Lucille 1957- *WhoAmW 91*
Wells, Dicky 1907-1985 *OxCPMus*
Wells, Donald Smith 1935- *WhoAm 90*
Wells, Donald Thomas 1931- *WhoSSW 91*
Wells, Donn Arthur 1938- *BiDrAPA 89*
Wells, Donna Frances 1948- *WhoAmW 91*
Wells, Donna Jo 1966- *WhoAmW 91*
Wells, Ed 1900-1986 *Ballpl 90*
Wells, Elaine Louise 1951- *WhoAmW 91*
Wells, Emmeline 1828-1921 *FemiCLE*
Wells, Eric *BioIn 16*
Wells, Everett Clayton, Jr. 1954- *WhoSSW 91*
Wells, Fay Gillis 1908- *WhoAmW 91, WhoWor 91*
Wells, Frank B. *EarBlAP*
Wells, Frank G. 1932- *WhoAm 90*
Wells, Gary 1950- *ODwPR 91*
Wells, George A 1926- *ConAu 32NR*
Wells, George Douglas 1935- *St&PR 91, WhoAm 90*
Wells, George H. 1944- *St&PR 91*
Wells, George Henry 1944- *WhoAm 90*
Wells, George M. 1936- *St&PR 91*
Wells, Gerald W. 1945- *St&PR 91*
Wells, Gordon E. 1928- *St&PR 91*
Wells, H. G. 1866-1946 *BioIn 16*
Wells, H G 1866-1946 *MajTwCW*
Wells, H. G. 1866-1946 *RGTwCSF*
Wells, H G 1866-1946 *ShSCr 6 [port]*
Wells, H. G. 1866-1946 *WorAlBi*
Wells, H. Rickey 1956- *St&PR 91*
Wells, Harold C. *WhoAm 90*
Wells, Harriet 1933- *BiDrAPA 89*
Wells, Helen 1910-1988 *BioIn 16*
Wells, Helen Frances 1910- *AuBYP 90*
Wells, Helena 1761?-1824 *FemiCLE*
Wells, Henry 1805-1878 *EncABHB 6 [port]*
Wells, Henry 1914- *WhoAm 90*
Wells, Henry M., III 1945- *St&PR 91*
Wells, Henry W. 1805-1878 *WorAlBi*
Wells, Herbert George 1866-1946 *BioIn 16*
Wells, Herman B. 1902- *St&PR 91, WhoAm 90, WhoWor 91*
Wells, Herschel James 1924- *WhoAm 90, WhoWor 91*
Wells, Howard Avery 1909- *St&PR 91*
Wells, Hoyt M. 1926- *WhoAm 90*
Wells, Huey Thomas, Jr. 1950- *WhoEmL 91, WhoSSW 91*
Wells, Hugh G. 1933- *St&PR 91*
Wells, Hugh H. 1949- *WhoSSW 91*
Wells, Ida B. 1862-1931 *BioIn 16*
Wells, J. *BiDWomA*
Wells, James Curtis, Jr. 1951- *WhoSSW 91*
Wells, James Edward 1836-1898 *DcCanB 12*
Wells, James H *BiDrAPA 89*
Wells, James R. 1947- *ODwPR 91*
Wells, James Shelton, Jr. 1947- *BiDrAPA 89*
Wells, Jane C. 1955- *BiDrAPA 89*
Wells, Jane Frances 1944- *WhoAmW 91*
Wells, Jane Kathleen Sinclair 1952- *IntWWM 90*
Wells, Jay *BioIn 16*
Wells, Jeremy 1945- *WhoSSW 91*
Wells, Joel Freeman 1930- *WhoAm 90, WhoWrEP 89*
Wells, Joel R. 1928- *St&PR 91*
Wells, Joel Reaves, Jr. 1928- *WhoAm 90, WhoSSW 91*

Wells, John A. 1946- *St&PR 91*
Wells, John C. 1940- *St&PR 91*
Wells, John C., Jr. 1941- *St&PR 91*
Wells, John L. 1942- *St&PR 91*
Wells, John Stewart 1934- *BiDrAPA 89*
Wells, John West 1907- *WhoAm 90*
Wells, Joseph W., Jr. 1954- *WhoE 91*
Wells, Karen Jeannine 1960- *WhoSSW 91*
Wells, Karen Kay 1956- *WhoAmW 91*
Wells, Kendra Buckel 1954- *WhoAmW 91*
Wells, Kenneth Brooks 1948- *BiDrAPA 89*
Wells, Kenneth Wayne *BiDrAPA 89*
Wells, Kimberley 1955- *ODwPR 91*
Wells, Kitty 1918- *OxCPMus*
Wells, L. Rosemary Siplon 1930- *WhoAmW 91*
Wells, Lane T. 1929- *St&PR 91*
Wells, Leonard Nathaniel David, Jr. 1914- *WhoAm 90*
Wells, Linda Alice 1957- *WhoE 91*
Wells, Lionelle D 1921- *BiDrAPA 89*
Wells, Lionelle Dudley 1951- *WhoEmL 91*
Wells, Lloyd Allan 1948- *BiDrAPA 89*
Wells, Lynton 1940- *WhoAmA 91*
Wells, Mac 1925- *WhoAmA 91*
Wells, Maie Lounsbury *AuBYP 90*
Wells, Mark Howard 1951- *WhoE 91*
Wells, Mary *BiDEWW, FemiCLE*
Wells, Mary 1943- *DrBlPA 90, EncPR&S 89*
Wells, Mary Elizabeth Thompson 1936- *WhoAmW 91, WhoSSW 91*
Wells, Mary Janet 1944- *WhoSSW 91*
Wells, Mary Layton 1958- *WhoAmW 91*
Wells, Maryann Michelle 1953- *WhoAmW 91, WhoE 91*
Wells, Maureen 1921- *BioIn 16*
Wells, Melissa Foelsch 1932- *WhoAm 90, WhoAmW 91, WhoWor 91*
Wells, Milton Thomas 1948- *WhoE 91*
Wells, Nancy Marie 1953- *WhoWrEP 89*
Wells, Pamela Kay 1948- *WhoE 91*
Wells, Patricia *BioIn 16*
Wells, Patricia 1946- *ConAu 132*
Wells, Patricia Bennett 1935- *WhoAmW 91*
Wells, Patricia Lee Kleiber 1946- *WhoWor 91*
Wells, Paul Francis 1951- *IntWWM 90*
Wells, Peter Boyd, Jr. 1915- *WhoWor 91*
Wells, Peter Scoville 1938- *WhoE 91*
Wells, Petrina *ODwPR 91*
Wells, Phil *NewAgMG*
Wells, Phillip C. 1932- *St&PR 91*
Wells, Phillip H *BiDrAPA 89*
Wells, Ralph M. 1935- *ODwPR 91*
Wells, Randall Hal *BiDrAPA 89*
Wells, Randall S. *BioIn 16*
Wells, Randall S. 1952- *St&PR 91*
Wells, Richard Arthur 1937- *St&PR 91*
Wells, Richard Marshall 1930- *St&PR 91*
Wells, Richard Paul 1959- *WhoEmL 91*
Wells, Robert A. 1930- *St&PR 91*
Wells, Robert Hyland 1938- *ODwPR 91*
Wells, Robert L. 1913- *AuBYP 90*
Wells, Robert Louis 1939- *WhoSSW 91*
Wells, Robert Lynn 1917- *WhoAm 90*
Wells, Robert Milton *BiDrAPA 89*
Wells, Robert Vale 1943- *WhoAm 90*
Wells, Robert W. 1926- *St&PR 91*
Wells, Robin John 1943- *IntWWM 90*
Wells, Rona Lee 1950- *WhoAmW 91, WhoSSW 91, WhoWor 91*
Wells, Ronald Austin 1933- *WhoE 91, WhoWor 91*
Wells, Rosalind Lea 1936- *WhoAmW 91*
Wells, Russell Frederick 1937- *WhoE 91*
Wells, Sabrina *BioIn 16*
Wells, Samuel Alonzo, Jr. 1936- *WhoAm 90*
Wells, Sandra 1948- *WhoAmW 91*
Wells, Stanley Dale 1944- *WhoWor 91*
Wells, Stephen A. 1943- *St&PR 91*
Wells, Stephen Earl 1944- *WhoSSW 91*
Wells, Steven Alan 1955- *WhoSSW 91*
Wells, Stuart P. 1931- *St&PR 91*
Wells, Susan D. 1949- *ODwPR 91*
Wells, Theodore Arthur 1907- *St&PR 91*
Wells, Thomas 1916- *WhoAmA 91*
Wells, Thomas Watkins 1951- *WhoAm 90*
Wells, Tim 1954- *ConAu 129*
Wells, Tobias *TwCCr&M 91*
Wells, Tony *NewAgMG*
Wells, Victor Hugh, Jr. 1924- *WhoAm 90*
Wells, William 1945- *ODwPR 91*
Wells, William Addison, III 1955- *WhoSSW 91*
Wells, William T. 1933- *St&PR 91*
Wells, William Thomas 1908-1990? *ConAu 130*
Wells, Willie 1905- *Ballpl 90*
Wells, Willie 1905-1989 *BioIn 16*
Wells-Barnett, Ida 1862-1931 *FemiCLE*
Wells-Barnett, Ida Bell 1862-1931 *HarlReB [port]*
Wells-Owens, Sarah Jean 1951- *WhoAmW 91*
Wellshear, Charles C 1930- *BiDrAPA 89*
Wellsluer, Charlotte 1959- *ODwPR 91*
Wellso, Charles G 1928- *BiDrAPA 89*
Wellwarth, George E. 1932- *WhoWrEP 89*
Welna, Cecilia 1927- *WhoAm 90*
Welna, Sharon Kay 1951- *WhoAmW 91*
Welnak, Llowell Albert 1926- *St&PR 91*
Welner, Renee *BiDrAPA 89*
Welner, Zila *BiDrAPA 89*
Welnhofer, Robert William 1933- *St&PR 91, WhoAm 90*
Welpott, Jack Warren 1923- *WhoAm 90, WhoAmA 91*
Welpton, Douglas F 1935- *BiDrAPA 89*
Wels, Marguerite Samet *WhoAmW 91*
Wels, Richard Hoffman *NewYTBS 90*
Wels, Richard Hoffman 1913-1990 *BioIn 16*
Welsby, Norman 1939- *IntWWM 90*
Welsby, Paul A 1920- *ConAu 129*
Welsch, Glenn Albert 1915- *WhoAm 90*
Welsch, James Lester 1917- *WhoWor 91*
Welsch, Jerome K. 1953- *St&PR 91*
Welsch, Moray 1947- *PenDiMP*
Welsch, Walter Nicholas 1924- *St&PR 91*
Welscher, George F 1922- *BiDrAPA 89*
Welser-Most, Franz 1960- *IntWWM 90*
Welsh, Alan L. *St&PR 91*
Welsh, Alan L. 1948- *WhoSSW 91*
Welsh, Alex 1929-1982 *OxCPMus*
Welsh, Arthur Craig 1947- *WhoWor 91*
Welsh, Chris 1955- *Ballpl 90*
Welsh, David Malcolm 1942- *St&PR 91*
Welsh, Dianne H.B. 1956- *WhoAmW 91*
Welsh, Donald Emory 1943- *WhoAm 90*
Welsh, Donna Barham 1956- *WhoAmW 91*
Welsh, Edward C 1909-1990 *CurBio 90N*
Welsh, Edward Cristy 1909-1990 *BioIn 16, NewYTBS 90*
Welsh, George William 1922- *St&PR 91*
Welsh, Greg Jon 1951- *WhoE 91*
Welsh, Herbert 1851-1941 *WhNaAH*
Welsh, Howard K *BiDrAPA 89*
Welsh, J. Erica 1947- *WhoAmW 91*
Welsh, Jimmy 1902-1970 *Ballpl 90*
Welsh, John 1805-1886 *BioIn 16*
Welsh, John Francis 1916- *WhoAm 90*
Welsh, Judith 1939- *WhoWrEP 89*
Welsh, Judith Schenck 1939- *WhoAmW 91*
Welsh, Lawrence H. 1935- *WhoAm 90*
Welsh, Mary Agnes 1948- *ODwPR 91*
Welsh, Matthew Empson 1912- *WhoAm 90*
Welsh, Moray 1947- *IntWWM 90*
Welsh, Patrick Thomas 1946- *WhoSSW 91*
Welsh, Paul D., Jr. 1926- *St&PR 91*
Welsh, Peter Corbett 1926- *WhoAm 90*
Welsh, Raymond H. 1931- *St&PR 91*
Welsh, Richard Donald 1931- *St&PR 91*
Welsh, Rita May 1942- *WhoAmW 91*
Welsh, Robert Francis 1925- *St&PR 91*
Welsh, Robert H. 1926- *St&PR 91*
Welsh, Robert J. 1926- *St&PR 91*
Welsh, Ronald Arthur 1926- *WhoAm 90*
Welsh, S. Patricia 1956- *WhoWrEP 89*
Welsh, Sachiko Ann 1931- *WhoAmW 91*
Welsh, Suzanne P. 1953- *WhoAmW 91*
Welsh, T. Ward 1932- *ODwPR 91*
Welsh, Thomas J. 1921- *WhoE 91*
Welsh, Thomas M. 1949- *ODwPR 91, St&PR 91*
Welsh, William 1810-1879 *WhNaAH*
Welsh, William Brownlee 1924- *WhoAm 90*
Welsh, William E. 1942- *St&PR 91*
Welsh, William F., II 1941- *St&PR 91*
Welsh, William Francis Anthony 1950- *WhoWrEP 89*
Welsh, William J. *BioIn 16*
Welsh, Wilmer Hayden 1932- *IntWWM 90, WhoSSW 91, WhoWor 91*
Welshans, Merle Talmadge 1918- *WhoWor 91*
Welsher, Donald F. 1937- *St&PR 91*
Welshhans, Richard W. 1947- *St&PR 91*
Welt, Frank A. *NewYTBS 90*
Welt, Henry 1946- *WhoE 91, WhoWor 91*
Weltch, J.W. 1910- *St&PR 91*
Weltchek, Paul Richard 1928- *WhoAm 90*
Welte, A. Theodore 1944- *WhoE 91*
Welter, Cole H 1952- *WhoAmA 91*
Welter, Vanessa Marie 1959- *WhoAmW 91*
Welter, William Michael 1946- *WhoAm 90*
Welteroth, Dick 1927- *Ballpl 90*
Welti, Walter 1919- *BiDrAPA 89*
Welting, Ruth 1949- *IntWWM 90*
Weltman, Harry *WhoAm 90, WhoE 91*
Weltman, Joseph S 1910- *BiDrAPA 89*
Weltman, Rosemary 1949- *WhoE 91*
Weltner, Betsey S. 1952- *ODwPR 91*
Weltner, Charles Longstreet 1927- *WhoAm 90*
Weltner, Gary Lee 1944- *St&PR 91*
Weltner, John S 1934- *BiDrAPA 89*
Welton, Charles Ephraim 1947- *WhoEmL 91, WhoWor 91*
Welton, Frederic Percy 1926- *IntWWM 90*
Welton, Jessica Wheat 1953- *WhoEmL 91*
Welton, Lynn 1960- *WhoAmW 91*
Welton, Michael Peter 1957- *WhoEmL 91*
Welton, Nancy Boardman 1946- *St&PR 91*
Welton, Oliver K. 1925- *St&PR 91*
Welton, Robert Breen 1938- *WhoAm 90*
Weltsch, Robert 1891-1982 *BioIn 16*
Welty, Anne Cassedy *BiDrAPA 89*
Welty, Charles I. 1927- *St&PR 91*
Welty, Daniel Bearden 1951- *WhoSSW 91*
Welty, Elmer Elias 1906- *WhoSSW 91*
Welty, Eudora *WhoAm 90, WhoAmW 91, WhoWor 91, WhoWrEP 89*
Welty, Eudora 1909- *BioAmW, BioIn 16, ConAu 32NR, DcLB 102 [port], FemiCLE, MajTwCW, WorAlBi*
Welty, John Donald 1944- *WhoAm 90, WhoE 91*
Welty, Kenneth Adam, Sr. *BiDrAPA 89*
Welty, Miriam Trangsrud *ODwPR 91*
Welty, Robert L. 1932- *St&PR 91*
Welty, Robert Vance 1942- *St&PR 91*
Welty, Stanley R., Jr. 1929- *St&PR 91*
Welty, Steven Philip 1951- *St&PR 91*
Welty, William John 1946- *St&PR 91*
Weltzin, Theodore Eldon *BiDrAPA 89*
Welu, James A. 1943- *WhoAm 90, WhoE 91*
Welytok, Walter Steven 1930- *St&PR 91*
Welz, Bettina Maxine 1960- *BiDrAPA 89*
Welz, Carl John 1913- *WhoAm 90*
Welz, Kurt Willy 1942- *WhoWor 91*
Welz, Robert Henry 1929- *St&PR 91*
Welzant, Lucille Carol 1947- *WhoSSW 91*
Welzel, Jane *BioIn 16*
Welzenbach, Lanora Frances 1932- *WhoWrEP 89*
Welzer, Tony 1899-1971 *Ballpl 90*
Wemeau, Jacques 1944- *WhoWor 91*
Wemple, Donna Wachter 1944- *WhoAmW 91*
Wemple, William 1912- *WhoAm 90*
Wemyss, Margaret, Countess of 1659-1705 *BiDEWW*
Wen, Guo-chun 1930- *WhoWor 91*
Wen, Shih-Liang *WhoAm 90*
Wen, Tien Kuang 1924- *WhoWor 91*
Wenawine, Bruce Harley 1949- *WhoAmA 91*
Wenberg, Richard Vincent 1932- *St&PR 91*
Wenc, Karen Marie 1954- *WhoAmW 91*
Wence, Gary Fred 1957- *WhoEmL 91*
Wencel, Emil Eugene 1919- *WhoSSW 91*
Wencelblat, Gustavo 1936- *BiDrAPA 89*
Wenck, Edwin O. 1936- *WhoE 91*
Wenckus, James R. 1941- *St&PR 91*
Wenczel, Chester L. 1917- *St&PR 91*
Wend, Joanne Lenore 1960- *WhoAmW 91*
Wendeborn, Richard Donald *WhoAm 90, WhoE 91, WhoWor 91*
Wendeborn, Richard Donald 1929- *St&PR 91*
Wendehorst, Alfred 1927- *WhoWor 91*
Wendekier, Raymond Joseph 1942- *St&PR 91*
Wendel, Christopher Mark 1954- *WhoE 91*
Wendel, Douglas John 1951- *WhoEmL 91*
Wendel, Faye F. 1928- *WhoAmW 91*
Wendel, Francois Augustin Marie de 1874-1949 *BiDFrPL*
Wendel, Pamela L. 1960- *WhoAmW 91*
Wendel, Richard Frederick 1930- *WhoAm 90*
Wendel, Thomas Michael 1936- *WhoAm 90*
Wendel, William Hall *NewYTBS 90 [port]*
Wendel, William Hall 1914- *WhoAm 90*
Wendelberger, Gustav 1915- *WhoWor 91*
Wendelberger, James George 1953- *WhoEmL 91*
Wendelberger, Joanne Roth 1959- *WhoEmL 91*
Wendelburg, Norma Ruth 1918- *IntWWM 90, WhoWor 91*
Wendelken, Robert T. 1939- *St&PR 91*
Wendell, David Taylor 1931- *WhoWor 91*
Wendell, Leilah 1958- *WhoWrEP 89*
Wendell, Lesley Mallow 1955- *WhoE 91*
Wendell, Margaret R *BiDrAPA 89*
Wendell, Matthew Simon 1921- *St&PR 91*
Wendell, Patricia Lynn *WhoAmW 91, WhoE 91*
Wendell, Roy E. 1924- *ODwPR 91*
Wendell, Stephen A. 1941- *St&PR 91*
Wendell, Wayne D. 1944- *St&PR 91*
Wendelowski, Lisa Kerstin 1955- *WhoEmL 91*
Wendelstedt, Harry *BioIn 16*
Wendelstedt, Harry Hunter, Jr. 1938- *WhoAm 90*
Wendenburg, Carl A. 1945- *St&PR 91*
Wender, Herbert 1937- *St&PR 91*
Wender, Ira Tensard 1927- *WhoAm 90*
Wender, Joseph Harris 1944- *WhoAm 90*
Wender, Paul H 1934- *BiDrAPA 89*
Wender, Phyllis Bellows 1934- *WhoAm 90*
Wenderoth, Donald Edward *St&PR 91*
Wenders, Wim *BioIn 16*
Wendkos, Paul 1922- *ConTFT 8*
Wendland, Erroll 1929- *St&PR 91*
Wendlandt, Gary Edward 1950- *St&PR 91*
Wendler, Guy H. 1952- *St&PR 91*
Wendler, Kristopher Kip *BiDrAPA 89*
Wendlestedt, Harry 1938- *Ballpl 90*
Wendleton, Tina Lynne 1961- *WhoAmW 91*
Wendling, Elizabeth Louise 1949- *WhoAmW 91*
Wendling, Pete 1888-1974 *BioIn 16, OxCPMus*
Wendling, William 1945- *ODwPR 91*
Wendorf, Denver Fred, Jr. 1924- *WhoAm 90*
Wendorf, Hulen Dee 1916- *WhoAm 90*
Wendroff, Dave P. 1961- *St&PR 91*
Wendrow, Sylvia Diann *WhoAmW 91*
Wendt, Charles William 1931- *WhoAm 90*
Wendt, Dieter Werner Friedrich 1947- *WhoE 91*
Wendt, E. Allan 1935- *WhoAm 90*
Wendt, Edward George, Jr. 1928- *St&PR 91, WhoAm 90*
Wendt, Frank P. 1925- *St&PR 91*
Wendt, Frank Paul 1925- *WhoAm 90*
Wendt, Gary Carl 1942- *WhoE 91*
Wendt, Gary Frederick 1951- *WhoEmL 91*
Wendt, Henry 1933- *St&PR 91*
Wendt, Henry, III 1933- *WhoE 91*
Wendt, Ingrid Darlene 1944- *WhoWrEP 89*
Wendt, Janice Louise Clemons 1939- *WhoSSW 91*
Wendt, Johann B. 1928- *St&PR 91*
Wendt, John Arthur Frederic, Jr. *WhoWor 91*
Wendt, Julia M. 1871-1942 *BiDWomA*
Wendt, Lloyd *AuBYP 90*
Wendt, Lloyd 1908- *WhoAm 90, WhoWrEP 89*
Wendt, Richard Kurt 1932- *St&PR 91, WhoAm 90*
Wendt, Thomas Gene 1951- *WhoEmL 91*
Wendy *WhoWrEP 89*
Weng, Byron Song Jan 1934- *WhoWor 91*
Weng, Lee Tung-Jen *BiDrAPA 89*
Weng, Will 1907?- *BioIn 16*
Wengel, Steven Phillip 1959- *BiDrAPA 89*
Wengenroth, Brian H. 1951- *WhoAm 90*
Wengenroth, Stow 1906-1978 *WhoAmA 91N*
Wenger, Bruce Edward 1948- *WhoAmA 91*
Wenger, Dorothy Mae 1917- *WhoAmW 91, WhoSSW 91*
Wenger, Galen Rosenberger 1946- *WhoSSW 91*
Wenger, Jane 1944- *WhoAmA 91*
Wenger, John Christian 1910- *WhoAm 90*
Wenger, Larry Bruce 1941- *WhoAm 90*
Wenger, Luke Huber 1939- *WhoAm 90*
Wenger, Muriel 1915-1989 *WhoAmA 91N*
Wenger, Robert Eric 1946- *BiDrAPA 89*
Wenger, Sidney U 1913- *BiDrAPA 89, WhoE 91*
Wenger, Sigmund 1910- *WhoAmA 91*
Wenger, Vicki 1928- *WhoAmW 91, WhoE 91, WhoWor 91*
Wengerd, Sherman Alexander 1915- *WhoAm 90*
Wengerd, Tim 1945-1989 *BioIn 16*
Wengert, James Warren 1934- *BiDrAPA 89*
Wengert, Norman Irving 1916- *WhoAm 90*
Wengert, Stanley A. 1931- *St&PR 91*
Wengler, Robert E. 1933- *St&PR 91*
Wengler, Robert Eugene 1933- *WhoAm 90*
Wenglowski, Gary Martin 1942- *WhoAm 90*
Wengrovitz, Judith 1931- *WhoAmA 91*
Wenie, Frederick T. M. 1859-1914 *BioIn 16*
Wenig, Harold G. 1924- *St&PR 91*
Wenig, Janice K. 1929- *St&PR 91*
Wenig, Lynne Gaye 1937- *WhoWor 91*
Wenig, Mary Moers *WhoAmW 91*
Wenig, Norman H. 1925- *St&PR 91*
Weniger, Frederick L *BiDrAPA 89*
Weniger, Nell 1931- *WhoAmW 91*
Weniger, Sidney N. 1920- *St&PR 91*
Wenk, Edward, Jr. 1920- *WhoAm 90*
Wenk, Klaus Otto 1927- *WhoWor 91*
Wenk, William Bruce 1928- *St&PR 91*
Wenkel, Ortrun 1942- *IntWWM 90*
Wenker, Shari Knotts 1962- *ODwPR 91*
Wenkert, Ernest 1925- *WhoAm 90*
Wenkert, Naomi Elizabeth *BiDrAPA 89*
Wenkle, Sara Jose 1915- *St&PR 91*
Wenkoff, Spas 1928- *IntWWM 90*
Wenley, Archibald Gibson 1898-1962 *WhoAmA 91N*
Wenman, Agnes *FemiCLE*
Wennemer, Manfred 1947- *St&PR 91*

Wennemer, Manfred Heinrich 1947- *WhoAm 90, WhoE 91*
Wenner, Erwin K. 1955- *St&PR 91*
Wenner, Gene Charles 1931- *WhoAm 90, WhoSSW 91*
Wenner, Herbert Allan 1912- *WhoAm 90*
Wenner, Jann S. 1946- *WhoWrEP 89*
Wenner, Jann Simon 1946- *WhoAm 90*
Wenner, Lettie McSpadden 1937- *WhoAmW 91*
Wenner, Naomi K 1914- *BiDrAPA 89*
Wennerberg, Gunnar Gunnarsson *PenDiDA 89*
Wennergren, L. Goran 1947- *WhoWor 91*
Wennerstrom, Donald *St&PR 91*
Wennhold, Ann Ruhmann 1932- *WhoAmW 91*
Wenning, Elisabeth *AuBYP 90*
Wenning, Jane 1948- *ODwPR 91*
Wennlund, Dolores Marie 1922- *WhoAmW 91*
Wenokor, William 1957- *BiDrAPA 89*
Wenrich, Jay H. 1929- *St&PR 91*
Wenrich, John William 1937- *WhoAm 90*
Wenrich, Percy 1880-1952 *BioIn 16, OxCPMus*
Wensel, Darrell W. 1934- *St&PR 91*
Wensel, Louise O *BiDrAPA 89*
Wensel, Marvin Max 1934- *St&PR 91*
Wensinger, Arthur S. 1926- *ConAu 33NR*
Wensinger, Arthur Stevens 1926- *WhoAm 90*
Wensley, William Charles *WhoAmA 91N*
Wensloff, Butch 1915- *Ballpl 90*
Wensrich, Margaret Fryer 1926- *WhoWrEP 89*
Wenstrom, David Walter 1948- *WhoE 91*
Wenstrup, H. Daniel 1934- *St&PR 91*
Wente, Patricia Ann 1954- *St&PR 91*
Wente, Van Arthur 1925- *WhoE 91*
Wentley, Richard Taylor 1930- *WhoAm 90, WhoWor 91*
Wentling, Rose Mary 1955- *WhoAmW 91*
Wentorf, Robert Henry 1926- *WhoAm 90*
Wentworth, Anne *BiDEWW, FemiCLE*
Wentworth, Bette Wilson 1938- *WhoSSW 91*
Wentworth, Clare G. 1939- *St&PR 91*
Wentworth, Henrietta Maria 1657?-1686 *BiDEWW*
Wentworth, Jack Roberts 1928- *WhoAm 90*
Wentworth, John 1737-1820 *EncCRAm*
Wentworth, John 1945- *WhoEmL 91*
Wentworth, John Warren 1925- *WhoAm 90*
Wentworth, Justin, III 1950- *WhoWor 91*
Wentworth, Malinda Ann Nachman *WhoAmW 91*
Wentworth, Murray Jackson 1927- *WhoAm 90, WhoAmA 91*
Wentworth, Nathaniel Newcomb, Jr. 1917- *St&PR 91*
Wentworth, Norman R. 1954- *St&PR 91*
Wentworth, Patricia 1878-1961 *FemiCLE, TwCCr&M 91*
Wentworth, Paul *EncCRAm*
Wentworth, Perley *MusmAFA*
Wentworth, Philadelphia *BiDEWW*
Wentworth, Ralph L. 1922- *St&PR 91*
Wentworth, Richard Leigh 1930- *WhoAm 90*
Wentworth, Theodore Sumner 1938- *WhoWor 91*
Wentworth, Thomas 1593-1641 *BioIn 16*
Wentworth, W Jack 1932- *BiDrAPA 89*
Wentworth, William Philip 1957- *WhoE 91*
Wentz, Bill M., Jr. 1953- *St&PR 91*
Wentz, Billy Melvin, Jr. 1953- *WhoAm 90*
Wentz, Dennis Keith 1935- *WhoWor 91*
Wentz, George Robinison 1929- *WhoE 91*
Wentz, Howard Beck, Jr. 1930- *St&PR 91, WhoAm 90*
Wentz, Jack Lawrence 1937- *WhoAm 90*
Wentz, Norman Jay 1945- *St&PR 91*
Wentz, Rodney 1943- *St&PR 91*
Wentz, Ronald Elliott 1951- *St&PR 91*
Wentz, Roy A. 1949- *St&PR 91*
Wentz, Sidney Frederick 1932- *WhoAm 90*
Wentz, Walter John 1928- *WhoAm 90*
Wentzel, Alan R. 1953- *St&PR 91*
Wentzel, Dale H. 1932- *WhoE 91*
Wentzel, Gregor 1898-1978 *DcScB S2*
Wentzien, Derald Edwin 1958- *WhoE 91*
Wenz, Richard Ernest 1949- *St&PR 91*
Wenz, Rodney E. 1935- *ODwPR 91*
Wenzel, Evelyn Maklary 1927- *WhoWrEP 89*
Wenzel, Fred H. 1939- *St&PR 91*
Wenzel, Fred W. 1916- *St&PR 91*
Wenzel, Heinz-Dieter 1946- *WhoWor 91*
Wenzel, James Gottlieb 1926- *WhoAm 90*
Wenzel, Joan Ellen *WhoAmA 91*
Wenzel, Johann *PenDiDA 89*
Wenzel, Lynn 1944- *WhoWrEP 89*
Wenzel, Sally Ellen 1956- *WhoAmW 91*
Wenzel, Steve Edwin 1951- *WhoEmL 91*
Wenzell, Phillip David 1962- *St&PR 91*
Wenzinger, August 1905- *IntWWM 90, PenDiMP*
Wenzl, Aloys 1887- *EncO&P 3*
Wenzl, James Emmett 1935- *WhoAm 90*
Wenzlau, Thomas Eugene 1927- *WhoAm 90*
Wenzler, Edward William 1954- *WhoEmL 91*
Wenzler, Joseph Paul 1942- *WhoAm 90*
Wenzler, Michael Paul 1953- *BiDrAPA 89*
Wenzler, William Paul 1929- *WhoAm 90*
Weores, Sandor 1913-1989 *AnObit 1989, BioIn 16*
Weppler, Jay Robert 1943- *WhoE 91*
Weppner, Benjamin H. 1933- *St&PR 91*
Wera, Anne Regina 1936- *WhoAmW 91*
Werba, Erik 1918- *PenDiMP*
Werba, Gabriel 1930- *ODwPR 91, WhoAm 90*
Werbach, Melvyn Roy 1940- *BiDrAPA 89*
Werbel, James David 1949- *WhoSSW 91*
Werber, Bill 1908- *Ballpl 90*
Werbil, Jennifer Lee Vinson 1952- *WhoAmW 91*
Werblowsky, Joshua Harold 1942- *BiDrAPA 89, WhoE 91*
Werbner, Isydor *BiDrAPA 89*
Werboff, Robert Gary *BiDrAPA 89*
Werbow, Stanley Newman 1922- *WhoAm 90*
Werby, Gibran Bernard 1938- *WhoSSW 91*
Werch, Chudley E. *BioIn 16*
Werchick, Jack 1913- *WhoAm 90*
Werchol, Marcia *BiDrAPA 89*
Werckenthien, Charles C. *St&PR 91*
Werckmeister, Otto Karl 1934- *WhoAm 90*
Werden, Jane *BioIn 16*
Werden, Perry 1865-1934 *Ballpl 90*
Werder, Felix 1922- *IntWWM 90*
Werder, Steven Francis *BiDrAPA 89*
Werderitsch, Thomas Franklin 1942- *St&PR 91*
Were, Miriam 1940- *FemiCLE*
Werefkin, Marianne Vladimirovna von 1860-1938 *BiDWomA*
Wereide, Thorstein 1882- *EncO&P 3*
Weremchuk, Mark 1956- *BiDrAPA 89*
Werenskiold, Marit 1942- *ConAu 130*
Werfel, Franz *BioIn 16*
Werfel, Gina S 1951- *WhoAmA 91*
Werfelman, William H., Jr. 1953- *ODwPR 91, WhoE 91*
Werff, Ivo-Jan van der *PenDiMP*
Werft, Frances Marie 1956- *WhoAmW 91*
Wergeland, Henrik 1808-1845 *DcScanL*
Werger, Art 1955- *WhoAmA 91*
Werger, Arthur Lawrence 1955- *WhoSSW 91*
Wergley, Albert N. 1947- *St&PR 91*
Werin, Lars Henrik Vitalis 1928- *WhoWor 91*
Werion, Rudi 1935- *IntWWM 90*
Werkema, Thomas Earl 1925- *WhoAm 90*
Werkhausen, Bernd 1940- *WhoWor 91*
Werkheiser, Steven Lawrence 1945- *WhoWor 91*
Werkheiser, William A. 1960- *WhoSSW 91*
Werkman, Arline Sue Louise 1945- *WhoAmW 91*
Werkman, Rosemarie Anne 1926- *WhoE 91*
Werkman, Sidney L 1927- *BiDrAPA 89*
Werkman, Sidney Lee 1927- *WhoAm 90*
Werkstell, Leslie J. 1945- *St&PR 91*
Werle, Bill 1920- *Ballpl 90*
Werle, C. R. 1936- *ODwPR 91*
Werle, Lars Johan 1926- *IntWWM 90*
Werle, Robert Geary 1944- *WhoSSW 91*
Werlein, Ewing, Jr. 1936- *WhoSSW 91*
Werler, John E. *WhoAm 90*
Werler, Paul F. *St&PR 91*
Werley, Anthony D. 1956- *St&PR 91*
Werley, Carolyn Corrine 1957- *WhoAmW 91*
Werlin, Lewis R. 1933- *St&PR 91*
Werlin, Sidney 1918- *St&PR 91*
Werlin, Stanley Howard 1949- *WhoE 91*
Werling, Norman Victor 1936- *St&PR 91*
Werlla, Vanessa Lynn 1953- *BiDrAPA 89*
Werman, David S 1922- *BiDrAPA 89*
Werman, David Sanford 1922- *WhoAm 90*
Werman, Thomas Ehrlich 1945- *WhoAm 90*
Wermecke, John D. *St&PR 91*
Wermer, Olga S *BiDrAPA 89*
Wermuth, Bruce Melvin 1944- *BiDrAPA 89*
Wermuth, Lora Dunnam Morgan 1929- *WhoAmW 91*
Wermuth, Manfred Jakob 1941- *WhoWor 91*
Wermuth, Paul Charles 1925- *WhoAm 90*
Werne, Joellen 1944- *BiDrAPA 89*
Werneburg, Kenneth Roger 1941- *St&PR 91*
Wernecke, Herbert Henry 1895- *AuBYP 90*
Werner 1909- *WhoAmA 91*
Werner, Alan Blair 1955- *St&PR 91*
Werner, Alfred 1866-1919 *BioIn 16*
Werner, Alfred 1911-1979 *WhoAmA 91N*
Werner, Arnold 1938- *BiDrAPA 89*
Werner, Bernard 1949- *WhoEmL 91*
Werner, Charles George 1909- *WhoAm 90*
Werner, Charles Spencer 1952- *St&PR 91*
Werner, Christian Thor 1916- *WhoE 91*
Werner, Curtis G. 1964- *St&PR 91*
Werner, Dagmar *BioIn 16*
Werner, Donald 1929- *WhoAmA 91*
Werner, Doris Theresa 1948- *WhoAmW 91*
Werner, Eric 1901-1988 *BioIn 16*
Werner, Frank D. 1922- *St&PR 91*
Werner, Frank Robert 1936- *WhoAmA 91*
Werner, Fred H. 1908- *WhoWrEP 89*
Werner, Fritz *WhoAm 90*
Werner, George F. 1931- *St&PR 91*
Werner, Gerhard 1921- *BiDrAPA 89, WhoAm 90*
Werner, Gloria S. 1940- *WhoAmW 91*
Werner, Graham A. 1938- *St&PR 91*
Werner, Hans 1946- *ConAu 131*
Werner, Hans-Peter 1947- *WhoWrEP 89*
Werner, Hazel Hawthorne *BioIn 16*
Werner, Hazen G. 1895-1988 *BioIn 16*
Werner, Herma 1926- *BioIn 16*
Werner, Herman S. 1920- *St&PR 91*
Werner, Howard 1951- *WhoAmA 91*
Werner, James J. 1934- *St&PR 91*
Werner, Jean-Jacques 1791-1849 *PenDiDA 89*
Werner, Jeffrey Smith 1945- *St&PR 91*
Werner, Joanne Lucille 1940- *WhoAmW 91*
Werner, John Ellis 1932- *WhoAm 90*
Werner, Julia Stewart 1936- *WhoAmW 91*
Werner, Karl Ferdinand 1924- *ConAu 131*
Werner, L. Raymond 1938- *St&PR 91*
Werner, Lawrence R. *ODwPR 91*
Werner, Michael F. 1945- *St&PR 91*
Werner, Mindy *BiDrAPA 89*
Werner, Mort 1916-1990 *BioIn 16*
Werner, Nat 1908- *WhoAmA 91*
Werner, Oskar 1922-1984 *WorAlBi*
Werner, Pat *AuBYP 90*
Werner, Philip M 1939- *BiDrAPA 89*
Werner, R.R. 1928- *St&PR 91*
Werner, Richard Budd 1931- *WhoAm 90*
Werner, Robert *BiDrAPA 89*
Werner, Robert Allen 1946- *St&PR 91, WhoAm 90*
Werner, Robert Joseph 1932- *WhoAm 90*
Werner, Robert L. 1913- *WhoAm 90*
Werner, Robert Morton *NewYTBS 90*
Werner, Roger Livington 1950- *BioIn 16*
Werner, Ronald L. 1945- *St&PR 91*
Werner, Seth *BioIn 16*
Werner, Sidney Charles 1909- *WhoAm 90*
Werner, Stuart Lloyd 1932- *WhoE 91, WhoWor 91*
Werner, Susan M. 1947- *WhoAmW 91*
Werner, Thomas Carl 1948- *St&PR 91*
Werner, Thomas R 1934- *BiDrAPA 89*
Werner, Tom *NewYTBS 90 [port]*
Werner, Tom G. 1942- *St&PR 91*
Werner, Vivian *AuBYP 90*
Werner, Vivienne Ellen 1948- *WhoAmW 91*
Werner, Warren Winfield 1952- *WhoWrEP 89*
Werner, William Ernest 1930- *WhoAm 90*
Werner, William Richard 1920- *St&PR 91*
Werner, Zacharias 1768-1823 *DcLB 94 [port]*
Werner-Jacobsen, Emmy Elisabeth 1929- *WhoAm 90*
Werner Vaughn, Salle *WhoAmA 91*
Wernert, John J, III 1959- *BiDrAPA 89*
Wernerus, Mathias 1873-1931 *MusmAFA*
Werness, Hope B 1943- *WhoAmA 91*
Werness, James L. 1953- *ODwPR 91*
Wernet, Louis Jacob, Jr. 1943- *WhoSSW 91*
Wernick, Jack Harry 1923- *WhoAm 90*
Wernick, Justin 1936- *WhoE 91*
Wernick, Kenneth A. 1946- *St&PR 91*
Wernick, Richard Frank 1934- *WhoAm 90*
Wernick, Robert *BioIn 16*
Wernick, Sandie 1944- *ODwPR 91*
Wernick, Sandie Margot 1944- *WhoAmW 91*
Wernick, Stanley 1928- *WhoAm 90*
Wernick, Stanley S. 1928- *St&PR 91*
Wernick, Ted 1930- *WhoSSW 91*
Wernicke, James Curtis 1952- *WhoSSW 91*
Wernikoff, Nancy Kasdon 1938- *WhoAmW 91*
Wernimont, Cheryl Ann 1944- *WhoAmW 91*
Wernke, Suzanne Marie 1957- *BiDrAPA 89*
Wernle, Helen Abigail 1952- *WhoWrEP 89*
Werries, E. Dean 1929- *St&PR 91, WhoAm 90, WhoSSW 91*
Werry, John Scott 1931- *BiDrAPA 89*
Wersba, Barbara 1932- *AuBYP 90, BioIn 16*
Wershba, Joseph 1920- *WhoAm 90*
Wershing, Susan Medler 1938- *WhoWrEP 89*
Wersig, Gernot 1942- *WhoWor 91*
Werson, James Byrd 1916- *WhoAm 90*
Werst, J.J., Jr. 1918- *St&PR 91*
Werstein, Irving 1914?-1971 *AuBYP 90*
Werstler, Ernest Warren, Jr. 1945- *WhoE 91*
Wert, Charles Allen 1919- *WhoAm 90*
Wert, Don 1938- *Ballpl 90*
Wert, Harry Emerson 1932- *St&PR 91, WhoWor 91*
Wert, James Junior 1933- *WhoAm 90*
Wert, James W. 1946- *St&PR 91*
Wert, Jonathan Maxwell, II 1939- *WhoAm 90*
Wert, Lucille Mathena 1919- *WhoAm 90*
Wert, Ned Oliver 1936- *WhoAmA 91, WhoE 91*
Wert, Robert Clifton 1944- *WhoE 91*
Wert, William George 1939- *WhoE 91*
Wertenbaker, Lael Tucker 1909- *BioIn 16*
Wertenbaker, Timberlake *FemiCLE*
Werth, Alexander *BioIn 16*
Werth, Andrew M. 1934- *WhoAm 90*
Werth, Claude James *BiDrAPA 89*
Werth, Glenn Conrad 1926- *WhoAm 90*
Werth, Gunter Heinz 1938- *WhoWor 91*
Werth, Hans Juergen 1948- *WhoWor 91*
Werth, Pamela A. 1954- *St&PR 91*
Werth, Paul M. *ODwPR 91*
Werth, Ronald Fred 1936- *St&PR 91*
Werth, Ronald Paul 1947- *St&PR 91*
Wertham, Fredric 1895-1981 *EncACom*
Werthan, Bernard, Jr. 1931- *St&PR 91*
Wertheim, Audrey D. 1933- *ODwPR 91*
Wertheim, Audrey Darwin 1933- *St&PR 91, WhoAmW 91*
Wertheim, John David 1945- *WhoE 91*
Wertheim, Mary Carole 1939- *WhoAmW 91*
Wertheim, Maurice, Mrs *WhoAmA 91N*
Wertheim, Mitzi Mallina *WhoAm 90*
Wertheim, Raymond Alan 1951- *BiDrAPA 89*
Wertheim, Raymond B *BiDrAPA 89*
Wertheim, Richard W. 1948- *ODwPR 91*
Wertheim, Robert Halley 1922- *WhoAm 90*
Wertheim, Sally Harris 1931- *WhoAmW 91*
Wertheimer, Barbara M 1926?-1983 *ConAu 129*
Wertheimer, Franc 1927- *WhoAm 90, WhoE 91*
Wertheimer, Fred *BioIn 16*
Wertheimer, Fredric Michael 1939- *WhoAm 90*
Wertheimer, Gregory L. 1957- *St&PR 91*
Wertheimer, Henry 1943- *St&PR 91*
Wertheimer, James Louis 1944- *St&PR 91, WhoAm 90*
Wertheimer, Marc Joel 1949- *WhoE 91*
Wertheimer, Richard James 1936- *WhoAm 90*
Wertheimer, Sydney Bernard 1914- *WhoAm 90*
Wertheimer, Thomas 1938- *St&PR 91, WhoAm 90*
Werther, Ellen *ODwPR 91*
Wertimer, Sidney, Jr. 1920- *WhoAm 90*
Wertman, Louis 1925- *St&PR 91*
Wertmuller, Lina *BioIn 16*
Wertmuller, Lina 1923- *EncCoWW*
Wertmuller, Lina 1928- *WorAlBi*
Wertsman, Vladimir 1929- *ConAu 31NR*
Wertz, Alta Happ 1921- *WhoAmW 91*
Wertz, Frederick J 1915- *BiDrAPA 89*
Wertz, Harrison George 1945- *St&PR 91*
Wertz, Jane Karr 1934- *WhoAmW 91*
Wertz, Johnny 1898- *Ballpl 90*
Wertz, Kenneth Dean 1946- *WhoAm 90*
Wertz, Larry Jean 1946- *St&PR 91*
Wertz, Richard Lawrence 1947- *St&PR 91*
Wertz, Spencer K. 1941- *WhoAm 90*
Wertz, Vic 1925-1983 *Ballpl 90*
Werum, Joseph Ralston 1920- *WhoAm 90*
Werz, Guenther Wolfram 1927- *WhoWor 91*
Werzberger, Chaskel 1932-1990 *BioIn 16*
Wesberry, James Pickett 1906- *WhoAm 90, WhoSSW 91, WhoWor 91*
Wesberry, James Pickett, Jr. 1934- *WhoAm 90*
Wesbury, Stuart Arnold, Jr. 1933- *WhoAm 90*
Weschcke, Carl L. 1930- *EncO&P 3*
Wesche, Katie Ann 1941- *WhoSSW 91*
Weschler, Anita *WhoAm 90, WhoAmA 91, WhoAmW 91*
Weschler, Barbara Rae *BiDrAPA 89*
Weschler, James Andrew 1937- *WhoAm 90*

Weschler, Lawrence Michael 1952- *WhoAm 90*
Weschler, Thomas R. *St&PR 91*
Wescoe, David B. 1954- *St&PR 91*
Wescoe, Sibyl Goetz 1953- *BiDrAPA 89*
Wescoe, W. Clarke 1920- *St&PR 91*
Wescoe, William Clarke 1920- *WhoAm 90*
Wescott, Bonnie Smith 1941- *WhoSSW 91*
Wescott, Glenway 1901-1987 *BioIn 16, DcLB 102 [port]*
Wescott, Paul 1904-1970 *WhoAmA 91N*
Wescott, Roger Williams 1925- *WhoAm 90*
Wesel, Charles William 1932- *St&PR 91*
Wesel, Genevieve Catherine *St&PR 91*
Wesel, Joseph Henry 1929- *St&PR 91*
Weseli, Roger William 1932- *WhoAm 90*
Wesely, Edwin Joseph 1929- *WhoAm 90*
Wesely, Yolanda Thereza 1927- *WhoE 91*
Wesemann, Wolfgang 1931- *WhoWor 91*
Wesenberg, David Gordon 1931- *St&PR 91*
Wesenberg, John Herman 1927- *WhoAm 90, WhoWor 91*
Wesener, Barbara 1948- *ODwPR 91*
Wesener, Gunter Ernst Helmuth 1932- *WhoWor 91*
Wesker, Arnold 1932- *ConAu 33NR, MajTwCW, WhoWor 91*
Weslager, Clinton Alfred 1909- *WhoAm 90, WhoE 91, WhoWor 91*
Wesler, Oscar 1921- *WhoAm 90*
Wesley, Charles 1707-1788 *BioIn 16, DcLB 95 [port]*
Wesley, Fern D. 1938- *WhoAmW 91*
Wesley, Frank A. 1924- *St&PR 91*
Wesley, George 1927- *St&PR 91*
Wesley, James Paul 1921- *WhoWor 91*
Wesley, John *EncPaPR 91*
Wesley, John 1703-1791 *BioIn 16, DcLB 104 [port], WorAlBi*
Wesley, John 1928- *WhoAmA 91*
Wesley, John Mercer 1928- *WhoAm 90*
Wesley, Mary 1912- *FemiCLE, MajTwCW*
Wesley, Newton K. *BioIn 16*
Wesley, Patricia A 1938- *BiDrAPA 89*
Wesley, Patricia Ann 1938- *WhoE 91*
Wesley, Richard 1945- *DrBlPA 90*
Wesley, Samuel *EncPaPR 91*
Wesley, Samuel 1662-1735 *BioIn 16*
Wesley, Samuel Sebastian 1810-1876 *BioIn 16*
Wesley, Susanna 1669-1742 *FemiCLE*
Wesley, Susanna Annesley 1670-1742 *BioIn 16*
Wesley, Susannah 1670?-1742 *BiDEWW*
Wesley-Furke, Lisbeth Scranton 1951- *WhoE 91*
Wesley-Hosford, Zia 1945- *WhoAmW 91*
Wesley-Smith, Martin 1945- *IntWWM 90*
Wesley-Smith, Peter 1945- *WhoWor 91*
Wesling, Donald Truman 1939- *WhoAm 90, WhoWrEP 89*
Wesling, Richard Michael 1932- *St&PR 91*
Weslowski, James J. 1950- *St&PR 91*
Wesner, John Oliver, Jr. 1916- *St&PR 91*
Wesner, John William 1936- *WhoE 91*
Wesnes, Keith Andrew 1950- *WhoWor 91*
Wesolow, Adam 1923- *WhoAm 90*
Wesolowski, Adolph John 1916- *WhoWor 91*
Wesolowski, Gerald F. 1946- *St&PR 91*
Wesolowski, Germaine Marie Velicer 1941- *WhoAmW 91*
Wesolowski, Paul G. 1956- *WhoWrEP 89*
Wesolowski, Sigmund Adam 1923- *WhoAm 90*
Wesp, Christian 1945- *BioIn 16*
Wesse, David Joseph 1951- *WhoEmL 91, WhoWor 91*
Wessel, Fred W 1946- *WhoAmA 91*
Wessel, Henry 1942- *WhoAm 90, WhoAmA 91*
Wessel, Horst 1907-1930 *BioIn 16*
Wessel, James R. 1940- *St&PR 91*
Wessel, Jeffrey Hall 1942- *WhoAm 90*
Wessel, Joan Strauss 1929- *WhoAmW 91*
Wessel, Johann Herman 1742-1785 *DcScanL*
Wessel, Kenneth C. 1928- *St&PR 91*
Wessel, Kenneth H. 1949- *St&PR 91*
Wessel, Ludwig *PenDiDA 89*
Wessel, Robert Hoover 1921- *WhoAm 90*
Wessel, Wessel 1920- *WhoWor 91*
Wesselenyi, Polixena 1801-1878 *EncCoWW*
Wesseling, Pieter 1942- *WhoWor 91*
Wesselink, David Duwayne 1942- *St&PR 91, WhoAm 90*
Wesselius, Cassie Lee 1946- *BiDrAPA 89*
Wesselius, Lewis F *BiDrAPA 89*
Wessell, David L. 1942- *St&PR 91*
Wessells, Norman Keith 1932- *WhoAm 90*
Wessells, William Craig 1953- *BiDrAPA 89*
Wesselmann, Glenn Allen 1932- *WhoAm 90, WhoWor 91*
Wesselmann, Robert A. *BioIn 16*
Wesselmann, Tom 1931- *WhoAm 90, WhoAmA 91*
Wessels, Glenn Anthony 1895-1982 *WhoAmA 91N*
Wessels, Jan Lucas 1938- *St&PR 91*
Wessels, Richard H. 1939- *St&PR 91*
Wessels, Richard Herbert 1939- *WhoAm 90*
Wessels, Wessel Hendrik 1933- *WhoWor 91*
Wessels, William Robert 1948- *WhoSSW 91*
Wessely, Helene 1924- *IntWWM 90*
Wessely, Othmar 1922- *IntWWM 90*
Wessendarp, Edward M. 1910- *St&PR 91*
Wessendorff, Robert Garrow 1927- *WhoSSW 91*
Wesser, Yvonne D 1935- *WhoAmA 91*
Wessin y Wessin, Elias *WhoWor 91*
Wessinger, Susan Cheryl 1962- *WhoSSW 91*
Wessler, Mary Hraha 1961- *WhoAmW 91*
Wessler, Richard Lee 1936- *WhoAm 90*
Wessler, Stanford 1917- *WhoAm 90, WhoWor 91*
Wessling, Donald Moore 1936- *WhoAm 90*
Wessling, Francis Christopher 1939- *WhoSSW 91*
Wessner, Deborah Marie 1950- *WhoAmW 91*
Wessner, Kenneth T. 1922- *St&PR 91*
Wessner, Kenneth Thomas 1922- *WhoAm 90*
Wesson, Bruce F. 1942- *St&PR 91*
Wesson, Lynn Elise *BiDrAPA 89*
Wesson, Robert G. 1920- *WhoAm 90*
Wesson, Robert Michael 1935- *WhoSSW 91*
Wesson, William Simpson 1929- *WhoAm 90*
West, Adam *BioIn 16*
West, Adam 1928- *ConTFT 8*
West, Alden Louis 1924- *WhoE 91*
West, Alfred Paul 1942- *St&PR 91*
West, Alfred Paul, Jr. 1942- *WhoAm 90*
West, Anna L. 1953- *ODwPR 91*
West, Anthony C 1910- *ConAu 31NR*
West, Arleigh Burton 1910- *WhoAm 90*
West, Arnold Sumner 1922- *WhoAm 90*
West, Arthur James, II 1927- *WhoAm 90*
West, B. Kenneth 1933- *St&PR 91*
West, Barbara Marie 1953- *St&PR 91*
West, Benjamin 1738-1820 *EncCRAm, IntDcAA 90, WorAlBi*
West, Bernard Hyland 1933- *WhoSSW 91*
West, Bettie Joan 1947- *WhoSSW 91*
West, Betty *AuBYP 90*
West, Billy Gene 1946- *WhoWor 91*
West, Bob 1931- *WhoE 91*
West, Bruce 1951- *SmATA 63*
West, Bruce Alan 1948- *WhoWor 91*
West, Byron Francis *BioIn 16*
West, C.P. *ConAu 33NR*
West, C. P. *MajTwCW*
West, Carol Catherine 1944- *WhoSSW 91*
West, Caryn *ConTFT 8 [port]*
West, Cathy Maynard 1945- *WhoEmL 91*
West, Charles Converse 1921- *WhoAm 90*
West, Charles H. 1934- *WhoAm 90*
West, Charles Laurence 1897- *IntWWM 90*
West, Charles Levonne 1943- *WhoSSW 91*
West, Chole Garibay 1954- *BiDrAPA 89*
West, Clara Faye Johnson 1923- *WhoAmA 91*
West, Clark Darwin 1918- *WhoAm 90*
West, Converse M. 1931- *St&PR 91*
West, Cynthya Thomas 1947- *WhoAmW 91*
West, D J 1924- *EncO&P 3*
West, Dan *BioIn 16*
West, Dan Carlos 1939- *WhoAm 90*
West, Dana L. 1944- *WhoAmW 91*
West, David Armstrong 1933- *WhoSSW 91*
West, Debra Lee 1953- *WhoAmW 91*
West, Delouris Jeanne 1943- *WhoSSW 91*
West, Dick Sheppard 1920-1989 *ConAu 130*
West, Don 1906- *EncAL*
West, Donald Allan 1938- *BiDrAPA 89*
West, Donald D. 1951- *ODwPR 91*
West, Donald J. 1924- *EncPaPR 91*
West, Donald V. 1930- *St&PR 91*
West, Dorothy 1907- *HarlReB*
West, Dorothy 1912- *FemiCLE*
West, Dorothy Mae 1942- *WhoSSW 91*
West, Dottie 1932- *OxCPMus*
West, Doug 1947- *BioIn 16*
West, E Gordon 1933- *WhoAmA 91*
West, Edward Charles 1928- *St&PR 91*
West, Edward E., Jr. 1927- *St&PR 91*
West, Edward Nason *NewYTBS 90*
West, Edward Nason 1909- *WhoE 91*
West, Edward Nason 1909-1990 *BioIn 16*
West, Edward P., Jr. 1950- *St&PR 91*
West, Edward Randall Kenneth 1944- *IntWWM 90*
West, Elizabeth *FemiCLE*
West, Elmer Gordon 1914- *WhoAm 90*
West, Emily 1919- *AuBYP 90*
West, Eric Fowler 1923- *St&PR 91*
West, Ernest Patrick, Jr. 1925- *WhoSSW 91*
West, Everett Wilson 1930- *St&PR 91*
West, Ewan Donald 1960- *IntWWM 90*
West, Felton 1926- *WhoAm 90*
West, Fowler Claude 1940- *WhoAm 90*
West, Franklin H 1921- *BiDrAPA 89*
West, Franklin Howard 1921- *WhoE 91*
West, Gail Berry 1942- *WhoAm 90*
West, Gary Richard 1954- *WhoSSW 91*
West, Gary Wayne 1941- *St&PR 91*
West, George R. 1920- *St&PR 91*
West, Georgina L. 1941- *ODwPR 91*
West, Gerard M 1938- *BiDrAPA 89*
West, Gregory Joseph 1950- *St&PR 91*
West, Gregory Scott 1957- *WhoSSW 91*
West, Harold E. 1926- *St&PR 91*
West, Harold M 1930- *BiDrAPA 89*
West, Harry Archibald, Jr. 1939- *WhoSSW 91*
West, Harvey Gordon, Jr. 1945- *WhoSSW 91*
West, Herbert Buell 1916- *WhoAm 90, WhoE 91, WhoWor 91*
West, Herbert Buell 1916-1990 *BioIn 16, NewYTBS 90*
West, Howard Norton 1919- *WhoAm 90*
West, Hugh Brian 1939- *St&PR 91*
West, Hugh Sterling 1930- *WhoWor 91*
West, Hylie A. 1960- *WhoE 91*
West, J. Robinson 1946- *WhoAm 90*
West, James *AuBYP 90, ConAu 30NR*
West, James Edward 1944- *WhoE 91*
West, James Enoch 1941- *WhoSSW 91*
West, James Franklin, Jr. 1947- *WhoSSW 91*
West, James Harold 1926- *WhoAm 90*
West, James Joseph 1945- *WhoEmL 91*
West, James Kenneth 1935- *St&PR 91*
West, James L W 1946- *ConAu 131*
West, James W 1914- *BiDrAPA 89*
West, Jane 1758-1852 *BioIn 16, FemiCLE*
West, Jean 1935- *WhoWrEP 89*
West, Jerry 1938- *WorAlBi*
West, Jerry Alan 1938- *WhoAm 90*
West, Jerry W. 1938- *WhoAm 90*
West, Jerry Wayne 1938- *St&PR 91*
West, Jessamyn *BioIn 16*
West, Jessamyn 1902-1984 *FemiCLE, MajTwCW*
West, Jessamyn 1907-1984 *BioAmW*
West, Jessie Stevenson 1891-1976 *BioIn 16*
West, Joe 1952- *Ballpl 90*
West, Joe Earl 1932- *WhoSSW 91, WhoWor 91*
West, John Burnard 1928- *WhoAm 90*
West, John C. 1908- *St&PR 91*
West, John Carl 1922- *WhoWor 91*
West, John Henry, III 1954- *WhoE 91*
West, John Merle 1920- *WhoAm 90*
West, John Oliver 1925- *WhoAm 90*
West, John Roderick 1941- *WhoAm 90*
West, John Thomas, IV 1946- *St&PR 91*
West, Karen Elizabeth 1946- *St&PR 91*
West, Kathleen Fisher 1960- *WhoAmW 91*
West, Kathleene K. *WhoWrEP 89*
West, Kathryn Marie 1935- *WhoAmW 91*
West, Kenneth *BioIn 16*
West, Kenneth Wayne 1950- *St&PR 91*
West, L. Adele *BiDrAPA 89*
West, Lee Roy 1929- *WhoAm 90, WhoSSW 91*
West, Lewis Albert, III 1956- *WhoSSW 91*
West, Lockwood 1905-1989 *AnObit 1989, ConTFT 8*
West, Lola C. 1947- *WhoAmW 91*
West, Loretta Marie 1950- *WhoAmW 91*
West, Louis Jolyon 1924- *BiDrAPA 89, WhoAm 90*
West, Mae 1892- *WorAlBi*
West, Mae 1892-1980 *BioIn 16, NotWoAT, OxCPMus*
West, Mae 1893-1980 *BioAmW*
West, Marge L. 1928- *St&PR 91*
West, Marilyn Bess 1941- *WhoAmW 91*
West, Mariquita 1937- *BiDrAPA 89*
West, Marjorie Edith 1940- *WhoAmW 91*
West, Marvin Leon 1934- *WhoAm 90*
West, Max 1916- *Ballpl 90*
West, Maxine Marilyn 1945- *WhoAmW 91*
West, Maxwell J 1930- *BiDrAPA 89*
West, Melissa A 1957- *BiDrAPA 89*
West, Michael Alan 1938- *WhoAm 90*
West, Michael Barry 1942- *WhoSSW 91*
West, Michael Davidson 1937- *WhoE 91*
West, Michael Philip 1888-1973 *BioIn 16*
West, Michelle Lynne 1961- *WhoAmW 91*
West, Millard Farrar, Jr. 1910- *WhoAm 90*
West, Morris 1916- *WorAlBi*
West, Morris L 1916- *MajTwCW*
West, Morris Langlo 1916- *SpyFic, WhoAm 90, WhoWor 91, WhoWrEP 89*
West, Nathanael 1903-1940 *MajTwCW, WorAlBi, WrPh*
West, Olin Leslie *BiDrAPA 89*
West, Owen *MajTwCW*
West, Paul 1930- *BioIn 16*
West, Paul Noden 1930- *WhoAm 90, WhoWrEP 89*
West, Pennerton *WhoAmA 91N*
West, Perry Douglas 1947- *St&PR 91*
West, Peter 1953- *WhoAmA 91*
West, Philip William 1913- *WhoAm 90, WhoSSW 91*
West, Phillip John 1936- *BiDrAPA 89*
West, Phyllis Ann 1940- *St&PR 91*
West, Pilar Ramirez 1935- *WhoHisp 91*
West, Ralph W., Jr. *WhoAm 90*
West, Rebecca 1892-1983 *BioIn 16, DcNaB 1981, FemiCLE, MajTwCW, WorAlBi*
West, Rexford Leon 1938- *St&PR 91, WhoAm 90*
West, Rhea Horace, Jr. 1920- *WhoSSW 91*
West, Richard A. 1925- *St&PR 91*
West, Richard Charles 1945- *WhoAm 90*
West, Richard Henry 1926- *St&PR 91*
West, Richard Luther 1925- *WhoAm 90*
West, Richard M. 1944- *St&PR 91*
West, Richard P. 1921- *St&PR 91*
West, Richard Rollin 1938- *WhoAm 90*
West, Richard Samuel 1955- *ConAu 130*
West, Richard Vincent 1934- *WhoAm 90, WhoAmA 91*
West, Robert C. 1920- *St&PR 91*
West, Robert Cooper 1913- *WhoAm 90*
West, Robert Culbertson 1928- *WhoAm 90*
West, Robert H. 1938- *St&PR 91, WhoAm 90*
West, Robert MacLellan 1942- *WhoAm 90*
West, Robert V., Jr. 1921- *St&PR 91*
West, Robert Van Osdell, Jr. 1921- *WhoAm 90, WhoSSW 91*
West, Roger *BioIn 16*
West, Roger S., III 1949- *St&PR 91*
West, Roy Owen 1868-1958 *BiDrUSE 89*
West, Ruth *BioIn 16*
West, S.R. 1939- *St&PR 91*
West, Salli Lou 1939- *WhoWrEP 89*
West, Sam Carroll, Jr. 1947- *BiDrAPA 89*
West, Sammy 1904-1985 *Ballpl 90*
West, Samuel 1730-1807 *EncCRAm*
West, Samuel Edward 1938- *WhoSSW 91*
West, Sandra La Vonne 1947- *WhoWrEP 89*
West, Sharon Anne 1944- *WhoAmW 91*
West, Stephen A. 1935- *St&PR 91*
West, Stephen Allan 1935- *WhoE 91*
West, Stephen Owen 1946- *St&PR 91, WhoEmL 91*
West, Stephen R. 1931- *St&PR 91*
West, Tami Linn 1959- *WhoSSW 91*
West, Terence Douglas 1948- *WhoWor 91*
West, Thomas Edward 1954- *WhoWrEP 89*
West, Thomas Lowell, Jr. 1937- *St&PR 91*
West, Thomas Meade 1940- *St&PR 91, WhoAm 90*
West, Togo Dennis, Jr. 1942- *WhoAm 90*
West, Ulla Christina 1944- *WhoAmW 91*
West, Victoria Sackville- 1892-1962 *BioIn 16*
West, Virginia M *WhoAmA 91*
West, W Richard 1912- *WhoAmA 91*
West, Walter L. 1943- *St&PR 91*
West, Warren Henry 1956- *WhoE 91*
West, William Beverley, III 1922- *WhoAm 90*
West, William Scott 1955- *BiDrAPA 89*
West, William Stuart 1927- *St&PR 91*
West, Wilmer A. 1939- *St&PR 91*
West-Eberhard, Mary Jane 1941- *WhoAm 90*
West-Gale, Doe 1951- *WhoE 91*
West-James, Patricia F *BiDrAPA 89*
Westall, Marta Susan Wolf 1946- *WhoEmL 91*
Westberg, Charlotte Gene *WhoAmW 91*
Westberg, Harold A. 1923- *St&PR 91*
Westberg, Janet Ugrob *BiDrAPA 89*
Westberg, John Augustin 1931- *WhoWor 91*
Westberg, Nils 1938- *WhoWor 91*
Westberry, Billy Murry 1926- *WhoAm 90*
Westberry, Mark A. *St&PR 91*
Westbrook, James Edwin 1934- *WhoAm 90*
Westbrook, Joel Whitsitt, III 1916- *WhoAm 90*
Westbrook, John 1922-1989 *AnObit 1989*
Westbrook, John 1947-1983 *BioIn 16*
Westbrook, Karin Luka 1943- *St&PR 91*
Westbrook, Karla Renee 1964- *WhoAmW 91*
Westbrook, Katherine McGarvey 1956- *WhoSSW 91*
Westbrook, LaDawn Kay 1955- *WhoAmW 91*
Westbrook, Marianne McIntire 1948- *WhoAmW 91*

Westbrook, Peter *BioIn 16*
Westbrook, W. L. 1939- *St&PR 91*
Westburg, John Edward 1918- *WhoWrEP 89*
Westbury, Richard G.S. 1926- *St&PR 91*
Westcombe, John Bertram 1937- *IntWWM 90*
Westcot, George Duane 1927- *St&PR 91*
Westcott, F. Howard 1902-1989 *BioIn 16*
Westcott, Nadine *AuBYP 90*
Westcott, Nadine Bernard 1949- *BioIn 16*
Westcott, Shirley Joyce 1926- *WhoAmW 91*
Westcott, Theresa Commerton 1954- *WhoAmW 91*
Westcott, William Wynn 1848-1925 *EncO&P 3*
Westenborg, Jack A. 1942- *St&PR 91*
Westenburg, Richard 1932- *IntWWM 90*
Westendorf, Craig J. 1953- *IntWWM 90*
Westendorf, Elaine Susan 1956- *WhoEmL 91*
Westendorf, Wolfhart Heinrich 1924- *WhoWor 91*
Westendorp, Floyd 1932- *BiDrAPA 89*
Westenholz, Piers von *BioIn 16*
Wester, Barbara Ann 1966- *WhoAmW 91*
Wester, Brooks Hardy, Jr. 1942- *WhoSSW 91*
Wester, John Francis 1923- *WhoE 91*
Wester, Keith Albert 1940- *WhoAm 90, WhoWor 91*
Wester, Mark W. 1954- *St&PR 91*
Wester, Mark William 1954- *WhoAm 90*
Wester, Natalie Y. 1960- *ODwPR 91*
Wester, Neil Charles 1940- *St&PR 91*
Wester, Per Olov 1929- *WhoWor 91*
Wester, William Daniel 1926- *WhoAm 90*
Westerbeck, David Francis 1945- *St&PR 91, WhoAm 90*
Westerbeck, Kenneth Edward 1919- *WhoAm 90*
Westerbeek, Elbert 1967- *WhoWor 91*
Westerberg, Arthur William 1938- *WhoAm 90*
Westerberg, Gunnar Olof 1920- *WhoWor 91*
Westerdahl, John Brian 1954- *WhoEmL 91, WhoWor 91*
Westerfield, Frank M. Jr. 1925- *BiDrAPA 89*
Westerfield, Holt Bradford 1928- *WhoAm 90*
Westerfield, Putney 1930- *St&PR 91, WhoAm 90*
Westergaard, Peter 1931- *IntWWM 90*
Westergaard, Peter Talbot 1931- *WhoAm 90*
Westergaard, Richard C. 1944- *St&PR 91*
Westerhaus, Douglas B. 1951- *St&PR 91*
Westerhaus, Douglas Bernard 1951- *WhoEmL 91*
Westerheide, Richard J. 1951- *St&PR 91*
Westerheide, William Joseph, Jr. 1945- *WhoSSW 91*
Westerhoff, Harold E. 1915- *WhoAm 90, WhoWor 91*
Westerhoff, Heinz 1928- *WhoWor 91*
Westerhoff, John Henry, III 1933- *WhoAm 90*
Westerhold, Ruth Elizabeth 1926- *WhoAmW 91*
Westerholm, Sune Sigfrid 1941- *WhoWor 91*
Westerhout, Gart 1927- *WhoAm 90*
Westerkamp, Robert John 1935- *St&PR 91*
Westerlund, David A. 1950- *St&PR 91*
Westerlund Roosen, Mia 1942- *WhoAmA 91*
Westerman, Albert Barry 1941- *WhoSSW 91*
Westerman, Arne 1927- *BioIn 16*
Westerman, Gayl Shaw 1939- *WhoE 91*
Westerman, George W. 1939- *St&PR 91*
Westerman, Howard G. 1928- *WhoSSW 91*
Westerman, Keith F. 1952- *ODwPR 91*
Westerman, Mark Lee 1954- *St&PR 91*
Westerman, Susan S. 1943- *WhoAm 90*
Westerman, Sylvia Hewitt *WhoAm 90*
Westerman, Wm. L. 1931- *St&PR 91*
Westermann, Anthony J. 1906- *St&PR 91*
Westermann, David 1920- *WhoAm 90*
Westermann, H C 1922- *WhoAmA 91*
Westermann, Horace Clifford 1922- *WhoAm 90*
Westermann, Horace Clifford 1922-1981 *WhoAmA 91N*
Westermann, Nancy M *BiDrAPA 89*
Westermark, Torbjorn Erik Gunnar 1923- *WhoWor 91*
Westermeier, John Thomas, Jr. 1941- *WhoE 91*
Westermeyer, Joseph John 1937- *BiDrAPA 89*
Westermeyer, Michael T. 1949- *St&PR 91*
Westermeyer, Paul 1940- *IntWWM 90*
Western Brothers, The *OxCPMus*
Western, George *OxCPMus*
Western, Kenneth *OxCPMus*
Westerstahl, Nils Erik Gustaf 1933- *WhoWor 91*
Westervelt, Peter Jocelyn 1919- *WhoAm 90*
Westervelt, Robert F 1928- *WhoAmA 91*
Westerweel, Joop 1899-1944 *BioIn 16*
Westfall, Bernard G. 1941- *WhoAm 90, WhoSSW 91*
Westfall, Carol Ann 1938- *WhoAmW 91*
Westfall, Carol D 1938- *WhoAmA 91*
Westfall, David 1927- *WhoAm 90*
Westfall, Helen Naomi 1933- *WhoAmW 91*
Westfall, Mary Glenda 1944- *WhoWrEP 89*
Westfall, Michael Peter 1933- *BiDrAPA 89*
Westfall, Phillip K. 1943- *St&PR 91*
Westfall, Richard Merrill 1956- *WhoWor 91*
Westfall, Richard Samuel 1924- *WhoAm 90, WhoWrEP 89*
Westfall, Robert E *BiDrAPA 89*
Westfall, Stephen V R 1953- *WhoAmA 91*
Westfall, Ted B. *BioIn 16*
Westgate, R. I. Wilfred *BioIn 16*
Westhafer, J. C. 1932- *St&PR 91*
Westhead, Valerie Ann 1958- *BiDrAPA 89*
Westheimer, David 1917- *WhoWrEP 89*
Westheimer, David Kaplan 1917- *WhoAm 90*
Westheimer, Frank Henry 1912- *WhoAm 90*
Westheimer, Gerald 1924- *WhoAm 90*
Westheimer, Mary Helen 1955- *WhoAmW 91, WhoWrEP 89*
Westheimer, Ruth *BioIn 16*
Westheimer, Ruth Siegel *WhoAmW 91*
Westheimer, Ruth Susan 1941- *BiDrAPA 89*
Westheimer, Ruth Welling 1922- *WhoAmW 91*
Westhoff, Clara 1878-1954 *BiDWomA*
Westhoff, David John 1942- *St&PR 91*
Westhoff, Dennis Charles 1942- *WhoAm 90*
Westin, Alan Furman 1929- *WhoAm 90*
Westin, Avram Robert 1929- *WhoAm 90*
Westin, Dennis C 1942- *BiDrAPA 89*
Westin, Richard S. 1932- *St&PR 91*
Westin, Robert H 1946- *WhoAmA 91*
Westin, Sharen *BiDrAPA 89*
Westing, Arthur Herbert 1928- *WhoWor 91*
Westinghouse, George 1846-1914 *BioIn 16, WorAlBi*
Westlake, Anthony L. *St&PR 91*
Westlake, Aubrey T 1893-1985 *EncO&P 3*
Westlake, Donald 1933- *WorAlBi*
Westlake, Donald E. 1933- *ConAu 13AS [port], TwCCr&M 91*
Westlake, Donald Edwin 1933- *WhoAm 90*
Westlake, Donald Edwin Edmund 1933- *WhoWrEP 89*
Westlake, James Roger 1928- *WhoSSW 91*
Westlake, Merle T. 1922- *St&PR 91*
Westlake, Robert Elmer, Sr. 1918- *WhoAm 90*
Westlake, Robert J 1935- *BiDrAPA 89*
Westlake, Wally 1920- *Ballpl 90*
Westley, Dennis J. 1959- *St&PR 91*
Westley, Glenn Douglas 1950- *WhoE 91*
Westley, Helen 1875-1942 *BioIn 16, NotWoAT*
Westley, John Richard 1939- *WhoE 91*
Westley, Richard Owen 1912- *WhoAm 90*
Westling, Jon 1942- *WhoAm 90*
Westlund, Harry E 1941- *WhoAmA 91*
Westlund, Leslie 1962- *BiDrAPA 89*
Westlund, Lois Christopher 1933- *WhoAmW 91*
Westlund, Nick N. 1940- *St&PR 91*
Westlund, Norman 1904- *BiDrAPA 89*
Westmaas, William J 1925- *BiDrAPA 89*
Westmacott, Mary *AuBYP 90, MajTwCW*
Westmacott, Richard 1775-1856 *BioIn 16*
Westman, Barbara 1929- *WhoE 91*
Westman, Carl Edward 1943- *WhoAm 90*
Westman, Jack C 1927- *BiDrAPA 89*
Westman, Jack Conrad 1927- *WhoAm 90*
Westman, Kathryn Louise 1930- *WhoAm 90*
Westman, Lincoln H 1925- *BiDrAPA 89*
Westman, Sten-Olof Vilhelm 1931- *WhoWor 91*
Westmeyer, Edward Anthony 1948- *St&PR 91*
Westmeyer, Francis Emery 1949- *St&PR 91*
Westmeyer, Troy R. 1916-1989 *BioIn 16*
Westminster, Gerald C Grosvenor, Duke of 1951- *BioIn 16*
Westmore, Michael George 1938- *WhoAm 90*
Westmoreland, Barbara Fenn 1940- *WhoAmW 91*
Westmoreland, Douglas Brian 1959- *WhoSSW 91*
Westmoreland, Irena S *BiDrAPA 89*
Westmoreland, Jeri Elizabeth Johnston 1948- *WhoSSW 91*
Westmoreland, Joyce N. 1938- *St&PR 91*
Westmoreland, O.R. 1948- *St&PR 91*
Westmoreland, Phillip Duane 1956- *WhoSSW 91*
Westmoreland, R. P. 1936- *St&PR 91*
Westmoreland, Reginald Conway 1926- *WhoSSW 91*
Westmoreland, William C. *BioIn 16*
Westmoreland, William C 1914- *SmATA 63 [port], WorAlBi*
Westmoreland, William Thomas 1947- *BiDrAPA 89*
Westoff, Charles Francis 1927- *WhoAm 90*
Weston, Allen *ConAu 31NR, MajTwCW*
Weston, Arthur Walter 1914- *WhoAm 90*
Weston, Burt H *BiDrAPA 89*
Weston, Christine Goutiere 1904-1989 *BioIn 16*
Weston, Daniel D. 1923- *St&PR 91*
Weston, Don L *BiDrAPA 89*
Weston, Donald Eugene 1935- *St&PR 91*
Weston, Edward 1886-1958 *BioIn 16, WorAlBi*
Weston, Elizabeth 1582-1612 *BiDEWW*
Weston, Garfield Howard 1927- *WhoWor 91*
Weston, Harold 1894-1972 *WhoAmA 91N*
Weston, Jack 1915- *ConTFT 8*
Weston, Jack 1924- *WorAlBi*
Weston, Janice Leah Colmer 1944- *WhoAmW 91*
Weston, John Colby 1926- *WhoE 91*
Weston, John Frederick 1916- *WhoAm 90*
Weston, Josh S. 1928- *St&PR 91, WhoAm 90, WhoE 91*
Weston, Kim 1939- *DrBlPA 90*
Weston, Laurel Andrea *BiDrAPA 89*
Weston, Linda Lee 1954- *WhoSSW 91*
Weston, Lynda Rigsbee *BiDrAPA 89*
Weston, Martha 1947- *BioIn 16, ConAu 129*
Weston, Mary 1712-1766 *FemiCLE*
Weston, Paul 1912- *OxCPMus*
Weston, Paul Holliday 1944- *St&PR 91*
Weston, Phyllis J. 1921- *WhoAmW 91*
Weston, R. P. 1878-1936 *OxCPMus*
Weston, Randy 1926- *DrBlPA 90, WhoAm 90*
Weston, Roy F. 1911- *St&PR 91*
Weston, Roy Francis 1911- *WhoAm 90*
Weston, Stanley *BioIn 16*
Weston, Stanton D. 1930- *St&PR 91*
Weston, Susan B. 1943- *WhoWrEP 89*
Weston, Thomas 1575?-1664? *EncCRAm*
Weston, W Donald *BiDrAPA 89*
Weston, Willard Galen 1940- *WhoAm 90, WhoWor 91*
Weston, William Isedore 1946- *WhoEmL 91*
Weston, William Lee 1938- *WhoAm 90*
Weston-Major, Deirdre May 1959- *WhoE 91*
Weston McDonald, Laurie 1951- *BiDrAPA 89*
Westover, Brooke N. 1926- *St&PR 91*
Westover, Charles 1939-1990 *BioIn 16*
Westover, Frank Thomas 1938- *St&PR 91*
Westover, Karl J. 1933- *St&PR 91*
Westover, Russ 1886-1966 *EncACom*
Westphal, Antoinette 1937- *St&PR 91*
Westphal, Arnold Carl 1897- *BioIn 16*
Westphal, David E. 1944- *St&PR 91*
Westphal, Douglas Herbert 1940- *WhoSSW 91*
Westphal, Gordon Edward 1940- *St&PR 91*
Westphal, James P. *BioIn 16*
Westphal, Katherine *BioIn 16*
Westphal, Mary Josephine 1956- *WhoAmW 91*
Westphal, Rainer John 1935- *St&PR 91*
Westphal, Ruth Lilly 1931- *WhoAmW 91*
Westphal, Steven D. 1955- *St&PR 91*
Westphalen, Henry, Jr. 1933- *St&PR 91*
Westphalen, Jules 1937- *St&PR 91*
Westra, Kraig A. 1943- *St&PR 91*
Westra, Verlyn L. 1936- *St&PR 91*
Westran, Roy A. 1925- *St&PR 91*
Westran, Roy Alvin 1925- *WhoAm 90, WhoWor 91*
Westrick, Edward Roy *BiDrAPA 89*
Westrick, Elsie Margaret 1910- *WhoWrEP 89*
Westrick, Robert J. 1941- *St&PR 91*
Westrope, Martha Randolph 1922- *WhoAmW 91*
Westrum, Dexter 1944- *WhoWrEP 89*
Westrum, Edgar Francis, Jr. 1919- *WhoAm 90*
Westrum, Wes 1922- *Ballpl 90*
Westwater, Angela King 1942- *WhoAmA 91*
Westwater, James William 1919- *WhoAm 90*
Westwater, Robert Stuart 1920- *St&PR 91*
Westwick, Carmen Rose 1936- *WhoAmW 91*
Westwood, Albert Ronald Clifton 1932- *WhoAm 90*
Westwood, Horace 1884-1956 *EncO&P 3*
Westwood, Jean Miles 1923- *WhoAmW 91*
Westwood, Jefferson 1949- *WhoEmL 91*
Westwood, Mary *BiDEWW*
Wetamoe 1650?-1676 *WhNaAH*
Wetamoo 1650?-1676 *WhNaAH*
Wetamoo, Queen 1650?-1676 *WhNaAH*
Wetamou 1650?-1676 *WhNaAH*
Wetcher, Goldie Rappaport 1939- *WhoAmW 91*
Wetcher, Kenneth 1941- *BiDrAPA 89*
Wetemoo 1650?-1676 *WhNaAH*
Wetesnik, Kim Marie 1958- *WhoSSW 91*
Wetherald, Agnes Ethelwyn 1857-1940 *DcLB 99 [port]*
Wetherald, Ethelwyn 1857-1940 *FemiCLE*
Wetherald, Margaret Elizabeth 1958- *WhoAmW 91*
Wetherald, Michele Warholic 1954- *WhoAmW 91*
Wetherald, William 1820-1898 *DcCanB 12*
Wetherall, Robert Shaw 1944- *WhoWor 91*
Wetherbee, Roberta Janis 1948- *WhoAmW 91*
Wethered, Roger Henry 1899-1983 *DcNaB 1981*
Wetherell, Claire 1919- *WhoAmW 91*
Wetherell, Jeffrey S. 1942- *St&PR 91*
Wetherill, Eikins 1919- *WhoAm 90*
Wetherill, Elkins 1919- *St&PR 91*
Wetherill, George West 1925- *WhoAm 90*
Wetherill, Linda *IntWWM 90*
Wetherill, Samuel 1736-1816 *EncCRAm*
Wetherington, James M. 1945- *St&PR 91*
Wetherington, W. J. *WhoSSW 91*
Wethey, Harold Edwin 1902-1984 *WhoAmA 91N*
Wethington, John Abner, Jr. 1921- *WhoAm 90*
Wethington, R.B. 1944- *St&PR 91*
Wethington, William Orville 1906- *WhoWor 91*
Wethington, Wilma Zella 1918- *WhoAmA 91*
Wethington-Hadley, Wilma Zella *WhoAmA 91*
Wethli, Mark 1949- *WhoAmA 91*
Wetlaufer, Donald Burton 1925- *WhoAm 90*
Wetli, Peggy Marie 1949- *WhoAmW 91*
Wetmore, Andrew Rainsford 1820-1892 *DcCanB 12*
Wetmore, Donald L. 1927- *St&PR 91*
Wetmore, Gordon 1938- *WhoAmA 91*
Wetmore, Joan 1911-1989 *BioIn 16*
Wetmore, Karen E. 1953- *WhoAmW 91*
Wetmore, Richard Donald *BiDrAPA 89*
Wetmore, Thomas Hall 1915- *WhoAm 90*
Wetmore, Thomas Trask, III 1925- *WhoAm 90*
Wetreich, William 1953- *St&PR 91*
Wetsel, Nelson Thomas 1922- *St&PR 91*
Wetstein, Gary M. *WhoAm 90*
Wetston, Howard Isadore 1947- *WhoAm 90*
Wetstone, Howard Jerome 1926- *WhoE 91*
Wetstone, Janet Meyerson 1928- *WhoAmW 91*
Wettack, F. Sheldon *WhoAm 90*
Wette, Eduard Wilhelm 1925- *WhoWor 91*
Wettenhall, Roger Llewellyn 1931- *WhoWor 91*
Wettenstein, Beverly *ODwPR 91*
Wetter, Edward 1919- *WhoAm 90*
Wetter, Friedrich 1928- *WhoWor 91*
Wetter, Larry V. 1933- *St&PR 91*
Wetterau, Theodore C. 1927- *St&PR 91, WhoAm 90*
Wetterberg, Per Gunnar 1953- *WhoWor 91*
Wetterer, Margaret K. *AuBYP 90*
Wetterhahn, Karen Elizabeth 1948- *WhoAmW 91*
Wetterling, Jacob *BioIn 16*
Wetters, Brian Dale 1957- *WhoSSW 91*
Wetterstrom, Keith Erwin 1932- *St&PR 91*
Wetther, Karen Lee 1948- *WhoAmW 91*
Wettig, Patricia *BioIn 16, WhoAm 90, WhoAmW 91*
Wetton, Rita *BiDrAPA 89*
Wettreich, Daniel *St&PR 91*
Wettstein, Diter Von 1929- *WhoWor 91*
Wettstein, Frederick Albert, III 1943- *WhoE 91*
Wettstein, Horst Dieter 1933- *WhoWor 91*
Wettstein, Minna Adelt 1867- *EncCoWW*
Wettstein, Peter 1939- *IntWWM 90*
Wettstein, Robert Mark 1950- *BiDrAPA 89, WhoE 91*
Wettstein, Wieland F. 1949- *St&PR 91*
Wetzel, Arthur Alfred 1903- *St&PR 91*
Wetzel, Barry Jay 1943- *St&PR 91*

Wetzel, Brian 1946- *WhoE 91*
Wetzel, Carroll Robbins 1906- *WhoAm 90*
Wetzel, David L. 1929- *St&PR 91*
Wetzel, Don *BioIn 16*
Wetzel, Don 1945- *WhoEmL 91*
Wetzel, Donald C. *St&PR 91*
Wetzel, Edward Thomas 1937- *WhoE 91, WhoWor 91*
Wetzel, Elizabeth 1930- *WhoWrEP 89*
Wetzel, Gary Erwin 1938- *St&PR 91*
Wetzel, Gloria Mae Hipps 1941- *WhoE 91*
Wetzel, Harry 1920- *St&PR 91*
Wetzel, Heinz 1935- *WhoAm 90*
Wetzel, Karen J. 1953- *WhoAmW 91*
Wetzel, Mary Goodwin 1939- *WhoE 91*
Wetzel, Paul J. 1937- *ODwPR 91*
Wetzel, Richard *WhoAm 90*
Wetzel, Robert A. 1937- *St&PR 91*
Wetzel, Robert E. 1937- *St&PR 91*
Wetzel, Robert George 1936- *WhoAm 90*
Wetzel, Robert Lewis 1947- *WhoSSW 91*
Wetzel, Stephen Alan 1962- *WhoSSW 91*
Wetzels, Walter Dominic 1930- *WhoAm 90*
Wetzler, James Warren 1947- *WhoAm 90, WhoE 91*
Wetzler, Monte Edwin 1936- *WhoAm 90*
Wetzler, Robert Allan 1914- *BiDrAPA 89*
Wever, Hans 1922- *WhoWor 91*
Wever, Walter 1887-1936 *BioIn 16*
Wevers, Francois Rene 1960- *WhoWor 91*
Wevers, John William 1919- *WhoAm 90*
Wewer, Mildred Elizabeth 1927- *WhoWrEP 89*
Wewer, William Paul 1947- *WhoE 91, WhoWor 91*
We'wha 1849?-1896 *BioIn 16*
Wex, Timothy George 1947- *WhoE 91*
Wexelbaum, Michael 1946- *WhoE 91*
Wexelman, Ronald 1934- *St&PR 91*
Wexler, Anne 1930- *ODwPR 91, WhoAm 90*
Wexler, Bernard Carl 1923- *WhoAm 90*
Wexler, Bruce Edward 1947- *BiDrAPA 89*
Wexler, Claire Thyra *WhoAmA 91*
Wexler, Donald 1923- *BiDrAPA 89*
Wexler, Elmer 1918- *EncACom*
Wexler, George 1925- *WhoAmA 91*
Wexler, Ginia Davis 1923- *WhoAm 90*
Wexler, Haskell *BioIn 16*
Wexler, Haskell 1922- *WhoAm 90*
Wexler, Helene Shelley 1956- *WhoAmW 91*
Wexler, Herbert I. 1916- *St&PR 91, WhoAm 90, WhoWor 91*
Wexler, Jacqueline Grennan 1926- *WhoAm 90, WhoAmW 91*
Wexler, Jan Joseph 1928- *BiDrAPA 89*
Wexler, Jerome Leroy 1923- *WhoAmA 91, WhoE 91*
Wexler, Jerrold *BioIn 16*
Wexler, Jerrold 1924- *WhoAm 90*
Wexler, Ken 1954- *St&PR 91*
Wexler, Lee Edward 1951- *WhoAmA 91*
Wexler, Leonard 1931- *WhoAm 90*
Wexler, Leonard D. 1924- *WhoAm 90*
Wexler, Michael 1945- *WhoWor 91*
Wexler, Norman 1926- *WhoE 91, WhoWrEP 89*
Wexler, Peter John 1936- *WhoAm 90*
Wexler, Philip 1950- *WhoWrEP 89*
Wexler, Sam O. 1935- *St&PR 91*
Wexner, Leslie 1937- *ConAmBL*
Wexner, Leslie Herbert 1937- *WhoAm 90*
Wey, John Joseph 1948- *BiDrAPA 89*
Wey Cooke, Sharon Kay 1954- *WhoAmW 91*
Weyand, Frederick Carlton 1916- *St&PR 91, WhoAm 90*
Weybret, Frederick Eugene 1923- *St&PR 91*
Weybret, Martin 1951- *St&PR 91*
Weydahl, Hanna Marie 1922- *IntWWM 90*
Weyden, Roger Van Der 1400-1464 *WorAlBi*
Weyen, Wendy Lee 1963- *WhoAmW 91*
Weyenberg, Donald Richard 1930- *St&PR 91, WhoAm 90*
Weyer, Florence *BiDEWW*
Weyer, Johan 1515-1588 *EncO&P 3*
Weyer, Lee 1936-1988 *Ballpl 90, BioIn 16*
Weyerhaeuser, Frederick Theodore 1931- *WhoAm 90*
Weyerhaeuser, George H. 1926- *St&PR 91*
Weyerhaeuser, George Hunt 1926- *WhoAm 90*
Weyers, Hans-Leo 1934- *WhoWor 91*
Weyers, Susan Joyce 1958- *WhoAmW 91*
Weyforth, Mimi 1944- *WhoAm 90, WhoAmW 91*
Weygand, Maxime 1867-1965 *BiDFrPL*
Weygant, Noemi *AuBYP 90*
Weyhe, Arthur *WhoAmA 91*
Weyher, Harry Frederick 1921- *WhoAm 90*
Weyher, Harry Frederick, III 1956- *WhoAm 90*
Weyhing, Gus 1886-1955 *Ballpl 90*
Weyl, Martin 1940- *WhoWor 91*
Weyl, Simon *BiDrAPA 89*
Weyland, Alphonse Joseph 1943- *WhoWor 91*
Weyler, Walter E. 1939- *St&PR 91*
Weyler, Walter Eugen 1939- *WhoAm 90*
Weyler y Nicolau, Valeriano 1839-1930 *BioIn 16*
Weymann, Albert Conrad, III 1943- *St&PR 91*
Weymann, Ray J. 1934- *WhoAm 90*
Weymar, F. Helmut 1936- *WhoAm 90*
Weymouth, George *EncCRAm*
Weymouth, Lawrence B., Jr. 1943- *St&PR 91*
Weymouth, Marion Z. 1912- *St&PR 91*
Weymouth, Yann 1941- *BioIn 16*
Weymouth, Yann Ralph 1941- *WhoWor 91*
Weymuller, Charles A. 1896-1989 *BioIn 16*
Weymuller, Ernest A. 1907-1989 *BioIn 16*
Weyn, Suzanne 1955- *SmATA 63 [port]*
Weynerowski, Hanka *WhoAmA 91*
Weyr, Garret *BioIn 16*
Weyr, Thomas Hector 1927- *WhoE 91*
Weyrauch, Walter Otto 1919- *WhoAm 90*
Weyrich, Paul *BioIn 16*
Weyrich, Paul Michael 1942- *WhoAm 90, WhoWor 91*
Weyrick, John Alfred 1948- *WhoSSW 91*
Weywadt, Lars Bo 1950- *WhoWor 91*
Wezel, Johann Karl 1747-1819 *DcLB 94 [port]*
Whala, Stacey Ann 1962- *WhoAmW 91*
Whale, Arthur Richard 1923- *WhoAm 90*
Whalen, Brian B. 1939- *WhoWor 91*
Whalen, Charles William, Jr. 1920- *WhoAm 90*
Whalen, Curtis E. 1947- *St&PR 91*
Whalen, David G. 1957- *St&PR 91*
Whalen, Edward John 1948- *St&PR 91*
Whalen, Edward M *BiDrAPA 89*
Whalen, Elizabeth Joan 1956- *WhoAmW 91*
Whalen, Henry Francis, Jr. 1935- *St&PR 91*
Whalen, James F. 1931- *St&PR 91*
Whalen, James Joseph 1927- *WhoAm 90, WhoE 91*
Whalen, James Lawrence 1956- *St&PR 91*
Whalen, Jerome J. 1942- *St&PR 91*
Whalen, John A. 1947- *St&PR 91*
Whalen, John D. 1938- *St&PR 91*
Whalen, John Michael 1945- *WhoE 91*
Whalen, John P. *BioIn 16*
Whalen, John Sydney 1934- *WhoAm 90*
Whalen, Joseph Philip 1933- *WhoAm 90, WhoE 91*
Whalen, Kenneth J. 1923- *St&PR 91*
Whalen, Kevin M. *ODwPR 91*
Whalen, Lawrence Alan 1933- *WhoE 91*
Whalen, Lawrence William, Jr. *St&PR 91N*
Whalen, Loretta Theresa 1940- *WhoAmW 91*
Whalen, Lucille 1925- *WhoAm 90, WhoAmW 91*
Whalen, Martin J. 1940- *WhoAm 90*
Whalen, Nana Lee 1937- *WhoAmW 91*
Whalen, Patricia May 1945- *WhoAmW 91, WhoE 91*
Whalen, Philip Glenn 1923- *WhoAm 90, WhoWrEP 89*
Whalen, Richard J 1935- *ConAu 32NR*
Whalen, Richard James 1935- *WhoAm 90, WhoWrEP 89*
Whalen, Richard Paul *BiDrAPA 89*
Whalen, Robert Michael 1946- *WhoE 91*
Whalen, Thomas Douglas 1948- *WhoWrEP 89*
Whalen, Thomas M., III 1934- *WhoE 91*
Whalen, Timothy John 1960- *WhoE 91*
Whalen-Cruz, Wanda Jo 1958- *WhoAmW 91*
Whaley, Betti S. *BioIn 16, NewYTBS 90*
Whaley, Carrol Wayne 1946- *WhoSSW 91*
Whaley, Charles Henry, IV 1958- *WhoE 91*
Whaley, Charlotte T. 1925- *WhoWrEP 89*
Whaley, Charlotte Totebusch 1925- *WhoAmW 91*
Whaley, Dawn Ellen 1953- *IntWWM 90*
Whaley, Henry P. 1925- *St&PR 91*
Whaley, John Alexander 1940- *St&PR 91, WhoAm 90*
Whaley, Marc Alan 1945- *BiDrAPA 89, WhoE 91*
Whaley, Mary Susan Maison 1953- *IntWWM 90*
Whaley, Paul Arthur 1922- *St&PR 91*
Whaley, Peggy Elaine 1939- *WhoAmW 91*
Whaley, Richard Smith 1874- *AmLegL*
Whaley, Robert D. 1942- *St&PR 91*
Whaley, Ronald L. *St&PR 91*
Whaley, Ross Samuel 1937- *WhoE 91*
Whaley, Storm Hammond 1916- *WhoAm 90, WhoWor 91*
Whaley, Thomas Patrick 1923- *WhoWor 91*
Whaling, Frank 1934- *ConAu 32NR*
Whalley, Edward 1925- *WhoAm 90*
Whalley, Joyce Irene 1923- *SmATA 61 [port]*
Whalley, Peter 1946- *TwCCr&M 91*
Whalley-Kilmer, Joanne *BioIn 16*
Whallon, Evan Arthur, Jr. 1923- *WhoAm 90*
Whallon, Robert Edward 1940- *WhoAm 90*
Whallon, William 1928- *WhoAm 90, WhoWrEP 89*
Wham *EncPR&S 89*
Wham, David Buffington 1937- *WhoWrEP 89*
Wham, Dorothy Stonecipher 1925- *WhoAmW 91*
Wham, George Sims 1920- *WhoAm 90*
Wham, William Neil 1934- *WhoAm 90, WhoWor 91*
Whang, Yun Chow 1931- *WhoAm 90*
Whanger, Alan D *BiDrAPA 89*
Whanger, Herbert N *BiDrAPA 89*
Whaples, Miriam K. 1929- *IntWWM 90*
Wharity, Barry 1946- *St&PR 91*
Wharley, Mary 1657-1726 *BiDEWW*
Wharmby, Margot *SmATA 63*
Wharram, Paul F. *St&PR 91*
Wharton, Annabel Jane *WhoAmA 91*
Wharton, Anne 1659-1685 *BiDEWW, BioIn 16, FemiCLE*
Wharton, Beverly Ann 1953- *St&PR 91, WhoAm 90*
Wharton, Carol Forbes 1907-1958 *WhoAmA 91N*
Wharton, Charles, II 1936- *WhoSSW 91*
Wharton, Charles Benjamin 1926- *WhoAm 90*
Wharton, Clifton R. *BioIn 16*
Wharton, Clifton R. 1899-1990 *BioIn 16, CurBio 90N, NewYTBS 90 [port]*
Wharton, Clifton R., Jr. 1926- *St&PR 91*
Wharton, Clifton Reginald, Jr. 1926- *WhoAm 90, WhoWrEP 89*
Wharton, Conrad Kemper 1962- *WhoSSW 91*
Wharton, Dave *BioIn 16*
Wharton, David Carrie 1930- *WhoAm 90*
Wharton, David W 1951- *WhoAmA 91*
Wharton, Dolores D. *BioIn 16*
Wharton, Edith 1862-1937 *BioAmW, BioIn 16, ConAu 132, FemiCLE, MajTwCW, ShSCr 6 [port], WorAlBi, WrPh*
Wharton, Garry Lee 1936- *St&PR 91*
Wharton, Gary Charles 1940- *St&PR 91*
Wharton, Hannah *FemiCLE*
Wharton, Ingrid Arnold *BiDrAPA 89*
Wharton, J. Ernest *NewYTBS 90*
Wharton, J. Ernest 1899-1990 *BioIn 16*
Wharton, James *MajTwCW*
Wharton, James Pearce 1893-1963 *WhoAmA 91N*
Wharton, Joseph 1826-1909 *WorAlBi*
Wharton, Lennard 1933- *WhoAm 90*
Wharton, Margaret Agnes 1943- *WhoAmA 91*
Wharton, Ralph Nathaniel 1932- *BiDrAPA 89, WhoE 91*
Wharton, Richard *EncCRAm*
Wharton, Richard Gloor 1932- *St&PR 91*
Wharton, Shirley Granger 1947- *WhoAmW 91*
Wharton, Thomas Patrick 1947- *WhoE 91*
Wharton, Tilford Girard 1904- *WhoAm 90*
Wharton, William *BioIn 16*
Wharton, William Polk *WhoE 91, WhoWor 91*
Whateley, Anne 1561-1601 *FemiCLE*
Whately, Mary *BioIn 16*
Whatley, Booker T. *BioIn 16*
Whatley, Jacqueline Beltram 1944- *WhoAmW 91, WhoWor 91*
Whatley, James L. 1946- *St&PR 91*
Whatley, James R. 1926- *St&PR 91*
Whatley, James Royce 1926- *WhoAm 90*
Whatley, James Wallace 1945- *WhoWrEP 89*
Whatley, Robert Southcott 1951- *St&PR 91*
Whatley, Thomas Jewel 1918- *WhoAm 90*
Whatmore, George Bernard 1917- *WhoWor 91*
Whatmough, Helen Darlene 1943- *St&PR 91*
Whatmough, J. Jeremy T. 1934- *WhoAm 90*
Whatmough, Jeremy T. 1934- *St&PR 91*
Wheadon, David Eugene 1957- *BiDrAPA 89*
Whealdon, Everett Whittier 1910- *WhoWrEP 89*
Wheale, H. Douglas 1920- *St&PR 91*
Whealon, John Francis 1921- *WhoAm 90, WhoE 91*
Whealy, John Fisher 1932- *St&PR 91, WhoAm 90*
Wheary, Eugene C. 1911- *St&PR 91*
Wheat, Alan Dupree 1951- *BlkAmsC [port], WhoAm 90*
Wheat, Carolyn *TwCCr&M 91*
Wheat, Francis Millspaugh 1921- *WhoAm 90*
Wheat, James C., Jr. 1920- *St&PR 91*
Wheat, Joe Ben 1916- *WhoAm 90*
Wheat, Joe Franklin 1939- *WhoSSW 91*
Wheat, John *BioIn 16*
Wheat, John Marc 1964- *WhoE 91*
Wheat, Josiah 1928- *WhoAm 90*
Wheat, William D 1927- *BiDrAPA 89*
Wheat, Willis J. 1926- *St&PR 91*
Wheat, Willis James 1926- *WhoAm 90*
Wheat, Zach 1888-1972 *Ballpl 90 [port]*
Wheatcroft, John Stewart 1925- *WhoAm 90, WhoWrEP 89*
Wheater, Tim *NewAgMG*
Wheathill, Anne *BiDEWW, FemiCLE*
Wheatland, Richard, II 1923- *WhoAm 90*
Wheatley, Lord 1908-1988 *AnObit 1988*
Wheatley, Bernard Alfredo 1948- *WhoE 91*
Wheatley, Briana Marie 1942- *WhoAmW 91*
Wheatley, Bruce C. 1942- *ODwPR 91*
Wheatley, Dennis 1897-1977 *EncO&P 3, MajTwCW, TwCCr&M 91*
Wheatley, Dennis Yates 1897-1977 *SpyFic*
Wheatley, Edmund 1792?-1841 *BioIn 16*
Wheatley, Edward Warren 1936- *WhoSSW 91*
Wheatley, Ernest Harold 1927- *WhoAm 90*
Wheatley, George Milholland, Jr. 1937- *St&PR 91*
Wheatley, Grayson Hubbard, Jr. 1934- *WhoSSW 91*
Wheatley, J M O 1924- *EncO&P 3*
Wheatley, James Edward 1949- *St&PR 91*
Wheatley, James Melville Owen 1924- *EncPaPR 91*
Wheatley, Margaret Bisson 1941- *WhoAmW 91*
Wheatley, Mary *BioIn 16*
Wheatley, Mary Burkes *BiDrAPA 89*
Wheatley, Mary Jane 1949- *WhoEmL 91*
Wheatley, Melvin Ernest, Jr. 1915- *WhoAm 90*
Wheatley, Paul 1921- *WhoAm 90*
Wheatley, Phillis 1753-1784 *BioAmW, BioIn 16, FemiCLE, WorAlBi*
Wheatley, Phillis 1754?-1784 *EncCRAm*
Wheatley, Robert Ray, III 1934- *WhoSSW 91*
Wheatley, Willard 1915- *BioIn 16*
Wheatley, William Ogden, Jr. 1944- *WhoAm 90*
Wheatley, William S., Jr. 1939- *St&PR 91*
Wheaton, Beryl McLeod 1925- *WhoE 91*
Wheaton, Bruce R. 1944- *WhoWrEP 89*
Wheaton, Carla Ann 1960- *WhoAmW 91*
Wheaton, David Joe 1940- *WhoAm 90*
Wheaton, Frank H., Jr. 1913- *St&PR 91*
Wheaton, Henry 1785-1848 *BioIn 16*
Wheaton, John S. 1928- *St&PR 91*
Wheaton, John Southworth 1928- *WhoAm 90, WhoWor 91*
Wheaton, Scott R. 1929- *St&PR 91*
Wheaton, Theodore D. *AmLegL*
Wheaton, Wil *BioIn 16*
Wheatstone, Charles 1802-1875 *WorAlBi*
Wheatt, Theodis M *BiDrAPA 89*
Whedon, Aida Anthony 1915- *WhoAmA 91*
Whedon, George Donald 1915- *WhoAm 90*
Whedon, Margaret Brunssen *WhoAm 90*
Whedon, Ralph Gibbs 1949- *WhoAm 90*
Wheelan, Ed 1888-1966 *EncACom*
Wheelan, Fairfax David 1955- *WhoE 91*
Wheelen, Thomas Leo 1935- *WhoSSW 91*
Wheeler, Agnes 1734-1804 *FemiCLE*
Wheeler, Albert Lee, III 1954- *WhoSSW 91*
Wheeler, Alfred Harvey *BioIn 16*
Wheeler, Anna 1785-1848? *FemiCLE*
Wheeler, Anne *BioIn 16*
Wheeler, Barbara Louise 1948- *IntWWM 90*
Wheeler, Betsy 1939- *WhoAmW 91*
Wheeler, Beverly G 1952- *BiDrAPA 89*
Wheeler, Britt Ingegerd 1935- *WhoWor 91*
Wheeler, Bruce 1948- *WhoHisp 91*
Wheeler, Burton 1927- *WhoAm 90*
Wheeler, Burton K. 1882-1975 *WorAlBi*
Wheeler, C. Herbert 1915- *WhoAm 90*
Wheeler, Carol Estelle 1936- *WhoAmW 91*
Wheeler, Carroll Ray *BiDrAPA 89*
Wheeler, Cathy Jo 1954- *WhoAmW 91*
Wheeler, Charles 1947- *BioIn 16*
Wheeler, Charles Bertan 1926- *WhoAm 90*
Wheeler, Charles Lynn 1943- *IntWWM 90*
Wheeler, Cindy 1955- *BioIn 16, ConAu 31NR*
Wheeler, Clarence Joseph, Jr. 1917- *WhoSSW 91*
Wheeler, Clayton Eugene, Jr. 1917- *WhoAm 90*

Wheeler, Clyde T. 1942- St&PR 91
Wheeler, Daniel Redfield BiDrAPA 89
Wheeler, Daniel Scott 1947- WhoAm 90, WhoWrEP 89
Wheeler, Darrell Deane 1939- WhoSSW 91
Wheeler, David James 1952- WhoSSW 91
Wheeler, David Laurie 1934- WhoAm 90
Wheeler, Dennis Earl 1942- St&PR 91
Wheeler, Donald O. 1938- St&PR 91
Wheeler, Donna Marie 1962- WhoAmW 91
Wheeler, Douglas Lanphier 1937- WhoE 91
Wheeler, Douglas Paul 1942- WhoAm 90
Wheeler, Duane E. 1932- St&PR 91
Wheeler, Dwight Clark, II 1943- St&PR 91
Wheeler, Earl Milton 1939- WhoSSW 91
Wheeler, Earl W. 1927- St&PR 91
Wheeler, Earle Gilmore 1908-1975 WorAlBi
Wheeler, Edward Kendall 1913- WhoAm 90
Wheeler, Elizabeth Eustis BiDrAPA 89
Wheeler, Frank R. BiDrAPA 89
Wheeler, George Montague 1842-1905 WhNaAH
Wheeler, George William 1924- WhoAm 90
Wheeler, Gerald F. BioIn 16
Wheeler, Grant Walton 1941- St&PR 91
Wheeler, Harold 1943- DrBlPA 90
Wheeler, Harold Alden 1903- WhoAm 90
Wheeler, Harold Austin, Sr. 1925- WhoSSW 91
Wheeler, Helen Rippier ConAu 31NR
Wheeler, Henry Clark 1916- St&PR 91, WhoAm 90
Wheeler, Hewitt Brownell 1929- WhoAm 90
Wheeler, Hugh TwCCr&M 91
Wheeler, Ira Francis 1920- WhoSSW 91
Wheeler, James Orton 1938- WhoSSW 91
Wheeler, Janie Mae 1934- WhoSSW 91
Wheeler, Jeffrey Allan 1944- WhoE 91
Wheeler, Joe Frank 1955- WhoSSW 91
Wheeler, Joe Lawrence 1936- WhoE 91
Wheeler, John 1937- St&PR 91
Wheeler, John Archibald 1911- WhoAm 90, WhoE 91
Wheeler, John Craig 1943- WhoAm 90
Wheeler, John Harvey 1918- WhoAm 90
Wheeler, John Hill 1806-1882 BioIn 16
Wheeler, John Hubbard 1926- St&PR 91
Wheeler, John Ingraham, Jr. 1925- WhoAm 90
Wheeler, John James 1942- St&PR 91
Wheeler, John M. 1956- St&PR 91
Wheeler, John N. Ballpl 90
Wheeler, John Oliver 1924- WhoAm 90
Wheeler, John Watson 1938- WhoSSW 91
Wheeler, Joseph 1836-1906 WorAlBi
Wheeler, Katherine Wells 1940- WhoAmW 91
Wheeler, Keith Allen 1950- St&PR 91
Wheeler, Kenneth William 1929- WhoAm 90, WhoWor 91
Wheeler, Kenny 1930- BioIn 16
Wheeler, Kyle Thorn 1952- WhoAmW 91
Wheeler, Ladd 1937- WhoAm 90
Wheeler, Larry W. St&PR 91
Wheeler, Leonard 1901- WhoAm 90
Wheeler, Linda ODwPR 91
Wheeler, Lloyd E. 1937- ODwPR 91
Wheeler, Louis O. 1917- St&PR 91
Wheeler, Lyle BioIn 16
Wheeler, Lyle 1905-1990 ConDes 90, NewYTBS 90
Wheeler, M. Catherine 1942- WhoAmW 91
Wheeler, Malcolm Edward 1944- WhoAm 90
Wheeler, Marilyn Miller 1955- WhoAmW 91
Wheeler, Mark 1943- WhoAmA 91
Wheeler, Marshall Ralph 1917- WhoAm 90
Wheeler, Mary WhoAmA 91
Wheeler, Mary Curtis 1869-1944 BioIn 16
Wheeler, Mary Harrison 1938- WhoE 91
Wheeler, Michael Burnett 1945- St&PR 91, WhoAm 90
Wheeler, Michael David 1947- WhoWor 91
Wheeler, Michael Simpson 1942- WhoAm 90
Wheeler, Monroe 1900-1988 BioIn 16
Wheeler, Mortimer 1890-1976 ConAu 32NR
Wheeler, Nancy Alice 1954- WhoAmW 91
Wheeler, Orson Shorey 1902- WhoAmA 91
Wheeler, Orville Eugene 1932- WhoAm 90
Wheeler, Otis Bullard 1921- WhoAm 90
Wheeler, Patricia Harriett Ann 1950- WhoAmW 91
Wheeler, Paul Leonard 1926- St&PR 91
Wheeler, Philip Norman 1952- WhoE 91
Wheeler, Porter King 1940- WhoE 91
Wheeler, Post 1869- AuBYP 90
Wheeler, Richard Kenneth 1934- WhoAm 90
Wheeler, Richard Kenneth 1944- BioIn 16
Wheeler, Richard Warren 1929- WhoAm 90
Wheeler, Robert A. 1942- St&PR 91
Wheeler, Roger Graydon 1934- WhoAm 90
Wheeler, Ruric E. 1923- WhoWor 91
Wheeler, Sam 1924-1989 BioIn 16
Wheeler, Samuel Metcalf 1823-1886 AmLegL
Wheeler, Sessions S. AuBYP 90
Wheeler, Sessions Samuel 1911- WhoAm 90, WhoWor 91
Wheeler, Stanton 1930- WhoAm 90
Wheeler, Susan 1955- WhoWrEP 89
Wheeler, Thomas Beardsley 1936- WhoAm 90, WhoE 91
Wheeler, Thomas Edgar 1946- WhoAm 90, WhoE 91
Wheeler, Thomas Francis 1937- WhoWor 91
Wheeler, Thomas Hutchin 1947- WhoWrEP 89
Wheeler, Thomas Lyndon 1951- WhoE 91
Wheeler, Trent H. 1959- WhoWrEP 89
Wheeler, Vivian Barbara 1927- WhoAmW 91
Wheeler, Warren Gage, Jr. 1921- WhoAm 90
Wheeler, Wendy Robin 1953- WhoAmW 91
Wheeler, William A. 1934- St&PR 91
Wheeler, William Almon 1819-1887 BiDrUSE 89
Wheeler, William Bryan, III 1940- WhoSSW 91
Wheeler, William Chamberlain, Jr. 1945- WhoEmL 91
Wheeler, William Crawford 1914- WhoSSW 91
Wheeler, William O 1930- BiDrAPA 89
Wheeler, Willis Boly 1938- WhoSSW 91
Wheeler, Wilmot Fitch, Jr. 1923- St&PR 91, WhoAm 90
Wheeler-Nicholson, Malcolm 1890-1968 EncACom
Wheeling, Lynn AuBYP 90
Wheeling, Robert Franklin 1923- WhoSSW 91
Wheelis, Allen B BiDrAPA 89
Wheelis, Joan 1955- BiDrAPA 89, WhoE 91
Wheelock, Arthur Kingsland, Jr. 1943- WhoAm 90, WhoAmA 91
Wheelock, Carolyn Minnette 1923- WhoAmW 91
Wheelock, Donald Franklin 1940- IntWWM 90
Wheelock, Eleazar 1711-1779 EncCRAm, WhNaAH, WorAlBi
Wheelock, John Brian 1952- WhoSSW 91
Wheelock, Keith Ward 1933- WhoE 91
Wheelock, Major William, Jr. 1936- WhoAm 90
Wheelock, Martha Ellen 1941- WhoAmW 91
Wheelock, Moira Myrl Brewer WhoSSW 91
Wheelock, Morgan Dix BioIn 16
Wheelock, Thomas R. St&PR 91
Wheelock, Warren F 1880-1960 WhoAmA 91N
Wheelock, William I., Jr. 1947- St&PR 91
Wheelwright, Alice 1959- WhoSSW 91
Wheelwright, Ann 1920- St&PR 91
Wheelwright, Betty 1947- WhoWrEP 89
Wheelwright, Harvey Pearse 1923- BiDrAPA 89
Wheelwright, Jere Hungerford AuBYP 90
Wheelwright, John 1592?-1679 EncCRAm
Wheelwright, Joseph Balch BiDrAPA 89
Wheelwright, Joseph Storer 1948- WhoAmA 91
Wheelwright, Julie 1960- ConAu 130
Wheelwright, Lorin F. 1909- St&PR 91
Wheelwright, Steven C. 1943- WhoAm 90
Whelahan, Yvette Ann 1943- WhoSSW 91
Whelan, Albert 1875-1961 OxCPMus
Whelan, Elizabeth Ann Murphy 1943- WhoAm 90
Whelan, Francis C. 1907- WhoAm 90
Whelan, Francis J 1938- BiDrAPA 89
Whelan, James P. 1916- St&PR 91
Whelan, James Robert 1933- WhoAm 90, WhoE 91, WhoWor 91
Whelan, John J 1937- BiDrAPA 89
Whelan, John Kenneth 1941- WhoWor 91
Whelan, John William 1922- WhoAm 90
Whelan, Joseph L. 1917- WhoAm 90, WhoWor 91
Whelan, Laura Dozier 1922- WhoAmW 91
Whelan, Lawrence James 1961- WhoE 91
Whelan, Martin J. 1943- St&PR 91
Whelan, Michael F. 1938- St&PR 91
Whelan, Nicholas J. 1869- AmLegL
Whelan, Richard J. 1931- WhoAm 90
Whelan, Richard Vincent, Jr. 1933- WhoAm 90
Whelan, Thomas Joseph 1921- WhoAm 90
Whelan, Virginia 1950- WhoAmW 91
Whelan, Ward Bernard 1949- St&PR 91
Whelan, William Joseph 1924- WhoAm 90
Whelan-Cota, Marie Elaine 1952- WhoAmW 91
Whelchel, Betty Anne 1956- WhoE 91
Whelchel, Harry J., Jr. 1945- St&PR 91
Whelchel, John Davis 1940- WhoAm 90
Whelchel, Lucy Beasley 1942- WhoAmW 91
Whelchel, Sandra 1944- WhoWrEP 89
Whelchel, Sandra Jane 1944- WhoAmW 91
Whelchel, Susan F. 1951- St&PR 91
Whelden, Frederick Howard, Jr. 1931- St&PR 91
Whelden, James 1927- St&PR 91
Wheldon, Graham Herbert 1935- St&PR 91
Whelehan, Patricia Elizabeth 1947- WhoAmW 91
Wheless, Nicholas Hobson, Jr. 1916- WhoAm 90
Whellan, Floyd 1937- St&PR 91
Whelpley, David Bullard 1928- St&PR 91
Wherry, Stephen R. 1958- St&PR 91
Whetsel, Jack Allen 1920- St&PR 91
Whetstone, Bobby Don 1932- WhoSSW 91
Whetstone, R. Terral 1938- St&PR 91
Whettam, Graham Dudley 1927- IntWWM 90
Whetten, John Theodore 1935- WhoAm 90
Whetten, Lawrence Lester 1932- WhoAm 90
Whetter, Marvin Edward 1932- St&PR 91
Whetzel, Herbert H. 1941- St&PR 91
Whichard, Willis Padgett 1940- WhoAm 90
Whickam, Katie E. BioIn 16
Whicker, Alan 1925- ConAu 130
Whicker, Hodd James 1947- WhoWor 91
Whicker, Lawrence R. 1934- WhoAm 90
Whidden, George BioIn 16
Whidden, Lynn 1946- IntWWM 90
Whidden, Ray Harvey 1913- WhoAm 90
Whidden, Stanley John 1947- WhoAm 90, WhoEmL 91
Whiddon, Carol Price 1947- WhoAmW 91
Whiddon, Frederick Palmer 1930- WhoAm 90, WhoSSW 91
Whieldon, Thomas 1719-1795 PenDiDA 89
Whiffen, James Douglass 1931- WhoAm 90
Whigham, Frank Frederick, Jr. 1946- WhoSSW 91
Whigham, Mark Anthony 1959- WhoSSW 91, WhoWor 91
Whigham, Mary Ellen Flowers 1963- WhoSSW 91
Whigham, Terri Lee 1953- WhoAmW 91
Whikehart, R. Eric BiDrAPA 89
Whilden, Richard Douglas Cassan 1933- St&PR 91
Whillock, Carl S. 1926- St&PR 91
Whillock, Carl Simpson 1926- WhoAm 90
Whimpey, Dennis John 1938- St&PR 91, WhoAm 90
Whinery, Charles B. 1926- St&PR 91
Whinery, Ramona Diane BiDrAPA 89
Whines, Nicholas BioIn 16
Whinnery, John Roy 1916- WhoAm 90
Whinston, Arthur Lewis 1925- WhoAm 90
Whipham, Thomas PenDiDA 89
Whipkey, Earl E., Jr. 1937- St&PR 91
Whipp, Charley Bell 1952- WhoSSW 91
Whipper, Leigh EarBlAP
Whipper, Leigh 1877-1975 DrBlPA 90
Whipperman, Ronald Lee 1937- St&PR 91
Whipple, A B C 1918- SmATA 64
Whipple, Amiel Weeks 1818-1863 BioIn 16
Whipple, Barbara WhoAmA 91N
Whipple, Beverly 1941- ConAu 30NR
Whipple, Brent Hanks 1954- St&PR 91
Whipple, Cal 1918- SmATA X
Whipple, Christopher George 1949- WhoEmL 91
Whipple, David C. 1945- St&PR 91
Whipple, Dorothy 1893-1966 FemiCLE
Whipple, Edwin Percy 1819-1886 BioIn 16
Whipple, Enez Mary WhoAmA 91
Whipple, Fred Lawrence 1906- WhoAm 90
Whipple, Frederick L BiDrAPA 89
Whipple, George Stephenson 1950- WhoWor 91
Whipple, Gladys R 1924- BiDrAPA 89
Whipple, Henry Benjamin 1822-1901 WhNaAH
Whipple, Jacqueline Conant 1921- WhoAmW 91
Whipple, Kenneth 1934- WhoAm 90
Whipple, Stephen B BiDrAPA 89
Whipple, William 1730-1785 EncCRAm, WorAlBi
Whipps, Edward Franklin 1936- WhoAm 90, WhoWor 91
Whisant, Larry Gene 1949- WhoEmL 91
Whisenand, James Dudley 1947- WhoSSW 91
Whisenant, Bert Roy, Jr. 1950- WhoSSW 91
Whisenant, Billy St&PR 91
Whisenant, Michael J. St&PR 91
Whisenant, Pete 1929- Ballpl 90
Whisenant, Richard Francis 1937- St&PR 91
Whisenant, Thelma St&PR 91
Whisenant, W.B. St&PR 91
Whisenhunt, Donald Wayne 1938- WhoAm 90
Whisenhunt, J. Daniel 1943- St&PR 91
Whisennand, Cynthia Simmons 1956- WhoSSW 91
Whisenton, Mildred James 1937- WhoAmW 91
Whisler, James Steven 1954- St&PR 91, WhoAm 90
Whisler, Kirk 1951- WhoEmL 91
Whisler, Walter William 1934- WhoAm 90
Whisman, Nancy 1948- WhoAmW 91
Whisnand, R.V. 1944- St&PR 91
Whisnand, Roy Van Arsdel 1944- WhoAm 90
Whisnant, Jack Page 1924- WhoAm 90
Whisner, William T. BioIn 16
Whispel, Barbara 1949- WhoSSW 91
Whispel, Barbara A. 1949- St&PR 91
Whispers, The EncPR&S 89
Whist, Andrew ODwPR 91
Whistler, Anna M. 1804-1881 BioAmW
Whistler, James Abbott McNeill 1834-1903 WorAlBi
Whistler, James McNeill 1834-1903 BioIn 16, IntDcAA 90
Whistler, Laurence 1912- PenDiDA 89
Whistler, Roy Lester 1912- WhoAm 90
Whiston, Richard Michael 1944- WhoE 91
Whitacre, Diane Louise 1953- WhoAmW 91
Whitacre, Edward E., Jr. 1941- WhoAm 90
Whitacre, Huntley Robert 1943- WhoSSW 91
Whitacre, J C, II BiDrAPA 89
Whitacre, John P. 1943- St&PR 91
Whitacre, Peggy Margaret Allen 1933- WhoSSW 91
Whitacre, William Lewis 1946- WhoSSW 91
Whitaker, Agnes H. 1949- BiDrAPA 89
Whitaker, Albert Duncan 1932- WhoAm 90, WhoE 91
Whitaker, Alexander 1585-1617 EncCRAm
Whitaker, Audie Dale 1949- WhoEmL 91, WhoWor 91
Whitaker, Benton F. 1919- St&PR 91
Whitaker, Bob BioIn 16
Whitaker, Bruce Ezell 1921- WhoAm 90, WhoWor 91
Whitaker, Bruce R. 1944- St&PR 91
Whitaker, Carl A 1912- BiDrAPA 89
Whitaker, Clem, Jr. 1922- WhoAm 90
Whitaker, Eileen Monaghan 1911- WhoAm 90, WhoAmA 91, WhoAmW 91
Whitaker, Elizabeth Diane 1945- WhoAmW 91
Whitaker, Ewing Brooke 1965- WhoE 91
Whitaker, Forest BioIn 16
Whitaker, Forest 1961- ConTFT 8
Whitaker, Frederic 1891-1980 WhoAmA 91N
Whitaker, George O. AuBYP 90
Whitaker, Gilbert Riley, Jr. 1931- WhoAm 90
Whitaker, Glenda Kay BiDrAPA 89
Whitaker, James Benjamin 1944- WhoSSW 91
Whitaker, Jerry R. 1950- WhoSSW 91
Whitaker, Jo Anne 1927- BiDrAPA 89
Whitaker, Joel 1942- WhoE 91
Whitaker, John Carlton 1953- St&PR 91
Whitaker, John F 1936- BiDrAPA 89
Whitaker, John Francis 1924- WhoAm 90
Whitaker, John King 1933- WhoAm 90
Whitaker, John Stone 1956- WhoSSW 91
Whitaker, John Thompson 1906-1946 BioIn 16
Whitaker, Leroy 1929- WhoWor 91
Whitaker, Lloyd Tait 1934- St&PR 91
Whitaker, Lou BioIn 16
Whitaker, Lou 1957- Ballpl 90 [port]
Whitaker, Louis Rodman 1957- WhoAm 90
Whitaker, Margaret Joy 1926- IntWWM 90
Whitaker, Mark 1951- BioIn 16
Whitaker, Mary 1947- WhoAmW 91
Whitaker, Meade 1919- WhoAm 90
Whitaker, Morris W. 1900- St&PR 91

Whitaker, O'Kelley 1926- WhoAm 90
Whitaker, Peggy A. 1931- St&PR 91
Whitaker, Penelope Ann 1941- WhoAmW 91
Whitaker, Richard Carlton 1949- WhoSSW 91
Whitaker, Robert C. 1941- ODwPR 91
Whitaker, Roger Page 1952- St&PR 91
Whitaker, Ruth Margaret 1935- WhoWrEP 89
Whitaker, Shirley Ann 1955- WhoAmW 91
Whitaker, Steve 1943- Ballpl 90
Whitaker, Susanne Kanis 1947- WhoAm 90, WhoAmW 91
Whitaker, Thomas Russell 1925- WhoAm 90
Whitaker, Thomas Wallace 1904- WhoAm 90
Whitaker, Urban George, Jr. 1924- WhoAm 90
Whitaker, William 1943- WhoAmA 91
Whitbeck, Frank Lynn, Jr. 1916- St&PR 91
Whitbread, David H 1931- BiDrAPA 89
Whitbread, Donald Walter 1936- IntWWM 90
Whitbread, Fatima BioIn 16
Whitbread, Thomas Bacon 1931- WhoAm 90, WhoWrEP 89
Whitburn, Joel 1939- ConAu 32NR
Whitby, Beatrice 1855?-1931 FemiCLE
Whitby, Von H. 1948- St&PR 91
Whitcher, Frances Miriam 1813-1852 FemiCLE
Whitchurch, Charles Randall 1946- St&PR 91
Whitcomb, Benjamin Bradford, Jr. 1908- WhoAm 90
Whitcomb, Clifford Harry 1923- WhoE 91
Whitcomb, James H. 1927- St&PR 91
Whitcomb, Jon 1906-1988 BioIn 16
Whitcomb, Kay 1921- WhoAmA 91
Whitcomb, Kenneth Floyd 1943- WhoSSW 91
Whitcomb, Marion Inez 1927- WhoAmW 91
Whitcomb, Mervin W. 1913- IntWWM 90
Whitcomb, Richard Travis 1921- WhoAm 90
Whitcomb, Skip 1946- WhoAmA 91
Whitcomb, Steven M. 1951- St&PR 91
Whitcomb, Therese Truitt 1930- WhoAmA 91
Whitcombe, David Niles 1927- St&PR 91, WhoE 91
Whitcraft, Edward C. R. 1914- St&PR 91, WhoAm 90
White Antelope 1796-1864 WhNaAH
White Bear WhNaAH
White Bird 1807?-1882 WhNaAH
White Calf DcCanB 12
White Cloud 1794?-1841? WhNaAH
White Eagle BioIn 16, WhNaAH
White Eyes 1730?-1778 WhNaAH
White Hair WhNaAH
White Hairs WhNaAH
White Horse WhNaAH
White Path 1763-1835 WhNaAH
White Plume WhNaAH
White Shell Old Man DcCanB 12
White Shield 1833?-1883 WhNaAH
White, A. Joe 1933- St&PR 91
White, Adrian Michael Stephen 1940- WhoAm 90, WhoWor 91
White, Aileen ODwPR 91
White, Alan David 1938- IntWWM 90
White, Albert WhoAmA 91
White, Albert Joseph 1933- St&PR 91
White, Albert Larrabee 1925- WhoE 91
White, Alberta LaVerne 1913- WhoAmW 91
White, Alfred T. 1846-1921 WorAlBi
White, Alice Virginia 1946- WhoAmW 91
White, Allen Collier 1940- BiDrAPA 89
White, Alvin Swauger 1918- WhoAm 90
White, Amos, IV WhoAmA 91
White, Andrea St&PR 91
White, Andrew NewAgMG
White, Andrew 1579-1656 EncCRAm
White, Andrew Dickson 1832-1918 BioIn 16, WorAlBi
White, Andrew Nathaniel 1942- IntWWM 90
White, Andrew Stewart 1941- St&PR 91
White, Andrew V. ODwPR 91
White, Ann 1916- WhoWrEP 89
White, Anne Terry 1896- AuBYP 90
White, Antonia 1899-1980 BioIn 16, FemiCLE
White, Arthur Clinton 1925- WhoAm 90
White, Arthur Walter 1911- St&PR 91
White, Augustus Aaron, III 1936- WhoAm 90
White, B J 1946- WhoAmA 91
White, B. Joseph St&PR 91
White, Barbara Buckman 1943- WhoWrEP 89
White, Barry 1944- DrBlPA 90, WorAlBi
White, Barry Bennett 1943- WhoAm 90
White, Barry David 1943- St&PR 91
White, Benjamin Franklin 1838- AmLegL
White, Bernard B. BioIn 16
White, Bernard J. 1944- St&PR 91
White, Bertram Milton 1923- WhoE 91
White, Bessie BioIn 16
White, Bessie 1892- AuBYP 90
White, Betty BioIn 16
White, Betty 1922- WhoAm 90
White, Betty 1924- WorAlBi
White, Betty Maynard 1922- WhoSSW 91, WhoWor 91
White, Beverly Anita 1960- WhoAmW 91
White, Beverly Jean 1928- WhoAmW 91
White, Bill BioIn 16
White, Bill 1934- Ballpl 90 [port]
White, Brenda Sue 1951- BiDrAPA 89
White, Bruce Deane 1930- WhoE 91
White, Bruce Emerson, Jr. 1961- WhoSSW 91
White, Bruce Hilding 1933- WhoAmA 91
White, Burton 1936- BiDrAPA 89
White, Burton Leonard 1929- WhoAm 90
White, Byron R. 1917- WhoAm 90, WhoE 91, WorAlBi
White, C. Dale 1925- WhoAm 90, WhoE 91
White, C Ronald 1941- BiDrAPA 89
White, C. Thomas 1928- WhoAm 90
White, Calvin John 1948- WhoAm 90
White, Calvin Lamont 1947- WhoEmL 91
White, Carl J. 1935- St&PR 91, WhoAm 90
White, Carmen Hudson- BioIn 16
White, Carol Elaine 1953- WhoAmW 91
White, Carol Martin 1946- WhoAmW 91
White, Caroline Taylor 1895-1989 BioIn 16
White, Carter H. 1916- St&PR 91
White, Catherine Payne BioAmW
White, Chaney Ballpl 90
White, Chappell 1920- IntWWM 90
White, Charles 1918-1979 BioIn 16
White, Charles 1958- BioIn 16
White, Charles Albert, Jr. 1922- WhoAm 90
White, Charles D. 1859-1937 Ballpl 90
White, Charles E. 1946- St&PR 91
White, Charles Edmund, Jr. 1956- WhoSSW 91
White, Charles Luken 1950- St&PR 91
White, Charles Wilbert 1918-1979 WhoAmA 91N
White, Christine 1905- WhoAmW 91
White, Christopher John 1930- WhoWor 91
White, Clair Fox 1949- WhoSSW 91
White, Claire Nicolas 1925- BioIn 16, WhoWrEP 89
White, Clara Jo 1927- WhoAmW 91
White, Clarence Cameron 1879-1960 DcAfAmP
White, Cloid 1952- WhoSSW 91
White, Cricket Geisinger 1950- WhoAmW 91
White, Curtis Keith 1951- WhoWrEP 89
White, Cynthia 1932- WhoWrEP 89
White, Cynthia Bernice 1951- BiDrAPA 89
White, Cynthia Carol 1943- WhoAmW 91
White, Cynthia Jane 1954- BiDrAPA 89
White, Dale AuBYP 90
White, Dale Andrew 1958- WhoWrEP 89
White, Dana Rae 1963- WhoAmW 91
White, Daniel Arthur 1951- WhoSSW 91
White, Daniel Price 1814-1890 AmLegL
White, Daryl Joseph 1947- St&PR 91, WhoAm 90
White, David Alan BiDrAPA 89
White, David Alan, Jr. 1942- St&PR 91
White, David Calvin 1922- WhoAm 90
White, David Erol 1940- WhoSSW 91
White, David G. 1947- St&PR 91
White, David Gaylord 1933- WhoWor 91
White, David Hywel 1931- WhoAm 90
White, David L. 1938- ODwPR 91
White, David L. 1953- St&PR 91
White, David Manning 1917- WhoAm 90
White, Deacon 1847-1939 Ballpl 90 [port]
White, Dean Tom 1941- St&PR 91
White, Deborah WhoAmA 91
White, Deborah Ann BiDrAPA 89
White, Deborah Lynn Vess 1957- IntWWM 90
White, Debra Lee 1953- WhoSSW 91
White, Denise 1950- WhoAmW 91
White, Dennis Allen 1946- WhoE 91
White, Derek Alan 1941- WhoAm 90
White, Devon 1962- Ballpl 90
White, Doc 1879-1969 Ballpl 90 [port]
White, Don Henry 1955- WhoWor 91
White, Donald Gordon 1948- WhoE 91
White, Donald H. 1921- IntWWM 90
White, Donald Harvey 1931- WhoAm 90
White, Donald Joseph 1922- WhoE 91
White, Donald Keys 1924- WhoAm 90
White, Donald Powell 1956- WhoE 91
White, Donald Ray, Jr. 1963- WhoSSW 91
White, Donald Richard, Jr. 1953- WhoSSW 91
White, Donald Royce Joseph 1926- St&PR 91
White, Doris Anne 1924- WhoAm 90, WhoAmW 91
White, Dorothy 1630?-1685 BiDEWW, FemiCLE
White, Dorothy T. 1923- WhoAmW 91
White, Dorset 1929- St&PR 91
White, Douglas J. ODwPR 91
White, Douglas James, Jr. 1934- WhoAm 90
White, Duane Earl 1955- St&PR 91
White, Dwight L. WhoAm 90
White, E. B. 1899-1985 BioIn 16
White, E B 1899-1985 ChlLR 21 [port], MajTwCW
White, E. B. 1899-1985 WorAlBi
White, Edgar 1947- BioIn 16
White, Edgar B 1947- DrBlPA 90
White, Edmund 1940- BioIn 16, MajTwCW, WorAu 1980 [port]
White, Edmund Valentine 1940- WhoAm 90, WhoWrEP 89
White, Edward A. 1928- St&PR 91
White, Edward A. 1935- St&PR 91
White, Edward D. 1845-1921 WorAlBi
White, Edward E. 1909-1988 BioIn 16
White, Edward F. 1928- St&PR 91
White, Edward Higgins 1930-1967 BioIn 16
White, Edward Lupton 1940- BiDrAPA 89
White, Edwin Wood 1950- BiDrAPA 89
White, Eliot Carter 1947- St&PR 91
White, Elizabeth BiDEWW
White, Elizabeth 1637?-1669 FemiCLE
White, Elizabeth D. 1921- St&PR 91
White, Elizabeth Loczi 1936- WhoAmW 91
White, Ellen Gould 1827-1915 BioAmW, WorAlBi
White, Elwyn Brooks 1899-1985 AuBYP 90, BioIn 16
White, Emil BioIn 16
White, Emil Henry 1926- WhoAm 90
White, Emily Thorn Vanderbilt Sloane 1852-1946 BioIn 16
White, Ernest J BiDrAPA 89
White, Ernie 1916-1974 Ballpl 90
White, Errol Ivor 1901-1985 DcNaB 1981
White, Erskine N., Jr. 1924- St&PR 91
White, Erskine Norman, Jr. 1924- WhoAm 90, WhoE 91
White, Ess A, Jr. 1920- BiDrAPA 89
White, Eugene B WhoAmA 91N
White, Eugene E. St&PR 91
White, Eugene Elliot 1854-1908 WhNaAH
White, Eugene James 1928- WhoAm 90
White, Eugene R. WhoAm 90
White, Eva A. 1913- St&PR 91
White, Everett Lowell 1943- St&PR 91
White, F. William 1938- St&PR 91
White, Ferrell E. 1934- ODwPR 91
White, Florence AuBYP 90
White, Floyd H. 1932- St&PR 91
White, Francis Edward 1915- WhoAm 90
White, Francis M. 1927- St&PR 91, WhoAm 90
White, Francis Vincent 1934- St&PR 91
White, Frank 1950- Ballpl 90 [port]
White, Frankie Lee 1945- WhoAmW 91
White, Franklin 1943- WhoAmA 91
White, Fred Rollin, Jr. 1913- WhoAm 90
White, Frederick 1909- St&PR 91
White, Frederick Andrew 1918- WhoAm 90
White, Frederick Rollin, Jr. 1913- St&PR 91
White, Fredrick John 1952- WhoEmL 91, WhoWor 91
White, Garland S. St&PR 91
White, Gary C. 1937- IntWWM 90
White, Gary L. 1932- St&PR 91
White, Gary M. 1935- St&PR 91
White, Gayle Clay 1944- WhoWor 91
White, Geneva M. 1958- WhoAmW 91
White, George 1890-1968 OxCPMus
White, George Cooke 1935- WhoAm 90
White, George Donnie 1945- WhoSSW 91
White, George Edward 1941- WhoAm 90, WhoE 91, WhoWor 91
White, George Henry 1852-1918 BlkAmsC [port]
White, George M. St&PR 91N
White, George Malcolm 1920- WhoAm 90, WhoE 91
White, George Stephen 1936- St&PR 91
White, George W., Jr. 1903-1970 MusmAFA
White, Gerald A. 1934- St&PR 91
White, Gerald Andrew 1934- WhoAm 90
White, Gilbert 1720-1793 BioIn 16
White, Gilbert Fowler 1911- WhoAm 90
White, Glenn E. 1926- St&PR 91
White, Glenn L. 1941- St&PR 91
White, Gloria Waters 1934- WhoAmW 91, WhoWor 91
White, Gordon Eliot 1933- WhoAm 90
White, Gordon Lindsay 1923- WhoAm 90, WhoE 91
White, Gwendolyn Leen BiDrAPA 89
White, H. Blair 1927- WhoAm 90
White, Hal 1919- Ballpl 90
White, Harlan Ray BiDrAPA 89
White, Harold E. 1913- St&PR 91
White, Harold Tredway, III 1947- WhoE 91
White, Harrison Colyar 1930- WhoWrEP 89
White, Harry 1958- IntWWM 90
White, Harry Bryant 1938- St&PR 91
White, Harry Clifford 1930- WhoSSW 91
White, Harry Dexter 1892-1948 BioIn 16, EncABHB 7 [port]
White, Harry Edward, Jr. 1939- WhoE 91
White, Harvey Lee 1938- BiDrAPA 89
White, Helen Magill 1853-1944 BioIn 16
White, Helen Patricia 1925- BiDrAPA 89
White, Henry 1850-1927 BioIn 16
White, Henry Kirke 1785-1806 DcLB 96 [port]
White, Henry S. 1908-1988 BioIn 16
White, Henry Samuel 1947- BiDrAPA 89
White, Henry Sumner BioIn 16
White, Herbert C. 1919- St&PR 91
White, Herbert Spencer 1927- WhoAm 90
White, Homer 1917- WhoAm 90
White, Horace 1834-1916 BioIn 16, EncABHB 6 [port]
White, Howard Ashley 1913- WhoAm 90
White, Hugh Lawson 1773-1840 EncABHB 6 [port]
White, Hugh Vernon, Jr. 1933- WhoAm 90
White, I. D. NewYTBS 90
White, I. D. 1901-1990 BioIn 16
White, Ian McKibbin 1929- WhoAm 90
White, Isaac D 1901-1990 CurBio 90N
White, Isaac Davis 1901-1990 BioIn 16
White, J Coleman 1923- WhoAm 90
White, J. Spratt 1941- St&PR 91
White, J.V. 1925- St&PR 91
White, Jack Edward 1921-1988 BioIn 16
White, Jameela Adams 1954- WhoE 91
White, James A. 1938- St&PR 91
White, James Alexander 1943- WhoAm 90
White, James Arthur 1933- WhoE 91, WhoSSW 91
White, James B. 1953- St&PR 91
White, James Barr 1941- WhoAm 90
White, James Boyd 1938- ConAu 30NR, WhoAm 90, WhoWrEP 89
White, James David 1942- St&PR 91
White, James Edward 1918- WhoAm 90
White, James George 1929- WhoAm 90
White, James H 1941- BiDrAPA 89
White, James H. 1942- St&PR 91
White, James M. 1921- WhoWrEP 89
White, James Mackey 1941- WhoE 91
White, James Patrick 1931- WhoAm 90
White, James Richard 1948- WhoSSW 91
White, James Richard 1950- WhoAmA 91
White, James William, Jr. 1934- WhoE 91
White, James Wilson 1941- WhoAm 90
White, Jan 1949- St&PR 91
White, Jan Tuttle 1943- WhoAmW 91, WhoE 91, WhoWor 91
White, Jane 1922- DrBlPA 90
White, Jane F. 1928- St&PR 91
White, Janet L. 1951- St&PR 91
White, Janet Murphree 1946- WhoAmW 91
White, Janice BioIn 16
White, Jeannine A. 1929- WhoAmW 91
White, Jeff V. BioIn 16
White, Jeff V. 1925- WhoAm 90, WhoSSW 91
White, Jerry 1952- Ballpl 90
White, Jerry E 1937- ConAu 129
White, Jerry S. 1946- ConAu 130
White, Jesse AmLegL
White, Jesse Marc WhoAm 90
White, Jimm F. 1944- WhoAm 90
White, Jo-Jo 1919- Ballpl 90
White, Joan Ellen 1945- WhoWrEP 89
White, Joan M. 1948- WhoAmW 91
White, Joe Dan 1939- St&PR 91
White, Joe Lloyd 1921- WhoAm 90
White, John EncCRAm, PenDiMP, WhNaAH
White, John 1938- IntWWM 90
White, John, Jr. 1930- WhoAm 90
White, John Arnold 1933- WhoAm 90
White, John Austin, Jr. 1939- WhoAm 90
White, John B. 1951- BiDrAPA 89
White, John Branum 1952- WhoSSW 91
White, John Campbell 1932- St&PR 91
White, John Charles 1939- WhoAm 90
White, John David 1931- IntWWM 90, WhoAm 90
White, John Francis 1917- WhoAm 90
White, John Francis 1929- WhoAm 90
White, John Francis 1945- WhoE 91
White, John Glenn, Jr. 1934- WhoE 91
White, John Glenn, Jr. 1949- WhoSSW 91
White, John Irwin 1902- BioIn 16, WhoWrEP 89

White, John J. 1909- *St&PR 91*
White, John M 1937- *WhoAmA 91*
White, John M., Jr. 1955- *St&PR 91*
White, John Michael 1938- *WhoAm 90*
White, John Paul *BiDrAPA 89*
White, John Richard 1930- *St&PR 91*
White, John Simon 1910- *WhoAm 90*
White, John W. 1939- *EncPaPR 91*
White, John Warren 1939- *WhoWrEP 89*
White, John Wesley 1928- *ConAu 31NR*
White, John Wesley, Jr. 1933- *WhoAm 90*
White, John William Loud 1923- *St&PR 91, WhoAm 90*
White, Jolly Hobart 1928- *St&PR 91*
White, Jon Burran 1936- *St&PR 91*
White, Jon Manchip *WhoWrEP 89*
White, Jon Manchip 1924- *ConAu 32NR, TwCCr&M 91*
White, Jon McClendon 1946- *WhoAm 90*
White, Jonathan Forbes 1944- *WhoWor 91*
White, Joseph Blanco 1775-1841 *BioIn 16*
White, Joseph Charles 1922- *WhoAm 90*
White, Joseph Lee 1951- *WhoSSW 91*
White, Joseph Mallie, Jr. 1921- *WhoAm 90*
White, Joseph Murray 1928- *St&PR 91*
White, Joseph Reeves, Jr. 1930- *WhoAm 90, WhoSSW 91*
White, Josh 1908-1969 *DrBlPA 90*
White, Josh 1915-1969 *OxCPMus*
White, Joy Mieko 1951- *WhoAmW 91*
White, Judi *BioIn 16*
White, Judith Fox 1943- *WhoAmW 91*
White, Judith Louise 1939- *WhoAmW 91*
White, Judy Mary 1933- *WhoWor 91*
White, Julia Seyfarth 1950- *WhoE 91*
White, Julia Zita 1951- *WhoAmW 91*
White, June Miller 1938- *WhoSSW 91*
White, Kande 1950- *WhoWor 91*
White, Karen J 1943- *WhoAmA 91*
White, Karyn *BioIn 16*
White, Kate *WhoAmW 91*
White, Katharine S. 1892-1977 *BioAmW*
White, Katharine Sergeant Angell 1892-1977 *BioIn 16*
White, Katherine Elizabeth 1920- *WhoAmW 91*
White, Katherine Patricia 1948- *WhoAmW 91, WhoE 91, WhoEmL 91, WhoWor 91*
White, Kathleen Mae 1941- *WhoAmW 91*
White, Kathy A. 1944- *WhoAmW 91*
White, Kenneth E *BiDrAPA 89*
White, Kenneth Thomas 1947- *WhoSSW 91*
White, Kerr Lachlan 1917- *WhoAm 90*
White, Kerrin Leon 1947- *BiDrAPA 89*
White, Kimberly Ames 1956- *BiDrAPA 89*
White, Kirby 1884-1943 *Ballpl 90*
White, Lana Joyce *WhoAmW 91*
White, Larry D. 1945- *St&PR 91*
White, Larry G. *WhoAm 90*
White, Larry L. 1937- *St&PR 91*
White, Larry Lee 1937- *WhoAm 90*
White, Lavarne 1952- *WhoAmW 91*
White, Lawrence E 1944- *BiDrAPA 89*
White, Lawrence J 1943- *ConAu 31NR, WhoAm 90*
White, Lee 1946- *WhoE 91*
White, Lee Calvin 1923- *WhoAm 90*
White, Lee Inman, II 1962- *WhoSSW 91*
White, Leland I. 1946- *WhoAm 90*
White, Leon 1935- *St&PR 91*
White, Leslie *BioIn 16*
White, Lewis Southall 1940- *St&PR 91*
White, Lezli Hope 1955- *WhoE 91*
White, Libby Kramer 1934- *WhoAmW 91*
White, Linda Hardy 1946- *WhoAmW 91*
White, Lionel 1905- *TwCCr&M 91*
White, Lloyd Michael 1949- *WhoEmL 91*
White, Lois M. 1931- *WhoAmW 91*
White, Lois R. *WhoAmW 91*
White, Lorelei Annette 1962- *WhoWrEP 89*
White, Louis K. 1937- *St&PR 91*
White, Lowell E., Jr. 1928- *WhoAm 90, WhoSSW 91*
White, Luther Wesley 1923- *WhoAm 90*
White, Lyndsay Pond 1938- *WhoSSW 91*
White, Lynn Townsend 1907-1987 *BioIn 16*
White, Lynn Townsend, III 1941- *WhoE 91*
White, Lynne M. *ODwPR 91*
White, Mahlon T. 1961- *St&PR 91*
White, Margaret Bourke- 1904-1971 *BioIn 16*
White, Margit Triska 1932- *WhoAmW 91*
White, Margita Eklund 1937- *WhoAm 90, WhoAmW 91*
White, Maria B. 1955- *WhoAmW 91*
White, Marilyn Elaine 1944- *WhoAmW 91*
White, Martha *BioIn 16*
White, Martha 1954- *WhoWrEP 89*
White, Martin 1943- *BioIn 16*
White, Martin Christopher 1943- *WhoAm 90*
White, Martin John 1941- *IntWWM 90*
White, Marvin Lee 1940- *WhoSSW 91*
White, Mary Jane 1953- *WhoWrEP 89*
White, Mary Jennie 1936- *WhoWrEP 89*
White, Mary Louise 1933- *WhoAmW 91, WhoSSW 91*
White, Mary Ransford 1941- *St&PR 91*
White, Mary Ruth Wathen 1927- *WhoAmW 91, WhoSSW 91*
White, Matthew 1956- *ConAu 129*
White, Mattie Mitchell *BiDrAPA 89*
White, Merit Penniman 1908- *WhoAm 90, WhoE 91*
White, Michael *BioIn 16*
White, Michael D. 1947- *WhoAm 90*
White, Michael J. 1956- *St&PR 91*
White, Michael K. 1938- *St&PR 91*
White, Michael L. 1946- *St&PR 91*
White, Michael Reed 1951- *WhoAm 90*
White, Michelle Jo 1945- *WhoAmW 91*
White, Minor 1908-1976 *WhoAmA 91N*
White, Morton Gabriel 1917- *WhoAm 90, WhoWrEP 89*
White, Nan *ODwPR 91*
White, Nancy 1916- *WhoAmW 91, WhoE 91*
White, Nancy A. 1959- *WhoAmW 91*
White, Nancy Ann 1949- *WhoE 91*
White, Nancy Bean 1922- *AuBYP 90*
White, Nancy-Cecile Jeep 1955- *WhoAmW 91*
White, Nancy Elaine 1952- *WhoAmW 91*
White, Nancy Helen 1959- *WhoAmW 91, WhoEmL 91*
White, Ned 1946- *ConAu 129*
White, Nelson Henry 1938- *WhoWrEP 89*
White, Nicholas I. 1950- *St&PR 91*
White, Nick J. 1945- *St&PR 91, WhoSSW 91*
White, Norman Lee 1955- *WhoSSW 91*
White, Norman S 1933- *BiDrAPA 89*
White, Norman Triplett 1938- *WhoAmA 91*
White, Norris 1944- *St&PR 91*
White, Norval Crawford 1926- *WhoAm 90*
White, Osmar 1909- *ConAu 130*
White, P. Mark 1948- *St&PR 91*
White, Pamela Joyce 1950- *WhoAmW 91*
White, Pat Joe 1950- *WhoSSW 91*
White, Patricia Ann 1942- *WhoAmW 91*
White, Patricia Smith 1928- *WhoAmW 91*
White, Patrick 1912- *MajTwCW, WhoAm 90, WhoWor 91, WorAlBi*
White, Patrick 1912-1990 *ConAu 132, CurBio 90N, NewYTBS 90 [port]*
White, Paul A. 1915- *WhoAm 90*
White, Paul Dunbar 1917- *WhoAm 90, WhoWor 91*
White, Paul Gaston, Jr. 1954- *WhoSSW 91*
White, Paul Joseph, III 1948- *St&PR 91*
White, Paul L *BiDrAPA 89*
White, Paul Richard, Sr. 1950- *WhoSSW 91*
White, Paul Ward 1939- *WhoAm 90*
White, Paul Welrose 1902-1955 *BioIn 16*
White, Pauline *AuBYP 90*
White, Pearl 1889-1938 *BioAmW, WorAlBi*
White, Peggy Gene 1932- *WhoSSW 91*
White, Pegi 1941- *WhoAmW 91*
White, Percival 1887-1970 *AuBYP 90*
White, Perry Elverado 1926- *WhoWrEP 89*
White, Perry Merrill, Jr. 1925- *WhoAm 90*
White, Peter Gilbert 1937- *IntWWM 90*
White, Philip Butler 1935- *WhoAm 90, WhoAmA 91*
White, Philip Hayden 1945- *WhoEmL 91, WhoSSW 91*
White, Philip I. 1936- *St&PR 91*
White, Philip V. *BioIn 16*
White, Phillip Laudell 1940- *St&PR 91*
White, Phyllis Dorothy James *BioIn 16*
White, Phyllis Dorothy James 1920- *MajTwCW*
White, Priscilla 1900-1989 *BioIn 16*
White, R. Elton 1942- *WhoAm 90*
White, R. Quincy 1933- *WhoAm 90*
White, Ralph 1921- *WhoAmA 91*
White, Ralph Dallas 1919- *WhoAm 90*
White, Ralph David 1931- *WhoAm 90*
White, Ralph Paul 1926- *WhoAm 90, WhoE 91*
White, Randall Francis *BiDrAPA 89*
White, Randall R. 1950- *St&PR 91*
White, Randy *BioIn 16*
White, Randy 1953- *WorAlBi*
White, Ray 1938- *St&PR 91*
White, Raymond M. 1931- *St&PR 91*
White, Raymond Petrie, Jr. 1937- *WhoAm 90*
White, Reggie *BioIn 16*
White, Reginald P 1927- *BiDrAPA 89*
White, Rene 1951- *ODwPR 91*
White, Renee Allyn 1945- *WhoWor 91*
White, Rhea A 1931- *EncO&P 3*
White, Rhea Amelia 1931- *EncPaPR 91, WhoAmW 91*
White, Rhea Anderson 1947- *WhoAmW 91*
White, Rhoda 1820?-1866 *FemiCLE*
White, Richard Alan 1935- *WhoAm 90*
White, Richard Booth 1930- *WhoAm 90*
White, Richard Clarence 1933- *WhoAm 90*
White, Richard Edmund 1944- *WhoE 91*
White, Richard F. *St&PR 91*
White, Richard Grant 1821-1885 *BioIn 16*
White, Richard Henry Reeve 1926- *WhoWor 91*
White, Richard Holbrook 1946- *WhoAm 90*
White, Richard J. 1943- *St&PR 91*
White, Richard L. 1939- *WhoAm 90*
White, Richard Stanton, Jr. 1934- *St&PR 91*
White, Richard Thomas 1941- *WhoE 91*
White, Richard Winfrey 1936- *WhoSSW 91*
White, Rita Alexandra 1941- *WhoWrEP 89*
White, Robb 1909- *AuBYP 90, WhoAm 90*
White, Robert 1921- *WhoAmA 91*
White, Robert 1940- *PenDiMP*
White, Robert Allan 1934- *WhoAm 90*
White, Robert B *BiDrAPA 89*
White, Robert B 1921- *BiDrAPA 89*
White, Robert Bruce 1937- *WhoSSW 91*
White, Robert Bruce 1942- *WhoSSW 91*
White, Robert Charles, Jr. 1936- *WhoE 91*
White, Robert E 1939- *BiDrAPA 89*
White, Robert E. 1943- *St&PR 91*
White, Robert Edward 1917- *WhoAm 90*
White, Robert Edward 1926- *WhoAm 90*
White, Robert F. 1912- *WhoAm 90*
White, Robert Frederick 1927- *WhoE 91*
White, Robert J. 1926- *WhoAm 90*
White, Robert James 1927- *WhoAm 90*
White, Robert James 1928- *St&PR 91, WhoAm 90*
White, Robert Joel 1946- *WhoEmL 91*
White, Robert Joseph, Jr 1943- *WhoE 91*
White, Robert L. *BioIn 16*
White, Robert Lee 1927- *WhoAm 90*
White, Robert Lemont 1927- *St&PR 91*
White, Robert M., II 1915- *WhoAm 90, WhoE 91*
White, Robert MacDonald 1942- *WhoSSW 91*
White, Robert Marshall 1938- *WhoAm 90*
White, Robert Mayer 1923- *WhoAm 90*
White, Robert Miles Ford 1928- *WhoSSW 91*
White, Robert Roy 1916- *WhoAm 90*
White, Robert S 1947- *BiDrAPA 89*
White, Robert Silliman 1947- *WhoE 91*
White, Robert Solomon 1956- *WhoSSW 91, WhoWor 91*
White, Robert Winslow 1934- *WhoAm 90, WhoSSW 91*
White, Roberta Louise 1936- *WhoAmW 91*
White, Rock E. 1956- *St&PR 91*
White, Roderick Macleod 1928- *WhoAm 90*
White, Roger John *WhoAm 90*
White, Roger K 1934- *BiDrAPA 89*
White, Rollin H. 1872-1962 *EncABHB 4 [port]*
White, Roma 1866-1930 *FemiCLE*
White, Ronald Lee 1950- *St&PR 91*
White, Ronald Leon 1930- *WhoAm 90, WhoWor 91*
White, Roseanne C. *ODwPR 91*
White, Rowena Ruth 1944- *BiDrAPA 89*
White, Roy 1943- *Ballpl 90*
White, Roy Bernard *WhoAm 90, WhoWor 91*
White, Russell *BioIn 16*
White, Russell Charles 1940- *St&PR 91*
White, Ruth 1911- *WhoAmA 91*
White, Ruth 1914-1969 *BioIn 16, NotWoAT*
White, Ruth Lillian 1924- *WhoAm 90*
White, Ruth O'Brien 1909- *WhoAm 90*
White, Ruth S. 1925- *IntWWM 90*
White, Ryan *BioIn 16*
White, Ryan *NewYTBS 90*
White, Ryan 1972?-1990 *News 90, -90-3*
White, Sallie Joy *BioIn 16*
White, Sally Ann 1946- *WhoSSW 91*
White, Sally Rey 1948- *WhoAmW 91*
White, Sam 1913-1988 *AnObit 1988*
White, Sammy 1928- *Ballpl 90*
White, Samuel Floyd 1940- *WhoSSW 91*
White, Samuel Knox 1918- *WhoAm 90*
White, Sandra Lavelle 1941- *WhoAmW 91*
White, Sandra Lee 1946- *WhoAmW 91*
White, Sandra R. 1948- *WhoEmL 91*
White, Saxon N. 1921- *WhoWrEP 89*
White, Scott Allyn 1958- *WhoSSW 91*
White, Sharon 1959- *WhoAmW 91*
White, Slappy *DrBlPA 90*
White, Sol 1868-1955 *Ballpl 90*
White, Stan 1941- *WhoAm 90*
White, Stanford 1853-1906 *BioIn 16, WorAlBi*
White, Stanley Archibald 1931- *WhoAm 90, WhoWor 91*
White, Stanley Everett 1951- *WhoE 91*
White, Stanley Oliver 1941- *St&PR 91*
White, Stephen 1915- *WhoAm 90*
White, Stephen A. 1949- *St&PR 91*
White, Stephen Halley 1940- *WhoAm 90*
White, Steve 1954- *WhoWrEP 89*
White, Steven Carl 1944- *WhoE 91*
White, Steven Douglas 1953- *WhoSSW 91*
White, Steven F 1955- *ConAu 30NR*
White, Steven Forsythe 1955- *WhoWrEP 89*
White, Steven V. 1928-1988 *BioIn 16*
White, Stewart Edward 1873-1946 *EncO&P 3*
White, Stuart James 1944- *WhoAmA 91*
White, Sumner W. *BioIn 16*
White, Susan Chrysler 1954- *WhoAmA 91*
White, Susan Waltz 1945- *WhoWrEP 89*
White, Susanne Tropez 1949- *WhoSSW 91*
White, Susie Mae 1914- *WhoAmW 91*
White, T. H. 1906-1964 *WorAlBi*
White, Teri 1946- *ConAu 132, TwCCr&M 91*
White, Terrell Hilda 1951- *BiDrAPA 89*
White, Terrence Harold 1943- *WhoAm 90*
White, Terry Dale 1942- *WhoWrEP 89*
White, Terry Gilbert 1933- *St&PR 91*
White, Terry Houston 1929- *WhoSSW 91*
White, Theodore H. 1915- *WorAlBi*
White, Theodore H. 1915-1986 *BioIn 16, ConAu 33NR, MajTwCW*
White, Thomas 1943- *WhoE 91*
White, Thomas A.H. 1958- *St&PR 91*
White, Thomas C. *ODwPR 91*
White, Thomas David, II 1946- *WhoE 91*
White, Thomas Edward 1933- *WhoAm 90*
White, Thomas Edward 1936- *WhoAm 90*
White, Thomas Harrington 1931- *WhoSSW 91*
White, Thomas James 1945- *WhoAm 90*
White, Thomas Joseph, Jr. 1936- *WhoWor 91*
White, Thomas Lester 1903- *WhoWor 91*
White, Thomas W. 1944- *St&PR 91*
White, Timothy 1952- *SmATA 60 [port]*
White, Timothy Douglas 1950- *WhoAm 90*
White, Tom Willingham 1943- *WhoSSW 91*
White, Tony Lee 1946- *St&PR 91*
White, Vanna *BioIn 16*
White, Vanna Marie 1957- *WhoHisp 91*
White, Verna Hesby 1919- *WhoAmW 91*
White, Virginia Joycelyn 1924- *WhoWor 91*
White, Virginia L. 1924- *St&PR 91*
White, Virginia Lou 1932- *WhoAmW 91*
White, W. Robin 1928- *WhoWrEP 89*
White, W. Ward *ODwPR 91*
White, Walter 1893-1955 *WorAlBi*
White, Walter C. 1876-1929 *EncABHB 4 [port]*
White, Walter L *WhoAmA 91N*
White, Walter L. 1940- *St&PR 91*
White, Walter Paul, Jr. 1930- *WhoSSW 91*
White, Ward Allen, III 1938- *WhoSSW 91*
White, Warren K. 1935- *St&PR 91*
White, Warren W. 1932- *St&PR 91*
White, Warren Wurtele 1932- *WhoAm 90*
White, Wayne Joseph 1938- *St&PR 91*
White, Wellington 1930- *St&PR 91*
White, Will 1854-1911 *Ballpl 90*
White, Will W., III 1930- *ODwPR 91*
White, Will Walter, III 1930- *WhoAm 90*
White, Willard 1946- *IntWWM 90, PenDiMP*
White, William 1897-1967 *WorAlBi*
White, William 1914-1990 *BioIn 16*
White, William 1928- *WhoAm 90*
White, William, Jr. 1934- *ConAu 31NR*
White, William Allen 1868-1944 *BioIn 16, WorAlBi*
White, William Allen 1906- *WhoAm 90*
White, William Arthur 1916- *WhoAm 90, WhoWor 91*
White, William Blaine 1934- *WhoAm 90*
White, William Clinton 1911- *WhoSSW 91*
White, William Gerald 1939- *WhoAm 90*
White, William Hale 1831-1913 *BioIn 16*
White, William Henry 1924-1989 *BioIn 16*
White, William J. 1932- *St&PR 91*
White, William James 1938- *WhoAm 90*
White, William Joseph 1942- *WhoHisp 91*
White, William Lindsay 1900-1973 *BioIn 16*
White, William North 1925- *WhoAm 90*
White, William Samuel 1937- *WhoAm 90, WhoWor 91*
White, William T., Jr. 1925- *St&PR 91*
White, William V. 1944- *St&PR 91*
White, Willis Sheridan, Jr. 1926- *St&PR 91, WhoAm 90, WhoSSW 91, WhoWor 91*
White, Willmon Lee 1932- *WhoAm 90, WhoWrEP 89*
White, Wilton G. *WhoSSW 91*

White, Windsor T. 1866-1958 *EncABHB 4 [port]*
White, Winifred V. 1953- *WhoAmW 91*
White, Xavier *BiDrAPA 89*
White-Hunt, Keith 1950- *WhoWor 91*
White-Hurst, John Marshall 1942- *WhoSSW 91*
White-Lathrop, Kathryn 1947- *WhoE 91*
White-Man-Runs-Him 1855?-1925 *WhNaAH [port]*
White-Thomson, Ian Leonard 1936- *St&PR 91, WhoAm 90*
Whiteaker, Gary Prinz 1944- *St&PR 91*
Whiteaker, James Dale 1952- *WhoSSW 91*
Whiteaker, John J. 1820-1902 *AmLegL*
Whitear, Sheelagh Lesley *IntWWM 90*
Whitecloud *WhoWrEP 89*
Whitecotton, James H. 1854-1944 *AmLegL*
Whitecross, Alan J. 1949- *St&PR 91*
Whited, Christina *BioIn 16*
Whited, Maureen R. 1960- *WhoAmW 91*
Whitefield, Alan C. 1944- *St&PR 91*
Whitefield, Ben Taylor 1937- *WhoSSW 91*
Whitefield, George 1714-1770 *BioIn 16, EncCRAm*
Whiteford, Andrew Hunter 1913- *WhoAm 90*
Whiteford, Kate 1952- *BiDWomA*
Whitehair, Jay Charles 1910- *WhoE 91*
Whitehead, Alfred North 1861-1947 *DcLB 100 [port], WorAlBi*
Whitehead, Anne 1624-1686 *BiDEWW, FemiCLE*
Whitehead, Ardelle Coleman 1917- *WhoAmW 91*
Whitehead, Burgess 1910- *Ballpl 90*
Whitehead, Carl Francis 1927- *St&PR 91, WhoAm 90*
Whitehead, Catherine Sarah 1960- *ConAu 131*
Whitehead, Charles Oliver 1918- *WhoAm 90*
Whitehead, Clay Carlton 1942- *BiDrAPA 89*
Whitehead, Clay Thomas 1938- *WhoAm 90*
Whitehead, David Barry 1946- *WhoWor 91*
Whitehead, Dollie Glover 1936- *WhoAmW 91*
Whitehead, Elizabeth *BiDEWW*
Whitehead, Ennis Clement 1895-1964 *BioIn 16*
Whitehead, Frances 1953- *WhoAmA 91*
Whitehead, Gail 1942- *WhoAmW 91*
Whitehead, Gillian *IntWWM 90*
Whitehead, Helen May 1951- *WhoAmW 91*
Whitehead, Henry 1810-1885 *BioIn 16*
Whitehead, J. Rennie *WhoAm 90*
Whitehead, James G. 1938- *St&PR 91*
Whitehead, Jane *BiDEWW*
Whitehead, Jaudon Copeland 1921- *St&PR 91, WhoAm 90*
Whitehead, Jennifer 1950- *WhoE 91*
Whitehead, John 1909-1964 *Ballpl 90*
Whitehead, John 1945- *St&PR 91*
Whitehead, John C. 1939- *WhoAm 90*
Whitehead, John Cunningham 1922- *WhoAm 90*
Whitehead, John Jed 1945- *WhoAm 90*
Whitehead, John W. 1946- *WhoEmL 91, WhoWor 91*
Whitehead, Kate *ConAu 131*
Whitehead, Kenneth Dean 1930- *WhoAm 90*
Whitehead, Leland E. 1936- *ODwPR 91*
Whitehead, Leston S *BiDrAPA 89*
Whitehead, Louise 1940- *WhoAmW 91*
Whitehead, Margaret Harold 1928- *WhoWrEP 89*
Whitehead, Marvin Delbert 1917- *WhoAm 90*
Whitehead, Mary Beth *BioIn 16*
Whitehead, Melissa Annette Slagle 1938- *WhoSSW 91*
Whitehead, Michael Anthony 1935- *WhoAm 90*
Whitehead, Milton Frank 1933- *St&PR 91*
Whitehead, Paul L 1936- *BiDrAPA 89*
Whitehead, Paxton 1937- *OxCCanT*
Whitehead, Richard L. 1927- *St&PR 91*
Whitehead, Richard Lee 1927- *WhoAm 90*
Whitehead, Robert 1916- *OxCCanT, WhoAm 90*
Whitehead, Ruth *AuBYP 90*
Whitehead, Susan 1945- *WhoAmW 91*
Whitehead, Walter Dexter, Jr. 1922- *WhoAm 90*
Whitehead, Willard 1954- *BiDrAPA 89*
Whitehead, William Cary, III 1949- *WhoSSW 91*
Whitehead, William John 1938- *WhoAm 90*
Whitehill, Clarence 1871-1932 *BioIn 16, PenDiMP*
Whitehill, Clifford Lane 1931- *St&PR 91, WhoAm 90, WhoHisp 91*
Whitehill, Earl 1899-1954 *Ballpl 90*
Whitehill, Walter Muir 1905-1978 *WhoAmA 91N*
Whitehill, Walter R. 1945- *St&PR 91*
Whitehorn, Nathaniel 1912- *St&PR 91*
Whitehorn, William Victor 1915- *WhoAm 90*
Whitehorne, Robert Alvin 1925- *St&PR 91*
Whitehouse, Alton Winslow, Jr. 1927- *WhoAm 90, WhoWor 91*
Whitehouse, Ann Maliniak 1959- *WhoAmW 91*
Whitehouse, Anne Cherner 1954- *WhoWrEP 89*
Whitehouse, Arch 1895-1979 *AuBYP 90*
Whitehouse, Arthur George *AuBYP 90*
Whitehouse, C. Thomas 1942- *St&PR 91*
Whitehouse, David 1941- *ConAu 131*
Whitehouse, David J M 1951- *BiDrAPA 89*
Whitehouse, David Rempfer 1929- *WhoAm 90*
Whitehouse, Frank, Jr. 1924- *IntWWM 90*
Whitehouse, Fred Waite 1926- *WhoAm 90*
Whitehouse, Gary 1938- *WhoSSW 91*
Whitehouse, Hugh L. 1924- *St&PR 91*
Whitehouse, J. David 1937- *St&PR 91*
Whitehouse, Jack Pendleton 1924- *WhoWor 91*
Whitehouse, John D 1916- *BiDrAPA 89*
Whitehouse, Julian Michael 1940- *WhoWor 91*
Whitehouse, Len 1957- *Ballpl 90*
Whitehouse, M Jody 1957- *BiDrAPA 89*
Whitehouse, Margaret Patricia *BioIn 16*
Whitehouse, Nancy Lenamay 1941- *WhoE 91*
Whitehouse, Paula Marie 1953- *WhoAmW 91*
Whitehouse-Tedd, Carl 1960- *WhoWor 91*
Whitehurst, Betty Campbell 1934- *WhoAmW 91*
Whitehurst, Brooks Morris 1930- *WhoSSW 91, WhoWor 91*
Whitehurst, William Oscar 1945- *WhoEmL 91*
Whitehurst, William Wilfred, Jr. 1937- *WhoE 91, WhoWor 91*
Whiteker, Roy Archie 1927- *WhoAm 90*
Whitelaw, Debra Ann 1957- *WhoE 91*
Whitelaw, Elizabeth Ann 1941- *WhoAmW 91*
Whitelaw, James T. 1845-1909 *BioIn 16*
Whitelaw, Nancy Eaton 1933- *WhoWrEP 89*
Whiteley, Benjamin Robert 1929- *St&PR 91, WhoAm 90*
Whiteley, George 1909?-1990 *ConAu 132*
Whiteley, Harold Edmond *BiDrAPA 89*
Whiteley, Harry 1930- *BiDrAPA 89*
Whiteley, Henry Ellen 1945- *WhoWrEP 89*
Whiteley, John Scott 1950- *IntWWM 90*
Whiteley, Martha Homma *ODwPR 91*
Whiteley, Norman Franklin, Jr. 1940- *WhoE 91*
Whiteley, Richard Clayton 1939- *St&PR 91*
Whiteley, Robert Claude, Jr. 1957- *WhoSSW 91*
Whitelock, Dorothy 1901-1982 *ConAu 129*
Whitelock, Paul Richard 1943- *BiDrAPA 89*
Whiteman, Bruce 1952- *ConAu 132*
Whiteman, Donald Ray 1941- *St&PR 91*
Whiteman, Douglas E. 1961- *WhoAm 90*
Whiteman, Edward Russell 1938- *WhoAmA 91*
Whiteman, George 1882-1947 *Ballpl 90*
Whiteman, Gilbert Lee 1931- *WhoE 91*
Whiteman, H. Clifton 1925- *St&PR 91*
Whiteman, Horace Clifton 1925- *WhoAm 90*
Whiteman, J H M 1906- *EncO&P 3*
Whiteman, Jack William 1914- *St&PR 91*
Whiteman, Jacob Harvey 1863-1928 *AmLegL*
Whiteman, John F. 1948- *St&PR 91*
Whiteman, Joseph David 1933- *St&PR 91, WhoAm 90*
Whiteman, Joseph Hilary Michael 1906- *EncPaPR 91*
Whiteman, Paul 1890-1967 *BioIn 16, OxCPMus, PenDiMP*
Whiteman, Paul 1891-1967 *WorAlBi*
Whiteman, Richard Frank 1925- *WhoAm 90*
Whiteman, Samuel Dickey, Jr. 1927- *St&PR 91*
Whitemore, Hugh 1936- *ConAu 132*
Whiten, Colette 1945- *WhoAmA 91*
Whiten, Eva *St&PR 91*
Whiten, Tim 1941- *WhoAmA 91*
Whitener, Barrett Simpson 1960- *WhoSSW 91*
Whitener, Bill L. 1925- *St&PR 91*
Whitener, Paul A W 1911-1959 *WhoAmA 91N*
Whitener, Robert W 1927- *BiDrAPA 89*
Whitener, William Garnett 1951- *WhoAm 90*
Whitescarver, Charles Kyle, III 1953- *WhoSSW 91*
Whitescarver, William A. 1930- *St&PR 91*
Whitesell, Dale Edward 1925- *WhoAm 90*
Whitesell, John D 1942- *WhoAmA 91*
Whitesell, John Edwin 1938- *WhoAm 90*
Whitesell, Kimberly Karen 1962- *BiDrAPA 89*
Whitesell, Nancy Jane 1953- *WhoAmW 91*
Whitesell, Nolan Gary 1953- *WhoSSW 91*
Whitesell, Terry G. 1939- *St&PR 91*
Whiteside, C Thomas 1943- *BiDrAPA 89*
Whiteside, Carol Gordon 1942- *WhoAm 90, WhoAmW 91*
Whiteside, Daniel Fowler 1931- *WhoAm 90*
Whiteside, David Powers, Jr. 1950- *WhoSSW 91*
Whiteside, Donald Campbell 1953- *WhoSSW 91*
Whiteside, Duncan 1935- *WhoE 91*
Whiteside, Elizabeth Ayres 1960- *WhoAmW 91, WhoWor 91*
Whiteside, James Brooks 1942- *WhoE 91*
Whiteside, John Henry 1938- *WhoAm 90*
Whiteside, Joseph J. 1941- *St&PR 91*
Whiteside, Joseph Stackhouse, III 1963- *WhoE 91*
Whiteside, Ninian E. *AmLegL*
Whiteside, Ralph Talbott 1933- *St&PR 91*
Whiteside, Richard Hartman 1926- *St&PR 91*
Whiteside, Robert Scott 1951- *WhoAm 90*
Whiteside, William Albert, II 1925- *WhoAmA 91*
Whitesides, Elizabeth Igler 1910- *WhoAmW 91*
Whitesides, George McClelland 1939- *WhoAm 90*
Whitesides, Jack Wayne 1945- *St&PR 91*
Whitesides, Robert Gene 1927- *St&PR 91*
Whitesides, Thomas Edward, Jr. 1929- *WhoAm 90, WhoSSW 91*
Whitesides-Woo, Rob *NewAgMG*
Whitesitt, Linda 1951- *ConAu 129, IntWWM 90*
Whitesitt, Linda Marie 1951- *WhoSSW 91*
Whitesnake *ConMus 5 [port]*
Whitestone, Todd A. 1954- *St&PR 91*
Whiteway, Douglas Alfred 1951- *WhoWrEP 89*
Whitfield, Cecil Wallace- 1930-1990 *BioIn 16*
Whitfield, Clyde H., Jr. 1935- *ODwPR 91*
Whitfield, David 1925-1980 *OxCPMus*
Whitfield, David Richard 1928- *WhoWor 91*
Whitfield, Edwin Wycliffe 1925- *WhoE 91, WhoWor 91*
Whitfield, Francis James 1916- *WhoAm 90*
Whitfield, Fred 1938- *Ballpl 90*
Whitfield, Graham Frank 1942- *WhoSSW 91, WhoWor 91*
Whitfield, H. Lewis 1942- *St&PR 91*
Whitfield, Harvey James 1940- *BiDrAPA 89*
Whitfield, Herschel Larry 1940- *WhoSSW 91*
Whitfield, Jack D. 1928- *St&PR 91*
Whitfield, Jack Duane 1928- *WhoAm 90, WhoSSW 91*
Whitfield, Jahnathon *BioIn 16*
Whitfield, James Edward, Jr. 1930- *St&PR 91*
Whitfield, Joanne Christian 1941- *WhoSSW 91*
Whitfield, John Peter 1957- *IntWWM 90*
Whitfield, Joseph A *BiDrAPA 89*
Whitfield, Josie *BioIn 16*
Whitfield, Leigh Cosby 1952- *WhoAmW 91*
Whitfield, Lynn *DrBIPA 90*
Whitfield, Marion S., Jr. 1945- *St&PR 91*
Whitfield, Martha Ann 1956- *WhoSSW 91*
Whitfield, Michael J 1944- *OxCCanT*
Whitfield, Needham Bryan 1936- *St&PR 91*
Whitfield, Norman 1943- *OxCPMus*
Whitfield, Raoul 1898-1945 *TwCCr&M 91*
Whitfield, Terry 1953- *Ballpl 90*
Whitham, Gerald Beresford 1927- *WhoAm 90*
Whitham, Kenneth 1927- *WhoAm 90*
Whiticker, Michael 1954- *IntWWM 90*
Whitin, Richard Courtney, Jr. 1921- *WhoAm 90*
Whiting, Adolph M 1918- *BiDrAPA 89*
Whiting, Albert Nathaniel 1917- *WhoAm 90*
Whiting, Allen Suess 1926- *WhoAm 90*
Whiting, Arthur Milton 1928- *St&PR 91, WhoAm 90*
Whiting, Basil John, Jr. 1938- *WhoE 91*
Whiting, Carson Ross 1910- *St&PR 91*
Whiting, Estelle Louise *WhoWrEP 89*
Whiting, Fred *ODwPR 91*
Whiting, Gaylord Peter 1950- *WhoSSW 91*
Whiting, Geoffrey 1919-1988 *BioIn 16*
Whiting, Henry H. *WhoAm 90*
Whiting, Jack 1901-1961 *OxCPMus*
Whiting, John Randolph 1914- *WhoAm 90*
Whiting, John Wesley Mayhew 1908- *WhoAm 90*
Whiting, Kenneth R. 1927- *St&PR 91*
Whiting, Lisa Lorraine 1959- *WhoAmW 91*
Whiting, Margaret 1924- *WorAlBi*
Whiting, Mary 1654-1676 *BiDEWW*
Whiting, Mary Alexandra 1952- *WhoAmW 91*
Whiting, Paul Leo 1943- *St&PR 91*
Whiting, Richard A. 1891-1938 *BioIn 16, OxCPMus*
Whiting, Richard Albert 1922- *WhoAm 90*
Whiting, Richard Brooke 1947- *WhoAm 90*
Whiting, Robert *BioIn 16*
Whiting, Susan H. 1945- *ODwPR 91*
Whiting, William Fairfield 1864-1936 *BiDrUSE 89*
Whitinger, Leila Lee 1941- *WhoAmW 91*
Whitinger, R. D. *AuBYP 90*
Whitis, Jessie Dillard 1937- *WhoSSW 91*
Whitis, Peter Roome 1933- *BiDrAPA 89*
Whitla, F.E. 1930- *BiDrAPA 89*
Whitlam, Nicholas *BioIn 16*
Whitlark, James Stuart 1948- *WhoSSW 91*
Whitlatch, Jo Bell 1943- *WhoAm 90*
Whitlaw, Michael D. 1951- *ODwPR 91*
Whitledge, James T. 1941- *WhoE 91*
Whitler, Sandra B. 1949- *St&PR 91*
Whitley, Agnes V 1937- *BiDrAPA 89*
Whitley, Ann Elizabeth 1947- *WhoEmL 91*
Whitley, Arthur Francis 1927- *WhoAm 90*
Whitley, Aubrey Russell, Jr. 1953- *WhoSSW 91*
Whitley, Ben Gordon 1960- *WhoSSW 91*
Whitley, Carolyn Davis 1933- *WhoAmW 91*
Whitley, Douglas Best, Jr. 1956- *WhoSSW 91*
Whitley, Frank Jackson, Jr. 1940- *St&PR 91*
Whitley, Gwendolyn Ruth *BiDrAPA 89*
Whitley, James Craig 1948- *WhoAm 90, WhoEmL 91*
Whitley, Joe Daly 1950- *WhoAm 90*
Whitley, John Calvin, Jr. *BiDrAPA 89*
Whitley, John Quention, Jr. 1955- *WhoSSW 91*
Whitley, Juana Lynn 1964- *WhoAmW 91*
Whitley, Kathleen Petrie *BiDrAPA 89*
Whitley, Keith *BioIn 16, WhoNeCM [port]*
Whitley, Mary A 1951- *SmATA 62*
Whitley, Mary Ann 1951- *WhoWrEP 89*
Whitley, Michael R. 1943- *St&PR 91*
Whitley, Nancy O'Neil 1932- *WhoAm 90, WhoAmW 91*
Whitley, Ralph Charles 1943- *St&PR 91*
Whitley, Richard James 1945- *WhoAm 90*
Whitley, Sandra Ann 1951- *WhoE 91*
Whitlinger, Gene P. 1933- *WhoAm 90*
Whitlinger, Gene Paul 1933- *St&PR 91*
Whitlock, Albert 1915- *ConDes 90*
Whitlock, Baird Woodruff 1924- *WhoAm 90*
Whitlock, Bennett Clarke, Jr. 1927- *WhoAm 90*
Whitlock, Brand 1869-1934 *BioIn 16*
Whitlock, C. William 1942- *WhoAm 90*
Whitlock, Charles Preston 1919- *WhoAm 90*
Whitlock, Darrell Dean 1941- *WhoSSW 91*
Whitlock, Denise Lucille 1959- *WhoAmW 91*
Whitlock, Foster Brand 1914- *WhoAm 90, WhoWor 91*
Whitlock, Jerry Dean 1932- *St&PR 91*
Whitlock, John Joseph 1935- *WhoAm 90, WhoAmA 91*
Whitlock, Mary Ellen Jenkins 1906- *WhoAmW 91*
Whitlock, Reverdy Robert Hale 1913- *St&PR 91*
Whitlock, Robert Henry 1941- *WhoE 91*
Whitlock, William Abel 1929- *WhoAm 90*
Whitlow, Donald R. 1932- *St&PR 91*
Whitlow, Michael D. 1952- *ODwPR 91*
Whitman, Alden 1913-1990 *ConAu 132, NewYTBS 90 [port]*
Whitman, Allen Earle, III 1934- *St&PR 91*
Whitman, Ann 1908- *BioIn 16*
Whitman, Ardis 1905?-1990 *ConAu 131*
Whitman, Ardis Rumsey *NewYTBS 90*
Whitman, Bert 1908- *EncACom*
Whitman, Bruce N. 1933- *St&PR 91*
Whitman, Bruce Nairn 1933- *WhoAm 90*
Whitman, Carl E. *St&PR 91*
Whitman, Carl Edward 1930- *WhoAm 90*
Whitman, Charles Henry 1933- *St&PR 91*
Whitman, Chester W. 1928- *St&PR 91*

Whitman, Dale Alan 1939- *WhoAm 90*
Whitman, Dick 1920- *Ballpl 90*
Whitman, Donald Ray 1931- *WhoAm 90*
Whitman, Ernest 1893-1954 *DrBlPA 90*
Whitman, Helen Herrick 1925- *WhoAmW 91*
Whitman, Howard *WhoAm 90*
Whitman, Howard Mitchell 1948- *St&PR 91*
Whitman, John M *BiDrAPA 89*
Whitman, Jules I. 1923- *WhoAm 90*
Whitman, Kenneth Jay 1947- *WhoEmL 91, WhoWor 91*
Whitman, Laura June 1959- *BiDrAPA 89*
Whitman, Marcus 1802-1847 *WhNaAH, WorAlBi*
Whitman, Marina von Neumann *BioIn 16*
Whitman, Marina Von Neumann 1935- *WhoAmW 91*
Whitman, Martin J. 1924- *St&PR 91*
Whitman, Nancy Ellin 1934- *IntWWM 90*
Whitman, Nancy Irene 1947- *WhoSSW 91*
Whitman, Narcissa 1808-1847 *FemiCLE*
Whitman, Narcissa P. 1808-1847 *BioAmW*
Whitman, Reginald Norman 1909- *WhoAm 90, WhoSSW 91, WhoWor 91*
Whitman, Richard L. 1947- *St&PR 91*
Whitman, Robert 1936- *WhoAm 90*
Whitman, Robert Harold 1930- *St&PR 91*
Whitman, Robert Van Duyne 1928- *WhoAm 90*
Whitman, Roch Gerard 1959- *WhoE 91*
Whitman, Roy M 1925- *BiDrAPA 89*
Whitman, Russell Brian 1944- *WhoAm 90*
Whitman, Ruth 1922- *ConAu 31NR, WhoAm 90, WhoWrEP 89, WorAu 1980 [port]*
Whitman, Sarah 1803-1878 *FemiCLE*
Whitman, Sarah P. 1803-1878 *BioAmW*
Whitman, Sigrid Taillon 1932- *WhoAmW 91*
Whitman, Slim 1924- *OxCPMus*
Whitman, Walt 1819-1892 *BioIn 16, WorAlBi, WrPh*
Whitman, William *BiDrAPA 89*
Whitman, Winfred G *BiDrAPA 89*
Whitmer, Gilbert N. 1942- *St&PR 91*
Whitmer, John Harrison 1923- *BiDrAPA 89*
Whitmer, Joseph Morton 1942- *WhoSSW 91*
Whitmer, Melvin Howard 1928- *WhoWrEP 89*
Whitmer, Ruth C. 1919- *WhoAmW 91*
Whitmer, William Eward 1933- *WhoSSW 91*
Whitmer, William R. 1933- *St&PR 91*
Whitmire, Florence Eileen 1942- *St&PR 91*
Whitmire, John 1927-1989 *BioIn 16*
Whitmire, John 1949- *WhoSSW 91*
Whitmire, Kathryn J. *BioIn 16*
Whitmire, Kathryn Jean 1946- *WhoAm 90, WhoAmW 91, WhoSSW 91*
Whitmire, Kenneth Neal 1938- *St&PR 91*
Whitmire, Leslie E *BiDrAPA 89*
Whitmore, Beatrice Eileen 1935- *WhoAmW 91, WhoE 91*
Whitmore, Charles H. 1914- *St&PR 91*
Whitmore, Charles Horace 1914- *WhoAm 90*
Whitmore, Dan C. 1932- *St&PR 91*
Whitmore, Donald Earl, Jr. 1935- *St&PR 91*
Whitmore, Edward Hugh 1926- *WhoAm 90*
Whitmore, Ernest Henry 1958- *WhoSSW 91*
Whitmore, Franklin E. 1935- *St&PR 91*
Whitmore, George 1945-1989 *BioIn 16, ConAu 30NR*
Whitmore, George Merle, Jr. 1928- *WhoAm 90*
Whitmore, Howard *BioIn 16*
Whitmore, Jacob Leslie, III 1939- *WhoE 91*
Whitmore, James 1921- *WorAlBi*
Whitmore, James Allen 1921- *WhoAm 90*
Whitmore, John Rogers 1933- *WhoAm 90*
Whitmore, Jon Scott 1945- *WhoAm 90*
Whitmore, Joshua David 1949- *WhoSSW 91*
Whitmore, Kay Rex 1932- *St&PR 91, WhoAm 90, WhoE 91, WhoWor 91*
Whitmore, Menandra M. *WhoAmW 91*
Whitmore, Michael Eugene 1946- *WhoSSW 91*
Whitmore, Ralph Ervin, Jr. 1932- *St&PR 91*
Whitmore, Sharp 1918- *WhoAm 90*
Whitmore, Susan *BioIn 16*
Whitmore, William Francis 1917- *WhoAm 90*
Whitmyer, Russell Eliot 1915- *WhoAm 90*
Whitmyre, Richard D. 1951- *ODwPR 91*
Whitmyre, Richard David 1951- *WhoE 91*
Whitnah, Donald Robert 1925- *WhoAm 90*
Whitner, George C. 1923- *St&PR 91*
Whitner, Lillian Maddox *WhoAmW 91*
Whitner, Thomas Church 1958- *WhoSSW 91*
Whitney, Alan John 1925- *WhoAm 90*
Whitney, Alden E 1934- *BiDrAPA 89*
Whitney, Alec *TwCCr&M 91*
Whitney, Anne 1821-1915 *BiDWomA*
Whitney, Carolyn Joyce 1933- *WhoSSW 91*
Whitney, Charles Allen 1929- *WhoAm 90*
Whitney, Charles E 1903-1977 *WhoAmA 91N*
Whitney, Charlotte Armide 1923- *WhoAmA 91*
Whitney, Constance Clein *WhoAmW 91*
Whitney, Cornelius Vanderbilt 1899- *WhoAm 90*
Whitney, Craig 1943- *BioIn 16*
Whitney, Craig Richard 1943- *ConAu 131, WhoAm 90, WhoWor 91*
Whitney, Daniel Eugene 1938- *WhoE 91*
Whitney, David C. 1921- *BioIn 16*
Whitney, Diane Foster 1946- *BiDrAPA 89*
Whitney, Dickson Loos 1927- *St&PR 91*
Whitney, Donald H. 1955- *WhoSSW 91*
Whitney, Dorothy 1887-1968 *BioAmW*
Whitney, Dorothy Ann Sullivan *WhoE 91*
Whitney, E.W., III 1947- *St&PR 91*
Whitney, Edgar Albert 1891- *WhoAmA 91N*
Whitney, Edward Bonner 1945- *WhoAm 90*
Whitney, Eli 1765-1825 *WorAlBi*
Whitney, Enoch Jonathan 1945- *WhoSSW 91*
Whitney, Eric H. 1946- *WhoE 91*
Whitney, George 1885-1963 *BioIn 16*
Whitney, George H., Jr. 1927- *St&PR 91*
Whitney, George Ward 1924- *WhoAm 90*
Whitney, Gertrude 1875-1942 *BiDWomA*
Whitney, Gertrude 1877-1942 *BioAmW*
Whitney, Gertrude Vanderbilt *BioIn 16*
Whitney, Gertrude Vanderbilt 1877-1942 *WorAlBi*
Whitney, Grace Lee *BioIn 16*
Whitney, Harry Payne 1872-1930 *BioIn 16*
Whitney, Hassler 1907-1989 *BioIn 16*
Whitney, Herbert N. 1940- *St&PR 91*
Whitney, Isabel Lydia *WhoAmA 91N*
Whitney, Isabella *BioIn 16, FemiCLE*
Whitney, J. D. 1940- *WhoWrEP 89*
Whitney, James S. 1925- *WhoAm 90*
Whitney, James Saunders 1925- *St&PR 91*
Whitney, Jane 1941- *WhoE 91, WhoWor 91*
Whitney, Jeffrey Garrett 1941- *St&PR 91*
Whitney, Jeffrey Michael 1955- *WhoSSW 91*
Whitney, Jim 1857-1891 *Ballpl 90*
Whitney, Joan 1914- *OxCPMus*
Whitney, John Clarence 1915- *WhoAm 90*
Whitney, John Hay 1904-1982 *BioIn 16, WhoAmA 91N*
Whitney, Jon R. *St&PR 91*
Whitney, Jon R. 1944- *WhoAm 90*
Whitney, Kayla *WhoWrEP 89*
Whitney, King, Jr. 1925- *St&PR 91*
Whitney, Leon Fradley 1894-1973 *AuBYP 90*
Whitney, Lester Frank 1928- *WhoE 91*
Whitney, Marylou *BioIn 16*
Whitney, Maynard Merle 1931- *WhoAmA 91*
Whitney, Michael Anthony 1941- *St&PR 91*
Whitney, Orson Ferguson 1855-1931 *BioIn 16*
Whitney, Patrick Foster 1951- *WhoAm 90*
Whitney, Philip Mather 1941- *St&PR 91*
Whitney, Philip Richardson 1878- *WhoAmA 91N*
Whitney, Phyllis 1903- *WorAlBi*
Whitney, Phyllis A 1903- *BestSel 90-3 [port], TwCCr&M 91*
Whitney, Phyllis Ayame 1903- *AuBYP 90, WhoAm 90, WhoAmW 91*
Whitney, Phyllis Burrill 1928- *WhoAmW 91*
Whitney, Pinky 1905- *Ballpl 90*
Whitney, Ralph Royal, Jr. 1934- *St&PR 91, WhoE 91, WhoWor 91*
Whitney, Richard 1888-1974 *BioIn 16*
Whitney, Richard Porter 1938- *St&PR 91*
Whitney, Richard Wheeler 1946- *WhoAmA 91, WhoE 91*
Whitney, Robert A., Jr. 1935- *WhoAm 90*
Whitney, Robert Avery 1912- *WhoAm 90, WhoWor 91*
Whitney, Robert L. 1931- *St&PR 91*
Whitney, Robert S. 1904-1986 *PenDiMP*
Whitney, Ruth Ann Rotundo 1945- *WhoE 91*
Whitney, Ruth Reinke 1928- *WhoAm 90, WhoAmW 91, WhoWrEP 89*
Whitney, Salem Tutt *EarBlAP*
Whitney, Sharon 1937- *SmATA 63 [port]*
Whitney, Thomas P. *AuBYP 90*
Whitney, Thomas Porter 1917- *WhoE 91, WhoWor 91*
Whitney, W. Beaumont, III 1922- *St&PR 91*
Whitney, Wallace French, Jr. 1943- *WhoAm 90*
Whitney, Wayne R. 1945- *St&PR 91*
Whitney, Wheelock *WhoAm 90*
Whitney, William Collins 1841-1902 *BiDrUSE 89*
Whitney, William Elliot, Jr. 1933- *WhoAm 90*
Whitney, William Gordon 1922- *WhoE 91*
Whitney, William Kuebler 1921-1985 *WhoAmA 91N*
Whitridge, Arnold 1891-1989 *BioIn 16*
Whitrow, Joan *BiDEWW, FemiCLE*
Whitrow, Susanna 1662-1677 *BiDEWW*
Whitsel, Agnes Booth 1931- *WhoSSW 91*
Whitsel, Robert Malcolm 1929- *St&PR 91, WhoAm 90*
Whitsell, Helen Jo 1938- *St&PR 91, WhoAm 90*
Whitsell, Leon J *BiDrAPA 89*
Whitsitt, Bob 1956- *WhoAm 90*
Whitsitt, Robert James 1956- *WhoAm 90*
Whitsitt, William F. 1945- *St&PR 91*
Whitsitt, William Heth 1841-1911 *BioIn 16*
Whitson 1941- *WhoAmA 91*
Whitson, Angela *BioIn 16*
Whitson, Angie *WhoAmA 91*
Whitson, Barbara Lee 1943- *WhoAmW 91*
Whitson, Betty Jo 1945- *WhoAmW 91*
Whitson, Ed 1955- *Ballpl 90*
Whitson, Harold A. 1940- *St&PR 91*
Whitson, James N. 1935- *St&PR 91*
Whitson, James Norfleet, Jr. 1935- *WhoAm 90*
Whitson, Laura Ann 1952- *WhoAmW 91*
Whitson, Robert Edd 1942- *St&PR 91*
Whitson, Shelby Alderman 1937- *WhoSSW 91*
Whitson, Susan Jean 1951- *WhoAmW 91*
Whitson, William Burroughs 1915- *St&PR 91*
Whitt, Barbara Sandra 1943- *WhoAmW 91*
Whitt, David Virgel 1935- *WhoAm 90*
Whitt, Ernie 1952- *Ballpl 90*
Whitt, Gregory Sidney 1938- *WhoAm 90*
Whitt, John Alan 1958- *BiDrAPA 89*
Whitt, John Robert 1946- *St&PR 91*
Whitt, Mary F. *WhoAmW 91*
Whitt, Michael Rayburn 1952- *WhoWor 91*
Whitt, Phillip Bryant, Sr. 1942- *WhoSSW 91*
Whitt, Richard Ernest 1944- *WhoAm 90*
Whitt, Walter F. 1943- *St&PR 91*
Whitt, William O'Neal 1923- *WhoAm 90*
Whittaker, Bob 1939- *WhoAm 90*
Whittaker, C R 1929- *ConAu 131*
Whittaker, Charles Joseph 1938- *WhoE 91*
Whittaker, Douglas Kirkland 1949- *WhoSSW 91*
Whittaker, Geoffrey Owen 1932- *WhoWor 91*
Whittaker, George Henry 1939- *St&PR 91*
Whittaker, Herbert 1910- *OxCCanT*
Whittaker, J.K. 1926- *St&PR 91*
Whittaker, Jeanne Evans 1934- *WhoAm 90*
Whittaker, Mary Frances 1926- *WhoSSW 91*
Whittaker, Patricia DiMaggio 1952- *WhoAmW 91*
Whittaker, Roger 1936- *OxCPMus*
Whittaker, Roy D. 1929- *St&PR 91*
Whittaker, Sheelagh Dillon 1947- *WhoAmW 91*
Whittaker, Steven Dale 1950- *St&PR 91*
Whittaker, W G 1876-1944 *PenDiMP*
Whittaker, Walter Hugh 1929- *St&PR 91*
Whittaker, William Russell 1957- *WhoSSW 91*
Whittall, Eliot *BioIn 16*
Whittall, H. Richard 1923- *St&PR 91*
Whittall, Hubert Richard 1923- *WhoAm 90*
Whittard, Walter Frederick 1902-1966 *DcScB S2*
Whitted, John B., Jr. 1924- *St&PR 91*
Whitted, Possum 1890-1962 *Ballpl 90*
Whittell, George 1882-1969 *BioIn 16*
Whittelsey, Souther *NewYTBS 90*
Whittelsey, Souther 1910- *WhoE 91*
Whittelsey, Stuart G., Jr. 1929- *St&PR 91*
Whittemore, Bert Robinson 1934- *WhoE 91*
Whittemore, Dexter D, Jr. *BiDrAPA 89*
Whittemore, Dorothy Jane 1920- *WhoAmW 91*
Whittemore, Edward Reed, II 1919- *WhoAm 90*
Whittemore, Frank Bowen 1916- *WhoE 91*
Whittemore, Frederick Brewster 1930- *WhoAm 90*
Whittemore, Helen Simpson *WhoAmA 91N*
Whittemore, Joan Margaret 1944- *IntWWM 90*
Whittemore, Laurence Frederick 1929- *St&PR 91, WhoAm 90*
Whittemore, Margaret Anne 1950- *WhoE 91*
Whittemore, Marjorie Maas 1947- *WhoAmW 91*
Whittemore, Ronald Clarence 1938- *WhoWor 91*
Whitten, Benjamin 1907-1989 *BioIn 16*
Whitten, Bertwell Kneeland 1941- *WhoAm 90*
Whitten, Charles Alexander, Jr. 1940- *WhoAm 90*
Whitten, David George 1938- *WhoAm 90*
Whitten, Dolphus, Jr. 1916- *WhoAm 90*
Whitten, Eric Harold Timothy 1927- *WhoAm 90*
Whitten, James R 1933- *BiDrAPA 89*
Whitten, Jamie Lloyd 1910- *WhoAm 90, WhoSSW 91*
Whitten, Jerry Lynn 1937- *WhoAm 90*
Whitten, Leslie Hunter, Jr. 1928- *WhoAm 90, WhoWrEP 89*
Whitten, Thomas B. 1939- *St&PR 91*
Whitten-Stovall, Richard Frank 1947- *BiDrAPA 89*
Whitters, Alan Christopher 1956- *BiDrAPA 89*
Whitters, James Payton, III 1939- *WhoAm 90*
Whitters, Joseph Edward 1958- *St&PR 91*
Whitthorne, Washington Curran 1825-1891 *AmLegL*
Whittier, John Greenleaf 1807-1892 *BioIn 16, WorAlBi*
Whittier, John R *BiDrAPA 89*
Whittier, John Rensselaer *NewYTBS 90*
Whittier, Max 1866?-1925? *BioIn 16*
Whittier, Michael Warren 1943- *WhoSSW 91*
Whittier, SaraJane 1912- *WhoAmW 91, WhoSSW 91, WhoWor 91*
Whittier, Susan J. *ODwPR 91*
Whittingham, Charles Arthur 1930- *WhoAm 90*
Whittingham, Charles Edward 1913- *WhoAm 90*
Whittingham, Charlie 1913- *BioIn 16*
Whittingham, Harry Edward, Jr. 1918- *WhoAm 90*
Whittingham, Michael Stanley 1941- *WhoE 91*
Whittingham, Thomas C. 1928- *St&PR 91*
Whittington, Aven 1917- *WhoAm 90*
Whittington, Bernard Wiley 1920- *WhoAm 90*
Whittington, Constance V. 1954- *ODwPR 91*
Whittington, Edward H. *WhoSSW 91*
Whittington, Floyd Leon 1909- *WhoAm 90, WhoWor 91*
Whittington, Harry 1915- *TwCCr&M 91*
Whittington, Horace G 1929- *BiDrAPA 89*
Whittington, John Jay 1947- *St&PR 91*
Whittington, Jon Hammon 1938- *WhoAmA 91*
Whittington, Robert Bruce 1927- *WhoAm 90*
Whittington, Stuart Gordon 1942- *WhoAm 90*
Whittington, Vanessa Elizabeth 1960- *WhoE 91*
Whittington, Vera J. 1929- *St&PR 91*
Whittle, Charles Edward 1938- *St&PR 91*
Whittle, Charles Edward, Jr. 1931- *WhoAm 90*
Whittle, Christopher *BioIn 16*
Whittle, D. Christopher 1928- *ODwPR 91*
Whittle, Douglas Alexander 1947- *WhoE 91*
Whittle, Elenor Willow 1944- *WhoE 91*
Whittle, Howard Palmer 1932- *St&PR 91*
Whittle, James *PenDiDA 89*
Whittle, John Joseph 1936- *St&PR 91, WhoAm 90*
Whittle, Mack Ira, Jr. 1948- *WhoSSW 91*
Whittlebot, Hernia *MajTwCW*
Whittlesey, John R. B. 1927- *EncO&P 3*
Whittlesey, John Williams 1917- *WhoE 91*
Whittlesey, Marjorie Tooker 1912- *WhoWrEP 89*
Whittlesey, Robert Hargreaves, II 1945- *St&PR 91*
Whittlesey, Susan 1938- *AuBYP 90*
Whittome, Irene F *WhoAmA 91*
Whitton, Charlotte Elizabeth 1896-1975 *BioIn 16*
Whitton, Hollis Dale 1925- *St&PR 91*
Whitton, Jeffrey Herschel 1957- *WhoSSW 91*
Whitton, Katherine *BiDEWW, FemiCLE*
Whitton, Kenneth S 1925- *ConAu 131*
Whitton, Walter E. 1911- *St&PR 91*
Whittow, Marion Frances 1947- *IntWWM 90*

Whittredge, Robert B., II 1944- *St&PR 91*
Whitty, Gerard Charles 1950- *WhoE 91*
Whitty, Larry Joe 1960- *St&PR 91*
Whitty, Lawrence J. 1937- *St&PR 91*
Whitty, May 1865-1948 *WorAlBi*
Whitty, Raymond John 1945- *St&PR 91*
Whitty, Thomas J. 1936- *St&PR 91*
Whitwam, David Ray 1942- *WhoAm 90*
Whitwell, George L. 1940- *St&PR 91*
Whitworth, Hall Baker 1919- *WhoAm 90*
Whitworth, J. Bryan 1938- *St&PR 91*
Whitworth, James Bruce *BiDrAPA 89*
Whitworth, Jerry A. *BioIn 16*
Whitworth, John 1945- *ConAu 131*
Whitworth, John Harvey, Jr. 1933- *WhoAm 90*
Whitworth, Kathrynne Ann 1939- *WhoAm 90, WhoAmW 91*
Whitworth, Kathy 1939- *WorAlBi*
Whitworth, Pamela Suzanne 1958- *WhoSSW 91*
Whitworth, William A. 1937- *WhoAm 90, WhoE 91*
Whiz Kids *Ballpl 90*
Whiz, Walter Raimu 1918- *WhoWrEP 89*
Who, The *EncPR&S 89, OxCPMus*
Whorf, John 1903-1959 *WhoAmA 91N*
Whoriskey, Robert Donald 1929- *WhoAm 90, WhoWor 91*
Whorton, Danna Binder 1905- *WhoSSW 91*
Whorton, M. Donald 1943- *WhoAm 90*
Whorton, Ronald Ellis 1936- *WhoAm 90*
Whritenour, Robert A. 1936- *St&PR 91*
Whyard, Florence 1917- *ConAu 129*
Whybrow, Peter Charles 1939- *BiDrAPA 89, WhoAm 90, WhoE 91*
Whyman, Herbert 1913-1990 *BioIn 16*
Whymant, Neville 1894- *EncO&P 3*
Whynot, D.A. 1961- *St&PR 91*
Whyte, Alec J 1931- *BiDrAPA 89*
Whyte, Bruce Lincoln 1941- *WhoAmA 91, WhoE 91, WhoWor 91*
Whyte, Donald Edward 1918- *St&PR 91*
Whyte, Eric H A *BiDrAPA 89*
Whyte, George Kenneth, Jr. 1936- *WhoAm 90*
Whyte, Hamilton *NewYTBS 90*
Whyte, Iain Boyd 1947- *ConAu 132*
Whyte, James L. 1927- *St&PR 91*
Whyte, James Primrose, Jr. 1921- *WhoAm 90*
Whyte, John D. 1940- *ConAu 129*
Whyte, King *BioIn 16*
Whyte, Mal 1933- *SmATA 62 [port]*
Whyte, Martin King 1942- *WhoAm 90*
Whyte, Raymond A 1923- *WhoAmA 91*
Whyte, Rogelio L *BiDrAPA 89*
Whyte, Ron *BioIn 16*
Whyte, Ron 1942?-1989 *ConAu 129, -132, SmATA 63*
Whyte, Thaddeus Everett, Jr. 1937- *WhoE 91*
Whyte, William Foote 1914- *WhoAm 90*
Whyte, William Hollingsworth *BioIn 16*
Whyte, William Hollingsworth 1917- *WhoAm 90, WhoWrEP 89*
Whyte, William R. 1947- *WhoSSW 91*
Wiaczek, Pamela Paxton 1961- *WhoAmW 91*
Wiaduck, James Patrick *BiDrAPA 89*
Wiant, Sarah Kirsten 1946- *WhoEmL 91*
Wiarda, Gerardus 1906-1988 *BioIn 16*
Wibaut, Frank 1945- *IntWWM 90*
Wibbelsman, Charles 1945- *BioIn 16*
Wibbelsman, Robert John 1939- *WhoWor 91*
Wibberley, Leonard *TwCCr&M 91*
Wibberley, Leonard 1915-1983 *AuBYP 90*
Wiber, Peter *PenDiDA 89*
Wiberg, Anders 1816-1887 *BioIn 16*
Wiberg, Donald Martin 1936- *WhoAm 90*
Wiberg, J Lawrence 1940- *BiDrAPA 89*
Wiberg, Kenneth Berle 1927- *WhoAm 90*
Wiberg, Richard L. 1930- *ODwPR 91*
Wiberg, Tore 1911- *IntWWM 90*
Wiberley, Stephen Edward 1919- *WhoAm 90*
Wible, Arthur E., Jr. 1937- *ODwPR 91*
Wible, Judith Laine 1940- *BiDrAPA 89*
Wible, Mary Grace *WhoAmA 91*
Wibmer, Fanny 1890- *EncCoWW*
Wiborg, James H. 1924- *St&PR 91*
Wice, Jeffrey Mark 1952- *WhoE 91*
Wich, Gunther 1928- *IntWWM 90, PenDiMP*
Wich, Robert T. 1927- *St&PR 91*
Wich, Robert Thomas 1927- *WhoAm 90, WhoSSW 91*
Wichard, Rudolf 1937- *WhoWor 91*
Wicher, Donna Christine 1951- *WhoAmW 91*
Wichern, Dean William 1942- *WhoAm 90*
Wichinsky, Glenn Ellis 1952- *WhoEmL 91*
Wichmann, Robert Karl 1937- *St&PR 91*
Wichser, Karl 1952- *St&PR 91*
Wichterman, Ralph 1907- *WhoE 91*
Wick, Arthur D. 1943- *St&PR 91*
Wick, Carter *ConAu 31NR, TwCCr&M 91, WhoWrEP 89*
Wick, Chad P. 1942- *St&PR 91*
Wick, Chad Philip 1942- *WhoAm 90*
Wick, Charles Z. *BioIn 16*
Wick, Douglas 1917- *St&PR 91*
Wick, Gary Allen 1942- *WhoSSW 91*
Wick, Hilton A. 1920- *St&PR 91*
Wick, Hilton Addison 1920- *WhoAm 90, WhoE 91*
Wick, Jeffrey W. 1948- *St&PR 91*
Wick, John B. 1907-1990 *BioIn 16*
Wick, John G. 1924- *St&PR 91*
Wick, Margaret 1942- *WhoAm 90, WhoAmW 91*
Wick, Myron A. *BioIn 16*
Wick, Paul Henry 1936- *BiDrAPA 89*
Wick, Richard 1946- *St&PR 91*
Wick, Stuart Mary *TwCCr&M 91*
Wickard, Claude Raymond 1893-1967 *BiDrUSE 89*
Wickard, Donald Clayton *St&PR 91N*
Wickard, Frank Oscar 1937- *WhoAm 90*
Wicke, Peter 1951- *IntWWM 90*
Wickel, Harrison *Ballpl 90*
Wickelgren, Wayne Allen 1938- *WhoE 91*
Wickenden, Dan 1913-1989 *BioIn 16, CurBio 90N*
Wickenden, John Wynn 1940- *WhoE 91*
Wickenden, Leonard Daniel 1913?-1989 *ConAu 130*
Wickenheiser, Robert J. 1942- *WhoAm 90*
Wickens, Aryness Joy 1901- *WhoAm 90*
Wickens, Delos D. *BioIn 16*
Wickens, Donald Lee 1934- *St&PR 91*
Wickens, Robert G. 1944- *St&PR 91*
Wicker, Alan 1926- *IntWWM 90*
Wicker, Bob 1878-1955 *Ballpl 90*
Wicker, Danny 1946- *St&PR 91*
Wicker, David Jennings 1925- *WhoSSW 91*
Wicker, Elizabeth Ann 1946- *WhoAmW 91*
Wicker, Elizabeth Ann 1954- *WhoWrEP 89*
Wicker, Ireene *AuBYP 90*
Wicker, Ireene 1900-1987 *BioIn 16*
Wicker, Kristin Lee 1953- *WhoAmW 91*
Wicker, Lisa Harper 1965- *WhoSSW 91*
Wicker, Marie Peachee 1925- *WhoSSW 91*
Wicker, Nina A. 1927- *WhoWrEP 89*
Wicker, Thomas 1926- *WorAlBi*
Wicker, Thomas Grey 1926- *WhoAm 90, WhoE 91*
Wicker, Tom *BioIn 16*
Wicker, Vernon Estil 1937- *IntWWM 90*
Wicker, Veronica DiCarlo *WhoAm 90, WhoAmW 91, WhoSSW 91*
Wickers, Roger T. 1935- *St&PR 91*
Wickersham, Dave 1935- *Ballpl 90*
Wickersham, Ellen Hancock 1947- *WhoSSW 91*
Wickersham, Erskine Brewster, Jr. 1943- *WhoSSW 91*
Wickersham, George 1858-1936 *BiDrUSE 89*
Wickert, Erwin 1915- *ConAu 132*
Wickert, William E. 1931- *St&PR 91*
Wickes, Diana C. 1930- *WhoWrEP 89*
Wickes, George 1698-1761 *PenDiDA 89*
Wickes, George 1923- *WhoAm 90, WhoWrEP 89*
Wickes, Lambert 1735-1777 *EncCRAm*
Wickes, Mary *WhoAm 90*
Wickes, Michael *BioIn 16*
Wickes, Richard Paul 1948- *WhoEmL 91*
Wickes, Thomas Lee 1947- *WhoSSW 91*
Wickesberg, Albert Klumb 1921- *WhoAm 90*
Wickesberg, Alfred 1908- *St&PR 91*
Wickesberg, Margaret *St&PR 91*
Wickesberg, Paul *St&PR 91*
Wickett, Martha Damron *BiDrAPA 89*
Wickett, William Herbert 1919- *IntWWM 90*
Wickey, Beth Margaret 1951- *WhoAmW 91*
Wickey, Edward Lewis 1942- *WhoWor 91*
Wickfield, Eric Nelson 1953- *WhoE 91*
Wickham Family *BioIn 16*
Wickham, Anna 1884-1947 *BioIn 16, FemiCLE*
Wickham, Clennel Wilsden 1895-1938 *BioIn 16*
Wickham, John Adams, Jr. 1928- *WhoAm 90, WhoWor 91*
Wickham, John Ewart Alfred 1927- *WhoWor 91*
Wickham, Kenneth Gregory 1913- *WhoAm 90*
Wickham, Patricia Maria-Claire 1951- *WhoAmW 91*
Wickham, Robert B. 1957- *St&PR 91*
Wicki, Dieter 1931- *WhoWor 91*
Wickings, William George 1928- *St&PR 91*
Wickiser, Ralph Lewanda 1910- *WhoAm 90, WhoAmA 91*
Wickizer, Cindy Louise 1946- *WhoAmW 91*
Wickizer, Mary Alice 1938- *WhoAm 90*
Wickkiser, Carol Busck 1938- *WhoWor 91*
Wickland, Al 1888-1980 *Ballpl 90*
Wickland, Carey Bradford 1941- *St&PR 91*
Wickland, Carl August 1861- *EncO&P 3*
Wicklander, Edward A 1952- *WhoAmA 91*
Wicklander, Philip J. 1938- *St&PR 91*
Wicklein, John Frederick 1924- *WhoAm 90*
Wicklife, Jack D. 1939- *St&PR 91*
Wickliffe, Charles Anderson 1788-1869 *BiDrUSE 89*
Wicklow, Joseph F. 1941- *St&PR 91*
Wicklund, Millie Mae 1936- *WhoWrEP 89*
Wicklund, Renae *BioIn 16*
Wickman, Carl E. 1887-1954 *WorAlBi*
Wickman, John Edward 1929- *WhoAm 90*
Wickman, Paul Everett 1912- *WhoAm 90*
Wickman, Robert Warren 1941- *WhoSSW 91*
Wickramanayake, Kosala Rohana 1953- *WhoWor 91*
Wicks, E. N. 1856- *BioIn 16*
Wicks, Elizabeth T. 1944- *ODwPR 91*
Wicks, Eugene Claude 1931- *WhoAm 90, WhoAmA 91*
Wicks, John Cox 1935- *BiDrAPA 89*
Wicks, Marie Mavis 1952- *WhoAmW 91*
Wicks, Wesley D. 1936- *WhoAm 90*
Wicks, William W. 1923- *ODwPR 91*
Wicks, William Withington 1923- *St&PR 91, WhoAm 90*
Wicksell, Johan Gustaf Knut 1851-1926 *BioIn 16*
Wicksell, Knut 1851-1926 *BioIn 16*
Wickser, John Philip 1922- *WhoAm 90*
Wicksteed, Philip Henry 1844-1927 *BioIn 16*
Wicksten, Mary Katherine 1948- *WhoAmW 91*
Wickstrom, Karl Youngert 1935- *WhoAm 90*
Wickstrom, Lois June 1948- *WhoWrEP 89*
Wickstrom, Rob *BioIn 16*
Wickware, Frank 1888- *Ballpl 90*
Wickwire, Patricia Joanne Nellor *WhoAmW 91*
Wicoff, James S 1947- *BiDrAPA 89*
Widawsky, Gerald J. 1924- *WhoE 91*
Widdemer, Mabel 1902-1964 *AuBYP 90*
Widder, David Roland 1947- *IntWWM 90*
Widder, Kenneth Jon 1953- *St&PR 91, WhoAm 90*
Widder, Theodore Carl, Jr. 1921- *WhoAm 90*
Widder, Willard Graves 1924- *WhoAm 90*
Widdess, Richard 1951- *IntWWM 90*
Widdicombe, Gillian 1943- *IntWWM 90*
Widdicombe, Richard Palmer 1941- *WhoAm 90*
Widdis, Marie *BioIn 16*
Widdop, Walter 1892-1949 *PenDiMP*
Widdrington, P.N.T. 1930- *St&PR 91*
Widdrington, Peter Nigel Tinling 1930- *WhoAm 90, WhoWor 91*
Widell, Carl Olaf 1935- *WhoWor 91*
Wideman, Jacob *BioIn 16*
Wideman, John Edgar *BioIn 16*
Wideman, John Edgar 1941- *WhoAm 90, WorAu 1980 [port]*
Widen, Arthur Garland 1951- *St&PR 91*
Widener, Gary Wayne 1946- *WhoWor 91*
Widener, Herbert Lloyd 1941- *WhoSSW 91*
Widener, Hiram Emory, Jr. 1923- *WhoAm 90*
Widener, James C. 1943- *St&PR 91*
Widener, James Curtis 1943- *WhoAm 90*
Widener, Peri Ann 1956- *WhoAmW 91*
Widener, Susan Dale 1951- *St&PR 91*
Widenmann, Faye 1948- *St&PR 91*
Widenmyer, David R. 1921- *St&PR 91*
Widenor, Malcolm Douglas 1923- *St&PR 91*
Widera, G. E. O. 1938- *WhoAm 90*
Widera, Georg Ernst Otto 1938- *WhoWor 91*
Widerberg, Bo 1930- *BioIn 16*
Widerberg, Siv 1931- *AuBYP 90*
Wides, Norman A. 1918- *St&PR 91*
Widgery, Jeanne-Anna 1920- *WhoAmW 91, WhoWrEP 89*
Widgery, John Passmore 1911-1981 *DcNaB 1981*
Widgoff, Mildred 1924- *WhoAm 90*
Widgren, Richard Roy 1942- *St&PR 91*
Widhe, Sten Olle Muhammad Yussif 1943- *WhoWor 91*
Widick, Robert E. 1937- *St&PR 91*
Widing, Carol Scharfe 1941- *WhoAmW 91*
Widing, Warren S. 1922- *St&PR 91*
Widiss, Alan I. 1938- *WhoAm 90*
Widlund, Olof Bertil 1938- *WhoAm 90*
Widlus, Hannah Beverly 1955- *WhoAmW 91*
Widmaier, Christopher *ODwPR 91*
Widmaier, Hans Peter 1934- *WhoWor 91*
Widmaier, Henry Joseph 1945- *St&PR 91*
Widman, Gary Lee 1936- *WhoAm 90*
Widman, Judith 1942- *WhoAm 90*
Widman, Richard Gustave 1922- *WhoAm 90*
Widmann, Chester H. 1923- *St&PR 91*
Widmann, Chester Henry 1923- *WhoAm 90*
Widmann, David Nicholas 1949- *St&PR 91*
Widmann, Donald E 1935- *BiDrAPA 89*
Widmann, Klaus-Peter 1943- *WhoE 91*
Widmann, Nancy *BioIn 16*
Widmann, Nancy C. *WhoAmW 91*
Widmann, Richard Dale 1926- *St&PR 91*
Widmann, Roger M. 1939- *St&PR 91*
Widmann, Roger Maurice 1939- *WhoAm 90, WhoE 91*
Widmar, Al 1925- *Ballpl 90*
Widmar, Russell Charles 1946- *St&PR 91*
Widmark, Cliffor Brian 1959- *BiDrAPA 89*
Widmark, Richard 1914- *BioIn 16, WhoAm 90, WorAlBi*
Widmayer, Francis J. 1929- *St&PR 91*
Widmayer, Gustav G. 1958- *St&PR 91*
Widmayer, Patricia 1943- *WhoAmW 91*
Widmer, Gwen Ellen 1945- *WhoAmA 91*
Widmer, Hans Michael 1933- *WhoWor 91*
Widmer, James A. 1949- *WhoSSW 91*
Widmer, Kemble 1913- *WhoAm 90*
Widmer, Raymond Arthur 1923- *WhoAm 90*
Widmer, Robert H. 1916- *WhoAm 90*
Widmer, Robert J. 1940- *St&PR 91*
Widmer, Ruth Lynn 1955- *WhoAmW 91*
Widmoyer, Fred Bixler 1920- *WhoAm 90*
Widnall, Sheila Evans 1938- *WhoAm 90, WhoAmW 91, WhoE 91*
Widner, Ralph Randolph 1930- *WhoAm 90*
Widness, Sara 1940- *ODwPR 91*
Widom, Benjamin 1927- *WhoAm 90*
Widor, Charles-Marie 1844-1937 *PenDiMP*
Widrig, Richard F. 1952- *St&PR 91*
Widroe, Harvey J *BiDrAPA 89*
Widrow, Bernard 1929- *WhoAm 90*
Widstrom, Edward Frederick 1903- *WhoAmA 91*
Widulski, Laura Jean 1961- *WhoAmW 91, WhoEmL 91*
Widup, Kim Richard 1957- *WhoSSW 91*
Widzer, Helen Magun 1950- *WhoAmW 91*
Widzer, Martin Ellis 1940- *BiDrAPA 89*
Wiebe, Charles M 1949- *WhoAmA 91*
Wiebe, Dallas Eugene 1930- *WhoWrEP 89*
Wiebe, Gerhard 1827-1900 *DcCanB 12*
Wiebe, Katie Funk *BioIn 16*
Wiebe, Katie Funk 1924- *ConAu 132*
Wiebe, Leonard Irving 1941- *WhoAm 90*
Wiebe, Rudy Henry 1934- *BioIn 16*
Wiebenga, William Martin 1938- *WhoAm 90*
Wiebenson, Dora Louise 1926- *WhoAm 90*
Wiebers, Herman Augustus 1925- *St&PR 91*
Wiebusch, Janice Marie 1946- *WhoAmW 91*
Wiebush, Joseph Roy 1920- *WhoAm 90*
Wiecek, William Michael 1938- *WhoAm 90*
Wiecha, Joseph Augustine 1926- *WhoAm 90, WhoWor 91*
Wiechert, Ernst Emil 1887-1950 *BioIn 16*
Wiechmann, Gordon Stuart 1920- *St&PR 91*
Wieck, Clara *PenDiMP*
Wieckert, Walter Bernard 1934- *St&PR 91*
Wiecki, Richard 1958- *WhoWor 91*
Wieczynski, Frank R. 1939- *St&PR 91*
Wieczynski, Frank Robert 1939- *WhoAm 90*
Wied, George Ludwig 1921- *WhoWor 91*
Wied, Gustav 1858-1914 *DcScanL*
Wied, Martina *EncCoWW*
Wiedefeld, Marcia Fenchak 1964- *WhoE 91*
Wiedel, William Conrad, Jr. 1959- *St&PR 91*
Wiedeman, Geoffrey Paul 1917- *WhoAm 90*
Wiedeman, George H 1912- *BiDrAPA 89*
Wiedeman, George Henkins 1912- *WhoAm 90*
Wiedeman, John Herman 1935- *WhoAm 90*
Wiedeman, Richard Lawrence 1945- *WhoE 91*
Wiedemann, Anita Melissa 1960- *WhoAmW 91*
Wiedemann, Anne *BioIn 16*
Wiedemann, Charles Louis 1936- *WhoE 91, WhoWor 91*
Wiedemann, Frederic Franklin 1923- *St&PR 91*
Wiedemann, George Stanhope 1944- *WhoAm 90*

Wiedemann, Joseph Robert 1928- *St&PR 91*
Wieden, Dan *BioIn 16, NewYTBS 90 [port]*
Wieden, Marion Anna 1937- *WhoAmW 91*
Wiedenbeck, Mary Ellen 1961- *ODwPR 91*
Wiedenhoeft, Renate 1942- *WhoAmA 91*
Wiedenmann, Eric William 1951- *St&PR 91*
Wiedenmann, Paul W. 1937- *St&PR 91*
Wiedenmayer, Christopher M. 1941- *St&PR 91, WhoAm 90*
Wiedenmayer, Gustave E. 1908- *St&PR 91*
Wieder, Bernard R. *NewYTBS 90*
Wieder, Bonnie Schulman 1957- *WhoE 91*
Wieder, Douglas M. 1952- *St&PR 91*
Wieder, Herbert 1921- *BiDrAPA 89*
Wieder, Laurance 1946- *WhoWrEP 89*
Wieder, Michael D. *St&PR 91*
Wieder, Stephen J 1948- *BiDrAPA 89*
Wieder, Thomas Herbert 1948- *St&PR 91*
Wiederhold, Paul B. 1943- *St&PR 91*
Wiederhold, Pieter R. 1928- *St&PR 91*
Wiederhold, Pieter Rijk 1928- *WhoE 91*
Wiederhold, Richard Edgar 1949- *WhoSSW 91*
Wiederkehr, Alvin M. 1923- *St&PR 91*
Wiederlight, Melvin *BiDrAPA 89*
Wiedershine, Leonard Jack 1921- *BiDrAPA 89*
Wiederspahn, Alvin Lee 1949- *WhoEmL 91*
Wiedl, MaryAnn 1945- *WhoAmW 91, WhoE 91*
Wiedl, Sheila Colleen 1950- *WhoAmW 91*
Wiedlin, Jane *BioIn 16*
Wiedlin, Paul E. 1945- *St&PR 91*
Wiedman, Wayne Rentchler 1928- *WhoAm 90*
Wiedorn, William S *BiDrAPA 89*
Wiedrich, Joyce Lorraine 1952- *WhoAmW 91*
Wiegand, Bruce 1947- *St&PR 91, WhoAm 90*
Wiegand, C. Monroe 1912- *WhoAm 90*
Wiegand, Charmion von 1899-1983 *BiDWomA*
Wiegand, Craig Loren 1933- *WhoSSW 91*
Wiegand, Frank L., Jr. 1912- *St&PR 91*
Wiegand, Phillips 1939- *St&PR 91*
Wiegand, Robert 1934- *WhoAmA 91*
Wiegand, Robert, II 1947- *WhoEmL 91*
Wiegand, Sylvia Margaret 1949- *WhoAmW 91*
Wiegand, Viola Lucille 1920- *BiDrAPA 89*
Wiegand, Warren 1945- *St&PR 91*
Wiegandt, Herbert Frederick 1917- *WhoAm 90*
Wiegel, Robert Louis 1922- *WhoAm 90*
Wiegenstein, John Gerald 1930- *WhoAm 90*
Wiegers, Eric C. 1957- *ODwPR 91*
Wiegers, George A. 1936- *St&PR 91*
Wiegers, George Anthony 1936- *WhoAm 90*
Wiegersma, Nan A. 1942- *WhoE 91*
Wiegersma, Sjoerd 1940- *WhoWor 91*
Wiegert, Rene 1930-1989 *BioIn 16*
Wieghardt, Karl Eugen Gottfried 1913- *WhoWor 91*
Wieghardt, Paul 1897-1969 *WhoAmA 91N*
Wieghart, James Gerard 1933- *WhoAm 90*
Wieghorst, Olaf 1899-1988 *BioIn 16*
Wiegman, Eugene William 1929- *WhoAm 90*
Wiegmann, Jenny 1895-1969 *BiDWomA*
Wiegmann, Roger Henry 1934- *WhoAm 90*
Wiegner, Allen Walter 1947- *WhoAm 90*
Wiegner, Edward Alex 1939- *WhoAm 90*
Wiegner, Elizabeth Ann 1949- *WhoAmW 91*
Wiegold, Peter John 1949- *IntWWM 90*
Wiekamp, Darwin L. 1914- *St&PR 91*
Wiekrykas, Daniel Edward 1960- *St&PR 91*
Wiel, Carol Lee 1943- *WhoAmW 91*
Wieland, Bob *BioIn 16*
Wieland, Christoph Martin 1733-1813 *DcLB 97 [port]*
Wieland, Clark D 1932- *BiDrAPA 89*
Wieland, Eloina S *BiDrAPA 89*
Wieland, Ferdinand 1943- *WhoAm 90, WhoWor 91*
Wieland, Gerhard *EncCoWW*
Wieland, Heinrich Frank 1947- *WhoWor 91*
Wieland, Heinrich Otto 1877-1957 *WorAlBi*
Wieland, Henry, Jr. *ODwPR 91*
Wieland, John 1936- *St&PR 91*
Wieland, Joyce 1931- *WhoAmA 91*
Wieland, Robert Richard 1937- *St&PR 91, WhoAm 90*
Wieland, Timothy E. 1953- *St&PR 91*
Wieland, Walter P. 1932- *St&PR 91*
Wieland, William Dean 1948- *WhoEmL 91, WhoSSW 91, WhoWor 91*
Wieland, William F 1934- *BiDrAPA 89*
Wieland, Wolfgang 1933- *WhoWor 91*
Wielech, Dennis David 1936- *WhoWor 91*
Wielepski, Eugene Carl 1946- *St&PR 91*
Wieler, Alvin L. 1946- *St&PR 91*
Wieler, Craig Samson 1925- *WhoWor 91*
Wielgus, Charles Joseph 1923- *WhoAm 90*
Wieloch, Tadeusz Wojciech *WhoWor 91*
Wieman, Robert John 1947- *WhoE 91*
Wiemann, George Frederick 1921- *St&PR 91*
Wiemann, John Moritz 1947- *WhoEmL 91*
Wiemann, Marion Russell, Jr. 1929- *WhoWor 91*
Wiemer, Robert Anthony 1931- *WhoE 91*
Wiemer, Robert Ernest 1938- *WhoAm 90, WhoWor 91*
Wiemer-Sumner, Anne-Marie 1938- *WhoAmW 91*
Wiemers, Eugene Lee *BiDrAPA 89*
Wiemers, Kurt 1920- *WhoWor 91*
Wien, Lawrence A. 1905-1988 *BioIn 16*
Wien, Richard William 1945- *WhoE 91*
Wien, Stuart Lewis 1923- *WhoAm 90*
Wien, Wilhelm 1864-1928 *WorAlBi*
Wienand, Marilyn M. 1942- *IntWWM 90*
Wienandt, Elwyn Arthur 1917- *WhoAm 90*
Wiencrot, Noni Lipson 1948- *BiDrAPA 89*
Wienecke, Robert Miller *BiDrAPA 89*
Wienecke, Rudolph Albert 1925- *WhoWor 91*
Wiener, Alfred 1927- *BiDrAPA 89*
Wiener, Annabelle 1922- *WhoAmW 91, WhoWor 91*
Wiener, Arthur Charles 1937- *St&PR 91*
Wiener, Daniel Eli 1959- *St&PR 91*
Wiener, Elizabeth Margaret 1948- *WhoAmW 91*
Wiener, Elliott Maxwell 1935- *St&PR 91*
Wiener, Ferdinand Joseph 1904- *WhoWrEP 89*
Wiener, Gabriele Kathryn 1938- *WhoAmW 91*
Wiener, George *WhoAmA 91N*
Wiener, Harry 1924- *WhoE 91, WhoWor 91*
Wiener, Herman *BioIn 16*
Wiener, Hesh 1946- *WhoAm 90, WhoWor 91*
Wiener, Isidor 1886-1970 *MusmAFA*
Wiener, Jack J *BiDrAPA 89*
Wiener, Jack Ralph 1958- *WhoE 91*
Wiener, James S 1930- *BiDrAPA 89*
Wiener, Jerry M 1933- *BiDrAPA 89*
Wiener, Joel H 1937- *ConAu 31NR*
Wiener, Joseph 1927- *WhoAm 90*
Wiener, Jude 1953- *St&PR 91*
Wiener, Karen Elaine 1949- *BiDrAPA 89*
Wiener, Louis 1925- *St&PR 91*
Wiener, Malcolm Hewitt 1935- *WhoAm 90*
Wiener, Martin Joel 1941- *WhoAm 90*
Wiener, Marvin S. 1925- *BioIn 16, WhoAm 90, WhoWrEP 89*
Wiener, Maurice 1942- *St&PR 91*
Wiener, Max 1918- *WhoE 91*
Wiener, Michele L *BiDrAPA 89*
Wiener, Norbert 1894-1964 *WorAlBi*
Wiener, Norma 1931- *St&PR 91*
Wiener, Otto 1911- *PenDiMP*
Wiener, Otto 1913- *IntWWM 90*
Wiener, Phyllis Ames 1921- *WhoAmA 91*
Wiener, Rene 1856-1939 *PenDiDA 89*
Wiener, Robert Alvin 1918- *WhoAm 90*
Wiener, Robert S. 1938- *ODwPR 91*
Wiener, Robin Kim 1963- *WhoAmW 91*
Wiener, Sam *ConAu 132*
Wiener, Sam 1928- *WhoAmA 91*
Wiener, Solomon 1915- *WhoE 91, WhoWor 91*
Wiener, Stanley Lewis 1930- *WhoAm 90*
Wiener, Stanley M 1927- *BiDrAPA 89*
Wiener, Stephen R 1947- *BiDrAPA 89*
Wiener, Theodore A. 1932- *St&PR 91*
Wiener, Thomas Eli 1940- *WhoAm 90*
Wiener, Valerie 1948- *WhoAmW 91, WhoEmL 91, WhoWor 91*
Wieners, John 1934- *WorAu 1980 [port]*
Wieniawski, Henryk 1835-1880 *PenDiMP*
Wieniawski, Jozef *PenDiMP*
Wienold, Gotz 1938- *WhoWor 91*
Wiens, Arthur Nicholai 1926- *WhoAm 90*
Wiens, Deborah 1956- *WhoAmW 91*
Wiens, Gloria Jean 1958- *WhoAmW 91*
Wienshienk, Ralph 1919- *WhoAm 90*
Wier, Allen 1946- *WhoWrEP 89*
Wier, Dara 1949- *WhoWrEP 89*
Wier, Ester 1910- *AuBYP 90*
Wier, James A. *St&PR 91*
Wier, John Rex, III 1949- *BiDrAPA 89*
Wier, Leighton Arthur 1943- *WhoSSW 91*
Wier, Patricia Ann 1937- *WhoAm 90, WhoAmW 91*
Wier, Patricia N. 1937- *St&PR 91*
Wier, Richard Royal, Jr. 1941- *WhoAm 90*
Wier, Robert Charles 1928- *St&PR 91*
Wierchowicz, Zofia 1924-1978 *ConDes 90*
Wieringa, Robert T. 1924-1988 *BioIn 16*
Wierling, Albert Reginald 1937- *WhoSSW 91*
Wierman, John Charles 1949- *WhoAm 90*
Wiernik, Peter Harris 1939- *WhoAm 90, WhoE 91*
Wiernik, Stan 1947- *St&PR 91*
Wiersbe, Warren Wendell 1929- *WhoAm 90*
Wiersma, Peggy Ann 1956- *WhoAmW 91*
Wiersum, Charles Chester 1940- *St&PR 91*
Wierum, Thornton Briggs 1925- *St&PR 91*
Wierwille, Ann Southard *BiDrAPA 89*
Wiesbeck, Werner 1942- *WhoWor 91*
Wieschenberg, Klaus 1932- *St&PR 91, WhoWor 91*
Wiese, Bruno K 1922- *ConDes 90*
Wiese, Dorothy Jean 1940- *WhoAmW 91*
Wiese, James Douglas 1939- *St&PR 91*
Wiese, John Paul 1934- *WhoAm 90*
Wiese, Kevin Glen 1960- *WhoEmL 91, WhoWor 91*
Wiese, Kurt 1887-1974 *AuBYP 90*
Wiese, Michael 1947- *WhoWrEP 89*
Wiese, Terry Eugene 1948- *WhoSSW 91, WhoWor 91*
Wiese, Wolfgang Lothar 1931- *WhoE 91*
Wiesehahn, Willem 1914- *IntWWM 90*
Wiesel, Benjamin 1911- *BiDrAPA 89*
Wiesel, Carl *BiDrAPA 89*
Wiesel, Elie 1928- *BioIn 16, MajTwCW, WhoAm 90, WhoE 91, WhoWor 91, WhoWrEP 89, WorAlBi*
Wiesel, Torsten N. 1924- *WorAlBi*
Wiesel, Torsten Nils 1924- *WhoAm 90, WhoE 91, WhoWor 91*
Wiesel, Uzi *PenDiMP*
Wieseltier, Leon 1952- *WhoWrEP 89*
Wieseman, Mary Folliard 1942- *WhoAmW 91*
Wiesen, Anne Rhoda 1926- *WhoAmW 91*
Wiesen, Donald Guy 1928- *WhoAm 90*
Wiesen, Trude *WhoAmA 91*
Wiesenberg, Jacqueline Leonardi 1928- *WhoAmW 91, WhoE 91, WhoWor 91*
Wiesenberg, Russel John 1924- *WhoE 91*
Wiesendanger, Martin Wolfgang 1908- *WhoAmA 91*
Wiesenfeld, Bess Gazevitz 1915- *WhoAmW 91*
Wiesenfeld, Joe 1947- *ConAu 131*
Wiesenfeld, John Richard 1944- *WhoAm 90*
Wiesenfeld, Paul 1942-1990 *WhoAmA 91N*
Wiesenthal, Marc A. 1959- *St&PR 91*
Wiesenthal, Richard Stanley 1929- *St&PR 91*
Wiesenthal, Simon *BioIn 16*
Wiesenthal, Simon 1908- *WhoWor 91*
Wieser, Charles Edward 1929- *St&PR 91, WhoAm 90*
Wieser, Friedrich von 1851-1926 *BioIn 16*
Wieser, Joan Elizabeth 1948- *WhoAmW 91*
Wiesert, Kenneth Niel 1950- *BiDrAPA 89*
Wiesinger, Alois 1885-1955 *EncO&P 3*
Wiesinger, Gwendolyn English 1956- *WhoWor 91*
Wiesinger, Heinz 1940- *WhoWor 91*
Wiesler, James Ballard 1927- *WhoAm 90*
Wiesler-Wuytack, Evelyn Lydia 1959- *WhoAmW 91*
Wiesman, Janice Faye 1958- *BiDrAPA 89*
Wiesner, Dallas Charles 1959- *WhoEmL 91, WhoWor 91*
Wiesner, David *AuBYP 90*
Wiesner, Don Robert *BiDrAPA 89*
Wiesner, Douglas Warren 1940- *St&PR 91*
Wiesner, Irving S 1940- *BiDrAPA 89*
Wiesner, Jerome Bert 1915- *WhoAm 90, WhoE 91, WhoWor 91*
Wiesner, Joan Ruth 1950- *WhoAmW 91*
Wiesner, John J. 1938- *St&PR 91*
Wiesner, John Joseph 1938- *WhoAm 90, WhoSSW 91*
Wiesner, Sharon Marie 1938- *WhoAmW 91, WhoWor 91*
Wiess, Bernard 1903-1989 *BioIn 16*
Wiess, G. Parry 1922- *St&PR 91*
Wiessler, David Albert 1942- *WhoAm 90*
Wiessner, Fritz *BioIn 16*
Wiest, Diane 1948- *WorAlBi*
Wiest, Dianne 1948- *WhoAm 90, WhoAmW 91*
Wiest, Roger Vaughn 1940- *St&PR 91*
Wiester, Linda Marie 1946- *WhoAmW 91*
Wietelmann, Whitey 1919- *Ballpl 90*
Wiethe, John A. 1912-1989 *BioIn 16*
Wietholter, William James, Jr. 1942- *St&PR 91*
Wieting, William Frank 1938- *WhoE 91*
Wietor, Michael George 1937- *WhoSSW 91*
Wietsma, Leigh 1962- *ODwPR 91*
Wiewel, Betty C. *WhoAmW 91*
Wiewel, Roger North 1927- *WhoAm 90*
Wig, Narendra N 1930- *BiDrAPA 89*
Wigan, Marcus Ramsay 1941- *WhoWor 91*
Wigand, Patricia Ann 1953- *WhoAmW 91*
Wigdahl, Lowell Carl *BiDrAPA 89*
Wigdale, James B. *WhoAm 90*
Wigdor, Lawrence A. 1941- *WhoAm 90*
Wigert, Walter S 1936- *BiDrAPA 89*
Wigg, Cindy Lou *BiDrAPA 89*
Wigg, George Edward Cecil 1900-1983 *DcNaB 1981*
Wigger, Diane Bisciotti 1951- *WhoSSW 91*
Wigger, G. Eugene 1944- *WhoSSW 91*
Wiggers, Charlotte Suzanne Ward 1943- *WhoAmW 91*
Wiggers, Harold Carl 1910- *WhoAm 90*
Wiggert, Barbara Norene 1938- *WhoAmW 91*
Wiggin, Blanton C. 1922- *St&PR 91*
Wiggin, Kate Douglas 1856-1923 *AuBYP 90, BioAmW, FemiCLE, WorAlBi*
Wiggin, William F. 1928- *St&PR 91*
Wiggins, Alan 1958- *Ballpl 90*
Wiggins, Albert H. 1938- *St&PR 91*
Wiggins, Allie Dell 1942- *WhoSSW 91*
Wiggins, Amelda Lees 1942- *WhoSSW 91*
Wiggins, Barbara *BioIn 16*
Wiggins, Bernice Love 1897- *HarlReB*
Wiggins, Bill 1917- *WhoAmA 91*
Wiggins, Bruce Gilbert 1949- *WhoSSW 91*
Wiggins, Charles 1938- *WhoE 91*
Wiggins, Charles Edward 1927- *WhoAm 90*
Wiggins, Charles Henry, Jr. 1939- *WhoAm 90*
Wiggins, Christopher David 1956- *IntWWM 90*
Wiggins, Constance Crabtree 1951- *WhoSSW 91*
Wiggins, Daniel Braxton, Jr. 1952- *WhoSSW 91*
Wiggins, Edmond Foster 1938- *WhoE 91*
Wiggins, Frances Knotts 1926- *WhoAmW 91*
Wiggins, Guy A 1920- *WhoAmA 91*
Wiggins, Guy C 1883-1962 *WhoAmA 91N*
Wiggins, Ida Silver *WhoAmW 91*
Wiggins, James Bryan 1935- *WhoAm 90, WhoE 91*
Wiggins, James Russell *BioIn 16*
Wiggins, James Russell 1903- *WhoAm 90, WhoE 91*
Wiggins, James Walter 1949- *WhoSSW 91*
Wiggins, Jerome Meyer 1940- *WhoAm 90*
Wiggins, K Douglas 1959- *WhoAmA 91*
Wiggins, Kathy *ODwPR 91*
Wiggins, Kenneth Marvin 1931- *BiDrAPA 89*
Wiggins, Marianne *BioIn 16*
Wiggins, Marianne 1947- *ConAu 130*
Wiggins, Michael C. 1948- *St&PR 91*
Wiggins, Myra Albert 1869-1956 *WhoAmA 91N*
Wiggins, Nancy Bowen 1948- *WhoAmW 91*
Wiggins, Norman Adrian 1924- *WhoAm 90*
Wiggins, Penny Kay 1948- *WhoAmW 91*
Wiggins, Samuel Paul 1919- *WhoAm 90*
Wiggins, Timothy J. 1956- *St&PR 91*
Wiggins, Walter James 1925- *St&PR 91*
Wiggins, Walton Wray 1924- *WhoAmA 91, WhoWor 91*
Wiggins, Wanda 1945- *WhoAmW 91*
Wiggins, William Bramwell 1921- *IntWWM 90*
Wigginton, Eugene H. 1935- *St&PR 91, WhoAm 90*
Wigginton, Madison Smartt 1901- *St&PR 91*
Wigginton, Ron *BioIn 16*
Wigglesworth, Edward 1693?-1765 *EncCRAm*
Wigglesworth, Edward 1732-1794 *EncCRAm*
Wigglesworth, Michael 1631-1705 *EncCRAm, WorAlBi*
Wiggs, David Harold, Jr. 1947- *WhoSSW 91*
Wiggs, Eugene Overbey 1928- *WhoAm 90*
Wiggs, Robert Howard 1947- *WhoSSW 91*
Wiggs, Shirley JoAnn 1940- *WhoSSW 91*
Wight, Bennett Allen, Jr. 1933- *BiDrAPA 89*
Wight, Bill 1922- *Ballpl 90*
Wight, Darlene 1926- *WhoAmW 91, WhoWor 91*
Wight, Doris Teresa 1929- *WhoWrEP 89*
Wight, Frederick S 1902-1986 *WhoAmA 91N*
Wight, James Alfred *AuBYP 90, BioIn 16*
Wight, James Alfred 1916- *WhoWor 91*
Wight, Sarah 1632?- *BiDEWW, FemiCLE*
Wight, Terry Eugene 1953- *WhoE 91*
Wight, Virginia Joy *BiDrAPA 89*
Wightman, Arthur Strong 1922- *WhoAm 90*
Wightman, Brian Robin 1942- *IntWWM 90*

Wightman, Ludmilla Popova 1933- *WhoE 91*
Wightman, Nancy Matthews 1941- *WhoWor 91*
Wightman, Patricia Anne *BiDrAPA 89*
Wigington, Jo Ann Rankin 1933- *WhoSSW 91*
Wigington, Leticia *BiDEWW*
Wigington, Ronald Lee 1932- *WhoAm 90*
Wiginton, Jay Spencer 1941- *WhoSSW 91, WhoWor 91*
Wiginton, Morris S., III 1950- *WhoEmL 91*
Wigler, Michael 1948- *WhoAm 90*
Wigler, Paul William 1928- *WhoSSW 91*
Wiglesworth, Michael Bland 1949- *WhoEmL 91, WhoWor 91*
Wigley, David Albert 1937- *IntWWM 90*
Wigley, Michael Robert 1954- *St&PR 91*
Wigman, James Francis 1935- *St&PR 91*
Wigmore, Ann 1909- *NewAgE 90*
Wigmore, Barrie Atherton 1941- *WhoAm 90*
Wigmore, Winifred *BiDEWW*
Wignall, Ernest Carl 1927- *St&PR 91*
Wignall, Jeffrey Frederic 1953- *WhoE 91*
Wigner, Eugene P. 1902- *WorAlBi*
Wigner, Eugene Paul 1902- *WhoAm 90, WhoE 91, WhoWor 91*
Wignesan, T. 1933- *WhoWor 91*
Wigny, Damien 1942- *WhoWor 91*
Wigodsky, Herman Saul 1915- *St&PR 91*
Wigren, Barbara Louise 1932- *WhoAmW 91*
Wigsten, Paul Bradley, Jr. 1947- *WhoE 91*
Wigton, George Lindbergh 1929- *WhoE 91*
Wigton, Paul N. 1932- *St&PR 91*
Wigton, Paul Norton 1932- *WhoAm 90*
Wigton, Robert Spencer *BiDrAPA 89*
Wigutow, Marcus 1933- *BiDrAPA 89*
Wihan, Hanus 1855-1920 *PenDiMP*
Wihlborg, Hans Ferdinand 1916- *IntWWM 90*
Wiig, Elisabeth Hemmersam 1935- *WhoAm 90, WhoAmW 91*
Wiik, Maria Katarina 1853-1928 *BiDWomA*
Wiin-Nielsen, Aksel Christopher 1924- *WhoAm 90*
Wiitala, Geri Colozzi *BioIn 16*
Wiitasalo, Shirley 1949- *WhoAmA 91*
Wijasuriya, Donald Earlian Kingsley 1934- *WhoWor 91*
Wijaya, Andi 1936- *WhoWor 91*
Wijaya, Don Henry *BiDrAPA 89*
Wijdeveld, Hendrikus Theodorus 1885-1987 *BioIn 16*
Wijenaike, Punyakante 1933- *FemiCLE*
Wijeratne, Ranjan 1931- *WhoWor 91*
Wijetunge, Dimbiri Banda 1922- *WhoWor 91*
Wijnen, Adeline Frances 1933- *WhoAmW 91*
Wijnholds, Johannes de Beaufort 1943- *WhoWor 91*
Wijnstroom, Margreet *BioIn 16*
Wikander, Lawrence Einar 1915- *WhoAm 90*
Wikant, Duane Edwin 1931- *St&PR 91*
Wike, Andrew 1952- *WhoSSW 91*
Wike, Connie Gathright 1938- *WhoSSW 91*
Wike, D. Elaine 1954- *WhoAmW 91, WhoEmL 91, WhoSSW 91*
Wike, DeJuana Deniece 1960- *WhoAmW 91*
Wike, James E. 1928- *St&PR 91*
Wiker, Nancy Eileen 1949- *WhoAmW 91*
Wikerd, Paul Hubert 1947- *WhoE 91*
Wiklund, K. Lars C. 1943- *WhoWor 91*
Wiklund, Lennart Stig 1950- *WhoWor 91*
Wikman, Andrew O. 1927- *St&PR 91*
Wikman, Georg Karl 1943- *WhoWor 91*
Wikner, Stephen Charles Nevill 1948- *WhoWor 91*
Wiksten, B. F. *ODwPR 91*
Wiksten, B.F. 1935- *St&PR 91*
Wiksten, Barry Frank 1935- *WhoAm 90*
Wikstrom, Gunnar, Jr. 1936- *WhoAm 90*
Wikstrom, Ingrid 1945- *WhoWor 91*
Wikstrom, Lars Erik 1931- *WhoWor 91*
Wikstrom, Loretta Wermerskirchen 1938- *WhoAmW 91*
Wikstrom, Thomas R 1952- *BiDrAPA 89*
Wiktorowicz, Andrew Charles 1945- *WhoEmL 91, WhoWor 91*
Wilander, Mats *BioIn 16*
Wilander, Sonya *BioIn 16*
Wilansky, Donald C 1924- *BiDrAPA 89*
Wilbanks, Darrel Jay 1944- *WhoSSW 91*
Wilbanks, Jan Joseph 1928- *WhoAm 90*
Wilbanks, Karen Courtney Kincannon 1945- *WhoSSW 91*
Wilbanks, Robert Smith 1947- *St&PR 91*
Wilber, Bob *BioIn 16*
Wilber, Bob 1928- *OxCPMus*
Wilber, Charles Grady 1916- *WhoAm 90*
Wilber, Clyde *WhoAm 90*
Wilber, Del 1919- *Ballpl 90*
Wilber, Donald Newton 1907- *AuBYP 90*
Wilber, Gary 1950- *WhoAm 90*
Wilber, Ken *EncO&P 3*
Wilber, Ken 1949- *NewAgE 90*
Wilber, Laura Ann 1934- *WhoAm 90, WhoWor 91*
Wilber, Philip Irving 1927- *St&PR 91, WhoAm 90*
Wilber, Robert E. 1932- *St&PR 91*
Wilber, Robert Edwin 1932- *WhoAm 90*
Wilber, Thomas Craig 1963- *WhoEmL 91*
Wilberforce, Samuel 1805-1873 *BioIn 16*
Wilberforce, William 1759-1833 *BioIn 16*
Wilbert, Donald Eugene 1942- *BiDrAPA 89*
Wilbert, Felicia Libo 1959- *WhoWrEP 89*
Wilbert, Marlin T. 1930- *St&PR 91*
Wilbert, Robert John 1929- *WhoAmA 91*
Wilborn, Richard E. 1945- *St&PR 91*
Wilbourn, Gordon Gene 1933- *St&PR 91*
Wilbourn, Jerry Sanford 1939- *WhoAm 90*
Wilbourne, Preston Holt 1925- *St&PR 91*
Wilbrecht, Jon Keehn 1942- *St&PR 91*
Wilbur, Bernard Freeborn, Jr. 1926- *St&PR 91*
Wilbur, Brayton, Jr. 1935- *WhoAm 90*
Wilbur, Cornelia B *BiDrAPA 89*
Wilbur, Curtis Dwight 1867-1954 *BiDrUSE 89*
Wilbur, D. Elliott, Jr. 1929- *St&PR 91*
Wilbur, David E. 1942- *St&PR 91*
Wilbur, E. Packer 1936- *WhoAm 90, WhoWor 91*
Wilbur, George Marvin 1951- *WhoE 91*
Wilbur, Georgia Delores 1926- *WhoAmW 91*
Wilbur, James Benjamin, III 1924- *WhoAm 90*
Wilbur, John Hearring 1929- *St&PR 91*
Wilbur, Karl Milton 1912- *WhoAm 90*
Wilbur, Lawrence Nelson 1897-1988 *BioIn 16, WhoAmA 91N*
Wilbur, Lee S. 1943- *WhoE 91*
Wilbur, Leslie Clifford 1924- *WhoAm 90*
Wilbur, Lyman Dwight 1900- *WhoAm 90*
Wilbur, Melissa Ellen 1944- *WhoE 91*
Wilbur, Michael F. 1945- *St&PR 91*
Wilbur, Patricia Lynn 1962- *WhoAmW 91*
Wilbur, Ralph Edwin 1932- *St&PR 91, WhoAm 90*
Wilbur, Ray Lyman 1875-1949 *BiDrUSE 89*
Wilbur, Richard 1921- *MajTwCW, WorAlBi*
Wilbur, Richard P. 1921- *AuBYP 90*
Wilbur, Richard Purdy 1921- *WhoAm 90, WhoWrEP 89*
Wilbur, Richard Sloan 1924- *WhoAm 90*
Wilbur, W. Allan 1937- *ODwPR 91*
Wilbur, William B. 1950- *St&PR 91*
Wilburn, Adolph Yarbrough 1932- *WhoE 91*
Wilburn, Barry *BioIn 16*
Wilburn, Leila Ross 1885-1967 *BioIn 16*
Wilburn, Mary Nelson 1932- *WhoAmW 91, WhoE 91, WhoWor 91*
Wilburn, Tyree Gary 1952- *WhoAm 90*
Wilby, James 1958- *ConTFT 8*
Wilchek, Meir 1935- *WhoWor 91*
Wilcher, Alfred P. 1941- *St&PR 91*
Wilcher, LaJuana Sue 1954- *WhoEmL 91*
Wilcher, Larry Keith 1950- *WhoAm 90*
Wilcher, Shirley J. 1951- *WhoAmW 91, WhoE 91*
Wilchins, Howard Martin 1945- *WhoE 91*
Wilcock, Bill Wayne 1943- *St&PR 91*
Wilcock, Donald Frederick 1913- *WhoAm 90*
Wilcock, James W. 1917- *St&PR 91*
Wilcock, James William 1917- *WhoAm 90, WhoE 91*
Wilcock, John *WhoWrEP 89*
Wilcocks, David 1919- *IntWWM 90*
Wilcockson, Craig J. 1935- *St&PR 91*
Wilcott, Scott J. 1938- *St&PR 91*
Wilcox, Adelaide 1960- *WhoSSW 91*
Wilcox, Arthur Manigault 1922- *WhoAm 90*
Wilcox, Barbara Montgomery 1939- *WhoSSW 91*
Wilcox, Bruce Gordon 1947- *WhoAm 90*
Wilcox, Calvin Hayden 1924- *WhoAm 90*
Wilcox, Charles William 1947- *WhoSSW 91*
Wilcox, Cheryl Ann 1948- *WhoEmL 91*
Wilcox, Colleen Bridget 1949- *WhoAmW 91*
Wilcox, Collin 1924- *ConAu 31NR, TwCCr&M 91*
Wilcox, Collin M. 1924- *WhoAm 90, WhoWrEP 89*
Wilcox, David Albertson 1938- *St&PR 91*
Wilcox, David Eric 1939- *WhoE 91*
Wilcox, David Wayne 1949- *WhoSSW 91*
Wilcox, Debra Kay 1955- *WhoEmL 91*
Wilcox, Delbert Estus 1922- *BiDrAPA 89*
Wilcox, Don *AuBYP 90*
Wilcox, Dora 1873-1953 *FemiCLE*
Wilcox, Earl V. *WhoHisp 91*
Wilcox, Ella 1850-1919 *FemiCLE*
Wilcox, Ella Wheeler 1850-1919 *BioAmW*
Wilcox, Fred A 1940- *ConAu 129*
Wilcox, Gail Patricia Waters 1957- *WhoAmW 91*
Wilcox, Gary Burl 1951- *WhoSSW 91*
Wilcox, Gordon Cumnock 1924- *WhoE 91*
Wilcox, Gordon Cumnock 1934- *WhoAmA 91*
Wilcox, Gregory G. 1949- *St&PR 91*
Wilcox, Harry Hammond 1918- *WhoAm 90*
Wilcox, Harry Roger 1936- *St&PR 91*
Wilcox, Harry Wilbur, Jr. 1925- *St&PR 91, WhoAm 90*
Wilcox, Harvey John 1937- *WhoAm 90*
Wilcox, Helen Elizabeth 1955- *WhoWor 91*
Wilcox, Jackson Burton 1918- *WhoWrEP 89*
Wilcox, James 1949- *ConAu 129, WorAu 1980 [port]*
Wilcox, James Allen *BiDrAPA 89*
Wilcox, James Kermit, III 1954- *WhoE 91, WhoWor 91*
Wilcox, James R. 1942- *St&PR 91*
Wilcox, James S. 1946- *St&PR 91, WhoAm 90*
Wilcox, Janice Horde 1940- *WhoE 91*
Wilcox, Jean Marie 1958- *WhoAmW 91*
Wilcox, Jeanne Burden 1948- *WhoAmW 91*
Wilcox, John Caven 1942- *St&PR 91*
Wilcox, Laird Maurice 1942- *WhoWrEP 89*
Wilcox, Larry 1947- *ConTFT 8*
Wilcox, Lucia *WhoAmA 91N*
Wilcox, Lynn E. 1935- *WhoAmW 91*
Wilcox, Marsha Ann 1956- *WhoE 91*
Wilcox, Mary Ann 1946- *WhoWrEP 89*
Wilcox, Mary Rose 1949- *WhoHisp 91*
Wilcox, Maud 1923- *WhoAm 90, WhoAmW 91*
Wilcox, Michael Wing 1941- *WhoAm 90*
Wilcox, Milt 1950- *Ballpl 90*
Wilcox, Patricia Anne 1932- *WhoWrEP 89*
Wilcox, Ralph 1818-1877 *AmLegL*
Wilcox, Robert Colton 1933- *St&PR 91*
Wilcox, Robert K. 1947- *WhoAm 90*
Wilcox, Ronald Bruce 1934- *WhoAm 90*
Wilcox, Ruth 1889-1958 *WhoAmA 91N*
Wilcox, Scott A. 1958- *St&PR 91*
Wilcox, Walter Jerome 1934- *BiDrAPA 89*
Wilcox, William L., Jr. 1945- *St&PR 91*
Wilcox, William Ross 1935- *WhoAm 90*
Wilcox, William Walter 1926- *WhoAm 90*
Wilcoxen, Joan Heeren 1948- *WhoAmW 91*
Wilcoxen, Shirley 1937- *WhoAmW 91*
Wilczak, Wayne Edward 1948- *St&PR 91*
Wilczek, Robert Joseph 1944- *WhoAm 90*
Wilczewski, Melvin Lee 1950- *St&PR 91*
Wilczynski, Donald James 1934- *St&PR 91*
Wilczynski, Janusz S. 1929- *WhoAm 90*
Wild Bill Hickok *WhNaAH*
Wild Cat 1816?-1857 *WhNaAH*
Wild, Earl 1915- *BioIn 16, IntWWM 90, PenDiMP*
Wild, Heidi Karin 1948- *WhoAmW 91*
Wild, James Robert 1945- *WhoSSW 91*
Wild, John Paul 1923- *WhoWor 91*
Wild, Nelson Hopkins 1933- *WhoAm 90*
Wild, Peter *BioIn 16*
Wild, Robert Arnold 1946- *WhoSSW 91*
Wild, Robert Lee 1921- *WhoAm 90*
Wild, Stephen Aubrey 1941- *IntWWM 90*
Wild, Victor Allyn 1946- *WhoEmL 91*
Wild-Barido, Michael Ray 1952- *WhoEmL 91*
Wildasin, J. J. *WhoSSW 91*
Wildauer, Werner 1934- *St&PR 91*
Wildavsky, Aaron 1930- *ConAu 30NR*
Wildbraham, John 1944- *IntWWM 90*
Wilde, Alan 1929- *ConAu 31NR, WhoWrEP 89*
Wilde, Carlton D. 1935- *WhoAm 90*
Wilde, Cornel 1915-1989 *AnObit 1989, BioIn 16, ConTFT 8, WorAlBi*
Wilde, Cornel Louis 1915- *WhoAm 90*
Wilde, Daniel Underwood 1937- *WhoAm 90*
Wilde, Darwin John 1944- *St&PR 91*
Wilde, David 1935- *PenDiMP*
Wilde, David Clark 1935- *IntWWM 90*
Wilde, Davis Stewart 1937- *WhoWrEP 89*
Wilde, Dawn Johnson 1934- *WhoAmA 91*
Wilde, Deborah Ann 1957- *WhoE 91*
Wilde, Donald Raymond 1926- *WhoAm 90*
Wilde, Edwin Frederick 1931- *WhoAm 90, WhoSSW 91*
Wilde, John 1919- *BioIn 16, WhoAm 90, WhoAmA 91*
Wilde, Larry 1928- *WhoWrEP 89*
Wilde, Louis J. 1865-1924 *BioIn 16*
Wilde, Norman Taylor, Jr. 1930- *St&PR 91, WhoAm 90*
Wilde, Oscar 1854-1900 *BioIn 16, WorAlBi*
Wilde, Patricia 1928- *WhoAmW 91*
Wilde, Richard Henry 1789-1847 *BioIn 16*
Wilde, Richard Lawrence 1944- *WhoAm 90*
Wilde, Robert Eugene 1923- *WhoWrEP 89*
Wilde, Shanley Joseph 1932- *St&PR 91*
Wilde, Stephanie 1952- *WhoAmA 91*
Wilde, Teruko 1945- *WhoEmL 91*
Wilde, Thomas Arthur 1932- *WhoSSW 91*
Wilde, William Key 1933- *St&PR 91, WhoAm 90*
Wilde, William Lawrence 1936- *WhoWrEP 89*
Wilde, Wilson 1927- *St&PR 91, WhoAm 90*
Wildebush, Joseph Frederick 1910- *WhoE 91*
Wildenhain, Frans 1905-1980 *WhoAmA 91N*
Wildenmann, Rudolf 1921- *WhoWor 91*
Wildenstein, Daniel Leopold 1917- *WhoWor 91*
Wildenstein, Felix *WhoAmA 91N*
Wildenstein, Georges 1892-1963 *WhoAmA 91N*
Wildenthal, Claud Kern 1941- *WhoAm 90*
Wildenvey, Herman Theodor 1886-1959 *DcScanL*
Wilder, Alec 1907-1980 *AuBYP 90, BioIn 16, OxCPMus*
Wilder, Alexander Lafayette Chew *AuBYP 90*
Wilder, Amos Tappan 1940- *WhoE 91*
Wilder, Anne *BiDrAPA 89*
Wilder, Annette Bedford *WhoSSW 91, WhoWor 91*
Wilder, Billy 1906- *BioIn 16, WhoAm 90, WorAlBi*
Wilder, Charles Willoughby 1929- *WhoAm 90*
Wilder, David Randolph 1929- *WhoAm 90*
Wilder, David S *BiDrAPA 89*
Wilder, Donald Martin 1927- *St&PR 91*
Wilder, Duane Edward 1929- *St&PR 91*
Wilder, Eleanor Marie 1950- *WhoAmW 91, WhoEmL 91*
Wilder, Elmon 1937- *WhoE 91*
Wilder, F. Daniel 1933- *WhoAm 90*
Wilder, Gene *BioIn 16*
Wilder, Gene 1935- *WhoAm 90, WorAlBi*
Wilder, J Lloyd 1917- *BiDrAPA 89*
Wilder, Jack F 1926- *BiDrAPA 89*
Wilder, James *BioIn 16*
Wilder, James D. 1935- *WhoWor 91*
Wilder, John Richard *WhoWrEP 89*
Wilder, John Shelton 1921- *WhoAm 90, WhoSSW 91*
Wilder, L. Douglas *BioIn 16, NewYTBS 90 [port]*
Wilder, L Douglas 1931- *CurBio 90 [port], News 90 [port], -90-3 [port]*
Wilder, Laura 1867-1957 *AuBYP 90, FemiCLE*
Wilder, Laura Ingalls 1867-1957 *BioAmW, BioIn 16, WorAlBi*
Wilder, Lawrence Douglas 1931- *WhoAm 90, WhoSSW 91*
Wilder, Leslie Norman 1935- *St&PR 91*
Wilder, Melissa Ann 1963- *WhoAmW 91*
Wilder, Mitchell Armitage 1913-1979 *WhoAmA 91N*
Wilder, Myron Farnham, Jr. 1934- *St&PR 91*
Wilder, Nicholas *BioIn 16, WhoAmA 91N*
Wilder, Pelham, Jr. 1920- *WhoAm 90*
Wilder, Philip Sawyer, Jr. 1924- *WhoAm 90, WhoE 91*
Wilder, Richard B. 1943- *St&PR 91*
Wilder, Robert Allen 1944- *WhoSSW 91*
Wilder, Robert David 1948- *WhoE 91*
Wilder, Robert George 1920- *St&PR 91, WhoAm 90*
Wilder, Robert O. 1927- *St&PR 91*
Wilder, Robert Vard 1939- *WhoSSW 91*
Wilder, Roland Percival, Jr. 1940- *WhoWor 91*
Wilder, Ronald 1937- *WhoAm 90*
Wilder, Ronald Parker 1941- *WhoAm 90*
Wilder, Thornton 1897-1975 *BioIn 16, MajTwCW, WorAlBi, WrPh*
Wilder, Valerie 1947- *WhoAm 90*
Wilder, Walter R. 1926- *St&PR 91*
Wilder, Webb, And The Beatnecks *WhoNeCM [port]*
Wilder, William Price 1922- *St&PR 91*
Wildermuth, Chris 1960- *ODwPR 91*
Wildermuth, Gordon Lee 1937- *WhoAm 90*
Wildermuth, Jo Voisard 1951- *WhoAmW 91*
Wildermuth, Ottilie 1817-1877 *EncCoWW*
Wildermuth, Robert Edward 1929- *St&PR 91*
Wildermuth, Roger Gregory 1944- *St&PR 91*

Wilderotter, James Arthur 1944- *WhoAm 90*
Wildes, Dudley Joseph 1935- *WhoAm 90*
Wildesen, Leslie Elizabeth 1944- *WhoAm 90*
Wildey, Doug *EncACom*
Wildey, William Edward 1952- *WhoE 91*
Wildfeuer, David 1920- *WhoSSW 91*
Wildfoerster, Christopher Justus 1958- *St&PR 91*
Wildgen, Mark Finley 1950- *BiDrAPA 89*
Wildhaber, Luzius 1937- *WhoWor 91*
Wildhack, William August, Jr. 1935- *St&PR 91, WhoAm 90, WhoE 91*
Wildi, Ernst *BioIn 16*
Wilding, Alison 1948- *BiDWomA*
Wilding, Diane 1942- *WhoAmW 91, WhoSSW 91, WhoWor 91*
Wilding, Henry Peter 1922- *St&PR 91*
Wilding, Michael 1912-1979 *WorAlBi*
Wildman, Caroline Lax *WhoAmA 91N*
Wildman, Donald C. 1932- *St&PR 91*
Wildman, Donna M. 1940- *WhoE 91*
Wildman, Eugene 1936- *WhoWrEP 89*
Wildman, Gary Cecil 1942- *WhoAm 90*
Wildman, Mark 1955- *IntWWM 90*
Wildman, Max Edward 1919- *WhoAm 90*
Wildman, R. Joseph 1938- *St&PR 91*
Wildman, Timothy James 1958- *WhoSSW 91*
Wildmon, Donald *BioIn 16*
Wildmon, Donald E. *NewYTBS 90 [port]*
Wildnauer, Richard Harry 1940- *WhoE 91*
Wildpret, Robert Frank 1946- *St&PR 91*
Wildrick, Laurence E 1930- *BiDrAPA 89*
Wilds, Benjamin James, Jr. 1944- *WhoSSW 91*
Wildsmith, Brian 1930- *AuBYP 90, BioIn 16*
Wile, Donald Clayton 1931- *St&PR 91*
Wile, Frederic William 1873-1941 *BioIn 16*
Wile, Joan 1931- *WhoAmW 91*
Wile, Julius 1915- *WhoAm 90*
Wile, Margery B *BiDrAPA 89*
Wilen, Israel 1914- *St&PR 91*
Wilen, Joseph M. 1950- *St&PR 91*
Wilen, Judith Beth 1954- *WhoAmW 91*
Wilen, Stanley Herbert 1919- *WhoAm 90*
Wilens, Timothy Edwin *BiDrAPA 89*
Wilenski, Peter Stephen 1939- *WhoWor 91*
Wilensky, Alvin 1921- *St&PR 91, WhoAm 90*
Wilensky, Gail Roggin 1943- *WhoAm 90, WhoAmW 91*
Wilensky, Harold L. 1923- *WhoAm 90*
Wilensky, Julius M. 1916- *WhoAm 90*
Wilensky, Moshe 1910- *IntWWM 90*
Wilentz, David Theodore 1894-1988 *BioIn 16*
Wilentz, Jacqueline Melino *BioIn 16*
Wilentz, Robert Nathan 1927- *WhoAm 90, WhoE 91*
Wiler, Edward A. 1927- *St&PR 91*
Wiles, C. David 1942- *St&PR 91*
Wiles, Charles Preston 1918- *WhoAm 90*
Wiles, Charles Preston 1956- *BiDrAPA 89*
Wiles, David Kimball 1942- *WhoSSW 91*
Wiles, Edward Joseph, Jr. 1948- *St&PR 91*
Wiles, Eugene F. 1922- *WhoAm 90*
Wiles, Irving R 1861-1948 *WhoAmA 91N*
Wiles, John Craig 1943- *St&PR 91*
Wiles, Margaret Jones 1911- *IntWWM 90*
Wiles, Q. T. *BioIn 16*
Wiles, Q.T. 1919- *St&PR 91*
Wiles, Quentin T. *BioIn 16*
Wiles, Quentin Thomas 1919- *WhoAm 90*
Wiles, Richard Chester 1934- *St&PR 91*
Wilets, Gregory A 1950- *BiDrAPA 89*
Wilets, Lawrence 1927- *WhoAm 90*
Wiley, Albert Lee, Jr. 1936- *WhoWor 91*
Wiley, Barry Holland 1936- *St&PR 91*
Wiley, Bonnie *BioIn 16*
Wiley, Bonnie Jean *WhoAmW 91*
Wiley, Carl Ross 1930- *St&PR 91, WhoAm 90*
Wiley, Charles Henry 1927- *St&PR 91*
Wiley, Charles J. 1924- *St&PR 91*
Wiley, Damon Lee 1956- *WhoSSW 91*
Wiley, Dana Lee *BiDrAPA 89*
Wiley, David B *BiDrAPA 89*
Wiley, Dayna Ann 1960- *WhoSSW 91*
Wiley, Dean L 1951- *BiDrAPA 89*
Wiley, Donovon Linn 1938- *WhoAm 90*
Wiley, Edwin Miller 1951- *WhoWor 91*
Wiley, Edwin P. 1929- *St&PR 91*
Wiley, Edwin Packard 1929- *WhoAm 90*
Wiley, Guilford M., Jr. 1924- *St&PR 91*
Wiley, Hannah Christine 1950- *WhoAmW 91*
Wiley, James Loman 1961- *WhoSSW 91*
Wiley, Jane Allen Walker 1944- *IntWWM 90*
Wiley, Jason LaRue, Jr. 1917- *WhoE 91*
Wiley, Jerold Wayne 1944- *WhoSSW 91*
Wiley, John P., Jr. *BioIn 16*
Wiley, Karla 1918- *AuBYP 90*
Wiley, Lee 1915-1975 *OxCPMus*
Wiley, Marquita Trenier 1950- *WhoAmW 91*
Wiley, Michael Eugene 1943- *WhoSSW 91*
Wiley, Patricia *BioIn 16*
Wiley, Peter 1942- *ConAu 131*
Wiley, Ralph *BioIn 16*
Wiley, Richard 1944- *ConAu 129*
Wiley, Richard Arthur 1928- *St&PR 91, WhoAm 90*
Wiley, Richard Emerson 1934- *WhoAm 90*
Wiley, Richard Gordon 1937- *WhoAm 90*
Wiley, Richard Haven 1913- *WhoAm 90*
Wiley, Robert A. 1934- *WhoAm 90*
Wiley, Robert David 1966- *WhoEmL 91*
Wiley, Robert F. 1946- *WhoWrEP 89*
Wiley, Robin Gail 1963- *WhoAmW 91*
Wiley, Ronald Gordon 1947- *WhoSSW 91*
Wiley, S. Donald 1926- *St&PR 91, WhoAm 90*
Wiley, Scott T. 1949- *St&PR 91*
Wiley, Susan Deaner 1953- *BiDrAPA 89*
Wiley, Thomas E. *St&PR 91*
Wiley, Thomas Glen 1928- *WhoAm 90*
Wiley, W. Bradford 1910- *St&PR 91*
Wiley, William *BioIn 16*
Wiley, William A 1931- *BiDrAPA 89*
Wiley, William Bradford 1910- *WhoAm 90*
Wiley, William Clay 1945- *WhoAm 90, WhoSSW 91*
Wiley, William R. 1931- *St&PR 91*
Wiley, William Rodney 1931- *WhoAm 90*
Wiley, William T. 1937- *WhoAm 90, WhoAmA 91*
Wilf, Andrew Jeffrey 1949-1982 *WhoAmA 91N*
Wilf, Frederic Marshal 1959- *WhoE 91*
Wilf, Theodore J 1941- *BiDrAPA 89*
Wilfinger, Rebecca Gail 1951- *WhoE 91*
Wilfley, Arthur R. 1927- *St&PR 91*
Wilfley, George M. 1924- *St&PR 91*
Wilfong, J. Scott 1950- *St&PR 91*
Wilfong, John Scott 1950- *WhoAm 90*
Wilfong, Rob 1953- *Ballpl 90*
Wilford, John Noble 1933- *AuBYP 90*
Wilford, John Noble, Jr. 1933- *WhoAm 90*
Wilford, Loran 1892-1972 *WhoAmA 91N*
Wilford, Walton Terry 1937- *WhoAm 90*
Wilfred, Thomas 1889-1968 *WhoAmA 91N*
Wilgarde, Ralph L. 1928- *WhoWor 91*
Wilgenbusch, Nancy *WhoAmW 91*
Wilgis, Herbert E., Jr. 1935- *St&PR 91*
Wilgocki, Theresa Ann 1965- *WhoAmW 91*
Wilgus, D K 1918-1989 *ConAu 130*
Wilgus, Joan Elizabeth 1947- *WhoAmW 91*
Wilgus, Ralph Edwin 1914- *St&PR 91*
Wilgus, Walter Stephen 1932- *St&PR 91*
Wilhelm II 1859-1941 *BioIn 16*
Wilhelm, Arthur Lee 1946- *St&PR 91*
Wilhelm, Brenda Lea 1960- *WhoAmW 91*
Wilhelm, Carl F. 1927- *St&PR 91*
Wilhelm, Gale 1908- *FemiCLE*
Wilhelm, Gayle Brian 1936- *WhoAm 90*
Wilhelm, Hans 1945- *BioIn 16*
Wilhelm, Hans Adolf 1919- *WhoWor 91*
Wilhelm, Hoyt 1923- *Ballpl 90 [port]*
Wilhelm, James Edward, Jr. 1945- *WhoSSW 91*
Wilhelm, James Francis 1924- *St&PR 91*
Wilhelm, James Jerome 1932- *ConAu 32NR*
Wilhelm, James K. 1927- *St&PR 91*
Wilhelm, Jim 1954- *WhoE 91*
Wilhelm, Joseph Lawrence 1909- *WhoAm 90*
Wilhelm, Kaiser 1874-1936 *Ballpl 90*
Wilhelm, Kate *BioIn 16, MajTwCW*
Wilhelm, Kate 1928- *FemiCLE, RGTwCSF, WhoAmW 91*
Wilhelm, Katie Gertrude 1928- *MajTwCW*
Wilhelm, Kurt, II *BiDrAPA 89*
Wilhelm, Kyle M. 1961- *St&PR 91*
Wilhelm, Luther Ray 1939- *WhoSSW 91*
Wilhelm, Max 1928- *WhoWor 91*
Wilhelm, Norman D. 1926- *St&PR 91*
Wilhelm, Richard Herman 1909-1968 *DcScB S2*
Wilhelm, Robert Oscar 1918- *WhoAm 90*
Wilhelm, Ronald Eugene 1947- *St&PR 91*
Wilhelm, Rudie 1914- *St&PR 91*
Wilhelm, Stephen Paul 1948- *WhoWor 91*
Wilhelm, Walter Eugene 1931- *WhoSSW 91*
Wilhelm, William Jean 1935- *WhoAm 90*
Wilhelmi, Henry Paul 1930- *WhoE 91*
Wilhelmi, William Merle 1939- *WhoAmA 91*
Wilhelmina 1880-1962 *WomWR [port]*
Wilhelmina, Queen of the Netherlands 1880-1962 *BioIn 16*
Wilhelmj, August 1845-1908 *PenDiMP*
Wilhelmsen, Alexandra Leonore 1947- *WhoSSW 91*
Wilhelmsen, Harold J. 1928- *St&PR 91*
Wilhelmsen, Harold John 1928- *WhoAm 90*
Wilhite, Clayton Edward 1945- *St&PR 91, WhoAm 90*
Wilhite, Jim O. 1938- *WhoAm 90*
Wilhite, Sam Yancey 1919- *St&PR 91*
Wilhoit, Henry Rupert, Jr. 1935- *WhoAm 90*
Wilhoit, Melvin Ross 1948- *IntWWM 90*
Wilhoit, Randall Kenneth 1958- *St&PR 91*
Wilinsky, Harriet *WhoAm 90*
Wilinsky, Howard C 1935- *BiDrAPA 89*
Wilis, Gerald 1938- *St&PR 91*
Wilja *EncCoWW*
Wilk, Gerald Michael 1937- *St&PR 91*
Wilk, Johannes F. 1937- *St&PR 91*
Wilk, Lynne Anne *BiDrAPA 89*
Wilk, Max 1920- *WhoWrEP 89*
Wilk, Peter David 1950- *BiDrAPA 89*
Wilk, Richard David 1957- *WhoE 91*
Wilke, Charles Robert 1917- *WhoAm 90*
Wilke, Charles S. 1942- *St&PR 91*
Wilke, Hannah 1940- *BioIn 16, WhoAmA 91*
Wilke, Harold 1914- *ConAu 132*
Wilke, Richard B. *WhoAm 90*
Wilke, Robert D. 1931- *St&PR 91*
Wilke, Ulfert S 1907-1988 *WhoAmA 91N*
Wilke, Wolfgang Rudolf 1934- *WhoWor 91*
Wilke Montemayor, Joanne Marie 1941- *WhoAmW 91*
Wilken, Arden *NewAgMG*
Wilken, Earl Weston 1923- *WhoE 91*
Wilken, Robert Louis 1936- *WhoAm 90*
Wilken, Tim *BioIn 16*
Wilkenfeld, Byron Eli *BiDrAPA 89*
Wilkening, Friedrich 1946- *WhoWor 91*
Wilkening, Laurel Lynn 1944- *WhoAm 90, WhoAmW 91*
Wilkening, Steven Lee 1945- *St&PR 91*
Wilkens, Anne 1948- *IntWWM 90*
Wilkens, Christopher William 1947- *WhoE 91*
Wilkens, George Robert 1949- *WhoWrEP 89*
Wilkens, Henry J. 1922- *St&PR 91*
Wilkens, Jane Rae 1952- *WhoAmW 91*
Wilkens, Lenny *BioIn 16*
Wilkens, Leonard Randolph, Jr. 1937- *WhoAm 90*
Wilkens, Robert Allen 1929- *St&PR 91, WhoAm 90*
Wilkens, Robert E. 1929- *St&PR 91*
Wilkens, Steven A. 1957- *WhoWrEP 89*
Wilker, Gertrud 1924- *EncCoWW*
Wilkerson, Calvin Walter 1934- *St&PR 91*
Wilkerson, Curtis 1961- *Ballpl 90*
Wilkerson, Cynthia *ConAu 31NR*
Wilkerson, D Clifton 1933- *BiDrAPA 89*
Wilkerson, David *BioIn 16*
Wilkerson, Donald Keith *BiDrAPA 89*
Wilkerson, Douglas 1948- *St&PR 91*
Wilkerson, Edward *BioIn 16*
Wilkerson, Floyd Monroe 1932- *WhoAm 90*
Wilkerson, Frank L. 1936- *St&PR 91*
Wilkerson, George Edward *BiDrAPA 89*
Wilkerson, James Douglas, Jr. 1942- *WhoSSW 91*
Wilkerson, James Edward 1945- *WhoSSW 91*
Wilkerson, James Neill 1939- *WhoWor 91*
Wilkerson, Janice Shipp 1935- *WhoAmW 91*
Wilkerson, Leo C. 1933- *St&PR 91*
Wilkerson, Lizzie 1901-1984 *MusmAFA*
Wilkerson, Lynda Hayes 1956- *WhoAmW 91*
Wilkerson, Marjorie JoAnn Madar 1930- *WhoAmW 91*
Wilkerson, Michael N. 1955- *WhoWrEP 89*
Wilkerson, O.A., III 1935- *St&PR 91*
Wilkerson, William Christopher *BiDrAPA 89*
Wilkerson, William Holton 1947- *St&PR 91, WhoAm 90, WhoEmL 91, WhoWor 91*
Wilkerson-Kassel, Tichi *St&PR 91*
Wilkes, Charles 1798-1877 *WorAlBi*
Wilkes, Charles D. 1920- *WhoWor 91*
Wilkes, Clem Cabell, Jr. 1953- *WhoSSW 91*
Wilkes, Corbin McCue 1946- *St&PR 91*
Wilkes, David R. 1922- *St&PR 91*
Wilkes, Delano Angus 1935- *WhoWor 91*
Wilkes, Franklin John, Jr. 1943- *WhoE 91*
Wilkes, G. S. *WhoAm 90*
Wilkes, Gary Mason *BiDrAPA 89*
Wilkes, James C. 1949- *St&PR 91*
Wilkes, James Oscroft 1932- *WhoAm 90*
Wilkes, John *PenDiDA 89*
Wilkes, John 1727-1797 *EncCRAm*
Wilkes, Joseph Allen 1919- *WhoAm 90*
Wilkes, Kenneth Roger *BiDrAPA 89*
Wilkes, Kevin *BioIn 16*
Wilkes, Larry Anthony 1951- *WhoE 91*
Wilkes, Laurie K. 1955- *WhoAmW 91*
Wilkes, Lowell Lyndon, Jr. 1919- *WhoE 91*
Wilkes, Marilyn Z. *AuBYP 90*
Wilkes, Paul 1938- *BioIn 16, WhoAm 90*
Wilkes, Penny F. 1946- *WhoWrEP 89*
Wilkes, Robert David 1934- *St&PR 91*
Wilkes, Robert Edmond 1933- *St&PR 91*
Wilkes, Sema *BioIn 16*
Wilkes, Shar 1951- *WhoAmW 91*
Wilkes, Thomas C R 1951- *BiDrAPA 89*
Wilkes, William 1951- *WhoSSW 91*
Wilkeson, Adela Gandia *BiDrAPA 89*
Wilkey, Jeffrey R. 1942- *St&PR 91*
Wilkey, Malcolm Richard 1918- *WhoAm 90, WhoSSW 91, WhoWor 91*
Wilkey, Yvonne Williams 1950- *WhoAmW 91*
Wilkie, David 1785-1841 *IntDcAA 90*
Wilkie, Donald Walter 1931- *WhoAm 90*
Wilkie, George H 1931- *BiDrAPA 89*
Wilkie, James Broadus 1956- *WhoSSW 91*
Wilkie, John Frederick 1951- *WhoE 91*
Wilkie, Jonathan Paul 1947- *St&PR 91*
Wilkie, Katharine Elliott 1904-1980 *AuBYP 90*
Wilkie, Kevin S. 1963- *St&PR 91*
Wilkie, Leighton A. 1900- *St&PR 91*
Wilkie, Leighton Allyn 1900- *WhoAm 90*
Wilkie, Michael Leighton 1941- *WhoAm 90*
Wilkie, Patricia Lynn 1948- *WhoSSW 91*
Wilkie, Robert Lee 1925- *St&PR 91*
Wilkie, Valleau, Jr. 1923- *WhoAm 90, WhoWor 91*
Wilkie, William Lawrence 1944- *WhoAm 90*
Wilkin, Charles M. *St&PR 91*
Wilkin, E. Ray 1926- *St&PR 91*
Wilkin, Eloise Burns 1904-1987 *BioIn 16*
Wilkin, Eugene Welch 1923- *WhoAm 90*
Wilkin, Jerome Russell 1947- *St&PR 91*
Wilkin, Karen *WhoAmA 91, WhoE 91*
Wilkin, Richard Edwin 1930- *WhoAm 90*
Wilking, Virginia N 1920- *BiDrAPA 89*
Wilkins, Alfred T., Jr. 1949- *ConAu 129*
Wilkins, Arlene 1936- *WhoAmW 91*
Wilkins, Barratt 1943- *WhoAm 90, WhoSSW 91*
Wilkins, Beriah 1846-1905 *BioIn 16*
Wilkins, Burleigh Taylor 1932- *WhoAm 90*
Wilkins, C. Howard, Jr. 1938- *WhoWor 91*
Wilkins, Caroline Hanke 1937- *WhoAm 90, WhoAmW 91*
Wilkins, Catherine Marie 1960- *WhoE 91*
Wilkins, Charles L. 1938- *WhoAm 90*
Wilkins, Charles Louis 1961- *WhoE 91*
Wilkins, Christina L. 1950- *St&PR 91, WhoAm 90*
Wilkins, Coleridge Anthony 1930- *WhoWor 91*
Wilkins, David George 1939- *WhoAm 90, WhoAmA 91, WhoE 91*
Wilkins, David John *BiDrAPA 89*
Wilkins, Dominique *BioIn 16*
Wilkins, Dominique 1960- *WorAlBi*
Wilkins, Earle Wayne, Jr. 1919- *WhoAm 90*
Wilkins, Floyd, Jr. 1925- *WhoAm 90*
Wilkins, Frances *AuBYP 90*
Wilkins, Frank J. 1931- *St&PR 91*
Wilkins, Fraser 1908-1989 *BioIn 16*
Wilkins, Frederick C. 1935- *WhoWrEP 89*
Wilkins, Frederick Charles 1935- *WhoE 91*
Wilkins, George Hubert 1888-1958 *WorAlBi*
Wilkins, Graham John 1924- *St&PR 91, WhoWor 91*
Wilkins, H. Andrew 1950- *WhoE 91*
Wilkins, Heath *BioIn 16*
Wilkins, Herbert Putnam 1930- *WhoAm 90, WhoE 91*
Wilkins, Hugh Percival 1896- *AuBYP 90*
Wilkins, Janet Rosemary 1917- *WhoAmW 91*
Wilkins, Jeffrey M. 1944- *St&PR 91*
Wilkins, Jerry Lynn 1936- *WhoSSW 91, WhoWor 91*
Wilkins, John Antoine 1943- *WhoSSW 91*
Wilkins, John Warren 1936- *WhoAm 90*
Wilkins, Josetta Edwards 1932- *WhoSSW 91*
Wilkins, Kent Myrup 1935- *St&PR 91*
Wilkins, Laura *BioIn 16*
Wilkins, Lawrence Newell 1953- *WhoSSW 91*
Wilkins, Margaret Lucy 1939- *IntWWM 90*
Wilkins, Martha Huddleston 1940- *WhoSSW 91*
Wilkins, Mary Calhoun 1926- *BioIn 16*
Wilkins, Mary H. *AuBYP 90*
Wilkins, Maurice Gray, Jr. 1931- *St&PR 91, WhoAm 90*
Wilkins, Maurice H. F. 1916- *WorAlBi*
Wilkins, Maurice Hugh Frederick 1916- *BioIn 16, WhoWor 91*
Wilkins, Paul Cole 1947- *BiDrAPA 89*

Wilkins, Ray, Jr. 1937- *St&PR 91, WhoSSW 91*
Wilkins, Raymond Gene *WhoSSW 91*
Wilkins, Richard *NewAgMG*
Wilkins, Rita Denise 1951- *WhoAmW 91*
Wilkins, Robert Earl 1925- *St&PR 91*
Wilkins, Robert L. 1925- *St&PR 91*
Wilkins, Robert Mason 1937- *WhoE 91*
Wilkins, Robert Pearce 1933- *WhoAm 90*
Wilkins, Roger Carson 1906- *WhoAm 90*
Wilkins, Roger W. 1932- *BioIn 16*
Wilkins, Roger Wood 1932- *WhoAm 90*
Wilkins, Roy 1901-1981 *BioIn 16, WorAlBi*
Wilkins, Skip *ConAu 129*
Wilkins, Susan Linda 1950- *WhoAmW 91*
Wilkins, Tracy Dale 1943- *WhoAm 90*
Wilkins, W. Gary 1945- *WhoHisp 91*
Wilkins, William 1779-1865 *BiDrUSE 89*
Wilkins, William S. 1942- *WhoWor 91*
Wilkins, William Walter, Jr. 1942- *WhoAm 90, WhoSSW 91*
Wilkinson, Albert Mims, Jr. 1925- *WhoAm 90*
Wilkinson, Ann Marie 1947- *WhoAmW 91*
Wilkinson, Anne 1910-1961 *FemiCLE*
Wilkinson, B. Andrew 1944- *St&PR 91*
Wilkinson, Barry *BioIn 16*
Wilkinson, Ben 1932- *WhoSSW 91*
Wilkinson, Bill 1964- *Ballpl 90*
Wilkinson, Brenda Scott 1946- *BioIn 16*
Wilkinson, Bruce W. 1944- *St&PR 91, WhoAm 90, WhoSSW 91*
Wilkinson, Burke 1913- *AuBYP 90*
Wilkinson, Cathy *ODwPR 91*
Wilkinson, Cecilia A. *ODwPR 91*
Wilkinson, Charles B 1922- *BiDrAPA 89*
Wilkinson, Christopher Foster 1938- *WhoAm 90, WhoSSW 91*
Wilkinson, David Anthony 1951- *St&PR 91*
Wilkinson, David Todd 1935- *WhoAm 90*
Wilkinson, Denys Haigh 1922- *WhoWor 91*
Wilkinson, Donald Ellsworth 1922- *WhoAm 90*
Wilkinson, Doris Yvonne 1936- *WhoAm 90, WhoAmW 91*
Wilkinson, Edward Anderson, Jr. 1933- *WhoAm 90*
Wilkinson, Eliza *FemiCLE*
Wilkinson, Elizabeth *FemiCLE*
Wilkinson, Geoffrey 1921- *WhoAm 90, WhoWor 91, WorAlBi*
Wilkinson, George L 1942- *BiDrAPA 89*
Wilkinson, Gerald *BioIn 16*
Wilkinson, Glovinia Phipps *WhoAmW 91*
Wilkinson, Gregg Stuart 1942- *WhoSSW 91*
Wilkinson, Gregor M *BiDrAPA 89*
Wilkinson, Harold Arthur 1935- *WhoAm 90*
Wilkinson, Harry J. 1937- *WhoAm 90*
Wilkinson, Harry John 1937- *St&PR 91*
Wilkinson, Harry R. 1942- *St&PR 91*
Wilkinson, Howard Neal 1930- *WhoSSW 91*
Wilkinson, Hutton *BioIn 16*
Wilkinson, Ivan Eugene 1941- *St&PR 91*
Wilkinson, J. Jay 1950- *St&PR 91*
Wilkinson, J. L. 1874-1964 *Ballpl 90*
Wilkinson, James 1757-1825 *WorAlBi*
Wilkinson, James Allan 1945- *WhoWor 91*
Wilkinson, James E. 1948- *St&PR 91*
Wilkinson, James Harvie, III 1944- *WhoAm 90, WhoSSW 91*
Wilkinson, Jane Insalaco 1939- *WhoAmW 91*
Wilkinson, Janet Worman 1944- *WhoAmW 91*
Wilkinson, Jemima 1752-1810 *FemiCLE*
Wilkinson, Jemima 1752-1819 *BioAmW, EncCRAm*
Wilkinson, Jessie Lenore 1957- *WhoAmW 91*
Wilkinson, John 1913-1973 *WhoAmA 91N*
Wilkinson, John 1940- *St&PR 91*
Wilkinson, John Burke 1913- *WhoAm 90*
Wilkinson, John H. *St&PR 91*
Wilkinson, John Hart 1940- *WhoAm 90*
Wilkinson, John M. 1948- *St&PR 91*
Wilkinson, John R. 1930- *IntWWM 90*
Wilkinson, Joseph Barbour, Jr. 1930- *WhoAm 90*
Wilkinson, Kenneth Herbert 1928- *WhoAm 90*
Wilkinson, King 1938- *WhoSSW 91*
Wilkinson, Linda Cornelia Painton 1927- *WhoAmW 91*
Wilkinson, Lisa *DrBlPA 90*
Wilkinson, Lloyd 1857- *AmLegL*
Wilkinson, Louise Cherry 1948- *WhoAm 90*
Wilkinson, Lynn 1951- *St&PR 91*
Wilkinson, Mark Lawrence 1950- *WhoWor 91*
Wilkinson, Mary Ellen 1947- *WhoAmW 91*
Wilkinson, Maurice Gilliam 1950- *WhoSSW 91*
Wilkinson, Michael Douglas 1949- *St&PR 91*
Wilkinson, Michael Kennerly 1921- *WhoAm 90*
Wilkinson, Milton James 1937- *WhoAm 90*
Wilkinson, Owen Inglis 1944- *St&PR 91*
Wilkinson, Paul 1937- *WhoWor 91*
Wilkinson, Philip George 1929- *IntWWM 90*
Wilkinson, Philip William 1927- *St&PR 91*
Wilkinson, Rachel Elizabeth Diggs 1913- *WhoAmW 91*
Wilkinson, Richard W. 1932- *St&PR 91, WhoSSW 91*
Wilkinson, Robert Eugene 1926- *WhoSSW 91*
Wilkinson, Robin Edwin 1942- *IntWWM 90*
Wilkinson, Rosemary 1924- *WhoWrEP 89*
Wilkinson, Roy 1893-1956 *Ballpl 90*
Wilkinson, Ruth *BioIn 16*
Wilkinson, S. H. *AmLegL*
Wilkinson, Samuel Vincent 1959- *WhoSSW 91*
Wilkinson, Sarah Scudgell *FemiCLE*
Wilkinson, Sylvia 1940- *BioIn 16*
Wilkinson, Theodore Stark 1934- *WhoE 91*
Wilkinson, Thomas Allan 1932- *WhoWor 91*
Wilkinson, Thomas Brame, IV 1948- *WhoSSW 91*
Wilkinson, Wallace, Jr. 1954- *MusmAFA*
Wilkinson, Wallace G. 1941- *WhoAm 90, WhoSSW 91, WhoWor 91*
Wilkinson, Warren 1945- *ConAu 132*
Wilkinson, Warren S. 1920- *St&PR 91*
Wilkinson, William Durfee 1924- *WhoAm 90*
Wilkinson, William Emmet, Jr. *BiDrAPA 89*
Wilkinson, William R. 1942- *St&PR 91*
Wilkinson, William Sherwood 1933- *St&PR 91, WhoAm 90*
Wilkinson, William Wells 1933- *St&PR 91*
Wilkirson, Deanna Jean 1948- *WhoAmW 91*
Wilkomirska, Maria 1904- *PenDiMP*
Wilkomirska, Wanda 1929- *IntWWM 90, PenDiMP*
Wilkomirski, Jozef 1926- *IntWWM 90*
Wilkomirski, Kazimierz 1900- *IntWWM 90, PenDiMP*
Wilkoski, Joseph S. 1952- *St&PR 91*
Wilkowski, Joseph Stephen 1952- *WhoE 91*
Wilks, Bradley D. *ODwPR 91*
Wilks, David M. 1946- *St&PR 91*
Wilks, Ivor Gordon Hughes 1928- *WhoAm 90*
Wilks, Joseph Wayne 1956- *St&PR 91*
Wilks, Judith *BiDEWW*
Wilks, Phillip 1934- *St&PR 91*
Wilks, Ted 1915- *Ballpl 90*
Wilks, William Lee 1931- *WhoAm 90*
Will, Bob 1931- *Ballpl 90*
Will, Edward Edmund 1952- *WhoSSW 91*
Will, Frederic B *BiDrAPA 89*
Will, George F. *BioIn 16*
Will, George F 1941- *BestSel 90-3 [port], ConAu 32NR, MajTwCW, WhoWrEP 89, WorAlBi*
Will, George Frederick 1941- *WhoAm 90, WhoE 91*
Will, Hubert Louis 1914- *WhoAm 90*
Will, James Fredrick 1938- *WhoAm 90, WhoE 91*
Will, Jerrie Ann 1950- *WhoAmW 91, WhoE 91*
Will, Jessie German 1912- *WhoAmW 91*
Will, Joanne M. *ODwPR 91*
Will, Joanne Marie 1937- *WhoAm 90*
Will, John 1917- *WhoAm 90*
Will, John A 1939- *WhoAmA 91*
Will, Michael Rudolf 1937- *WhoWor 91*
Will, Michael Vincent *BiDrAPA 89*
Will, Montford S. 1943- *St&PR 91*
Will, Otto A, Jr. 1910- *BiDrAPA 89*
Will, Peter 1935- *St&PR 91*
Will, Robert C. 1922- *ODwPR 91*
Will, Robert Erwin 1928- *WhoAm 90*
Will, Rosalyn Nell 1933- *WhoAmW 91*
Will, Susan Jean 1949- *WhoAmW 91*
Will, Thomas Joseph 1939- *St&PR 91*
Will-Sparber, Elaine Ingeborg 1954- *WhoWrEP 89*
Willadsen, Kay A. 1947- *WhoAmW 91*
Willaert, Johan Leo Gabriel 1950- *WhoWor 91*
Willam, Kaspar Jodok 1940- *WhoAm 90*
Willan, John Anthony 1943- *WhoWor 91*
Willand, Lois Carlson 1935- *WhoWrEP 89*
Willans, Jean Stone 1924- *WhoWor 91*
Willard, Barbara 1909- *BioIn 16*
Willard, Betty Riner 1948- *WhoAmW 91*
Willard, Charles Grayson 1924- *St&PR 91*
Willard, Corinne Wadhams 1920- *WhoAmW 91*
Willard, Daniel 1861-1942 *WorAlBi*
Willard, Daniel, III 1926- *WhoE 91*
Willard, Davis Wesley 1948- *WhoE 91*
Willard, Dean Marvin 1946- *St&PR 91*
Willard, Donald Smith 1924- *WhoAm 90*
Willard, Edward Nason 1945- *WhoSSW 91*
Willard, Emma 1787-1870 *BioIn 16, FemiCLE, WorAlBi*
Willard, Emma Hart 1787-1870 *BioAmW*
Willard, Frances 1839-1898 *EncAL, FemiCLE, WorAlBi*
Willard, Frances E. 1839-1898 *BioAmW*
Willard, Frank 1893-1958 *EncACom*
Willard, Frank H 1893-1958 *WhoAmA 91N*
Willard, Harrison Robert 1933- *WhoWor 91*
Willard, Helen *WhoAmA 91N*
Willard, James Douglas 1945- *WhoAm 90*
Willard, Jerry 1960- *Ballpl 90*
Willard, John Gerard 1952- *WhoEmL 91*
Willard, Joseph Edward 1865-1924 *BioIn 16*
Willard, Josiah Flynt 1869-1907 *BioIn 16*
Willard, Louis Charles 1937- *WhoAm 90*
Willard, Nancy 1936- *AuBYP 90, MajTwCW*
Willard, Nancy Margaret *WhoAm 90, WhoAmW 91*
Willard, Norman, Jr. 1924- *St&PR 91*
Willard, Patricia Rae 1949- *WhoAmW 91*
Willard, Ralph Lawrence 1922- *WhoAm 90, WhoWor 91*
Willard, Richard Kennon 1948- *WhoAm 90*
Willard, Robert Edgar 1929- *WhoAm 90*
Willard, Rodlow 1911- *EncACom*
Willard, Samuel 1640-1707 *EncCRAm*
Willard, Sherwood Skelton 1941- *St&PR 91, WhoAm 90*
Willard, Simon 1753-1848 *PenDiDA 89*
Willard, Thomas Maxwell 1937- *WhoSSW 91*
Willard, Timothy Holmes 1951- *WhoWrEP 89*
Willard, Walter V. 1934- *St&PR 91*
Willard-Gallo, Karen Elizabeth 1953- *WhoAmW 91*
Willardson, Kimberly Ann Carey 1959- *WhoAmW 91*
Willauer, George Jacob 1935- *WhoE 91*
Willauer, Whiting Russell 1931- *WhoAm 90*
Willauer, William Bradford 1944- *St&PR 91*
Willaume, David 1658-1741 *PenDiDA 89*
Willax, Paul A. *BioIn 16*
Willax, Paul Anthony 1939- *WhoAm 90*
Willbanks, Roger Paul 1934- *WhoWor 91*
Willbanks, Sue Sutton 1935- *WhoAmW 91*
Willbern, York 1915- *WhoAm 90*
Willbrandt, Barry William 1947- *WhoSSW 91*
Willcocks, David 1919- *IntWWM 90, PenDiMP*
Willcocks, Jonathan Peter 1953- *IntWWM 90*
Willcox, Frederick Preston 1910- *WhoE 91, WhoWor 91*
Willcox, Georgie Bain 1930- *WhoSSW 91*
Willcox, Hugh L. 1905- *St&PR 91*
Willcox, Peter *BioIn 16*
Willcox, Peter John 1945- *WhoWor 91*
Willcox, Toyah 1958- *BioIn 16*
Wille, Eberhard 1942- *WhoWor 91*
Wille, Frank 1931-1988 *BioIn 16*
Wille, Gunnar Edvard 1937- *WhoWor 91*
Wille, Janet Neipris 1936- *ConAu 30NR*
Wille, Lois Jean 1932- *WhoAm 90, WhoAmW 91*
Wille, Marc A. 1962- *WhoE 91*
Wille, Warren S 1924- *BiDrAPA 89*
Wille, Wayne Martin 1930- *WhoAm 90*
Willebrands, Johannes 1909- *WorAlBi*
Willebrands, Johannes Gerardus Maria 1909- *WhoWor 91*
Willebrandt, Mabel W. 1889-1963 *BioAmW*
Willeford, Betsy Ann 1939- *ConAu 132*
Willeford, Carl Ernest 1943- *WhoSSW 91*
Willeford, Charles Ray 1919-1988 *BioIn 16*
Willeford, George 1921- *BiDrAPA 89*
Willemer, Marianne von 1784-1860 *EncCoWW*
Willems, Jan Camiel 1939- *WhoWor 91*
Willems, Joseph 1715?-1766 *PenDiDA 89*
Willemstyn, Willem 1927- *St&PR 91*
Willenbecher, John 1936- *WhoAm 90, WhoAmA 91*
Willenbring, Mark Leon *BiDrAPA 89*
Willenbrink, Rose Ann 1950- *St&PR 91*
Willenbrock, Frederick Karl 1920- *WhoAm 90*
Willens, Harold 1914- *ConAu 132*
Willens, Howard Penney 1931- *WhoAm 90*
Willens, Rita Jacobs *BioIn 16, NewYTBS 90*
Willens, Tina Kirkwood 1962- *WhoAmW 91*
Willensky, Elliot *NewYTBS 90 [port]*
Willensky, Elliot 1933-1990 *BioIn 16, ConAu 131*
Willenson, Kim Jeremy 1937- *WhoAm 90*
Willenz, June Adele *WhoAmW 91*
Willenz, Nicole Valli 1958- *WhoAmW 91*
Willer, Edward Herman 1941- *WhoSSW 91*
Willer, Gary Alan *BiDrAPA 89*
Willer, Lee H 1924- *BiDrAPA 89*
Willerding, Margaret Frances 1919- *WhoAm 90*
Willerman, Lee 1939- *WhoAm 90*
Willert, August W. 1910- *St&PR 91*
Willert, Gregory R. 1943- *St&PR 91*
Willert, John A. 1930- *St&PR 91*
Willert, St. Joan 1924- *WhoAmW 91*
Willes, Jean *BioIn 16*
Willes, Mark Hinckley 1941- *St&PR 91, WhoAm 90*
Willet, E. Crosby 1929- *St&PR 91*
Willet, Henry Lee 1899-1983 *WhoAmA 91N*
Willet, Richard A. *WhoSSW 91*
Willeto, Charlie 1905?-1965 *MusmAFA*
Willeto, Leonard 1955-1984 *MusmAFA*
Willett, Mrs. *EncO&P 3*
Willett, Mrs. 1874-1956 *EncPaPR 91*
Willett, A. L. Thompson 1909- *WhoWor 91*
Willett, Allan Brock 1941- *BiDrAPA 89*
Willett, Allan Robert 1936- *St&PR 91*
Willett, Christine Robin 1961- *WhoE 91*
Willett, David A. 1935- *St&PR 91*
Willett, Ed 1884-1934 *Ballpl 90*
Willett, Edward Farrand, Jr. 1933- *WhoAm 90*
Willett, Fehrunissa Maureen 1953- *WhoSSW 91*
Willett, Jacques 1882-1958 *WhoAmA 91N*
Willett, John E. 1930- *St&PR 91*
Willett, Kenneth B. 1901- *St&PR 91*
Willett, Michael Scott 1958- *WhoSSW 91*
Willett, Robert Bynum 1939- *St&PR 91*
Willett, Robert E., Jr. 1941- *ODwPR 91*
Willett, Roslyn *ODwPR 91*
Willett, T Gregory 1942- *BiDrAPA 89*
Willett, Vincent Roger, Jr. 1948- *WhoSSW 91*
Willette, Edward David 1935- *St&PR 91*
Willette, Leslie Ray 1927- *St&PR 91*
Willetts, Susan A. 1955- *St&PR 91*
Willey, C.S. *St&PR 91*
Willey, Calvert Livingston 1920- *WhoAm 90*
Willey, Carl 1931- *Ballpl 90*
Willey, Charles Wayne 1932- *WhoWor 91*
Willey, Chloe 1760- *FemiCLE*
Willey, Gordon Randolph 1913- *WhoAm 90*
Willey, Grafton H., III 1923- *St&PR 91*
Willey, H. David 1930- *WhoE 91*
Willey, James Henry 1939- *IntWWM 90*
Willey, James Lee 1953- *WhoEmL 91*
Willey, John C. 1914-1990 *BioIn 16, ConAu 131, NewYTBS 90*
Willey, John Douglas 1917- *WhoAm 90*
Willey, Paul Wayne 1938- *WhoAm 90*
Willey, Philo Levi 1887-1980 *MusmAFA*
Willey, Phyllis D. 1945- *St&PR 91*
Willey, Robert *AuBYP 90*
Willham, Richard Lewis 1932- *WhoAm 90*
Willhite, Donald H. 1936- *St&PR 91*
Willhite, Nick 1941- *Ballpl 90*
Willhite-Wright, Jeanne Elmore 1946- *WhoAmW 91*
Willhoit-Rudt, Marilyn Jean 1947- *WhoEmL 91*
Willhouse, Donald Edwin 1944- *WhoE 91*
Willi, Jim Henry 1948- *WhoSSW 91*
William I 1028?-1087 *WorAlBi*
William II 1859-1941 *BioIn 16*
William III and Mary II *PenDiDA 89*
William, Archbishop of Tyre 1130?-1190? *BioIn 16*
William III, King of Great Britain 1650-1702 *BioIn 16*
William II of England 1056?-1100 *EncO&P 3*
William, Prince of Great Britain 1982- *BioIn 16*
William Rufus 1056?-1100 *EncO&P 3*
William I, the Conqueror 1027?-1087 *BioIn 16*
William, Gordon L. *St&PR 91*
William, Wayne 1942- *St&PR 91*
Williams' Jubilee Singers *DcAfAmP*
Williams, Adrian 1956- *IntWWM 90*
Williams, Al 1954- *Ballpl 90*
Williams, Alan 1935- *SpyFic*

Williams, Alan 1952- *WhoSSW 91*
Williams, Alan Davison 1925- *WhoAm 90*
Williams, Alan Gentry 1951- *St&PR 91*
Williams, Alan Harold 1927- *WhoWor 91*
Williams, Albert E. 1940- *St&PR 91*
Williams, Albert Frank, III 1957- *WhoSSW 91*
Williams, Albert Norman 1935- *WhoAm 90*
Williams, Albert Paine 1935- *WhoAm 90*
Williams, Albert Theophilus Wadi 1922- *WhoSSW 91*
Williams, Alberta Norine 1908- *WhoWrEP 89*
Williams, Alexander Johnston 1943- *WhoAm 90*
Williams, Alfred Blythe 1940- *WhoWor 91*
Williams, Alfred Vaughn *BiDrAPA 89*
Williams, Alice Noel Tuckerman 1918- *WhoE 91*
Williams, Alwyn 1921- *WhoWor 91*
Williams, Alyson *BioIn 16*
Williams, Andy 1928- *OxCPMus*
Williams, Andy 1930- *WorAlBi*
Williams, Angela 1966- *WhoAmW 91*
Williams, Angela Carol 1970- *WhoAmW 91*
Williams, Angelia Evette 1960- *WhoSSW 91*
Williams, Angie C. 1927- *St&PR 91*
Williams, Ann C. 1949- *WhoAmW 91*
Williams, Ann Houston 1943- *WhoAmW 91*
Williams, Ann Meagher 1929- *WhoAmW 91*
Williams, Anna 1706-1783 *FemiCLE*
Williams, Anna Fay 1935- *WhoAmW 91*
Williams, Anne *ConAu 32NR, NewAgMG*
Williams, Anne Douglas 1943- *WhoE 91*
Williams, Annie John 1913- *WhoAmW 91, WhoSSW 91, WhoWor 91*
Williams, Art *BioIn 16*
Williams, Arthur 1904- *WhoAm 90*
Williams, Arthur Cozad 1926- *WhoAm 90*
Williams, Arthur Middleton, Jr. 1914- *WhoAm 90*
Williams, Arvin Samuel 1920- *WhoAm 90*
Williams, Aubrey Willis 1924- *WhoAm 90*
Williams, Avon Nyanza, Jr. 1921- *WhoSSW 91*
Williams, Barbara *BioIn 16*
Williams, Barbara 1925- *AuBYP 90*
Williams, Barbara 1937- *SmATA 62 [port]*
Williams, Barbara Anne 1938- *WhoAmW 91, WhoE 91*
Williams, Barbara Ellen 1933- *WhoSSW 91*
Williams, Barbara Ivory 1936- *WhoAmW 91, WhoE 91*
Williams, Barbara Jean 1948- *WhoAmW 91*
Williams, Barbara Jean May 1927- *WhoAm 90*
Williams, Barbara Joann 1933- *WhoWrEP 89*
Williams, Barbara Joanne K *BiDrAPA 89*
Williams, Barbara June 1948- *WhoE 91*
Williams, Barbara Lou 1927- *WhoAmW 91*
Williams, Barbara R. 1933- *St&PR 91*
Williams, Barry *BioIn 16*
Williams, Barry 1954- *ConTFT 8*
Williams, Barry Neil *BiDrAPA 89*
Williams, Barry Richard 1949- *WhoE 91*
Williams, Ben Ames 1889-1953 *DcLB 102 [port]*
Williams, Ben Franklin, Jr. 1929- *WhoAm 90*
Williams, Ben Wayne 1932- *St&PR 91*
Williams, Benjamin Davis, III 1936- *WhoAm 90*
Williams, Benjamin Forrest 1925- *WhoAmA 91*
Williams, Benjamin Tallifaro 1931- *WhoAm 90*
Williams, Bernard 1929- *ConAu 130*
Williams, Bernard Arthur Owen 1929- *WhoAm 90*
Williams, Bernard Moore *BiDrAPA 89*
Williams, Bernard Norman 1932- *WhoWor 91*
Williams, Bert 1874-1922 *DrBlPA 90, OxCPMus*
Williams, Bert 1875-1922 *BioIn 16*
Williams, Bessie *EncO&P 3*
Williams, Betsy Lynn 1950- *WhoAmW 91*
Williams, Betty 1943- *BioIn 16, WhoWor 91*
Williams, Beverly D 1954- *BiDrAPA 89*
Williams, Beverly Jean 1945- *St&PR 91*
Williams, Bill 1939- *WhoWrEP 89*
Williams, Billy 1916-1972 *DrBlPA 90*
Williams, Billy 1930- *Ballpl 90*
Williams, Billy 1938- *Ballpl 90 [port]*
Williams, Billy Brinn 1941- *St&PR 91*
Williams, Billy Dee *BioIn 16*
Williams, Billy Dee 1937- *ConTFT 8 [port], DrBlPA 90, WhoAm 90, WorAlBi*
Williams, Billy Leo 1938- *WhoAm 90*
Williams, Bradley Verne 1950- *BiDrAPA 89*
Williams, Brandt Hugh 1950- *WhoSSW 91*
Williams, Brenda Joan 1965- *WhoAmW 91*
Williams, Brenda Wilcox *ODwPR 91*
Williams, Brian 1943- *BioIn 16*
Williams, Brian Thomas 1948- *St&PR 91*
Williams, Bruce *BioIn 16*
Williams, Bruce David 1932- *St&PR 91*
Williams, Bruce Edward 1931- *WhoE 91*
Williams, Bruce K. 1948- *St&PR 91*
Williams, Bruce Livingston 1945- *WhoSSW 91*
Williams, Bruce S. *St&PR 91*
Williams, Bryan *WhoAm 90*
Williams, Bryn Terence 1939- *WhoWor 91*
Williams, Buff 1882-1933 *Ballpl 90*
Williams, C. James, III 1960- *WhoEmL 91*
Williams, C. K. 1936- *BioIn 16*
Williams, C. Terry 1944- *St&PR 91*
Williams, Camilla *DrBlPA 90, IntWWM 90, WhoAm 90*
Williams, Camilla 1922- *BioIn 16*
Williams, Camilla Ella 1922- *DcAfAmP*
Williams, Carl Chanson 1937- *St&PR 91, WhoAm 90*
Williams, Carl E., Sr. *WhoAm 90*
Williams, Carl Harwell 1915- *WhoAm 90*
Williams, Carl Leslie 1938- *WhoSSW 91*
Williams, Carlton Hinkle 1914- *WhoAm 90*
Williams, Carol Jorgensen 1944- *WhoAmW 91, WhoE 91, WhoWor 91*
Williams, Carol Kennedy 1956- *WhoSSW 91*
Williams, Carolyn Antonides 1939- *WhoAmW 91*
Williams, Carolyn Elizabeth 1943- *St&PR 91, WhoAmW 91*
Williams, Carolyn Knight 1945- *WhoAmW 91*
Williams, Carolyn Ruth Armstrong 1944- *WhoAmW 91*
Williams, Carrie Patricia 1960- *BiDrAPA 89*
Williams, Carroll Milton 1916- *WhoAm 90*
Williams, Casey 1947- *WhoAmA 91*
Williams, Charles *AuBYP 90, ConAu 33NR, EncO&P 3*
Williams, Charles 1850?- *EncPaPR 91*
Williams, Charles 1886-1945 *DcLB 100 [port]*
Williams, Charles 1893-1978 *OxCPMus*
Williams, Charles 1908- *WorAlBi*
Williams, Charles 1909-1975 *TwCCr&M 91*
Williams, Charles D *BiDrAPA 89*
Williams, Charles D. 1935- *ODwPR 91*
Williams, Charles David 1935- *WhoAm 90*
Williams, Charles Dudley 1933- *St&PR 91, WhoAm 90*
Williams, Charles Edward 1946- *WhoE 91*
Williams, Charles Finn 1954- *St&PR 91*
Williams, Charles G. *WhoSSW 91*
Williams, Charles G. 1933- *St&PR 91*
Williams, Charles J. *AmLegL*
Williams, Charles Kenneth 1936- *BioIn 16, WhoAm 90, WhoWrEP 89*
Williams, Charles Laval, Jr. 1916- *WhoAm 90*
Williams, Charles Lee 1947- *WhoE 91*
Williams, Charles Linwood 1960- *WhoAm 90*
Williams, Charles M. *St&PR 91*
Williams, Charles M. 1912- *St&PR 91*
Williams, Charles Marvin 1917- *WhoAm 90*
Williams, Charles Murray 1931- *WhoSSW 91*
Williams, Charles N. 1946- *WhoSSW 91*
Williams, Charles Oliver, Jr. 1939- *WhoSSW 91*
Williams, Charles Pickens 1926- *WhoAm 90*
Williams, Charles R. 1947- *St&PR 91*
Williams, Charles Raymond 1945- *WhoSSW 91*
Williams, Charles Stanley, Jr. 1921- *WhoAm 90*
Williams, Charles Wesley *WhoAm 90*
Williams, Charlie 1947- *Ballpl 90*
Williams, Charlotte Bell 1944- *WhoAmW 91, WhoSSW 91*
Williams, Charlotte Evelyn Forrester 1905- *WhoAmW 91, WhoSSW 91, WhoWor 91*
Williams, Charlton H. 1915- *St&PR 91*
Williams, Chee Chee *DrBlPA 90*
Williams, Chester Arthur, Jr. 1924- *WhoAm 90*
Williams, Chester Lee 1944- *WhoAmA 91*
Williams, Christian 1943- *ConAu 130*
Williams, Christopher Alan 1962- *IntWWM 90*
Williams, Christopher Brian 1950- *St&PR 91*
Williams, Christopher Roland 1956- *IntWWM 90*
Williams, Chuck *BioIn 16*
Williams, Cicely D. 1893- *BioIn 16*
Williams, Cindy *BioIn 16*
Williams, Cindy 1947- *WorAlBi*
Williams, Cindy J. 1947- *WhoEmL 91*
Williams, Cindy Lee 1958- *WhoAmW 91*
Williams, Clarence *EarBlAP*
Williams, Clarence 1893-1965 *DrBlPA 90*
Williams, Clarence 1898-1965 *OxCPMus*
Williams, Clarence, III 1939- *DrBlPA 90*
Williams, Clarke McRae 1922- *St&PR 91*
Williams, Claude 1893-1977 *EncAL*
Williams, Clayton Wheat, Jr. *BioIn 16*
Williams, Clifford T. 1955- *St&PR 91*
Williams, Clyde C. 1881-1974 *AuBYP 90*
Williams, Clyde E., Jr. 1919- *St&PR 91, WhoAm 90*
Williams, Coe *AuBYP 90*
Williams, Colin David 1948- *WhoSSW 91*
Williams, Collin Peter 1941- *St&PR 91*
Williams, Constance I A *BiDrAPA 89*
Williams, Cootie 1908-1985 *BioIn 16, DrBlPA 90, OxCPMus*
Williams, Craig Lamar 1952- *WhoSSW 91*
Williams, Cranston 1895-1989 *BioIn 16*
Williams, Cranston, Jr. 1926- *St&PR 91*
Williams, Cy 1887-1974 *Ballpl 90*
Williams, Dale C. 1955- *St&PR 91*
Williams, Dale Philip 1928- *St&PR 91*
Williams, Dan Edward 1950- *WhoEmL 91*
Williams, Daniel Douglas 1962- *WhoEmL 91*
Williams, Daniel T 1944- *BiDrAPA 89*
Williams, Daniel Turk 1944- *WhoE 91*
Williams, Darnell 1955- *DrBlPA 90*
Williams, Darrell E. *ODwPR 91*
Williams, Darryl Marlowe 1938- *WhoAm 90*
Williams, Dave Harrell 1932- *WhoAm 90, WhoAmA 91*
Williams, Davey 1927-1955 *Ballpl 90*
Williams, David 1904- *WhoE 91*
Williams, David 1926- *TwCCr&M 91*
Williams, David Alan 1928- *WhoSSW 91*
Williams, David Allan 1949- *WhoEmL 91*
Williams, David Benton 1920- *WhoAm 90*
Williams, David Brian 1943- *IntWWM 90*
Williams, David C. 1928- *WhoE 91*
Williams, David Earl 1953- *WhoSSW 91*
Williams, David Fulton 1926- *St&PR 91, WhoAm 90*
Williams, David Harold *BiDrAPA 89*
Williams, David Henry, Jr. 1931- *St&PR 91, WhoAm 90*
Williams, David Irvin 1942- *WhoAm 90*
Williams, David Jon 1944- *WhoAmA 91*
Williams, David Overton, Jr. 1925- *WhoSSW 91*
Williams, David Perry 1934- *St&PR 91, WhoAm 90*
Williams, David R. 1943- *St&PR 91*
Williams, David R., Jr. 1921- *St&PR 91*
Williams, David Rogerson, Jr. 1921- *WhoAm 90*
Williams, David Russell 1932- *IntWWM 90, WhoAm 90*
Williams, David Welford 1910- *WhoAm 90*
Williams, Deborah Lynn 1946- *WhoE 91*
Williams, Deborah Spiceland 1958- *WhoSSW 91*
Williams, Deborah White 1954- *St&PR 91*
Williams, Debra Ann 1954- *WhoAmW 91*
Williams, Debra W. 1959- *St&PR 91*
Williams, Delwin *BiDrAPA 89*
Williams, Delwyn Charles 1936- *WhoAm 90*
Williams, Deniece *BioIn 16*
Williams, Deniece 1951- *DrBlPA 90, WhoAmW 91*
Williams, Dennis A. *BioIn 16*
Williams, Dennis Thomas 1925- *WhoE 91*
Williams, Dennis Vaughn 1946- *WhoE 91, WhoEmL 91, WhoWor 91*
Williams, Diane *WhoWrEP 89*
Williams, Diane Lynn 1951- *WhoAmW 91*
Williams, Diane Theresa 1955- *WhoE 91*
Williams, Diane Wray 1938- *WhoAmW 91*
Williams, Dib 1910- *Ballpl 90*
Williams, Dick 1928- *Ballpl 90 [port]*
Williams, Dick Anthony 1938- *DrBlPA 90*
Williams, Dolores Louise 1937- *WhoAmW 91*
Williams, Don 1939- *ConMus 4 [port]*
Williams, Don E. 1923- *St&PR 91*
Williams, Donald Clyde 1939- *WhoAm 90*
Williams, Donald E. *St&PR 91N*
Williams, Donald Elmer 1930- *WhoSSW 91*
Williams, Donald H 1936- *BiDrAPA 89*
Williams, Donald Herbert 1936- *WhoAm 90*
Williams, Donald Jarvis 1940- *BiDrAPA 89*
Williams, Donald John 1933- *WhoAm 90*
Williams, Donald R. 1946- *St&PR 91*
Williams, Donald Shand 1930- *WhoAm 90*
Williams, Doreen 1949- *WhoAmW 91*
Williams, Doris Terry 1951- *WhoEmL 91*
Williams, Dorothea Webb 1948- *WhoAmW 91*
Williams, Dorothy Elizabeth *BioIn 16*
Williams, Dorothy Washington 1946- *WhoAmW 91*
Williams, Doug *BioIn 16*
Williams, Doug 1955- *WorAlBi*
Williams, Douglas George 1932- *WhoAm 90*
Williams, Doyce Vann 1952- *WhoSSW 91*
Williams, Doyle Z. 1939- *WhoAm 90*
Williams, Drew Davis 1935- *WhoAm 90, WhoWor 91*
Williams, Dudley 1912- *WhoAm 90*
Williams, Dudley D. 1939- *St&PR 91*
Williams, Earl 1948- *Ballpl 90*
Williams, Earl Duane 1929- *WhoWor 91*
Williams, Earl Glynn 1949- *WhoWor 91*
Williams, Earl Patrick, Jr. 1950- *WhoE 91*
Williams, Earle Carter 1929- *St&PR 91, WhoAm 90, WhoSSW 91*
Williams, Ebenezer David, Jr. 1927- *WhoE 91*
Williams, Eda Dunstan *WhoAmW 91*
Williams, Eddie C. 1958- *WhoSSW 91*
Williams, Eddie Nathan 1932- *WhoAm 90*
Williams, Eddie Ruth 1947- *WhoAmW 91*
Williams, Edgar *AuBYP 90*
Williams, Edgar 1926- *IntWWM 90*
Williams, Edgar A. 1911- *St&PR 91*
Williams, Edgar Gene 1922- *WhoAm 90*
Williams, Edgar Warren 1949- *IntWWM 90*
Williams, Edna Aleta Theadora Johnston 1923- *WhoAmW 91*
Williams, Edson Poe 1923- *WhoAm 90*
Williams, Edward Bennett *BioIn 16*
Williams, Edward Bennett 1920-1988 *WorAlBi*
Williams, Edward Christopher 1871-1929 *EarBlAP*
Williams, Edward David 1932- *WhoE 91*
Williams, Edward Earl, Jr. 1945- *WhoAm 90, WhoWor 91*
Williams, Edward F., III 1935- *WhoWrEP 89*
Williams, Edward Foster, III 1935- *WhoSSW 91*
Williams, Edward G. 1929- *AuBYP 90, WhoWrEP 89*
Williams, Edward Gilman 1926- *WhoAm 90*
Williams, Edward Jones, IV 1961- *WhoSSW 91*
Williams, Edward Joseph 1942- *WhoAm 90*
Williams, Edward K 1870- *WhoAmA 91N*
Williams, Edward Thomas 1854-1944 *BioIn 16*
Williams, Edward Vinson 1935- *WhoAm 90*
Williams, Edwin William 1912- *WhoAm 90*
Williams, Elaine 1953- *WhoAmW 91*
Williams, Eleanor Joyce 1936- *WhoAmW 91*
Williams, Eleazar 1788-1858 *WhNaAH*
Williams, Elisabeth Green 1915- *WhoAmW 91*
Williams, Elizabeth 1948- *WhoAmW 91*
Williams, Elizabeth Gertner 1927- *WhoAmW 91*
Williams, Elizabeth Gundlach 1944- *WhoAmW 91*
Williams, Elliot Joseph 1939- *St&PR 91*
Williams, Elwyn Gildas 1946- *IntWWM 90*
Williams, Elynor Alberta 1946- *WhoAmW 91*
Williams, Emlyn 1905- *WorAlBi*
Williams, Emlyn 1905-1987 *MajTwCW*
Williams, Emory 1911- *St&PR 91, WhoAm 90*
Williams, Erastus Appleman 1850-1930 *AmLegL*
Williams, Eric Ernest 1911-1983 *AuBYP 90, DcNaB 1981*
Williams, Eric Eustace 1911-1981 *BioIn 16*
Williams, Eric Joseph 1945- *WhoEmL 91, WhoWor 91*
Williams, Eric Stanton 1958- *WhoSSW 91*
Williams, Erma Brooks 1957- *WhoAmW 91*
Williams, Ernest *WhoSSW 91*
Williams, Ernest E. 1916-1989 *BioIn 16*
Williams, Ernest Edward 1914- *WhoAm 90*
Williams, Ernest Going 1915- *St&PR 91, WhoAm 90*
Williams, Ernest William, Jr. 1916- *WhoAm 90*

Williams, Ernest Y BiDrAPA 89
Williams, Ernest Y. NewYTBS 90
Williams, Esther 1923- WorAlBi
Williams, Ethel Frances 1928- WhoAmW 91
Williams, Eugene D. 1921- St&PR 91
Williams, Eugene F., Jr. 1923- St&PR 91
Williams, Eugene Flewellyn, Jr. 1923- WhoAm 90
Williams, Evan Michael 1945- WhoWor 91
Williams, Evelyn 1929- BiDWomA
Williams, Everett W BiDrAPA 89
Williams, Fiona BioIn 16
Williams, Flora Leona 1937- WhoAmW 91
Williams, Forman Arthur 1934- WhoAm 90
Williams, Francis Leon 1918- WhoWor 91
Williams, Francis Michael 1941- St&PR 91
Williams, Frank 1958- Ballpl 90
Williams, Frank Evan 1934- WhoWor 91
Williams, Frank J. 1940- WhoWor 91
Williams, Frank J., Jr. 1938- ODwPR 91
Williams, Frank James, Jr. 1938- St&PR 91, WhoAm 90
Williams, Frank Mathews 1938- WhoSSW 91
Williams, Frank R. 1948- St&PR 91
Williams, Frank S BiDrAPA 89
Williams, Frank Talton, Jr. 1941- WhoSSW 91
Williams, Frankie E BiDrAPA 89
Williams, Franklin H. BioIn 16
Williams, Franklin H. NewYTBS 90 [port]
Williams, Franklin John 1940- WhoAmA 91
Williams, Fred A. 1938- St&PR 91
Williams, Fred Alton, Jr. 1923- WhoSSW 91, WhoWor 91
Williams, Fred B. St&PR 91
Williams, Fred Devoe, III 1936- WhoAm 90
Williams, Frederic Allen 1898-1958 WhoAmA 91N
Williams, Frederick 1922- WhoAm 90
Williams, Frederick Ballard 1871-1956 WhoAmA 91N
Williams, Frederick D. WhoAm 90
Williams, Frederick DeForrest 1918- WhoAm 90
Williams, Frederick Park 1924- IntWWM 90
Williams, Fredrick Elbert 1939- WhoSSW 91
Williams, G. Bretnell 1929- St&PR 91
Williams, G. Mont 1944- WhoAm 90
Williams, Gail Ann 1953- WhoAmW 91
Williams, Garth 1912- BioIn 16
Williams, Garth Montgomery 1912- AuBYP 90, WhoAm 90
Williams, Gary Alan 1962- WhoSSW 91
Williams, Gary Murray 1940- WhoAm 90
Williams, Gavin Rodney 1942- IntWWM 90
Williams, Gene Troy 1940- St&PR 91
Williams, George 1821-1905 BioIn 16
Williams, George 1910- MusmAFA
Williams, George Abiah 1931- WhoAm 90
Williams, George Cabell 1926- St&PR 91
Williams, George Christopher 1926- WhoAm 90, WhoE 91
Williams, George Connor 1929- St&PR 91
Williams, George Doyne, Jr. 1935- WhoAm 90
Williams, George Earnest 1923- WhoAm 90
Williams, George H. 1932- St&PR 91
Williams, George Henry 1823-1910 BiDrUSE 89
Williams, George Howard 1918- WhoAm 90
Williams, George Huntston 1914- WhoAm 90
Williams, George James 1920- St&PR 91
Williams, George Leo 1931- WhoE 91
Williams, George Masayasu 1930- WhoAm 90
Williams, George Rafter 1914- St&PR 91
Williams, George Rainey 1926- WhoAm 90
Williams, George Randall BiDrAPA 89
Williams, George Thomas, Jr. 1959- WhoE 91
Williams, George Valentine 1883-1946 SpyFic
Williams, George W., III 1930- St&PR 91
Williams, George Walton 1922- WhoAm 90
Williams, George Washington 1849-1891 BioIn 16
Williams, George Zur 1907- WhoAm 90
Williams, Gerhard Mennen 1911-1988 BioIn 16
Williams, Gerhard Mennen, Jr. 1941- St&PR 91
Williams, Gertie Boothe WhoAmW 91
Williams, Glen Morgan 1920- WhoAm 90, WhoSSW 91
Williams, Glenn Carber 1914- WhoAm 90
Williams, Gordon ConAu 130, TwCCr&M 91
Williams, Gordon Bretnell 1929- WhoAm 90
Williams, Gordon Harold 1937- WhoAm 90
Williams, Gordon Lee 1947- WhoSSW 91
Williams, Gordon M 1934?- ConAu 130
Williams, Gordon Roland 1914- WhoAm 90
Williams, Graham 1931- WhoE 91
Williams, Gregory 1948- WhoE 91
Williams, Gregory Howard 1943- WhoAm 90
Williams, Gretchen Minyard 1956- WhoSSW 91
Williams, Gunther Gebel- BioIn 16
Williams, Gurney, III 1941- ConAu 30NR
Williams, Gus 1888-1964 Ballpl 90
Williams, Guy 1924-1989 BioIn 16
Williams, Guy R 1920- ConAu 31NR
Williams, Gwendolen 1870-1955 BiDWomA
Williams, H. Kirk, III 1924- St&PR 91
Williams, Hal DrBIPA 90
Williams, Hamilton Wayne 1942- St&PR 91
Williams, Hampton Murray 1931- WhoSSW 91
Williams, Hank WhoNeCM C [port]
Williams, Hank 1923-1953 OxCPMus, WorAlBi
Williams, Hank 1949- BioIn 16
Williams, Hank, Jr. WhoNeCM [port]
Williams, Hank, Jr. 1949- OxCPMus, WhoAm 90, WorAlBi
Williams, Hank, Sr. 1923-1953 ConMus 4 [port]
Williams, Harold 1914-1990 ConAu 131
Williams, Harold 1934- WhoAm 90
Williams, Harold Anthony 1916- WhoAm 90
Williams, Harold David 1952- WhoSSW 91
Williams, Harold Duane 1942- St&PR 91
Williams, Harold L. 1926- St&PR 91
Williams, Harold Marvin 1928- WhoAm 90
Williams, Harold Milton 1907- WhoAm 90
Williams, Harold Roger 1935- WhoAm 90
Williams, Harold William 1920- WhoE 91
Williams, Harriet Clarke 1922- WhoAmW 91, WhoE 91, WhoWor 91
Williams, Harriet Elizabeth 1918- WhoAmW 91
Williams, Harry Edward 1925- WhoWor 91
Williams, Harry John, Jr. 1924- WhoSSW 91
Williams, Harry Leverne 1916- WhoAm 90
Williams, Heather Niles 1962- WhoAmW 91, WhoE 91
Williams, Helen Margaret 1947- WhoAmW 91
Williams, Helen Maria 1762?-1827 BioIn 16, FemiCLE
Williams, Helen Morgan 1933- WhoWrEP 89
Williams, Henry Rudolph 1919- WhoSSW 91
Williams, Henry Thomas 1932- WhoAm 90
Williams, Henry Ward, Jr. 1930- St&PR 91, WhoE 91
Williams, Herbert B. 1933- St&PR 91
Williams, Hermann Warner, Jr 1908-1975 WhoAmA 91N
Williams, Hermine Weigel 1933- IntWWM 90
Williams, Hiram Draper 1917- WhoAm 90, WhoAmA 91
Williams, Hope 1897-1990 BioIn 16, NewYTBS 90 [port]
Williams, Howard 1947- IntWWM 90
Williams, Howard Russell 1915- WhoAm 90
Williams, Howard Walter 1937- WhoWor 91
Williams, Hugh Alexander, Jr. 1926- WhoAm 90
Williams, Hugh C. 1930- St&PR 91
Williams, Hugh Steadman 1935- ConAu 132
Williams, Hulen Brown 1920- WhoAm 90
Williams, Idaherma WhoAmA 91, WhoE 91
Williams, Irene E.G. 1951- WhoWrEP 89
Williams, Irene Mae 1943- WhoWrEP 89
Williams, Irving BioIn 16
Williams, J. D. 1937- WhoAm 90
Williams, J. Hulon, III 1952- St&PR 91
Williams, J. Linda 1945- WhoEmL 91
Williams, J. R. EncACom
Williams, J. Robert BioIn 16
Williams, J.T., Jr. 1933- St&PR 91
Williams, J. Vernon 1921- WhoAm 90
Williams, J.W., Jr. 1925- St&PR 91
Williams, J. Walker ConAu 33NR, MajTwCW
Williams, Jack L. 1944- St&PR 91
Williams, Jack Marvin 1938- WhoAm 90
Williams, Jack Murphy 1934- WhoSSW 91
Williams, Jack R. 1929- St&PR 91
Williams, Jack Raymond 1923- WhoWor 91
Williams, James BioIn 16
Williams, James 1796-1869 BioIn 16
Williams, James Alexander 1929- WhoAm 90
Williams, James Arthur 1932- WhoAm 90
Williams, James B. 1945- WhoAm 90
Williams, James Bryan 1933- St&PR 91, WhoAm 90, WhoSSW 91
Williams, James Case 1938- WhoAm 90, WhoWor 91
Williams, James Edgar 1924- St&PR 91
Williams, James Eugene, Jr. 1927- WhoAm 90
Williams, James Francis, Jr. 1938- WhoSSW 91
Williams, James Franklin, II 1944- WhoAm 90
Williams, James Garth 1938- BiDrAPA 89
Williams, James Howard 1920- WhoSSW 91
Williams, James J. ODwPR 91
Williams, James Kay 1931- WhoE 91
Williams, James Kelley 1934- St&PR 91, WhoAm 90, WhoSSW 91
Williams, James Kendrick WhoAm 90
Williams, James Lee 1941- WhoAm 90
Williams, James Lee, Sr. 1939- WhoSSW 91
Williams, James Lloyd 1940- St&PR 91
Williams, James Lynn 1943- St&PR 91
Williams, James Marshall 1947- WhoSSW 91
Williams, James O. 1931- St&PR 91
Williams, James Orrin 1937- WhoAm 90, WhoSSW 91
Williams, James P., Jr. 1944- WhoAm 90
Williams, James Robert 1947- St&PR 91, WhoE 91
Williams, James Stanley 1934- St&PR 91
Williams, James William 1825?-1892 DcCanB 12
Williams, Jana Montice BiDrAPA 89
Williams, Jane 1806-1885 FemiCLE
Williams, Jane Almena 1957- WhoE 91
Williams, Jane Ann 1952- WhoEmL 91
Williams, Janelle Evon 1959- WhoAmW 91
Williams, Janet B. W. 1947- BiDrAPA 89
Williams, Janet Elaine BiDrAPA 89
Williams, Janet Faye 1934- WhoAmW 91
Williams, Janet Jean Deare 1946- WhoSSW 91
Williams, Janice Denise 1951- WhoAmW 91
Williams, Janice E WhoAmA 91
Williams, Janie BioIn 16
Williams, Jay 1914-1978 AuBYP 90
Williams, Jay Kevin 1950- WhoSSW 91
Williams, Jay Stephen 1949- WhoE 91
Williams, Jean Myers 1948- WhoAmW 91
Williams, Jean Shipp 1946- WhoE 91
Williams, Jeanne BioIn 16
Williams, Jeanne Freeman 1924- WhoAmW 91
Williams, Jeffery 1920- ConAu 132
Williams, Jeffrey Scott 1952- WhoSSW 91
Williams, Jenny 1939- SmATA 60
Williams, Jerre Stockton 1916- WhoAm 90
Williams, Jerry 1932- St&PR 91
Williams, Jerry Arthur 1925- St&PR 91
Williams, Jerry David 1930- WhoSSW 91
Williams, Jerry Mayer 1934- St&PR 91
Williams, Jerry O. 1938- BioIn 16, St&PR 91
Williams, Jim ODwPR 91
Williams, Jimmy 1876-1965 Ballpl 90
Williams, Jimy BioIn 16
Williams, Jimy 1943- Ballpl 90
Williams, Joan 1927- BioIn 16
Williams, Joan 1928- BioIn 16, WhoWrEP 89
Williams, Joe BioIn 16
Williams, Joe 1891-1972 Ballpl 90
Williams, Joe 1918- DrBIPA 90, WhoAm 90, WorAlBi
Williams, Joe Anderson 1958- WhoSSW 91
Williams, Joe Ed 1945- St&PR 91
Williams, Joel AuBYP 90
Williams, Joel Jay 1948- WhoEmL 91
Williams, John BioIn 16, ODwPR 91
Williams, John BioIn 16
Williams, John 1664-1729 EncCRAm
Williams, John 1932- OxCPMus, PenDiMP, WorAlBi
Williams, John 1941- IntWWM 90, PenDiMP, WhoWor 91
Williams, John 1954- ConAu 129
Williams, John A. 1925- WhoAm 90, WhoWrEP 89
Williams, John A. 1955- St&PR 91
Williams, John Alden 1928- WhoAmA 91
Williams, John Andrew 1941- WhoAm 90
Williams, John Autry BiDrAPA 89
Williams, John Barry TwCCr&M 91
Williams, John Brooks 1921- St&PR 91
Williams, John Burr 1900-1989 BioIn 16, ConAu 129
Williams, John Carl 1952- WhoSSW 91
Williams, John Chamberlin 1919- WhoE 91
Williams, John Cornelius 1903- WhoAm 90
Williams, John David 1923- ODwPR 91
Williams, John Dickinson 1923- St&PR 91
Williams, John Dickinson, Jr. 1952- St&PR 91
Williams, John Edwin 1928- WhoAm 90
Williams, John F. 1828- AmLegL
Williams, John H. BioIn 16
Williams, John H. 1918- St&PR 91
Williams, John Hartley 1942- ConAu 130
Williams, John Horter 1918- WhoAm 90
Williams, John Howard 1942- St&PR 91
Williams, John Irving, Jr. 1954- WhoE 91
Williams, John J. 1904-1988 BioIn 16
Williams, John James, Jr. 1949- WhoEmL 91
Williams, John Kelvin 1932- St&PR 91
Williams, John Krueger 1956- WhoE 91
Williams, John Lawrence 1951- WhoE 91
Williams, John Lee 1942- WhoSSW 91
Williams, John M. 1944- WhoSSW 91
Williams, John Martyn 1947- IntWWM 90
Williams, John Pattison, Jr. 1941- WhoAm 90
Williams, John T. 1932- BioIn 16
Williams, John Tilman 1925- WhoAm 90
Williams, John Tolliver 1944- WhoSSW 91
Williams, John Towner 1932- WhoE 91, WhoWor 91
Williams, John Wesley 1928- WhoAm 90, WhoAmA 91
Williams, Jon Edward 1937- WhoE 91
Williams, Jonathan 1929- ConAu 12AS [port]
Williams, Joseph Benjamin 1933- IntWWM 90
Williams, Joseph Dalton 1926- St&PR 91, WhoAm 90, WhoE 91
Williams, Joseph H. 1933- St&PR 91
Williams, Joseph Hill 1933- WhoAm 90, WhoSSW 91
Williams, Joseph John 1832- AmLegL
Williams, Joseph Lanier 1921- WhoSSW 91
Williams, Joseph R. 1931- WhoAm 90
Williams, Joseph Theodore 1937- WhoAm 90, WhoSSW 91
Williams, Joseph Wesley 1938- WhoSSW 91
Williams, Josie R. 1941- WhoSSW 91
Williams, Joy 1944- BioIn 16, WhoWrEP 89
Williams, Joy Rhonda 1945- WhoAmW 91
Williams, Joyce Ann 1944- WhoAmW 91
Williams, Joyce White 1929- WhoE 91
Williams, Judith Ann 1954- WhoAmW 91
Williams, Judith L. 1948- WhoSSW 91
Williams, Judson F. 1913- St&PR 91
Williams, Julia Tochie 1887-1948 WhoAmA 91N
Williams, Julian Benjamin BioIn 16
Williams, Julie Belle 1950- WhoAmW 91
Williams, Julie F. 1948- St&PR 91
Williams, Julie Ford 1948- WhoAm 90
Williams, Julius Penson 1954- IntWWM 90
Williams, June Vanleer ConAu 131
Williams, Justin W. 1942- WhoAm 90
Williams, Karen BioIn 16
Williams, Karen A. 1956- WhoSSW 91
Williams, Karen B. 1956- WhoAmW 91
Williams, Karen Grava 1952- WhoE 91
Williams, Kate ConAu 30NR
Williams, Katharine K 1951- BiDrAPA 89
Williams, Kathleen Hopson 1958- WhoSSW 91
Williams, Kathryn Fraser BiDrAPA 89
Williams, Kay Nobile 1948- BiDrAPA 89
Williams, Keith Shaw 1905-1951 WhoAmA 91N
Williams, Ken 1890-1959 Ballpl 90
Williams, Ken 1964- Ballpl 90
Williams, Ken Michael 1944- WhoWor 91
Williams, Kenneth 1926-1988 AnObit 1988, BioIn 16
Williams, Kenneth B. 1954- BiDrAPA 89
Williams, Kenneth Edward 1928- IntWWM 90
Williams, Kenneth Franklin 1945- St&PR 91
Williams, Kenneth Merald, Jr. 1957- WhoSSW 91

Williams, Kenneth Raynor 1912- WhoAm 90
Williams, Kenneth Scott 1955- WhoAm 90
Williams, Kenneth Stewart 1940- WhoWor 91
Williams, Kent Alan 1946- WhoSSW 91
Williams, Kimmika Lyvette Hawes 1959- WhoWrEP 89
Williams, Kitty St&PR 91
Williams, Koren Debi A. 1958- WhoWor 91
Williams, L. Stanton 1919- St&PR 91
Williams, La Ronnia Vernon Dobson 1934- WhoAmW 91
Williams, Langbourne Meade 1903- WhoAm 90
Williams, Larry 1935-1980 OxCPMus
Williams, Larry Bill 1945- WhoAm 90
Williams, Larry E. 1936- St&PR 91
Williams, Larry Michael 1939- St&PR 91
Williams, Laura Lee 1956- WhoAm 90
Williams, Laverne IntWWM 90
Williams, Lavinia BioIn 16
Williams, Lawrence Eugene 1949- WhoAm 90
Williams, Lawrence Soper 1917- WhoE 91
Williams, Lea Everard 1924- WhoAm 90
Williams, Lee Dwain 1950- WhoEmL 91
Williams, Lefty 1893-1959 Ballpl 90
Williams, Leon Vincent 1949- WhoSSW 91
Williams, Leonard Todd, Jr. 1947- WhoEmL 91, WhoWor 91
Williams, Leslie Howard, Jr. 1942- WhoAm 90
Williams, Leslie Pearce 1927- WhoAm 90
Williams, Lewis Edmund 1939- WhoE 91
Williams, Lewis Lanier 1929- St&PR 91
Williams, Lewis M BiDrAPA 89
Williams, Lewis W, II 1918-1990 WhoAmA 91N
Williams, Lillie B. 1945- WhoAmW 91
Williams, Linda AuBYP 90, BioIn 16
Williams, Linda Mangham 1945- WhoAmW 91
Williams, Linda Turner 1941- WhoAmW 91
Williams, Lisa BioIn 16
Williams, Lois 1953- BiDWomA
Williams, Loraine Plant 1929- WhoSSW 91
Williams, Lorelle 1945- WhoAmW 91, WhoWor 91
Williams, Loretta Walton 1938- WhoAmW 91
Williams, Louis C., Jr. 1940- ODwPR 91
Williams, Louis Gressett 1913- WhoAm 90
Williams, Louis Stanton 1919- WhoAm 90
Williams, Louise PenDiMP
Williams, Lowell K 1921- BiDrAPA 89
Williams, Lucia Lorain 1815-1874 BioIn 16
Williams, Lucinda BioIn 16
Williams, Lucious Lawrence 1932- WhoSSW 91
Williams, Luke G. 1923- St&PR 91
Williams, Lula Agnes 1904- WhoAmW 91
Williams, Lula Mae 1947- WhoAmW 91
Williams, Luther Steward 1940- WhoAm 90
Williams, Lydia Frances 1949- WhoAmW 91
Williams, Lyman Neil, Jr. 1936- WhoAm 90
Williams, Lynda Elaine 1951- WhoAmW 91, WhoEmL 91
Williams, Lynn AuBYP 90, BioIn 16
Williams, Lynne Huie 1943- BiDrAPA 89
Williams, M. A., Mrs. EncO&P 3
Williams, M. Jane 1955- WhoAmW 91
Williams, M. Suzanne 1963- WhoAmW 91
Williams, M. V. Seton- 1910- BioIn 16
Williams, Madeleine Crozat- BioIn 16
Williams, Marcille G. 1947- ODwPR 91
Williams, Margaret Helen 1926- WhoAmW 91
Williams, Margaret Jean BiDrAPA 89
Williams, Margaret Kay 1946- WhoAmW 91
Williams, Margaret Lu Wertha Hiett 1938- WhoAmW 91, WhoSSW 91, WhoWor 91
Williams, Mari Melanie 1965- WhoAmW 91
Williams, Marilyn 1950- WhoAmW 91
Williams, Marilyn Janet 1929- St&PR 91
Williams, Marion 1927- DrBlPA 90
Williams, Marion Elizabeth 1941- WhoAmW 91
Williams, Marjorie J. WhoAm 90
Williams, Marjory BioIn 16
Williams, Mark Carmichael 1963- WhoSSW 91
Williams, Mark Douglas BiDrAPA 89
Williams, Marlys J. 1932- WhoAmW 91
Williams, Marsha Rhea 1948- WhoEmL 91
Williams, Marshall Henry, Jr. 1924- WhoAm 90
Williams, Marshall MacKenzie 1923- St&PR 91
Williams, Martha Daugherty 1938- WhoE 91
Williams, Martha Ethelyn 1934- WhoAm 90, WhoAmW 91
Williams, Martha G. 1942- St&PR 91
Williams, Martha Jane Shipe 1935- WhoAm 90
Williams, Martin 1924- IntWWM 90
Williams, Martin Keith 1962- BiDrAPA 89
Williams, Martin Tridor 1924- WhoAm 90
Williams, Martyn John 1953- IntWWM 90
Williams, Marvin 1944- WhoSSW 91
Williams, Marvin Justine 1958- WhoSSW 91
Williams, Mary Alice BioIn 16, WhoAmW 91
Williams, Mary Beth 1956- WhoAmW 91
Williams, Mary Catherine BiDrAPA 89
Williams, Mary Elmore 1931- WhoAmW 91, WhoSSW 91, WhoWor 91
Williams, Mary Irene 1944- WhoAmW 91
Williams, Mary Lou 1910-1981 BioIn 16, DrBlPA 90, OxCPMus
Williams, Mary Macaulay 1959- St&PR 91
Williams, Mary Pearl 1928- WhoAm 90
Williams, Marylou Lord Study WhoAmA 91
Williams, Matt 1965- Ballpl 90
Williams, Maurice 1938- EncPR&S 89
Williams, Maurice Jacoutot 1920- WhoAm 90
Williams, Max Lea, Jr. 1922- WhoAm 90
Williams, Maxine Eleanor 1940- WhoAmW 91
Williams, Melborne A 1945- BiDrAPA 89
Williams, Melissa 1951- WhoAmA 91
Williams, Melva Jean 1935- WhoAmW 91, WhoWor 91
Williams, Melva Maureen 1958- WhoAmW 91
Williams, Melvenia Corean 1945- WhoAmW 91
Williams, Melvin Gilbert 1937- WhoE 91
Williams, Melvin John 1915- WhoAm 90
Williams, Melvin Walker BiDrAPA 89
Williams, Meredith Jane 1947- WhoAmW 91
Williams, Michael Alan 1948- WhoEmL 91
Williams, Michael Allan 1933- WhoAm 90
Williams, Michael Anthony 1932- WhoAm 90
Williams, Michael Charles 1952- WhoSSW 91
Williams, Michael D. 1915-1989 BioIn 16
Williams, Michael David 1947- WhoE 91
Williams, Michael Edward 1954- WhoWrEP 89
Williams, Michael Erwin 1948- WhoSSW 91
Williams, Michael Judson 1937- St&PR 91
Williams, Michael L NewYTBS 90 [port]
Williams, Michael Roy 1946- WhoSSW 91
Williams, Michael S. 1946- St&PR 91
Williams, Michele Olga 1949- WhoAmW 91
Williams, Mikki Terry 1943- WhoAmW 91
Williams, Mildred Jane 1944- WhoAmW 91, WhoE 91, WhoSSW 91
Williams, Miller 1930- DcLB 105 [port], WhoAm 90, WhoSSW 91, WhoWor 91, WhoWrEP 89
Williams, Milton Craig 1945- BiDrAPA 89
Williams, Milton W. 1949- St&PR 91
Williams, Miriam M BiDrAPA 89
Williams, Mitch BioIn 16
Williams, Mitch 1964- Ballpl 90
Williams, Moke W BiDrAPA 89
Williams, Morgan Lloyd 1935- St&PR 91, WhoAm 90
Williams, Murat Willis 1914- WhoAm 90
Williams, N. Jane 1955- WhoAmW 91
Williams, Nancy Ellen-Webb WhoAmW 91, WhoWor 91, WhoWrEP 89
Williams, Neil WhoAmA 91N
Williams, Neil 1934-1988 BioIn 16
Williams, Noel A BiDrAPA 89
Williams, Noreen 1955- WhoAmW 91
Williams, Norman 1915- WhoE 91
Williams, Norton L BiDrAPA 89
Williams, Olan Dale 1944- St&PR 91
Williams, Oni 1943- WhoWrEP 89
Williams, Oscar 1939- DrBlPA 90
Williams, Otis 1941- ConAu 130
Williams, Pamela Bernice 1948- WhoAmW 91
Williams, Parham Wilson 1938- St&PR 91
Williams, Pat 1937- WhoAm 90
Williams, Pat Ward 1948- WhoAmA 91
Williams, Patricia Ann BiDrAPA 89
Williams, Patricia Ann 1950- St&PR 91, WhoAmW 91
Williams, Patricia Ann 1951- WhoAmW 91
Williams, Patricia W BiDrAPA 89
Williams, Patrick 1950- ConAu 129
Williams, Patrick Moody 1939- WhoAm 90
Williams, Paul 1940- BioIn 16, ConMus 5 [port], WorAlBi
Williams, Paul Alan 1934- WhoAmA 91
Williams, Paul Anthony, II 1946- St&PR 91
Williams, Paul Chester 1926- St&PR 91
Williams, Paul Hamilton 1940- WhoAm 90
Williams, Paul Robert 1937- WhoWor 91
Williams, Paul T. 1934- St&PR 91
Williams, Paul Thomas 1934- WhoSSW 91
Williams, Paul Vincent 1941- BiDrAPA 89
Williams, Paul W. 1957- St&PR 91
Williams, Paul X. St&PR 91
Williams, Penny 1937- WhoAmW 91
Williams, Percy Don 1922- WhoAm 90, WhoSSW 91
Williams, Peter C. 1946- St&PR 91
Williams, Peter Fredric 1937- IntWWM 90
Williams, Peter H. C. 1935- St&PR 91
Williams, Peter Maclellan 1931- WhoE 91, WhoWor 91
Williams, Peter W 1944- ConAu 30NR
Williams, Peter Welles 1948- BiDrAPA 89, WhoE 91
Williams, Petra Schatz 1913- WhoAmW 91
Williams, Philip Copelain 1917- WhoWor 91
Williams, Philip Eugene 1923- WhoWor 91
Williams, Philip H. 1953- St&PR 91
Williams, Philip Lee 1950- ConAu 129
Williams, Philip Mitchell 1933- St&PR 91
Williams, Phillip L. WhoAm 90
Williams, Phillip L. 1922- St&PR 91
Williams, Phillip Stephen 1949- WhoAm 90
Williams, Phillip Wayne 1939- WhoSSW 91
Williams, Phyllis Cutforth 1917- WhoAmW 91
Williams, Phyllis Eleanor 1920- WhoAmW 91
Williams, Pop 1874-1959 Ballpl 90
Williams, Preston C., Jr. 1925- St&PR 91
Williams, Preston Clark, Jr. 1925- WhoAm 90
Williams, Preston Noah 1926- WhoAm 90
Williams, Quinn Patrick 1949- St&PR 91
Williams, R Hallock 1929- BiDrAPA 89
Williams, R. Hallock 1929- WhoE 91
Williams, R. Leon 1909- St&PR 91
Williams, R. Owen 1952- WhoWor 91
Williams, R. P. BioIn 16
Williams, Ralph A BiDrAPA 89
Williams, Ralph Chester, Jr. 1928- WhoAm 90
Williams, Ralph L 1952- BiDrAPA 89
Williams, Ralph Vaughan PenDiMP A
Williams, Ralph Vaughan 1872-1958 BioIn 16
Williams, Ralph Watson, Jr. 1933- WhoAm 90
Williams, Randall 1951- BioIn 16
Williams, Ray Anthony DrBlPA 90
Williams, Raymond 1921-1988 AnObit 1988, BioIn 16, ConAu 33NR, MajTwCW
Williams, Raymond 1935- ConAu 132
Williams, Raymond F. St&PR 91
Williams, Raymond Lester 1926- WhoAmA 91
Williams, Redford Brown 1940- WhoAm 90
Williams, Reggie BioIn 16
Williams, Reginald Victor, III 1956- WhoAm 90
Williams, Reynear 1840- AmLegL
Williams, Rhona Loraine 1953- WhoAmW 91
Williams, Rhys 1929- WhoAm 90
Williams, Richard BioIn 16
Williams, Richard Bruce 1947- WhoE 91
Williams, Richard Clarence 1923- WhoAm 90
Williams, Richard D. 1926- St&PR 91
Williams, Richard Donald 1926- WhoAm 90
Williams, Richard Dwayne 1944- WhoAm 90
Williams, Richard Eaton 1930- WhoAm 90
Williams, Richard Eldon 1934- WhoAmA 91
Williams, Richard J. 1936- St&PR 91
Williams, Richard James 1942- WhoWor 91
Williams, Richard Leroy 1923- WhoAm 90, WhoSSW 91
Williams, Richard Lloyd 1934- St&PR 91
Williams, Richard Lucas, III 1940- WhoAm 90
Williams, Richard N. 1957- WhoSSW 91
Williams, Richard Rhys 1923- WhoAm 90
Williams, Richard Warren BiDrAPA 89
Williams, Richmond Dean 1925- WhoAm 90
Williams, Rick 1952- Ballpl 90
Williams, Robert A 1942- BiDrAPA 89
Williams, Robert A. 1944- ODwPR 91
Williams, Robert C. 1930- WhoAm 90, WhoSSW 91
Williams, Robert C. 1934- WhoAm 90
Williams, Robert Carlton 1948- WhoSSW 91, WhoWor 91
Williams, Robert Chadwell 1938- WhoAm 90
Williams, Robert Coleman 1940- WhoWor 91
Williams, Robert E. St&PR 91N
Williams, Robert Edward 1933- IntWWM 90
Williams, Robert Eugene 1940- WhoAm 90
Williams, Robert F. 1925- BioIn 16
Williams, Robert Frank 1916- St&PR 91
Williams, Robert Gordon 1934- St&PR 91
Williams, Robert Hope, Jr. 1910- WhoAm 90
Williams, Robert Jene 1931- St&PR 91, WhoAm 90
Williams, Robert Jerrell 1932- BiDrAPA 89
Williams, Robert K 1924- BiDrAPA 89
Williams, Robert L 1922- BiDrAPA 89
Williams, Robert Leon 1922- WhoAm 90
Williams, Robert Luther 1923- WhoAm 90
Williams, Robert Lyle 1942- WhoAm 90
Williams, Robert M. 1941- St&PR 91
Williams, Robert Mann 1940- WhoE 91
Williams, Robert Martin 1913- WhoAm 90
Williams, Robert Nowell 1930- St&PR 91
Williams, Robert O. St&PR 91
Williams, Robert Stewart 1944- WhoE 91, WhoWor 91
Williams, Robert Thomas, Jr. 1946- St&PR 91
Williams, Robert Walter 1920- WhoAm 90
Williams, Robin NewYTBS 90 [port]
Williams, Robin 1952- BioIn 16, WhoAm 90, WorAlBi
Williams, Robin Joy 1964- WhoAmW 91
Williams, Robin-Marie 1960- WhoAmW 91
Williams, Robin Murphy, Jr. 1914- WhoAm 90
Williams, Rodney John 1941- IntWWM 90
Williams, Rodney Thomas 1944- WhoWor 91
Williams, Roger 1603-1683 EncCRAm [port], WorAlBi
Williams, Roger 1603?-1684 WhNaAH [port]
Williams, Roger 1604?-1683 BioIn 16
Williams, Roger 1924- WhoAm 90
Williams, Roger 1939- St&PR 91
Williams, Roger Allen 1955- WhoSSW 91
Williams, Roger J. 1893-1988 BioIn 16
Williams, Roger Lawrence 1923- WhoAm 90
Williams, Roger M. BioIn 16
Williams, Roger Wright 1918- WhoAm 90
Williams, Roland Charles 1928- St&PR 91, WhoWor 91
Williams, Ronald Doherty 1927- WhoE 91, WhoWor 91
Williams, Ronald John 1927- WhoSSW 91, WhoWor 91
Williams, Ronald L. 1935- WhoAm 90
Williams, Ronald Oscar 1940- WhoWor 91
Williams, Ronald Ray 1929- IntWWM 90
Williams, Ronald Raymond 1942- St&PR 91
Williams, Rosalind Dodie 1947- WhoSSW 91
Williams, Rosana Frische 1937- WhoAmW 91
Williams, Rose ConAu 32NR
Williams, Ross Merlin 1931- St&PR 91
Williams, Roy Henry 1936- WhoE 91
Williams, Roy L. BioIn 16
Williams, Ruby Elizabeth 1933- WhoSSW 91
Williams, Russell Eugene 1951- WhoE 91
Williams, Russell I., Jr. 1917- St&PR 91
Williams, Ruth Ann 1958- WhoAmW 91
Williams, Ruth Arlene 1956- WhoWrEP 89
Williams, Ruth Evelyn 1952- WhoAmW 91
Williams, Ruth H. 1938- WhoAmW 91
Williams, Ruth Lee 1944- WhoWor 91
Williams, S. Bradford, Jr. 1944- WhoWrEP 89
Williams, S. Linn 1946- WhoE 91

Williams, Sally Mae 1954- *WhoAmW 91*
Williams, Samm *ConTFT 8*
Williams, Samm Art 1942?- *DrBlPA 90*
Williams, Samm-Art 1946- *ConTFT 8*
Williams, Samuel D, Sr. *BiDrAPA 89*
Williams, Samuel Dunstan 1936- *St&PR 91*
Williams, Sandra Keller 1944- *WhoAmW 91*
Williams, Sandra Wheeler 1957- *WhoAmW 91*
Williams, Sarah 1841-1868 *FemiCLE*
Williams, Shelley Suezanne 1964- *WhoEmL 91*
Williams, Sherley Anne 1944- *FemiCLE*
Williams, Sherry Lynne 1952- *WhoAm 90, WhoSSW 91*
Williams, Shirley Mae 1954- *WhoSSW 91*
Williams, Shirley Vivian Teresa Brittain 1930- *WhoWor 91*
Williams, Shirley Y *BiDrAPA 89*
Williams, Sioned 1953- *IntWWM 90*
Williams, Slim *AuBYP 90*
Williams, Smokey Joe 1886-1946 *Ballpl 90*
Williams, Sonja D *BiDrAPA 89*
Williams, Sophia Wells Royce 1850-1928 *BioIn 16*
Williams, Spencer 1889-1965 *DrBlPA 90, OxCPMus*
Williams, Spencer 1893-1969 *DrBlPA 90, EarBlAP*
Williams, Spencer M. 1922- *WhoAm 90*
Williams, Stan 1936- *Ballpl 90*
Williams, Stanley 1925- *WhoAm 90*
Williams, Stanley Alan 1934- *WhoAm 90*
Williams, Stefana *ODwPR 91*
Williams, Stephen 1926- *WhoAm 90*
Williams, Stephen Arthur 1952- *WhoWrEP 89*
Williams, Stephen Fain 1936- *WhoE 91*
Williams, Sterling Lee 1943- *WhoAm 90*
Williams, Steven *BioIn 16*
Williams, Steven Randell 1954- *WhoSSW 91*
Williams, Steven Roger 1951- *St&PR 91*
Williams, Steven Wilson 1955- *WhoSSW 91*
Williams, Sue Darden 1943- *WhoAm 90, WhoAmW 91, WhoSSW 91*
Williams, Susan Eileen 1952- *WhoAmW 91, WhoWor 91*
Williams, Susan M. 1961- *WhoAmW 91*
Williams, Sylvia H 1936- *WhoAmA 91*
Williams, Sylvia Hill 1936- *WhoAm 90, WhoAmW 91*
Williams, T. H. Lee 1951- *WhoSSW 91*
Williams, T. Lynn *St&PR 91*
Williams, Talcott 1849-1928 *BioIn 16*
Williams, Talmage Theodore, Jr. 1933- *WhoSSW 91*
Williams, Ted *BioIn 16*
Williams, Ted 1918- *Ballpl 90 [port], BioIn 16, WhoAm 90, WorAlBi*
Williams, Temple Weatherly, Jr. 1934- *WhoAm 90*
Williams, Tennessee 1911-1983 *BioIn 16, ConAu 31NR, MajTwCW, WorAlBi*
Williams, Terry Wesley 1952- *St&PR 91*
Williams, Theodore Clayton 1947 *St&PR 91*
Williams, Theodore E. *BioIn 16*
Williams, Theodore E. 1943- *WhoAm 90*
Williams, Theodore Earle 1920- *St&PR 91, WhoAm 90*
Williams, Theodore Joseph 1923- *WhoAm 90*
Williams, Thomas *WhNaAH*
Williams, Thomas *NewYTBS 90 [port]*
Williams, Thomas 1926- *WhoAm 90, WhoWrEP 89*
Williams, Thomas 1926-1990 *ConAu 132, WorAu 1980 [port]*
Williams, Thomas A. 1936- *St&PR 91*
Williams, Thomas Allison 1936- *WhoAm 90, WhoE 91*
Williams, Thomas Arthur 1936- *BiDrAPA 89*
Williams, Thomas C. 1939- *St&PR 91*
Williams, Thomas Carl 1940- *St&PR 91*
Williams, Thomas E. 1948- *St&PR 91*
Williams, Thomas Eugene 1936- *WhoSSW 91, WhoWor 91*
Williams, Thomas Eugene 1961- *WhoSSW 91*
Williams, Thomas Ffrancon 1928- *WhoAm 90*
Williams, Thomas Franklin 1921- *WhoAm 90*
Williams, Thomas Harold, Jr. 1934- *BiDrAPA 89*
Williams, Thomas L, Jr. 1925- *BiDrAPA 89*
Williams, Thomas Lanier 1911-1983 *BioIn 16, WrPh*
Williams, Thomas Lee 1945- *St&PR 91*
Williams, Thomas P. *BiDrAPA 89*
Williams, Thomas Rice 1928- *St&PR 91*
Williams, Thomas Stafford 1930- *WhoWor 91*
Williams, Thomas Thackery 1925- *WhoSSW 91*
Williams, Timothy John 1966- *WhoSSW 91*
Williams, Timothy Shaler 1928- *WhoAm 90*
Williams, Tonda 1949- *WhoAmW 91, WhoE 91*
Williams, Tony *BioIn 16*
Williams, Treat 1951- *ConTFT 8 [port], WhoAm 90*
Williams, Trevor G 1924- *BiDrAPA 89*
Williams, Tyler Edward, Jr. 1926- *WhoE 91, WhoWor 91*
Williams, Valena Marie 1948- *WhoAmW 91*
Williams, Valentine 1883-1946 *TwCCr&M 91*
Williams, Valerie Christine 1944- *St&PR 91*
Williams, Van *BioIn 16*
Williams, Vanessa *BioIn 16, DrBlPA 90*
Williams, Vera B. *BioIn 16*
Williams, Vera B. 1927- *AuBYP 90*
Williams, Vergil Lewis 1935- *WhoAm 90*
Williams, Vernon *BioIn 16*
Williams, Veronica Ann 1956- *WhoAmW 91, WhoE 91, WhoEmL 91, WhoWor 91*
Williams, Veronica Myres 1947- *WhoAmW 91*
Williams, Victoria Anne Vilchez 1955- *WhoWor 91*
Williams, Virginia Sue 1931- *WhoSSW 91*
Williams, Vivian *BioIn 16*
Williams, Vivian Lewie 1923- *WhoAmW 91*
Williams, W. Clyde *WhoAm 90*
Williams, Walt 1943- *Ballpl 90*
Williams, Walter Baker 1921- *WhoWor 91*
Williams, Walter Fred 1929- *St&PR 91, WhoAm 90, WhoE 91, WhoWor 91*
Williams, Walter Hudson 1910- *St&PR 91*
Williams, Walter Jackson, Jr. 1925- *WhoAm 90*
Williams, Walter Joseph 1918- *WhoAm 90*
Williams, Walter Randolph 1939- *WhoWor 91*
Williams, Walter W. *WhoAm 90*
Williams, Walter Waylon 1933- *WhoAm 90*
Williams, Warner 1903-1982 *WhoAmA 91N*
Williams, Warren Herbert 1951- *BiDrAPA 89*
Williams, Wayne C., Jr. 1928- *St&PR 91*
Williams, Wayne De Armond 1914- *WhoAm 90*
Williams, Wayne Francis 1937- *WhoAmA 91*
Williams, Wesley Nathaniel, Jr. 1946- *WhoSSW 91*
Williams, Wesley Samuel, Jr. 1942- *WhoAm 90*
Williams, Wheeler 1897-1972 *WhoAmA 91N*
Williams, Wilbur K. 1927- *St&PR 91*
Williams, Wilho Edward 1922- *WhoAm 90*
Williams, William *WhoAm 90*
Williams, William 1731-1811 *EncCRAm*
Williams, William Appleman *EncAL*
Williams, William Appleman *NewYTBS 90 [port]*
Williams, William Appleman 1921-1990 *BioIn 16, ConAu 131*
Williams, William Arnold 1922- *WhoAm 90*
Williams, William Bryant, Jr. 1940- *WhoSSW 91*
Williams, William C. *MajTwCW*
Williams, William Carlos 1883-1963 *BioIn 16, MajTwCW, WorAlBi*
Williams, William Earle 1950- *WhoAmA 91, WhoE 91*
Williams, William Gordon 1935- *WhoE 91*
Williams, William Harrison 1924- *WhoAm 90*
Williams, William Henry, II 1931- *WhoE 91, WhoWor 91*
Williams, William Ivor 1923- *WhoAm 90*
Williams, William John 1928- *St&PR 91*
Williams, William John, Jr. 1937- *WhoAm 90, WhoE 91*
Williams, William Joseph 1926- *WhoAm 90*
Williams, William Lane 1914- *WhoAm 90*
Williams, William Martin 1935- *St&PR 91*
Williams, William Orville 1940- *WhoAm 90*
Williams, William Ralph 1917- *St&PR 91*
Williams, William Ralston 1910- *WhoAm 90*
Williams, William Robert 1949- *WhoE 91*
Williams, William S. 1787-1849 *WhNaAH*
Williams, William Thomas 1942- *WhoAm 90, WhoAmA 91*
Williams, William Walter, Jr. 1927- *St&PR 91*
Williams, Willie, Jr. 1947- *WhoAm 90, WhoE 91*
Williams, Willie Biggs 1949- *WhoSSW 91*
Williams, Wilmer Dempsey 1937- *WhoSSW 91*
Williams, Woody 1912- *Ballpl 90*
Williams, Wyman 1928- *St&PR 91*
Williams, Wythe 1881-1956 *BioIn 16*
Williams, Yvonne Elaine 1944- *WhoSSW 91*
Williams, Zack 1888- *DrBlPA 90*
Williams-Ashman, Howard Guy 1925- *WhoAm 90*
Williams-Breese, Marilyn Olive 1942- *WhoAmW 91, WhoWor 91*
Williams-Cacicedo, Jean *BioIn 16*
Williams-Ellis, Amabel 1894-1984 *FemiCLE*
Williams-Hall, Jill Denise 1959- *WhoE 91*
Williams-King, Anne *IntWWM 90*
Williams-Sanchez, Toni Adella 1952- *WhoAmW 91*
Williams-Steinwender, Karin Mae 1948- *WhoAmW 91*
Williams-Thorpe, Elisabeth Faye 1962- *WhoWrEP 89*
Williams-Tims, Lillie Althea 1951- *WhoSSW 91*
Williamsen, Walter John 1941- *St&PR 91*
Williamson, Ada C 1883-1958 *WhoAmA 91N*
Williamson, Alexander W. 1824-1904 *WorAlBi*
Williamson, Alistair David 1962- *WhoE 91*
Williamson, Alyce L. 1935- *WhoAmW 91*
Williamson, Andrew 1730?-1786 *EncCRAm*
Williamson, Arlene 1947- *WhoSSW 91*
Williamson, Barbara Diane 1950- *WhoAmW 91*
Williamson, Barbara Jane 1963- *WhoAmW 91*
Williamson, Barbara Lewis 1941- *WhoSSW 91*
Williamson, Barbara Williams 1945- *WhoAmW 91*
Williamson, Bruce Monroe 1947- *St&PR 91*
Williamson, C. Dickie 1931- *St&PR 91*
Williamson, Cecil H. *EncO&P 3*
Williamson, Charles DeMontel 1946- *St&PR 91*
Williamson, Chet 1948- *WhoWrEP 89*
Williamson, Clara 1875-1976 *MusmAFA*
Williamson, Clara McDonald *WhoAmA 91N*
Williamson, Clarence Kelly 1924- *WhoAm 90*
Williamson, Cy M. 1922- *St&PR 91*
Williamson, David, Jr. 1930- *WhoAm 90*
Williamson, David Douglas 1945- *WhoSSW 91*
Williamson, David Francis 1934- *WhoWor 91*
Williamson, Dennis W. 1941- *St&PR 91*
Williamson, Donna C. Erickson 1952- *St&PR 91*
Williamson, Douglas Franklin, Jr. 1930- *WhoAm 90, WhoWor 91*
Williamson, E.L. 1924- *St&PR 91*
Williamson, Edith 1938- *WhoSSW 91*
Williamson, Edythe Evelyn 1925- *BiDrAPA 89*
Williamson, Ernest Lavone 1924- *WhoAm 90, WhoSSW 91*
Williamson, Evangeline FloAnn 1934- *WhoWor 91*
Williamson, Fletcher Phillips 1923- *WhoE 91, WhoWor 91*
Williamson, Fred 1938- *DrBlPA 90*
Williamson, Frederick B., III 1918- *St&PR 91*
Williamson, Frederick Beasley, III 1918- *WhoAm 90*
Williamson, G. Robert, III 1947- *St&PR 91*
Williamson, George Andrew 1946- *WhoSSW 91*
Williamson, George Evans 1887- *EncO&P 3*
Williamson, Gerald Neal 1932- *WhoWrEP 89*
Williamson, Geraldine Clift 1936- *WhoSSW 91*
Williamson, Gilbert D. 1936- *St&PR 91*
Williamson, Gilbert Pemberton *BioIn 16*
Williamson, Gilbert Pemberton 1937- *St&PR 91*
Williamson, Gilbert Pemberton, Jr. 1937- *WhoAm 90*
Williamson, Handy, Jr. 1945- *WhoSSW 91*
Williamson, Harwood Danford 1932- *St&PR 91, WhoAm 90*
Williamson, Henry 1895-1977 *MajTwCW*
Williamson, Henry G., Jr. 1947- *St&PR 91*
Williamson, Henry Gaston, Jr. 1947- *WhoAm 90, WhoSSW 91*
Williamson, Herbert C., III 1948- *St&PR 91*
Williamson, Herbert M. 1951- *St&PR 91*
Williamson, Horace Hampton 1924- *WhoAm 90*
Williamson, Hugh 1735-1819 *BioIn 16, EncCRAm*
Williamson, Hugh Jackson 1943- *WhoSSW 91*
Williamson, Isabel K. *BioIn 16*
Williamson, J. N. *WhoWrEP 89*
Williamson, Jack 1908- *RGTwCSF, WhoAm 90*
Williamson, James 1806-1895 *DcCanB 12*
Williamson, Janet A. 1934- *WhoAmW 91*
Williamson, Jason H 1926- *WhoAmA 91*
Williamson, Jay Reed 1953- *WhoSSW 91*
Williamson, Jeffrey Gale 1935- *WhoE 91*
Williamson, Jeffrey Phillips 1945- *WhoE 91*
Williamson, Jewel 1965- *WhoAmW 91*
Williamson, Joanne Small 1926- *AuBYP 90*
Williamson, Jody Lynn 1959- *WhoEmL 91*
Williamson, John 1908- *WorAlBi*
Williamson, John 1937- *WhoE 91*
Williamson, John A. 1927- *St&PR 91*
Williamson, John Alexander 1918- *WhoSSW 91*
Williamson, John Fletcher 1818-1889 *AmLegL*
Williamson, John Pritchard 1922- *WhoAm 90*
Williamson, John Ramsden 1929- *IntWWM 90*
Williamson, Joseph Dallas, II 1945- *St&PR 91*
Williamson, Juanita V. *WhoAmW 91, WhoSSW 91, WhoWor 91*
Williamson, Keith Harvey 1952- *WhoE 91*
Williamson, Kenneth Dale 1920- *WhoSSW 91*
Williamson, Kenneth Lee 1934- *WhoAm 90*
Williamson, L. Paul 1946- *WhoSSW 91*
Williamson, Laird 1937- *WhoAm 90*
Williamson, Liz *WhoAm 90, WhoE 91*
Williamson, Malcolm 1931- *PenDiMP A*
Williamson, Malcolm Benjamin Graham C. 1931- *IntWWM 90*
Williamson, Margaret 1924- *AuBYP 90*
Williamson, Margery Paysinger 1927- *WhoAmW 91*
Williamson, Marilyn Lammert 1927- *WhoAm 90*
Williamson, Mark 1959- *Ballpl 90*
Williamson, Marlene M. 1955- *ODwPR 91*
Williamson, Maynard Burden 1922- *WhoE 91*
Williamson, Michael Joe 1944- *St&PR 91*
Williamson, Miriam Bedinger 1919- *WhoAmW 91*
Williamson, Mykel T *DrBlPA 90*
Williamson, Myrna Hennrich 1937- *WhoAm 90, WhoAmW 91*
Williamson, Nancy Danowitz 1950- *WhoAmW 91*
Williamson, Nancy Lee 1939- *WhoE 91*
Williamson, Ned 1857-1894 *Ballpl 90*
Williamson, Neil Seymour, III 1935- *WhoWor 91*
Williamson, Nicol 1938- *ConTFT 8, WhoAm 90, WhoWor 91, WorAlBi*
Williamson, Oliver Eaton 1932- *WhoAm 90*
Williamson, Patricia M. 1952- *St&PR 91*
Williamson, Peter Charles 1953- *BiDrAPA 89*
Williamson, Peter David 1944- *WhoAm 90*
Williamson, Peter Woollard 1938- *St&PR 91*
Williamson, R. Max 1937- *St&PR 91*
Williamson, Ralph Edward 1949- *WhoSSW 91*
Williamson, Richard 1946- *WhoWrEP 89*
Williamson, Richard Cardinal 1939- *WhoAm 90*
Williamson, Richard Dale 1947- *WhoE 91*
Williamson, Richard Hall 1940- *WhoAm 90*
Williamson, Richard Salisbury 1949- *WhoAm 90*
Williamson, Robert Charles 1925- *WhoSSW 91, WhoWor 91*
Williamson, Robert Elmore 1937- *WhoSSW 91*
Williamson, Robert Paul 1944- *WhoAm 90*
Williamson, Robert Thomas 1946- *WhoE 91*
Williamson, Robert W. 1942- *St&PR 91*
Williamson, Roberta Ann *BiDrAPA 89*
Williamson, Ronald Frank 1941- *WhoAm 90*
Williamson, Rushton Marot, Jr. 1948- *WhoE 91*

Williamson, Sam 1910- WhoAm 90
Williamson, Samuel Ruthven, Jr. 1935- WhoAm 90
Williamson, Sandra D. 1942- St&PR 91
Williamson, Sherri Redies 1953- WhoAmW 91
Williamson, Steven Douglas 1944- St&PR 91
Williamson, Terry E. 1959- St&PR 91
Williamson, Thomas Arnold 1939- St&PR 91, WhoAm 90
Williamson, Thomas Garnett 1934- WhoAm 90
Williamson, Truman Dale, Jr. 1913- St&PR 91
Williamson, Vikki Lyn 1956- WhoAmW 91, WhoEmL 91, WhoWor 91
Williamson, Walker Kendrick 1924- WhoSSW 91
Williamson, Walter Bland 1938- WhoWor 91
Williamson, Walter L. 1928- St&PR 91
Williamson, Warren B. 1928- St&PR 91
Williamson, Warren Pyatt, Jr. 1900- WhoAm 90
Williamson, William A., Jr. 1936- St&PR 91
Williamson, William Floyd, Jr. 1924- WhoAm 90
Williamson, William Paul, Jr. 1929- WhoAm 90, WhoSSW 91
Williamson-Hunt, Barbara 1951- WhoE 91
Williamsons WorAlBi
Willian, Suzanne Spiller 1962- WhoAmW 91
Williar, Sara Bertha BiDrAPA 89
Willick, Martin S 1933- BiDrAPA 89
Willie, Charles V 1927- ConAu 31NR
Willie, Charles Vert 1927- WhoAm 90
Willie, Frederick MajTwCW
Willies, Douglas B. 1950- St&PR 91
Williford, Clifford Frederick 1950- WhoWor 91
Williford, Donald Bratton 1936- St&PR 91
Williford, Hollis 1940- BioIn 16
Williford, Hollis R 1940- WhoAmA 91
Williford, John Hugo 1930- St&PR 91
Williford, Lawrence H. 1929- ODwPR 91
Williford, Mabon Leslie, II 1950- WhoSSW 91
Williford, Richard Allen 1934- St&PR 91
Williford, William Bailey 1921- WhoSSW 91
Willig, Billy Winston 1929- WhoWor 91
Willig, Doris BiDrAPA 89
Willig, Karl Victor 1944- WhoAm 90
Willig, Leslie A. 1926- St&PR 91
Willig, Robert Daniel 1947- WhoAm 90, WhoE 91
Willig, Wanda 1903- BiDrAPA 89
Willigan, Richard Joseph 1965- WhoSSW 91
Willihnganz, Paul W. 1937- St&PR 91
Willihnganz, Paul Waddell 1937- WhoSSW 91
Willimas, Caesar St&PR 91
Willimon, William H. BioIn 16
Willims, Henry L. 1941- St&PR 91
Willing, Thomas 1731-1821 EncCRAm
Willinganz, Gregory R. 1946- WhoSSW 91
Willinger, Geoffrey Lee 1944- WhoSSW 91
Willinger, Ken 1957- WhoE 91
Willinger, Laszlo BioIn 16
Willinger, Laszlo 1906-1989 AnObit 1989
Willinger, Rhonda Zwern 1962- WhoAmW 91
Willingham, Calder 1922- MajTwCW
Willingham, Calder Baynard, Jr. 1922- WhoWrEP 89
Willingham, Clark Suttles 1944- WhoAm 90
Willingham, Jeanne Maggart 1923- WhoAmW 91, WhoSSW 91
Willingham, Mary Maxine 1928- WhoAmW 91
Willingham, Sharon Givens 1954- BiDrAPA 89
Willingham, Susan Elizabeth G. 1957- WhoAmW 91
Willingham, T.K. St&PR 91
Willingham, Thomas A, III 1942- BiDrAPA 89
Willingham, Thomas Wasson 1945- St&PR 91
Willingham, Warren Willcox 1930- WhoAm 90, WhoWor 91
Willis, Albert Shelby 1843-1897 BioIn 16
Willis, Allen B. 1948- St&PR 91
Willis, Anne-Marie 1954- WhoWor 91
Willis, Barbara Cummings 1949- WhoAmW 91
Willis, Barbara Florence 1932- WhoAmA 91, WhoE 91
Willis, Benjamin Coppage 1901-1988 BioIn 16
Willis, Betty Jo 1942- WhoWrEP 89
Willis, Beverly 1928- WomArch [port]
Willis, Beverly Ann WhoAm 90
Willis, Bill BioIn 16
Willis, Bobby J. 1936- St&PR 91
Willis, Bruce BioIn 16
Willis, Bruce Walter 1955- WhoAm 90
Willis, Carl 1960- Ballpl 90
Willis, Carol Lee BiDrAPA 89
Willis, Catherine-Elizabeth 1960- WhoAmW 91
Willis, Charles AuBYP 90, MajTwCW
Willis, Charles E. 1915- St&PR 91
Willis, Chuck 1928-1958 BioIn 16
Willis, Clyde Arnold 1922- St&PR 91
Willis, Corrine AuBYP 90
Willis, Craig Dean 1935- WhoAm 90
Willis, David Edwin 1926- WhoAm 90
Willis, David Lee 1927- WhoAm 90
Willis, Dawn Louise 1959- WhoAmW 91
Willis, Deborah Bledsoe 1956- WhoAmW 91
Willis, Diana May 1943- WhoAmW 91
Willis, Donald J. 1919- BioIn 16
Willis, Donald Sigurdson 1917- WhoAm 90
Willis, Edgar Ernest 1913- WhoAm 90
Willis, Edward 1835-1891 DcCanB 12
Willis, Edward Henry 1918- SpyFic
Willis, Eleanor Lawson 1936- WhoAmW 91
Willis, Elizabeth 1936- WhoAmW 91
Willis, Elizabeth Barker 1959- WhoSSW 91
Willis, Elizabeth Bayley WhoAmA 91
Willis, Elizabeth Firestone BioIn 16
Willis, Emily Pispeky 1955- WhoAmW 91
Willis, Ernest W. 1934- St&PR 91
Willis, Everett Irving 1908- WhoAm 90
Willis, F. L. H. EncO&P 3
Willis, Frank Roy 1930- WhoAm 90
Willis, Franklin Knight 1942- WhoAm 90
Willis, Gary R. 1951- St&PR 91
Willis, George E. 1944- St&PR 91
Willis, George Edmund 1920- WhoAm 90
Willis, George Henry 1941- WhoE 91
Willis, Gerald 1938- St&PR 91
Willis, Glenn Harry 1922- WhoWor 91
Willis, Gordon WhoAm 90
Willis, Gordon A. 1938- St&PR 91
Willis, Gordon C. 1920- St&PR 91
Willis, Harold Wendt, Sr. 1927- WhoWor 91
Willis, Helen 1959- IntWWM 90
Willis, Henry BioIn 16
Willis, Ida Dennie 1929- WhoAmW 91
Willis, Isaac 1940- WhoSSW 91, WhoWor 91
Willis, Jakie Arleta WhoE 91
Willis, James Herbert 1928- BiDrAPA 89
Willis, Jan Burt 1951- St&PR 91
Willis, Jane Marlow 1942- WhoAmW 91
Willis, Jay Stewart 1940- WhoAmA 91
Willis, Jeanne 1959- SmATA 61
Willis, Jeffrey Harold 1949- WhoSSW 91
Willis, Jerry Weldon 1943- WhoSSW 91, WhoWor 91
Willis, John Alvin 1916- WhoAm 90, WhoWrEP 89
Willis, Judith Laura Levine 1941- WhoWrEP 89
Willis, Ken ODwPR 91
Willis, Kenneth R. 1932- St&PR 91
Willis, Kenneth Walter 1952- BiDrAPA 89
Willis, Kirby Roger 1951- St&PR 91
Willis, L. Clayton 1933- WhoAm 90
Willis, Laura Smith 1934- WhoAmW 91
Willis, Lisa Hart 1958- WhoAmW 91
Willis, Louise McKinney 1924- WhoWor 91
Willis, Lucille Reed 1939- WhoAmW 91
Willis, Luster 1913- MusmAFA
Willis, Lydia 1707-1767 FemiCLE
Willis, Maud ConAu 30NR
Willis, Maxine Frasure 1933- WhoAmW 91
Willis, Meredith Sue 1946- WhoWrEP 89
Willis, Meryll Meachum 1948- WhoAmW 91
Willis, Michael 1942- St&PR 91
Willis, Mike 1950- Ballpl 90
Willis, Nathaniel Parker 1806-1867 BioIn 16
Willis, Paul Allen 1941- WhoAm 90
Willis, Paul Wayne 1932- St&PR 91
Willis, Priscilla D. AuBYP 90
Willis, Ralph Houston 1942- WhoSSW 91
Willis, Raymond Edson 1930- WhoAm 90
Willis, Richard Hutchinson 1933- St&PR 91
Willis, Richard Murat 1929- WhoAm 90
Willis, Robert D. 1936- St&PR 91
Willis, Robert E 1922- WhoAmA 91N
Willis, Robert H. 1921- St&PR 91
Willis, Robert Howard 1938- BiDrAPA 89
Willis, Robert J. AuBYP 90
Willis, Robert James 1940- WhoAm 90
Willis, Robert T. 1927- St&PR 91
Willis, Ron 1943-1977 Ballpl 90
Willis, Samuel ConAu 30NR
Willis, Shirley Ann 1938- WhoAmW 91
Willis, Sid Frank 1930- WhoE 91
Willis, Sidney F 1930- WhoAmA 91
Willis, Stanley E 1923- BiDrAPA 89
Willis, Susan Hayes 1955- BiDrAPA 89
Willis, Ted 1918- TwCCr&M 91
Willis, Thornton 1936- WhoAmA 91
Willis, Thornton Wilson 1936- WhoAm 90
Willis, Val AuBYP 90
Willis, Val 1946- ConAu 130
Willis, Vic 1876-1947 Ballpl 90 [port]
Willis, Wesley R. 1941- St&PR 91
Willis, William Allen BiDrAPA 89
Willis, William Burchett 1948- WhoE 91
Willis, William Darrell, Jr. 1934- WhoAm 90
Willis, William Ervin 1926- WhoAm 90
Willis, William H., Jr. 1927- St&PR 91
Willis, William Harold, Jr. 1927- WhoAm 90
Willis, William Henry 1951- WhoAm 90
Willis, William Henry, Jr 1940- WhoAmA 91
Willis, William Scott 1921- WhoAm 90
Willis, Yvonne Francis 1940- WhoAmW 91
Williscroft, Beverly Ruth 1945- WhoAmW 91
Willison, Bruce Gray 1948- St&PR 91
Willison, Charles 1935- St&PR 91
Willke, John Charles 1925- WhoE 91
Willke, Thomas Aloys 1932- WhoAm 90
Willkie, Wendell L. 1892-1944 WorAlBi
Willkie, Wendell Lewis, II 1951- WhoAm 90, WhoEmL 91
Willman, John Norman 1915- WhoAm 90
Willman, Noel 1918-1988 BioIn 16, ConTFT 8
Willmarth, William Walter 1924- WhoAm 90
Willmes, Francis Edwin 1929- St&PR 91
Willmore, Robert Louis 1955- WhoAm 90
Willmot, Donald G. 1916- St&PR 91
Willmot, Donald Gilpin 1916- WhoAm 90
Willmot, William Clarence 1925- WhoSSW 91, WhoWrEP 89
Willmott, Enrique A BiDrAPA 89
Willmott, Paul Kenneth 1939- WhoAm 90
Willmott, Peter Sherman 1937- St&PR 91
Willms, Emilie 1888-1969 BioIn 16
Willmschen, Robert W. 1947- St&PR 91
Willmuth, Lewis Ragon 1938- BiDrAPA 89
Willner, Ann Ruth 1924- WhoAm 90
Willner, Channan 1951- IntWWM 90
Willner, Dorothy 1927- WhoAm 90
Willner, Eugene Burton 1934- WhoSSW 91
Willner, Gerda Franziska 1911- WhoE 91
Willner, Gerda P 1911- BiDrAPA 89
Willner, Gerte 1894-1990 BioIn 16
Willner, Hal BioIn 16
Willner, Herman H BiDrAPA 89
Willner, Larry Elliott 1932- WhoSSW 91
Willner, Mark Steven BiDrAPA 89
Willner, Morris Stephen 1946- WhoE 91
Willoch, Kare 1928- WhoWor 91
Willoch, Raymond 1933- St&PR 91
Willock, Marcelle Monica 1938- WhoAm 90
Willock, Roland D. 1936- St&PR 91
Willock, William Charles, Jr. 1952- WhoSSW 91
Willocks, Robert Max 1924- WhoAm 90
Willoughby, Carroll V. 1913- St&PR 91
Willoughby, Carroll Vernon 1913- WhoAm 90
Willoughby, Claude 1898-1973 Ballpl 90
Willoughby, Doris Mellott 1936- WhoWrEP 89
Willoughby, Edward 1926- St&PR 91
Willoughby, Gary Lawrence 1950- St&PR 91
Willoughby, George BioIn 16
Willoughby, George Vernon, Jr. 1933- St&PR 91
Willoughby, Harvey William 1946- WhoAm 90
Willoughby, Hugh ConAu 30NR
Willoughby, Jane Baker WhoAmA 91
Willoughby, John Wallace 1932- WhoAm 90
Willoughby, Lillian BioIn 16
Willoughby, Michael James 1945- WhoE 91
Willoughby, R. J., Mrs. 1927- St&PR 91
Willoughby, Rodney Erwin 1925- St&PR 91, WhoAm 90
Willoughby, Russell J. 1914- St&PR 91
Willoughby, Stephen Schuyler 1932- WhoAm 90, WhoWor 91
Willoughby, William E. 1920- St&PR 91
Willour, Byron J. 1936- St&PR 91
Willow, Judith Ann Loye 1939- WhoE 91
Willrich, Mason 1933- St&PR 91, WhoAm 90
Wills, Alma Jean 1947- St&PR 91
Wills, Arthur 1926- IntWWM 90
Wills, Audrey Elizabeth 1930- WhoAmW 91, WhoE 91
Wills, Barbara Y. 1940- WhoSSW 91
Wills, Benjamin C BiDrAPA 89
Wills, Bob WhoNeCM C
Wills, Bob 1905-1975 BioIn 16, OxCPMus
Wills, Bump 1952- Ballpl 90
Wills, Cecil M. 1891- TwCCr&M 91
Wills, Charles Francis 1914- WhoAm 90
Wills, Childe Harold 1878-1940 EncABHB 4 [port]
Wills, Chill 1902-1978 WorAlBi
Wills, Christopher 1938- ConAu 132
Wills, Craig R. 1948- St&PR 91
Wills, David Arthur 1952- WhoWrEP 89
Wills, Donna M. 1946- WhoAmW 91
Wills, E. William 1943- St&PR 91
Wills, Frank 1958- Ballpl 90
Wills, Garry 1934- WhoAm 90, WhoWrEP 89
Wills, Helen 1905- BioAmW, BioIn 16
Wills, Helen 1906- WorAlBi
Wills, J. Robert 1940- WhoAm 90
Wills, John Gordon 1931- WhoAm 90
Wills, John Henry 1942- WhoSSW 91
Wills, Katherine Vasilios 1957- WhoAmW 91
Wills, Lisa Christine Illing 1962- WhoSSW 91
Wills, Maury 1932- Ballpl 90 [port]
Wills, Nancy Kay 1949- WhoAmW 91
Wills, Reid Nash 1933- St&PR 91
Wills, Robert Hamilton 1926- St&PR 91, WhoAm 90
Wills, Shirley ODwPR 91
Wills, Sidney Hayward 1926- WhoAm 90
Wills, Sylvia Lucy 1964- WhoAmW 91
Wills, Ted 1934- Ballpl 90
Wills, Thomas TwCCr&M 91
Wills, Walter Joe 1915- WhoAm 90
Wills, William Ridley, II 1934- WhoAm 90
Wills-Raftery, Dorothy 1959- WhoWrEP 89
Willse, James Patrick 1944- WhoAm 90
Willsey, Lynn Willcox 1933- St&PR 91
Willsie, Debra Ann 1955- BiDrAPA 89
Willson, Alan Neil, Jr. 1939- WhoAm 90
Willson, Brian BioIn 16
Willson, Dixie AuBYP 90
Willson, James Douglas 1915- WhoAm 90
Willson, Julie 1958- WhoAmW 91
Willson, Kenneth B. BioIn 16
Willson, L.H. 1935- St&PR 91
Willson, Laura Faulk 1937- WhoAmW 91
Willson, Margaret Pace 1919- WhoAmA 91
Willson, Mary F 1938- ConAu 129, WhoAm 90, WhoAmW 91
Willson, Meredith 1902-1984 OxCPMus, WorAlBi
Willson, Philip James 1923- WhoAm 90
Willson, Robert 1912- WhoAmA 91, WhoWrEP 89
Willson, Robert Alan 1918- WhoAm 90
Willson, Robert Frank 1939- WhoWrEP 89
Willson, Susan 1952- WhoAmW 91
Willson, William Harry 1920- St&PR 91
Willumsen, Dorrit 1940- ConAu 131, DcScanL, EncCoWW
Willumsen, Maria Jose 1939- WhoSSW 91
Willvonseder, Robert 1939- WhoWor 91
Willy ConAu 131, MajTwCW
Willy, Colette ConAu 131, MajTwCW
Willy, Warren B. 1943- St&PR 91
Willys, John N. 1873-1935 WorAlBi
Willys, John North 1873-1935 EncABHB 4 [port]
Wilmer, Charlotte M. 1946- WhoAmW 91
Wilmer, Clive 1945- ConAu 130
Wilmer, Dale TwCCr&M 91
Wilmer, Harry A 1917- BiDrAPA 89
Wilmer, Harry Aron 1917- WhoSSW 91, WhoWor 91
Wilmer, Harry Aron 1945- St&PR 91
Wilmer, James Albert 1936- St&PR 91
Wilmer, Mary Charles 1930- WhoAmW 91, WhoWor 91
Wilmerding, Harold Pratt 1937- St&PR 91, WhoAm 90
Wilmerding, John 1938- WhoAm 90, WhoAmA 91
Wilmering, Kathy 1958- WhoAmW 91
Wilmers, Frank William 1925- WhoWor 91
Wilmers, Robert G. 1934- St&PR 91
Wilmers, Robert George 1934- WhoAm 90
Wilmes, Gerald William BiDrAPA 89
Wilmeth, Ernest, II 1952- WhoAmA 91
Wilmeth, Harvey Delbert 1918- St&PR 91
Wilmore, Jack H 1938- ConAu 129
Wilmoski, Scott Emery 1953- St&PR 91
Wilmot, Catherine 1773?-1824 FemiCLE
Wilmot, Elizabeth BiDEWW
Wilmot, Fred Woodfin 1924- St&PR 91
Wilmot, Gretchen Kathryn 1939- St&PR 91
Wilmot, Irvin Gorsage 1922- WhoAm 90

Wilmot, John 1647-1680 *BioIn 16*
Wilmot, Martha 1775-1873 *FemiCLE*
Wilmot, Paul George 1946- *WhoEmL 91*
Wilmot, Richard E. *ODwPR 91*
Wilmot, Robert Duncan 1809-1891 *DcCanB 12*
Wilmot, Samuel 1822-1899 *DcCanB 12*
Wilmoth, Ralph Eugene 1927- *St&PR 91*
Wilmotte, Raymond M. 1901- *WhoAm 90*
Wilmouth, Robert K. 1928- *WhoAm 90*
Wilmouth, Robert Kearney 1928- *St&PR 91*
Wilmowski, Wendy Ann 1962- *WhoAmW 91*
Wilms, Albert *PenDiDA 89*
Wilms, John Henry 1925- *BiDrAPA 89*
Wilner, Alvin G. 1940- *St&PR 91*
Wilner, Arie 1917-1943 *BioIn 16*
Wilner, Lois Annette 1935- *WhoAmW 91*
Wilner, Lynne Ann 1962- *WhoAmW 91*
Wilner, Martin T *BiDrAPA 89*
Wilner, Morton Harrison 1908- *WhoAm 90*
Wilner, Philip J. 1957- *BiDrAPA 89*
Wiloch, Thomas 1953- *WhoWrEP 89*
Wilowsky, Jacob David 1845-1913 *BioIn 16*
Wilroy, Hiaburnia Gaines 1929- *WhoAmW 91*
Wilsey, H. Lawrence 1923- *WhoSSW 91*
Wilshire, Everett S. 1946- *St&PR 91*
Wilshire, H. Gaylord 1861-1927 *EncAL*
Wilsie, Ronald Thomas 1951- *St&PR 91*
Wilske, Jack Charles 1925- *WhoAm 90*
Wilske, Kenneth Ray 1935- *WhoAm 90*
Wilson Phillips *ConMus 5*
Wilson, A. N. 1950- *BioIn 16*
Wilson, A N 1950- *WorAu 1980 [port]*
Wilson, A. W. *BioIn 16*
Wilson, Abbott E. 1931- *St&PR 91*
Wilson, Abraham 1922- *WhoE 91, WhoWor 91*
Wilson, Adam 1814-1891 *DcCanB 12*
Wilson, Addison Graves 1947- *WhoSSW 91*
Wilson, Adrian 1923-1988 *BioIn 16, ConAu 132*
Wilson, Al 193-?- *EncPR&S 89*
Wilson, Albert Eugene 1927- *WhoAm 90*
Wilson, Albert J. 1932- *St&PR 91*
Wilson, Albert John Endsley, III 1934- *WhoSSW 91*
Wilson, Alexander Erwin, III 1937- *WhoAm 90*
Wilson, Alexander Galbraith 1924- *IntWWM 90*
Wilson, Alexander Murray 1922- *WhoAm 90*
Wilson, Alice Bland 1938- *WhoAmW 91*
Wilson, Allan Byron 1948- *St&PR 91, WhoAm 90*
Wilson, Allan Charles 1934- *WhoAm 90*
Wilson, Allison 1953- *WhoWrEP 89*
Wilson, Alma D. 1917- *WhoAmW 91, WhoSSW 91*
Wilson, Almon Chapman 1924- *WhoAm 90*
Wilson, Alvernia Barbara 1945- *WhoSSW 91*
Wilson, Andrew Marion 1957- *WhoSSW 91*
Wilson, Andrew Norman 1950- *BioIn 16*
Wilson, Andrew R. 1941- *St&PR 91*
Wilson, Angus *BioIn 16*
Wilson, Angus 1913- *MajTwCW, WhoWor 91*
Wilson, Ann D. 1950- *WhoAm 90, WhoAmW 91, WhoWor 91*
Wilson, Anne Deirdre 1934- *WhoWor 91*
Wilson, Anne Gawthrop 1949- *WhoAmA 91*
Wilson, Anthony Aaron 1966- *WhoWrEP 89*
Wilson, Anthony Parks 1941- *WhoE 91*
Wilson, Anthony Vincent 1936- *WhoAm 90*
Wilson, Arnold W *BiDrAPA 89*
Wilson, Art 1885-1960 *Ballpl 90*
Wilson, Arthur 1595-1652 *BioIn 16*
Wilson, Arthur Richard 1924- *St&PR 91*
Wilson, Arthur Theodore 1945- *WhoWor 91*
Wilson, Arthur William 1961- *WhoE 91*
Wilson, Artie 1920- *Ballpl 90*
Wilson, August *BioIn 16*
Wilson, August 1945- *ConLC 63 [port], DrBlPA 90, MajTwCW, NewYTBS 90, WhoAm 90, WorAlBi, WorAu 1980 [port]*
Wilson, Augusta Evans 1835-1909 *BioAmW*
Wilson, Barbara *BiDrAPA 89*
Wilson, Barbara 1937- *SmATA X*
Wilson, Barbara 1950- *TwCCr&M 91*
Wilson, Barbara Ann 1962- *WhoAmW 91*
Wilson, Barbara Helen 1959- *WhoAmW 91*
Wilson, Barbara Joyce 1947- *WhoAmW 91*
Wilson, Barbara Louise 1952- *WhoAmW 91*
Wilson, Basil Wrigley 1909- *WhoAm 90*
Wilson, Ben 1913- *WhoAmA 91, WhoE 91*
Wilson, Ben F. *AmLegL*
Wilson, Berkeley B. 1926- *St&PR 91*
Wilson, Bernard J. 1949- *St&PR 91*
Wilson, Bertha 1923- *WhoAm 90, WhoAmW 91, WhoE 91*
Wilson, Bertina Iolia 1938- *WhoAmW 91*
Wilson, Beth *AuBYP 90*
Wilson, Beth P. *BioIn 16*
Wilson, Bette *BioIn 16*
Wilson, Betty M. 1947- *St&PR 91*
Wilson, Betty May 1947- *WhoAmW 91*
Wilson, Beverley Faye *BiDrAPA 89*
Wilson, Bill 1928- *Ballpl 90*
Wilson, Bill 1942- *Ballpl 90*
Wilson, Billy 1935- *DrBlPA 90*
Wilson, Blakely 1923- *St&PR 91*
Wilson, Blenda Jacqueline 1941- *WhoAm 90, WhoAmW 91*
Wilson, Brad Marshall 1951- *St&PR 91*
Wilson, Bradley, Jr. 1928- *St&PR 91*
Wilson, Brenda C. *BioIn 16*
Wilson, Brian *BioIn 16*
Wilson, Brian Douglas 1942- *WhoAm 90*
Wilson, Bruce Brighton 1936- *St&PR 91, WhoAm 90*
Wilson, Budge 1927- *BioIn 16*
Wilson, Byron Eric 1957- *WhoE 91*
Wilson, C. Daniel, Jr. 1941- *WhoAm 90, WhoSSW 91*
Wilson, C. Dexter, Jr. *St&PR 91*
Wilson, C. Edwin 1947- *St&PR 91*
Wilson, C. Philip *BiDrAPA 89*
Wilson, Carl Lee 1940- *St&PR 91*
Wilson, Carl W., Jr. 1933- *St&PR 91*
Wilson, Carl Weldon, Jr. 1933- *WhoSSW 91, WhoWor 91*
Wilson, Carlos Guillermo 1941- *WhoHisp 91*
Wilson, Carnie 1969?- *ConMus 5*
Wilson, Carolyn Taylor 1936- *WhoAmW 91*
Wilson, Carolyn Ziegler *BiDrAPA 89*
Wilson, Carrie Lois 1944- *WhoAmA 91*
Wilson, Carter 1941- *AuBYP 90*
Wilson, Cassandra *BioIn 16*
Wilson, Catherine 1936- *IntWWM 90*
Wilson, Catherine 1951- *ConAu 132*
Wilson, Catherine Cooper 1955- *WhoAmW 91, WhoWrEP 89*
Wilson, Catherine Mary 1957- *WhoAmW 91*
Wilson, Cecil 1961- *WhoEmL 91*
Wilson, Cedric W M 1925- *EncO&P 3*
Wilson, Charlene Willa 1943- *WhoAmW 91*
Wilson, Charles 1933- *BioIn 16, WhoAm 90, WhoSSW 91*
Wilson, Charles Alden 1943- *WhoE 91*
Wilson, Charles Banks 1918- *BioIn 16, WhoAm 90, WhoAmA 91*
Wilson, Charles E. 1890-1961 *WorAlBi*
Wilson, Charles Elmer 1955- *WhoE 91*
Wilson, Charles Erwin 1890-1961 *BiDrUSE 89, EncABHB 5 [port]*
Wilson, Charles Fox 1949- *St&PR 91*
Wilson, Charles Glen 1948- *WhoAm 90, WhoSSW 91*
Wilson, Charles H 1937- *WhoAmA 91*
Wilson, Charles L *BiDrAPA 89*
Wilson, Charles Morrow 1905-1977 *AuBYP 90*
Wilson, Charles Reginald 1904- *WhoAm 90*
Wilson, Charles Stuart, Mrs. 1870-1956 *EncPaPR 91*
Wilson, Charles T. R. 1869-1959 *WorAlBi*
Wilson, Charles Thomas 1907- *St&PR 91*
Wilson, Charles William 1916- *WhoAm 90*
Wilson, Charles Zachary, Jr. 1929- *WhoAm 90*
Wilson, Charlie *BioIn 16*
Wilson, Charlotte 1854-1944 *BioIn 16*
Wilson, Cheryl Lee 1956- *WhoWrEP 89*
Wilson, Chris *NewYTBS 90*
Wilson, Chuck W. 1939- *St&PR 91*
Wilson, Cindy *BioIn 16*
Wilson, Clarence Ivan 1927- *WhoAm 90, WhoSSW 91*
Wilson, Claude Raymond, Jr. 1933- *WhoAm 90, WhoWor 91*
Wilson, Clifford D., Jr. 1928- *St&PR 91*
Wilson, Colin 1931- *BioIn 16, ConAu 33NR, EncO&P 3, MajTwCW, TwCCr&M 91*
Wilson, Colin Henry 1931- *WhoAm 90, WhoWor 91*
Wilson, Constance Kramer 1959- *WhoAmW 91*
Wilson, Curtis Wayne 1941- *WhoSSW 91*
Wilson, Cynthia Diane 1954- *WhoEmL 91*
Wilson, Cynthia Lindsay 1945- *WhoAmA 91*
Wilson, Cynthia Marie 1954- *WhoAmW 91*
Wilson, D. James 1939- *St&PR 91*
Wilson, Dana Lynn Bartlett *WhoE 91*
Wilson, Dana Richard 1946- *IntWWM 90*
Wilson, Daniel 1816-1892 *DcCanB 12*
Wilson, Daniel Richard *BiDrAPA 89*
Wilson, David 1947- *WhoWor 91*
Wilson, David Bruce 1927- *WhoAm 90*
Wilson, David Clive 1935- *WhoWor 91*
Wilson, David H *BiDrAPA 89*
Wilson, David Henry 1937- *ConAu 32NR*
Wilson, David James 1930- *WhoAm 90*
Wilson, David Jefferies 1939- *WhoE 91*
Wilson, David Mackenzie 1931- *WhoWor 91*
Wilson, David Merl 1941- *WhoSSW 91*
Wilson, David Philip 1909- *WhoAmA 91*
Wilson, David Randall 1933- *St&PR 91*
Wilson, David William 1958- *WhoWor 91*
Wilson, Deborah Kay Pultz 1956- *WhoSSW 91*
Wilson, Delano Dee 1934- *WhoAm 90*
Wilson, Delbert Ray 1926- *WhoAm 90, WhoWrEP 89*
Wilson, Demond 1946- *DrBlPA 90*
Wilson, Denise Jane 1958- *WhoWrEP 89*
Wilson, Dennis Robert 1949- *St&PR 91*
Wilson, Dewey Errol 1950- *WhoSSW 91*
Wilson, Diane Baer 1949- *WhoSSW 91*
Wilson, Diane Lyn 1949- *BiDrAPA 89*
Wilson, Dierdre 1945- *WhoEmL 91, WhoWor 91*
Wilson, Dirk *MajTwCW*
Wilson, Don 1945-1975 *Ballpl 90*
Wilson, Don E. 1944- *WhoE 91*
Wilson, Don Whitman 1942- *WhoAm 90*
Wilson, Donald Alfred 1941- *WhoE 91*
Wilson, Donald Douglas 1930- *WhoWrEP 89*
Wilson, Donald Edward 1936- *WhoAm 90*
Wilson, Donald Grey 1917- *WhoAm 90*
Wilson, Donald King, Jr. 1935- *St&PR 91*
Wilson, Donald Malcolm 1925- *WhoAm 90, WhoE 91*
Wilson, Donald P 1925- *BiDrAPA 89*
Wilson, Donald Wallin 1938- *WhoAm 90*
Wilson, Dooley 1894-1953 *DrBlPA 90*
Wilson, Doric 1939- *ConAu 129*
Wilson, Doris Fanuzzi 1935- *WhoAmW 91, WhoE 91, WhoWor 91*
Wilson, Doris Faye Blackwell 1937- *WhoAmW 91*
Wilson, Dorothy Clarke 1904- *WhoAm 90*
Wilson, Doug *BioIn 16*
Wilson, Douglas Edwin 1917- *WhoWor 91*
Wilson, Douglas Fenn 1953- *WhoAmA 91*
Wilson, Douglas J. 1939- *St&PR 91*
Wilson, Douglas Lawson 1935- *WhoAm 90*
Wilson, Dudley Keith 1936- *IntWWM 90*
Wilson, Dwight Liston 1931- *WhoAm 90*
Wilson, E. O. *NewYTBS 90 [port]*
Wilson, E. Paul *St&PR 91*
Wilson, Earl *BioIn 16*
Wilson, Earl 1904-1990 *BioIn 16*
Wilson, Earl 1934- *Ballpl 90*
Wilson, Earle Frederick, Jr. 1932- *St&PR 91*
Wilson, Earle Lawrence 1934- *WhoAm 90*
Wilson, Edgar Bright 1874-1953 *AmLegL*
Wilson, Edgar Hunter 1923- *WhoAm 90*
Wilson, Edith 1896-1981 *BioIn 16, DrBlPA 90*
Wilson, Edith Bolling 1872-1961 *BioAmW*
Wilson, Edith Bolling Galt 1872-1961 *BioIn 16*
Wilson, Edmund 1895-1972 *BioIn 16, MajTwCW, WorAlBi*
Wilson, Edward Converse, Jr. 1928- *WhoAm 90*
Wilson, Edward George 1909- *WhoAm 90*
Wilson, Edward John 1946- *WhoWor 91*
Wilson, Edward Lawrence 1931- *WhoAm 90*
Wilson, Edward N 1925- *WhoAmA 91*
Wilson, Edward Nathan 1941- *WhoAm 90*
Wilson, Edward Nathaniel 1925- *WhoE 91*
Wilson, Edward O. 1929- *BioIn 16, MajTwCW*
Wilson, Edward Osborne 1929- *WhoAm 90*
Wilson, Edward T 1941- *ConAu 129*
Wilson, Edwin Graves *WhoAm 90, WhoSSW 91*
Wilson, Eileen Partlow 1903- *WhoSSW 91*
Wilson, Elaine Carol 1948- *WhoSSW 91*
Wilson, Eleanore Hubbard *AuBYP 90*
Wilson, Elizabeth 1921- *ConTFT 8 [port]*
Wilson, Elizabeth Dolan Nolan 1909- *WhoAmW 91*
Wilson, Elizabeth S *BiDrAPA 89*
Wilson, Ellen Axson *BioIn 16*
Wilson, Ellen Axson 1860-1914 *BioAmW*
Wilson, Ellen Janet *AuBYP 90*
Wilson, Ellery H. 1848-1906 *AmLegL*
Wilson, Emanuel Willis 1854-1905 *AmLegL*
Wilson, Emery Allen 1942- *WhoAm 90*
Wilson, Eric 1938- *WhoWrEP 89*
Wilson, Erica *BioIn 16*
Wilson, Ethel 1888-1980 *BioIn 16, FemiCLE*
Wilson, Ethel Davis 1888?-1980 *MajTwCW*
Wilson, Eugene Rolland 1938- *WhoAm 90*
Wilson, EvaLyn Leonard 1951- *WhoAmW 91*
Wilson, Evan Carter 1953- *WhoAmA 91*
Wilson, Evan M 1910-1984 *ConAu 129*
Wilson, Eve 188-?-1935? *FemiCLE*
Wilson, Evelyn Olga 1915- *WhoSSW 91*
Wilson, Everett Lee 1947- *WhoWor 91*
Wilson, Ewen Maclellan 1944- *WhoAm 90*
Wilson, Felicia Ann 1961- *WhoE 91*
Wilson, Flip *BioIn 16*
Wilson, Flip 1933- *DrBlPA 90, WorAlBi*
Wilson, Fran *ConAu 130*
Wilson, Frances Engle 1922- *ConAu 130*
Wilson, Frances Helen 1929- *WhoAmW 91*
Wilson, Francis Mairs Huntington 1875-1946 *BioIn 16*
Wilson, Francis Servis 1906- *WhoAm 90*
Wilson, Frank 1886-1956 *EarBlAP*
Wilson, Frank Elmore 1909- *WhoAm 90*
Wilson, Frank G. 1919- *St&PR 91*
Wilson, Frank H 1886-1956 *DrBlPA 90*
Wilson, Frank J. 1926- *St&PR 91*
Wilson, Frank Lyndall 1926- *WhoSSW 91*
Wilson, Frank Maxwell, Jr. 1922- *St&PR 91*
Wilson, Frederic B 1927- *BiDrAPA 89*
Wilson, Frederic Rowland 1947- *WhoEmL 91*
Wilson, Frederick Allen 1937- *WhoAm 90*
Wilson, Frederick Calvin 1932- *St&PR 91*
Wilson, Garff Bell 1909- *WhoAm 90*
Wilson, Gary Charles 1949- *St&PR 91*
Wilson, Gary E. 1939- *St&PR 91*
Wilson, Gary Lee 1940- *BioIn 16, St&PR 91, WhoAm 90*
Wilson, George 1947- *IntWWM 90*
Wilson, George Andrew 1925- *WhoAm 90*
Wilson, George F 1943- *BiDrAPA 89*
Wilson, George Hugh 1922- *WhoAm 90*
Wilson, George Patton 1943- *WhoSSW 91*
Wilson, George Peter 1935- *WhoAm 90*
Wilson, George Simpson 1876- *AmLegL*
Wilson, George Wharton 1923- *WhoAm 90*
Wilson, George Wilton 1928- *WhoAm 90*
Wilson, Gerald Einar 1922- *WhoAm 90*
Wilson, Gerald L. 1939- *BioIn 16*
Wilson, Gerald Loomis 1939- *WhoAm 90*
Wilson, Geroge Lewis 1930- *WhoAmA 91*
Wilson, Gladys Marie 1913- *WhoWrEP 89*
Wilson, Glen Parten 1922- *WhoE 91*
Wilson, Glen Wesley 1930- *St&PR 91*
Wilson, Glenn *BioIn 16*
Wilson, Glenn 1929- *WhoAm 90*
Wilson, Glenn 1958- *Ballpl 90*
Wilson, Glenn E. 1926- *St&PR 91*
Wilson, Graham 1940- *EncO&P 3*
Wilson, Graham MacGregor 1944- *St&PR 91*
Wilson, Gregory K. 1952- *St&PR 91*
Wilson, Gwendolyn Dianne 1945- *WhoSSW 91*
Wilson, H. Brian 1928- *ODwPR 91, St&PR 91*
Wilson, Hack 1900-1948 *Ballpl 90 [port]*
Wilson, Hamilton Buntin Gillies 1921- *WhoE 91*
Wilson, Hamline C. 1937- *St&PR 91*
Wilson, Harold 1916- *BioIn 16, WorAlBi*
Wilson, Harold Albert 1874-1964 *DcScB S2*
Wilson, Harold Charles 1931- *WhoWrEP 89*
Wilson, Harold Frederick 1922- *WhoAm 90*
Wilson, Harold Graham 1931- *St&PR 91, WhoAm 90*
Wilson, Harold Hiller, Jr. 1930- *St&PR 91*
Wilson, Harold Kermit 1940- *St&PR 91*
Wilson, Harriet E. 1807?-1870? *FemiCLE*
Wilson, Harriette 1786-1845 *FemiCLE*
Wilson, Harrison B. 1928- *WhoSSW 91*
Wilson, Harry B. 1917- *WhoAm 90*
Wilson, Harry Cochrane 1945- *WhoAm 90*
Wilson, Harry E *BiDrAPA 89*
Wilson, Hazel 1898- *AuBYP 90*
Wilson, Headley Egerton 1951- *WhoE 91*
Wilson, Heather Ann 1960- *WhoE 91*
Wilson, Heidi Renee 1956- *WhoSSW 91*
Wilson, Helen 1884-1974 *WhoAmA 91N*
Wilson, Helen Marie 1930- *WhoAmW 91*
Wilson, Helena *WhoAmA 91*
Wilson, Henry 1812-1875 *BiDrUSE 89, BioIn 16*
Wilson, Henry 1864-1934 *PenDiDA 89*
Wilson, Henry Arthur, Jr. 1939- *WhoWor 91*
Wilson, Henry Lane 1857-1932 *BioIn 16*
Wilson, Herman *BioIn 16, NewYTBS 90*
Wilson, Herman Bernard 1929- *St&PR 91*
Wilson, Highball 1878-1934 *Ballpl 90*
Wilson, Hillsman Vaughan 1928- *WhoAm 90*

Wilson, Holly *AuBYP 90*
Wilson, Horace *BioIn 16*
Wilson, Howard I 1933- *BiDrAPA 89*
Wilson, Hugh *BioIn 16*
Wilson, Hugh 1943- *WhoAm 90*
Wilson, Hugh Robert 1885-1946 *BioIn 16*
Wilson, Hugh Shannon 1926- *WhoAm 90*
Wilson, Ian Holroyde 1925- *WhoWor 91*
Wilson, Ian Robert 1929- *WhoAm 90*
Wilson, Ira Lee 1927- *WhoAmW 91, WhoWor 91*
Wilson, Irene K. *WhoWrEP 89*
Wilson, Iron Jaw *BioIn 16*
Wilson, Isaiah Herbert *BioIn 16*
Wilson, Isaiah Herbert 1909-1990 *ConAu 131*
Wilson, J. Lawrence 1936- *St&PR 91*
Wilson, J. Robert 1927- *St&PR 91*
Wilson, J. Steven *St&PR 91*
Wilson, J. Tylee 1931- *St&PR 91, WhoAm 90*
Wilson, Jack *WhNaAH*
Wilson, Jack 1912- *Ballpl 90*
Wilson, Jack Alexander 1924- *WhoWor 91*
Wilson, Jack Fredrick 1920- *WhoAm 90*
Wilson, Jack Harold Jay 1943- *St&PR 91*
Wilson, Jack Martin 1945- *WhoAm 90*
Wilson, Jack Russell 1921- *St&PR 91*
Wilson, Jackie *BioIn 16*
Wilson, Jackie 1934-1984 *DrBlPA 90, EncPR&S 89, OxCPMus*
Wilson, Jacqueline *BioIn 16*
Wilson, Jacqueline 1945- *SmATA 61 [port]*
Wilson, James 1742-1798 *BioIn 16, EncCRAm*
Wilson, James 1835-1920 *AmLegL, BiDrUSE 89*
Wilson, James Charles, Jr. 1947- *WhoSSW 91, WhoWor 91*
Wilson, James Crocket 1841-1899 *DcCanB 12*
Wilson, James Dacus, Sr. 1947- *WhoSSW 91*
Wilson, James Edward 1935- *St&PR 91*
Wilson, James Edward 1938- *BiDrAPA 89*
Wilson, James Ernest 1915- *WhoAm 90*
Wilson, James Hargrove, Jr. 1920- *WhoAm 90*
Wilson, James Harris 1945- *WhoSSW 91*
Wilson, James Harrison 1837-1925 *WorAlBi*
Wilson, James John 1933- *WhoSSW 91, WhoWor 91*
Wilson, James L. 1935- *St&PR 91*
Wilson, James Larry 1942- *WhoSSW 91*
Wilson, James Lawrence 1936- *WhoAm 90, WhoE 91*
Wilson, James Madison 1916- *St&PR 91*
Wilson, James Milton, III 1934- *St&PR 91, WhoAm 90*
Wilson, James Oliver 1926- *St&PR 91*
Wilson, James Quinn *WhoAm 90*
Wilson, James R. 1941- *WhoAm 90*
Wilson, James Reid, Jr. 1934- *WhoE 91*
Wilson, James Robert 1927- *WhoAm 90*
Wilson, James Rodney 1937- *WhoWor 91*
Wilson, James Steven 1951- *WhoSSW 91*
Wilson, James V. *St&PR 91*
Wilson, James William 1928- *St&PR 91, WhoAm 90*
Wilson, James William 1936- *WhoSSW 91*
Wilson, Jane 1924- *WhoAmA 91*
Wilson, Janet Harsha 1948- *WhoSSW 91*
Wilson, Janet Sue 1934- *WhoAmW 91*
Wilson, Janice Darlene 1955- *WhoAmW 91*
Wilson, Janie Menchaca 1936- *WhoHisp 91*
Wilson, Jean Avis 1924- *WhoWrEP 89*
Wilson, Jean Donald 1932- *WhoAm 90*
Wilson, Jean L. 1928- *WhoAmW 91*
Wilson, Jean Marie Haley 1921- *WhoAmW 91*
Wilson, Jean S *WhoAmA 91*
Wilson, Jeannette Solomon 1915- *WhoAmW 91*
Wilson, Jeff *St&PR 91*
Wilson, Jeffery John 1957- *IntWWM 90*
Wilson, Jeffrey Charles *BiDrAPA 89*
Wilson, Jeffrey W 1940- *BiDrAPA 89*
Wilson, Jeffrey Wellington 1946- *WhoSSW 91*
Wilson, Jennifer Joy 1953- *WhoAm 90*
Wilson, Jennifer Lee 1963- *WhoSSW 91*
Wilson, Jerome Martin 1916- *St&PR 91*
Wilson, Jerri *St&PR 91*
Wilson, Jim 1922-1986 *Ballpl 90*
Wilson, Jimmie 1900-1947 *Ballpl 90*
Wilson, John *WhoSSW 91*
Wilson, John 1922- *WhoAm 90, WhoAmA 91*
Wilson, John 1940- *IntWWM 90*
Wilson, John A *BiDrAPA 89*
Wilson, John Alan 1917- *WhoAm 90*
Wilson, John Anthony Burgess 1917- *BioIn 16*
Wilson, John Arthur 1921- *St&PR 91*
Wilson, John Burgess 1917- *MajTwCW*
Wilson, John C. *EncO&P 3*
Wilson, John Cowles 1921- *WhoAm 90*
Wilson, John D. 1931- *WhoAm 90, WhoSSW 91*
Wilson, John David 1934- *WhoAmA 91*
Wilson, John David 1946- *WhoE 91*
Wilson, John Donald 1913- *WhoAm 90*
Wilson, John E., Jr. 1928- *St&PR 91*
Wilson, John Eric 1919- *WhoAm 90, WhoWor 91*
Wilson, John Fletcher 1923- *WhoE 91*
Wilson, John Foster 1919- *WhoWor 91*
Wilson, John Frederick 1933- *WhoAm 90*
Wilson, John G. 1947- *St&PR 91*
Wilson, John Hill Tucker 1934- *WhoAm 90*
Wilson, John Louis 1899-1989 *BioIn 16*
Wilson, John M *BiDrAPA 89*
Wilson, John Marshall 1958- *WhoSSW 91*
Wilson, John Morgan 1942- *WhoSSW 91*
Wilson, John Oliver 1938- *ConAu 129, St&PR 91*
Wilson, John Page 1922- *St&PR 91*
Wilson, John Rex Storm, III 1955- *WhoEmL 91*
Wilson, John Ross 1920- *WhoAm 90*
Wilson, John S., Jr. 1942- *St&PR 91*
Wilson, John Samuel 1916- *WhoAm 90*
Wilson, John Samuel 1933- *St&PR 91*
Wilson, John Steuart 1913- *WhoAm 90*
Wilson, John T 1914-1990 *ConAu 132*
Wilson, John W. 1938- *St&PR 91*
Wilson, Joseph Dennis 1949- *WhoE 91*
Wilson, Joseph Lopez 1960- *WhoWor 91*
Wilson, Joseph V., III 1949- *St&PR 91*
Wilson, Joyce Lynn 1961- *WhoAmW 91*
Wilson, Jud 1899-1963 *Ballpl 90*
Wilson, Julia Page 1926- *WhoSSW 91*
Wilson, June 1946- *WhoAmA 91*
Wilson, June Gail 1946- *WhoE 91*
Wilson, June Taylor 1959- *WhoAmW 91*
Wilson, Katherine Schmitkons 1913- *WhoAmW 91*
Wilson, Kathleen Jane 1951- *WhoAmW 91*
Wilson, Kathleen Stevens 1951- *WhoE 91*
Wilson, Kathy Shores 1955- *WhoAmW 91*
Wilson, Keith 1927- *BioIn 16*
Wilson, Keith Charles 1927- *WhoWrEP 89*
Wilson, Kemmons *BioIn 16*
Wilson, Kemmons 1913- *St&PR 91, WorAlBi*
Wilson, Kendrick R., III 1947- *St&PR 91*
Wilson, Kenneth G. 1936- *WorAlBi*
Wilson, Kenneth Geddes 1936- *WhoAm 90, WhoWor 91*
Wilson, Kenneth Jay 1944- *WhoAm 90*
Wilson, Kermit H. 1916- *St&PR 91*
Wilson, Lana Yvonne 1969- *WhoAmW 91*
Wilson, Lance Henry 1948- *WhoAm 90*
Wilson, Lanford 1937- *BioIn 16, WhoAm 90, WorAlBi*
Wilson, Larry *BioIn 16*
Wilson, Larry Joseph 1948- *WhoSSW 91*
Wilson, Laura Sue 1943- *WhoSSW 91*
Wilson, Lauren Ross 1936- *WhoAm 90*
Wilson, LaVerne 1931- *WhoSSW 91*
Wilson, Lawrence Alexander 1935- *St&PR 91*
Wilson, Lawrence G 1940- *BiDrAPA 89*
Wilson, Lawrence Graham, III 1944- *WhoWor 91*
Wilson, Leigh *BioIn 16*
Wilson, Leland D. 1927- *St&PR 91*
Wilson, Lennox Norwood 1932- *WhoAm 90*
Wilson, Leonard Gilchrist 1928- *WhoAm 90*
Wilson, Leonard Richard 1906- *WhoWor 91*
Wilson, Leroy 1928- *WhoAm 90*
Wilson, Leslie 1941- *WhoAm 90*
Wilson, Levanna Mildred 1940- *WhoAmW 91*
Wilson, LeVon Edward 1954- *WhoEmL 91, WhoSSW 91, WhoWor 91*
Wilson, Lewis Dunbar 1840-1922 *BioIn 16*
Wilson, Lewis Lansing 1932- *WhoE 91*
Wilson, Linda Ann 1947- *WhoAmW 91*
Wilson, Linda Cheryl 1963- *WhoAmW 91*
Wilson, Linda Lee 1943- *WhoAmW 91*
Wilson, Linda Smith 1936- *WhoAm 90, WhoAmW 91*
Wilson, Lisa Ann 1958- *WhoAmW 91*
Wilson, Lisle 1943- *DrBlPA 90*
Wilson, Lloyd Bonner 1947- *WhoSSW 91*
Wilson, Lloyd Lee 1947- *WhoAm 90*
Wilson, Logan *NewYTBS 90*
Wilson, Lois *BioIn 16*
Wilson, Lois Burnham *BioIn 16*
Wilson, Lois M. 1927- *WhoAm 90, WhoWor 91*
Wilson, Lonnie Edward 1930- *St&PR 91*
Wilson, Lori Lynn 1954- *WhoAmW 91*
Wilson, Louis H. *St&PR 91*
Wilson, Louita Dodson 1917- *WhoAmW 91*
Wilson, Lowell M *BiDrAPA 89*
Wilson, Lucius Roy, Jr. 1926- *WhoSSW 91*
Wilson, Luther 1944- *WhoWrEP 89*
Wilson, Lynn Howard 1954- *WhoSSW 91*
Wilson, Lynn R. 1913- *St&PR 91*
Wilson, Lynton Ronald 1940- *WhoAm 90*
Wilson, M. Thomas, Jr. *WhoE 91*
Wilson, Major Loyce 1926- *WhoSSW 91*
Wilson, Malcolm 1914- *St&PR 91, WhoAm 90*
Wilson, Malcolm Campbell 1942- *WhoAm 90, WhoE 91*
Wilson, Malcolm E., Jr. 1925- *St&PR 91*
Wilson, Malcolm John 1924-1989 *BioIn 16*
Wilson, Malcolm M. 1922- *St&PR 91*
Wilson, Malicia Howard 1960- *WhoAmW 91*
Wilson, Malin 1947- *WhoAmA 91*
Wilson, Marc F 1941- *WhoAmA 91*
Wilson, Marc Fraser 1941- *WhoAm 90*
Wilson, Marcella Maria *BiDrAPA 89*
Wilson, Marcia Carol Wiles 1947- *WhoSSW 91*
Wilson, Margaret 1882-1973 *FemiCLE*
Wilson, Margaret Ann 1931- *WhoSSW 91*
Wilson, Margaret Bush 1919- *WhoAm 90*
Wilson, Margaret Dauler 1939- *WhoAm 90*
Wilson, Margaret Elizabeth 1935- *WhoE 91*
Wilson, Margaret Scarbrough 1930- *WhoAm 90*
Wilson, Margo 1942- *ConAu 31NR*
Wilson, Margot Lois 1957- *WhoSSW 91*
Wilson, Marily Sharronn 1942- *WhoAmW 91*
Wilson, Marion S. *AmLegL*
Wilson, Marjorie Price *WhoAm 90, WhoAmW 91*
Wilson, Mark Ferlin 1939- *WhoE 91*
Wilson, Mark Glen 1943- *WhoE 91*
Wilson, Mark Randall 1965- *WhoEmL 91*
Wilson, Marolyn Caldwell 1934- *WhoWrEP 89*
Wilson, Martha 1947- *BiDWomA*
Wilson, Martin Paul 1939- *WhoSSW 91*
Wilson, Mary 1944- *DrBlPA 90*
Wilson, Mary Elizabeth 1942- *WhoAmW 91*
Wilson, Mary Ellen 1953- *WhoAmW 91*
Wilson, Mary Lawrence 1907- *WhoAm 90*
Wilson, Mary Louise 1940- *WhoAm 90*
Wilson, Mary Therese *BiDrAPA 89*
Wilson, Mathew Kent 1920- *WhoAm 90*
Wilson, Matthew Frederick 1956- *WhoAm 90*
Wilson, Maura *BioIn 16*
Wilson, Melanie *BioIn 16*
Wilson, Melanie Ann 1952- *WhoAmW 91*
Wilson, Melissa Anne 1968- *WhoAmA 91*
Wilson, Michael 1937- *CurBio 90 [port]*
Wilson, Michael Brian *BiDrAPA 89*
Wilson, Michael Burl 1945- *WhoSSW 91*
Wilson, Michael H. *BioIn 16*
Wilson, Michael Holcombe 1937- *WhoE 91, WhoWor 91*
Wilson, Michael Joseph 1953- *WhoWor 91*
Wilson, Michael Moureau *BiDrAPA 89*
Wilson, Michael Robert 1954- *WhoE 91*
Wilson, Mike L. 1940- *St&PR 91*
Wilson, Miles Scott 1943- *WhoWrEP 89*
Wilson, Millie 1948- *WhoAmA 91*
Wilson, Milner Bradley, III 1933- *St&PR 91, WhoAm 90*
Wilson, Minter Lowther, Jr. 1925- *WhoAm 90*
Wilson, Miriam Geisendorfer 1922- *WhoAm 90, WhoAmW 91*
Wilson, Mitchell David 1957- *BiDrAPA 89*
Wilson, Mollie Cross Haley 1942- *WhoAmW 91*
Wilson, Mookie 1956- *Ballpl 90*
Wilson, Murray S 1927- *BiDrAPA 89*
Wilson, Myron Robert, Jr. 1932- *WhoWor 91*
Wilson, Nancy 1937- *DrBlPA 90, WhoAm 90*
Wilson, Nancy 1949- *IntWWM 90*
Wilson, Nancy Keeler 1937- *WhoAmW 91, WhoSSW 91*
Wilson, Nancy L. *WhoAmW 91*
Wilson, Nancy Parsons 1941- *WhoAmW 91*
Wilson, Nathanial Junior 1960- *WhoSSW 91*
Wilson, Nelson 1945- *WhoSSW 91*
Wilson, Newton W., III 1950- *St&PR 91*
Wilson, Nicholas Jon 1947- *WhoAmA 91*
Wilson, Norma F. 1940- *WhoHisp 91*
Wilson, Norman Louis 1937- *WhoE 91*
Wilson, Olin Chaddock 1909- *WhoAm 90*
Wilson, Orme 1885-1966 *WhoAmA 91N*
Wilson, Orme, Jr. 1920- *WhoAm 90*
Wilson, Orrin A. 1940- *St&PR 91*
Wilson, Otis *BioIn 16*
Wilson, Owen 1883-1954 *Ballpl 90*
Wilson, Pat Leighton 1939- *St&PR 91*
Wilson, Patricia Ann 1937- *WhoWrEP 89*
Wilson, Patricia Boyd 1911- *WhoAmW 91*
Wilson, Patricia Jane 1946- *WhoAmW 91, WhoWor 91*
Wilson, Patricia Poplar 1931- *WhoAmW 91*
Wilson, Patrick Elliott 1934- *St&PR 91*
Wilson, Patrick R. 1940- *ODwPR 91*
Wilson, Paul Edwin 1913- *WhoAm 90*
Wilson, Paul F 1922- *BiDrAPA 89*
Wilson, Paul Lowell 1951- *WhoSSW 91*
Wilson, Paul T 1932- *BiDrAPA 89*
Wilson, Paul Tyler 1932- *WhoE 91*
Wilson, Paula Rea *BiDrAPA 89*
Wilson, Percy 1893- *EncO&P 3*
Wilson, Perkins 1929- *WhoSSW 91, WhoWor 91*
Wilson, Pete *BioIn 16*
Wilson, Pete 1933- *WhoAm 90, WhoWor 91, WorAlBi*
Wilson, Peter Cecil 1913-1984 *DcNaB 1981*
Wilson, Peter G 1932- *BiDrAPA 89, WhoE 91*
Wilson, Peter Gardner Woltherspoon 1936- *IntWWM 90*
Wilson, Peter Leighton 1940- *WhoE 91*
Wilson, Philip T 1956- *BiDrAPA 89*
Wilson, Phillip R. 1945- *St&PR 91*
Wilson, Phyllis A. 1941- *WhoAmW 91*
Wilson, Phyllis Starr 1928- *WhoWrEP 89*
Wilson, Phyllis Starr 1928-1988 *BioIn 16*
Wilson, Porterfield *BioIn 16*
Wilson, R. Dale 1949- *WhoEmL 91*
Wilson, Rachel 1720-1775 *FemiCLE*
Wilson, Ralph Cookerly, Jr. 1918- *WhoE 91*
Wilson, Ralph Edwin 1921- *WhoAm 90*
Wilson, Ramon B. 1922- *WhoAm 90*
Wilson, Randal D. 1950- *WhoSSW 91*
Wilson, Ransom 1951- *ConMus 5 [port]*
Wilson, Ray *BioIn 16*
Wilson, Ray C. 1929- *St&PR 91*
Wilson, Raymond Clark 1915- *WhoAm 90*
Wilson, Red 1929- *Ballpl 90*
Wilson, Reginald 1927- *WhoE 91*
Wilson, Rhea 1946- *WhoAm 90*
Wilson, Rhys Thaddeus 1955- *WhoEmL 91, WhoSSW 91*
Wilson, Richard *BioIn 16, NewYTBS 90*
Wilson, Richard 1714-1782 *IntDcAA 90*
Wilson, Richard 1926- *EncO&P 3, WhoAm 90*
Wilson, Richard Alan 1956- *WhoE 91*
Wilson, Richard Allan 1927- *WhoAm 90*
Wilson, Richard Brian 1944- *WhoAmA 91*
Wilson, Richard Brown 1942- *St&PR 91*
Wilson, Richard Charles 1945- *WhoE 91*
Wilson, Richard Christian 1921- *WhoAm 90*
Wilson, Richard E. 1928-1989 *BioIn 16*
Wilson, Richard Edward 1941- *WhoAm 90*
Wilson, Richard Franklin 1936- *WhoAm 90*
Wilson, Richard Harold 1930- *WhoAm 90*
Wilson, Richard Lee 1944- *WhoSSW 91*
Wilson, Richard M. 1932- *St&PR 91*
Wilson, Richard Randolph 1950- *WhoEmL 91*
Wilson, Richard V 1922- *BiDrAPA 89*
Wilson, Rick D. 1948- *WhoWrEP 89*
Wilson, Rickey Lee *BiDrAPA 89*
Wilson, Rita Ann 1947- *WhoAmW 91*
Wilson, Robert *WhoAm 90, WhoAmA 91*
Wilson, Robert 1941- *BioIn 16*
Wilson, Robert A. *ODwPR 91*
Wilson, Robert Alan 1949- *WhoAmA 91*
Wilson, Robert Albert 1936- *WhoE 91*
Wilson, Robert Allen 1947- *BiDrAPA 89*
Wilson, Robert Anton 1932- *WhoWrEP 89*
Wilson, Robert B. 1936- *St&PR 91*
Wilson, Robert Burns 1850-1916 *LiHiK*
Wilson, Robert Burton 1936- *WhoAm 90*
Wilson, Robert Edward 1951- *WhoSSW 91, WhoWrEP 89*
Wilson, Robert Edward 1958- *WhoSSW 91*
Wilson, Robert Elden *BiDrAPA 89*
Wilson, Robert Eldon 1959- *WhoEmL 91*
Wilson, Robert Eugene 1932- *WhoSSW 91*
Wilson, Robert Foster 1926- *WhoWor 91*
Wilson, Robert Gordon 1933- *WhoSSW 91*
Wilson, Robert Henry 1909- *WhoAm 90*
Wilson, Robert J. 1928- *St&PR 91*
Wilson, Robert James Montgomery 1920- *WhoAm 90*
Wilson, Robert Kenneth 1937- *WhoSSW 91*
Wilson, Robert Lake 1924- *WhoSSW 91*
Wilson, Robert M. 1941- *WhoAm 90*
Wilson, Robert M 1944- *MajTwCW*
Wilson, Robert McLiam 1964- *ConAu 132, ConLC 59 [port]*
Wilson, Robert Nathan 1940- *WhoAm 90*
Wilson, Robert Neal 1924- *WhoAm 90*
Wilson, Robert Oliver 1927- *WhoSSW 91*
Wilson, Robert Patterson Clark 1834-1916 *AmLegL*

Wilson, Robert R. 1914- *BioIn 16*
Wilson, Robert Sidney 1947- *WhoEmL 91, WhoWor 91*
Wilson, Robert Spencer 1951- *WhoAm 90*
Wilson, Robert W. R. 1929- *IntWWM 90*
Wilson, Robert Walter 1936- *St&PR 91*
Wilson, Robert Wayne 1957- *BiDrAPA 89*
Wilson, Robert William 1935- *St&PR 91, WhoAm 90*
Wilson, Robert Woodrow 1936- *WhoAm 90, WhoE 91, WhoWor 91, WorAlBi*
Wilson, Roberta May 1943- *WhoAmW 91*
Wilson, Robin Scott 1928- *WhoAm 90*
Wilson, Robley Conant, Jr. 1930- *WhoAm 90, WhoWrEP 89*
Wilson, Rodgers McKinley *BiDrAPA 89*
Wilson, Rodney Estes 1930- *St&PR 91*
Wilson, Roger Charles 1949- *St&PR 91*
Wilson, Roger Goodwin 1950- *WhoEmL 91*
Wilson, Roger Howard 1926- *St&PR 91*
Wilson, Roger M 1940- *BiDrAPA 89*
Wilson, Romer 1891-1930 *FemiCLE*
Wilson, Ronald J. 1934- *St&PR 91*
Wilson, Rosalind Baker 1923- *BioIn 16, ConAu 132*
Wilson, Rosemary Virginia *BiDrAPA 89*
Wilson, Roy Craig 1955- *BiDrAPA 89*
Wilson, Roy Edward *BiDrAPA 89*
Wilson, Roy Gardiner 1932- *WhoAm 90*
Wilson, Roy Kenneth 1913- *WhoAm 90*
Wilson, Ruby Leila 1931- *WhoAm 90*
Wilson, Ruth *AuBYP 90*
Wilson, Sally K. *ODwPR 91*
Wilson, Samuel, Jr. 1911- *WhoAm 90*
Wilson, Samuel Lamar 1936- *BiDrAPA 89*
Wilson, Samuel Mack 1921- *WhoAm 90*
Wilson, Samuel R. 1948- *St&PR 91*
Wilson, Sandy 1924- *OxCPMus*
Wilson, Sara Redding 1950- *WhoAm 90*
Wilson, Sarah 1934- *BioIn 16*
Wilson, Sarah J. 1942- *WhoAmW 91*
Wilson, Scott Numo *BiDrAPA 89*
Wilson, Selma M. *St&PR 91*
Wilson, Selma Pierce 1956- *WhoAmW 91*
Wilson, Shanice *BioIn 16*
Wilson, Sharonn 1951- *WhoAmW 91*
Wilson, Sherrie Darlene 1950- *WhoAmW 91*
Wilson, Sherwood E 1936- *BiDrAPA 89*
Wilson, Shirl Neal 1938- *WhoSSW 91*
Wilson, Skeeter J.H. 1952- *WhoAmW 91*
Wilson, Sloan 1920- *WhoAm 90*
Wilson, Sloan Jacob 1910- *WhoAm 90*
Wilson, Sol 1896-1974 *WhoAmA 91N*
Wilson, Stanley P. 1922- *St&PR 91, WhoAm 90*
Wilson, Stephanie Y. 1952- *St&PR 91*
Wilson, Stephen Douglas 1952- *WhoSSW 91*
Wilson, Stephen Edward 1945- *WhoEmL 91*
Wilson, Stephen Jay 1940- *BiDrAPA 89*
Wilson, Stephen L. *St&PR 91*
Wilson, Stephen Ray 1948- *St&PR 91*
Wilson, Stephen Roy 1946- *St&PR 91*
Wilson, Steven B. 1941- *St&PR 91*
Wilson, Steven Eugene 1948- *St&PR 91*
Wilson, Stuart Kay *BiDrAPA 89*
Wilson, Stuart R. 1932- *ODwPR 91*
Wilson, Sule Greg C. 1957- *WhoE 91*
Wilson, Susan 1943- *ODwPR 91*
Wilson, Sybil 1923- *WhoAmA 91*
Wilson, T. A. *BioIn 16*
Wilson, Teddy 1912-1986 *BioIn 16, DrBlPA 90, OxCPMus*
Wilson, Teddy 1938- *WhoAmW 91*
Wilson, Terrence Raymond 1943- *WhoE 91*
Wilson, Terry L. 1962- *WhoE 91*
Wilson, Terry W. 1934- *ODwPR 91*
Wilson, Terry Wayne 1934- *St&PR 91*
Wilson, Theodore 1943- *DrBlPA 90*
Wilson, Theodore Alexander 1935- *WhoAm 90*
Wilson, Theodore Allen 1940- *WhoAm 90*
Wilson, Thomas *BioIn 16*
Wilson, Thomas A. *BioIn 16*
Wilson, Thomas Alexander *BiDrAPA 89*
Wilson, Thomas Arthur 1935- *WhoAm 90*
Wilson, Thomas Booth 1949- *WhoE 91*
Wilson, Thomas Brendan 1927- *IntWWM 90*
Wilson, Thomas Daniel 1953- *St&PR 91*
Wilson, Thomas E 1933- *BiDrAPA 89*
Wilson, Thomas Francis 1923- *St&PR 91*
Wilson, Thomas Gross, III 1946- *WhoSSW 91*
Wilson, Thomas H. 1938- *St&PR 91*
Wilson, Thomas Hastings 1925- *WhoAm 90*
Wilson, Thomas Henry 1931- *WhoE 91*
Wilson, Thomas Jerome 1945- *BiDrAPA 89*
Wilson, Thomas Leon 1942- *WhoWor 91*
Wilson, Thomas Matthew, III 1936- *WhoE 91, WhoWor 91*
Wilson, Thomas N., Jr. 1929- *St&PR 91*
Wilson, Thomas Raiford, Jr. 1930- *WhoSSW 91*
Wilson, Thomas William 1935- *WhoAm 90, WhoWor 91*
Wilson, Thornton A. *BioIn 16*
Wilson, Thornton Arnold 1921- *WhoAm 90*
Wilson, Timothy Stearns 1957- *WhoE 91*
Wilson, Todd Dorian 1953- *WhoWrEP 89*
Wilson, Tom 1931- *WhoAmA 91*
Wilson, Tom Muir 1930- *WhoAmA 91*
Wilson, Tracy *BioIn 16*
Wilson, Trevor 1966- *Ballpl 90*
Wilson, Trey *BioIn 16*
Wilson, Trey 1948-1989 *ConTFT 8*
Wilson, Verna Jean 1937- *WhoAmW 91*
Wilson, Victoria Wiegand 1957- *WhoSSW 91*
Wilson, Vincent Joseph, Jr. 1921- *WhoE 91, WhoWor 91*
Wilson, Virginia A. 1932- *St&PR 91*
Wilson, W. Stephen 1946- *WhoE 91*
Wilson, Wallace 1947- *WhoAm 90, WhoAmA 91*
Wilson, Wallace S. 1929- *St&PR 91*
Wilson, Walter Edward 1949- *WhoSSW 91*
Wilson, Wanda Lee 1950- *WhoAmW 91*
Wilson, Warner Rushing 1935- *WhoAm 90*
Wilson, Warren Bingham 1920- *WhoAmA 91*
Wilson, Warren Brett 1953- *WhoSSW 91*
Wilson, Wayne M. 1948- *WhoEmL 91*
Wilson, Wayne R. 1943- *St&PR 91*
Wilson, Wendy 1970?- *ConMus 5*
Wilson, Wilburn Leroy 1913- *WhoAm 90*
Wilson, Wilburn Martin 1930- *WhoWrEP 89*
Wilson, Wilfred James 1922- *WhoAm 90*
Wilson, William A. 1933- *St&PR 91*
Wilson, William Albert 1933- *WhoAm 90, WhoE 91*
Wilson, William Bauchop 1862-1934 *BiDrUSE 89*
Wilson, William Craig 1951- *St&PR 91*
Wilson, William E. 1906-1988 *BioIn 16*
Wilson, William G. 1864- *AmLegL*
Wilson, William G. 1895-1971 *WorAlBi*
Wilson, William Griffith *BioIn 16*
Wilson, William H. *BioIn 16*
Wilson, William H 1951- *BiDrAPA 89*
Wilson, William Hall, Jr. 1942- *WhoE 91*
Wilson, William Howard 1924- *WhoAm 90*
Wilson, William J. 1932- *WhoSSW 91*
Wilson, William James 1936- *St&PR 91*
Wilson, William Julius *BioIn 16*
Wilson, William Julius 1935- *WhoAm 90*
Wilson, William K. 1913- *St&PR 91*
Wilson, William Lyne 1843-1900 *BiDrUSE 89*
Wilson, William Maxwell 1927- *St&PR 91*
Wilson, William P 1922- *BiDrAPA 89*
Wilson, William Preston 1922- *WhoAm 90*
Wilson, William R. 1954- *WhoSSW 91*
Wilson, William R S 1913- *BiDrAPA 89*
Wilson, William S. 1932- *WhoWrEP 89, WorAu 1980 [port]*
Wilson, William S, III 1932- *WhoAmA 91*
Wilson, William Smith, III 1932- *WhoE 91*
Wilson, William W *BiDrAPA 89*
Wilson, William Wartman 1917- *WhoE 91*
Wilson, William Wheaton 1930- *WhoE 91*
Wilson, Willie 1955- *Ballpl 90 [port]*
Wilson, Wilma Ruth 1950- *WhoAmW 91*
Wilson, Woodrow 1856-1924 *BiDrUSE 89, BioIn 16, WorAlBi*
Wilson, Woodrow, Mrs. 1872-1961 *BioIn 16*
Wilson, Woodrow S. 1915- *St&PR 91*
Wilson, Worth B., Jr. 1952- *St&PR 91*
Wilson, York 1907- *WhoAmA 91*
Wilson, Yvonne Marie 1937- *WhoSSW 91*
Wilson, Zelma Gussin 1918- *WhoAm 90*
Wilson-Butler, Joyce Ann 1944- *WhoAmW 91*
Wilson-Felder, Cynthia Ann 1951- *IntWWM 90*
Wilson-Hammond, Charlotte Emily 1941- *WhoAmA 91*
Wilson-Hopkins, Deborah Dana 1955- *WhoAmW 91*
Wilson-Hurey, Carolyn Ann 1956- *WhoAmW 91*
Wilson-Johnson, David 1950- *IntWWM 90*
Wilson-Simpson, Dorothy Andrea 1945- *WhoAmW 91*
Wilt, Alan Freese 1937- *WhoAm 90*
Wilt, F. R. 1946- *BiDrAPA 89*
Wilt, Stevan J. 1945- *St&PR 91*
Wiltberger, Mary E 1913- *BiDrAPA 89*
Wilthew, Robert M. 1931- *St&PR 91*
Wilton, Anna Keener 1895- *WhoAmA 91N*
Wilton, Frank Putnam 1930- *St&PR 91*
Wilton, Hal 1910-1988 *SmATA X*
Wilton, Joseph 1722-1803 *BioIn 16*
Wilton, Marie 1839-1921 *BioIn 16*
Wilton, Robert Frederick 1953- *WhoE 91*
Wiltraut, Douglas *BioIn 16*
Wiltraut, Douglas Scott 1951- *WhoAmA 91*
Wiltrout, Ann Elizabeth 1939- *WhoSSW 91*
Wilts, Merle David 1938- *St&PR 91*
Wiltse, Charles M 1907-1990 *ConAu 131*
Wiltse, Charles Maurice 1907- *WhoAm 90*
Wiltse, Charles Maurice 1907-1990 *BioIn 16*
Wiltse, Hal 1903-1983 *Ballpl 90*
Wiltse, Hooks 1880-1959 *Ballpl 90 [port]*
Wiltse, Snake 1871-1928 *Ballpl 90*
Wiltsek, Kenneth M. 1942- *St&PR 91*
Wiltshire, James Merrill, Jr. 1925- *St&PR 91*
Wiltshire, Richard W. 1921- *St&PR 91*
Wiltshire, Richard Watkins, Jr. 1945- *St&PR 91, WhoAm 90, WhoSSW 91*
Wiltshire, Richard Watkins, Sr. 1921- *WhoAm 90, WhoSSW 91*
Wiltz, Hector R 1926- *BiDrAPA 89*
Wiltz, James Wesley 1945- *St&PR 91*
Wiltz, Louis Alfred 1843-1881 *AmLegL*
Wiltz, Magdalena 1952- *BiDrAPA 89*
Wiltz, Robert E. 1936- *St&PR 91*
Wilusz, Melisse Debra 1955- *WhoAmW 91*
Wilver, Wayne Riegel 1933- *St&PR 91*
Wilwers, Edward Mathias 1918- *WhoAmA 91*
Wilwerth, Claude 1937- *WhoWor 91*
Wilzack, Adele *WhoAmW 91*
Wiman, Bill 1940- *WhoAmA 91*
Wimar, Charles 1828-1862 *WhNaAH*
Wimberg, Elizabeth 1931- *BiDrAPA 89*
Wimberger, Herbert C *BiDrAPA 89*
Wimberger, Peter 1940- *IntWWM 90*
Wimberley, Frank Walden 1926- *WhoAmA 91*
Wimberley, Geraldine Joubert 1943- *WhoSSW 91*
Wimberly, Beadie Reneau 1937- *WhoAmW 91, WhoWor 91*
Wimberly, Don Adger *WhoAm 90*
Wimberly, Elliott 1954- *WhoE 91*
Wimberly, George James 1915- *WhoAm 90*
Wimberly, W. Carl 1924- *WhoAm 90*
Wimbish, Richard S. 1934- *St&PR 91*
Wimbish, Shack Burke, Jr. 1935- *St&PR 91*
Wimble, William R. 1932- *St&PR 91*
Wimer, Mary Catherine 1954- *BiDrAPA 89*
Wimer, Sarah Joyce 1951- *WhoEmL 91*
Wimer, William John 1934- *St&PR 91*
Wimmer, Billie Kops 1956- *WhoAmW 91*
Wimmer, Dorn C. 1946- *St&PR 91*
Wimmer, Gayle 1943- *WhoAmA 91*
Wimmer, Rene W. 1955- *St&PR 91*
Wimmer, William Carey 1939- *BiDrAPA 89*
Wimpee, Andy C. 1946- *St&PR 91*
Wimperis, Arthur 1874-1953 *OxCPMus*
Wimpey, Perry A. 1931- *St&PR 91*
Wimpfheimer, Charles Anthony 1928- *WhoAm 90*
Wimpfheimer, Jacques D. 1918- *St&PR 91*
Wimpfheimer, Michael Clark 1944- *WhoWor 91*
Wimpress, Gordon Duncan, Jr. 1922- *WhoAm 90, WhoSSW 91, WhoWor 91*
Wimsatt, William K. 1907-1975 *BioIn 16*
Win, Maung Htein *BiDrAPA 89*
Winahradsky, Michael F. 1948- *St&PR 91*
Winahradsky, Michael Francis 1948- *WhoAm 90*
Winaker, Kenneth Lee 1945- *BiDrAPA 89*
Winand, Rene Fernand Paul 1932- *WhoWor 91*
Winandy, John Pierre 1926- *St&PR 91, WhoAm 90*
Winans, Allan Davis 1936- *WhoWrEP 89*
Winans, Barbara Ann 1939- *WhoAmW 91*
Winans, Gary L. 1949- *St&PR 91*
Winans, Margaret Lucille 1955- *WhoE 91*
Winant, John Gilbert 1889-1947 *BioIn 16*
Winawer, Sidney Jerome 1931- *WhoAm 90*
Winberg, Jack S *BiDrAPA 89*
Winbergh, Gosta 1943- *IntWWM 90*
Winbigler, Leon Francis 1926- *St&PR 91, WhoE 91*
Winburn, Hardy L., Jr. 1932- *St&PR 91*
Wince-Smith, Deborah L. *WhoAm 90, WhoAmW 91*
Wincentz, Peer 1944- *WhoWor 91*
Winch, David Monk 1933- *WhoAm 90*
Winch, Peter Guy 1926- *WhoAm 90*
Winchar, Fred Daniel 1959- *WhoSSW 91*
Winchel, Ron M *BiDrAPA 89*
Winchell, Margaret Webster St. Clair 1923- *WhoAmW 91*
Winchell, Michael George 1949- *WhoWor 91*
Winchell, Walter 1897-1972 *BioIn 16, WorAlBi*
Winchell, William Olin 1933- *WhoWor 91*
Winchelsea, Anne, Countess of *BiDEWW*
Winchester, Albert McCombs 1908- *WhoAm 90*
Winchester, Alice 1907- *WhoAmA 91*
Winchester, Alma Elizabeth Tatsch 1907- *WhoWor 91*
Winchester, Clarence Floyd 1901- *WhoE 91*
Winchester, Elhanan 1751-1797 *BioIn 16*
Winchester, Elizabeth Young 1934- *WhoE 91*
Winchester, Jacqueline Canton 1930- *WhoAmW 91, WhoSSW 91*
Winchester, Jeanette M. 1953- *WhoAmW 91*
Winchester, Kirk Handley 1952- *St&PR 91*
Winchester, Robert Joseph 1937- *WhoAm 90*
Winchester, Rush B. 1924- *St&PR 91*
Winchester-Vega, Michele Renee 1960- *WhoAmW 91*
Winchevsky, Morris 1856-1932 *EncAL*
Winchilsea, Anne Finch, Countess of 1661-1720 *BioIn 16*
Winckel, Fritz 1907- *IntWWM 90*
Winckelmann, Johann Joachim 1717-1768 *DcLB 97 [port]*
Winckler, Robert E. 1934- *St&PR 91*
Wincor, Michael Z. 1946- *WhoEmL 91*
Wincott, Gerald Jay 1935- *St&PR 91*
Wincup, G. Kim 1944- *WhoAm 90*
Wind, Herbert Warren 1916- *WhoAm 90*
Wind, Marlise Wabun 1945- *WhoWrEP 89*
Wind, Moe 1924- *St&PR 91*
Wind, William Joseph 1934- *St&PR 91*
Windal, Floyd Wesley 1930- *WhoAm 90*
Windauer, Hans 1945- *WhoWor 91*
Windaus, Adolf O. R. 1876-1959 *WorAlBi*
Windbichler, Christine 1950- *WhoWor 91*
Windeknecht, Margaret Brake 1936- *WhoAmA 91*
Windelev, Claus 1943- *WhoE 91*
Windell, Violet Bruner *WhoAmA 91*
Windels, Carol Elizabeth 1948- *WhoAmW 91*
Windels, Paul, Jr. 1921- *St&PR 91, WhoAm 90*
Winder, Barbara Dietz 1927- *WhoWrEP 89*
Winder, Clarence Leland 1921- *WhoAm 90*
Winder, David William 1947- *WhoSSW 91*
Winder, R. Bayly 1920-1988 *BioIn 16*
Winder, Richard Bayly 1920-1988 *BioIn 16*
Winder, Robert Owen 1934- *WhoAm 90*
Winder, Robert William 1933- *IntWWM 90*
Winder, Viola Hitti *AuBYP 90*
Windfuhr, Gernot Ludwig 1938- *WhoAm 90*
Windgassen, Fritz 1883-1963 *PenDiMP*
Windgassen, Wolfgang 1914-1974 *BioIn 16, PenDiMP*
Windhager, Erich Ernst 1928- *WhoAm 90*
Windhager, Evelyn Ann 1959- *WhoE 91*
Windhager, Juliane 1912-1986 *EncCoWW*
Windham, Basil *ConAu 33NR, MajTwCW*
Windham, C. Richard *ODwPR 91*
Windham, Charles Parker *BiDrAPA 89*
Windham, Donald 1920- *BioIn 16*
Windham, Edward James 1950- *WhoWor 91*
Windham, Kathryn Tucker *BioIn 16*
Windham, Revish 1949- *WhoWrEP 89*
Windham, Thomas *WhoSSW 91*
Windhausen, John Daniel *WhoE 91*
Windhausen, Rodolfo A. 1944- *WhoHisp 91*
Windhauser, John William 1943- *WhoSSW 91*
Windheim, Daniel Robert 1930- *St&PR 91*
Windholz, Francis Leo 1932- *WhoAm 90*
Windhorst, Dave Alan 1953- *St&PR 91*
Winding, Charles A. 1907- *St&PR 91*
Winding, Kai 1922-1983 *BioIn 16*
Winding, Walter G. 1941- *St&PR 91*
Windisch, E.C. 1927- *St&PR 91*
Windish, George Elliott 1939- *WhoSSW 91*
Windish, John Joseph, III 1947- *WhoE 91*
Windle, Jonathan W. 1936- *St&PR 91*
Windle, Melville P. 1926- *St&PR 91*
Windler, Gerald 1941- *BiDrAPA 89*
Windman, Arnold Lewis 1926- *St&PR 91, WhoAm 90*
Windmuller, John Philip 1923- *WhoAm 90*
Windolph, Gary Robert 1942- *St&PR 91*
Windom, William 1827-1891 *BiDrUSE 89*
Windom, William 1923- *WorAlBi*
Windrich, Elaine 1921- *ConAu 131*
Windrow, Patricia 1923- *WhoAmA 91*

Windsor, Anthony Beck 1950- WhoSSW 91
Windsor, Charles Everette 1927- WhoAm 90
Windsor, Edward, Duke of 1894-1972 BioIn 16
Windsor, Gerard Charles 1944- WhoWor 91
Windsor, John Robert WhoE 91
Windsor, Laurence Charles, Jr. 1935- WhoAm 90
Windsor, Natalie Precker WhoAmW 91
Windsor, Patricia 1938- WhoAm 90
Windsor, Robert Kennedy 1933- WhoAm 90, WhoE 91
Windsor, Wallis Simpson 1896-1986 BioAmW
Windsor, Wallis Warfield, Duchess of 1896-1986 BioIn 16
Windsor-Liscombe, Rhodri 1946- ConAu 129
Windt, Arnold 1924- BiDrAPA 89
Windy Boy, Janine Pease- BioIn 16
Wine, Bobby 1938- Ballpl 90
Wine, Donald Arthur 1922- WhoAm 90, WhoWor 91
Wine, James W. NewYTBS 90 [port]
Wine, James Wilmer 1918- WhoAm 90
Wine, Sherwin Theodore 1928- WhoAm 90
Wine-Banks, Jill Susan 1943- WhoAm 90, WhoAmW 91
Wineapple, Ed 1906- BioIn 16
Winearls, Christopher Good 1949- WhoWor 91
Winebarger, Estel C. 1946- St&PR 91
Winebarger, Joe P. 1948- St&PR 91
Winebrenner, Douglas Joseph 1942- St&PR 91
Winebrenner, Hugh 1937- BioIn 16
Winebrenner, Janis L. 1949- WhoWrEP 89
Wineburg, Elliot N BiDrAPA 89
Winegar, Albert Lee 1931- St&PR 91, WhoAm 90
Winegar, William 1953- WhoSSW 91
Winegard, William Charles 1924- WhoAm 90, WhoE 91
Winegarden, Joel I. 1938- St&PR 91
Winegarner, Ralph 1909- Ballpl 90
Winegrad, Dilys Veronica 1937- WhoAmW 91
Winegrad, Gerald William 1944- WhoE 91
Winekoff, Connie J. 1962- WhoAmW 91
Wineland, Robert L. 1955- St&PR 91
Winema 1836-1920 WhNaAH
Wineman, Alan Stuart 1937- WhoAm 90
Wineman, James Martin 1949- St&PR 91
Winenger, Dwight Irvin 1936- IntWWM 90
Winer, Bart BioIn 16
Winer, Donald Arthur 1927- WhoAmA 91
Winer, Harold 1910- WhoAm 90
Winer, Helene 1936- WhoAmA 91
Winer, Irwin Basil 1920- St&PR 91
Winer, Jay D. 1950- WhoSSW 91
Winer, Jerome A 1938- BiDrAPA 89
Winer, Melvin L BiDrAPA 89
Winer, Michael Raymond 1957- St&PR 91
Winer, Morton J. 1914- St&PR 91
Winer, Nahum J. 1907-1990 BioIn 16
Winer, Richard 1916- WhoAm 90
Winer, Richard Steven BiDrAPA 89
Winer, Robert Harry 1933- St&PR 91
Winer, Robert Joseph 1940- BiDrAPA 89
Winer, Stephen J. 1954- St&PR 91
Winer, Ward Otis 1936- WhoAm 90, WhoSSW 91
Winer, Warren James 1946- WhoWor 91
Wines, Fred James 1931- St&PR 91
Wines, James N. 1932- WhoAm 90, WhoAmA 91
Wines, Richard 1946- ODwPR 91
Wines, Roger R. 1942- St&PR 91
Winesanker, Michael Max 1913- IntWWM 90
Winesett, R. Davis, Jr. 1941- St&PR 91
Winestock, Major BiDrAPA 89
Winett, Samuel Joseph 1934- St&PR 91, WhoAm 90
Winey, William Kenneth 1926- St&PR 91
Winfield, Arlene V BiDrAPA 89
Winfield, Bruce W.D. 1947- St&PR 91
Winfield, Dave NewYTBS 90 [port]
Winfield, Dave 1951- Ballpl 90 [port], BioIn 16
Winfield, David Mark 1951- WhoAm 90
Winfield, Donald H. 1942- St&PR 91
Winfield, John A. 1922- St&PR 91
Winfield, John Buckner 1942- WhoAm 90
Winfield, Mary Beth 1957- WhoAmW 91
Winfield, Michael David 1939- St&PR 91
Winfield, Paul BioIn 16
Winfield, Paul 1941- DrBlPA 90, WorAlBi
Winfield, Richard Neill 1933- WhoE 91, WhoWor 91
Winfield, Rodney M 1925- WhoAmA 91
Winfield, Stephen NewAgMG
Winford, Jim 1909-1970 Ballpl 90
Winford, Maria 1945- WhoWor 91
Winfree, Arthur Taylor 1942- WhoAm 90
Winfrey, Carey Wells 1941- WhoAm 90
Winfrey, Charles Jack 1946- BiDrAPA 89
Winfrey, Dorman Hayward 1924- WhoAm 90, WhoSSW 91
Winfrey, John Crawford 1935- WhoAm 90
Winfrey, LaPearl Logan 1952- WhoAmW 91
Winfrey, Marion Lee 1932- WhoAm 90
Winfrey, Oprah BioIn 16
Winfrey, Oprah 1953- DrBlPA 90
Winfrey, Oprah 1954- WhoAm 90, WhoAmW 91, WorAlBi
Winfrey, Shirley Maureen 1956- WhoAmW 91
Wing, Adrien Katherine 1956- WhoWor 91
Wing, Christopher D. 1954- St&PR 91
Wing, Edward Joseph 1945- WhoE 91
Wing, Elizabeth Schwarz 1932- WhoAmW 91
Wing, George Lee BiDrAPA 89
Wing, James 1929- WhoE 91
Wing, James Erwin 1958- WhoWor 91
Wing, Janet Eleanor Sweedyk Bendt 1925- WhoAmW 91
Wing, Jasper WhoWrEP 89
Wing, John Adams 1935- St&PR 91, WhoAm 90
Wing, John F. 1934- St&PR 91
Wing, Kylene Scarborough WhoAmW 91
Wing, Martin Richard 1954- WhoSSW 91
Wing, Michael C. 1948- ODwPR 91
Wing, Rena Rimsky 1945- WhoAmW 91
Wing, Robert L. 1929- St&PR 91
Wing, Roger C. 1932- St&PR 91
Wing, Sidney E. St&PR 91
Wing, Thomas 1929- WhoWor 91
Wingard, Ernie 1900-1977 Ballpl 90
Wingard, George Clifton 1963- WhoSSW 91
Wingard, Peggy BiDrAPA 89
Wingard, Raymond Randolph 1930- WhoWor 91
Wingart, Cleland J. 1921- St&PR 91
Wingate, Arline WhoAmA 91
Wingate, Arline 1906- WhoAm 90
Wingate, Barbara Ann 1955- WhoAmW 91
Wingate, Charles Douglas 1953- WhoE 91
Wingate, David A. 1921- St&PR 91
Wingate, Edwin Henry 1932- WhoAm 90
Wingate, George B 1941- WhoAmA 91
Wingate, Henry Travillion 1947- WhoAm 90, WhoSSW 91
Wingate, John 1921- BioIn 16
Wingate, Orde Charles 1903-1944 WorAlBi
Wingate, Paul D. 1921- St&PR 91
Wingate, Rebecca Gomez 1954- St&PR 91
Wingate, Robert Bray 1925- WhoAmA 91
Wingate, Robert Lee, Jr. 1936- WhoSSW 91
Wingate, Tessa Elizabeth 1947- WhoAmW 91
Wingate, William Peter 1944- WhoAm 90, WhoE 91
Winger, Charles Edwin 1940- St&PR 91
Winger, Charles Joseph 1945- St&PR 91
Winger, Debra BioIn 16
Winger, Debra 1955- WhoAm 90, WhoAmW 91, WorAlBi
Winger, Dennis Lawrence 1947- WhoAm 90
Winger, Eric R. 1941- St&PR 91
Winger, Howard Woodrow 1914- WhoAm 90
Winger, Maurice, Jr. 1917- St&PR 91
Winger, Ralph O. 1919- WhoAm 90
Wingerson, Dane Kurt 1960- BiDrAPA 89
Wingert, Dick 1919- EncACom
Wingert, Hannelore Christiane WhoE 91
Wingert, John B. 1934- St&PR 91
Wingert, Paul Stover 1900-1974 WhoAmA 91N
Wingerter, John Parker 1940- WhoAmA 91, WhoE 91
Wingerter, Laurence Adrian 1942- St&PR 91
Wingerter, Roger Allen 1939- WhoSSW 91
Winges, Mark David 1951- IntWWM 90
Wingfield, Alexander Hamilton 1828-1896 DcCanB 12
Wingfield, C. E. EncPaPR 91
Wingfield, Charles Michael 1952- WhoSSW 91
Wingfield, David Brian 1946- WhoSSW 91
Wingfield, George 1876-1959 EncABHB 7 [port]
Wingfield, Kate EncO&P 3
Wingfield, Sheila 1906- BioIn 16, ConAu 130
Wingfield, Ted 1899-1975 Ballpl 90
Winglass, Robert Joseph 1935- WhoAm 90
Wingo, Al Ballpl 90
Wingo, Charles William 1931- St&PR 91
Wingo, Ivy 1890-1941 Ballpl 90
Wingo, Michael B 1941- WhoAmA 91
Wingo, Pamela Denise 1959- WhoSSW 91
Wingo, Wendell BioIn 16
Wingrove, Robert C. 1932- St&PR 91
Wings OxCPMus
Wings Over Jordan DcAfAmP
Wings, Mary 1949- TwCCr&M 91
Wingstrand, Hans Anders 1949- WhoWor 91
Wingti, Paias WhoWor 91
Winham, Gilbert Rathbone 1938- WhoAm 90
Winhold, Duncan Ramsay 1932- St&PR 91, WhoAm 90
Winholtz, Howard Messick 1918- WhoAm 90
Winiarczyk, Marek 1947- WhoWor 91
Winiarski, Thaddeus Joseph 1928- St&PR 91
Winiarz, Witold V 1905- BiDrAPA 89
Winick, Alfred Zell 1941- St&PR 91
Winick, Charles 1922- WhoAm 90
Winick, Darvin M. 1929- St&PR 91
Winick, Myron 1929- WhoAm 90
Winick, Theodore 1935- St&PR 91
Winick, Veta Lois 1931- WhoSSW 91
Winick, William BiDrAPA 89
Winig, Hugh R 1943- BiDrAPA 89
Winik, Jay B. 1957- WhoAm 90
Winikoff, Beverly 1945- WhoAmW 91
Winikoff, Marcia 1923- St&PR 91
Winikoff, Stanley 1917- St&PR 91
Winikow, Linda 1940- WhoE 91
Wininger, Deborah Kay 1950- WhoWrEP 89
Winings, Michael Harry 1952- St&PR 91
Wink, David A. St&PR 91
Wink, Don 1938- WhoAmA 91
Winkel, Nina 1905-1990 WhoAmA 91N
Winkel, Raymond Norman 1928- WhoAm 90
Winkelhake, Jean Kathryn 1937- WhoAmW 91
Winkelhaus, John William 1950- St&PR 91
Winkelman, Babe BioIn 16
Winkelman, Earl L. 1927- St&PR 91
Winkelman, Edward E. 1938- St&PR 91
Winkelman, John Weyl 1956- BiDrAPA 89
Winkelman, Stanley J. 1922- St&PR 91
Winkelmann, John Paul 1933- WhoWrEP 89
Winkelmayer, Richard 1930- BiDrAPA 89
Winkelsas, Dennis James 1950- WhoSSW 91
Winkelstein, Charles 1926- BiDrAPA 89
Winkelstein, Norman BiDrAPA 89
Winkelstern, Philip Norman 1930- St&PR 91
Winker, James Anthony 1928- St&PR 91
Winkin, John BioIn 16
Winkin, Justin Philip 1922- St&PR 91, WhoAm 90
Winkleblack, Jack Dean 1928- WhoSSW 91
Winkleman, John S. 1955- ODwPR 91
Winkler, Agnieszka M. 1946- WhoAmW 91
Winkler, Allan Michael 1945- WhoEmL 91
Winkler, Amelia Bleicher 1933- WhoAmW 91
Winkler, Arthur 1944- St&PR 91
Winkler, Cuno 1919- WhoWor 91
Winkler, Edward D. 1942- St&PR 91
Winkler, Fred Martin 1943- WhoSSW 91
Winkler, Helmut Gustav Franz 1915-1980 DcScB S2
Winkler, Henry 1945- WorAlBi
Winkler, Henry Franklin 1945- WhoAm 90
Winkler, Henry Ralph 1916- WhoAm 90
Winkler, Herbert M. 1933- St&PR 91
Winkler, Hermann 1936- IntWWM 90
Winkler, Howard Leslie 1950- WhoWor 91
Winkler, Irwin BioIn 16
Winkler, Irwin 1931- WhoAm 90
Winkler, John Harbit 1942- WhoAm 90
Winkler, John J. BioIn 16
Winkler, John J 1943-1990 ConAu 131
Winkler, John L 1925- BiDrAPA 89
Winkler, Joseph Conrad 1916- WhoAm 90
Winkler, Kenneth M. 1928- St&PR 91
Winkler, Laura 1948- WhoAmW 91
Winkler, Lee B. 1925- WhoAm 90
Winkler, Lewis Alan BiDrAPA 89
Winkler, Lyle D. 1939- St&PR 91
Winkler, Maria Paula 1945- WhoAmA 91
Winkler, Martin Kenneth 1943- WhoAm 90
Winkler, Michael 1952- WhoAmA 91
Winkler, Nancy Ann 1952- WhoAmW 91
Winkler, Oskar Werner 1959- WhoWor 91
Winkler, Paul Frank, Jr. 1942- WhoAm 90
Winkler, Peter M. 1946- WhoSSW 91
Winkler, Robert Charles 1927- St&PR 91
Winkler, Robert Lewis 1943- WhoAm 90
Winkler, Sheldon 1932- WhoAm 90
Winkler, William F. 1956- St&PR 91
Winkles, Stuart WhoWrEP 89
Winklevoss, Carl R. 1919- St&PR 91
Winks, Robin W 1930- SmATA 61 [port]
Winks, Robin William 1930- ConAu 30NR, WhoAm 90
Winkworth, Catherine 1827-1878 BioIn 16
Winland, Denise Lynn 1951- WhoAmW 91
Winmill, Bassett S. 1930- St&PR 91
Winn, Albert Curry 1921- WhoAm 90
Winn, Casey 1966- IntWWM 90
Winn, Charles Scott Brent 1961- WhoSSW 91
Winn, David B. 1937- WhoAm 90
Winn, David Baker 1937- St&PR 91
Winn, Edward Burton 1920- WhoAm 90
Winn, Evelyn Dawson BioIn 16, NewYTBS 90
Winn, Ewa 1938- WhoAmW 91
Winn, George Michael 1944- St&PR 91
Winn, Harold 1927- BiDrAPA 89
Winn, Herschel C. 1931- St&PR 91
Winn, Herschel Clyde 1931- WhoAm 90
Winn, Jane Kaufman 1957- WhoAmW 91
Winn, Jerry Ray 1939- St&PR 91
Winn, Jill Kanaga Kline 1944- WhoAmW 91
Winn, Jim 1959- Ballpl 90
Winn, John A. 1946- St&PR 91
Winn, John Arthur, Jr. 1945- WhoE 91
Winn, Judith Katz 1938- WhoAmW 91
Winn, Judith Lynn 1949- WhoSSW 91
Winn, Kitty 1944- ConTFT 8
Winn, Margaret E BiDrAPA 89
Winn, Marie AuBYP 90
Winn, Paul J. 1940- St&PR 91
Winn, Philip D. 1925- WhoAm 90, WhoWor 91
Winn, Raymond Webster 1945- WhoSSW 91
Winn, Rowland Denys Guy 1916-1984 DcNaB 1981
Winn, Stewart Dowse, Jr. 1936- WhoE 91
Winn, Walter Vincent 1963- WhoEmL 91
Winn, Wandal W BiDrAPA 89
Winnberg, Siv 1944- IntWWM 90
Winne, Mark George 1950- WhoE 91
Winne, Mark T. 1950- St&PR 91
Winnebago Prophet WhNaAH
Winnefeld, James Alexander 1929- WhoAm 90
Winneg, Andrew Stephen BiDrAPA 89
Winnemucca WhNaAH [port]
Winnemucca, Sarah 1844-1891 BioAmW, BioIn 16, WhNaAH, WorAlBi
Winner, Albertine 1907-1988 AnObit 1988
Winner, Ellen 1947- WhoE 91
Winner, Ellen Plucknett 1943- WhoAmW 91
Winner, Larry J. 1947- St&PR 91
Winner, Michael 1935- WorAlBi
Winner, Michael Robert 1935- WhoAm 90, WhoWor 91
Winner, Nathalie WhoAmW 91
Winner, Septimus 1827-1902 OxCPMus
Winner, Thomas G. 1917- WhoAm 90
Winnerman, Robert H. 1921- St&PR 91
Winnerman, Robert Henry 1921- WhoAm 90, WhoE 91
Winnert, Franklin Roy 1932- WhoAm 90
Winneshiek 1812-1872 WhNaAH
Winnet, Nochem Samuel 1898- WhoAm 90
Winnett, Asa George 1923- WhoE 91
Winney, Ronald Dean 1942- St&PR 91
Winnick, Karen B. 1946- BioIn 16
Winnick, Maurice 1902-1962 OxCPMus
Winnie, Alon Palm 1932- WhoAm 90
Winnie, Dayle David 1935- WhoSSW 91
Winnikoff, Alan ODwPR 91
Winning, John Patrick 1952- WhoEmL 91
Winning, Joseph S. 1930- St&PR 91
Winninger, Charles 1884-1969 OxCPMus, WorAlBi
Winningham, Clarence Glenn 1940- WhoSSW 91
Winningham, Geoff 1943- WhoAmA 91
Winningham, Herm 1961- Ballpl 90
Winningstad, C. Norman 1925- St&PR 91
Winningstad, Chester Norman 1925- WhoAm 90
Winnington-Ingram, R P 1904- ConAu 129
Winnowski, T.R. 1942- St&PR 91
Winny, George C 1954- BiDrAPA 89
Winocur, Emanuel M 1928- BiDrAPA 89
Winograd, Arthur PenDiMP
Winograd, Audrey Lesser 1933- WhoAmW 91, WhoE 91
Winograd, Florence L. 1923- St&PR 91
Winograd, Harold S. 1921- St&PR 91
Winograd, Nicholas 1945- WhoAm 90
Winograd, Shmuel 1936- WhoAm 90
Winograd, Terry Allen 1946- WhoAm 90
Winogrand, Garry 1928-1984 BioIn 16, ModArCr 1 [port], WhoAmA 91N
Winoker, Diana Lee 1953- WhoSSW 91
Winokur, Anita D 1952- BiDrAPA 89
Winokur, Barton Joel 1940- WhoE 91

Winokur, Dena 1949- ODwPR 91
Winokur, George 1925- BiDrAPA 89, WhoAm 90
Winokur, Harvey Jay 1950- WhoSSW 91
Winokur, Herbert Simon, Jr. 1943- WhoAm 90
Winokur, James L. 1922- St&PR 91, WhoAmA 91
Winokur, Jon 1947- ConAu 132, WhoWrEP 89
Winokur, Matthew N 1951- ODwPR 91
Winokur, Neil S 1945- WhoAmA 91
Winokur, Paula Colton 1935- WhoAmA 91
Winokur, Robert M. 1924- WhoAm 90
Winokur, Robert Mark 1933- WhoAmA 91
Winquist, Vernon Nathaniel 1921- WhoSSW 91
Winsberg, Bertrand G 1936- BiDrAPA 89
Winsby, Roger Merritt 1951- St&PR 91
Winschel, Diane Perron BioIn 16
Winschel, James Francis 1949- St&PR 91
Winship, Albert Edward 1845-1933 BioIn 16
Winship, Frederick Moery 1924- WhoAm 90
Winship, G Montgomery 1919- BiDrAPA 89
Winship, Gary M. 1945- St&PR 91
Winship, H. Dillon, Jr. 1929- St&PR 91
Winship, Henry Dillon, Jr. 1929- WhoAm 90, WhoSSW 91
Winship, James D. 1948- St&PR 91
Winship, Leslie BioIn 16
Winship, M. Douglas 1949- WhoE 91
Winship, Thomas 1920- WhoE 91
Winship, Wadleigh Chichester 1940- WhoAm 90, WhoSSW 91
Winsky, Gregory J. 1949- St&PR 91
Winsky, Robert Leonard, Jr. BiDrAPA 89
Winsloe, Christa 1888-1944 EncCoWW
Winslow, Anne Branan 1920- WhoAmW 91
Winslow, Charles Ellis, Jr. 1928- WhoSSW 91
Winslow, Debra L. 1954- St&PR 91
Winslow, Edward 1595-1655 EncCRAm, WhNaAH
Winslow, Edward 1669-1753 PenDiDA 89
Winslow, Frances Edwards 1948- WhoAmW 91
Winslow, Francis Dana 1939- WhoWor 91
Winslow, Frank J. ODwPR 91
Winslow, Gail H. 1929- St&PR 91
Winslow, Helen WhoAmA 91
Winslow, Helen Maria 1851-1938 FemiCLE
Winslow, Henry Nichols 1938- St&PR 91
Winslow, John 1703-1774 EncCRAm
Winslow, Joseph C. 1913- St&PR 91
Winslow, Josiah 1629?-1680 EncCRAm, WhNaAH
Winslow, Julian Dallas 1914- WhoE 91
Winslow, Michael 1960- DrBIPA 90
Winslow, Pauline Glen TwCCr&M 91
Winslow, Philip BioIn 16
Winslow, Ralph E 1902-1978 WhoAmA 91N
Winslow, Richard E, III 1934- ConAu 129
Winslow, Richard Sears, Jr. 1942- BiDrAPA 89
Winslow, Robert Albert 1922- WhoAm 90
Winslow, Russell A. 1934- WhoAm 90
Winslow, Russell Austin 1934- St&PR 91
Winslow, Vernon BioIn 16
Winslow, Walter Keith 1947- IntWWM 90
Winslow, Walter W 1925- BiDrAPA 89
Winslow, Walter William 1925- WhoAm 90
Winsor, Barbara Ann 1943- WhoAmW 91, WhoE 91
Winsor, Curtin, Jr. 1939- WhoE 91
Winsor, Diana 1946- SpyFic
Winsor, Edward 1902- St&PR 91
Winsor, Eleanor Webster 1941- WhoE 91
Winsor, Henry C. 1928- WhoSSW 91
Winsor, Jacque 1941- WhoAmA 91
Winsor, Jacqueline 1941- BiDWomA
Winsor, Kathleen WhoAm 90, WhoWrEP 89
Winsor, Ralph 1936-1989 BioIn 16
Winsor, Robert AuBYP 90
Winsor, Robert David 1958- WhoSSW 91
Winsor, Travis Walter 1914- WhoWor 91
Winstanley, Gerrard 1609-1676 BioIn 16
Winstanley, John Breyfogle 1874-1947 WhoAmA 91N
Winstanley, Michael J. 1949- ConAu 129
Winstanley, Peter F. 1944- St&PR 91
Winstead, Betsy Barnes 1936- St&PR 91
Winstead, Daniel Keith 1944- BiDrAPA 89
Winstead, David Legender 1947- WhoE 91
Winstead, Elisabeth Weaver 1926- WhoWrEP 89
Winstead, George Alvis 1916- WhoWor 91
Winstead, George Ashby 1950- WhoSSW 91
Winstead, Meldrum Barnett, Jr. 1926- WhoAm 90
Winstead, Nash Nicks 1925- WhoAm 90
Winstead, Ray L. 1909- St&PR 91
Winstead, Steven Howard 1953- WhoSSW 91
Winstead, Terri Lee 1953- WhoAmW 91
Winstead, William Owen 1942- IntWWM 90
Winstein, Saul 1912-1969 DcScB S2
Winsten, Archer 1904- WhoAm 90
Winston, Arnold 1935- BiDrAPA 89
Winston, Bob 1948- BiDrAPA 89
Winston, Bruce H. 1948- St&PR 91
Winston, Chriss Hurst 1948- WhoAm 90, WhoAmW 91, WhoE 91
Winston, Claire 1961- ODwPR 91
Winston, Clara 1921-1983 BioIn 16
Winston, Frank 1920- BiDrAPA 89
Winston, George BioIn 16, NewAgMG
Winston, Gordon Chester 1929- WhoAm 90
Winston, Harry 1896-1978 WorAlBi
Winston, Hattie 1945- DrBIPA 90
Winston, Henry 1911-1986 EncAL
Winston, Herbert Saul BiDrAPA 89
Winston, Irwin BioIn 16
Winston, James BiDrAPA 89
Winston, James O., Jr. 1902- St&PR 91
Winston, Jane Ellen 1944- WhoAmW 91
Winston, Janet Margaret 1937- WhoAmW 91
Winston, Jaron Lerner 1956- BiDrAPA 89
Winston, Jeffrey Lee 1953- BiDrAPA 89
Winston, Joseph Mosby, Jr. 1916- WhoSSW 91
Winston, Judith Ann 1943- WhoAmW 91
Winston, Julia L. 1957- BiDrAPA 89
Winston, Lena WhoWrEP 89
Winston, Lindley M 1928- BiDrAPA 89
Winston, Lydia BioIn 16
Winston, Marshall G. St&PR 91
Winston, Mary G. BioIn 16
Winston, Michael G. 1951- WhoEmL 91
Winston, Michael Russell 1941- WhoAm 90, WhoE 91, WhoWor 91
Winston, Patrick Henry, Jr. 1935- St&PR 91
Winston, Peter R. St&PR 91
Winston, Reginald Michael 1953- WhoWor 91
Winston, Richard 1917-1979 AuBYP 90, BioIn 16
Winston, Robert Alan BiDrAPA 89
Winston, Roland 1936- WhoAm 90
Winston, Ronald St&PR 91
Winston, Sanford H. 1920- ODwPR 91
Winston, Sarah 1912- WhoWrEP 89
Winston, Sherry E. BioIn 16
Winston, Stephen Edward 1949- WhoWrEP 89
Winston, Susan Amy 1961- WhoE 91
Winston, Thomas Coleman 1943- WhoAm 90, WhoSSW 91
Winstone, Eric 1915-1974 OxCPMus
Wint, Dennis Michael 1943- WhoAm 90
Wintels, Theodorus-Gertrudis 1924- WhoWor 91
Winter, A Scott BiDrAPA 89
Winter, Alan 1937- WhoAm 90
Winter, Alison A. 1946- St&PR 91
Winter, Andrew 1892-1958 WhoAmA 91N
Winter, Arch Reese 1913- WhoAm 90
Winter, Barbara Ann 1957- WhoAmW 91
Winter, Calvin Arnold, Jr. 1955- WhoSSW 91
Winter, Caryl 1944- WhoWrEP 89
Winter, Chester Caldwell 1922- WhoAm 90
Winter, Chester Norman 1931- St&PR 91
Winter, Daniel Wallace 1928- IntWWM 90
Winter, David Ferdinand 1920- WhoAm 90
Winter, David L 1954- WhoAmA 91
Winter, David Leon 1933- WhoAm 90
Winter, Dennis W. 1937- St&PR 91
Winter, Edgar 1946- EncPR&S 89
Winter, Edward H. BioIn 16, NewYTBS 90
Winter, Edwin Thomas 1936- St&PR 91
Winter, Ezra 1886-1949 WhoAmA 91N
Winter, Fred David 1921- St&PR 91
Winter, Fred Joseph 1950- WhoE 91
Winter, Frederick Elliot 1922- WhoAm 90
Winter, Frederick William, Jr. 1945- WhoAm 90
Winter, Friedrich PenDiDA 89
Winter, George 1878-1951 Ballpl 90
Winter, Gerald Glen 1936- WhoAmA 91
Winter, Gibson 1916- WhoAm 90
Winter, Ginny Linville 1925- AuBYP 90
Winter, Harrison L. 1921-1990 BioIn 16
Winter, Harvey John 1915- WhoAm 90
Winter, Helmut 1935- WhoWor 91
Winter, Herbert Robert 1928- WhoE 91
Winter, J. Burgess 1933- St&PR 91
Winter, J.W. 1953- St&PR 91
Winter, Jacqueline Marie 1932- WhoSSW 91
Winter, James Burgess 1933- St&PR 91
Winter, Jeanette AuBYP 90
Winter, Jerry Alan 1937- WhoE 91
Winter, Joan Elizabeth 1947- WhoAmW 91, WhoWor 91
Winter, John WhoAm 90
Winter, John Dawson, III 1944- WhoAm 90
Winter, John Harold 1952- IntWWM 90
Winter, John Rinn, Jr. 1925- WhoAm 90
Winter, John Strange 1856-1911 FemiCLE
Winter, Johnny 1944- ConMus 5 [port], EncPR&S 89
Winter, Knut Rochus Roland 1927- WhoWor 91
Winter, Larry Eugene 1950- WhoEmL 91, WhoSSW 91
Winter, Mark Lee 1950- WhoSSW 91
Winter, Paul NewAgE 90, NewAgMG
Winter, Paul 1939- News 90 [port]
Winter, Paul Theodore 1939- WhoAm 90
Winter, Paula 1929- BioIn 16
Winter, Peter Michael 1934- WhoAm 90, WhoWor 91
Winter, Phillip Emil 1935- WhoSSW 91
Winter, Richard Lawrence 1945- WhoEmL 91, WhoWor 91
Winter, Richard Nelson 1944- WhoSSW 91
Winter, Robert 1938- WhoE 91
Winter, Robert Bruce 1932- WhoAm 90
Winter, Roger 1934- WhoAmA 91
Winter, Roger C. 1946- St&PR 91
Winter, Roger Paul 1942- WhoAm 90
Winter, Rolf Gerhard 1928- WhoAm 90
Winter, Ronald E. 1926- St&PR 91
Winter, Ruth 1913- WhoAmA 91, WhoE 91
Winter, Ruth Grosman 1930- WhoAm 90
Winter, Sidney Graham, Jr. 1935- WhoAm 90
Winter, Steve 1955- WhoE 91
Winter, Terry BioIn 16
Winter, Werner 1923- WhoWor 91
Winter, William E. 1920- St&PR 91
Winter, William Earl 1920- WhoAm 90
Winter, William Forrest 1923- WhoAm 90
Winter, William John 1912- AuBYP 90
Winter, William R., Jr. 1942- St&PR 91
Winter-Switz, Cheryl Donna 1947- WhoAmW 91
Winterbauer, John E. 1938- St&PR 91
Winterbauer, Richard Hill 1936- WhoAm 90
Winterberger, Suzanne 1952- WhoAmA 91
Winterble, Charles B. 1947- WhoAm 90
Winterbotham, F. W. NewYTBS 90
Winterbotham, F. W. 1897-1990 BioIn 16
Winterbotham, F W 1897-1990 ConAu 130
Winterbotham, Frederick William 1897-1990 BioIn 16
Winterbotham, Russ 1904-1971 EncACom
Winterbottom OxCPMus
Winterbottom, Frank 1861-1930 OxCPMus
Winterbottom, Henry OxCPMus
Winterbottom, Herbert Wager 1921- IntWWM 90
Winterbottom, John OxCPMus
Winterbottom, John 1817-1897 OxCPMus
Winterbottom, Thomas OxCPMus
Winterbottom, William 1822-1889 OxCPMus
Winterer, Philip Steele 1931- WhoAm 90
Winterfeld, Henry 1901- BioIn 16
Winterfeldt, Ursula 1920- WhoE 91
Winterflood, Brian BioIn 16
Winterhalter, Franz Xavier 1805-1873 BioIn 16
Winterhalter, Hugo 1909-1973 OxCPMus
Winterkamp, Fred Henry 1927- WhoE 91
Winterling, Mary Ann 1943- WhoE 91
Wintermute, Marjorie McLean 1919- WhoAm 90
Winternitz, Sarah Frances 1954- BiDrAPA 89
Winternitz, Sherry R BiDrAPA 89
Winterowd, Walter Ross 1930- WhoAm 90, WhoWrEP 89
Winters, Alice Graham Butler 1907- WhoAmW 91
Winters, Anne K. 1937- WhoWrEP 89
Winters, Barbara Jo WhoAm 90, WhoAmW 91
Winters, Christina Margaret 1947- WhoAmW 91
Winters, David Allen 1942- St&PR 91
Winters, Donald Wayne 1949- WhoWrEP 89
Winters, Edward William 1947- WhoWor 91
Winters, Frederick Peter 1929- St&PR 91, WhoAm 90
Winters, Gail Petrina BioIn 16
Winters, J. C. 1939- SmATA X [port]
Winters, J. Otis 1932- St&PR 91, WhoAm 90
Winters, James Robert 1947- St&PR 91
Winters, Janet Lewis 1899- WhoWrEP 89
Winters, Jayshree 1951- BiDrAPA 89, WhoE 91
Winters, Jesse 1893-1986 Ballpl 90
Winters, John BioIn 16
Winters, John David 1928- WhoAm 90
Winters, John E. 1931- St&PR 91
Winters, Jon 1939- SmATA X [port]
Winters, Jonathan 1925- BioIn 16, WhoAm 90, WorAlBi
Winters, Kent D. 1943- St&PR 91
Winters, Lawrence 1915-1965 DcAfAmP, DrBIPA 90
Winters, Leonard Alan 1950- WhoWor 91
Winters, Mary Ann 1937- WhoAmW 91
Winters, Mary-Frances 1951- WhoAmW 91
Winters, Matthew Littleton 1926- WhoE 91
Winters, Mel 1936- WhoAm 90
Winters, Michelle G. 1953- WhoAmW 91
Winters, Murl Mather 1939- WhoSSW 91
Winters, Nathan 1921- St&PR 91
Winters, Nina 1944- SmATA 62
Winters, Nip 1899-1971 Ballpl 90
Winters, Nola Frances 1925- WhoAm 90
Winters, Paul E. 1944- St&PR 91
Winters, Peter H V 1929- BiDrAPA 89
Winters, Phyllis Jean 1945- WhoAmW 91
Winters, Richard Allan 1947- BiDrAPA 89
Winters, Richard Bruce 1953- WhoSSW 91
Winters, Robert C. 1931- St&PR 91
Winters, Robert Charles 1946- WhoAm 90
Winters, Robert Cushing 1931- WhoAm 90, WhoE 91, WhoWor 91
Winters, Roland 1905-1989 BioIn 16
Winters, Sandy 1949- WhoAmA 91
Winters, Sharon K. BiDrAPA 89
Winters, Shelley BioIn 16
Winters, Shelley 1922- WhoAm 90, WhoAmW 91, WorAlBi
Winters, Shirley Royce 1922- WhoWrEP 89
Winters, Sidney A. 1921- St&PR 91
Winters, Stephen Henry 1949- WhoSSW 91
Winters, Sylvia Dahl BiDrAPA 89
Winters, Wendi 1953- ODwPR 91
Winters, William C. BiDrAPA 89
Winters, Yvor 1900-1968 MajTwCW
Wintersheimer, Donald Carl 1932- WhoAm 90
Wintersmith, Charles Godfrey 1810?-1881 AmLegL
Winterson, Jeanette 1959- BioIn 16, ConLC 64 [port], FemiCLE
Wintersteen, Bernice McIlhenny 1903-1986 WhoAmA 91N
Winterton, Joseph Henry 1948- WhoE 91
Winterton, Paul 1908- SpyFic
Wintgens, Randolph Walter 1948- WhoE 91
Winther, Michael BioIn 16
Winther, Niels 1948- IntWWM 90
Winther, Sophus Keith 1893-1983 DcScanL
Winther, William Paul 1944- St&PR 91
Winther-Schorsch, Lynn 1947- BiDrAPA 89
Winthrop, Elizabeth 1948- AuBYP 90
Winthrop, Fitz-John 1638-1707 EncCRAm
Winthrop, John 1588-1649 EncCRAm [port], WorAlBi
Winthrop, John 1606-1676 EncCRAm
Winthrop, John 1714-1778 EncCRAm
Winthrop, John 1936- WhoAm 90
Winthrop, John 1947- WhoAm 90
Winthrop, Margaret 1591?-1647 BioAmW
Winthrop, Sherman 1931- WhoWor 91
Wintman, Melvin R. 1918- St&PR 91
Wintman, Melvin Robert 1918- WhoAm 90
Winton, Alexander 1860-1932 EncABHB 4 [port]
Winton, Calhoun 1927- WhoWrEP 89
Winton, Craig Brewster 1951- WhoE 91
Winton, David Michael 1928- WhoAm 90
Winton, George J BiDrAPA 89
Winton, Herschel Benson, III 1959- WhoSSW 91
Winton, Robert Emmett BiDrAPA 89
Winton, Stanley J. 1923- St&PR 91, WhoAm 90
Wintour, Anna 1949- CurBio 90 [port], News 90 [port], WhoAm 90, WhoAmW 91
Wintrob, Benjamin 1907- BiDrAPA 89
Wintrob, Jay S. 1957- St&PR 91
Wintrob, Ronald M BiDrAPA 89
Wintrode, Ralph Charles 1942- WhoWor 91
Wintroub, Bruce Urich 1943- WhoAm 90
Wintsch, H. Frederick 1940- St&PR 91

Wintz, Cary Decordova 1943- *WhoSSW 91*
Wintz, Joseph Anthony, III 1946- *WhoWor 91*
Wintz, Lester Merrill 1927- *St&PR 91*
Winuk, Jay Steven 1958- *ODwPR 91*
Winwar, Frances 1900- *AuBYP 90*
Winwood, Stephen Lawrence 1948- *WhoAm 90*
Winwood, Steve *BioIn 16*
Winwood, Steve 1948- *EncPR&S 89, WorAlBi*
Winyard, Lori Kaye 1958- *WhoE 91*
Winzeler, John H., Jr. 1943- *St&PR 91*
Winzeler, John Harold 1916- *St&PR 91*
Winzeler, Robert Cameron 1931- *St&PR 91*
Winzeler, Ted J. 1948- *WhoSSW 91*
Winzell, Debra Kay 1951- *WhoAmW 91*
Winzenreid, James Ernest 1951- *WhoEmL 91, WhoWor 91*
Winzenried, Barbara E. 1935- *St&PR 91*
Winzenried, Jesse David 1922- *WhoAm 90*
Winzenried, Ora A. 1933- *St&PR 91*
Winzenz, Karon Hagemeister 1941- *WhoAmA 91*
Winzler, John R. 1930- *St&PR 91*
Wion, John Hamilton 1937- *IntWWM 90*
Wior, Carol *BioIn 16*
Wiora, Walter 1906- *IntWWM 90*
Wiot, Jerome Francis 1927- *WhoAm 90*
Wipke, W. Todd 1940- *WhoAm 90*
Wippern, Ronald Frank 1933- *WhoE 91*
Wirahadikusumah, Umar 1924- *WhoWor 91*
Wirawan, Purnadi Setia 1965- *WhoEmL 91*
Wirch, Sue *BioIn 16*
Wire, Teddy Kermit 1936- *WhoSSW 91*
Wire, William Shidaker, II 1932- *St&PR 91, WhoAm 90, WhoSSW 91*
Wirecki, Theodore S 1948- *BiDrAPA 89*
Wireman, Billy Overton 1932- *WhoAm 90*
Wiren, Dag 1905-1986 *PenDiMP A*
Wirges, Manford Frank 1925- *WhoAm 90*
Wirick, Elizabeth Ellen 1940- *WhoAmW 91*
Wirick, Weldon J., III 1951- *St&PR 91*
Wirkkala, Brian M. 1941- *St&PR 91*
Wirkkala, Tapio 1915-1985 *ConDes 90, PenDiDA 89*
Wironen, Robert Alan 1955- *WhoE 91*
Wirsching, Charles Philipp, Jr. 1935- *WhoWor 91*
Wirsching, Michael Hilmar 1947- *WhoWor 91*
Wirsig, Claus Adolf 1933- *WhoAm 90*
Wirsig, Woodrow 1916- *WhoAm 90*
Wirsing, Martin Hermann Friedrich 1948- *WhoWor 91*
Wirsum, Karl 1939- *WhoAmA 91*
Wirszup, Izaak 1915- *WhoAm 90, WhoWor 91*
Wirt, Frederick Marshall 1924- *ConAu 31NR, WhoAm 90*
Wirt, George H. 1943- *St&PR 91*
Wirt, Mildred 1905- *AuBYP 90*
Wirt, Sherwood Eliot 1911- *ConAu 33NR*
Wirt, William 1772-1834 *BiDrUSE 89*
Wirtanen, P.L. 1944- *St&PR 91*
Wirtenberg, Thelma Jean 1950- *WhoAmW 91*
Wirth, Arthur George 1919- *WhoAm 90*
Wirth, Barry Dennis 1953- *St&PR 91*
Wirth, Beverly 1938- *SmATA 63 [port]*
Wirth, Christian 1885-1944 *BioIn 16*
Wirth, Harold Edward 1905- *WhoE 91*
Wirth, Irwin *BiDrAPA 89*
Wirth, James Burnham *BiDrAPA 89*
Wirth, John Davis 1936- *WhoAm 90*
Wirth, John Francis 1929- *St&PR 91*
Wirth, Louis 1897-1952 *BioIn 16*
Wirth, Otto Howard 1935- *St&PR 91*
Wirth, Peter Theodor 1934- *WhoWor 91*
Wirth, Timothy Endicott 1939- *WhoAm 90, WhoWor 91*
Wirth, Willard Ralph, Jr. 1930- *WhoAm 90*
Wirth, Winifred Prozeller 1916- *WhoAmW 91, WhoWor 91*
Wirthlin, David Bitner 1935- *WhoAm 90*
Wirthlin, Richard Bitner 1931- *WhoAm 90*
Wirths, Claudine G 1926- *SmATA 64*
Wirths, Claudine Gibson 1926- *WhoWrEP 89*
Wirths, Theodore William 1924- *WhoAm 90*
Wirtschafter, Bud 1924- *WhoAmA 91*
Wirtschafter, Jonathan Dine 1935- *WhoAm 90*
Wirtz, Arthur Michael, Jr. *WhoAm 90*
Wirtz, Dianne Dempsey 1945- *WhoAmW 91*
Wirtz, Dorothea 1953- *IntWWM 90*
Wirtz, John W. 1925- *St&PR 91*
Wirtz, Norman Richard 1944- *WhoAm 90*
Wirtz, Stephen Carl 1945- *WhoAmA 91*
Wirtz, Willem Kindler 1912- *WhoAm 90*
Wirtz, William Willard 1912- *BiDrUSE 89, WhoAm 90*
Wirum, Mary Lou 1937- *WhoAmW 91*
Wirz, Pascal F. 1943- *St&PR 91*
Wisa, Louis, Sr *WhoAmA 91N*
Wisbauer, Robert Alois 1941- *WhoWor 91*
Wisbaum, Wayne David 1935- *WhoAm 90*
Wisberg, Aubrey *NewYTBS 90*
Wisberg, Aubrey 1909-1990 *BioIn 16, ConAu 131*
Wisberg, Folke Bernadotte 1895-1948 *BioIn 16*
Wisch, Marilyn Joan 1942- *WhoAmW 91*
Wischnitzer, Rachel 1885?-1989 *ConAu 130*
Wischnitzer, Rachel Bernstein 1885-1989 *BioIn 16*
Wischnowsky, Richard J. 1929- *St&PR 91*
Wisdom, Daniel W. 1952- *St&PR 91*
Wisdom, Guyrena Knight 1923- *WhoAmW 91, WhoWor 91*
Wisdom, Jack Leach 1953- *WhoAm 90*
Wisdom, John Minor 1905- *WhoAm 90*
Wisdom, Joyce 1940- *WhoAmA 91*
Wisdom, Michael Ray 1951- *WhoSSW 91*
Wise, Aaron Medalie 1913- *BioIn 16*
Wise, Allen Floyd 1942- *WhoAm 90*
Wise, Arthur Edward 1942- *WhoE 91*
Wise, Bernard O *BiDrAPA 89*
Wise, Bill McFarland 1936- *WhoAm 90*
Wise, Blanche Ann 1929- *WhoAmW 91*
Wise, Charles Conrad, Jr. 1913- *WhoAm 90*
Wise, Cindy Sue 1955- *WhoAmW 91*
Wise, Cynthia 1944- *WhoAmW 91*
Wise, Darlene Faye 1931- *WhoAmW 91*
Wise, David *PenDiMP*
Wise, David 1930- *SpyFic, WhoAm 90, WhoWrEP 89*
Wise, Dewey D. 1926- *St&PR 91*
Wise, Dewey Dennis 1926- *St&PR 91*
Wise, Edmund Allen, Jr. 1967- *WhoWrEP 89*
Wise, Edward Jean, Jr. 1953- *WhoSSW 91*
Wise, Erbon Wilbur 1920- *WhoAm 90, WhoWrEP 89*
Wise, Ernie *ConAu 129*
Wise, Ferdinand Andre 1926- *St&PR 91*
Wise, Gary Lamar 1945- *WhoAm 90, WhoEmL 91, WhoSSW 91, WhoWor 91*
Wise, Geneva H *WhoAmA 91*
Wise, George Edward 1924- *WhoAm 90*
Wise, George Urban 1945- *WhoAm 90*
Wise, George Wilkinson 1915- *WhoSSW 91*
Wise, Gerald Lee 1941- *WhoAmA 91*
Wise, Gordon H. 1934- *St&PR 91*
Wise, Gwendolyn Elliott *WhoSSW 91*
Wise, Harry H. 1938- *WhoE 91, WhoWor 91*
Wise, Helena Sunny 1954- *WhoEmL 91*
Wise, Howard 1903-1989 *BioIn 16, WhoAmA 91N*
Wise, Irving *BioIn 16*
Wise, Isaac Mayer 1819-1900 *BioIn 16, WorAlBi*
Wise, Jack Kenneth 1936- *St&PR 91*
Wise, Janet Eugenia Wherry 1942- *WhoAmW 91*
Wise, Janie Denise 1945- *WhoAmW 91*
Wise, Janieth K 1949- *BiDrAPA 89*
Wise, Jeremy Lambert 1942- *St&PR 91*
Wise, Jim P. 1943- *St&PR 91*
Wise, Jim Price 1943- *WhoAm 90*
Wise, John 1652-1725 *EncCRAm*
Wise, John Augustus 1938- *WhoAm 90*
Wise, John Hice 1920- *WhoAm 90*
Wise, John James 1932- *WhoAm 90*
Wise, Joseph Powell 1946- *WhoSSW 91*
Wise, Joseph Stephen 1939- *WhoAmA 91*
Wise, K. Kelly 1932- *WhoWrEP 89*
Wise, Kenneth Kelly 1932- *WhoAm 90, WhoAmA 91, WhoE 91*
Wise, Kenneth Tod 1949- *WhoE 91*
Wise, Lawrence Charles 1942- *St&PR 91*
Wise, Lawrence George 1946- *WhoSSW 91*
Wise, Louis J *BiDrAPA 89*
Wise, Louise Waterman *WhoAmA 91N*
Wise, Marvin Jay 1926- *WhoAm 90*
Wise, Maureen Kamen 1946- *WhoAmW 91*
Wise, Michael G 1944- *BiDrAPA 89*
Wise, Miguel David 1960- *WhoSSW 91, WhoWor 91*
Wise, Milton B. 1929- *WhoAm 90*
Wise, Mintron Suzanne 1946- *WhoSSW 91*
Wise, Patricia 1943- *IntWWM 90*
Wise, Patricia Ann 1944- *WhoAm 90*
Wise, Paul Schuyler 1920- *WhoAm 90*
Wise, Richard Evans 1947- *WhoE 91, WhoWor 91*
Wise, Rick 1945- *Ballpl 90*
Wise, Robert 1914- *BioIn 16, WhoAm 90, WhoWor 91, WorAlBi*
Wise, Robert Arthur *BiDrAPA 89*
Wise, Robert Edward 1918- *WhoAm 90*
Wise, Robert Ellsworth, Jr. 1948- *WhoAm 90, WhoSSW 91*
Wise, Robert L. 1943- *St&PR 91*
Wise, Robert Lester 1943- *WhoAm 90*
Wise, Robert Powell 1951- *WhoEmL 91*
Wise, Ronald Lee 1936- *St&PR 91*
Wise, S. H. 1955- *St&PR 91*
Wise, Samuel P, III 1921- *BiDrAPA 89*
Wise, Samuel P., III 1921- *WhoE 91*
Wise, Sherwood Willing 1910- *WhoAm 90, WhoWor 91*
Wise, Stephen Carl 1954- *St&PR 91*
Wise, Stephen Samuel 1874-1949 *BioIn 16*
Wise, Sue 1921- *WhoAmA 91*
Wise, Susan Tamsberg 1945- *WhoAmW 91, WhoSSW 91*
Wise, Suzanne Tanderup 1952- *WhoAmA 91*
Wise, Sybil Zulalian 1935- *WhoAmW 91, WhoE 91*
Wise, Takouhy *WhoAmA 91*
Wise, Thomas Alonzo 1920- *WhoAm 90*
Wise, Thomas Nathan 1943- *BiDrAPA 89*
Wise, Urban Gregg 1943- *St&PR 91*
Wise, Vernon Laing, Jr. 1929- *St&PR 91*
Wise, Walter L., Jr. 1912- *St&PR 91*
Wise, Warren R. 1929- *St&PR 91*
Wise, Warren Roberts 1929- *WhoAm 90*
Wise, Watson William 1899-1989 *BioIn 16*
Wise, William 1923- *AuBYP 90*
Wise, William Allan 1945- *St&PR 91, WhoAm 90, WhoSSW 91*
Wise, William Dean 1931- *St&PR 91*
Wise, William Jerrard 1934- *WhoAm 90*
Wise, Winifred E. *AuBYP 90*
Wise-Ciobotaru, G. *BiDWomA*
Wisecarver, Keith Douglas 1957- *WhoSSW 91*
Wisecarver, William D. *St&PR 91*
Wisehart, Arthur McKee 1928- *WhoAm 90*
Wisehart, Mary Ruth 1932- *WhoAmW 91*
Wisekal, Frank William 1934- *St&PR 91, WhoAm 90*
Wiseman, Adele 1928- *FemiCLE*
Wiseman, Bernard 1922- *AuBYP 90*
Wiseman, Carl Donald 1925- *WhoAm 90*
Wiseman, Dana 1954- *WhoE 91*
Wiseman, David 1916- *ConAu 30NR*
Wiseman, Ernest 1925- *ConAu 129*
Wiseman, Eve Jessica *BiDrAPA 89*
Wiseman, Floyd Charles 1950- *BiDrAPA 89*
Wiseman, Frederick *BioIn 16*
Wiseman, Frederick 1930- *WhoAm 90*
Wiseman, Fredrick 1930- *ConTFT 8*
Wiseman, Howard Willard 1928- *WhoE 91*
Wiseman, James Richard 1934- *WhoAm 90, WhoWor 91*
Wiseman, Jane *BiDEWW, FemiCLE*
Wiseman, Jay Donald 1952- *WhoEmL 91*
Wiseman, Laurence D. 1947- *St&PR 91*
Wiseman, Laurence Donald 1947- *WhoAm 90*
Wiseman, Michael L. 1952- *St&PR 91*
Wiseman, Nicholas Patrick 1802-1865 *BioIn 16*
Wiseman, Robert E. J. 1924- *St&PR 91*
Wiseman, Shirley *BioIn 16*
Wiseman, Shirley McVay 1937- *WhoAm 90, WhoAmW 91*
Wiseman, Thomas Anderson, Jr. 1930- *WhoSSW 91*
Wiseman, Thomas Lynn 1944- *WhoWrEP 89*
Wiseman, Walter S. 1945- *St&PR 91*
Wiseman, William Scott 1957- *WhoSSW 91*
Wisener, Robert A. 1927- *St&PR 91*
Wisener, William H. 1812-1882 *AmLegL*
Wiser, Celeste Beryl *BiDrAPA 89*
Wiser, George L. 1925- *St&PR 91*
Wiser, James Louis 1945- *WhoAm 90*
Wish, Jay Barry 1950- *WhoWor 91*
Wish, Paul E. 1937- *St&PR 91*
Wish, Richard 1935- *St&PR 91*
Wisham, Lawrence Herman 1918- *WhoAm 90*
Wishart, Joyce 1942- *WhoAmW 91*
Wishart, Leonard Plumer, III 1934- *WhoAm 90*
Wishart, Robert A. *BioIn 16*
Wishart, Ronald Sinclair 1925- *WhoAm 90*
Wishart, Steven William 1943- *St&PR 91*
Wishart, Trevor 1946- *IntWWM 90*
Wishaw, Susan Diane 1956- *WhoEmL 91*
Wishek, Max A. 1901- *St&PR 91*
Wishert, Jo Ann Chappell 1951- *WhoAmW 91*
Wishner, Howard E. 1952- *ODwPR 91*
Wishner, Maynard Ira 1923- *WhoAm 90*
Wishner, Steven R. 1950- *St&PR 91, WhoE 91, WhoEmL 91*
Wishnick, Marcia Margolis 1938- *WhoAmW 91*
Wishnick, William 1924- *St&PR 91, WhoAm 90, WhoE 91*
Wishnie, Howard Allen *BiDrAPA 89*
Wishnietsky, Dan Harvey 1950- *WhoSSW 91*
Wishnoff, Stanley 1935- *St&PR 91*
Wishnow, Emanuel 1910- *WhoAm 90*
Wisinger-Florian, Olga 1844-1926 *BioIn 16*
Wiskich, Joseph Tony 1935- *WhoWor 91*
Wiskind, Milton Ira 1925- *St&PR 91*
Wiskowski, John P. 1938- *St&PR 91*
Wisler, Charles Clifton, Jr. 1926- *WhoAm 90*
Wisler, G. Clifton 1950- *BioIn 16*
Wisler, G Clifton 1950- *ConAu 129*
Wisler, Rae *BiDrAPA 89*
Wisler, Willard Eugene 1933- *WhoSSW 91*
Wisliceny, Dieter 1911-1948 *BioIn 16*
Wislocki, Stanislaw *PenDiMP*
Wislocki, Stanislaw 1921- *IntWWM 90*
Wisman, Jack F *BiDrAPA 89*
Wismer, David Joseph 1950- *St&PR 91*
Wismer, Donald 1946- *BioIn 16*
Wismer, Harvey G. 1916- *St&PR 91*
Wismer, Robert Kingsley 1945- *WhoE 91*
Wismer, Stephen Hanawalt 1946- *St&PR 91*
Wisner, E. James 1942- *St&PR 91*
Wisner, Frank George 1938- *WhoAm 90, WhoWor 91*
Wisner, George 1812-1849 *BioIn 16*
Wisner, Jesse Oldfield 1811-1897 *DcCanB 12*
Wisner, John Henry, Jr. 1946- *BiDrAPA 89*
Wisner, Katherine Leah *BiDrAPA 89*
Wisner, Linda Ann 1951- *WhoAmW 91*
Wisner, William L. 1914?-1983 *AuBYP 90*
Wisneski, Mary Jo Elizabeth 1938- *WhoAmW 91*
Wisneski, William John 1946- *WhoAm 90*
Wisnewski, Robert *BioIn 16*
Wisnia, Kelman 1942- *WhoWor 91*
Wisniewski, Czeslaw 1932- *WhoWor 91*
Wisniewski, David 1953- *ConAu 132*
Wisniewski, Henryk Miroslaw 1931- *WhoAm 90*
Wisniewski, John Sigmund 1947- *St&PR 91*
Wisniewski, Judith Lee 1941- *WhoAmW 91*
Wisniewski, Thomas Joseph 1926- *IntWWM 90, WhoAm 90*
Wisnosky, John G 1940- *WhoAmA 91*
Wisocki, Patricia A. 1943- *WhoAmW 91*
Wisot, Richard Alan 1946- *St&PR 91*
Wisott, Richard L. 1933- *St&PR 91*
Wiss, Marcia A. 1947- *WhoE 91*
Wiss, Teri Francine 1958- *WhoAmW 91*
Wisse, Eddie 1938- *WhoWor 91*
Wisse, Frederik 1947- *WhoWor 91*
Wisse, Ruth R. *BioIn 16*
Wissemann, Andrew Frederick 1928- *WhoAm 90*
Wissemann-Widrig, Nancy *WhoAmA 91*
Wisser, Lawrence 1922- *WhoE 91*
Wisser, Richard L. R. 1927- *WhoWor 91*
Wisser, William P. *St&PR 91*
Wissing, Neil Phillip 1931- *St&PR 91*
Wissler, Eugene Harley 1927- *WhoAm 90*
Wissler-Thomas, Carrie 1946- *WhoAmW 91*
Wissmann, Carol Renee 1946- *WhoAmW 91*
Wissmann, Ruth H. *AuBYP 90*
Wissmer, Pierre 1915- *IntWWM 90*
Wissner, Robert C. 1924- *St&PR 91*
Wissner, Seth Ernst 1922- *WhoAm 90*
Wissolik, Raymond A. 1923- *St&PR 91*
Wissore, Eileen Frances 1944- *WhoAmW 91*
Wist, Abund Ottokar 1926- *WhoSSW 91*
Wistar, Caspar 1696-1752 *EncCRAm, PenDiDA 89*
Wistar, Richard *PenDiDA 89*
Wister, Owen 1860-1938 *BioIn 16, SmATA 62 [port], WorAlBi*
Wister, Sarah 1761-1804 *FemiCLE*
Wister, William David 1938- *St&PR 91*
Wistisen, Martin J. 1938- *St&PR 91, WhoAm 90*
Wistreich, Hugo E. 1930- *St&PR 91*
Wiswall, Frank Lawrence, Jr. 1939- *WhoAm 90, WhoWor 91*
Wiswell, Andrew Peters 1852-1906 *AmLegL*
Wiswell, Emily Mary Hull 1918- *WhoAmW 91, WhoSSW 91*
Wiswesser, George Andrew *BiDrAPA 89*
Wit, Anna Augusta Henrietta de 1864-1939 *EncCoWW*
Wit, Anton *PenDiMP*
Wit, Antoni 1944- *IntWWM 90*
Wit, Daniel 1923- *WhoAm 90*
Wit, Harold Maurice 1928- *WhoAm 90*
Witajewski, Robert M. 1946- *WhoSSW 91*
Witbeck, Norman C. 1925- *St&PR 91*
Witchel, Sam 1924- *ODwPR 91*
Witcher, Daniel Dougherty 1924- *WhoAm 90*
Witcher, David L. 1939- *St&PR 91*

Witcher, Robert Campbell 1926- *WhoAm 90, WhoE 91*
Witcher, Rodney Fernell 1953- *WhoSSW 91*
Witcoff, Sheldon William 1925- *St&PR 91, WhoAm 90*
Witcombe, R T 1943- *ConAu 132*
Witcover, Jules Joseph 1927- *WhoAm 90*
Witeck, Robert V. 1951- *ODwPR 91*
Witek, James Eugene 1932- *WhoAm 90*
Witek, Mickey 1915- *Ballpl 90*
Witenberg, Earl G 1917- *BiDrAPA 89*
Witenberg, Earl George 1917- *WhoWor 91*
With, Beverly Carol 1947- *WhoE 91*
With, Daphne Marina 1939- *WhoAmW 91*
With, Elizabeth *BiDEWW*
Withaeger, Rosemary Ann 1949- *WhoAmW 91*
Withall, Gary A. 1949- *St&PR 91*
Withall, William John 1814-1898 *DcCanB 12*
Withalm, Claudio Immanuel 1943- *WhoWor 91*
Witham, Eleanor Elizabeth 1933- *WhoSSW 91*
Witham, Peter Martin 1933- *WhoAm 90*
Witham, Richard Nicholas 1938- *St&PR 91*
Witham, Rodney Arthur 1924- *St&PR 91*
Witham, Vernon Clint 1925- *WhoAmA 91*
Witherbee-Olson, Vickie Dianne 1953- *WhoAmW 91*
Witherby, Frederick R.H., Jr. 1943- *St&PR 91*
Withered, Dennis Forrest 1948- *WhoSSW 91*
Witherel, Michael Joseph 1953- *WhoE 91*
Witherell, Peter Charles 1943- *WhoE 91*
Witheridge, Elizabeth P. *AuBYP 90*
Witherow, Richard I. 1949- *St&PR 91*
Withers, Alton M. 1926- *St&PR 91*
Withers, Alton Merrill 1926- *WhoAm 90*
Withers, B. M., Jr. 1927- *WhoSSW 91*
Withers, Barbara Ann 1939- *WhoAmW 91, WhoE 91*
Withers, Bill 1938- *DrBlPA 90, EncPR&S 89*
Withers, Carl 1900-1970 *AuBYP 90*
Withers, Carl A 1900-1970 *ConAu 30NR*
Withers, Cheryl Ann 1958- *WhoE 91*
Withers, Debra Manning 1961- *WhoSSW 91*
Withers, Jane 1927- *WorAlBi*
Withers, Josephine 1938- *WhoAmA 91*
Withers, Kenneth Joel 1956- *WhoE 91*
Withers, Linda Carol 1948- *WhoAmW 91*
Withers, Marshall Scott 1954- *St&PR 91*
Withers, Ramsey Muir 1930- *WhoAm 90*
Withers, Robert Wayne 1932- *St&PR 91*
Withers, W. Russell, Jr. 1936- *WhoAm 90*
Withers, W. Wayne 1940- *WhoAm 90*
Withers, Welty Kenney 1927- *WhoAm 90*
Withers, William Marlin 1954- *St&PR 91*
Witherspoon, Audrey Goodwin 1949- *WhoAmW 91*
Witherspoon, Fredda Lilly *WhoAmW 91*
Witherspoon, Jimmy 1923- *OxCPMus*
Witherspoon, John 1723-1794 *BioIn 16, EncCRAm, WorAlBi*
Witherspoon, John Knox, Jr. 1928- *WhoAm 90*
Witherspoon, John Marshall 1945- *WhoSSW 91*
Witherspoon, Jonathan H. 1942- *St&PR 91*
Witherspoon, Lynn Ralph 1942- *WhoSSW 91*
Witherspoon, Richard Wayne 1943- *St&PR 91*
Witherspoon, Walter Pennington, Jr. 1938- *WhoSSW 91, WhoWor 91*
Witherspoon, William 1909- *WhoWor 91*
Withersty, David James 1941- *BiDrAPA 89*
Witherup, William Allen 1935- *WhoWrEP 89*
Withgott, James William 1945- *St&PR 91*
Withington, Frederic Burnham 1922- *WhoE 91*
Withrow, John Jacob 1833-1900 *DcCanB 12*
Withrow, Lucille Monnot 1923- *WhoAmW 91*
Withrow, Lydia Brizicky 1958- *WhoAmW 91*
Withrow, Mary Ellen 1930- *WhoAm 90, WhoAmW 91*
Withrow, Robert Parker 1942- *BiDrAPA 89*
Withrow, Tommy Austin 1949- *St&PR 91*
Withrow, William Henry 1839-1908 *DcLB 99 [port]*
Withrow, William J 1926- *WhoAmA 91*
Withrow, William John 1926- *WhoAm 90, WhoE 91*
Withrow-Gallanter, Sherrie Anne 1960- *WhoAmW 91*
Withuhn, William Lawrence 1941- *WhoE 91, WhoWor 91*
Witiak, Donald Theodore 1935- *WhoAm 90*
Witiak, Joanne *BioIn 16*
Witkam, Willem-Joris 1939- *WhoWor 91*
Witkay, Paul Richard 1954- *St&PR 91*
Witke, David Rodney 1937- *WhoAm 90*
Witke, Edward Charles 1931- *WhoAm 90*
Witken, Beatrice *NewYTBS 90*
Witker, Jim *AuBYP 90*
Witkie, Susan Marie *BiDrAPA 89*
Witkin, Beatrice 1916-1990 *BioIn 16*
Witkin, Evelyn Maisel 1921- *WhoAm 90, WhoAmW 91*
Witkin, Isaac 1936- *WhoAmA 91*
Witkin, Jerome 1939- *WhoAmA 91*
Witkin, Joel-Peter 1939- *WhoAm 90, WhoAmA 91*
Witkin, Mildred Hope Fisher *WhoAmW 91, WhoE 91, WhoWor 91*
Witkin, Miriam *BioIn 16*
Witkin, Nathan *NewYTBS 90*
Witkin-Lanoil, Georgia Hope *WhoAmW 91, WhoWor 91*
Witko, Frank P. *St&PR 91*
Witkojc, Mina 1893-1975 *EncCoWW*
Witkop, Bernhard 1917- *WhoAm 90*
Witkop, Carl Jacob 1920- *WhoAm 90*
Witkop, Robert 1948- *St&PR 91*
Witkoski, Robert Henry 1954- *WhoE 91*
Witkow, Stanley P. 1948- *St&PR 91*
Witkowski, Henry Joseph 1920- *St&PR 91*
Witkowski, James Joseph 1949- *WhoE 91*
Witkowski, John 1949- *St&PR 91*
Witkowski, Ronald Joseph 1944- *St&PR 91*
Witkowski, Walter Joseph 1950- *WhoE 91*
Witkowsky, Gizella *BioIn 16*
Witlox, Marc Charles 1957- *WhoWor 91*
Witmark, Isidore 1869-1941 *BioIn 16*
Witmark, Jay 1877-1950 *BioIn 16*
Witmark, Julius 1870-1929 *BioIn 16*
Witmer, Albert L. 1920- *St&PR 91*
Witmer, G. Robert 1904- *WhoAm 90*
Witmer, George Robert, Jr. 1937- *WhoAm 90*
Witmer, Harriette F. 1921- *St&PR 91*
Witmer, John Albert 1920- *WhoAm 90*
Witmer, John E., Jr. 1935- *WhoE 91*
Witmer, John H., Jr. 1940- *St&PR 91*
Witmer, John Harper, Jr. 1940- *WhoAm 90*
Witmer, John Light 1908- *St&PR 91*
Witmer, Melvin P., Sr. 1940- *St&PR 91*
Witmer, Stephen B. 1941- *ODwPR 91*
Witmeyer, Stanley Herbert 1913- *WhoAmA 91*
Witmond, Bartholomeus Johannes 1964- *WhoWor 91*
Witnauer, Ericka *WhoAmW 91*
Witnauer, Ericka Anne *St&PR 91*
Witold-K 1932- *WhoAmA 91*
Witomski, Theodore Raymond 1953- *WhoWrEP 89*
Witorsch, Philip 1937- *WhoE 91, WhoWor 91*
Witover, M. Kenneth 1947- *WhoE 91*
Witover, Stephen Barry 1941- *WhoE 91*
Witowski, Patrick A. 1946- *St&PR 91*
Witrick, Joseph J. 1937- *St&PR 91*
Witry, Bernard J. 1925- *St&PR 91*
Witschel, Gunter 1927- *WhoWor 91*
Witschy, James Kenton *BiDrAPA 89*
Witsil, Elizabeth Smith Alison 1909- *WhoAmW 91*
Witsil, John Palmer 1923- *WhoE 91*
Witsken, Clarence H. 1933- *St&PR 91*
Witsman, Karl Robert 1959- *WhoWrEP 89*
Witsman, Starla DiAnne 1952- *WhoAmW 91*
Witt, Alan Michael 1952- *WhoEmL 91*
Witt, Barry Michael 1958- *St&PR 91*
Witt, Bobby 1964- *Ballpl 90*
Witt, Cathleen M. 1964- *WhoAmW 91*
Witt, Charles E. 1917- *WhoAm 90*
Witt, Clarke Dean 1942- *BiDrAPA 89*
Witt, Dan Franklin 1938- *St&PR 91*
Witt, David L 1951- *WhoAmA 91*
Witt, Debora Esensee 1956- *WhoSSW 91*
Witt, Donald James 1949- *WhoSSW 91*
Witt, Dorleen Emma 1923- *WhoAmW 91*
Witt, Edward A 1939- *BiDrAPA 89*
Witt, Fred William 1932- *St&PR 91*
Witt, Frederick W 1925- *BiDrAPA 89*
Witt, George 1933- *Ballpl 90*
Witt, Georgia Strong 1923- *WhoAmW 91*
Witt, Harold Vernon 1923- *WhoWrEP 89*
Witt, Helen Mercer 1933- *WhoAm 90, WhoAmW 91*
Witt, Hugh Ernest 1921- *WhoAm 90*
Witt, Johan de 1625-1672 *BioIn 16*
Witt, John 1940- *WhoAmA 91*
Witt, John Leonard 1934- *St&PR 91*
Witt, John P 1919- *BiDrAPA 89*
Witt, Katarina *BioIn 16*
Witt, Katarina 1965- *WorAlBi*
Witt, Kathryn Lisa 1963- *WhoAmW 91*
Witt, Mike 1960- *Ballpl 90*
Witt, Nancy Camden 1930- *WhoAmA 91*
Witt, Nancy Garrett *BiDrAPA 89*
Witt, Norbert A. *NewYTBS 90*
Witt, Paul Junger *BioIn 16*
Witt, Paul M. 1943- *St&PR 91*
Witt, Peter A. 1943- *BioIn 16*
Witt, Peter Christian Konrad 1943- *WhoWor 91*
Witt, Raymond Buckner, Jr. 1915- *WhoAm 90*
Witt, Richard Allen 1951- *St&PR 91*
Witt, Robert Charles 1941- *WhoAm 90*
Witt, Robert Edward 1909- *St&PR 91*
Witt, Robert Louis 1940- *St&PR 91, WhoAm 90*
Witt, Robert Wayne 1937- *WhoSSW 91*
Witt, Ruth Elizabeth 1922- *WhoAm 90*
Witt, Sally Eleanor *WhoAmW 91*
Witt, Samuel Brown, III 1935- *St&PR 91*
Witt, Sandra Lea 1949- *WhoWrEP 89*
Witt, Sandra Smith 1944- *WhoAmW 91*
Witt, Stephen Joseph 1934- *WhoAm 90*
Witt, Tom 1944- *WhoSSW 91*
Witt, Whitey 1895- *Ballpl 90*
Witta, George Thermes 1947- *St&PR 91*
Wittanen, Etolin 1907- *BioIn 16*
Wittbrodt, Edwin Stanley 1918- *WhoAm 90*
Wittcoff, Harold Aaron 1918- *WhoAm 90*
Witte, Betty J. *AuBYP 90*
Witte, Dale Frederick 1951- *St&PR 91*
Witte, David William 1942- *St&PR 91*
Witte, David Wynn 1942- *St&PR 91*
Witte, Edwin E. 1887-1960 *WorAlBi*
Witte, Emanuel de 1617?-1691? *IntDcAA 90*
Witte, Erich 1911- *IntWWM 90, PenDiMP*
Witte, Margaret *BioIn 16*
Witte, Mary Stieglitz *WhoAmA 91*
Witte, Merlin Michael 1926- *WhoAm 90*
Witte, Sergei 1849-1915 *WorAlBi*
Wittebol, Paul 1923- *WhoWor 91*
Wittekindt, John Roy 1942- *BiDrAPA 89*
Wittels, Howard Bernard 1950- *St&PR 91*
Witteman, Charles R. 1884-1967 *WorAlBi*
Witteman, Wilhelmus Jacobus 1933- *WhoWor 91*
Wittemans, Jacques Werner 1933- *WhoWor 91*
Witten, Charles Henry 1918- *WhoSSW 91*
Witten, David Melvin 1926- *WhoAm 90*
Witten, Edward *WhoAm 90*
Witten, Lillian L. *St&PR 91*
Witten, Louis 1921- *WhoAm 90*
Witten, Thomas David 1943- *WhoWor 91*
Witten Born, George 1905-1974 *WhoAmA 91N*
Wittenauer, Bill 1944- *St&PR 91*
Wittenberg, Bernard H 1931- *BiDrAPA 89*
Wittenberg, Ernest 1920- *ODwPR 91, WhoAm 90*
Wittenberg, Howard Ira 1930- *St&PR 91*
Wittenberg, Jan *PenDiMP*
Wittenberg, Jean-Victor P 1946- *BiDrAPA 89*
Wittenberg, Ralph E 1934- *BiDrAPA 89*
Wittenberg, Ruth *NewYTBS 90 [port]*
Wittenberg, Yitzhak 1907-1943 *BioIn 16*
Wittenberns, Michelle-May 1960- *WhoAmW 91*
Wittenborn, August F. 1923- *St&PR 91*
Wittenmeyer, Charles E. 1903- *WhoAm 90*
Wittenmyer, Annie Turner 1827-1906 *WorAlBi*
Wittenstein, Arthur 1926- *WhoAm 90*
Wittenstein, Arthur 1926-1989 *BioIn 16*
Wittenstein, Michael David 1958- *WhoSSW 91*
Wittenwyler, Ronald Paul 1947- *St&PR 91*
Witter, Aaron C. 1850-1891 *AmLegL*
Witter, Diana Gonser 1930- *WhoAmW 91*
Witter, Evelyn *BioIn 16*
Witter, Gerd Karl 1944- *St&PR 91*
Witter, Jill 1954- *St&PR 91*
Witter, Lee F. 1935- *WhoE 91*
Witter, Richard Lawrence 1936- *WhoAm 90*
Witter, Robert Nelson, Jr. 1932- *St&PR 91*
Witter, Thomas W. 1928- *St&PR 91*
Witter, Thomas Winship 1928- *WhoAm 90*
Witter, Warren Rusty 1953- *WhoSSW 91*
Witter, William D. 1929- *St&PR 91*
Witterholt, Suzanne Teresa 1961- *BiDrAPA 89*
Witteveen, Sibble Jozef 1956- *WhoWor 91*
Wittfogel, Karl August 1896-1988 *BioIn 16*
Wittgenstein, Carolyne de Sayn- 1819-1887 *BioIn 16*
Wittgenstein, Ludwig 1889-1951 *BioIn 16*
Wittgenstein, Ludwig Josef Johann 1889-1951 *WorAlBi*
Wittgenstein, Paul 1887-1961 *PenDiMP*
Witthuhn, Burton Orrin 1934- *WhoAm 90*
Witthuhn, Kay Lynn 1957- *WhoAmW 91*
Wittich, John Jacob 1921- *WhoAm 90*
Wittich, Marie 1868-1931 *PenDiMP*
Wittig, Georg 1897-1987 *WorAlBi*
Wittig, Heinz Joseph 1921-1988 *BioIn 16*
Wittig, Johnnie 1914- *Ballpl 90*
Wittig, Linda Beth *BiDrAPA 89*
Wittig, Monique 1935- *FemiCLE*
Wittig, Philip Martin 1934- *St&PR 91*
Wittig, Raymond Shaffer 1944- *WhoE 91, WhoWor 91*
Wittig, Richard E. 1934- *St&PR 91*
Wittig, Robert Link *BiDrAPA 89*
Wittinbel, Gregory A. 1953- *St&PR 91*
Witting, Chris J. 1915- *St&PR 91, WhoWor 91*
Wittink, Dick Roelof 1945- *WhoEmL 91*
Wittke, Dayton D. 1932- *St&PR 91*
Wittke, James P. *BioIn 16*
Wittkemper, Gerd 1943- *St&PR 91*
Wittkopp, George Fred 1945- *BiDrAPA 89*
Wittkopp, Thomas Arno 1944- *BiDrAPA 89*
Wittkower, Robert Steven 1951- *WhoEmL 91*
Wittkower, Rudolf 1901-1971 *WorAu 1980 [port]*
Wittler, Janet Marie 1947- *WhoAmW 91*
Wittler, Shirley Joyce 1927- *WhoAm 90*
Wittlich, Gary Eugene 1934- *WhoAm 90*
Wittlich, Jae L. 1942- *St&PR 91*
Wittlin, Byron Jay 1946- *BiDrAPA 89*
Wittlinger, Timothy David 1940- *WhoAm 90*
Wittmack, Edgar Franklin 1894-1956 *WhoAmA 91N*
Wittman, Connie Susan 1956- *WhoAmW 91*
Wittman, Edward S. 1947- *St&PR 91*
Wittman, Gordon R. 1930- *St&PR 91*
Wittman, John Edward 1929- *WhoAm 90*
Wittman, Paul 1931- *WhoWor 91*
Wittman, Robert Emil 1940- *St&PR 91*
Wittmann, Otto 1911- *WhoAm 90, WhoAmA 91*
Wittmann, Robert Z. 1960- *WhoWor 91*
Wittmer, Donald George 1935- *St&PR 91*
Wittmeyer, Kenneth E. 1929- *St&PR 91*
Wittner, Lawrence S. 1941- *ConAu 33NR*
Wittner, Loren A. 1938- *ODwPR 91*
Wittner, Loren Antonow 1938- *WhoAm 90*
Wittner, Ted Philip 1928- *WhoAm 90*
Wittner, William K *BiDrAPA 89*
Witton, Dorothy *AuBYP 90*
Witton, Kurt *BiDrAPA 89*
Wittouck, Eric 1946- *WhoWor 91*
Wittreich, Joseph Anthony, Jr. 1939- *WhoAm 90, WhoWrEP 89*
Wittrock, Merlin Carl 1931- *WhoAm 90, WhoWor 91*
Wittry, David Beryle 1929- *WhoAm 90*
Witts, Leslie John 1898-1982 *DcNaB 1981*
Wittson, Cecil L *BiDrAPA 89*
Wittstadt, Klaus 1936- *WhoWor 91*
Wittstein, Edwin Frank 1929- *WhoAm 90*
Wittwer, Chester Allen, Jr. 1937- *St&PR 91*
Wittwer, John W. 1945- *St&PR 91*
Wittwer, Uwe 1954- *BioIn 16*
Witty, Frederic N. *BioIn 16*
Witty, John Barber 1946- *WhoSSW 91*
Witty, Lela Dawn 1943- *St&PR 91*
Witty, Paul A. 1898-1976 *BioIn 16*
Witty, Paul Andrew 1898-1976 *AuBYP 90*
Witwer, Andrew S. 1920?-1990 *ConAu 132*
Witwer, Samuel Weiler 1908- *WhoAm 90*
Witz, Allen Barry 1941- *WhoAm 90*
Witz, Konrad 1400?-1445? *IntDcAA 90*
Witzel, Detlef 1942- *WhoWor 91*
Witzel, E. J. Michael 1943- *WhoAm 90*
Witzel, Frederick Chase 1923- *St&PR 91*
Witzel, Herbert G. 1924- *WhoWor 91*
Witzeman, Frank Charles 1926- *St&PR 91*
Witzenmann, Wolfgang 1937- *IntWWM 90*
Witzig, Gene R. 1929- *St&PR 91*
Witzig, Harold L. 1927- *St&PR 91*
Witzig, Scott A. 1959- *St&PR 91*
Witzig, Warren Frank 1921- *WhoAm 90*
Witzman, Audrey Loraine 1937- *WhoAmW 91*
Witztum, Harry *BiDrAPA 89*
Wivallius, Lars 1604?-1669 *DcScanL*
Wivel, Ole 1921- *DcScanL*
Wivell, William Edward 1932- *St&PR 91*
Wiwi, Robert P. 1941- *St&PR 91*
Wiwi, Robert Paul 1941- *WhoAm 90*
Wix, Emma Lou 1924- *St&PR 91*
Wixell, Ingvar 1931- *IntWWM 90, PenDiMP*
Wixen, Burton N 1931- *BiDrAPA 89*
Wixom, Chuck *ODwPR 91*
Wixom, G.R. *St&PR 91*
Wixom, William D 1929- *WhoAmA 91*
Wixom, William David 1929- *WhoAm 90, WhoE 91*
Wixon, Rufus 1911- *WhoAm 90*
Wixon, William N. 1930- *St&PR 91*
Wixson, Bobby Guinn 1931- *WhoSSW 91*
Wixson, Douglas Charles 1933- *WhoWrEP 89*
Wizmur, Judith H. 1949- *WhoAmW 91*
Wizner, William Wolfgang 1928- *WhoSSW 91*
Wiznia, Andrew Alan 1954- *WhoE 91*
Wiznia, Robert Abraham 1943- *WhoE 91*

Wiznitzer, Manuel 1919- *WhoWor 91*
Wizon, Tod 1952- *WhoAmA 91*
Wizorek, Martin William 1948- *WhoSSW 91*
Wlast *EncCoWW*
Wleugel, Johan Peter 1929- *WhoAm 90*
Wloka, Joseph Theodor 1929- *WhoWor 91*
Wlosok, Antonie Elisabeth 1930- *WhoWor 91*
Wluka, David 1946- *WhoE 91*
Wnorowski, Elaine Marie 1954- *WhoSSW 91*
Wnuk, Wade Joseph 1944- *St&PR 91, WhoSSW 91*
Wobbeking, Ronald Lee 1943- *St&PR 91*
Wobschall, Darold Clarence 1932- *WhoE 91*
Wobst, Frank 1933- *St&PR 91*
Wobus, Reinhard Arthur 1941- *WhoAm 90*
Wochinger, Marilynn Turnbull 1923- *WhoAmW 91*
Wockenfuss, John 1949- *Ballpl 90*
Wodehouse, P. G. 1881-1975 *BioIn 16*
Wodehouse, P.G. 1881-1975 *ConAu 33NR, MajTwCW*
Wodehouse, P. G. 1881-1975 *OxCPMus, WorAlBi*
Wodehouse, Pelham Grenville 1881-1975 *BioIn 16*
Wodge, Dreary *ConAu 30NR*
Wodlinger, Mark Louis 1922- *WhoAm 90*
Wodnicki, Moises *BiDrAPA 89*
Wodzislawska, Maia 1942- *WhoWor 91*
Woehrle, Charles *BioIn 16*
Woehrle, Richard *BioIn 16*
Woehrlen, Arthur Edward, Jr. 1947- *WhoEmL 91, WhoWor 91*
Woelfel, James Warren 1937- *WhoAm 90*
Woelfel, Mary Teresa 1941- *WhoSSW 91*
Woelfel, Robert William 1944- *WhoWor 91*
Woelffer, Emerson 1914- *BioIn 16, WhoAmA 91*
Woelffer, Emerson Seville 1914- *WhoAm 90*
Woelffer, Neill Carl 1935- *WhoSSW 91*
Woelflein, Ann Buckley 1933- *WhoE 91*
Woelflein, Kevin Gerard 1933- *WhoAm 90*
Woelfling, Maxine Marie 1949- *WhoE 91*
Woelk, Guy G. *St&PR 91*
Woeller, David John 1926- *WhoAm 90*
Woellhof, A.W. 1932- *St&PR 91*
Woerdehoff, Valorie Anne 1954- *WhoWrEP 89*
Woerner, Fred F., Jr. 1933- *WhoAm 90*
Woerner, Philip Irvin 1935- *BiDrAPA 89*
Woerner, Robert Lester 1925- *WhoAm 90*
Woerpel, Dwayne R. 1939- *ODwPR 91*
Woesner, Mary Elizabeth 1949- *BiDrAPA 89*
Woessner, Frederick T. 1935- *WhoWor 91*
Woessner, Garry Lee 1955- *WhoSSW 91*
Woeste, John Theodore 1934- *WhoAm 90*
Woestenburg, Laurent Cornelius 1932- *WhoWor 91*
Woestendiek, John, Jr. 1953- *WhoAm 90*
Woestendiek, William John 1924- *WhoAm 90*
Woetzel, Damian *BioIn 16*
Woetzel, Damian Abdo 1967- *WhoAm 90*
Wofford, Harris 1926- *ConAu 129*
Wofford, Harris Llewellyn 1926- *WhoAm 90*
Wofford, Patricia Ann Madonna 1961- *WhoAmW 91*
Wofford, Philip 1935- *WhoAmA 91*
Wofford, Randall H. *ODwPR 91*
Wofford, Sandra Smith 1952- *WhoAmW 91*
Wofsey, Alan Ross 1946- *BiDrAPA 89*
Wofsy, Leon 1921- *WhoAm 90*
Wogan, Amelie 1947- *St&PR 91*
Wogan, Gerald Norman 1930- *WhoAm 90*
Wogan, Robert 1925- *WhoAm 90*
Wogen, Warren Ronald 1943- *WhoAm 90*
Woggon, Elmer *EncACom*
Wogsland, James Willard 1931- *St&PR 91, WhoAm 90*
Wogstad, James Everet 1939- *WhoAmA 91*
Woh, Edgar Augusto 1955- *WhoE 91*
Wohl, Armand Jeffrey 1946- *WhoWor 91*
Wohl, David 1950- *WhoSSW 91*
Wohl, Lisa Gay 1953- *WhoAmW 91*
Wohl, Norma S *BiDrAPA 89*
Wohl, Patricia Jeanne 1959- *WhoSSW 91*
Wohl, Robert Allen 1931- *WhoAm 90*
Wohlauer, Peter Frank *BiDrAPA 89*
Wohlberg, Meg *NewYTBS 90*
Wohleber, Robert Michael 1951- *WhoSSW 91*
Wohlenhaus, Grace Forcier 1919- *WhoAmA 91*
Wohlers, Debra Louise 1955- *WhoAmW 91*
Wohlers, Rudiger 1943- *IntWWM 90*
Wohlfarth, David Warren 1946- *St&PR 91*
Wohlford, Jeffrey Stephen 1946- *St&PR 91*
Wohlford, Jim 1951- *Ballpl 90*
Wohlforth, Robert 1904- *St&PR 91*
Wohlforth, Robert M. 1925- *St&PR 91*
Wohlgelernter, Joseph I Ozer 1946- *BiDrAPA 89*
Wohlgemuth, George Francis 1924- *St&PR 91*
Wohlgemuth, Roderich 1940?-1988 *BioIn 16*
Wohlgenant, Richard Glen 1930- *WhoAm 90*
Wohlhauser, Rene Claude 1954- *IntWWM 90*
Wohlheter, Susan Hazel 1948- *WhoAmW 91*
Wohlmut, Thomas Arthur 1953- *WhoWor 91*
Wohlpart, Alfred 1937- *WhoAm 90*
Wohlrabe, Heidi Ruth *BiDrAPA 89*
Wohlrabe, John C 1927- *BiDrAPA 89*
Wohlrabe, Raymond A. 1900-1977 *AuBYP 90*
Wohlreich, George M 1942- *BiDrAPA 89*
Wohlreich, Jack Jay 1946- *WhoWor 91*
Wohlreich, Madelaine M 1950- *BiDrAPA 89*
Wohlschlag, Donald Eugene 1918- *WhoAm 90*
Wohlstetter, Albert J. 1913- *ConAu 129*
Wohlstetter, Charles *BioIn 16*
Wohlstetter, Charles 1910- *WhoSSW 91*
Wohltmann, Hulda Justine 1923- *WhoAmW 91*
Wohlust, Ronald E. 1937- *St&PR 91*
Wohlwill, Joachim F. 1928-1987 *BioIn 16*
Wohlworth, Ivan H. *BioIn 16*
Wohmann, Gabriele 1932- *EncCoWW*
Wohn, Patricia Joy 1943- *St&PR 91*
Woicik, Edward Charles *BiDrAPA 89*
Woide, Robert E 1927- *WhoAmA 91*
Woima, T. Robert 1944- *St&PR 91*
Woit, Bonnie Ford 1931- *WhoAmA 91*
Woit, Erik Peter 1931- *St&PR 91, WhoAm 90*
Woitach, Richard 1935- *WhoAm 90*
Woitena, Ben S 1942- *WhoAmA 91*
Woitkoski, Joseph Paul 1947- *St&PR 91*
Woiwode, Larry *BioIn 16*
Wojahn, R. Lorraine *WhoAmW 91*
Wojak, Joseph Gregory 1937- *St&PR 91*
Wojcicki, Andrew Adalbert 1935- *WhoAm 90*
Wojcicki, Antoni B. *BioIn 16, NewYTBS 90*
Wojcicki, Stanley George 1937- *WhoAm 90*
Wojcie, Stanley 1927- *St&PR 91*
Wojciechowicz, Alex 1938- *St&PR 91*
Wojciechowska, Maia 1927- *AuBYP 90, WhoWrEP 89*
Wojciechowski, Franz Laurens 1951- *WhoWor 91*
Wojcik, Anthony Stephen 1945- *WhoAm 90*
Wojcik, John Michael 1953- *St&PR 91*
Wojcik, Joseph *St&PR 91*
Wojcik, Mark Edmund 1961- *WhoE 91*
Wojcik, Martin Henry 1948- *WhoAm 90*
Wojcik, Richard Thomas 1938- *St&PR 91*
Wojda, Peter Joseph 1931- *St&PR 91*
Wojnarowicz, David 1954- *BioIn 16, WhoAmA 91*
Wojnilower, Albert Martin 1930- *WhoAm 90*
Wojnowski, Leon A. 1948- *St&PR 91*
Wojtach, Mary Ann 1954- *WhoAmW 91*
Wojtila, James A. 1961- *St&PR 91*
Wojtyla, Haase 1933- *WhoAmA 91*
Wojtyla, Karol 1920- *BioIn 16*
Wojtyla, Karol Jozef 1920- *WhoWor 91*
Wokke, Eduard Andries 1928- *WhoWor 91*
Wolaner, Robin Peggy 1954- *WhoAm 90*
Wolanic, Susan Seseske 1947- *WhoAmA 91*
Wolanin, Barbara A 1943- *WhoAmA 91*
Wolanin, Barbara Ann Boese 1943- *WhoAmW 91*
Wolanin, Sophie Mae 1915- *WhoAmW 91, WhoWor 91*
Wolanin, Vincent Martin 1947- *St&PR 91*
Wolansky, Oleh M 1914- *BiDrAPA 89*
Wolansky, Raymond 1926- *IntWWM 90*
Wolas, Herbert 1933- *WhoAm 90*
Wolaver, John H *BiDrAPA 89*
Wolbach, William Wellington, Sr. 1915- *WhoAm 90*
Wolbarsht, Myron Lee 1924- *WhoSSW 91*
Wolber, Paul J 1935- *WhoAmA 91*
Wolberg, Arlene Robbins *BioIn 16*
Wolberg, Arlene Robbins 1907-1989 *ConAu 130*
Wolbers, Paul Arthur 1954- *IntWWM 90*
Wolbert, James Vincent 1939- *St&PR 91*
Wolbrink, Donald Henry 1911- *WhoAm 90*
Wolbrink, James Francis 1942- *WhoAm 90*
Wolbrom, Irving M. 1934- *St&PR 91*
Wolchansky, Dorothy Louise Laves 1942- *WhoAmW 91*
Wolchansky, Louise G. 1911- *St&PR 91*
Wolcin, Joseph John, III 1946- *WhoE 91*
Wolck, Wolfgang Hans-Joachim 1932- *WhoAm 90*
Wolcott, Arthur S. 1926- *St&PR 91*
Wolcott, Carolyn Muller *AuBYP 90*
Wolcott, Darrell 1935- *St&PR 91*
Wolcott, Darwin F. 1925- *St&PR 91*
Wolcott, David Rittenhouse 1949- *WhoE 91*
Wolcott, Deane Leroy *BiDrAPA 89*
Wolcott, Eugene Aaron 1923- *St&PR 91*
Wolcott, Hugh Dixon 1946- *WhoSSW 91*
Wolcott, Joanne Moreau *WhoSSW 91*
Wolcott, John *AuBYP 90*
Wolcott, John Winthrop, III 1924- *WhoAm 90*
Wolcott, Leonard Thompson *AuBYP 90*
Wolcott, Louis H. 1927- *St&PR 91*
Wolcott, Marion Post *WhoAmA 91*
Wolcott, Marion Scott Post 1910- *BioIn 16*
Wolcott, Mark Walton 1915- *WhoAm 90*
Wolcott, Oliver 1726-1797 *EncCRAm, WorAlBi*
Wolcott, Oliver 1760-1833 *BiDrUSE 89*
Wolcott, Oliver 1930- *BiDrAPA 89*
Wolcott, Oliver Dwight 1918- *WhoAm 90*
Wolcott, Robert B., Jr. 1920- *ODwPR 91*
Wolcott, Robert Boynton, Jr. 1920- *WhoAm 90*
Wolcott, Robert Wilson, Jr. 1926- *St&PR 91, WhoAm 90*
Wolcott, Samuel H., III 1935- *WhoAm 90*
Wolcott, Samuel H., Jr. 1910- *St&PR 91*
Wolcott, Samuel Huntington, III 1935- *St&PR 91*
Wolcowitz, Jeffrey 1952- *WhoE 91*
Wold, Allen L. 1943- *SmATA 64 [port]*
Wold, Allen Lester 1943- *WhoSSW 91*
Wold, Arden Bernard 1919- *St&PR 91*
Wold, Emma 1871-1950 *WorAlBi*
Wold, Finn 1928- *WhoAm 90*
Wold, Jeffrey Wayne *BiDrAPA 89*
Wold, Jeffrey Wayne 1947- *WhoE 91*
Wold, John Schiller 1916- *WhoAm 90*
Wold, Nana Beha 1943- *WhoAmW 91*
Wold, Patricia N 1927- *BiDrAPA 89*
Wold, Patricia Neely 1927- *WhoE 91*
Wold, Richard O. 1934- *St&PR 91*
Wold, Richard Otto 1934- *WhoAm 90*
Wold, Robert Lee 1931- *WhoAm 90*
Wolda, Hindrik 1931- *WhoSSW 91*
Woldenberg, Harry C. 1917- *St&PR 91*
Wolderling, Johannes Alex 1927- *WhoWor 91*
Woldike, Mogens 1897-1988 *PenDiMP*
Wolding, Carlyle Manferd 1944- *WhoSSW 91*
Woldrich, John David 1943- *St&PR 91*
Woldt, Harold Frederick, Jr. 1947- *WhoAm 90*
Wolejko, Janusz Ambrozy 1945- *WhoE 91*
Wolek, Ronald Andrew 1947- *WhoWor 91*
Woleslagle, Mildred Marie 1937- *WhoAmW 91*
Wolf, Albert Edmund 1929- *St&PR 91*
Wolf, Alexander 1907- *BiDrAPA 89*
Wolf, Alfred 1915- *WhoAm 90*
Wolf, Alfred 1936- *St&PR 91*
Wolf, Alfred Clarence 1911- *WhoWor 91*
Wolf, Alfred Peter 1923- *WhoAm 90*
Wolf, Alice K. 1933- *WhoE 91*
Wolf, Anna Dryden 1890-1985 *BioIn 16*
Wolf, Arnold S. 1928- *St&PR 91*
Wolf, Aron S 1937- *BiDrAPA 89, WhoWor 91*
Wolf, Barry 1947- *WhoAm 90*
Wolf, Bernice Fix *WhoAmW 91*
Wolf, Bill 1940- *ODwPR 91*
Wolf, Brian David 1959- *WhoWor 91*
Wolf, Brian George 1962- *WhoE 91*
Wolf, Bruce *BioIn 16*
Wolf, Bruce L. 1936- *St&PR 91*
Wolf, Burt *BioIn 16*
Wolf, Carol Euwema 1936- *WhoAmW 91*
Wolf, Charles, Jr. 1924- *WhoAm 90*
Wolf, Charles Robert 1933- *WhoAm 90*
Wolf, Charles S. 1921- *St&PR 91*
Wolf, Charlotte Elizabeth 1926- *WhoAm 90*
Wolf, Cheryl Jeane 1951- *WhoAmW 91*
Wolf, Chicken 1862-1903 *Ballpl 90*
Wolf, Christa *BioIn 16*
Wolf, Christa 1929- *EncCoWW, FemiCLE, MajTwCW*
Wolf, Christopher 1954- *WhoE 91*
Wolf, Claire 1961- *WhoE 91*
Wolf, Claire Ruth Marie 1930- *WhoAmW 91*
Wolf, Clarence, Jr. 1908- *WhoAm 90, WhoSSW 91, WhoWor 91*
Wolf, Dale Edward 1924- *WhoAm 90, WhoE 91*
Wolf, Dale Joseph 1939- *St&PR 91*
Wolf, David 1927- *WhoAm 90*
Wolf, Dennis Edward *BiDrAPA 89*
Wolf, Don Allen 1929- *WhoAm 90*
Wolf, Dorothy Ann 1954- *WhoEmL 91*
Wolf, Duane Carl 1946- *WhoSSW 91*
Wolf, Edward Christopher 1932- *IntWWM 90*
Wolf, Edward Dean 1935- *WhoAm 90*
Wolf, Edward Earl 1928- *St&PR 91*
Wolf, Edward Lincoln 1936- *WhoAm 90*
Wolf, Edwin, II 1911- *WhoAm 90*
Wolf, Eelco *ODwPR 91*
Wolf, Elliott M 1943- *BiDrAPA 89*
Wolf, Emanuel L. 1927- *St&PR 91*
Wolf, Emil 1922- *WhoAm 90*
Wolf, Emma 1865- *FemiCLE*
Wolf, Eric Robert 1923- *WhoAm 90*
Wolf, Erica Pachtman 1950- *BiDrAPA 89*
Wolf, Ernest S *BiDrAPA 89*
Wolf, Erving 1926- *WhoAm 90, WhoSSW 91*
Wolf, Estelle *BioIn 16*
Wolf, Esther Valladolid 1940- *WhoHisp 91*
Wolf, Evan Williams 1947- *WhoE 91*
Wolf, Frances *WhoWrEP 89*
Wolf, Frank Gerald 1922- *St&PR 91*
Wolf, Frank R. 1939- *WhoAm 90, WhoSSW 91*
Wolf, Frederic Eastman 1909- *WhoAm 90*
Wolf, Frederick George 1952- *WhoEmL 91*
Wolf, Fredric M. 1945- *WhoWor 91*
Wolf, Friedrich 1935- *IntWWM 90*
Wolf, Gary L. 1944- *St&PR 91*
Wolf, Gary Wickert 1938- *WhoAm 90*
Wolf, George Anthony, Jr. 1914- *WhoAm 90*
Wolf, George Van Velsor 1908- *WhoAm 90*
Wolf, Gerald Leo 1931- *St&PR 91*
Wolf, Gerald P. 1925- *St&PR 91*
Wolf, Gerrit 1941- *WhoAm 90*
Wolf, Hans Abraham 1928- *WhoAm 90*
Wolf, Harold Arthur 1923- *WhoAm 90*
Wolf, Harold Herbert 1934- *WhoAm 90*
Wolf, Harry Frances Schlesinger *WhoE 91*
Wolf, Hazel *BioIn 16*
Wolf, Henry 1925- *ConDes 90, WhoAm 90, WhoE 91*
Wolf, Hugo 1860-1903 *BioIn 16, WorAlBi*
Wolf, Irving 1924- *WhoAm 90*
Wolf, Isabel Drane 1933- *WhoAmW 91*
Wolf, Jack Keil 1935- *WhoAm 90*
Wolf, Jack Stanley 1934- *WhoWor 91*
Wolf, James Anthony 1945- *WhoAm 90*
Wolf, James Everett 1941- *St&PR 91*
Wolf, James Henry 1952- *St&PR 91*
Wolf, Jane Margaret 1950- *BiDrAPA 89*
Wolf, Jerome Arthur 1943- *WhoSSW 91*
Wolf, Joan Silverman 1936- *WhoAmW 91*
Wolf, John A. 1928- *St&PR 91*
Wolf, John D. 1947- *St&PR 91*
Wolf, John H. 1932- *St&PR 91*
Wolf, John H. 1936- *St&PR 91*
Wolf, John J. 1937- *St&PR 91*
Wolf, John M. 1920- *St&PR 91*
Wolf, John M., Jr. 1946- *St&PR 91*
Wolf, John W. 1939- *St&PR 91*
Wolf, John William 1940- *St&PR 91*
Wolf, Jonathan Lee 1954- *WhoSSW 91*
Wolf, Joseph Albert 1936- *WhoAm 90*
Wolf, Judith C. *ODwPR 91*
Wolf, Julie 1868-1944 *BiDWomA*
Wolf, Julius 1918- *WhoAm 90*
Wolf, Karl Everett 1921- *St&PR 91, WhoAm 90*
Wolf, Katharine P 1936- *BiDrAPA 89*
Wolf, Kathleen Ellen 1945- *WhoAmW 91*
Wolf, Lawrence Morton 1931- *St&PR 91*
Wolf, Lee J. 1915- *St&PR 91*
Wolf, Lewis Isidore 1933- *WhoE 91, WhoWor 91*
Wolf, Linda Joyce 1955- *WhoSSW 91*
Wolf, Lothar Jakob 1938- *WhoWor 91*
Wolf, Marion Ester *BiDrAPA 89*
Wolf, Mark Lawrence 1946- *WhoAm 90*
Wolf, Markus *NewYTBS 90 [port]*
Wolf, Markus 1962- *IntWWM 90*
Wolf, Marvin H. 1924- *St&PR 91*
Wolf, Mary 1938- *WhoAmW 91*
Wolf, Mary Jean 1936- *St&PR 91*
Wolf, Melvin L. 1944- *St&PR 91*
Wolf, Michael Jay *BiDrAPA 89*
Wolf, Milton Albert 1924- *WhoAm 90, WhoWor 91*
Wolf, Monica Theresia 1943- *WhoAmW 91*
Wolf, Nancy Schoenholz 1954- *WhoAmW 91*
Wolf, Norbert Richard 1943- *WhoWor 91*
Wolf, Patricia Allison 1963- *WhoE 91*
Wolf, Peter Michael 1935- *WhoAm 90*
Wolf, Philip R. 1935- *St&PR 91*
Wolf, R Peter 1942- *IntWWM 90*
Wolf, Ralph Steven 1950- *BiDrAPA 89*
Wolf, Reinhold Michael 1956- *IntWWM 90*
Wolf, Richard E *BiDrAPA 89*
Wolf, Richard L. 1935- *St&PR 91*
Wolf, Richard Lloyd 1935- *WhoAm 90*
Wolf, Richard Samuel 1936- *St&PR 91*

Wolf, Robert *ODwPR 91*
Wolf, Robert B. 1914- *St&PR 91, WhoAm 90*
Wolf, Robert Farkas 1932- *WhoE 91*
Wolf, Robert Howard 1942- *WhoAm 90*
Wolf, Roger D. *St&PR 91*
Wolf, Rosalie Joyce 1941- *WhoAm 90*
Wolf, Ruth Rochelle 1937- *WhoAmW 91*
Wolf, S. K. *ConAu 132*
Wolf, Sanford R *BiDrAPA 89*
Wolf, Sara Straight 1947- *St&PR 91*
Wolf, Sarah 1936- *ConAu 132*
Wolf, Sheila 1934- *WhoWrEP 89*
Wolf, Stephen M. *BioIn 16*
Wolf, Steven Mitchell 1963- *WhoE 91*
Wolf, Steven P. 1945- *St&PR 91*
Wolf, Stewart *BiDrAPA 89*
Wolf, Stewart George, Jr. 1914- *WhoAm 90, WhoWor 91*
Wolf, Terry 1947- *WhoAmW 91*
Wolf, Thomas 1945- *IntWWM 90*
Wolf, Thomas Mark 1944- *WhoSSW 91*
Wolf, Thomas Walter 1954- *WhoE 91*
Wolf, Virginia Simmons 1915- *WhoWrEP 89*
Wolf, Walter 1931- *WhoAm 90*
Wolf, Warner William 1937- *WhoAm 90*
Wolf, Werner Paul 1930- *WhoAm 90*
Wolf, William Penn 1833-1896 *AmLegL*
Wolf, William Scott 1961- *WhoSSW 91*
Wolf-Ferrari, Ermanno 1876-1948 *PenDiMP A*
Wolf-Schatz, Ann Marie C *BiDrAPA 89*
Wolfard, Larry L. 1932- *St&PR 91*
Wolfart, H. Christoph 1943- *WhoAm 90*
Wolfbein, Seymour Louis 1915- *WhoAm 90*
Wolfberg, Bernard Behr 1943- *BiDrAPA 89*
Wolfberg, Judith R 1938- *BiDrAPA 89*
Wolfberg, Melvin Donald 1926- *WhoAm 90*
Wolfberg, Steven S. 1946- *St&PR 91*
Wolfe, Al 1932- *WhoAm 90*
Wolfe, Albert Blakeslee 1909- *WhoAm 90*
Wolfe, Alexander McW., Jr. 1926- *St&PR 91*
Wolfe, Ann *WhoAmA 91*
Wolfe, Arnold B 1934- *BiDrAPA 89*
Wolfe, Barbara A. 1943- *St&PR 91*
Wolfe, Barbara Joyce 1932- *BiDrAPA 89*
Wolfe, Bertram 1927- *WhoAm 90*
Wolfe, Bill 1876-1953 *Ballpl 90*
Wolfe, Brenda L. 1956- *WhoAmW 91*
Wolfe, Caroline Margaret 1943- *WhoAmW 91*
Wolfe, Charles Morgan 1935- *WhoAm 90*
Wolfe, Corinne Howell 1912- *WhoAmW 91, WhoWor 91*
Wolfe, Dale E. *St&PR 91*
Wolfe, Damon Ian *BiDrAPA 89*
Wolfe, David Joe 1938- *WhoSSW 91*
Wolfe, David Louis 1951- *WhoEmL 91*
Wolfe, Deborah Cannon Patridge *WhoAm 90, WhoAmW 91*
Wolfe, Diane Honore 1954- *BiDrAPA 89*
Wolfe, Donald H. 1926- *St&PR 91*
Wolfe, Douglas P. 1925- *St&PR 91*
Wolfe, Edgar F. *Ballpl 90*
Wolfe, Edward Emmett, Jr 1947- *WhoAm 90*
Wolfe, Edward Harvey 1945- *WhoEmL 91, WhoSSW 91, WhoWor 91*
Wolfe, Ethyle Renee 1919- *WhoAm 90*
Wolfe, Frederic D. 1929- *St&PR 91*
Wolfe, Gail J. *St&PR 91*
Wolfe, Gary Donald 1941- *WhoE 91*
Wolfe, Gary K 1946- *ConAu 129*
Wolfe, Gene 1931- *ConAu 32NR, RGTwCSF, WorAu 1980 [port]*
Wolfe, George 1922- *St&PR 91*
Wolfe, Gordon H. 1924- *ODwPR 91*
Wolfe, Gregory Baker 1922- *WhoAm 90, WhoSSW 91*
Wolfe, Harold Joel 1940- *St&PR 91, WhoAm 90*
Wolfe, Harriet Leeds *BiDrAPA 89*
Wolfe, Harry F., Jr. 1931- *St&PR 91*
Wolfe, Ira Steven 1951- *WhoE 91*
Wolfe, Irma L. 1928- *ODwPR 91*
Wolfe, J. Matthew 1956- *WhoE 91, WhoWor 91*
Wolfe, Jacob Merle 1924- *St&PR 91*
Wolfe, James 1727-1759 *BioIn 16, EncCRAm, WhNaAH, WorAlBi*
Wolfe, James 1944- *WhoAmA 91*
Wolfe, James Franklin 1936- *WhoAm 90*
Wolfe, James Martin 1944- *WhoE 91*
Wolfe, James Richard 1929-1988 *BioIn 16*
Wolfe, James Ronald 1932- *WhoAm 90, WhoE 91, WhoWor 91*
Wolfe, Jason Stuart 1941- *WhoAm 90*
Wolfe, Jean Elizabeth 1925- *WhoAmW 91*
Wolfe, John Thomas, Jr. 1942- *WhoAm 90*
Wolfe, John Walton 1928- *WhoAm 90*
Wolfe, Jonathan Scott 1950- *WhoEmL 91, WhoWor 91*
Wolfe, Judith Ann 1946- *WhoAmW 91*
Wolfe, Karl Eric 1954- *WhoE 91*
Wolfe, Kenneth Gilbert 1920- *WhoAm 90*
Wolfe, Kenneth L. 1939- *WhoAm 90, WhoE 91*
Wolfe, Larry T. 1948- *St&PR 91*
Wolfe, Laura Carnes 1936- *WhoAmW 91*
Wolfe, Lawrence Irving 1924- *WhoWor 91*
Wolfe, Leonhard Scott 1926- *WhoAm 90*
Wolfe, Linda *ConAu 129*
Wolfe, Linda Press 1953- *WhoAmW 91*
Wolfe, Lisa Ann 1962- *WhoAmW 91*
Wolfe, Louis 1905- *AuBYP 90*
Wolfe, Louise Dahl- *BioIn 16*
Wolfe, Lynn Robert 1917- *WhoAmA 91*
Wolfe, Margaret Ripley 1947- *WhoAmW 91*
Wolfe, Matthew *St&PR 91*
Wolfe, Maurice G. 1931- *WhoWor 91*
Wolfe, Maurice Raymond 1924- *WhoAmA 91*
Wolfe, Merle D. *St&PR 91*
Wolfe, Michael David 1950- *WhoSSW 91*
Wolfe, Mildred Nungester 1912- *WhoAmA 91*
Wolfe, Nancy Beals 1933- *ODwPR 91*
Wolfe, Norma Lee 1932- *WhoAmW 91*
Wolfe, Norman 1926- *St&PR 91*
Wolfe, Peter *BioIn 16*
Wolfe, Ralph Stoner 1921- *WhoAm 90*
Wolfe, Raphael David 1917- *WhoAm 90*
Wolfe, Richard J 1928- *ConAu 30NR*
Wolfe, Robert, Jr 1930- *WhoAmA 91*
Wolfe, Robert J. 1936- *WhoE 91*
Wolfe, Robert Richard 1937- *WhoAm 90*
Wolfe, Rodney Delyn 1936- *WhoAm 90*
Wolfe, Russell Bryan 1952- *BiDrAPA 89*
Wolfe, Russell Marshall 1925- *St&PR 91*
Wolfe, Russell Simmons, Jr. 1952- *WhoE 91*
Wolfe, Saul 1933- *WhoAm 90*
Wolfe, Sheila *WhoAm 90*
Wolfe, Sheldon *BiDrAPA 89*
Wolfe, Sheldon H. 1933- *WhoAm 90*
Wolfe, Sidney Manuel 1937- *WhoAm 90*
Wolfe, Stanley 1924- *WhoAm 90*
Wolfe, Stuart 1930- *BiDrAPA 89*
Wolfe, Theodore Joseph 1935- *St&PR 91, WhoAm 90*
Wolfe, Thomas 1900-1938 *BioIn 16, ConAu 132, DcLB 102 [port], MajTwCW, WorAlBi, WrPh*
Wolfe, Thomas Kennerly, Jr. 1930- *ConAu 33NR*
Wolfe, Thomas Kennerly, Jr. 1931- *MajTwCW, WhoAm 90, WhoE 91, WhoWrEP 89*
Wolfe, Tom *BioIn 16, ConAu 33NR, MajTwCW*
Wolfe, Tom 1931- *WorAlBi*
Wolfe, Tom J. 1958- *St&PR 91*
Wolfe, Townsend, III 1935- *WhoAmA 91*
Wolfe, Townsend Durant, III 1935- *WhoAm 90, WhoSSW 91*
Wolfe, Tracey Dianne 1951- *WhoAmW 91, WhoEmL 91*
Wolfe, Virginia Kay *BiDrAPA 89*
Wolfe, Warren Dwight 1926- *WhoAm 90*
Wolfe, Warren E *BiDrAPA 89*
Wolfe, Wayne *BioIn 16*
Wolfe, William Downing 1947- *WhoEmL 91*
Wolfe, William Gerald 1917- *WhoAm 90*
Wolfe-Cundiff, Leslie *BioIn 16*
Wolfe Graubard, Ann *WhoAmA 91*
Wolfen, Werner F. 1930- *WhoAm 90*
Wolfenbarger, Penny Sue 1959- *WhoEmL 91*
Wolfenden, James Douglas 1938- *St&PR 91*
Wolfenden, John Frederick 1906-1985 *DcNaB 1981*
Wolfenden, Richard Vance 1935- *WhoAm 90*
Wolfenden, Terry Lyn *WhoAmW 91*
Wolfensohn, James David 1933- *BioIn 16, St&PR 91*
Wolfenson, Azi U. 1933- *WhoWor 91*
Wolfenson, Elena Hernandez *BiDrAPA 89*
Wolfers, Alan M. 1961- *St&PR 91*
Wolfers, Philippe 1858-1929 *PenDiDA 89*
Wolferstan, Elizabeth Pipe 1763- *FemiCLE*
Wolfert, Hubert H. 1916- *St&PR 91*
Wolfert, Jerry *AuBYP 90*
Wolfert, Karen Barrett 1959- *WhoAmW 91*
Wolfert, Laurence Mark 1947- *WhoE 91*
Wolfert, Ruth 1933- *WhoAmW 91, WhoE 91, WhoWor 91*
Wolff, Aaron Sidney 1930- *WhoAm 90*
Wolff, Alan William 1942- *WhoAm 90*
Wolff, Albert 1884-1970 *PenDiMP*
Wolff, Alexander 1957- *SmATA 63*
Wolff, Ann 1937- *ConDes 90*
Wolff, Anna K *BiDrAPA 89*
Wolff, Armin Henry 1904- *BiDrAPA 89*
Wolff, Ashley *AuBYP 90*
Wolff, Ashley 1956- *BioIn 16*
Wolff, Beverly 1928- *IntWWM 90*
Wolff, Bob *Ballpl 90*
Wolff, Carl T 1931- *BiDrAPA 89*
Wolff, Charles Godfrey 1934- *St&PR 91*
Wolff, Christian 1934- *IntWWM 90*
Wolff, Christoph Johannes 1940- *WhoAm 90*
Wolff, Christopher 1949- *WhoAm 90*
Wolff, Cynthia Griffin 1936- *WhoAm 90*
Wolff, Cyril M. 1944- *St&PR 91*
Wolff, Daniel J. *WhoWrEP 89*
Wolff, Darryl J. 1958- *St&PR 91*
Wolff, David 1732-1798 *PenDiDA 89*
Wolff, David Marc 1956- *BiDrAPA 89*
Wolff, David Stephen 1940- *WhoSSW 91*
Wolff, Dee I 1948- *WhoAmA 91*
Wolff, Derish Michael 1935- *WhoAm 90*
Wolff, Edward A. 1929- *WhoAm 90, WhoE 91*
Wolff, Edward N 1946- *ConAu 132*
Wolff, Egon *BioIn 16*
Wolff, Egon 1926- *HispWr 90*
Wolff, Elroy Harris 1935- *WhoAm 90*
Wolff, Emanuel C *BiDrAPA 89*
Wolff, Fritz Konrad 1935- *WhoWor 91*
Wolff, Geoffrey 1937- *BioIn 16*
Wolff, Geoffrey Ansell 1937- *WhoAm 90, WhoWrEP 89*
Wolff, Gerhart 1931- *WhoWor 91*
Wolff, Gunther Arthur 1918- *WhoAm 90*
Wolff, Hans Walter 1911- *ConAu 130*
Wolff, Harold D 1930- *BiDrAPA 89*
Wolff, Helen B *BiDrAPA 89*
Wolff, Henry *NewAgMG*
Wolff, Herbert Eric 1925- *WhoAm 90, WhoWor 91*
Wolff, Howard Keith 1948- *WhoEmL 91*
Wolff, Hugh *BioIn 16*
Wolff, Hugh 1953- *IntWWM 90*
Wolff, Hugh MacPherson 1953- *WhoAm 90, WhoE 91*
Wolff, Ivan Lawrence 1944- *WhoAm 90*
Wolff, Jesse David 1913- *WhoAm 90*
Wolff, Joachim Rudolf 1935- *WhoWor 91*
Wolff, Joel C. 1929- *St&PR 91*
Wolff, Johann *PenDiDA 89*
Wolff, Julian *NewYTBS 90*
Wolff, Julian 1905-1990 *BioIn 16*
Wolff, Karl 1900-1984 *BioIn 16*
Wolff, Konrad 1907-1989 *BioIn 16, ConAu 130*
Wolff, Kurt Jakob 1936- *WhoE 91*
Wolff, Linda M. 1953- *WhoAmW 91*
Wolff, Lothar 1909-1988 *BioIn 16*
Wolff, Manfred Ernst 1930- *WhoAm 90*
Wolff, Martha Anne Wood 1949- *WhoAm 90*
Wolff, Michael *BioIn 16*
Wolff, Miles *BioIn 16*
Wolff, Millie Bender *WhoAmW 91*
Wolff, Moss Leonardus Herman 1907- *IntWWM 90*
Wolff, Patrick Marie Francois Albert 1944- *WhoWor 91*
Wolff, Paul Davis 1954- *St&PR 91*
Wolff, Peter 1933- *WhoWor 91*
Wolff, Peter Adalbert 1923- *WhoAm 90*
Wolff, Peter Hartwig 1926- *BiDrAPA 89*
Wolff, Randall P. 1950- *St&PR 91*
Wolff, Raymond Eugene 1945- *WhoE 91*
Wolff, Richard Carl 1933- *WhoE 91*
Wolff, Richard H 1928- *BiDrAPA 89*
Wolff, Robert Jay 1905-1978 *WhoAmA 91N*
Wolff, Robert Paul 1933- *WhoAm 90*
Wolff, Robert S. 1925- *St&PR 91*
Wolff, Robert W, Jr 1947- *WhoAmA 91*
Wolff, Roger 1911- *Ballpl 90*
Wolff, Russell B., Jr. 1953- *St&PR 91*
Wolff, Sanford Irving 1915- *WhoAm 90*
Wolff, Sheldon 1928- *WhoAm 90*
Wolff, Sheldon Malcolm 1930- *WhoAm 90*
Wolff, Sidney Carne 1941- *WhoAm 90, WhoAmW 91*
Wolff, Sonia *ConAu 32NR*
Wolff, Susan 1944- *WhoAmW 91*
Wolff, Susan 1953- *BiDrAPA 89*
Wolff, Theodore M 1931- *BiDrAPA 89*
Wolff, Thomas John 1928- *WhoAm 90*
Wolff, Timothy Kane 1957- *BiDrAPA 89*
Wolff, Tobias 1945- *BioIn 16, ConLC 64 [port], WhoWrEP 89*
Wolff, Werner 1929- *St&PR 91*
Wolff, William H 1906- *WhoAmA 91*
Wolff-Bekker, Elizabeth 1738-1804 *EncCoWW*
Wolff von Amerongen, Otto 1918- *WhoWor 91*
Wolffl, Josef 1773-1812 *BioIn 16*
Wolffl, Joseph 1773-1812 *PenDiMP*
Wolfgang, Jerald Ira 1938- *WhoE 91*
Wolfgang, Marvin Eugene 1924- *WhoAm 90*
Wolfgang, Mellie 1890-1947 *Ballpl 90*
Wolfgang, Steven Lewis *BiDrAPA 89*
Wolfgang, Steven Lewis 1942- *WhoE 91*
Wolfgram, Edwin D 1932- *BiDrAPA 89*
Wolfin, Louis *St&PR 91*
Wolfinbarger, Lloyd, Jr. 1943- *WhoSSW 91*
Wolfinbarger, Steve Michael 1957- *IntWWM 90*
Wolfinger, Barbara Kaye *WhoAmW 91*
Wolfinger, Raymond Edwin 1931- *WhoAm 90*
Wolfinger, Robert C. 1950- *St&PR 91*
Wolfkill, Ronald V. 1938- *St&PR 91*
Wolfl, Joseph 1773-1812 *PenDiMP*
Wolfle, Dael Lee 1906- *WhoAm 90*
Wolfley, Alan 1923- *WhoAm 90*
Wolfley, Vern Alvin 1912- *WhoWor 91*
Wolfman Jack 1938- *BioIn 16, WhoAm 90*
Wolfman, Bernard 1924- *WhoAm 90*
Wolfman, Brunetta Reid 1931- *WhoAmW 91, WhoE 91*
Wolfman, Cyrus 1928- *BiDrAPA 89*
Wolfman, Earl Frank, Jr. 1926- *WhoAm 90*
Wolfman, Ira Joel 1950- *WhoAm 90*
Wolfman, Marvin *BiDrAPA 89*
Wolford, Cheryl Lynn 1964- *WhoSSW 91*
Wolford, Eileen J. 1938- *St&PR 91*
Wolford, Elizabeth Jule Johnson 1960- *WhoAmW 91*
Wolford, Farley Edwin 1934- *WhoSSW 91*
Wolford, Jack A 1917- *BiDrAPA 89*
Wolford, Larry Eugene 1952- *WhoE 91*
Wolford, Roy, Jr. 1946- *WhoEmL 91*
Wolford-Barnard, Eileen Joyce 1938- *WhoWrEP 89*
Wolfort, Louis Philip 1916- *St&PR 91*
Wolfort, Louis Phillip, III 1943- *WhoSSW 91*
Wolfowitz, Brian Lester 1942- *WhoWor 91*
Wolfowitz, Jacob 1910-1981 *DcScB S2*
Wolfowitz, Paul Dundes 1943- *WhoAm 90, WhoWor 91*
Wolfram von Eschenbach 1170?-1220? *ClMLC 5, WorAlBi*
Wolfram, Annemarie *BioIn 16*
Wolfram, Charles William 1937- *WhoAm 90*
Wolfram, Stephen *BioIn 16*
Wolfram, Thomas 1936- *WhoAm 90*
Wolfreston, Francis 1607-1677 *BiDEWW*
Wolfrom, Howard E. 1948- *St&PR 91*
Wolfrom, Joan Margaret 1930- *WhoAmW 91*
Wolfrom, Melville Lawrence 1900-1969 *DcScB S2*
Wolfrum, Blaise Joseph 1960- *BiDrAPA 89*
Wolfrum, C. Rudiger 1941- *WhoWor 91*
Wolfsberg, Max 1928- *WhoAm 90*
Wolfsburg, Carl Ferdinand von 1692-1764 *PenDiDA 89*
Wolfsheimer, Ronald M. 1952- *St&PR 91*
Wolfslayer, Donald R. 1926- *St&PR 91*
Wolfson, Alan William 1951- *WhoWor 91*
Wolfson, Alfred *EncO&P 3*
Wolfson, Dirk Jacob 1933- *WhoWor 91*
Wolfson, Evelyn *AuBYP 90*
Wolfson, Evelyn 1937- *SmATA 62 [port]*
Wolfson, Harry Austryn 1887-1974 *BioIn 16*
Wolfson, Ivan Richard 1945- *St&PR 91*
Wolfson, James Kenneth *BiDrAPA 89*
Wolfson, Jay 1952- *WhoSSW 91*
Wolfson, Joel *BiDrAPA 89*
Wolfson, Lawrence Scott 1960- *WhoSSW 91*
Wolfson, Leonard Arthur 1935- *St&PR 91, WhoAm 90*
Wolfson, Mark Alan 1952- *WhoAm 90*
Wolfson, Martin 1936- *St&PR 91*
Wolfson, Mast, II *BiDrAPA 89*
Wolfson, Michael George 1938- *WhoAm 90*
Wolfson, Michele Karen 1946- *St&PR 91*
Wolfson, Milton Jay 1942- *St&PR 91*
Wolfson, Mitchell 1939- *BioIn 16*
Wolfson, Neil I. 1938- *WhoE 91*
Wolfson, Nessa *BioIn 16*
Wolfson, Richard F. 1923- *St&PR 91*
Wolfson, Richard Frederick 1923- *WhoAm 90*
Wolfson, Robert Pred 1926- *WhoWor 91*
Wolfson, Saul David 1939- *BiDrAPA 89*
Wolfson, Sidney 1911-1973 *WhoAmA 91N*
Wolfson, Victor *NewYTBS 90*
Wolfson, Victor 1910-1990 *BioIn 16, ConAu 131*
Wolfson, Warren David 1949- *St&PR 91, WhoAm 90*
Wolfson, William Q *BiDrAPA 89*
Wolfthorn, Julie 1868-1944 *BiDWomA*
Wolga, George Jacob 1931- *WhoAm 90*
Wolgamott, Robert 1926- *BiDrAPA 89*
Wolgast, Donald Richard 1931- *St&PR 91*
Wolgemut, Michael 1434-1519 *IntDcAA 90*
Wolgin, Richard Ira 1949- *St&PR 91*
Wolicki, Nancy Frieda 1953- *WhoAmW 91*
Wolin, Doris Diamond 1929- *WhoE 91*
Wolin, Howard Evan 1940- *BiDrAPA 89*
Wolin, Jeffrey Alan 1951- *WhoAmA 91*
Wolin, Neal Steven 1961- *WhoE 91*

Wolin, Richard E 1938- *BiDrAPA 89*
Wolin, Robert Harvey 1925- *WhoE 91*
Wolin, Ron *BioIn 16, NewYTBS 90*
Wolin, Steven Joel 1940- *BiDrAPA 89*
Wolinetz, Alan 1945- *St&PR 91*
Wolins, Joseph 1915- *WhoAm 90, WhoAmA 91*
Wolinski, Diane Marie 1956- *WhoE 91*
Wolinski, Henryk 1901-1986 *BioIn 16*
Wolinsky, Emanuel 1917- *WhoAm 90*
Wolintz, Arthur Harry 1937- *WhoAm 90*
Wolis, Steven Evan 1960- *St&PR 91*
Woliston, Jack *BioIn 16*
Woliston, Jack 1916?-1990 *ConAu 131*
Wolitarsky, James W. 1946- *St&PR 91*
Wolitarsky, James William 1946- *WhoAm 90*
Wolitzer, Hilma 1930- *WhoWrEP 89*
Wolitzer, Meg 1959- *Au&Arts 6 [port]*
Wolitzer, Steven *BioIn 16*
Wolk, Alan Scott 1957- *WhoE 91*
Wolk, Beryl J. 1929- *St&PR 91*
Wolk, Bruce Alan 1946- *WhoEmL 91*
Wolk, Elliot K. 1935- *St&PR 91*
Wolk, Elliot Samuel 1919- *WhoAm 90*
Wolk, Gary Norman *BiDrAPA 89*
Wolk, Herbert 1932- *St&PR 91*
Wolk, Howard Marvin 1920- *WhoAm 90, WhoWrEP 89*
Wolk, Howard William 1938- *St&PR 91*
Wolk, Joan Marcia 1947- *WhoAmW 91*
Wolk, John Paul 1948- *WhoAm 90*
Wolk, Paula Carol 1945- *BiDrAPA 89*
Wolken, Jerome Jay 1917- *WhoAm 90*
Wolkin, Paul Alexander 1917- *WhoAm 90*
Wolking, Henry C. 1948- *IntWWM 90*
Wolking, Joseph Anthony 1934- *St&PR 91*
Wolkoff, Albert 1940- *BiDrAPA 89*
Wolkoff, Eugene Arnold 1932- *WhoAm 90*
Wolkoff, Irvin Isidor 1952- *BiDrAPA 89*
Wolkomir, Joyce Rogers 1942- *WhoWrEP 89*
Wolkomir, Richard 1943- *WhoWrEP 89*
Wolkow, Alan Edward 1946- *WhoSSW 91*
Wolkow-Krupnikova, Nadia *BiDrAPA 89*
Wolkowitz, Benjamin 1945- *WhoE 91*
Wolkowitz, Owen Mark 1952- *BiDrAPA 89*
Wolkowski, Leszek August 1941- *WhoWor 91*
Wolkstein, Andrew Irving 1951- *WhoE 91*
Wolkstein, Diane *WhoWrEP 89*
Wolkstein, Diane 1942- *ConAu 32NR*
Woll, Harry J. 1920- *WhoAm 90*
Woll, Moises 1915- *WhoWor 91*
Woll, Patricia Ann 1956- *WhoE 91*
Woll, Peter 1933- *WhoE 91*
Woll, Richard Henry 1963- *WhoSSW 91*
Woll, Robert Nicolas 1936- *WhoWor 91*
Woll, S. Raymond 1919- *St&PR 91*
Wollaeger, Timothy John 1943- *St&PR 91*
Wollan, Gerald Casper 1922- *WhoAm 90*
Wolle, Charles Robert 1935- *WhoAm 90*
Wolle, Eduardo 1954- *WhoHisp 91*
Wolle, June Rose Bush 1941- *WhoAmW 91*
Wolle, Muriel Sibell 1898-1977 *WhoAmA 91N*
Wolle, William Down 1928- *WhoAm 90*
Wollemborg, Leo Joseph 1912- *WhoWor 91*
Wollen, Nalla 1942- *St&PR 91*
Wollenberg, Fred A. 1937- *St&PR 91*
Wollenberg, J. Roger 1919- *WhoAm 90*
Wollenberg, Jorg 1937- *WhoWor 91*
Wollenberg, Lynn A. 1964- *WhoAmW 91*
Wollenberg, Richard Peter 1915- *St&PR 91, WhoAm 90*
Wollenberg, Susan Lesley Freda 1949- *IntWWM 90*
Wollenberger, Albert 1912- *WhoWor 91*
Wollensack, Frank Eugene 1920- *St&PR 91*
Wollensak, John Charles 1932- *WhoSSW 91*
Wollensak, Richard John 1930- *St&PR 91*
Wollersheim, Janet Puccinelli 1936- *WhoAmW 91*
Wollert, Gerald Dale 1935- *St&PR 91, WhoAm 90*
Wolley, Hannah 1621?-1674 *BiDEWW*
Wolley, Hannah 1621?-1676? *FemiCLE*
Wollheim, Donald Allen 1914- *AuBYP 90, WhoWrEP 89*
Wollin, Lucy Ann 1939- *WhoAmW 91*
Wollin, Richard Anderson 1952- *St&PR 91*
Wollman, Eric 1951- *WhoE 91*
Wollman, Fred William 1930- *St&PR 91*
Wollman, Harry 1932- *WhoAm 90, WhoWor 91*
Wollman, June Rose 1929- *WhoE 91*
Wollman, Leo 1914- *WhoAm 90*
Wollman, Nathaniel 1915- *WhoAm 90*
Wollmer, R.J. 1920- *St&PR 91*
Wollner, Barry Stuart 1953- *WhoE 91*
Wollner, Thomas Edward 1936- *WhoAm 90*
Wollowick, Isidore J. 1909- *St&PR 91*
Wollrab, Adalbert Paul Richard 1928- *WhoWor 91*
Wollschlaeger, Gertraud 1924- *WhoAmW 91*
Wollstadt, Paul 1910-1988 *BioIn 16*
Wollstonecraft, Mary 1759-1797 *BioIn 16, DcLB 104 [port], FemiCLE, WorAlBi*
Wollum, Raymond M. *St&PR 91*
Wolman, Abel 1892-1989 *BioIn 16*
Wolman, Carol Stone 1941- *BiDrAPA 89*
Wolman, Harold M *BiDrAPA 89*
Wolman, J. Martin 1919- *St&PR 91, WhoAm 90*
Wolman, M. Gordon 1924- *WhoAm 90*
Wolman, Stuart Alan *BiDrAPA 89*
Wolman, Tara Sophia 1948- *WhoAmW 91*
Wolman, Thomas S 1946- *BiDrAPA 89*
Wolman, Walter *BiDrAPA 89*
Wolnek, Stephen S. 1938- *St&PR 91*
Wolner, Rena Meryl 1945- *WhoAm 90*
Wolner, Ron Kevin 1956- *BiDrAPA 89*
Wolodzko, Joseph 1932- *BiDrAPA 89*
Wolohan, James L. 1951- *St&PR 91*
Wolohan, Richard Vincent 1915- *St&PR 91*
Woloshin, Gabrielle S 1931- *BiDrAPA 89*
Woloshin, Marvin 1934- *St&PR 91*
Woloshin, Melvyn A. 1939- *WhoE 91*
Wolosky, Joel Martin 1942- *WhoAm 90*
Wolosz, Richard Anthony 1957- *WhoE 91*
Woloszyk, Holly Arlene 1960- *WhoAmW 91*
Wolotkiewicz, Marian M. 1954- *WhoAmW 91, WhoE 91*
Wolotkiewicz, Marian Margaret 1954- *WhoWrEP 89*
Woloy, Eleanora M 1932- *BiDrAPA 89*
Wolozen, John Joseph, Jr. 1952- *WhoE 91*
Wolpe, Berthold 1905-1989 *AnObit 1989, ConAu 129*
Wolpe, Berthold Ludwig 1905-1989 *BioIn 16*
Wolpe, Howard *BioIn 16*
Wolpe, Howard Eliot 1939- *WhoAm 90*
Wolpe, Joseph 1915- *BiDrAPA 89*
Wolper, Allan L. *WhoE 91*
Wolper, Barry Mark 1955- *St&PR 91*
Wolper, David L. *BioIn 16*
Wolper, David Lloyd 1928- *WhoAm 90, WhoWor 91*
Wolper, Marshall 1922- *WhoAm 90, WhoWor 91*
Wolpert, Arthur 1932- *BiDrAPA 89*
Wolpert, Clive 1935- *WhoWor 91*
Wolpert, Edward A 1930- *BiDrAPA 89*
Wolpert, Edward Alan 1930- *WhoAm 90*
Wolpert, Etta *WhoAmA 91*
Wolpert, Julian 1932- *WhoAm 90*
Wolpert, Julie 1950- *WhoAmW 91*
Wolpert, Richard W. 1926- *St&PR 91*
Wolpert, William Henry 1954- *WhoSSW 91*
Wolpin, Albert Lawrence 1925- *St&PR 91*
Wolpoff, Alvin S. 1926- *St&PR 91*
Wolpoff, Alvin Sidney 1926- *WhoE 91*
Wolsey, Thomas 1475?-1530 *WorAlBi*
Wolshaw, Dorene Lee *WhoWrEP 89*
Wolsiffer, Patricia Rae 1933- *WhoAm 90*
Wolski, Donna Catherine 1942- *WhoE 91*
Wolski, Lawrence George 1944- *St&PR 91*
Wolski, Patrick Edward 1939- *WhoAm 90*
Wolski, Robert Lawrence *BiDrAPA 89*
Wolski, Werner Edward 1947- *WhoWor 91*
Wolsky, Jack 1930- *WhoAmA 91*
Wolsky, Murray 1931- *St&PR 91, WhoAm 90*
Wolson, Craig Alan 1949- *WhoAm 90, WhoE 91, WhoWor 91*
Wolsson, Kenneth 1933- *WhoE 91*
Wolstat, Henry 1934- *BiDrAPA 89*
Wolstenholme, William 1865-1931 *PenDiMP*
Wolstenholme-Elmy, Elizabeth Clark *BioIn 16*
Wolston, Edward Jonathan 1949- *BiDrAPA 89, WhoE 91*
Wolter, Duane Roland 1948- *St&PR 91, WhoAm 90*
Wolter, Elise H. *ODwPR 91*
Wolter, Harry 1884-1970 *Ballpl 90*
Wolter, John Amadeus 1925- *WhoAm 90*
Wolter, Jurgen Reimer 1924- *WhoAm 90*
Wolterbeek, Jacob C *BiDrAPA 89*
Woltering, David F. 1946- *St&PR 91*
Woltering, Margaret Mae 1913- *WhoAmW 91*
Wolterink, Lester Floyd 1915- *WhoAm 90*
Wolters, Curt Cornelis Frederik 1938- *WhoE 91*
Wolters, Oliver William 1915- *WhoAm 90*
Wolters, Raymond 1938- *WhoAm 90*
Wolthausen, Reed C. 1947- *St&PR 91*
Wolton, Georgie 1934- *WomArch [port]*
Woltz, Alan E. 1932- *St&PR 91*
Woltz, Charles Killian 1914- *WhoAm 90*
Woltz, Howard Osler 1925- *St&PR 91*
Woltz, Howard Osler, Jr. 1925- *WhoAm 90, WhoSSW 91*
Woltz, Mary Lynn Monaco 1951- *WhoAmW 91*
Wolverton, Basil 1909-1979 *EncACom*
Wolverton, Byron A. 1934- *IntWWM 90*
Wolverton, David 1940- *St&PR 91*
Wolverton, Harry 1873-1937 *Ballpl 90*
Wolverton, Linda May 1943- *WhoAmW 91*
Wolverton, Robert Earl 1925- *WhoAm 90*
Wolverton, William T. 1937- *St&PR 91*
Wolvesperges, Albert E. 1934- *WhoWor 91*
Wolynes, Peter Guy 1953- *WhoAm 90*
Wolynic, Edward Thomas 1948- *St&PR 91, WhoAm 90*
Wolz, Henry George 1905- *WhoAm 90*
Wolz, Larry Robert 1951- *IntWWM 90*
Wolzien, Thomas *BioIn 16*
Wolzogen, Karoline von 1763-1847 *EncCoWW*
Womach, Emily Hitch 1927- *WhoAm 90*
Womach, Merrill P. 1927- *St&PR 91*
Womack, Ana Maria *BiDrAPA 89*
Womack, Bill B. 1938- *WhoSSW 91*
Womack, Bob 1843-1909 *BioIn 16*
Womack, Bobbi Hackett 1951- *WhoAmW 91*
Womack, Bobby *BioIn 16*
Womack, Bobby 1944- *ConMus 5 [port], DrBlPA 90, EncPR&S 89*
Womack, Brian Edward 1964- *WhoSSW 91*
Womack, C. Michael 1943- *St&PR 91*
Womack, Craig Paul 1950- *St&PR 91*
Womack, Dooley 1939- *Ballpl 90*
Womack, Doug C. 1950- *WhoEmL 91*
Womack, Edgar Allen, Jr. 1942- *WhoAm 90*
Womack, Eric 1959- *WhoWrEP 89*
Womack, Idalah Demina 1943- *WhoE 91*
Womack, James Scott 1928- *St&PR 91*
Womack, Jimmy *BioIn 16*
Womack, Kathryn Joanne 1938- *WhoSSW 91*
Womack, Lowell Asher 1938- *St&PR 91*
Womack, Pamela *WhoAmW 91*
Womack, Richard Marvin 1936- *WhoAm 90*
Womack, Richard Muse 1928- *St&PR 91*
Womack, Richard R. 1936- *St&PR 91*
Womack, Sharon Gennelle *WhoAmW 91*
Womack, Steven James 1952- *WhoWrEP 89*
Womack, Walter Charles 1947- *St&PR 91*
Womack, William M *BiDrAPA 89*
Wombacher, Gerald Thomas 1929- *St&PR 91*
Womble, George Morgan 1926- *St&PR 91, WhoAm 90*
Womble, Patrice Torres 1955- *BiDrAPA 89*
Womble, William Fletcher 1916- *WhoAm 90*
Wombwell, George B. 1931- *St&PR 91*
Wombwell, George Burkley 1931- *WhoAm 90*
Womeldorf, Donald W. 1933- *St&PR 91*
Womeldorff, Porter John 1933- *St&PR 91, WhoAm 90*
Womelsdorf, L. Kenneth 1934- *St&PR 91*
Womer, Charles Berry 1926- *WhoAm 90*
Womer, Jan Linwood 1939- *WhoWor 91*
Wommack, Barbara Kay 1946- *WhoAmW 91*
Wommack, Janice Marie 1939- *WhoWor 91*
Wommack, William W. 1922- *St&PR 91*
Wommack, William Walton 1922- *WhoAm 90*
Wonak, Daniel C. 1948- *St&PR 91*
Wonder, David Royden 1958- *WhoSSW 91*
Wonder, John Paul 1921- *WhoAm 90*
Wonder, Stevie *BioIn 16*
Wonder, Stevie 1950- *DrBlPA 90, EncPR&S 89, OxCPMus, WhoAm 90, WhoWor 91, WorAlBi*
Wondergem, Casey 1929- *ODwPR 91*
Wonderlic, Charles Frederick 1938- *St&PR 91*
Wonders, Alan George 1952- *WhoSSW 91*
Wonders, William Clare 1924- *WhoAm 90*
Wondra, Janet C. 1952- *WhoWrEP 89*
Wondriska, William *BioIn 16*
Wondriska, William Allen 1931- *AuBYP 90*
Wong Kan Seng 1946- *WhoWor 91*
Wong, Alfred Yiu-fai 1937- *WhoAm 90*
Wong, Anna May 1907-1961 *BioIn 16, WorAlBi*
Wong, Anthony C 1954- *BiDrAPA 89*
Wong, Brian Ming 1954- *St&PR 91*
Wong, Calvin Robert 1958- *St&PR 91*
Wong, Chak-Kuen 1938- *WhoAm 90*
Wong, Chin Wah 1954- *WhoWor 91*
Wong, Ching-Ping 1947- *WhoAm 90*
Wong, Chorng-Huey 1940- *WhoE 91*
Wong, David T. 1935- *WhoWor 91*
Wong, David Yaukar 1957- *WhoE 91*
Wong, David Yue 1934- *WhoAm 90*
Wong, Dennis 1954- *BiDrAPA 89*
Wong, Donald 1957- *St&PR 91*
Wong, Edward Chor-Cheung 1952- *WhoE 91*
Wong, Edward Wai Che 1936- *WhoAm 90*
Wong, Edwin Sau Nin 1929- *St&PR 91*
Wong, Elaine Dang 1936- *WhoAmW 91, WhoSSW 91*
Wong, Eugene 1934- *WhoAm 90*
Wong, Felix Siumon 1956- *WhoSSW 91*
Wong, Frederick 1929- *WhoAmA 91*
Wong, Gene 1922- *St&PR 91*
Wong, Grace H. 1926- *St&PR 91*
Wong, Harry 1933- *St&PR 91*
Wong, Helen Ka-ning 1963- *WhoAmW 91*
Wong, Henry Li-Nan 1940- *WhoWor 91*
Wong, Ho Sang 1943- *WhoWor 91*
Wong, Howard Joseph 1940- *St&PR 91*
Wong, Jade Snow *BioIn 16*
Wong, James Bok 1922- *WhoWor 91*
Wong, Jason 1934- *WhoAmA 91*
Wong, Jim 1931- *St&PR 91*
Wong, John Lui 1940- *WhoSSW 91*
Wong, John W C 1934- *BiDrAPA 89*
Wong, Jon *BiDrAPA 89*
Wong, Kellogg H. 1928- *WhoAm 90*
Wong, Kin-Ping 1941- *WhoAm 90*
Wong, Kuang Chung 1936- *WhoAm 90*
Wong, Kwok Kay Evan 1957- *WhoWor 91*
Wong, Lan Kan 1950- *WhoE 91*
Wong, Linda Seid 1953- *WhoAm 90*
Wong, Ling 1946- *WhoWor 91*
Wong, Lum Kong 1940- *WhoWor 91*
Wong, Lydia 1960- *IntWWM 90*
Wong, Ma-Li *BiDrAPA 89, WhoE 91*
Wong, Maria Mei 1959- *St&PR 91*
Wong, Marie Lisa 1965- *WhoE 91*
Wong, Martin *BioIn 16*
Wong, Mary Ann 1953- *WhoWor 91*
Wong, Maurice King Fan 1932- *WhoE 91*
Wong, Mel *BioIn 16*
Wong, Nancy 1949- *WhoWrEP 89*
Wong, Nellie *FemiCLE*
Wong, Nellie 1934- *WhoWrEP 89*
Wong, Normund 1934- *BiDrAPA 89*
Wong, Ovid K. *AuBYP 90*
Wong, Patrick *BiDrAPA 89*
Wong, Patrick Man-ning 1955- *WhoWor 91*
Wong, Paul Kan 1951- *WhoAmA 91*
Wong, Penelope Lynn 1945- *WhoAmW 91*
Wong, Po Kee 1934- *WhoAm 90*
Wong, Priscilla Devarakonda 1962- *WhoE 91*
Wong, Raylice Yuk Kwon 1943- *WhoAmW 91*
Wong, Raymond Roy 1937- *WhoWor 91*
Wong, Richard Yue-Chim 1952- *WhoWor 91*
Wong, Robert William 1955- *WhoE 91*
Wong, Roger Frederickson 1945- *WhoAmA 91*
Wong, Ruth 1920- *BiDrAPA 89, WhoE 91*
Wong, Stephanie Lam 1949- *WhoEmL 91*
Wong, Suzanne Crawbuck 1957- *WhoAmW 91*
Wong, Tak Lam 1936- *WhoWor 91*
Wong, Victor Kenneth 1938- *WhoAm 90*
Wong, Wally 1949- *St&PR 91*
Wong, Wing Keung 1933- *WhoWor 91*
Wong, Ying Wood 1950- *WhoWor 91*
Wong-Ryan, Lillian R *BiDrAPA 89*
Wongsarnpigoon, Lerwut 1949- *BiDrAPA 89*
Wongwantanee, Lucksmee Ongkasuwan 1940- *WhoWor 91*
Wonham, Frederick Stapley 1931- *WhoAm 90*
Wonham, Walter Murray 1934- *WhoAm 90*
Wonka, Richard A 1923- *BiDrAPA 89*
Wonnacott, James Brian 1945- *WhoSSW 91*
Wonnacott, Paul 1933- *WhoAm 90, WhoE 91*
Wonnacott, Ronald Johnston 1930- *WhoAm 90*
Wonner, Paul 1920- *WhoAmA 91*
Woo, Anthony Dah-Huang 1952- *WhoAm 90*
Woo, David Charles 1956- *St&PR 91*
Woo, Frances Mei Soo 1949- *WhoAmW 91, WhoE 91*
Woo, Gerry *BioIn 16*
Woo, Helen Jane 1955- *WhoE 91*
Woo, Jung Woo 1933- *WhoSSW 91*
Woo, S. B. 1937- *WhoAm 90*
Woo, Shien-biau *BioIn 16*
Woo, Stephen Kendall 1957- *BiDrAPA 89*
Woo, William Franklin 1936- *WhoAm 90*
Wood, Aaron 1717-1785 *PenDiDA 89*
Wood, Abraham *EncCRAm, WhNaAH*
Wood, Alan 1935- *WhoAmA 91*
Wood, Alfred McCreary 1896- *WhoSSW 91*
Wood, Allen John 1925- *WhoAm 90, WhoE 91*
Wood, Andrew McLean, III 1949- *WhoSSW 91*

Wood, Angela Margaret 1948- *BiDrAPA 89*
Wood, Anne 1937- *SmATA 64 [port]*
Wood, Antonio J *BiDrAPA 89*
Wood, Arthur 1875-1953 *OxCPMus*
Wood, Arthur MacDougall 1913- *WhoAm 90*
Wood, Audrey *AuBYP 90, BioIn 16*
Wood, Audrey 1905-1985 *BioIn 16, NotWoAT*
Wood, Barbara 1947- *WhoAmW 91*
Wood, Barbara Jane *BiDrAPA 89*
Wood, Barbara Louise Champion 1924- *WhoAmW 91*
Wood, Barrie Ross 1934- *St&PR 91*
Wood, Barry W. 1958- *St&PR 91*
Wood, Beatrice *BioIn 16, WhoAmA 91*
Wood, Beatrice 1892?- *BiDWomA*
Wood, Benjamin O. 1936- *St&PR 91*
Wood, Berenice Howland 1910- *WhoE 91*
Wood, Betty A. 1943- *WhoAmW 91*
Wood, Beverly Ann *BiDrAPA 89*
Wood, Billy Henry, Jr. 1950- *WhoSSW 91*
Wood, Bob 1865-1943 *Ballpl 90*
Wood, Bob Lee 1944- *WhoSSW 91*
Wood, C. E. 1854- *EncO&P 3*
Wood, Carole Dee 1939- *WhoAmW 91*
Wood, Charles Drury, III 1934- *WhoAm 90*
Wood, Charles Martin, III 1943- *St&PR 91*
Wood, Charles R. 1933- *St&PR 91*
Wood, Charles T 1933- *ConAu 30NR*
Wood, Charles Tuttle 1933- *WhoAm 90*
Wood, Charles Winter 1870-1952 *EarBlAP*
Wood, Christie Ann 1955- *WhoAmW 91*
Wood, Claude Barton 1942- *WhoSSW 91*
Wood, Clinton Wayne 1954- *WhoSSW 91*
Wood, Curtis L. *WhoWrEP 89*
Wood, Daniel Gordon 1937- *St&PR 91*
Wood, Daniel Raymie 1942- *WhoSSW 91*
Wood, Darlene Sprinkle 1954- *WhoAmW 91*
Wood, David 1944- *IntWWM 90*
Wood, David Alvra 1904- *WhoWor 91*
Wood, David C. 1921-1988 *BioIn 16*
Wood, David Charles 1943- *St&PR 91, WhoAm 90*
Wood, David John 1942- *BiDrAPA 89*
Wood, David Kennedy Cornell 1925- *WhoAm 90*
Wood, David R. 1943- *St&PR 91*
Wood, David Robert 1952- *St&PR 91*
Wood, Dee J. 1929- *WhoAmW 91*
Wood, Delmas Byrom 1938- *St&PR 91*
Wood, Derek L. 1939- *St&PR 91*
Wood, Don 1945- *BioIn 16*
Wood, Don James 1936- *WhoAm 90*
Wood, Donald Craig 1937- *WhoE 91*
Wood, Donald Euriah 1935- *WhoAm 90*
Wood, Donald W. 1925- *WhoAm 90*
Wood, Dorothy Carrico *AuBYP 90*
Wood, Dorothy Lee 1954- *St&PR 91*
Wood, Duncan Wilson 1948- *St&PR 91*
Wood, E. Scott *ODwPR 91*
Wood, Earl Howard 1912- *WhoAm 90*
Wood, Edward D. 1933- *WhoAm 90*
Wood, Edwin C 1925- *BiDrAPA 89*
Wood, Elizabeth A 1912- *ConAu 30NR*
Wood, Ellen 1814-1887 *FemiCLE*
Wood, Ellen Price 1814-1887 *BioIn 16*
Wood, Emma Caroline 1802-1879 *FemiCLE*
Wood, Enoch 1759-1840 *PenDiDA 89*
Wood, Eric *St&PR 91*
Wood, Eric Franklin 1947- *WhoAm 90*
Wood, Erskine Biddle 1911- *WhoAm 90*
Wood, Ervin L. 1946- *WhoSSW 91*
Wood, Esther 1905-1989 *BioIn 16*
Wood, Eve Allison *BiDrAPA 89*
Wood, Evelyn Nielsen 1909- *WhoAm 90, WhoAmW 91*
Wood, F. A. 1932-1985 *BioIn 16*
Wood, Fay S. *WhoAmW 91*
Wood, Fergus James 1917- *WhoWor 91*
Wood, Frances E *BiDrAPA 89*
Wood, Francis C. *NewYTBS 90*
Wood, Frank A. 1927- *St&PR 91*
Wood, Frank Bradshaw 1915- *WhoAm 90*
Wood, Frank M. 1935- *St&PR 91*
Wood, Frank Preuit 1916- *WhoAm 90*
Wood, Frederick Harrison 1936- *WhoSSW 91*
Wood, Frederick S. 1928- *WhoAm 90*
Wood, G. Pierce 1927- *St&PR 91*
Wood, Gavin Antony 1954- *WhoWor 91*
Wood, George H. 1946- *WhoAm 90*
Wood, Gerald Carl 1944- *WhoSSW 91*
Wood, Gerald David 1947- *WhoSSW 91*
Wood, Gordon Stewart 1933- *WhoAm 90*
Wood, Grant 1892-1942 *WorAlBi*
Wood, H. Graham 1910- *St&PR 91*
Wood, Hap 1941- *St&PR 91*
Wood, Harland Goff 1907- *WhoAm 90*
Wood, Harleston Read 1913- *WhoAm 90*
Wood, Harlington, Jr. 1920- *WhoAm 90*
Wood, Harry 1870-1943 *EncACom*
Wood, Harry Emsley, Jr 1910- *WhoAmA 91*
Wood, Harvey Joseph 1919- *WhoWrEP 89*
Wood, Haydn 1882-1959 *OxCPMus*
Wood, Henry, Mrs. 1814-1887 *BioIn 16, TwCCr&M 91A*
Wood, Henry J 1869-1944 *PenDiMP*
Wood, Howard Eugene 1932- *St&PR 91*
Wood, Howard Graham 1910- *WhoAm 90*
Wood, Howard P 1923- *BiDrAPA 89*
Wood, Hugh 1932- *IntWWM 90*
Wood, Hugh B. *BioIn 16*
Wood, Isaac Keith 1955- *BiDrAPA 89*
Wood, J. Howard 1901-1988 *BioIn 16*
Wood, J. Kenneth 1935- *St&PR 91*
Wood, Jacalyn Kay 1949- *WhoAmW 91*
Wood, Jack Auburn 1951- *WhoSSW 91*
Wood, Jack Calvin 1933- *WhoAm 90*
Wood, Jack W. 1925- *St&PR 91*
Wood, Jackie C. 1963- *WhoAmW 91*
Wood, Jake 1937- *Ballpl 90*
Wood, James *BioIn 16*
Wood, James *BioIn 16*
Wood, James 1927- *WhoAm 90*
Wood, James 1930- *BioIn 16, St&PR 91, WhoAm 90, WhoE 91*
Wood, James Allen 1906- *WhoAm 90*
Wood, James Arthur 1927- *WhoAmA 91*
Wood, James E., Jr. 1922- *WhoAm 90, WhoWor 91*
Wood, James Nowell 1941- *WhoAmA 91*
Wood, James Peter 1953- *IntWWM 90*
Wood, James Playsted 1905- *AuBYP 90*
Wood, Jane Semple 1940- *WhoAmW 91*
Wood, Jean Kathleen 1940- *WhoAmW 91*
Wood, Jeanne Clarke 1916- *WhoAm 90*
Wood, Jeannette Griffin 1928- *WhoAmW 91*
Wood, Jeannette Suzon 1967- *WhoAmW 91*
Wood, Jeff J. 1932- *St&PR 91*
Wood, Jeffrey Charles 1940- *WhoE 91*
Wood, Jeffrey Gilchrist 1940- *WhoSSW 91*
Wood, Jeffrey Neal 1954- *IntWWM 90*
Wood, Jeremy Scott 1941- *WhoE 91*
Wood, Joanna 1867-1927 *FemiCLE*
Wood, Joanna E 1867-1927 *DcLB 92 [port]*
Wood, Joe 1889-1985 *Ballpl 90 [port]*
Wood, John 1938- *OxCCanT*
Wood, John, Mrs. 1831-1915 *BioIn 16, NotWoAT*
Wood, John A. 1937- *St&PR 91*
Wood, John Armstead 1932- *WhoAm 90*
Wood, John Denison 1931- *WhoAm 90*
Wood, John F. 1940- *St&PR 91*
Wood, John Fisher 1850?-1899 *DcCanB 12*
Wood, John Frank 1908-1989 *BioIn 16*
Wood, John George 1827-1889 *BioIn 16*
Wood, John H. 1936- *ODwPR 91*
Wood, John Herbert 1936- *St&PR 91*
Wood, John Lewis 1912- *WhoAm 90*
Wood, John McGee 1854-1926 *AmLegL*
Wood, John Shirley 1888-1966 *BioIn 16*
Wood, John Thornton *BiDrAPA 89*
Wood, John Thurston 1928- *WhoSSW 91*
Wood, Joseph George 1928- *WhoAm 90*
Wood, Joseph Roberts 1915- *IntWWM 90*
Wood, Joshua Warren, III 1941- *WhoAm 90, WhoE 91*
Wood, Juliene Jensen 1945- *St&PR 91*
Wood, Karen Ann *BioIn 16*
Wood, Katherine Leslie 1950- *IntWWM 90*
Wood, Keith S. 1917- *St&PR 91*
Wood, Ken 1924- *Ballpl 90*
Wood, Kenneth Arthur 1926- *WhoAm 90*
Wood, Kenneth Laverne 1936- *WhoSSW 91*
Wood, Kevin *BioIn 16*
Wood, Kevin Joseph 1947- *IntWWM 90, WhoE 91*
Wood, Kimba M. 1944- *WhoAmW 91*
Wood, Larry *WhoAm 90, WhoAmW 91, WhoWor 91*
Wood, Laura Gale *St&PR 91*
Wood, Laura Newbold 1911- *AuBYP 90*
Wood, Leo 1882-1929 *OxCPMus*
Wood, Leonard 1860-1927 *BioIn 16, WorAlBi*
Wood, Leonard Alton 1922- *WhoE 91*
Wood, Leonard T. 1930- *WhoAm 90*
Wood, Leslie Ann 1957- *WhoAmW 91*
Wood, Leslie Carol 1955- *WhoWrEP 89*
Wood, Lew *ODwPR 91*
Wood, Lillian E. *HarlReB*
Wood, Linda C. 1945- *BioIn 16*
Wood, Linda Doris 1953- *WhoAmW 91*
Wood, Linda Gaye 1959- *WhoAmW 91*
Wood, Linda May 1942- *WhoAm 90, WhoAmW 91*
Wood, Loren Morris 1930- *St&PR 91*
Wood, Louise Aletha 1910-1988 *BioIn 16*
Wood, Lyman Phillips 1910- *St&PR 91*
Wood, Marcia Joan 1933- *WhoAmA 91*
Wood, Margaret Gray 1918- *WhoAmW 91*
Wood, Marian Starr 1938- *WhoAm 90*
Wood, Marilyn Susan 1950- *WhoAmW 91*
Wood, Martha M. 1929- *WhoSSW 91*
Wood, Martha Swain 1943- *WhoAmW 91*
Wood, Mary *BioIn 16*
Wood, Mary Catherine 1957- *WhoSSW 91*
Wood, Matilda Charlotte Vining 1831-1915 *BioIn 16*
Wood, Maurice 1922- *WhoAm 90*
Wood, McCrystle 1947- *WhoAmA 91*
Wood, Michael Curtise 1946- *St&PR 91*
Wood, Michael Joseph *BiDrAPA 89*
Wood, Michael Lane 1956- *WhoSSW 91*
Wood, Michael Lewis 1951- *WhoSSW 91*
Wood, Michael Stephen 1954- *WhoE 91*
Wood, Michael T 1943- *BiDrAPA 89*
Wood, Nancy Elizabeth *WhoAm 90, WhoAmW 91*
Wood, Nancy K. 1955- *WhoAmW 91*
Wood, Natalie *BioIn 16*
Wood, Natalie 1938-1981 *WorAlBi*
Wood, Natalie 1939-1981 *BioAmW*
Wood, Neil Roderick 1931- *St&PR 91, WhoAm 90*
Wood, Nicholas Wheeler 1946- *WhoAmA 91*
Wood, Norman Dwight 1941- *WhoE 91*
Wood, Norman S. 1928- *St&PR 91*
Wood, Oliver Gillan, Jr. 1937- *WhoWor 91*
Wood, Owen 1929- *SmATA 64 [port]*
Wood, Patricia Ann 1953- *WhoAmW 91*
Wood, Patricia Eileen 1952- *ODwPR 91*
Wood, Patricia Myers 1946- *WhoSSW 91*
Wood, Paul Donald 1945- *WhoSSW 91*
Wood, Paul Edward *BiDrAPA 89*
Wood, Paul R. 1929- *St&PR 91*
Wood, Peggy 1892-1978 *BioIn 16, NotWoAT, OxCPMus*
Wood, Phillip C *BiDrAPA 89*
Wood, Phyllis Anderson 1923- *AuBYP 90*
Wood, Quentin Eugene 1923- *St&PR 91, WhoAm 90*
Wood, R. Lyman 1937- *St&PR 91*
Wood, R. Ray 1942- *St&PR 91*
Wood, Ralph 1715-1772 *PenDiDA 89*
Wood, Ralph, II 1748-1795 *PenDiDA 89*
Wood, Reba Maxine 1919- *WhoAmW 91*
Wood, Renate 1938- *WhoWrEP 89*
Wood, Rene Modesto 1949- *St&PR 91*
Wood, Rex B. 1942- *St&PR 91*
Wood, Richard 1943- *ODwPR 91*
Wood, Richard Courtney 1943- *WhoSSW 91*
Wood, Richard Donald 1926- *St&PR 91, WhoAm 90*
Wood, Richard Eugene 1943- *WhoSSW 91*
Wood, Richard J. *WhoAm 90*
Wood, Richard P. 1945- *St&PR 91*
Wood, Richard Robert 1950- *St&PR 91*
Wood, Richard W. 1943- *St&PR 91*
Wood, Robert Charles 1939- *St&PR 91*
Wood, Robert Charles 1956- *WhoSSW 91, WhoWor 91*
Wood, Robert Coldwell 1923- *BiDrUSE 89, WhoAm 90*
Wood, Robert E. 1879-1969 *WorAlBi*
Wood, Robert E 1926- *WhoAmA 91*
Wood, Robert Edward 1941- *WhoAm 90*
Wood, Robert Elkington, II 1938- *WhoAm 90*
Wood, Robert Hart 1910- *WhoAm 90*
Wood, Robert Hemsley 1932- *WhoAm 90*
Wood, Robert J. *NewYTBS 90*
Wood, Robert J. 1918-1990 *BioIn 16*
Wood, Robert James 1918- *WhoAm 90*
Wood, Robert Kenneth 1940- *WhoE 91*
Wood, Robert L. 1939- *St&PR 91*
Wood, Robert Lee 1940- *WhoSSW 91*
Wood, Robert S. 1928- *St&PR 91*
Wood, Robert Warren 1955- *WhoEmL 91, WhoWor 91*
Wood, Robert William 1926- *St&PR 91*
Wood, Robert William, Jr. 1931- *WhoSSW 91*
Wood, Roberta Susan 1948- *WhoAmW 91*
Wood, Roderick M. *St&PR 91*
Wood, Roger S. 1927- *St&PR 91*
Wood, Ron *BioIn 16*
Wood, Ronald 1947- *WhoAm 90*
Wood, Ronald H. *St&PR 91*
Wood, Ronald Henry 1934- *WhoAm 90*
Wood, Roy Clay 1942- *WhoSSW 91*
Wood, Roy Vaughn 1939- *WhoAm 90*
Wood, Russell Lewis 1927- *St&PR 91, WhoAm 90*
Wood, Ruth C. *AuBYP 90*
Wood, Ruth Lundgren Williamson *WhoAmW 91, WhoWor 91*
Wood, Sally 1759-1854 *FemiCLE*
Wood, Sally Ann 1949- *WhoWrEP 89*
Wood, Samuel *PenDiDA 89*
Wood, Samuel Eugene 1934- *WhoWor 91*
Wood, Samuel Newitt 1825-1891 *AmLegL*
Wood, Sharon 1957- *WhoAmW 91*
Wood, Shelton Eugene 1938- *WhoWor 91*
Wood, Shirley *BioIn 16*
Wood, Silviana 1940- *WhoHisp 91*
Wood, Stanley George 1919- *WhoAm 90*
Wood, Stella L. 1865-1949 *BioAmW*
Wood, Stephen V. 1936- *St&PR 91*
Wood, Steven Albert 1950- *WhoE 91*
Wood, Steven Charles 1960- *WhoEmL 91*
Wood, Steven Quiring 1941- *WhoSSW 91*
Wood, Susan Macduff 1941- *ConAu 132*
Wood, Sydney 1935- *ConAu 31NR*
Wood, Ted 1931- *TwCCr&M 91*
Wood, Thomas 1815-1898 *DcCanB 12*
Wood, Thomas A. 1926- *St&PR 91*
Wood, Thomas Archie 1945- *WhoSSW 91*
Wood, Thomas Bond 1844-1922 *BioIn 16*
Wood, Thomas Kemble 1919- *WhoAm 90*
Wood, Thomas Marion 1952- *St&PR 91*
Wood, Thor E. 1932-1988 *BioIn 16*
Wood, Timothy McDonald 1947- *St&PR 91, WhoAm 90*
Wood, Tyrus Cobb, Jr. 1945- *WhoWrEP 89*
Wood, Virginia Margaret 1936- *WhoAmW 91*
Wood, Virginia Riley 1938- *WhoAmW 91*
Wood, Vivian Poates 1923- *WhoAmW 91*
Wood, Vivian Poates 1928- *IntWWM 90*
Wood, W. Carlton 1939- *St&PR 91*
Wood, Wally 1927-1981 *EncACom*
Wood, Wayne Barry 1958- *WhoEmL 91, WhoWor 91*
Wood, Wendy Deborah 1940- *WhoE 91*
Wood, Wilbur 1941- *Ballpl 90*
Wood, William *EncCRAm*
Wood, William Andrew, Jr. 1919- *St&PR 91*
Wood, William Barry, III 1938- *WhoAm 90*
Wood, William Charles, Jr. 1952- *BiDrAPA 89*
Wood, William Ezekiel, III 1942- *St&PR 91*
Wood, William G 1941- *BiDrAPA 89*
Wood, William Jerome 1928- *WhoAm 90*
Wood, William John 1929- *WhoE 91*
Wood, William Lawrence 1927- *WhoSSW 91*
Wood, William M 1924- *BiDrAPA 89*
Wood, William McBrayer 1942- *WhoWor 91*
Wood, William Philler 1927- *WhoAm 90*
Wood, William Ransom 1907- *WhoAm 90, WhoWor 91*
Wood, Willie *BioIn 16*
Wood, Willis B., Jr. 1934- *St&PR 91*
Wood, Willis Bowne, Jr. 1934- *WhoAm 90*
Wood, Yvonne Roberta 1951- *WhoAmW 91*
Wood Prince, William Norman 1942- *St&PR 91*
Wood-Smith, Donald 1931- *WhoWor 91*
Woodall, Charlotte Dee 1945- *WhoAmW 91*
Woodall, Charlotte Glenn 1916- *WhoSSW 91*
Woodall, Edwin Augustus 1925- *WhoSSW 91*
Woodall, George 1850-1925 *PenDiDA 89*
Woodall, Hubert C., Jr. 1918- *St&PR 91*
Woodall, J Martin *BiDrAPA 89*
Woodall, Jesse C., III 1964- *WhoSSW 91*
Woodall, John 1940- *WhoAmA 91*
Woodall, John P. *BiDrAPA 89*
Woodall, John William 1949- *WhoSSW 91*
Woodall, Larry 1894-1963 *Ballpl 90*
Woodall, Lowery A. 1929- *WhoSSW 91*
Woodall, Marvin Leonard 1937- *WhoE 91, WhoWor 91*
Woodall, Norman Eugene 1916- *WhoAm 90*
Woodall, Robert E. 1926- *St&PR 91*
Woodall, Ronald Lee 1941- *St&PR 91*
Woodall, Samuel Roy, Jr. 1936- *WhoAm 90*
Woodall, Thomas 1849-1926 *PenDiDA 89*
Woodall, William L. 1923- *St&PR 91*
Woodall, William Leon 1923- *WhoAm 90*
Woodard, Alfre *BioIn 16*
Woodard, Alfre 1953- *DrBlPA 90, WhoAmW 91*
Woodard, Alva Abe 1928- *WhoWor 91*
Woodard, Anne Taylor 1953- *WhoAmW 91*
Woodard, Carol Jane 1929- *WhoAm 90, WhoAmW 91*
Woodard, Charlaine *BioIn 16, DrBlPA 90*
Woodard, Charles Clifton, Jr. 1923- *WhoAm 90*
Woodard, Cheri Faith *BioIn 16*
Woodard, Clarence J. 1923- *St&PR 91*
Woodard, Clarence James 1923- *WhoAm 90*
Woodard, Dorothy Marie 1932- *WhoAmW 91, WhoWor 91*
Woodard, Duane 1938- *WhoAm 90*
Woodard, George Dewey 1931- *St&PR 91*
Woodard, George Hatfield 1906- *St&PR 91, WhoAm 90*
Woodard, George Sawyer, Jr. 1924- *WhoAm 90*
Woodard, Harold Raymond 1911- *WhoAm 90*
Woodard, Henry Herman, Jr. *BioIn 16*
Woodard, James A. 1930- *St&PR 91*
Woodard, James Philips 1929- *IntWWM 90*
Woodard, Jeff Neil 1955- *WhoSSW 91*
Woodard, John Roger 1932- *WhoAm 90*

Woods, John Merle 1943- *WhoSSW 91*
Woods, John Simon 1953- *WhoEmL 91*
Woods, John W. 1931- *St&PR 91*
Woods, John William 1912- *WhoAm 90*
Woods, John William 1943- *WhoAm 90*
Woods, John Witherspoon 1931- *WhoAm 90, WhoSSW 91, WhoWor 91*
Woods, Jonathan K. 1928- *St&PR 91*
Woods, Joseph Jacob 1851- *AmLegL*
Woods, Karen Marguerite 1945- *WhoWor 91*
Woods, Katherine Pearson 1853-1923 *FemiCLE*
Woods, Kenneth 1954- *WhoWrEP 89*
Woods, Kenneth M. 1935- *St&PR 91*
Woods, Laurie 1947- *WhoAmW 91*
Woods, Lawrence Milton 1932- *St&PR 91, WhoAm 90*
Woods, Lindsay Elizabeth 1948- *WhoAmW 91*
Woods, M. Malloy 1951- *St&PR 91*
Woods, Marcus E. 1930- *St&PR 91*
Woods, Margaret 1748-1821 *FemiCLE*
Woods, Margaret 1856-1945 *FemiCLE*
Woods, Mary 1955- *ODwPR 91*
Woods, Mary Dawson 1955- *WhoSSW 91*
Woods, Merilyn Baron 1927- *WhoAmW 91*
Woods, Michael Alan *BioIn 16*
Woods, Millie Hampton 1936- *WhoE 91*
Woods, Norman E., Jr. 1943- *St&PR 91*
Woods, Norman James 1934- *WhoAm 90*
Woods, Parnell 1912-1977 *Ballpl 90*
Woods, Patrick Henry 1931- *St&PR 91*
Woods, Pendleton 1923- *WhoSSW 91, WhoWor 91*
Woods, Phil *BioIn 16*
Woods, Philip *BioIn 16*
Woods, Philip Wells 1931- *WhoAm 90*
Woods, Phineas Skinner, Jr. 1922- *WhoE 91*
Woods, Pinky 1915-1982 *Ballpl 90*
Woods, Raymond Lynn 1931- *WhoSSW 91*
Woods, Reginald Foster 1939- *WhoAm 90*
Woods, Richard Seavey 1919- *WhoAm 90*
Woods, Rip 1933- *WhoAmA 91*
Woods, Robert Archer 1920- *WhoAm 90*
Woods, Robert Lawrence 1911- *WhoWor 91*
Woods, Robin Funnell 1943- *WhoAmW 91*
Woods, Rodney Ian 1941- *WhoAm 90*
Woods, Ron 1943- *Ballpl 90*
Woods, Ronald Noel 1958- *WhoWor 91*
Woods, Rose Mary 1917- *WhoAm 90*
Woods, Sandra Kay 1944- *St&PR 91, WhoAmW 91*
Woods, Sara 1922-1985 *TwCCr&M 91*
Woods, Sarah Ladd 1895-1980 *WhoAmA 91N*
Woods, Seborn Enloe 1931- *WhoSSW 91*
Woods, Sherwyn M 1932- *BiDrAPA 89*
Woods, Stephen Charles 1942- *WhoAm 90*
Woods, Stockton *TwCCr&M 91*
Woods, Susanne 1943- *WhoAm 90, WhoAmW 91, WhoE 91*
Woods, Sylvia *NewAgMG*
Woods, Thomas Alan *BiDrAPA 89*
Woods, Thomas Cochrane, Jr. *St&PR 91N*
Woods, Thomas James, Jr. 1922- *WhoSSW 91, WhoWor 91*
Woods, Thomas Lee 1937- *WhoE 91*
Woods, Thomas Seth 1954- *IntWWM 90*
Woods, Walt 1875-1951 *Ballpl 90*
Woods, Walter Ralph 1931- *WhoAm 90*
Woods, Ward Wilson, Jr. 1942- *WhoAm 90*
Woods, Wendell David 1932- *WhoSSW 91*
Woods, Wendy *BioIn 16*
Woods, William A F 1944- *BiDrAPA 89*
Woods, William Burnham 1824-1887 *AmLegL*
Woods, William Ellis 1917- *WhoAm 90*
Woods, William Hervey 1931-1976 *BioIn 16*
Woods, Willie G. 1943- *WhoAmW 91, WhoE 91*
Woods, Willis Franklin 1920-1988 *WhoAmA 91N*
Woods-Smith, Sybil 1954- *WhoWrEP 89*
Woodside, Bertram John 1946- *WhoWor 91*
Woodside, D Blake 1957- *BiDrAPA 89*
Woodside, Gordon William *WhoAmA 91*
Woodside, Howard Bush 1921- *St&PR 91*
Woodside, Lisa Nicole 1944- *WhoAmW 91*
Woodside, Nina Bencich 1931- *BiDrAPA 89*
Woodside, Robert Elmer 1904- *WhoAm 90*
Woodside, Samuel Talgart 1953- *St&PR 91*
Woodside, William S. 1922- *St&PR 91*
Woodside, William Stewart 1922- *WhoAm 90, WhoE 91*
Woodson, Benjamin N. 1908- *St&PR 91*
Woodson, Benjamin Nelson, III 1908- *WhoAm 90*
Woodson, Carter G. 1875-1950 *WorAlBi*
Woodson, Carter Godwin 1875-1950 *BioIn 16*
Woodson, Cheryl Anne 1959- *WhoAmW 91*
Woodson, Cynthia *BiDrAPA 89*
Woodson, David 1934- *St&PR 91*
Woodson, Dennis Marshall, II 1949- *WhoSSW 91*
Woodson, Dick 1945- *Ballpl 90*
Woodson, Doris 1929- *WhoAmA 91*
Woodson, Ernest Lyle 1937- *WhoHisp 91*
Woodson, Frederick G *BiDrAPA 89*
Woodson, Herbert Horace 1925- *WhoAm 90*
Woodson, James Charles 1942- *St&PR 91*
Woodson, Joseph B *BiDrAPA 89*
Woodson, Loren Dexter *BiDrAPA 89*
Woodson, Richard Peyton, III 1923- *St&PR 91, WhoAm 90*
Woodson, Robert Ray 1932- *St&PR 91*
Woodson, Shirley Ann 1936- *WhoAmA 91*
Woodson, Stephen William 1950- *WhoWor 91*
Woodson-Howard, Marlene Erdley 1937- *WhoAmW 91, WhoSSW 91*
Woodsum, Gayle M. 1956- *WhoAmW 91*
Woodsworth, Anne 1941- *WhoAm 90, WhoAmW 91, WhoE 91*
Woodward, Anita Barrett 1950- *WhoAmW 91*
Woodward, Bart 1953- *WhoE 91*
Woodward, Bob *ConAu 31NR, MajTwCW*
Woodward, Bob 1943- *BioIn 16*
Woodward, Burns 1945- *BiDrAPA 89*
Woodward, C. Vann 1908- *BioIn 16, WhoWrEP 89*
Woodward, Charles C.M. 1929- *St&PR 91*
Woodward, Charles Namby Wynn 1924- *WhoAm 90*
Woodward, Cleveland 1900-1986 *BioIn 16*
Woodward, Comer Vann 1908- *BioIn 16, WhoAm 90*
Woodward, Daniel Holt 1931- *WhoAm 90*
Woodward, David Luther 1942- *WhoSSW 91*
Woodward, Diana *BioIn 16*
Woodward, Doris J *BiDrAPA 89*
Woodward, Edward 1930- *WhoAm 90*
Woodward, Edward Roy 1916- *WhoAm 90*
Woodward, Ellsworth *PenDiDA 89*
Woodward, F. Robert, Jr. 1936- *St&PR 91*
Woodward, Fae Blanche 1925- *WhoAmW 91*
Woodward, Frederick Miller 1943- *WhoAm 90*
Woodward, George D *BiDrAPA 89*
Woodward, Greta Charmaine 1930- *WhoAmW 91*
Woodward, Gwenda Mary 1927- *IntWWM 90*
Woodward, Hanna Liisa *BiDrAPA 89*
Woodward, Harold Edward 1888-1988 *BioIn 16*
Woodward, Helen De Long 1896- *WhoWrEP 89*
Woodward, Henry 1646?-1686 *EncCRAm*
Woodward, Herbert Norton 1911- *St&PR 91*
Woodward, Hildegard 1898- *AuBYP 90*
Woodward, Isabel Avila 1906- *WhoAmW 91, WhoWor 91*
Woodward, J. Taylor, III 1940- *St&PR 91*
Woodward, James Arthur 1934- *St&PR 91*
Woodward, James Hoyt, Jr. 1939- *WhoAm 90*
Woodward, Jerome Paul *BiDrAPA 89*
Woodward, Joanne 1930- *BioIn 16, WorAlBi*
Woodward, Joanne Gignilliat 1930- *WhoAm 90, WhoAmW 91*
Woodward, John 1921-1988 *BioIn 16*
Woodward, John Taylor, III 1940- *WhoAm 90*
Woodward, Kesler Edward 1951- *WhoAmA 91*
Woodward, Lawrence J. *ODwPR 91*
Woodward, Lester Ray 1932- *WhoAm 90*
Woodward, Linda L. 1946- *WhoAmW 91*
Woodward, M. Cabell, Jr. 1929- *St&PR 91, WhoAm 90*
Woodward, Madison Truman, Jr. 1908- *WhoAm 90, WhoWor 91*
Woodward, Mark Stephen 1953- *WhoSSW 91*
Woodward, Michael R. 1946- *St&PR 91*
Woodward, Patricia Beal 1949- *WhoWrEP 89*
Woodward, Ralph Lee, Jr. 1934- *WhoAm 90, WhoWrEP 89*
Woodward, Richard B. *St&PR 91*
Woodward, Richard H., Jr. 1947- *St&PR 91*
Woodward, Richard Joseph, Jr. 1907- *WhoAm 90, WhoWor 91*
Woodward, Rob 1962- *Ballpl 90*
Woodward, Robert 1943- *WorAlBi*
Woodward, Robert B. 1917-1979 *WorAlBi*
Woodward, Robert D 1925- *BiDrAPA 89*
Woodward, Robert Forbes 1908- *WhoAm 90*
Woodward, Robert Strong 1885-1957 *WhoAmA 91N*
Woodward, Robert Upshur 1943- *ConAu 31NR, MajTwCW, WhoAm 90, WhoWrEP 89*
Woodward, Roger 1942- *PenDiMP*
Woodward, Roger Robert 1942- *IntWWM 90*
Woodward, Stanley 1890-1970 *WhoAmA 91N*
Woodward, Steven P 1953- *WhoAmA 91*
Woodward, Susan Ellen 1949- *WhoAm 90, WhoAmW 91, WhoE 91*
Woodward, Theodore Englar 1914- *WhoAm 90*
Woodward, Thomas Aiken 1933- *WhoAm 90*
Woodward, Thomas Morgan 1925- *WhoAm 90, WhoWor 91*
Woodward, William 1935- *WhoAmA 91*
Woodward, William C. 1913-1989 *BioIn 16*
Woodward, William J.D. 1952- *St&PR 91*
Woodward, William P. 1939- *St&PR 91*
Woodward, Woody 1942- *Ballpl 90*
Woodward-Stadtmueller, Donna Lynn 1946- *IntWWM 90*
Woodwell, George M. *BioIn 16*
Woodwell, George Masters 1928- *WhoAm 90*
Woodwell, Margot Bell 1936- *WhoAmW 91*
Woodworth, Donald Duryea 1935- *WhoE 91*
Woodworth, Fred Lowe 1940- *WhoWor 91*
Woodworth, G Wallace 1902-1969 *PenDiMP*
Woodworth, Henry Forrest *BiDrAPA 89*
Woodworth, James Richard 1918- *WhoAm 90*
Woodworth, Leslie R. 1917- *St&PR 91*
Woodworth, Lynne Marie 1953- *WhoAmW 91*
Woodworth, Peter Walker 1946- *St&PR 91*
Woodworth, Ralph Leon 1933- *WhoWrEP 89*
Woodworth, Robert Cummings 1930- *WhoE 91*
Woodworth-Etter, Maria B. 1844-1924 *BioAmW*
Woody, A-Young Moon 1934- *WhoAmW 91*
Woody, Carol Clayman 1949- *WhoAmW 91*
Woody, Catherine Evelyn 1943- *WhoAmW 91*
Woody, Clyde Woodrow 1920- *WhoSSW 91*
Woody, George Edward 1938- *BiDrAPA 89*
Woody, Howard 1935- *WhoAmA 91*
Woody, Jacquelyn Kay 1955- *WhoAmW 91*
Woody, Julie 1939- *WhoAmW 91*
Woody, Kathleen Joanna 1949- *WhoAmW 91*
Woody, Kennerly 1902-1989 *BioIn 16*
Woody, Regina Llewellyn 1894- *AuBYP 90*
Woody, Victor Morton, III 1943- *WhoSSW 91*
Woody, Walter Ruffin, Jr. 1933- *St&PR 91*
Woodyard, Cynthia Lee 1960- *WhoAmW 91*
Woodyard, Edward Lender *BioIn 16*
Woodyard, Russell D. 1939- *St&PR 91*
Woodyard, Sam 1925-1988 *AnObit 1988, BioIn 16*
Woodyear, John M 1923- *BiDrAPA 89*
Woof, Maija Gegeris Zack *WhoAmA 91*
Woofter, R.D. 1923- *St&PR 91*
Woofter, R. D. 1923- *WhoSSW 91*
Wool, Alexandra 1927- *WhoE 91*
Wool, Carol Anne 1945- *BiDrAPA 89*
Wool, Christoper *WhoAmA 91*
Wool, Glorye *BiDrAPA 89*
Wool, Harlene E. 1930- *St&PR 91*
Wool, Ira Goodwin 1925- *WhoAm 90*
Wool, John Ellis 1784-1869 *WhNaAH*
Wool, Marvin S. 1928- *St&PR 91*
Woolam, Gerald Lynn 1937- *WhoAm 90*
Wooland, Norman 1905-1989 *ConTFT 8*
Woolard, Alan J. 1948- *St&PR 91*
Woolard, Deborah Jean 1953- *WhoAmW 91*
Woolard, Edgar S., Jr. 1934- *WhoAm 90, WhoE 91, WhoWor 91*
Woolard, Edgar Smith, Jr. 1934- *St&PR 91*
Woolard, Roderick Staton 1950- *St&PR 91*
Woolbert, Richard E. 1933- *St&PR 91*
Woolcock, Alan R. 1944- *St&PR 91*
Wooldredge, William Dunbar 1937- *WhoAm 90*
Wooldridge, Bruce Alan 1939- *St&PR 91*
Wooldridge, Dean Everett 1913- *WhoAm 90*
Wooldridge, Ewart *BioIn 16*
Wooldridge, George John 1936- *St&PR 91*
Wooldridge, James Walter, Jr. *BiDrAPA 89*
Wooldridge, Jane 1958- *WhoAmW 91*
Wooldridge, John R. 1939- *St&PR 91*
Wooldridge, Rhode 1906- *AuBYP 90*
Wooldridge, Sandra Sue 1946- *WhoSSW 91*
Wooldridge, Susan *ConTFT 8 [port]*
Wooldridge, Thomas Wright 1949- *WhoSSW 91*
Woolery, George William 1931- *WhoWrEP 89*
Woolever, Naomi Louise 1922- *WhoAm 90, WhoAmW 91, WhoWrEP 89*
Wooley, Bruce Allen 1943- *WhoAm 90*
Wooley, Donald Alan 1926- *WhoAm 90*
Wooley, John P. 1928- *St&PR 91*
Wooley, Kenneth Virgil 1938- *WhoWor 91*
Wooley, Richard Earl 1965- *WhoE 91*
Woolf, Barbara S *BiDrAPA 89*
Woolf, Brian Patrick 1943- *St&PR 91, WhoAm 90*
Woolf, F. X. *TwCCr&M 91*
Woolf, Geoff *BioIn 16*
Woolf, Harry 1923- *WhoAm 90*
Woolf, Jack 1936- *St&PR 91*
Woolf, Jack J. 1933- *St&PR 91*
Woolf, James Tennyson 1933- *St&PR 91*
Woolf, Larry J. 1944- *WhoAm 90*
Woolf, Leonard 1880-1969 *BioIn 16, DcLB 100 [port]*
Woolf, Nancy Slater *BiDrAPA 89*
Woolf, Robert Leslie 1929- *St&PR 91*
Woolf, Robert W. 1942- *St&PR 91*
Woolf, Ronald Alan 1862- *WhoSSW 91*
Woolf, Samuel J 1880-1948 *WhoAmA 91N*
Woolf, Sheldon M. 1932- *St&PR 91*
Woolf, Virginia 1882-1941 *BioIn 16, ConAu 130, DcLB 100 [port], FemiCLE, MajTwCW, ShSCr 7 [port], WorAlBi, WrPh*
Woolf, William B. 1927- *St&PR 91*
Woolf, William Blauvelt 1932- *WhoAm 90*
Woolfenden, Guy Anthony 1937- *IntWWM 90*
Woolfenden, Milton, Jr. 1925- *WhoAm 90*
Woolfenden, William Edward 1918- *WhoAm 90, WhoAmA 91*
Woolford, Delia Osborne 1931- *IntWWM 90*
Woolford, John R. 1934- *St&PR 91*
Woolfson, William C. *BioIn 16*
Woolheater, Robert Leroy 1930- *St&PR 91, WhoAm 90*
Woollacott, Robert A. 1949- *St&PR 91*
Woollam, Kenneth Geoffrey 1937- *IntWWM 90*
Woollams, Henry *PenDiDA 89*
Woollams, Stanley J 1932- *BiDrAPA 89*
Woollams, William *PenDiDA 89*
Woollams, William 1782-1840 *PenDiDA 89*
Woollcott, Alexander 1887-1943 *BioIn 16, WorAlBi*
Woollcott, Philip, Jr. 1928- *BiDrAPA 89*
Woolley, Alma Schelle 1931- *WhoAm 90*
Woolley, Barbara Ellen 1951- *WhoAmW 91*
Woolley, Catherine 1904- *AuBYP 90, WhoAm 90, WhoAmW 91*
Woolley, Dennis Robert 1940- *St&PR 91*
Woolley, Donald Eugene 1922- *WhoE 91*
Woolley, Donna P. 1926- *St&PR 91*
Woolley, Edward Timothy Starbuck 1942- *WhoWor 91*
Woolley, George Walter 1904- *WhoAm 90*
Woolley, Jonathan Michael 1958- *WhoE 91*
Woolley, Kenneth Frank 1933- *WhoWor 91*
Woolley, Margaret Anne 1946- *WhoAmW 91*
Woolley, Mary 1630-1710 *BiDEWW*
Woolley, Mary Elizabeth 1947- *WhoAm 90*
Woolley, Mary Emma 1863-1947 *BioAmW*
Woolley, Robert *BioIn 16*
Woolley, Robert Barkley 1952- *BiDrAPA 89*
Woolley, Samuel H. 1909- *St&PR 91*
Woolley, Steven E. 1943- *WhoE 91*
Woolls, Esther Blanche 1935- *WhoAm 90*
Woolman, Ann *ODwPR 91*
Woolman, John 1720-1772 *EncCRAm, WhNaAH*
Woolman, Maurice John 1953- *WhoEmL 91*
Woolman, Michael Louis 1944- *St&PR 91*
Woolman, Morris 1918- *St&PR 91*
Woolnough, James Porter 1934- *St&PR 91*
Woolpert, Laura Diane 1960- *WhoAmW 91, WhoWor 91*
Woolpert, Mary Elizabeth 1926- *St&PR 91*
Woolrich, Cornell 1903-1968 *BioIn 16, TwCCr&M 91*

Wortley, Thomas C. 1931- St&PR 91
Wortman, Alex BioIn 16
Wortman, Denys 1886-1958 WhoAmA 91N
Wortman, Denys 1887-1958 EncACom
Wortman, Gisela Laufer BiDrAPA 89
Wortman, Richard N BiDrAPA 89
Wortman, Richard S. 1938- WhoAm 90
Wortman, Victor D. ODwPR 91
Worton, Geoffrey Peter 1947- WhoE 91
Worton-Steward, Andrew 1948- IntWWM 90
Wortz, Melinda Farris 1940- WhoAmA 91
Wortzel, Adrianne 1941- WhoAmA 91
Wortzel, Lawrence Herbert 1932- WhoAm 90, WhoE 91
Wortzel, Murray N. 1923- WhoE 91, WhoWor 91
Wortzelius, Fredrik Inge 1951- IntWWM 90
Worzel, John Lamar 1919- WhoAm 90
Wos, Carol Elaine 1957- WhoAmW 91
Wos, Susan Marie 1955- WhoAmW 91
Wosgien, Bernd Klaus-Peter 1939- WhoSSW 91
Woskow, Marvin Z. 1929- St&PR 91
Woskow, Marvin Zane 1929- WhoAm 90
Wosmek, Frances 1917- AuBYP 90
Woss, Kurt 1914-1978 PenDiMP
Wostrel, Nancy J WhoAmA 91
Wothers, Deborah Lois BiDrAPA 89
Wotiz, Herbert Henry 1922- WhoAm 90
Wotiz, John Henry 1919- WhoAm 90
Wotman, Stephen 1931- WhoAm 90
Wou, Leo S. 1927- WhoAm 90
Wou, Tia BioIn 16
Woudhuysen, Lewis 1912-1985 ConDes 90
Woudstra, Frank Robert WhoAm 90
Woudstra, Frank Robert 1945- St&PR 91
Wouk, Herman 1915- ConAu 33NR, MajTwCW, WhoAm 90, WhoWor 91, WhoWrEP 89, WorAlBi
Woulf, James A. 1935- St&PR 91
Woundy, Douglas Stanley 1939- WhoSSW 91
Wouters, Freerk W BiDrAPA 89
Wouters, Joyce ODwPR 91
Wouters, Labora M BiDrAPA 89
Wouters, Liliane 1930- EncCoWW
Wovoka 1856?-1932 WhNaAH
Wowtschuk, Walter 1924- St&PR 91
Woy, Frank Van 1930- St&PR 91
Woycehoski, Thomas L. St&PR 91
Woyczynski, Wojbor Andrzej 1943- WhoAm 90
Woyski, Margaret Skillman 1921- WhoAmW 91
Woytassek, Leonard Erwin BiDrAPA 89
Woytek, David G. 1944- St&PR 91
Woythal, Constance Lee 1954- WhoAmW 91
Wozencraft, Kim BioIn 16
Woznak, George Brian 1949- WhoEmL 91
Wozniak, Albert James 1938- St&PR 91
Wozniak, David Frank 1950- WhoE 91
Wozniak, Debra Gail 1954- WhoAmW 91
Wozniak, Donald Albert 1933- St&PR 91
Wozniak, Joyce Marie 1955- WhoAmW 91
Wozniak, Stephen BioIn 16
Woznicki, Robert Michael BiDrAPA 89
Woznicki-Likavec, Marie Elaine 1952- WhoWrEP 89
Wozny, Joseph Edward 1951- St&PR 91
Wraase, Dennis Richard 1944- St&PR 91, WhoAm 90
Wrabel, Joseph John 1939- St&PR 91
Wraga, William G. 1957- WhoE 91
Wragg, Joanna DiCarlo 1941- WhoAmW 91
Wragg, Laishley Palmer, Jr. 1933- WhoAm 90, WhoE 91, WhoWor 91
Wragg, Otis, III 1939- ODwPR 91
Wragg, S. R. BioIn 16
Wragge, Connie Gail 1947- WhoE 91
Wrancher, Elizabeth Ann 1930- WhoSSW 91
Wrangel, Ferdinand, Baron Von 1797-1870 WorAlBi
Wrangel, Peter 1878-1928 WorAlBi
Wrangel, Pytor Nikolayevich 1878-1928 BioIn 16
Wranglen, Karl Gustaf 1923- WhoWor 91
Wrape, Eric Wayne 1959- WhoSSW 91
Wrather, Christopher Covington 1952- St&PR 91
Wratten, Ian Denis BioIn 16
Wratten, Richard W. 1938- St&PR 91
Wray, Bettye K. 1926- BioIn 16
Wray, Cecil, Jr. 1934- WhoAm 90
Wray, Charles W. 1919- St&PR 91
Wray, Charles Williamson, Jr. 1933- WhoAm 90
Wray, Dick 1933- WhoAmA 91
Wray, Edwin BioIn 16
Wray, Edwin Newton 1917- St&PR 91
Wray, Fay 1907- BioIn 16, ConTFT 8, WorAlBi
Wray, Frank Junior 1921- WhoAm 90
Wray, Gilbert Andrew 1940- WhoE 91
Wray, J. Edward 1874-1961 Ballpl 90
Wray, Janet Genevra 1935- WhoAmW 91
Wray, Karl 1913- WhoAm 90, WhoWor 91
Wray, Marc F. BioIn 16
Wray, Marc Frederick WhoAm 90
Wray, Marc Frederick 1932- St&PR 91
Wray, Margaret Masle WhoAmA 91N
Wray, Newton BioIn 16
Wray, Robert H 1939- BiDrAPA 89
Wray, Robert L. 1925- St&PR 91
Wray, Ronald Edmonds 1949- WhoWrEP 89
Wreaks, Charles Fitzwilliam 1963- WhoWor 91
Wrede, Barbara 1931- WhoWrEP 89
Wrede, Harold Franz 1939- St&PR 91
Wrede, Patricia Collins 1953- WhoWrEP 89
Wrede, Rabbe Kenneth 1944- WhoWor 91
Wrede, Stuart 1944- BioIn 16
Wrede, Stuart Henrik 1944- WhoAm 90
Wreden, Nicholas Roman, III 1953- WhoEmL 91
Wreford, David Mathews 1943- WhoAm 90
Wreford, Debra Renee 1955- WhoAmW 91
Wreford, James ConAu 132
Wrege, Beth Marie 1954- WhoWrEP 89
Wrege, Charles Deck 1924- WhoE 91
Wrege, Julia Bouchelle 1944- WhoAmW 91
Wreggit, John David 1940- BiDrAPA 89
Wren, Christopher 1632-1723 WorAlBi
Wren, Colin Ward 1943- St&PR 91
Wren, Dahlia Allen 1942- WhoSSW 91
Wren, Frances J BiDrAPA 89
Wren, Harold Gwyn 1921- WhoAm 90
Wren, Jill Robinson 1954- WhoWrEP 89
Wren, Joe Richard 1944- WhoSSW 91
Wren, Paul Ingraham 1906- WhoAm 90
Wren, Rosemary BioIn 16
Wren, T.W. St&PR 91
Wren, Thomas Wayne 1922- WhoAm 90
Wren, William C. St&PR 91
Wren, William C. 1944- ODwPR 91
Wren, William Marcel 1906- WhoSSW 91
Wrenick, Rudy E., Jr. 1944- St&PR 91
Wrenn, James Joseph 1926- WhoAm 90
Wrenn, Richard Barry 1944- St&PR 91
Wrenn, Robert B. 1927- St&PR 91
Wrenn, Thomas G. 1944- St&PR 91
Wrenn, Tony Pentecost 1933- WhoE 91
Wrenn, William James, Jr. 1932- WhoSSW 91
Wrensch, Dana Louise 1946- WhoAmW 91
Wresinski, Margot Bloch- BioIn 16
Wretlind, Karl Arvid Johannes 1919- WhoWor 91
Wride, Anh Thu 1955- WhoAmW 91
Wriedt, Etta 1859?-1942 EncO&P 3, EncPaPR 91
Wright Brothers BioIn 16
Wright, A. D. 1947- ConAu 129
Wright, A. J., III 1952- WhoWrEP 89
Wright, Albert Jay, III 1927- WhoE 91
Wright, Alfred George James 1916- WhoAm 90, WhoWor 91
Wright, Alice L 1933- BiDrAPA 89
Wright, Alice Morgan 1881-1975 BiDWomA
Wright, Allen 1825-1885 WhNaAH
Wright, Allen Ted, Sr. 1937- WhoSSW 91
Wright, Alonzo 1821-1894 DcCanB 12
Wright, Amy BioIn 16
Wright, Andrew 1923- WhoAm 90
Wright, Anita St&PR 91
Wright, Ann Follinger 1927- WhoAmW 91
Wright, Ann Misty 1961- WhoSSW 91
Wright, Arthur Dotson 1944- WhoSSW 91
Wright, Arthur E., Jr. 1919- ODwPR 91
Wright, Arthur Frederick 1913-1976 ConAu 33NR
Wright, Arthur M. 1930- St&PR 91
Wright, Austin M. 1922- WhoWrEP 89
Wright, Barbara Brown 1946- WhoAmW 91
Wright, Barbara Evelyn 1926- WhoAmW 91
Wright, Barbara J. 1956- WhoAmW 91
Wright, Barbara S. Marks BioIn 16
Wright, Barton Allen 1920- WhoAmA 91
Wright, Basil 1907-1987 BioIn 16
Wright, Benjamin Drake 1926- WhoAm 90
Wright, Bernard 1938- WhoAmA 91
Wright, Betty Ren AuBYP 90, BioIn 16
Wright, Betty Ren 1927- SmATA 63
Wright, Beverly L. St&PR 91
Wright, Bill Ballpl 90
Wright, Bill Acton 1923- WhoAm 90
Wright, Blair Lanston 1958- WhoSSW 91
Wright, Bobbie Jean 1933- WhoAmW 91, WhoSSW 91
Wright, Brian James 1946- IntWWM 90
Wright, Bruce 1918- BioIn 16
Wright, Bruce A BiDrAPA 89
Wright, Bruce A. 1962- WhoE 91
Wright, Byron T. 1917- WhoAm 90
Wright, C. D. 1949- WhoWrEP 89
Wright, C. Lamar 1940- St&PR 91
Wright, Caleb Merrill 1908- WhoAm 90
Wright, Calvin Persinger 1928- WhoSSW 91
Wright, Calvin Ray, Jr. 1958- WhoSSW 91
Wright, Carole Yvonne 1932- WhoAmW 91, WhoWor 91
Wright, Catharine Morris 1899-1988 WhoAmA 91N
Wright, Cecil A. 1904-1967 BioIn 16
Wright, Cecil M. 1942- St&PR 91
Wright, Celeste Turner 1906- WhoWrEP 89
Wright, Charles 1935- BioIn 16, MajTwCW
Wright, Charles, III 1916- St&PR 91
Wright, Charles Alan 1927- WhoAm 90, WhoWor 91
Wright, Charles Conrad 1917- WhoAm 90
Wright, Charles D 1950- BiDrAPA 89
Wright, Charles Edward 1906- WhoAm 90
Wright, Charles Penzel, Jr. 1935- WhoAm 90, WhoWrEP 89
Wright, Charles Richard 1941- WhoAm 90
Wright, Charlotte Hughes 1939- WhoWrEP 89
Wright, Chatt Grandison 1941- WhoAm 90
Wright, Christopher BioIn 16
Wright, Christopher George 1954- IntWWM 90
Wright, Clare BioIn 16
Wright, Clarence 1878-1930 Ballpl 90
Wright, Clark Phillips 1942- WhoSSW 91
Wright, Claude Holtman 1946- St&PR 91
Wright, Clifford 1919- WhoAmA 91
Wright, Clyde 1941- Ballpl 90
Wright, Colin 1936- WhoAm 90
Wright, Colin M. 1945- WhoSSW 91
Wright, Curtiss B BiDrAPA 89
Wright, Daniel 1931- WhoSSW 91
Wright, Dare 1926?- AuBYP 90
Wright, David 1920- BioIn 16
Wright, David A. 1933- St&PR 91
Wright, David Arthur 1934- IntWWM 90
Wright, David B. 1933- St&PR 91
Wright, David Burton 1933- WhoAm 90
Wright, David George 1931- WhoAm 90
Wright, David L. 1949- WhoAm 90
Wright, David Lee 1949- St&PR 91
Wright, David Mahan 1955- WhoSSW 91
Wright, David Morris 1931- St&PR 91
Wright, David Thomas 1947- WhoAmA 91
Wright, Dean Greg 1954- St&PR 91
Wright, Deil Spencer 1930- WhoAm 90
Wright, Dexter Russell 1821-1886 AmLegL
Wright, Diana Louise 1946- WhoAmW 91
Wright, Dianne Chandler 1944- WhoSSW 91
Wright, Dianne Hamby 1941- WhoAmW 91, WhoSSW 91
Wright, Dixie Lee 1953- WhoSSW 91
Wright, Don C. 1934- WhoAm 90
Wright, Don G. 1942- St&PR 91
Wright, Donald C. 1931- St&PR 91
Wright, Donald Eugene 1930- WhoAm 90
Wright, Donald F. 1940-1989 BioIn 16
Wright, Donald Franklin 1934- BioIn 16, WhoAm 90
Wright, Donald Gene 1938- WhoSSW 91
Wright, Donald Ian 1934- WhoWor 91
Wright, Donald Kenneth 1945- WhoSSW 91, WhoWor 91
Wright, Donald Kenneth 1951- WhoSSW 91
Wright, Donovan G 1913- BiDrAPA 89
Wright, Douglas Chandler, Jr. 1934- WhoAm 90
Wright, Douglas Tyndall 1927- WhoAm 90
Wright, Douglass Brownell 1912- WhoAm 90
Wright, Early BioIn 16
Wright, Ed 1827-1895 AmLegL
Wright, Ed 1919- Ballpl 90
Wright, Edith Sanders 1933- WhoSSW 91
Wright, Edred John 1911- IntWWM 90
Wright, Edward 1912-1988 BioIn 16
Wright, Edward Benton, Jr. 1938- WhoWrEP 89
Wright, Edward Galbraith 1948- St&PR 91
Wright, Edward Reynolds 1931-1988 BioIn 16
Wright, Eldon Edward 1930- St&PR 91
Wright, Eleanor Straub 1923- WhoAmW 91
Wright, Eleanore R 1915- BiDrAPA 89
Wright, Elisabeth Nancy BiDrAPA 89
Wright, Elizur 1804-1885 BioIn 16
Wright, Ellen Marie 1953- WhoWrEP 89
Wright, Enid Meadowcroft AuBYP 90
Wright, Eric 1929- ConAu 132, TwCCr&M 91
Wright, Erma Naomi 1930- WhoAmW 91
Wright, Ernest Marshall 1940- WhoAm 90
Wright, Eugene Allen 1913- WhoAm 90
Wright, Faith-Dorian 1934- WhoAmA 91, WhoAmW 91
Wright, Fanny Amelia 1813?-1891 DcCanB 12
Wright, Farrin Scott 1936- WhoSSW 91
Wright, Felix E. 1935- WhoAm 90
Wright, Flavel Allen 1913- WhoAm 90
Wright, Frances 1795-1852 BioIn 16, FemiCLE, WorAlBi
Wright, Frances 1897- AuBYP 90
Wright, Frances Jane 1943- WhoAmW 91
Wright, Frances Woodworth 1897-1989 BioIn 16
Wright, Francis McGill 1928- BiDrAPA 89
Wright, Frank 1932- WhoAmA 91
Wright, Frank Gardner 1931- WhoAm 90
Wright, Frank Lloyd EncJap
Wright, Frank Lloyd 1867-1959 BioIn 16, PenDiDA 89, WorAlBi
Wright, Frank Lloyd 1869?-1959 ModArCr 1 [port]
Wright, Fred 1907-1984 EncAL
Wright, Frederic A. 1935- St&PR 91
Wright, Frederick Arthur, Jr. 1936- St&PR 91
Wright, G Alan 1927- WhoAmA 91N
Wright, Gail Blake 1943- WhoSSW 91
Wright, Gary Alan 1950- WhoAm 90
Wright, Gary C. 1950- St&PR 91
Wright, Geoffrey John Bradford 1912- IntWWM 90
Wright, George 1803-1865 BioIn 16
Wright, George 1847-1937 Ballpl 90 [port]
Wright, George 1958- Ballpl 90
Wright, George Frederick 1838-1921 BioIn 16
Wright, George Hand 1872-1951 WhoAmA 91N
Wright, George Thaddeus 1925- WhoAm 90
Wright, George Washington 1816-1885 BioIn 16
Wright, Gerald F. BioIn 16
Wright, Gladys Stone 1925- WhoAmW 91
Wright, Glenn 1901-1984 Ballpl 90
Wright, Glenn E BiDrAPA 89
Wright, Glenn Eugene 1914- WhoAm 90
Wright, Gordon BioIn 16
Wright, Gordon 1912- WhoAm 90
Wright, Gordon Brooks 1934- IntWWM 90, WhoAm 90
Wright, Gordon Kennedy 1920- WhoAm 90
Wright, Gordon Lee 1942- St&PR 91
Wright, Gordon Pribyl 1938- WhoAm 90
Wright, Gustavus Blinn 1830-1898 DcCanB 12
Wright, Guy Darrell 1922- WhoAm 90
Wright, Gwendolyn 1946- WhoAm 90
Wright, H. Dudley 1921- St&PR 91
Wright, H Norman 1937- ConAu 32NR
Wright, Hardy WhoWrEP 89
Wright, Harlan Tonie 1941- WhoSSW 91
Wright, Harold David 1942- WhoAmA 91
Wright, Harold Madison WhoAm 90
Wright, Harold S 1914- BiDrAPA 89
Wright, Harold Samuel 1914- WhoE 91
Wright, Harrison Morris 1928- WhoAm 90
Wright, Harrold Eugene 1924- WhoSSW 91
Wright, Harry 1835-1895 Ballpl 90 [port]
Wright, Harry, III 1925- WhoAm 90
Wright, Harry D. 1932- St&PR 91
Wright, Harry Forrest, Jr. 1931- WhoAm 90
Wright, Harry H BiDrAPA 89
Wright, Harry Hercules 1948- WhoEmL 91, WhoSSW 91
Wright, Hastings Kemper 1928- WhoAm 90
Wright, Helen 1914- WhoAm 90
Wright, Helen Kennedy 1927- WhoAmW 91, WhoWor 91
Wright, Helen Patton 1919- WhoAm 90, WhoWor 91
Wright, Helena Rosa 1887-1982 DcNaB 1981
Wright, Helene Segal 1955- WhoAmW 91, WhoEmL 91
Wright, Herbert Edgar, Jr. 1917- WhoAm 90
Wright, Howard E. AmLegL
Wright, Howard Walter, Jr. 1922- St&PR 91
Wright, Hugh Elliott, Jr. 1937- WhoAm 90, WhoWrEP 89
Wright, Irving Sherwood 1901- WhoAm 90
Wright, J.A., Jr. 1916- St&PR 91
Wright, J. Skelly 1911-1988 BioIn 16
Wright, Jackson Atchison 1918- WhoAm 90
Wright, James 1927-1980 MajTwCW

Wright, James Arlington 1927-1980 *BioIn 16*
Wright, James Bowers 1950- *WhoWrEP 89*
Wright, James C., Jr. 1922- *WhoAm 90, WhoSSW 91, WhoWor 91, WorAlBi*
Wright, James Carter 1924- *WhoSSW 91*
Wright, James Claud 1942- *WhoSSW 91*
Wright, James Claude 1922- *BioIn 16*
Wright, James David 1947- *WhoAm 90*
Wright, James Dorsey 1944- *WhoAm 90*
Wright, James Edward 1921- *WhoAm 90*
Wright, James Hendon 1931- *WhoAm 90*
Wright, James Houston 1954- *WhoSSW 91*
Wright, James J 1935- *BiDrAPA 89*
Wright, James O. 1921- *St&PR 91*
Wright, James Richard 1934- *WhoSSW 91*
Wright, James Robert 1950- *BiDrAPA 89*
Wright, James Roscoe 1922- *WhoAm 90*
Wright, James S *BiDrAPA 89*
Wright, James Skelly *BioIn 16*
Wright, Jane Cooke 1919- *WhoAm 90*
Wright, Janet H. 1936- *WhoAmW 91, WhoWor 91*
Wright, Janet Lynne 1963- *WhoAmW 91*
Wright, Jean S 1922- *BiDrAPA 89*
Wright, Jeanette Tornow 1927- *WhoAm 90*
Wright, Jeanne Elizabeth Jason 1934- *WhoAm 90, WhoAmW 91, WhoE 91, WhoWrEP 89*
Wright, Jeffrey Joseph 1951- *WhoSSW 91*
Wright, Jerry R. 1935- *St&PR 91*
Wright, Jerry Raymond 1935- *WhoAm 90*
Wright, Jesse Graham, Jr 1939- *WhoAmA 91*
Wright, Jim *BioIn 16*
Wright, Jim 1922- *BioIn 16*
Wright, Jim 1950- *Ballpl 90*
Wright, Joe *NewYTBS 90 [port]*
Wright, John 1941- *WhoAm 90*
Wright, John C. 1925- *St&PR 91*
Wright, John Charles 1951- *St&PR 91*
Wright, John Charles Young 1925- *WhoAm 90, WhoSSW 91*
Wright, John Collins 1927- *WhoAm 90*
Wright, John Emerson 1937- *WhoAm 90*
Wright, John George 1923- *St&PR 91*
Wright, John L. 1937- *ConAu 131*
Wright, John M. 1916- *BioIn 16*
Wright, John M. 1930- *St&PR 91*
Wright, John MacNair, Jr. 1916- *WhoAm 90*
Wright, John Michael 1617?-1694? *BioIn 16*
Wright, John Pardee 1957- *WhoE 91*
Wright, John Peale 1924- *WhoAm 90*
Wright, John Robert 1935- *WhoAm 90*
Wright, John Winthrop 1912- *St&PR 91*
Wright, Jonathan Clifford 1949- *St&PR 91*
Wright, Jonathan Courtney 1936- *WhoWor 91*
Wright, Joseph 1734-1797 *IntDcAA 90*
Wright, Joseph Albert 1810-1867 *BioIn 16*
Wright, Joseph Robert, Jr. 1938- *WhoAm 90, WhoWor 91*
Wright, Josephine L 1948- *BiDrAPA 89*
Wright, Josephine Rosa Beatrice 1942- *WhoAmW 91*
Wright, Joshua Butler 1877-1939 *BioIn 16*
Wright, Joyce Louise 1947- *WhoAmW 91*
Wright, Judith 1915- *ConAu 31NR, FemiCLE, MajTwCW*
Wright, Judith Margaret 1944- *WhoAm 90*
Wright, Judy Helm 1944- *WhoAmW 91*
Wright, Karen Marquerite 1964- *WhoAmW 91*
Wright, Katharine Miranda 1945- *WhoWrEP 89*
Wright, Katie Harper 1923- *WhoAmW 91*
Wright, Kay Morrow 1942- *WhoAmW 91*
Wright, Keith Melville 1940- *St&PR 91*
Wright, Keith Robert 1925- *St&PR 91*
Wright, Ken 1946- *Ballpl 90*
Wright, Kenneth *AuBYP 90, MajTwCW*
Wright, Kenneth Brooks 1934- *WhoAm 90*
Wright, Kenneth E. 1952- *WhoSSW 91*
Wright, Kenneth Lyle 1926- *WhoWor 91*
Wright, Kenneth Osborne 1911- *WhoAm 90*
Wright, Kieth Carter 1933- *WhoAm 90*
Wright, L Alan 1937- *BiDrAPA 89*
Wright, L Hart 1917-1983 *ConAu 32NR*
Wright, L R 1939- *TwCCr&M 91*
Wright, Lance S 1923- *BiDrAPA 89*
Wright, Lanita S *BiDrAPA 89*
Wright, Larry 1935- *St&PR 91*
Wright, Larry 1940- *EncACom*
Wright, Laurali 1939- *FemiCLE*
Wright, Laurali R. 1939- *WhoAmW 91*
Wright, Laurence Sedgwick, II 1935- *St&PR 91*
Wright, Lawrence A. 1927- *WhoAm 90*
Wright, Lawrence Alan 1937- *WhoE 91*
Wright, Lawrence Dean 1940- *WhoAm 90*
Wright, Lee *BioIn 16*
Wright, Leslie Jean Erway 1947- *WhoE 91*
Wright, Lewis Jones 1927- *St&PR 91*
Wright, Leyton L. 1937- *St&PR 91*
Wright, Lilyan Boyd 1920- *WhoAmW 91*
Wright, Linda *WhoSSW 91*
Wright, Linda Diane 1948- *WhoAmW 91*
Wright, Linda Jean 1949- *WhoAmW 91, WhoSSW 91, WhoWor 91*
Wright, Linsey Hardy 1928- *WhoWrEP 89*
Wright, Linus D. 1927- *WhoAm 90*
Wright, Lisa Marlene 1954- *WhoAmW 91*
Wright, Lloyd 1890-1978 *WhoAmA 91N*
Wright, Lloyd George 1922- *St&PR 91*
Wright, Lois Maxine 1923- *WhoWrEP 89*
Wright, Luke Edward 1846-1922 *BiDrUSE 89, BioIn 16*
Wright, M R *ConAu 131*
Wright, Machaelle Small 1945- *BioIn 16*
Wright, Margaret Taylor 1949- *WhoAmW 91*
Wright, Marie Anne 1953- *WhoAmW 91*
Wright, Mark Kemper 1955- *WhoEmL 91, WhoSSW 91, WhoWor 91*
Wright, Marshall 1926- *ODwPR 91, St&PR 91, WhoAm 90*
Wright, Mary *PenDiDA 89*
Wright, Mary Beth 1952- *WhoAmW 91*
Wright, Mary L. 1934- *WhoAmW 91*
Wright, Mary McKenzie 1945- *WhoAmW 91, WhoSSW 91*
Wright, Mary Ruth 1922- *WhoAmW 91*
Wright, Mary Van Lear 1956- *WhoAmW 91*
Wright, Max 1943- *ConTFT 8*
Wright, Mehetabel 1697?-1750 *FemiCLE*
Wright, Michael *ODwPR 91*
Wright, Michael Frank 1947- *WhoE 91*
Wright, Michael George 1939- *WhoAm 90*
Wright, Michael Gordon 1935- *WhoAm 90*
Wright, Michael W. 1938- *St&PR 91*
Wright, Michael William 1938- *WhoAm 90*
Wright, Michael William 1947- *St&PR 91*
Wright, Mickey 1935- *WorAlBi*
Wright, Mildred Whatley *AuBYP 90*
Wright, Milton 1920- *WhoAmA 91*
Wright, Minturn Tatum, III 1925- *WhoAm 90*
Wright, Morris H. 1913- *St&PR 91*
Wright, Myron Arnold 1911- *WhoAm 90*
Wright, N. Mark *St&PR 91*
Wright, Nancy Diane 1947- *WhoAmW 91*
Wright, Nancy Howell 1932- *WhoAmW 91, WhoE 91, WhoWor 91*
Wright, Nancy Means *WhoWrEP 89*
Wright, Nannie Bell 1934- *WhoAmW 91*
Wright, Nathalia 1913- *WhoWrEP 89*
Wright, Neil Richard 1946- *St&PR 91*
Wright, Nina Kaiden *BioIn 16*
Wright, Oliver 1921- *WhoAm 90*
Wright, Orville 1871-1948 *BioIn 16, WorAlBi*
Wright, Otis Clarence, Jr. 1940- *WhoE 91*
Wright, Patience 1725-1786 *BioAmW*
Wright, Patience Lovell 1725-1786 *EncCRAm*
Wright, Patricia 1931- *WhoAmW 91*
Wright, Patricia Ann *BiDrAPA 89*
Wright, Patricia Ann 1934- *St&PR 91*
Wright, Patricia D 1951- *BiDrAPA 89*
Wright, Patricia Dillin 1951- *WhoE 91*
Wright, Paul, Jr. 1911- *WhoAm 90*
Wright, Paul E. 1931- *WhoAm 90*
Wright, Paula Christine 1955- *WhoAmW 91*
Wright, Peggy Ann 1935- *WhoAmW 91*
Wright, Peter *BioIn 16*
Wright, Peter Michael 1954- *IntWWM 90*
Wright, Philip Lincoln 1914- *WhoAm 90*
Wright, Princa McManus 1931- *WhoSSW 91*
Wright, Raleigh Lewis 1931- *WhoSSW 91*
Wright, Ralph Roland, Jr. 1948- *WhoSSW 91*
Wright, Randolph Earle 1920- *WhoAm 90*
Wright, Rasty 1895-1948 *Ballpl 90*
Wright, Rayburn 1922-1990 *BioIn 16, NewYTBS 90*
Wright, Rayburn B. 1922-1990 *ConAu 131*
Wright, Raymond Robert 1934- *St&PR 91*
Wright, Richard 1908-1960 *Au&Arts 5 [port], BioIn 16, DcLB 102 [port], DrBlPA 90, EncAL, MajTwCW, WorAlBi, WrPh*
Wright, Richard 1909-1960 *EarBlAP*
Wright, Richard Donald 1936- *St&PR 91, WhoE 91, WhoWor 91*
Wright, Richard John 1951- *WhoAm 90*
Wright, Richard L. 1932- *St&PR 91*
Wright, Richard Lee 1951- *BiDrAPA 89*
Wright, Richard Newport, III 1932- *WhoAm 90*
Wright, Richardson L. 1820- *AmLegL*
Wright, Robert 1914- *OxCPMus*
Wright, Robert 1957- *ConAu 129*
Wright, Robert A 1900-1958 *WhoAmA 91N*
Wright, Robert Burroughs 1916- *WhoAm 90*
Wright, Robert C. 1943- *WhoAm 90, WhoE 91*
Wright, Robert Charles *BioIn 16*
Wright, Robert E. 1914- *St&PR 91*
Wright, Robert Earl, Jr. 1945- *WhoSSW 91*
Wright, Robert F. *WhoAm 90, WhoE 91*
Wright, Robert F. 1925- *St&PR 91*
Wright, Robert G 1927- *BiDrAPA 89*
Wright, Robert Joseph 1949- *WhoEmL 91*
Wright, Robert Lawrence 1931- *WhoE 91*
Wright, Robert Lee 1919- *WhoAm 90*
Wright, Robert Marlow 1956- *WhoEmL 91, WhoSSW 91*
Wright, Robert N. 1932- *St&PR 91*
Wright, Robert Stephen 1946- *WhoAm 90*
Wright, Robin *BioIn 16*
Wright, Robin 1948- *ConAu 131*
Wright, Rodger Lee 1944- *St&PR 91*
Wright, Rodney H. 1931- *WhoAm 90*
Wright, Roger Ellerton 1946- *St&PR 91*
Wright, Ron *BiDrAPA 89*
Wright, Ronald A. 1932- *WhoAm 90*
Wright, Ronald A. 1935- *St&PR 91*
Wright, Rosalie Muller 1942- *WhoAm 90, WhoAmW 91*
Wright, Rowland *TwCCr&M 91*
Wright, Russel 1904-1976 *ConDes 90, PenDiDA 89, WhoAmA 91N*
Wright, Russell D. 1946- *St&PR 91*
Wright, Samuel E *DrBlPA 90*
Wright, Samuel Howard 1946- *WhoAm 90*
Wright, Sara-Alyce Parson 1918- *WhoAm 90*
Wright, Sarah Bird 1933- *WhoAmW 91, WhoSSW 91*
Wright, Scott Olin 1923- *WhoAm 90*
Wright, Sewall 1889-1988 *BioIn 16*
Wright, Sharon L. 1945- *St&PR 91*
Wright, Stanley Marc 1911- *WhoAmA 91, WhoE 91*
Wright, Stephen 1922- *WhoWrEP 89*
Wright, Stephen C 1922- *BiDrAPA 89*
Wright, Stephen Gailord 1943- *WhoAm 90*
Wright, Stephen W. 1935- *St&PR 91*
Wright, Steven *BioIn 16*
Wright, Stuart Thurman 1948- *WhoEmL 91*
Wright, Susan Lockwood *BioIn 16*
Wright, Susan Lynne 1964- *WhoAmW 91*
Wright, Susan Webber 1948- *WhoAmW 91*
Wright, Susanna 1697-1784 *FemiCLE*
Wright, Sydney Thurman, Jr. 1946- *BiDrAPA 89*
Wright, Sylvia Hart 1936- *WhoE 91*
Wright, Taffy 1911-1981 *Ballpl 90*
Wright, Tamela Jean 1962- *WhoAmW 91*
Wright, Ted 1937- *WhoSSW 91*
Wright, Teresa 1918- *WorAlBi*
Wright, Terry Alan 1952- *WhoWrEP 89*
Wright, Theodore Paul, Jr. 1926- *WhoAm 90*
Wright, Thomas 1840?-1892 *BioIn 16*
Wright, Thomas Alden 1945- *WhoSSW 91*
Wright, Thomas David 1937- *WhoAm 90*
Wright, Thomas F. 1945- *St&PR 91*
Wright, Thomas H., Jr. 1918- *St&PR 91*
Wright, Thomas Henry 1904- *WhoAm 90*
Wright, Thomas James 1932- *St&PR 91*
Wright, Thomas Jon 1958- *WhoEmL 91, WhoSSW 91*
Wright, Thomas S 1924- *BiDrAPA 89*
Wright, Thomas William 1941- *WhoAm 90*
Wright, Thomas William Dunstan 1919- *WhoAm 90*
Wright, Timothy T. *St&PR 91*
Wright, Tom 1923- *Ballpl 90*
Wright, Tom Z. 1908- *WhoAm 90*
Wright, Vernon Orville 1920- *St&PR 91, WhoAm 90*
Wright, Victor R. 1945- *St&PR 91*
Wright, Wallace Mathias 1928- *WhoAm 90*
Wright, Wayne Kenneth 1944- *WhoSSW 91*
Wright, Wayne Paul 1936- *IntWWM 90*
Wright, Wilbur 1867-1912 *BioIn 16, WorAlBi*
Wright, Willard Huntington *TwCCr&M 91*
Wright, Willard Jurey 1914- *WhoAm 90*
Wright, William *BioIn 16*
Wright, William Bigelow 1924- *St&PR 91*
Wright, William Charles 1921- *St&PR 91*
Wright, William Cook 1939- *WhoE 91*
Wright, William E. 1938- *St&PR 91*
Wright, William Kirby, III 1960- *WhoSSW 91*
Wright, William M. 1947- *St&PR 91*
Wright, William Michael 1955- *WhoSSW 91*
Wright, William Michael, Jr. 1952- *WhoSSW 91*
Wright, William T, Jr. 1946- *BiDrAPA 89*
Wright, Willie L. *ODwPR 91*
Wright, Wilson 1948- *WhoSSW 91*
Wright, Yvonne Febres Cordero De *WhoHisp 91*
Wright, Yvonne Gibson 1921- *WhoAmW 91*
Wright, Zara *HarlReB*
Wright-Frierson, Virginia 1949- *BioIn 16*
Wright-Mescher, Pamela J 1954- *BiDrAPA 89*
Wright-Stevenson, Linda Mae 1948- *WhoE 91*
Wrighton, Mark S. 1949- *BioIn 16*
Wrighton, Mark Stephen 1949- *WhoAm 90, WhoE 91*
Wrightson, Clarence Monroe, Jr. 1950- *WhoE 91*
Wrightson, John Chaffe 1923- *St&PR 91*
Wrightson, Patricia 1921- *Au&Arts 5 [port], AuBYP 90*
Wrightstone, Russ 1893-1969 *Ballpl 90*
Wrigley, Chris 1947- *ConAu 129*
Wrigley, Donald E. *WhoAm 90, WhoSSW 91*
Wrigley, E A 1931- *ConAu 129*
Wrigley, Elizabeth Springer 1915- *WhoAmW 91, WhoWor 91*
Wrigley, P. K. 1894-1977 *WorAlBi*
Wrigley, Peter Francis Martyn 1939- *WhoWor 91*
Wrigley, Philip K. 1894-1977 *Ballpl 90*
Wrigley, Rick *BioIn 16*
Wrigley, Rick 1955- *WhoAmA 91*
Wrigley, Robert Alan 1951- *WhoWrEP 89*
Wrigley, William 1933- *St&PR 91, WhoAm 90*
Wrigley, William, Jr. 1861-1932 *WorAlBi*
Wrinch, Dorothy 1894-1976 *BioIn 16*
Wrinkle, John Newton 1929- *WhoSSW 91*
Wrist, Peter Ellis 1927- *St&PR 91, WhoAm 90*
Wriston, Barbara 1917- *WhoAm 90, WhoAmA 91*
Wriston, Kathryn Dineen *WhoAmW 91*
Wriston, Walter B. 1919- *EncABHB 7 [port], St&PR 91*
Wriston, Walter Bigelow 1919- *WhoAm 90*
Wrobbel, Patricia Ann 1959- *WhoAmW 91*
Wrobel, Donald Joseph 1938- *WhoAm 90*
Wrobel, Robert F. 1944- *St&PR 91*
Wrobel, Robert Franklin 1944- *WhoAm 90*
Wrobleski, Harry F *BiDrAPA 89*
Wrobleski, Jeanne Pauline 1942- *WhoAmW 91*
Wroblewski, Celeste J. *ODwPR 91*
Wroblewski, Celeste Judine *WhoAm 90*
Wroblewski, Kenneth J. 1958- *St&PR 91*
Wrobley, Ralph Gene 1935- *WhoAm 90*
Wroblowa, Halina Stefania 1925- *WhoAmW 91, WhoWor 91*
Wrolsen, Jean Losee 1920- *WhoWrEP 89*
Wrolstad, Merald Ernest 1923-1987 *BioIn 16*
Wrong Way Corrigan *BioIn 16*
Wrong, Colin B. 1927- *St&PR 91*
Wrong, Dennis Hume 1923- *BioIn 16, WhoAm 90*
Wronski, Craig Joseph *BiDrAPA 89*
Wroth, James Melvin 1929- *WhoAm 90*
Wroth, Lawrence Kinvin 1932- *WhoAm 90*
Wroth, Mary 1586?-1652? *BiDEWW*
Wroth, Mary 1587?-1651? *FemiCLE*
Wroth, Mary Sidney *BioIn 16*
Wrubel, Allie 1905-1973 *OxCPMus*
Wruble, Brian Frederick 1943- *WhoAm 90*
Wruck, Erich-Oskar 1928- *WhoSSW 91*
Wrves, Orestes G. 1951- *WhoHisp 91*
Wryde, Dogear *ConAu 30NR*
Wrye, John Cameron *BiDrAPA 89*
Wrzeszcz, Barbara Elaine 1958- *WhoE 91*
Wu Chao 625-705? *WomWR*
Wu Guanzhong 1919- *BioIn 16*
Wu Hou 625-705? *WomWR*
Wu Tso Tien 625-705? *WomWR*
Wu Xueqian 1922- *WhoWor 91*
Wu, Allison Meta 1958- *WhoAmW 91*
Wu, Anna Fang 1940- *WhoAmW 91*
Wu, Arlouine Goodjohn 1918- *IntWWM 90*
Wu, Arthur Hannan 1932- *WhoAm 90*
Wu, Carl Cherng-Miin 1938- *WhoE 91*
Wu, Chien Shiung 1913- *BioIn 16*
Wu, Ching-Mai 1947- *WhoWor 91*
Wu, Dao-Tsing 1933- *WhoE 91*
Wu, Feng-Shan 1945- *WhoWor 91*
Wu, Geraldine *BiDrAPA 89*
Wu, Harry Pao-Tung 1932- *WhoWor 91*
Wu, Haw Chyr *BiDrAPA 89*
Wu, Hsiu Kwang 1935- *WhoAm 90*
Wu, James Chen-Yuan 1931- *WhoAm 90*
Wu, Jin 1934- *WhoAm 90*
Wu, Jonathan Charnghau 1953- *WhoWor 91*
Wu, Joseph C *BiDrAPA 89*
Wu, Julian Juh-Ren 1935- *WhoSSW 91*
Wu, Katherine G 1956- *BiDrAPA 89*
Wu, Kathleen Johnson 1940- *WhoSSW 91*
Wu, Kuan-chung 1919- *BioIn 16*

Wu, Kung Chao 1922- *WhoWor 91*
Wu, L.P. 1934- *St&PR 91*
Wu, Lilian Shiao-Yen 1947- *WhoAmW 91*
Wu, Linda Yee Chau 1919- *WhoAmA 91*
Wu, Ming-yen 1939- *WhoWor 91*
Wu, Miranda Lai-Yeung 1954- *WhoWor 91*
Wu, Nan Faion 1943- *WhoAmW 91*
Wu, Nelson Ikon 1919- *WhoAm 90, WhoWor 91*
Wu, Po-Shun 1947- *WhoWor 91*
Wu, Ray Jui 1928- *WhoAm 90*
Wu, Shi Tsan 1933- *WhoSSW 91*
Wu, Shien-Ming 1924- *WhoAm 90*
Wu, Silas Hsiu-Liang 1929- *WhoAm 90*
Wu, Stephen S. 1922- *WhoE 91*
Wu, Tai Te 1935- *WhoAm 90*
Wu, Tai Tsun 1933- *WhoAm 90*
Wu, Teresita Go *BiDrAPA 89*
Wu, Theodore Wai 1936- *WhoAm 90*
Wu, Tse Cheng 1923- *WhoWor 91*
Wu, Tung 1940- *WhoAm 90*
Wu, Wai-on Thomas 1945- *WhoWor 91*
Wu, Wayne Wen-Yau 1935- *WhoAmA 91*
Wu, Wen Chuan 1931- *WhoWor 91*
Wu, William Lung-Shen 1921- *WhoWrEP 89*
Wu, Xiao-Lei Charley 1958- *WhoE 91*
Wu, Ying Chu Lin Susan 1932- *WhoAmW 91*
Wu, Yongshi 1927- *WhoWor 91*
Wu, Zuqiang 1927- *IntWWM 90*
Wubbels, Theo 1949- *WhoWor 91*
Wubbena, Jan Helmut 1947- *IntWWM 90*
Wubbena, Kurt Wilharm 1949- *WhoEmL 91*
Wubbenhorst, William H. 1928- *ODwPR 91*
Wuchenich, Allen Samuel 1939- *WhoE 91*
Wucherer, Ruth Marie 1948- *WhoWrEP 89*
Wuchiski, Walter A. 1945- *St&PR 91*
WuDunn, Sheryl 1959- *ConAu 132, WhoAm 90, WhoWor 91*
Wuensch, Bernhardt John 1933- *WhoAm 90*
Wuensche, Vernon Edgar 1945- *WhoSSW 91*
Wuenscher, David E. 1936- *St&PR 91*
Wuer Kaixi *BioIn 16*
Wuerfele, Alberta Irene 1918- *St&PR 91*
Wuerkaixi *BioIn 16*
Wuerl, Donald W. 1940- *WhoAm 90, WhoE 91*
Wuerpel, Edmund Henry 1886-1958 *WhoAmA 91N*
Wuertenbaecher, H.E., Jr. 1926- *St&PR 91*
Wuerthner, J.J., Jr. 1924- *St&PR 91*
Wuertz, John Paul *BiDrAPA 89*
Wuertz, Robert Eugene 1947- *WhoE 91*
Wuerzl, Eberhard 1915- *IntWWM 90*
Wuest, George W. 1925- *WhoAm 90*
Wuest, Ronald Jay *BiDrAPA 89*
Wueste, Ward W., Jr. 1937- *St&PR 91*
Wuesthoff, Hubert Ernest 1921- *BiDrAPA 89*
Wuestman, Tony 1933- *St&PR 91*
Wuethrich, Hugo 1927- *OxCCanT*
Wuetig, Joyce Linda 1938- *WhoAmW 91*
Wuhl, Charles M 1943- *BiDrAPA 89*
Wuhl, Charles Michael 1943- *WhoE 91, WhoWor 91*
Wuhl, Robert *BioIn 16*
Wuhrer, Friedrich 1900-1975 *PenDiMP*
Wuiet, Caroline 1766?-1835? *EncCoWW*
Wujciak, Sandra Criscuolo 1949- *WhoAmW 91, WhoE 91*
Wujcik, Theo *WhoAmA 91*
Wujek, Marianne Feltz 1959- *WhoAmW 91*
Wukasch, Doris Lucille Stork 1924- *WhoWor 91*
Wulach, Sandra Hicks 1946- *BiDrAPA 89*
Wulbern, John C. 1936- *St&PR 91*
Wulbern, John Cummins 1936- *WhoAm 90*
Wulbert, Daniel Eliot 1941- *WhoAm 90*
Wulf, Christoph 1944- *WhoWor 91*
Wulf, Jerold W. 1931- *St&PR 91*
Wulf, Melvin Lawrence 1927- *WhoAm 90*
Wulf, Sharon Ann 1954- *WhoAmW 91*
Wulf, William Allan 1939- *WhoE 91*
Wulfe, Carl E. 1932- *St&PR 91*
Wulfe, Jesse E. 1924- *St&PR 91*
Wulff, Geraldine Schepker 1947- *WhoAmW 91*
Wulff, John K. 1948- *St&PR 91*
Wulff, John Kenneth 1948- *WhoE 91*
Wulff, Robert King 1938- *St&PR 91*
Wulff, Roger LaVern 1940- *WhoE 91*
Wulfing, George A. 1925- *St&PR 91*
Wuliger, Ernest M. 1920- *WhoAm 90*
Wulkan, Barry Warren 1939- *WhoE 91*
Wullaert, Pierre 1926- *WhoWor 91*
Wullner, Franz 1832-1902 *PenDiMP*
Wullner, Ludwig 1858-1938 *PenDiMP*
Wulsin, Howard E 1926- *BiDrAPA 89*
Wulsin, Lawson Reed 1951- *BiDrAPA 89*
Wulstan, David 1937- *IntWWM 90*
Wunch, Karen Elizabeth 1953- *WhoAmW 91*
Wunder, Charles Alan 1933- *WhoSSW 91*
Wunder, Charles Cooper 1928- *WhoAm 90*
Wunder, Gene Carroll 1939- *WhoSSW 91*
Wunder, George 1912-1987 *EncACom*
Wunder, Gustave Frederick 1926- *St&PR 91*
Wunder, Haroldene Fowler 1944- *WhoAmW 91*
Wunder, Jean Baker 1934- *WhoAmW 91*
Wunder, Richard Paul 1923- *WhoAmA 91*
Wunderle, Ann Kathryn 1953- *WhoAmW 91*
Wunderle, Joseph Mackie, Jr. 1949- *WhoSSW 91*
Wunderle, Robert E. 1944- *WhoE 91*
Wunderlich, Alfred Leon 1939- *WhoAm 90*
Wunderlich, Bernhard 1931- *WhoAm 90, WhoSSW 91*
Wunderlich, Eileen *ODwPR 91*
Wunderlich, Frances Maria 1953- *WhoE 91*
Wunderlich, Fritz 1930-1966 *PenDiMP*
Wunderlich, Hermann *WhoAm 90, WhoE 91*
Wunderlich, P.K. *St&PR 91*
Wunderlich, Peggy Duke 1951- *St&PR 91*
Wunderlich, Ray C., Jr. 1929- *WhoWrEP 89*
Wunderlich, Rudolf G 1920- *WhoAmA 91*
Wunderlich, Susan Clay 1942- *WhoAmA 91*
Wunderlich, William Israel 1947- *St&PR 91*
Wunderman, Jan 1921- *WhoAmA 91*
Wunderman, Jan Darcourt 1921- *WhoE 91*
Wunderman, Lester 1920- *WhoAm 90*
Wundt, Wilhelm Max 1832-1920 *WorAlBi*
Wunnicke, Brooke 1918- *WhoAmW 91*
Wunsch, Carl Isaac 1941- *WhoAm 90*
Wunsch, Charles A 1920- *BiDrAPA 89*
Wunsch, James Stevenson 1946- *WhoAm 90*
Wunsch, Josephine 1914- *AuBYP 90, SmATA 64 [port]*
Wunsch, Kathryn Sutherland 1935- *WhoAmW 91*
Wunschel, Ronald Louis 1946- *St&PR 91*
Wunschel, Siegfried Hermann 1941- *WhoWor 91*
Wuolijoki, Hella 1886-1954 *DcScanL*
Wuolijoki, Hella Maria 1886-1954 *EncCoWW*
Wuori, Matti Ossian 1945- *WhoWor 91*
Wuorinen, Charles 1938- *IntWWM 90, PenDiMP A, WhoAm 90*
Wuorio, Eva-Lis *AuBYP 90*
Wurdeman, Lew Edward 1949- *WhoEmL 91*
Wurdemann, Helen *WhoAmA 91N*
Wurfel, Walter W. *ODwPR 91*
Wurgler, Niels Arne 1943- *IntWWM 90*
Wurlitzer, Rudolph 1831-1914 *WorAlBi*
Wurm, Marie 1860-1938 *PenDiMP*
Wurm, Theophil 1868-1953 *BioIn 16*
Wurman, Richard Saul 1935- *WhoAm 90*
Wurmbrand, Harry George 1938- *WhoAm 90*
Wurmfeld, Charles J. *BioIn 16*
Wurmfeld, Sanford 1942- *WhoAmA 91*
Wurmser, Leon 1931- *BiDrAPA 89*
Wursig, Bernd Gerhard 1948- *WhoAm 90, WhoSSW 91*
Wurst, Milan 1929- *WhoWor 91*
Wurst, Paul Henry 1959- *BiDrAPA 89*
Wurst, Robert Arthur 1922- *St&PR 91*
Wurster, Charles Frederick 1930- *WhoAm 90*
Wurster, Dale Erwin 1918- *WhoWor 91*
Wurster, Donald F. 1953- *St&PR 91*
Wurster, George R 1935- *BiDrAPA 89*
Wurster, James C. 1947- *St&PR 91*
Wurster, Lauren 1905- *St&PR 91*
Wurster, Michael 1940- *WhoWrEP 89*
Wurster, Ralph 1930- *WhoWrEP 89*
Wurster, Stephen Harry 1941- *WhoAm 90*
Wurtele, C. Angus 1934- *St&PR 91*
Wurtele, Christopher Angus 1934- *WhoAm 90*
Wurtele, Morton Gaither 1919- *WhoAm 90*
Wurth, Ignaz Joseph *PenDiDA 89*
Wurth, Ignaz Sebastian von 1746-1834 *PenDiDA 89*
Wurth, Joseph *PenDiDA 89*
Wurtman, Judith Joy 1937- *WhoAmW 91*
Wurtman, Richard Jay 1936- *WhoAm 90*
Wurts, John S. 1948- *St&PR 91*
Wurtz, James 1934- *St&PR 91*
Wurtz, Lyle Dean 1931- *St&PR 91*
Wurtz, Merryrose 1936- *St&PR 91, WhoAm 90, WhoAmW 91*
Wurtz, Robert Henry 1936- *WhoAm 90*
Wurtzburger, Janet E C 1908- *WhoAmA 91N*
Wurtzel, Alan Henry 1947- *St&PR 91, WhoE 91*
Wurtzel, Alan Leon 1933- *St&PR 91, WhoAm 90, WhoSSW 91*
Wurtzler, Stephen D. 1947- *St&PR 91*
Wurzbach, Natascha 1933- *WhoWor 91*
Wurzbacher, Terrie 1948- *WhoAmW 91*
Wurzberger, Bezalel 1945- *BiDrAPA 89, WhoE 91*
Wurzberger, Suzanne Alice Wells 1938- *WhoAmW 91*
Wurzburg, Reginald 1901- *St&PR 91*
Wurzburg, Richard 1934- *St&PR 91*
Wurzburg, Warren Seymour 1926- *St&PR 91*
Wurzburger, John 1945- *St&PR 91*
Wurzburger, Stuard A. 1907- *WhoSSW 91*
Wurzburger, Walter Samuel 1920- *WhoAm 90, WhoE 91, WhoWor 91*
Wurzel, Leonard 1918- *WhoAm 90*
Wurzel, Stephen Berke 1947- *St&PR 91, WhoAm 90*
Wurzer, Henry Kahl 1936- *WhoAm 90*
Wurzlow, Gayle Frances 1940- *BiDrAPA 89*
Wussler, Marilyn Theresa 1938- *WhoAmW 91*
Wussler, Robert Joseph 1936- *WhoAm 90*
Wussow, Roland D. 1942- *ODwPR 91*
Wust, Carl John 1928- *WhoSSW 91*
Wustrack, Paul Karl, Jr. 1943- *St&PR 91*
Wuthrich, Hans 1937- *IntWWM 90*
Wuthrich, Kurt 1938- *WhoWor 91*
Wuttke, Dieter 1929- *WhoWor 91*
Wutzler, Jerry A. 1937- *St&PR 91*
Wuzik, Martin 1954- *WhoWor 91*
Wyan, Anthony Joseph 1937- *WhoE 91*
Wyand, Anne Lewis 1943- *WhoAmW 91*
Wyandance 1600?-1659 *WhNaAH*
Wyandanch 1600?-1659 *WhNaAH*
Wyandt, Steven P. 1944- *St&PR 91*
Wyant, Clyde 1938- *St&PR 91*
Wyant, Clyde W., Jr. 1938- *WhoAm 90, WhoSSW 91*
Wyant, Gregory Erich 1956- *WhoSSW 91*
Wyant, Joseph Andrew 1949- *WhoEmL 91, WhoWor 91*
Wyant, Mary *BioIn 16*
Wyant, Mary Lynn *BiDrAPA 89*
Wyant, Rowena *BioIn 16*
Wyat, Hester *BiDEWW*
Wyatt, Alfred Dyonisius 1928- *IntWWM 90*
Wyatt, Bruce H. 1946- *St&PR 91*
Wyatt, Carl Van 1947- *WhoSSW 91*
Wyatt, Curtis E. 1929- *St&PR 91*
Wyatt, David Kent 1937- *WhoAm 90*
Wyatt, David M. 1948- *ConAu 132*
Wyatt, Dorothy Katharine Wolf 1947- *WhoE 91*
Wyatt, Edgar *AuBYP 90*
Wyatt, Edith Elizabeth 1914- *WhoAmW 91*
Wyatt, Edith Franklin 1873-1958 *FemiCLE*
Wyatt, Faricita Hall 1912- *WhoAmW 91, WhoWor 91*
Wyatt, Forest Kent 1934- *WhoAm 90*
Wyatt, Francis 1588-1644 *EncCRAm*
Wyatt, Geoffrey James 1943- *WhoWor 91*
Wyatt, George Millard 1929- *WhoSSW 91*
Wyatt, Geraldine 1907- *AuBYP 90*
Wyatt, Greg Alan 1949- *WhoAmA 91*
Wyatt, Huey Pierce 1933- *BiDrAPA 89*
Wyatt, Inzer B. *NewYTBS 90*
Wyatt, Inzer B. 1907-1990 *BioIn 16*
Wyatt, Isabel *AuBYP 90*
Wyatt, J. Allen 1945- *St&PR 91*
Wyatt, Jack Hoover 1929- *St&PR 91*
Wyatt, Jack Miller 1918- *St&PR 91*
Wyatt, James A. 1945- *St&PR 91*
Wyatt, James Frank, Jr. 1922- *WhoAm 90*
Wyatt, James Franklin 1934- *WhoAm 90*
Wyatt, James L. 1924- *St&PR 91*
Wyatt, James Luther 1924- *WhoAm 90*
Wyatt, Jane 1911- *WorAlBi*
Wyatt, Janice Barber 1947- *WhoAm 90*
Wyatt, Jeanine Moesser *WhoAmW 91*
Wyatt, Jenta Rae 1935- *WhoAmW 91*
Wyatt, Joan Portis 1931- *WhoAmW 91*
Wyatt, Joe Billy 1935- *WhoAm 90, WhoSSW 91, WhoWor 91*
Wyatt, John 1935- *Ballpl 90*
Wyatt, Joseph Lucian, Jr. 1924- *WhoAm 90*
Wyatt, Juanita Graham 1929- *WhoAmW 91*
Wyatt, Julie 1939- *WhoAmW 91*
Wyatt, Kathleen Ann 1951- *WhoAmW 91*
Wyatt, Kathryn Elizabeth Benton 1928- *WhoAmW 91, WhoSSW 91, WhoWor 91*
Wyatt, Leland Wayne 1942- *St&PR 91*
Wyatt, Lowry 1918- *St&PR 91*
Wyatt, M. Mildred *ODwPR 91*
Wyatt, Marsha Kapnicky 1956- *WhoAmW 91*
Wyatt, Marta Villalpando 1940- *WhoHisp 91*
Wyatt, Mary 1958- *ODwPR 91*
Wyatt, Mary Catherine 1958- *WhoAmW 91*
Wyatt, Mary Jean *ODwPR 91*
Wyatt, Michael A. 1932- *St&PR 91*
Wyatt, Morris Lucius, II 1947- *WhoSSW 91*
Wyatt, Oscar Sherman, Jr. *BioIn 16*
Wyatt, Oscar Sherman, Jr. 1924- *St&PR 91, WhoAm 90, WhoSSW 91*
Wyatt, Peter Edward 1950- *St&PR 91*
Wyatt, Phillipa Kathleen *WhoAmW 91, WhoWor 91*
Wyatt, Rachel 1929- *OxCCanT*
Wyatt, Raymond Michael 1946- *WhoSSW 91, WhoWor 91*
Wyatt, Richard Jed 1939- *BiDrAPA 89, WhoAm 90*
Wyatt, Robert Odell 1946- *WhoSSW 91*
Wyatt, Sandra Mitchell 1945- *St&PR 91*
Wyatt, W. Whitlow 1948- *St&PR 91*
Wyatt, Whit 1907- *Ballpl 90*
Wyatt, Wilson Watkins 1905- *WhoAm 90*
Wyatt-Brown, Bertram 1932- *WhoAm 90, WhoWrEP 89*
Wybierala, Alice Sophie 1939- *St&PR 91*
Wybierala, Richard Anthony 1932- *St&PR 91*
Wyble, George F. 1931- *St&PR 91*
Wyble, James Stanley 1925- *St&PR 91*
Wybran, Joseph *BioIn 16*
Wyche, Henry Blanchard 1914- *St&PR 91*
Wyche, Sam *BioIn 16*
Wyche, Samuel David 1945- *WhoAm 90*
Wyche, Samuel P, Jr. *BiDrAPA 89*
Wycherley, Ronald 1941-1983 *DcNaB 1981*
Wycherly, Margaret 1884-1956 *BioIn 16, NotWoAT*
Wychulis, Adam Robert 1935- *WhoWor 91*
Wyckoff, Alexander 1898- *WhoWor 91*
Wyckoff, DeWitte Campbell 1918- *WhoAm 90*
Wyckoff, Donald 1926-1989 *BioIn 16*
Wyckoff, Edward Lisk, Jr. 1934- *WhoAm 90*
Wyckoff, James M. 1918- *AuBYP 90*
Wyckoff, Jean Bratton 1932- *WhoAm 90*
Wyckoff, John 1892-1961 *Ballpl 90*
Wyckoff, Julie Ann 1952- *WhoWrEP 89*
Wyckoff, Linda S. 1948- *WhoAmW 91*
Wyckoff, Linda Sue 1948- *St&PR 91*
Wyckoff, Lorna Matheson 1949- *WhoSSW 91*
Wyckoff, Margo Gail 1941- *WhoAmW 91, WhoWor 91*
Wyckoff, Raymond W. 1923- *St&PR 91, WhoAm 90, WhoSSW 91*
Wyckoff, Richard Darrel, Sr. 1944- *WhoE 91*
Wyckoff, Richard Hunt 1933- *St&PR 91*
Wyckoff, Stuart M 1949- *BiDrAPA 89*
Wyckoff, Susan 1941- *WhoAmW 91*
Wyckoff, Sylvia Spencer 1915- *WhoAmA 91*
Wycliffe, John *BioIn 16*
Wycliffe, John 1320?-1384 *WorAlBi*
Wycoff, Charles Coleman 1918- *WhoWor 91*
Wycoff, Robert E. 1930- *WhoAm 90, WhoWor 91*
Wycoff, Robert Elmer 1930- *St&PR 91*
Wycoff, W.A. 1947- *St&PR 91*
Wycoff, Winfield Scott 1937- *WhoE 91*
Wyden, Ronald Lee 1949- *WhoAm 90*
Wydick, Richard Crews 1937- *WhoAm 90*
Wydler, Hans Ulrich 1923- *WhoE 91, WhoWor 91*
Wydman, Marcy R. 1958- *St&PR 91*
Wydman, Mary Witt 1925- *St&PR 91*
Wydra, Clement John 1935- *WhoSSW 91*
Wydra, Frank Thomas 1939- *WhoWrEP 89*
Wyer, James Ingersoll 1923- *WhoAm 90*
Wyer, Jean Conover 1950- *WhoE 91*
Wyer, John *BioIn 16*
Wyer, John 1909-1989 *AnObit 1989*
Wyer, William Clarke 1946- *WhoAm 90, WhoE 91*
Wyers, Charles H. *St&PR 91*
Wyeth, Andrew 1917- *BioIn 16, WhoAm 90, WorAlBi*
Wyeth, Andrew Newell 1917- *WhoAmA 91*
Wyeth, Buz *BioIn 16*
Wyeth, Henriette 1907- *WhoAmA 91*
Wyeth, James 1946- *WorAlBi*
Wyeth, James Browning 1946- *WhoAm 90, WhoAmA 91*
Wyeth, Marion Sims *BioIn 16*
Wyeth, N. C. 1882-1945 *WorAlBi*
Wyeth, Nathaniel C. *NewYTBS 90*
Wyeth, Willard Hiram 1924- *St&PR 91*
Wyetzner, Beatrice *ODwPR 91*
Wygal, Deborah Anne *WhoE 91*
Wygant, Foster Laurance 1920- *WhoAm 90*
Wygant, James Peter 1926- *WhoAm 90*

Wygnanski, Israel Jerzy 1935- *WhoAm 90*
Wyke, Robert James 1933- *St&PR 91*
Wyker, Judith Charach *BioIn 16*
Wyker, Robert 1935- *St&PR 91*
Wykes, Edmund Harold 1928- *St&PR 91, WhoAm 90*
Wykoff, Frank Champion 1942- *WhoAm 90*
Wyland, Robert *BioIn 16*
Wyld, Lionel Darcy 1925- *WhoE 91*
Wylde, Henry 1822-1890 *PenDiMP*
Wylde, Sam M. 1914- *St&PR 91*
Wylde, Sam Mayo, III 1951- *St&PR 91*
Wyle, Frank S. 1919- *St&PR 91*
Wyle, Frederick S. 1928- *WhoAm 90*
Wyler, Leopold S. 1922- *St&PR 91*
Wyler, Marjorie Goldwasser 1915- *WhoE 91*
Wyler, Michael Gabriel 1947- *WhoWor 91*
Wyler, Rose 1909- *AuBYP 90*
Wyler, Seymour B. *BioIn 16*
Wyler, William 1902-1981 *BioIn 16, WorAlBi*
Wylie, Albert Sidney 1924- *WhoAm 90*
Wylie, Andrew *BioIn 16*
Wylie, Betty Jane 1931- *BioIn 16, OxCCanT*
Wylie, Cathy Lynn 1964- *WhoAmW 91*
Wylie, Chalmers Pangburn 1920- *WhoAm 90*
Wylie, Clarence Raymond, Jr. 1911- *WhoAm 90*
Wylie, Elinor 1885-1928 *FemiCLE*
Wylie, Elinor Hoyt 1885-1928 *BioAmW*
Wylie, Evan Benjamin 1931- *WhoAm 90*
Wylie, Grace Scott 1925- *WhoAmW 91*
Wylie, Harold W, Jr. 1931- *BiDrAPA 89*
Wylie, Howard L *BiDrAPA 89*
Wylie, I. A. R. 1885-1959 *FemiCLE*
Wylie, James Vivian David 1937- *IntWWM 90*
Wylie, John, II 1953- *WhoSSW 91*
Wylie, John Voorhees 1941- *BiDrAPA 89*
Wylie, Kenneth Millar, Jr. 1927- *WhoWrEP 89*
Wylie, Laura *MajTwCW*
Wylie, Paul Edward *BiDrAPA 89*
Wylie, Philip *TwCCr&M 91*
Wylie, Philip Gordon 1902-1971 *SpyFic*
Wylie, Roger L. *St&PR 91*
Wylie, Russell L. 1936- *ODwPR 91*
Wylie, Ted David 1945- *WhoSSW 91*
Wyller, Arne August 1927- *WhoWor 91*
Wyllie, Alfred Linn 1949- *WhoSSW 91, WhoWor 91*
Wyllie, Edward 1848-1911 *EncO&P 3*
Wyllie, Peter John 1930- *WhoAm 90*
Wyllie, Stuart Sloan 1954- *St&PR 91*
Wyllys, Ronald Eugene 1930- *WhoAm 90*
Wyly, Charles J., Jr. 1933- *St&PR 91*
Wyly, James K *BiDrAPA 89*
Wyly, Robert Henry 1920- *St&PR 91*
Wyly, Sam E. 1934- *St&PR 91*
Wyman, Alan Duane 1949- *St&PR 91*
Wyman, Anne F. 1926- *St&PR 91*
Wyman, Bill *BioIn 16*
Wyman, David Sword 1929- *WhoAm 90, WhoE 91*
Wyman, Debra Jean 1952- *WhoWrEP 89*
Wyman, Donald Paul 1931- *St&PR 91*
Wyman, Douglas Philip 1955- *WhoWor 91*
Wyman, Franklin, Jr. 1921- *St&PR 91*
Wyman, Gail Trask 1957- *WhoSSW 91*
Wyman, Georgina 1946- *WhoAm 90*
Wyman, Hastings, Jr. 1939- *WhoE 91*
Wyman, Henry W. 1919- *St&PR 91*
Wyman, Henry Walter 1919- *WhoAm 90, WhoE 91*
Wyman, Herbert M 1935- *BiDrAPA 89*
Wyman, James T. 1920- *St&PR 91*
Wyman, James Thomas 1920- *WhoAm 90*
Wyman, James V. 1923- *St&PR 91*
Wyman, James Vernon 1923- *WhoAm 90*
Wyman, Jane *BioIn 16*
Wyman, Jane 1914- *BioAmW, WhoAm 90, WhoAmW 91, WorAlBi*
Wyman, Jeffrey Alan 1945- *WhoAm 90*
Wyman, Lance 1937- *ConDes 90*
Wyman, Leland Clifton 1897-1988 *BioIn 16*
Wyman, Lotte Ann Novak 1925- *WhoAmW 91*
Wyman, Louis Crosby 1917- *WhoAm 90*
Wyman, M. Richard 1928- *St&PR 91*
Wyman, Morton 1922- *St&PR 91*
Wyman, Paul Lindsey 1952- *BiDrAPA 89*
Wyman, Ralph M. 1926- *St&PR 91*
Wyman, Ralph Mark 1926- *WhoAm 90*
Wyman, Richard L. 1946- *WhoE 91*
Wyman, Richard Vaughn 1927- *St&PR 91, WhoAm 90*
Wyman, Robert *St&PR 91*
Wyman, Robert J. 1940- *WhoAm 90*
Wyman, Stanley Moore 1913- *WhoAm 90*
Wyman, Stephen Marc *BiDrAPA 89*
Wyman, Thomas Hunt 1929- *St&PR 91*
Wyman, William 1922-1980 *WhoAmA 91N*
Wyman, William George 1941- *WhoAm 90*
Wymark, Olwen 1929- *FemiCLE*
Wymer, Norman 1911- *AuBYP 90*
Wymes, Michael R 1954- *BiDrAPA 89*
Wymor, Larry L. 1936- *St&PR 91, WhoWor 91*
Wymore, Albert Wayne 1927- *WhoAm 90*
Wynar, Bohdan Stephen 1926- *WhoAm 90, WhoWrEP 89*
Wynar, Lubomyr R 1932- *ConAu 31NR*
Wynblatt, Paul Pinhas 1935- *WhoAm 90*
Wynbrandt, Gary David *BiDrAPA 89*
Wynbush, Octavia Beatrice 1894-1972? *HarlReB*
Wyncott, April Frances 1958- *WhoAmW 91*
Wyndaele, Jean Jacques 1949- *WhoWor 91*
Wynder, Ernst Ludwig 1922- *WhoAm 90*
Wyndham, Anne 1632-1698 *BiDEWW*
Wyndham, Charles 1837-1919 *BioIn 16*
Wyndham, Charles L. 1933- *St&PR 91*
Wyndham, Francis 1924- *ConAu 131*
Wyndham, Harald P. 1946- *WhoWrEP 89*
Wyndham, John 1903- *WorAlBi*
Wyndham, John 1903-1969 *RGTwCSF*
Wyndham, John S. 1915- *St&PR 91*
Wyndham, Lee 1912-1978 *AuBYP 90*
Wyndham, Robert 1906?-1973 *AuBYP 90*
Wyndrum, Ralph W., Jr. 1937- *WhoAm 90*
Wynegar, Butch 1956- *Ballpl 90*
Wyner, Aaron Daniel 1939- *WhoAm 90*
Wyner, Donald Stewart 1947- *WhoE 91*
Wyner, Genevieve G. 1930- *St&PR 91*
Wyner, Justin L. 1925- *St&PR 91*
Wyner, Susan Davenny 1945- *IntWWM 90*
Wyner, Yehudi 1929- *IntWWM 90, WhoAm 90*
Wynette, Tammy *BioIn 16*
Wynette, Tammy 1942- *OxCPMus, WhoAm 90, WorAlBi*
Wyngaard, Susan Elizabeth *WhoAmA 91*
Wyngaarden, James Barnes 1924- *WhoAm 90*
Wynkoop, Edward 1836-1891 *WhNaAH*
Wynkoop, Henry 1737-1816 *BioIn 16*
Wynkoop, Roger D. 1948- *St&PR 91*
Wynn, Carlton Terrell, Jr. 1942- *WhoSSW 91*
Wynn, Cordell *WhoAm 90*
Wynn, Coy Wilton 1920- *WhoAm 90*
Wynn, Dale Richard 1918- *WhoAm 90, WhoWrEP 89*
Wynn, Deborah 1645?-1727 *BiDEWW*
Wynn, Donald James 1942- *WhoAmA 91*
Wynn, Early 1920- *Ballpl 90 [port], WorAlBi*
Wynn, Ed 1886-1966 *BioIn 16, OxCPMus, WorAlBi*
Wynn, George Richard 1942- *WhoE 91*
Wynn, Jimmy 1942- *Ballpl 90 [port]*
Wynn, Joe Allen 1953- *WhoWrEP 89*
Wynn, John 1920- *WhoWrEP 89*
Wynn, John Charles 1920- *WhoAm 90*
Wynn, John David 1957- *BiDrAPA 89*
Wynn, John Thomas 1938- *WhoSSW 91, WhoWor 91*
Wynn, Katherine *BiDEWW*
Wynn, Keenan 1916-1986 *BioIn 16, WorAlBi*
Wynn, Kenneth Richard 1952- *St&PR 91, WhoAm 90*
Wynn, Patricia W. 1947- *WhoAmW 91*
Wynn, Robert Raymond 1929- *WhoWor 91*
Wynn, Ronnie *BioIn 16*
Wynn, Si Richard 1923- *St&PR 91*
Wynn, Stephen A. *BioIn 16*
Wynn, Thomas Joseph 1918- *WhoAm 90*
Wynn, Tracy Keenan 1945- *ConTFT 8*
Wynn, William Harrison 1931- *WhoAm 90*
Wynn Williams, Peter 1957- *WhoWor 91*
Wynne, Albert Givens 1922- *WhoAmA 91*
Wynne, Arthur Vincent, Jr. 1933- *WhoE 91*
Wynne, Billy 1943- *Ballpl 90*
Wynne, Brian James 1950- *WhoAm 90*
Wynne, Carol Joan 1960- *WhoE 91*
Wynne, Edward A. 1928- *ConAu 130*
Wynne, Elise Marcia *WhoWrEP 89*
Wynne, Frank *WhoWrEP 89*
Wynne, Greville *NewYTBS 90 [port]*
Wynne, Greville 1919-1990 *ConAu 131*
Wynne, Greville Maynard 1919-1990 *BioIn 16*
Wynne, Harrison K *BiDrAPA 89*
Wynne, Joan 1932- *WhoAmW 91*
Wynne, John B. 1930- *St&PR 91*
Wynne, John Benedict 1930- *WhoAm 90*
Wynne, John Oliver 1945- *St&PR 91, WhoAm 90, WhoSSW 91*
Wynne, John Watterson 1933- *St&PR 91*
Wynne, Joseph J. 1936- *St&PR 91*
Wynne, Lyman C 1923- *BiDrAPA 89*
Wynne, Lyman Carroll 1923- *WhoAm 90*
Wynne, Marvell 1959- *Ballpl 90*
Wynne, Michael Walter 1944- *WhoAm 90*
Wynne, Paul *NewYTBS 90 [port]*
Wynne, Paul 1943?-1990 *ConAu 132*
Wynne, Paul Emmett 1940- *St&PR 91*
Wynne, Robert John 1851-1922 *BiDrUSE 89*
Wynne, Ronald David 1934- *WhoE 91*
Wynne, Susan Winchester 1943- *WhoAmW 91*
Wynne-Edwards, Hugh Robert 1934- *WhoAm 90*
Wynne-Jones, Tim *BioIn 16*
Wynne-Jones, Tim 1948- *ChlLR 21 [port]*
Wynsma, James Burton 1936- *St&PR 91*
Wynstra, Nancy Ann 1941- *WhoAmW 91, WhoWor 91*
Wynter, Dana 1930- *WhoAm 90*
Wynter, Hector Lincoln 1926- *WhoWor 91*
Wynter, Sylvia 1930?- *FemiCLE*
Wyre, John *BioIn 16*
Wyrick, Charles Lloyd, Jr. 1939- *WhoAm 90, WhoAmA 91*
Wyrick, Cheryl Renee 1960- *WhoAmW 91*
Wyrick, Jesse Eugene 1928- *St&PR 91*
Wyrick, Priscilla Blakeney 1940- *WhoAmW 91*
Wyrostek, Johnny 1919-1986 *Ballpl 90*
Wyrsch, James Robert 1942- *WhoWor 91*
Wyschogrod, Michael 1928- *WhoAm 90*
Wyse, Bonita Wensink 1945- *WhoAmW 91*
Wyse, Denton H 1943- *BiDrAPA 89*
Wyse, Geraldine C. 1947- *WhoAmW 91*
Wyse, Hank 1918- *Ballpl 90*
Wyse, Holly Marie 1960- *WhoE 91*
Wyse, L Arnold 1937- *BiDrAPA 89*
Wyse, Lois *BioIn 16, WhoAm 90, WhoAmW 91*
Wyse, Sheila Ruth 1950- *St&PR 91, WhoAmW 91*
Wyse, William Walker 1919- *WhoAm 90*
Wyshak, Georgette Taffy 1953- *WhoAmW 91*
Wysinski, Robert M. 1948- *St&PR 91*
Wysocki, Ann M. 1956- *St&PR 91*
Wysocki, Boleslaw Antoni 1912- *WhoE 91*
Wysocki, Conrad E. 1927- *St&PR 91*
Wysocki, Felix Michael 1947- *WhoEmL 91*
Wysocki, Jerzy *BiDrAPA 89*
Wysocki, Matthew *BioIn 16*
Wysocki, Nancy 1940- *WhoWrEP 89*
Wysocki, Sharon Ann 1955- *WhoWrEP 89*
Wysolmerski, Theresa 1932- *WhoE 91*
Wysong, Ronald Eugene 1943- *St&PR 91*
Wysor, Bettie *WhoWrEP 89*
Wyss, David A. 1944- *St&PR 91*
Wyss, Dianne Dunlop 1950- *WhoAmW 91*
Wyss, James Michael 1948- *WhoSSW 91*
Wyss, Kurt 1943- *WhoWor 91*
Wyss, Michael Wayne 1952- *WhoSSW 91*
Wyss, Norma Rose Topping 1919- *WhoAmW 91, WhoSSW 91*
Wyss, Orville 1912- *WhoAm 90*
Wyss, Sophie 1897-1983 *PenDiMP*
Wyszomirski, Margaret Jane 1949- *WhoAmW 91*
Wyszynski, Antoinette Ambrosino 1954- *BiDrAPA 89*
Wyszynski, Valentine Anthony 1941- *WhoWor 91*
Wythe, George *NewYTBS 90*
Wythe, George 1726-1806 *BioIn 16, EncCRAm, WorAlBi*
Wythens, Lady *BiDEWW*
Wythes, Paul M. 1933- *St&PR 91*
Wyton, Alec 1921- *WhoAm 90*
Wyttenbach, Charles Richard 1933- *WhoAm 90*
Wywoda, Daniel Walter 1932- *St&PR 91*
Wyzner, Eugeniusz 1931- *WhoWor 91*

X

X *EncCoWW, EncPR&S 89*
X, Mr. *TwCCr&M 91*
Xagas, Steven George James 1951- *WhoEmL 91*
Xander, Al 1921- *St&PR 91*
Xanrof, Leon 1867-1953 *OxCPMus*
Xanta *EncCoWW*
Xanthaky, Nicholas 1911- *St&PR 91*
Xanthopoulos, Diomedes 1926- *WhoWor 91*
Xanthopoulos, Harry C 1917- *BiDrAPA 89*
Xanthopoulos, Philip 1944- *WhoSSW 91*
Xanto Avelli, Francesco, of Rovigo *PenDiDA 89*
Xavier, Francis 1506-1552 *EncJap*
Xavier, Francis 1916- *WhoE 91*
Xavier, Francisco Candido 1910- *EncO&P 3*
Xavier, Narithookil S 1945- *BiDrAPA 89*
Xceron, Jean 1890-1967 *WhoAmA 91N*
Xenakis, Francoise 1930- *EncCoWW*
Xenakis, Iannis 1922- *IntWWM 90, PenDiMP A, WhoWor 91*
Xenakis, Stephen N 1948- *BiDrAPA 89*
Xenakis, Stephen Nicholas 1948- *WhoAm 90*
Xenophon 431?BC-350?BC *WorAlBi*
Xenopol, Adela *EncCoWW*
Xerxes 519?BC-465BC *WorAlBi*
Xerxes I, King of Persia 519BC-465?BC *BioIn 16*
Xhrouet *PenDiDA 89*
Xia, Eugene Zhu 1963- *WhoE 91*
Xiang, Longwan 1941- *WhoWor 91*
Xiao Jingguang 1904-1989 *BioIn 16*
Xie Xide *BioIn 16*
Xie, Ganquan 1943- *WhoWor 91*
Ximenes, Vicente Trevino 1919- *BioIn 16, WhoHisp 91*
Xin, Yuan-Long 1943- *WhoWor 91*
Xiong, Bonnie Z. 1956- *WhoE 91*
Xochimoki *NewAgMG*
XTC *EncPR&S 89*
Xu Jiatun *BioIn 16*
Xu Xiangqian 1901-1990 *NewYTBS 90*
Xu, Bai-yi 1911- *WhoWor 91*
Xu, Jingi *WhoAmA 91*
Xuan Tong 1906-1967 *BioIn 16*
Xuande, Emperor *PenDiDA 89*
Xucaro, Kate *EncCoWW*
Xuereb, Angelo 1952- *WhoWor 91*
Xuereb, Charles E *BiDrAPA 89*
Xuereb, Paul 1923- *WhoWor 91*
Xyttas, Nicholas C. 1946- *WhoWor 91*
XYZ der Jungere *EncCoWW*

Y

Yaa Akyaa 1837?- *WomWR*
Yaa Asantewaa 1850?- *WomWR*
Yablans, Frank 1935- *ConTFT 8*
Yablans, Irwin 1934- *ConTFT 8*
Yablecki, Edward J. 1940- *St&PR 91*
Yablon, Leonard H. 1929- *St&PR 91*
Yablon, Leonard Harold 1929- *WhoAm 90*
Yablon, Marvin 1935- *WhoE 91*
Yablonsk'a, Tetiana Nilivna 1917- *BiDWomA*
Yablonskaia, Tatyana Nilovna 1917- *BiDWomA*
Yablonsky, Dennis *BioIn 16*
Yablonsky, Dennis 1952- *WhoAm 90*
Yabsley, James 1934- *St&PR 91*
Yach, Carla Jean 1954- *WhoAmW 91*
Yachnes, Eleanor *BiDrAPA 89*
Yachnin, Stanley 1930- *WhoAm 90*
Yacht, Irving 1946- *WhoAm 90*
Yacine, Kateb *BioIn 16*
Yacine, Kateb 1929-1989 *AnObit 1989*
Yackel, Kenneth Raymond 1946- *St&PR 91*
Yackira, Michael W. 1951- *St&PR 91*
Yackow, Cynthia Ludemann 1963- *WhoSSW 91*
Yacktman, Donald Arthur 1941- *St&PR 91*
Yackulic, Charles Fred 1947- *BiDrAPA 89*
Yacobi, Avraham 1945- *WhoE 91*
Yacobi, Stephen 1955- *WhoSSW 91*
Yacobian, Sonia Simone 1943- *WhoAmW 91*
Yacona, Anthony F 1946- *BiDrAPA 89*
Yaconetti, Dianne M. 1946- *St&PR 91*
Yaconetti, Dianne Mary 1946- *WhoAm 90, WhoAmW 91, WhoEmL 91*
Yacoub, Ignatius I. 1937- *WhoAm 90*
Yacoub, Talaat *BioIn 16*
Yacoubian, Jean H 1926- *BiDrAPA 89*
Yacovone, Ellen Elaine 1951- *WhoAmW 91*
Yacura, Sandra Leigh 1964- *WhoAmW 91*
Yacyshyn, Joseph Leon 1951- *WhoE 91*
Yadalam, Kashinath G 1954- *BiDrAPA 89*
Yadalam, Kashinath Gangadhara 1954- *WhoE 91*
Yadati, Santharam 1949- *BiDrAPA 89*
Yadin, Yigael 1917-1984 *BioIn 16*
Yaeger, Alan Martin 1946- *St&PR 91*
Yaeger, Billie Patricia 1949- *WhoAmW 91, WhoEmL 91, WhoSSW 91, WhoWor 91*
Yaeger, Deborah Sue *BiDrAPA 89*
Yaeger, Dewey R. 1940- *St&PR 91*
Yaeger, Edgar Louis 1904- *WhoAmA 91*
Yaeger, James Amos 1928- *WhoAm 90*
Yaffe, Harold J. 1947- *St&PR 91*
Yaffe, Harvey Morton 1931- *St&PR 91*
Yaffe, James 1927- *WhoAm 90, WhoWrEP 89*
Yaffe, Joseph X. 1913- *WhoAm 90*
Yaffe, Michael Charles 1951- *IntWWM 90*
Yaffe, Robert Norton 1933- *St&PR 91*
Yaffe, Sherwin Abe *BiDrAPA 89*
Yaffe, Sumner Jason 1923- *WhoAm 90*
Yaffee, Edith Widing 1895-1961 *WhoAmA 91N*
Yager, Ann Marie 1945- *WhoAmW 91*
Yager, Barry E. 1944- *St&PR 91*
Yager, Cinda 1954- *WhoWrEP 89*
Yager, David 1949- *WhoAmA 91*
Yager, Elizabeth Anne *BiDrAPA 89*
Yager, Helmut 1934- *BiDrAPA 89*
Yager, Hunter 1929- *WhoAm 90*
Yager, Jan 1948- *ConAu 30NR*
Yager, Jay Jerome 1947- *St&PR 91*
Yager, Joel 1941- *BiDrAPA 89*
Yager, John Warren 1920- *St&PR 91, WhoAm 90, WhoWor 91*
Yager, Joseph Arthur, Jr. 1916- *WhoAm 90*
Yager, Pamela Hall 1953- *St&PR 91*
Yager, Vincent Cook 1928- *St&PR 91*
Yaghi, Husam M. 1961- *WhoSSW 91*
Yaghjian, Edmund *WhoAmA 91*
Yagi, Kazufumi 1921- *WhoWor 91*
Yagi, Robert S. 1946- *St&PR 91*
Yago, Bernard 1916- *WhoWor 91*
Yago, C.E. 1934- *St&PR 91*
Yago, Glenn Harvey 1950- *WhoE 91*
Yagoda, Louis *NewYTBS 90*
Yagoda, Richard 1941- *St&PR 91*
Yague, Angeline Sirineo 1952- *BiDrAPA 89*
Yahagi, Tsuneo 1942- *WhoWor 91*
Yahaya, Jahara 1948- *WhoWor 91*
Yahia, Abraham *BiDrAPA 89*
Yahia, Mohamed *BiDrAPA 89*
Yahiro, Toshikuni 1915- *WhoWor 91*
Yahr, Melvin David 1917- *WhoAm 90*
Yahya 1869-1948 *PolLCME*
Yakar, Rachel 1938- *IntWWM 90*
Yakatan, Stan 1942- *St&PR 91*
Yake, William Harry 1926- *St&PR 91*
Yakel, Louella Marie 1956- *WhoAmW 91*
Yaker, Lynda E. 1945- *WhoAmW 91*
Yakey, Paula Sue 1953- *WhoAmW 91*
Yakhmi, Damanjit *BiDrAPA 89*
Yakhmi, Devinder 1934- *BiDrAPA 89*
Yakimowski-Zumwalt, Josephine Rose 1953- *WhoAmW 91*
Yakira, Joseph 1949- *BiDrAPA 89*
Yaklich, F. J., Jr. *WhoAm 90*
Yakos, Barbara Verlee 1912- *WhoWrEP 89*
Yakovetic 1952- *BioIn 16*
Yakovlev, Aleksander *BioIn 16*
Yakovlev, Aleksandr Nikolayevich 1923- *WhoWor 91*
Yakovlev, Aleksandr Sergeevich 1906-1989 *BioIn 16*
Yakovlev, Alexander 1906-1989 *AnObit 1989*
Yakovlev, Yegor Vladimirovich 1930- *BioIn 16*
Yakovleva, Galina Alexandrovna 1939- *WhoWor 91*
Yaku, Takeo 1947- *WhoWor 91*
Yakubu, Abdul-Aziz 1958- *WhoEmL 91*
Yalamanchili, Krishna Gopala *BiDrAPA 89*
Yaldwyn, John Cameron 1929- *WhoWor 91*
Yale, Andy *BioIn 16*
Yale, Charles E. 1925- *WhoAm 90*
Yale, Donald E. 1945- *St&PR 91*
Yale, Elihu 1649-1721 *EncCRAm, WorAlBi*
Yale, Pierre-Paul 1948- *BiDrAPA 89*
Yale, Seymour Hershel 1920- *WhoAm 90, WhoWor 91*
Yalen, Gary N. 1942- *WhoAm 90*
Yalkovsky, Rafael 1917- *WhoWrEP 89*
Yalkut, Arlen Spencer 1945- *WhoAmW 91*
Yallapragada, Rammohan Rao 1933- *WhoSSW 91*
Yalman, Ann 1948- *WhoAmW 91*
Yalom, Irvin David *BiDrAPA 89*
Yalow, Benjamin Michael 1952- *WhoE 91*
Yalow, Rosalyn 1921- *WorAlBi*
Yalow, Rosalyn Sussman 1921- *WhoAm 90, WhoAmW 91, WhoE 91, WhoWor 91*
Yamabayashi, Hajime 1926- *WhoWor 91*
Yamada, Ayako 1963- *WhoAmW 91*
Yamada, Eiji 1935- *WhoWor 91*
Yamada, Hisatoshi 1932- *WhoWor 91*
Yamada, Makiko 1938- *WhoWor 91*
Yamada, Mitsuye 1925- *FemiCLE*
Yamada, Mitsuye May 1923- *WhoWrEP 89*
Yamada, Ryoji 1928- *WhoWor 91*
Yamada, Satoshi 1934- *WhoWor 91*
Yamada, Shinichi 1937- *WhoWor 91*
Yamada, T. Albert 1938- *ODwPR 91*
Yamada, Taro 1934- *WhoAm 90, WhoWor 91*
Yamada, Tomohiko Albert 1938- *WhoE 91*
Yamada, William Yukio 1951- *WhoAm 90*
Yamada, Yastel 1939- *WhoWor 91*
Yamada, Yasuhiko 1927- *WhoWor 91*
Yamada, Yoichi 1955- *IntWWM 90*
Yamada, Yoshimasa 1924- *WhoWor 91*
Yamada, Yutaka 1926- *WhoWor 91*
Yamagata Aritomo 1838-1922 *EncJap*
Yamagata, Aritomo 1838-1922 *WorAlBi*
Yamagata, Taketora 1926- *WhoWor 91*
Yamaguchi, Ellen Diane 1957- *WhoWrEP 89*
Yamaguchi, Hiroshi 1928- *WhoWor 91*
Yamaguchi, Kristi *BioIn 16*
Yamaguchi, Takeaki 1935- *WhoWor 91*
Yamaguchi, Tamotsu 1930- *WhoAm 90*
Yamaguchi, Yoichi 1942- *WhoWor 91*
Yamakawa, David Kiyoshi, Jr. 1936- *WhoWor 91*
Yamakawa, Hiromi 1931- *WhoWor 91*
Yamakawa, Katsumi 1932- *WhoWor 91*
Yamakawa, Kikue 1890-1980 *BioIn 16*
Yamakawa, Masaru 1937- *WhoWor 91*
Yamakawa, Thomas Takamasa 1930- *WhoAm 90*
Yamakoshi, Lois 1954- *WhoAmW 91*
Yamakura, Motoo 1943- *WhoSSW 91*
Yamamoto Isoroku 1884-1943 *EncJap*
Yamamoto, Hiro-Aki 1947- *WhoWor 91*
Yamamoto, Hisaye *BioIn 16*
Yamamoto, Hisaye 1921- *FemiCLE*
Yamamoto, Isoroku 1884-1943 *WorAlBi*
Yamamoto, Joe 1924- *BiDrAPA 89, WhoAm 90, WhoWor 91*
Yamamoto, Kansai 1944- *ConDes 90*
Yamamoto, Kazuyoshi 1937- *St&PR 91*
Yamamoto, Kenichi *BioIn 16*
Yamamoto, Koji 1947- *Ballpl 90*
Yamamoto, Masaharu 1943- *WhoWor 91*
Yamamoto, Michiko 1936- *ConAu 132*
Yamamoto, Mikio 1913- *WhoWor 91*
Yamamoto, Shigeru 1929- *WhoWor 91*
Yamamoto, Sobeh 1926- *WhoWor 91*
Yamamoto, Tadatoyo *BioIn 16*
Yamamoto, Toshio 1921- *WhoWor 91*
Yamamoto, Yukoh 1939- *WhoWor 91*
Yamamura, Harry Tadashi 1941- *St&PR 91*
Yamamura, Kohtaroh 1933- *WhoWor 91*
Yamana, Hideaki 1949- *WhoWor 91*
Yamana, Shoji 1941- *WhoWor 91*
Yamanaka, Einosuke 1928- *WhoWor 91*
Yamanaka, Hiroshi 1913- *WhoWor 91*
Yamanaka, Kei-ichi 1940- *WhoWor 91*
Yamanaka, Shigehiro 1940- *St&PR 91*
Yamanaka, Teruo 1944- *St&PR 91*
Yamanaka, Tetsuo 1921- *BioIn 16*
Yamane, George Mitsuyoshi 1924- *WhoAm 90*
Yamane, Mitsuyoshi 1927- *WhoWor 91*
Yamane, Shu 1931- *WhoWor 91*
Yamane, Stanley Joel 1943- *WhoAm 90*
Yamani, Ahmed Zaki *BioIn 16*
Yamani, Elaine Reiko 1945- *WhoAmW 91*
Yamaoka, Seigen H. *WhoAm 90*
Yamashina, Yoshimaro 1900-1989 *BioIn 16*
Yamashiro, Jane Mieko 1939- *WhoAmW 91*
Yamashiro, Tomoe 1912- *BioIn 16*
Yamashita, Elizabeth Swayne 1927- *WhoAm 90*
Yamashita, Fumio 1927- *WhoWor 91*
Yamashita, Kazuhito 1961?- *ConMus 4*
Yamashita, Shinichi 1950- *WhoWor 91*
Yamashita, Susumu *BioIn 16*
Yamashita, Tadashi 1938- *WhoWor 91*
Yamashita, Tomoyuki 1885-1946 *WorAlBi*
Yamashita, Toyoko S 1944- *WhoAmW 91*
Yamashita, Yuya 1926- *WhoWor 91*
Yamashta, Stomu *NewAgMG*
Yamash'ta, Stomu 1947- *PenDiMP*
Yamato, Kei C. 1921- *WhoAm 90*
Yamatotakeru, Prince *EncJap*
Yamaura, Shun 1935- *St&PR 91*
Yamazaki, Genji 1946- *WhoWor 91*
Yamazaki, Mikiya 1924- *WhoWor 91*
Yamazaki, Ryuzo 1920- *WhoWor 91*
Yamazaki, Toshimitsu 1934- *WhoWor 91*
Yambor, Mari M *BiDrAPA 89*
Yambrusic, Edward Slavko 1933- *WhoWor 91*
Yamin, Michael Geoffrey 1931- *WhoE 91, WhoWor 91*
Yamin, Steven Edward 1946- *WhoAmA 91*
Yamini-Sharif, Bahman *BiDrAPA 89*
Yamins, David Matthew *BiDrAPA 89*
Yammine, Riad Nassif 1934- *WhoWor 91*
Yampolsky, Mariana *BioIn 16*
Yamron, Joseph 1928- *St&PR 91*
Yan Yangchu 1893-1990 *BioIn 16*
Yan, Hong 1959- *WhoWor 91*
Yan Naing, U *BioIn 16*
Yana 1932-1989 *AnObit 1989*
Yanagi Soetsu 1889-1961 *EncJap*
Yanagi, Amy Tsuki 1954- *WhoE 91*
Yanagi, Ruth Midori *BiDrAPA 89*
Yanagi, Sori 1915- *ConDes 90, PenDiDA 89*
Yanagisawa, Samuel Tsuguo 1922- *WhoAm 90*
Yanagita Kunio 1875-1962 *EncJap*
Yanagita, Masako 1944- *IntWWM 90, WhoE 91*
Yanagitani, Elizabeth 1953- *WhoAmW 91*
Yanase, Naoki 1943- *WhoWor 91*
Yanbennekom, Pieter W. 1945- *St&PR 91*
Yance, James Alexander 1946- *WhoSSW 91*
Yancey, Asa Greenwood, Jr. *BiDrAPA 89*
Yancey, Asa Greenwood, Sr. 1916- *WhoAm 90*

Yancey, Bert 1938- *BioIn 16*
Yancey, Bessie Woodson 1882-1958 *HarlReB [port]*
Yancey, Bill 1904-1971 *Ballpl 90*
Yancey, J. Curtis 1929- *St&PR 91*
Yancey, Jimmie Isaac 1935- *WhoSSW 91, WhoWor 91*
Yancey, Jimmy 1898-1951 *OxCPMus*
Yancey, Lee M. 1942- *St&PR 91*
Yancey, Orson Pierre 1955- *WhoE 91*
Yancey, Philip David 1949- *WhoAm 90, WhoWrEP 89*
Yancey, Richard Charles 1926- *WhoAm 90*
Yancey, Robert E., Jr. 1946- *St&PR 91*
Yancey, Robert E., Sr. 1921- *St&PR 91*
Yancey, Robert Earl, Jr. 1945- *WhoAm 90, WhoSSW 91*
Yancey, Wallace Glenn 1930- *St&PR 91, WhoAm 90, WhoWor 91*
Yancey, William Lowndes 1814-1863 *BioIn 16*
Yancher, Arville Noel 1927- *St&PR 91*
Yancik, Joseph John 1930- *WhoAm 90*
Yancy, Emily 1939- *DrBlPA 90*
Yancy, Isaiah Andrew 1946- *WhoSSW 91*
Yancy, Richard Charles 1926- *St&PR 91*
Yancy, Robert James 1944- *WhoSSW 91*
Yandell, Donnetta Kay 1953- *WhoAmW 91*
Yandell, Enid 1870-1934 *BiDWomA*
Yandell, George Wilson 1924- *BiDrAPA 89*
Yandell, Lunsford P. 1902- *WhoAm 90*
Yanders, Armon Frederick 1928- *WhoAm 90*
Yandle, Richard 1956- *WhoSSW 91*
Yandow, Valery Worth *BiDrAPA 89*
Yandow, Valery Worth 1930- *WhoAmW 91, WhoE 91*
Yaneff, Chris 1928- *WhoAmA 91*
Yaney, George 1930- *WhoAm 90*
Yaney, Lucile *BioIn 16*
Yaney, Ralph D *BiDrAPA 89*
Yanez, Agustin 1904-1980 *BioIn 16, ConAu 131, HispWr 90*
Yanez, Frank John 1962- *WhoHisp 91*
Yanez, Jose Donoso *MajTwCW*
Yang Baibing 1920- *BioIn 16*
Yang Chengzhong 1913-1987 *BioIn 16*
Yang Jiang 1911- *BioIn 16, WorAu 1980 [port]*
Yang Jikang 1911- *WorAu 1980 [port]*
Yang Shangkun *BioIn 16*
Yang Shangkun 1907- *WhoWor 91*
Yang Shihui 1911- *BioIn 16*
Yang Zhong Mei 1945- *ConAu 132*
Yang, Anthony Tsu-Ming 1944- *WhoWor 91*
Yang, C. C. 1927- *WhoWor 91*
Yang, Charles Qi-Xiang 1944- *WhoSSW 91*
Yang, Chen Ning 1922- *WhoAm 90, WhoE 91, WhoWor 91, WorAlBi*
Yang, Ch'eng-chung 1913-1987 *BioIn 16*
Yang, Cheng-Zhi 1938- *WhoWor 91*
Yang, Chiang 1911- *BioIn 16*
Yang, Edward S. 1937- *WhoAm 90*
Yang, Hayng-Sung 1944- *BiDrAPA 89*
Yang, Henry Hanalei *BiDrAPA 89*
Yang, Henry Tsu Yow 1940- *WhoAm 90*
Yang, Hsi Kun 1912- *WhoWor 91*
Yang, Jay 1946- *ConDes 90*
Yang, John Eric 1958- *WhoE 91*
Yang, Kichoon 1955- *WhoSSW 91*
Yang, Lien-Sheng *NewYTBS 90*
Yang, Monica Wu 1938- *WhoE 91*
Yang, Peter Quay 1922- *WhoWor 91*
Yang, Shih-hui 1911- *BioIn 16*
Yang, Song-Yu 1938- *WhoWor 91*
Yang, Ti Liang 1929- *WhoWor 91*
Yang, Tony Tien Sheng 1928- *WhoAm 90*
Yang, Vivian 1937- *WhoAmW 91*
Yang, William 1948- *WhoE 91, WhoWor 91*
Yang, William Norman 1948- *WhoSSW 91*
Yang, Won Tack 1924- *WhoAm 90*
Yang, Xiaokai 1948- *WhoWor 91*
Yang Ko, Lillian Yang 1944- *WhoWor 91*
Yanguas, Lourdes M. 1965- *WhoHisp 91*
Yanik, Stephen J. 1941- *St&PR 91*
Yanish, Elizabeth *WhoAmA 91*
Yanity, Eugene J 1931- *BiDrAPA 89*
Yaniv, Zvi 1946- *St&PR 91*
Yaniz, Antonio M 1939- *BiDrAPA 89*
Yaniz, Henry 1917- *WhoHisp 91*
Yankauer, Alfred 1913- *WhoWrEP 89*
Yanke, Eliza Belle 1939- *WhoSSW 91*
Yankee, William Joseph 1948- *St&PR 91*
Yankelovich, Daniel 1924- *WhoAm 90*
Yanklowitz, Stephen Michael 1944- *WhoE 91*
Yanko, John Bernard 1935- *St&PR 91*
Yankovic, Al 1959- *WorAlBi*
Yankovic, Judith E. 1947- *WhoAm 90*
Yankovic, Judith Elaine 1947- *St&PR 91*
Yankowich, George Paul 1948- *St&PR 91*
Yankowitz, Susan 1941- *BioIn 16, FemiCLE, NotWoAT*
Yankowski, Carl James 1948- *WhoWor 91*
Yankwich, Peter Ewald 1923- *WhoAm 90*
Yann, Arthur, III *ODwPR 91*
Yannas, Ioannis Vassilios 1935- *WhoAm 90, WhoWor 91*
Yannes, John F. 1927- *St&PR 91*
Yanni *NewAgMG*
Yannielli, John Thomas 1942- *St&PR 91*
Yannios, Christos 1913- *BiDrAPA 89*
Yanniotis, Alexander Nicholas 1924- *WhoWor 91*
Yannoulopoulos, Peter Apostolos 1948- *WhoWor 91*
Yannuzzi, Miguel M. 1941- *WhoE 91*
Yano, Brian Sueo *BiDrAPA 89*
Yano, Katsumi 1928- *WhoWor 91*
Yanof, Judith Ann *BiDrAPA 89*
Yanoff, Arthur 1939- *WhoAmA 91*
Yanoff, Arthur Samuel 1939- *WhoE 91*
Yanoff, Marc S. *St&PR 91*
Yanoff, Myron 1936- *WhoAm 90*
Yanofsky, Charles 1925- *WhoAm 90*
Yanok, Linda Naylor 1953- *WhoAmW 91*
Yanos, Theodore 1923- *BiDrAPA 89*
Yanoski, Edith M. 1944- *WhoAmW 91*
Yanovshtchinsky, Vera 1952- *WomArch [port]*
Yanovsky, Basile S. *ConAu 129*
Yanovsky, Tatiana N *BiDrAPA 89*
Yanovsky, V. S. 1906-1989 *BioIn 16*
Yanovsky, V S 1906-1989 *ConAu 129*
Yanow, Rhoda *BioIn 16*
Yanow, Rhoda Mae *WhoAmA 91, WhoE 91*
Yanowitz, Irwin M. 1926- *St&PR 91*
Yans, Frank M. 1935- *St&PR 91, WhoE 91*
Yansha, Beverly Ann 1947- *WhoAmW 91*
Yansons, Arvid 1914-1984 *PenDiMP*
Yantis, John M. 1918- *St&PR 91*
Yantis, Judith Barbara 1948- *BiDrAPA 89*
Yantis, Phillip Alexander 1928- *WhoAm 90*
Yantis, Richard William 1923- *WhoAm 90*
Yantis, Stanley Mark 1947- *BiDrAPA 89*
Yantis, Thomas G. 1956- *St&PR 91*
Yanuck, Cheryl Hoffman *BiDrAPA 89*
Yao Yilin 1917- *WhoWor 91*
Yao, Andrew Chi-Chih *WhoAm 90*
Yao, Clara Sai-Hsi 1938- *WhoAmW 91*
Yao, Dennis Alden 1953- *WhoE 91*
Yao, Di-Xiong 1949- *WhoWor 91*
Yao, Edward York-Peng 1940- *St&PR 91*
Yao, Fred York-Sung 1939- *St&PR 91*
Yao, Kathy York-Bing 1941- *St&PR 91*
Yao, Lily King 1943- *WhoAmW 91*
Yao, Shih-Chin 1913- *St&PR 91*
Yap Ah Loy 1837-1885 *BioIn 16*
Yap, Alfredo T *BiDrAPA 89*
Yap, Alvin Tan 1960- *WhoWor 91*
Yap, Bing Kie 1922- *BiDrAPA 89*
Yap, Caroll Anne 1937- *BiDrAPA 89*
Yap, Dedenia Dy *BiDrAPA 89*
Yap, Dolorosa B 1940- *BiDrAPA 89*
Yap, John Roger 1935- *St&PR 91*
Yap, Kie-Han 1925- *WhoWor 91*
Yap, Romeo Sy *BiDrAPA 89*
Yap, Swee-Hee 1955- *WhoWor 91*
Yapa, Wima 1937- *BiDrAPA 89*
Yapalater, Alvin R 1923- *BiDrAPA 89*
Yapor, Alfredo 1948- *WhoE 91*
Yaqub, Adil Mohamed 1928- *WhoAm 90*
Yaqub, Fawzi Mohamad 1931- *WhoE 91*
Yaqub-Khan, Sahabzada 1920- *WhoWor 91*
Yarabek, Jennifer Johnson 1961- *WhoEmL 91*
Yarbo, Lillian *DrBlPA 90*
Yarborough, Cale 1940- *WorAlBi*
Yarborough, Christine Troutman 1925- *WhoAmA 91*
Yarborough, David Miller 1950- *St&PR 91*
Yarborough, Glenn 1930- *WorAlBi*
Yarborough, Gordon Wilson 1940- *St&PR 91*
Yarborough, Judith Ann 1949- *WhoAmW 91*
Yarborough, Katherine 1950- *BiDrAPA 89*
Yarborough, Lavinia Williams *BioIn 16*
Yarborough, N. Patricia 1936- *WhoAmW 91*
Yarborough, Ronald Gayle 1948- *WhoSSW 91*
Yarborough, Sara 1951- *DrBlPA 90*
Yarborough, Valerie Louise 1928- *WhoAmW 91*
Yarborough, William 1926- *IntWWM 90, WhoE 91*
Yarborough, William Glenn, Jr. 1940- *WhoE 91, WhoWor 91*
Yarborough, William Pelham 1912- *WhoAm 90, WhoWor 91*
Yarborough-Hall, Gwendolyn 1948- *WhoSSW 91*
Yarbro, Alan David 1941- *WhoAm 90*
Yarbrough, Amelia Hergystine Burgess 1939- *WhoAmW 91*
Yarbrough, Billy A. 1939- *St&PR 91*
Yarbrough, Camille 1948- *BioIn 16*
Yarbrough, Charles A. 1935- *St&PR 91*
Yarbrough, Charles Gerald, Jr. 1961- *WhoSSW 91*
Yarbrough, Dena Cox 1933- *WhoAmW 91*
Yarbrough, Desiree Simone 1964- *WhoAmW 91*
Yarbrough, Jerry A. 1938- *St&PR 91*
Yarbrough, Joyce Lenore 1948- *WhoAmW 91*
Yarbrough, Leila Kepert 1932- *WhoAmA 91*
Yarbrough, Marilyn *BioIn 16*
Yarbrough, Marilyn Virginia 1945- *WhoAm 90, WhoSSW 91*
Yarbrough, Martha Cornelia 1940- *WhoAmW 91*
Yarbrough, Robert E., Jr. 1928- *St&PR 91*
Yarbrough, Sonja Dianne 1948- *WhoAmW 91*
Yarbrugh, Henrietta Maria 1694-1776 *BiDEWW*
Yard, Molly *BioIn 16, WhoAmW 91*
Yard, Rix Nelson 1917- *WhoAm 90*
Yard, Sally Elizabeth 1951- *WhoAmA 91*
Yardan, Shana 1942- *FemiCLE*
Yardbirds, The *EncPR&S 89*
Yarden, Paul E. *BiDrAPA 89*
Yardis, Pamela Hintz 1944- *WhoE 91*
Yardis-Vignola, Pamela Hintz 1944- *WhoAmW 91*
Yardley, Andrea 1955- *WhoAmW 91*
Yardley, Edna Ramsaier *BioIn 16, NewYTBS 90*
Yardley, John Finley 1925- *St&PR 91, WhoAm 90*
Yardley, John Howard 1926- *WhoAm 90*
Yardley, Jonathan *BioIn 16*
Yardley, Jonathan 1939- *WhoAm 90*
Yardley, Norman 1915-1989 *AnObit 1989*
Yardley, Richard Quincy 1903-1979 *WhoAmA 91N*
Yardley, Rosemary Roberts 1938- *WhoAmW 91*
Yardley, Samuel *PenDiDA 89*
Yardumian, John *BiDrAPA 89*
Yared, Paul David 1949- *St&PR 91*
Yared, Thomas Albert 1947- *BiDrAPA 89*
Yaremko, Peter William 1942- *WhoE 91*
Yarger, Sam Jacob 1937- *WhoAm 90*
Yarington, Charles Thomas, Jr. 1934- *WhoAm 90*
Yariv, Amnon 1930- *WhoAm 90*
Yarker, John 1833-1913 *EncO&P 3*
Yarletts, Carol Lynne 1959- *WhoAmW 91*
Yarling, John Lewis 1935- *BiDrAPA 89*
Yarmolinsky, Adam 1922- *WhoAm 90, WhoE 91*
Yarmon, Betty *WhoAm 90*
Yarmon, Morton 1916- *ODwPR 91*
Yarmus, James Jay 1941- *WhoE 91*
Yarnal, James Rodgers 1948- *WhoE 91*
Yarnall, D. Robert, Jr. 1925- *WhoAm 90*
Yarne, Geraldine F 1940- *BiDrAPA 89*
Yarnell, Kenneth A., Jr. *St&PR 91*
Yarnell, Richard Asa 1929- *WhoAm 90*
Yarnell, Stephen K 1943- *BiDrAPA 89*
Yarnold, Barbara Maria 1961- *WhoAmW 91*
Yaros, Constance G *WhoAmA 91*
Yarosewick, Stanley J. 1939- *WhoAm 90*
Yarosky, Harvey William 1934- *WhoAm 90*
Yarost, Nancy E. *ODwPR 91*
Yarotsky, Lori 1955- *WhoAmA 91*
Yarow, Natalie 1916- *BiDrAPA 89*
Yarp, H. Richard *St&PR 91*
Yarra, Nirmala K 1944- *BiDrAPA 89*
Yarra, Nirmala Karnam 1944- *WhoE 91*
Yarrell, Thomas C. 1934- *St&PR 91*
Yarrell, Zuleika *BiDrAPA 89*
Yarrigle, Charlene Sandra Shuey 1940- *WhoAmW 91, WhoWor 91*
Yarrington, Hugh J. 1942- *St&PR 91*
Yarrow, Peter 1938- *WhoAm 90, WorAlBi*
Yarsinske, Amy Melissa 1963- *WhoSSW 91*
Yarus, Mike *St&PR 91*
Yarusinski, Joseph John 1948- *WhoSSW 91*
Yarvis, Richard M 1938- *BiDrAPA 89*
Yarwood, Cecil Edmund 1907-1981 *BioIn 16*
Yarwood, Charles Thomas, Jr. 1952- *WhoSSW 91*
Yarwood, Dean Lesley 1935- *WhoAm 90*
Yarymovych, Michael Ihor 1933- *WhoAm 90*
Yaryura-Tobias, Jose A 1934- *BiDrAPA 89, WhoHisp 91*
Yas, S.M. 1941- *St&PR 91*
Yas, Solomon M. 1941- *WhoE 91*
Yas-Kaz *NewAgMG*
Yasar, Tug 1941- *St&PR 91*
Yaschik, Henry 1910- *WhoSSW 91*
Yaseen, Leonard C. 1912-1989 *BioIn 16, ConAu 129*
Yashima, Taro *AuBYP 90*
Yashon, David 1935- *WhoAm 90*
Yasiejko, Myron 1946- *WhoE 91*
Yasin, Fazle Mobin *BiDrAPA 89*
Yasinitsky, Gregory Walter 1953- *IntWWM 90*
Yaskin, H Edward 1909- *BiDrAPA 89*
Yasko, Caryl Anne 1941- *WhoAmA 91*
Yasmin Aga Khan *BioIn 16*
Yasnovsky, Tatyana *BiDrAPA 89*
Yassa, Guirguis Fahmy 1930- *WhoE 91, WhoWor 91*
Yassa, Ramzy Yassa A 1940- *BiDrAPA 89*
Yassin, Robert Alan 1941- *WhoAm 90, WhoAmA 91*
Yassine, Khair Nimer 1934- *WhoWor 91*
Yassky, Harold 1930- *WhoSSW 91*
Yassky, Lester 1941- *WhoAm 90*
Yassky, Lester Harvey 1941- *St&PR 91*
Yassukovich, Dimitri M. *BioIn 16*
Yast, Patricia Ann 1961- *BiDrAPA 89*
Yastrzemski, Carl *BioIn 16*
Yastrzemski, Carl 1939- *Ballpl 90 [port], WorAlBi*
Yastrzemski, Carl Michael 1939- *WhoAm 90*
Yastrzemski, J. Richard 1943- *St&PR 91*
Yasuda, Cathy Tomi 1957- *WhoAmW 91*
Yasuda, Hirotsugu Koge 1930- *WhoAm 90*
Yasuda, Robert 1940- *WhoAmA 91*
Yasugi, Tadao 1929- *WhoWor 91*
Yasumoto, Takeshi 1935- *WhoWor 91*
Yasumuro, Kenichi 1947- *WhoWor 91*
Yasuo, Kimoto 1929- *WhoWor 91*
Yasuoka Shotaro 1920- *WorAu 1980 [port]*
Yasuoka, Akio 1927- *WhoWor 91*
Yatabe, Atsuhiko 1929- *WhoWor 91*
Yater, George D. 1910- *WhoE 91*
Yater, George David 1910- *WhoAmA 91*
Yates, Alayne 1929- *BiDrAPA 89*
Yates, Albert Carl 1941- *WhoAm 90*
Yates, Alden P. *BioIn 16*
Yates, Arthur Edward, Jr. 1943- *WhoE 91*
Yates, Barry Cordell 1939- *BiDrAPA 89*
Yates, Bill 1921- *EncACom*
Yates, Brock Wendel 1933- *AuBYP 90*
Yates, Bruce L. 1940- *St&PR 91*
Yates, Carol B. 1952- *ODwPR 91*
Yates, Charles D. 1936- *IntWWM 90*
Yates, Charles Richardson 1913- *WhoAm 90*
Yates, David John C. 1927- *WhoAm 90*
Yates, Donald Glen 1939- *St&PR 91, WhoSSW 91*
Yates, Dornford 1885-1960 *TwCCr&M 91*
Yates, Douglas Martin 1943- *St&PR 91*
Yates, Dudley Vernon 1932- *WhoAm 90*
Yates, Edmund 1831-1894 *BioIn 16*
Yates, Elizabeth 1905- *AuBYP 90, WhoAm 90*
Yates, Ella Gaines 1927- *WhoAm 90, WhoAmW 91, WhoSSW 91*
Yates, Elton G. 1935- *St&PR 91, WhoAm 90*
Yates, Frances A 1899-1981 *ConAu 30NR*
Yates, Frances Amelia *BioIn 16*
Yates, Frances Amelia 1899-1981 *DcNaB 1981*
Yates, Frances R. 1935- *St&PR 91*
Yates, G. Neil 1950- *WhoSSW 91*
Yates, Gayle Graham 1940- *WhoAmW 91*
Yates, George *BioIn 16*
Yates, Hazel A. 1925- *St&PR 91*
Yates, Helen Eva *WhoAm 90*
Yates, Herbert Spencer 1942- *St&PR 91*
Yates, J. Michael 1938- *BioIn 16*
Yates, James E 1923- *BiDrAPA 89*
Yates, Jeffrey McKee 1948- *WhoAm 90*
Yates, Jeffrey W. 1941- *St&PR 91*
Yates, Jessie Ward 1929- *WhoAmW 91*
Yates, Jo Ann Ruth 1931- *WhoAm 90, WhoAmW 91*
Yates, Joe Elton 1938- *WhoSSW 91*
Yates, John Mike 1941- *BiDrAPA 89*
Yates, John Robert, Jr. 1930- *WhoE 91*
Yates, John Thomas, Jr. 1935- *WhoAm 90*
Yates, Juanita 1924- *WhoWrEP 89*
Yates, Kathryn A. *ODwPR 91*
Yates, Kathryn Anne 1950- *WhoE 91*
Yates, Keith 1928- *WhoAm 90*
Yates, Keith David 1950- *WhoSSW 91*
Yates, Laurie *BioIn 16*
Yates, Leigh Thomas 1942- *St&PR 91*
Yates, Lenore Easley 1945- *WhoAmW 91*
Yates, Lori *WhoNeCM [port]*
Yates, Margaret B 1926- *BiDrAPA 89*
Yates, Marie 1940- *BiDWomA*
Yates, Marvin Clarence 1943- *WhoAmA 91*
Yates, Marypaul 1957- *WhoE 91*
Yates, Maurice Marvin, III 1954- *WhoSSW 91*
Yates, Michael Francis 1946- *WhoE 91, WhoWor 91*
Yates, Peter *BioIn 16*
Yates, Peter 1924- *WhoAm 90*
Yates, Peter 1929- *WhoAm 90, WhoWor 91*
Yates, Raymond Francis 1895-1966 *AuBYP 90*

Yates, Richard L. 1950- *St&PR 91*
Yates, Robert 1738-1801 *BioIn 16*
Yates, Robert Doyle 1931- *WhoAm 90, WhoSSW 91*
Yates, Robin 1965- *ODwPR 91*
Yates, Ronald Eugene 1941- *WhoAm 90*
Yates, Samuel 1919- *WhoSSW 91, WhoWrEP 89*
Yates, Sandra *BioIn 16*
Yates, Sidney Richard 1909- *WhoAm 90*
Yates, Simon *BioIn 16*
Yates, Steven A *WhoAmA 91*
Yates, Steven Winfield 1946- *WhoSSW 91*
Yates, William A. 1835-1871 *AmLegL*
Yates, William Eugene 1938- *WhoSSW 91*
Yates, William Harrison, Jr. 1930- *St&PR 91*
Yates, William Robert 1951- *BiDrAPA 89*
Yates-Buckles, Jeannette Keber 1942- *WhoE 91, WhoWor 91*
Yatron, Gus 1927- *WhoAm 90, WhoE 91*
Yatsevitch, Gratian Michael 1911- *WhoE 91, WhoWor 91*
Yatsu, John Shigeru 1953- *WhoEmL 91, WhoSSW 91*
Yau, Cheuk Chung 1950- *WhoSSW 91*
Yau, Joseph K 1949- *BiDrAPA 89*
Yau, Jot Kai-Hong 1957- *WhoE 91*
Yau, Shing-Tung 1949- *WhoE 91*
Yau, Stephen Sik-sang 1935- *WhoAm 90, WhoWor 91*
Yauger, Margaret 1947- *IntWWM 90*
Yaukey, Grace 1899- *AuBYP 90*
Yaus, Holly Nill 1964- *WhoAmW 91*
Yavitz, Boris 1923- *St&PR 91, WhoAm 90*
Yavorsky, Stanislav *BioIn 16*
Yaw, Elbert M. 1940- *St&PR 91*
Yawkey, Jean R. 1909- *WhoAm 90, WhoAmW 91, WhoE 91*
Yawkey, Tom 1903-1976 *Ballpl 90, BioIn 16*
Yaworski, Alex F 1907- *WhoAmA 91*
Yaworsky, George Myroslaw 1940- *WhoWor 91*
Yaworsky, Walter 1934- *BiDrAPA 89*
Yaxley, Jack Thomas 1943- *WhoSSW 91, WhoWor 91*
Yaylayan, Shahnour 1956- *BiDrAPA 89*
Yaz, Engin 1954- *WhoSSW 91*
Yazbak, Eugene Paul 1960- *WhoE 91*
Yazel, John Joe 1945- *BiDrAPA 89*
Yazov, Dmitri Timofeevich 1923- *WhoWor 91*
Yballe, Sonia B 1940- *BiDrAPA 89*
Ybanez, John P. 1946- *WhoHisp 91*
Ybarnegaray, Michel Albert Jean Joseph 1883-1956 *BiDFrPL*
Ybarra, Miguel de Oriol e *BioIn 16*
Ybarra, Shirley J. 1945- *St&PR 91*
Ybarrondo, L. J. *WhoHisp 91*
Ycaza Baquerizo, Rosanna Asuncion 1960- *WhoWor 91*
Yde, Emil 1900-1968 *Ballpl 90*
Ye Jianying *BioIn 16*
Ye, Xiaogang 1955- *IntWWM 90*
Ye, Zhongxing 1946- *WhoE 91*
Ye-lu Shih *WomWR*
Yeager, Bernice Whittaker 1915- *WhoAmW 91*
Yeager, C. Clayton 1942- *St&PR 91*
Yeager, Carole Garrahan 1949- *WhoE 91*
Yeager, Charles 1923- *WorAlBi*
Yeager, Charles Elwood 1923- *WhoAm 90*
Yeager, Charles L *BiDrAPA 89*
Yeager, Chuck 1923- *BioIn 16*
Yeager, Clyde E., Jr. 1932- *St&PR 91*
Yeager, Dennis Randall 1941- *WhoE 91*
Yeager, Ernest Bill 1924- *WhoAm 90*
Yeager, G. Thomas, III 1927- *St&PR 91*
Yeager, George *BioIn 16*
Yeager, George Michael 1934- *WhoAm 90*
Yeager, Jacques Stadler, Sr. 1921- *WhoAm 90*
Yeager, Jacques Stalder 1921- *St&PR 91*
Yeager, Jeana *BioIn 16*
Yeager, Joe 1873-1940 *Ballpl 90*
Yeager, John S. 1940- *St&PR 91*
Yeager, John Spencer 1940- *WhoAm 90*
Yeager, Joseph Harold 1950- *St&PR 91*
Yeager, Joseph Henry 1920- *WhoAm 90*
Yeager, Julie *ODwPR 91*
Yeager, Pamela Crowl 1949- *WhoAmW 91*
Yeager, Paul David 1938- *St&PR 91, WhoAm 90*
Yeager, Peter C 1949- *ConAu 131*
Yeager, Phyllis Diane 1949- *WhoWrEP 89*
Yeager, Randolph O. 1912- *ConAu 130*
Yeager, Riff 1953- *ODwPR 91*
Yeager, Robert L. 1907-1988 *BioIn 16*
Yeager, Ronald Kent 1935- *St&PR 91*
Yeager, Steve 1948- *Ballpl 90*
Yeager, Waldo E. 1936- *St&PR 91*
Yeagle, Paul Harry 1939- *St&PR 91*
Yeagley, J. Walter 1909-1990 *BioIn 16*
Yeago, R.S. 1925- *St&PR 91*
Yeakel, Joseph Hughes 1928- *WhoAm 90, WhoE 91*
Yeakley, M. H. *AuBYP 90*
Yeakley, Mark *BiDrAPA 89*
Yeamans, Isabel 1637?-1704 *BiDEWW, FemiCLE*
Yeardley, George 1587?-1627 *EncCRAm*
Yeargain, Dallas G. 1922- *St&PR 91*
Yeargin, Robert Harper 1926- *St&PR 91, WhoAm 90*
Yeargin-Allsopp, Marshalyn 1948- *WhoAmW 91*
Yearley, Douglas Cain 1936- *St&PR 91, WhoAm 90*
Yearling, Loweta Lee 1939- *WhoAmW 91*
Yearsley, Ann 1752-1806 *FemiCLE*
Yearsley, Ann Cromartie 1752-1806 *BioIn 16*
Yearwood, Collins *BioIn 16*
Yearwood, Donald R. 1939- *St&PR 91*
Yearwood, Donald Robert 1939- *WhoAm 90*
Yeater, David Allan 1947- *St&PR 91, WhoE 91*
Yeates, Zeno Lanier 1915- *WhoAm 90*
Yeatman, C. James *St&PR 91*
Yeatman, Harry Clay 1916- *WhoAm 90*
Yeatman, Trezevant Player, III 1951- *WhoWrEP 89*
Yeats, Robert Sheppard 1931- *WhoAm 90*
Yeats, W. B. 1865-1939 *BioIn 16*
Yeats, W B 1865-1939 *EncO&P 3*
Yeats, William Butler 1865-1939 *BioIn 16, DcLB 98 [port], EncPaPR 91, MajTwCW, WorAlBi, WrPh*
Yeats-Brown, Francis 1886-1944 *EncO&P 3*
Yeatts, George Dewey 1957- *WhoSSW 91*
Yeatts, Guillermo M. 1937- *WhoWor 91*
Yeazell, Ruth Bernard 1947- *WhoAmW 91*
Yecies, Paul Richard 1945- *St&PR 91*
Yecies, Susan *ODwPR 91*
Yeddis, Abe 1917- *St&PR 91*
Yedinsky, Sylvia Schein 1935- *BiDrAPA 89*
Yedlicka, William George 1922- *WhoWor 91*
Yedlik, Edwon G. 1945- *WhoWor 91*
Yedlin, Nancy M. *BioIn 16*
Yedra, Jose 1936- *WhoSSW 91*
Yee, Albert Hoy 1929- *WhoAm 90*
Yee, Alfred Alphonse 1925- *WhoAm 90*
Yee, Chiang 1903-1977 *WhoAmA 91N*
Yee, Darlene 1958- *WhoAmW 91*
Yee, Eugene *ODwPR 91*
Yee, Jordan *BiDrAPA 89*
Yee, Maria Ruiza *BiDrAPA 89*
Yee, Raymond *BiDrAPA 89*
Yee, Raymond 1960- *WhoE 91*
Yee, Susan G. 1948- *WhoAmW 91*
Yee, William R *BiDrAPA 89*
Yee, Willie Kai 1944- *BiDrAPA 89*
Yefimov, Igor 1937- *WhoWrEP 89*
Yeganeh, Albert *BioIn 16*
Yeganeh, Mehdi L 1925- *BiDrAPA 89*
Yegge, Robert Bernard 1934- *WhoAm 90, WhoWor 91*
Yegorov, Yuri 1954-1988 *PenDiMP*
Yegul, Fikret Kutlu 1941- *WhoAmA 91*
Yeh, Carol 1938- *WhoAmA 91*
Yeh, Chai 1911- *WhoAm 90*
Yeh, Charlotte Shawing 1952- *WhoAmW 91*
Yeh, Engg-Kung *BiDrAPA 89*
Yeh, Gar-on-Anthony 1952- *WhoWor 91*
Yeh, George Hon Cheng 1948- *WhoSSW 91*
Yeh, Joanne I-ti 1966- *WhoE 91*
Yeh, Kung Chie 1930- *WhoAm 90*
Yeh, Raymond Wei-Hwa 1942- *WhoAm 90*
Yeh, Walter Huai-teh 1911- *WhoSSW 91*
Yeh, William Wen-Gong 1938- *WhoAm 90*
Yeh, Yu-shuan 1939- *WhoAm 90*
Yehl, Suzy Perkins 1945- *WhoWor 91*
Yehoshua, Abraham B. *BioIn 16*
Yehudai, Yosef *BioIn 16*
Yeiser, Charles William 1925- *WhoAmA 91*
Yeiser, Charles William, Jr. 1925- *WhoE 91*
Yeiser, Doris Beverly 1920- *WhoAmW 91*
Yeiser, Idabelle 1897?- *HarlReB*
Yeisley, Rexford A. 1947- *St&PR 91*
Yeiter, Patti 1917-1989 *BioIn 16*
Yekta, Timucin 1935- *WhoWor 91*
Yektai, Manoucher 1922- *WhoAm 90, WhoAmA 91*
Yektai, Niki *AuBYP 90*
Yeldell, James Willis, Jr. 1936- *St&PR 91*
Yelena Glinskaya 1506?-1538 *WomWR*
Yelencsics, Anthony M. *BioIn 16*
Yelenick, Mary Therese 1954- *WhoAmW 91*
Yelin, Gershon *BiDrAPA 89*
Yelin, Haim 1913-1944 *BioIn 16*
Yelin, Robert Bruce 1944- *WhoE 91*
Yelinek, Laura *BiDrAPA 89*
Yelity, Stephen C. 1949- *WhoAm 90*
Yell, Archibald 1797-1847 *BioIn 16*
Yelle, Christine Eveline 1952- *WhoE 91*
Yelle, George Francis 1913- *St&PR 91*
Yelle, Richard J. 1936- *St&PR 91*
Yelle, Richard Wilfred 1951- *WhoAm 90*
Yellen, Jack 1892- *OxCPMus, WorAlBi*
Yellen, Linda Beverly 1949- *WhoAmW 91*
Yellen, Maurice 1943- *St&PR 91*
Yellen, Steven L. *St&PR 91*
Yellin, Victor Fell 1924- *IntWWM 90, WhoAm 90*
Yellott, Roberta Kim 1952- *WhoSSW 91*
Yellow Hair 1850?-1876 *WhNaAH*
Yellow Hand *WhNaAH*
Yellow Thunder 1774?-1874 *WhNaAH*
Yellow Wolf *WhNaAH*
Yellow Wolf 1856-1935 *WhNaAH*
Yellowtail, Robert Summers *BioIn 16*
Yeltatzie, James Allen 1959- *BiDrAPA 89*
Yelton, Richard Allen 1965- *WhoSSW 91*
Yeltsin, Boris *BioIn 16*
Yeltsin, Boris 1931- *News 91-1 [port], WorAlBi*
Yeltsin, Boris N. *NewYTBS 90 [port]*
Yel'tsin, Boris Nikolayevich 1931- *WhoWor 91*
Yelvington, David Benjamin *BiDrAPA 89*
Yen, David Chi-Chung 1953- *WhoEmL 91*
Yen, Douglas Ernest 1924- *WhoWor 91*
Yen, Julia Lai-Teh *BiDrAPA 89*
Yen, Samuel Show-Chih 1927- *WhoAm 90*
Yen, Teh Fu 1927- *WhoAm 90*
Yen, Victor L. 1938- *St&PR 91*
Yen, Wen-hsiung 1934- *IntWWM 90*
Yen, Y. C. James 1893-1990 *BioIn 16, NewYTBS 90*
Yen, Y C James 1894?-1990 *CurBio 90N*
Yenawine, Philip 1942- *WhoAmA 91*
Yencho, George, Jr. 1924- *St&PR 91*
Yendell, Robert William 1927- *St&PR 91*
Yendo, Masayoshi 1920- *WhoWor 91*
Yengo, John W. 1915-1988 *BioIn 16*
Yeni, Leo 1920- *WhoAm 90*
Yenkin, Bernard K. 1930- *St&PR 91*
Yenkin, Fred 1911- *St&PR 91*
Yenne, Allen Wayne 1906- *St&PR 91*
Yenne, Charles Richard 1930- *St&PR 91*
Yensen, Arthur 1898- *WhoWrEP 89*
Yentis, Richard David 1938- *BiDrAPA 89*
Yeo, Douglas 1955- *IntWWM 90*
Yeo, Edwin Harley, III 1934- *WhoAm 90, WhoE 91*
Yeo, Jong-Kee 1946- *WhoWor 91*
Yeo, Ron 1933- *WhoAm 90*
Yeo, Ronald Frederick 1923- *WhoAm 90*
Yeoman, Lynn Chalmers 1943- *WhoSSW 91*
Yeomans, Donald Ralph 1925- *WhoAm 90*
Yeomans, Frank Elton 1949- *BiDrAPA 89*
Yeomans, Jay Anthony 1950- *BiDrAPA 89*
Yeon, Woon Bok *BiDrAPA 89*
Yeosock, Michael Michael 1962- *WhoE 91*
Yep, Laurence *BioIn 16*
Yep, Laurence 1948- *Au&Arts 5 [port]*
Yep, Laurence Michael 1948- *WhoAm 90*
Yepes, Narciso 1927- *PenDiMP*
Yepes De Acevedo, Fabio 1937- *IntWWM 90*
Yepsen, Harold Louis 1928- *St&PR 91*
Yepsen, Roger B. *BioIn 16*
Yeragani, Vikram Kumar *BiDrAPA 89*
Yerant, Gene Stephen 1947- *St&PR 91*
Yerasi, Bhaskar R. 1955- *BiDrAPA 89*
Yerazunis, Stephen 1922- *WhoAm 90*
Yerby, Frank *EarBlAP*
Yerby, Frank 1916- *WhoAm 90, WhoWrEP 89*
Yerby, Frank G 1916- *MajTwCW*
Yerbysmith, Ernest Alfred *WhoAmA 91N*
Yeretsian, Ara Khoren 1947- *BiDrAPA 89*
Yerevanian, Boghos Isahag 1949- *BiDrAPA 89*
Yerganian, Rosa *BioIn 16*
Yerger, Eloise Barrangon 1915- *EncO&P 3*
Yerger, John R. 1946- *St&PR 91*
Yerger, Ralph William 1922- *WhoAm 90*
Yergin, Daniel Howard 1947- *WhoAm 90*
Yergin, Marc Lawrence 1944- *WhoE 91*
Yerkes, David Norton 1911- *WhoAm 90*
Yerkes, Robert H. 1962- *St&PR 91*
Yerkes, Robert Mearns 1876-1956 *WorAlBi*
Yerkes, Stan 1874-1940 *Ballpl 90*
Yerkes, Steve 1888-1971 *Ballpl 90*
Yerkes, Susan Gamble 1951- *WhoAmW 91*
Yerkow, Charles *AuBYP 90*
Yerlich, Jean E. *ODwPR 91*
Yeroushalmi, Parviz *BiDrAPA 89*
Yerow, Mara H. 1951- *WhoE 91*
Yershov, Ivan 1867-1943 *PenDiMP*
Yerushalmi, Yosef Hayim 1932- *WhoAm 90*
Yes *EncPR&S 89, OxCPMus*
Yes, Phyllis A 1941- *WhoAmA 91*
Yesavage, Jerome Albert 1949- *BiDrAPA 89*
Yeshion, Theodore Elliot 1951- *WhoSSW 91*
Yeshurun, Avot 1904- *ConAu 132*
Yesipova, Anna 1851-1914 *PenDiMP*
Yesner, A. Glenn 1958- *St&PR 91*
Yessa, John M. 1939- *St&PR 91*
Yessin, George *BiDrAPA 89*
Yessler, Paul G 1922- *BiDrAPA 89*
Yester, Roselyn 1926- *WhoSSW 91*
Yeston, Maury 1945- *WhoAm 90*
Yestramski, Joanne L. 1953- *St&PR 91*
Yetka, Lawrence Robert 1924- *WhoAm 90*
Yetman, Gerald George 1929- *WhoSSW 91*
Yetnikoff, Walter R. *BioIn 16*
Yetnikoff, Walter R. 1933- *WhoAm 90*
Yetska 1940- *SmATA X [port]*
Yett, Fowler Redford 1919- *WhoSSW 91, WhoWor 91*
Yett, Rich 1962- *Ballpl 90*
Yetter, Thomas G. 1952- *St&PR 91*
Yetter, William Albert *BiDrAPA 89*
Yeu, Hokun *BiDrAPA 89*
Yeung, Chap-Yung 1936- *WhoWor 91*
Yeung, Edward Szeshing 1948- *WhoAm 90*
Yeung, Pat Hok-Kwong 1965- *WhoEmL 91, WhoWor 91*
Yeung, William 1947- *St&PR 91*
Yeung, Wing Hon 1947- *BiDrAPA 89*
Yeutter, Clayton K. *BioIn 16*
Yeutter, Clayton Keith 1930- *BiDrUSE 89, WhoAm 90, WhoE 91, WhoWor 91*
Yeutter, Laura P. *BioIn 16*
Yevtushenko, Yevgeniy Aleksandrovich 1933- *WhoWor 91*
Yevtushenko, Yevgeny 1933- *ConAu 33NR, MajTwCW, WorAlBi*
Yevtushenko, Yevgeny Aleksandrovich 1933- *BioIn 16*
Yewaisis, Joseph Stephen 1939- *St&PR 91*
Yezback, Steven A. 1943- *AuBYP 90*
Yezerski, Howard J 1941- *WhoAmA 91*
Yezierska, Anzia 1880?-1970 *FemiCLE*
Yezierska, Anzia 1885?-1970 *MajTwCW*
Yffer, Louis Alexander *IntWWM 90*
Yglesias, Helen 1915- *FemiCLE, MajTwCW*
Yglesias, Helen Bassine 1915- *WhoAm 90*
Yglesias, Jose 1919- *ConAu 32NR, HispWr 90, WhoHisp 91*
Yglesias Castro, Rafael 1861-1924 *BioIn 16*
Yhap, Laetitia 1941- *BiDWomA*
Yi Chong-ok *WhoWor 91*
Yi, Donna D 1957- *BiDrAPA 89*
Yi, Kang *BioIn 16*
Yiannakos, Andrew E. K. 1960- *WhoE 91*
Yiannes 1943- *WhoE 91*
Yiannopoulos, Athanassios Nicholas 1928- *WhoAm 90*
Yick, Paulina Y. 1961- *WhoAmW 91*
Yielding, K. Lemone 1931- *WhoAm 90*
Yien, Edward C. 1925- *St&PR 91*
Yih, Chia-Shun 1918- *WhoAm 90, WhoSSW 91*
Yih, Mae Dunn 1928- *WhoAmW 91*
Yillar, Mehmet K 1933- *BiDrAPA 89*
Yilma, Adamu Belay *WhoWor 91*
Yilmaz, Ahmet Mesut 1947- *WhoWor 91*
Yim, Jay Alan 1958- *IntWWM 90*
Yim, Mary Ancilla 1927- *WhoAmW 91*
Yim, Vera S. W. 1950- *WhoWrEP 89*
Yim, Won-Bin 1956- *IntWWM 90*
Yin, George Kuo-Ming 1949- *WhoEmL 91*
Yin, Gerald Zheyao 1944- *WhoWor 91*
Yin, Paul Yuen-Chen 1941- *BiDrAPA 89*
Yin, Ts'ao 1658-1712 *BioIn 16*
Ying Ruocheng 1929- *WhoWor 91*
Ying, John Jeffrey 1962- *WhoE 91*
Ying, John L. 1948- *WhoEmL 91, WhoWor 91*
Ying, Tian *BioIn 16*
Yinger, J. Milton 1916- *WhoAm 90*
Yingling, Adrienne Elizabeth 1959- *WhoAmW 91, WhoEmL 91*
Yingling, Earl 1888-1962 *Ballpl 90*
Yingling, Julie Margaret 1948- *WhoAmW 91*
Yingst, Beverly Ann 1955- *WhoAmW 91*
Yingst, Diane Marie 1961- *WhoAmW 91*
Yingst, Thomas E. 1950- *St&PR 91*
Yip, Alexander WaiHung 1948- *WhoEmL 91, WhoWor 91*
Yip, Cecil Cheung-Ching 1937- *WhoAm 90*
Yip, Pau-Wah 1937- *WhoWor 91*
Yip, Wai-Hong 1930- *WhoWor 91*
Yiptong, Charles Chan *BiDrAPA 89*
Yizar, Donald *St&PR 91*
Yizar, Jeanette *St&PR 91*
Yizar, Marvin 1950- *St&PR 91*
Yizar, Raymond *St&PR 91*
Yliheljo, Pentti Olavi 1945- *WhoWor 91*
Ylla *AuBYP 90*
Ylvisaker, Jane Penelope Mitchell 1946- *WhoAmW 91*
Ylvisaker, Paul Norman 1921- *WhoAm 90*
Ylvisaker, William T. 1924- *St&PR 91*
Ylvisaker, William Townend 1924- *WhoAm 90*
Ynclan, Nery 1959- *WhoHisp 91*
Yngve, John Anton 1924- *St&PR 91*
Yniguez, Linda Ellen 1960- *WhoAmW 91*

Yntema, Mary Katherine 1928- *WhoAmW 91*
Yoakam, Dwight *BioIn 16, WhoNeCM [port]*
Yoakum, Del 1915- *WhoAmA 91*
Yoakum, Gerald *BioIn 16*
Yoakum, Joseph Elmer 1886?-1972 *MusmAFA*
Yocam, Delbert Wayne 1943- *WhoAm 90*
Yoch, Florence *BioIn 16*
Yochelson, Ellis Leon 1928- *WhoAm 90*
Yochelson, John 1944- *WhoE 91*
Yochelson, Kathryn Mersey 1910- *WhoAmW 91, WhoE 91*
Yochem, August S, Jr. 1922- *BiDrAPA 89*
Yochem, Barbara June 1945- *WhoAmW 91, WhoWor 91*
Yochim, Louise Dunn 1909- *WhoAmA 91*
Yochim, Marie Hirst *WhoAmW 91, WhoE 91*
Yochum, Leo William 1927- *St&PR 91*
Yochum, Philip Theodore 1924- *WhoAm 90*
Yock, Robert John 1938- *WhoAm 90*
Yockel, Jane *BioIn 16*
Yockey, Anthony Scott 1956- *WhoEmL 91, WhoWor 91*
Yocom, John E. 1922- *St&PR 91*
Yocum, Frederic William, Jr. 1942- *St&PR 91*
Yocum, Ronald C. *BioIn 16*
Yocum, Ronald H. 1939- *St&PR 91*
Yocum, Ronald Harris 1939- *WhoAm 90*
Yoder, Allen 1927- *St&PR 91*
Yoder, Amos 1921- *WhoAm 90*
Yoder, Anna A. 1934- *WhoAmW 91*
Yoder, Carl W. 1937- *WhoAm 90*
Yoder, Carolyn Patricia 1953- *WhoAmW 91, WhoWrEP 89*
Yoder, Dan Samuel 1937- *St&PR 91*
Yoder, Daryl Hoak 1947- *BiDrAPA 89*
Yoder, Debra Marie 1955- *WhoSSW 91*
Yoder, Douglas O. 1918- *WhoAm 90*
Yoder, Edwin Milton 1934- *WhoAm 90, WhoWrEP 89*
Yoder, Eileen Rhude 1946- *WhoWrEP 89*
Yoder, Evelyn R. 1949- *St&PR 91*
Yoder, Frederick Floyd 1935- *WhoAm 90*
Yoder, Hatten Schuyler, Jr. 1921- *WhoAm 90*
Yoder, Margaret Ann 1963- *WhoEmL 91*
Yoder, Michael C. 1949- *St&PR 91*
Yoder, Nelson Brent 1944- *WhoSSW 91*
Yoder, Orus R *BiDrAPA 89*
Yoder, Patricia D. 1939- *ODwPR 91*
Yoder, Patricia Doherty 1942- *WhoAm 90, WhoAmW 91*
Yoder, Richard Allen 1947- *WhoAmA 91*
Yoder, Richard Franklin 1930- *St&PR 91, WhoAm 90*
Yoder, Robert Lee 1935- *WhoAm 90*
Yoder, Robert R 1922- *BiDrAPA 89*
Yoder, Ronnie A. 1937- *WhoAm 90*
Yoder, Sharon Kathleen 1942- *WhoAmW 91*
Yoder, Vernon Eli 1931- *BiDrAPA 89*
Yoder Wise, Patricia Snyder 1941- *WhoAmW 91*
Yodice, Lawrence Anthony 1941- *WhoE 91*
Yoe, Harry Warner 1912- *WhoAm 90*
Yoe, William Thomas 1952- *WhoSSW 91*
Yoel, Marcel M. 1931- *ODwPR 91*
Yoelson, Asa *BioIn 16*
Yoerg, Robert Louis 1940- *BiDrAPA 89*
Yoerger, Roger Raymond 1929- *WhoAm 90*
Yoffe, Stuart Alan 1936- *St&PR 91, WhoAm 90*
Yogananda, Paramahansa 1893-1952 *EncO&P 3, NewAgE 90*
Yogendra, Shri 1897- *NewAgE 90*
Yogev, Sara 1946- *WhoAmW 91*
Yogman, Jack 1920- *St&PR 91*
Yoh, Harold L., Jr. 1936- *St&PR 91*
Yoh, Harold Lionel, III 1960- *St&PR 91*
Yoh, Michael Hulme 1962- *St&PR 91*
Yoh, Shoei 1940- *ConDes 90*
Yohalem, Alan Daniel 1940- *St&PR 91*
Yohalem, David *BioIn 16*
Yohalem, Rona A. 1946- *WhoAmW 91*
Yohalem, Stephen Bennett 1916-1990 *BioIn 16*
Yohann, Monica Jean 1953- *WhoAmW 91*
Yohanna, Daniel *BiDrAPA 89*
Yohannan, Kohle *BioIn 16*
Yohe, Charles D 1922- *BiDrAPA 89*
Yohe, Frank James *BiDrAPA 89*
Yohe, John Christopher 1943- *St&PR 91*
Yohe, Linda J. 1949- *St&PR 91*
Yohe, Robert L. 1936- *WhoAm 90*
Yohman, Edward J. 1932- *St&PR 91*
Yohn, David Stewart 1929- *WhoAm 90*
Yohn, Sharon A. 1952- *WhoAmW 91*
Yokan, Melvyn R *BiDrAPA 89*
Yokell, David 1943- *BiDrAPA 89*
Yokell, Michael David 1946- *St&PR 91, WhoAm 90*
Yokely, Ronald Eugene 1942- *WhoWor 91*
Yokem, James William 1929- *St&PR 91*
Yoken, Deborah K. 1950- *ODwPR 91*
Yokley, Arlen G. 1937- *St&PR 91*
Yokley, Richard Clarence 1942- *WhoWor 91*
Yoko Ono *EncJap*
Yokobori, Takeo 1917- *WhoWor 91*
Yokobori, Yasumasa 1949- *WhoSSW 91*
Yokogawa, Kiyoshi 1946- *WhoWor 91*
Yokoi, Yoshinori 1932- *WhoWor 91*
Yokomi, Richard Koji 1944- *WhoAmA 91*
Yokoo, Tadanori 1936- *ConDes 90*
Yokosaka, Yasuhiko 1956- *IntWWM 90*
Yokum, Kenneth 1951- *WhoSSW 91*
Yolanda 1212-1228 *WomWR*
Yolande *WomWR*
Yolande de Bourgogne *WomWR*
Yolanta 1212-1228 *WomWR*
Yolen, Jane *BioIn 16*
Yolen, Jane 1939- *AuBYP 90, WhoWrEP 89*
Yolen, Jane Hyatt 1939- *WhoAm 90*
Yolles, Jennifer Cindy *BiDrAPA 89*
Yolles, Stanley F *BiDrAPA 89*
Yolles, Stanley Fausst 1919- *WhoAm 90*
Yolton, John William 1921- *WhoAm 90*
Yom, Peter Dongjun 1960- *WhoE 91*
Yomantas, Gary Charles 1949- *St&PR 91*
Yomazzo, Michael Joseph 1942- *St&PR 91*
Yon Hyong-muk 1925- *WhoWor 91*
Yon, Eugene T. 1936- *St&PR 91, WhoE 91*
Yon, Joseph L. 1912- *WhoAm 90*
Yon, Laura Troy 1957- *WhoSSW 91*
Yon, R.B. 1942- *St&PR 91*
Yonadi, Albert Joseph 1929- *St&PR 91*
Yonaguska 1760?-1839 *WhNaAH*
Yonagusta 1760?-1839 *WhNaAH*
Yonamine, Wally 1925- *Ballpl 90*
Yonas, Martin I. 1938- *St&PR 91*
Yonce, Samuel McClay 1931- *St&PR 91*
Yonda, Alfred William 1919- *WhoE 91, WhoWor 91*
Yoneda, Elaine 1906-1988 *BioIn 16*
Yoneda, Fumio 1929- *WhoWor 91*
Yoneda, Kimimaru 1931- *WhoWor 91*
Yoneda, Tetsuya *Ballpl 90*
Yonemura, Earl Tsuneki 1939- *WhoWor 91*
Yoneoka, Elaine Sayoko 1955- *WhoE 91*
Yonetani, Kaoru 1938- *WhoWor 91*
Yonezawa, Shigeru 1911- *WhoWor 91*
Yonezawa, Yoh 1929- *WhoWor 91*
Yong Zhen, Emperor *PenDiDA 89*
Yong, Junesik Nuri 1929- *BiDrAPA 89*
Yong, Raymond Nen-Yiu 1929- *WhoAm 90*
Yongchaiyut, Chaovalit *BioIn 16*
Yonge, Charlotte 1823-1901 *FemiCLE*
Yonge, Charlotte Mary 1823-1901 *BioIn 16*
Yonge, Denise Champagne 1952- *WhoSSW 91*
Yonge, Juliana *FemiCLE*
Yonge, Keith A 1910- *BiDrAPA 89*
Yongue, Alfred H 1932- *BiDrAPA 89*
Yongue, Judith Salle 1936- *BiDrAPA 89*
Yonker, Theresa Marie 1957- *BiDrAPA 89*
Yonkers, Anthony James 1938- *WhoAm 90*
Yonkers, Kimberly Ann 1957- *BiDrAPA 89*
Yonkers, Winifred Frances 1939- *WhoE 91*
Yonkman, Fredrick Albers 1930- *WhoAm 90*
Yonto, Anthony J. 1921- *St&PR 91*
Yontz, Kenneth Frederic 1944- *St&PR 91*
Yontz, Kenneth Fredric 1944- *WhoAm 90*
Yontz, William Lee 1938- *WhoE 91*
Yonusaitis, Linda Susan 1954- *WhoAmW 91*
Yoo, Dong Ho 1943- *BiDrAPA 89*
Yoo, John Hyun Soo *BiDrAPA 89*
Yoo, Paul J. 1939- *St&PR 91*
Yoo, Petrus S *BiDrAPA 89*
Yoo, Sang Wook *BiDrAPA 89*
Yoo, Sook Hee Lee *BiDrAPA 89*
Yoo, Suz Coover 1964- *WhoEmL 91*
Yoo, Tai Pyung 1945- *BiDrAPA 89*
Yood, Bernard *BiDrAPA 89*
Yoon, Albert S 1939- *BiDrAPA 89*
Yoon, Dosyng *BiDrAPA 89*
Yoon, Eui-Sun Lee *BiDrAPA 89*
Yoon, Hoil 1943- *WhoWor 91*
Yoon, Katherine C *BiDrAPA 89*
Yoon, Nam Im 1930- *BiDrAPA 89*
Yoon, Yeomin 1942- *WhoE 91*
Yoon, Young Shup 1938- *BiDrAPA 89*
Yoors, Jan 1922-1977 *WhoAmA 91N*
Yopp, Johanna Futchs 1938- *WhoAmW 91*
Yopp, Suzanne Anderson 1948- *WhoAmW 91*
Yopps, Fredric Robert 1945- *St&PR 91*
Yorburg, Betty 1926- *WhoAmW 91*
Yordan, Carlos Manuel 1925- *WhoAm 90*
Yordan, Philip 1913?- *ConAu 129*
Yorgo 1929- *WhoAmA 91*
Yori, Lawrence George 1950- *St&PR 91*
Yori, Robert Lance 1949- *St&PR 91*
Yorinks, Arthur 1953- *BioIn 16*
Yorio, Carlos Alfredo *BioIn 16*
Yorio, Frank A. 1947- *St&PR 91*
Yorio, Judith Mary 1952- *WhoAmW 91*
York, Albert 1928- *BioIn 16*
York, Alexandra *BioIn 16*
York, Alvin 1887-1964 *WorAlBi*
York, Andrew 1930- *TwCCr&M 91*
York, Anne Halstead 1945- *WhoAmW 91*
York, Anne Hyde, Duchess of 1637-1671 *BiDEWW, BioIn 16*
York, Anthony James 1948- *St&PR 91*
York, Arthur M. *ODwPR 91*
York, Beryl Roxanne 1938- *WhoAmW 91*
York, Beth *NewAgMG*
York, Billie Murray, Jr. 1948- *WhoSSW 91*
York, Carol 1928- *AuBYP 90*
York, Consuella *BioIn 16*
York, David Stanley 1920- *IntWWM 90*
York, Dick *BioIn 16*
York, E. Malcolm 1936- *St&PR 91*
York, E. Travis, Jr. 1922- *WhoAm 90*
York, Elizabeth Jane 1934- *WhoAmW 91*
York, Frederick, III *St&PR 91*
York, Harry Lawrence 1944- *WhoAm 90*
York, Herbert F. *BioIn 16*
York, Herbert Frank 1921- *WhoAm 90*
York, James Orison 1927- *WhoAm 90*
York, James Wesley 1912- *BioIn 16, St&PR 91*
York, James Wesley, Jr. 1939- *WhoAm 90*
York, Janet Brewster 1941- *WhoAmW 91, WhoE 91*
York, Jeremy *MajTwCW, TwCCr&M 91*
York, Jim 1947- *Ballpl 90*
York, John 1949- *IntWWM 90*
York, John Christopher 1946- *WhoEmL 91, WhoWor 91*
York, John Thomas 1953- *WhoWrEP 89*
York, Judith Ann 1955- *WhoAmW 91*
York, Linda Kaye 1948- *WhoAmW 91*
York, Lorraine 1958- *ConAu 129*
York, Michael 1942- *WhoAm 90, WorAlBi*
York, Michael Otto 1939- *WhoWor 91*
York, Nancy Ann 1947- *WhoAmW 91*
York, Philip Wylie 1942- *WhoSSW 91*
York, Phyllis 1937- *BioIn 16, ConAu 132*
York, Richard Travis 1950- *WhoAmA 91*
York, Robert 1919-1975 *WhoAmA 91N*
York, Rudy 1913-1970 *Ballpl 90*
York, Sarah, Duchess of 1959- *BioIn 16*
York, Simon *AuBYP 90, MajTwCW*
York, Stephen Stanier 1949- *WhoEmL 91*
York, Susannah 1941?- *BioIn 16, ConAu 130, WorAlBi*
York, Susannah 1942- *WhoAm 90, WhoWor 91*
York, Theodore C. 1942- *St&PR 91*
York, Tina 1951- *WhoAmA 91, WhoEmL 91*
York, Troy David 1944- *WhoSSW 91*
York, W. Thomas 1933- *St&PR 91*
Yorke, Aaron Jones, IV 1931- *WhoAm 90*
Yorke, Colin 1941- *IntWWM 90*
Yorke, Joseph 1724-1792 *BioIn 16*
Yorke, Malcolm 1938- *ConAu 131*
Yorke, Margaret 1924- *TwCCr&M 91*
Yorke, Marianne 1948- *WhoAmW 91, WhoE 91*
Yorke, Peter 1902-1966 *OxCPMus*
Yorke, Stephen 1840-1891 *FemiCLE*
Yorkin, Bud 1926- *WhoAm 90, WorAlBi*
Yorkston, Neil James 1928- *WhoAm 90*
Yorra, David Ian 1923- *St&PR 91*
Yorshis, Morris 1903- *BiDrAPA 89*
Yorty, Samuel 1909- *WhoAm 90*
Yoseloff, Julien David 1941- *WhoAm 90*
Yoseloff, Lee Daniels 1944- *BiDrAPA 89*
Yoseloff, Mark Laurance 1946- *WhoAm 90*
Yoseloff, Martin 1919- *WhoAm 90, WhoWrEP 89*
Yoseloff, Thomas 1913- *WhoAm 90, WhoWor 91, WhoWrEP 89*
Yosheda, Yoshio 1933- *Ballpl 90*
Yoshiaki, Taketa 1934- *WhoWor 91*
Yoshida Shigeru 1878-1967 *EncJap*
Yoshida, Masafumi 1946- *WhoWor 91*
Yoshida, Noriyoshi 1931- *WhoWor 91*
Yoshida, Ray Kakuo 1930- *WhoAmA 91*
Yoshida, Shigeru 1878-1967 *BioIn 16*
Yoshida, Shiro 1951- *WhoWor 91*
Yoshida, Takeshi *BiDrAPA 89*
Yoshida, Yukio 1925- *WhoWor 91*
Yoshida, Zen-Ichi 1925- *WhoWor 91*
Yoshihara, Ronald T. 1955- *St&PR 91*
Yoshihito, Emperor *EncJap*
Yoshii, Eiichi 1931- *WhoWor 91*
Yoshii, Rika 1959- *WhoAmW 91*
Yoshikawa, Masanosuke 1934- *WhoWor 91*
Yoshikawa, Viveca Ruth 1944- *WhoAmW 91*
Yoshikuni, Jiro 1919- *WhoWor 91*
Yoshimizou, Minoru 1939- *St&PR 91*
Yoshimoto, Haruhiko 1923- *WhoWor 91*
Yoshimura, Fumio 1926- *BioIn 16, WhoAmA 91*
Yoshimura, Hiroshi *NewAgMG*
Yoshimura, Junzo 1908- *WhoWor 91*
Yoshinaga, Ben K. 1922- *St&PR 91*
Yoshino Sakuzo 1878-1933 *EncJap*
Yoshino, Hiroyuki *BioIn 16*
Yoshioka, Kaoru David 1936- *St&PR 91*
Yoshioka, Masanori 1941- *WhoWor 91*
Yoshioka, Morimasa 1921- *WhoWor 91*
Yoshiyuki Junnosuke 1924- *WorAu 1980*
Yoshizawa, Hidenari 1941- *WhoWor 91*
Yoshizawa, Masakazu *NewAgMG*
Yoskowitz, Irving B. 1945- *St&PR 91*
Yoskowitz, Irving Benjamin 1945- *WhoAm 90*
Yosowitz, Sanford 1939- *St&PR 91, WhoAm 90*
Yosry, Mohamed Hussein *BiDrAPA 89*
Yoss, David 1946- *IntWWM 90*
Yossif, George *BiDrAPA 89*
Yossif, George 1939- *WhoSSW 91, WhoWor 91*
Yossifova, Ekaterina 1941- *EncCoWW*
Yost, Bernice *WhoAmW 91*
Yost, Byron Lee 1939- *St&PR 91*
Yost, Charles Woodruff 1907-1981 *BioIn 16*
Yost, Donald H. 1927- *St&PR 91*
Yost, Eddie 1926- *Ballpl 90*
Yost, Edna 1889-1971 *AuBYP 90*
Yost, Ellen Ginsberg 1945- *WhoAmW 91*
Yost, Erma Martin 1947- *WhoAmA 91*
Yost, Frank A. 1902- *St&PR 91*
Yost, Fred J 1888-1968 *WhoAmA 91N*
Yost, Frederick Maurice 1914- *St&PR 91*
Yost, Graham 1959- *ConAu 129*
Yost, H Hunter 1951- *BiDrAPA 89*
Yost, Henry Frank *BiDrAPA 89*
Yost, James Everett 1925- *WhoAm 90*
Yost, John F 1933- *BiDrAPA 89*
Yost, L. Morgan 1908- *WhoAm 90*
Yost, Leon C 1943- *WhoAmA 91*
Yost, Lyle E. 1913- *St&PR 91*
Yost, Lyle Edgar 1913- *BioIn 16, WhoAm 90*
Yost, Marlene J. 1934- *WhoAmW 91*
Yost, Miriam Kahn *BiDrAPA 89*
Yost, Murray A *BiDrAPA 89*
Yost, Nancy Runyon 1933- *WhoAmW 91, WhoWor 91*
Yost, Ned 1955- *Ballpl 90*
Yost, Nellie Irene Snyder 1905- *BioIn 16*
Yost, Nicholas Churchill 1938- *WhoE 91*
Yost, Patricia Ann 1937- *IntWWM 90*
Yost, Paul Alexander, Jr. 1929- *WhoAm 90*
Yost, Paul Wesley 1920- *BiDrAPA 89*
Yost, Pauline Chambers 1916- *St&PR 91*
Yost, R. David 1947- *St&PR 91*
Yost, Richard Alan 1953- *WhoSSW 91*
Yost, Robert L. 1922-1990 *BioIn 16*
Yost, William Albert 1944- *WhoAm 90*
Yost, William Arthur, III 1935- *St&PR 91, WhoAm 90, WhoWor 91*
Yoste, Charles Todd 1948- *WhoSSW 91*
Yothers, Tina 1973- *WhoHisp 91*
Yotsuuye, Elsie Leilani 1936- *WhoAmW 91*
Yotsuyanagi, Takao 1938- *WhoWor 91*
Youd, C. S. 1922- *BioIn 16*
Youdelman, Jeffrey David 1947- *WhoE 91*
Youdovin, Susan W. 1941- *ODwPR 91*
Youdovin, Susan Welber 1941- *WhoE 91*
Youel, Kenneth 1901- *WhoAm 90*
Youell, Mary Louise 1957- *WhoAmW 91*
Youf, Jean-Baptiste-Gilles 1762-1838 *PenDiDA 89*
Youkeles, Anne *WhoAmA 91*
Youkeoma 1835?-1929 *WhNaAH*
Youkioma 1835?-1929 *WhNaAH*
Youman, Lillian Hobson Lincoln 1940- *WhoAmW 91*
Youman, Robert Inis 1928- *St&PR 91*
Youman, Roger Jacob 1932- *WhoAm 90*
Youmans, Claire *WhoWrEP 89*
Youmans, Floyd 1964- *Ballpl 90*
Youmans, Julian Ray 1928- *WhoAm 90*
Youmans, Letitia *DcCanB 12*
Youmans, Rich 1960- *WhoWrEP 89*
Youmans, Vincent 1898-1946 *BioIn 16, OxCPMus, WorAlBi*
Younce, Huston Howard 1936- *St&PR 91*
Young Bear 1868-1933 *WhNaAH*
Young Lady, A *BiDEWW*
Young, Lord 1932- *WhoWor 91*
Young M.C. 1968- *ConMus 4 [port]*
Young, A S 1924- *DrBIPA 90*
Young, A. Thomas 1938- *WhoE 91*
Young, Alan 1919- *WorAlBi*
Young, Alan 1949- *WhoAmA 91*
Young, Albert Frederick, Jr. 1946- *WhoE 91*
Young, Albert James 1939- *WhoWrEP 89*
Young, Alexander 1920- *IntWWM 90, PenDiMP*
Young, Allen 1941- *WhoWrEP 89*
Young, Andrew *NewYTBS 90 [port]*
Young, Andrew 1932- *BioIn 16, WhoAm 90, WhoSSW 91, WorAlBi*
Young, Andrew B. 1907- *St&PR 91*
Young, Andrew Brodbeck 1907- *WhoAm 90*

Young, Andrew Jackson, Jr. 1932- *BlkAmsC [port]*
Young, Andrew Sturgeon Nash 1924- *BioIn 16*
Young, Ann Eliza 1844-1908? *BioAmW*
Young, Ann Elizabeth O'Quinn *WhoAmW 91*
Young, Anne Steele 1923- *ConAu 129*
Young, Ardell Moody 1911- *WhoAm 90*
Young, Arnold L. 1932- *St&PR 91*
Young, Art 1866-1943 *BioIn 16, EncAL*
Young, Arthur Gordon 1921- *WhoAm 90*
Young, Arthur Henry 1866-1943 *BioIn 16*
Young, Arthur Price 1940- *WhoAm 90, WhoSSW 91*
Young, Arthur R. 1925- *St&PR 91*
Young, Augustus J. 1922- *St&PR 91*
Young, Austin Prentiss 1940- *St&PR 91*
Young, Babe 1915-1983 *Ballpl 90*
Young, Babette Spero 1918- *St&PR 91*
Young, Barbara 1920- *BiDrAPA 89, WhoAm 90, WhoAmA 91*
Young, Barbara Aldie 1964- *WhoAmW 91*
Young, Barbara N 1939- *BiDrAPA 89*
Young, Barbara Neil 1943- *WhoAmA 91*
Young, Barbara Pisaro 1939- *WhoAmW 91*
Young, Barney Thornton 1934- *WhoAm 90, WhoWor 91*
Young, Bascom B *BiDrAPA 89*
Young, Bernice Elizabeth 1931- *AuBYP 90, BioIn 16*
Young, Beverly Ann *WhoSSW 91*
Young, Beverly J. 1934- *St&PR 91*
Young, Bill *BioIn 16*
Young, Billie 1933- *WhoE 91*
Young, Bobby 1925-1985 *Ballpl 90*
Young, Bracebridge Hemyng 1956- *WhoAm 90*
Young, Bradley 1955- *St&PR 91*
Young, Brian Richard *BiDrAPA 89*
Young, Brian W. 1939- *St&PR 91*
Young, Brigham 1801-1877 *WhNaAH, WorAlBi*
Young, Bruce Jay 1941- *St&PR 91*
Young, Bryant Llewellyn 1948- *WhoAm 90*
Young, Burt 1927- *WorAlBi*
Young, Burt 1940- *WhoAm 90*
Young, C. B. Fehrler 1908- *WhoSSW 91*
Young, C. Clifton 1922- *WhoAm 90*
Young, C. Fredric 1938- *St&PR 91*
Young, C. W. Bill 1930- *WhoAm 90, WhoSSW 91*
Young, Carol Ann 1933- *WhoAmW 91*
Young, Carol Ann Morizot 1944- *WhoWrEP 89*
Young, Carole J. 1950- *WhoAmW 91*
Young, Cathy *BioIn 16*
Young, Cecilia 1710?-1789 *PenDiMP*
Young, Chad 1954- *St&PR 91*
Young, Charles Alexander 1930- *WhoAmA 91, WhoE 91*
Young, Charles Edward 1931- *WhoAm 90, WhoWor 91*
Young, Charles Edward 1942- *WhoSSW 91*
Young, Charles Morris 1869-1964 *WhoAmA 91N*
Young, Charles R *BiDrAPA 89*
Young, Charles Richard *BiDrAPA 89*
Young, Charles Smith 1943- *WhoSSW 91*
Young, Chester George 1944- *St&PR 91*
Young, Chic 1901-1973 *EncACom, WhoAmA 91N*
Young, Chloe Hamilton 1927-1985 *BioIn 16*
Young, Chris *BioIn 16*
Young, Chris 1971- *ConTFT 8 [port]*
Young, Christine Brooks 1944- *WhoAmW 91*
Young, Cliff 1905-1985 *WhoAmA 91N*
Young, Clyde William 1919- *IntWWM 90*
Young, Coleman *BioIn 16*
Young, Coleman A. 1918- *WorAlBi*
Young, Coleman Alexander 1918- *WhoAm 90*
Young, Collier *TwCCr&M 91*
Young, Connie Paraskevin- *BioIn 16*
Young, Conrad Scotland 1921- *St&PR 91*
Young, Curt 1960- *Ballpl 90*
Young, Curtis James 1949- *WhoSSW 91*
Young, Cy 1867-1955 *Ballpl 90 [port], WorAlBi*
Young, Daisy Fuller *BioIn 16*
Young, Dale L. 1928- *St&PR 91*
Young, Dale Lee 1928- *WhoAm 90*
Young, Dallas M 1914- *WhoAm 90*
Young, Daniel Test 1923- *WhoAm 90*
Young, Darlene Lynelle 1963- *WhoAmW 91*
Young, David A *BiDrAPA 89*
Young, David Alexander 1942- *WhoSSW 91*
Young, David John 1962- *WhoE 91*
Young, David Lincoln 1929- *WhoAm 90*
Young, David Maynard 1928- *WhoE 91*
Young, David Michael 1935- *WhoAm 90*
Young, David Michael 1949- *St&PR 91*
Young, David Pollock 1936- *WhoAm 90, WhoWrEP 89*
Young, David Reginald 1936- *WhoWor 91*
Young, David William 1942- *WhoE 91*
Young, Davis 1939- *ODwPR 91*
Young, Deablo *BioIn 16*
Young, Dean 1938- *ConAu 130*
Young, Deborah *BiDrAPA 89*
Young, Deborah Nelson 1961- *WhoE 91*
Young, Del 1912-1979 *Ballpl 90*
Young, Dennis Eugene 1943- *St&PR 91, WhoAm 90*
Young, Dennis Michael *BiDrAPA 89*
Young, Dick 1918-1987 *Ballpl 90*
Young, Don J. 1910- *WhoAm 90*
Young, Dona D. 1954- *St&PR 91*
Young, Dona Davis Gagliano 1954- *WhoAmW 91*
Young, Donald A. *ODwPR 91*
Young, Donald Alan 1939- *WhoAm 90*
Young, Donald E. 1933- *WhoAm 90*
Young, Donald Francis 1944- *WhoSSW 91*
Young, Donald Fredrick 1928- *WhoAm 90*
Young, Donald L 1934- *BiDrAPA 89*
Young, Donald Roy 1935- *WhoE 91*
Young, Donald Stirling 1933- *WhoAm 90*
Young, Dorothy Theressa 1929- *WhoWor 91*
Young, Douglas 1947- *IntWWM 90*
Young, Douglas E. 1949- *St&PR 91*
Young, Douglas F. 1911-1989 *BioIn 16*
Young, Douglas Logan 1938- *St&PR 91*
Young, Dwight Wayne 1925- *WhoAm 90*
Young, E. H. 1880-1949 *FemiCLE*
Young, Ed *BioIn 16*
Young, Ed 1931- *ConAu 130*
Young, Edna E 1936- *WhoAmA 91*
Young, Edward *AuBYP 90*
Young, Edward 1683-1765 *BioIn 16, DcLB 95 [port]*
Young, Edward 1927- *WhoWor 91*
Young, Edward G. 1939- *St&PR 91*
Young, Edward S. 1926- *St&PR 91*
Young, Edwin Harold 1918- *WhoAm 90*
Young, Edwin S. W. 1943- *WhoWor 91*
Young, Elaine Claire 1931- *WhoE 91*
Young, Elisabeth Larsh 1910- *WhoWrEP 89*
Young, Ella 1867-1956 *AuBYP 90*
Young, Ella Flagg 1845-1918 *BioAmW*
Young, Eric 1912-1986 *BioIn 16*
Young, Eric A. 1958- *St&PR 91*
Young, Eric Alan 1958- *WhoSSW 91*
Young, Ernestina Munoz 1954- *WhoAmW 91*
Young, Faron 1932- *OxCPMus*
Young, Florence H. 1923- *St&PR 91*
Young, Florence M *BiDrAPA 89*
Young, Francis A 1907- *ConAu 130*
Young, Francis Allan 1918- *WhoAm 90*
Young, Frank, Jr. 1925- *WhoWrEP 89*
Young, Frank B., Jr. 1951- *St&PR 91*
Young, Frank E. *BioIn 16*
Young, Frank Edward 1931- *WhoAm 90*
Young, Frank Mitchell 1940- *IntWWM 90*
Young, Frank Nelson, Jr. 1915- *WhoAm 90*
Young, Frank Sharp 1933- *WhoAm 90*
Young, Fredda Florine 1937- *WhoSSW 91*
Young, Frederic Hisgin 1936- *WhoWor 91*
Young, Frederica *AuBYP 90*
Young, Frederick Hugh 1936- *St&PR 91*
Young, Gail Adaline 1948- *WhoEmL 91*
Young, Garry Gean 1951- *WhoWor 91*
Young, Gary Eugene 1951- *WhoWrEP 89*
Young, Gary M. *BioIn 16, NewYTBS 90*
Young, Gary Thomas 1946- *WhoSSW 91*
Young, Gavin 1928- *BioIn 16*
Young, Genevieve Leman 1930- *St&PR 91, WhoAm 90*
Young, Genevieve Marie 1963- *WhoE 91*
Young, George Adams 1958- *WhoE 91*
Young, George Bernard, Jr. 1930- *WhoAm 90, WhoE 91*
Young, George Cressler 1916- *WhoAm 90*
Young, George Haywood, Jr. 1921- *WhoAm 90, WhoWor 91*
Young, George Kennedy 1911-1990 *ConAu 131*
Young, George M. 1949- *St&PR 91*
Young, Gerald 1964- *Ballpl 90*
Young, Gerry *BioIn 16*
Young, Gig 1917-1978 *WorAlBi*
Young, Gloria Rose 1947- *WhoWrEP 89*
Young, Gordon Alan 1920- *WhoWor 91*
Young, Gordon Ellsworth 1919- *IntWWM 90, WhoAm 90*
Young, Grace Oralee *BiDrAPA 89*
Young, Gregory G 1929- *BiDrAPA 89*
Young, H.R. 1918- *St&PR 91*
Young, Harold Chester 1932- *ConAu 129*
Young, Harvey Michael 1937- *St&PR 91*
Young, Henry Vival 1936- *WhoSSW 91*
Young, Herbert Floyd 1929- *St&PR 91*
Young, Herbert J. 1931- *St&PR 91, WhoAm 90*
Young, Herrick B. *NewYTBS 90*
Young, Herrick B. 1904-1990 *BioIn 16*
Young, Holly Peacock 1949- *WhoAmW 91*
Young, Howard How-wah 1948- *WhoWor 91*
Young, Howard Seth 1924- *WhoAm 90*
Young, Howard Thomas 1926- *WhoAm 90*
Young, Hubert Howell, Jr. 1945- *WhoSSW 91*
Young, Hugh David 1930- *WhoAm 90*
Young, Hugh Howard *BiDrAPA 89*
Young, Ian Musgrave 1941- *WhoAm 90*
Young, Irv 1877-1935 *Ballpl 90*
Young, J. Anthony *WhoAm 90*
Young, J. Givens 1921- *St&PR 91*
Young, J. Michael 1943- *WhoSSW 91*
Young, J. Will 1906- *St&PR 91*
Young, James Allan 1934- *WhoAm 90*
Young, James Arthur 1926- *WhoAm 90*
Young, James Bradford 1951- *IntWWM 90*
Young, James E 1921- *BiDrAPA 89*
Young, James E. 1941- *WhoWor 91*
Young, James Earl 1922- *WhoAm 90*
Young, James Fred 1934- *WhoAm 90*
Young, James H. 1932- *St&PR 91*
Young, James Harry 1936- *WhoAm 90, WhoSSW 91*
Young, James Harvey 1915- *WhoAm 90*
Young, James Heyward, Jr. 1937- *WhoAm 90*
Young, James Joseph *BiDrAPA 89*
Young, James Julius 1926- *WhoAm 90*
Young, James Morningstar 1929- *WhoAm 90*
Young, James Nolen 1924- *WhoSSW 91*
Young, James Oliver 1945- *WhoEmL 91, WhoSSW 91, WhoWor 91*
Young, James Richard 1945- *BiDrAPA 89*
Young, James Richard 1960- *St&PR 91*
Young, James Scott 1956- *WhoWrEP 89*
Young, Jan *AuBYP 90*
Young, Janet Cheryl 1960- *WhoAmW 91*
Young, Janet Randall *AuBYP 90*
Young, Janie Chester 1949- *WhoAmA 91, WhoE 91*
Young, Jay Alfred 1920- *WhoE 91*
Young, Jeffery Thomas 1955- *BiDrAPA 89*
Young, Jeffrey 1942- *St&PR 91*
Young, Jere Arnold 1936- *WhoAm 90*
Young, Jerome Melvyn 1941- *BiDrAPA 89*
Young, Jess R. 1928- *WhoAm 90*
Young, Jess Wollett 1926- *WhoSSW 91, WhoWor 91*
Young, Jesse Colin *EncPR&S 89*
Young, Jesse Robert 1938- *St&PR 91*
Young, Jimmie Eugene 1944- *WhoWor 91*
Young, Joan Carol 1928- *WhoSSW 91*
Young, Joan Crawford 1931- *WhoAmW 91, WhoWor 91*
Young, Joe 1889-1939 *OxCPMus*
Young, John 1930- *BioIn 16*
Young, John A. *BioIn 16, St&PR 91*
Young, John Alan 1932- *WhoAm 90*
Young, John Edward 1935- *WhoAm 90, WhoE 91, WhoWor 91*
Young, John F. 1957- *St&PR 91*
Young, John Falkner 1940- *WhoSSW 91*
Young, John Gerald *BiDrAPA 89*
Young, John H 1922- *BiDrAPA 89*
Young, John Hardin 1948- *WhoAm 90, WhoE 91, WhoEmL 91, WhoWor 91*
Young, John Hendricks 1912- *WhoAm 90, WhoWor 91*
Young, John Henry 1955- *WhoE 91*
Young, John Jeffrey 1951- *WhoSSW 91*
Young, John Leonard 1943- *BiDrAPA 89, WhoE 91*
Young, John Marvin 1941- *St&PR 91*
Young, John Michael 1944- *WhoAm 90*
Young, John Morgan 1941- *St&PR 91, WhoAm 90*
Young, John Paul, II 1945- *St&PR 91*
Young, John Richard *AuBYP 90*
Young, John Russell 1840-1899 *BioIn 16*
Young, John T 1954- *WhoAmA 91*
Young, John W. 1930- *WorAlBi*
Young, John Watts 1930- *WhoAm 90*
Young, John William 1912- *WhoSSW 91*
Young, Jordan R. 1950- *WhoWrEP 89*
Young, Joseph Beverly 1934- *St&PR 91*
Young, Joseph E 1939- *WhoAmA 91*
Young, Joseph H. 1922- *WhoAm 90*
Young, Joseph Laurie 1924- *WhoAm 90*
Young, Joseph Louis 1919- *WhoAm 90, WhoAmA 91*
Young, Joseph Lum-Jip 1935- *St&PR 91*
Young, Joseph-Marie 1820-1897 *DcCanB 12*
Young, Joseph Samuel, Jr. 1932- *WhoWrEP 89*
Young, June Magna 1936- *WhoAmW 91*
Young, Kara *BioIn 16*
Young, Karen *ConTFT 8*
Young, Karl Frederick 1931- *WhoSSW 91*
Young, Kathy Ann 1948- *WhoE 91*
Young, Kenneth 1927- *WhoAm 90*
Young, Kenneth Earl 1925- *St&PR 91*
Young, Kenneth Evans 1922- *WhoAm 90*
Young, Kenneth Victor 1933- *WhoAmA 91*
Young, Kip 1954- *Ballpl 90*
Young, Laura 1947- *WhoAm 90*
Young, Laurence Byron 1932- *St&PR 91*
Young, Laurence Retman 1935- *WhoAm 90, WhoE 91*
Young, Laurens Dolan 1942- *BiDrAPA 89*
Young, Lauretta Lee *BiDrAPA 89*
Young, Lawrence 1925- *WhoAm 90*
Young, Lawrence J. 1944- *St&PR 91*
Young, Leah Ruth 1942- *WhoE 91*
Young, Legrande L. 1936- *St&PR 91*
Young, Leianna Mary 1944- *WhoAmW 91*
Young, Leo 1926- *WhoAm 90*
Young, Leontine Ruth *BioIn 16*
Young, Lesley Margaret 1954- *IntWWM 90*
Young, Lester *BioIn 16*
Young, Lester 1909-1959 *DrBIPA 90, OxCPMus, WorAlBi*
Young, Linda O. *BioIn 16*
Young, Lionel Wesley 1932- *WhoAm 90*
Young, Lisa 1960- *BiDrAPA 89*
Young, Lisa Sperber 1952- *WhoAmW 91*
Young, Lloyd *BiDrAPA 89*
Young, Lois 1911-1981 *AuBYP 90*
Young, Lois Anne 1936- *WhoAmW 91*
Young, Lois Catherine 1930- *WhoAmW 91, WhoWor 91*
Young, Lois Moran *NewYTBS 90 [port]*
Young, Loretta 1913- *BioAmW, BioIn 16, ConTFT 8, WhoAm 90, WhoAmW 91, WorAlBi*
Young, Loretta A. 1962- *WhoAmW 91*
Young, Lorraine K. 1935- *St&PR 91*
Young, Louise B. 1919- *SmATA 64 [port]*
Young, Louise Dillon Gray 1935- *WhoAmW 91*
Young, Lucy Cleaver 1943- *WhoAmW 91*
Young, Lyman 1893-1984 *EncACom*
Young, M. Clemewell 1925- *WhoWrEP 89*
Young, Mahonri M 1877-1957 *WhoAmA 91N*
Young, Mahonri S 1911- *WhoAmA 91*
Young, Mahonri Sharp 1911- *WhoAm 90*
Young, Malcolm Black 1940- *St&PR 91*
Young, Margaret Aletha McMullen 1916- *WhoAmW 91, WhoSSW 91*
Young, Margaret B. 1922- *BioIn 16*
Young, Margaret Buckner *WhoAmW 91, WhoE 91, WhoWor 91*
Young, Margaret Ellen 1934- *St&PR 91*
Young, Margaret Hays 1954- *WhoAmW 91*
Young, Margaret Mary *BioIn 16*
Young, Margaret Mary 1909- *NotWoAT*
Young, Margaret Ruth 1953- *WhoAmW 91*
Young, Marguerite 1909- *FemiCLE*
Young, Marianne P *BiDrAPA 89*
Young, Marianne Pollak 1915- *WhoE 91*
Young, Marie Theresa 1952- *WhoE 91*
Young, Marion Marshall *BiDrAPA 89*
Young, Marjabelle *AuBYP 90*
Young, Marjorie H. 1946- *WhoAmW 91*
Young, Marjorie W. *WhoSSW 91*
Young, Marjorie Ward 1910- *WhoAmA 91*
Young, Marjorie Willis *WhoAm 90*
Young, Mark E. 1957- *St&PR 91*
Young, Mark James 1966- *WhoE 91*
Young, Mark Jeffrey 1949- *BiDrAPA 89*
Young, Marlene Annette 1946- *WhoAmW 91*
Young, Marvin O. 1929- *St&PR 91*
Young, Marvin Oscar 1929- *WhoAm 90*
Young, Mary Elizabeth 1929- *WhoAm 90, WhoAmW 91*
Young, Mary Ellen 1949- *WhoWrEP 89*
Young, Mary Julia *FemiCLE*
Young, Mary Louise 1920- *WhoE 91, WhoWrEP 89*
Young, Mary Sophie 1872-1919 *WomFie [port]*
Young, Matt 1958- *Ballpl 90*
Young, Matt Norvel, Jr. 1915- *WhoAm 90*
Young, Maurice Alan 1914- *St&PR 91*
Young, Maurice Isaac 1927- *WhoAm 90*
Young, Melanie A. 1959- *ODwPR 91*
Young, Melanie Sue 1961- *WhoAmW 91*
Young, Melinda Louise *BiDrAPA 89*
Young, Melville Curtis 1935- *St&PR 91*
Young, Meredith Anne 1952- *WhoAmW 91*
Young, Meredith Lady *EncPaPR 91*
Young, Merwin Crawford 1931- *WhoAm 90*
Young, Michael Cochise 1957- *WhoSSW 91*
Young, Michael David 1939- *WhoE 91*
Young, Michael Minkyo *BiDrAPA 89*
Young, Michael R. 1945- *WhoAm 90*
Young, Michael Richard 1956- *WhoE 91, WhoEmL 91, WhoWor 91*
Young, Michael Warren 1947- *St&PR 91*
Young, Michael William 1951- *WhoE 91*
Young, Mike 1960- *Ballpl 90*
Young, Milton Earl 1929- *WhoAm 90*
Young, Milton R. 1897-1983 *WorAlBi*
Young, Miriam 1913-1974 *AuBYP 90*
Young, Mitchell Alan *BiDrAPA 89*
Young, Monika Jane 1952- *ODwPR 91*
Young, Nancy *ODwPR 91*

Young, Nancy 1954- *WhoAm 90, WhoAmW 91, WhoEmL 91*
Young, Nancy J 1939- *WhoAmA 91*
Young, Neal E. 1943- *St&PR 91*
Young, Neil *BioIn 16*
Young, Neil 1945- *EncPR&S 89, News 91-2 [port], WhoAm 90, WorAlBi*
Young, Nicholas *BiDrAPA 89*
Young, Nicholas Edwyn 1945- *WhoWor 91*
Young, Noel B. 1922- *WhoWrEP 89*
Young, Norma 1928- *WhoSSW 91*
Young, Olivia Knowles 1922- *WhoAm 90*
Young, Oran Reed 1941- *WhoAm 90*
Young, Otis 1932- *DrBlPA 90*
Young, Owen D. 1874-1962 *BioIn 16, EncABHB 7 [port]*
Young, P. B. 1884-1962 *BioIn 16*
Young, Pamela Thorpe 1959- *WhoAmW 91*
Young, Parry 1943- *St&PR 91*
Young, Patrick *AuBYP 90*
Young, Patrick G 1955- *BiDrAPA 89*
Young, Paul *WhoHisp 91*
Young, Paul 1956- *EncPR&S 89*
Young, Paul Allen 1898-1979 *BioIn 16*
Young, Paul Andrew 1926- *WhoAm 90*
Young, Paul Ruel 1936- *WhoAm 90*
Young, Pep 1907-1962 *Ballpl 90*
Young, Percy M 1912- *ConAu 31NR*
Young, Percy Marshall 1912- *AuBYP 90, IntWWM 90*
Young, Peter A. *St&PR 91*
Young, Peter Alfred, Jr. 1943- *WhoE 91*
Young, Peter Edmund 1948- *WhoWor 91*
Young, Peter Ford 1940- *WhoAmA 91*
Young, Peter John *St&PR 91N*
Young, Peter V. 1936- *St&PR 91*
Young, Philip 1948- *IntWWM 90*
Young, Philip Baker 1950- *WhoSSW 91*
Young, Philip Mayo 1940- *WhoAm 90*
Young, Philip Pratt 1918- *WhoAm 90*
Young, Philip Stuart 1947- *St&PR 91*
Young, Plummer Bernard 1884-1962 *BioIn 16*
Young, Polly 1749?-1799 *PenDiMP*
Young, Quentin Hayes 1944- *St&PR 91*
Young, Ralph 1889-1965 *Ballpl 90*
Young, Ralph Alden 1920- *WhoAm 90*
Young, Ralph Eugene 1923- *WhoAm 90*
Young, Ralph O. 1931- *St&PR 91*
Young, Ralph W. 1928- *St&PR 91*
Young, Raymond Henry 1927- *WhoAm 90*
Young, Raymond Holmes 1928- *St&PR 91*
Young, Raymond N. 1938- *St&PR 91*
Young, Rebecca Mary Conrad 1934- *WhoAmW 91*
Young, Reginald J *BiDrAPA 89*
Young, Revel Paul 1944- *St&PR 91*
Young, Richard 1919- *WhoAm 90*
Young, Richard Alan 1935- *WhoAm 90*
Young, Richard Allen 1915- *St&PR 91, WhoAm 90*
Young, Richard Emerson 1932- *WhoAm 90*
Young, Richard Michael 1941- *WhoWor 91*
Young, Richard Stuart 1927- *WhoAm 90*
Young, Richard W. 1929- *St&PR 91*
Young, Richard William 1926- *St&PR 91, WhoAm 90, WhoE 91*
Young, Rida 1875-1926 *FemiCLE*
Young, Rida Johnson *BioIn 16*
Young, Rida Johnson 1869-1926 *OxCPMus*
Young, Rida Johnson 1875?-1926 *NotWoAT*
Young, Robert *ConAu 31NR*
Young, Robert 1907- *WhoAm 90, WorAlBi*
Young, Robert A. 1952- *St&PR 91*
Young, Robert A., III 1940- *St&PR 91, WhoAm 90, WhoSSW 91*
Young, Robert Alan 1921- *WhoAm 90*
Young, Robert Andrew 1964- *WhoEmL 91*
Young, Robert B. 1929- *St&PR 91*
Young, Robert Britton 1955- *BiDrAPA 89, WhoE 91*
Young, Robert Bruno *BiDrAPA 89*
Young, Robert C 1947- *BiDrAPA 89*
Young, Robert C. 1960- *WhoE 91*
Young, Robert Crabill 1940- *WhoAm 90*
Young, Robert Francis 1919- *WhoAm 90*
Young, Robert G 1929- *WhoAmA 91*
Young, Robert Harris 1947- *St&PR 91*
Young, Robert John 1938- *WhoAmA 91*
Young, Robert Lerton 1936- *St&PR 91*
Young, Robert M. 1924- *BioIn 16*
Young, Robert M 1954- *BiDrAPA 89*
Young, Robert Marshall 1933- *WhoSSW 91*
Young, Robert N. 1926- *St&PR 91*
Young, Robert S W 1948- *WhoAmA 91*
Young, Robert Truman 1919- *WhoSSW 91*
Young, Robert William 1916-1969 *AuBYP 90*
Young, Robin Ray 1952- *St&PR 91*
Young, Roger Austin 1946- *St&PR 91, WhoAm 90*
Young, Roland 1887-1953 *WorAlBi*
Young, Ronald A. 1928- *St&PR 91*
Young, Ronald C *BiDrAPA 89*
Young, Ronald Carl 1955- *WhoEmL 91*
Young, Ronald Faris 1939- *WhoAm 90*
Young, Ronnie Lee 1943- *St&PR 91*
Young, Rose *ConAu 30NR*
Young, Roy Alton 1921- *WhoAm 90*
Young, Roy Reid, III 1948- *WhoWor 91*
Young, Roy Robert 1917- *St&PR 91*
Young, Ruby Jean 1923- *WhoWrEP 89*
Young, Samuel A. 1940- *St&PR 91*
Young, Sandra Betty 1940- *WhoAmW 91*
Young, Sandra Cooper 1939- *WhoAmW 91*
Young, Sandra Kay 1961- *WhoAmW 91*
Young, Sarah Margaret *BiDrAPA 89*
Young, Scott 1946- *St&PR 91*
Young, Scott Alexander 1918- *WhoAm 90*
Young, Scott Arnold *BiDrAPA 89*
Young, Sean *BioIn 16*
Young, Sharon Ann 1959- *WhoAmW 91*
Young, Sharon Lee 1955- *WhoAmW 91*
Young, Shin *BioIn 16*
Young, Shirley 1935- *St&PR 91, WhoAm 90, WhoAmW 91*
Young, Shirley Jean 1944- *WhoAmW 91, WhoSSW 91*
Young, Shirley June 1937- *WhoAmW 91, WhoSSW 91*
Young, Shirley Lou 1944- *WhoAmW 91*
Young, Stanley 1906-1975 *AuBYP 90*
Young, Stark 1881-1963 *DcLB 102 [port]*
Young, Stephanie Dee 1948- *WhoAmW 91*
Young, Stephen Wesley 1946- *WhoE 91*
Young, Steven Alan *BiDrAPA 89*
Young, Steven Dale 1948- *St&PR 91*
Young, Steven James *BiDrAPA 89*
Young, Steven Scott 1966- *WhoEmL 91*
Young, Stuart F., Jr. 1950- *St&PR 91*
Young, Sue Duncan 1953- *WhoSSW 91*
Young, Susan Elizabeth 1946- *WhoAmW 91*
Young, Susan Frances *WhoAmW 91*
Young, Susan Rodbard 1941- *BiDrAPA 89*
Young, Sutton E. 1847- *AmLegL*
Young, Terence 1915- *WhoAm 90*
Young, Teresa Moran *BiDrAPA 89*
Young, Terry Alan 1954- *WhoSSW 91*
Young, Thomas 1731-1777 *BioIn 16*
Young, Thomas 1773-1829 *WorAlBi*
Young, Thomas Daniel 1919- *BioIn 16, WhoAm 90*
Young, Thomas Ganley *WhoE 91*
Young, Thomas Richard 1942- *WhoSSW 91*
Young, Thomas Richard 1959- *WhoSSW 91*
Young, Tom 1924- *WhoAmA 91*
Young, Tommie Morton *WhoAmW 91*
Young, Trummy 1912-1984 *BioIn 16, OxCPMus*
Young, Valarie C *BiDrAPA 89*
Young, Vera Lee Hall 1944- *WhoAmW 91*
Young, Vera Miller 1927- *WhoSSW 91*
Young, Victor 1900-1956 *OxCPMus*
Young, Virginia Brady 1918- *WhoWrEP 89*
Young, Virginia S. 1944- *St&PR 91*
Young, Wallace C. 1928- *St&PR 91*
Young, Walter Bramwell *BioIn 16*
Young, Walter C. 1927- *St&PR 91*
Young, Walter C 1940- *BiDrAPA 89*
Young, Walter Martin 1922- *St&PR 91*
Young, Walter Reed 1923- *WhoAm 90*
Young, Walter Richard 1947- *WhoAm 90, WhoSSW 91*
Young, Walter Russell, Jr. 1944- *St&PR 91*
Young, Webster Axline 1950- *IntWWM 90*
Young, Wesley Eugene 1930- *St&PR 91*
Young, Whitney M., Jr. 1921-1971 *WorAlBi*
Young, Whitney Moore 1921-1971 *BioIn 16*
Young, Wilhelmina G. 1938- *WhoWrEP 89*
Young, William Allen 1953?- *DrBlPA 90*
Young, William Charles 1940- *St&PR 91*
Young, William Dale 1953- *WhoSSW 91*
Young, William Dean 1946- *WhoSSW 91*
Young, William Edgar 1930- *WhoSSW 91*
Young, William G *BiDrAPA 89*
Young, William Glover 1940- *WhoAm 90*
Young, William H. *WhoAm 90*
Young, William H, Jr. 1920- *BiDrAPA 89*
Young, William J. *BioIn 16*
Young, William J. 1927- *St&PR 91*
Young, William James 1927- *WhoAm 90*
Young, William John 1925- *WhoAm 90*
Young, William Johnson 1928- *WhoAm 90*
Young, William Lee 1960- *WhoE 91*
Young, William Lewis 1929- *WhoE 91, WhoWor 91*
Young, William M *BiDrAPA 89*
Young, William Maurice 1924- *St&PR 91*
Young, William P. 1943- *St&PR 91*
Young, William T. 1918- *St&PR 91*
Young, William Thomas 1924- *WhoSSW 91*
Young, William Thomas 1928- *IntWWM 90*
Young, William V. 1937- *St&PR 91*
Young, Wills Morrison 1935- *St&PR 91*
Young, Wilson Wing sun 1939- *WhoWor 91*
Young, Zora Oral 1922- *BiDrAPA 89*
Young-Bruehl, Elisabeth *BioIn 16*
Young-Bruehl, Elisabeth 1946- *ConAu 131, WhoE 91*
Young Lively, Sandra Lee 1943- *WhoAmW 91, WhoWor 91*
Young Scott, Frances 1954- *WhoAmA 91*
Youngberg, Charlotte Anne 1937- *WhoAmW 91*
Youngberg, David Arthur 1955- *St&PR 91*
Youngberg, Oscar J. *BioIn 16*
Youngblade, Charles John 1926- *WhoAm 90*
Youngblood, Benjamin Franklin, III 1954- *WhoSSW 91*
Youngblood, Daisy *BioIn 16*
Youngblood, Franklin Hugh Lee 1923- *WhoE 91*
Youngblood, Jack *BioIn 16*
Youngblood, James Wesley 1935- *WhoSSW 91*
Youngblood, Jess *WhoSSW 91*
Youngblood, Joel 1951- *Ballpl 90*
Youngblood, John C. 1926- *St&PR 91*
Youngblood, John Curtis, Jr. 1949- *St&PR 91*
Youngblood, John L. 1941- *St&PR 91*
Youngblood, Judy *WhoAmA 91*
Youngblood, Michelle Karen Wolstein 1958- *WhoAmW 91*
Youngblood, Nat 1916- *WhoAmA 91*
Youngblood, Nat Howard, Jr. 1916- *WhoAm 90*
Youngblood, Ray W. 1931- *St&PR 91*
Youngblood, Ronald F 1931- *ConAu 30NR*
Youngblood, Samuel C. 1955- *St&PR 91*
Youngblood, Spencer L. 1945- *St&PR 91*
Youngblood, William Lester, Jr. 1948- *WhoSSW 91*
Youngblood, William Randolph 1957- *WhoSSW 91*
Youngbloods, The *EncPR&S 89*
Youngclaus, William P. 1939- *WhoAm 90*
Youngclaus, William Paul 1939- *St&PR 91*
Youngdahl, James Edward 1926- *WhoAm 90*
Youngdahl, Patricia Lucy 1927- *WhoAmW 91*
Youngdahl, Russell Charles 1924- *WhoAm 90*
Younger, Dan Forrest 1954- *WhoAmA 91*
Younger, Deborah Anne *BiDrAPA 89*
Younger, Doris Anne 1924- *WhoAm 90*
Younger, Evelle Jansen 1918-1989 *BioIn 16*
Younger, Gary Paul 1947- *St&PR 91*
Younger, George Kenneth Hotson 1931- *WhoWor 91*
Younger, Gordon Myles 1938- *St&PR 91*
Younger, Irving *BioIn 16*
Younger, J. C. *WhoWrEP 89*
Younger, J. Michael 1930- *St&PR 91*
Younger, John M.D. 1946- *St&PR 91*
Younger, Judith Tess 1933- *WhoAm 90, WhoAmW 91*
Younger, Julian William 1950- *WhoE 91*
Younger, Kenneth G. 1925- *WhoAm 90, WhoSSW 91*
Younger, Kenneth Maurice 1952- *WhoEmL 91, WhoSSW 91*
Younger, Kenneth Wayne 1951- *WhoWor 91*
Younger, Mary Sue 1944- *WhoAmW 91*
Younger, Susan C 1957- *BiDrAPA 89*
Younger, William Carl 1919- *WhoSSW 91, WhoWor 91*
Youngerman, Jack 1926- *WhoAm 90, WhoAmA 91*
Youngerman, Joseph Kuhn 1942- *BiDrAPA 89*
Youngers, Marion Anthony 1930- *St&PR 91*
Youngert, Barbara Ann 1938- *WhoWrEP 89*
Younghans, Carol Lou 1943- *WhoAmW 91*
Younghusband, Eileen Louise 1902-1981 *DcNaB 1981*
Younghusband, Francis 1863-1942 *EncO&P 3*
Youngken, Heber Wilkinson, Jr. 1913- *WhoAm 90*
Youngkin, Jack Glenn 1951- *WhoSSW 91*
Youngleson, Sharon S *BiDrAPA 89*
Younglove, Ruth Ann 1909- *WhoAmA 91*
Younglove, Truman G. 1815-1882 *AmLegL*
Youngman, Chris *BioIn 16*
Youngman, Henny *BioIn 16, WhoAm 90*
Youngman, Henny 1906- *WorAlBi*
Youngman, John Crawford 1903- *WhoWor 91*
Youngman, Nan 1906- *BiDWomA, BioIn 16*
Youngman, Vincent 1911- *BiDrAPA 89*
Youngman, William Sterling 1907- *WhoAm 90*
Youngner, Julius Stuart 1920- *WhoAm 90*
Youngner, Philip Genevus 1920- *WhoAm 90*
Youngner, Stuart James 1944- *BiDrAPA 89*
Youngquist, Alvin Menvid, Jr. 1925- *WhoAm 90, WhoWrEP 89*
Youngquist, Amy B. 1952- *St&PR 91*
Youngquist, David Jack 1932- *St&PR 91*
Youngquist, Erick H. *BioIn 16*
Youngquist, Jack 1918- *WhoAmA 91*
Youngquist, John Anthony 1931- *WhoSSW 91*
Youngren, Ralph Park 1924- *St&PR 91, WhoAm 90*
Youngs, Betty 1934-1985 *BioIn 16*
Youngs, David D 1937- *BiDrAPA 89*
Youngs, John 1623-1698 *EncCRAm*
Youngs, John Robert 1950- *St&PR 91*
Youngs, Joseph Harry 1930- *St&PR 91*
Youngs, Joyce Ann 1938- *WhoAmW 91*
Youngs, Ross 1897-1927 *Ballpl 90 [port], BioIn 16*
Youngs, Shirley Cean 1939- *WhoAmW 91*
Youngs, Wallace I. 1931- *St&PR 91*
Youngson, James, Jr. 1937- *WhoSSW 91*
Youngster, Ardithe 1947- *WhoAmW 91*
Youngstrum, David Mansfield 1942- *WhoSSW 91*
Youngwerth, Peter William 1938- *St&PR 91*
Youngwood, Alfred Donald 1938- *WhoAm 90*
Younis, Mahmoud Rachid 1948- *WhoWor 91*
Younk, James L. 1942- *St&PR 91*
Younker, Fred D. 1949- *St&PR 91*
Younker, Pamela Godfrey 1955- *WhoAmW 91*
Younkin, David Joseph 1940- *WhoE 91*
Younkin, Gregory Wayne 1953- *WhoWor 91*
Yount, David 1934- *ODwPR 91*
Yount, David Eugene 1935- *WhoAm 90*
Yount, Florence Jane 1926- *WhoAm 90, WhoAmW 91*
Yount, George Stuart 1949- *St&PR 91, WhoEmL 91, WhoWor 91*
Yount, George W. 1929- *St&PR 91*
Yount, John Alonzo 1935- *WhoWrEP 89*
Yount, Kenneth Harold 1947- *WhoSSW 91*
Yount, Marvin Edward, Jr. 1920- *WhoSSW 91*
Yount, Philip Richard 1937- *St&PR 91*
Yount, Robin *BioIn 16*
Yount, Robin 1955- *Ballpl 90 [port], WorAlBi*
Yount, Stanley G. 1903- *St&PR 91*
Younts, Elizabeth Mendenhall 1919- *WhoSSW 91*
Younts, Gerlind *BioIn 16*
Younts, Jack *BioIn 16*
Younts, Melvin K. 1929- *St&PR 91*
Younts, Patty Lou 1950- *WhoAmW 91*
Younts, Sanford Eugene 1930- *WhoAm 90*
Youra, Daniel George 1944- *WhoWrEP 89*
Yourcenar, Marguerite *BioIn 16*
Yourcenar, Marguerite 1903- *EncCoWW*
Yourcenar, Marguerite 1903-1987 *EuWr 12, MajTwCW*
Youritzin, Victor Koshkin 1942- *WhoAmA 91*
Youse, Glad Robinson 1898- *IntWWM 90*
Yousef, Fathi Salaama 1934- *WhoWor 91*
Youshock, Eva Lynn 1955- *WhoAmW 91*
Youssef, Hanafy Ahmed 1939- *WhoWor 91*
Youssef, Ibrahim *BiDrAPA 89*
Youssef, Nasr H. 1945- *St&PR 91*
Yousten, Allan Arthur 1936- *WhoSSW 91*
Yousuf, Mohammed Shahid *BiDrAPA 89*
Yousuf, Nigar 1959- *BiDrAPA 89*
Yousuf, Zahra 1949- *BiDrAPA 89*
Youtan, Norman 1938- *WhoAm 90*
Youtcheff, John Sheldon 1925- *WhoE 91, WhoWor 91*
Youtt, Stanley Addison 1946- *St&PR 91*
Youtz, Richard P. 1910-1986 *BioIn 16*
Youville, Marguerite d' 1701-1771 *BioIn 16*
Yovanovich, Deborah Theresa 1953- *WhoAmW 91*
Yovich, Daniel John 1930- *WhoAm 90*
Yovicich, George Steven Jones 1927- *WhoAm 90*
Yovicsin, John *BioIn 16*
Yovits, Marshall Clinton 1923- *WhoAm 90*
Yovovich, Paul G. 1953- *St&PR 91*
Yow, Kay *BioIn 16*
Yow, Raymond Murray 1924- *St&PR 91*
Yowell, William C., Jr. 1926- *St&PR 91*
Yoxall, G. Patrick 1934- *St&PR 91*

Yoxall, Patricia A. 1958- *ODwPR 91*
Yozgatlioglu, Cuneyt A *BiDrAPA 89*
Yozwiak, Bernard James 1919- *WhoAm 90*
Yperen, Pieternella Cornelia van *EncCoWW*
Yradier, Sebastian de 1809-1865 *OxCPMus*
Yram 1884-1917 *EncO&P 3, EncPaPR 91*
Yrarrazaval, Arturo C. 1946- *WhoWor 91*
Yrigoyen, Hipolito 1852-1933 *BioIn 16*
Yrjola, Erkki Pentti Juhani 1941- *WhoWor 91*
Ysaye Quartet *PenDiMP*
Ysaye, Eugene 1858-1931 *PenDiMP*
Ysaye, Theophile 1865-1918 *PenDiMP*
Yska, Dugald 1954- *WhoE 91*
Ysseldyke, James Edward 1944- *WhoAm 90*
Ystueta, Mary Caroline 1964- *WhoAmW 91*
Ytreberg, F.M. 1942- *St&PR 91*
Ytterberg, Donald Victor 1926- *St&PR 91*
Ytterberg, Ralph Warren 1927- *St&PR 91*
Yttrehus, Rolv 1926- *IntWWM 90*
Yttri, Diane Fowler *ODwPR 91*
Yturbe, Jean de *BioIn 16*
Yturbe, Sandy de *BioIn 16*
Yturria, Paul 1937- *WhoSSW 91*
Yu Kuo-Hwa 1914- *WhoWor 91*
Yu Zhuoyun 1918- *ConAu 132*
Yu, Aiting Tobey 1921- *WhoAm 90*
Yu, Albert Y.C. 1941- *St&PR 91*
Yu, Anne Ramona Wing-mui 1948- *WhoEmL 91*
Yu, Anthony C. 1938- *WhoAm 90*
Yu, Cha Jong 1944- *BiDrAPA 89*
Yu, Choon Shik *BiDrAPA 89*
Yu, Chun-Yee 1936- *IntWWM 90*
Yu, Chyang John 1948- *WhoWor 91*
Yu, Francis Tiong Suy 1932- *WhoAm 90*
Yu, George Tzuchiao 1931- *WhoAm 90*
Yu, Jen 1943- *WhoAm 90*
Yu, John Yuh-Lin 1937- *WhoWor 91*
Yu, Julie Hung-Hsua 1954- *WhoAmW 91, WhoEmL 91, WhoWor 91*
Yu, Kang Yun *BiDrAPA 89*
Yu, Keun Ho 1939- *BiDrAPA 89*
Yu, Kitson Szewai 1950- *WhoEmL 91*
Yu, Lily 1950- *St&PR 91*
Yu, Linda 1946- *WhoAmW 91*
Yu, Lydia T *BiDrAPA 89*
Yu, Paul Nangan 1915- *WhoAm 90*
Yu, Po Lung 1940- *WhoAm 90*
Yu, Shao-Chen *BiDrAPA 89*
Yu, Shao-Chi *BiDrAPA 89*
Yu, Simon Shyi-Jian 1935- *WhoSSW 91*
Yu, Sui *ConAu 132*
Yu, Timothy Pan 1974- *WhoWrEP 89*
Yu, Yi-Yuan 1923- *WhoAm 90*
Yu, Ying Shih 1930- *WhoAm 90*
Yu, Yuh-chao 1941- *WhoWor 91*
Yu-Chin, Rose 1950- *BiDrAPA 89*
Yu Hussein, Pattie 1956- *ODwPR 91, WhoAmW 91*
Yuan *PenDiDA 89*
Yuan Yu *WomWR*
Yuan, Lily 1962- *IntWWM 90*
Yuan, Shao Wen 1914- *WhoAm 90*
Yuan, Sidney Wei Kwun 1957- *WhoEmL 91*
Yudain, Carole Gewirtz *WhoE 91*
Yudell, Charlotte D 1911- *BiDrAPA 89*
Yudell, Richard L 1941- *BiDrAPA 89*
Yudenich, Alexei 1943-1990 *BioIn 16*
Yudenich, Nikolay Nikolayevich 1862-1933 *BioIn 16*
Yudina, Maria 1899-1970 *PenDiMP*
Yudkin, Gerald S *BiDrAPA 89*
Yudkowsky, Rachel P 1955- *BiDrAPA 89*
Yudof, Mark G. 1944- *WhoAm 90*
Yudofsky, Beth Koster 1952- *BiDrAPA 89*
Yudofsky, Stuart C 1944- *BiDrAPA 89*
Yudowitz, Bernard S *BiDrAPA 89*
Yue, Alfred Shui-choh 1920- *WhoAm 90*
Yue, Charlotte *AuBYP 90*
Yue, David *AuBYP 90*
Yue, William W.L. 1944- *St&PR 91*
Yuelys, Alexander 1926- *WhoAm 90*
Yuen, Chung Kwong 1947- *WhoWor 91*
Yuen, Darrel 1951- *St&PR 91*
Yuen, Gregory Ew M *BiDrAPA 89*
Yuen, Tom 1951- *WhoE 91*
Yuen, William 1929- *St&PR 91*
Yuenger, James Laury 1939- *WhoAm 90*
Yugovich, John Paul 1946- *WhoSSW 91*
Yuhas, Eddie 1924-1986 *Ballpl 90*
Yuhn, Robert B *BiDrAPA 89*
Yui, George Micheal 1942- *St&PR 91*
Yuill, P. B. *ConAu 130, TwCCr&M 91*
Yukawa, Hideki 1907-1981 *DcScB S2, WorAlBi*
Yukawa, Setsuko 1941- *WhoWor 91*
Yukelson, Ron 1956- *ODwPR 91*
Yuker, Harold Elwood 1924- *WhoAm 90*
Yukl, Trudy Ann 1947- *WhoAmW 91*
Yule, Andrew 1936- *ConAu 129*
Yule, John 1834-1888 *AmLegL*
Yule, Pamelia Sarah *DcCanB 12*
Yulish, Charles B. 1936- *ODwPR 91*
Yulish, Charles Barry 1936- *WhoAm 90, WhoWor 91*
Yum, Jung Hae *BiDrAPA 89*
Yum, Jung Hae 1942- *WhoE 91*
Yumino, Masahiko 1940- *St&PR 91*
Yumul, Fe Anastacio 1941- *BiDrAPA 89*
Yun Po Sun *NewYTBS 90*
Yun, Daniel Duwhan 1933- *WhoE 91, WhoWor 91*
Yun, Isang 1917- *IntWWM 90, PenDiMP A*
Yun, James Myung Ju 1938- *WhoE 91, WhoWor 91*
Yun, Jin Ha *BiDrAPA 89*
Yun, Young Sun *BiDrAPA 89*
Yuna, Joelle 1935- *ODwPR 91*
Yunck, Donald A. 1927- *St&PR 91*
Yuncker, Barbara *WhoAm 90*
Yund, Theodore Joseph 1947- *WhoWrEP 89*
Yundt, Delbert G. *St&PR 91*
Yundt, Jeffrey W. 1945- *St&PR 91*
Yung Cheng *PenDiDA 89*
Yung, Christoph 1935- *BiDrAPA 89*
Yung-Fatah, Ellen Meefong 1953- *WhoAmW 91*
Yungbluth, Thomas Alan 1934- *WhoSSW 91*
Yunich, David L. 1917- *St&PR 91*
Yunich, David Lawrence 1917- *WhoAm 90*
Yunick, Robert Peter 1935- *St&PR 91*
Yunis, Jorge Jose *WhoAm 90, WhoWor 91*
Yunkel, Ramar *HispWr 90*
Yunker, Ronald Charles 1927- *St&PR 91*
Yunker, Todd Elliott 1960- *WhoWrEP 89*
Yunkers, Adja 1900-1983 *WhoAmA 91N*
Yunying, Aisin Gioro *BioIn 16*
Yuodelis, Christine Elizabeth 1957- *BiDrAPA 89*
Yup, Paula Anne 1957- *WhoWrEP 89*
Yuracko, Ellen B. 1939- *St&PR 91*
Yurchenco, Henrietta Weiss 1916- *WhoAm 90*
Yurchenko, Henrietta 1916- *AuBYP 90*
Yurchuck, Roger Alexander 1938- *WhoAm 90*
Yurchyshyn, George Bohdan 1940- *St&PR 91*
Yurcon, George Edward 1929- *St&PR 91*
Yurek, Allen Lang 1948- *WhoSSW 91*
Yurevich, Nina *BiDrAPA 89*
Yurick, Sol 1925- *WhoWrEP 89*
Yurieff, Zoya Osipovna 1922- *EncCoWW*
Yurka, Blanche 1887-1974 *BioIn 16, NotWoAT*
Yurko, Mike 1924- *St&PR 91*
Yurkovic, Leonard Stephen 1937- *St&PR 91*
Yurovich, Douglas Paul 1957- *WhoWor 91*
Yurow, John Jesse 1931- *WhoAm 90*
Yurowski, G. Edmund 1931- *St&PR 91*
Yurugor, Yuksel E 1928- *BiDrAPA 89*
Yuschak, William 1925- *St&PR 91*
Yuschok, Theresa A *BiDrAPA 89*
Yusim, Rakhil *BiDrAPA 89*
Yusim, Solomon *BiDrAPA 89*
Yusk, Janice Woods 1942- *WhoAmW 91*
Yusko, Edward Michael, Jr. 1957- *WhoEmL 91*
Yusko, Gary John 1955- *St&PR 91*
Yuspeh, Alan Ralph 1949- *WhoAm 90*
Yuspeh, Sonia E. 1928- *St&PR 91*
Yuspeh, Sonia Elizabeth 1928- *WhoAm 90*
Yuss, Irene A. 1932- *WhoAm 90*
Yust, David E 1939- *WhoAmA 91*
Yuster, Leigh Carol 1949- *WhoE 91*
Yusty, Maria *BioIn 16*
Yutalo, Rodney W. *St&PR 91*
Yuthasastrkosol, Charin 1930- *WhoAmW 91, WhoE 91*
Yutzy, Sean Hearn *BiDrAPA 89*
Yuzon, Ricardo A 1936- *BiDrAPA 89*
Yvain, Maurice 1891-1965 *OxCPMus*
Yves, Martin 1929- *WhoAm 90*
Yvon, Klaus *WhoWor 91*
Yzaguirre, Raul 1939- *WhoHisp 91*
Yzaguirre, Raul Humberto 1939- *BioIn 16*
Yzaguirre, Ruben Antonio 1947- *WhoHisp 91*
Yzerman, Steve *BioIn 16*
Yzerman, Steve 1965- *News 91-2 [port], WorAlBi*

Z

Zaaiman, Reginald Brandt 1922- *WhoWor 91*
Zaback, Ayn S *BiDrAPA 89*
Zaback, Carol Fay 1942- *WhoAmW 91*
Zaback, Robert C. 1931- *St&PR 91*
Zabaknikov, Nikolay *PenDiMP*
Zabaleta, Nicanor 1907- *IntWWM 90, PenDiMP*
Zaban, Erwin 1921- *St&PR 91, WhoAm 90, WhoSSW 91*
Zabarsky, Marsha Ann 1952- *WhoE 91*
Zabarsky, Melvin Joel 1932- *WhoAmA 91*
Zabawa, Robert Thomas 1941- *St&PR 91*
Zabecki, David Tadeusz 1947- *WhoWor 91*
Zabel *WomWR*
Zabel, Edward 1927- *WhoAm 90*
Zabel, Fern I. Rookstool 1945- *WhoAmW 91*
Zabel, Robert Alger 1917- *WhoAm 90*
Zabel, Sheldon Alter 1941- *WhoAm 90*
Zabel, William David 1936- *WhoAm 90, WhoE 91*
Zabelsky, Robert *St&PR 91*
Zabibi *WomWR*
Zabinski, Jan 1897- *BioIn 16*
Zablan, Lilia Lacsina *BiDrAPA 89*
Zable, David 1936- *St&PR 91*
Zable, Marian Magdelen 1933- *WhoAmW 91*
Zable, Norman Arnold 1934- *WhoSSW 91*
Zable, Walter C. 1946- *St&PR 91*
Zable, Walter Joseph 1915- *St&PR 91*
Zablocki, Jerzy 1928- *IntWWM 90*
Zablotny, Raymond 1947- *BiDrAPA 89*
Zablow, Leonard 1927- *WhoE 91*
Zablow, Sheldon Blake 1951- *BiDrAPA 89*
Zaboly, Bill 1910-1985 *EncACom*
Zaborney, Kevin *BioIn 16*
Zaborowski, Dennis J 1943- *WhoAmA 91*
Zaborowski, Richard Paul 1951- *WhoE 91*
Zabors, Thomas E *BiDrAPA 89*
Zabrack, Harold A. 1928- *IntWWM 90*
Zabriskie, Dale O. 1935- *ODwPR 91*
Zabriskie, Grace *ConTFT 8*
Zabriskie, Louise 1887-1957 *BioIn 16*
Zabriskie, Stewart Clark 1936- *WhoAm 90*
Zabriskie, Virginia M. *WhoAm 90, WhoAmA 91*
Zabron, Floyd Stanley 1940- *St&PR 91*
Zabukovec, Jamie Jo 1954- *WhoAmW 91*
Zacaire, Denis 1510- *EncO&P 3*
Zacarias, David James 1949- *St&PR 91*
Zacarias, Rebecca Anne 1961- *WhoAmW 91*
Zaccaglin, Victor 1921- *St&PR 91*
Zaccagnini, Benigno 1912-1989 *BioIn 16*
Zaccarello, Michael D. 1947- *St&PR 91*
Zaccaria, Jerome John 1930- *St&PR 91*
Zaccaria, Joseph A. 1942- *ODwPR 91*
Zaccaria, Nicola 1923- *PenDiMP*
Zaccone, Robert Michael 1946- *WhoE 91*
Zaccone, Suzanne Maria 1957- *WhoAmW 91, WhoEmL 91, WhoWor 91*
Zacek, Joseph Frederick 1930- *WhoAm 90*
Zach, Bob *BioIn 16*
Zach, Cheryl 1947- *BioIn 16*
Zach, Franz Xaver, Freiherr von 1754-1832 *BioIn 16*
Zach, Jan 1914-1986 *BioIn 16*
Zach, Jonathan I *BiDrAPA 89*
Zach, Miriam Susan 1954- *WhoAmW 91*
Zacha, William 1920- *WhoAmA 91*
Zachar, Joel Stephen 1948- *St&PR 91*
Zacharia, Friedrich Wilhelm 1726-1777 *DcLB 97 [port]*
Zachariah, Michael Russel 1957- *WhoE 91*
Zachariah, Susan *BiDrAPA 89*
Zacharias, Athanasios 1927- *WhoAmA 91*
Zacharias, Athos 1927- *WhoE 91*
Zacharias, Christian 1950- *IntWWM 90*
Zacharias, Donald Wayne 1935- *WhoAm 90, WhoSSW 91*
Zacharias, Edwin H., Sr. 1910- *St&PR 91*
Zacharias, Helmut W. 1942- *St&PR 91*
Zacharias, James 1912- *St&PR 91*
Zacharias, John Spero 1932- *St&PR 91*
Zacharias, Lela Ann 1944- *WhoWrEP 89*
Zacharias, Richard M. 1914- *St&PR 91*
Zacharias, Thomas Elling 1954- *WhoE 91*
Zachariasen, William Houlder 1906-1979 *DcScB S2*
Zachariou, Nicola 1923- *PenDiMP*
Zacharius, Walter 1923- *WhoAm 90*
Zacharkow, George S. 1927- *St&PR 91*
Zachary, Alan M. *ODwPR 91*
Zachary, Andrea Anne 1946- *WhoAmW 91*
Zachary, Chris 1944- *Ballpl 90*
Zachary, Domna 1957- *WhoAmW 91*
Zachary, Fay N. 1931- *WhoWrEP 89*
Zachary, Frank 1914- *BioIn 16*
Zachary, Hugh D. 1928- *WhoSSW 91*
Zachary, James Luther 1932- *WhoSSW 91*
Zachary, Norman 1926- *St&PR 91*
Zachary, Phillip Eugene 1934- *St&PR 91*
Zachary, Ronald F. 1938- *St&PR 91*
Zachary, Saul 1934- *ConAu 129*
Zachary, Tom 1896-1969 *Ballpl 90*
Zachary, Woodford William 1935- *WhoE 91*
Zacheis, Carleton F. 1933- *St&PR 91*
Zachem, Harry M. 1944- *WhoAm 90*
Zacher, Allan Norman, Jr. 1928- *WhoWor 91*
Zacher, Gerd 1929- *PenDiMP*
Zacherl, Anita Marie 1946- *WhoAmW 91*
Zachert, Martha Jane 1920- *WhoAm 90*
Zachert, Virginia 1920- *WhoAm 90, WhoAmW 91*
Zachik, Albert Anthony 1951- *BiDrAPA 89*
Zachmann, Dorothy *BiDrAPA 89*
Zachmann, Virginia Joyce 1933- *WhoWrEP 89*
Zachmann, William Francis 1942- *WhoAm 90, WhoE 91, WhoWor 91*
Zachos, Kimon Stephen 1930- *St&PR 91, WhoE 91*
Zachreson, Nick Bernard 1952- *WhoWrEP 89*
Zachrisson, K. Sune R. 1932- *WhoWor 91*
Zachry, Henry Bartell, Jr. 1933- *St&PR 91, WhoAm 90*
Zachry, Pat 1952- *Ballpl 90*
Zack, Anthony J. 1941- *St&PR 91*
Zack, Arnold Marshall 1931- *WhoAm 90*
Zack, Badanna Bernice *WhoAmA 91*
Zack, David 1917- *St&PR 91*
Zack, George J. 1936- *WhoSSW 91*
Zack, Kenneth R 1938- *BiDrAPA 89*
Zack, Thomas J. *ODwPR 91*
Zackery, Bennie Lee 1946- *WhoAmW 91*
Zackheim, Adrian Walter 1951- *WhoAm 90*
Zackheim, Marc Allen 1950- *WhoEmL 91*
Zackler, Lester M *BiDrAPA 89*
Zacks, Gordon 1933- *St&PR 91*
Zacks, Gordon Benjamin 1933- *WhoAm 90*
Zacks, Irene *AuBYP 90*
Zacks, Philip H. 1948- *St&PR 91*
Zacks, Samuel Jacob 1904-1970 *WhoAmA 91N*
Zacks, Sumner Irwin 1929- *WhoAm 90*
Zacky, Dolores 1947- *WhoAmW 91*
Zacny, R.J. *St&PR 91*
Zadeh, Stella 1947- *WhoAmW 91*
Zadek, Hilde 1917- *PenDiMP*
Zadek, Robert L. 1940- *St&PR 91*
Zaderenko, Sergio Manuel *BiDrAPA 89*
Zadikow, Victor H. 1943- *St&PR 91*
Zadkiel 1795-1874 *EncO&P 3*
Zadkine, Ossip 1890-1967 *IntDcAA 90*
Zadora, Pia *BioIn 16*
Zadra, Joseph James 1922- *St&PR 91*
Zadra, Larry 1961- *St&PR 91*
Zadravec, Edward John 1937- *St&PR 91*
Zadravec, Katharine *BioIn 16*
Zadrozny, W.T. 1945- *St&PR 91*
Zadylak, Connie Lorraine 1947- *WhoAmW 91*
Zadylak, Robert G 1947- *BiDrAPA 89*
Zaehringer, Mary Veronica 1911- *WhoAmW 91*
Zaenglein, William George 1929- *St&PR 91*
Zaenglein, William George, Jr. 1929- *WhoAm 90*
Zaentz, Saul *WhoAm 90*
Zaepfel, Glenn Peter 1951- *WhoEmL 91, WhoSSW 91*
Zaepfel, John Bruce 1936- *St&PR 91*
Zaferiou, Paul John 1934- *WhoE 91*
Zaffaroni, Alejandro C. 1923- *St&PR 91*
Zaffe, Gwen 1949- *St&PR 91*
Zaffirini, Judith 1946- *WhoAmW 91, WhoSSW 91*
Zaffirni, Judith 1946- *WhoHisp 91*
Zaffo, George J. *AuBYP 90*
Zaffos, Gerald 1950- *WhoEmL 91*
Zafran, Eric Myles 1946- *WhoAmA 91*
Zafrani, Michael Bruce 1953- *BiDrAPA 89*
Zafren, Herbert Cecil 1925- *WhoAm 90*
Zagalsky, Nelson Ray 1942- *WhoAm 90*
Zagame, Susan Koerber 1951- *WhoAmW 91*
Zagami, Anthony James 1951- *WhoWor 91*
Zagan, Shakhne 1892-1942 *BioIn 16*
Zagar, Peter 1961- *IntWWM 90*
Zagare, Isabella Maria 1955- *WhoAmW 91*
Zagasbaldan, Damiranjavyn 1931- *WhoWor 91*
Zagel, James Block 1941- *WhoAm 90*
Zager, Arnold S 1944- *BiDrAPA 89*
Zager, Ruth P *BiDrAPA 89*
Zagier, Helene De B 1918- *BiDrAPA 89*
Zagier-Roberts, Vega Johanna 1948- *BiDrAPA 89*
Zagnoli, Roland Candiano 1931- *WhoSSW 91, WhoWor 91*
Zago, Tino 1937- *WhoAmA 91*
Zagoloff, Anna *BiDrAPA 89*
Zagoloff, Helen *BiDrAPA 89*
Zagoloff, Murat L *BiDrAPA 89*
Zagorac, Michael, Jr. 1941- *St&PR 91*
Zagoren, Allen Jeffrey 1947- *WhoEmL 91*
Zagoren, Marc Alan 1940- *ConAu 132*
Zagoren, Ruby 1922-1974 *AuBYP 90*
Zagoria, Sam David 1919- *WhoAm 90*
Zagorin, Perez 1920- *WhoAm 90*
Zagorski, Krzysztof Hubert 1941- *WhoWor 91*
Zagorsky, Carol Lacci 1942- *WhoE 91*
Zagorzycki, Maria Teresa 1953- *WhoAmW 91*
Zagotta, Anthony James 1966- *WhoEmL 91*
Zagrodnik, Diane Jeanne 1950- *WhoWrEP 89*
Zagrosek, Lothar 1942- *IntWWM 90, PenDiMP*
Zagst-Feldman, Joanne Marie 1934- *IntWWM 90*
Zagursky, George Palmer 1943- *WhoSSW 91*
Zagzebski, Edwin Joseph 1935- *St&PR 91*
Zaharia, Eric Stafford 1948- *WhoAm 90*
Zaharias, Babe 1914-1956 *WorAlBi*
Zaharias, Babe Didrikson 1911-1956 *BioIn 16*
Zaharias, Mildred 1912-1956 *BioAmW*
Zahavy, Reuvain 1953- *WhoE 91*
Zaher, Celia Ribeiro 1931- *WhoWor 91*
Zaher, Rafik Abbass 1924- *WhoWor 91*
Zahid, Mussarat Yasmin *BiDrAPA 89*
Zahir Shah 1914- *BioIn 16*
Zahka, George J. 1922- *St&PR 91*
Zahka, William Joseph 1929- *WhoE 91*
Zahler, Karen 1950- *WhoEmL 91*
Zahler, Mary Lynne Quinnan 1960- *WhoAmW 91*
Zahler, Michael Joseph 1942- *WhoE 91*
Zahm, Robert H 1921- *BiDrAPA 89*
Zahn, Albert 1864-1953 *MusmAFA*
Zahn, Anton James 1941- *St&PR 91*
Zahn, Carl Frederick 1928- *WhoAm 90, WhoAmA 91, WhoE 91*
Zahn, Curtis Langalier 1912- *WhoWrEP 89*
Zahn, Erich Otto Karl 1940- *WhoWor 91*
Zahn, Geoff 1945- *Ballpl 90*
Zahn, George F. *BioIn 16*
Zahn, John Joseph 1930- *St&PR 91*
Zahn, Leonard *BioIn 16*
Zahn, Louis Jennings 1922- *WhoSSW 91*
Zahn, Paul Hugh 1944- *WhoWor 91*
Zahn, Paula *BioIn 16*
Zahnd, Richard Hugo 1946- *WhoAm 90*
Zahner, Jane Elizabeth 1951- *WhoSSW 91*
Zahner, Sally Lovett 1953- *WhoAmW 91*
Zahniser, Frank Stewart 1927- *St&PR 91*
Zahniser, James A. 1946- *St&PR 91*
Zahniser, Jill Diane 1951- *WhoAmW 91*
Zahniser, Marvin Ralph 1934- *WhoAm 90*
Zahniser, Paul 1896-1964 *Ballpl 90*
Zahodnick, John Dennis 1950- *WhoWor 91*
Zahorchak, Gerald Lee 1957- *WhoE 91*
Zahorchak, Michael 1929- *WhoWrEP 89*
Zahorian, Stephen Glen 1938- *St&PR 91, WhoAm 90, WhoSSW 91*
Zahos, Efrosine 1961- *WhoAmW 91*
Zahourek, Jon Gail 1940- *WhoAmA 91*
Zahra, Susan Gore 1950- *WhoWrEP 89*
Zahradnik, Julia Anne 1964- *WhoEmL 91*
Zahradnik, Richard *ODwPR 91*
Zahrn, James Frederick 1950- *St&PR 91, WhoAm 90*

Zahurullah, Abdul Rahman M 1943- *BiDrAPA 89*
Zaid, Barry 1938- *BioIn 16*
Zaidel, Nahum 1933- *IntWWM 90*
Zaidenberg, Arthur 1903- *AuBYP 90*
Zaidenberg, Arthur 1908-1990 *BioIn 16, ConAu 131*
Zaidenweber, Jose C. 1935- *WhoWor 91*
Zaidi, Mahmood A. 1930- *WhoAm 90*
Zaidi, Munsif 1953- *WhoWor 91*
Zaidi, Sajjad Abid *BiDrAPA 89*
Zaidi, Samina *BiDrAPA 89*
Zaidi, Shuja Haider 1952- *WhoEmL 91*
Zaidman, Gerald L. 1937- *St&PR 91*
Zaik, Carol Ford 1955- *WhoAmW 91, WhoE 91*
Zaik, Margaret Ford 1920- *WhoE 91*
Zaikine, Zak 1941- *WhoAmA 91*
Zaikov, Lev Nikolayevich 1923- *WhoWor 91*
Zaim, Semih 1926- *St&PR 91*
Zaima, Stephen Gyo 1947- *WhoAmA 91*
Zaimont, Judith Lang 1945- *BioIn 16, IntWWM 90*
Zain, C. C. *NewAgE 90*
Zain, C. C. 1882-1951 *EncO&P 3*
Zainaldin, Jamil Shaheen 1948- *WhoE 91*
Zaininger, Karl Heinz 1929- *WhoAm 90*
Zaino, Russell B. 1948- *St&PR 91*
Zais, Bernard H. *WhoE 91*
Zaiser, Sally Solemma Vann 1917- *WhoAmW 91*
Zaitlin, Michael A. 1956- *St&PR 91*
Zaitlin, Robert 1923- *BiDrAPA 89*
Zaitsev, Vyacheslav *BioIn 16*
Zaitsoff, I.M. 1943- *St&PR 91*
Zaitz, Joan Salwen 1951- *WhoAmW 91*
Zajac, Barbara Ann 1937- *WhoAmW 91*
Zajac, Christine *BioIn 16*
Zajac, Isaslawa *BiDrAPA 89*
Zajac, Jack 1929- *WhoAm 90, WhoAmA 91*
Zajac, John 1946- *WhoEmL 91*
Zajac, Joseph Michael 1966- *WhoEmL 91*
Zajan, Paula L. *BioIn 16*
Zajecka, John Michael 1958- *BiDrAPA 89*
Zajic, Donna Jean 1951- *WhoAmW 91*
Zajicek, Iva Marie 1925- *WhoAmW 91*
Zajicek, Lynn Engelbrecht 1950- *WhoAmW 91*
Zajick, Dolora *BioIn 16*
Zajonc, Robert Boleslaw 1923- *WhoAm 90*
Zak, A. Jeanne 1932- *St&PR 91*
Zak, Cheryl Marie 1952- *WhoAmW 91*
Zak, Dorothy Zerykier 1950- *WhoAmW 91*
Zak, Jerzy 1954- *IntWWM 90*
Zak, John Paul 1946- *BiDrAPA 89*
Zak, Thomas C. 1938- *St&PR 91*
Zak-Cerhova, Eva 1940- *BiDrAPA 89*
Zakakis, Dimitrios Paul 1945- *WhoWor 91*
Zakala, Marina Lisa 1962- *BiDrAPA 89*
Zakanitch, Robert S. 1935- *WhoAm 90, WhoAmA 91*
Zakaria, Bilal Ahmed *BiDrAPA 89*
Zakarian, Albert 1940- *WhoAm 90*
Zakarian, John J. 1937- *ConAu 132*
Zaken, Kenneth Allen 1958- *WhoSSW 91*
Zakharia, Manell Elias 1955- *WhoWor 91*
Zakhary, Rafat Reed *BiDrAPA 89*
Zakheim, Barbara Jane 1953- *WhoAmW 91, WhoE 91*
Zakheim, Dov Solomon 1948- *WhoAm 90*
Zakhem, Sam *BioIn 16*
Zakhem, Sam Hanna 1935- *WhoAm 90, WhoWor 91*
Zaki, Saleh Abbas 1935- *WhoSSW 91*
Zaki, Sayed M *BiDrAPA 89*
Zakibe, Thomas Anthony 1947- *St&PR 91*
Zakim, David 1935- *WhoAm 90*
Zakim, Gerald 1928- *WhoE 91*
Zakin, Jacques Louis 1927- *WhoAm 90*
Zakin, Mikhail *WhoAmA 91*
Zakiya *BioIn 16*
Zakkay, Victor 1927- *WhoAm 90*
Zakko, Hazim Yousif *BiDrAPA 89*
Zaklow, Jill L. *WhoE 91*
Zakon, Alan J. 1935- *WhoE 91*
Zakris, James Joseph 1957- *BiDrAPA 89*
Zakrzewski, Vladimir 1946- *WhoAmA 91*
Zakrzewski, Vladimir Jan 1946- *WhoE 91*
Zaks, Arthur *BiDrAPA 89*
Zaks, Jerry 1946- *WhoAm 90, WhoE 91*
Zaks, Paula Kay S. 1949- *WhoAmW 91*
Zal, H Michael 1941- *BiDrAPA 89*
Zal, H. Michael 1941- *WhoE 91*
Zal, Roxana *BioIn 16*
Zalaha, John Charles 1916- *St&PR 91*
Zalamia, Louisa Calayag *WhoSSW 91*
Zalazar, Daniel 1928- *WhoE 91*
Zalaznick, Sheldon 1928- *WhoAm 90, WhoWrEP 89*
Zalben, Jane Breskin 1950- *WhoWrEP 89*
Zalben, Simon 1917- *St&PR 91*
Zalce, Alfredo 1908- *ArtLatA*
Zaldastani, Guivy 1919- *WhoE 91, WhoWor 91*
Zaldastani, Othar 1922- *WhoWor 91*
Zaldin, Arthur H. 1916- *St&PR 91*
Zaldivar, Fulgencio Batista y 1901-1973 *BioIn 16*
Zaldivar, Gilberto 1934- *WhoHisp 91*
Zaldo, Bruno 1946- *WhoHisp 91*
Zalecki, Paul Henry 1931- *St&PR 91*
Zales, Michael R 1937- *BiDrAPA 89*
Zaleski, Andrew B. 1938- *St&PR 91*
Zaleski, James Vincent 1943- *WhoWor 91*
Zaleski, Jean *WhoAmA 91, WhoAmW 91, WhoE 91*
Zaleski, Marek Bohdan 1936- *WhoAm 90*
Zaleski, Michael Louis 1941- *WhoAm 90*
Zalewski, C.V. 1937- *St&PR 91*
Zaleznik, Abraham 1924- *WhoAm 90*
Zalieckas, Joseph John 1943- *St&PR 91*
Zalinski, Edmund L.G. 1915- *St&PR 91*
Zalinski, Edmund Louis Gray 1915- *WhoAm 90*
Zaliouk, Yuval Nathan 1939- *WhoAm 90*
Zalis, Orestes S *BiDrAPA 89*
Zalk, Charles Leonard 1923- *St&PR 91*
Zalka, Lori Marlene 1955- *WhoAmW 91*
Zalkikar, Jyoti Narayan 1962- *WhoSSW 91*
Zalkin, Larry 1942- *St&PR 91*
Zalkind, Norman 1914- *WhoE 91*
Zall, Alex 1920- *St&PR 91*
Zall, Harry 1938- *BiDrAPA 89*
Zall, Paul Maxwell 1922- *WhoAm 90, WhoWrEP 89*
Zall, Robert J. 1923- *St&PR 91*
Zall, Robert Rouben 1925- *WhoAm 90*
Zalla, James Albert 1940- *WhoSSW 91*
Zallen, Harold 1926- *WhoAm 90, WhoWor 91*
Zaller, Eli J *BiDrAPA 89*
Zaller, Robert 1940- *ConAu 32NR*
Zaller, Robert Michael 1940- *WhoWrEP 89*
Zallinger, Jean Day 1918- *WhoAmA 91*
Zallinger, Peter 1943- *BioIn 16*
Zallinger, Rudolph Franz 1919- *WhoAmA 91*
Zalm, William Vander *BioIn 16*
Zalokar, Robert Frank 1931- *WhoAm 90*
Zalokar, Robert H. 1927- *WhoSSW 91*
Zaloom, John B. 1941- *St&PR 91*
Zaloom, Richard Joseph 1925- *WhoWor 91*
Zaloudek, Duane 1931- *WhoAmA 91*
Zalta, Edward 1930- *WhoAm 90*
Zaluk, Ellen Louise 1948- *St&PR 91*
Zalusky, Lawrence 1926- *St&PR 91*
Zalut, Warren Jay 1949- *BiDrAPA 89*
Zalutsky, Audrey Englebardt 1935- *WhoAmW 91*
Zalutsky, Morton Herman 1935- *WhoAm 90*
Zamani *EncCoWW*
Zamaria, Abdallah E 1948- *BiDrAPA 89*
Zamarripa, Robert S. 1955- *WhoHisp 91*
Zambaco, Maria Terpithea 1843-1914 *BiDWomA*
Zambarano, William J. 1944- *St&PR 91*
Zambelli, Francesco *PenDiDA 89*
Zambello, Francesca 1956- *IntWWM 90*
Zambetti, Marc A. *BioIn 16*
Zamble, Allan J. 1935- *St&PR 91*
Zambie, Allan John 1935- *WhoAm 90*
Zambito, Charles Anthony 1947- *St&PR 91*
Zambito, Raymond Francis 1926- *WhoE 91*
Zambo, Paul W. 1944- *WhoE 91*
Zamboldi, Robert Joseph 1940- *St&PR 91*
Zamboni, Frank J. *BioIn 16*
Zamboni, Frank Joseph 1921- *WhoAm 90*
Zamboni, Luigi 1767-1837 *PenDiMP*
Zambonini, Giuseppe *NewYTBS 90 [port]*
Zamboukos, Cynthia Soteria 1957- *WhoAmW 91*
Zambrana, Rafael 1931- *WhoHisp 91*
Zambrano, Oscar *BiDrAPA 89*
Zambrona, Tito *WhoHisp 91*
Zambrowski, Stephane 1914- *WhoWor 91*
Zameck, Harvey Jason 1943- *WhoWor 91*
Zamecnik, Susan Marie 1960- *WhoAmW 91*
Zamek, Seth 1960- *WhoSSW 91*
Zamenhof, Ludwik Lejzer 1859-1917 *WorAlBi*
Zames, George David 1934- *WhoAm 90*
Zametkin, Alan Joel 1950- *BiDrAPA 89*
Zamfir, Gheorgie *NewAgMG*
Zamiatin, Evgenii Ivanovich 1884-1937 *BioIn 16*
Zamiatin, Yvgenij 1884-1937 *RGTwCSF*
Zamiska, Marie Catherine 1954- *WhoE 91*
Zamlowski, Peter Steven 1958- *WhoE 91*
Zammitt, Norman 1931- *WhoAm 90, WhoAmA 91*
Zamor, Joseph L 1941- *BiDrAPA 89*
Zamora, Anthony 1948- *WhoHisp 91*
Zamora, Bernice 1938- *HispWr 90*
Zamora, Emil N *BiDrAPA 89*
Zamora, Maria Helena Paluch 1906- *WhoWrEP 89*
Zamora, Mario Dimarucut 1935- *WhoAm 90*
Zamora, Marjorie Dixon 1933- *WhoAmW 91*
Zamora, Oscar 1944- *Ballpl 90*
Zamora-Cope, Rosie 1935- *WhoHisp 91*
Zamore, Ellen Rubinson 1938- *WhoAmW 91*
Zamoyski, Tomasz Jozef 1935- *WhoWor 91*
Zampa, Robbie C. 1947- *WhoAmW 91*
Zampano, Robert Carmine 1929- *WhoAm 90*
Zampelas, Michael Herodotou 1937- *WhoWor 91*
Zampiello, Richard Sidney 1933- *WhoAm 90, WhoE 91, WhoWor 91*
Zampieri, Maria 1941- *IntWWM 90*
Zamuco, Leonara M *BiDrAPA 89*
Zamvil, Linda Susan 1951- *BiDrAPA 89*
Zamyatin, Leonid Mitrofanovich 1922- *WhoWor 91*
Zamyatin, Yevgeny 1884-1937 *TwCLC 37 [port], WorAlBi*
Zan, Bernhard *PenDiDA 89*
Zanakis, Steve H. 1940- *WhoSSW 91*
Zanardelli, Italia 1872?-1944 *BiDWomA*
Zanardelli, John Joseph 1950- *WhoE 91*
Zanartu, Federico Errazuriz 1825-1877 *BioIn 16*
Zanasi, Mario 1927- *IntWWM 90*
Zanca, Joseph Bruce 1945- *WhoE 91*
Zanca, Minerva Martinez *WhoWrEP 89*
Zancan, Glaci Theresinha 1934- *WhoWor 91*
Zancanaro, Giorgio 1941- *IntWWM 90*
Zancanata, Harold W. *BioIn 16*
Zanchuk, Walter Andrew 1950- *St&PR 91*
Zancig, Julius 1857-1929 *EncO&P 3*
Zancig, Julius, Mrs. *EncO&P 3*
Zand, Dale Ezra 1926- *WhoAm 90*
Zand, Lloyd Craig 1942- *WhoSSW 91*
Zande, Anthony Louis 1954- *WhoSSW 91*
Zande, Susan Elaine 1959- *WhoAmW 91*
Zander, Alvin Frederick 1913- *WhoAm 90*
Zander, Benjamin 1939- *WhoE 91*
Zander, Edward J. *BioIn 16*
Zander, Janet Adele *BiDrAPA 89*
Zander, Josef 1918- *WhoWor 91*
Zander, Peter 1922- *IntWWM 90*
Zandi, Ava Sonya Nelson 1954- *WhoAmW 91*
Zandi, Mahin 1939- *BiDrAPA 89*
Zandin, Kjell Bertil 1937- *St&PR 91*
Zandjani, Tubagus Chairul Amachi 1949- *WhoWor 91*
Zandman, Felix 1928- *St&PR 91*
Zando, Peter Anthony 1941- *WhoSSW 91*
Zandt, Marie van *PenDiMP*
Zandveld, Frederik 1939- *WhoWor 91*
Zane, Arnie *BioIn 16*
Zane, Elizabeth 1766?-1831? *EncCRAm*
Zane, James Orville 1933- *St&PR 91*
Zane, Manuel D 1913- *BiDrAPA 89*
Zane, Raymond J. 1939- *WhoE 91*
Zanella, Africa Garcia 1949- *WhoWor 91*
Zanelli, Renato 1892-1935 *PenDiMP*
Zanelli Morales, Renato 1892-1935 *PenDiMP*
Zaner, Claudia Manning 1949- *ODwPR 91*
Zanes, George William 1926- *WhoSSW 91*
Zanetta Hurtado, Sergio M. 1942- *WhoWor 91*
Zanetti, Alexander Henry 1944- *WhoE 91*
Zanetti, Joseph Maurice, Jr. 1928- *St&PR 91*
Zanettovich, Renato 1921- *IntWWM 90*
Zang, Allen 1927- *St&PR 91*
Zang, Edward *BioIn 16*
Zang, Gerald Lee 1931- *St&PR 91*
Zang, William L. 1953- *St&PR 91*
Zangara, Giuseppe 1900-1933 *WorAlBi*
Zangari, Rose Marie 1917- *WhoAmW 91*
Zangeneh, Fereydoun 1937- *WhoSSW 91*
Zanger, Allene C. *St&PR 91*
Zanger, Andre Louis *BiDrAPA 89*
Zangerle, Helmut 1930- *IntWWM 90*
Zanghi, Santo Anthony 1955- *St&PR 91*
Zanghi, William Anthony 1936- *St&PR 91*
Zangwill, Israel 1864-1926 *BioIn 16, TwCCr&M 91A*
Zani, Frederick Caesar 1929- *WhoWor 91*
Zani, Gerald Andrew 1934- *St&PR 91*
Zanin, Joseph D. 1935- *St&PR 91*
Zanini, Bernardino *BiDrAPA 89*
Zanini, Eugenio A *BiDrAPA 89*
Zanini, Gianni 1954- *WhoE 91*
Zanini, Marco *PenDiDA 89*
Zanino di Pietro *PenDiDA 89*
Zanke, Jorg 1945- *WhoWor 91*
Zankel, Arthur 1932- *St&PR 91, WhoAm 90*
Zanker, Bill *BioIn 16*
Zanker, Theodore 1936- *BiDrAPA 89*
Zankofski, Deborah Ann 1955- *WhoAmW 91*
Zankowski, Doreen Marie 1959- *WhoE 91*
Zanni, Anthony L 1913- *BiDrAPA 89*
Zanni, Dom 1932- *Ballpl 90*
Zannieri, Nina 1955- *WhoAmW 91*
Zannoni, Peter J. 1921- *St&PR 91*
Zanone, Valerio 1936- *WhoWor 91*
Zanoni, Mickey G. 1945- *St&PR 91*
Zanoni, Ronald Albert 1942- *St&PR 91, WhoAm 90*
Zanot, Craig Allen 1955- *WhoEmL 91, WhoWor 91*
Zanotelli, Hans 1927- *IntWWM 90*
Zanotti, Luciano 1932- *WhoWor 91*
Zanotti, Marie Louise 1954- *WhoAmW 91*
Zanotti, Martin P. 1932- *St&PR 91, WhoAm 90*
Zanow, Lois A. 1933- *WhoAmW 91*
Zansky, Jeanette Uretzky 1923- *WhoAmW 91*
Zant, Robert Franklin 1943- *WhoAm 90*
Zantman, J B 1919- *WhoAmA 91*
Zanuck, Darryl *BioIn 16*
Zanuck, Darryl F. 1902-1979 *WorAlBi*
Zanuck, Richard D. 1934- *BioIn 16, St&PR 91*
Zanuck, Richard Darryl 1934- *WhoAm 90*
Zanuso, Marco 1916- *ConDes 90, PenDiDA 89*
Zanussi, Krzysztof 1939- *BioIn 16, ConTFT 8, WhoWor 91*
Zanville, Stephen Alan *BiDrAPA 89*
Zanzi, James Michael 1940- *WhoAm 90*
Zao, Wou-ki 1921- *BioIn 16*
Zapalac, Robert L 1940- *BiDrAPA 89*
Zapanta, Al *WhoHisp 91*
Zapanta, Conrad Ronquillo 1941- *WhoSSW 91*
Zapapas, James Richard 1926- *WhoAm 90*
Zapata, Ariel F. 1958- *WhoHisp 91*
Zapata, Carlos Eduardo 1961- *WhoHisp 91*
Zapata, Carmen 1927- *BioIn 16*
Zapata, Carmen Margarita 1927- *WhoHisp 91*
Zapata, Elssy-Fedora 1950- *WhoAmW 91*
Zapata, Emiliano 1879-1919 *BioIn 16*
Zapata, Emiliano 1883-1919 *WorAlBi*
Zapata, Javier Angel *BiDrAPA 89*
Zapata, Jose Angel, Jr. 1958- *WhoHisp 91*
Zapata, Leoncio *BiDrAPA 89*
Zapata, M. Nelson, Jr. 1950- *WhoHisp 91*
Zapata, Sabas, III 1945- *WhoHisp 91*
Zapata Olivella, Manuel 1920- *HispWr 90*
Zapel, Wesley Clair 1954- *WhoE 91*
Zapf, Charles Alger 1949- *BiDrAPA 89*
Zapf, Hermann 1918- *ConDes 90, WhoAm 90*
Zapf, John G. 1915- *St&PR 91*
Zapfe, Guillermo 1933- *WhoAmA 91*
Zapffe, Carl Andrew 1912- *WhoE 91*
Zaphiropoulos, Miltiades L 1914- *BiDrAPA 89*
Zapiain, Norman Gerard 1962- *WhoHisp 91*
Zapicchi, Michael Vincent 1955- *WhoE 91*
Zapkus, Kes 1938- *WhoAmA 91*
Zapolska, Gabriela 1857-1921 *EncCoWW*
Zappa, Dweezil *BioIn 16*
Zappa, Frank *BioIn 16*
Zappa, Frank 1940- *CurBio 90 [port], EncPR&S 89, OxCPMus, WhoAm 90, WorAlBi*
Zappa, James Victor 1964- *WhoE 91*
Zappa, Moon Unit *BioIn 16*
Zappala, Anthony *BiDrAPA 89*
Zappala, Joseph *WhoWor 91*
Zappala, Stephen A. 1932- *WhoE 91*
Zappas, Hubert F 1929- *BiDrAPA 89*
Zappella, David G 1924- *BiDrAPA 89*
Zappetti, Thomas A. 1942- *St&PR 91*
Zappi, Faustina 1679-1745 *EncCoWW*
Zappia, Dominic Carmen 1929- *WhoE 91*
Zappler, Lisbeth 1930- *AuBYP 90*
Zappone, Mary Slagle 1964- *WhoAmW 91*
Zappone, Ronald A *BiDrAPA 89*
Zappulla, Lawrence Joseph 1936- *St&PR 91, WhoAm 90*
Zapun, Simone *AuBYP 90*
Zar, Carol B. 1945- *WhoAmW 91*
Zar, Jerrold Howard 1941- *WhoAm 90*
Zara, Louis 1910- *WhoAm 90, WhoWrEP 89*
Zarabet, Joseph 1932- *St&PR 91*
Zarafonetis, Chris John Dimiter 1914- *WhoAm 90*
Zaragoza, Blanca *WhoHisp 91*
Zaragoza, Rogelio Soria 1958- *BiDrAPA 89*
Zarakas, Peter 1928- *St&PR 91*
Zaraleya-Harari, Sarah 1926- *WhoAmW 91*
Zarand, Julius John 1913- *WhoAmA 91*
Zarangas, Leonidas Pantelis 1949- *WhoWor 91*
Zaranka, Albert J. 1949- *WhoSSW 91, WhoWor 91*
Zaraspe, Hector *BioIn 16*
Zarate, Lenore Beatrice 1937- *WhoAmW 91*
Zarate, Narcisa 1925- *WhoHisp 91*
Zarb, Frank Gustave 1935- *St&PR 91, WhoAm 90*

Zarchy, Harry 1912- *AuBYP 90*
Zarcone, Vincent Peter, Jr. 1937- *WhoAm 90*
Zardari, Asif Ali *BioIn 16*
Zardiackas, Lyle Dean 1944- *WhoSSW 91*
Zardis, Chester *NewYTBS 90*
Zardoya, Concha 1914- *EncCoWW*
Zare, Richard Neil 1939- *WhoAm 90*
Zare-Parsi, Mojgan *BiDrAPA 89*
Zarecor, William Donald 1930- *WhoAm 90*
Zarefsky, David Harris 1946- *WhoAm 90*
Zareh, Mo 1943- *WhoSSW 91*
Zarem, Abe Mordecai 1917- *WhoAm 90*
Zarem, Lewis *AuBYP 90*
Zarem, Norton Lewis 1937- *BiDrAPA 89*
Zaremba, Carolyn Weis 1953- *WhoAmW 91*
Zaremba, Karen Ann 1954- *WhoAmW 91*
Zarembina, Ewa Szelburg- 1899-1986 *BioIn 16*
Zarembka, Paul 1942- *WhoE 91*
Zaremski, Miles Jay 1948- *WhoAm 90*
Zarenko, Ronald P. 1946- *St&PR 91*
Zaret, Barry Lewis 1940- *WhoAm 90*
Zaretsky, Alan *St&PR 91*
Zaretsky, Marilyn Lee 1945- *WhoAmW 91*
Zargaj, Tomislav 1933- *BiDrAPA 89*
Zarges, Thomas Henry 1948- *St&PR 91*
Zarghamee, Mehdi S. 1941- *St&PR 91*
Zarif, Shabbir *BiDrAPA 89*
Zariffa, Kamal-Joseph 1937- *BiDrAPA 89*
Zarilla, Al 1919- *Ballpl 90*
Zarin, Deborah Ann 1956- *BiDrAPA 89*
Zarin, Gerald 1941- *WhoAm 90*
Zaring, Jane 1936- *BioIn 16*
Zaring Thayer, Barbara *BioIn 16*
Zarins, Bertram 1942- *WhoAm 90*
Zarins, Joyce Audy 1949- *BioIn 16*
Zariphes, Constantine, Jr. 1932- *BiDrAPA 89*
Zaris, David *BiDrAPA 89*
Zaritt, Judy *BioIn 16*
Zarky, Karen Jane 1948- *WhoAmW 91*
Zarle, Thomas H. *WhoAm 90*
Zarlenga, Carol A. *St&PR 91*
Zarling, Craig Frederic 1958- *BiDrAPA 89*
Zarling, Robert Stanley 1931- *St&PR 91*
Zarnick, Bernard F. 1936- *St&PR 91*
Zarnick, Genny R. 1939- *St&PR 91*
Zarnick, Laura Lynn 1968- *St&PR 91*
Zarnow, William Robert, Jr. 1934- *St&PR 91*
Zarnowitz, Victor 1919- *WhoAm 90*
Zarnowski, Chester Frank 1943- *WhoE 91*
Zarnowski, James David 1950- *WhoEmL 91*
Zaro, Ambrose *BioIn 16*
Zarobe, Christina Maria 1961- *WhoHisp 91*
Zaroff, Ralph *BiDrAPA 89*
Zaroulis, Charles George 1937- *WhoE 91*
Zarr, Melvyn 1936- *WhoAm 90*
Zarr, Michael L 1949- *BiDrAPA 89*
Zarraonandia, David *WhoHisp 91*
Zarrella, Ronald L. 1949- *St&PR 91*
Zarrella, Vincent Joseph 1925- *St&PR 91*
Zarrett, Linda Pauline 1956- *WhoAmW 91, WhoEmL 91, WhoWor 91*
Zarrett, Mary Ann 1949- *WhoAmW 91*
Zarriello, Richard Anthony *BiDrAPA 89*
Zarrilli, Gary Anthony 1947- *St&PR 91*
Zarro, Janice *BioIn 16*
Zarro, Janice Anne 1947- *WhoAm 90, WhoAmW 91*
Zarrow, Herbert Daniel 1933- *St&PR 91*
Zarse, Leigh Bryant 1930- *WhoWor 91*
Zarsky, Edward L 1923- *BiDrAPA 89*
Zarsky, Norman Isaiah 1955- *BiDrAPA 89*
Zartman, David Lester 1940- *WhoAm 90*
Zartman, Joann M. 1938- *St&PR 91*
Zartman, Richard E. 1946- *WhoSSW 91*
Zartovnicka, Milka *EncCoWW*
Zaruby, Walter Stephen 1930- *WhoAm 90*
Zarudsky, Nikolaus *BiDrAPA 89*
Zarur, Pedro 1947- *St&PR 91*
Zarutskie, Paul Walter 1951- *WhoEmL 91, WhoWor 91*
Zarwan, John 1949- *WhoE 91*
Zarwell, David Harvey 1939- *BiDrAPA 89*
Zarwyn, Berthold 1921- *WhoAm 90*
Zarzar, Michael Nakhleh *BiDrAPA 89*
Zarzar, Nakhleh P 1932- *BiDrAPA 89*
Zarzar, Nicholas Saleh *BiDrAPA 89*
Zarzycki-Berg, Donna 1948- *WhoAmW 91*
Zaslavskaia, Tat'iana I. *BioIn 16*
Zaslavskiy, Ilya *BioIn 16*
Zaslavsky, Thomas 1944- *WhoE 91*
Zasloff, J. J. *ConAu 129*
Zasloff, Joseph J 1925- *ConAu 129*
Zaslove, Phoebe *BioIn 16, WhoAm 90, WhoAmW 91, WhoE 91, WhoWor 91*
Zaslow, Edmund Morris 1917- *WhoWrEP 89*
Zaslow, Jeffrey *BioIn 16*
Zaslow, Jeffrey Lloyd 1958- *WhoAm 90*
Zaslow, Stephen L 1936- *BiDrAPA 89*
Zaslow, Stephen Lee 1936- *WhoE 91*
Zaslowe, Peter Bruce 1946- *WhoE 91*
Zassenhaus, Hiltgunt Margret 1916- *WhoAm 90*
Zastro, Kathryn Anna 1951- *St&PR 91*
Zastrow, Gregg *BioIn 16*
Zastrow, John Thurman 1937- *WhoWor 91*
Zastrow, Klaus D. 1929- *St&PR 91*
Zateli, Zyranna 1951- *EncCoWW*
Zatezalo, Sandy *BioIn 16*
Zatkins, Karen Marie 1950- *WhoE 91*
Zatkoff, Lawrence P. *WhoAm 90*
Zatkova, Rougena 1885-1923 *BiDWomA*
Zatlin, Gabriel Stanley 1935- *WhoE 91*
Zatopek, Emil 1922- *WhoWor 91*
Zatuchni, Gerald Irving 1933- *WhoAm 90*
Zaturenska, Marya 1902-1982 *FemiCLE*
Zatz, Arline 1937- *WhoWrEP 89*
Zatz, Irving J. 1953- *WhoEmL 91*
Zauchin, Norm 1929- *Ballpl 90*
Zauderer, Mark Carl 1946- *WhoEmL 91*
Zauditu *WomWR*
Zaugg, Georges 1951- *IntWWM 90*
Zaugg, Robert *St&PR 91*
Zaun, Bruce G. 1930- *St&PR 91*
Zaun, P.S. 1954- *St&PR 91*
Zaunemann, Sidonia Hedwig 1714-1740 *EncCoWW*
Zauner, Christian Walter 1930- *WhoAm 90*
Zaur, Alan Leonard *BiDrAPA 89*
Zaur, Alan Leonard 1947- *WhoE 91*
Zausner, L. Andrew 1949- *WhoAm 90*
Zausner, Sol *BioIn 16*
Zavada, Mary Roberta 1936- *WhoAmW 91*
Zavada, Michael Stephan 1952- *WhoSSW 91*
Zavala, Adina de 1861-1955 *BioIn 16*
Zavala, Eduardo Alberto 1960- *WhoHisp 91*
Zavala, Iris M. 1935- *WhoWor 91*
Zavala, Iris M 1936- *ConAu 32NR, HispWr 90*
Zavala, Lorenzo de 1788-1836 *BioIn 16*
Zavala, Maria Elena 1950- *WhoHisp 91*
Zavala, Valerie Renee 1955- *WhoHisp 91*
Zavala-Alvarado, Lauro 1954- *WhoWor 91*
Zavarine, Carolyn J. 1936- *BiDrAPA 89*
Zavattini, Cesare 1902-1989 *AnObit 1989, BioIn 16, ConAu 130*
Zaveri, Nirmal Gopaldas 1952- *WhoWor 91*
Zaveri, Salil Ashok 1960- *WhoE 91*
Zavertal, Ladislao 1849-1942 *PenDiMP*
Zavijava Orchestra *NewAgMG*
Zavis, Michael William 1937- *WhoAm 90*
Zavitz, Ronald Vernon 1947- *WhoSSW 91*
Zavitzianos, George 1909- *BiDrAPA 89*
Zavodnick, Jacquelyn M 1945- *BiDrAPA 89*
Zavodnick, Jacquelyn Miller 1945- *WhoE 91*
Zavodnick, Steven 1948- *BiDrAPA 89*
Zavoina, Andrew M. 1958- *St&PR 91*
Zavon, N.H. 1918- *St&PR 91*
Zavorski, Lisa Marie 1960- *WhoAmW 91*
Zavrian, Suzanne Ostro *WhoWrEP 89*
Zavrski, Josip 1917- *WhoWor 91*
Zawacki, John Edward 1949- *St&PR 91*
Zawacki, Joseph Edward, Jr. 1957- *WhoE 91*
Zawada, Edward Thaddeus, Jr. 1947- *WhoEmL 91, WhoWor 91*
Zawadzka-Golosz, Anna 1955- *IntWWM 90*
Zawadzki, Joseph Nathan 1949- *St&PR 91*
Zawatsky, Julia Jones 1953- *BiDrAPA 89*
Zawinul, Joe *BioIn 16*
Zawinul, Josef 1932- *WhoAm 90, WhoWor 91*
Zawisha, Richard Garry 1956- *St&PR 91*
Zawistowska, Kazimiera 1870-1902 *EncCoWW*
Zawodny, Albert Michael 1927- *St&PR 91*
Zawodzinski, Stefan 1928- *WhoWor 91*
Zax, Jeffrey Stephen 1954- *WhoE 91*
Zax, Kenneth Charles 1924- *St&PR 91*
Zax, Melvin 1928- *WhoAm 90*
Zax, Ruth B. *ODwPR 91*
Zax, Ruth Barbara 1947- *WhoE 91*
Zax, Stanley R. *WhoAm 90*
Zax, Stanley R. 1937- *St&PR 91*
Zay, Jean Elie Paul 1904-1944 *BiDFrPL*
Zay, Thomas Charles 1932- *WhoSSW 91*
Zayachek, Mary Katherine 1943- *WhoAmW 91*
Zayan, Mohamed Ameen 1949- *St&PR 91*
Zayas, Miguel Angel 1949- *WhoHisp 91*
Zayas-Bazan, Eduardo 1935- *WhoAm 90*
Zayas y Alfonso, Alfredo 1861-1934 *BioIn 16*
Zayas y Sotomayor, Maria de 1590-1661? *EncCoWW*
Zaydon, Jemille Ann 1940- *WhoAmW 91*
Zaydon, Thomas John, Jr. 1952- *WhoSSW 91*
Zayed bin Sultan Al-Nahayan, Sheikh 1918- *WhoWor 91*
Zayed Bin Sultan Al Nuhayyan 1918?- *PolLCME*
Zayek, Francis Mansour 1920- *WhoAm 90, WhoE 91*
Zaylor, Charles Leonard 1952- *BiDrAPA 89*
Zazanis, Marina P. 1938- *St&PR 91*
Zazas, George John 1926- *WhoAm 90*
Zazik, Jesse 1938- *St&PR 91*
Zazow, Paul Leslie 1950- *BiDrAPA 89*
Zazueta, Fernando *WhoHisp 91*
Zazulia, Irwin *WhoSSW 91*
Zazzali, George Peter 1939- *St&PR 91*
Zazzera, Edmund *St&PR 91*
Zbarsky, John Jacob 1946- *St&PR 91*
Zbarsky, Sidney Howard 1920- *WhoAm 90*
Zblewski, Randall Joseph 1955- *BiDrAPA 89*
Zborowski, R.W. 1951- *St&PR 91*
Zboyovsky, James F. 1926- *St&PR 91*
Zbuzek, Vlasta Kmentova 1933- *WhoAmW 91*
Zdanis, Richard Albert 1935- *WhoAm 90*
Zdellar, R.D. 1944- *St&PR 91*
Zdobylak, Andrew Martin 1951- *WhoAm 90*
Zdon, Joseph Paul, Jr. 1941- *St&PR 91*
Zea, Kristi *BioIn 16*
Zea Aguilar, Leopoldo 1912- *WhoWor 91*
Zealberg, Joseph James 1950- *BiDrAPA 89*
Zeami 1363-1443 *EncJap*
Zeami, Motokiyo 1363-1443 *WorAlBi*
Zeanah, Charles H, Jr. 1951- *BiDrAPA 89*
Zeanah, Robert Clyde 1951- *WhoSSW 91*
Zeani, Virginia 1928- *IntWWM 90, PenDiMP*
Zeares, Melinda Ann 1947- *WhoAmW 91*
Zearfoss, Herbert Keyser 1929- *WhoWor 91*
Zeavin, Bernard Harold 1926- *WhoSSW 91*
Zebauers, Vladimirs Valdis 1903- *WhoWrEP 89*
Zebedee, William Arthur 1937- *St&PR 91*
Zebley, Arthur 1923- *St&PR 91*
Zebley, Joseph Wildman, Jr. 1914- *WhoE 91, WhoWrEP 89*
Zebot, Cyril A. 1914-1989 *BioIn 16*
Zebraski, Kathleen 1950- *WhoAmW 91*
Zebroski, Edwin Leopold 1921- *WhoAm 90*
Zebrowitz, Leslie Ann 1944- *WhoAm 90*
Zebrowski, Edward A. 1931- *St&PR 91*
Zebrowski, Edward Richard 1921- *St&PR 91*
Zebrowski, Ernest, Jr. 1944- *WhoWrEP 89*
Zebrowski, George 1945- *ConAu 30NR*
Zebrowski, Joseph J. 1947- *WhoE 91*
Zebrowski, Marilyn Frances *WhoAmW 91*
Zebrowski, Mary Theodorette 1916- *WhoE 91*
Zebrowski, Sandra Marie *BiDrAPA 89*
Zec, Philip 1909-1983 *DcNaB 1981*
Zecca, John Andrew 1914- *WhoAm 90*
Zecchi, Carlo 1903-1984 *PenDiMP*
Zecchini, Salvatore R. 1943- *WhoWor 91*
Zech, Lando William 1923- *BioIn 16*
Zech, Paul 1881-1946 *BioIn 16*
Zech, Ronald H. 1943- *St&PR 91*
Zecha, Austen Victor Lauw 1940- *WhoWor 91*
Zechella, Alexander Philip 1920- *WhoAm 90*
Zechello, Anni L. 1943- *WhoAmW 91*
Zecher, J. Richard 1940- *St&PR 91*
Zecher, Joseph Richard 1940- *WhoAm 90*
Zecher, Nat *BioIn 16*
Zecher, Scott J. 1959- *St&PR 91*
Zecher, Thomas R. 1953- *WhoWor 91*
Zechiel, William A. 1951- *St&PR 91*
Zechman, Fred William, Jr. 1928- *WhoAm 90*
Zechmeister, Laszlo K. E. 1889-1972 *BioIn 16*
Zechter, Sol 1926- *St&PR 91*
Zeckel, Harold R *BiDrAPA 89*
Zeckel, Johann 1660?-1728 *PenDiDA 89*
Zeckendorf, William 1905-1976 *WorAlBi*
Zeckendorf, William, Jr. 1929- *St&PR 91, WhoAm 90*
Zeckhauser, Richard Jay 1940- *WhoAm 90*
Zed, Aggie 1952- *WhoAmA 91*
Zedda, Alberto 1928- *IntWWM 90, PenDiMP*
Zedek, Nehemia *BiDrAPA 89*
Zedekias *EncO&P 3*
Zeder, Fred Monroe, II 1921- *WhoAm 90*
Zeder, Fred Morrell 1886-1951 *EncABHB 5 [port]*
Zednik, Heinz 1940- *IntWWM 90*
Zedrosser, Joseph John 1938- *WhoAm 90, WhoE 91*
Zee, Hugo J 1930- *BiDrAPA 89*
Zeeble, Bill T. 1957- *WhoSSW 91*
Zeeman, Joan Javits 1928- *WhoAmW 91, WhoWor 91*
Zeeman, Pieter 1865-1943 *WorAlBi*
Zeff, Arnold Eugene 1936- *BiDrAPA 89*
Zeff, Edward W *BiDrAPA 89*
Zeff, Karl Norman *BiDrAPA 89*
Zeff, Mark *BioIn 16*
Zeff, Richard Lee 1949- *WhoE 91*
Zeff, Stephen Addam 1933- *WhoAm 90*
Zeff, Susan Leah 1945- *WhoAmW 91*
Zeffer, Alan E. 1952- *St&PR 91*
Zeffirelli, Franco *BioIn 16*
Zeffirelli, Franco 1923- *ConDes 90, WhoAm 90, WhoWor 91, WorAlBi*
Zeffirelli, G. Franco 1923- *IntWWM 90*
Zeffren, Eugene 1941- *St&PR 91*
Zegadlo, Ray *St&PR 91*
Zegans, Leonard S *BiDrAPA 89*
Zegar, Frank Anthony 1938- *St&PR 91*
Zegarelli, Edward Victor 1912- *WhoAm 90*
Zegart, Arthur *BioIn 16*
Zegers, Christopher J 1960- *BiDrAPA 89*
Zegers, Kip 1943- *WhoWrEP 89*
Zegiob-Devereaux, Leslie Elaine 1948- *WhoAmW 91*
Zeglen, Kurt Thomas 1953- *WhoE 91*
Zegler, Chester J. 1936- *St&PR 91*
Zegler, Chester Joseph 1936- *WhoAm 90*
Zegota, Robert Thompson 1948- *WhoSSW 91*
Zegrea, Nick George 1936- *WhoSSW 91*
Zeh, Geoffrey N. 1943- *WhoAm 90*
Zeh, Raymond F, Jr. 1944- *BiDrAPA 89*
Zehfuss, Lawrence Thomas 1938- *WhoAm 90*
Zehler, Edward Joseph 1940- *WhoE 91*
Zehler, Edward M *BiDrAPA 89*
Zehner, Marsha Louise 1951- *WhoE 91*
Zehner, Richard N. 1953- *St&PR 91*
Zehner, Richard Norman 1953- *WhoWor 91*
Zehr, Dale R. *St&PR 91*
Zehr, Eldon Irvin 1935- *WhoSSW 91*
Zehr, Robert F. 1950- *St&PR 91*
Zehring, John William 1947- *WhoWrEP 89*
Zehring, Karen 1945- *WhoAmW 91, WhoE 91*
Zei, Alki *AuBYP 90*
Zeichner, Ben 1938- *BiDrAPA 89*
Zeichner, Oscar 1916- *WhoAm 90*
Zeid Bin Shaker, Sharif 1934- *WhoWor 91*
Zeidenberg, Phillip 1932- *BiDrAPA 89*
Zeidenbergs, Olafs 1936- *WhoAmA 91*
Zeidenfeld, David 1909- *St&PR 91*
Zeidenstein, George 1929- *WhoAm 90*
Zeider, Rollie 1883-1967 *Ballpl 90*
Zeidler, Eberhard Heinrich 1926- *WhoAmA 91, WhoWor 91*
Zeidler, Frank *EncAL*
Zeidler, Frank P. 1912- *WhoAm 90*
Zeidler, Robert Bernard 1943- *WhoSSW 91*
Zeidman, Heywood W 1941- *BiDrAPA 89*
Zeidman, R Amos *BiDrAPA 89*
Zeidman, Sylvan Arnold 1947- *WhoEmL 91*
Zeidner, Lisa A. 1955- *WhoWrEP 89*
Zeien, Alfred M. 1930- *WhoAm 90*
Zeien, Alfred Michael 1930- *St&PR 91*
Zeifman, Israel 1926- *BiDrAPA 89*
Zeiger, Delbert Lee 1941- *WhoWor 91*
Zeiger, Henry Anthony 1930- *AuBYP 90*
Zeiger, Lila L. 1927- *WhoWrEP 89*
Zeiger, Martin 1937- *St&PR 91*
Zeigfreid, Karl *ConAu 32NR*
Zeigler, Alan 1951- *St&PR 91*
Zeigler, Bernard Phillip 1940- *WhoAm 90*
Zeigler, Charles E., Sr. 1925- *St&PR 91*
Zeigler, Donald Jay 1951- *WhoSSW 91*
Zeigler, Earle Frederick 1919- *WhoAm 90*
Zeigler, George 1934- *WhoSSW 91*
Zeigler, George M. 1934- *St&PR 91*
Zeigler, Jon Glass 1936- *St&PR 91*
Zeigler, Judy Rose 1946- *WhoEmL 91*
Zeigler, Kenneth Baron 1948- *St&PR 91*
Zeigler, Lee Woodward 1868-1952 *WhoAmA 91N*
Zeigler, Luther Harmon 1936- *WhoAm 90*
Zeigler, Michael C. 1946- *St&PR 91*
Zeigler, Stephen F. 1951- *St&PR 91*
Zeiguer, Luis Valentin *BiDrAPA 89*
Zeihen, Lester Gregory 1913- *WhoWor 91*
Zeikowitz, Benson J. 1926- *St&PR 91*
Zeilberger, Doron 1950- *WhoE 91*
Zeileis, Friedrich Georg 1939- *WhoWor 91*
Zeiler, Christian 1936- *WhoWor 91*
Zeiler, Michael Donald 1933- *WhoAm 90*
Zeilig, Nancy Meeks 1943- *WhoAmW 91, WhoWrEP 89*
Zeilinger, Alan F. 1937- *St&PR 91*
Zeiller, Warren 1929- *WhoAm 90*
Zeilmaker, Gerardus Hendrikus 1936- *WhoWor 91*
Zeilman, William Whitney 1939- *St&PR 91*

Zein-Eldin, E Ahmed 1925- *BiDrAPA 89*
Zeiner, Ann Oreski 1939- *WhoAmW 91*
Zeiner, Lukas *PenDiDA 89*
Zeinert, Karen Kay 1942- *WhoWrEP 89*
Zeisberger, David 1721-1808 *EncCRAm, WhNaAH*
Zeisel, Eva 1906- *ConDes 90*
Zeisel, Hans 1905- *WhoAm 90*
Zeisler, Claire 1903- *WhoAm 90, WhoAmA 91*
Zeisler, Fannie 1863-1927 *PenDiMP*
Zeisler, Fannie Bloomfield 1863-1927 *BioIn 16*
Zeisler, John E. *BioIn 16*
Zeisler, Richard Spiro 1916- *WhoAm 90, WhoAmA 91*
Zeisler, Robert H. 1933- *St&PR 91*
Zeiss, Clifford John 1920- *BiDrAPA 89, WhoE 91*
Zeissig, Johann Elias *PenDiDA 89*
Zeit, Ruth Mae 1945- *WhoAmW 91, WhoE 91*
Zeiter, William Emmet 1934- *WhoAm 90*
Zeitinger, Robert Carl 1927- *St&PR 91*
Zeitlan, Marilyn Labb 1938- *WhoAmW 91*
Zeitler, Deborah Leila 1952- *WhoAmW 91*
Zeitler, Herbert 1923- *WhoWor 91*
Zeitler, Robert G 1929- *BiDrAPA 89*
Zeitler, Rudolf Walter 1912- *BioIn 16*
Zeitlin, Bruce Allen 1943- *St&PR 91*
Zeitlin, Dennis Jay 1938- *BiDrAPA 89*
Zeitlin, Denny *BioIn 16, NewAgMG*
Zeitlin, Eugenia Pawlik *WhoAmW 91*
Zeitlin, Froma I. 1933- *WhoAm 90*
Zeitlin, Gerald Mark 1937- *WhoWor 91*
Zeitlin, Harriet 1929- *WhoAmA 91*
Zeitlin, Herbert Zakary *WhoAm 90*
Zeitlin, Hillel 1871-1942 *BioIn 16*
Zeitlin, Jacob Israel 1902- *BioIn 16*
Zeitlin, Joseph 1906- *BioIn 16*
Zeitlin, Marilyn A 1941- *WhoAmA 91*
Zeitlin, Maurice 1935- *WhoWor 91*
Zeitlin, Maurice I 1941- *BiDrAPA 89*
Zeitlin, Stanley S. 1937- *ODwPR 91*
Zeitlin, Zvi 1923- *IntWWM 90, PenDiMP, WhoAm 90*
Zeitman, Lea S. 1947- *St&PR 91*
Zeitner, June Culp *WhoWrEP 89*
Zeitz, Abraham *BioIn 16*
Zeitz, Elizabeth B *BiDrAPA 89*
Zeitz, John A *BiDrAPA 89*
Zeitz, Kenneth 1927- *St&PR 91*
Zekan, William C. 1920- *WhoAm 90*
Zekan, William Charles *BioIn 16*
Zekan, William Charles 1919- *St&PR 91*
Zekind, Diane Marie 1961- *WhoAmW 91*
Zekiyan, Boghos Levon 1943- *WhoWor 91*
Zekman, Pamela Lois 1944- *WhoAm 90*
Zekman, Terri Margaret 1950- *WhoAm 90, WhoAmW 91*
Zekowski, Arlene 1922- *WhoWrEP 89*
Zelanski, Paul John 1931- *WhoAmA 91, WhoE 91*
Zelasko, Barbara *ODwPR 91*
Zelaya, Jose Santos 1853-1919 *BioIn 16*
Zelazny, Roger *BioIn 16*
Zelazny, Roger 1937- *MajTwCW, RGTwCSF, WorAlBi*
Zelazny, Roger Joseph 1937- *WhoAm 90, WhoWrEP 89*
Zelazo, Helene 1920- *St&PR 91*
Zelazo, Nathaniel K. 1918- *St&PR 91, WhoAm 90*
Zelazo, Ronald Elliott 1946- *St&PR 91*
Zelby, Leon Wolf 1925- *WhoAm 90*
Zelby, Rachel 1930- *WhoAmW 91*
Zelda *EncCoWW*
Zeldes, Ilya Michael 1933- *WhoWor 91*
Zeldes, Stephen Paul 1956- *WhoE 91*
Zeldin, Edmond Toby *BiDrAPA 89*
Zeldin, Richard Packer 1918- *WhoAm 90*
Zeldis, Malcah 1931- *BioIn 16, MusmAFA*
Zel'dovich, Iakov Borisovich *BioIn 16*
Zeldowicz, Henry C *BiDrAPA 89*
Zelen, Herbert Jack 1931- *WhoE 91*
Zelenak, Edward John 1940- *WhoAmA 91*
Zelenka, Jan 1923- *WhoWor 91*
Zelenka, Ladislav *PenDiMP*
Zelenovic, Dragutin *WhoWor 91*
Zelenski, Steven G 1944- *BiDrAPA 89*
Zeleny, Jindrich 1922- *ConAu 132*
Zeleny, Marjorie Pfeiffer 1924- *WhoAmW 91, WhoSSW 91*
Zeleny, Robert Owen 1930- *St&PR 91, WhoAm 90*
Zelepos, Steve *BioIn 16*
Zelevansky, Paul 1946- *WhoWrEP 89*
Zelewski, Erich Bach- 1899-1972 *BioIn 16*
Zelezny, William Francis 1918- *WhoWor 91*
Zelig, Irma *BiDrAPA 89*
Zeligman, Sergio 1949- *WhoHisp 91*
Zelikoff, Murray 1922- *WhoAm 90*
Zelikow, Howard Monroe 1934- *WhoAm 90*
Zelin, Jerome 1930- *St&PR 91, WhoAm 90*
Zelinka, David *BioIn 16*
Zelinsky, Deborah Gail 1960- *WhoSSW 91*
Zelinsky, Paul O. *AuBYP 90, BioIn 16*
Zelis, Robert Felix 1939- *WhoAm 90*
Zelisko, Mark 1951- *St&PR 91*
Zelitch, Israel 1924- *WhoE 91*
Zelitzky, Gail P. 1941- *WhoAmW 91*
Zelizer, Nathan 1907- *BioIn 16*
Zell, Donald David 1928- *WhoSSW 91*
Zell, Hans M 1940- *ConAu 32NR*
Zell, John R 1927- *BiDrAPA 89*
Zell, Mary Alice 1948- *St&PR 91*
Zell, Ronald A. 1939- *St&PR 91*
Zell, Samuel *BioIn 16*
Zell, Samuel 1941- *WhoAm 90*
Zell, Steven Peter 1946- *WhoAm 90*
Zellars, John Broadus 1924- *St&PR 91*
Zelle, Charles A. 1955- *St&PR 91*
Zelle, Louis N. 1924- *St&PR 91*
Zellen, Carol Ann 1947- *WhoAmW 91*
Zeller, Barbara Ann 1945- *WhoAmW 91*
Zeller, Barton Wallace 1941- *WhoWor 91*
Zeller, Brenda Lynn 1964- *WhoAmW 91*
Zeller, C. Nick 1949- *St&PR 91*
Zeller, Clifford L 1947- *BiDrAPA 89*
Zeller, Earnest Jerome 1925- *WhoAm 90*
Zeller, Edward Jacob 1925- *WhoAm 90*
Zeller, Fred E. 1923- *WhoSSW 91*
Zeller, Frederic 1924- *ConAu 132, WhoAmA 91*
Zeller, Gary *BioIn 16*
Zeller, Hector C *BiDrAPA 89*
Zeller, Karl 1842-1898 *OxCPMus*
Zeller, Mark C. 1948- *St&PR 91*
Zeller, Michael Edward 1939- *WhoAm 90*
Zeller, Paul William 1948- *St&PR 91, WhoE 91, WhoWor 91*
Zeller, Richard A. 1934- *St&PR 91*
Zeller, Robert Lee, Jr. 1951- *St&PR 91*
Zeller, William W 1921- *BiDrAPA 89*
Zellerbach, Harold L 1895-1978 *WhoAmA 91N*
Zellerbach, William Joseph 1920- *WhoAm 90*
Zellers, C.F., Jr. 1932- *St&PR 91*
Zellers, Carl Fredrick, Jr. 1932- *WhoAm 90*
Zellers, Harold George 1948- *WhoSSW 91*
Zellers, Roger William 1945- *St&PR 91*
Zelli, Mary Diane 1957- *WhoAmW 91*
Zellman, Ande 1952- *WhoAm 90, WhoE 91*
Zellman, Sela Ann 1946- *WhoE 91*
Zellner, Arnold 1927- *WhoAm 90*
Zelman, Arthur B 1939- *BiDrAPA 89*
Zelman, Martin Ira 1952- *WhoE 91*
Zelman, Marvin *BiDrAPA 89*
Zelman, Patricia Grace 1944- *WhoAmW 91*
Zelmanowitz, Julius Martin 1941- *WhoAm 90*
Zelmer, Amy Elliott 1935- *WhoAm 90*
Zelner, Marjorie Swirsky 1950- *WhoAm 90*
Zelnick, Carl Robert 1940- *WhoAm 90*
Zelnick, David R. 1929- *St&PR 91*
Zelnick, Peter 1957- *St&PR 91*
Zelnick, Robert W. *ODwPR 91*
Zelnick, Strauss 1957- *WhoAm 90*
Zelov, Randolph Dickinson 1925- *St&PR 91*
Zelov, V.H. 1923- *St&PR 91*
Zelov, V. Scott 1957- *St&PR 91*
Zelt, Martha 1930- *WhoAmA 91*
Zeltins, Teodors 1914- *WhoWrEP 89*
Zeltzerman, Israel *BiDrAPA 89*
Zeluck, Roy S. 1952- *St&PR 91*
Zelver, Patricia 1923- *WhoWrEP 89*
Zelvin, Elizabeth 1944- *WhoWrEP 89*
Zelvin, Robert 1923- *St&PR 91*
Zemach, Harve 1933-1974 *AuBYP 90*
Zemach, Margot *BioIn 16*
Zemach, Margot 1931-1989 *AnObit 1989*
Zemach-Bersin, Kaethe 1958- *BioIn 16*
Zemaite 1845-1921 *EncCoWW*
Zeman, Anton Leonard 1930- *St&PR 91*
Zeman, Charles Joseph 1927- *St&PR 91*
Zeman, Herbert David 1944- *WhoE 91*
Zeman, Ivo 1931- *WhoWor 91*
Zeman, Jarold Knox 1926- *WhoAm 90, WhoWrEP 89*
Zeman, John Robert 1940- *St&PR 91, WhoAm 90, WhoE 91*
Zeman, Paula Redd 1956- *WhoAmW 91*
Zeman, Peter Michael 1941- *BiDrAPA 89*
Zeman, Raymond John 1939- *WhoE 91*
Zeman, Ruth E *BiDrAPA 89*
Zemanek, Kenneth James 1960- *BiDrAPA 89*
Zemanick, Karen Beth *BiDrAPA 89*
Zemann, Josef 1923- *WhoWor 91*
Zemans, Joyce L 1940- *WhoAmA 91*
Zemanski, Kevin M. 1958- *St&PR 91*
Zemba, Dorothy Irene 1928- *WhoAmW 91*
Zembala, Dennis 1942- *WhoE 91*
Zembrod, Evelyn *BioIn 16*
Zemcuznikov, Nicolas 1919- *BiDrAPA 89*
Zemeckis, Robert *BioIn 16*
Zemeckis, Robert L. 1952- *WhoAm 90*
Zemel, Carol Moscovitch 1941- *WhoE 91*
Zemel, Jay Norman 1928- *WhoAm 90*
Zemelman, James Louis 1931- *WhoWor 91*
Zemenick, James Michael 1947- *St&PR 91*
Zeminski, Joseph J., Jr. 1943- *St&PR 91*
Zemke, Hub 1914- *BioIn 16*
Zemke, Joseph *WhoAm 90*
Zemke, Lorna 1933- *IntWWM 90*
Zemlinsky, Alexander von 1871-1942 *PenDiMP A*
Zemmer, Joseph Lawrence, Jr. 1922- *WhoAm 90*
Zemmers, Robert M 1937- *BiDrAPA 89*
Zemmin, Richard W. 1941- *ODwPR 91*
Zemmin, Richard William 1941- *St&PR 91*
Zemojtel, Alexander Michael 1952- *WhoE 91*
Zemp, John Workman 1931- *WhoAm 90*
Zempel, Clare W. 1946- *St&PR 91*
Zemplenyi, Tibor Karol 1916- *WhoAm 90*
Zemsky, Samuel Paul 1951- *St&PR 91*
Zemurray, Samuel 1877-1961 *BioIn 16*
Zemyan, Stephen Michael 1948- *WhoE 91*
Zen, Carlo 1851-1918 *PenDiDA 89*
Zen, E-an 1928- *WhoAm 90*
Zen, Mark King Kim *BiDrAPA 89*
Zenatello, Giovanni 1876-1949 *PenDiMP*
Zenaty, Jayne *BioIn 16*
Zencker, Ernest Bernard 1929- *WhoE 91*
Zendejas, Esperanza 1952- *WhoHisp 91*
Zendejas, Luis *WhoHisp 91*
Zender, Hans 1936- *PenDiMP, WhoWor 91*
Zender, Johannes Wolfgang Hans 1936- *IntWWM 90*
Zendle, Howard Mark 1949- *WhoE 91, WhoWor 91*
Zendt, Esther Virginia 1914- *WhoAmW 91*
Zener, Karl A 1932- *BiDrAPA 89*
Zener, Karl E. 1903-1963 *EncPaPR 91*
Zenere, R.P. 1929- *St&PR 91*
Zeng Yi *BioIn 16*
Zenger, Anna Catherine 1704?-1751 *BioIn 16*
Zenger, John Peter 1697-1746 *BioIn 16, EncCRAm, WorAlBi*
Zengo, George Victor 1934- *St&PR 91*
Zeni, Jane Elizabeth 1945- *WhoAmW 91*
Zenios, Marios Chris 1951- *WhoWor 91*
Zeniya, Toru 1930- *WhoWor 91*
Zenke, Karl G. 1939- *WhoWor 91*
Zenker, Richard C. 1954- *St&PR 91*
Zenkovich, Brian 1956- *St&PR 91*
Zenkovich, Victor 1925- *St&PR 91*
Zenkovsky, Betty Jean 1927- *WhoAmW 91*
Zenn, Richard David *BiDrAPA 89*
Zenner, Ronald Peter 1938- *St&PR 91*
Zeno 490?BC-430?BC *WorAlBi*
Zeno, Jo Ann 1952- *WhoAmW 91*
Zeno, Phyllis Wolfe *WhoAm 90, WhoSSW 91*
Zeno Gandia, Manuel 1855-1930 *BioIn 16*
Zenobia *WomWR [port]*
Zenobia, Queen of Palmyra *BioIn 16*
Zenor, Cathryn Lenora 1955- *WhoAmW 91*
Zenowitz, Allan Ralph 1928- *WhoAm 90*
Zens, Patricia Martin 1926-1972 *BioIn 16*
Zentella, Yoly Gabriela 1949- *WhoWrEP 89*
Zentmyer, George Aubrey 1913- *WhoAm 90*
Zentner, Arnold S 1925- *BiDrAPA 89*
Zentner, Arnold Stuart 1925- *WhoE 91*
Zentner, Scott David *BiDrAPA 89*
Zenzie, Henry 1929- *St&PR 91*
Zeo, Frank James 1910- *WhoE 91*
Zeolla, Connie *WhoAmW 91*
Zepeda, Maria Angelica 1952- *WhoHisp 91*
Zepf, Edward Charles 1938- *St&PR 91*
Zepf, Thomas Herman 1935- *WhoAm 90, WhoWor 91*
Zepht, Fritz H. 1923- *St&PR 91*
Zepht, Peter 1963- *St&PR 91*
Zeplin, Rosemarie 1939- *EncCoWW*
Zepp, Bill 1946- *Ballpl 90*
Zeppa, Robert 1924- *WhoAm 90*
Zeppelin, Ferdinand, Graf Von 1838-1917 *WorAlBi*
Zeppetella, Anthony John 1949- *WhoE 91*
Zeps, Aivars A *BiDrAPA 89*
Zeps, Valdis Juris 1932- *WhoAm 90*
Zera, Carol Joyce 1943- *WhoAmW 91*
Zeranti, Cheryl Ann 1948- *WhoE 91*
Zeratsky, John Gibbons 1939- *St&PR 91*
Zeray, Peter *BioIn 16*
Zerba, Janet Ann 1941- *WhoAmW 91*
Zerbe, Anthony *WhoAm 90*
Zerbe, Brian Paul 1962- *WhoSSW 91*
Zerbe, D.G. 1946- *St&PR 91*
Zerbe, Jerome 1904-1988 *BioIn 16*
Zerbe, John B. 1929- *St&PR 91*
Zerbe, Karl 1903-1972 *WhoAmA 91N*
Zerbe, Kathryn Jane 1951- *BiDrAPA 89*
Zerbe, Pamela Lynn 1959- *WhoAmW 91*
Zerbey, Joseph Henry, IV 1942- *St&PR 91*
Zerbo, Rita Michaelle 1946- *WhoAmW 91*
Zerby, Judy Ann 1941- *WhoAmW 91*
Zercher, David Lynn 1960- *WhoE 91*
Zerella, Joseph T. 1941- *WhoAm 90*
Zerella, William Robert 1956- *St&PR 91*
Zerfoss, David B. 1948- *St&PR 91*
Zerfoss, Lester Frank 1903- *WhoSSW 91, WhoWor 91*
Zerfoss, Linda Louise 1953- *WhoAmW 91*
Zerin, Steven David 1953- *WhoAm 90*
Zeritsky, Samuel A *BiDrAPA 89*
Zerkel, Fred H. 1940- *St&PR 91*
Zerkel, Jacqulyn Wade 1961- *WhoEmL 91*
Zerkin, E. Leif 1949- *WhoWrEP 89*
Zerla, Aurelio Sergio *BiDrAPA 89*
Zerlaut, Gene Arlis 1930- *WhoWor 91*
Zerman, William Sheridan 1924- *WhoAm 90*
Zerna, Wolfgang 1916- *WhoWor 91*
Zerner, Henri Thomas 1939- *WhoAmA 91*
Zerner, Michael Charles 1940- *WhoSSW 91*
Zernhelt, Francis L. 1938- *St&PR 91*
Zernial, Gus 1923- *Ballpl 90*
Zernike, Elisabeth 1891-1982 *EncCoWW*
Zero, Jose Rodolfo 1962- *WhoE 91*
Zerounian, Ara 1926- *IntWWM 90*
Zerounian, Peruz 1924- *IntWWM 90*
Zerr, George C 1935- *BiDrAPA 89*
Zerrenner, John J. 1934- *St&PR 91*
Zerrudo, Chito Duenas 1950- *BiDrAPA 89*
Zertsalova, Natalya *PenDiMP*
Zertuche, Antonio *WhoHisp 91*
Zervas, Ioannis M 1959- *BiDrAPA 89*
Zervas, Leonidas 1902-1980 *DcScB S2*
Zervas, Nicholas Themistocles 1929- *WhoAm 90*
Zerweck, Charles W. 1908- *St&PR 91*
Zerwekh, Robert 1939- *BioIn 16*
Zerwekh, Robert Paul 1939- *WhoAm 90*
Zesch, Gene 1932- *BioIn 16*
Zeschinger, Johannes *PenDiDA 89*
Zesiewicz, Mary F *BiDrAPA 89*
Zesk, Richard S. 1930- *St&PR 91*
Zethelius, Sven Magnus *BiDrAPA 89*
Zetley, Linda 1953- *BiDrAPA 89*
Zetlin, Lev 1918- *WhoAm 90*
Zetlin, Valentine W 1912- *BiDrAPA 89*
Zetmeir, Norris Dean 1940- *WhoSSW 91*
Zettek, Chris R. 1960- *St&PR 91*
Zettelmaier, Ann Eleanor *BiDrAPA 89*
Zetterberg, Peder Arne 1951- *WhoWor 91*
Zetterling, Mai *BioIn 16*
Zetterling, Mai Elisabeth 1925- *WhoWor 91*
Zettlein, George 1844-1905 *Ballpl 90*
Zettlemoyer, Albert Charles 1915- *WhoAm 90*
Zettlemoyer, Ave Jeanne 1953- *WhoWrEP 89*
Zettler, Vallorie Raye 1961- *WhoAmW 91*
Zetumer, Matthew Robert 1947- *BiDrAPA 89*
Zetzer, Marlene Judith *BiDrAPA 89*
Zetzer, Stuart Irwin *BiDrAPA 89*
Zetzmann, Robert E. 1929- *St&PR 91*
Zeug, Mark E. 1943- *ODwPR 91*
Zeugheer, Jakob 1803-1865 *PenDiMP*
Zeugner, John Finn 1938- *WhoAm 90*
Zeuschner, Erwin Arnold 1935- *WhoAm 90*
Zevi, Bruno 1918- *WhoWor 91*
Zevin, Robert B. 1936- *St&PR 91*
Zevon, Irene 1918- *WhoAmA 91*
Zevon, Susan Jane 1944- *WhoAmW 91*
Zevon, Warren *BioIn 16*
Zevon, Warren 1947- *EncPR&S 89, WhoAm 90*
Zewail, Ahmed Hassan 1946- *WhoAm 90*
Zeybekoglu, Ilhan I. 1939- *WhoWor 91*
Zeynel, Sefik Charles 1949- *WhoE 91*
Zezza, Margaret Ann 1962- *WhoAmW 91*
Zfass, Isadore S 1910- *BiDrAPA 89*
Zgambo, Thomas Patrick 1953- *WhoE 91*
Zgoda, Larry 1950- *WhoAmA 91*
Zgodava, Richard A. *IntWWM 90*
Z'graggen, John Anton 1932- *WhoWor 91*
Z'Graggen, Yvette 1920- *EncCoWW*
Zgusta, Ladislav 1924- *WhoAm 90*
Zhabotinskii, Vladimir Evgen'evich 1880-1940 *BioIn 16*
Zhadovskaia, Iulia 1824-1883 *EncCoWW*
Zhang Aiping 1908- *WhoWor 91*
Zhang Bingyao *BioIn 16*
Zhang Daqian 1899-1983 *BioIn 16*
Zhang Guoxi *BioIn 16*
Zhang Jie 1937- *WorAu 1980 [port]*
Zhang Liyin *BioIn 16*
Zhang Weiguo *BioIn 16*
Zhang Xianliang 1936- *WorAu 1980*
Zhang Yimou *BioIn 16*
Zhang, Guo-xi 1952- *WhoWor 91*
Zhang, Theodore Tian-ze 1920- *WhoWor 91*
Zhang, Wenpu 1927- *WhoWor 91*
Zhang, Zhongfu 1938- *WhoWor 91*
Zhang, Zicun 1918- *WhoWor 91*

Zhao Zhangguang *BioIn 16*
Zhao Zhongxian 1941- *BioIn 16*
Zhao Zhunwang *BioIn 16*
Zhao Ziyang 1919- *WhoWor 91*
Zhao, Yi-Chun 1933- *WhoSSW 91*
Zhao, Zijun 1962- *WhoE 91*
Zharkov, Dimitrii Sergeevich 1924- *BioIn 16*
Zhdanov, Andrei 1896-1948 *WorAlBi*
Zhelev, Zhelyu 1923- *WhoWor 91*
Zhelezniakov, Anatoli 1895-1919 *BioIn 16*
Zheludev, Ivan Stepanovich 1921- *WhoWor 91*
Zheng Tuobin *WhoWor 91*
Zheng, Dechao 1961- *WhoE 91*
Zheng, Fangyang 1962- *WhoE 91*
Zheutlin, Abraham 1920- *BiDrAPA 89*
Zheutlin, Dale R 1948- *WhoAmA 91*
Zhi-Jian, Wang 1934- *IntWWM 90*
Zhitlovsky, German 1942- *BiDrAPA 89*
Zhivkov, Todor Khristov 1911- *WhoWor 91*
Zhordaniia, Noi Nikolaevich 1870-1953 *BioIn 16*
Zhou *PenDiDA 89*
Zhou Duo *BioIn 16*
Zhou Enlai 1898-1976 *BioIn 16*
Zhou Jue 1927- *WhoWor 91*
Zhou Yang 1907-1989 *BioIn 16*
Zhou, Guangzhao 1929- *WhoWor 91*
Zhu Da 1624?-1705? *BioIn 16*
Zhu, Ai-Lan 1956- *WhoAm 90*
Zhu, Jian-er 1922- *IntWWM 90*
Zhu, Jianchao 1952- *WhoSSW 91*
Zhu, Jianping 1958- *WhoEmL 91*
Zhu, Rongji 1928- *WhoWor 91*
Zhu, Tong Bo 1938- *WhoWor 91*
Zhu, Wei-Jing 1969- *WhoEmL 91*
Zhu, Zheng 1922- *WhoWor 91*
Zhuang, Zixin 1936- *WhoWor 91*
Zhukov, Georgi 1896-1974 *WorAlBi*
Zhukova, Maria 1804-1851 *EncCoWW*
Zhurakovski, Galina Dmitrievna 1952- *BiDrAPA 89*
Zia, Fereydoon Bob 1945- *St&PR 91*
Zia, Muhammad S *BiDrAPA 89*
Zia, Rashid *BiDrAPA 89*
Zia Ul-Haq, General Muhammad 1924-1988 *AnObit 1988*
Zia-ul-Haq, Mohammad *BioIn 16*
Ziadeh, Farhat J. 1917- *WhoAm 90*
Ziaie, Bahram *BiDrAPA 89*
Ziance, James P. 1947- *St&PR 91*
Zianitzka, K. Th. *EncCoWW*
Ziavras, Charles Efthemios 1921- *WhoWrEP 89*
Zib, Tom *WhoAmA 91*
Zibart, Michael Alan 1947- *WhoAm 90*
Zibbell, David R. 1939- *St&PR 91*
Zibelli, Thomas A *WhoAmA 91*
Zibelman, Robert Stephen *BiDrAPA 89*
Ziccardi, Karen M. Myers *WhoAmW 91*
Ziccarelli, Joseph M *BiDrAPA 89*
Zich, Sue Schaab 1946- *WhoAmW 91*
Zichek, Melvin Eddie 1918- *WhoWor 91*
Zichy, Geza 1849-1924 *PenDiMP*
Zick, David Gerald 1957- *BiDrAPA 89*
Zick, Janice Lee 1958- *WhoAmW 91*
Zick, Januarius *PenDiDA 89*
Zick, John Walter 1925- *WhoAm 90*
Zick, Leonard Otto 1905- *WhoWor 91*
Zickau, William E. 1936- *St&PR 91*
Zickel, John 1919- *WhoAm 90*
Zickler, Leo E. 1936- *St&PR 91*
Zicklin, Lawrence 1936- *St&PR 91*
Zide-Booth, Rochelle 1938- *BioIn 16*
Zide-Booth, Rochelle Deena 1938- *WhoAmW 91, WhoE 91*
Zidek, James Victor 1939- *WhoAm 90*
Zidelis, Rosa *BiDrAPA 89*
Zider, Robert Warren 1950- *St&PR 91, WhoE 91*
Ziebarth, E. William 1910- *WhoAm 90*
Ziebarth, Karl R. 1938- *St&PR 91*
Ziebarth, Karl Rex 1938- *WhoAm 90*
Ziebarth, Robert Charles 1936- *WhoAm 90*
Ziebarth, Steven William 1953- *WhoE 91*
Ziedins, Visvaldis *BiDrAPA 89*
Ziedonis, Douglas Michael *BiDrAPA 89*
Ziefert, Harriet *AuBYP 90*
Zieff, Leah Rose 1941- *WhoAmW 91*
Ziefle, Helmut W 1939- *ConAu 130*
Zieg, Kermit C., Jr. *St&PR 91*
Ziegaus, Alan J. *ODwPR 91*
Ziege, Roland Wacker 1914- *WhoSSW 91*
Ziegel, Bari Ann 1959- *WhoAmW 91*
Ziegele, William John 1940- *St&PR 91*
Ziegelheim, Irwin L. 1931- *St&PR 91*
Ziegelman, Robert Lee 1936- *WhoAm 90*
Ziegelmeier, Robert E. 1954- *St&PR 91*
Ziegenfuss, Douglas Edwin 1955- *WhoSSW 91*
Ziegfeld, Florenz 1867-1932 *OxCPMus*
Ziegfeld, Florenz 1869-1932 *WorAlBi*
Ziegler, Arthur B. 1930- *St&PR 91, WhoAm 90*
Ziegler, Bette J. 1940- *WhoWrEP 89*
Ziegler, Beverly Ann 1934- *WhoAmW 91*
Ziegler, Christiana Mariana 1695-1760 *EncCoWW*
Ziegler, Daniel Martin 1927- *WhoAm 90*
Ziegler, Delores *WhoAm 90*
Ziegler, Dewey Kiper 1920- *WhoAm 90*
Ziegler, Dhyana 1949- *WhoAmW 91*
Ziegler, Donald E. 1949- *St&PR 91*
Ziegler, Donald Emil 1936- *WhoAm 90, WhoE 91*
Ziegler, Donald Robert 1932- *WhoAm 90*
Ziegler, Edward Paul 1951- *St&PR 91*
Ziegler, Ekhard Erich 1940- *WhoAm 90*
Ziegler, Eldon Arthur 1939- *St&PR 91*
Ziegler, Frederick J 1924- *BiDrAPA 89*
Ziegler, Frederick Joseph, III 1951- *WhoE 91*
Ziegler, George Herbert 1951- *St&PR 91*
Ziegler, Heide 1943- *WhoWor 91*
Ziegler, Henry Steinway 1933- *WhoAm 90*
Ziegler, Hubert Andreas Maximilian 1924- *WhoWor 91*
Ziegler, Jack 1942- *SmATA 60, WhoAm 90*
Ziegler, James Russell 1922- *WhoWor 91*
Ziegler, Jan 1953- *WhoAmW 91*
Ziegler, Janet Cassaro 1946- *WhoAmW 91*
Ziegler, Jesse H. 1913- *WhoAm 90*
Ziegler, John Alan 1933- *WhoSSW 91*
Ziegler, John Augustus, Jr. 1934- *WhoAm 90*
Ziegler, John K. 1937- *St&PR 91*
Ziegler, Jules-Claude 1804-1856 *PenDiDA 89*
Ziegler, Karl Waldemar 1898-1973 *DcScB S2*
Ziegler, Kurt 1942- *St&PR 91*
Ziegler, Leonard Charles 1931- *St&PR 91*
Ziegler, Lynda K. 1964- *WhoAmW 91*
Ziegler, M.S. 1921- *St&PR 91*
Ziegler, Penelope P *BiDrAPA 89*
Ziegler, R.D. 1927- *St&PR 91*
Ziegler, Raymond Stewart 1919- *WhoAm 90*
Ziegler, Reinard 1935- *WhoWor 91*
Ziegler, Robert Baldwin 1932- *St&PR 91*
Ziegler, Robert George 1941- *BiDrAPA 89*
Ziegler, Robert Holton, Sr. 1921- *WhoAm 90*
Ziegler, Ronald L. *BioIn 16*
Ziegler, Ronald Louis 1939- *WhoAm 90, WhoWor 91*
Ziegler, Sandra Kay 1938- *WhoAmW 91*
Ziegler, Sheila Gerber 1949- *WhoAmW 91*
Ziegler, Theresa W. 1935- *St&PR 91*
Ziegler, Ursina *AuBYP 90*
Ziegler, Vincent E *BiDrAPA 89*
Ziegler, William, III 1928- *St&PR 91, WhoAm 90, WhoE 91*
Ziegler, William Alexander 1924- *WhoAm 90*
Ziegler, William Paul 1922- *St&PR 91*
Ziegler-Driscoll, Genevra 1916- *WhoE 91*
Ziegman, Ronald Allan 1951- *WhoEmL 91*
Ziegner, Edward Henry 1920- *WhoAm 90*
Ziegra, Alice Stevenson 1927- *WhoAmW 91*
Ziehm, Richard W. 1948- *St&PR 91*
Ziehrer, Karl Michael 1843-1922 *OxCPMus*
Ziel, Charles D. 1923- *St&PR 91*
Ziel, Patricia Ann 1943- *BiDrAPA 89*
Zieleck, Karin Laura Lee 1948- *WhoAmW 91*
Zielinska, Irene Zofia *BiDrAPA 89*
Zielinska, Lidia 1953- *IntWWM 90*
Zielinski, David 1953- *ConAu 132*
Zielinski, Diethart 1941- *WhoWor 91*
Zielinski, Joan 1948- *WhoE 91*
Zielinski, Kathryn Manfredi 1959- *St&PR 91*
Zielinski, Leszek 1948- *WhoWrEP 89*
Zielinski, Mark Henry *BiDrAPA 89*
Zielinski, Peter A. 1929- *St&PR 91*
Zielinski, Robert James *BiDrAPA 89*
Zielke, Roland Jurgen 1946- *WhoWor 91*
Zielonko, Walter 1931- *BiDrAPA 89*
Zielski, Glenda Joyce 1952- *WhoAmW 91*
Ziemann, Edward F. 1944- *St&PR 91*
Ziemann, Richard Claude 1932- *WhoAmA 91*
Ziemba, Eugene Stanley 1946- *St&PR 91*
Ziemba, Ronald S. 1943- *ODwPR 91*
Ziemer, James L. 1950- *St&PR 91*
Ziemer, Paul D. *St&PR 91*
Ziemer, Paul Frederick *BiDrAPA 89*
Ziemer, Rodger Edmund 1937- *WhoAm 90*
Zientara, Benny 1920-1985 *Ballpl 90*
Zients, Alan Barry 1939- *BiDrAPA 89*
Zier, Adolfo *BiDrAPA 89*
Zier, Alex Richard 1949- *St&PR 91*
Zier, Ronald E. 1931- *ODwPR 91*
Zier, Ronald Edward 1931- *St&PR 91*
Zierau, Harold K. 1922- *St&PR 91*
Ziercher, Julia Ann 1937- *WhoAmW 91*
Zierden, William Ernest 1938- *St&PR 91*
Zierdt, Charles Henry 1922- *WhoWor 91*
Ziereis, Franz Xaver 1905-1945 *BioIn 16*
Ziering, Sigi 1928- *St&PR 91*
Ziering, William Mark 1931- *WhoAm 90*
Zierk, Carey Vigor 1952- *BiDrAPA 89*
Zierler, Neal 1926- *WhoAm 90, WhoE 91*
Zierold, Maria Reyes *EncO&P 3*
Zierold, Maria Reyes de *EncPaPR 91*
Zieroth, Dale 1946- *BioIn 16*
Ziervogel, Josef 1937- *WhoWor 91*
Zieseniss, Hubert Frederick 1941- *WhoWor 91*
Ziesing, Hibben *BioIn 16*
Zieske, Scott H. 1948- *ODwPR 91*
Zietz, Joachim 1953- *WhoSSW 91*
Zietz, Karyl Lynn Kopelman 1943- *WhoE 91*
Zieve, Leonard S. 1920- *St&PR 91*
Zieve, Morton I. 1927- *St&PR 91*
Zieve, Morton L. 1932- *St&PR 91, WhoE 91*
Zieverink, William Donelan 1943- *BiDrAPA 89*
Zievers, Marilee Kinney *BiDrAPA 89*
Ziferstein, Isidore *BiDrAPA 89*
Ziff, Irma 1915- *St&PR 91*
Ziff, Jerrold 1928- *WhoAmA 91*
Ziff, Larzer 1927- *WhoAm 90*
Ziff, Lloyd Richard 1942- *WhoAm 90, WhoE 91, WhoWor 91*
Ziff, Morris 1913- *WhoAm 90*
Ziff, Paul 1922- *WhoAm 90*
Ziff, Robert Alan 1952- *WhoSSW 91, WhoWor 91*
Ziff, Roy Edward 1938- *WhoWor 91*
Ziff, Ruth 1924- *St&PR 91*
Ziff, William Bernard, Jr. 1930- *WhoAm 90*
Ziffren, Lester 1906- *ODwPR 91*
Ziffren, Lester 1925- *WhoAm 90*
Ziffren, Paul 1913- *WhoAm 90, WhoWor 91*
Ziffrin, Marilyn Jane 1926- *IntWWM 90*
Zigal, Thomas 1948- *WhoWrEP 89*
Zigarelli, Joseph F *BiDrAPA 89*
Zigarlick, John *BioIn 16*
Zigarlick, John 1937- *St&PR 91*
Zigelbaum, Sheldon D 1931- *BiDrAPA 89*
Ziglar, James W. 1945- *WhoAm 90*
Zigler, Edward F. 1930- *ConAu 33NR*
Zigler, Edward Frank 1930- *WhoAm 90*
Zigman, Harvey Lee 1942- *BiDrAPA 89*
Zigman, Marvin Seymour 1938- *WhoE 91*
Zigman, Robert S. 1919- *ODwPR 91, WhoAm 90*
Zigment, Robert A. 1956- *St&PR 91*
Zigmond, Sally Householder 1944- *WhoAmW 91*
Zigner, Gloria *ODwPR 91*
Zigrosser, Carl 1891-1975 *WhoAmA 91N*
Zigun, Charles *BiDrAPA 89*
Zigun, Jeffrey Robert 1958- *BiDrAPA 89*
Zigun, Sylvia Helene 1934- *WhoAmW 91, WhoE 91, WhoWor 91*
Ziito *EncO&P 3*
Zijderveld, Hendrik Johan 1927- *WhoWor 91*
Zikakis, John P. 1933- *WhoAm 90*
Zikken, Aya 1919- *EncCoWW*
Zikmund, Barbara Brown 1939- *WhoAm 90, WhoAmW 91*
Zikmundova, Eva 1932- *IntWWM 90*
Zikry, Yasser S *BiDrAPA 89*
Zil, John Stephen 1947- *BiDrAPA 89, WhoWor 91*
Zilbach, Joan J 1927- *BiDrAPA 89, WhoE 91*
Zilber, Maurice Leonard 1938- *St&PR 91*
Zilczer, Judith Katy 1948- *WhoAmA 91*
Zile, Ronald L. 1933- *St&PR 91*
Zilenziger, Rodman J. *St&PR 91*
Zilinskaite, Vytaute 1930- *EncCoWW*
Zilis, Milton Charles 1928- *St&PR 91*
Zilius, Vladas 1939- *WhoAmA 91*
Zilke, Timothy A. 1957- *St&PR 91*
Zilkha, Donald Elias 1951- *WhoE 91*
Zilkha, Ezra Khedouri 1925- *St&PR 91, WhoAm 90*
Zill, Arthur C. 1927- *St&PR 91*
Zill, Egon *BioIn 16*
Ziller, Richard Patrick 1941- *St&PR 91*
Zilli, Harry A., Jr. 1930- *St&PR 91*
Zilli, Harry Angelo, Jr. 1930- *WhoAm 90*
Zilligen, Joseph H. 1941- *St&PR 91*
Zilling, George R. 1932- *St&PR 91*
Zillmann, Robert Edward 1929- *WhoAm 90*
Ziloti, Alexander 1863-1945 *PenDiMP*
Zilversmit, Donald Berthold 1919- *WhoAm 90*
Zilz, David Arthur 1937- *WhoAm 90*
Zilzer, Gyula 1898-1969 *WhoAmA 91N*
Zim, Alyosha 1943- *BiDrAPA 89*
Zim, Herbert Spencer 1909- *AuBYP 90, WhoAm 90*
Zima, Bonnie *BiDrAPA 89*
Zimanas, Genrikas 1910-1987 *BioIn 16*
Zimand, Harvey Folks 1928- *WhoAm 90*
Zimansky, Robert 1948- *IntWWM 90*
Zimbalist, Efrem 1889-1985 *PenDiMP, WorAlBi*
Zimbalist, Efrem, Jr. 1923- *WorAlBi*
Zimbardo, Philip George 1933- *WhoAm 90*
Zimbelman, Robert George 1930- *WhoE 91*
Zimbelmann, Henry Peter 1935- *St&PR 91*
Zimberg, Gary Bryant *BiDrAPA 89*
Zimberg, Laura Louise 1961- *WhoE 91*
Zimberg, Sheldon 1936- *BiDrAPA 89*
Zimble, James Allen 1933- *WhoAm 90*
Zimbroff, Dan Louis *BiDrAPA 89*
Zimburean, John Michael *BiDrAPA 89*
Zimcosky, James 1948- *St&PR 91*
Zimdars-Orthman, Marjorie A. 1949- *St&PR 91*
Zimelman, Nathan *AuBYP 90*
Zimerman, Krystian *BioIn 16*
Zimerman, Krystian 1956- *IntWWM 90, PenDiMP*
Zimet, Carl N. *BioIn 16*
Zimet, Carl Norman 1925- *WhoAm 90*
Zimet, Irvin M. 1925- *St&PR 91*
Zimetbaum, Mala 1922-1944 *BioIn 16*
Zimiles, M Robert *BiDrAPA 89*
Zimiles, Murray 1941- *WhoAmA 91, WhoE 91*
Zimlich, Albert Leo, Jr. 1930- *St&PR 91*
Zimm, Bruno Hasbrouck 1920- *WhoAm 90*
Zimmar, George Peter 1937- *WhoAm 90*
Zimmer, Alan Mark 1959- *St&PR 91*
Zimmer, Albert Arthur 1918- *WhoAm 90*
Zimmer, Art 1938- *WhoWor 91*
Zimmer, Basil George 1920- *WhoAm 90*
Zimmer, Ben 1952- *BiDrAPA 89*
Zimmer, Charles Edward 1924- *St&PR 91*
Zimmer, Chief 1860-1949 *Ballpl 90*
Zimmer, Clifford G. 1924- *St&PR 91*
Zimmer, Dirk *BioIn 16*
Zimmer, Don 1931- *Ballpl 90, BioIn 16*
Zimmer, Donald William 1931- *WhoAm 90*
Zimmer, Edward Michael 1937- *St&PR 91*
Zimmer, Edward Paul 1949- *St&PR 91*
Zimmer, Elizabeth Ann 1940- *WhoWrEP 89*
Zimmer, Fritz *WhoAmA 91N*
Zimmer, Gregory F. 1944- *St&PR 91*
Zimmer, Hans Willi 1921- *WhoAm 90*
Zimmer, Jack Anthony 1932- *St&PR 91*
Zimmer, Jan 1926- *IntWWM 90*
Zimmer, Jay Alan 1952- *WhoE 91*
Zimmer, Jeremy *BioIn 16*
Zimmer, John Herman 1922- *WhoWor 91*
Zimmer, Karl R. 1926- *St&PR 91*
Zimmer, Lawrence Joseph 1946- *BiDrAPA 89*
Zimmer, Nancy Child 1932- *WhoAmW 91*
Zimmer, Norman Cunningham 1924- *WhoAm 90*
Zimmer, Paul H. 1929- *St&PR 91*
Zimmer, Paul J. 1934- *WhoWrEP 89*
Zimmer, Richard B *BiDrAPA 89*
Zimmer, Richard P. 1945- *St&PR 91*
Zimmer, Robert James 1942- *St&PR 91*
Zimmer, Roberta G. 1924- *St&PR 91*
Zimmer, Sheila Kirchenbauer 1941- *WhoE 91*
Zimmer, Stanley 1926- *St&PR 91*
Zimmer, Thomas R. 1931- *St&PR 91*
Zimmer, Walter C. 1935- *St&PR 91*
Zimmer, William H. 1953- *St&PR 91*
Zimmer, William H., Jr. 1930- *St&PR 91*
Zimmer, William R. *St&PR 91*
Zimmer-Long, Janie Louise 1943- *WhoE 91*
Zimmerberg, Hyman Joseph 1921- *WhoE 91*
Zimmerer, Anna Morgan 1923- *WhoAm 90*
Zimmerer, Carl Gerhard 1926 *WhoWor 91*
Zimmerer, Vincent Hugh 1926- *St&PR 91*
Zimmerli, Alice 1906- *St&PR 91*
Zimmerli, Louis E. 1919- *St&PR 91*
Zimmerlin, Alfred Peter 1955- *IntWWM 90*
Zimmerman, Aaron Mark 1953- *WhoEmL 91*
Zimmerman, Adam Hartley 1927- *WhoAm 90*
Zimmerman, Alan K. 1925- *St&PR 91*
Zimmerman, Alice A 1939- *WhoAmA 91*
Zimmerman, Alisa Jeanne 1959- *WhoAmW 91*
Zimmerman, Amy J. 1967- *WhoAmW 91*
Zimmerman, Arnold *PenDiDA 89*
Zimmerman, Arnold 1954- *WhoAmA 91*
Zimmerman, Arnold E. 1909- *BioIn 16*
Zimmerman, Arthur Baird 1955- *WhoSSW 91*
Zimmerman, Arthur T. 1945- *ODwPR 91*
Zimmerman, Austin Manlove 1909- *WhoAm 90, WhoWor 91*
Zimmerman, Barry 1938- *St&PR 91, WhoE 91*
Zimmerman, Ben, Jr. 1916- *St&PR 91*
Zimmerman, Bernard 1932- *WhoE 91*
Zimmerman, Bernard 1946- *WhoEmL 91*

Zimmerman, Betty Janet 1918- WhoAmW 91
Zimmerman, Bill J. 1932- St&PR 91, WhoAm 90
Zimmerman, Billy Raymond 1941- WhoWrEP 89
Zimmerman, Bonnie Jean BiDrAPA 89
Zimmerman, Bruce 1952- ConAu 131
Zimmerman, Bryant Kable 1922- St&PR 91, WhoAm 90
Zimmerman, Carol Jean 1951- WhoAmW 91
Zimmerman, Carole Lee 1948- WhoE 91
Zimmerman, Carrie Englert 1957- ODwPR 91
Zimmerman, Cathie S. 1956- WhoE 91
Zimmerman, Charles Daniel, III 1941- St&PR 91
Zimmerman, Charles Edward 1958- WhoSSW 91
Zimmerman, Charles Hinckley 1905- WhoAm 90
Zimmerman, Clarence D. 1936- St&PR 91
Zimmerman, Daniel John 1930- St&PR 91
Zimmerman, David Radoff 1934- WhoAm 90, WhoWrEP 89
Zimmerman, Derk BioIn 16
Zimmerman, Diane Leenheer 1941- WhoAmW 91
Zimmerman, Diane Marie 1957- WhoAmW 91
Zimmerman, Donald Joseph 1937- St&PR 91
Zimmerman, Donald Patrick 1942- WhoE 91
Zimmerman, Drake H. 1954- WhoEmL 91
Zimmerman, E. Paul 1919- St&PR 91
Zimmerman, Earl Abram 1937- WhoAm 90
Zimmerman, Edward Kline 1936- WhoAm 90
Zimmerman, Edwin Morton 1924- WhoAm 90, WhoE 91
Zimmerman, Elaine 1950- WhoAmW 91
Zimmerman, Elyn 1945- WhoAmA 91
Zimmerman, Erik Eugene 1949- BiDrAPA 89
Zimmerman, Eugene 1862-1935 BioIn 16
Zimmerman, Eugene Walter 1909- WhoWor 91
Zimmerman, Evelyn Nellie 1922- WhoAmW 91
Zimmerman, Everett Lee 1936- WhoAm 90
Zimmerman, Faith 1960- WhoAmW 91
Zimmerman, Florence Arline 1924- WhoAmW 91
Zimmerman, Frank William, Jr. 1933- BiDrAPA 89
Zimmerman, Franklin B. 1923- IntWWM 90
Zimmerman, Franklin Bershir 1924- WhoAm 90
Zimmerman, Fred T 1902- BiDrAPA 89
Zimmerman, Frederick A 1886-1974 WhoAmA 91N
Zimmerman, Gail Marie 1945- WhoAm 90
Zimmerman, Gary Alan 1938- WhoAm 90
Zimmerman, George St&PR 91
Zimmerman, George Ogurek 1935- WhoAm 90
Zimmerman, Gideon K. 1920- WhoAm 90
Zimmerman, Guy, Jr. 1921- BiDrAPA 89
Zimmerman, Heinie 1887-1969 Ballpl 90
Zimmerman, Helene Loretta 1933- WhoAmW 91
Zimmerman, Howard Elliot 1926- WhoAm 90
Zimmerman, Howard Eric 1932- St&PR 91
Zimmerman, Hyman Joseph 1914- WhoAm 90
Zimmerman, James M. 1944- WhoAm 90
Zimmerman, Janice Marie 1958- WhoAmW 91
Zimmerman, Jean 1947- WhoAmW 91, WhoE 91, WhoEmL 91, WhoWor 91
Zimmerman, Jeanne Bailey 1956- BiDrAPA 89
Zimmerman, Jerry 1934- Ballpl 90
Zimmerman, Jo Ann 1936- WhoAm 90, WhoAmW 91
Zimmerman, John H. 1932- St&PR 91, WhoAm 90
Zimmerman, John Max 1950- WhoE 91
Zimmerman, Jon Lewis 1947- WhoE 91
Zimmerman, Joseph Dale 1934- St&PR 91, WhoAm 90
Zimmerman, Joseph Francis 1928- WhoAm 90, WhoWrEP 89
Zimmerman, Jules 1934- St&PR 91
Zimmerman, Justin Fred 1912- St&PR 91
Zimmerman, Karen Michelle 1957- WhoEmL 91
Zimmerman, Kathleen Marie 1923- WhoAm 90, WhoAmA 91, WhoAmW 91
Zimmerman, Keith W. 1947- St&PR 91
Zimmerman, Kent A BiDrAPA 89
Zimmerman, Laurie Twila BiDrAPA 89
Zimmerman, Lenore Stenzel 1919- WhoAmW 91
Zimmerman, LeRoy S. 1934- WhoAm 90
Zimmerman, Linda Fran 1946- WhoAmW 91
Zimmerman, M. Paul 1934- WhoAm 90
Zimmerman, Margaret Catherine 1915- WhoWrEP 89
Zimmerman, Mari Sperry 1942- WhoAmW 91
Zimmerman, Mark 1957- BiDrAPA 89
Zimmerman, Martha Rosenberger 1937- WhoAmW 91
Zimmerman, Martin E. 1938- St&PR 91
Zimmerman, Mary Ann ODwPR 91
Zimmerman, Mary Ganson WhoSSW 91
Zimmerman, Michael David 1943- WhoAm 90
Zimmerman, Michael G. 1957- ODwPR 91
Zimmerman, Michael S. 1951- WhoSSW 91
Zimmerman, Milton J. St&PR 91
Zimmerman, Mortimer Fred 1922- St&PR 91, WhoAm 90
Zimmerman, Muriel Elaine 1942- WhoAmW 91
Zimmerman, Paul Albert 1918- WhoAm 90
Zimmerman, Paul Louis 1951- WhoE 91
Zimmerman, Paul Warren 1921- WhoAmA 91
Zimmerman, Peter C. 1946- St&PR 91
Zimmerman, Philip Louis 1943- St&PR 91
Zimmerman, Raymond 1923- WhoSSW 91
Zimmerman, Richard Anson 1932- St&PR 91, WhoAm 90, WhoE 91
Zimmerman, Richard C 1932- BiDrAPA 89
Zimmerman, Richard E. 1940- St&PR 91
Zimmerman, Richard Gayford 1934- WhoAm 90
Zimmerman, Richard Orin 1956- WhoSSW 91
Zimmerman, Robert A. 1930- St&PR 91
Zimmerman, Robert Allen 1941- BioIn 16
Zimmerman, Robert Amelin 1924- BiDrAPA 89
Zimmerman, Robert Dingwall 1952- WhoWrEP 89
Zimmerman, Robert E. 1928- St&PR 91
Zimmerman, Robert Earl 1928- WhoAm 90
Zimmerman, Robert M 1931- BiDrAPA 89
Zimmerman, Robert Raymond 1919- St&PR 91
Zimmerman, Robert Scott 1951- WhoE 91
Zimmerman, Ronald 1940- St&PR 91
Zimmerman, Russell Richard 1942- WhoWor 91
Zimmerman, S. LaNette 1944- St&PR 91
Zimmerman, S. Mort 1927- St&PR 91
Zimmerman, Samuel Morton 1927- WhoSSW 91
Zimmerman, Sarah E. 1937- WhoAmW 91
Zimmerman, Scott Franklin 1935- WhoAm 90
Zimmerman, Solomon 1948- WhoSSW 91
Zimmerman, Stanley Elliot, Jr. 1947- St&PR 91
Zimmerman, Stephen D. 1942- St&PR 91
Zimmerman, Susan G. 1952- WhoAmW 91
Zimmerman, Theodore S. 1937-1988 BioIn 16
Zimmerman, Thom Jay 1942- WhoAm 90
Zimmerman, Thomas A. 1953- St&PR 91
Zimmerman, Thomas Fletcher 1912- WhoAm 90
Zimmerman, Timothy Karl 1951- St&PR 91
Zimmerman, Udo 1943- ConMus 5
Zimmerman, Veva H 1937- BiDrAPA 89
Zimmerman, Vickie Lynn 1955- St&PR 91
Zimmerman, Warren 1934- WhoAm 90, WhoWor 91
Zimmerman, William Edwin 1941- WhoAm 90, WhoWrEP 89
Zimmerman, William Frederick 1938- WhoAm 90
Zimmerman, William Harold 1937- WhoAmA 91
Zimmerman, William R. 1927- St&PR 91
Zimmerman, William Robert 1927- WhoAm 90
Zimmerman, Winona Estelle 1941- WhoWrEP 89
Zimmerman, Yale 1945- St&PR 91
Zimmerman, Zelma Lucille WhoAmW 91
Zimmermann, Agnes 1845-1925 PenDiMP
Zimmermann, Alan Lewis 1950- WhoAm 90
Zimmermann, Bernd Alois 1918-1970 PenDiMP A
Zimmermann, David Scott 1955- WhoEmL 91
Zimmermann, Don E. 1935- WhoAm 90
Zimmermann, Don G. 1940- St&PR 91
Zimmermann, Ekkart 1946- WhoWor 91
Zimmermann, Eleonore M. 1931- WhoAm 90
Zimmermann, Ethel Agnes 1909-1984 ConAu 129
Zimmermann, Frederick Karl 1952- St&PR 91
Zimmermann, G. Floyd, III 1944- WhoSSW 91
Zimmermann, Gail St&PR 91
Zimmermann, Gerald St&PR 91
Zimmermann, Harald Volkmar 1926- WhoWor 91
Zimmermann, Horst Ernst Friedrich 1934- WhoWor 91
Zimmermann, Johann Baptist 1680-1758 PenDiDA 89
Zimmermann, John 1937- St&PR 91, WhoAm 90
Zimmermann, John Joseph 1939- WhoWor 91
Zimmermann, Margrit 1927- IntWWM 90
Zimmermann, Marie BioIn 16
Zimmermann, Mark Hutchings 1952- WhoWor 91
Zimmermann, R. Peter 1940- WhoAm 90
Zimmermann, Reinhardt 1936- ConDes 90
Zimmermann, Robert Laurence 1932- WhoWor 91
Zimmermann, Robert Walter 1919- WhoAm 90, WhoE 91
Zimmermann, Steven G. 1950- St&PR 91
Zimmermann, T. C. Price 1934- WhoAm 90
Zimmermann, Udo 1943- IntWWM 90
Zimmermann, Walter 1892-1980 DcScB S2
Zimmermann, Wolfram 1920- IntWWM 90
Zimmerschied, Dieter 1934- IntWWM 90
Zimmet, Suzanna Viola BiDrAPA 89
Zimmett, Mark Paul 1950- WhoAm 90, WhoWor 91
Zimnik, Reiner 1930- AuBYP 90
Zimny, Marilyn Lucile 1927- WhoAm 90
Zimolo, Armando Di Val Giurata 1938- WhoWor 91
Zimon, Kathy Elizabeth 1941- WhoAmA 91
Zimonick, Frank Edward 1928- St&PR 91
Zimowski, Joyce Ann 1955- WhoAmW 91
Zimpelmann, Uwe Jorg 1943- WhoWor 91
Zimring, Lois Eileen Jacobs 1923- WhoAm 90
Zimroth, Evan 1943- WhoWrEP 89
Zin, Sung Tae 1942- BiDrAPA 89
Zinaman, Helaine Madeleine 1951- WhoAmW 91
Zinbarg, Edward Donald 1934- St&PR 91
Zinberg, Dorothy Shore 1928- WhoAm 90
Zinberg, Norman E BiDrAPA 89
Zinberg, Norman Earl 1921-1989 BioIn 16
Zinchuk, Aleksander Ivanovich 1920- WhoWor 91
Zinck, Louis Richmond 1927- WhoSSW 91
Zindel, Bonnie 1943- ConAu 31NR
Zindel, Paul BioIn 16
Zindel, Paul 1936- AuBYP 90, ConAu 31NR, MajTwCW, WhoAm 90, WhoWrEP 89, WorAlBi
Zindel, William 1934- St&PR 91
Zinder, Hanina BioIn 16
Zinder, Newton Donald 1927- WhoAm 90
Zinder, Norton David 1928- WhoAm 90
Zine, Larry Joseph 1954- St&PR 91, WhoAm 90
Ziner, Florence Katz 1921- AuBYP 90
Ziner, Robert J. 1945- St&PR 91
Zingale, Donald Paul 1946- WhoEmL 91
Zingale, Lawrence 1938- WhoAmA 91
Zingale, Mary Genevieve 1928- WhoAmW 91
Zingale, Roxanne 1961- WhoAmW 91
Zinger, Freddy 1954- WhoWor 91
Zingerline, Arthur William 1950- WhoE 91
Zingher, Edy B. 1944- St&PR 91
Zingle, Mark R. 1952- St&PR 91
Zingraff, Michael, Jr. 1920- WhoAm 90
Zinicola, Anthony Vincent 1963- WhoE 91
Zink, Charles Talbott 1937- WhoAm 90
Zink, John H., Jr. 1918- St&PR 91
Zink, Joseph Paul, III 1945- WhoWrEP 89
Zink, Lubor Jan 1920- WhoE 91
Zink, Melissa BioIn 16
Zink, Philip Ripley 1947- St&PR 91
Zink, Robert Lee 1935- St&PR 91
Zink, Walter Earl, II 1947- WhoEmL 91
Zink, William Pirotte 1951- WhoSSW 91
Zinkan, K. James 1938- St&PR 91
Zinke, Ernest Albert BiDrAPA 89
Zinke, Michael Duane 1954- WhoSSW 91
Zinke, Myra Rose 1926- BiDrAPA 89
Zinkeisen, Anna Katarina 1902-1976 BiDWomA
Zinkeisen, Doris Clare 1898- BiDWomA
Zinkil, George A., Jr. 1944- St&PR 91
Zinkoff, Dave AuBYP 90
Zinkow, William Arthur 1948- WhoSSW 91
Zinman, David BioIn 16
Zinman, David 1936- PenDiMP
Zinman, David Joel 1936- IntWWM 90, WhoAm 90, WhoE 91
Zinman, Jacques 1922- WhoWor 91
Zinman, Philip 1904- St&PR 91
Zinn, Alice 1948- WhoSSW 91
Zinn, Ben T. 1937- WhoAm 90
Zinn, Chester A., Jr. 1934- St&PR 91
Zinn, David Benjamin 1953- WhoE 91
Zinn, Domby Lloyd 1924- St&PR 91
Zinn, Donald J. 1954- St&PR 91
Zinn, E. Z. BioIn 16
Zinn, Edward 1940- BiDrAPA 89
Zinn, Elias BioIn 16
Zinn, Elias Paul 1954- St&PR 91, WhoAm 90
Zinn, Frank Kleman 1934- WhoAm 90
Zinn, Fredric M. 1951- St&PR 91
Zinn, Grover Alfonso, Jr. 1937- WhoAm 90
Zinn, Guy 1887-1949 Ballpl 90
Zinn, Howard 1922- ConAu 33NR, WhoAm 90
Zinn, Jimmy 1895- Ballpl 90
Zinn, Karl Georg 1939- WhoWor 91
Zinn, Keith A. 1955- St&PR 91
Zinn, Keith Marshall 1940- WhoAm 90
Zinn, Lynwood David 1940- BiDrAPA 89
Zinn, Maxine Baca 1942- BioIn 16
Zinn, Michael F. 1952- St&PR 91
Zinn, Raymond D. 1937- St&PR 91
Zinn, Sanford M. 1933- St&PR 91
Zinn, Stephen Blake 1944- BiDrAPA 89
Zinn, Terry Leigh 1951- St&PR 91, WhoSSW 91
Zinn, Thomas Roger 1949- St&PR 91
Zinn, Walter H. 1906- WorAlBi
Zinn, William 1924- IntWWM 90, WhoAm 90, WhoE 91, WhoWor 91
Zinna, Rosario F BiDrAPA 89
Zinnecker, Robert Wallace 1938- WhoAm 90, WhoE 91
Zinnemann, Fred 1907- WhoAm 90, WorAlBi
Zinnen, Robert Oliver 1929- WhoAm 90
Zinner, Donald Alan 1956- WhoSSW 91
Zinner, Gilbert Paul 1935- WhoSSW 91
Zinner, John 1937- BiDrAPA 89
Zinner, Michael Jeffrey 1945- WhoAm 90
Zinner, Ronald J 1933- BiDrAPA 89
Zinnes, Harriet F. WhoWrEP 89
Zinober, Peter Wolfson 1943- WhoSSW 91
Zinola, Maria WhoHisp 91
Zinov'eva-Annibal, Lidia Dmitrievna 1866-1907 EncCoWW
Zinoviev, Grigori 1883-1936 WorAlBi
Zinov'yev, Grigorii Yeseyevich 1883-1936 BioIn 16
Zins-Penninck, Judith FemiCLE
Zinselmeyer, Arthur G. 1920- St&PR 91
Zinsenheim, Joyce Renee BiDrAPA 89
Zinser, Elisabeth Ann BioIn 16
Zinser, Elisabeth Ann 1940- WhoAm 90, WhoAmW 91
Zinski, Lawrence W. 1940- St&PR 91
Zinsky, Lentha Louise 1965- WhoE 91
Zinsli, Paul 1906- WhoWor 91
Zinspenninck, Judith BiDEWW
Zinspinning, Judith FemiCLE
Zinsser, August 1941- St&PR 91
Zinsser, William 1922- ConAu 31NR
Zinsser, William Knowlton 1922- WhoAm 90
Zinsstag, Gerard 1941- IntWWM 90
Zintgraff, Edward Forrest 1950- WhoSSW 91
Zinz, David Albert 1952- WhoE 91
Zinzow, Lee Alan 1947- St&PR 91
Zinzuvadia, Kishor N BiDrAPA 89
Ziobro, John Martin 1962- WhoE 91
Ziock, Klaus Otto Heinrich 1925- WhoAm 90
Ziolko, Mary Ellen 1948- WhoSSW 91
Ziolkowski Family BioIn 16
Ziolkowski, Bruno E. 1939- St&PR 91
Ziolkowski, Korczak 1908-1982 BioIn 16, WhoAmA 91N
Ziolkowski, Theodore Joseph 1932- WhoAm 90, WhoWrEP 89
Ziomek, Alberta Ann 1931- BiDrAPA 89
Ziomek, Henry Stanley, Jr. 1950- WhoE 91
Ziomek, Henryk 1922- ConAu 30NR
Zion, Gene 1913-1975 AuBYP 90
Zion, Leela Clarice 1929- WhoAmW 91
Zion, Robert 1921- BioIn 16
Zion, Roger H. 1921- WhoAm 90
Zion, Sidney BioIn 16
Ziperski, James R. 1932- St&PR 91
Ziperski, James Richard 1932- WhoAm 90
Zipes, Douglas Peter 1939- WhoAm 90
Zipfinger, Frank Peter 1953- WhoEmL 91
Zipkin, D.W. 1945- St&PR 91
Zipkin, Jerome BioIn 16
Zipkin, Sheldon Lee 1951- WhoSSW 91
Zipkiyah WhNaAH
Zipko, Raymond Edward 1946- St&PR 91
Zipoli, Domenico 1688-1726 BioIn 16
Ziporyn, Marvin C BiDrAPA 89

Zipp, Arden Peter 1938- *WhoAm 90*
Zipp, Brian Roger 1953- *WhoE 91*
Zipp, Joel Frederick 1948- *WhoAm 90, WhoE 91, WhoEmL 91, WhoWor 91*
Zipp, Raymond D *BiDrAPA 89*
Zipp, Ronald Duane 1946- *WhoEmL 91*
Zippelius, Reinhold Walter 1928- *WhoWor 91*
Zipper, Herbert 1904- *WhoAm 90*
Zipperer, Laura Love 1959- *WhoAmW 91, WhoSSW 91*
Zipperman, Louts 1915- *St&PR 91*
Zippi, Barbara Ann 1953- *WhoE 91*
Zippin, Calvin 1926- *WhoAm 90*
Zipprodi-Zonka, Constance *WhoAmW 91*
Zipprodt, Patricia *BioIn 16, WhoAmW 91*
Zipprodt, Patricia 1925- *ConDes 90, NotWoAT*
Ziprik, Kathleen S. *ODwPR 91*
Zipser, Janet Rose 1952- *WhoAmW 91*
Zipursky, Robert Baruch 1956- *BiDrAPA 89*
Zipursky, Sheldon *BiDrAPA 89*
Zirbel, Ronald DuWayne 1937- *St&PR 91*
Zirbes, Laura *AuBYP 90*
Zirin, Harold 1929- *WhoAm 90*
Zirin, James David 1940- *WhoAm 90*
Zirin, Jane E. *BiDrAPA 89*
Zirin, Nola 1943- *WhoAmA 91*
Zirkel, Don 1927- *WhoAm 90*
Zirkelbach, Alan P. 1962- *WhoSSW 91*
Zirkelbach, Werner Karl 1929- *St&PR 91*
Zirker, Elizabeth Ann *BiDrAPA 89*
Zirker, Joseph 1924- *WhoAmA 91*
Zirkes, Al 1935- *WhoE 91*
Zirkind, Ralph 1918- *WhoAm 90*
Zirkle, L.G. 1946- *St&PR 91*
Zirkle, Lewis Greer 1940- *WhoAm 90*
Zirkowa, Elisaveta 1888-1949 *EncCoWW*
Zirnis, Monika M *BiDrAPA 89*
Ziroli, Angelo Gerardo 1899-1948 *WhoAmA 91N*
Ziros, Christos Konstantinos *WhoWrEP 89*
Zirpoli, Robert M *BiDrAPA 89*
Ziruk, Carolyn J. 1948- *WhoAmW 91*
Zischke, Douglas Arthur 1929- *WhoAm 90*
Zisk, Richie 1949- *Ballpl 90*
Ziska, David Lee 1931- *WhoSSW 91*
Ziska, Deborah *ODwPR 91*
Ziskin, Barry 1952- *St&PR 91*
Ziskind, Burton Leslie 1949- *WhoSSW 91*
Ziskind, Eugene 1900- *BiDrAPA 89*
Zisla, Harold 1925- *WhoAmA 91*
Zislis, Paul David 1952- *BiDrAPA 89*
Zisman, Barry Stuart 1937- *WhoSSW 91*
Zisman, Daniel *PenDiMP*
Zisook, Sidney 1943- *BiDrAPA 89*
Zisselman, Marc Howard *BiDrAPA 89*
Zissis, George John 1922- *WhoAm 90*
Zissman, Lorin 1930- *St&PR 91, WhoE 91*
Zisson, James Stern 1952- *WhoSSW 91*
Zissos, Stephen Nick 1947- *St&PR 91*
Zissu, Frederick 1913- *St&PR 91*
Zistler, Betty A. 1930- *St&PR 91*
Zita, Empress 1892-1989 *AnObit 1989, BioIn 16*
Zitani, Alfred M, Sr. *BiDrAPA 89*
Zitarelli, David Earl 1941- *WhoE 91*
Zitek, Brook Elizabeth *BiDrAPA 89*
Zitello, Mary Catherine 1954- *WhoAmW 91*
Zitin, Barry Rossman 1947- *BiDrAPA 89*
Zitin, Gilbert N. 1937- *St&PR 91*
Zitner, George Louis 1930- *BiDrAPA 89*
Zito, J Anthony 1941- *BiDrAPA 89*
Zito, James Anthony 1931- *WhoAm 90*
Zito, Joseph 1957- *WhoAmA 91*
Zito, Robert Thomas 1953- *WhoE 91*
Zito, Ross Alan 1952- *WhoE 91*
Zitrin, Arthur 1918- *BiDrAPA 89, WhoAm 90*
Zitrin, Charlotte M *BiDrAPA 89*
Zitrin, Charlotte Marker 1918- *WhoAmW 91*
Zitter, Martha Elisabeth 16--?- *EncCoWW*
Zitterin, Martha Elisabeth 16--?- *EncCoWW*
Zitterkopf, Irvin Leroy 1933- *St&PR 91*
Zitz-Halein, Kathinka Rosa Pauline M 1801-1877 *EncCoWW*
Zitzelsberger, Otto Joseph 1929- *WhoE 91*
Zitzewitz, Augusta von 1880-1960 *BiDWomA*
Zitzmann, Billy 1897-1985 *Ballpl 90*
Zitzmann, Friedrich *PenDiDA 89*
Zitzmann, Michael Georg 1947- *St&PR 91*
Ziulek, Richard Stanley, Jr. 1949- *St&PR 91*
Ziv, Seymore Leonard 1925- *WhoAm 90*
Zivian, Charles H. 1944- *St&PR 91*
Zivic, William Thomas 1930- *WhoAmA 91*
Zivin, Norman H. 1944- *WhoE 91*
Zivkovic, Marina 1953- *WhoAmW 91*
Zivley, Gloria June 1949- *WhoAmW 91*
Zivoni, Yossi 1939- *IntWWM 90*
Zizza, Salvatore J. 1945- *St&PR 91*
Zizzo, Alicia Theodoratos 1945- *WhoAm 90*
Zjawin, Dorothy Arlene 1945- *WhoWrEP 89*
Zlatar, Jaksa 1947- *IntWWM 90*
Zlatkis, Albert 1924- *WhoAm 90*
Zlatoff-Mirsky, Everett Igor 1937- *WhoAm 90, WhoWor 91*
Zlevor, William L. 1930- *St&PR 91*
Zloch, William J. 1944- *WhoAm 90*
Zlokower, Harry 1942- *ODwPR 91*
Zlomek, Joseph Michael 1955- *WhoEmL 91*
Zlotin, Patricia A. 1946- *St&PR 91*
Zlotolow-Stambler, Ernest 1943- *WhoE 91*
Zlowe, Florence M *WhoAmA 91*
Zlowe, Florence Markowitz *WhoAm 90*
Zmach, Thomas B. 1937- *St&PR 91*
Zmed, Adrian 1954- *ConTFT 8 [port]*
Zmichowska, Narcyza 1819-1876 *EncCoWW*
Zmitrovich, Ann Carroll 1961- *WhoAmW 91*
Zmora, Ohad 1933- *WhoWor 91*
Zmuda, Sharon Louise 1942- *WhoAmW 91*
Zobel, Gerald 1929- *St&PR 91*
Zobel, Hiller Bellin 1932- *WhoAm 90*
Zobel, Jill Anne Hausrath 1949- *WhoAm 90*
Zobel, Richard Julius 1945- *WhoWor 91*
Zobel, Robert Edward 1948- *WhoSSW 91*
Zobel, Rya W. 1931- *WhoAm 90, WhoAmW 91*
ZoBell, Claude E. 1904-1989 *BioIn 16*
ZoBell, Karl 1932- *WhoAm 90*
Zober, Jerry Martin 1948- *BiDrAPA 89*
Zoberman, Martin 1939- *St&PR 91*
Zoble, Adrienne Kaplan 1940- *WhoAmW 91*
Zobor, Kerry Green *ODwPR 91*
Zobrist, Benedict Karl 1921- *WhoAm 90*
Zobrist, George Winston 1934- *WhoAm 90*
Zobrist, Gerald J. 1943- *St&PR 91*
Zocchi, Louis Joseph 1935- *WhoSSW 91*
Zoch, Carl Robert, Jr. 1953- *St&PR 91*
Zoch, Richmond Tucker 1903- *WhoSSW 91*
Zocholl, Stanley Ernest 1929- *WhoAm 90*
Zock, George J. 1950- *St&PR 91*
Zodhiates, Spiros George 1922- *WhoAm 90*
Zodiacs, The *EncPR&S 89*
Zodrow, Charles Francis 1922- *St&PR 91*
Zodrow, George Roy 1950- *WhoSSW 91*
Zody, Richard Eugene 1937- *WhoSSW 91*
Zoe 980-1050 *WomWR [port]*
Zoega, Tomas 1946- *BiDrAPA 89*
Zoege von Manteuffel, Clause 1926- *WhoWor 91*
Zoeller, Carl Joseph 1920- *St&PR 91*
Zoeller, David Louis 1949- *WhoAm 90*
Zoeller, Donald J. 1930- *WhoAm 90*
Zoeller, Jack Carl 1949- *WhoE 91, WhoWor 91*
Zoeller, Laurence W. 1936- *ODwPR 91*
Zoellick, Glenn Walter 1943- *St&PR 91*
Zoellick, Pauline Angione 1944- *WhoAmW 91*
Zoellner, James W. 1941- *St&PR 91*
Zoellner, Sandra Ann 1964- *WhoAmW 91*
Zoetemelk, Joop *BioIn 16*
Zoffany, Johann 1733-1810 *IntDcAA 90*
Zoffer, H. Jerome 1930- *WhoAm 90*
Zoffmann, Elisabeth *BiDrAPA 89*
Zofkie, Marcia Mary 1929- *IntWWM 90*
Zofnass, Paul Jesse 1947- *WhoAm 90*
Zog, King of Albania 1895-1961 *BioIn 16*
Zogbaum, Wilfrid *WhoAmA 91N*
Zogby, James Edward 1948- *St&PR 91*
Zogg, Chris John 1929- *St&PR 91*
Zoghbi, Habib George 1955- *WhoE 91*
Zoghby, Guy A. 1934- *St&PR 91*
Zoghby, Linda 1949- *IntWWM 90*
Zoghi, Behbood 1960- *WhoSSW 91*
Zografos, Dorothea Stephen 1933- *St&PR 91*
Zografos, James Michael 1923- *St&PR 91*
Zohn, Fred *St&PR 91*
Zohn, Harry 1923- *WhoAm 90*
Zohn, Nagaere Macray *BioIn 16*
Zoilus *MajTwCW*
Zokol, Richard *BioIn 16*
Zokosky, Peter L 1957- *WhoAmA 91*
Zola, Emile 1840-1902 *BiDFrPL, BioIn 16, WorAlBi*
Zola, Lisa 1958- *WhoAm 90, WhoAmW 91*
Zola, Mazzi Cameo 1952- *St&PR 91*
Zola, Michael S. 1942- *WhoWor 91*
Zolan, Harold *BiDrAPA 89*
Zolan, Robert Edward 1936- *St&PR 91*
Zolar *EncO&P 3*
Zolber, Kathleen Keen 1916- *WhoAmW 91*
Zolberg, Aristide Rodolphe 1931- *WhoAm 90*
Zoldak, Sam 1918-1966 *Ballpl 90*
Zoldy, Sandor *PenDiMP*
Zoley, George C. 1950- *St&PR 91*
Zolides, William H. 1930- *St&PR 91*
Zoline, Pamela 1941- *ConLC 62 [port]*
Zolkind, Neil Arther *BiDrAPA 89*
Zoll, Lawrence J. 1933- *St&PR 91*
Zoll, Paul Maurice 1911- *WhoAm 90*
Zoll, Steven Daniel 1963- *St&PR 91*
Zollar, Carolyn Catherine 1947- *WhoSSW 91*
Zollar, Michael Edward 1944- *St&PR 91*
Zoller, George G. 1951- *St&PR 91*
Zoller, Gerhard H. 1939- *St&PR 91*
Zoller, Richard Bernard 1929- *St&PR 91, WhoAm 90*
Zoller, Robert 1946- *St&PR 91*
Zollinger, Gary 1948- *St&PR 91*
Zollinger, Jack J. 1937- *St&PR 91*
Zollinger, John J., Jr. 1911- *St&PR 91*
Zollinger, Philip I. 1952- *St&PR 91*
Zollinger, William Daniel 1940- *St&PR 91*
Zollman, Ronald 1950- *IntWWM 90*
Zollner, Edward J. *St&PR 91*
Zollner, Johann C. F. 1834-1882 *EncO&P 3*
Zollner, Johann K. F. 1834-1882 *EncPaPR 91*
Zollo, Frederick *BioIn 16*
Zollweg, Aileen Boules *WhoAmA 91, WhoE 91*
Zolner, Eric Charles 1949- *WhoSSW 91*
Zolomij, John Joseph 1947- *WhoE 91*
Zolomy, Jack 1948- *St&PR 91*
Zolotas, Xenophon Efthymios 1904- *WhoWor 91*
Zolotow, Charlotte 1915- *AuBYP 90, St&PR 91*
Zolotow, Charlotte Shapiro 1915- *WhoAm 90, WhoAmW 91, WhoWrEP 89*
Zolotow, Maurice 1913- *WhoAm 90*
Zoltai, Tibor Zoltan 1925- *WhoAm 90*
Zoltak, John Louis 1939- *WhoWor 91*
Zoltok-Seltzer, Harriet *WhoWrEP 89*
Zombankais, Minos Andreas 1926- *St&PR 91*
Zombies, The *EncPR&S 89*
Zomick, David Alan 1941- *WhoAm 90*
Zomorodi, Ali 1942- *BiDrAPA 89*
Zona, Louis A 1944- *WhoAmA 91*
Zona, Louis Albert 1944- *WhoAm 90*
Zona, Richard A. 1944- *St&PR 91*
Zonana, Howard V 1938- *BiDrAPA 89*
Zonarich, Frank J. 1945- *St&PR 91*
Zonaro, Fausto 1854-1929 *BioIn 16*
Zondag, Cornelius Henry 1913- *WhoAm 90*
Zondag, Sharon Jones 1954- *St&PR 91*
Zondervan, Peter J. 1909- *St&PR 91*
Zondervan, Peter John 1909- *WhoAm 90*
Zondervan, Robert L *BiDrAPA 89*
Zonia, Dhimitri 1921- *WhoAmA 91*
Zonis, Marvin 1936- *WhoAm 90*
Zonnebelt-Smeenge, Susan Jean 1948- *WhoAmW 91*
Zonnis, Marian E *BiDrAPA 89*
Zontal, Jorge *WhoAmA 91*
Zoobkoff, Anthony A. 1949- *St&PR 91*
Zook, Amy Jo Schoonover 1937- *WhoWrEP 89*
Zook, Donovan Quay 1918- *WhoAm 90*
Zook, Elvin Glenn 1937- *WhoAm 90*
Zook, Martha Frances Harris 1921- *WhoAmW 91*
Zook, Robert Gerald 1964- *WhoE 91*
Zook, Woodrow J. 1915- *St&PR 91*
Zoon, William K. 1943- *WhoAm 90*
Zoon, William Kenneth 1943- *St&PR 91*
Zopf, Paul Edward 1931- *WhoAm 90*
Zopfi, Anne Katherine 1945- *WhoAmW 91*
Zopfi, John Peter 1957- *WhoEmL 91*
Zopp, E. Frederick 1932- *St&PR 91*
Zopp, Eberhard Frederick 1932- *WhoAm 90*
Zoppa, Richard Mario *BiDrAPA 89*
Zora, Stefan *BiDrAPA 89*
Zorab, George A M 1898- *EncO&P 3*
Zorab, George Avetoom Marterus 1898- *EncPaPR 91*
Zorach, Marguerite 1887-1966 *BiDWomA*
Zorach, Marguerite T 1887-1968 *WhoAmA 91N*
Zorach, Peter 1943- *BiDrAPA 89*
Zorach, William 1887-1966 *WhoAmA 91N*
Zorc, Hrvoje 1951- *WhoWor 91*
Zore, Edward John 1945- *St&PR 91, WhoAm 90*
Zoretich, George Stephen 1918- *WhoAmA 91*
Zorian, Olive 1916-1965 *PenDiMP*
Zoric, Christina 1946- *WhoWor 91*
Zorick, Frank John 1941- *BiDrAPA 89*
Zorie, Stephanie Marie 1951- *WhoEmL 91, WhoSSW 91*
Zorin, Shalom 1902-1974 *BioIn 16*
Zorinsky, Edward *BioIn 16*
Zorn, Edward 1926- *St&PR 91*
Zorn, Eric J. 1958- *WhoAm 90*
Zorn, Eric Stuart 1948- *WhoAm 90*
Zorn, John *BioIn 16*
Zorn, Richard Laurence 1940- *St&PR 91*
Zorn, Stephen Alan 1943- *WhoE 91*
Zornack, Annemarie 1932- *EncCoWW*
Zornberg, Gwen Lois 1955- *BiDrAPA 89*
Zorner, Karl-Heinz 1936- *WhoWor 91*
Zornes, Milford 1908- *WhoAm 90*
Zornitzer, Michael R 1946- *BiDrAPA 89*
Zornow, Peter L. 1955- *St&PR 91*
Zornow, William Frank 1920- *WhoAm 90, WhoWor 91*
Zoroaster 660?BC-583?BC *WorAlBi*
Zorrilla de San Martin, Juan 1855-1931 *BioIn 16*
Zorthian, Barry 1920- *ODwPR 91, WhoAm 90, WhoE 91*
Zorumski, Charles Francis, Jr. *BiDrAPA 89*
Zosel, Frederick R. *ODwPR 91*
Zoss, Dean L. 1939- *St&PR 91*
Zotom 1853-1913 *WhNaAH*
Zottola, Carla Jean 1959- *WhoAmW 91*
Zottoli, Danny A. 1946- *St&PR 91*
Zottoli, Robert A 1939- *WhoE 91*
Zou Jiahua 1927- *WhoWor 91*
Zouary, Maurice H. 1921- *WhoAm 90, WhoE 91*
Zoubek, Charles Edward 1913- *WhoAm 90*
Zoubok, Boris *BiDrAPA 89*
Zoumas, Barry Lee 1942- *WhoAm 90*
Zoungrana, Paul 1917- *WhoWor 91*
Zoupanos, Theodore S. 1935- *WhoWor 91*
Zousmer, William J. 1940- *WhoAm 90*
Zovko, Michael John 1951- *WhoE 91*
Zowaski, Katharine Abbott *ODwPR 91*
Zox, Larry 1936- *WhoAm 90, WhoAmA 91*
Zoyhofski, Sharron Anne 1961- *WhoAmW 91*
Zraket, Charles Anthony 1924- *WhoAm 90, WhoWor 91*
Zraly, Kevin *BioIn 16*
Zrinyi, Miklos 1620-1664 *BioIn 16*
Zrudlo, Leo Raymond 1934- *WhoAm 90*
Zrull, Joel P 1932- *BiDrAPA 89*
Zschau, Marilyn 1944- *IntWWM 90*
Zschokke, Heinrich 1771-1848 *DcLB 94 [port], EncO&P 3*
Zsenyuk, Aileen Murphy 1936- *WhoAmW 91*
Zsigmond, Vilmos 1930- *ConTFT 8 [port], WhoAm 90*
Zsigmond, William *ConTFT 8*
Zsigmondy, Denes 1922- *IntWWM 90*
Zsigmondy, Richard A. 1865-1929 *WorAlBi*
Zsolnay, Ignaz *PenDiDA 89*
Zsolnay, Miklos *PenDiDA 89*
Zsolnay, Vilmos *PenDiDA 89*
Zsuzsa, J. I. Gardi 1934- *WhoWor 91*
Zuanich, Anthony J. 1943- *St&PR 91*
Zuazo, Hernan Siles *BioIn 16*
Zuazo, Rene Alberto 1949- *WhoHisp 91*
Zubair, Habeeba Hussain Habeeb 1930- *WhoWor 91*
Zubchevich, Emira D *BiDrAPA 89*
Zube, Ervin Herbert 1931- *WhoAm 90*
Zubenko, George Stephen *BiDrAPA 89*
Zuber, Bill 1913-1982 *Ballpl 90*
Zuber, Jean *PenDiDA 89*
Zuber, Michael Stephen 1954- *St&PR 91*
Zuber, Norma Keen 1934- *WhoAmW 91*
Zubi, Mahmoud 1938- *WhoWor 91*
Zubillaga, Jose Gustavo 1945- *WhoSSW 91*
Zubin, Joseph *NewYTBS 90*
Zubin, Joseph 1900- *BiDrAPA 89, ConAu 30NR, WhoE 91*
Zubizarreta, Teresa A. 1937- *WhoHisp 91*
Zubkoff, Michael 1944- *WhoAm 90*
Zubowicz, George 1916- *BiDrAPA 89*
Zubowicz, Vincent Nicholas 1951- *WhoSSW 91*
Zubroff, Leonard Saul 1925- *WhoWor 91*
Zubulake, Laura Anne 1960- *WhoE 91*
Zucaro, Aldo Charles 1939- *St&PR 91, WhoAm 90*
Zuccarelli, Frank Edward 1921- *WhoAmA 91, WhoE 91*
Zuccari, Anna Radius *EncCoWW*
Zuccarini, Amedee *EncO&P 3*
Zuccaro, Kate *EncCoWW*
Zuccaro, Robert S. 1957- *St&PR 91*
Zuccaro, Taddeo 1529-1566 *IntDcAA 90, PenDiDA 89*
Zucchi, Gian Giacomo 1933- *WhoWor 91*
Zucchini, Michael Rinaldo 1946- *WhoAm 90*
Zucchino, David Alan 1951- *WhoAm 90, WhoE 91*
Zucconi, Vittorio Guido 1944- *WhoE 91*
Zuccotti, John Eugene 1937- *WhoAm 90*
Zuch, Joseph H 1933- *BiDrAPA 89*
Zuck, Alfred Christian 1924- *WhoAm 90, WhoWor 91*
Zuck, Thomas Frank 1933- *WhoAm 90*

Zuck, Wynona Colleen 1939- WhoAm 90, WhoAmW 91
Zucker, Alexander 1924- WhoAm 90
Zucker, Arnold H 1930- BiDrAPA 89
Zucker, Arnold Harris 1930- WhoE 91
Zucker, Barbara M 1940- WhoAmA 91
Zucker, Barbara S. 1929- St&PR 91
Zucker, Bob 1946- WhoAmA 91
Zucker, David Hard 1938- WhoE 91
Zucker, David K 1948- BiDrAPA 89
Zucker, Edward M BiDrAPA 89
Zucker, Herbert 1928- WhoE 91, WhoWor 91
Zucker, Howard D 1916- BiDrAPA 89
Zucker, Irwin ODwPR 91
Zucker, Jack S. 1935- WhoWrEP 89
Zucker, Jacques 1900-1981 WhoAmA 91N
Zucker, James William 1948- WhoE 91
Zucker, Jean Maxson 1925- WhoAmW 91
Zucker, Jerry 1949- WhoAm 90
Zucker, Jerry 1950- ConTFT 8
Zucker, Joseph I 1941- WhoAmA 91
Zucker, Joseph M BiDrAPA 89
Zucker, Malcolm 1914- St&PR 91
Zucker, Marjorie Bass 1919- WhoAmW 91
Zucker, Marshall J. 1954- WhoE 91
Zucker, Martin 1937- ConAu 30NR
Zucker, Murray Harvey 1920- WhoAmA 91
Zucker, Murray L BiDrAPA 89
Zucker, Naomi Flink 1938- WhoWrEP 89
Zucker, Nathan BioIn 16
Zucker, Norman Livingston 1933- WhoAm 90, WhoWrEP 89
Zucker, Robert Alpert 1935- WhoAm 90
Zucker, Robert Lewis 1928- St&PR 91
Zucker, Robert Stephen 1945- WhoEmL 91
Zucker, Rudolph 1896- St&PR 91
Zucker, Scott H. 1961- WhoSSW 91
Zucker, Stefan IntWWM 90, WhoE 91, WhoWor 91
Zucker, Susan Shapiro 1941- WhoE 91
Zucker, William 1917- WhoAm 90
Zucker-Franklin, Dorothea 1929- WhoAmW 91
Zucker-Maltese, Cher R. 1949- St&PR 91
Zuckerberg, David Alan 1946- St&PR 91, WhoAm 90
Zuckerberg, Roy J. 1936- WhoAm 90
Zuckerberg, Stanley M 1919- WhoAmA 91
Zuckerkandl, Emile 1922- WhoAm 90
Zuckerman, Anna Elaine 1958- WhoWrEP 89
Zuckerman, Burt M. 1933- St&PR 91
Zuckerman, Edward Paul 1942- WhoE 91
Zuckerman, Frederick P BiDrAPA 89
Zuckerman, Frederick William 1934- St&PR 91, WhoAm 90
Zuckerman, Gilbert George 1932- St&PR 91
Zuckerman, Harriet 1937- WhoAm 90
Zuckerman, Ira Laurence 1947- WhoWor 91
Zuckerman, Jan Goren BioIn 16
Zuckerman, Jeffrey Ira 1950- WhoAm 90, WhoE 91
Zuckerman, Joseph 1938- WhoAm 90
Zuckerman, Kenneth Stuart 1946- WhoSSW 91
Zuckerman, Leo 1930- St&PR 91
Zuckerman, Madeline 1947- ODwPR 91
Zuckerman, Marc A. 1951- St&PR 91
Zuckerman, Marilyn 1925- WhoWrEP 89
Zuckerman, Martin H. 1942- St&PR 91
Zuckerman, Martin Harvey 1942- WhoAm 90
Zuckerman, Marvin 1928- WhoAm 90
Zuckerman, Mitchell 1946- St&PR 91, WhoAm 90, WhoE 91
Zuckerman, Mortimer 1937- CurBio 90 [port]
Zuckerman, Mortimer B. BioIn 16
Zuckerman, Mortimer Benjamin 1937- WhoAm 90
Zuckerman, Paul BioIn 16
Zuckerman, Perry Philip BiDrAPA 89
Zuckerman, Philip 1930- BiDrAPA 89, WhoE 91
Zuckerman, Ronald K. 1942- St&PR 91
Zuckerman, Ruth Victor 1933- WhoAmA 91
Zuckerman, Solly 1904- BioIn 16
Zuckerman, Stephen 1954- WhoE 91
Zuckerman, Stuart 1933- BiDrAPA 89, WhoAm 90
Zuckerman, Susan Lynn BiDrAPA 89
Zuckerman, Yitzhak 1915-1981 BioIn 16
Zuckermandel, James William 1947- WhoSSW 91
Zuckermann, Doron Peter 1952- WhoWor 91
Zuckermann, Wolfgang Joachim 1922- IntWWM 90
Zuckernik, Burton 1925- St&PR 91
Zuckert, Donald Mack 1934- St&PR 91, WhoAm 90
Zuckert, Eugene M. 1911- St&PR 91
Zuckman, Harvey Lyle 1934- WhoAm 90
Zuckman, Saul 1940- St&PR 91
Zuckmayer, Alice Herdan- BioIn 16
Zuckmayer, Carl 1896-1977 BioIn 16
Zuckrow, Edward 1941- WhoWrEP 89
Zudeck, Darryl 1961- SmATA 61 [port]
Zuege, David A. 1941- St&PR 91
Zuehlke, Clarence Edgar WhoAmA 91N
Zuehlke, Gus A. 1921- St&PR 91
Zuehlke, Martha Ellen 1949- BiDrAPA 89
Zuehlke, Richard William 1933- WhoAm 90
Zuelzer, Mary Elizabeth BiDrAPA 89
Zuendt, William F. 1946- WhoAm 90
Zuercher, Joseph Clement 1956- St&PR 91
Zuercher, William Thomas 1933- St&PR 91
Zuern, David E. 1949- St&PR 91
Zuern, David Ernest 1949- WhoAm 90
Zufryden, Fred S. 1943- WhoAm 90
Zugby, Robert Coury 1941- WhoE 91
Zuger, Bernard 1905- BiDrAPA 89
Zuger, Max BiDrAPA 89
Zuger, Max 1903-1989 BioIn 16
Zugor, Sandor 1923- WhoAmA 91
Zugsmith, Leane 1903-1969 FemiCLE, LiHiK
Zugun, Eleonore 1913- EncPaPR 91
Zugun, Eleonore 1914- EncO&P 3
Zuhdi, Mohamed Nazih 1925- WhoSSW 91, WhoWor 91
Zuhn, Cheryl 1959- WhoAmA 91
Zuidema, David Jay 1956- WhoE 91
Zuidema, George Dale 1928- WhoAm 90
Zuk, Benjamin Richard 1951- St&PR 91
Zuk, William 1924- WhoAm 90
Zukas, Julius 1925- St&PR 91
Zukas, Thomas Joseph 1943- St&PR 91
Zukauckas, Anthony Victor 1937- St&PR 91
Zuke, Leslie C. 1946- ODwPR 91
Zuker, Michael 1949- WhoAm 90
Zukerman, Allan Benjamin 1938- St&PR 91
Zukerman, Eugenia 1944- IntWWM 90, PenDiMP
Zukerman, Jay 1938- St&PR 91
Zukerman, Lori Jean 1956- BiDrAPA 89
Zukerman, Michael 1940- WhoE 91, WhoWor 91
Zukerman, Morris E. 1944- WhoAm 90, WhoE 91
Zukerman, Pinchas 1948- ConMus 4 [port], IntWWM 90, PenDiMP, WhoAm 90, WhoWor 91
Zukerman, Sidney 1929- St&PR 91
Zukin, Jane 1948- WhoWrEP 89
Zukin, Sharon ConAu 131
Zukin, Stephen R 1948- BiDrAPA 89
Zukin, Stephen Randolph 1948- WhoE 91
Zukof, Debra BiDrAPA 89
Zukofsky, Louis 1904-1978 BioIn 16, MajTwCW
Zukofsky, Paul BioIn 16
Zukofsky, Paul 1943- IntWWM 90, PenDiMP
Zukor, Adolph 1873-1976 WorAlBi
Zukowski, Virginia A. 1950- WhoAmW 91
Zukowski, Walter Henry 1914- WhoAm 90
Zukowski, Walter Jon 1954- WhoEmL 91
Zukowsky, David John 1953- BiDrAPA 89, WhoE 91
Zukowsky, John Robert 1948- WhoAm 90
Zukrigl, Kurt 1931- WhoWor 91
Zukrowski, Wojciech 1916- WhoWor 91
Zulch, Joan Carolyn 1931- WhoAm 90
Zuleg, Colleen Geralyn 1963- WhoE 91
Zulema 1947?- DrBlPA 90
Zulficar, Safinaz 1921-1988 BioIn 16
Zulker, Charles Bates 1926- WhoAm 90
Zullig, Irwin P. 1927- St&PR 91
Zulu, Alexander Grey 1924- WhoWor 91
Zulu, Alphaeus 1905-1988 AnObit 1988
Zulu, Itibari Masekela 1953- WhoWrEP 89
Zulueta, Philip de 1925-1989 AnObit 1989
Zulver, Julius M. 1922- St&PR 91
Zumalacarregui, Tomas 1788-1835 BioIn 16
Zumalt, Joanna Maudie 1942- WhoAmW 91
Zuman, Petr 1926- WhoE 91
Zumarraga, Luis Noble 1936- BiDrAPA 89
Zumaya, David G. 1931- WhoHisp 91
Zumba, Charles F. 1931- St&PR 91
Zumberge, James Herbert 1923- WhoAm 90, WhoWor 91
Zumbiel, Robert W. 1932- St&PR 91
Zumbiel, Thomas James 1933- St&PR 91
Zumeta, Bertram William 1919- St&PR 91, WhoAm 90
Zumfelde, Donald Barthold 1936- St&PR 91
Zumino, Bruno 1923- WhoAm 90
Zummer, Katerina 1937- WhoWor 91
Zumo, Billie Thomas 1936- WhoAmW 91
Zumpe, Doris 1940- WhoAmW 91
Zumsteg, Stephan William 1946- St&PR 91
Zumwalt, Elmo, III BioIn 16
Zumwalt, Elmo R. BioIn 16
Zumwalt, Elmo R., Jr. 1920- WorAlBi
Zumwalt, Elmo Russell, Jr. 1920- St&PR 91, WhoAm 90
Zumwalt, Glen Wallace 1926- WhoAm 90
Zumwalt, Judith Ann Atkins 1939- WhoWrEP 89
Zumwalt, Richard Dowling 1912- WhoAm 90
Zumwalt, Roger Carl 1943- WhoAm 90
Zunde, Pranas 1923- WhoWor 91
Zunde, Steven 1955- St&PR 91
Zundel, Carolyn Steidley 1940- WhoAmW 91
Zundel, Georg 1931- WhoWor 91
Zundt, Mathias 1498?-1572 PenDiDA 89
Zung, Thomas Tse-Kwai 1933- WhoWor 91
Zuniga, Alonso de Ercilla y 1533-1584 BioIn 16
Zuniga, Daphne BioIn 16, ConTFT 8
Zuniga, Jo Ann 1958- WhoHisp 91
Zuniga, Jorge S BiDrAPA 89
Zuniga, Marta Cecilia 1950- WhoHisp 91
Zuniga, Mary Diane BiDrAPA 89
Zuniga, Richard A. WhoHisp 91
Zunin, Leonard M 1936- BiDrAPA 89
Zunino, Frank Joseph 1933- St&PR 91
Zunker, Sharon Jienell 1943- WhoAmW 91
Zunz, Lyonel E. 1921- St&PR 91
Zupan, Bruno 1939- WhoAmA 91
Zupan, Frank Louis 1924- St&PR 91
Zupanic, Richard Louis 1944- St&PR 91
Zupko, Alan John 1946- WhoE 91
Zupko, Arthur George 1916- WhoAm 90
Zupko, Karen Anne 1950- WhoAmW 91
Zupko, Ramon 1932- IntWWM 90
Zupnick, Elliot 1923- WhoAm 90
Zupon, Karen Elizabeth 1954- WhoAmW 91
Zupsic, Matthew Michael 1950- WhoE 91, WhoEmL 91, WhoWor 91
zu Putlitz, Gisbert 1931- WhoWor 91
Zur, Janice Mae 1942- WhoAmW 91
Zur, Menachem 1942- IntWWM 90
Zurav, Edward H. 1956- WhoE 91, WhoWor 91
Zuraw, Kathleen Ann 1960- WhoAmW 91, WhoEmL 91, WhoWor 91
Zurawski, Robert Lawrence 1961- WhoE 91
Zurbaran, Francisco de 1598?-1664 IntDcAA 90, WorAlBi
Zurbriggen, Pirmin BioIn 16
Zurcher, Louis A. 1936-1987 BioIn 16
Zu Reventlow, Franziska 1871-1918 BioIn 16
Zurfluh, Charles Victor 1942- St&PR 91
Zurheide, Charles Henry 1923- WhoAm 90
Zurhellen, Joseph Owen, Jr. NewYTBS 90
Zurhellen, Joseph Owen, Jr. 1920- WhoAm 90
Zuriarrain, Amaury Juan 1955- WhoHisp 91
Zurier, Robert Burton 1934- WhoAm 90
Zurik, Jesselyn Benson 1916- WhoAmA 91
Zurilla, William A. 1952- St&PR 91
Zuris, Donald P 1944- WhoAmA 91
Zurita, Raul 1951- ConAu 131, HispWr 90
Zurkammer, LaVeta Faye 1916- WhoAmW 91, WhoWor 91
Zurkowski, Paul George 1932- WhoAm 90
Zurkowski, Thomas Mark BiDrAPA 89
Zurliene, Donald H., Jr. 1955- St&PR 91
zur Loye, Dieter 1928- WhoAm 90, WhoE 91
Zurmuhle, Robert Walter 1933- WhoAm 90
Zur Muhlen, Hermynia 1883-1951 BioIn 16
Zur Muhlen, Raimund von 1854-1931 PenDiMP
Zurn, David Melvin 1938- WhoAm 90
Zuromski, Paul 1952- WhoEmL 91
Zuromskis, Diane ConAu 32NR
Zuromskis, Diane Stanley ConAu 32NR
Zurschmiede, W. Tom, Jr. 1926- St&PR 91
Zurzolo, Antonio 1923- WhoWor 91
Zuschlag, Richard Emery 1948- WhoSSW 91
Zusman, Jack 1934- BiDrAPA 89
Zusman, Lee St&PR 91
Zusman, Zeev 1955- BiDrAPA 89
Zuspan, Frederick Paul 1922- WhoAm 90
Zuspan, William Harris 1939- St&PR 91, WhoSSW 91
Zussman, Marc 1946- BiDrAPA 89
Zussman, Yale Martin 1952- WhoE 91
Zussy, Nancy Louise 1947- WhoAm 90, WhoAmW 91
Zutter, John D., Jr. 1948- St&PR 91
Zutz, Denise M. 1951- ODwPR 91
Zutz, Harry David 1917- WhoE 91
Zutz, Kenneth Aubrey 1953- St&PR 91
Zuur, Aad Pieter 1928- WhoWor 91
Zuverink, George 1924- Ballpl 90
Zuzelo, Edward A. 1924- St&PR 91
Zuzinec, Pat BioIn 16
Zvelebil, Kamil Veith 1927- WhoWor 91
Zvelebil, Marek 1952- WhoWor 91
Zver, James M 1935- WhoAmA 91
Zvereva, Galina G BiDrAPA 89
Zvereva, Irina BioIn 16
Zvereva, Natalia BioIn 16
Zvezdin, Vasilii Vasil'evich 1896-1943 BioIn 16
Zvirbulis, Jacob 1936- BiDrAPA 89
Zvonik, Loekie 1933- EncCoWW
Zwaan, Garnetta Sue 1951- WhoAmW 91
Zwack, Henry Francis 1952- WhoEmL 91
Zwack, Michael 1949- WhoAmA 91
Zwaenepoel, Jozef Camille 1922- WhoWor 91
Zwahlen, Fred Casper, Jr. 1924- WhoWor 91
Zwain, Laurence Michael 1952- St&PR 91
Zwakenberg, Larry W. 1947- St&PR 91
Zwanenburg, Wiecher 1933- WhoWor 91
Zwang, David Lawrence 1950- WhoE 91
Zwanzig, Robert W. 1928- BioIn 16
Zwanzig, Robert Walter 1928- WhoAm 90
Zwar, Charles 1911-1989 OxCPMus
Zwart, Piet 1885-1977 ConDes 90
Zwass, Vladimir 1946- WhoAm 90
Zwaveling, Albert 1927- WhoWor 91
Zwecker, Irving 1927- St&PR 91
Zweerts, Arnold 1918- WhoAmA 91
Zweiback, A. Martin 1939- WhoWor 91
Zweibel, Joel Burton 1935- WhoAm 90
Zweifach, Mark BiDrAPA 89
Zweifel, Richard George 1926- WhoAm 90
Zweig, Arnold 1887-1968 BioIn 16
Zweig, Ellen 1947- WhoWrEP 89
Zweig, Lisa E. 1960- ODwPR 91
Zweig, Ronald William 1949- WhoWor 91
Zweig, Stanley 1929- St&PR 91
Zweigart, Jacqueline 1934- St&PR 91
Zweigart, Pierre Max 1925- St&PR 91
Zweigenthal, Gail 1944- WhoAmW 91
Zweiman, Beverly Heafitz 1944- WhoAmW 91
Zweiman, Burton 1931- WhoAm 90
Zwerdling, Alex 1932- WhoAm 90
Zwerdling, David Mark 1944- BiDrAPA 89
Zwerenz, Bruno Heinz BiDrAPA 89
Zwerenz, Gottfried O. 1943- WhoWor 91
Zwerg, Charles Alvin 1936- St&PR 91
Zwerg, Daniel Robert 1961- WhoSSW 91
Zwerger, Lisbeth BioIn 16
Zwerin, Jeffrey Howard 1947- BiDrAPA 89
Zwerling, Charles M. 1925- St&PR 91
Zwerling, Frederick 1931- St&PR 91
Zwerling, Gary L. 1949- St&PR 91
Zwerling, Gary Leslie 1949- WhoAm 90, WhoE 91
Zwerling, Israel 1917- BiDrAPA 89, WhoAm 90, WhoE 91
Zwerling, Margaret Jane BiDrAPA 89
Zwern, Richard N. 1955- ODwPR 91
Zwiacher, Kaye Freeman BiDrAPA 89
Zwick, Charles J. 1926- St&PR 91
Zwick, Charles John 1926- WhoAm 90, WhoSSW 91
Zwick, Edward BioIn 16
Zwick, Paul A BiDrAPA 89
Zwick, Rosemary G 1925- WhoAmA 91
Zwicke, Dianne Lynn 1952- WhoAmW 91
Zwicky, Fay 1933- FemiCLE
Zwicky, Fritz 1898-1974 DcScB S2, WorAlBi
Zwicky, Gary 1934- IntWWM 90
Zwicky, Kathleen M. 1946- St&PR 91
Zwicky, Peter Ernst 1953- WhoWor 91
Zwiebe, Sherman 1942- St&PR 91
Zwiebel, Arthur 1923- WhoE 91
Zwiebel, Imre 1932- WhoAm 90
Zwiebel, James Andrew 1949- WhoE 91
Zwiebel, Malvina Dee 1943- St&PR 91
Zwiebel, Sherman 1942- St&PR 91
Zwiener, David K. 1954- St&PR 91
Zwiener, Robert Joseph 1937- WhoE 91
Zwiep, Donald Nelson 1924- WhoAm 90
Zwiercan, Gary A. 1942- St&PR 91
Zwietnig-Rotterdam, Paul WhoAmA 91
Zwilgmeyer, Dikken 1853-1913 EncCoWW
Zwilich, Ellen 1939- News 90 [port]
Zwilich, Ellen Taaffe 1939- BioIn 16, IntWWM 90, WhoAm 90, WhoAmW 91
Zwilling, Dutch 1888-1978 Ballpl 90
Zwilling, Jane Riegelhaupt 1957- WhoAmW 91
Zwinger, Ann 1925- ConAu 30NR
Zwingli, Huldrych 1484-1531 WorAlBi
Zwingli, John C. 1956- St&PR 91
Zwink, Timothy Ashley 1949- WhoWrEP 89
Zwirn, Paul Henri 1925- WhoWor 91
Zwirn, Robert 1948- WhoEmL 91
Zwirz, Jankiel 1903- MusmAFA
Zwislocki, Jozef John 1922- WhoAm 90
Zwissler, Alexander M.F. 1957- St&PR 91

Zwolinski, Bruno John 1919- *WhoAm 90*
Zworykin, Vladimir K. 1889-1982 *WorAlBi*
Zwoyer, Eugene Milton 1926- *WhoAm 90*
Zych, Leonard A. 1948- *St&PR 91*
Zychowicz, Ralph Charles 1948- *WhoEmL 91*
Zygelbojm, Samuel Artur 1895-1943 *BioIn 16*
Zygmont, Christina *BioIn 16*
Zygmund, Antoni 1900- *WhoAm 90*
Zygmunt, W. John 1945- *St&PR 91*
Zykan, Mary Susan 1946- *WhoAmW 91*
Zykorie, David 1942- *BiDrAPA 89*
Zyla, Gregory Joseph 1949- *WhoWrEP 89*
Zyla, Mark Lawrence 1960- *WhoSSW 91*
Zylawy, Roman 1939- *WhoSSW 91*
Zylis-Gara, Teresa 1935- *IntWWM 90, PenDiMP*
Zylis-Gara, Teresa Gerarda 1935- *WhoAm 90*
Zylstra, Stanley James 1943- *WhoAm 90*
Zymierski, Michal 1890-1989 *BioIn 16*
Zyroff, Ellen Slotoroff 1946- *WhoAmW 91*
Zyromski, Jean 1890-1975 *BiDFrPL*
Zysblat, William Larry 1950- *WhoE 91*
Zyskind, Harold *BioIn 16, NewYTBS 90*
Zyskind, Harold 1917-1990 *ConAu 130*
Zytaruk, George John 1927- *WhoWrEP 89*
Zytowski, Carl Byrd 1921- *IntWWM 90*
Zywicki, Robert Albert 1930- *WhoAm 90*
ZZ Top *EncPR&S 89*
Zzagar, Zzivojin 1925- *WhoWor 91*